NELSON'S COMPLETE CONCORDANCE OF THE NEW AMERICAN BIBLE

NELSON'S COMPLETE CONCORDANCE OF THE NEW AMERICAN BIBLE

Fr. Stephen J. Hartdegen, O.F.M., L.S.S.

General Editor

The Liturgical Press

Collegeville • Minnesota

NIHIL OBSTAT
Fr. Stephen J. Hartdegen, O.F.M., L.S.S.
Censor Deputatus

IMPRIMATUR:
William Cardinal Baum
Archbishop of Washington

June 6, 1977

Published by Thomas Nelson Inc., Publishers, in Nashville, Tennessee. Manufactured in the United States of America.

Library of Congress Cataloging in Publication Data

Hartdegen, Stephen J
Complete concordance of the New American Bible.

1. Bible—Concordances, English—New American Bible.
I. Baum, William W., joint author. II. Bible.
English. New American. III. Title.
BS425.H27 220.2 77–22170
ISBN 0–8407–4900–7

PREFACE

A verbal concordance of the Bible comprises three elements: 1) a listing in alphabetical order of the words of the Bible; 2) all references to book, chapter, and verse in which each listed word is found; and 3) sense quotations in which the key word is embodied. It differs from a topical or thematic concordance, which lists biblical references dealing with the same topic, theme, or subject matter.

The first verbal concordance was the *Concordantiae Sancti Jacobi* of the Latin Vulgate Bible (c.1230). Its form, to which was added sense quotations in two later thirteenth century works, became the model of all verbal concordances even to the present time. The later works were *Concordantiae Anglicanae* (1250) and *Concordantiae Bibliorum* of Conrad of Halberstadt (1290).

Many biblical concordances both of original texts and of ancient and modern versions have since been compiled. Their value depends on the text underlying the concordance and on the fidelity of the translation. They have been very useful for exegetical studies, textual criticism, every kind of Bible study, and for preaching the word of God.

From the sixteenth to the nineteenth centuries, concordances in English of both Testaments were made of the Authorized (King James) Version. Among them, Cruden's Concordance (1737) gained wide acceptance because of its accuracy. Young's Analytical Concordance to the Bible (1873) includes Hebrew and Greek equivalents to English words. Strong's Exhaustive Concordance (1894) adds the feature of a comparison between the Authorized and the Revised Version. The American Standard Version is the basis of Hazard's Concordance (1932), and the Douay-Rheims (Catholic) Version underlies Thompson and Stock's Complete Concordance (1942-1945). It includes the words of the deuterocanonical books of the Catholic Bible. In 1957 the Concordance of the Revised Standard Version became the first to be produced by an electronic computer.

In 1970 an entirely new translation of the whole Bible, including the deuterocanonical books, was completed by Catholic scholars who were joined by several non-Catholic colleagues. It is entitled the *New American Bible.* The translation made critical use of all the ancient sources, including the Dead Sea Scrolls of Qumran and the Masada texts. In view of this, the translation has been referred to as "the most up-to-date [translation] that has appeared in the United States" (*The Catechist*).

The broad distribution of the *New American Bible* with its numerous editions, its use in reading, study, and public worship, and the growing familiarity with its wording, calls for a new verbal concordance to facilitate the location of words in this modern translation and to guide its use in study.

More than 300,000 entries are listed in this Complete Concordance, covering 18,000 key words. The notation next to each word heading indicates how many times the word is found in the *New American Bible*.

The widespread use of electronic equipment and the problem of time made the use of a computer in the production of the NAB Concordance a practical necessity. Human and mechanical means combined to guarantee the accuracy of the work. Obviously, the use of a computer to produce the Concordance precluded the analysis of the precise Hebrew or Greek words underlying the listings. Such aids are to be found in concordances of the original languages of Sacred Scripture.

Frequently occurring common words unlikely to be sought as key words of a biblical text are not included in the NAB Concordance. The words omitted are:

a	**and**	**before**	**go**	**however**	**my**
about	**any**	**but**	**goes**	**I**	**no**
above	**are**	**by**	**going**	**if**	**not**
across	**around**	**can**	**gone**	**in**	**now**
after	**aren't**	**could**	**had**	**into**	**O**
again	**as**	**did**	**has**	**is**	**of**
against	**ask**	**do**	**have**	**it**	**oh**
ago	**asks**	**does**	**having**	**its**	**on**
all	**asked**	**done**	**he**	**like**	**one**
almost	**asking**	**doing**	**her**	**may**	**or**
also	**at**	**down**	**hers**	**me**	**ought**
am	**be**	**even**	**him**	**meanwhile**	**our**
among	**because**	**for**	**his**	**might**	**ours**
an	**been**	**from**	**how**	**mine**	**out**

over
reply
replies
replied
replying
said
saw
say
says
saying
see
seeing
seen
shall
she
should
so
than
that
the
their
them
then
there
therefore
therein
thereof
thereon
thereupon
therewith
these
they
this
those
thought
through
thus
to
too
under
unto
up
upon
us
very
was
we
went
were
what
when
where
which
while
who
whom
whose
why
will
with
within
without
would
yet
you
your
yours

Excluded also are titles—e.g., of psalms—and the wordings of footnotes. Their omission is thought not to reduce the usefulness of the Concordance.

In each quotation the key word is abbreviated by using the initial letter followed by a period.

The editor expresses his appreciation and esteem for his colleague, Fr. Christopher Rehwinkel, O.F.M. who some years ago undertook singlehandedly the laborious task of preparing a concordance of the *New American Bible* only to be obliged to relinquish it because of ill health. Sincere thanks are due for the unfailing cooperation of Thomas Nelson Publishers—of Sam Moore, president, Bernard Deeter, vice-president, John Kincer, C. Franklin Hiam, Jeff Miller, and the editorial staff—and for the tireless help of the General Editor's assistant, Nancy Fascelli, and the supportive efforts of Charles A. Buggè of the Confraternity of Christian Doctrine, U.S. Catholic Conference. Through the mutual cooperation of many, the work of compiling a COMPLETE CONCORDANCE OF THE NEW AMERICAN BIBLE has become a reality.

Stephen J. Hartdegen, O.F.M., L.S.S.
General Editor

Washington, D.C.
June 8, 1977

1 2 3 4 5 6 7 8 9

A

A-GALLOP (1)

Na 3: 2 rumbling sound of wheels; horses *a,*

AARON (318)

Ex 4:14 "Have you not your brother, *A* the Levite?
4:27 The LORD said to *A,* "Go into the desert
4:27 met at the mountain of God, *A* kissed him.
4:29 Then Moses and *A* went and assembled all
4:30 *A* told them everything the LORD had said
5: 1 that, Moses and *A* went to Pharaoh and said,
5: 4 them, "What do you mean, Moses and *A,*
5:20 left Pharaoh and came upon Moses and *A,*
6:13 spoke to Moses and *A* and gave them his
6:20 married his aunt Jochebed, who bore him *A,*
6:23 *A* married Amminadab's daughter,
6:26 This is the *A* and this the Moses
6:27 the same Moses and *A.*
7: 1 *A* your brother shall act as your prophet.
7: 2 your brother *A* shall tell Pharaoh to let
7: 6 and *A* did as the LORD had commanded them.
7: 7 *A* eighty-three when they spoke to Pharaoh.
7: 8 The LORD told Moses and *A,*
7: 9 work a sign or wonder, you shall say to *A:*
7:10 Then Moses and *A* went to Pharaoh and did
7:10 *A* threw his staff down before Pharaoh and
7:19 The LORD then said to Moses, "Say to *A:*
7:20 *A* did as the LORD had commanded.
7:20 *A* raised his staff and struck the waters
7:22 and would not listen to Moses and *A,*
8: 1 The LORD then told Moses, "Say to *A:*
8: 2 *A* stretched out his hand over the waters
8: 4 Pharaoh summoned Moses and *A* and said,
8: 8 After Moses and *A* left Pharaoh's presence,
8:12 "Tell *A* to stretch out his staff and
8:13 *A* stretched out his hand,
8:21 summoned Moses and *A* and said to them,
9: 8 Then the LORD said to Moses and *A,*
9:27 summoned Moses and *A* and said to them,
10: 3 Moses and *A* went to Pharaoh and told him,
10: 8 Moses and *A* were brought back to Pharaoh,
10:16 Pharaoh summoned Moses and *A* and said,
10:24 then summoned Moses and *A* and said,
11:10 although Moses and *A* performed these
12: 1 said to Moses and *A* in the land of Egypt,
12:28 did as the LORD had commanded Moses and *A.*
12:31 Pharaoh summoned Moses and *A* and said,
12:43 The LORD said to Moses and *A,*
12:50 just as the LORD had commanded Moses and *A.*
16: 2 community grumbled against Moses and *A.*
16: 6 So Moses and *A* told all the Israelites,
16: 9 Then Moses said to *A,*
16:10 When *A* announced this to the whole
16:33 Moses then told *A,* "Take an urn
16:34 So *A* placed it in front of the
17:10 to the top of the hill with *A* and Hur.
17:12 Meanwhile *A* and Hur supported his hands,
18:12 and *A* came with all the elders of Israel
19:24 Then come up again along with *A.*
24: 1 told, "Come up to the LORD, you and *A,*
24: 9 Moses then went up with *A,*
24:14 *A* and Hur are staying with you.
27:21 From evening to morning *A* and his sons
28: 1 among the Israelites have your brother *A,*
28: 2 *A* you shall have sacred vestments made.
28: 3 such vestments for *A* as will set him apart
28: 4 brother *A* and his sons are to wear in serving
28:12 Thus *A* shall bear their names on his
28:29 "Whenever *A* enters the sanctuary,
28:35 *A* shall wear it when ministering,
28:38 Since *A* bears whatever guilt the
28:41 shall clothe your brother *A* and his sons.
28:43 *A* and his sons shall wear them whenever
29: 4 *A* and his sons you shall also bring to the
29: 5 the vestments and clothe *A* with the tunic,
29: 9 and thus shall you ordain *A* and his sons.
29:10 There *A* and his sons shall lay their hands
29:15 and after *A* and his sons have laid their
29:19 and when *A* and his sons have laid their
29:21 and sprinkle this on *A* and his vestments,
29:24 shall put into the hands of *A* and his sons,
29:27 else belonging to *A* or to his sons.
29:28 Such things are due to *A* and his sons from
29:29 *A* shall be passed down to his descendants,
29:32 At the entrance of the meeting tent *A* and
29:35 Carry out all these orders in regard to *A*
29:44 consecrate *A* and his sons to be my priests.
30: 7 "On it *A* shall burn fragrant incense.
30:10 Once a year *A* shall perform the atonement
30:19 *A* and his sons shall use it in washing
30:30 *A* and his sons you shall also anoint and
31:10 the sacred vestments for *A* the priest,
32: 1 they gathered around *A* and said to him,
32: 2 *A* replied, "Have your wives and sons
32: 3 off their earrings and brought them to *A,*
32: 5 *A* built an altar before the calf and
32:21 Moses asked *A,* "What did this people
32:22 *A* replied, "Let not my lord be angry.
32:25 their foes, *A* had let the people run wild,
32:35 for having had *A* make the calf for them.
34:30 When *A,* then, and the other Israelites saw
34:31 Only after Moses called to them did *A* and
35:19 the sacred vestments for *A,*
38:21 direction of Ithamar, son of *A* the priest.
39: 1 as well as the sacred vestments for *A,*
39:27 For *A* and his sons there were also woven
39:41 the sacred vestments for *A* the priest,
40:12 "Then bring *A* and his sons to the entrance
40:13 *A* with the sacred vestments and anoint him,
40:31 Moses and *A* and his sons used to wash

Lv 2: 3 cereal offering belongs to *A* and his sons.
2:10 cereal offering belongs to *A* and his sons.
6: 2 *A* and his sons the following command:
6: 9 The rest of it *A* and his sons may eat;
6:11 All the male descendants of *A* may partake
6:13 "This is the offering that *A* and his sons
6:18 LORD said to Moses, "Tell *A* and his sons:
7:31 but the breast belongs to *A* and his sons.
7:33 The descendant of *A* who offers up the
7:34 is raised up, and I have given them to *A,*
7:35 allotted to *A* and his sons on the day he
8: 2 LORD said to Moses, "Take *A* and his sons,
8: 6 Bringing forward *A* and his sons,
8: 7 Then he put the tunic on *A,*
8:14 *A* and his sons laid their hands on its
8:18 and *A* and his sons laid their hands on its
8:22 and *A* and his sons laid their hands on
8:24 Moses had the sons of *A* also come forward,
8:27 things into the hands of *A* and his sons,
8:30 sprinkled with it *A* and his vestments,
8:30 thus consecrating both *A* and his vestments
8:31 Finally, Moses said to *A* and his sons,
8:31 *A* and his sons shall eat of it.'
8:36 So *A* and his sons did all that the LORD
9: 1 eighth day Moses summoned *A* and his sons,
9: 2 with the elders of Israel, and said to *A,*
9: 7 Come up to the altar," Moses then told *A,*
9: 8 *A* first slaughtered the calf that was his
9:12 Then *A* slaughtered his holocaust.
9:18 *A* splashed it on all sides of the altar.
9:22 *A* then raised his hands over the people
9:23 Moses and *A* went into the meeting tent.
10: 3 Moses then said to *A,*
10: 3 But *A* said nothing.
10: 6 said to *A* and his sons Eleazar and Ithamar,
10: 8 The LORD said to *A,* "When you are to go
10:12 Moses said to *A* and his surviving sons,
10:16 he was angry with the surviving sons of *A,*
10:19 *A* answered Moses,
11: 1 Moses and *A,* "Speak to the Israelites
13: 1 The LORD said to Moses and *A,*
13: 2 he shall be brought to *A,* the priest
14:33 Moses and *A,* "When you come
15: 1 The LORD said to Moses and *A,*
16: 2 "Tell your brother *A* that he is not to
16: 3 Only in this way may *A* enter the sanctuary.
16: 6 *A* shall bring in the bullock,
16: 9 *A* shall bring in and offer up as a sin
16:11 "Thus shall *A* offer up the bullock,
16:20 altar, *A* shall bring forward the live goat.
16:23 *A* has again gone into the meeting tent,
17: 2 said to Moses, "Speak to *A* and his sons,
21:17 said to Moses, "Speak to *A* and tell him:
21:21 No descendant of *A* the priest who has any
21:24 *A* and his sons and to all the Israelites.
22: 2 "Tell *A* and his sons to respect the
22: 4 of *A* who is stricken with leprosy,
22:18 *A* and his sons and to all the Israelites,
24: 3 *A* shall set up the lamps to burn before
24: 9 It shall belong to *A* and his sons,

Nm 1: 3 You and *A* shall enroll in companies all
1:17 *A* took these men who had been designated,
1:44 and *A* and the twelve princes of Israel.
2: 1 The LORD said to Moses and *A:*
3: 1 The following were the descendants of *A*
3: 2 The sons of *A* were Nadab his first-born,
3: 3 These are the names of the sons of *A,*
3: 4 under the direction of their father *A.*
3: 6 of Levi and present them to *A* the priest,
3: 9 shall give the Levites to *A* and his sons;
3:10 But only *A* and his descendants shall you
3:32 however, was Eleazar, son of *A* the priest;
3:38 camped Moses and *A* and the latter's sons.
3:48 Give this silver to *A* and his sons as
3:51 gave this ransom silver to *A* and his sons,
4: 1 Moses and *A:* "Among the Levites
4: 5 *A* and his sons shall go in and take down
4:15 "Only after *A* and his sons have finished
4:16 "Eleazar, son of *A* the priest,
4:17 The LORD said to Moses and *A:*
4:19 *A* and his sons shall go in and assign to
4:27 under the direction of *A* and his sons,
4:28 of Ithamar, son of *A* the priest.
4:33 of Ithamar, son of *A* the priest."
4:34 So Moses and *A* and the princes of the
4:37 tent, which Moses took, together with *A,*
4:41 tent, which Moses took, together with *A,*
4:45 clans which Moses took, together with *A,*
4:46 when Moses and *A* and the Israelites
6:23 "Speak to *A* and his sons and tell them:
7: 8 of Ithamar, son of *A* the priest.
8: 2 to Moses, and said, "Give *A* this command:
8: 3 *A* did so, setting up the lamps to face
8:11 Let *A* then offer the Levites before the
8:13 the Levites stand before *A* and his sons,
8:19 dedicated Israelites to *A* and his sons
8:20 did Moses and *A* and the whole community
8:21 *A* offered them as a wave offering before
8:22 under the supervision of *A* and his sons.
9: 6 up to Moses and *A* that same day and said,
10: 8 "It is the sons of *A,*
12: 1 Miriam and *A* spoke against Moses on the
12: 4 the LORD said to Moses and *A* and Miriam,
12: 5 entrance of the tent, called *A* and Miriam.
12:10 When *A* turned and saw her a leper,
13:26 met Moses and *A* and the whole community
14: 2 Israelites grumbled against Moses and *A,*
14: 5 But Moses and *A* fell prostrate before the
14:26 The LORD also said to Moses and *A:*
15:33 him to Moses and *A* and the whole assembly.
16: 3 and held an assembly against Moses and *A,*
16:11 *A* done that you should grumble against him?"
16:16 you and they and *A* too.
16:17 you and *A,* each with his own censer
16:18 of the meeting tent along with Moses and *A.*
16:20 and the LORD said to Moses and *A,*
17: 2 Moses, "Tell Eleazar, son of *A* the priest,
17: 5 no one who was not a descendant of *A,*
17: 6 community grumbled against Moses and *A,*
17: 7 Moses and *A* turned toward the meeting tent,
17: 8 *A* came to the front of the meeting tent,
17: 9 tent, and the LORD said to Moses and *A,*
17:11 Then Moses said to *A,*
17:12 *A* took his censer and ran in among the
17:15 *A* returned to Moses at the entrance of the
18: 1 The LORD said to *A,* "You and your sons
18: 8 The LORD said to *A,* "I myself have given
18:20 LORD said to *A,* "You shall not have
18:28 handing over to *A* the priest the part to
19: 1 The LORD said to Moses and *A:*
20: 2 they held a council against Moses and *A.*
20: 6 But Moses and *A* went away from the
20: 8 the community, you and your brother *A,*
20:10 He and *A* assembled the community in front
20:12 But the LORD said to Moses and *A,*
20:23 of Edom, the LORD said to Moses and *A,*
20:24 *A* is about to be taken to his people,
20:25 Take *A* and his son Eleazar and bring them
20:26 Then strip *A* of his garments and put them
20:26 for there *A* shall be taken in death."
20:28 Moses stripped *A* of his garments and put
20:28 Then *A* died there on top of the mountain.
20:29 understood that *A* had passed away;
25: 7 son of Eleazar, son of *A* the priest,
25:11 son of Eleazar, son of *A* the priest,
26: 1 to Moses and Eleazar, son of *A* the priest,
26: 9 revolted against Moses and *A* [like Korah's
26:59 bore *A* and Moses and their sister Miriam.
26:60 To *A* were born Nadab and Abihu,
26:64 by Moses and the priest *A* in the census
27:13 to your people, as was your brother *A,*
33: 1 of Egypt under the guidance of Moses and *A.*
33:38 *A* the priest ascended Mount Hor at the
33:39 *A* was a hundred and twenty-three years old

AARON (cont.)

Dt 9:20 With *A*, too, the LORD was deeply angry
10: 6 for Moserah, where *A* died and was buried,
32:50 just as your brother *A* died on Mount Hor
Jos 21: 4 the descendants of *A* the priest obtained
21:10 of *A* in the Kohathite clan of the Levites,
21:13 Thus to the descendants of *A* the priest
21:19 belonged to the priestly descendants of *A*,
24: 5 "Then I sent Moses and *A*,
24:33 When Eleazar, son of *A*,
Jgs 20:28 and Phinehas, son of Eleazar, son of *A*,
1Sm 12: 6 is witness, who appointed Moses and *A*,
12: 8 Moses and *A* to bring them out of Egypt,
1Chr 5:29 The children of Amram were *A*,
5:29 The sons of *A* were Nadab,
6:34 it was *A* and his descendants who burnt the
6:35 These were the descendants of *A*:
6:39 *A* who belonged to clan of the Kohathites,
6:42 were assigned to the descendants of *A*:
12:28 with Jehoiada, leader of the line of *A*,
15: 4 together the sons of *A* and the Levites:
23:13 The sons of Amram were *A* and Moses.
23:13 *A* was set apart to be consecrated as most
23:28 *A* in the service of the house of the LORD,
23:32 tent, the sanctuary, and the sons of *A*,
24: 1 of *A* also were divided into classes.
24: 1 The sons of *A* were Nadab,
24:19 keeping with the precepts given them by *A*,
24:31 as their relatives, the descendants of *A*,
27:17 son of Kemuel; for *A*, Zadok
2Chr 13: 9 the priests of the LORD, the sons of *A*,
13:10 ministering to the LORD are sons of *A*,
26:18 LORD, but for the priests, the sons of *A*,
29:21 for Judah, and he ordered the sons of *A*,
31:19 The sons of *A*,
35:14 Indeed the priests, the sons of *A*,
35:14 and for the priests, the sons of *A*.
Ezr 7: 5 son of Eleazar, son of the high priest *A*—
Neh 12:47 the Levites made theirs to the sons of *A*.
1Mc 7:14 of the line of *A* has come with the army,
Ps(s) 77:21 like a flock under the care of Moses and *A*.
99: 6 Moses and *A* were among his priests,
105:26 He sent Moses his servant; *A*,
106:16 Moses in the camp, and *A*, the holy one
115:10 The house of *A* trusts in the LORD;
115:12 he will bless the house of *A*;
118: 3 Let the house of *A* say,
133: 2 runs down over the beard, the beard of *A*,
135:19 of Israel, bless the LORD, house of *A*,
Sir 45: 6 like Moses in holiness, his brother *A*,
45:20 of *A* and bestowed upon him his inheritance:
45:25 heritage of *A* is for all his descendants.
50:13 All the sons of *A* in their dignity
50:16 God, The sons of *A* would sound a blast,
Mi 6: 4 And I sent before you Moses, *A*,
Lk 1: 5 wife was a descendant of *A* named Elizabeth.
Acts 7:40 that will be our leaders,' they said to *A*.
Heb 5: 4 but only when called by God as *A* was.
7:11 a priest according to the order of *A*?
9: 4 manna, the rod of *A* which had blossomed,

AARONITE (1)

Neh 10:39 An *A* priest shall be with the Levites when

AARON'S (31)

Ex 6:25 *A* son, Eleazar, married one of Putiel's
7:12 But *A* staff swallowed their staffs.
15:20 The prophetess Miriam, *A* sister,
28:30 that they may be over *A* heart whenever he
28:38 on the front of the miter, over *A* forehead.
28:40 for the glorious adornment of *A* sons
29:20 put on the tip of *A* right ear
29:26 take the breast of *A* ordination ram and
Lv 1: 5 the bull before the LORD, but *A* sons,
1: 7 After *A* sons, the priests
1:11 Then *A* sons, the priests, shall splash
2: 2 When he has brought it to *A* sons,
3: 2 but *A* sons, the priests, shall splash
3: 5 All this *A* sons shall then burn on the
3: 8 but *A* sons shall splash its blood on the
3:13 but *A* sons shall splash its blood on the
6: 7 One of *A* sons shall first present it
6:15 *A* descendant who succeeds him as the
7:10 to all of *A* sons without distinction.
8:12 poured some of the anointing oil on *A* head,
8:13 Moses likewise brought forward *A* sons,
8:23 blood and put it on the tip of *A* right ear,
10: 1 During this time *A* sons Nadab and Abihu
10: 4 and Elzaphan, the sons of *A* uncle Uzziel,
16: 1 After the death of *A* two sons,
21: 1 The LORD said to Moses, "Speak to *A* sons,
Nm 17:18 and mark *A* name on Levi's staff,
17:21 and *A* staff was with them.
17:23 day, when Moses entered the tent, *A* staff,
17:25 back *A* staff in front of the commandments,
Tb 1: 7 and present them to the priests, *A* sons,

ABACK (4)

Mt 22:22 Taken *a* by this reply, they went off
Mk 6:51 They were taken *a* by these happenings,
Acts 9:21 Any who heard it were greatly taken *a*.
Rv 17: 7 "Why are you so taken *a*?

ABADDON (3)

Jb 26: 6 is the nether world, and *A* has no covering.
28:22 *A* and Death say,
Rv 9:11 name in Hebrew is *A* and in Greek Apollyon.

ABAGTHA (1)

Est 1:10 Mehuman, Biztha, Harbona, Bigtha, *A*,

ABANA (1)

2Kgs 5:12 rivers of Damascus, the *A* and the Pharpar,

ABANDON (37)

Dt 4:31 God, he will not *a* and destroy you,
Jos 10: 6 "Do not *a* your servants.
23:12 For if you ever *a* him and ally yourselves
Ru 1:16 said, "Do not ask me to *a* or forsake you!
1Sm 12:22 great name the LORD will not *a* his people,
2Sm 6:14 came dancing before the LORD with *a*,
1Chr 28: 9 if you *a* him, he will cast you off forever
28:20 He will not fail you or *a* you before you
2Chr 15: 2 but if you *a* him, he will abandon you
Tb 4: 3 and do not *a* her as long as she lives.
14: 6 all shall *a* their idols which have
2Mc 6: 1 force the Jews to *a* the customs
6:16 misfortunes, he does not *a* his own people.
7:24 happy if he would *a* his ancestral customs:
Ps(s) 16:10 you will not *a* my soul to the nether world,
85: 5 savior, and *a* your displeasure against us.
94:14 cast off his people, nor *a* his inheritance;
Prv 28: 4 Those who *a* the law praise the wicked man,
Wis 10:13 did not *a* the just man when he was sold,
12: 2 may *a* their wickedness and believe in you,
12:20 time and opportunity to *a* wickedness,
Sir 4:19 she will *a* him and deliver him into the
13: 4 but when you are exhausted, he will *a* you.
23: 4 of my life, *a* me not into their control!
46:11 were not deceived, Who did not *a* God:
51:10 Do not *a* me in time of trouble,
Jer 12:12 I *a* my house,
Lam 5:20 should you forget us, *a* us so long a time?
Bar 6:41 unable to reflect and *a* these gods,
Ez 20: 8 eyes, they did not *a* the idols of Egypt.
Acts 2:27 you will not *a* my soul to the nether world,
7:19 He forced our fathers to *a* their infants
21:21 who live among the Gentiles to *a* Moses,
27:30 Then the sailors tried to *a* ship.
2Tm 2:19 who professes the name of the Lord *a* evil."
Heb 12: 3 do not grow despondent or *a* the struggle.

ABANDONED (65)

Jos 22: 3 years now you have not once *a* your kinsmen,
Jgs 2:13 *a* him and served Baal and the Ashtaroth,
2:17 *a* themselves to the worship of other gods.
6:13 For now the LORD has *a* us and has
8:33 Israelites again *a* themselves to the Baals,
10: 6 had *a* the LORD and would not serve him,
1Sm 23:13 escaped from Kielah, he *a* the expedition.
28:15 are waging war against me and God has *a* me.
28:16 LORD has *a* you and is with your neighbor?
30:13 My master *a* me because I fell sick three
31: 7 dead, they too *a* their cities and fled.
2Sm 5:21 They *a* their gods there,
2Kgs 7:13 let some of us take five of the *a* horses
21:22 He *a* the LORD,
25: 5 desert near Jericho, *a* by his whole army.
2Chr 12: 1 become powerful, he *a* the law of the LORD,
12: 5 'You have *a* me,
12: 5 I have *a* you to the power of Shishak.' "
13:11 to the LORD, our God, but you have *a* him.
24:20 you have abandoned the LORD, he has *a* you.' "
24:24 their power, because Judah had *a* the LORD,
28: 6 valiant men, because they had *a* the LORD,
29: 6 They *a* him, turned away their faces
34:25 Because they have *a* me and have offered
Ezr 9: 9 but in our servitude our God has not *a* us;
9:10 For we have *a* your commandments,
Neh 9:28 you *a* them to the power of their enemies,
13:11 demanding, "Why is the house of God *a*?"
Jdt 5: 8 Since they *a* the way of their ancestors,
1Mc 1:15 their circumcision and *a* the holy covenant;
1:52 Many of the people, those who *a* the law,
10:14 who had *a* the law and the commandments,
2Mc 10:13 called a traitor for having *a* Cyprus,
Ps(s) 78:62 He *a* his people to the sword and was
Sir 47:19 But you *a* yourself to women and gave them
49: 4 They *a* the Law of the Most High,
Is 2: 6 You have *a* your people,
6:12 far away, and the land is *a* more and more.
17: 2 Her cities shall be forever *a*,
17: 9 cities shall be like those *a* by the Hivites
27:10 city shall be desolate, an *a* pasture,
54: 7 For a brief moment I *a* you,
58: 2 is just and not *a* the law of their God;
Jer 4:29 All the cities are *a*,
9:12 Because they have *a* my law,
Lam 5:14 The old men have *a* the gate,
Ez 36: 4 valleys, the desolate ruins and *a* cities,
Hos 4:10 they have *a* the LORD to practice harlotry.
Am 5: 2 She lies *a* upon her land,
Mt 4:20 *a* their nets and became his followers.
4:22 they *a* boat and father to follow him.
Mk 1:18 *a* their nets and became his followers.
1:20 They *a* their father Zebedee,
Lk 13:35 Your temple will be *a*.
Acts 2:31 said that he was not *a* to the nether world,
7:21 father's house, but afterward he was *a*,
7:42 But God turned away from them and *a* them
27:20 Toward the end, we *a* any hope of survival.
27:40 loose the anchors and *a* them to the sea.
2Cor 4: 9 We are persecuted but never *a*;
Eph 4:19 without remorse they have *a* themselves to
2Tm 4:16 In fact, everyone *a* me.
2Pt 2:15 They have *a* the straight road and wander
Jude 1:11 *a* themselves to Balaam's error for pay,

ABANDONING (4)

Jgs 2:12 *A* the LORD, the God of their fathers
2Kgs 7: 7 in the twilight they fled, *a* their tents,
1Mc 1:42 one people, each *a* his particular customs.
Ez 31:12 of the land withdrew from its shade, *a* it.

ABANDONS (3)

Jb 12:23 he spreads peoples abroad and he *a* them.
Sir 29:16 and the ingrate *a* his protector;
Lk 9:39 then *a* him in his shattered condition.

ABARIM (6)

Nm 27:12 "Go up here into the *A* Mountains and view
33:47 camped in the *A* Mountains opposite Nebo.
33:48 Setting out from the *A* Mountains,
Dt 32:49 here in the *A* Mountains [it is in the land
Jer 22:20 Cry out from *A*,
Ez 39:11 the Valley of *A* east of the sea [it is

ABASE (1)

Sir 4:27 Do not *a* yourself before an impious man,

ABASED (4)

Is 2: 9 But man is *a*, each one brought low.
2:11 lowered, the arrogance of men will be *a*,
2:17 Human pride will be *a*,
5:15 Men shall be *a*,

ABASHED (2)

Jer 50:12 to shame, she that bore you shall be *a*;
Ez 36:32 Be ashamed and *a* because of your conduct,

ABATE (2)

Jer 23:20 The anger of the LORD shall not *a* until he
30:24 The anger of the LORD will not *a* until he

ABATED (3)

Est 7:10 for Mordecai, and the anger of the king *a*.
Is 12: 1 have been angry with me, your anger has *a*,
Jon 1:15 him into the sea, and the sea's raging *a*.

ABATES (2)

Eccl 10: 4 for mildness *a* great offenses.
Sir 18:15 Like dew that *a* a burning wind,

ABBA (3)

Mk 14:36 He kept saying, *A* (O Father),
Rom 8:15 of adoption through which we cry out, *A*!"
Gal 4: 6 the spirit of his Son which cries out *A*!"

ABBREVIATE (1)

2Mc 2:32 to a story and then *a* the story itself.

ABDA (2)

1Kgs 4: 6 and Adoniram, son of *A*,
Neh 11:17 and *A*, son of Shammua, son of Galal

ABDEEL (1)

Jer 36:26 son of Azriel, and Shelemiah, son of *A*,

ABDI (3)

1Chr 6:29 Ethan, son of Kishi, son of *A*,
2Chr 29:12 Kish, son of *A*,
Ezr 10:26 Mattaniah, Zechariah, Jehiel, *A*,

ABDIEL (1)

1Chr 5:15 Ahi, son of *A*, son of Guni,

ABDOMEN (4)

1Sm 31: 3 he was pierced through the *a*.
2Sm 2:23 him in the *a* with the heel of his javelin,
3:27 There he stabbed him in the *a*,
20:10 hand, Joab stabbed him in the *a* with it,

ABDON (9)

Jos 19:28 Neiel, it extended to Cabul, Mishal, *A*,
21:30 pasture lands, *A* with its pasture lands,
Jgs 12:13 After him the Pirathonite *A*,

12:15 for eight years, the Pirathonite A,
1Chr 6:59 pasture lands, A with its pasture lands,
8:23 sons of Shimei, Ishpan, Eber, Eliel, A,
8:30 also his first-born son, A,
9:36 His first-born son was A;
2Chr 34:20 Hilkiah, to Ahikam, son of Shaphan, to A,

ABEDNEGO (14)

Dn 1: 7 Mishael to Meshach, and Azariah to A.
2:49 and A administrators of the province of
3:12 Shadrach, Meshach, A;
3:13 and sent for Shadrach, Meshach, and A,
3:14 "Is it true, Shadrach, Meshach, and A,
3:16 and A answered King Nebuchadnezzar,
3:19 rage against Shadrach, Meshach, and A.
3:20 army bind Shadrach, Meshach, and A
3:22 who threw Shadrach, Meshach, and A into it.
3:93 and called to Shadrach, Meshach, and A:
3:93 Meshach, and A came out of the fire.
3:95 be the God of Shadrach, Meshach, and A,
3:96 and A shall be cut to pieces and his house
3:97 Meshach, and A in the province of Babylon.

ABEL (16)

Gn 4: 2 Next she bore his brother A.
4: 2 A became a keeper of flocks,
4: 4 God from the fruit of the soil, while A,
4: 4 looked with favor on A and his offering,
4: 8 Cain said to his brother A,
4: 8 Cain attacked his brother A and killed him.
4: 9 LORD asked Cain, "Where is your brother A?"
4:25 granted me more offspring in place of A,"
2Sm 20:14 all the tribes of Israel to A Beth-maacah.
20:15 came and besieged him in A Beth-maacah.
20:18 'Let them ask if they will in A or in Dan
Mt 23:35 from the blood of holy A to the blood of
Lk 11:51 the blood of A to the blood of Zechariah,
Heb 11: 4 By faith A offered God a sacrifice greater
11: 4 although A is dead, he still speaks
12:24 speaks more eloquently than that of A.

ABEL-BETH-MAACAH (2)

1Kgs 15:20 They attacked Ijon, Dan, A,
2Kgs 15:29 king of Assyria, came and took Ijon, A,

ABEL-KERAMIM (1)

Jgs 11:33 (twenty cities in all) and as far as A.

ABEL-MAIM (1)

2Chr 16: 4 They attacked Ijon, Dan, A,

ABEL-MEHOLAH (3)

Jgs 7:22 Zarethan, near the border of A
1Kgs 4:12 below Jezreel from Beth-shean to A;
19:16 of Israel, and Elisha, son of Shaphat of A,

ABEL-MIZRAIM (1)

Gn 50:11 That is why the place was named A.

ABEL-SHITTIM (1)

Nm 33:49 of Moab extended from Beth-jeshimoth to A.

ABETTING (1)

2Mc 4: 4 and Phoenicia, was a Simon's wickedness.

ABHOR (17)

Dt 7:26 and a it utterly as a thing that is doomed.
23: 8 But do not a the Edomite,
Est C:26 and a the bed of the uncircumcised or of
C:27 that I a the sign of grandeur which rests
C:27 a it like a polluted rag,
Jb 9:31 the ditch, so that my garments would a me.
30:10 They a me, they stand aloof from me
Ps(s) 119:163 Falsehood I hate and a; your law I love.
Prv 8: 7 recounts, but the wickedness my lips a.
Sir 13:19 so does the rich man a the poor.
Is 49: 7 To the one despised, whom the nations a,
Hos 1: 6 rather, I a them utterly.
Am 5:10 the gate and a him who speaks the truth.
6: 8 I a the pride of Jacob,
Mi 3: 9 You who a what is just,
Rom 2:22 You who a idols, do you rob temples?
Jude 1:23 a so much as their flesh-stained clothing.

ABHORRED (4)

Lv 26:43 spurned my precepts and a my statutes.
2Mc 5: 8 a as the butcher of his country and his
Jb 19:17 My breath is a by my wife;
Ps(s) 106:40 with his people, and a his inheritance;

ABHORRENCE (2)

Lv 26:30 In my a of you,
Jdt 9: 4 a of the defilement of their kinswoman,

ABHORRENT (6)

Gn 43:32 that is a to them.)
46:34 since all shepherds are a to the Egyptians."
Lv 18:23 such things are a.
20:12 since they have committed an a deed,
Is 66:24 and they shall be a to all mankind.
Hos 9:10 they became as a as the thing they loved.

ABHORS (2)

Ps(s) 5: 7 bloodthirsty and the deceitful the LORD a.
Sir 13:19 A proud man a lowliness;

ABI (1)

2Kgs 18: 2 His mother's name was A,

ABIA (1)

2Chr 29: 1 His mother was named A,

ABIASAPH (2)

Ex 6:24 sons of Korah were Assir, Elkanah and A.
1Chr 26: 1 the son of Kore, one of the sons of A.

ABIATHAR (29)

1Sm 22:20 son of Ahimelech, son of Ahitub, named A,
22:21 When A told David that Saul had slain the
23: 6 A, son of Ahimelech,
23: 9 to harm him, he said to the priest A,
30: 7 in the LORD his God, David said to A,
30: 7 When A brought him the ephod,
2Sm 8:17 son of Ahitub, and Ahimelech, son of A,
15:24 and A brought the ark of God to a halt
15:27 that you and A return to the city in peace,
15:29 So Zadok and A took the ark of God back to
15:35 the priests Zadok and A there with you.
15:35 report it to the priests Zadok and A,
17:15 Hushai said to the priests Zadok and A:
19:12 David sent word to the priests Zadok and A:
20:25 Zadok and A were priests.
1Kgs 1: 7 son of Zeruiah, and with A the priest,
1:19 invited all the king's sons, A the priest,
1:25 commanders of the army, and A the priest,
1:42 speaking, Jonathan, son of A the priest,
2:22 and has with him A the priest and Joab,
2:26 The king said to A the priest:
2:27 A from his office of priest of the LORD,
2:35 and put Zadok the priest in place of A.
4: 4 Zadok and A, priests
1Chr 15:11 David summoned the priests Zadok and A,
18:16 son of Ahitub, and Ahimelech, son of A,
24: 6 the priest, and of Ahimelech, son of A,
27:34 came Jehoiada, the son of Benaiah, and A.
Mk 2:26 God's house in the days of A the high priest

ABIATHAR'S (2)

2Sm 15:27 your own son Ahimaaz, and A son Jonathan.
15:36 Zadok's son Ahimaaz and A son Jonathan.

ABIB (6)

Ex 13: 4 day of your departure is in the month of A.
23:15 at the prescribed time in the month of A,
34:18 month of A you are to eat unleavened bread,
34:18 in the month of A you came out of Egypt.
Dt 16: 1 of A by keeping the Passover of the LORD,
16: 1 since it was in the month of A that he

ABIBAAL (1)

2Sm 23:31 A from Beth-arabah;

ABIDA (2)

Gn 25: 4 of Midian were Ephah, Epher, Hanoch, A,
1Chr 1:33 of Midian were Ephah, Epher, Hanoch, A,

ABIDAN (5)

Nm 1:11 A, son of Gideoni; from Dan:
2:22 [Their prince was A,
7:60 On the ninth day it was the turn of A,
7:65 This was the offering of A,
10:24 the host of the tribe of Manasseh, and A,

ABIDE (28)

Ex 23:33 They must not a in your land,
1Kgs 8:13 house, a dwelling where you may a forever."
1Chr 17:24 God of Israel, may be great and a forever,
29:15 on earth is like a shadow that does not a.
2Chr 6: 2 and dwelling, where you may a forever."
Jb 14: 2 fades, swift as a shadow that does not a.
24:13 they a not in its paths.
Ps(s) 37:27 evil and do good, that you may a forever;
49:13 man, for all his splendor, does not a;
91: 1 High, who a in the shadow of the Almighty,
102:13 But you, O LORD, a forever,
102:29 The children of your servants shall a,
140:12 of wicked tongue shall not a in the land;
Prv 10:30 but the wicked will not a in the land.
15:31 to salutary reproof will a among the wise.
21:16 sense will a in the assembly of the shades.
Wis 3: 9 and the faithful shall a with him in love:
8:12 would a my silence and attend my utterance;
Sir 6:21 The fool cannot a her.
24: 7 in whose inheritance should I a?
50:23 you joy of heart and may peace a among you;
Is 32:16 in the desert and justice a in the orchard.
Jer 15:18 a treacherous brook, whose waters do not a!
Jl 4:20 But Judah shall a forever,
Zec 12: 6 but Jerusalem shall not a on its own site.
14:11 Jerusalem shall a in security.
Gal 3:10 "Cursed is he who does not a by
1Jn 2: 6 a in him to conduct himself just as he did.

ABIDES (16)

Dt 33:12 the day while he a securely at his breast."
2Chr 6:11 in which a the covenant of the LORD which
Jb 41:14 Strength a in his neck,
Ps(s) 16: 9 and my soul rejoices, my body, too, a,
25:13 He a in prosperity,
74: 7 your name a they have razed and profaned.
Prv 14:33 In the heart of the intelligent wisdom a,
Wis 11:21 For with you great strength a always;
Sir 1:13 and with their children her beneficence a.
41: 6 and reproach a with their descendants.
42:24 The universe lives and a forever;
Jas 1:25 peers into freedom's ideal law and a by it.
1Jn 3:15 that eternal life a in no murder's heart.
4:16 love, and he who abides in love a in God,
2Jn 1: 2 that a in us and will be with us forever.

ABIDING (2)

Eccl 2:16 of the fool will there be an a remembrance,
Jn 5:38 neither do you have his word a in your

ABIEL (3)

1Sm 9: 1 Benjamin named Kish, who was the son of A,
14:51 and Ner, Abner's father, were sons of A.
1Chr 11:32 A, from Beth-arabah

ABIEZER (8)

Nm 26:30 through A the clan of the Abiezrites,
Jos 17: 2 descendants of Manasseh, the clans of A,
Jgs 6:34 the horn that summoned A to follow him.
8: 2 of Ephraim better than the vintage of A?
2Sm 23:27 A from Anathoth;
1Chr 7:18 His sister Molecheth bore Ishhod, A,
11:28 A, from Anathoth
27:12 for the ninth month, was A from Anathoth,

ABIEZRITE (1)

Jgs 6:11 in Ophrah that belonged to Joash the A.

ABIEZRITES (3)

Nm 26:30 through Abiezer the clan of the A,
Jgs 6:24 To this day it is still in Ophrah of the A.
8:32 of his father Joash in Ophrah of the A.

ABIGAIL (16)

1Sm 25: 3 The man was named Nabal, his wife A.
25:14 But Nabal's wife A was informed of this by
25:18 A quickly got together two hundred loaves,
25:23 As soon as A saw David,
25:32 David said to A: "Blessed be the LORD
25:36 When A came to Nabal,
25:39 then sent a proposal of marriage to A.
25:40 When David's servants came to A in Carmel,
27: 3 his two wives, Ahinoam from Jezreel and A,
30: 5 two wives, Ahinoam of Jezreel and A,
2Sm 2: 2 his two wives, Ahinoam of Jezreel and A,
3: 3 Chileab, of A the widow of Nabal of Carmel;
17:25 Ishamelite named Ithra, who had married A,
1Chr 2:16 Their sisters were Zeruiah and A.
2:17 A bore Amasa, whose father was Jether
3: 1 the second, Daniel, by A of Carmel;

ABIHAIL (6)

Nm 3:35 the clans of Merari was Zuriel, son of A.
1Chr 2:29 Abishur's wife, who was named A,
5:14 These were the sons of A,
2Chr 11:18 of Jerimoth, son of David and of A,
Est 2:15 daughter of A and adopted daughter of his
9:29 daughter of A and of Mordecai the Jew,

ABIHU (12)

Ex 6:23 she bore him Nadab, A,
24: 1 to the LORD, you and Aaron, with Nadab, A,
24: 9 Moses then went up with Aaron, Nadab, A,
28: 1 Aaron, together with his sons Nadab, A,
Lv 10: 1 sons Nadab and A took their censers and,
Nm 3: 2 sons of Aaron were Nadab his first-born, A,
3: 4 But when Nadab and A offered profane fire
26:60 To Aaron were born Nadab and A,
26:61 But Nadab and A died when they offered
1Chr 5:29 The sons of Aaron were Nadab, A,
24: 1 The sons of Aaron were Nadab, A,
24: 2 Nadab and A died before their father,

ABIJAH (25)

1Sm 8: 2 was named Joel, his second son, A;
1Kgs 14: 1 At that time A, son of Jeroboam
1Chr 3:10 of Solomon was Rehoboam, whose son was A,

ABIJAH (cont.)

6:13 Joel, the first-born, and *A*, the second
7: 8 Eliezer, Elioenai, Omri, Jeremoth, *A*,
24:10 the seventh to Hakkoz, the eighth to *A*,
2Chr 11:20 daughter of Absalom, who bore him *A*,
11:22 Rehoboam constituted *A*,
12:16 His son *A* succeeded him as king.
13: 1 of King Jeroboam, *A* became king of Judah;
13: 2 There was war between *A* and Jeroboam.
13: 3 *A* joined battle with a force of four
13: 4 *A* stood on Mount Zemariam,
13:15 Jeroboam and all Israel before *A* and Judah.
13:17 *A* and his people inflicted a severe defeat
13:19 *A* pursued Jeroboam and took cities from him:
13:20 did not regain power during the time of *A;*
13:21 died, while *A* continued to grow stronger.
13:23 *A* rested with his ancestors;
Neh 10: 8 Daniel, Ginnethon, Baruch, Meshullam, *A*,
12: 4 Rehum, Meremoth, Iddo, Ginnethon, *A*,
12:17 for *A*, Zichri
Mt 1: 7 the father of Abijah, *A* the father of Asa.
Lk 1: 5 Zechariah of the priestly class of *A;*

ABIJAH'S (1)

2Chr 13:22 The rest of *A* acts, his deeds and his words

ABIJAM (4)

1Kgs 14:31 His son *A* succeeded him as king.
15: 1 son of Nebat, *A* became king of Judah;
15: 6 There was war between *A* and Jeroboam.
15: 8 *A* rested with his ancestors;

ABIJAM'S (1)

1Kgs 15: 7 The rest of *A* acts,

ABILENE (1)

Lk 3: 1 Trachonitis, and Lysanias tetrarch of *A*,

ABILITIES (1)

Mt 25:14 over to them according to each man's *a*.

ABILITY (1)

Ex 35:34 of the tribe of Dan, the *a* to teach others.

ABIMAEL (2)

Gn 10:28 Jerah, Hadoram, Uzal, Diklah, Obal, *A*,
1Chr 1:22 Jerah, Hadoram, Uzal, Diklah, Ebal, *A*,

ABIMELECH (57)

Gn 20: 2 So *A*, king of Gerar, sent and took Sarah.
20: 3 to *A* in a dream one night and said to him,
20: 4 *A*, who had not approached her, said:
20: 8 Early the next morning *A* called all his
20: 9 Then *A* summoned Abraham and said to him:
20:14 Then *A* took flocks and herds and male and
20:17 with God, and God restored health to *A*,
21:22 About that time *A*, accompanied by Phicol
21:25 reproached *A* about a well that Abimelech's
21:26 "I have no idea who did that," *A* replied.
21:27 and gave them to *A* and the two made a pact.
21:29 ewe lambs of the flock, and *A* asked him,
21:32 pact in Beer-sheba, *A* along with Phicol,
26: 1 days of Abraham), and Isaac went down to *A*,
26: 8 *A*, king of the Philistines
26:10 "How could you do this to us!" exclaimed *A*
26:11 *A* therefore gave this warning to all his
26:16 So *A* said to Isaac, "Go away from us;
26:26 *A* had meanwhile come to him from Gerar,
Jgs 8:31 also bore him a son, whom he named *A*.
9: 1 *A*, son of Jerubbaal, went to his mother's
9: 3 the citizens of Shechem sympathized with *A*,
9: 4 with which *A* hired shiftless men and
9: 6 proceeded to make *A* king by the terebinth
9:16 and honorably in appointing *A* your king,
9:18 sons upon one stone, and have made *A*,
9:19 rejoice in *A* and may he in turn rejoice
9:20 let fire come forth from *A* to devour the
9:20 of Shechem and Beth-millo, to devour *A*."
9:21 he remained for fear of his brother *A*.
9:22 When *A* had ruled Israel for three years,
9:23 between *A* and the citizens of Shechem,
9:23 of Shechem, who rebelled against *A*.
9:24 avenge their blood upon their brother *A*,
9:25 But it was reported to *A*.
9:27 god, where they ate and drank and cursed *A*.
9:28 Gaal, son of Ebed, said, "Who is *A?*
9:29 I would depose *A*.
9:29 I would say to *A*,
9:31 to *A* in Arumah with the information:
9:34 During the night *A* advanced with all his
9:35 When *A* and his soldiers rose from their
9:38 'Who is *A* that we should serve him?'
9:39 citizens of Shechem and fought against *A*.
9:40 But *A* routed him,
9:41 *A* returned to Arumah,
9:42 taking the field, it was reported to *A*,
9:44 *A* and the company with him dashed in and
9:45 That entire day *A* fought against the city,
9:47 It was reported to *A* that all the citizens
9:49 cut down brushwood, and following *A*,
9:50 *A* proceeded to Thebez,
9:52 *A* came up to the tower and fought against
9:55 When the Israelites saw that *A* was dead,
9:56 Thus did God requite the evil *A* had done
10: 1 After *A* there rose to save Israel the
2Sm 11:21 Who killed *A*, son of Jerubbaal?

ABIMELECH'S (3)

Gn 20:18 closed every womb in *A* household
21:25 a well that *A* men had seized by force.
Jgs 9:53 upper part of a millstone down on *A* head,

ABINADAB (12)

1Sm 7: 1 brought it into the house of *A* on the hill,
16: 8 called *A* and presented him before Samuel,
17:13 the first-born Eliab, the second son *A*,
31: 2 and his sons closely, and slew Jonathan, *A*,
2Sm 6: 3 taken away from the house of *A* on the hill.
6: 3 Uzzah and Ahio, sons of *A*,
1Kgs 4:11 the son of *A*,
1Chr 2:13 the father of Eliab, his first-born, of *A*,
8:33 the father of Jonathan, Malchishua, *A*,
9:39 the father of Jonathan, Malchishua, *A*,
10: 2 the Philistines had killed Jonathan, *A*,
13: 7 of God on a new cart from the house of *A;*

ABINOAM (4)

Jgs 4: 6 She sent and summoned Barak, son of *A*,
4:12 reported to Sisera that Barak, son of *A*,
5: 1 [and Barak, son of *A* sang this song:
5:12 make despoilers your spoil, son of *A*.

ABIRAM (11)

Nm 16: 1 [and Dathan and *A*, sons of Eliab
16:12 Moses summoned Dathan and *A*,
16:24 the Dwelling" [of Korah, Dathan and *A*.
16:25 arose and went to Dathan and *A*
16:27 When Dathan and *A* had come out and were
16:35 the Dwelling [of Korah, Dathan and *A*.
26: 9 descendants of Eliab were Dathan and *A*—
26: 9 the same Dathan and *A*,
Dt 11: 6 he did to the Reubenites Dathan and *A*,
1Kgs 16:34 He lost his first-born son, *A*,
Ps(s) 106:17 up Dathan, and covered the faction of *A*.
Sir 45:18 desert, The followers of Dathan and *A*,

ABISHAG (5)

1Kgs 1: 3 of Israel, and found *A* the Shunamite,
1:15 while *A* the Shunamite was attending him
2:17 to give me *A* the Shunamite for my wife."
2:21 "Let *A* the Shunamite be given to your
2:22 do you ask *A* the Shunamite for Adonijah?"

ABISHAI (25)

1Sm 26: 6 David asked Ahimelech the Hittite, and *A*,
26: 6 *A* replied, "I will."
26: 7 So David and *A* went among Saul's soldiers
26: 8 *A* whispered to David: "God has delivered
26: 9 But David said to *A*,
2Sm 2:18 Joab, *A*, and Asahel.
2:24 Joab and *A*, however, continued
3:30 [Joab and his brother *A* had lain in wait
10:10 under the command of his brother *A*,
10:14 fled from *A* and withdrew into the city.
16: 9 *A*, son of Zeruiah, said to the king:
16:11 the king said to *A* and to all his servants:
18: 2 command, a third under command of *A*,
18: 5 gave this command to Joab, *A* and Ittai:
18:12 for the king charged you and *A* and Ittai
19:22 But *A*, son of Zeruiah, countered:
20: 6 Then David said to *A:*
20: 7 marched out behind *A* from Jerusalem
20:10 Then Joab and his brother *A* pursued Sheba,
21:17 sword and planned to kill David, but *A*,
23:18 *A*, brother of Joab,
1Chr 2:16 *A*, Joab, and Asahel.
18:12 *A*, the son of Zeruiah,
19:11 placed under the command of his brother *A*,
19:15 also took to flight before his brother *A*,

ABISHALOM (2)

1Kgs 15: 2 mother's name was Maacah, daughter of *A*.
15:10 name was Maacah, daughter of *A*.

ABISHUA (5)

1Chr 5:30 Phinehas became the father of *A*.
5:31 *A* became the father of Bukki.
6:35 whose son was Phinehas, whose son was *A*,
8: 4 The sons of Ehud were *A*,
Ezr 7: 5 son of Uzzi, son of Bukki, son of *A*,

ABISHUR (1)

1Chr 2:28 The sons of Shammai were Nadab and *A*.

ABISHUR'S (1)

1Chr 2:29 *A* wife, who was named Abihail,

ABITAL (2)

2Sm 3: 4 the fifth, Shephatiah, son of *A;*
1Chr 3: 3 the fifth, Shephatiah, by *A;*

ABITUB (1)

1Chr 8:11 he became the father of *A* and Elpaal.

ABIUD (2)

Mt 1:13 father of Abiud, *A* the father of Eliakim,

ABJECTION (1)

Ps(s) 136:23 Who remembered us in our *a*,

ABJECTLY (1)

2Chr 33:12 He humbled himself *a* before the God of his

ABLAZE (12)

Dt 5:23 while the mountain was *a* with fire,
2Kgs 22:13 LORD has been set furiously *a* against us,
22:17 my anger is *a* against this place and it
2Chr 34:21 LORD has been set furiously *a* against us,
34:25 my anger is *a* against this place and
Est D: 7 *a* with the height of majestic anger,
2Mc 14:41 and calling for fire to set the door *a*,
Ps(s) 83:15 as a flame setting the mountains *a*,
Prv 29: 8 Arrogant men set the city *a*,
Is 64: 1 As when brushwood is set *a*,
Ob 1:18 and they shall set them *a* and devour them;
Jas 3: 5 the spark is that sets a huge forest *a!*

ABLE (106)

Gn 42:24 When he was *a* to speak to them again,
45:15 then were his brothers *a* to talk with him.
Ex 18:21 all the people for *a* and God-fearing men,
18:23 orders you will be *a* to stand the strain,
18:25 He picked out *a* men from all Israel and
32:30 I may be *a* to make atonement for your sin."
Lv 10:10 You must be *a* to distinguish between what
Nm 5:28 and will still be *a* to bear children.
14:16 'The LORD was not *a* to bring this people
22: 6 We may then be *a* to defeat them and drive
22:11 we may then be *a* to give them battle and
Dt 7:24 No man will be *a* to stand up against you,
9:28 'The LORD was not *a* to bring them into the
14:24 you and you are not *a* to bring your tithe,
19: 3 every homicide will be *a* to find a refuge.
31: 2 and am no longer *a* to move about freely;
Jos 6: 5 they will be *a* to make a frontal attack."
10: 8 Not one of them will be *a* to withstand you."
14:12 is with me I shall be *a* to drive them out,
24:19 "You may not be *a* to serve the LORD,
Jgs 2:14 whom they were no longer *a* to withstand.
8: 3 have I been *a* to do in comparison with you?"
11: 6 that we may be *a* to fight the Ammonites."
12: 6 being *a* to give the proper pronunciation,
20:16 every one of them *a* to sling a stone at a
1Sm 12:11 so that you were *a* to live in security.
14:24 I am *a* to avenge myself on my enemies."
14:45 were *a* to rescue Jonathan from death.
16:18 soldier, besides being an *a* speaker,
2Sm 3:11 was no longer *a* to say a word to him.
1Kgs 3: 9 is *a* to govern this vast people of yours?"
13: 6 that I may be *a* to withdraw my hand."
17:15 She was *a* to eat for a year,
1Chr 29: 2 the house of my God, as far as I was *a*,
2Chr 2: 5 Yet who is really *a* to build him a house,
29:34 few in number to be *a* to skin all the victims
32:13 lands *a* to save their lands from my hand?
32:14 ban was *a* to save his people from my hand?
32:14 god, then, be *a* to save you from my hand?
32:15 *a* to save his people from my hand
Neh 4: 4 Never shall we be *a* the wall to rebuild."
4:10 only half my *a* men took a hand in the work,
5: 8 "As far as we were *a*,
Tb 1:22 behalf, and I was *a* to return to Nineveh.
5: 2 shall I be *a* to obtain the money from him,
11: 8 will again be *a* to see the light of day."
Jdt 5:20 we shall be *a* to go up and conquer them.
11:18 not one of them will be *a* to withstand you.
1Mc 3:53 we be *a* to resist them unless you help us?"
5:40 us first, we shall not be *a* to resist him;
6:27 these, and you will not be *a* to stop them."
9:60 They were not *a* to do this,
13:10 So Simon mustered all the men *a* to fight,
Jb 33: 5 If you are *a*, refute me
Prv 27:11 and I will be *a* to rebut him who taunts me.
Wis 17: 5 force, even of fire, was *a* to give light,
Sir 29: 6 If the lender is *a* to recover barely half,
48:12 nor was any man *a* to intimidate his will.
Is 7: 1 but they were not *a* to conquer it.
Jer 13:23 As easily would you be *a* to do good,
Dn 2:47 is why you were *a* to reveal this mystery."
4:34 those who walk in pride he is *a* to humble.
5:16 if you are *a* to read the writing and tell
6:21 been *a* to save you from the lions?"
Zep 1:18 silver nor their gold shall be *a* to save them
Mt 17:20 you would be *a* to say to this mountain,
Mk 3: 2 to be *a* to bring an accusation against him.
16:18 they will be *a* to handle serpents,

16:18 be *a* to drink deadly poison without harm,
16:20 be *a* to drink deadly poison without harm,
Lk 7:42 Since neither was *a* to repay,
14:29 and then not being *a* to complete the work;
Jn 5:13 great that Jesus had been *a* to slip away.
9: 7 off and washed, and came back *a* to see.
9:11 When I did go and wash, I was *a* to see."
Acts 5:39 you will not be *a* to destroy them without
15:10 neither we nor our fathers were *a* to bear?
20:12 they were *a* to take the boy away alive.
25: 7 him, none of which they were *a* to prove.
26: 2 I count myself fortunate to be *a* to make
27:16 we *a* to gain control of the ship's boat.
Rom 2:18 you know his will and are *a* to make sound
8:39 will be *a* to separate us from the love of
11:23 grafted back on, for God is *a* to do this.
14: 4 will, for the Lord is *a* to make him stand.
15:14 you are *a* to give advice to one another.
16:25 Now to him who is *a* to strengthen you in
1Cor 10:13 of it so that you may be *a* to endure it.
14:16 be *a* to say "Amen" to your thanksgiving?
16: 2 put aside whatever he has been *a* to save,
Eph 3:18 Thus you will be *a* to grasp fully,
6:11 that you may be *a* to stand firm
1Tm 2: 2 that we may be *a* to lead undisturbed and
2Tm 1:12 and I am confident that he is *a* to guard
2: 2 men who will be *a* to teach others.
3: 7 never *a* to reach a knowledge of the truth.
Ti 1: 9 so that he will be *a* both to encourage men
2: 8 be *a* to find anything bad to say about us,
Heb 2:18 he is *a* to help those who are tempted.
5: 2 is *a* to deal patiently with erring sinners,
5: 7 to God, who was *a* to save him from death,
7:25 Therefore he is always *a* to save those who
10: 1 it was never *a* to perfect the worshipers
11:19 that God was *a* to raise from the dead,
13:23 If he is *a* to join me soon,
1Pt 4: 7 remain calm so that you will be *a* to pray.

ABLE-BODIED (3)

Gn 34:24 All the *a* men of the town agreed with
34:24 including every *a* man in the community,
Jdt 14: 2 and let all the *a* men rush out of the city

ABLUTIONS (2)

Ex 30:18 "For *a* you shall make a bronze laver with
Lk 11:38 performed the *a* prescribed before eating.

ABNER (58)

1Sm 14:50 The name of his general was *A*,
17:55 Philistine, he asked his general Abner, "*A*,
17:55 *A* replied, "As truly as your majesty
17:57 *A* took him and presented him to Saul.
20:25 facing him, while *A* sat at the king's side,
26: 5 Saul and *A*, son of Ner, the general
26: 7 *A* and his men sleeping around him.
26:13 remote hilltop at a great distance from *A*,
26:14 He then shouted, "Will you not answer, *A*?"
26:14 *A* answered, "Who is it that calls me?"
26:15 David said to *A*: "Are you not a man
2Sm 2: 8 *A*, son of Ner, Saul's general,
2:12 Now *A*, son of Ner
2:14 Then *A* said to Joab,
2:17 *A* and the men of Israel were defeated by
2:19 in the open field, set out after *A*,
2:20 *A* turned around and said,
2:21 *A* said to him, "Turn right or left;
2:22 Once more *A* said to Asahel:
2:23 So *A* struck him in the abdomen with the
2:24 however, continued the pursuit of *A*.
2:25 Here the Benjaminites rallied around *A*,
2:26 Then *A* called to Joab and said:
2:29 *A* and his men marched all night long
2:30 Joab, after interrupting the pursuit of *A*,
2:31 and sixty men of Benjamin, followers of *A*.
3: 6 *A* was gaining power in the house of Saul.
3: 7 And Ishbaal, son of Saul, said to *A*,
3: 8 Enraged at the words of Ishbaal, *A* said,
3: 9 May God do thus and so to *A* if I do not
3:11 In his fear of *A*,
3:12 Then *A* sent messengers to David in Telam,
3:16 But *A* said to him, "Go back!"
3:17 *A* then said in discussion with the elders
3:19 *A* also spoke personally to Benjamin,
3:20 When *A*, accompanied by twenty men
3:20 for *A* and for the men who were with him.
3:21 Then *A* said to David, "I will now go
3:21 So David bade *A* farewell,
3:22 *A*, having been dismissed by David,
3:23 had with him arrived, he was informed, *A*,
3:24 *A* came to you.
3:25 Are you not aware that *A* came to deceive
3:26 David's knowledge sent messengers after *A*,
3:27 When *A* returned to Hebron,
3:29 full responsibility for the death of *A*,
3:30 Abishai had lain in wait for *A*
3:31 with sackcloth, and mourn over *A*."
3:32 When they had buried *A* in Hebron,
3:32 the king wept aloud at the grave of *A*,
3:33 And the king sang this elegy over *A*:
3:33 "Would *A* have died like a fool?
3:37 the king had no part in the killing of *A*,
4: 1 of Saul, heard that *A* had died in Hebron,
1Kgs 2: 5 the two generals of Israel's armies, *A*,
2:32 *A*, son of Ner, general of Israel's army
1Chr 26:28 *A*, son of Ner
27:21 for Benjamin, Jaasiel, son of *A*;

ABNER'S (2)

1Sm 14:51 Kish, Saul's father, and Ner, *A* father,
2Sm 4:12 Ishbaal and buried it in *A* grave in Hebron.

ABOARD (6)

1Mc 15:37 gotten *a* a ship and escaped to Orthosia.
Jon 1: 3 went *a* to journey with them to Tarshish,
Jn 21:11 Simon Peter went *a* and hauled ashore the
Acts 20:14 Assos we took him *a* and sailed to Mitylene.
27: 6 bound for Italy, and he ordered us *a*.
27:17 They hoisted it *a* and then made use of

ABODE (26)

Gn 28:17 This is nothing else but an *a* of God,
28:22 up as a memorial stone shall be God's *a*.
Lv 13:46 dwell apart, making his *a* outside the camp.
Nm 24:21 Your *a* is enduring,
Dt 12:21 chooses for the *a* of his name is too far,
14:24 for the *a* of his name is too far for you,
26:15 Look down, then, from heaven, your holy *a*,
Tb 3: 6 let me go to the everlasting *a*;
4:10 and keeps one from going into the dark *a*.
Jdt 5: 9 their *a* and proceed to the land of Canaan.
1Mc 1:38 away, and she became the *a* of strangers.
2Mc 6:23 to send him at once to the *a* of the dead,
Jb 18:15 over his *a* brimstone is scattered.
38:19 of light, and where is the *a* of darkness,
Ps(s) 27: 5 hide me in his *a* in the day of trouble;
31:21 within your *a* from the strife of tongues.
74: 2 where you took up your *a*
76: 3 In Salem is his *a*;
Sir 24:10 before him, and in Zion I fixed my *a*.
Is 33:20 let your eyes see Jerusalem as a quiet *a*,
34:13 an *a* for jackals and a haunt for ostriches.
35: 7 The *a* where jackals lurk will be a marsh
Jer 31:23 bless you, holy mountain, *a* of justice!"
50: 7 hope of their fathers, their *a* of justice."
Ob 1: 3 of the rock, whose *a* is in the heights,
Lk 16:23 the *a* of the dead where he was in torment,

ABOLISH (6)

Dn 9:27 the week he shall *a* sacrifice and oblation;
Mi 5:11 *a* the means of divination from your use,
5:12 I will *a* your carved images and the sacred
Na 1:14 I will *a* the carved and the molten image;
Mt 5:17 I have come to *a* the law and the prophets.
5:17 I have come, not to *a* them,

ABOLISHED (5)

1Mc 6:59 was on account of their laws, which we *a*,
2Mc 2:22 the laws that were in danger of being *a*,
Dn 12:11 the daily sacrifice is *a*
Jl 1: 9 *A* are offering and libation from the house
Eph 2:15 *a* the law with its commands and precepts,

ABOLISHING (3)

1Mc 3:29 brought upon the land by *a* the laws
Dn 11:31 *a* the daily sacrifice and setting up the
Rom 3:31 Are we then *a* the law by means of faith?

ABOMINABLE (48)

Lv 18:30 defile yourselves by observing the *a* customs
20:13 shall be put to death for their *a* deed;
Dt 7:26 not bring any *a* thing into your house,
14: 3 "You shall not eat any *a* thing.
20:18 *a* offerings as they make to their gods,
32:16 strange gods and angered him with *a* idols.
1Kgs 14:24 Judah imitated all the *a* practices of the
21:26 He became completely *a* by following idols,
2Kgs 16: 3 in accordance with the *a* practice of the
21: 2 following the *a* practices of the nations
2Chr 28: 3 according to the *a* practice of the nations
33: 2 following the *a* practices of the nations
34:33 Josiah removed every *a* thing from all the
36: 8 of Jehoiakim, the *a* things that he did,
Ezr 9:14 by intermarrying with these *a* peoples?
2Mc 6: 5 with *a* offerings prohibited by the laws.
10:34 blasphemies and uttering *a* words.
Jb 15:16 in his sight, How much less so is the *a*,
Ps(s) 14: 1 they do *a* deeds;
53: 2 they do *a* deeds;
Prv 12:28 is life, but the *a* way leads to death.
24: 9 and sin, it is arrogance that men find *a*.
Wis 14:11 since they have become *a* amid God's works,
Sir 15:13 *A* wickedness the LORD hates,
49: 2 our betrayals, and destroyed the *a* idols.
Jer 6:15 they have done *a* things,
7:30 my name by setting up in it their *a* idols.
8:12 they have done *a* things,
Ez 7:20 made of them their *a* images [their idols].
8: 9 see the *a* evils which they are doing here.
8:17 to do the *a* things they have done here
16:36 your harlotry with your lovers and *a* idols,
16:43 add lewdness to the rest of your *a* deeds?
16:50 and committed *a* crimes in my presence;
16:51 You have done more *a* things than they,
16:51 just, with all the *a* deeds you have done.
16:52 of your sinful deeds, more *a* than theirs,
18:12 raises his eyes to idols, does *a* things,
18:24 kind of *a* things that the wicked man does,
22:11 *a* things with the wives of their neighbors,
33:26 You rely on your sword, you do *a* things,
33:29 because of all the *a* things they have done.
43: 8 profaned my holy name by their *a* deeds;
44:13 disgrace because of all their *a* deeds.
Mal 2:11 an *a* thing has been done in Israel and in
Mt 24:15 "When you see the *a* and destructive thing
Mk 13:14 "When you see the *a* and destructive
Rv 17: 4 the *a* and sordid deeds of her lewdness.

ABOMINABLY (1)

Ez 16:47 did you walk, and act as *a* as they did;

ABOMINATION (41)

Ex 8:22 LORD, our God, are an *a* to the Egyptians.
8:22 we offer sacrifices which are an *a* to them,
Lv 18:22 such a thing is an *a*.
Dt 7:25 for it is an *a* to the LORD,
12:31 their gods every *a* that the LORD detests,
13:15 this *a* has been committed in your midst,
17: 1 that would be an *a* to the LORD,
17: 4 that this *a* has been committed in Israel,
18:12 who does such things is an *a* to the LORD,
22: 5 who does such things is an *a* to the LORD,
23:19 both these things are an *a* to the LORD,
24: 4 That would be an *a* before the LORD,
25:16 any of these matters is an *a* to the LORD,
27:15 an *a* to the LORD,
1Mc 1:48 defiled with every kind of impurity and *a*,
1:54 horrible *a* upon the altar of holocausts,
4:43 the stones of the *A* to an unclean place.
6: 7 pulled down the *A* which he had built
Ps(s) 88: 9 you have made me an *a* to them;
Prv 3:32 To the LORD the perverse man is an *a*,
6:16 the LORD hates, yes, seven are an *a* to him;
11: 1 False scales are an *a* to the LORD,
11:20 The depraved in heart are an *a* to the LORD,
12:22 Lying lips are an *a* to the LORD,
15: 8 of the wicked is an *a* to the LORD,
15: 9 The way of the wicked is an *a* to the LORD,
15:26 wicked man's schemes are an *a* to the LORD,
16: 5 Every proud man is an *a* to the LORD;
17:15 the just, are both an *a* to the LORD.
20:10 measures, are both an *a* to the LORD.
20:23 Varying weights are an *a* to the LORD,
21:27 The sacrifice of the wicked is an *a*,
28: 9 hearing the law, even his prayer is an *a*.
29:27 The evildoer is an *a* to the just,
29:27 who walks uprightly is an *a* to the wicked.
Sir 1:22 but fear of the LORD is an *a* to the sinner.
Is 41:24 To choose you is an *a*.
44:19 Shall I then make an *a* out of the rest,
Dn 9:27 temple wing shall be the horrible *a*
11:31 sacrifice and setting up the horrible *a*.
12:11 is abolished and the horrible *a* is set up,

ABOMINATIONS (44)

Lv 18:26 decrees forbidding all such *a*
18:29 *a* shall be cut off from among his people.
Dt 18: 9 to imitate the *a* of the peoples there.
18:12 the LORD, and because of such *a* the LORD,
2Kgs 21:11 has practiced these *a* and has done greater
2Chr 36:14 practicing all the *a* of the nations and
Ezr 9: 1 of the land and their *a* [Canaanites,
9:11 with the *a* with which they have filled it
Prv 26:25 him not, for seven *a* are in his heart.
Wis 12:23 folly, you tormented through their own *a*.
Is 66: 3 ways and taken pleasure in their own *a*,
Jer 7:10 we can commit all these *a* again"?
16:18 and filling my heritage with their *a*.
32:35 my mind that they should practice such *a*.
Ez 5: 9 Because of all your *a* I will do with you
5:11 my sanctuary with all your detestable *a*,
6: 9 because of their evil deeds, all their *a*.
6:11 of all the *a* of the house of Israel,
7: 3 upon you the consequences of all your *a*.
7: 4 of your *a* shall be in your midst;
7: 8 upon you the consequences of all your *a*.
7: 9 consequences of your *a*
8: 6 Do you see the great *a* that the house of
8: 6 But you shall see still greater *a*!
8:13 still greater *a* that they are practicing.
8:15 You shall see other *a*, greater than these!
9: 4 all the *a* that are practiced within it.
11:18 it and remove from it all its detestable *a*.
11:21 hearts are devoted to their detestable *a*,
12:16 tell of all their *a* among the nations
14: 6 turn yourselves away from all your *a*.
16: 2 Son of man, make known to Jerusalem her *a*:
16:22 And through all your *a* and harlotries you
16:58 The penalty of your lewdness and your *a*—
18:13 Because he practiced all these *a*,
20: 4 the *a* of their ancestors in these words:
22: 2 Then make known all her *a*, and say:

ABOMINATIONS (cont.)

23:36 Then make known to them their a.
36:31 loathe yourselves for your sins and your a.
37:23 themselves with their idols, their a,
44: 6 Enough of all these a of yours,
44: 7 you have broken my covenant by all your a.
Zec 9: 7 meat, and his a from between his teeth:
Rv 17: 5 mother of harlots and all the world's a."

ABOUND (10)

Gn 8:17 and let them a on the earth,
9: 7 a on earth and subdue it."
Ps(s) 4: 8 my heart, more than when grain and wine a.
62:11 take no empty pride; though wealth a,
94:19 When cares a within me,
Is 40:29 for the weak he makes vigor a.
Rom 5:15 of the one man, Jesus Christ, a for all.
6: 1 us continue in sin that grace may a"?
2Cor 8: 7 we bear you, so may you a in this charity.
Phil 1: 9 is that your love may more and more a,

ABOUNDING (5)

Ps(s) 37:11 the land, they shall delight in a peace.
86: 5 a in kindness to all who call upon you.
86:15 slow to anger, a in kindness and fidelity.
103: 8 the LORD, slow to anger and a in kindness.
Sir 44: 2 The a glory of the Most High's portion,

ABOUNDS (1)

Jb 20:22 When he a to overflowing,

ABRAHAM (235)

Gn 17: 5 your name shall be A,
17: 9 God also said to A: "On your part
17:15 God further said to A: "As for your wife
17:17 A prostrated himself and laughed as he
17:18 Then A said to God,
17:22 speaking with him, God departed from A.
17:23 A took his son Ishmael and all his slaves,
17:24 A was ninety-nine years old when the flesh
17:26 day A and his son Ishmael were circumcised;
18: 1 appeared to A by the terebinth of Mamre,
18: 6 A hastened into the tent and told Sarah,
18:11 Now A and Sarah were old,
18:13 But the LORD said to A:
18:16 A was walking with them,
18:17 I hide from A what I am about to do,
18:19 for A the promises he made about him."
18:22 Sodom, the LORD remained standing before A.
18:23 Then A drew nearer to him and said:
18:27 A spoke up again:
18:29 But A persisted,
18:33 speaking with Abraham, and A returned home.
19:27 early the next morning A went
20: 1 A journeyed on to the region of the Negeb,
20: 9 Abimelech summoned A and said to him:
20:11 "I was afraid," answered A,
20:14 male and female slaves and gave them to A;
20:17 A then interceded with God,
21: 2 pregnant and bore A a son in his old age,
21: 3 A gave the name Isaac to this son of his
21: 4 was eight days old, A circumcised him,
21: 5 A was a hundred years old when his son
21: 7 Who would have told A,"
21: 8 the child's weaning, A held a great feast.
21: 9 had borne to A playing with her son Isaac;
21:10 so she demanded of A:
21:11 A was greatly distressed,
21:12 But God said to A: "Do not be distressed
21:14 Early the next morning A got some bread
21:22 the commander of his army, said to A:
21:24 To this A replied, "I so swear."
21:25 A, however, reproached Abimelech
21:27 Then A took sheep and cattle and gave them
21:28 A also set apart seven ewe lambs of the
21:30 A answered, "The seven ewe lambs
21:33 A planted a tamarisk at Beer-sheba,
21:34 A resided in the land of the Philistines
22: 1 after these events, God put A to the test.
22: 1 He called to him, A!"
22: 3 the next morning A saddled his donkey,
22: 4 day A got sight of the place from afar.
22: 6 Thereupon A took the wood for the
22: 7 on together, Isaac spoke to his father A.
22: 8 "Son," A answered,
22: 9 A built an altar there and arranged the
22:11 called to him from heaven, "Abraham, A!"
22:13 As A looked about,
22:14 A named the site Yahweh-yireh;
22:15 messenger called to A from heaven and said:
22:19 A then returned to his servants,
22:19 for Beer-sheba, where A made his home.
22:20 Some time afterward, the news came to A:
23: 2 and A performed the customary mourning
23: 5 The Hittites answered A:
23: 7 A, however, began to bow low
23:10 So Ephron the Hittite replied to A in the
23:12 But A, after bowing low
23:14 Ephron replied to A, "Please.
23:16 A accepted Ephron's terms;
23:18 was conveyed to A by purchase in the
23:19 A buried his wife Sarah in the cave of the
23:20 from the Hittites to A as a burial place.
24: 1 A had now reached a ripe old age,
24: 2 A said to the senior servant of his
24: 6 back there for any reason," A told him.
24: 9 A and swore to him in this undertaking.
24:12 "LORD, God of my master A,
24:12 and thus deal graciously with my master A.
24:27 be the LORD, the God of my master A,
24:42 'LORD, God of my master A,
24:48 blessing the LORD, the God of my master A,
25: 1 A married another wife,
25: 5 A deeded everything that he owned to his
25:10 field that A had bought from the Hittites;
25:11 After the death of A, God blessed his son
25:12 the Egyptian, Sarah's slave, bore to A.
25:19 family history of Isaac, son of A; Abraham
26: 1 one that had occurred in the days of A),
26: 3 of the oath that I swore to your father A.
26: 5 this because A obeyed me,
26:15 had dug back in the days of his father A.)
26:18 dug back in the days of his father A
26:24 "I am the God of your father A.
26:24 descendants for the sake of my servant A."
28: 4 descendants the blessing he gave to A,
28: 4 you are staying, which he assigned to A."
28:13 of your forefather A and the God of Isaac;
31:42 the God of A and the Awesome One of Isaac,
31:53 May the God of A and the god of Nahor
32:10 of my father A and God of my father Isaac!
35:12 once gave to A and Isaac I now give to you;
35:27 is, Hebron], where A and Isaac had stayed.
48:15 whose ways my fathers A and Isaac walked,
48:16 and the names of my fathers A and Isaac,
49:30 the field that A bought from Ephron the
49:31 There A and his wife Sarah are buried,
50:13 the field that A had bought for a burial
50:24 to the land that he promised on oath to A,
Ex 2:24 and was mindful of his covenant with A,
3: 6 father," he continued, "the God of A,
3:15 the God of your fathers, the God of A,
3:16 the God of your fathers, the God of A,
4: 5 the God of their fathers, the God of A,
6: 3 As God the Almighty I appeared to A,
6: 8 into the land which I swore to give to A,
32:13 Remember your servants A,
33: 1 from here to the land which I swore to A,
Lv 26:42 with Isaac, and my covenant with A;
Nm 32:11 under oath to A and Isaac and Jacob.
Dt 1: 8 the land I swore to your fathers, A,
6:10 land which he swore to your fathers, A,
9: 5 which he made on oath to your fathers, A,
9:27 Remember your servants, A, Isaac
29:12 you and as he swore to your fathers A,
30:20 LORD swore he would give to your fathers A,
34: 4 "This is the land which I swore to A,
Jos 24: 2 down to Terah, father of A and Nahor,
24: 3 But I brought your father A from the
1Kgs 18:36 came forward and said, "LORD, God of A,
2Kgs 13:23 compassion because of his covenant with A,
1Chr 1:27 Reu, Serug, Nahor, Terah, Abram, who was A.
1:28 The sons of A were Isaac and Ishmael.
1:34 A became the father of Isaac.
16:16 into with A and by his oath to Isaac;
29:18 O LORD, God of our fathers A,
2Chr 20: 7 gave it forever to the descendants of A,
30: 6 return to the LORD, the God of A,
Neh 9: 7 from Ur of the Chaldees, and named him A.
Tb 4:12 My boy, keep in mind Noah, A,
14: 7 shall they dwell forever in the land of A,
Jdt 8:26 Recall how he dealt with A,
Est C: 8 And now, Lord God, King, God of A,
C:29 had no joy except in you, O Lord, God of A.
1Mc 2:52 Was not A found faithful in trial,
12:21 both nations descended from A.
2Mc 1: 2 his covenant with his faithful servants, A,
Ps(s) 47:10 together with the people of the God of A.
105: 6 You descendants of A,
105: 9 into with A and by his oath to Isaac;
105:42 remembered his holy word to his servant A.
Sir 44:19 A, father of many peoples,
44:22 he renewed the same promise because of A,
Is 29:22 God of the house of Jacob, who redeemed A:
41: 8 offspring of A my friend
51: 2 Look to A, your father,
63:16 Were A not to know us,
Jer 33:26 his descendants rulers for the race of A,
Bar 2:34 oath I promised to their fathers, to A,
Ez 33:24 A, though but a single individual,
Dn 3:35 your mercy from us, for the sake of A,
Mi 7:20 faithfulness to Jacob, and grace to A,
Mt 1: 1 of Jesus Christ, son of David, son of A.
1: 2 A was the father of Isaac,
1:17 from A to David, fourteen generations;
3: 9 yourselves on the claim, A is our father.'
3: 9 up children to A from these very stones.
8:11 the banquet in the kingdom of God with A,
22:32 what God said to you, 'I am the God of A,
Mk 12:26 bush, how God told him, 'I am the God of A,
Lk 1:55 promised A and his descendants forever."
1:73 he swore to A our father he would grant us:
3: 8 by saying to yourselves, A is our father.'
3: 8 raise up children to A from these stones.
3:34 son of Jacob, son of Isaac, son of A,
13:16 Should not this daughter of A here who has
13:28 and grinding of teeth when you see A,
16:22 carried by angels to the bosom of A.
16:23 he raised his eyes and saw A afar off,
16:24 "He called out, 'Father A, have pity on me.
16:25 'My child,' replied A,
16:29 A answered, 'They have Moses
16:30 'No, Father A,' replied the rich man.
16:31 A said to him, 'If they do not listen
19: 9 for this is what it means to be a son of A.
20:37 when he called the Lord the God of A,
Jn 8:33 "We are descendants of A,"
8:39 They retorted, "Our father is A."
8:40 A did nothing like that.
8:52 A is dead.
8:53 pretend to be greater than our father A,
8:56 father A rejoiced that he might see my day.
8:57 How can you have seen A?"
8:58 before A came to be, I AM."
Acts 3:13 The God of A,
3:25 made with your fathers when he said to A,
7: 2 The God of glory appeared to our father A
7: 8 circumcision with him, and A
7:16 in the tomb which A had bought
7:17 of the promise made by God to A,
7:32 am the God of your fathers, the God of A,
13:26 children of the family of A
Rom 4: 1 What, then, shall we say of A,
4: 2 Certainly if A was justified by his deeds
4: 3 A believed God,
4:12 which A walked while still uncircumcised.
4:13 Certainly the promise made to A and his
4:18 A believed and so became the father of
11: 1 I myself am an Israelite, descended from A,
2Cor 11:22 Are they the seed of A?
Gal 3: 6 Consider the case of A:
3: 7 means that those who believe are sons of A.
3: 8 faith, it foretold this good news to A:
3: 9 all who believe are blessed along with A,
3:14 blessing bestowed on A might descend
3:16 spoken to A and to his "descendant."
3:18 promise that God granted A his privilege.
3:29 to Christ you are the descendants of A,
4:22 There it is written that A had two sons,
Heb 2:16 angels, but rather the children of A;
6:13 When God made his promise to A,
6:15 waiting, A obtained what God had promised.
7: 1 met A returning from his defeat of the
7: 2 And A apportioned to him one tenth of all
7: 4 See the greatness of this man to whom A
7: 5 though all of them are descendants of A;
7: 6 received tithes of A and blessed him who
7:10 his father's loins when Melchizedek met A.
11: 8 By faith A obeyed when he was called,
11:17 By faith A, when put to the test,
Jas 2:21 Was not our father A justified by his
2:23 was fulfilled which says, A believed God,
1Pt 3: 6 was subject to A and called him her master.

ABRAHAM'S (19)

Gn 17:23 male among the members of A household
20:18 household on account of A wife Sarah.
22:23 eight Milcah bore to A brother Nahor.
24:15 the wife of A brother Nahor) came out with
24:34 "I am A servant," he began.
24:52 When A servant heard their answer,
24:59 leave, along with A servant and his men.
25: 7 The whole span of A life was one hundred
25:12 These are the descendants of A son Ishmael,
26:18 Philistines had stopped up after A death;
28: 9 of A son Ishmael and sister of Nebaioth.
1Chr 1:32 The descendants of Keturah, A concubine:
Jn 8:37 I realize you are one of A stock.
8:39 "If you were A children,
8:39 children, you would be following A example.
Acts 7: 6 A posterity will be strangers in a foreign
Rom 4: 9 say that A faith was "credited as justice."
4:16 promise holds true for all A descendants,
9: 7 nor are all A descendants his children,

ABRAM (58)

Gn 11:26 years old, he became the father of A,
11:27 Terah became the father of A,
11:29 A and Nahor took wives;
11:31 Terah took his son A,
11:31 Sarai, the wife of his son A,
12: 1 The LORD said to A: "Go forth
12: 4 in you," A went as the LORD directed him,
12: 4 A was seventy-five years old when he left
12: 5 A took his wife Sarai, his brother's son
12: 6 A passed through the land as far as the
12: 7 The LORD appeared to A and said,
12: 7 So A built an altar there to the LORD who
12: 9 Then A journeyed on by stages to the Negeb.
12:10 so A went down to Egypt to sojourn there,
12:14 When A came to Egypt,
12:16 On her account it went very well with A,
12:18 Then Pharaoh summoned A and said to him:
13: 1 From Egypt A went up to the Negeb with his
13: 2 Now A was very rich in livestock,
13: 5 Lot, who went with A,

13: 8 *A* said to Lot: "Let there be no strife
13:12 *A* stayed in the land of Canaan,
13:14 After Lot had left, the LORD said to *A:*
13:18 *A* moved his tents and went on to settle
14:13 came and brought the news to *A* the Hebrew,
14:13 these were in league with *A.*
14:14 *A* heard that his nephew had been captured,
14:17 When *A* returned from his victory over
14:18 Most High, he blessed *A* with these words:
14:19 "Blessed be *A* by God Most High,
14:20 Then *A* gave him a tenth of everything.
14:21 The king of Sodom said to *A,*
14:22 But *A* replied to the king of Sodom:
14:23 yours, lest you should say, 'I made *A* rich.'
15: 1 word of the LORD came to *A* in a vision:
15: 1 "Fear not, *A!* I am your shield."
15: 2 But *A* said, "O Lord GOD,
15: 3 *A* continued, "See, you have given me no
15: 6 *A* put his faith in the LORD,
15:11 on the carcasses, but *A* stayed with them.
15:12 was about to set, a trance fell upon *A,*
15:13 the LORD said to *A:* "Know for certain
15:18 that the LORD made a covenant with *A,*
16: 2 Sarai said to *A:* "The LORD has kept me
16: 2 *A* heeded Sarai's request.
16: 3 after *A* had lived ten years in the land of
16: 3 her to her husband *A* to be his concubine.
16: 5 So Sarai said to *A:* "You are responsible
16: 6 *A* told Sarai: "Your maid is in your power
16:15 Hagar bore *A* a son, and Abram named
16:16 *A* was eighty-six years old when Hagar bore
17: 1 When *A* was ninety-nine years old,
17: 3 When *A* prostrated himself,
17: 5 No longer shall you be called *A;*
19:29 he was mindful of *A* by sending Lot away
1Chr 1:27 Eber, Peleg, Reu, Serug, Nahor, Terah, *A,*
Neh 9: 7 "You, O LORD, are the God who chose *A,*

ABRAM'S (5)

Gn 11:29 the name of *A* wife was Sarai,
12:17 severe plagues because of *A* wife Sarai.
13: 7 herdsmen of *A* livestock and those of Lot's.
14:12 their way, taking with them *A* nephew Lot,
16: 1 *A* wife Sarai had borne him no children.

ABREAST (3)

Jgs 19:14 when they were *a* of Gibeah of Benjamin.
2Sm 16:13 Shimei kept *a* of them on the hillside,
Jdt 4: 7 the defile was only wide enough for two *a.*

ABREK (1)

Gn 41:43 chariot of his vizier, and they shouted *A!*"

ABROAD (17)

Dt 6: 7 Speak of them at home and *a,*
11:19 children, speaking of them at home and *a,*
Jos 10: 2 them and that there was great fear *a,*
1Chr 14:17 fame was spread *a* through every land,
1Mc 3: 3 He spread *a* the glory of his people,
Jb 12:23 he spreads peoples *a* and he abandons them.
38:41 out to God, and they rove *a* without food?
Ps(s) 31:12 they who see me *a* flee from me.
77:18 your arrows also sped *a.*
Prv 5:16 How may your water sources be dispersed *a,*
Sg 4:16 my garden that its perfumes may spread *a.*
Wis 2: 3 will be poured *a* like unresisting air.
Is 54: 3 spread *a* to the right and to the left;
Hos 7: 1 thieves break in, bandits plunder *a.*
Mk 13:34 It is like a man traveling *a.*
2Cor 9: 9 "He scattered *a* and gave to the poor,
Jude 1:13 their shameless deeds *a* like foam,

ABROGATED (1)

2Mc 4:11 he *a* the lawful institutions and

ABRON (1)

Jdt 2:24 down every fortified city along the Wadi *A,*

ABRONAH (2)

Nm 33:34 out from Jotbathah, they camped at *A.*
33:35 Setting out from *A,* they camped

ABRUPTLY (5)

Ps(s) 140:12 evil shall *a* entrap the violent man.
Wis 3:18 While should they die *a,*
5:13 *a* came to nought and held no sign of
5:22 them and the streams shall *a* overflow;
Mt 16: 4 With that he left them *a.*

ABSALOM (95)

2Sm 3: 3 the third, *A,* son of Maacah
13: 1 son *A* had a beautiful sister named Tamar,
13:20 Her brother *A* said to her:
13:20 and forlorn in the house of her brother *A.*
13:22 *A,* moreover, said nothing at all to Amnon,
13:23 *A* had shearers in Baal-hazor near Ephraim,
13:24 *A* went to the king and said:
13:25 the King said to *A,* "No, my son, all of us
13:25 And though *A* urged him,
13:26 *A* then said, "If you will not come
13:27 *A* prepared a banquet fit for royalty.
13:29 servants did to Amnon as *A* had commanded,
13:30 a report reached David that *A* had killed
13:32 for *A* was determined on this ever since
13:34 Meanwhile, *A* had taken flight.
13:37 *A,* who had taken flight, went to Talmai
13:39 but his longing reached out for *A* as he
14: 1 observed how the king felt toward *A,*
14:21 Go, therefore, and bring back young *A.*"
14:23 off to Geshur and brought *A* to Jerusalem.
14:24 So *A* went off to his house and did not
14:25 could so be praised for his beauty as *A,*
14:27 *A* had three sons born to him,
14:28 *A* lived in Jerusalem for two years without
14:31 Joab went to *A* in his house and asked him,
14:32 *A* answered Joab: "I was summoning you
14:33 The king then called *A,*
15: 1 this *A* provided himself with chariots,
15: 2 *A* used to rise early and stand alongside
15: 2 by the king, *A* would call to him and say,
15: 3 a tribe of Israel," *A* would say to him,
15: 6 *A* was stealing away the loyalties of the
15: 7 a period of four years, *A* said to the king:
15:10 Then *A* sent spies throughout the tribes of
15:10 of the horn, declare *A* king in Hebron."
15:11 men had accompanied *A* from Jerusalem.
15:12 *A* also sent to Ahithophel the Gilonite,
15:12 and the people with *A* increased in numbers.
15:13 have transferred their loyalty to *A.*"
15:14 flight, or none of us will escape from *A.*
15:31 was among the conspirators with *A,*
15:34 if you return to the city and say to *A,*
15:37 of Jerusalem as *A* was about to enter it.
16: 8 has given over the kingdom to your son *A.*
16:15 *A,* accompanied by Ahithophel
16:16 friend Hushai the Archite came to *A,*
16:17 But *A* asked Hushai: "Is this your devotion
16:18 Hushai replied to *A:* "On the contrary
16:20 Then *A* said to Ahithophel,
16:21 Ahithophel replied to *A:*
16:22 So a tent was pitched on the roof for *A,*
16:23 was all his counsel both to David and to *A.*
17: 1 Ahithophel went on to say to *A:*
17: 4 to *A* and to all the elders of Israel.
17: 5 *A* said, "Now call Hushai the Archite
17: 6 When Hushai came to *A,*
17: 7 Hushai replied to *A,*
17:14 Then *A* and all the Israelites pronounced
17:14 counsel, in order thus to bring *A* to ruin.
17:15 Ahithophel gave *A* and the elders of Israel,
17:18 But an attendant saw them and informed *A.*
17:24 Now David had gone to Mahanaim when *A*
17:25 *A* had put Amasa in command of the army in
17:26 and *A* encamped in the territory of Gilead.
18: 5 "Be gentle with young *A* for my sake."
18: 5 the various leaders with regard to *A.*
18: 9 *A* unexpectedly came up against David's
18:10 he had seen *A* hanging from a terebinth.
18:12 to protect the youth *A* for his sake.
18:14 in hand, he thrust for the heart of *A,*
18:15 Joab's young armor-bearers closed in on *A,*
18:17 *A* was taken up and cast into a deep pit in
18:18 During his lifetime *A* had taken a pillar
18:29 But the king asked, "Is the youth *A* safe?"
18:32 king asked the Cushite, "Is young *A* safe?"
19: 1 He said as he wept, "My son *A!*
19: 1 If only I had died instead of you, *A,*
19: 2 the king was weeping and mourning for *A;*
19: 5 "My son *A!* Absalom!
19: 7 if *A* were alive today and all of us dead,
19:10 now he has fled from the country before *A,*
19:11 from the country before Absalom, and *A,*
20: 6 may now do us more harm than *A* did.
1Kgs 1: 6 and next in age to *A* by the same mother.
2: 7 kindly when I was fleeing your brother *A.*
2:28 sided with Adonijah, though not with *A,*
1Chr 3: 2 the third, *A,* son of Maacah,
2Chr 11:20 her, he married Maacah, daughter of *A,*
11:21 Rehoboam loved Maacah, daughter of *A,*
1Mc 11:70 the army commanders Mattathias, son of *A,*
13:11 He sent Jonathan, son of *A,*
2Mc 11:17 John and *A,* your envoys,

ABSALOM'S (5)

2Sm 13: 4 am in love with Tamar, my brother *A* sister."
13:27 At *A* urging, however, he sent Amnon
14:30 And so *A* servants set the field on fire.
17: 9 say, *A* followers have been slaughtered.'
17:20 *A* servants came to the woman at the house,

ABSENCE (5)

Mt 25:19 After a long *a,* the master of those servants
Acts 24:17 "After several years' *a,* I had come to bring
1Cor 16:17 Achaicus, because they made up for your *a.*
2Cor 10:11 are by word, in the letters during our *a,*
13: 2 and I repeat it now in my *a*

ABSENT (11)

Nm 9:10 of a corpse, or if he is *a* on a journey,
2Kgs 10:19 See that no one is *a,*
10:19 Whoever is *a* shall not live."
Wis 14:17 honor, out of zeal to flatter him when *a,*
Sir 38:16 the body, *a* not yourself from his burial:
Jn 20:24 means "Twin"), was *a* when Jesus came.
1Cor 5: 3 though *a* in body I am present in spirit,
2Cor 10: 1 am lowly, but when *a* am bold toward you.
Phil 2:12 with you but all the more now that I am *a.*
Col 2: 5 be *a* in body but I am with you in spirit,
Heb 10:25 should not *a* ourselves from the assembly,

ABSOLUTE (7)

Sir 37:18 and life, their *a* mistress is the tongue.
Dn 6:13 The king answered them, "The decree is *a,*
7:26 is taken away by final and *a* destruction,
2Cor 11:21 I speak with *a* foolishness now
Col 1:19 It pleased God to make *a* fullness reside
1Tm 5: 2 younger women as sisters, with *a* purity.
Heb 10:22 near in utter sincerity and *a* confidence,

ABSOLUTELY (1)

Ex 21:11 things, she shall be given her freedom *a,*

ABSOLVE (2)

Dt 21: 8 *A,* O LORD, your people Israel
Jb 10:14 me, and from my guilt you would not *a* me.

ABSOLVED (1)

Dt 21: 8 shall be *a* from the guilt of bloodshed,

ABSOLVING (1)

2Chr 6:23 but *a* the innocent and rewarding him

ABSORB (2)

1Cor 7:34 has the cares of this world to *a* her and
1Tm 4:15 let them *a* you,

ABSORBED (3)

Mk 1:35 there he was *a* in prayer.
Acts 18: 5 Paul was *a* in preaching and giving
2Cor 5: 4 so that what is mortal may be *a* by life.

ABSTAIN (8)

Nm 6: 3 he shall *a* from wine and strong drink;
Dt 12:25 *A* from it, that you and your children
Jgs 13:13 "Your wife is to *a* from all the things of
Zec 7: 3 "Must I mourn and *a* in the fifth month as
Acts 15:20 to *a* from anything contaminated by idols,
15:29 namely, to *a* from meat sacrificed to idols,
1Thes 4: 3 that you *a* from immorality,
Ti 3: 9 *a* from stupid arguments and genealogies,

ABSTAINED (2)

1Sm 21: 5 if the men have *a* from women,
Rom 14:21 be acting nobly if you *a* from eating meat,

ABSTAINING (1)

Jer 17:24 the sabbath holy and *a* from all work on it,

ABSTAINS (3)

Rom 14: 3 not ridicule him who *a* from certain foods;
14: 3 the man who *a* must not sit in judgment
14: 6 man who does not eat *a* to honor the Lord,

ABSTEMIOUS (1)

Sir 37:30 have died, but the *a* man prolongs his life.

ABSTINENCE (2)

Nm 30: 3 binds himself under oath to a pledge of *a,*
1Tm 4: 3 require *a* from foods which God created

ABSURD (1)

1Cor 1:27 the world considers *a* to shame the wise;

ABSURDITY (5)

1Cor 1:18 *a* to those who are headed for ruin,
1:21 the *a* of the preaching of the gospel.
1:23 block to Jews, and an *a* to Gentiles;
2:14 For him, that is *a.* He cannot come to know
3:19 for the wisdom of this world is *a* with God.

ABUBUS (2)

1Mc 16:11 Ptolemy, son of *A,* had been appointed
16:15 The son of *A* gave them a deceitful welcome

ABUNDANCE (43)

Gn 1:20 water teem with an *a* of living creatures,
27:28 fertility of the earth *a* of grain and wine.
33:11 been generous toward me, and I have an *a.*"
41:29 Seven years of great *a* are now coming
41:30 *a* in the land of Egypt will be forgotten.
41:31 no trace of the *a* will be found in the
41:34 the land during the seven years of *a.*
41:53 When the seven years of *a* enjoyed by the
Lv 25:19 its fruit and you will have food in *a,*
26: 5 and you will have food to eat in *a,*

ABUNDANCE (cont.)

Nm 20:11 and water gushed out in *a* for the
Dt 28:47 with joy and gratitude for *a* of every kind,
33:19 Because you suck up the *a* of the seas and
Ru 1:21 I went away with an *a*,
1Kgs 10:10 Never again did anyone bring such an *a* of
1Chr 22: 5 his death David laid up materials in *a*.
2Chr 11:23 and sought an *a* of wives for them.
18: 1 therefore had wealth and glory in *a*;
20:25 found an *a* of cattle and personal property,
32: 4 of Assyria come and find an *a* of water?"
Neh 5:18 all kinds of wine in *a* every ten days,
9:25 olive groves, and fruit trees in *a*.
Tb 4: 8 great wealth, give alms out of your *a*;
12: 8 is better than *a* with wickedness.
Jdt 5: 9 gold, silver, and a great *a* of livestock.
Jb 31:25 was great, or that my hand had acquired *a*—
36:31 the nations, and gives them food in *a*.
Ps(s) 17:14 and bequeath their *a* to their little ones.
49: 7 the *a* of their riches is their boast.
72:16 May there be an *a* of grain upon the earth;
Eccl 5:11 but the rich man's *a* allows him no sleep.
Is 30:33 it is piled with dry grass and wood in *a*,
Jer 33: 6 and reveal to them an *a* of lasting peace.
Lam 3:32 he takes pity, in the *a* of his mercies;
Hos 2:10 the wine, and the oil, And her *a* of silver,
Zec 14:14 gold, silver, and garments, in great *a*.
Lk 6:45 Each man speaks from his heart's *a*.
Rom 15:13 of the Holy Spirit you may have hope in *a*.
2Cor 4:15 so that the grace bestowed in *a* may bring
9:10 and bread for the eater will provide in *a*;
Phil 4:12 low, yet I know what it is to have an *a*.
1Pt 1: 2 Favor and peace be yours in *a*.
2Pt 1: 2 may grace be yours and peace in *a* through

ABUNDANT (31)

Gn 41:47 of plenty, when the land produced *a* crops,
1Chr 4:40 They found *a* and good pastures,
Jdt 2:18 *a* provisions for each man,
1Mc 6: 6 and *a* possessions taken from the armies
2Mc 2:24 narratives where the material is *a*,
Ps(s) 5: 8 But I, because of your *a* kindness,
106: 7 They remembered not your *a* kindness,
106:45 covenant and relented, in his *a* kindness,
132:15 I will bless her with *a* provision,
145: 7 They publish the fame of your *a* goodness
Prv 20:13 eyes wide open mean *a* food.
Wis 10:10 labors and made *a* the fruit of his works,
11: 7 gave them *a* water in an unhoped-for way,
Sir 20:27 He who works his land has *a* crops,
Is 7:22 *a* yield of milk he shall live on curds:
9: 2 brought them *a* joy and great rejoicing,
30:23 that the soil produces will be rich and *a*.
35: 2 They will bloom with *a* flowers,
66:11 may nurse with delight at her *a* breasts!
Ez 19:10 and branchy was she because of the *a* water.
31: 5 longer of branch because of the *a* water.
31: 7 for its roots were turned toward *a* water.
32:13 of her animals perish beside her *a* waters;
36:29 I will order the grain to be *a*,
47: 9 shall live, and there shall be *a* fish,
Dn 3:98 wherever they dwell on earth *a* peace!
4: 9 Its leaves were beautiful and its fruit *a*,
4:18 which had beautiful foliage and *a* fruit,
11:39 him he shall provide with *a* honor;
Hos 10: 1 The more *a* his fruit, the more altars
2Cor 8: 2 poverty have produced an *a* generosity.

ABUNDANTLY (5)

Gn 22:17 I will bless you *a* and make your
24:35 so *a* that he has become a wealthy man;
Dt 15: 4 will bless you *a* in the land he will give
Jn 15: 5 lives in me and I am him, will produce *a*,
2Cor 1: 5 Christ do we share *a* in his consolation.

ABUSE (12)

Jgs 19:22 "Bring out your guest, that we may *a* him."
Tb 3: 7 daughter Sarah also had to listen to *a*,
Sir 22:24 so does *a* come before bloodshed.
27:28 Mockery and *a* will be the lot of the proud,
29: 6 pays him back, with *a* instead of honor.
29:28 *a* at home and insults from his creditors.
Am 4: 1 You who oppress the weak and *a* the needy;
Lk 12:45 begins to *a* the housemen and servant girls,
Acts 13:45 with violent *a* whatever Paul said.
14: 5 with their leaders, to *a* and stone them.
1Tm 6: 1 of God and the church's teaching suffer *a*.
2Pt 2:12 *a* on things of which they are ignorant.

ABUSED (3)

Gn 16: 6 *a* her so much that Hagar ran away from her.
Jgs 19:25 *a* her all night until the following dawn,
20: 5 and my concubine they *a* so that she died.

ABUSIVE (5)

Gn 16: 9 mistress and submit to her *a* treatment.
Sir 23:15 A man who has the habit of *a* language will
Mt 5:22 any man who uses *a* language toward his
1Cor 5:11 covetous, an idolater, an *a* person,
2Tm 3: 2 of self and of money, proud, arrogant, *a*,

ABYSMAL (1)

Ps(s) 69: 3 in the *a* swamp where there is no foothold;

ABYSS (33)

Gn 1: 2 wasteland, and darkness covered the *a*,
7:11 the fountains of the great *a* burst forth,
8: 2 The fountains of the *a* and the floodgates
49:25 the blessings of the *a* that crouches below,
Dt 33:13 skies above and of the *a* crouching beneath;
Tb 13: 2 world, and he brings up from the great *a*.
Jb 28:14 The *a* declares, "It is not in me"
31:12 fire that should burn down to the *a*
38:16 or walked about in the depths of the *a*?
Ps(s) 69:16 overwhelm me, nor the *a* swallow me up,
88: 7 the bottom of the pit, into the dark *a*.
107:24 works of the LORD and his wonders in the *a*.
Prv 15:11 world and the *a* lie open before the LORD;
27:20 nether world and the *a* are never satisfied;
Sir 1: 3 earth's breadth, the depths of the *a*:
12:16 heart he schemes to plunge you into the *a*.
16:16 earth and the *a* tremble at his visitation;
24: 5 alone, through the deep *a* I wandered.
24:27 her counsels, than the great *a*.
Ez 26:19 when I churn up the *a* against you,
31: 4 made it grow, the *a* made it flourish,
31:15 world I made the *a* close up over him;
Am 7: 4 It had devoured the great *a*,
Jon 2: 6 the *a* enveloped me;
Lk 8:31 with him not to order them back to the *a*.
16:26 you and us there is fixed a great *a*,
Rom 10: 7 down), or "Who shall go down into the *a*?'
Rv 9: 1 was given the key to the shaft of the *a*;
9:11 king was the angel in charge of the *a*,
11: 7 wild beast that comes up from the *a*
17: 8 the *a* once more before going to final ruin.
20: 1 key to the *a* and a huge chain in his hand.
20: 3 The angel hurled him into the *a*,

ACACIA (28)

Ex 25: 5 *a* wood; oil for the light;
25:10 "You shall make an ark of *a* wood,
25:13 poles of *a* wood and plate them with gold.
25:23 "You shall also make a table of *a* wood,
25:28 shall make of *a* wood and plate with gold.
26:15 boards of *a* wood as walls for the Dwelling.
26:26 Also make bars of *a* wood:
26:32 hung on four gold-plated columns of *a* wood,
26:37 five columns of *a* wood for this curtain;
27: 1 "You shall make an altar of *a* wood,
27: 6 also make poles of *a* wood for the altar,
30: 1 incense you shall make an altar of *a* wood,
30: 5 Make the poles, too, of *a* wood
35: 7 *a* wood; oil for light
35:24 to have *a* wood for any part of the work,
36:20 *a* wood were made as walls for the Dwelling.
36:31 Bars of *a* wood were also made,
36:36 Four gold-plated columns of *a* wood,
37: 1 Bezalel made the ark of *a* wood,
37: 4 of *a* wood were made and plated with gold;
37:10 The table was made of *a* wood,
37:15 were made of *a* wood and plated with gold.
37:25 The altar of incense was made of *a* wood,
37:28 were made of *a* wood and plated with gold.
38: 1 The altar of holocausts was made of *a* wood,
38: 6 were made of *a* wood and plated with bronze.
Dt 10: 3 So I made an ark of *a* wood,
Is 41:19 I will plant in the desert the cedar, *a*,

ACCAD (1)

Gn 10:10 of his kingdom were Babylon, Erech, and *A*,

ACCEDE (1)

Jgs 20:13 to *a* to the demand of their brothers,

ACCEDED (1)

Dn 1:14 He *a* to this request, and tested them

ACCEDING (1)

2Chr 10: 7 and give in to them, *a* to their request,

ACCENT (1)

Mt 26:73 Even your *a* gives you away!"

ACCEPT (78)

Gn 21:30 seven ewe lambs you shall *a* from me
23:13 *A* it from me,
33:10 me the favor, please *a* this gift from me,
33:11 Do *a* the present I have brought you;
Ex 22:10 the owner must *a* the oath,
25: 2 From every man you shall *a* the
25: 3 the contributions you shall *a* from them:
Lv 26:31 to *a* your sweet-smelling offerings.
Nm 7: 5 LORD then said to Moses, *A* their offering,
35:31 "You shall not *a* indemnity in place of
35:32 Nor shall you *a* indemnity to allow a
Dt 33:11 and *a* the ministry of his hands.
1Sm 2:15 He will not *a* boiled meat from you,
9:16 their misery and *a* their cry for help."
25:27 *A* this present,
2Sm 24:23 "May the LORD your God *a* your offering."
1Kgs 2:38 Shimei answered the king: "I *a*.
2:42 And you answered, "I *a* and obey.'
2Kgs 5:15 Please *a* a gift from your servant."
5:17 "If you will not *a*,
1Mc 15:20 also decided to *a* the shield from them.
15:27 But he refused to *a* the aid;
2Mc 1:26 *a* this sacrifice on behalf of all your
7:29 but be worthy of your brothers and *a* death,
15:16 said, *A* this holy sword as a gift from God;
Jb 2:10 We *a* good things from God;
2:10 and should we not *a* evil?"
42: 8 for his prayer I will *a*,
Ps(s) 20: 4 offerings and graciously *a* your holocaust.
51:18 I offer a holocaust, you would not *a* it.
Prv 5:20 wife and *a* the embraces of an adulteress?
Sir 2: 4 *A* whatever befalls you,
7: 9 the Most High will *a* my offerings."
18:13 Merciful to those who *a* his guidance,
32:14 He who would find God must *a* discipline:
35:11 But offer no bribes, these he does not *a*!
51:26 yoke, that your mind may *a* her teaching.
Jer 14:12 or cereal offerings, I will not *a* them.
44: 5 they would not listen or *a* the warning to
Ez 20:40 there I will *a* them,
20:41 As a pleasing odor I will *a* you,
43:27 Then I will *a* you, says the Lord GOD.
Am 5:22 Your cereal offerings I will not *a*,
Zep 3: 7 you will fear me, you will *a* correction";
Mal 1: 8 see if he will *a* it,
1:10 will I *a* any sacrifice from your hands,
1:13 Shall I *a* it from your hands?
Mt 11:14 If you are prepared to *a* it,
19:11 said, "Not everyone can *a* this teaching,
19:12 Let him *a* this teaching who can."
Mk 4:16 to the word *a* it joyfully at the outset.
10:15 I assure you that whoever does not *a* the
12:38 robes and *a* marks of respect in public,
Lk 7:35 God's wisdom is vindicated by all who *a* it."
18:17 whoever does not *a* the kingdom of God
Jn 1:11 his own he came, yet his own did not *a* him.
1:12 Any who did *a* him he empowered to become
3:11 have seen, but you do not *a* our testimony.
3:33 Whoever does *a* this testimony certifies
5:34 (Not that I myself *a* such human testimony
5:41 "It is not that I *a* human praise
5:43 in my Father's name, yet you do not *a* me.
5:43 come in his own name, and him you will *a*.
5:44 when you *a* praise from one another yet do
12:48 does not *a* my words already has his judge,
14:17 Spirit of truth, whom the world cannot *a*,
Acts 16:14 opened her heart to *a* what Paul was saying.
22:18 they will not *a* your testimony about me.'
Rom 15: 7 *A* one another,
1Cor 2:14 not *a* what is taught by the Spirit of God.
6: 4 do you *a* as judges those who have no
2Cor 11:16 then *a* me as a fool all the way and let me
Gal 6:13 The very ones who *a* circumcision do not
1Jn 5: 9 Do we not *a* human testimony?
Rv 13:16 to *a* a stamped image on their right hand
14:11 or its image or *a* the mark of its name."
19:20 making them *a* the mark of the beast and
22:17 desire it *a* the gift of life-giving water.

ACCEPTABLE (28)

Lv 1: 4 that it may be *a* to make atonement for him.
19: 5 to the LORD, if you wish it to be *a*,
22:19 offering to the LORD, if it is to be *a*,
22:20 for such a one would not be *a* for you.
22:23 but it will not be *a* as a votive offering.
22:25 or defective, they will not be *a* for you."
22:27 from the eighth day onward will it be *a*,
22:29 LORD, so offer it that it may be *a* for you;
23:11 before the LORD that it may be *a* for you.
1Sm 29: 9 answered David, "that you are *a* to me.
29:10 you are as *a* to me as an angel of God.
Neh 2: 6 I set a date that was *a* to him,
Est 3: 4 see whether Mordecai's explanation was *a*,
2Mc 11:18 and the things that were *a* he has granted.
Prv 21: 3 just is more *a* to the LORD than sacrifice.
Wis 9:12 Thus my deeds will be *a*,
Is 56: 7 and sacrifices will be *a* on my altar,
58: 5 you call this a fast, a day *a* to the LORD?
60: 7 They will be *a* offerings on my altar,
Acts 10:35 fears God and acts uprightly is *a* to him.
Rom 12: 1 as a living sacrifice holy and *a* to God,
2Cor 6: 2 he says, "In an *a* time I have heard you;
6: 2 Now is the *a* time!
Phil 4:18 a sacrifice *a* and pleasing to God.
Col 3:20 in everything as the *a* way in the Lord.
Heb 12:28 worship *a* to him in reverence and awe.
1Pt 2: 5 sacrifices *a* to God through Jesus Christ.
2:20 what is right, this is *a* in God's eyes.

ACCEPTANCE (6)

Lv 22:21 a free-will offering, if it is to find *a*,
Est 1:21 found *a* with the king and the officials,
Lk 4:24 "no prophet gains *a* in his native place.
Rom 11:15 for the world, what will their *a* mean?
1Tm 1:15 You can depend on this as worthy of full *a*:
4: 9 can depend on this as worthy of complete *a*.

ACCEPTED (38)

Gn 23:16 Abraham *a* Ephron's terms;
33:11 Since he so urged him, Esau *a*.
Ex 32: 4 them to Aaron, who *a* their offering,
Nm 7: 6 So Moses *a* the wagons and oxen,
31:51 the priest Eleazar *a* this gold from them,
31:54 and the priest Eleazar *a* the gold from the
Jgs 13:23 he would not have *a* a holocaust and cereal
1Sm 8: 3 but sought illicit gain and *a* bribes,
12: 3 have I *a* a bribe and overlooked his guilt?
12: 4 oppressed us, nor *a* anything from anyone."
1Kgs 12:24 They *a* this message of the LORD and gave
Jdt 15:11 dishes, and all his furniture, which she *a*.
1Mc 6:61 sent peace terms to the Jews, and they *a*.
9:31 From that moment Jonathan *a* the leadership,
10: 1 He was *a* and began to reign there.
10:46 words, they neither believed nor *a* them,
14:47 Simon *a* and agreed to act as high priest,
2Mc 12: 4 live on friendly terms, *a* the invitation,
Jb 42: 9 And the LORD *a* the intercession of Job.
Ps(s) 6:10 the LORD has *a* my prayer.
61: 6 You indeed, O God, have *a* my vows;
Prv 27: 6 from a friend may be *a* as well meant,
Sir 36:21 Though any man may be *a* as a husband,
Jer 32:11 on the scales, I *a* the deed of purchase,
Lk 22: 6 He *a*, then kept looking for an opportunity
Acts 2:41 Those who *a* his message were baptized;
6: 5 was unanimously *a* by the community.
8:12 Christ, men and women alike *a* baptism.
8:14 heard that Samaria had *a* the word of God,
11: 1 that Gentiles, too, had *a* the word of God.
Rom 13:11 is closer than when we first *a* the faith.
15: 7 Accept one another, then, as Christ *a* you,
2Cor 11: 4 or a gospel other than the gospel you *a*,
11: 8 I *a* support from them in order to minister
Phil 4: 9 according to what you have learned and *a*,
Rv 3: 3 Call to mind how you *a* what you heard;
16: 2 men who had *a* the mark of the beast
20: 4 nor *a* its mark on their foreheads

ACCEPTING (5)

2Kgs 5:20 this Aramean Naaman, not *a* what he brought.
Am 5:12 Oppressing the just, *a* bribes,
Jn 13:20 me, and in *a* me accepts him who sent me."
Phil 2: 8 humbled himself, obediently *a* even death,
3Jn 1: 7 and they are *a* nothing from the pagans.

ACCEPTS (13)

Dt 10:17 awesome, who has no favorites, *a* no bribes;
27:25 who *a* payment for slaying an innocent man!'
Ps(s) 15: 5 usury and *a* no bribe against the innocent.
Prv 17:23 The wicked man *a* a concealed bribe to
Ez 18:17 off from evildoing, *a* no interest or usury,
Zep 3: 2 She hears no voice, *a* no correction;
Mal 2:13 nor *a* it favorably from your hand;
Mk 16:16 believes in it and *a* baptism will be saved;
Jn 3:32 seen and heard, but no one *a* his testimony.
13:20 you, he who *a* anyone I send accepts me,
13:20 you, he who accepts anyone I send *a* me,
13:20 me, and in accepting me *a* him who sent me."
Rv 14: 9 or *a* its mark on his forehead or hand,

ACCESS (10)

Jdt 4: 7 passes, since these offered *a* to Judea.
2Mc 14: 3 position and regain *a* to the holy altar.
Prv 18:16 way for him, and gains him *a* to great men.
Sir 38: 2 and gives him *a* to those in authority.
Is 58: 2 what is due them, pleased to gain *a* to God.
Zec 3: 7 will give you *a* among these standing here.
Lk 11:52 You yourselves have not gained *a*,
Rom 5: 2 Through him we have gained *a* by faith to
Eph 2:18 we both have *a* in one Spirit to the Father.
Rv 22:14 have free *a* to the tree of life

ACCESSIBLE (1)

Sir 6:23 is like her name, she is not *a* to many.

ACCIDENT (2)

1Sm 6: 9 struck us, but that an *a* happened to us."
20:26 "He must have become unclean by *a*,

ACCIDENTAL (1)

Jos 20: 3 to which one guilty of *a* and unintended

ACCIDENTALLY (2)

Nm 35:22 man pushes another *a* and not out of enmity,
Jos 20: 9 killed a person *a* might flee to escape death

ACCLAIM (7)

2Chr 23:13 musical instruments were leading the *a*.
Jdt 16: 1 to him a new song, exalt and *a* his name.
Est C:21 of the heathen to *a* their false gods,
Ps(s) 81: 2 *a* the God of Jacob.
95: 1 let us *a* the Rock of our salvation.
Is 12: 4 Give thanks to the LORD, *a* his name;
24:14 These lift up their voice in *a*;

ACCLAIMING (1)

2Chr 23:12 din of the people running and *a* the king,

ACCLAMATIONS (1)

2Mc 4:22 who escorted him with torchlights and *a*;

ACCO (2)

Jos 19:30 Thus, with Mahalab, Achzib, Ummah, *A*,
Jgs 1:31 out the inhabitants of *A* or those of Sidon,

ACCOMPANIED (58)

Gn 13: 1 all that belonged to him, and Lot *a* him.
21:22 About that time Abimelech, *a* by Phicol,
26:26 come to him from Gerar, *a* by Ahuzzath,
32: 7 coming to meet you, *a* by four hundred men."
33: 1 and saw Esau coming, *a* by four hundred men.
43:15 of money with them, and, *a* by Benjamin,
Ex 1: 1 sons of Israel who, *a* by their households,
Nm 22:22 along on his ass, *a* by two of his servants.
Jos 8:35 and the strangers who had *a* Israel.
Ru 1:22 who *a* her back from the plateau of Moab.
1Sm 10:26 *a* by warriors whose hearts the LORD had
30:22 those who had *a* David spoke up to say,
2Sm 2: 2 So David went up there *a* by his two wives,
3:20 When Abner, *a* by twenty men,
15:11 hundred men had *a* Absalom from Jerusalem.
15:16 king set out, *a* by his entire household,
15:18 men of Gath who had *a* him from that city,
16:15 In the meantime Absalom, *a* by Ahithophel,
17:24 the Jordan *a* by all the Israelites.
19:18 David, *a* by a thousand men from Benjamin.
19:18 *a* by his fifteen sons and twenty servants,
19:41 king crossed over to Gilgal, *a* by Chimham.
1Kgs 16:17 marched up from Gibbethon, *a* by all Israel,
20: 1 and *a* by thirty-two kings with horses and
2Kgs 3: 9 *a* by the king of Judah and the king of
2Chr 1: 3 and, *a* by the whole assembly,
8:18 who *a* Solomon's servants to Ophir and
9: 1 *a* by a very numerous retinue and by camels
22: 5 following their counsel when he *a* Jehoram,
Ezr 4: 7 in Aramaic and was *a* by a translation.
10:14 *a* by the elders and magistrates of each
Neh 4:17 bodyguard that *a* me took off his clothes;
Tb 6: 2 When the boy left home, *a* by the angel,
12: 8 either is almsgiving *a* by righteousness.
Jdt 7: 2 baggage train or the men who *a* it on foot
1Mc 6:56 and Media with the army that *a* the king,
9:65 city, Jonathan, *a* by a small group of men,
11: 7 Jonathan *a* the king as far as the river
12:47 to Galilee while one thousand *a* him.
Is 30:29 of Israel, *a* by the timbrels and lyres.
Mt 16:27 with his Father's glory *a* by his angels.
20:20 sons came up to him *a* by her sons,
22:16 to him, *a* by Herodian sympathizers,
26:47 *a* by a great crowd with swords and clubs.
26:51 who *a* Jesus put his hand to his sword,
Mk 4:36 was sitting, while the other boats *a* him.
11:11 he went out to Bethany *a* by the Twelve.
14:43 *a* by a crowd with swords and clubs;
16:20 the message through the signs which *a* them.
Lk 7:11 and his disciples and a large crowd *a* him.
8: 1 The Twelve *a* him,
20: 1 priests and Pharisees, *a* by the elders,
22:39 his disciples *a* him.
23:49 All his friends and the women who had *a*
Jn 11:33 and the Jews who had *a* her also weeping,
Acts 10:23 them, *a* by some of the brothers from Joppa.
10:45 The circumcised believers who had *a* Peter
2Thes 2: 9 *a* by all the power and signs and wonders

ACCOMPANIES (1)

Wis 7: 2 of man, and the pleasure that *a* marriage.

ACCOMPANIMENT (7)

1Chr 16:42 forever," with trumpets and cymbals for *a*,
25: 1 to the *a* of lyres and harps and cymbals.
25: 3 who sang inspired songs to the *a* of a lyre,
25: 6 the house of the LORD to the *a* of cymbals,
2Chr 29:27 to the *a* of the trumpets and the
Eccl 8:15 for this is the *a* of his toil during the
Am 6: 5 harp, like David, they devise their own *a*.

ACCOMPANY (18)

Ex 10: 9 as well as our flocks and herds must *a* us."
Jgs 1: 3 *a* you into the territory allotted to you."
1Sm 30:22 spoke up to say, "Since they did not *a* us,
1Kgs 5:20 My servants shall *a* yours,
22:50 my servants *a* your servants in the ships."
2Kgs 6: 3 "Please agree to *a* your servants,"
2Chr 7: 6 when David used them to *a* the hymns.
Tb 4:15 nor let drunkenness *a* you on your way.
5:17 and may his angel *a* you for safety,
Jdt 10:15 our men will *a* you to present you to him.
2Mc 2: 4 tent and the ark should *a* him
Sir 13:13 and take care never to *a* men of violence.
Mk 5:18 had been possessed was pressing to *a* him.
16:17 *a* those who have professed their faith:
Acts 11:12 instructed me to *a* them without hesitation.
15:40 part, chose Silas to *a* him on his journey,

1Cor 16: 4 that I should go myself, they will *a* me.
Rv 14:13 their labors, for their good works *a* them."

ACCOMPANYING (3)

2Sm 15:17 left the city, with all his officers *a* him,
Acts 13: 5 synagogues, John *a* them as an assistant.
20: 4 *A* him were Sopater,

ACCOMPLICE (1)

Prv 29:24 The *a* of a thief is his own enemy:

ACCOMPLICES (1)

Est E: 5 become *a* in the shedding of innocent blood,

ACCOMPLISH (12)

1Sm 9: 6 Perhaps he can tell us how to *a* our errand."
12:16 the LORD is about to *a* before your eyes.
1Kgs 9:21 doom the Israelites had been unable to *a*,
Jdt 2:12 what I have spoken I will *a* by my power.
Is 46:10 my plan shall stand, I *a* my every purpose.
46:11 Yes, I have spoken, I will *a* it;
60:22 *a* these things when their time comes.
Mi 2: 1 they *a* it when it lies within their power.
Jn 5:36 the works the Father has given me to *a*.
Acts 14:27 related all that God had helped them *a*,
15: 4 reported all that God had helped them *a*.
Ti 1: 5 that you might *a* what had been left undone,

ACCOMPLISHED (20)

Jgs 8: 2 "What have I *a* now in comparison with you?"
2Kgs 10:10 The LORD has *a* all that he foretold
2Chr 7:11 he successfully *a* everything he had
Tb 14: 4 that whatever God has spoken will be *a*.
Jdt 8:34 will not tell you until my plan has been *a*."
Est B: 3 my counselors as to how this might be *a*,
1Mc 14:35 all he had *a* and the loyalty and justice
2Mc 13:17 *a* with the help and protection of the LORD.
Is 26:12 for it is you who have *a* all we have done.
53:10 will of the LORD shall be *a* through him.
Dn 3:99 which the most high God has *a* in my regard.
Mk 6: 2 such miraculous deeds are *a* by his hands?
Lk 9:10 return related to Jesus all they had *a*.
13:32 and on the third day my purpose is *a*.
18:31 concerning the Son of Man may be *a*.
Acts 2:11 his own tongue about the marvels God has *a*."
21:19 *a* among the Gentiles through his ministry.
Eph 2: 9 is it a reward for anything you have *a*,
Rv 10: 7 servants the prophets, shall be *a* in full."
17:17 on the beast until his will is *a*.

ACCOMPLISHES (4)

Jdt 12: 4 Lord *a* by my hand what he has determined."
Sir 43:27 succeeds, and at his bidding *a* his will.
Acts 15:18 *a* these things known to him from of old.'
1Cor 12: 6 the same God who *a* all of them in everyone.

ACCOMPLISHING (3)

Eccl 11: 5 work of God which he is *a* in the universe.
Lk 13:17 else rejoiced at the marvels Jesus was *a*.
Jn 14:10 is the Father who lives in me *a* his works.

ACCOMPLISHMENTS (12)

1Kgs 15:23 the acts of Asa, with all his valor and *a*,
16: 5 acts of Baasha, with all his valor and *a*,
16:27 acts of Omri, with all his valor and *a*,
2Kgs 10:34 the acts of Jehu, his valor and all his *a*,
13: 8 of Jehoahaz, with all his valor and *a*,
13:12 Amaziah, king of Judah, and all his *a*,
14:28 acts of Jeroboam, his valor and all his *a*,
15: 6 of the acts of Azariah, and all his *a*,
15:21 of the acts of Menahem, and all his *a*,
15:26 of the acts of Pekahiah, and all his *a*,
15:31 rest of the acts of Pekah, and all his *a*,
15:36 rest of the acts of Jotham, and all his *a*,

ACCORD (32)

Nm 24:13 gold, I could not of my own *a* to anything,
35:26 If the homicide of his own *a* leaves the
2Kgs 23:25 in *a* with the entire law of Moses;
Jdt 4:12 and with one *a* they cried out fervently to
7:29 All in the assembly with one *a* broke into
13:17 down and worshiped God, saying with one *a*,
15: 5 this, all the Israelites, with one *a*,
15: 9 visited her, all with one *a* blessed her,
1Mc 14:46 the right to act in *a* with these decisions,
2Mc 6:19 of his own *a* to the instrument of torture,
Jb 36: 3 afar, and to my Maker I will *a* the right.
Wis 18: 9 effect with one *a* the divine institution,
Sir 50:17 Then all the people with one *a* would
Zep 3: 9 name of the LORD, to serve him with one *a*;
Lk 2:20 seen, in *a* with what had been told them.
2:24 *a* with the dictate in the law of the Lord.
Jn 12:14 in *a* with Scripture:
Rom 8:20 its own *a* but by him who once subjected it;
14:23 does not *a* with one's belief is sinful.
15: 3 Thus, in *a* with Scripture,
15:27 They did so of their own *a*,
2Cor 6:15 What *a* is there between Christ and Belial,
8:12 to give should *a* with one's means,

ACCORD (cont.)

Gal 1: 6 in *a* with his gracious design in Christ,
1: 8 not in *a* with the one we delivered to you,
5:16 My point is that you should live in *a* with
Eph 3:11 of heaven, in *a* with his age-old purpose,
4:21 you in *a* with the truth that is in Jesus:
Phil 1:27 with one *a* for the faith of the gospel.
2Thes 1:12 in *a* with the gracious gift of our God and
1Pt 2:24 to sin, could live in *a* with God's will.
1Jn 5: 8 and these three are of one *a*.

ACCORDANCE (27)

Ex 24: 8 with you in *a* with all these words of his."
34:27 for in *a* with them I have made a covenant
Lv 26: 3 "If you live in *a* with my precepts and
Nm 3:16 *a* with the command the LORD had given him.
35:24 the avenger of blood in *a* with these norms,
Dt 24: 8 *a* with the instructions I have given them.
Jos 14: 2 in *a* with the instructions the LORD had
2Sm 3:39 the evildoer in *a* with his evil deed."
2Kgs 16: 3 in *a* with the abominable practice of the
17:13 in *a* with the entire law which I enjoined
1Chr 11: 3 in *a* with the word of the LORD as revealed
2Chr 30:12 the princes in *a* with the word of the LORD.
Ezr 7:25 in *a* with the wisdom of your God which is
Neh 12:45 in *a* with the prescriptions of David
13:22 mercy on me in *a* with your great mercy!
1Mc 14:22 In *a* with what they said we have recorded
Ez 25:14 with Edom in *a* with my anger and my fury;
Zec 5: 3 *a* with it shall every thief be swept away,
5: 3 and in *a* with it shall every perjurer be
Lk 23:56 as a day of rest, in *a* with the law.
Jn 19:40 and in *a* with Jewish burial custom bound
Rom 2:12 by the law will be judged in *a* with it.
2:16 day when, in *a* with the gospel I preach,
14:23 is not acting in *a* with what he believes.
1Cor 15: 3 died for our sins in *a* with the Scriptures;
15: 4 was buried and, in *a* with the Scriptures,
1Tm 1:18 *a* with the prophecies made in your regard,

ACCORDED (3)

1Mc 10:88 these events, he *a* new honors to Jonathan.
2Mc 2:21 heavenly manifestations *a* to the heroes
Sir 15: 9 lips, for it is not *a* to him by God.

ACCORDING (270)

Gn 10:20 of Ham, *a* to their clans and languages,
10:31 *a* to their clans and languages by their
10:32 *a* to their origins and by their nations.
36:19 of Esau [that is, Edom] *a* to their clans.
36:40 *a* to their subdivisions and localities:
36:43 *a* to their settlements in their
43:33 seated by his directions *a* to their age,
Ex 25: 9 *a* to the pattern that I will now show you.
25:40 *a* to the pattern shown you on the mountain.
26:30 *a* to the pattern shown you on the mountain.
30:13 *a* to the standard of the sanctuary shekel,
30:24 *a* to the standard of the sanctuary shekel;
38:24 *a* to the standard of the sanctuary shekel;
38:25 *a* to the standard of the sanctuary shekel;
38:26 *a* to the standard of the sanctuary shekel,
Lv 5:15 *a* to the standard of the sanctuary shekel.
27:16 *a* to the amount of seed required to sow it,
27:18 money value *a* to the number of years
27:25 *a* to the standard of the sanctuary shekel.
Nm 1:18 and lineage *a* to clan and ancestral house,
1:44 registered, each *a* to his ancestral house,
2:34 man *a* to his clan and his ancestral house.
3:47 *a* to the standard of the sanctuary shekel,
3:50 shekels *a* to the sanctuary standard.
4:49 *A* to the LORD's bidding to Moses,
7:13 thirty shekels *a* to the sanctuary standard
7:19 thirty shekels *a* to the sanctuary standard
7:25 thirty shekels *a* to the sanctuary standard
7:31 thirty shekels *a* to the sanctuary standard
7:37 thirty shekels *a* to the sanctuary standard
7:43 thirty shekels *a* to the sanctuary standard
7:49 thirty shekels *a* to the sanctuary standard
7:55 thirty shekels *a* to the sanctuary standard
7:61 thirty shekels *a* to the sanctuary standard
7:67 thirty shekels *a* to the sanctuary standard
7:73 thirty shekels *a* to the sanctuary standard
7:79 thirty shekels *a* to the sanctuary standard
7:85 shekels, *a* to the sanctuary standard.
7:86 apiece, *a* to the sanctuary standard,
8: 4 *a* to the pattern which the LORD had shown
18:16 silver shekels *a* to the sanctuary standard,
36: 5 *a* to the instructions of the LORD:
Dt 6:18 of the LORD, that you may, *a* to his word,
17:10 *A* to this decision that they give you in
Jos 4: 8 placed them, *a* to the LORD's direction.
8:27 *a* to the command of the LORD issued to
22: 9 *a* to the LORD's command through Moses.
1Sm 10:19 before the LORD *a* to tribes and families."
2Sm 14:26 hundred shekels *a* to the royal standard.
22:21 "The LORD rewarded me *a* to my justice;
22:21 *a* to the cleanness of my hands he requited
22:25 *a* to my justice, according to my innocence
1Kgs 6:38 in all particulars, exactly *a* to plan,
8:39 to each one of them *a* to his conduct;
11:33 to me *a* to my statutes and my decrees,
15:29 *a* to the warning which the LORD had
2Kgs 16:11 Uriah the priest built an altar *a* to the
17:34 day they worship *a* to their ancient rites.
1Chr 5: 1 in the family records *a* to birthright.
5: 7 the family records *a* to their descendants,
6: 4 of Levi, distributed *a* to their ancestors:
15:15 had ordained *a* to the word of the LORD.
16:37 the ark regularly *a* to the daily ritual;
23: 6 them into classes *a* to the sons of Levi:
23:24 sons of Levi *a* to their ancestral houses,
23:24 were enrolled one by one *a* to their names.
24:30 of the Levites *a* to their ancestral houses.
26:31 was their chief *a* to their family records.
2Chr 3: 3 was sixty cubits *a* to the old measure,
4:20 *a* to prescription before the sanctuary,
6:16 conduct so as always to live *a* to my law,
6:23 innocent and rewarding him *a* to his virtue.
6:30 heart, render to everyone *a* to his conduct,
8:13 day by day *a* to the command of Moses,
8:14 And *a* to the ordinance of his father David
8:14 and the Levites *a* to their functions of
10:14 to them *a* to the advice of the young men:
17:14 mustering *a* to their ancestral houses.
24:13 the house of God *a* to its original form,
25: 4 he acted *a* to what is written in the law,
25: 5 and Benjamin *a* to their ancestral houses,
26:11 divided into bands *a* to the number
28: 3 sons by fire *a* to the abominable practice
29:25 and lyres *a* to the prescriptions of David,
30:16 prescribed for them *a* to the law of Moses,
31: 2 Levites *a* to their former classification,
31:15 great and small alike, *a* to their classes.
31:16 house of the LORD *a* to the daily rule
31:17 family records *a* to their ancestral houses,
31:17 *a* to their various offices and classes.
35: 4 *a* to the prescriptions of King David
35: 5 Stand in the sanctuary *a* to the divisions
35: 6 that all may be carried out *a* to the word
35:10 in their classes *a* to the king's command.
Ezr 2:69 *A* to their means they contributed to the
6: 9 *a* to the requirements of the priests who
6:14 They finished the building *a* to the
10: 8 *a* to the judgment of the leaders and
Neh 9:27 and *a* to your great mercy give them
9:28 heaven and delivered them *a* to your mercy,
12:47 their portions, *a* to their daily needs.
Tb 6:13 crime *a* to the decree in the Book of Moses,
7:11 yours *a* to the decree of the Book of Moses.
7:12 "Take her *a* to the law.
7:12 *A* to the decree written in the Book of
7:13 his wife *a* to the decree of the Mosaic law.
8:16 have dealt with us *a* to your great mercy.
Est 9:13 again tomorrow to act *a* to today's decree,
1Mc 1:14 in Jerusalem *a* to the Gentile custom.
1:50 Whoever refused to act *a* to the command of
2:23 the altar in Modein *a* to the king's order.
2:29 Many who sought to live *a* to righteousness
3:39 Judah and ravage it *a* to the king's orders.
3:56 each return to his home, *a* to the law.
4:47 Then they took uncut stones, *a* to the law,
4:53 they arose and offered sacrifice *a* to the law
6:59 to live *a* to their own laws as formerly;
7:16 in one day, *a* to the text of Scripture:
7:42 judge him *a* to his wickedness."
10:58 great splendor *a* to the custom of kings.
13:46 "Do not treat us *a* to our evil deeds,"
13:46 deeds," they said, "but *a* to your mercy."
15:21 so that he may punish them *a* to their law."
2Mc 12:38 *a* to custom and kept the sabbath there.
Jb 37:12 who changes their rounds, *a* to his plans,
Ps(s) 17: 4 *a* to the words of your lips I have kept
18:21 The LORD rewarded me *a* to my justice;
18:21 *a* to the cleanness of my hands he
18:25 And the LORD requited me *a* to my justice,
18:25 *a* to the cleanness of my hands in his
62:13 that you render to everyone *a* to his deeds.
78:10 *a* to his law they would not walk;
81:13 they walked *a* to their own counsels.
89:31 my law and walk not *a* to my ordinances,
103:10 Not *a* to our sins does he deal with us,
103:10 nor does he requite us *a* to our crimes.
110: 4 forever, *a* to the order of Melchizedek."
119:25 give me life *a* to your word.
119:28 strengthen me *a* to your words.
119:41 O LORD, your salvation *a* to your promise.
119:58 heart, have pity on me *a* to your promise.
119:65 to your servant, O LORD, *a* to your word.
119:76 me *a* to your promise to your servants.
119:91 *A* to your ordinances they still stand firm:
119:107 O LORD, give me life *a* to your word.
119:124 Deal with your servant *a* to your kindness,
119:133 Steady my footsteps *a* to your promise,
119:149 Hear my voice *a* to your kindness,
119:149 *a* to your ordinance give me life.
119:156 *a* to your ordinances give me life.
119:170 rescue me *a* to your promise.
122: 4 of the LORD, *A* to the decree for Israel,
Prv 12: 8 *A* to his good sense a man is praised,
24:12 and he will repay each one *a* to his deeds.
24:29 I will repay the man *a* to his deeds."
26: 4 Answer not the fool *a* to his folly,
26: 5 Answer the fool *a* to his folly,
Wis 2:20 for *a* to his own words, God will take care of
6: 4 the law, nor walk *a* to the will of God,
16:25 bounty *a* to what they needed and desired;
Sir 1: 8 upon every living thing *a* to his bounty;
8:14 judge, for he will settle it *a* to his whim.
11:26 day of death to repay man *a* to his deeds.
16:12 he judges men, each *a* to his deeds.
16:14 reward, which each receives *a* to his deeds.
29:20 surety for your neighbor *a* to your means,
33:13 a potter, to be molded *a* to his pleasure,
35: 9 given to you, generously, *a* to your means.
35:22 Till he requites mankind *a* to its deeds,
35:22 deeds, and repays men *a* to their thoughts;
38:11 petition, a rich offering *a* to your means.
41:14 judge of disgrace only *a* to my rules,
50:22 womb, and fashions them *a* to his will!
Is 63: 7 us *a* to him mercy and his great kindness.
Jer 17:10 reward everyone *a* to his ways, according
18:12 *a* to the stubbornness of his evil heart!"
21: 2 deal with us *a* to all his wonderful works,
25:14 and thus I will repay them *a* to their own
25:14 own deeds and *a* to their own handiwork.
26: 4 not living *a* to the law I placed before
32:19 *a* to his ways, according to the fruit
Lam 3:64 as they deserve, O LORD, *a* to their deeds;
Ez 5: 7 but acting *a* to the ordinances of the
7: 3 judge you *a* to your conduct
7: 8 I will judge you *a* to your conduct and lay
7: 9 I will deal with you *a* to your conduct,
7:27 *a* to their conduct, and according to their
11:12 you have acted *a* to the ordinances of the
11:20 so that they will live *a* to my statutes,
16:59 will deal with you *a* to what you have done,
18:30 house of Israel, each one *a* to his ways,
20:44 *a* to your evil conduct and corrupt actions,
33:20 will judge every one of you *a* to his ways,
35:11 I will deal with you *a* to your anger and
36:19 *a* to their conduct and deeds I judged them.
39:24 *A* to their uncleanness and their
44:24 as judges, judging them *a* to my decrees.
45: 8 to the house of Israel *a* to their tribes.
47:21 among yourselves *a* to the tribes of Israel.
Dn 1:13 and treat your servants *a* to what you see."
13: 3 their daughter *a* to the law of Moses.
13:61 *A* to the law of Moses,
Hos 13: 2 images, Silver idols *a* to their fancy,
Jon 3: 3 went to Nineveh, *a* to the LORD's bidding.
Zec 1: 6 has treated us *a* to our ways and deeds,
Mt 16:27 he will repay each man *a* to his conduct.
25:14 over to them *a* to each man's abilities.
Mk 3:25 If a household is divided *a* to loyalties,
Lk 1: 9 it fell to him by lot *a* to priestly usage
2:22 came to purify them *a* to the law of Moses,
Jn 6:31 *a* to Scripture,
8:15 You pass judgment *a* to appearances but I
8:31 "If you live *a* to my teaching,
18:31 and pass judgment on him *a* to your law?"
19: 7 "and *a* to that law he must die because he
Acts 4:35 be distributed to everyone *a* to his need.
7:44 to make it *a* to the pattern he had seen.
9: 2 man or woman, living *a* to the new way.
11:29 set something aside, each *a* to his means,
13:23 *A* to his promise,
13:33 *a* to what is written in the second psalm,
15: 1 you are circumcised *a* to Mosaic practice,
23: 3 You sit there judging men *a* to the law,
23:31 *A* to their orders,
24:14 I admit to you that it is *a* to the new way
Rom 1: 3 who was descended from David *a* to the
1: 4 God in power *a* to the spirit of holiness,
4: 1 of Abraham, our ancestor *a* to the flesh?
8: 4 not *a* to the flesh, but according to
8: 5 Those who live *a* to the flesh are intent
8: 5 the flesh, those who live *a* to the spirit,
8:12 so that we should live *a* to the flesh.
8:13 If you live *a* to the flesh,
8:28 who have been called *a* to his decree.
12: 6 *a* to the favor bestowed on each of us.
15: 5 another *a* to the spirit of Christ Jesus,
1Cor 10:18 Look at Israel *a* to the flesh and see if
14:34 *A* to the rule observed in all the assemblies
2Cor 5:10 good or bad, *a* to his life in the body.
8: 3 *A* to their means
8:11 may be matched by giving *a* to your means.
9: 7 give *a* to what he has inwardly decided;
Gal 2:14 *a* to Gentile ways rather than Jewish,
Eph 1:11 everything *a* to his will and counsel,
Phil 3:21 it *a* to the pattern of his glorified body,
4: 9 *a* to what you have learned and accepted,
2Tm 1: 9 any merit of ours but *a* to his own design
4:14 the Lord will repay him *a* to his deeds.
Heb 5: 6 forever, *a* to the order of Melchizedek."
5:10 high priest *a* to the order of Melchizedek.
6:20 forever *a* to the order of Melchizedek.
7:11 a priest *a* to the order of Melchizedek,
7:11 choosing a priest *a* to the order of Aaron?
7:15 appointed *a* to the likeness of Melchizedek:
7:17 forever *a* to the order of Melchizedek."
7:21 forever, *a* to the order of Melchizedek.'"
8: 5 "See that you make everything *a* to the
9:22 *A* to the law almost everything is purified
10: 8 offered *a* to the prescriptions of the law.)
1Pt 1: 2 *a* to the foreknowledge of God the Father,
2Pt 3:13 and a new earth where, *a* to his promise,

1Jn 5:14 whenever we ask for anything *a* to his will.
2Jn 1: 6 involves our walking *a* to the commandments,
Rv 20:12 The dead were judged *a* to their conduct as
20:13 Each person was judged *a* to his conduct.

ACCORDINGLY (34)

Gn 24:49 I can then proceed *a*."
45:21 The sons of Israel acted *a*.
Ex 1:11 *A*, taskmasters were set over the
Nm 21: 9 Moses *a* made a bronze serpent and mounted
23: 5 to him, "Go back to Balak, and speak *a*."
23:16 to him, "Go back to Balak, and speak *a*."
Jos 11:15 Moses commanded Joshua, and Joshua acted *a*.
Ru 4: 4 it, tell me so, that I may be guided *a*,
1Sm 9: 4 *A* they went through the hill country of
12:11 *A*, the LORD sent Jerubbaal.
14:11 *A*, the two of them appeared before the
16:19 *A*, Saul dispatched messengers to ask Jesse
18:13 *A*, Saul removed him from his presence by
27: 2 *A*, David departed with his six hundred men
2Sm 20: 5 *A* Amasa set out to summon Judah,
24: 2 *A* the king said to Joab and the leaders of
1Kgs 12:24 of the LORD and gave up the expedition *a*.
20: 9 *A* he directed the couriers of Ben-hadad,
2Kgs 12: 8 *A*, King Joash summoned the priest Jehoiada
1Chr 15:14 *A*, the priests and the Levites sanctified
21:11 *A*, Gad went to David and said to him;
2Chr 30: 6 *A* the couriers, with the letters written
Est 2: 4 pleased the king, and he acted *a*.
1Mc 10: 7 *A* Jonathan went up to Jerusalem and read
2Mc 11:26 *A*, please send them messengers to give
Jb 33:27 did wrong, yet he has not punished me *a*.
Sir 6:17 For he who fears God behaves *a*,
Lk 22: 8 *A*, Jesus sent Peter and John off with the
22:13 and *a* they prepared the Passover supper.
Jn 19:32 *A*, the soldiers came and broke the legs of
Acts 5:21 *A* they went into the temple at dawn and
15: 6 *a* convened to look into the matter.
21:26 *A*, Paul gathered the men together and went
1Pt 4:19 *A*, let those who suffer as God's will

ACCORDS (1)

Lk 20:44 Now if David *a* him the title 'lord,'

ACCOS (1)

1Mc 8:17 chose Eupolemus, son of John, son of *A*,

ACCOUNT (94)

Gn 12:13 that it may go well with me on your *a*
12:16 On her *a* it went very well with Abram,
20:11 and so they would kill me on *a* of my wife.
20:18 household on *a* of Abraham's wife Sarah.
21:11 especially on *a* of his son Ishmael.
26: 7 the place would kill him on *a* of Rebekah,
26: 9 "I thought I might lose my life on her *a*."
43:18 "on *a* of the money put back in our bags
Ex 38:21 The following is an *a* of the various
Lv 21:21 on *a* of his defect he may not draw near to
21:23 nor go up to the altar on *a* of his defect;
Dt 1:37 was angered against me also on your *a*,
3:26 with me on your *a* and would not hear me.
4:21 LORD was angered against me on your *a*
9: 5 on *a* of their wickedness
Ru 2:11 "I have had a complete *a* of what you have
1Sm 15: 9 only what was worthless and of no *a*.
20:34 month, for he was grieved on David's *a*,
23:10 to Keilah, to destroy the city on my *a*.
1Kgs 9:15 This is an *a* of the forced labor which
2Chr 9: 5 "The *a* I heard in my country about your
24:27 *a* in the midrash of the book of the kings.
Neh 5: 7 I called the nobles and magistrates to *a*,
9:32 *a* all the disasters that have befallen us,
Jdt 5: 5 "My lord, hear this *a* from your servant;
6:17 He replied by giving them an *a* of what was
14: 9 When she finished her *a*, the people cheered
Est 10: 2 a detailed *a* of the greatness of Mordecai,
1Mc 1:28 land was shaken on *a* of its inhabitants,
6:59 it was on *a* of their laws,
10:70 I am laughed at and put to shame on your *a*.
13:15 brother Jonathan on *a* of the money
16:18 wrote an *a* of this and sent it to the king,
2Mc 2:32 we shall begin our *a* without further ado;
5: 8 Called to *a* before Aretas,
7:18 We suffer these things on our own *a*,
8:35 help by those whom he had thought of no *a*,
11: 4 He did not take God's power into *a* at all,
Jb 9:19 and if of judgment, who will call him to *a*?
18: 4 earth be neglected on your *a*
27: 5 Far be it from me to *a* you right;
31:14 what could I answer when he demanded an *a*?
31:37 Of all my steps I should give him an *a*;
33:13 him that he gives no *a* of his doings?
40: 4 Behold, I am of little *a*;
Ps(s) 38:17 I say, "Let them not be glad on my *a* who,
106:32 Meribah, and Moses fared ill on their *a*,
119:119 You *a* all the wicked of the earth as dross;
Wis 4:14 understand, nor did they take this into *a*.
10: 4 When on his *a* the earth was flooded,
18:13 at every turn on *a* of sorceries,
Jer 1:17 Be not crushed on their *a*,
9:24 *a* of all those circumcised in their flesh:
23:10 on their *a* the land mourns,
49:19 who can call me to *a*?
50:44 who calls me to *a*?
Ez 31:15 all the trees in the land dropped on his *a*.
32: 8 in the heavens I will darken on your *a*,
Dn 7: 1 Then he wrote down the dream; the *a* began:
9:16 On *a* of our sins and the crimes of our
Jon 1: 7 whose *a* we have met with this misfortune."
Mt 10:18 them and before the Gentiles on my *a*.
10:22 You will be hated by all on *a* of me.
14: 3 in chains, and imprisoned on *a* of Herodias,
24:10 you will be hated by all nations on my *a*.
Mk 6:17 chained, and imprisoned on *a* of Herodias,
13: 9 governors and kings on my *a*
Lk 9:48 this little child on my *a* welcomes me,
11:50 generation will have to *a* for the blood
11:51 you, this generation will have to *a* for it.
14:21 master of the house grew angry at the *a*.
16: 2 Give me an *a* of your service,
21:13 will be brought to give witness on *a* of it.
Jn 9:19 do you *a* for the fact that now he can see?"
12:11 Jesus and believing in him on *a* of Lazarus.
Acts 1: 1 In my first *a*, Theophilus, I dealt with all
Rom 2:24 "On your *a* the name of God is held in
11:20 Do not be haughty on that *a*, but fearful.
14:12 have to give an *a* of himself before God.
1Cor 1:26 Not many of you are wise, as men *a* wisdom;
3: 7 nor he who waters is of any special *a*,
4:10 We are fools on Christ's *a*.
10:28 to it and on *a* of the conscience issue
14:24 to task by all and called to *a* by all,
Gal 1:24 and they gave glory to God on my *a*.
Phil 4:17 is for the ever-growing balance in your *a*.
1Tm 1:16 on that very *a* I was dealt with mercifully,
6: 2 not take liberties with them on that *a*.
Heb 4:13 eyes of him to whom we must render an *a*.
11: 4 borne witness to him on *a* of his gifts;
13:17 watch over you as men who must render an *a*.
Jas 3: 1 who do so will be called to the stricter *a*.
2Pt 3: 5 they do not take into *a* that of old there
Rv 18:20 has exacted punishment from her on your *a*.

ACCOUNTABLE (2)

Dn 6: 3 these were *a* to three supervisors,
Mt 12:36 held *a* for every unguarded word they speak.

ACCOUNTED (7)

Jb 9:29 If I must be *a* guilty,
18: 3 Why are we *a* like the beasts,
Wis 5: 4 His life we *a* madness,
5: 5 See how he is *a* among the sons of God;
7: 9 and before her, silver is to be *a* mire.
Bar 3:11 *a* with those destined for the nether world?
Phil 3: 8 I have *a* all else rubbish so that Christ

ACCOUNTING (4)

Gn 9: 5 own lifeblood, too, I will demand an *a*:
9: 5 man I will demand an *a* for human life.
Jb 37:23 his great justice owes no one an *a*.
1Pt 4: 5 They shall give an *a* to him who stands

ACCOUNTS (5)

Gn 27:42 to settle *a* with you by killing you.
Tb 1:21 son, in charge of all the *a* of his kingdom,
Is 40:17 as nought, as nothing and void he *a* them.
Mt 18:23 decided to settle *a* with his officials.
25:19 servants came home and settled *a* with them.

ACCREDITED (1)

1Sm 3:20 that Samuel was an *a* prophet of the LORD.

ACCRUE (1)

Nm 18: 9 shares shall *a* to you and to your sons.

ACCUMULATE (1)

Dt 17:17 he *a* a vast amount of silver and gold.

ACCUMULATED (2)

Gn 12: 5 Lot, all the possessions that they had *a*,
31: 1 and he has *a* all this wealth of his by

ACCURACY (1)

Sir 42: 4 Of *a* of scales and balances,

ACCURATE (1)

Sir 16:23 measured wisdom, and impart *a* knowledge.

ACCURATELY (4)

Ezr 7:21 heaven, requests of you, dispense to him *a*,
Mt 15: 7 How *a* did Isaiah prophesy about you when
Mk 7: 6 "How *a* Isaiah prophesied about you
Acts 18:25 He spoke and taught *a* about Jesus,

ACCURSED (21)

Jos 9:23 For this are you *a*:
1Sm 2:30 me, but those who spurn me shall be *a*.
2Kgs 9:34 "Attend to that *a* woman and bury her;
Tb 13:12 *A* are all who speak a harsh word against
13:12 *a* are all who destroy you and pull down
2Mc 7: 9 "You *a* fiend, you are depriving us
8:34 The *a* Nicanor,
Jb 24:18 Their portion in the land is *a*,
Ps(s) 119:21 You rebuke the *a* proud,
Wis 3:12 *a* is their brood.
12:11 for they were a race *a* from the beginning.
14: 8 but the handmade idol is *a*,
Sir 3:16 *a* of his Creator,
23:26 She will leave an *a* memory;
Is 65:20 who fails of a hundred shall be thought *a*.
Jer 44:22 desert, a thing *a* and without inhabitants,
Mi 6:10 hoarding and the meager ephah that is *a*?
Mal 3: 9 You are indeed *a*,
Mk 14:21 *a* be that man by whom the Son of Man is
Gal 3:13 *A* is anyone who is hanged on a tree."
2Pt 2:14 An *a* lot are they!

ACCUSATION (13)

1Kgs 21:13 came in and confronted him with the *a*,
Ezr 4: 6 prepared a written *a* against the inhabitants
1Mc 7: 6 made this *a* to the king against the people:
2Mc 4: 1 made false *a* that it was Onias who
Is 54:17 prove false that launches an *a* against you.
58: 9 oppression, false *a* and malicious speech;
Dn 6: 5 find grounds for *a* against Daniel
6: 6 no grounds for *a* against this Daniel
13:36 The elders made this *a*:
Mt 12:10 to Jesus, hoping to bring an *a* against him:
Mk 3: 2 to be able to bring an *a* against him.
Jn 18:29 "What *a* do you bring against this man?"
1Tm 5:19 Pay no attention to an *a* against a

ACCUSATIONS (6)

Ps(s) 89:51 I bear in my bosom all the *a* of the
Prv 10:18 but he who spreads *a* is a fool.
Dn 13:27 At the *a* by the old men,
Mk 15: 3 meanwhile, brought many *a* against him.
15: 4 how many *a* they are leveling against you."
Acts 28:19 no cause to make *a* against my own people.

ACCUSE (16)

Dt 19:16 a man to *a* him of a defection from the law,
1Sm 22:15 Let not the king *a* his servant or anyone
1Kgs 21:10 and *a* him of having cursed God and king.
1Mc 10:61 of the law, united against him to *a* him,
Is 3:13 The LORD rises to *a*,
57:16 I will not *a* forever,
Jer 2: 9 Therefore will I yet *a* you,
2: 9 and even your children's children I will *a*.
Dn 6: 5 But they could *a* him of no wrongdoing;
Zec 3: 1 Satan stood at his right hand to *a* him.
Lk 23:10 scribes were at hand to *a* him vehemently.
Jn 5:45 the one to *a* you is Moses on whom you have
8: 6 that they could have something to *a* him of.)
Rom 2:15 will *a* or defend them on the day when,
3: 8 that some slanderously *a* us of teaching;
2Cor 10: 2 ones who *a* us of weak human behavior.

ACCUSED (13)

Dt 19:18 witness and has *a* his kinsman falsely,
1Mc 7:25 to the king and *a* them of grave crimes.
2Mc 10:13 was *a* before Eupator by the King's Friends.
10:21 *a* those men of having sold their kinsmen
Dn 3: 8 came and *a* the Jews to King Nebuchadnezzar:
6:25 king then ordered the men who had *a* Daniel,
Mt 27:12 he was *a* by the chief priests and elders,
Acts 5:34 *a* ordered out of court for a few minutes,
19:40 *a* of rioting because of today's conduct.
23:29 I subsequently discovered that he was *a* in
25:16 not the Roman practice to hand an *a* man
26: 7 Your Majesty, that I stand *a* by the Jews.
Rv 12:10 who night and day *a* them before our God.

ACCUSER (6)

2Mc 4: 5 to the king, not as an *a* of his countrymen,
Jb 31:35 that my *a* would write out his indictment!
Ps(s) 109: 6 him, and let the *a* stand at his right hand.
Zep 3: 8 LORD, against the day when I arise as *a*;
Jn 5:45 that I will be your *a* before the Father;
Rv 12:10 For the *a* of our brothers is cast out,

ACCUSERS (8)

1Mc 10:64 When his *a* saw the honor paid to him in
Ps(s) 109:20 recompense from the LORD upon my *a*
109:29 Let my *a* be clothed with disgrace and let
Acts 23:30 his *a* to take the matter up with you."
23:35 your case," he said, "when your *a* arrive."
24:12 did my *a* find me debating with anyone or
25:16 before he had been confronted with his *a*
25:18 His *a* surrounded him but they did not

ACCUSING (2)

1Mc 11:11 His real reason for *a* Alexander,
Acts 24: 8 and learn for yourself why we are *a* him."

ACCUSTOMED (9)

Lv 5: 4 or evil, such as men are *a* to utter rashly,

ACCUSTOMED (cont.)

Jdt 13:10 together as they were *a* to do for prayer.
Is 53: 3 by men, a man of suffering, *a* to infirmity,
Jer 9: 4 They have *a* their tongues to lying,
13:23 be able to do good, *a* to evil as you are.
Lam 4: 5 *a* to dainty food perish in the streets;
Mt 27:15 procurator was *a* to release one prisoner,
Mk 2:18 disciples and the Pharisees were *a* to fast.
Jn 9: 8 had been *a* to see him begging began to ask,

ACHAIA (10)

Acts 18:12 During Gallio's proconsulship in *A*,
18:27 He wanted to go on to *A*,
19:21 to travel through Macedonia and *A* again,
Rom 15:26 Macedonia and *A* have kindly decided to
1Cor 16:15 Stephanas is the first fruits of *A*
2Cor 1: 1 the holy ones of the church who live in *A*.
9: 2 that *A* has been ready since last year.
11:10 of mine will not cease in the regions of *A*!
1Thes 1: 7 for all the believers of Macedonia and *A*.
1: 8 This is true not only in Macedonia and *A*;

ACHAICUS (1)

1Cor 16:17 arrival of Stephanas, Fortunatus, and *A*,

ACHAN (6)

Jos 7: 1 *A*, son of Carmi, son of Zerah,
7:18 and *A*, son of Carmi, son of Zabdi,
7:19 Joshua said to *A*, "My son, give to the LORD
7:20 *A* answered Joshua, "I have indeed sinned
7:24 Then Joshua and all Israel took *A*,
22:20 When *A*, son of Zerah, violated the ban

ACHAR (1)

1Chr 2: 7 *A*, who brought trouble upon Israel by

ACHBOR (6)

Gn 36:38 When Shaul died, Baal-hanan, son of *A*,
2Kgs 22:12 *A*, son of Micaiah,
22:14 So Hilkiah the priest, Ahikam, *A*,
1Chr 1:49 When Shaul died, Baal-hanan, son of *A*,
Jer 26:22 King Jehoiakim sent Elnathan, son of *A*,
36:12 son of Shemaiah, Elnathan, son of *A*,

ACHIEVE (9)

Gn 49:16 "Dan shall *a* justice for his kindred like
50:20 meant it for good, to *a* his present end,
1Mc 5:62 it was granted to *a* Israel's salvation.
2Mc 7: 2 do you expect to *a* by questioning us?
Jb 5:12 cunning, so that their hands *a* no success;
Jer 22:30 No descendant of his shall *a* a seat on the
Lk 19:48 people, but they had no idea how to *a* it,
Phil 2:12 with anxious concern to *a* your salvation,
2Thes 2:14 might *a* the glory of our Lord Jesus Christ.

ACHIEVED (5)

1Mc 3: 6 By his hand redemption was happily *a*,
Is 26:18 Salvation we have not *a* for the earth,
Col 1:22 But now Christ has a reconciliation
Heb 7:11 perfection had been *a* through the
9:12 his own blood, and *a* eternal redemption.

ACHIEVEMENT (5)

Sir 29: 6 barely half, he considers this an *a*;
39:18 nothing can limit his *a*.
Is 12: 5 praise to the LORD for his glorious *a*;
Gal 6: 4 be because the *a* is his and not another's.
Phil 2:13 begets in you any measure of desire or *a*.

ACHIEVEMENTS (2)

2Sm 23:20 from Kabzeel, was a man of great *a*.
1Mc 16:23 and his other *a* these things are recorded

ACHIEVES (1)

Col 2:19 *a* a growth from this source which comes

ACHIEVING (2)

Is 55:11 do my will, *a* the end for which I sent it.
1Pt 1: 9 with glory because you are *a* faith's goal,

ACHIM (2)

Mt 1:14 the father of Zadok, Zadok the father of *A*,
1:14 the father of Achim, *A* the father of Eliud.

ACHIOR (12)

Jdt 5: 5 Then *A*, the leader of all the Ammonites
5:22 when *A* had concluded his recommendation,
6: 1 in chief of the Assyrian army, said to *A*,
6: 2 "Who are you, *A*, to prophesy among us
6: 5 As for you, *A*,
6:10 were standing by in his tent to seize *A*,
6:13 where they bound *A* and left him lying at
6:16 They placed *A* in the center of the throng,
6:20 they reassured *A* and praised him highly.
14: 5 doing this, summon for me *A* the Ammonite,
14: 6 So they called *A* from the house of Uzziah.
14:10 Now *A*, seeing all that the God of Israel

ACHIOR'S (1)

Jdt 11: 9 "As for *A* speech in your council,

ACHISH (20)

1Sm 21:11 David took to flight from Saul, going to *A*,
21:12 But the servants of *A* said,
21:13 remarks and became very much afraid of *A*,
21:15 Finally *A* said to his servants:
27: 2 his six hundred men and went over to *A*,
27: 3 David and his men lived in Gath with *A*;
27: 5 David said to *A*:
27: 6 That same day *A* gave him Ziklag,
27: 9 On his return he brought these to *A*,
27:12 And *A* trusted David,
28: 1 So *A* said to David, "You realize, of course,
28: 2 David answered *A*, "Good!
28: 2 Then *A* said to David,
29: 2 men were marching in the rear guard with *A*.
29: 3 And *A* answered them:
29: 6 So *A* summoned David and said to him:
29: 8 But David said to *A*: "What have I done?"
29: 9 "You know," *A* answered David,
1Kgs 2:39 two of Shimei's servants ran away to *A*,
2:40 to *A* in Gath in search of his servants,

ACHOR (5)

Jos 7:24 and led them off to the Valley of *A*.
7:26 is called the Valley of *A* to this day.
15: 7 climbed to Debir, north of the vale of *A*,
Is 65:10 valley of *A* a resting place for the cattle
Hos 2:17 had, and the valley of *A* as a door of hope.

ACHSAH (5)

Jos 15:16 "I will give my daughter *A* in marriage to
15:17 Caleb gave him his daughter *A* in marriage.
Jgs 1:12 "I will give my daughter *A* in marriage to
1:13 Caleb gave him his daughter *A* in marriage.
1Chr 2:49 *A* was Caleb's daughter.

ACHSHAPH (3)

Jos 11: 1 to the king of Shimron, to the king of *A*,
12:20 Aphek, Lasharon, Madon, Hazor, Shimron, *A*,
19:25 included Helkath, Hali, Beten, *A*,

ACHZIB (3)

Jos 15:44 Ashan, Iphtah, Ashnah, Nezib, Keilah, *A*,
19:29 Thus, with Mahalab, *A*,
Jgs 1:31 of Sidon, or take possession of Mahaleb, *A*,

ACKNOWLEDGE (30)

Dt 26: 3 and say to him, 'Today I *a* to the LORD,
33: 9 his brothers he would not *a*,
Jos 23:14 So now *a* with your whole heart and soul
1Kgs 8:43 and may *a* that this temple which I have
Tb 12: 6 *a* the many good things he has done for
12:22 and they continued to *a* these marvelous
Jdt 8:20 But since we *a* no other god but the Lord,
Jb 40: 8 Would you refuse to *a* my right?
40:14 *a* that your own right hand can save you.
Ps(s) 38:19 Indeed, I *a* my guilt;
51: 5 For I *a* my offense,
79: 6 your wrath upon the nations that *a* you not,
119:79 turn to me who fear you and *a* your decrees.
Sir 4:26 Be not ashamed to *a* your guilt,
Is 33:13 you who are near, *a* my might.
61: 9 *a* them as a race the LORD has blessed.
63:16 Abraham not to know us, nor Israel to *a* us,
Bar 4:13 law of God, and did not *a* his statutes;
Mt 10:32 men I will *a* before my Father in heaven.
Lk 12: 8 of Man will *a* him before the angels of God.
Acts 24: 3 and everywhere *a* our deep gratitude to you.
Rom 1:28 They did not see fit to *a* God,
Gal 4: 8 In the past, when you did not *a* God,
2Thes 1: 8 punishment on those who do not *a* God
Heb 3: 1 apostle and high priest whom we *a* in faith,
13:15 fruit of lips which *a* his name.
1Jn 1: 9 But if we *a* our sins,
4: 3 that fails to *a* him does not belong to God.
2Jn 1: 7 not *a* Jesus Christ as coming in the flesh.
Rv 3: 5 but will *a* him in the presence of my

ACKNOWLEDGED (9)

Ezr 10: 1 While Ezra prayed and *a* their guilt,
Jdt 5: 8 *a* with divine worship the God of heaven,
Ps(s) 32: 5 Then I *a* my sin to you,
Wis 4: 1 because both by God is it *a*, and by men.
18:13 they *a* that the people was God's son.
Sir 44:23 God *a* him as the first-born,
Jn 9:22 that anyone who *a* Jesus as the Messiah
Acts 6: 3 men *a* to be deeply spiritual and prudent,
Gal 2: 9 on me, those who were the *a* pillars,

ACKNOWLEDGES (7)

Ps(s) 91:14 will set him on high because he *a* my name.
Dn 11:39 *a* him he shall provide with abundant honor;
Mt 10:32 Whoever *a* me before men I will
Lk 12: 8 "I tell you, whoever *a* me before men
1Jn 2:23 who *a* the Son can claim the Father as well.
4: 2 every spirit that *a* Jesus Christ come in
4:15 When anyone *a* that Jesus is the Son of God,

ACKNOWLEDGING (1)

Heb 11:13 By *a* themselves to be strangers and

ACKNOWLEDGMENT (1)

Gn 21:30 have your *a* that the well was dug by me."

ACQUAINT (2)

Prv 1:23 you my spirit, I will *a* you with my words.
Sir 8: 8 wise, but *a* yourself with their proverbs;

ACQUAINTANCE (2)

2Mc 6:21 because of their long *a* with him,
Sir 51:20 At first *a* with her, I gained understanding

ACQUAINTANCES (3)

Jb 42:11 sisters came to him, and all his former *a*,
Sir 6: 6 Let your *a* be many,
Lk 2:44 for him among their relatives and *a*.

ACQUAINTED (5)

2Chr 8:18 sent him ships and crewmen *a* with the sea,
Tb 5: 4 Tobiah went to look for someone *a* with the
Acts 26: 5 *a* with me for a long time and can testify,
26:26 The king here is well *a* with these matters.
2Cor 8: 9 You are well *a* with the favor shown you by

ACQUIRE (21)

Gn 34:10 freely in it, and *a* a landed property here."
Lv 25:28 *a* sufficient means to buy back his land,
Dt 8:18 God, who gives you the power to *a* wealth,
17:16 people go back again to Egypt to *a* them,
Ru 4: 4 for it if you wish to *a* it as next of kin.
4: 5 "Once you *a* the field from Naomi,
4: 8 in saying to Boaz, *A* it for yourself,"
2Chr 1:16 would *a* them by purchase from Cilicia,
Prv 16:16 How much better to *a* wisdom than gold!
16:16 To *a* understanding is more desirable than
Eccl 7:23 I said, "I will *a* wisdom";
Sir 6: 1 A bad name and disgrace will you *a*:
8: 8 From them you will *a* the training to serve
25: 3 your youth, how will you *a* in your old age?
51:28 *A* but a little instruction;
Is 29:24 who err in spirit shall *a* understanding,
Dn 10:12 made up your mind to *a* understanding
11: 2 fourth shall *a* the greatest riches of all.
Mi 6:14 What you *a*, you cannot save;
Eph 4:23 through illusion and desire, and *a* a fresh,
Jas 4: 2 You envy and you cannot *a*,

ACQUIRED (27)

Gn 12: 5 and the persons they had *a* in Haran,
17:12 houseborn slaves and those *a* with money
17:13 and those *a* with money must be circumcised.
17:23 born in his house or *a* with his money
17:27 house or *a* with his money from foreigners,
26:14 He *a* such flocks and herds,
31:18 all the property he had *a* in Paddan-aram,
34:23 Would not the livestock they have *a*—
36: 6 property he had *a* in the land of Canaan,
46: 6 they had *a* in the land of Canaan.
47:20 *a* all the farm land of Egypt for Pharaoh,
47:23 I have *a* you and your land for Pharaoh,
47:27 There they *a* property,
Ru 4: 9 *a* from Naomi all the holdings of Elimelech,
1Sm 18:30 officers, and as a result *a* great fame.]
1Kgs 1: 5 He *a* chariots,
2Chr 32:29 and he *a* sheep and oxen in great numbers,
Neh 5:16 Moreover, though I had *a* no land of my own,
Jdt 15: 6 plundered it, and *a* great riches.
Jb 31:25 was great, or that my hand had *a* abundance
Eccl 2: 7 I *a* male and female slaves,
Sir 33:31 for you have *a* him with your life's blood;
Is 15: 7 So now whatever they have *a* or stored away
Jer 48:36 the wealth they *a* has perished.
Mk 4:21 "Is a lamp *a* to be put under a bushel
Acts 20:28 he has *a* at the price of his own blood.
2Pt 2: 1 to deny the Master who *a* them for his own,

ACQUIRES (6)

Lv 22:11 But a slave whom a priest *a* by purchase or
25:26 but later on *a* sufficient means to buy it
25:49 or, if he *a* the means,
Prv 1:19 gain takes away the life of him who *a* it.
Sir 29: 6 wealth and *a* an enemy at no extra charge;
Jer 17:11 her own is the man who *a* wealth unjustly:

ACQUIRING (2)

Sir 42: 5 Of *a* much or little,
1Thes 5: 9 *a* salvation through our Lord Jesus Christ.

ACQUIT (5)

Ex 23: 7 put to death, nor shall you *a* the guilty.
1Kgs 8:32 but *a* the just and establish his innocence.
Sir 10:28 Who will *a* him who condemns himself?
Is 5:23 To those who *a* the guilty for bribes,
Mi 6:11 Shall I *a* criminal balances,

ACQUITS (1)

Wis 1: 6 *a* not the blasphemer of his guilty lips;

ACQUITTAL (2)

Rom 5:16 came after many offenses and brought *a*.
5:18 righteous act brought all men *a* and life.

ACQUITTED (5)

Ex 21:19 the one who struck the blow shall be *a*,
2Mc 4:47 all the trouble, the king *a* of the charges,
Mt 12:37 By your words you will be *a*,
Acts 13:38 could never be *a* of under the law of Moses.
13:39 In him, every believer is *a*.

ACQUITTING (1)

Dt 25: 1 *a* the innocent party and condemning

ACREAGE (1)

Lv 27:16 the *a* sown with a homer of barley seed

ACRES (1)

Is 5:10 Ten *a* of vineyard shall yield but one

ACROPOLIS (1)

2Mc 4:12 a gymnasium at the very foot of the *a*,

ACT (90)

Gn 15: 6 it to him as an *a* of righteousness.
18:25 the judge of all the world *a* with justice?"
21:23 but will *a* as loyally toward me and the
26:29 you shall not *a* unkindly toward us,
44:17 "Far be it from me to *a* thus!"
Ex 1:16 "When you *a* as midwives for the Hebrew
7: 1 Aaron your brother shall *a* as your prophet.
18:19 *A* as the people's representative before God,
21:13 down, but caused his death by an *a* of God,
22: 1 the *a* of housebreaking and beaten to death,
22:24 you shall not *a* like an extortioner toward
Lv 19:15 not *a* dishonestly in rendering judgment.
19:35 "Do not *a* dishonestly in using measures
Nm 5:13 who might have caught her in the *a*;
23:19 Is he one to speak and not *a*,
27:17 who shall *a* as their leader in all things,
Dt 17:10 place which the LORD chooses, you shall *a*,
24: 8 Take care to *a* in accordance with the
Jos 22:16 What *a* of treachery is this you have
22:31 this *a* of treachery against the LORD,
Jgs 6:31 destroyed is a god, let him *a* for himself!"
6:31 him, "Do you intend to *a* in Baal's stead,
15: 7 said to them, "If this is how you *a*,
2Sm 5:24 the tops of the mastic trees, *a* decisively,
13:28 Be resolute and *a* manfully."
1Kgs 2: 6 *A* with the wisdom you possess;
3: 7 a mere youth, not knowing at all how to *a*.
11:10 him this very *a* of following strange gods,
2Chr 19: 7 *A* carefully,
19: 9 "You shall *a* faithfully and
19:11 *A* firmly,
22: 3 his mother counseled him to *a* sinfully.
27: 2 people, however, continued to *a* sinfully.
Neh 5:15 I, because I feared God, did not *a* thus.
6:13 *a* on it out of fear and commit this sin.
13:18 Did not your fathers *a* in this same way,
Tb 3:14 I am innocent of any impure *a* with a man,
Jdt 11:15 response reaches them and they *a* upon it,
Est 9:13 tomorrow to *a* according to today's decree,
1Mc 1:50 Whoever refused to *a* according to the
14:42 He shall *a* as governor general over them,
14:46 right to *a* in accord with these decisions,
14:47 accepted and agreed to *a* as high priest,
16:17 *a* of treason he repaid good with evil.
2Mc 3:29 hope of aid, due to an *a* of God's power,
6: 8 to *a* in the same way against the Jews:
14: 9 *a* in the interest of our country and its
Jb 34:12 Surely, God cannot *a* wickedly,
Ps(s) 31:24 more than requites those who *a* proudly
37: 5 trust in him, and he will *a*.
119:126 It is time for the LORD to *a*:
Sir 12: 3 nor is it an *a* of mercy that he does.
37:16 a thought, of every *a*.
Ez 8:18 Therefore I in turn will *a* furiously:
16:47 you walk, and *a* as abominably as they did;
22:14 I, the LORD, have spoken, and I will *a*.
36:22 Not for your sakes do I *a*,
36:32 Not for your sakes do I *a*,
Dn 9:19 O Lord, be attentive and *a* without delay,
Mt 15: 2 "Why do your disciples *a* contrary to the
15: 3 "Why do you for your part *a* contrary to
22:16 favor and do not *a* out of human respect.
Mk 12:14 It is evident you do not *a* out of human
Lk 6:39 a blind man *a* as guide to a blind man?
8:21 who hear the word of God and *a* upon it."
8:47 saw that her *a* had not gone unnoticed,
11:19 In such case, let them *a* as your judges.
20: 8 will I tell you by whose authority I *a*."
Jn 8: 4 woman has been caught in the *a* of adultery.
Acts 8: 1 his part, concurred in the *a* of killing.
26:20 *a* in conformity with their change of heart.
Rom 5:18 *a* brought all men acquittal and life.
7:16 When I *a* against my own will,
1Cor 16:13 stand firm in the faith, and *a* like men.
2Cor 10: 2 I am there, I may not have to *a* boldly,
12:18 Did we not *a* in the one spirit,
Eph 5:15 Do not *a* like fools,
6: 9 *a* in a similar way toward your slaves.
Phil 1:16 Some *a* from unaffected love,
2: 3 Never *a* out of rivalry or conceit;
2:14 you do, *a* without grumbling or arguing:
1Tm 2:12 I do not permit a woman to *a* as teacher,
5:21 prejudice, *a* with complete impartiality!
Heb 13:17 So *a* that they may fulfill their task with
13:18 as we do, to *a* rightly in every respect.
Jas 1:22 *A* on this word.
2:12 Always speak and *a* as men destined for
2Pt 2:12 They *a* like creatures of instinct,
1Jn 1: 6 we are liars and do not *a* in truth.
Rv 21:27 who is a liar or has done a detestable *a*.

ACTED (38)

Gn 21:23 in which you stay as I have *a* toward you."
22:16 that because you *a* as you did in not
26:29 but have always *a* kindly toward you and
45:21 The sons of Israel *a* accordingly.
Ex 1:18 and asked them, "Why have you *a* thus,
Nm 5:20 have *a* impurely by letting a man
22:29 "You have *a* so willfully against me,"
Jos 9:24 great fear for our lives, we *a* as we did.
11:15 commanded Joshua, and Joshua *a* accordingly.
22:22 If now we have *a* out of rebellion or
Jgs 9:16 if you have *a* in good faith and honorably
9:19 you have *a* in good faith and with honor
1Sm 6:10 They *a* upon this advice.
21:14 and *a* like a madman in their hands,
2Sm 17:23 saw that his counsel was not *a* upon,
1Chr 21: 8 guilt, for I have *a* very foolishly."
2Chr 11:23 He *a* prudently,
16: 9 You have *a* foolishly in this matter,
25: 4 *a* according to what is written in the law,
29: 6 Our fathers *a* faithlessly and did evil in
Est 1:21 and the king *a* on the advice of Memucan.
2: 4 pleased the king, and he *a* accordingly.
C: 5 pride or desire for fame that I *a* thus
C: 7 But I *a* as I did so as not to place the
1Mc 6:25 have *a* aggressively not only against us,
8: 1 and *a* amiably to all who took their side.
2Mc 12:43 he *a* in a very excellent and noble way,
Ez 11:12 you have *a* according to the ordinances of
20: 9 but I *a* for my name's sake,
20:14 an end to them, but I *a* for my name's sake,
23:39 Thus they *a* within my house.]
25:15 the Philistines have *a* revengefully,
Dn 13:57 is how you *a* with the daughters of Israel,
Hos 2: 7 she that conceived them has *a* shamefully.
Lk 24:28 and he *a* as if he were going farther.
Acts 3:17 my brothers, that you *a* out of ignorance,
2Cor 1:12 *a* from God-given holiness and candor;
1Thes 1: 5 while still among you, we *a* on your behalf.

ACTING (16)

Gn 34:19 young man lost no time in *a* in the matter,
Ex 18:17 "You are not *a* wisely,"
Est C: 7 It is not out of pride that I am *a* thus.
2Mc 14:30 *a* with unaccustomed rudeness when they met;
Ez 5: 7 but *a* according to the ordinances of the
16:30 things, *a* like a shameless prostitute,
20:22 but I stayed my hand, *a* for my name's sake,
Mi 2:11 If one, *a* on impulse,
Lk 1:25 "In these days the Lord is *a* on my behalf;
Rom 14:21 *a* nobly if you abstained from eating meat,
14:23 not *a* in accordance with what he believes.
2Cor 1:17 in making those plans I was *a* insincerely?
6: 4 God, *a* with patient endurance amid trials,
2Thes 3:11 not keeping busy but *a* like busybodies.
Jas 2: 8 You are *a* rightly,
Rv 9:11 *A* as their king was the angel in charge of

ACTION (25)

Gn 41:34 should also take *a* to appoint overseers,
Jgs 6:32 the words, "Let Baal take *a* against him,
1Sm 24:14 So I will take no *a* against you.
2Sm 3:18 Now take *a*,
1Kgs 8:32 take *a* and pass judgment on your servants.
2Chr 6:23 take *a* and pass judgment on your servants,
Ezr 10: 4 stand by you, so have courage and take *a*!"
Jdt 7: 2 day all their fighting men went into *a*.
Est 4: 5 *a* of Mordecai meant and the reason for it.
2Mc 5:18 presumptuous *a* as soon as he approached.
Is 9:10 them and stirs up their enemies to *a*:
48: 3 then suddenly I took *a* and they came to be.
Jer 14: 7 take *a*, O LORD, for the honor
29:26 to take *a* against all madmen and those who
Dn 11:32 loyal to their God shall take strong *a*.
Jl 4: 4 take vengeance upon me by some *a*?
4: 4 But if you do take *a* against me,
Mal 3:17 special possession, on the day I take *a*.
3:21 soles of your feet, on the day I take *a*,
Mt 27: 1 formal *a* against Jesus to put him to death.
27: 3 condemned, began to regret his *a* deeply.
Lk 23:51 been associated with their plan or their *a*.
2Cor 10:11 we mean to be in *a* when we are present.
Col 3:17 Whatever you do, whether in speech or in *a*,
Ti 1:16 and thoroughly incapable of any decent *a*.

ACTIONS (17)

Gn 18:21 see whether or not their *a* fully correspond
Nm 27:17 all things, to guide them in all their *a*;
27:21 as a whole shall perform all their *a*."
Est A:16 at the court, and rewarded him for his *a*.
1Mc 3: 4 In his *a* he was like a lion,
Ps(s) 139:16 Your eyes have seen my *a*;
Sir 17:15 All their *a* are clear as the sun to him,
Ez 14:22 see their conduct and their *a*
14:23 you when you see their conduct and *a*,
20:44 to your evil conduct and corrupt *a*,
Jon 3:10 *a* how they turned from their evil way,
Zep 3:11 your deeds, your rebellious *a* against me;
Jn 7: 4 to be known publicly keeps his *a* hidden.
Rom 7:15 I cannot even understand my own *a*.
Ti 1:16 but by their *a* they deny that he exists.
1Pt 1:17 each one justly on the basis of his *a*.
1Jn 3:10 No one whose *a* are unholy belongs to God,

ACTIVE (3)

Nm 31:27 *a* part in the war by going out to combat,
1Sm 29: 6 pleased to have you *a* with me in the camp,
Wis 16:17 quenches anything, the fire grew more *a*;

ACTIVITIES (2)

2Chr 27: 7 of the acts of Jotham, his wars and his *a*,
28:26 The rest of his deeds and his *a*,

ACTIVITY (2)

Mt 19:12 men are incapable of sexual *a* from birth;
Acts 5:38 their purpose or *a* is human in its origins,

ACTS (80)

Gn 32:11 I am unworthy of all the *a* of kindness
Ex 6: 6 arm and with mighty *a* of judgment.
7: 4 great *a* of judgment I will bring the hosts
Lv 20:27 "A man or a woman who *a* as a medium or
Nm 5:29 authority of her husband and *a* impurely,
Jgs 6:31 If anyone *a* for him,
1Sm 12: 7 and shall recount for you all the *a* of
25:25 Fool is his name, and he *a* the fool.
1Kgs 11:41 The rest of the *a* of Solomon,
14:19 The rest of the *a* of Jeroboam,
14:29 The rest of the *a* of Rehoboam,
15: 7 The rest of Abijam's *a*,
15:23 The rest of the *a* of Asa,
15:31 The rest of the *a* of Nadab,
16: 5 The rest of the *a* of Baasha,
16:14 The rest of the *a* of Elah,
16:20 The rest of the *a* of Zimri,
16:27 The rest of the *a* of Omri,
22:39 The rest of the *a* of Ahab,
22:46 The rest of the *a* of Jehoshaphat,
2Kgs 1:18 The rest of the *a* of Ahaziah are recorded
8:23 The rest of the *a* of Jehoram,
10:34 The rest of the *a* of Jehu,
12:20 The rest of the *a* of Joash,
13: 8 The rest of the *a* of Jehoahaz,
13:12 [The rest of the *a* of Joash,
14:15 The rest of the *a* of Jehoash,
14:18 The rest of the *a* of Amaziah are written
14:28 The rest of the *a* of Jeroboam,
15: 6 The rest of the *a* of Azariah,
15:11 The rest of the *a* of Zechariah are
15:15 The rest of the *a* of Shallum,
15:21 The rest of the *a* of Menahem,
15:26 The rest of the *a* of Pekahiah,
15:31 son of Uzziah] The rest of the *a* of Pekah,
15:36 The rest of the *a* of Jotham,
16:19 The rest of the *a* of Ahaz are recorded in
20:20 The rest of the *a* of Hezekiah,
21:17 The rest of the *a* of Manasseh,
21:25 The rest of the *a* that Amon did are
23:28 The rest of the *a* of Josiah,
24: 5 The rest of the *a* of Jehoiakim,
2Chr 9:29 The rest of the *a* of Solomon,
9:29 well known, in the *a* of Nathan the prophet,
12:15 The *a* of Rehoboam,
13:22 The rest of Abijah's *a*,
16:11 Now the *a* of Asa,
20:34 The rest of the *a* of Jehoshaphat,
25:26 The rest of the *a* of Amaziah,
26:22 of Amos, wrote the rest of the *a* of Uzziah,
27: 7 The rest of the *a* of Jotham,
32:32 The rest of Hezekiah's *a*,
33:18 The rest of the *a* of Manasseh,
35:26 written in the law of the LORD, and his *a*,
36: 8 The rest of the *a* of Jehoiakim,
Tb 2:14 Where are your virtuous *a*?
Est 10: 2 All the *a* of his power and valor,
1Mc 9:22 The other *a* of Judas,
14:45 Whoever *a* otherwise or violates any of
2Mc 8:18 "They trust in weapons and *a* of daring,"
Prv 19: 2 and he who *a* hastily,
21:24 pride who *a* with scornful effrontery.
Sir 12:11 he *a* humbly and peaceably toward you,
Is 26:10 in an upright land he *a* perversely,

ACTS (cont.)

Ez 25:17 will execute great *a* of vengeance on them,
Mt 5:16 *a* and give praise to your heavenly Father.
6: 1 performing religious *a* for people to see.
Mk 7:21 *a* of fornication,
Jn 3:21 But he who *a* in truth comes into the light,
Acts 9:36 by constant good deeds and *a* of charity.
10:35 God and *a* uprightly is acceptable to him.
Rom 3:12 not one of them *a* uprightly,
1Cor 7:37 mind to keep his virgin, also *a* rightly.
7:38 man who marries his virgin, *a* fittingly;
Col 3:25 Whoever *a* unjustly will be repaid for the
Heb 2: 4 it by signs, miracles, varied *a* of power,
1Jn 2:29 who *a* in holiness has been begotten by him.
3: 4 Everyone who sins *a* lawlessly,
3: 7 the man who *a* in holiness is holy indeed,
3: 9 No one begotten of God *a* sinfully because

ACTUAL (1)

Dt 2:31 Sihon and his land, begin the *a* occupation.'

ACTUALLY (8)

Nm 5:14 his wife, whether she was *a* impure or not:
2Mc 9:22 *A*, I do not despair about my health since
Jn 2:21 *A* he was talking about the temple of his
11:30 *A* Jesus had not yet come into the village
21: 8 *A* they were not far from land
Acts 21:35 he *a* had to be carried up by the soldiers
1Cor 5: 1 It is *a* reported that there is lewd
1Tm 1: 7 teachers of the law but *a* not understanding

ADADAH (1)

Jos 15:22 Kabzeel, Eder, Jagur, Kinah, Dimonah, *A*,

ADAH (8)

Gn 4:19 the name of the first was *A*,
4:20 *A*, gave birth to Jabal,
4:23 *A* and Zillah, hear my voice;
36: 2 *A*, daughter of Elon the Hittite;
36: 4 *A* bore Eliphaz to Esau;
36:10 Eliphaz, son of Esau's wife *A*;
36:12 These are the descendants of Esau's wife *A*.
36:16 they are descended from *A*.

ADAIAH (9)

2Kgs 22: 1 name was Jedidah, daughter of *A* of Bozkath.
1Chr 6:26 son of Ethni, son of Zerah, son of *A*,
8:21 Zabdi, Elienai, Zillethai, Eliel, *A*,
9:12 *A*, son of Jeroham, son of Pashhur,
2Chr 23: 1 Masseiah, son of *A*;
Ezr 10:29 Meshullam, Malluch, *A*;
10:39 Shimei, Shelemiah, Nathan, and *A*;
Neh 11: 5 son of Colhozeh, son of Hazaiah, son of *A*,
11:12 *A*, son of Jeroham, son of Pelaliah,

ADALIA (1)

Est 9: 8 Dalphon, Aspatha, Porathai, *A*,

ADAM (19)

Gn 4:25 *A* again had relations with his wife,
5: 1 This is the record of the descendants of *A*.
5: 3 *A* was one hundred and thirty years old
5: 4 *A* lived eight hundred years after the
5: 5 of *A* was nine hundred and thirty years;
Dt 32: 8 when he parceled out the descendants of *A*,
Jos 3:16 for a very great distance indeed, from *A*,
1Chr 1: 1 *A*, Seth, Enosh, Kenan, Mahalalel,
Tb 8: 6 You made *A* and you gave him his wife Eve
Sir 49:16 of any living being was the splendor of *A*.
Lk 3:38 son of Enos, son of Seth, son of *A*,
Rom 5:14 I say, from *A* to Moses death reigned,
5:14 not sinned by breaking a precept as did *A*,
1Cor 15:22 Just as in *A* all die,
15:45 the last *A* has become a life-giving spirit.
15:45 Scripture has it that *A*,
1Tm 2:13 For *A* was created first,
2:14 was not *A* who was deceived but the woman.
Jude 1:14 the seventh generation descended from *A*,

ADAMAH (1)

Jos 19:36 Zer, Hammath, Rakkath, Chinnereth, *A*,

ADAMI-NEKEB (1)

Jos 19:33 to Lakkum, including *A* and Jabneel,

ADAPTATION (1)

2Mc 2:31 but the man who is making an *a* should be

ADAR (15)

Ezr 6:15 house on the third day of the month *A*,
Est 3: 7 the thirteenth day of the twelfth month, *A*.
3:13 thirteenth day of the twelfth month, *A*,
B:6 fourteenth day of the twelfth month, *A*,
8:12 the thirteenth of the twelfth month, *A*.
E:20 thirteenth day of the twelfth month, *A*,
9: 1 thirteenth day of the twelfth month, *A*,
9:15 fourteenth of the month of *A* and killed
9:17 on the thirteenth day of the month of *A*.
9:19 of *A* as a day of rejoicing and feasting,
9:21 fifteenth of the month of *A* as the days
F:10 month *A* throughout all future generations
1Mc 7:43 on the thirteenth day of the month *A*.
7:49 observed every year on the thirteenth of *A*.
2Mc 15:36 of the twelfth month, called *A* in Aramaic,

ADASA (3)

1Mc 7:40 Judas camped in *A* with three thousand men.
7:45 a day's journey, from *A* to near Gazara,
2Mc 14:16 came upon the enemy at the village of *A*.

ADBEEL (2)

Gn 25:13 Nebaioth (Ishmael's first-born), Kedar, *A*,
1Chr 1:29 the first-born of Ishmael, then Kedar, *A*,

ADD (25)

Gn 30:24 the LORD *a* another son to this one for me!"
32:21 and be sure to *a*, 'Your servant Jacob
Nm 32:14 *a* still more to the LORD's blazing wrath
Dt 4: 2 you shall not *a* to what I command you nor
19: 9 then *a* three cities to these three.
Jos 22:18 must you now *a* to it?
2Kgs 20: 6 I will *a* fifteen years to your life.
1Chr 22:14 up wood and stones, to which you must *a*.
Neh 13:18 Would you *a* to the wrath against Israel by
Tb 5:16 son, I will even *a* a bonus to your wages!"
1Mc 8:30 decide to *a* or take away anything,
8:30 they shall *a* or take away shall be valid.
11: 1 Alexander's kingdom and *a* it to his own.
Ps(s) 61: 7 *A* to the days of the king's life;
Prv 30: 6 *A* nothing to his words,
Sir 18:14 My son, to your charity *a* no reproach,
43:28 More than this we need not *a*;
Is 29: 1 *A* year to year,
38: 5 I will *a* fifteen years to your life.
Ez 16:43 For did you not *a* lewdness to the rest of
Am 8: 5 will diminish the ephah, *a* to the shekel,
Mt 6:27 worrying can *a* a moment to his life-span?
Lk 12:25 worrying can *a* a moment to his life-span?
Gal 2: 6 God plays no favorites), made me *a* nothing.
3:15 You cannot *a* anything to a man's will or

ADDAN (1)

Ezr 2:59 from Tel-melah, Tel-harsha, Cherub, *A*,

ADDAR (2)

Jos 15: 3 across to Hezron, and up to *A*;
1Chr 8: 3 The sons of Bela were *A* and Gera,

ADDAX (1)

Dt 14: 5 the gazelle, the roe deer, the ibex, the *a*,

ADDED (41)

Gn 9:12 God *a*: "This is the sign
15: 5 Just so," he *a*,
16:10 so numerous," *a* the LORD's messenger,
21: 7 Who would have told Abraham," she *a*,
24:25 of straw and fodder at our place," she *a*,
38:25 Please verify," she *a*,
Ex 3:14 Then he *a*, "This is what you shall tell
9: 5 And setting a definite time, the LORD *a*,
19:10 the response of the people, the LORD *a*,
Nm 36: 3 will be *a* to that of the tribe
36: 4 these women will be permanently *a*
Ru 2:21 "He even told me," *a* Ruth the Moabite,
1Sm 10:12 And someone from that district *a*,
12:19 not die for having *a* to all our other sins
1Kgs 2:14 "Yes," he answered, and *a*,
11:25 this *a* to the harm done by Hadad,
2Kgs 11:15 If anyone follows her," he *a*,
2Chr 2:11 He *a*: "Blessed be the LORD
36:14 and the people *a* infidelity to infidelity,
Ezr 10:10 women as wives has *a* to Israel's guilt.
Tb 5:15 Then he *a*: "For each day
10:14 to Raguel and his wife Edna, and *a*,
Est 5:12 "Moreover," Haman *a*, "Queen Esther
1Mc 10:38 three districts that have been *a* to Judea
2Mc 3:12 He *a* that it was utterly unthinkable to
14:11 quickly *a* fuel to Demetrius' indignation.
Ps(s) 69:27 and *a* to the pain of him you wounded.
Sir 42:22 With nothing *a*, nothing taken away
47: 9 He *a* beauty to the feasts and solemnized
Zec 1:15 was but a little angry, they *a* to the harm,
Mk 4: 9 Having spoken this parable, he *a*:
6:10 not bring a second tunic," he said, and *a*:
Lk 3:20 He *a* to his guilt by shutting John up in
Jn 11:11 After uttering these words, he *a*,
Acts 1:26 Matthias who was *a* to the eleven apostles.
2:41 some three thousand were *a* that day.
2:47 Day by day the Lord *a* to their number
5:14 numbers, were continually *a* to the Lord.
11:24 Thereby large numbers were *a* to the Lord.
28:25 Then Paul *a* one final word:
Rv 14:13 The Spirit *a*, "Yes, they shall find rest

ADDER (2)

Prv 23:32 like a serpent, or like a poisonous *a*.
Is 14:29 out of the serpent's root shall come an *a*,

ADDER'S (2)

Is 11: 8 and the child lay his hand on the *a* lair.
59: 5 They hatch *a* eggs,

ADDI (1)

Lk 3:28 son of Neri, son of Melchi, son of *A*,

ADDICTED (1)

1Tm 3: 3 He must not be *a* to drink.

ADDING (7)

Lv 5:16 sanctuary, *a* to it a fifth of its value.
Dt 13: 1 neither *a* to it nor subtracting from it.
Jb 34:37 For he is *a* rebellion to his sin by
Eccl 3:14 there is no *a* to it,
7:27 *a* one thing to another that I might
Sir 5: 5 be not overconfident, *a* sin upon sin.
Is 30: 1 are not inspired by me, *a* sin upon sin.

ADDITION (33)

Gn 28: 9 to Ishmael, and in *a* to the wives he had,
Lv 5:24 restitution of the thing itself, and in *a*,
23:38 day, in *a* to those of the LORD's sabbaths,
Nm 5: 7 and in *a* give one fifth of their value to
17:14 in *a* to those who died because of Korah.
28:10 holocaust in *a* to the established holocaust
28:15 These are to be offered in *a* to the
28:23 in *a* to the established morning holocaust;
28:24 in *a* to the established holocaust with its
28:31 in *a* to the established holocaust with its
29: 6 These are to be offered in *a* to the
29: 6 and in *a* to the established holocaust with
29:11 offered in *a* to the atonement sin offering,
29:16 These are to be offered in *a* to the
35: 6 refuge, and in *a* forty-two other cities
Dt 28:69 in *a* to the covenant which he made with
Jos 22:19 of your own in *a* to the altar of the LORD,
22:29 or sacrifice in *a* to the altar of the LORD,
Jgs 8:26 in *a* to the crescents and pendants,
20:15 in *a* to the inhabitants of Gibeah.
1Sm 14:21 In *a*, the Hebrews
1Kgs 3:13 In *a*, I give you what you have not asked
5:30 In *a* to three thousand three hundred
10:15 in *a* to what came from the Tarshish fleet,
10:21 In *a*, all King Solomon's drinking vessels
2Kgs 21:16 In *a* to the sin which he caused Judah to
1Chr 3: 9 of David, in *a* to other sons by concubines;
11:42 son of Ahlai, and, in *a* to the Thirty,
12: 4 of the Thirty, and in *a* to their number;
29: 3 in *a* to all that I stored up for the holy
2Chr 9:14 in *a* to what was collected from travelers
17:19 in *a* were those whom the king had placed
Jer 36:32 and many others of the same kind in *a*.

ADDITIONAL (7)

Jos 13: 2 This *a* land includes all Geshur and all
15:19 She answered, "Give me an *a* gift!
Jgs 1:15 Give me an *a* gift," she answered.
1Kgs 11:18 through Paran, where they picked up *a* men,
1Mc 10:41 All the *a* funds that the officials did not
Ez 44:26 cleansed, he must wait an *a* seven days,
Mt 25:20 thousand came forward bringing the *a* five.

ADDON (1)

Neh 7:61 from Tel-melah, Tel-harsha, Cherub, *A*,

ADDRESS (25)

1Mc 10:47 he had been the first to *a* them peaceably,
Jb 40:27 after time, or *a* you with tender words?
Wis 13:17 not ashamed to *a* the thing without a soul.
Dn 6: 8 no one is to *a* any petition to god or man
6:13 *a* a petition to god or man for thirty days,
Mt 22: 1 Jesus began to *a* them,
Mk 12: 1 He began to *a* them once more in parables:
Lk 14: 7 He went on to *a* a parable to the guests,
Jn 13:13 You *a* me as 'Teacher' and 'Lord,'
Acts 10:34 Peter proceeded to *a* them in these words:
11:15 to *a* them the Holy Spirit came upon them,
13:15 have any exhortation to *a* to the people,
17:22 up in the Areopagus and delivered this *a*:
20:18 When they came to him he delivered this *a*:
21:39 I beg you, let me *a* these people."
1Cor 10:15 I *a* you as one addresses sensible people.
2Cor 1:20 *a* our Amen to God when we worship together.
Col 4: 6 to respond properly to all who *a* you.
1Jn 2:12 Little ones, I *a* you,
2:13 Fathers, I *a* you,
2:13 Young men, I *a* you,
2:14 I *a* you, children,
2:14 I *a* you, fathers, for you have known
2:14 him who is from the beginning, I *a* you,
Rv 2:24 And now I *a* myself to you others in

ADDRESSED (39)

Gn 23: 3 side of his dead one and *a* the Hittites:
23:12 *a* Ephron in the hearing of these men:
Jos 24: 2 ranks before God, Joshua *a* all the people:
1Sm 10:18 to the LORD at Mizpah and *a* the Israelites:
12: 1 Samuel *a* all Israel:

1Chr 12:18 out to meet them and *a* them in these words:
Ezr 8:28 I *a* them in these words:
Neh 4: 8 then *a* these words to the nobles,
1Mc 2:17 Then the officers of the king *a* Mattathias:
12: 4 *a* to the authorities in the various places,
14:40 that the Romans had *a* the Jews as friends,
15:15 as this *a* to various kings and countries:
Jb 32:14 For had he *a* his words to me,
38: 1 the LORD *a* Job out of the storm and said:
40: 6 the LORD *a* Job out of the storm and said:
Wis 6: 9 are my words *a* that you may learn wisdom
Mt 13: 3 He *a* them at length in parables,
26:62 The high priest rose to his feet and *a* him:
28:18 came forward and *a* them in these words:
Mk 1:40 with a request, kneeling down as he *a* him:
3: 3 He *a* the man with the shriveled hand:
Lk 4:39 stood over her and *a* himself to the fever,
5:24 he then *a* the paralyzed man:
14: 5 Then he *a* himself to them:
15: 3 Then he *a* this parable to them:
18: 9 He then spoke this parable *a* to those who
23:20 Pilate *a* them again, for he wanted Jesus
Jn 9:17 Then they *a* the blind man again:
10:35 those men gods to whom God's word was *a*—
11:49 priest that year, *a* them at this point:
13:27 Jesus *a* himself to him:
Acts 2:14 the Eleven, raised his voice, and *a* them:
3:12 saw this, he *a* the people as follows:
8:26 angel of the Lord then *a* himself to Philip:
9:29 He even *a* the Greek-speaking Jews and
12:21 seat on the rostrum and publicly *a* them.
Rom 3:19 is *a* to those who are under its authority.
Heb 12: 5 the encouraging words *a* to you as sons:
12:19 heard begged that they be not *a* to them,

ADDRESSES (2)

Mk 12:37 If David himself *a* him as 'Lord,'
1Cor 10:15 and I address you as one *a* sensible people.

ADDRESSING (12)

Nm 7:89 he heard the voice *a* him from above the
Ezr 5: 9 the elders, *a* to them the following words:
Jb 32: 4 than he, Elihu bided his time before *a* Job.
34:37 off our arguments and *a* many words to God.
Mt 12:46 He was still *a* the crowds when his mother
28: 5 Then the angel spoke, *a* the women:
Mk 11:14 Then *a* it he said, "Never again shall anyone
14:48 *A* himself to them, Jesus said:
Acts 4: 1 Peter and John were still *a* the crowd,
22: 2 When they heard him *a* them in Hebrew,
24: 2 Tertullus began his prosecution by *a* Felix:
Eph 5:19 *a* one another in psalms and hymns and

ADDS (7)

Prv 19: 4 Wealth *a* many friends,
Wis 8: 3 She *a* to nobility the splendor of
Sir 21:15 of wisdom, he approves them and *a* to them;
29: 4 *a* to the burdens of those who help him;
34:10 with travel a man *a* to his resourcefulness.
Jer 45: 3 the LORD *a* grief to my pain;
Rv 22:18 If anyone *a* to these words,

ADHERES (4)

Lv 3: 3 organs, and all the fat that *a* to them,
3: 9 organs, and all the fat that *a* to them,
3:14 organs, and all the fat that *a* to them,
4: 8 organs, and all the fat that *a* to them,

ADIDA (2)

1Mc 12:38 Simon likewise built up *A* in the Shephelah,
13:13 But Simon pitched his camp at *A*,

ADIEL (3)

1Chr 4:36 Jaakobath, Jeshohaiah, Asaiah, *A*,
9:12 Maasai, son of *A*,
27:25 of the king was Azmaveth, the son of *A*.

ADIN (4)

Ezr 2:15 sons of *A*, four hundred and fifty-four
8: 6 of the sons of *A*, Ebed, son of Jonathan,
Neh 7:20 sons of *A*, six hundred and fifty-five;
10:17 Bunni, Azgad, Bebai, Adonijah, Bigvai, *A*,

ADINA (1)

1Chr 11:42 Ahlai, and, in addition to the Thirty, *A*,

ADITHAIM (1)

Jos 15:36 Adullam, Socoh, Azekah, Shaaraim, *A*,

ADJACENT (6)

Jos 17:18 Its *a* land shall also be yours if,
21:11 region of Judah, with the *a* pasture lands,
1Kgs 7:21 then erected *a* to the porch of the temple,
1Chr 6:40 its *a* pasture lands in the land of Judah,
2Mc 12:16 slaughter on it that the *a* pool,
Mk 6:55 The crowds scurried about the *a* area and

ADJOINING (15)

Jos 13: 3 stream *a* Egypt to the boundary of Ekron
1Kgs 6: 5 the temple, and *a* the wall of the temple,
8: 8 part of the holy place *a* the sanctuary;
2Chr 26:23 them in the field *a* the royal cemetery,
Neh 3:11 The *a* sector, as far as the Oven Tower
3:19 of Mizpah, who repaired the *a* sector,
3:20 repaired the *a* sector from the Corner to
3:21 repaired the *a* sector from the entrance of
3:24 repaired the *a* sector from the house of
3:27 the Tekoites repaired the *a* sector
3:30 sixth son of Zalaph, repaired the *a* sector;
3:30 son of Berechiah, repaired the *a* sector;
Ez 40: 7 The threshold of the gate *a* the vestibule
40:14 *a* the court on either side were six cubits.
48: 1 at the northern extremity, *a* Hamath,

ADJOINS (1)

Nm 13:21 Zin as far as where Rehob *a* Labo of Hamath.

ADJOURNED (1)

Acts 24:22 when he heard these words he *a* the trial,

ADJURE (12)

Nm 5:19 Then he shall *a* the woman,
5:21 *a* the woman with this oath of imprecation
1Kgs 22:16 "How many times must I *a* you to tell me
2Chr 18:15 "How many times must I *a* you to tell me
Jdt 7:28 We *a* you by heaven and earth,
Sg 2: 7 I *a* you, daughters of Jerusalem,
3: 5 I *a* you, daughters of Jerusalem,
5: 8 I *a* you, daughters of Jerusalem,
5: 9 differ from any other, that you *a* us so?
8: 4 I *a* you, daughters of Jerusalem,
Acts 19:13 "I *a* you by the Jesus whom Paul preaches."
1Thes 5:27 I *a* you by the Lord that this letter be

ADJURED (3)

Lv 5: 1 has seen or learned, he has been *a* to give,
Neh 13:25 and I *a* them by God:
Jer 40: 9 *a* them and their men not to be afraid to

ADJUTANT (7)

2Kgs 5:18 to worship there, then, I, too, as his *a*,
7: 2 But the *a* on whose arm the king leaned,
7:17 of the gate the officer who was his *a*;
7:19 The *a* had answered the man of God.
9:25 Then Jehu said to his *a* Bidkar,
15:25 His *a* Pekah,
Sir 48:18 led an invasion and sent his *a*;

ADJUTANTS (1)

1Kgs 9:22 force, his ministers, commanders, *a*,

ADLAI (1)

1Chr 27:29 in the valleys was Shaphat, the son of *A*;

ADMAH (5)

Gn 10:19 the way to Sodom, Gomorrah, *A* and Zeboiim,
14: 2 Birsha king of Gomorrah, Shinab king of *A*,
14: 8 the king of Gomorrah, the king of *A*,
Dt 29:22 like Sodom and Gomorrah, *A* and Zeboiim,
Hos 11: 8 How could I treat you as *A*,

ADMATHA (1)

Est 1:14 He summoned Carshena, Shethar, *A*,

ADMIN (1)

Lk 3:33 of Nahshon, son of Amminadab, son of *A*,

ADMINISTER (5)

Dt 1:16 and *a* true justice to both parties even if
16:18 your tribes to *a* true justice for the people
2Chr 9: 8 over them as king to *a* right and justice."
Ezr 7:25 magistrates and judges to *a* justice
Neh 5:12 had them *a* an oath to these men

ADMINISTERED (3)

Lk 7:29 received from John the baptismal bath he *a*.
Col 2:11 not with the circumcision *a* by hand but
Heb 12:11 At the time it is *a*,

ADMINISTERING (2)

2Sm 8:15 judging and *a* justice to all his people.
2Cor 9:12 The *a* of this public benefit not only

ADMINISTERS (1)

Eph 1:11 who *a* everything according to his will and

ADMINISTRATION (6)

1Chr 26:30 had the *a* of Israel on the western side of
26:32 appointed them to the *a* of the Reubenites,
Tb 1:21 so that he took control over the entire *a*.
Est B: 6 of the *a* and is a second father to us,
8:12 entrusted with the *a* of affairs
Dn 6: 5 accusation against Daniel as regards the *a*.

ADMINISTRATOR (2)

Tb 1:22 chief cupbearer, keeper of the seal, *a*,
1Cor 4: 2 of an *a* is that he prove trustworthy.

ADMINISTRATORS (5)

Dn 2:49 and Abednego *a* of the province of Babylon,
3:12 you have made *a* of the province of Babylon:
1Cor 4: 1 of Christ and *a* of the mysteries of God.
12:28 miracle workers, healers, assistants, *a*,
Gal 4: 2 and *a* until the time set by his father.

ADMIRABLE (3)

2Mc 6:23 of the *a* life he had lived from childhood;
7:20 Most *a* and worthy of everlasting
Phil 4: 8 respect, all that is honest, pure, *a*,

ADMIRATION (2)

Est 2:15 Yet she won the *a* of all who saw her.
Lk 8:25 Filled with fear and *a*,

ADMIRE (1)

Sir 11:21 *A* not how sinners live,

ADMIRES (1)

Sir 27:23 uses honeyed talk, and *a* your every word,

ADMIT (6)

2Mc 6: 6 feasts, nor even *a* that he was a Jew.
Wis 6:23 shall I *a* consuming jealousy to my company,
Is 48: 6 must you not *a* it?
60:11 But shall *a* to you the wealth of nations,
Jn 12:42 refused to *a* it because of the Pharisees,
Acts 24:14 I *a* to you that it is according to the new

ADMITS (1)

Sir 20: 2 who *a* his fault will be kept from disgrace.

ADMITTED (13)

Dt 23: 2 may be *a* into the community of the LORD.
23: 3 may be *a* into the community of the LORD,
23: 4 ever be *a* into the community of the LORD,
23: 9 be *a* into the community of the LORD.
Neh 13: 1 may ever be *a* into the assembly of God;
Est 8: 1 and Mordecai was *a* to the king's presence,
Bar 6:56 can it be *a* or thought that they are gods?
Ez 44: 5 those who are to be *a* to the temple
44: 7 You have *a* foreigners,
Dn 13:14 They *a* their lust,
Zec 1: 6 Then they repented and *a*:
Lk 11:10 whoever knocks, is *a*.
Acts 26:31 matters over among themselves and *a*,

ADMITTING (1)

Mt 23:13 nor *a* those who are trying to enter.

ADMONISH (13)

Dt 25: 8 of his city shall summon him and *a* him.
Ps(s) 81: 9 Hear, my people, and I will *a* you;
Sir 19:12 *A* your friend—he may not have done it;
19:13 *A* your neighbor—he may not have said
19:14 *A* your friend—often it may be slander;
19:16 *A* your neighbor before you break with him;
20: 2 much better to *a* than to lose one's temper,
1Cor 4:14 you but to *a* you as my beloved children.
Col 1:28 This is the Christ we proclaim while we *a*
3:16 made perfect, instruct and *a* one another.
1Thes 5:12 exercise authority in the Lord and *a* you;
5:14 We exhort you to *a* the unruly;
Ti 1:13 *A* them sharply,

ADMONISHED (1)

2Mc 2: 2 *a* them not to forget the commandments of

ADMONISHES (1)

Sir 4:11 her children and *a* those who seek her.

ADMONISHING (2)

Wis 11:10 latter you tested, *a* them as a father;
Sir 18:12 Reproving, *a*, teaching, as a shepherd

ADMONITION (6)

Jdt 8:27 It is by way of *a* that he chastises those
Prv 10:17 A path to life is his who heeds *a*,
15: 5 The fool spurns his father's *a*,
15:32 He who rejects *a* despises his own soul,
Sir 20: 1 An *a* can be inopportune,
Mk 8:26 Jesus sent him home with the *a*,

ADNA (2)

Ezr 10:30 *A*, Chelal,
Neh 12:15 for Harim, *A*; for Meremoth,

ADNAH (2)

1Chr 12:21 *A*, Jozabad,
2Chr 17:14 *A* the commander,

ADO (2)

2Mc 2:32 shall begin our account without further *a;*
6:17 further *a* we must go on with our story.

ADONIBEZEK (3)

Jgs 1: 5 they came upon *A* and fought against him.
1: 6 the Canaanites and Perizzites, *A* fled.
1: 7 At this *A* said,

ADONIJAH (24)

2Sm 3: 4 the fourth, *A,* son of Haggith;
1Kgs 1: 6 *A* was also very handsome,
1: 8 pick of David's army, did not side with *A.*
1: 9 near En-rogel, *A* invited all his brothers,
1:11 "Have you not heard that *A,*
1:13 Why, then, has *A* become king?'
1:18 But now *A* has become king,
1:24 that *A* is to reign after you and sit on
1:25 his company and saying, 'Long live King *A!'*
1:41 *A* and all the guests who were with him
1:42 "Come," said *A,* "you are a man of worth
1:49 All the guests of *A* left in terror,
1:50 *A,* in fear of Solomon, also left;
1:51 It was reported to Solomon that *A,*
2:13 his sovereignty firmly established, *A,*
2:19 to King Solomon to speak to him for *A,*
2:21 be given to your brother *A* for his wife."
2:22 why do you ask Abishag the Shunamite for *A?"*
2:23 and more besides if *A* has not proposed
2:24 promised, this day shall *A* be put to death."
2:28 news came to Joab, who had sided with *A,*
1Chr 3: 2 the fourth, *A,* son of Haggith;
2Chr 17: 8 Shemiramoth, Jehonathan, *A* and Tobijah,
Neh 10:17 Elam, Zattu, Bani, Bunni, Azgad, Bebai, *A,*

ADONIKAM (3)

Ezr 2:13 sons of *A,* six hundred and sixty-six;
8:13 of the sons of *A,* younger sons
Neh 7:18 sons of *A,* six hundred and sixty-seven

ADONIRAM (2)

1Kgs 4: 6 and *A,* son of Abda,
5:28 *A* was in charge of the draft.

ADONIZEDEK (2)

Jos 10: 1 Now *A,* king of Jerusalem,
10: 3 So *A,* king of Jerusalem,

ADOPT (4)

2Mc 6: 9 not consent to *a* the customs of the Greeks.
Acts 16:21 not lawful for us Romans to *a* or practice."
Gal 2:14 do you force the Gentiles to *a* Jewish ways?"
5:10 the Lord, you will not *a* a different view.

ADOPTED (9)

Ex 2:10 who *a* him as her son and called him Moses;
1Kgs 9: 9 they *a* strange gods which they worshiped
2Kgs 17: 9 They *a* unlawful practices toward the LORD,
2Chr 7:22 and they *a* strange gods and worshiped them
Est 2:15 and *a* daughter of his nephew Mordecai,
Wis 19: 3 of the dead, They *a* another senseless plan;
Acts 7:21 *a* him and brought him up as her own son.
Gal 4: 5 that we might receive our status as *a* sons.
Eph 1: 5 us through Christ Jesus to be his *a* sons

ADOPTION (2)

Rom 8:15 but a spirit of *a* through which we cry out,
9: 4 Theirs were the *a,* the glory, the covenants,

ADORA (1)

1Mc 13:20 went around by the road that leads to *A,*

ADORAIM (1)

2Chr 11: 9 Soco, Adullam, Gath, Mareshah, Ziph, *A,*

ADORAM (2)

2Sm 20:24 *A* was in charge of the forced labor.
1Kgs 12:18 King Rehoboam then sent out *A,*

ADORATION (1)

Sir 50:17 to the ground In *a* before the Most High,

ADORE (14)

Dt 30:17 are led astray and *a* and serve other gods,
Ps(s) 29: 2 *a* the LORD in holy attire.
Jer 13:10 follow strange gods to serve and *a* them,
25: 6 follow strange gods to serve and *a* them,
Dn 14: 4 worshiped it and went every day to *a* it;
14: 5 the king asked him, "Why do you not *a* Bel?"
14:24 deny that this is a living god, so *a* it."
14:25 But Daniel answered, "I *a* the Lord,
Mi 5:12 shall no longer *a* the works of your hands.
Zep 1: 5 who *a* the host of heaven on the roofs,
1: 5 those who *a* the LORD but swear by Milcom;
2:11 the coastlands of the nations shall *a* him.
Mt 4:10 him alone shall you *a.'"*
Lk 4: 8 him alone shall you *a.'"*

ADORED (6)

Dt 29:25 they went and served other gods and *a* them,
2Chr 7: 3 with their faces to the earth and *a,*
1Mc 4:55 themselves and *a* and praised Heaven,
Ps(s) 106:19 made a calf in Horeb and *a* a molten image;
Dn 14: 4 but Daniel *a* only his God.
2Thes 1:10 holy ones and *a* by all who have believed

ADORES (1)

Is 44:15 another part he makes a god which he *a,*

ADORING (3)

Dt 4:19 be led astray into *a* them and serving them.
1Kgs 11: 5 By *a* Astarte,
Jer 1:16 to strange gods and *a* their own handiwork.

ADORN (5)

2Mc 9:16 he would *a* with the finest offerings the
Jb 40:10 *A* yourself with grandeur and majesty,
Sir 43: 9 *a* with their sparkling the heights of God,
Ti 2:10 so as to *a* in every way possible the
1Pt 3: 5 past ages used to *a* themselves in this way,

ADORNED (11)

2Kgs 9:30 Jezreel, she shadowed her eyes, *a* her hair,
Sg 5:14 arms are rods of gold *a* with chrysolites.
Sir 45: 8 and *a* him with the glorious vestments:
45:13 Before him, no one was *a* with these,
Is 61:10 justice, Like a bridegroom *a* with a diadem,
Jer 10: 4 with the adze, *a* with silver and gold.
Ez 16:11 I *a* you with jewelry:
16:13 Thus you were *a* with gold and silver;
Lk 21: 5 temple was *a* with precious stones
Rv 17: 4 *a* with gold and pearls and other jewels.
18:16 *A* all in gold and jewels and pearls!

ADORNMENT (8)

Ex 28: 2 For the glorious *a* of your brother Aaron
28:40 for the glorious *a* of Aaron's sons you
1Mc 2:11 All her *a* has been taken away.
Prv 3:22 life to your soul, and an *a* for your neck.
14:18 The *a* of simpletons is folly,
Bar 6:23 Despite the gold that covers them for *a,*
1Tm 2:10 be religious, their *a* should be good deeds.
1Pt 3: 4 Your *a* is rather the hidden character of

ADORNMENTS (3)

Jdt 12:15 festive garments and all her feminine *a.*
Est C:13 all her festive *a* were put aside,
Is 49:18 shall be arrayed with them all as with *a,*

ADORNS (2)

Ps(s) 73: 6 So pride *a* them as a necklace;
149: 4 people, and he *a* the lowly with victory.

ADRAMMELECH (2)

2Kgs 19:37 his sons *A* and Sharezer slew him with the
Is 37:38 his sons *A* and Sharezer slew him with the

ADRAMYTTIUM (1)

Acts 27: 2 *A* bound for ports in the province of Asia,

ADRIEL (2)

1Sm 18:19 in marriage to *A* the Meholathite instead.]
2Sm 21: 8 daughter Merob that she had borne to *A,*

ADUEL (1)

Tb 1: 1 son Tobiel, son of Hananiel son of *A,*

ADULLAM (8)

Jos 12:15 Debir, Geder, Hormah, Arad, Libnah, *A,*
15:35 Engannim, Tappuah, Enam, Jarmuth, *A,*
2Sm 23:13 went down to David in the cave of *A,*
1Chr 11:15 who was in the cave of *A* while the
2Chr 11: 7 Bethlehem, Etam, Tekoa, Beth-zur, Soco, *A,*
Neh 11:30 in En-rimmon, Zorah, Jarmuth, Zanoah, *A,*
2Mc 12:38 rallied his army and went to the city of *A.*
Mi 1:15 Even to *A* shall go the glory of Israel.

ADULLAMITE (3)

Gn 38: 1 his tent near a certain *A* named Hirah.
38:12 in company with his friend Hirah the *A.*
38:20 the *A* to recover the pledge from the woman;

ADULTERER (2)

Lv 20:10 *a* and the adulteress shall be put to death.
Jb 24:15 The eye of the *a* watches for the twilight;

ADULTERERS (7)

Ps(s) 50:18 with him, and with *a* you throw in your lot.
Wis 3:16 children of *a* will remain without issue,
Jer 9: 1 They are all *a,* a faithless band.
23:10 With *a* the land is filled;
Mal 3: 5 to bear witness Against the sorcerers, *a,*
1Cor 6: 9 no fornicators, idolaters, or *a,*
Heb 13: 4 for God will judge fornicators and *a.*

ADULTERESS (10)

Lv 20:10 adulterer and the *a* shall be put to death.
Prv 2:16 another, from the *a* with her smooth words,
5: 3 The lips of an *a* drip with honey,
5:20 wife and accept the embraces of an *a?*
6:24 wife, from the smooth tongue of the *a.*
7: 5 wife, from the *a* with her smooth words.
22:14 The mouth of the *a* is a deep pit;
23:27 is a deep ditch, and the *a* a narrow pit;
Is 1:21 How has she turned *a,*
Rom 7: 3 She will be called an *a* if,

ADULTERESSES (3)

Ez 16:38 on you the sentence of *a* and murderesses;
23:45 sentence meted out to *a* and murderesses,
Hos 4:13 harlot, and your daughters-in-law are *a.*

ADULTERIES (3)

Jer 3: 8 all the *a* rebellious Israel had committed,
13:27 Your *a,* your neighings,
Ez 23:43 "Oh, this woman jaded with *a!*

ADULTEROUS (7)

Prv 30:20 Such is the way of an *a* woman:
Is 57: 3 you, draw near, you sons of a sorceress, *a,*
Ez 6: 9 after I have broken their *a* hearts that
16:32 The *a* wife receives, instead of her husband,
Mt 15:19 murder, *a* conduct, fornication, stealing
Mk 7:22 of fornication, theft, murder, *a* conduct,
Lk 18:11 the rest of men—grasping, crooked, *a*—

ADULTERY (39)

Ex 20:14 "You shall not commit *a.*
Lv 20:10 a man commits *a* with his neighbor's wife,
Dt 5:18 'You shall not commit *a.*
Prv 6:32 But he who commits *a* is a fool;
Wis 14:24 kills his neighbor, or aggrieves him by *a.*
14:26 disorder in marriage, *a* and shamelessness.
Sir 23:23 in her wanton *a* she has borne children
Jer 3: 9 the land, committing *a* with stone and wood.
5: 7 I fed them, but they committed *a;*
7: 9 to steal and murder, commit *a* and perjury,
23:14 *A,* living in lies,
29:23 committing *a* with their neighbors' wives,
Ez 23:37 For they committed *a,*
23:37 They committed *a* with their idols;
23:45 and murderesses, for they have committed *a,*
Hos 2: 4 before her, her *a* from between her breasts,
4: 2 swearing, lying, murder, stealing and *a!*
4:14 your daughters-in-law for their *a?*
Mt 5:27 the commandment, 'You shall not commit *a.'*
5:28 committed *a* with her in his thoughts.
5:32 forces her to commit *a.*
5:32 a divorced woman likewise commits *a.*
19: 9 case) and marries another commits *a,*
19: 9 who marries a divorced woman commits *a."*
19:18 'You shall not commit *a';*
Mk 10:11 and marries another commits *a* against her;
10:12 her husband and marries another commits *a."*
10:19 You shall not commit *a;*
Lk 16:18 his wife and marries another commits *a.*
16:18 from her husband likewise commits *a.*
18:20 "You shall not commit *a.*
Jn 8: 3 a woman forward who had been caught in *a.*
8: 4 woman has been caught in the act of *a.*
Rom 2:22 You who forbid adultery, do you commit *a?*
7: 3 commit *a* by consorting with another man.
13: 9 commandments, "You shall not commit *a;*
Jas 2:11 For he who said, "You shall not commit *a,"*
2:11 you do not commit *a* but do commit murder,

ADULTRESS (1)

Hos 3: 1 to a woman beloved of a paramour, an *a;*

ADUMMIM (2)

Jos 15: 7 of the Gilgal that faces the pass of *A,*
18:17 to Geliloth, opposite the pass of *A.*

ADVANCE (32)

Nm 20:18 do, I will *a* against you with the sword."
24:17 A star shall *a* from Jacob,
Dt 2:24 *A* now across the Wadi Arnon.
12:29 from your way as you *a* to dispossess them,
28:25 you *a* against them from one direction,
Jos 9:24 Since, therefore, at your *a,*
13: 6 At the *a* of the Israelites I will drive
2Kgs 20:10 "It is easy for the shadow to *a* ten steps,"
1Chr 14:10 God, "Shall I *a* against the Philistines,
14:10 The LORD answered him, *A,*
2Chr 6:41 And now, *A,* LORD God,
Jdt 2:19 expedition in *a* of King Nebuchadnezzar,
11:19 was told me, and announced to me in *a,*
14: 2 plain against the *a* guard of the Assyrians,
2Mc 8:12 When Judas learned of Nicanor's *a* and
Jb 19:12 His troops *a* as one man;
30:14 as through a wide breach they *a.*

Ps(s) 132: 8 A, O LORD, to your resting place
Prv 1: 5 man by hearing them will a in learning,
9: 6 a in the way of understanding.
Wis 8: 8 in a and the outcome of times and ages.
Is 46:10 I foretell the outcome; in a,
Jer 46:13 concerning the a of Nebuchadnezzar,
50: 9 from there they a,
Bar 5: 7 Israel may a secure in the glory of God.
Dn 11:10 armed host, which shall a like a flood,
Jl 2: 7 They a, each in his own lane
2Cor 9: 5 arrange in a for the bountiful gift
Gal 3: 8 Because Scripture saw in a that God's way
Eph 2:10 good deeds which God prepared for us in a.
Heb 6: 1 teaching about Christ and a to maturity,
6: 3 And, God permitting, we shall a!

ADVANCED (51)

Gn 18:11 Now Abraham and Sarah were old, a in years,
34:25 a against the city without any trouble,
Nm 20:20 and a against them with a large and
21:23 and a into the desert against Israel.
21:33 a against them with all his people to give
Dt 2:32 a against us to join battle at Jahaz;
3: 1 a against us with all his people to give
33: 2 Mount Paran and a from Meribath-kadesh.
Jos 13: 1 When Joshua was old and a in years,
13: 1 "Though now you are old and a in years,
23: 1 and when Joshua was old and a in years,
23: 2 "I am old and a in years.
Jgs 6:35 and these tribes a to meet the others.
9:34 During the night Abimelech a with all his
20:19 Israelites a on Gibeah with their forces.
20:34 all Israel, and a against the city itself.
1Sm 7:10 Philistines a to join battle with Israel.
17:41 also a closer and closer to David.
28: 4 Philistine levies a to Shunem and encamped.
2Sm 6:13 of the ark of the LORD had a six steps,
1Kgs 1: 1 When King David was old and a in years,
1:15 was attending him because of his a age.
2Kgs 14:11 King Jehoash of Israel then a,
17: 3 king of Assyria, a against him,
25: 1 and his whole army a against Jerusalem,
1Chr 14:11 They a, therefore, to Baal-perazim,
19:14 Joab therefore a with his men to engage
2Chr 25:21 Therefore King Joash of Israel a and he
Jdt 16:23 reaching the a age of a hundred and five.
1Mc 1: 3 He a to the ends of the earth,
3:15 And again a large company of renegades a
3:37 crossed the Euphrates River and a inland.
6:42 Judas with his army a to fight,
10:77 but at the same time he a into the plain,
2Mc 4:40 a man as a in folly as he was in years.
6:18 a man of a age and noble appearance,
6:23 of his years, the dignity of his a age,
10:27 a a considerable distance from the city,
11:10 they a in battle order with the aid of
15:25 Nicanor and his men a to the sound of
Jb 15:10 among us more a in years than your father.
Eccl 9:14 city with few men in it a a mighty king,
Is 38: 8 of Ahaz go back the ten steps it has a."
38: 8 the sun came back the ten steps it had a.
Jer 52: 4 and his whole army a against Jerusalem,
Dn 2:48 He a Daniel to a high post,
Zec 2: 7 Then the angel who spoke with me a,
Mt 26:39 He a a little and fell prostrate in prayer.
Mk 14:35 He a a little and fell to the ground,
Lk 1: 7 moreover, both were a in years.
1:18 I am an old man; my wife too is a in age."

ADVANCEMENT (1)

2Mc 5:16 offerings made by other kings for the a,

ADVANCES (9)

2Mc 8: 8 successful a were becoming more frequent,
Ps(s) 68:18 the Lord a from Sinai to the sanctuary.
Prv 9: 9 teach a just man, and he a in learning.
Sir 20:26 A wise man a himself by his words,
Jer 4:13 like storm clouds he a,
48:15 The ravager of Moab and his cities a,
50: 3 A people from the north a against her to
Jl 2: 8 crowds another, each a in his own track;
Na 2: 1 mountains there a the bearer of good news,

ADVANCING (5)

Jgs 9:52 a to the very entrance of the tower to set
1Sm 12:12 king of the Ammonites, a against you,
2Mc 13: 9 The king was a,
Jer 5:28 justice they do not defend By a the claim
Ez 38: 9 storm, a like a cloud to cover the earth,

ADVANTAGE (28)

Est E: 9 taking a of changing conditions and
2Mc 11:36 so that we may present them to your a,
Jb 22: 3 Is it of a to the Almighty if you are just?
35: 3 what a have I more than if I had sinned?"
Prv 9:12 If you are wise, it is to your own a;
Eccl 2:13 And I saw that wisdom has the a over folly
2:13 as much as light has the a over darkness.
3: 9 What a has the worker from his toil?
3:19 and man has no a over the beast;
5: 8 Yet an a for a country in every respect is
6: 8 For what a has the wise man over the fool,
6: 8 or what a has the poor man in knowing how
7:11 good, and an a to those that see the sun.
7:12 and the a of knowledge is that wisdom
10:10 but the craftsman has the a of his skill.
10:11 then there is no a for the charmer.
Sir 3:15 tribulation it will be recalled to your a,
19:23 when not observed, he will take a of you:
37:21 When a man is wise to his own a,
37:22 When a man is wise to his people's a,
38:13 There are times that give him an a,
Bar 6:27 resell their sacrifices for their own a.
Jn 18:14 the a of having one man die for the people.)
Rom 3: 1 What is the a, then, of being a Jew,
1Cor 10:33 in any way I can by seeking, not my own a,
2Cor 12:17 Did I ever take a of you through any of
12:18 Did Titus take a of you in any way?
1Thes 4:15 an a over those who have fallen asleep.

ADVANTAGEOUS (2)

1Cor 10:23 things are lawful" but not all are a.
Ti 3: 8 This is what is good and a for men.

ADVERSARIES (21)

Ex 15: 7 your great majesty you overthrew your a;
Dt 33:11 Break the backs of his a and of his foes,
2Sm 22:40 you subdued my a beneath me.
22:49 Above my a you exalt me and from the
2Mc 15:16 with it you shall crush your a."
Ps(s) 3: 2 O LORD, how many are my a!
18:40 you subdued my a beneath me.
18:49 Truly above my a you exalt me and from the
27:11 lead me on a level path, because of my a.
44: 6 through your name we trampled down our a.
56: 3 My a trample upon me all the day;
59: 2 from my a defend me.
92:12 ears have heard of the fall of my wicked a.
109:28 may my a be put to shame,
Wis 11: 8 they then had how you punished their a.
18: 8 For when you punished our a,
Sir 51: 2 you have been my helper against my a.
Jer 18:19 me, O LORD, and listen to what my a say.
Na 1: 2 The LORD brings vengeance on his a,
Lk 21:15 your a can take exception to or contradict.
Heb 10:27 and a flaming fire to consume the a of God.

ADVERSARY (6)

1Kgs 11:14 The LORD then raised up an a to Solomon:
11:23 God raised up against Solomon another a,
1Mc 1:36 and a wicked a to Israel at all times.
Jb 27: 7 be as the wicked and my a as the unjust!
Sir 21:27 man curses his a he really curses himself.
2Thes 2: 4 that son of perdition and a who exalts

ADVERSITY (10)

2Chr 15: 6 for God destroyed them by every kind of a.
Tb 4: 9 treasure for yourself against the day of a.
2Mc 1: 5 to you, and never forsake you in time of a.
12:30 their kind treatment even in times of a,
Prv 24:10 If you remain indifferent in time of a,
Sir 2: 2 and steadfast, undisturbed in time of a.
11:25 The day of prosperity makes one forget a;
11:25 the day of a makes one forget prosperity.
12: 8 in a an enemy will not remain concealed.
12: 9 in a even his friend disappears.

ADVICE (37)

Gn 41:37 a pleased Pharaoh and all his officials.
Ex 18:19 listen to me, and I will give you some a,
18:24 Moses followed the a of his father-in-law
Nm 31:16 very ones who on Balaam's a prompted
Jos 9:14 without seeking the a of the LORD.
1Sm 6:10 They acted upon this a.
2Sm 20:22 She went to all the people with her a,
1Kgs 12: 8 he ignored the a the elders had given him,
12:13 Ignoring the a the elders had given him,
20:25 He took their a and did this.
2Chr 10: 8 But he ignored the a the elders had given
10:13 Ignoring the a the elders had given him,
10:14 them according to the a of the young men:
Tb 4:18 think lightly of any a that can be useful.
Est 1:21 and the king acted on the a of Memucan.
Jb 6:13 Have I no helper, and has a deserted me?
26: 3 how profuse is the a you offer!
Prv 3:21 keep a and counsel in view;
4: 2 Yes, excellent a I give you;
8:14 Mine are counsel and a;
12:15 own eyes, but he who listens to a is wise.
20:18 Plans made after a succeed;
31: 1 The a which his mother gave him:
Sir 6:24 Listen, my son, and heed my a;
12:12 seat, And in the end you appreciate my a,
16:22 Hearken to me, my son, take my a,
31:22 later you will find my a good.
37: 8 Be on the alert when one proffers a,
37:10 a from one who regards you with hostility;
37:11 pay no attention to any a they give.
Jer 35:14 The a of Jonadab,
Dn 4:24 Therefore, O king, take my a;
Acts 5:38 My a is that you have nothing to do with
27:21 taken my a and not set sail from Crete.
Rom 15:14 that you are able to give a to one another.
2Cor 8:10 you some a on this matter of rich and poor.
Rv 3:18 Take my a. Buy from me gold refined

ADVISE (8)

Ru 3: 5 "I will do whatever you a,"
1Kgs 1:12 let me a you so that you may save your
12: 6 answer do you a me to give this people?"
12: 9 answer do you a me to give this people,
2Chr 10: 6 answer do you a me to give this people?"
10: 9 answer do you a me to give this people,
Ezr 10: 3 in keeping with what you, my lord, a,
2Mc 7:25 urging her to a her boy to save his life.

ADVISED (6)

Jos 7: 3 Ai, they returned to Joshua and a,
9:21 the community did as the princes a them.
1Kgs 12:14 He said to them, as the young men had a:
1Mc 9:69 men who had a him to invade the province.
Lk 9: 3 Jesus a them: "Take nothing
Acts 15:29 You will be well a to avoid these things.

ADVISER (1)

Jb 12:20 He silences the trusted a,

ADVISERS (3)

Est 6:13 him, his a and his wife Zeresh said to him,
Is 19:11 wisest of Pharaoh's a give stupid counsel.
Gal 1:16 without seeking human a or even going to

ADVISING (1)

Acts 19:31 him a him not to venture into the theater.

ADVOCATE (3)

Jb 13: 8 Do you play a on behalf of God?
Mal 2:12 witness and a out of the tents of Jacob,
Acts 16:21 which means they a customs which are not

ADZE (1)

Jer 10: 3 forest, Wrought by craftsmen with the a,

AENEAS (2)

Acts 9:33 There he found a man named A,
9:34 Peter said to him, A, Jesus Christ cures you!

AENON (1)

Jn 3:23 at A near Salim where water was plentiful,

AESORA (1)

Jdt 4: 4 Belmain, and Jericho, to Choba and A,

AFAR (33)

Gn 22: 4 day Abraham got sight of the place from a.
Dt 28:49 will raise up against you a nation from a,
Ezr 3:13 a mighty clamor which was heard a off.
Neh 12:43 at Jerusalem could be heard from a off.
Tb 13:11 many nations shall come to you from a,
Jb 36: 3 I will bring my knowledge from a,
36:25 man beholds it from a.
39:25 Even from a he scents the battle,
39:29 his eyes behold it a off.
Ps(s) 38:12 my neighbors stand a off.
138: 6 he sees, and the proud he knows from a.
139: 2 you understand my thoughts from a.
Prv 31:14 ships, she secures her provisions from a.
Wis 11:11 a off and those close by were afflicted:
Sir 24:30 like the dawn, to become known a off.
37: 4 but in time of trouble he stands a off.
Is 10: 3 day of punishment, when ruin comes from a?
22: 3 leaders fled away together, fled a off;
30:27 of the LORD coming from a in burning wrath,
43: 6 Bring back my sons from a,
49:12 See, some shall come from a,
60: 4 Your sons come from a,
60: 9 children from a with their silver and gold,
Jer 5:15 I will bring against you a nation from a,
31: 3 his rest, the LORD appears to him from a:
51:50 Remember the LORD from a,
51:55 waters, and their clamor was heard a.
Bar 4:15 has brought against them a nation from a,
Ez 23:40 they sent for men who had to come from a,
Hb 1: 8 horses prance, his horsemen come from a:
Zec 6:15 And they who are from a shall come and
Lk 16:23 he raised his eyes and saw Abraham a off,
Heb 11:13 promised but saw and saluted it from a.

AFFAIR (18)

Ex 2:14 thought, "The a must certainly be known."
2:15 of the a and sought to put him to death.
Nm 31:16 Israelites toward the LORD in the Peor a,
2Sm 13:20 Do not take this a to heart."
13:21 King David, who got word of the whole a,
19:43 Why are you angry over this a?
2Chr 24: 5 You must hasten this a."
Ezr 10:14 us our God's burning anger over this a."

AFFAIR (cont.)

Est 9:26 had witnessed and experienced in this *a*,
2Mc 4: 1 and instigated the whole miserable *a*.
4:31 went off in haste to settle the *a*,
4:43 about this *a* were brought against Menelaus.
Eccl 3: 1 and a time for every *a* under the heavens.
3:17 for every *a* and on every work a judgment.
Mt 27: 4 It is your *a*!"
Acts 5:24 priests did not know what to make of the *a*.
8:21 You can have no portion or lot in this *a*.
11: 4 *a* to them step by step from the beginning:

AFFAIRS (30)

Jgs 11:11 Jephthah settled all his *a* before the LORD.
1Chr 26:29 Israel's civil *a* as officials and judges.
29: 6 overseers of the king's *a* came forward
Neh 11:16 over the external *a* of the house of God;
11:24 deputy in all *a* that concerned the people.
Jdt 8:12 yourselves in the place of God in human *a*?
Est B: 7 *a* stable and undisturbed for the future."
E: 5 administration of *a* has induced many
1Mc 3:32 in charge of the king's *a* from the
6:57 duty to take care of the *a* of the kingdom.
10:37 positions of trust in the *a* of the kingdom.
2Mc 9:20 are well and your *a* are going as you wish,
11:23 be undisturbed in conducting their own *a*.
11:29 to return home and attend to your own *a*.
Ps(s) 112: 5 and lends, who conducts his *a* with justice;
Wis 9:11 in my *a* and safeguard me by her glory;
11: 1 their *a* prosper through the holy prophet.
Sir 3:17 My son, conduct your *a* with humility,
10:25 Flaunt not your wisdom in managing your *a*,
11:15 and understanding and knowledge of *a*,
33:23 Keep control over all your *a*;
Dn 8:27 then I arose and took care of the king's *a*.
Mt 25:21 I will put you in charge of larger *a*.
25:23 I will put you in charge of larger *a*.
Rom 6:19 human *a* because of your weak human nature.)
1Cor 4:13 that is the present state of *a*.
6: 3 then, we are up to deciding everyday *a*.
7:32 unmarried man is busy with the Lord's *a*,
1Thes 4:11 remain at peace and attend to your own *a*.
2Tm 2: 4 entangled in the *a* of civilian life;

AFFECT (2)

Jb 35: 8 wickedness can *a* only a man like yourself;
Gal 5: 9 "A little yeast can *a* the entire dough."

AFFECTATION (1)

1Pt 3: 3 The *a* of an elaborate hairdress,

AFFECTED (3)

1Chr 29:30 and of the events that *a* him and all
2Cor 11:29 Who is weak that I am not *a* by it?
Col 2:23 a certain show of wisdom in their *a* piety,

AFFECTION (8)

Gn 34: 3 with the girl, he endeavored to win her *a*.
43:30 for he was so overcome with *a* for his
2Mc 9:21 *a* the esteem and good will you bear me.
14:24 for he had a cordial *a* for the man.
15:30 from youth his *a* for his countrymen,
Rom 1:31 conscience, without loyalty, without *a*,
12:10 Love one another with the *a* of brothers.
Phil 1: 8 each of you with the *a* of Christ Jesus!

AFFECTS (1)

Nm 15:26 the fault of inadvertence *a* all the people.

AFFIRM (2)

Dt 28: 8 The LORD will *a* his blessing upon you,
Rom 15: 8 I *a* that Christ became the servant of the

AFFIRMS (1)

Sir 35:18 responds, judges justly and *a* the right.

AFFIXED (2)

Tb 7:13 the contract, to which they *a* their seals.
1Mc 14:26 which they *a* to pillars on Mount Zion.

AFFLICT (18)

Ex 9: 3 will *a* all your livestock in the field
15:26 I will not *a* you with any of the diseases
Dt 7:15 he will not *a* you with any of the
8:16 fathers, that he might *a* you and test you,
28:60 He will again *a* you with all the diseases
1Sm 6: 3 and will learn why he continues to *a* you."
6: 5 Perhaps then he will cease to *a* you,
2Sm 7:10 continue to *a* them as they did of old,
1Kgs 8:35 have sinned against you and you *a* them,
17:20 will you *a* even the widow with whom I am
1Chr 21:17 but do not *a* your people with this plague!"
2Chr 6:26 they withdraw from sin because you *a* them,
Ps(s) 89:23 deceive him, nor shall the wicked *a* him.
94: 5 they trample down, your inheritance they *a*.
Is 58: 3 *a* ourselves, and you take no note of it?"
64:11 you remain silent, and *a* us so severely?
Ez 22:29 they *a* the poor and the needy,

Rv 11: 6 turn water into blood and to *a* the earth

AFFLICTED (96)

Ex 15:26 the diseases with which I *a* the Egyptians;
Lv 14:32 This is the law for one *a* with leprosy who
15: 2 Every man who is *a* with a chronic flow
15: 4 bed on which the man *a* with the flow lies,
15: 6 furniture on which the *a* man was sitting,
15: 7 body of the *a* man shall wash his garments,
15: 8 If the *a* man spits on a clean man,
15: 9 Any saddle on which the *a* man rides,
15:11 Anyone whom the *a* man touches with
15:12 touched by the *a* man shall be broken;
15:13 man who has been *a* with a flow
15:25 "When a woman is *a* with a flow of blood
15:32 for the man who is *a* with a chronic flow,
15:33 period, or who is *a* with a chronic flow;
21:20 or walleyed, or who is *a* with eczema,
Dt 8: 3 He therefore let you be *a* with hunger,
Jos 7:25 today the misery with which you have *a* us!"
Jgs 10: 8 *a* and oppressed the Israelites in Bashan,
1Sm 5: 6 He ravaged and *a* the city and its vicinity
5: 9 he *a* its inhabitants, young and old,
5:12 who escaped death were *a* with hemorrhoids,
6:19 calamity with which the LORD had *a* them.
2Sm 19: 8 that has *a* you from your youth until now."
2Kgs 15: 5 The LORD *a* the king, and he was a leper
17:20 He *a* them and delivered them over to
2Chr 21:18 the LORD *a* him with an incurable disease
26:20 fled willingly, for the LORD had *a* him.
Tb 6: 8 a woman who is *a* by a demon or evil spirit,
7: 7 charitable man should be *a* with blindness!"
Jdt 16: 7 widow's garb to raise up the *a* in Israel.
Est C:13 She *a* her body severely;
1Mc 3: 7 was happily achieved, and he *a* many kings;
10:46 in Israel, and how sorely he had *a* them.
Jb 34:28 him, so that he heard the plea of the *a*.
Ps(s) 9:13 he has not forgotten the cry of the *a*.
9:14 see how I am *a* by my foes,
9:19 nor shall the hope of the *a* forever perish.
10: 2 Proudly the wicked harass the *a*,
10: 9 he lies in wait to catch the *a*;
10: 9 the *a* and drags them off in his net.
10:12 Forget not the *a*!
10:17 The desire of the *a* you hear,
12: 6 "Because they rob the *a*, and the needy
14: 6 You would confound the plans of the *a*,
25:16 have pity on me, for I am alone and *a*
34: 7 When the *a* man called out,
35:10 of the *a* man from those too strong for him,
35:10 the *a* and the needy from their despoilers?"
35:13 I *a* myself with fasting and poured forth
37:14 their bow to bring down the *a* and the poor,
40:18 Though I am *a* and poor,
69:30 But I am *a* and in pain;
70: 6 But I am *a* and poor; O God, hasten to me!
72: 2 with justice and your *a* ones with judgment.
72: 4 He shall defend the *a* among the people,
72:12 and the *a* when he has no one to help him.
73: 5 and are not *a* like the rest of men.
74:19 unmindful of the lives of your *a* ones.
74:21 may the *a* and the poor praise your name.
76:10 judgment, to save all the *a* of the earth.
82: 3 render justice to the *a* and the destitute.
86: 1 answer me, for I am *a* and poor.
88:16 I am *a* and in agony from my youth;
90:15 Make us glad, for the days when you *a* us,
107:17 wicked ways and *a* because of their sins,
116:10 even when I said, "I am greatly *a*";
119:67 Before I was *a* I went astray,
119:71 It is good for me that I have been *a*,
119:75 and in your faithfulness you have *a* me.
119:107 I am very much *a*;
140:13 that the LORD renders justice to the *a*,
Wis 11:11 those afar off and those close by were *a*:
14:15 For a father, *a* with untimely mourning,
Sir 30:20 So it is with the *a* man who groans at the
Is 11: 4 and decide aright for the land's *a*.
14:32 and in her the *a* of his people find refuge."
41:17 The *a* and the needy seek water in vain,
49:13 his people and shows mercy to his *a*.
51:21 But now, hear this, O *a* one,
53: 4 as stricken, as one smitten by God and *a*.
54:11 O *a* one, storm-battered and unconsoled,
58:10 bread on the hungry and satisfy the *a*;
66: 2 lowly and *a* man who trembles at my word.
Lam 1:12 LORD *a* me on the day of his blazing wrath.
Bar 3: 1 *a* souls and dismayed spirits call to you.
Mi 4: 6 the outcasts, and those whom I have *a*.
Mt 4:24 They carried to him all those *a* with
8:16 a simple command and cured all who were *a*,
14:35 People brought him all the *a*,
Mk 1:34 Those whom he cured, who were variously *a*,
5:25 been *a* with a hemorrhage for a dozen years.
Lk 9: 2 proclaim the reign of God and heal the *a*.
2Cor 1: 6 If we are *a* it is for your encouragement
4: 8 We are *a* in every way possible,
Heb 11:37 in the skins of sheep or goats, needy, *a*,

AFFLICTING (1)

Lam 3:33 no joy in *a* or grieving the sons of men.

AFFLICTION (52)

Gn 41:52 has made me fruitful in the land of my *a*."
Ex 3: 7 "I have witnessed the *a* of my people in
4:31 concerned about them and had seen their *a*,
Lv 15:13 with a flow becomes free of his *a*,
15:28 "If she becomes freed from her *a*,
Dt 8: 2 so as to test you by *a* and find out
16: 3 it only unleavened bread, the bread of *a*,
26: 7 and he heard our cry and saw our *a*,
Jgs 2:18 cries of *a* under their oppressors.
2Sm 16:12 Perhaps the LORD will look upon my *a* and
2Kgs 14:26 the LORD saw the very bitter *a* of Israel,
2Chr 6:29 kind, and in awareness of his *a* and pain,
20: 9 house, and we will cry out to you in our *a*,
Neh 9: 9 "You saw the *a* of our fathers in Egypt,
Tb 6: 8 spirit, the *a* will leave him completely,
1Mc 1:63 Terrible *a* was upon Israel.
2Mc 7:31 contrived every kind of *a* for the Hebrews,
8:17 Place and the *a* of the humiliated city,
14: 8 great *a* from the unreasonable conduct
Jb 10:15 filled with ignominy and sodden with *a*!
30:27 days of *a* have overtaken me.
36: 8 with fetters and held fast by bonds of *a*,
36:15 he saves the unfortunate through their *a*,
36:21 for you have preferred carousal to *a*.
Ps(s) 25:18 Put an end to my *a* and my suffering,
31: 8 my *a* and watched over me in my distress,
31:11 My strength has failed through *a*,
38:12 my companions stand back because of my *a*;
73:14 For I suffer *a* day after day and
88:10 My eyes have grown dim through *a*;
91:10 you, nor shall *a* come near your tent,
106:44 regard for their *a* when he heard their cry;
107:39 low through oppression, *a* and sorrow.
119:50 in my *a* is that your promise gives me life.
119:92 my delight, I should have perished in my *a*.
119:153 Behold my *a*, and rescue me,
Eccl 8: 6 it is a great *a* for man that he is
Wis 3: 2 passing away was thought an *a*
Sir 3:27 the *a* of the proud man there is no cure;
11:27 *a* brings forgetfulness of past delights;
23:11 just, and all his house will suffer *a*.
Is 48:10 silver, tested you in the furnace of *a*.
53:11 Because of his *a* he shall see the light in
63: 9 he became their savior in their every *a*.
Jer 51: 2 besiege her from all sides on the day of *a*.
Lam 3: 1 man who knows *a* from the rod of his anger,
Dn 9:25 With streets and trenches, in time of *a*.
Zec 9: 8 again, for now I have regard for their *a*.
Mk 5:29 cured of her *a* ran through her whole body.
Acts 7:34 I have witnessed the *a* of my people in
Rom 2: 9 *a* and anguish will come upon every man who
5: 3 We know that *a* makes for endurance,

AFFLICTIONS (9)

2Mc 7:37 and by *a* and blows to make you confess
Ps(s) 71:20 you have made me feel many bitter *a*,
141: 5 but I will still pray under these *a*.
Sir 10:13 unheard-of *a* and brings men to utter ruin.
Mk 3:10 had *a* kept pushing toward him to touch him.
Lk 7:21 he was curing many of their diseases, *a*,
Rom 5: 3 But not only that—we even boast of our *a*!
2Cor 1: 4 He comforts us in all our *a* and thus
7: 4 despite my many *a* my joy knows no bounds.

AFFORD (8)

Lv 5: 7 he cannot *a* an animal of the flock,
5:11 to *a* even two turtledoves or two pigeons,
12: 8 If, however, she cannot *a* a lamb,
14:21 "If a man is poor and cannot *a* so much,
14:22 or pigeons, which he can more easily *a*,
14:30 or pigeons, such as the man can *a*,
Neh 2: 7 *a* me safe-conduct till I arrive in Judah;
Lk 21: 4 her want has given what she could not *a*—

AFFORDED (1)

Wis 5: 8 What have wealth and its boastfulness *a* us?

AFFORDING (1)

Ps(s) 144:13 our garners be full, *a* every kind of store;

AFFORDS (2)

1Jn 2:15 the world, nor the things that the world *a*.
2:16 that the world *a* comes from the Father.

AFFRIGHT (4)

Jb 3: 5 upon it, the blackness of night *a* it!
7:14 Then you *a* me with dreams and with visions
13:11 *a* you and the dread of him fall upon you.
18:11 On every side terrors *a* him;

AFIRE (5)

Jos 8: 8 it *a* in obedience to the LORD's command.
2Chr 36:19 walls of Jerusalem, set all its palaces *a*,
Jb 41:13 His breath sets coals *a*;
Sir 11:31 with a spark he sets many coals *a*.
Is 30:33 like a stream of sulphur, will set it *a*.

AFLAME (5)

Sir 43: 4 it sets the mountains *a* with its rays;
Is 13: 8 look aghast at each other, their faces *a.*
Na 1:10 As when a tangle of thornbushes is set *a,*
Jn 5:35 He was the lamp, set *a* and burning bright,
2Cor 11:29 that I am not *a* with indignation?

AFOOT (1)

Jn 11:53 day onward there was a plan *a* to kill him.

AFOREMENTIONED (2)

2Mc 2: 1 to take some of the *a* fire with them,
4:23 sent Menelaus, brother of the *a* Simon,

AFORESAID (1)

2Mc 3: 7 instructions to expropriate the *a* wealth.

AFRAID (103)

Gn 3:10 but I was *a,* because I was naked,
18:15 Because she was *a,* Sarah dissembled,
19:30 Since Lot was *a* to stay in Zoar,
20:10 What were you *a* of,"
20:11 "I was *a,*" answered Abraham,
21:17 Don't be *a;* God has heard the boy's cry
26: 7 He was *a,* if he called her his wife
46: 3 Do not be *a* to go down to Egypt,
Ex 2:14 Then Moses became *a* and thought,
3: 6 hid his face, for he was *a* to look at God.
20:20 Moses answered the people, "Do not be *a,*
34:30 had become, they were *a* to come near him.
Nm 14: 9 need not be *a* of the people of that land;
14: 9 Therefore, do not be *a* of them."
21:34 said to Moses, "Do not be *a* of him;
Dt 2: 4 Though they are *a* of you,
3: 2 however, said to me, 'Do not be *a* of him,
5: 5 Since you were *a* of the fire and would not
7:18 But do not be *a* of them.
7:19 to all the nations of whom you are now *a.*
20: 1 greater than your own, do not be *a* of them,
20: 3 Be not weakhearted or *a;*
20: 8 'Is there anyone who is *a* and weakhearted?
Jos 8: 1 "Do not be *a* or dismayed.
10:25 said to them, "Do not be *a* or dismayed,
Jgs 4:18 do not be *a.*"
7: 3 the soldiers, 'If anyone is *a* or fearful,
7:10 If you are *a* to attack,
8:20 a boy, he was *a* and did not draw his sword.
1Sm 7: 7 *a* of the Philistines and said to Samuel,
17:24 they all retreated before him, very much *a.*
21:13 remarks and became very much *a* of Achish,
23: 3 "We are *a* here in Judah.
2Sm 1:14 "How is it that you were not *a* to put
10:19 *a* to give further aid to the Ammonites.
12:18 were *a* to tell him that the child was dead,
13:28 Do not be *a,* for it is I who order you
1Kgs 17:13 "Do not be *a,*" Elijah said to her.
19: 3 Elijah was *a* and fled for his life,
2Kgs 1:15 you need not be *a* of him."
6:16 "Do not be *a,*" Elisha answered.
25:24 "Do not be *a* of the Chaldean officials,"
1Chr 13:12 David was now *a* of God,
2Chr 32: 7 do not be *a* or dismayed because of the
Tb 6:15 So now I too am *a* of this demon.
6:18 But do not be *a,* for she was set apart
Jdt 1:11 They were not *a* of him but regarded him
5:23 "We are not *a* of the Israelites,"
1Mc 3:22 so do not be *a* of them."
3:56 planting vineyards, and those who were *a,*
4: 8 *a* of their numbers or dread their attack.
5:41 *a* and camps on the other side of the river,
7:30 Judas was *a* and would not meet him again.
8:12 all who heard of their fame were *a* of them.
9: 6 of the troops, they were very much *a,*
10:76 of the city became *a* and opened the gates,
12:40 was *a* that Jonathan would not permit him,
12:42 large army he was *a* to offer him violence.
16: 6 that his men were *a* to cross the stream,
2Mc 7:29 Do not be *a* of this executioner,
Jb 6:21 you see a terrifying thing and are *a.*
9:35 that I might speak without being *a* of him.
19:29 Be *a* of the sword for yourselves,
32: 6 and was *a* to declare to you my knowledge.
41:17 When he rises up, the mighty are *a;*
Prv 3:24 When you lie down, you need not be *a,*
3:25 Be not *a* of sudden terror,
Wis 8:15 princes, hearing of me, would be *a;*
Sir 34:14 fears the LORD is never alarmed, never *a;*
Is 57:11 Of whom were you *a?*
Jer 38:19 "I am *a* of the men of Judah who have
39:17 handed over to the men of whom you are *a.*
40: 9 men not to be *a* to serve the Chaldeans:
41:18 They were *a* of the Chaldeans,
42:11 of Babylon, before whom you are now *a;*
Dn 1:10 to Daniel, "I am *a* of my lord the king;
Am 3: 8 The lion roars— who will not be *a!*
Zec 9: 5 Ashkelon shall see it and be *a;* Gaza also:
Mt 2:22 of Judea, and he was *a* to go back there.
10:31 so do not be *a* of anything.
14: 5 to kill John but was *a* of the people,
14:27 It is I. Do not be *a!*"
17: 7 Get up! Do not be *a.*"
28:10 At this Jesus said to them, "Do not be *a!*
Mk 6:50 It is I. Do not be *a!*"
9:32 his words, they were *a* to question him.
11:18 They were at the same time *a* of him
Lk 2: 9 around them, and they were very much *a.*
5:10 Jesus said to Simon, "Do not be *a.*
9:45 were *a* to question him about the matter.
12: 4 Do not be *a* of those who kill the body and
19:21 I was *a* of you because you are a hard man.
20:19 on him, but they were *a* of the people.
22: 2 but they were *a* of the people.
Jn 6:20 do not be *a.*"
9:22 fashion because they were *a* of the Jews,
19: 8 this kind of talk, he was more *a* than ever.
Acts 9:26 it turned out that they were all *a* of him.
18: 9 "Do not be *a.* Go on speaking
27:24 'Do not be *a,* Paul,' he said.
Rom 13: 4 Only if you do wrong ought you to be *a.*
Heb 13: 6 "The Lord is my helper, I will not be *a;*
1Jn 4:18 love is not yet perfect in one who is *a.*

AFRESH (1)

Lv 24: 8 bread shall be set out *a* before the LORD,

AFTERBIRTH (1)

Dt 28:57 the *a* that issues from her womb

AFTERGROWTH (5)

Lv 25: 5 The *a* of your harvest you shall not reap,
25:11 nor shall you reap the *a* or pick the
2Kgs 19:29 this year you shall eat the *a,*
Prv 27:25 the grass is taken away and the *a* appears,
Is 37:30 this year you shall eat the *a,*

AFTERNOON (7)

Jgs 19: 8 "Fortify yourself and tarry until the *a.*"
Mt 20: 6 *a* he found still others standing around.
20: 9 *a* came up they received a full day's pay,
Mk 11:11 but since it was already late in the *a,*
Jn 1:39 (It was about four in the *a.*)
4:52 "The fever left him yesterday *a* about one."
Acts 10: 3 One *a* at about three he had a vision in

AFTERWARD (69)

Gn 10:18 *A,* the clans of the Canaanites spread out,
18: 5 and *a* you may go on your way."
22:20 Some time *a,* the news came to Abraham:
38:30 *A* his brother came out;
40: 1 Some time *a,* the royal cupbearer
48: 1 Some time *a,* Joseph was informed,
Lv 6:21 shall be scoured *a* and rinsed with water.
Nm 19: 7 and only *a* may he return to the camp.
Dt 17: 7 *a* all the people are to join in.
23:14 dig a hole and *a* cover up your excrement.
Jos 1:15 *A* you may return and occupy your own land,
24: 6 *A* I led you out of Egypt,
Jgs 1: 9 *A* the Judahites went down to fight against
1Sm 15:32 *A* Samuel commanded,
24: 6 *A,* however, David regretted
2Sm 2:26 not know that *a* there will be bitterness?
24:10 *A,* however, David regretted
1Kgs 18: 1 Long *a,* in the third year,
2Kgs 4: 8 *A,* whenever he passed by,
10:25 *A* they went into the inner shrine of the
1Chr 19: 1 *A* Nahash, king of the Ammonites, died
20: 4 *A* there was another battle with the
28: 8 possess this good land and *a* leave it
2Chr 6:24 but *a* they return and praise your name,
33:14 *A* he built an outer wall for the City of
35:14 *A* they prepared the Passover for
Neh 2:17 *A* I said to them:
Tb 1:20 *A,* all my property was confiscated;
6: 7 *A* they traveled on together till they were
7: 9 *A,* Raguel slaughtered a ram from the flock
7:14 *A* they began to eat and drink.
14: 5 *A* all of them shall return from their exile,
Jdt 13: 9 Soon *a,* she came out and handed over
1Mc 4:18 *A* you can freely take the plunder."
2Mc 5:20 *a* participated in their good fortune;
11: 1 Very soon *a,* Lysias,
Prv 20:17 but *a* his mouth will be filled with gravel.
24:27 *a* you can establish your house.
Eccl 9: 3 and *a* they go to the dead.
Wis 4:19 And they shall *a* become dishonored
5:11 *a* no mark of passage can be found in it.
Sir 3:30 He who does a kindness is remembered *a;*
6:29 Thus will you *a* find rest in her,
Is 41:23 Foretell the things that shall come *a,*
Jer 34:11 *a* they took back their male and female
49: 6 *a* I will change the lot of the Ammonites,
Jl 3: 1 Then *a* I will pour out my spirit upon all
Mt 4: 2 days and forty nights, and *a* was hungry.
14:12 *A,* they came and informed Jesus.
14:22 Immediately *a,* while dismissing
19:21 *A,* come back and follow me."
21:30 but *a* he regretted it and went.
27:30 *A* they took hold of the reed and kept
Mk 1:21 Shortly *a* they came to Capernaum,
6:45 Immediately *a* he insisted that his
Lk 1:24 *A,* his wife Elizabeth conceived.
5:27 *A* he went out and saw a tax collector
7:11 Soon *a* he went to a town called Naim,
8:37 Shortly *a,* the entire population
17: 8 You can eat and drink *a'?*
Jn 19:38 *A,* Joseph of Arimathea,
Acts 5:40 the name of Jesus, and *a* dismissed them.
7:21 his father's house, but *a* he was abandoned,
16:40 *a* they departed.
20:11 *A* Paul went upstairs again,
1Tm 2:13 For Adam was created first, Eve *a;*
Heb 4: 7 when long *a* he spoke through David the
4: 8 God would not have spoken *a* of another day.
12:17 You know that *a* he wanted to inherit his

AGABUS (2)

Acts 11:28 One of them named *A* was inspired to stand
21:10 stay, a prophet named *A* arrived from Judea.

AGAG (6)

1Sm 15: 8 He took *A,*
15: 9 *A* and the best of the fat sheep and oxen,
15:20 I have brought back *A,*
15:32 Afterward Samuel commanded, "Bring *A,*
15:32 *A* came to him struggling and saying,
15:33 he cut *A* down before the LORD in Gilgal.

AGAGITE (6)

Est A:17 Haman, however, son of Hammedatha the *A,*
3: 1 raised Haman, son of Hammedatha the *A,*
3:10 gave it to Haman, son of Hammedatha the *A,*
8: 3 to revoke the harm done by Haman the *A,*
8: 5 schemer Haman, son of Hammedatha the *A,*
9:24 Haman, son of Hammedatha the *A,*

AGAMA (1)

Lv 11:30 lizards, the gecko, the chameleon, the *a,*

AGAPE (1)

Jb 16:10 their mouths are *a* to bite me.

AGATE (2)

Ex 28:19 third row, a jacinth, an *a* and an amethyst;
39:12 third row a jacinth, an *a* and an amethyst;

AGE (129)

Gn 6: 9 Noah, a good man and blameless in that *a,*
7: 1 in this *a* have I found to be truly just.
15:15 you shall be buried at a contented old *a.*
21: 2 and bore Abraham a son in his old *a,*
21: 7 Yet I have borne him a son in his old *a.*"
24: 1 Abraham had now reached a ripe old *a,*
24:36 bore a son to my master in her old *a,*
25: 8 breathed his last, dying at a ripe old *a,*
37: 3 sons, for he was the child of his old *a;*
43:33 by his directions according to their *a,*
44:20 a young brother, the child of his old *a.*
48:10 (Now Israel's eyes were dim from *a,*
50:26 Joseph died at the *a* of a hundred and ten.
Nm 4: 3 between thirty and fifty years of *a;*
4:23 men between thirty and fifty years of *a;*
4:30 men between thirty and fifty years of *a;*
4:35 men between thirty and fifty years of *a.*
4:39 men between thirty and fifty years of *a.*
4:43 the men from thirty up to fifty years of *a.*
4:47 men between thirty and fifty years of *a*
26:62 of male Levites one month or more of *a,*
Dt 31:29 future *a* because you have done evil
32: 7 of old, reflect on the years of age upon *a.*
Jos 5: 4 every man of military *a* had died in the
24:29 LORD, died at the *a* of a hundred and ten.
Jgs 8:32 At a good old *a* Gideon,
Ru 4:15 comfort and the support of your old *a,*
1Sm 2:31 no man in your family shall reach old *a.*
8: 1 In his old *a* Samuel appointed his sons
2Sm 19:34 for your old *a* as my guest in Jerusalem."
1Kgs 1: 6 next in *a* to Absalom by the same mother.
1:15 attending him because of his advanced *a.*
2: 6 to go down to the grave in peaceful old *a.*
14: 4 not see because *a* had dimmed his sight.
15:23 In his old *a,* Asa had an infirmity
1Chr 23:24 of the LORD from twenty years of *a* upward,
27:23 who were twenty years of *a* or younger,
29:28 He died at a ripe old *a,*
2Chr 24:15 Jehoiada lived to a ripe old *a;*
26: 1 though he was but sixteen years of *a,*
31:16 houses of males thirty years of *a* and over,
Ezr 3: 8 Levites twenty years of *a* and over
Neh 10:29 all who are of the *a* of discretion,
Tb 3:10 cause my father in his old *a* to go down
8: 7 allow us to live together to a happy old *a.*"
14: 1 at the *a* of a hundred and twelve,
14:14 the venerable *a* of a hundred and seventeen.
Jdt 16:23 the advanced *a* of a hundred and five.
2Mc 6:18 a man of advanced *a* and noble appearance,
6:23 his years, the dignity of his advanced *a,*
6:24 "At our *a* it would be unbecoming to make
6:25 would bring shame and dishonor on my old *a.*
6:27 I will prove myself worthy of my old *a,*
7:27 and supported you to your present *a.*

AGE (cont.)

Jb 12:12 So with old *a* is wisdom,
41:24 think the deep had the hoary head of *a*.
Ps(s) 10: 6 *a* to age I shall be without misfortune."
71: 9 Cast me not off in my old *a;*
92:15 They shall bear fruit even in old *a;*
Prv 27:24 forever, nor even a crown from *a* to age.
Eccl 6: 3 many years, no matter to what great *a,*
Wis 3:17 and dishonored will their old *a* be at last;
4: 8 For the *a* that is honorable comes not with
4: 9 an unsullied life, the attainment of old *a*.
7:27 And passing into holy souls from age to *a,*
Sir 25: 3 youth, how will you acquire in your old *a?*
30:24 life, worry brings on premature old *a*.
46: 9 Caleb remained with him even in his old *a*
Is 13:20 be inhabited, nor dwelt in, from *a* to age;
46: 4 Even to your old *a* I am the same,
Jer 41: 3 slew all the men of Judah of military *a*
50:39 it be peopled, or lived in, from *a* to age.
Lam 5:19 your throne stands from *a* to age.
Bar 4:15 for *a* nor tenderness for childhood;
Ez 16: 7 developed, you came to the *a* of puberty;
26:20 into the pit, those of the bygone *a;*
Dn 1:10 with the other young men of your *a,*
6: 1 to the kingdom at the *a* of sixty-two.
13:50 God has given you the prestige of old *a*."
13:52 "How you have grown evil with *a!*
Zec 8: 4 each with staff in hand because of old *a,*
Mt 12:32 either in this *a* or in the age to come.
12:39 evil and unfaithful *a* is eager for a sign!
16: 4 An evil, faithless *a* is eager for a sign,
19:28 in the new *a* when the Son of Man takes his
Mk 8:12 he said, "Why does this *a* seek a sign?
8:38 corrupt *a* is ashamed of me and my doctrine,
10:30 present *a* a hundred times as many homes,
10:30 and in the *a* to come,
16:20 lawless and faithless *a* is under Satan,
Lk 1:18 my wife too is advanced in *a*."
1:36 has conceived a son in her old *a;*
1:50 His mercy is from *a* to age on those
2:52 wisdom and *a* and grace before God and men.
3:23 his work he was about thirty years of *a,*
11:29 "This is an evil *a*.
11:30 the Son of Man be a sign for the present *a*.
17:25 much and be rejected by the present *a*.
18:30 plentiful return in this *a*
18:30 age and life everlasting in the *a* to come."
20:34 of this *a* marry and are given in marriage,
20:35 a place in the *a* to come
Jn 9:23 was why his parents said, "He is of *a*—
Acts 4:22 cured was more than forty years of *a*.
Rom 12: 2 Do not conform yourselves to this *a* but be
1Cor 2: 6 It is not a wisdom of this *a,*
2: 6 age, however, not of the rulers of this *a,*
2: 8 of the rulers of this *a* knew the mystery;
2Cor 4: 4 blinded by the god of the present *a*
Gal 1: 4 to rescue us from the present evil *a,*
4: 1 as long as a designated heir is not of *a*
4: 3 while we were not yet of *a* we were like
Eph 1:21 be given in this *a* or in the age to come.
2: 2 the present *a* and to the prince of the air,
1Tm 5: 9 should be not less than sixty years of *a*.
Ti 2:12 in this *a* as we await our blessed hope,
Heb 1: 2 in this, the final *a,*
6: 5 of God and the powers of the *a* to come,
11:11 to conceive though she was past the *a,*

AGE-OLD (7)

Dt 33:15 With the finest gifts of the *a* mountains
Ps(s) 37:35 and stalwart as a flourishing, *a* tree.
Sir 14:17 the *a* law is: All must die
Jer 31: 3 With *a* love I have loved you;
Bar 5: 7 And that the *a* depths and gorges be filled
Hb 3: 6 the *a* hills bow low along his ancient ways.
Eph 3:11 of heaven, in accord with his *a* purpose,

AGED (14)

Gn 43:27 he asked them, "And how is your *a* father,
44:20 we said to my lord, 'We have an *a* father,
Lv 19:32 "Stand up in the presence of the *a,*
Dt 28:50 respect for the *a* nor pity for the young.
2Chr 36:17 nor maiden, neither the *a* nor the decrepit;
2Mc 8:30 persecuted, to orphans, widows, and the *a*.
Jb 12:20 adviser, and takes discretion from the *a*.
32: 9 wise, nor the *a* who understand the right.
Ps(s) 6: 8 they have *a* because of all my foes.
Prv 30:17 that mocks a father, or scorns an *a* mother,
Sir 9:10 you drink with pleasure only when it has *a*.
25: 5 How becoming to the *a* is wisdom,
25:19 to *a* feet is a railing wife to a quiet man.
42: 8 *a* and infirm answering for wanton conduct.

AGEE (1)

2Sm 23:11 to him was Shammah, son of *A* the Hararite.

AGENT (1)

Tb 1:13 I became purchasing *a* for all his needs.

AGENTS (3)

1Kgs 10:28 Cilicia, where the king's *a* purchased them.
2Chr 1:16 The king's *a* would acquire them by
Ezr 4: 9 officials, and *a* from among the Persian,

AGES (49)

Gn 9:12 sign that I am giving for all *a* to come,
17: 7 throughout the *a* as an everlasting pact,
17: 9 you must keep my covenant throughout the *a*.
17:12 Throughout the *a,*
Lv 27: 3 persons between the *a* of twenty and sixty,
27: 5 persons between the *a* of five and twenty,
27: 6 between the *a* of one month and five years,
Tb 11:14 holy name be praised throughout all the *a,*
13: 1 because his kingdom lasts for all *a*.
13: 6 righteousness, and exalt the King of the *a*.
13:10 his goodness, and bless the King of the *a,*
13:11 you the chosen one, through all *a* forever.
13:13 together and shall bless the Lord of the *a*.
13:18 may he be blessed for all *a!*"
14: 7 bless the God of the *a* in righteousness.
Ps(s) 145:13 Your kingdom is a kingdom for all *a,*
Eccl 1:10 already existed in the *a* that preceded us.
Wis 8: 8 in advance and the outcome of times and *a*.
Sir 24: 9 Before all *a,*
24: 9 and through all *a* I shall not cease to be.
39:20 His gaze spans all the *a;*
40:12 be wiped out, but loyalty remains for *a*.
51: 8 of the LORD, his kindness through *a* past;
Is 45:17 be put to shame or disgrace in future *a*."
51: 9 Awake as in the days of old, in *a* long ago!
58:12 foundations from *a* past you shall raise up;
60:15 Now I will make you the pride of the *a,*
Dn 3:52 and exalted above all for all *a*.
Mt 24:21 of the world until now or in all *a* to come.
Lk 1:48 all *a* to come shall call me blessed.
Acts 14:16 In past *a* he let the Gentiles go their way.
Rom 16:25 reveals the mystery hidden for many *a*
16:27 given through Jesus Christ unto endless *a*.
1Cor 2: 7 God planned it before all *a* for our glory.
10:11 to us, upon whom the end of the *a* has come.
Gal 1: 5 to him be glory for endless *a*.
Eph 2: 7 that in the *a* to come he might display the
3: 5 unknown to men in former *a* but now
3: 9 design which for *a* was hidden in God,
Phil 4:20 glory to our God and Father for unending *a!*
Col 1:26 that mystery hidden from *a* and generations
1Tm 1:17 To the King of *a,*
Ti 1: 2 who cannot lie, promised in endless *a* past.
Heb 9:26 end of the *a* to take away sins
1Pt 3: 5 *a* used to adorn themselves in this way,
4:11 him be glory and dominion throughout the *a*.
5:11 Dominion be his throughout the *a!*
Jude 1:25 too, be his, might and power from *a* past,
1:25 from ages past, now and for *a* to come.

AGGRESSIVELY (1)

1Mc 6:25 They have acted *a* not only against us,

AGGRIEVES (1)

Wis 14:24 kills his neighbor, or *a* him by adultery.

AGHAST (6)

Lv 26:32 live there will stand *a* at the sight of it.
Is 13: 8 They look *a* at each other,
Jer 49:20 own pasture shall be *a* because of them.
50:45 own pasture shall be *a* because of them.
Ez 27:35 who dwell on the coastlands are *a* over you,
28:19 peoples, all who knew you stand *a* at you;

AGILE (1)

Wis 7:22 holy, unique, Manifold, subtle, *a,*

AGING (1)

Tb 14:13 of his *a* father-in-law and mother-in-law;

AGITATED (2)

Gn 41: 8 Next morning his spirit was *a*.
2Thes 2: 2 not to be so easily *a* or terrified,

AGITATORS (1)

Acts 16:20 men are *a* disturbing the peace of our city!

AGONY (4)

1Mc 9:56 Finally he died in great *a*.
2Mc 15:19 remained in the city suffered a like *a,*
Ps(s) 88:16 I am afflicted and in *a* from my youth;
Rom 8:22 creation groans and is in *a* even until now.

AGREE (16)

Gn 34:15 We will *a* with you only on this condition,
34:22 But the men will *a* to live with us and
39:10 day, he would not *a* to lie beside her,
Dt 1:14 me, 'We *a* to do as you have proposed.'
1Sm 30:24 Who could *a* with this proposal of yours?
1Kgs 5:22 Solomon, "I *a* to the proposal you sent me,
22:50 But Jehoshaphat would not *a*.
2Kgs 6: 3 "Please *a* to accompany your servants,"
2Mc 11:24 We understand that the Jews do not *a* with
Mk 14:56 under oath but their testimony did not *a*.
14:59 Even so, their testimony did not *a*.
Acts 15:15 The words of the prophets *a* with this,
Rom 7:16 by that very fact I *a* that the law is good.
1Cor 1:10 Lord Jesus Christ, to *a* in what you say.
Phlm 1:19 I *a* to pay
Rv 17:17 by making them *a* to bestow their

AGREEABLE (7)

1Sm 18: 5 soldiers, and this was *a* to the whole army,
2Sm 3:19 concerning all that would be *a* to Israel
17: 4 This plan was *a* to Absalom and to all the
1Mc 1:12 The proposal was *a;*
Jb 6:25 How *a* are honest words;
Prv 23: 8 up, and you will have wasted your *a* words.
Sir 36:18 yet some foods are more *a* than others;

AGREED (38)

Gn 29:28 Jacob *a*. He finished the bridal
30:34 "Very well," *a* Laban.
34:24 the town *a* with Hamor and his son Shechem,
37:27 His brothers *a*.
42:20 To this they *a*.
Ex 2:21 Moses *a* to live with him,
Jgs 20:38 the other Israelites had *a* with the men in
1Sm 12: 5 "He is witness," they *a*.
1Kgs 15:20 Ben-hadad *a* with King Asa and sent the
18:24 All the people answered, *A!*"
2Kgs 3:12 word of the LORD," the king of Judah *a*.
12: 9 So the priests *a* that they would neither
1Chr 13: 4 And the whole assembly *a* to do this,
2Chr 16: 4 Ben-hadad *a* to King Asa's request and sent
18:21 The LORD *a:* You shall succeed
30: 2 assembly in Jerusalem had *a* to celebrate
30:23 assembly *a* to celebrate another seven days.
Ezr 10:16 The exiles did as *a*.
Neh 2: 6 to him, and the king *a* that I might go.
10:31 *A,* that we will not marry our daughters to
10:36 We have *a* to bring each year to the house
11: 2 *a* to take up residence in Jerusalem.
1Mc 6:23 We *a* to serve your father and to follow
9:71 He *a* to do as Jonathan had asked.
11:29 The king *a* and wrote the following letter
14:47 Simon accepted and *a* to act as high priest,
2Mc 4: 9 this he *a* to pay a hundred and fifty more,
11:15 common good, *a* to all that Lysias proposed;
12:12 respects, Judas *a* to make peace with them.
Wis 19: 2 That though they themselves had *a* to the
Jer 34:10 But though they *a* and freed them,
Dn 6: 8 and governors are *a* that the following
13:14 and then they *a* to look for an occasion
Am 3: 3 Do two walk together unless they have *a?*
Mt 20:13 You *a* on the usual wage, did you not?
Lk 22: 5 were delighted, and *a* to give him money.
Jn 9:22 who had already *a* among themselves that
Acts 23:20 "The Jews have *a* among themselves to ask

AGREEING (2)

Dt 1:23 *A* with the proposal,
Jgs 18:20 The priest, *a,* took the ephod,

AGREEMENT (36)

Gn 26:28 there be a sworn *a* between our two sides
Lv 24: 8 part of the Israelites by an everlasting *a*.
Dt 26:17 Today you are making this *a* with the LORD:
26:18 today the LORD is making this *a* with you:
Jos 9:15 them and entered into an *a* to spare them,
9:16 Three days after the *a* was entered into,
1Sm 22: 8 my son has made an *a* with the son of Jesse?
23:18 made a joint *a* before the LORD in Horesh,
2Sm 3:12 at the moment, to say, "Make an *a* with me,
3:13 "Very well, I will make an *a* with you.
3:21 the king, that they may make an *a* with you;
5: 3 made an *a* with them there before the LORD,
1Kgs 20:34 made an *a* with him and then set him free.
1Mc 7:12 Alcimus and Bacchides to ask for a just *a*.
7:18 the *a* and the oath that they swore."
8:29 have made an *a* with the Jewish people.
2Mc 13:23 Having come to this *a,*
14:19 Theodotus and Mattathias to arrange an *a*.
14:20 and when general *a* was expressed,
14:28 his *a* with a man who had done no wrong.
Jb 31: 1 If I have made an *a* with my eyes and
40:28 Will he make an *a* with you that you may
Sir 41:17 disloyalty, and of breaking an oath or *a*.
44:18 A lasting *a* was made with him,
44:20 Most High, and entered into an *a* with him;
Jer 34: 8 Zedekiah had made an *a* with all the people
34:10 others who entered the *a* consented
34:15 making an *a* before me in the house
34:18 terms of the *a* which they made before me,
Dn 11:17 He shall conclude an *a* with him and give
Mt 20: 2 an *a* with them for the usual daily wage,
Acts 5:12 *a* they used to meet in Solomon's Portico.
15:22 in *a* with the whole Jerusalem church,
28:25 Without reaching any *a* among themselves,
2Cor 6:16 Tell me what *a* there is between the temple
Rv 17:13 Then they will come to *a* and bestow their

AGREEMENTS (2)

1Mc 15:27 he broke all the *a* he had previously made

2Mc 12: 1 After these *a* were made,

AGREES (2)

Dt 20:11 If it *a* to your terms of peace and opens
Rom 7:22 My inner self *a* with the law of God,

AGRIPPA (11)

Acts 25:13 A few days later King *A* and Bernice
25:22 *A* said to Festus,
25:23 So the next day *A* and Bernice came with
25:24 *A* and all you who are here present with us,
25:26 you, and in particular before you, King *A*,
26: 1 *A* now spoke to Paul:
26: 2 leveled against me by the Jews, King *A*.
26:19 "King *A*, I could not disobey
26:27 Do you believe the prophets, King *A?*
26:28 At this, *A* said,
26:32 *A* further remarked to Festus,

AGROUND (3)

Jn 6:21 *a* on the shore they had been approaching.
Acts 27:39 to run the ship *a* on it if possible.
27:41 but the ship hit a sandbar and ran *a*.

AGUR (1)

Prv 30: 1 The words of *A*, son of Jakeh the Massaite:

AH (26)

Gn 23:13 *A*, if only you would please listen to me!
27:27 With that, he blessed him, saying, *A*,
27:39 *A*, far from the fertile earth shall be
Ex 32:31 Moses went back to the LORD and said, *A*,
Nm 12:11 When Aaron turned and saw her a leper, *A*,
Dt 3:25 *A*, let me cross over and see this good
Jb 6: 2 *A*, could my anguish but be measured and my
Sg 1:15 *A*, you are beautiful, my beloved
1:15 *a*, you are beautiful; your eyes are doves!
1:16 Ah, you are beautiful, my lover
3: 7 *A*, it is the litter of Solomon;
4: 1 *A*, you are beautiful, my beloved, ah,
Is 1: 4 *A!* sinful nation,
1:24 *A!* I will take vengeance
17:12 *A!* the roaring of many peoples
18: 1 *A*, land of buzzing insects,
41:29 *A*, all of them are nothing,
44:16 full, and then warms himself and says, *A!*
Jer 1: 6 *A*, Lord GOD!" I said,
4:31 *A*, woe is me!
14:13 *A!* LORD GOD, I replied,
32:17 *A*, LORD GOD, you have made
Dn 9: 4 to the LORD, my God, and confessed, *A*,
Acts 22:28 *A*," said Paul,
1Cor 4:10 *A*, but in Christ you are wise!

AHA (9)

Jb 39:25 trumpet, but at each blast he cries, *A!*"
Ps(s) 35:21 wide their mouths against me, saying, *A*,
35:21 their mouths against me, saying, "Aha, *a!*
35:25 Let them not say in their hearts, *A!*
40:16 dismayed in their shame who say to me, *A*,
40:16 in their shame who say to me, "Aha, *a!*"
70: 4 their shame who say to me, *A*, aha!"
Ez 26: 2 *A!* it is broken, the gateway

AHAB (79)

1Kgs 16:28 and his son *A* succeeded him as king.
16:29 year of Asa, king of Judah, *A* son of Omri,
16:30 *A*, son of Omri,
16:32 *A* erected an altar to Baal in the temple
17: 1 Tishbite, from Tishbe in Gilead, said to *A:*
18: 1 to Elijah, "Go, present yourself to *A*,"
18: 2 So Elijah went to present himself to *A*.
18: 4 was bitter, and *A* had summoned Obadiah,
18: 5 *A* said to Obadiah,
18: 6 between them, *A* went one way by himself,
18: 9 are handing me over to *A* to have me killed?
18:12 I go to inform *A* and he does not find you,
18:16 Obadiah went to meet *A* and informed him.
18:16 *A* came to meet Elijah,
18:20 So *A* sent to all the Israelites and had
18:41 Elijah then said to *A*,
18:42 So *A* went up to eat and drink,
18:44 Elijah said, "Go and say to *A*,
18:45 *A* mounted his chariot and made for Jezreel.
18:46 *A* as far as the approaches to Jezreel.
19: 1 *A* told Jezebel all that Elijah had done
20: 2 He sent couriers to *A*,
20:13 Then a prophet came up to *A*,
20:14 But *A* asked,
20:14 Then *A* asked, "Who is to attack?"
20:15 So *A* called up the retainers of the
20:34 "On these terms," *A* replied,
21: 1 in Jezreel next to the palace of *A*,
21: 2 of Ahab, king of Samaria, *A* said to Naboth,
21: 4 *A* went home disturbed and angry at the
21:15 had been stoned to death, she said to *A*,
21:16 *A* started off on his way down to the
21:18 "Start down to meet *A*,
21:20 *A* said to Elijah.
21:25 of evil in the sight of the LORD as did *A*,
21:27 When *A* heard these words,
21:29 seen that *A* has humbled himself before me?
22:20 The LORD asked, 'Who will deceive *A*,
22:39 The rest of the acts of *A*,
22:40 *A* rested with his ancestors,
22:41 reign over Judah in the fourth year of *A*,
22:50 Then Ahaziah, son of *A*,
22:52 Ahaziah, son of *A*,
2Kgs 3: 1 Joram, son of *A*,
3: 5 But when *A* died,
8:16 In the fifth year of Joram, son of *A*,
8:18 like the kings of Israel of the line of *A*,
8:18 Ahab, since the sister of *A* was his wife;
8:25 in the twelfth year of Joram, son of *A*,
8:27 He conducted himself like the house of *A*,
8:28 He joined Joram, son of *A*,
9: 7 shall destroy the house of *A* your master;
9: 8 and by all the rest of the family of *A*.
9: 9 of *A* as I dealt with the house of Jeroboam,
9:25 we were driving teams behind his father *A*,
9:29 in the eleventh year of Joram, son of *A*.
10: 1 *A* had seventy descendants in Samaria.
10:10 the house of *A* shall go unfulfilled.
10:11 were left of the family of *A* in Jezreel,
10:18 *A* served Baal to some extent,
10:30 have treated the house of *A* as I desire,
21: 3 Baal, and also set up a sacred pole, as *A*,
21:13 with the plummet I used for the house of *A*.
2Chr 18: 1 but he became related to *A* by marriage.
18: 2 went down to *A* at Samaria; Ahab offered
18: 3 *A*, king of Israel,
18:19 The LORD asked, 'Who will deceive *A*,
21: 6 like the kings of Israel of the line of *A*,
21:13 into idolatry, as did the house of *A*,
22: 3 too, followed the ways of the house of *A*,
22: 4 sight of the LORD, as did the house of *A*,
22: 5 when he accompanied Jehoram, son of *A*,
22: 6 went down to visit Jehoram, son of *A*,
22: 7 had anointed to cut down the house of *A*.
22: 8 was executing judgment on the house of *A*,
Jer 29:21 who prophesy lies to you in my name, *A*,
29:22 the LORD make you like Zedekiah and *A*,
Mi 6:16 Omri, and all the works of the house of *A*,

AHAB'S (8)

1Kgs 21: 8 So she wrote letters in *A* name and,
21:21 you and will cut off every male in *A* line,
21:24 "When one of *A* line dies in the city,
2Kgs 1: 1 After *A* death,
9: 8 I will cut off every male in *A* line,
10: 1 the guardians of *A* descendants in Samaria.
10:17 Jehu slew all who remained there of *A* line,
2Chr 21: 6 because one of *A* daughters was his wife.

AHARAH (1)

1Chr 8: 1 his first-born, Ashbel, the second son, *A*,

AHARHEL (1)

1Chr 4: 8 and Zobebah, as well as of the clans of *A*,

AHASABI (1)

1 Chr 11:36 Elipheleth, son of *A*, from Beth-maacah

AHASBAI (1)

2Sm 23:34 Sharar the Hararite, Eliphelet, son of *A*,

AHASHTARITES (1)

1Chr 4: 6 Ahuzzam, Hepher, the Temenites and the *A*.

AHASHUERUS (1)

Ezr 4: 6 Also at the beginning of the reign of *A*

AHASUERUS (33)

Est A: 1 year of the reign of the great King *A*,
A:13 they were preparing to lay hands on King *A*.
1: 1 During the reign of *A*—
1: 1 this was the *A* who ruled over a hundred
1: 9 women inside the royal palace of King *A*.
1:10 the seven eunuchs who attended King *A*,
1:15 order of King *A* issued through the eunuchs?"
1:16 throughout the provinces of King *A*.
1:17 'King *A* commanded that Queen Vashti be
1:19 to come into the presence of King *A*
2: 1 After this, when King *A*' wrath had cooled,
2:12 Each girl went in turn to visit King *A*
2:16 to King *A* in his palace in the tenth month,
2:21 plotted in anger to lay hands on King *A*.
3: 1 After these events King *A* raised Haman,
3: 6 people, throughout the realm of King *A*.
3: 7 Nisan, in the twelfth year of King *A*,
3: 8 Then Haman said to King *A:*
3:12 *A* and sealed with the royal signet ring.
B: 1 "The great King *A* writes to the satraps
6: 2 for seeking to lay hands on King *A*.
7: 5 and where," said King *A* to Queen Esther,
8: 1 That day King *A* gave the house of Haman,
8: 7 King *A* then said to Queen Esther and to
8:10 *A* and sealed with the royal signet ring,
8:12 spoil throughout the provinces of King *A;*
E: 1 "King *A* the Great to the governors of the
9: 2 throughout the provinces of King *A*
9:20 and far, in all the provinces of King *A*.
9:30 and twenty-seven provinces of *A*' kingdom.
10: 1 King *A* laid tribute on the land and on the
10: 3 Jew Mordecai was next in rank to King *A*,
Dn 9: 1 was the first year that Darius, son of *A*,

AHAVA (3)

Ezr 8:15 assemble by the river that flows toward *A*,
8:21 a fast, there by the river of *A*,
8:31 of *A* on the twelfth day of the first month.

AHAZ (43)

2Kgs 15:38 His son *A* succeeded him as king.
16: 1 year of Pekah, son of Remaliah, *A*,
16: 2 *A* was twenty years old when he became king,
16: 5 Although they besieged *A*,
16: 7 *A* sent messengers to Tiglath-pileser,
16: 8 *A* took the silver and gold that were in
16:10 *A* went to Damascus to meet Tiglath-pileser,
16:10 King *A* sent to Uriah the priest a model of
16:11 plans which King *A* sent him from Damascus,
16:15 King *A* commanded Uriah the priest,
16:16 priest did just as King *A* had commanded.
16:17 King *A* detached the frames from the bases
16:19 The rest of the acts of *A* are recorded in
16:20 *A* rested with his ancestors and was buried
17: 1 In the twelfth year of *A*,
18: 1 Elah, king of Israel, Hezekiah, son of *A*,
20:11 on the staircase to the terrace of *A*.
23:12 Judah on the roof (the roof terrace of *A)*,
1Chr 3:13 whose son was Jotham, whose son was *A*,
8:35 of Micah were Pithon, Melech, Tarea, and *A*.
8:36 *A* became the father of Jehoaddah,
9:41 Micah were Pithon, Melech, Tahrea, and *A*.
9:42 *A* became the father of Jehoaddah,
2Chr 27: 9 David, and his son *A* succeeded him as king.
28: 1 *A* was twenty years old when he became king,
28:16 At that time King *A* sent an appeal for
28:19 LORD had brought Judah low because of *A*,
28:21 Though *A* plundered the LORD's house and
28:22 *A* became even more unfaithful to the LORD.
28:24 *A* gathered up the utensils of God's house
28:27 *A* rested with his ancestors and was buried
29:19 All the articles which King *A* during his
Is 1: 1 the days of Uzziah, Jotham, *A* and Hezekiah,
7: 1 In the days of *A*,
7: 3 Go out to meet *A*,
7:10 Again the LORD spoke to *A:*
7:12 But *A* answered, "I will not ask!
14:28 In the year that King *A* died,
38: 8 of *A* go back the ten steps it has advanced."
Hos 1: 1 Beeri, in the days of Uzziah, Jotham, *A*,
Mi 1: 1 of Moresheth in the days of Jotham, *A*,
Mt 1: 9 father of Jotham, Jotham the father of *A*,
1: 9 father of Ahaz, *A* the father of Hezekiah.

AHAZIAH (35)

1Kgs 22:40 and his son *A* succeeded him as king.
22:50 Then *A*, son of Ahab, said
22:52 *A*, son of Ahab,
2Kgs 1: 2 *A* had fallen through the lattice of his
1: 5 The messengers then returned to *A*,
1:11 *A* sent another captain with his company of
1:13 *A* sent a captain with his company of fifty
1:17 *A* died in fulfillment of the prophecy of
1:18 The rest of the acts of *A* are recorded in
8:24 His son *A* succeeded him as king.
8:25 *A*, son of Jehoram,
8:29 Then *A*, son of Jehoram,
9:16 to Jezreel, where Joram lay ill and *A*,
9:21 had done so, Joram, king of Israel, and *A*,
9:23 Joram reigned about and fled, crying to *A*,
9:23 and fled, crying to Ahaziah, "Treason, *A!*"
9:27 Seeing what was happening, *A*,
9:29 *A* had become king of Judah in the eleventh
10:13 on the way, he came across kinsmen of *A*,
10:13 "We are kinsmen of *A*," they replied.
11: 1 mother of *A*, saw that her son was dead
11: 2 daughter of King Jehoram and sister of *A*,
12:19 forebears, Jehoshaphat, Jehoram, and *A*,
13: 1 the twenty-third year of Joash, son of *A*,
14:13 captured Amaziah, son of Jehoash, son of *A*,
1Chr 3:11 whose son was Joram, whose son was *A*,
2Chr 20:35 Judah allied himself with King *A* of Israel,
20:37 saying, "Because you have joined with *A*,
22: 1 Then the inhabitants of Jerusalem made *A*,
22: 1 Thus *A*, son of Jehoram,
22: 6 Because of this illness, *A*,
22: 8 the nephews of *A* who were his attendants,
22: 9 Then he looked for *A* himself.
22:10 When Athaliah, mother of *A*,
22:11 daughter of King Jehoram, a sister of *A*,

AHAZIAH'S (3)

2Chr 22: 7 for *A* downfall that he should join Jehoram,
22: 9 There remained in *A* house no one powerful
22:11 secretly took *A* son Joash from among the

AHBAN (1)

1Chr 2:29 was named Abihail, bore him *A* and Molid.

AHEAD (64)

Gn 19:20 this town *a* is near enough to escape to.
32: 4 *a* to his brother Esau in the land of Seir,
32:17 and he told the servants, "Go on *a* of me,
32:18 To whom do these animals *a* of you belong?'
32:22 So the gifts went on *a* of him,
33: 3 He himself went on *a* of them,
33:14 Let my lord, then, go on *a* of me,
45: 5 lives that God sent me here *a* of you.
45: 7 sent me on *a* of you to ensure for you a
45:11 Since five years of famine still lie *a,*
46:28 Israel had sent Judah *a* to Joseph,
Ex 23:28 and *a* of you I will send hornets to drive
Nm 22:26 The angel of the LORD then went *a,*
Dt 1:22 'Let us send men *a* to reconnoiter the land
Jos 1:14 cross over armed *a* of your kinsmen
3: 6 of the covenant and go on *a* of the people;
3:14 carrying the ark of the covenant *a* of them.
6: 4 priests carrying ram's horns *a* of the ark.
6: 7 troops marching *a* of the ark of the LORD.
6:13 *A* of these marched the picked troops,
24:12 *a* of you which drove them [the Amorites,
1Sm 9:12 "Yes, there—straight *a.*
9:19 Go up *a* of me to the high place and eat
9:27 Saul, "Tell the servant to go on *a* of us,
10: 8 Now go down *a* of me to Gilgal,
23:24 So they went off to Ziph *a* of Saul.
25:19 She then said to her servants, "Go on *a;*
2Sm 15:23 on *a* of him by way of the Mount of Olives,
2Kgs 4:31 on *a* and had laid the staff upon the boy,
6:32 man *a* before he himself should come to him.
Tb 11: 3 Let us hurry on *a* of your wife to prepare
11: 4 both went on *a* and Raphael said to Tobiah,
Jdt 11:22 done well in sending you *a* of your people,
12:15 Meanwhile her maid went *a* and spread out
1Mc 4:17 the plunder, for there is a fight *a* of us,
5:30 *a* and saw a countless multitude of people,
9:11 and the archers came on *a* of the army,
10:23 "Why have we allowed Alexander to get *a*
16:21 But someone ran *a* and brought word to John
2Mc 12:21 he sent on *a* of him the women and children,
Ps(s) 137: 6 not, If I place not Jerusalem *a* of my joy.
Prv 4:25 *a* and your glance be directly forward.
Mt 2: 9 observed at its rising went *a* of them
11:10 says, 'I send my messenger *a* of you,
21: 2 "Go into the village straight *a* of you
26:32 raised up, I will go to Galilee *a* of you."
28: 7 the dead and now goes *a* of you to Galilee,
Mk 6:33 on foot to the place, arriving *a* of them.
11: 2 "Go to the village straight *a* of you,
14:28 raised up, I will go to Galilee *a* of you."
16: 7 Peter, 'He is going *a* of you to Galilee,
Lk 7:27 *a* of you to prepare your way before you.'
9:51 Jerusalem, and sent messengers on *a* of him.
19:28 he went *a* with his ascent to Jerusalem.
19:30 "Go into the village straight *a* of you.
Jn 1:15 'The one who comes after me ranks *a* of me,
1:30 me is to come a man who ranks *a* of me,
5: 7 there, someone else has gone in *a* of me."
Acts 8:30 Philip ran *a* and heard the man reading the
19:22 and Erastus, into Macedonia *a* of him,
20: 5 went on *a* and waited for us in Troas.
20:13 on *a* to the ship and set sail for Assos,
Phil 3:13 what lies behind but push on to what is *a.*
Heb 12: 1 in running the race which lies *a;*

AHI (2)

1Chr 5:15 *A,* son of Abdiel,
7:34 The sons of Shomer were *A,*

AHIAH (1)

Neh 10:27 Shobek, Rehum, Hashabnah, Maaseiah, *A,*

AHIAM (2)

2Sm 23:33 *A,* son of Sharar the Hararite,
1Chr 11:35 *A,* son of Sachar,

AHIAN (1)

1Chr 7:19 The sons of Shemida were *A,*

AHIEZER (6)

Nm 1:12 *A,* son of Ammishaddai;
2:25 [Their prince was *A,*
7:66 On the tenth day it was the turn of *A,*
7:71 This was the offering of *A,*
10:25 and arranged in companies, with *A,*
1Chr 12: 3 *A* was their chief,

AHIHUD (2)

Nm 34:27 *A,* son of Shelomi;
1Chr 8: 7 exile, became the father of Uzza and *A.*

AHIJAH (21)

1Sm 14: 3 *A,* son of Ahitub,
14:18 Saul then said to *A,*
14:18 *A* was wearing the ephod in front of the
1Kgs 4: 3 Elihoreph and *A,*
11:29 *A* the Shilonite met him on the road.
11:30 *A* took off his new cloak,
12:15 son of Nebat, through *A* the Shilonite.
14: 2 Shiloh, where you will find the prophet *A.*
14: 4 and entered the House of *A*
14: 5 The LORD had said to *A:*
14: 6 So *A,* hearing the sound
14:18 through his servant the prophet *A.*
15:27 Baasha, son of *A,*
15:29 through his servant, *A* the Shilonite,
15:33 of Asa, king of Judah, Baasha, son of *A,*
21:22 Nebat, and like that of Baasha, son of *A,*
2Kgs 9: 9 and with the house of Baasha, son of *A.*
1Chr 8: 7 Also Naaman, *A,* and Gera.
11:36 *A,* from Gilo; Hezro, from Carmel;
2Chr 9:29 in the prophecy of *A* the Shilonite,
10:15 the son of Nebat, through *A* the Shilonite.

AHIKAM (21)

2Kgs 22:12 this command to Hilkiah the priest, *A,*
22:14 So Hilkiah the priest, *A,*
25:22 as their governor Gedaliah, son of *A,*
25:30 governor Gedaliah, son of *A,*
2Chr 34:20 and issued this command to Hilkiah, to *A,*
Jer 26:24 But *A,* son of Shaphan,
39:14 guard, and entrusted to Gedaliah, son of *A,*
40: 5 "or go to Gedaliah, son of *A,*
40: 6 Jeremiah went to Gedaliah, son of *A,*
40: 7 of Babylon had given Gedaliah, son of *A,*
40: 9 Gedaliah, son of *A,*
40:11 appointed over them Gedaliah, son of *A,*
40:15 But Gedaliah, son of *A,*
40:16 Nevertheless, Gedaliah, son of *A,*
41: 1 came with ten men to Gedaliah, son of *A,*
41: 2 attacked with swords Gedaliah, son of *A,*
41: 7 "Come to Gedaliah, son of *A,*"
41:10 had confided to Gedaliah, son of *A.*
41:16 Mizpah after he killed Gedaliah, son of *A,*
41:18 Nethaniah, had slain Gedaliah, son of *A,*
43: 6 had entrusted to Gedaliah, son of *A,*

AHILUD (5)

2Sm 8:16 Jehoshaphat, son of *A,* was chancellor.
20:24 Jehoshaphat, son of *A,* was the chancellor.
1Kgs 4: 3 Jehoshaphat, son of *A,*
4:12 Baana, son of *A,*
1Chr 18:15 Jehoshaphat, son of *A,*

AHIMAAZ (16)

1Sm 14:50 was named Ahinoam, was the daughter of *A.*
2Sm 15:27 both your sons with you, your own son *A,*
15:36 Zadok's son *A* and Abiathar's son Jonathan.
17:17 Jonathan and *A* were staying at En-rogel,
17:20 they asked, "Where are *A* and Jonathan?"
17:21 *A* and Jonathan came up out of the cistern
18:19 Then *A,* son of Zadok, said, "Let me
18:22 But *A,* son of Zadok, said to Joab again,
18:23 *A* sped off by way of the Jordan plain and
18:27 "I notice that the first one runs like *A,*
18:28 Then *A* called out and greeted the king.
18:29 *A* replied, "I saw a great disturbance
1Kgs 4:15 *A,* who was married to Basemath,
1Chr 5:34 Zadok became the father of *A.*
5:35 *A* became the father of Azariah.
6:38 whose son was Zadok, whose son was *A.*

AHIMAN (4)

Nm 13:22 of Negeb, they reached Hebron, where *A,*
Jos 15:14 Sheshai, *A* and Talmai.
Jgs 1:10 and defeated Sheshai, *A* and Talmai.
1Chr 9:17 were Shallum, Akkub, Talmon, *A,*

AHIMELECH (15)

1Sm 21: 2 David went to *A,*
21: 9 David then asked *A:*
22: 9 "I saw the son of Jesse come to *A,*
22:11 the king sent a summons to *A* the priest,
22:14 *A* answered the king:
22:16 But the king said, "You shall die, *A,*
22:20 One son of *A,*
23: 6 Abiathar, son of *A,*
26: 6 David asked *A* the Hittite,
30: 7 said to Abiathar, the priest, son of *A,*
2Sm 8:17 Zadol, son of Ahitub, and *A,*
1Chr 18:16 Zadok, son of Ahitub, and *A,*
24: 3 Zadok, a descendant of Eleazar, and *A,*
24: 6 leaders, of Zadok the priest, and of *A,*
24:31 in the presence of King David, Zadok, *A,*

AHIMOTH (1)

1Chr 6:10 The sons of Elkanah were Amasai and *A,*

AHINADAB (1)

1Kgs 4:14 *A,* son of Iddo, in Mahanaim;

AHINOAM (7)

1Sm 14:50 Saul's wife, who was named *A,*
25:43 wife, and David also married *A* of Jezreel.
27: 3 his two wives, *A* from Jezreel and Abigail,
30: 5 two wives, *A* of Jezreel and Abigail,
2Sm 2: 2 by his two wives, *A* of Jezreel and Abigail,
3: 2 his first-born, Amnon, of *A* from Jezreel;
1Chr 3: 1 the first-born, Amnon, by *A* of Jezreel;

AHIO (5)

2Sm 6: 3 Uzzah and *A,*
6: 4 guided the cart, with *A* walking before it,
1Chr 8:31 and Zur, Kish, Baal, Ner, Nadab, Gedor, *A,*
9:37 came Zur, Kish, Baal, Ner, Nadab, Gedor, *A,*
13: 7 Uzzah and *A* were guiding the cart,

AHIQAR (10)

Tb 1:21 who succeeded him as king, placed *A,*
1:22 Then *A* interceded on my behalf,
1:22 of Assyria, *A* had been chief cupbearer,
2:10 *A,* however,
11:18 *A* and his nephew Nadab also came to
14:10 Think, my son, of all that Nadab did to *A,*
14:10 *A* went down alive into the earth!
14:10 *A* came out again into the light,
14:10 darkness, for he had tried to kill *A.*
14:10 Because *A* had given alms to me,

AHIRA (5)

Nm 1:15 *A,* son of Enan."
2:29 [Their prince was *A,*
7:78 On the twelfth day it was the turn of *A,*
7:83 This was the offering of *A,* son of Enan.
10:27 the host of the tribe of Asher, and *A,*

AHIRAM (2)

Gn 46:21 Bela, Becher, Ashbel, Gera, Naaman, *A,*
Nm 26:38 through *A* the clan of the Ahiramites,

AHIRAMITES (1)

Nm 26:38 through Ahiram the clan of the *A,*

AHISAMACH (3)

Ex 31: 6 I have appointed Oholiab, son of *A,*
35:34 also given both him and Oholiab, son of *A,*
38:23 and he was assisted by Oholiab, son of *A,*

AHISHAHAR (1)

1Chr 7:10 Ehud, Chenaanah, Zethan, Tarshish, and *A.*

AHISHAR (1)

1Kgs 4: 6 *A,* major-domo of the palace;

AHITHOPHEL (18)

2Sm 15:12 Absalom also sent to *A* the Gilonite,
15:31 *A* was among the conspirators with Absalom,
15:31 "O LORD, turn the counsel of *A* to folly!"
15:34 you will undo for me the counsel of *A.*
16:15 In the meantime Absalom, accompanied by *A,*
16:20 Then Absalom said to *A,*
16:21 *A* replied to Absalom:
16:23 Now the counsel given by *A* at that time
17: 1 *A* went on to say to Absalom:
17: 6 "This is what *A* proposed.
17: 7 "This time *A* has not given good counsel."
17:14 Hushai the Archite better than that of *A.*
17:15 *A* gave Absalom and the elders of Israel,
17:21 for *A* has given the following counsel in
17:23 *A* saw that his counsel was not acted upon,
23:34 Eliam, son of *A,*
1Chr 27:33 *A* was also the king's counselor,
27:34 After *A* came Jehoiada,

AHITHOPHEL'S (1)

2Sm 17:14 LORD had decided to undo *A* good counsel,

AHITOB (1)

Jdt 8: 1 son of Gideon, son of Raphain, son of *A,*

AHITUB (15)

1Sm 14: 3 Ahijah, son of *A,*
22: 9 son of Jesse come to Ahimelech, son of *A,*
22:11 summons to Ahimelech the priest, son of *A,*
22:12 Then Saul said, "Listen, son of *A!*"
22:20 One son of Ahimelech, son of *A,*
2Sm 8:17 Zadok, son of *A,*
1Chr 5:33 Amariah became the father of *A.*
5:34 *A* became the father of Zadok.
5:37 Amariah became the father of *A.*
5:38 *A* became the father of Zadok.
6:37 whose son was Amariah, whose son was *A,*
9:11 son of Zadok, son of Meraioth, son of *A,*
18:16 Zadok, son of *A,*
Ezr 7: 2 son of Shallum, son of Zadok, son of *A,*
Neh 11:11 son of Zadok, son of Meraioth, son of *A,*

AHLAI (2)

1Chr 2:31 The sons of Sheshan: *A*
11:41 Zabad, son of *A,*

AHOAH (1)

1Chr 8: 4 The sons of Ehud were Abishua, Naaman, *A,*

AHOH (3)

2Sm 23:28 Zalmon from *A;*
1Chr 11:29 Ilai, from *A;*
27: 4 month was Eleazar, son of Dodo, from *A,*

AHOHITE (2)

2Sm 23: 9 warriors, was Eleazar, son of Dodo the *A.*
1Chr 11:12 Next to him Eleazar, the son of Dodo the *A,*

AHUMAI (1)

1Chr 4: 2 Jahath became the father of *A* and Lahad.

AHUZZAM (1)

1Chr 4: 6 Naarah bore him *A,*

AHUZZATH (1)

Gn 26:26 come to him from Gerar, accompanied by *A,*

AHZAI (1)

Neh 11:13 and Amasai, son of Azarel, son of *A,*

AI (30)

Gn 12: 8 with Bethel to the west and *A* to the east.
13: 3 and *A* where his tent had formerly stood,
Jos 7: 2 Joshua next sent men from Jericho to *A,*
7: 2 When they had explored *A,*
7: 3 three thousand go up, they can overcome *A.*
7: 4 but they were defeated by those at *A,*
8: 1 the army with you and prepare to attack *A.*
8: 1 delivered the king of *A* into your power,
8: 2 Do to *A* and its king what you did to
8: 3 and all the soldiers prepared to attack *A.*
8: 9 taking up their position to the west of *A,*
8:10 the army and went up to *A* at its head,
8:11 the city, they pitched camp north of *A,*
8:12 set them in ambush between Bethel and *A,*
8:14 The king of *A* saw this,
8:17 not a soldier remained in *A* [or Bethel],
8:18 out the javelin in your hand toward *A,*
8:20 By the time the men of *A* looked back,
8:21 in smoke, they struck back at the men of *A.*
8:22 the men of *A* were hemmed in by Israelites
8:24 All the inhabitants of *A* who had pursued
8:25 men and women, the entire population of *A.*
8:26 the doom on all the inhabitants of *A.*
8:29 king of *A* hanged on a tree until evening;
9: 3 what Joshua had done to Jericho and *A,*
10: 1 that, in the capture and destruction of *A,*
10: 2 royal city, larger even than the city of *A,*
12: 9 kings of Jericho, *A* (which is near Bethel),
Ezr 2:28 men of Bethel and *A,*
Neh 7:32 men of Bethel and *A,*

AIAH (3)

Gn 36:24 Zibeon's descendants were *A* and Anah.
2Sm 3: 7 had a concubine, Rizpah, the daughter of *A.*
1Chr 1:40 The sons of Zibeon were *A* and Anah.

AIAH'S (3)

2Sm 21: 8 that *A* daughter Rizpah had borne to Saul,
21:10 Then Rizpah, *A* daughter,
21:11 was informed of what Rizpah, *A* daughter,

AIATH (1)

Is 10:28 he has reached *A,*

AID (34)

Dt 22:27 help, there was no one to come to her *a.*
28:29 continually, with no one to come to your *a.*
28:31 enemies, with no one to come to your *a.*
Jos 10: 4 to come to his *a* for an attack on Gibeon,
Jgs 18:28 No one came to their *a,*
2Sm 3:12 *a* you by bringing all Israel over to you."
8: 5 of Damascus came to the *a* of Hadadezer,
10:19 afraid to give further *a* to the Ammonites.
22:30 with your *a* I run against an armed band,
1Chr 18: 5 of Damascus came to the *a* of Hadadezer,
19:19 refused to come to the *a* of the Ammonites.
Jdt 8:11 within that time the Lord comes to our *a,*
8:15 wish to come to our *a* within the five days,
1Mc 10:24 and gifts, so that they may be an *a* to me."
11:47 So the king called the Jews to his *a.*
15:27 But he refused to accept the *a;*
2Mc 3:29 speechless and deprived of all hope of *a,*
8: 8 to come to the *a* of the king's government.
11:10 order with the *a* of their heavenly ally.
12:15 the *a* of the great Sovereign of the world,
14:15 who always comes to the *a* of his heritage.
Ps(s) 18:30 with your *a* I run against an armed band,
22:20 O my help, hasten to *a* me.
59: 5 Rouse yourself to see it, and *a* me,
59:11 May God come to my *a;*
60:13 Give us *a* against the foe,
108:13 Give us *a* against the foe,
Prv 19:23 The fear of the LORD is an *a* to life;
Wis 13:18 for *a* he beseeches the wholly incompetent,
Sir 36: 1 Come to our *a,*
Lam 3:57 You came to my *a* when I called to you;
4:17 ever wasted away, looking in vain for *a;*
Acts 7:24 he went to his *a* and avenged the victim by
Phil 4: 3 fellow worker, to go to their *a;*

AIDE (6)

Ex 24:13 So Moses set out with Joshua, his *a,*
Nm 11:28 Nun, who from his youth had been Moses' *a,*
Dt 1:38 you shall enter there, but your *a* Joshua,
Jos 1: 1 had died, the LORD said to Moses' *a* Joshua,
Jgs 7:10 go down to the camp with your *a* Purah.
7:11 his *a* Purah to the outposts of the camp.

AIDES (1)

Ez 12:14 All his retinue, his *a,*

AIDING (1)

Jdt 13: 5 now is the time for *a* your heritage and

AIJA (1)

Neh 11:31 Benjaminites were in Geba, Michmash, *A,*

AIJALON (9)

Jos 10:12 sun, at Gibeon, O moon, in the valley of *A!*
19:42 Zorah, Eshtaol, Ir-shemesh, Shaalabbin, *A,*
21:24 pasture lands, *A* with its pasture lands,
Jgs 1:35 a firm hold in Har-heres, *A* and Shaalbim,
1Sm 14:31 were routed that day from Michmash to *A,*
1Chr 6:54 pasture lands, *A* with its pasture lands,
8:13 were family heads of those who dwelt in *A,*
2Chr 11:10 Ziph, Adoraim, Lachish, Azekah, Zorah, *A,*
28:18 they captured Beth-shemesh, *A,*

AILMENT (2)

Ps(s) 41: 4 he will take away all his *a* when he is ill.
Gal 4:13 You are aware that it was a bodily *a* that

AIM (8)

Dt 16:20 Justice and justice alone shall be your *a,*
2Mc 2:31 be allowed to *a* at brevity
Ps(s) 7:13 he will bend and *a* his bow,
21:13 you shall *a* your shafts against them.
64: 4 who *a* like arrows their bitter words,
Is 1:17 Make justice your *a:*
Rom 14:19 make it our *a* to work for peace and to
2Cor 5: 9 we make it our *a* to please him whether we

AIMED (2)

2Mc 2:25 we have *a* to please those who prefer
1Tm 1: 9 is, with the understanding that it is *a,*

AIMING (2)

1Sm 20:20 will shoot arrows, as though *a* at a target.
1Tm 1: 5 What we are *a* at in this warning is the

AIMLESSLY (2)

Gn 21:14 roamed *a* in the wilderness of Beer-sheba,
Ex 14: 3 are wandering about *a* in the land.

AIN (2)

Nm 34:11 shall go down to Ar-Baal, east of *A,*
1Chr 4:32 Etam, also, and *A,*

AIR (58)

Gn 1:26 the fish of the sea, the birds of the *a,*
1:28 the fish of the sea, the birds of the *a,*
1:30 of the land, all the birds of the *a,*
2:19 wild animals and various birds of the *a,*
2:20 to all the cattle, all the birds of the *a,*
6: 7 the creeping things and the birds of the *a,*
7: 3 likewise, of every clean bird of the *a,*
7:23 the creeping things and the birds of the *a;*
9: 2 of the earth and all the birds of the *a,*
Dt 28:26 of the *a* and for the beasts of the field,
1Sm 17:44 birds of the *a* and the beasts of the field."
17:46 birds of the *a* and the beasts of the field;
Jdt 11: 7 and the cattle and the birds of the *a,*
2Mc 4:24 he flattered him with such an *a* of
4:46 a colonnade, as if to get some fresh *a,*
15:13 and with an *a* about him of extraordinary,
Jb 12: 7 you, and the birds of the *a* to tell you;
28:21 from the birds of the *a* it is concealed.
Ps(s) 8: 9 beasts of the field, The birds of the *a,*
50:11 I know all the birds of the *a,*
Prv 11:29 his household has empty *a* for a heritage;
30:19 The way of an eagle in the *a,*
Eccl 10:20 the birds of the *a* may carry your voice,
Wis 2: 3 will be poured abroad like unresisting *a.*
5:11 Or like a bird flying through the *a;*
5:11 But the fluid *a,*
5:12 the parted *a* straightway flows together
7: 3 I too, when born, inhaled the common *a,*
13: 2 But either fire, or wind, or the swift *a,*
15:15 for vision, nor nostrils to snuff the *a,*
17:10 even the *a* that they could nowhere escape.
Jer 4:25 even the birds of the *a* had flown away!
8: 7 Even the stork in the *a* knows it seasons;
9: 9 Birds of the *a* as well as beasts,
34:20 birds of the *a* and the beasts of the field.
Lam 4:19 were swifter than eagles in the *a,*
Ez 8: 3 Spirit lifted me up in the *a* and brought
29: 5 and the birds of the *a* I give you as food,
31: 6 its boughs nested all the birds of the *a,*
31:13 trunk rested all the birds of the *a,*
32: 4 have all the birds of the *a* alight on you,
38:20 fish of the sea and the birds of the *a,*
Dn 2:38 men, wild beasts, and birds of the *a,*
3:80 All you birds of the *a,*
4: 9 in its branches the birds of the *a* nested;
4:18 in whose branches the birds of the *a* dwelt
Hos 2:20 of the field, With the birds of the *a,*
4: 3 beasts of the field, the birds of the *a,*
7:12 like birds in the *a* I will bring them down,
Zec 5: 9 As they lifted up the bushel into the *a,*
Lk 8: 5 walked on and the birds of the *a* ate it up.
13:19 the birds of the *a* nested in its branches."
Acts 22:23 their cloaks and flung dirt through the *a.*
1Cor 14: 9 You will be talking to the *a.*
Eph 2: 2 present age and to the prince of the *a,*
1Thes 4:17 in the clouds to meet the Lord in the *a.*
Rv 9: 2 The sun and the *a* were darkened by the
16:17 angel poured out his bowl upon the empty *a.*

AIRS (2)

1Cor 13: 4 Love is not jealous, it does not put on *a,*
2Cor 11:20 you, who impose upon you and put on *a,*

AIRY (2)

Jb 15: 2 Should a wise man answer with *a* opinions,
Jer 22:14 myself a spacious house, with *a* rooms,"

AKAN (1)

Gn 36:27 of Ezer were Bilhan, Zaavan, and *A.*

AKELDAMA (1)

Acts 1:19 Field of Blood *A'* in their own language.

AKKUB (8)

1Chr 3:24 were Hodaviah, Eliashib, Pelaiah, *A,*
9:17 The gatekeepers were Shallum, *A,*
Ezr 2:42 sons of Ater, sons of Talmon, sons of *A,*
2:45 of Lebanah, sons of Hagabah, sons of *A,*
Neh 7:45 sons of Ater, sons of Talmon, sons of *A,*
8: 7 Levites Jeshua, Bani, Sherebiah, Jamin, *A,*
11:19 The gatekeepers were *A,*
12:25 Meshullam, Talmon, and *A* were gatekeepers.

AKRABATTENE (1)

1Mc 5: 3 attacked the sons of Esau at *A* in Idumea,

AKRABBIM (3)

Nm 34: 4 Salt Sea, and turning south of the *A* Pass,
Jos 15:3 Southward below the pass of *A*
Jgs 1:36 from the *A* pass to Sela and beyond

ALABASTER (1)

Mk 14: 3 a woman entered carrying an *a* jar of

ALAMOTH (1)

1Chr 15:20 and Benaiah, played on harps set to *"A."*

ALARM (18)

Nm 10: 5 When you sound the first *a,*
10: 6 when you sound the second *a,*
10: 6 when you sound the third *a,*
10: 6 when you sound the fourth *a,*
10: 6 shall the *a* be sounded for them to depart.
10: 7 an ordinary blast, without sounding the *a.*
10: 9 you, you shall sound the *a* on the trumpets,
31: 6 and the trumpets for sounding the *a.*
Tb 6: 3 He shouted in *a.*
Ps(s) 116:11 I said in my *a,*
Jer 4:19 the sound of the trumpet, the *a* of war.
42:14 more of war, hear the trumpet *a* no longer,
49: 2 the Ammonites I will sound the battle *a;*
50:22 Battle *a* in the land, dire destruction!
Hos 5: 8 Sound the *a* in Beth-aven:
Jl 2: 1 in Zion, sound the *a* on my holy mountain!
Zep 1:16 and battle *a* Against fortified cities,
1Pt 3: 6 do what is right and let no fears *a* you.

ALARMED (8)

Dt 20: 3 be neither *a* nor frightened by them.
2Sm 4: 1 he ceased to resist and all Israel was *a.*
Jdt 4: 2 *a* for Jerusalem and the temple of the Lord,
Sir 34:14 He who fears the LORD is never *a,*
Mt 24: 6 Do not be *a.*
Acts 16:38 *a* at hearing they were Roman citizens.
20:10 "Don't be *a!"*
22:29 The commander became *a* because he realized

ALARMS (1)

Jer 20:16 cries in the morning, battle *a* at noonday,

ALAS (36)

Gn 42:21 *A,* we are being punished because of our
Nm 24:23 *A,* who shall survive of Ishmael,
Jos 7: 7 *A,* O Lord GOD ,"
Jgs 6:22 had been the angel of the LORD, said, *A,*
11:35 saw her, he rent his garments and said, *A,*
2Sm 1:19 *A!* the glory of Israel
14: 5 *A,* I am a widow; my husband is dead.
1Kgs 13:30 *A,* my brother!"
2Kgs 3:10 *A!"* exclaimed the king of Israel
6:15 *A!"* he said to Elisha
Tb 10: 5 *A,* my child,
Jb 10:15 If I should be wicked, *a* for me!
Sir 37: 3 *A,* my companion!
Jer 4:10 *A!* LORD GOD,"
6: 4 *A!* the day is waning,
22:18 They shall not lament him, *A!*
22:18 my brother"; *A!*
22:18 They shall not lament him, *A,* Lord!
22:18 *a,* Majesty!"
45: 3 to you, Baruch, because you said, *A!*
47: 6 *A,* sword of the LORD!
Ez 6:11 your hands, stamp your feet, and cry *A!"*
9: 8 I fell prone, crying out, *A,* Lord GOD!
11:13 *A,* Lord GOD!
21: 5 But I said, *A!*
Jl 1:15 *A,* the day!
Am 5:16 they shall cry, Alas! *A*
Mi 7: 1 *A!* I am as when the fruit
Na 3:18 *A!* how your shepherds slumber
Rv 18:10 *A,* alas, great city that you are, Babylon
18:16 *A,* alas, the great city, dressed in fine
18:19 *A,* alas, the great city, in which

ALCIMUS (13)

1Mc 7: 5 They were led by *A,*
7: 9 He sent him and the impious *A,*
7:12 gathered about *A* and Bacchides to ask for
7:20 he handed the province over to *A,*
7:21 *A* spared no pains to maintain his high
7:23 When Judas saw all the evils that *A* and
7:25 But when *A* saw that Judas and his
9: 1 Bacchides and *A* into the land of Judah,
9:54 *A* ordered the wall of the inner court of
9:57 Seeing that *A* was dead,
2Mc 14: 3 A certain *A,* a former high priest,
14:13 up *A* as high priest of the great temple.
14:26 When *A* saw their friendship for each other,

ALEMA (2)

1Mc 5:26 imprisoned in Bozrah, in Bosor near *A,*
5:35 toward *A* and attacked and captured it;

ALEMETH (3)

1Chr 7: 8 Omri, Jeremoth, Abijah, Anathoth, and *A*—
8:36 and Jehoaddah became the father of *A,*
9:42 and Jehoaddah became the father of *A,*

ALERT (5)

2Kgs 6:10 the man of God had indicated, and *a* it;
Sir 37: 8 Be on the *a* when one proffers advice,
Is 29:20 All who are *a* to do evil will be cut off,
1Thes 5: 8 We who live by day must be *a,*
1Pt 5: 8 Stay sober and *a.*

ALERTED (2)

1Sm 15: 4 Saul *a* the soldiers,
Acts 27:31 *a* the centurion and the soldiers to this:

ALEXANDER (29)

1Mc 1: 1 After *A* the Macedonian,
1: 7 *A* had reigned twelve years when he died.
6: 2 breastplates, and weapons left there by *A,*
10: 1 In the year one hundred and sixty, *A,*
10: 4 he makes peace with *A* against us,
10:15 King *A* heard of the promises that
10:18 *A* sends greetings to his brother Jonathan.
10:23 "Why have we allowed *A* to get ahead of us
10:47 They therefore decided in favor of *A,*
10:48 King *A* gathered together a large army and
10:49 the army of Demetrius fled, *A* pursued him,
10:51 *A* sent ambassadors to Ptolemy,
10:58 There King *A* met him,
10:59 King *A* also wrote to Jonathan to come and
10:68 King *A* heard of it he was greatly troubled,
10:88 When King *A* heard of these events,
11: 2 him, as King *A* had ordered them to do,
11: 8 Plotting evil against *A,*
11: 9 give you my daughter whom *A* has married,
11:11 His real reason for accusing *A,*
11:12 her to Demetrius, Ptolemy broke with *A;*
11:14 King *A* was in Cilicia at that time,
11:15 When *A* heard the news,
11:16 *A* fled to Arabia to seek protection.
Mk 15:21 Simon of Cyrene, the father of *A* and Rufus,
Acts 4: 6 Annas the high priest, Caiaphas, John, *A,*
19:33 Some brought out of the crowd *A,*
1Tm 1:20 their faith, among them Hymenaeus and *A;*
2Tm 4:14 *A* the coppersmith did me a great deal of

ALEXANDER'S (5)

1Mc 11: 1 to take *A* kingdom and add it to his own.
11:11 however, was that he coveted *A* kingdom.
11:17 cut off *A* head and sent it to Ptolemy.
11:39 who had previously belonged to *A* party,
11:39 who was bringing up *A* young son Antiochus.

ALEXANDRIA (2)

Acts 6: 9 Jews from Cyrene, *A,* Cilicia and Asia
18:24 a native of *A* and a man of eloquence,

ALEXANDRIAN (2)

Acts 27: 6 discovered an *A* vessel bound for Italy,
28:11 It was an *A* vessel with the "Heavenly

ALIAH (1)

1Chr 1:51 the chiefs of Timna, *A,*

ALIAN (1)

1Chr 1:40 The sons of Shobal were *A,*

ALIEN (69)

Gn 23: 4 "Although I am a resident *a* among you,
Ex 12:19 Anyone, be he a resident *a* or a native,
12:45 *a* or hired servant may partake of it.
12:49 same for the resident *a* as for the native."
20:10 your beast, or by the *a* who lives with you.
22:20 "You shall not molest or oppress an *a,*
23: 9 You shall not oppress an *a;*
23: 9 you well know how it feels to be an *a,*
23:12 maidservant and the *a* may be refreshed.
Lv 16:29 of you, whether a native or a resident *a,*
17:12 No one among you, not even a resident *a,*
17:15 "Everyone, whether a native or an *a,*
19:10 you shall leave for the poor and the *a.*
19:33 "When an *a* resides with you in your land,
19:34 You shall treat the *a* who resides with
20: 2 an Israelite or an *a* residing in Israel,
22:18 of Israel, or any *a* residing in Israel,
23:22 you shall leave for the poor and the *a.*
24:16 *a* and native alike must be put to death
24:22 have but one rule, for *a* and native alike.
25:35 to him the privileges of an *a* or a tenant,
25:47 sells himself to a wealthy *a*
25:53 The *a* shall treat him as a servant hired
Nm 9:14 "If an *a* who lives among you wishes to
9:14 resident *a* as for the native of the land."
15:14 any *a* residing with you permanently or for
15:15 one rule for you and for the resident *a,*
15:15 Before the LORD you and the *a* are alike,
15:16 the *a* residing among you as for yourselves."
15:29 native Israelite or an *a* residing with you.
15:30 defiantly, whether he be a native or an *a,*
Dt 1:16 both parties even if one of them is an *a.*
5:14 your beasts, or the *a* who lives with you.
10:18 orphan and the widow, and befriends the *a,*
10:19 So you too must befriend the *a,*
14:21 it to an *a* who belongs to your community,
14:29 in the heritage with you, and also the *a,*
16:11 to your community, as well as the *a,*
16:14 female slave, and also the Levite, the *a,*
23: 8 since you were an *a* in his country.
24:17 the rights of the *a* or of the orphan,
24:19 let it be for the *a,*
24:20 let what remains be for the *a,*
24:21 let what remains be for the *a,*
26: 5 a small household and lived there as an *a.*
26:12 you have given them to the Levite, the *a,*
26:13 and I have given it to the Levite, the *a,*
27:19 be he who violates the rights of the *a,*
28:43 The *a* residing among you will rise higher
2Chr 2:16 all the *a* men who were in the land of Israel
Est B: 5 all men, lives by divergent and *a* laws,
2Mc 6:24 Eleazar had gone over to an *a* religion.
Jb 19:15 I am an *a* in their sight.
Ps(s) 81:10 among you nor shall you worship any *a* god.
114: 1 house of Jacob from a people of *a* tongue,
Sir 10:21 Be it tenant or wayfarer, *a* or pauper,
Is 33:19 people of *a* tongue you will look no more,
Jer 7: 6 you no longer oppress the resident *a,*
22: 3 Do not wrong or oppress the resident *a,*
Bar 4: 3 to another, your privileges to an *a* race.
4:15 afar, a nation ruthless and of *a* speech,
6: 4 their *a* example and stand in fear of them,
Ez 14: 7 *a* resident in Israel is estranged from me,
22: 7 midst, they extort from the resident *a;*
22:29 and oppress the resident *a* without justice.
47:23 In whatever tribe the *a* may be resident,
Zec 7:10 the widow or the orphan, the *a* or the poor;
Acts 7:29 residence as an *a* in the land of Midian,
1Cor 14:21 in *a* speech I will speak to this people,

ALIENATE (1)

Ez 48:14 They may not sell or exchange or *a* this,

ALIENATED (2)

Jer 19: 4 they have forsaken me and *a* this place
Col 1:21 You yourselves were once *a* from him;

ALIENS—ALIEN'S (32)

Gn 15:13 shall be *a* in a land not their own,
Ex 6: 4 the land in which they were living as *a.*
12:48 If any *a* living among you wish to
22:20 once *a* yourselves in the land of Egypt.
23: 9 once *a* yourselves in the land of Egypt.
Lv 17: 8 of Israel or of the *a* residing among them,
17:10 of Israel or of the *a* residing among them,
17:13 Israelites or of the *a* residing among them,
18:26 however, whether natives or resident *a,*
19:34 you too were once *a* in the land of Egypt.
25:23 you are but *a* who have become my tenants.
25:45 You may also buy them from among the *a*
Nm 15:26 but also the *a* residing among you,
19:10 and for the *a* residing among them.
35:15 all the resident or transient *a* among them,
Dt 10:19 once *a* yourselves in the land of Egypt.
24:14 one of the *a* who live in your communities.
26:11 the Levite and the *a* who live among you,
29:10 children and the *a* who live in your camp,
31:12 well as the *a* who live in your communities
2Sm 4: 3 they have been resident *a* to this day.
1Chr 22: 2 David then ordered that all the *a* who
29:15 For we stand before you as *a:*
Jdt 4:10 All their resident *a,*
Ps(s) 144: 7 me from many waters, from the hands of *a,*
144:11 and rescue me from the hands of *a,*
Prv 5:10 your hard-won earnings go to an *a* house;
Is 14: 1 the *a* will join them and be counted with
Ez 20:38 they sojourned as *a* I will bring them out,
47:22 and for the *a* resident in your midst
Ob 1:11 the day when *a* carried off his possessions,
Eph 2:19 that you are strangers and *a* no longer.

ALIGHT (4)

Gn 8: 9 dove could find no place to *a* and perch,
Dt 29:19 curse mentioned in this book will *a* on him.
Bar 6:21 *a* on their bodies and on their heads;
Ez 32: 4 have all the birds of the air *a* on you,

ALIGHTED (6)

Gn 24:64 she *a* from her camel and asked the servant,
Jos 15:18 Then, as she *a* from the ass,
Jgs 1:14 Then, as she *a* from the ass,
2Kgs 5:21 Naaman *a* from his chariot to wait for him.
5:26 the man *a* from his chariot to wait for you?
Wis 18:16 And as he *a,*

ALIGHTS (3)

2Sm 17:12 down upon him as dew *a* on the ground.
Sir 5: 7 upon the wicked *a* his wrath.
16:11 forgives, though on the wicked *a* his wrath.

ALIGNED (1)

Acts 4:26 The kings of the earth were *a,*

ALIGNMENT (1)

1Kgs 7: 4 at either end, with windows in strict *a.*

ALIKE (53)

Gn 18:25 innocent and the guilty would be treated *a!*
Lv 7: 7 sin offering and the guilt offering are *a,*
24:16 alien and native *a* must be put to death
24:22 have but one rule, for alien and native *a.*
Nm 5: 3 Male and female *a,*
15:15 you and the alien are *a*
Dt 1:17 give ear to the lowly and to the great *a,*
12:22 the unclean and the clean eating it *a.*
15:22 it, the unclean and the clean eating it *a,*
32:25 home Shall be the youth and the maiden *a,*
32:36 protected and unprotected *a* disappearing,
Jos 8:33 And all Israel, stranger and native *a,*
1Sm 30:24 they shall share *a."*
1Chr 25: 8 equally, young and old, master and pupil *a.*
26:13 gate, the small and the large families *a.*
2Chr 31:15 to their brethren great and small *a,*
Jdt 5:22 of Moab *a* said he should be cut to pieces.
Jb 21:26 *A* they lie down in the dust,
Ps(s) 14: 3 All *a* have gone astray;
37:38 Sinners shall all *a* be destroyed;
49: 3 birth or high degree, rich and poor *a.*
53: 4 All *a* have gone astray;
Eccl 9:11 for a time of calamity comes to all *a.*
11: 6 or whether both *a* will turn out well.
Wis 6: 7 as the small, and he provides for all *a;*
15: 7 clean purposes and their opposites, all *a;*
15:13 he creates fragile vessels and idols *a.*
18: 9 share *a* the same good things and dangers,
18:12 all *a* by a single death had countless dead;
Sir 5: 7 For mercy and anger *a* are with him;
16:11 *a* are with him who remits and forgives,
Is 1:28 Rebels and sinners *a* shall be crushed,
24: 2 Layman and priest *a,*
46: 5 or match me against, as though we were *a?*
65:25 The wolf and the lamb shall graze *a,*

Jer 6:13 Small and great *a*,
6:21 Fathers and sons *a*,
8:10 Small and great *a*,
Bar 1: 4 and the whole people, small and great *a*—
Ez 14:10 and the prophet shall be punished *a*,
Jn 2:15 sheep and oxen *a* out of the temple area,
Acts 8:12 Christ, men and women *a* accepted baptism.
19:10 of the province of Asia, Jews and Greeks *a*,
20:21 With Jews and Greeks *a* I insisted solemnly
24:15 resurrection of the good and the wicked *a*.
26:22 stand here to testify to great and small *a*.
Rom 1:14 non-Greeks, to learned and unintelligent *a*.
3: 9 charge against Jews and Greeks *a*
3:12 wrong course, all *a* have become worthless;
14: 5 someone else considers all days *a*.
1Cor 1:24 those who are called, Jews and Greeks *a*,
4: 9 to the universe, to angels and men *a*.
12:19 If all the members were *a*,
Rv 11:18 who revere you, the great and the small *a*;

ALIVE (90)

Gn 6:19 female, that you may keep them *a* with you.
6:20 come into the ark with you, to stay *a*.
7: 3 will keep their issue *a* over all the earth.
9: 3 creature that is *a* shall be yours to eat;
16:13 seen God and remained *a* after my vision?"
31:32 one you find them with shall not remain *a*!
42: 2 we may stay *a* rather than die of hunger."
45:26 When they told him, "Joseph is still *a*—
45:28 "My son Joseph is still *a*!
46:30 seen for myself that Joseph is still *a*."
Ex 22: 3 what he stole is found *a* in his possession,
Lv 16:10 for Azazel he shall set *a* before the LORD,
Nm 16:30 swallows them *a* down into the nether world,
16:33 They went down *a* to the nether world with
Dt 4: 4 to the LORD, your God, are all *a* today.
5: 3 with us, all of us who are *a* here this day.
20:16 you shall not leave a single soul *a*.
31:27 Why, even now, while I am *a* among you,
Jos 8:23 whom they took *a* and brought to Joshua.
11:11 there to the sword, till none was left *a*.
11:14 the last of them, leaving none *a*.
1Sm 15: 8 He took Agag, king of Amalek, *a*,
17:55 replied, "As truly as your majesty is *a*,
20:14 if I am still *a*,
25:22 male *a* among all those who belong to him."
25:34 not have had a single man or boy left *a*."
27: 9 David would not leave a man or woman *a*,
27:11 a man or woman *a* to be brought to Gath,
2Sm 1: 9 for I am in great suffering, yet fully *a*.'
12:18 "When the child was *a*,
18:14 of Absalom, still hanging from the tree *a*.
19: 7 if Absalom were *a* today and all of us dead,
1Kgs 12: 6 in his father's service while he was *a*,
17:23 Elijah said to her, "your son is *a*."
20:18 peace or for war, in any case take them *a*."
20:32 "Is he still *a*?"
21:15 to sell you, because Naboth is not *a*,
2Kgs 7:12 us *a* and enter our city when we leave it."
10:14 "Take them *a*," Jehu ordered.
10:14 They were taken *a*,
2Chr 25:12 also brought back another ten thousand *a*,
Tb 5:10 Though *a*, I am among the dead.
7: 5 They answered, "Yes, he is *a* and well."
8:12 in to see whether Tobiah is *a* or dead,
8:14 told the girl's parents that Tobiah was *a*,
14:10 Ahiqar went down *a* into the earth!
Jdt 10:19 It is not wise to leave one man of them *a*,
1Mc 1: 6 kingdom among them while he was still *a*.
2:13 Why are we still *a*?"
8: 7 They had taken him *a* and obliged him and
10:85 together with those who were burned *a*,
14: 2 he sent one of his generals to take him *a*.
2Mc 6:26 of men, I shall never, whether *a* or dead,
7:24 As the youngest brother was still *a*,
9: 9 while he was still *a* in hideous torments,
10:36 the fire and burned the blasphemers *a*.
12:35 intending to capture the vile wretch *a*,
Jb 30:23 death to the destined place of everyone *a*.
33: 4 me, the breath of the Almighty keeps me *a*.
Ps(s) 49:10 remain *a* always and not see destruction.
55:16 let them go down *a* to the nether world,
124: 3 us, then would they have swallowed us *a*.
Prv 1:12 them up, as the nether world does, *a*,
Eccl 4: 2 in death than are the living to be still *a*.
Sir 17:23 they glorify the LORD who are *a* and well.
Jer 49:11 your orphans behind, I will keep them *a*;
Lam 3:53 They struck me down *a* in the pit,
Ez 13:18 lives of my people, yet keep yourselves *a*?
13:19 and keeping *a* those who should not live,
33:12 the virtuous man, when he sins, remain *a*.
37:10 they came *a* and stood upright,
Dn 3:90 sing, and astonished at seeing them *a*,
Jon 4: 8 "I would be better off dead than *a*."
Mt 27:63 while he was still *a* made the claim,
Mk 16:11 that he was *a* and had been seen by her,
Lk 20:38 All are *a* for him."
24:23 a vision of angels who declared he was *a*.
Jn 11:26 is *a* and believes in me will never die.
Acts 1: 3 in many convincing ways that he was *a*,
9:41 and the widows to show them that she was *a*.
20:12 they were able to take the boy away *a*.
25:19 who had died but who Paul claimed is *a*.
Rom 6:11 dead to sin but *a* for God in Christ Jesus.
7: 3 if, while her husband is still *a*,
1Cor 15: 6 brothers at once, most of whom are still *a*,
2Cor 6: 9 dead, yet here we are, *a*;
Phil 1:24 more urgent that I remain *a* for your sakes.
Heb 9:17 it has no force while the testator is *a*.
Rv 3: 1 I know the reputation you have of being *a*,
19:20 *a* into the fiery pool of burning sulphur.

ALL-BEAUTIFUL (2)

Sg 4: 7 You are *a*, my beloved,
Lam 2:15 "Is this the *a* city,

ALL-EMBRACING (1)

Wis 1: 7 spirit of the Lord fills the world, is *a*,

ALL-HEALING (1)

Wis 16:12 application cured them, but your *a* word,

ALL-KNOWING (1)

1Sm 2: 3 For an *a* God is the LORD,

ALL-NIGHT (2)

Jos 10: 9 upon them after an *a* march from Gilgal,
2Sm 2:32 Joab and his men made an *a* march,

ALL-NOURISHING (1)

Wis 16:25 it was serving your *a* bounty according to

ALL-POWERFUL (2)

Wis 7:23 kindly, Firm, secure, tranquil, *a*,
18:15 *a* word from heaven's royal throne bounded,

ALL-SEEING (8)

Est D: 2 after invoking the *a* God and savior,
E: 4 the vindictive judgment of the *a* God.
2Mc 7:35 the judgment of the almighty and *a* God.
9: 5 the *a* Lord, the God of Israel, struck him
12:22 and terror at the manifestation of the *A*.
15: 2 respect for the day which the *A* has exalted
Wis 7:23 Firm, secure, tranquil, all-powerful, *a*,
Sir 15:18 he is mighty in power, and *a*.

ALL-VIOLET (1)

Nm 4: 6 skin, and on top of this spread an *a* cloth.

ALLAMMELECH (1)

Jos 19:26 Helkath, Hali, Beten, Achshaph, *A*,

ALLAY (1)

Is 47:11 shall befall you which you cannot *a*.

ALLAYS (2)

Prv 15:18 up strife, but a patient man *a* discord.
21:14 A secret gift *a* anger,

ALLEGATIONS (1)

Lk 23:14 no charge against him arising from your *a*.

ALLEGE (1)

Ex 23: 2 Neither shall you *a* the example of the

ALLEGED (1)

2Thes 2: 2 or rumor, or a letter *a* to be ours,

ALLEGIANCE (4)

1Chr 12:30 them had held their *a* to the house of Saul.
29:24 of King David, swore *a* to King Solomon.
1Cor 1:12 still another, "Cephas has my *a*."
Eph 2: 2 as you gave *a* to the present age and to

ALLEGING (2)

Jer 29:23 and *a* in my name things I did not command.
Mk 14:57 taking the stand, testified falsely by *a*,

ALLEGORY (1)

Gal 4:24 All this is an *a*:

ALLELUIA (15)

1Chr 16:36 Let all the people say, Amen! *A*
Tb 13:18 and all her houses shall cry out, *A*!
Ps(s) 104:35 Bless the LORD, O my soul! *A*
105:45 and observe his laws. *A*.
106: 1 *A*. Give thanks to the LORD
106:48 Let all the people say, Amen! *A*.
146:10 through all generations. *A*
147:20 made known to them. *A*
148:14 people close to him. *A*
149: 9 glory of all his faithful. *A*.
150: 6 Praise the LORD, *A*.
Rv 19: 1 *A*! Salvation, glory and might
19: 3 Once more they sang *A*!"
19: 4 and sang, "Amen! *A*!"
19: 6 *A*! The LORD is king.

ALLEY (1)

Acts 12:10 emerged and made their way down a narrow *a*,

ALLEYS (1)

Lk 14:21 streets and *a* of the town

ALLIANCE (20)

Jos 9: 2 they all formed an *a* to launch a common
9: 6 land to propose that you make an *a* with us."
9: 7 How, then, can we make an *a* with you?"
9:11 we propose that you make an *a* with us.'
9:15 So Joshua made an *a* with them and entered
Jgs 3:13 In *a* with the Ammonites and Amalekites,
1Mc 1:11 make an *a* with the Gentiles all around us;
8: 1 a friendly *a* with all who applied to them.
8:17 to establish an *a* of friendship with them.
8:20 us to you to make a peaceful *a* with you,
8:22 with the Jews as a record of peace and *a*:
12: 3 friendship and *a* between you and them."
12: 8 which clearly referred to *a* and friendship.
12:16 our former friendship and *a* with them.
14:18 friendship and *a* that they had established
14:24 minas, to confirm the *a* with the Romans.
15:17 us to renew their earlier *a* of friendship.
Is 8:12 Call not *a* what this people calls alliance,
8:12 not alliance what this people calls *a*,
8:13 But with the LORD of hosts make your *a*—

ALLIANCES (2)

Dn 2:43 they shall seal their *a* by intermarriage,
Hos 10: 4 promises, swear false oaths, and make *a*,

ALLIED (9)

Gn 14: 5 Chedorlaomer and the kings *a* with him
14:17 and the kings who were *a* with him,
1Kgs 3: 1 Solomon *a* himself by marriage with Pharaoh,
2Chr 20:35 *a* himself with King Ahaziah of Israel,
Jdt 7: 1 the *a* troops that had come to his support,
1Mc 1:15 they *a* themselves with the Gentiles and
Ps(s) 83: 6 with one mind, and against you they are *a*:
Sir 13:16 Is a wolf ever *a* with a lamb?
Ez 30: 5 and people of the *a* territory shall fall

ALLIES (14)

1Kgs 20:16 with the thirty-two kings who were his *a*.
1Mc 8:20 enroll ourselves among your *a* and friends."
8:24 or any of its *a* in any of their dominions,
8:31 yoke heavy upon our friends and *a* the Jews?
9:60 letters secretly to all his *a* in Judea,
10:47 remained his *a* for the rest of his life.
11:60 forces of Syria espoused his cause as *a*.
12:14 rest of our *a* and friends in these wars;
14:40 had addressed the Jews as friends, *a*,
15:17 envoys of the Jews, our friends and *a*,
Jer 47: 4 from Tyre and Sidon the last of their *a*.
Ez 32:21 Come down, you and your *a*,
Dn 11: 6 After some years they shall become *a*:
Ob 1: 7 all your *a*;

ALLOCATED (1)

1Kgs 10:26 these he *a* among the chariot cities and to

ALLON (1)

1Chr 4:37 Benaiah, Ziza, son of Shiphi, son of *A*,

ALLON-BACUTH (1)

Gn 35: 8 oak below Bethel, and so it was called *A*.

ALLOT (4)

Neh 8:10 and *a* portions to those who had nothing
Is 49: 8 the land and *a* the desolate heritages,
Ez 4: 5 their sins I *a* you the same number of days,
47:22 You shall *a* it as inheritances for

ALLOTED (3)

Ps(s) 11: 6 a burning blast is their *a* cup.
16: 5 O LORD, my *a* portion and my cup,
2Cor 10:16 already done by another in his *a* territory.

ALLOTMENT (1)

Jos 17: 2 the *a* was now made to the other

ALLOTS (1)

Jb 21:17 upon them, the portion he *a* in his anger?

ALLOTTED (18)

Lv 7:35 *a* to Aaron and his sons on the day he
Jos 18:11 The territory *a* them lay between the
21: 8 pasture lands the Israelites *a* to the Levites
21:40 cities which were *a* to the Merarite clans,
Jgs 1: 3 up with me into the territory *a* to me,
1: 3 accompany you into the territory *a* to you."
1Chr 16:18 the land of Canaan as your *a* inheritance."
2Chr 31: 3 wealth the king *a* a portion for holocausts,
Neh 13: 5 in grain, wine, and oil *a* to the Levites,

ALLOTTED (cont.)
1Mc 5:20 Three thousand men were *a* to Simon,
Ps(s) 105:11 the land of Canaan as your *a* inheritance."
Sir 10:18 Insolence is not *a* to a man,
11:18 a miser's life, and this is his *a* reward:
40: 1 A great anxiety has God *a*,
45:20 The sacred offerings he *a* to him,
Ez 4: 6 one day for each year I have *a* you.
Dn 1: 5 The king *a* them a daily portion of food
1:10 it is he who *a* your food and drink.

ALLOTTING (1)
2Mc 8:30 *a* half to themselves and the rest to the

ALLOW (46)
Gn 23: 8 you will *a* me room for burial of my dead,
31:28 You did not even *a* me a parting kiss to my
Ex 3:19 will not *a* you to go unless he is forced.
Lv 22:15 priests shall not *a* to be profaned
Nm 6:21 from anything else which his means may *a*.
30:14 *a* to remain valid or render null and void.
33:55 those whom you *a* to remain will become as
35:32 Nor shall you accept indemnity to *a* a
Jos 7: 7 ever *a* this people to pass over the Jordan,
10:19 Do not *a* them to escape to their cities,
Ru 2: 2 field of anyone who will *a* me that favor."
1Sm 16:22 message, *A* David to remain in my service,
18: 2 not *a* him to return to his father's house.
2Sm 15: 7 *A* me to go to Hebron and fulfill a vow I
1Kgs 2: 6 you must not *a* him to go down to the grave
20:31 *A* us, therefore, to garb ourselves
2Kgs 21: 8 I will not in future *a* Israel to be driven
2Chr 20:10 you did not *a* Israel to invade
33: 8 I will not again *a* Israel's feet to leave
Tb 8: 7 *a* us to live together to a happy old age."
Jdt 4:12 not to *a* their children to be seized,
1Mc 5:42 "Do not *a* any man to pitch a tent;
2Mc 12: 2 would not *a* them to live in peace.
13:11 and not to *a* this nation,
Sir 23: 5 A brazen look *a* me not;
25:24 *A* water no outlet,
37:26 so that you *a* it not what is bad for you;
Is 66: 9 Or shall I who *a* her to conceive,
Jer 13: 9 So also I will *a* the pride of Judah to rot,
31:18 If you *a* me,
Ez 4:15 I *a* you cow's dung in place of human
14: 3 should I *a* myself to be consulted by them?
20: 3 I will not *a* myself to be consulted by you,
22:16 In you I will *a* myself to be profaned in
39: 7 no longer *a* my holy name to be profaned.
Dn 2: 3 "I had a dream which will *a* my spirit no
13: 9 would not *a* their eyes to look to heaven,
Hos 5: 4 deeds do not *a* them to return to their God;
Mt 24:43 eye and not *a* his house to be broken into.
Mk 7:12 you *a* him to do nothing more for his
16:20 who does not *a* what is unclean and
Lk 4:41 He rebuked them and did not *a* them to
Acts 16: 7 again the Spirit of Jesus would not *a* them.
Rom 14:16 neither may you *a* your privilege to become
Jas 2: 1 Lord Jesus Christ must not *a* of favoritism.
Rv 13:16 it did not *a* a man to buy or sell anything

ALLOWANCE (9)
Gn 47:22 Since the priests had a fixed *a* from
47:22 lived off the *a* Pharaoh had granted them,
2Kgs 25:30 The *a* granted him by the king was a
25:30 granted him by the king was a perpetual *a*,
Neh 5:14 my brethren lived from the governor's *a*.
5:18 this I did not claim the governor's *a*,
Jer 52:34 The *a* given him by the king of Babylon was
52:34 by the king of Babylon was a perpetual *a*,
Ez 16:27 I diminished your *a* and delivered you over

ALLOWANCES (1)
1Mc 10:36 in the king's army and *a* be given them,

ALLOWED (38)
Gn 3:22 he must not be *a* to put out his hand to
24:59 At this they *a* their sister Rebekah and
48:11 has *a* me to see your descendants as well!"
Ex 19:13 a one, man or beast, must not be *a* to live.
26:12 which shall be *a* to hang down over the
Nm 16:10 He has *a* you and your kinsmen,
30:15 he has *a* them to remain valid,
Dt 4:35 All this you were *a* to see that you might
Jgs 2:14 He *a* them to fall into the power of their
2:23 therefore the LORD *a* them to remain
3: 1 are the nations which the LORD *a* to remain,
3: 8 and he *a* them to fall into the power of
4: 2 So the LORD *a* them to fall into the power
10: 7 became angry with Israel and *a* them to fall
1Sm 12: 9 *a* them to fall into the clutches of Sisera,
20:16 The name of Jonathan must never be *a* by
2Kgs 25:22 he had *a* to remain in the land of Judah,
2Chr 1: 8 and you have *a* me to succeed him as king.
34:11 the kings of Judah had *a* to fall into ruin.
Ezr 9:13 deserved and have *a* us to survive as we do
Est 2:13 she was *a* to take with her from the harem
1Mc 10:23 "Why have we *a* Alexander to get ahead of
2Mc 2:31 should be *a* to aim at brevity of expression
10:20 they *a* a number of them to escape.
Jb 31:16 or *a* the eyes of the widow to languish
Jer 40:15 Why should he be *a* to kill you?
Lam 5: 5 we are worn out, but *a* no rest.
Ez 7:19 They shall not be *a* to satisfy their
Lk 6: 4 even though only priests are *a* to eat it?"
13:33 be *a* to die anywhere except in Jerusalem.'
Jn 5:10 and you are not *a* to carry that mat around."
Acts 23:16 They *a* him to enter,
24:23 to be kept in custody but *a* some freedom,
27: 3 where Julius kindly *a* Paul to visit some
28:16 Paul was *a* to take a lodging of his own,
Rv 9: 5 The locusts were not *a* to kill them but
13: 7 The beast was *a* to wage war against God's
13:14 Because of the prodigies it was *a* to

ALLOWING (2)
Ex 1:18 have you acted thus, *a* the boys to live?"
Rv 6: 4 of peace by *a* men to slaughter one another.

ALLOWS (2)
Nm 30:15 he thereby *a* as valid any vow or any
Eccl 5:11 the rich man's abundance *a* him no sleep.

ALLOY (1)
Is 1:25 dross in the furnace, removing all your *a*.

ALLURE (1)
Hos 2:16 So I will *a* her;

ALLUREMENTS (1)
1Jn 2:16 Carnal *a*, enticements for the eye

ALLURES (1)
Prv 16:29 A lawless man *a* his neighbor,

ALLY (8)
Jos 23:12 For if you ever abandon him and *a*
1Mc 10: 6 gather an army and procure arms as his *a*;
10:16 Let us now make him our friend and *a*."
2Mc 8:24 With the Almighty as their *a*,
10:16 public prayers asking God to be their *a*,
11:10 order with the aid of their heavenly *a*.
11:13 because the mighty God was their *a*.
12:36 himself their *a* and leader in the battle.

ALLYING (1)
Dn 11:23 After *a* with him,

ALMIGHTY (82)
Gn 17: 1 "I am God the *A*.
28: 3 May God *A* bless you and make you fertile,
35:11 "I am God *A*; be fruitful and multiply.
43:14 May God *A* dispose the man to be merciful
48: 3 "God *A* appeared to me at Luz in the land
49:25 God of your father, who helps you, God *A*,
Ex 6: 3 As God the *A* I appeared to Abraham,
Nm 24: 4 knows, Of one who sees what the *A* sees,
24:16 knows, Of one who sees what the *A* sees,
Ru 1:20 for the *A* has made it very bitter for me.
1:21 me and the *A* has brought evil upon me?"
Tb 3:16 heard in the glorious presence of *A* God.
Jdt 4:13 the sanctuary of the Lord *A* in Jerusalem.
8:13 *A* for whom you are laying down conditions;
15:10 be blessed by the Lord *A* forever and ever!"
16: 5 "But the Lord *A* thwarted them,
16:17 the Lord *A* will requite them;
Est C: 2 "O Lord God, *a* King,
2Mc 1:25 who alone are gracious, just, *a*,
3:22 While they were imploring the *a* Lord to
3:30 now that the *a* Lord had manifested himself.
5:20 and what the *A* had forsaken in his anger
6:26 alive or dead, escape the hands of the *A*.
7:35 the judgment of the *a* and all-seeing God.
7:38 wrath of the *A* that has justly fallen
8:11 that was to fall upon him from the *A*.
8:18 daring," he said, "but we trust in *a* God,
8:24 With the *A* as their ally,
15: 8 too, victory would be given them by the *A*.
15:32 out against the holy dwelling of the *A*.
Jb 6: 4 For the arrows of the *A* pierce me,
6:14 though he have forsaken the fear of the *A*.
8: 3 judgment, and does the *A* distort justice?
8: 5 to God and make supplication to the *A*,
11: 7 Dare you vie with the perfection of the *A*?
13: 3 But I would speak with the *A*;
15:25 against God and bade defiance to the *A*,
21:15 What is the *A* that we should serve him?
21:20 and the wrath of the *A* let him drink!
22: 3 it of advantage to the *A* if you are just?
22:17 and, "What can the *A* do to us?"
22:23 If you return to the *A*,
22:25 Then the *A* himself shall be your gold and
22:26 For then you shall delight in the *A* and
23:16 the *A* has put me in dismay.
24: 1 Why are not times set by the *A*,
27: 2 lives, who withholds my deserts, the *A*,
27:10 in the *A* and call upon him constantly?
27:11 and the way of the *A* I will not conceal.
27:13 an oppressor receives from the *A*:
29: 5 When the *A* was yet with me,
31: 2 above, his inheritance from the *A* on high?
31:37 let the *A* answer me!
32: 8 it is a spirit in man, the breath of the *A*,
33: 4 me, the breath of the *A* keeps me alive.
34:10 far from the *A* to do wrong!
34:12 act wickedly, the *A* cannot violate justice.
35:13 hear or that the *A* does not take notice.
37:23 The *A*! we cannot discover him
40: 2 we have arguing with the *A* by the critic?
Ps(s) 68:15 While the *A* dispersed the kings there,
91: 1 High, who abide in the shadow of the *A*,
Wis 7:25 and a pure effusion of the glory of the *A*:
11:17 For not without means was your *a* hand,
Sir 39: 6 Then, if it pleases the LORD *A*,
42:21 Perennial is his *a* wisdom;
Is 13: 6 as destruction from the *A* it comes.
Bar 3: 1 "Lord *A*, God of Israel,
3: 4 Lord *A*, God of Israel, hear the prayer
Ez 1:24 of mighty waters, like the voice of the *A*.
10: 5 like the voice of God the *A* when he speaks.
Jl 1:15 the LORD, and it comes as ruin from the *A*.
2Cor 6:18 be my sons and daughters,' says the Lord *A*."
Rv 1: 8 is and who was and who is to come, the *A*!"
4: 8 "Holy, holy, holy, is the Lord God *A*,
11:17 you, the Lord God *A* who is and who was.
15: 3 and wonderful are your works, Lord God *A*!
16: 7 "Yes, Lord God *A*,
16:14 for battle on the great day of God the *A*.
19: 6 The Lord is king, our God, the *A*!
19:15 winepress the blazing wrath of God the *A*.
21:22 The Lord, God the *A*,

ALMIGHTY'S (1)
Jb 5:17 The *A* chastening do not reject.

ALMODAD (2)
Gn 10:26 Joktan became the father of *A*,
1Chr 1:20 Joktan became the father of *A*,

ALMON (2)
Jos 21:18 lands, and *A* with its pasture lands.
1Chr 6:45 pasture lands, *A* with its pasture lands,

ALMON-DIBLATHAIM (2)
Nm 33:46 out from Dibon-gad, they camped at *A*.
33:47 Setting out from *A*,

ALMOND (8)
Gn 30:37 fresh shoots of poplar, *a* and plane trees,
Ex 25:33 to be three cups, shaped like *a* blossoms,
25:33 to be three cups, shaped like *a* blossoms,
25:34 to be four cups, shaped like *a* blossoms,
37:19 were three cups, shaped like *a* blossoms,
37:19 were three cups, shaped like *a* blossoms,
37:20 were four cups, shaped like *a* blossoms,
Eccl 12: 5 When the *a* tree blooms,

ALMONDS (2)
Gn 43:11 honey, gum and resin, and pistachios and *a*.
Nm 17:23 but blossoms as well, and even bore ripe *a*!

ALMS (23)
Tb 4: 7 "Give *a* from your possessions.
4: 8 Son, give *a* in proportion to what you own.
4: 8 great wealth, give *a* out of your abundance;
4: 8 But do not hesitate to give *a*;
4:11 *A* are a worthy offering in the sight of
4:16 you have left over, give away as *a*;
4:16 and do not begrudge the *a* you give.
12: 8 is better to give *a* than to store up gold;
12: 9 regularly give *a* shall enjoy a full life;
14: 2 giving *a* and continually blessing God and
14: 9 to do what is upright and to give *a*,
14:10 Because Ahiqar had given *a* to me,
Sir 3:29 a flaming fire, and *a* atone for sins.
7:10 prayers, and neglect not the giving of *a*.
29: 8 keep him not waiting for your *a*;
35: 2 when he gives *a* he presents his sacrifice
Mt 6: 2 When you give *a*,
6: 3 In giving *a* you are not to let your left
Lk 11:41 But if you give what you have as *a*,
12:33 Sell what you have and give *a*.
Acts 3: 3 on their way in, he begged them for an *a*.
24:17 *a* to my own people and to make
Rom 12: 8 He who gives *a* should do so generously;

ALMSGIVING (5)
Tb 4:10 *A* frees one from death,
12: 8 either is *a* accompanied by righteousness.
12: 9 for *a* saves one from death and expiates
14:11 So, my children, note well what *a* does,
Sir 29:12 Store up *a* in your treasure house,

ALOES (4)
Ps(s) 45: 9 and *a* and cassia your robes are fragrant;
Prv 7:17 I have sprinkled my bed with myrrh, with *a*,
Sg 4:14 Myrrh and *a*,

Jn 19:39 and *a* which weighed about a hundred pounds.

ALOFT (9)

Jb 39:27 fly up at your command to build his nest *a*?
Sir 24:13 "Like a cedar on Lebanon I am raised *a*,
34: 1 and fools are borne *a* by dreams.
48: 9 You were taken *a* in a whirlwind,
Is 6: 2 their feet, and with two they hovered *a*.
Jer 49:22 like an eagle he soars *a*,
Bar 5: 6 you borne *a* in glory as on royal thrones.
Zec 9:16 jewels in a crown raised *a* over his land.
1Tm 2: 8 offer prayers with blameless hands held *a*,

ALONE (183)

Gn 2:18 "It is not good for the man to be *a*.
7: 1 for you *a* in this age have I found to be
32:25 his possessions, Jacob was left there *a*.
Ex 14:12 'Leave us *a*.
18:14 Why do you sit *a* while all the people have
18:18 you cannot do it *a*.
21: 3 If he comes into service *a*,
21: 3 into service alone, he shall leave *a*;
21: 4 property and the man shall leave *a*.
22:19 to any god, except to the LORD *a*,
24: 2 but Moses *a* is to come close to the LORD;
32:10 "Let me *a*,
Nm 1:49 "The tribe of Levi *a* you shall not enroll
12: 2 it through Moses *a* that the LORD speaks?
18: 1 shall rest on you and your sons *a*.
18:23 tent, and they *a* shall be held responsible;
Dt 1: 9 "At that time I said to you, *A*,
1:12 I *a* bear the crushing burden that you are,
6: 4 The LORD is our God, the LORD *a*!
8: 3 show you that not by bread *a* does man live,
13: 5 serving him and holding fast to him *a*.
16:20 Justice and justice *a* shall be your aim,
19:15 "One witness *a* shall not take the stand
22:25 relations with her, the man *a* shall die.
29:13 with you *a* that I am making this covenant,
32:12 The LORD *a* was their leader,
32:39 "Learn then that I, I *a*,
Jos 22:20 man, he did not perish *a* for his guilt!"
Jgs 3:20 him where he sat *a* in his cool upper room,
6:37 If dew comes on the fleece *a*,
6:39 Let the fleece *a* be dry,
6:40 the fleece *a* was dry,
1Sm 5: 4 lying on the threshold, his trunk *a* intact.
6: 3 the God of Israel, you must not send it *a*,
7: 3 yourselves to the LORD, and worship him *a*.
7: 4 and Ashtaroth, and worshiped the LORD *a*.
21: 2 to meet him and asked, "Why are you *a*?
2Sm 2:10 The Judahites *a* followed David.
13:32 Amnon *a* is dead,
13:33 Amnon *a* is dead."
16:11 Let him *a* and let him curse,
17: 2 him flee, I shall strike down the king *a*.
18:24 looked about and saw a man running all *a*.
18:25 to inform the king, who said, "If he is *a*,
20:21 Surrender him *a*,
1Kgs 3:18 We were *a* in the house;
8:39 You who *a* know the hearts of all men,
11:29 The two were *a* in the area,
12:20 David's house except the tribe of Judah *a*.
14:13 for he *a* of Jeroboam's line will be laid
14:13 since in him *a* of Jeroboam's house has
19:10 I *a* am left,
19:14 I *a* am left,
2Kgs 4:27 "Let her *a*,
19:15 You *a* are God over all the kingdoms of the
19:19 kingdoms of the earth may know that you *a*,
1Chr 6:34 they *a* had charge of the holy of holies
29: 1 "My son Solomon, whom *a* God has chosen,
2Chr 6:30 conduct, for you *a* know the hearts of men.
32:12 only, and on it *a* you shall offer incense"?
Ezr 4: 3 God, but we *a* must build it for the LORD,
Tb 1: 6 would often make the pilgrimage *a* to
8: 6 said, 'It is not good for the man to be *a*;
Jdt 3: 8 nation might worship Nebuchadnezzar *a*,
9:14 the people of Israel but you *a*
11: 8 the kingdom you *a* are competent,
12:10 gave a banquet for his servants *a*,
13: 2 was left *a* in the tent with Holofernes,
Est 1:16 "Queen Vashti has not wronged the king *a*,
3: 6 was not enough to lay hands on Mordecai *a*.
4:13 palace, you *a* of all the Jews will escape.
C:14 "My Lord, our King, you *a* are God.
C:14 Help me, who am *a* and have no help but you,
C:25 help me, who am *a* and have no one but you,
1Mc 13: 4 my brothers have perished, and I *a* am left.
2Mc 1:25 king and benefactor, who *a* are gracious,
7:37 blows to make you confess that he *a* is God.
8:35 fled *a* across country like a runaway slave,
15:38 is harmful to drink wine *a* or water alone,
15:38 is harmful to drink wine alone or water *a*,
Jb 1:15 sword, and I *a* have escaped to tell you."
1:16 and I *a* have escaped to tell you."
1:17 sword, and I *a* have escaped to tell you."
1:19 and I *a* have escaped to tell you."
7:16 let me *a*, for my days are but a breath.
7:19 let me *a* long enough to swallow my spittle?
9: 8 He *a* stretches out the heavens and treads
10:20 Let me *a*, that I may recover
13:13 Be silent, let me *a*!
15:19 fathers, To whom *a* the land was given,
31:17 to languish While I ate my portion *a*,
Ps(s) 4: 9 down, I fall peacefully asleep, for you *a*,
22:30 To him *a* shall bow down all who sleep in
25:16 for I am *a* and afflicted Relieve the
72:18 God of Israel, who *a* does wondrous deeds.
83:19 perish, Knowing that you *a* are the LORD,
86:10 you *a* are God.
102: 8 I am like a sparrow *a* on the housetop.
136: 4 I Who *a* does great wonders,
148:13 of the LORD, for his name *a* is exalted;
Prv 5:17 Let your fountain be yours *a*,
9:12 if you are arrogant, you *a* shall bear it.
17:11 On rebellion *a* is the wicked man bent,
Eccl 4:11 How can one *a* keep warm?
Sg 6: 9 One *a* is my dove,
Wis 10: 1 of the world when he *a* had been created;
17:21 Over them *a* was spread oppressive night,
Sir 18: 1 the LORD *a* is just.
24: 5 The vault of heaven I compassed *a*,
37: 8 For he may be thinking of himself *a*;
45:13 be worn by any Except his sons and them *a*,
45:25 an individual heritage through one son *a*;
Is 2:11 be abased, and the LORD *a* will be exalted,
2:17 low, And the LORD *a* will be exalted,
2:22 As for you, let man *a*,
5: 8 left to dwell *a* in the midst of the land!
10:14 As one takes eggs left *a*,
28:19 terror *a* shall convey the message.
29:13 only and honors me with their lips *a*,
37:16 You *a* are God over all the kingdoms of the
37:20 earth may know that you, O LORD, *a* are God."
44:24 things, who *a* stretched out the heavens;
49:21 I was left all *a*;
63: 3 "The wine press I have trodden *a*,
Jer 3:23 our God, *a* is the salvation of Israel.
14:22 Is it not you *a*,
14:22 You *a* have done all these things.
15:17 *a* because you filled me with indignation.
17:10 LORD, *a* probe the mind and test the heart,
34: 7 since these *a* were left of the fortified
49:31 That has no gates or bars, and dwells *a*.
Lam 3: 3 Against me *a* he brings back his hand again
3:28 Let him sit *a* and in silence,
Ez 9: 8 As they began to strike, I was left *a*.
14:16 they *a* would be saved,
14:18 they *a* would be saved.
37: 3 GOD," I answered, "you *a* know that."
Dn 3:45 Let them know that you *a* are the Lord God,
10: 7 I *a*, Daniel, saw the vision
10: 8 So I was left *a*, seeing this great vision.
13:14 for an occasion when they could meet her *a*.
13:36 "As we were walking in the garden *a*,
14:14 the king *a* was present.
Hos 4:17 is an associate of idols, let him *a*!
Am 3: 2 You *a* have I favored,
Mt 4: 4 'Not on bread *a* is man to live but on
4:10 him *a* shall you adore.' "
14:24 pray, remaining there *a* as evening drew on.
27:49 Meanwhile the rest said, "Leave him *a*.
Mk 2: 7 Who can forgive sins except God *a*?"
6:47 out on the lake while he was *a* on the land.
10:18 No one is good but God *a*.
12:29 The Lord our God is Lord *a*!
14: 6 Jesus said, "Let her *a*.
Lk 4: 4 has it, 'Not on bread *a* shall man live.' "
4: 8 him *a* shall you adore.' "
4:34 "Leave us *a*! What do you want?
5:21 Who can forgive sins but God *a*?"
9:36 the voice fell silent, Jesus was there *a*.
10:40 left me to do the household tasks all *a*?
11: 7 he from inside should reply, 'Leave me *a*.
18:19 None is good but God *a*.
Jn 6:15 king, so he fled back to the mountain *a*.
8: 9 This left him *a* with the woman,
8:16 of mine is valid because I am not *a*:
12: 7 "Leave her *a*.
16:32 each will go his way, leaving me quite *a*.
16:32 (Yet I can never be *a*;
17:20 "I do not pray for them *a*.
Acts 5:38 Let them *a*. If their purpose
Rom 3:29 Does God belong to the Jews *a*?
4:23 him," were not written with him *a* in view;
11: 3 I *a* am left and they are seeking my life."
14: 4 *a* can judge whether he stands or falls.
16:27 to him, the God who *a* is wise,
1Thes 3: 1 to remain *a* at Athens and send you Timothy.
1Tm 5: 3 that is, who are *a* and bereft.
6:16 Lord of lords who *a* has immortality
Heb 5:13 *a* is ignorant of the word that sanctifies,
Jas 2:24 justified by his works and not by faith *a*.
Rv 15: 4 Since you *a* are holy,
19:10 Worship God *a*. The prophetic spirit
22: 9 Worship God *a*!"

ALONG (293)

Gn 14:16 *a* with the women and the other captives.
21:32 in Beer-sheba, Abimelech *a* with Phicol,
24:59 *a* with Abraham's servant and his men.
32:32 Penuel, Jacob limped *a* because of his hip.
43:12 Also take extra money *a*,
46:15 in Paddan-aram, *a* with his daughter Dinah
48: 1 So he took *a* with him his two sons,
Ex 2: 5 while her maids walked *a* the river bank.
13:19 Moses also took Joseph's bones *a*,
17: 5 *a* with some of the elders of Israel,
18: 2 his father-in-law Jethro took *a* Zipporah,
18: 6 to you, *a* with your wife and her two sons."
19:24 Then come up again *a* with Aaron.
26: 4 *a* the edge of the end sheet in one set,
26: 4 and the same *a* the edge of the end sheet
26: 5 There are to be fifty loops *a* the edge of
26: 5 and fifty loops *a* the edge of the
26:10 *a* the edge of the end sheet in one set,
26:10 and fifty loops *a* the edge of the end
29: 3 them *a* with the bullock and the two rams.
33:14 myself," the LORD answered, "will go *a*,
34: 4 him, taking *a* the two stone tablets.
34: 9 with you, O Lord, do come *a* in our company.
36:11 Loops of violet yarn were made *a* the edge
36:11 and the same *a* the edge of the end sheet
36:17 *a* the edge of the end sheet in one set,
36:17 and fifty loops *a* the edge of the
Lv 7:13 loaves of leavened bread *a* with the victim
9: 4 *a* with a cereal offering mixed with oil;
14:12 as a guilt offering, *a* with the log of oil,
14:24 guilt-offering lamb, *a* with the log of oil,
14:31 as a holocaust, *a* with the cereal offering.
14:52 the spring water, *a* with the living bird,
23:18 *a* with their cereal offering and libations,
Nm 1:49 in the census *a* with the other Israelites.
5:15 shall take *a* as an offering
6:14 *a* with their cereal offerings and
6:20 *a* with the breast of the wave offering and
8: 8 *a* with its cereal offering of fine flour
9: 7 proper time *a* with the other Israelites?"
11:30 to the camp, *a* with the elders of Israel.
13:29 and Canaanites *a* the seacoast and the
15:24 *a* with its prescribed cereal offering and
16:18 of the meeting tent *a* with Moses and Aaron.
20:17 but we will go straight *a* the royal road
20:19 "We want only to go up *a* the highway.
21: 1 were coming *a* the way of Atharim,
21:22 but we will go straight *a* the royal road
21:33 turned and went up *a* the road to Bashan.
22:22 hinder him as he was riding *a* on his ass,
26: 3 Moab *a* the Jericho stretch of the Jordan,
26:63 Moab *a* the Jericho stretch of the Jordan.
31:12 Moab, *a* the Jericho stretch of the Jordan.
33:48 Moab *a* the Jericho stretch of the Jordan.
33:49 Their camp *a* the Jordan on the plains of
34: 3 at the desert of Zin *a* the border of Edom;
34:12 boundary shall continue *a* the Jordan
35: 5 cubits outside the city *a* each side
Dt 1:12 burden that you are, *a* with your bickering?
1:25 taking *a* some of the fruit of the land,
1:31 all *a* your journey until you arrived at
2:27 I will go *a* it without turning aside to
12:18 he chooses, *a* with your son and daughter,
18: 8 *a* with his monetary offerings and
22: 6 "If, while walking *a*,
22: 6 take away the mother bird *a* with her brood;
23:15 journeys *a* within your camp to defend you
25:18 fear of any god he harassed you *a* the way,
31:29 aside from the way *a* which I directed you,
Jos 2: 7 out *a* the way to the fords of the Jordan,
2:22 them all *a* the road without finding them,
4: 8 and carried them *a* to the camp site,
9: 1 and *a* the coast of the Great Sea as far as
9:11 'Take *a* provisions for the journey and go
10:11 Israel *a* the descent from Beth-horon,
15:11 extended *a* the northern flank of Ekron,
18:16 *a* the southern flank of the Jebusites,
22: 7 *a* with their kinsmen west of the Jordan.)
24:17 protected us *a* our entire journey
Jgs 5:17 Asher, who dwells *a* the shore,
14: 9 out into his palms and ate it as he went *a*.
Ru 4: 1 relative of whom he had spoken come *a*,
1Sm 1:24 up with her, *a* with a three-year-old bull,
6: 9 *a* the route to his own territory,
6:11 *a* with the box containing the golden mice
6:12 to Beth-shemesh and continued *a* this road,
16: 2 "Take a heifer *a* and say,
17:52 and Philistines fell wounded *a* the road
18: 4 it to David, *a* with his military dress,
21: 9 brought *a* neither my sword nor my weapons,
23:26 As Saul moved *a* one rim of the gorge,
24: 4 When he came to the sheepfolds *a* the way,
30:22 Let them take those *a* and be on their way."
31: 7 those *a* the Jordan saw that the men
2Sm 11: 1 David sent out Joab *a* with his officers
19:42 across the Jordan, *a* with all David's men?"
1Kgs 4:16 of Hushai, in Asher and *a* the rocky coast;
5:32 and Hiram's builders, *a* with the Gebalites,
6: 3 from side to side, *a* the width of the nave,
6: 6 because there were offsets *a* the outside
6:10 was built all *a* the outside of the temple,
14: 3 Take *a* ten loaves,
17:11 after her, "Please bring *a* a bit of bread."
2Kgs 5: 5 will send *a* a letter to the king of Israel."
5: 5 set out, taking *a* ten silver talents,
10: 5 city, *a* with the elders and the guardians,
10:16 And he took him *a* in his own chariot.
11: 2 and spirited him away, *a* with his nurse,

ALONG (cont.)

23: 9 but they, *a* with their relatives,
25:25 *a* with the Jews and Chaldeans who were in
1Chr 5:21 *A* with one hundred thousand men they also
12: 3 Ahiezer was their chief, *a* with Joash,
12:28 four thousand six hundred, *a* with Jehoiada,
14: 1 to David *a* with masons and carpenters,
15:12 must sanctify yourselves *a* with your
18:11 to the LORD *a* with all the silver and gold
19: 7 *a* with the king of Maacah and his army,
2Chr 3: 4 before the nave *a* the width of the house
21:17 palace, *a* with his sons and his wives;
29:35 *a* with the fat of the peace offerings and
36:10 *a* with precious vessels from the temple of
Ezr 8:22 to protect us against enemies *a* the way,
8:24 of the priestly leaders *a* with Sherebiah,
8:31 us from enemies and bandits *a* the way.
Neh 4:13 separated from one another *a* the wall;
12:31 to the right, *a* the top of the wall,
12:33 half the princes of Judah, *a* with Azariah,
12:37 continued *a* the top of the wall
12:38 *a* the top of the wall past the Oven Tower
Tb 9: 2 take *a* with you four servants and two
9: 2 him *a* with you to the wedding celebration.
11: 4 And the dog ran *a* behind them.
11:16 of Nineveh saw him walking *a* briskly,
Jdt 1: 6 region, all who dwelt *a* the Euphrates,
1: 7 to all who dwelt *a* the seacoast,
2:17 He took *a* a very large number of camels,
2:20 or the dust of the earth, went *a* with them.
2:24 down every fortified city *a* the Wadi Abron,
4:10 they, *a* with their wives,
5: 4 meet me *a* with all the other inhabitants
5:14 *a* the route to Sinai and Kadesh-barnea.
6: 7 leave you at one of the towns *a* the ascent.
15: 2 in all directions, and fled *a* every road,
Est 8:11 wipe out, *a* with their wives and children,
1Mc 5: 4 the people by ambushing them *a* the roads.
5: 5 the towers *a* with all the persons in them.
5:46 and strongly fortified city *a* the way,
6:33 force hastily *a* the road to Beth-zechariah;
6:35 beasts were distributed *a* the phalanxes,
9: 1 Judah, *a* with the right wing of his army.
11: 4 in the war and stacked up *a* his route.
11: 8 possession of the cities *a* the seacoast
13:20 moved *a* opposite him everywhere he went.
15:14 the city, his ships closed in *a* the coast,
2Mc 8:20 fought *a* with four thousand Macedonians;
10:19 and Joseph, *a* with Zacchaeus and his men,
10:37 killed him, *a* with his brother Chaereas,
12:35 cloak and dragged him *a* by main strength,
Jb 34: 8 with evildoers and goes *a* with wicked men,
Ps(s) 85:14 him, and salvation, *a* the way of his steps.
142: 4 *a* which I walk they have hid a trap for me.
Prv 1:11 entice you, and say, "Come *a* with us!
7: 8 sense, Going *a* the street near the corner,
8: 2 On the top of the heights *a* the road,
8:20 way of duty I walk, *a* the paths of justice,
Sir 40:14 Which, in its rising, rolls *a* the stones,
Is 14: 2 take them and bring them *a* to its place,
19: 7 land *a* the Nile shall dry up and blow away,
30:29 as one marching *a* with a flute Toward the
49: 9 *A* the ways they shall find pasture,
59:10 Like blind men we grope *a* the wall,
60: 8 What are these that fly *a* like clouds,
Jer 17:25 or upon their horses, *a* with their princes,
19: 1 Take *a* some of the elders of the people
27:20 *a* with all the nobles of Judah and
38:10 the Cushite to take three men *a* with him,
38:11 Ebed-melech took the men *a* with him,
43: 5 and all the army leaders took *a* the whole
49: 3 into exile *a* with his priests and captains.
Ez 10:19 the earth, the wheels rising *a* with them.
11:22 wings, and the wheels went *a* with them,
16:53 I will restore your fortune *a* with them],
23:23 Shoa and Koa, *a* with all those of Assyria,
25:10 I will hand her over, *a* with the Ammonites,
29: 4 midst of your Niles *a* with all the fish
33:30 *a* the walls and in the doorways of houses.
40:40 *A* the wall of the vestibule,
41:14 façade of the temple, *a* with the free area,
42: 7 parallel to the chambers *a* the outer court;
42: 8 but *a* its entire length the wall measured
42:10 To the south *a* the side of the free area
47: 7 *A* the bank of the river I saw very many
47:10 be standing *a* it from En-gedi to En-eglaim,
47:12 *A* both banks of the river,
47:16 *a* the frontiers of Hamath and Damascus,
47:22 *a* with you they shall receive inheritances
48: 1 all *a* from the approaches to Hethlon
48:11 *a* with the Israelites as the Levites did,
48:15 The remaining five thousand cubits *a* the
48:18 shall remain an area *a* the sacred tract,
48:21 extending *a* the twenty-five-thousand-cubit
48:21 and westward *a* the
48:28 *A* the frontier of Gad shall be the
Dn 6:25 *a* with their children and their wives,
Hb 3: 6 age-old hills bow low *a* his ancient ways.
Mt 4:15 of Naphtali *a* the sea beyond the Jordan,
4:18 As he was walking *a* the Sea of Galilee he
4:21 He walked *a* farther and caught sight of
8:28 that no one could travel *a* that road.
13: 2 a boat while the crowd stood *a* the shore.
13:19 The seed *a* the path is the man who hears
13:29 and you might take the wheat *a* with them.
15:29 that place and passed *a* the Sea of Galilee.
16: 1 The Pharisees and Sadducees came *a*,
16: 5 they had forgotten to bring any bread *a*.
18:25 ordered him to be sold, *a* with his wife,
20: 4 'You too go *a* to my vineyard and I will
21: 8 from the trees and lay them *a* his path.
25: 3 in taking their torches, brought no oil *a*,
26:37 He took *a* Peter and Zebedee's two sons,
27:38 Two insurgents were crucified *a* with him,
Mk 1:16 As he made his way *a* the Sea of Galilee,
1:19 Proceeding a little farther *a*,
2:13 while he went walking *a* the lakeshore,
2:23 to pull off heads of grain as they went *a*.
4: 4 where the birds came *a* and ate it.
8:14 They had forgotten to bring any bread *a*;
9: 4 Elijah appeared to them *a* with Moses;
11:20 next morning, as they were walking *a*,
14:33 at the same time he took *a* with him Peter,
14:42 Rouse yourselves and come *a*.
14:66 servant girls of the high priest came *a*.
15: 7 Barabbas jailed *a* with the rebels
16:12 were walking *a* on their way to the country,
Lk 5:18 men came *a* carrying a paralytic on a mat.
9:57 As they were making their way *a*,
10: 4 wear no sandals and greet no one *a* the way.
10:33 But a Samaritan who was journeying *a* came
11:31 judgment *a* with the men of this generation,
11:32 will rise *a* with the present generation,
14:17 servant to say to those invited, 'Come *a*,
14:23 *a* the hedgerows and force them to come in.
17:11 *a* the borders of Samaria and Galilee.
19: 4 a sycamore tree which was *a* Jesus' route,
19:36 their cloaks on the roadway as he moved *a*;
23:26 shoulder for him to carry *a* behind Jesus.
23:32 were led *a* with him to be crucified.
23:55 with him from Galilee followed *a* behind.
24:15 approached and began to walk *a* with them.
Jn 2:12 *a* with his mother and brothers [and his
9: 1 As he walked *a*,
11:16 to his fellow disciples, "Let us go *a*,
20: 6 came *a* behind him and entered the tomb.
Acts 7:43 You took *a* the tent of Moloch and the star
8:36 moved *a* the road they came to some water,
9: 3 he traveled *a* and was approaching Damascus,
9:25 took him *a* the wall one night and lowered
10: 9 were traveling *a* and approaching the city,
11:12 These six brothers came *a* with me,
15:22 sent to Antioch *a* with Paul and Barnabas.
15:25 you, *a* with our beloved Barnabas and Paul,
15:35 continued in Antioch, *a* with many others,
15:37 Barnabas wanted to take *a* John,
15:38 mission, he was not fit to be taken *a* now.
15:39 took Mark *a* with him and sailed for Cyprus.
16: 3 anxious to have him come *a* on the journey.
16:39 They came *a* and tried to quiet them;
18: 8 Crispus, *a* with his whole household,
21:16 came *a* to escort us to the house of Mnason,
21:24 Take them *a* with you and join with them in
21:36 A crowd of people was following *a* shouting,
22: 6 As I was traveling *a*,
27: 8 *a* the coast to a place called Fair Havens,
27:17 moving the ship and the ship was carried *a*.
1Cor 10:13 *A* with the test he will give you a way out
2Cor 1:21 firmly establishes us *a* with you in Christ;
4:14 will raise us up *a* with Jesus
8:18 We have sent *a* with him that brother whom
8:22 We have sent *a* that brother whose
Gal 3: 9 all who believe are blessed *a* with Abraham,
Phil 2:22 father's side serving the gospel *a* with me.
4: 3 *a* with Clement and the others who have
4:10 You had been concerned all *a*,
Col 4:10 Aristarchus, who is a prisoner *a* with me,
1Tm 1:14 *a* with the faith and love which are in
2Tm 2: 3 Bear hardship *a* with me as a good soldier
2:22 *a* with those who call on the Lord in
Heb 11:25 he wished to be ill-treated *a* with God's
Rv 5: 8 *A* with their harps,
8: 7 *a* with a third of the trees and every
10: 6 earth and sea *a* with everything in them:
17:12 possess royal authority *a* with the beast,
19:20 The beast was captured *a* with the false

ALONGSIDE (12)

Gn 33:12 I will travel *a* you."
Ex 37:14 The rings were *a* the frame as holders for
40:20 *a* the ark and set the propitiatory upon it.
Jos 15:46 the sea, all the towns that lie *a* Ashdod,
2Sm 15: 2 and stand *a* the road leading to the gate.
1Chr 5:11 The Gadites lived *a* them in the land of
2Chr 8:14 of praise and ministry *a* the priests,
Neh 3:23 of Annaniah, made the repairs *a* his house.
13:21 "Why do you spend the night *a* the wall?
1Mc 13:52 of the temple hill *a* the citadel,
Ez 3:13 one another, and by the wheels *a* them,
40:18 The pavement lay *a* the gates,

ALOOF (6)

2Sm 18:13 of the king, and you would stand *a*."
Ezr 9: 1 kept themselves *a* from the peoples
Jb 30:10 They abhor me, they stand *a* from me,
Ps(s) 10: 1 Why, O LORD, do you stand *a*?
Wis 2:16 *a* from our paths as from things impure.
Sir 22:26 friend all will stand *a* who hear of it.

ALOUD (41)

Gn 27:38 and Esau wept *a*.
Ex 24: 7 the covenant, he read it *a* to the people,
Dt 27:14 shall proclaim *a* to all the men of Israel:
31:11 this law *a* in the presence of all Israel.
Jos 6: 5 that signal, all the people shall shout *a*.
8:34 Then were read *a* all the words of the law,
8:35 Joshua read *a* to the entire community,
Jgs 2: 4 to all the Israelites, the people wept *a*,
Ru 1:14 Again they sobbed *a* and wept;
1Sm 11: 4 the news to the people, all of whom wept *a*.
20:41 They kissed each other and wept *a* together.
24:17 And he wept *a*.
30: 4 him wept *a* until they could weep no more.
2Sm 3:32 the king wept *a* at the grave of Abner,
13:36 than the princes came in, weeping *a*.
15:23 wept *a* as the last of the soldiers went by,
2Kgs 22:10 him a book, and then read it *a* to the king.
2Chr 34:30 and he had read *a* to them the entire text
Tb 3: 1 in spirit, I groaned and wept *a*.
7: 7 his eyesight, he was grieved and wept *a*.
10: 4 began to weep *a* and to wail over her son:
11: 9 And she sobbed *a*.
1Mc 3:50 And they cried *a* to Heaven:
Jb 2:12 not recognize him, they began to weep *a*;
Ps(s) 77: 2 *A* to God I cry; aloud to God
Prv 1:20 Wisdom cries *a* in the street,
8: 3 of the city, in the entryways she cries *a*:
Sir 20:14 often, and like a crier he shouts *a*.
Jer 51:61 see that you read *a* all these words,
Dn 3:25 In the fire Azariah stood up and prayed *a*:
13:42 But Susanna cried *a*:
13:46 a young boy named Daniel, and he cried *a*:
13:60 The whole assembly cried *a*,
14:18 the king looked at the table and cried *a*,
14:41 The king cried *a*,
Jn 12:44 Jesus proclaimed *a*:
Acts 7:57 The onlookers were shouting *a*,
15:21 read *a* in the synagogues on every sabbath."
Jas 5: 4 Here, crying *a*,
Rv 5:13 everything in the universe cried *a*:
12: 2 *a* in pain as she labored to give birth.

ALPHA (3)

Rv 1: 8 Lord God says, "I am the *A* and the Omega,
21: 6 I am the *A* and the Omega,
22:13 I am the *A* and the Omega,

ALPHAEUS (5)

Mt 10: 3 James, son of *A*,
Mk 2:14 the son of *A* at his tax collector's post,
3:18 Matthew, Thomas, James son of *A*;
Lk 6:15 Matthew and Thomas, James son of *A*,
Acts 1:13 James son of *A*;

ALREADY (119)

Gn 19:19 "You have *a* thought enough of your
27:37 "I have *a* appointed him your master,
28:11 a certain shrine, as the sun had *a* set,
Ex 1: 5 Joseph was *a* in Egypt.
5: 5 how numerous the people of the land are *a*,"
14:10 Pharaoh was *a* near when the Israelites
36: 7 there was *a* enough at hand,
Lv 13:21 deeper than the skin and is *a* dying out,
13:26 deeper than the skin and is *a* dying out,
13:28 spreading on the skin and is *a* dying out,
13:39 on the skin are white and *a* dying out,
19:20 female slave who has *a* been living
27:26 which as such *a* belongs to the LORD,
Nm 14:22 times *a* and have failed to heed my voice,
17:12 where the blow was *a* falling on the people.
19:14 the tent, as well as everyone *a* in it,
34:14 Manasseh, have *a* received their heritage;
Dt 2: 5 since I have *a* given Esau possession of
2:31 'Now that I have *a* begun to hand over to
9:12 they have *a* turned aside from the way I
9:16 you had *a* turned aside from the way which
29:28 [Both what is still hidden and what has *a*
30:14 you, *a* in your mouths and in your hearts;
31:27 For I *a* know how rebellious and
Jos 8:20 the smoke from the city was *a* sky-high.
14: 3 had *a* given a heritage beyond the Jordan;
17: 1 who had *a* obtained Gilead and Bashan,
18: 7 Manasseh have *a* received the heritage
Jgs 8: 6 of Zebah and Zalmunna *a* in your possession,
8:15 of Zebah and Zalmunna *a* in your possession,
16:15 Three times *a* you have mocked me,
18:22 The Danites had *a* gone some distance,
19: 9 father said to him, "It is *a* growing dusk.
2Sm 18:12 "Even if I *a* held a thousand pieces of
2Kgs 1:14 *A* fire has come down from heaven,
1Chr 14:15 for God has *a* gone before you to strike
2Chr 20: 2 are *a* in Hazazon-tamar" (which is Engedi).
28:13 Our guilt is *a* great,
28:22 While he was *a* in distress,
Ezr 4:12 and the foundations have *a* been laid.
Neh 9:25 with all good things, cisterns *a* dug,

Tb 3: 8 You have *a* been married seven times,
3:15 I have *a* lost seven husbands;
5: 3 have *a* passed since I deposited that money!
6:14 this woman has *a* been married seven times,
10: 7 I have *a* told you how I left him."
12:11 I have *a* said to you,
2Mc 4:32 he had *a* sold some other vessels in Tyre
12:18 for he had *a* departed from there without
15: 9 them of the battles they had *a* won,
15:20 The enemy were *a* drawing near with their
Eccl 1:10 has *a* existed in the ages that preceded us.
2:12 What men have *a* done!
3:15 What now is has *a* been;
3:15 what is to be, *a* is;
Wis 18:23 had *a* fallen one on another in heaps,
Sir 34: 5 what you *a* expect,
Is 56: 8 I gather to him besides those *a* gathered.
Jer 32:25 has *a* been handed over to the Chaldeans!
46:14 the sword has *a* devoured your neighbors.
Zec 2:12 LORD of hosts (after he had *a* sent me)
Mal 2: 2 Yes, I have *a* cursed it,
Mt 5:28 lustfully at a woman has *a* committed
6: 2 be sure of this much, they are *a* repaid.
6: 5 I give you my word, they are *a* repaid.
6:16 I assure you, they are *a* repaid.
14:15 is a deserted place and it is *a* late.
14:24 *a* several hundred yards out from shore,
17:12 assure you, though, that Elijah has *a* come,
27:17 Since they were *a* assembled,
Mk 6:35 is a deserted place and it is *a* late.
7:29 The demon has *a* left your daughter."
9:13 Let me assure you, Elijah has *a* come.
11:11 but since it was *a* late in the afternoon,
15:44 and inquired whether Jesus was *a* dead.
Lk 17:21 The reign of God is *a* in your midst."
19:25 'Yes, but he *a* has ten,' they said.
Jn 3:18 whoever does not believe is *a* condemned
4:23 Yet an hour is coming, and is *a* here,
4:36 The reaper *a* collects his wages and
9:22 who had *a* agreed among themselves that
11:17 Lazarus had *a* been in the tomb four days.
12:48 does not accept my words *a* has his judge,
13: 2 The devil had *a* induced Judas,
15: 3 You are clean *a*,
16:27 The Father *a* loves you,
16:32 has indeed *a* come
19:33 came to Jesus and saw that he was *a* dead,
Acts 3:20 you Jesus, *a* designated as your Messiah.
6: 8 The Stephen *a* spoken of was a man filled
16:14 She *a* reverenced God,
Rom 3: 9 We have *a* brought the charge against Jews
14:23 misgivings about eating, he is *a* condemned,
15:20 in places where Christ's name was *a* known,
1Cor 5: 3 and have *a* passed sentence in the name of
12:24 which the more presentable *a* have.
2Cor 1:13 just as you know us to a certain degree *a*,
2: 6 The punishment *a* inflicted by the majority
7: 3 I have *a* said that you are in our hearts,
7: 7 Titus had *a* received from you,
8: 6 had *a* begun this work of charity among you,
9: 2 I *a* know your willingness,
9: 5 for the bountiful gift you have *a* promised.
10:16 *a* done by another in his alloted territory.
Phil 3:12 it yet, or have *a* finished my course;
2Thes 1:10 for you *a* have our witness to you.
2: 7 secret force of lawlessness is *a* at work,
1Tm 5:15 *A*, some have turned away to follow Satan.
2Tm 2:18 that the resurrection has *a* taken place.
4: 6 part am *a* being poured out like a libation.
Heb 8: 4 for there are priests *a* offering the gifts
1Pt 4: 3 *A* you have devoted enough time to what the
2Pt 1:12 even though you *a* understand and are
1Jn 2: 7 now old, is the word you have *a* heard.
4: 3 in fact, it is in the world *a*.
Jude 1: 3 I was *a* fully intent on writing you,
1: 5 you may *a* be very well aware of them.
Rv 17:10 five have *a* fallen,
21: 6 "These words are *a* fulfilled!

ALTAR (422)

Gn 8:20 Then Noah built an *a* to the LORD,
8:20 clean bird, he offered holocausts on the *a*.
12: 7 So Abram built an *a* there to the LORD who
12: 8 He built an *a* there to the LORD and
13: 4 the site where he had first built the *a*;
13:18 There he built an *a* to the LORD.
22: 9 an *a* there and arranged the wood on it.
22: 9 and put him on top of the wood on the *a*.
26:25 an *a* there and invoked the LORD by name.
35: 1 Settle there and build an *a* there to the
35: 3 and I will build an *a* there to the God who
35: 7 he built an *a* and named the place Bethel,
Ex 17:15 Moses also built an *a* there,
20:24 "An *a* of earth you shall make for me,
20:25 If you make an *a* of stone for me,
20:26 You shall not go up by steps to my *a*,
21:14 him even from my *a* and put him to death.
24: 4 foot of the mountain an *a* and twelve pillars
24: 6 the other half he splashed on the *a*.
27: 1 "You shall make an *a* of acacia wood,
27: 2 made that they spring directly from the *a*.
27: 5 Put it down around the *a*, on the ground.
27: 5 network is to be half as high as the *a*.
27: 6 also make poles of acacia wood for the *a*,
27: 7 on either side of the *a* when it is carried.
27: 8 the *a* itself in the form of a hollow box,
28:43 the *a* to minister in the sanctuary,
29:12 your finger put it on the horns of the *a*.
29:12 you shall pour out at the base of the *a*.
29:13 on them, you shall take and burn on the *a*.
29:16 take and splash on all the sides of the *a*.
29:18 entire ram shall then be burned on the *a*,
29:20 of the blood on all the sides of the *a*.
29:21 take some of the blood that is on the *a*,
29:25 *a* as a sweet-smelling oblation to the LORD.
29:36 you purge the *a* in making atonement for it;
29:37 atonement for the *a* and in consecrating it.
29:37 Then the *a* will be most sacred,
29:38 this is what you shall offer on the *a*:
29:43 at the *a*, I will meet the Israelites;
29:44 consecrate the meeting tent and the *a*,
30: 1 incense you shall make an *a* of acacia wood,
30: 6 This *a* you are to place in front of the
30: 9 On this *a* you shall not offer up any
30:10 This *a* is most sacred to the LORD."
30:18 it between the meeting tent and the *a*,
30:20 when they approach the *a* in their ministry,
30:27 the *a* of incense and the altar of
30:28 *a* of holocausts with all its appurtenances,
31: 8 all its appurtenances, the *a* of incense,
31: 9 *a* of holocausts with all its appurtenances,
32: 5 built an *a* before the calf and proclaimed,
35:15 the *a* of incense,
35:16 the *a* of holocausts,
37:25 The *a* of incense was made of acacia wood,
38: 1 *a* of holocausts was made of acacia wood,
38: 2 were made that sprang directly from the *a*.
38: 3 All the utensils of the *a*,
38: 4 was made for the *a* and placed round it,
38: 4 the ground, half as high as the *a* itself.
38: 7 on the sides of the *a* for carrying it.
38: 7 The *a* was made in the form
38:30 the bronze *a* with its bronze gratings and
38:30 and all the appurtenances of the *a*,
39:38 the oil for the light, the golden *a*,
39:39 the *a* of bronze with its bronze grating,
40: 5 Put the golden *a* of incense in front of
40: 6 Put the *a* of holocausts in front of the
40: 7 laver between the meeting tent and the *a*,
40:10 *a* of holocausts and all its appurtenances,
40:26 He placed the golden *a* in the meeting tent,
40:29 He put the *a* of holocausts in front of the
40:30 the laver between the meeting tent and *a*,
40:32 into the meeting tent or approached the *a*,
40:33 around the Dwelling and the *a*
Lv 1: 5 splashing it on the sides of the *a*
1: 7 embers on the *a* and laid some wood on them,
1: 8 on top of the wood and embers on the *a*.
1: 9 the whole offering on the *a* as a holocaust,
1:11 before the LORD at the north side of the *a*.
1:11 splash its blood on the sides of the *a*.
1:12 on top of the wood and the fire on the *a*.
1:13 the whole offering on the *a* as a holocaust,
1:15 it to the *a* where it is to be burned,
1:15 out its blood against the side of the *a*.
1:16 on the ash heap at the east side of the *a*.
1:17 halves, the priest shall burn it on the *a*,
2: 2 he shall burn on the *a* as a token offering,
2: 8 to the priest, who shall take it to the *a*.
2: 9 *a* as a sweet-smelling oblation to the LORD.
2:12 to be placed on the *a* for a pleasing odor.
3: 2 splash its blood on the sides of the *a*.
3: 5 then burn on the *a* with the holocaust,
3: 8 splash its blood on the sides of the *a*.
3:11 the *a* as the food of the LORD's oblation.
3:13 splash its blood on the sides of the *a*.
3:16 All this the priest shall burn on the *a* as
4: 7 horns of the *a* of fragrant incense
4: 7 base of the *a* of holocausts
4:10 shall burn it on the *a* of holocausts.
4:18 horns of the *a* of fragrant incense
4:18 base of the *a* of holocausts
4:19 he shall take from it and burn on the *a*,
4:25 put it on the horns of the *a* of holocausts.
4:25 he shall pour out at the base of this *a*.
4:26 the *a* like the fat of the peace offering.
4:30 put it on the horns of the *a* of holocausts.
4:30 he shall pour out at the base of the *a*.
4:31 on the *a* for an odor pleasing to the LORD.
4:34 put it on the horns of the *a* of holocausts.
4:34 he shall pour out at the base of the *a*.
4:35 the *a* with the other oblations of the LORD.
5: 9 the sin offering against the side of the *a*.
5: 9 be squeezed out against the base of the *a*.
5:12 the *a* with the other oblations of the Lord.
6: 2 of the *a* all night until the next morning,
6: 2 the fire is to be kept burning on the *a*.
6: 3 fire has reduced the holocaust on the *a*,
6: 3 altar, and lay them at the side of the *a*.
6: 5 The fire on the *a* is to be kept burning;
6: 6 to be kept burning continuously on the *a*;
6: 7 it before the LORD, in front of the *a*.
6: 8 shall burn on the *a* as its token offering,
7: 2 shall be splashed on the sides of the *a*.
7: 5 burn on the *a* as an oblation to the LORD.
7:31 The priest shall burn the fat on the *a*,
8:11 times on the *a*, and anointed the altar,
8:15 around the *a*, thus purifying the altar.
8:15 He also made atonement for the *a* by
8:16 with their fat, Moses burned them on the *a*.
8:19 splashed its blood on all sides of the *a*.
8:21 parts of the ram on the *a* as a holocaust,
8:24 blood he splashed on the sides of the *a*.
8:28 on the *a* as the ordination offering,
8:30 and some of the blood that was on the *a*,
9: 7 Come up to the *a*,"
9: 8 Going up to the *a*,
9: 9 the blood and put it on the horns of the *a*.
9: 9 blood he poured out at the base of the *a*.
9:10 He then burned on the *a* the fat,
9:12 he splashed it on all sides of the *a*.
9:13 the holocaust, and he burned them on the *a*.
9:14 these also with the holocaust on the *a*.
9:17 a handful of it, he burned it on the *a*.
9:18 Aaron splashed it on all sides of the *a*.
9:20 of the breasts and burned them on the *a*,
9:24 and the remnants of the fat on the *a*.
10:12 the *a* in the form of unleavened cakes.
14:20 cereal offering, on the *a* before the LORD.
16:12 glowing embers from the *a* before the LORD,
16:18 he shall come out to the *a* before the
16:18 he shall put it on the horns around the *a*,
16:20 sanctuary, the meeting tent and the *a*,
16:25 burn the fat of the sin offering on the *a*.
16:33 sanctuary, the meeting tent and the *a*,
17: 6 blood on the *a* of the LORD
17:11 blood, I have made you put it on the *a*,
21:23 go up to the *a* on account of his defect;
22:22 animal on the *a* as an oblation to the LORD.
Nm 3:26 enclosing both the Dwelling and the *a*,
4:11 golden *a* they shall spread a violet cloth,
4:13 After cleansing the *a* of its ashes,
4:14 basins, and all the utensils of the *a*.
4:26 that encloses both the Dwelling and the *a*,
5:25 before the LORD, shall put it near the *a*,
5:26 as its token offering and burn it on the *a*.
7: 1 (as well as the *a* with all its equipment),
7:10 For the dedication of the *a* also,
7:10 before the *a* on the day it was anointed.
7:11 his offering for the dedication of the *a*."
7:84 the offerings for the dedication of the *a*,
7:88 dedication of the *a* after it was anointed.
17: 3 them hammered into plates to cover the *a*,
17: 4 hammered into a covering for the *a*,
17: 5 the *a* to offer incense before the LORD,
17:11 your censer, put fire from the *a* in it,
18: 3 not come near the sacred vessels or the *a*,
18: 5 have charge of the sanctuary and of the *a*,
18: 7 the *a* and the room within the veil.
18:17 Their blood you must splash on the *a*
23: 2 offering a bullock and a ram on each *a*.
23:30 offering a bullock and a ram on each *a*.
Dt 12:27 of your holocausts on the *a* of the LORD,
12:27 be poured out against the *a* of the LORD,
16:21 any kind of wood beside the *a* of the LORD,
26: 4 shall set it in front of the *a* of the LORD,
27: 5 an *a* made of stones that no iron tool has
27: 6 You shall make this *a* of the LORD,
33:10 nostrils, and burnt offerings to your *a*.
Jos 8:30 Later Joshua built an *a* to the LORD,
8:31 On this *a* they offered holocausts and
9:27 the community and for the *a* of the LORD,
22:10 at the Jordan a conspicuously large *a*.
22:11 Manasseh had built an *a*
22:16 against him by building an *a* of your own!
22:19 an *a* of your own in addition to the altar
22:23 an *a* of our own to secede from the LORD,
22:26 interests by building this *a* of our own:
22:28 the *a* of the LORD which our fathers made,
22:29 the LORD by building an *a* for holocaust,
22:29 sacrifice in addition to the *a* of the LORD,
22:34 Gadites gave the *a* its name
Jgs 6:24 *a* to the LORD and called it Yahweh-shalom.
6:25 destroy your father's *a* to Baal
6:26 instead, the proper kind of *a* to the LORD,
6:28 that the *a* of Baal had been destroyed,
6:28 bullock offered on the *a* that was built.
6:30 for he has destroyed the *a* of Baal and has
6:31 If he whose *a* has been destroyed is a god,
6:32 against him, since he destroyed his *a*."
13:20 as the flame rose to the sky from the *a*,
13:20 of the LORD ascended in the flame of the *a*.
21: 4 Early the next day the people built an *a*
1Sm 2:28 Israel to be my priests, to go up to my *a*,
2:33 some of your family to remain at my *a*,
7:17 judged Israel and built an *a* to the LORD.
14:35 and Saul built an *a* to the LORD
14:35 the first time he built an *a* to the LORD.
2Sm 24:18 "Go up and build an *a* to the LORD on the
24:21 floor from you to build an *a* to the LORD,
24:25 Then David built an *a* there to the LORD,
1Kgs 1:50 he went and seized the horns of the *a*.
1:51 had seized the horns of the *a* and said,
1:53 sent to have him brought down from the *a*,
2:28 of the LORD and seized the horns of the *a*.
2:29 to the tent of the LORD and was at the *a*.
3: 4 *a* Solomon offered a thousand holocausts.
6:21 made in front of the sanctuary a cedar *a*,

ALTAR (cont.)

6:22 the whole *a* before the sanctuary was also
7:48 the golden *a*;
8:22 Solomon stood before the *a* of the LORD in
8:31 the oath before your *a* in this temple,
8:54 he rose from before the *a* of the LORD,
8:64 because the bronze *a* before the LORD was
9:25 on the *a* which he had built to the LORD,
12:33 Jeroboam ascended the *a* he built in Bethel
13: 1 was standing at the *a* to offer sacrifice.
13: 2 out against the *a* the word of the LORD:
13: 2 "O *a*, altar, the LORD says, 'A child shall
13: 3 The *a* shall break up and the ashes on it
13: 4 man of God was crying out against the *a*,
13: 4 forth his hand from the *a* and said,
13: 5 the *a* broke up and the ashes from it were
13:32 against the *a* in Bethel
16:32 Ahab erected an *a* to Baal in the temple of
18:26 they hopped around the *a* they had prepared.
18:30 the *a* of the LORD which had been destroyed.
18:32 an *a* in honor of the LORD with the stones,
18:32 the *a* large enough for two seahs of grain.
18:35 The water flowed around the *a*,
2Kgs 11:11 the *a* and the temple on the king's behalf.
16:10 When he saw the *a* in Damascus,
16:10 model of the *a* and a detailed design
16:11 Uriah the priest built an *a* according to
16:12 from Damascus, the king inspected this *a*,
16:13 the blood of his peace-offerings on the *a*.
16:14 The bronze *a* that stood before the LORD he
16:14 the new *a* and the temple of the LORD
16:14 and set it on the north side of his *a*.
16:15 "Upon the large *a*," King Ahaz
16:15 bronze *a* shall be mine for consultation."
18:22 to worship before this *a* in Jerusalem?'
23: 9 function at the *a* of the LORD in Jerusalem;
23:15 Likewise the *a* which was at Bethel,
23:15 this same *a* and high place he tore down,
23:16 taken from the graves and burned on the *a*,
23:16 was standing by the *a* on the feast day.
23:17 things you have done to the *a* of Bethel."
1Chr 6:34 offerings on the *a* of holocausts
6:34 of holocausts and on the *a* of incense;
16:40 the LORD on the *a* of holocausts regularly,
21:18 erect an *a* to the LORD
21:22 that I may build on it an *a* to the LORD.
21:26 David then built an *a* there to the LORD,
21:26 fire from heaven upon the *a* of holocausts.
21:29 and the *a* of holocausts were at that time
22: 1 and this is the *a* of holocausts for Israel."
28:18 weight, to be used for the *a* of incense;
2Chr 1: 5 The bronze *a* made by Bezalel,
1: 6 on the bronze *a* at the meeting tent;
4: 1 Then he made a bronze *a* twenty cubits long,
4:19 the golden *a*,
5:12 harps and lyres, stood east of the *a*,
6:12 Solomon then took his place before the *a*
6:22 for the oath before your *a* in this temple,
7: 7 since the bronze *a* which Solomon had made
7: 9 dedication of the *a* for seven days
8:12 holocausts to the LORD upon the *a*
15: 8 and to restore the *a* of the LORD which was
23:10 the *a* and the temple on the king's behalf.
26:16 to make an offering on the *a* of incense.
26:19 house of the LORD beside the *a* of incense,
29:18 the *a* of holocausts with all its utensils,
29:19 and they are now before the LORD's *a*."
29:21 to offer them on the *a* of the LORD.
29:22 collected the blood and cast it on the *a*.
29:22 the rams and cast the blood on the *a*;
29:22 and cast the blood on the *a*.
29:24 the *a* to atone for the sin of all Israel;
29:27 the holocaust to be sacrificed on the *a*,
32:12 prostrate yourselves before one *a* only,
33:16 He restored the *a* of the LORD,
35:16 holocausts offered on the *a* of the LORD,
Ezr 3: 2 set about rebuilding the *a* of the God of
3: 3 they replaced the *a* on its foundations and
7:17 *a* of the house of your God in Jerusalem.
Neh 10:35 year, to be burnt on the *a* of the LORD,
Tb 1: 7 to the priests, Aaron's sons, at the *a*.
Jdt 4: 3 gathered together, and the vessels, the *a*,
4:12 The *a*, too, they draped in sackcloth;
4:14 attendance on the Lord who served his *a*,
8:24 the temple, and the *a* rests with us.
9: 8 to overthrow with iron the horns of your *a*.
Est C:20 the glory of your temple and your *a*;
1Mc 1:21 the sanctuary and took away the golden *a*,
1:54 abomination upon the *a* of holocausts,
1:59 the *a* erected over the altar of holocausts.
2:23 *a* in Modein according to the king's order.
2:24 sprang forward and killed him upon the *a*.
2:25 them to sacrifice, and he tore down the *a*.
4:38 the sanctuary desolate, the *a* desecrated,
4:44 *a* of holocausts that had been desecrated.
4:45 so they tore down the *a*.
4:47 law, and built a new *a* like the former one.
4:49 brought the lampstand, the *a* of incense,
4:50 *a* and lighted the lamps on the lampstand,
4:53 the new *a* of holocausts that they had made.
4:56 celebrated the dedication of the *a*
4:59 dedication of the *a* should be observed
5: 1 heard that the *a* had been rebuilt
6: 7 which he had built upon the *a* in Jerusalem;
7:36 and stood before the *a* and the sanctuary.
2Mc 1:18 the rebuilder of the temple and the *a*,
1:19 fire from the *a* and hid it
1:32 the brilliance cast from a light on the *a*.
2: 5 the tent, the ark, and the *a* of incense;
2:19 the great temple, the dedication of the *a*,
3:15 in their priestly robes before the *a*,
4:14 no longer cared about the service of the *a*.
6: 5 so that the *a* was covered with abominable
10: 3 purifying the temple, they made a new *a*.
10:26 Lying prostrate at the foot of the *a*,
13: 8 sins against the *a* with its pure fire
14: 3 position and regain access to the holy *a*.
14:33 I will tear down the *a*,
15:31 stationed the priests before the *a*,
Ps(s) 26: 6 in innocence, and I go around your *a*,
43: 4 Then will I go in to the *a* of God,
51:21 shall they offer up bullocks on your *a*.
118:27 with leafy boughs up to the horns of the *a*.
Wis 9: 8 *a* in the city that is your dwelling place.
Sir 35: 5 The just man's offering enriches the *a* and
47: 9 each year With string music before the *a*,
50:11 As he ascended the glorious *a* and lent
50:14 services at the *a* with the arranging
50:15 And poured it out at the foot of the *a*,
50:19 *a* by presenting to God the sacrifice due;
Is 6: 6 which he had taken with tongs from the *a*.
19:19 be an *a* to the LORD in the land of Egypt,
36: 7 and Jerusalem to worship before this *a*?'
56: 7 and sacrifices will be acceptable on my *a*,
60: 7 They will be acceptable offerings on my *a*,
Lam 2: 7 The Lord has disowned his *a*,
Bar 1:10 offer these on the *a* of the Lord our God,
Ez 8: 5 the gate the *a* of the statue of jealousy.
8:16 temple, between the vestibule and the *a*,
9: 2 They entered and stood beside the bronze *a*.
40:46 for the priests who have charge of the *a*.
40:47 The *a* stood in front of the temple.
41:22 was something that looked like a wooden *a*,
43:13 These were the measurements of the *a* in
43:13 The height of the *a* itself was as follows:
43:15 the hearth of the *a* was four cubits high,
43:15 of the hearth were the four horns of the *a*.
43:17 The steps of the *a* face the east.
43:18 These are the statutes for the *a* when it
43:20 and put it on the four horns of the *a*,
43:22 to purify the *a* as was done with the bull.
43:26 Thus atonement shall be made for the *a*,
43:27 holocausts and peace offerings on the *a*.
45:19 on the four corners of the ledge of the *a*,
47: 1 side of the temple, south of the *a*.
Jl 1:13 wail, O ministers of the *a*!
2:17 the porch and the *a* let the priests,
Am 2: 8 taken in pledge they recline beside any *a*;
3:14 The horns of the *a* shall be broken off and
9: 1 I saw the Lord standing beside the *a*,
Zec 9:15 libation bowls, like the corners of the *a*.
14:20 be as the libation bowls before the *a*.
Mal 1: 7 By offering polluted food on my *a*!
1:10 you from kindling fire on my *a* in vain!
2:13 the *a* of the LORD you cover with tears,
Mt 5:23 If you bring your gift to the *a* and there
5:24 against you, leave your gift at the *a*,
23:18 'If a man swears by the *a* it means nothing,
23:18 by the gift on the *a* he is obligated.'
23:19 or the *a* which makes the offering sacred?
23:20 The man who swears by the *a* is swearing by
23:35 between the temple building and the *a*.
Lk 1:11 standing at the right of the *a* of incense.
11:51 his death between the *a* and the sanctuary!
Acts 17:23 shrines, I even discovered an *a* inscribed,
1Cor 9:13 at the *a* share the offerings of the altar?
10:18 eat the sacrifices do not share in the *a*!
Heb 7:13 of whose members ever officiated at the *a*.
9: 4 in which were the golden *a* of incense and
13:10 We have an *a* from which those who serve
Jas 2:21 when he offered his son Isaac on the *a*?
Rv 6: 9 I saw under the *a* the spirits of those who
8: 3 He took his place at the *a* of incense and
8: 3 on the *a* of gold in front of the throne,
8: 5 filled it with live coals from the *a*,
9:13 horns of the *a* of gold in God's presence.
11: 1 the measurements of God's temple and *a*,
14:18 in charge of the fire at the *a* of incense,
16: 7 Then I heard the *a* cry out:

ALTARS (62)

Ex 34:13 Tear down their *a*;
Nm 3:31 the ark, the table, the lampstand, the *a*,
23: 1 Balaam said to Balak, "Build me seven *a*,
23: 2 said to him, "I have erected the seven *a*,
23:14 where he built seven *a* and offered a
23:29 then said to him, "Here build me seven *a*;
Dt 7: 5 Tear down their *a*,
12: 3 Tear down their *a*,
Jgs 2: 2 land, and you were to pull down their *a*.
1Kgs 19:10 forsaken your covenant, torn down your *a*,
19:14 forsaken your covenant, torn down your *a*,
2Kgs 11:18 They shattered its *a* and images completely,
11:18 Mattan, the priest of Baal, before the *a*.
18:22 high places and *a* Hezekiah has removed,
21: 3 He erected *a* to Baal,
21: 4 He built *a* in the temple of the LORD,
21: 5 *a* for the whole host of heaven,
23:12 He also demolished the *a* made by the kings
23:12 and the *a* made by Manasseh in the two
23:20 He slaughtered upon the *a* all the priests
2Chr 14: 2 removing the heathen *a* and the high places,
23:17 They smashed its *a* and images,
23:17 Mattan, the priest of Baal, before the *a*.
28:24 had *a* made for himself in every corner
30:14 to take down the *a* that were in Jerusalem;
30:14 also they removed all the *a* of incense and
31: 1 the high places and *a* throughout Judah,
32:12 and *a* and commanded Judah and Jerusalem,
33: 3 had torn down, erected *a* for the Baals,
33: 4 He even built *a* in the temple of the LORD,
33: 5 he built *a* to the whole host of heaven in
33:15 all the *a* he had built on the mount
34: 4 the *a* of the Baals were destroyed;
34: 5 of the priests he burned upon their *a*.
34: 7 he destroyed the *a*,
1Mc 1:47 to build pagan *a* and temples and shrines,
1:54 cities of Judah they built pagan *a*.
2:45 went about and tore down the pagan *a*;
5:68 *a* and burned the statues of their gods;
2Mc 10: 2 they destroyed the *a* erected by the
Ps(s) 84: 4 Your *a*, O LORD of hosts,
Is 17: 8 He shall not look to the *a*,
27: 9 the stones of the *a* like pieces of chalk;
27: 9 no sacred poles or incense *a* shall stand.
36: 7 whose high places and *a* Hezekiah removed,
Jer 2:28 are the *a* you have set up for Baal.
11:13 are the *a* for offering sacrifice to Baal.
17: 1 [And the horns of their *a*,
17: 2 remember their *a* and their sacred poles,
Ez 6: 4 Your *a* shall be laid waste,
6: 5 will scatter their bones all around your *a*.
6: 6 *a* will be made desolate and laid waste,
6:13 lie amid their idols, all about their *a*,
Hos 4:19 they shall have only shame from their *a*.
8:11 many *a* to expiate sin, his altars became
10: 1 abundant his fruit, the more *a* he built;
10: 2 their *a* and destroy their sacred pillars.
10: 8 thorns and thistles shall overgrow their *a*.
12:12 Their *a* are like heaps of stones in the
Am 3:14 crimes, I will visit also the *a* of Bethel:
Rom 11: 3 your prophets, they have torn down your *a*;

ALTER (4)

Ezr 6:12 undertake to *a* this
Ps(s) 89:35 the promise of my lips I will not *a*.
Gal 1: 7 Some who wish to *a* the gospel of Christ
Heb 12:17 he had no opportunity to *a* his choice,

ALTERED (1)

Dn 3:94 been singed, nor were their garments *a*;

ALTERNATE (1)

Jer 33:20 that day and night no longer *a* in sequence,

ALTERNATED (1)

Ezr 3:11 They *a* in songs of praise and thanksgiving

ALTERNATELY (1)

2Cor 1:19 Son of God, was not *a* "yes" and "no";

ALTERNATING (2)

Ex 28:34 and thus *a* all around the hem of the robe.
39:26 and thus *a* all around the hem of the robe

ALTERNATIVES (2)

2Sm 24:12 I offer you three *a*;
1Chr 21:10 I offer you three *a*;

ALTHOUGH (74)

Gn 23: 4 *A* I am a resident alien among you,
27:22 felt him, he said, *A* the voice is Jacob's,
28:16 LORD is in this spot, *a* I did not know it!"
32:11 *a* I crossed the Jordan here with nothing
38:14 was aware that, *a* Shelah was now grown up,
39:10 *A* she tried to entice him day after day,
41:54 *A* there was famine in all the other
42: 8 his brothers, *a* they did not recognize him,
48:14 the head of Ephraim, *a* he was the younger,
48:14 head of Manasseh, *a* he was the first-born.
Ex 11:10 *a* Moses and Aaron performed these various
16:27 out to gather it, *a* they did not find any.
Lv 7:24 *A* the fat of an animal that has died a
Nm 9: 7 said, *A* we are unclean because of a corpse,
27: 3 *A* he did not join those who banded
35:23 *a* he was not his enemy nor seeking to harm
Dt 22: 7 let her go, *a* you may take her brood away.
Jos 14:10 and *a* I am now eighty-five years old,
17: 8 *a* Tappuah itself was an Ephraimite city on
21:12 *a* the open country and villages belonging
Jgs 13:16 the LORD answered Manoah, *A* you press me,
14: 6 came upon Samson, and *a* he had no weapons,
1Sm 13: 7 *a* all his followers were seized with fear.
2Sm 3:39 *A* I am the anointed king,

13:22 a he hated him for having shamed his
14:29 A he summoned him a second time,
21: 2 a the Israelites had given them their oath,
23:21 A the Egyptian was armed with a spear,
2Kgs 10: 9 a I conspired against my lord and slew him,
16: 5 A they besieged Ahaz,
17:12 and served idols, a the LORD had told them,
1Chr 6:41 a the open country and the villages
2Chr 15:17 A the high places did not disappear from
24:19 A prophets were sent to them to convert
1Mc 2:19 A all the Gentiles in the king's realm
8: 4 a it was very remote from their own.
11:25 A some impious men of his own nation
13:17 A Simon knew that they were speaking
13:22 A Trypho got all his cavalry ready to go,
2Mc 4:27 A Menelaus had obtained the office,
6:16 A he disciplines us with misfortunes,
6:30 well that, a I could have escaped death,
Jb 2: 3 He still holds fast to his innocence a you
16:17 my eyes, A my hands are free from violence,
Ps(s) 126: 6 A they go forth weeping,
Prv 28: 1 The wicked man flees a no one pursues him;
Is 19:22 A the LORD shall smite Egypt severely,
46: 7 A they cry out to it, it cannot answer;
Jer 35:14 a I spoke to you untiringly and
Ez 22:28 the Lord GOD," a the LORD has not spoken.
35:10 we shall possess them a the LORD was there
Dn 4:15 A none of the wise men in my kingdom can
10: 7 themselves, a they did not see the vision.
13:53 and freeing the guilty, a the Lord says,
Mt 21:46 A they sought to arrest him,
Jn 19:38 Jesus a a secret one for fear of the Jews),
Acts 7: 5 him as a possession a he had no child.
16:37 us into jail, a we are Roman citizens!
18:25 Jesus, a he knew only of John's baptism.
28:16 a a soldier was assigned to keep guard
Rom 2:14 these men a without the law serve as a law
8:23 a we have the Spirit as first fruits,
1Cor 7:12 a I know of nothing the Lord has said,
9: 2 A I may not be an apostle for others,
9:19 A I am not bound to anyone,
9:20 is bound a in fact I am not bound by it),
15: 6 are still alive, a some have fallen asleep.
1Tm 3:14 A I hope to visit you soon,
Phlm 1: 8 a I feel that I have every right to
Heb 5:12 A by this time you should be teaching
11: 4 therefore, a Abel is dead,
1Pt 1: 8 A you have never seen him,
4: 6 a condemned in the flesh in the eyes of
Rv 12: 7 A the dragon and his angels fought back,

ALTOGETHER (6)

Dt 18:13 however, must be a sincere toward the LORD,
1Mc 12:10 so as not to become strangers to you a;
2Mc 13: 8 It was a just that he who had committed so
Jb 13: 5 Oh, that you would be a silent!
Mt 13:57 They found him a too much for them.
2Pt 1:19 prophetic message as something a reliable.

ALUSH (2)

Nm 33:13 Setting out from Dophkah, they camped at A.
33:14 Setting out from A,

ALVAH (1)

Gn 36:40 the clans of Timna, A,

ALVAN (1)

Gn 36:23 Shobal's descendants were A,

ALWAYS (135)

Gn 24:40 LORD, in whose presence I have a walked,
26:29 but have a acted kindly toward you and
42:36 Why must such things a happen to me?"
Ex 19: 9 you, they may a have faith in you also."
25:30 you shall a keep showbread set before me.
28:30 Thus he shall a bear the decisions for the
28:38 this plate must a be over his forehead,
Lv 25:32 "In levitical cities the Levites shall a
25:34 it must a remain their hereditary property.
Nm 9:16 It was a so:
9:23 it was a at the bidding of the LORD that
22:30 have you not a ridden upon me until now?
Dt 5:29 Would that they might a be of such a mind,
6:24 that we may a have as prosperous and happy
11: 1 your God, therefore, and a heed his charge:
12:28 that you and your descendants may a
14:23 that you may learn a to fear the LORD,
18: 5 your tribes to be a in attendance
28:13 you will a mount higher and not decline,
Jos 9:23 every one of you shall a be a slave
1Sm 5: 5 they a step over it.
2Sm 9: 7 Saul, and you shall a eat at my table."
9:10 your lord's son, shall a eat at my table."
9:13 because he a ate at the king's table.
1Kgs 2: 4 you shall a have someone of your line on
5:15 for Hiram had a been David's friend.
8:25 'You shall a have someone from your line
9: 3 and my eyes and my heart shall be there a.
9: 5 'You shall a have someone from your line
10: 8 before you a and listen to your wisdom.
11:36 may a have a lamp before me in Jerusalem,
1Chr 17:20 God but you, just as we have a understood.
23:31 they must a be present before the LORD.
2Chr 6:16 'You shall a have someone from your line
6:16 so as a to live according to my law,
7:16 my eyes and my heart also shall be there a.
9: 7 before you a and listen to your wisdom.
18: 7 he prophesies not good but a evil about me.
Est B: 2 but a to deal fairly and with clemency;
E: 9 deciding a with equitable treatment
1Mc 2:65 listen to him a,
2Mc 14:15 and who a comes to the aid of his heritage.
14:24 but he a kept Judas in his company,
Jb 23:11 My foot has a walked in his steps;
Ps(s) 9:19 For the needy shall not a be forgotten,
12: 8 us and preserve us a from this generation,
38:18 near to falling, and my grief is with me a.
44: 9 your name we praised a.
49:10 to remain alive a and not see destruction.
50: 8 you, for your holocausts are before me a.
51: 5 my offense, and my sin is before me a:
52:11 I will thank you a for what you have done,
69:24 cannot see, and keep their backs a feeble.
71:14 a hope and praise you ever more and more.
73:12 then, are the wicked; a carefree,
73:23 Yet with you I shall a be;
89:22 him, That my hand may be a with him,
103: 9 He will not a chide,
106: 3 what is right, who do a what is just.
109:19 him, like a girdle which is a about him.
119:112 in my heart to fulfill your statutes a,
Prv 5:19 Her love will invigorate you a,
6:14 in his heart, is a plotting evil,
6:21 Keep them fastened over your heart a,
17:17 He who is a friend is a a friend,
23:17 but be zealous for the fear of the LORD a;
28:14 Happy the man who is a on his guard;
Wis 11:21 For with you great strength abides a;
17:11 conscience, a magnifies misfortunes.
Sir 20:18 the unruly are a ready to offer it.
29: 3 him and you will a come by what you need.
35:10 For the Lord is one who a repays,
38:29 He is a concerned for his products,
41: 1 For the man unruffled and a successful,
41: 2 failing strength, Tottering and a rebuffed,
41:14 rules, For it is not a well to be ashamed,
41:14 nor is it a the proper thing to blush:
49: 9 to JOB, who a persevered in the right path.
Is 28:24 a loosening and harrowing his land for
47: 7 remain a a sovereign mistress forever!"
57:16 I will not accuse forever, nor a be angry;
58:11 Then the LORD will guide you a and give
60:21 all be just, they shall a possess the land,
65:18 there shall a be rejoicing and happiness
Jer 32:39 I will give them, that they may fear me a,
Ez 33:31 My people come to you as people a do;
46: 8 The prince shall a enter and depart by the
Dn 14:13 which they a came in to consume the food.
Hos 12: 7 loyal and do right and a hope in your God.
Mt 6:32 are a running after these things.
26:11 The poor you will a have with you but you
26:11 have with you but you will not a have me.
28:20 And know that I am with you a,
Mk 14: 7 The poor you will a have with you and you
14: 7 you wish, but you will not a have me.
Lk 12:30 world are a running after these things.
15:31 replied the father, 'you are with me a,
18: 1 of praying a and not losing heart:
Jn 6:34 "Sir, give us this bread a,"
7: 6 me, whereas the time is a right for you.
8:29 deserted me since I a do what pleases him."
11:42 I know that you a hear me but I have said
12: 8 The poor you a have with you,
12: 8 have with you, but me you will not a have."
14:16 to be with you a:
18:20 I a taught in a synagogue or in the temple
Acts 7:51 you are a opposing the Holy Spirit just as
20:35 I have a pointed out to you that it is by
24: 3 Therefore we must a and everywhere
24:16 In this regard I too a strive to keep my
Rom 1:10 a pleading that somehow by God's will I
7:21 leads to wrongdoing is a ready at hand.
1Cor 11: 2 I praise you because you a remember me and
2Cor 1:12 a acted from God-given holiness and candor;
6:10 sorrowful, though we are a rejoicing;
9: 8 may a have enough of everything
Eph 5:20 Give thanks to God the Father a and for
Phil 1:20 now as a Christ will be exalted through me,
2:12 dearly beloved, obedient as a to my urging,
4: 4 Rejoice in the Lord a!
Col 1: 3 We a give thanks to God,
4: 6 speech be a gracious and in good taste,
4:12 He is a servant of Christ Jesus who is a
1Thes 5:15 a seek one another's good and,
5:16 Rejoice a,
2Thes 1:11 We pray for you a that our God may make
2:13 We are bound to thank God for you a,
2Tm 2:25 in the hope a that God will enable them to
3: 7 a learning but never able to reach a
Phlm 1: 4 I thank God a,
Heb 3:10 I said, 'They have a been of erring heart,
7:25 Therefore he is a able to save those who
13: 1 Love your fellow Christians a.
Jas 2:12 A speak and act as men destined for
Rv 21: 3 he shall be their God who is a with them.

AMAD (1)

Jos 19:26 Beten, Achshaph, Allammelech, A and Mishal,

AMAL (1)

1Chr 7:35 Hotham were Zophah, Imna, Shelesh, and A.

AMALEK (29)

Gn 36:12 concubine Timna, and she bore A to Eliphaz.)
36:16 Omar, Zepho, Kenaz, Korah, Gatam, and A.
Ex 17: 8 A came and waged war against Israel.
17: 9 and tomorrow go out and engage A in battle.
17:10 he engaged A in battle after Moses had
17:11 hands rest, A had the better of the fight.
17:13 And Joshua mowed down A and his people
17:14 out the memory of A from under the heavens."
17:16 will war against A through the centuries."
Nm 24:20 Upon seeing A,
24:20 First of the peoples was A,
Dt 25:17 "Bear in mind what A did to you on the
25:19 out the memory of A from under the heavens.
Jgs 6: 3 Midian, A and the Kedemites would come up,
6:33 Then all Midian and A and the Kedemites
1Sm 14:48 He defeated A and delivered Israel from
15: 2 'I will punish what A did to Israel when
15: 3 Go, now, attack A,
15: 5 Saul went to the city of A,
15: 6 Leave A and withdraw,
15: 7 A from Havilah to the approaches of Shur,
15: 8 He took Agag, king of A,
15:15 "They were brought from A.
15:20 Agag, and I have destroyed A under the ban.
15:32 Samuel commanded, "Bring Agag, king of A,
28:18 not carry out his fierce anger against A,
1Chr 1:36 Omar, Zephi, Gatam, Kenaz, [Timna,] and A.
18:11 the Ammonites, the Philistines, and A.
Ps(s) 83: 8 people of Hagar, Gebal and Ammon and A,

AMALEKITE (3)

1Sm 30:13 "I am an Egyptian, the slave of an A.
2Sm 1: 8 and I replied, 'An A.'
1:13 replied, "I am the son of an A immigrant."

AMALEKITES (19)

Gn 14: 7 both of the A and of the Amorites
Nm 13:29 A live in the region of the Negeb;
14:25 A and Canaanites are living in the valleys,
14:43 For there the A and Canaanites face you,
14:45 And the A and Canaanites who dwelt in that
Jgs 1:16 they later left and settled among the A.
3:13 In alliance with the Ammonites and A,
7:12 The Midianites, A,
10:12 the Philistines, the Sidonians, the A,
12:15 land of Ephraim on the mountain of the A.
1Sm 15:18 the sinful A under a ban of destruction.
27: 8 raids on the Geshurites, Girzites, and A—
30: 1 day, the A had raided the Negeb and Ziklag,
30:16 were the A scattered all over the ground,
30:18 David recovered everything the A had taken,
30:19 or daughters, of all that the A had taken.
2Sm 1: 1 of the A and spent two days in Ziklag.
8:12 from the Philistines, from the A,
1Chr 4:43 attacked the surviving A who had escaped,

AMAM (1)

Jos 15:26 A, Shema, Moladah.

AMANA (1)

Sg 4: 8 Descend from the top of A,

AMARIAH (16)

1Chr 5:33 Meraioth became the father of A.
5:33 A became the father of Ahitub.
5:37 Azariah became the father of A.
5:37 A became the father of Ahitub.
6:37 whose son was Meraioth, whose son was A,
23:19 Jeriah, the chief, A,
24:23 of Hebron were Jeriah, the chief, A,
2Chr 19:11 A is high priest over you in everything
31:15 Jeshua, Shemaiah, A and Shecaniah,
Ezr 7: 3 son of Zadok, son of Ahitub, son of A,
10:42 Azarel, Shelemiah, Shemariah, Shallum, A,
Neh 10: 4 Seraiah, Azariah, Jeremiah, Pashhur, A,
11: 4 son of Uzziah, son of Zechariah, son of A,
12: 2 Seraiah, Jeremiah, Ezra, A,
12:13 for A, Jehohanan
Zep 1: 1 Cushi, the son of Gedaliah, the son of A,

AMASA (15)

2Sm 17:25 A in command of the army in Joab's place.
17:25 A was the son of an Ishmaelite named Ithra,
19:14 Also say to A: Are you not my bone
20: 4 Then the king said to A:
20: 5 Accordingly A set out to summon Judah,
20: 8 the great stone in Gibeon when A met them.
20: 9 Joab asked A, "How are you, my brother?"
20:10 And since A was not on his guard against

AMASA (cont.)

20:11 of Joab's attendants stood by A and said,
20:12 A lay covered with blood in the middle of
20:12 So he removed A from the road to the field
1Kgs 2: 5 Israel's armies, Abner, son of Ner, and A,
2:32 of Ner, general of Israel's army, and A,
1Chr 2:17 Abigail bore A, whose father was Jether
2Chr 28:12 Jehizkiah, son of Shallum, and A,

AMASAI (5)

1Chr 6:10 The sons of Elkanah were A and Ahimoth,
12:19 Then spirit enveloped A,
15:24 Shebaniah, Joshaphat, Nethanel, A,
2Chr 29:12 Mahath, son of A, and Joel,
Neh 11:13 and A, son of Azarel, son of Ahzai,

AMASA'S (1)

2Sm 20: 9 hand Joab held A beard as if to kiss him.

AMASI (1)

1Chr 6:20 son of Elkanah, son of Mahath, son of A,

AMASIAH (1)

2Chr 17:16 Next to him, A, son of Zichri,

AMASSED (2)

Prv 13:11 dwindles away, but a little by little,
Eccl 2: 8 I a for myself silver and gold,

AMAWITES (1)

Nm 22: 5 on the Euphrates, in the land of the A,

AMAZED (21)

Gn 29:25 In the morning Jacob was a:
2Chr 7:21 everyone passing by it will be a and ask:
Tb 11:16 one leading him by the hand, they were a.
Jdt 15: 1 those still in their tents were a,
1Mc 15:32 and the rest of his rich display, he was a.
Wis 5: 2 fear, and a at the unlooked-for salvation.
Is 52:14 Even as many were a at him
Jer 2:12 Be a at this, O heavens, and shudder
4: 9 the priests will be a,
18:16 All passers-by will be a,
19: 8 will be a and will catch his breath.
Hb 1: 5 over the nations and see, and be utterly a!
Mk 1:27 All who looked on were a.
5:20 They were all a at what they heard.
6: 2 in a way that kept his large audience a.
16: 6 "You need not be a!
Lk 2:47 were a at his intelligence and his answers.
11:14 The crowds were a at this.
Acts 4:13 men of no standing, the questioners were a.
Gal 1: 6 I am a that you are so soon deserting him
Rv 17: 8 world shall be a when they see the beast,

AMAZEMENT (16)

Gn 43:33 youngest, they looked at one another in a;
Dt 28:37 of wood and stone, and will call forth a,
1Kgs 9: 8 passer-by shall catch his breath in a
Sir 11:13 head and exalts him to the a of the many.
Jer 19: 8 make this city an object of a and derision.
Mt 8:10 Jesus showed a on hearing this and
13:54 They were filled with a,
Mk 7:37 Their a went beyond all bounds:
12:17 Their a at him knew no bounds.
Lk 5: 9 a at the catch they had made seized him
7: 9 Jesus showed a on hearing this,
9:43 midst of their a at all that he was doing,
24:12 went away full of a at what had occurred.
Jn 7:15 The Jews were filled with a and said,
Acts 2: 7 They asked in utter a,
13:41 'Look on in a, you cynics, then disappear!

AMAZIAH (43)

2Kgs 12:22 David, and his son A succeeded him as king.
13:12 the valor with which he fought against A,
14: 1 Joash, son of Jehoahaz, king of Israel, A,
14: 5 When A had the kingdom firmly in hand,
14: 7 A slew ten thousand Edomites in the Salt
14: 8 Then A sent messengers to Jehoash,
14:11 But A would not listen.
14:11 and he and King A of Judah met in battle
14:13 King Jehoash of Israel captured A,
14:15 Jehoash, his valor, and how he fought A,
14:17 A, son of Joash,
14:18 The rest of the acts of A are written in
14:21 him king to succeed his father A.
14:22 after King A rested with his ancestors.
14:23 In the fifteenth year of A,
15: 1 Azariah, son of A,
15: 3 the LORD just as his father A had done.
1Chr 3:12 whose son was Joash, whose son was A,
4:34 Meshobab, Jamlech, Joshah, son of A,
6:30 of Malluch, son of Hashabiah, son of A,
2Chr 24:27 His son A succeeded him as king.
25: 1 A was twenty-five years old when he
25: 5 A mustered Judah and placed them,
25: 9 A answered the man of God,
25:10 A then disbanded the troops that had come
25:11 A now assumed command of his army.
25:13 the mercenaries whom A had dismissed from
25:14 When A returned from his conquest
25:15 anger of the LORD blazed out against A,
25:17 King A of Judah sent messengers to Joash,
25:18 Israel sent this reply to King A of Judah:
25:20 But A would not listen,
25:21 A met in battle at Beth-shemesh of Judah.
25:23 King Joash of Israel captured A,
25:25 A, son of Joash,
25:26 The rest of the acts of A,
25:27 the time that A ceased to follow the LORD,
26: 1 him king to succeed his father A.
26: 2 King A had gone to rest with his ancestors.
26: 4 the LORD, just as his father A had done.
Am 7:10 A, the priest of Bethel,
7:12 To Amos, A said: "Off with you, visionary
7:14 Amos answered A,

AMAZING (1)

Sir 43:26 In it are his creatures, stupendous, a,

AMBASSADOR (2)

Eph 6:20 that mystery for which I am an a in chains.
Phlm 1: 9 a of Christ and now a prisoner for him,

AMBASSADORS (9)

2Sm 5:11 Hiram, king of Tyre, sent a to David;
2Chr 32:31 in respect to the a [princes] sent to him
1Mc 9:70 Jonathan learned of this and sent a to
10:51 Alexander sent a to Ptolemy,
11: 9 He sent a to King Demetrius, saying:
Is 18: 2 the rivers of Ethiopia, Sending a by sea,
57: 9 While you sent your a far away,
Jer 27: 3 a who have come to Jerusalem to Zedekiah,
2Cor 5:20 This makes us a for Christ,

AMBITION (4)

1Kgs 1: 5 Haggith, began to display his a to be king.
2Chr 25:19 and thus a makes you proud.
Wis 14:18 the artisan's a provided a stimulus.
Jas 3:14 jealousy and selfish a in your hearts,

AMBITIONS (1)

2Cor 12:20 jealousy, outbursts of anger, selfish a,

AMBITIOUS (4)

2Kgs 14:10 conquered Edom, and you have become a.
Est E: 2 "Many have become the more a the more
1Mc 16:13 a and sought to get control of the country.
Rom 12:16 Put away a thoughts and associate with

AMBROSIAL (1)

Wis 19:21 the icelike, quick-melting kind of a food.

AMBUSH (39)

Jos 8: 2 Set an a behind the city."
8: 4 "See that you a the city from the rear,
8: 7 from a and take possession of the city,
8: 9 They went to the place of a,
8:12 and set them in a between Bethel and Ai,
8:13 north of the city and the a west of it,
8:14 that there was an a behind the city.
8:19 did so, the men in a rose from their post,
8:21 taken from a and was going up in smoke,
Jgs 9:25 set men in a for him on the mountaintops,
9:32 set an a tonight in the fields,
9:34 set up an a for Shechem in four companies.
9:35 his soldiers rose from their place of a,
9:43 companies, and set up an a in the fields.
16: 2 with an a at the city gate all night long.
20:29 So Israel set men in a around Gibeah.
20:33 a rushed from their place west of Gibeah,
20:36 trusting in the a they had set at Gibeah.
20:37 men in a made a sudden dash into Gibeah,
20:38 men in a on a smoke signal
1Sm 15: 5 Amalek, and after setting an a in the wadi,
2Chr 13:13 But Jeroboam had an a go around them to
13:13 army faced Judah, his a lay behind them.
20:22 the LORD laid an a against the Ammonites,
1Mc 1:36 citadel became an a against the sanctuary,
9:40 against them from their a and killed them.
10:80 discovered that there was an a behind him,
11:68 detached an a against him in the mountains.
11:69 Then the men in a rose out of their places
Ps(s) 10: 8 He lurks in a near the villages;
64: 5 Shooting from a at the innocent man,
Prv 7:12 and at every corner she lurks in a—
12: 6 The words of the wicked are a deadly a,
Wis 10:12 him from foes, and secured him against a,
Sir 8:11 it will set him in a against you.
28:26 and fall victim to your foe waiting in a.
Jer 9: 7 his friends, but in his heart he lays an a!
Lam 3:10 bear he has been to me, a lion in a!
Hos 6: 9 As brigands a a man,

AMBUSHES (1)

Jer 51:12 Post sentries, arrange a!

AMBUSHING (1)

1Mc 5: 4 to the people by a them along the roads.

AMEN (62)

Nm 5:22 And the woman shall say, 'Amen, a!'
Dt 27:15 And all the people shall answer, A!'
27:16 And all the people shall answer, A!'
27:17 And all the people shall answer, A!'
27:18 And all the people shall answer, A!'
27:19 And all the people shall answer, A!'
27:20 And all the people shall answer, A!'
27:21 And all the people shall answer, A!'
27:22 And all the people shall answer, A!'
27:23 And all the people shall answer, A!'
27:24 And all the people shall answer, A!'
27:25 And all the people shall answer, A!'
27:26 And all the people shall answer, A!'
1Chr 16:36 Let all the people say, A!
Neh 5:13 And the whole assembly answered, A,"
8: 6 hands raised high, answered, "Amen, a!"
Tb 8: 8 They said together, "Amen, a."
14:15 They said together, "A.
Jdt 13:20 And all the people answered, A!
15:10 And all the people answered, A!"
Ps(s) 41:14 eternity and forever. Amen. A.
72:19 filled with his glory. Amen. A.
89:53 A, and amen!
106:48 Let all the people say, A!
Jer 11: 5 A, LORD," I answered.
28: 6 A! thus may the LORD do!
Rom 1:25 blessed be he forever, a!
9: 5 God who is over all! A.
11:36 To him be glory forever. A.
15:33 God of peace be with you all. A.
16:27 unto endless ages. A.
1Cor 14:16 be able to say A" to your thanksgiving?
2Cor 1:20 our A to God when we worship together.
Gal 1: 5 glory for endless ages. A.
6:18 Jesus Christ be with your spirit. A.
Eph 3:21 world without end. A.
Phil 4:20 for unending ages! A.
4:23 Christ be with your spirit. A.
1Tm 1:17 glory forever and ever! A.
6:16 honor and everlasting rule! A.
2Tm 4:18 glory forever and ever. A.
Heb 13:21 To Christ be glory forever! A.
1Pt 4:11 dominion throughout the ages. A.
5:11 throughout the ages! A.
2Pt 3:18 to the day of eternity! A.
Jude 1:25 for ages to come. A.
Rv 1: 6 power forever and ever! A.
1: 7 So it is to be! A!
3:14 "'The A, the faithful Witness and true,
5:14 The four living creatures answered, A,"
7:12 A!" Praise and glory,
7:12 forever and ever, A!"
19: 4 God seated on the throne and sang, A!
22:20 A! Come, LORD Jesus
22:21 Jesus be with you all. A!

AMEN-EM-OPE (1)

Prv 22:19 LORD, I make known to you the words of A.

AMENDS (6)

Lv 26:41 humbled and they make a for their guilt,
Nm 5: 8 the priest makes a for the guilty man.
25:13 his God and thus made a for the Israelites."
1Sm 6: 3 make a to him through a guilt offering.
6: 4 guilt offering should be our a to him?",
6: 8 that you are offering, as a for your guilt.

AMETHYST (3)

Ex 28:19 third row, a jacinth, an agate and an a;
39:12 third row a jacinth, an agate and an a;
Rv 21:20 the eleventh hyacinth, and the twelfth a.

AMI (1)

Ezr 2:57 sons of Pochereth-hazzebaim, sons of A.

AMIABLY (1)

1Mc 8: 1 and acted a to all who took their side.

AMID (30)

2Sm 6:12 into the City of David a festivities.
1Chr 13: 8 enthusiasm, a songs and music on lyres,
Jb 30:14 A the uproar they come on in waves;
Ps(s) 42: 5 God, A loud cries of joy and thanksgiving,
47: 6 God mounts his throne a shouts of joy;
47: 6 the LORD, a trumpet blasts.
73:19 They are completely wasted away a horrors.
120: 5 Meshech, that I dwell a the tents of Kedar!
138: 7 Though I walk a distress,
Prv 27:22 with the pestle, a the grits in a mortar,
Wis 14:11 they have become abominable a God's works,
Sir 31:29 disgrace is wine drunk a anger and strife.
41: 4 you for the man at peace a his possessions,
Is 44: 4 They shall spring up a the verdure like
Jer 32:21 Egypt a signs and wonders and great terror.
32:24 Chaldeans who are attacking it, a sword,

32:36 handed over to the king of Babylon *a* sword,
Ez 6:13 when their slain shall lie *a* their idols,
19:11 Stately was her height *a* the dense foliage;
26:10 cover you with dust, *a* the noise of steeds,
31: 3 *a* the very clouds lifted its crest.
Am 1:14 and it will devour her castles *A* clamor on
2: 2 Moab shall meet death *a* uproar
Hb 3:15 steeds *a* the churning of the deep waters.
Zec 4: 7 out the capstone *a* exclamations of 'Hail,
Mk 5: 5 and day, *a* the tombs and on the hillsides,
2Cor 6: 4 acting with patient endurance *a* trials,
1Tm 6:10 faith, and have come to grief *a* great pain.
Jas 1:11 rich man wither away *a* his many projects.
Rv 1: 7 See, he comes *a* the clouds!

AMIDST (1)

Ez 29: 3 Great crouching monster *a* your Niles:

AMITTAI (2)

2Kgs 14:25 his servant, the prophet Jonah, son of *A*,
Jon 1: 1 of the LORD that came to Jonah, son of *A*:

AMITY (1)

1Mc 10:20 after our interests and preserve *a* with us."

AMMAH (1)

2Sm 2:24 hill of *A* which lies east of the valley

AMMI (1)

Hos 2: 3 Say to your brothers, *A*,"

AMMIEL (6)

Nm 13:12 for the Josephites, with *A*, son of
2Sm 9: 4 "He is in the house of Machir, son of *A*,
9: 5 brought from the house of Machir, son of *A*,
17:27 Ammonites, Machir, son of *A* from Lodebar,
1Chr 3: 5 by Bathsheba, the daughter of *A*;
26: 5 the fourth, Nethanel, the fifth, *A*,

AMMIHUD (10)

Nm 1:10 Elishama, son of *A*, and from Manasseh:
2:18 [Their prince was Elishama, son of *A*,
7:48 day it was the turn of Elishama, son of *A*,
7:53 was the offering of Elishama, son of *A*.
10:22 in companies, with Elishama, son of *A*,
34:20 Samuel, son of *A*
34:28 Pedahel, son of *A*."
2Sm 13:37 taken flight, went to Talmai, son of *A*,
1Chr 7:26 whose son was Ladan, whose son was *A*,
9: 4 Among the Judahites was Uthai, son of *A*,

AMMINADAB (14)

Nm 1: 7 Nahshon, son of *A*
2: 3 of the Judahites was Nahshon, son of *A*,
7:12 on the first day was Nahshon, son of *A*,
7:17 This was the offering of Nahshon, son of *A*.
10:14 Nahshon, son of *A*,
Ru 4:19 father of Ram, Ram was the father of *A*,
4:20 of Amminadab, *A* was the father of Nahshon,
1Chr 2:10 the father of *A*, and Amminadab became
6: 7 his son *A*, whose son was Korah,
15:10 of the sons of Uzziel, *A*, their chief,
15:11 Asaiah, Joel, Shemaiah, Eliel, and *A*,
Mt 1: 4 the father of *A*, Amminadab the father
Lk 3:33 son of Sala, son of Nahshon, son of *A*,

AMMINADAB'S (1)

Ex 6:23 Aaron married *A* daughter,

AMMISHADDAI (5)

Nm 1:12 Ahiezer, son of *A*
2:25 [Their prince was Ahiezer, son of *A*,
7:66 day it was the turn of Ahiezer, son of *A*,
7:71 This was the offering of Ahiezer, son of *A*.
10:25 in companies, with Ahiezer, son of *A*,

AMMIZABAD (1)

1Chr 27: 6 His son *A* was over his division.

AMMON (6)

Gn 19:38 gave birth to a son, and she named him *A*,
2Chr 24:26 Zabad, son of Shimeath from *A*,
Jdt 1:12 his sword all the inhabitants of Moab, *A*,
Ps(s) 83: 8 people of Hagar, Gebal and *A* and Amalek,
Dn 11:41 except Edom, Moab, and the chief part of *A*,
Zep 2: 9 like Sodom, the land of *A* like Gomorrah:

AMMONITE (20)

Dt 2:37 did not encroach upon any of the *A* land,
23: 4 No *A* or Moabite may ever be admitted into
1Sm 11: 1 *A* went up and laid siege to Jabesh-gilead.
11: 2 But Nahash the *A* replied,
2Sm 10: 3 the *A* princes said to their lord Hanun:
12:31 This is what he did to all the *A* cities.
23:37 Zelek the *A*;
1Kgs 14:21 His mother was the *A* named Naamah.
14:31 His mother was the *A* named Naamah.
1Chr 11:39 Zelek the *A*;
19: 3 comfort Hanun, the *A* princes said to Hanun,
2Chr 12:13 Rehoboam's mother was named Naamah, an *A*.
Neh 2:10 and Tobiah the *A* slave had heard of this,
2:19 Sanballat the Horonite, Tobiah the *A* slave,
3:35 Tobiah the *A* was beside him, and he said:
13: 1 "no *A* or Moabite may ever be admitted
13:23 I saw Jews who had married Ashdodite, *A*,
Jdt 6: 1 of the Moabites, and of the *A* mercenaries:
6: 5 As for you, Achior, you *A* mercenary,
14: 5 doing this, summon for me Achior the *A*,

AMMONITES (106)

Gn 19:38 He is the ancestor of the *A* of today.
Nm 21:24 Jabbok and as far as the country of the *A*,
Dt 2:19 As you come opposite the *A*,
2:19 give you possession of any land of the *A*,
2:20 inhabitants, whom the *A* called Zamzummim,
2:21 the LORD cleared out of the way for the *A*,
3:11 still preserved in Rabbah of the *A*
3:16 Wadi Jabbok, which is the border of the *A*,
Jos 13:10 in Heshbon, to the boundary of the *A*;
13:25 and half the land of the *A* as far as Aroer,
Jgs 3:13 In alliance with the *A* and Amalekites,
10: 6 Sidon, the gods of Moab, the gods of the *A*,
10: 7 the power of [the Philistines and] the *A*.
10: 9 The *A* also crossed the Jordan to fight
10:11 not the Egyptians, the Amorites, the *A*,
10:17 The *A* had gathered for war and encamped in
10:18 war against the *A* shall be leader
11: 4 Some time later, the *A* warred on Israel.
11: 6 that we may be able to fight the *A*."
11: 8 if you go with us to fight against the *A*,
11: 9 the *A* and the LORD delivers them up to me,
11:12 messengers to the king of the *A* to say,
11:14 sent messengers to the king of the *A*,
11:15 take the land of Moab or the land of the *A*.
11:27 this day between the Israelites and the *A*!"
11:28 But the king of the *A* paid no heed to the
11:29 well, and from there he went on to the *A*.
11:30 "If you deliver the *A* into my power,"
11:31 from the *A* shall belong to the LORD.
11:32 went on to the *A* to fight against them,
11:33 Thus were the *A* brought into subjection by
11:36 vengeance for you on your enemies the *A*."
12: 1 the *A* without calling us to go with you?
12: 2 engaged in a critical contest with the *A*.
12: 3 life in my own hand and went on to the *A*,
1Sm 11:11 slaughtered *A* until the heat of the day;
12:12 Yet, when you saw Nahash, king of the *A*,
14:47 Moab, the *A*,
2Sm 8:12 from Edom and Moab, from the *A*,
10: 1 Some time later the king of the *A* died,
10: 2 servants entered the country of the *A*,
10: 6 the *A* sent for and hired twenty thousand
10: 8 The *A* came out and drew up in battle
10:10 Abishai, who arrayed them against the *A*.
10:11 But if the *A* are stronger than you,
10:14 The *A*, seeing that the Arameans had fled
10:14 attack on the *A* and returned to Jerusalem.
10:19 were afraid to give further aid to the *A*.
11: 1 they ravaged the *A* and besieged Rabbah.
12: 9 and him you killed with the sword of the *A*.
12:26 of the *A* and captured this royal city.
17:27 Shobi, son of Nahash from Rabbah of the *A*,
1Kgs 11: 1 the daughter of Pharaoh (Moabites, *A*,
11: 5 Sidonians, and Milcom, the idol of the *A*,
11: 7 Moab, and to Molech, the idol of the *A*,
11:33 god of Moab, and Milcom, god of the *A*;
2Kgs 23:13 horror, and of Milcom, the idol of the *A*.
24: 2 of Chaldeans, Arameans, Moabites, and *A*;
1Chr 18:11 from Edom, Moab, the *A*,
19: 1 Afterward Nahash, king of the *A*,
19: 2 entered the land of the *A* to comfort Hanun,
19: 6 When the *A* realized that they had put
19: 6 Hanun and the *A* sent a thousand talents of
19: 7 The *A* also assembled from their cities and
19: 9 The *A* marched out and lined up for a
19:11 Abishai, then lined up to oppose the *A*.
19:12 and if the *A* prove too strong for you,
19:15 when the *A* saw that the Arameans had fled,
19:19 refused to come to the aid of the *A*.
20: 1 in force, laid waste the land of the *A*,
20: 3 David dealt with all the cities of the *A*.
2Chr 20: 1 After this the Moabites, the *A*,
20:10 And now, see the *A*,
20:22 the LORD laid an ambush against the *A*,
20:23 For the *A* and Moabites set upon the
26: 8 The *A* paid tribute to Uzziah and his fame
27: 5 with the king of the *A* and conquered them.
27: 5 *A* paid him one hundred talents of silver,
Ezr 9: 1 Hittites, Perizzites, Jebusites, *A*,
Neh 4: 1 When Sanballat, Tobiah, the Arabs, the *A*,
Jdt 5: 2 of the Moabites, the generals of the *A*,
5: 5 the leader of all the *A* said to him:
7: 8 the Edomites and all the leaders of the *A*,
7:18 The Edomites and the *A* went up and
1Mc 5: 6 Then he crossed over to the *A*,
2Mc 4:26 out as a fugitive to the country of the *A*.
5: 7 again took refuge in the country of the *A*.
Is 11:14 possessions, and the *A* their subjects.
Jer 9:25 Egypt and Judah, Edom and the *A*,
25:21 Edom, Moab, and the *A*;
27: 3 to the kings of Edom, of Moab, of the *A*,
40:11 of Judah in Moab, those among the *A*,
40:14 not know that Baalis, the king of the *A*,
41:10 set out to make his way to the *A*.
41:15 Johanan and fled to the *A* with eight men.
49: 1 Concerning the *A*, thus says the LORD:
49: 2 of the *A* I will sound the battle alarm;
49: 6 afterward I will change the lot of the *A*,
Ez 21:25 to Rabbah of the *A* or to Judah's capital,
21:33 Lord GOD against the *A* and their insults:
25: 2 toward the *A* and prophesy against them.
25: 3 Say to the *A*: "Hear the word of the LORD!
25: 5 of the *A* a resting place for flocks.
25:10 I will hand her over, along with the *A*,
Am 1:13 For three crimes of the *A*,
Zep 2: 8 uttered by Moab, and the insults of the *A*,

AMNESTY (1)

Wis 12:11 for anyone did you grant *a* for their sins.

AMNON (27)

2Sm 3: 2 his first-born, *A*, of Ahinoam from Jezreel;
13: 1 named Tamar, and David's son *A* loved her.
13: 2 *A* thought it impossible to carry out his
13: 3 Now *A* had a friend named Jonadab,
13: 4 So *A* said to him,
13: 6 So *A* lay down and pretended to be sick.
13: 6 king came to visit him, *A* said to the king,
13: 7 *A* and prepare some nourishment for him."
13: 8 Tamar went to the house of her brother *A*,
13: 9 But *A* would not eat;
13:10 *A* said to Tamar, "Bring the nourishment
13:10 them to her brother *A* in the bedroom.
13:15 Then *A* conceived an intense hatred for her,
13:20 "Has your brother *A* been with you?
13:21 spark the resentment of his son *A*,
13:22 moreover, said nothing at all to *A*,
13:26 please let my brother *A* come to us."
13:27 sent *A* and all the other princes with him.
13:28 When *A* is merry with wine and I say to you,
13:28 I say to you, 'Kill *A*,' put him to death.
13:29 servants did to *A* as Absalom had commanded,
13:32 *A* alone is dead, for Absalom
13:32 this ever since *A* shamed his sister Tamar.
13:33 *A* alone is dead."
13:39 as he became reconciled to the death of *A*.
1Chr 3: 1 the first-born, *A*, by Ahinoam of Jezreel;
4:20 The sons of Shimon were *A*,

AMOK (2)

Neh 12: 7 Shemaiah, and Joiarib, Jedaiah, Sallu, *A*,
12:20 for *A*, Eber; for Hilkiah, Hashabiah;

AMOMUM (1)

Rv 18:13 cinnamon and *a*,

AMON (18)

1Kgs 22:26 "Seize Micaiah and take him back to *A*,
2Kgs 21:18 His son *A* succeeded him as king.
21:19 *A* was twenty-two years old when he began
21:23 Subjects of *A* conspired against him and
21:24 slew all who had conspired against King *A*,
21:25 The rest of the acts that *A* did are
1Chr 3:14 whose son was Manasseh, whose son was *A*,
2Chr 18:25 "Seize Micaiah and take him back to *A*,
33:20 His son *A* succeeded him as king.
33:21 *A* was twenty-two years old when he became
33:22 *A* offered sacrifice to all the idols which
33:23 the contrary, *A* only increased his guilt.
33:25 those who had conspired against King *A*,
Neh 7:59 sons of Pochereth-hazzebaim, sons of *A*.
Jer 1: 2 to him in the days of Josiah, son of *A*,
25: 3 the thirteenth year of Josiah, son of *A*,
46:25 I will punish *A* of Thebes,
Zep 1: 1 in the days of Josiah, the son of *A*,

AMORITE (11)

Gn 14:13 camping at the terebinth of Mamre the *A*,
Nm 21:29 be taken captive by the *A* king Sihon.
Dt 2:24 your hands Sihon, the *A* king of Heshbon,
33:27 out of your way and the *A* he destroyed.
Jos 10: 5 The five *A* kings,
10: 6 because all the *A* kings of the mountain
13:21 This *A* king, who reigned in Heshbon,
Jgs 10: 8 in the *A* land beyond the Jordan in Gilead.
1Chr 1:14 and Heth, and the Jebusite, the *A*,
Ez 16: 3 father was an *A* and your mother a Hittite.
16:45 mother was a Hittite and your father an *A*.

AMORITES (78)

Gn 10:16 also of the Jebusites, the *A*,
14: 7 and of the *A* who dwelt in Hazazon-tamar.
15:16 the wickedness of the *A* will not have
15:21 the Perizzites, the Rephaim, the *A*,
48:22 captured from the *A* with my sword and bow."
Ex 3: 8 the country of the Canaanites, Hittites, *A*,
3:17 the land of the Canaanites, Hittites, *A*,

AMORITES (cont.)

13: 5 the land of the Canaanites, Hittites, *A,*
23:23 will go before you and bring you to the *A,*
33: 2 Driving out the Canaanites, *A,*
34:11 "I will drive out before you the *A,*
Nm 13:29 Jebusites and *A* dwell in the highlands,
21:13 territory of the *A;* for the Arnon
21:21 Israel sent men to Sihon, king of the *A,*
21:25 here and settled in these towns of the *A,*
21:26 was the capital of Sihon, king of the *A,*
21:31 Israel had settled in the land of the *A,*
21:32 and dispossessed the *A* who were there.
21:34 to him as you did to Sihon, king of the *A,*
22: 2 Zippor, saw all that Israel did to the *A.*
32:33 the kingdom of Sihon, king of the *A,*
32:39 it, driving out the *A* who were there.
Dt 1: 4 he had defeated Sihon, king of the *A,*
1: 7 the *A* and to all the surrounding regions,
1:19 the direction of the hill country of the *A.*
1:20 have come to the hill country of the *A,*
1:27 us into the hands of the *A* and destroy us.
1:44 *A* living there came out against you and,
3: 2 to him as you did to Sihon, king of the *A,*
3: 8 two kings of the *A* beyond the Jordan
3: 9 by the Sidonians and Senir by the *A,*
4:46 in the land of Sihon, king of the *A,*
4:47 of the *A* in the region east of the Jordan:
7: 1 the Hittites, Girgashites, *A,*
20:17 the Hittites, *A,*
31: 4 Og, the kings of the *A* whom he destroyed,
Jos 2:10 the two kings of the *A* beyond the Jordan,
3:10 Perizzites, Girgashites, *A* and Jebusites.
5: 1 When all the kings of the *A* to the west of
7: 7 delivering us into the power of the *A,*
9: 1 Hittites, *A,*
9:10 the two kings of the *A* beyond the Jordan,
10:12 LORD delivered up the *A* to the Israelites,
11: 3 were Canaanites to the east and west, *A,*
12: 2 First, Sihon, king of the *A,*
12: 8 the Negeb, belonging to the Hittites, *A,*
13: 4 to Aphek, and the boundaries of the *A;*
13:10 of the cities of Sihon, king of the *A,*
24: 8 land of the *A* who lived east of the Jordan.
24: 8 them [the two kings of the *A* before you.
24:12 ahead of you which drove them [the *A,*
24:15 of the *A* in whose country you are dwelling.
24:18 including] the *A* who dwelt in the land.
Jgs 1:34 The *A* hemmed in the Danites in the
1:35 The *A* had a firm hold in Har-heres,
1:36 The territory of the *A* extended from the
3: 5 living among the Canaanites, Hittites, *A,*
6:10 of the *A* in whose land you are dwelling.
10:11 "Did not the Egyptians, the *A,*
11:19 sent messengers to Sihon, king of the *A,*
11:21 the land of the *A* dwelling in that region,
11:23 cleared the *A* out of the way of his people,
1Sm 7:14 there was peace between Israel and the *A.*
2Sm 21: 2 not Israelites, but survivors of the *A;*
1Kgs 4:19 of Gilea, the land of Sihon, king of the *A,*
9:20 in the land, descendants of the *A,*
21:26 by following idols, just as the *A* had done,
2Kgs 21:11 than all that was done by the *A* before him,
2Chr 8: 7 people that remained of the Hittites, *A,*
Ezr 9: 1 Ammonites, Moabites, Egyptians, and *A;*
Neh 9: 8 the land of the Canaanites, Hittites, *A,*
Jdt 5:15 then they settled in the land of the *A,*
Ps(s) 135:11 Sihon, king of the *A,*
136:19 Sihon, king of the *A,*
Is 17: 9 *A* When faced with the children of Israel:
Am 2: 9 it was I who destroyed the *A* before them,
2:10 forty years, to occupy the land of the *A:*

AMOS (14)

2Chr 26:22 The prophet Isaiah, son of *A,*
32:20 Hezekiah and the prophet Isaiah, son of *A,*
32:32 Vision of the Prophet Isaiah, son of *A,*
Tb 2: 6 pronounced by the prophet *A* against Bethel:
Am 1: 1 The words of *A,* a shepherd from Tekoa
7: 8 The LORD asked me, "What do you see, *A?*"
7:10 *A* has conspired against you here within
7:11 For this is what *A* says: Jeroboam shall die
7:12 To *A,* Amaziah said: "Off with you, visionary,
7:14 *A* answered Amaziah,
8: 2 "What do you see, *A?*"
Mt 1:10 the father of Amos, *A* the father of Josiah,
Lk 3:25 of Joseph, son of Mattathias, son of *A,*

AMOUNT (30)

Gn 43:12 for you must return the *a* that was put
43:15 took double the *a* of money with them,
43:21 our money in the full *a!*
47: 9 as a wayfarer *a* to a hundred and thirty.
Ex 5:13 daily *a* as when your straw was supplied."
5:14 prescribed *a* of bricks yesterday and today,
5:19 told not to reduce the daily *a* of bricks.
16:17 Some gathered a large and some a small *a.*
16:18 gathered a large *a* did not have too much,
16:18 gathered a small *a* did not have too little.
21:30 for his life whatever *a* is imposed on him.
30:23 half the *a,* that is, two hundred and fifty
38:25 The *a* of the silver received from the
Lv 22:14 with an increment of one fifth of the *a.*
25: 8 the seven cycles *a* to forty-nine years.
27:16 to the *a* of seed required to sow it,
Dt 17:17 he accumulate a vast *a* of silver and gold.
1Kgs 10: 2 camels bearing spices, a large *a* of gold,
2Kgs 12:11 there was a large *a* of silver in the chest,
12:12 The *a* thus realized they turned over to
23:35 the land to raise the *a* Pharaoh demanded.
1Chr 20: 2 out a great *a* of booty from the city.
28:17 the *a* of gold for each golden bowl and the
2Chr 3: 8 fine gold to the *a* of six hundred talents.
Est 4: 7 as well as the exact *a* of silver Haman had
Is 44: 9 Idol makers all *a* to nothing,
Mt 18:24 one was brought in who owed him a huge *a.*
Lk 3:13 nothing over and above your fixed *a.*"
Acts 5: 8 piece of property for such and such an *a?*"
Rv 18: 6 into her cup twice the *a* she concocted!

AMOUNTED (21)

Gn 46:27 come to Egypt *a* to seventy persons in all.
Ex 38:24 *a* to twenty-nine talents and seven hundred
38:29 *a* to seventy talents and two thousand four
Nm 2: 4 and his soldiers *a* in the census to
2: 6 and his soldiers *a* in the census to
2: 8 and his soldiers *a* in the census to
2:11 and his soldiers *a* in the census to
2:13 and his soldiers *a* in the census to
2:15 and his soldiers *a* in the census to
2:19 and his soldiers *a* in the census to forty
2:21 and his soldiers *a* in the census to
2:23 and his soldiers *a* in the census to
2:26 and his soldiers *a* in the census to
2:28 and his soldiers *a* in the census to
2:30 and his soldiers *a* in the census to
7:85 *a* to two thousand four hundred shekels,
7:86 cups *a* to one hundred and twenty shekels.
31:32 *a* to six hundred and seventy-five thousand
31:52 contribution to the LORD *a* in all
Neh 7:71 *a* to twenty thousand drachmas of gold,
2Mc 3:11 the total *a* to four hundred talents of

AMOUNTING (1)

2Mc 12:43 *a* to two thousand silver drachmas,

AMOUNTS (7)

Ex 38:21 of the various *a* used on the Dwelling,
2Kgs 25:30 a perpetual allowance, in fixed daily *a,*
Ezr 8:26 I consigned it to them in these *a:*
Jer 52:34 a perpetual allowance, in fixed daily *a,*
Mk 12:41 Many of the wealthy put in sizable *a;*
Gal 6: 3 If anyone thinks he *a* to something,
Rv 8: 3 given large *a* of incense to deposit

AMOZ (10)

2Kgs 19: 2 to tell the prophet Isaiah, son of *A,*
19:20 Then Isaiah, son of *A,* sent this message
20: 1 mortally ill, the prophet Isaiah, son of *A,*
Is 1: 1 The vision which Isaiah, son of *A,*
2: 1 This is what Isaiah, son of *A,* saw
13: 1 a vision of Isaiah, son of *A.*
20: 2 a warning through Isaiah, the son of *A:*
37: 2 to tell the prophet Isaiah, son of *A:*
37:21 Isaiah, son of *A,* sent this message
38: 1 mortally ill, the prophet Isaiah, son of *A,*

AMPHIPOLIS (1)

Acts 17: 1 *A* and Apollonia and came to Thessalonica,

AMPLE (6)

Gn 26:22 said, "The LORD has now given us *a* room,
34:21 there is *a* room in the country for them.
Jgs 18:10 are a trusting people, and the land is *a.*
Ps(s) 80: 6 and given them tears to drink in *a* measure.
Prv 15: 6 house of the just there are *a* resources,
27:27 there will be *a* goat's milk to supply you,

AMPLIATUS (1)

Rom 16: 8 Greetings to *A,* who is dear to me

AMPLY (3)

Jdt 12: 2 but I shall be *a* supplied from the things
Prv 11:25 He who confers benefits will be *a* enriched,
13: 4 but the diligent soul is *a* satisfied.

AMRAM (13)

Ex 6:18 The sons of Kohath were *A,*
6:20 *A* married his aunt Jochebed,
6:20 *A* lived one hundred and thirty-seven years.
Nm 3:19 descendants of Kohath, by clans, were *A,*
26:58 Among the descendants of Kohath was *A,*
26:59 To *A* she bore Aaron and Moses and their
1Chr 5:28 The sons of Kohath were *A,*
5:29 The children of *A* were Aaron,
6: 3 The sons of Kohath were *A,*
23:12 *A,* Izhar, Hebron, and Uzziel:
23:13 The sons of *A* were Aaron and Moses.
24:20 were Shubael, of the descendants of *A,*
Ezr 10:34 Maadai, *A,*

AMRAMITES (2)

Nm 3:27 To Kohath belonged the clans of the *A,*
1Chr 26:23 From the *A,* Izharites, Hebronites

AMRAPHEL (2)

Gn 14: 1 *A* king of Shinar,
14: 9 Tidal king of Goiim, *A* king of Shinar,

AMULETS (2)

2Mc 12:40 they found *a* sacred to the idols of Jamnia,
Is 3:20 bangles, cinctures, perfume boxes, and *a;*

AMUSE (1)

Jgs 16:25 they said, "Call Samson that he may *a* us."

AMUSED (2)

2Mc 6: 4 they *a* themselves with prostitutes and had
Lk 22:63 guarding Jesus *a* themselves at his expense.

AMUSEMENT (1)

Jgs 16:27 and women looked on as Samson provided *a.*

AMZI (2)

1Chr 6:31 son of Amaziah, son of Hilkiah, son of *A,*
Neh 11:12 son of Jeroham, son of Pelaliah, son of *A,*

ANAB (2)

Jos 11:21 the Anakim in Hebron, Debir, *A,*
15:50 Kiriath-sannah (that is, Debir), *A,*

ANAEL'S (1)

Tb 1:21 as king, placed Ahiqar, my brother *A* son,

ANAH (12)

Gn 36: 2 through *A* of Zibeon the Hivite;
36:14 granddaughter through *A* of Zibeon
36:18 of Esau's wife Oholibamah, daughter of *A.*
36:20 Lotan, Shobal, Zibeon, *A,*
36:24 Zibeon's descendants were Aiah and *A.*
36:24 (He is the *A* who found water in the desert
36:25 of *A* were Dishon and Oholibamah,
36:25 were Dishon and Oholibamah, daughter of *A.*
36:29 the clans of Lotan, Shobal, Zibeon, *A,*
1Chr 1:38 of Seir were Lotan, Shobal, Zibeon, *A,*
1:40 The sons of Zibeon were Aiah and *A.*
1:41 The sons of *A:*

ANAHARATH (1)

Jos 19:19 Chesulloth, Shunem, Hapharaim, Shion, *A,*

ANAIAH (2)

Neh 8: 4 his right side stood Mattithiah, Shema, *A,*
10:23 Zadok, Jaddua, Pelatiah, Hanan, *A,*

ANAK (4)

Jos 15:13 Kiriath-arba (Arba was the father of *A),*
15:14 the three Anakim, the descendants of *A:*
21:11 Kiriath-arba (Arba was the father of *A),*
Jgs 1:20 who then drove from it the three sons of *A.*

ANAKIM (13)

Nm 13:22 Sheshai and Talmai, descendants of the *A,*
13:28 Besides, we saw descendants of the *A* there.
13:33 giants [the *A* were a race of giants];
Dt 1:28 besides, they saw the *A* there.'
2:10 strong and numerous and tall like the *A;*
2:21 strong and numerous and tall like the *A.*
9: 2 the *A,* a people great and tall.
9: 2 of them, 'Who can stand up against the *A?*'
Jos 11:21 regions and exterminated the *A* in Hebron,
11:22 *A* were left in the land of the Israelites.
14:12 True, the *A* are there,
14:15 from Arba, the greatest among the *A.*
15:14 And Caleb drove out from there the three *A,*

ANALOGY (1)

Wis 13: 5 created things their original author, by *a,*

ANAMIM (2)

Gn 10:13 became the father of the Ludim, the *A,*
1Chr 1:11 Mesraim became the father of the Ludim, *A,*

ANAN (1)

Neh 10:27 Hashabnah, Maaseiah, Ahiah, Hanan, *A,*

ANANI (1)

1Chr 3:24 Pelaiah, Akkub, Johanan, Delaiah, and *A—*

ANANIAH (2)

Neh 3:23 son of *A,* made the repairs
11:32 and its dependencies, Anathoth, Nob, *A,*

ANANIAS (13)

Jdt 8: 1 son of Oziel, son of Elkiah, son of *A*,
Acts 5: 1 Another man named *A* and his wife Sapphira
5: 3 *A*, why have you let Satan fill your heart
5: 5 At the sound of these words, *A* fell dead.
5: 7 Three hours later *A'* wife came in,
9:10 *A*!" he said. "Here I am LORD,"
9:10 There was a disciple in Damascus named *A*
9:12 (Saul saw in a vision a man named *A* coming
9:13 But *A* protested: "LORD, I have heard
9:17 With that *A* left.
22:12 "A certain *A*,
23: 2 the high priest *A* ordered his attendants
24: 1 the high priest *A* came down to Caesarea

ANATH (3)

Jgs 3:31 After him there was Shamgar, son of *A*,
5: 6 In the days of Shamgar, son of *A*,
2Kgs 17:31 city gods, King Hadad and his consort *A*.

ANATHOTH (20)

Jos 21:18 pasture lands, *A* with its pasture lands,
2Sm 23:27 Abiezer from *A*;
1Kgs 2:26 "Go to your land in *A*.
1Chr 6:45 pasture lands, *A* with its pasture lands.
7: 8 Elioenai, Omri, Jeremoth, Abijah, *A*,
11:28 Abiezer, from *A*;
12: 3 Jehu from *A*;
27:12 for the ninth month, was Abiezer from *A*,
Ezr 2:23 men of *A*, one hundred and twenty-eight;
Neh 7:27 men of *A*, one hundred and twenty-eight;
10:20 Azzur, Hodiah, Hashum, Bezai, Hariph, *A*,
11:32 Aija, Bethel and its dependencies, *A*,
Is 10:30 Answer her, *A*!
Jer 1: 1 son of Hilkiah, of a priestly family in *A*,
11:21 concerning the men of *A* who seek your life,
11:23 I will bring misfortune upon the men of *A*,
29:27 of *A* who poses as a prophet among you?
32: 7 "Buy for yourself my field in *A*,
32: 8 and said, "Please buy my field in *A*,
32: 9 the field in *A* from my cousin Hanamel,

ANCESTOR (15)

Gn 4:20 the *a* of all who dwell in tents and keep
4:21 *a* of all who play the lyre and the pipe.
4:22 the *a* of all who forge instruments of
10:21 and the *a* of all the children of Eber,
19:37 He is the *a* of the Moabites of today.
19:38 He is the *a* of the Ammonites of today.
36: 9 the descendants of Esau, *a* of the Edomites,
Jos 19:47 renamed the settlement after their *a* Dan.
Jgs 18:29 They named it Dan after their *a* Dan,
2Kgs 22: 2 unswervingly just as his *a* David had done.
1Chr 2:55 from Hammath of the *a* of the Rechabites.
2Chr 21:12 says the LORD, the God of your *a* David:
34: 2 LORD, following the path of his *a* David.
Jn 4:12 not pretend to be greater than our *a* Jacob,
Rom 4: 1 of Abraham, our *a* according to the flesh?

ANCESTORS (76)

Gn 46:34 answer, 'We your servants, like our *a*,
47: 3 answered, "We your servants, like our *a*,
47: 9 the years that my *a* lived as wayfarers."
47:30 When I lie down with my *a*,
Lv 25:41 his kindred and to the property of his *a*.
Dt 10:22 Your *a* went down to Egypt seventy strong,
2Sm 7:12 your time comes and you rest with your *a*,
1Kgs 2:10 his *a* and was buried in the City of David.
11:21 that David rested with his *a* and that Joab,
11:43 Solomon rested with his *a*;
13:22 not be brought to the grave of your *a*.' "
14:20 He rested with his *a*,
14:31 Rehoboam rested with his *a*;
15: 8 Abijam rested with his *a*;
15:24 He rested with his *a*;
16: 6 Baasha rested with his *a*;
16:28 Omri rested with his *a*;
22:40 Ahab rested with his *a*,
22:51 Jehoshaphat rested with his *a*;
2Kgs 8:24 Jehoram rested with his *a* and was buried
9:28 in the tomb of his *a* in the City of David.
10:35 with his *a* and was buried in Samaria.
13: 9 with his *a* and was buried in Samaria.
13:13 Joash rested with his *a*,
14:16 Jehoash rested with his *a*;
14:20 his *a* in the City of David in Jerusalem.
14:22 after King Amaziah rested with his *a*.
14:29 Jeroboam rested with his *a*,
15: 7 Azariah rested with his *a*,
15:22 Menahem rested with his *a*,
15:38 Jotham rested with his *a* and was buried
16:20 Ahaz rested with his *a* and was buried with
20:21 Hezekiah rested with his *a* and his son
21:18 his *a* and was buried in his palace garden,
22:20 I will therefore gather you to your *a*;
24: 6 Jehoiakim rested with his *a*,
1Chr 6: 4 of Levi, distributed according to their *a*:
2Chr 9:31 He rested with his *a*;
12:16 Rehoboam rested with his *a*;
13:23 Abijah rested with his *a*;
16:13 Asa rested with his *a*;
21: 1 Jehoshaphat rested with his *a*;
25:28 buried him with his *a* in the City of Judah.
26: 2 King Amaziah had gone to rest with his *a*.
26:23 Uzziah rested with his *a*;
27: 9 his *a* and was buried in the City of David,
28:27 with his *a* and was buried in Jerusalem
32:33 Hezekiah rested with his *a*;
33:20 his *a* and was buried in his own palace.
34:28 I will gather you to your *a* and you shall
35:24 He was buried in the tombs of his *a*,
Neh 2: 3 city where my *a* are buried lies in ruins,
2: 5 me to Judah, to the city of my *a'* graves,
Jdt 5: 8 Since they abandoned the way of their *a*,
Est C:16 and our fathers from among all their *a*,
1Mc 7: 2 to enter the royal palace of his *a*,
15: 3 gained control of the kingdom of my *a*,
15:10 Antiochus invaded the land of his *a*,
15:34 we are holding on to the heritage of our *a*.
2Mc 4:15 what their *a* had regarded as honors,
5:10 any kind or any place in the tomb of his *a*.
6: 1 *a* and live no longer by the laws of God;
7: 2 rather than transgress the laws of our *a*."
8:19 times when help had been given their *a*;
11:25 in keeping with the customs of their *a*.
Sir 44: 1 Now will I praise those godly men, our *a*,
Ez 20: 4 the abominations of their *a* in these words:
Dn 11:37 his *a* or for the one in whom women delight;
Mt 15: 2 act contrary to the tradition of our *a*?
Mk 7: 3 cling to the custom of their *a* and never
7: 5 not follow the tradition of our *a*,
Jn 4:20 Our *a* worshiped on this mountain,
6:31 Our *a* had manna to eat in the desert;
6:49 Your *a* ate manna in the desert,
6:58 Unlike your *a* who ate and died nonetheless,
Gal 1:14 to live out all the traditions of my *a*.

ANCESTRAL (106)

Gn 31:42 If my *a* God,
31:53 *a* deities] maintain justice between us!"
Ex 6:14 These are the heads of the *a* houses.
6:25 the heads of the *a* clans of the Levites.
Nm 1: 2 of the Israelites, by clans and *a* houses,
1: 4 from each tribe, the head of his *a* house.
1:16 the community, princes of their *a* tribes,
1:18 and lineage according to clan and *a* house,
1:20 Reuben, . . . in clans and *a* houses:
1:22 Simeon, . . . in clans and *a* houses:
1:24 Gad, . . . in clans and *a* houses:
1:26 Judah, . . . in clans and *a* houses:
1:28 Issachar, . . . in clans and *a* houses:
1:30 Zebulun, . . . in clans and *a* houses:
1:32 Ephraim, . . . in clans and *a* houses:
1:34 Manasseh, . . . in clans and *a* houses:
1:36 Benjamin, . . . in clans and *a* houses:
1:38 Dan, . . . in clans and *a* houses:
1:40 Asher, . . . in clans and *a* houses:
1:42 Naphtali, . . . in clans and *a* houses:
1:44 registered, each according to his *a* house,
1:45 military service, registered by *a* houses,
1:47 not registered by *a* tribe with the others.
2: 2 under the ensigns of their *a* houses.
2:32 census of the Israelites taken by *a* houses.
2:34 man according to his clan and his *a* house.
3:15 of the Levites by *a* houses and clans,
3:20 were the clans of the Levites by *a* houses.
3:24 The prince of their *a* house was Eliasaph,
3:30 The prince of their *a* house was Elizaphan,
3:35 *a* house of the clans of Merari was Zuriel,
4: 2 of the Kohathites, by clans and *a* houses,
4:22 Gershonites also, by *a* houses and clans,
4:29 you shall enroll by clans and *a* houses all
4:34 the Kohathites, by clans and *a* houses,
4:38 the Gershonites, by clans and *a* houses,
4:40 tent, as registered by clans and *a* houses,
4:42 among the Merarites, by clans and *a* houses,
4:46 among the Levites, by clans and *a* houses,
7: 2 of Israel, who were heads of *a* houses;
13: 2 You shall send one man from each *a* tribe,
17:17 get one staff from them for each *a* house,
17:18 of Levi's *a* house shall also have a staff.
18: 1 other members of your *a* house
18: 2 kinsmen of the tribe of Levi, your *a* tribe,
25:14 prince of an *a* house of the Simeonites.
25:15 of Zur, who was head of a clan, an *a* house,
26: 2 the priest, "Take a census, by *a* houses,
26:55 as the heritage of the various *a* tribes.
31:26 Eleazar and of the heads of the *a* houses,
32:28 heads of the *a* tribes of the Israelites:
33:54 be within the heritage of his *a* tribe.
34:14 all the *a* houses of the tribe of Reuben,
34:14 and the *a* houses of the tribe of Gad,
36: 1 The heads of the *a* houses in the clan of
36: 1 of the *a* houses of the other Israelites.
36: 3 withdrawn from our *a* heritage
36: 4 will be withdrawn from that of our *a* tribe."
36: 6 they marry into a clan of their *a* tribe,
36: 7 will retain their own *a* heritage.
36: 8 belonging to a clan of her own *a* tribe,
36: 8 in possession of their own *a* heritage.
36: 9 tribes will retain their own *a* heritage."
36:13 will be withdrawn from that of our *a* tribe."
Jos 22:14 prince and military leader of his *a* house.
Jgs 9: 5 He then went to his *a* house in Ophrah,
1Kgs 8: 1 princes in the *a* houses of the Israelites,
21: 3 "that I should give you my *a* heritage."
21: 4 "I will not give you my *a* heritage."
1Chr 4:38 and their *a* houses spread out to such an
5:13 brothers, corresponding to their *a* houses,
5:15 of Guni, was the head of their *a* houses.
5:24 following were the heads of their *a* houses:
5:24 famous men, and heads over their *a* houses.
7: 2 warrior heads of the *a* houses of Tola.
7: 4 Their kindred, by *a* houses,
7: 7 were heads of their *a* houses and warriors.
7: 9 were heads of their *a* houses and warriors.
7:11 of Jediael, heads of *a* houses and warriors.
7:40 descendants of Asher, heads of *a* houses,
9: 9 those named were heads of their *a* houses.
9:13 Their brethren, heads of their *a* houses,
9:19 and his brethren of the same *a* house of
12:31 warriors, men renowned in their *a* houses.
23:24 sons of Levi according to their *a* houses,
24: 6 *a* houses of the priests and of the Levites,
24:30 of the Levites according to their *a* houses.
2Chr 5: 2 the princes of the Israelite *a* houses,
17:14 mustering according to their *a* houses.
25: 5 and Benjamin according to their *a* houses,
31:16 There was also a register by *a* houses of
31:17 family records according to their *a* houses,
35: 4 Prepare yourselves in your *a* houses and
35: 5 divisions of the *a* houses of your brethren,
35:12 various groups of the *a* houses
Ezr 2:59 *a* houses and their descent were Israelite:
Neh 7:61 *a* houses and their descent were Israelite:
1Mc 15:33 but our *a* heritage which for a time had
2Mc 7:24 happy if he would abandon his *a* customs:
7:37 up my body and my life for our *a* laws,
8:17 as the subversion of their *a* way of life.
8:33 celebrating the victory in their *a* city,
12:37 raising a battle cry in his *a* language,
12:39 them with their kinsmen in their *a* tombs.
14: 7 now that I am deprived of my *a* dignity,
Acts 28:17 against our people or our *a* customs;

ANCESTRY (3)

Ex 12:38 A crowd of mixed *a* also went up with them,
Heb 7: 3 Without father, mother or *a*,
7: 6 but Melchizedek, who was not of their *a*,

ANCHOR (3)

Acts 27:13 for, so they weighed *a* and proceeded,
27:17 they lowered the small *a* used for moving
Heb 6:19 Like a sure and firm *a*,

ANCHORS (3)

Acts 27:29 *a* from the stern and prayed for daylight.
27:30 to run out *a* from the bow of the ship,
27:40 loose the *a* and abandoned them to the sea.

ANCIENT (32)

Dt 33:27 he extended the *a* canopy.
2Sm 20:18 "There is an *a* saying,
2Kgs 17:34 they worship according to their *a* rites.
Ezr 4:15 has been fostered there since *a* times.
4:19 it was verified that from *a* times this
Est E: 7 *a* stories that have been handed down to us,
Jb 22:15 keep to the *a* way trodden by worthless men,
Ps(s) 24: 7 reach up, you *a* portals,
24: 9 *a* portals, that the king of glory may come
68:34 who rides on the heights of the *a* heavens.
89:50 Where are your *a* favors,
Prv 22:28 the *a* landmark which your fathers set up.
23:10 Remove not the *a* landmark,
Wis 12: 3 truly, the *a* inhabitants of your holy land,
13:10 or useless stone, the work of an *a* hand.
Sir 38:34 Yet they maintain God's *a* handiwork,
Is 19:11 "I am a disciple of wise men, of *a* kings?"
24: 5 violated statutes, broken the *a* covenant.
58:12 The *a* ruins shall be rebuilt for your sake,
61: 4 They shall rebuild the *a* ruins,
Jer 5:15 A long-lived nation, an *a* nation,
6:11 taken, husband and wife, graybeard with *a*.
Ez 38:17 I spoke in *a* times through my servants,
Dn 7: 9 were set up and the *A* One took his throne.
7:13 the *A* One and was presented before him,
7:22 and was victorious until the *A* One arrived;
Mi 5: 1 Whose origin is from of old, from *a* times.
Hb 3: 6 the age-old hills bow low along his *a* ways.
Lk 1:70 of his holy ones, the prophets of *a* times:
2Pt 2: 5 Nor did he spare the *a* world
Rv 12: 9 the *a* serpent known as the devil or Satan,
20: 2 He seized the dragon, the *a* serpent,

ANCIENTS (1)

Lk 22:52 the chiefs of the temple guard, and the *a*—

ANDREW (13)

Mt 4:18 now known as Peter, and his brother *A*,
10: 2 now known as Peter, and his brother *A*;
Mk 1:16 brother *A* casting their nets into the sea;
1:29 house of Simon and *A* with James and John.

ANDREW (cont.)

3:18 A, Philip, Bartholomew, Matthew,
13: 3 and A began to question him privately.
Lk 6:14 he gave the name Peter, and A his brother,
Jn 1:40 hearing John was Simon Peter's brother A.
1:44 Bethsaida, the same town as A and Peter.
6: 8 Jesus' disciples, A, Simon Peter's brother,
12:22 went to tell A; Philip and Andrew in turn
Acts 1:13 Peter and John and James and A;

ANDRONICUS (7)

2Mc 4:31 in haste to settle the affair, leaving A,
4:32 from the temple and presented them to A;
4:34 Thereupon Menelaus approached A privately
4:34 So A went to Onias,
4:38 immediately stripped A of his purple robe,
5:23 at Mount Gerizim, A;
Rom 16: 7 worked hard for you, and to A and Junias,

ANER (2)

Gn 14:13 the Amorite, a kinsman of Eshcol and A;
14:24 that is due to the men who joined me A,

ANEW (7)

Nm 6:12 begin a the period of his dedication
Jb 29: 1 Job took up his theme a and said;
Ps(s) 90: 6 changing grass, Which at dawn springs up a,
Wis 19: 6 its several kinds, was being made over a,
Lam 5:21 give us a such days as we had of old.
Gal 6:15 All that matters is that one is created a.
Col 3:10 he is formed a in the image of his Creator.

ANGEL (206)

Gn 48:16 The A who has delivered me from all harm,
Ex 3: 2 There an a of the LORD appeared to him in
14:19 The a of God, who had been leading
23:20 "See, I am sending an a before you,
23:23 "My a will go before you and bring you to
32:34 My a will go before you.
33: 2 I will send an a before you to the land
Nm 20:16 cry and sent an a who led us out of Egypt.
22:22 and the a of the LORD stationed himself on
22:23 When the ass saw the a of the LORD
22:24 Then the a of the LORD took his stand in a
22:25 When the ass saw the a of the LORD there,
22:26 The a of the LORD then went ahead,
22:27 When the ass saw the a of the LORD there,
22:31 saw the a of the LORD standing
22:32 But the a of the LORD said to him,
22:34 Then Balaam said to the a of the LORD,
22:35 But the a of the LORD said to Balaam,
Jgs 2: 1 An a of the LORD went up from Gilgal to
2: 4 When the a of the LORD had made these
6:11 Then the a of the LORD came and sat under
6:12 the a of the LORD appeared to him and said,
6:20 The a of God said to him,
6:21 the a of the LORD stretched out the tip of
6:21 the a of the LORD disappeared from sight.
6:22 aware that it had been the a of the LORD,
6:22 I have seen the a of the LORD face to face!"
13: 3 An a of the LORD appeared to the woman and
13: 6 he had the appearance of an a of God,
13: 9 and the a of God came again to the woman
13:13 The a of the LORD answered Manoah,
13:15 Then Manoah said to the a of the LORD,
13:16 But the a of the LORD answered Manoah,
13:16 knowing that it was the a of the LORD,
13:18 The a of the LORD answered him,
13:20 the a of the LORD ascended in the flame of
13:21 but the a of the LORD was seen no more by
13:21 realizing that it was the a of the LORD,
1Sm 29:10 you are as acceptable to me as an a of God.
2Sm 14:17 my lord the king is like an a of God,
14:20 But my lord is as wise as an a of God,
19:28 But my lord the king is like an a of God.
24:16 But when the a stretched forth his hand
24:16 a causing the destruction among the people,
24:16 The a of the LORD was then standing at the
24:17 saw the a who was striking the people,
1Kgs 13:18 and an a told me in the word of the LORD
19: 5 but then an a touched him and ordered him
19: 7 the a of the LORD came back a second time,
2Kgs 1: 3 a of the LORD said to Elijah the Tishbite:
1:15 Then the a of the LORD said to Elijah,
19:35 That night the a of the LORD went forth
1Chr 21:12 destroying a in every part of Israel?
21:15 God also sent an a to destroy Jerusalem;
21:15 the calamity, and said to the destroying a,
21:15 The a of the LORD was then standing by the
21:16 he saw the a of the LORD standing between
21:18 Then the a of the LORD commanded Gad to
21:27 to the a to return his sword to its sheath.
21:30 fearful of the sword of the a of the LORD.
2Chr 32:21 Then the LORD sent an a,
Tb 5: 4 he found the a Raphael standing before him,
5: 4 he did not know that this was an a of God.
5:17 and may his a accompany you for safety,
5:22 For a good a will go with him,
6: 2 the boy left home, accompanied by the a,
6: 4 But the a said to him,
6: 5 The a then told him:
6: 7 The boy asked the a this question:
12:22 done when the a of God appeared to them.
Est D:13 "I saw you, my lord, as an a of God,
1Mc 7:41 your a went out and killed a hundred and
2Mc 11: 6 and tears to send a good a to save Israel.
15:22 a in the days of King Hezekiah of Judea,
15:23 send a good a now to spread fear
Jb 33:23 If then there be for him an a,
Ps(s) 34: 8 The a of the LORD encamps around those who
35: 5 with the a of the LORD driving them on.
35: 6 with the a of the LORD pursuing them.
Is 37:36 The a of the LORD went forth and struck
63: 9 It was not a messenger or an a,
Bar 6: 6 for my a is with you,
Dn 3:49 But the a of the Lord went down into the
3:95 who sent his a to deliver the servants
6:23 My God has sent his a and closed the
13:55 "for the a of God shall receive the
13:59 "for the a of God waits with a sword to
14:34 the field, when an a of the Lord told him,
14:36 The a of the Lord seized him by the crown
14:39 the a of the Lord at once brought Habakkuk
Hos 12: 5 He contended with the a and triumphed,
Zec 1: 9 and the a who spoke with me answered me,
1:11 And they answered the a of the LORD who
1:12 Then the a of the LORD spoke out and said,
1:13 To the a who spoke with me,
1:14 And the a who spoke with me said to me,
2: 2 the a who spoke with me what these were.
2: 7 Then the a who spoke with me advanced,
2: 7 and another a came out to meet him,
3: 1 priest standing before the a of the LORD,
3: 2 And the a of the LORD said to Satan,
3: 3 Now Joshua was standing before the a,
3: 5 Then the a of the LORD,
3: 6 The a of the LORD then gave Joshua this
4: 1 Then the a who spoke with me returned
4: 4 Then I said to the a who spoke with me,
4: 5 And the a who spoke with me replied,
5: 5 Then the a who spoke with me came forward
5:10 the air, I said to the a who spoke with me,
6: 4 I asked the a who spoke with me,
6: 5 The a said to me in reply,
12: 8 godlike, like an a of the LORD before them.
Mt 1:20 suddenly the a of the Lord appeared
1:24 When Joseph awoke he did as the a of the
2:13 the a of the Lord suddenly appeared in a
2:19 the a of the Lord appeared in a dream to
28: 2 as the a of the Lord descended from heaven.
28: 5 Then the a spoke, addressing the women:
Lk 1:11 hour, an a of the Lord appeared to him,
1:13 The a said to him: "Do not be frightened,
1:18 Zechariah said to the a: "How am I to know
1:19 The a replied: "I am Gabriel,
1:26 the a Gabriel was sent from God to a town
1:28 Upon arriving, the a said to her:
1:30 The a went on to say to her:
1:34 Mary said to the a, "How can this be
1:35 The a answered her: "The Holy Spirit
1:38 With that the a left her.
2: 9 The a of the Lord appeared to them as the
2:10 The a said to them: "You have nothing to fear
2:13 the a a multitude of the heavenly host,
2:21 a had given him before he was conceived.
22:43 An a then appeared to him from heaven to
Jn 12:29 maintained, "An a was speaking to him."
Acts 5:19 a of the Lord opened the gates of the jail,
6:15 Stephen's face seemed like that of an a.
7:30 "Forty years later an a appeared to him
7:35 the a appearing to him in the thornbush,
7:38 the a on Mount Sinai and with our fathers;
8:26 An a of the Lord then addressed himself to
11:13 He informed us that he had seen an a
11:13 in his house and that the a had said:
12: 7 Suddenly an a of the Lord stood nearby and
12: 8 The a said, "Put on your belt
12: 8 the a told him, "Now put on your cloak
12:10 narrow alley, when suddenly the a left him.
12:11 Lord has sent his a to rescue me
12:15 All they could say was, "It must be his a."
12:23 The a of the Lord struck Herod down at
23: 9 If a spirit or an a has spoken to him.
1Cor 10:10 them did, to be killed by the destroying a.
2Cor 11:14 Satan disguises himself as an a of light.
12: 7 an a of Satan to beat me and keep me from
Gal 1: 8 For even if we, or an a from heaven,
4:14 you took me to yourselves as an a of God,
Heb 11:28 a might not touch the first-born of Israel.
Rv 1: 1 known by sending his a to his servant John,
5: 2 a mighty a who proclaimed in a loud voice:
7: 2 I saw another a come up from the east
8: 3 Another a came in holding a censer of gold.
8: 5 Then the a took the censer,
8: 7 When the first a blew his trumpet,
8: 8 When the second a blew his trumpet,
8:10 When the third a blew his trumpet,
8:12 When the fourth a blew his trumpet,
9: 1 Then the fifth a blew his trumpet,
9:11 king was the a in charge of the abyss,
9:13 Then the sixth a blew his trumpet,
9:14 It said to the sixth a,
10: 1 a come down from heaven wrapped in a cloud,
10: 5 Then the a whom I saw standing on the sea
10: 7 for the seventh a to blow his trumpet,
10: 8 the a standing on the sea and on the land."
10: 9 I went up to the a and said to him,
11:15 Then the seventh a blew his trumpet.
14: 6 Then I saw another a flying in midheaven,
14: 8 A second a followed and cried out:
14: 9 A third a followed the others and said in
14:15 Another a came out of the temple and in a
14:17 out of the temple in heaven came another a,
14:18 second a, who was in charge of the fire
14:19 So the a wielded his sickle over the earth
16: 2 The first a went out,
16: 3 second a poured out his bowl on the sea.
16: 4 The third a poured out his bowl on the
16: 5 the a in charge of the waters cry out:
16: 8 fourth a poured out his bowl on the sun.
16:10 The fifth a poured out his bowl on the
16:12 The sixth a poured out his bowl on the
16:17 a poured out his bowl upon the empty air.
17: 3 The a then carried me away in spirit to a
17: 7 The a said to me: "Why are you so taken
17:15 The a then said to me:
18: 1 I saw another a coming down from heaven.
18:21 A powerful a picked up a stone like a
19: 9 The a then said to me:
19: 9 The a continued, "These words are true
19:17 Next I saw an a standing on the sun.
20: 1 Then I saw an a come down from heaven,
20: 3 The a hurled him into the abyss,
21:17 by the unit of measurement the a used.
22: 1 The a then showed me the river of
22: 6 a said to me: "These words are trustworthy
22: 6 has sent his a to show his servants what
22: 8 at the feet of the a who showed them to me.
22:16 who have sent my a to give you this

ANGELIC (3)

1Cor 13: 1 I speak with human tongues and a as well,
1Pt 3:22 with a rulers and powers subjected to him.
Jude 1: 8 God's dominion and revile the a beings.

ANGELS (99)

Gn 19: 1 The two a reached Sodom in the evening,
19:12 Then the a said to Lot:
19:15 As dawn was breaking the a urged Lot on,
Dt 32:43 you heavens, glorify him, all you a of God;
1Chr 12:23 a vast encampment, like an encampment of a.
Tb 11:14 great name, and blessed be all his holy a.
12:15 one of the seven a who enter and serve
Jb 4:18 servants, and with his a he can find fault.
Ps(s) 8: 6 You have made him little less than the a,
91:11 to his a he has given command about you,
103:20 Bless the LORD, all you his a,
138: 1 presence of the a I will sing your praise;
148: 2 Praise him, all you his a,
Wis 16:20 of a and furnished them bread from heaven,
Dn 3:58 A of the Lord, bless the Lord,
Mt 4: 6 'He will bid his a take care of you;
4:11 left him, and a came and waited on him.
13:39 the world, while the harvesters are the a.
13:41 The Son of Man will dispatch his a to
13:42 The a will hurl them into the fiery
13:49 A will go out and separate the wicked from
16:27 his Father's glory accompanied by his a.
18:10 their a in heaven constantly behold my
22:30 in marriage but live like a in heaven.
24:31 his a 'with a mighty trumpet blast,
24:36 it, neither the a in heaven nor the Son,
25:31 his glory, escorted by all the a of heaven,
25:41 fire prepared for the devil and his a!
26:53 notice more than twelve legions of a?
Mk 1:13 with the wild beasts, and a waited on him.
8:38 with the holy a in his Father's glory."
12:25 in marriage but live like a in heaven.
13:27 He will dispatch his a and assemble his
13:32 neither the a in heaven nor even the Son,
Lk 2:15 When the a had returned to heaven,
4:10 has it, 'He will bid his a watch over you';
9:26 and that of his Father and his holy a.
12: 8 will acknowledge him before the a of God.
12: 9 disowned in the presence of the a of God.
15:10 the a of God over one repentant sinner."
16:22 was carried by a to the bosom of Abraham.
20:36 like a and are no longer liable to death.
24:23 a vision of a who declared he was alive.
Jn 1:51 the a of God ascending and descending
20:12 and there she saw two a in dazzling robes.
Acts 7:53 the ministry of a have not observed it."
12: 9 this was taking place through the a help.
23: 8 and that there are neither a nor spirits,
Rom 8:38 nor life, neither a nor principalities,
1Cor 4: 9 to the universe, to a and men alike.
6: 3 Do you not know that we are to judge a?
11:10 submission on her head, because of the a.
Gal 3:19 of transgressions and promulgated by a,
Col 2:18 insisting on servility in the worship of a.
2Thes 1: 7 is revealed from heaven with his mighty a;
1Tm 3:16 Seen by the a;
5:21 before God, Christ Jesus, and the chosen a:
Heb 1: 4 as far superior to the a as the name he
1: 5 To which of the a did God ever say,
1: 6 says, "Let all the a of God worship him."

1: 7 Of the *a* he says, "He makes his angels
1:13 To which of the *a* has God ever said,
2: 2 the word spoken through *a* stood unchanged,
2: 5 subject to *a*.
2: 7 him for a little while lower than the *a*;
2: 9 made for a little while lower than the *a*,
2:16 Surely he did not come to help *a*,
12:22 to myriads of *a* in festal gathering,
13: 2 some have entertained *a* without knowing it.
1Pt 1:12 Into these matters *a* long to search.
2Pt 2: 4 Did God spare even the *a* who sinned?
2:11 reviling celestial beings, on whom *a*,
Jude 1: 6 There were *a*, too, who did not keep
1: 7 indulged in lust, just as those *a* did;
Rv 3: 5 him in the presence of my Father and his *a*.
5:11 I heard the voices of many *a* who
7: 1 After this I saw four *a* standing at the
7: 2 four *a* who were given power
7:11 All the *a* who were standing around the
8: 2 the seven *a* who minister in God's presence
8: 4 From the *a* hand the smoke of the incense
8: 6 The seven *a* with the seven trumpets made
8:13 blasts the other three *a* are about to blow!"
9:14 "Release the four *a* who are tied up on
9:15 So the four *a* were released;
10:10 little scroll from the *a* hand and ate it.
12: 7 and his *a* battled against the dragon.
12: 7 Although the dragon and his *a* fought back,
14:10 before the holy *a* and before the Lamb,
15: 1 seven *a* holding the seven final plagues
15: 6 came the seven *a* holding the seven plagues.
15: 6 The *a* were dressed in pure white linen,
15: 7 gave to the seven *a* seven golden bowls
15: 8 plagues of the seven *a* had come to an end.
16: 1 from the sanctuary say to the seven *a*,
17: 1 Then one of the seven *a* who were holding
21: 9 One of the seven *a* who held the seven
21:12 gates at which twelve *a* were stationed.

ANGER (240)

Gn 27:45 your brother's *a* against you subsides]
30: 2 In *a* Jacob retorted,
Ex 11: 8 that he left Pharaoh's presence in hot *a*.
15: 8 At a breath of your *a* the waters piled up,
19:22 else he will vent his *a* upon them."
19:24 else he will vent his *a* upon them."
34: 6 to *a* and rich in kindness and fidelity,
Nm 14:18 LORD is slow to *a* and rich in kindness,
22:22 the *a* of God flared up at him for going,
22:27 So, in *a*, he again beat the ass
24:10 in a blaze of *a* at Balaam and said to him,
25: 3 the LORD's *a* flared up against Israel.
25:11 has turned my *a* from the Israelites by his
32:13 So in his *a* with the Israelites the LORD
Dt 9:19 the fierce *a* of the LORD against you:
9:22 likewise, you provoked the LORD to *a*.
19: 6 in the heat of his *a* pursue the homicide
29:27 furious wrath and tremendous *a* the LORD
31:17 that time my *a* will flare up against them;
32:19 and *a* toward his sons and daughters.
32:21 with a foolish nation I will *a* them.
Jos 7: 1 and the *a* of the LORD flared up against
7:26 Then the *a* of the LORD relented.
23:16 the *a* of the LORD will flare up against
Jgs 2:14 the *a* of the LORD flared up against Israel,
2:20 In his *a* toward Israel the LORD said,
3: 8 the *a* of the LORD flared up against them,
8: 3 he said this, their *a* against him subsided.
14:19 Then he went off to his own family in *a*,
1Sm 20:34 sprang up from the table in great *a*
28:18 not carry out his fierce *a* against Amalek,
2Sm 6: 8 because the LORD had vented his *a* on Uzzah.
24: 1 The LORD's *a* against Israel flared again,
1Kgs 8:46 and in your *a* against them you deliver
15:30 provoked the LORD, the God of Israel, to *a*.
16: 2 to sin, provoking me to *a* by their sins,
16: 7 LORD, provoking him to *a* by his evil deeds,
16:13 the God of Israel, to *a* by their idols.
16:26 the God of Israel, to *a* by their idols.
16:33 He did more to *a* the LORD,
2Kgs 5:12 With this, he turned about in *a* and left.
17:18 him till, in his great *a* against Israel,
21: 6 in the LORD's sight and provoked him to *a*.
22:13 for the *a* of the LORD has been set
22:17 my *a* is ablaze against this place and it
23:26 from his fiercely burning *a* against Judah.
24:20 The LORD's *a* befell Jerusalem and Judah
1Chr 5:26 Israel incited against them the *a* of Pul,
13:11 the LORD's *a* had broken out against Uzzah.
2Chr 6:36 and in your *a* against them you deliver
12:12 the *a* of the LORD turned from him so that
25:15 *a* of the LORD blazed out against Amaziah,
26:19 the moment he showed his *a* to the priests,
28:11 for the burning *a* of the LORD is upon you."
28:13 and there is a burning *a* upon Israel."
29: 8 Therefore the *a* of the LORD has come upon
29:10 that his burning *a* may withdraw from us.
30: 8 he may turn away his burning *a* from you.
32:25 Therefore *a* descended upon him and upon
32:26 his *a* on them during the time of Hezekiah.
34:21 For the *a* of the LORD has been set
34:25 my *a* is ablaze against this place and
36:16 until the *a* of the LORD against his people
Ezr 10:14 us our God's burning *a* over this affair."
Neh 3:33 his *a* and he became very much incensed.
9:17 compassionate, slow to *a* and rich in mercy;
Jdt 5: 2 In great *a* he summoned all the rulers of
8:14 my brothers, do not *a* the Lord our God.
Est 2:21 in *a* to lay hands on King Ahasuerus.
3: 5 and bow down to him, he was filled with *a*.
D: 7 ablaze with the height of majestic *a*,
D: 8 But God changed the king's *a* to gentleness.
5: 9 of him, he was filled with *a* toward him.
7: 7 *a* and went into the garden of the palace,
7:10 for Mordecai, and the *a* of the king abated.
1Mc 2:44 in their *a* and lawbreakers in their wrath,
2:49 it is a time of disaster and violent *a*.
7:35 He went away in great *a*.
15:36 no reply, but returned to the king in *a*.
2Mc 4:38 Inflamed with *a*,
5:20 in his *a* was restored in all its glory,
9: 4 Overcome with *a*,
13: 4 the *a* of Antiochus against the scoundrel.
14:45 Still breathing, and inflamed with *a*,
Jb 9: 5 he overturns them in his *a*.
15:13 So that you turn your *a* against God and
18: 4 You who tear yourself in your *a*,
20:28 waters that run off in the day of God's *a*.
21:17 upon them, the portion he allots in his *a*?
32: 2 But the *a* of Elihu,
35:15 you have done otherwise, God's *a* punishes,
36:13 impious in heart lay up *a* for themselves;
Ps(s) 2: 5 Then in *a* he speaks to them;
2:12 from the way, when his *a* blazes suddenly.
6: 2 O LORD, reprove me not in your *a*,
7: 7 Rise up, O LORD, in your *a*;
21:10 May the LORD consume them in his *a*;
27: 9 do not in *a* repel your servant.
30: 6 For his *a* lasts but a moment;
37: 8 Give up your *a*, and forsake wrath;
38: 2 O LORD, in your *a* punish me not,
69:25 let the fury of your *a* overtake them.
74: 1 does your *a* smolder against the sheep of
76: 8 can withstand you for the fury of your *a*?
77:10 Does he in *a* withhold his compassion?"
78:21 against Jacob, and *a* rose against Israel,
78:31 When the *a* of God rose against them and
78:38 his *a* and let none of his wrath be roused.
78:49 He loosed against them his fierce *a*,
78:50 of his *a* he spared them not from death,
80: 5 you burn with *a* while your people pray?
85: 4 you have revoked your burning *a*.
85: 6 us, prolonging your *a* to all generations?
86:15 are a God merciful and gracious, slow to *a*,
90: 7 Truly we are consumed by your *a*,
90:11 Who knows the fury of your *a* or your
95:11 Therefore I swore in my *a*:
103: 8 LORD, slow to *a* and abounding in kindness.
138: 7 the *a* of my enemies you raise your hand;
145: 8 merciful, slow to *a* and of great kindness.
Prv 12:16 The fool immediately shows his *a*,
15: 1 calms wrath, but a harsh word stirs up *a*.
19:11 It is good sense in a man to be slow to *a*,
20: 2 he who incurs his *a* forfeits his life.
21:14 A secret gift allays *a*,
27: 4 *A* is relentless,
29:11 The fool gives vent to all his *a*;
30:33 and the stirring of *a* brings forth blood.
Eccl 10: 4 Should the *a* of the ruler burst upon you,
Wis 5:20 shield and whet his sudden *a* for a sword,
10: 3 the unjust man withdrew from her in his *a*,
10:10 the just man fled from his brother's *a*,
11: 9 recognized how the wicked, condemned in *a*,
15: 1 you, our God, are good and true, slow to *a*,
16: 5 serpents, your *a* endured not the end.
18:20 Yet not for long did the *a* last.
18:23 he stood in the midst and checked the *a*,
18:25 for the mere trial of *a* was enough.
Sir 1:19 cannot justify unjust *a*; anger plunges
4: 2 A hungry man grieve not, a needy man *a* not;
5: 7 For mercy and *a* alike are with him;
10:18 a man, nor stubborn *a* to one born of woman.
16:11 For mercy and *a* alike are with him who
26: 8 A drunken wife arouses great *a*,
27:30 Wrath and *a* are hateful things,
28: 3 Should a man nourish *a* against his fellows
28:10 a man's strength, the sterner his *a*,
30:24 Envy and *a* shorten one's life,
31:29 disgrace is wine drunk amid *a* and strife.
36: 6 Rouse your *a*, pour out wrath,
39:28 force and appease the *a* of their Maker.
46: 7 Averted God's *a* from the people and
Is 7: 4 [the blazing *a* of Rezin and the Arameans,
10: 5 My rod in *a*, my staff in wrath.
10:25 brief moment more, and my *a* shall be over;
11:15 hand over the Euphrates in his fierce *a*
12: 1 have been angry with me, your *a* has abated,
13: 3 warriors, eager and bold to carry out my *a*.
13: 9 comes cruel, with wrath and burning *a*;
13:13 LORD of hosts on the day of his burning *a*.
14: 6 That beat down the nations in *a*,
41:11 and disgrace who vent their *a* against you;
42:25 So he poured out wrath upon them, his *a*,
45:16 and disgrace who vent their *a* against him;
45:24 come all who vent their *a* against him.
48: 9 For the sake of my name I restrain my *a*,
63: 3 I trod them in my *a*,
63: 6 I trampled down the peoples in my *a*,
Jer 2:35 at least, his *a* is turned away from me."
4: 4 Lest my *a* break out like fire,
7:20 my *a* and my wrath will pour out upon this
10:10 King, Before whose *a* the earth quakes,
10:24 us, O LORD, but with equity, not in *a*,
12:13 their harvest, the flaming *a* of the LORD.
18:23 proceed against them in the time of your *a*.
21: 5 outstretched hand and mighty arm, in *a*,
23:20 The *a* of the LORD shall not abate until he
30:24 The *a* of the LORD will not abate until he
32:31 day, this city has excited my *a* and wrath,
32:37 together from all the lands to which in *a*,
33: 5 of those whom I slay in my *a* and wrath,
36: 7 for great is the fury of *a* with which the
42:18 Just as my furious *a* was poured out upon
42:18 so shall my *a* be poured out on you when
44: 6 Therefore the fury of my *a* poured forth in
Lam 2: 2 in his *a* the fortresses of daughter Judah;
3: 1 knows affliction from the rod of his *a*,
4:11 The LORD has spent his *a*,
Bar 1:13 and the wrath and *a* of the Lord have not
2:13 Let your *a* be withdrawn from us,
2:20 have brought your wrath and *a* down upon us,
4: 9 indeed saw coming upon you the *a* of God;
4:25 the *a* that has come from God upon you;
Ez 5:13 Thus shall my *a* spend itself,
5:15 *a* and fury and with furious chastisements,
7: 3 I will unleash my *a* against you and judge
7: 8 my fury upon you and spend my *a* upon you;
13:13 of my *a* there shall be a flooding rain,
16:26 so many times that I was provoked to *a*.
20: 8 my *a* on them there in the land of Egypt;
20:21 of spending my *a* on them in the desert;
22:21 the fire of my *a* and smelt you with it.
25:14 Edom in accordance with my *a* and my fury;
35:11 according to your *a* and your envy
38:18 In my *a* and in my jealousy,
Dn 9:16 let your *a* and your wrath be turned away
Hos 7: 6 All the night their *a* sleeps;
11: 9 I will not give vent to my blazing *a*,
13:11 I give you a king in my *a*,
Jl 2:13 gracious and merciful is he, slow to *a*,
Am 1:11 in his *a* and kept his wrath to the end,
Jon 4: 2 are a gracious and merciful God, slow to *a*,
Mi 5:14 I will wreak vengeance in *a* and wrath upon
7:18 Who does not persist in *a* forever,
Na 1: 3 The LORD is slow to *a*,
1: 6 stand firm, and who can face his blazing *a*?
Hb 3: 8 Is your *a* against the streams, O LORD?
Zep 2: 2 comes upon you the blazing *a* of the LORD:
2: 2 comes upon you the day of the LORD's *a*.
2: 3 be sheltered on the day of the LORD's *a*.
3: 8 out upon them my wrath, all my blazing *a*;
Zec 1:12 that have felt your *a* these seventy years?"
7:13 the LORD of hosts in his great *a* said that,
Mt 18:34 Then in *a* the master handed him over to
Mk 3: 5 He looked around at them with *a*,
Acts 7:54 they ground their teeth in *a* at him.
1Cor 10:22 we mean to provoke the Lord to jealous *a*?
13: 5 is not self-seeking, it is not prone to *a*;
2Cor 12:20 find discord, jealousy, outbursts of *a*,
Eph 4:31 rid of all bitterness, all passion and *a*,
6: 4 Fathers, do not *a* your children.
Col 3: 8 all the *a* and quick temper,
1Tm 2: 8 aloft, and be free from *a* and dissension.
Heb 3:11 "Thus I swore in my *a*,
4: 3 "Thus I swore in my *a*.
Jas 1:19 be quick to hear, slow to speak, slow to *a*.
1:20 a man's *a* does not fulfill God's justice.
Rv 11:18 The nations have raged in *a*,
14:10 poured full strength into the cup of his *a*.

ANGERED (17)

Dt 1:37 LORD was *a* against me also on your account,
4:21 Since the LORD was *a* against me on your
9: 7 mind and do not forget how you *a* the LORD,
32:16 gods and *a* him with abominable idols.
32:21 'no-god' and *a* me with their vain idols,
1Sm 29: 4 chiefs were *a* at this and said to him:
1Kgs 14:22 and by their sins *a* him even more than
2Chr 28:25 Thus he *a* the LORD, the God of his fathers.
Ezr 9:14 Would you not become so *a* with us as to
2Mc 10:35 army of Maccabeus, *a* over such blasphemies,
13:25 of that city were *a* by the peace treaty;
Ps(s) 78:58 They *a* him with their high places and with
106:32 They *a* him at the waters of Meribah,
Eccl 5: 5 lest God be *a* by such words and destroy
Jer 52: 3 so *a* the LORD that he cast them
Bar 4: 6 It was because you *a* God that you were
Heb 3:10 I was *a* with that generation and I said,

ANGERS (1)

Sir 3:16 of his Creator, he who *a* his mother.

ANGLE (4)

2Chr 26: 9 Gate, at the Valley Gate, and at the *A*,
Neh 3:24 Azariah to the Corner [that is, to the *A*.
3:31 and as far as the upper chamber of the *A*.

ANGLE (cont.)
3:32 upper chamber of the *A* and the Sheep Gate,

ANGLES (1)
2Chr 26:15 stand on the towers and at the *a* of the walls

ANGRY (100)
Gn 18:32 Lord grow *a* if I speak up this last time.
40: 2 Pharaoh was *a* with his two courtiers,
41:10 Once, when Pharaoh was *a*,
44:18 and do not become *a* with your servant,
Ex 4:14 Then the LORD became *a* with Moses and said,
32:22 Aaron replied, "Let not my lord be *a*.
Lv 10:16 he was *a* with the surviving sons of Aaron,
Nm 11:10 tents, so that the LORD became very *a*,
12: 9 So *a* was the LORD against them that when
16:15 Moses became very *a* and said to the LORD,
16:22 sin make you *a* with the whole community?"
31:14 became *a* with the officers of the army,
Dt 1:34 When the LORD heard your words, he was *a*;
3:26 But the LORD was *a* with me on your account
9: 8 LORD that he was *a* enough to destroy you,
9:20 With Aaron, too, the LORD was deeply *a*,
29:26 that is why the LORD was *a* with this land
Jos 22:18 be *a* with the whole community of Israel!
Jgs 6:39 "Do not be *a* with me if I speak once more.
9:30 was *a* and sent messengers to Abimelech in
10: 7 the LORD became *a* with Israel and allowed
1Sm 11: 6 God rushed upon him and he became very *a*.
15:11 grew *a* and cried out to the LORD all night.
17:28 the men, he grew *a* with David and said:
18: 8 Saul was very *a* and resentful of the song,
20: 7 But if he becomes quite *a*,
20:30 extremely *a* with Jonathan and said to him:
2Sm 6: 7 But the LORD was *a* with Uzzah;
11:20 the king may become *a* and say to you:
12: 5 very *a* with that man and said to Nathan:
13:21 word of the whole affair, became very *a*.
19:43 Why are you *a* over this affair?
1Kgs 11: 9 The LORD, therefore, became *a* with Solomon,
20:43 Disturbed and *a*,
21: 4 Ahab went home disturbed and *a* at the
21: 5 "Why are you so *a* that you will not eat?"
2Kgs 5:11 But Naaman went away *a*,
13: 3 The LORD was *a* with Israel and for a long
13:19 *A* with him, the man of God said:
1Chr 13:10 LORD became *a* with Uzzah and struck him;
2Chr 16:10 But Asa became *a* with the seer and
25:10 however, became furiously *a* with Judah,
26:19 censer for burning the incense, became *a*,
28: 9 was *a* with Judah that he delivered them
Neh 4: 1 they became extremely *a*.
5: 6 I was extremely *a* when I heard the reasons
Tb 2:14 I became very *a* with her over this.
1Mc 3:27 heard about these events, he was *a*;
5: 1 consecrated as before, they were very *a*.
6:28 When the king heard this he was *a*,
6:59 they became *a* and did all these things."
9:69 he was *a* with the lawless men who had
2Mc 4:35 and *a* over the unjust murder of the man.
5:17 the Lord was *a* for a little while
Jb 26:13 With his *a* breath he scatters the waters,
32: 2 He was *a* with Job for considering himself
32: 3 He was *a* also with the three friends
37: 2 *a* voice as it rumbles forth from his mouth!
42: 7 am *a* with you and with your two friends;
Ps(s) 2:12 Lest he be *a* and you perish from the way,
60: 3 you have been *a*;
79: 5 Will you be *a* forever?
85: 6 Will you be ever *a* with us,
106:40 And the LORD grew *a* with his people,
Prv 22:14 with whom the LORD is *a* will fall into it.
25:23 and a backbiting tongue an *a* countenance.
Sg 1: 6 My brothers have been *a* with me;
Sir 43:17 drives on the south wind, the *a* north wind,
45:19 But the LORD saw this and became *a*,
Is 12: 1 though you have been *a* with me,
27: 4 I am not *a*,
34: 2 The LORD is *a* with all the nations and is
47: 6 *A* at my people,
54: 9 So I have sworn not to be *a* with you,
57:16 will not accuse forever, nor always be *a*;
57:17 Because of their wicked avarice I was *a*,
64: 4 Behold, you are *a*,
64: 8 Be not so very *a*,
Jer 3:12 the LORD, I will not remain *a* with you;
Dn 2:12 At this the king became violently *a* and
14:21 The *a* king arrested the priests,
14:28 they were *a* and turned against the king.
Jon 4: 1 displeasing to Jonah, and he became *a*.
4: 4 the LORD asked, "Have you reason to be *a*?"
4: 9 "Have you reason to be *a* over the plant?"
4: 9 reason to be *a*," Jonah answered, "angry
Na 1: 2 the LORD, an avenger is the LORD, and *a*;
Zec 1: 2 The LORD was indeed *a* with your fathers . . .
1:15 exceedingly *a* with the complacent nations;
1:15 whereas I was but a little *a*,
Mal 1: 4 the people with whom the LORD is *a* forever.
Mt 5:22 everyone who grows *a* with his brother
Lk 14:21 master of the house grew *a* at the account.
15:28 The son grew *a* at this and would not go in;
Jn 7:23 how is it you are *a* with me for curing a
Acts 4: 2 *a* because they were teaching the people
Rom 10:19 with a senseless nation I will make you *a*."
Eph 4:26 If you are *a*, let it be without sin.
Heb 3:17 With whom was God *a* for forty years?

ANGUISH (49)
Gn 42:21 the *a* of his heart when he pleaded with us,
42:21 that is why this *a* has now come upon us."
44:34 to see the *a* that would overcome my father."
Ex 15:14 *a* gripped the dwellers in Philistia.
1Kgs 3:26 whose son it was, in the *a* she felt for it,
2Kgs 4:27 "Let her alone, she is in bitter *a*;
Tb 3: 6 command me to be delivered from such *a*;
Est 4: 4 Overwhelmed with *a*,
C:12 Queen Esther, seized with mortal *a*,
2Mc 3:16 of his face manifested the *a* of his soul.
3:21 and the high priest full of dread and *a*.
Jb 6: 2 could my *a* but be measured and my calamity
7:11 I will speak in the *a* of my spirit;
15:24 distress and *a* overpower him.
17: 7 My eye has grown blind with *a*,
Ps(s) 31:23 Once I said in my *a*, "I am cut off
38: 9 I roar with *a* of heart.
48: 7 *a*, like a woman's in labor,
119:143 Though distress and *a* have come upon me,
Prv 1:27 when distress and *a* befall you.
15:13 face, but by mental *a* the spirit is broken.
Wis 5: 3 rueful and groaning through *a* of spirit:
Sir 31:20 Distress and *a* and loss of sleep,
48:19 and they were in *a* like that of childbirth.
Is 8:23 *A* has taken wing, dispelled is darkness:
21: 3 Therefore my loins are filled with *a*,
23: 5 they shall be in *a* at the news of Tyre.
26:16 we cried out in *a* under your chastising.
65:14 grief of heart and howl for *a* of spirit.
Jer 4:31 the *a* of a mother with her first child
6:24 fall our hands, *A* takes hold of us,
14: 2 from Jerusalem ascends a cry of *a*.
15: 8 Suddenly I struck her with *a* and terror.
15:11 with you in the time of misfortune and *a*?
50:43 *A* seizes him,
Bar 2:25 They died in dire *a*,
Ez 7:25 When *a* comes they shall seek peace,
27:31 put on sackcloth, For you they weep in *a*,
30: 4 upon Egypt, and *a* shall be in Ethiopia,
30: 9 they shall be in *a* on the day of Egypt,
30:16 Syene shall writhe in *a*;
Zep 1:15 wrath is that day a day of *a* and distress,
Zec 9: 5 she shall be in great *a*;
Mt 24:21 those days will be more filled with *a*
Lk 12:50 What *a* I feel till it is over!
21:25 On the earth, nations will be in *a*,
22:44 *a* he prayed with all the greater intensity,
Rom 2: 9 affliction and *a* will come upon every man
2Cor 2: 4 is why I wrote you in great sorrow and *a*,

ANGUISHED (2)
Dt 28:65 LORD will give you an *a* heart
Dn 7:15 my spirit *a* within its sheath of flesh,

ANGULAR (1)
1Kgs 7:31 work at the opening, on panels that were *a*,

ANIAM (1)
1Chr 7:19 Shemida were Ahian, Shechem, Likhi, and *A*.

ANIM (1)
Jos 15:50 (that is, Debir), Anab, Eshtemoh, *A*,

ANIMAL (63)
Gn 7: 2 Of every clean *a*, take with you seven
7:14 of wild beast, every kind of domestic *a*,
8:20 from every clean *a* and every clean bird,
9: 5 from every *a* I will demand it,
30:32 every dark *a* among the sheep
30:33 any *a* in my possession that is not a
31:39 never brought you an *a* torn by wild beasts;
43:16 and have an *a* slaughtered and prepared,
Ex 10:26 Not an *a* must be left behind.
21:34 restoring the value of the *a* to its owner;
21:34 the dead *a*, however, he may keep.
21:35 as well as the dead *a* equally between them.
21:36 but the dead *a* he may keep.
22: 9 or any other *a* to another for safekeeping,
22:12 not make restitution for the mangled *a*.
22:13 a man borrows an *a* from his neighbor,
22:18 who lies with an *a* shall be put to death.
Lv 1: 2 wishes to bring an *a* offering to the LORD,
3: 1 the LORD either a male or a female *a*,
3: 6 he may offer either a male or a female *a*,
5: 2 as the carcass of an unclean wild *a*,
5: 2 animal, or that of an unclean domestic *a*,
5: 6 to the LORD a female *a* from the flock,
5: 7 he cannot afford an *a* of the flock,
7:21 uncleanness be of human or of *a* origin
7:24 Although the fat of an *a* that has died a
7:25 If anyone eats the fat of an *a* from which
7:26 of any blood, be it of bird or of *a*.
11: 3 any *a* that has hoofs you may eat,
17:13 catches an *a* or a bird that may be eaten,
17:15 who eats of an *a* that died of itself or
18:23 shall not have carnal relations with an *a*,
18:23 herself in front of an *a* to mate with it;
20:15 If a man has carnal relations with an *a*,
20:15 be put to death, and the *a* shall be slain.
20:16 a woman goes up to any *a* to mate with it,
20:16 it, the woman and the *a* shall be slain;
22: 8 by eating of any *a* that has died
22:22 *a* on the altar as an oblation to the LORD.
24:18 *a* shall make restitution of another animal.
24:21 Whoever slays an *a* shall make restitution,
27: 9 to the LORD is an *a* that may be sacrificed,
27: 9 every such *a*, when vowed to the LORD,
27:10 to offer one *a* in place of another,
27:11 If the *a* vowed to the LORD is unclean and
27:13 If the offerer wishes to redeem the *a*,
27:26 "Note that a first-born *a*,
27:27 but if it is an unclean *a*,
27:28 human being or an *a* or a hereditary field,
27:32 every tenth *a* as they are counted
27:33 both the original *a* and its substitute
Dt 4:17 of any *a* on the earth or of any bird that
14: 6 Any *a* that has hoofs you may eat,
14:21 must not eat any *a* that has died of itself,
17: 1 the flock an *a* with any serious defect;
21: 3 been put to work as a draft *a* under a yoke,
27:21 'Cursed be he who has relations with any *a*!'
2Kgs 14: 9 but an *a* of Lebanon passed by and trampled
2Mc 5:11 Raging like a wild *a*,
Mal 1: 8 When you offer a blind *a* for sacrifice,
Lk 19:35 Then they led the *a* to Jesus,
Heb 12:20 "If even an *a* touches the mountain,
Jas 3:15 It is earthbound, a kind of *a*,

ANIMALS (83)
Gn 1:24 creeping things, and wild *a* of all kinds."
1:25 God made all kinds of wild *a*,
1:26 and over all the wild *a* and all the
1:30 be your food, and to all the *a* of the land,
2:19 wild *a* and various birds of the air,
2:20 the birds of the air, and all the wild *a*;
3: 1 of all the *a* that the LORD God had made.
3:14 all the *a* and from all the wild creatures;
7: 2 and of the unclean *a*,
7: 8 Of the clean *a* and the unclean,
7:21 birds, cattle, wild *a*,
8: 1 then God remembered Noah and all the *a*,
8:17 birds or *a* or creeping things of the earth
8:19 and all the *a*, wild and tame,
9: 2 all the *a* of the earth and all the birds
9:10 and the various tame and wild *a* that were
26:14 such flocks and herds, and so many work *a*,
29: 7 it is hardly the time to bring the *a* home.
30:32 Only such *a* shall be my wages.
30:38 the *a* were in heat as they came to drink,
30:38 front of the *a* that drank from the troughs.
30:40 and he set these *a* to face the streaked or
30:40 streaked or fully dark-colored *a* of Laban.
30:41 whenever the hardier *a* were in heat,
30:41 in the troughs in full view of these *a*,
30:42 weaker *a* he would not put the rods there.
30:42 So the feeble *a* would go to Laban,
31: 8 said, 'The speckled *a* shall be your wages,'
31: 8 said, 'The streaked *a* shall be your wages,'
32:17 He put these *a* in charge of his servants,
32:18 To whom do these *a* ahead of you belong?'
34:23 all their *a*— then be ours?
36: 6 comprising various *a* and all the property
45:17 Load up your *a* and go without delay to the
Ex 11: 5 as well as all the first-born of the *a*.
11: 7 and their *a* not even a dog shall growl,
12:29 as well as all the first-born of the *a*.
13:12 of your *a* shall belong to the LORD.
22: 3 he shall restore two *a* for each one stolen.
Lv 11: 2 all land *a* these are the ones you may eat:
11:26 All hoofed *a* that are not cloven-footed or
11:39 one of the *a* that you could otherwise eat,
11:46 "This is the law for *a* and birds and for
19:19 *a* with others of a different species;
20:25 apart, then, the clean *a* from the unclean,
22:25 such *a* to offer up as the food of your God;
25: 7 livestock and for the wild *a* on your land.
Nm 7:87 The *a* for the holocausts were,
7:88 The *a* for the peace offerings were,
18:15 first-born of man, as well as of unclean *a*,
35: 3 serve their herds and flocks and other *a*.
Dt 11:15 forth grass in your fields for your *a*.
14: 4 These are the *a* you may eat:
1Sm 9: 4 of Benjamin, but they failed to find the *a*.
2Sm 21:10 on them by day, and the wild *a* by night.
1Kgs 5: 8 For the chariot horses and draft *a* also,
2Kgs 3: 9 out for the army and for the *a* with them.
3:17 your livestock and your pack *a* to drink.'
Neh 2:12 and with no other *a* but my own mount.
10:37 the first-born of our children and our *a*,
Jdt 4:10 their wives, and children, and domestic *a*.
11:12 ran low, they decided to kill their *a*,
1Mc 1:47 shrines, to sacrifice swine and unclean *a*,
2Mc 5:27 companions lived like wild *a* in the hills,
9:15 to be eaten by vultures and wild *a*;
10: 6 like wild *a* in caves on the mountains.
Jb 1: 3 she-asses, and a great number of work *a*,

40:20 to him, and of all wild *a* he makes sport.
Ps(s) 50:10 For mine are all the *a* of the forests,
148:10 You wild beasts and all tame *a*,
Wis 7:20 positions of the stars, natures of *a*,
17:19 rocks, Or the unseen gallop of bounding *a*,
19:10 young of *a* the land brought forth gnats,
19:21 the perishable *a* that went about in them,
Is 40:16 fuel, nor its *a* be enough for holocausts.
Ez 32:13 of her *a* perish beside her abundant waters;
Acts 15:20 sexual union, from the meat of strangled *a*,
15:29 from blood, from the meat of strangled *a*,
21:25 to idols, blood, the flesh of strangled *a*,
1Cor 15:39 Men have one kind of body, *a* another.
Heb 13:11 The bodies of the *a* whose blood is brought
2Pt 2:12 brute *a* born to be caught and destroyed.
Jude 1:10 things they know by instinct, like brute *a*.

ANIMOSITY (1)

2Chr 21:16 *a* of the Philistines

ANKLE-DEEP (1)

Ez 47: 3 had me wade through the water, which was *a*.

ANKLE-LENGTH (1)

Rv 1:13 One like a Son of Man wearing an *a* robe,

ANKLES (1)

Acts 3: 7 the beggar's feet and *a* became strong;

ANKLET (1)

Nm 31:50 article he has picked up, such as an *a*,

ANKLETS (3)

Jdt 10: 4 sandals for her feet, and put on her *a*,
Is 3:16 they go, their *a* tinkling with every step,
3:18 will do away with the finery of the *a*,

ANNA (8)

Tb 1: 9 When I reached manhood I married *A*,
1:20 except for my wife *A* and my son Tobiah.
2: 1 *A* and my son Tobiah were restored to me.
2:11 my wife *A* worked for hire at weaving cloth,
10: 4 His wife *A* said,
11: 5 *A* sat watching the road by which her son
11: 9 Then *A* ran up to her son,
Lk 2:36 was also a certain prophetess, *A* by name,

ANNALS (1)

Est 2:23 was written in the *a* for the king's use.]

ANNAS (4)

Lk 3: 2 the high-priesthood of *A* and Caiaphas,
Jn 18:13 They led him first to *A*,
18:24 *A* next sent him,
Acts 4: 6 next day in Jerusalem, *A* the high priest,

ANNEX (3)

1Kgs 6: 5 an *a* of several stories was built.
6: 8 the *a* was at the right side of the temple,
6:10 The *a*, with its lowest story

ANNEXED (1)

1Mc 10:30 or from the three districts *a* from Samaria.

ANNIHILATE (1)

2Thes 2: 8 and *a* him by manifesting his own presence.

ANNIHILATED (2)

Dt 7:23 will rout them utterly until they are *a*.
Sir 41:11 but a virtuous name will never be *a*.

ANNIHILATION (1)

1Mc 5: 5 he vowed their *a* and burned down the

ANNIVERSARY (4)

Dt 16: 6 on the *a* of your departure from Egypt,
1Mc 4:54 On the *a* of the day on which the Gentiles
4:59 on the *a* every year for eight days,
2Mc 10: 5 On the *a* of the day on which the temple

ANNOUNCE (35)

Lv 23:44 Thus did Moses *a* to the Israelites the
Nm 25:12 *A*, therefore, that I hereby give
Dt 5: 5 time, to *a* to you these words of the LORD:
1Sm 3:13 I *a* to him that I am condemning his family
1Chr 16:23 the LORD, all the earth, *a* his salvation,
Ps(s) 96: 2 *a* his salvation,
Is 42: 9 they spring into being, I *a* them to you.
43:21 for myself, that they might *a* my praise.
44: 8 did I not *a* and foretell it long ago?
48: 6 From now on I *a* new things to you,
61: 2 To *a* a year of favor from the LORD and a
63: 1 "It is I, I who *a* vindication,
Jer 4:15 Dan, from Mount Ephraim they *a* destruction:
4:16 known to the nations, *a* it to Jerusalem:
5:20 *A* this to the house of Jacob,
23:18 Who has heeded his word, so as to *a* it?
46:14 *A* it in Egypt,
50: 2 *A* and publish it among the nations;
50:28 They *a* in Zion the vengeance of the LORD,
Dn 9:23 an answer was given which I have come to *a*,
Hos 5: 9 tribes of Israel I *a* what is sure to be.
Jon 3: 2 *a* to it the message that I will tell you."
Mi 3: 5 teeth have something to bite, *a* peace,
Mt 13:35 I will *a* what has lain hidden since the
Mk 16:10 went to *a* the good news to his followers,
Lk 4:19 To *a* a year of favor from the Lord."
4:43 I must *a* the good news of the reign of God,
Jn 16:13 and will *a* to you the things to come.
16:14 received from me what he will *a* to you.
16:15 what he will *a* to you he will have from me.
Acts 13:32 "We ourselves *a* to you the good news that
16:32 They proceeded to *a* the word of God to him
Rom 10:15 are the feet of those who *a* good news!"
Heb 2:12 "I will *a* your name to my brothers,
1Jn 1: 5 we have heard from him and *a* to you:

ANNOUNCED (26)

Ex 16:10 *a* this to the whole Israelite community,
1Kgs 1:23 When he had been *a*,
2Kgs 3:16 of the LORD came upon Elisha and he *a*:
7:11 The gatekeepers *a* this and it was reported
2Chr 34:18 Then Shaphan the scribe *a* to the king,
Jdt 10:22 When they *a* her to him,
11:19 This was told me, and *a* to me in advance,
Ps(s) 40:10 I *a* your justice in the vast assembly;
Is 21:10 hosts, The God of Israel, I have *a* to you.
41:26 Who *a* this from the beginning,
44: 7 Who of old *a* future events?
44:26 I carry out the plan *a* by my messengers;
45:21 Who *a* this from the beginning and foretold
Mi 7: 4 The day *a* by your watchmen!
Mk 16:13 steps and *a* the good news to the others;
16:20 his companions all that had been *a* to them.
Lk 24:25 to believe all that the prophets have *a*!
Jn 20:18 "I have seen the Lord!" she *a*.
Acts 3:18 he *a* long ago through all the prophets:
3:24 onward, have *a* the events of these days.
12:14 but ran in and *a* that Peter was outside.
Eph 2:17 He came and *a* the good news of peace to
Col 1:23 has been *a* to every creature under heaven,
Heb 2: 3 *A* first by the Lord,
4: 6 it was first *a* did not because of unbelief,
Rv 10: 7 which he *a* to his servants the prophets,

ANNOUNCEMENT (2)

Mt 10: 7 As you go, make this *a*:
Lk 8:49 came from the ruler's house with the *a*,

ANNOUNCING (7)

Is 52: 7 of him who brings glad tidings, *A* peace,
52: 7 peace, bearing good news, *a* salvation,
Jon 3: 4 and had gone but a single day's walk *a*,
Na 2: 1 advances the bearer of good news, *a* peace!
Acts 8:40 and he went about *a* the good news in all
11:20 *a* the good news of the Lord Jesus to them.
20:27 from *a* to you God's design in its entirety.

ANNOYED (1)

Acts 16:18 several days until finally Paul became *a*,

ANNUAL (2)

Lv 25:53 treat him as a servant hired on an *a* basis,
2Kgs 17: 4 pay the *a* tribute to his Assyrian overlord.

ANNUL (1)

2Mc 13:25 that they wanted to *a* its provisions.

ANNULLED (2)

Nm 30:13 since her husband has *a* them,
Heb 7:18 *a* because of its weakness and uselessness,

ANNULS (2)

Nm 30: 9 he thereby *a* the vow she had made or the
30:13 day he learns of them her husband *a* them,

ANOINT (29)

Ex 28:41 *A* and ordain them,
29: 7 take the anointing oil and *a* him with it,
29:36 you shall *a* it in order to consecrate it.
30:26 shall *a* the meeting tent and the ark
30:30 shall also *a* and consecrate as my priests.
40: 9 and *a* the Dwelling and everything in it,
40:10 *A* the altar of holocausts and all its
40:11 Likewise, *a* the laver with its base,
40:13 Aaron with the sacred vestments and *a* him,
40:15 their father, *a* them also as my priests.
Jgs 9: 8 the trees went to *a* a king over themselves.
9:15 wish to *a* me king over you in good faith,
Ru 3: 3 So bathe and *a* yourself;
1Sm 9:16 are to *a* as commander of my people Israel.
15: 1 sent to *a* you king over his people Israel.
16: 3 are to *a* for me the one I point out to you."
16:12 *a* him, for this is he!"
2Sm 14: 2 apparel and do not *a* yourself with oil,
1Kgs 1:34 the prophet are to *a* him king of Israel,
19:15 arrive, you shall *a* Hazael as king of Aram.
19:16 Then you shall *a* Jehu,
2Kgs 9: 3 I *a* you king over Israel
9: 6 I *a* you king over the people of the LORD
9:12 'I *a* you king over Israel.' "
Ps(s) 23: 5 You *a* my head with oil;
Dn 10: 3 and I did not *a* myself at all until the
Am 6: 6 bowls and *a* themselves with the best oils;
Mk 16: 1 with which they intended to go and *a* Jesus.
Lk 7:46 You did not *a* my head with oil,

ANOINTED (107)

Gn 31:13 *a* a memorial stone and made a vow to me.
Ex 29:29 that in them they may be *a* and ordained.
40:15 As you have *a* their father,
40:15 Thus, by being *a*,
Lv 4: 3 if it is the *a* priest who thus sins and
4: 5 The *a* priest shall then take some of the
4:16 the *a* priest shall bring some of its blood
6:13 present to the LORD [on the day he is *a*:
6:15 him as the *a* priest shall do likewise.
7:36 on the day he *a* them the LORD ordered the
8:10 oil, Moses *a* and consecrated the Dwelling,
8:11 seven times on the altar, and *a* the altar,
16:32 priest who has been *a* and ordained
Nm 3: 3 the *a* priests who were ordained to
7: 1 had *a* and consecrated it
7:10 before the altar on the day it was *a*.
7:88 the dedication of the altar after it was *a*.
35:25 high priest who has been *a* with sacred oil.
1Sm 2:10 to his king, and exalt the horn of his *a*!"
2:35 function in the presence of my *a* forever.
10: 1 has *a* you commander over his heritage:
12: 3 in the presence of the LORD and of his *a*.
12: 5 against you this day, and his *a* as well,
15:17 The LORD *a* you king of Israel and sent you
16: 6 "Surely the LORD'S *a* is here before him."
16:13 hand, *a* him in the midst of his brothers;
24: 7 such a thing to my master, the LORD'S *a*,
24: 7 lay a hand on him, for he is the Lord's *a*."
24:11 for he is the LORD's *a* and a father to me.'
26: 9 on the LORD's *a* and remain unpunished?
26:11 But the LORD forbid that I touch his *a*!
26:16 have not guarded your lord, the LORD's *a*.
26:23 my grasp, I would not harm the LORD's *a*.
2Sm 1:14 forth your hand to desecrate the LORD's *a*?"
1:16 when you said, 'I dispatched the LORD's *a*.' "
1:21 the shield of Saul, no longer *a* with oil.
2: 4 there and *a* David king of the Judahites.
2: 7 dead, the Judahites have *a* me their king."
3:39 Although I am the *a* king,
5: 3 the LORD, and they *a* him king of Israel.
5:17 heard that David had been *a* king of Israel,
12: 7 'I *a* you king of Israel.'
12:20 the ground, David washed and *a* himself,
19:11 Absalom, and Absalom, whom we *a* over us,
19:22 He cursed the LORD's *a*."
22:51 to your king and showed kindness to your *a*.
23: 1 man God raised up, *A* of the God of Jacob,
1Kgs 1:39 horn of oil from the tent and *a* Solomon.
1:45 and Nathan the prophet *a* him king at Gihon,
5:15 had been *a* king in place of his father,
2Kgs 11:12 They proclaimed him king and *a* him,
23:30 land took Jehoahaz, son of Josiah, *a* him,
1Chr 11: 3 and they *a* him king over Israel,
14: 8 that David was *a* king over all Israel,
16:22 "Touch not my *a*,
29:22 king, and they *a* him as the LORD'S prince,
2Chr 6:42 LORD God, reject not the plea of your *a*,
22: 7 LORD had *a* to cut down the house of Ahab.
23:11 Jehoiada and his sons *a* him,
28:15 feet, gave them food and drink, *a* them,
Tb 2:10 more they *a* my eyes with various salves,
Jdt 10: 3 with water, and *a* it with rich ointment.
16: 7 She *a* her face with fragrant oil;
2Mc 1:10 and member of the family of the *a* priests,
Ps(s) 2: 2 against the LORD and against his *a*:
18:51 to your king and showed kindness to your *a*,
20: 7 that the LORD has given victory to his *a*,
28: 8 of his people, the saving refuge of his *a*.
45: 8 has *a* you with the oil of gladness above
84:10 shield, and look upon the face of your *a*.
89:21 with my holy oil I have *a* him,
89:39 and spurned and been enraged at your *a*.
89:52 which they have reviled your *a* on his way!
92:11 you have *a* me with rich oil.
105:15 "Touch not my *a*,
132:10 servant, reject not the plea of your *a*.
132:17 I will place a lamp for my *a*.
Sir 45:15 ordained him and *a* him with the holy oil,
46:13 kingdom and *a* princes to rule the people.
46:19 testified before the LORD and his *a* prince,
48: 8 You *a* kings who should inflict vengeance,
Is 45: 1 Thus says the LORD to his *a*,
61: 1 GOD is upon me, because the LORD has *a* me;
Lam 4:20 The *a* one of the LORD,
Ez 16: 4 you were neither washed with water nor *a*,

ANOINTED (cont.)

16: 9 washed away your blood, and *a* you with oil.
Dn 9:24 ratified, and a most holy will be *a*.
9:25 be rebuilt Until one who is *a* and a leader,
9:26 After the sixty-two weeks an *a* shall be
Hb 3:13 to save your people, to save your *a* one.
Zec 4:14 *a* who stand by the LORD of the whole earth."
Mk 6:13 expelled many demons, *a* the sick with oil,
Lk 2:26 death until he had seen the *A* of the Lord.
4:18 therefore, he has *a* me.
7:46 oil, but she has *a* my feet with perfume.
Jn 1:41 The Messiah, . . . (This term means the *A.)*
4:25 Messiah coming. (This term means *A.)*
11: 2 who *a* the Lord with perfume
12: 3 nard, with which she *a* Jesus' feet.
Acts 4:26 against the Lord and against his *a*.'
4:27 your holy Servant, Jesus, whom you *a*—
10:38 God *a* him with the Holy Spirit and power.
2Cor 1:21 it is he who *a* us and has sealed us,
Heb 1: 9 has *a* you with the oil of gladness above
11:26 God's *A* greater riches
Rv 11:15 now belongs to our Lord and to his *A* One,
12:10 of our God and the authority of his *A* One.

ANOINTING (28)

Ex 25: 6 for the *a* oil and for the fragrant incense;
29: 7 Then take the *a* oil and anoint him with it,
29:21 the altar, together with some of the *a* oil,
30:25 and blend them into sacred *a* oil,
30:26 With this sacred *a* oil you shall anoint
30:31 As sacred *a* oil this shall belong to me
30:32 not be used in any ordinary *a* of the body,
31:11 for his sons in their ministry, the *a* oil,
35: 8 for the *a* oil and for the fragrant incense;
35:15 the *a* oil,
35:28 as spices, and oil for the light, *a* oil,
37:29 The sacred *a* oil and the fragrant incense
39:38 for the light, the golden altar, the *a* oil,
40: 9 "Take the *a* oil and anoint the Dwelling
Lv 8: 2 together with the vestments, the *a* oil,
8:10 Taking the *a* oil, Moses anointed
8:12 poured some of the *a* oil on Aaron's head,
8:30 Taking some of the *a* oil and some of the
10: 7 for the *a* oil of the LORD is upon you."
21:10 upon whose head the *a* oil has been poured
21:12 of his God, for with the *a* oil upon him,
Nm 4:16 established cereal offering, and the *a* oil.
7:84 princes of Israel on the occasion of its *a:*
Jas 5:14 *a* him with oil in the Name [of the Lord].
1Jn 2:20 have the *a* that comes from the Holy One,
2:27 the *a* you received from him remains in
2:27 *a* teaches you about all things and is true
2:27 remain in him as that *a* taught you.

ANOINTS (1)

1Sm 10: 1 LORD *a* you commander over his heritage.

ANOTHER (465)

Gn 8:12 He waited still *a* seven days and then
8:19 the earth left the ark, one kind after *a*.
9:11 not be *a* flood to devastate the earth."
11: 3 They said to one *a*, "Come, let us mold
11: 7 that one will not understand what *a* says."
25: 1 Abraham married *a* wife,
26:21 Then they dug *a* well,
26:22 moved on from there, he dug still *a* well;
29:27 for *a* seven years of service with me."
29:30 remained in Laban's service *a* seven years.
30:24 the LORD add *a* son to this one for me!"
37: 9 Then he had *a* dream,
37: 9 "I had *a* dream,"
37:19 They said to one *a:*
38: 5 Then she bore still *a* son,
41: 5 He fell asleep again and had *a* dream.
41:22 In *a* dream I saw seven ears of grain,
41:38 "Could we find *a* like him,"
42: 1 "Why do you keep gaping at one *a?*
42:21 To one *a*, however, they said:
42:28 Trembling, they asked one *a*,
43: 6 by telling the man that you had *a* brother?"
43: 7 Do you have *a* brother?'
43:33 they looked at one *a* in amazement;
44:19 servants, 'Have you a father, or *a* brother?'
Ex 4:11 one man speech and makes *a* deaf and dumb?
4:11 who gives sight to one and makes *a* blind?
10:23 Men could not see one *a*,
16:15 On seeing it, the Israelites asked one *a*,
21:10 If he takes *a* wife,
21:14 *a* after maliciously scheming to do so,
22: 6 article to *a* for safekeeping
22: 8 where *a* claims that the thing is his,
22: 9 or any other animal to *a* for safekeeping,
26: 9 set, and the other six sheets into *a* set.
33:11 Moses face to face, as one man speaks to *a*.
36:16 and the other six sheets into *a* set.
Lv 13: 5 shall quarantine him for *a* seven days,
13:33 shall quarantine him for *a* seven days.
13:54 and then quarantined for *a* seven days.
19:11 shall not lie or speak falsely to one *a*.
19:20 living with *a* man
24:11 This man quarreled publicly with *a*
24:18 animal shall make restitution of *a* animal
24:20 *a* shall be inflicted on him in return.
26:21 me, I will multiply my blows *a* sevenfold,
26:37 over one *a* as if to escape a weapon,
27:10 to offer one animal in place of *a*,
Nm 5:13 to him by having intercourse with *a* man,
8: 8 shall take *a* young bull for a sin offering.
14: 4 So they said to one *a*,
23:13 "Please come with me to *a* place from
23:27 "Come, let me bring you to *a* place;
35:15 *a* unintentionally may take refuge there.
35:16 "If a man strikes *a* with an iron
35:17 If a man strikes *a* with a death-dealing
35:18 If a man strikes *a* with a death-dealing
35:20 "If a man pushes *a* out of hatred,
35:21 *a* out of enmity and causes his death,
35:22 *a* accidentally and not out of enmity,
35:30 "Whenever someone kills *a*,
36: 7 Israelites will pass from one tribe to *a*,
36: 9 no heritage can pass from one tribe to *a*,
Dt 4:34 for himself from the midst of *a* nation,
20: 5 lest he die in battle and *a* dedicate it.
20: 6 battle and *a* enjoy its fruits in his stead.
20: 7 he die in battle and *a* take her to wife.'
22:22 with a woman who is married to *a*,
24: 2 she goes and becomes the wife of *a* man,
28:30 you betroth a wife, *a* man will have her.
Jos 17: 7 *a* boundary ran southward to include the
Jgs 4:17 the Kenite Heber were at peace with one *a*.
6:29 They asked one *a*, "Who did this?"
7:13 one man was telling *a* about a dream.
7:22 the LORD set the sword of one against *a*.
10:18 the princes of Gilead said to one *a*,
11: 2 our family, for you are the son of *a* woman."
17: 8 he set out to find *a* place of residence.
19:10 The man, however, refused to stay *a* night;
20:45 Gidom, killed *a* two thousand of them there.
Ru 3:12 to you, you have *a* relative still closer.
3:14 but rose before men could recognize one *a*.
1Sm 2:25 If a man sins against *a* man,
10: 3 three kids, *a* three loaves of bread,
10: 6 state and will be changed into *a* man.
10: 9 to leave Samuel, God gave him *a* heart.
10:11 among the prophets, they said to one *a*,
13:18 *a* turned in the direction of Beth-horon;
14:20 confused, were thrusting swords at one *a*.
17:30 from him to *a* and asked the same question;
2Sm 14:12 say still *a* word to my lord the king."
18:26 coming nearer, the lookout spied *a* runner.
18:26 out, "There is *a* man running by himself."
19:10 arguing among themselves, saying to one *a:*
21:15 There was *a* battle between the Philistines
21:18 was *a* battle with the Philistines in Gob.
21:19 was *a* battle with the Philistines in Gob,
21:20 There was *a* battle at Gath in which there
1Kgs 4:15 married to Basemath, *a* daughter of Solomon,
7: 8 His living quarters were in *a* court,
11:23 God raised up against Solomon *a* adversary,
13:10 So he departed by *a* road and did not go
18: 6 way by himself, Obadiah *a* way by himself.
20:37 The prophet met *a* man and said,
22:20 And one said this, *a* that,
2Kgs 1:11 Ahaziah sent *a* captain with his company of
3:23 fought among themselves and killed one *a*.
4: 6 she said to her son, "Bring me *a* vessel."
7: 8 Back they came into *a* tent,
7: 9 Then they said to one *a:*
11: 6 *a* third shall be at the gate Sur;
11:17 and *a* covenant,
1Chr 2:26 Jerahmeel also had *a* wife,
12:28 Aaron, with *a* three thousand seven hundred,
16:20 to nation, from one kingdom to *a* people.
17:21 *a* nation on earth whom a god went to
20: 4 there was *a* battle with the Philistines,
20: 6 In still *a* battle, at Gath,
2Chr 6:36 that their captors deport them to *a* land,
18: 7 *a* through whom we may consult the LORD,
18:19 And one said this, *a* that,
23: 5 *a* third must be at the king's palace and
25:12 also brought back *a* ten thousand alive,
30:23 assembly agreed to celebrate *a* seven days.
32: 5 towers upon it, and built *a* wall outside.
35:21 you this day, for my war is with *a* kingdom,
35:24 chariot, placed him in *a* he had in reserve,
Neh 4: 6 had come to us from one place after *a*,
4:13 widely separated from one *a* along the wall;
7:34 sons of *a* Elam,
9: 3 and during *a* fourth part they made their
Tb 2: 8 The neighbors mocked me, saying to one *a:*
6:13 you or let her become engaged to *a* man;
6:16 do not give *a* thought to this demon,
Jdt 7: 4 were, they said to one *a* in great dismay:
10:19 because of her, and they said to one *a*,
Est 4:14 will come to the Jews from *a* source;
8: 3 In *a* audience with the king,
9:19 on which they send gifts of food to one *a*.
9:22 food to one *a* and gifts to the poor.
1Mc 2:40 kinsmen have done," they said to one *a*,
3:43 So they said to one *a*,
5:37 *a* army and camped opposite Raphon,
7:29 to Judas, and they greeted one *a* peaceably.
10:16 said, "Shall we ever find *a* man like him?
12:50 encouraged one *a* and went out in compact
13:28 He set up seven pyramids facing one *a* for
2Mc 4: 8 as eighty talents from *a* source of income.
4:26 and now saw himself cheated by *a* man,
7: 5 mother encouraged one *a* to die bravely,
12:22 that in many cases they wounded one *a*,
15:13 Then in the same way *a* man appeared,
Jb 1:16 *a* came and said, "Lightning has fallen
1:17 While he was yet speaking, *a* came and said,
1:18 While he was yet speaking, *a* came and said,
8:19 the road, and out of the soil *a* sprouts.
21:25 *A* dies in bitterness of soul,
31: 8 my hands, Then may I sow, but *a* eat of it,
31:10 Then may my wife grind for *a*,
41: 9 *a* that they hold fast and cannot be parted.
Ps(s) 75: 8 *a* he lifts up.
105:13 to nation and from one kingdom to *a* people,
109: 8 may *a* take his office.
Prv 2:16 Saving you from the wife of *a*,
6: 1 neighbor, given your hand in pledge to *a*,
11:15 is in a bad way who becomes surety for *a*,
11:24 *a* is too sparing,
13: 7 *a* pretends to be poor,
20:16 Take his garment who becomes surety for *a*,
25: 9 but *a* man's secret do not disclose;
27: 2 Let *a* praise you
27:13 Take his garment who becomes surety for *a*,
27:19 As one face differs from *a*,
27:19 another, so does one human heart from *a*.
Eccl 1: 4 One generation passes and *a* comes,
2:21 wisdom and knowledge and skill, and to *a*,
4: 4 work is the rivalry of one man for *a*.
5: 7 for the high official has *a* higher than he
6: 1 is *a* evil which I have seen under the sun,
7:27 adding one thing to *a* that I might
8: 9 one man tyrannizes over *a* to his hurt.
10: 5 I have seen under the sun *a* evil,
Wis 18:18 And cast half-dead, one here, *a* there,
18:23 had already fallen one on *a* in heaps,
19: 3 of the dead, They adopted *a* senseless plan;
Sir 6: 9 *A* is a friend who becomes an enemy,
6:10 *A* is a friend,
10: 8 *a* because of the violence of the arrogant.
11:12 *A* goes his way a weakling and a failure,
14:18 one falls off and *a* sprouts
14:18 one dies and *a* is born.
20: 4 wise, *a* is talkative and is disliked.
20: 5 *a* is silent,
23:23 adultery she has borne children by *a* man.
33: 7 Why is one day more important than *a*,
33:21 Give not to *a* your wealth,
34:23 If one man builds up and *a* tears down,
34:24 If one man prays and *a* curses,
36:21 yet one girl will be more suitable than *a:*
41:19 of defrauding *a* of his appointed share,
42:25 All of them differ, one from *a*,
Is 2: 4 nation shall not raise the sword against *a*,
3: 5 them, And the people shall oppress one *a*,
21:16 In *a* year, like those of a hireling,
23:15 With the days of *a* king,
34:14 desert beasts, satyrs shall call to one *a;*
41: 6 One man helps *a*,
44: 5 the LORD's," *a* shall be named after Jacob,
44:15 with *a* part he makes a god which he adores,
48:11 My glory I will not give to *a*.
65:15 servants shall be called by *a* name
66:23 From one new moon to *a*,
66:23 to another, and from one sabbath to *a*,
Jer 3: 1 and, after leaving him, she marries *a* man,
3:16 it, or remember it, or miss it, or make *a*.
18: 4 clay *a* object of whatever sort he pleased.
22: 8 will pass by this city and ask one *a:*
23:35 Thus you shall ask, when speaking to one *a*,
26: 6 of the earth shall refer to when cursing *a*.
26:20 There was *a* man who prophesied in the name
36:16 they were frightened and said to one *a*,
36:28 Take *a* scroll, and write on it everything
36:32 Jeremiah took *a* scroll,
46:16 They said one to *a*, "Up!
48:11 He was not poured from one flask to *a*,
51:31 One runner meets *a*,
Bar 2: 3 that one after *a* of us should eat the
4: 3 Give not your glory to *a*,
Ez 1: 8 and the wings of one touched those of *a*.
1:16 as though one wheel were within *a*.
3:13 of the living creatures striking one *a*,
5: 2 place *a* third around the city and strike
5:12 *a* third shall fall by the sword all around
12: 3 on, migrate from where you live to *a* place;
17: 7 But there was *a* great eagle,
19: 5 She took *a* of her whelps,
24:23 because of your sins and groan one to *a*.
33:30 They say to one *a*, "Come and hear
34:17 GOD, I will judge between one sheep and *a*,
34:22 and I will judge between one sheep and *a*.
37:16 Then take *a* stick and write on it:
41:11 entrance on the north and *a* on the south.
46:21 saw that in each corner there was *a* court:
47: 4 He measured off *a* thousand and once more
Dn 2:39 *A* kingdom shall take your place,
2:44 be destroyed or delivered up to *a* people;
7: 6 After this I looked and saw *a* beast,
7: 8 the ten horns it had, when suddenly *a*,
7:24 *a* shall rise up after them,

8: 1 After this first vision, I, Daniel, had *a*,
8:13 *a* said to whichever one it was that spoke,
11:13 the king of the north shall raise *a* army,
13:51 two far from one *a* that I may examine them."
Jl 2: 8 No one crowds *a*,
Am 4: 7 I sent rain upon one city but not upon *a*;
4: 7 by rain, but *a* without rain dried up;
5: 3 *A* that marched out with a hundred shall be
Jon 1: 7 Then they said to one *a*,
Mi 4: 3 nation shall not raise the sword against *a*,
Hg 2:16 *a* went to the vat to draw fifty measures,
Zec 2: 7 advanced, and *a* angel came out to meet him,
3:10 one *a* under your vines and fig trees."
7:10 not plot evil against one *a* in your hearts.
8:16 Speak the truth to one *a*;
8:17 of you plot evil against *a* in his heart,
8:21 of one city shall approach those of *a*,
Mal 3:16 they who fear the LORD spoke with one *a*,
Mt 2:12 went back to their own country by *a* route.
8: 9 If I say to *a*, 'Come here,' he comes.
8:21 *A*, a disciple,
11: 3 'He who is to come' or do we look for *a*?"
13:24 He proposed to them *a* parable:
13:31 He proposed still *a* parable:
13:33 He offered them still *a* image:
13:54 filled with amazement, and said to one *a*,
15:14 If one blind man leads *a*,
18:16 If he does not listen, summon *a*,
19: 9 case) and marries *a* commits adultery,
19:16 *A* time a man came up to him and said,
21:33 "Listen to *a* parable.
21:35 They beat one, killed *a*,
21:38 saw the son, the tenants said to one *a*,
22: 5 way, one to his farm, *a* to his business.
24: 2 you, not one stone will be left on *a*—
24: 7 rise against nation, one kingdom against *a*.
24:10 falter then, betraying and hating one *a*.
25:16 thousand went to invest it and made *a* five.
26:22 this, they began to say to him one after *a*,
26:71 *a* girl saw him and said to those nearby,
27:57 He was *a* of Jesus' disciples,
Mk 1:27 They began to ask one *a*:
2:13 *A* time, while he went walking
4: 1 On *a* occasion he began to teach beside the
4:18 Those sown among thorns are *a* class.
4:24 He said to them *a* time:
4:41 They kept saying to one *a*,
7:10 and in *a* place,
8: 1 At about that time *a* large crowd assembled,
9:50 hearts and you will be at peace with one *a*."
10:11 and marries *a* commits adultery against her;
10:12 her husband and marries *a* commits adultery."
10:26 at this, and exclaimed to one *a*,
12: 4 The second time he sent them *a* servant;
12: 5 He sent yet *a* and they killed him.
12: 7 But those tenants said to one *a*,
13: 2 Not one stone will be left upon *a*—
13: 8 rise against nation, one kingdom against *a*.
14:58 I will construct *a* not made by human hands.'"
15:43 *a* who looked forward to the reign of God.
16: 3 They were saying to one *a*,
Lk 2:15 to heaven, the shepherds said to one *a*:
4:13 he left him, to await *a* opportunity.
4:36 and they began saying to one *a*:
6: 6 On *a* sabbath he came to teach in a
6:11 asking one *a* what could be done to Jesus.
7: 8 to *a*, 'Come here,' and he comes;
8: 4 resorting to him from one town after *a*.
8:25 fear and admiration, they said to one *a*,
9:56 Then they set off for *a* town.
9:59 To *a* he said, "Come after me."
9:61 Yet *a* said to him,
12: 1 so dense that they were treading on one *a*.
13: 8 the man said, 'Sir, leave it *a* year,
14:19 *A* said, 'I have bought five yoke of oxen
14:31 to march on *a* king to do battle with him,
16: 1 *A* time he said to his disciples:
16:18 his wife and marries *a* commits adultery.
19:16 the sum you gave me has earned you *a* ten.'
21: 6 come when not one stone will be left on *a*,
22:59 hour after that *a* spoke more insistently:
24:32 They said to one *a*,
Jn 4:33 At this the disciples said to one *a*,
4:37 'One man sows; *a* reaps.'
5:32 there is *a* who is testifying on my behalf,
5:44 accept praise from one *a*
12:19 The Pharisees remarked to one *a*,
13:22 The disciples looked at one *a*,
13:34 Love one *a*
13:35 your love for one *a*."
14:16 Father and he will give you *a* Paraclete
15:12 love one *a* as I have loved you.
15:17 I give you is this, that you love one *a*.
16:17 At this, some of his disciples asked one *a*:
16:19 "You are asking one *a* about my saying,
18:15 Simon Peter, in company with *a* disciple,
19:37 is still *a* Scripture passage which says:
21:18 and *a* will tie you fast and carry you off
Acts 1:20 And again, 'May *a* take his office.'
2:12 they asked one *a*,
5: 1 *A* man named Ananias and his wife Sapphira
5:15 his shadow might fall on one or *a* of them.
12:17 said, then left them to go off to *a* place.
13:35 That is why he said in still *a* place,
19:14 *A* time, when the seven sons of Sceva,
21: 5 After we had said good-bye to one *a*,
28: 4 from his hand, the natives said to one *a*,
Rom 1:27 with women and burned with lust for one *a*.
2: 1 one of you who judges *a* is inexcusable.
3: 7 *A* question: If my falsehood
7: 3 is still alive, she gives herself to *a*.
7: 3 commit adultery by consorting with *a* man.
7:23 *a* law at war with the law of my mind;
9:21 for a lofty purpose and *a* for a humble one?
12: 5 Christ and individually members one of *a*.
12:10 Love one *a* with the affection of brothers.
13: 8 the debt that binds us to love one *a*.
14:13 we must no longer pass judgment on one *a*.
14:19 to work for peace and to strengthen one *a*.
15: 5 *a* according to the spirit of Christ Jesus,
15: 7 Accept one *a*,
15:14 that you are able to give advice to one *a*.
15:20 build on a foundation laid by *a*
16:16 Greet one *a* with a holy kiss.
1Cor 1:12 of you will say, "I belong to Paul," *a*,
1:12 another, "I belong to Apollos," still *a*,
4: 6 association with one person rather than *a*.
6: 1 How can anyone with a case against *a* dare
6: 5 between one member of the church and *a*?
6: 7 against one *a* is disastrous for you.
7: 5 Do not deprive one *a*,
7: 5 Then return to one *a*,
7: 7 his own gift from God, one this and *a* that.
7:18 come to *a* who had never been circumcised?
10:29 be restricted by *a* man's conscience?
11:21 One person goes hungry while *a* gets drunk.
11:33 you assemble for the meal, wait for one *a*.
12: 8 to *a* the power to express knowledge.
12: 9 same Spirit *a* is given the gift of healing,
12:10 to *a* power to distinguish one spirit from
12:10 power to distinguish one spirit from *a*.
12:10 of healing, and still *a* miraculous powers.
12:10 *a* that of interpreting the tongues.
12:25 all the members may be concerned for one *a*.
14:26 has a psalm, *a* some instruction to give,
14:26 to give, still *a* a revelation to share;
14:26 one speaks in a tongue, *a* interprets.
14:27 with *a* to interpret what they are saying.
14:30 If *a*, sitting by, should happen to receive
15:39 Men have one kind of body, animals *a*.
15:40 bodies is one thing, that of the earthly *a*.
15:41 stars, one differs from *a* in brightness.
16:20 Greet one *a* with a holy kiss.
2Cor 10:12 comparing themselves with one *a*,
10:16 already done by *a* in his alloted territory.
11: 4 preaching *a* Jesus than the one we preached,
13:11 Encourage one *a*.
13:12 Greet one *a* with a holy kiss.
Gal 1: 6 in Christ, and are going over to *a* gospel.
5:15 go on biting and tearing one *a* to pieces,
5:26 or challenging, or jealous toward one *a*.
Eph 4: 2 and patience, bearing with one *a* lovingly.
4:25 his neighbor, for we are members of one *a*.
4:32 In place of these, be kind to one *a*,
5:19 *a* in psalms and hymns and inspired songs.
5:21 Defer to one *a* out of reverence for Christ.
Phil 2:27 too, so as to spare me one sorrow after *a*.
3:15 If you see it *a* way,
Col 3: 9 Stop lying to one *a*.
3:13 Bear with one *a*;
3:13 whatever grievances you have against one *a*.
3:16 made perfect, instruct and admonish one *a*.
1Thes 3:12 overflow with love for one *a* and for all,
4: 9 God himself has taught you to love one *a*,
4:17 Console one *a* with this message.
5:11 Therefore, comfort and upbuild one *a*,
5:13 Remain at peace with one *a*.
Ti 3: 3 envy, hateful ourselves and hating one *a*.
Heb 3:13 one *a* daily while it is still "today,"
4: 8 would not have spoken afterward of *a* day.
5: 6 just as he says in *a* place,
7:15 The matter is clearer still if *a* priest is
10:25 assembly, as some do, but encourage one *a*;
Jas 4:11 Do not, my brothers, speak ill of one *a*.
5: 9 Do not grumble against one *a*,
5:16 sins to one another, and pray for one *a*,
5:19 the truth, and of *a* bringing him back.
1Pt 1:22 love one *a* constantly from the heart.
3: 8 sympathetic, loving toward one *a*,
4: 8 all, let your love for one *a* be constant,
4:10 put your gifts at the service of one *a*,
5: 5 In your relations with one *a*,
5:14 Greet one *a* with the embrace of true love.
1Jn 1: 7 the light, we have fellowship with one *a*,
3:11 we should love one *a*.
3:23 we are to love one *a* as he commanded us.
4: 7 let us love one *a* because love is of God;
4:11 so, we must have the same love for one *a*.
4:12 Yet if we love one *a* God dwells in us,
2Jn 1: 5 let us love one *a*.
Rv 4: 1 After this I had *a* vision:
6: 4 *A* horse came forth, a red one.
6: 4 peace by allowing men to slaughter one *a*.
7: 2 I saw *a* angel come up from the east
8: 3 *A* angel came in holding a censer of gold.
10: 1 Then I saw *a* mighty angel come down from
12: 3 Then *a* sign appeared in the sky:
13:11 saw *a* wild beast come up out of the earth;
14: 6 Then I saw *a* angel flying in midheaven,
14:15 *A* angel came out of the temple and in a
14:17 out of the temple in heaven came *a* angel,
15: 1 I saw in heaven *a* sign,
15: 5 After this I had *a* vision.
18: 1 this I saw *a* angel coming down from heaven.
18: 4 Then I heard *a* voice from heaven say:

ANOTHER'S (20)

Ex 21:35 man's ox hurts *a* ox so badly that it dies,
22: 4 fire spread so that it burns in *a* field,
Jb 19:27 my own eyes, not *a*,
Prv 5:20 should you go astray for *a* wife and accept
7: 5 That they may keep you from *a* wife,
Sir 9: 8 gaze not upon the beauty of *a* wife
21: 8 He who builds his house with *a* money is
40:29 When one has to look to *a* table,
41:21 and of entertaining thoughts about *a* wife;
Jer 5: 8 they are, each neighs after *a* wife.
19: 9 they shall eat one *a* flesh during the
Ez 1:11 out above so that they touched one *a*,
Hg 2:22 their horses shall go down by one *a* sword.
Zec 11: 9 let those that are left devour one *a* flesh."
Rom 14: 4 Who are you to pass judgment on *a* servant?
Gal 5:13 of love, place yourselves at one *a* service.
6: 2 Help carry one *a* burdens;
6: 4 because the achievement is his and not *a*.
1Thes 5:15 always seek one *a* good and,
1Pt 4:15 a malefactor, or a destroyer of *a* rights.

ANSWER (224)

Gn 24:52 When Abraham's servant heard their *a*,
32:19 Then you shall *a*,
41:16 God who will give Pharaoh the right *a*."
43: 7 We had to *a* his questions.
45: 3 But his brothers could give him no *a*,
46:34 asks what your occupation is, you must *a*,
Lv 5:17 that he incurs guilt for which he must *a*,
Nm 14:10 In *a*, the whole community
22: 8 will give you whatever *a* the LORD gives me."
Dt 18:19 my name, I myself will make him *a* for it.
27:15 And all the people shall *a*, 'Amen!'
27:16 And all the people shall *a*, 'Amen!'
27:17 And all the people shall *a*, 'Amen!'
27:18 And all the people shall *a*, 'Amen!'
27:19 And all the people shall *a*, 'Amen!'
27:20 And all the people shall *a*, 'Amen!'
27:21 And all the people shall *a*, 'Amen!'
27:22 And all the people shall *a*, 'Amen!'
27:23 And all the people shall *a*, 'Amen!'
27:24 And all the people shall *a*, 'Amen!'
27:25 And all the people shall *a*, 'Amen!'
27:26 And all the people shall *a*, 'Amen!'
29:24 And the *a* will be,
Jos 4: 7 these stones mean to you, you shall *a* them,
22:28 to us or to our descendants, we could *a*:
Jgs 14:13 But if you cannot *a* it for me,
14:15 After three days' failure to *a* the riddle,
14:15 "Coax your husband to *a* the riddle for us,
14:16 my countrymen, but have not told me the *a*."
14:17 she importuned him, he told her the *a*,
19:28 but there was no *a*.
1Sm 8: 7 prayed to the LORD, however, who said in *a*:
8:18 but on that day the LORD will not *a* you."
12: 3 *A* me in the presence of the LORD and of
14:37 But he received no *a* on this occasion.
14:41 "Why did you not *a* your servant this time?
17:30 and everyone gave him the same *a* as before.
18:24 reported to him the nature of David's *a*,
20:10 tell me if your father gives you a harsh *a*?"
20:16 you, or the LORD will make you *a* for it."
26:14 He then shouted, "Will you not *a*,
28: 6 but the LORD gave no *a*,
1Kgs 1:36 In *a* to the king,
9: 9 Men will *a*:
12: 6 *a* do you advise me to give this people?"
12: 7 submit to them, giving them a favorable *a*,
12: 9 *a* do you advise me to give this people,
12:13 him, the king gave the people a harsh *a*.
18:21 The people, however, did not *a* him.
18:26 on Baal from morning to noon, saying, *A* us,
18:37 *A* me, LORD!
18:37 *A* me, that this people
21: 4 *a* Naboth the Jezreelite had made to him:
2Kgs 4:29 him, and if anyone greets you, do not *a*.
6:18 And in *a* to the prophet's prayer the LORD
18:36 remained silent and did not *a* him one word,
18:36 for the king had ordered them not to *a* him.
19:20 in *a* to your prayer for help against
1Chr 21:12 What *a* am I to give him who sent me?"
2Chr 2:10 Tyre, wrote an *a* which he sent to Solomon:
7:22 And men will *a*:
10: 6 *a* do you advise me to give this people?"
10: 9 *a* do you advise me to give this people,
10:10 "This is the *a* you should give to this
10:13 given him, the king gave them a harsh *a*,
18: 3 "You and I are as one," was his *a*;
Ezr 4:17 The king sent this *a*:
5:11 This was their *a* to us:
10:12 In *a*, the whole assembly cried out

ANSWER (cont.)

Neh 2:20 My *a* to them was this:
5: 8 remained silent, for they could find no *a.*
6: 8 I sent him this *a:*
6:11 My *a* was: "A man like me
1Mc 12:18 kindly send us an *a* on this matter."
Jb 9: 3 could not *a* him once in a thousand times.
9:14 How much less shall I give him any *a,*
9:15 though I were right, I could not *a* him,
9:32 not a man like myself, that I should *a* him,
11: 6 that God will make you *a* for your guilt.
13:22 or let me speak first, and *a* me.
14:15 You would call, and I would *a* you;
15: 2 Should a wise man *a* with airy opinions,
19:16 I call my servant, but he gives no *a,*
20: 2 So now my thoughts provide me with an *a,*
23: 5 learn the words with which he would *a,*
30:20 I cry to you, but you do not *a* me;
31:14 what could I *a* when he demanded an account?
31:37 let the Almighty *a* me!
32: 1 Then the three men ceased to *a* Job,
32: 3 found a good *a* and had not condemned Job.
33:32 If you have aught to say, then *a* me.
40: 2 Let him who would correct God give *a!*
40: 4 what can I *a* you?
Ps(s) 4: 2 I When I call, *a* me,
13: 4 Look, *a* me, O LORD, my God!
17: 6 I call upon you, for you will *a* me,
20: 2 I The LORD *a* you in time of distress;
20:10 the king, and *a* us when we call upon you.
22: 3 O my God, I cry out by day, and you *a* not;
27: 7 have pity on me, and *a* me.
38:16 you, O LORD my God, will *a* When I say,
55: 3 give heed to me, and *a* me.
60: 7 help us by your right hand, and *a* us!
65: 6 awe-inspiring deeds of justice you *a* us,
69:14 kindness *a* me with your constant help.
69:17 *A* me. O LORD,
69:18 in my distress, make haste to *a* me.
69:19 as an *a* for my enemies,
86: 1 *a* me, for I am afflicted and poor.
86: 7 I call upon you, for you will *a* me.
91:15 He shall call upon me, and I will *a* him;
102: 3 in the day when I call, *a* me speedily.
108: 7 help us by your right hand, and *a* us.
119:42 I have an *a* for those who reproach me,
119:145 *a* me, O LORD; I will observe
143: 1 in your justice *a* me.
143: 7 Hasten to *a* me, O LORD,
Prv 1:28 "Then they call me, but I *a* not;
15: 1 A mild *a* calms wrath,
26: 4 *A* not the fool according to his folly,
26: 5 *A* the fool according to his folly,
26:16 wiser than seven men who *a* with good sense.
Eccl 7:27 discover the *a* which my soul still seeks
Sg 5: 6 I called to him but he did not *a* me.
Sir 5:13 Be swift to hear, but slow to *a.*
5:14 If you have the knowledge, *a* your neighbor;
8: 9 the knowledge how to *a* in time of need,
11: 8 Before hearing, *a* not,
33: 4 upon your training, and then give your *a.*
46: 5 *a* to him in hailstones of tremendous power,
Is 3: 7 Then shall he *a* in that day:
10:30 *A* her, Anathoth!
14:32 will one *a* the messengers of the nation?
30:19 cry out, as soon as he hears he will *a* you.
36:21 remained silent and did not *a* him one word,
36:21 for the king had ordered them not to *a* him.
37:21 In *a* to your prayer for help against
40: 6 I *a,* "What shall I cry out?"
41:17 I, the LORD, will *a* them;
41:28 counsel, to make an *a* when I question them.
46: 7 Although they cry out to it, it cannot *a;*
49: 8 In a time of favor I *a* you,
50: 2 Why did no one *a* when I called?
58: 9 Then you shall call, and the LORD will *a,*
65:12 Since I called and you did not *a,*
65:24 Before they call, I will *a;*
Jer 7:13 because you did not *a,*
7:27 call to them, they will not *a* you.
16:11 you shall *a* them:
22: 9 And the *a* will be given:
23:33 you shall *a,* "You are the burden,
23:35 to one another, "What *a* did the LORD give?"
23:37 the prophet, "What *a* did the LORD give?"
26:12 this *a* to the princes and all the people:
33: 3 Call to me, and I will *a* you;
35:17 did not obey, when I called they did not *a.*
37: 7 Give this *a* to the king of Judah who sent
38:26 give them this *a:*
44:15 and Upper Egypt, Jeremiah received this *a:*
44:20 people, men and women, who gave him this *a,*
Bar 3:35 When he calls them they *a,*
Ez 14: 4 his *a* in person because of his many idols.
14: 7 him, I, the LORD, will be his *a* in person.
33:11 *A* them: As I live,
33:25 Give them this *a:*
37:19 *a* them: Thus says the LORD GOD.
Dn 7:16 in *a,* he made known
9:23 *a* was given which I have come to announce,
9:23 mark the *a* and understand the vision.
Mi 3: 4 they cry to the LORD, he shall not *a* them;
3: 7 because there is no *a* from God.
6: 3 have I wearied you? *A* me!
Hb 2: 1 and what *a* he will give to my complaint.
2:11 and the beam in the woodwork shall *a* it!
Zec 13: 6 he shall *a,*
Mt 13:37 He said in *a:* "The farmer sowing
21:24 If you *a* it for me,
21:27 So their *a* to Jesus was,
22:46 No one could give him an *a;*
25:40 The king will *a* them:
25:45 He will *a* them:
26:62 no *a* to the testimony leveled against you?"
27:14 He did not *a* him on a single count,
Mk 11:29 If you give me an *a,*
11:33 So their *a* to Jesus was,
12:34 the insight of this *a* and told him,
14:60 no *a* to what these men testify against you?"
15: 4 "Surely you have some *a?*
Lk 7:40 In *a* to his thoughts,
10:37 The *a* came, "The one who treated him
13: 8 In *a,* the man said,
13:27 But he will *a,*
13:32 His *a* was: "Go tell that fox
14: 6 This they could not *a.*
16: 7 The *a* came, 'A hundred measures
18:29 His *a* was, "I solemnly assure you,
18:37 The *a* came that Jesus of Nazareth was
20: 3 "Let me put a question for you to *a:*
20: 5 during which someone said, "If we *a,*
20:26 His *a* completely disconcerted them and
22:51 Jesus said in *a* to their question,
22:68 me, and if I question you, you will not *a.*
23: 9 considerable length, but Jesus made no *a.*
Jn 1:22 we can give some *a* to those who sent us.
2:19 "Destroy this temple," was Jesus' *a,*
3: 3 Jesus gave him this *a:*
5:17 But he had an *a* for them:
5:19 This was Jesus' *a:* "I solemnly
7:16 This was Jesus' *a:* "My doctrine
8:33 are descendants of Abraham," was their *a.*
18:22 "Is that the way to *a* the high priest?"
19: 9 Jesus would not give him any *a.*
20:25 His *a* was, "I will never believe it
Acts 1: 7 His *a* was: "The exact time
4: 9 If we must *a* today for a good deed done to
8:20 Peter said in *a:*
9:10 "Here I am, Lord," came the *a.*
10: 4 The *a* came:
12:13 door and a maid named Rhoda came to *a* it.
16:31 Their *a* was,
Rom 3: 2 The *a* is, much in every respect.
9:20 Friend, who are you to *a* God back?
11: 4 How does God *a* him?
Rv 22:17 Let him who hears *a,* "Come!"

ANSWERABLE (2)

1Kgs 5:30 *a* to Solomon's prefects for the work,
Mt 5:22 his brother shall be *a* to the Sanhedrin,

ANSWERED (512)

Gn 3: 2 The woman *a* the serpent:
3:10 He *a,* "I heard you in the garden;
3:13 The woman *a,* "The serpent tricked
4: 9 He *a,* "I do not know.
15: 9 He *a* him,
16: 8 She *a,* "I am running away
16:11 For the LORD has heard you, God has *a* you.
18:28 "I will not destroy it," he *a,*
18:31 "I will not destroy it," he *a,*
20: 6 God *a* him in the dream:
20:11 "I was afraid," *a* Abraham,
21:30 Abraham *a,* "The seven ewe lambs
22: 8 "Son," Abraham *a,*
22:11 "Yes, Lord," he *a.*
23: 5 The Hittites *a* Abraham:
24:24 She *a:* "I am the daughter
24:47 she *a,* 'The daughter of Bethuel,
24:57 They *a,* "Let us call the girl
24:58 She *a,* "I do."
25:23 She went to consult the LORD, and he *a* her:
26: 7 place asked questions about his wife, he *a,*
26:28 They *a:* "We are convinced
27:19 Jacob *a* his father:
27:20 He *a,* "The LORD, your God
29: 5 "We do," they *a.*
29: 6 "He is," they *a;*
29:18 had fallen in love with Rachel, he *a* Laban,
30:15 Rachel *a.* "In exchange
30:27 Laban *a* him:
30:31 Laban asked. Jacob *a:*
31:14 Rachel and Leah *a* him:
32:28 He *a,* "Jacob."
32:30 He *a,* "Why should you want
33: 5 Jacob *a,* "They are the children
33: 8 Jacob *a,* "It was to gain my lord's favor."
35: 3 God who *a* me in my hour of distress
37:13 "I am ready," Joseph *a.*
37:16 "I am looking for my brothers," he *a.*
38:17 He *a,* "I will send you a kid
38:18 She *a,* "Your seal and cord,
38:21 But they *a,*
40: 8 They *a* him,
42: 7 They *a,* "From the land of Canaan
42:12 But he *a* them:
43: 7 They *a:* "The man kept
46: 2 "Here I am," he *a.*
47: 3 them what their occupation was, they *a,*
47:25 saved our lives!" they *a.*
48: 9 "They are my sons," Joseph *a* his father,
Ex 1:19 The midwives *a* Pharaoh,
2: 8 "Yes, do so," she *a.*
2:19 They *a,* "An Egyptian saved us
3: 4 He *a,* "Here I am."
3:12 He *a,* "I will be with you;
4: 2 "A staff," he *a.*
5: 2 Pharaoh *a,* "Who is the LORD,
5: 4 The king of Egypt *a* them,
5:17 Pharaoh *a,* "It is just because
6: 1 Then the LORD *a* Moses,
7: 1 The LORD *a* him, "See!
8: 5 " Moses *a* Pharaoh,
8:25 Moses *a,* "As soon as I leave
10: 9 and old must go with us," Moses *a,*
14:13 But Moses *a* the people, "Fear not!
17: 5 The LORD *a* Moses,
18:15 Moses *a* his father-in-law,
19: 8 to tell them, the people all *a* together,
20:20 Moses *a* the people,
24: 3 of the LORD, they all *a* with one voice,
24: 7 he read it aloud to the people, who *a,*
32:18 But Moses *a,*
32:33 The LORD *a,*
33:14 "I myself," the LORD *a,*
33:19 He *a,* "I will make all my beauty pass
Lv 10:19 Aaron *a* Moses,
Nm 9: 8 Moses *a* them,
10:30 But he *a,* "No, I will not come.
11:23 The LORD *a* Moses,
11:29 But Moses *a* him,
12:14 But the LORD *a* Moses,
14:20 The LORD *a:* "I pardon them
16:12 and Abiram, sons of Eliab, but they *a,*
16:23 The LORD *a* Moses,
20:18 But Edom *a* him,
22:10 Balaam *a* God,
22:38 Balaam *a* him,
23:26 But Balaam *a* Balak,
32: 6 But Moses *a* the Gadites and Reubenites:
32:25 The Gadites and Reubenites *a* Moses,
Dt 1:14 You *a* me,
Jos 1:16 all you have commanded us," they *a* Joshua,
2:14 our lives for yours," the men *a* her.
2:17 The men *a* her,
7:20 Achan *a* Joshua,
9: 8 But they *a* Joshua,
9: 9 They *a* him,
9:24 They *a* Joshua,
15:19 She *a,* "Give me an additional gift!
17:15 the LORD has blessed us" Joshua *a* them,
24:16 But the people *a,*
24:21 But the people *a* Joshua,
Jgs 1: 2 The LORD *a,* "Judah shall attack:
1:15 Give me an additional gift," she *a.*
4: 8 But Barak *a* her,
6:15 But he *a* him,
6:17 He *a* him,
6:18 He *a,* "I will await your return."
6:23 The LORD *a* him, "Be calm, do not fear.
8: 2 he *a* them.
8: 8 of Penuel *a* him as had the men of Succoth.
8:23 But Gideon *a* them,
9: 9 But the olive tree *a* them,
9:11 But the fig tree *a* them,
9:13 But the vine *a* them,
9:36 But Zebul *a* him,
10:11 The LORD *a* the Israelites:
11: 9 Jephthah *a* the elders of Gilead,
11:13 He *a* the messengers of Jephthah,
12: 2 Jephthah *a* them,
12: 5 If he *a,* "No!"
13:11 "Yes," he *a.*
13:13 The angel of the LORD *a* Manoah,
13:16 But the angel of the LORD *a* Manoah,
13:18 The angel of the LORD *a* him,
14: 3 But Samson *a* his father,
14:19 garments to those who had *a* the riddle.
15:10 they *a,* "To take Samson prisoner;
15:11 He *a* them,
16: 7 which have not dried," Samson *a* her,
16:11 which no work has been done," he *a* her,
17: 9 He *a* him, "I am a Levite
18:24 gone off with my priest as well," he *a.*
20:22 and the LORD *a* that they should.
Ru 2: 6 The overseer of the harvesters *a,*
2:11 Boaz *a* her:
4: 4 He *a,* "I will put in my claim."
1Sm 1:15 "It isn't that my lord," Hannah *a.*
1:23 Her husband Elkanah *a* her:
3: 4 The LORD called to Samuel, who *a,*
3: 6 But he *a,* "I did not call you, my son.
3:10 Samuel *a,* "Speak,
3:18 Eli *a,* "He is the LORD.
4:17 And the messenger *a:* "Israel fled
4:20 Yet she neither *a* nor paid any attention.
9: 8 Again the servant *a* Saul,
9:12 The girls *a,* "Yes, there—straight ahead.

9:19 Samuel *a* Saul: "I am the seer.
10:22 The LORD *a*,
12:20 "Do not fear," Samuel *a* them.
14:39 But none of the people *a* him.
15:20 Saul *a* Samuel: "I did indeed obey
15:30 But he *a*: "I have sinned,
16: 2 To this the LORD *a*:
17:33 But Saul *a* David,
17:37 Saul *a* David, "Go!
17:45 David *a* him:
18:18 But David *a* Saul:
19:17 Michal *a* Saul:
20: 2 Jonathan *a* him:
20: 5 David *a*: "Tomorrow is
20: 9 But Jonathan *a*:
20:28 Jonathan *a* Saul:
21: 3 David *a* the priest:
21: 6 David *a* the priest:
22:14 Ahimelech *a* the king:
23: 2 The LORD *a*, "Go, for you will defeat
23: 4 Again David consulted the LORD, who *a*,
23:11 The LORD *a*, "He will come down."
23:12 And the LORD *a*, "Yes."
24:17 saying these things to Saul, Saul *a*,
25:10 But Nabal *a* the servants of David:
25:41 Rising and bowing to the ground, she *a*,
26:14 And Abner *a*, "Who is it that calls me?"
26:17 David *a*, "Yes, my lord the king."
26:22 But David *a*: "Here is the king's spear
27:10 And David *a*, "The Negeb of Judah,"
28: 2 David *a* Achish, "Good!
28: 7 His servants *a* him,
28: 9 But the woman *a* him,
28:11 to conjure up and he *a*, "Samuel."
28:13 The woman *a* Saul,
29: 3 And Achish *a* them:
29: 9 "You know," Achish *a* David,
30: 8 The LORD *a* him,
30:15 He *a*, "Swear to me
2Sm 1: 4 He *a* that the soldiers had fled the battle
7: 3 Nathan *a* the king,
9: 3 Ziba *a* the king,
9: 4 and Ziba *a*,
9: 6 David said, "Meribbaal," and he *a*,
9: 8 Bowing low, he *a*,
11: 7 was going, and Uriah *a* that all was well.
11:11 Uriah *a* David,
12:13 Nathan *a* David:
13:12 But she *a* him, "No my brother!
14: 9 The woman of Tekoa *a* him,
14:18 The king *a* the woman,
14:19 And the woman *a*: "As you live
14:32 Absalom *a* Joab:
15:15 The king's officers *a* him,
15:21 But Ittai *a* the king,
16: 3 Ziba *a* the king,
19:31 Meribbaal *a* the king,
19:35 But Barzillai *a* the king:
19:44 The Israelites *a* the Judahites:
20:20 Joab *a*, "Not at all, not at all!
21: 4 The Gibeonites *a* him,
22:42 but he *a* them not.
24:14 David *a* Gad: I am in very serious
1Kgs 1:17 She *a* him: "My lord, you swore to me
1:28 King David *a*, "Call Bathsheba here."
1:43 Jonathan *a* him. "Our lord, King David
1:52 Solomon *a*, "If he proves himself
2:13 "Yes," he *a*, and added,
2:22 King Solomon *a* his mother.
2:30 But he *a*, "No!
2:31 The king *a* him:
2:38 Shimei *a* the king:
2:42 And you *a*, "I accept and obey.'
3: 6 Solomon *a*: "You have shown
3:22 The other woman *a*, "It is not so!
3:27 The king then *a*,
12: 5 back to me in three days," he *a* them.
12:16 not listen to them, the people *a* the king:
13:14 he *a*, "Yes."
13:16 water with you in this place," he *a*,
17:12 "As the LORD, your God lives," she *a*,
18: 8 "Yes," he *a*.
18:15 Elijah *a*, "As the LORD of hosts lives
18:18 "It is not I who disturb Israel," he *a*,
18:24 All the people *a*, "Agreed!"
18:29 no one *a*,
19:10 He *a*: "I have been zealous
19:20 Elijah *a*. "Have I done
20: 4 The king of Israel *a*,
20:14 He *a*, "The LORD says,
20:18 He *a*, "Whether they have
20:33 He *a*, "Go and get him."
21: 3 Naboth *a* him,
21: 6 He *a* her, "Because I spoke to Naboth
21:20 "Yes," he *a*.
22: 4 Jehoshaphat *a* the king of Israel,
22: 6 "Go up," they *a*.
22: 8 The king of Israel *a*,
22:14 "As the LORD lives," Micaiah *a*,
22:15 "Go up," he *a*, "you shall succeed!
22:16 But the king *a* him,
22:22 He *a*, 'I will go forth
2Kgs 1: 6 "A man came up to us," they *a*,
1:10 I am a man of God," Elijah *a* the captain,
1:12 "If I am a man of God," Elijah *a* him,
2: 9 Elisha *a*, "May I receive a double portion
2:16 "Do not send them," he *a*.
4: 2 Elisha *a* her. "Tell me what you have
4: 6 "There is none left," he *a* her.
4:14 Gehazi *a*. "She has no son,
5:25 He *a*, "Your servant has not gone
6:12 one, my lord king," *a* one of the officers.
6:16 "Do not be afraid," Elisha *a*.
7: 2 arm the king leaned, *a* the man of God,
7:19 The adjutant had *a* the man of God.
8:10 "Go and tell him," Elisha *a*,
9: 5 "For you, commander," he *a*.
20:10 shadow to advance ten steps," Hezekiah *a*.
20:15 saw everything in my house," *a* Hezekiah.
1Chr 14:10 The LORD *a* him, "Advance,
14:14 But God *a* him: "Do not try
21:26 he *a* him by sending down fire from heaven
2Chr 1: 8 Solomon *a* God: "You have shown great
10: 5 "In three days," he *a* them,
10:16 not listen to them, the people *a* the king.
18: 5 "Go up," they *a*.
18: 7 The king of Israel *a* Jehoshaphat,
18:13 "As the LORD lives," Micaiah *a*,
18:14 "Go up," he *a*,
18:16 Then Micaiah *a*:
18:21 He *a*, 'I will go forth
25: 9 Amaziah *a* the man of God,
31:10 Azariah, head of the house of Zadoc, *a* him,
32:24 the LORD, who *a* him by giving him a sign.
Ezr 4: 3 rest of the family heads of Israel *a* them,
Neh 1: 3 and about Jerusalem, and they *a* me:
2: 3 I was seized with great fear, I *a* the king:
2: 5 to the God of heaven and then *a* the king:
5:12 They *a*: "We will return
5:13 And the whole assembly *a*,
8: 6 all the people, their hands raised high, *a*,
9: 5 The Israelites *a* with the blessing,
Tb 2: 3 He *a*, "Father, one of our people
5: 3 Tobit *a* his son Tobiah:
5:10 Raphael *a*: "Yes, I can go
5:13 Raphael *a*, "I am Azariah,
6: 8 He *a*: "As regards the fish's
6:11 He *a*, "Yes, what is it?"
7: 3 They *a*, "We are of the exiles
7: 4 They *a*, "Indeed we do!"
7: 5 They *a*, "Yes, he is alive and well."
7:11 Tobiah *a*, "I will eat or drink nothing
12: 4 Tobit *a*, "It is only fair,
Jdt 11: 5 Judith *a* him:
12: 4 Judith *a* him,
13:20 And all the people *a*, "Amen!
14:15 As no one *a*,
15:10 And all the people *a*, "Amen!"
Est 1:16 the king and of the officials, Memucan *a*:
6: 5 The king's servants *a* him,
7: 9 The king *a*, "Hang him on it."
1Mc 2:19 But Mattathias *a* in a loud voice:
10:55 King Ptolemy *a* in these words:
2Mc 3:37 man to be sent to Jerusalem next, he *a*:
Jb 1: 7 Then Satan *a* the LORD and said,
1: 9 But Satan *a* the LORD and said,
2: 2 And Satan *a* the LORD and said,
2: 4 And Satan *a* the LORD and said,
6: 1 Then Job *a* and said: Ah, could
9: 1 Then Job *a* and said: I know well
9:16 If I appealed to him and he *a* my call,
11: 2 Should not the man of many words be *a*,
16: 1 Then Job *a* and said: I have heard this
19: 1 Then Job *a* and said: How long
22: 1 Then Eliphaz the Temanite *a* and said:
23: 1 Again Job *a* and said:
25: 1 Then Bildad the Shuhite *a* and said:
32:14 not then have *a* him as you have done.
40: 3 Then Job *a* the LORD and said: Behold,
42: 1 Job *a* the LORD and said: I know that
Ps(s) 18:42 but he *a* them not.
20: 7 that he has *a* him from his holy heaven
34: 5 he *a* me and delivered me from all my fears.
81: 8 Unseen, I *a* you in thunder;
99: 6 they called upon the LORD, and he *a* them.
99: 8 O LORD, our God, you *a* them;
118: 5 the LORD *a* me and set me free.
118:21 for you have *a* me and have been my savior.
119:26 I declared my ways, and you *a* me;
120: 1 distress I called to the LORD, and he *a* me.
138: 3 When I called, you *a* me;
Is 7:12 But Ahaz *a*, "I will not ask!
38: 7 [Isaiah *a*: "This will be the sign
39: 3 Hezekiah *a*, "They came
66: 4 Because, when I called, no one *a*,
Jer 1: 7 But the LORD *a* me,
9:12 The LORD *a*: Because they have
11: 5 "Amen, LORD," I *a*.
15:19 Thus the LORD *a* me:
21: 3 But Jeremiah *a* them:
22:21 to you when you were secure, but you *a*,
28: 5 The prophet Jeremiah *a* the prophet
36:18 all these words to me," Baruch *a* them,
37:14 Jeremiah *a*, "I am not deserting
37:17 Jeremiah *a*: you shall be handed over
38: 5 King Zedekiah *a*:
38:14 Jeremiah *a* Zedekiah:
38:20 You will not be handed over, Jeremiah *a*.
38:27 and he *a* them in the very words the king
40:16 Gedaliah, son of Ahikam, *a* Johanan,
42: 4 the prophet Jeremiah *a* them:
Ez 9: 9 He *a* me: The sins of the house
37: 3 "Lord GOD," I *a*,
Dn 2: 4 The Chaldeans *a* the king [Aramaic]:
2: 5 The king *a* the Chaldeans,
2: 7 Again they *a*,
2:10 The Chaldeans *a* the king:
3:16 and Abednego *a* King Nebuchadnezzar,
3:91 "Assuredly, O king," they *a*.
5:17 Daniel *a* the king:
6:13 The king *a* them,
6:22 Daniel *a* the king:
7:23 He *a* me thus:
8:14 He *a* him,
13:55 "Under a mastic tree," he *a*.
14:17 And Daniel *a*, "They are unbroken,
14:25 But Daniel *a*, "I adore the Lord,
14:35 But Habakkuk *a*,
Jl 2:19 The LORD *a* and said to his people:
Am 7: 8 And when I *a*,
7:14 Amos *a* Amaziah,
8: 2 I *a*, "A basket of ripe fruit."
Jon 1: 9 Jonah *a* them; "I worship the LORD,
2: 3 distress I called to the LORD, and he *a* me;
4: 9 "I have reason to be angry," Jonah *a*,
Mi 6: 5 and how Balaam, the son of Beor, *a* him . . .
Hb 2: 2 Then the LORD *a* me and said:
Hg 2:12 "No," the priests *a*.
2:13 The priests *a*, "They become unclean."
Zec 1: 9 and the angel who spoke with me *a* me,
1:11 And they *a* the angel of the LORD who was
2: 2 He *a* me,
2: 6 "To measure Jerusalem," he *a*;
4: 5 "No, my lord," I *a*.
4:13 "No, my lord," I *a* him.
5: 2 I *a*, "I see a scroll flying;
5: 6 And he *a*,
Mt 3:15 Jesus *a*: "Give in for now.
4: 7 Jesus *a* him, "Scripture also has it:
8:32 He *a*, "Out with you!"
12:39 He *a*: "An evil and unfaithful
13:11 He *a*: "To you has been given
13:28 He *a*, 'I see an enemy's hand in this.'
13:51 "Yes," they *a*:
15:26 But he *a*, "It is not right
16:16 "You are the Messiah," Simon Peter *a*,
19:17 He *a*, "Why do you question me
20:21 She *a*, "Promise me
21:24 Jesus *a*: "I too will ask
22:42 "David's," they *a*.
25:12 But he *a*, 'I tell you, I do not know you.'
26:25 Jesus *a*, "It is you who have said it."
26:50 Jesus *a*, "Friend, do what you are here for!"
26:64 Jesus *a*: "It is you who
26:66 They *a*, "He deserves death!"
Mk 5: 9 "Legion is my name," he *a*.
6:24 The mother *a*,
6:38 When they learned the number they *a*,
8:19 They *a*, "Twelve."
8:20 They *a*, "Seven."
8:29 Peter *a* him, "You are the Messiah!"
10: 4 They *a*, "Moses permitted divorce
10:18 Jesus *a*, "Why do you call me good?
10:29 Jesus *a*: "I give you my word,
11: 6 They *a* as Jesus had told them to,
12:28 he realized how skillfully Jesus *a* them.
14:30 Jesus *a*, "I give you my assurance,
14:62 Then Jesus *a*: "I am;
Lk 1:35 The angel *a* her: "The Holy Spirit
3:13 He *a* them, "Exact nothing over
3:16 John *a* them all by saying:
4: 4 Jesus *a* him, "Scripture has it,
5: 5 Simon *a*, "Master, we have been hard
5:22 knew their reasoning and *a* them by saying:
7:43 Simon *a*, "He, I presume,
8:30 "Legion," he *a*,
9:13 He *a* them,
9:62 Jesus *a* him, "Whoever puts his hand
10:26 Jesus *a* him: "What is written
10:28 Jesus said, "You have *a* correctly.
11:46 Jesus *a*: "Woe to you
15:27 The servant *a*, 'Your brother
16:29 Abraham *a*, 'They have Moses
17: 6 the Lord, "Increase our faith," and he *a*:
17:37 they asked him, and he *a*,
18:41 "Lord," he *a*, "I want to see."
22:38 He *a*, "Enough."
22:70 He *a*, "It is you who say I am."
23: 3 He *a*, "That is your term."
Jn 1:21 "I am not Elijah," he *a*.
1:26 John *a* them: "I baptize
1:39 "Come and see," he *a*.
1:48 "Before Philip called you," Jesus *a*,
3:27 John *a*: "No one can lay
4:19 "Sir," *a* the woman,
5: 7 "Sir," the sick man *a*,
6:26 Jesus *a* them: "I assure you,
6:68 Simon Peter *a* him,
7: 6 Jesus *a* them:

ANSWERED (cont.)

7:21 Jesus *a:* "I have performed
8:11 "No one, sir," she *a.*
8:14 Jesus *a:* "What if I am
8:25 Jesus *a:* "What I have
8:34 Jesus *a* them:
8:42 Jesus *a:* "Were God your father
8:48 The Jews *a,*
8:54 Jesus *a:* "If I glorify
8:58 Jesus *a* them:
9: 3 "Neither," *a* Jesus:
9:11 He *a:* "That man they
9:20 The parents *a:*
9:22 (His parents *a* in this fashion because
9:25 whether his is a sinner or not," he *a.*
9:27 you would not listen to me," he *a* them.
9:36 He *a,* "Who is he, sir,
10:25 Jesus *a:* "I did tell you
10:34 Jesus *a:* "Is it not written
11: 9 Jesus *a:* "Are there not
12:23 Jesus *a* them:
12:30 Jesus *a,* "That voice
12:35 Jesus *a:* "The light is among
13: 7 Jesus *a,* "You may not realize
13: 8 "If I do not wash you," Jesus *a,*
13:26 Jesus *a,* "The one to whom
13:36 Jesus *a:* "I am going
13:38 Jesus *a.* "I tell you truly,
14:23 Jesus *a:* "Anyone who loves me
16:31 Jesus *a* them:
18: 5 "I am he," he *a.*
18:20 Jesus *a* by saying:
18:31 may not put anyone to death," the Jews *a.*
18:34 Jesus *a,* "Are you saying
18:36 Jesus *a:* "My kingdom does
19:11 Jesus *a:* "You would have
19:22 to be King of the Jews'" Pilate *a,*
20:13 She *a* them,
21: 5 "Not a thing," they *a.*
Acts 2:38 Peter *a:* "You must reform
4:19 Peter and John *a,*
5: 8 She *a,* "Yes, that was the sum."
9: 5 The voice *a,*
10:14 He *a:* "Sir, it is unthinkable!
10:22 They *a:* "The centurion
19: 2 They *a,* "We have not so much as heard
19:15 were doing this, the evil spirit *a,*
21:13 He *a* with a question:
22: 8 I *a,* 'Who are you, sir?'
22:19 I *a:* 'Lord, it is because
22:27 "I am," Paul *a.*
23: 5 Paul *a:* "My brothers,
25: 4 But Festus *a* that Paul was being kept in
25:10 Paul *a:* "I stand before
26:15 and the Lord *a:*
26:25 "No, Your Excellency," *a* Paul,
1Pt 3: 7 will keep your prayers from being *a.*
Rv 5:14 The four living creatures *a,*

ANSWERING (6)

Ex 19:19 was speaking and God *a* him with thunder.
Jgs 5:29 answers her, and she, too, keeps *a* herself:
1Kgs 18:26 But there was no sound, and no one *a.*
2Mc 7: 8 *A* in the language of his forefathers,
Sir 42: 8 the aged and infirm *a* for wanton conduct.
Mt 21:11 And the crowd kept *a,*

ANSWERS (21)

Gn 24:14 your jug, that I may drink,' and she *a,*
24:44 a little water from your jug, and she *a,*
Jgs 5:29 The wisest of her princesses *a* her,
1Sm 28:15 longer *a* me through prophets or in dreams,
1Kgs 3:23 The other *a,* 'No! The dead one
18:24 The God who *a* with fire is God."
Jb 12: 4 one whom God *a* when he calls upon him,
21:34 comfort, while in your *a* perfidy remains?
34:36 since his *a* are those of the impious;
35:12 he *a* not against the pride of the wicked.
38: 3 I will question you, and you tell me the *a!*
40: 7 will question you, and you tell me the *a!*
Ps(s) 3: 5 the LORD, he *a* me from his holy mountain.
Prv 18:13 He who *a* before he hears
18:23 man implores, but the rich man *a* harshly.
Eccl 10:19 living glad, but money *a* for everything.
Sir 47:17 song and story and riddle, and with your *a,*
Jer 42: 4 whatever the LORD *a* you,
Am 6:10 and he *a,*
Lk 2:47 were amazed at his intelligence and his *a.*
Acts 21:34 in the crowd shouted out different *a.*

ANT (1)

Prv 6: 6 Go to the *a,*

ANTECHAMBER (1)

Jdt 10:22 her to him, he came out to the *a,*

ANTELOPES (1)

Is 51:20 at every street corner like *a* in a net.

ANTHOTHIJAH (1)

1Chr 8:24 Abdon, Zichri, Hanan, Hananiah, Elam, *A,*

ANTI-LEBANON (1)

Jdt 1: 7 of Cilicia and Damascus, Lebanon and *A,*

ANTICHRIST (4)

1Jn 2:18 just as you heard that the *a* was coming,
2:22 He is the *a,*
4: 3 Such is the spirit of the *a* which,
2Jn 1: 7 This is the *a!*

ANTICHRISTS (1)

1Jn 2:18 coming, so now many such *a* have appeared.

ANTICIPATE (2)

Rom 12:10 *A* each other in showing respect.
Phil 1:20 I firmly trust and *a* that I shall never be

ANTICIPATED (1)

1Mc 6:36 These *a* the beast wherever it was;

ANTICIPATING (1)

Mk 14: 8 body she is *a* its preparation for burial.

ANTICIPATION (3)

Wis 6:13 to make herself known in *a* of men's desire;
Lk 3:15 The people were full of *a,*
21:26 in *a* of what is coming upon the earth.

ANTIDOTE (1)

Wis 16:10 for your mercy brought the *a* to heal them.

ANTIOCH (34)

1Mc 3:37 half of the army and set out from *A,*
4:35 he withdrew to *A* and began to recruit
6:63 he departed in haste and returned to *A,*
10:68 he was greatly troubled, and returned to *A.*
11:13 entered *A* and assumed the crown of Asia;
11:44 thousand good fighting men to him at *A.*
11:56 captured the elephants and occupied *A.*
2Mc 4:33 the inviolable sanctuary at Daphne, near *A.*
5:21 from the temple, and hurried back to *A.*
8:35 like a runaway slave, until he reached *A.*
11:36 your advantage, for we are on our way to *A.*
13:23 charge of the government in *A* had rebelled.
13:26 gaining their good will, he returned to *A.*
14:27 Maccabeus as a prisoner to *A* without delay.
Acts 6: 5 Timon, Parmenas, and Nicolaus of *A,*
11:19 went as far as Phoenicia, Cyprus and *A,*
11:20 come to *A* began to talk even to the Greeks,
11:22 resulting in Barnabas' being sent to *A.*
11:26 he had found him, he brought him back to *A.*
11:26 It was in *A* that the disciples were called
11:27 prophets came down from Jerusalem to *A.*
13: 1 church at *A* certain prophets and teachers:
13:14 on from Perga and came to *A* in Pisidia.
14:19 some Jews from *A* and Iconium arrived and
14:21 to Lystra and Iconium first, then to *A.*
14:26 From there they sailed back to *A,*
15: 1 Some men came down to *A* from Judea and
15:22 and sent to *A* along with Paul and Barnabas.
15:23 to the brothers of Gentile origin in *A,*
15:30 representatives sent on their way to *A;*
15:35 Paul and Barnabas continued in *A,*
18:22 the congregation, and then went down to *A.*
Gal 2:11 Cephas came to *A* I directly withstood him,
2Tm 3:11 through persecutions and sufferings in *A,*

ANTIOCHIANS (2)

2Mc 4: 9 for it and to enroll men in Jerusalem as *A.*
4:19 as representatives of the *A* of Jerusalem,

ANTIOCHIS (1)

2Mc 4:30 their cities had been given as a gift to *A,*

ANTIOCHUS (57)

1Mc 1:10 from these a sinful offshoot, *A* Epiphanes,
1:10 Antiochus Epiphanes, son of King *A,*
1:16 secure, *A* proposed to become king of Egypt,
1:19 and *A* plundered the land of Egypt.
1:20 After *A* had defeated Egypt in the year one
3:27 When *A* heard about these events,
3:33 care of his son *A* until his own return.
6: 1 King *A* was traversing the inland provinces,
6:15 king's son *A* and bring him up to be king.
6:16 King *A* died in Persia in the year one
6:17 king was dead, he set up the king's son *A,*
6:55 Lysias heard that Philip, whom King *A,*
6:55 appointed to train his son *A* to be king,
7: 2 seized *A* and Lysias to bring them to him.
8: 6 *A* the Great, king of Asia,
10: 1 who was called Epiphanes, son of *A,*
11:39 was bringing up Alexander's young son *A.*
11:54 and brought with him the young boy *A,*
11:55 around *A* and fought against Demetrius,
11:57 Then young *A* wrote to Jonathan:
12:16 So we have chosen Numenius, son of *A,*
12:39 assume the crown, and do away with King *A.*
13:31 dealt treacherously with the young King *A.*
14:22 Since Numenius, son of *A,*
15: 1 *A,* son of King Demetrius,
15: 2 "King *A* sends greetings to Simon,
15:10 *A* invaded the land of his ancestors,
15:11 Pursued by *A,* Trypho fled to Dor,
15:13 *A* encamped before Dor with a hundred and
15:25 When King *A* was encamped before Dor,
15:26 to *A'* support two thousand elite troops,
2Mc 1:14 *A* with his Friends had come to the place
1:15 *A* with a few attendants came to the temple
2:20 against *A* Epiphanes and his son Eupator,
4: 7 and when *A* surnamed Epiphanes succeeded
4:21 *A* learned that the king was opposed to his
4:37 *A* was deeply grieved and full of pity;
5: 1 *A* sent his second expedition into Egypt.
5: 5 a false rumor circulated that *A* was dead.
5:17 *A* did not realize that it was because of
5:21 *A* carried off eighteen hundred talents
7:24 *A,* suspecting insult in her words,
9: 1 About that time *A* retreated in disgrace
9: 2 recourse to arms, and *A'* men were routed,
9: 2 so that in the end *A* was put to flight by
9:19 "To my esteemed Jewish citizens, *A,*
9:25 have therefore appointed as king my son *A,*
9:29 but fearing *A'* son,
10: 9 Such was the end of *A* surnamed Epiphanes.
10:10 shall relate what happened under *A* Eupator,
10:13 and for having gone over to *A* Epiphanes.
11:22 *A* sends greetings to his brother Lysias.
11:27 "King *A* sends greetings to the Jewish
13: 1 *A* Eupator was invading Judea
13: 3 and with great duplicity kept urging *A* on,
13: 4 the anger of *A* against the scoundrel.
14: 2 doing away with *A* and his guardian Lysias.

ANTIPAS (1)

Rv 2:13 have in me, not even at the time when *A,*

ANTIPATER (2)

1Mc 12:16 chosen Numenius, son of Antiochus, and *A,*
14:22 Since Numenius, son of Antiochus, and *A,*

ANTIPATRIS (1)

Acts 23:31 and escorted him that night as far as *A.*

ANTIQUATED (1)

Rom 7: 6 serve in the new spirit, not the *a* letter.

ANTS (1)

Prv 30:25 *A*— a species not strong,

ANUB (1)

1Chr 4: 8 Koz became the father of *A* and Zobebah,

ANVIL (2)

Sir 38:28 So with the smith standing near his *a,*
Is 41: 7 with the hammer, him who strikes on the *a;*

ANXIETIES (2)

Mk 4:19 to the word, but *a* over life's demands,
Phil 2:28 seeing him, and my own *a* may be lessened.

ANXIETY (15)

Gn 32: 8 In his *a,*
Lv 26: 6 that you may lie down to rest without *a.*
1Sm 13:12 So in my *a* I offered up the holocaust."
Est D: 8 In great *a* he sprang from his throne,
1Mc 6:10 my eyes, for my heart is sinking with *a.*
Prv 12:25 *A* in a man's heart depresses it,
15:16 of the LORD than a great fortune with *a.*
23:29 Who have *a?*
Eccl 2:22 all the toil and *a* of heart
Sir 40: 1 A great *a* has God allotted,
Ez 12:18 and drink your water shaking with *a.*
12:19 bread in *a* and drink their water in horror,
Mt 13:22 *a* and the lure of money choke it off.
2Cor 11:28 pressing on me, my *a* for all the churches.
Phil 4: 6 Dismiss all *a* from your minds.

ANXIOUS (12)

Jos 22:24 We did it rather out of our *a* concern lest
1Sm 9: 5 about the asses and become *a* about us."
10: 2 the asses, but is *a* about you and says,
23:26 David was in *a* flight to escape Saul,
2Mc 15:19 *a* as they were about the battle in the
Lk 10:41 you are *a* and upset about many things;
12:26 beyond your power, why be *a* about the rest?
Acts 13: 7 and Saul and was *a* to hear the word of God.
16: 3 *a* to have him come along on the journey.
27:43 because the centurion was *a* to save Paul,
28:22 we are *a* to hear you present your views.
Phil 2:12 with *a* concern to achieve your salvation,

ANXIOUSLY (3)

Wis 19: 2 departure and had *a* sent them on their way,

Bar 3:18 They schemed *a* for money,
Ez 4:16 eat bread which they have weighed out *a*,

ANYBODY'S (1)

2Kgs 4:39 pot of vegetable stew without *a* knowing it.

ANYONE (304)

Gn 4:14 on the earth, *a* may kill me at sight."
4:15 "If *a* kills Cain,
4:15 on Cain, lest *a* should kill him at sight.
9: 6 If *a* sheds the blood of man,
13:16 if *a* could count the dust of the earth,
26:11 *A* who molests this man or his wife shall
34:19 highly respected than *a* else in his clan.
43:34 was five times as large as *a* else's.
Ex 12:19 *A*, be he a resident alien or a native,
19:12 If *a* touches the mountain,
22: 9 away, without *a* witnessing the fact,
22:18 *A* who lies with an animal shall be put to
23: 1 your hand, as an unjust witness, upon *a*.
24:14 If *a* has a complaint,
31:14 If *a* does work on that day,
31:15 *A* who does work on the sabbath day shall
32:24 'Let *a* who has gold jewelry take it off.'
33: 7 *A* who wished to consult the LORD would go
35: 2 *A* who does work on that day shall be put
Lv 2: 1 "When *a* wishes to bring a cereal offering
7:12 *a* makes a peace offering in thanksgiving,
7:18 and *a* who eats of it shall have his guilt
7:25 If *a* eats the fat of an animal from which
11:39 *a* who touches its dead body shall be
11:40 and *a* who eats of its dead body shall wash
11:40 *a* who removes its dead body shall wash his
15: 5 *A* who touches his bed shall wash his
15:11 *A* whom the afflicted man touches with
15:19 *A* who touches her shall be unclean until
15:21 *A* who touches her bed shall wash his
15:27 *A* who touches them becomes unclean;
17: 8 *A*, whether of the house of Israel or of
17:10 And if *a*, whether of the house
17:13 *A* hunting, whether of the Israelites
17:14 *a* who partakes of it shall be cut off.
20: 2 *A*, whether an Israelite or an alien
20: 6 Should *a* turn to mediums and
20: 9 *A* who curses his father or mother shall be
22: 4 if *a* touches a person who has become
22: 4 or if *a* has had an emission of seed,
22: 5 or if *a* touches any swarming creature or
22:18 When *a* of the house of Israel,
22:21 When *a* presents a peace offering to the
23:29 *A* who does not mortify himself on this day
23:30 people, and if *a* does any work on this day,
24:15 *A* who curses his God shall bear the
24:19 *A* who inflicts an injury on his neighbor
27: 2 When *a* fulfills a vow of offering one or
Nm 9:13 *a* who is clean and not away on a journey,
15:30 "But *a* who sins defiantly,
17:28 time *a* approaches the Dwelling of the LORD,
19:17 For *a* who is thus unclean,
19:21 and *a* who comes in contact with this water
19:22 and *a* who touches it becomes unclean until
21: 8 and if *a* who has been bitten looks at it,
21: 9 and whenever *a* who had been bitten by a
31:19 who have slain *a* or touched anyone slain
35:15 so that *a* who has killed another
36: 6 They may marry *a* they please,
Dt 18:10 Let there not be found among you *a* who
18:12 *A* who does such things is an abomination
20: 5 'Is there *a* who has built a new house and
20: 6 Is there *a* who has planted a vineyard and
20: 7 Is there *a* who has betrothed a woman and
20: 8 'Is there *a* who is afraid and weakhearted?
22: 5 for *a* who does such things is an
25: 5 shall not marry *a* outside the family;
Jos 1:18 If *a* rebels against your orders and does
2:19 if *a* in the house with you is harmed.
Jgs 4:20 "If *a* comes and asks,
6:31 If *a* acts for him,
7: 3 the soldiers, 'If *a* is afraid or fearful,
21: 1 daughter in marriage to *a* from Benjamin.
21: 5 For they had taken a solemn oath that *a*
21: 8 And when they asked whether *a* among the
Ru 2: 2 field of *a* who will allow me that favor."
2: 8 Do not go to glean in *a* else's field;
1Sm 9: 9 *a* who went to consult God used to say,
11: 7 "If *a* does not come out to follow Saul
12: 4 oppressed us, nor accepted anything from *a*."
17:25 If *a* should kill him,
22:15 servant or *a* in my family of such a thing.
25:29 If *a* rises to pursue you and to seek your
2Sm 14:10 the king said, "If *a* says a word to you,
14:14 take thought how not to banish *a* from him.
19:23 Should *a* die today in Israel?
1Kgs 3:12 there has never been *a* like you up to now,
10:10 Never again did *a* bring such an abundance
16: 4 If *a* of Baasha's line dies in the city,
19:17 If *a* escapes the sword of Hazael,
22:31 with *a* at all except the king of Israel."
2Kgs 4:29 if you meet *a*,
4:29 do not greet him, and if *a* greets you,
9:32 "Who is on my side? *A*?"
10:24 "If one of you lets *a* escape of those
11: 8 and if *a* tries to approach the cordon,
11:15 If *a* follows her,"
18: 5 *a* like him among all the kings of Judah.
18:21 pierces the hand of *a* who leans on it.
21:12 and Judah that, whenever *a* hears of it,
2Chr 15: 5 there was no peace for *a* to go or come,
23:14 the ranks, and if *a* tries to follow her,
Ezr 3: 5 and those which *a* might offer as a
7:13 that *a* in my kingdom belonging to the
Neh 2:12 (for I had not told *a* what my God
Tb 1:18 I also buried *a* whom Sennacherib slew when
7:10 I have the right to give her to *a* but you,
Jdt 11: 1 harmed *a* who chose to serve Nebuchadnezzar,
Est C: 7 I will not bow down to *a* but you, my Lord.
1Mc 2:41 against *a* who attacks us on the sabbath,
15:25 by preventing *a* from going in or out.
2Mc 1:19 sure that the place would be unknown to *a*.
Jb 4: 2 For how can *a* refrain from speaking?
5: 1 Will *a* respond to you?
13:19 If *a* can make a case against me,
21:22 Can *a* teach God knowledge,
32:21 I would not be partial to *a*,
34:31 When *a* says to God,
Ps(s) 109:12 him a kindness, nor *a* to pity his orphans.
Wis 2: 1 nor is *a* known to have come back from the
12:11 for *a* did you grant amnesty for their sins.
Sir 2:10 *a* hoped in the LORD and been disappointed?
2:10 *a* persevered in his fear and been forsaken?
2:10 has *a* called upon him and been rebuffed?
12:13 is bitten, or *a* who goes near a wild beast?
Is 27: 3 Lest *a* harm it,
34:10 never again shall *a* pass through her.
36: 6 pierces the hand of *a* who leans on it.
44:10 all the associates of *a* who forms a god,
50: 8 if *a* wishes to oppose me,
Jer 2: 3 Should *a* presume to partake of them,
23:34 *a* else mentions "the burden of the LORD,"
31:30 but through his own fault only shall *a* die:
41: 4 murder of Gedaliah, before *a* knew of it,
Lam 3:34 When *a* tramples underfoot all the
Bar 6:33 Whether they are treated well or ill by *a*,
6:34 they cannot give *a* riches or coppers;
Ez 12:12 and covering his face lest he be seen by *a*.
14: 4 If *a* of the house of Israel,
14: 7 For if *a* of the house of Israel or any
18: 3 I swear that there shall no longer be *a*
18:16 who does not oppress *a*,
18:32 no pleasure in the death of *a* who dies,
33: 4 *a* hearing but not heeding the warning of
33: 6 so that the sword comes and takes *a*,
44: 2 is not to be opened for *a* to enter by it;
Am 6:10 to a man inside a house, "Is *a* with you?"
Zec 13: 6 And if *a* asks him,
Mal 2:12 *a* to offer sacrifice to the LORD of hosts!
Mt 5:28 *a* who looks lustfully at a woman has
5:40 If *a* wants to go to law over your shirt,
5:41 *a* press you into service for one mile,
7:11 Father give good things to *a* who asks him!
7:24 *A* who hears my words and puts them into
7:26 *A* who hears my words but does not put them
10:14 If *a* does not receive you or listen to
11:27 and *a* to whom the Son wishes to reveal him.
12: 4 to him and his men or *a* other than priests?
12:29 "How can *a* enter a strong man's house and
16:20 not to tell *a* that he was the Messiah.
17: 8 looked up they did not see *a* but Jesus.
17: 9 "Do not tell *a* of the vision until the
18: 6 it would be better for *a* who leads astray
20:26 *A* among you who aspires to greatness must
21: 3 If *a* says a word to you,
22: 9 and invite to the wedding *a* you come upon.'
23: 9 Do not call *a* on earth your father.
24:23 If *a* tells you at that time,
Mk 1:44 "Not a word to *a*, now," he said.
5:37 not permit *a* to follow him except Peter,
5:43 them strictly not to let *a* know about it,
7:36 he enjoined them strictly not to tell *a*;
8: 4 "How can *a* give these people sufficient
8:30 them strict orders not to tell *a* about him.
8:38 If *a* in this faithless and corrupt age is
9: 8 around they no longer saw *a* with them
9: 9 them not to tell *a* what they had seen,
9:30 but he did not want *a* to know about it.
9:35 him and said, "If *a* wishes to rank first,
9:40 *A* who is not against us is with us.
9:42 But it would be better if *a* who leads
10:43 *A* among you who aspires to greatness must
11: 3 If *a* says to you,
11:14 "Never again shall *a* eat of your fruit!"
11:16 *a* to carry things through the temple area.
11:25 forgive *a* against whom you have a
13:21 If *a* tells you at that time,
16: 8 their great fear, they said nothing to *a*.
Lk 3:14 He told them, "Don't bully *a*.
6:49 *a* who has heard my words but not put them
8:56 them not to tell *a* what had happened.
9:21 He strictly forbade them to tell this to *a*.
9:36 of what they had seen at that time to *a*.
10:22 and *a* to whom the Son wishes to reveal him."
12:10 *A* who speaks against the Son of Man will
13: 4 guilty than *a* else who lived in Jerusalem?
14:26 "If *a* comes to me without turning his
14:27 *A* who does not take up his cross and
16:10 while *a* unjust in a slight matter is also
16:26 so, nor can *a* cross from your side to us.'
19: 8 If I have defrauded *a* in the least,
19:31 If *a* should ask you,
20:18 It will make dust of *a* on whom it falls."
Jn 5: 7 "I do not have *a* to plunge me into the
6:46 Not that *a* has seen the Father
6:51 If *a* eats this bread he shall live forever;
6:60 How can *a* take it seriously?"
7:37 "If *a* thirsts,
8:33 "Never have we been slaves to *a*.
9:22 *a* who acknowledged Jesus as the Messiah
9:32 It is unheard of that *a* ever gave sight to
11:57 *a* who knew where he was should report it,
12:26 If *a* would serve me,
12:26 If *a* serves me, him the Father will honor.
12:46 to keep *a* who believes in me from
12:47 If *a* hears my words and does not keep them,
13:20 you, he who accepts *a* I send accepts me,
14:23 *A* who loves me will be true to my word,
16: 2 a time will come when *a* who puts you to
16:30 is no need for *a* to ask you questions.
18:31 "We may not put *a* to death,"
18:37 *A* committed to the truth hears my voice."
19:12 *A* who makes himself a king becomes
Acts 3:23 *A* who does not listen to that prophet
4:12 There is no salvation in *a* else,
4:17 to mention that man's name to *a* again."
4:34 nor was there *a* needy among them,
8:19 hands on *a* he will receive the Holy Spirit."
9: 2 and bring to Jerusalem *a* he might find,
19:38 craftsmen want to bring charges against *a*,
23:22 tell *a* that you gave me this information."
24:12 find me debating with *a* or inciting a mob.
Rom 5: 7 *a* should lay down his life for a just man,
8: 9 If *a* does not have the Spirit of Christ,
13: 8 Owe no debt to *a* except the debt that
1Cor 1:16 I am not aware of having baptized *a* else.
3:17 If *a* destroys God's temple,
5:11 not associating with *a* who bears the title
6: 1 How can *a* with a case against another dare
7:36 If *a* thinks he is behaving dishonorably
8: 3 But if *a* loves God,
9:15 rather die than let *a* rob me of my boast!
9:19 Although I am not bound to *a*,
10:12 let *a* who thinks he is standing upright
11:16 If *a* wants to argue about this,
11:34 If *a* is hungry let him eat at home,
14: 7 how will *a* know what is being played if
14: 9 how will *a* know what you are saying?
14:37 If *a* thinks he is a prophet or a man of
14:38 If *a* ignores it,
16:22 If *a* does not love the Lord,
2Cor 2: 5 If *a* has given offense he has hurt not
2:16 a mission as this, is *a* really qualified?
5:16 look on *a* in terms of mere human judgment.
5:17 This means that if *a* is in Christ,
6: 3 We avoid giving *a* offense,
10: 6 *a* else once your own obedience is perfect.
10: 7 *a* is convinced that he belongs to Christ,
11:21 But what *a* else dares to claim
12: 7 lest *a* think more of me than what he sees
Gal 1: 9 if *a* preaches a gospel to you other than
3:13 "Accursed is *a* who is hanged on a tree."
6: 3 If *a* thinks he amounts to something,
Phil 3: 4 If *a* thinks he has a right to put his
2Thes 3: 8 were among you, nor depend on *a* for food.
3:10 that *a* who would not work should not eat.
3:14 If *a* will not obey our injunction,
1Tm 5: 8 If *a* does not provide for his own
5:22 Never lay hands hastily on *a*,
2Tm 3:12 *A* who wants to live a godly life in Christ
Ti 3: 2 not to speak evil of *a* or be quarrelsome.
Heb 10:28 *A* who rejects the law of Moses is put to
11: 6 *A* who comes to God must believe that he
Jas 5:13 If *a* among you is suffering hardship,
5:14 Is there *a* sick among you?
1Pt 3:15 Should *a* ask you the reason for this hope
4:16 If *a* suffers for being a Christian,
2Pt 2:19 for surely *a* is the slave of that by which
1Jn 2: 1 But if *a* should sin,
2:15 If *a* loves the world,
2:23 *A* who denies the Son has no claim on the
2:27 means you have no need for *a* to teach you.
3:10 God, nor *a* who fails to love his brother.
3:15 *A* who hates his brother is a murderer,
4: 6 We belong to God and *a* who has knowledge
4: 6 *a* who is not of God refuses to hear us.
4:15 When *a* acknowledges that Jesus is the Son
4:20 If *a* says,
5:16 *A* who sees his brother sinning,
2Jn 1: 9 *A* who is so "progressive" that he does
1: 9 while *a* who remains rooted in the teaching
1:10 If *a* comes to you who does not bring this
Rv 3:20 If *a* hears me calling and opens the door,
11: 5 If *a* tries to harm them,
11: 5 *A* attempting to harm them will surely be
13:15 to death *a* who refused to worship it.
13:18 *a* can calculate the number of the beast,
14: 9 "If *a* worships the beast or its image,
20:15 *a* whose name was not found inscribed in
21: 6 To *a* who thirsts I will give to drink
21:27 nor *a* who is a liar or has done a

ANYONE (cont.)

22:18 If *a* adds to these words,
22:19 If *a* takes from the words of this

ANYONE'S (7)

Nm 33:54 Wherever *a* lot falls,
1Sm 26:12 without *a* seeing or knowing or awakening.
Tb 8:12 we may bury him without *a* knowing about it."
Jdt 7:13 there to guard against *a* leaving the city.
Mk 12:14 truthful man, unconcerned about *a* opinion.
12:19 *a* brother dies leaving a wife but no child,
Acts 20:33 Never did I set my heart on *a* silver or

ANYTHING (164)

Gn 6: 5 his heart conceived was ever *a* but evil,
14:23 or a sandal strap from *a* that is yours,
18:14 Is *a* too marvelous for the LORD to do?
19: 8 But don't do *a* to these men,
19:22 I cannot do *a* until you arrive there."
30:31 "You do not have to pay me *a* outright.
31:32 you identify *a* here as belonging to you,
31:39 responsible for *a* stolen by day or night.
39: 6 Joseph there, to *a* but the food he ate.
39: 8 not concern himself with *a* in the house,
39:23 with *a* at all that was in Joseph's charge,
40:15 and here I have not done *a* for which I
Ex 20: 4 shape of *a* in the sky
20:17 ox or ass, nor *a* else that belongs to him."
20:23 Do not make *a* to rank with me;
22: 8 a garment, or *a* else that has disappeared,
23: 7 You shall keep away from *a* dishonest.
23:24 their gods, nor shall you make *a* like them;
29:27 *a* else belonging to Aaron or to his sons.
Lv 7:19 Should the flesh touch *a* unclean,
7:21 Likewise, if someone touches *a* unclean,
12: 4 she shall not touch *a* sacred nor enter the
13:48 or wool, or on a hide or *a* made of leather,
15:10 Whoever touches *a* that was under him shall
15:20 *A* on which she lies or sits during her
Nm 6: 4 shall not eat *a* of the produce of the vine;
6:21 from *a* else which his means may allow.
16:26 men and do not touch *a* that is theirs:
22:17 handsomely and will do *a* you ask of me.
22:18 full of silver and gold, I could not do *a*,
22:38 But what power have I to say *a*?
24:13 gold, I could not of my own accord to *a*,
Dt 4:18 of *a* that crawls on the ground or of any
4:32 Did *a* so great ever happen before?
5: 8 shape of *a* in the sky above
5:21 his ox or ass, nor *a* that belongs to him.'
13:18 You shall not retain *a* that is doomed,
14:26 or strong drink, or *a* else you would enjoy,
22: 3 or *a* else which your kinsman loses and you
23:15 if he sees *a* indecent in your midst,
23:20 food or of *a* else on which interest
28:57 uses them for food for want of *a* else,
Jos 6:18 in your greed, *a* that is under the ban;
Jgs 13:14 must not eat *a* that comes from the vine,
13:14 wine or strong drink, nor eat *a* unclean.
1Sm 3: 7 the LORD had not revealed *a* to him as yet.
12: 4 oppressed us, nor accepted *a* from anyone."
15: 9 out the doom on *a* that was worthwhile,
19: 3 If I learn *a*, I will let you know."
21: 3 let no one know *a* about the business
25: 7 miss *a* all the while they were in Carmel.
25:15 neither did we miss *a* all the while we
30:22 us, we will not give them *a* from the booty,
2Sm 3:35 me if I eat bread or *a* else before sunset."
14:18 do not conceal from me *a* I may ask you!"
15:35 If you hear *a* from the royal palace,
19:39 And *a* else you would like me to do for you,
19:43 Have we had *a* to eat at the king's expense?
20:20 I do not wish to destroy or to ruin *a*.
1Kgs 19:20 "Have I done *a* to you?"
2Kgs 4:41 there was no longer *a* harmful in the pot.
8:13 like me, your servant, do *a* so important?"
Jdt 8:13 will you never understand *a*?
Est 2:15 ask for *a* but what the royal eunuch Hegai,
6:10 Do not omit *a* you proposed."
1Mc 1:62 in their hearts not to eat *a* unclean;
3:28 and commanded them to be prepared for *a*.
8:30 hereafter decide to add or take away *a*,
2Mc 9:24 if *a* unexpected happened or any unwelcome
12:18 without having done *a* except
Jb 1:11 forth your hand and touch *a* that he has,
1:22 sin, nor did he say *a* disrespectful of God.
6:22 Have I asked you to give me *a*,
31:16 If I have denied *a* to the poor,
Prv 13: 5 *A* deceitful the just man hates,
Eccl 7:14 that man cannot find fault with him in *a*.
9: 5 are to die, but the dead no longer know *a*.
9: 6 have part in *a* that is done under the sun.
9:10 *A* you can turn your hand to,
Wis 16:17 expectation, in water which quenches *a*,
Sir 13: 5 you have *a* he will speak fair words to you,
17:26 Is *a* brighter than the sun?
19: 9 Let *a* you hear die within you;
50:29 them into practice, he can cope with *a*,
Is 44: 9 their shame, they neither see nor know *a*;
Jer 32:27 Is *a* impossible to me?
38:15 If I tell you *a*,
Bar 6:23 nor did they feel *a* when they were molded.
Ez 12:22 drag on, and no vision ever comes to *a*"?
15: 3 Can you use its wood to make *a* worthwhile?
15: 4 middle is scorched, is it still good for *a*?
15: 5 and scorched it, can it be used for *a*!
33: 7 when you hear me say *a*,
44:17 they shall not put on *a* woolen when they
44:18 gird themselves with *a* that causes sweat.
44:31 The priests shall not eat *a*,
Am 3: 5 up from the ground without catching *a*?
Jon 3: 7 neither cattle nor sheep, shall taste *a*;
Mt 5:23 recall that your brother has *a* against you,
5:37 *A* beyond that is from the evil one.
10:31 so do not be afraid of *a*.
12:32 *a* against the Son of Man will be forgiven,
12:32 but whoever says *a* against the Holy Spirit
12:34 How can you utter *a* good,
14: 7 swore he would grant her *a* she asked for.
18:19 voices on earth to pray for *a* whatever,
24:17 not come down to get *a* out of his house.
Mk 2:12 saying, "We have never seen *a* like this!"
6:22 for *a* you want and I will give it to you."
7: 4 they never eat *a* from the market without
8: 1 assembled, and they were without *a* to eat.
8:23 hands on him and asked, "Can you see *a*?"
9:22 of your heart you can do *a* to help us,
11:13 went over to see if he could find *a* on it.
13:15 down or enter his house to get *a* out of it.
Lk 15:16 pigs, but no one made a move to give him *a*.
20:40 They did not dare ask him *a* else.
22:35 bag or sandals, were you in need of *a*?"
23:22 I have not discovered *a* about him that
24:41 he said to them, "Have you *a* here to eat?"
Jn 1:46 that was, "Can *a* good come from Nazareth?"
3:27 on *a* unless it is given him from on high.
5:19 assure you, the Son cannot do *a* by himself
5:30 I cannot do *a* of myself.
14:14 *A* you ask me in my name I will do,
16:24 now you have not asked for *a* in my name.
18:20 There was nothing secret about *a* I said.
18:23 "If I said *a* wrong produce the evidence,
21: 5 them, "Children, have you caught *a* to eat?"
Acts 4:32 None of them ever claimed *a* as his own;
10:14 never eaten *a* unclean or impure in my life."
15:20 to abstain from *a* contaminated by idols,
19:36 you must calm yourselves and not do *a* rash.
23:29 of *a* deserving death or imprisonment.
25:25 find that he had done *a* deserving of death,
Rom 11:35 has given him *a* so as to deserve return?"
14: 2 A man of sound faith knows he can eat *a*,
14: 3 The man who will eat *a* must not ridicule
14:21 or *a* else that offers your brother an
15:18 I will not dare to speak of *a* except what
16: 2 If she needs help in *a*,
1Cor 6:12 but I will not let myself be enslaved by *a*.
9:15 to see to it that *a* should be done for me.
14:35 If they want to learn *a*,
2Cor 1:13 *a* that you cannot read and understand.
1:19 he was never *a* but "yes."
2:10 If you forgive a man *a*, so do I.
3: 5 entitled of ourselves to take credit for *a*.
13: 8 We cannot do *a* against the truth,
Gal 3:15 You cannot add *a* to a man's will or set it
5: 6 nor the lack of it counts for *a*;
6: 4 if he has reason to boast of *a*,
6:14 *a* but the cross of our Lord Jesus Christ!
Eph 2: 9 is it a reward for *a* you have accomplished,
5:27 without stain or wrinkle or *a* of that sort.
1Thes 1: 8 makes it needless for us to say *a* more.
1Tm 6: 7 world, nor have we the power to take *a* out.
Ti 2: 8 will be able to find *a* bad to say about us,
Phlm 1:14 did not want to do *a* without your consent,
1:18 If he has done you an injury or owes you *a*,
Jas 1: 7 must not expect to receive *a* from the Lord.
1Jn 2:21 that no lie has *a* in common with the truth.
5:14 we ask for *a* according to his will.
Rv 13:16 did not allow a man to buy or sell *a*

ANYWAY (2)

Jos 23: 6 law of Moses, not straying from it in *a*,
Jn 7:49 and they are lost *a*!"

ANYWHERE (13)

Gn 19:17 Don't look back or stop *a* on the Plain.
23:17 cave and all the trees *a* within its limits,
Ex 9:14 know that there is none like me *a* on earth.
34:10 been wrought in any nation *a* on earth,
Nm 18:31 families, as well as you, may eat them *a*,
Dt 18: 6 *a* in Israel in which he ordinarily resides,
1Kgs 2:36 Do not go *a* else.
2:42 warning that, if you left and went *a* else,
2Kgs 5:25 He answered, "Your servant has not gone *a*."
Jdt 1:12 and those living *a* in Egypt as far as the
Bar 2: 2 has not been done *a* under heaven
Lk 13:33 be allowed to die *a* except in Jerusalem.'
Acts 24:12 in the synagogue, nor *a* else in the city,

APACE (2)

Jer 48:16 is Moab's ruin, his disaster hastens *a*.
2Thes 1: 3 grows *a* and your mutual love increases;

APART (57)

Gn 21:28 also set *a* seven ewe lambs of the flock,
21:29 these seven ewe lambs that you have set *a*?"
30:40 sheep, on the other hand, Jacob kept *a*,
Ex 21:13 place which I will set *a* for this purpose.
28: 3 him *a* for his sacred service as my priest.
Lv 13:46 He shall dwell *a*,
20:24 who has set you *a* from the other nations.
20:25 You, too, must set *a*,
20:25 in the land that I have set *a* for you.
20:26 you *a* from the other nations to be my own.
Nm 5: 8 this is *a* from the atonement ram with
6:21 vow of dedication *a* from anything else
16:21 Moses and Aaron, "Stand *a* from this band,
23: 9 Here is a people that lives *a* and does not
Dt 4:41 Then Moses set *a* three cities in the
10: 8 "At that time the LORD set *a* the tribe of
19: 2 *a* three cities in the land which the LORD,
19: 7 is why I order you to set *a* three cities.
Jos 17: 5 Thus ten shares fell to Manasseh *a* from
20: 7 So they set *a* Kedesh in Galilee in the
2Sm 10: 8 and Maacah remained *a* in the open country.
1Kgs 8:53 because you have set them *a* among all the
2Kgs 15: 5 He lived in a house *a*,
1Chr 19: 9 to their help remained *a* in the open field.
23:13 was set *a* to be consecrated as most holy,
25: 1 set *a* for service the descendants of Asaph,
Tb 6:18 was set *a* for you before the world existed.
Est 3: 8 there is a certain people living *a*,
1Mc 2:16 and his sons gathered in a group *a*.
Ps(s) 16: 2 *A* from you I have no good."
Eccl 2:25 For who can eat or drink *a* from him?
Is 24:19 burst asunder, the earth will be shaken *a*,
Jer 12: 3 set them *a* for the day of carnage.
Ez 45: 1 set *a* a sacred tract of land for the LORD,
48: 8 shall be the tract which you shall set *a*,
48:20 set *a* the sacred tract
Mi 7:14 inheritance, That dwells *a* in a woodland,
Zec 12:12 And the land shall mourn, each family *a*;
12:14 each family *a*, and the wives apart.
Mt 15:38 four thousand, *a* from women and children.
Mk 5: 4 the chains *a* and smashed the fetters.
6: 5 *a* from curing a few who were sick by
Jn 1: 3 being, and *a* from him nothing came to be.
15: 4 can bear fruit of itself *a* from the vine,
15: 4 the vine, can you bear fruit *a* from me.
15: 5 for *a* from me you can do nothing.
Acts 10:42 one set *a* by God as judge of the living
13: 2 "Set *a* Barnabas and Saul for me to do the
Rom 1: 1 called to be an apostle and set *a* to
3:20 Justice *A* from the Law.
3:21 of God has been manifested *a* from the law,
3:28 by faith *a* from observance of the law.
Gal 1:15 set me *a* before I was born
Eph 2:14 the barrier of hostility that kept us *a*.
2Thes 1: 9 eternal ruin *a* from the presence
1Pt 3: 1 gospel may be won over *a* from preaching,

APARTMENTS (3)

2Kgs 23: 7 He tore down the *a* of the cult prostitutes
Ez 16:41 They shall burn your *a* with fire and
Am 3:15 The ivory *a* shall be ruined,

APELLES (1)

Rom 16:10 Greetings to *A*,

APES (3)

1Kgs 10:22 with a cargo of gold, silver, ivory, *a*,
2Chr 9:21 of gold and silver, ivory, *a* and monkeys.
Jer 9: 3 Every brother *a* Jacob,

APHAIREMA (1)

1Mc 11:34 but also of the three districts of *A*,

APHEC (1)

2Kgs 13:17 You will completely conquer Aram at *A*."

APHEK (7)

Jos 12:18 Makkedah, Bethel, Tappuah, Hepher, *A*,
13: 4 from Mearah of the Sidonians to *A*,
19:30 Mahalab, Achzib, Ummah, Acco, *A*
1Sm 4: 1 while the Philistines camped at *A*.
29: 1 had mustered all their forces in *A*,
1Kgs 20:26 and went up to *A* to fight against Israel.
20:30 thousand of them, fled into the city of *A*,

APHEKAH (1)

Jos 15:53 Arab, Dumah, Eshan, Janim, Bethtappuah, *A*,

APHIAH (1)

1Sm 9: 1 son of Zeror, son of Becorath, son of *A*,

APHIK (1)

Jgs 1:31 of Mahaleb, Achzib, Helbah, *A* or Rehob.

APIECE (8)

Ex 12: 3 itself a lamb, one *a* for each household.
38:26 one bekah *a*, that is, a half-shekel apiece

Nm 7:86 filled with incense weighed ten shekels *a*,
Jos 4: 5 lift to your shoulders one stone *a*,
Jgs 21:22 since we did not take a woman *a* in the war.
2Kgs 6: 2 *a* we can build ourselves a place to live."

APIS (1)

Jer 46:15 Why has *A* fled,

APOLLONIA (1)

Acts 17: 1 Amphipolis and *A* and came to Thessalonica,

APOLLONIUS (14)

1Mc 3:10 Then *A* gathered the Gentiles,
3:12 and the sword of *A* was taken by Judas,
10:69 appointed *A* governor of Coelesyria.
10:69 *A* pitched his camp at Jamnia.
10:74 When Jonathan heard the message of *A*,
10:75 him out because *A* had a garrison there.
10:77 When *A* heard of it,
10:79 *A*, however,
2Mc 3: 5 against Onias, he went to *A* of Tarsus,
3: 7 When *A* had an audience with the king,
4: 4 the opposition was serious and that *A*,
4:21 When *A*,
5:24 for the Jewish citizens, the King sent *A*
12: 2 of the local governors, Timothy and *A*,

APOLLOPHANES (1)

2Mc 10:37 along with his brother Chaereas, and *A*.

APOLLOS (11)

Acts 18:24 A Jew named *A*,
18:25 *A* was a man full of spiritual fervor.
19: 1 While *A* was in Corinth,
1Cor 1:12 to Paul," another, "I belong to *A*,"
3: 4 Paul," and someone else, "I belong to *A*,"
3: 5 After all, who is *A*?
3: 6 I planted the seed and *A* watered it,
3:22 are yours, whether it be Paul, or *A*,
4: 6 and *A* by way of example for your benefit.
16:12 As for our brother *A*,
Ti 3:13 Zenas the lawyer and *A* on their journey,

APOLLYON (1)

Rv 9:11 name in Hebrew is Abaddon and in Greek *A*.

APOSTASY (9)

Dt 13: 6 to take, he has preached *a* from the LORD,
2Chr 29:19 reign had thrown away because of his *a*,
Ezr 9: 2 rulers have taken a leading part in this *a*!"
9: 4 the God of Israel on this *a* of the exiles,
1Mc 2:15 in charge of enforcing the *a*
Is 59:13 our God, Threatening outrage, and *a*,
Ez 37:23 deliver them from all their sins of *a*,
Mt 13:41 from his kingdom all who draw others to *a*,
2Thes 2: 3 Since the mass *a* has not yet occurred nor

APOSTATES (1)

Ps(s) 119:158 I beheld the *a* with loathing,

APOSTATIZE (1)

Dn 11:32 some who were disloyal to the covenant *a*;

APOSTATIZED (1)

Is 1: 4 LORD, spurned the Holy One of Israel, *a*.

APOSTLE (20)

Rom 1: 1 called to be an *a* and set apart to
11:13 Inasmuch as I am the *a* of the Gentiles,
1Cor 1: 1 by God's will to be an *a* of Christ Jesus,
9: 1 Am I not an *a*?
9: 2 Although I may not be an *a* for others,
2Cor 1: 1 Paul, by God's will an *a* of Jesus Christ,
12:12 great patience the signs that show the *a*,
Gal 1: 1 Paul, an *a* sent not by men or by any man,
2: 8 Peter as his *a* among the Jews
Eph 1: 1 by the will of God an *a* of Jesus Christ,
Col 1: 1 an *a* of Christ Jesus by the will of God,
1Tm 1: 1 an *a* of Christ Jesus by command of God our
2: 7 been made its herald and *a* (believe me,
2Tm 1: 1 by the will of God an *a* of Christ Jesus
1:11 been appointed preacher and *a* and teacher,
Ti 1: 1 sent as an *a* of Jesus Christ for the sake
Heb 3: 1 the *a* and high priest whom we acknowledge
Jas 5:20 mulgated by blessed James the *a*."
1Pt 1: 1 Peter, an *a* of Jesus Christ,
2Pt 1: 1 Peter, servant and *a* of Jesus Christ,

APOSTLES—APOSTLES' (59)

Mt 10: 2 The names of the twelve *a* are these:
Mk 6:30 The *a* returned to Jesus and reported to
6:32 So Jesus and the *a* went off in the boat by
Lk 6:13 and selected twelve of them to be his *a*:
9:10 The *a* on their return related to Jesus all
11:49 said, 'I will send them prophets and *a*,
17: 5 The *a* said to the Lord,
22:14 his place at table, and the *a* with him.
24:10 The other women with them also told the *a*,
Acts 1: 2 *a* he had chosen through the Holy Spirit.
1:26 to Matthias who was added to the eleven *a*.
2:37 They asked Peter and the other *a*,
2:42 the *a* instruction and the communal life,
2:43 wonders and signs were performed by the *a*.
4:33 With power the *a* bore witness to the
4:35 feet of the *a* to be distributed
4:36 to whom the *a* gave the name Barnabas
4:37 of the money, laying it at the *a*' feet.
5: 2 rest he took and laid at the feet of the *a*.
5:12 Through the hands of the *a*,
5:18 the *a* and threw them into the public jail.
5:29 To this, Peter and the *a* replied:
5:40 called in the *a* and had them whipped.
5:41 The *a* for their part left the Sanhedrin
6: 6 They presented these men to the *a*,
8: 1 All except the *a* scattered throughout the
8:14 When the *a* in Jerusalem heard that Samaria
8:18 of hands that the *a* conferred the Spirit,
9:27 him in charge and introduced him to the *a*.
11: 1 the *a* and the brothers heard that Gentiles,
14: 4 siding with the Jews and others with the *a*.
14:14 When the *a* Barnabas and Paul heard of this,
15: 2 see the *a* and presbyters
15: 4 as well as by the *a* and the presbyters,
15: 6 The *a* and the presbyters accordingly
15:22 It was resolved by the *a* and the
15:23 "The *a* and the presbyters,
16: 4 the *a* and presbyters had made in Jerusalem.
Rom 16: 7 they are outstanding *a*,
1Cor 4: 9 God has put us *a* at the end of the line,
9: 5 *a* and the brothers of the Lord and Cephas?
12:28 God has set up in the church first *a*,
12:29 Are all *a*?
15: 7 then by all the *a*.
15: 9 I am the least of the *a*;
2Cor 8:23 our brothers too are *a* of the churches,
11:13 Such men are false *a*.
11:13 deceit in their disguise as *a* of Christ.
Gal 1:17 to see those who were *a* before me,
1:19 I did not meet any other *a* except James,
Eph 2:20 on the foundation of the *a* and prophets,
3: 5 by the Spirit to the holy *a* and prophets.
4:11 It is he who gave *a*, prophets,
1Thes 2: 7 on our own importance as *a* of Christ.
2Pt 3: 2 Lord and Savior preached to you by the *a*.
Jude 1:17 words of the *a* of our Lord Jesus Christ;
Rv 2: 2 self-styled *a* who are nothing of the sort,
18:20 you heavens, you saints, *a* and prophets!
21:14 the names of the twelve *a* of the Lamb.

APOSTLESHIP (1)

Rom 1: 5 Through him we have been favored with *a*,

APOSTOLATE (1)

1Cor 9: 2 You are the very seal of my *a* in the Lord.

APOSTOLIC (1)

Acts 1:25 these two you choose for this *a* ministry,

APPAIM (2)

1Chr 2:30 The sons of Nadab were Seled and *A*.
2:31 The sons of *A*: Ishi.

APPALLED (13)

Jdt 16:10 at her daring, the Medes *a* at her boldness.
Jb 18:20 They who come after shall be *a* at his fate;
Ps(s) 143: 4 faint within me, my heart within me is *a*.
Is 8: 9 Know, O peoples, and be *a*!
59:16 and was *a* that there was none to intervene;
63: 5 *a* that there was no one to lend support;
Jer 49:17 *a* and catch his breath at all her wounds.
50:13 by Babylon will be *a* and catch his breath,
Ez 19: 7 all in it were *a* at the noise of his roar.
32:10 Many peoples shall be *a* at you,
Dn 4:16 name was Belteshazzar, was *a* for a while,
8:27 But I was *a* at the vision,
Jl 1:11 Be *a*, you husbandmen!

APPALLING (1)

Dn 12: 6 shall it be to the end of these *a* things?"

APPAREL (9)

2Sm 14: 2 *a* and do not anoint yourself with oil,
1Mc 11:24 He brought with him silver, gold *a*,
14: 9 the young men wore the glorious *a* of war.
Ps(s) 45:15 embroidered *a* she is borne in to the king;
Sir 45: 8 He clothed him with splendid *a*,
Is 63: 2 Why is your *a* red,
63: 3 all my *a* I stained.
Ez 28: 7 shall run them through your splendid *a*.
Zep 1: 8 sons, and all that dress in foreign *a*.

APPARENT (2)

2Kgs 3:27 So he took his first-born, his heir *a*,
Eccl 4:15 the heir *a* who will succeed to his place.

APPARITIONS (2)

Wis 17: 3 in fearful trembling, terrified by *a*.
17:15 Were partly smitten by fearsome *a* and

APPEAL (19)

Ex 5:15 foremen came and made this *a* to Pharaoh:
Nm 5:15 offering for an *a* in a question of guilt.
5:18 in her hands the cereal offering of her *a*,
Jos 10: 6 sent an *a* to Joshua in his camp at Gilgal:
2Sm 19:29 I still have to make further *a* to the king?"
2Chr 28:16 sent an *a* for help to the kings of Assyria.
Ezr 10: 2 of the sons of Elam, made this *a* to Ezra:
Jb 5: 1 To which of the holy ones will you *a*?
5: 8 In your place, I would *a* to God,
Prv 8: 4 my *a* is to the children of men.
Sir 51:11 LORD heard my voice, he listened to my *a*;
Mk 5:23 fell at his feet and made this earnest *a*:
Acts 25:11 I *a* to the emperor!"
28:19 objected, I was forced to *a* to the emperor,
2Cor 8:17 Not only did he welcome our *a*,
1Tm 5: 1 an older man, but *a* to him as to a father.
Phlm 1: 9 be done, I prefer to *a* in the name of love.
1:10 a prisoner for him, *a* to you for my child,
1Pt 5: 1 glory that is to be revealed, make this *a*.

APPEALED (18)

Gn 23: 8 citizens, the Hittites, while he *a* to them:
34: 8 Hamor *a* to them, saying:
34:11 too, *a* to Dinah's father and brothers:
Ex 15:25 he *a* to the LORD,
1Sm 12: 8 oppressed them, your fathers *a* to the LORD,
12:10 Each time they *a* to the LORD and said,
1Kgs 13: 6 Then the king *a* to the man of God.
18:21 Elijah *a* to all the people and said,
1Mc 11:62 Then the people of Gaza *a* to him for mercy,
2Mc 7:24 brother was still alive, the king *a* to him,
7:25 to him at all, the king *a* to the mother,
Jb 9:16 If I *a* to him and he answered my call,
Ps(s) 66:17 When I *a* to him in words,
Acts 25:12 "You have *a* to the emperor.
25:21 Paul *a* to be kept here until there could
25:24 and in Jerusalem, has *a* to me about him,
25:25 so when he *a* to His Majesty the Emperor,
26:32 at liberty, if he had not *a* to the emperor!"

APPEALING (5)

Mt 8:31 The demons kept *a* to him,
Lk 4:22 the *a* discourse which came from his lips.
Acts 28:23 by *a* to the law of Moses and the prophets.
2Cor 5:20 for Christ, God as it were *a* through us.
2Tm 4: 2 correcting, reproving, *a*—

APPEALS (1)

Ti 2:15 Make our *a* and corrections with the

APPEAR (63)

Gn 1: 9 a single basin, so that the dry land may *a*."
43: 3 'You shall not *a* in my presence unless
43: 5 'You shall not *a* in my presence unless
Ex 4: 1 they may say, 'The LORD did not *a* to you.'"
4: 5 of Isaac, the God of Jacob, did *a* to you."
10:28 to it that you do not *a* before me again!
10:28 The day you *a* before me you shall die!"
10:29 I will never *a* before you again."
23:15 No one shall *a* before me empty-handed.
23:17 shall all your men *a* before the Lord GOD.
34:20 "No one shall *a* before me empty-handed.
34:23 year all your men shall *a* before the Lord,
34:24 up three times a year to *a* before the LORD,
Nm 16:16 your band shall *a* before the LORD tomorrow
Dt 16:16 male among you shall *a* before the LORD,
16:16 one shall *a* before the LORD empty-handed,
19:17 shall *a* before the LORD
31:11 when all Israel goes to *a* before the LORD,
Jos 20: 9 until he could *a* before the community.
1Sm 1:22 I will take him to *a* before the LORD and
2Sm 3:13 *a* before me unless you bring back Michal,
14: 2 that you may *a* to be a woman who has been
14:24 he shall not *a* before me."
14:24 to his house and did not *a* before the king.
14:32 Now, let me *a* before the king.
Ezr 10: 8 failed to *a* within three days would,
10:14 women for wives *a* at appointed times,
Neh 10: 1 sealed document *a* the names of our princes,
Tb 10: 1 of days was reached and his son did not *a*,
Est C:27 which rests on my head when I *a* in public;
1Mc 9:27 time prophets ceased to *a* among the people.
Jb 19:18 when I *a*,
33:21 be seen, and his bones, once invisible, *a*;
Ps(s) 21:10 as though in a fiery furnace, when you *a*.
Eccl 9: 1 both *a* equally vain,
Sg 2:12 The flowers *a* on the earth,
Wis 8:15 in the assembly I should *a* noble,
Sir 27: 4 When a sieve is shaken, the husks *a*;
35: 4 *A* not before the LORD empty-handed,
Is 50: 8 wishes to oppose me, let us *a* together.
Jer 13:26 skirts from you, so that your shame will *a*.
Ez 16:51 and have even made your sisters *a* just,
16:52 theirs, they *a* just in comparison with you.
16:52 shame of having made your sisters *a* just.

APPEAR (cont.)

Dn 11: 3 king shall *a* and rule with great might,
11: 4 No sooner shall he *a* than his kingdom
Zec 9:14 The LORD shall *a* over them,
Mt 24:24 False messiahs and false prophets will *a*,
24:30 sign of the Son of Man will *a* in the sky,
Mk 13:22 *a* performing signs and wonders to mislead,
Lk 12:58 your opponent to *a* before a magistrate,
19:11 that the reign of God was about to *a*.
Acts 27:24 'You are destined to *a* before the emperor.
Rom 14:10 have to *a* before the judgment seat of God.
15:12 Isaiah says, "The root of Jesse will *a*,
2Cor 13: 7 not in order that we may *a* approved but
Col 3: 4 then you shall *a* with him in glory.
2Thes 2: 9 will *a* as part of the workings of Satan,
1Tm 5:24 while other men's sins will *a* only later.
6:14 until our Lord Jesus Christ shall *a*.
Heb 9:24 he might *a* before God now on our behalf.
9:28 he will *a* a second time not to take away
2Pt 1:19 streaks of dawn *a* and the morning star

APPEARANCE (51)

Lv 13:43 same pink *a* as that of skin leprosy
13:55 If the infection has not changed its *a*,
Nm 9:15 it took on the *a* of fire over the Dwelling.
9:16 cloud, which at night had the *a* of fire.
11: 7 coriander seed and had the *a* of bdellium.
Jgs 13: 6 he had the *a* of an angel of God,
1Sm 16: 7 judge from his *a* or from his lofty stature,
16: 7 the *a* but the LORD looks into the heart."
16:12 handsome to behold and making a splendid *a*.
17:42 was youthful, and ruddy, and handsome in *a*,
2Chr 20:21 *A* as it went forth at the head of the army.
Est D: 2 In making her state *a*,
2Mc 3:16 Whoever saw the *a* of the high priest was
6:18 a man of advanced age and noble *a*,
14:17 *a* of the enemy suffered a slight repulse.
15:12 a good and virtuous man, modest in *a*,
Jb 14:20 with changed *a* you send him away.
26: 9 He holds back the *a* of the full moon by
Wis 11:19 even their frightful *a* itself could slay.
14:17 copied the *a* of the distant king
Sir 11: 2 despise not a man for his *a*.
19:25 One can tell a man by his *a*;
Is 11: 3 Not by *a* shall he judge,
44:13 making it like a man in *a* and dignity,
52:14 of man, and his *a* beyond that of mortals
53: 2 at him, nor *a* that would attract us to him.
Lam 4: 8 Now their *a* is blacker than soot,
Ez 1:16 wheels had the sparkling *a* of chrysolite,
1:26 up above, one who had the *a* of a man.
40: 3 I saw a man whose *a* was that of bronze;
Dn 2:31 terrifying in *a* as it stood before you.
Jl 2: 4 Their *a* is that of horses;
Mt 2: 7 from them the exact time of the star's *a*.
3: 1 his *a* as a preacher in the desert of Judea,
6:16 They change the *a* of their faces so that
13:26 grain, the weeds made their *a* as well.
28: 3 In *a* he resembled a flash of lightning
Mk 6:56 Wherever he put in an *a*,
12:40 widows and recite long prayers for *a* sake;
14:43 made his *a* accompanied by a crowd with
16:12 revealed to them completely changed in *a*.
Lk 1:80 day when he made his public *a* in Israel.
9:29 *a* and his clothes became dazzlingly white.
Jn 21: 1 This is how the *a* took place.
Rom 2:28 *A* does not make a Jew.
1Cor 3:13 That day will make its *a* with fire,
Eph 6: 6 service for *a* only and to please men,
1Tm 6:15 This *a* God will bring to pass at his
2Tm 1:10 made manifest through the *a* of our Savior.
Rv 4: 3 One whose *a* had a gemlike sparkle
9: 7 In *a* the locusts were like horses equipped

APPEARANCES (4)

Lk 20:47 they recite long prayers to keep up *a*.
Jn 7:24 judging by *a* and make an honest judgment.
8:15 to *a* but I pass judgment on no man.
2Cor 5:12 say to those who take pride in external *a*,

APPEARED (111)

Gn 1: 9 into its basin, and the dry land *a*.
6: 4 the Nephilim *a* on earth (as well as later),
8: 5 tenth month the tops of the mountains *a*.
12: 7 The LORD *a* to Abram and said,
12: 7 altar there to the LORD who had *a* to him.
15:17 *a* a smoking brazier and a flaming torch,
17: 1 years old, the LORD *a* to him and said:
18: 1 *a* to Abraham by the terebinth of Mamre,
26: 2 The LORD *a* to him and said:
26:24 The same night the LORD *a* to him and said:
31:13 I am the God who *a* to you in Bethel,
31:24 But that night God *a* to Laban the Aramean
35: 1 God who *a* to you while you were fleeing
35: 9 God *a* to him again and blessed him.
48: 3 *a* to me at Luz in the land of Canaan,
Ex 3: 2 *a* to him in fire flaming out of a bush.
3:16 Isaac and Jacob, has *a* to me and said:
6: 3 As God the Almighty I *a* to Abraham,
16:10 lo, the glory of the LORD *a* in the cloud!
24:10 his feet there *a* to be sapphire tilework,
Nm 14:10 But then the glory of the LORD *a* at the
16:19 of the LORD *a* to the entire community,
17: 7 now covered it and the glory of the LORD *a*.
20: 6 Then the glory of the LORD *a* to them,
Dt 31:15 LORD *a* at the tent in a column of cloud,
Jgs 6:12 the angel of the LORD *a* to him and said,
8:18 "They *a* to be princes."
13: 3 of the LORD *a* to the woman and said to her,
13:10 who came to me the other day has *a* to me,"
1Sm 1:18 with her husband, and no longer *a* downcast.
14:11 *a* before the outpost of the Philistines,
2Sm 22:16 Then the wellsprings of the sea *a*,
1Kgs 3: 5 the LORD *a* to Solomon in a dream at night.
9: 2 planned, the LORD *a* to him a second time,
9: 2 second time, as he had *a* to him in Gibeon.
11: 9 who had *a* to him twice (for though the
2Kgs 11:13 *a* before them in the temple of the LORD.
2Chr 1: 7 night God *a* to Solomon and said to him,
7:12 The LORD *a* to Solomon during the night and
Tb 12:22 had done when the angel of God *a* to them.
Jdt 10:14 face, which *a* wondrously beautiful to them,
Est A: 9 there *a* to come forth a great river,
1Mc 1:11 In those days there *a* in Israel men who
4: 6 *a* in the plain with three thousand men,
4:19 was finishing this speech, a detachment *a*,
9:23 of Israel, and all kinds of evildoers *a*.
2Mc 1:18 and of the fire that *a* when Nehemiah,
2: 8 just as it *a* in the time of Moses and when
3:25 There *a* to them a richly caparisoned horse,
3:26 and splendidly attired, *a* before him.
3:33 again *a* and stood before Heliodorus.
5: 2 days, there *a* horsemen charging in midair,
10:24 then he *a* in Judea,
10:29 there *a* to the enemy from the heavens five
11: 8 near Jerusalem, a horseman *a* at their head,
12:22 But when Judas' first cohort *a*,
15:13 Then in the same way another man *a*,
Ps(s) 18:16 Then the bed of the sea *a*,
102:17 LORD has rebuilt Zion and *a* in his glory;
Wis 17: 4 and mute phantoms with somber looks *a*.
Sir 48: 1 Till like a fire there *a* the prophet whose
50: 5 How splendid he was as he *a* from the tent,
Bar 3:38 Since then she has *a* on earth,
Ez 8: 2 He stretched out what *a* to be a hand and
10: 1 the cherubim what *a* to be a sapphire stone;
10: 9 *a* to have the luster of chrysolite stone.
Dn 5: 5 lampstand, the fingers of a human hand *a*,
7:20 which *a* greater than its fellows.
Zec 1: 8 There *a* the driver of a red horse,
Mt 1:20 of the Lord *a* in a dream and said to him:
2:13 *a* in a dream to Joseph with the command:
2:19 the angel of the Lord *a* in a dream to
3:13 *a* before John at the Jordan to be baptized
11:18 words, John *a* neither eating nor drinking,
11:19 The Son of Man *a* eating and drinking,
12:46 his brothers *a* outside to speak with him.
17: 3 and Elijah *a* to them conversing with him.
20:10 group *a* they supposed they would get more;
27:53 and entered the holy city and *a* to many.
Mk 1: 4 was that John the Baptizer *a* in the desert,
1:14 Jesus *a* in Galilee proclaiming the good
1:23 There *a* in their synagogue a man with an
9: 4 Elijah *a* to them along with Moses;
16: 9 He first *a* to Mary Magdalene,
Lk 1:11 hour, an angel of the Lord *a* to him,
2: 9 The angel of the Lord *a* to them as the
9: 8 others, "Elijah has *a*";
9:31 They *a* in glory and spoke of his passage,
22:43 *a* to him from heaven to strengthen him.
24:34 He has *a* to Simon."
Jn 21:14 This marked the third time that Jesus *a* to
Acts 2: 3 Tongues as of fire *a*,
7: 2 The God of glory *a* to our father Abraham
7:26 He *a* the next day while some of them were
7:30 "Forty years later an angel *a* to him in
9:10 Ananias to whom the Lord had *a* in a vision.
9:17 Lord Jesus who *a* to you on the way here,
13:31 thereafter Jesus *a* to those who had come
23:11 night the Lord *a* at Paul's side and said:
25: 7 When Paul *a*,
26:16 I have *a* to you to designate you as my
Ti 2:11 The grace of God has *a*,
3: 4 the kindness and love of God our savior *a*,
Heb 9:26 But now he has *a* at the end of the ages to
1Jn 2:18 so now many such antichrists have *a*.
4: 1 many false prophets have *a* in the world.
Rv 12: 1 A great sign *a* in the sky,
12: 3 Then another sign *a* in the sky:
14: 1 Then the Lamb *a* in my vision.
14:14 Then, as I watched, a white cloud *a*,
19:11 and as I looked on, a white horse *a*;

APPEARING (7)

2Sm 14:28 for two years without *a* before the king.
Sir 50: 7 like the rainbow *a* in the cloudy sky;
Acts 1: 3 *a* to them over the course of forty days
7:35 the angel *a* to him in the thornbush,
2Tm 4: 1 dead, and by his *a* and his kingly power,
4: 8 have looked for his *a* with eager longing.
Ti 2:13 the *a* of the glory of the great God and of

APPEARS (18)

Gn 9:14 the earth, and the bow *a* in the clouds,
9:16 As the bow *a* in the clouds,
Lv 13: 2 blotch which *a* to be the sore of leprosy,
13:14 But as soon as raw flesh *a* on him,
13:57 the infection again *a* on the garment,
Prv 27:25 grass is taken away and the aftergrowth *a*,
Wis 6:16 her, and graciously *a* to them in the ways,
Is 60: 2 the LORD shines, and over you *a* his glory.
Jer 1:13 I replied, "that *a* from the north."
31: 3 his rest, the LORD *a* to him from afar:
Ez 1:28 Like the bow which *a* in the clouds on a
Mal 3: 2 And who can stand when he *a*?
Eph 5:13 light of day, and all that then *a* is light.
Col 3: 4 When Christ our life *a*,
Jas 4:14 are a vapor that *a* briefly and vanishes.
1Pt 1: 7 glory, and honor when Jesus Christ *a*.
1:13 to be conferred on you when Jesus Christ *a*.
5: 4 so that when the chief Shepherd *a* you will

APPEASE (7)

Gn 32:21 I first *a* him with gifts that precede me,
1Sm 26:19 you against me, let an offering *a* him;
2Chr 33:12 In this distress, he began to *a* the LORD,
Jb 38:39 the lioness or *a* the hunger of her cubs,
Wis 19:12 to *a* them quail came to them from the sea.
Sir 39:28 their force and *a* the anger of their Maker.
Dn 9:13 As we did not *a* the LORD,

APPEASED (2)

Prv 13:25 When the just man eats, his hunger is *a*;
Ez 5:13 will wreak my fury upon them till I am *a*;

APPEASING (3)

Ez 6:13 they offered *a* odors to any of their gods.
16:19 fed you, you set before them as an *a* odor,
20:28 offerings], there they sent up *a* odors,

APPEND (1)

2Thes 3:17 I *a* this signature to every letter I write.

APPETITE (6)

Jb 33:20 So that to his *a* food becomes repulsive,
Prv 6:30 steals to satisfy his *a* when he is hungry;
16:26 The laborer's *a* labors for him,
23: 2 to your throat if you have a ravenous *a*.
Sir 37:26 govern your *a* so that you allow it not
Rv 18:14 "The fruit your *a* craved has deserted you.

APPETITES (1)

Sir 18:31 If you satisfy your lustful *a* they will

APPETIZING (7)

Gn 27: 4 With your catch prepare an *a* dish for me,
27: 7 with it prepare an *a* dish for me to eat,
27: 9 I will prepare an *a* dish for your father,
27:14 and with them she prepared an *a* dish,
27:17 the *a* dish and the bread she had prepared.
27:31 he too prepared an *a* dish with his game,
2Sm 13: 5 If she prepares something *a* in my presence,

APPHIA (1)

Phlm 1: 2 fellow worker Philemon, to *A* our sister,

APPHUS (1)

1Mc 2: 5 and Jonathan, who was called *A*.

APPIUS (1)

Acts 28:15 of *A* and the Three Taverns to meet us.

APPLAUD (1)

Eccl 4:16 yet the later generations will not *a* him.

APPLAUDED (1)

Neh 11: 2 The people *a* all those men who willingly

APPLAUSE (1)

Mt 6: 2 and streets like hypocrites looking for *a*.

APPLE (8)

Dt 32:10 them, guarding them as the *a* of his eye.
Ps(s) 17: 8 Keep me as the *a* of your eye;
Prv 7: 2 and live, my teaching as the *a* of your eye;
Sg 2: 3 As an *a* tree among the trees of the woods,
8: 5 Under the *a* tree I awakened you;
Sir 17:17 a man's virtue, like the *a* of his eye.
Jl 1:12 the date palm also, and the *a*,
Zec 2:12 touches you touches the *a* of my eye.

APPLES (3)

Prv 25:11 Like golden *a* in silver settings are words
Sg 2: 5 me with raisin cakes, refresh me with *a*,
7: 9 and the fragrance of your breath like *a*,

APPLICATION (2)

Nm	15:16	same law and the same *a* of it
Wis	16:12	For indeed, neither herb nor *a* cured them,

APPLIED (14)

1Kgs	6:35	open flowers, over which gold was evenly *a*.
2Kgs	20: 7	of figs to be brought and *a* to the boil,
1Mc	8: 1	a friendly alliance with all who *a* to them.
2Mc	4:20	was in fact *a* by those who brought it,
Eccl	1:13	and I *a* my mind to search and investigate
	1:17	I *a* my mind to know wisdom and knowledge,
	8: 9	All these things I considered and I *a* my
	8:16	When I *a* my heart to know wisdom and to
Is	38:21	of figs to be taken and *a* to the boil,
Ez	28: 5	By your great wisdom *a* to your trading you
Acts	19:12	had touched his skin were *a* to the sick,
1Cor	4: 6	I have *a* all this to myself and Apollos by
Gal	3:16	as if it *a* to many, but as if it applied

APPLIES (2)

Ex	21:31	This law *a* if it is a boy or a girl that
Nm	31:19	This *a* both to you and to your captives.

APPLY (11)

Ex	12: 7	They shall take some of its blood and *a* it
Nm	5:30	the priest shall *a* this law in full to her.
Prv	22:17	my words, and *a* your heart to my doctrine;
	23:12	*A* your heart to instruction,
Sir	6:32	if you *a* yourself,
	16:22	take my advice, *a* your mind to my words,
	23: 2	Who will *a* the lash to my thoughts,
Is	8:19	*a* to the dead on behalf of the living?"
Jl	4:13	*A* the sickle,
Rom	4: 9	this blessedness *a* only to the circumcised,
1Tm	5:21	*a* these rules without prejudice,

APPOINT (26)

Gn	41:34	should also take action to *a* overseers,
Nm	3:10	*a* to have charge of the priestly functions.
	14: 4	"Let us *a* a leader and go back to Egypt."
Dt	1:13	tribes, that I may *a* them as your leaders.'
	16:18	"You shall *a* judges and officials
1Sm	2:36	*A* me, I beg you, to a priestly function,
	8: 5	not follow your example, *a* a king over us,
	8:12	He will also *a* from among them his
	8:22	their request and *a* a king to rule them."
	10:19	'Not so, but you must *a* a king over us.'
	28: 2	"I shall *a* you my permanent bodyguard."
1Chr	15:16	Levites to *a* their brethren as chanters,
Ezr	7:25	*a* magistrates and judges to administer
Neh	7: 3	*A* as watchmen the inhabitants of Jerusalem,
Est	2: 3	Let the king *a* commissaries in all the
1Mc	11:57	priesthood and *a* you ruler
Is	7: 6	force, and *a* the son of Tabeel king there."
	60:17	I will *a* peace your governor,
Jer	3:15	*a* over you shepherds after my own heart,
	23: 4	I will *a* shepherds for them who will
	51:27	*A* recruiting officers against her,
Ez	34:23	*a* one shepherd over them to pasture them,
Dn	6: 2	Darius decided to *a* over his entire
Hos	2: 2	They shall *a* for themselves one head and
Acts	6: 3	prudent, and we shall *a* them to this task.
Heb	7:11	*a* a priest according to the order of

APPOINTED (120)

Gn	18:14	At the *a* time,
	27:37	"I have already *a* him your master,
Ex	2:14	"Who has *a* you ruler and judge over us?
	13:10	rite at its *a* time from year to year.
	31: 6	As his assistant I have *a* Oholiab,
Nm	28: 2	At the times I have *a*,
Dt	20: 9	military officers shall be *a* over the army.
1Sm	8: 1	age Samuel *a* his sons judges over Israel.
	11:11	On the *a* day,
	12: 6	LORD is witness, who *a* Moses and Aaron,
	13:14	and has *a* him commander of his people,
2Sm	6:21	he *a* me commander of the LORD's people,
	7:11	I first *a* judges over my people Israel.
	15: 4	"If only I could be *a* judge in the land!
	24:15	over Israel from morning until the time *a*,
1Kgs	2:35	The king *a* Benaiah,
	11:18	who gave Hadad a house, *a* him rations,
	22:48	There was no king in Edom, but an *a* regent.
2Kgs	23: 5	had *a* to burn incense
	23:34	Pharaoh Neco then *a* Eliakim,
	24:17	king of Babylon *a* his uncle Mattaniah king,
	25:22	of Babylon, *a* as their governor Gedaliah,
	25:23	king of Babylon had *a* Gedaliah governor,
1Chr	6:33	Their brother Levites were *a* to all the
	9:29	Others were *a* to take care of the utensils
	15:17	Therefore the Levites *a* Heman,
	16: 4	He now *a* certain Levites to minister
	16: 7	David *a* Asaph and his brethren to sing for
	17:10	time when I *a* judges over my people Israel.
	22: 2	and he *a* them stonecutters to hew out
	24:19	This was the *a* order of their service when
	26:32	King David *a* them to the administration of
2Chr	2: 6	and Jerusalem, whom my father David *a*.
	8:14	David he *a* the various classes
	9: 8	he has *a* you over them as king to
	11:15	he himself *a* priests for the high places
	19: 5	He *a* judges in the land,
	19: 8	Jehoshaphat *a* some Levites and priests and
	20:21	he *a* some to sing to the LORD and some to
	32: 6	he *a* army commanders over the people.
	33: 6	and *a* necromancers and diviners of spirits,
Ezr	8:20	David and the princes *a* to serve
	10:14	foreign women for wives appear at *a* times,
	10:16	Ezra *a* as his assistants men who were
Neh	5:14	*a* me governor in the land of Judah,
	11:22	*a* to the service of the house of God
	11:23	for they had been *a* by royal decree,
	12:44	*a* over the chambers set aside for stores,
	12:44	For Judah rejoiced in its *a* priests and
	13:13	of the storerooms I *a* the priest Shelemiah,
	13:30	and Levites, so that each had his *a* task.
Tb	14: 4	shall take place in the time *a* for it.
	14: 5	era when the *a* times shall be completed.
Est	A:16	king also *a* Mordecai to serve at the court,
	9:27	by this letter, and at the time *a*.
	9:31	Thus were established, for their *a* time,
1Mc	1:51	He *a* inspectors over all the people,
	3:55	this Judas *a* officers among the people,
	4:41	Judas *a* men to attack those in the citadel,
	6:55	*a* to train his son Antiochus to be king,
	10:20	We have therefore *a* you today to be high
	10:34	days, sabbaths, new moon festivals, *a* days,
	10:69	*a* Apollonius governor of Coelesyria.
	15:38	Then the king *a* Cendebeus
	16:11	been *a* governor of the plain of Jericho,
2Mc	3: 4	had been *a* superintendent of the temple,
	5:22	more cruel than the man who *a* him;
	9:25	have therefore *a* as king my son Antiochus,
	14:12	the elephants, and *a* him governor of Judea.
	14:26	against the state, and that he had *a* Judas,
Jb	3: 8	the sea, the *a* disturbers of Leviathan!
	20:29	wicked man, and the heritage *a* him by God.
	23:14	For he will carry out what is *a* for me;
Ps(s)	75: 3	"When I seize the *a* time,
	102:14	time to pity her, for the *a* time has come.
Eccl	1:13	task God has *a* for men to be busied about.
	3: 1	There is an *a* time for everything,
	3:10	which God has *a* for men to be busied about.
Sir	14:12	nor have you been told the grave's *a* time.
	41:19	of defrauding another of his *a* share,
Jer	1: 5	you, a prophet to the nations I *a* you.
	5:24	watches for us over the *a* weeks of harvest."
	6:27	A tester among my people I have *a* you,
	29:26	"The LORD has *a* you priest in place of
	40: 5	has *a* ruler over the cities of Judah;
	40:11	in Judah, and had *a* over them Gedaliah,
	47: 7	Ashkelon and the seashore he has *a* it.
Ez	3:17	*a* you a watchman for the house of Israel.
	21:20	gates I have *a* the sword for slaughter,
	33: 7	I have *a* watchman for the house of Israel;
	44: 8	you have *a* such as these to serve me in my
Dn	2:24	had *a* to destroy the wise men of Babylon,
	8:19	for at the *a* time,
	11:27	no success, because the *a* end is not yet.
	11:29	time *a* he shall come again to the south,
	11:35	the end time which is still *a* to come.
	11:40	"At the *a* time the king of the south
	13: 5	two elders of the people were *a* judges,
Hos	6:11	you also, O Judah, a harvest has been *a*.
	12:10	have you live in tents, as in that *a* time.
Mt	8:29	you come to torture us before the *a* time?"
	26:18	'The Teacher says, My *a* time draws near.
Mk	3:16	He *a* the Twelve as follows:
	13:33	You do not know when the *a* time will come.
Lk	10: 1	the Lord *a* a further seventy-two and sent
	22: 7	it was *a* to sacrifice the paschal lamb.
	22:22	Son of Man is following out his *a* course,
Acts	7:27	'And who has *a* you ruler and judge over us?'
	7:35	the words, 'Who has *a* you ruler and judge?',
	12:21	On an *a* day Herod,
	17:31	with justice' through a man he has *a*—
Rom	5: 6	At the *a* time,
2Cor	8:19	*a* our traveling companion by the churches,
2Tm	1:11	been *a* preacher and apostle and teacher,
Heb	3: 2	faith, who was faithful to him who *a* him.
	7:15	*a* according to the likeness of Melchizedek:
	8: 3	priest is *a* to offer gifts and sacrifices;
	9:27	Just as it is *a* that men die once,
Rv	1: 3	is written in it, for the *a* time is near!
	22:10	words of this book, for the *a* time is near!

APPOINTING (6)

Ex	8: 5	"Do me the favor of *a* the time when I am
Jgs	9:16	and honorably in *a* Abimelech your king,
1Sm	7: 1	*a* his son Eleazar as guardian of the ark
	18:13	from his presence by *a* him a field officer.
2Kgs	11:18	*a* a detachment for the temple of the LORD,
Ezr	3: 8	began by *a* the Levites twenty years of age

APPOINTMENT (3)

1Sm	20:35	with a little boy for his *a* with David.
2Chr	31:13	by *a* of King Hezekiah and of Azariah,
Ti	1: 5	the *a* of presbyters in every town.

APPOINTS (3)

1Sm	25:30	you, and *a* you as commander over Israel,
Dn	5:21	kingdom of men and *a* over it whom he will.
Heb	7:28	came after the law *a* as priest the Son,

APPORTION (9)

Nm	33:54	shall *a* the land among yourselves by lot,
	34:17	of the men who shall *a* the land among you:
	36: 2	to *a* the land by lot among the Israelites;
Jos	13: 7	*a* among the nine tribes and the half-tribe
Ps(s)	60: 8	"Exultantly I will *a* Shechem,
	108: 8	"Exultantly I will *a* Shechem,
Ez	45: 1	When you *a* the land into inheritances,
	47:13	shall *a* the land among the twelve tribes
	48:29	Such is the land which you shall *a* as

APPORTIONED (5)

Nm	34:13	is the land, to be *a* among you by lot,
Jos	12: 7	Seir, Joshua *a* to the tribes of Israel.
	23: 4	Bear in mind that I have *a* among your
Rom	12: 3	the measure of faith that God has *a* him.
Heb	7: 2	*a* to him one tenth of all his booty.

APPORTIONING (2)

Jos	11:23	as their heritage, *a* it among the tribes.
	14: 5	Thus, in *a* the land,

APPRAISE (1)

1Cor	2:15	man, on the other hand, can *a* everything,

APPRAISED (3)

Jb	28:27	thunderbolts, Then he saw wisdom and *a* it,
1Cor	2:14	because it must be *a* in a spiritual way.
	2:15	though he himself can be *a* by no one.

APPRAISERS (1)

2Cor	10:12	Since people like that are their own *a*,

APPRAISES (1)

Prv	21:12	The just man *a* the house of the wicked:

APPRECIATE (5)

Nm	14:31	in, and they shall *a* the land you spurned.
2Sm	19:36	*a* the voices of singers and songstresses?
Prv	1: 2	That men may *a* wisdom and discipline,
Sir	7: 9	"He will *a* my many gifts;
	12:12	your seat, And in the end you *a* my advice,

APPRECIATES (1)

Sir	3:28	The mind of a sage *a* proverbs,

APPREHEND (3)

Jn	7:44	Some of them even wanted to *a* him.
	11:57	should report it, so that they could *a* him.)
Acts	9:21	Did he not come here purposely to *a* such

APPREHENDED (4)

Dt	21:19	shall have him *a* and brought
Sir	23:21	when he least expects it, he will be *a*.
Mt	26:57	Those who had *a* Jesus led him off to
Acts	24: 6	desecrate our temple, but we *a* him in time.

APPREHENSIVE (2)

Gn	43:18	on being led to his house, they became *a*.
1Sm	23:15	David was *a* because Saul had come out to

APPRISE (1)

1Sm	20:13	if I do not *a* you of it

APPROACH (43)

Ex	19:22	who *a* the LORD must sanctify themselves;
	28:43	*a* the altar to minister in the sanctuary,
	30:20	when they *a* the altar in their ministry,
Lv	10: 3	who *a* me I will manifest my sacredness;
	18: 6	"None of you shall *a* a close relative to
	18:19	"You shall not *a* a woman to have
	21:23	he may not *a* the veil nor go up to the
Nm	4:19	die when they *a* the most sacred objects,
	16:10	kinsmen, the descendants of Levi, to *a* him,
	17: 5	should *a* the altar to offer incense before
	18:22	may no longer *a* the meeting tent;
Jos	3:10	at your *a* will dispossess the Canaanites,
	5: 1	disheartened and lost courage at their *a*.
	23: 5	them out and dislodge them at your *a*,
	23: 9	At your *a* the LORD has driven out large
	24:18	our *a* the LORD drove out [all the peoples,
Jgs	11:33	from Aroer to the *a* of Minnith (twenty
1Sm	1: 7	of the LORD, Peninnah would *a* her,
	18: 6	At the *a* of Saul and David (on David's
	27: 8	the land between Telam, on the *a* to Shur,
2Kgs	11: 8	and if anyone tries to *a* the cordon,
2Chr	29:31	*A*, and bring forward the sacrifices and
	32:33	*a* to the tombs of the descendants of David.
Jdt	3: 9	*a* to the main ridge of the Judean mountain,
2Mc	8:12	his companions about the *a* of the army,
	10:25	At his *a*,
	12:21	When Timothy learned of the *a* of Judas,
Jb	5:26	You shall *a* the grave in full vigor,
Prv	5: 8	far from her, *a* not the door of her house,

APPROACH (cont.)

Eccl 4:17 Let your *a* be obedience,
8:10 Meanwhile I saw wicked men *a* and enter;
12: 1 come And the years *a* of which you will say,
Sir 1:25 the LORD, nor *a* it with duplicity of heart.
9:13 But if you *a* him,
Jer 30:21 When I summon him, he shall *a* me;
35: 2 *A* the Rechabites and speak to them;
Ez 42:14 then *a* the place destined for the people."
44:16 who shall *a* my table to minister to me,
Hos 7: 6 the plotters *a* with hearts like ovens.
Zec 8:21 of one city shall *a* those of another,
Lk 19:37 on his *a* to the descent from Mount Olivet,
Heb 4:16 So let us confidently *a* the throne of
7:25 able to save those who *a* God through him,

APPROACHED (54)

Gn 20: 4 Abimelech, who had not *a* her, said:
47:29 When the time *a* for Israel to die,
50:16 So they *a* Joseph and said:
Ex 20:21 while Moses *a* the cloud where God was.
40:32 went into the meeting tent or *a* the altar,
Lv 16: 1 who died when they *a* the LORD's presence,
Jgs 4:21 she stealthily *a* him and drove the peg
1Sm 1:25 bull, Hannah, his mother, *a* Eli and said:
17:40 also ready to hand, he *a* the Philistine.
2Sm 10:13 were with him *a* the Arameans for battle,
15: 5 Whenever a man *a* him to show homage,
2Kgs 2: 5 the guild prophets *a* Elisha and asked him.
Ezr 4: 2 they *a* Zerubbabel and the family heads and
9: 1 the leaders *a* me with this report:
Tb 6:14 On the very night they *a* her,
7:11 and all died on the very night they *a* her.
Jdt 13:10 As they *a* its gates,
2Mc 4:34 Thereupon Menelaus *a* Andronicus privately
5:18 his presumptuous action as soon as he *a*.
Sir 1:29 Because you *a* the fear of the LORD with
46:19 When Samuel *a* the end of his life,
Is 57: 9 it While you *a* the king with scented oil,
Jer 42: 1 and low, *a* the prophet Jeremiah and said,
Lam 2: 3 of his right hand when the enemy *a*;
Dn 7:16 I *a* one of those present and asked him
8: 6 It *a* the two-horned ram I had seen
Mt 4: 3 The tempter *a* and said to him,
8: 5 a centurion *a* him with this request:
8:19 A scribe *a* him and said,
8:28 As he *a* the Gadarene boundary,
15: 1 from Jerusalem *a* Jesus with the question:
15:12 His disciples *a* him and said,
17:14 As they *a* the crowd,
17:19 The disciples *a* Jesus at that point and
17:24 of the temple tax *a* Peter and said,
21:28 He *a* the elder and said,
Mk 1:40 A leper *a* him with a request,
5:15 As they *a* Jesus,
5:38 they *a* the house of the synagogue leader,
7:25 She *a* him and crouched at his feet.
9:14 As they *a* the disciples,
10:35 Zebedee's sons, James and John, *a* him.
11:27 and the elders *a* him and said to him,
Lk 7:12 As he *a* the gate of the town a dead man
9:12 sunset *a* the Twelve came and said to him,
9:51 *a* when he was to be taken from this world,
10:34 He *a* him and dressed his wounds,
19:29 As he *a* Bethphage and Bethany on the mount
20: 1 by the elders, *a* him with the question,
22:47 He *a* Jesus to embrace him.
23:52 *a* Pilate with a request for Jesus' body.
24:15 Jesus *a* and began to walk along with them.
Jn 11:38 again troubled in spirit, Jesus *a* the tomb.
12:21 They *a* Philip,

APPROACHES (17)

Nm 17:28 time anyone *a* the Dwelling of the LORD,
1Sm 15: 7 Amalek from Havilah to the *a* of Shur,
17:52 to the *a* of Gath and to the gates of Ekron,
1Kgs 18:46 ran before Ahab as far as the *a* to Jezreel.
1Chr 4:39 an extent that they went to the *a* of Gedor,
Jdt 7: 7 He reconnoitered the *a* to their city and
Jb 30:12 they build their *a* for my ruin.
Prv 1:27 a storm, and your doom *a* like a whirlwind;
8: 3 By the gates at the *a* of the city,
Sir 42:11 no place that overlooks the *a* to the house.
Jer 49: 3 Howl, Heshbon, for the ravager *a*,
Ez 27: 3 Tyre that is situated at the *a* of the sea,
48: 1 all along from the *a* to Hethlon through
Mt 13:19 The evil one *a* him to steal away what was
Lk 14:10 so that when your host *a* you he will say,
22:37 All that has to do with me *a* its climax."
Jn 12:15 Your king *a* you on a donkey's colt."

APPROACHING (17)

Gn 24:63 around, he noticed that camels were *a*.
Dt 31:14 Moses, "The time is now *a* for you to die.
1Sm 9:27 As they were *a* the edge of town,
2Sm 16: 5 As David was *a* Bahurim,
Tb 11:15 shortly, for she was *a* the gate of Nineveh.
1Mc 5:40 and his army were *a* the running stream,
13:23 When he was *a* Baskama,
2Mc 3:24 he was *a* the treasury with his bodyguards,
Jb 5:21 shall be hidden, and shall not fear *a* ruin.
17:12 there is darkness they talk of *a* light.
Jer 30:21 should one take the deadly risk of *a* me?
Lk 7: 4 Upon *a* Jesus they petitioned him earnestly.
Jn 6:19 four miles, they sighted Jesus *a* the boat,
6:21 came aground on the shore they had been *a*.
Acts 9: 3 As he traveled along and was *a* Damascus,
10: 9 men were traveling along and *a* the city,
22: 6 traveling along, *a* Damascus around noon,

APPROPRIATE (5)

Gn 49:28 and gave to each of them an *a* message,
1Mc 10:40 out of the royal revenues, from *a* places.
12:11 we offer on our feasts and other *a* days,
Eccl 3:11 He has made everything *a* to its time,
Sir 50:27 Wise instruction, *a* proverbs,

APPROPRIATED (1)

Gn 31:19 meanwhile *a* her father's household idols.

APPROPRIATION (1)

Ex 22: 8 In every question of dishonest *a*,

APPROVAL (16)

Gn 27: 7 my blessing with the LORD's *a* before I die.'
41:44 "that without your *a* no one shall move
1Sm 16:22 in my service, for he meets with my *a*."
27: 5 "If I meet with your *a*,
2Sm 3:36 All the people noted this with *a*,
2Mc 4:10 received the king's *a* and came into office,
Wis 15:19 escaped both the *a* of God and his blessing.
Sir 13:21 though what he says is odious, it wins *a*.
Hos 8: 4 they established princes, but without my *a*.
Acts 2:47 God and winning the *a* of all the people.
15: 8 showed his *a* by granting the Holy Spirit
Rom 13: 3 Do what is right and you will gain its *a*,
2Cor 8:21 *a* but also for the good esteem of men.
Gal 1:10 If I were trying to win man's *a*,
6:12 circumcised are making a play for human *a*—
2Tm 2:15 hard to make yourself worthy of God's *a*,

APPROVE (4)

Nm 23:27 *a* of your cursing them for me from there."
2Mc 11:35 of the king, has granted you, we also *a*.
Is 66: 2 This is the one whom I *a*:
Rom 1:32 they not only do them but *a* them in others.

APPROVED (12)

2Chr 30: 4 been *a* by the king and the entire assembly,
1Mc 14:46 "'All the people *a* of granting Simon the
2Mc 13:24 He *a* of Maccabeus and left him as military
14:35 you have *a* of a temple for your dwelling
Mk 12:34 *a* the insight of this answer and told him,
Acts 22:20 was being shed, I stood by and *a* it.
2Cor 10:18 is *a* but the man whom the Lord recommends.
13: 7 *a* but simply that you may do what is good,
Heb 11: 2 of faith the men of old were *a* by God.
11:39 all of these were *a* because of their faith,
1Pt 2: 4 a living stone, rejected by men but *a*,
2: 6 laying a cornerstone in Zion, an *a* stone,

APPROVES (3)

Ps(s) 37:23 steps of a man made firm, and he *a* his way.
Sir 21:15 of wisdom, he *a* them and adds to them;
34:19 Most High *a* not the gifts of the godless,

APPURTENANCES (18)

Ex 25:39 pure gold for the lampstand and all its *a*.
30:27 the table and all its *a*,
30:27 appurtenances, the lampstand and its *a*,
30:28 and the altar of holocausts with all its *a*,
31: 8 the table with its *a*,
31: 8 the pure gold lampstand with all its *a*,
31: 9 the altar of holocausts with all its *a*,
35:13 the table, with its poles and all its *a*,
35:14 the lampstand, with its *a*,
35:16 bronze grating, its poles, and all its *a*;
37:24 used for the lampstand and its various *a*.
38:30 bronze gratings and all the *a* of the altar,
39:33 the Dwelling, the tent with all its *a*,
39:36 the table with all its *a* and the showbread,
39:37 its lamps set up on it and with all its *a*,
39:39 bronze grating, its poles and all its *a*,
40:10 the altar of holocausts and all its *a*,
Lv 8:11 and anointed the altar, with all its *a*,

APRON (4)

1Sm 2:18 the boy Samuel, girt with a linen *a*,
2Sm 6:14 Then David, girt with a linen *a*,
Lk 12:37 I tell you, he will put on an *a*,
17: 8 *a* and wait on me while I eat and drink.

APT (2)

Sir 33:28 for idleness is an *a* teacher of mischief.
2Tm 2:24 He must be an *a* teacher,

AQUEDUCT (1)

Neh 3:15 He also repaired the wall of the *A* Pool

AQUILA (7)

Acts 18: 2 There he found a Jew named *A*,
18:18 Syria, in the company of Priscilla and *A*.
18:19 he left Priscilla and *A* behind and entered
18:26 When Priscilla and *A* heard him,
Rom 16: 3 Give my greetings to Prisca and *A*;
1Cor 16:19 *A* and Prisca,
2Tm 4:19 Prisca and *A* and the family of Onesiphorus.

AR (6)

Nm 21:15 site of *A* and slant to the border of Moab."
21:30 *A* is laid waste;
Dt 2: 9 *A* to the descendants of lot as their own.
2:18 leave *A* and the territory of Moab behind.
2:29 and the Moabites who dwell in *A* have done,
Is 15: 1 waste in a night, *A* of Moab is destroyed;

AR-BAAL (1)

Nm 34:11 Shepham the boundary shall go down to *A*,

ARA (1)

1Chr 7:38 of Jether were Jephunneh, Pispa, and *A*.

ARAB (7)

Jos 15:52 *A*, Dumah, Eshan, Janim, Bethtappuah,
Neh 2:19 Geshem the *A* mocked us and ridiculed us.
6: 1 to Sanballat, Tobiah, Geshem the *A*,
1Mc 11:17 when the *A* Zabdiel cut off
11:39 at Demetrius, he went to Imalkue the *A*,
Is 13:20 The *A* shall not pitch his tent there,
Jer 3: 2 waited for them like an *A* in the desert.

ARABAH (26)

Dt 1: 1 the Jordan [in the desert, in the *A*,
1: 7 the land of the Canaanites in the *A*,
2: 8 "Then we left behind us the *A* route,
3:17 as well as the *A* with the Jordan
3:17 from Chinnereth to the Salt Sea of the *A*,
4:49 Hermon) and all the *A* east of the Jordan,
4:49 as the *A* Sea under the slopes of Pisgah.
11:30 of the Canaanites who live in the *A*,
Jos 3:16 the Salt Sea of the *A* disappeared entirely.
8:14 in battle at the descent toward the *A*,
11: 2 regions and in the *A* near Chinnereth,
11:16 the land of Goshen, the foothills, the *A*,
12: 2 all the eastern of the *A*
12: 3 as well as the *A* from the eastern side of
12: 3 the *A* in the direction of Beth-jeshimoth,
12: 8 the mountain regions and foothills, the *A*,
18:18 of the *A* overlook, down into the Arabah.
1Sm 23:24 Maon, in the *A* south of the wasteland.
2Sm 2:29 marched all night long through the *A*
4: 7 traveled on the *A* road all night long.
2Kgs 14:25 from Labo of Hamath to the sea of the *A*,
25: 4 they went in the direction of the *A*.
Jer 39: 4 He went in the direction of the *A*.
52: 7 city, they went in the direction of the *A*.
Ez 47: 8 into the eastern district down upon the *A*,
Am 6:14 you from Labo of Hamath even to the Wadi *A*.

ARABIA (12)

1Kgs 10:15 of *A* and the governors of the country.
2Chr 9:14 All the kings of *A* also,
Jdt 2:25 the southern borders of Japheth, toward *A*.
1Mc 11:16 Alexander fled to *A* to seek protection.
Ps(s) 72:10 kings of *A* and Seba shall bring tribute.
72:15 May he live to be given the gold of *A*,
Is 21:13 Oracle on *A*:
Jer 25:24 [all the kings of *A* all the kings of Zimri,
Ez 27:21 The trade of *A* and of all the sheikhs of
30: 5 Ethiopia, Put, Lud, all *A*,
Gal 1:17 were apostles before me, I went off to *A*;
4:25 The mountain Sinai [Hagar] is in *A* and

ARABIAN (1)

Jb 28:19 it surpasses pearls and *A* topaz.

ARABLE (1)

Eccl 5: 8 in every respect is a king for the *a* land.

ARABS (11)

2Chr 17:11 and the *A* also brought him a flock of
21:16 of the *A* who bordered on the Ethiopians.
22: 1 that had come into the fort with the *A*.
26: 7 against the *A* who dwelt in Gurbaal,
Neh 4: 1 When Sanballat, Tobiah, the *A*,
1Mc 5:39 they have also hired *A* to help them,
12:31 against the *A* who are called Zabadeans,
2Mc 5: 8 to account before Aretas, king of the *A*,
12:10 they were attacked by *A* numbering at least
12:12 exchanged, the *A* withdrew to their tents.
Acts 2:11 Cretans and *A* too.

ARAD (7)

Nm 21: 1 When the Canaanite king of *A*,
26:40 The descendants of Bela were *A* and Naaman:
26:40 through *A* the clan of the Aradites,
33:40 Now, when the Canaanite king of *A*,

Jos 12:14 Eglon, Gezer, Debir, Geder, Hormah, *A*,
Jgs 1:16 to the desert at *A* [which is in the Negeb].
1Chr 8:15 Zebadiah, *A*, Eder, Michael,

ARADITES (1)

Nm 26:40 through Arad the clan of the *A*,

ARADUS (1)

1Mc 15:23 Rhodes, Phaselis, Cos, Side, *A*,

ARAH (4)

1Chr 7:39 The sons of Ulla were *A*,
Ezr 2: 5 sons of *A*,
Neh 6:18 was the son-in-law of Shecaniah, son of *A*,
7:10 sons of *A*,

ARAM (83)

Gn 10:22 Elam, Asshur, Arpachshad, Lud, and *A*.
10:23 The descendants of *A*:
22:21 his brother Buz, Kemuel (the father of *A*),
24:10 his way to the city of Nahor in *A* Naharaim.
Nm 23: 7 From *A* has Balak brought me here,
Dt 23: 5 son of Beor, from Pethor in *A* Naharaim,
Jgs 3: 8 of Cushan-rishathaim, king of *A* Naharaim,
3:10 delivered Cushan-rishathaim, king of *A*,
10: 6 the Baals and Ashtaroth, the gods of *A*,
1Sm 14:47 Moab, the Ammonites, *A*,
2Sm 8: 6 then placed garrisons in *A* of Damascus,
15: 8 For while living in Geshur in *A*,
1Kgs 15:18 son of Tabrimmon, son of Hezion, king of *A*,
19:15 you shall anoint Hazael as king of *A*.
20: 1 Ben-hadad, king of *A*,
20:20 pursuing them, while Ben-hadad, king of *A*,
20:21 and inflicted a severe defeat on *A*.
20:22 of the year the king of *A* will attack you."
20:23 the servants of the king of *A* said to him:
20:26 Ben-hadad mobilized *A* and went up to Aphek
20:27 of goats, while *A* covered the countryside.
20:28 *A* has said the LORD is a god of mountains,
20:29 thousand foot soldiers of *A* in one day.
22: 1 passed without war between *A* and Israel.
22: 3 nothing to take it from the king of *A*?"
22:11 shall gore *A* until you have destroyed them.' "
22:31 In the meantime the king of *A* had given
2Kgs 3:26 to break through to the king of *A*,
5: 1 the army commander of the king of *A*,
5: 1 him the LORD had brought victory to *A*.
5: 5 "Go," said the king of *A*.
6: 8 the king of *A* was waging war on Israel,
6: 9 by this place, for *A* will attack there."
6:11 the king of *A* called together his officers.
6:24 After this, Ben-hadad, king of *A*,
8: 7 at a time when Ben-hadad, king of *A*,
8: 9 and said, "Your son Ben-hadad, king of *A*,
8:13 LORD has showed you to me as king over *A*,"
8:28 Ahab, in battle against Hazael, king of *A*,
8:29 in his battle against Hazael, king of *A*.
9:14 Ramoth-gilead against Hazael, king of *A*,
9:15 in the battle against Hazael, king of *A*.
12:18 of *A* mounted a siege against Gath.
12:19 palace, and sent them to King Hazael of *A*,
13: 3 them in the power of Hazael, king of *A*,
13: 4 which the king of *A* had subjected Israel.
13: 5 the Israelites, freed from the power of *A*,
13: 7 since the king of *A* had destroyed them and
13:17 The arrow of victory over *A*!
13:17 You will completely conquer *A* at Aphec."
13:19 you would have defeated *A* completely.
13:19 Now, you will defeat *A* only three times."
13:22 King Hazael of *A* oppressed Israel during
13:24 So when King Hazael of *A* died and his son
15:37 the LORD first loosed Rezin, king of *A*,
16: 5 Then Rezin, king of *A*,
16: 7 of the king of *A* and the king of Israel,
1Chr 1:17 were Elam, Asshur, Arpachshad, Lud, and *A*.
1:17 The descendants of *A* were Uz,
2:23 and *A* took from them the villages of Jair,
7:34 Shomer were Ahi, Rohgah, Jehubbah, and *A*.
18: 6 up garrisons in the Damascus region of *A*,
19: 6 hire chariots and horsemen from *A* Naharaim,
2Chr 16: 2 and sent them to Ben-hadad, king of *A*,
16: 7 the king of *A* and did not rely on the LORD,
16: 7 of the king of *A* has escaped your hand.
18:10 shall gore *A* until you have destroyed them.' "
18:30 the king of *A* had given his chariot
22: 5 to battle against Hazael, king of *A*,
22: 6 in his battle against Hazael, king of *A*.
28: 5 him into the power of the king of *A*.
28:23 the gods of the kings of *A* who helped them,
Is 7: 1 Jotham, son of Uzziah, Rezin, king of *A*,
7: 2 of David that *A* was encamped in Ephraim,
7: 5 because of the mischief that *A* [Ephraim
7: 8 Damascus is the capital of *A*,
9:11 *A* on the east and the Philistines on the
17: 3 The remnant of *A* shall have the same glory
22: 6 takes up the quivers, *A* mounts the horses,
Jer 35:11 army of the Chaldeans and the army of *A*;
Hos 12:13 When Jacob fled to the land of *A*,
Am 1: 5 the people of *A* shall be exiled to Kir,
Zec 9: 1 place, For the cities of *A* are the LORD's,

ARAM-MAACAH (1)

1Chr 19: 6 and horsemen from Aram Naharaim, from *A*,

ARAMAIC (6)

2Kgs 18:26 "Please speak to your servants in *A*;
Ezr 4: 7 in *A* and was accompanied by a translation.
4: 7 *A* and was accompanied
2Mc 15:36 day of the twelfth month, called Adar in *A*,
Is 36:11 "Please speak to your servants in *A*;
Dn 2: 4 The Chaldeans answered the king *A*:

ARAMEAN (15)

Gn 25:20 the daughter of Bethuel the *A* of
25:20 Paddan-aram and the sister of Laban the *A*.
28: 5 to Laban, son of Bethuel the *A*,
31:20 Jacob had hoodwinked Laban the *A* by not
31:24 to Laban the *A* in a dream and warned him,
Dt 26: 5 'My father was a wandering *A* who went down
2Sm 10: 6 *A* foot soldiers from Beth-rehob and Zobah,
10:18 and forty thousand of the *A* foot soldiers.
1Kgs 10:29 these rates to all the Hittite and *A* kings.
2Kgs 5:20 master was too easy with this *A* Naaman,
6:23 *A* raiders came into the land of Israel.
7:14 king sent them to reconnoiter the *A* army.
1Chr 7:14 of Manasseh, whom his *A* concubine bore:
2Chr 1:17 middlemen for all the Hittite and *A* kings.
24:24 Though the *A* force came with few men,

ARAMEANS (46)

2Sm 8: 5 *A* of Damascus came to the aid of Hadadezer,
8: 6 of Damascus, and the *A* became subjects,
10: 8 while the *A* of Zobah and Rehob and the men
10: 9 of Israel and arrayed them against the *A*.
10:11 Joab said, "If the *A* are stronger than I,
10:13 were with him approached the *A* for battle,
10:14 The Ammonites, seeing that the *A* had fled,
10:15 Then the *A* responded to their defeat by
10:16 and enlisted *A* from beyond the Euphrates.
10:17 The *A* drew up in formation against David
10:18 But the *A* gave way before Israel,
10:19 And the *A* were afraid to give further aid
1Kgs 20:20 The *A* fled with Israel pursuing them,
22:35 was propped up in his chariot facing the *A*,
2Kgs 5: 2 Now the *A* had captured from the land of
6:18 When the *A* came down to get him,
7: 4 Come, let us desert to the camp of the *A*.
7: 5 At twilight they left for the *A*;
7: 6 *A* to hear the sound of chariots and horses,
7:10 "We went to the camp of the *A*,"
7:12 me tell you what the *A* have done to us.
7:15 They followed the *A* as far as the Jordan,
7:15 that the *A* had thrown away in their haste.
7:16 went out and plundered the camp of the *A*;
8:28 Ramoth-gilead, where the *A* wounded Joram.
8:29 wounds which the *A* had inflicted
9:15 wounds the *A* had inflicted
24: 2 loosed against him bands of Chaldeans, *A*,
1Chr 18: 5 *A* of Damascus came to the aid of Hadadezer,
18: 6 of Aram, and the *A* became his subjects,
19:10 and set them in array against the *A*;
19:12 "If the *A* prove too strong for me,
19:14 with his men to engage the *A* in battle;
19:15 when the Ammonites saw that the *A* had fled,
19:16 the *A* sent messengers to bring out the
19:16 out the *A* from the other side of the River,
19:17 the army of David drawn up to fight the *A*,
19:18 But the *A* fled before Israel,
19:19 the *A* refused to come to the aid of the
2Chr 18:34 on his chariot facing the *A* until evening.
22: 5 There Jehoram was wounded by the *A*.
24:23 year a force of *A* came up against Joash.
24:25 After the *A* had departed from him,
28: 5 The *A* defeated him and carried away
Is 7: 4 [the blazing anger of Rezin and the *A*,
Am 9: 7 from Caphtor and the *A* from Kir?

ARAN (2)

Gn 36:28 The descendants of Dishan were Uz and *A*.
1Chr 1:42 The sons of Dishan were Uz and *A*.

ARARAT (5)

Gn 8: 4 the ark came to rest on the mountains of *A*.
2Kgs 19:37 with the sword and fled into the land of *A*.
Tb 1:21 who then escaped into the mountains of *A*.
Is 37:38 with the sword and fled into the land of *A*.
Jer 51:27 her, summon against her the kingdoms, *A*,

ARAUNAH (8)

2Sm 24:16 at the threshing floor of *A* the Jebusite.
24:18 on the threshing floor of *A* the Jebusite
24:20 Now *A* looked down and noticed
24:21 Then *A* asked,
24:22 But *A* said to David:
24:23 All this does *A* give to the king."
24:23 *A* then said to the king,
24:24 The king, however, replied to *A*,

ARBA (3)

Jos 14:15 was formerly called Kiriath-arba, for *A*,
15:13 Kiriath-arba *A* was the father of Anak),
21:11 Kiriath-arba *A* was the father of Anak),

ARBATTA (1)

1Mc 5:23 him the Jews who were in Galilee and in *A*,

ARBELA (1)

1Mc 9: 2 and camping opposite the ascent at *A*,

ARBITE (1)

2Sm 23:35 Paarai the *A*; Igal, son of Nathan

ARBITER (2)

Jb 9:33 Would that there were an *a* between us,
Lk 12:14 who has set me up as your judge or *a*?"

ARBITRARILY (1)

1Kgs 12:33 the month in which he *a* chose to

ARCH-REBELS (1)

Jer 6:28 *A* are they all,

ARCHANGEL (1)

Jude 1: 9 Even the *a* Michael,

ARCHANGELS (1)

1Thes 4:16 the sound of the *a* voice and God's trumpet;

ARCHCRIMINAL (1)

Est E:15 who were doomed to extinction by this *a*,

ARCHELAUS (1)

Mt 2:22 that *A* had succeeded his father Herod as

ARCHER (2)

Prv 26:10 Like an *a* wounding all who pass by is he
26:18 Like a crazed *a* scattering firebrands and

ARCHERS (12)

Gn 49:23 Harrying and attacking, the *a* opposed him;
1Sm 31: 3 raged around Saul, and the *a* hit him;
2Sm 11:24 Then the *a* shot at your servants from the
1Chr 8:40 The sons of Ulam were combat *a*,
10: 3 Then the *a* found him,
12: 2 They were *a* who could use either the right
2Chr 14: 7 Benjamin who carried bucklers and were *a*,
35:23 Then the *a* shot King Josiah,
Jdt 2:15 commanded, and twelve thousand mounted *a*,
1Mc 9:11 and the *a* came on ahead of the army,
Is 21:17 Few of Kedar's stalwart *a* shall remain,
Jer 50:29 Call up against Babylon *a*,

ARCHIPPUS (2)

Col 4:17 To *A* say,
Phlm 1: 2 our sister, to our fellow soldier *A*,

ARCHITE (5)

2Sm 15:32 God, Hushai the *A* was there to meet him,
16:16 friend Hushai the *A* came to Absalom,
17: 5 Absalom said, "Now call Hushai the *A* also;
17:14 the *A* better than that of Ahithophel.
1Chr 27:33 and Hushai the *A* was the king's confidant.

ARCHITECT (1)

2Mc 2:29 As the *a* of a new house must give

ARCHITES (1)

Jos 16: 2 ridge to the border of the *A* at Ataroth,

ARCHIVES (3)

Ezr 5:17 let a search be made in the royal *a* of
6: 1 issued an order to search the *a*
1Mc 14:23 a copy of their words in the public *a*,

ARD (1)

Gn 46:21 Naaman, Ahiram, Shupham, Hupham, and *A*.

ARDENT (3)

2Mc 14:38 risked body and life in his *a* zeal for it.
2Cor 7: 7 your grief, and your *a* concern for me,
7:11 *a* desire to restore the balance of justice!

ARDENTLY (1)

1Sm 9:20 *a* if not you and your father's family?"

ARDON (1)

1Chr 2:18 Her sons were Jesher, Shobab, and *A*.

ARDOR (3)

1Mc 6:47 of the royal army and the *a* of its forces,
Is 42:13 a hero, like a warrior he stirs up his *a*;
Jer 2:24 the desert, Snuffing the wind in her *a*—

AREA (31)

2Sm 5: 9 he built up the *a* from Millo to the palace.
1Kgs 11:29 The two were alone in the *a*,
Ez 41:12 The building fronting the free *a* on the
41:13 The free *a*,
41:14 of the temple, along with the free *a*,
41:15 lay the length of the free *a* and behind it,
42: 1 that lay across the free *a*
42:10 To the south along the side of the free *a*
42:13 on the free *a* are the sanctuary chambers;
42:15 had finished measuring the inner temple *a*,
43:12 *a* on the mountain top shall be most sacred.
45: 1 its whole *a* shall be sacred.
48:18 shall remain an *a* along the sacred tract,
Mt 9:31 and spread word of him through the whole *a*.
21:14 him inside the temple *a* and he cured them.
24: 1 out to him the buildings of the temple *a*.
Mk 5:25 There was a woman in the *a* who had been
6:55 The crowds scurried about the adjacent *a*
11:16 to carry things through the temple *a*.
13: 1 he was making his way out of the temple *a*,
Lk 19:47 teaching in the temple *a* from day to day.
Jn 2:15 sheep and oxen alike out of the temple *a*,
7:14 went into the temple *a* and began to teach.
7:28 Jesus, who was teaching in the temple *a*,
8: 2 At daybreak he reappeared in the temple *a*;
10:23 Jesus was walking in the temple *a*,
18:20 temple *a* where all the Jews come together.
Acts 2:46 went to the temple *a* together every day,
13:49 of the Lord was carried throughout that *a*.
21:28 *a* and thus profaned this sacred place."
24:12 Neither in the temple *a*,

AREAS (1)

Jos 13: 6 at least include these *a* in the division

ARELI (2)

Gn 46:16 Haggi, Shuni, Ezbon, Eri, Arod, and *A*.
Nm 26:17 through *A* the clan of the Arelites.

ARELITES (1)

Nm 26:17 Arodites, through Areli the clan of the *A*.

ARENA (1)

1Cor 4: 9 the line, like men doomed to die in the *a*.

AREOPAGUS (3)

Acts 17:19 Then they led him off to the *A*,
17:22 up in the *A* and delivered this address:
17:34 a member of the court of the *A*,

ARETAS (2)

2Mc 5: 8 Called to account before *A*,
2Cor 11:32 In Damascus the ethnarch of King *A* was

ARGOB (4)

Dt 3: 4 eluding our grasp, the whole region of *A*,
3:13 the kingdom of Og, the whole *A* region,
3:14 took all the region of *A* as far as the
1Kgs 4:13 and of the district of *A* in Bashan

ARGUE (5)

Jb 15: 3 Should he *a* in speech which does not avail,
Mk 8:11 came forward and began to *a* with him.
Lk 22:23 Then they began to *a* among themselves as
Acts 19:38 Let the parties *a* their case.
1Cor 11:16 If anyone wants to *a* about this,

ARGUED (1)

1Kgs 3:22 Thus they *a* before the king.

ARGUING (5)

2Sm 19:10 all the people were *a* among themselves,
Jb 40: 2 we have *a* with the Almighty by the critic?
Mk 9:34 been *a* about who was the most important.
12:28 and when he heard them *a* he realized how
Phil 2:14 you do, act without grumbling or *a*:

ARGUMENT (5)

Jb 6:25 yet how unconvincing is your *a*!
24:25 will confute me, and reduce my *a* to nought?
Ez 16:52 you are an *a* in favor of your sisters!
1Cor 1:20 Where is the master of worldly *a*?
Heb 6:16 to a promise and puts an end to all *a*.

ARGUMENTATION (1)

1Cor 2: 4 of the persuasive force of "wise" *a*,

ARGUMENTS (11)

Jb 9:14 any answer, or choose out *a* against him!
21:27 and the *a* you rehearse against me.
23: 4 before him, and fill my mouth with *a*;
32:11 discourses, and have given ear to your *a*.
33: 5 draw up your *a* and stand forth.
34:37 off our *a* and addressing many words to God.
Acts 2:40 of his testimony he used many other *a*,
19: 8 debated fearlessly, with persuasive *a*,
Eph 5: 6 Let no one deceive you with worthless *a*.
Col 2: 4 that no one may delude you with specious *a*.
Ti 3: 9 you abstain from stupid *a* and genealogies,

ARIARTHES (1)

1Mc 15:22 to Kings Demetrius, Attalus, *A* and Arsaces;

ARID (5)

Jer 51:43 parched and *a* land Where no man lives,
Hos 2: 5 like the desert, reduce her to an *a* land,
Jl 2:20 and drive him out into a land *a* and waste,
Mt 12:43 it roams through *a* wastes searching for a
Lk 11:24 *a* wastes searching for a resting-place;

ARIDAI (1)

Est 9: 9 Adalia, Aridatha, Parmashta, Arisai, *A*,

ARIDATHA (1)

Est 9: 8 Porathai, Adalia, *A*, Parmashta,

ARIEL (8)

1Chr 11:22 He killed the two sons of *A* of Moab,
Ezr 8:16 Therefore I sent Eliezer, *A*,
Is 29: 1 Woe to *A*, Ariel, the city where
29: 2 But I will bring distress upon *A*,
29: 2 You shall be to me like *A*,
29: 7 *A* with all the earthworks of her besiegers.
33: 7 See, the men of *A* cry out in the streets,

ARIGHT (6)

1Chr 15:13 burst upon us, for we did not seek him *a*."
Jdt 11: 7 who has sent you to set all creatures *a*!
Jb 11:13 *a* and stretch out your hands toward him,
Ps(s) 90:12 Teach us to number our days *a*,
Wis 2: 1 who said among themselves, thinking not *a*:
Is 11: 4 and decide *a* for the land's afflicted.

ARIMATHEA (4)

Mt 27:57 evening fell, a wealthy man from *A* arrived,
Mk 15:43 eve of the sabbath), Joseph from *A* arrived
Lk 23:51 He was from *A*,
Jn 19:38 Afterward, Joseph of *A*,

ARIOCH (7)

Gn 14: 1 Amraphel king of Shinar, *A* king of Ellasar,
14: 9 king of Shinar, and *A* king of Ellasar
Jdt 1: 6 the Hydaspes, and King *A* of the Elamites,
Dn 2:14 Then Daniel prudently took counsel with *A*,
2:15 When *A* told him,
2:24 So Daniel went to *A*,
2:24 *A* quickly brought Daniel to the king and

ARISAI (1)

Est 9: 9 Parmashta, *A*, Aridai, and Vaizatha,

ARISE (34)

Gn 21:18 *A*, lift up the boy and hold him by the hand;
Nm 10:35 the ark set out, Moses would say, *A*,
Jgs 5:12 *a*, Barak, make despoilers
7:15 to the camp of Israel, he said, *A*,
Neh 9: 5 Hodiah, Shebaniah, and Pethahiah said, *A*,
Jb 7: 4 If in bed I say, "When shall I *a*?"
Ps(s) 12: 6 and the needy sigh, now will I *a*,"
44:24 *A*! Cast us not off
44:27 *A*, help us!
59: 6 *A*; punish all the nations;
73:20 awakened, O Lord, so will you, when you *a*,
74:22 *A*, O God:
88:11 Will the shades *a* to give you thanks?
102:14 You will *a* and have mercy on Zion,
Sg 2:10 he says to me, *A*,
2:13 *A*, my beloved,
4:16 *A*, north wind!
Is 23:12 *A*, pass over to the Kittim,
51:17 *A*, O Jerusalem,
Ez 38:10 At that time thoughts shall *a* in your mind,
Dn 7:17 four kingdoms which shall *a* on the earth.
8:23 their measure, There shall *a* a king,
11:20 In his stead one shall *a* who will send a
12: 1 "At that time there shall *a* Michael,
Mi 4:13 *A* and thresh,
6: 1 *A*, present your plea before the mountains,
7: 8 though I have fallen, I will *a*;
Hb 2:19 to dumb stone, *A*!"
Zep 3: 8 LORD, against the day when I *a* as accuser;
Mal 3:20 *a* the sun of justice with its healing rays;
Lk 17: 1 "Scandals will inevitably *a*,
Eph 5:14 "Awake, O sleeper, *a* from the dead,
Jas 5:19 the case may *a* among you of someone
Rv 18: 9 her when they see the smoke *a* as she burns.

ARISEN (2)

Dt 34:10 then no prophet has *a* in Israel like Moses,
Mt 4:16 a land overshadowed by death, light has *a*."

ARISES (7)

Dt 13: 2 "If there *a* among you a prophet or a
1Mc 14:41 and high priest until a true prophet *a*.
Ps(s) 68: 2 God *a*; his enemies are scattered,
82: 1 God *a* in the divine assembly;
Prv 24:22 For suddenly *a* the destruction they send,
Is 2:19 majesty, when he *a* to overawe the earth.
2:21 majesty, when he *a* to overawe the earth.

ARISING (1)

Lk 23:14 charge against him *a* from your allegations.

ARISTARCHUS (5)

Acts 19:29 the theater and dragged in Gaius and *A*,
20: 4 *A* and Secundus from Thessalonica;
27: 2 us was a Macedonian, *A* of Thessalonica.
Col 4:10 *A*, who is a prisoner along with me,
Phlm 1:24 Christ Jesus, greets you, as do Mark, *A*,

ARISTOBULUS (2)

2Mc 1:10 Judas send greetings and good wishes to *A*,
Rom 16:10 to all who belong to the household of *A*.

ARISTOCRACY (1)

Est 1: 3 the Persian and Median *a*,

ARIUS (2)

1Mc 12: 7 was sent to the high priest Onias from *A*,
12:20 *A*, king of the Spartans,

ARK (221)

Gn 6:14 "Make yourself an *a* of gopherwood,
6:15 of the *a* shall be three hundred cubits,
6:16 for daylight in the *a*, and finish the ark
6:16 Put an entrance in the side of the *a*,
6:18 and your sons' wives, shall go into the *a*.
6:19 creatures you shall bring two into the *a*,
6:20 two of each shall come into the *a* with you,
7: 1 "Go into the *a*,
7: 7 the *a* because of the waters of the flood.
7: 9 male and female entered the *a* with Noah,
7:13 wives of Noah's sons had entered the *a*,
7:15 the breath of life entered the *a* with Noah.
7:17 As the waters increased, they lifted the *a*,
7:18 the *a* floated on the surface of the waters.
7:23 Noah and those with him in the *a* were left.
8: 1 wild and tame, that were in the *a*
8: 4 *a* came to rest on the mountains of Ararat.
8: 6 opened the hatch he had made in the *a*,
8: 9 perch, and it returned to him in the *a*,
8: 9 dove and drew it back to him inside the *a*.
8:10 and again sent the dove out from the *a*.
8:13 Noah then removed the covering of the *a*
8:16 "Go out of the *a*,
8:19 creeping creatures of the earth left the *a*,
9:10 that were with you and came out of the *a*.
9:18 of Noah who came out of the *a* were Shem,
Ex 25:10 "You shall make an *a* of acacia wood,
25:12 fasten them on the four supports of the *a*,
25:14 through the rings on the sides of the *a*,
25:15 the rings of the *a* and never be withdrawn.
25:16 In the *a* you are to put the commandments
25:21 you shall then place on top of the *a*.
25:21 In the *a* itself you are to put the
25:22 two cherubim on the *a* of the commandments.
26:33 The *a* of the commandments you shall bring
26:34 Set the propitiatory on the *a* of the
30: 6 *a* of commandments where I will meet you.
30:26 meeting tent and the *a* of the commandments,
31: 7 the *a* of the commandments with the
35:12 the *a*, with its poles,
37: 1 Bezalel made the *a* of acacia wood,
37: 5 through the rings on the sides of the *a*,
39:35 the *a* of the commandments with its poles,
40: 3 Put the *a* of the commandments in it,
40: 3 in it, and screen off the *a* with the veil.
40: 5 in front of the *a* of the commandments,
40:20 the commandments and put them in the *a*;
40:20 the *a* and set the propitiatory upon it.
40:21 He brought the *a* into the Dwelling and
40:21 screening off the *a* of the commandments,
Lv 16: 2 in front of the propitiatory of the *a*;
Nm 3:31 had charge of whatever pertained to the *a*,
4: 5 cover the *a* of the commandments with it.
7:89 propitiatory on the *a* of the commandments,
10:33 and the *a* of the covenant of the LORD
10:35 Whenever the *a* set out,
14:44 even though neither the *a* of the covenant
Dt 10: 1 Also make an *a* of wood.
10: 2 broke, and you shall place them in the *a*.'
10: 3 So I made an *a* of acacia wood,
10: 5 and placed the tablets in the *a* I had made.
10: 8 to carry the *a* of the covenant of the LORD,
31: 9 carry the *a* of the covenant of the LORD,
31:25 *a* of the covenant of the LORD this order:
31:26 beside the *a* of the covenant of the LORD,
Jos 3: 3 you see the *a* of the covenant of the LORD,
3: 4 two thousand cubits between you and the *a*.
3: 6 take up the *a* of the covenant

3: 8 Now command the priests carrying the *a* of
3:11 The *a* of the covenant of the Lord of the
3:13 of the priests carrying the *a* of the LORD,
3:14 the *a* of the covenant ahead of them.
3:15 bearers of the *a* waded into the waters
3:17 the priests carrying the *a* of the covenant
4: 5 the Jordan in front of the *a* of the LORD,
4: 7 flow before the *a* of the covenant
4: 9 who were carrying the *a* of the covenant.
4:10 The priests carrying the *a* remained in the
4:11 reached the other side, the *a* of the LORD,
4:16 carrying the *a* of the commandments
4:18 and when the priests carrying the *a* of the
6: 4 carrying ram's horns ahead of the *a*.
6: 6 then ordered them to take up the *a* of the
6: 6 ram's horns in front of the *a* of the LORD.
6: 7 troops marching ahead of the *a* of the LORD.
6: 8 and the *a* of the covenant of the LORD
6: 9 the rear guard followed the *a*,
6:11 he had the *a* of the LORD circle the city,
6:12 had the priests take up the *a* of the LORD.
6:13 marched in front of the *a* of the LORD,
6:13 the rear guard followed the *a* of the LORD,
7: 6 before the *a* of the LORD until evening;
8:33 stood on either side of the *a* facing the
8:33 carrying the *a* of the covenant of the LORD.
Jgs 20:27 *a* of the covenant of God
1Sm 3: 3 temple of the LORD where the *a* of God was.
4: 3 Let us fetch the *a* of the LORD from Shiloh
4: 4 from there the *a* of the LORD of hosts,
4: 4 and Phinehas, were with the *a* of God.
4: 5 When the *a* of the LORD arrived in the camp,
4: 6 the *a* of the LORD had come into the camp,
4:11 The *a* of God was captured,
4:13 was troubled at heart about the *a* of God.
4:17 dead, and the *a* of God has been captured."
4:18 At this mention of the *a* of God,
4:19 capture of the *a* and the deaths
4:21 capture of the *a* of God
4:22 because the *a* of God had been captured.
5: 1 Philistines, having captured the *a* of God,
5: 2 They then took the *a* of God and brought it
5: 3 on the ground before the *a* of the LORD.
5: 4 on the ground before the *a* of the LORD,
5: 7 "The *a* of the God of Israel must not
5: 8 we do with the *a* of the God of Israel?"
5: 8 "Let them move the *a* of the God of Israel
5: 9 moved the *a* of the God of Israel to Gath!
5:10 The *a* of God was next sent to Ekron;
5:10 "Why have they brought the *a* of the God
5:11 "Send away the *a* of the God of Israel.
6: 1 The *a* of the LORD had been in the land of
6: 2 "What shall we do with the *a* of the LORD?
6: 3 to send away the *a* of the God of Israel,
6: 8 the *a* of the LORD and place it on the cart,
6:11 they placed the *a* of the LORD on the cart,
6:13 When they looked up and spied the *a*,
6:15 down the *a* of God and the box beside it,
6:18 The large stone on which the *a* of the LORD
6:19 when they greeted the *a* of the LORD,
6:21 have returned the *a* of the LORD;
7: 1 came for the *a* of the LORD
7: 1 Eleazar as guardian of the *a* of the LORD.
7: 2 From the day the *a* came to rest in
2Sm 6: 2 Judah to bring up from there the *a* of God,
6: 3 The *a* of God was placed on a new cart and
6: 6 his hand to the *a* of God and steadied it,
6: 9 "How can the *a* of the LORD come to me?"
6:10 So David would not have the *a* of the
6:11 The *a* of the LORD remained in the house of
6:12 David went to bring up the *a* of God from
6:13 the *a* of the LORD had advanced six steps,
6:15 bringing up the *a* of the LORD
6:16 As the *a* of the LORD was entering the City
6:17 The *a* of the LORD was brought in and set
7: 2 cedar, while the *a* of God dwells in a tent!"
11:11 *a* and Israel and Judah are lodged in tents,
15:24 bearers of the *a* of the covenant of God],
15:24 and Abiathar brought the *a* of God to a
15:25 "Take the *a* of God back to the city.
15:29 So Zadok and Abiathar took the *a* of God
1Kgs 2:26 because you carried the *a* of the Lord GOD
3:15 before the *a* of the covenant of the Lord,
6:19 to house the *a* of the LORD's covenant,
8: 1 to bring up the *a* of the LORD's covenant
8: 3 had arrived, the priests took up the *a*;
8: 4 they carried the *a* of the LORD and the
8: 5 before the *a* sheep and oxen
8: 6 The priests brought the *a* of the covenant
8: 7 over the place of the *a*, sheltering the ark
8: 9 There was nothing in the *a* but the two
8:21 the *a* in which is the covenant of the LORD,
1Chr 6:16 *a* had obtained a permanent resting place.
13: 3 us bring the *a* of our God here among us,
13: 5 to bring the *a* of God from Kiriath-jearim.
13: 6 of Judah, to bring back the *a* of God,
13: 7 They transported the *a* of God on a new
13: 9 stretched out his hand to steady the *a*,
13:10 because he had laid his hand on the *a*.
13:12 "How can I bring the *a* of God with me?"
13:13 the *a* back with him to the City of David,
13:14 The *a* of God remained in the house of
15: 1 and prepared a place for the *a* of God,
15: 2 may carry the *a* of God except the Levites,
15: 2 carry the *a* of the LORD
15: 3 bring the *a* of the LORD
15:12 your brethren and bring the *a* of the LORD,
15:14 themselves to bring up the *a* of the LORD,
15:15 the *a* of God on their shoulders with poles,
15:23 and Elkanah were gatekeepers before the *a*.
15:24 sounded the trumpets before the *a* of God.
15:24 Jeiel were also gatekeepers before the *a*.
15:25 bring up the *a* of the covenant
15:26 bearing the *a* of the covenant of the LORD,
15:27 as were all the Levites who carried the *a*,
15:28 Thus all Israel brought back the *a* of the
15:29 But as the *a* of the covenant of the LORD
16: 1 They brought in the *a* of God and set it
16: 4 to minister before the *a* of the LORD,
16: 6 before the *a* of the covenant of God.
16:37 brethren there before the *a* of the covenant
16:37 *a* regularly according to the daily ritual;
17: 1 but the *a* of the covenant of the LORD
22:19 that the *a* of the covenant of the LORD and
28: 2 for the *a* of the covenant of the LORD,
28:18 covered the *a* of the covenant of the LORD.
2Chr 1: 4 (The *a* of God,
5: 2 *a* of the LORD's covenant
5: 4 had arrived, the Levites took up the *a*,
5: 5 and they carried the *a* and the meeting
5: 6 before the *a* were sacrificing sheep
5: 7 The priests brought the *a* of the covenant
5: 8 over the place of the *a*, sheltering the ark
5: 9 The *a* has remained there to this day.
6:11 And I have placed there the *a*,
6:41 place, you and the *a* of your majesty.
8:11 where the *a* of the LORD has come are holy."
35: 3 the holy *a* in the house built by Solomon,
2Mc 2: 4 *a* should accompany him
2: 5 in a cave in which he put the tent, the *a*,
Ps(s) 132: 8 place you and the *a* of your majesty.
Jer 3:16 say, "The *a* of the covenant of the LORD!"
Mt 24:38 right up to the day Noah entered the *a*.
Lk 17:27 right up to the day Noah entered the *a*—
Heb 9: 4 incense and the *a* of the covenant
9: 4 *a* were the golden jar containing the manna,
9: 5 Above the *a* were the cherubim of glory
11: 7 an *a* that his household might be saved.
1Pt 3:20 God patiently waited until the *a* was built.
3:20 in all, escaped in the *a* through the water.
Rv 11:19 temple could be seen the *a* of the covenant.

ARKITE (1)

1Chr 1:15 the Girgashite, the Hivite, the *A*,

ARKITES (1)

Gn 10:17 the Girgashites, the Hivites, the *A*,

ARM (84)

Ex 6: 1 compelled by my outstretched *a*,
6: 6 *a* and with mighty acts of judgment.
15:16 of your *a* they were frozen like stone,
Nm 31: 3 men from your midst and *a* them for war,
Dt 4:34 with his strong hand and outstretched *a*,
5:15 with his strong hand and outstretched *a*.
7:19 and outstretched *a* with which the LORD,
9:29 great power and with your outstretched *a*.
11: 2 his strong hand and outstretched *a*;
26: 8 with his strong hand and outstretched *a*,
33:20 that has seized the *a* and head of the prey.
2Sm 1:10 his *a* and brought them here to my lord."
23: 7 He who wishes to touch them must *a* himself
1Kgs 8:42 your mighty hand and your outstretched *a*),
10:19 top, and an *a* on each side of the seat.
10:19 Next to each *a* stood a lion;
2Kgs 7: 2 the adjutant on whose *a* the king leaned,
17:36 Egypt with great power and outstretched *a*:
2Chr 6:32 mighty power, and your outstretched *a*,
9:18 there was an *a* on each side of the seat,
32: 8 For he has only an *a* of flesh,
1Mc 3:58 *A* yourselves and be brave;
7:47 cut off Nicanor's head and his right *a*,
9:47 Jonathan raised his *a* to strike Bacchides,
2Mc 12:35 and cut off his *a* at the shoulder.
15:24 By the might of your *a* may those be struck
15:30 *a* to be cut off and taken to Jerusalem.
15:32 blasphemer's *a* that had been boastfully
Jb 26: 2 powerless, what strength to the feeble *a*!
31:22 Then may my *a* fall from the shoulder,
38:15 withheld, and the *a* of pride is shattered.
40: 9 Have you an *a* like that of God,
Ps(s) 44: 4 nor did their own *a* make them victorious,
44: 4 But it was your *a* and your right hand and
77:16 your strong *a* you redeemed your people,
89:11 strong *a* you have scattered your enemies.
89:14 Yours is a mighty *a*;
89:22 him, and that my *a* may make him strong.
98: 1 hand has won victory for him, his holy *a*.
136:12 With a mighty hand and an outstretched *a*,
Sg 2: 6 under my head and his right *a* embraces me.
8: 3 under my head and his right *a* embraces me.
8: 6 a seal on your heart, as a seal on your *a*;
Wis 5:16 right hand, and protect them with his *a*.
5:17 he shall *a* creation to requite the enemy;
11:21 who can resist the might of your *a*?
16:16 you were punished by the might of your *a*,
Sir 21:21 a wise man, like a bracelet on his right *a*.
36: 5 the splendor of your right hand and *a*;
46: 2 What glory was his when he raised his *a*,
47: 5 who gave strength to his right *a* To defeat
Is 8: 9 *A*, but be crushed! *A*, but be crushed!
30:30 and let it be seen how his *a* descends In
40:10 the Lord GOD, who rules by his strong *a*;
44:12 hammers, and forges it with his strong *a*.
45: 5 It is I who *a* you,
49: 2 and concealed me in the shadow of his *a*.
51: 5 forth [and my *a* shall judge the nations];
51: 5 coastlands hope, and my *a* they shall await.
51: 9 awake, put on strength, O *a* of the LORD!
52:10 his holy *a* in the sight of all the nations;
53: 1 whom has the *a* of the LORD been revealed?
59:16 So his own *a* brought about the victory,
62: 8 by his right hand and by his mighty *a*:
63: 5 So my own *a* brought about the victory and
63:12 glorious *a* was the guide at Moses' right;
Jer 21: 5 you with outstretched hand and mighty *a*,
27: 5 by my great power, with my outstretched *a*;
32:17 your great might, with your outstretched *a*;
32:21 With strong hand and outstretched *a* you
Bar 2:11 and great might, and with your upraised *a*,
Ez 4: 7 with bared *a* you shall prophesy against it.
17: 9 of a mighty *a* or many people to do this.]
20:33 with a mighty hand and outstretched *a*,
20:34 outstretched *a*, with poured-out wrath,
30:21 Son of man, I have broken the *a* of Pharaoh,
30:22 I will break his strong *a*,
Zec 9:13 as my bow, I will *a* myself with Ephraim;
11:17 fall upon his *a* and upon his right eye;
11:17 Let his *a* wither away entirely,
Lk 1:51 "He has shown might with his *a*;
Acts 13:17 an outstretched *a* he led them out of it.
1Pt 4: 1 *a* yourselves with his same mentality.

ARMAGEDDON (1)

Rv 16:16 the kings in a place called in Hebrew *A*."

ARMED (42)

Nm 20:20 them with a large and heavily *a* force.
22:32 It is I who have come *a* to hinder you
31: 5 there were twelve thousand men *a* for war.
32:27 as *a* troops to battle before the LORD,
Jos 1:14 cross over *a* ahead of your kinsmen
4:12 Gadites, and half-tribe of Manasseh, *a*,
Jgs 18:11 the Danites, fully *a* with weapons of war,
2Sm 22:30 For with your aid I run against an *a* band,
23:21 Although the Egyptian was *a* with a spear,
1Chr 12:24 muster of the detachments of *a* troops
12:25 six thousand eight hundred *a* troops.
12:35 and with them, *a* with shield and lance,
2Chr 17: 2 He placed *a* forces in all the fortified
17:17 hundred thousand *a* with bow and buckler.
Neh 4:10 work, while the other half, *a* with spears,
4:11 The load carriers, too, were *a*;
Jdt 7: 7 stationing *a* detachments around them,
Est 8:11 every *a* group of any nation or province
1Mc 3: 3 He *a* himself with weapons of war;
12:27 his men to be on guard and to remain *a*,
14:32 *a* forces and giving them their pay.
2Mc 4:40 *a* men under the leadership of Auranus,
5: 2 fully *a* with lances and drawn swords;
5:25 work, he ordered his men to parade fully *a*.
5:26 and running through the city with *a* men,
8: 9 twenty thousand *a* men of various nations
13: 2 and three hundred chariots *a* with scythes.
14:22 Judas had posted *a* men in readiness at
15:11 When he had *a* each of them,
Jb 29:25 I took a king's place in the *a* forces.
Ps(s) 18:30 For with your aid I run against an *a* band,
Prv 6:11 like a highway man, and want like an *a* man.
24:34 like a highwayman, and want like an *a* man.
Sir 36:26 an *a* band that shifts from city to city?
Dn 11:10 shall prepare and assemble a great *a* host,
11:22 *A* might shall be completely overwhelmed by
11:31 *A* forces shall move at his command and
Mt 26:55 come *a* with swords and clubs to arrest me?
Mk 14:48 "You have come out to arrest me *a* with
Lk 11:21 a strong man fully *a* guards his courtyard,
22:52 come out after me *a* with swords and clubs?
Acts 26:12 *a* with the authority and commission

ARMFUL (1)

Is 17: 5 Like the reaper's mere *a* of stalks when

ARMIES (20)

1Sm 17:26 he should insult the *a* of the living God?"
17:36 he has insulted the *a* of the living God."
17:45 of the *a* of Israel that you have insulted.
1Kgs 2: 5 he slew the two generals of Israel's *a*,

ARMIES (cont.)

1Mc 3:42 *a* were encamped within their territory;
6: 5 news that the *a* sent into the land of Judah
6: 6 taken from the *a* they had destroyed;
6:33 and the *a* prepared for battle,
7:43 The *a* met in battle on the thirteenth day
9:13 The earth shook with the noise of the *a*,
16: 5 and between the two *a* was a stream.
2Mc 10:28 As soon as dawn broke, the *a* joined battle,
Ps(s) 44:10 disgrace, and you go not forth with our *a*.
60:12 that you go not forth, O God, with our *a*?
108:12 that you go not forth, O God, with our *a*?
Jer 34: 1 *a* and the earth's kingdoms subject to him,
34: 7 while the *a* of the king of Babylon were
40:13 and all the leaders of the *a* in the field
Rv 19:14 The *a* of heaven were behind him riding
19:19 and the *a* they had mustered to do battle

ARMING (1)

1Sm 17:38 on his head and *a* him with a coat of mail.

ARMLET (1)

2Sm 1:10 crown from his head and the *a* from his arm

ARMONI (1)

2Sm 21: 8 But the king took *A* and Meribbaal,

ARMOR (23)

1Sm 17: 5 of scale *a* weighing five thousand shekels,
17:39 however, since he had never tried *a* before.
17:54 but he kept Goliath's *a* in his own tent.
31: 9 off Saul's head and stripped him of his *a*,
31:10 They put his *a* in the temple of Astarte,
1Kgs 20:11 man who is buckling his *a*
1Chr 10: 9 him, cut off his head, and took his *a*;
10:10 His *a* they put in the house of their gods,
Jdt 14: 3 They will seize their *a* and hurry to their
15:13 the men of Israel followed in their *a*,
1Mc 4: 6 *a* and swords as they would have wished.
6:43 any of the others and covered with royal *a*,
13:29 carved suits of *a* as a perpetual memorial,
13:29 and next to the *a* he placed carved ships,
2Mc 3:25 The rider was seen to be wearing golden *a*.
5: 3 ornaments, together with *a* of every sort.
10:30 and shielding him with their own *a*,
15:28 Nicanor lying there in all his *a*,
Jb 41: 4 his strength, and the fitness of his *a*.
Wis 5:17 He shall take his zeal for *a* and he shall
Rom 13:12 of darkness and put on the *a* of light.
Eph 6:11 Put on the *a* of God so that you may be
6:13 You must put on the *a* of God if you are to

ARMOR-BEARER (22)

Jgs 9:54 immediately called his *a* and said to him,
1Sm 14: 1 day Jonathan, son of Saul, said to his *a*,
14: 6 Jonathan said to his *a*:
14: 7 *a* replied, "Do whatever you are inclined
14:12 the outpost called to Jonathan and his *a*.
14:12 So Jonathan said to his *a*, "Climb up
14:13 clambered up with his *a* behind him;
14:13 his *a* followed him and finished them off.
14:14 In this first exploit Jonathan and his *a*
14:17 they found Jonathan and his *a* missing.
16:21 became very fond of him, made him his *a*,
31: 4 Then Saul said to his *a*
31: 4 his *a*, badly frightened, refused to do it.
31: 5 When the *a* saw that Saul was dead,
31: 6 and his *a* died together on that same day.
2Sm 11: 3 and wife of [Joab's *a* Uriah the Hittite."
23:37 Naharai from Beeroth, *a* of Joab,
1Chr 10: 4 Saul said to his *a*, "Draw your sword
10: 4 But the *a*, in great fear, refused.
10: 5 the *a* also fell on his sword and died.
11:39 Naharai, from Beeroth, the *a* of Joab,
1Mc 4:30 of Jonathan, the son of Saul, and his *a*

ARMOR-BEARERS (1)

2Sm 18:15 ten of Joab's young *a* closed in on Absalom,

ARMORY (3)

2Kgs 20:13 silver, gold, spices and fine oil, his *a*,
Is 39: 2 the spices and fine oil, his whole *a*,
Jer 50:25 The LORD opens his *a* and brings forth the

ARMPITS (1)

Jer 38:12 tattered rags between your *a* and the ropes."

ARMS (78)

Gn 45:14 and wept, and Benjamin wept in his *a*.
46:29 on his neck and wept a long time in his *a*.
49:24 remained stiff, as their *a* were unsteady,
Ex 26:17 Each board shall have two *a* that shall
26:20 pedestals under each board, at its two *a*;
36:22 Each board had two *a*,
36:24 pedestals under each board, at its two *a*;
Jgs 7:23 Israelites were called to *a* from Naphtali,
7:24 So all the Ephraimites were called to *a*,
15:14 the ropes around his *a* became as flax that
16:12 But he snapped them off his *a* like thread.
18:22 that of Micah took up *a* and overtook them.
18:23 do you want, that you have taken up *a*?"
1Sm 21: 6 so today, when they are consecrated at *a*!"
2Sm 22:35 war till my *a* could bend a bow of brass.
1Kgs 20:27 called to *a* and supplied with provisions;
2Kgs 3:21 every man capable of bearing *a* was called
2Chr 9:18 seat, with two lions standing beside the *a*.
Ezr 4:23 and stopped their work by force of *a*.
Tb 7: 7 to weep in the *a* of his kinsman Tobiah.
11: 9 ran up to her son, threw her *a* around him,
11:13 son, he threw his *a* around him and wept.
Jdt 11:22 of your people, to bring victory to our *a*,
14:11 *a* and went to the slopes of the mountain.
Est D: 8 held her in his *a* until she recovered,
1Mc 5:43 they threw away their *a* and fled to the
6: 6 they had grown strong by reason of the *a*,
6:41 their marching, and the clashing of the *a*,
7:44 was dead, they threw down their *a* and fled.
8:26 they shall not give nor provide grain, *a*,
8:28 them there shall not be given grain, *a*,
10: 6 gather an army and procure *a* as his ally;
10:21 he gathered an army and procured many *a*.
11:50 So they threw down their *a* and made peace.
14:33 previously the enemy's *a* had been stored.
2Mc 8:27 They collected the enemy's *a* and stripped
9: 2 the people had swift recourse to *a*,
10:23 successful at *a* in all his undertakings,
10:27 they took up their *a* and advanced a
11: 7 himself was the first to take up *a*,
11:12 away were wounded and stripped of their *a*,
15: 5 up *a* and carry out the king's business."
15:12 *a* for the whole Jewish community.
15:21 not through *a* but through the LORD's
Ps(s) 18:35 for war and my *a* to bend a bow of brass.
59: 5 no guilt of mine they hurry to take up *a*.
129: 7 hand, nor the gatherer of sheaves his *a*;
Prv 6:10 slumber, a little folding of the *a* to rest
24:33 slumber, a little folding of the *a* to rest
31:17 about with strength, and sturdy are her *a*.
31:20 the poor, and extends her *a* to the needy.
Eccl 4: 5 folds his *a* and consumes his own flesh"
Sg 5:14 His *a* are rods of gold adorned with
Wis 18:22 not by bodily strength, nor by force of *a*;
Sir 12: 5 No *a* for combat should you give him,
Is 3:12 a babe in *a* will be their tyrant,
40:11 in his *a* he gathers the lambs,
49:22 They shall bring your sons in their *a*,
60: 4 your daughters in the *a* of their nurses.
66:12 nurslings, you shall be carried in her *a*,
Lam 2:12 And breathe their last in their mothers' *a*.
Ez 13:20 their *a* and set free those you have caught.
16:11 I put bracelets on your *a*,
23:42 *a* and splendid diadems on their heads.
30:24 strengthen the *a* of the king of Babylon,
30:25 make the *a* of the king of Babylon strong,
30:25 strong, but the *a* of Pharaoh shall drop.]
Dn 2:32 was pure gold, its chest and *a* were silver,
10: 6 *a* and feet looked like burnished bronze,
Hos 7:15 Though I trained and strengthened their *a*,
11: 3 Ephraim to walk, who took them in my *a*;
Jl 4: 9 proclaim a war, rouse the warriors to *a*!
Mk 9:36 their midst, and putting his *a* around him,
Lk 2:28 in his *a* and blessed God in these words:
11:22 such a one carries off the *a* on which he
15:20 to meet him, threw his *a* around his neck,
Acts 20:37 their *a* around him and kissing him,
Phil 2:25 my brother, co-worker, and comrade in *a*,

ARMY (309)

Gn 21:22 by Phicol, the commander of his *a*,
21:32 along with Phicol, the commander of his *a*,
26:26 and Phicol, the general of his *a*.
Ex 14: 4 glory through Pharaoh and all his *a*,
14: 9 Pharaoh's whole *a*,
14:17 glory through Pharaoh and all his *a*,
14:28 charioteers of Pharaoh's whole *a*
15: 4 chariots and *a* he hurled into the sea;
Nm 31:14 became angry with the officers of the *a*,
31:48 of the *a* came up to Moses and said to him,
Dt 11: 4 *a* and to their horses and chariots,
20: 1 chariots and an *a* greater than your own,
20: 9 officers shall be appointed over the *a*.
Jos 8: 1 the *a* with you and prepare to attack Ai.
8:10 the *a* and went up to Ai at its head,
8:14 and he and all his *a* came out very early
10:21 all the *a* returned safely to Joshua and
11: 4 an *a* numerous as the sands on the seashore,
11: 7 Joshua with his whole *a* came upon them at
Jgs 4: 2 The general of his *a* was Sisera,
4: 7 lead Sisera, the general of Jabin's *a*,
4:16 and the *a* as far as Haro-sheath-ha-goiim.
4:16 entire *a* of Sisera fell beneath the sword,
7:22 The *a* fled as far as Beth-shittah in the
8: 6 that we should give food to your *a*?"
8:10 all who were left of the whole Kedemite *a*,
8:12 captive, throwing the entire *a* into panic.
9:29 to Abimelech, 'Get a larger *a* and come out!' "
20:26 the entire Israelite *a* went up to Bethel,
21: 9 A roll call of the *a* established that none
1Sm 12: 9 of Sisera, the captain of the *a* of Jabin,
14:15 spread to the *a* and to the countryside,
14:38 said, "Come here, all officers of the *a*.
14:45 But the *a* said to Saul:
17:20 the barricade of the camp just as the *a*,
17:46 corpses of the Philistine *a* for the birds
18: 5 and this was agreeable to the whole *a*,
28:19 have delivered the *a* of Israel
2Sm 8:16 son of Zeruiah, was in command of the *a*.
10:16 with Shobach, general of Hadadezer's *a*,
10:18 Shobach, general of the *a*,
11: 1 with his officers and the *a* of Israel,
11:17 Joab, some officers of David's *a* fell,
15:18 while the whole *a* marched past him.
17:25 Amasa in command of the *a* in Joab's place.
18: 6 *a* then took the field against Israel,
19: 3 mourning for the whole *a*
20:23 was in command of the whole *a* of Israel.
24: 2 and the leaders of the *a* who were with him,
24: 4 overruled Joab and the leaders of the *a*,
1Kgs 1: 8 and his companions, the pick of David's *a*,
1:10 Nathan, or Benaiah, or the pick of the *a*,
1:19 the priest, and Joab, the general of the *a*,
1:25 the king's sons, the commanders of the *a*,
2:32 Abner, son of Ner, general of Israel's *a*,
2:32 Amasa, son of Jether, general of Judah's *a*.
2:35 son of Jehoiada, over the *a* in his place,
4: 4 son of Jehoiada, commander of the *a*;
11:15 Edom, Joab, the general of the *a*,
11:21 and that Joab, the general of the *a*,
16:15 The *a* was besieging Gibbethon of the
16:16 Israel proclaimed Omri, general of the *a*,
20:13 LORD says, 'Do you see all this huge *a*?
20:19 the provinces with the *a* following them
20:25 Mobilize an *a* as large as the army that
20:28 I will deliver up to you all this large *a*,
22:36 At sunset a cry went through the *a*,
2Kgs 3: 9 for the *a* and for the animals with them.
4:13 to the king or to the commander of the *a*?' "
5: 1 the *a* commander of the king of Aram,
6:24 his whole *a* and laid siege to Samaria.
7: 6 The LORD had caused the *a* of the Arameans
7: 6 chariots and horses, the din of a large *a*,
7:14 sent them to reconnoiter the Aramean *a*.
8:21 Then his *a* fled homeward.
9: 5 the commanders of the *a* were in session.
18:17 a great *a* to King Hezekiah at Jerusalem.
24:14 all the officers and men of the *a*,
24:16 Babylon all seven thousand men of the *a*,
25: 1 and his whole *a* advanced against Jerusalem,
25: 5 But the Chaldean *a* pursued the king and
25: 5 near Jericho, abandoned by his whole *a*.
25:19 in the city, the scribe of the *a* commander,
25:23 all the *a* commanders with their men came
25:26 left with the *a* commanders and went to
1Chr 12:15 These Gadites were *a* commanders,
12:22 warriors and became commanders of his *a*.
14:15 you to strike the *a* of the Philistines."
14:16 the Philistine *a* from Gibeon to Gezer.
18: 9 had defeated the entire *a* of Hadadezer,
18:15 son of Zeruiah, was in command of the *a*;
19: 7 along with the king of Maacah and his *a*,
19: 8 and his whole *a* of warriors against them.
19:11 the rest of the *a*,
19:16 Shophach, the general of Hadadezer's *a*,
19:17 *a* of David drawn up to fight the Arameans,
19:18 also killed Shophach, the general of the *a*.
20: 1 go to war, Joab led the *a* out in force,
20: 3 he and his whole *a* returned to Jerusalem.
21: 2 Joab and to the other generals of the *a*,
26:26 of hundreds, and the commanders of the *a*,
27: 3 commanders of the *a* for the first month.
27: 5 The third *a* commander,
27:34 The commander of the king's *a* was Joab.
2Chr 12: 3 the *a* that came with him from Egypt
13:13 so that while his *a* faced Judah,
14: 7 Asa had an *a* of three hundred thousand
14:12 were crushed before the LORD and his *a*,
16: 7 the *a* of the king of Aram has escaped your
16: 8 not the Ethiopians and Libyans a vast *a*,
20:21 as it went forth at the head of the *a*.
23:14 the captains who were in command of the *a*;
25: 7 king, let not the *a* of Israel go with you,
25:11 Amaziah now assumed command of his *a*.
26:11 Uzziah also had a standing *a* of fit
26:13 at their disposal was a mighty *a*
26:14 for the entire *a*— bucklers, lances,
28: 9 *a* returning to Samaria and said to them:
32: 6 he appointed *a* commanders over the people.
33:11 them the *a* commanders of the Assyrian king;
33:14 He stationed *a* officers in all the
Neh 2: 9 also sent with me *a* officers and cavalry.
Jdt 1:13 proceeded with his *a* against King Arphaxad,
1:16 and there he and his *a* relaxed and feasted
2:14 generals and officers of the Assyrian *a*.
2:19 Then he and his whole *a* proceeded on their
3: 6 he went down with his *a* to the seacoast,
3:10 to refurbish all the equipment of his *a*.
5: 1 commander in chief of the Assyrian *a*,
5: 3 How large is their *a*?
5: 3 up as their king and the leader of their *a*?
5:24 your great *a*,
6: 1 commander in chief of the Assyrian *a*,
6: 6 the sword of my *a* or the spear of my
7: 1 day Holofernes ordered his whole *a*,
7: 2 a very great *a*.

7:18 the Assyrian *a* was encamped in the plain,
13:15 general in charge of the Assyrian *a*,
14: 3 to awaken the generals of the Assyrian *a*.
14:19 of the Assyrian *a* heard these words,
1Mc 1: 4 a very strong *a* and conquered provinces,
2:44 They gathered an *a* and struck down sinners
2:66 *a* and direct the war against the nations.
3:10 together with a large *a* from Samaria,
3:13 But Seron, commander of the Syrian *a*,
3:17 when they saw the *a* coming against them,
3:19 does not depend upon the size of the *a*,
3:23 he rushed suddenly upon Seron and his *a*,
3:27 the forces of his kingdom, a very strong *a*.
3:34 He entrusted to him half of the *a*,
3:35 Lysias was to send an *a* against them to
3:37 half of the *a* and set out from Antioch,
3:57 Then the *a* moved off,
4: 3 soldiers to attack the king's *a* at Emmaus,
4: 7 They saw the *a* of the Gentiles,
4: 9 Sea, when Pharaoh pursued them with an *a*.
4:10 and destroy this *a* before us today.
4:16 Judas and the *a* returned from the pursuit,
4:18 and his *a* are near us on the mountain.
4:20 They saw that their *a* had been put to
4:21 *a* of Judas in the plain ready to attack,
4:30 Seeing that the *a* was strong,
4:31 *a* into the hands of your people Israel;
4:37 So the whole *a* assembled,
5: 6 where he found a strong *a* and a large body
5:11 Timothy is the leader of their *a*.
5:18 people, with the rest of the *a* to guard it.
5:28 suddenly changed direction with his *a*,
5:29 He led his *a* from that place by night,
5:32 loud shouting, he said to the men of his *a*,
5:34 When the *a* of Timothy realized that it was
5:37 another *a* and camped opposite Raphon,
5:40 his *a* were approaching the running stream,
5:40 Timothy said to the officers of his *a*:
5:50 the men of the *a* took up their positions,
5:56 and Azariah, the leaders of the *a*,
5:58 to the men of their *a* who were with them,
6: 6 *a* and been driven back by the Israelites;
6:28 all his Friends, the officers of his *a*,
6:30 His *a* numbered a hundred thousand
6:38 or the other of the two flanks of the *a*,
6:40 of the king's *a* extended over the heights,
6:41 for the *a* was very great and strong.
6:42 Judas with his *a* advanced to fight,
6:42 and six hundred men of the king's *a* fell.
6:47 of the royal *a* and the ardor of its forces,
6:48 *a* went up to Jerusalem to attack them,
6:56 Media with the *a* that accompanied the king,
6:57 He said to the king, the leaders of the *a*,
7:10 in the land of Judah with a great *a*,
7:11 seeing that they had come with a great *a*.
7:14 of the line of Aaron has come with the *a*,
7:32 About five hundred men of Nicanor's *a* fell;
7:35 and his *a* are not delivered to me at once,
7:38 Take revenge on this man and his *a*,
7:39 Beth-horon, where the Syrian *a* joined him.
7:42 the same way, crush this *a* before us today,
7:43 Nicanor's *a* was crushed,
7:44 When his *a* saw that Nicanor was dead,
8: 6 cavalry and chariots and a very great *a*,
9: 1 Nicanor and his *a* had fallen in battle,
9: 1 Judah, along with the right wing of his *a*.
9: 7 As Judas saw that his *a* was melting away
9:11 Then the *a* of Bacchides moved out of camp
9:11 and the archers came on ahead of the *a*,
9:14 the right, with the main force of his *a*,
10: 2 *a* and marched out to engage him in combat.
10: 6 gather an *a* and procure arms as his ally;
10: 8 had given him authority to gather an *a*.
10:21 he gathered an *a* and procured many arms.
10:36 the king's *a* and allowances be given them,
10:48 a large *a* and encamped opposite Demetrius.
10:49 battle, and when the *a* of Demetrius fled,
10:53 him in battle, defeated him and his *a*,
10:69 Having gathered a large *a*,
10:80 an ambush behind him, his *a* was surrounded.
11:38 no opposition, he dismissed his entire *a*,
11:67 Jonathan and his *a* pitched their camp near
11:68 on the plain, was the *a* of the foreigners.
11:68 This *a* attacked him in the open,
11:70 stayed except the *a* commanders Mattathias,
12:24 attack him with a stronger *a* than before.
12:42 *a* he was afraid to offer him violence.
13: 1 *a* to invade and ravage the land of Judah,
13:12 with a large *a* to invade the land of Judah,
13:20 but Simon and his *a* moved along opposite
14: 1 assembled his *a* and marched into Media
14: 3 went forth and defeated the *a* of Demetrius;
16: 5 an immense *a* of foot soldiers and horsemen,
16: 8 and Cendebeus and his *a* were put to flight;
16:19 To the *a* officers he sent letters inviting
2Mc 1:13 Persia with his seemingly irresistible *a*,
4:22 this, he led his *a* into Phoenicia.
5:24 head of an *a* of twenty-two thousand men,
8:12 companions about the approach of the *a*,
8:21 Then Judas divided his *a* into four,
8:24 disabled the greater part of Nicanor's *a*,
8:35 successful in destroying his own *a*.
9: 9 so that the entire *a* was sickened by the
10:35 twenty young men in the *a* of Maccabeus,
12:20 Maccabeus divided his *a* into cohorts,
12:27 of these, he moved his *a* to Ephron,
12:38 his *a* and went to the city of Adullam.
13: 2 They led a Greek *a* of one hundred and ten
13:13 before the king's *a* could invade Judea and
13:21 men inside, but Rhodocus, of the Jewish *a*,
14: 1 of Tripolis with a powerful *a* and a fleet,
15:22 thousand men of Sennacherib's *a*.
15:26 met the *a* with supplication and prayers.
Ps(s) 27: 3 Though an *a* encamp against me,
33:16 A king is not saved by a mighty *a*,
68:12 women bear the glad tidings, a vast *a*:
136:15 swept Pharaoh and his *a* into the Red Sea,
Wis 12: 8 wasps as forerunners of your *a*
Sir 46: 6 *a* till on the slope he destroyed the foe;
Is 13: 4 LORD of hosts is mustering an *a* for battle.
36: 2 a great *a* to King Hezekiah in Jerusalem.
40:26 He leads out their *a* and numbers them,
43:17 out chariots and horsemen, a powerful *a*,
Jer 8: 2 sun and the moon and the whole *a* of heaven,
32: 2 At that time the *a* of the king of Babylon
35:11 *a* of the Chaldeans and the army of Aram;
37: 5 Also, Pharaoh's *a* had set out from Egypt,
37: 7 Pharaoh's *a* which has set out to help you
37:10 the whole Chaldean *a* now attacking you,
37:11 When the Chaldean *a* lifted the siege of
37:11 at the threat of the *a* of Pharaoh,
38: 3 over to the *a* of the king of Babylon;
39: 1 and all his *a* marched against Jerusalem
39: 5 Arabah, but the Chaldean *a* pursued them,
40: 7 When the *a* leaders who were still in the
41:11 and the other *a* leaders with him heard of
41:13 son of Kareah, and the other *a* leaders,
41:16 and all his *a* leaders took charge of the
42: 1 Then all the *a* leaders,
42: 8 Johanan, son of Kareah, his *a* leaders,
43: 5 and all the *a* leaders took along the whole
46: 2 Against the *a* of Pharaoh Neco,
51: 3 Spare not her young men, doom her entire *a*.
52: 4 and his whole *a* advanced against Jerusalem,
52: 8 But the Chaldean *a* pursued the king and
52: 8 Jericho, while his whole *a* fled from him.
52:25 and the scribe of the *a* commander who
Lam 1:15 an *a* against me to crush my young men;
Ez 1:24 of the tumult was like the din of an *a*.
17:15 to Egypt to obtain horses and a great *a*.
17:17 Pharaoh with a great *a* and numerous troops.
26: 7 with cavalry and a great and mighty *a*.
27:10 and Lud and Put were in your *a* as warriors;
29:18 *a* in an exhausting campaign against Tyre.
29:18 but neither he nor his *a* received any
32:31 Pharaoh and all his *a*,
37:10 came alive and stood upright, a vast *a*.
38: 4 I will lead you forth with all your *a*,
38:15 on horses, a great horde and a mighty *a*?
Dn 3:20 the strongest men in his *a* bind Shadrach,
11:13 king of the north shall raise another *a*,
11:13 with this large *a* and great resources.
11:25 meet the king of the south with a great *a*;
11:25 for battle with a very large and strong *a*,
11:26 to destroy him, his *a* shall be overwhelmed,
Hos 8:10 with the nations, I will now gather an *a*;
Jl 2:11 raises his voice at the head of his *a*;
2:25 cutter, my great *a* which I sent among you.
Zec 4: 6 Not by an *a*,
Mt 22: 7 sent his *a* to destroy those murderers
Rv 19:19 the One riding the horse, and with his *a*.

ARNAN (1)

1Chr 3:21 were Pelatiah, Jeshaiah, Rephaiah, *A*,

ARNI (1)

Lk 3:33 son of Amminadab, son of Admin, son of *A*,

ARNON (25)

Nm 21:13 they encamped on the other side of the *A*,
21:13 *A* forms Moab's boundary with the Amorites.
21:15 *A* and the wadi gorges That reach back
21:24 land from the *A* to the Jabbok
21:26 seized all his land from Jazer to the *A*.
21:28 and swallowed up the high places of the *A*.
22:36 the *A* at the end of the Moabite territory.
Dt 2:24 " 'Advance now across the Wadi *A*.
2:36 *A* and from the city in the wadi itself,
3: 8 from the Wadi *A* to Mount Hermon
3:12 from Aroer, on the edge of the Wadi *A*,
3:16 the territory from Gilead to the Wadi *A*—
4:48 from Aroer on the edge of the Wadi *A* to
Jos 12: 1 Jordan, from the River *A* to Mount Hermon,
12: 2 Aroer, which is on the bank of the Wadi *A*,
13: 9 the Wadi *A* and the city in the wadi itself,
13:16 from Aroer, on the bank of the Wadi *A*,
Jgs 11:13 took away my land from the *A* to the Jabbok
11:18 the land of Moab and encamped across the *A*.
11:18 of Moab, for the *A* is the boundary of Moab.
11:22 whole territory from the *A* to the Jabbok,
11:26 and all the cities on the banks of the *A*?
2Kgs 10:33 the river *A* up through Gilead and Bashan.
Is 16: 2 daughters of Moab at the fords of the *A*.
Jer 48:20 Publish it at the *A*,

AROD (2)

Gn 46:16 Zephon, Haggi, Shuni, Ezbon, Eri, *A*,
Nm 26:17 Erites, through *A* the clan of the Arodites,

ARODITES (1)

Nm 26:17 Erites, through Arod the clan of the *A*,

AROER (16)

Nm 32:34 the fortified towns of Dibon, Ataroth, *A*,
Dt 2:36 From *A* on the edge of the Wadi Arnon and
3:12 gave Reuben and Gad the territory from *A*,
4:48 from *A* on the edge of the Wadi Arnon to
Jos 12: 2 His domain extended from *A*,
13: 9 from *A* on the bank of the Wadi Arnon and
13:16 Their territory reached from *A*,
13:25 the land of the Ammonites as far as *A*,
Jgs 11:26 and its villages, *A* and its villages,
11:33 from *A* to the approach of Minnith (twenty
1Sm 30:28 to those in Jattir, to those in *A*,
2Sm 24: 5 Crossing the Jordan, they began near *A*,
2Kgs 10:33 from *A* on the river Arnon up through
1Chr 5: 8 in *A* and as far as Nebo and Baal-meon;
11:44 Shama and Jeiel, sons of Hotham, from *A*;
Jer 48:19 watch closely, you that dwell in *A*;

AROMA (1)

2Cor 2:15 We are an *a* of Christ for God's sake,

AROMATIC (6)

Ex 30:34 LORD told Moses, "Take these *a* substances:
Sg 5:13 like beds of spice with ripening *a* herbs.
Ez 27:19 and *a* cane from Uzal for your wares.
Mk 14: 3 jar of perfume made from expensive *a* nard.
Jn 12: 3 of costly perfume made from genuine *a* nard,
Rv 5: 8 vessels of gold filled with *a* spices,

AROMATICS (1)

2Chr 16:14 kinds of *a* compounded into an ointment.

AROSE (31)

Gn 32:23 course of that night, however, Jacob *a*,
Ex 12:30 Pharaoh *a* in the night,
Nm 11:31 There *a* a wind sent by the LORD,
16:25 of Israel, *a* and went to Dathan and Abiram.
22:13 Balaam *a* and told the princes of Balak,
22:21 So the next morning when Balaam *a*,
Jgs 2:10 generation *a* that did not know the LORD,
1Sm 5: 4 But the next morning early, when they *a*,
10:12 Thus the proverb *a*,
2Kgs 4:35 He *a*, paced up and down the room,
6:15 attendant of the man of God *a* and went out,
8:21 He *a* by night and broke through the
2Chr 21: 9 He *a* by night and broke through the
29:12 Then the Levites *a*: Mahath
Tb 8: 4 Tobiah *a* from bed and said to his wife,
Jdt 14:19 Loud screaming and howling *a* in the camp.
1Mc 4:53 they *a* and offered sacrifice according to
Ps(s) 76:10 and was silent When God *a* for judgment,
Sir 47:23 Until one *a* who should not be remembered,
Dn 8:27 I *a* and took care of the king's affairs.
Jon 1: 4 *a* the ship was on the point of breaking up.
4: 8 And when the sun *a*,
Lk 9:46 A discussion *a* among them as to which of
22:24 A dispute *a* among them about who should be
Jn 3:25 A controversy about purification *a* between
Acts 11:19 persecution that *a* because of Stephen
13:16 So Paul *a*, motioned to them for silence,
23: 7 a dispute *a* between Pharisees and
23: 9 Pharisee party *a* and declared emphatically:
1Cor 10: 7 and drink, and *a* to take their pleasure."
Rv 15: 8 smoke which *a* from God's glory

AROUSE (5)

Nm 24: 9 who shall *a* him?
Sg 2: 7 and hinds of the field, Do not *a*,
3: 5 Do not *a*, do not stir up love
8: 4 gazelles and hinds of the field, Do not *a*,
Zec 9:13 I will *a* your sons,

AROUSED (7)

Nm 23:18 Be *a*, O Balak, and hearken;
1Mc 2:24 heart was moved and his just fury was *a*;
2Mc 13: 4 But the King of kings *a* the anger of
Jb 17: 8 and the innocent *a* against the wicked.
41: 2 Is he not relentless when *a*;
Ez 38:18 says the Lord GOD, my fury shall be *a*.
Acts 17: 5 This only *a* the resentment of the Jews,

AROUSES (3)

Wis 15: 5 of which *a* yearning in the senseless man,
Sir 26: 8 A drunken wife *a* great anger,
26:19 to my heart, and the third *a* my horror:

ARPACHSHAD (9)

Gn 10:22 Elam, Asshur, *A*, Lud, and Aram.
10:24 *A* became the father of Shelah,
11:10 years old, he became the father of *A*,
11:11 five hundred years after the birth of *A*,

ARPACHSHAD (cont.)

11:12 When *A* was thirty-five years old,
11:13 *A* lived four hundred and three years after
1Chr 1:17 descendants of Shem were Elam, Asshur, *A*,
1:18 *A* became the father of Shelah,
1:24 Shem, *A*, Shelah, Eber,

ARPAD (6)

2Kgs 18:34 Where are the gods of Hamath and *A*?
19:13 are the king of Hamath, the king of *A*,
Is 10: 9 Calno like Carchemish, Or Hamath like *A*,
36:19 Where are the gods of Hamath and *A*?
37:13 is the king of Hamath, the king of *A*,
Jer 49:23 Hamath and *A* are covered with shame,

ARPHAXAD (6)

Jdt 1: 1 time *A* ruled over the Medes in Ecbatana.
1: 5 waged war against King *A* in the vast plain,
1:13 he proceeded with his army against King *A*,
1:13 He routed the whole force of *A*,
1:15 *A* himself he overtook in the mountains of
Lk 3:36 son of Shelah, son of Cainan, son of *A*,

ARRAIGN (1)

1Sm 12: 7 stand, and I shall *a* you before the LORD,

ARRAIGNED (2)

Mt 27:11 Jesus was *a* before the procurator,
Mk 13: 9 You will be *a* before governors and kings

ARRANGE (8)

Dt 19: 3 and so *a* the routes that every homicide
1Kgs 5:23 and I will *a* them into rafts in the sea
2Kgs 4:10 let us *a* a little room on the roof and
2Mc 14:19 Theodotus and Mattathias to *a* an agreement.
Prv 24:27 tasks, and *a* your work in the field;
Jer 51:12 Post sentries, *a* ambushes!
Dn 11:28 he shall *a* matters and return to his land.
2Cor 9: 5 go to you and *a* in advance

ARRANGED (23)

Gn 22: 9 built an altar there and *a* the wood on it.
Ex 40:23 and *a* the bread on it before the LORD,
Nm 2: 3 divisional camp of Judah, *a* in companies.
2:10 divisional camp of Reuben, *a* in companies.
2:18 divisional camp of Ephraim, *a* in companies.
2:25 the divisional camp of Dan, *a* in companies.
10:14 under its own standard and *a* in companies,
10:18 under its own standard and *a* in companies,
10:22 under its own standard and *a* in companies,
10:25 under its own standard and *a* in companies,
1Sm 11:11 Saul *a* his troops in three companies and
21: 3 I have *a* a meeting place with my men.
1Kgs 18:33 When he had *a* the wood,
2Chr 35:10 When the service had been *a*,
35:16 Thus the entire service of the LORD was *a*
Neh 12:31 mount the wall, and I *a* two great choirs.
Jdt 10: 3 She *a* her hair and bound it with a fillet,
Est F: 7 For this purpose he *a* two lots:
Eccl 12: 9 weighed, scrutinized and *a* many proverbs.
Mt 26:48 His betrayer had *a* to give them a signal,
Mk 6:40 and fifties, neatly *a* like flower beds.
14:44 The betrayer had *a* a signal for them,
Acts 28:23 they *a* a day with him and came to his

ARRANGEMENT (1)

Acts 20:13 This was the *a* he had made,

ARRANGEMENTS (1)

Heb 9: 6 These were the *a* for worship.

ARRANGING (1)

Sir 50:14 the *a* of the sacrifices for the Most High,

ARRAY (13)

Gn 2: 1 the earth and all their *a* were completed.
Ex 13:18 *a* the Israelites marched out of Egypt.
Jgs 20:20 *a* at Gibeah for the combat with Benjamin,
1Sm 17:21 drew up opposite each other in battle *a*.
1Chr 12:34 battle *a* with every kind of weapon for war:
12:36 Of the Danites, set in battle *a*:
12:37 for military service and set in battle *a*:
19:10 and set them in *a* against the Arameans;
2Chr 14: 9 in battle *a* in the valley of Zephathah,
2Mc 5: 3 squadrons of cavalry in battle *a*,
Jb 40:10 and *a* yourself with glory and splendor.
Prv 30:27 have no king, yet they migrate all in *a*;
Ez 23:24 they shall *a* against you everywhere.

ARRAYED (11)

2Sm 10: 9 of Israel and *a* them against the Arameans.
10:10 Abishai, who *a* them against the Ammonites.
Est D: 1 garments and *a* herself in her royal attire.
Jb 6: 4 the terrors of God are *a* against me.
Ps(s) 3: 7 of people *a* against me on every side.
Is 49:18 be *a* with them all as with adornments,
63: 1 This one *a* in majesty,
Jl 2: 5 Like a mighty people *a* for battle.
Mt 6:29 all his splendor was *a* like one of these.
Lk 12:27 splendor was not *a* like any one of them.
Acts 12:21 an appointed day Herod, *a* in royal robes,

ARREST (20)

Gn 42:16 while the rest of you stay here under *a*.
1Sm 19:14 When Saul sent messengers to *a* David,
19:20 near Ramah, he sent messengers to *a* David.
2Mc 14:39 more than five hundred soldiers to *a* him.
Jer 36:26 and Shelemiah, son of Abdeel, to *a* Baruch,
Mt 21:46 Although they sought to *a* him,
26: 4 to *a* Jesus by some trick and kill him;
26:55 come armed with swords and clubs to *a* me?
Mk 1:14 After John's *a*,
12:12 They wanted to *a* him at this,
14: 1 a way to *a* him by some trick and kill him.
14:44 *a* him and lead him away,
14:48 "You have come out to *a* me armed with
Lk 22:54 They led him away under *a* and brought him
Jn 7:32 together sent temple guards to *a* him.
10:39 At these words they again tried to *a* him,
Acts 9: 2 empower him to *a* and bring to Jerusalem
9:14 priests to *a* any who invoke your name."
22: 5 I would *a* back to Jerusalem for punishment.
2Cor 11:32 a close watch on the city in order to *a* me,

ARRESTED (26)

2Kgs 17: 5 king of Assyria *a* and imprisoned Hoshea;
25: 6 The king was therefore *a* and brought to
25:20 *a* these and brought them to the king of
1Mc 7:16 *a* sixty of them and killed them
7:19 had many of the men *a* who deserted to him,
16:22 kill him, he had them *a* and put to death,
2Mc 6:10 two women who were *a* for having
7: 1 seven brothers with their mother were *a*
13:21 He was found out, *a*, and imprisoned.
Jer 52: 9 therefore, was *a* and brought to Riblah,
52:26 *a* these and brought them to the king of
Dn 14:21 The angry king *a* the priests,
Mt 4:12 When Jesus heard that John had been *a*,
14: 3 Recall that Herod had had John *a*,
26:50 forward to lay hands on Jesus, and *a* him.
26:55 the temple precincts, yet you never *a* me.
Mk 6:17 Herod was the one who had ordered John *a*,
14:46 At this, they laid hands on him and *a* him.
14:49 the temple precincts, yet you never *a* me.
Jn 18:12 the Jewish guards *a* Jesus and bound him.
Acts 1:16 the one who guided those that *a* Jesus.
4: 3 *a* them and put them in jail for the night.
5:18 *a* the apostles and threw them into the
12: 4 Bread he had him *a* and thrown into prison,
21:33 *a* Paul and had him bound with double irons.
22: 4 I *a* and imprisoned both men and women.

ARRESTING (1)

2Mc 14:40 He thought that by *a* such a man he would

ARRIVAL (33)

Gn 35: 9 On Jacob's *a* from Paddan-aram,
43:25 their gifts to await Joseph's *a* at noon,
46:28 On his *a* in the region of Goshen,
Nm 10:21 which was to be erected before their *a*.
Jgs 3:27 On his *a* he sounded the horn in the
Ru 1: 2 time after their *a* on the Moabite plateau,
1:19 On their *a* there,
1Sm 9:15 The day before Saul's *a*, the LORD
9:24 Eat, for it was kept for you until your *a*;
26: 4 who confirmed Saul's *a* David himself then
29: 6 you from the day of your *a* to this day.
2Sm 11:22 and on his *a* he relayed to David all the
1Kgs 12:21 On his *a* in Jerusalem,
2Kgs 5:15 On his *a* he stood before him and said,
8: 9 On his *a*,
16:12 On his *a* from Damascus,
18:17 They went up, and on their *a* in Jerusalem,
2Chr 11: 1 On his *a* in Jerusalem Rehoboam gathered
22: 7 his *a* he rode out with Jehoram to Jehu,
Jdt 10:18 the news of her *a* spread among the tents,
1Mc 11:44 the king, he was delighted over their *a*,
2Mc 9: 3 On his *a* in Ecbatana,
Mt 8:33 and upon their *a* in the town related
Acts 9:39 his *a* they took him upstairs to the room.
11:23 On his *a* he rejoiced to see the evidence
13: 5 On their *a* in Salamis they proclaimed the
14:27 On their *a*, they called the congregation
15:30 and upon their *a* there they called the
17:10 On their *a*, they went to the Jewish
21:17 On our *a* in Jerusalem, the brothers
1Cor 16:17 I was very happy at the *a* of Stephanas,
2Cor 7: 6 gave me strength with the *a* of Titus.
7: 7 not only by his *a* but by the reinforcement

ARRIVE (15)

Gn 19:22 I cannot do anything until you *a* there."
Ex 10:26 to him until we *a* at the place itself."
1Sm 10: 3 on, when you *a* at the terebinth of Tabor,
13: 8 When Samuel did not *a* at Gilgal,
1Kgs 19:15 "When you *a*,
Neh 2: 7 afford me safe-conduct till I *a* in Judah;
Tb 11:15 daughter Sarah, who would *a* shortly,
2Mc 9: 4 graveyard of the Jews as soon as I *a* there."
Jer 42:15 to go to Egypt, when you *a* there to stay,
Acts 23:35 case," he said, "when your accusers *a*."
Rom 9:31 justice would come, did not *a* at that law?
1Cor 16: 2 will not have to be taken up after I *a*.
Phil 3:11 that I may *a* at resurrection from the dead.
1Tm 4:13 Until I *a*, devote yourself to the reading
2Pt 3: 3 by their passions will *a* on the scene.

ARRIVED (106)

Gn 19:23 rising over the earth as Lot *a* in Zoar,
29: 9 them, Rachel *a* with her father's sheep;
33:18 Jacob *a* safely at the city of Shechem,
35: 6 people who were with him *a* in Luz [that is,
43:21 But when we *a* at a night's encampment and
46: 1 When he *a* at Beer-sheba,
50:10 When they *a* at Goren-ha-atad,
Ex 15:23 without finding water, they *a* at Marah,
Nm 20: 1 *a* in the desert of Zin in the first month,
Dt 1:31 your journey until you *a* at this place.'
9: 7 land of Egypt until you *a* in this place,
11: 5 in the desert until you *a* in this place;
32:17 had not known before, To newcomers just *a*,
Jos 5:14 of the host of the LORD and I have just *a*."
Jgs 7:13 When Gideon *a*,
Ru 1:22 They *a* in Bethlehem at the beginning of
1Sm 4: 5 When the ark of the LORD *a* in the camp,
4:13 When he *a*,
11: 4 When the messengers *a* at Gibeah of Saul,
13:10 just finished this offering when Samuel *a*.
25: 9 When David's young men *a*,
30: 3 David and his men *a* at the city to find it
2Sm 3:23 and the whole force he had with him *a*,
16:14 with him *a* at the Jordan tired out,
1Kgs 1:42 Jonathan, son of Abiathar the priest, *a*.
8: 3 When all the elders of Israel had *a*,
10: 2 She *a* in Jerusalem with a very numerous
17:10 As he *a* at the entrance of the city,
2Kgs 1:13 When the third captain *a*,
4:11 Elisha *a* and stayed in the room overnight.
6: 4 *a* at the Jordan they began to fell trees.
6:14 They *a* by night and surrounded the city.
9: 5 When he *a*,
9:30 Jezebel learned that Jehu had *a* in Jezreel,
10: 7 When the letter *a*,
10:17 When he *a* in Samaria,
24:11 himself *a* at the city while his servants
2Chr 5: 4 When all the elders of Israel had *a*,
23:15 and when she *a* at the entrance to the
29:17 month they *a* at the vestibule of the LORD;
Ezr 2:68 *a* at the house of the LORD in Jerusalem,
4:12 *a* at Jerusalem and are now rebuilding
7: 9 day of the fifth month he *a* at Jerusalem,
8:32 Thus we *a* in Jerusalem,
Neh 2:11 When I had *a* in Jerusalem,
Est 6:14 the king's eunuchs *a* and hurried Haman off
8:17 every city, wherever the king's order *a*,
9: 1 When the day *a* on which the order decreed
1Mc 5:14 *a* from Galilee to deliver a similar
7: 1 *a* with a few men in a city on the seacoast,
11:60 When he *a* at Ashkalon,
12:42 But when Trypho saw that Jonathan had *a*
2Mc 1:13 When their leader *a* in Persia with his
2: 5 When Jeremiah *a* there,
3: 9 When he *a* in Jerusalem and had been
5:25 When this man *a* in Jerusalem,
12:31 Finally they *a* in Jerusalem,
15:31 When he *a* there,
Jer 32:24 have *a* at this city to breach it;
43: 7 they went to Egypt, and *a* at Tahpanhes. . . .
Ez 33:22 me the evening before the fugitive *a*,
Dn 7:22 was victorious until the Ancient One *a*;
Mt 2: 1 the east *a* one day in Jerusalem inquiring,
9:23 When Jesus *a* at the synagogue leader's
16: 5 The disciples discovered when they *a* at
21:34 When vintage time *a* he dispatched his
25:10 While they went off to buy it the groom *a*,
26:47 *a* accompanied by a great crowd with swords
27:57 fell, a wealthy man from Arimathea *a*,
Mk 2: 3 people *a* bringing a paralyzed man to him.
3:22 the scribes who *a* from Jerusalem asserted,
3:31 His mother and his brothers *a*,
5:35 people from the official's house *a* saying,
8:22 When they *a* at Bethsaida,
9:28 When Jesus *a* at the house his disciples
14:17 As it grew dark he *a* with the Twelve.
15:43 of the sabbath), Joseph from Arimathea *a*—
Lk 1:57 When Elizabeth's time for delivery *a*,
2:21 When the eighth day *a* for his circumcision,
8:51 Once he had *a* at the house,
15: 6 Once *a* home,
22: 7 The day of Unleavened Bread *a* on which it
22:14 When the hour *a*,
Jn 4:45 When he *a* in Galilee,
11:17 When Jesus *a* at Bethany,
20: 8 who had *a* first at the tomb went in.
Acts 5:21 supporters *a* they convoked the Sanhedrin,
9:26 When he *a* back in Jerusalem he tried to
10:17 the men sent by Cornelius *a* at the gate
10:24 The following day, he *a* in Caesarea.
14:19 and Iconium *a* and won the people over.
15: 4 When they *a* in Jerusalem they were

16: 1 Paul *a* first at Derbe;
18: 2 *a* from Italy with his wife Priscilla.
18:24 a man of eloquence, *a* by ship at Ephesus.
18:27 When he *a*,
20: 2 Finally he *a* in Greece,
21:10 stay, a prophet named Agabus *a* from Judea.
21:33 Then, when the commander *a* on the scene,
23:33 When the cavalrymen *a* in Caesarea,
25: 1 days after Festus had *a* in the province,
25:13 King Agrippa and Bernice *a* in Caesarea
28:13 we sailed around the toe and *a* at Rhegium.
28:21 *a* with a report or rumor to your discredit.
2Cor 7: 5 When I *a* in Macedonia I was restless and
Gal 2:12 But when they *a* he drew back to avoid

ARRIVES (6)

Ex 1:19 robust and give birth before the midwife *a*."
1Sm 9:13 The people will not eat until he *a*;
16:11 the sacrificial banquet until he *a* here."
Prv 26: 2 its flight, a curse uncalled-for *a* nowhere.
Lk 12:36 a wedding, so that when he *a* and knocks,
Acts 24:22 the case when Lysias the commander *a*."

ARRIVING (7)

1Sm 19:22 *A* at the cistern of the threshing floor on
1Mc 7:10 *a* in the land of Judah with a great army,
Mt 27:33 Upon *a* at a site called Golgotha (a name
Mk 6:33 on foot to the place, *a* ahead of them.
Lk 1:28 Upon *a*, the angel said to her:
Acts 8:17 The pair upon *a* imposed hands on them and
27: 7 headway, *a* at Cnidus only with difficulty.

ARROGANCE (29)

1Sm 2: 3 longer, nor let *a* issue from your mouths.
17:28 I know your *a* and your evil intent.
Tb 4:13 in such *a* there is ruin and great disorder.
Jdt 6:19 "Lord, God of heaven, behold their *a!*
1Mc 1:24 spoken with great *a* and shed much blood.
2:49 *A* and scorn have now grown strong;
2Mc 5:21 In his *a* he planned to make the land
7:36 shall receive just punishments for your *a*.
9: 4 rode with him, since he said in his *a*,
9: 7 he was all the more filled with *a*.
9:11 he began to give up his excessive *a*,
15: 6 In his utter boastfulness and *a* Nicanor
Ps(s) 59:13 their lips let them be caught in their *a*,
Prv 1:30 And in their *a* they preferred arrogance.
8:13 Pride, *a*, the evil way,
24: 9 and sin, it is *a* that men find abominable.
Sir 10: 6 neighbor, and do not walk the path of *a*.
10: 7 Odious to the LORD and to men is *a*.
21: 4 Violence and *a* wipe out wealth;
Is 2:11 be lowered, the *a* of men will be abased,
2:17 will be abased, the *a* of men brought low,
9: 8 those who say in *a* and pride of heart,
Jer 48:30 I know, says the LORD, his *a*;
Hos 4:18 in their *a* they love shame.
5: 5 The *a* of Israel bears witness against him;
7:10 The *a* of Israel bears witness against him;
Mk 7:22 deceit, sensuality, envy, blasphemy, *a*,
1Tm 1:13 a persecutor, a man filled with *a*;

ARROGANT (36)

Est E: 4 with the *a* boastfulness of those to whom
1Mc 1: 3 him, and his heart became proud and *a*.
2:47 They put to flight the *a*,
Ps(s) 5: 6 the *a* may not stand in your sight.
73: 3 Because I was envious of the *a* when I saw
123: 4 more than sated with the mockery of the *a*,
Prv 3:34 When he is dealing with the *a*,
9: 7 He who corrects an *a* man earns insult;
9: 8 Reprove not an *a* man,
9:12 and if you are *a*,
14: 9 Guilt lodges in the tents of the *a*,
19:25 If you beat an *a* man,
19:29 Rods are prepared for the *a*,
20: 1 Wine is *a*,
21:11 When the *a* man is punished,
21:24 *A* is the name for the man of overbearing
22:10 Expel the *a* man and discord goes out;
29: 8 *A* men set the city ablaze,
Sir 10: 8 another because of the violence of the *a*.
10:14 The thrones of the *a* God overturns and
11: 9 in the strife of the *a* take no part.
23: 8 the railer and the *a* man fall thereby.
Is 2:12 his day against all that is proud and *a*,
13:11 I will put an end to the pride of the *a*,
16: 6 *a* insolence that his empty words do not
28:14 hear the word of the LORD, you *a*,
28:22 be *a* no more lest your bonds be tightened,
29: 5 horde of your *a* shall be like fine dust,
29:20 will be no more and the *a* will have gone;
Dn 7:11 first of the *a* words which the horn spoke,
2Tm 3: 2 be lovers of self and of money, proud, *a*,
Ti 1: 7 He may not be self-willed or *a*,
Jas 3:14 from *a* and false claims against the truth.
4:16 can do is make *a* and pretentious claims.
1Pt 5: 5 the *a* but to the humble he shows kindness."
2Pt 2:10 These bold and *a* men have no qualms

ARROGANTLY (5)

Dt 1:43 you *a* marched off into the hill country.
1Mc 7:47 his right arm, which he had lifted up so *a*.
2Mc 1:28 who tyrannize over us and *a* mistreat us.
Dn 7: 8 eyes like a man, and a mouth that spoke *a*.
7:20 with the eyes and the mouth that spoke *a*,

ARROW (27)

1Sm 20:21 to him, 'Look, the *a* is this side of you;
20:22 say to the boy, 'Look, the *a* is beyond you,'
20:36 he said to the boy, "Run and fetch the *a*."
20:36 *a* beyond him in the direction of the city.
20:37 had shot the *a* Jonathan called after him,
20:37 called after him, "The *a* is farther on!"
20:38 up the *a* and brought it to his master.
2Kgs 9:24 so that the *a* went through his heart and
13:17 exclaimed, "The LORD's *a* of victory!
13:17 The *a* of victory over Aram!
19:32 not reach this city, nor shoot an *a* at it,
Jb 34: 6 in my wound the *a* rankles,
41:20 The *a* will not put him to flight;
Ps(s) 11: 2 they place the *a* on the string to shoot
91: 5 of the night nor the *a* that flies by day;
Prv 7:23 the net, till an *a* pierces its liver;
25:18 Like a club, or a sword, or a sharp *a*,
Wis 5:12 Or as, when an *a* has been shot at a mark,
Sir 19:11 Like an *a* lodged in a man's thigh is
26:12 tent peg and opens her quiver for every *a*.
Is 37:33 not reach this city, nor shoot an *a* at it,
49: 2 He made me a polished *a*,
Jer 9: 7 A murderous *a* is his tongue,
Lam 3:12 bow, and set me up as the target for his *a*.
Ez 21:27 hand is the divining *a* marked "Jerusalem,"
21:28 and the *a* taken in hand marks their guilt.
Zec 9:14 and his *a* shall shoot forth as lightning;

ARROWS (45)

Ex 19:13 must be stoned to death or killed with *a*.
Dt 32:23 upon woe and exhaust all my *a* against them:
32:42 I will make my *a* drunk with blood,
1Sm 20:20 the third day of the month I will shoot *a*,
20:21 send my attendant to go and recover the *a*.
2Sm 22:15 He sent forth *a* to put them to flight;
2Kgs 13:15 "Take a bow and some *a*,"
13:18 said to the king of Israel, "Take the *a*,"
1Chr 10: 3 found him, and wounded him with their *a*.
12: 2 stones and in shooting *a* with the bow.
2Chr 26:15 the walls to shoot *a* and cast large stones.
1Mc 6:51 bows for shooting *a* and slingstones.
10:80 until evening they showered his men with *a*.
2Mc 5: 3 flights of *a* and flashes of gold ornaments,
10:30 *a* and hurled thunderbolts at the enemy,
Jb 6: 4 For the *a* of the Almighty pierce me,
16:13 his *a* strike me from all directions,
Ps(s) 7:14 against them, and use fiery darts for *a*.
18:15 He sent forth his *a* to put them to flight,
38: 3 For your *a* have sunk deep in me,
45: 6 Your *a* are sharp;
57: 5 Their teeth are spears and *a*,
58: 8 the bow, let their *a* be headless shafts.
64: 4 swords, who aim like *a* their bitter words,
64: 8 But God shoots his *a* at them;
77:18 your *a* also sped abroad.
120: 4 Sharp *a* of a warrior with fiery coals of
127: 4 Like *a* in the hand of a warrior are the
144: 6 and put them to flight, shoot your *a*,
Prv 26:18 *a* Is the man who deceives his neighbor,
Sir 43:13 speeds the *a* of his judgment to their goal.
51: 6 of lies, from the *a* of dishonest tongues.
Is 5:28 Their *a* are sharp,
7:24 Men shall go there with bow and *a*;
Jer 50: 9 Their *a* are arrows of the skilled warrior;
50:14 Shoot at her, spare not your *a*,
51:11 Sharpen the *a*,
Lam 2: 4 with his *a* in his right hand He took his
Ez 5:16 you the cruel, destructive *a* of hunger,
21:26 he has shaken the *a*,
39: 3 hand, and make the *a* drop from your right.
39: 9 [shields and bucklers,] bows and *a*,
Hb 3: 9 is your bow, filled with *a* is your quiver.
3:11 its shelter, At the light of your flying *a*,

ARSACES (3)

1Mc 14: 2 When *A*, king of Persia and Media,
14: 3 he captured him and brought him to *A*,
15:22 Kings Demetrius, Attalus, Ariarthes and *A*;

ARSENAL (1)

Neh 3:19 the Corner, opposite the ascent to the *a*.

ART (6)

2Mc 8: 9 commander, well-versed in the *a* of war.
Wis 13:10 Gold and silver, the product of *a*,
13:11 off all its bark, And deftly plying his *a*,
17: 7 mockeries of the magic *a* were in readiness,
Mk 7: 9 "You have made a fine *a* of setting aside
Acts 17:29 stone, a product of man's genius and his *a*.

ARTAXERXES (15)

Ezr 4: 7 Again, in the time of *A*,
4: 7 and the rest of his fellow officials to *A*,
4: 8 letter against Jerusalem to King *A*:
4:11 "To King *A*, your servants, the men
4:23 King *A*' letter had been read before Rehum,
6:14 the decrees of Cyrus and Darius [and of *A*,
7: 1 After these events, during the reign of *A*,
7: 7 to Jerusalem in the seventh year of King *A*.
7:11 King *A* gave to Ezra the priest-scribe,
7:12 *A*, king of kings, to Ezra the priest,
7:21 I, *A* the king, issue this decree
8: 1 me from Babylon during the reign of King *A*:
Neh 2: 1 Nisan of the twentieth year of King *A*,
5:14 King *A* appointed me governor in the land
13: 6 for in the thirty-second year of *A*,

ARTEMAS (1)

Ti 3:12 When I send *A* to you,

ARTEMIS (5)

Acts 19:24 Demetrius who made miniature shrines of *A*
19:27 the great goddess *A* will count for nothing.
19:28 began to shout, "Long live *A* of Ephesus!"
19:34 chant in unison, "Long live *A* of Ephesus!"
19:35 custodian of the temple of the great *A*,

ARTICLE (25)

Ex 22: 6 "When a man gives money or an *a* to
Lv 5:21 a deposit or a pledge or a stolen *a*,
5:22 unjustly, or if, having found a lost *a*,
5:23 the deposit left with him or the lost *a*
11:32 *a* that men use, whether it be an article
13:49 or on any leather *a* is greenish or reddish,
13:50 quarantine the infected *a* for seven days.
13:51 is malignant leprosy, and the *a* is unclean.
13:52 of wool or linen, or the leather *a*,
13:53 or knitted material, or on the leather *a*,
13:54 give orders to have the infected *a* washed
13:55 the infected *a* after it has been washed.
13:55 the *a* is unclean and shall be destroyed by
13:57 or knitted material, or on the leather *a*,
13:58 or knitted material, or the leather *a*,
13:59 or knitted material, or on any leather *a*,
15:12 every wooden *a* shall be rinsed with water.
15:22 *a* of furniture on which she was sitting,
15:26 and any *a* of furniture on which she sits
Nm 31:20 You shall also purify every *a* of cloth,
31:50 to the LORD some gold *a* he has picked up,
Dt 22: 5 woman shall not wear an *a* proper to a man,
2Kgs 12:14 basins, trumpets, or any gold or silver *a*.
Wis 15: 7 molds for our service each several *a*:

ARTICLES (22)

Gn 24:53 objects of silver and gold and *a* of clothing
Ex 3:22 her house guest for silver and gold *a*
11: 2 for silver and gold *a* and for clothing."
12:35 for *a* of silver and gold and for clothing.
35:22 rings, necklaces and various other gold *a*.
Nm 31:51 from them, all of it in well-wrought *a*.
Jos 6:19 and gold, and the *a* of bronze or iron,
6:24 the silver, gold, and *a* of bronze and iron,
1Sm 6: 8 it the golden *a* that you are offering,
6:15 box beside it, in which the golden *a* were,
2Sm 8:10 Hadoram also brought with him *a* of silver,
1Kgs 7:45 All these *a* which Hiram made for King
7:47 all the *a* because they were so numerous;
7:48 Solomon had all the *a* made for the
7:51 and other *a* in the treasuries of the
10:25 silver or gold *a*,
2Chr 4:16 Huram-abi made all these *a* for King
4:19 had all these *a* made for the house of God:
5: 1 *a* in the treasuries of the house of God.
9:24 bring his tribute—silver and gold *a*,
29:19 All the *a* which King Ahaz during his reign
Ez 27:13 slaves and *a* of bronze for your goods.

ARTIFICER (2)

Wis 7:22 for Wisdom, the *a* of all,
14: 2 this latter, and Wisdom the *a* produced it.

ARTIFICIAL (1)

Neh 3:16 as far as the *a* pool and the barracks.

ARTILLERY (1)

1Mc 6:51 the sanctuary, setting up *a* and machines,

ARTISAN (4)

Wis 13: 1 studying the works did not discern the *a*:
Jer 10:14 every *a* is put to shame by his idol:
51:17 every *a* is put to shame by his idol:
Hos 8: 6 The work of an *a* no god at all,

ARTISANS (11)

2Kgs 25:11 the king of Babylon, and the last of the *a*.
1Chr 29: 5 and for every work that is to be done by *a*.
Neh 11:35 Lod, Ono, and the Valley of the *A*.
Wis 14:18 the *a* ambition provided a stimulus.

ARTISANS (cont.)

Sir 9:17 Skilled *a* are esteemed for their deftness;
Jer 10: 9 all of them the work of *a.*
24: 1 of Judah, the *a* and the skilled workers,
29: 2 the *a* and the skilled workmen had left
52:15 the king of Babylon, and the rest of the *a.*
Ez 21:36 you over to ravaging men, *a* of destruction.
Hos 13: 2 their fancy, all of them the work of *a.*

ARTIST (1)

Sg 7: 2 are like jewels, the handiwork of an *a.*

ARTISTIC (1)

2Chr 2:13 devise every type of *a* work that may be

ARTS (5)

Ex 7:11 of Egypt, did likewise by their magic *a.*
7:22 magicians did the same by their magic *a.*
8: 3 magicians did the same by their magic *a.*
8:14 to bring forth gnats by their magic *a,*
35:35 weaving, and all other *a* and crafts.

ARUBBOTH (1)

1Kgs 4:10 the son of Hesed in *A* as well as in Socoh

ARUMAH (2)

Jgs 9:31 to Abimelech in *A* with the information:
9:41 Abimelech returned to *A,*

ARVAD (2)

Ez 27: 8 of Sidon and *A* served as your oarsmen;
27:11 The men of *A* were all about your walls,

ARVADITE (1)

1Chr 1:16 the Hivite, the Arkite, the Sinite, the *A,*

ARVADITES (1)

Gn 10:18 Hivites, the Arkites, the Sinites, the *A,*

ARZA (1)

1Kgs 16: 9 drinking to excess in the house of *A,*

ASA (54)

1Kgs 15: 8 David, and his son *A* succeeded him as king.
15: 9 year of Jeroboam, king of Israel, *A,*
15:11 *A* pleased the LORD like his forefather
15:13 *A* cut down this object and burned it in
15:16 There was war between *A* and Baasha,
15:17 Ramah to prevent communication with *A,*
15:18 *A* then took all the silver and gold
15:18 ministers, King *A* sent them to Ben-hadad,
15:20 Ben-hadad agreed with King *A* and sent the
15:22 *A* summoned all Judah without exception,
15:22 King *A* built Geba of Benjamin and Mizpeh.
15:23 The rest of the acts of *A,*
15:23 old age, *A* had an infirmity in his feet.
15:25 In the second year of *A,*
15:28 Baasha killed him in the third year of *A,*
15:32 [There was war between *A* and Baasha,
15:33 In the third year of *A,*
16: 8 In the twenty-sixth year of *A,*
16:10 him in the twenty-seventh year of *A,*
16:15 In the twenty-seventh year of *A,*
16:23 In the thirty-first year of *A,*
16:29 In the thirty-eighth year of *A,*
22:41 Jehoshaphat, son of *A,*
22:43 all the ways of his father *A* unswervingly,
22:47 had remained in the reign of his father *A.*
1Chr 3:10 son was Abijah, whose son was *A,*
9:16 and Berechiah, son of *A,*
2Chr 13:23 His son *A* succeeded him as king.
14: 1 *A* did what was good and pleasing to the
14: 7 *A* had an army of three hundred thousand
14: 9 *A* went out to meet him and set himself in
14:10 *A* called upon the LORD, his God, praying:
14:11 defeated the Ethiopians before *A* and Judah,
14:12 *A* and those with him pursued them as far
15: 2 He went forth to meet *A* and said to him:
15: 2 "Hear me, *A* and all Judah and Benjamin!
15: 8 When *A* heard these words and the prophecy
15:16 Maacah, the mother of King *A,*
15:16 *A* cut this down,
16: 1 Ramah to prevent any communication with *A,*
16: 2 *A* then brought out silver and gold from
16: 6 Then King *A* commandeered all of Judah to
16: 7 At that time Hanani the seer came to *A,*
16:10 But *A* became angry with the seer and
16:10 *A* also oppressed some of his people at
16:11 Now the acts of *A,*
16:12 *A* contracted a serious disease in his feet.
16:13 *A* rested with his ancestors;
17: 2 of Ephraim which his father *A* had taken.
20:32 the path of his father *A* unswervingly,
21:12 path of your father Jehoshaphat, nor of *A,*
Jer 41: 9 by King *A* to defend himself against Baasha,
Mt 1: 7 father of Abijah, Abijah the father of *A.*
1: 8 *A* was the father of Jehoshaphat,

ASAHEL (17)

2Sm 2:18 Abishai, and *A.* Asahel, who was as fleet
2:20 turned around and said, "Is that you, *A?*"
2:21 But *A* would not desist from his pursuit.
2:22 Once more Abner said to *A:*
2:23 to the place where *A* had fallen and died,
2:30 Besides *A,* nineteen other servants
2:32 They took up *A* and buried him in his
3:27 for the killing of Joab's brother *A.*
3:30 killed their brother *A* in battle at Gibeon.]
23:24 *A,* brother of Joab. . . .
1Chr 2:16 Abishai, Joab, and *A.*
11:26 *A,* the brother of Joab;
27: 7 Fourth, for the fourth month, was *A,*
2Chr 17: 8 Levites, Shemaiah, Nethaniah, Zebadiah, *A,*
31:13 Jehiel, Azaziah, Nahath, *A,*
Ezr 10:15 Only Jonathan, son of *A,*

ASAIAH (8)

2Kgs 22:12 scribe Shaphan, and the king's servant *A:*
22:14 and *A* betook themselves to the Second
1Chr 4:36 Asiel, Elioenai, Jaakobath, Jeshohaiah, *A,*
6:15 whose son was Haggiah, whose son was *A.*
9: 5 Among the Shelanites were *A,*
15: 6 of the sons of Merari, *A,*
15:11 and Abiathar, and the Levites Uriel, *A,*
2Chr 34:20 of Michah, to Shaphan the scribe, and to *A,*

ASAPH (32)

2Kgs 18:18 and the herald Joah, son of *A.*
18:37 the scribe, and the herald Joah, son of *A,*
1Chr 6:24 His brother *A* stood at his right hand.
6:24 *A* was the son of Berechiah,
9:15 of Mica, son of Zichri, a descendant of *A;*
15:17 son of Joel, and, among his brethren, *A,*
15:19 The chanters, Heman, *A,*
16: 5 *A* was their chief,
16: 5 lyres, while *A* was to sound the cymbals,
16: 7 David appointed *A* and his brethren to sing
16:37 Then David left *A* and his brethren there
25: 1 apart for service the descendants of *A,*
25: 2 Of the sons of *A*
25: 2 sons of *A,* under the direction of *A*
25: 6 All these, whether of *A,*
25: 9 The first lot fell to *A,*
2Chr 5:12 who were singers, all who belonged to *A,*
20:14 of Mattaniah, a Levite of the clan of *A,*
29:13 Shimri and Jeuel; of the sons of *A:*
29:30 in the words of David and of *A* the seer.
35:15 The singers, the sons of *A,*
35:15 *A,* Heman and Jeduthun, the king's seer.
Ezr 2:41 sons of *A,* one hundred and twenty-eight.
3:10 the trumpets and the Levites, sons of *A,*
Neh 2: 8 also a letter for *A,*
7:44 sons of *A,* one hundred and forty-eight.
11:17 son of Zabdi, son of *A,*
11:22 he was one of the sons of *A,*
12:35 son of Micaiah, son of Zaccur, son of *A,*
12:46 the days of David and *A* in times of old.
Is 36: 3 the scribe, and the herald Joah, son of *A.*
36:22 the scribe, and the herald Joah, son of *A,*

ASARAMEL (1)

1Mc 14:27 year under Simon the high priest in *A,*

ASAREL (1)

1Chr 4:16 Jehallelel were Ziph, Ziphah, Tiria, and *A.*

ASA'S (6)

1Kgs 15:14 yet *A* heart was entirely with the LORD as
2Chr 15:10 month of the fifteenth year of *A* reign,
15:17 *A* heart was undivided as long as he lived.
15:19 war until the thirty-fifth year of *A* reign.
16: 1 In the thirty-sixth year of *A* reign,
16: 4 Ben-hadad agreed to King *A* request and

ASCALON (1)

Jdt 2:28 in Azotus and *A* also feared him greatly.

ASCEND (7)

Tb 12:20 Behold, I am about to *a* to him who sent me;
Jdt 10:13 show him the route by which he can *a*
Ps(s) 24: 3 Who can *a* the mountain of the LORD?
Is 14:14 I will *a* above the tops of the clouds;
52: 2 Shake off the dust, *a* to the throne,
Ob 1:21 *a* Mount Zion to rule the mount of Esau,
Jn 6:62 the Son of Man *a* to where he was before . . .

ASCENDED (13)

Nm 33:38 priest *a* Mount Hor at the LORD's command,
Jgs 13:20 of the LORD *a* in the flame of the altar.
1Kgs 12:33 Jeroboam *a* the altar he built in Bethel on
2Chr 6:13 Having *a* it,
Tb 12:21 When Raphael *a* they rose to their feet and
1Mc 5:54 They *a* Mount Zion in joy and gladness and
Ps(s) 68:19 You have *a* on high,
Sir 50:11 As he *a* the glorious altar and lent
Ez 40:26 It was *a* by seven steps;
Jn 20:17 to me, for I have not yet *a* to the Father.
Eph 4: 8 "When he *a* on high,
4: 9 "He *a*— what does this mean
4:10 the very one who *a* high above the heavens,

ASCENDING (3)

1Chr 26:16 with the Shallecheth gate at the *a* highway.
Jn 1:51 of God *a* and descending on the Son of Man."
20:17 them, 'I am *a* to my Father and your Father,

ASCENDS (1)

Jer 14: 2 from Jerusalem *a* a cry of anguish.

ASCENT (11)

1Sm 9:11 As they were going up the *a* to the city,
2Sm 15:17 opposite the *a* of the Mount of Olives,
2Chr 20:16 will see them coming up by the *a* of Ziz,
Neh 3:19 the Corner, opposite the *a* to the arsenal.
Jdt 6: 7 leave you at one of the towns along the *a.*
6:12 and all the slingers blocked the *a* of
1Mc 3:16 When he reached the *a* of Beth-horon,
9: 2 and camping opposite the *a* at Arbela,
Is 15: 5 The *a* of Luhith they climb weeping;
Jer 48: 5 The *a* of Luhith they climb weeping;
Lk 19:28 thus he went ahead with his *a* to Jerusalem.

ASCERTAINED (1)

2Chr 4:18 that the weight of the bronze was not *a.*

ASCRIBE (1)

Acts 12:23 once because he did not *a* the honor to God,

ASCRIBED (3)

2Sm 4: 2 [Beeroth, too, was *a* to Benjamin;
2Chr 26:15 *a* to the marvelous help he had received.
Sir 47: 6 his praises and *a* to him tens of thousands.

ASENATH (3)

Gn 41:45 on Joseph, and he gave him in marriage *A,*
41:50 the father of two sons, borne to him by *A,*
46:20 father of Manasseh and Ephraim, whom *A,*

ASH (4)

Lv 1:16 the *a* heap at the east side of the altar.
4:12 At the place of the *a* heap,
1Sm 2: 8 from the *a* heap he lifts up the poor,
Lam 4: 5 up in purple now cling to the *a* heaps.

ASHAMED (49)

2Sm 10: 5 word to them, since the men were quite *a.*
2Kgs 19:26 shorn of power, are dismayed and *a,*
Ezr 8:22 For I would have been *a* to ask the king
9: 6 *a* and confounded to raise my face to you,
1Mc 4:31 them *a* of their troops and their cavalry.
Ps(s) 119:46 your decrees before kings without being *a.*
Wis 13:17 not *a* to address the thing without a soul.
Sir 4:26 Be not *a* to acknowledge your guilt,
4:26 guilt, but of your ignorance rather be *a.*
41:14 rules, For it is not always well to be *a,*
41:15 father and mother be *a* of immorality,
41:18 Be *a* of theft from the people where you
42: 1 But of these things be not *a,*
51:29 of God, and be not *a* to give him praise.
Is 1:29 be *a* of the terebinths which you prized,
20: 5 be dismayed and *a* because of Ethiopia,
29:22 Now Jacob shall have nothing to be *a* of,
30: 5 be *a* of a people that gain them nothing,
37:27 shorn of power, are dismayed and *a,*
Jer 6:15 things, yet they are not at all *a,*
8:12 things, yet they are not at all *a,*
9:18 Ruined we are, and greatly *a;*
14: 3 *A,* despairing, they cover their heads
14: 4 is no rain in the land the farmers are *a,*
22:22 Surely then you shall be *a* and confounded
51:51 We are *a* because we have heard taunts,
Ez 16:61 conduct and be *a* when I take your sisters,
36:32 Be *a* and abashed because of your conduct,
43:10 Israel [that they may be *a* of their sins],
43:11 if they are *a* of all that they have done,]
Dn 13:11 for they were *a* to reveal their lustful
13:27 old men, the servants felt very much *a,*
Zep 3:11 day You need not be *a* of all your deeds,
Zec 13: 4 prophet shall be *a* to prophesy his vision,
Mk 8:38 and corrupt age is *a* of me and my doctrine,
8:38 the Son of Man will be *a* of him when he
Lk 9:26 If a man is *a* of me and my doctrine,
9:26 the Son of Man will be *a* of him when he
16: 3 I am *a* to go begging.
Rom 1:16 I am not *a* of the gospel.
6:21 Things you are now *a* of,
2Thes 3:14 ostracized that he may be *a* of his conduct.
2Tm 1: 8 never be *a* of your testimony to our Lord,
1:12 But I am not *a,*
1:16 me new heart and has not been *a* of me,
2:15 a workman who has no cause to be *a,*
Heb 2:11 he is not *a* to call them brothers,
11:16 God is not *a* to be called their God,
1Pt 4:16 a Christian, however, he ought not to be *a.*

ASHAN (5)

Jos 15:42 and their villages, Libnah, Ether, *A*,
19: 7 Also En-rimmon, Ether and *A*;
21:16 pasture lands, *A* with its pasture lands,
1Chr 4:32 also, and Ain, Rimmon, Tochen, and *A*—
6:44 pasture lands, *A* with its pasture lands,

ASHARELAH (1)

1Chr 25: 2 Zaccur, Joseph, Nethaniah, and *A*,

ASHBEL (3)

Gn 46:21 Bela, Becher, *A*,
Nm 26:38 through *A* the clan of the Ashbelites,
1Chr 8: 1 the father of Bela, his first-born, *A*,

ASHBELITES (1)

Nm 26:38 through Ashbel the clan of the *A*,

ASHDOD (19)

Jos 11:22 some survived in Gaza, in Gath, and in *A*.
13: 3 five lords of the Philistines in Gaza, *A*,
15:46 sea, all the towns that lie alongside *A*,
15:47 *A* and its towns and villages;
1Sm 5: 1 of God, transferred it from Ebenezer to *A*.
5: 3 people of *A* rose early the next morning,
5: 5 threshold of Dagon in *A* to this very day;
5: 6 LORD dealt severely with the people of *A*.
5: 7 how matters stood, the men of *A* decided,
6:17 one for *A*, one for Gaza, one for Ashkelon,
2Chr 26: 6 Jabneh and *A* [and built cities in the
26: 6 in the district of *A* and in Philistia].
Is 20: 1 Assyria, fought against *A* and captured it,
Jer 25:20 and the remnant of *A*
47: 5 *A*, the remnant of their strength,
Am 1: 8 I will root out those who live in *A*,
3: 9 Proclaim this in the castles of *A*,
Zep 2: 4 a waste, *A* they shall drive out at midday,
Zec 9: 6 inhabited, and the baseborn shall occupy *A*.

ASHDODITE (2)

Neh 13:23 in those days I saw Jews who had married *A*,
13:24 Of their children, half spoke *A*,

ASHDODITES (1)

Neh 4: 1 and the *A* heard that the restoration of

ASHEN (1)

Dn 5: 9 his face went *a*,

ASHER (37)

Gn 30:13 So she named him *A*.
35:26 Gad and *A*.
46:17 The sons of *A*: Imnah, Ishvah,
Ex 1: 4 Gad and *A*.
Nm 1:13 Ahiezer, son of Ammishaddai;from *A*:
1:40 Of the descendants of *A*,
1:41 hundred were enrolled in the tribe of *A*.
2:27 the tribe of *A* [Their prince was Pagiel,
10:26 Ochran, over the host of the tribe of *A*.
26:47 These were the clans of *A*,
34:27 from the tribe of *A*: Ahihud, son of Shelomi
Dt 27:13 over the people, while Reuben, Gad, *A*,
33:24 Of *A* he said: "More blessed than
33:24 "More blessed than the other sons be *A*!
Jos 17: 7 Manasseh bordered on *A*.
17:10 *A* on the north and Issachar on the east.
17:11 in Issachar and in *A* Manasseh was awarded
19:34 Zebulun on the south, *A* on the west,
21: 6 tribe of Issachar, from the tribe of *A*,
21:29 from the tribe of *A*,
Jgs 1:31 Nor did *A* drive out the inhabitants of
5:17 *A*, who dwells along the shore,
6:35 through *A*, Zebulun and Naphtali,
7:23 were called to arms from Naphtali, from *A*,
1Kgs 4:16 of Hushai, in *A* and along the rocky coast;
1Chr 2: 2 Joseph, Benjamin, Naphtali, Gad, and *A*.
6:47 cities from the tribes of Issachar, *A*,
6:59 From the tribe of *A*: Mashal
7:30 The sons of *A* were Imnah,
7:40 All these were descendants of *A*,
12:37 From *A*, fit for military service
2Chr 30:11 Nevertheless, some from *A*,
Ez 48: 2 *A*: on the frontier of Dan
48: 3 on the frontier of *A*,
48:34 the gate of Gad, the gate of *A*,
Lk 2:36 daughter of Phanuel of the tribe of *A*.
Rv 7: 6 Gad, twelve thousand from the tribe of *A*,

ASHERAH (7)

1Kgs 15:13 she had made an outrageous object for *A*.
18:19 prophets of *A* who eat at Jezebel's table."
2Kgs 21: 7 The *A* idol he had made,
23: 4 the objects that had been made for Baal, *A*,
23: 7 in which the women wove garments for the *A*.
23:15 grinding them to powder, and burning the *A*.
2Chr 15:16 she had made an outrageous object for *A*;

ASHERAHS (1)

Jgs 3: 7 God, and serving the Baals and the *A*,

ASHERITES (5)

Nm 7:72 of Pagiel, son of Ochran, prince of the *A*.
26:44 The *A* by clans were:
Jos 19:24 fell to the clans of the tribe of the *A*.
19:31 of the clans of the tribe of the *A*.
Jgs 1:32 The *A* live among the Canaanite natives of

ASHER'S (2)

Gn 49:20 *A* produce is rich,
Nm 26:46 The name of *A* daughter was Serah.

ASHES (51)

Gn 18:27 to my Lord, though I am but dust and *a*!
Ex 27: 3 Make pots for removing the *a*,
Lv 4:12 a clean place where the *a* are deposited
6: 3 shall take away the *a* to which the fire
6: 4 the *a* to a clean place outside the camp.
Nm 4:13 After cleansing the altar of its *a*,
19: 9 a man who is clean shall gather up the *a*
19:10 He who has gathered up the *a* of the heifer
19:17 *a* from the sin offering shall be put in a
2Sm 13:19 Tamar put *a* on her head and tore the long
1Kgs 13: 3 up and the *a* on it shall be strewn about."
13: 5 up and the *a* from it were strewn about
2Kgs 23: 4 of the Kidron and their *a* carried to Bethel.
Jdt 4:11 building, with *a* strewn on their heads,
4:15 With *a* upon their turbans,
9: 1 prostrate, with *a* strewn upon her head,
Est 4: 1 tore his garments, put on sackcloth and *a*,
4: 3 they all slept on sackcloth and *a*.)
4:16 she covered her head with dirt and *a*.
1Mc 3:47 *a* on their heads and tore their clothes.
4:39 *a* and fell with their faces to the ground.
2Mc 4:41 pieces of wood or handfuls of the *a* lying
13: 5 a tower seventy-five feet high, full of *a*,
13: 5 down steeply on all sides toward the *a*.
13: 8 fire and *a* should meet his death in ashes.
13: 8 fire and ashes should meet his death in *a*.
Jb 2: 8 to scrape himself, as he sat among the *a*.
30:19 I am leveled with the dust and *a*.
42: 6 what I have said, and repent in dust and *a*.
Ps(s) 102:10 For I eat *a* like bread and mingle my
147:16 frost he strews like *a*.
Wis 2: 3 our body will be *a* and our spirit will be
15:10 *A* his heart is!
Sir 10: 9 Why are dust and *a* proud?
17:27 heaven, while all men are dust and *a*.
40: 3 a lofty throne or grovels in dust and *a*,
Is 44:20 He is chasing *a*—
58: 5 like a reed, and lie in sackcloth and *a*?
61: 3 who mourn in Zion a diadem instead of *a*,
Jer 6:26 people, gird on sackcloth, roll in the *a*.
31:40 The whole valley of corpses and *a*,
Ez 27:30 dust on their heads, rolling in the *a*.
Dn 9: 3 prayer, with fasting, sackcloth, and *a*.
14:14 ordered his servants to bring some *a*,
Am 2: 1 he burned to *a* the bones of Edom's king,
Jon 3: 6 himself with sackcloth, and sat in the *a*.
Mal 3:21 will become *a* under the soles of your feet,
Mt 11:21 have reformed in sackcloth and *a* long ago.
Lk 10:13 long ago have reformed in sackcloth and *a*.
Heb 9:13 the sprinkling of a heifer's *a* can sanctify
2Pt 2: 6 in *a* and condemned them to destruction,

ASHHUR (2)

1Chr 2:24 of his father Hezron, and she bore him *A*,
4: 5 *A*, the father of Tekoa

ASHIMA (1)

2Kgs 17:30 the men of Hamath made *A*,

ASHKALON (3)

1Mc 10:86 left there and pitched his camp at *A*,
11:60 When he arrived at *A*,
12:33 far as *A* and its neighboring strongholds.

ASHKELON (13)

Jos 13: 3 of the Philistines in Gaza, Ashdod, *A*,
Jgs 1:18 with its territory, *A* with its territory,
14:19 LORD came upon him, and he went down to *A*,
1Sm 6:17 one for Ashdod, one for Gaza, one for *A*,
2Sm 1:20 Gath, herald it not in the streets of *A*,
Jer 25:20 *A*, Gaza, Ekron
47: 5 is shaved bald, *A* is reduced to silence;
47: 7 *A* and the seashore he has appointed it.
Am 1: 8 in Ashdod, and the sceptered ruler of *A*;
Zep 2: 4 shall be forsaken, and *A* shall be a waste,
2: 7 *A* at evening they shall couch their flocks,
Zec 9: 5 *A* shall see it and be afraid; Gaza also:
9: 5 from Gaza, and *A* shall not be inhabited,

ASHKENAZ (3)

Gn 10: 3 *A*, Riphath, and Togarmah.
1Chr 1: 6 The descendants of Gomer were *A*,
Jer 51:27 her the kingdoms, Ararat, Minni, and *A*;

ASHNAH (2)

Jos 15:33 Eshtaol, Zorah, *A*,
15:43 villages, Libnah, Ether, Ashan, Iphtah, *A*,

ASHORE (4)

Mt 13:48 When it was full they hauled it *a* and sat
Mk 6:53 the crossing they came *a* at Gennesaret,
Jn 21:11 hauled *a* the net loaded with sizable fish
Acts 27:44 In this way all came safely *a*.

ASHPENAZ (1)

Dn 1: 3 The king told *A*, his chief chamberlain,

ASHTAROTH (11)

Dt 1: 4 of Bashan, who lived in *A* and in Edrei.
Jos 9:10 and Og, king of Bashan, who lived in *A*.
12: 4 of the Rephaim, who lived at *A* and Edrei.
13:12 of the Rephaim, who reigned at *A* and Edrei.
13:31 Half of Gilead, with *A* and Edrei,
Jgs 2:13 abandoned him and served Baal and the *A*,
10: 6 the LORD, serving the Baals and *A*,
1Sm 7: 3 put away your foreign gods and your *A*,
7: 4 the Israelites put away their Baals and *A*,
12:10 the LORD and worshiping Baals and *A*;
1Chr 6:56 pasture lands and *A* with its pasture lands.

ASHTERATH (1)

1Chr 11:44 Uzzia, from *A*;

ASHTEROTH-KARNAIM (1)

Gn 14: 5 him came and defeated the Rephaim in *A*,

ASHURITES (1)

2Sm 2: 9 where he made him king over Gilead, the *A*,

ASHVATH (1)

1Chr 7:33 sons of Japhlet were Pasach, Bimhal, and *A*;

ASHY (1)

Jb 13:12 Your reminders are *a* maxims,

ASIA (26)

1Mc 8: 6 Antiochus the Great, king of *A*,
11:13 Antioch and assumed the crown of *A*;
11:13 on his head, that of Egypt and that of *A*.
12:39 Trypho was determined to become king of *A*,
13:32 in his place, putting on the crown of *A*.
2Mc 3: 3 Thus Seleucus, king of *A*,
10:24 a large number of cavalry from *A*;
Acts 2: 9 Cappadocia, Pontus, the province of *A*,
6: 9 Cilicia and *A*) would undertake to engage
16: 6 preaching the message in the province of *A*.
19:10 all the inhabitants of the province of *A*,
19:22 while he himself stayed on for a time in *A*.
19:26 but throughout most of the province of *A*,
19:27 she whom *A* and all the world revere may
20: 4 Tychicus and Trophimus from *A*.
20:16 past Ephesus so as not to lose time in *A*,
20:18 first day I set foot in the province of *A*—
21:27 Jews from the province of *A* recognized Paul
24:19 province of *A* are the ones who found me.
27: 2 bound for ports in the province of *A*.
Rom 16: 5 the first offering that *A* made to Christ.
1Cor 16:19 The churches of *A* send you greetings.
2Cor 1: 8 in the dark about the trouble we had in *A*;
2Tm 1:15 You know that all in *A*,
1Pt 1: 1 throughout Pontus, Galatia, Cappadocia, *A*,
Rv 1: 4 the seven churches in the province of *A*;

ASIARCHS (1)

Acts 19:31 Even some of the *A* who were friends of

ASIDE (87)

Gn 19: 2 *a* into your servant's house for the night,
19: 3 *a* to his place and entered his house.
Ex 29:27 "Thus shall you set *a* the breast of
32: 8 *a* from the way I pointed out to them,
33: 6 the Israelites laid *a* their ornaments.
Lv 19: 4 "Do not turn *a* to idols,
Nm 3: 9 they have been set *a* from among the
8:14 and thus shall you set *a* the Levites from
21:22 will not turn *a* into any field or vineyard,
24: 1 did not go *a* as before to seek omens,
Dt 2:27 without turning *a* to the right or the left.
5:32 not turning *a* to the right or to the left,
9:12 they have already turned *a* from the way I
9:16 you had already turned *a* from the way
11:28 turn *a* from the way I ordain for you today,
17:11 without turning *a* to the right or to the
17:20 nor turn *a* to the right or to the left
21:13 her nails and lay *a* her captive's garb.
23:13 have a place set *a* to be used as a latrine.
26:12 "When you have finished setting *a* all the
28:14 not turning *a* to the right or to the left
31:29 *a* from the way along which I directed you,
Jos 16: 9 to each city set *a* for the Ephraimites
Jgs 14: 8 he stepped *a* to look at the remains of the

ASIDE (cont.)

1Sm 9:23 portion I gave you and told you to put *a.*"
2Sm 3:27 Joab took him *a* within the city gate as
18:30 "Step *a* and remain in attendance here."
18:30 So he stepped *a* and remained there.
2Kgs 4: 4 vessels, and as each is filled, set it *a.*"
Neh 12:44 over the chambers set *a* for stores,
13: 5 had set *a* for the latter's use a large
13: 7 in setting *a* for him a chamber in the
Tb 6: 6 had cut the fish open, he put *a* the gall,
7:11 nothing until you set *a* what belongs to me."
12: 6 the two men *a* privately and said to them:
Jdt 10: 3 on, laid *a* the garments of her widowhood,
Est C:13 all her festive adornments were put *a,*
1Mc 12:31 So Jonathan turned *a* against the Arabs who
2Mc 4:11 He set *a* the royal concessions granted to
6:21 ritual meal took the man *a* privately,
8:35 laid *a* his fine clothes and fled alone
Jb 6:18 Caravans turn *a* from their routes;
9:27 will lay *a* my sadness and be of good cheer,
23:11 his way I have kept and have not turned *a.*
Ps(s) 44:19 nor our steps turned *a* from your path,
125: 5 But such as turn *a* to crooked ways may the
Prv 4: 5 forget or turn *a* from the words I utter.
4:15 Shun it, cross it not, turn *a* from it,
Sir 6:22 and he will not delay in casting her *a.*
7: 2 wickedness, and it will turn *a* from you.
28: 6 Remember your last days, set enmity *a;*
31: 8 without fault, who turns not *a* after gain!
32:17 The sinner turns *a* reproof and distorts
51:23 Come *a* to me,
Lam 3: 9 with fitted stones, and turned my paths *a.*
Bar 6:43 drawn *a* by some passer-by who lies with her,
Ez 26:16 down from their thrones, lay *a* their robes,
48: 9 The tract that you set *a* for the LORD
Jon 3: 6 he rose from his throne, laid *a* his robe,
Mal 2: 8 But you have turned *a* from the way,
3: 5 those who turn *a* the stranger,
3: 7 fathers you have turned *a* from my statutes,
Mt 2: 7 Herod called the astrologers *a* and found
16:22 him *a* and began to remonstrate with him.
19:27 we have put everything *a* to follow you.
20:17 the Twelve *a* on the road and said to them:
Mk 7: 9 "You have made a fine art of setting *a*
8:32 him *a* and began to remonstrate with him.
10:28 "We have put *a* everything to follow you!"
10:32 Taking the Twelve *a* once more,
10:50 He threw *a* his cloak,
Lk 18:31 Taking the Twelve *a,* he said to them:
Acts 5: 2 put *a* a part of the proceeds for himself;
7:27 was wronging his neighbor pushed Moses *a.*
7:39 thrust him *a* and longed to return to Egypt.
11:29 disciples determine to set something *a,*
23:19 the hand and drew him *a* to ask privately,
1Cor 13:11 When I became a man I put childish ways *a.*
16: 2 put *a* whatever he has been able to save,
Gal 3:15 or set it *a* once it is legally validated.
3:17 God is not set *a* as invalid by any law
4:14 you did not despise or brush *a* in disgust.
Eph 4:22 that you must lay *a* your former way of
Col 3: 8 You must put that *a* now:
3: 9 What you have done is put *a* your old self
Heb 12: 1 let us lay *a* every encumbrance of sin which
Rv 2: 4 you have turned *a* from your early love.

ASIEL (2)

1Chr 4:35 of Joshibiah, son of Seraiah, son of *A,*
Tb 1: 1 Aduel, son of Gabael of the family of *A,*

ASLEEP (44)

Gn 2:21 deep sleep on the man, and while he was *a,*
41: 5 He fell *a* again and had another dream.
Jos 2: 8 Before the spies fell *a,*
Jgs 4:21 While Sisera was sound *a,*
1Sm 3: 2 One day Eli was *a* in his usual place.
26: 7 found Saul lying *a* within the barricade,
26:12 All remained *a,*
2Sm 4: 6 dozed off while sifting wheat, and was *a.*
4: 7 while Ishbaal was lying *a* in his bedroom.
1Kgs 18:27 Perhaps he is *a* and must be awakened."
19: 5 lay down and fell *a* under the broom tree,
Tb 8:13 went in, and found them sound *a* together.
Ps(s) 4: 9 soon as I lie down, I fall peacefully *a,*
44:24 Why are you *a,* O LORD?
Jon 1: 5 hold of the ship, and lay there fast *a.*
1: 6 to him and said, "What are you doing *a?*
Mt 9:24 She is *a.*"
13:25 While everyone was *a,*
25: 5 so they all began to nod, then to fall *a.*
26:40 returned to his disciples, he found them *a.*
26:43 Once more, on his return, he found them *a;*
27:53 of saints who had fallen *a* were raised.
28:13 the night and stole him while we were *a.*'
Mk 4:38 stern through it all, sound *a* on a cushion.
5:39 She is *a.*"
13:36 not let him come suddenly and catch you *a.*
14:37 When he returned he found them *a.*
14:37 He said to Peter, *A,* Simon?
14:40 Once again he found them *a* on his return.
Lk 8:52 "Stop crying for she is not dead but *a.*"
22:45 came to his disciples, only to find them *a,*
Jn 11:11 added, "Our beloved Lazarus has fallen *a,*
11:12 "Lord, if he is *a* his life will be saved."
Acts 13:36 God's will, fell *a* and joined his fathers,
20: 9 He finally went sound *a,*
1Cor 15: 6 still alive, although some have fallen *a.*
15:18 *a* in Christ are the deadest of the dead.
15:20 first fruits of those who have fallen *a.*
15:51 Not all of us shall fall *a,*
1Thes 4:14 also who have fallen *a* believing in him.
4:15 an advantage over those who have fallen *a.*
5: 6 therefore let us not be *a* like the rest,
5:10 us, that all of us, whether awake or *a,*
2Pt 2: 3 their destruction is not *a.*

ASMODEUS (2)

Tb 3: 8 but the wicked demon *A* killed them off
3:17 and then drive the wicked demon *A* from her.

ASNAH (1)

Ezr 2:50 sons of Paseah, sons of Besai, sons of *A,*

ASP (1)

Ps(s) 91:13 You shall tread upon the *a* and the viper;

ASPATHA (1)

Est 9: 7 They also killed Parshandatha, Dalphon, *A,*

ASPECT (1)

1Pt 1:15 holy yourselves in every *a* of your conduct,

ASPENS (1)

Ps(s) 137: 2 On the *a* of that land we hung up our harps,

ASPHAR (1)

1Mc 9:33 and camped by the waters of the pool of *A.*

ASPIRATIONS (1)

Ez 17:14 would remain a modest one, without *a,*

ASPIRES (3)

Mt 20:26 you who *a* to greatness must serve the rest,
Mk 10:43 you who *a* to greatness must serve the rest;
1Tm 3: 1 wants to be a bishop *a* to a noble task.

ASPS (4)

Jb 20:14 it shall be venom of *a* inside him.
20:16 The poison of *a* he shall drink in;
Ps(s) 140: 4 the venom of *a* is under their lips.
Rom 3:13 The venom of *a* lies behind their lips,

ASRIEL (2)

Nm 26:31 through *A* the clan of the Asrielites,
Jos 17: 2 Manasseh, the clans of Abiezer, Helek, *A,*

ASRIELITES (1)

Nm 26:31 through Asriel the clan of the *A,*

ASS (73)

Gn 16:12 He shall be a wild *a* of a man,
49:11 vine, his purebred *a* to the choicest stem.
49:14 "Issachar is a rawboned *a,*
49:22 colt by a spring, a wild *a* on a hillside.
Ex 4:20 the land of Egypt, with them riding the *a.*
13:13 of an *a* you shall redeem with a sheep.
20:17 male or female slave, nor his ox or *a,*
21:33 again, should an ox or an *a* fall into it,
22: 3 possession, be it an ox, an *a* or a sheep,
22: 8 whether it be about an ox, or an *a,*
22: 9 "When a man gives an *a,*
23: 4 upon your enemy's ox or *a* going astray,
23: 5 When you notice the *a* of one who hates you
23:12 your ox and your *a* may also have rest,
34:20 *a* you shall redeem with one of the flock;
Nm 16:15 I have never taken a single *a* from them,
22:21 when Balaam arose, he saddled his *a*
22:22 hinder him as he was riding along on his *a,*
22:23 When the *a* saw the angel of the LORD
22:25 When the *a* saw the angel of the LORD there,
22:27 When the *a* saw the angel of the LORD there,
22:27 anger, he again beat the *a* with his stick.
22:28 now the LORD opened the mouth of the *a,*
22:29 against me," said Balaam to the *a,*
22:30 But the *a* said to Balaam,
22:32 have you beaten your *a* these three times?
22:33 When the *a* saw me,
Dt 5:14 or your ox or *a* or any of your beasts,
5:21 his male or female slave, nor his ox or *a,*
22: 3 You shall do the same with his *a,*
22: 4 You shall not see your kinsman's *a* or ox
22:10 with an ox and an *a* harnessed together.
28:31 Your *a* will be stolen in your presence,
Jos 7:24 and daughters, his ox, his *a* and his sheep,
15:18 Then, as she alighted from the *a,*
Jgs 1:14 Then, as she alighted from the *a,*
15:15 Near him was the fresh jawbone of an *a;*
15:16 of an *a* I have piled them in a heap;
15:16 of an *a* I have slain a thousand men."
19:28 her on an *a* and started out again for home.
1Sm 12: 3 Whose *a* have I taken?
25:20 through a mountain defile riding on an *a,*
25:23 she dismounted quickly from the *a* and,
25:42 She got up immediately, mounted an *a,*
2Sm 17:23 acted upon, he saddled his *a* and departed,
19:27 is lame, said to him, 'Saddle the *a* for me,
1Kgs 2:40 So Shimei rose, saddled his *a,*
13:13 he said to his sons, "Saddle the *a* for me."
13:23 and drunk water, the *a* was saddled for him,
13:24 road, and the *a* remained standing by it,
13:27 he said to his sons, "Saddle the *a* for me."
13:28 with the *a* and the lion standing beside it.
13:28 not eaten the body nor had it harmed the *a.*
13:29 of the man of God and put it on the *a,*
Jb 6: 5 Does the wild *a* bray when he has grass?
39: 5 Who has given the wild *a* his freedom,
Prv 26: 3 whip for the horse, the bridle for the *a,*
Sir 33:25 Fodder and whip and loads for an *a;*
Is 1: 3 An ox knows its owner, and an *a,*
21: 7 a pair of horses, Someone riding an *a,*
32:20 stream, and let the ox and the *a* go freely!
Jer 22:19 The burial of an *a* shall he be given,
48: 6 to survive like the wild *a* in the desert!"
Ez 23:20 whose members are like that of an *a,*
Hos 8: 9 a wild *a* off on its own
Zec 9: 9 on an *a,* on a colt, the foal of an ass.
Mt 21: 2 find an *a* tethered and her colt with her.
21: 5 comes to you without display astride an *a,*
21: 7 they brought the *a* and the colt and laid
Lk 13:15 Which of you does not let his ox or *a* out
19:30 *a* tied there which no one has yet ridden.
19:33 As they untied the *a,*

ASSAILED (4)

Jb 19: 3 have reviled me, have *a* me without shame!
41: 3 Who has *a* him and come off safe
Wis 18:17 perturbed them and unexpected fears *a* them;
19: 1 wicked, merciless wrath *a* until the end.

ASSAILS (2)

Jb 16: 9 I am the prey his wrath *a,*
Is 21: 4 My mind reels, shuddering *a* me;

ASSASSINATE (1)

Jer 40:14 sent Ishmael, son of Nethaniah, to *a* him.

ASSASSINATED (1)

Tb 1:21 later the king was *a* by two of his sons,

ASSAULT (3)

1Kgs 20:12 "Prepare the *a,*" he commanded
2Mc 11: 9 that they were ready to *a* not only men,
Jl 2: 9 They *a* the city, they run upon the wall,

ASSAULTED (2)

1Mc 5:50 he *a* the city all that day and night,
15:25 he *a* it continuously both with troops and

ASSAULTING (1)

Acts 21:32 him and the soldiers, they stopped *a* Paul.

ASSEMBLAGE (1)

Lk 8:47 she related before the whole *a* why she had

ASSEMBLE (36)

Gn 49: 2 *A* and listen, sons of Jacob, listen to Israel,
Ex 3:16 "Go and *a* the elders of the Israelites,
Lv 8: 3 Then *a* the whole community at the entrance
Nm 8: 9 where you shall *a* also the whole community
11:16 *A* for me seventy of the elders of Israel,
20: 8 "Take the staff and *a* the community,
Dt 4:10 and he said to me, *A* the people for me;
31:12 *A* the people—men, women and children,
31:28 *a* all your tribal elders and your
2Sm 3:21 go to *a* all Israel for my lord the king,
12:28 Therefore, *a* the rest of the soldiers,
1Kgs 18:20 and had the prophets *a* on Mount Carmel.
Ezr 8:15 *a* by the river that flows toward Ahava,
Est 4:16 "Go and *a* all the Jews who are in Susa;
Ps(s) 48: 5 the kings *a,* they come on together;
Is 11:12 shall *a* from the four corners of the earth.
34:15 There shall the kites *a,*
43: 9 gather together, let the peoples *a!*
44:11 they will all *a* and stand forth,
45:20 Come and *a,*
48:14 All of you *a* and listen:
Ez 11:17 will gather you from the nations and *a* you
Dn 11:10 shall prepare and *a* a great armed host,
Jl 2:16 *A* the elders, gather the children
4: 2 I will *a* all the nations and bring them
4:11 all you neighboring peoples, *a* there!
Mi 2:12 one, I will *a* all the remnant of Israel;
4: 6 gather the lame, And I will *a* the outcasts,
Zep 3: 8 together the nations, to *a* the kingdoms,
3:19 I will save the lame, and *a* the outcasts;
Mt 24:31 they will *a* his chosen from the four winds,
Mk 13:27 and *a* his chosen from the four winds,
1Cor 11:20 you *a* it is not to eat the Lord's Supper,
11:33 my brothers, when you *a* for the meal,

14:26 When you *a,* one has a psalm,
Rv 16:14 They went out to *a* all the kings of the

ASSEMBLED (79)

Gn 29: 3 Only when all the shepherds were *a* there
Ex 4:29 and *a* all the elders of the Israelites.
35: 1 Moses *a* the whole Israelite community and
Lv 8: 4 had *a* at the entrance of the meeting tent,
Nm 1:18 and *a* the whole community on the first day
14: 5 the whole *a* community of the Israelites;
16:19 when Korah had *a* all his band against them
20:10 Aaron *a* the community in front of the rock,
Dt 33: 5 When the chiefs of the people *a* and the
Jos 18: 1 community of the Israelites *a* at Shiloh,
22:12 and therefore they *a* their whole community
Jgs 4:13 So Sisera *a* from Harosheth-ha-goiim at the
10:17 the Israelites *a* and encamped in Mizpah.
16:23 The lords of the Philistines *a* to offer a
20:14 *a* from their other cities to Gibeah,
1Sm 13: 5 The Philistines also *a* for battle,
13:11 and with the Philistines *a* at Michmash,
2Sm 2:30 the pursuit of Abner, *a* all the men.
6: 1 David again *a* all the picked men of Israel,
10:17 On receiving this news, David *a* all Israel,
12:29 So David *a* the rest of the soldiers and
20:14 *a* and they too entered the city after him.
23: 9 when the Philistines *a* there for battle.
23:11 The Philistines had *a* at Lehi,
1Kgs 8: 2 All the men of Israel *a* before King
8:65 who had *a* in large numbers from Labo of
1Chr 13: 5 Then David *a* all Israel,
15: 3 Then David *a* all Israel in Jerusalem to
19: 7 *a* from their cities and came out for war.
28: 1 *a* at Jerusalem all the leaders of Israel,
2Chr 5: 3 All the men of Israel *a* before the king
7: 8 who had *a* in very large numbers from Labo
Jdt 13:13 the least to the greatest, hurriedly *a,*
Est F: 5 who *a* to destroy the name of the Jews,
1Mc 3:46 they *a* and went to Mizpah near Jerusalem,
3:58 fight these Gentiles who have *a* against us
4:37 So the whole army *a,*
5: 9 The Gentiles in Gilead *a* to attack and
5:37 *a* another army and camped opposite Raphon,
5:45 Then he *a* all the Israelites,
6:20 and fifty they *a* and stormed the citadel,
12:35 returned, he *a* the elders of the people,
13: 2 There he *a* the people and exhorted them in
14: 1 King Demetrius *a* his army and marched into
2Mc 4:39 the people *a* in protest against Lysimachus.
6:11 who had *a* in nearby caves to observe the
8: 1 to Judaism, *a* about six thousand men.
8:16 Maccabeus *a* his men,
10:21 he *a* the rulers of the people and accused
15:31 When he arrived there, he *a* his countrymen,
Is 13: 4 the noise of kingdoms, nations *a!*
31: 4 With a band of shepherds *a* against it,
60: 9 All the vessels of the sea are *a,*
Jer 26:17 came forward and said to all the people *a,*
28: 5 all the people *a* in the house of the LORD,
Ez 22:21 When I have *a* you,
38: 7 ready, you and all your horde *a* about you,
38: 8 which has been *a* from many peoples [on the
Mt 22:34 silenced the Sadducees, they *a* in a body;
22:41 Jesus put a question to the *a* Pharisees,
25:32 and all the nations will be *a* before him.
26: 3 were *a* in the palace of the high priest,
27:17 Since they were already *a,*
Mk 3:20 the house with them and again the crowd *a,*
8: 1 At about that time another large crowd *a,*
15:16 at the same time they *a* the whole cohort.
Lk 1:59 When they *a* for the circumcision of the
22:66 the chief priests, and the scribes *a* again.
23:48 *a* for this spectacle saw what had happened,
24:33 the Eleven and the rest of the company *a.*
Jn 21: 2 *A* were Simon Peter, Thomas (the "Twin"),
Acts 2: 6 heard the sound, and *a* in a large crowd.
4: 5 the scribes *a* the next day in Jerusalem,
6: 2 *a* the community of the disciples and said,
10:27 He found many people *a* there,
12:22 The *a* crowd shouted back,
20: 8 lamps in the upstairs room where we were *a.*
1Cor 14:23 is *a* and everyone is speaking in tongues,
Rv 16:16 The devils then *a* the kings in a place

ASSEMBLIES (3)

Ps(s) 26:12 in the *a* I will bless the LORD.
Is 1:13 New moon and sabbath, calling of *a,*
1Cor 14:34 rule observed in all the *a* of believers,

ASSEMBLING (1)

Nm 10: 2 in *a* the community and in breaking camp.

ASSEMBLY (157)

Gn 28: 3 you that you may become an *a* of peoples.
35:11 A nation, indeed an *a* of nations,
48: 4 numerous and raise you into an *a* of tribes,
Ex 12: 6 then, with the whole *a* of Israel present,
12:16 On the first day you shall hold a sacred *a,*
Lv 23: 2 which you shall celebrate with a sacred *a.*
23: 3 is the sabbath rest, a day for sacred *a,*
23: 4 at their proper time with a sacred *a.*
23: 7 hold a sacred *a* and do no sort of work.
23: 8 hold a sacred *a* and do no sort of work."
23:21 you shall by proclamation have a sacred *a,*
23:24 with a sacred *a* and with the trumpet
23:27 when you shall hold a sacred *a* and mortify
23:35 On the first day there shall be a sacred *a,*
23:36 sacred *a* and offer an oblation to the LORD.
23:37 on which you shall proclaim a sacred *a,*
Nm 10: 7 an *a* you are to blow an ordinary blast,
15:33 him to Moses and Aaron and the whole *a.*
16: 3 and held an *a* against Moses and Aaron,
20: 6 the *a* to the entrance of the meeting tent,
25: 7 Aaron the priest, saw this, he left the *a,*
28:18 of these days you shall hold a sacred *a,*
28:25 the seventh day you shall hold a sacred *a,*
28:26 cereal offering, you shall hold a sacred *a,*
29: 1 seventh month you shall hold a sacred *a,*
29: 7 seventh month you shall hold a sacred *a,*
29:12 seventh month you shall hold a sacred *a,*
Dt 5:22 spoke with a loud voice to your entire *a*
9:10 the midst of the fire on the day of the *a.*
10: 4 the midst of the fire on the day of the *a.*
18:16 your God, at Horeb on the day of the *a,*
31:30 to end, for the whole *a* of Israel to hear:
Jgs 20: 2 themselves in the *a* of the people of God.
21: 5 did not come up to the LORD for the *a?"*
21: 8 had come to the encampment for the *a.*
1Kgs 12:20 to an *a* and made him king over all Israel.
2Kgs 10:20 "Proclaim a solemn *a* in honor of Baal."
1Chr 13: 2 leaders, he said to the whole *a* of Israel:
13: 4 And the whole *a* agreed to do this,
28: 8 presence of all Israel, the *a* of the LORD,
29: 1 King David then said to the whole *a:*
29:10 the LORD in the presence of the whole *a,*
29:20 Then David besought the whole *a,*
29:20 And the whole *a* blessed the LORD,
2Chr 1: 3 and, accompanied by the whole *a,*
1: 5 There Solomon and the *a* consulted the LORD,
10: 3 Jeroboam was summoned to the *a,*
20: 5 Jehoshaphat stood up in the *a* of Judah
20:14 the clan of Asaph, in the midst of the *a,*
20:26 they held an *a* in the Valley of Beracah
23: 3 the whole *a* made a covenant with the king
24: 6 of the LORD, and by the *a* of Israel,
28:14 plunder before the princes and the whole *a.*
29:23 were led before the king and the *a,*
29:28 The entire *a* prostrated itself,
29:31 Then the *a* brought forward the sacrifices
29:32 the *a* brought forward was seventy oxen,
30: 2 and the entire *a* in Jerusalem had agreed
30: 4 approved by the king and the entire *a,*
30:13 it was a very great *a.*
30:17 in the *a* had not sanctified themselves,
30:23 *a* agreed to celebrate another seven days.
30:24 bulls and seven thousand sheep to the *a,*
30:24 *a* a thousand bulls and ten thousand sheep.
30:25 and the whole *a* of Judah rejoiced,
30:25 rest of the *a* that had come from Israel,
31:18 thus for the entire *a,*
Ezr 2:64 The entire *a* taken together came to
10: 1 large *a* of Israelites gathered about him,
10: 8 be excluded from the *a* of the exiles.
10:12 the whole *a* cried out with a loud voice:
10:14 Let our leaders represent the whole *a;*
Neh 5:13 And the whole *a* answered, "Amen,"
7:66 The entire *a* taken together came to
8: 2 the priest brought the law before the *a,*
8:17 Thus the entire *a* of the returned exiles
8:18 days, and the solemn *a* on the eighth day,
13: 1 may ever be admitted into the *a* of God;
Jdt 6:16 women, gathered in haste at the place of *a.*
6:21 Uzziah brought him from the *a* to his home,
7:29 All in the *a* with one accord broke into
14: 6 of one of the men in the *a* of the people,
1Mc 2:56 Caleb, for bearing witness before the *a,*
3:13 him, an *a* of faithful men ready for war.
3:44 The *a* gathered together to prepare for
5:16 a great *a* convened to consider what they
14:19 These were read before the *a* in Jerusalem.
14:28 in Asaramel, in a great *a* of priests,
14:44 an *a* in the country without his consent,
Ps(s) 1: 5 nor shall sinners, in the *a* of the just.
7: 8 Let the *a* of the peoples surround you;
22:23 in the midst of the *a* I will praise you:
22:26 gift will I utter praise in the vast *a;*
26: 5 I hate the *a* of evildoers,
35:18 I will give you thanks in the vast *a,*
40:10 I announced your justice in the vast *a;*
40:11 kindness and your truth in the vast *a.*
82: 1 God arises in the divine *a;*
89: 6 faithfulness, in the *a* of the holy ones.
107:32 Let them extol him in the *a* of the people
111: 1 my heart in the company and *a* of the just.
149: 1 song of praise in the *a* of the faithful.
Prv 5:14 to utter ruin, condemned by the public *a!"*
21:16 sense will abide in the *a* of the shades.
26:26 but his malice will be revealed in the *a.*
Wis 8:15 in the *a* I should appear noble,
Sir 4: 7 Endear yourself to the *a;*
7: 7 nor disgrace yourself before the *a.*
15: 5 in the *a* she will make him eloquent.
21:17 views of a prudent man are sought in an *a,*
23:24 Such a woman will be dragged before the *a,*
24: 2 the *a* of the Most High she opens her mouth,
31:11 secure, and the *a* recounts his praises.
33:19 O rulers of the *a,* give ear!
38:33 bench, nor are they prominent in the *a;*
39:10 of his wisdom, and in *a* sing his praises.
41:16 before the public *a,* of crime;
44:15 retold, and the *a* proclaims their praise.
46: 7 Jephunneh, when they opposed the rebel *a,*
50:13 in the presence of the whole *a* of Israel.
Is 4: 5 of Mount Zion and over her place of *a,*
14:13 I will take my seat on the Mount of *A,*
Jer 30:20 of old, his *a* before me shall stand firm;
Lam 1:10 Whom you forbade to come into your *a.*
Bar 1:14 on the feast day and during the days of *a:*
Ez 16:40 They shall lead an *a* against you to stone
23:46 Summon an *a* against them,
23:47 The *a* shall stone them and hack them to
Dn 13:41 The *a* believed them, since they were
13:60 The whole *a* cried aloud,
Jl 1:14 Proclaim a fast, call an *a;*
2:15 proclaim a fast, call an *a;*
Mi 2: 5 out boundaries by lot in the *a* of the LORD.
Lk 1:10 While the full *a* of people was praying
23: 1 entire *a* rose up and led him before Pilate.
Acts 5:35 for a few minutes, and then said to the *a,*
7:38 In that desert *a,*
15:12 At that the whole *a* fell silent.
15:30 the *a* together to deliver the letter.
17: 5 bring Paul and Silas before the people's *a.*
19: 9 of the new way in the presence of the *a,*
19:32 with the whole *a* in chaos and the majority
19:39 it ought to be settled in the lawful *a.*
23: 7 and Sadducees which divided the whole *a.*
1Cor 11:34 that your *a* may not deserve condemnation.
14:28 there should be silence in the *a,*
14:35 is a disgrace when a woman speaks in the *a.*
16:19 with the *a* that meets in their house,
Col 4:15 Nymphas and the *a* that meets at his house.
4:16 is read in the *a* of the Laodiceans as well,
Heb 2:12 sing your praise in the midst of the *a";*
10:25 We should not absent ourselves from the *a,*
12:23 the *a* of the first-born enrolled in heaven,
Jas 2: 2 come into your *a* a man fashionably dressed,
Rv 2: 9 nothing other than members of Satan's *a.*
3: 9 I mean to make some of Satan's *a,*
19: 1 like the loud song of a great *a* in heaven.

ASSENTED (2)

2Mc 14:20 was expressed, they *a* to the treaty.
Heb 10:34 *a* to the confiscation of your goods,

ASSER (1)

Tb 1: 2 upper Galilee, above and to the west of *A,*

ASSERT (1)

Jn 9:16 This prompted some of the Pharisees to *a,*

ASSERTED (1)

Mk 3:22 the scribes who arrived from Jerusalem *a,*

ASSES (56)

Gn 12:16 male and female slaves, male and female *a,*
24:35 male and female slaves, and camels and *a.*
30:43 male and female servants and camels and *a.*
32: 6 I own cattle, *a* and sheep,
34:28 They seized their flocks, herds and *a,*
36:24 was pasturing the *a* of his father Zibeon.)
Ex 9: 3 your horses, *a,* camels, herds and flocks
Nm 31:28 *a* and sheep in their half of the spoil you
31:30 the different beasts, oxen, *a* and sheep,
31:34 thousand oxen, sixty-one thousand *a,*
31:39 thirty thousand five hundred *a,*
31:45 oxen, thirty thousand five hundred *a,*
Jos 6:21 and old, as well as oxen, sheep and *a,*
9: 4 making use of old sacks for their *a,*
Jgs 5:10 They who ride on white *a,*
6: 4 sustenance in Israel, nor sheep, oxen or *a.*
19: 3 set out with his servant and a pair of *a,*
19:10 set out with a pair of saddled *a,*
19:19 We have straw and fodder for our *a,*
19:21 to his house and provided fodder for the *a.*
1Sm 8:16 as well as your best oxen and your *a,*
9: 3 Now the *a* of Saul's father,
9: 3 with you and go out and hunt for the *a."*
9: 5 about the *a* and become anxious about us."
9:20 As for the *a* you lost three days ago,
10: 2 *a* you went to look for have been found.
10: 2 father is no longer worried about the *a,*
10:14 Saul replied, "To look for the *a.*
10:16 "He assured us that the *a* had been found."
15: 3 and infants, oxen and sheep, camels and *a.'"*
22:19 and infants, and oxen, *a* and sheep.
25:18 of pressed figs, and loaded them on *a.*
27: 9 alive, but would carry off sheep, oxen, *a,*
2Sm 16: 1 *a* laden with two hundred loaves of bread,
16: 2 *a* are for the king's household to ride on.
2Kgs 7: 7 their tents, their horses, and their *a,*
7:10 voice, only the horses and *a* tethered,
1Chr 5:21 fifty thousand sheep, and two thousand *a.*
12:41 and Naphtali came bringing food on *a,*

ASSES (cont.)
2Chr 28:15 them, and all who were weak they set on *a*.
Ezr 2:67 *a* six thousand seven hundred and twenty.
Neh 7:68 *a* six thousand seven hundred and twenty.
13:15 sheaves of grain, loading them on their *a*,
Tb 10:10 slaves, oxen and sheep, *a* and camels,
Jdt 2:17 along a very large number of camels, *a*,
Jb 1:14 were plowing and the *a* grazing beside them,
24: 3 The *a* of orphans they drive away;
24: 5 Like wild *a* in the desert,
Ps(s) 104:11 field, till the wild *a* quench their thirst.
Sir 13:18 Lion's prey are the wild *a* of the desert;
Is 30: 6 They carry their riches on the backs of *a*
30:24 The oxen and the *a* that till the ground
32:19 wasteland forever for wild *a* to frolic in,
Jer 14: 6 The wild *a* stand on the bare heights,
Dn 5:21 he lived with wild *a*,
Zec 14:15 plague upon the horses, mules, camels, *a*,

ASSESSED (1)
Acts 19:19 When the value of these was *a*,

ASSHUR (7)
Gn 2:14 it is the one that flows east of *A*.
10:11 From that land he went forth to *A*,
10:22 Elam, *A*, Arpachshad, Lud, and Aram.
25:18 on the border of Egypt, all the way to *A*;
Nm 24:24 they have conquered *A* and conquered Eber,
1Chr 1:17 The descendants of Shem were Elam, *A*,
Ez 27:23 and Eden, the merchants of Sheba, *A*,

ASSHURIM (1)
Gn 25: 3 descendants of Dedan were the *A*

ASSIGN (14)
Gn 45:18 I will *a* you the best land in Egypt,
Nm 3:41 Then *a* the Levites to me,
4:19 Aaron and his sons shall go in and *a* to
7: 5 *A* them to the Levites,
18:21 I hereby *a* all tithes in Israel as their
26:54 a large group you shall *a* a large heritage,
34:29 the LORD commanded to *a* the Israelites
35:13 Six cities of asylum shall you *a*:
Dt 30: 7 will *a* to your enemies and the foes who
Jos 20: 4 *a* him a place in which to live among them.
1Sm 8:11 sons and *a* them to his chariots and horses,
1Chr 17: 9 I will *a* a place for my people Israel and
Ez 47:23 there you shall *a* him his inheritance,
Lk 22:29 I for my part *a* to you the dominion my

ASSIGNED (60)
Gn 27:37 *a* to him all his kinsmen as his slaves;
28: 4 you are staying, which he *a* to Abraham."
29:24 (Laban *a* his slave girl Zilpah to his
29:29 (Laban *a* his slave girl Bilhah to his
39: 2 *a* to the household of his Egyptian master.
40: 4 The chief steward *a* Joseph to them,
Lv 10:14 for these have been *a* to you and your
Nm 7: 6 wagons and oxen, and *a* them to the Levites.
18: 8 I have *a* them to you and to your sons
18:11 I have *a* it to you and to your sons
18:12 I have also *a* to you all the best of the
18:19 By perpetual ordinance I have *a* to you and
18:24 for I have *a* to them as their heritage the
18:26 I have *a* you from them as your heritage,
26:56 group, large or small, be *a* its heritage."
35: 4 The pasture lands of the cities to be *a*
35: 7 their pasture lands to be *a* the Levites.
Dt 32: 8 the Most High *a* the nations their heritage,
33:21 be his when the princely portion was *a*,
Jos 12: 6 them, he *a* their land to the Reubenites,
13:14 tribe of Levi Moses *a* no heritage since,
15:19 Since you have *a* to me land in the Negeb,
19:49 *a* a heritage in their midst to Joshua,
21:10 and *a* them to the descendants of Aaron in
21:21 They were *a*,
22: 7 of Manasseh Moses had *a* land
24: 4 To Esau I *a* the mountain region of Seir in
Jgs 1:15 "Since you have *a* land in the Negeb to me,
1Sm 2:28 and I *a* all the oblations of the
2Sm 11:16 he *a* Uriah to a place where he knew the
12:31 inhabitants, whom he *a* to work with saws,
1Kgs 11:18 appointed him rations, and *a* him land.
1Chr 6:40 was *a* Hebron with its adjacent pasture
6:42 There were *a* to the descendants of Aaron:
6:49 The Israelites *a* these cities with their
6:52 They were *a*: Shechem in the mountain
9:19 house of the Korahites had as their *a* task
24: 3 *a* the functions for the priestly service.
24: 5 Their functions were *a* impartially by lot,
26:12 were *a* watches in the service of the house
2Chr 9:25 which he *a* to the chariot cities and to
11:14 for the Levites left their *a* pasture lands
23:18 to whom David had *a* turns in the temple
33: 8 leave the land which I *a* to your fathers,
Neh 12:44 legally *a* to the priests and Levites.
1Mc 6:35 *a* to it a thousand men in coats of mail,
Jb 7: 3 So I have been *a* months of misery,
Sir 16:24 works and, as he made them, *a* their tasks,
33:13 Creator, to be *a* by him their function.
Is 53: 9 A grave was *a* him among the wicked and a
Ez 45: 2 fifty cubits, shall be *a* to the sanctuary.
48:15 *a* to the City for dwellings and pasture;
Mt 8: 9 myself and I have troops *a* to me.
Lk 22:29 to you the dominion my Father has *a* to me.
Jn 5:22 no one, but has *a* all judgment to the Son,
Acts 20:24 to which I have been *a* by the Lord Jesus,
28:16 a soldier was *a* to keep guard over him.
1Cor 3: 5 of them doing only what the Lord *a* him.
7:17 should lead the life the Lord has *a* him,
1Pt 5: 3 flock, not lording it over those *a* to you,

ASSIGNING (7)
Nm 33:54 *a* a large heritage to a large group and a
35: 8 In *a* the cities from the property of the
1Chr 6:50 designating them by name and *a* them by lot
2Chr 31: 2 *a* to each priest and Levite his proper
Neh 4: 7 *a* them by family groups with their swords,
11:23 for the singers *a* them their daily duties.
2Mc 8:22 a division, *a* to each fifteen hundred men.

ASSIGNMENTS (2)
Nm 4:49 individual *a* for service and for transport;
Sir 39:31 in their *a* they disobey not his command.

ASSIR (4)
Ex 6:24 The sons of Korah were *A*,
1Chr 6: 7 whose son was Korah, whose son was *A*,
6: 8 whose son was Ebiasaph, whose son was *A*,
6:22 son of Zaphaniah, son of Tahath, son of *A*,

ASSIST (7)
Ex 4:12 It is I who will *a* you in speaking and
4:15 I will *a* both you and him in speaking and
Nm 1: 4 *a* you there shall be a man from each tribe,
1: 5 are the names of those who are to *a* you:
1Chr 23:28 their duty shall be to *a* the sons of Aaron
1Mc 15:19 are not to *a* those who fight against them.
1Tm 5:16 relatives who are widows, she must *a* them.

ASSISTANCE (4)
2Sm 21:17 his *a* and struck and killed the Philistine.
2Kgs 15:19 *a* in strengthening his hold on the kingdom.
2Mc 2:22 Lord favored them with all his generous *a*.
Rom 15:25 for Jerusalem to bring *a* to the saints.

ASSISTANT (7)
Gn 37: 2 he was an *a* to the sons of his father's
Ex 31: 6 As his *a* I have appointed Oholiab,
33:11 then return to the camp, but his young *a*,
Neh 13:13 of Zaccur, son of Mattaniah, as their *a*;
Sir 46: 1 of Nun, *a* to Moses in the prophetic office,
Lk 4:20 he gave it back to the *a* and sat down.
Acts 13: 5 synagogues, John accompanying them as an *a*.

ASSISTANTS (6)
Nm 3: 6 present them to Aaron the priest, as his *a*.
18: 2 ancestral tribe, as your associates and *a*,
1Chr 18:17 David's sons were the chief *a* to the king.
Ezr 10:16 as his *a* men who were family heads,
Acts 19:22 So he sent two of his *a*,
1Cor 12:28 then miracle workers, healers, *a*,

ASSISTED (6)
Ex 38:23 commanded Moses, and he was *a* by Oholiab,
1Sm 22:17 the priests of the LORD, for they *a* David.
2Chr 29:34 their brethren the Levites *a* them until
Ezr 1: 4 *a* by the people of that place with silver,
8:33 son of Uriah, who was *a* by Eleazar,
8:33 they were *a* by the Levites Jozabad,

ASSISTING (3)
1Chr 9:25 took turns in *a* them for seven-day periods,
Lk 8: 3 others who were *a* them out of their means.
Jas 2:22 *a* his works and implemented by his works.

ASSOCIATE (9)
1Chr 26:25 His *a* pertained to Eliezer,
Neh 13: 4 of our God and who was an *a* of Tobiah,
Sir 9:14 neighbors' measure, and *a* with the wise.
37:12 Instead, *a* with a religious man,
Hos 4:17 Ephraim is an *a* of idols, let him alone!
Zec 13: 7 my shepherd, against the man who is my *a*,
Acts 10:28 not proper for a Jew to *a* with a Gentile
Rom 12:16 thoughts and *a* with those who are lowly.
1Cor 5: 9 my letter not to *a* with immoral persons.

ASSOCIATED (6)
2Mc 8: 9 With him he *a* Gorgias,
Ez 37:16 and those Israelites who are *a* with him.
37:16 and all the house of Israel *a* with him.
37:19 and of the tribes of Israel *a* with him,
Lk 23:51 not been *a* with their plan or their action.
Heb 10:33 at other times you *a* yourselves with those

ASSOCIATES (7)
Nm 18: 2 ancestral tribe, as your *a* and assistants,
18: 4 As your *a* they shall have charge of all
Ps(s) 55:21 Each one lays hands on his *a*,
Sir 13: 1 who *a* with an impious man learns his ways.
13:15 with his own kind every man *a*.
Is 44:10 all the *a* of anyone who forms a god,
Zec 3: 8 *a* who sit before you are men of good omen.

ASSOCIATING (1)
1Cor 5:11 What I really wrote about was your not *a*

ASSOCIATION (3)
Wis 8:16 For *a* with her involves no bitterness and
1Cor 4: 6 his *a* with one person rather than another.
5:10 of *a* with immoral people in this world,

ASSOS (2)
Acts 20:13 on ahead to the ship and set sail for *A*,
20:14 When he met us at *A* we took him aboard and

ASSRYIA (1)
Mi 5: 5 And we shall be delivered from *A*,

ASS'S (1)
2Kgs 6:25 an *a* head sold for eighty pieces of silver,

ASSUAGE (1)
Jer 33: 6 I will treat and *a* the city's wounds;

ASSUAGEMENT (1)
Wis 11: 4 *a* for their thirst from the hard stone.

ASSUME (2)
1Mc 12:39 to become king of Asia, *a* the crown,
Zec 13: 4 shall he *a* the hairy mantle to mislead,

ASSUMED (8)
2Chr 25:11 Amaziah now *a* command of his army.
1Mc 11:13 entered Antioch and *a* the crown of Asia;
13:32 killed him and *a* the kingship in his place,
Prv 12: 9 than one of *a* importance who lacks bread.
Sir 47: 6 When he *a* the royal crown,
Acts 7:25 He *a* that his kinsmen would understand
21:29 so they now *a* that Paul had brought him
Rv 11:17 You have *a* your great power,

ASSURANCE (15)
2Mc 11:30 Xanthicus will have our *a* of full permission
Jb 24:22 *a* of his life he gives safety and support.
Wis 5: 1 Then shall the just one with great *a*
Zec 3: 6 angel of the LORD then gave Joshua this *a*:
Mk 14:30 Jesus answered, "I give you my *a*,
Jn 8:34 "I give you my *a*,
16:23 I give you my *a*,
Acts 4:29 complete *a* by stretching forth your hand
15:41 giving the churches there renewed *a*.
28:31 With full *a*, and without any hindrance
2Cor 10: 2 with that *a* I might dare to use
Col 2: 2 enriched with full *a* by their knowledge
1Tm 1: 7 less the matters they discuss with such *a*.
3:13 and much *a* in their faith in Christ Jesus.
Heb 11: 1 is confident *a* concerning what we hope for,

ASSURANCES (1)
2Mc 11:26 to give them our *a* of friendship,

ASSURBANIPAL (1)
Ezr 4:10 the great and illustrious *A* transported

ASSURE (66)
Prv 16: 5 I *a* you that he will not go unpunished.
Mt 5:18 Of this much I *a* you:
6:16 I *a* you, they are already repaid.
6:29 Yet I *a* you,
8:10 and remarked to his followers, "I *a* you,
10:15 I *a* you, it will go easier
10:23 I solemnly *a* you, you will not
11:11 "I solemnly *a* you, history has not known
11:22 I *a* you, it will go easier for Tyre
11:24 I *a* you, it will go easier for Sodom
12: 6 I *a* you, there is something greater
12:31 "That, I *a* you, is why every sin
12:36 I *a* you, on judgment day
13:17 I *a* you, many a prophet
16:28 I *a* you, among those standing here
17:12 I *a* you, though, that Elijah has already
17:20 "I *a* you, if you had faith the size
18: 3 "I *a* you, unless you change
18:10 I *a* you, their angels in heaven
18:18 I *a* you, whatever you declare bound
19:23 "I *a* you, only with difficulty will a rich
21:31 "I *a* you that tax collectors and
23:36 All this, I *a* you, will be the fate
24: 2 I *a* you, not one stone will be left
24:34 I *a* you, the present generation
24:47 I *a* you, he will put him in charge of all
25:40 'I *a* you, as often as you did it for one
25:45 'I *a* you, as often as you neglected to do

26:13 I *a* you, wherever the good news
26:21 the course of the meal he said, "I *a* you,
Mk 8:12 I *a* you, no such sign will be given it!"
9: 1 "I *a* you, among those standing here
9:13 Let me *a* you, Elijah has already come.
9:41 you belong to Christ will not, I *a* you,
10:15 I *a* you that whoever does not accept the
11:23 I solemnly *a* you,
13:30 I *a* you, this generation will not pass away
14: 9 I *a* you, wherever the good news
14:25 I solemnly *a* you, I will never again drink
Lk 7:26 He is that, I *a* you, and something more.
7:28 I *a* you, there is no man born of woman
9:27 I *a* you, there are some standing here
10:12 I *a* you, on that day the fate of Sodom
12:51 I *a* you, the contrary is true;
18:29 His answer was, "I solemnly *a* you,
21: 3 "I *a* you, this poor widow has put in more
23:43 And Jesus replied, "I *a* you:
Jn 1:51 went on to tell them, "I solemnly *a* you,
3: 3 "I solemnly *a* you, no one can see the reign
3: 5 "I solemnly *a* you, no one can enter
3:11 "I solemnly *a* you, we are talking about
5:19 "I solemnly *a* you, the Son cannot do
5:24 I solemnly *a* you, the man who hears
5:25 I solemnly *a* you, an hour is coming,
6:26 "I *a* you, you are not looking for me
6:32 "I solemnly *a* you, it was not Moses
6:47 Let me firmly *a* you, he who believes
6:53 "Let me solemnly *a* you, if you do not eat
8:51 I solemnly *a* you, if a man is true
10: 1 "Truly I *a* you:
11:40 "Did I not *a* you that if you believed you
12:24 I solemnly *a* you, unless the grain
13:16 I solemnly *a* you, no slave is greater
13:20 I solemnly *a* you, he who accepts anyone
14:12 I solemnly *a* you, the man who has faith
Gal 1:11 I *a* you, brothers, the gospel I proclaimed

ASSURED (10)

Jos 2:24 They *a* Joshua, "The LORD has delivered
Ru 3:11 So be *a*, daughter, I will do for you
1Sm 9:17 caught sight of Saul, the LORD *a* him,
10:16 "He *a* us that the asses had been found."
Sir 19: 9 be *a* it will not make you burst.
Is 55: 3 covenant, the benefits *a* to David.
Jn 11:23 brother will rise again," Jesus *a* her.
Acts 13:34 the benefits *a* to David under the covenant.'
Heb 6:11 end, fully *a* of that for which you hope.
Jas 2:26 Be *a*, then, that faith without works

ASSUREDLY (4)

Prv 23: 5 for *a* it grows wings,
Dn 3:91 *A*, O king," they answered.
Lk 12:44 *A*, his master will put him in charge of
Rom 3: 6 *A* not!

ASSURES (1)

Heb 10:19 since the blood of Jesus *a* our entrance

ASSYRIA (131)

2Kgs 15:19 During his reign, Pul, king of *A*,
15:20 money to give to the king of *A* by exacting
15:20 The king of *A* did not remain in the
15:29 of Israel, Tiglath-pileser, king of *A*,
15:29 Galilee, deporting the inhabitants to *A*.
16: 7 messengers to Tiglath-pileser, king of *A*,
16: 8 sent them as a present to the king of *A*.
16:10 to meet Tiglath-pileser, king of *A*.
16:18 In deference to the king of *A* he removed
17: 3 Shalmaneser, king of *A*,
17: 4 But the king of *A* found Hoshea guilty of
17: 5 king of *A* arrested and imprisoned Hoshea;
17: 6 year of Hoshea, the king of *A* took Samaria,
17: 6 Samaria, and deported the Israelites to *A*,
17:23 into exile from their native soil to *A*,
17:24 The king of *A* brought people from Babylon,
17:26 A report reached the king of *A*:
17:27 The king of *A* gave the order,
18: 7 the king of *A* and did not serve him.
18: 9 king of Israel, Shalmaneser, king of *A*,
18:11 The king of *A* then deported the Israelites
18:11 Israelites to *A* and settled them in Halah,
18:13 of King Hezekiah, Sennacherib, king of *A*,
18:14 this message to the king of *A* at Lachish:
18:14 The king of *A* exacted three hundred
18:16 gold, and gave the gold to the king of *A*.
18:17 The king of *A* sent the general,
18:19 'Thus says the great king, the king of *A*:
18:23 make a wager with my lord, the king of *A*:
18:28 the words of the great king, the king of *A*.
18:30 will not be handed over to the king of *A*.
18:31 listen to Hezekiah, for the king of *A* says:
18:33 his land from the hand of the king of *A*?
19: 4 commander, whom his master, the king of *A*,
19: 6 of the king of *A* have blasphemed me.
19: 8 the king of *A* had withdrawn from Lachish,
19: 9 The king of *A* heard a report that Tirhakah,
19:10 will not be handed over to the king of *A*.
19:11 of *A* have done to all other countries:
19:17 the kings of *A* have laid waste the nations
19:20 for help against Sennacherib, king of *A*:
19:32 says the LORD concerning the king of *A*:
19:36 So Sennacherib, the king of *A*,
20: 6 this city from the hand of the king of *A*;
23:29 the river Euphrates to the king of *A*.
1Chr 5: 6 whom Tiglath-pileser, the king of *A*,
5:26 against them the anger of Pul, king of *A*,
5:26 and of Tiglath-pileser, king of *A*,
2Chr 28:16 sent an appeal for help to the kings of *A*.
28:20 Tilgath-pilneser, king of *A*,
28:21 princes to make payment to the king of *A*,
32: 1 by such deeds, Sennacherib, king of *A*,
32: 4 of *A* come and find an abundance of water?"
32: 7 dismayed because of the king of *A*
32: 9 After this, while Sennacherib, king of *A*,
32:10 "King Sennacherib of *A* has this to say:
32:11 save us from the grasp of the king of *A*'?
32:22 from the hand of Sennacherib, king of *A*,
Ezr 4: 2 since the days of Esarhaddon, king of *A*,
6:22 by making the king of *A* favorable to them,
Neh 9:32 the time of the kings of *A* until this day!
Tb 1: 2 the reign of Shalmaneser, king of *A*,
1: 3 had been deported with me to Nineveh, in *A*.
1:22 For under Sennacherib, king of *A*,
14: 4 happen, and shall overtake *A* and Nineveh;
14: 4 be safer in Media than in *A* or Babylon.
14:15 done against the citizens of Nineveh and *A*.
Is 7:17 [This means the king of *A*
7:18 of Egypt, and for the bee in the land of *A*.
7:20 the River [with the king of *A* the head,
8: 4 shall be carried off by the king of *A*.
8: 7 mighty [the king of *A* and all his power].
10: 5 Woe to *A*! My rod in anger
11:11 his people that is left from *A* and Egypt,
11:16 remnant of his people that is left from *A*,
19:23 there shall be a highway from Egypt to *A*;
19:23 enter Assyria, and Egypt shall serve *A*.
19:24 shall be a third party with Egypt and *A*,
19:25 people Egypt, and the work of my hands *A*,
20: 1 the general sent by Sargon, king of *A*,
20: 4 king of *A* lead away captives from Egypt,
20: 6 help and deliverance from the king of *A*;
23:13 the land of the Chaldeans, not *A*
27:13 and the lost in the land of *A* and the
30:31 When the LORD speaks, *A* will be shattered,
31: 8 *A* shall fall by a sword not wielded by man,
36: 1 of King Hezekiah, Sennacherib, king of *A*,
36: 2 From Lachish the king of *A* sent his
36: 4 Thus says the great king, the king of *A*,
36: 8 make a wager with my lord the king of *A*:
36:13 the words of the great king, the king of *A*.
36:15 will not be handed over to the king of *A*."'
36:16 listen to Hezekiah, for the king of *A* says:
36:18 his land from the hand of the king of *A*?
37: 4 commander, whom his master, the king of *A*,
37: 6 of the king of *A* have blasphemed me.
37: 8 heard that the king of *A* had left there,
37: 9 The king of *A* heard a report that Tirhakah,
37:10 will not be handed over to the king of *A*.
37:11 kings of *A* have done to all the countries:
37:18 the kings of *A* have laid waste all the
37:21 for help against Sennacherib, king of *A*,
37:33 says the LORD concerning the king of *A*:
37:37 So Sennacherib, the king of *A*,
38: 6 this city from the hand of the king of *A*;
52: 4 *A*, too, oppressed them for nought.
Jer 2:18 Why go to *A*, to drink the waters
2:36 you be shamed, as you were shamed by *A*.
50:17 Formerly the king of *A* devoured her,
50:18 land, as once I punished the king of *A*;
Lam 5: 6 To Egypt we submitted, and to *A*,
Ez 23:23 Shoa and Koa, along with all those of *A*,
32:22 There is *A* with all her company,
Hos 5:13 and Judah his sore, Ephraim went to *A*,
7:11 They call upon Egypt, they go to *A*.
8: 9 They went up to *A*—
9: 3 and in *A* they shall eat unclean food.
10: 6 It too shall be carried to *A*,
11: 5 the land of Egypt, and *A* shall be his king;
11:11 like sparrows, from the land of *A*,
12: 2 he comes to terms with *A*,
14: 4 *A* will not save us,
Mi 5: 4 If *A* invades our country and treads upon
5: 5 shall tend the land of *A* with the sword,
7:12 shall come to you from *A* and from Egypt,
Na 3:18 how your shepherds slumber, O king of *A*,
Zep 2:13 his hand against the north, to destroy *A*;
Zec 10:10 the land of Egypt, and gather them from *A*.
10:11 The pride of *A* shall be cast down,

ASSYRIAN (20)

2Kgs 17: 4 pay the annual tribute to his *A* overlord.
19:35 and eighty-five thousand men in *A* camp.
2Chr 30: 6 remnant left from the hands of the *A* kings.
32:21 and commander in the camp of the *A* king,
33:11 them the army commanders of the *A* king;
Jdt 2:14 the generals and officers of the *A* army.
5: 1 commander in chief of the *A* army,
6: 1 commander in chief of the *A* army,
6:17 of all his own words among the *A* officers,
7:18 of the *A* army was encamped in the plain,
7:20 The whole *A* camp,
10:11 the valley, they encountered the *A* outpost.
12:13 and to be like one of the *A* women who live
13:15 general in charge of the *A* army,
14: 3 camp to awaken the generals of the *A* army.
14:19 commanders of the *A* army heard these words,
16: 3 *A* came from the mountains of the north,
Is 10:24 who dwell in Zion, do not fear the *A*,
14:25 I will break the *A* in my land and trample
37:36 and eighty-five thousand in the *A* camp.

ASSYRIANS (21)

Jdt 1: 1 of the *A* in the great city of Nineveh.
1: 7 Now Nebuchadnezzar, king of the *A*,
1:11 summons of Nebuchadnezzar, king of the *A*,
2: 1 palace of Nebuchadnezzar, king of the *A*,
2: 4 his plan, Nebuchadnezzar, king of the *A*,
4: 1 in chief of Nebuchadnezzar, king of the *A*,
7:17 moved camp, together with five thousand *A*.
7:24 injustice in not making peace with the *A*.
8: 9 the city to the *A* at the end of five days,
9: 7 "Here are the *A*, a vast force,
14: 2 plain against the advance guard of the *A*,
14:12 When the *A* saw them, they notified
15: 6 Bethulia swept down on the camp of the *A*,
Ps(s) 83: 9 The *A*, too, are leagued with them
Sir 48:21 of the *A* and routed them with a plague.
Is 19:23 the *A* shall enter Egypt,
Ez 16:28 You also played the harlot with the *A*,
23: 5 she lusted after her lovers, the *A*,
23: 7 harlot to them, to all the elite of the *A*,
23: 9 her lovers, the *A* for whom she had lusted.
23:12 She too lusted after the *A*,

ASSYRIA'S (1)

Is 10:12 the utterance of the king of *A* proud heart,

ASTARTE (4)

1Sm 31:10 They put his armor in the temple of *A*,
1Kgs 11: 5 By adoring *A*, the goddess of the Sidonians,
11:33 he has forsaken me and has worshiped *A*,
2Kgs 23:13 king of Israel, had built in honor of *A*,

ASTIR (2)

Ru 1:19 there, the whole city was *a* over them,
Is 14: 9 below is all *a* preparing for your coming;

ASTONISHED (13)

Jdt 11:16 the world will be *a* on hearing of them.
13:17 All the people were greatly *a*.
Jb 17: 8 Upright men are *a* at this,
21: 5 Look at me and be *a*,
Sir 40: 7 wakes up *a* that there was nothing to fear.
Dn 3:90 them sing, and *a* at seeing them alive,
Mt 12:23 All in the crowd were *a*.
Lk 1:63 This *a* them all.
2:18 All who heard of it were *a* at the report
2:48 When his parents saw him they were *a*,
Acts 2: 7 The whole occurrence *a* them.
12:16 opened the door and were *a* to see him.
Rv 17: 6 When I saw her I was greatly *a*.

ASTONISHING (2)

2Mc 7:18 is why such *a* things have happened to us.
Lk 24:22 our group have just brought us some *a* news.

ASTONISHMENT (8)

2Chr 29: 8 them an object of terror, *a* and mockery,
Jer 29:18 kingdoms of the earth, of malediction, *a*,
Mt 15:31 The result was great *a* in the crowds as
Mk 5:42 At this the family's *a* knew no bounds.
Lk 4:36 All were struck with *a*,
5:26 At this they were all seized with *a*.
Jn 7:21 a single work and you profess *a* over it.
Acts 3:10 They were struck with *a*—

ASTOUNDED (4)

Jdt 10: 7 very much *a* at her beauty and said to her,
1Mc 16:22 On hearing this, John was utterly *a*.
Sir 47:17 and with your answers, you *a* the nations.
Lk 8:56 Her parents were *a*, but he ordered them

ASTOUNDING (2)

Ps(s) 46: 9 LORD, the *a* things he has wrought on earth:
Lam 1: 9 *A* is her downfall,

ASTRAY (64)

Ex 23: 4 come upon your enemy's ox or ass going *a*,
Nm 5:12 If a man's wife goes *a* and becomes
5:19 and you have not gone *a* by impurity while
5:20 But if you have gone *a* while under the
5:29 When a woman goes *a* while under the
15:39 without going wantonly *a* after the desires
Dt 4:19 led *a* into adoring them and serving them.
13: 6 to lead you *a* from the way which the LORD,
13:11 he sought to lead you *a* from the LORD,
13:14 have led *a* the inhabitants of their city
22: 1 driven *a* without showing concern about it;
30:17 are led *a* and adore and serve other gods,

ASTRAY (cont.)

2Mc 2: 2 of the Lord or be led *a* in their thoughts,
6:25 moment of life, they would be led *a* by me,
Ps(s) 14: 3 All alike have gone *a;*
53: 4 All alike have gone *a;*
58: 4 *a* from birth have the liars gone.
107: 4 They went *a* in the desert wilderness;
107:40 and sends them *a* through a trackless waste,
119:67 Before I was afflicted I went *a,*
119:176 I have gone *a* [like a lost sheep];
Prv 5: 7 to me, go not *a* from the words of my mouth.
5:20 should you go *a* for another's wife and
7:21 with her smooth lips she leads him *a;*
7:25 turn to her ways, go not *a* in her paths;
10:17 but he who disregards reproof goes *a.*
12:26 but the way of the wicked leads them *a.*
14:22 Do not those who plot evil go *a?*
15:10 is in store for the man who goes *a;*
20: 1 none who goes *a* for it is wise.
Wis 12:24 For they went far *a* in the paths of error,
13: 6 For they indeed have gone *a* perhaps,
Sir 15:12 "It was he who set me *a";*
31: 5 for he who pursues wealth is led *a* by it.
34: 7 For dreams have led many *a,*
Is 19:13 The chiefs of her tribes have led Egypt *a,*
28: 7 Led *a* by strong drink,
30:28 on the jaws of the peoples to send them *a.*
35: 8 may pass over it, nor fools go *a* on it.
47:10 Your wisdom and your knowledge led you *a,*
53: 6 We had all gone *a* like sheep,
Jer 8: 4 if he goes *a,* does he not turn back?
23:13 by Baal and led my people Israel *a.*
23:32 and who lead my people *a* by recounting
Lam 3:11 He deranged my ways, set me *a,*
Ez 13:10 the very reason that they led my people *a,*
Dn 9:11 Israel transgressed your law and went *a,*
Hos 4:12 For the spirit of harlotry has led them *a;*
Am 2: 4 their fathers followed have led them *a,*
Mi 3: 5 the prophets who lead my people *a;*
Mt 18: 6 it would be better for anyone who leads *a*
Mk 9:42 it would be better if anyone who leads *a*
13: 6 he,' they will claim, and will lead many *a.*
Acts 2:40 from this generation which has gone *a."*
20:30 truth and leading *a* any who follow them.
1Cor 12: 2 were pagans you were led *a* to mute idols,
15:33 Do not be led *a* any longer.
1Tm 2:14 It was she who was led *a* and fell into sin.
2Pt 3:17 you be led *a* by the error of the wicked,
Rv 13:14 beast, it led *a* the earth's inhabitants,
18:23 you led all nations *a* by your sorcery.
19:20 its presence the prodigies that led men *a,*
20: 3 *a* until the thousand years are over.
20:10 The devil who led them *a* was hurled into

ASTRIDE (3)

Neh 2:14 room here for my mount to pass with me *a,*
Mt 21: 5 without display *a* an ass, astride a colt,

ASTROLOGERS (9)

Is 47:13 Let the *a* stand forth to save you,
Dn 2:27 and *a* could not explain to the king.
4: 4 enchanters, Chaldeans, and *a* had come in,
5: 7 Chaldeans, and *a* to be brought in.
5:11 magicians, enchanters, Chaldeans, and *a,*
Mt 2: 1 *a* from the east arrived one day in
2: 7 Herod called the *a* aside and found out
2:16 realized that he had been deceived by the *a,*
2:16 of the date he had learned from the *a.*

ASTUTE (2)

2Sm 22:27 but toward the crooked you are *a.*
Ps(s) 18:27 but toward the crooked you are *a;*

ASTYAGES (1)

Dn 14: 1 After King *A* was laid with his fathers,

ASUNDER (9)

Ps(s) 107:14 darkness and gloom and broke their bonds *a.*
Prv 27: 9 the heart, but by grief the soul is torn *a.*
Is 7: 6 saying, "Let us go up and tear Judah *a,*
24:19 The earth will burst *a,*
Dn 14:27 and when the dragon ate them, he burst *a.*
Na 1: 6 fire, and the rocks are rent *a* before him.
1:13 yoke from off you, and burst *a* your bonds.
Zec 11:10 took my staff "Favor" and snapped it *a,*
11:14 Then I snapped *a* my other staff,

ASYLUM (18)

Nm 35: 6 the six cities of *a* which you must
35:11 yourselves cities to serve as cities of *a,*
35:12 as places of *a* from the avenger of blood,
35:13 Six cities of *a* shall you assign:
35:15 These six cities of *a* shall serve not only
35:25 him to the city of *a* where he took refuge;
35:26 of the city of *a* where he has taken refuge,
35:28 of *a* until the death of the high priest.
35:32 to allow a refugee to leave his city of *a*
Jos 20: 3 may flee for *a* from the avenger of blood.
21:13 the city of *a* for homicides at Hebron,
21:21 the city of *a* for homicides at Shechem in
21:27 the city of *a* for homicides at Golan,
21:32 of *a* for homicides at Kedesh in Galilee,
21:36 the city of *a* for homicides at Bezer with
21:38 the city of *a* for homicides at Ramoth in
1Chr 6:42 Hebron a city of *a,*
6:52 mountain region of Ephraim, a city of *a,*

ASYNCRITUS (1)

Rom 16:14 Greetings to *A,* Phlegon, Hermes,

ATARAH (1)

1Chr 2:26 Jerahmeel also had another wife, *A* by name,

ATARGATIS (1)

2Mc 12:26 marched to Karnion and the shrine of *A,*

ATAROTH (4)

Nm 32: 3 the community and said, "The region of *A,*
32:34 rebuilt the fortified towns of Dibon, *A,*
Jos 16: 2 ridge to the border of the Archites at *A,*
16: 7 from there it descended to *A* and Naarah,

ATAROTH-ADDAR (2)

Jos 16: 5 ran from east of *A* to Upper Beth-horon
18:13 Then it ran down to *A,*

ATE (95)

Gn 3: 6 So she took some of its fruit and *a* it;
3: 6 her husband, who was with her, and he *a* it.
3:12 gave me fruit from the tree, and so I *a* it."
3:13 serpent tricked me into it, so I *a* it."
3:17 "Because you listened to your wife and *a*
18: 8 waited on them under the tree while they *a.*
25:34 and Esau *a,*
26:30 a feast for them, and they *a* and drank.
27:25 Jacob served it to him, and Isaac *a;*
39: 6 there, to anything but the food he *a.*
41: 4 ugly, gaunt cows *a* up the seven handsome,
41:20 ugly cows *a* up the first seven fat cows.
Ex 10:15 They *a* up all the vegetation in the land
16: 3 by our fleshpots and *a* our fill of bread!
16:35 Israelites *a* this manna for forty years,
16:35 they *a* manna until they reached the
Nm 25: 2 and the people *a* of the sacrifices and
Dt 32:15 So Jacob *a* his fill,
32:38 Let those who *a* the fat of your sacrifices
Jos 5:11 On the day after the Passover they *a* of
5:12 on which they *a* of the produce of the land,
5:12 year *a* of the yield of the land of Canaan.
Jgs 9:27 they *a* and drank and cursed Abimelech.
14: 9 into his palms and *a* it as he went along.
19: 6 and the two men *a* and drank together.
19:21 they washed their feet, and *a* and drank.
Ru 2:14 and she *a* her fill and had some left over.
3: 7 Boaz *a* and drank to his heart's content.
1Sm 1:18 her quarters, *a* and drank with her husband,
28:25 before Saul and his servants, and they *a.*
30:11 He was provided with food, which he *a,*
2Sm 9:11 And so Meribbaal *a* at David's table like
9:13 because he always *a* at the king's table.
11:13 him, and he *a* and drank with David,
12:20 request food was set before him, and he *a.*
1Kgs 4:20 they *a* and drank and made merry.
13:19 and *a* bread and drank water in his house.
13:22 but returned and *a* bread and drank water
19: 6 After he *a* and drank, he lay down again
19: 8 He got up, *a* and drank;
2Kgs 6:29 So we boiled my son and *a* him.
7: 8 they went first into one tent, *a* and drank,
23: 9 their relatives, *a* the unleavened bread.
25:29 *a* at the king's table as long as he lived.
1Chr 29:22 and on that day they *a* and drank in the
2Chr 30:18 Nevertheless they *a* the Passover,
Tb 1: 8 and we *a* it in keeping with the decree of
1:10 and relatives *a* the food of heathens,
2: 5 I washed myself and *a* my food in sorrow.
6: 6 Then he broiled and *a* part of the fish;
10: 7 road her son had taken, and she *a* nothing.
Jdt 12:19 prepared, and *a* and drank in his presence.
Jb 31:17 to languish While I *a* my portion alone,
Ps(s) 78:29 So they *a* and were wholly surfeited;
106:28 of Peor and *a* the sacrifices of dead gods.
Is 44:19 I baked bread and roasted meat which I *a.*
Jer 31:29 longer say, "The fathers *a* unripe grapes,
52:33 *a* at the king's table as long as he lived.
Ez 3: 3 I *a* it, and it was as sweet as honey
Dn 1:15 the young men who *a* from the royal table.
4: 9 all men *a* of it.
4:30 out from among men, he *a* grass like an ox,
5:21 with wild asses, and *a* grass like an ox;
10: 3 I *a* no savory food,
14:15 children, and they *a* and drank everything.
14:27 of the dragon, and when the dragon *a* them,
Hos 13: 6 They *a* their fill;
Zec 7: 6 was it not for yourselves that you *a,*
Mt 12: 4 entered God's house and *a* the holy bread,
13: 4 a footpath, where birds came and *a* it up.
14:20 All those present *a* their fill.
14:21 Those who *a* were about five thousand,
15:37 All *a* until they were full.
Mk 2:26 *a* the holy bread which only the priests
4: 4 where the birds came along and *a* it.
6:42 them and they *a* until they had their fill.
8: 8 in the crowd *a* until they had their fill;
Lk 4: 2 During that time he *a* nothing,
6: 4 *a* the holy bread and gave it to his men,
7:34 Son of Man came and he both *a* and drank,
8: 5 walked on and the birds of the air *a* it up.
9:17 They all *a* until they had enough.
13:26 to say, 'We *a* and drank in your company.
17:27 They *a* and drank, they took husbands
17:28 they *a* and drank, they bought and sold,
24:43 which he took and *a* in their presence.
Jn 6:49 Your ancestors *a* manna in the desert,
6:58 your ancestors who *a* and died nonetheless,
13:23 loved, reclined close to him as they *a.*
Acts 9: 9 during which time he neither *a* nor drank.
10:41 by us who *a* and drank with him after he
11: 3 house of uncircumcised men and *a* with them."
20:11 went upstairs again, broke bread, and *a.*
1Cor 10: 3 All *a* the same spiritual food.
Rv 10:10 scroll from the angel's hand and *a* it.

ATER (5)

Ezr 2:16 sons of *A,* who were sons of Hezekiah,
2:42 sons of Shallum, sons of *A,*
Neh 7:21 sons of *A* who were sons of Hezekiah,
7:45 sons of Shallum, sons of *A,*
10:18 Azgad, Bebai, Adonijah, Bigvai, Adin, *A,*

ATHACH (1)

1Sm 30:30 to those in Borashan, to those in *A,*

ATHAIAH (1)

Neh 11: 4 *A,* son of Uzziah,

ATHALIAH (15)

2Kgs 8:26 His mother's name was *A;*
11: 1 When *A,* the mother of Ahaziah, saw
11: 2 She concealed him from *A,*
11: 3 temple of the LORD, while *A* ruled the land.
11:13 *A* heard the noise made by the people,
11:20 now that *A* had been slain with the sword
1Chr 8:26 Shamsherai, Shehariah, *A.*
2Chr 22: 2 His mother was named *A,* daughter of Omri.
22:10 When *A,* mother of Ahaziah, learned
22:12 house of God, while *A* ruled over the land.
23:12 When *A* heard the din of the people running
23:13 *A* tore her garments and cried out,
23:21 that *A* had been put to death by the sword.
24: 7 For the wicked *A* and her sons had damaged
Ezr 8: 7 Jeshaiah, son of *A,*

ATHALIAH'S (1)

2Chr 22:11 the priest, hid the child from *A* sight,

ATHARIM (1)

Nm 21: 1 Israelites were coming along the way of *A,*

ATHENIAN (2)

2Mc 6: 1 Not long after this the king sent an *A*
Acts 17:21 (Indeed, all *A* citizens,

ATHENIANS (1)

2Mc 9:15 perfect equality with the *A* all the Jews,

ATHENOBIUS (3)

1Mc 15:28 He sent *A,* one of his Friends
15:32 So *A,* the king's Friend,
15:36 *A* made no reply,

ATHENS (5)

Acts 17:15 Paul was taken as far as *A* by his escort,
17:16 While Paul was waiting for them in *A,*
17:22 "Men of *A,* I note that in every respect
18: 1 that, Paul left *A* and went to Corinth.
1Thes 3: 1 to remain alone at *A* and send you Timothy.

ATHIRST (1)

Ps(s) 42: 3 *A* is my soul for God, the living god.

ATHLAI (1)

Ezr 10:28 Jehohanan, Hananiah, Zabbai, and *A;*

ATHLETES (1)

1Cor 9:25 *A* deny themselves all sorts of things.

ATHLETIC (2)

2Mc 4:14 in the unlawful exercises on the *a* field.
2Tm 2: 5 if one takes part in an *a* contest,

ATONE (6)

Lv 16: 6 to *a* for himself and for his household.
16:11 to *a* for himself and for his family.
2Chr 29:24 the altar to *a* for the sin of all Israel;
Sir 3:29 a flaming fire, and alms *a* for sins.

45:16 and to *a* for the people of Israel.
Dn 4:24 *a* for your sins by good deeds,

ATONED (1)

Sir 45:23 noble heart, *a* for the children of Israel.

ATONEMENT (82)

Ex 29:33 eat of these things by which *a* was made
29:36 each day as a sin offering, to make *a*.
29:36 you purge the altar in making *a* for it;
29:37 *a* for the altar and in consecrating it.
30:10 shall perform the *a* rite on its horns.
30:10 Throughout your generations this *a* is to
32:30 I may be able to make *a* for your sin."
Lv 1: 4 it may be acceptable to make *a* for him.
4:20 Thus the priest shall make *a* for them,
4:26 priest shall make *a* for the prince's sin,
4:31 Thus the priest shall make *a* for him,
4:35 the priest shall make *a* for the man's sin,
5: 6 The priest shall then make *a* for his sin.
5:10 shall make *a* for the sin the man committed,
5:13 Thus the priest shall make *a* for the sin
5:16 make *a* for him with the guilt-offering ram,
5:18 The priest shall then make *a* for the fault
5:26 shall make *a* for him before the LORD,
6:23 meeting tent to make *a* in the sanctuary;
7: 7 belongs to the priest who makes *a* with it.
8:15 He also made *a* for the altar by pouring
8:34 been done today be done to make *a* for you.
9: 7 in *a* for yourself and for your family;
9: 7 the offering of the people in *a* for them,
10:17 and make *a* for them before the LORD.
12: 7 them up before the LORD to make *a* for her,
12: 8 The priest shall make *a* for her,
14:18 the priest make *a* for him before the LORD.
14:19 offering in *a* for the man's uncleanness
14:20 When the priest has thus made *a* for him,
14:21 used as a wave offering in *a* for himself,
14:29 shall he make *a* for him before the LORD.
14:31 Thus shall the priest make *a* before the
14:53 When he has thus made *a* for it,
15:15 make *a* before the LORD for the man's flow.
15:30 *a* before the LORD for her unclean flow.
16:10 so that with it he may make *a* by sending
16:16 Thus he shall make *a* for the sanctuary
16:17 the sanctuary to make *a* until he departs.
16:17 has made *a* for himself and his household,
16:18 before the LORD and make *a* for it also.
16:20 has completed the *a* rite for the sanctuary,
16:24 in *a* for himself and for the people,
16:27 was brought into the sanctuary to make *a*,
16:30 day *a* is made for you to make you clean,
16:32 "This *a* is to be made by the priest who
16:33 and make *a* for the sacred sanctuary,
16:34 once a year *a* shall be made for all the
17:11 *a* may thereby be made for your own lives,
17:11 blood, as the seat of life, that makes *a*.
19:22 With this ram the priest shall make *a*
23:27 of this seventh month is the Day of *A*,
23:28 it is the Day of *A*, when atonement
25: 9 trumpet resound; on this, the Day of *A*,
Nm 5: 8 this is apart from the *a* ram with which
6:11 thus making *a* for him for the sin he has
8:12 to the LORD, in *a* for the Levites.
8:19 in the meeting tent and to make *a* for them,
8:21 LORD, and made *a* for them to purify them.
15:25 make *a* for the whole Israelite community;
15:28 and the priest shall make *a* before the
15:28 when *a* has been made for him,
17:11 to the community to make *a* for them;
17:12 the incense and made *a* for the people,
28:22 goat as a sin offering in *a* for yourselves.
28:30 as a sin offering in *a* for yourselves.
29: 5 as a sin offering in *a* for yourselves.
29:11 offered in addition to the *a* sin offering,
31:50 to make *a* for ourselves before the LORD,
35:33 the land can have no *a* for the blood shed
2Sm 21: 3 must I do for you and how must I make *a*,
1Chr 6:34 holy of holies and of making *a* for Israel,
Neh 10:34 for sin offerings to make *a* for Israel,
2Mc 3:33 priest was offering the sacrifice of *a*,
12:46 Thus he made *a* for the dead that they
Sir 35: 3 the LORD, and to avoid injustice is an *a*.
Ez 43:20 Thus you shall purify it and make *a* for it.
43:26 Thus *a* shall be made for the altar,
45:15 and peace offerings and *a* sacrifices,
45:17 to make *a* on behalf of the house of Israel.
45:20 thus you shall make *a* for the temple.

ATONES (1)

Sir 3: 3 He who honors his father *a* for sins;

ATONING (1)

Ex 30:10 year with the blood of the *a* sin offering.

ATOP (1)

2Sm 18:26 From his place *a* the gate he cried out,

ATROTH-BETH-JOAB (1)

1Chr 2:54 were Bethlehem, the Netophathites, *A*

ATROTH-SHOPHAN (1)

Nm 32:35 towns of Dibon, Ataroth, Aroer, *A*,

ATTACHED (8)

Gn 29:34 at last my husband will become *a* to me,
Ex 28:25 are *a* to the shoulder straps of the ephod.
39:18 *a* to the shoulder straps of the ephod.
Dt 10:15 the LORD was so *a* to them as to choose you,
2Chr 31:19 who lived on the lands *a* to their cities,
1Mc 12: 7 you are our brothers, as the *a* copy shows.
Lk 15:15 So he *a* himself to one of the propertied
Acts 13: 7 He was *a* to the court of the proconsular

ATTACHING (1)

Lv 8: 9 the miter on his head, *a* the gold plate,

ATTACK (115)

Gn 32: 9 "If Esau should *a* and overwhelm one camp,"
34:30 if these people unite against me and *a* me,
43:18 they want to use it as a pretext to *a* us
Nm 13:31 with him said, "We cannot *a* these people;
31: 3 to *a* the Midianites and execute the LORD'S
32:17 towns, safe from *a* by the natives.
Dt 20:10 "When you march up to *a* a city,
24: 8 "In an *a* of leprosy you shall be careful
Jos 6: 5 and they will be able to make a frontal *a*."
6:20 the city in a frontal *a* and took it.
7: 4 three thousand of the people made the *a*,
8: 1 all the army with you and prepare to *a* Ai.
8: 3 and all the soldiers prepared to *a* Ai.
9: 2 a common *a* against Joshua and Israel.
9:18 and Kiriath-jearim, but did not *a* them,
10: 4 to come to his aid for an *a* on Gibeon,
10: 9 And when Joshua made his surprise *a* upon
10:31 where they set up a camp during the *a*.
11: 7 at the waters of Merom in a surprise *a*.
Jgs 1: 1 asking "Who shall be first among us to *a*
1: 2 The LORD answered, "Judah shall *a*:
7:10 If you are afraid to *a*, go down
9:43 city, and then rose against them for the *a*.
18: 9 they replied, "Come, let us *a* them,
20:18 go first in the *a* on the Benjaminites,
20:28 the LORD said, *A!*
1Sm 4: 1 Philistines gathered for an *a* on Israel.
15: 3 Go, now, *a* Amalek, and deal with him
17:35 *a* it and rescue the prey from its mouth.
24: 8 men and would not permit them to *a* Saul.
31: 1 As they pressed their *a* on Israel,
2Sm 5: 8 "All who wish to *a* the Jebusites must
5:19 of the LORD, "Shall I *a* the Philistines
5:19 The LORD replied to David, *A*,
5:23 "You must not *a* frontally,
5:24 you to *a* the camp of the Philistines."
10:14 Joab then ceased his *a* on the Ammonites
11:25 your *a* on the city and destroy it.'
17: 9 our soldiers should fall at the first *a*,
17:12 We can then *a* him wherever we find him,
1Kgs 20: 1 proceeded to invest and *a* Samaria.
20:14 Then Ahab asked, "Who is to *a*?"
20:22 of the year the king of Aram will *a* you."
22: 6 I go to *a* Ramoth-gilead or shall I refrain?"
2Kgs 3: 8 They discussed the route for their *a*,
6: 8 with his servants to *a* a particular place.
6: 9 pass by this place, for Aram will *a* there."
12:18 it, Hazael decided to go on to *a* Jerusalem.
16: 5 of Israel, came up to Jerusalem to *a* it.
2Chr 13:12 with trumpets to sound the *a* against you.
18: 5 them, "Shall we go to *a* Ramoth-gilead,
Neh 4: 6 times over that they were about to *a* us,
Jdt 5:24 Let us therefore *a* them;
6: 4 Not a trace of them shall survive our *a*:
7:11 sir, do not *a* them in regular formation;
16: 6 bring him low, nor huge giants *a* him;
Est 8:11 any nation or province which should *a* them,
8:12 defend themselves against those who *a* them.
9: 2 to *a* those who sought to do them harm,
1Mc 2:32 and prepared to *a* them on the sabbath.
4: 2 set out at night in order to *a* the camp
4: 3 soldiers to *a* the king's army at Emmaus,
4: 8 afraid of their numbers or dread their *a*.
4:21 the army of Judas in the plain ready to *a*,
4:41 appointed men to *a* those in the citadel,
5: 9 The Gentiles in Gilead assembled to *a* and
5:27 Tomorrow their enemies plan to *a* the
5:30 and beginning to *a* the people within.
5:39 camped beyond the stream, ready to *a* you."
5:39 So Judas went forward to *a* them.
5:43 He was the first to cross to the *a*,
5:49 make an *a* from the place where he was.
6:48 king's army went up to Jerusalem to *a* them,
11:20 men of Judea to *a* the citadel in Jerusalem,
12:24 to *a* him with a stronger army than before.
12:26 made ready to *a* the Jews that very night.
14:13 No one was left to *a* them in their land;
2Mc 4:40 Lysimachus launched an unjustified *a*
4:41 Reacting against Lysimachus' *a*,
8:18 a mere nod destroy not only those who *a* us,
10:14 and used every opportunity to *a* the Jews.
11: 5 Jerusalem, launched a strong *a* against it.
12: 6 In a night *a* he set the harbor on fire,
13:15 he made a night *a* on the king's pavilion
13:26 is how the king's *a* and withdrawal went.
15: 1 to *a* them in all safety on the day of rest.
Jb 7:12 Why have you set me up as an object of *a*;
10:17 You renew your *a* upon me and
19:12 they build up their road to *a* me,
30:13 destroy me, they *a* with none to stay them;
Ps(s) 56: 2 all the day they press their *a* against me.
71:13 be put to shame and consumed who *a* my life;
94:21 Though they *a* the life of the just and
Wis 11:19 could these *a* and completely destroy them;
Sir 22:22 a treacherous *a* will drive away any friend.
Is 7: 1 son of Remaliah, went up to *a* Jerusalem,
54:15 Should there be any *a*,
Jer 21:13 You who say, "Who will *a* us,
34:22 They shall *a* and capture it,
37:20 of Babylon would not *a* you or this land?
41:12 all their men and set out to *a* Ishmael,
46:13 king of Babylon, to *a* the land of Egypt:
46:22 like woodchoppers, they *a* her with axes.
49:28 Rise up, *a* Kedar, ravage the Easterners.
50:21 *A* the land of Merathaim,
Ez 13: 5 firm against *a* on the day of the LORD.
38:11 *a* the peaceful people who are living in
Dn 8: 7 *a* the ram with furious blows when they met,
11:13 *a* with this large army and great resources.
11:16 He shall *a* him and do as he pleases,
Hos 13: 8 *a* them like a bear robbed of its young,
Am 7: 9 *a* the house of Jeroboam with the sword.
Hb 3:16 that will come upon the people who *a* us.
Acts 16:22 The crowd joined in the *a* on them,
18:10 No one will *a* you or harm you.

ATTACKED (66)

Gn 4: 8 Cain *a* his brother Abel and killed him.
Jos 10:29 Israel from Makkedah to Libnah, which he *a*.
10:34 it, they *a* it and captured it the same day,
10:36 to Hebron, which they *a* and captured.
10:38 all Israel turned back to Debir and *a* it,
19:47 so the Danites marched up and *a* Leshem,
Jgs 1: 4 When the forces of Judah *a*,
3:13 and Amalekites, he *a* and defeated Israel,
8:11 and *a* the camp when it felt secure.
9:44 upon all who were in the field and *a* them.
18:27 and the priest he had had, they *a* Laish,
1Sm 17:35 If it *a* me, I would seize it by the jaw,
30:17 From dawn to sundown David *a* them,
2Sm 8: 1 David *a* the Philistines and conquered them,
22:19 They *a* me on my day of calamity,
1Kgs 14:25 Shishak, king of Egypt, *a* Jerusalem.
15:17 *a* Judah and fortified Ramah to prevent
15:20 They *a* Ijon,
2Kgs 3:24 the Israelites rose up and *a* the Moabites,
15:10 Zechariah, *a* and killed him at Ibleam,
15:14 to Samaria, where he *a* and killed Shallum,
15:30 he *a* and killed him,
17: 5 then occupied the whole land and *a* Samaria,
18: 9 Shalmaneser, king of Assyria, *a* Samaria,
24:10 king of Babylon, *a* Jerusalem,
25:25 with ten men, *a* Gedaliah and killed him,
1Chr 4:41 and *a* the tents of Ham (for Hamites dwelt
4:43 *a* the surviving Amalekites who had escaped,
20: 1 When Joab had *a* Rabbah and destroyed it,
2Chr 12: 2 Shishak, king of Egypt, *a* Jerusalem,
12: 9 *a* Jerusalem and carried off the treasures
14:14 They *a* also the tents of the
16: 1 *a* Judah and fortified Ramah to prevent any
16: 4 They *a* Ijon,
28:17 The Edomites had returned, *a* Judah,
Neh 3:35 *a* it would breach their wall of stones!"
Jdt 15: 5 *a* them and cut them down as far as Choba.
Est 8: 7 him on the gibbet because he *a* the Jews,
1Mc 1:30 Then he *a* the city suddenly,
2:35 Then the enemy *a* them at once;
2:38 and soldiers *a* them on the sabbath,
5: 3 Then Judas *a* the sons of Esau at
5:16 kinsmen who were being *a* by enemies.
5:35 turned toward Alema and *a* and captured it;
5:65 brothers went out and *a* the sons of Esau
6:31 For many days they *a* it;
9:12 the phalanx *a* as they blew their trumpets.
10:82 were exhausted, Simon *a* the phalanx,
11:65 besieged Beth-zur, *a* it for many days,
11:68 This army *a* him in the open,
12:13 us, and the kings around us have *a* us.
13:43 city, and *a* and captured one of the towers.
2Mc 3:25 horse *a* Heliodorus with its front hoofs.
5: 5 a thousand men and suddenly *a* the city.
12: 9 them, he *a* the Jamnian populace by night,
12:10 they were *a* by Arabs numbering at least
12:13 He also *a* a certain city called Caspin,
12:35 when a Thracian horseman *a* Dositheus and
13:23 he withdrew and *a* Judas and his men.
Ps(s) 18:19 They *a* me in the day of my calamity,
106:29 him by their deeds, and a plague *a* them.
109: 3 have encompassed me and *a* me without cause.
119:150 I am *a* by malicious persecutors who are
Jer 41: 2 him, rose up and *a* with swords Gedaliah,
47: 1 the Philistines, before Pharaoh *a* Gaza:
Jon 4: 7 at dawn God sent a worm which *a* the plant,

ATTACKING (18)

Gn 49:23 Harrying and *a*, the archers opposed him;

ATTACKING (cont.)

Nm 10: 9 go to war against an enemy that is *a* you,
1Sm 23: 1 Philistines were *a* Keilah and plundering
27: 9 In *a* the land David would not leave a man
2Kgs 3:25 slingers had surrounded it and were *a* it.
16: 7 Aram and the king of Israel, who are *a* me."
2Chr 32: 2 coming with the intention of *a* Jerusalem,
Jdt 4: 7 It would be easy to ward off the *a* forces,
1Mc 8:28 are *a* them there shall not be given grain,
11:50 and let the Jews stop *a* us and our city."
2Mc 8:16 number of the Gentiles *a* them unjustly,
10:17 *A* vigorously, they gained control
Jer 21: 2 Nebuchadnezzar, king of Babylon, is *a* us.
32:24 handed over to the Chaldeans who are *a* it,
32:29 The Chaldeans who are *a* it shall enter
34: 1 were all *a* Jerusalem and all her cities:
34: 7 armies of the king of Babylon were *a*
37:10 defeat the whole Chaldean army now *a* you,

ATTACKS (8)

Jos 15:16 one who *a* Kiriath-sepher and captures it."
Jgs 1:12 one who *a* Kiriath-sepher and captures it."
1Mc 2:41 against anyone who *a* us on the sabbath,
15:39 could launch *a* against the Jewish people.
2Mc 8: 7 as being especially helpful for such *a*.
Jb 16:14 he *a* me like a warrior.
Is 54:15 whoever *a* you shall fall before you.
Gal 5:11 circumcision, why do the *a* on me continue?

ATTAI (4)

1Chr 2:35 to his slave Jarha, and she bore him *A*.
2:36 *A* became the father of Nathan.
12:12 Mishmannah fourth, Jeremiah fifth, *A* sixth,
2Chr 11:20 of Absalom, who bore him Abijah, *A*,

ATTAIN (16)

Jos 1: 8 then you will successfully *a* your goal.
2Sm 23:19 However, he did not *a* to the Three.
23:23 However, he did not *a* to the Three.
1Chr 11:21 commander, but he did not *a* to the Three.
11:25 the Thirty, but he did not *a* to the Three.
Ps(s) 69:28 guilt, and let them not *a* to your reward.
139: 6 too lofty for me to *a*.
Prv 5: 5 to death, to the nether world her steps *a*;
8: 9 and right to those who *a* knowledge.
8:12 experience, and judicious knowledge I *a*.
Wis 3:17 will disappear For should they *a* long life,
Sir 15: 7 Worthless men will not *a* to her,
27: 8 If you strive after justice you will *a* it,
Hos 8: 5 they be unable to *a* innocence in Israel?
Eph 3:19 you may *a* to the fullness of God himself.
Col 1: 9 asking that you may *a* full knowledge

ATTAINED (4)

Est E:11 he *a* the rank second to the royal throne.
Wis 8:20 rather, being noble, I *a* an unsullied body.
Sir 51:20 purified my hands in cleanness I *a* to her.
Rom 9:30 who were not seeking justice, *a* it

ATTAINING (1)

Sir 40:18 name, but better than either, *a* wisdom.

ATTAINMENT (1)

Wis 4: 9 and an unsullied life, the *a* of old age.

ATTAINMENTS (1)

Sir 34:12 of death, but by these *a* I was saved.

ATTAINS (1)

Sir 18:28 he who *a* to her should declare her praise;

ATTALIA (1)

Acts 14:25 the message in Perga, they went down to *A*.

ATTALUS (1)

1Mc 15:22 similar letters to Kings Demetrius, *A*,

ATTEMPT (8)

1Mc 11:45 the center of the city in an *a* to kill him.
2Mc 13:22 *a* by negotiating with the men of Beth-zur.
Zec 12: 3 *a* to lift it shall injure themselves badly,
Mt 22:35 of them, a lawyer, in an *a* to trip him up,
Acts 9:24 day and night in an *a* to do away with him.
17: 5 marched on the house of Jason in an *a*
1Cor 6: 5 I say this in an *a* to shame you.
Ti 1:13 in an *a* to keep them close to sound faith,

ATTEMPTED (7)

Lv 27:33 If any exchange is *a*,
Jgs 20: 5 Me they *a* to kill,
2Sm 21: 2 Saul had *a* to kill them off in his zeal
2Mc 9: 2 *a* to rob the temple and gain control
Acts 12:20 chamberlain Blastus and *a* to placate him,
Heb 11:29 *a* the same thing they were drowned.

ATTEMPTING (4)

1Sm 23:26 and Saul and his men were *a* to outflank
Mt 24: 5 Many will come *a* to impersonate me.
Mk 13: 6 Any number will come *a* to impersonate me.
Rv 11: 5 Anyone *a* to harm them will surely be slain

ATTEMPTS (5)

Lv 27:10 *a* to offer one animal in place of another,
Jos 6:26 LORD be the man who *a* to rebuild this city,
Jb 4: 2 If someone *a* a word with you,
Acts 21:31 *A* were being made on his life when a
2Tm 4:18 rescue me from all *a* to do me harm

ATTEND (17)

1Kgs 1: 2 "Let a young virgin be sought to *a* you,
2Kgs 9:34 *A* to that accursed woman and bury her;
2Mc 11:29 to return home and *a* to your own affairs.
Jb 27: 9 *a* to his cry when calamity comes upon him?
Ps(s) 5: 2 to my words, O LORD, *a* to my sighing.
17: 1 *a* to my outcry; harken to my prayer
86: 6 prayer and *a* to the sound of my pleading.
142: 7 *A* to my cry, for I am brought low indeed.
Wis 8:12 would abide my silence and *a* my utterance;
Sir 3:21 What is committed to you, *a* to;
Jer 32: 5 There he shall remain, until I *a* to him,
Mt 25:44 or in prison and not *a* you in your needs?'
27:55 Jesus from Galilee to *a* to his needs.
Lk 8: 8 who has ears *a* to what he has heard."
1Thes 4:11 remain at peace and *a* to your own affairs.
1Tm 4:15 *A* to your duties; let them absorb you,
Heb 2: 1 must *a* all the more to what we have heard,

ATTENDANCE (14)

Dt 10: 8 in *a* before the LORD and minister to him,
18: 5 in *a* to minister in the name of the LORD.
18: 7 Levites who are in *a* there before the LORD.
1Sm 16:16 it, we, your servants here in *a* on you,
18:10 David was in *a*, playing the harp
25:42 her five maids following in *a* upon her.
2Sm 16:19 as I was in *a* upon your father,
18:30 said, "Step aside and remain in *a* here."
1Kgs 10: 5 ministers, the *a* and garb of his waiters,
2Chr 9: 4 the *a* of his servants and their dress,
Jdt 4:14 in *a* on the Lord who served his altar,
Sir 39: 4 He is in *a* on the great,
Jer 36:21 all the princes who were in *a* on the king.
Lk 1:19 "I am Gabriel, who stand in *a* before God.

ATTENDANT (16)

Gn 39: 4 to Joseph and made him his personal *a*;
40: 4 Joseph to them, and he became their *a*.
Lv 16:21 then have it led into the desert by an *a*.
Jgs 9:54 So his *a* ran him through and he died.
16:26 said to the *a* who was holding his hand,
1Sm 20:21 send my *a* to go and recover the arrows.
26:22 Let an *a* come over to get it.
2Sm 9: 9 The king then called Ziba, Saul's *a*,
13:17 called the youth who was his *a* and said,
13:18 When his *a* put her out and barred the door
17:18 But an *a* saw them and informed Absalom.
1Kgs 19:21 Then he left and followed Elijah as his *a*.
2Kgs 6:15 the *a* of the man of God arose and went out,
Neh 4:16 inside Jerusalem, each man with his own *a*,
Wis 9: 4 Give me Wisdom, the *a* at your throne,
Is 41: 2 of justice, and summoned him to be his *a*?

ATTENDANTS (19)

Gn 45: 1 himself in the presence of all his *a*,
Jgs 3:19 Then when all his *a* had left his presence,
2Sm 1:15 then called one of the *a* and said to him,
20:11 One of Joab's *a* stood by Amasa and said,
1Kgs 1:33 "Take with you the royal *a*.
1Chr 18: 7 *a* and brought them to Jerusalem.
2Chr 22: 8 and the nephews of Ahaziah who were his *a*,
Neh 4:17 I, nor my kinsmen, nor any of my *a*,
5:10 and my *a* have lent the people money and
Jdt 13: 1 the *a* from their master's presence.
Est 2: 2 Then the king's personal *a* suggested:
4:30 troubled and all his *a* tried to revive her.
6: 3 The king's *a* replied, "Nothing was done
2Mc 1:15 with a few *a* came to the temple precincts.
7:12 his *a* marveled at the young man's courage,
Is 60:10 walls, and their kings shall be your *a*;
Mt 22:13 The king then said to the *a*,
Acts 23: 2 ordered his *a* to strike Paul on the mouth.
23: 4 At this, the *a* protested, "How dare you

ATTENDED (5)

Est 1:10 the seven eunuchs who *a* King Ahasuerus,
7: 9 Harbona, one of the eunuchs who *a* the king,
Dn 7:10 to him, and myriads upon myriads *a* him.
Mk 15:41 when he was in Galilee and *a* to his needs.
Acts 8: 6 performed *a* closely to what he had to say.

ATTENDING (1)

1Kgs 1:15 was *a* him because of his advanced age.

ATTENDS (1)

Wis 12:18 for power, whenever you will, *a* you.

ATTENTION (47)

Ex 5: 9 mind on it and pay no *a* to lying words."
Dt 13: 4 pay no *a* to the words of that prophet or
1Sm 4:20 Yet she neither answered nor paid any *a*.
25:25 my lord pay *a* to that worthless man Nabal,
2Sm 9: 8 you should pay *a* to a dead dog like me?"
18:13 would have come to the *a* of the king,
1Kgs 17:18 to call *a* to my guilt and to kill my son?"
2Chr 33:10 and his people, but they paid no *a*.
Neh 9:34 they paid no *a* to your commandments and
Est B: 4 in the kingdom, brought it to our *a* that,
E: 9 treatment matters coming to our *a*.
1Mc 7:11 But these paid no *a* to their words,
2Mc 2:29 must give his *a* to the whole structure,
7:25 When the youth paid no *a* to him at all,
11:18 be referred to the king I called to his *a*,
Jb 6:28 Come now, give me your *a*;
Prv 16:17 who pays *a* to his way safeguards his life.
27:23 your flocks, give careful *a* to your herds;
Sir 13:21 he speaks wisely and no *a* is paid him.
37:11 pay no *a* to any advice they give.
Is 28:23 my voice, pay *a* and listen to what I say:
Jer 5:21 Pay *a* to this,
9:16 *A!* tell the wailing women
31:21 Turn your *a* to the highway,
Ez 21:29 Because you have drawn *a* to your guilt,
21:29 revealed (because *a* has been drawn to you),
22:26 they pay no *a* to my sabbaths,
40: 4 pay strict *a* to all that I will show you,
44: 5 Son of man, pay strict *a*,
Dn 3:12 these men, O king, have paid no *a* to you;
6:14 the Jewish exile, has paid no *a* to you,
Hos 5: 1 Hear this, O priests, Pay *a*,
Jl 1: 2 Pay *a*, all you who dwell in the land!
Mi 6: 2 O mountains, the plea of the LORD, pay *a*,
Zec 1: 4 But they would not listen or pay *a* to me,
Lk 9:44 "Pay close *a* to what I tell you:
Jn 10:20 Why pay any *a* to him?"
Acts 3: 5 The cripple gave them his whole *a*,
8:10 every rank of society were paying *a* to him.
9:24 to kill Saul, but their plot came to his *a*.
18:17 but Gallio paid no *a* to it.
1Cor 10:28 for the sake of the one who called *a* to it
Gal 5: 2 Pay close *a* to me, Paul, when I tell you
Phil 3:14 My entire *a* is on the finish line as I run
Col 3:22 not with the purpose of attracting *a*
1Tm 5:19 Pay no *a* to an accusation against a
2Pt 1:19 Keep your *a* closely fixed on it,

ATTENTIVE (22)

Ex 23:21 Be *a* to him and heed his voice.
2Chr 6:40 your ears *a* to the prayer of this place.
7:15 and my ears *a* to the prayer of this place.
Neh 1: 6 keep your commandments, may your ear be *a*,
1:11 may your ear be *a* to my prayer and that of
Jb 33:31 Be *a*, O Job; listen to me!
Ps(s) 130: 2 your ears be *a* to my voice in supplication:
Prv 4: 1 O children, a father's instruction, be *a*,
4:20 My son, to my words be *a*,
5: 1 My son, to my wisdom be *a*,
7:24 to me, be *a* to the words of my mouth!
27:18 he who is *a* to his master will be enriched.
Sir 3:28 and an *a* ear is the wise man's joy.
25: 9 finds a friend and he who speaks to *a* ears.
Is 32: 3 the ears of those who hear will be *a*.
34: 1 Come near, O nations, and hear, be *a*,
51: 4 Be *a* to me, my people;
Ez 44: 5 be *a* in regard to those who are to be
Dn 9:19 O Lord, be *a* and act without delay,
Mt 6:24 other or be *a* to one and despise the other.
Lk 16:13 or be *a* to the one and despise the other.
Col 4: 2 Pray perseveringly, be *a* to prayer,

ATTENTIVELY (4)

Neh 8: 3 people listened *a* to the book of the law.
Jb 32:12 you *a* as you searched out what to say;
Mal 3:16 with one another, and the LORD listened *a*;
Eph 6:18 and *a* for all in the holy company.

ATTEST (2)

Jn 9:19 if so, do you *a* that he was blind at birth?
Eph 4:17 I declare and solemnly *a* in the Lord that

ATTESTATION (1)

Ru 4: 7 This was the form of *a* in Israel.

ATTESTED (3)

1Tm 2: 6 This truth was *a* at the fitting time.
5:10 character will be *a* to by her good deeds.
Heb 11: 4 Because of this he was *a* to be just,

ATTESTING (1)

Rom 4:11 sign of circumcision as a seal *a* to the justice

ATTESTS (1)

Heb 10:15 The Holy Spirit *a* this to us,

ATTIRE (9)

Ru 3: 3 best *a* and go down to the threshing floor.

2Sm 1:24 who decked your *a* with ornaments of gold.
1Chr 16:29 worship the LORD in holy *a*.
Jdt 10: 3 festive *a* she had worn while her husband,
Est 4:30 and arrayed herself in her royal *a*.
Ps(s) 29: 2 adore the LORD in holy *a*.
96: 9 worship the LORD in holy *a*.
Sir 19:26 A man's *a*, his hearty laughter and his gait
Is 23:18 fill and clothe themselves in choice *a*.

ATTIRED (1)

2Mc 3:26 strikingly beautiful, and splendidly *a*,

ATTITUDE (5)

Gn 31: 2 that Laban's *a* toward him was not what it
31: 5 *a* toward me is not as it was in the past;
Rom 12:16 Have the same *a* toward all.
Phil 2: 5 Your *a* must be that of Christ:
3:15 are spiritually mature must have this *a*.

ATTORNEY (1)

Acts 24: 1 of the elders and an *a* named Tertullus.

ATTRACT (1)

Is 53: 2 him, nor appearance that would *a* us to him.

ATTRACTED (3)

Gn 34: 3 Since he was strongly *a* to Dinah,
Phil 1:23 I am strongly *a* by both:
2Pt 2:15 He was a man *a* to dishonest gain,

ATTRACTING (1)

Col 3:22 not with the purpose of *a* attention and

ATTRACTION (1)

Mk 6:20 yet he felt the *a* of his words.

ATTRACTIVE (4)

1Sm 25: 3 The woman was intelligent and *a*,
Ez 23: 6 and officers, all of them *a* young men,
23:12 mounted on horses, all of them *a* young men.
23:23 with all those of Assyria, *a* young men,

AUDIENCE (11)

1Kgs 10:24 And the whole world sought *a* with Solomon,
2Chr 9:23 kings of the earth sought *a* with Solomon,
Est 5: 1 on his royal throne in the *a* chamber,
8: 3 In another *a* with the king,
2Mc 3: 7 When Apollonius had an *a* with the king,
Mt 2: 9 After their *a* with the king, they set out.
Mk 6: 2 in a way that kept his large *a* amazed.
15:43 He was bold enough to seek an *a* with
Lk 4:28 At these words the whole *a* in the
Jn 8: 9 Then the *a* drifted away one by one,
Acts 25:23 entered the *a* chamber in the company

AUDITING (1)

Mt 18:24 When he began his *a*, one was brought in

AUGHT (3)

Ru 1:17 if *a* but death separates me from you!"
Jb 33:32 If you have *a* to say, then answer me.
Sir 30:23 is there *a* to be gained from resentment.

AUGMENTS (1)

Prv 16:23 and *a* the persuasiveness of his lips.

AUGURY (1)

2Chr 33: 6 He practiced *a*, divination and magic

AUGUSTA (1)

Acts 27: 1 named Julius from the cohort known as *A*.

AUGUSTUS (1)

Lk 2: 1 In those days Caesar *A* published a decree

AUNT (3)

Ex 6:20 Amram married his *a* Jochebed,
Lv 18:14 with his wife, since she, too, is your *a*.
20:20 *a* shall pay the penalty by dying childless.

AURA (1)

Wis 7:25 For she is an *a* of the might of God and a

AURANUS (1)

2Mc 4:40 armed men under the leadership of *A*,

AUSTERITY (1)

Col 2:23 affected piety, humility, and bodily *a*,

AUTHENTIC (2)

Jn 4:23 when *a* worshipers will worship the Father
Ti 1: 9 he must hold fast to the *a* message,

AUTHOR (4)

Jdt 9: 5 It is you who were the *a* of those events
2Mc 2:28 for exact details to the original *a*,
Wis 13: 5 beauty of created things their original *a*,
Acts 3:15 You put to death the *A* of life.

AUTHORITIES (6)

Nm 11:16 for true elders and *a* among the people,
1Mc 12: 4 addressed to the *a* in the various places,
Lk 12:11 bring you before synagogues, rulers and *a*,
Jn 7:26 *a* have decided that this is the Messiah.
Acts 16:19 into the main square before the local *a*.
Rom 13: 1 Let everyone obey the *a* that are over him,

AUTHORITY (91)

Gn 39: 9 wields no more *a* in this house than I do,
41:35 collecting the grain under Pharaoh's *a*,
Ex 23:21 My *a* resides in him.
Nm 5:19 impurity while under the *a* of your husband,
5:20 if you have gone astray while under the *a*
5:29 the *a* of her husband and acts impurely,
Est E: 5 many placed in *a* to become accomplices
E: 7 influence of those undeserving of *a*.
9:29 with full *a* this second letter about Purim,
1Mc 10: 8 the king had given him *a* to gather an army.
10:32 yield my *a* over the citadel in Jerusalem,
10:35 Let no man have *a* to exact payment from
10:38 and obey no other *a* than the high priest.
14:47 priests and to exercise supreme *a* over all.'"
2Mc 4: 9 if he were given *a* to establish a
4:24 he flattered him with such an air of *a*
15:13 air about him of extraordinary, majestic *a*.
Wis 6: 3 Because *a* was given you by the Lord and
10:14 of royalty and *a* over his oppressors,
Sir 3: 2 a mother's *a* he confirms over her sons.
7: 4 Seek not from the LORD *a*,
20: 7 he who pretends to *a* is hated.
38: 2 and gives him access to those in *a*.
45:17 his laws, and *a* to prescribe and to judge:
45:26 should ever be forgotten, or your *a*,
Is 22:21 your sash, and give over to him your *a*.
Jer 29:25 your own *a* to all the people of Jerusalem,
Dn 6: 4 of giving him *a* over the entire kingdom.
Hos 8: 4 They made kings, but not by my *a*;
Mi 3: 8 spirit of the LORD, with *a* and with might;
Mt 7:29 taught with *a* and not like their scribes.
8: 9 *a* myself and I have troops assigned to me.
9: 6 of Man has *a* on earth to forgive sins"
9: 8 they praised God for giving such *a* to men.
10: 1 gave them *a* to expel unclean spirits
20:25 *a* among the Gentiles lord it over them;
21:23 "On what *a* are you doing these things?
21:24 tell you on what *a* I do the things I do.
21:27 I tell you on what *a* I do the things I do."
28:18 "Full *a* has been given to me both in
Mk 1:22 by his teaching because he taught with *a*,
1:27 A completely new teaching in a spirit of *a*!
2:10 you may know that the Son of Man has *a*
3:15 were likewise to have *a* to expel demons.
6: 7 by two, giving them *a* over unclean spirits.
10:42 who seem to exercise *a* lord it over them;
11:28 "On what *a* are you doing these things?
11:29 tell you on what *a* I do the things I do.
11:33 I tell you on what *a* I do the things I do."
16:20 said to Christ, "reveal your just *a* now."
Lk 4:32 by his teaching, for his words had *a*.
4:36 the unclean spirits with *a* and power,
5:24 of Man has *a* on earth to forgive sins"
9: 1 gave them power and *a* to overcome
20: 2 us, by what *a* do you do these things?
20: 8 neither will I tell you by whose *a* I act."
20:20 over to the office and *a* of the procurator.
22:25 *a* over them are called their benefactors.
Jn 17: 2 as you have given him *a* over all mankind,
Acts 18:24 He was both an *a* on Scripture and
26:10 the *a* I received from the chief priests,
26:12 the *a* and commission of the chief priests.
Rom 3:19 is addressed to those who are under its *a*.
12: 8 who rules should exercise his *a* with care;
13: 1 him, for there is no *a* except from God,
13: 1 all *a* that exists is established by God.
13: 2 *a* rebels against the ordinance of God;
13: 3 Do you wish to be free from the fear of *a*?
14:14 I know with certainty on the *a* of the Lord
1Cor 9:18 make full use of the *a* the gospel gives me.
15:24 having destroyed every sovereignty, *a*,
2Cor 13:10 with severity the *a* the Lord has given me
13:10 me *a* to build up rather than to destroy.
1Thes 5:12 to exercise *a* in the Lord and admonish you;
1Tm 2: 2 men, especially for kings and those in *a*,
2:12 or in any way to have *a* over a man;
Ti 2:15 and corrections with the *a* of command.
2Pt 2:10 for whatever corrupts, and who despise *a*.
Rv 2:26 the end, I will give *a* over the nations
2:26 the same *a* I received from my Father.
6: 8 were given *a* over one quarter of the earth,
12:10 of our God and the *a* of his Anointed One.
13: 2 power and throne, together with great *a*.
13: 4 the dragon for giving his *a* to the beast;
13: 5 but the *a* it received was to last only
13: 7 granted *a* over every race and people,
13:12 It used the *a* of the first beast to
13:14 allowed to perform by *a* of the first beast,
17:12 will possess royal *a* along with the beast,
17:13 and bestow their power and *a* on the beast.
18: 1 His *a* was so great that all the earth was

AUTHORIZATION (2)

Jdt 11:14 to them *a* from the council of the elders;
Acts 9:14 He is here now with *a* from the chief

AUTHORIZE (1)

1Mc 15: 6 I *a* you to coin your own money,

AUTHORIZED (7)

Lv 10: 1 LORD profane fire, such as he had not *a*.
Ezr 3: 7 of Joppa, as Cyrus, king of Persia, had *a*.
Est 8:11 In these letters the king *a* the Jews in
1Mc 1:13 and he *a* them to introduce the way of
10: 6 So Demetrius *a* him to gather an army and
2Mc 11:20 these matters I have *a* my representatives,
Lk 20: 2 In other words, who has *a* you?"

AUTHORIZING (2)

Est 1:19 *a* the king to give her royal dignity
Jn 2:18 can you show us *a* you to do these things?"

AUTHORS (1)

Sir 44: 4 *A* skilled in composition,

AUTOMATIC (1)

Est 4:11 summoned, suffers the *a* penalty of death,

AUTUMN (1)

Acts 27: 9 The *a* fast was over,

AUXILIARIES (2)

Jdt 3: 6 from them he impressed picked troops as *a*.
Na 3: 9 Put and the Libyans were her *a*.

AVAIL (12)

Jb 15: 3 Should he argue in speech which does not *a*,
41:18 Should the sword reach him, it will not *a*;
Wis 4: 3 progeny of the wicked shall be of no *a*;
5: 8 What did our pride *a* us?
Is 16:12 to pray, but it shall *a* him nothing.
44: 9 and their precious works are of no *a*,
47:12 Perhaps you can make them *a*,
Jer 5:22 Toss though it may, it is to no *a*;
8: 9 of the LORD, of what *a* is their wisdom?
8:15 We wait for peace to no *a*;
14:19 We wait for peace, to no *a*;
Hb 2:18 Of what *a* is the carved image,

AVAILABLE (7)

Gn 41:54 food was *a* throughout the land of Egypt.
42: 1 learned that grain rations were *a* in Egypt,
42: 2 on, "that rations of grain are *a* in Egypt.
2Kgs 22: 9 servants have smelted down the metals *a*
1Chr 22:15 you have *a* an unlimited supply of workmen,
1Mc 14:49 they would be *a* to Simon and his sons.
Gal 2:21 If justice is *a* through the law,

AVAILED (1)

2Chr 28:21 to the king of Assyria, it *a* him nothing.

AVARAN (2)

1Mc 2: 5 Eleazar, who was called *A*;
6:43 Eleazar called *A*, saw one of the beasts

AVARICE (2)

Prv 21:26 Some are consumed with *a* all the day,
Is 57:17 Because of their wicked *a* I was angry,

AVARICIOUS (2)

Prv 28:22 The *a* man is perturbed about his wealth,
Lk 16:14 The Pharisees, who were *a* men,

AVEN (2)

Hos 10: 8 The high places of *A* shall be destroyed,
Am 1: 5 out those who live in the Valley of *A*,

AVENGE (19)

Nm 31: 2 "*A* the Israelites on the Midianites,
Jgs 9:24 to *a* their blood upon their brother
16:28 I may *a* myself once and for all
1Sm 14:24 before I am able to *a* myself on my enemies."
2Kgs 9: 7 I *a* the blood of my servants the prophets,
2Chr 24:22 dying, he said, "May the LORD see and *a*."
Jdt 1:12 he would *a* himself on all the territories
Est 8:13 that day to *a* themselves on their enemies.
1Mc 2:67 and you shall *a* the wrongs of your people.
6:22 you fail to do justice and *a* our kinsmen?
13: 6 will I *a* my nation and the sanctuary,
Ps(s) 10: 4 wicked man boasts, "He will not *a* it";
10:13 saying in his heart, "He will not *a* it"?
79:10 you *a* the shedding of your servants' blood.

AVENGE (cont.)
Jer 15:15 Lord, visit me, and *a* me on my persecutors.
51:36 I will defend your cause, I will *a* you;
Jl 4:21 I will *a* their blood,
Rom 12:19 Beloved, do not *a* yourselves;
Rv 6:10 before you judge our cause and *a* our blood

AVENGED (6)
Gn 4:15 kills Cain, Cain shall be *a* sevenfold."
4:24 If Cain is *a* sevenfold,
1Sm 25:31 for having *a* yourself personally.
2Sm 4: 8 Thus has the Lord this day *a* my lord the
Acts 7:24 and *a* the victim by slaying the Egyptian.
Rv 19: 2 He has *a* the blood of his servants which

AVENGER (21)
Lv 26:25 will make the sword, the *a* of my covenant,
Nm 35:12 as places of asylum from the *a* of blood,
35:19 The *a* of blood may execute the murderer,
35:21 The *a* of blood may execute the murderer on
35:24 *a* of blood in accordance with these norms,
35:25 shall free the homicide from the *a* of
35:27 and the *a* of blood finds him beyond these
35:27 and kills him, the *a* incurs no bloodguilt;
Dt 19: 6 the *a* of blood may in the heat of his
19:12 him over to be slain by the *a* of blood.
Jos 20: 3 may flee for asylum from the *a* of blood.
20: 5 Though the *a* of blood pursues him,
20: 9 escape death at the hand of the *a* of blood,
2Sm 14:11 that the *a* of blood may not go too far in
Ps(s) 9:13 For the *a* of blood has remembered;
44:17 and in the presence of the enemy and the *a*.
Sir 30: 6 The *a* he leaves against his foes,
Jer 30:17 they have called you, "with no *a*."
50:34 Strong is their *a*, whose name is Lord
Na 1: 2 avenging God is the Lord, an *a* is the Lord,
1Thes 4: 6 for the Lord is an *a* of all such things,

AVENGES (1)
Dt 32:43 For he *a* the blood of his servants and

AVENGING (6)
1Sm 25:26 blood and from *a* yourself personally.
25:33 blood and from *a* myself personally.
Sir 39:30 and the *a* sword to exterminate the wicked;
48: 7 threats at Sinai, at Horeb *a* judgments.
Na 1: 2 A jealous and *a* God is the Lord,
Rom 13: 4 to inflict his *a* wrath upon the wrongdoer.

AVERT (3)
Sir 4: 4 *a* not your face from the poor.
9: 8 *A* your eyes from a comely woman;
Lam 2:14 not lay bare your guilt, to *a* your fate;

AVERTED (2)
Jdt 13:20 being oppressed, and you *a* our disaster,
Sir 46: 7 *A* God's anger from the people and

AVID (2)
Sir 11:10 who is *a* for wealth will not be blameless?
31: 7 stumbling block to those who are *a* for it,

AVIDLY (1)
Wis 2: 6 real, and use the freshness of creation *a*.

AVITH (2)
Gn 36:34 the name of his city was *A*.
1Chr 1:46 plateau, and the name of his city was *A*.

AVOID (37)
Gn 4:14 and I must *a* your presence and become a
38: 9 *a* contributing offspring for his brother.
Tb 4:21 be a rich man if you fear God, *a* all sin,
2Mc 5:27 what grew wild to *a* sharing the defilement.
6:26 the time being, I *a* the punishment of men,
Prv 13:14 life, that a man may *a* the snares of death.
14: 7 To *a* the foolish man, take steps!
14:27 life, that a man may *a* the snares of death.
15:24 that he may *a* the nether world below.
Sir 7: 2 *a* wickedness,
7:34 *A* not those who weep,
11:33 *A* a wicked man, for he breeds only evil,
17:12 He says to them, *A* all evil";
28: 8 *A* strife and your sins will be fewer,
35: 3 Lord, and to *a* injustice is an atonement.
41:24 the things you should rightly *a* as shameful
Mt 7: 1 "If you want to *a* judgment,
23: 8 As to you, *a* the title 'Rabbi.'
23:10 *A* being called teachers.
Mk 3: 9 could *a* the press of the crowd against him.
Lk 12:15 to the crowd, *A* greed in all its forms.
Jn 8:11 But from now on, *a* this sin."]
18:28 for they had to *a* ritual impurity if they
Acts 15:29 You will be well advised to *a* these things.
21:25 were merely to *a* meat sacrificed to idols,
Rom 16:17 *A* their company.
1Cor 5:10 To *a* them, you would have to leave
7: 2 But to *a* immorality, every man should
2Cor 6: 3 We *a* giving anyone offense,
8:20 There is one thing I wish to *a*,
Gal 2:12 *a* trouble with those who were circumcised.
6: 1 to *a* falling into temptation himself.
Eph 5:18 *A* getting drunk on wine;
Col 3:19 *A* any bitterness toward them.
1Thes 5:22 *A* any semblance of evil.
2Thes 3: 6 to *a* any brother who wanders from the
2Tm 2:16 *A* worldly, idle talk, for those who indulge

AVOIDED (2)
Jb 1: 1 man named Job, who feared God and *a* evil.
Is 53: 3 He was spurned and *a* by men,

AVOIDING (3)
Jb 1: 8 and upright, fearing God and *a* evil?"
2: 3 and upright, fearing God and *a* evil?
28:28 and *a* evil is understanding.

AVOIDS (5)
Prv 16: 6 and by the fear of the Lord man *a* evil.
16:17 The path of the upright *a* misfortune;
Sir 6:12 he turns against you and *a* meeting you.
Jn 3:18 Whoever believes in him *a* condemnation,
2Tm 2: 4 he *a* this in order to please his

AVVA (4)
2Kgs 17:24 brought people from Babylon, Cuthah, *A*,
17:31 the men of *A* made Nibhaz and Tartak;
18:34 are the gods of Sepharvaim, Hena, and *A*?
19:13 kings of the cities Sepharvaim, Hena and *A*?' "

AVVIM (3)
Dt 2:23 from Caphtor, cleared away the *A*,
Jos 13: 3 also where the *A* are in the south;
18:23 Beth-arabah, Zemaraim, Bethel, *A*,

AWAIT (15)
Gn 43:25 their gifts to *a* Joseph's arrival at noon,
Jgs 6:18 He answered, "I will *a* your return."
Sir 6:19 then *a* her bountiful crops.
Is 38:18 who go down into the pit *a* your kindness.
51: 5 coastlands hope, and my arm they shall *a*.
Hb 3:16 I *a* the day of distress that will come
Lk 4:13 he left him, to *a* another opportunity.
Acts 20:23 to city that chains and hardships *a* me.
Rom 8:23 while we *a* the redemption of our bodies.
Gal 5: 5 we eagerly *a* the justification we hope for,
Phil 3:20 that we eagerly *a* the coming of our Savior,
1Thes 1:10 and to *a* from heaven the Son he raised
Ti 2:13 in this age as we *a* our blessed hope,
Heb 9:28 bring salvation to those who eagerly *a* him.
2Pt 3:13 we *a* are new heavens and a new earth where,

AWAITED (3)
2Mc 15:20 Everyone now *a* the decisive moment.
Wis 18: 7 Your people *a* the salvation of the just
Lk 2:25 and pious, and *a* the consolation of Israel,

AWAITING (2)
Lk 12:36 men *a* their master's return from a wedding,
Rom 8:25 see means *a* it with patient endurance.

AWAITS (7)
2Mc 12:45 *a* those who had gone to rest in godliness,
Jb 12: 5 a disgrace such as *a* unsteady feet;
Sir 7:17 what *a* man is worms.
9:11 fame, for you know not what disaster *a* him.
Rom 8:19 *a* the revelation of the sons of God.
2Tm 4: 8 From now on a merited crown *a* me;
Jas 5: 7 farmer *a* the precious yield of the soil.

AWAKE (36)
Jgs 5:12 *A*, awake, Deborah! awake, awake, strike up
Jb 8: 6 *a* for you and restore your rightful domain;
14:12 the heavens are no more, they shall not *a*,
Ps(s) 35:23 *A*, and be vigilant in my defense;
44:24 *A*! Why are you asleep
57: 9 *A*, O my soul; awake, lyre and harp!
108: 3 *A*, O my soul; awake, lyre and harp;
Prv 23:35 When shall I *a* to seek wine once again?"
Is 26:19 *a* and sing,
51: 9 *A*, awake, put on strength,
51: 9 *A* as in the days of old,
51:17 *A*, awake! Arise O Jerusalem,
52: 1 *A*, awake! Put on your strength
Dn 12: 2 sleep in the dust of the earth shall *a*;
Hb 2: 7 Shall not they who make you tremble *a*?
2:19 Woe to him who says to wood, *A*!"
Zec 13: 7 *A*, O sword, against my shepherd,
Mt 24:42 Stay *a*, therefore!
26:38 Remain here and stay *a* with me."
26:40 could not stay *a* with me for even an hour?
Mk 13:33 Stay *a*!
14:34 Remain here and stay *a*."
14:37 You could not stay *a* for even an hour?
Lk 12:37 whom the master finds wide *a*
Eph 5:14 *A*, O sleeper, arise from the dead,
1Thes 5: 6 be asleep like the rest, but *a* and sober!
5:10 us, that all of us, whether *a* or asleep,
Rv 16:15 Happy the man who stays wide *a* and fully

AWAKEN (4)
Jdt 14: 3 to *a* the generals of the Assyrian army.
Jer 51:39 overcome with perpetual sleep, never to *a*,
51:57 they sleep an eternal sleep, never to *a*,
Lk 8:24 They came to *a* him, saying, "Master,

AWAKENED (6)
1Kgs 18:27 Perhaps he is asleep and must be *a*."
2Kgs 4:31 and informed him that the boy had not *a*.
Ps(s) 73:20 they were the dream of one who had *a*,
Sg 8: 5 Under the apple tree I *a* you;
Zec 4: 1 returned and *a* me, like a man awakened

AWAKENING (3)
Jgs 16:14 *A* from his sleep,
1Sm 26:12 without anyone's seeing or knowing or *a*.
Lk 9:32 but *a*, they saw his glory

AWAKENS (3)
Is 14: 9 It *a* the shades to greet you,
29: 8 he is eating and *a* with an empty stomach,
29: 8 dreams he is drinking and *a* faint and dry,

AWARD (2)
1Cor 9:24 part in the race, the *a* goes to one man.
2Tm 4: 8 just judge that he is, will *a* it to me

AWARDED (1)
Jos 17:11 Manasseh was *a* Beth-shean and its towns,

AWARE (51)
Gn 16: 4 When she became *a* of her pregnancy,
16: 5 ever since she became *a* of her pregnancy,
19:33 not *a* of her lying down or her getting up.
19:35 not *a* of her lying down or her getting up.
38:14 for she was *a* that, although Shelah
Ex 32: 1 When the people became *a* of Moses' delay
Lv 4:13 without even being *a* of it does something
5: 2 or if someone, without being *a* of it,
5: 3 or if someone, without being *a* of it,
5: 4 or if someone, without being *a* of it,
5:17 "If someone, without being *a* of it,
Jgs 6:22 *a* that it had been the angel of the Lord,
1Sm 13: 6 *a* of the danger and of the difficult
20: 3 *a* that I am favored with your friendship,
28: 9 "You are surely *a* of what Saul has done,
2Sm 3:25 Are you not *a* that Abner came to deceive
19:23 Am I not *a* that today I am king of Israel?"
1Kgs 22:33 *a* that he was not the king of Israel,
2Kgs 5:21 *A* that someone was running after him,
19:27 I am *a* whether you stand or sit;
2Chr 18:32 The chariot commanders became *a* that he
Neh 4: 5 "Before they are *a* of it or see us,
4: 9 When our enemies became *a* that we had been
Jdt 11: 8 and all the world is *a* that throughout
1Mc 7:30 When he became *a* that Nicanor had come to
Jb 9:11 should he pass by, I am not *a* of him;
14:21 If his sons are honored, he is not *a* of it;
Is 37:28 I am *a* whether you stand or sit;
Dn 13:42 are *a* of all things before they come to be:
Mt 9: 4 was *a* of what they were thinking and said:
12:15 Jesus was *a* of this,
26:10 Jesus became *a* of this and said to them:
Mk 2: 8 Jesus was immediately *a* of their reasoning,
8:17 *A* of this he said to them,
15:10 He was *a*, of course, that it was out
Lk 20:19 They were well *a* that he had told the
Jn 2:25 He was well *a* of what was in man's heart.
6:61 Jesus was fully *a* that his disciples were
13: 3 fully *a* that he had come from God and was
16:19 was *a* that they wanted to question him,
18: 4 Jesus, *a* of all that would happen to him,
Acts 23: 6 was *a* that some of them were Sadducees and
Rom 6: 3 Are you not *a* that we who were baptized
7: 1 Are you not *a*,
1Cor 1:16 I am not *a* of having baptized anyone else.
3:16 you not *a* that you are the temple of God,
8: 7 meat, fully *a* that it has been sacrificed,
Gal 4:13 You are *a* that it was a bodily ailment
Phil 1:16 *a* that my circumstances provide an
Jas 4: 4 *a* that love of the world is enmity to God?
Jude 1: 5 you may already be very well *a* of them.

AWARENESS (2)
2Chr 6:29 kind, and in *a* of his affliction and pain,
1Pt 2:19 hardship through his *a* of God's presence,

AWAY (701)
Gn 6:21 food that is to be eaten, and store it *a*,
16: 6 her so much that Hagar ran *a* from her.
16: 8 "I am running *a* from my mistress,
17:14 flesh of his foreskin has not been cut *a*,
18:23 you sweep *a* the innocent with the guilty?
19:12 take them *a* from it!
19:15 be swept *a* in the punishment of the city."
19:17 the hills at once, or you will be swept *a*."

19:29 by sending Lot *a* from the upheaval
21:14 the child on her back, he sent her *a*.
21:16 sat down opposite him, about a bowshot *a;*
25: 6 still living, as he sent them *a* eastward,
25: 6 to the land of Kedem, *a* from his son Isaac.
26:16 So Abimelech said to Isaac, "Go *a* from us;
26:27 you hate me and have driven me *a* from you?"
27:36 First he took *a* my birthright,
27:36 and now he has taken *a* my blessing."
29: 3 could they roll the stone *a* from the mouth
29: 8 the stone *a* from the mouth of the well;
29:10 the stone *a* from the mouth of the well,
30:15 it not enough for you to take *a* my husband,
31:19 Now Laban had gone *a* to shear his sheep,
31:27 Why did you dupe me by stealing *a* secretly?
31:31 take your daughters *a* from me by force.
31:42 you would now have sent me *a* empty-handed.
34:17 we will take our daughter and go *a*."
37:27 instead of doing *a* with him ourselves.
38:19 When she went *a*, she took off her shawl
39:12 hand, he got *a* from her and ran outside.
39:15 left his cloak beside me and ran *a* outside."
42:24 But turning *a* from them, he wept.
42:36 is gone, and now you would take *a* Benjamin!
44:29 If you now take this one *a* from me too,
Ex 2:17 But some shepherds came and drove them *a*.
3:20 After that he will send you *a*.
4: 3 into a serpent, and Moses shied *a* from it.
5: 4 by taking the people *a* from their work?
6: 1 by my mighty hand, he will send them *a;*
7:23 He turned *a* and went into his house,
8: 5 that the frogs may be taken *a* from you and
8:24 not go too far *a* and that you pray for me."
11: 1 he will drive you *a*.
13: 3 a strong hand that the LORD brought you *a*.
13:19 they would carry his bones *a* with them.
14: 8 even while they were marching *a* in triumph.
15:15 All the dwellers in Canaan melted *a;*
16:21 when the sun grew hot, the manna melted *a*.
16:23 is left put *a* and keep for the morrow."
16:24 When they put it *a* for the morrow,
20:18 position much farther *a* and said to Moses,
22: 9 if it dies, or is maimed or snatched *a*,
23: 7 You shall keep *a* from anything dishonest.
33: 7 Moses used to pitch at some distance *a*,
Lv 6: 3 shall take *a* the ashes to which the fire
14: 7 the living bird fly *a* over the countryside.
14:45 *a* to an unclean place outside the city.
14:53 *a* over the countryside outside the city.
16:22 region, it must be sent *a* into the desert.
16:26 "The man who has led *a* the goat for
26:22 dwindles *a* and your roads become deserted.
26:39 *a* for their own and their fathers' guilt.
Nm 5:21 thighs to waste *a* and your belly to swell!
5:22 your belly swell and your thighs waste *a!'*
5:27 will swell and her thighs will waste *a*,
9:13 anyone who is clean and not *a* on a journey,
14:25 turn *a* tomorrow and set out in the desert
16:13 *a* from a land flowing with milk and honey,
16:26 "Keep *a* from the tents of these wicked
16:26 will be swept *a* because of all their sins."
17: 2 and scatter the fire some distance *a*,
20: 6 But Moses and Aaron went *a* from the
20:29 understood that Aaron had passed *a;*
22:33 me, she turned *a* from me these three times.
22:33 If she had not turned *a* from me,
25: 4 blazing wrath may be turned *a* from Israel."
32:15 If you turn *a* from following him,
Dt 2:23 from Caphtor, cleared *a* the Avvim,
11:16 be careful lest your heart be so lured *a*
13: 8 any other nations, near at hand or far *a*,
15:13 so, you shall not send him *a* empty-handed,
22: 6 *a* the mother bird along with her brood;
22: 7 her go, although you may take her brood *a*.
29:17 now turn *a* their hearts from the LORD,
29:18 as though to sweep *a* both the watered soil
30:17 you turn *a* your hearts and will not listen,
32:25 "Snatched *a* by the sword in the street
Jos 7: 5 of the people melted *a* like water.
8: 6 until we have drawn them *a* from the city,
8: 9 Then Joshua sent them *a*.
8:17 Since they were drawn *a* from the city,
22: 6 them and sent them *a* to their own tents.
24:23 put *a* the strange gods that are among you
Jgs 2:21 I for my part will not clear *a* for them
5:21 The Wadi Kishon swept them *a;*
11: 2 sons of the wife had driven Jephthah *a*,
11:13 "Israel took *a* my land from the Arnon to
11:38 he replied, and sent her *a* for two months.
15:14 fire and his bonds melted *a* from his hands.
20:32 them *a* from the city onto the highways.
20:32 drawn *a* from the city onto the highways,
Ru 1:21 I went *a* with an abundance,
1Sm 2:30 But now,' the LORD declares, *a* with this!
5:11 "Send *a* the ark of the God of Israel.
6: 3 to send *a* the ark of the God of Israel,
6: 7 but drive their calves indoors *a* from them.
7: 3 put *a* your foreign gods and your Ashtaroth,
7: 4 Israelites put *a* their Baals and Ashtaroth,
13: 8 Gilgal, the men began to slip *a* from Saul.
13:11 I saw that the men were slipping *a* from me,
19:10 struck only the wall, and David got *a* safe.
19:17 You have helped my enemy to get *a!"*

19:18 Thus David got safely *a;*
20:22 beyond you,' go, for the LORD sends you *a*.
21: 7 by fresh bread when it was taken *a*.
24:20 his enemy, does he send him *a* unharmed?
25:10 many servants who run *a* from their masters.
26:12 and they got *a* without anyone's seeing or
2Sm 3:10 take *a* the kingdom from the house of Saul
3:15 and took her *a* from her husband Paltiel,
3:21 Abner farewell, and he went *a* in peace.
5: 6 the blind and the lame will drive you *a!"*
5:21 and David and his men carried them *a*.
6: 3 *a* from the house of Abinadab on the hill.
8: 7 David also took *a* the golden shields used
8: 7 took *a* when he came to Jerusalem in the
10: 4 cutting *a* the lower halves of their garments
10: 4 garments at the buttocks, sent them *a*.
12:31 the city, and also led *a* the inhabitants,
13:17 and said, "Put her outside, *a* from me,
13:19 to her head, she went *a* crying loudly.
14:11 and that my son may not be done *a* with."
15: 6 *a* the loyalties of the men of Israel.
16: 7 *A*, away, you murderous and wicked man!
18:21 The Cushite bowed to Joab and sped *a*.
19:42 our brothers the Judahites steal you *a*
23: 6 wicked are all like thorns to be cast *a;*
1Kgs 2:39 two of Shimei's servants ran *a* to Achish,
11: 9 his heart was turned *a* from the LORD,
11:13 Nor will I take *a* the whole kingdom.
11:31 'I will tear *a* the kingdom from Solomon's
15:22 and they carried *a* the stones and beams
18: 4 hid them *a* fifty each in two caves,
20: 6 and take *a* whatever they consider valuable.'"
21: 4 he turned *a* from food and would not eat.
2Kgs 2:16 him *a* to some mountain or some valley."
3: 2 He did *a* with the pillar of Baal,
4:27 Gehazi came near to push her *a*,
5:11 But Naaman went *a* angry,
6:23 they had eaten and drunk he sent them *a*,
7:15 the Arameans had thrown *a* in their haste.
9: 2 Enter and take him *a* from his companions
10:17 doing *a* with them completely and thus
11: 2 took Joash, his son, and spirited him *a*,
12:19 who then led his forces *a* from Jerusalem.
17:18 the LORD put them *a* out of his sight.
17:21 he tore Israel *a* from the house of David,
17:21 he drove the Israelites *a* from the LORD,
17:23 the LORD put Israel *a* out of his sight as
18: 6 the LORD, Hezekiah never turned *a* from him,
23:11 He did *a* with the horses which the kings
23:24 Josiah did *a* with the consultation of
23:34 Jehoahaz he took *a* with him to Egypt,
25:13 they carried *a* the bronze to Babylon.
1Chr 7:21 had gone down to take *a* their livestock.
8: 8 he had put *a* his wives Hushim and Baara.
18: 1 *a* from the control of the Philistines.
18: 8 He likewise took *a* from Tibhath and Cun,
19: 4 Then he sent them *a*.
21: 8 Take *a* your servant's guilt,
2Chr 7:19 But if you turn *a* and forsake my statutes
9: 4 house of the LORD, it took her breath *a*.
14:12 his army, which carried *a* enormous spoils.
16: 6 Asa commandeered all of Judah to carry *a*
21:17 and carried *a* all the wealth found in the
24:23 did *a* with all the princes of the people,
25:13 of the inhabitants and took *a* much booty.
25:24 He took *a* all the gold and silver and all
28: 5 *a* captive a large number of his people,
28: 8 The Israelites took *a* as captives two
29: 6 *a* their faces from the LORD's dwelling,
29:19 reign had thrown *a* because of his apostasy,
30: 8 he may turn *a* his burning anger from you.
30: 9 he will not turn *a* his face from you
35:23 who said to his servants, "Take me *a*,
36: 4 Jehoahaz *a* and brought him to Egypt.
36: 7 Nebuchadnezzar also carried *a* to Babylon
Ezr 1: 7 Nebuchadnezzar had taken *a* from Jerusalem
2: 1 king of Babylon, had carried *a* to Babylon,
6: 1 the Babylonian records were stored *a;*
10:14 till we have turned *a* from us our God's
10:44 but they sent them *a*, both the women
Neh 3:36 them be carried *a* to a land of captivity!
7: 6 king of Babylon, had carried *a*,
9:35 nor did they turn *a* from their evil deeds.
Tb 1: 4 of my forefather Naphtali had broken *a*
4: 7 not turn your face *a* from any of the poor,
4: 7 God's face will not be turned *a* from you.
4:16 you have left over, give *a* as alms;
5:15 you are *a* I will give you the normal wages,
5:18 "Why have you decided to send my child *a?*
6: 4 hold of the fish and don't let it get *a!"*
6: 5 but throw *a* the entrails.
7:16 over her, she wiped *a* the tears and said:
10:12 he said good-bye to them and sent them *a*.
10:13 kissed them both and sent them *a* in peace.
14: 4 and led *a* into exile from the Good Land.
Jdt 1:11 them, and turned *a* his envoys empty-handed,
2: 3 They decided to do *a* with all those who
7:22 Their children fainted *a*,
Est B: 2 to be carried *a* with the sense of power,
C: 1 *a* and did exactly as Esther had commanded.
C:20 do *a* with the decree you have pronounced,
1Mc 1:21 the sanctuary and took *a* the golden altar,
1:23 and took *a* the gold and silver and the

1:38 them the inhabitants of Jerusalem fled *a*,
2:11 All her adornment has been taken *a*.
3: 8 He turned *a* wrath from Israel
4: 4 forces were still scattered *a* from the camp.
4:43 carried *a* the stones of the Abomination
5:13 *a* their wives and children and their goods,
5:43 they threw *a* their arms and fled to the
6:12 when I carried *a* all the vessels of gold
6:32 Then Judas marched *a* from the citadel and
7:35 He went *a* in great anger.
8:30 hereafter decide to add or take *a* anything,
8:30 they shall add or take *a* shall be valid.
9: 6 afraid, and many slipped *a* from the camp,
9: 7 *a* just when the battle was imminent,
9:47 Bacchides, but Bacchides backed *a* from him.
11:12 his daughter *a* and giving her to Demetrius,
11:73 were running *a* saw it and returned to him;
12:39 the crown, and do *a* with King Antiochus.
16:13 plans to do *a* with Simon and his sons.
16:19 sent other men to Gazara to do *a* with John.
2Mc 3:24 at God's power and fainted *a* in terror.
3:28 his whole bodyguard was carried *a* helpless,
5:21 on foot, so carried *a* was he with pride.
8:13 faith in God's justice deserted and got *a*.
11:12 *a* were wounded and stripped of their arms,
12: 9 as far as Jerusalem, thirty miles *a*.
12:22 they rushed *a* in such headlong flight that
14: 2 *a* with Antiochus and his guardian Lysias.
14:34 With these words he went *a*.
Jb 1:21 The LORD gave and the LORD has taken *a;*
3:16 was I not buried *a* like an untimely birth,
5: 5 [or God shall take it *a* by blight;]
6:27 the orphan, and would barter *a* your friend!
7:16 I waste *a:* I cannot live forever;
7:19 long will it be before you look *a* from me,
7:21 not pardon my offense, or take *a* my guilt?
8:20 Behold, God will not cast *a* the upright;
9:25 are swifter than a runner, they flee *a;*
11:16 or recall it like waters that have ebbed *a*.
12:17 He sends counselors *a* barefoot,
12:19 lets their never-failing waters flow *a*.
14: 6 Look *a* from him and let him be,
14:19 As waters wear *a* the stones and floods
14:19 and floods wash *a* the soil of the land,
14:20 with changed appearance you send him *a*.
15: 4 You in fact do *a* with piety,
15:12 Why do your notions carry you *a*,
17:11 My days are passed *a*,
20: 8 he fades *a* like a vision of the night.
20:28 The flood shall sweep *a* his house with the
21:18 and like chaff which the storm snatches *a!*
22: 9 You have sent widows *a* empty-handed,
22:16 Who were snatched *a* before their time;
22:16 whose foundations a flood swept *a?*
24: 2 they steal *a* herds and pasture them.
24: 3 The asses of orphans they drive *a;*
27:16 like dust and store *a* mounds of clothing,
30:16 My soul ebbs *a* from me;
30:30 My blackened skin falls *a* from me;
32:22 if I did, my Maker would soon take me *a*.
33:17 man from evil and keeping pride *a* from him,
34:20 He brings on nobles, and takes them *a*,
34:27 *a* from him and heeded none of his ways,
37:21 the wind comes by and sweeps the clouds *a*.
Ps(s) 1: 4 are like chaff which the wind drives *a*.
22:15 become like wax melting *a* within my bosom.
22:25 Nor did he turn his face *a* from him,
25:18 and my suffering, and take *a* all my sins.
28: 3 Drag me not *a* with the wicked,
32: 1 I Happy is he whose fault is taken *a*,
32: 3 wasted *a* with my groaning all the day,
32: 5 LORD," and you took *a* the guilt of my sin.
39:11 Take *a* your scourge from me;
39:11 at the blow of your hand I wasted *a*.
40:15 confusion who seek to snatch *a* my life.
41: 4 will take *a* all his ailment when he is ill.
43: 2 Why do you keep me so far *a?*
46: 7 his voice resounds, the earth melts *a*,
49:11 the senseless and the stupid pass *a*,
51:11 Turn *a* your face from my sins,
55: 2 turn not *a* from my pleading;
55: 7 like a dove, I would fly *a* and be at rest.
55: 8 Far *a* I would flee;
58:10 thistles, let the whirlwind carry them *a*.
68: 3 As smoke is driven *a*,
73:19 They are completely wasted *a* amid horrors.
73:26 Though my flesh and my heart waste *a*,
80: 9 you drove *a* the nations and planted it.
88: 9 You have taken my friends *a* from me;
88:19 and neighbor you have taken *a* from me;
90: 9 our days have passed *a* in your indignation;
90:10 toil, for they pass quickly and we drift *a*.
104:29 if you take *a* their breath, they perish
107: 5 their life was wasting *a* within them.
107:26 their hearts melted *a* in their plight.
109:23 I pass *a;* I am swept away like the locust.
112:10 he shall gnash his teeth and pine *a;*
119:21 proud, who turn *a* from your commands.
119:22 Take *a* from me reproach and contempt,
119:37 Turn *a* my eyes from seeing what is vain;
119:39 Turn *a* from me the reproach which I dread,
119:51 bitterly at me, I turn not *a* from your law.
119:102 From your ordinances I turn not *a*,

AWAY (cont.)

119:157 are many, I turn not *a* from your decrees.
125: 5 may the LORD lead *a* with the evildoers!
148: 6 he gave them a duty which shall not pass *a*.
Prv 1:19 takes *a* the life of him who acquires it.
1:23 how long will you turn *a* at my reproof?
3: 7 fear the LORD and turn *a* from evil;
4:16 made no one stumble steals *a* their sleep.
4:24 Put *a* from you dishonest talk,
6:33 get, and his disgrace will not be wiped *a*;
11:30 a tree of life, but violence takes lives *a*.
13:11 Wealth quickly gotten dwindles *a*,
19:26 his father, or drives *a* his mother,
20:30 Evil is cleansed *a* by bloody lashes,
21: 7 of the wicked will sweep them *a*,
27:10 neighbor near at hand than a brother far *a*.
27:25 is taken *a* and the aftergrowth appears,
28: 9 one turns *a* his ear from hearing the law,
Eccl 3: 6 a time to keep, and a time to cast *a*.
11:10 heart and put *a* trouble from your presence,
Sg 8: 7 cannot quench love, nor floods sweep it *a*.
Wis 2: 4 will pass *a* like the traces of a cloud,
3: 2 and their passing *a* was thought an
4:11 Snatched *a*, lest wickedness pervert
7:13 her riches I do not hide *a*;
14:17 Men who lived so far *a* that they could not
16:14 malice, but when the spirit has come *a*,
19: 3 those whom they had sent *a* with entreaty,
Sir 2: 7 for his mercy, turn not *a* lest you fall.
3:15 warmth upon frost it will melt *a* your sins.
4: 1 force not the eyes of the needy to turn *a*.
4:23 proper time, and hide not *a* your wisdom;
6:13 Keep *a* from your enemies;
6:36 let your feet wear *a* his doorstep!
9:13 offend him not, lest he take *a* your life;
10:17 The traces of the proud God sweeps *a* and
13:10 keep not too far *a* lest you be forgotten.
15:11 "It was God's doing that I fell *a*";
17:21 Turn again to the Most High and *a* from sin,
22:13 Turn *a* from him and you will find rest and
22:20 who throws stones at birds drives them *a*,
22:22 treacherous attack will drive *a* any friend.
25:25 walks not by your side, cut her *a* from you.
27:20 Follow him not, for he is far *a*,
29: 9 their want, do not send them *a* empty-handed.
29:27 *A*, stranger, for one more worthy;
30:23 courage, drive resentment far *a* from you;
31: 1 and the care of wealth drives *a* rest.
33:33 If you mistreat him and he runs *a*,
38:28 flesh, yet he toils *a* in the furnace heat.
42: 9 wakeful, and worry over her drives *a* rest:
42:22 same, With nothing added, nothing taken *a*;
44:14 Their bodies are peacefully laid *a*,
Is 1:16 Put *a* your misdeeds from before my eyes;
3: 1 shall take *a* from Jerusalem and from Judah
3:18 will do *a* with the finery of the anklets,
4: 4 *a* the filth of the daughters of Zion,
5: 5 Take *a* its hedge, give it to grazing,
6:12 Until the LORD removes men far *a*,
11:13 The envy of Ephraim shall pass *a*,
14:31 Philistia, all of you melts *a*!
15: 7 whatever they have acquired or stored *a*
16:10 the orchards are taken *a* joy and gladness,
17:13 rebuke them, and they shall flee far *a*;
19: 3 of the Egyptians ebbs *a* within them,
19: 6 Reeds and rushes shall wither *a*,
19: 7 along the Nile shall dry up and blow *a*,
19: 8 their nets in the water shall pine *a*.
20: 4 king of Assyria lead *a* captives from Egypt,
22: 3 All your leaders fled *a* together,
22: 4 Turn *a* from me, let me weep bitterly;
22:25 that hung on it shall be done *a* with;
23:18 It shall not be stored up or laid *a*,
24:16 But I said, "I am wasted, wasted *a*.
25: 8 GOD will wipe *a* the tears from all faces;
28:17 Hail shall sweep *a* the refuge of lies,
30:22 them *a* like filthy rags to which you say,
34: 4 scroll, and all their host shall wither *a*,
38:12 tent, is struck down and borne *a* from me;
40:24 the stormwind carries them *a* like straw.
42:14 I have looked *a*, and kept silence,
42:22 them trapped in holes, hidden *a* in prisons.
44:22 have brushed *a* your offenses like a cloud,
45: 3 and riches that have been hidden *a*,
49:19 those who swallowed you up will be far *a*.
52: 5 people have been taken *a* without redress;
53: 8 Oppressed and condemned, he was taken *a*,
53:12 And he shall take *a* the sins of many,
57: 1 Devout men are swept *a*,
57: 1 he is taken *a* from the presence of evil,
57: 9 While you sent your ambassadors far *a*,
57:13 shall carry off, the breeze shall bear *a*.
64: 5 and our guilt carries us *a* like the wind.
Jer 2:24 and far, breaking *a* toward the desert,
2:35 at least, his anger is turned *a* from me."
2:37 shall you go *a* with hands upon your head;
3: 1 If man sends *a* his wife and,
3: 8 I put her *a* and gave her a bill of divorce,
4: 8 wrath of the LORD is not turned *a* from us."
4:25 even the birds of the air had flown *a*!
5:10 Tear *a* her tendrils,
5:23 they turn and go *a*,
7:15 I will cast you *a* from me,
7:15 from me, as I cast *a* all your brethren,
7:29 Cut off your dedicated hair and throw it *a*!
7:33 of the field, which no one will drive *a*.
10:18 I will sling *a* the inhabitants of the land;
10:24 not in anger, lest you have us dwindle *a*.
11:15 meat turn *a* your misfortune from you?
13:17 tears for the LORD's flock, led *a* to exile.
13:22 skirts are stripped *a* and you are violated.
15: 1 Send them *a* from me.
15: 9 The mother of seven swoons *a*,
17: 5 flesh, whose heart turns *a* from the LORD.
18:20 behalf, to turn *a* your wrath from them.
18:21 to famine, do *a* with them by the sword.
20: 5 shall seize it and carry it *a* to Babylon.
22:10 Weep rather for him who is going *a*;
23: 2 have scattered my sheep and driven them *a*.
24: 5 Judah's exiles whom I sent *a* from this place
28: 3 Babylon, took *a* from this place to Babylon.
28:11 At that, the prophet Jeremiah went *a*.
29:20 whom I sent *a* from Jerusalem to Babylon.
37: 5 this report they marched *a* from the city.
38:22 feet are stuck in the mud, they slink *a*."
41:10 led *a* the remnant of the people left in
41:14 brought *a* from Mizpah went over to Johanan,
41:16 *a* from Mizpah after he killed Gedaliah,
44: 5 accept the warning to turn *a* from the evil
44:12 I will take *a* the remnant of Judah who
46:16 own people, *a* from the destroying sword."
49:20 They shall be dragged *a*,
49:29 Their tents and herds shall be taken *a*,
50: 3 there, because man and beast have fled *a*.
50:45 They shall be dragged *a*,
52:17 they carried *a* all the bronze to Babylon.
52:28 people whom Nebuchadnezzar led *a* captive:
Lam 1: 5 Her little ones have gone *a*,
1: 8 She herself groans and turns *a*.
1:15 ones in my midst the LORD has cast *a*;
2:11 faint *a* in the open spaces of the town.
2:12 As they faint *a* like the wounded in the
3: 4 He has worn *a* my flesh and my skin,
4: 9 for those who die of hunger, Who waste *a*,
4:15 *A* you unclean!"
4:15 they cried to them, "Away, *a*,
4:17 Our eyes ever wasted *a*,
Bar 2:29 great and numerous throng will dwindle *a*
3:30 her, bearing her *a* rather than choice gold?
4:16 have led *a* this widow's cherished sons,
5: 6 *a* on foot by their enemies they left you:
6:13 does *a* with those that offend against it.
6:19 it is said their hearts are eaten *a*.
6:23 unless someone wipes *a* the corrosion,
6:57 go *a* with the clothing that was on them,
Ez 3:19 yet he has not turned *a* from his evil nor
3:20 If a virtuous man turns *a* from virtue and
4:17 terror and waste *a* because of his sins.
6: 9 their adulterous hearts that turned *a*
7:22 I will turn *a* my face from them,
11:15 say, "They are far *a* from the LORD;
14: 6 yourselves *a* from all your abominations.
16: 9 bathed you with water, washed *a* your blood,
16:39 and take *a* your splendid ornaments,
17:12 *a* its king and princes with him to Babylon.
18:21 man turns *a* from all the sins he committed,
18:26 man turns *a* from virtue to commit iniquity,
18:28 *a* from all the sins which he committed,
18:31 Cast *a* from you all the crimes you have
19: 4 took him *a* with hooks to the land of Egypt.
19: 9 cage and took him *a* to the king of Babylon,
20: 7 Throw *a*, each of you,
20: 8 none of them threw *a* the detestable things
21:31 Off with the turban and *a* with the crown!
23:10 her sons and daughters they took *a*,
23:25 They shall take *a* your sons and daughters,
24:16 taking *a* from you the delight of your eyes,
24:23 but you shall rot *a* because of your sins
24:25 the day I take *a* from them their bulwark,
33:10 we are rotting *a* because of them.
33:14 if he turns *a* from his sin and does what
33:18 turns *a* from what is right and does wrong,
33:19 But when a wicked man turns *a* from
36:24 I will take you *a* from among the nations,
38:13 and gold, to take *a* cattle and goods,
45: 9 Put *a* violence and oppression,
Dn 1:16 *a* the food and wine they were to receive,
2:35 wind blew them *a* without leaving a trace.
3:35 Do not take *a* your mercy from us,
7: 8 horns were torn *a* to make room for it.
7:14 dominion that shall not be taken *a*,
7:26 taken *a* by final and absolute destruction,
9:16 wrath be turned *a* from your city Jerusalem,
11: 8 gold, he shall carry *a* as booty into Egypt.
12: 4 many shall fall *a* and evil shall increase."
Hos 1: 2 to harlotry, turning *a* from the Lord.
2:11 I will snatch *a* my wool and my flax,
5:13 he cannot heal you nor take *a* your sore.
5:14 carry it *a* and no one can save it from me.
6: 4 cloud, like the dew that early passes *a*.
8: 3 men of Israel have thrown *a* what is good;
8: 5 Cast *a* your calf, O Samaria!
9:11 The glory of Ephraim flies *a* like a bird:
9:12 Woe to them when I turn *a* from them!
13: 3 cloud or like the dew that early passes *a*,
13:11 in my anger, and I take him *a* in my wrath.
13:12 Israel is wrapped up, his sin is stored *a*.
14: 5 for my wrath is turned *a* from them.
Jl 1:12 Yes, joy has withered *a* from among mankind.
Am 4: 2 you When they shall drag you *a* with hooks,
4: 7 when the harvest was still three months *a*;
5:23 *A* with your noisy songs!
5:26 You will carry *a* Sakkuth,
6: 7 their wanton revelry shall be done *a* with.
9: 3 too I will hunt them and take them *a*;
Jon 1: 3 ready to flee to Tarshish *a* from the LORD.
1: 3 with them to Tarshish, *a* from the LORD.
Mi 2: 9 you take *a* forever the honor I gave them.
7:11 on that day the boundary shall be taken *a*.
Na 3:11 too, shall drink of this till you faint *a*;
Hb 1:15 his hook, he hauls them *a* with his net,
Zep 1: 2 *a* all things from the face of the earth,
1: 3 I will sweep *a* man and beast,
1: 3 beast, I will sweep *a* the birds of the sky,
1: 6 And those who have fallen *a* from the LORD,
1:11 all who weigh out silver, done *a* with.
2: 2 Before you are driven *a*, like chaff
2:11 he makes all the gods of earth to waste *a*;
3:15 against you, he has turned *a* your enemies;
Hg 1: 9 and what you brought home, I blew *a*.
Zec 3: 5 said, "See, I have taken *a* your guilt."
3: 9 take *a* the guilt of the land in one day.
5: 3 with it shall every thief be swept *a*,
10:11 down, and the scepter of Egypt taken *a*.
11: 8 month I did *a* with the three shepherds.
11:17 Let his arm wither *a* entirely,
13: 2 I will also take *a* the prophets and the
Mal 2: 6 uprightness, and turned many *a* from evil.
Mt 4:10 At this, Jesus said to him, *A* with you,
5:18 until heaven and earth pass *a*,
5:18 be done *a* with until it all comes true.
5:29 your trouble, gouge it out and throw it *a*!
5:30 is your trouble, cut it off and throw it *a*!
8:30 *a* a large herd of swine was feeding.
9:15 the day comes that the groom is taken *a*,
13:19 him to steal *a* what was sown in his mind.
13:48 What was useless they threw *a*.
14:12 themselves to carry his body *a* and bury it.
14:23 When he had sent them *a*,
15:32 I do not wish to send them *a* hungry,
18:12 a hundred sheep and one of them wanders *a*;
18:13 the ninety-nine that did not wander *a*.
19:22 these words, the young man went *a* sad,
20: 5 At that they went *a*.
21:43 the kingdom of God will be taken *a* from
24:34 will not pass *a* until all this takes place.
24:35 will pass *a* but my words will not pass.
25:15 Then he went *a*.
25:28 Take the thousand *a* from him and give it
25:38 When did we welcome you *a* from home or
25:43 *a* from home and you gave me no welcome,
25:44 hungry or thirsty or *a* from home
26:73 Even your accent gives you *a*!"
27: 2 They bound him and led him *a* to be handed
27:60 across the entrance of the tomb and went *a*.
28: 8 hurried *a* from the tomb half-overjoyed,
Mk 2:20 when the groom will be taken *a* from them;
2:21 has used to cover the hole would pull *a*—
4:10 Now when he was *a* from the crowd,
4:25 not, what little they have will be taken *a*."
4:36 him *a* in the boat in which he was sitting,
5:10 not to drive them *a* from that neighborhood.
5:17 begging him to go *a* from their district.
6:29 carried his body *a* and laid it in a tomb.
7:17 When he got home, *a* from the crowd,
7:33 took him off by himself *a* from the crowd.
10:22 He went *a* sad, for he had many
13:30 pass *a* until all these things take place.
13:31 will pass *a* but my words will not pass.
14:36 Take this cup *a* from me.
14:44 arrest him and lead him *a*,
15: 1 They bound Jesus, led him *a*,
15:16 *a* into the hall known as the praetorium;
Lk 1:53 thing, while the rich he has sent empty *a*.
4:30 straight through their midst and walked *a*.
8:13 a while, but fall *a* in time of temptation.
8:39 with him, but he sent him *a* with the words,
9:60 come *a* and proclaim the kingdom of God."
11:52 You have taken *a* the key of knowledge.
13:27 *A* from me, you evildoers!'
14:35 it has to be thrown *a*.
15:18 I will break *a* and return to my father,
16:17 for the heavens and the earth to pass *a*
20: 9 tenant farmers, and went *a* for a long time.
20:10 they beat him and sent him *a* empty-handed.
20:11 Him too they sent *a* empty-handed,
20:12 likewise maltreated before driving him *a*.
21:32 will not pass *a* until all this takes place.
21:33 The heavens and the earth will pass *a*,
22:54 They led him *a* under arrest and brought
23:18 The whole crowd cried out, *A* with this man;
23:26 As they led him *a*,
24:12 *a* full of amazement at what had occurred.
Jn 1:29 of God who takes *a* the sin of the world!
5:13 great that Jesus had been able to slip *a*.
6:66 many of his disciples broke *a* and would
7:33 you, then I am going *a* to him who sent me.
8: 9 Then the audience drifted *a* one by one,
8:21 "I am going *a*.

10:12 sight of the wolf coming and runs *a*,
11:39 "Take *a* the stone," Jesus directed.
11:41 They then took *a* the stone and Jesus
11:48 and sweep *a* our sanctuary and our nation."
14:28 You have heard me say, 'I go *a* for a while,
15: 2 He prunes *a* every barren branch,
19:15 At this they shouted, *A* with him!
19:15 *A* with him!
19:16 Jesus was led *a*,
19:31 legs be broken and the bodies be taken *a*.
19:38 it, so they came and took the body *a*.
20: 1 She saw that the stone had been moved *a*,
20:13 them, "Because the Lord has been taken *a*,
20:15 you have laid him and I will take him *a*."
Acts 1:12 a mere sabbath's journey *a*.
3:19 Turn to God, that your sins may be wiped *a*!
7:42 But God turned *a* from them and abandoned
8:13 as they occurred, and was quite carried *a*.
8:39 Philip *a* and the eunuch saw him no more.
9:24 and night in an attempt to do *a* with him.
13: 8 to turn the governor *a* from the faith.
20:12 they were able to take the boy *a* alive.
21:34 ordered Paul to be led *a* to headquarters.
22:16 wash *a* your sins as you call upon his name.'
22:29 who were about to interrogate him backed *a*.
23:22 commander sent the boy *a* with the order,
27:42 so that none might swim *a* and escape;
Rom 11:27 make with them when I take *a* their sins."
12:16 Put *a* ambitious thoughts and associate
1Cor 6:13 God will do *a* with them both in the end"
7:31 for the world as we know it is passing *a*.
13: 8 will be silent, knowledge will pass *a*.
13:10 perfect comes, the imperfect will pass *a*.
2Cor 3:11 was destined to pass *a* was given in glory,
3:14 it is only in Christ that it is taken *a*.
5: 6 dwell in the body we are *a* from the Lord.
5: 8 *a* from the body and at home with the Lord.
5: 9 him whether we are with him or *a* from him.
5:17 The old order has passed *a*;
11: 3 you may fall *a* from your sincere
13:10 I am writing in this way while *a* from you,
Gal 2:13 Barnabas was swept *a* by their pretense.
1Tm 4: 1 in later times some will turn *a* from the faith
5:15 some have turned *a* to follow Satan.
Heb 2: 1 to what we have heard, lest we drift *a*.
3:12 spirit and fall *a* from the living God.
6: 6 the age to come, and then have fallen *a*,
7:24 has a priesthood which does not pass *a*.
9:26 take *a* sins once for all by his sacrifice.
9:28 offered up once to take *a* the sins of many;
9:28 will appear a second time not to take *a* sin
10: 4 blood of bulls and goats to take sins *a*.
10: 9 he takes *a* the first covenant to establish
10:11 sacrifices which can never take *a* sins.
11: 5 By faith Enoch was taken *a* without dying,
12:15 that no man falls *a* from the grace of God;
12:25 we turn *a* from him who speaks from heaven!
12:27 that shaken, created things will pass *a*,
13: 9 carried *a* by all kinds of strange teaching.
Jas 1:11 rich man wither *a* amid his many projects.
1:21 Strip *a* all that is filthy,
1Pt 2: 1 So strip *a* everything vicious,
2Pt 2: 2 Their lustful ways will lure many *a*.
3:12 and the elements will melt *a* in a blaze.
1Jn 2:17 world with its seductions is passing *a*
3: 5 he revealed himself was to take *a* sins;
Rv 12:15 to search out the woman and sweep her *a*.
16:11 did not turn *a* from their wicked deeds.
17: 3 The angel then carried me *a* in spirit to a
21: 1 heavens and the former earth had passed *a*,
21: 4 or pain, for the former world has passed *a*."
21:10 He carried me *a* in spirit to the top of a
22:19 God will take *a* his share in the tree of

AWE (22)

Dt 28:10 of the LORD, they will stand in *a* of you.
32:17 of whom their fathers had never stood in *a*.
1Kgs 3:28 the king had given, they were in *a* of him,
Est D: 6 stones, so that he inspired great *a*.
Ps(s) 40: 4 shall look on in *a* and trust in the LORD.
52: 8 The just shall look on with *a*;
119:161 but my heart stands in *a* of your word.
Is 8:12 fear not, nor stand in *a* of what they fear.
8:13 for him be your fear and your *a*.
29:23 of Jacob, and be in *a* of the God of Israel.
41:23 or evil, that will put us in *a* and in fear.
Mal 2: 5 he feared me, and stood in *a* of my name.
3:14 dress in *a* of the LORD of hosts?
Mt 9: 8 sight, a feeling of *a* came over the crowd,
Mk 4:41 A great *a* overcame them at this.
9: 6 to say, for they were all overcome with *a*.
9:15 Jesus, the whole crowd was overcome with *a*.
Lk 5:26 Full of *a*, they gave praise to God,
2Cor 5:11 in *a* of the Lord we try to persuade men,
Eph 6: 5 human masters with the reverence, the *a*,
Heb 12:28 acceptable to him in reverence and *a*.
1Pt 3:14 not stand in *a* of what this people fears."

AWE-INSPIRING (7)

Ex 34:10 live may see how *a* are the deeds which I,
2Sm 7:23 and by doing *a* things as you cleared
Ps(s) 65: 6 With *a* deeds of justice you answer us,
Sg 6: 4 as Jerusalem, as *a* as bannered troops,
6:10 as the sun, as *a* as bannered troops?
Sir 1: 6 There is but one, wise and truly *a*,
Rv 15: 1 I saw in heaven another sign, great and *a*;

AWESOME (22)

Gn 28:17 "How *a* is this shrine!
31:42 the God of Abraham and the *A* One of Isaac,
31:53 Jacob took the oath by the *A* One of Isaac.
Dt 7:21 who is in your midst, is a great and *a* God.
10:17 of lords, the great God, mighty and *a*,
28:58 revere the glorious and *a* name of the LORD,
1Chr 16:25 and *a* is he,
17:21 won for yourself a name for great and *a*
Neh 1: 5 "O LORD, God of heaven, great and *a* God,
9:32 O our God, great, mighty, and *a* God,
Est D:14 For you are *a*, my lord,
2Mc 1:24 God, creator of all things, *a* and strong,
Jb 37:22 comes, surrounding God's *a* majesty!
Ps(s) 47: 3 For the LORD, the Most High, the *a*,
68:36 *A* in his sanctuary is God,
89: 8 is great and *a* beyond all round about him.
96: 4 *a* is he, beyond all gods
99: 3 Let them praise your great and *a* name;
111: 9 holy and *a* is his name.
Sir 48: 4 How *a* are you, ELIJAH, Whose glory
Is 64: 2 you wrought *a* deeds we could not hope for,
Dn 9: 4 and confessed, "Ah, Lord, great and *a* God,

AWESOMENESS (1)

Jb 25: 2 Dominion and *a* are his who brings about

AWESTRUCK (1)

Mk 2:12 They were *a*; all gave praise to God,

AWFUL (2)

Wis 19:16 oppressed with *a* toils those who now
Sir 43:30 *A* indeed is the LORD's majesty,

AWHILE (2)

Jn 2:10 then when the guests have been drinking *a*,
4:40 him, they begged him to stay with them *a*.

AWL (2)

Ex 21: 6 he shall pierce his ear with an *a*,
Dt 15:17 you shall take an *a* and thrust it through

AWOKE (8)

Gn 28:16 When Jacob *a* from his sleep,
1Kgs 3:15 When Solomon *a* from his dream,
Est A:11 and what God intended to do, Mordecai *a*.
Ps(s) 78:65 Then the Lord *a*, as wakes from sleep
Jer 31:26 Upon this I *a* and opened my eyes;
Mt 1:24 When Joseph *a* he did as the angel of the
Mk 4:39 *a* and rebuked the wind and said to the sea:
Lk 8:24 He *a* and rebuked the wind and the

AX—AXE (10)

Dt 19: 5 and as he swings his *a* to fell a tree,
20:19 destroy its trees by putting an *a* to them.
Jgs 9:48 all his soldiers, took his *a* in his hand,
1Kgs 6: 7 at the quarry, so that no hammer, *a*,
Is 10:15 the *a* boast against him who hews with it?
10:34 The forest thickets are felled with the *a*,
Jer 22: 7 I will send destroyers, each with his *a*:
Bar 6:14 Each has in its right hand an *a* or dagger,
Mt 3:10 now the *a* is laid to the root of the tree.
Lk 3: 9 now the *a* is laid to the root of the tree.

AXES (6)

1Sm 13:20 to sharpen their plowshares, mattocks, *a*,
13:21 the *a* and for setting the oxgoads.
2Sm 12:31 to work with saws, iron picks, and iron *a*,
1Chr 20: 3 them to work with saws, iron picks, and *a*.
Ps(s) 74: 5 men coming up with *a* to a clump of trees;
Jer 46:22 like woodchoppers, they attack her with *a*.

AXHEAD (1)

2Kgs 6: 5 trunk, the iron *a* slipped into the water.

AXLES (2)

1Kgs 7:30 stand had four bronze wheels and bronze *a*.
7:33 their *a*, fellies, spokes, and hubs

AXLETREES (1)

1Kgs 7:32 and the *a* of the wheels and the stand were

AYYAH (1)

1Chr 7:28 and its towns as far as *A* and its towns.

AZALIAH (2)

2Kgs 22: 3 Josiah sent the scribe Shaphan, son of *A*,
2Chr 34: 8 as the land, he sent Shaphan, son of *A*,

AZANIAH (1)

Neh 10:10 Jeshua, son of *A*; Binnui, of the sons

AZAREL (5)

1Chr 12: 7 Elkanah, Isshiah, *A*, Joezer, and Ishbaal,
27:22 for Dan, *A*, son of Jeroham
Ezr 10:41 Shashai, Sharai, *A*, Shelemiah, Shemariah,
Neh 11:13 and Amasai, son of *A*, son of Ahzai,
12:36 of Asaph, and his brethren Shemaiah, *A*,

AZARIAH (65)

1Kgs 4: 2 *A*, son of Zadok, priest;
4: 5 *A*, son of Nathan, chief of the
2Kgs 14:21 of Judah took the sixteen-year-old *A*
14:22 It was *A* who rebuilt Elath and restored it
15: 1 *A*, son of Amaziah, king of Judah,
15: 6 The rest of the acts of *A*,
15: 7 *A* rested with his ancestors,
15: 8 In the thirty-eighth year of *A*,
15:17 In the thirty-ninth year of *A*,
15:23 In the fiftieth year of *A*,
15:27 In the fifty-second year of *A*,
1Chr 2: 8 The sons of Ethan: *A*.
2:38 Jehu became the father of *A*.
2:39 *A* became the father of Helez.
3:12 whose son was Amaziah, whose son was *A*,
5:35 Ahimaaz became the father of *A*.
5:35 *A* became the father of Johanan.
5:36 Johanan became the father of *A*,
5:37 *A* became the father of Amariah.
5:39 Hilkiah became the father of *A*.
5:40 *A* became the father of Seraiah.
6:21 son of Elkanah, son of Joel, son of *A*,
8:38 his first-born, Ishmael, Sheariah, *A*,
9:11 *A*, son of Hilkiah,
9:44 his first-born, Ishmael, Sheariah, *A*,
2Chr 15: 1 Upon *A*, son of Oded, came the spirit
21: 2 His brothers, sons of Jehoshaphat, were *A*,
21: 2 were Azariah, Jehiel, Zechariah, *A*,
23: 1 *A*, son of Jehoram;
23: 1 *A*, son of Obed;
26:17 But *A* the priest, and with him eighty
26:20 *A* the chief priest and all the other
28:12 this, some of the Ephraimite leaders, *A*,
29:12 Mahath, son of Amasai, and Joel, son of *A*,
29:12 Kish, son of Abdi, and *A*,
31:10 concerning the heaps, and the priest *A*,
31:13 by appointment of King Hezekiah and of *A*,
Ezr 7: 1 of Persia, Ezra, son of Seraiah, son of *A*,
7: 3 son of Ahitub, son of Amariah, son of *A*,
Neh 3:23 after them, *A*, son of Maaseiah,
3:24 from the house of *A* to the Corner [that is,
7: 7 with Zerubbabel, Jeshua, Nehemiah, *A*,
8: 7 Shabbethai, Hodiah, Maaseiah, Kelita, *A*,
10: 3 Seraiah, *A*, Jeremiah, Pashhur, Amariah,
12:33 half the princes of Judah, along with *A*,
Tb 5:13 Raphael answered, "I am *A*,
6: 7 "Brother *A*, what medicinal value is there
6:14 "Brother *A*, I have heard that this woman
7: 1 Ecbatana, Tobiah said, "Brother *A*,
7: 9 eat, Tobiah said to Raphael, "Brother *A*,
9: 2 "Brother *A*, take along with you
1Mc 2:59 Hananiah, *A* and Mishael,
5:18 he left Joseph, son of Zechariah, and *A*,
5:56 Joseph, son of Zechariah, and *A*,
5:60 Joseph and *A* were beaten,
Jer 42: 1 army leaders, Johanan, son of Kareah, *A*,
43: 2 which the LORD has sent him to them, *A*,
Dn 1: 6 Daniel, Hananiah, Mishael, and *A*.
1: 7 Mishael to Meshach, and *A* to Abednego.
1:11 of Daniel, Hananiah, Mishael, and *A*,
1:19 equal to Daniel, Hananiah, Mishael, and *A*;
2:17 his companions Hananiah, Mishael, and *A*,
3:25 In the fire *A* stood up and prayed aloud:
3:49 into the furnace with *A* and his companions,
3:88 Hananiah, *A*, Mishael, bless the Lord;

AZAZ (1)

1Chr 5: 8 chief, and Zechariah, and Bela, son of *A*,

AZAZEL (4)

Lv 16: 8 which one is for the LORD and which for *A*.
16:10 for *A* he shall set alive before the LORD,
16:10 by sending it off to *A* in the desert.
16:26 "The man who has led away the goat for *A*

AZAZIAH (2)

1Chr 27:20 for the sons of Ephraim, Hoshea, son of *A*;
2Chr 31:13 Jehiel, *A*, Nahath, Asahel, Jerimoth,

AZBUK (1)

Neh 3:16 was carried out by Nehemiah, son of *A*,

AZEKAH (7)

Jos 10:10 harassing them as far as *A* and Makkedah.
10:11 from the sky above them all the way to *A*,
15:35 Tappuah, Enam, Jarmuth, Adullam, Socoh, *A*,
1Sm 17: 1 between Socoh and *A* at Ephes-dammim.
2Chr 11: 9 Gath, Mareshah, Ziph, Adoraim, Lachish, *A*,
Neh 11:30 its countryside, *A* and its dependencies.
Jer 34: 7 remaining cities of Judah, Lachish and *A*,

AZEL (6)

1Chr 8:37 whose son was Eleasah, whose son was A.
8:38 A had six sons,
8:38 all these were the sons of A.
9:43 whose son was Eleasah, whose son was A.
9:44 A had six sons,
9:44 these were the sons of A.

AZGAD (4)

Ezr 2:12 sons of A, one thousand two hundred
8:12 of the sons of A, Johanan, son of Hakkatan;
Neh 7:16 sons of A, two thousand three hundred
10:16 Pahath-moab, Elam, Zattu, Bani, Bunni, A,

AZIZA (1)

Ezr 10:27 Mattaniah, Jeremoth, Zabad, and A;

AZMAVETH (7)

2Sm 23:31 A from Bahurim; Eliahba from Shaalbon;
1Chr 8:36 Jehoaddah became the father of Alemeth, A,
9:42 Jehoaddah became the father of Alemeth, A,
11:33 A, from Bahurim; Eliahba, from Shaalbon;
12: 3 also Jeziel and Pelet, sons of A;
27:25 Over the treasures of the king was A,
Neh 12:29 and from the plains of Geba and A

AZMON (3)

Nm 34: 4 thence it shall cross to A,
34: 5 and turning from A to the Wadi of Egypt,
Jos 15: 4 it crossed to A and then joined the Wadi

AZNOTH-TABOR (1)

Jos 19:34 A and from there extended to Hukkok;

AZOR (2)

Mt 1:13 father of Eliakim, Eliakim the father of A.
1:14 A was the father of Zadok,

AZOTUS (12)

Jdt 2:28 in A and Ascalon also feared him greatly.
1Mc 4:15 and the plains of Judea, to A and Jamnia.
5:68 toward A in the land of the Philistines.
10:77 He marched on A as though he were going on
10:78 Jonathan followed him to A,
10:83 The enemy fled to A and entered Beth-dagon,
10:84 and plundered A with its neighboring towns,
11: 4 When he reached A, he was shown
11: 4 by fire, A and its suburbs demolished,
14:34 by the sea and Gazara on the border of A,
16:10 refuge in the towers on the plain of A,
Acts 8:40 Philip found himself at A next,

AZRIEL (3)

1Chr 5:24 Epher, Ishi, Eliel, A, Jeremiah, Hodaviah,
27:19 for Naphtali, Jeremoth, son of A;
Jer 36:26 a royal prince, and Seraiah, son of A,

AZRIKAM (6)

1Chr 3:23 of Neariah were Elioenai, Hizkiah, and A—
8:38 Azel had six sons, whose names were A,
9:14 were Shemaiah, son of Hasshub, son of A,
9:44 Azel had six sons, whose names were A,
2Chr 28: 7 killed Maaseiah, the king's son, and A,
Neh 11:15 were Shemaiah, son of Hasshub, son of A,

AZUBAH (4)

1Kgs 22:42 His mother's name was A,
1Chr 2:18 By his wife A, Caleb, son of Hezron,
2:19 When A died, Caleb married Ephrath,
2Chr 20:31 His mother was named A,

AZZAN (1)

Nm 34:26 Paltiel, son of A from the tribe of Asher:

AZZUR (3)

Neh 10:18 Adonijah, Bigvai, Adin, Ater, Hezekiah, A,
Jer 28: 1 year, the prophet Hananiah, son of A,
Ez 11: 1 men, among whom were Jaazaniah, son of A,

B

BAAL (67)

Nm 25: 3 thus submitted to the rites of B of Peor,
25: 5 have submitted to the rites of B of Peor."
Dt 4: 3 midst everyone that followed the B of Peor;
Jgs 2:13 him and served B and the Ashtaroth,
6:25 destroy your father's altar to B
6:28 that the altar of B had been destroyed,
6:30 for he has destroyed the altar of B and
6:32 the words, "Let B take action against him,
8:33 making B of Berith their god and
9: 4 shekels from the temple of B of Berith,
1Kgs 16:31 over to the veneration and worship of B.
16:32 Ahab erected an altar to B in the temple
16:32 the temple of B which he built in Samaria,
18:19 the four hundred and fifty prophets of B
18:21 if B, follow him
18:22 are four hundred and fifty prophets of B.
18:25 Elijah then said to the prophets of B,
18:26 it and called on B from morning to noon,
18:26 morning to noon, saying, "Answer us, B!"
18:40 said to them, "Seize the prophets of B.
19:18 who have not knelt to B or kissed him."
22:54 He served and worshiped B,
2Kgs 3: 2 He did away with the pillar of B,
10:18 "Ahab served B to some extent,
10:19 absent, for I have a great sacrifice for B.
10:19 that he might destroy the worshipers of B.
10:20 "Proclaim a solemn assembly in honor of B."
10:21 All the worshipers of B without exception
10:21 exception came into the temple of B,
10:22 the garments for all the worshipers of B."
10:23 of Baal and said to the worshipers of B,
10:23 here with you, but only worshipers of B."
10:25 into the inner shrine of the temple of B,
10:26 temple of Baal, took out the stele of B,
10:27 Then they smashed the stele of B,
10:28 rooted out the worship of B from Israel.
11:18 went to the temple of B and demolished it.
11:18 and slew Mattan, the priest of B,
17:16 all the host of heaven, and served B.
21: 3 He erected altars to B,
23: 4 all the objects that had been made for B,
23: 5 as well as those who burned incense to B,
1Chr 4:33 all their outlying villages as far as B.
5: 5 whose son was Reaiah, whose son was B,
8:30 first-born son, Abdon, and Zur, Kish, B,
9:36 then came Zur, Kish, B,
2Chr 23:17 went to the temple of B and tore it down.
23:17 and they slew Mattan, the priest of B,
Ps(s) 106:28 they submitted to the rites of B of Peor
Jer 2: 8 The prophets prophesied by B,
2:28 are the altars you have set up for B.
7: 9 adultery and perjury, burn incense to B,
11:13 are the altars for offering sacrifice to B.
11:17 Judah, who provoked me by sacrificing to B.
12:16 formerly taught my people to swear by B
19: 5 They have built high places for B to
19: 5 their sons in fire as holocausts to B:
23:13 by B and led my people Israel astray.
23:27 just as their fathers forget my name for B.
32:29 roofs of which incense was burned to B
32:35 places to B in the Valley of Ben-hinnom,
Hos 2:10 and of gold, which they used for B,
2:18 me "My husband," and never again "My b."
13: 1 but he sinned through B and died.
Zep 1: 4 from this place the last vestige of B,
Rom 11: 4 men who have not bowed the knee to B."

BAAL-GAD (3)

Jos 11:17 Halak that rises toward Seir as far as B
12: 7 from B in the Lebanon valley
13: 5 from B at the foot of Mount Hermon to Labo

BAAL-HAMON (1)

Sg 8:11 Solomon had a vineyard at B;

BAAL-HANAN (5)

Gn 36:38 When Shaul died, B, son of Achbor,
36:39 When B died, Hadar succeeded him
1Chr 1:49 When Shaul died, B, son of Achbor,
1:50 B died and Hadad succeeded him.
1Chr 27:28 of the foothills was B the Gederite,

BAAL-HAZOR (1)

2Sm 13:23 Absalom had shearers in B near Ephraim,

BAAL-HERMON (2)

Jgs 3: 3 between B and the entrance to Hamath.
1Chr 5:23 lived in the land of Bashan as far as B,

BAAL-MEON (4)

Nm 32: 3 Heshbon, Elealeh, Sebam, Nebo and B,
32:38 Kiriathaim, Nebo, B [names to be changed!],
1Chr 5: 8 lived in Aroer and as far as Nebo and B;
Ez 25: 9 Beth-jesimoth, B, and Kiriathaim.

BAAL-PEOR (2)

Dt 4: 3 with your own eyes what the LORD did at B:
Hos 9:10 B and consecrated themselves to the Shame,

BAAL-PERAZIM (4)

2Sm 5:20 David then went to B,
5:20 That is why the place is called B.
1Chr 14:11 They advanced, therefore, to B,
14:11 Therefore that place was called B.

BAAL-SHALISHAH (1)

2Kgs 4:42 A man came from B bringing the man of God

BAAL-TAMAR (1)

Jgs 20:33 They reformed their ranks at B,

BAAL-ZEBUB (4)

2Kgs 1: 2 "Go and inquire of B,
1: 3 Israel that you are going to inquire of B,
1: 6 that you are sending to inquire of B,
1:16 you sent messengers to inquire of B,

BAAL-ZEPHON (3)

Ex 14: 2 You shall camp in front of B,
14: 9 by the sea, at Pi-hahiroth, in front of B.
Nm 33: 7 back to Pi-hahiroth, which is opposite B,

BAALA (1)

2Sm 6: 2 people who were with him set out for B

BAALAH (5)

Jos 15: 9 cities of Mount Ephron, and continued to B,
15:10 From B the boundary curved westward to
15:11 through Shikkeron, and across to Mount B,
15:29 B, Iim, Ezem, Eltolad, Chesil, Hormah,
1Chr 13: 6 David and all Israel went up to B,

BAALATH (3)

Jos 19:44 Elon, Timnah, Ekron, Eltekoh, Gibbethon, B,
1Kgs 9:18 then rebuilt Gezer), Lower Beth-horon, B,
2Chr 8: 6 also B, all the supply cities belonging to

BAALATH-BEER (1)

Jos 19: 8 around these cities as far as B (that is,

BAALIADA (1)

2Sm 5:16 Elishua, Nepheg, Japhia, Elishama, B,

BAALIS (1)

Jer 40:14 asked him whether he did not know that B,

BAALS—BAAL'S (20)

Jgs 2:11 offended the LORD by serving the B.
3: 7 God, and serving the B and the Asherahs,
6:31 him, "Do you intend to act in B stead,
8:33 again abandoned themselves to the B,
10: 6 the LORD, serving the B and Ashtaroth,
10:10 forsaken our God and have served the B."
1Sm 7: 4 Israelites put away their B and Ashtaroth,
12:10 the LORD and worshiping B and Ashtaroth;
1Kgs 18:18 commands of the LORD and following the B.
2Kgs 10:19 Now summon for me all B prophets,
2Chr 17: 3 beginning, and he did not consult the B.
24: 7 turned over to the B the dedicated resources
28: 2 Israel and even made molten idols of the B.
33: 3 had torn down, erected altars for the B,
34: 4 the altars of the B were destroyed;
Jer 2:23 not defiled, I have not gone after the B"?
9:13 the hardness of their hearts and the B,
Hos 2:15 I will punish her for the days of the B,
2:19 remove from her mouth the names of the B,
11: 2 to the B and burning incense to idols.

BAANA (3)

1Kgs 4:12 B, son of Ahilud, in Taanach
4:16 B, son of Hushai, in Asher
Neh 3: 4 and next to him was Zadok, son of B.

BAANAH (9)

2Sm 4: 2 two company leaders named B and Rechab,
4: 5 of Rimmon the Beerothite, Rechab and B,
4: 6 So Rechab and his brother B slipped past
4: 9 David replied to Rechab and his brother B,
23:29 Heled, son of B, from Netophah;
1Chr 11:30 Heled, son of B, from Netophah;
Ezr 2: 2 Bilshan, Mispereth, Bigvai, Rehum, and B):
Neh 7: 7 Bilshan, Mispereth, Bigvai, Nehum, and B).
10:28 Ahiah, Hanan, Anan, Malluch, Harim, B.

BAARA (1)

1Chr 8: 8 he had put away his wives Hushim and B.

BAASEIAH (1)

1Chr 6:25 son of Shimea, son of Michael, son of B,

BAASHA (27)

1Kgs 15:16 There was war between Asa and B,
15:17 B, king of Israel, attacked Judah
15:19 Go, break your treaty with B,
15:21 When B heard of it
15:22 beams with which B was fortifying Ramah.
15:27 B, son of Ahijah,
15:28 B killed him in the third year of Asa,
15:32 [There was war between Asa and B,
15:33 the third year of Asa, king of Judah, B,
16: 1 The LORD spoke against B to Jehu,
16: 3 by their sins, I will destroy you, B,
16: 5 The rest of the acts of B,
16: 6 B rested with his ancestors;
16: 7 the LORD had threatened B and his house
16: 7 the evil B did in the sight of the LORD,
16: 8 of Asa, king of Judah, Elah, son of B,

16:11 he killed off the whole house of B,
16:12 Zimri destroyed the entire house of B,
16:12 prophesied to B through the prophet Jehu,
16:13 because of all the sins which B and his
21:22 son of Nebat, and like that of B,
2Kgs 9: 9 son of Nebat, and with the house of B,
2Chr 16: 1 the thirty-sixth year of Asa's reign, B,
16: 3 Go, break your treaty with B,
16: 5 When B heard of it, he left off
16: 6 with which B had been fortifying Ramah,
Jer 41: 9 by King Asa to defend himself against B,

BAASHA'S (1)

1Kgs 16: 4 If anyone of B line dies in the city,

BABBLER (1)

Prv 20:19 so have nothing to do with a b!

BABBLINGS (1)

Jb 11: 3 Shall your b keep men silent,

BABE (3)

Nm 12:12 Let her not thus be like the stillborn b
Dt 32:25 nursing b as well as the hoary old man
Is 3:12 a b in arms will be their tyrant,

BABEL (1)

Gn 11: 9 That is why it was called B,

BABES (4)

Jdt 16: 4 to the sword, Dash my b to the ground,
Jb 3:16 like b that have never seen the light?
Ps(s) 8: 3 Out of the mouths of b and sucklings you
Lam 4: 4 The b cry for food,

BABIES (4)

1Mc 1:61 decree, with the b hung from their necks;
2Mc 6:10 paraded about the city with their b
Lk 18:15 They even brought b to be touched by him.
1Pt 2: 2 Be as eager for milk as newborn b—

BABY (6)

Ex 2: 6 it, she looked, and lo, there was a b boy,
2Kgs 4:16 next year you will be fondling a b son."
Is 11: 8 The b shall play by the cobra's den,
Lk 1:41 Mary's greeting, the b leapt in her womb.
1:44 in my ears, the b leapt in my womb for joy.
2:16 and Joseph, and the b lying in the manger;

BABYLON (300)

Gn 10:10 The chief cities of his kingdom were B,
2Kgs 17:24 The king of Assyria brought people from B,
20:12 son of Baladan, king of B,
20:14 "They came from a distant land, from B,"
20:17 until this day, shall be carried off to B;
20:18 servants in the palace of the king of B."
24: 1 his reign Nebuchadnezzar, king of B,
24: 7 for the king of B had taken all that
24:10 officials of Nebuchadnezzar, king of B,
24:11 Nebuchadnezzar, king of B,
24:12 surrendered to the king of B,
24:15 He deported Jehoiachin to B,
24:15 Jerusalem to B the king's mother and wives,
24:16 The king of B also led captive to Babylon
24:17 of B appointed his uncle Mattaniah king,
24:20 Zedekiah rebelled against the king of B.
25: 1 of the month, Nebuchadnezzar, king of B,
25: 6 and brought to Riblah to the king of B,
25: 7 him with fetters, and had him brought to B.
25: 8 year of Nebuchadnezzar, king of B),
25: 8 as the representative of the king of B.
25:11 those who had deserted to the king of B,
25:13 they carried away the bronze to B.
25:20 brought them to the king of B at Riblah,
25:22 land of Judah, Nebuchadnezzar, king of B,
25:23 king of B had appointed Gedaliah governor,
25:24 in the country and serve the king of B,
25:27 twelfth month, Evil-merodach, king of B,
25:28 of the other kings who were with him in B.
1Chr 9: 1 in captivity to B because of its rebellion.
2Chr 32:31 ambassadors [princes] sent to him from B
33:11 him with chains, and transported him to B.
36: 6 Nebuchadnezzar, king of B, came up
36: 6 and bound him with chains to take him to B.
36: 7 Nebuchadnezzar also carried away to B some
36: 7 the LORD and put them in his palace in B.
36:10 sent for him and had him brought to B,
36:18 his princes, all these he brought to B.
36:20 escaped the sword he carried captive to B,
Ezr 1:11 were brought back from B to Jerusalem.
2: 1 exiles, whom Nebuchadnezzar, king of B,
2: 1 king of Babylon, had carried away to B,
5:12 the Chaldean, Nebuchadnezzar, king of B,
5:12 this house and led the people captive to B.
5:13 in the first year of Cyrus, king of B,
5:14 and carried off to the temple in B,
5:14 B and consigned to a certain Sheshbazzar,
5:17 search be made in the royal archives of B
6: 5 and brought to B are to be sent back:
7: 6 this Ezra came up from B.
7: 9 he resolved on the journey up from B,
7:16 may receive throughout the province of B,
8: 1 from B during the reign of King Artaxerxes:
Neh 7: 6 the exiles whom Nebuchadnezzar, king of B,
13: 6 year of Artaxerxes, king of B,
Tb 14: 4 be safer in Media than in Assyria or B.
Est A: 3 captives whom Nebuchadnezzar, king of B,
2: 6 of Judah, whom Nebuchadnezzar, king of B,
1Mc 6: 4 dismay withdrew from there to return to B.
Ps(s) 87: 4 Egypt and B among those that know the LORD;
137: 1 B we sat and wept when we remembered Zion.
137: 8 O daughter of B, you destroyer,
Is 13: 1 An oracle concerning B;
13:19 And B, the jewel of kingdoms,
14: 4 up this taunt-song against the king of B:
14:22 hosts, and cut off from B name and remnant,
21: 9 calls out and says, 'Fallen, fallen is B,
39: 1 son of Baladan, king of B,
39: 3 came to me from a distant land, from B."
39: 6 until this day, shall be carried off to B;
39: 7 servants in the palace of the king of B."
43:14 For your sakes I send to B;
47: 1 sit in the dust, O virgin daughter B;
48:14 will against B and the progeny of Chaldea.
48:20 Go forth from B, flee from Chaldea!
Jer 20: 4 All Judah I will deliver to the king of B,
20: 4 captive to B or slay them with the sword.
20: 5 who shall seize it and carry it away to B.
20: 6 To B you shall go,
21: 2 LORD, because Nebuchadnezzar, king of B,
21: 4 which you intend to fight the king of B
21: 7 the hand of Nebuchadnezzar, king of B,
21:10 the king of B who shall burn it with fire.
22:25 the hands of Nebuchadnezzar, king of B,
24: 1 This was after Nebuchadnezzar, king of B,
24: 1 the skilled workers, and brought them to B—
25: 1 first year of Nebuchadnezzar, king of B).
25: 9 I will send to Nebuchadnezzar, king of B,
25:11 shall be enslaved to the king of B;
25:12 I will punish the king of B and the nation
27: 6 the hand of Nebuchadnezzar, king of B,
27: 8 will not serve Nebuchadnezzar, king of B,
27: 8 its neck under the yoke of the king of B,
27: 9 to you, "You need not serve the king of B."
27:11 its neck to the yoke of the king of B
27:12 your necks to the yoke of the king of B;
27:13 nation that will not serve the king of B?
27:14 say, "You need not serve the king of B,"
27:16 LORD will be brought back from B soon now,"
27:17 Serve the king of B that you may live;
27:18 and in Jerusalem might not be taken to B.
27:20 city, which Nebuchadnezzar, king of B,
27:20 king of Judah, from Jerusalem to B,
27:22 To B they shall be brought,
28: 2 'I will break the yoke of the king of B.
28: 3 of Babylon, took away from this place to B.
28: 4 and all the exiles of Judah who went to B,'
28: 4 I will break the yoke of the king of B.'"
28: 6 all the exiles back from B to this place!
28:11 the yoke of Nebuchadnezzar, king of B,
28:14 nations serving Nebuchadnezzar, king of B,
29: 1 by Nebuchadnezzar from Jerusalem to B.
29: 3 Delivered in B by Elasah,
29: 3 king of Judah, sent to the king of B,
29: 4 exiles whom I exiled from Jerusalem to B:
29:10 after seventy years have elapsed for B
29:15 has raised up for us prophets here in B—
29:20 whom I sent away from Jerusalem to B.
29:21 them over to Nebuchadnezzar, king of B,
29:22 Judah in B will pattern a curse after them:
29:22 whom the king of B roasted in the flames."
29:28 For he sent us in B this message:
32: 2 of the king of B was besieging Jerusalem,
32: 3 am handing over this city to the king of B,
32: 4 shall he be handed over to the king of B.
32: 5 to face, and Zedekiah shall be taken to B.
32:28 Chaldeans, for Nebuchadnezzar, king of B,
32:36 is handed over to the king of B amid sword,
34: 1 the LORD while Nebuchadnezzar, king of B,
34: 2 am handing this city over to the king of B;
34: 3 king of B and speak to him face to face.
34: 3 Then you shall be taken to B.
34: 7 while the armies of the king of B
34:21 B who have at present withdrawn from you.
35:11 But when Nebuchadnezzar, king of B,
37: 1 land of Judah by Nebuchadnezzar, king of B.
37:17 you shall be handed over to the king of B.
37:20 of B would not attack you or this land?
38: 3 handed over to the army of the king of B;
38:23 you shall be handed over to the king of B,
39: 1 king of Judah, Nebuchadnezzar, king of B,
39: 3 of B came and occupied the middle gate:
39: 3 and all the other princes of the king of B.
39: 5 king of B pronounced sentence upon him.
39: 6 slain at Riblah by order of the king of B,
39: 7 and bound him in chains to bring him to B.
39: 9 B the rest of the people left in the city,
39:11 Jeremiah, Nebuchadnezzar, king of B,
39:13 and all the nobles of the king of B,
40: 1 and Judah who were being exiled to B.
40: 4 it seems good to you to come with me to B,
40: 4 But if it does not please you to come to B,
40: 5 whom the king of B has appointed ruler
40: 7 that the king of B had given Gedaliah,
40: 7 poor who had not been led captive to B,
40: 9 in the land and submit to the king of B,
40:11 the king of B had left a remnant in Judah,
41: 2 the king of B had made ruler over the land;
41:18 of B had made ruler in the land of Judah.
42:11 Do not fear the king of B,
43: 3 the Chaldeans to be killed or exiled to B."
43:10 for my servant Nebuchadnezzar, king of B,
44:30 and mortal foe, Nebuchadnezzar, king of B.
46: 2 Euphrates by Nebuchadnezzar, king of B,
46:13 the advance of Nebuchadnezzar, king of B,
46:26 their lives, to Nebuchadnezzar, king of B,
49:28 defeated by Nebuchadnezzar, king of B,
49:30 against you [Nebuchadnezzar, king of B.
50: 1 The word which the LORD spoke against B,
50: 2 B is taken, Bel confounded,
50: 8 Flee from B,
50: 9 B a band of great nations from the north;
50:13 by B will be appalled and catch his breath,
50:14 Take your posts encircling B,
50:16 Cut off from B the sower and him who
50:17 now Nebuchadnezzar of B gnaws her bones.
50:18 I will punish the king of B and his land,
50:23 of horror B has become among the nations!
50:24 ensnared yourself, and were caught, O B,
50:28 fugitives, the escaped from the land of B:
50:29 Call up against B archers,
50:34 earth, but unrest to those who live in B.
50:42 place for battle against you, daughter B.
50:43 The king of B hears news of them,
50:45 of the LORD which he has taken against B;
50:46 At the cry B is captured!"
51: 1 I rouse against B,
51: 2 Against B I will send winnowers to winnow
51: 6 Flee out of B; let each one save his life,
51: 7 B was a golden cup in the hand of the LORD
51: 8 B suddenly falls and is crushed:
51: 9 "We have tried to heal B,
51:11 B he is resolved to destroy.
51:12 Against the walls of B raise a signal,
51:12 his threat against the inhabitants of B.
51:24 Thus will I repay B,
51:29 the LORD's plan against B is carried out,
51:29 land of B into a desert where no one lives.
51:31 the king of B that all his city is taken.
51:33 Daughter B is like a threshing floor at
51:34 of B he has left me as an empty vessel;
51:35 My torn flesh be upon B,
51:37 B shall become a heap of ruins,
51:41 What a horror has B become among nations:
51:42 against B the sea rises,
51:44 I will punish Bel in B,
51:44 The wall of B falls!
51:47 coming when I will punish the idols of B;
51:48 in them shall shout over B with joy,
51:49 B, too, must fall, O slain of Israel
51:49 B have fallen the slain of all the earth.
51:53 Though B scale the heavens,
51:54 loud cries from B, dire destruction
51:55 For the LORD lays B waste,
51:56 comes upon her, B her heroes are captured,
51:58 of spacious B shall be leveled utterly;
51:59 when he went to B for the king in the
51:60 that was to befall B in a single book:
51:60 these words that were written against B.
51:61 When you reach B,
51:64 Thus shall B sink.
52: 3 Zedekiah rebelled against the king of B.
52: 4 of the month, Nebuchadnezzar, king of B,
52: 9 in the land of Hamath, to the king of B,
52:10 the king of B slew his sons as well as all
52:11 and had him brought to B and kept in
52:12 year of Nebuchadnezzar, king of B),
52:12 as the representative of the king of B.
52:15 those who had deserted to the king of B,
52:17 they carried away all the bronze to B.
52:26 brought them to the king of B at Riblah,
52:31 twelfth month, Evil-merodach, king of B,
52:32 of the other kings who were with him in B.
52:34 by the king of B was a perpetual allowance,
Bar 1: 1 of Hasadiah, son of Hilkiah, wrote in B,
1: 4 all who lived in B by the river Sud.
1: 9 had made after Nebuchadnezzar, king of B,
1: 9 as captives, and brought them to B
1:11 for the life of Nebuchadnezzar, king of B,
1:12 shadow of Nebuchadnezzar, king of B,
2:21 shoulders to the service of the king of B,
2:22 Lord's voice so as to serve the king of B.
2:24 heed your voice, or serve the king of B,
6: 1 to B by the king of the Babylonians,
6: 1 being led captive to B by Nebuchadnezzar,
6: 2 you reach B you will be there many years,
6: 3 And now in B you will see borne upon men's
Ez 12:13 I will bring him to B,
17:12 The king of B came to Jerusalem and took
17:12 away its king and princes with him to B.
17:16 he broke, there in B I swear he shall die!
17:20 I will bring him to B and enter into
19: 9 a cage and took him away to the king of B,
21:24 which the sword of the king of B can come.
21:26 the two roads divide stands the king of B,
23:23 the men of B and all of Chaldea,

BABYLON (cont.)

24: 2 day the king of *B* has invested Jerusalem.
26: 7 the north Nebuchadnezzar the king of *B*,
29:18 Son of man, Nebuchadnezzar, the king of *B*,
29:19 land of Egypt to Nebuchadnezzar, king of *B*.
30:10 by the hand of Nebuchadnezzar, king of *B*.
30:24 will strengthen the arms of the king of *B*,
30:25 will make the arms of the king of *B* strong,
30:25 put my sword in the hand of the king of *B*
32:11 sword of the king of *B* shall come upon you.
Dn 1: 1 of *B* came and laid siege to Jerusalem.
2:12 all the wise men of *B* to be put to death.
2:14 who had set out to kill the wise men of *B*:
2:18 perish with the rest of the wise men of *B*.
2:24 appointed to destroy the wise men of *B*,
2:24 "Do not put the wise men of *B* to death.
2:48 made him ruler of the whole province of *B*
2:48 chief prefect over all the wise men of *B*.
2:49 administrators of the province of *B*,
3: 1 in the plain of Dura in the province of *B*.
3:12 made administrators of the province of *B*:
3:97 Meshach, and Abednego in the province of *B*.
4: 3 a decree that all the wise men of *B*
4:26 on the roof of the royal palace in *B*,
4:27 in Babylon, the king said, *B* the great!
5: 7 it means," he said to the wise men of *B*,
7: 1 In the first year of King Belshazzar of *B*,
13: 1 In *B* there lived a man named Joakim,
13: 5 Lord said, "Wickedness has come out of *B*:
14:34 you have to Daniel in the lions' den at *B*."
14:35 But Habakkuk answered, *B*,
14:36 wind, he set him down in *B* above the den.
Mi 4:10 To *B* shall you go,
Zec 2:11 you who dwell in daughter *B*.
6:10 son of Zephaniah (these had come from *B*).
Acts 7:43 For that I will exile you beyond *B*.'
1Pt 5:13 The church that is in *B*,
Rv 14: 8 "Fallen, fallen is *B* the great,
16:19 God remembered *B* the great,
17: 5 was written a symbolic name, *B* the great,
18: 2 "Fallen, fallen is *B* the great!
18:10 great city that you are, *B* the mighty!
18:21 *B* the great city shall be cast down like

BABYLONIA (1)

2Mc 8:20 of the battle in *B* against the Galatians,

BABYLONIAN (7)

Jos 7:21 the spoils, I saw a beautiful *B* mantle,
Ezr 4: 9 agents from among the Persian, Urukian, *B*,
6: 1 in which the *B* records were stored away;
Mt 1:11 his brothers at the time of the *B* exile.
1:12 After the *B* exile Jechoniah was the father
1:17 from David to the *B* captivity,
1:17 from the *B* captivity to the Messiah,

BABYLONIANS (8)

2Kgs 17:30 Thus the *B* made Marduk and his consort;
Bar 6: 1 captive to Babylon by the king of the *B*,
6: 1 Babylon by Nebuchadnezzar, king of the *B*.
Ez 23:15 chariot warriors, the portraits of *B*,
23:17 Then the *B* came to her,
Dn 14: 3 The *B* had an idol called Bel,
14:23 was a great dragon which the *B* worshiped.
14:28 When the *B* heard this,

BABYLON'S (6)

Jer 36:29 *B* king shall surely come and lay waste
38:17 If you surrender to the princes of *B* king,
38:18 do not surrender to the princes of *B* king,
38:22 be brought out to the princes of *B* king,
50:35 Chaldeans, says the LORD, upon *B* people,
51:30 *B* warriors have ceased to fight,

BACCHIDES (24)

1Mc 7: 8 Then the king chose *B*,
7:12 Alcimus and *B* to ask for a just agreement.
7:19 *B* withdrew from Jerusalem and pitched his
9: 1 sent *B* and Alcimus into the land of Judah,
9:11 Then the army of *B* moved out of camp and
9:12 *B* was on the right wing.
9:14 Seeing that *B* was on the right,
9:22 *B* and Jonathan.
9:25 *B* chose impious men and made them masters
9:26 the friends of Judas and brought them to *B*,
9:29 *B* and those who are hostile to our nation.
9:32 When *B* learned of it, he sought to kill
9:43 When *B* heard of it,
9:47 Bacchides, but *B* backed away from him.
9:49 A thousand men on *B*' side fell that day.
9:50 to Jerusalem, *B* built strongholds in Judea:
9:57 Alcimus was dead, *B* returned to the king,
9:58 Now then, let us have *B* return,
9:60 When *B* was setting out with a large force,
9:63 When *B* learned of this,
9:68 They fought against *B*, and he was beaten.
10:12 in the strongholds that *B* had built,
2Mc 8:30 challenged the forces of Timothy and *B*,

BACENOR'S (1)

2Mc 12:35 a powerful horseman and one of *B* men,

BACK (643)

Gn 8: 2 and the downpour from the sky was held *b*.
8: 7 It flew *b* and forth until the waters dried
8: 9 dove and drew it *b* to him inside the ark.
8:11 In the evening the dove came *b* to him,
8:12 and this time it did not come *b*.
14: 7 turned *b* and came to Enmishpat (that is,
14:16 *b* his kinsman Lot and his possessions,
15:16 time-span the others shall come *b* here;
16: 9 "Go *b* to your mistress and submit to her
19: 9 They replied, "Stand *b*!
19:17 Don't look *b* or stop anywhere on the Plain.
19:26 But Lot's wife looked *b*,
21:14 Then, placing the child on her *b*,
22: 5 We will worship and then come *b* to you."
24: 5 son *b* to the land from which you migrated?"
24: 6 "Never take my son *b* there for any reason,"
24: 8 But never take my son *b* there!"
24:20 and ran *b* to the well to draw more water,
24:56 let me go *b* to my master."
26:15 dug *b* in the days of his father Abraham.)
26:18 his father's servants had dug *b* in the days
27:30 when his brother Esau came *b* from his hunt.
27:45 Then I will send for you and bring you *b*.
28:15 you go, and bring you *b* to this land.
28:21 and I come *b* safe to my father's house,
29: 3 stone *b* again over the mouth of the well.
32: 1 then he set out on his journey *b* home,
32:10 O LORD, 'Go *b* to the land of your birth,
33:16 day that Esau began his journey *b* to Seir,
37:14 brothers and the flocks and bring *b* word."
37:29 When Reuben went *b* to the cistern and saw
38:22 He went *b* to Judah and told him,
42:20 come *b* to me with your youngest brother.
42:29 When they got *b* to their father Jacob in
42:34 come *b* to me with your youngest brother,
42:37 in my care, and I will bring him *b* to you.
43: 2 "Go *b* and procure us a little more food."
43: 9 If I fail to bring him *b*,
43:10 could have been there and *b* twice by now!"
43:12 that was put *b* in the mouths of your bags;
43:13 too, and be off on your way *b* to the man.
43:18 the money put *b* in our bags the first time,
43:21 We have now brought it *b*.
44: 8 We even brought *b* to you from the land of
44:17 you may go *b* safe and sound to your father."
44:23 your youngest brother comes *b* with you,
44:25 to come *b* and buy some food for the family.
44:30 us when I go *b* to your servant my father,
44:32 saying, 'If I fail to bring him *b* to you,
44:33 and let the boy go *b* with his brothers.
44:34 *b* to my father if the boy were not with me?
45: 9 "Hurry *b*,
45:18 your families, and then come *b* here to me;
45:19 transport your father on your way *b* here.
46: 4 I will also bring you *b* here,
50: 5 up there to bury my father and then come *b*?"
50:15 us *b* in full for all the wrong we did him!"
Ex 4: 7 said, "Now, put your hand *b* in your bosom."
4: 7 Moses put his hand *b* in his bosom,
4:18 Jethro and said to him, "Let me go *b*,
4:19 the LORD said to Moses, "Go *b* to Egypt,
4:20 sons, and started *b* to the land of Egypt,
10: 8 Moses and Aaron were brought *b* to Pharaoh,
14:26 the water may flow *b* upon the Egyptians,
14:27 dawn the sea flowed *b* to its normal depth.
14:28 As the water flowed *b*,
15:19 the waters of the sea flow *b* upon them,
18: 2 Moses' wife, whom Moses had sent *b* to him,
19: 8 *b* to the LORD the response of the people.
29:25 you have received them *b* from their hands,
32:15 were written on both sides, front and *b*;
32:31 So Moses went *b* to the LORD and said,
33:23 remove my hand, so that you may see my *b*;
34:31 the rulers of the community come *b* to him.
Lv 8:28 When he had received them *b*,
25:25 may go and buy *b* what his kinsman has sold.
25:26 means to buy it *b* in his own name,
25:27 and then pay *b* the balance to the one to
25:28 acquire sufficient means to buy *b* his land,
25:29 he has the right to buy it *b* during the
25:51 of the sale price he shall pay *b* as ransom;
27:31 someone wishes to buy *b* any of his tithes,
27:33 without the right of being bought *b*."
Nm 12:14 only then may she be brought *b*."
12:15 start out again until she was brought *b*.
14: 4 us appoint a leader and go *b* to Egypt."
14:43 You have turned *b* from following the LORD;
14:45 them, beating them *b* as far as Hormah.
17:25 "Put *b* Aaron's staff in front of the
21:15 That reach *b* toward the site of Ar
22:13 of Balak, "Go *b* to your own country,
22:14 of Moab went *b* to Balak with the report,
22:23 had to beat her to bring her *b* on the road.
22:34 it has displeased you, I will go *b* home."
23: 5 the LORD said to him, "Go *b* to Balak,
23: 6 So he went *b* to Balak,
23:16 his mouth, he said to him, "Go *b* to Balak,
23:17 So he went *b* to Balak,
33: 7 from Etham, they turned *b* to Pi-hahiroth,
Dt 17:16 people go *b* again to Egypt to acquire them,
17:16 that you must never go *b* that way again.
22: 2 then give it *b* to him.
23:12 sun has set, he may come *b* into the camp.
24:19 sheaf there, you shall not go *b* to get it;
28:68 LORD will send you *b* in galleys to Egypt,
30: 4 even from there will he bring you *b*.
32: 7 Think *b* on the days of old,
Jos 2:23 Then the two came *b* down from the hills,
7: 5 They pressed them *b* across the clearing in
7: 8 Israel has turned its *b* to its enemies?
7:12 enemies, but must turn their *b* to them,
8:20 By the time the men of Ai looked *b*,
8:21 in smoke, they struck *b* at the men of Ai.
10:38 Israel turned *b* to Debir and attacked it,
11:10 At that time Joshua, turning *b*,
14: 7 I brought *b* to him a conscientious report.
19:29 Then the boundary turned *b* to Ramah and
19:29 it cut *b* to Hosah and ended at the sea.
20: 6 *b* home to his own city from which he fled."
Jgs 6:18 until I come *b* to you and bring out my
8:29 son of Joash, went *b* home to stay.
11: 8 "In any case, we have now come *b* to you;
11: 9 "If you bring me *b* to fight against the
19: 3 after her to forgive her and take her *b*.
19: 7 him he went *b* and spent the night there.
19:18 Bethlehem of Judah and am now going *b*
20:40 It was when Benjamin looked *b* and saw the
21:23 dancers, and went *b* to their own territory,
Ru 1: 6 She then made ready to go *b* from the
1: 7 were on the road *b* to the land of Judah,
1: 8 said to her two daughters-in-law, "Go *b*,
1:11 "Go *b*, my daughters!" said Naomi.
1:12 Go *b*, my daughters!
1:15 has gone *b* to her people and her god.
1:15 Go *b* after your sister-in-law!"
1:21 but the LORD has brought me *b* destitute.
1:22 accompanied her *b* from the plateau of Moab.
3: 1 When she was *b* with her mother-in-law,
3:17 come *b* to my mother-in-law empty-handed!"
4: 3 who has come *b* from the Moabite plateau,
1Sm 3: 5 "Go *b* to sleep."
3: 5 So he went *b* to sleep.
3: 6 Go *b* to sleep."
3:18 told him everything, and held nothing *b*.
6: 2 Tell us what we should send *b* with it."
6:17 golden hemorrhoids the Philistines sent *b*
9: 5 who was with him, "Come, let us turn *b*,
13: 2 the rest of the people *b* to their tents.
15:20 I have brought *b* Agag,
18:27 he brought *b* their foreskins and counted
19:15 *b* to see David and commanded them,
21: 1 way, while Jonathan went *b* into the city.
23:23 Then come *b* to me with sure information,
24: 9 When Saul looked *b*,
26:21 Come *b*, my son David,
29: 4 "Send that man *b*!
29: 4 how else can he win *b* his master's favor,
30:19 David brought *b* everything.
2Sm 1:22 The bow of Jonathan did not turn *b*,
2:23 and the weapon protruded from his *b*.
3:13 appear before me unless you bring *b* Michal,
3:16 But Abner said to him, "Go *b*!"
3:16 And he turned *b*.
3:26 brought him *b* from the cistern of Sirah.
5: 2 led the Israelites out and brought them *b*.
10: 5 beards grow," he said, "and then come *b*."
11:15 *b* and leave him to be struck down dead."
11:23 them *b* to the entrance of the city gate.
12:23 Can I bring him *b* again?
14:13 for not bringing *b* his own banished son.
14:14 Yet, though God does not bring *b* life,
14:21 Go, therefore, and bring *b* young Absalom."
14:32 'Why did I come *b* from Geshur?
15: 8 'If the LORD ever brings me *b* to Jerusalem,
15:19 Go *b* and stay with the king,
15:25 "Take the ark of God *b* to the city.
15:25 *b* and permit me to see it and its lodging.
15:29 of God *b* to Jerusalem and remained there.
17: 3 can bring *b* the rest of the people to you,
18:16 *b* from the pursuit of the Israelites,
19:38 Please let your servant go *b* to die in his
23:10 the soldiers turned *b* after Eleazar,
1Kgs 1:35 When you come *b* in his train,
2:34 Benaiah, son of Jehoiada, went *b*,
2:40 search of his servants, whom he brought *b*.
5:16 Solomon sent *b* this message to Hiram:
6:34 was banded by a metal strap, front and *b*,
7: 9 to size and trimmed front and *b* with a saw,
8:34 them *b* to the land you gave their fathers.
8:48 their whole heart and soul they turn *b*
9:28 and brought *b* four hundred and twenty
10:19 throne had six steps, a *b* with a round top,
12: 5 "Come *b* to me in three days,"
12:12 day all Israel came *b* to King Rehoboam,
13: 4 withered, so that he could not draw it *b*.
13:10 did not go *b* the way he had come to Bethel.
13:16 "I cannot go *b* with you,
13:17 water here, and not to go *b* the way I came,"
13:18 word of the LORD to bring you *b* with me
13:19 So he went *b* with him,
13:20 to the prophet who had brought him *b*,

13:26 had brought him *b* from his journey said:
13:29 and brought it *b* to the city to mourn over
14: 9 but me you have cast behind your *b*.
14:17 So Jeroboam's wife started *b*;
18:37 you have brought them *b* to their senses."
19: 7 the angel of the LORD came *b* a second time,
19:15 the road *b* to the desert near Damascus,"
19:20 "Go *b*!" Elijah answered.
22:17 Let each of them go *b* home in peace.' "
22:26 "Seize Micaiah and take him *b* to Amon,
2Kgs 1: 6 *b* to the king who sent you and tell him:
2:13 went *b* and stood at the bank of the Jordan.
4: 4 Then come *b* and close the door on yourself
4:22 quickly to the man of God, and I will be *b*."
4:30 So he started to go *b* with her.
6:22 and drink, and then go *b* to their master."
6:23 them away, and they went *b* to their master.
7: 8 *B* they came into another tent,
13:21 he came *b* to life and rose to his feet.
13:25 son of Jehoahaz, took *b* from Ben-hadad,
14:20 He was brought *b* on horses and buried with
14:28 Damascus and turned *b* Hamath from Israel,
17:27 *b* one of the priests whom I deported,
19:36 broke camp, and went *b* home to Nineveh.
20: 5 "Go *b* and tell Hezekiah,
20: 9 Shall the shadow go forward or *b* ten steps?"
20:10 "Rather, let it go *b* ten steps."
1Chr 11:18 at Bethlehem, and carried it *b* to David.
13: 6 of Judah, to bring *b* the ark of God,
13:13 the ark *b* with him to the City of David,
15:28 Thus all Israel brought *b* the ark of the
19: 5 and then you may come *b* here."
21: 2 *b* to me that I may know their number."
21:12 the sword of your foes ever at your *b*;
2Chr 6:25 and bring them *b* to the land which you
6:38 with their whole soul they turn *b* to you
7:10 month he sent the people *b* to their tents,
8:18 brought *b* from there four hundred
10: 5 days," he answered them, "come *b* to me."
10:12 Jeroboam and all the people came *b* to King
18:16 Let each of them go *b* home in peace.' "
18:25 "Seize Micaiah and take him *b* to Amon,
19: 4 of Ephraim and brought them *b* to the LORD,
20:27 turned *b* toward Jerusalem celebrating the
24:11 took it *b* and returned it to its place.
25:12 also brought *b* another ten thousand alive,
25:14 *b* with him the gods of the people of Seir,
25:28 They brought him *b* on horses and buried
28:11 send *b* the captives you have carried off
34:28 They brought *b* this message to the king.
Ezr 1:11 were brought *b* from Babylon to Jerusalem.
2: 1 and who came *b* to Jerusalem and Judah,
5: 5 order be sent *b* concerning this matter.
6: 5 and brought to Babylon are to be sent *b*:
Neh 1: 9 and bring them *b* to the place which I have
2:15 the Valley Gate, by which I went *b* in.
3:36 Turn *b* their derision upon their own heads
4: 9 God had upset their plan, we all went *b*,
5: 8 we bought *b* our fellow Jews who had been
5: 8 own brothers, to have them bought *b* by us."
7: 6 and who came *b* to Jerusalem and Judah,
9:26 them in order to bring them *b* to you,
9:28 would go *b* to doing evil in your sight.
9:29 them, in order to bring them *b* to your law.
13: 6 king of Babylon, I had gone *b* to the king.
Tb 2: 2 worshiper of God, bring him *b* with you,
2: 2 son, I shall wait for you to come *b*."
2:12 When she sent *b* the goods to their owners,
2:12 the cloth and sent it *b* to the owners.
2:13 Give it *b* to its owners,
2:14 and told her to give it *b* to its owners.
5: 3 but get *b* that money from Gabael."
5: 7 young man, till I go *b* and tell my father;
5: 9 Tobiah went *b* to tell his father Tobit
5:17 way and bring you *b* to me safe and sound;
5:21 health and come *b* to us in good health.
6:13 her and bring her *b* with us to your house."
7:12 Take her and bring her *b* safely
8:11 went *b* into the house and called his wife,
8:21 you go *b* in good health to your father;
10: 7 At sunset she would go *b* home to wail and
10: 7 beg you, father, let me go *b* to my father.
10: 9 I beg you to let me go *b* to my father."
10:13 kinsman, may the Lord bring you *b* safely,
11:15 Then Tobit went *b* in,
11:15 that he had brought *b* the money;
12: 2 of all the wealth he brought *b* with me.
12: 3 He led me *b* safe and sound;
12: 3 he brought the money *b* with me:
12: 4 receive half of all that he brought *b*."
12: 5 wages half of all that you have brought *b*,
13: 6 When you turn *b* to him with all your heart,
13: 6 before him, Then He will turn *b* to you,
13: 6 "Turn *b*, you sinners!
14: 5 and bring them *b* to the land of Israel.
Jdt 5:19 they have come *b* from the Dispersion
11:14 Jerusalem to bring *b* to them authorization
16:21 *b* to Bethulia and remained on her estate.
Est 4:15 Esther sent *b* to Mordecai the response:
1Mc 1:24 all this, he went *b* to his own country,
2:68 Pay *b* the Gentiles what they deserve,
4:23 Then Judas went *b* to plunder the camp,
5:34 it was Maccabeus, they fell *b* before him,
6: 6 army and been driven *b* by the Israelites;
6:45 that they fell *b* from him on both sides.
9: 9 our lives now, and come *b* with our kinsmen,
9:15 drove *b* the right wing and pursued them as
9:16 wing saw that the right wing was driven *b*,
10: 9 and he gave them *b* to their parents.
11:72 Then he went *b* to the combat and so
12:26 spies he had sent into their camp came *b*
12:45 men to stay with you, send the rest *b* home,
12:51 to fight for their lives, they turned *b*.
13:27 monument of stones, polished front and *b*,
13:49 the country and *b* for the purchase of food;
2Mc 3:38 and you will receive him *b* well-flogged,
5: 5 *b* and the city was finally being taken,
5:18 would have been flogged and turned *b*
5:21 from the temple, and hurried *b* to Antioch.
7:23 will give you *b* both breath and life,
10:17 places, drove *b* all who manned the walls,
12: 7 intending to come *b* later and wipe out the
13:19 but he was driven *b*,
14:44 as they quickly drew *b* and left an opening,
14:46 and of spirit to give these *b* to him again.
Jb 1:21 womb, and naked shall I go *b* again.
12:15 He holds *b* the waters and there is drought;
20:25 The dart shall come out of his *b*;
26: 9 He holds *b* the appearance of the full moon
30:23 Indeed I know you will turn me *b* in death
32: 6 therefore I held *b* and was afraid to
33:23 for him and bring the man *b* to justice,
33:30 *b* his soul from the pit to the light,
34:14 If he were to take *b* his spirit to himself,
36:10 and exhorts them to turn *b* from evil.
39:22 he turns not *b* from the sword.
39:24 he holds not *b* at the sound of the trumpet,
41: 7 Rows of scales are on his *b*,
41:17 the waves of the sea fall *b*.
Ps(s) 6:11 they shall fall *b* in sudden shame.
9: 4 High, Because my enemies are turned *b*,
9:18 the nether world the wicked shall turn *b*,
35: 4 *b* and confounded who plot evil against me.
38:12 stand *b* because of my affliction;
40:15 turned *b* in disgrace who desire my ruin.
40:18 O my God, hold not *b*!
44:11 You have let us be driven *b* by our foes;
44:19 Our hearts have not shrunk *b*,
51:14 Give me *b* the joy of your salvation,
54: 7 Turn *b* the evil upon my foes;
56:10 Then do my enemies turn *b*,
68:23 "I will fetch them *b* from Bashan;
68:23 fetch them *b* from the depths of the sea,
70: 3 be turned *b* in disgrace who desire my ruin.
70: 6 O LORD, hold not *b*!
74:11 Why draw *b* your hand and keep your right
78:38 Often he turned *b* his anger and let none
78:57 *b* and were faithless like their fathers;
89:44 You have turned *b* his sharp sword and have
90: 3 You turn man *b* to dust,
106:23 the breach to turn *b* his destructive wrath.
114: 3 The sea beheld and fled; Jordan turned *b*.
114: 5 O Jordan, that you turn *b*?
126: 1 the LORD brought *b* the captives of Zion,
126: 6 to be sown, They shall come *b* rejoicing,
129: 3 Upon my *b* the plowers plowed;
129: 5 be put to shame and fall *b* that hate Zion.
Prv 1:15 them, hold *b* your foot from their path!
2:19 None who enter thereon come *b* again,
6:31 if he be caught he must pay *b* sevenfold;
10: 6 the just, but a rod for the *b* of the fool.
12:14 work of his hands comes *b* to reward him.
14: 3 the mouth of the fool is a rod for his *b*,
26: 3 the ass, and the rod for the *b* of fools.
26:27 and a stone comes *b* upon him who rolls it.
Wis 2: 1 known to have come *b* from the nether world.
15: 8 the life that was lent him is demanded *b*.
16:13 the gates of the nether world, and lead *b*.
16:14 he bring *b* the soul once it is confined.
Sir 1:20 time, and then contentment comes *b* to him.
1:21 For a while he holds *b* his words,
4:18 Then she comes *b* to bring him happiness
12:15 but if you slip, he cannot hold *b*.
17:19 But to the penitent he provides a way *b*,
20: 9 no good, and some must be paid *b* double.
20:14 He lends today, he asks it *b* tomorrow;
21:15 with scorn and casts them behind his *b*.
27:25 As a stone falls *b* on him who throws it up,
29: 2 pay *b* your neighbor when a loan falls due;
29: 6 curses and insults the borrower pays him *b*,
35:10 and he will give *b* to you sevenfold.
48: 5 a dead man *b* to life from the nether world,
48:10 *b* the hearts of fathers toward their sons,
48:13 beneath him flesh was brought *b* into life.
48:23 In his lifetime he turned *b* the sun and
51: 2 death, and kept *b* my body from the pit,
51:19 with desire for her, never turning *b*.
Is 5:25 For all this, his wrath is not turned *b*,
9:11 For all this, his wrath is not turned *b*,
9:16 For all this, his wrath is not turned *b*,
9:20 For all this, his wrath is not turned *b*,
10: 4 For all this, his wrath is not turned *b*,
14:27 who can turn it *b*?
21:12 If you will ask, ask; come *b* again."
28: 6 to those who turn *b* the battle at the gate.
37:37 broke camp and went *b* home to Nineveh.
38: 8 of Ahaz go *b* the ten steps it has advanced."
38: 8 sun came *b* the ten steps it had advanced.
38:17 When you cast behind your *b* all my sins.
42:17 turned *b* in utter shame who trust in idols;
43: 5 the east I will bring *b* your descendants,
43: 6 Hold not *b*!
43: 6 Bring *b* my sons from afar,
44:25 men *b* and make their knowledge foolish.
48: 9 the sake of my renown I hold it *b* from you,
49: 5 that Jacob may be brought *b* to him
50: 5 And I have not rebelled, have not turned *b*.
50: 6 I gave my *b* to those who beat me,
51:23 While you offered your *b* like the ground,
54: 6 The LORD calls you *b*,
54: 7 with great tenderness I will take you *b*.
55:12 depart, in peace you shall be brought *b*;
58: 7 them, and not turning your *b* on your own.
58:13 If you hold *b* your foot on the sabbath
59:13 the LORD, turning *b* from following our God,
63:15 O Lord, hold not *b*,
64:11 Can you hold *b*, O LORD, after all this?
65: 5 in their dishes, Crying out, "Hold *b*,
Jer 3: 1 man, Does the first husband come *b* to her?
4:28 repent, I have resolved, I will not turn *b*.
5:25 have turned *b* these blessings from you.
8: 4 if he goes astray, does he not turn *b*?
8: 5 cling to deceptive idols, refuse to turn *b*?
12:15 I will pity them again and bring them *b*,
15: 6 me, says the LORD, turned your *b* upon me;
16:15 *b* to the land which I gave their fathers.
18:17 I will show them my *b*,
21: 4 I will turn *b* in your hands the weapons
22:27 come *b* to the land for which they yearn.
23: 3 them and bring them *b* to their meadow;
23:22 They would have brought them *b* from evil
24: 6 their good, and bring them *b* to this land,
25: 5 Turn *b*, each of you, from your evil way
26: 3 Perhaps they will listen and turn *b*,
26:23 into Egypt to bring Uriah *b* to the king,
27:16 will be brought *b* from Babylon soon now,"
27:22 them *b* and restore them to this place.
28: 4 And I will bring *b* to this place Jeconiah,
28: 6 the exiles *b* from Babylon to this place!
29:10 my promise to bring you *b* to this place.
29:14 and bring you *b* to the place from which I
30: 3 and bring them *b* to the land which I have
31: 8 bring them *b* from the land of the north;
31:21 Turn *b*, O virgin Israel, turn back
32:37 I will bring them *b* to this place and
34:11 afterward they took *b* their male and
34:16 profaned my name by taking *b* your male
34:22 the LORD, and bring them *b* to this city.
35:15 the prophets, telling you to turn *b*,
36: 3 they will turn *b* each from his evil way,
36: 7 and will all turn *b* from their evil way;
37:20 me *b* into the house of Jonathan the scribe,
38:26 send me *b* to Jonathan's house to die there.' "
46: 5 With broken ranks They fall *b*;
48:10 cursed he who holds *b* his sword from blood.]
48:39 How he turns his *b* in shame!
50:19 But I will bring *b* Israel to her fold,
Lam 3: 3 *b* his hand again and again all the day.
5:21 Lead us *b* to you,
Bar 2:33 *b* from their stiff-necked stubbornness,
2:34 And I will bring them *b* to the land which
4:23 you *b* to me with enduring gladness and joy.
4:29 in saving you, bring you *b* enduring joy."
5: 6 but God will bring them *b* to you borne
6: 2 I will bring you *b* from there in peace.
Ez 2:10 It was covered with writing front and *b*,
11:24 me *b* to the exiles in Chaldea [in a vision,
14: 5 *b* to their senses the house of Israel,
18: 7 gives *b* the pledge received for a debt,
18:12 commits robbery, does not give *b* a pledge,
20:37 the staff and bring *b* but a small number.
20:42 when I bring you *b* to the land of Israel,
23:35 forgotten me and cast me behind your *b*,
29:14 bringing them *b* to the land of Pathros,
31:15 so that the deep waters were held *b*.
33:15 what is right and just, giving *b* pledges,
34: 4 not bring *b* the strayed nor seek the lost,
34:13 I will bring them *b* to their own country
34:16 will seek out, the strayed I will bring *b*,
36:24 lands, and bring you *b* to your own land.
37:12 and bring you *b* to the land of Israel.
37:21 all sides to bring them *b* to their land.
39:27 When I bring them *b* from among the peoples,
39:28 nations, will gather them *b* on their land,
40:13 He measured the gate from the *b* wall of
40:13 *b* wall of the cell on the opposite side:
41:12 west side was seventy cubits front to *b*;
42:12 of the way which led to the *b* wall,
44: 1 me *b* to the outer gate of the sanctuary,
47: 1 brought me *b* to the entrance of the temple,
Dn 7: 6 its *b* were four wings like those of a bird,
9:13 by turning *b* from our wickedness and
11:28 turn *b* toward his land with great riches,
13:14 but both turned *b*,
14:39 once brought Habakkuk *b* to his own place.
Hos 2: 9 say, "I will go *b* to my first husband,
2:11 I will take *b* my grain in its time,
3: 5 of Israel shall turn *b* and seek the LORD,
5:15 I will go *b* to my place until they pay for

BACK (cont.)

Am 8: 8 and settles b like the river of Egypt?
9: 5 and settles b like the river of Egypt;
Ob 1:15 deed shall come b upon your own head;
Mi 2: 4 measured out, and no one can get them b!"
Na 2: 9 but none turns b.
Zec 8: 8 bring them b to dwell within Jerusalem.
10: 6 I will bring them b,
10:10 I will bring them b from the land of Egypt,
Mt 2:12 b to their own country by another route.
2:22 of Judea, and he was afraid to go b there.
5:42 Do not turn your b on the borrower.
9: 1 the crossing, and came b to his own town.
9:18 hand on her and she will come b to life."
11: 4 b and report to John what you hear and see:
12:44 it says, 'I will go b where I came from,'
12:45 Off it goes again to bring b with it this
13:15 with their hearts, and turn b to me,
13:46 he went b and put up for sale all that he
18:26 with me and I will pay you b in full.'
18:28 'Pay b what you owe,' he demanded.
18:29 give me time and I will pay you b in full.'
18:30 put in jail until he paid b what he owed.
18:34 torturers until he paid b all that he owed.
19:21 Afterward, come b and follow me."
21: 2 Untie them and lead them b to me.
24:18 he must not turn b to pick up his cloak.
25:11 Later the other bridesmaids came b.
25:25 Here is your money b.'
25:27 return I could have had it b with interest.
26:52 "Put b your sword where it belongs.
27: 3 b to the chief priests and elders and said,
28: 2 He came to the stone, rolled it b,
Mk 2: 1 He came b to Capernaum after a lapse of
5:21 b to the other side again in the boat,
6:25 At that the girl hurried b to the king's
6:27 him to bring b the Baptizer's head.
10:10 B in the house again, the disciples
11: 2 Untie it and bring it b.
11: 3 it but he will send it b here at once.'"
11: 7 Jesus and threw their cloaks across its b,
12:23 resurrection, when they all come b to life,
13:16 he must not turn b to pick up his cloak.
14:39 b again he began to pray in the same words.
15:13 They shouted b, "Crucify him!"
16: 3 "Who will roll b the stone for us from
16: 4 found that the stone had been rolled b.
Lk 1:16 will he bring b to the Lord their God.
4:20 he gave it b to the assistant and sat down.
6:30 takes what is yours, do not demand it b.
6:38 you measure with will be measured b to you.
7:15 Then Jesus gave him b to his mother.
8:31 with him not to order them b to the abyss.
8:37 into the boat and went b across the lake.
8:39 "Go b home and recount all that God has
9:62 looking b is unfit for the reign of God."
10: 6 if not, it will come b to you.
10:35 expense I will repay you on my way b.'
11:24 it says, 'I will go b to where I came from.'
12:46 b on a day when he does not expect him,
14:26 turning his b on his father and mother,
15:24 of mine was dead and has come b to life.
15:27 calf because he has him b in good health.'
15:32 of yours was dead, and has come b to life.
17: 4 seven times a day turns b to you saying,
17:15 cured, came b praising God in a loud voice.
19: 8 anyone in the least, I pay him b fourfold."
19:13 saying to them, 'Invest this until I get b.'
19:23 my return I could get it b with interest?'
19:30 Untie it and lead it b.
23:11 robe on him and sent him b to Pilate.
23:15 Herod, who therefore has sent him b to us;
23:21 they shouted b, "Crucify him, crucify him!"
24: 2 found the stone rolled b from the tomb;
24: 8 this reminder, his words came b to them.
Jn 4: 3 left Judea and started b for Galilee again.
4:16 call your husband, and then come b here."
4:47 Jesus had come b from Judea to Galilee,
6:15 king, so he fled b to the mountain alone.
7:45 When the temple guards came b,
9: 7 off and washed, and came b able to see.
9:30 He came b at them: "Well, this is news!
10:40 Then he went b across the Jordan to the
11: 7 to his disciples, "Let us go b to Judea."
11: 8 stone you, you are going b up there again?"
11:28 this she went b and called her sister Mary.
13:12 cloak b on and reclined at table once more.
13:25 b against Jesus' chest and said to him,
14: 3 then I shall come b to take you with me,
14:18 I will come b to you.
14:28 go away for a while, and I come b to you.'
16: 5 Now that I go b to him who sent me,
16:17 not say that he is going b to the Father?"
18:11 to Peter, "Put your sword b in its sheath.
18:33 b into the praetorium and summoned Jesus.
18:40 They shouted b, "We want Barabbas,
19: 9 Going b into the praetorium,
20:10 With this, the disciples went b home.
Acts 4:18 So they called them b and made it clear
4:23 the two went b to their own people and
5:23 find them, and hurried b with the report,
8:25 they went b to Jerusalem bringing the good
9:26 When he arrived b in Jerusalem he tried to
11:26 had found him, he brought him b to Antioch.
12:22 The assembled crowd shouted b,
14:20 long he got up and went b into the town.
14:26 From there they sailed b to Antioch,
15:33 they were sent b with greetings from the
15:36 "Let us go b now and see how the brothers
18:21 "God willing, I will come b to you again."
22: 5 would arrest b to Jerusalem for punishment.
23:10 their midst and take him b to headquarters.
Rom 6:13 men who have come b from the dead to life,
8:15 spirit of slavery leading you b into fear,
9:20 Friend, who are you to answer God b?
11:10 Bow down their b forever."
11:23 their unbelief they will be grafted b on,
2Cor 5:13 and when we are brought b to our senses,
Gal 2:12 But when they arrived he drew b to avoid
4:19 and you put me b in labor pains until
2Thes 2: 7 but there is one who holds him b until
Heb 10:38 if he draws b I take no pleasure in him.
10:39 are not among those who draw b and perish,
11:15 b to the place from which they had come,
11:19 and so he received Isaac b as a symbol.
11:34 in battle, and turned b foreign invaders.
11:35 received b their dead through resurrection.
Jas 5:19 the truth, and of another bringing him b.
5:20 the person who brings a sinner b from his
Rv 4: 6 creatures covered with eyes front and b.
12: 7 the dragon and his angels fought b,
18: 6 Pay her b as she has paid others;

BACKBITING (1)

Prv 25:23 rain, and a b tongue an angry countenance.

BACKED (3)

1Mc 9:47 Bacchides, but Bacchides b away from him.
Sir 22:17 A resolve that is b by prudent
Acts 22:29 who were about to interrogate him b away.

BACKER (1)

Sir 29:15 Forget not the kindness of your b,

BACKING (1)

Jos 3:16 b up in a solid mass for a very great

BACKS (18)

Gn 9:23 took a robe, and holding it on their b,
Dt 33:11 the b of his adversaries and of his foes,
2Chr 4: 4 the sea rested on their b.
29: 6 LORD's dwelling, and turned their b on him.
Neh 9:26 they cast your law behind their b,
9:29 They turned stubborn b,
Ps(s) 66:11 you laid a heavy burden on our b.
69:24 Keep their b always feeble
Prv 19:29 the arrogant, and blows for the b of fools.
Sir 35:20 Till he breaks the b of the merciless
Is 30: 6 They carry their riches on the b of asses
Jer 2:27 They turn to me their b,
7:24 of their evil hearts and turned their b,
32:33 They turned their b to me,
Ez 8:16 with their b to the LORD's temple
Zec 7:11 b and stopped their ears so as not to hear.
2Tm 1:15 and Hermogenes, have turned their b on me.
2Pt 2:21 their b on the holy law handed on to them,

BACKSLIDERS (1)

Jas 4: 8 purify your hearts, you b.

BACKWARD (4)

Gn 9:23 b and covered their father's nakedness;
49:17 horse's heel, so that the rider tumbles b.
1Sm 4:18 Eli fell b from his chair into the gateway;
Is 28:13 So that when they walk, they stumble b,

BAD (57)

Gn 2: 9 the tree of the knowledge of good and b.
2:17 except the tree of knowledge of good and b.
3: 5 gods who know what is good and what is b."
3:22 of us, knowing what is good and what is b!
37: 2 he brought his father b reports about them.
Ex 5:21 You have brought us into b odor with
33: 4 When the people heard this b news,
Lv 27:12 in keeping with its good or b qualities,
27:14 value in keeping with its good or b points,
27:33 good ones or b ones are thus chosen,
Nm 13:19 the country in which they live good or b?
14:37 these men who had given out the b report
Dt 1:39 who as yet do not know good from b—
Jgs 9:23 God put b feelings between Abimelech and
2Sm 14:17 an angel of God, evaluating good and b.
19:36 Can I distinguish between good and b?
2Kgs 2:19 but the water is b and the land unfruitful."
1Chr 19: 6 had put themselves in b odor with David,
Jdt 8: 8 No one had a b word to say about her,
Est B: 4 the world, there is one people of b will,
1Mc 5:61 It was a b defeat for the people,
Prv 11:15 in a b way who becomes surety for another,
20:14 "Bad, b!" says the buyer;
21:27 so when they offer it with a b intention.
Eccl 9: 2 and the wicked, for the good and the b,
12:14 its hidden qualities, whether good or b.
Sir 6: 1 A b name and disgrace will you acquire:
26: 7 A b wife is a chafing yoke;
37:26 so that you allow it not what is b for you;
39:25 but for the wicked good things and b.
Is 7:15 learns to reject the b and choose the good.
7:16 learns to reject the b and choose the good,
Jer 24: 2 contained very b figs, so bad they could
24: 3 the b ones very bad, so bad they cannot
24: 8 that are bad, so b they cannot be eaten
29:17 them like rotten figs, too b to be eaten.
49:23 covered with shame, they have heard b news;
Lam 3:38 Most High, whether the thing be good or b!
Ez 16:56 Was not your sister Sodom kept in b repute
Mt 5:45 for his sun rises on the b and the good,
6:23 if your eyes are b,
7:17 fruit, while a decayed tree bears b fruit.
7:18 A sound tree cannot bear b fruit any more
21:41 "He will bring that wicked crowd to a b end
22:10 up everyone they met, b as well as good.
22:18 recognized their b faith and said to them,
Mk 4:37 It happened that a b squall blew up.
Lk 11:34 is lighted up, but when your eyesight is b,
1Cor 15:33 B company corrupts good morals."
2Cor 5:10 one may receive his recompense, good or b,
2Tm 3:13 men and charlatans will go from b to worse,
Ti 2: 8 be able to find anything b to say about us,

BADE (19)

Gn 26:31 Then Isaac b them farewell,
32:30 With that, he b him farewell.
47:10 Then Jacob b Pharaoh farewell and withdrew
49:28 as he b them farewell and gave to each of
Ex 18:27 Then Moses b farewell to his father-in-law,
Nm 4:37 together with Aaron, as the LORD b him.
4:45 together with Aaron, as the LORD b him.
Jos 2:21 say," she replied, and b them farewell.
2Sm 1: 4 "Tell me what happened," David b him.
3:21 So David b Abner farewell,
19:40 he kissed Barzillai and b him Godspeed as
1Kgs 8:66 who b the king farewell and went to their
2Kgs 4:23 But she b him good-bye,
Neh 9:15 You b them enter and occupy the land which
Jdt 5: 9 Their God b them leave their abode and
12: 1 and b them set a table for her with his
2Mc 3:35 had spared his life, he b Onias farewell,
Jb 15:25 against God and b defiance to the Almighty,
Jer 26: 8 the LORD b him speak to all the people,

BADGER (2)

Lv 11: 5 the rock b, which indeed chews the cud,
Dt 14: 7 the camel, the hare and the rock b,

BADLY (19)

Ex 5:22 "Lord, why do you treat this people so b?
21:35 ox hurts another's ox so b that it dies,
Nm 11:11 "Why do you treat your servant so b?"
1Sm 28:20 for he was b shaken by Samuel's message.
31: 4 But his armor-bearer, b frightened,
Prv 10: 9 but he whose ways are crooked will fare b.
13:20 but the companion of fools will fare b.
Sir 3:25 A stubborn man will fare b in the end,
49: 7 for they had treated him b who even in the
Jer 18: 4 he was making turned out b in his hand,
Zec 11: 8 of them, and they behaved b toward me.
12: 3 to lift it shall injure themselves b,
Mt 18:31 saw what had happened they were b shaken,
22:29 "You are b misled because you fail to
Mk 4:37 over the boat and it began to ship water b.
12:24 "You are b misled,
13:17 It will go b with pregnant and nursing
Lk 13:11 She was b stooped
21:23 at the breast will fare b in those days!

BAEAN (1)

1Mc 5: 4 remembered the malice of the sons of B,

BAFFLED (1)

Sir 43:19 the eyes, the mind is b by its steady fall.

BAG (21)

Gn 42:27 his b to give his donkey some fodder,
42:27 to see his money in the mouth of his b.
42:28 "Here it is in my b!"
43:21 was each man's money in the mouth of his b—
44: 1 put each man's money in the mouth of his b.
44: 2 youngest one's b put also my silver goblet,
44:11 lowered his b to the ground and opened it,
44:12 the goblet turned up in Benjamin's b.
Dt 25:13 not keep two differing weights in your b,
1Sm 17:40 put them in the pocket of his shepherd's b.
17:49 his hand into the b and took out a stone,
Tb 8: 2 and heart from the b which he had with him,
Jdt 10: 5 She filled a b with roasted grain,
Prv 7:20 A b of money he took with him,
Hg 1: 6 wages earned them for a b with holes in it.

Mt 10:10 no traveling *b,* no change of shirt,
Mk 6: 8 no food, no traveling *b,*
Lk 9: 3 neither walking staff nor traveling *b;*
10: 4 not carry a walking staff or traveling *b;*
22:35 without purse or traveling *b* or sandals,
22:36 the same with the traveling *b.*

BAGATHAN (3)

Est A:12 lodged at the court with *B* and Thares,
2:21 spent at the king's gate, *B* and Thares,
6: 2 in which Mordecai reported *B* and Teresh,

BAGGAGE (16)

Gn 43:11 *b* and take them down to the man as gifts:
Nm 7: 3 consisted of six *b* wagons and twelve oxen,
Jos 7:11 and have deceitfully put them in their *b.*
1Sm 10:22 LORD answered, "He is hiding among the *b.*"
17:22 of the *b* and hastened to the battle line,
25:13 while two hundred remained with the *b.*
30:24 who remains with the *b* shall be the same;
Jdt 2:17 of camels, asses, and mules for their *b;*
7: 2 not counting the *b* train or the men who
1Mc 9:35 with them their great quantity of *b.*
9:39 and suddenly saw a noisy crowd with *b;*
2Mc 12:21 the women and children, as well as the *b,*
Jer 46:19 Pack your *b* for exile,
Ez 12: 3 on, prepare your *b* as though for exile,
12: 4 You shall bring out your *b* like an exile
12: 7 my *b* as though it were that of an exile,

BAGOAS (6)

Jdt 12:11 And he said to *B,* the eunuch
12:13 So *B* left the presence of Holofernes,
12:15 the fleece *B* had furnished for her daily use
13: 1 *B* closed the tent from the outside and
13: 3 To *B* she had said this also.
14:14 *B* went in, and knocked at the entry

BAGPIPE (4)

Dn 3: 4 trumpet, flute, lyre, harp, psaltery, *b,*
3: 7 *b,* and all the other musical instruments,
3:10 trumpet, flute, lyre, harp, psaltery, *b,*
3:15 trumpet, flute, lyre, harp, psaltery, *b,*

BAGS (10)

Gn 43:12 that was put back in the mouths of your *b;*
43:18 the money put back in our *b* the first time,
43:21 at a night's encampment and opened our *b,*
43:22 not know who put the first money in our *b.*"
43:23 must have put treasures in your *b* for you.
44: 1 *b* with as much food as they can carry,
44: 8 money that we found in the mouths of our *b.*
1Sm 9: 7 There is no bread in our *b,*
2Kgs 5:23 up these silver talents in *b* and gave them,
Mi 6:11 criminal balances, *b* of false weights?

BAHURIM (9)

2Sm 3:16 who followed her weeping as far as *B.*
13:34 down the slope from the direction of *B.*
13:34 the mountainside from the direction of *B.*
16: 5 As David was approaching *B,*
17:18 in *B* who had a cistern in his courtyard.
19:17 son of Gera, the Benjaminite from *B,*
23:31 Azmaveth from *B;*
1Kgs 2: 8 Shimei, son of Gera, the Benjaminite of *B,*
1Chr 11:33 Azmaveth, from *B;*

BAIL (1)

Acts 17: 9 they released Jason and the others on *b.*

BAITING (1)

2Pt 2:18 bombast while *b* their hooks with passion,

BAKBAKKAR (1)

1Chr 9:15 the descendants of Merari; *B;* Heresh;

BAKBUK (2)

Ezr 2:51 sons of the Nephusites, sons of *B,*
Neh 7:53 sons of the Nephusites, sons of *B,*

BAKBUKIAH (3)

Neh 11:17 *B,* second in rank among his brethren;
12: 9 while *B* and Unno and their brethren
12:25 opposite the other, were Mattaniah, *B,*

BAKE (6)

Ex 16:23 You may either *b* or boil the manna,
Lv 24: 5 take fine flour and *b* it into twelve cakes,
Tb 8:19 asked his wife to *b* many loaves of bread;
Ez 4:12 For your food you must *b* barley loaves
4:15 *b* your bread on that.
46:20 sin offerings, and *b* the cereal offerings,

BAKED (10)

Ex 12:39 leavened, they *b* it into unleavened loaves.
Lv 2: 4 offering you present is *b* in an oven,
6:10 It shall not be *b* with leaven.
7: 9 every cereal offering that is *b* in an oven
23:17 an ephah of fine flour and *b* with leaven.
1Sm 28:24 she kneaded it and *b* unleavened bread.
1Kgs 17:12 lives," she answered, "I have nothing *b;*
Ps(s) 22:16 My throat is dried up like *b* clay,
Is 44:19 I *b* bread and roasted meat which I ate.
Jer 44:19 consent that we *b* for her cakes in her image

BAKER (8)

Gn 40: 1 cupbearer and *b* gave offense to their lord,
40: 5 the cupbearer and the *b* of the king of
40:16 When the chief *b* saw that Joseph had given
40:20 the chief cupbearer and the chief *b*
40:20 heads of the chief cupbearer and chief *b.*
40:22 but the chief *b* he impaled
41:10 he put me and the chief *b* in custody in
Hos 7: 4 Whose fire the *b* desists from stirring

BAKERS—BAKER'S (2)

1Sm 8:13 as ointment-makers, as cooks, and as *b.*
Jer 37:21 a loaf of bread each day from the *b'* shop

BAKERY (1)

Gn 40:17 were all kinds of *b* products for Pharaoh,

BAKING (4)

Gn 19: 3 a meal for them, *b* cakes without leaven,
Lv 26:26 ten women will need but one oven for *b*
1Chr 23:29 unleavened bread, and of the *b* and mixing,
Is 44:15 warms himself, or makes a fire for *b* bread;

BALAAM (60)

Nm 22: 5 Moab at that time, sent messengers to *B,*
22: 7 the divination fee in hand and went to *B.*
22: 8 So the princes of Moab lodged with *B.*
22: 9 Then God came to *B* and said,
22:10 *B* answered God, "Balak, son of Zippor,
22:12 But God said to *B,* "Do not go with them
22:13 *B* arose and told the princes of Balak,
22:14 with the report, *B* refused to come with us."
22:16 On coming to *B* they told him,
22:18 But *B* replied to Balak's officials,
22:20 That night God came to *B* and said to him,
22:21 So the next morning when *B* arose,
22:23 and *B* had to beat her to bring her back on
22:27 of the LORD there, she cowered under *B.*
22:28 the mouth of the ass, and she asked *B,*
22:29 willfully against me," said *B* to the ass,
22:30 But the ass said to *B,*
22:30 "No," replied *B.*
22:34 Then *B* said to the angel of the LORD,
22:35 But the angel of the LORD said to *B,*
22:35 So *B* went on with the princes of Balak.
22:36 When Balak heard that *B* was coming,
22:37 he said to *B,* "I sent an urgent summons
22:38 *B* answered him, "Well, I have come
22:39 Then *B* went with Balak,
22:40 to *B* and to the princes who were with him.
22:41 morning Balak took *B* up on Bamoth-baal,
23: 1 *B* said to Balak, "Build me seven altars,
23: 2 So he did as *B* had ordered,
23: 3 *B* then said to him, "Stand here by your
23: 7 Then *B* gave voice to his oracle:
23:11 What have you done to me?" cried Balak to *B.*
23:12 *B* replied, "Is it not what the LORD puts
23:15 *B* then said to Balak, "Stand here by
23:16 Then the LORD met *B,*
23:18 *B* gave voice to his oracle: "Be aroused,
23:25 you cannot curse them," said Balak to *B,*
23:26 But *B* answered Balak, "Did I not warn
23:27 Then Balak said to *B,* "Come, let me bring
23:28 So he took *B* to the top of Peor,
23:29 *B* then said to him, "Here build me seven
23:30 And Balak did as *B* had ordered,
24: 1 *B,* however, preceiving that the LORD
24: 3 The utterance of *B,* son of Beor,
24:10 in a blaze of anger at *B* and said to him,
24:12 *B* replied to Balak, "Did I not warn
24:15 Then *B* gave voice to his oracle:
24:15 The utterance of *B,*
24:20 seeing Amalek, *B* gave voice to his oracle:
24:25 Then *B* set out on his journey home;
31: 8 and they also executed *B,* son of Beor,
Dt 23: 5 you left Egypt, and because Moab hired *B,*
23: 6 would not listen to *B* and turned his curse
Jos 13:22 put to the sword also the soothsayer *B,*
24: 9 He summoned *B,* son of Beor, to curse you;
24:10 but I would not listen to *B.*
Neh 13: 2 and water, but they hired *B* to curse them,
Mi 6: 5 what Moab's King Balak planned, and how *B,*
2Pt 2:15 road and wander off on the path taken by *B,*
Rv 2:14 among you who follow the teaching of *B,*

BALAAM'S (5)

Nm 22:25 and since she squeezed *B* leg against it,
22:31 Then the LORD removed the veil from *B* eyes
23: 5 When he had put an utterance in *B* mouth,
31:16 they are the very ones who on *B* advice
Jude 1:11 abandoned themselves to *B* error for pay,

BALADAN (2)

2Kgs 20:12 time, when Merodach-baladan, son of *B,*
Is 39: 1 that time when Merodach-baladan, son of *B,*

BALAH (1)

Jos 19: 3 Beersheba, Shema, Moladah, Hazar-shual, *B,*

BALAK (37)

Nm 22: 2 Now *B,* son of Zippor, saw all that Israel
22: 4 And *B,* Zippor's son who was king
22:10 Balaam answered God, *B,* son of Zippor
22:13 Balaam arose and told the princes of *B,*
22:14 of Moab went back to *B* with the report,
22:15 *B* again sent princes,
22:16 to Balaam they told him, "This is what *B,*
22:18 "Even if *B* gave me his house full of
22:35 So Balaam went on with the princes of *B.*
22:36 When *B* heard that Balaam was coming,
22:39 Then Balaam went with *B,*
22:40 Here *B* slaughtered oxen and sheep,
22:41 morning *B* took Balaam up on Bamoth-baal,
23: 1 Then Balaam said to *B,* "Build me seven
23: 2 *B* said to him, "I have erected the seven
23: 5 the LORD said to him, "Go back to *B,*
23: 6 So he went back to *B,*
23: 7 From Aram has *B* brought me here,
23:11 have you done to me?" cried *B* to Balaam
23:13 Then *B* said to him, "Please come with me
23:15 Balaam then said to *B,* "Stand here by
23:16 his mouth, he said to him, "Go back to *B,*
23:17 So he went back to *B,* who was still
23:17 *B* asked him, "What did the LORD say?"
23:18 Be aroused, O *B,* and hearken; give ear
23:25 you cannot curse them," said *B* to Balaam,
23:26 But Balaam answered *B,* "Did I not warn
23:27 Then *B* said to Balaam, "Come, let me
23:30 And *B* did as Balaam had ordered,
24:10 *B* beat his palms together in a blaze of
24:12 Balaam replied to *B,* "Did I not warn
24:13 Even if *B* gave me his house full of silver
24:25 and *B* also went his way.
Jos 24: 9 Then *B,* son of Zippor, king of Moab,
Jgs 11:25 Again, are you any better than *B,*
Mi 6: 5 remember what Moab's King *B* planned,
Rv 2:14 who instructed *B* to throw a stumbling

BALAK'S (2)

Nm 22: 7 When they had given him *B* message,
22:18 But Balaam replied to *B* officials,

BALAMON (1)

Jdt 8: 3 in the field between Dothan and *B.*

BALANCE (11)

Lv 25:27 back the *b* to the one to whom he sold it,
Ps(s) 62:10 In a *b* they prove lighter,
73: 2 But, as for me, I almost lost my *b;*
Prv 16:11 *B* and scales belong to the LORD;
Wis 11:22 the whole universe is as a grain from a *b.*
Sir 6:15 is beyond price, no sum can *b* his worth.
28:25 silver and gold, so *b* and weigh your words.
Is 40:12 mountains in scales and the hills in a *b?*
Hos 12: 8 A merchant who holds a false *b,*
2Cor 7:11 ardent desire to restore the *b* of justice!
Phil 4:17 is for the ever-growing *b* in your account.

BALANCES (2)

Sir 42: 4 Of accuracy of scales and *b,*
Mi 6:11 Shall I acquit criminal *b,*

BALBAIM (1)

Jdt 7: 3 out in breadth toward Dothan as far as *B,*

BALD (10)

Lv 13:40 not unclean merely because of his *b* crown.
13:41 unclean merely because of his *b* forehead.
13:42 pink sore on his bald crown or *b* forehead,
13:43 and if the scab on the sore of the *b* spot
Jer 47: 5 Gaza is shaved *b,* Ashkelon is reduced
48:37 Every head has been made *b,*
Ez 29:18 became *b* and their shoulders were galled;
Am 8:10 all with sackcloth and make every head *b.*
Mi 1:16 Make yourself *b,* pluck out your hair,

BALDHEAD · (1)

2Kgs 2:23 up, baldhead," they shouted, "go up, *b!*"

BALDNESS (3)

Is 3:24 girdle, a rope, And for the coiffure, *b;*
Ez 7:18 all their faces and *b* on all their heads.
Mi 1:16 Let your *b* be as the eagle's,

BALDRIC (1)

1Sm 17: 6 and had a bronze scimitar slung from a *b.*

BALEFULLY (1)

1Kgs 2: 8 cursed me *b* when I was going to Mahanaim.

BALL (1)

Is 22:18 like a *b* into an open land To perish there,

BALLAD (1)

Ez 33:32 For them you are only a *b* singer,

BALM (7)

Gn 37:25 gum, *b* and resin to be taken down to Egypt.
43:11 some *b* and honey, gum and resin,
Sir 24:15 Like cinnamon, or fragrant *b*,
Jer 8:22 Is there no *b* in Gilead,
46:11 Go up to Gilead, and take *b*,
51: 8 Bring *b* for her wounds,
Ez 27:17 figs, honey, oil, and *b* for your goods.

BAMOTH (2)

Nm 21:19 from Nahaliel to *B*, from Bamoth to the cleft
21:20 Bamoth, from *B* to the cleft in the plateau

BAMOTH-BAAL (2)

Nm 22:41 next morning Balak took Balaam up on *B*,
Jos 13:17 which are on the tableland, Dibon, *B*,

BAN (28)

Gn 24:41 Then you shall be released from my *b*.
24:41 then, too, you shall be released from my *b*.'
Jos 6:17 It is under the LORD's *b*.
6:18 your greed, anything that is under the *b*;
6:18 camp of Israel this *b* and the misery of it.
6:21 They observed the *b* by putting to the
7: 1 But the Israelites violated the *b*;
7: 1 Judah, took goods that were under the *b*,
7:11 stealthily taken goods subject to the *b*,
7:12 them, it is because they are under the *b*.
7:12 from among you whoever has incurred the *b*.
7:13 You are under the *b*, O Israel.
7:13 from among you whoever has incurred the *b*.
7:15 incurred the *b* shall be destroyed by fire,
22:20 When Achan, son of Zerah, violated the *b*,
Jgs 21:11 They were told to include under the *b* all
1Sm 14:24 that day, putting the people under this *b*:
15: 3 with him and all that he has under the *b*.
15: 8 effect the *b* of destruction by the sword.
15:15 but we have carried out the *b* on the rest."
15:18 sinful Amalekites under a *b* of destruction.
15:20 and I have destroyed Amalek under the *b*.
30:17 putting them under the *b* so that none
1Chr 2: 7 trouble upon Israel by violating the *b*.
4:41 They pronounced against them the *b* that is
2Chr 32:14 *b* was able to save his people from my hand?
Is 43:28 the holy gates, put Jacob under the *b*,
Ez 44:29 is under the *b* in Israel shall be theirs.

BAND (32)

Nm 16: 5 Then he said to Korah and to all his *b*,
16: 6 take your censers [Korah and all his *b* and
16:11 that you and all your *b* are conspiring.
16:16 "You and all your *b* shall appear before
16:19 when Korah had assembled all his *b* against
16:21 Moses and Aaron, "Stand apart from this *b*,
17: 5 lest he meet the fate of Korah and his *b*.
26: 9 *b* when it rebelled against the LORD].
26:10 as a warning [Korah too and the *b* that died
27: 3 together against the LORD [in Korah's *b*,
31: 4 shall send a *b* of one thousand men to war."
Jgs 18:20 idol and went off in the midst of the *b*.
1Sm 10: 5 that city, you will meet a *b* of prophets,
10:10 there to Gibeah, a *b* of prophets met him,
13:17 One *b* took the Ophrah road toward the
19:20 But when they saw the *b* of prophets,
30:23 into our grip the *b* that came against us.
2Sm 22:30 with your aid I run against an armed *b*,
1Kgs 11:24 men about him and became leader of a *b*,
2Kgs 13:21 when suddenly they spied such a raiding *b*.
2Chr 22: 1 slain by the *b* that had come into the fort
Ps(s) 18:30 with your aid I run against an armed *b*,
Sir 16: 6 Against a sinful *b* fire is enkindled,
21: 9 A *b* of criminals is like a bundle of tow;
36:26 an armed *b* that shifts from city to city?
45:18 and the *b* of Korah in their defiance.
Is 11: 5 Justice shall be the *b* around his waist,
31: 4 With a *b* of shepherds assembled against it,
Jer 9: 1 They are all adulterers, a faithless *b*.
50: 9 a *b* of great nations from the north;
Hos 6: 9 a *b* of priests slay on the way to Shechem,
Acts 21:38 and led a *b* of four thousand cutthroats out

BANDAGE (3)

1Kgs 20:38 disguised himself with a *b* over his eyes.
20:41 He immediately removed the *b* from his eyes,
Sir 30: 7 who spoils his son will have wounds to *b*,

BANDAGED (1)

Is 1: 6 welt and gaping gash, not drained, or *b*,

BANDAGES (1)

Ez 30:21 it has not been bound up with *b* and

BANDED (3)

Ex 38:17 columns of the court were *b* with silver.
Nm 27: 3 Although he did not join those who *b*
1Kgs 6:34 each door was *b* by a metal strap,

BANDING (1)

Ex 38:28 the capitals, and for *b* them with silver.

BANDITS (3)

Ezr 8:31 us from enemies and *b* along the way.
Bar 6:56 They are safe from neither thieves nor *b*,
Hos 7: 1 thieves break in, *b* plunder abroad.

BANDS (17)

Ex 27:10 and *b* on the columns shall be of silver.
27:11 and *b* on the columns shall be of silver.
27:17 the court shall have *b* and hooks of silver,
36:38 hooks as well as their capitals and *b*,
38:10 hooks and *b* of the columns being of silver.
38:11 hooks and *b* of the columns being of silver.
38:12 hooks and *b* of the columns being of silver.
38:17 hooks and *b* of the columns were of silver;
1Sm 13:17 the camp of the Philistines in three *b*.
2Kgs 13:20 *b* of Moabites used to raid the land each
24: 2 The LORD loosed against him *b* of Chaldeans,
2Chr 26:11 army of fit soldiers divided into *b* according
Jb 38: 9 garment and thick darkness its swaddling *b*?
Jer 27: 2 Make for yourself *b* and yoke bars and put
Ez 13:18 Woe to those who sew *b* for everyone's
13:20 *b* of yours in which you entrap men's lives:
Hos 11: 4 drew them with human cords, with *b* of love;

BANEFUL (1)

Wis 7:22 agile, clear, unstained, certain, Not *b*,

BANGLES (1)

Is 3:20 bracelets, and veils; the headdresses, *b*,

BANI (13)

2Sm 23:36 *B* the Gadite; Zelek the Ammonite;
1Chr 6:31 son of Hilkiah, son of Amzi, son of *B*,
9: 4 son of Omri, son of Imri, son of *B*,
Ezr 2:10 sons of *B*, six hundred and forty-two;
8:10 the sons of *B*, Shelomith, son of Josiphiah,
10:29 of the sons of *B*: Meshullam, Malluch,
Neh 3:17 Rehum, son of *B*.
8: 7 [The Levites Jeshua, *B*, Sherebiah, Jamin,
9: 4 Kadmiel, Shebaniah, Bunni, Sherebiah, *B*,
9: 5 *The Levites Jeshua, Kadmiel, *B*,
10:14 Zaccur, Sherebiah, Shebaniah, Hodiah, *B*,
10:15 Parosh, Pahath-moab, Elam, Zattu, *B*,
11:22 Levites in Jerusalem was Uzzi, son of *B*,

BANISH (11)

2Sm 14:14 take thought how not to *b* anyone from him.
Ps(s) 109:15 till he *b* the memory of these parents from
Wis 17: 8 For they who undertook to *b* fears and
Sir 8:19 heart to no man, and *b* not your happiness.
Jer 8: 3 in any of the places to which I *b* them,
15:15 Because of your long-suffering *b* me not;
27:10 to make me *b* you so that you will perish.
27:15 my name, with the result that I must *b* you,
29:18 all the nations among which I will *b* them.
32:37 in anger, wrath, and great rage I *b* them;
Zec 9:10 He shall *b* the chariot from Ephraim,

BANISHED (13)

Gn 3:23 therefore *b* him from the garden of Eden,
4:14 Since you have now *b* me from the soil,
2Sm 14:13 for not bringing back his own *b* son.
2Mc 14:14 from Judea, who would have *b* Judas,
Jb 18:18 into darkness, and *b* out of the world.
30: 5 They were *b* from among men,
Jer 7:27 the word itself is *b* from their speech.
13:19 All Judah is *b* in universal exile,
16:15 all the countries to which he had *b* them."
23: 8 from all the lands to which I *b* them;
29:14 and all the places to which I have *b* you,
Jon 2: 5 Then I said, "I am *b* from your sight!
Zec 9:10 The warrior's bow shall be *b*,

BANISHES (1)

Sir 31: 2 Concern for one's livelihood *b* slumber;

BANISHING (1)

1Kgs 15:12 *b* the temple prostitutes from the land and

BANISHMENT (1)

1Chr 12: 1 while he was still under *b* from Saul,

BANK (20)

Gn 41: 3 on the *b* of the Nile beside the others,
41:17 dream, I was standing on the *b* of the Nile,
Ex 2: 3 placed it among the reeds on the river *b*.
2: 5 while her maids walked along the river *b*.
7:15 go and present yourself by the river *b*,
Jos 3:13 down from upstream will halt in a solid *b*."
12: 2 Aroer, which is on the *b* of the Wadi Arnon,
13: 9 from Aroer on the *b* of the Wadi Arnon and
13:16 from Aroer, on the *b* of the Wadi Arnon,
13:23 of the Reubenites was the *b* of the Jordan.
13:27 with the *b* of the Jordan to the
2Kgs 2:13 went back and stood at the *b* of the Jordan.
Jb 40:22 all about him are the poplars on the *b*.
Is 19: 7 away, and bulrushes on the *b* of the Nile;
Jer 46: 6 There in the north, on the Euphrates' *b*,
Ez 47: 6 Then he brought me to the *b* of the river,
47: 7 Along the *b* of the river I saw very many
Dn 10: 4 month I was on the *b* of the great river,
12: 5 one standing on either *b* of the river.
Acts 16:13 the city gate to the *b* of the river,

BANKED (1)

Jb 37:16 Do you know how the clouds are *b*,

BANKERS (1)

Mt 25:27 reason to deposit my money with the *b*,

BANKS (12)

Nm 13:29 along the seacoast and the *b* of the Jordan."
Dt 3:16 including the wadi bed and its *b*—
3:17 Arbah with the Jordan and its eastern *b*
Jos 3:15 *b* during the entire season of the harvest,
4:18 course and as before overflowed all its *b*.
Jgs 11:26 and all the cities on the *b* of the Arnon?
1Chr 12:16 overflowing both its *b* in the first month,
1Mc 9:43 to the *b* of the Jordan with a large force.
Sir 50: 8 like a lily on the *b* of a stream;
Is 8: 7 all its channels, and overflow all its *b*;
Ez 47:12 Along both *b* of the river,
Rv 9:14 up on the *b* of the great river Euphrates!"

BANNED (4)

Gn 3:14 you shall be *b* from all the animals and
4:11 Therefore you shall be *b* from the soil
1Sm 15:21 and oxen, the best of what had been *b*,
Ez 28:16 Then I *b* you from the mountain of God;

BANNER (3)

Ex 17:16 he said, "The LORD takes in hand his *b*;
Ps(s) 60: 6 have raised for those who fear you a *b*
Ez 27: 7 became your sail [to serve you as a *b*.

BANNERED (2)

Sg 6: 4 Jerusalem, as awe-inspiring as *b* troops,
6:10 as the sun, as awe-inspiring as *b* troops?

BANQUET (35)

Gn 40:20 when he gave a *b* to all his staff,
Jgs 14:10 to the woman, and Samson gave a *b* there,
1Sm 16: 5 yourselves and join me today for the *b*."
16:11 the sacrificial *b* until he arrives here."
2Sm 13:27 Absalom prepared a *b* fit for royalty.
1Kgs 1:41 him heard it, just as they ended their *b*.
3:15 and gave a *b* for all his servants.
10: 5 and garb of his waiters, his *b* service,
Jdt 6:21 his home, where he gave a *b* for the elders.
12:10 Holofernes gave a *b* for his servants alone,
13: 1 they were all tired from the prolonged *b*.
Est C:28 nor have I graced the *b* of the king or
5: 4 today with Haman to a *b* I have prepared."
5: 5 with Haman to the *b* Esther had prepared.
5: 8 to a *b* which I shall prepare for you;
5:12 no one but me to the *b* with the king;
5:14 go to the *b* with the king in good cheer."
6:14 Haman off to the *b* Esther had prepared.
7: 1 of Haman went to the *b* with Queen Esther.
7: 7 The king left the *b* in anger and went into
7: 8 the garden of the palace to the *b* hall,
1Mc 16:15 While serving them a sumptuous *b*,
16:16 in hand, rushed upon Simon in the *b* hall,
2Mc 2:27 preparation of a festive *b* is no light matter
Ps(s) 63: 6 riches of a *b* shall my soul be satisfied,
Sg 1:12 *b* my nard gives forth its fragrance.
2: 4 the *b* hall and his emblem over me is love.
Sir 49: 1 like honey to the taste, like music at a *b*.
Bar 6:31 their gods as others do at a funeral *b*.
Dn 5: 1 gave a great *b* for a thousand of his lords,
5:10 his lords, she entered the *b* hall and said,
Mt 8:11 the *b* in the kingdom of God with Abraham,
22: 2 to a king who gave a wedding *b* for his son.
22: 8 'The *b* is ready, but those who were invited
Jn 12: 2 gave him a *b*, at which Martha served.

BANQUETERS (1)

Mt 22:10 This filled the wedding hall with *b*.

BANQUETING (1)

Est 8:17 exultation, *b* and feasting for the Jews.

BANQUETS (5)

Sir 29:22 roof than sumptuous *b* among strangers.
Mt 23: 6 at *b* and the front seats in synagogues,
Mk 12:39 the synagogues, and places of honor at *b*.
Lk 20:46 in synagogues, and places of honor at *b*.

Jude 1:12 These men are blotches on your Christian *b.*

BAPTISM (21)

Mt 21:25 What was the origin of John's *b?*
Mk 1: 4 proclaiming a *b* of repentance which led to
11:30 *b* of divine origin or merely from men?"
16:16 believes in it and accepts *b* will be saved;
Lk 3: 3 of the Jordan proclaiming a *b* of repentance
7:30 his *b* defeated God's plan in their regard.
12:50 I have a *b* to receive.
20: 4 the *b* of John come from God or from men?"
Acts 1:22 from the *b* of John until the day he was
8:12 Christ, men and women alike accepted *b.*
10:37 in Galilee with the *b* John preached;
13:24 by proclaiming a *b* of repentance to all
18:25 Jesus, although he knew only of John's *b.*
19: 3 They replied, "With the *b* of John."
19: 4 "John's *b* was a baptism of repentance.
Rom 6: 4 *b* into his death we were buried with him,
Eph 4: 5 There is one Lord, one faith, one *b;*
Col 2:12 In *b* you were not only buried with him but
Ti 3: 5 He saved us through *b* of new birth and
1Pt 3:21 This *b* is no removal of physical stain,

BAPTISMAL (2)

Lk 7:29 from John the *b* bath he administered.
1Pt 3:21 *b* bath which corresponds to this exactly.

BAPTISMS (1)

Heb 6: 2 instruction about *b* and laying-on of hands,

BAPTIZE (10)

Mt 3:11 I *b* you in water for the sake of reform,
3:11 who will *b* you in the Holy Spirit and fire.
28:19 *B* them in the name of the Father,
Mk 1: 8 he will *b* you in the Holy Spirit."
Lk 3:16 will *b* you in the Holy Spirit and in fire.
Jn 1:25 nor Elijah, nor the Prophet, why do you *b?*"
1:26 "I *b* with water.
1:33 one who sent me to *b* with water told me,
1:33 it is he who is to *b* with the Holy Spirit.'
1Cor 1:17 For Christ did not send me to *b,*

BAPTIZED (45)

Mt 3: 6 They were being *b* by him in the Jordan
3:13 before John at the Jordan to be *b* by him.
3:14 with the protest, "I should be *b* by you,
3:16 After Jesus was *b,* he came directly out of
Mk 1: 5 They were being *b* by him in the Jordan
1: 8 I have *b* you in water;
1: 9 in Galilee and was *b* in the Jordan by John.
10:38 or be *b* in the same bath of pain as I?"
Lk 3: 7 to the crowds that came out to be *b* by him:
3:12 Tax collectors also came to be *b,*
3:21 When all the people were *b,*
3:21 was at prayer after likewise being *b,*
Jn 3:23 plentiful, and people kept coming to be *b.*
4: 2 however, it was not Jesus himself who *b,*
Acts 1: 5 John *b* with water, but within a few days
1: 5 days you will be *b* with the Holy Spirit."
2:38 "You must reform and be *b,*
2:41 Those who accepted his message were *b;*
8:13 He was *b* like the rest and became a
8:16 only been *b* in the name of the Lord Jesus.
8:37 What is to keep me from being *b?*"
8:38 into the water with the eunuch and *b* him.
9:18 He got up and was *b,*
10:47 even as we have, from being *b* with water?"
10:48 that they be *b* in the name of Jesus Christ.
11:16 'John *b* with water but you will be baptized
16:15 After she and her household had been *b,*
16:33 then he and his whole household were *b.*
18: 8 too, who heard Paul believed and were *b.*
19: 3 "Well, how were you *b?*"
19: 5 they were *b* in the name of the Lord Jesus.
22:16 Be *b* at once and wash away your sins as
Rom 6: 3 were *b* into Christ Jesus were baptized
1Cor 1:13 Was it in Paul's name that you were *b?*
1:14 I *b* none of you except Crispus and Gaius,
1:15 who can say that you were *b* in my name.
1:16 Oh, and I *b* the household of Stephanas.
1:16 I am not aware of having *b* anyone else.
10: 2 and the sea all of them were *b* into Moses.
12:13 Greek, slave or free, were *b* into one body.
15:29 have themselves *b* on behalf of the dead?
15:29 is not a reality, why be *b* on their behalf?
Gal 3:27 All of you who have been *b* into Christ

BAPTIZER (14)

Mt 3: 1 When John the *B* made his appearance as a
11:11 man born of woman greater than John the *B.*
14: 2 his courtiers, "This man is John the *B*—
14: 8 me the head of John the *B* on a platter."
16:14 They replied, "Some say John the *B,*
17:13 had been speaking to them about John the *B.*
Mk 1: 4 was that John the *B* appeared in the desert,
6:14 "John the *B* has been raised from the dead;
6:24 mother answered, "The head of John the *B.*"
6:25 once, the head of John the *B* on a platter."
8:28 They replied, "Some, John the *B,*
Lk 7:20 the *B* sends us to you with this question:
7:33 I mean that John the *B* came neither eating
9:19 "John the *B,*"

BAPTIZER'S (2)

Mt 11:12 From John the *B* time until now the kingdom
Mk 6:27 ordering him to bring back the *B* head.

BAPTIZING (8)

Lk 3:16 "I am *b* you in water,
Jn 1:28 across the Jordan, where John was *b.*
1:31 though the very reason I came *b* with water
3:22 and he spent some time with them there *b.*
3:23 John too was *b* at Aenon near Salim where
3:26 is *b* now,
4: 1 and *b* more disciples than John (in fact,
10:40 to the place where John had been *b* earlier,

BAR (10)

Ex 26:28 The center *b,* at the middle of the boards
36:33 The center *b,* at the middle of the boards
Jos 7:21 and a *b* of gold fifty shekels in weight;
7:24 the silver, the mantle, and the *b* of gold,
Jgs 16: 3 gateposts, and tore them loose, *b* and all.
2Sm 13:17 away from me, and *b* the door after her."
Neh 7: 3 shining they shall shut and *b* the doors.
Jb 38:10 for it and fastened the *b* of its door,
Am 1: 5 I will break the *b* of Damascus,
Acts 24: 2 Following Paul's summons to the *b,*

BAR-JESUS (1)

Acts 13: 6 magician named *B* who posed as a prophet.

BARABBAS (12)

Mt 27:16 at the time a notorious prisoner named *B.*
27:17 for you, *B* or Jesus the so-called Messiah?"
27:20 ask for *B* and have Jesus put to death.
27:21 wish me to release for you?" they said, "*B.*"
27:26 At that, he released *B* to them.
Mk 15: 7 There was a prisoner named *B* jailed along
15:11 the crowd to have him release *B* instead.
15:15 to satisfy the crowd, released *B* to them;
Lk 23:18 "Away with this man; release *B* for us!"
23:19 This *B* had been thrown in prison for
Jn 18:40 They shouted back, "We want *B,*
18:40 *B* was an insurrectionist.)

BARACHEL (2)

Jb 32: 2 the anger of Elihu, son of *B* the Buzite,
32: 6 So Elihu, son of *B* the Buzite,

BARACHIAH (1)

Mt 23:35 Abel to the blood of Zechariah son of *B,*

BARAK (15)

Jgs 4: 6 She sent and summoned *B,*
4: 8 *B* answered her, "If you come with me,
4: 9 joined *B* and journeyed with him to Kedesh.
4:10 *B* summoned Zebulun and Naphtali to Kedesh,
4:12 It was reported to Sisera that *B,*
4:14 Deborah then said to *B,*
4:14 So *B* went down Mount Tabor,
4:15 and all his forces to rout before *B.*
4:16 *B,* however, pursued the chariots
4:22 Then when *B* came in pursuit of Sisera,
5: 1 On that day Deborah [and *B,*
5:12 arise, *B,* make despoilers your spoil,
5:15 *B,* too, was in the valley,
1Sm 12:11 *B,* Jephthah, and Samson, he delivered
Heb 11:32 I have no time to tell of Gideon, *B,*

BARBARIAN (2)

2Mc 2:21 the whole land, put to flight the *b* hordes,
15: 2 them in that way, like a savage *b,*

BARBAROUS (6)

2Mc 9: 6 the bowels of others with many *b* torments.
10: 4 them over to blasphemous and *b* Gentiles.
12: 5 *b* deed perpetrated against his countrymen,
Ez 3: 5 speech and *b* language am I sending you,
3: 6 [with difficult speech and *b* language]
28: 7 you foreigners, the most *b* of nations.

BARBED (1)

Dt 28:37 reproach and *b* scorn from all the nations

BARBER'S (1)

Ez 5: 1 a sharp sword and use it like a *b* razor,

BARBS (2)

Nm 33:55 as *b* in your eyes and thorns in your sides,
Jb 40:31 Can you fill his hide with *b,*

BARE (37)

Lv 10: 6 not *b* your heads or tear your garments,
13:45 keep his garments rent and his head *b,*
19:10 you shall not pick your vineyard *b,*
20:18 laid *b* the flowing fountain of her blood.
21: 5 shall not make *b* the crown of the head,
21:10 shall not *b* his head or rend his garments,
Nm 24: 8 like grass, their bones he shall strip *b.*
1Sm 19:22 of the threshing floor on the *b* hilltop,
2Sm 22:16 the foundations of the earth were laid *b,*
1Kgs 21:27 and put on sackcloth over his *b* flesh.
2Kgs 9:13 spread it under Jehu on the *b* steps,
Ps(s) 18:16 the foundations of the world were laid *b,*
142: 3 before him I lay *b* my distress.
Sir 19: 1 the little he has will be stripped *b.*
Is 3:17 scabs, and the LORD shall *b* their heads.
13: 2 Upon the *b* mountains set up a signal;
32:11 Strip yourselves *b,*
33: 9 steppe, Bashan and Carmel are stripped *b.*
41:18 I will open up rivers on the *b* heights,
47: 2 Strip off your train, *b* your legs,
49: 9 on every *b* height shall their pastures be.
Jer 14: 6 The wild asses stand on the *b* heights,
Lam 2:14 They did not lay *b* your guilt,
4: 3 *b* their breasts and suckle their young;
4:22 he will punish, he will lay *b* your sins.
Ez 13:14 it to the ground, laying *b* its foundations.
21:29 with your crimes laid *b* and your
24: 7 she poured it on the *b* rock;
24: 8 vengeance, she put her blood on the *b* rock,
26: 4 the ground from her and leave her a *b* rock;
26:14 I will make you a *b* rock;
Hos 2:12 *b* her shame before the eyes of her lovers,
Mi 1: 6 her stones, and lay *b* her foundations.
Hb 3:13 wicked, you lay *b* their bases at the neck.
Lk 2:35 the thoughts of many hearts may be laid *b.*"
1Cor 14:25 and the secret of his heart will be laid *b.*
Heb 4:13 all lies *b* and exposed to the eyes of him

BARED (3)

Is 52:10 The LORD has *b* his holy arm in the sight
Ez 4: 7 with *b* arm you shall prophesy against it.
Hb 3: 9 *B* and ready is your bow,

BAREFOOT (6)

2Sm 15:30 His head was covered, and he was walking *b.*
Jb 12:17 He sends counselors away *b,*
Is 20: 2 This he did, walking naked and *b.*
20: 3 Isaiah has gone naked and *b* for three years
20: 4 from Ethiopia, young and old, naked and *b,*
Mi 1: 8 reason I lament and wail, I go *b* and naked;

BARELY (4)

Gn 40:10 It had *b* budded when its blossoms came out,
2Kgs 4:42 twenty *b* loaves made from the first fruits,
Sir 29: 6 If the lender is able to recover *b* half,
Rom 5: 7 though it is *b* possible that for a good

BARES (1)

Sir 22:19 he who pierces the heart *b* its feelings.

BARGAIN (2)

Jb 40:30 Will the traders *b* for him?
Hos 8:10 Even though they *b* with the nations,

BARGAINED (1)

Hos 8: 9 Ephraim *b* for lovers.

BARGAINING (2)

Sir 42: 5 little, or of *b* in dealing with a merchant;
Dn 2: 8 know for certain that you are *b* for time,

BARIAH (1)

1Chr 3:22 Shecaniah were Shemiah, Hattush, Igal, *B,*

BARK (4)

Gn 30:37 the *b* down to the white core of the shoots.
Wis 13:11 tree and skillfully scrape off all its *b,*
Is 56:10 They are all dumb dogs, they cannot *b;*
Jl 1: 7 He has stripped it, sheared off its *b;*

BARKOS (2)

Ezr 2:53 sons of Mehida, sons of Harsha, sons of *B,*
Neh 7:55 sons of Mehida, sons of Harsha, sons of *B,*

BARLEY (36)

Ex 9:31 *b* were ruined, because the barley was
Lv 27:16 the acreage sown with a homer of *b* seed
Nm 5:15 for her a tenth of an ephah of *b* meal.
Dt 8: 8 hills and valleys, a land of wheat and *b,*
Jgs 7:13 "that a round loaf of *b* bread was rolling
Ru 1:22 at the beginning of the *b* harvest.
2:17 gleaned it came to about an ephah of *b,*
2:23 until the end of the *b* and wheat harvests.
3: 2 will be winnowing *b* at the threshing floor.
3:15 did so, he poured out six measures of *b,*
3:17 "He gave me these six measures of *b*
2Sm 14:30 field that borders mine, on which he has *b.*
17:28 and earthenware, as well as wheat, *b,*
21: 9 that is, at the beginning of the *b* harvest.
1Kgs 5: 8 quota of *b* and straw to the required place.
2Kgs 7: 1 a shekel, and two seahs of *b* for a shekel,

BARLEY (cont.)

7:16 a shekel and two seahs of *b* for a shekel,
7:18 "Two seahs of *b* will sell for a shekel,
1Chr 11:13 The plow-land was fully planted with *b*,
2Chr 2: 9 kors of wheat, twenty thousand kors of *b*,
2:14 my lord send to his servants the wheat, *b*,
27: 5 kors of wheat and ten thousand of *b*.
Jdt 8: 2 had died at the time of the *b* harvest.
Jb 31:40 of wheat and noxious weeds instead of *b*!
Is 28:25 gith and sow cumin, Put in wheat and *b*,
Jer 41: 8 wheat and *b*, oil and honey."
Ez 4: 9 Again, take wheat and *b*,
4:12 For your food you must bake *b* loaves over
13:19 with handfuls of *b* and crumbs of bread,
45:13 one sixth of an ephah from each homer of *b*.
Hos 3: 2 of silver and a homer and a lethech of *b*.
Jl 1:11 Over the wheat and the *b*,
Jn 6: 9 five *b* loaves and a couple of dried fish,
6:13 who had been fed with the five *b* loaves.
Rv 6: 6 of wheat and the same for three of *b*!

BARN (5)

Lv 11:18 the cormorant, the screech owl, the *b* owl,
Mt 3:12 floor and gather his grain into the *b*,
13:30 to burn, then gather the wheat into my *b*.'"
Lk 3:17 floor and gather the wheat into his *b*;
12:24 not reap, they have neither cellar nor *b*—

BARNABAS (31)

Acts 4:36 name *B* (meaning "son of encouragement").
9:27 Then *B* took him in charge and introduced
11:22 resulting in *B*' being sent to Antioch.
11:25 Then *B* went off to Tarsus to look for Saul;
11:30 the presbyters in the care of *B* and Saul.
12:25 *B* and Saul returned to Jerusalem upon
13: 1 *B*, Symeon known as Niger,
13: 2 "Set apart *B* and Saul for me to do the
13: 7 a man of intelligence who had summoned *B*
13:43 Jewish converts followed Paul and *B*,
13:46 Paul and *B* spoke out fearlessly,
13:50 a persecution started against Paul and *B*.
14: 3 Paul and *B* spent considerable time there
14: 6 When Paul and *B* learned of this,
14:12 They named *B* Zeus;
14:14 When the apostles *B* and Paul heard of this,
14:20 The next day he left with *B* for Derbe.
15: 2 controversy between them and Paul and *B*.
15: 2 Finally it was decided that Paul, *B*,
15:12 They listened to *B* and Paul as the two
15:22 and sent to Antioch along with Paul and *B*.
15:25 to you, along with our beloved *B* and Paul,
15:35 Paul and *B* continued in Antioch,
15:36 After a certain time Paul said to *B*,
15:37 *B* wanted to take along John, called Mark.
15:39 *B* took Mark along with him and sailed for
1Cor 9: 6 and *B* who are forced to work for a living?
Gal 2: 1 years, I went up to Jerusalem again with *B*,
2: 9 gave *B* and me the handclasp of fellowship,
2:13 even *B* was swept away by their pretense.
Col 4:10 So does Mark, the cousin of *B*.

BARNS (5)

Dt 28: 8 on your *b* and on all your undertakings,
2Chr 32:28 and *b* for the various kinds of cattle and
Prv 3:10 Then will your *b* be filled with grain,
Jl 1:17 are destroyed, The *b* are broken down,
Mt 6:26 sow or reap, they gather nothing into *b*;

BARRACKS (1)

Neh 3:16 as far as the artificial pool and the *b*.

BARRED (6)

1Sm 15: 2 *b* his way as he was coming up from Egypt.
2Sm 13:18 put her out and *b* the door after her,
1Kgs 4:13 walled cities with gates *b* with bronze;
Jb 19: 8 He has *b* my way and I cannot pass;
Sir 28:24 with thorns, set *b* doors over your mouth;
Mt 25:10 Then the door was *b*.

BARRELS (1)

Dn 14: 3 they provided for it six *b* of fine flour,

BARREN (23)

Gn 11:30 Sarai was *b*; she had no child.
29:31 made her fruitful, while Rachel remained *b*.
Ex 23:26 woman in your land will be *b* or miscarry;
Nm 13:20 Is the soil fertile or *b*, wooded or clear?
23: 3 He went out on the *b* height,
Dt 7:14 be childless nor shall your livestock be *b*.
Jgs 13: 2 His wife was *b* and had borne no children.
13: 3 you are *b* and have had no children,
1Sm 1: 5 loved her, though the LORD had made her *b*.
1: 6 to her that the LORD had left her *b*.
2: 5 The *b* wife bears seven sons,
23:14 desert, or in the *b* hill country near Ziph.
Jb 3: 7 May that night be *b*;
Ps(s) 113: 9 *b* wife as the joyful mother of children.
Prv 30:16 The nether world, and the *b* womb;
Sg 4: 2 big with twins, none of them thin and *b*.
6: 6 big with twins, none of them thin and *b*.
Is 49:21 I was bereft and *b* [exiled and repudiated];
54: 1 a glad cry, you *b* one who did not bear,
Jer 17: 6 He is like a *b* bush in the desert that
Mal 3:11 And the vine in the field will not be *b*,
Jn 15: 2 He prunes away every *b* branch,
Gal 4:27 "Rejoice, you *b* one who bears no children;

BARRENS (1)

1Sm 23:15 while he was at Horesh in the *b* near Ziph,

BARRICADE (3)

1Sm 17:20 reached the *b* of the camp just as the army,
26: 5 Saul's were within the *b*,
26: 7 and found Saul lying asleep within the *b*,

BARRIER (2)

1Mc 12:36 a high *b* between the citadel and the city,
Eph 2:14 down the *b* of hostility that kept us apart.

BARRIERS (1)

Jb 12:21 He breaks down the *b* of the streams and

BARS (37)

Ex 26:26 Also make *b* of acacia wood:
26:29 gold rings on them as holders for the *b*,
35:11 covering, its clasps, its boards, its *b*,
36:31 *B* of acacia wood were also made,
36:34 were made on them as holders for the *b*,
39:33 the clasps, the boards, the *b*,
40:18 pedestals, set up its boards, put in its *b*,
Nm 3:36 to the boards of the Dwelling, its *b*,
4:31 the boards of the Dwelling with its *b*,
Dt 3: 5 fortified with high walls and gates and *b*.
1Sm 23: 7 for he has entered a city with gates and *b*."
2Chr 8: 5 fortified cities with walls, gates and *b*;
14: 6 them with walls, towers, gates and *b*.
Neh 3: 1 set up its doors, its bolts, and its *b*,
3: 3 and set up its doors, its bolts, and its *b*.
3: 6 and set up its doors, its bolts, and its *b*.
3:13 and set up its doors, its bolts, and its *b*.
3:14 and set up its doors, its bolts, and its *b*.
3:15 and set up its doors, its bolts, and its *b*.
1Mc 9:50 Tephon, with high walls and gates and *b*.
12:38 by providing them with gates and *b*.
13:33 towers, thick walls, and gates with *b*,
Ps(s) 68:31 them prostrate themselves with *b* of silver;
107:16 the gates of brass and burst the *b* of iron.
147:13 For has strengthened the *b* of your gates;
Prv 18:19 and a friend is like the *b* of a castle.
Sir 49:13 shattered defenses, and set up gates and *b*.
Is 43:14 I will lower all the *b*,
45: 2 I will shatter, and iron *b* I will snap.
Jer 27: 2 yoke *b* and put them over your shoulders.
49:31 says the LORD, That has no gates or *b*,
51:30 Burned are their homes, and broken their *b*.
Lam 2: 9 he has removed and broken her *b*.
Bar 6:17 their houses with gates and *b* and bolts,
Ez 38:11 without walls, having neither *b* nor gates,
Jon 2: 7 the *b* of the nether world were closing
Na 3:13 are open wide, fire has consumed their *b*.

BARSABBAS (2)

Acts 1:23 that they nominated two, Joseph (called *B*,
15:22 men of the community, Judas, known as *B*,

BARTER (2)

Jb 6:27 the orphan, and would *b* away your friend!
Sir 7:18 *B* not a friend for money,

BARTERING (1)

Jb 15:31 for vain shall be his *b*.

BARTHOLOMEW (4)

Mt 10: 3 Philip and *B*, Thomas and Matthew
Mk 3:18 Andrew, Philip, *B*, Matthew, Thomas,
Lk 6:14 his brother, James and John, Philip and *B*,
Acts 1:13 Philip and Thomas, *B* and Matthew;

BARTIMAEUS (1)

Mk 10:46 there was a blind beggar *B* ("son of

BARUCH (26)

Neh 3:20 After him, *B*, son of Zabbai,
10: 7 Meremoth, Obadiah, Daniel, Ginnethon, *B*,
11: 5 Maaseiah, son of *B*, son of Colhozeh,
Jer 32:12 This deed of purchase I gave to *B*,
32:13 In their presence I gave *B* this charge:
32:16 After giving the deed of purchase to *B*,
36: 4 So Jeremiah called *B*, son of Neriah
36: 5 Then Jeremiah charged *B*:
36: 8 *B*, son of Neriah,
36:10 that *B* publicly read the words of Jeremiah
36:13 he had heard *B* read publicly from his book.
36:14 son of Cushi, to *B* with the order:
36:14 Scroll in hand, *B*, son of Neriah,
36:15 *B* read it to them,
36:17 Then they asked *B*: "Tell us, please,
36:18 all these words to me," *B* answered them,
36:19 At this the princes said to *B*,
36:26 Shelemiah, son of Abdeel, to arrest *B*,
36:27 with the text Jeremiah had dictated to *B*:
36:32 scroll, and gave it to his secretary, *B*,
43: 3 It is *B*, son of Neriah,
43: 6 also Jeremiah, the prophet, and *B*,
45: 1 that the prophet Jeremiah gave to *B*,
45: 2 says the LORD, God of Israel, to you, *B*,
Bar 1: 1 these are the words of the scroll which *B*,
1: 3 And *B* read the words of this scroll for

BARZILLAI (12)

2Sm 17:27 Machir, son of Ammiel from Lodebar, and *B*,
19:32 *B* the Gileadite also came down from
19:33 It was *B*, a very old man of eighty
19:34 The king said to *B*, "Cross over with me
19:35 But *B* answered the king: "How much longer
19:40 he kissed *B* and bade him Godspeed as he
21: 8 borne to Adriel, son of *B* the Meholathite,
1Kgs 2: 7 be kind to the sons of *B* the Gileadite,
Ezr 2:61 sons of *B* (he had married one of the
2:61 (he had married one of the daughters of *B*
Neh 7:63 sons of *B* (he had married one of the
7:63 one of the daughters of *B* the Gileadite

BASE (36)

Ex 19:12 go up the mountain, or even to touch its *b*.
29:12 you shall pour out at the *b* of the altar.
30:18 shall make a bronze laver with a bronze *b*.
30:28 appurtenances, and the laver with its *b*.
31: 9 its appurtenances, the laver with its *b*,
32:19 and broke them on the *b* of the mountain.
35:16 the laver, with its *b*;
38: 8 The bronze laver, with its bronze *b*,
39:39 its appurtenances, the laver with its *b*,
40:11 Likewise, anoint the laver with its *b*,
Lv 4: 7 blood he shall pour out at the *b* of the altar
4:18 blood he shall pour out at the *b* of the altar
4:25 he shall pour out at the *b* of this altar.
4:30 he shall pour out at the *b* of the altar.
4:34 he shall pour out at the *b* of the altar.
5: 9 be squeezed out against the *b* of the altar.
8:11 appurtenances, and the laver, with its *b*,
8:15 the blood at its *b* when he consecrated it.
9: 9 blood he poured out at the *b* of the altar.
21:15 he will have *b* off-spring among his people.
2Kgs 18:19 On what do you *b* this confidence of yours?
Jdt 1: 3 with a thickness of sixty cubits at the *b*.
7:12 that flows out at the *b* of the mountain,
Ps(s) 101: 3 I will not set before my eyes any *b* thing.
Eccl 8: 3 do not join in with a *b* plot,
Is 3: 5 the elder, and the *b* toward the honorable.
29: 4 and from the *b* dust your words shall come.
36: 4 'On what do you *b* this confidence of yours?
Jer 2:36 *b* you have become in changing your course!
Bar 2:19 do we *b* our plea for mercy in your sight,
Ez 41:22 corners, and its *b* and sides were of wood.
43:13 *b* was one cubit high and one cubit deep,
43:14 from its *b* at the bottom up to the lower
43:17 And there was a *b* of one cubit all around.
Mal 2: 9 contemptible and *b* before all the people,
Rv 6:14 and island was uprooted from its *b*.

BASEBORN (1)

Zec 9: 6 inhabited, and the *b* shall occupy Ashdod.

BASED (11)

Gn 49:13 ships], and his flank shall be *b* on Sidon.
Sir 22:18 Neither can a timid resolve *b* on foolish
Mt 22:40 these two commandments the whole law is *b*,
Jn 8:44 and has never *b* himself on truth;
Phil 3: 6 when it came to justice *b* on the law.
3: 9 of my own *b* on observance of the law.
3: 9 It has its origin in God and is *b* on faith.
Col 2: 8 *b* on cosmic powers rather than on Christ.
2:22 *b* on merely human precepts and doctrines.
1Jn 3: 3 has this hope *b* on him keeps himself pure,
2Jn 1: 2 This love is *b* on the truth that abides in

BASELY (1)

Dt 32: 5 Yet *b* has he been treated by his

BASEMATH (7)

Gn 26:34 daughter of Beeri the Hittite, and *B*,
36: 3 and *B*, daughter of Ishmael and sister
36: 4 *B* bore Reuel;
36:10 and Reuel, son of Esau's wife *B*.
36:13 These are the descendants of Esau's wife *B*.
36:17 they are descended from Esau's wife *B*.
1Kgs 4:15 Ahimaaz, who was married to *B*,

BASES (6)

2Kgs 16:17 the *b* and removed the lavers from them;
Jdt 16:15 The mountains to their *b*,
Sg 5:15 are columns of marble resting on golden *b*.
Sir 26:18 *b* are her shapely limbs and steady feet.
Am 9: 1 Strike the *b*, so that the doorjambs totter
Hb 3:13 wicked, you lay bare their *b* at the neck.

BASEST (1)

Ps(s) 12: 9 strut and in high place are the *b* of men.

BASHAN (58)

Nm 21:33 turned and went up along the road to *B*.
21:33 But Og, king of *B*, advanced against them
32:33 king of *B* the land with its towns and the
Dt 1: 4 who lived in Heshbon, and Og, king of *B*,
3: 1 "Then we turned and proceeded toward *B*.
3: 1 But Og, king of *B*, advanced against us
3: 3 delivered into our hands Og, king of *B*,
3: 4 region of Argob, the kingdom of Og in *B*:
3:10 of Og in *B* including Salecah and Edrei.
3:11 [Og, king of *B*, was the last remaining
3:13 The rest of Gilead and all of *B*,
3:13 of *B* was once called a land of the Rephaim.
3:14 called it after his own name *B* Havvothjair,
4:43 and Golan in *B* for the Manassehites.
4:47 his land and the land of Og, king of *B*,
29: 6 Sihon, king of Heshbon, and Og, king of *B*,
32:14 Its *B* bulls and its goats,
33:22 a lion's whelp, that springs forth from *B*!"
Jos 9:10 Sihon, king of Heshbon, and Og, king of *B*,
12: 4 Og, king of *B*, a survivor of the Rephaim
12: 5 and all *B* as far as the boundary of the
13:11 Mount Hermon, and all *B* as far as Salecah,
13:12 as Salecah, the entire kingdom in *B* of Og,
13:30 territory included Mahanaim, all of *B*,
13:30 the entire kingdom of Og, king of *B*,
13:30 of Jair, which are sixty cities in *B*.
13:31 Edrei, once the royal cities of Og in *B*,
17: 1 who had already obtained Gilead and *B*,
17: 5 the land of Gilead and *B* beyond the Jordan,
20: 8 and Golan in *B* in the tribe of Manasseh.
22: 7 of Manasseh Moses had assigned land in *B*;
Jgs 10: 8 and oppressed the Israelites in *B*,
1Kgs 4:13 and of the district of Argob in *B*—
4:19 king of the Amorites, and of Og, king of *B*.
2Kgs 10:33 the river Arnon up through Gilead and *B*.
1Chr 5:11 them in the land of *B* as far as Salecah.
5:12 in command, and Janai was judge in *B*.
5:16 They dwelt in Gilead, in *B* and its towns,
5:23 in the land of *B* as far as Baal-hermon,
6:47 and from the half-tribe of Manasseh in *B*.
6:56 Golan in *B* with its pasture lands and
Neh 9:22 of Heshbon, and the land of Og, king of *B*.
Ps(s) 22:13 the strong bulls of *B* encircle me.
68:16 High the mountains of *B*;
68:16 rugged the mountains of *B*.
68:23 "I will fetch them back from *B*;
135:11 king of the Amorites, and Og, king of *B*,
136:20 And Og, king of *B*,
Is 2:13 cedars of Lebanon and all the oaks of *B*,
33: 9 the steppe, *B* and Carmel are stripped bare.
Jer 22:20 and cry out, in *B* lift up your voice;
50:19 to her fold, to feed on Carmel and *B*,
Ez 27: 6 the highest oaks of *B* they made your oars;
39:18 lambs, and goats, bullocks, fatlings of *B*,
Am 4: 1 of the mountain of Samaria, you cows of *B*,
Mi 7:14 Let them feed in *B* and Gilead,
Na 1: 4 Withered are *B* and Carmel,
Zec 11: 2 Wail, you oaks of *B*,

BASIC (1)

Heb 5:12 again the *b* elements of the oracles of God;

BASIN (21)

Gn 1: 9 under the sky be gathered into a single *b*,
1: 9 under the sky was gathered into its *b*,
1:10 and the *b* of the water he called "the sea."
Ex 12:22 dipping it in the blood that is in the *b*,
Nm 7:13 and one silver *b* weighing seventy shekels,
7:19 and one silver *b* weighing seventy shekels,
7:25 and one silver *b* weighing seventy shekels,
7:31 and one silver *b* weighing seventy shekels,
7:37 and one silver *b* weighing seventy shekels,
7:43 and one silver *b* weighing seventy shekels,
7:49 and one silver *b* weighing seventy shekels,
7:55 and one silver *b* weighing seventy shekels,
7:61 and one silver *b* weighing seventy shekels,
7:67 and one silver *b* weighing seventy shekels,
7:73 and one silver *b* weighing seventy shekels,
7:79 and one silver *b* weighing seventy shekels,
7:85 thirty shekels, and each silver *b* seventy,
1Sm 2:14 boiling, and would thrust it into the *b*,
1Kgs 7:33 had cast braces, which were under the *b*;
7:38 *b* for the top of each of the ten stands.
Jn 13: 5 Then he poured water into a *b* and began to

BASINS (15)

Ex 27: 3 removing the ashes, as well as shovels, *b*,
38: 3 of the altar, the pots, shovels, *b*,
Nm 4:14 the fire pans, forks, shovels, *b*,
7:84 twelve silver plates, twelve silver *b*,
2Sm 17:28 couches, coverlets, *b* and earthenware,
1Kgs 7:38 Ten bronze *b* were then made,
7:43 columns, ten stands, ten *b* on the stands,
7:50 *b*, snuffers, bowls, cups, and fire pans
2Kgs 3:16 LORD, 'Provide many catch *b* in this wadi.'
12:14 there to make silver cups, snuffers, *b*,
2Chr 4: 6 Then he made ten *b* for washing,
4:14 made the stands, and the *b* on the stands;
24:14 and *b* and other gold and silver utensils.
Neh 7:69 one thousand drachmas of gold, fifty *b*,
Jer 52:19 The *b* also, the fire holders, the bowls,

BASIS (10)

Lv 25:15 On the *b* of the number of years since the
25:15 on the *b* of the number of years for crops,
25:53 him as a servant hired on an annual *b*,
Wis 6:18 her laws is the *b* for incorruptibility;
Mt 2:16 making his calculations on the *b* of the date
20:12 but you have put them on the same *b* as us
Acts 2:45 everything on the *b* of each one's need.
Rom 3:30 and the uncircumcised on the *b* of faith.
Heb 7:11 *b* of which the people received the law),
1Pt 1:17 each one justly on the *b* of his actions.

BASKAMA (1)

1Mc 13:23 When he was approaching *B*,

BASKET (27)

Gn 40:17 pecking at them out of the *b* on my head."
Ex 2: 3 hide him no longer, she took a papyrus *b*,
2: 5 Noticing the *b* among the reeds,
29: 3 and put them in a *b*.
29: 3 Take the *b* of them along with the bullock
29:23 out of the *b* of unleavened food that you
29:32 of the ram and the bread that is in the *b*.
Lv 8: 2 the two rams, and the *b* of unleavened food.
8:26 from the *b* of unleavened food that was set
8:31 is in the *b* of the ordination offering,
Nm 6:15 and a *b* of unleavened cakes of fine flour
6:17 libation, and the *b* of unleavened cakes.
6:19 cake and one unleavened wafer from the *b*,
Dt 23:25 as you wish, but do not put them in your *b*.
26: 2 God, gives you, and putting them in a *b*,
26: 4 The priest shall then receive the *b* from
Jgs 6:19 the meat in a *b* and the broth in a pot,
Ps(s) 81: 7 his hands were freed from the *b*.
Jer 24: 2 One *b* contained excellent figs,
24: 2 But the other *b* contained very bad figs,
Am 8: 1 a *b* of ripe fruit.
8: 2 I answered, "A *b* of ripe fruit."
Mt 5:15 a lamp and then put it under a bushel *b*.
Mk 4:21 under a bushel *b* or hidden under a bed?
Lk 8:16 puts it under a bushel *b* or under a bed;
11:33 put it in the cellar or under a bushel *b*,
2Cor 11:33 but I was lowered in a *b* through a window

BASKETS (10)

Gn 40:16 In it I had three wicker *b* on my head;
40:18 The three *b* are three days;
2Kgs 10: 7 all seventy of them, put their heads in *b*,
Jer 24: 1 The LORD showed me two *b* of figs placed
Mt 14:20 when gathered up, filled twelve *b*.
Mk 6:43 up enough leftovers to fill twelve *b*,
8: 8 gathered up seven wicker *b* of leftovers.
8:19 how many *b* of fragments you gathered up?"
Lk 9:17 had left, over and above, filled twelve *b*.
Jn 6:13 they gathered twelve *b* full of pieces left

BASKETS-FULL (1)

Mt 16: 9 five thousand and how many *b* you picked up?

BASTARDS (1)

Heb 12: 8 discipline of sons, you are not sons but *b*.

BASTIONS (2)

Jdt 7: 5 their weapons, lighted fires on their *b*,
Jer 50:15 on all sides, She surrenders, her *b* fall,

BAT (2)

Lv 11:19 species of herons, the hoopoe, and the *b*.
Dt 14:18 species of herons, the hoopoe, and the *b*.

BAT-GADER (1)

Mi 4:14 Now fence yourself in, *B*!

BATCH (3)

Nm 15:20 of a cake of your first *b* of dough.
15:21 to the LORD from your first *b* of dough.
Neh 10:38 The first *b* of our dough,

BATH (6)

Mt 3: 7 Sadducees were stepping forward for this *b*,
Mk 10:38 or be baptized in the same *b* of pain as I?"
10:39 the *b* I am immersed in you shall share.
Lk 7:29 from John the baptismal *b* he administered.
Eph 5:26 in the *b* of water by the power of the word,
1Pt 3:21 *b* which corresponds to this exactly.

BATH-RABBIM (1)

Sg 7: 5 like the pools in Heshbon by the gate of *B*.

BATHE (32)

Gn 18: 4 water be brought, that you may *b* your feet,
19: 2 house for the night, and *b* your feet;
24:32 water was brought to *b* his feet and the
43:24 He gave them water to *b* their feet,
Ex 2: 5 daughter came down to the river to *b*,
Lv 14: 8 and shave off all his hair and *b* in water;
14: 9 wash his garments and *b* his body in water;
15: 5 bed shall wash his garments, *b* in water,
15: 6 shall wash his garments, *b* in water,
15: 7 man shall wash his garments, *b* in water,
15: 8 latter shall wash his garments, *b* in water,
15:10 thing shall wash his garments, *b* in water,
15:11 hands shall wash his garments, *b* in water,
15:13 garments and *b* his body in fresh water,
15:16 he shall *b* his whole body in water and be
15:18 *b* in water and be unclean until evening.
15:21 bed shall wash his garments, *b* in water,
15:22 shall wash his garments, *b* in water,
15:27 he shall wash his garments, *b* in water,
16:26 wash his garments and *b* his body in water;
16:28 wash his garments and *b* his body in water;
17:15 beast, shall wash his garments, *b* in water,
17:16 If he does not wash or does not *b* his body,
Nm 19: 7 wash his garments and *b* his body in water.
19: 8 wash his garments, *b* his body in water,
19:19 wash his garments and *b* his body in water,
Ru 3: 3 So *b* and anoint yourself;
2Sm 11: 8 "Go down to your house and *b* your feet."
Ps(s) 58:11 *b* his feet in the blood of the wicked.
68:24 sea, So that you will *b* your feet in blood;
Dn 13:15 She decided to *b*, for the weather was warm.
13:17 "and shut the garden doors while I *b*."

BATHED (20)

Lv 16: 4 on until he has first *b* his body in water.
22: 6 until he has first *b* his body in water,
Dt 23:12 until, toward evening, he has *b* in water;
1Kgs 22:38 licked up his blood and harlots *b* there,
Tb 2: 9 That same night I *b*, and went to sleep
7: 9 When they had *b* and reclined to eat,
Jb 29: 6 When my footsteps were *b* in milk,
Sg 5: 3 I have *b* my feet, am I then to soil them?
5:12 waters, His teeth would seem *b* in milk,
Sir 34:25 man again touches a corpse after he has *b*,
Ez 16: 9 Then I *b* you with water,
23:40 and for them you *b* yourself,
Dn 4:12 Let him be *b* with the dew of heaven;
4:20 let him be *b* with the dew of heaven,
4:22 like an ox and be *b* with the dew of heaven;
4:30 and his body was *b* with the dew of heaven,
5:21 his body was *b* with the dew of heaven,
Jn 11: 9 because he sees the world *b* in light.
13:10 "The man who has *b* has no need to wash
Acts 16:33 night he took them in and *b* their wounds;

BATHES (1)

2Pt 2:22 and, "A sow *b* by wallowing in the mire."

BATHING (3)

Lv 16:24 *b* his body with water in a sacred place,
2Sm 11: 2 From the roof he saw a woman *b*,
Jdt 12: 8 After *b*, she besought the Lord,

BATHS (2)

Ezr 7:22 one hundred *b*; oil, one hundred baths;

BATHSHEBA (11)

2Sm 11: 3 about the woman and was told, "She is *B*,
12:24 Then David comforted his wife *B*.
1Kgs 1:11 Then Nathan said to *B*, Solomon's mother:
1:15 So *B* visited the king in his room,
1:16 *B* bowed in homage to the king,
1:28 King David answered, "Call *B* here."
1:31 to the floor in homage to the king, *B* said,
2:13 Adonijah, son of Haggith, went to *B*,
2:18 "Very well," replied *B*,
2:19 So *B* went to King Solomon to speak to him
1Chr 3: 5 four by *B*, the daughter of Ammiel;

BATHSHUA (1)

1Chr 2: 3 these three were born to him of *B*,

BATS (2)

Is 2:20 will throw to the moles and the *b* the idols
Bar 6:21 *B* and swallows alight on their bodies and

BATTEN (1)

1Sm 2: 5 out for bread, while the hungry *b* on spoil.

BATTERED (3)

Jdt 2:24 and *b* down every fortified city along the
Ps(s) 62: 4 though he were a sagging fence, a *b* wall?
Is 24:12 its gates are *b* and desolate.

BATTERING (2)

2Sm 20:15 Joab began *b* the wall to throw it down.
Ez 4: 2 pitch camps, and set up *b* rams all around.

BATTERING-RAM (1)

2Mc 12:15 Jericho without *b* or siege machine;

BATTERING-RAMS (2)

Ez 21:27 in the battle cry, to post *b* at the gates,
26: 9 He shall pound your walls with *b* and break

BATTLE (221)

Gn 14: 8 of Siddim they went into *b* against them:
Ex 13:18 In *b* array the Israelites marched out of
17: 9 and tomorrow go out and engage Amalek in *b.*
17:10 he engaged Amalek in *b* after Moses had
32:17 to Moses, "That sounds like a *b* in camp."
Nm 21: 1 them in *b* and took some of them captive.
21:23 he reached Jahaz, he engaged Israel in *b.*
21:33 with all his people to give *b* at Edrei.
22:11 be able to give them *b* and drive them out.' "
31: 8 Besides those slain in *b,*
31:19 or touched anyone slain in *b* shall purify
32:27 as armed troops to *b* before the LORD,
Dt 2: 9 to the Moabites or engage them in *b,*
2:24 Begin the occupation; engage him in *b.*
2:32 advanced against us to join *b* at Jahaz;
3: 1 us with all his people to give *b* at Edrei.
3:18 But all you troops equipped for *b* must
20: 2 "When you are about to go into *b,*
20: 3 you are going into *b* against your enemies.
20: 5 lest he die in *b* and another dedicate it.
20: 6 lest he die in *b* and another enjoy its
20: 7 he die in *b* and another take her to wife.'
20:12 peace with you and instead offers you *b,*
29: 6 of Bashan, came out to engage us in *b,*
Jos 4:13 forty thousand troops equipped for *b*
8:14 in *b* at the descent toward the Arabah,
11:19 all were taken in *b.*
Jgs 1: 1 the Canaanites and to do *b* with them?"
1: 3 me, and let us engage the Canaanites in *b,*
3: 1 [just to instruct, by training them in *b,*
8:13 returned from *b* by the pass of Heres.
20:14 to Gibeah, to do *b* with the Israelites.
20:17 hundred thousand swordsmen ready for *b,*
20:20 On the day the Israelites drew up in *b*
20:22 I again engage my brother Benjamin in *b?"*
20:28 "Shall I go out again to *b* with Benjamin,
20:30 line of *b* at Gibeah as on other occasions.
20:34 In a fierce *b,* the LORD defeated Benjamin
1Sm 4: 1 to engage them in *b* and camped at Ebenezer,
4: 2 then drew up in *b* formation against Israel.
4: 3 LORD from Shiloh that it may go into *b*
7:10 Philistines advanced to join *b* with Israel.
13: 5 The Philistines also assembled for *b,*
13:22 And so on the day of *b* neither sword nor
14:23 The *b* continued past Beth-horon;
17: 1 Philistines rallied their forces for *b*
17: 2 up their *b* line to meet the Philistines.
17: 8 "Why come out in *b* formation?
17:20 battleground, were shouting their *b* cry.
17:21 drew up opposite each other in *b* array.
17:22 of the baggage and hastened to the *b* line,
17:28 You came down to enjoy the *b!"*
17:47 For the *b* is the LORD'S and he shall
17:48 *b* line in the direction of the Philistine.
26:10 to die, or he goes out and perishes in *b.*
29: 4 into *b* with us, lest during the battle he
29: 9 you are not to go up with us to *b.*
30:24 the share of the one who goes down to *b*
31: 3 The *b* raged around Saul,
31: 8 The day after the *b* the Philistines came
2Sm 1: 4 answered that the soldiers had fled the *b*
1:25 in the thick of the *b,*
2:17 After a very fierce *b* that day,
3:30 killed their brother Asahel in *b* at Gibeon.]
8:10 him for his victory over Hadadezer in *b,*
10: 8 The Ammonites came out and drew up in *b*
10: 9 Joab saw the *b* lines drawn up against him,
10:13 with him approached the Arameans for *b,*
11:18 a report of all the details of the *b,*
11:19 giving the king all the details of the *b,*
18: 6 a *b* was fought in the forest near Mahanaim.
18: 8 The *b* spread out over that entire region,
19: 4 that day like men shamed by flight in *b.*
19:11 whom we anointed over us, died in *b.*
21:15 *b* between the Philistines and Israel.
21:17 "You must not go out to *b* with us again
21:18 was another *b* with the Philistines in Gob.
21:19 was another *b* with the Philistines in Gob,
21:20 There was another *b* at Gath in which there
23: 9 when the Philistines assembled there for *b.*
1Kgs 20:29 On the seventh day *b* was joined,
20:39 servant went into the thick of the *b,*
22:30 "I will disguise myself and go into *b,*
22:32 But Jehoshaphat shouted his *b* cry,
22:35 The *b* grew fierce during the day,
2Kgs 3: 7 Will you join me in *b* against Moab?"
3:21 that the kings had come to give them *b;*
3:26 When he saw that he was losing the *b,*
8:28 Joram, son of Ahab, in *b* against Hazael,
8:29 on him at Ramah in his *b* against Hazael,
9:15 inflicted on him in the *b* against Hazael,
13:25 had taken in *b* from his father Jehoahaz.
14: 7 in the Salt Valley, and took Sela in *b.*
14:11 of Judah met in *b* at Beth-shemesh of Judah.
1Chr 5:20 For during the *b* they called on God,
5:22 Many had fallen in *b,*
10: 3 the whole fury of the *b* descended upon Saul.
11:13 where the Philistines had massed for *b.*
12:20 with the Philistines to *b* against Saul.
12:26 Of the Simeonites, warriors fit for *b:*
12:34 *b* array with every kind of weapon for war:
12:36 Of the Danites, set in *b* array:
12:37 for military service and set in *b* array:
12:39 All these soldiers, drawn up in *b* order,
14:15 of the mastic trees, then go forth to *b,*
19: 9 lined up for a *b* at the gate of the city,
19:10 a *b* line both in front of and behind him,
19:14 with his men to engage the Arameans in *b;*
19:17 up to fight the Arameans, they gave *b.*
20: 4 there was another *b* with the Philistines,
20: 6 In still another *b,* at Gath,
2Chr 13: 3 Abijah joined *b* with a force of four
13: 3 while Jeroboam lined up against him in *b*
13:12 Do not *b* against the LORD,
13:14 and saw that they had to *b* on both fronts,
14: 9 in *b* array in the valley of Zephathah,
18: 3 We will be with you in the *b."*
18:29 Jehoshaphat, "I will go into *b* disguised,
18:34 The *b* grew fierce during the day,
20:15 for the *b* is not yours but God's.
22: 5 Ahab, king of Israel, to *b* against Hazael,
22: 6 received at Rama in his *b* against Hazael,
25:13 Amaziah had dismissed from *b* service
25:21 Amaziah met in *b* at Beth-shemesh of Judah.
Jdt 5: 1 that the Israelites were ready for *b,*
7: 1 passes, and engage the Israelites in *b.*
14:13 slaves have dared come down to give us *b,*
1Mc 3:44 prepare for *b* and to pray and implore mercy
3:59 It is better for us to die in *b* than to
4:13 them, they came out of their camp for *b,*
4:14 The *b* was joined and the Gentiles were
4:34 Then they engaged in *b,*
5:31 the noise of the *b* was resounding to heaven
5:42 all must go into *b."*
5:59 men came out of the city to meet them in *b.*
5:67 At that time some priests fell in *b* who
6: 4 of the city who rose up in *b* against him.
6:33 and the armies prepared for *b,*
7:43 *b* on the thirteenth day of the month Adar.
7:43 he himself was the first to fall in the *b.*
8: 5 in *b* had been overwhelmed and subjugated.
9: 1 that Nicanor and his army had fallen in *b,*
9: 7 melting away just when the *b* was imminent,
9:13 and the *b* raged from morning until evening.
9:17 The *b* was fought desperately,
9:30 leader in his place, and to fight our *b."*
9:45 The *b* is before us,
9:47 they joined *b,* Jonathan raised his arm
10:49 The two kings joined *b,*
10:50 He pressed the *b* hard until sunset,
10:53 for I engaged him in *b,* defeated him
10:78 him to Azotus, and they engaged in *b.*
11:15 news, he came to challenge Ptolemy in *b.*
11:69 out of their places and joined in the *b.*
12:28 that Jonathan and his men were ready for *b,*
2Mc 5: 3 squadrons of cavalry in *b* array,
8:20 the *b* in Babylonia against the Galatians,
8:23 division and joined in *b* with Nicanor.
10:28 soon as dawn broke, the armies joined *b,*
10:29 In the midst of the fierce *b,*
11:10 they advanced in *b* order with the aid of
12:34 ensuing *b,* a few of the Jews were slain.
12:36 himself their ally and leader in the *b.*
12:37 raising a *b* cry in his ancestral language,
13:15 Giving his men the *b* cry "God's Victory,"
15:19 they were about the *b* in the open country.
15:20 near with their troops drawn up in *b* line,
15:25 to the sound of trumpets and *b* songs.
15:28 When the *b* was over and they were joyfully
Jb 38:23 of stress, for the days of war and of *b?*
39:25 Even from afar he scents the *b,*
Ps(s) 24: 8 strong and mighty, the LORD, mighty in *b.*
78: 9 ranks of bowmen, retreated in the day of *b.*
89:44 sword and have not sustained him in *b.*
140: 8 you are my helmet in the day of *b!*
144: 1 LORD, my rock, who trains my hands for *b,*
Prv 21:31 The horse is equipped for the day of *b,*
Eccl 9:11 won by the swift, nor the *b* by the valiant,
Sg 3: 8 them expert with the sword, skilled in *b,*
Wis 12: 9 the wicked vanquished in *b* by the just,
Sir 4:28 and the LORD your God will *b* for you.
37: 6 Forget not your comrade during the *b,*
Is 9: 4 For every boot that trampled in *b,*
13: 4 LORD of hosts is mustering an army for *b.*
16: 9 fruits and harvests the *b* cry has fallen.
21:15 From the taut bow, from the fury of *b.*
22: 2 not slain with the sword, nor killed in *b.*
27: 4 thorns, In *b* I should march against them;
28: 6 to those who turn back the *b* at the gate.
30:28 repeated winnowings will he *b* against them
41:12 be as nothing at all who do *b* with you.
42:13 He shouts out his *b* cry,
42:25 upon them, his anger, and the fury of *b;*
Jer 6:23 Each in his place, for *b* against you,
8: 6 his course, like a steed dashing into *b.*
18:21 their young men be slain by the sword in *b.*
20:16 cries in the morning, *b* alarms at noonday,
33: 5 men come to *b* the Chaldeans,
46: 3 shield and buckler! march to *b!*
49: 2 of the Ammonites I will sound the *b* alarm;
49:14 together, move against her, rise up for *b.*
50:22 *B* alarm in the land, dire destruction!
50:42 Each in his place for *b* against you,
Ez 21:27 slaying, to raise his voice in the *b* cry,
Dn 11:20 destroyed, though not in conflict or in *b.*
11:25 for *b* with a very large and strong army,
Jl 2: 5 Like a mighty people arrayed for *b.*
Am 1:14 of *b* and stormwind in a time of tempest.
Zep 1:16 and *b* alarm Against fortified cities,
Zec 10: 5 trampling the mire of the streets in *b;*
14: 2 all the nations against Jerusalem for *b:*
14: 3 those nations, fighting as on a day of *b.*
Lk 14:31 to march on another king to do *b* with him,
1Cor 14: 8 is uncertain, who will get ready for *b?*
Eph 6:12 Our *b* is not against human forces but
Heb 11:34 were made powerful, became strong in *b,*
Rv 9: 7 locusts were like horses equipped for *b.*
9: 9 many chariots and horses charging into *b.*
16:14 for *b* on the great day of God the Almighty.
19:19 to do *b* with the One riding the horse,

BATTLE-AX (1)

2Sm 23: 8 It was he who brandished his *b* over eight

BATTLED (2)

Sir 47: 6 *b* 7 and subdued the enemy on every side.
Rv 12: 7 and his angels *b* against the dragon.

BATTLEFIELD (3)

1Sm 4: 2 who slew about four thousand men on the *b.*
4:12 the *b* and reached Shiloh that same day,
4:16 said, "It is I who have come from the *b;*

BATTLEGROUND (1)

1Sm 17:20 just as the army, on their way to the *b,*

BATTLEMENTS (5)

Tb 13:16 with gold, and their *b* with pure gold.
Sg 4: 4 neck is like David's tower girt with *b;*
Is 54:12 I will make your *b* of rubies,
Zep 1:16 fortified cities, against *b* on high.
3: 6 destroyed nations, their *b* are laid waste;

BATTLES (21)

Jgs 3: 1 of the *b* with Canaan [just to instruct,
1Sm 8:20 and to lead us in warfare and fight our *b."*
18:17 my champion and fight the *b* of the LORD.
25:28 lordship is fighting the *b* of the LORD,
2Sm 8:10 Toi had been in many *b* with Hadadezer.
1Chr 11: 2 it was you who led Israel in all its *b.*
12: 1 among the warriors who helped him in his *b.*
2Chr 32: 8 our God, to help us and to fight our *b."*
1Mc 3: 3 *b* and protected the camp with his sword.
3:26 the Gentiles talked about the *b* of Judas.
5: 7 He fought many *b* with them,
5:21 and fought many *b* with the Gentiles.
8: 2 He was also told of their *b* and the brave
9:22 The other acts of Judas, his *b,*
10:15 he was also told of the *b* and valiant
13: 3 what *b* and disasters we have been through.
13: 9 Fight our *b,* and we will do everything
16: 2 the *b* of Israel from our youth until today,
2Mc 15: 9 them of the *b* they had already won,
Sir 46: 3 him when he fought the *b* of the LORD?
46: 6 the LORD was watching over his people's *b.*

BAY (4)

Jos 15: 2 The boundary there ran from the *b* that
15: 6 from the *b* where the Jordan meets the sea,
Ps(s) 59: 8 Though they *b* with their mouths,
Acts 27:39 They could make out a *b* with a sandy beach,

BAZAARS (1)

1Kgs 20:34 and you may make yourself *b* in Damascus,

BAZLITH (1)

Neh 7:54 sons of Hakupha, sons of Harhur, sons of *B,*

BAZLUTH (1)

Ezr 2:52 of Hakupha, sons of Harhur, sons of *B,*

BDELLIUM (2)

Gn 2:12 *b* and lapis lazuli are also there.
Nm 11: 7 coriander seed and had the appearance of *b.*

BEACH (3)

Acts 21: 5 off, and we knelt down on the *b* and prayed.
27:39 They could make out a bay with a sandy *b,*
27:40 into the wind, and made for the *b;*

BEAD (1)

Sg 4: 9 of your eyes, with one *b* of your necklace.

BEALIAH (1)

1Chr 12: 6 *B;*

BEALOTH (1)

Jos 15:24 Ziph, Telem, *B,*

BEAM (4)

2Kgs 6: 2 where by getting one *b* apiece we can build
Ezr 6:11 edict, a *b* is to be taken from his house,
Bar 6:19 They are like any *b* in the house;
Hb 2:11 and the *b* in the woodwork shall answer it!

BEAMS (15)

Lv 14:45 *b* and mortar shall be hauled away to an
1Kgs 6: 6 the *b* would not be fastened into the walls
6:10 temple, to which it was joined by cedar *b.*
6:15 floor to ceiling *b* with cedar paneling,
6:36 of hewn stones and one course of cedar *b.*
7: 3 cedar above the *b* resting on the columns;
7: 3 these *b* numbered forty-five,
7: 7 paneled with cedar from floor to ceiling *b.*
7:12 stones and a bonding course of cedar *b.*
15:22 *b* with which Baasha was fortifying Ramah.
2Chr 3: 7 The house, its *b* and thresholds,
34:11 buy hewn stone and timber for the tie *b*
Sg 1:17 the *b* of our house are cedars,
Sir 22:16 wooden *b* is not loosened by an earthquake;
Bar 6:54 themselves are burnt up in the fire like *b.*

BEANS (2)

2Sm 17:28 as wheat, barley, flour, roasted grain, *b,*
Ez 4: 9 take wheat and barley, and *b* and lentils,

BEAR (182)

Gn 4:13 "My punishment is too great to *b.*
16:11 "You are now pregnant and shall *b* a son;
17:19 your wife Sarah is to *b* you a son,
17:21 shall *b* to you by this time next year."
18:13 laugh and say, 'Shall I really *b* a child,
20:17 so that they could *b* children;
21:12 Isaac that descendants shall *b* your name.
30: 1 saw that she failed to *b* children to Jacob,
30: 9 Leah saw that she had ceased to *b* children,
31: 8 the entire flock would *b* speckled young;
31: 8 the entire flock would *b* streaked young.
44:34 I could not *b* to see the anguish that
47:20 with the famine too much for them to *b,*
Ex 18:22 lightened, since they will *b* it with you.
20:16 not *b* false witness against your neighbor.
28:12 Thus Aaron shall *b* their names on his
28:29 he will thus *b* the names of the sons of
28:30 Thus he shall always *b* the decisions for
Lv 5: 1 and thus commits a sin and has guilt to *b;*
7:18 who eats of it shall have his guilt to *b.*
10:17 It has been given to you that you might *b*
17:16 his body, he shall have the guilt to *b.*"
19:17 *b* hatred for your brother in your heart.
24:15 his God shall *b* the penalty of his sin;
26: 4 season, so that the land will *b* its crops,
26:20 your land will *b* no crops,
Nm 5:28 and will still be able to *b* children.
5:31 woman shall *b* such guilt as she may have."
9:13 man shall *b* the consequences of his sin.
11:17 You will then not have to *b* it by yourself.
Dt 1:12 I alone *b* the crushing burden that you are,
5:20 *b* dishonest witness against your neighbor.
9: 7 *B* in mind and do not forget how you
21:15 and if both *b* him sons,
25:17 *B* in mind what Amalek did to you on the
29:17 would *b* such poison and wormwood among
31:21 to recite, will *b* witness against them.
Jos 23: 4 *B* in mind that I have apportioned among
Jgs 13: 3 yet you will conceive and *b* a son.
13: 5 As for the son you will conceive and *b,*
13: 7 'You will be with child and will *b* a son.
1Sm 17:34 *b* came to carry off a sheep from the flock,
17:36 servant has killed both a lion and a *b,*
17:37 me from the claws of the lion and the *b,*
2Sm 17: 8 as a *b* in the wild robbed of her cubs.
2Kgs 19:30 shall again strike root below and *b* fruit
Jdt 11:10 not disregard his word, but *b* it in mind,
1Mc 7:37 have chosen this house to *b* your name,
2Mc 9:12 When he could no longer *b* his own stench,
9:21 the esteem and good will you *b* me.
Jb 9: 9 He made the *B* and Orion,
21: 3 *B* with me while I speak;
38:32 season, or guide the *B* with its train?
39: 3 They crouch down and *b* their young;
Ps(s) 68:12 women *b* the glad tidings,
69: 8 of Israel, Since for your sake I *b* insult,
89:51 I *b* in my bosom all the accusations of the
91:12 Upon their hands they shall *b* you up,
92:15 They shall *b* fruit even in old age;
Prv 9:12 if you are arrogant, you alone shall *b* it.
17:12 Face a *b* robbed of her cubs,
18:14 but a broken spirit who can *b?*
28:15 *b* is a wicked ruler over a poor people.
30:21 trembles, yes, under four it cannot *b* up:
Wis 3:13 shall *b* fruit at the visitation of souls.
Sir 6:31 of glory, *b* her as your splendid crown.
11:22 man, and in due time his hopes *b* fruit.
13: 2 *B* no burden too heavy for you;
22:15 mass are easier to *b* than a stupid man.
25:16 looks, and makes her sullen as a female *b.*
26: 5 lying testimony are harder to *b* than death,
43: 3 of the earth, and who can *b* its fiery heat?
Is 1:13 octaves with wickedness: these I cannot *b.*
7:14 virgin shall be with child, and *b* a son,
11: 7 The cow and the *b* shall be neighbors,
37:31 again strike root below and *b* fruit above.
45:20 They are without knowledge who *b* wooden
46: 2 unable to save those who *b* them,
46: 4 even when your hair is gray I will *b* you;
46: 8 this and be firm, *b* it well in mind,
53:11 justify many, and their guilt he shall *b.*
54: 1 a glad cry, you barren one who did not *b,*
57:13 shall carry off, the breeze shall *b* away;
59:12 are many, our sins *b* witness against us.
63:19 you do not rule, who do not *b* your name.
Jer 4: 6 *B* the standard to Zion,
10:19 if I make light of my wound, I can *b* it.
14: 7 though our crimes *b* witness against us,
14: 9 are in our midst, O LORD, your name we *b:*
29: 6 that they may *b* sons and daughters.
30: 6 since when do men *b* children?
31:19 with shame, I *b* the disgrace of my youth.
44:22 The LORD could no longer *b* your evil deeds,
Lam 3:10 A lurking *b* he has been to me,
3:27 for a man to *b* the yoke from his youth.
5: 7 but we *b* their guilt.
Bar 2:15 Israel and his descendants *b* your name.
4:25 *b* patiently the anger that has come from
5: 2 *b* on your head the miter that displays the
Ez 4: 4 as you lie thus, you shall *b* their sins.
4: 5 you will *b* the sins of the house of Israel.
4: 6 and *b* the sins of the house of Judah forty
16:52 You, then, *b* your shame;
16:52 and *b* the shame of having made your
16:54 that you may *b* your shame and be disgraced
16:58 you must *b* it all, says the LORD.
17: 8 it was planted, to grow branches, *b* fruit,
17:23 It shall put forth branches and *b* fruit,
23:35 it is for you to *b* the penalty of your
32:24 and they *b* their disgrace with those who
32:30 slain by the sword and *b* their disgrace
34:27 trees of the field shall *b* their fruits,
34:29 land, or *b* the reproaches of the nations.
36: 7 nations shall *b* their own reproach.
36: 8 branches and *b* fruit for my people Israel,
36:15 of nations, or *b* insults from peoples,
36:30 *b* among the nations the reproach of famine.
44:10 they shall *b* the consequences of their sin.
44:12 they shall *b* the consequences of their sin.
44:13 Thus they shall *b* their disgrace because
47:12 Every month they shall *b* fresh fruit,
Dn 7: 5 The second was like a *b;*
9:19 this city and your people *b* your name!"
Hos 9:11 Were they to *b* children,
9:16 they shall *b* no fruit.
13: 8 attack them like a *b* robbed of its young,
14: 9 Because of me you *b* fruit!
Jl 2:11 and exceedingly terrible; who can *b* it?
Am 3:13 and *b* witness against the house of Jacob,
5:19 flee from a lion, and a *b* should meet him;
9:12 Edom and all the nations shall *b* my name,
Mi 6:10 Am I to *b* any longer criminal hoarding and
6:16 you shall *b* the reproach of the nations.
Na 1:14 no descendant shall come to *b* your name;
Zec 8:12 its fruit, the land shall *b* its crops,
Mal 3: 5 swift to *b* witness Against the sorcerers,
Mt 7:18 A sound tree cannot *b* bad fruit any more
7:18 more than a decayed tree can *b* good fruit.
7:19 Every tree that does not *b* good fruit is
19:18 'You shall not *b* false witness';
Mk 10:19 You shall not *b* false witness;
Lk 1:13 shall *b* a son whom you shall name John.
1:31 and *b* a son and give him the name Jesus.
8:15 it, and *b* fruit through perseverance.
13: 9 then perhaps it will *b* fruit.
18:20 You shall not *b* dishonest witness.
Jn 8:43 It is because you cannot *b* to hear my word.
15: 4 can *b* fruit of itself apart from the vine,
15: 4 the vine, can you *b* fruit apart from me.
15:16 I who chose you to go forth and *b* fruit.
15:26 he will *b* witness on my behalf.
15:27 You must *b* witness as well,
16:12 more to tell you, but you cannot *b* it now.
Acts 10:42 us to preach to the people and to *b* witness
15:10 neither we nor our fathers were able to *b?*
15:14 among the Gentiles a people to *b* his name.
15:17 that *b* my name may seek out the Lord.
22: 5 whole council of elders can *b* me witness,
Rom 1: 9 the gospel of his Son will *b* witness
2:17 Let us suppose you *b* the name of "Jew"
3:21 both law and prophets *b* witness to it
7: 4 the dead, so that we might *b* fruit for God.
1Cor 4:12 Persecution comes our way; we *b* it
15:49 we *b* the likeness of the man from heaven.
2Cor 2: 4 to help you realize the great love I *b* you.
8: 7 in total concern, and in the love we *b* you,
Gal 6: 5 Everyone should *b* his own responsibility.
6:17 I *b* the brand marks of Jesus in my body.
Col 1: 4 and the love you *b* toward all the saints
3:13 *B* with one another; forgive whatever
2Tm 1: 8 *b* your share of the hardship
2: 3 *B* hardship along with me as a good soldier
2:10 Therefore I *b* with all of this for the
3:11 know what persecutions I have had to *b,*
Heb 12:20 for they could not *b* to hear the command:
13:22 you to *b* with this word of encouragement,
2Pt 1: 8 they *b* fruit in true knowledge of our Lord
1Jn 1: 1 we have seen and *b* witness to it,
3Jn 1: 3 great joy to have the brothers *b* witness
Jude 1:12 trees at the year's end they *b* no fruit,
Rv 13: 2 had paws like a *b* and the mouth of a lion.
22: 4 to face and *b* his name on their foreheads.

BEARD (16)

Lv 13:45 and his head bare, and shall muffle his *b;*
14: 9 shave off all the hair of his head, his *b,*
19:27 the temples, nor trim the edges of your *b.*
21: 5 of the head, nor shave the edges of the *b,*
1Sm 21:14 doors of the gate and drooling onto his *b.*
2Sm 20: 9 hand Joab held Amasa's *b* as if to kiss him.
Ezr 9: 3 my mantle, plucked hair from my head and *b,*
Ps(s) 133: 2 runs down over the beard, the *b* of Aaron,
Is 7:20 It shall also shave off the *b.*
15: 2 Every head is shaved, every *b* sheared off.
50: 6 me, my cheeks to those who plucked my *b;*
Jer 48:37 head has been made bald, every *b* shaved;
Bar 6:30 with torn tunic and with shaven hair and *b,*
Ez 5: 1 razor, passing it over your head and *b.*
24:17 sandals on your feet, do not cover your *b,*

BEARDS (5)

2Sm 10: 4 after shaving off half their *b* and cutting
10: 5 "Stay in Jericho until your *b* grow,"
1Chr 19: 5 told them, "until your *b* have grown again;
Jer 41: 5 knew of it, eighty men with *b* shaved off,
Ez 24:22 your *b* nor eating the customary bread.

BEARER (4)

1Sm 17: 7 His shield *b* went before him.
2Sm 4:10 thinking himself the *b* of good news for
Is 41:27 I will pick out a *b* of the glad tidings."
Na 2: 1 there advances the *b* of good news,

BEARERS (7)

Jos 3:15 No sooner had these priestly *b* of the ark
Jgs 3:18 presentation went off with the tribute *b.*
2Sm 6:13 As soon as the *b* of the ark of the LORD
15:24 *b* of the ark of the covenant of God],
Neh 4: 4 "Slackened is the *b*' strength,
2Mc 4:19 But the *b* themselves decided that the
Lk 7:14 at this, the *b* halted.

BEARING (35)

Gn 16: 2 "The LORD has kept me from *b* children.
24:10 and *b* all kinds of gifts from his master,
29:35 Then she stopped *b* children.
Dt 28:10 the earth see you *b* the name of the LORD,
Jos 6:13 The seven priests *b* the ram's horns
1Kgs 10: 2 numerous retinue, and with camels *b* spices,
2Kgs 3:21 every man capable of *b* arms was called up
1Chr 12:25 Judahites *b* shields and spears:
15:26 were *b* the ark of the covenant of the LORD,
2Chr 9: 1 numerous retinue and by camels *b* spices,
12:11 of the LORD, the troops would come *b* them,
Ezr 2:63 should be a priest *b* the Urim and Thummim.
Neh 7:65 should be a priest *b* the Urim and Thummim.
9:30 *b* witness against them through your spirit,
Tb 13:11 *B* in their hands their gifts for the King
Est D: 4 while the other followed her, *b* her train.
E: 3 incapable of *b* such greatness,
1Mc 2:56 Caleb, for *b* witness before the assembly,
2Mc 9:25 also *b* in mind that the neighboring rulers,
Wis 10: 7 desert, Plants *b* fruit that never ripens,
18:16 *b* the sharp sword of your inexorable
18:21 *b* the weapon of his special office,
Is 52: 7 tidings, Announcing peace, *b* good news,
53: 2 in him no stately *b* to make us look at him,
60: 6 Sheba shall come *b* gold and frankincense,
Jer 12: 2 root, they keep on growing and *b* fruit.
46: 9 warriors, Cush and Put, *b* your shields,
Bar 3:30 her, *b* her away rather than choice gold?
Na 3:12 are but fig trees, *b* early figs That fall,
Jn 15: 8 *b* much fruit and becoming my disciples.
Acts 20:24 *b* witness to the gospel of God's grace.
28:23 *b* witness to the reign of God among men.
Eph 4: 2 and patience, *b* with one another lovingly.
1Tm 6:13 who in *b* witness made his noble profession
Heb 13:13 the camp, *b* the insult which he bore.

BEARS (42)

Gn 1:11 every kind of plant that *b* seed and every
1:11 on earth that *b* fruit with its seed in it."
1:12 brought forth every kind of plant that *b* seed
1:12 on earth that *b* fruit with its seed in it.
Ex 21: 4 him a wife and she *b* him sons or daughters,
28:38 Since Aaron *b* whatever guilt the
Lv 13:45 "The one who *b* the sore of leprosy shall
Nm 6: 7 since his head *b* his dedication to God.
12: 7 Throughout my house he *b* my trust:

BEARS (cont.)

Dt 3:14 Bashan Havvothjair, the name it *b* today.]
25: 6 The first-born son she *b* shall continue
1Sm 2: 5 The barren wife *b* seven sons,
2Sm 6: 2 which *b* the name of the LORD of hosts
Ps(s) 68:20 day by day be the Lord, who *b* our burdens;
Prv 25:18 who *b* false witness against his neighbor.
Wis 11:17 upon them a drove of *b* or fierce lions,
14: 1 wood more unsound than the boat that *b* him.
Sir 40: 4 Whether he *b* a splendid crown or is
47: 3 lions as though they were kids, and of *b*,
Is 3: 9 Their very look *b* witness against them;
59:11 We all growl like *b*,
Jer 7:10 before me in this house which *b* my name,
7:11 Has this house which *b* my name become in
7:30 They have defiled the house which *b* my
17: 8 it shows no distress, but still *b* fruit.
Bar 2:26 which *b* your name to what it is today,
Dn 9:18 our ruins and the city which *b* your name.
Hos 5: 5 arrogance of Israel *b* witness against him;
7:10 arrogance of Israel *b* witness against him;
Jl 2:22 The tree *b* its fruit
Mt 7:17 Any sound tree *b* good fruit,
7:17 fruit, while a decayed tree *b* bad fruit.
10:41 He who welcomes a prophet because he *b* the
13:23 He it is who *b* a yield of a hundred- or
Mk 4:19 it *b* no yield.
Rom 2:15 *b* witness together with that law,
9: 1 My conscience *b* me witness in the Holy
1Cor 5:11 *b* the title "brother" if he is immoral,
Gal 4:27 you barren one who *b* no children;
2Tm 2:19 It *b* this inscription: "The LORD knows
Heb 6: 8 But if it *b* thorns and thistles,
Rv 1: 2 who in reporting all he saw *b* witness to

BEAST (116)

Gn 7:14 ark, together with every kind of wild *b*,
37:20 we could say that a wild *b* devoured him.
37:33 A wild *b* has devoured him!
Ex 8:13 of the earth and gnats came upon man and *b*.
8:14 As the gnats infested man and *b*,
9: 6 but not one *b* belonging to the Israelites.
9: 7 one *b* belonging to the Israelites had died,
9: 9 boils on man and *b* throughout the land."
9:10 and it caused festering boils on man and *b*.
9:19 Whatever man or *b* remains in the fields
9:22 on man and *b* and every growing thing in
9:25 It struck down every man and *b* that was in
12:12 first-born of the land, both man and *b*,
13: 2 among the Israelites, both of man and *b*,
13:15 of Egypt, every first-born of man and of *b*.
19:13 man or *b*, must not be allowed to live.
20:10 or your male or female slave, or your *b*,
22:12 If it has been killed by a wild *b*,
Lv 17:15 died of itself or was killed by a wild *b*,
20:25 with the uncleanness of any *b* or bird
Nm 3:13 Israel sacred to me, both of man and of *b*,
8:17 the Israelites, both of man and of *b*,
18:15 opens the womb, whether of man or of *b*,
22:30 ass said to Balaam, "Am I not your own *b*,
1Mc 6:36 These anticipated the *b* wherever it was;
6:46 The *b* fell to the ground on top of him,
2Mc 4:25 of a cruel tyrant and the rage of a wild *b*.
Jb 28:21 It is hid from the eyes of any *b*;
Ps(s) 36: 7 man and *b* you save,
68:31 Rebuke the wild *b* of the reeds,
73:22 I was like a brute *b* in your presence.
104:11 And give drink to every *b* of the field,
135: 8 first-born in Egypt, both of man and of *b*.
Prv 12:10 The just man takes care of his *b*,
Eccl 3:19 For the lot of man and of *b* is one lot;
3:19 and man has no advantage over the *b*;
Wis 13:14 man or makes it resemble some worthless *b*.
Sir 12:13 bitten, or anyone who goes near a wild *b*?
40: 8 it is with all flesh, with man and with *b*,
Is 35: 9 nor *b* of prey go up to be met upon it.
Jer 7:20 pour out upon this place, upon man and *b*,
21: 6 inhabitants of this city, both man and *b*;
27: 5 and man and *b* on the face of the earth,
31:27 with the seed of man and the seed of *b*.
32:43 which you call a desert, without man or *b*,
33:10 desolate it is, without man, without *b*!"
33:10 without man, without citizen, without *b*,
33:12 place, now desolate, without man or *b*,
36:29 waste this land and empty it of man and *b*?"
50: 3 there, because man and *b* have fled away.
51:62 that neither man nor *b* should dwell in it,
Ez 14:13 it and cut off from it both man and *b*;
14:17 the land cutting off from it man and *b*,
14:19 fury, cutting off from it man and *b*,
14:21 pestilence, to cut off from it man and *b*,
25:13 against Edom and cut off from it man and *b*.
29: 8 you, and cut off from you both man and *b*,
29:11 No foot of man or *b* shall pass through it;
32:13 nor shall the hoof of *b* disturb them.
34: 8 sheep have become food for every wild *b*,
Dn 4:13 let him be given the sense of a *b*,
5:21 among men and was made insensate as a *b*;
7: 6 After this I looked and saw another *b*,
7: 6 To this *b* dominion was given.
7: 7 visions of the night I saw the fourth *b*,
7:11 until the *b* was slain and its body thrown
7:19 wished to make certain about the fourth *b*,
7:23 *b* shall be a fourth kingdom on earth,
8: 4 No *b* could withstand it or be rescued from
Hos 13: 8 lion, as though a wild *b* were to rend them.
Jon 3: 7 "Neither man nor *b*, neither cattle nor
3: 8 Man and *b* shall be covered with sackcloth
Zep 1: 3 I will sweep away man and *b*,
Mt 21: 5 astride a colt, the foal of a *b* of burden."
Lk 10:34 on his own *b* and brought him to an inn,
19:31 should ask you, 'Why are you untying the *b*?'
2Pt 2:16 A mute *b* spoke with a human voice to
Rv 11: 7 the wild *b* that comes up from the abyss
13: 1 Then I saw a wild *b* come out of the sea
13: 2 The *b* I saw was like a leopard,
13: 3 the whole world followed after the *b*.
13: 4 dragon for giving his authority to the *b*;
13: 4 they also worshiped the *b* and said,
13: 4 and said, "Who can compare with the *b*,
13: 5 The *b* was given a mouth for uttering proud
13: 7 The *b* was allowed to wage war against
13: 8 The *b* will be worshiped by all those
13:11 another wild *b* come up out of the earth;
13:12 It used the authority of the first *b* to
13:12 all its inhabitants worship the first *b*,
13:14 to perform by authority of the first *b*,
13:14 them to make an idol in honor of the *b*
13:15 The second wild *b* was then permitted to
13:17 was first marked with the name of the *b*
13:18 anyone can calculate the number of the *b*,
14: 9 "If anyone worships the *b* or its image,
14:11 the *b* or its image or accept the mark of its
15: 2 won the victory over the *b* and its image,
16: 2 the mark of the *b* or worshiped its image.
16:10 poured out his bowl on the throne of the *b*.
16:13 of the dragon, from the mouth of the *b*,
17: 3 *b* which was covered with blasphemous names.
17: 3 This *b* had seven heads and ten horns.
17: 7 seven-headed and ten-horned *b* carrying her.
17: 8 The *b* you saw existed once but now exists
17: 8 world shall be amazed when they see the *b*,
17:11 The *b* which existed once but now exists no
17:12 possess royal authority along with the *b*,
17:13 bestow their power and authority on the *b*.
17:16 *b* will turn against the harlot with hatred;
17:17 on the *b* until his will is accomplished.
19:19 I saw the *b* and the kings of the earth,
19:20 The *b* was captured along with the false
19:20 the mark of the *b* and worship its image.
20: 4 those who had never worshiped the *b* or its
20:10 where the *b* and the false prophet had also

BEASTS (141)

Gn 6: 7 but also the *b* and the creeping things and
6:20 Of all kinds of birds, of all kinds of *b*,
31:39 never brought you an animal torn by wild *b*;
44:28 he must have been torn to pieces by wild *b*;
49: 9 like a lion recumbent, the king of *b*—
Ex 23:11 *b* of the field may eat what the poor leave.
23:29 that the wild *b* will multiply against you.
Lv 7:24 by wild *b* may be put to any other use,
22: 8 of itself or has been killed by wild *b*.
26: 6 I will rid the country of ravenous *b*,
26:22 I will unleash the wild *b* against you,
Nm 31:11 with the people and *b* they had captured,
31:26 captives and the *b* that have been taken;
31:30 and the same from the different *b*,
31:47 of every fifty, both of persons and of *b*,
Dt 5:14 slave, or your ox or ass or any of your *b*,
7:22 the wild *b* become too numerous for you.
28:26 of the air and for the *b* of the field,
32:24 the teeth of wild *b* I will send among them,
1Sm 17:44 birds of the air and the *b* of the field."
17:46 birds of the air and the *b* of the field;
1Kgs 5:13 out of the wall, and he spoke about *b*,
18: 5 shall not have to slaughter any of the *b*."
2Chr 25:18 But the wild *b* of the Lebanon passed by
Jdt 11: 7 *b* and the cattle and the birds of the air,
Est E:24 even shunned by wild *b* and birds forever."
1Mc 6:35 The *b* were distributed along the phalanxes,
6:43 saw one of the *b* bigger than any of the
2Mc 11: 9 not only men, but the most savage *b*,
Jb 4:10 lion roars, though the king of *b* cries out,
5:22 the *b* of the earth you need not dread.
5:23 and the wild *b* shall be at peace with you.
12: 7 But now ask the *b* to teach you,
18: 3 Why are we accounted like the *b*,
28: 8 The proud *b* have not trodden it,
35:11 Taught us rather than the *b* of the earth,
37: 8 the wild *b* take to cover and remain
39:15 them, that the wild *b* may trample them,
41:26 he is king over all proud *b*.
Ps(s) 8: 8 and oxen, yes, and the *b* of the field,
35:17 Save me from the roaring *b*;
49:13 he resembles the *b* that perish.
49:21 not prudence, resembles the *b* that perish.
50:10 forests, *b* by the thousand on my mountains.
78:48 their *b* and their flocks to the lightning.
78:50 death, and delivered their *b* to the plague.
79: 2 your faithful ones to the *b* of the earth.
80:14 waste, and the *b* of the field feed upon it?
104:20 then all the *b* of the forest roam about;
148:10 You wild *b* and all tame animals,
Prv 30:30 The lion, mightiest of *b*,
Eccl 3:18 showing that they are in themselves like *b*.
3:21 and the life-breath of *b* goes earthward?
Wis 7:20 stars, natures of animals, tempers of *b*,
11:18 unknown *b* to breathe forth fiery breath,
12: 9 once by terrible *b* or by one decisive word;
12:24 gods the worthless and disgusting among *b*,
13:10 the product of art, and likenesses of *b*,
15:18 they worship the most loathsome *b*—
15:19 their looks are they good or desirable *b*,
16: 5 For when the dire venom of *b* came upon
16:18 tempered so that the *b* might not be burnt
17:19 or the roaring cry of the fiercest *b*,
Sir 17: 4 flesh, and gives him rule over *b* and birds.
38:26 he keeps a watch on the *b* in the stalls.
39:30 and hail, famine, disease, Ravenous *b*,
Is 13:22 Desert *b* shall howl in her castles,
18: 6 birds of prey, and to the *b* in the land;
18: 6 them all the *b* of the earth shall winter.
34:14 Wildcats shall meet with desert *b*,
43:20 Wild *b* honor me,
46: 1 stoops, their idols are upon *b* and cattle;
56: 9 All you wild *b* of the field,
56: 9 come and eat, all you *b* in the forest!
Jer 2:24 No *b* need tire themselves seeking her;
7:33 of the sky and for the *b* of the field,
9: 9 Birds of the air as well as *b*,
12: 4 who dwell in it *b* and birds disappear,
12: 9 gather together, all you *b* of the field,
15: 3 *b* of the earth to devour and destroy them.
16: 4 birds of the sky and the *b* of the field.
19: 7 birds of the sky and the *b* of the field.
27: 6 even the *b* of the field I have given him
28:14 even the *b* of the field I give him.
34:20 birds of the air and the *b* of the field.
50:39 wildcats and desert *b* shall dwell there,
Bar 3:16 who lorded it over the wild *b* of the earth,
3:32 time, and filled it with four-footed *b*;
6:67 The *b* which can help themselves by fleeing
Ez 4:14 carrion flesh or that torn by wild *b*;
5:17 wild *b* that shall rob you of your children.
8:10 *b* [all the idols of the house of Israel].
14:15 I were to cause wild *b* to prowl the land,
14:15 traversed by none because of the wild *b*,
14:21 punishments, the sword, famine, wild *b*,
29: 5 To the *b* of the earth and the birds of the
31: 6 its branches all *b* of the field gave birth,
31:13 its branches were all the *b* of the field.
32: 4 the *b* of the earth eat their fill of you.
33:27 field I have given to the wild *b* for food;
34: 5 and became food for all the wild *b*.
34:25 them, and rid the country of ravenous *b*,
34:28 the nations or devoured by *b* of the earth,
36:11 I will settle crowds of men and *b* upon you,
38:20 the *b* of the field and all the reptiles
39: 4 to the wild *b* I am giving you to be eaten.
39:17 birds of every kind and to all the wild *b*:
44:31 of itself or has been killed by wild *b*.
Dn 2:38 men, wild *b*, and birds of the air,
3:81 All you *b*, wild and tame, bless the Lord;
4: 9 Under it the wild *b* found shade,
4:11 let the *b* flee its shade,
4:12 his lot be to eat, among *b*,
4:18 food for all, under which the wild *b* lived,
4:20 wild *b* till seven years pass over him'
4:22 out from among men and dwell with wild *b*;
4:29 among men, and shall dwell with wild *b*;
7: 3 sea, from which emerged four immense *b*,
7:12 The other *b*, which also their dominion
7:17 "These four great *b* stand for four
Hos 2:14 rank growth and wild *b* shall devour them.
2:20 them on that day, with the *b* of the field,
4: 3 The *b* of the field,
Jl 1:18 How the *b* groan!
1:20 Even the *b* of the field cry out to you;
2:22 Fear not, *b* of the field!
Mi 5: 7 peoples, Like a lion among *b* of the forest,
Hb 2:17 the destruction of the *b* shall terrify you;
Zep 2:15 has she become a waste, a lair for wild *b*?
Hg 1:11 Upon men and upon *b*,
Zec 2: 8 of the multitude of men and *b* in her midst.
8:10 were no wages for men, or hire for *b*;
14:15 and upon all the *b* that are in those camps.
Mk 1:13 He was with the wild *b*,
Acts 11: 6 of the earth, wild *b* and reptiles,
Rom 1:23 images representing mortal man, birds, *b*,
1Cor 15:32 *b* at Ephesus for purely human motives,
Ti 1:12 "Cretans have ever been liars, *b*,
Rv 6: 8 and plague and the wild *b* of the earth.
13: 3 I noticed that one of the *b* heads seemed
13:15 then permitted to give life to the *b* image,

BEAT (52)

Ex 9:25 it *b* down every growing thing and
Nm 22:23 had to *b* her to bring her back on the road.
22:25 Balaam's leg against it, he *b* her again.
22:27 anger, he again *b* the ass with his stick.
22:28 you that you should *b* me these three times?"
24:10 Balak *b* his palms together in a blaze of
Dt 28: 7 will *b* down before you the enemies that
Jgs 19:22 surrounded the house and *b* on the door.
Ru 2:17 and when she *b* out what she had gleaned it

1Sm 17: 9 but if I *b* him and kill him,
2Sm 20:19 *b* down a city that is a mother in Israel.
1Kgs 12:11 My father *b* you with whips,
12:11 whips, but I will *b* you with scorpions.' "
12:14 My father *b* you with whips,
12:14 whips, but I will *b* you with scorpions."
2Chr 10:11 My father *b* you with whips,
10:11 whips, but I will *b* you with scorpions!' "
10:14 My father *b* you with whips,
10:14 whips, but I will *b* you with scorpions."
34: 7 and carved images and *b* them into dust,
Tb 3: 9 Why do you *b* us?
2Mc 9: 2 natives and forced to *b* a shameful retreat.
Jb 39:13 The wings of the ostrich *b* idly;
Ps(s) 62: 4 you set upon a man and all together *b* him
Prv 19:25 If you *b* an arrogant man,
23:13 if you *b* him with the rod,
23:14 *B* him with the rod,
23:35 They *b* me, but I felt it not;
Wis 5:11 the fluid air, lashed by the *b* of pinions,
Is 2: 4 They shall *b* their swords into plowshares
14: 6 That *b* down the nations in anger,
27:12 The LORD shall *b* out the grain between the
32:12 *B* your breasts for the pleasant fields,
50: 6 I gave my back to those who *b* me,
Jer 5:17 They will *b* flat with the sword the
Dn 7:23 It shall devour the whole earth, *b* it down,
Jl 4:10 *B* your plowshares into swords,
Jon 4: 8 *b* upon Jonah's head
Mi 4: 3 They shall *b* their swords into plowshares,
Mt 21:35 They *b* one, killed another, and stoned
24:49 and begins to *b* his fellow servants,
Mk 12: 3 But they seized him, *b* him,
12: 4 *b* over the head and treated shamefully.
12: 5 some they *b*; some they killed.
Lk 10:30 They stripped him, *b* him,
18:13 All he did was *b* his breast and say,
20:10 they *b* him and sent him away empty-handed.
20:11 He sent a second servant whom they also *b*.
23:27 who *b* their breasts and lamented over him.
Acts 18:17 and *b* him in full view of the bench;
2Cor 12: 7 to *b* me and keep me from getting proud.
Rv 7:16 shall the sun or its heat *b* down on them,

BEATEN (40)

Ex 5:14 of Pharaoh had placed over them, were *b*,
5:16 Look how your servants are *b*!
22: 1 in the act of housebreaking and *b* to death,
22: 2 But if after sunrise he is thus *b*,
25:18 Make two cherubim of *b* gold for the two
25:31 shall make a lampstand of pure *b* gold
25:36 form but a single piece of pure *b* gold.
37: 7 Two cherubim of *b* gold were made for the
37:17 The lampstand was made of pure *b* gold
37:22 formed but a single piece of pure *b* gold.
Lv 26:17 till you are *b* down before your enemies
Nm 8: 4 *b* gold in both its shaft and its branches,
10: 2 "Make two trumpets of *b* silver,
14:42 go, you will be *b* down before your enemies.
22:32 have you *b* your ass these three times?
Dt 1:42 lest you be *b* down before your enemies,
25: 3 if he were *b* with more stripes than these,
28:25 will let you be *b* down before your enemies;
1Kgs 10:16 Solomon made two hundred shields of *b* gold
10:17 shield) and three hundred bucklers of *b* gold
2Kgs 23: 6 there he had it burned and *b* to dust,
2Chr 9:15 made two hundred large shields of *b* gold,
9:15 shekels of *b* gold going into each shield,
9:16 and three hundred bucklers of *b* gold,
25:19 You are thinking, 'See, I have *b* Edom!',
34: 4 images were shattered and *b* into dust,
Neh 13:25 some of them *b* and their hair pulled out;
1Mc 5:60 Joseph and Azariah were *b*,
9:68 fought against Bacchides, and he was *b*.
Sir 50: 9 Like a vessel of *b* gold,
50:16 the priests, on their trumpets of *b* metal;
Is 17: 6 As when an olive tree has been *b*,
21:10 been threshed, *b* on my threshing floor!
24:13 As with an olive tree after it is *b*,
28:27 But gith is *b* out with a staff,
Jer 18:15 old, To travel on bypaths, not the *b* track.
37:15 and had Jeremiah *b* and thrown into prison
Mk 13: 9 You will be *b* in synagogues.
2Cor 11:25 three times I was *b* with rods;
1Pt 2:20 If you do wrong and get *b* for it,

BEATING (10)

Nm 14:45 them, *b* them back as far as Hormah.
Dt 25: 3 disgraced because of the severity of the *b*.
Jgs 6:11 While his son Gideon was *b* out wheat in
Prv 6:33 A degrading *b* will he get,
18: 6 into strife, and his mouth provokes a *b*.
Wis 2: 2 reason is a spark at the *b* of our hearts,
Sir 42: 5 or of *b* the sides of a disloyal servant;
Na 2: 8 guard, Moaning like doves, *b* their breasts.
Lk 12:47 to fulfill them will get a severe *b*,
23:48 happened, they went home *b* their breasts.

BEATINGS (2)

2Cor 6: 5 *b*, imprisonments, and riots;
11:23 worse *b* and frequent brushes with death.

BEATS (3)

1Sm 17: 9 If he *b* me in combat and kills me,
Is 41: 7 goldsmith, the one who *b* with the hammer,
Jer 4:19 My heart *b* wildly, I cannot be still

BEAUTEOUS (3)

Wis 5:16 receive the splendid crown, the *b* diadem,
Ez 28: 7 draw their swords against your *b* wisdom,
Hos 9:13 I saw, was like Tyre, planted in a *b* spot;

BEAUTIFUL (54)

Gn 6: 2 the sons of heaven saw how *b* the daughters
12:11 how *b* a woman you are
12:14 the Egyptians saw how *b* the woman was;
24:16 The girl was very *b*, a virgin, untouched
26: 7 account of Rebekah, since she was very *b*.
29:17 eyes, but Rachel was well formed and *b*.
Jos 7:21 the spoils, I saw a *b* Babylonian mantle,
Jgs 15: 2 Her younger sister is more *b* than she;
2Sm 11: 2 he saw a woman bathing, who was very *b*.
13: 1 son Absalom had a *b* sister named Tamar,
14:27 a daughter named Tamar, who was a *b* woman.
1Kgs 1: 3 *b* girl throughout the territory of Israel,
1: 4 maiden, who was very *b*, nursed the king
Tb 6:12 girl is sensible, courageous, and very *b*;
Jdt 10: 4 made herself very *b*, to captivate the eyes
10:14 face, which appeared wondrously *b* to them,
11:21 the other looks so *b* and speaks so wisely!"
Est 2: 2 *b* young virgins be sought for the king.
2: 3 bring together all *b* young virgins to
2Mc 3:26 men, remarkably strong, strikingly *b*,
Jb 42:15 women were as *b* as the daughters of Job;
Prv 11:22 is a *b* woman with a rebellious disposition.
Sg 1: 8 If you do not know, O most *b* among women,
1:15 are beautiful, my beloved, ah, you are *b*;
1:16 you are *b*, my lover—yes, you are lovely.
2:10 says to me, "Arise, my beloved, my *b* one,
2:13 Arise, my beloved, my *b* one, and come!
4: 1 are beautiful, my beloved, ah, you are *b*!
4:10 How *b* is your love,
5: 9 from any other, O most *b* among women?
6: 1 has your lover gone, O most *b* among women?
6: 4 You are as *b* as Tirzah,
6:10 forth like the dawn, as *b* as the moon,
7: 2 How *b* are your feet in sandals,
7: 7 How *b* you are, how pleasing,
Sir 42:23 How *b* are all his works,
Is 52: 7 How *b* upon the mountains are the feet of
Jer 3:19 land, a heritage most *b* among the nations!
Ez 16:13 You were exceedingly *b*,
31: 3 a cypress [cedar] in Lebanon, *b* of branch,
31: 7 *b* and stately in its spread of foliage,
31: 9 I made it *b*, with much foliage,
Dn 4: 9 Its leaves were *b* and its fruit abundant,
4:18 which had *b* foliage and abundant fruit,
13: 2 who married a very *b* and God-fearing woman,
13:31 Susanna, very delicate and *b*, was veiled;
Mt 23:27 *b* to look at on the outside but inside
Acts 3: 2 the temple gate called "the *B*"
3:10 used to sit at the *B* Gate of the temple.
Rom 10:15 "How *b* are the feet of those who announce
Heb 11:23 because they saw that he was a *b* child.
Rv 21: 2 *b* as a bride prepared to meet her husband.

BEAUTIFULLY (2)

Jdt 8: 7 She was *b* formed and lovely to behold.
Est 2: 7 The girl was *b* formed and lovely to behold.

BEAUTIFYING (2)

Est 2:12 Of this period of *b* treatment,
Jer 4:30 eyes with cosmetics, *b* yourself in vain?

BEAUTY (53)

Ex 33:19 "I will make all my *b* pass before you,
2Sm 14:25 could so be praised for his *b* as Absalom,
Jdt 10: 7 much astounded at her *b* and said to her,
10:19 They marveled at her *b*,
10:23 they all marveled at the *b* of her face.
16: 6 by the *b* of her countenance disabled him.
16: 9 his eyes, and her *b* captivated his mind.
Est 1:11 her *b* to the populace and the officials,
C:30 She glowed with the perfection of her *b*
1Mc 1:26 and the *b* of the women was disfigured.
2:12 and our *b* and our glory laid waste,
Ps(s) 37:20 of the LORD, like the *b* of the meadows,
45: 3 Fairer in *b* are you than the sons of men;
45:12 So shall the king desire your *b*;
50: 2 From Zion, perfect in *b*, God shines forth.
Prv 6:25 Lust not in your heart after her *b*,
31:30 Charm is deceptive and *b* fleeting;
Wis 8: 2 her for my bride and was enamored of her *b*.
13: 3 of joy in their *b* they thought them gods,
13: 3 the original source of *b* fashioned them.
13: 5 *b* of created things their original author,
Sir 9: 8 gaze not upon the *b* of another's wife
9: 8 Through woman's *b* many perish,
25:20 Stumble not through a woman's *b*,
26:16 the *b* of a virtuous wife is the radiance
26:17 are her *b* of face and graceful figure.
36:22 *b* makes her husband's face light up,
40:22 Charm and *b* delight the eye,
43: 9 The *b*, the glory, of the heavens are the
45:12 splendor, a delight to the eyes, *b* supreme.
47: 9 He added *b* to the feasts and solemnized
51:14 She came to me in her *b*,
Is 3:24 a sackcloth skirt. Then, instead of *b*:
28: 1 To the fading blooms of his glorious *b*,
28: 4 The fading blooms of his glorious *b* on the
60:13 and the pine, To bring *b* to my sanctuary,
Jer 13:11 be my people, my renown, my praise, my *b*.
Bar 6:62 not their equal, whether in *b* or in power;
Ez 7:20 *b* of their ornaments they put their pride:
16:14 renowned among the nations for your *b*,
16:15 But you were captivated by your own *b*,
16:25 dais for yourself to use your *b* obscenely,
27: 3 you said, "I am a ship, perfect in *b*."
27: 4 your builders placed you, perfected your *b*.
27:11 on your walls, and made perfect your *b*.
28:12 of complete wisdom and perfect *b*,
28:17 became haughty of heart because of your *b*;
31: 8 no tree in the garden of God matched its *b*.
32:19 "Whom do you excel in *b*?
Dn 13:32 face so as to sate themselves with her *b*.
13:56 Daniel said to him, *b* has seduced you,
Zec 9:17 For what wealth is theirs, and what *b*!
1Pt 3: 4 *b* of a calm and gentle disposition.

BEBAI (6)

Ezr 2:11 sons of *B*, six hundred and twenty-three
8:11 of the sons of *B*, Zechariah, son of Bebai,
10:28 of the sons of *B*:
Neh 7:16 sons of *B*, six hundred and twenty-eight;
10:16 Elam, Zattu, Bani, Bunni, Azgad, *B*,

BECAME (447)

Gn 2: 7 of life, and so man *b* a living being.
3:20 because she *b* the mother of all the living.
4: 2 Abel *b* a keeper of flocks,
4:17 Cain also *b* the founder of a city,
4:18 Irad, and Irad *b* the father of Mehujael;
4:18 Mehujael *b* the father of Methusael,
4:18 and Methusael *b* the father of Lamech.
5: 6 five years old, he *b* the father of Enosh.
5: 9 ninety years old, he *b* the father of Kenan.
5:12 years old, he *b* the father of Mahalalel.
5:15 years old, he *b* the father of Jared.
5:18 years old, he *b* the father of Enoch.
5:21 years old, he *b* the father of Methuselah.
5:25 years old, he *b* the father of Lamech.
5:32 hundred years old, he *b* the father of Shem,
9:21 he *b* drunk and lay naked inside his tent.
10: 8 Cush *b* the father of Nimrod,
10:13 Mizraim *b* the father of the Ludim,
10:15 Canaan *b* the father of Sidon,
10:24 Arpachshad *b* the father of Shelah,
10:24 of Shelah, and Shelah *b* the father of Eber.
10:26 Joktan *b* the father of Almodad,
11:10 years old, he *b* the father of Arpachshad,
11:12 years old, he *b* the father of Shelah.
11:14 thirty years old, he *b* the father of Eber.
11:16 years old, he *b* the father of Peleg.
11:18 thirty years old, he *b* the father of Reu.
11:20 years old, he *b* the father of Serug.
11:22 thirty years old, he *b* the father of Nahor.
11:24 years old, he *b* the father of Terah.
11:26 years old, he *b* the father of Abram,
11:27 Terah *b* the father of Abram,
11:27 and Haran, and Haran *b* the father of Lot.
16: 4 intercourse with her, and she *b* pregnant.
16: 4 When she *b* aware of her pregnancy,
16: 5 ever since she *b* aware of her pregnancy,
19:36 Lot's daughters *b* pregnant by their father.
20:12 and so she *b* my wife.
21: 2 Sarah *b* pregnant and bore Abraham a son in
21:20 in the wilderness and *b* an expert bowman,
22:23 Bethuel *b* the father of Rebekah.
24:67 he married her, and thus she *b* his wife.
25: 3 Jokshan *b* the father of Sheba and Dedan.
25:21 heard his entreaty, and Rebekah *b* pregnant.
25:27 the boys grew up, Esau *b* a skillful hunter,
26:13 him, he *b* richer and richer all the time,
26:14 that the Philistines *b* envious of him.
26:35 But they *b* a source of embitterment to
30: 1 to Jacob, she *b* envious of her sister.
36:32 Bela, son of Beor, *b* king in Edom;
39:19 his slave had treated her, he *b* enraged.
40: 4 Joseph to them, and he *b* their attendant.
41:50 set in, Joseph *b* the father of two sons,
43:18 led to his house, they *b* apprehensive.
46:20 *b* the father of Manasseh and Ephraim,
49:15 to the burden and *b* a toiling serf.
50:15 Joseph's brothers *b* fearful and thought,
Ex 1: 7 They *b* so numerous and strong that the
2:14 Then Moses *b* afraid and thought,
4: 4 hold of it, and it *b* a staff in his hand.
4:14 Then the LORD *b* angry with Moses and said,
7:21 and the river itself *b* so polluted that
8:11 he *b* obdurate and would not listen to them
8:28 *b* obdurate and would not let the people go.
9:24 seen in the land since Egypt *b* a nation.
9:34 he with his servants *b* obdurate,
14:20 But the cloud now *b* dark,

BECAME (cont.)

15:25 this into the water, the water *b* fresh.
16:20 following morning, it *b* wormy and rotten.
32: 1 When the people *b* aware of Moses' delay in
Nm 6:12 because his dedicated head *b* unclean.
11:10 their tents, so that the LORD *b* very angry,
16:15 Moses *b* very angry and said to the LORD,
31:14 *b* angry with the officers of the army,
Dt 26: 5 But there he *b* a nation great,
32:15 you *b* fat and gross and gorged.
33: 5 his domain, and he *b* king of his darling.
Jgs 10: 7 the LORD *b* angry with Israel and allowed
11:39 then it *b* a custom in Israel
15:14 the ropes around his arms *b* as flax that
17: 5 one of his sons, who *b* his priest.
17:11 man, to whom he *b* as one of his own sons.
17:12 the young Levite, who *b* his priest,
Ru 4:16 placed him on her lap, and *b* his nurse.
4:22 of Jesse, and Jesse *b* the father of David.
1Sm 7: 7 the Israelites *b* afraid of the Philistines
11: 6 of God rushed upon him and he *b* very angry.
13: 1 he *b* king and he reigned . . . (two) years
16:21 Saul *b* very fond of him,
21:13 remarks and *b* very much afraid of Achish,
22: 2 who were embittered, and he *b* their leader.
25:37 died within him, and he *b* like a stone.
25:42 She *b* his wife, and David also married
2Sm 2:10 forty years old when he *b* king over Israel,
4: 4 in their hasty flight, he fell and *b* lame.]
5: 4 David was thirty years old when he *b* king,
8: 2 Thus the Moabites *b* tributary to David.
8: 6 of Damascus, and the Arameans *b* subjects,
8:13 David *b* famous for having slain eighteen
8:14 Thus all the Edomites *b* David's subjects,
10:19 with the Israelites and *b* their subjects.
11:27 She *b* his wife and bore him a son.
12:15 borne to David, and it *b* desperately ill.
13: 2 over his sister Tamar that he *b* sick;
13:21 got word of the whole affair, *b* very angry.
13:39 as he *b* reconciled to the death of Amnon.
14:26 year, because his hair *b* too heavy for him
16: 8 family of Saul, in whose stead you *b* king,
22:44 A people I had not known *b* my slaves;
23:10 until his hand grew tired and *b* cramped,
1Kgs 2:15 the kingdom escaped me and *b* my brother's,
11: 9 The LORD, therefore, *b* angry with Solomon,
11:24 men about him and *b* leader of a band,
11:24 settled there, and *b* king in Damascus.
13:33 and *b* a priest of the high places.
14:21 He was forty-one years old when he *b* king,
15: 1 son of Nebat, Abijam *b* king of Judah;
15:25 Nadab, son of Jeroboam, *b* king of Israel;
16: 7 so that he *b* like the house of Jeroboam;
16:22 Tibni died and Omri *b* king.
16:23 year of Asa, king of Judah, Omri *b* king;
16:29 Judah, Ahab son of Omri, *b* king of Israel;
21:26 *b* completely abominable by following idols,
2Kgs 3: 1 *b* king of Israel in Samaria [in the
4:34 himself over the child, the body *b* warm.
5: 2 girl, who *b* the servant of Naaman's wife.
5:14 *b* again like the flesh of a little child,
8:11 stared him down until Hazael *b* ill at ease.
8:16 son of Jehoshaphat, king of Judah, *b* king.
8:25 Judah, *b* king in the twelfth year of Joram,
12: 1 Joash was seven years old when he *b* king.
14: 2 was twenty-five years old when he *b* king,
15: 1 *b* king in the twenty-seventh year of
15:13 *b* king in the thirty-ninth year of Uzziah,
15:33 was twenty-five years old when he *b* king,
16: 2 Ahaz was twenty years old when he *b* king,
17: 3 Hoshea *b* his vassal and paid him tribute.
17:15 The vanity they pursued, they themselves *b:*
18: 2 was twenty-five years old when he *b* king,
24: 1 and Jehoiakim *b* his vassal for three years.
24:18 was twenty-one years old when he *b* king,
1Chr 1:10 Cush *b* the father of Nimrod,
1:11 Mesraim *b* the father of the Ludim,
1:13 Canaan *b* the father of Sidon,
1:18 Arpachshad *b* the father of Shelah,
1:18 of Shelah, and Shelah *b* the father of Eber.
1:20 Joktan *b* the father of Almodad,
1:34 Abraham *b* the father of Isaac.
2:10 Ram *b* the father of Amminadab,
2:10 and Amminadab *b* the father of Nahshon,
2:11 Nahshon *b* the father of Salma.
2:11 Salma *b* the father of Boaz.
2:12 Boaz *b* the father of Obed.
2:12 Obed *b* the father of Jesse.
2:13 Jesse *b* the father of Eliab,
2:18 son of Hezron, *b* the father of a daughter,
2:20 Hur *b* the father of Uri,
2:20 of Uri, and Uri *b* the father of Bezalel.
2:22 Segub *b* the father of Jair,
2:36 Attai *b* the father of Nathan.
2:36 Nathan *b* the father of Zabad.
2:37 Zabad *b* the father of Ephlal.
2:37 Ephlal *b* the father of Obed.
2:38 Obed *b* the father of Jehu.
2:38 Jehu *b* the father of Azariah.
2:39 Azariah *b* the father of Helez.
2:39 Helez *b* the father of Eleasah.
2:40 Eleasah *b* the father of Sismai.
2:40 Sismai *b* the father of Shallum.
2:41 Shallum *b* the father of Jekamiah.
2:41 Jekamiah *b* the father of Elishama.
2:44 Shema *b* the father of Raham,
2:44 Rekem *b* the father of Shammai.
2:46 Haran *b* the father of Gazez.
4: 2 the son of Shobal, *b* the father of Jahath,
4: 2 Jahath *b* the father of Ahumai and Lahad.
4: 8 Koz *b* the father of Anub and Zobebah,
4:11 brother of Shuhah, *b* the father of Mehir,
4:12 Eshton *b* the father of Bethrapha,
4:14 Meonothai *b* the father of Ophrah.
4:14 Seraiah *b* the father of Joab,
4:17 Jether *b* the father of Miriam,
5: 2 in fact, *b* powerful among his brothers,
5:30 Eleazar *b* the father of Phinehas.
5:30 Phinehas *b* the father of Abishua.
5:31 Abishua *b* the father of Bukki.
5:31 Bukki *b* the father of Uzzi.
5:32 Uzzi *b* the father of Zerahiah.
5:32 Zerahiah *b* the father of Meraioth.
5:33 Meraioth *b* the father of Amariah.
5:33 Amariah *b* the father of Ahitub.
5:34 Ahitub *b* the father of Zadok.
5:34 Zadok *b* the father of Ahimaaz.
5:35 Ahimaaz *b* the father of Azariah.
5:35 Azariah *b* the father of Johanan.
5:36 Johanan *b* the father of Azariah,
5:37 Azariah *b* the father of Amariah.
5:37 Amariah *b* the father of Ahitub.
5:38 Ahitub *b* the father of Zadok.
5:38 Zadok *b* the father of Shallum.
5:39 Shallum *b* the father of Hilkiah.
5:39 Hilkiah *b* the father of Azariah.
5:40 Azariah *b* the father of Seraiah.
5:40 Seraiah *b* the father of Jehozadak.
7:32 Heber *b* the father of Japhlet,
8: 1 Benjamin *b* the father of Bela,
8: 7 exile, *b* the father of Uzza and Ahihud.
8: 8 Shaharaim *b* a father on the Moabite
8: 9 his wife Hodesh he *b* the father of Jobab,
8:11 he *b* the father of Abitub and Elpaal.
8:32 Mikloth *b* the father of Shimeah.
8:33 Ner *b* the father of Kish,
8:33 of Kish, and Kish *b* the father of Saul.
8:33 Saul *b* the father of Jonathan,
8:34 and Merribbaal *b* the father of Micah.
8:36 Ahaz *b* the father of Jehoaddah,
8:36 and Jehoaddah *b* the father of Alemeth,
8:36 Zimri *b* the father of Moza.
8:37 Moza *b* the father of Binea,
9:18 now they *b* gatekeepers for the encampments
9:38 Mikloth *b* the father of Shimeah.
9:39 Ner *b* the father of Kish,
9:39 of Kish, and Kish *b* the father of Saul.
9:39 Saul *b* the father of Jonathan,
9:40 and Meribbaal *b* the father of Micah.
9:42 Ahaz *b* the father of Jehoaddah,
9:42 and Jehoaddah *b* the father of Alemeth,
9:42 Zimri *b* the father of Moza.
9:43 Moza *b* the father of Binea,
11: 6 and so he *b* chief.
11: 9 David *b* more and more powerful,
11:21 as any of the Thirty and *b* their commander,
12:22 all warriors and *b* commanders of his army.
13:10 the LORD *b* angry with Uzzah and struck him;
14: 3 *b* the father of more sons and daughters.
17:22 own forever, and you, O LORD, *b* their God.
18: 2 Moab, and the Moabites *b* his subjects,
18: 6 of Aram, and the Arameans *b* his subjects,
18:13 and all the Edomites *b* David's subjects.
19:19 made peace with David and *b* his subjects.
2Chr 1:13 the meeting tent, and *b* king over Israel.
1:15 while cedars *b* as numerous as the
8: 9 *b* soldiers, commanders of his warriors,
9:27 while cedars *b* as numerous as the
12:13 he was forty-one years old when he *b* king,
13: 1 of King Jeroboam, Abijah *b* king of Judah;
16:10 But Asa *b* angry with the seer and
18: 1 but he *b* related to Ahab by marriage.
18:32 The chariot commanders *b* aware that he was
20:31 was thirty-five years old when he *b* king,
21: 5 was thirty-two years old when he *b* king,
21:20 He was thirty-two years old when he *b* king,
22: 2 He was twenty-two years old when he *b* king,
24: 1 Joash was seven years old when he *b* king,
24: 3 and he *b* the father of sons and daughters.
25: 1 was twenty-five years old when he *b* king,
25:10 however, *b* furiously angry with Judah,
26: 3 was sixteen years old when he *b* king,
26:16 he *b* proud to his own destruction and
26:19 a censer for burning the incense, *b* angry,
27: 1 was twenty-five years old when he *b* king,
27: 8 was twenty-five years old when he *b* king,
28: 1 Ahaz was twenty years old when he *b* king,
28:22 Ahaz *b* even more unfaithful to the LORD.
29: 1 was twenty-five years old when he *b* king,
32:24 In those days Hezekiah *b* mortally ill.
33: 1 was twelve years old when he *b* king,
33:21 was twenty-two years old when he *b* king,
34: 1 Josiah was eight years old when he *b* king,
36: 2 was twenty-three years old when he *b* king,
36: 5 was twenty-five years old when he *b* king,
36: 9 was eighteen years old when he *b* king,
36:11 was twenty-one years old when he *b* king,
36:13 He *b* stiffnecked and hardened his heart
36:20 where they *b* his and his sons' servants
Ezr 2:61 the Gileadite and *b* known by his name).
Neh 3:33 his anger and he *b* very much incensed.
4: 1 they *b* extremely angry.
4: 9 When our enemies *b* aware that we had been
7:63 the Gileadite and *b* known by his name).
12:10 Jeshua *b* the father of Joiakim,
12:10 Joiakim, Joiakim *b* the father of Eliashib,
12:10 and Eliashib *b* the father of Joiada.
12:11 Joiada *b* the father of Johanan,
12:11 and Johanan *b* the father of Jaddua.
Tb 1:13 I *b* purchasing agent for all his needs.
1:15 him as king, the roads to Media *b* unsafe,
2:10 various salves, the worse the cataracts *b,*
2:14 I *b* very angry with her over this.
6:18 love with her, and his heart *b* set on her.
Est 2:22 When the plot *b* known to Mordecai,
D:16 The king *b* troubled and all his attendants
9: 1 the Jews *b* masters of their enemies.
1Mc 1: 1 Persians and Medes, he *b* king in his place,
1: 3 him, and his heart *b* proud and arrogant.
1: 4 and rulers, and they *b* his tributaries.
1:10 He *b* king in the year one hundred and
1:33 and strong towers, and it *b* their citadel.
1:35 And they *b* a great threat.
1:36 citadel *b* an ambush against the sanctuary,
1:38 away, and she *b* the abode of strangers.
1:38 She *b* a stranger to her own offspring,
2:53 the commandment, and he *b* master of Egypt.
2:55 his commission, *b* a judge in Israel.
6: 3 because his plan *b* known to the people of
6:59 that they *b* angry and did all these things."
7:30 When he *b* aware that Nicanor had come to
8:13 they desired to help to a kingdom *b* kings,
9:60 this, however, because their plot *b* known.
10:76 of the city *b* afraid and opened the gates,
10:81 whereas the enemy's horses *b* tired out.
11:12 broke with Alexander; their enmity *b* open.
11:19 Thus Demetrius *b* king in the year one
11:51 and they *b* renowned throughout his kingdom.
11:53 his promises and *b* estranged from Jonathan.
11:54 who *b* king and wore the royal crown.
15:27 made with Simon and *b* hostile toward him.
16:13 But he *b* ambitious and sought to get
2Mc 1:33 When the event *b* known and the king of the
4:16 thing, *b* their enemies and oppressors.
4:50 where he grew in wickedness and *b* the
5:20 once the great Sovereign *b* reconciled.
6:29 now *b* hostile toward him because what he
7:39 the king *b* enraged and treated him even
10:14 When Gorgias *b* governor of the region,
14:27 villain's calumnies, the king *b* enraged.
Ps(s) 18:44 A people I had not known *b* my slaves;
69:12 my garment, and I *b* a byword for them.
83:11 they *b* dung on the ground.
106:36 their idols, which *b* a snare for them.
106:39 They *b* defiled by their works,
107:38 He blessed them, and they *b* very many;
114: 2 of alien tongue, Judah *b* his sanctuary,
Eccl 2: 9 I *b* great, and stored up more than all
Wis 10:17 and *b* a shelter for them by day and a
14:21 And this *b* a snare for mankind,
Sir 24:29 suddenly this rivulet of mine *b* a river,
45:19 But the LORD saw this and *b* angry,
46: 4 power stop the sun, so that one day *b* two?
51:18 I *b* resolutely devoted to her
51:19 I *b* preoccupied with her,
Is 57:11 that you *b* false And did not remember me
63: 8 So he *b* their savior 9 in their every
Jer 2: 5 after empty idols, and *b* empty themselves?
15:16 *b* my joy and the happiness of my heart,
44: 6 they *b* the ruinous waste they are today.
44:22 and so your land *b* a waste,
52: 1 was twenty-one years old when he *b* king,
Ez 14:15 land, depopulating it so that it *b* a waste,
16: 8 you *b* mine, says the LORD GOD
16:15 on every passer-by, whose own you *b.*
16:47 *b* more corrupt in all your ways than they.
16:50 they *b* haughty and committed abominable
16:57 yourself, before your wickedness *b* evident?
17: 6 Thus it *b* a vine, produced branches
19: 3 whelp she raised up, a young lion he *b;*
19: 6 among the lions, a young lion he *b;*
23: 4 They *b* mine and bore sons and daughters.
23: 5 Oholah *b* a harlot faithless to me;
23:10 Thus she *b* a byword for women,
23:17 defiled by them, she *b* disgusted with them.
23:18 and I *b* disgusted with her as I had become
27: 7 *b* your sail [to serve you as a banner].
28:17 *b* haughty of heart because of your beauty;
29:18 *b* bald and their shoulders were galled;
31: 7 It *b* beautiful and stately in its spread
31:10 Because it *b* lofty in stature,
31:10 because it *b* proud in heart at its height,
34: 5 and *b* food for all the wild beasts.
44:12 and *b* an occasion of sin to the house of
Dn 2:12 At this the king *b* violently angry and
2:35 But the stone that struck the statue *b* a
3:19 *b* livid with utter rage against Shadrach,
4:33 my kingdom, and *b* much greater than before.
5:20 But when his heart *b* proud and his spirit

8: 4 it did what it pleased and *b* very powerful.
8: 8 The he-goat *b* very powerful,
Hos 8:11 expiate sin, his altars *b* occasions of sin.
9:10 *b* as abhorrent as the thing they loved.
13: 6 they *b* proud of heart and forgot me.
Jon 1: 5 *b* frightened and each one cried to his god.
4: 1 displeasing to Jonah, and he *b* angry.
4: 8 beat upon Jonah's head till he *b* faint.
Zec 11: 7 So I *b* the shepherd of the flock to be
Mt 1:11 Josiah *b* the father of Jechoniah and his
2: 3 this news King Herod *b* greatly disturbed,
2:16 deceived by the astrologers, he *b* furious.
4:20 abandoned their nets and *b* his followers.
12:13 it *b* as sound as the other.
17: 2 His face *b* as dazzling as the sun,
20:24 this, *b* indignant at the two brothers.
20:34 and they *b* his followers.
21:15 The chief priests and the scribes *b*
26:10 Jesus *b* aware of this and said to them:
Mk 1:18 abandoned their nets and *b* his followers.
2:14 Levi got up and *b* his follower.
9: 3 eyes and his clothes *b* dazzlingly white
9:26 the boy *b* like a corpse,
10:14 Jesus *b* indignant when he noticed it and
10:41 this, *b* indignant at James and John.
Lk 5:11 land, left everything, and *b* his followers.
5:28 behind, Levi stood up and *b* his follower.
6:11 At this they *b* frenzied and began asking
9:29 and his clothes *b* dazzlingly white.
13:19 It grew and *b* a large shrub and the birds
22:44 and his sweat *b* like drops of blood
23:12 each other, *b* friends from that day.
Jn 1:14 *b* flesh and made his dwelling among us,
4:53 his whole household thereupon *b* believers.
20:29 "You *b* a believer because you saw me.
Acts 3: 7 the beggar's feet and ankles *b* strong;
7:13 and his family ties *b* known to the Pharaoh.
7:29 Midian, where he *b* the father of two sons.
8:13 rest and *b* a devoted follower of Philip.
9:42 This *b* known all over Joppa,
10:10 He *b* hungry and asked for some food,
13:45 they *b* very jealous and countered with
16:18 several days until finally Paul *b* annoyed,
19: 2 the Holy Spirit when you *b* believers?"
19:17 When this *b* known to the Jews and Greeks
20: 9 on the window-sill *b* drowsier and drowsier.
22:29 The commander *b* alarmed because he
24:25 the coming judgment, Felix *b* frightened.
Rom 4:18 and so *b* the father of many nations,
5:19 one man's disobedience all *b* sinners,
6:18 from your sin, you *b* slaves of justice.
11: 8 The rest *b* blind, as Scripture says:
15: 8 I affirm that Christ *b* the servant of the
1Cor 3: 5 ministers through whom you *b* believers,
9:20 I *b* like a Jew to the Jews in order to win
9:20 To those bound by the law I *b* like one who
9:21 To those not subject to the law I *b* like
9:22 To the weak I *b* a weak person with a view
13:11 When I *b* a man I put childish ways aside.
15:45 that Adam, the first man, *b* a living soul;
Gal 4:12 to become like me as I *b* like you.
Eph 3: 7 of his power, I *b* a minister of the gospel.
Col 1:25 I *b* a minister of this church through the
1Thes 1: 6 in turn, *b* imitators of us and of the Lord,
1: 7 Thus you *b* a model for all the believers
Heb 5: 9 he *b* the source of eternal salvation for
7:20 the old covenant *b* priests without an oath,
11:34 were made powerful, *b* strong in battle,
1Pt 2: 7 the builders rejected that *b* a cornerstone."
1Jn 1: 1 (This life *b* visible;
1: 1 present to the Father and *b* visible to us.)
Rv 15: 8 Then the sanctuary *b* so filled with the

BECHER (5)

Gn 46:21 Bela, *B*, Ashbel, Gera, Naaman,
Nm 26:35 through *B* the clan of the Bechrites,
1Chr 7: 6 The sons of Benjamin were Bela, *B*,
7: 8 The sons of *B* were Zemirah,
7: 8 all these were sons of *B*.

BECHRITES (1)

Nm 26:35 through Becher the clan of the *B*,

BECOME (407)

Gn 2:24 his wife, and the two of them *b* one body.
3:22 The man has *b* like one of us,
4:12 shall *b* a restless wanderer on the earth."
4:14 and *b* a restless wanderer on the earth,
6:12 When God saw how corrupt the earth had *b*,
9:15 *b* a flood to destroy all mortal beings.
17: 4 are to *b* the father of a host of nations.
17:20 He shall *b* the father of twelve chieftains,
18:18 he is to *b* a great and populous nation,
24:35 so abundantly that he has *b* a wealthy man;
24:51 she may *b* the wife of your master's son,
26:16 you have *b* far too numerous for us."
27:40 But when you *b* restive,
28: 3 you that you may *b* an assembly of peoples.
29:34 at last my husband will *b* attached to me,
34:15 that you *b* like us by having every male
34:16 you and *b* one kindred people with you.
36: 7 had *b* too great for them to dwell together,
38:23 "otherwise we shall *b* a laughingstock.
44: 9 rest of us, we shall *b* my lord's slaves."
44:10 who is found to have it shall *b* my slave,
44:17 the goblet was found shall *b* my slave;
44:18 lord, and do not *b* angry with your servant,
47:19 and we will *b* Pharaoh's slaves and our
48:16 may *b* teeming multitudes upon the earth!"
48:19 That one too shall *b* a tribe,
48:19 descendants shall *b* a multitude of nations."
Ex 4: 9 the river will *b* blood on the dry land."
7:18 and the river itself shall *b* so polluted
7:19 that they may *b* blood.
16:24 commanded, it did not *b* rotten or wormy.
23:29 else the land will *b* so desolate that the
29:37 and whatever touches it will *b* sacred.
32: 7 land of Egypt, for they have *b* depraved.
34:12 else they will *b* a snare among you.
34:29 *b* radiant while he conversed with the LORD.
34:30 how radiant the skin of his face had *b*,
Lv 4: 3 and thereby makes the people also *b* guilty,
4:14 on *b* known that the sin was committed,
4:22 of the LORD, his God, and thus *b* guilty,
6:20 Whatever touches its flesh shall *b* sacred.
11:34 men drink, in any such vessel *b* unclean.
11:38 but if the grain has *b* moistened it
13: 6 man shall wash his garments and so *b* clean.
14:36 lest everything in the house *b* unclean.
18:25 Because their land has *b* defiled,
19:29 land will *b* corrupt and full of lewdness.
21:11 he thus *b* unclean or leave the sanctuary;
22: 4 who has *b* unclean by contact with a corpse,
25:23 you are but aliens who have *b* my tenants.
26:21 *b* defiant in your unwillingness to obey me,
26:22 dwindles away and your roads *b* deserted.
27:21 is doomed, it shall *b* priestly property.
Nm 5: 2 who has *b* unclean by contact with a corpse.
5:10 they *b* the property of the priest to whom
5:27 so that she will *b* an example of
6: 7 brother, should they die, may he *b* unclean,
6:20 *b* sacred and shall belong to the priest,
17: 3 before the LORD they have *b* sacred.
19:12 on the seventh day, he will not *b* clean.
21:29 He let his sons *b* fugitives and his
31:23 put into the fire, that it may *b* clean;
33:55 allow to remain will *b* as barbs in your eyes
Dt 1:39 little ones, who you said would *b* booty,
7:22 the wild beasts *b* too numerous for you.
8:14 you then *b* haughty of heart and unmindful
9:12 have brought out of Egypt have *b* depraved;
17:20 Let him not *b* estranged from his
19:10 and you will not *b* guilty of bloodshed.
21:11 captives and *b* so enamored of her
22: 9 if you do, its produce shall *b* forfeit,
24: 4 her as his wife after she has *b* defiled.
27: 9 This day you have *b* the people of the LORD,
28:25 so that you will *b* a terrifying example to
28:26 Your carcasses will *b* food for all the
28:44 He will *b* the head, you the tail.
31:17 so that they will *b* a prey to be devoured,
31:29 after my death you are sure to *b* corrupt
32:20 said, "and see what will then *b* of them.
Jos 14: 9 land where you have set foot shall *b* your
Jgs 1:30 among them, but have *b* forced laborers.
1:33 Beth-anath have *b* forced laborers for them.
2: 3 you and their gods shall *b* a snare for you."
6: 5 their tents would *b* as numerous as locusts;
17:13 me, since the Levite has *b* my priest."
Ru 1:11 sons in my womb who may *b* your husbands?
4:12 may your house *b* like the house of Perez,
4:14 May he *b* famous in Israel!
1Sm 4: 9 otherwise you will *b* slaves to the Hebrews,
6: 6 Why should you *b* stubborn,
8:17 and you yourselves will *b* his slaves.
9: 5 about the asses and *b* anxious about us."
18: 1 Jonathan had *b* as fond of David as if his
18:17 give you in marriage if you *b* my champion
18:18 that I should *b* the king's son-in-law?"
18:21 will offer her to him to *b* a snare for him,
18:21 David, "You shall *b* my son-in-law today."]
18:22 You should *b* the king's son-in-law."
18:23 think it easy to *b* the king's son-in-law?
18:27 that he might thus *b* the king's son-in-law.
19: 5 should you *b* guilty of shedding innocent
20:26 "He must have *b* unclean by accident,
22:13 he might rebel against me and *b* my enemy,
25:26 those who seek to harm my lord *b* as Nabal!
25:37 But then, when Nabal had *b* sober,
25:41 "Your handmaid would *b* a slave to wash
29: 4 us, lest during the battle he *b* our enemy.
2Sm 7:24 forever, and you, LORD, have *b* their God.
11:20 the king may *b* angry and say to you:
19:14 if you do not *b* my general permanently in
1Kgs 1:11 has *b* king without the knowledge of our
1:13 Why, then, has Adonijah *b* king?'
1:18 But now Adonijah has *b* king,
9: 7 *b* a proverb and a byword among all nations,
9: 8 and this temple shall *b* a heap of ruins.
11:37 that you desire and shall *b* king of Israel.
22:22 'I will go forth and *b* a lying spirit in
2Kgs 9:29 Ahaziah had *b* king of Judah in the
14:10 conquered Edom, and you have *b* ambitious.
21:14 *b* a prey and a booty for all their enemies,
22:19 would *b* a desolation and a curse;
1Chr 17: 7 you might *b* ruler over my people Israel.
2Chr 12: 1 consolidated his rule and had *b* powerful,
18:21 'I will go forth and *b* a lying spirit in
19:10 warn them lest they *b* guilty before the
26:16 But after he had *b* strong,
32:25 his debt of gratitude, for he had *b* proud.
Ezr 9:14 Would you not *b* so angered with us as to
Neh 9:21 their garments did not *b* worn,
9:21 worn, and their feet did not *b* swollen.
9:36 see, we have *b* slaves upon it!
Tb 4:15 Do not drink wine till you *b* drunk,
6:13 you or let her *b* engaged to another man;
14: 4 entire country of Israel shall *b* desolate;
14: 4 Samaria and Jerusalem shall *b* desolate!
14: 7 but those who *b* guilty of sin shall
Jdt 5:21 *b* the laughing stock of the whole world."
7:27 we would be better off to *b* their prey.
Est 1:17 conduct will *b* known to all the women,
2:11 Esther was faring and what was to *b* of her.
E: 2 "Many have *b* the more ambitious the more
E: 5 many placed in authority to *b* accomplices
9: 1 the Jews had expected to *b* masters of them,
1Mc 1:16 Antiochus proposed to *b* king of Egypt,
2: 8 "Her temple has *b* like a man disgraced,
2:11 From being free, she has *b* a slave.
3:42 brothers saw that the situation had *b* critical
5: 4 who had *b* a snare and a stumblingblock to
6:24 the sons of our people have *b* our enemies;
10:56 and I will *b* your father-in-law as you
12:10 so as not to *b* strangers to you altogether;
12:39 Trypho was determined to *b* king of Asia,
14:30 rallied his nation and *b* their high priest,
2Mc 5:18 they had not *b* entangled in so many sins,
9:17 he would *b* a Jew himself and visit every
11:14 also, and to induce him to *b* their friend.
12:39 day, since the task had now *b* urgent,
Jb 6:21 It is thus that you have now *b* for me;
11:17 its gloom shall *b* as the morning,
12: 4 I have *b* the sport of my neighbors:
17: 6 their object lesson I have *b*.
21: 7 wicked surive, grow old, *b* mighty in power?
30: 9 I am *b* a byword among them.
30:29 I have *b* the brother of jackals,
33:25 Then his flesh shall *b* soft as a boy's;
37:10 frost, and the broad waters *b* congealed.
Ps(s) 7: 3 rescue me, Lest I *b* like the lion's prey,
14: 3 they have *b* perverse;
22:15 *b* like wax melting away within my bosom.
28: 1 I *b* one of those going down into the pit.
38:15 I am *b* like a man who neither hears nor
53: 4 they have *b* perverse;
69: 9 I have *b* an outcast to my brothers,
69:26 Let their encampment *b* desolate;
79: 4 We have *b* the reproach of our neighbors,
102: 7 I have *b* like an owl among the ruins.
109:25 And I am *b* a mockery to them;
118:22 builders rejected has *b* the cornerstone.
119:70 Their heart has *b* gross and fat;
143: 7 I *b* like those who go down into the pit.
Prv 6: 1 son, if you have *b* surety to your neighbor,
11:16 [The slothful *b* impoverished,
11:29 and the fool will *b* slave to the wise man.
13:20 Walk with wise men and you will *b* wise,
19:20 that you may eventually *b* wise.
22:26 in pledge, of those who *b* surety for debts;
25:16 lest you *b* glutted with it and vomit it up.
26: 4 to his folly, lest you too *b* like him.
26: 5 his folly, lest he *b* wise in his own eyes.
29:12 to lying words, his servants all *b* wicked.
29:18 Without prophecy the people *b* demoralized;
Eccl 1: 7 to the sea, yet never does the sea *b* full.
1:16 I have *b* great and stored up wisdom beyond
7: 9 Do not in spirit *b* quickly discontented,
Sg 8:10 in his eyes I have *b* one to be welcomed.
Wis 4:13 Having *b* perfect in a short while,
4:19 And they shall afterward *b* dishonored
8:11 I should *b* keen in judgment,
14:11 they have *b* abominable amid God's works,
16:11 and *b* unresponsive to your beneficence.
Sir 6:29 find rest in her, and she will *b* your joy.
7: 6 Seek not to *b* a judge if you have not
11:18 A man may *b* rich through a miser's life,
18:33 *B* not a glutton and a winebibber with
19: 8 it against you, and in time *b* your enemy.
23:13 Let not your mouth *b* used to coarse talk,
24:17 vine, my blossoms *b* fruit fair and rich.
24:30 shining like the dawn, to *b* known afar off.
30:12 he is still small, Lest he *b* stubborn,
37:28 neither *b* a glutton for choice foods,
38:24 whoever is free from toil can *b* a wise man.
38:25 How can he *b* learned who guides the plow,
39:17 his word the waters *b* still as in a flask;
41: 9 at death, you *b* a curse.
Is 1: 9 us a scanty remnant, We had *b* as Sodom,
1:18 be like scarlet, they may *b* white as snow;
1:18 be crimson red, they may *b* white as wool.
1:30 shall *b* like a tree with falling leaves,
1:31 turn to tow, and his work shall *b* a spark;
5:24 Even so their root shall *b* rotten and
8:21 and in his hunger he shall *b* enraged
10:17 The light of Israel will *b* a fire,
14:10 say to you, "You too have *b* weak like us,

BECOME (cont.)

15: 6 The waters of Nimrim have b a waste;
17: 1 shall cease to be a city and b a ruin;
19: 6 Its streams shall b foul,
19:13 The princes of Zoan have b fools,
29:11 has b like the words of a sealed scroll.
29:13 And their reverence for me has b routine
32: 4 The flighty will b wise and capable,
32:15 Then will the desert b an orchard and the
32:19 Hill and tower will b wasteland forever
34: 9 and her land shall b burning pitch;
34:13 She shall b an abode for jackals and a
35: 7 The burning sands will b pools,
54: 5 he who has b your husband is your Maker;
58:10 and the gloom shall b for you like midday;
60:22 The smallest shall b a thousand,
64: 5 all of us have b like unclean men,
64: 9 Your holy cities have b a desert,
Jer 2:14 Why then has he b booty?
2:36 base you have b in changing your course!
3:16 you multiply and b fruitful in the land,
5:13 The prophets have b wind,
6:10 the LORD has b for them an object of scorn,
7:11 my name b in your eyes a den of thieves?
13:27 how long will it yet be before you b clean!
15:18 have indeed b for me a treacherous brook,
16: 4 and their corpses will b food for the
22: 5 this palace shall b rubble.
23:12 their way shall b for them slippery ground.
25:27 b drunk and vomit;
26:18 Zion shall b a plowed field,
27:17 else this city will b a heap of ruins.
42:18 b an example of malediction and horror,
44: 8 Will you be rooted out and b a curse and a
44:12 by hunger, and b an example of malediction,
46:19 Memphis shall b a desert,
48:39 Moab has b a laughingstock and a horror to
49: 2 She shall b a mound of ruins,
49: 7 the prudent, has their wisdom b corrupt?
49:13 Bozrah shall b an object of horror
49:13 and all her cities shall b ruins forever.
49:17 Edom shall b an object of horror.
49:33 Hazor shall b a haunt of jackals,
50:13 she shall be empty, and b a total desert;
50:23 of horror Babylon has b among the nations!
50:36 the soothsayers, that they may b fools!
50:37 her motley throng, that they may b women!
51: 7 drank its wine, with this they have b mad.
51:30 up is their strength, they have b women.
51:37 Babylon shall b a heap of ruins,
51:41 What a horror has Babylon b among nations:
51:43 Her cities have b a desert,
Lam 1: 2 have all betrayed her and b her enemies.
1:11 O LORD, and see how worthless I have b!
1:17 has b in their midst a thing unclean.
2: 5 The Lord has b an enemy,
3:14 I have b a laughingstock for all nations,
4: 3 b as cruel as the ostrich in the desert.
4:21 you shall b drunk and naked.
5: 3 We have b orphans, fatherless;
Ez 14: 5 who have b estranged from me through all
16:20 Was it not enough that you had b a harlot?
17: 8 bear fruit, and b a majestic vine.
17:23 and bear fruit, and b a majestic cedar.
20:26 I let them b defiled by their gifts,
22: 4 with the idols you made you have b defiled;
22:18 the house of Israel has b dross for me.
22:18 dross from silver have they b.
22:19 Because all of you have b dross,
23:18 her as I had b disgusted with her sister.
27:36 You have b a horror,
28:19 You have b a horror,
29: 9 The land of Egypt shall b a desolate waste;
34: 8 my sheep have b food for every wild beast,
35:10 two nations and the two lands have b mine;
36: 2 the everlasting heights have b our
36: 3 b a possession for the rest of the nations,
36: 3 and have b a byword and a popular jeer;
47: 5 water had risen so high it had b a river
Dn 3:33 revere you, have b a shame and a reproach.
4:19 has b so great as to touch the heavens,
9:16 have b the reproach of all our neighbors.
11: 6 After some years they shall b allies:
11:33 a time they will b victims of the sword,
14:28 "The king has b a Jew,"
Hos 4:15 harlot, O Israel, let not Judah b guilty!
5: 1 For you have b a snare at Mizpah,
5: 9 shall b a waste on the day of chastisement:
5:10 b like those that move a boundary line;
7:16 They have again b useless,
12: 9 Though Ephraim says, "How rich I have b;
Am 5: 5 led into exile, and Bethel shall b nought.
8: 3 temple songs shall b wailings on that day,
Ob 1:16 and shall b as though they had not been.
Mi 7:16 their ears shall b deaf.
Hb 2: 7 You shall b their spoil!
Zep 2: 6 the Cretans shall b fields for shepherds,
2: 9 the God of Israel, Moab shall b like Sodom,
2:15 How has she b a waste,
Hg 2:12 or any other food, do they b sanctified?
2:13 touches any of these, do they b unclean?
2:13 The priests answered, "They b unclean."
Zec 2:13 they b plunder for their slaves.
8:19 shall b occasions of joy and gladness,
9: 7 He also shall b a remnant for our God,
11: 5 say, "Blessed be the LORD, I have b rich!"
14: 9 The LORD shall b king over the whole earth;
Mal 3:21 will b ashes under the soles of your feet,
Mt 10:25 pupil should be glad to b like his teacher,
10:26 and nothing hidden that will not b known.
18: 3 you change and b like little children,
19: 5 to his wife, and the two shall b as one"?
21:42 has b the keystone of the structure.
Mk 4:32 springs up to b the largest of shrubs,
6:14 had b widespread and people were saying,
10: 8 and mother and the two shall b as one.
12:10 has b the keystone of the structure.
Lk 18:28 have left all we own to b your followers."
19:12 went to a faraway country to b its king,
20:17 has b the keystone of the structure"?
20:36 They b like angels and are no longer
21:34 "Be on guard lest your spirits b bloated
Jn 1:12 him he empowered to b children of God.
4:14 water I give shall b a fountain within him,
9:27 tell me you want to b his disciples too?"
12:36 thus you will b sons of light."
Acts 4:11 the builders which has b the cornerstone.'
7: 8 Abraham, who had b the father of Isaac,
7:52 turn have b his betrayers and murderers.
17:34 few did join him, however, to b believers.
18:27 who through God's favor had b believers.
19:18 Many who had b believers came forward and
26:29 who listen to me today might b what I am
27: 9 of the year sailing had b hazardous.
Rom 1:20 eternal power and divinity, have b visible,
3:12 wrong course, all alike have b worthless;
5:19 one man's obedience all shall b just.
6:22 freed from sin and have b slaves of God,
7:13 Did this good thing then b death for me?
9:29 us a remnant, we should have b as Sodom,
11: 9 "Let their table b a snare and a trap,
11:31 disobedience, so they have b disobedient
14:16 privilege to b an occasion for blasphemy.
1Cor 3:18 in a worldly way, he had better b a fool.
4: 9 We have b a spectacle to the universe,
4:13 We have b the world's refuse,
6:16 says, "The two shall b one flesh."
7:11 remain single or b reconciled to him again.
8: 9 right you b an occasion of sin to the weak.
10: 7 Do not b idolaters, as some of them did.
10:20 I do not want you to b sharers with demons.
15:45 the last Adam has b a life-giving spirit.
2Cor 5:21 in him we might b the very holiness of God.
8: 9 so that you might b rich by his poverty.
12: 7 in order that I might not b conceited I
12:11 Corinthian ChurchWhat a fool I have b!
Gal 4:12 to b like me as I became like you.
4:16 Have I b your enemy just because I tell
Eph 2:22 b a dwelling place for God in the Spirit.
4:13 till we b one in faith and in the
Phil 1:13 My imprisonment in Christ's cause has b
1Thes 2: 8 our very lives, so dear had you b to us.
1Tm 1:16 and that I might b an example to those who
3: 6 lest he b conceited and thus incur the
5:16 not let them b a burden to the church,
2Tm 2:16 who indulge in it b more and more godless,
Ti 3: 7 be justified by his grace and b heirs,
Phlm 1:11 He has b in truth Onesimus [Useful],
Heb 2:17 he had to b like his brothers in every way,
3:14 We have b partners of Christ if only we
5:11 difficult to explain, for you have b deaf.
6: 4 gift and b sharers in the Holy Spirit,
7:16 one who has b a priest,
7:22 Jesus b the guarantee of a better covenant.
8:13 And what has b obsolete and has grown old
12:15 up through which many may b defiled;
Jas 2:10 remainder, has b guilty on all counts.
2:11 you have b a transgressor of the law.
3: 1 Not many of you should b teachers,
1Pt 1:15 b holy yourselves in every aspect of your
4:18 what is to b of the godless and the sinner?
2Pt 1: 4 lust might b sharers of the divine nature.
Rv 2: 3 Moreover, you do not b discouraged.
18: 2 She has b a dwelling place for demons.

BECOMES (70)

Gn 2:10 there it divides and b four branches.
Lv 4:27 of the LORD, and thus b guilty,
5: 2 creature, and thus b unclean and guilty;
6:11 Whatever touches the oblations b sacred."
11:26 everyone who touches them b unclean.
11:32 one of them falls when dead b unclean.
11:32 until evening, when it again b clean.
11:33 a clay vessel, everything in it b unclean,
11:35 one of their dead bodies falls, b unclean;
11:36 whoever touches the dead body b unclean.
11:38 it b unclean when one of these falls on it.
13:24 of the burn now b a pink or a white blotch,
15:13 with a flow b free of his affliction,
15:24 bed on which he then lies also b unclean.
15:26 she lies during such a flow b unclean,
15:26 b unclean just as during her menstruation.
15:27 Anyone who touches them b unclean;
15:28 "If she b freed from her affliction,
15:32 an emission of seed, and thereby b unclean;
22: 4 sacred offerings, unless he again b clean.
22: 7 then when the sun sets, he again b clean.
25:39 your countryman b so impoverished beside
27: 9 animal, when vowed to the LORD, b sacred.
27:28 is thus doomed b most sacred to the LORD.
Nm 5:12 If a man's wife goes astray and b
5:30 a man that he b suspicious of his wife,
6: 9 so that his dedicated head b unclean,
11:20 your very nostrils and b loathsome to you.
15:24 b guilty of the fault of inadvertence,
19:22 unclean person touches b unclean itself,
19:22 who touches it b unclean until evening."
30: 6 or any pledge she has made b null and void;
30:13 her vow or in her pledge b null and void;
Dt 23:11 b unclean because of a nocturnal emission,
24: 2 she goes and b the wife of another man,
1Sm 20: 7 But if he b quite angry,
2Chr 13: 9 bull and seven rams b a priest of no-gods.
Jb 33:20 So that to his appetite food b repulsive,
Ps(s) 49:17 rich, when the wealth of his house b great,
Prv 9: 9 Instruct a wise man, and he b still wiser;
11:15 is in a bad way who b surety for another,
17:18 in pledge, who b surety for his neighbor.
20:16 Take his garment who b surety for another,
27:13 Take his garment who b surety for another,
30:22 Under a slave when he b king,
Eccl 10:10 If the iron b dull,
Sir 4:24 it is through speech that wisdom b known,
6: 9 Another is a friend who b an enemy,
14: 3 Wealth ill b the mean man;
16: 4 through a clan of rebels it b desolate.
19: 2 and the companion of harlots b reckless.
22: 4 daughter b a treasure to her husband,
33:29 if he b unruly, load him with chains.
36:25 a man with no wife b a homeless wanderer.
37: 2 when your bosom companion b your enemy?
Is 44:12 and weak, drinks no water and b exhausted.
Jer 20: 9 then it b like fire burning in my heart,
23:36 For each man his own word b the burden so
48:26 and vomits, and he too b a laughingstock.
Mt 12:45 state of that man b worse than the first.
13:32 It b so big a shrub that the birds of the
Mk 9:18 the mouth and grinds his teeth and b rigid.
9:50 but if salt b tasteless, how can you season
Jn 19:12 who makes himself a king b Caesar's rival."
Rom 4:14 then faith b an empty word and the promise
14:14 something unclean that it b so for him.
1Cor 6:16 joined to a prostitute b one body with her?
6:17 joined to the Lord b one spirit with him.
1Tm 2:10 as b women who profess to be religious,
2Tm 2: 4 No soldier b entangled in the affairs of

BECOMING (19)

Lv 12: 4 days more in b purified of her blood;
12: 5 sixty-six days in b purified of her blood.
1Sm 18:26 the prospect of b the king's son-in-law.
2Sm 23:19 respect than the Thirty, b their leader.
1Kgs 11:25 made a rift in Israel by b king over Edom.
2Kgs 19:26 ashamed, B like the plants of the field,
2Mc 8: 8 successful advances were b more frequent,
14:30 was b cool in his dealings with him,
Sir 23: 9 or b too familiar with the Holy Name.
25: 4 How b to the gray-haired is judgment,
25: 5 How b to the aged is wisdom,
Is 37:27 ashamed, B like the plants of the field,
56: 6 the name of the LORD and b his servants,
Mt 14:30 how strong the wind was, b frightened,
18: 4 makes himself lowly, b like this child,
Jn 6:18 a strong wind blowing, the sea was b rough.
15: 8 your bearing much fruit and b my disciples.
Gal 3:13 law's curse by himself b a curse for us,
1Tm 5:13 to house b not only time-wasters but gossips

BECORATH (1)

1Sm 9: 1 the son of Abiel, son of Zeror, son of B,

BECTILETH (2)

Jdt 2:21 from Nineveh, they reached the plain of B,
2:21 and from B they next encamped near the

BED (91)

Gn 19: 4 Before they went to b,
47:31 Then Israel bowed at the head of the b.
48: 2 he rallied his strength and sat up in b.
49: 4 b and defiled my couch to my sorrow.
49:33 to his sons, he drew his feet into the b,
Ex 7:28 and into your bedroom and onto your b,
21:18 not mortally, but enough to put him in b,
Lv 15: 4 Any b on which the man afflicted with the
15: 5 who touches his b shall wash his garments,
15:21 who touches her b shall wash his garments,
15:23 on the b or on the seat when he touches it,
15:24 every b on which he then lies also becomes
15:26 Any b on which she lies during such a flow
Dt 3:11 He had a b of iron,
3:16 including the wadi b and its banks
23: 1 wife, nor shall he dishonor his father's b.
27:20 wife, for he dishonors his father's b!'
Jos 3:17 on dry ground in the b of the Jordan
4: 3 stones from this spot in the b of the Jordan
4: 5 "Go to the b of the Jordan in front of

4: 8 they took up as many stones from the *b* of
4: 9 twelve stones set up in the *b* of the Jordan
4:10 the ark remained in the *b* of the Jordan
4:18 LORD had come up from the *b* of the Jordan,
1Sm 19:13 the household idol and laid it in the *b*,
19:15 them, "Bring him up to me in the *b*,
19:16 they found the household idol in the *b*,
2Sm 4:11 have slain an innocent man in *b* at home,
11:13 sleep on his *b* among his lord's servants,
13: 5 down on your *b* and pretend to be sick.
13: 8 house of her brother Amnon, who was in *b*.
1Kgs 1:47 And the king in his *b* worshiped God,
17:19 he was staying, and laid him on his own *b*.
21: 4 Lying down on his *b*,
2Kgs 1: 4 shall not leave the *b* upon which you lie;
1: 6 shall not leave the *b* upon which you lie;
1:16 shall not leave the *b* upon which you lie;
4:10 the roof and furnish it for him with a *b*,
4:21 and laid him on the *b* of the man of God.
4:34 Then he lay upon the child on the *b*,
Tb 7:16 She went and made the *b* in the room,
8: 4 Tobiah arose from *b* and said to his wife,
8: 9 and went to *b* for the night.
Jdt 9: 3 blood the *b* in which they lay deceived,
9: 3 the same *b* that had felt the shame of
10:21 Now Holofernes was reclining on his *b*
13: 2 Holofernes, who lay prostrate on his *b*,
13: 4 by Holofernes' *b* and said within herself;
13: 7 his sword from it, drew close to the *b*,
13: 9 *b* and took the canopy from its supports.
Est C:26 *b* of the uncircumcised or of any foreigner.
1Mc 1: 5 But after all this he took to his *b*,
6: 8 his designs had failed, he took to his *b*.
Jb 7: 4 If in *b* I say, "When shall I arise?"
7:13 When I say, "My *b* shall comfort me,
33:19 Or a man is chastened on his *b* by pain and
Ps(s) 6: 7 every night I flood my *b* with weeping;
18:16 Then the *b* of the sea appeared,
36: 5 He plans wickedness in his *b*;
Prv 7:17 I have sprinkled my *b* with myrrh,
22:27 pay, your *b* will be taken from under you.
26:14 on its hinges, the sluggard, on his *b*!
Sg 3: 1 On my *b* at night I sought him whom my
Wis 3:13 knew not transgression of the marriage *b*;
3:16 and the progeny of an unlawful *b* will
Sir 23:18 *b* and says to himself "Who can see me?
24:29 my plants, my flower *b* I will drench";
40: 5 Even when he lies on his *b* to rest,
Is 28:20 the *b* shall be too short to stretch out in,
57: 7 a high and lofty mountain you made your *b*,
57: 8 me, you spread out your high, wide *b*;
Ez 17: 7 freely than the *b* where it was planted.
17:10 by the east wind, in the *b* where it grew?
Dn 2:28 this was the dream you saw as you lay in *b*.
2:29 To you in your *b* there came thoughts about
4: 2 I had a terrifying dream as I lay in *b*,
4: 7 "These were the visions I saw while in *b*:
4:10 In the vision I saw while in *b*,
7: 1 Daniel had a dream as he lay in *b*,
Mt 8: 6 my serving boy is at home in *b* paralyzed,
8:14 Peter's mother-in-law in *b* with a fever.
Mk 4:21 under a bushel basket or hidden under a *b*?
4:27 He goes to *b* and gets up day after day.
7:30 the child lying in *b* and the demon gone.
Lk 8:16 it under a bushel basket or under a *b*;
11: 7 shut now and my children and I are in *b*.
17:34 that night there will be two men in one *b*;
Acts 9:34 Get up and make your *b*."
28: 8 that Publius' father was sick in *b*,
Heb 13: 4 way and the marriage *b* be kept undefiled,
Rv 2:22 I mean to cast her down on a *b* of pain;

BEDAD (2)

Gn 36:35 When Husham died, Hadad, son of *B*,
1Chr 1:46 Husham died and Hadad, son of *B*,

BEDAN (1)

1Chr 7:17 The sons of Ulam: *B*

BEDECKED (1)

Is 61:10 a diadem, like a bride *b* with her jewels.

BEDECKING (1)

Jer 4:30 by putting on purple, *b* yourself with gold,

BEDEIAH (1)

Ezr 10:35 Maadai, Amram, Uel, Benaiah, *B*,

BEDPOST (1)

Jdt 13: 6 went to the *b* near the head of Holofernes,

BEDRIDDEN (1)

Acts 9:33 a paralytic who had been *b* for eight years.

BEDROLLS (1)

Mk 6:55 on *b* to the place where they heard he was.

BEDROOM (16)

Ex 7:28 palace and into your *b* and onto your bed,
2Sm 4: 7 while Ishbaal was lying asleep in his *b*.
13:10 Tamar, "Bring the nourishment into the *b*,
13:10 brought them to her brother Amnon in the *b*.
2Kgs 6:12 Israel the very words you speak in your *b*."
11: 2 *b* where the princes were about to be slain.
2Chr 22:11 be slain, and put him and his nurse in a *b*.
Tb 7:15 the other *b* and bring the girl there."
8: 1 of the dining room and led him into the *b*.
8: 4 left the *b* and closed the door behind them,
8:13 maid, who lit a lamp, opened the *b* door,
Jdt 13: 3 her maid to stand outside the *b* and wait,
13: 4 no one, small or great, was left in the *b*,
14:15 he parted the curtains, entered the *b*,
16:19 that she herself had taken from his *b*.
Eccl 10:20 in the privacy of your *b* revile the rich.

BEDS (10)

Jdt 13: 1 They went off to their *b*,
Jb 33:15 upon men] as they slumber in their *b*,
Ps(s) 4: 5 reflect, upon your *b*,
Sg 5:13 *b* of spice with ripening aromatic herbs.
6: 2 down to his garden, to the *b* of spice,
Sir 48: 6 and nobles, from their *b* of sickness.
Ez 32: 6 river *b* shall be filled with your blood.
Hos 7:14 hearts when they wailed upon their *b*;
Am 6: 4 Lying upon *b* of ivory,
Mk 6:40 and fifties, neatly arranged like flower *b*.

BEE (2)

Sir 11: 3 Least is the *b* among winged things,
Is 7:18 and for the *b* in the land of Assyria.

BEEF (1)

Neh 5:18 one *b*, six choice muttons, poultry

BEELIADA (1)

1Chr 14: 7 Nogah, Nepheg, Japhia, Elishama, *B*,

BEELZEBUL (6)

Mt 10:25 If they call the head of the house *B*,
12:24 can expel demons only with the help of *B*,
Mk 3:22 asserted, "He is possessed by *B*,"
Lk 11:15 Some of them said, "It is by *B*,
11:18 you say it is by *B* that I cast out devils.
11:19 If I cast out devils by *B*,

BEELZEBUL'S (1)

Mt 12:27 If I expel demons with *B* help,

BEER (4)

Nm 21:16 From there they went to *B*,
21:18 From *B* they went to Mattanah,
Dt 29: 5 not your food, nor wine or *b* your drink.
Jgs 9:21 Then Jotham went in flight to *B*,

BEER-ELIM (1)

Is 15: 8 As far as Eglaim the wailing, and to *B*,

BEER-LAHAI-ROI (3)

Gn 16:14 That is why the well is called *B*.
24:62 Meanwhile Isaac had gone from *B* and was
25:11 who made his home near *B*

BEER-SHEBA (33)

Gn 21:14 roamed aimlessly in the wilderness of *B*,
21:31 This is why the place is called *B*;
21:32 When they had thus made the pact in *B*,
21:33 Abraham planted a tamarisk at *B*,
22:19 servants, and they set out together for *B*,
26:23 From there Isaac went up to *B*.
26:33 hence the name of the city, *B*,
28:10 departed from *B* and proceeded toward Haran.
46: 1 When he arrived at *B*, he offered sacrifices
46: 5 So Jacob departed from *B*,
Jos 15:28 Beth-pelet, Hazar-shual, *B* and Biziothiah;
19: 2 they received *B*, Shema, Moladah
Jgs 20: 1 from Dan to *B*,
1Sm 3:20 Thus all Israel from Dan to *B* came to know
8: 2 his second son, Abijah; they judged at *B*.
2Sm 3:10 over Israel and over Judah from Dan to *B*."
17:11 Let all Israel from Dan to *B*,
24: 2 from Dan to *B* and register the people,
24: 7 and ending up at *B* in the Negeb of Judah.
24:15 thousand of the people from Dan to *B* died.]
1Kgs 5: 5 vine or under his fig tree from Dan to *B*,
19: 3 and fled for his life, going to *B* of Judah.
2Kgs 12: 2 mother, who was named Zibiah, was from *B*.
23: 8 Judah, and then defiled, from Geba to *B*,
1Chr 4:28 They dwelt in *B*,
21: 2 the number of the Israelites from *B* to Dan,
2Chr 19: 4 he went out again among the people from *B*
24: 1 His mother, named Zibiah, was from *B*.
30: 5 throughout all Israel from *B* to Dan,
Neh 11:27 in Hazar-shual, in *B* and its dependencies,
11:30 They were settled from *B* to Ge-hinnom.
Am 5: 5 not come to Gilgal, and do not cross to *B*.
8:14 "By the life of your love, O *B*!"

BEERA (1)

1Chr 7:37 Shilshah, Ithran, and *B*

BEERAH (1)

1Chr 5: 6 whose son was Baal, whose son was *B*,

BEERI (2)

Gn 26:34 married Judith, daughter of *B* the Hittite,
Hos 1: 1 Lord that came to Hosea, the son of *B*,

BEEROTH (8)

Dt 10: 6 set out from *B* Bene-jaakan for Moserah,
Jos 9:17 of Gibeon, Chephirah, *B* and Kiriath-jearim,
18:25 Ramah, *B*, Mizpeh, Chephirah, Mozah,
2Sm 4: 2 *B*, too, was ascribed to Benjamin;
23:37 Naharai from *B*, armor-bearer of Joab
1Chr 11:39 Naharai, from *B*, the armor-bearer of Joab
Ezr 2:25 men of Kiriath-jearim, Chephirah, and *B*,
Neh 7:29 men of Kiriath-jearim, Chephirah, and *B*,

BEEROTHITE (3)

2Sm 4: 2 of Rimmon the *B*, of the tribe of
4: 5 The sons of Rimmon the *B*,
4: 9 his brother Baanah, sons of Rimmon the *B*:

BEEROTHITES (1)

2Sm 4: 3 the *B* fled to Gittaim,

BEERSHEBA (1)

Jos 19: 2 For their heritage they received *B*,

BEES (3)

Dt 1:44 there came out against you and, like *b*,
Jgs 14: 8 swarm of *b* and honey in the lion's carcass.
Ps(s) 118:12 They encompassed me like *b*,

BEFALL (23)

Gn 42: 4 for he thought some disaster might *b* him.
42:38 should *b* him on the journey you must make,
Dt 31:17 and many evils and troubles will *b* them.
31:21 then, when many evils and troubles *b* them,
31:29 so that evil will *b* you in some future age
Est 8: 6 I witness the evil that is to *b* my people,
Ps(s) 91:10 No evil shall *b* you,
Prv 1:27 when distress and anguish *b* you.
10:24 What the wicked man fears will *b* him,
11:27 he who pursues evil will have evil *b* him.
13:18 shame *b* the man who disregards correction,
Eccl 2:15 myself, if the fool's lot is to *b* me also,
Sir 15:13 he does not let it *b* those who fear him.
31:22 be moderate, and no sickness will *b* you.
Is 47:11 shall *b* you which you cannot allay.
Jer 2: 3 to partake of them, evil would *b* him,
5:12 No evil shall *b* us,
13:22 ask in your heart why these things *b* you:
14:13 famine shall not *b* you.
14:15 "Sword and famine shall not *b* this land":
32:23 Hence you let all these evils *b* them.
39:12 let no harm *b* him,
51:60 that was to *b* Babylon in a single book:

BEFALLEN (11)

Lv 10:19 LORD today, yet this misfortune has *b* me.
Nm 20:14 know of all the hardships that have *b* us,
Dt 31:17 is not among us that these evils have *b* us?'
Jos 2:23 of Nun, and reported all that had *b* them.
1Chr 7:23 named Beriah, since evil had *b* his house.
Neh 9:32 account all the disasters that have *b* us,
Wis 19: 4 and made them forgetful of what had *b* them,
Sir 5: 4 "I have sinned, yet what has *b* me?"
Jer 40: 3 not obey his voice, this fate has *b* you.
44:23 this evil has *b* you at the present day.
Lam 5: 1 Remember, O LORD, what has *b* us,

BEFALLS (6)

Gn 44:29 away from me too, and some disaster *b* him,
Prv 12:21 No harm *b* the just,
27:10 if ruin *b* you, enter not a kinsman's house.
Eccl 2:14 Yet I knew that one lot *b* both of them.
Sir 2: 4 Accept whatever *b* you,
Am 3: 6 If evil *b* a city, has not the LORD caused

BEFELL (2)

2Kgs 24: 3 This *b* Judah because the LORD had stated
24:20 The LORD's anger *b* Jerusalem and Judah

BEFIT (1)

Ti 2: 3 in ways that *b* those who belong to God.

BEFITS (4)

Ps(s) 93: 5 holiness *b* your house,
Sir 31:17 Be the first to stop, as *b* good manners:
33:29 Put him to work, for that is what *b* him;
1Tm 3:15 of conduct *b* a member of God's household,

BEFITTED (1)

Est 1: 7 flowed freely, as *b* the king's munificence.

BEFITTING (3)

Prv 19:10 Luxury is not *b* a fool;
Mt 19:28 takes his seat upon a throne *b* his glory,
Eph 6: 4 the training and instruction *b* the Lord.

BEFOREHAND (11)

Wis 18: 6 That night was known *b* to our fathers,
18:19 that disturbed them had proclaimed this *b*,
19: 1 For he knew *b* what they were yet to do:
Is 41:26 *b*,
48: 8 nor knew, they did not reach your ears *b*.
Mt 24:25 Remember, I have told you all about it *b*;
Mk 13:11 custody, do not worry *b* about what to say.
13:23 I have told you about it *b*.
Lk 21:14 resolve not to worry about your defense *b*,
Acts 2:31 *b* the resurrection of the Messiah.
10:41 such witnesses as had been chosen *b* by God

BEFORETIME (1)

Is 48: 7 into being, and *b* you did not hear of them,

BEFRIEND (1)

Dt 10:19 So you too must *b* the alien,

BEFRIENDS (1)

Dt 10:18 the orphan and the widow, and *b* the alien,

BEG (45)

Gn 19: 7 behind him, he said, "I *b* you my brothers,
33:10 "No, I *b* you!" said Jacob.
44:18 "I *b* you, my lord, let your servant speak
Ex 11: 8 and prostrate before me, they shall *b* me,
1Sm 2:36 Appoint me, I *b* you,
2Kgs 4:28 "Did I not *b* you not to deceive me?"
Tb 3:10 myself, but to *b* the Lord to have me die,
6:18 *B* the Lord of heaven to show you mercy and
8: 4 Let us pray and *b* our LORD to have mercy
8: 5 and *b* that deliverance might be theirs.
10: 7 So I *b* you, father, let me go back
10: 9 I *b* you to let me go back to my father."
Est 7: 3 I *b* that you spare the lives of my people.
7: 7 stayed to *b* Queen Esther for his life,
2Mc 6:12 Now I *b* those who read this book not to be
7:28 I *b* you, child, to look at the heavens
9:26 Therefore I *b* and entreat each of you to
Jb 9:15 but should rather *b* for what was due me.
Sir 40:28 life of a beggar, better to die than to *b*;
Mt 9:38 *B* the harvest master to send out laborers
Mk 7:26 *b* him to expel the demon from her daughter.
Lk 6:30 Give to all who *b* from you.
8:28 Do not torment me, I *b* you."
9:38 "Teacher, I *b* you to look at my son;
Jn 9: 8 this the fellow who used to sit and *b*?"
Acts 3: 2 to *b* from the people as they entered.
21:39 I *b* you, let me address these people."
24: 4 I *b* your indulgence for a brief hearing of
26: 3 I *b* you to listen to me patiently.
Rom 12: 1 I *b* you through the mercy of God to offer
15:30 I *b* you, brothers, for the sake of our
16:17 I *b* you to be on the watch against those
1Cor 1:10 I *b* you, brothers, in the name of our
4:16 I *b* you, then, be imitators of me.
2Cor 2: 8 *b* you to reaffirm your love for him.
6: 1 As your fellow workers we *b* you not to
10: 2 I *b* you that when I am there,
11: 1 Put up with me, I *b* you!
Gal 4:12 I *b* you, brothers, to become like me as I
Eph 3:13 I *b* you not to be disheartened by the
Phil 2: 1 in spirit, compassion, and pity, I *b* you:
1Thes 4: 1 we *b* and exhort you in the Lord Jesus that
5:12 We *b* you, brothers, respect those among
2Thes 2: 1 and our being gathered to him, we *b* you,
Heb 13:22 I *b* you to bear with this word of

BEGAN (307)

Gn 4:26 that time men *b* to invoke the LORD by name.
6: 1 When men *b* to multiply on earth and
8: 1 the earth, and the waters *b* to subside.
8:13 month, the water *b* to dry up on the earth.
21:16 As she sat opposite him, he *b* to cry.
23: 7 *b* to bow low before the local citizens,
24:34 "I am Abraham's servant," he *b*.
26:25 there, his servants *b* to dig a well nearby.
33:16 day that Esau *b* his journey back to Seir,
35:16 Rachel *b* to be in labor and to suffer
39: 7 wife *b* to look fondly at him and said,
Nm 31:16 *b* the slaughter of the LORD's community.
Dt 1: 5 Moses *b* to explain the law in the land of
Jos 6:20 As the horns blew, the people *b* to shout.
18:12 Their northern boundary *b* at the Jordan
18:15 The southern boundary *b* at the limits of
Jgs 16:19 Then she *b* to mistreat him,
16:22 *b* to grow as soon as it was shaved off.
20:40 signal column *b* to rise up from the city.
1Sm 7: 6 that Samuel *b* to judge the Israelites.
13: 8 Gilgal, the men *b* to slip away from Saul.
18:12 Saul then *b* to fear David,
2Sm 13:25 he refused to go and *b* to bid him good-bye.
19:42 *b* coming to the king and saying,
20:15 Joab *b* battering the wall to throw it down.
24: 5 Crossing the Jordan, they *b* near Aroer,
1Kgs 1: 5 *b* to display his ambition to be king.
15: 9 of Israel, Asa, king of Judah, *b* to reign;
15:33 *b* his twenty-four-year reign over Israel
16: 8 *b* his two-year reign over Israel in Tirzah.
22:41 *b* to reign over Judah in the fourth year
22:42 thirty-five years old when he *b* to reign,
22:52 *b* to reign over Israel in Samaria in the
2Kgs 4:40 the men to eat, but when they *b* to eat it,
6: 4 arrived at the Jordan they *b* to fell trees.
8:17 thirty-two years old when he *b* to reign,
8:26 twenty-two years old when he *b* his reign,
10:32 that time the LORD *b* to dismember Israel.
11: 1 she *b* to kill off the whole royal family.
12: 2 *b* to reign in the seventh year of Jehu,
13: 1 *b* his seventeen-year reign over Israel in
13:10 *b* his sixteen-year reign over Israel in
14: 1 son of Joash, king of Judah, *b* to reign.
14:23 *b* his forty-one-year reign in Samaria.
15: 2 was sixteen years old when he *b* to reign,
15:17 of Gadi, *b* his ten year reign over Samaria.
15:23 *b* his two-year reign over Israel in
15:27 *b* his twenty-year reign over Israel in
15:32 son of Uzziah, king of Judah, *b* to reign.
16: 1 son of Jotham, king of Judah, *b* to reign.
17: 1 *b* his nine-year reign over Israel in
17:29 But these peoples *b* to make their own gods
18: 1 son of Ahaz, king of Judah, *b* to reign.
21: 1 was twelve years old when he *b* to reign,
21:19 twenty-two years old when he *b* to reign,
22: 1 was eight years old when he *b* to reign,
23:31 twenty-three years old when he *b* to reign,
23:36 twenty-five years old when he *b* to reign,
24: 8 was eighteen years old when he *b* to reign,
1Chr 21: 7 displeased God, who *b* to punish Israel.
27:24 son of Zeruiah, *b* to take the census,
2Chr 3: 1 Then Solomon *b* to build the house of the
3: 2 He *b* to build in the second month of the
13:23 time, ten years of peace *b* in the land.
20:22 At the moment they *b* their jubilant hymn,
20:23 of Seir, they *b* to destroy each other.
24:18 *b* to serve the sacred poles and the idols;
29:17 They *b* the work of consecration on the
29:27 began, they also *b* the song of the LORD,
31: 7 month that they *b* to establish these heaps,
31:10 "Since they *b* to bring the offerings to
33:12 In this distress, he *b* to appease the LORD,
34: 3 he *b* to seek after the God of his
34: 3 and in his twelfth year he *b* to purge
Ezr 3: 6 they *b* to offer holocausts to the LORD,
3: 8 *b* by appointing the Levites twenty years
5: 1 *b* to prophesy to the Jews in Judah and
5: 2 *b* again to build the house of God in
Neh 1: 4 I *b* to weep and continued mourning for
Tb 2:13 On entering my house the goat *b* to bleat.
3: 1 Then with sobs I *b* to pray:
5:18 But his mother *b* to weep.
7: 8 and even their daughter Sarah *b* to weep.
7:14 Afterward they *b* to eat and drink.
8: 5 He *b* with these words:
8:19 So the servants *b* to prepare the feast.
10: 3 And he *b* to worry.
10: 4 *b* to weep aloud and to wail over her son:
11: 1 Then they left and *b* their return journey.
Jdt 14: 8 left till the time she *b* speaking to them.
1Mc 3:25 Then Judas and his brothers *b* to be feared,
4: 5 so he *b* to hunt for them in the mountains,
4:35 he withdrew to Antioch and *b* to recruit
5: 2 *b* to massacre and persecute the people.
7: 1 city on the seacoast, and *b* to rule there.
9:54 But he only *b* to tear it down.
9:73 he *b* to judge the people and he destroyed
10: 1 He was accepted and *b* to reign there.
10:10 and *b* to build and restore the city.
11:46 control of the main streets and *b* to fight.
13:20 Next he *b* to invade and ravage the country.
13:42 *b* to write in their records and contracts,
15:40 he *b* to harass the people and to make
2Mc 1:22 which had been clouded over, *b* to shine,
1:30 Then the priests *b* to sing hymns.
4:40 crowds, now thoroughly enraged, *b* to riot,
9:11 he *b* to give up his excessive arrogance,
Jb 1:20 *b* to tear his cloak and cut off his hair.
2:12 not recognize him, they *b* to weep aloud;
Ez 9: 6 So they *b* with the men [the elders] who
9: 8 As they *b* to strike, I was left alone.
23:27 and to the harlotry you *b* in Egypt;
42:10 outer court where the wall of the court *b*.
Dn 7: 1 he wrote down the dream; the account *b*:
9:23 When you *b* your petition,
12: 1 distress since nations *b* until that time.
13: 8 day for her walk, they *b* to lust for her.
14: 7 Daniel *b* to laugh.
14:39 While Daniel *b* to eat,
Am 7: 1 when the late growth *b* to come up
Jon 3: 4 Jonah *b* his journey through the city,
Mt 4:17 time on Jesus *b* to proclaim this theme:
5: 2 around him, and he *b* to teach them:
8:15 She got up at once and *b* to wait on him.
8:24 and the boat *b* to be swamped by the waves.
9:24 At this they *b* to ridicule him.
9:33 the demon was expelled the mute *b* to speak,
11: 7 Jesus *b* to speak to the crowds about John:
11:20 He *b* to reproach the towns
12: 1 so they *b* to pull off the heads of grain
12:14 When the Pharisees were outside they *b* to
13: 6 it, it *b* to wither for lack of roots.
13:26 When the crop *b* to mature and yield grain,
13:33 the whole mass of dough *b* to rise."
14:26 said, and in their fear they *b* to cry out.
14:29 out of the boat and *b* to walk on the water,
14:30 frightened, he *b* to sink and cried out,
15:23 His disciples came up and *b* to entreat him,
16:22 him aside and *b* to remonstrate with him.
18:24 When he *b* his auditing,
18:29 to his knees and *b* to plead with him,
19:13 The disciples *b* to scold them,
20:30 that Jesus was passing by, *b* to shout,
20:31 The crowd *b* to scold them in an effort to
21: 8 while some *b* to cut branches from the
22: 1 Jesus *b* to address them,
22:15 Then the Pharisees went off and *b* to plot
25: 5 delayed his coming, so they all *b* to nod,
26: 7 him at table and *b* to pour it on his head.
26:22 they *b* to say to him one after another,
26:37 and *b* to experience sorrow and distress.
26:42 Withdrawing a second time, he *b* to pray:
26:44 somewhat, and *b* to pray a third time,
26:67 they *b* to spit in his face and hit him.
26:74 At that he *b* cursing,
26:74 Just then a cock *b* to crow and Peter
26:75 He went out and *b* to weep bitterly.
27: 3 condemned, *b* to regret his action deeply.
27:29 Then they *b* to mock him by dropping to
Mk 1:21 he entered the synagogue and *b* to teach.
1:27 They *b* to ask one another:
1:31 She immediately *b* to wait on them.
1:45 and *b* to proclaim the whole matter freely,
2: 2 At that they *b* to gather in great numbers.
2: 4 so they *b* to open up the roof over the
2:23 and his disciples *b* to pull off heads of
3: 6 they immediately *b* to plot with the
3:23 then *b* to speak to them by way of examples:
4: 1 occasion he *b* to teach beside the lake.
4: 2 He *b* to instruct them at great length,
4: 6 it, it *b* to wither for lack of roots.
4:37 over the boat and it *b* to ship water badly.
5:13 bluff into the lake, where they *b* to drown.
5:20 At that the man went off and *b* to proclaim
5:30 Wheeling about in the crowd, he *b* to ask,
5:40 At this they *b* to ridicule him.
5:42 stood up immediately and he *b* to walk around.
6: 2 When the sabbath came he *b* to teach in the
6: 7 Twelve and *b* to send them out two by two,
6:34 and he *b* to teach them at great length.
6:49 it was a ghost and they *b* to cry out.
6:55 and *b* to bring in the sick on bedrolls
7:26 a Syro-Phoenician by birth *b* to beg him to
7:35 the impediment, and *b* to speak plainly.
8:11 came forward and *b* to argue with him.
8:31 He *b* to teach them that the Son of Man had
8:32 him aside and *b* to remonstrate with him.
9:20 he *b* to roll around and foam at the mouth.
9:28 house his disciples *b* to ask him privately,
9:30 district and *b* a journey through Galilee,
9:33 once inside the house, *b* to ask them,
10: 1 him, and as usual he *b* to teach them.
10: 2 Pharisees came up and as a test *b* to ask him
10:10 the disciples *b* to question him about this.
10:32 he *b* to tell them what was going to happen
10:47 it was Jesus of Nazareth, he *b* to call out,
11:15 entered the temple precincts and *b* to drive
11:17 Then he *b* to teach them:
11:18 and *b* to look for a way to destroy him.
12: 1 He *b* to address them once more in parables:
13: 3 and Andrew *b* to question him privately.
13: 5 Jesus *b* his discourse:
14: 1 scribes *b* to look for a way to arrest him
14: 3 jar, she *b* to pour the perfume on his head.
14:19 They *b* to say to him sorrowfully,
14:34 he *b* to be filled with fear and distress.
14:39 back again he *b* to pray in the same words.
14:54 guard and *b* to warm himself at the fire.
14:60 the court and *b* to interrogate Jesus:
14:65 Some of them *b* to spit on him.
14:71 He *b* to curse, and to swear
14:72 He broke down and *b* to cry.
15:18 and put it on him, and *b* to salute him,
Lk 1:64 loosed, and he *b* to speak in praise of God.
1:65 *b* to be recounted to the last detail.
3:23 When Jesus *b* his work he was about thirty
4:21 Then he *b* by saying to them,
4:31 he *b* instructing them on the sabbath day.
4:36 and they *b* saying to one another:
5:21 scribes and the Pharisees *b* a discussion,
6:11 At this they became frenzied and *b* asking
7:15 The dead man sat up and *b* to speak.
7:16 seized them all and they *b* to praise God.
7:24 Jesus *b* to speak about him to the crowds.
7:49 fellow guests *b* to ask among themselves,
8: 9 His disciples *b* asking him what the
8:23 they *b* to ship water and to be in danger.

8:28 On seeing Jesus he *b* to shriek;
11:29 him he *b* to speak to them in these words:
11:53 the scribes and Pharisees *b* to manifest
12: 1 He *b* to speak first to his disciples:
13:13 she stood up straight and *b* thanking God.
13:21 until the whole mass of dough *b* to rise."
14:18 But they *b* to excuse themselves,
14:30 man *b* to build what he could not finish.'
15:24 Then the celebration *b*.
15:28 father came out and *b* to plead with him.
16:14 men, heard all this and *b* to deride him.
18:43 he was given his sight and *b* to follow him,
19: 7 this was observed, everyone *b* to murmur,
19:37 the entire crowd of disciples *b* to rejoice
19:45 temple and *b* ejecting the traders saying:
20: 9 *b* to tell the people the following parable:
22: 2 *b* to look for some way to dispose of him;
22:23 Then they *b* to argue among themselves as
23: 5 whole of Judea, from Galilee, where he *b*,
24:15 approached and *b* to walk along with them.
24:30 the bread and *b* to distribute it to them.
Jn 5: 9 he picked up his mat and *b* to walk.
5:10 Jews *b* telling the man who had been cured,
5:16 the sabbath that they *b* to persecute him.
6:14 the sign he had performed they *b* to say,
7:14 went into the temple area and *b* to teach.
7:40 the crowd who heard these words *b* to say,
8: 2 to him, he sat down and *b* to teach them.
8:22 At this some of the Jews *b* to ask,
9: 8 accustomed to see him begging *b* to ask,
9:15 *b* to inquire how he had recovered his
11:35 Jesus *b* to weep,
13: 5 Then he poured water into a basin and *b* to
17: 5 a glory I had with you before the world *b*.
17:24 of the love you bore me before the world *b*.
18:27 At that moment a cock *b* to crow.
Acts 2: 4 They *b* to express themselves in foreign
3: 8 stood for a moment, then *b* to walk around.
4: 7 and *b* the interrogation in this fashion:
5:27 priest *b* the interrogation in this way:
7:32 Moses *b* to tremble and dared look no more.
7:58 him out of the city, and *b* to stone him.
8: 3 After that, Saul *b* to harass the church.
8:12 but once they *b* to believe in the good
8:26 Philip *b* the journey.
9:20 and soon *b* to proclaim in the synagogues
10:28 there, and he *b* speaking to them thus:
11:15 As I *b* to address them the Holy Spirit
11:18 instead *b* to glorify God in these words:
11:20 to Antioch *b* to talk even to the Greeks,
13:16 arose, motioned to them for silence, and *b*:
14:10 The man jumped up and *b* to walk around.
15: 1 from Judea and *b* to teach the brothers:
16:17 The girl *b* to follow Paul and the rest of
18:26 He too *b* to express himself fearlessly in
19: 6 they *b* to speak in tongues and to utter
19:28 were overcome with fury and *b* to shout,
20:37 They *b* to weep without restraint,
21:27 and *b* to stir up the whole crowd there.
21:40 on them as he *b* to speak to them in Hebrew.
22:22 listening to Paul, but now they *b* to shout,
24: 2 *b* his prosecution by addressing Felix:
25:24 The governor *b* to speak:
26: 1 stretched out his hand and *b* his defense.
27:13 When a gentle south wind *b* to blow,
27:27 sailors *b* to suspect that land was near.
27:35 before all of them, broke it, and *b* to eat.
28: 2 for it had *b* to rain and was growing cold.
28: 6 their minds and *b* to say that he was a god.
28: 9 *b* to come to Paul and they too were healed.
28:13 A day later a south wind *b* to blow which
28:25 among themselves, they *b* to leave.
Rom 5:17 If death *b* its reign through one man
2Cor 8:10 help you who *b* this good work last year,
Eph 1: 4 God chose us in him before the world *b*,
2Tm 1: 9 to us in Christ Jesus before the world *b* but
Heb 3:14 to the end that confidence with which we *b*.
Rv 13: 6 It *b* to hurl blasphemies against God,
19: 3 smoke *b* to rise from her forever and ever,

BEGET (6)

Dt 28:41 Though you *b* sons and daughters,
2Chr 6: 9 you will *b* shall build the temple to my honor.'
Sir 41: 9 you will *b* them only for groaning.
Is 65:23 nor *b* children for sudden destruction;
Jer 16: 3 the fathers who will *b* them in this land:
29: 6 Take wives and *b* sons and daughters;

BEGETS (8)

Jb 5: 7 But man himself *b* mischief,
Prv 23:24 he who *b* a wise son will have joy in him.
Ez 18:10 But if he *b* a son who is a thief,
18:14 On the other hand, if a man *b* a son who,
Jn 3: 6 Flesh *b* flesh, Spirit begets spirit.
Phil 2:13 *b* in you any measure of desire or
Jas 1:15 and when sin reaches maturity it *b* death.

BEGETTING (1)

Is 45:10 to him who asks a father, "What are you *b?*"

BEGGAR (6)

Sir 4: 4 A *b* in distress do not reject;
40:28 My son, live not the life of a *b*,
Mk 10:46 there was a blind *b* Bartimaeus ("son of
Lk 16:20 *b* named Lazarus who was covered with sores.
16:22 Eventually, the *b* died.
Acts 3:10 they recognized him as that *b* who used to

BEGGARS—BEGGAR'S (3)

Ps(s) 109:10 his children be roaming vagrants and *b;*
Lk 14:13 a reception, invite *b* and the crippled,
Acts 3: 7 the *b* feet and ankles became strong;

BEGGED (24)

Gn 27:34 "Father bless me too!" he *b*.
1Sm 11: 1 All the men of Jabesh *b* Nahash,
20:29 'Please let me go,' he *b*,
2Mc 3:15 and loudly *b* him in heaven who had given
3:31 Heliodorus *b* Onias to invoke the Most High,
8:15 They *b* the Lord to do this,
10: 4 they prostrated themselves and *b* the Lord
10:26 altar, they *b* him to be gracious to them,
11: 6 they and all the people *b* the Lord with
12:11 The defeated nomads *b* Judas to make
Dn 1: 8 so he *b* the chief chamberlain to spare him
Mt 8:34 they *b* him to leave their neighborhood.
Mk 5:12 "Send us into the swine," they *b* him.
6:56 sick in the market places and *b* him
7:32 and *b* him to lay his hand on him.
8:22 him a blind man and *b* him to touch him.
Jn 4:40 him, they *b* him to stay with them awhile.
4:47 he went to him and *b* him to come down and
Acts 3: 3 on their way in, he *b* them for an alms.
7:46 who found favor with God and *b* that he
13:28 death, they *b* Pilate to have him executed.
2Cor 8: 4 they *b* us insistently for the favor of
12: 8 I *b* the Lord that this might leave me.
Heb 12:19 heard *b* that they be not addressed to them,

BEGGING (8)

1Mc 13:45 loud voices, *b* Simon to grant them peace.
Ps(s) 37:25 man forsaken nor his descendants *b* bread.
Sir 40:30 the mouth of the shameless man *b* is sweet,
Mk 5:17 were *b* him to go away from their district.
Lk 8:41 *b* that he come to his home because his
16: 3 I am ashamed to go *b*.
18:35 a blind man sat at the side of the road *b*.
Jn 9: 8 been accustomed to see him *b* began to ask,

BEGIN (31)

Lv 26:29 till you *b* to eat the flesh of your own
Nm 6:12 and *b* anew the period of his dedication
15:19 you and *b* to eat of the food of that land,
34: 3 east it shall *b* at the end of the Salt Sea,
Dt 2:24 *B* the occupation; engage him in battle.
2:25 This day I will *b* to put a fear and dread
2:31 and his land, *b* the actual occupation.'
Jos 3: 7 *b* to exalt you in the sight of all Israel,
18: 4 commission them to *b* a survey of the land,
Jgs 13: 5 It is he who will *b* the deliverance of
1Sm 16:11 we will not *b* the sacrificial banquet
Tb 8:21 Take, to *b* with, half of whatever I own
Jdt 7:13 Then thirst will *b* to carry them off,
Est E: 3 *b* plotting against their own benefactors.
2Mc 2:32 we shall *b* our account without further ado;
Ps(s) 56: 4 O Most High, when I *b* to fear,
Jer 25:29 is called by my name, I *b* to inflict evil,
Ez 9: 6 *b* at my sanctuary.
27:28 of your mariners, the shores *b* to quake.
Hos 11: 6 The sword shall *b* with his cities and end
Mi 6:13 Rather I will *b* to strike you with
Mt 16:24 his cross, and *b* to follow in my footsteps.
20: 8 but *b* with the last group and end with the
Lk 3: 8 Do not *b* by saying to yourselves,
13:26 Then you will *b* to say,
21:28 When these things *b* to happen,
23:30 Then they will *b* saying to the mountains,
23:54 and the sabbath was about to *b*.
Acts 10:34 "I *b* to see how true it is that God shows
2Cor 5:12 not *b* to recommend ourselves to you again,
Jas 4: 9 *B* to lament, to mourn, and to weep;

BEGINNING (99)

Gn 1: 1 In the *b*, when God created the heavens
46:34 keepers of livestock from the *b* until now,'
Lv 23:15 *B* with the day after the sabbath,
23:32 *B* on the evening of the ninth of the month,
27:17 field is made at the *b* of a jubilee period,
Dt 11:12 from the *b* of the year to the end.
31:30 the words of this song from *b* to end,
Jos 6:15 On the seventh day, *b* at day-break,
Jgs 7:19 of the camp at the *b* of the middle watch,
18: 9 *b* your expedition to possess the land.
20:31 and in the *b* they killed off about thirty
Ru 1:22 Bethlehem at the *b* of the barley harvest.
2Sm 21: 9 that is, at the *b* of the barley harvest.
21:10 from the *b* of the harvest until rain came
1Kgs 20:22 for at the *b* of the year the king of Aram
20:26 At the *b* of the year, Ben-hadad mobilized
1Chr 20: 1 At the *b* of the following year,
2Chr 17: 3 the ways his father had pursued in the *b*,
Ezr 4: 6 Also at the *b* of the reign of Ahashuerus
10:16 *b* with the first day of the tenth month.
Neh 4: 1 for the gaps were *b* to be closed up
Tb 11:13 Then, *b* at the corners of Tobit's eyes,
Est C:8 the inheritance that was yours from the *b*.
6:13 Mordecai, before whom you are *b* to decline,
1Mc 4:35 When Lysias saw his ranks *b* to give way,
5:30 and *b* to attack the people within.
2Mc 7:23 of the universe who shapes each man's *b*,
Jb 40:19 He came at the *b* of God's ways,
Ps(s) 111:10 The fear of the LORD is the *b* of wisdom;
Prv 1: 7 The fear of the LORD is the *b* of knowledge;
4: 7 The *b* of wisdom is:
9:10 The *b* of wisdom is the fear of the LORD,
Eccl 3:11 men's ever discovering, from *b* to end,
7: 8 Better is the end of speech than its *b;*
10:13 The *b* of his words is folly,
Wis 6:22 But from the very *b* I shall search out and
7:18 *b* and the end and the midpoint of times,
12:11 for they were a race accursed from the *b*.
14:13 For in the *b* they were not,
Sir 1:12 The *b* of wisdom is fear of the LORD,
10:12 The *b* of pride is man's
15:14 When God, in the *b*, created man,
18: 5 When a man ends he is only *b*,
24: 9 Before all ages, in the *b*, he created me,
25:23 In woman was sin's *b*,
39:25 for the good he provided from the *b*
Is 1:26 at first, and your counselors as in the *b;*
40:21 Was it not foretold you from the *b?*
41: 4 called forth the generations since the *b*.
41:26 Who announced this from the *b*,
45:21 from the *b* and foretold it from of old?
46:10 At the *b* I foretell the outcome;
48:16 Not from the *b* did I speak it in secret;
52: 4 To Egypt in the *b* my people went down,
Jer 7:12 the dwelling place of my name in the *b*.
17:12 A throne of glory, exalted from the *b*,
26: 1 In the *b* of the reign of Jehoiakim,
27: 1 [In the *b* of the reign of Jehoiakim,
28: 1 year, in [the *b* of] the reign of Zedekiah,
49:34 Jeremiah at the *b* of the reign of Zedekiah,
Lam 2:19 in the night, at the *b* of every watch;
Ez 36:11 and be more generous to you than in the *b;*
40: 1 month *b* the twenty-fifth year of our exile,
42:12 *b* of the way which led to the back wall,
Hos 1: 2 In the *b* of the Lord's speaking to Hosea,
Mi 1:13 Lachish, the *b* of sin for daughter Zion,
Mt 19: 4 "Have you not read that at the *b* the Creator
19: 8 "but at the *b* it was not that way.
24:21 from the *b* of the world until now or in all
Mk 5:33 Fearful and *b* to tremble now as she
10: 6 At the *b* of creation God made them male
Lk 1: 3 the whole sequence of events from the *b*,
24:27 *B*, then, with Moses and all the prophets,
24:47 to all the nations, *b* at Jerusalem.
Jn 1: 1 In the *b* was the Word;
1: 2 He was present to God in the *b*.
8: 9 drifted away one by one, *b* with the elders.
8:25 "What I have been telling you from the *b*.
8:44 He brought death to man from the *b*,
15:27 well, for you have been with me from the *b*.
Acts 8: 1 That day saw the *b* of a great persecution
10:37 *b* in Galilee with the baptism John
11: 4 affair to them step by step from the *b*:
11:15 upon them, just as it had upon us at the *b*.
26: 4 people from the *b* and later at Jerusalem,
2Cor 3: 1 Am I *b* to speak well of myself again?
Gal 3: 3 After *b* in the spirit,
Col 1:18 he who is the *b*, the first-born of the dead,
Heb 7: 3 ancestry, without *b* of days or end of life,
1Jn 2:13 for you have known him who is from the *b*.
2:14 for you have known him who is from the *b*.
2:24 you heard from the *b* remain in your hearts.
2:24 from the *b* does remain in your hearts,
3: 8 because the devil is a sinner from the *b*.
3:11 is the message you heard from the *b*:
2Jn 1: 6 and as you have heard from the *b*,
Rv 13: 8 at the world's *b* in the book of the living,
21: 6 the Alpha and the Omega, the *B* and the End.
22:13 the First and the Last, the *B* and the End!

BEGINNINGS (1)

Zec 4:10 scornful on that day of small *b* shall rejoice

BEGINS (11)

Jgs 10:18 "The one who *b* the war against the
Prv 17:14 therefore, check a quarrel before it *b!*
Sg 8: 8 we do for our sister when her courtship *b?*
Mt 24:49 coming,' and *b* to beat his fellow servants,
Mk 1: 1 Here *b* the gospel of Jesus Christ,
13:28 runs high and it *b* to sprout leaves,
Lk 12:45 *b* to abuse the housemen and servant girls,
Rom 1:17 justice of God which *b* and ends with faith;
1Tm 5: 4 let these learn that piety *b* at home
1Pt 4:17 If it *b* this way with us,
1Jn 2: 8 is over and the real light *b* to shine.

BEGONE (1)

Is 30:22 away like filthy rags to which you say, *B!*"

BEGOT (7)

Gn 5: 3 years old when he *b* a son in his likeness,
5:28 years old, he *b* a son and named him Noah,
6:10 age, for he walked with God, *b* three sons:
Dt 32:18 You were unmindful of the Rock that *b* you,
Prv 8:22 "The LORD *b* me, the first-born of his ways,
23:22 Listen to your father who *b* you,
1Cor 4:15 It was I who *b* you in Christ Jesus through

BEGOTTEN (25)

Gn 25:19 Abraham had *b* Isaac.
Jb 38:28 or who has *b* the drops of dew?
Ps(s) 2: 7 this day I have *b* you.
90: 2 Before the mountains were *b* and the earth
110: 3 the daystar, like the dew, I have *b* you."
Hos 5: 7 for they have *b* illegitimate children;
Jn 1:13 who were *b* not by blood,
3: 3 the reign of God unless he is *b* from above."
3: 5 without being *b* of water and Spirit.
3: 7 I tell you you must all be *b* from above.
3: 8 So it is with everyone *b* of the Spirit."
Acts 13:33 'You are my son; this day I have *b* you.'
Gal 4:23 girl had been *b* in the course of nature,
Phlm 1:10 whom I have *b* during my imprisonment.
Heb 1: 5 "You are my son; today I have *b* you"?
5: 5 "You are my son; today I have *b* you";
1Jn 2:29 who acts in holiness has been *b* by him.
3: 9 No one *b* of God acts sinfully because he
3: 9 he cannot sin because he is *b* of God.
4: 7 loves is *b* of God and has knowledge of God.
5: 1 that Jesus is the Christ has been *b* of God.
5: 1 loves the father loves the child he has *b*.
5: 4 Everyone *b* of God conquers the world,
5:18 We know that no one *b* of God commits sin;
5:18 rather, God protects the one *b* by him,

BEGRIMED (1)

2Sm 1:21 Upon you lie *b* the warriors' shields,

BEGRUDGE (3)

Dt 28:54 fastidious man among you will *b* his brother
28:56 will *b* her beloved husband and her son and
Tb 4:16 and do not *b* the alms you give.

BEGS (3)

Gn 50:17 Jacob *b* you to forgive the criminal
Sir 13: 3 the poor man is wronged and *b* forgiveness.
Mt 5:42 Give to the man who *b* from you.

BEGUILE (7)

Dt 29:18 should *b* himself into thinking that he can
Jgs 16: 5 *B* him and find out the secret of his great
Jdt 10:19 to be spared they could *b* the whole world."
16: 8 tresses, and put on a linen robe to *b* him.
Ps(s) 59:12 O God, slay them, lest they *b* my people;
Wis 4:11 pervert his mind or deceit *b* his soul;
Sir 13: 7 While it serves his purpose he will *b* you,

BEGUILED (3)

Jer 49:16 The terror you spread *b* you,
Ez 14: 9 prophet, if he is *b* into speaking a word,
14: 9 I, the LORD, shall have *b* that prophet;

BEGUILES (1)

Ps(s) 36: 3 For he *b* himself with the thought that his

BEGUILING (1)

Eccl 2: 3 I thought of *b* my senses with wine,

BEGUN (14)

Dt 2:31 *b* to hand over to you Sihon and his land,
3:24 you have *b* to show to your servant your
Jgs 20:39 And though the men of Benjamin had *b* by
1Kgs 6: 1 of the temple of the LORD was *b*.
1Mc 5:31 Judas perceived that the struggle had *b*
2Mc 13:11 this nation, which had just *b* to revive,
Ez 23: 8 up the harlotry which she had *b* in Egypt,
Jn 9:18 really been born blind and had *b* to see,
1Cor 4: 8 Would that you had really *b* to reign,
2Cor 8: 6 already *b* this work of charity among you,
Phil 1: 6 that he who has *b* the good work in you
1Pt 4:17 has begun, and *b* with God's own household.
Rv 11:17 your great power, you have *b* your reign.

BEHALF (62)

Gn 25:21 Isaac entreated the LORD on *b* of his wife,
Nm 25:13 because he was zealous on *b* of his God and
Jos 22:27 you on *b* of ourselves and our descendants,
Jgs 9: 3 kin repeated these words to them on his *b*,
2Sm 12:25 to name him Jedidiah, on *b* of the LORD.
14: 8 I will issue a command on your *b*."
1Kgs 2: 4 the promise he made on my *b* when he said,
2Kgs 11:11 the altar and the temple on the king's *b*.
2Chr 19: 6 on behalf of man, but on *b* of the LORD;
23:10 the altar and the temple on the king's *b*.
34:21 "On *b* of myself and those who are left in
Tb 1:22 Then Ahiqar interceded on my *b*,
Est 4: 8 and intercede with him in *b* of her people.
4:16 fast on my *b*, all of you, not eating
1Mc 10:27 favors in return for what you do in our *b*.
2Mc 1:26 accept this sacrifice on *b* of all your
11:15 granted in *b* of the Jews all the written
Jb 13: 8 Do you play advocate on *b* of God?
17: 3 Grant me one to offer you a pledge on my *b*:
36: 2 are still words to be said on God's *b*.
Ps(s) 74: 9 Deeds on our *b* we do not see;
Prv 31: 8 Open your mouth in *b* of the dumb,
Wis 12:14 you on *b* of those you have punished.
16:17 For the universe fights on *b* of the just.
Sir 29:16 turn a pledge on their *b* into misfortune,
Is 8:19 gods, apply to the dead on *b* of the living?"
Jer 7:16 raise not in their *b* a pleading prayer!
11:14 Do not intercede on *b* of this people,
18:20 I stood before you to speak in their *b*,
Ez 27:30 shore, Making their voice heard on your *b*,
45:17 make atonement on *b* of the house of Israel.
45:22 day the prince shall offer on his own *b*,
45:22 and on *b* of all the people of the land,
Dn 9:20 LORD, my God, on *b* of his holy mountain
Jl 4: 2 there on *b* of my people and my inheritance,
Mt 26:28 in *b* of many for the forgiveness of sins.
Mk 14:24 covenant, to be poured out on *b* of many.
Lk 1:25 these days the Lord is acting on my *b*;
Jn 5:31 "If I witness on my own *b*,
5:32 is another who is testifying on my *b*,
5:36 on my *b* that the Father has sent me.
5:37 me has himself given testimony on my *b*.
5:39 they also testify on my *b*.
8:18 I am one of those testifying in my *b*,
15:26 he will bear witness on my *b*.
Acts 12: 5 church prayed fervently to God on his *b*.
13:22 on his *b* God testified,
Rom 15:30 struggle by your prayers to God on my *b*.
1Cor 15:29 have themselves baptized on *b* of the dead?
15:29 not a reality, why be baptized on their *b*?
2Cor 1:11 so that on our *b* God may be thanked for
8:23 my companion and fellow worker in your *b*;
Gal 4:15 I can testify on your *b* that if it were
Eph 3: 1 for Christ Jesus on *b* of you Gentiles,
Phil 1: 4 rejoicing, as I plead on your *b*,
1Thes 1: 5 while still among you, we acted on your *b*.
Heb 2:17 faithful high priest before God on their *b*,
6:20 our forerunner, has entered on our *b*,
9:24 he might appear before God now on our *b*.
1Jn 5: 9 testimony God has given on his own Son's *b*.
5:10 testimony he has given on his own Son's *b*.

BEHAVE (6)

Tb 4:14 If you thus *b* as God's servant,
Sir 31:16 *B* at table like a favored guest,
Jer 18:12 each one of us will *b* according to the
Mal 1:12 But you *b* profanely toward me by thinking
Mt 6: 5 do not *b* like the hypocrites who love to
Ti 2: 3 the older women must *b* in ways that befit

BEHAVED (2)

1Kgs 3: 6 David, because he *b* faithfully toward you,
Zec 11: 8 of them, and they *b* badly toward me.

BEHAVES (1)

Sir 6:17 For he who fears God *b* accordingly,

BEHAVING (3)

2Sm 15: 6 By *b* in this way toward all the Israelites
1Kgs 22:53 the sight of the LORD, *b* like his father,
1Cor 7:36 If anyone thinks he is *b* dishonorably

BEHAVIOR (7)

1Sm 25: 3 was harsh and ungenerous in his *b*.
1Cor 3: 3 And is not your *b* that of ordinary men?
2Cor 1:12 testimony to the boast that in our *b* toward
10: 2 certain ones who accuse us of weak human *b*.
Phil 1:27 or hear about your *b* from a distance,
Jas 3:16 are inconstancy and all kinds of vile *b*.
1Pt 2:15 talk of foolish men by your good *b*.

BEHEADED (5)

Mt 14:10 He sent the order to have John *b* in prison.
Mk 6:28 The man went and *b* John in the prison.
Lk 9: 9 But Herod said, "John I *b*.
Acts 12: 2 He *b* James the brother of John,
Rv 20: 4 who had been *b* for their witness to Jesus

BEHELD (12)

Ex 14:31 *b* the great power that the LORD had shown
24:10 of Israel, and they *b* the God of Israel.
Jdt 10:23 when Holofernes and his servants *b* Judith,
Ps(s) 102:20 holy height, from heaven he *b* the earth,
114: 3 The sea *b* and fled; Jordan turned back.
119: 6 be put to shame when I *b* all your commands.
119:158 I *b* the apostates with loathing,
Wis 19: 8 your hand, after they *b* stupendous wonders.
Sir 17:11 His majestic glory their eyes *b*,
49: 8 EZEKIEL *b* the vision and described the
Lam 2:14 They *b* for you in vision false and
Mt 15:31 in the crowds as they *b* the mute speaking,

BEHEMOTH (1)

Jb 40:15 See, besides you I made *B*,

BEHIND (111)

Gn 18:10 at the entrance of the tent, just *b* him.
19: 6 When he had shut the door *b* him,
32:19 and Jacob himself is right *b* us.'"
32:20 all the others who followed *b* the droves,
32:21 to add, 'Your servant Jacob is right *b* us.'"
41: 3 *B* them seven other cows,
41: 6 *B* them sprouted seven ears of grain,
41:19 *B* them came seven other cows,
41:23 *B* them sprouted seven ears of grain,
Ex 10:26 Not an animal must be left *b*.
14:19 camp, now moved and went around *b* them.
14:19 the front, took up its place *b* them,
26:33 *b* this veil which divides the holy place
Lv 14:38 he shall close the door of the house *b* him
26:36 fainthearted that, if leaves rustle *b* them,
Nm 3:23 of the Gershonites camped *b* the Dwelling,
Dt 2: 8 "Then we left *b* us
2:18 to leave Ar and the territory of Moab *b*.
3:19 remain *b* in the towns I have given you,
25:18 cut off at the rear all those who lagged *b*.
Jos 8: 2 Set an ambush *b* the city."
8:14 that there was an ambush *b* the city.
Jgs 5:14 *b* you was Benjamin, among your troops.
1Sm 11: 5 Saul came in from the field, *b* his oxen.
14:13 clambered up with his armor-bearer *b* him;
21:10 is here [wrapped in a mantle] *b* an ephod.
24: 1 there and stayed in the refuges *b* Engedi.
30: 9 where those who were to remain *b* halted.
30:10 to cross the Wadi Besor and remained *b*.
30:21 and whom he had left *b* at the Wadi Besor,
2Sm 15:16 ten concubines whom he left *b*
16:21 whom he left *b* to take care of the palace.
20: 3 the ten concubines whom he had left *b*
20: 7 and all the warriors marched out *b* Abishai
1Kgs 14: 9 but me you have cast *b* your back.
20:15 *B* them he mustered all the Israelite
2Kgs 3:25 Kir-hareseth was left *b* its stone walls,
6:32 His master's footsteps are echoing *b* him."
9:18 Jehu said, "Get *b* me."
9:19 Jehu replied, "Get *b* me."
9:25 we were driving teams *b* his father Ahab,
11: 6 third shall be at the gate *b* the guards.
19:21 *B* you she wags her head,
25:12 guard, left *b* as vinedressers and farmers.
1Chr 19:10 a battle line both in front of and *b* him,
2Chr 13:13 army faced Judah, his ambush lay *b* them.
Neh 4: 7 I stationed guards down below, *b* the wall,
4:10 stood guard *b* the whole house of Judah as
9:26 they cast your law *b* their backs,
Tb 8: 4 the bedroom and closed the door *b* them,
11: 4 And the dog ran along *b* them.
1Mc 2:28 *b* in the city all their possessions.
5:33 He came up *b* them with three columns
5:43 to the attack, with all the people *b* him,
7:45 blowing the trumpets *b* them as signals.
9:45 and *b* us are the waters of the Jordan on
10:79 left a thousand cavalry in hiding *b* them.
10:80 discovered that there was an ambush *b* him,
2Mc 12:18 *b* in one place a very strong garrison.
Jb 41:24 *B* him he leaves a shining path;
Ps(s) 45:15 *b* her the virgins of her train are brought
50:17 hate discipline and cast my words *b* you?
139: 5 *B* me and before, you hem me in and
Sg 2: 9 Here he stands *b* our wall,
4: 1 Your eyes are doves *b* your veil.
4: 3 is like a half-pomegranate *b* your veil.
6: 7 is like a half-pomegranate *b* your veil.
Sir 21:15 them with scorn and casts them *b* his back.
44: 8 Some of them have left *b* a name and men
47:23 his father, and left *b* him one of his sons,
Is 2:10 Get *b* the rocks,
26:20 your chambers, and close your doors *b* you;
30:21 you shall see your Teacher, While from *b*,
37:22 *B* you she wags her head,
38:17 When you cast *b* your back all my sins.
57: 5 the wadies, *b* the crevices in the cliffs?
57: 8 *B* the door and the doorpost you placed
Jer 9:21 on a field, Like sheaves *b* the harvester,
48: 2 *b* you stalks the sword.
49:11 Leave your orphans *b*, I will keep them
52:16 guard, left *b* as vinedressers and farmers.
Bar 6: 5 crowd before them and *b* worshiping them.
Ez 3:12 and I heard *b* me the noise of a loud
23:35 have forgotten me and cast me *b* your back,
24:21 you left *b* shall fall by the sword.
39:28 on their land, not leaving any of them *b*.
41:15 lay the length of the free area and *b* it,
Hos 5: 8 "Look *b* you, O Benjamin!"
Jl 2:14 again relent and leave *b* him a blessing.
Jon 2: 7 the nether world were closing *b* me forever,
Zec 1: 8 trees in a shady place, and *b* him were red,
Mt 9:20 *b* him and touched the tassel on his cloak.
Mk 5:27 She had heard about Jesus and came up *b*
12:22 fact none of the seven left any children *b*.
14:52 him he left the cloth *b* and ran off naked.
Lk 2:43 Jesus remained *b* unknown to his parents.
5:28 Leaving everything *b*, Levi stood up
7:38 perfumed oil and stood *b* him at his feet,

8:44 *b* him and touched the tassel on his cloak.
11:48 that you stand *b* the deeds of your fathers:
23:26 shoulder for him to carry along *b* Jesus.
23:55 with him from Galilee followed along *b*.
Jn 20: 6 came along *b* him and entered the tomb.
Acts 17:14 the sea, while Silas and Timothy stayed *b*.
18:19 he left Priscilla and Aquila *b* and entered
25:14 he said, "whom Felix left *b* in custody.
Rom 3:13 The venom of asps lies *b* their lips,
Phil 3:13 what lies *b* but push on to what is ahead.
Heb 9: 3 *B* the second veil was the tabernacle
Rv 1:10 and I heard *b* me a piercing voice like the
19:14 The armies of heaven were *b* him riding

BEHOLD (122)

Nm 23: 9 crags I see him, from the heights I *b* him.
23:23 and of Israel, *B* what God has wrought!"
24:17 I *b* him, though not near:
Dt 4:19 And when you look up to the heavens and *b*
1Sm 16:12 to *b* and making a splendid appearance.
Tb 11:15 *B*, I now see my son Tobiah!"
12:20 *B*, I am about to ascend to him who sent me;
13:14 in you as they *b* all your joy forever.
Jdt 6:19 "Lord, God of heaven, *b* their arrogance!
7:27 and not have to *b* our little ones dying
8: 7 She was beautifully formed and lovely to *b*.
11:23 You are fair to *b*,
Est 1:11 and the officials, for she was lovely to *b*.
2: 7 was beautifully formed and lovely to *b*.
8: 6 and how can I *b* the destruction of my race?"
Jb 1:12 And the LORD said to Satan, *B*,
4: 3 *B*, you have instructed many,
7: 8 eye that now sees me shall no more *b* me;
8:20 *B*, God will not cast away the upright;
13:18 *B*, I have prepared my case,
16:19 Even now, *b*, my witness is in heaven,
19:27 my own eyes, not another's, shall *b* him,
20: 9 nor shall his dwelling again *b* him.
21:27 *B*, I know your thoughts,
22:12 in the heights of the heavens, *b* the stars,
23: 9 Where the north enfolds him, I *b* him not;
25: 5 *B*, even the moon is not bright and the
27:12 *B*, you yourselves have all seen it;
28:10 his eyes *b* all that is precious.
28:28 *B*, the fear of the LORD is wisdom;
32:11 *B*, I have waited for your discourses,
32:12 *b*, there is none who has convicted Job,
33: 2 *B*, now I open my mouth;
33: 6 *B* I, like yourself, have been taken
33:28 to the pit, and I *b* the light of life."
34:29 If he hides his face, who then can *b* him?
35: 5 Look up to the skies and *b*;
36: 5 *B*, God rejects the obstinate in heart;
36:22 *B*, God is sublime in his power.
39:29 his eyes *b* it afar off.
40: 4 *B*, I am of little account;
40:16 *B* the strength in his loins,
Ps(s) 8: 4 *b* your heavens, the work of your fingers,
10:14 You do see, for you *b* misery and sorrow,
11: 4 *b*, his searching glance is on mankind.
17: 2 your eyes *b* what is right.
17:15 But I in justice shall *b* your face;
25:19 *B*, my enemies are many,
40: 8 then said I, *B* I come;
42: 3 When shall I go and *b* the face of God?
46: 9 *b* the deeds of the LORD,
51: 8 *B*, you are pleased with sincerity of heart,
54: 6 *B*, God is my helper;
59: 4 For *b*, they lie in wait for my life;
68:34 *B*, his voice resounds, the voice of power
83: 3 For *b*, your enemies raise a tumult,
84:10 O God, *b* our shield,
91: 8 you *b* and see the requital of the wicked,
92:10 For behold, your enemies, O LORD, for *b*,
119:40 *B*, I long for your precepts;
119:153 *B* my affliction, and rescue me
123: 2 *B*, as the eyes of servants are on the
127: 3 *B*, sons are a gift from the LORD;
128: 4 *B*, thus is the man blessed who fears the
132: 6 *B*, we heard of it in Ephrathah;
133: 1 *B*, how good it is,
139: 4 Even before a word is on my tongue, *b*,
Prv 23:33 Your eyes *b* strange sights,
24:31 And *b*! it was all overgrown
29:16 but their downfall the just will *b*.
Eccl 1:14 things that are done under the sun, and *b*,
1:16 Though I said to myself, *B*,
2: 1 But *b*, this too was vanity.
2:11 toil at which I had taken such pains, *b*!
7:27 *B*, this have I found, says Qoheleth,
7:29 *B*, only this have I found out:
Sir 15: 7 attain to her, haughty men will not *b* her.
16:16 *B*, the heavens, the heaven of heavens,
30:20 who groans at the good things his eyes *b*!
43:11 firmament by its brilliance, *B* the rainbow!
Is 10:33 *B*, the Lord, the LORD of hosts,
25: 9 *B* our God, to whom we looked to save us!
26:11 your hand is uplifted, but they *b* it not;
28: 2 *B*, the LORD has a strong one and a mighty,
38:11 No longer shall I *b* my fellow men among
39: 6 *B*, the days shall come when all that is in
40:15 Power of the Creator *B*,
52:10 the earth will *b* the salvation of our God.
62: 2 Nations shall *b* your vindication,
64: 4 *B*, you are angry, and we are sinful;
Jer 2:35 *B*, I will judge you on that word of yours,
4:25 I looked and *b*, there was no man;
4:26 *b*, the garden land was a desert,
5:14 *B*, I make my words in your mouth, a fire,
10:18 *B*, this time I will sing away the
11:16 A spreading olive tree, goodly to *b*,
23: 5 *B*, the days are coming, says the LORD
23:15 *B*, I will give them wormwood to eat,
30: 3 For *b*, the days will come, says the LORD
30:10 *B*, I will deliver you from the far-off land,
31: 8 *B*, I will bring them back from the land of
32:37 *B*, I will gather them together from all
33: 6 *B*, I will treat and assuage the city's
39:16 *B*, I am now fulfilling the words I spoke
46:27 *B*, I will deliver you from the far-off land,
47: 2 *B*: waters are rising from the north,
48:40 *B*, like an eagle he soars,
49:35 *B*, I will break the bow of Elam,
51:47 *b*, the days are coming when I will punish
51:52 But *b*, the days are coming, says the LORD,
Lam 1:18 all you peoples, and *b* my suffering:
Bar 2:17 Look directly at us, and *b*:
3: 8 *B* us today in our captivity,
4:36 *b* the joy that comes to you from God.
Ez 31: 3 *B*, a cypress [cedar] in Lebanon,
Mi 2: 3 *B*, I am planning against this race an evil
7:16 The nations shall *b* and be put to shame,
Mt 18:10 constantly *b* my heavenly Father's face.
21:42 did this and we find it marvelous to *b*'?
Mk 12:11 who did it and we find it marvelous to *b*'?"
Rom 9:33 *B*, I am placing in Zion a stone to make

BEHOLDING (1)

Wis 17: 6 And in their terror they thought *b* these

BEHOLDS (5)

Nm 12: 8 The presence of the LORD he *b*.
Jb 28:24 For he *b* the ends of the earth and sees
34:21 the ways of man, and he *b* all his steps.
36:25 man *b* it from afar.
Ps(s) 33:14 throne he *b* all who dwell on the earth,

BEING (272)

Gn 2: 7 of life, and so man became a living *b*.
10:12 and Calah, the latter *b* the principal city.
14:18 and wine, and *b* a priest of God Most High,
15: 2 if I keep on *b* childless and have as my
24:32 and while the camels were *b* unloaded and
42:21 we are *b* punished because of our brother.
43:18 But on *b* led to his house,
47:14 for the rations that were *b* dispensed,
Ex 3:16 about the way you are *b* treated in Egypt;
10: 7 not yet realize that Egypt is *b* destroyed?"
18:11 for he took occasion of their *b* dealt with
28:25 the other two ends of the cords *b* fastened
28:32 opening of a shirt, to keep it from *b* torn.
30:12 plague may come upon them for *b* registered.
38:10 hooks and bands of the columns *b* of silver.
38:11 hooks and bands of the columns *b* of silver.
38:12 hooks and bands of the columns *b* of silver.
39:23 around the opening to keep it from *b* torn.
40:15 Thus, by *b* anointed,
Lv 4:13 inadvertently and without even *b* aware of it
5: 2 or if someone, without *b* aware of it,
5: 3 or if someone, without *b* aware of it,
5: 4 or if someone, without *b* aware of it,
5:17 "If someone, without *b* aware of it,
11:43 creature through *b* contaminated by them.
14: 8 The man *b* purified shall then wash his
14:11 shall place the man who is *b* purified,
14:18 put on the head of the man *b* purified.
14:25 tip of the right ear of the man *b* purified,
18:14 brother by *b* intimate with his wife,
24:17 life of any human *b* shall be put to death;
27:16 seed *b* valued at fifty silver shekels.
27:28 human *b* or an animal or a hereditary field,
27:33 sacred, without the right of *b* bought back."
Nm 17: 3 because in *b* presented before the LORD
19: 6 the fire in which the heifer is *b* burned.
19:11 human *b* shall be unclean for seven days;
Dt 17: 4 and if, on *b* informed of it,
17:10 *b* careful to do exactly as they direct.
29:22 its soil *b* nothing but sulphur and salt,
31: 7 for you must *b* this people into the land
Jos 9:26 saved them from *b* killed by the Israelites,
22:14 each one *b* both prince and military leader
Jgs 8:14 who upon *b* questioned listed for him the
8:24 *b* Ishmaelites, the enemy had gold rings.)
12: 6 *b* able to give the proper pronunciation,
15:18 *B* very thirsty, he cried to the LORD
20:42 with the fight *b* pressed against them.
Ru 2:16 them for her to glean without *b* rebuked.
1Sm 16:18 soldier, besides *b* an able speaker,
28: 3 died and, after *b* mourned by all Israel,
28:13 a preternatural *b* rising from the earth."
2Sm 14: 6 There *b* no one to part them,
17:17 could not risk *b* seen entering the city.
1Kgs 1:27 my royal master's order without my *b* told
7:26 resembled that of a cup, *b* lily-shaped.
14:10 completely, as though dung were *b* burned.
2Chr 4: 5 was made like that of a cup, *b* lily-shaped.
Ezr 3:12 the foundation of the present house *b* laid.
4:14 to look on while the king is *b* dishonored.
5: 8 it is *b* rebuilt of cut stone and the walls
5: 8 and the walls are *b* reinforced with timber;
5: 8 the work is *b* carried on diligently and is
Neh 13:10 due the Levites were no longer *b* given,
Tb 13: 4 Exalt him before every living *b*,
Jdt 9: 1 While the incense was *b* offered in the
9: 5 Whatever you devise comes into *b*;
10:18 while he was *b* informed about her.
13:20 life when your people were *b* oppressed,
Est 2:20 she had when she was *b* brought up by him.
4:11 king in the inner court without *b* summoned,
6: 1 While this was *b* read to him,
1Mc 2: 6 were *b* committed in Judah and in Jerusalem,
2:11 From *b* free, she has become a slave.
4:20 put to flight and their camp was *b* burned.
5:16 kinsmen who were *b* attacked by enemies.
7:33 holocaust that was *b* offered for the king.
16:12 gold, *b* the son-in-law of the high priest.
2Mc 1:19 When our fathers were *b* exiled to Persia,
1:23 While the sacrifice was *b* burned,
2:22 laws that were in danger of *b* abolished,
2:26 this digest, the task, far from *b* easy,
3:18 the Place was in danger of *b* profaned.
4: 3 were *b* committed by one of his henchmen,
5: 5 back and the city was finally *b* taken,
5: 8 After *b* driven into Egypt,
5:14 and the same number *b* sold into slavery.
6:18 was *b* forced to open his mouth to eat pork.
6:26 Even if, for the time *b*,
7: 4 While they were *b* quickly heated,
7:14 hope of *b* restored to life by him;
7:24 in her words, thought he was *b* ridiculed.
8: 2 people, who were *b* oppressed on all sides;
8: 3 which was *b* destroyed and about to be
8: 7 as *b* especially helpful for such attacks.
8:35 after *b* humbled through the Lord's help by
10:30 their own armor, kept him from *b* wounded.
11: 1 *b* greatly displeased at what had happened,
13: 3 but in the hope of *b* established in office.
Jb 9:35 I might speak without *b* afraid of him.
19:26 my inmost *b* is consumed with longing.
35: 8 and your justice only a fellow human *b*.
37:20 or when a man says he is *b* destroyed?
Ps(s) 35:10 my *b* shall say, "O LORD, who is like you,
44:23 for your sake we are *b* slain all the day;
51: 8 and in my inmost *b* you teach me wisdom.
78:38 Yet he, *b* merciful, forgave their sin
103: 1 and all my *b*, bless his holy name.
119:46 decrees before kings without *b* ashamed.
139:13 Truly you have formed my inmost *b*;
Prv 4:22 them, to man's whole *b* they are health.
18: 8 morsels that sink into one's inmost *b*.
19:23 and sleeps without *b* visited by misfortune.
20:27 it searches through all his inmost *b*.
20:30 lashes, and a scourging to the inmost *b*.
23:16 And my inmost *b* will exult,
24:11 Rescue those who are *b* dragged to death,
26:22 morsels that sink into one's inmost *b*.
26:24 but in his inmost *b* he maintains deceit;
30: 9 Lest, *b* full,
30: 9 Or, *b* in want, I steal,
Eccl 12: 9 Besides *b* wise, Qoheleth taught the people
Wis 1:14 all things that they might have *b*;
8:20 *b* noble, I attained an unsullied body.
10: 6 from among the wicked who were *b* destroyed,
11: 9 condemned in anger, were *b* tormented.
12:22 and, when *b* judged, may look for mercy.
14: 6 when the proud giants were *b* destroyed,
15:17 *b* mortal, he makes a dead thing
16: 4 shown how their enemies were *b* tormented.
19: 6 in its several kinds, was *b* made over anew,
Sir 13: 8 Guard against *b* presumptuous;
13:15 Every *b* is drawn to its own kind;
29: 7 of meanness, but from fear of *b* cheated.
32: 3 *B* older, you may talk;
33:30 But never lord it over any human *b*,
40: 6 mind's eye sees, like a fugitive *b* pursued;
42:15 God's word were his works brought into *b*;
42:18 their innermost *b* he understands.
47: 8 With his whole *b* he loved his Maker and
47:21 Thus two governments came into *b*,
49:16 of any living *b* was the splendor of ADAM.
50:25 My whole *b* loathes two nations,
51:21 whole *b* was stirred as I learned about her;
Is 42: 9 Before they spring into *b*,
48: 7 not long ago, they are brought into *b*,
Jer 7:11 I too see what is *b* done, says the LORD.
7:20 it will burn without *b* quenched.
21:12 like fire which burns without *b* quenched,
33: 4 which are *b* destroyed in the face of
40: 1 and Judah who were *b* exiled to Babylon.
44:18 are *b* destroyed by the sword and by hunger.
49:33 Where no man lives, no human *b* stays.
50:40 dwell there, no human *b* shall tarry there.
Bar 6: 1 those who were *b* led captive to Babylon
6: 1 *b* led captive to Babylon by Nebuchadnezzar,
Ez 3:26 to rebuke them for *b* a rebellious house.
33:24 we, therefore, *b* many,

BEING (cont.)

40: 2 seemed to be a city b built before me.
40: 5 each cubit b a cubit and a handbreadth;
Dn 2:34 from a mountain without a hand b put to it,
2:45 the mountain without a hand b put to it,
8:25 he shall be broken without a hand b raised.
13:45 As she was b led to execution,
Mi 6:14 You shall eat, without b satisfied,
Hb 1: 5 For a work is b done in your days that you
Zec 6: 5 b reviewed by the Lord of all the earth."
Mal 2:15 Did he not make one b,
Mt 3: 6 They were b baptized by him in the Jordan
12:12 more precious a human b is than a sheep.
14:24 was b tossed about in the waves raised by
23: 7 respect in public and of b called 'Rabbi.'
23:10 Avoid b called teachers.
24:22 shortened, not a human b would be saved.
24:38 and drinking, marrying and b married,
Mk 1: 5 They were b baptized by him in the Jordan
4:17 B rootless, they last only a while.
7:19 It does not penetrate his b,
Lk 1:25 "My b proclaims the greatness of the Lord,
2:33 marveling at what was b said about him.
3:21 was at prayer after likewise b baptized,
3:23 work he was about thirty years of age, b—
7:12 of the town a dead man was b carried out,
8:53 laughed at him, b certain she was dead.
9:42 As he was b brought, the spirit threw him
14:29 and then not b able to complete the work;
16: 8 devious employee credit for b enterprising!
17:20 on b asked by the Pharisees when the reign
19: 3 Jesus was like, but b small of stature,
Jn 1: 3 Through him all things came into b,
3: 5 without b begotten of water and Spirit.
7:42 say that the Messiah, b of David's family,
16: 1 all this to keep your faith from b shaken.
16:13 b the Spirit of truth he will guide you to
18:36 to save me from b handed over to the Jews.
21:14 the disciples after b raised from the dead.
Acts 2:47 to their number those who were b saved.
3: 2 a man crippled from birth was b carried in.
4:23 After b released, the two went back to
5:26 force, for fear of b stoned by the crowd.
6: 1 were b neglected in the daily distribution
7:59 was b stoned he could be heard praying,
8:37 What is to keep me from b baptized?"
9:31 It was b built up and was making steady
10:10 it was b prepared he fell into a trance.
10:47 as we have, from b baptized with water?"
11:22 resulting in Barnabas' b sent to Antioch.
13:38 forgiveness of sins is b proclaimed to you,
17:28 'In him we live and move and have our b,'
19:40 we run the risk of b accused of rioting
21:31 Attempts were b made on his life when a
22:20 blood of your witness Stephen was b shed,
25: 4 Paul was b kept in custody at Caesarea,
27:18 We were b pounded by the storm so
27:27 were still b driven across the Ionian Sea,
Rom 1:18 The wrath of God is b revealed from heaven
3: 1 What is the advantage, then, of b a Jew,
4:17 into b those things which had not been.
8:36 your sake we are b slain all the day long;
13: 6 magistrates b God's ministers who devote
15:24 the joy of b with you for a little while.
1Cor 3: 3 b still very much in a natural condition.
11:32 b condemned with the rest of the world.
14: 7 how will anyone know what is b played if
15: 2 You are b saved by it at this very moment
2Cor 2:15 both among those who are b saved and those
3:12 hope b such, we speak with full confidence.
3:18 are b transformed from glory to glory into
4:11 b delivered to death for Jesus' sake,
4:16 because our inner b is renewed each day
4:16 our body is b destroyed at the same time.
5: 9 This b so, we make it our aim to please
8:17 but b very eager he has gone to you freely.
11: 9 I kept myself from b burdensome to you,
11:19 B wise yourselves,
12:16 b crafty, you say, I caught you by guile.
Gal 2: 3 circumcision, despite his b a Greek.
2:14 were not b straightforward about the truth
3:17 into b four hundred and thirty years later,
Eph 1:12 his glory by b the first to hope in Christ.
2:22 in him you are b built into this temple,
Phil 1:18 or genuine ones, Christ is b proclaimed!
1:26 My b with you once again should make you
2: 7 of a slave, b born in the likeness of men.
3: 5 b of the stock of Israel and the tribe of
3:10 by b formed into the pattern of his death.
4:12 I am experienced in b brought low,
Col 1:17 In him everything continues in b.
3:23 you do, work at it with your whole b.
2Thes 2: 1 Jesus Christ and our b gathered to him,
1Tm 2:15 her chastity b taken for granted.
6:16 whom no human b has ever seen or can see.
2Tm 2: 9 even to the point of b thrown into chains
4: 6 am already b poured out like a libation.
Heb 1: 3 exact representation of the Father's b,
6:20 b made high priest forever according to
10:14 perfected those who are b sanctified.
10:33 with those who were b so dealt with.
11: 3 visible came into b through the invisible.
11:30 fell after b encircled for seven days.
11:31 from b destroyed with the unbelievers,
Jas 1:13 is free to say, "I am b tempted by God."
1Pt 3: 7 will keep your prayers from b answered.
4:15 that none of you suffers for b a murderer,
4:16 If anyone suffers for b a Christian,
2Pt 3: 5 all brought into b by the word of God.
3Jn 1: 9 but Diotrephes, who enjoys b their leader,
Jude 1: 9 when his case with the devil was b judged
1:12 they bear no fruit, b dead and uprooted.
Rv 3: 1 I know the reputation you have of b alive,
6:14 as if it were a scroll b rolled up;
21:16 its length and its width b the same.

BEINGS (9)

Gn 8:21 will I ever again strike down all living b,
9:15 made between me and you and all living b,
9:15 become a flood to destroy all mortal b.
9:16 established between God and all living b—
32:29 with divine and human b and have prevailed."
Lv 27:29 All human b that are doomed lose the right
Jer 17: 5 Cursed is the man who trusts in human b,
2Pt 2:10 whatever about reviling celestial b,
Jude 1: 8 God's dominion and revile the angelic b.

BEKAH (1)

Ex 38:26 one b apiece, that is, a half-shekel apiece,

BEL (17)

Is 46: 1 B bows down, Nebo stoops,
Jer 50: 2 Babylon is taken, B confounded,
51:44 I will punish B in Babylon,
Bar 6:40 forward B and ask the god to make noise,
Dn 14: 3 The Babylonians had an idol called B,
14: 5 king asked him, "Why do you not adore B?"
14: 6 "You do not think B is a living god?
14: 9 But if you can show that B consumes them,
14: 9 them, Daniel shall die for blaspheming B."
14:10 There were seventy priests of B,
14:10 went with Daniel into the temple of B,
14:11 the temple of Bel, the priests of B said,
14:12 If you do not find that B has eaten it all
14:14 departed the king set the food before B,
14:18 and cried aloud, "Great you are, O B;
14:22 them to death, and handed B over to Daniel,
14:28 "he has destroyed B,

BELA (14)

Gn 14: 2 of Zeboiim, and the king of B (that is,
14: 8 of Zeboiim, and the king of B (that is,
36:32 B, son of Beor, became king in Edom;
36:33 When B died, Jobab, son of Zerah,
46:21 B, Becher, Ashbel, Gera, Naaman,
Nm 26:38 through B the clan of the Belaites,
26:40 The descendants of B were Arad and Naaman:
1Chr 1:43 B, son of Beor,
1:44 When B died, Jobab, son of Zerah,
5: 8 Jeiel, the chief, and Zechariah, and B,
7: 6 The sons of Benjamin were B,
7: 7 The sons of B were Ezbon,
8: 1 Benjamin became the father of B,
8: 3 The sons of B were Addar and Gera,

BELAITES (1)

Nm 26:38 through Bela the clan of the B,

BELIAL (1)

2Cor 6:15 What accord is there between Christ and B,

BELIE (1)

Ps(s) 89:34 from him, nor will I b my faithfulness.

BELIEF (3)

2Mc 15:11 a dream, a kind of vision, worthy of b.
Acts 15:11 Our b is rather that we are saved by the
Rom 14:23 does not accord with one's b is sinful.

BELIEVE (149)

Gn 45:26 he could not b them.
Ex 4: 1 Moses, "suppose they will not b me,
4: 5 "This will take place so that they may b,"
4: 8 "If they will not b you,
4: 8 they should b the message of the second.
4: 9 if they will not b even these two signs,
Nm 14:11 How long will they refuse to b in me,
1Kgs 10: 7 "Though I did not b the report until I
2Chr 9: 6 "Yet I did not b the report until I came
32:15 Do not b him!
Tb 2:14 Yet I would not b her,
10: 7 do not b they will ever see me again.
14: 4 flee into Media for I b God's word
14: 4 For I know and b that whatever God has
Jb 9:16 not b that he would hearken to my words;
Ps(s) 27:13 I b that I shall see the bounty of the
Wis 12: 2 may abandon their wickedness and b in you,
16:26 your word that preserves those who b you!
Sir 19:14 every story you must not b.
Is 43:10 and b in me and understand that it is I.
53: 1 Who would b what we have heard?
Jer 12: 6 Do not b them, even if they are friendly
40:15 Gedaliah, son of Ahikam, would not b them.
Lam 4:12 The kings of the earth did not b,
Mt 18: 6 one of these little ones who b in me,
18:13 b me he is happier about this one than
21:21 B me, if you trust and do not falter,
21:32 and the prostitutes did b in him.
21:32 saw that, you did not repent and b in him."
24:23 is here,' or 'He is there,' do not b it.
24:26 is in the innermost rooms,' do not b it.
27:42 from that cross and then we will b in him.
Mk 1:15 Reform your lives and b in the gospel!"
9:24 father immediately exclaimed, "I do b!
11:24 if you are ready to b that you will
13:21 'Look, he is there!'—do not b it.
15:32 and now so that we can see it and b in him!"
16:11 had been seen by her, they refused to b it.
16:16 who refuses to b in it will be condemned.
Lk 8:12 of their hearts lest they b and be saved.
8:13 they b for a while, but fall away in time
18:14 B me, this man went home from the
20: 5 he will say, 'Then why do you not b in it?';
22:67 "If I tell you, you will not b me,
24:11 like nonsense and they refused to b them.
24:25 to b all that the prophets have announced!
Jn 1: 7 so that through him all men might b—
1:12 These are they who b in his name
1:50 "Do you b just because I told you I saw
2:22 b the Scripture and the word he had spoken.
3:12 not b when I tell you about earthly things,
3:12 to b when I tell you about those of heaven?
3:15 all who b may have eternal life in him.
3:18 but whoever does not b is already
4:21 B me, woman, an hour is coming when
4:48 people see signs and wonders, you do not b."
5:38 because you do not b the One he has sent.
5:44 How can people like you b,
5:46 If you believed Moses you would then b me,
5:47 But if you do not b what he wrote,
5:47 what he wrote, how can you b what I say?"
6:36 you have seen me, you still do not b.
6:64 Yet among you there are some who do not b."
6:64 of course, the ones who refused to b,
6:69 We have come to b; we are convinced
7:31 Many in the crowd came to b in him.
7:39 that came to b in him were to receive.
8:24 your sins unless you come to b that I AM."
8:30 he spoke this way, many came to b in him.
8:46 am telling the truth, why do you not b me?
9:18 The Jews refused to b that he had really
9:35 asked him, "Do you b in the Son of Man?"
9:36 "Who is he, sir, that I may b in him?"
9:38 [I do b, Lord," he said, and bowed down
10:25 "I did tell you, but you do not b.
10:26 refuse to b because you are not my sheep.
10:42 In that place, many came to b in him.
11:15 I was not there, that you may come to b.
11:26 will never die. Do you b this?"
11:27 have come to b that you are the Messiah,
11:42 crowd, that they may b that you sent me."
11:48 like this, the whole world will b in him.
12:37 their presence, they refused to b in him.
12:39 The reason they could not b was that,
13:19 when it takes place you may b that I AM.
14:10 Do you not b that I am in the Father and
14:11 B me that I am in the Father and the
14:11 me, or else, b because of the works I do.
14:29 so that when it takes place you may b.
16: 9 in that they refuse to b in me;
16:30 We do indeed b you came from God."
16:31 Jesus answered them, "Do you really b?
17:20 those who will b in me through their word,
17:21 us, that the world may b that you sent me.
19:35 what he knows is true, so that you may b.)
20:25 "I will never b it without probing the
20:27 Do not persist in your unbelief, but b!"
20:31 to help you b that Jesus is the Messiah,
Acts 8:12 but once they began to b in the good news
9:26 even refused to b that he was a disciple.
9:42 because of it, many came to b in the Lord.
15: 7 would hear the message of the gospel and b.
16:15 you are convinced that I b in the Lord,
16:31 B in the Lord Jesus and you will be saved,
17:12 Many of them came to b,
19: 4 come after him in whom they were to b—
19: 9 When some in their obstinacy would not b,
21:20 how many thousands of Jews have come to b,
23: 8 while the Pharisees b in all these things.)
24:14 I b all that is written in the law and the
26: 8 hard to b that God raises dead men to life.
26:27 Do you b the prophets, King Agrippa?
28:24 others would not b.
28:31 others would not b.
Rom 3:22 faith in Jesus Christ for all who b.
3:25 him the means of expiation for all who b.
3:26 and might justify those who b in Jesus.
4:11 the father of all the uncircumcised who b,
4:24 faith will be credited to us also if we b in
6: 8 we b that we are also to live with him.
10: 9 and b in your heart that God raised him
10:14 can they b unless they have heard of him?
16:26 all the Gentiles that they may b and obey
1Cor 1:21 who b through the absurdity of the preaching
11:18 among you, and I am inclined to b it.

14:22 who believe but for those who do not *b*,
2Cor 4:13 We *b* and so we speak,
Gal 3: 7 means that those who *b* are sons of Abraham.
3: 9 all who *b* are blessed along with Abraham,
3:22 might be fulfilled in those who *b*,
Eph 1:19 scope of his power in us who *b*.
Phil 1:29 to *b* in him but also to suffer for him.
4:22 send you theirs, as do all those who *b*,
1Thes 2:13 the word of God at work within you who *b*.
4:14 For if we *b* that Jesus died and rose,
1Tm 2: 7 have been made its herald and apostle (*b* me,
4:10 of all men, but especially of those who *b*.
Heb 11: 6 who comes to God must *b* that he exists,
Jas 2:19 Do you *b* that God is one?
2:19 The demons *b* that, and shudder.
1Pt 1: 8 him, and without seeing you now *b* in him,
3: 1 who do not *b* in the word of the gospel
1Jn 3:23 we are to *b* in the name of his Son,
4:16 know and to *b* in the love God has for us.
5:10 Whoever does not *b* God has made God a liar
5:10 God a liar by refusing to *b* in the testimony
5:13 you who *b* in the name of the Son of God.
Jude 1: 5 but later destroyed those who refused to *b*.

BELIEVED (59)

Ex 4:31 The people *b*,
14:31 LORD and *b* in him and in his servant Moses.
2Kgs 17:14 their fathers, who had not *b* in the LORD,
Jdt 14:10 God of Israel had done, *b* firmly in him.
1Mc 10:46 words, they neither *b* nor accepted them,
12:46 Jonathan *b* him and did as he said.
Ps 78:22 they *b* not God nor trusted in his help.
78:32 sinned still more and *b* not in his wonders.
106:12 Then they *b* his words and sang his praises.
106:24 they *b* not his word.
116:10 I *b*, even when I said, "I am greatly
Sir 34: 7 and those who *b* in them have perished.
Dn 13:41 The assembly *b* them,
Jon 3: 5 when the people of Nineveh *b* God;
Hb 1: 5 in your days that you would not have *b*,
Lk 18: 9 those who *b* in their own self-righteousness
Jn 2:11 his glory, and his disciples *b* in him.
2:23 the Passover festival, many *b* in his name,
4:39 Many Samaritans from that town *b* in him on
5:46 If you *b* Moses you would then believe me,
8:31 went on to say to those Jews who *b* in him:
11:40 *b* you would see the glory of God displayed?"
12:38 who has *b* what has reached our ears?
12:42 even among the Sanhedrin, who *b* in him;
16:27 loved me and have *b* that I came from God.
17: 8 you, they have *b* it was you who sent me.
20: 8 He saw and *b*.
20:29 are they who have not seen and have *b*."
Acts 2:44 Those who *b* shared all things in common;
4: 4 many of those who had heard the speech *b*;
8:13 Even Simon *b*.
11:17 when we first *b* in the Lord Jesus Christ,
11:21 of them *b* and were converted to the Lord.
13:12 the governor saw what had happened, he *b*,
13:41 would have *b* even if you had been told.' "
13:48 destined for life everlasting *b* in it.
18: 8 too, who heard Paul *b* and were baptized.
22:19 they know that I imprisoned those who *b*
Rom 3: 3 may ask, what if some of them have not *b*?
4: 3 "Abraham *b* God,
4:17 father in the sight of God in whom he *b*,
4:18 Abraham *b* and so became the father of many
10:14 they call on him in whom they have not *b*?
10:16 But not all have *b* the gospel.
10:16 who has *b* what he has heard from us?"
1Cor 15: 2 Otherwise you have *b* in vain.
15:11 is what we preach and this is what you *b*.
2Cor 4:13 of which the Scripture says, "Because I *b*,
Gal 2:16 we too have *b* in him in order to be
3: 6 *b* God, and it was credited to him as justice."
Eph 1:13 salvation, the word of truth, and *b* in it,
Col 2:12 raised to life with him because you *b*
2Thes 1:10 holy ones and adored by all who have *b*—
2:12 so that all who have not *b* the truth but
1Tm 3:16 the Gentiles, *B* in throughout the world,
2Tm 1:12 ashamed, for I know him in whom I have *b*,
3:14 faithful to what you have learned and *b*,
Heb 4: 3 is we who have *b* who enter into that rest,
Jas 2:23 was fulfilled which says, "Abraham *b* God,

BELIEVER (4)

Jn 20:29 "You became a *b* because you saw me.
Acts 13:39 In him, every *b* is acquitted.
16: 1 Timothy, whose mother was Jewish and a *b*,
2Cor 6:15 what common lot between *b* and unbeliever?

BELIEVERS (23)

Mk 9:42 these simple *b* were to be plunged in the sea
Jn 4:53 and his whole household thereupon became *b*.
Acts 4:32 of *b* were of one heart and one mind.
5:14 Nevertheless more and more *b*,
9:41 call in those who were *b* and the widows
10:45 The circumcised *b* who had accompanied
17:34 A few did join him, however, to become *b*.
18:27 those who through God's favor had become *b*.
19: 2 receive the Holy Spirit when you became *b*?"
19:18 Many who had become *b* came forward and
1Cor 3: 5 ministers through whom you became *b*,
6: 2 not know that the *b* will judge the world?
14:34 rule observed in all the assemblies of *b*,
Eph 1: 1 holy ones [at Ephesus], *b* in Christ Jesus.
3: 8 To me, the least of all *b*,
1Thes 1: 7 for all the *b* of Macedonia and Achaia.
2:10 our conduct was toward you who are *b*.
1Tm 4: 3 with thanksgiving by *b* who know the truth.
4:12 example of love, faith, and purity to *b*.
6: 2 from their work are *b* and beloved brothers.
Ti 1: 6 the father of children who are *b* and are
1Pt 1:21 It is through him that you are *b* in God,
5: 9 realizing that the brotherhood of *b* is

BELIEVES (25)

Prv 14:15 The simpleton *b* everything,
Sir 34: 2 the wind, is the one who *b* in dreams.
Mk 11:23 doubts but *b* that what he says will happen,
16:16 *b* in it and accepts baptism will be saved;
Jn 3:16 that whoever *b* in him may not die but may
3:18 Whoever *b* in him avoids condemnation,
3:36 Whoever *b* in the Son has life eternal.
6:35 no one who *b* in me shall ever thirst.
6:40 Son and *b* in him shall have eternal life.
6:47 assure you, he who *b* has eternal life.
7:38 let him drink who *b* in me.
11:26 whoever *b* in me, though he should die,
11:26 is alive and *b* in me will never die.
12:44 *b* not so much in me as in him who sent me;
12:46 who *b* in me from remaining in the dark.
Acts 10:43 saying that everyone who *b* in him has
Rom 1:16 leading everyone who *b* in it to salvation,
4: 5 yet *b* in him who justifies the sinful,
9:33 he who *b* in him will not be put to shame."
10: 4 him, justice comes to everyone who *b*.
10:11 "No one who *b* in him will be put to shame."
14:23 is not acting in accordance with what he *b*.
1Jn 5: 1 Everyone who *b* that Jesus is the Christ
5: 5 The one who *b* that Jesus is the Son of God.
5:10 Whoever *b* in the Son of God possesses that

BELIEVING (11)

Jn 3:18 for not *b* in the name of God's only Son.
7:48 do not see any of the Sanhedrin *b* in him,
12:11 Jesus and *b* in him on account of Lazarus.
Rom 15:13 fill you with all joy and peace in *b* so that
1Cor 7:14 husband is consecrated by his *b* wife;
7:14 wife is consecrated by her *b* husband.
7:15 The *b* husband or wife is not bound in such
9: 5 Do we not have the right to marry a *b*
1Thes 4:14 those also who have fallen asleep *b* in him.
2Thes 2: 2 into *b* that the day of the Lord is here.
2Pt 3: 5 In *b* this, they do not take into account

BELL (2)

Ex 28:34 first a gold *b*, then a pomegranate,
39:26 first a *b*, then a pomegranate,

BELLIES (3)

Ps(s) 17:14 where with your treasures you fill their *b*.
Ez 7:19 to satisfy their craving or fill their *b*,
Rom 16:18 not Christ our Lord, but their own *b*,

BELLOWS (2)

Prv 26:21 What a *b* is to live coals,
Jer 6:29 The *b* roars, the lead is consumed

BELLS (4)

Ex 28:33 linen twined, with gold *b* between them;
39:25 *b* of pure gold were also made and put
Sir 45: 9 the hem, And a rustle of *b* round about,
Zec 14:20 there shall be upon the *b* of the horses,

BELLY (20)

Gn 3:14 On your *b* shall you crawl,
Lv 11:42 Whether it crawls on its *b*,
Nm 5:21 thighs to waste away and your *b* to swell!
5:22 your *b* swell and your thighs waste away!'
5:27 and her *b* will swell and her thighs will
Jgs 3:21 right thigh, and thrust it into Eglon's *b*.
1Mc 6:46 under the elephant and stabbed it in the *b*,
Jb 20:15 God shall compel his *b* to disown them.
40:16 and his vigor in the sinews of his *b*.
41:22 His *b* is sharp as pottery fragments;
Prv 13:25 but the *b* of the wicked suffers want.
Sir 51: 5 fire, from the deep *b* of the nether world;
Jer 51:34 filled his *b* with my delights,
Ez 3: 3 feed your *b* and fill your stomach with
Dn 2:32 arms were silver, its *b* and thighs bronze,
Jon 2: 1 *b* of the fish three days and three nights.
2: 2 From the *b* of the fish Jonah said this
Mt 12:40 and three nights in the *b* of the whale,
Lk 15:16 He longed to fill his *b* with the husks
Phil 3:19 their *b* and their glory is in their shame.

BELMAIN (1)

Jdt 4: 4 region of Samaria, to Kona, Beth-horon, *B*,

BELONG (96)

Gn 19:12 daughters and all who *b* to you in the city
32:18 To whom do these animals ahead of you *b*?'
32:19 answer, 'They *b* to your brother Jacob,
38:25 whom these things *b* that I am with child.
Ex 13:12 of your animals shall *b* to the LORD.
30:31 shall *b* to me throughout your generations.
Lv 5:13 cereal offerings, shall *b* to the priest."
7: 9 shall *b* to the priest who offers it,
7:10 mixed with oil shall *b* to all of Aaron's sons
7:14 this shall *b* to the priest who splashes
10:15 Then they shall *b* to you and your children
23: 3 shall *b* to the LORD wherever you dwell.
23:20 be sacred to the LORD and *b* to the priest.
24: 9 It shall *b* to Aaron and his sons,
25:30 it shall *b* in perpetuity to the purchaser
25:55 For to me the Israelites *b* as servants;
27:30 or in fruit from the trees, *b* to the LORD,
Nm 3:13 They *b* to me; I am the LORD."
3:45 their cattle, that the Levites may *b* to me.
6:20 become sacred and shall *b* to the priest,
8:17 both of man and of beast, *b* to me;
18:10 As sacred, they *b* to you.
18:18 right leg of the wave offering *b* to you.
Dt 10:14 highest heavens, *b* to the LORD your God,
14:29 and the widow who *b* to your community,
16:14 and the widow who *b* to your community.
20:15 does not *b* to the peoples of this land.
21:17 and to him *b* the rights of the first-born.
33: 8 "To Levi *b* your Thummim,
Jgs 11:31 from the Ammonites shall *b* to the LORD.
19:18 the mountain region of Ephraim, where I *b*.
1Sm 25: 6 your family, and with all who *b* to you.
25:22 male alive among all those who *b* to him."
30:13 Then David asked him, "To whom do you *b*,
Neh 5: 5 our fields and our vineyards *b* to others."
Tb 8:21 and we *b* to you and to your beloved now
Jdt 10:12 and asked her, "To what people do you *b*?
1Mc 5:62 But they did not *b* to the family of those
10:42 *b* to the priests who perform the services.
Prv 16:11 Balance and scales *b* to the LORD;
Sg 7:11 I *b* to my lover and for me he yearns.
Wis 15: 2 we will not sin, knowing that we *b* to you.
Is 45:14 Shall come over to you and *b* to you;
Jer 5:10 her tendrils, they do not *b* to the LORD.
Ez 13: 9 shall not *b* to the community of my people,
44:30 of every kind, shall *b* to the priests;
45: 6 this shall *b* to the whole house of Israel.
46:16 to any of his sons, it shall *b* to his sons;
46:17 it shall *b* to the latter only until the
48:21 The remainder shall *b* to the prince:
48:22 and of Benjamin shall *b* to the prince.
Dn 11: 4 torn to pieces and *b* to others than they.
Hos 3: 3 shall not play the harlot Or *b* to any man;
Jon 1: 8 your country, and to what people do you *b*?"
Zep 2: 7 *b* to the remnant of the house of Judah;
Mk 9:41 of water because you *b* to Christ will not,
Jn 8:23 "You *b* to what is below;
8:23 I *b* to what is above.
8:23 You *b* to this world
10:16 other sheep that do not *b* to this fold.
15:19 you is that you do not *b* to the world.
17:14 they do not *b* to the world [any more than
17:14 the world [any more than I *b* to the world].
17:16 the world, any more than I *b* to the world.
18:36 "My kingdom does not *b* to this world.
Rom 1: 6 who have been called to *b* to Jesus Christ.
3:29 Does God *b* to the Jews alone?
7: 4 that you might *b* to that Other who was
8: 9 Spirit of Christ, he does not *b* to Christ.
11:24 so much the more will they who *b* to it by
16:10 all who *b* to the household of Aristobulus.
1Cor 1:12 One of you will say, "I *b* to Paul,"
1:12 to Paul," another, "I *b* to Apollos,"
1:12 and the fourth, "I *b* to Christ."
3: 4 When someone says, "I *b* to Paul,"
3: 4 Paul," and someone else, "I *b* to Apollos,"
7: 4 does not *b* to herself but to her husband;
7: 4 does not *b* to himself but to his wife.
12:15 I am not a hand I do not *b* to the body,"
12:15 would it then no longer *b* to the body?
12:16 I am not an eye I do not *b* to the body,"
12:16 would it then no longer *b* to the body?
15:23 at his coming, all those who *b* to him.
2Cor 10: 7 he may *b* to Christ but just as much do we.
Gal 3:29 if you *b* to Christ you are the descendants
5:24 Those who *b* to Christ Jesus have crucified
1Thes 1: 1 church of the Thessalonians who *b* to God
5: 5 We *b* neither to darkness nor to night;
2Thes 1: 1 church of the Thessalonians who *b* to God
Ti 2: 3 in ways that befit those who *b* to God.
1Jn 4: 1 spirits to a test to see if they *b* to God,
4: 3 fails to acknowledge him does not *b* to God.
4: 5 Those others *b* to the world;
4: 6 We *b* to God and anyone who has knowledge
5:19 We know that we *b* to God,
Rv 19: 1 Salvation, glory and might *b* to our God,

BELONGED (42)

Gn 12:20 way, with his wife and all that *b* to him.
13: 1 Negeb with his wife and all that *b* to him,
31: 1 has taken everything that *b* to our father,

BELONGED (cont.)

Nm 3:21 To Gershon *b* the clan of the Libnites and
3:27 To Kohath *b* the clans of the Amramites,
3:33 To Merari *b* the clans of the Mahlites and
Dt 11:6 and every living thing that *b* to them.
Jos 16:9 the villages that *b* to each city set aside
17:8 the district of Tappuah *b* to Manasseh,
17:9 The cities that *b* to Ephraim from among
17:10 The land on the south *b* to Ephraim and
18:14 which city *b* to the Judahites.
21:19 *b* to the priestly descendants of Aaron,
21:26 pasture lands *b* to the rest of the Kohathite
21:33 with their pasture lands *b* to the Gershonite
21:41 with their pasture lands, *b* to the Levites,
Jgs 6:11 in Ophrah that *b* to Joash the Abiezrite.
9:1 whole clan to which his mother's family *b*,
Ru 4:3 of land that *b* to our kinsman Elimelech,
1Sm 27:6 *b* to the kings of Judah up to the present
2Sm 6:12 family of Obed-edom and all that *b* to him,
9:9 all that *b* to Saul and to all his family.
2Kgs 12:17 they *b* to the priests.
24:7 all that *b* to the king of Egypt from the Wadi
25:13 pillars that *b* to the house of the LORD,
1Chr 2:23 in all, which had *b* to the sons of Machir,
5:7 His brothers who *b* to his clans,
6:39 of Aaron who *b* to clan of the Kohathites,
6:55 These *b* to the rest of the Kohathite clan.
23:7 To the Gershonites *b* Ladan and Shimei.
2Chr 5:12 who were singers, all who *b* to Asaph,
1Mc 11:39 who had previously *b* to Alexander's party,
Jb 22:8 As if the land *b* to the man of might,
Jer 52:17 pillars that *b* to the house of the LORD,
Ez 27:21 and of all the sheikhs of Kedar *b* to you;
Am 7:14 nor have I *b* to a company of prophets;
Mk 2:16 When the scribes who *b* to the Pharisee
Jn 15:19 If you *b* to the world, it would love you
2Tm 1:5 faith which first *b* to your grandmother
1Jn 2:19 not that they really *b* to us;
2:19 for if they had *b* to us,
3:12 *b* to the evil one and killed his brother.

BELONGING (27)

Gn 31:32 on, you identify anything here as *b* to you,
Ex 9:4 so that none *b* to the Israelites will die."
9:6 but not one beast *b* to the Israelites.
9:7 one beast *b* to the Israelites had died,
29:27 or anything else *b* to Aaron or to his sons.
Lv 7:20 flesh of a peace offering *b* to the LORD,
7:21 eats of a peace offering *b* to the LORD,
25:31 as *b* to the surrounding farm land;
25:34 *b* to their cities shall not be sold at all;
Nm 16:30 into the nether world, with all *b* to them,
16:33 to the nether world with all *b* to them;
36:8 *b* to a clan of her own ancestral tribe,
Jos 12:8 desert, and the Negeb, *b* to the Hittites,
18:21 Now the cities *b* to the clans of the tribe
21:12 *b* to the city had been given to Caleb,
Jgs 12:4 in territory *b* to Ephraim and Manasseh."
Ru 2:3 section *b* to Boaz of the clan of Elimelech.
1Sm 6:18 of the Philistines *b* to the five lords,
1Chr 6:41 *b* to the city had been given to Caleb,
2Chr 8:6 all the supply cities *b* to Solomon,
34:33 from all the territory *b* to the Israelites,
Ezr 7:13 in my kingdom *b* to the people of Israel,
Is 8:1 *B* to Maher-shalal-hash-baz."
Ez 42:8 *b* to the outer court was fifty cubits,
45:4 sacred part of the land *b* to the priests,
Lk 5:3 into one of the boats, the one *b* to Simon,
Heb 9:11 by hands, that is, not *b* to this creation.

BELONGINGS (6)

Gn 31:37 found a single object taken from your *b*?
45:20 Do not be concerned about your *b*,
Ps(s) 109:11 May the usurer ensnare all his *b*,
Lk 15:13 all his *b* and went off to a distant land,
17:31 on the rooftop and his *b* are in the house,
19:8 "I give half my *b*, Lord, to the poor.

BELONGS (46)

Gn 19:12 "Who else *b* to you here?
26:20 servants, saying, "The water *b* to us!"
31:16 our father really *b* to us and our children.
31:43 everything you see *b* to me.
Ex 13:2 both of man and beast, for it *b* to me."
20:17 ox or ass, nor anything else that *b* to him."
34:19 "To me *b* every first-born male that opens
Lv 2:3 cereal offering *b* to Aaron and his sons.
2:10 cereal offering *b* to Aaron and his sons.
3:16 All the fat *b* to the LORD.
7:7 the guilt offering likewise *b* to the
7:31 but the breast *b* to Aaron and his sons.
14:13 *b* to the priest and is most sacred.)
27:26 which as such already *b* to the LORD,
Nm 1:50 all its equipment and all that *b* to it.
16:5 who *b* to him and who is the holy one
Dt 5:21 his ox or ass, nor anything that *b* to him.'
12:12 as well as with the Levite who *b* to your
12:18 and the Levite who *b* to your community;
14:21 it to an alien who *b* to your community,
14:27 the Levite who *b* to your community,
16:11 and the Levite who *b* to your community,
Jgs 18:28 was in the valley that *b* to Beth-rehob,
2Chr 36:23 among you *b* to any part of his people,
Ezr 1:3 among you *b* to any part of his people,
Tb 7:11 nothing until you set aside what *b* to me."
Ps(s) 50:11 and whatever stirs in the plains, *b* to me.
62:12 that power *b* to God,
89:19 For to the LORD *b* our shield,
Sg 2:16 My lover *b* to me and I to him;
6:3 My lover *b* to me and I to him;
Mt 19:14 The kingdom of God *b* to such as these."
26:52 "Put back your sword where it *b*.
Mk 10:14 such as these that the kingdom of God *b*.
Lk 18:16 The reign of God *b* to such as these.
Jn 16:15 All that the Father has *b* to me.
17:10 (Just as all that *b* to me is yours,
17:10 me is yours, so all that *b* to you is mine.)
2Cor 10:7 If anyone is convinced that he *b* to Christ,
1Pt 2:8 it *b* to their destiny to do so.
1Jn 3:8 The man who sins *b* to the devil,
3:10 No one whose actions are unholy *b* to God,
4:2 Jesus Christ come in the flesh *b* to God,
3Jn 1:11 Whoever does what is good *b* to God;
Rv 11:15 now *b* to our Lord and to his Anointed One,
13:8 living, which *b* to the Lamb who was slain.

BELOVED (82)

Gn 22:12 did not withhold from me your own *b* son."
22:16 did in not withholding from me your *b* son,
Dt 13:7 or your son or daughter, or your *b* wife,
28:54 and his *b* wife and his surviving children,
28:56 will begrudge her *b* husband and her son
33:12 "Benjamin is the *b* of the LORD,
2Sm 1:23 Saul and Jonathan, *b* and cherished,
Neh 13:26 and though he was *b* of his God and God had
Tb 3:10 'You had only one *b* daughter,
7:11 now on you are her love, and she is your *b*.
8:21 to you and to your *b* now and forever.
10:13 "My child and *b* kinsman,
10:13 on I am your mother, and Sarah is your *b*.
1Mc 6:12 Yet I was kindly and *b* in my rule.'
Ps(s) 127:2 bread, for he gives to his *b* in sleep.
Sg 1:9 chariots would I liken you, my *b*:
1:15 Ah, you are beautiful, my *b*,
2:2 lily among thorns, so is my *b* among women.
2:10 he says to me, "Arise, my *b*,
2:13 Arise, my *b*, my beautiful one, and come!
4:1 Ah, you are beautiful, my *b*,
4:7 You are all-beautiful, my *b*,
5:2 "Open to me, my sister, my *b*,
6:4 You are as beautiful as Tirzah, my *b*,
Sir 46:13 *B* of his people,
Jer 11:15 What right has my *b* in my house,
12:7 The *b* of my soul I deliver into the hand
Bar 3:37 Jacob, his servant, to Israel, his *b* son.
Dn 3:35 from us, for the sake of Abraham, your *b*,
9:23 I have come to announce, because you are *b*.
10:11 "Daniel, *b*," he said to me,
10:19 strengthened me, saying, "Fear not, *b*,
Hos 3:1 Give your love to a woman *b* of a paramour,
Mt 3:17 from the heavens said, "This is my *b* Son.
17:5 "This is my *b* Son on whom my favor rests.
Mk 1:11 "You are my *b* Son.
9:7 "This is my Son, my *b*.
Lk 3:22 "You are my *b* Son.
Jn 11:11 added, "Our *b* Lazarus has fallen asleep,
Acts 15:25 to you, along with our *b* Barnabas and Paul,
Rom 1:7 in Rome, *b* of God and called to holiness,
9:25 those who were not loved I will call *B*';
11:28 are *b* by him because of the patriarchs.
12:19 *B*, do not avenge yourselves;
16:5 Greetings to my *b* Epaenetus;
16:9 and to my *b* Stachys.
1Cor 4:14 you but to admonish you as my *b* children.
4:17 Timothy, my *b* and faithful son in the Lord.
15:58 steadfast and persevering, my *b* brothers,
2Cor 7:1 Since we have these promises, *b*,
Eph 1:6 favor he has bestowed on us in his *b*.
Phil 2:12 So then, my dearly *b*,
Col 1:13 brought us into the kingdom of his *b* Son.
3:12 you are God's chosen ones, holy and *b*,
1Thes 1:4 We know, too, brothers *b* of God,
2Thes 2:13 God for you always, *b* brothers in the Lord,
1Tm 6:2 their work are believers and *b* brothers.
Phlm 1:1 to our *b* friend and fellow worker Philemon,
1:16 but as more than a slave, a *b* brother,
Heb 6:9 *B*, even though we speak in this way,
1Pt 2:11 *B*, you are strangers and in exile;
4:12 Do not be surprised, *b*,
2Pt 1:17 "This is my *b* Son,
3:14 So, *b*, while waiting for this,
3:15 Paul, our *b* brother, wrote you this in
3:17 You are forewarned, *b* brothers.
1Jn 2:7 Dearly *b*, it is no new commandment
3:2 Dearly *b*, we are God's children now;
3:21 *B*, if our consciences have nothing to
4:1 *B*, do not trust every spirit,
4:7 *B*, let us love one another because love is
4:11 *B*, if God has loved us so,
3Jn 1:1 The elder to the *b* Gaius,
1:2 *B*, I hope you are in good health
1:5 *B*, you demonstrate fidelity by all that
1:11 *B*, do not imitate what is evil but what is
1:15 The *b* here send you their greetings;
1:15 greet the *b* there, each by name
Jude 1:3 was already fully intent on writing you, *b*,
1:17 Remember, *b*, all of you, the prophetic
1:20 But you, *b*, grow strong in your holy faith
Rv 20:9 *b* city where God's people were encamped;

BELOW (47)

Gn 1:7 water above the dome from the water *b* it.
35:8 she was buried under the oak *b* Bethel,
49:25 blessings of the abyss that crouches *b*,
Ex 20:4 earth *b* or in the waters beneath the earth;
25:35 including a knob *b* each of the three pairs
37:21 including a knob *b* each of the three pairs
Lv 13:3 shows that it has penetrated *b* the skin,
13:4 not seem to have penetrated *b* the skin,
13:25 this seems to have penetrated *b* the skin,
13:30 find that the sore has penetrated *b* the
13:31 that it has not penetrated *b* the skin,
13:32 not seem to have penetrated *b* the skin,
13:34 and that it has not penetrated *b* the skin,
Dt 4:39 is God in the heavens above and on earth *b*,
5:8 earth *b* or in the waters beneath the earth;
Jos 2:11 God, is God in heaven above and on earth *b*.
15:3 Sea, southward *b* the pass of Arkrabbim,
1Sm 23:24 and his men were in the desert *b* Maon.
23:25 down to the gorge in the desert *b* Maon.
23:25 and pursued David into the desert *b* Maon.
2Sm 24:6 Gilead and to the district *b* Mount Hermon.
1Kgs 4:12 *b* Jezreel from Beth-shean to Abel-meholah;
7:29 likewise, above and *b* the lions and oxen,
7:32 The four wheels were *b* the paneling,
8:23 like you in heaven above or on earth *b*;
2Kgs 19:30 shall again strike root *b* and bear fruit
2Chr 4:3 *b* the rim a ring of figures of oxen
Neh 4:7 to attack us, I stationed guards down *b*,
Jdt 6:11 till they reached the springs *b* Bethulia.
6:13 So they took cover *b* the mountain,
2Mc 3:19 girded with sackcloth *b* their breasts,
9:25 I have written to him the letter copied *b*.
Jb 18:16 *B*, his roots dry up,
Ps(s) 113:6 looks upon the heavens and the earth *b*?
Prv 15:24 that he may avoid the nether world *b*.
20:5 heart is like water far *b* the surface,
Is 14:9 *b* is all astir preparing for your coming;
37:31 again strike root *b* and bear fruit above.
51:6 to the heavens, and look at the earth *b*;
Jer 31:37 or the foundations *b* the earth be sounded,
Ez 31:14 are destined for death, for the land *b*,
31:16 the land *b*, all Eden's trees were consoled,
31:18 down with the trees of Eden to the land *b*.
42:9 *B* these chambers there was the way in from
42:12 *B* the chambers to the south there was an
Jn 8:23 "You belong to what is *b*;
Acts 2:19 the heavens above and signs on the earth *b*:

BELSHAZZAR (9)

Bar 1:11 king of Babylon, and that of *B*,
1:12 king of Babylon, and that of *B*,
Dn 5:1 King *B* gave a great banquet for a thousand
5:9 Then King *B* was greatly terrified;
5:22 his son, *B*, have not humbled your heart,
5:29 order of *B* they clothed Daniel in purple,
5:30 *B*, the Chaldean King, was slain
7:1 In the first year of King *B* of Babylon,
8:1 in the third year of the reign of King *B*.

BELT (22)

Ex 28:8 The embroidered *b* of the ephod shall
28:27 in front, just above its embroidered *b*.
28:28 *b* of the ephod and not swing loose from it.
29:5 the embroidered *b* of the ephod around him.
39:5 *b* on the ephod extended out from it,
39:20 in front, just above its embroidered *b*.
39:21 right above the embroidered *b* of the ephod
Lv 8:7 him with the embroidered *b* of the ephod,
1Sm 18:4 dress, and his sword, his bow and his *b*.
2Sm 18:11 to give you fifty pieces of silver and a *b*."
20:8 Now Joab had a *b* over his tunic,
1Kgs 2:5 *b* about my waist and the sandal on my foot.
Is 5:27 None will have his waist *b* loose,
11:5 waist, and faithfulness a *b* upon his hips.
Dn 10:5 with a *b* of fine gold around his waist.
Mt 3:4 and wore a leather *b* around his waist.
Mk 1:6 and wore a leather *b* around his waist.
Jn 21:18 your *b* and went about as you pleased;
Acts 12:8 said, "Put on your *b*
21:11 He came up to us, and taking Paul's *b*,
21:11 this *b* and hand him over to the Gentiles.'"
Eph 6:14 with the truth as the *b* around your waist,

BELTESHAZZAR (10)

Dn 1:7 Daniel to *B*,
2:26 The king asked Daniel, whose name was *B*,
4:5 whose name is *B* after the name of my god,
4:6 *B*, chief of the magicians,
4:15 Now, *B*, tell me its meaning.
4:16 Then Daniel, whose name was *B*,
4:16 *B*," the king said to him,
4:17 "My lord," *B* replied,
5:12 by this Daniel, whom the king named *B*.

10: 1 was given to Daniel, who had been named *B.*

BELTS (4)

Prv 31:24 them, and stocks the merchants with *b.*
Mt 10: 9 gold nor silver nor copper in your *b;*
Mk 6: 8 bag, not a coin in the purses in their *b.*
Lk 12:35 "Let your *b* be fastened around your

BEN-HADAD (27)

1Kgs 15:18 to his ministers, King Asa sent them to *B,*
15:20 *B* agreed with King Asa and sent the
20: 1 *B,* king of Aram, gathered all his forces,
20: 9 Accordingly he directed the couriers of *B,*
20:10 *B* then sent him the message,
20:12 *B* was drinking in the pavilions with the
20:16 while *B* was drinking heavily in the
20:17 *B* received word that some men had marched
20:20 while *B,* king of Aram, escaped
20:26 *B* mobilized Aram and went up to Aphek to
20:30 *B,* too, fled, and took refuge
20:32 "Your servant *B* pleads for his life,"
20:33 at his word and said, *B* is your brother."
20:33 When *B* came out to him,
20:34 *B* said to him, "I will restore the cities
2Kgs 6:24 After this, *B,* king of Aram,
8: 7 Elisha came to Damascus at a time when *B,*
8: 9 before the prophet and said, "Your son *B,*
8:14 "What did Elisha tell you?" asked *B.*
13: 3 power of Hazael, king of Aram, and of *B,*
13:24 died and his son *B* succeeded him as king,
13:25 Joash, son of Jehoahaz, took back from *B,*
13:25 Joash defeated *B* three times,
2Chr 16: 2 of the royal palace and sent them to *B,*
16: 4 *B* agreed to King Asa's request and sent
Jer 49:27 and it shall devour the palaces of *B,*
Am 1:4 of Hazael, to devour the castles of *B*

BEN-HADAD'S (2)

1Kgs 20: 3 "This is *B* message: 'Your silver and gold
20: 5 came again and said, "This is *B* message:

BEN-HAIL (1)

2Chr 17: 7 of his reign he sent his leading men, *B,*

BEN-HINNOM (10)

Jos 15: 8 Climbing again to the Valley of *B* on the
18:16 Rephaim, where it faces the Valley of *B;*
2Kgs 23:10 also defiled Topheth in the Valley of *B,*
2Chr 28: 3 he offered sacrifice in the Valley of *B,*
33: 6 his sons by fire in the Valley of *B.*
Jer 7:31 In the Valley of *B* they have built the
7:32 Valley of *B* will no longer be called such,
19: 2 and go out toward the Valley of *B,*
19: 6 be called Topheth, or the Valley of *B,*
32:35 high places to Baal in the Valley of *B,*

BEN-ONI (1)

Gn 35:18 at the point of death—she called him *B;*

BENAIAH (43)

2Sm 8:18 *B,* son of Jehoiada, was in command
20:23 *B,* son of Jehoiada, was in command
23:20 *B,* son of Jehoiada, a stalwart
23:22 Such were the deeds performed by *B,*
23:30 *B* from Pirathon;
1Kgs 1: 8 Zadok the priest, *B,* son of Jehoiada,
1:10 did not invite the prophet Nathan, or *B,*
1:26 nor Zadok the priest, nor *B,*
1:32 the priest, Nathan the prophet, and *B,*
1:36 In answer to the king, *B,*
1:38 Zadok the priest, Nathan the prophet, *B,*
1:44 Zadok the priest, Nathan the prophet, *B,*
2:25 Then King Solomon sent *B,*
2:29 He sent *B,* son of Jehoiada,
2:30 *B* went to the tent of the LORD and said to
2:30 *B* reported to the king,
2:34 *B,* son of Jehoiada,
2:35 The king appointed *B,* son of Jehoiada,
2:46 The king then gave the order to *B,*
4: 4 *B,* son of Jehoiada, commander of the army;
1Chr 4:36 Jeshohaiah, Asaiah, Adiel, Jesimiel, *B,*
9:32 *B* the Kohathite, one of their brethren,
11:22 *B,* son of Jehoiada,
11:24 deeds as these of *B,* the son of Jehoiada
11:31 *B,* from Pirathon;
15:18 Shemiramoth, Jehiel, Unni, Eliab, *B,*
15:20 Jehiel, Unni, Eliab, Maaseiah, and *B,*
15:24 Joshaphat, Nethanel, Amasai, Zechariah, *B,*
16: 5 Shemiramoth, Jehiel, Mattithiah, Eliab, *B,*
16: 6 and the priests *B* and Jahaziel were to be
18:17 *B,* son of Jehoiada, was in command
27: 5 chief for the third month, was *B,*
27: 6 This *B* was a warrior among the Thirty and
27:14 the eleventh month, was *B* the Pirathonite,
27:34 Ahithophel came Jehoiada, the son of *B,*
2Chr 20:14 upon Jahaziel, son of Zechariah, son of *B,*
31:13 Mahath and *B* were supervisors subject to
Ezr 10:25 Mijamin, Eleazar, Malchijah, and *B;*
10:30 Adna, Chelal, *B,*
10:35 Maadai, Amram, Uel, *B,*
10:43 Mattithiah, Zabad, Zebina, Jaddai, Joel, *B.*
Ez 11: 1 son of Azzur, and Pelatiah, son of *B,*
11:13 I was prophesying, Pelatiah, the son of *B,*

BENCH (8)

Sir 38:33 They do not occupy the judge's *b,*
Mt 27:19 While he was still presiding on the *b,*
Jn 19:13 a judge's *b* at the place called the Stone
Acts 18:12 against Paul and brought him before the *b.*
18:17 and beat him in full view of the *b;*
25: 6 on the *b* and ordered Paul to be brought in.
25:10 "I stand before the imperial *b;*
25:17 on the *b* and ordered the man brought in.

BEND (16)

2Sm 22:35 war till my arms could *b* a bow of brass.
Ps(s) 7:13 he will *b* and aim his bow,
11: 2 For, see, the wicked *b* the bow;
18:35 for war and my arms to *b* a bow of brass.
22:30 him shall *b* all who go down into the dust.
37:14 they *b* their bow to bring down the
Sir 7:23 *b* their necks from childhood.
30:12 *B* him to the yoke when he is young,
Is 45:23 To me every knee shall *b;*
Jer 27: 8 or will not *b* its neck under the yoke of
50:14 encircling Babylon, you who *b* the bow;
50:29 against Babylon archers, all who *b* the bow;
Bar 2:21 *B* your shoulders to the service of the
Zec 9:13 For I will *b* Judah as my bow,
Rom 14:11 every knee shall *b* before me and every
Phil 2:10 name every knee must *b* in the heavens,

BENE-BERAK (1)

Jos 19:45 Eltekoh, Gibbethon, Baalath, Jehud, *B,*

BENE-JAAKAN (3)

Nm 33:31 out from Moseroth, they camped at *B.*
33:32 Setting out from *B,*
Dt 10: 6 set out from Beeroth *B* for Moserah,

BENEATH (38)

Gn 1:20 earth let birds fly *b* the dome of the sky."
Ex 20: 4 earth below or in the waters *b* the earth;
Nm 16:31 all this than the ground *b* them split open,
Dt 5: 8 earth below or in the waters *b* the earth;
33:13 skies above and of the abyss crouching *b;*
Jgs 4:16 The entire army of Sisera fell *b* the sword,
7: 8 the camp of Midian was *b* him in the valley.
2Sm 22:39 they fell *b* my feet.
22:40 you subdued my adversaries *b* me.
1Kgs 8: 6 to its place *b* the wings of the cherubim
19: 4 until he came to a broom tree and sat *b* it.
2Chr 5: 7 to its place *b* the wings of the cherubim
Jb 9: 6 of its place, and the pillars *b* it tremble.
9:13 the helpers of Rahab bow *b* him.
26: 5 The shades *b* writhe in terror,
Ps(s) 18:39 they fell *b* my feet.
18:40 you subdued my adversaries *b* me.
74:11 and keep your right hand idle *b* your cloak?
Wis 17: 2 they lay confined *b* their own roofs as
Sir 48:13 *b* him flesh was brought back into life.
Is 10: 4 *b* the captive or fall beneath the slain?
10: 4 beneath the captive or fall *b* the slain?
14:11 The couch *b* you is the maggot,
Jer 10:11 from the earth, and from *b* these heavens!
Ez 1:23 *B* the firmament their wings were stretched
6:13 *b* every green tree and leafy oak,
10:20 *b* the God of Israel by the river Chebar,
13:14 When it falls, you shall be crushed *b* it;
17:23 Birds of every kind shall dwell *b* it,
24: 5 Then pile the wood *b* it;
46:23 were built *b* the stones all the way around.
47: 1 water flowing out from *b* the threshold
Hos 4:13 incense, *B* oak and poplar and terebinth,
Am 2: 9 their fruit above, and their roots *b.*
Ob 1: 7 Those who eat your bread lay snares *b* you:
Hb 3:16 invades my bones, my legs tremble *b* me.
Mt 22:44 until I humble your enemies *b* your feet"?
Heb 10:13 until his enemies are placed *b* his feet.

BENEDICTION (1)

Sir 45: 1 and men, MOSES, whose memory is held in *b.*

BENEFACTOR (4)

Est E:13 of Mordecai, our savior and constant *b,*
2Mc 1:24 just and merciful, the only king and *b,*
4: 2 government the man who was a *b* of the city,
Ps(s) 57: 3 I call to God the Most High, to God, my *b.*

BENEFACTORS (2)

Est E: 3 even begin plotting against their own *b.*
Lk 22:25 authority over them are called their *b.*

BENEFICENCE (2)

Wis 16:11 and become unresponsive to your *b.*
Sir 1:13 old, and with their children her *b* abides.

BENEFICENT (2)

Wis 7:22 loving the good, keen, unhampered, *b,*
19:14 but these were enslaving *b* guests.

BENEFIT (17)

1Sm 25:31 the LORD confers this *b* on your lordship,
Jdt 8:23 enslavement will not be turned to our *b,*
Eccl 6: 3 if he has not the full *b* of his goods,
Wis 11:13 their own torments was a *b* to these others,
16:24 is relaxed in *b* for those who trust in you.
Sir 30: 2 He who disciplines his son will *b* from him,
37:19 A man may be wise and *b* many,
Is 30: 5 that gain them nothing, Neither help nor *b,*
Bar 6:37 neither pity the widow nor *b* the orphan.
6:63 can neither execute judgment, nor *b* man.
Rom 6:21 What *b* did you then enjoy?
6:22 your *b* is sanctification as you tend
1Cor 4: 6 and Apollos by way of example for your *b.*
2Cor 4:15 Indeed, everything is ordered to your *b,*
9:12 The administering of this public *b* not
Gal 2: 5 the gospel might survive intact for your *b.*
Jas 1:17 gift, every genuine *b* comes from above,

BENEFITED (3)

Est 7: 9 who gave the report that *b* the king."
Wis 11: 5 were punished they in their need were *b.*
16: 2 you *b* your people with a novel dish,

BENEFITS (14)

1Sm 2:32 rival all the *b* enjoyed by Israel,
2Sm 16:12 *b* for the curses he is uttering this day."
1Mc 11:33 decided to bestow *b* on the Jewish nation,
2Mc 9:26 general and individual *b* you have received,
Ps(s) 71:21 Renew your *b* toward me,
85:13 The LORD himself will give his *b;*
103: 2 O my soul, and forget not all his *b;*
Prv 11:17 A kindly man *b* himself,
11:25 He who confers *b* will be amply enriched,
Sir 30:25 and gay while at table *b* from his food.
Is 55: 3 covenant, the *b* assured to David.
Jer 33: 9 over all the peaceful *b* I will give her.
Acts 13:34 the *b* assured to David under the covenant.'
14:17 Yet in bestowing his *b,*

BENEVOLENCE (1)

Est 2:17 of all the virgins she won his favor and *b.*

BENGUI (1)

Ezr 10:34 of the sons of *B:*

BENHANAN (1)

1Chr 4:20 The sons of Shimon were Amnon, Rinnah, *B,*

BENINU (1)

Neh 10:14 Sherebiah, Shebaniah, Hodiah, Bani, *B.*

BENJAMIN (135)

Gn 35:18 his father, however, named him *B.*
35:24 Joseph and *B;*
42: 4 *B* that Jacob did not send with the rest,
42:36 is gone, and now you would take away *B!*
43:14 let your other brother go, as well as *B.*
43:15 of money with them, and, accompanied by *B,*
43:16 When Joseph saw *B* with them,
43:29 Joseph's eye fell on his full brother *B,*
45:12 for yourselves, and *B* can see for himself,
45:14 Benjamin and wept, and *B* wept in his arms.
45:22 but to *B* he gave three hundred shekels of
46:19 Joseph and *B.*
46:21 The sons of *B:* Bela, Becher, Ashbel,
49:27 *B* is a ravenous wolf;
Ex 1: 2 3 Issachar, Zebulun and *B;*
Nm 1:11 descendants of Joseph from *B:*
1:36 Of the descendants of *B,*
1:37 hundred were enrolled in the tribe of *B.*
2:22 the tribe of *B.* Their prince was Abidan,
10:24 Gideoni, over the host of the tribe of *B.*
34:21 the tribe of *B:*
Dt 27:12 Joseph and *B* shall stand on Mount Gerizim
33:12 Of *B* he said:
33:12 *B* is the beloved of the LORD,
Jos 21: 4 lot from the tribes of Judah, Simeon and *B.*
21:17 From the tribe of *B* they obtained the four
Jgs 5:14 behind you was *B,* among your troops.
10: 9 the Jordan to fight against Judah, *B,*
19:14 them when they were abreast of Gibeah of *B.*
20: 4 and I went into Gibeah of *B* for the night.
20:10 of *B* for the crime it committed in Israel."
20:12 sent men throughout the tribe of *B* to say,
20:17 the other Israelites who, without *B,*
20:20 array at Gibeah for the combat with *B,*
20:22 I again engage my brother *B* in battle?"
20:28 "Shall I go out again to battle with *B,*
20:35 battle, the LORD defeated *B* before Israel;
20:35 twenty-five thousand one hundred men of *B,*
20:36 for the men of Israel gave ground to *B,*
20:39 And though the men of *B* had begun by
20:40 It was when *B* looked back and saw the
20:41 the men of *B* were thrown into confusion,

BENJAMIN (cont.)

20:43 The men of *B* had been surrounded,
20:46 Those of *B* who fell on that day were in
21: 1 his daughter in marriage to anyone from *B.*
21: 6 disconsolate over their brother *B* and said,
21:14 When *B* returned at that time,
21:15 The people were still disconsolate over *B*
21:16 For every woman in *B* has been put to death."
21:17 "Those of *B* who survive must have heirs,
21:18 'Cursed be he who gives a woman to *B!*' "
21:21 Shiloh for a wife, and go to the land of *B.*
1Sm 9: 1 There was a stalwart man from *B* named Kish,
9: 4 They also went through the land of *B,*
9:16 I will send you a man from the land of *B*
9:21 least among the clans of the tribe of *B?*
10: 2 tomb at Zelzah in the territory of *B,*
10:20 forward, and the tribe of *B* was chosen.
10:21 had the tribe of *B* come forward in clans,
13: 2 were with Jonathan in Gibeah of *B.*
13:15 soldiers, going from Gilgal to Gibeah of *B.*
13:16 with them were now occupying Geba of *B,*
14:16 The lookouts of Saul in Geba of *B* saw that
22: 7 "Listen, men of *B!*
2Sm 2: 9 Gilead, the Ashurites, Jezreel, Ephraim, *B,*
2:31 wounded three hundred and sixty men of *B,*
3:19 Abner also spoke personally to *B,*
3:19 to Israel and to the whole house of *B.*
4: 2 Rimmon the Beerothite, of the tribe of *B.*
4: 2 [Beeroth, too, was ascribed to *B;*
19:18 accompanied by a thousand men from *B.*
20: 1 rebellious individual from *B* named Sheba,
21:14 father Kish at Zela in the territory of *B.*
1Kgs 4:18 Shimei, son of Ela, in *B;*
12:21 all the house of Judah and the tribe of *B*—
12:23 Judah, and to the house of Judah and to *B,*
15:22 them King Asa built Geba of *B* and Mizpeh.
1Chr 2: 2 Judah, Issachar, Zebulun, Dan, Joseph, *B,*
6:45 Also from the tribe of *B:* Gibeon
7: 6 The sons of *B* were Bela,
7:10 The sons of Bilhan were Jeush, *B,*
8: 1 *B* became the father of Bela,
8:40 All these were the descendants of *B.*
11:31 Ithai, son of Ribai, from Gibeah of *B;*
12: 2 They were some of Saul's kinsmen, from *B.*
21: 6 Levi and *B,* however, he did not include
27:12 month, was Abiezer from Anathoth, of *B,*
27:21 for *B,* Jaasiel, son of Abner;
2Chr 11: 1 together the house of Judah and *B,*
11: 3 and to all the Israelites in Judah and *B:*
11:10 these were fortified cities in Judah and *B.*
11:12 Thus Judah and *B* remained his.
11:23 all the districts of Judah and *B,*
14: 7 *B* who carried bucklers and were archers,
15: 2 "Hear me, Asa and all Judah and *B!*
15: 8 land of Judah and *B* and from the cities
15: 9 Then he convened all Judah and *B,*
17:17 From *B:* Eliada, a valiant warrior,
25: 5 and *B* according to their ancestral houses,
31: 1 places and altars throughout Judah, *B,*
34: 9 of Israel, as well as from all of Judah, *B,*
34:32 committed all who were of Jerusalem and *B,*
Ezr 1: 5 of Judah and *B* and the priests and Levites
4: 1 When the enemies of Judah and *B* heard that
10: 9 All the men of Judah and *B* gathered
10:32 Isshijah, Malchijah, Shemaiah, Shimeon, *B,*
Neh 3:23 *B* and Hasshub carried out the repair in
11:36 of the Levites from Judah settled in *B.*
12:34 with Azariah, Ezra, Meshullam, Judah, *B,*
Est A: 1 of Shimei, son of Kish, of the tribe of *B,*
Ps(s) 68:28 There is *B,* the youngest, leading them;
80: 3 forth before Ephraim, *B* and Manasseh.
Jer 1: 1 family in Anathoth, in the land of *B.*
6: 1 Flee, sons of *B,* out of Jerusalem!
17:19 Go, stand at the Gate of *B,*
17:26 from the land of *B* and from the foothills,
20: 2 upper Gate of *B* in the house of the LORD.
32: 8 field in Anathoth, in the district of *B;*
32:44 witnesses shall be used in the land of *B,*
33:13 the land of *B* and the suburbs of Jerusalem,
37:12 out from Jerusalem for the District of *B,*
37:13 But when he reached the Gate of *B,*
38: 7 happened just then to be at the Gate of *B,*
Ez 48:22 Judah and of *B* shall belong to the prince.
48:23 *B:* from the eastern to the western boundary
48:24 on the frontier of *B,*
48:32 the gate of Joseph, the gate of *B,*
Hos 5: 8 "Look behind you, O *B!*"
Ob 1:19 of Samaria, And *B* shall occupy Gilead.
Zec 14:10 Gate of *B* to the place of the First Gate,
Acts 13:21 them Saul son of Kish, of the tribe of *B,*
Rom 11: 1 descended from Abraham, of the tribe of *B.*
Phil 3: 5 of the stock of Israel and the tribe of *B,*
Rv 7: 8 and twelve thousand from the tribe of *B.*

BENJAMINITE (10)

Jgs 3:15 he raised up for them a savior, the *B* Ehud,
19:16 he lived among the *B* townspeople of Gibeah.
20:15 The number of the *B* swordsmen from the
1Sm 4:12 A *B* fled from the battlefield and reached
9: 1 Zeror, son of Becorath, son of Aphiah, a *B.*
9:21 "Am I not a *B,*
2Sm 16:11 my life, how much more might this *B* do so!
19:17 Shimei, son of Gera, the *B* from Bahurim,
1Kgs 2: 8 you Shimei, son of Gera, the *B* of Bahurim,
Est 2: 5 of Jair, son of Shimei, son of Kish, a *B,*

BENJAMINITES (35)

Nm 7:60 of Abidon, son of Gideoni, prince of the *B*
26:38 The *B* by clans were: through Bela
26:41 These were the *B* by clans,
Jos 18:11 lot fell to the clans of the tribe of *B.*
18:20 clans of the *B* was bounded on all sides.
18:21 to the clans of the tribe of the *B* were:
18:28 This was the heritage of the clans of *B.*
Jgs 1:21 The *B* did not dislodge the Jebusites who
1:21 Jerusalem beside the *B* to the present day.
20: 3 the *B* heard that the Israelites had gone
20:13 But the *B* refused to accede to the demand
20:14 the *B* assembled from their other cities to
20:18 should go first in the attack on the *B,*
20:21 the *B* came out of the city and felled
20:24 when they met the *B* for the second time,
20:25 once again the *B* who came out of Gibeah
20:30 The Israelites went up against the *B* for
20:31 The *B* went out to meet them,
20:32 Therefore the *B* thought,
20:36 To the *B* it had looked as though the enemy
20:48 withdrew through the territory of the *B,*
21:13 sent a message to the *B* at the rock Rimmon,
21:20 And they instructed the *B,*
21:23 The *B* did this; they carried off a wife
2Sm 2:15 twelve of the *B* of Ishbaal,
2:25 Here the *B* rallied around Abner,
23:29 Ittai, son of Ribai, from Gibeah of the *B;*
1Chr 6:50 tribes of the Judahites, Simeonites, and *B.*
9: 3 In Jerusalem lived Judahites and *B;*
9: 7 Among the *B* were Sallu, son of Meshullam,
12:17 Some *B* and Judahites also came to David at
12:30 Of the *B,* the brethren of Saul:
Neh 11: 4 In Jerusalem dwelt both Judahites and *B.*
11: 7 These were the *B:* Sallu, son of Meshullam
11:31 *B* were in Geba,

BENJAMIN'S (2)

Gn 43:34 *B* portion was five times as large as
44:12 youngest, the goblet turned up in *B* bag.

BENT (13)

Gn 49:15 He *b* his shoulder to the burden and became
Est C: 8 and are *b* upon destroying the inheritance
Prv 17:11 On rebellion alone is the wicked man *b,*
Eccl 12: 3 house tremble, and the strong men are *b,*
Sir 27: 6 a man's speech disclose the *b* of his mind.
43:12 this bow *b* by the mighty hand of God.
Is 5:28 arrows are sharp, and all their bows are *b.*
Lam 3:12 He *b* his bow, and set me up as the target
Ez 17: 7 To him this vine *b* its roots,
Jn 7:18 on his own is *b* on self-glorification.
8: 6 Jesus *b* down and started tracing on the
8: 8 time he *b* down and wrote on the ground.
20: 5 He did not enter but *b* down to peer in,

BENUMBED (1)

Hb 1: 4 This is why the law is *b,*

BEOR (11)

Gn 36:32 Bela, son of *B,* became king in Edom;
Nm 22: 5 time, sent messengers to Balaam, son of *B,*
24: 3 The utterance of Balaam, son of *B,*
24:15 The utterance of Balaam, son of *B,*
31: 8 and they also executed Balaam, son of *B,*
Dt 23: 5 and because Moab hired Balaam, son of *B,*
Jos 13:22 sword also the soothsayer Balaam, son of *B.*
24: 9 He summoned Balaam, son of *B,*
1Chr 1:43 Bela, son of *B,*
Mi 6: 5 planned, and how Balaam, the son of *B,*
2Pt 2:15 off on the path taken by Balaam, son of *B.*

BEQUEATH (2)

Dt 21:16 when he comes to *b* his property to his
Ps(s) 17:14 and *b* their abundance to their little ones.

BERA (1)

Gn 14: 2 king of Goiim made war on *B* king of Sodom,

BERACAH (3)

1Chr 12: 3 *B;* Jehu from Anathoth;
2Chr 20:26 they held an assembly in the Valley of *B*—
20:26 has ever since been called the Valley of *B.*

BERAIAH (1)

1Chr 8:21 Elienai, Zillethai, Eliel, Adaiah, *B,*

BEREA (1)

1Mc 9: 4 Then they set out for *B* with twenty

BEREAVED (1)

Jer 16: 7 the *b* to console them in their bereavement;

BEREAVEMENT (5)

Gn 43:14 As for me, if I am to suffer *b,*
Ps(s) 35:12 me evil for good, bringing *b* to my soul.
Is 47: 9 Complete *b* and widowhood shall come upon
Jer 15: 7 I destroyed my people through *b;*
16: 7 the bereaved to console them in their *b;*

BEREAVES (1)

Lam 1:20 In the streets the sword *b,*

BERECHIAH (12)

1Chr 3:20 sons of Meshullam were Hashubah, Ohel, *B,*
6:24 Asaph was the son of *B,*
9:16 and *B,* son of Asa, son of Elkanah,
15:17 and, among his brethren, Asaph, son of *B;*
15:23 *B* and Elkanah were gatekeepers before the
2Chr 28:12 *B,* son of Meshillemoth,
Neh 3: 4 next to him was Meshullam, son of *B,*
3:30 after them, Meshullam, son of *B,*
6:18 the daughter of Meshullam, son of *B.*
Zec 1: 1 came to the prophet Zechariah, son of *B,*
1: 7 came to the prophet Zechariah, son of *B,*

BERED (2)

Gn 16:14 It is between Kadesh and *B.*
1Chr 7:20 Shuthelah, whose son was *B,*

BEREFT (4)

Wis 10: 8 first were *b* of knowledge of the right,
Is 49:21 I was *b* and barren [exiled and repudiated];
Bar 4:12 no one gloat over me, a widow, *b* of many:
1Tm 5: 3 widows—that is, who are alone and *b.*

BERI (1)

1Chr 7:36 of Zophah were Suah, Harnepher, Shual, *B,*

BERIAH (9)

Gn 46:17 Imnah, Ishvah, Ishvi, and *B,*
46:17 and the sons of *B:* Heber and Malchiel
Nm 26:44 through *B* the clan of the Beriites,
1Chr 7:23 conceived and bore a son whom he named *B,*
7:30 of Asher were Imnah, Iishvah, Ishvi, and *B;*
8:13 built Ono and Lod with its nearby towns, *B,*
8:16 Ishpah, and Joha were the sons of *B.*
23:10 Shimei were Jahath, Zizah, Jeush, and *B;*
23:11 but Jeush and *B* had not many sons,

BERIAH'S (1)

1Chr 7:31 *B* sons were Heber and Malchiel,

BERIITES (1)

Nm 26:44 through Beriah the clan of the *B,*

BERITH (2)

Jgs 8:33 of *B* their god and forgetting the LORD,
9: 4 shekels from the temple of Baal of *B,*

BERNICE (3)

Acts 25:13 A few days later King Agrippa and *B*
25:23 So the next day Agrippa and *B* came with
26:30 governor and *B* and the rest of the company.

BEROEA (4)

2Mc 13: 4 he ordered him to be taken to *B* and
Acts 17:10 the brothers sent Paul and Silas off to *B.*
17:13 God had been proclaimed by Paul in *B* also,
20: 4 him were Sopater, son of Pyrrhus, from *B;*

BEROTHAH (1)

Ez 47:16 Hethlon, past Labo of Hamath, to Zedad, *B,*

BEROTHAI (1)

2Sm 8: 8 From Tebah and *B,* towns of Hadadezer,

BERRY (1)

Eccl 12: 5 sluggish and the caper *b* is without effect,

BERYL (4)

Ex 28:18 second row, a garnet, a sapphire and a *b;*
39:11 second row, a garnet, a sapphire and a *b;*
Ez 28:13 your covering [carnelian, topaz, and *b,*
Rv 21:20 the seventh chrysolite, the eighth *b,*

BESAI (2)

Ezr 2:49 sons of Uzza, sons of Paseah, sons of *B,*
Neh 7:52 sons of Uzza, sons of Paseah, sons of *B,*

BESEECH (4)

Jgs 13: 8 "O Lord, I *b* you,"
Ps(s) 142: 2 with a loud voice I *b* the LORD.
Jon 1:14 "We *b* you, O LORD, let us not perish
4: 2 "I *b* you, LORD," he prayed,

BESEECHES (2)

Wis 13:18 And for aid he *b* the wholly incompetent,
Sir 38:14 and he too *b* God That his diagnosis may

BESET (6)

1Mc 12:13 But many hardships and wars have *b* us,
Ps(s) 17: 9 My ravenous enemies *b* me;
Wis 2:12 Let us *b* the just one,
Sir 46: 5 God when his enemies *b* him on all sides,
Lam 3: 5 He has *b* me round about with poverty and
Heb 5: 2 for he himself is *b* by weakness and so

BESIDE (88)

Gn 28:13 was the LORD standing *b* him and saying:
39:10 after day, he would not agree to lie *b* her,
39:15 left his cloak *b* me and ran away outside."
39:18 he left his cloak *b* me and fled outside."
41: 3 on the bank of the Nile *b* the others,
Lv 10:12 and eat it *b* the altar in the form of
25:35 to poverty and is unable to hold out *b* you,
25:39 *b* you that he sells you his services,
Nm 2:12 *B* them shall camp the tribe of Simeon
2:20 *B* them shall camp the tribe of Manasseh
2:27 *B* them shall camp the tribe of Asher
11:16 When they are in place *b* you,
24: 6 They are like gardens *b* a stream,
33:10 out from Elim, they camped *b* the Red Sea.
33:50 the plains of Moab *b* the Jericho stretch
35: 1 Moab *b* the Jericho stretch of the Jordan:
36:13 Moab *b* the Jericho stretch of the Jordan.
Dt 11:30 the Gilgal *b* the terebinth of Moreh?]
16:21 any kind of wood *b* the altar of the LORD,
31:26 it *b* the ark of the covenant of the LORD,
Jos 15:63 *b* the Judahites to the present day.]
Jgs 1:21 *b* the Benjaminites to the present day.
5:16 Why do you stay *b* your hearths listening
14:17 But she wept *b* him during the seven days
Ru 4: 1 called to him by name, "Come and sit *b* me!"
1Sm 4:13 Eli was sitting in his chair *b* the gate,
5: 2 the temple of Dagon, placing it *b* Dagon.
6: 8 putting in a box *b* it the golden articles
6:15 taken down the ark of God and the box *b* it,
19: 3 will go out and stand *b* my father in the
20:41 David rose from *b* the mound and prostrated
26: 3 camped *b* the road on the hill of Hachilah,
2Sm 12:17 *b* him urging him to rise from the ground:
1Kgs 13:25 in the road, with the lion standing *b* it,
13:28 with the ass and the lion standing *b* it.
13:31 Lay my remains *b* his.
2Kgs 12:10 a hole in its lid, and set it *b* the stele,
2Chr 9:18 seat, with two lions standing *b* the arms.
23:13 king standing *b* his pillar at the entrance,
26:19 house of the LORD *b* the altar of incense,
Neh 2: 6 Then the king, and the queen seated *b* him,
3:35 Tobiah the Ammonite was *b* him,
4:13 Also, a trumpeter stood *b* me,
Tb 6: 2 and made camp *b* the Tigris River.
Jdt 6: 2 What god is there *b* Nebuchadnezzar?
1Mc 5:42 *b* the stream and gave them this order:
Jb 1:14 were plowing and the asses grazing *b* them,
8:19 There he lies rotting *b* the road,
Ps(s) 23: 2 *B* restful waters he leads me;
104:12 *B* them the birds of heaven dwell;
121: 5 he is *b* you at your right hand.
Prv 8:30 Then was I *b* him as his craftsman,
Sg 5:12 His eyes are like doves *b* running waters,
Wis 8:16 my dwelling, I should take my repose *b* her;
Sir 14:25 Who pitches his tent *b* her,
24:14 like a plane tree growing *b* the water.
Is 32:20 Happy are you who sow *b* every stream,
44: 4 verdure like poplars *b* the flowing waters.
49:10 them and guides them *b* springs of water.
Jer 6:16 Stand *b* the earliest roads,
17: 2 and their sacred poles, *b* the green trees,
17: 8 He is like a tree planted *b* the waters
Bar 6:26 one puts gifts beside them as *b* the dead.
Ez 1:15 one *b* each of the four living creatures.
9: 2 They entered and stood *b* the bronze altar.
10: 9 four wheels *b* them, one wheel beside each
10:16 the cherubim moved, the wheels went *b* them;
32:13 her animals perish *b* her abundant waters;
39:15 human bone, let them put up a marker *b* it,
40:44 were two chambers, one *b* the north gate,
40:44 south, and the other *b* the south gate,
43: 6 from the temple, while the man stood *b* me.
Dn 8: 2 I was *b* the river Ulai.
Am 2: 8 in pledge they recline *b* any altar;
9: 1 I saw the Lord standing *b* the altar,
Hb 3: 4 rays shine forth from *b* him,
Zec 4: 3 their tubes, and *b* it are two olive trees,
Mk 4: 1 occasion he began to teach *b* the lake.
Lk 9:47 took a little child and placed it *b* him,
22:55 of the courtyard and were sitting *b* it,
24: 4 two men in dazzling garments stood *b* them.
Jn 20:11 Meanwhile, Mary stood weeping *b* the tomb.
Acts 1:10 when two men dressed in white stood *b* them.
5:10 carried her out for burial *b* her husband.
8:31 Philip to get in and sit down *b* him.
Rv 3:21 and took my seat *b* my Father on his throne.

BESIDES (84)

Gn 14:16 *b* bringing back his kinsman Lot and his
16:11 *B*," the LORD's messenger said to her:
20:12 *B*, she is in truth my sister,
27:37 *b*, I have enriched him with grain and wine.
31:50 or take other wives *b* my daughters,
33:13 *B*, I am encumbered with the flocks and
38:22 *b*, the men of the place said there was no
44:32 *B*, I, your servant, got the boy from
Ex 4:14 *B*, he is now on his way to meet you.
12:38 also went up with them, *b* their livestock,
20: 3 You shall not have other gods *b* me.
Lv 18: 7 *B*, since she is your own mother,
23:18 *B* the bread, you shall offer to the LORD
Nm 13:28 *B*, we saw descendants of the Anakim there.
29:19 *b* the established holocaust with its
29:22 *b* the established holocaust with its
29:25 *b* the established holocaust with its
29:28 *b* the established holocaust with its
29:31 *b* the established holocaust with its
29:34 *b* the established holocaust with its
29:38 *b* the established holocaust with its
29:39 on your festivals, *b* whatever holocausts,
31: 8 *B* those slain in battle,
Dt 1:28 *b*, they saw the Anakim there.
5: 7 You shall not have other gods *b* me.
22:19 *b* fining him one hundred silver shekels,
27: 4 *b* setting up on Mount Ebal these stones
31: 2 *b* the LORD has told me that I shall not
32:39 I alone, am God, and there is no god *b* me.
Jos 19: 8 *b* all the villages around these cities as
Jgs 3: 5 *B*, the Israelites were living among the
11:34 he had neither son nor daughter *b* her.
20:26 *b* offering holocausts and peace offerings
Ru 1:17 the LORD do so and so to me, and more *b*,
1Sm 16:18 stalwart soldier, *b* being an able speaker,
18:28 *b*, his own daughter Michal loved David.
2Sm 2:30 *B* Asahel, nineteen other servants of David
14:27 sons born to him, *b* a daughter named Tamar,
19:33 very old man of eighty and very wealthy *b*,
1Kgs 1:46 *B*, Solomon took his seat on the royal
2:23 and more *b* if Adonijah has not proposed
4:19 There was one prefect *b*,
10:13 *b* such presents as were given her from
11: 1 women *b* the daughter of Pharaoh (Moabites,
15:20 all Chinnereth, *b* all the land of Naphtali.
Ezr 1: 6 gifts *b* all their freewill offerings.
10:13 *b*, this is not a task that can be performed
Neh 5:18 poultry *b* all kinds of wine in abundance
Tb 7:10 *B*, not even I have the right to give her
Jdt 8:25 *B* all this, we should be grateful
1Mc 3:17 *B*, we are weak today from fasting."
6:37 it by a harness, held, *b* the Indian mahout,
2Mc 2:13 *B* these things, it is also told in the records
4: 9 *B* this he agreed to pay a hundred and
5:23 and *b* these, Menelaus, who lorded it over
9:17 *B* all this, he would become a Jew himself
Jb 40:15 See, *b* you I made Behemoth,
Ps(s) 120: 3 What will he inflict on you, with more *b*,
Eccl 12: 9 *B* being wise, Qoheleth taught the people
Wis 12:13 any god *b* you who have the care of all,
15:18 *b*, they worship the most loathsome beasts—
Sir 28:21 *b* which even the nether world is a gain;
29:25 *b*, you will hear these bitter words:
36:23 And if, *b*, her speech is kindly,
Is 44: 8 Is there a God or any Rock *b* me?
45: 5 there is no other, there is no God *b* me.
45: 6 sun men may know that there is none *b* me.
45:21 I, the LORD, *b* whom there is no other God?
56: 8 I gather to him *b* those already gathered.
Dn 14:10 priests of Bel, *b* their wives and children.
14:41 God of Daniel, and there is no other *b* you!"
Hos 13: 4 You know no God *b* me,
Mt 6:33 and all these things will be given you *b*.
15:30 the blind, the mute, and many others *b*.
Mk 4:24 you give you shall receive, and more *b*.
6:43 baskets, *b* what remained of the fish.
7:13 And you have many other such practices *b*."
10:30 persecution *b*— and in the age to come,
Lk 24:21 *B* all this, today, the third day since these
Jn 8:48 you are a Samaritan, and possessed *b*?"
Rom 8:32 of us will all not grant us all things *b*?
1Cor 10:13 *B*, God keeps his promise.
1Tm 5:13 *B*, they learn to be ladies of leisure,
2Pt 1:19 *B*, we possess the prophetic message as

BESIEGE (12)

Dt 28:52 will *b* you in each of your communities,
28:52 They will so *b* you in every community
1Sm 23: 8 go down to Keilah and *b* David and his men.
1Chr 20: 1 of the Ammonites, and went on to *b* Rabbah,
2Chr 6:28 their enemies *b* them at any of their gates;
1Mc 6:19 all the people together to *b* them
2Mc 10:19 his men, in sufficient numbers to *b* them,
12:21 which was hard to *b* and even hard to reach
Is 21: 2 *b*, O Media; I will put an end to all
Jer 21: 4 the Chaldeans who *b* you outside the walls.
51: 2 They shall *b* her from all sides on the day
Ez 4: 3 in the state of siege, and you shall *b* it.

BESIEGED (21)

2Sm 11: 1 they ravaged the Ammonites and *b* Rabbah.
20:15 came and *b* him in Abel Beth-maacah.
2Kgs 16: 5 Although they *b* Ahaz,
17: 5 Samaria, which he *b* for three years.
2Chr 32: 1 He invaded Judah, *b* the fortified cities,
1Mc 5: 5 them to take refuge in towers, which he *b*;
6:21 Some of the *b* escaped,
6:26 They have now *b* the citadel in Jerusalem
6:31 but the *b* made a sortie and burned these
6:51 For many days he *b* the sanctuary,
10:75 When the Jews *b* it,
11:61 *b* it and burned and plundered its suburbs.
11:65 Simon *b* Beth-zur,
13:43 *b* Gazara and surrounded it with troops.
2Mc 10:33 and his men eagerly *b* the fortress.
10:36 on the defenders, taking the *b* in the rear;
12:14 *b* treated Judas and his men with contempt,
Jer 13:19 The cities of the Negeb are *b*,
39: 1 army marched against Jerusalem and *b* it.
Ez 6:12 and he that is *b* shall perish by famine;
Zec 12: 2 [Judah will be *b*, even Jerusalem.]

BESIEGERS (3)

Ps(s) 53: 6 For God has scattered the bones of your *b*;
Is 29: 7 Ariel with all the earthworks of her *b*.
Jer 4:16 The *b* are coming from the distant land,

BESIEGES (1)

1Kgs 8:37 your people *b* them in one of their cities;

BESIEGING (13)

2Sm 11:16 So while Joab was *b* the city,
1Kgs 15:27 which Nadab and all Israel were *b*.
16:15 army was *b* Gibbethon of the Philistines
2Kgs 9:14 had been *b* Ramoth-gilead against Hazael,
19: 8 from Lachish, he found him *b* Libnah.
24:11 at the city while his servants were *b* it.
1Mc 6:57 are scanty, the place we are *b* is strong,
11:21 him that Jonathan was *b* the citadel.
2Mc 11: 6 learned that Lysias was *b* the strongholds,
Is 37: 8 had left there, he found him *b* Libnah.
Jer 21: 9 leaves and surrenders to the *b* Chaldeans
32: 2 of the king of Babylon was *b* Jerusalem,
37: 5 when the Chaldeans who were *b* Jerusalem

BESMIRCHES (1)

Sir 21:28 A slanderer *b* himself,

BESMIRCHING (1)

Wis 14:26 good men, neglect of gratitude, *b* of souls,

BESODEIAH (1)

Neh 3: 6 and Meshullam, son of *B*;

BESOR (3)

1Sm 30: 9 hundred men and came as far as the Wadi *B*,
30:10 to cross the Wadi *B* and remained behind.
30:21 and whom he had left behind at the Wadi *B*,

BESOUGHT (7)

Dt 3:23 "And it was then that I *b* the LORD,
2Sm 12:16 David *b* God for the child.
1Chr 29:20 Then David *b* the whole assembly,
Jdt 12: 8 After bathing, she *b* the Lord,
2Mc 8:14 and at the same time *b* the Lord to deliver
Wis 8:21 I went to the Lord and *b* him,
Jn 6:34 give us this bread always," they *b* him.

BEST (71)

Gn 4: 4 one of the *b* firstlings of his flock.
27:15 Rebekah then took the *b* clothes of her
37: 3 Israel loved Joseph *b* of all his sons,
37: 4 their father loved him *b* of all his sons,
43:11 Put some of the land's *b* products in your
45:18 I will assign you the *b* land in Egypt,
45:20 for the *b* in the whole land of Egypt shall
Ex 22: 4 the *b* produce of his own field or vineyard.
35:29 voluntary offerings as they thought *b*,
Nm 13:20 *b* to get some of the fruit of the land."
18:12 I have also assigned to you all the *b* of
18:29 that you receive, and from the *b* parts,
18:30 made your contribution from the *b* part,
18:32 as you make a contribution of the *b* part.
Dt 33:13 his land with the *b* of the skies above
33:14 With the *b* of the produce of the year,
33:15 and the *b* from the timeless hills;
33:16 With the *b* of the earth and its fullness,
33:21 He saw that the *b* should be his when the
Jgs 9:33 against you, deal with him as *b* you can."
14:20 the one who had been *b* man at his wedding.
15: 2 so I gave her to your *b* man.
15: 6 his wife was taken and given to his *b* man."
17: 6 everyone did what he thought *b*.
21:25 everyone did what he thought *b*.
Ru 3: 3 then put on your *b* attire and go down to
1Sm 1:23 "Do what you think is *b*;
3:18 He will do what he judges *b*."

BEST (cont.)
8:14 He will take the *b* of your fields,
8:16 as well as your *b* oxen and your asses,
14:36 They replied, "Do what you think *b.*"
14:40 people responded, "Do what you think *b.*"
15: 9 Agag and the *b* of the fat sheep and oxen,
15:15 *b* sheep and oxen to sacrifice to the LORD,
15:21 and oxen, the *b* of what had been banned,
2Sm 10:12 the LORD will do what he judges *b.*"
18: 4 to them, "I will do what you think *b*";
19:28 Do what you judge *b.*
2Kgs 8: 9 camel loads of the *b* goods of Damascus.
10: 3 you decide which is the *b* and the fittest
10: 5 do whatever you think *b.*"
1Chr 19:10 he chose some of the *b* fighters among the
19:13 then may the LORD do what seems *b* to him."
21:23 my lord the king do what seems *b* to him.
2Chr 31: 5 in great quantities, the *b* of their grain,
Ezr 7:18 your brethren may do whatever seems *b*
Est 2: 9 and her maids to the *b* place in the harem.
1Mc 8: 8 and Lydia from among their *b* provinces.
2Mc 9:19 *b* wishes for their health and happiness.
15:38 and mediocre, that is the *b* I could do.
Ps(s) 78:31 God rose against them and slew their *b* men,
81:17 Israel I would feed with the *b* of wheat,
147:14 with the *b* of wheat he fills you.
Prv 19: 8 who gains intelligence is his own *b* friend;
Eccl 2: 3 until I should understand what is *b* for men
Wis 14:19 over the likeness to the *b* of his skill;
Sir 9:14 As *b* you can,
14:11 you have and enjoy it as *b* you can;
Jer 9:16 women to come, summon the *b* of them;
Ez 31:16 were consoled, Lebanon's choice and *b,*
34:18 enough for you to graze on the *b* pasture,
44:30 all the *b* of your offerings of every kind,
44:30 likewise the *b* of your dough you shall
48:14 or alienate this, the *b* part of the land,
Am 6: 6 and anoint themselves with the *b* oils;
Mi 7: 4 he pleases, The *b* of them is like a brier,
Mt 7: 6 They will trample them under foot, at *b,*
27:65 Go and secure the tomb as *b* you can."
Jn 3:29 The groom's *b* man waits there listening
Col 4:15 Give our *b* wishes to the brothers at
2Tm 4: 9 Do your *b* to join me soon,

BESTIR (3)
Is 28:21 *b* himself as in the Valley of Gibeon,
Ez 38:14 will you not *b* yourself and come from your
Jl 4:12 Let the nations *b* themselves and come up

BESTOW (17)
Lv 25:21 I will *b* such blessings on you in the
Nm 10:32 you the prosperity the LORD will *b* on us."
11:17 that is on you and will *b* it on them,
11:29 the LORD might *b* his spirit on them all!"
1Chr 22: 9 I will *b* peace and tranquillity on Israel.
1Mc 10:28 many exemptions and will *b* gifts on you.
11:33 decided to *b* benefits on the Jewish nation,
2Mc 1:35 To those on whom the king wished to *b*
Prv 4: 9 a glorious crown will she *b* on you."
Sir 1:23 and the LORD will *b* her upon you;
24:31 prophecy and *b* it on generations to come.
Is 58:10 If you *b* your bread on the hungry and
Mt 4: 9 "All these will I *b* on you if you
Jn 17: 2 may *b* eternal life on those you gave him.
Eph 3:16 and I pray that he will *b* on you gifts in
Rv 17:13 *b* their power and authority on the beast.
17:17 by making them agree to *b* their

BESTOWED (27)
Gn 33: 5 whom God has graciously *b* on your servant."
41:45 *b* the name of Zaphenath-paneah on Joseph,
Nm 11:25 on Moses, he *b* it on the seventy elders;
Dt 15:14 blessing the LORD, your God, has *b* on you.
16:10 blessing the LORD, your God, has *b* on you.
16:17 which the LORD, your God, has *b* on you.
Neh 9:20 "Your good spirit you *b* on them,
Ps(s) 44: 5 king and my God, who *b* victories on Jacob.
Sir 26: 3 gift *b* upon him who fears the LORD;
45: 7 he *b* on him the priesthood of his people;
45:20 of Aaron and *b* upon him his inheritance:
Ez 16:14 of my splendor which I had *b* on you,
16:33 you rather *b* your gifts on all your lovers,
Rom 12: 6 according to the favor *b* on each of us.
1Cor 1: 4 the favor he has *b* on you in Christ Jesus,
2Cor 4:15 so that the grace *b* in abundance may bring
Gal 2: 9 and recognizing, too, the favor *b* on me,
3:14 the blessing *b* on Abraham might descend
Eph 1: 3 who has *b* on us in Christ every spiritual
1: 6 favor he has *b* on us in his beloved.
3: 7 *b* on me by the exercise of his power,
Phil 2: 9 *b* on him the name above every other name,
2Tm 1: 6 of God *b* when my hands were laid on you.
Phlm 1:14 not be forced on you but might be freely *b.*
2Pt 1: 3 That divine power of his has freely *b* on
1: 4 By virtue of them he has *b* on us the great
1Jn 3: 1 See what love the Father has *b* on us in

BESTOWER (1)
Is 23: 8 such a thing against Tyre, the *b* of crowns,

BESTOWING (5)
Ex 20: 6 *b* mercy down to the thousandth generation,
Dt 5:10 third and fourth generation but *b* mercy,
Est 2:18 provinces and *b* gifts with royal bounty.
Acts 14:17 Yet in *b* his benefits,
1Cor 12:24 thus *b* on the less presentable a propriety

BESTOWS (6)
Ps(s) 42: 9 By day the LORD *b* his grace,
84:12 grace and glory he *b*;
Sir 4:13 wherever he dwells, the LORD *b* blessings.
Eph 4: 7 favor in the measure in which Christ *b* it.
Jas 4: 6 Yet he *b* a greater gift,
4: 6 the proud but *b* his favor on the lowly."

BESTRIDE (1)
Hb 3:12 In wrath you *b* the earth,

BETAKE (1)
Ez 20:29 sort of high place do you *b* yourselves?—and

BETEN (1)
Jos 19:25 Their territory included Helkath, Hali, *B,*

BETH-ACHZIB (1)
Mi 1:14 *B* is a deception to the kings of Israel.

BETH-ANATH (3)
Jos 19:38 Yiron, Migdal-el, Horem, *B* and Bethshemesh;
Jgs 1:33 inhabitants of Beth-shemesh or those of *B,*
1:33 and *B* have become forced laborers for them.

BETH-ANOTH (1)
Jos 15:59 Beth-zur, Gedor, Maarath, *B* and Eltekon;

BETH-ARABAH (5)
Jos 15: 6 up to Beth-hoglah, and ran north of *B*
15:61 *B,* Middin,
18:22 Jericho, Beth-hoglah, Emek-keziz, *B,*
2Sm 23:31 Abibaal from *B;*
1Chr 11:32 Abiel, from *B;*

BETH-ARBEL (1)
Hos 10:14 ravaged As Salman ravaged *B* in time of war,

BETH-ASTHAROTH (1)
Jos 21:27 and also *B* with its pasture lands.

BETH-AVEN (5)
Jos 18:12 mountains, till it reached the desert of *B.*
1Sm 13: 5 they encamped in Michmash, east of *B.*
Hos 4:15 Come not to Gilgal, nor up to *B,*
5: 8 Sound the alarm in *B:*
10: 5 of Samaria fear for the calf of *B;*

BETH-AZMAVETH (2)
Ezr 2:24 men of *B,* forty-two; men
Neh 7:28 men of *B,* forty-two; men

BETH-BAAL-MEON (1)
Jos 13:17 on the tableland, Dibon, Bamoth-baal, *B,*

BETH-BARAH (2)
Jgs 7:24 the water courses against them as far as *B,*
7:24 they seized the water courses as far as *B,*

BETH-CAR (1)
1Sm 7:11 Philistines, harrying them down beyond *B.*

BETH-DAGON (3)
Jos 15:41 Cabbon, Lahmam, Chitlish, Gederoth, *B,*
19:27 the other direction, it ran eastward of *B,*
1Mc 10:83 The enemy fled to Azotus and entered *B,*

BETH-DIBLATHAIM (1)
Jer 48:22 and Mephaath, on Dibon, Nebo, and *B,*

BETH-EDEN (1)
Am 1: 5 of Aven, And the sceptered ruler of *B;*

BETH-EKED (1)
2Kgs 10:14 in number, then slain at the pit of *B.*

BETH-EKED-HAROIM (1)
2Kgs 10:12 set out for Samaria, and at *B* on the way,

BETH-EMEK (1)
Jos 19:27 then north of *B* and Neiel,

BETH-EZEL (1)
Mi 1:11 lamentation of *B* finds in you its grounds.

BETH-GAMUL (1)
Jer 48:23 and Beth-diblathaim, on Kiriathaim, *B,*

BETH-GILGAL (1)
Neh 12:29 from *B,* and from the plains

BETH-HACCHEREM (2)
Neh 3:14 of Rechab, leader of the district of *B;*
Jer 6: 1 trumpet in Tekoa, raise a signal over *B;*

BETH-HAGGAN (1)
2Kgs 9:27 Ahaziah, king of Judah, fled toward *B.*

BETH-HANAN (1)
1Kgs 4: 9 Makaz, Shaalbim, Beth-shemesh, Elon and *B;*

BETH-HARAM (1)
Jos 13:27 *B,* Beth-nimrah,

BETH-HARAN (1)
Nm 32:36 Jazer, Jogbehah, Beth-nimrah and *B,*

BETH-HOGLAH (3)
Jos 15: 6 where the Jordan meets the sea, up to *B,*
18:19 continued across the northern flank of *B*
18:21 Jericho, *B,*

BETH-HORON (20)
Jos 10:10 Gibeon and pursued them down the *B* slope,
10:11 before Israel along the descent from *B,*
16: 3 the Japhletites, to that of the Lower *B,*
16: 5 to Upper *B* and thence to the sea.
18:13 on the mountaintop south of Lower *B.*
18:14 *B* till it reached Kiriath-baal (that is,
21:22 with its pasture lands, and *B*
1Sm 13:18 another turned in the direction of *B;*
14:23 The battle continued past *B;*
1Kgs 9:17 Solomon then rebuilt Gezer), Lower *B,*
1Chr 6:53 lands, and *B* with its pasture lands.
7:24 built lower and upper *B* and Uzzensheerah.
2Chr 8: 5 He built Upper *B* and Lower Beth-horon,
25:13 the cities of Judah from Samaria to *B.*
Jdt 4: 4 the whole region of Samaria, to Kona, *B,*
1Mc 3:16 When he reached the ascent of *B,*
3:24 Seron down the descent of *B* into the plain.
7:39 left Jerusalem and pitched his camp at *B,*
9:50 Jericho fortress, as well as Emmaus, *B,*

BETH-JESHIMOTH (3)
Nm 33:49 of Moab extended from *B* to Abel-shittim.
Jos 12: 3 Sea of the Arabah in the direction of *B,*
13:20 Beth-peor, the slopes of Pisgah, *B,*

BETH-JESIMOTH (1)
Ez 25: 9 *B,* Baal-meon, and Kiriathaim.

BETH-LEAPHRAH (1)
Mi 1:10 In *B* roll in the dust.

BETH-LEBAOTH (1)
Jos 19: 6 Hazar-susah, *B* and Sharuhen;

BETH-MAACAH (7)
2Sm 20:14 through all the tribes of Israel to Abel *B.*
20:15 servants came and besieged him in Abel *B.*
23:34 Eliphelet, son of Ahasbai, from *B;*
2Kgs 25:23 the Netophathite, and Jaazaniah, from *B.*
1Chr 11:36 Elipheleth, son of Ahasabi, from *B;*
11:43 Hanan, from *B;*
Jer 40: 8 and Jezaniah of *B.*

BETH-MARCABOTH (2)
Jos 19: 5 Ezem, Eltolad, Bethul, Hormah, Ziklag, *B,*
1Chr 4:31 Ezem, Tolad, Bethuel, Hormah, Ziklag, *B,*

BETH-MEON (1)
Jer 48:23 on Kiriathaim, Beth-gamul, and *B,*

BETH-MILLO (3)
Jgs 9: 6 citizens of Shechem and all *B* came together
9:20 from the citizens and from *B,*
2Kgs 12:21 a plot against him and killed him at *B.*

BETH-NIMRAH (2)
Nm 32:36 Jazer, Jogbehah, *B* and Beth-haran,
Jos 13:27 Beth-haran, *B,* Succoth,

BETH-PAZZEZ (1)
Jos 19:21 Ebez, Remeth, En-gannim, En-haddah and *B.*

BETH-PELET (3)
Jos 15:27 Hazar-gaddah, Heshmon, *B,*
2Sm 23:26 Helez from *B;*
Neh 11:26 and its villages, in Jeshua, Moladah, *B,*

BETH-PEOR (4)

Dt 3:29 was while we were in the ravine opposite *B.*
4:46 the Jordan in the ravine opposite *B,*
34: 6 the ravine opposite *B* in the land of Moab,
Jos 13:20 on the knoll within the valley, *B,*

BETH-PHELET (1)

1Chr 27:10 for the seventh month, was Hellez, from *B,*

BETH-REHOB (3)

Jgs 18:28 which was in the valley that belongs to *B,*
1Sm 14:47 Moab, the Ammonites, Aram, *B,*
2Sm 10: 6 Aramean foot soldiers from *B* and Zobah,

BETH-SHAN (6)

1Sm 31:10 but impaled his body on the wall of *B.*
31:12 of Saul and his sons from the wall of *B,*
2Sm 21:12 off secretly from the public square of *B,*
1Mc 5:52 Jordan to the great plain in front of *B,*
12:40 and kill him, he set out and reached *B.*
12:41 thousand picked fighting men and came to *B.*

BETH-SHEAN (6)

Jos 17:11 Asher Manasseh was awarded *B* and its towns,
17:16 in particular those in *B* and its towns,
Jgs 1:27 Manasseh did not take possession of *B*
1Kgs 4:12 Megiddo, and beyond Jokmeam, and in all *B,*
4:12 below Jezreel from *B* to Abel-meholah;
1Chr 7:29 however, had possession of *B* and its towns

BETH-SHEMESH (18)

Jos 15:10 thence it descended to *B,*
19:38 Migda-el, Horem, Beth-anath and *B*
19:22 boundary reached Tabor, Shahazumah and *B,*
21:16 lands, and *B* with its pasture lands:
Jgs 1:33 inhabitants of *B* or those of Beth-anath,
1:33 the inhabitants of *B* and Beth-anath have
1Sm 6: 9 to *B* along the route to his own territory,
6:12 route to *B* and continued along this road,
6:12 followed them as far as the border of *B.*
6:13 *B* were harvesting the wheat in the valley.
6:15 The men of *B* also offered other holocausts
6:19 of *B* when they greeted the ark of the LORD,
6:20 The men of *B* asked,
1Kgs 4: 9 the son of Deker in Makaz, Shaalbim, *B,*
2Kgs 14:11 of Judah met in battle at *B* of Judah.
14:13 son of Ahaziah, king of Judah, at *B.*
1Chr 6:44 lands, and *B* with its pasture lands.
2Chr 25:21 King Amaziah met in battle at *B* of Judah.
25:23 at *B* and brought him to Jerusalem.
28:18 they captured *B,* Aijalon, Gederoth,

BETH-SHEMITE (2)

1Sm 6:14 field of Joshua the *B* and stopped there.
6:18 field of Joshua the *B* at the present time.

BETH-SHITTAH (1)

Jgs 7:22 as far as *B* in the direction of Zarethan,

BETH-TAPPUAH (1)

Jos 15:53 Arab, Dumah, Eshan, Janim, *B*

BETH-TOGARMAH (2)

Ez 27:14 From *B* horses, steeds, and mules were
38: 6 *B* from the recesses of the north with all

BETH-ZAITH (1)

1Mc 7:19 from Jerusalem and pitched his camp in *B.*

BETH-ZECHARIAH (2)

1Mc 6:32 from the citadel and moved his camp to *B,*
6:33 his force hastily along the road to *B;*

BETH-ZUR (19)

Jos 15:58 Halhul, *B,*
1Chr 2:45 Maon, who was the father of *B.*
2Chr 11: 7 He built up Bethlehem, Etam, Tekoa, *B,*
Neh 3:16 Azbuk, leader of half the district of *B,*
1Mc 4:29 They came into Idumea and camped at *B,*
4:61 to protect it, and likewise fortified *B,*
6: 7 as it had been before, and his city of *B.*
6:26 they have fortified the sanctuary and *B.*
6:31 passed through Idumea and camped before *B.*
6:49 He made peace with the men of *B,*
6:50 The king took *B* and stationed a garrison
9:52 He fortified the city of *B,*
10:14 Only in *B* did some remain of those who had
11:65 Simon besieged *B,*
14: 7 war and made himself master of Gazara, *B,*
14:33 Judea, especially the frontier city of *B,*
2Mc 11: 5 he invaded Judea, and when he reached *B,*
13:19 So he marched against *B,*
13:22 attempt by negotiating with the men of *B.*

BETHANY (13)

Jdt 1: 9 west of the Jordan as far as Jerusalem, *B,*
Mt 21:17 he left them and went out of the city to *B,*
26: 6 was in *B* at the house of Simon the leper,
Mk 11: 1 Bethphage and *B* on the Mount of Olives,
11:11 he went out to *B* accompanied by the Twelve.
11:12 when they were leaving *B* he felt hungry.
14: 3 When Jesus was in *B* reclining at table in
Lk 19:29 Bethphage and *B* on the mount called Olivet,
24:50 Then he led them out near *B,*
Jn 1:28 This happened in *B,* across the Jordan,
11: 1 He was from *B,* the village of Mary
11:17 When Jesus arrived at *B,*
12: 1 Six days before Passover Jesus came to *B,*

BETHBASI (2)

1Mc 9:62 companions withdrew to *B* in the desert;
9:64 He came and pitched his camp before *B,*

BETHBIRI (1)

1Chr 4:31 Ziklag, Beth-marcaboth, Hazar-susim, *B,*

BETHEL (72)

Gn 12: 8 he moved on to the hill country east of *B,*
12: 8 tent with *B* to the west and Ai to the east.
13: 3 toward *B,* to the place between Bethel
28:10 at *B* When he came upon a certain shrine,
28:19 He called that site *B,*
31:13 I am the God who appeared to you in *B,*
35: 1 "Go up now to *B.*
35: 3 We are now to go up to *B,*
35: 6 in Luz [that is, *B* in the land of Canaan.
35: 7 he built an altar and named the place *B,*
35: 8 she was buried under the oak below *B,*
35:15 Jacob named the site *B,*
35:16 Then they departed from *B;*
Jos 7: 2 to Ai, which is near *B* on its eastern side,
8: 9 position to the west of Ai, toward *B,*
8:12 and set them in ambush between *B* and Ai,
8:17 not a soldier remained in Ai [or *B,*
12: 9 the kings of Jericho, Ai (which is near *B),*
12:16 Arad, Libnah, Adullam, Makkedah, *B,*
16: 1 went up from Jericho to the heights at *B.*
16: 2 Leaving *B* for Luz,
18:13 to the southern flank of Luz (that is, *B).*
18:22 Emek-keziz, Beth-arabah, Zemaraim, *B,*
Jgs 1:22 house of Joseph, too, marched up against *B,*
1:23 of Joseph had a reconnaissance made of *B,*
4: 5 and *B* in the mountain region of Ephraim,
20:18 battle, moved on to *B* and consulted God.
20:26 So the entire Israelite army went up to *B,*
20:32 the highways, of which the one led to *B,*
21: 2 So the people went to *B* and remained there
21:19 feast of the LORD at Shiloh, north of *B,*
21:19 the highway that goes up from *B* to Shechem,
1Sm 7:16 made a yearly journey, passing through *B,*
10: 3 be met by three men going up to God at *B;*
13: 2 in Michmash and in the hill country of *B,*
30:27 to those in *B,* to those in Ramoth-negeb,
1Kgs 12:29 And he put one in *B,* the other in Dan.
12:30 frequented these calves in *B* and in Dan.
12:32 in *B* the pilgrimage feast of Judah,
12:32 *B* priests of the high places he had built.
12:33 Jeroboam ascended the altar he built in *B*
13: 1 from Judah to *B* by the word of the LORD,
13:10 did not go back the way he had come to *B.*
13:11 that the man of God had done that day in *B.*
13:32 he proclaimed against the altar in *B*
16:34 his reign, Hiel from *B* rebuilt Jericho.
2Kgs 2: 2 "The LORD has sent me on to *B.*"
2: 2 So they went down to *B,*
2:23 From there Elisha went up to *B.*
10:29 regards the golden calves at *B* and at Dan.
17:28 from Samaria returned and settled in *B,*
23: 4 of the Kidron and their ashes carried to *B.*
23:15 Likewise the altar which was at *B,*
23:17 things you have done to the altar of *B.*"
23:19 the very same to them as he had done in *B.*
1Chr 7:28 their dwellings were in *B* and its towns.
2Chr 13:19 *B* and its dependencies,
Ezr 2:28 men of *B* and Ai,
Neh 7:32 men of *B* and Ai,
11:31 Michmash, Aija, *B* and its dependencies,
Tb 2: 6 pronounced by the prophet Amos against *B:*
1Mc 9:50 as well as Emmaus, Beth-horon, *B,*
Jer 48:13 disappointed by *B* in which they trusted.
Hos 10:15 So shall it be done to you, *B,*
12: 5 *B* he met God and there he spoke with him;
Am 3:14 crimes, I will visit also the altars of *B:*
4: 4 Come to *B,* and sin, to Gilgal,
5: 5 me, that you may live, but do not seek *B;*
5: 5 led into exile, and *B* shall become nought.
7:10 Amaziah, the priest of *B,*
7:12 but never again prophesy in *B;*

BETHELSAREZER (1)

Zec 7: 2 *B* sent Regemmelech and his men to implore

BETHER (2)

Jos 15:59 Tatam, Zores, Karim, Gallim, *B* and Manoko;
Sg 2:17 or a young stag upon the mountains of *B.*

BETHESDA (1)

Jn 5: 2 there is a place with the Hebrew name *B.*

BETHGADER (1)

1Chr 2:51 of Bethlehem, and Hareph, the father of *B.*

BETHLEHEM (51)

Gn 35:19 buried on the road to Ephrath [that is, *B.*
48: 7 there on the way to Ephrath [that is, *B.*"
Jos 15:59 Tekoa, Ephrathah (that is, *B),*
19:15 Kattah, Nahalal, Shimron, Idalah and *B,*
Jgs 12: 8 After him Ibzan of *B* judged Israel.
12:10 years, Ibzan died and was buried in *B.*
17: 7 within the tribe of Judah at *B* of Judah.
17: 9 him, "I am a Levite from *B* in Judah,
19: 1 for himself a concubine from *B* of Judah.
19: 2 him for her father's house in *B* of Judah,
19:18 "We are traveling from *B* of Judah far up
19:18 to *B* of Judah and am now going back home;
Ru 1: 2 they were Ephrathites from *B* of Judah.
1:19 they went on together till they reached *B.*
1:22 *B* at the beginning of the barley harvest.
2: 4 came from *B* and said to the harvesters,
4:11 you do well in Ephrathah and win fame in *B.*
1Sm 16: 1 I am sending you to Jesse of *B,*
16: 4 When he entered *B,* the elders of the city
16:18 sons of Jesse of *B* is a skillful harpist.
17:12 named Jesse, who was from *B* in Judah.
17:15 from Saul to tend his father's sheep at *B.*
17:58 "I am the son of your servant Jesse of *B.*"
20: 6 let him go on short notice to his city *B,*
20:28 asked me to let him go to his city, *B.*
2Sm 2:32 and buried him in his father's tomb in *B.*
21:19 Gob, in which Elhanan, son of Jair from *B,*
23:14 there was a garrison of Philistines in *B.*
23:15 from the cistern that is by the gate of *B!*"
23:16 from the cistern that is by the gate of *B.*
23:24 Elhanan, son of Dodo, from *B;*
1Chr 2:51 of Kiriath-jearim, Salma, the father of *B,*
2:54 The descendants of Salma were *B,*
4: 4 first-born of Ephrathah, the father of *B.*
4:22 held property in Moab, but returned to *B.*
11:16 and a Philistine garrison was at *B.*
11:17 from the cistern that is by the gate at *B!*"
11:18 water from the cistern by the gate at *B,*
11:26 Elhanan, son of Dodo, from *B,*
2Chr 11: 6 He built up *B,*
Ezr 2:21 sons of *B,* one hundred and twenty-three
Neh 7:26 men of *B* and Netophah,
Jer 41:17 to the lodging place of Chimham near *B,*
Mt 2: 1 *B* of Judea during the reign of King Herod,
2: 5 "In *B* of Judea," they informed him.
2: 6 'And you, *B,* land of Judah,
2: 8 Then he sent them to *B,*
2:16 years old and under in *B* and its environs,
Lk 2: 4 in Galilee to Judea, to David's town of *B*—
2:15 "Let us go over to *B* and see this event
Jn 7:42 being of David's family, is to come from *B,*

BETHLEHEM-EPHRATHAH (1)

Mi 5: 1 *B* too small to be among the clans of Judah,

BETHPHAGE (3)

Mt 21: 1 entering *B* on the Mount of Olives,
Mk 11: 1 *B* and Bethany on the Mount of Olives,
Lk 19:29 *B* and Bethany on the mount called Olivet,

BETHRAPHA (1)

1Chr 4:12 Eshton became the father of *B,*

BETHSAIDA (7)

Mt 11:21 And just as ill with you, *B!*
Mk 6:45 and precede him to the other side toward *B,*
8:22 When they arrived at *B,*
Lk 9:10 with him, he retired to a town called *B,*
10:13 And just as ill with you *B!*
Jn 1:44 Now Philip was from *B,*
12:21 Philip, who was from *B* in Galilee,

BETHUEL (9)

Gn 22:22 Chesed, Hazo, Pildash, Jidlaph, and *B.*"
22:23 *B* became the father of Rebekah.
24:15 words when Rebekah (who was born to *B,*
24:24 "I am the daughter of *B* the son of Milcah,
24:47 she answered, 'The daughter of *B,*
25:20 the daughter of *B* the Aramean of
28: 2 to the home of your mother's father *B,*
28: 5 to Laban, son of *B* the Aramean,
1Chr 4:30 Hazar-shual, Bilhah, Ezem, Tolad, *B,*

BETHUL (1)

Jos 19: 4 Hazar-shual, Balah, Ezem, Eltolad, *B,*

BETHULIA (20)

Jdt 4: 6 to the inhabitants of *B* [and Betomesthaim],
6:10 his tent to seize Achior, conduct him to *B,*
6:11 till they reached the springs below *B.*
6:14 city, loosed him, and brought him into *B.*

BETHULIA (cont.)

7: 1 come to his support, to move against *B*,
7: 3 at the spring in the valley near *B*,
7: 3 as Balbaim, and in length from *B* to Cyamon,
7: 6 the sight of the Israelites who were in *B*.
7:13 where the inhabitants of *B* get their water.
7:20 of water failed the inhabitants of *B*,
8: 3 and he died of this illness in *B*,
8:11 to me, you rulers of the people of *B*.
10: 6 went out to the gate of the city of *B*
11: 9 When the men of *B* spared him,
12: 7 night she went out to the ravine of *B*,
13:10 the ravine, reached *B* on the mountain.
15: 3 mountain district around *B* took to flight.
15: 6 *B* swept down on the camp of the Assyrians,
16:21 went back to *B* and remained on her estate.
16:23 She died in *B*, where they buried her

BETOKENED (1)

2Mc 14:30 he concluded that this coldness *b* no good.

BETOMASTHAIM (1)

Jdt 15: 4 Uzziah sent messengers to *B*,

BETOMESTHAIM (1)

Jdt 4: 6 to the inhabitants of Bethulia [and *B*,

BETONIM (1)

Jos 13:26 is, from Heshbon to Ramath-mizpeh and *B*,

BETOOK (1)

2Kgs 22:14 Asaiah *b* themselves to the Second Quarter

BETRAY (12)

Jos 2:14 "If you do not *b* this errand of ours,
2:20 If, however, you *b* this errand of ours,
1Sm 27:11 fearing that they would *b* him by saying,
1Chr 12:18 But if you have come to *b* me to my enemies
Sir 27:17 but if you *b* his confidence,
Is 24:16 The traitors *b*: with treachery
Jer 12: 6 the members of your father's house, *b* you;
Ob 1:14 *B* not his fugitives on the day of distress!
Mt 26:21 assure you, one of you is about to *b* me."
Mk 14:18 you my word, one of you is about to *b* me,
Lk 22:48 would you *b* the Son of Man with a kiss?"
Jn 13:21 tell you solemnly, one of you will *b* me."

BETRAYAL (1)

Ezr 10: 6 was in mourning over the *b* by the exiles.

BETRAYALS (1)

Sir 49: 2 For he grieved over our *b*,

BETRAYED (15)

2Sm 19:27 "My lord the king, my servant *b* me.
Ezr 10: 2 "We have indeed *b* our God by taking
2Mc 6:11 were *b* to Philip and all burned to death.
13:21 army, *b* military secrets to the enemy.
Is 24:16 with treachery have the traitors *b*!
33: 1 never destroyed, O traitor never *b*!
33: 1 when wearied with betraying you will be *b*.
Jer 38:22 "They *b* you, outdid you,
Lam 1: 2 have all *b* her and become her enemies.
Mt 10: 4 member, and Judas Iscariot, who *b* him.
26:24 to that man by whom the Son of Man is *b*.
Mk 3:19 Party, and Judas Iscariot, who *b* him.
14:21 be that man by whom the Son of Man is *b*.
Lk 22:22 but woe to that man by whom he is *b*."
1Cor 11:23 on the night in which he was *b* took bread,

BETRAYER (8)

Prv 14:25 saves lives, but he who utters lies is a *b*.
Mt 26:25 Then Judas, his *b*, spoke:
26:46 See, my *b* is here."
26:48 His *b* had arranged to give them a signal,
Mk 14:42 My *b* is near."
14:44 The *b* had arranged a signal for them,
Lk 22:21 the hand of my *b* is with me at this table.
Jn 13:11 are washed clean," was that he knew his *b*.)

BETRAYERS (1)

Acts 7:52 your turn have become his *b* and murderers.

BETRAYING (4)

Neh 13:27 evil, *b* our God by marrying foreign women?"
Sir 41:23 repeating what you hear, and of *b* secrets
Is 33: 1 when wearied with *b* you will be betrayed.
Mt 24:10 falter then, *b* and hating one another.

BETRAYS (5)

Prv 20:11 Even by his manners the child *b* whether
Sir 26:11 bold, and be not surprised if she *b* you;
27:16 He who *b* a secret cannot be trusted,
27:21 but he who *b* secrets does hopeless damage.
Is 21: 2 the traitor *b*, the despoiler spoils.

BETROTH (1)

Dt 28:30 Though you *b* a wife,

BETROTHED (9)

Ex 22:15 a man seduces a virgin who is not *b*,
Dt 20: 7 Is there anyone who has *b* a woman and not
22:23 city a man comes upon a maiden who is *b*,
22:25 that a man comes upon such a *b* maiden,
22:27 the *b* maiden may have cried out for help,
22:28 a man comes upon a maiden that is not *b*,
Ps(s) 78:63 young men, and their maidens were not *b*.
Mal 2:14 though she is your companion, your *b* wife.
Lk 1:27 to a virgin *b* to a man named Joseph,

BETTER (167)

Ex 14:12 Far *b* for us to be the slaves of the
17:11 raised up, Israel had the *b* of the fight,
17:11 hands rest, Amalek had the *b* of the fight.
Lv 27:10 for it by exchanging either a *b* for a worse
27:10 for a worse one or a worse for a *b* one.
Nm 14: 3 it not be *b* for us to return to Egypt?"
Jgs 8: 2 of Ephraim *b* than the vintage of Abiezer?
9: 2 'Which is *b* for you:
11:25 Again, are you any *b* than Balak,
18:19 Is it *b* for you to be priest for the
1Sm 15:22 Obedience is *b* than sacrifice,
15:28 to a neighbor of yours, who is *b* than you.
16:16 over you, he will play and you will feel *b*."
16:23 and Saul would be relieved and feel *b*,
2Sm 14:32 I would be *b* off if I were still there!'
17:14 the Archite *b* than that of Ahithophel.
18: 3 Therefore it is *b* that we have you to help
1Kgs 2:32 down two men *b* and more just than himself,
19: 4 my life, for I am no *b* than my fathers."
21: 2 I will give you a *b* vineyard in exchange,
2Kgs 5:12 Pharpar, *b* than all the waters of Israel?
7:13 those who are left in the city are no *b* off
2Chr 21:13 of your father's house who were *b* than you,
Tb 3: 6 It is *b* for me to die than to live,
3: 6 For it is *b* for me to die than to endure
3:10 It is far *b* for me not to hang myself,
12: 8 but *b* than either is almsgiving
12: 8 is *b* than abundance with wickedness.
12: 8 It is *b* to give alms than to store up gold;
Jdt 7:27 we would be *b* off to become their prey.
1Mc 3:59 It is *b* for us to die in battle than to
13: 5 distress, for I am not *b* than my brothers.
Ps(s) 4: 7 Many say, "Oh, that we might see *b* times!"
37:16 *B* is the scanty store of the just than the
118: 8 It is *b* to take refuge in the LORD than
118: 9 It is *b* to take refuge in the LORD than to
Prv 3:14 For her profit is *b* than profit in silver,
3:14 in silver, and *b* than gold is her revenue;
8:11 [For Wisdom is *b* than corals,
8:19 My fruit is *b* than gold,
12: 9 *B* a lowly man who supports himself than
15:16 *B* a little with fear of the LORD than a
15:17 *B* a dish of herbs where love is than a
16: 8 *B* a little with virtue,
16:16 How much *b* to acquire wisdom than gold!
16:19 It is *b* to be humble with the meek than to
16:32 A patient man is *b* than a warrior,
17: 1 *B* a dry crust with peace than a house full
18:19 brother is a *b* defense than a strong city,
19: 1 *B* a poor man who walks in his integrity
21: 9 It is *b* to dwell in a corner of the
21:19 It is *b* to dwell in a wilderness than with
25: 7 For it is *b* that you be told,
25:24 It is *b* to dwell in a corner of the
27: 5 *B* is an open rebuke than a love that
27:10 *B* is a neighbor near at hand than a
28: 6 *B* a poor man who walks in his integrity
Eccl 2:24 There is nothing *b* for man than to eat and
3:12 I recognized that there is nothing *b* than
3:22 *b* for a man than to rejoice in his work;
4: 3 And *b* off than both is the yet unborn,
4: 6 *B* is one handful with tranquility than
4: 9 Two are *b* than one:
4:13 *B* is a poor but wise youth than an old but
5: 4 You had *b* not make a vow than make it and
6: 9 is *b* than what the desires wander after."
7: 1 A good name is *b* than good ointment,
7: 2 It is *b* to go to the house of mourning
7: 3 Sorrow is *b* than laughter,
7: 5 It is *b* to hearken to the wise man's rebuke
7: 8 *B* is the end of speech than its beginning;
7: 8 *b* is the patient spirit than the lofty
7:10 is it that former times were *b* than these?
7:19 Wisdom is a *b* defense for the wise man
9: 4 a live dog is *b* off than a dead lion.
9:16 I had said, "Wisdom is *b* than force,"
9:17 "The quiet words of the wise are *b* heeded
Wis 4: 1 *B* is childlessness with virtue;
8: 6 who in the world is a *b* craftsman than she?
15:17 For he is *b* than the things he worships;
Sir 7:16 Do not esteem yourself *b* than your fellows;
10:26 *B* the worker who has plenty of everything
16: 3 For one can be *b* than a thousand;
20: 2 *b* to admonish than to lose one's temper,
20:24 *B* a thief than an inveterate liar,
20:30 *B* the man who hides his folly than the one
23:27 nothing is *b* than the fear of the LORD,
24:19 than honey, *b* to have than the honeycomb.
29:13 *B* than a stout shield and a sturdy spear
29:22 *B* a poor man's fare under the shadow of
30:14 *B* a poor man strong and robust,
33:22 Far *b* that your children plead with you
37:14 *b* than seven watchmen in a lofty tower.
40:17 but *b* than either is finding a treasure.
40:18 preserve one's name, but *b* than either,
40:19 but *b* than either, a devoted wife;
40:20 music delight the soul, but *b* than either,
40:21 harp offer sweet melody, but *b* than either,
40:22 beauty delight the eye, but *b* than either,
40:23 are timely guides, but *b* than either,
40:24 but *b* than either, charity that rescues.
40:25 make one's way secure, but *b* than either,
40:26 build up confidence, but *b* than either,
40:28 the life of a beggar, *b* to die than to beg;
41:12 for it will stand by you *b* than precious
42:14 *B* a man's harshness than a woman's
Is 56: 5 and a name *B* than sons and daughters;
Lam 4: 9 *B* for those who perish by the sword than
Bar 6:58 much *b* to be a king displaying his valor,
6:67 by fleeing to shelter are *b* than they are.
6:72 The *b* for the just man who has no idols:
Ez 15: 2 the wood of the vine *b* than any other wood?
Dn 1:15 they looked healthier and *b* fed than any
1:20 he found them ten times *b* than all the
13:23 Yet it is *b* for me to fall in your power
Hos 2: 9 for it was *b* with me then than now."
4: 9 priests shall fare no *b* than the people:
Am 6: 2 Are you *b* than these kingdoms,
Jon 4: 3 for it is *b* for me to die than to live."
4: 8 saying, "I would be *b* off dead than alive."
Na 3: 8 Are you *b* than No-amon that was set among
Mt 5:29 *B* to lose part of your body than to have
5:30 *B* to lose part of your body than to have
8: 8 Just give an order and my boy will get *b*.
8:13 That very moment the boy got *b*.
15:28 That very moment her daughter got *b*.
18: 6 it would be *b* for anyone who leads astray
18: 8 *B* to enter life maimed or crippled than be
18: 9 *B* to enter life with one eye than be
19:10 between man and wife, it is *b* not to marry."
25: 9 You had *b* go to the dealers and buy
26:24 *B* for him if he had never been born."
Mk 9:42 But it would be *b* if anyone who leads
9:43 *B* for you to enter life maimed than to
9:45 *B* for you to enter life crippled than to
9:47 *B* for you to enter the kingdom of God with
14:21 It were *b* for him had he never been born."
Lk 5:39 He says, 'I find the old wine *b*.'"
10:42 Mary has chosen the *b* portion and she
17: 2 He would be *b* off thrown into the sea with
Jn 8:55 do not know him, I would be no *b* than you
11:50 Can you not see that it is *b* for you to
16: 7 It is much *b* for you that I go.
Acts 5:29 *B* for us to obey God than men!
17:11 were *b* disposed than those in Thessalonica,
Rom 14: 5 One man regards this day as *b* than that;
1Cor 3:18 in a worldly way, he had *b* become a fool.
7: 1 is *b* off having no relations with a woman.
7: 9 It is *b* to marry than to be on fire.
7:21 be *b* off making the most of your slavery.
7:38 the one who does not, will do *b*.
Phil 1:23 with Christ, for that is the far *b* thing;
2Tm 1:18 Christ in Ephesus you know even *b* than I.
4:15 Meanwhile, you too had *b* be on guard,
Heb 6: 9 are persuaded of *b* things in your regard,
7:19 But a *b* hope has supervened,
7:22 Jesus become the guarantee of a *b* covenant.
8: 6 a *b* covenant, founded on better promises.
9:23 themselves called for *b* sacrifices.
10:34 you had *b* and more permanent possessions.
11:16 But they were searching for a *b*,
11:35 in order to obtain a *b* resurrection.
11:40 God had made a *b* plan,
1Pt 3:17 it is *b* to do so for good deeds than for
2Pt 2:21 It would have been *b* for them not to have
Rv 7:14 to him, "Sir, you should know *b* than I."

BETWEEN (233)

Gn 3:15 *b* you and the woman, and between your
9:12 of the covenant *b* me and you and every
9:13 a sign of the covenant *b* me and the earth.
9:15 made *b* me and you and all living beings,
9:16 established *b* God and all living beings
9:17 established *b* me and all mortal creatures
10:12 as well as Resen, *b* Nineveh and Calah,
13: 3 to the place *b* Bethel and Ai where his
13: 7 There were quarrels *b* the herdsmen of
13: 8 no strife *b* you and me, or between your
15:17 flaming torch, which passed *b* those pieces.
16: 5 May the LORD decide *b* you and me!"
16:14 It is *b* Kadesh and Bered.
17: 2 *B* you and me I will establish my covenant,
17:11 be the mark of the covenant *b* you and me.
20: 1 Negeb, where he settled *b* Kadesh and Shur.
23:15 what is that *b* you and me,
26:28 agreement *b* our two sides —between you
30:36 a three days' journey *b* himself and Jacob,
31:37 and mine, and let them decide *b* us two.

31:44 the LORD shall be a witness *b* us."
31:48 be a witness from now on *b* you and me."
31:49 "May the LORD keep watch *b* you and me
31:50 is about, God will be witness *b* you and me."
31:51 stone that I have set up *b* you and me.
31:53 ancestral deities] maintain justice *b* us!"
32:17 but keep a space *b* one drove and the next."
49:10 from Judah, or the mace from *b* his legs,
49:14 a rawboned ass, crouching *b* the saddlebags.
Ex 8:19 distinction *b* my people and your people.
9: 4 But the LORD will distinguish *b* the
11: 7 *b* the Egyptians and the Israelites.
14: 2 before Pi-hahiroth, *b* Migdol and the sea.
14:20 so that it came *b* the camp of the
16: 1 desert of Sin, which is *b* Elim and Sinai,
18:16 to have me settle the matter *b* them
21:35 as well as the dead animal equally *b* them.
25:22 *b* the two cherubim on the ark of the
28:33 fine linen twined, with gold bells *b* them;
30:18 Place it *b* the meeting tent and the altar,
31:13 *b* you and me throughout the generations,
31:17 *B* me and the Israelites it is to be an
39:25 put *b* the pomegranates all around the hem
40: 7 the laver *b* the meeting tent and the altar,
40:30 the laver *b* the meeting tent and altar,
Lv 10:10 *b* what is sacred and what is profane,
10:10 *b* what is clean and what is unclean;
11:47 distinguish *b* the clean and the unclean,
11:47 *b* creatures that may be eaten and those
26:46 in the pact *b* himself and the Israelites.
27: 3 for persons *b* the ages of twenty and sixty,
27: 5 for persons *b* the ages of five and twenty,
27: 6 *b* the ages of one month and five years,
Nm 4: 3 Kohathites *b* thirty and fifty years of age;
4:23 the men *b* thirty and fifty years of age;
4:30 their men *b* thirty and fifty years of age;
4:35 the men *b* thirty and fifty years of age.
4:39 the men *b* thirty and fifty years of age.
4:47 of all the men *b* thirty and fifty years of
7:89 the commandments, from *b* the two cherubim;
11: 8 it *b* millstones or pound it in a mortar,
11:33 But while the meat was still *b* their teeth,
17:13 standing there *b* the living and the dead,
22:24 *b* vineyards with a stone wall on each side.
30:17 the relationship *b* a husband and his wife,
30:17 as well as *b* a father and his daughter
35:24 deciding the case *b* the slayer and the
Dt 1: 1 Arabah, opposite Suph, *b* Paran and Tophel,
2:14 Thirty-eight years had elapsed *b* our
5: 5 I stood *b* the LORD and you at that time,
Jos 3: 4 of two thousand cubits *b* you and the ark.
8:12 men and set them in ambush *b* Bethel and Ai,
13: 6 regions *b* Lebanon and Misrephoth-maim;
18:11 The territory allotted them lay *b* the
22:25 the Jordan as a boundary *b* you and us.
22:28 sacrifices, but to witness *b* you and us.'
23: 4 *b* the Jordan and the Great Sea in the west.
24: 7 darkness *b* your people and the Egyptians,
Jgs 3: 3 *b* Baal-hermon and the entrance to Hamath.
4: 5 situated *b* Ramah and Bethel in the
9:23 *b* Abimelech and the citizens of Shechem,
11:10 is witness *b* us that we will do as you say."
11:27 day *b* the Israelites and the Ammonites!"
13:25 Mahaneh-dan, which is *b* Zorah and Eshtaol.
15: 4 he tied *b* each pair of tails one of the
16:24 Then they stationed him *b* the columns.
16:31 of his father Manoah *b* Zorah and Eshtaol.
Ru 4:11 who *b* them built up the house of Israel.
1Sm 7:12 stone and placed it *b* Mizpah and Jeshanah;
7:14 there was peace *b* Israel and the Amorites.
14:42 "Cast lots *b* me and my son Jonathan."
17: 1 *b* Socoh and Azekah at Ephes-dammim.
17: 3 on an opposite hill, with a valley *b* them.
20: 3 live, there is but a step *b* me and death."
20: 8 servant because of the LORD's bond *b* us,
20:23 the LORD shall be *b* you and me forever."
20:42 LORD shall be *b* you and me, and between
24:13 The LORD will judge *b* me and you,
24:16 he will decide *b* me and you.
27: 8 peoples living in the land *b* Telam,
2Sm 3: 1 war *b* the house of Saul and that of David,
3: 6 war *b* the house of Saul and that of David,
18: 9 He hung *b* heaven and earth while the mule
18:24 Now David was sitting *b* the two gates,
19:23 "What has come *b* you and me,
19:36 Can I distinguish *b* good and bad?
21: 7 a bond *b* David and Saul's son Jonathan.
21:15 battle *b* the Philistines and Israel.
1Kgs 5:26 and there was peace *b* Hiram and Solomon,
7:29 the panels *b* the frames there were lions,
7:46 the clayey ground *b* Succoth and Zarethan.
14:30 constant warfare *b* Rehoboam and Jeroboam.
15: 6 There was war *b* Abijam and Jeroboam.
15:16 There was war *b* Asa and Baasha,
15:19 *b* you and me, as there was between your
15:32 [There was war *b* Asa and Baasha,
18: 6 Dividing the land to explore *b* them,
18:42 to the earth, and put his head *b* his knees.
22: 1 years passed without war *b* Aram and Israel.
22:34 of Israel *b* the joints of his breastplate.
2Kgs 2:11 chariot and flaming horses came *b* them,
9:24 his bow and shot Joram *b* the shoulders,
11:17 Then Jehoiada made a covenant *b* the LORD

11:17 covenant, *b* the king and the people.
16:14 from the space *b* the new altar and the
25: 4 by night through the gate *b* the two walls
1Chr 21:16 of the LORD standing *b* earth and heaven,
2Chr 4:17 in the clayey ground *b* Succoth and Zeredah.
12:15 war continually *b* Rehoboam and Jeroboam.
13: 2 There was war *b* Abijah and Jeroboam.
16: 3 *b* you and me, as there was between your
18:33 of Israel *b* the joints of his breastplate.
23:16 *b* himself and all the people and the king,
35:21 "What quarrel is *b* us, king of Judah?
Neh 3:32 *B* the upper chamber of the Angle and the
Jdt 3:10 he set up his camp *b* Geba and Scythopolis,
7:24 "God judge *b* you and us!
8: 3 in the field *b* Dothan and Balamon.
8:11 you interposed *b* God and yourselves this
1Mc 1: 9 Pact *b* Jews and Gentiles.
3:18 difference *b* deliverance by many or by few,
7:28 "Let there be no fight *b* me and you.
12: 3 friendship and alliance *b* you and them."
12:36 a high barrier *b* the citadel and the city,
13:40 Let there be peace *b* us."
16: 5 and *b* the two armies was a stream.
16: 7 into two corps and put his cavalry *b* them,
Jb 9:33 Would that there were an arbiter *b* us,
13:14 I will carry my flesh *b* my teeth,
16:21 and decide *b* a man and his neighbor.
19:20 I have escaped with my flesh *b* my teeth.
24:11 *B* the rows they press out the oil;
34: 4 let us learn *b* us what is good.
Prv 18:18 is decisive in a controversy *b* the mighty.
Wis 18: 2 for the sake of the difference *b* them.
Sir 13:17 Can there be peace *b* the hyena and the dog?
13:17 *b* the rich and the poor can there be peace?
18:26 *B* morning and evening the weather changes;
27: 2 peg driven *b* fitted stones, between buying
Is 2: 4 He shall judge *b* the nations,
5: 3 men of Judah, judge *b* me and my vineyard:
7:20 Assyria] the head, and the hair *b* the legs.
22:11 you made a reservoir *b* the two walls for
27:12 *b* the Euphrates and the Wadi of Egypt,
Jer 21: 8 I am giving you a choice *b* life and death.
34:18 cut in two, *b* those two parts they passed.
34:19 people, who passed *b* the parts of the calf,
38:12 tattered rags *b* your armpits and the ropes."
39: 4 Road through the gate *b* the two walls.
52: 7 by night through the gate *b* the two walls
Bar 6:54 they are like crows *b* heaven and earth.
Ez 4: 3 it up as an iron wall *b* you and the city.
8:16 temple, *b* the vestibule and the altar,
18: 8 judges fairly *b* a man and his opponent;
20:12 my sabbaths to be a sign *b* me and them,
20:20 *b* me and you to show that I am the LORD,
22:26 distinguish *b* the sacred and the profane,
22:26 the difference *b* the unclean and the clean;
34:17 judge *b* one sheep and another, between
34:20 will I judge *b* the fat and the lean sheep.
34:22 and I will judge *b* one sheep and another.
40: 7 pilasters *b* the cells measured five cubits.
40:19 it was one hundred cubits *b* them.
41: 8 *B* the side chambers of the temple and the
41:18 a palmtree *b* every two cherubim.
42: 5 than the closest chambers and those in *b*;
43: 8 next to mine, so that only a wall was *b* us,
44:23 distinguish *b* the sacred and the profane,
44:23 the difference *b* the clean and the unclean.
47:18 *b* the Hauran —toward Damascus—
48:22 the territory *b* the portions of Judah and
Dn 5:10 of the discussion *b* the king and his lords,
11:45 *b* the sea and the glorious holy mountain,
Hos 2: 4 her, her adultery from *b* her breasts,
Jl 2:17 *B* the porch and the altar let the priests,
Mi 4: 3 He shall judge *b* many peoples and impose
Zec 6: 1 chariots coming out from *b* two mountains;
6:13 and *b* the two of them there shall be
9: 7 and his abominations from *b* his teeth:
11:14 off the brotherhood *b* Judah and Israel.
Mal 2:14 witness *b* you and the wife of your youth,
3:18 the distinction *b* the just and the wicked;
3:18 *B* him who serves God,
Mt 18:15 his fault, but keep it *b* the two of you.
19:10 him, "If that is the case *b* man and wife,
23:35 *b* the temple building and the altar.
Mk 6:48 time was *b* three and six in the morning.
13:19 than any *b* God's work of creation and now,
Lk 11:51 his death *b* the altar and the sanctuary!
16:26 *B* you and us there is fixed a great abyss,
Jn 3:25 arose *b* John's disciples and a certain Jew.
Acts 1:26 Then they drew lots *b* the two men.
12: 6 trial, Peter was sleeping *b* two soldiers,
15: 2 controversy *b* them and Paul and Barnabas.
15: 9 He made no distinction *b* them and us,
23: 7 a dispute arose *b* Pharisees and Sadducees
Rom 10:12 there is no difference *b* Jew and Greek;
1Cor 6: 5 *b* one member of the church and another?
2Cor 6:15 What accord is there *b* Christ and Belial,
6:15 what common lot *b* believer and unbeliever?
6:16 there is *b* the temple of God and idols.
1Tm 2: 5 One also is the mediator *b* God and men,
2Pt 3: 5 of the waters and standing *b* the waters,
Rv 5: 6 *b* the throne with the four living creatures
9:13 I heard a voice coming from *b* the horns

BEVELED (1)

1Kgs 6:31 the doorframes had *b* posts.

BEWAILED (2)

1Mc 9:20 All Israel *b* him in great grief.
13:26 All Israel *b* him with solemn lamentation,

BEWAILING (3)

Ps(s) 35:14 like one *b* a mother, I was bowed down
Mt 2:18 Rachel *b* her children; no comfort for her
Acts 8: 2 Stephen, *b* him loudly as they did so,

BEWARE (14)

Eccl 12:12 As to more than these, my son, *b*.
Sir 22:13 *B* of him lest you have trouble and be
Jer 5:15 *B*, I will bring against you a nation from
6:25 into the street, *B* of the enemy's sword;
7:32 Therefore, *b!* days will come, says the Lord
13:13 *B!* I am filling with drunkenness
21:13 *B!* I am against you.
51:25 *B!* I am against you,
Am 2:13 *B*, I will crush you into the ground as a
6:14 *B*, I am raising up against you,
Lk 20:46 *B* of the scribes, who like to parade
Phil 3: 2 *B* of unbelieving dogs.
Rv 9:12 The first woe is past, but *b!*
11:14 The second woe is past, but *b!*

BEWILDERED (5)

2Mc 10:30 at the enemy, who were *b* and blinded,
Sir 18: 5 beginning, and when he stops he is still *b*.
Is 21: 3 I am too *b* to hear, too dismayed to look.
Jl 1:18 The herds of cattle are *b!*
Mk 16: 8 out and fled from the tomb *b* and trembling;

BEYOND (128)

Gn 2:10 *b* there it divides and becomes four
31:52 I pass *b* this mound into your territory,
31:52 territory, nor may you pass *b* it into mine.
35:21 on and pitched his tent *b* Migdal-eder.
41:49 stopped measuring it, for it was *b* measure.
50:10 at Goren-ha-atad, which is *b* the Jordan,
50:11 It is *b* the Jordan.
Ex 12:10 None of it must be kept *b* the next morning;
18:11 that the LORD is a deity great *b* any other;
38:15 other side, *b* the entrance of the court,
Lv 10: 7 not you go *b* the entry of the meeting tent,
15:25 her flow continues *b* the ordinary period,
Nm 11:23 Moses, "Is this *b* the LORD's reach?
35:14 three *b* the Jordan,
35:27 finds him *b* these bounds and kills him,
Dt 1: 1 to all Israel *b* the Jordan [in the desert,
1: 5 the law in the land of Moab *b* the Jordan,
3: 8 the two kings of the Amorites *b* the Jordan
3:25 over and see this good land *b* the Jordan,
4:46 come out of Egypt and were *b* the Jordan
11:30 [Are they not *b* the Jordan,
Jos 1:14 the land Moses gave you here *b* the Jordan.
2:10 the two kings of the Amorites *b* the Jordan,
9:10 the two kings of the Amorites *b* the Jordan,
13:32 of Moab, *b* the Jordan east of Jericho.
14: 3 had already given a heritage *b* the Jordan;
17: 5 the land of Gilead and Bashan *b* the Jordan,
20: 8 And *b* the Jordan east of Jericho they
22: 4 may now return to your tents *b* the Jordan;
24: 2 dwelt *b* the River and served other gods.
24: 3 Abraham from the region *b* the River
24:14 fathers served *b* the River and in Egypt,
24:15 the gods your fathers served *b* the River
Jgs 1:36 from the Akrabbim pass to Sela and *b*.
5: 7 Gone was freedom *b* the walls,
5:17 Gilead, *b* the Jordan,
7:25 of Oreb and Zeeb to Gideon *b* the Jordan.
10: 8 in the Amorite land *b* the Jordan in Gilead.
1Sm 7:11 Philistines, harrying them down *b* Beth-car.
14:15 so that the panic was *b* human endurance.
20:22 say to the boy, 'Look, the arrow is *b* you,'
20:36 arrow *b* him in the direction of the city.
24:16 my part, and grant me justice *b* your reach!"
2Sm 10:16 and enlisted Arameans from *b* the Euphrates.
16: 1 had gone a little *b* the top when Ziba,
20: 5 delayed *b* the time set for him by David.
1Kgs 4:12 in Taanach and Megiddo, and *b* Jokmeam,
8: 8 however, they could not be seen *b*.
14:15 their fathers, scattering them *b* the River,
16:25 the LORD's sight *b* any of his predecessors.
1Chr 16:25 and awesome is he, *b* all gods.
2Chr 5: 9 however, they could not be seen *b*.
Jdt 1:10 the land of Goshen, Tanis, Memphis and *b*,
15: 5 even *b* Damascus and its territory.
1Mc 5:39 to help them, and have camped *b* the stream,
Jb 8:16 and *b* his garden his shoots go forth;
9:10 finding out, marvelous things *b* reckoning.
36:26 Lo, God is great *b* our knowledge;
37: 5 He does great things *b* our knowing;
Ps(s) 38: 5 are like a heavy burden, *b* my strength.
40:13 For all about me are evils *b* reckoning;
89: 8 is great and awesome *b* all round about him.
96: 4 awesome is he, *b* all gods.
Prv 6:15 in an instant he is crushed *b* cure.

BEYOND (cont.)

17:26 man, but *b* reason to scourge princes.
24: 9 *B* intrigue and folly and sin,
29: 1 rebuke will be crushed suddenly *b* cure.
31:10 a worthy wife, her value is far *b* pearls.
Eccl 1:16 *b* all who were before me in Jerusalem,
7:23 but it was *b* me.
Wis 7:10 *B* health and comeliness I loved her,
7:24 For Wisdom is mobile *b* all motion,
16:19 fire blazed *b* its strength so as to
Sir 3:20 into things *b* your strength search not.
3:22 when shown things *b* human understanding.
6:15 A faithful friend is *b* price,
8:13 Go not surety *b* your means;
25:11 its possessor is *b* compare.
36:23 is kindly, his lot is *b* that of mortal men.
43:31 though he is still *b* your power to praise;
43:34 *B* these, many things lie hid;
48:13 Nothing was *b* his power;
49:16 but *b* that of any living being was the
Is 18: 1 buzzing insects, *b* the rivers of Ethiopia,
30:14 like a potter's jar smashed *b* rescue,
40:28 weary, and his knowledge is *b* scrutiny.
52:14 so marred was his look *b* that of man,
52:14 man, and his appearance *b* that of mortals
Jer 17: 9 than all else is the human heart, *b* remedy;
22:19 and cast out *b* the gates of Jerusalem.
25:22 of Sidon, and of the shores *b* the sea;
33: 3 you things great *b* reach of your knowledge.
48:29 heard of the pride of Moab, pride *b* bounds:
Ez 9: 9 of the house of Israel are great *b* measure;
28: 3 Daniel, there is no secret that is *b* you.
41: 3 Then he went in *b* and measured the
41: 4 He measured the space *b* the nave,
Dn 3:37 we are reduced, O Lord, *b* any other nation,
Am 5:27 For I will exile you *b* Damascus,
Zep 3:10 From *b* the rivers of Ethiopia and as far
Mal 1: 5 is the LORD, even *b* the land of Israel."
Mt 4:15 of Naphtali along the sea *b* the Jordan,
5:37 Anything *b* that is from the evil one.
14:33 declaring, *B* doubt you are the Son of God!"
Mk 7:37 Their amazement went *b* all bounds:
Lk 12:26 If the smallest things are *b* your power,
Acts 2:36 house of Israel know *b* any doubt that God
7:43 For that I will exile you *b* Babylon.'
15:28 burden *b* that which is strictly necessary,
19:36 Since this is *b* question,
1Cor 1:16 *B* that, I am not aware of having baptized
4: 6 learn from us not to go *b* what is set down,
10:13 will not let you be tested *b* your strength.
2Cor 1: 8 we were crushed *b* our strength,
4:17 eternal weight of glory *b* all comparison.
7:13 *B* this consolation, we have rejoiced
8: 3 indeed I can testify even *b* their means
8: 5 *B* our hopes they first gave themselves to
8:12 accord with one's means, not go *b* them.
10:16 we hope to preach the gospel even *b* your
Gal 1:14 observance far *b* most of my contemporaries,
Phil 2:15 children of God *b* reproach in the midst of
4: 7 own peace, which is *b* all understanding,
Col 1:27 the glory *b* price which this mystery brings
Heb 6: 1 go *b* the initial teaching about Christ and
6:19 extends *b* the veil through which Jesus,
Jas 1:13 Surely God, who is *b* the grasp of evil,
1Pt 1:19 or gold, but by Christ's blood *b* all price:

BEZAI (3)

Ezr 2:17 sons of *B*, three hundred and twenty-three;
Neh 7:23 sons of *B*, three hundred and twenty-four;
10:19 Ater, Hezekiah, Azzur, Hodiah, Hashum, *B*,

BEZALEL (9)

Ex 31: 2 said to Moses, "See, I have chosen *B*,
35:30 Israelites, "See, the LORD has chosen *B*,
36: 1 *B*, therefore, will set to work
36: 2 Moses then called *B* and Oholiab and all
37: 1 *B* made the ark of acacia wood,
38:22 However, it was *B*, son of Uri, son of Hur,
1Chr 2:20 of Uri, and Uri became the father of *B*.
2Chr 1: 5 The bronze altar made by *B*,
Ezr 10:30 Chelal, Benaiah, Maaseiah, Mattaniah, *B*,

BEZEK (3)

Jgs 1: 4 and they slew ten thousand of them in *B*.
1: 5 It was in *B* that they came upon Adonibezek
1Sm 11: 8 When he reviewed them in *B*,

BEZER (5)

Dt 4:43 *B* in the desert,
Jos 20: 8 they designated *B* on the open tableland
21:36 for homicides at *B* with its pasture lands,
1Chr 6:63 *B* in the desert with its pasture lands,
7:37 Suah, Harnepher, Shual, Beri, Imrah, *B*,

BICHRI (8)

2Sm 20: 1 from Benjamin named Sheba, the son of *B*,
20: 2 Israelites left David for Sheba, son of *B*.
20: 6 "Sheba, son of *B*,
20: 7 to campaign in pursuit of Sheba, son of *B*.
20:10 brother Abishai pursued Sheba, son of *B*.
20:13 after Joab in pursuit of Sheba, son of *B*.
20:21 A man named Sheba, son of *B*,
20:22 they cut off the head of Sheba, son of *B*,

BICHRITES (1)

2Sm 20:14 Then all the *B* assembled and they too

BICKERING (4)

Dt 1:12 burden that you are, along with your *b*?
Rom 1:29 greed, ill will, envy, murder, *b*,
Gal 5:20 idolatry, sorcery, hostilities, *b*,
1Tm 6: 5 the *b* of men with twisted minds who have

BID (9)

2Sm 13:25 refused to go and began to *b* him good-bye.
Tb 3:13 *B* me to depart from the earth,
Ps(s) 61: 8 *b* kindness and faithfulness preserve him.
Wis 9: 8 You have *b* me build a temple on your holy
Dn 11: 6 But her *b* for power shall fail:
Mt 4: 6 'He will *b* his angels take care of you;
Lk 4:10 it, 'He will *b* his angels watch over you';
7:14 He said, "Young man, I *b* you get up."
21:14 I *b* you resolve not to worry about your

BIDDEN (1)

Nm 9:23 the LORD, as he had *b* them through Moses.

BIDDING (21)

Nm 4:41 took, together with Aaron, at the LORD's *b*.
4:49 eighty, According to the LORD's *b* to Moses,
9:18 the *b* of the LORD the Israelites moved on,
9:18 moved on, and at his *b* they encamped.
9:20 the *b* of the LORD that they stayed in camp,
9:20 and it was at his *b* that they departed.
9:23 at the *b* of the LORD that they encamped,
9:23 encamped, and at his *b* that they set out;
10:13 camp at the *b* of the LORD through Moses,
Ru 4: 4 you, *b* you before those here present,
2Sm 24:19 Following Gad's *b*, David went up
Tb 10:11 *B* them farewell, he let them go.
Ps(s) 103:20 you mighty in strength, who do his *b*,
Prv 6:20 Observe, my son, your father's *b*,
6:23 the *b* is a lamp, and the teaching a light,
Sir 39:31 In doing his *b* they rejoice,
43:27 and at his *b* accomplishes his will.
Jer 4:12 this wind from the heights come at my *b*;
Ez 21:27 *b* him to give the order for slaying,
Jl 2:11 his camp, yes, mighty, and it does his *b*.
Jon 3: 3 went to Nineveh, according to the LORD's *b*.

BIDE (1)

Tb 3:15 relative whom I might *b* my time to marry.

BIDED (1)

Jb 32: 4 he, Elihu *b* his time before addressing Job.

BIDES (1)

Sir 5: 4 for the LORD *b* his time.

BIDING (3)

Jdt 12:16 for he had been *b* his time to seduce her
Prv 29:11 but by *b* his time, the wise man calms it.
Sir 20: 5 another is silent, *b* his time.

BIDKAR (1)

2Kgs 9:25 Then Jehu said to his adjutant *B*,

BIER (1)

2Sm 3:31 King David himself followed the *b*.

BIG (15)

Lv 8:23 hand, and on the *b* toe of his right foot.
8:24 and on the *b* toes of their right feet.
14:14 hand, and the *b* toe of his right foot.
14:17 hand, and the *b* toe of his right foot,
14:25 hand, and on the *b* toe of his right foot.
14:28 hand, and the *b* toe of his right foot,
Jgs 1: 6 him, cut off his thumbs and his *b* toes.
1: 7 with their thumbs and *b* toes cut off,
1Mc 13:29 pyramids he devised a setting of *b* columns,
Sg 4: 2 the washing, All of them *b* with twins,
6: 6 from the washing, All of them *b* with twins,
Mt 13:32 It becomes so *b* a shrub that the birds of
Mk 4:32 with branches *b* enough for the birds of
Acts 10:11 come down that looked like a *b* canvas.
11: 5 An object like a *b* canvas came down;

BIGGER (1)

1Mc 6:43 saw one of the beasts *b* than any of the

BIGTHA (1)

Est 1:10 he instructed Mehuman, Biztha, Harbona, *B*,

BIGVAI (6)

Ezr 2: 2 Reelaiah, Mordecai, Bilshan, Mispereth, *B*,
2:14 sons of *B*, two thousand and fifty-six;
8:14 of the sons of *B*, Uthai, son of Zakkur,
Neh 7: 7 Nahamani, Mordecai, Bilshan, Mispereth, *B*,
7:19 sons of *B*, two thousand and sixty-seven;
10:17 Bani, Bunni, Azgad, Bebai, Adonijah, *B*,

BILDAD (5)

Jb 2:11 Eliphaz from Teman, *B* from Shuh,
8: 1 *B* the Shuhite spoke out and said:
18: 1 Then *B* the Shuhite replied and said:
25: 1 Then *B* the Shuhite answered and said:
42: 9 Eliphaz the Temanite, and *B* the Shuhite,

BILGAH (4)

1Chr 24:14 fourteenth to Ishbaal, the fifteenth to *B*,
Neh 12: 5 Ginnethon, Abijah, Mijamin, Maadiah, *B*,
12:18 for *B*, Shammua;
2Mc 3: 4 Simon, of the priestly course of *B*,

BILGAI (1)

Neh 10: 9 Meshullam, Abijah, Mijamin, Maaziah, *B*,

BILHAH (11)

Gn 29:29 (Laban assigned his slave girl *B* to his
30: 3 She replied, "Here is my maidservant *B*.
30: 4 gave him her maidservant *B* as a consort,
30: 5 When *B* conceived and bore a son,
30: 7 *B* conceived again and bore a second son,
35:22 in that region, Reuben went and lay with *B*,
35:25 the sons of Rachel's maid *B*:
37: 2 sons of his father's wives *B* and Zilpah,
46:25 These were the sons of *B*,
1Chr 4:29 in Beer-sheba, Moladah, Hazar-shual, *B*,
7:13 These were descendants of *B*.

BILHAN (4)

Gn 36:27 The descendants of Ezer were *B*,
1Chr 1:42 The sons of Ezer were *B*,
7:10 The sons of Jediael: *B*.
7:10 The sons of *B* were Jeush,

BILIOUSNESS (1)

Sir 37:29 with overeating, and gluttony brings on *b*.

BILL (5)

Gn 8:11 in its *b* was a plucked-off olive leaf!
Dt 24: 1 out a *b* of divorce and hands it to her,
24: 3 by handing her a written *b* of divorce;
Is 50: 1 Where is the *b* of divorce with which I
Jer 3: 8 I put her away and gave her a *b* of divorce,

BILLOWING (2)

Jer 46: 7 like the Nile, like rivers of *b* waters?
46: 8 like the Nile, like rivers of *b* waters.

BILLOWS (5)

Ps(s) 42: 8 All your breakers and your *b* pass over me.
88: 8 and with all your *b* you overwhelm me.
107:29 breeze, and the *b* of the sea were stilled;
Jer 5:22 though its *b* roar, they cannot pass.
Jon 2: 4 your breakers and your *b* passed over me.

BILSHAN (2)

Ezr 2: 2 Nehemiah, Seraiah, Reelaiah, Mordecai, *B*,
Neh 7: 7 Azariah, Raamiah, Nahamani, Mordecai, *B*,

BIMHAL (1)

1Chr 7:33 The sons of Japhlet were Pasach, *B*,

BIN (2)

Dt 28: 5 be your grain *b* and your kneading bowl!
28:17 be your grain *b* and your kneading bowl!

BIND (24)

Ex 28:28 Violet ribbons shall *b* the rings of the
Dt 6: 8 *B* them at your wrist as a sign and let
11:18 *B* them at your wrist as a sign,
Jgs 15:13 only *b* you and deliver you over to them."
16: 5 and *b* him so as to keep him helpless.
16: 7 "If they *b* me with seven fresh bowstrings
16:11 "If they *b* me tight with new ropes,
Jdt 8:30 and to *b* ourselves by an oath that we
Jb 12:18 but a waistcloth to *b* the king's own loins.
39:10 Will a rope *b* him in the furrow,
Ps(s) 149: 8 To *b* their kings with chains,
Prv 3: 3 *b* them around your neck;
7: 3 *B* them on your fingers,
Jer 40: 4 today from the fetters that *b* your hands;
Ez 3:25 put cords upon you and *b* you with them,
4: 8 I will *b* you with cords so that you cannot
24:17 no lament for the dead, *b* on your turban,
34: 4 nor heal the sick nor *b* up the injured.
34:16 I will bring back, the injured I will *b* up,
Dn 3:20 the strongest men in his army *b* Shadrach,
Hos 6: 1 he has struck us, but he will *b* our wounds.
Mt 22:13 *B* him hand and foot and throw him out into
23: 4 They *b* up heavy loads,
Acts 21:11 'This is how the Jews in Jerusalem will *b*

BINDING (6)

Gn 37: 7 There we were, *b* sheaves in the field,
Ru 4: 7 *b* a contract of redemption or exchange,
1Chr 16:15 which he made *b* for a thousand generations
Ps(s) 105: 8 which he made *b* for a thousand generations
Ez 17:13 whom he made a covenant, *b* him under oath,
Eph 4: 3 as its origin and peace as its *b* force.

BINDS (10)

Nm 30: 3 When a man makes a vow to the LORD or *b*
30: 4 vow to the LORD, or *b* herself to a pledge,
30:10 any pledge to which such a woman *b* herself,
30:11 a vow or *b* herself under oath to a pledge,
Jb 5:18 For he wounds, but he *b* up;
26: 8 He *b* up the waters in his clouds,
Ps(s) 147: 3 the brokenhearted and *b* up their wounds.
Is 30:26 day the LORD *b* up the wounds of his people,
Rom 13: 8 the debt that *b* us to love one another.
Col 3:14 *b* the rest together and makes them perfect.

BINEA (2)

1Chr 8:37 Moza became the father of *B*,
9:43 Moza became the father of *B*,

BINNUI (13)

Ezr 2:40 sons of Jeshua, Kadmiel, *B*,
3: 9 his sons and brethren, with Kadmiel and *B*,
8:33 son of Jeshua, and Noadiah, son of *B*.
10:30 Benaiah, Maaseiah, Mattaniah, Bezalel, *B*,
10:38 Mattenai, and Jaasu; of the sons of *B*:
Neh 3:18 *B*, son of Henadad,
3:24 After him, *B*, son of Henadad,
7:15 sons of *B*, six hundred and forty-eight;
7:43 sons of Jeshua, Kadmiel, *B*,
9: 4 platform of the Levites were Jeshua, *B*,
10:10 *B*, of the sons of Henadad;
12: 8 The Levites were Jeshua, *B*,
12:24 were Hashabiah, Sherebiah, Jeshua, *B*,

BINS (1)

Lk 12:18 pull down my grain *b* and build larger ones.

BIRD (42)

Gn 7: 3 likewise, of every clean *b* of the air,
7:14 thing of the earth, and every kind of *b*.
8:20 from every clean animal and every clean *b*,
Lv 1:14 he offers a *b* as a holocaust to the LORD,
1:17 having split the *b* down the middle without
5:10 The other *b* shall be offered as a
7:26 of any blood, be it of *b* or of animal.
14: 6 Taking the living *b* with the cedar wood,
14: 6 the *b* that was slain over the spring water,
14: 7 the living *b* fly away over the countryside.
14:51 scarlet yarn, together with the living *b*,
14:51 blood of the slain *b* and the spring water,
14:52 the spring water, along with the living *b*,
14:53 He shall then let the living *b* fly away
17:13 catches an animal or a *b* that may be eaten,
20:25 any beast or *b* or of any swarming creature
Dt 4:17 earth or of any *b* that flies in the sky,
22: 6 and the mother *b* is sitting on them,
22: 6 away the mother *b* along with her brood;
Jb 28: 7 The path to it no *b* of prey knows,
40:29 Can you play with him, as with a *b*?
Ps(s) 11: 1 say to me, "Flee to the mountain like a *b*!
124: 7 rescued like a *b* from the fowlers' snare;
Prv 1:17 a net is spread before the eyes of any *b*—
6: 5 or as a *b* from the hand of the fowler.
7:23 Like a *b* that rushes into a snare,
27: 8 Like a *b* that is far from its nest is a
Eccl 12: 4 When one waits for the chirp of a *b*,
Wis 5:11 Or like a *b* flying through the air;
19:11 later they saw also a new kind of *b* when,
Sir 11:30 Though he seem like a *b* confined in a cage,
27:19 Like a *b* released from the hand,
Is 46:11 I call from the east a *b* of prey,
Lam 3:52 without cause hunted me down like a *b*;
Bar 6:70 a garden on which perches every kind of *b*,
Dn 4:30 eagle, and his nails like the claws of a *b*.
7: 6 its back were four wings like those of a *b*,
Hos 9:11 The glory of Ephraim flies away like a *b*:
Am 3: 5 Is a *b* brought to earth by a snare when
Mt 23:37 mother *b* gathers her young under her wings,
Lk 13:34 *b* collects her young under her wings,
Rv 18: 2 a cage for every filthy and disgusting *b*:

BIRD-CAGE (1)

Jer 5:27 as full of treachery as a *b* is of birds;

BIRDS (108)

Gn 1:20 let *b* fly beneath the dome of the sky."
1:21 the water teems, and all kinds of winged *b*.
1:22 and let the *b* multiply on the earth."
1:26 over the fish of the sea, the *b* of the air,
1:28 over the fish of the sea, the *b* of the air,
1:30 animals of the land, all the *b* of the air,
2:19 wild animals and various *b* of the air,
2:20 to all the cattle, all the *b* of the air,
6: 7 the creeping things and the *b* of the air,
6:20 Of all kinds of *b*,
7: 3 and a female, and of all the unclean *b*,
7: 8 clean animals and the unclean, of the *b*,
7:21 *b*, cattle, wild animals,
7:23 the creeping things and the *b* of the air;
8:17 be they *b* or animals or creeping things of
8:19 all the animals, wild and tame, all the *b*,
9: 2 of the earth and all the *b* of the air,
9:10 *b*, and the various tame and wild animals
15:10 but the *b* he did not cut up.
15:11 *B* of prey swooped down on the carcasses,
40:17 but the *b* were pecking at them out of the
40:19 *b* will be pecking the flesh from your body."
Lv 11:13 "Of the *b*, these you shall loathe and,
11:46 "This is the law for animals and *b* and
14: 4 to be purified, to get two live, clean *b*,
14: 5 to slay one of the *b* over an earthen vessel
14:49 To purify the house, he shall take two *b*,
14:50 One of the *b* he shall slay over an earthen
14:52 with the *b* blood and the spring water,
20:25 unclean, and the clean *b* from the unclean,
Dt 14:11 "You may eat all clean *b*.
22: 6 a *b* nest with young birds or eggs in it,
22: 6 a bird's nest with young *b* or eggs in it,
28:26 will become food for all the *b* of the air
1Sm 17:44 *b* of the air and the beasts of the field."
17:46 *b* of the air and the beasts of the field;
2Sm 21:10 *b* of the sky from settling on them by day,
1Kgs 5:13 of the wall, and he spoke about beasts, *b*,
14:11 he will be devoured by the *b* of the sky.
16: 4 he shall be devoured by the *b* of the sky."
21:24 field, the *b* of the sky will devour him."
Tb 2:10 there were *b* perched on the wall above me,
Jdt 11: 7 beasts and the cattle and the *b* of the air,
Est E:24 even shunned by wild beasts and *b* forever."
2Mc 15:33 he would feed it piecemeal to the *b*
Jb 12: 7 you, and the *b* of the air to tell you;
28:21 from the *b* of the air it is concealed.
35:11 us wise rather than the *b* of the heavens?"
Ps(s) 8: 9 the beasts of the field, The *b* of the air,
50:11 I know all the *b* of the air,
79: 2 your servants as food to the *b* of heaven,
104:12 Beside them the *b* of heaven dwell;
104:17 In them the *b* build their nests;
Eccl 9:12 the fatal net, or *b* trapped in the snare;
10:20 the *b* of the air may carry your voice,
Wis 17:18 song of *b* in the spreading branches,
Sir 17: 4 and gives him rule over beasts and *b*.
22:20 He who throws stones at *b* drives them away,
27: 9 *B* nest with their own kind,
43:18 He sprinkles the snow like fluttering *b*;
Is 16: 2 Like flushed *b*, like startled nestlings,
18: 6 all be left to the mountain *b* of prey,
18: 6 The *b* of prey shall summer on them and on
31: 5 Like hovering *b*,
Jer 4:25 even the *b* of the air had flown away!
5:27 full of treachery as a bird-cage is of *b*;
7:33 food for the *b* of the sky and for the beasts
9: 9 *B* of the air as well as beasts,
12: 4 who dwell in it beasts and *b* disappear,
15: 3 the *b* of the sky and the beasts of the
16: 4 *b* of the sky and the beasts of the field.
19: 7 *b* of the sky and the beasts of the field.
34:20 *b* of the air and the beasts of the field.
Bar 3:17 and made sport of the *b* of the heavens:
6:21 and cats as well as *b*.
Ez 17:23 *B* of every kind shall dwell beneath it,
29: 5 and the *b* of the air I give you as food,
31: 6 In its boughs nested all the *b* of the air,
31:13 fallen trunk rested all the *b* of the air,
32: 4 have all the *b* of the air alight on you,
38:20 the fish of the sea and the *b* of the air,
39: 4 To *b* of prey of every kind and to the wild
39:17 *b* of every kind and to all the wild beasts:
Dn 2:38 men, wild beasts, and *b* of the air,
3:80 All you *b* of the air,
4: 9 in its branches the *b* of the air nested;
4:11 flee its shade, and the *b* its branches.
4:18 in whose branches the *b* of the air dwelt
Hos 2:20 beasts of the field, With the *b* of the air,
4: 3 The beasts of the field, the *b* of the air,
7:12 like *b* in the air I will bring them down,
Zep 1: 3 beast, I will sweep away the *b* of the sky,
Mt 6:26 "Look at the *b* in the sky.
8:20 have lairs, the *b* in the sky have nests,
13: 4 on a footpath, where *b* came and ate it up.
13:32 It becomes so big a shrub that the *b* of
Mk 4: 4 where the *b* came along and ate it.
4:32 *b* of the sky to build nests in its shade."
Lk 8: 5 walked on and the *b* of the air ate it up.
9:58 have lairs, the *b* of the sky have nests,
12:24 much more important you are than the *b*!
13:19 the *b* of the air nested in its branches."
Acts 10:12 creatures and reptiles and *b* of the sky.
11: 6 wild beasts and reptiles, and *b* of the sky.
Rom 1:23 God for images representing mortal man, *b*,
1Cor 15:39 *B* are of their kind, fish are of theirs.
Rv 19:17 voice to all the *b* flying in midheaven.
19:21 and all the *b* gorged themselves on the

BIRSHA (1)

Gn 14: 2 on Bera king of Sodom, *B* king of Gomorrah,

BIRTH (132)

Gn 4:20 Adah, gave *b* to Jabal,
4:22 Zillah, on her part, gave *b* to Tubalcain,
4:25 she gave *b* to a son whom she called Seth.
5: 4 eight hundred years after the *b* of Seth,
5: 7 and seven years after the *b* of Enosh,
5:10 and fifteen years after the *b* of Kenan,
5:13 and forty years after the *b* of Mahalalel,
5:16 and thirty years after the *b* of Jared,
5:19 eight hundred years after the *b* of Enoch,
5:22 hundred years after the *b* of Methuselah,
5:26 and eighty-two years after the *b* of Lamech,
5:30 and ninety-five years after the *b* of Noah,
11:11 hundred years after the *b* of Arpachshad,
11:13 and three years after the *b* of Shelah,
11:15 and three years after the *b* of Eber,
11:17 and thirty years after the *b* of Peleg,
11:19 hundred and nine years after the *b* of Reu,
11:21 and seven years after the *b* of Serug,
11:23 two hundred years after the *b* of Nahor,
11:25 and nineteen years after the *b* of Terah,
17:17 Or can Sarah give *b* at ninety?"
19:37 one gave *b* to a son whom she named Moab,
19:38 The younger one, too, gave *b* to a son,
25:13 sons, listed in the order of their *b*:
30: 3 with her, and let her give *b* on my knees,
30:21 Finally, she gave *b* to a daughter,
30:25 After Rachel gave *b* to Joseph,
31:13 this land and return to the land of your *b*.'"
32:10 me, O LORD, 'Go back to the land of your *b*,
38:28 While she was giving *b*,
48:15 has been my shepherd from my *b* to this day,
Ex 1:16 the Hebrew women and see them giving *b*,
1:19 and give *b* before the midwife arrives."
28:10 the other stone, in the order of their *b*.
Lv 12: 2 a woman has conceived and gives *b* to a boy,
12: 5 If she gives *b* to a girl,
12: 7 woman who gives *b* to a boy or a girl child.
Nm 11:12 or was it I who gave them *b*,
Dt 32:18 you, You forgot the God who gave you *b*.
Ru 2:11 and your mother and the land of your *b*,
1Sm 2:21 *b* to three more sons and two daughters,
4:19 with child and at the point of giving *b*.
4:19 seized with the pangs of labor, and gave *b*.
4:20 You have given *b* to a son."
1Kgs 3:17 gave *b* in the house while she was present.
3:18 after I gave *b* this woman also gave birth.
2Kgs 4:17 following year she had given *b* to a son,
19: 3 Children are at the point of *b*,
2Mc 5:22 at Jerusalem, Philip, a Phrygian by *b*,
14:42 suffer outrages unworthy of his noble *b*.
Jb 3:11 Why did I not perish at *b*,
3:16 was I not buried away like an untimely *b*,
15:35 they give *b* to failure.
31:15 not the same One fashion us before our *b*?
38:29 who gives the hoarfrost its *b* in the skies,
39: 1 you know about the *b* of the mountain goats,
39: 1 goats, watch for the *b* pangs of the hinds,
Ps(s) 22:11 To you I was committed at *b*,
49: 3 in the world, Of lowly *b* or high degree,
58: 4 astray from *b* have the liars gone.
58: 9 like an untimely *b* that never sees the sun.
71: 6 On you I depend from *b*;
110: 3 is princely power in the day of your *b*,
Eccl 4:14 since even in his royalty he was poor at *b*.
7: 1 and the day of death than the day of *b*.
10:17 are you, O land, whose king is of noble *b*,
Wis 7: 5 For no king has any different origin or *b*,
Sir 11:16 were formed with sinners from their *b*,
19:10 in labor, like a woman giving *b* to a child.
23:14 been born or cursing the day of your *b*.
Is 23: 4 "I have not been in labor, nor given *b*,
26:17 give *b* writhes and cries out in her pains,
26:18 and writhed in pain, giving *b* to wind;
26:19 of light, and the land of shades gives *b*.
37: 3 Children are at the point of *b*,
45:10 or a woman, "What are you giving *b* to?"
46: 3 house of Israel, My burden since your *b*,
48: 8 a rebel you were called from *b*.
49: 1 The LORD called me from *b*,
51: 2 your father, and to Sarah, who gave you *b*;
66: 7 Before she comes to labor, she gives *b*;
66: 8 in labor when she gives *b* to her children.
66: 9 Shall I bring a mother to the point of *b*,
Jer 2:14 Is Israel a slave, a bondman by *b*?
2:27 father," and to a stone, "You gave me *b*."
13:21 seize you like those of a woman giving *b*?
15:10 Woe to me, mother, that you gave me *b*!
16: 3 place, the mothers who will give them *b*,
20:14 day my mother gave me *b* never be blessed!
22:10 never again will he see the land of his *b*.
46:16 to our own people, To the land of our *b*
Ez 16: 3 origin and *b* you are of the land of Canaan;
16: 4 As for your *b*, the day you were born
31: 6 branches all beasts of the field gave *b*,
Hos 2: 5 naked, leaving her as on the day of her *b*;
9:11 no *b*, no carrying in the womb,
13:13 The *b* pangs shall come for him,
Mi 5: 2 time when she who is to give *b* has borne,
Mt 1:18 is how the *b* of Jesus Christ came about.
1:23 shall be with child and give *b* to a son,
2: 1 After Jesus' *b* in Bethlehem of Judea

BIRTH (cont.)

19:12 are incapable of sexual activity from *b*;
24: 8 These are the early stages of the *b* pangs.
Mk 7:26 a Syro-Phoenician by *b*—
Lk 1:14 be yours, and many will rejoice at his *b*;
1:57 for delivery arrived, she gave *b* to a son.
2: 7 She gave *b* to her first-born son and
19:12 "A man of noble *b* went to a faraway
Jn 9: 1 he saw a man who had been blind from *b*.
9:19 so, do you attest that he was blind at *b*?
9:20 is our son, and we know he was blind at *b*.
9:32 ever gave sight to a person blind from *b*.
9:34 "You are steeped in sin from your *b*,
Acts 3: 2 a man crippled from *b* was being carried in.
14: 8 there was a man who was lame from *b*;
22:28 said Paul, "but I am a citizen by *b*!"
Gal 2:15 We are Jews by *b*,
4:29 the one whose *b* was in the realm of spirit,
Ti 3: 5 of new *b* and renewal by the Holy Spirit.
Heb 11:23 hid him for three months after his *b*,
Jas 1:15 passion has conceived, it gives *b* to sin,
1:18 He wills to bring us to *b* with a word
3: 6 Its flames encircle our course from *b*,
1Pt 1: 3 he who in his great mercy gave us new *b*;
1: 3 a *b* unto hope which draws its life from
1: 4 a *b* to an imperishable inheritance,
1: 5 a *b* to a salvation which stands ready to
Rv 12: 2 aloud in pain as she labored to give *b*.
12: 4 stood before the woman about to give *b*,
12: 5 She gave *b* to a son
12:13 the woman who had given *b* to the boy.

BIRTHDAY (4)

Gn 40:20 on the third day, which was Pharaoh's *b*,
2Mc 6: 7 celebration of the king's *b* the Jews had,
Mt 14: 6 Then on Herod's *b* Herodias' daughter
Mk 6:21 Herod held a *b* dinner for his court circle,

BIRTHPANGS (1)

Sir 7:27 your mother's *b* forget not.

BIRTHRIGHT (9)

Gn 25:31 "First give me your *b* in exchange for it."
25:32 What good will any *b* do me?"
25:33 So he sold Jacob his *b* under oath.
25:34 Esau cared little for his *b*.
27:36 First he took away my *b*,
1Chr 5: 1 his *b* was given to the sons of Joseph,
5: 1 in the family records according to *b*.
5: 2 from him, though the *b* had been Joseph's.)
Heb 12:16 like Esau, who sold his *b* for a meal.

BIRZAITH (1)

1Chr 7:31 and Malchiel, who was the father of *B*.

BISHOP (3)

1Tm 3: 1 wants to be a *b* aspires to a noble task.
3: 2 A *b* must be irreproachable,
Ti 1: 7 The *b* as God's steward must be blameless.

BISHOPS (1)

Phil 1: 1 with their *b* and deacons in Christ Jesus.

BIT (11)

Nm 21: 6 *b* the people so that many of them died.
1Kgs 17:11 her, "Please bring along a *b* of bread."
2Kgs 19:28 hook in your nose and my *b* in your mouth,
Jb 40:25 with a hook, or curb his tongue with a *b*?
Ps(s) 32: 9 *b* and bridle their temper must be curbed,
Wis 12:10 But condemning them *b* by bit,
Is 37:29 hook in your nose and my *b* in your mouth,
Jn 13:26 I give the *b* of food I dip in the dish."
Acts 16:37 Not a *b* of it!
Rv 16:10 men *b* their tongues in pain and blasphemed

BITE (8)

Jb 16:10 their mouths are agape to *b* me.
Wis 16: 5 were dying from the *b* of crooked serpents,
Sir 21: 2 that will *b* you if you go near it;
Jer 8:17 which no charm will work when they *b* you,
Am 5:19 against the wall, and a snake should *b* him.
9: 3 I will command the serpent there to *b* them;
Mi 3: 5 Who, when their teeth have something to *b*,
Acts 28: 5 and suffered no ill effects from the *b*.

BITES (4)

Gn 49:17 viper by the path, That *b* the horse's heel,
Prv 23:32 But in the end it *b* like a serpent,
Eccl 10:11 serpent *b* because it has not been charmed,
Wis 16: 9 the *b* of locusts and of flies slew them,

BITHIAH (1)

1Chr 4:18 These were the sons of *B*,

BITHYNIA (2)

Acts 16: 7 came to Mysia they tried to go on into *B*,
1Pt 1: 1 Pontus, Galatia, Cappadocia, Asia, and *B*;

BITING (1)

Gal 5:15 go on *b* and tearing one another to pieces,

BITS (5)

Prv 27:22 should pound the fool to *b* with the pestle,
Ez 6: 6 and your incense stands smashed to *b*.
Am 6:11 command to shatter the great house to *b*,
Mt 21:44 upon that stone will be smashed to *b*;
Jas 3: 3 When we put *b* into the mouths of horses to

BITTEN (4)

Nm 21: 8 and if anyone who has been *b* looks at it,
21: 9 and whenever anyone who had been *b* by a
Eccl 10: 8 through a wall may be *b* by a serpent.
Sir 12:13 Who pities a snake charmer when he is *b*,

BITTER (61)

Gn 27:34 words, Esau burst into loud, *b* sobbing.
Ex 1:14 making life *b* for them with hard work in
12: 8 flesh with unleavened bread and *b* herbs.
15:23 not drink the water, because it was too *b*.
Nm 5:18 shall hold the *b* water that brings a curse.
5:19 to the curse brought by this *b* water.
5:23 shall then wash them off into the *b* water,
5:24 it may go into her with all its *b* curse.
5:27 this *b* water that brings a curse will go
9:11 it with unleavened bread and *b* herbs,
Dt 32:24 and consuming fever and *b* prestilence,
32:32 are their grapes and *b* their clusters.
Jgs 21: 2 evening, raising their voices in *b* lament.
Ru 1:13 my lot is too *b* for you,
1:20 for the Almighty has made it very *b* for me.
1Sm 15:32 struggling and saying, "So it is *b* death!"
30: 6 so *b* were they over the fate of their sons
1Kgs 14: 6 have been commissioned to give you *b* news.
18: 3 Now the famine in Samaria was *b*,
2Kgs 4:27 "Let her alone, she is in *b* anguish;
14:26 LORD saw the very *b* affliction of Israel,
Est C:19 they are not satisfied with our *b* servitude,
1Mc 6:13 and now I am dying, in *b* grief,
7:26 officers, who was a *b* enemy of Israel,
2Mc 6: 7 birthday the Jews had, from *b* necessity,
Jb 3:20 the toilers, and life to the *b* in spirit?
9:18 breath, but might fill me with *b* griefs.
13:26 For you draw up *b* indictments against me,
23: 2 Though I know my complaint is *b*,
27: 2 the Almighty, who has made *b* my soul,
Ps(s) 64: 4 swords, who aim like arrows their *b* words,
71:20 you have made me feel many *b* afflictions,
Prv 5: 4 But in the end she is as *b* as wormwood,
17:25 father, and *b* sorrow to her who bore him.
27: 7 man who is hungry, any *b* thing is sweet.
Eccl 7:26 More *b* than death I find the woman who is
Sir 11: 4 the worn cloak and jibe at no man's *b* day:
21:12 but one form of shrewdness is thoroughly *b*.
25:17 neighbors, a *b* sigh escapes him unawares.
29:25 besides, you will hear these *b* words:
30:17 Preferable is death to a *b* life,
38:16 one who is dead with wailing and *b* lament;
41: 1 how *b* the thought of you for the man at
51:24 how long will you endure such *b* thirst?
Is 5:20 change *b* into sweet, and sweet into bitter!
24: 9 drink is *b* to those who partake of it.
Jer 2:19 how evil and *b* is your forsaking the LORD,
4:18 how *b* is this disaster of yours,
6:26 Mourn as for an only child with *b* wailing,
31:15 heard the sound of moaning, of *b* weeping!
Lam 1: 4 she is in *b* grief.
3:15 He has sated me with *b* food,
Ez 27:30 heard on your behalf, shouting *b* cries,
27:31 you they weep in anguish, with *b* lament.
Am 8:10 only son, and bring their day to a *b* end.
Hb 1: 6 up Chaldea, that *b* and unruly people,
Zep 1:14 *b*, then, the warrior's cry.
Acts 2:24 God freed him from death's *b* pangs,
Heb 12:15 that no *b* root springs up through which
Jas 3:14 Should you instead nurse *b* jealousy and

BITTERLY (18)

Jgs 8: 1 And they quarreled *b* with him.
2Sm 13:36 all his servants wept very *b*
2Kgs 20: 3 And Hezekiah wept *b*.
Est 4: 1 through the city crying out loudly and *b*.
1Mc 2:14 garments, put on sackcloth, and mourned *b*.
2Mc 7:39 since he *b* resented the boy's contempt.
Ps(s) 119:51 Though the proud scoff *b* at me,
Sir 38:17 Weeping *b*, mourning fully,
Is 22: 4 Turn away from me, let me weep *b*;
33: 7 streets, the messengers of Shalem weep *b*.
38: 3 And Hezekiah wept *b*.
Lam 1: 2 *B* she weeps at night,
Ez 21:11 strength groan *b* while they look on.
Mt 26:75 He went out and began to weep *b*.
Mk 6:26 The king *b* regretted the request;
Lk 22:62 He went out and wept *b*.
Rv 1: 7 peoples of the earth shall lament him *b*.
5: 4 I wept *b* because no one could be found

BITTERNESS (15)

1Sm 1:10 In her *b* she prayed to the LORD,
2Sm 2:26 not know that afterward there will be *b*?
Jb 7:11 I will complain in the *b* of my soul.
10: 1 I will speak from the *b* of my soul.
21:25 Another dies in *b* of soul,
Prv 14:10 The heart knows its own *b*,
Wis 8:16 involves no *b* and living with her no grief,
18:22 he overcame the *b* not by bodily strength,
Sir 4: 6 For if in the *b* of his soul he curse you,
31:29 *b* and disgrace is wine drunk amid anger
Is 38:15 all my years despite the *b* of my soul.
38:17 thus is my *b* transformed into peace.
Rom 3:14 Their mouths are full of curses and *b*.
Eph 4:31 Get rid of all *b*, all passion and anger
Col 3:19 Avoid any *b* toward them.

BITUMEN (3)

Gn 11: 3 used bricks for stone, and *b* for mortar.
14:10 the Valley of Siddim was full of *b* pits;
Ex 2: 3 papyrus basket, daubed it with *b* and pitch,

BIZIOTHIAH (1)

Jos 15:28 Beth-pelet, Hazar-shual, Beer-sheba and *B*;

BIZTHA (1)

Est 1:10 merry with wine, he instructed Mehuman, *B*,

BLACK (15)

Ex 10:15 of the whole land, till it was *b* with them.
Lv 13:31 skin, though the hair on it may not be *b*,
13:37 its place and that *b* hair has grown on it,
Dt 4:11 fire and was enveloped in a dense *b* cloud.
Jb 6:16 Though they may be *b* with ice,
10:22 the land of darkness and of gloom, The *b*,
Prv 23:29 Who have *b* eyes?
Sg 5:11 his locks are palm fronds, *b* as the raven.
Jer 13:16 turns to darkness, changes into *b* clouds.
Zep 1:15 and gloom, A day of thick *b* clouds,
Zec 6: 2 red horses, the second chariot *b* horses,
6: 6 The chariot with the *b* horses was turning
Mt 5:36 (you cannot make a single hair white or *b*).
Rv 6: 5 This time I saw a *b* horse,
6:12 the sun turned *b* as a goat's-hair

BLACKED (1)

Is 8:22 with the light *b* out by its clouds.

BLACKENED (2)

Jb 30:30 My *b* skin falls away from me;
Bar 6:20 faces are *b* by the smoke of the house.

BLACKENS (1)

Sir 13: 1 He who touches pitch *b* his hand;

BLACKER (1)

Lam 4: 8 Now their appearance is *b* than soot,

BLACKNESS (1)

Jb 3: 5 settle upon it, the *b* of night affright it!

BLACKSMITHS (1)

Zec 2: 3 Then the LORD showed me four *b*.

BLADE (4)

Dt 29:22 and unfruitful, without a *b* of grass,
Jgs 3:22 The hilt also went in after the *b*,
3:22 and the fat closed over the *b* because he
Mk 4:28 The soil produces of itself first the *b*,

BLADES (1)

Ez 32:12 cut down your horde with the *b* of warriors,

BLAME (16)

Lv 20:27 no one but themselves to *b* for their death."
Nm 15:31 He has only himself to *b*."
Jgs 15: 3 the Philistines cannot *b* me if I harm them."
1Sm 14:41 If the *b* for this resides in me or my son
25:24 "My lord, let the *b* be mine.
28:10 LORD lives, you shall incur no *b* for this."
2Sm 14: 9 him, "Let me and my family be to *b*,
2Mc 13: 4 that Menelaus was to *b* for all the trouble,
Wis 12:15 power to punish one who has incurred no *b*.
13: 6 But yet, for these the *b* is less;
Acts 18: 6 I am not to *b*!
20:26 that I take the *b* for no man's conscience,
2Cor 8:20 namely any *b* over my handling of this
Col 1:22 you to God holy, free of reproach and *b*.
1Tm 5: 7 about widows, so that no one may incur *b*.
6:14 keep God's command without *b* or reproach

BLAMED (3)

2Kgs 7: 9 wait until morning breaks, we shall be *b*.
1Cor 10:30 be *b* for the food over which I gave thanks?
2Cor 6: 3 offense, so that our ministry may not be *b*.

BLAMELESS (23)

Gn 6: 9 Noah, a good man and *b* in that age,

17: 1 Walk in my presence and be *b*.
Est E:13 and of Esther, our *b* royal consort,
1Mc 4:42 He chose *b* priests, devoted to the law;
Jb 1: 1 Uz there was a *b* and upright man named Job,
1: 8 is no one on earth like him, *b* and upright,
4:17 Can a mortal be *b* against his Maker?
8: 6 the Almighty, Should you be *b* and upright,
15:14 What is a man that he should be *b*,
Ps(s) 19:14 shall I be *b* and innocent of serious sin.
119: 1 Happy are they whose way is *b*,
Prv 28:10 [And *b* men will gain prosperity.]
Wis 10: 5 knew the just man, kept him *b* before God,
10:15 The holy people and *b* race
18:21 the *b* man hastened to be their champion,
Sir 11:10 he who is avid for wealth will not be *b*?
Ez 28:15 *B* you were in your conduct from the day
1Cor 1: 8 be *b* on the day of our Lord Jesus [Christ].
Eph 1: 4 world began, to be holy and *b* in his sight,
Phil 1:10 so that with a clear conscience and *b*
1Thes 3:13 making them *b* and holy before our God and
1Tm 2: 8 offer prayers with *b* hands held aloft,
Ti 1: 7 The bishop as God's steward must be *b*.

BLAMELESSLY (5)

Est B: 4 *b* designed by us cannot be established
Ps(s) 15: 2 He who walks *b* and does justice;
Prv 11:20 LORD, but those who walk *b* are his delight.
Lk 1: 6 *b* following all the commandments and
1Pt 2:12 conduct yourselves *b* among them.

BLANCHED (3)

Dn 5: 6 the wrist and hand that wrote, his face *b*;
7:28 terrified by my thoughts, and my face *b*,
Na 2:11 Writhing in every frame, every face *b*!

BLANCHES (1)

Jl 2: 6 them peoples are in torment, every face *b*.

BLANDISHMENTS (1)

Sir 20:12 but fools pour forth their *b* in vain.

BLANKET (1)

Sir 37: 3 you created to *b* the earth with deceit?"

BLANKETED (2)

Ps(s) 65:14 with flocks and the valleys *b* with grain.
2Pt 2: 6 He *b* the cities of Sodom and Gomorrah in

BLASPHEME (7)

Jb 1:11 has, and surely he will *b* you to your face."
2: 5 and surely he will *b* you to your face."
Ps(s) 69:10 insults of those who *b* you fall upon me.
74:10 How long, O God, shall the foe *b*?
Acts 26:11 synagogue, I compelled them by force to *b*.
1Tm 1:20 to Satan so that they may learn not to *b*.
Jas 2: 7 who *b* that noble name which has made you

BLASPHEMED (16)

Lv 24:11 Israelite and cursed and *b* the LORD's name.
2Kgs 19: 6 servants of the king of Assyria have *b* me.
19:22 Whom have you insulted and *b*,
1Mc 7:41 "When they who were sent by the king *b*,
Jb 1: 5 sons have sinned and *b* God in their hearts."
Ps(s) 74:18 Remember how the enemy has *b* you,
Sir 48:18 his fist at Zion and *b* God in his pride.
Is 37: 6 servants of the king of Assyria have *b* me.
37:23 Whom have you insulted and *b*,
Ez 20:27 In this way also your fathers *b* me,
Mt 26:65 "He has *b*!
Lk 23:39 the criminals hanging in crucifixion *b* him:
Jn 10:36 do you claim that I *b* when,
Rv 16: 9 by the intense heat *b* the name of God
16:11 men bit their tongues in pain and *b* the God
16:21 and men *b* God for the plague of hailstones,

BLASPHEMER (6)

Lv 24:14 to Moses, "Take the *b* outside the camp,
24:23 took the *b* outside the camp and stoned him;
2Mc 9:28 So this murderer and *b*,
Wis 1: 6 she acquits not the *b* of his guilty lips;
Sir 3:16 A *b* is he who despises his father;
1Tm 1:13 I was once a *b*,

BLASPHEMERS (3)

2Mc 10:36 spread the fire and burned the *b* alive.
15:32 wretched *b* arm that had been boastfully
1Pt 4: 4 It is no wonder that those *b* are surprised

BLASPHEMES (10)

Lv 24:16 whoever *b* the name of the LORD shall be
Ps(s) 10: 3 glories in his greed, and the covetous *b*,
44:17 face At the voice of him who mocks and *b*,
74:22 remember how the fool *b* you day after day.
Prv 14:31 He who oppresses the poor *b* his Maker,
17: 5 He who mocks the poor *b* his Maker;
Dn 3:96 that whoever *b* the God of Shadrach,
Mt 9: 3 scribes said to themselves, "The man *b*."
Mk 3:29 but whoever *b* against the Holy Spirit will
Lk 12:10 *b* the Holy Spirit will never be forgiven.

BLASPHEMIES (14)

Tb 1:18 King because of the *b* he had uttered.
1Mc 7:38 Remember their *b*,
2Mc 8: 4 and the *b* uttered against his name;
10:34 outrageous *b* and uttering abominable words.
10:35 army of Maccabeus, angered over such *b*,
12:14 them and even uttering *b* and profanity.
Jb 34: 7 He drinks in *b* like water,
Ps(s) 59: 8 their mouths, and *b* are on their lips
Dn 11:36 utter dreadful *b* against the God of gods.
Mk 3:28 forgiven mankind and all the *b* men utter,
Lk 5:21 "Who is this man who utters *b*?
Acts 6:11 heard him speaking *b* against Moses and God,
Rv 13: 5 a mouth for uttering proud boasts and *b*,
13: 6 It began to hurl *b* against God,

BLASPHEMING (4)

Lv 24:16 must be put to death for *b* the LORD's name.
1Sm 3:13 though he knew his sons were *b* God,
Dn 14: 9 consumes them, Daniel shall die for *b* Bel."
Jn 10:33 you," the Jews retorted, "but for *b*.

BLASPHEMOUS (4)

2Mc 10: 4 hand them over to *b* and barbarous Gentiles.
13:11 to be subjected again to *b* Gentiles.
Rv 13: 1 were ten diadems and on its heads *b* names.
17: 3 beast which was covered with *b* names.

BLASPHEMOUSLY (1)

2Mc 15:24 who have *b* come against your holy people!"

BLASPHEMY (9)

Mt 12:31 I assure you, is why every sin, every *b*,
12:31 *b* against the Spirit will not be forgiven.
15:19 fornication, stealing, false witness, *b*.
26:66 Remember, you heard the *b*.
Mk 2: 7 He commits *b*!
7:22 maliciousness, deceit, sensuality, envy, *b*,
14:64 You have heard the *b*.
Rom 14:16 your privilege to become an occasion for *b*.
Jude 1: 9 did not venture to charge him with *b*.

BLAST (21)

Ex 19:16 the mountain, and a very loud trumpet *b*,
19:19 The trumpet *b* grew louder and louder,
20:18 the trumpet *b* and the mountain smoking,
Lv 25: 9 *b* shall re-echo throughout your land.
Nm 10: 7 an assembly you are to blow an ordinary *b*,
Jos 6: 5 When they give a long *b* on the ram's horns
2Sm 22:16 LORD, at the *b* of the wind of his wrath.
Jb 4: 9 by the *b* of his wrath they are consumed.
39:25 of the trumpet, but at each *b* he cries,
Ps(s) 11: 6 a burning *b* is their alloted cup.
18:16 LORD, at the *b* of the wind of his wrath.
150: 3 Praise him with the *b* of the trumpet,
Wis 11:20 they could have been killed at a single *b*,
Sir 50:16 The sons of Aaron would sound a *b*,
50:16 A *b* to resound mightily as a reminder
Is 4: 4 her midst with the *b* of searing judgment,
58: 1 lift up your voice like a trumpet *b*;
Ez 22:21 I will *b* you with the fire of my anger and
33: 5 the trumpet *b* yet refused to take warning;
Mt 24:31 his angels 'with a mighty trumpet *b*,
Heb 12:19 gloomy darkness and storm and trumpet *b*,

BLASTED (2)

Gn 41: 6 ears of grain, thin and *b* by the east wind;
41:23 shriveled and thin and *b* by the east wind,

BLASTS (8)

Lv 23:24 and with the trumpet *b* as a reminder;
1Mc 5:31 to heaven with trumpet *b* and loud shouting,
Ps(s) 47: 6 the LORD, amid trumpet *b*.
Sir 43:21 Cold northern *b* he sends that turn the
Lam 5:10 by a furnace, with the searing *b* of famine.
Am 2: 2 amid uproar and shouts and trumpet *b*.
Zep 1:16 a day of trumpet *b* and battle alarm
Rv 8:13 from the trumpet *b* the other three angels

BLASTUS (1)

Acts 12:20 chamberlain *B* and attempted to placate him,

BLAZE (9)

Ex 32:10 may *b* up against them to consume them.
32:11 your wrath *b* up against your own people,
Nm 21:28 Heshbon and a *b* from the city of Sihon;
21:30 fires *b* as far as Medeba."
24:10 in a *b* of anger at Balaam and said to him,
Jer 48:45 Heshbon, and a *b* from the house of Sihon:
Lk 12:49 How I wish the *b* were ignited!
2Pt 3:12 and the elements will melt away in a *b*.
Rv 2:18 whose eyes *b* like fire and whose feet

BLAZED (14)

Dt 4:11 which *b* to the very sky with fire and was
33: 2 While at his right hand a fire *b* forth and
2Chr 25:15 anger of the LORD *b* out against Amaziah,
1Mc 6:39 brightness and *b* like flaming torches.
2Mc 1:22 began to shine, a great fire *b* up,
1:32 As soon as this was done, a flame *b* up,
Ps(s) 39: 4 in my thoughts, a fire *b* forth.
78:21 and fire *b* up against Jacob,
Wis 16:19 fire *b* beyond its strength so as to
16:22 Were consumed by a fire that *b* in the hail
Is 42:25 It *b* round about them,
Lam 2: 3 He *b* up in Jacob like a flaming fire
Rv 1:14 snow-white wool and his eyes *b* like fire.
19:12 His eyes *b* like fire,

BLAZES (2)

Ps(s) 2:12 from the way, when his anger *b* suddenly.
Is 5:25 the wrath of the LORD *b* against his people,

BLAZING (26)

Ex 32:12 Let your *b* wrath die down;
Nm 25: 4 his *b* wrath may be turned away from Israel."
32:14 the LORD's *b* wrath against the Israelites.
Dt 9:15 "When I had come down again from the *b*,
13:18 that the *b* wrath of the LORD may die down
2Chr 25:10 Judah, and returned home *b* with resentment.
Sg 8: 6 its flames are a *b* fire.
Sir 23:16 For burning passion is a *b* fire,
43: 4 Like a *b* furnace of solid metal,
Is 7: 4 [the *b* anger of Rezin and the Arameans,
Jer 4: 8 "The *b* wrath of the LORD is not turned
4:26 before the LORD, before his *b* wrath.
Lam 1:12 afflicted me on the day of his *b* wrath.
4:11 spent his anger, poured out his *b* wrath;
Ez 21: 3 The *b* flame shall not be quenched,
Hos 7: 4 are all kindled to wrath like a *b* oven,
7: 6 in the morning it flares like a *b* fire.
11: 9 I will not give vent to my *b* anger,
Jon 3: 9 and forgive, and withhold his *b* wrath,
Na 1: 6 stand firm, and who can face his *b* anger?
Zep 2: 2 comes upon you the *b* anger of the LORD:
3: 8 out upon them my wrath, all my *b* anger;
Mal 3:19 For lo, the day is coming, *b* like an oven,
Heb 12:18 to an untouchable mountain and a *b* fire,
Rv 16:19 cup filled with the *b* wine of his wrath.
19:15 winepress the *b* wrath of God the Almighty.

BLEACHER (1)

Mk 9: 3 than the work of any *b* could make them.

BLEAT (2)

Tb 2:13 On entering my house the goat began to *b*.
Jer 9: 9 them, unheard is the *b* of the flock;

BLEATING (1)

1Sm 15:14 of this *b* of sheep that comes to my ears,

BLEEDING (1)

Lk 8:44 Immediately her *b* stopped.

BLEMISH (12)

Ex 12: 5 lamb must be a year-old male and without *b*.
Lv 1: 3 from the herd, it must be a male without *b*.
1:10 or a goat, he must bring a male without *b*.
3: 1 a female animal, but it must be without *b*.
3: 6 a female animal, but it must be without *b*.
9: 2 and a ram for a holocaust, both without *b*,
Nm 19: 2 heifer that is free from every *b* and defect
2Sm 14:25 who was without *b* from the sole of his
Sg 4: 7 my beloved, and there is no *b* in you.
Wis 13:14 red stain, and daubed over every *b* in it,
Ez 45:23 LORD seven bulls and seven rams without *b*,
46: 6 bull, also six lambs and a ram without *b*,

BLEND (2)

Ex 30:25 and *b* them into sacred anointing oil,
30:35 and *b* them into incense.

BLENDED (4)

Prv 23:30 wine, those who engage in trials of *b* wine.
Wis 16:21 was *b* to whatever flavor each one wished,
Sir 49: 1 The name JOSIAH is like *b* incense,
Is 65:11 and fill cups of *b* wine for Destiny,

BLESS (166)

Gn 12: 2 of you a great nation, and I will *b* you;
12: 3 I will *b* those who bless you and curse
17:16 I will *b* her, and I will give you a son by her.
17:16 Him also will I *b*;
17:20 I hereby *b* him. I will make him fertile
22:17 I will *b* you abundantly and make your
26: 3 land, and I will be with you and *b* you;
26:24 I will *b* you and multiply your descendants
27:10 to eat, that he may *b* you before he dies."
27:29 curse you, and blessed be those who *b* you."
27:34 "Father, *b* me too," he begged
27:38 father? *B* me too!"
28: 3 God Almighty *b* you and make you fertile,
32:27 "I will not let you go until you *b* me."
48: 9 me," said his father, "that I may *b* them."

BLESS (cont.)

48:16 *b* these boys That in them my name be
Ex 20:24 of my name I will come to you and *b* you.
23:25 then I will *b* your food and drink,
Nm 6:23 This is how you shall *b* the Israelites.
6:24 The LORD *b* you and keep you!
6:27 upon the Israelites, and I will *b* them."
22: 6 For I know that whoever you *b* is blessed
23:25 Balak to Balaam, "at least do not *b* them."
24: 1 that the LORD was pleased to *b* Israel,
Dt 1:11 times over, and *b* you as he promised!
7:13 He will love and *b* and multiply you;
7:13 he will *b* the fruit of your womb and the
8:10 have eaten your fill, you must *b* the LORD,
14:29 God, may *b* you in all that you undertake.
15: 4 will *b* you abundantly in the land he will
15: 6 LORD, your God, will *b* you as he promised.
15:10 will *b* you for this in all your works and
15:18 your God, will *b* you in everything you do.
23:21 may *b* you in all your undertakings on the
24:13 Then he will *b* you,
24:19 God, may *b* you in all your undertakings.
26:15 and *b* your people Israel and the soil you
30:16 will *b* you in the land you are entering to
33:11 *B*, O LORD, his possessions
Jos 24:10 On the contrary, he had to *b* you,
Jgs 5: 2 noble deeds by the people who *b* the LORD,
5: 9 nobles of the people who *b* the LORD;
17: 4 his mother said, "May the LORD *b* my son!
Ru 2: 4 and they replied, "The LORD *b* you!"
3:10 He said, "May the LORD *b* you,
1Sm 2:20 And Eli would *b* Elkanah and his wife,
15:13 "The LORD *b* you!
23:21 LORD *b* you for your sympathy toward me.
2Sm 6:20 When David returned to *b* his own family,
7:29 *b* the house of your servant that it may be
21: 3 that you may *b* the inheritance of the LORD?"
1Chr 4:10 may truly *b* me and extend my boundaries!
16:43 home, David returned to *b* his household.
17:27 deigned to *b* the house of your servant,
23:13 minister to him, and to *b* his name forever.
29:20 whole assembly, "Now *b* the LORD your God!"
Neh 9: 5 and Pethahiah said, "Arise, *b* the LORD,
Tb 4:19 At all times *b* the Lord God,
5:17 Tobit said, "God *b* you, brother."
7: 7 "My child, God *b* you!
8:15 let them *b* you forever!
13: 6 *B* the Lord of righteousness,
13:10 his goodness, and *b* the King of the ages,
13:13 together and shall *b* the Lord of the ages.
14: 7 *b* the God of the ages in righteousness.
14: 9 at all times to *b* his name sincerely
2Mc 1: 2 May God *b* you and remember his covenant
Ps(s) 5:13 For you, O LORD, *b* the just man;
16: 7 I *b* the LORD who counsels me;
26:12 in the assemblies I will *b* the LORD.
28: 9 Save your people, and *b* your inheritance;
29:11 may the LORD *b* his people with peace!
34: 2 I will *b* the LORD at all times;
62: 5 They *b* with their mouths,
63: 5 Thus will I *b* you while I live;
66: 8 *B* our God, you peoples,
67: 2 May God have pity on us and *b* us;
67: 8 May God *b* us,
68:27 *b* God; bless the Lord, you of Israel's
72:15 day by day shall they *b* him.
96: 2 *b* his name; announce his salvation,
100: 4 *b* his name, for he is good:
103: 1 *B* the LORD, O my soul
103: 1 and all my being, *b* his holy name.
103: 2 *B* the LORD, O my soul,
103:20 *B* the LORD, all you his angels,
103:21 *B* the LORD, all you his hosts
103:22 *B* the LORD, all his works
103:22 *B* the LORD, O my soul!
104: 1 *B* the LORD, O my soul!
104:35 *B* the LORD, O my soul!
109:28 Let them curse, but do you *b*;
115:12 The LORD remembers us and will *b* us:
115:12 he will *b* the house of Israel;
115:12 he will *b* the house of Aaron;
115:13 He will *b* those who fear the LORD,
115:14 May the LORD *b* you more and more,
115:18 But we *b* the LORD, both now and forever.
118:26 we *b* you from the house of the LORD.
128: 5 The LORD *b* you from Zion:
129: 8 We *b* you in the name of the LORD!"
132:15 I will *b* her with abundant provision,
134: 1 Come, *b* the LORD, all you servants
134: 2 hands toward the sanctuary, and *b* the LORD.
134: 3 May the LORD *b* you from Zion,
135:19 House of Israel, *b* the LORD,
135:19 house of Aaron, *b* the LORD,
135:20 House of Levi, *b* the LORD;
135:20 you who fear the LORD, *b* the LORD.
145: 1 and I will *b* your name forever and ever.
145: 2 Every day will I *b* you,
145:10 O LORD, and let your faithful ones *b* you.
145:21 all flesh *b* his holy name forever and ever.
Sir 39:14 *b* the LORD for all he has done!
39:35 proclaim and *b* the name of the Holy One.
43:11 Then *b* its Maker,
45:15 priesthood and *b* his people in his name.
45:26 *b* the LORD who has crowned you with glory!
50:22 And now, *b* the God of all,
51:12 I *b* the name of the LORD.
Jer 18:10 of the good with which I promised to *b* it.
31:23 "May the LORD *b* you,
Bar 6:65 Kings they neither curse nor *b*.
Dn 3:57 *B* the Lord, all you works of the Lord,
3:58 Angels of the Lord, *b* the Lord,
3:59 You heavens, *b* the Lord,
3:60 you waters above the heavens, *b* the Lord,
3:61 All you hosts of the Lord, *b* the Lord;
3:62 Sun and moon, *b* the Lord;
3:63 Stars of heaven, *b* the Lord;
3:64 Every shower and dew, *b* the Lord;
3:65 All you winds, *b* the Lord;
3:66 Fire and heat, *b* the Lord;
3:67 [Cold and chill, *b* the Lord;
3:68 Dew and rain, *b* the Lord;
3:69 Frost and chill, *b* the Lord;
3:70 Ice and snow, *b* the Lord;
3:71 Nights and days, *b* the Lord;
3:72 Light and darkness, *b* the Lord;
3:73 Lightnings and clouds, *b* the Lord;
3:74 Let the earth *b* the Lord,
3:75 Mountains and hills, *b* the Lord;
3:76 growing from the earth, *b* the Lord;
3:77 You springs, *b* the Lord;
3:78 Seas and rivers, *b* the Lord;
3:79 and all water creatures, *b* the Lord,
3:80 All you birds of the air, *b* the Lord;
3:81 All you beasts, wild and tame, *b* the Lord;
3:82 You sons of men, *b* the Lord;
3:83 O Israel, *b* the Lord;
3:84 Priests of the Lord, *b* the Lord;
3:85 Servants of the Lord, *b* the Lord;
3:86 Spirits and souls of the just, *b* the Lord;
3:87 Holy men of humble heart, *b* the Lord;
3:88 Hananiah, Azariah, Mishael, *b* the Lord;
3:90 *B* the God of gods,
Hg 2:19 From this day, I will *b*!
Mt 10:12 As you enter his home *b* it.
Lk 6:28 *b* those who curse you and pray for those
Acts 3:26 *b* you by turning you from your evil ways."
Rom 12:14 *B* your persecutors; bless and do not curse
1Cor 10:16 we *b* a sharing in the blood of Christ?
Heb 6:14 and said, "I will indeed *b* you,

BLESSED (235)

Gn 1:22 God saw how good it was, and God *b* them,
1:28 God *b* them, saying:
2: 3 So God *b* the seventh day and made it holy,
5: 2 created, he *b* them and named them "man."
9: 1 God *b* Noah and his sons and said to them:
9:26 *B* be the LORD, the God of Shem!
14:18 God Most High, he *b* Abram with these words:
14:19 *B* be Abram by God Most High,
14:20 And *b* be God Most High,
24: 1 age, and the LORD had *b* him in every way.
24:27 *B* be the LORD,
24:31 "Come, *b* of the LORD!
24:35 "The LORD has *b* my master so abundantly
25:11 the death of Abraham, God *b* his son Isaac,
26:12 Since the LORD *b* him,
27:27 With that, he *b* him,
27:27 fragrance of a field that the LORD has *b*!
27:29 curse you, and *b* be those who bless you."
27:33 it just before you came, and I *b* him.
27:33 Now he must remain *b*!"
28: 6 Esau noted that Isaac had *b* Jacob when he
30:27 it is because of you that God has *b* me.
35: 9 God appeared to him again and *b* him.
39: 5 *b* the Egyptian's house for Joseph's sake;
48:15 Then he *b* them with these words:
48:20 So when he *b* them that day and said,
Ex 18:10 *B* be the LORD,"
20:11 has *b* the sabbath day and made it holy.
39:43 just as the Lord had commanded, he *b* them.
Lv 9:22 his hands over the people and *b* them.
9:23 On coming out they again *b* the people.
Nm 22: 6 bless is *b* and whoever you curse is cursed."
22:12 do not curse this people, for they are *b*."
23:11 instead, you have even *b* them."
24: 9 *B* is he who blesses you,
24:10 times now you have even *b* them instead!
Dt 2: 7 God, has *b* you in all your undertakings;
7:14 You will be *b* above all peoples;
12: 7 because the LORD, your God, has *b* you.
12:15 meat as the LORD, your God, has *b* you with;
14:24 you, considering how the LORD has *b* you,
16:15 has *b* you in all your crops and in all
28: 3 *b* in the city, and blessed in the country!
28: 4 *B* be the fruit of your womb,
28: 5 *B* be your grain bin and your kneading bowl!
28: 6 "May you be *b* in your coming in,
28: 6 in your coming in, and *b* in your going out!
33:13 *B* by the LORD is his land with the best of
33:20 *B* be he who has made Gad so vast!
33:24 "More *b* than the other sons be Asher!
Jos 14:13 Joshua *b* Caleb,
17:14 the LORD has *b* us" Joshua answered them,
22: 6 Joshua then *b* them and sent them away to
22:33 who *b* God and decided against declaring
Jgs 5:24 *B* among women be Jael, blessed among
13:24 The boy grew up and the LORD *b* him;
Ru 2:19 May he who took notice of you be *b*!"
2:20 "May he be *b* by the LORD,
4:14 *B* is the LORD who has not failed to
1Sm 25:32 *B* be the LORD, the God of Israel,
25:33 *B* be your good judgment and blessed be you
25:39 *B* be the LORD, who has requited the insult
26:25 *B* are you, my son David!
2Sm 2: 5 "May you be *b* by the LORD for having done
6:11 the LORD *b* Obed-edom and his whole house.
6:12 the LORD had *b* the family of Obed-edom
6:18 he *b* the people in the name of the LORD of
7:29 house of your servant shall be *b* forever."
18:28 the king and said, *B* be the LORD your God,
22:47 And *b* be my Rock!
1Kgs 1:48 *B* be the LORD, the God of Israel,
2:45 But King Solomon shall be *b*,
5:21 pleased and said, *B* be the LORD this day,
8:15 *B* be the LORD, the God of Israel,
8:55 stood and *b* the whole community of Israel,
8:56 *B* be the LORD who has given rest to his
10: 9 *B* be the LORD, your God,
1Chr 13:14 and the LORD *b* Obed-edom's household and
16: 2 he *b* the people in the name of the LORD,
16:36 *B* be the LORD, the God of Israel,
17:27 since it is you, O LORD, who *b* it,
17:27 O LORD, who blessed it, it is *b* forever."
26: 5 Peullethai, the eighth, for God *b* him.
29:10 Then David *b* the LORD in the presence of
29:10 *B* may you be, O LORD, God of Israel
29:20 And the whole assembly *b* the LORD,
2Chr 2:11 *B* be the LORD, the God of Israel,
6: 4 *B* be the LORD, the God of Israel,
9: 8 *B* be the LORD, your God,
20:26 for there they *b* the LORD;
30:27 levitical priests rose and *b* the people;
31: 8 they *b* the LORD and his people Israel.
31:10 left over, for the LORD has *b* his people.
Ezr 7:27 *B* be the LORD, THE GOD of our fathers,
Neh 8: 6 Ezra *b* the LORD, the great God,
9: 5 the blessing, *B* is your glorious name,
Tb 4:12 own kinsmen and were *b* in their children.
8: 5 *B* are you, O God of our fathers
8:15 *B* are you, O God,
8:16 *B* are you, who have made me glad
8:17 *B* are you, for you were merciful
9: 6 and greeted Gabael, who wept and *b* him,
9: 6 *B* be God, because I have seen the
10:14 joy, and he *b* the Lord of heaven and earth,
11:14 *B* be God, and praised be his great name,
11:14 great name, and *b* be all his holy angels.
11:17 *B* be your God for bringing you to us,
11:17 *B* are your father and your mother.
11:17 *B* is my son Tobiah, and blessed are you,
13: 1 *B* be God who lives forever,
13:12 forever *b* are all those who build you up.
13:18 *B* be God who has raised you up!
13:18 may he be *b* for all ages!"
14:15 and he *b* the Lord God forever and ever.
Jdt 13:17 God, saying with one accord, *B* are you,
13:18 *B* are you, daughter, by the Most High
13:18 and *b* be the Lord God,
14: 7 *B* are you in every tent of Judah;
15: 9 had visited her, all with one accord *b* her,
15:10 be *b* by the Lord Almighty forever and ever!"
15:12 *b* her and performed a dance in her honor.
1Mc 2:69 Then he *b* them,
3: 7 by his deeds, and his memory is *b* forever.
4:30 *B* are you, O Savior of Israel,
2Mc 1:17 Forever *b* be our God,
10:38 On completing these exploits, they *b*,
15:34 *B* be he who has kept his own Place
Jb 1:10 You have *b* the work of his hands,
1:21 *b* be the name of the LORD!"
29:11 Whoever heard of me *b* me;
31:20 Whose limbs have not *b* me when warmed
42:12 Thus the LORD *b* the latter days of Job
Ps(s) 18:47 And *b* be my Rock!
28: 6 *B* be the LORD, for he has heard
31:22 *B* be the LORD whose wondrous kindness he
37:26 and lends, and his descendants shall be *b*.
41:14 *B* be the LORD, the God of Israel,
45: 3 thus God has *b* you forever.
49:19 in his lifetime he counted himself *b*.
66:20 *B* be God who refused me not my prayer or
67: 7 God, our God, has *b* us.
68:20 *b* day by day be the Lord,
68:36 *B* be God!
72:17 May his name be *b* forever;
72:17 shall all the tribes of the earth be *b*;
72:18 *B* be the LORD, the God of Israel,
72:19 And *b* forever be his glorious name;
89:53 *B* be the LORD forever.
106:48 *B* be the LORD, the God of Israel,
107:38 He *b* them, and they became very many;
112: 2 the upright generation shall be *b*.
113: 2 *B* be the name of the LORD both now and
115:15 May you be *b* by the LORD,
118:26 *B* is he who comes in the name of the LORD;
119:12 *B* are you, O LORD; teach me your statutes.
124: 6 *B* be the LORD, who did not leave us
128: 4 thus is the man *b* who fears the LORD.

135:21 B from Zion be the LORD,
144: 1 B be the LORD, my rock,
147:13 he has b your children within you.
Prv 10: 7 The memory of the just will be b,
20:21 at the outset will in the end not be b.
22: 9 The kindly man will be b,
28:20 The trustworthy man will be richly b;
Eccl 10:17 B are you, O land,
Sg 6:12 had made me the b one of my kinswomen.
Wis 3: 5 a little, they shall be greatly b,
3:13 Yes, b is she who, childless and undefiled,
Sir 1:11 even on the day of his death he will be b.
25: 7 There are nine who come to my mind as b,
44:21 in his descendants the nations would be b,
46:11 may their memory be ever b,
48:11 B is he who shall have seen you before he
Is 19:25 B be my people Egypt,
30:18 b are all who wait for him!
51: 2 I called him, I b him and made him many.
61: 9 acknowledge them as a race the LORD has b.
65:16 he will be b on whom a blessing is invoked
65:23 b by the LORD are they and their offspring.
Jer 17: 7 B is the man who trusts in the LORD,
20:14 the day my mother gave me birth never be b!
Bar 4: 4 B are we, O Israel;
Dn 2:19 in a vision, and he b the God of heaven:
2:20 B be the name of God forever and ever,
3:26 B are you, and praiseworthy, O Lord,
3:52 B are you, O Lord, the God of our fathers
3:52 And b is your holy and glorious name,
3:53 B are you in the temple of your holy glory,
3:54 B are you on the throne of your kingdom,
3:55 B are you who look into the depths from
3:56 B are you in the firmament of heaven,
3:95 exclaimed, B be the God of Shadrach,
4:31 was restored to me, and I b the Most High,
12:12 B is the man who has patience and
Zec 11: 5 those who sell them say, B be the LORD,
Mal 3:12 Then all nations will call you b,
3:15 Rather must we call the proud b;
Mt 14:19 b and broke them and gave the loaves to
21: 9 B is he who comes in the name of the Lord!
23:39 B is he who comes in the name of the
26:26 During the meal Jesus took bread, b it,
Mk 10:16 Then he embraced them and b them,
11: 9 B is he who comes in the name of the Lord!
11:10 B is the reign of our father David to come!
14:22 the meal he took bread, b and broke it,
14:61 you the Messiah, the Son of the B One?"
Lk 1:28 B are you among women."
1:48 all ages to come shall call me b.
1:68 B be the Lord the God of Israel because he
2:28 him in his arms and b God in these words:
2:34 Simeon b them and said to Mary his mother:
13:35 B is he who comes in the name of the
19:38 B is he who comes as king in the name of
24:50 Bethany, and with hands upraised, b them.
24:51 As he b, he left them,
Jn 12:13 B is he who comes in the name of the Lord!
12:13 B is the King of Israel!"
Acts 3:25 all the families of the earth shall be b.'
Rom 1:25 the Creator— b be he forever,
9: 5 B forever be God who is over all!
2Cor 11:31 of the Lord Jesus knows b be he forever
Gal 3: 8 "All nations shall be b in you."
3: 9 all who believe are b along with Abraham,
1Tm 1:11 to the glorious gospel of God b be he
6:15 He is the b and only ruler,
Ti 2:13 in this age as we await our b hope,
Heb 7: 1 from his defeat of the kings and b him.
7: 6 and b him who had received God's promises.
7: 7 that a lesser person is b by a greater.
11:21 when dying, b each of the sons of Joseph,
Jas 5:11 Those who have endured we call b.

BLESSEDNESS (1)

Rom 4: 9 Does this b apply only to the circumcised,

BLESSES (10)

Gn 49:25 who helps you, God Almighty, who b you,
Nm 24: 9 Blessed is he who b you,
1Sm 2: 8 vower his vow, and b the sleep of the just.
9:13 only after he b the sacrifice will the
Tb 13:15 My spirit b the Lord,
Ps(s) 37:22 But those whom he b shall possess the land,
Prv 3:33 wicked, but the dwelling of the just he b;
30:11 curses its father, and b not its mother.
Sir 33:12 Some he b and makes great,
Is 19:25 of the land, when the LORD of hosts b it:

BLESSING (108)

Gn 12: 2 your name great, so that you will be a b.
12: 3 of the earth shall find b in you,"
18:18 nations of the earth are to find b in him?
22:18 all the nations of the earth shall find b—
24:48 down in worship to the LORD, b the LORD,
24:60 Invoking a b on Rebekah, they said:
26: 4 all the nations of the earth shall find b—
26:29 Henceforth, 'The LORD's b be upon you!'"
27: 4 I may give you my special b before I die."
27: 7 my b with the LORD's approval before I die.'
27:12 bring on myself a curse instead of a b."
27:19 so that you may give me your special b."
27:23 so in the end he gave him his b.)
27:25 I may eat of it and then give you my b."
27:30 just after Isaac had finished b him,
27:31 that you may then give me your special b."
27:35 here by a ruse and carried off your b,"
27:36 birthright, and now he has taken away my b."
27:36 he pleaded, "Haven't you saved a b for me?"
27:38 his father, "Have you only that one b,
27:41 because of the b his father had given him.
28: 1 called Jacob, greeted him with a b,
28: 4 your descendants the b he gave to Abraham,
28: 6 there, charging him, as he gave him his b,
28:14 all the nations of the earth shall find b.
39: 5 the LORD's b was on everything he owned,
48: 3 me at Luz in the land of Canaan, and b me,
Ex 32:29 to bring a b upon yourselves this day."
Nm 23:20 It is a b I have been given to pronounce;
23:20 a b which I cannot restrain.
Dt 11:26 before you here, this day, a b and a curse:
11:27 b for obeying the commandments of the LORD,
11:29 you shall pronounce the b on Mount Gerizim,
15:14 press, in proportion to the b the LORD,
16:10 shall be in proportion to the b the LORD,
23: 6 and turned his curse into a b for you,
28: 8 The LORD will affirm his b upon you,
28: 8 b you in the land that the LORD,
28:12 in due season, b all your undertakings,
30:19 you life and death, the b and the curse.
33: 1 This is the b which Moses,
Jos 8:33 for the b of the people of Israel on this
22: 7 sent them off to their tents with his b
1Sm 13:12 and I have not yet sought the LORD's b.'
2Sm 7:29 and by your b the house of your servant
14:22 to the ground in homage and b the king,
Neh 9: 5 The Israelites answered with the b,
9: 5 name, and exalted above all b and praise."
13: 2 though our God turned the curse into a b."
Tb 8:15 are you, O God, with every holy and pure b!
9: 6 grant heavenly b to you and to your wife,
11:17 Welcome to your home with b and joy.
12: 6 you, by b and extolling his name in song.
14: 2 b God and praising the divine Majesty.
Jb 29:13 The b of those in extremity came upon me,
Ps(s) 3: 9 Upon your people be your b.
21: 7 For you made him a b forever;
24: 5 He shall receive a b from the LORD,
65:11 Softening it with showers, b its yield.
109:17 he took no delight in b;
129: 8 say not, "The b of the LORD be upon you!
133: 3 For there the LORD has pronounced his b,
Prv 10:22 It is the LORD's b that brings wealth,
11:11 the b of the righteous the city is exalted,
24:25 and on them will come the b of prosperity.
Wis 15:19 escaped both the approval of God and his b.
Sir 3: 8 your father that his b may come upon you;
3: 9 For a father's b gives a family firm roots,
7:32 your hand, that your b may be complete;
11:22 God's b is the lot of the just man,
33:17 Since by the LORD's b I have made progress
34:17 to the eyes, gives health and life and b.
39:22 His b overflows like the Nile;
44:22 and the b rested upon the head of JACOB.
50:20 The b of the LORD would be upon his lips,
50:21 to receive from him the b of the Most High.
Is 19:24 and Assyria, a b in the midst of the land,
44: 3 offspring, and my b upon your descendants.
65:16 blessed on whom a b is invoked in the land.
Jer 4: 2 Then shall the nations use his name in b,
Ez 34:26 season, rains that shall be a b to them.
44:30 priests to bring a b down upon your house.
Dn 3:24 the flames, singing to God and b the Lord.
3:51 with one voice sang, glorifying and b God:
13:60 b God who saves those that hope in him.
Jl 2:14 will again relent and leave behind him a b.
Zec 8:13 so will I save you that you may be a b;
Mal 2: 2 upon you and of your b I will make a curse.
3:10 to pour down b upon you without measure?
Mt 10:13 is deserving, your b will descend on it.
10:13 If it is not, your b will return to you.
25:34 You have my Father's b!
Mk 6:41 his eyes to heaven, pronounced a b,
8: 7 asking a b on the fish,
Lk 9:16 eyes to heaven, pronounced a b over them,
22:17 a cup he offered a b in thanks and said:
24:30 to eat, he took bread, pronounced the b,
Rom 15:29 you, I shall come with Christ's full b.
1Cor 4:12 When we are insulted we respond with a b.
10:16 Is not the cup of b we bless a sharing in
Gal 3:14 Christ Jesus the b bestowed on Abraham
Eph 1: 3 in Christ every spiritual b in the heavens!
Heb 6: 7 it is cultivated, receives the b of God.
12:17 he wanted to inherit his father's b,
12:17 even though he sought the b with tears.
Jas 3:10 B and curse come out of the same mouth.
1Pt 3: 9 Return a b instead.
3: 9 you may receive a b as your inheritance.

BLESSINGS (33)

Gn 30:30 the LORD's b came upon you in my company.
48:20 shall the people of Israel pronounce b;
49:25 With the b of the heavens above,
49:25 the b of the abyss that crouches below,
49:25 crouches below, The b of breasts and womb,
49:26 the b of fresh grain and blossoms,
49:26 The b of the everlasting mountains,
Lv 25:21 I will bestow such b on you in the sixth
Dt 10: 8 minister to him, and to give b in his name,
16:17 in proportion to the b which the LORD,
21: 5 minister to him and to give b in his name,
27:12 Gerizim to pronounce b over the people,
28: 2 b will come upon you and overwhelm you:
30: 1 have set before you, the b and the curses,
33:23 favors and filled with the b of the LORD;
Jos 8:34 the words of the law, the b and the curses,
1Kgs 8:66 rejoicing and happy over all the b the
Jdt 13:20 everlasting honor, rewarding you with b,
Ps(s) 21: 4 For you welcomed him with goodly b,
Prv 10: 6 B are for the head of the just,
11:26 b upon the head of him who distributes it!
Sir 4:13 wherever he dwells, the LORD bestows b.
16:27 upon the earth, and filled it with his b.
26:15 Choicest of b is a modest wife,
31:23 On a man generous with food, b are invoked,
40:27 The fear of God is a paradise of b;
Jer 5:25 sins have turned back these b from you.
31:12 they shall come streaming to the LORD's b:
31:14 and my people shall be filled with my b,
Lk 12:19 You have b in reserve for years to come.
Rom 15:27 have shared in the spiritual b of the Jews,
1Cor 9:23 in the hope of having a share in its b.
Heb 11:20 for Jacob and Esau b that were still to be.

BLEST (32)

Wis 2:16 He calls b the destiny of the just and
14: 7 For b is the wood through which justice
18: 1 themselves had suffered, called them b;
Mt 5: 3 "How b are the poor in spirit:
5: 4 B too are the sorrowing;
5: 5 B are the lowly;
5: 6 B are they who hunger and thirst for
5: 7 B are they who show mercy;
5: 8 B are the single-hearted for they shall
5: 9 B too the peacemakers;
5:10 B are those persecuted for holiness' sake;
5:11 B are you when they insult you and
11: 6 B is the man who finds no stumbling block
13:16 "But b are your eyes because they see and
13:16 see and b are your ears because they hear.
16:17 Jesus replied, B are you, Simon son of Jonah!
Lk 1:42 B are you among women and blest is the
1:42 women and b is the fruit of your womb.
1:45 B is she who trusted that the Lord's words
6:20 B are you poor;
6:20 B are you who hunger;
6:21 B are you who are weeping;
6:22 B shall you be when men hate you,
7:23 B is that man who finds no stumbling block
10:23 B are the eyes that see what you see.
11:27 B is the womb that bore you and the
11:28 b are they who hear the word of God and
Jn 13:17 b will you be if you put them into
20:29 B are they who have not seen and have
Rom 4: 7 B are they whose iniquities are forgiven,
4: 8 B is the man to whom the Lord imputes no
Jas 1:25 B will this man be in whatever he does.

BLEW (29)

Gn 2: 7 and b into his nostrils the breath of life,
Ex 15:10 When your wind b,
Jos 6:16 b the horns and Joshua said to the people,
6:20 As the horns b, the people began to shout.
Jgs 6:34 he b the horn that summoned Abiezer to
7:19 They b the horns and broke the jars they
7:20 companies b horns and broke their jars.
1Kgs 1:39 They b the horn and all the people shouted,
2Kgs 9:13 Jehu on the bare steps, b the trumpet,
2Chr 7: 6 b the trumpets and all Israel stood.
Tb 11:11 and holding him firmly, b into his eyes.
1Mc 3:54 they b the trumpets and cried out loudly.
4:13 and the men with Judas b the trumpet.
9:12 phalanx attacked as they b their trumpets.
9:12 were on Judas' side also b their trumpets.
16: 8 They b the trumpets,
Dn 2:35 wind b them away without leaving a trace.
Hg 1: 9 and what you brought home, I b away.
Mt 7:25 and the winds b and buffeted his house.
7:27 the winds b and lashed against his house.
Mk 4:37 It happened that a bad squall b up.
Rv 7: 1 wind b on land or sea or through any tree.
8: 7 When the first angel b his trumpet,
8: 8 the second angel b his trumpet,
8:10 When the third angel b his trumpet,
8:12 When the fourth angel b his trumpet,
9: 1 Then the fifth angel b his trumpet,
9:13 Then the sixth angel b his trumpet,
11:15 Then the seventh angel b his trumpet.

BLIGHT (7)

Dt 28:22 fiery drought, with b and searing wind,
1Kgs 8:37 or if b comes, or mildew,
2Chr 6:28 the land, when there is pestilence, or b,

BLIGHT (cont.)

Jb 5: 5 for God shall take it away by *b* and the
Is 17:11 day of the grievous blow, the incurable *b.*
Am 4: 9 I struck you with *b* and searing wind;
Hg 2:17 you in all the works of your hands with *b,*

BLIGHTED (1)

Jl 1: 7 has laid waste my vine, and *b* my fig tree;

BLIND (87)

Ex 4:11 who gives sight to one and makes another *b?*
Lv 19:14 or put a stumbling block in front of the *b,*
21:18 *b,* or lame, or who has any disfigurement
22:22 One that is *b* or crippled or maimed,
Dt 15:21 lame or *b* or has any other serious defect,
27:18 be he who misleads a *b* man on his way!'
28:29 you will grope like a *b* man in the dark,
2Sm 5: 6 the *b* and the lame will drive you away!"
5: 8 *b* shall be the personal enemies of David."
5: 8 *b* and the lame shall not enter the palace."
2Kgs 6:18 prayed to the LORD, "Strike this people *b,*
6:18 prophet's prayer the LORD struck them *b.*
Tb 5:10 am, a *b* man who cannot see God's sunlight,
Jb 17: 7 My eye has grown *b* with anguish,
29:15 I was eyes to the *b,*
Ps(s) 146: 8 the LORD gives sight to the *b.*
Eccl 12: 3 they who look through the windows grow *b;*
Sir 20:28 Favors and gifts *b* the eyes;
Is 29: 9 *b* yourselves and stay blind!
29:18 and darkness, the eyes of the *b* shall see.
33:23 Then the *b* will divide great spoils and
35: 5 Then will the eyes of the *b* be opened,
42: 7 the nations, To open the eyes of the *b,*
42:16 I will lead the *b* on their journey;
42:18 You who are deaf, listen, you who are *b,*
42:19 Who is *b* but my servant,
43: 8 the people who are *b* though they have eyes,
56:10 My watchmen are *b,*
59:10 Like *b* men we grope along the wall,
Jer 31: 8 with the *b* and the lame in their midst,
Bar 6:36 To no *b* man do they restore his sight,
Zep 1:17 will hem men in till they walk like the *b,*
Zec 11:17 entirely, and his right eye be *b* forever!
12: 4 strike *b* all the horses of the peoples,
Mal 1: 8 When you offer a *b* animal for sacrifice,
Mt 9:27 there, two *b* men came after him crying out,
9:28 to the house, the *b* men caught up with him.
11: 5 the *b* recover their sight,
12:22 man who was brought to him was *b* and mute.
15:14 they are *b* leaders of the blind.
15:14 If one *b* man leads another,
15:30 with them cripples, the deformed, the *b,*
15:31 cripples walking about, and the *b* seeing.
20:30 suddenly two *b* men sitting by the roadside,
21:14 The *b* and the lame came to him inside the
23:16 It is an evil day for you, *b* guides!
23:17 *B* fools! which is more important
23:19 How *b* you are!
23:24 *B* guides! You strain out the gnat
23:26 *B* Pharisee! First cleanse the inside
Mk 8:22 him a *b* man and begged him to touch him.
8:23 Jesus took the *b* man's hand and led him
10:46 there was a *b* beggar Bartimaeus ("son of
10:49 So they called the *b* man over,
10:51 "Rabboni," the *b* man said,
Lk 4:18 of sight to the *b* and release to prisoners,
6:39 "Can a *b* man act as guide to a blind man?
7:21 he also restored sight to many who were *b.)*
7:22 The *b* recover their sight,
14:13 and the crippled, the lame and the *b.*
14:21 poor and the crippled, the *b* and the lame.'
18:35 *b* man sat at the side of the road begging.
Jn 5: 3 crowded with sick people lying there *b,*
9: 1 he saw a man who had been *b* from birth.
9: 2 his parents that caused him to be born *b?"*
9:13 man who had been born *b* to the Pharisees.
9:17 Then they addressed the *b* man again:
9:18 really been born *b* and had begun to see,
9:19 so, do you attest that he was *b* at birth?
9:20 is our son, and we know he was *b* at birth.
9:24 man who had been born *b* and said to him,
9:25 I was *b* before; now I can see."
9:32 ever gave sight to a person *b* from birth.
9:39 to make the sightless see and the seeing *b."*
9:40 up, saying, "You are not calling us *b,*
9:41 you were *b* there would be no sin in that.
10:21 a devil cannot open the eyes of the *b!"*
11:37 said, "He opened the eyes of that *b* man.
Acts 9: 9 For three days he continued *b,*
13:11 For a time you shall be *b,*
Rom 2:19 the *b* and enlighten those in darkness,
11: 7 The rest became *b,*
11: 8 *b* eyes and deaf ears,
Rv 3:17 how pitiable and poor, how *b* and naked!

BLINDED (10)

2Kgs 25: 7 Then he *b* Zedekiah,
2Mc 10:30 at the enemy, who were bewildered and *b,*
Jb 15:27 he has *b* himself with his crassness,
Wis 2:21 for their wickedness *b* them,
Jer 39: 7 He then *b* Zedekiah,
52:11 Then he *b* Zedekiah, bound him with fetters,
Mk 8:17 Are your minds completely *b?*
Jn 12:40 "He has *b* their eyes,
2Cor 4: 4 Their unbelieving minds have been *b* by the
1Jn 2:11 he is going, since the dark has *b* his eyes.

BLINDFOLDED (2)

Mk 14:65 They *b* him and hit him,
Lk 22:64 They *b* him first,

BLINDING (1)

Gn 19:11 with such a *b* light that they were utterly

BLINDLY (1)

Lam 4:14 They staggered *b* in the streets,

BLINDNESS (5)

Dt 28:28 will strike you with madness, *b* and panic.
Tb 7: 7 charitable man should be afflicted with *b!"*
Wis 19:17 And they were struck with *b,*
Rom 11:25 *b* has come upon part of Israel until the
2Pt 1: 9 is shortsighted to the point of *b.*

BLINDS (4)

Ex 23: 8 for a bribe *b* even the most clear-sighted
Dt 16:19 for a bribe *b* the eyes even of the wise
Sir 27: 1 and the struggle for wealth *b* the eyes.
43:19 Its shining whiteness *b* the eyes,

BLINK (1)

Jb 15:12 carry you away, and why do your eyes *b,*

BLOATED (1)

Lk 21:34 "Be on guard lest your spirits become *b*

BLOCK (15)

Ex 9:17 Will you still *b* the way for my people by
Lv 19:14 or put a stumbling *b* in front of the blind,
1Mc 5: 4 become a snare and a stumbling *b*
Ps(s) 35: 3 and *b* the way in the face of my pursuers;
119:165 and for them there is no stumbling *b.*
Sir 31: 7 a stumbling *b* to those who are avid for it,
Is 44:19 out of the rest, or worship a *b* of wood?"
Ez 3:20 when I place a stumbling *b* before him,
Dn 6:18 been brought to *b* the opening of the den.
Mt 11: 6 is the man who finds no stumbling *b* in me."
Lk 7:23 is that man who finds no stumbling *b* in me."
Rom 14:13 *b* or hindrance in your brother's way.
1Cor 1:23 Christ crucified—a stumbling *b* to Jews,
Gal 5:11 the cross would be a stumbling *b* no more.
Rv 2:14 a stumbling *b* in the way of the Israelites

BLOCKADED (4)

1Mc 11:65 it for many days, and *b* the inhabitants.
15:14 so that he *b* it by land and sea and let no
15:25 He *b* Trypho by preventing anyone from
Is 1: 8 a shed in a melon patch, like a city *b.*

BLOCKADING (1)

1Mc 5: 3 in Idumea, because they were *b* Israel;

BLOCKED (10)

Lv 15: 3 whether the flow drains off or is *b* up;
Jdt 5: 1 for battle, and had *b* the mountain passes,
6:12 and all the slingers *b* the ascent of
16: 3 Their numbers *b* the torrents,
1Mc 2:36 stones, nor *b* up their own hiding places.
5:47 them out and *b* up the gates with stones.
2Mc 2: 5 then he *b* up the entrance.
Lam 3: 9 He has *b* my ways with fitted stones,
Ez 39:11 east of the sea [it is *b* to travelers].
1Thes 2:18 but Satan *b* the way.

BLOCKS (6)

1Kgs 5:31 large *b* were quarried to give the temple a
7:10 (The foundation was made of fine, large *b,*
1Chr 22: 2 out stone *b* for building the house of God.
Jdt 1: 2 this city he built a wall of *b* of stone,
Is 57:14 the stumbling *b* from my people's path.
Mk 13: 1 huge *b* of stone and the enormous buildings!"

BLOOD (402)

Gn 4:10 brother's *b* cries out to me from the soil!
4:11 to receive your brother's *b* from your hand.
9: 6 If anyone sheds the *b* of man,
9: 6 blood of man, by man shall his *b* be shed;
17:12 from any foreigner who is not of your *b.*
29:14 to him, "You are indeed my flesh and *b."*
37:22 Instead of shedding *b,"*
37:26 killing our brother and concealing his *b?*
37:31 a goat, dipped the tunic in its *b.*
42:22 Now comes the reckoning for his *b."*
49:11 his garments, his robe in the *b* of grapes.
Ex 4: 9 the river will become *b* on the dry land."
4:25 she said, "You are a spouse of *b* to me."
4:26 At that time she said, "A spouse of *b,"*
7:17 I hold, and it shall be changed into *b.*
7:19 supplies of water—that they may become *b.*
7:19 the land of Egypt there shall be *b,*
7:20 the water of the river was changed into *b.*
7:21 There was *b* throughout the land of Egypt.
12: 7 They shall take some of its *b* and apply it
12:13 the *b* will mark the houses where you are.
12:13 Seeing the *b,* I will pass over you;
12:22 dipping it in the *b* that is in the basin,
12:22 lintel and the two doorposts with this *b.*
12:23 the *b* on the lintel and the two doorposts,
23:18 the *b* of my sacrifice with leavened bread;
24: 6 half of the *b* and put it in large bowls;
24: 8 took the *b* and sprinkled it on the people,
24: 8 "This is the *b* of the covenant which the
29:12 Take some of its *b* and with your finger
29:12 All the rest of the *b* you shall pour out
29:16 The *b* you shall take and splash on all the
29:20 Some of its *b* you shall take and put on
29:20 of the *b* on all the sides of the altar.
29:21 take some of the *b* that is on the altar,
30:10 with the *b* of the atoning sin offering.
34:25 me the *b* of sacrifice with leavened bread,
Lv 1: 5 shall offer up its *b* by splashing it on
1:11 splash its *b* on the sides of the altar.
1:15 out its *b* against the side of the altar.
3: 2 splash its *b* on the sides of the altar.
3: 8 splash its *b* on the sides of the altar.
3:13 splash its *b* on the sides of the altar.
3:17 You shall not partake of any fat or any *b."*
4: 5 *b* and bring it into the meeting tent,
4: 6 tent, where, dipping his finger in the *b,*
4: 7 The priest shall also put some of the *b* on
4: 7 The rest of the bullock's *b* he shall pour
4:16 bring some of its *b* into the meeting tent,
4:17 tent, and dipping his finger in the *b,*
4:18 He shall also put some of the *b* on the
4:18 The rest of the *b* he shall pour out at the
4:25 The priest shall then take some of the *b*
4:25 The rest of the *b* he shall pour out at the
4:30 The priest shall then take some of its *b*
4:30 The rest of the *b* he shall pour out at the
4:34 The priest shall then take some of the *b*
4:34 The rest of the *b* he shall pour out at the
5: 9 sprinkle some of the *b* of the sin offering
5: 9 The rest of the *b* shall be squeezed out
6:20 If any of its *b* is spilled on a garment,
6:23 offering of which some *b* has been brought
7: 2 Its *b* shall be splashed on the sides of
7:14 who splashes the *b* of the peace offering.
7:26 you dwell, you shall not partake of any *b,*
7:27 of any *b* shall be cut off from his people."
7:33 offers up the *b* and fat of the peace offering
8:15 slaughtered it, and taking some of its *b,*
8:15 the *b* at its base when he consecrated it.
8:19 splashed its *b* on all sides of the altar.
8:23 Moses took some of its *b* and put it on the
8:24 of the *b* on the tips of their right ears,
8:24 *b* he splashed on the sides of the altar.
8:30 and some of the *b* that was on the altar,
9: 9 When his sons presented the *b* to him,
9: 9 the *b* and put it on the horns of the altar.
9: 9 *b* he poured out at the base of the altar.
9:12 When his sons brought him the *b,*
9:18 When his sons brought him the *b,*
10:18 If its *b* was not brought into the inmost
12: 4 days more in becoming purified of her *b;*
12: 5 days in becoming purified of her *b.*
12: 7 will be clean again after her flow of *b.*
14: 6 priest shall dip them all in the *b* of the bird
14:14 Then the priest shall take some of the *b*
14:17 foot, over the *b* of the guilt offering.
14:25 lamb, he shall take some of its *b,*
14:28 foot, over the *b* of the guilt offering.
14:51 *b* of the slain bird and the spring water,
14:52 with the bird's *b* and the spring water,
15:25 a woman is afflicted with a flow of *b*
16:14 Taking some of the bullock's *b,*
16:14 sprinkle some of the *b* with his finger
16:15 goat, and bringing its *b* inside the veil,
16:15 do with it as he did with the bullock's *b,*
16:18 some of the bullock's and the goat's *b,*
16:19 sprinkle some of the *b* on it seven times.
16:27 The sin-offering bullock and goat whose *b*
17: 6 The priest shall splash the *b* on the altar
17:10 residing among them, partakes of any *b,*
17:10 one who partakes of *b* and will cut him off
17:11 the life of a living body is in its *b,*
17:11 for your own lives, because it is the *b,*
17:12 even a resident alien, may partake of *b.*
17:13 pour out its *b* and cover it with earth.
17:14 the life of every living body is its *b,*
17:14 You shall not partake of the *b* of any meat.
17:14 the life of every living body is its *b,*
19:26 "Do not eat meat with the *b* still in it.
20:18 laid bare the flowing fountain of her *b.*
Nm 18:17 Their *b* you must splash on the altar of
19: 4 priest shall take some of its *b* on his finger
19: 5 with its hide and flesh, its *b* and offal;
23:24 its prey and has drunk the *b* of the slain.
35:12 as places of asylum from the avenger of *b,*
35:19 The avenger of *b* may execute the murderer,
35:21 of *b* may execute the murderer on sight.
35:24 of *b* in accordance with these norms,

35:25 free the homicide from the avenger of *b*
35:27 and the avenger of *b* finds him beyond
35:33 can have no atonement for the *b* shed on it
35:33 it except through the *b* of him who shed it.
Dt 12:16 Only you shall not partake of the *b*,
12:23 for *b* is life, and you shall not consume this
12:24 Do not partake of the *b*,
12:27 you must offer both the flesh and the *b*
12:27 of your other sacrifices the *b* indeed
15:23 Only, you shall not partake of its *b*,
19: 6 the avenger of *b* may in the heat of his
19:10 innocent *b* will not be shed and you will
19:12 him over to be slain by the avenger of *b*.
19:13 Israel the stain of shedding innocent *b*,
21: 7 declare, 'Our hands did not shed this *b*,
21: 8 let not the guilt of shedding innocent *b*
21: 9 from your midst the guilt of innocent *b*,
32:14 and the foaming *b* of its grapes you drank.
32:42 I will make my arrows drunk with *b*,
32:42 With the *b* of the slain and the captured,
32:43 For he avenges the *b* of his servants and
Jos 20: 3 may flee for asylum from the avenger of *b*.
20: 5 Though the avenger of *b* pursues him,
20: 9 death at the hand of the avenger of *b*.
Jgs 9:24 their *b* upon their brother Abimelech,
1Sm 14:32 on the ground and eating the flesh with *b*.
14:33 the LORD by eating the flesh with *b*,
14:34 the LORD by eating the flesh with *b*."
19: 5 innocent *b* by killing David without cause?"
25:26 *b* and from avenging yourself personally.
25:31 for having shed innocent *b*
25:33 *b* and from avenging myself personally.
26:20 Do not let my *b* flow to the ground far
2Sm 1:22 "From the *b* of the slain,
14:11 that the avenger of *b* may not go too far
20:12 with *b* in the middle of the highroad,
23:17 Can I drink the *b* of these men who went at
1Kgs 2: 5 for the *b* of war in a time of peace,
2: 9 send down his hoary head in *b* to the grave."
2:31 the *b* which Joab shed without provocation.
2:32 will hold him responsible for his own *b*,
2:33 shall be responsible forever for their *b*.
2:37 You shall be responsible for your own *b*."
18:28 was their custom, until *b* gushed over them.
21:19 where the dogs licked up the *b* of Naboth,
21:19 of Naboth, the dogs shall lick up your *b*,
22:35 The *b* from his wound flowed to the bottom
22:38 licked up his *b* and harlots bathed there,
2Kgs 3:22 saw the water at a distance as red as *b*.
3:23 "This is *b*!", they exclaimed.
9: 7 I avenge the *b* of my servants the prophets,
9: 7 and the *b* of all the other servants of the
9:26 the *b* of Naboth and the blood of his sons,'
9:26 the blood of Naboth and the *b* of his sons,'
9:33 and some of her *b* spurted against the wall
16:13 the *b* of his peace-offerings on the altar.
16:15 it all the *b* of holocausts and sacrifices.
21:16 shedding so much innocent *b* as to fill the
24: 4 because of the innocent *b* he shed,
1Chr 11:19 the *b* of these men who risked their lives?"
22: 8 'You have shed much *b*,
22: 8 shed too much *b* upon the earth in my sight.
28: 3 you are a man who fought wars and shed *b*.'
2Chr 29:22 priests collected the *b* and cast it
29:22 slaughtered the rams and cast the *b*
29:22 the lambs and cast the *b* on the altar.
29:24 offered their *b* on the altar to atone
30:16 sprinkled the *b* given them by the Levites;
35:11 priests sprinkled some of the *b*
Jdt 6: 4 the mountains shall be drunk with their *b*,
8:21 pay for its profanation with our life's *b*.
9: 3 their *b* the bed in which they lay deceived,
Est E: 5 accomplices in the shedding of innocent *b*,
E:10 a Macedonian, certainly not of Persian *b*,
1Mc 1:24 with great arrogance and shed much *b*.
1:37 they shed innocent *b* around the sanctuary;
3:32 He left Lysias, a nobleman of royal *b*,
7:17 *b* they have shed round about Jerusalem,
9:38 Remembering the *b* of John their brother,
9:42 their revenge for the *b* of their brother,
2Mc 1: 8 to the gatehouse and shedding innocent *b*.
8: 3 to hearken to the *b* that cried out to him;
12:16 be filled with the *b* that flowed into it.
14:45 with *b* gushing from his frightful wounds.
14:46 steep rock, as he lost the last of his *b*,
Jb 16:18 O earth, cover not my *b*,
39:30 His young ones greedily drink *b*;
Ps(s) 9:13 For the avenger of *b* has remembered;
16: 4 *B* libations to them I will not pour out,
26: 9 of sinners, nor with men of *b* my life.
50:13 bulls, or is the *b* of goats my drink?
51:16 Free me from *b* guilt,
55:24 Men of *b* and deceit shall not live out
58:11 bathe his feet in the *b* of the wicked.
68:24 So that you will bathe your feet in *b*;
72:14 and precious shall their *b* be in his sight.
78:44 of Zoan, And changed into *b* their streams
79: 3 their *b* like water round about Jerusalem,
79:10 avenge the shedding of your servants' *b*.
94:21 life of the just and condemn innocent *b*,
105:29 their waters into *b* and killed their fish.
106:38 shed innocent *b*, the blood of their sons
139:19 and the men of *b* were to depart from me!
Prv 1:16 they hasten to shed *b*
1:18 These men lie in wait for their own *b*,
6:17 tongue, and hands that shed innocent *b*;
28:17 with human *b* were to flee to the grave,
30:33 and the stirring of anger brings forth *b*.
Wis 7: 2 body and *b*, from the seed of man,
11: 6 river was troubled with impure *b*
12: 5 a cannibal feast of human flesh and of *b*,
14:25 And all is confusion *b* and murder,
Sir 9: 9 to her and you go down in *b* to the grave.
11:32 The evil man lies in wait for *b*,
12:16 he will never have enough of your *b*.
14:18 So with the generations of flesh and *b*:
17:26 obscure then the thoughts of flesh and *b*!
33:31 you have acquired him with your life's *b*;
34:21 he who withholds it is a man of *b*.
34:22 sheds *b* who denies the laborer his wages.
39:26 wheat, milk and honey, the *b* of the grape,
50:15 hand for the cup, to offer *b* of the grape,
Is 1:11 In the *b* of calves, lambs and goats
1:15 Your hands are full of *b*!
4: 4 And purges Jerusalem's *b* from her midst
9: 4 in battle, every cloak rolled in *b*,
15: 9 The waters of Dimon are filled with *b*,
26:21 The earth will reveal the *b* upon her,
34: 3 The mountains shall run with their *b*,
34: 6 The LORD has a sword filled with *b*,
34: 6 with fat, With the *b* of lambs and goats,
34: 7 Their land shall be soaked with *b*,
49:26 their own *b* as with the juice of the grape.
59: 3 For your hands are stained with *b*,
59: 7 and they are quick to shed innocent *b*;
63: 3 Their *b* spurted on my garments;
63: 6 and I let their *b* run out upon the ground."
66: 3 cereal offering, like offering swine's *b*;
Jer 7: 6 no longer shed innocent *b* in this place,
19: 4 this place with the *b* of the innocent.
22: 3 and do not shed innocent *b* in this place.
22:17 on your own gain, On shedding innocent *b*,
26:15 it is innocent *b* you bring on yourselves,
46:10 devours, is sated, drunk with their *b*:
48:10 cursed he who holds back his sword from *b*
51:35 My *b* upon the people of Chaldea,
Lam 4:13 Who shed in her midst the *b* of the just!—
4:14 blindly in the streets, soiled with *b*,
Ez 16: 6 passed by and saw you weltering in your *b*.
16: 6 your *b* and grow like a plant in the field.
16: 9 bathed you with water, washed away your *b*,
16:22 girl, stark naked and weltering in your *b*.
21:37 your *b* shall flow throughout the land.
22: 3 *b* within herself so that her time has come,
22: 4 *b* which you shed you have been made guilty,
22:12 are those in you take brides to shed *b*.
22:27 *b* and destroying lives to get unjust gain.
23:37 adultery, and *b* is on their hands.
23:45 adultery, and *b* is on their hands.
24: 7 For the *b* she shed is in her midst:
24: 8 vengeance, she put her *b* on the bare rock,
28:23 and *b* shall flow in its streets.
32: 6 the river beds shall be filled with your *b*.
33:25 raise your eyes to your idols, you shed *b*—
35: 6 the Lord GOD, you have been guilty of *b*,
35: 6 GOD, you have been guilty of blood, and *b*,
36:18 the *b* which they poured out on the ground,
39:17 you shall have flesh to eat and *b* to drink.
39:18 the *b* of the princes of the land [rams,
39:19 are filled and drink *b* until you are drunk.
43:18 it and for the sprinkling of *b* against it.
43:20 Take some of its *b* and put it on the four
44: 7 it when you offered me food, fat, and *b*;
44:15 stand before me to offer me fat and *b*,
45:19 Then the priest shall take some of the *b*
Dn 1: 3 Israelites of royal *b* and of the nobility,
13:62 Thus was innocent *b* spared that day.
Hos 6: 8 is a city of evildoers, tracked with *b*.
Jl 3: 3 in the heavens and on the earth, *b*,
3: 4 be turned to darkness, and the moon to *b*.
4:19 because they shed innocent *b* in their land.
4:21 I will avenge their *b*,
Jon 1:14 do not charge us with shedding innocent *b*,
Mi 7: 2 They all lie in wait to shed *b*,
Hb 2: 8 Because of men's *b* shed,
2:17 Because of men's *b* shed,
Zep 1:17 And their *b* shall be poured out like dust,
Zec 9:11 you, for the *b* of your covenant with me,
9:15 They shall drink *b* like wine,
Mt 23:30 joined them in shedding the prophets' *b*.'
23:35 all the *b* of the just ones shed on earth,
23:35 from the *b* of holy Abel to the blood of
26:28 this is my *b*, the blood of the covenant,
27: 6 in the temple treasury since it is *b* money."
27: 8 that field, even today, is called *B* Field.
27:24 "I am innocent of the *b* of this just man.
27:25 "Let his *b* be on us and on our children."
Mk 5:29 Immediately her flow of *b* dried up and the
14:24 "This is my *b*, the blood of the covenant,
Lk 11:50 to account for the *b* of all the prophets shed
11:51 the *b* of Abel to the blood of Zechariah,
13: 1 *b* Pilate had mixed with their sacrifices.
22:20 "This cup is the new covenant in my *b*,
22:44 like drops of *b* falling to the ground.
Jn 1:13 who were begotten not by *b*,
6:53 flesh of the Son of Man and drink his *b*,
6:54 He who feeds on my flesh and drinks my *b*
6:55 my flesh is real food and my *b* real drink.
6:56 on my flesh and drinks my *b* remains in me,
19:34 and immediately *b* and water flowed out.
Acts 1:19 who named the property Field of *B*—
2:19 *b*, fire, and a cloud of smoke.
2:20 be turned to darkness and the moon to *b*
5:28 to make us responsible for that man's *b*."
7:26 'Friends, you are *b* brothers.
15:20 of strangled animals, and from eating *b*.
15:29 from meat sacrificed to idols, from *b*,
18: 6 "Your *b* be on your own heads.
20:28 he has acquired at the price of his own *b*.
21:25 to avoid meat sacrificed to idols, *b*,
22:20 *b* of your witness Stephen was being shed,
Rom 3:15 Swiftly run their feet to shed *b*;
3:25 Through his *b*, God made him the means
5: 9 Now that we have been justified by his *b*,
1Cor 10:16 we bless a sharing in the *b* of Christ?
11:25 "This cup is the new covenant in my *b*.
11:27 sins against the body and *b* of the Lord.
15:50 and *b* cannot inherit the kingdom of God;
Eph 1: 7 It is in Christ and through his *b* that we
2:13 been brought near through the *b* of Christ.
Col 1:20 making peace through the *b* of his cross.
Heb 2:14 since the children are men of *b* and flesh,
9: 7 with the *b* which he offered for himself
9:12 not with the *b* of goats and calves,
9:12 of goats and calves, but with his own *b*,
9:13 For if the *b* of goats and bulls and the
9:14 how much more will the *b* of Christ,
9:18 first covenant was inaugurated without *b*.
9:19 people, he took the *b* of goats and calves,
9:20 "This is the *b* of the covenant which God
9:21 and all the vessels of worship with *b*.
9:22 law almost everything is purified by *b*,
9:22 the shedding of *b* there is no forgiveness.
9:25 the sanctuary with *b* that is not his own;
10: 4 the *b* of bulls and goats to take sins away.
10:19 since the *b* of Jesus assures our entrance
11:28 the Passover and sprinkled the lamb's *b*,
12: 4 yet resisted to the point of shedding *b*.
12:24 and to the sprinkled *b* which speaks more
13:11 The bodies of the animals whose *b* is
13:12 gate, to sanctify the people by his own *b*.
13:20 the sheep by the *b* of the eternal covenant,
1Pt 1: 2 Jesus Christ and purification with his *b*.
1:19 but by Christ's *b* beyond all price:
1:19 the *b* of a spotless, unblemished lamb
1Jn 1: 7 and the *b* of his Son Jesus cleanses us
5: 6 Christ it is who came through water and *b*—
5: 6 not in water only, but in water and in *b*.
5: 8 the Spirit and the water and the *b*—
Rv 1: 5 and freed us from our sins by his own *b*,
5: 9 With your *b* you purchased for God men of
6:10 our *b* among the inhabitants of the earth?"
6:12 tentcloth and the moon grew red as *b*.
7:14 and made them white in the *b* of the Lamb.
8: 7 there came hail and then fire mixed with *b*,
8: 8 A third of the sea turned to *b*,
11: 6 They also have power to turn water into *b*
12:11 They defeated him by the *b* of the Lamb and
14:20 and so much *b* poured out of the winepress
16: 3 The sea turned to *b* like that of a corpse,
16: 4 These also turned to *b*.
16: 6 who shed the *b* of saints and prophets,
16: 6 and prophets, you have given *b* to drink;
17: 6 I saw that the woman was drunk with the *b*
17: 6 *b* of those martyred for their faith in Jesus.
18:24 "In her was found the *b* of prophets and
19: 2 He has avenged the *b* of his servants which
19:13 He wore a cloak that had been dipped in *b*,

BLOODGUILT (7)

Ex 22: 1 beaten to death, there is no *b* involved.
22: 2 after sunrise he is thus beaten, there is *b*
Nm 35:27 and kills him, the avenger incurs no *b*;
Dt 22: 8 off, you will bring *b* upon your house.
2Sm 21: 1 "There is *b* on Saul and his family
2Chr 19:10 whether it concerns *b* or questions of law,
Hos 12:15 *b* upon him and repay him for his outrage

BLOODIED (1)

Ez 28: 8 down to the pit, there to die a *b* corpse,

BLOODSHED (28)

Lv 17: 4 his Dwelling, shall be judged guilty of *b*;
Nm 35:33 Since *b* desecrates the land,
Dt 17: 8 *b* or of civil rights or of personal injury,
19:10 shed and you will not become guilty of *b*.
21: 8 shall be absolved from the guilt of *b*,
2Sm 16: 8 you for all the *b* in the family of Saul,
1Kgs 2: 5 and put *b* without provocation on the belt
2Mc 14:18 he shrank from deciding the issue by *b*.
Ps(s) 106:38 of Canaan, desecrating the land with *b*;
Sir 8:16 For *b* is nothing to him;
22:24 so does abuse come before *b*.
27:15 Wrangling among the haughty ends in *b*,
28:11 flare up, and insistent quarrels provoke *b*.
40: 9 Plague and *b*, wrath and the sword,
Is 5: 7 He looked for judgment, but see, *b*!

BLOODSHED (cont.)
33:15 stopping his ears lest he hear of *b*,
Ez 5:17 Pestilence and *b* shall stalk through you,
7:23 with *b* and the city full of violence.
9: 9 the land is filled with *b*,
22: 6 family by family, are in you only for *b*.
22: 9 are those in you who slander to cause *b*;
22:13 made and because of the *b* in your midst.
38:21 judgment with him in pestilence and *b*;
Hos 1: 4 I will punish the house of Jehu for the *b*
4: 2 in their lawlessness, *b* follows bloodshed.
Mi 3:10 Who build up Zion with *b*,
Hb 2:12 Woe to him who builds a city by *b*,

BLOODTHIRSTY (4)
Ps(s) 5: 7 The *b* and the deceitful the LORD abhors.
59: 3 from *b* men save me.
Prv 29:10 *B* men hate the honest man,
Ez 14:19 this land, pouring out upon it my *b* fury,

BLOODY (5)
Prv 20:30 Evil is cleansed away by *b* lashes,
Ez 22: 2 you judge, would you judge the *b* city?
24: 6 Woe to the *b* city, a pot containing rust,
Na 3: 1 Woe to the *b* city, all lies, full of plunder,
Zec 9: 7 and take from his mouth his *b* meat,

BLOOM (10)
Jb 15:33 and like an olive tree casting off its *b*.
Sg 2:13 puts forth its figs, and the vines, in *b*,
2:15 for our vineyards are in *b*!
6:11 the valley, To see if the vines were in *b*.
7:13 vineyards, and see if the vines are in *b*,
Is 35: 1 the steppe will rejoice and *b*.
35: 2 They will *b* with abundant flowers,
Ez 7:10 Lawlessness is in full *b*,
17:24 green tree, and make the withered tree *b*.
Na 1: 4 and Carmel, and the *b* of Lebanon fades;

BLOOMS (7)
Jb 38:27 ground till the desert *b* with verdure?
Ps(s) 103:15 like a flower of the field he *b*;
Eccl 12: 5 When the almond tree *b*,
Is 18: 5 and the *b* are succeeded by ripening grapes,
28: 1 To the fading *b* of his glorious beauty,
28: 4 The fading *b* of his glorious beauty on the
Mt 6:30 *b* today and is thrown on the fire tomorrow,

BLOSSOM (8)
Wis 2: 7 and let no springtime *b* pass us by;
Is 5:24 rotten and their *b* scatter like dust;
11: 1 of Jesse, and from his roots a bud shall *b*.
17:11 make your sprouts *b* on the next morning,
27: 6 shall take root, Israel shall sprout and *b*,
Hos 14: 6 he shall *b* like the lily;
14: 8 They shall *b* like the vine,
Hb 3:17 fig tree *b* not nor fruit be on the vines,

BLOSSOMED (3)
Sg 6:11 if the pomegranates had *b*.
7:13 have opened if the pomegranates have *b*;
Heb 9: 4 the manna, the rod of Aaron which had *b*,

BLOSSOMS (17)
Gn 40:10 It had barely budded when its *b* came out,
49:26 womb, the blessings of fresh grain and *b*,
Ex 25:33 to be three cups, shaped like almond *b*,
25:33 to be three cups, shaped like almond *b*,
25:34 are to be four cups, shaped like almond *b*,
37:19 were three cups, shaped like almond *b*,
37:19 were three cups, shaped like almond *b*,
37:20 were four cups, shaped like almond *b*,
Nm 17:23 put forth not only shoots, but *b* as well,
Jb 15:30 and with the wind his *b* shall disappear.
Sg 5:13 His lips are red *b*;
Sir 1:16 LORD, with *b* of peace and perfect health.
24:17 the vine, my *b* become fruit fair and rich.
39:14 of incense, break forth in *b* like the lily.
43:20 it shines like *b* on the thornbush.
50: 8 Like the *b* on the branches in springtime,
51:15 As the *b* yielded to ripening grapes,

BLOT (10)
Ex 17:14 I will completely *b* out the memory of
Dt 9:14 *b* out their name from under the heavens.
25:19 you shall *b* out the memory of Amalek from
29:19 The LORD will *b* out his name from under
32:26 and *b* out their name from men's memories,'
1Sm 24:22 that you will not *b* out my name and family."
2Kgs 14:27 Since the LORD had not determined to *b* out
Ps(s) 51:11 face from my sins, and *b* out all my guilt.
Sir 20:23 A lie is a foul *b* in a man,
Jer 18:23 crime, *b* not out their sin in your sight!

BLOTCH (8)
Lv 13: 2 *b* which appears to be the sore of leprosy,
13: 4 If, however, the *b* on the skin is white,
13:19 of the boil have a white scab or a pink *b*,
13:23 *b* remains in its place without spreading,
13:24 the burn now becomes a pink or a white *b*,
13:25 If the hair has turned white on the *b* and
13:26 that there is no white hair on the *b*
13:28 But if the *b* remains in its place without

BLOTCHES (4)
Lv 13:38 a man or a woman is spotted with white *b*,
13:39 If the *b* on the skin are white and already
14:56 as well as for scabs, pustules and *b*,
Jude 1:12 These men are *b* on your Christian banquets.

BLOTTED (9)
Dt 25: 6 that his name may not be *b* out from Israel.
Neh 3:37 let not their sin be *b* out in your sight,
2Mc 12:42 that the sinful deed might be fully *b* out.
Ps(s) 9: 6 their name you *b* out forever and ever.
109:13 next generation may their name be *b* out.
109:14 let not his mother's sin be *b* out;
Sir 23:26 her disgrace will never be *b* out.
44:13 endure, their glory will never be *b* out;
Is 48:19 never cut off or *b* out from my presence.

BLOW (47)
Ex 12:13 Egypt, no destructive *b* will come upon you.
21:12 a man a mortal *b* must be put to death.
21:19 one who struck the *b* shall be acquitted,
Nm 10: 7 an assembly you are to *b* an ordinary blast,
10: 8 the priests, who shall *b* the trumpets;
10:10 you shall *b* the trumpets over your
17:11 forth from the LORD and the *b* is falling."
17:12 the *b* was already falling on the people.
Dt 19: 5 handle and hits his neighbor a mortal *b*,
Jos 6: 4 times, and have the priests *b* the horns.
Jgs 7:18 with me *b* horns, you too must blow
2Sm 1:15 and the youth struck him a mortal *b*.
1Kgs 1:34 of Israel, and you shall *b* the horn and cry,
20:37 The man struck him a *b* and wounded him.
Jdt 13:18 *b* at the head of the chief of our enemies.
2Mc 9: 5 him down with an unseen but incurable *b*;
14:40 such a man he would deal the Jews a hard *b*.
Ps(s) 39:11 at the *b* of your hand I wasted away.
81: 4 *B* the trumpet at the new moon,
89:11 You have crushed Rahab with a mortal *b*;
147:18 he lets his breeze *b* and the waters run.
Sg 4:16 *b* upon my garden that its perfumes may
Sir 27:25 so a *b* struck in treachery injures more
28:12 If you *b* upon a spark,
28:17 A *b* from a whip raises a welt,
28:17 but a *b* from the tongue smashes bones;
Is 17:11 disappear on the day of the grievous *b*,
19: 7 along the Nile shall dry up and *b* away,
27:13 On that day, A great trumpet shall *b*,
Jer 4: 5 *B* the trumpet through the land,
6: 1 *B* the trumpet in Tekoa,
14:19 you struck us a *b* that cannot be healed?
51:27 the earth, *b* the trumpet among the nations;
Ez 24:16 by a sudden *b* I am taking away from you
33: 6 coming and fails to *b* the warning trumpet,
Hos 5: 8 *B* the horn in Gibeah,
Jl 2: 1 *B* the trumpet in Zion,
2:15 *B* the trumpet in Zion!
Mi 1: 9 is no remedy for the *b* she has been struck;
Mt 6: 2 do not *b* a horn before you in synagogues
Jn 18:22 nearby gave Jesus a sharp *b* on the face.
Acts 27:13 When a gentle south wind began to *b*,
28:13 A day later a south wind began to *b* which
Rv 8: 6 the seven trumpets made ready to *b* them.
8:13 the other three angels are about to *b*!"
10: 7 for the seventh angel to *b* his trumpet,

BLOWING (16)
Ex 10:13 and the LORD set an east wind *b* over the
Jos 6: 8 ram's horns before the LORD *b* their horns,
6: 9 and the *b* of horns was kept up continually
6:13 of the ark of the LORD, *b* their horns.
6:13 and the *b* of horns was kept up continually.
Jgs 7:20 and in their right the horns they were *b*,
7:22 But the three hundred men kept *b* the horns,
2Kgs 11:14 of the land rejoicing and *b* trumpets,
2Chr 5:12 a hundred and twenty priests *b* trumpets.
23:13 of the land rejoicing and *b* trumpets,
Tb 6: 9 *b* into his eyes right on the cataracts,
1Mc 5:33 *b* their trumpets and shouting in prayer.
7:45 *b* the trumpets behind them as signals.
Eccl 1: 6 *B* now toward the south,
Dn 3:50 a dew-laden breeze were *b* through it.
Jn 6:18 moreover, with a strong wind *b*,

BLOWN (3)
Nm 10: 3 When both are *b*,
10: 4 but when one of them is *b*,
Jude 1:12 They are *b* on the wind like clouds that

BLOWS (25)
Ex 9:14 or this time I will hurl all my *b* upon you
Lv 26:21 me, I will multiply my *b* another sevenfold,
Dt 25:11 her husband from the *b* of his opponent,
28:59 descendants with severe and constant *b*,
Jos 10:20 the last *b* in this very great slaughter,
Jgs 15: 8 And with repeated *b*,
2Sm 18:15 on Absalom, and killed him with further *b*.
2Mc 3:26 until they had given him innumerable *b*.
6:30 When he was about to die under the *b*,
7:37 *b* to make you confess that he alone is God.
Prv 19:29 the arrogant, and *b* for the backs of fools.
Wis 12:22 our enemies with a thousand *b* you punish,
Sir 22:18 height will not remain when the wind *b*;
Is 14: 6 struck the peoples in wrath relentless *b*;
18: 3 When the trumpet *b*, listen!
30:26 he will heal the bruises left by his *b*.
40: 7 when the breath of the LORD *b* upon it.
54:16 I have created the craftsman who *b* on the
Jer 6: 7 ever before me are wounds and *b*.
13:24 chaff that flies when the desert wind *b*.
Bar 6:60 and the same wind *b* over all the land.
Ez 33: 3 country, *b* the trumpet to warn the people,
Dn 8: 7 the ram with furious *b* when they met,
Lk 12:55 When the wind *b* from the south,
Jn 3: 8 The wind *b* where it will.

BLUE (1)
Rv 9:17 they wore were fiery red, deep *b*,

BLUFF (3)
Mt 8:32 down the *b* into the sea and were drowned.
Mk 5:13 went rushing down the *b* into the lake,
Lk 8:33 the herd charged down the *b* into the lake,

BLUNDER (1)
Sir 23:14 commit a *b* and disgrace your upbringing,

BLUNDERS (1)
Prv 19: 2 and he who acts hastily, *b*.

BLUSH (11)
Ps(s) 34: 6 joy, and your faces may not *b* with shame.
69: 7 Let not those who seek you *b* for me,
Sir 41:14 nor is it always the proper thing to *b*:
Is 1:29 and *b* for the groves which you chose.
24:23 Then the moon will *b* and the sun grow pale,
54: 4 you need not *b*, for you shall not be disgraced.
Jer 3: 3 you have a harlot's brow, you refused to *b*.
6:15 not at all ashamed, they know not how to *b*.
8:12 not at all ashamed, they know not how to *b*.
31:19 I *b* with shame,
Ez 16:52 *B* for shame, and bear the shame

BOANERGES (1)
Mk 3:17 of James (he gave these two the name *B*,

BOAR (1)
Ps(s) 80:14 fruit, The *b* from the forest lays it waste,

BOARD (13)
Gn 43:32 and to the Egyptians who partook of his *b*.
Ex 26:16 The length of each *b* is to be ten cubits,
26:17 Each *b* shall have two arms that shall
26:19 that there are two pedestals under each *b*,
26:21 forty silver pedestals, two under each *b*;
26:25 pedestals, two pedestals under each *b*.
36:21 The length of each *b* was ten cubits,
36:22 Each *b* had two arms,
36:24 there were two pedestals under each *b*,
36:26 forty silver pedestals, two under each *b*;
36:30 pedestals, two pedestals under each *b*.
Acts 27:33 dawn Paul urged all on *b* to take some food:
27:37 two hundred and seventy-six of us on *b*.)

BOARDED (3)
Acts 21: 2 for Phoenicia, we *b* it and sailed off.
21: 6 we *b* the ship and they returned home.
27: 2 We *b* a ship from Adramyttium bound for

BOARDS (33)
Ex 26:15 *b* of acacia wood as walls for the Dwelling.
26:17 that shall serve to fasten the *b* in line.
26:17 all the *b* of the Dwelling are to be made.
26:18 Set up the *b* of the Dwelling as follows:
26:18 twenty *b* on the south side,
26:19 forty silver pedestals under the twenty *b*,
26:20 twenty *b* on the other side of the Dwelling,
26:22 six *b* for the rear of the Dwelling,
26:23 and two *b* for the corners at the rear of
26:24 how both *b* in the corners are to be made.
26:25 Thus, there shall be in the rear eight *b*,
26:26 five for the *b* on one side of the Dwelling,
26:28 The center bar, at the middle of the *b*,
26:29 Plate the *b* with gold,
35:11 its tent, its covering, its clasps, its *b*,
36:20 *B* of acacia wood were made as walls for
36:22 way all the *b* of the Dwelling were made.
36:23 twenty *b* on the south side,
36:24 forty silver pedestals under the twenty *b*,
36:25 twenty *b* on the other side of the Dwelling,
36:27 six *b* at the rear of the Dwelling,

36:28 and two *b* at the corners in the rear of
36:29 is how both *b* in the corners were made.
36:30 Thus, there were in the rear eight *b*,
36:31 five for the *b* on one side of the Dwelling,
36:33 The center bar, at the middle of the *b*,
36:34 The *b* were plated with gold,
39:33 all its appurtenances, the clasps, the *b*,
40:18 He placed its pedestals, set up its *b*,
Nm 3:36 pertained to the *b* of the Dwelling,
4:31 the *b* of the Dwelling with its bars,
1Kgs 6: 9 was roofed in with rafters and *b* of cedar.
2Chr 2: 7 Also send me *b* of cedar,

BOAST (47)

Dt 32:27 feared that these foes would mistakenly *b*,
Jgs 9:38 to him, "Where now is the *b* you uttered,
1Kgs 20:11 armor to *b* as though he were taking it off.' "
Jdt 15: 9 You are the splendid *b* of our people.
Ps(s) 49: 7 the abundance of their riches is their *b*.
75: 5 *B* not; and to the wicked:
Prv 27: 1 *B* not of tomorrow,
Sir 10:25 affairs, and *b* not in your time of need.
30: 2 from him, and *b* of him among his intimates.
Is 10:15 the axe *b* against him who hews with it?
20: 5 their hope, and because of Egypt, their *b*.
52: 5 their rulers make a *b* of it,
61: 6 of the nations and *b* of riches from them.
Jer 48:30 his arrogance; liar in *b*, liar in deed.
Hb 3:14 their princes whose *b* would be of devouring
Rom 5: 2 and we *b* of our hope for the glory of God.
5: 3 we even *b* of our afflictions!
5:11 God our *b* through our Lord Jesus Christ,
11:17 the olive, do not *b* against the branches.
11:18 If you do *b*,
1Cor 1:31 "Let him who would *b*, boast in the Lord."
9:15 rather die than let anyone rob me of my *b!*
9:16 the gospel is not the subject of a *b;*
2Cor 1:12 Conscience gives testimony to the *b* that
1:14 will recognize that we shall be your *b*,
5:12 an opportunity to *b* about us
7: 4 with utter frankness and *b* much about you.
8:24 proof of your love, and why we *b* about you,
9: 2 and *b* about you to the Macedonians with
10:15 not *b* immoderately of the work of others;
10:16 without having to *b* of work already done
10:17 "Let him who would *b*, boast in the Lord."
11:10 the Christ who is in me that this *b* of mine
11:18 their human distinctions, I too will *b*.
11:30 If I must *b*,
12: 5 About this man I will *b;*
12: 6 And even if I were to *b* it would not be
12: 9 so I willingly *b* of my weaknesses instead,
Gal 6: 4 if he has reason to *b* of anything,
6:13 they may *b* about your bodily observance.
6:14 May I never *b* of anything but the cross of
Phil 2:16 you give me cause to *b* that I did not run
1Thes 2:20 You are our *b* and our delight.
2Thes 1: 4 we can *b* of your constancy and your faith
Heb 3: 6 our confidence and the hope of which we *b*.

BOASTED (6)

Ex 15: 9 The enemy *b*, "I will pursue
Jer 48:26 Because he *b* against the LORD,
48:42 a people, because he *b* against the LORD.
Dn 8:11 It *b* even against the prince of the host,
Zep 2:10 *b* against the people of the LORD of hosts.
2Cor 7:14 For though I had *b* to him about you,

BOASTER (1)

Sir 10:26 everything than the *b* who is without bread.

BOASTFUL (6)

Jb 36: 9 they have done and their sins of *b* pride.
Ps(s) 12: 4 the LORD destroy all smooth every *b* tongue,
75: 5 I say to the *b:* Boast not;
Sir 21: 7 Widely known is the *b* speaker but the wise
Rom 1:30 they hate God, are insolent, haughty, *b*,
Gal 5:26 Let us never be *b*, or challenging,

BOASTFULLY (3)

1Sm 2: 3 "Speak *b* no longer,
2Mc 15:32 blasphemer's arm that had been *b* stretched
Prv 25:14 the man who *b* promises what he never gives.

BOASTFULNESS (4)

Est E: 4 *b* of those to whom goodness has no meaning,
2Mc 15: 6 In his utter *b* and arrogance Nicanor had
Wis 5: 8 What have wealth and its *b* afforded us?
Is 10:13 proud heart, and the *b* of his haughty eyes.

BOASTING (18)

Jdt 6:17 and of all the *b* threats of Holofernes
9: 7 rider, *b* of the power of their infantry,
Ps(s) 94: 4 glory, Mouthing insolent speeches, *b*,
Sir 20: 6 but a *b* fool ignores the proper time.
Jer 23:32 recounting their lies and by their empty *b*.
Rom 3:27 What occasion is there then for *b?*
4: 2 by his deeds he has grounds for *b*,
1Cor 1:29 so that mankind can do no *b* before God.
3:21 Let there be no *b* about men.
4: 7 it, why are you *b* as if it were your own?
5: 6 This *b* of yours is an ugly thing.
2Cor 7:14 my *b* to Titus has been proved equally true.
11:16 fool all the way and let me do a little *b*.
11:17 I am about to say in this self-assured *b*,
12: 1 I must go on *b*, however useless it may be
12: 5 but I will do no *b* about myself unless it
Jas 4:16 All such *b* is reprehensible.
Rv 18: 7 In proportion to her *b* and sensuality,

BOASTS (7)

Ps(s) 10: 4 The wicked man *b*,
Prv 20:14 but once he has gone his way, he *b*.
Wis 2:16 of the just and *b* that God is his Father.
Sir 13: 3 The rich man does wrong and *b* of it,
Zep 2: 8 people and made *b* against their territory.
Rv 13: 5 mouth for uttering proud *b* and blasphemies,

BOAT (45)

Wis 14: 1 more unsound than the *b* that bears him.
Sir 33: 2 and is tossed about like a *b* in a storm.
Is 33:21 and wide streams on which no *b* is rowed,
Mt 4:21 They too were in their *b*,
4:22 they abandoned *b* and father to follow him.
8:23 into the *b* and his disciples followed him.
8:24 and the *b* began to be swamped by the waves.
9: 1 Then he reentered the *b*,
13: 2 a *b* while the crowd stood along the shore.
14:13 he withdrew by *b* from there to a deserted
14:22 the *b* and precede him to the other side.
14:24 the *b*, already several hundred yards out
14:29 of the *b* and began to walk on the water,
14:32 Once they had climbed into the *b*,
14:33 who were in the *b* showed him reverence,
15:39 the *b* and went to the district of Magadan.
Mk 1:19 in their *b* putting their nets in order.
1:20 who was in the *b* with the hired men,
3: 9 he told his disciples to have a fishing *b* ready
4: 1 that he went and sat in a *b* on the water,
4:36 him away in the *b* in which he was sitting,
4:37 the *b* and it began to ship water badly.
5: 2 As he got out of the *b*,
5:18 As Jesus was getting into the *b*,
5:21 back to the other side again in the *b*,
6:32 in the *b* by themselves to a deserted place.
6:45 his disciples get into the *b* and precede him
6:47 the *b* was far out on the lake while he was
6:51 the *b* with them and the wind died down.
6:54 the *b* people immediately recognized him.
8:10 He dismissed them and got into the *b* with
8:13 Then he left them, got into the *b* again,
8:14 one loaf they had none with them in the *b*.
Lk 5: 3 continued to teach the crowds from the *b*.
5: 7 mates in the other *b* to come and help them.
8:22 a *b* with his disciples and said to them,
8:37 into the *b* and went back across the lake.
Jn 6:19 they sighted Jesus approaching the *b*,
6:21 They wanted to take him into the *b*,
6:22 realized that there had been only one *b* there
21: 3 replied, and went off to get into their *b*.
21: 8 the other disciples came in the *b*,
Acts 27:16 we able to gain control of the ship's *b*.
27:30 they let the ship's *b* down into the sea.
27:32 soldiers cut the ropes and let the *b* drift.

BOATS (10)

2Mc 12: 3 to embark on *b* which they had provided.
12: 6 he set the harbor on fire, burnt the *b*,
Is 18: 2 by sea, in papyrus *b* on the waters!
Mk 4:36 sitting, while the other *b* accompanied him.
Lk 5: 2 saw two *b* moored by the side of the lake;
5: 3 He got into one of the *b*,
5: 7 filled the two *b* until they nearly sank.
5:11 With that they brought their *b* to land,
Jn 6:23 Then some *b* came out from Tiberias near
6:24 *b* and went to Capernaum looking for Jesus.

BOAZ (28)

Ru 2: 1 Naomi had a prominent kinsman named *B*,
2: 3 belonging to *B* of the clan of Elimelech.
2: 4 *B* himself came from Bethlehem and said to
2: 5 *B* asked the overseer of his harvesters,
2: 8 *B* said to Ruth, "Listen, my daughter!
2:11 *B* answered her: "I have had a complete
2:14 At mealtime *B* said to her,
2:15 and *B* instructed his servants to let her
2:19 at whose place I worked today is named *B*,"
2:23 stayed gleaning with the servants of *B*
3: 2 is not *B*, with whose servants you were,
3: 7 *B* ate and drank to his heart's content.
3:14 *B* said, "Let it not be known
4: 1 *B* went and took a seat at the gate;
4: 2 Then *B* picked out ten of the elders of the
4: 5 *B* continued, "Once you acquire the field
4: 8 So the near relative, in saying to *B*,
4: 9 *B* then said to the elders and to all the
4:13 *B* took Ruth.
4:21 was the father of *B*, Boaz was the father
1Kgs 7:21 and the other to the left, called *B*.
1Chr 2:11 Salma became the father of *B*.
2:12 *B* became the father of Obed.
2Chr 3:17 the right Jachin and the one to the left *B*.
Mt 1: 5 Salmon was the father of *B*,
1: 5 mother was Rahab, *B* was the father of Obed,
Lk 3:32 son of Jesse, son of Obed, son of *B*,

BOCHIM (2)

Jgs 2: 1 the LORD went up from Gilgal to *B* and said,
2: 5 and so that place came to be called *B*.

BODIES (52)

Gn 47:18 disposal except our *b* and our farm land.
Lv 11: 8 eat, and their dead *b* you shall not touch;
11:11 not eat, and their dead *b* you shall loathe.
11:24 dead *b* shall be unclean until evening,
11:25 who picks up any part of their dead *b*
11:27 dead *b* shall be unclean until evening,
11:28 who picks up their dead *b* shall wash
11:35 object on which one of their dead *b* falls,
11:37 though one of their dead *b* falls on it;
19:28 Do not lacerate your *b* for the dead,
Nm 8: 7 shave their whole *b* and wash their clothes,
14:29 Here in the desert shall your dead *b* fall.
14:32 you, your *b* shall fall here in the desert,
Dt 14: 8 eat, and their dead *b* you shall not touch.
1Sm 31:12 removed the *b* of Saul and his sons from
2Sm 1:22 of the slain, from the *b* of the valiant,
1Chr 10:12 man, recovered the *b* of Saul and his sons,
Neh 9:37 over our *b* and our cattle as they please.
Tb 1:18 to take their *b* by stealth and bury them;
1Mc 11: 4 and the charred *b* of those burned by
2Mc 1:16 They dismembered the *b*,
12:39 gather up the *b* of the slain and bury
Ps(s) 44:26 the dust, our *b* are pressed to the earth.
73: 4 their *b* are sound and sleek;
Sir 44:14 Their *b* are peacefully laid away,
Is 66:14 rejoice and your *b* flourish like the grass;
Jer 41: 5 with gashes on their *b* came from Shechem,
Bar 6:21 alight on their *b* and on their heads;
Ez 11:19 will remove the stony heart from their *b*,
36:26 taking from your *b* your stony hearts and
Dn 3:94 had had no power over the *b* of these men;
3:95 yielded their *b* rather than serve or worship
Na 3: 3 corpses, the endless *b* to stumble upon!
Mt 27:53 Many *b* of saints who had fallen asleep
Jn 19:31 the *b* left on the cross during the sabbath,
19:31 the legs be broken and the *b* be taken away.
Rom 1:24 in the mutual degradation of their *b*,
6:13 and your *b* to God as weapons for justice.
6:19 Just as formerly you enslaved your *b* to
8:11 dead will bring your mortal *b* to life also,
8:23 while we await the redemption of our *b*.
12: 1 offer your *b* as a living sacrifice
1Cor 6:15 not see that your *b* are members of Christ?
15:40 heavenly *b* and there are earthly bodies.
15:40 splendor of the heavenly *b* is one thing,
2Cor 4:10 we carry about in our *b* the dying of Jesus,
4:10 *b* the life of Jesus may also be revealed.
Eph 5:28 love their wives as they do their own *b*.
Heb 10:22 conscience and our *b* washed in pure water.
13:11 The *b* of the animals whose blood is
Jas 3: 3 them obey us, we guide the rest of their *b*.

BODILY (15)

Gn 8:17 all *b* creatures,
9:11 that never again shall all *b* creatures be
1Sm 28:20 Moreover, he had no *b* strength left,
2Kgs 20:18 Some of your own *b* descendants shall be
2Mc 3:17 The terror and *b* trembling that had come
Wis 18:22 overcame the bitterness not by *b* strength,
Sir 49:14 the equal of ENOCH, for he was taken up *b*.
Is 39: 7 Some of your own *b* descendants shall be
Jn 9:34 With that they threw him out *b*.
1Cor 15:39 Not all *b* nature is the same.
Gal 4:13 You are aware that it was a *b* ailment that
6:13 they may boast about your *b* observance.
Col 2: 9 the fullness of deity resides in *b* form.
2:23 affected piety, humility, and *b* austerity,
Jas 2:16 well fed," but do not meet their *b* needs,

BODY (234)

Gn 1: 6 to separate one *b* of water from the other."
2:24 his wife, and the two of them become one *b*.
25:25 and his whole *b* was like a hairy mantle;
39: 6 strikingly handsome in countenance and *b*.
40:19 will be pecking the flesh from your *b*."
Ex 4: 7 it was again like the rest of his *b*.
22:26 his is the only covering he has for his *b*.
30:32 used in any ordinary anointing of the *b*,
Lv 6: 3 robe and wearing linen drawers on his *b*,
11:36 whoever touches the dead *b* becomes unclean.
11:39 its dead *b* shall be unclean until evening.
11:40 and anyone who eats of its dead *b* shall
11:40 anyone who removes its dead *b* shall wash
13:13 that the leprosy does cover his whole *b*,
13:43 skin leprosy of the fleshy part of the *b*,
14: 9 wash his garments and bathe his *b* in water;
15: 7 Whoever touches the *b* of the afflicted man
15:13 garments and bathe his *b* in fresh water,
15:16 he shall bathe his whole *b* in water
16: 4 until he has first bathed his *b* in water.
16:24 bathing his *b* with water in a sacred place,

BODY (cont.)

16:26 wash his garments and bathe his *b* in water;
16:28 wash his garments and bathe his *b* in water;
17:11 the life of a living *b* is in its blood,
17:14 the life of every living *b* is its blood,
17:14 the life of every living *b* is its blood,
17:16 he does not wash or does not bathe his *b*,
20: 3 and cut him off from the *b* of his people;
21: 5 the edges of the beard, nor lacerate the *b*.
22: 6 until he has first bathed his *b* in water,
Nm 4:18 clans perish from the *b* of the Levites.
5:22 enter your *b* to make your belly swell and
18: 6 the Levites, from the *b* of the Israelites;
19: 7 wash his garments and bathe his *b* in water.
19: 8 wash his garments, bathe his *b* in water,
19:11 "Whoever touches the dead *b* of any human
19:13 touching the *b* of any deceased person,
19:18 a bone, a slain person or other dead *b*,
19:19 wash his garments and bathe his *b* in water,
Jos 8:13 with the main *b* north of the city and the
8:15 Joshua and the main *b* of the Israelites
8:21 for when Joshua and the main *b* of
8:29 Joshua ordered the *b* removed
Jgs 3:22 he did not withdraw the dagger from his *b*.
19:29 he took a knife to the *b* of his concubine,
1Sm 8: 4 in a *b* to Samuel at Ramah and said to him,
31:10 impaled his *b* on the wall of Beth-shan.
1Kgs 12:10 finger is thicker than my father's *b*.
13:25 passers-by saw the *b* lying in the road,
13:28 he went off and found the *b* lying in the
13:28 not eaten the *b* nor had it harmed the ass.
13:29 *b* of the man of God and put it on the ass,
13:30 He laid the man's *b* in his own grave,
17:21 life breath return to the *b* of this child."
17:22 returned to the child's *b* and he revived.
2Kgs 4:34 himself over the child, the *b* became warm.
9:33 Jehu rode in over her *b* and,
23:30 *b* on a chariot from Megiddo to Jerusalem,
2Chr 10:10 finger is thicker than my father's *b*.
Tb 2: 3 His *b* lies in the market place where he
Jdt 9: 2 thighs, and disgracefully violated her *b*.
10: 3 of her widowhood, washed her *b* with water,
13: 9 She rolled his *b* off the bed and took the
Est C:13 She afflicted her *b* severely;
1Mc 5: 6 *b* of people with Timothy as their leader.
12:50 and went out in compact *b* ready to fight.
2Mc 6:30 terrible pain in my *b* from this scourging,
7: 7 than have your *b* tortured limb by limb?"
7:37 up my *b* and my life for our ancestral laws,
9: 7 of his *b* was racked by the violent fall.
9: 9 *b* of this impious man swarmed with worms,
9:29 foster brother Philip brought the *b* home;
14:38 *b* and life in his ardent zeal for it.
15:30 who was ever in *b* and soul the chief
Ps(s) 6: 3 heal me, O LORD, for my *b* is in terror;
16: 9 my soul rejoices, my *b*, too, abides,
31:10 my soul also, and my *b*.
68:28 the princes of Judah in a *b*,
Prv 5:11 when your flesh and your *b* are consumed;
14:30 A tranquil mind gives life to the *b*,
16:24 sweet to the taste and healthful to the *b*.
17:22 A joyful heart is the health of the *b*,
Sg 5:14 His *b* is a work of ivory covered with
7: 3 *b* is a heap of wheat encircled with lilies.
Wis 1: 4 nor dwells she in a *b* under debt of sin.
2: 3 our *b* will be ashes and our spirit will be
7: 2 flesh in a ten-months' period *b* and blood,
8:20 being noble, I attained an unsullied *b*.
9:15 For the corruptible *b* burdens the soul and
Sir 10: 9 even during life man's *b* decays;
30:16 No treasure greater than a healthy *b*;
38:16 As is only proper, prepare the *b*,
41:11 Man's *b* is a fleeting thing,
43:21 He freezes over every *b* of water,
47:19 women and gave them dominion over your *b*.
49:15 Even his dead *b* was provided for.
51: 2 death, and kept back my *b* from the pit,
Is 10:18 will be consumed, soul and *b*;
17: 4 Jacob shall fade, and his full *b* grow thin,
Ez 1:11 the other two wings of each covered his *b*.
1:23 [Each of them had two covering his *b*
Dn 4:30 his *b* was bathed with the dew of heaven,
5:21 his *b* was bathed with the dew of heaven,
7:11 its *b* thrown into the fire to be burnt up.
10: 6 His *b* was like chrysolite,
Mi 6: 7 the fruit of my *b* for the sin of my soul?
Hb 3:16 I hear, and my *b* trembles;
Mt 5:29 *b* than to have it all cast into Gehenna.
5:30 Better to lose part of your *b*
6:22 are good, your *b* will be filled with light;
6:23 eyes are bad, your *b* will be in darkness.
6:25 Is not the *b* more valuable than clothes?
10:28 the *b* of life but cannot destroy the soul.
10:28 who can destroy both *b* and soul in Gehenna.
14:12 themselves to carry his *b* away and bury it.
22:34 the Sadducees, they assembled in a *b*;
26:12 By pouring this perfume on my *b*,
26:26 this and eat it," he said, "this is my *b*."
27:58 and had gone to request the *b* of Jesus.
27:59 Taking the *b*,
Mk 5:29 of her affliction ran through her whole *b*.
6:29 carried his *b* away and laid it in a tomb.
14: 8 By perfuming my *b* she is anticipating its
14:22 "Take this," he said, "this is my *b*."
15:43 and urgently requested the *b* of Jesus.
Lk 11:34 The eye is the lamp of your *b*.
11:34 is sound, your whole *b* is lighted up,
11:34 eyesight is bad, your *b* is in darkness.
11:36 *b* is lighted up and not partly in darkness,
12: 4 of those who kill the *b* and can do no more.
12:22 life, what you are to eat, or for your *b*,
12:23 than food and the *b* more than clothing.
22:19 "This is my *b* to be given for you.
23:52 Pilate with a request for Jesus' *b*.
23:55 They saw the tomb and how his *b* was buried.
24: 3 they did not find the *b* of the Lord Jesus.
24:23 tomb before dawn and failed to find his *b*,
Jn 2:21 he was talking about the temple of his *b*.
19:38 Pilate's permission to remove Jesus' *b*.
19:38 it, so they came and took the *b* away.
19:40 They took Jesus' *b*,
20:12 foot of the place where Jesus' *b* had lain.
Acts 1:18 His *b* burst wide open,
2:26 has rejoiced, my *b* will live on in hope,
2:31 world, nor did his *b* undergo corruption,
5: 6 young men came forward, wrapped up the *b*,
9:37 her *b* and laid it out in an upstairs room.
9:40 Turning to the dead *b*, he said, "Tabitha,
18:12 the Jews rose in a *b* against Paul and
Rom 4:19 weak in faith he thought of his own *b*,
6: 6 that the sinful *b* might be destroyed
6:12 your mortal *b* and make you obey its lusts;
6:13 of your *b* to sin as weapons for evil.
7: 4 died to the law through the *b* of Christ,
7:24 me from this *b* under the power of death?
8:10 is in you, the *b* is dead because of sin,
8:13 you put to death the evil deeds of the *b*,
12: 4 as each of us has one *b* with many members,
12: 5 are one *b* in Christ and individually
1Cor 5: 3 though absent in *b* I am present in spirit,
6:13 but the *b* is not for immorality;
6:13 is for the Lord, and the Lord is for the *b*.
6:16 to a prostitute becomes one *b* with her?
6:18 other sin a man commits is outside his *b*,
6:18 but the fornicator sins against his own *b*.
6:19 that your *b* is a temple of the Holy Spirit,
6:20 So glorify God in your *b*.
7:34 in pursuit of holiness in *b* and spirit.
9:27 I do is discipline my own *b* and master it,
10:16 we break a sharing in the *b* of Christ?
10:17 is one, we, many though we are, are one *b*,
11:24 thanks, broke it and said, "This is my *b*,
11:27 sins against the *b* and blood of the Lord.
11:29 *b* eats and drinks a judgment on himself.
12:12 The *b* is one and has many members,
12:12 members, many though they are, are one *b*;
12:13 slave or free, were baptized into one *b*.
12:14 Now the *b* is not one member, it is many.
12:15 I am not a hand I do not belong to the *b*,"
12:15 would it then no longer belong to the *b*?
12:16 I am not an eye I do not belong to the *b*,"
12:16 would it then no longer belong to the *b*?
12:17 If the *b* were all eye,
12:18 of the *b* in the place he wanted it to be.
12:19 members were alike, where would the *b* be?
12:20 indeed, many different members, but one *b*.
12:22 Even those members of the *b* which seem
12:24 God has so constructed the *b* as to give
12:25 that there may be no dissension in the *b*,
12:27 You, then, are the *b* of Christ.
13: 3 the poor and hand over my *b* to be burned,
15:35 What kind of *b* will they have?"
15:38 God gives *b* to it as he pleases
15:39 Men have one kind of *b*, animals another.
15:44 natural *b* is put down and a spiritual body
15:44 *b*, be sure there is also a spiritual body.
15:53 *b* must be clothed with incorruptibility,
15:53 this mortal *b* with immortality.
2Cor 4:16 our *b* is being destroyed at the same time.
5: 6 dwell in the *b* we are away from the Lord.
5: 8 away from the *b* and at home with the Lord.
5:10 or bad, according to his life in the *b*.
10: 3 We do indeed live in the *b* but we do not
12: 2 he was in or outside his *b* I cannot say,
12: 3 whether in or outside his *b* I do not know,
Gal 6:17 I bear the brand marks of Jesus in my *b*.
Eph 1:23 head of the church, which is his *b*:
2:16 of us to God in one *b* through his cross,
3: 6 members of the same *b* and sharers of the
4: 4 There is but one *b* and one Spirit,
4:12 the faithful to build up the *b* of Christ,
4:16 Through him the whole *b* grows,
5:23 just as Christ is head of his *b* the church,
5:30 for we are members of his *b*.
Phil 3:21 He will give a new form to this lowly *b* of
3:21 to the pattern of his glorified *b*,
Col 1:18 It is he who is head of the *b*,
1:22 for you in his mortal *b* by dying,
1:24 sufferings of Christ for the sake of his *b*,
2: 5 be absent in *b* but I am with you in spirit,
2:11 which strips off the carnal *b* completely.
2:17 the reality is the *b* of Christ.
2:19 The whole *b*, mutually supported
3:15 one *b* you have been called to that peace.
1Thes 5:23 you whole and entire, spirit, soul, and *b*,
Heb 10: 5 desire, but a *b* you have prepared for me;
10:10 of the *b* of Jesus Christ once for all.
Jas 2:26 works is as dead as a *b* without breath.
3: 2 sense, because he can control his entire *b*.
3: 6 The tongue defiles the entire *b*.
1Pt 2:24 own *b* he brought your sins to the cross,
Jude 1: 9 a dispute over Moses' *b*—

BODYGUARD (18)

1Sm 22:14 the king's son-in-law, captain of your *b*,
28: 2 "I shall appoint you my permanent *b*."
2Sm 23:23 David put him in command of his *b*.
2Kgs 25: 8 Babylon), Nebuzaradan, captain of the *b*,
1Chr 11:25 David put him in charge of his *b*.
Neh 4:17 *b* that accompanied me took off his clothes;
Jdt 12: 7 Holofernes ordered his *b* not to hinder her.
2Mc 3:28 and his whole *b* was carried away helpless,
Jer 39: 9 Nebuzaradan, chief of the *b*,
39:10 of Judah by Nebuzaradan, chief of the *b*,
39:11 orders through Nebuzaradan, chief of the *b*:
39:13 Thereupon Nebuzaradan, chief of the *b*,
40: 1 LORD, after Nebuzaradan, captain of the *b*,
40: 2 captain of the *b* took charge of Jeremiah,
40: 5 *b* gave him food and gifts and let him go.
41:10 whom Nebuzaradan, captain of the *b*,
43: 6 whom Nebuzaradan, captain of the *b*,
52:12 Babylon), Nebuzaradan, captain of the *b*,

BODYGUARDS (1)

2Mc 3:24 was approaching the treasury with his *b*,

BODY'S (2)

Mt 6:22 The eye is the *b* lamp.
Rom 7:23 but I see in my *b* members another law at

BOIL (17)

Ex 16:23 You may either bake or *b* the manna,
23:19 shall not *b* a kid in its mother's milk.
29:31 ordination ram and *b* it in the holy place.
34:26 shall not *b* a kid in its mother's milk."
Lv 8:31 "*B* the flesh at the entrance of the meeting
13:18 who had a *b* on his skin which later healed,
13:19 the *b* have a white scab or a pink blotch,
13:20 of leprosy that has broken out in the *b*.
13:23 spreading, it is merely the scar of the *b*;
Dt 14:21 shall not *b* a kid in its mother's milk.
1Kgs 19:21 equipment for fuel to *b* their flesh,
2Kgs 20: 7 of figs to be brought and applied to the *b*,
Jb 41:23 He makes the depths *b* like a pot;
Is 38:21 of figs to be taken and applied to the *b*,
64: 1 is set ablaze, or fire makes the water *b*!
Jer 1:14 will *b* over upon all who dwell in the land.
Ez 24: 5 bring to a *b* these pieces and the joints

BOILED (8)

Ex 12: 9 It shall not be eaten raw or *b*,
Nm 6:19 priest shall take a *b* shoulder of the ram,
1Sm 2:15 He will not accept *b* meat from you,
2Kgs 6:29 So we *b* my son and ate him.
Lam 4:10 compassionate women *b* their own children,
Ez 24:10 meat has been cooked, till the broth has *b*.
Dn 14:27 these he *b* together and made into cakes.
14:33 bread in a bowl with the stew he had *b*,

BOILING (2)

1Sm 2:13 fork, while the meat was still *b*,
Jer 1:13 "I see a *b* cauldron,"

BOILS (8)

Ex 9: 9 *b* on man and beast throughout the land."
9:10 and it caused festering *b* on man and beast.
9:11 for there were *b* on the magicians no less
Dt 28:27 strike you with Egyptian *b* and with tumors,
28:35 malignant *b* of which you cannot be cured,
Jb 2: 7 smote Job with severe *b* from the soles
Rv 16: 2 severe and festering *b* broke out on the
16:11 because of their suffering and their *b*.

BOLD (13)

1Chr 17:25 your servant has made *b* to pray before you.
2Mc 3:24 been *b* enough to follow Heliodorus
Sir 12:15 While you stand firm, he makes no *b* move;
13:10 Be not *b* with him lest you be rebuffed,
26:11 Follow close if her eyes are *b*,
Is 3: 5 The child shall be *b* toward the elder,
13: 3 eager and *b* to carry out my anger.
Mt 23: 4 Their words are *b* but their deeds are few.
Mk 15:43 He was *b* enough to seek an audience with
Acts 2: 4 make *b* proclamations as the Spirit
2Cor 10: 1 am lowly, but when absent am *b* toward you.
10:12 We are not so *b*,
2Pt 2:10 These *b* and arrogant men have no qualms

BOLDLY (4)

Sir 21:22 The fool steps *b* into a house,
Rom 10:20 Then Isaiah says *b*,
15:15 Yet I have written to you rather *b* in
2Cor 10: 2 when I am there, I may not have to act *b*,

BOLDNESS (3)

Jdt 16:10 at her daring, the Medes appalled at her *b.*
1Mc 4:32 with fear, weaken the *b* of their strength,
4:35 to give way, and the increased *b* of Judas,

BOLTS (9)

Dt 33:25 May your *b* be of iron and bronze;
Neh 3: 1 timbered it and set up its doors, its *b,*
3: 3 timbered it and set up its doors, its *b,*
3: 6 timbered it and set up its doors, its *b,*
3:13 rebuilt it and set up its doors, its *b,*
3:14 he rebuilt it and set up its doors, its *b,*
3:15 it over, and set up its doors, its *b,*
Bar 6:17 their houses with gates and bars and *b,*
Na 2: 5 like firebrands, flashing like lightning *b.*

BOMBAST (2)

2Pt 2:18 *b* while baiting their hooks with passion,
Jude 1:16 They live by their passions, uttering *b.*

BOND (9)

1Sm 18: 3 And Jonathan entered into a *b* with David,
20: 8 servant because of the LORD's *b* between us,
2Sm 21: 7 a *b* between David and Saul's son Jonathan.
Tb 9: 2 Go to Gabael's house and give him this *b.*
9: 5 *b* and told him about Tobit's son Tobiah,
Prv 22: 2 Rich and poor have a common *b:*
29:13 poor and the oppressor have a common *b:*
Wis 17:18 all were bound by the one *b* of darkness.
Col 2:14 He canceled the *b* that stood against us

BONDAGE (2)

Lk 13:16 been in the *b* of Satan for eighteen years
Jude 1: 6 These the Lord has kept in perpetual *b,*

BONDED (1)

Sir 22:16 Masonry *b* with wooden beams is not

BONDING (2)

1Kgs 7: 9 a saw, from the foundation to the *b* course.
7:12 hewn stones and a *b* course of cedar beams.

BONDMAN (1)

Jer 2:14 Is Israel a slave, a *b* by birth?

BONDS (23)

Jgs 15:14 fire and his *b* melted away from his hands.
Jb 12:18 He loosens the *b* imposed by kings and
30:11 Indeed, they have loosed their *b;*
36: 8 fetters and held fast by *b* of affliction,
38:31 the Pleiades, or loosened the *b* of Orion?
39: 5 his freedom, and who has loosed him from *b?*
Ps(s) 2: 3 their fetters and cast their *b* from us!"
69:34 and his own who are in *b* he spurns not.
107:14 and gloom and broke their *b* asunder.
116:16 you have loosed my *b.*
Eccl 7:26 is a snare and whose hands are prison *b.*
Wis 10:14 dungeon, and did not desert him in his *b,*
Sir 6:26 and be not irked at her *b.*
6:30 her *b,* your purple cord.
Is 28:22 arrogant no more lest your *b* be tightened,
52: 2 Loose the *b* from your neck,
Jer 2:20 you broke your yoke, you tore off your *b.*
30: 8 yoke from off your necks and snap your *b.*"
Ez 34:27 when I break the *b* of their yoke
Na 1:13 from off you, and burst asunder your *b.*
Zec 11: 7 which I called "Favor," and the other, *B,*"
11:14 Then I snapped asunder my other staff, *B,*"
Lk 8:29 but he would break his *b* and the demon

BONDSMEN (1)

Ps(s) 107:10 and gloom, *b* in want and in chains,

BONDWOMEN (1)

2Chr 28:10 of Judah and Jerusalem your slaves and *b.*

BONE (14)

Gn 2:23 is *b* of my bones and flesh of my flesh;
Nm 19:16 or who touches a human *b* or a grave,
19:18 were in it, or on him who touched a *b,*
Jgs 9: 2 remember that I am your own flesh and *b.*"
2Sm 5: 1 "Here we are, your *b* and your flesh.
19:13 are my brothers, you are my *b* and flesh.
19:14 'Are you not my *b* and flesh?
1Chr 11: 1 we are of the same *b* and flesh as you.
Jb 2: 5 your hand and touch his *b* and his flesh,
Ps(s) 102: 6 sighing I am reduced to skin and *b.*
Prv 25:15 and a soft tongue will break a *b.*
Ez 37: 7 as the bones came together, *b* joining bone.
39:15 pass through, should they see a human *b,*

BONES (81)

Gn 2:23 is bone of my *b* and flesh of my flesh;
50:25 bring my *b* up with you from this place."
Ex 12:46 You shall not break any of its *b.*
13:19 Moses also took Joseph's *b* along,
13:19 they would carry his *b* away with them.
Nm 9:12 till morning, nor breaking any of its *b,*
24: 8 like grass, their *b* he shall strip bare.
Jos 24:32 The *b* of Joseph,
1Sm 31:13 Then they took their *b* and buried them
2Sm 21:12 he went and obtained the *b* of Saul and of
21:13 the *b* of Saul and of his son Jonathan,
21:13 the *b* of those who had been dismembered
21:14 Then the *b* of Saul and of his son Jonathan
1Kgs 13: 2 you, and he shall burn human *b* upon you.'"
2Kgs 13:21 man came in contact with the *b* of Elisha,
23:14 places where they had been with human *b.*
23:16 he ordered the *b* taken from the graves and
23:18 him be," he said, "let no one move his *b.*"
23:18 *b* undisturbed together with the bones
23:20 the shrines, and burned human *b* upon them.
1Chr 10:12 buried their *b* under the oak of Jabesh,
2Chr 34: 5 and the *b* of the priests he burned upon
Jb 4:14 and shuddering, that terrified me to the *b.*
10:11 me, with *b* and sinews knit me together.
19:20 My *b* cleave to my skin,
21:24 nourished, and his *b* are rich in marrow.
33:21 so that it cannot be seen, and his *b,*
40:18 His *b* are like tubes of bronze;
Ps(s) 22:15 all my *b* are racked.
22:18 I can count all my *b.*
31:11 through affliction, and my *b* are consumed.
32: 3 *b* wasted away with my groaning all the day,
34:21 He watches over all his *b;*
38: 4 is no wholeness in my *b* because of my sin,
42:11 It crushes my *b* that my foes mock me,
51:10 the *b* you have crushed shall rejoice.
53: 6 God has scattered the *b* of your besiegers;
102: 4 vanish like smoke, and my *b* burn like fire.
109:18 like water and like oil into his *b;*
141: 7 so their *b* are strewn by the edge of the
Prv 3: 8 health for your flesh and vigor for your *b.*
12: 4 but a disgraceful one is like rot in his *b.*
14:30 life to the body, but jealousy rots the *b.*
15:30 good news invigorates the *b.*
17:22 but a depressed spirit dries up the *b.*
Sir 26:13 her thoughtfulness puts flesh on his *b;*
28:17 but a blow from the tongue smashes *b;*
46:12 *b* return to life from their resting place,
49:10 *b* return to life from their resting place!—
Is 38:13 Like a lion he breaks all my *b;*
Jer 8: 1 the *b* of the kings and princes of Judah,
8: 1 the *b* of the priests and the prophets,
8: 1 and the *b* of the citizens of Jerusalem
20: 9 burning in my heart, imprisoned in my *b;*
23: 2 within me is broken, my *b* all tremble;
50:17 now Nebuchadnezzar of Babylon gnaws her *b.*
Lam 3: 4 my flesh and my skin, he has broken my *b;*
4: 8 Their skin shrinks on their *b,*
Bar 2:24 to have the *b* of our kings and the bones
Ez 6: 5 scatter their *b* all around your altars.
32:27 and whose shields were laid over their *b,*
37: 1 of the plain, which was now filled with *b.*
37: 3 Son of man, can these *b* come to life?
37: 4 Prophesy over these *b,* and say to them:
37: 4 Dry *b,* hear the word of the LORD!
37: 5 Thus says the Lord GOD to these *b:*
37: 7 it was a rattling as the *b* came together,
37:11 these *b* are the whole house of Israel.
37:11 have been saying, "Our *b* are dried up,
Dn 6:25 overpowered them and crushed all their *b.*
Am 2: 1 he burned to ashes the *b* of Edom's king,
Mi 3: 2 from them, and their flesh from their *b!*
3: 3 their skin from them, and break their *b.*
Hb 3:16 Decay invades my *b,*
Zep 3: 3 that have had no *b* to gnaw by morning.
Mt 23:27 but inside full of filth and dead men's *b.*
Lk 24:39 a ghost does not have flesh and *b* as I do."
24:53 a ghost does not have flesh and *b* as I do."
Jn 19:36 "Break none of his *b.*"

BONFIRE (1)

Ez 24: 9 I, too, will heap up a great *b,*

BONUS (4)

Tb 2:14 given to me as a *b* over and above my wages."
5:16 my son, I will even add a *b* to your wages!"
12: 1 give him a *b* too."
12: 3 How much of a *b* should I give him?"

BOOK (149)

Ex 24: 7 Taking the *b* of the covenant,
32:32 me out of the *b* that you have written."
32:33 against me will I strike out of my *b.*
Nm 21:14 is said in the *B* of the Wars of the LORD":
Dt 28:58 of the law which is written in this *b,*
28:61 not mentioned in this *b* of the law,
29:19 mentioned in this *b* will alight on him.
29:20 covenant inscribed in this *b* of the law.
29:26 it all the imprecations listed in this *b;*
30:10 that are written in this *b* of the law,
Jos 1: 8 Keep this *b* of the law on your lips.
8:31 the LORD, as recorded in the *b* of the law.
8:34 exactly as written in the *b* of the law.
10:13 Is this not recorded in the *B* of Jashar?
23: 6 is written in the *b* of the law of Moses,
24:26 he recorded in the *b* of the law of God.
1Sm 10:25 the law of royalty and wrote it in a *b,*
2Sm 1:18 *B* of Jashar to be taught to the Judahites.
1Kgs 11:41 in the *b* of the chronicles of Solomon.
14:19 *b* of the chronicles of the kings of Israel.
14:29 *b* of the chronicles of the kings of Judah.
15: 7 *b* of the chronicles of the kings of Judah.
15:23 *b* of the chronicles of the kings of Judah.
15:31 *b* of the chronicles of the kings of Israel.
16: 5 *b* of the chronicles of the kings of Israel.
16:14 *b* of the chronicles of the kings of Israel.
16:20 *b* of the chronicles of the kings of Israel.
16:27 *b* of the chronicles of the kings of Israel.
22:39 *b* of the chronicles of the kings of Israel.
22:46 *b* of the chronicles of the kings of Judah.
2Kgs 1:18 the *b* of chronicles of the kings of Israel.
8:23 *b* of the chronicles of the kings of Judah.
10:34 *b* of the chronicles of the kings of Israel.
12:20 *b* of the chronicles of the kings of Judah.
13: 8 *b* of the chronicles of the kings of Israel.
13:12 *b* of the chronicles of the kings of Israel.
14: 6 written in the *b* of the law of Moses,
14:15 *b* of the chronicles of the kings of Israel.
14:18 *b* of the chronicles of the kings of Judah.
14:28 *b* of the chronicles of the kings of Israel.
15: 6 *b* of the chronicles of the kings of Judah.
15:11 *b* of the chronicles of the kings of Israel.
15:15 *b* of the chronicles of the kings of Israel.
15:21 *b* of the chronicles of the kings of Israel.
15:26 *b* of the chronicles of the kings of Israel.
15:31 *b* of the chronicles of the kings of Israel.
15:36 *b* of the chronicles of the kings of Judah.
16:19 *b* of the chronicles of the kings of Judah.
20:20 *b* of the chronicles of the kings of Judah.
21:17 *b* of the chronicles of the kings of Judah.
21:25 *b* of the chronicles of the kings of Judah.
22: 8 the *b* of the law in the temple of the LORD."
22: 8 Hilkiah gave the *b* to Shaphan,
22:10 that the priest Hilkiah had given him a *b,*
22:11 had heard the contents of the *b* of the law,
22:13 stipulations of this *b* that has been found,
22:13 did not obey the stipulations of this *b,*
22:16 in the *b* which the king of Judah has read.
23: 2 He had the entire contents of the *b* of the
23: 3 the covenant which were written in this *b.*
23:21 was prescribed in that *b* of the covenant.
23:24 law written in the *b* that the priest
23:28 *b* of the chronicles of the kings of Judah.
24: 5 *b* of the chronicles of the kings of Judah.
1Chr 9: 1 recorded in the *b* of the kings of Israel.
27:24 into the *b* of chronicles of King David.
2Chr 16:11 in the *b* of the kings of Judah and Israel.
17: 9 them the *b* containing the law of the LORD;
20:34 inserted in the *b* of the kings of Israel.
24:27 in the midrash of the *b* of the kings.
25: 4 is written in the law, in the *B* of Moses,
25:26 in the *b* of the kings of Judah and Israel.
27: 7 in the *b* of the kings of Israel and Judah.
28:26 in the *b* of the kings of Judah and Israel.
32:32 in the *b* of the kings of Judah and Israel.
34:14 Hilkiah the priest found the *b* of the law
34:15 the *b* of the law in the house of the LORD."
34:15 Hilkiah gave the *b* to Shaphan,
34:18 "Hilkiah the priest has given me a *b.*"
34:21 the words of the *b* that has been found.
34:21 not done all that is written in this *b.*"
34:24 curses written in the *b* that has been read
34:30 entire text of the *b* of the covenant
34:31 terms of the covenant written in this *b.*
35:12 LORD, as is prescribed in the *b* of Moses.
35:26 in the *b* of the kings of Israel and Judah.
36: 8 in the *b* of the kings of Israel and Judah.
Ezr 6:18 as is prescribed in the *b* of Moses.
Neh 8: 1 bring forth the *b* of the law of Moses
8: 3 out of the *b* from daybreak till midday,
8: 3 listened attentively to the *b* of the law.
8: 8 read plainly from the *b* of the law of God,
8:18 from the *b* of the law of God day after day,
9: 3 the *b* of the law of the LORD their God,
12:22 were written down in the *B* of Chronicles,
12:23 were written down in the *B* of Chronicles,
13: 1 *b* of Moses in the hearing of the people,
Tb 1: 1 This *b* tells the story of Tobit,
6:13 according to the decree in the *B* of Moses,
7:11 according to the decree of the *B* of Moses.
7:12 written in the *B* of Moses she is your wife.
Est 9:32 for Purim and was recorded in the *b.*
2Mc 2:23 we will try to condense into a single *b.*
6:12 Now I beg those who read this *b* not to be
8:23 the holy *b* and giving them the watchword,
Ps(s) 56: 9 are they not recorded in your *b?*
69:29 they be erased from the *b* of the living,
139:16 in your *b* they are all written;
Sir 24:22 true of the *b* of the Most High's covenant,
50:27 proverbs, I have written in this *b,*
Is 29:18 day the deaf shall hear the words of a *b;*
34:16 Look in the *b* of the LORD and read:
Jer 25:13 against it [all that is written in this *b,*
30: 2 all the words I have spoken to you in a *b:*
36:10 read the words of Jeremiah from his *b.*
36:11 all the words of the LORD read from the *b.*
36:13 had heard Baruch read publicly from his *b.*
36:18 "and I wrote them down with ink in the *b.*"
36:32 words contained in the *b* which Jehoiakim,

BOOK (cont.)
45: 1 when he wrote in a *b* the prophecies that
51:60 that was to befall Babylon in a single *b*:
51:63 When you have finished reading this *b*,
Bar 4: 1 She is the *b* of the precepts of God,
Dn 10:21 tell you what is written in the truthful *b*.
12: 1 everyone who is found written in the *b*.
12: 4 message and seal the *b* until the end time;
Na 1: 1 The *b* of the vision of Nahum of Elkosh.
Mal 3:16 And a record *b* was written before him of
Mk 12:26 dead, have you not read in the *b* of Moses,
Lk 3: 4 the *b* of the words of Isaiah the prophet:
4:17 the *b* of the prophet Isaiah was handed him,
Acts 1:20 "It is written in the *B* of Psalms.
7:42 find it written in the *B* of the Prophets:
Rom 9:25 As it says in the *B* of Hosea:
Gal 3:10 in the *b* of the law and carry it out."
Phil 4: 3 with me, whose names are in the *b* of life.
Heb 9:19 and sprinkled the *b* and all the people
10: 7 I said, 'As is written of me in the *b*,
Rv 3: 5 erase his name from the *b* of the living,
13: 8 world's beginning in the *b* of the living,
17: 8 written in the *b* of the living
20:12 scrolls, the *b* of the living was opened.
20:15 not found inscribed in the *b* of the living
21:27 in the *b* of the living kept by the Lamb.
22: 7 who heeds the prophetic message of this *b*!"
22: 9 and those who heed the message of this *b*.
22:10 not seal up the prophetic words of this *b*,
22:18 all who hear the prophetic words of this *b*.
22:19 takes from the words of this prophetic *b*,

BOOK-SCROLL (1)
Jer 36: 8 from the *b* he read the LORD's words in the

BOOKS (8)
1Mc 12: 9 the sacred *b* that are in our possession,
2Mc 2:13 how he collected the *b* about the kings,
2:14 Judas also collected for us the *b*
Eccl 12:12 Of the making of many *b* there is no end,
Dn 7:11 court was convened, and the *b* were opened.
Jn 21:25 entire world to hold the *b* to record them.
Acts 19:19 their *b* and burned them in public.
2Tm 4:13 I left in Troas with Carpus, and the *b*,

BOON (2)
Sir 6:10 Another is a friend, a *b* companion,
41:13 The *b* of life is for limited days,

BOOR (1)
Sir 21:23 A *b* peeps through the doorway of a house,

BOOT (1)
Is 9: 4 For every *b* that trampled in battle,

BOOTH (2)
Jb 27:18 or like a *b* put up by the vine-keeper.
Lam 2: 6 demolished his shelter like a garden *b*,

BOOTHS (25)
Gn 33:17 for himself and made *b* for his livestock.
Lv 23:34 seventh month is the LORD's feast of *B*,
23:42 Israelite among you shall dwell in *b*,
23:43 the land of Egypt, I made them dwell in *b*.
Dt 16:13 celebrate the feast of *B* for seven days,
16:16 the feast of Weeks, and at the feast of *B*.
31:10 "On the feast of *B*,
2Chr 8:13 the feast of Weeks and the feast of *B*.
Ezr 3: 4 the feast of *B* in the manner prescribed,
Neh 8:14 in *b* during the feast of the seventh month;
8:15 palm and other leafy trees, to make *b*,
8:16 with which they made *b* for themselves,
8:17 returned exiles made *b* and dwelt in them.
1Mc 10:21 one hundred and sixty at the feast of *B*,
2Mc 1: 9 the feast of *B* in the month of Chislev.
1:18 celebrate the feast of *B* and of the fire
10: 6 for eight days as on the feast of *B*,
10: 6 they had spent the feast of *B* living like
Zec 14:16 of hosts, and to celebrate the feast of *B*.
14:18 do not come up to celebrate the feast of *B*.
14:19 do not come up to celebrate the feast of *B*.
Mt 17: 4 your permission I will erect three *b* here,
Mk 9: 5 Let us erect three *b* on this site,
Lk 9:33 Let us set up three *b*,
Jn 7: 2 as the Jewish feast of *B* drew near,

BOOTY (49)
Nm 14: 3 wives and little ones will be taken as *b*.
14:31 however, who you said would be taken as *b*,
31:11 Then they took all the *b*,
31:11 captives, together with the spoils and *b*,
31:32 This *b*, what was left of the loot
Dt 1:39 little ones, who you said would become *b*,
2:35 Our only *b* was the livestock and the loot
3: 7 of each city we took as *b* for ourselves.
20:14 worth plundering you may take as your *b*,
Jos 8: 2 you may take its spoil and livestock as *b*.
8:27 *b* the livestock and the spoil of that city,
11:14 and livestock of these cities as their *b*;
Jgs 5:19 no silver *b* did they take.
8:24 Will each of you give me a ring from his *b*?"
8:25 which everyone threw a ring from his *b*.
1Sm 14:30 their enemy's *b* when they came across it,
30:16 rich *b* they had taken from the land
30:19 small or great, *b* or sons or daughters,
30:22 we will not give them anything from the *b*,
2Sm 12:30 He brought out immense *b* from the city,
2Kgs 21:14 a prey and a *b* for all their enemies,
1Chr 20: 2 out a great amount of *b* from the city.
26:27 from the *b* they had taken in the wars,
2Chr 14:13 the cities, for there was much *b* in them.
15:11 thousand sheep of the *b* they had brought.
25:13 of the inhabitants and took away much *b*.
28:15 who were naked they clothed from the *b*;
Jdt 7:26 deliver the whole city as *b* to the troops
15: 7 the enormous quantity of *b* they had seized.
1Mc 7:47 the Jews collected the spoils and the *b*;
10:87 returned to Jerusalem, laden with much *b*.
2Mc 8:20 thousand and took a great quantity of *b*,
8:28 they gave a share of the *b* to the
Prv 1:13 we gain, we shall fill our houses with *b*;
Is 42:22 They are taken as *b*,
49:24 Can *b* be taken from a warrior?
49:25 a warrior, and *b* be rescued from a tyrant;
Jer 2:14 Why then has he become *b*?
21: 9 shall live and have his life as *b*.
38: 2 his life shall be spared him as *b*,
39:18 Your life shall be spared as *b*,
45: 5 LORD, but your life I will leave you as *b*,
49:32 Their camels shall be your *b*,
Ez 7:21 I will hand them over as *b* to foreigners,
26: 5 and she shall be *b* for the nations.
Dn 11: 8 gold, he shall carry away as *b* into Egypt.
11:24 he shall distribute spoil, *b*,
Heb 7: 2 apportioned to him one tenth of all his *b*.
7: 4 the patriarch gave one tenth of his *b*!

BORASHAN (1)
1Sm 30:30 cities, to those in Hormah, to those in *B*,

BORDER (28)
Gn 25:18 which is on the *b* of Egypt,
Nm 20:23 at Mount Hor, on the *b* of the land of Edom,
21:15 the site of Ar and slant to the *b* of Moab."
33:37 at Mount Hor on the *b* of the land of Edom.
33:44 they camped at Iye-abarim on the *b* of Moab.
34: 3 at the desert of Zin along the *b* of Edom;
Dt 3:14 as the *b* of the Geshurites and Maacathites,
3:16 Jabbok, which is the *b* of the Ammonites,
Jos 16: 2 ridge to the *b* of the Archites at Ataroth,
16: 3 westward to the *b* of the Japhletites,
17: 8 an Ephraimite city on the *b* of Manasseh.
18:14 For the western *b*,
Jgs 7:22 near the *b* of Abel-meholah at Tabbath.
1Sm 6:12 them as far as the *b* of Beth-shemesh.
1Kgs 5: 1 of the Philistines, down to the *b*
2Kgs 3:21 arms was called up and stationed at the *b*.
2Chr 9:26 the Philistines and down to the *b* of Egypt.
Neh 9:22 which you divided up among them as *b* lands.
Jdt 2:23 Ishmaelites on the *b* of the desert toward
1Mc 14:34 by the sea and Gazara on the *b* of Azotus,
Is 28:25 in wheat and barley, with spelt as its *b*?
Ez 40:12 The *b* before each of the cells on both
42:13 chambers which *b* on the free area
47:16 Hazar-enon which is on the *b* of the Hauran.
47:17 *b* shall extend from the sea to Hazar-enon,
48: 1 on the northerly *b* with Damascus,
Ob 1: 7 To the *b* they drive you
Zec 9: 2 tribes of Israel, Hamath also, on its *b*,

BORDERED (2)
Jos 17: 7 Manasseh *b* on Asher.
2Chr 21:16 and of the Arabs who *b* on the Ethiopians.

BORDERING (2)
Dt 2:37 neither the region *b* on the Wadi Jabbok,
Ez 45: 7 The prince shall have a section *b* on both

BORDERLANDS (1)
2Kgs 7: 6 and the kings of the *b* to fight us."

BORDERS (23)
Gn 10:19 *b* extended from Sidon all the way to Gerar,
Ex 16:35 manna until they reached the *b* of Canaan.
Jgs 2: 9 and they buried him within the *b* of his
2Sm 14:30 "You see Joab's field that *b* mine,
1Kgs 5: 4 and he had peace on all his *b* round about.
1Chr 5:16 all the pasture lands of Sirion to the *b*.
Jdt 1:10 of Egypt as far as the *b* of Ethiopia.
1:12 in Egypt as far as the *b* of the two seas.
2:25 he proceeded to the southern *b* of Japheth,
Est B: 2 humane and effective as far as the *b*,
1Mc 7:24 he went about all the *b* of Judea and took
14: 6 He enlarged the *b* of his nation and gained
2Mc 9:25 especially those on the *b* of our kingdom,
Ps(s) 105:31 gnats, throughout all their *b*.
105:33 and shattered the trees throughout their *b*.
147:14 He has granted peace in your *b*;
Sir 47:13 of peace, for God made tranquil all his *b*.
Is 26:15 and extended far all the *b* of the land.
Jer 17: 3 for all your sins throughout your *b*,
31:17 Your sons shall return to their own *b*.
Mi 5: 5 it invades our land and treads upon our *b*.
Lk 17:11 passed along the *b* of Samaria and Galilee.
2Cor 10:16 beyond your *b* without having to boast

BORE (115)
Gn 4: 1 his wife Eve, and she conceived and *b* Cain,
4: 2 Next she *b* his brother Abel.
4:17 his wife, and she conceived and *b* Enoch.
6: 4 with the daughters of man, who *b* them sons.
16:15 Hagar *b* Abram a son,
16:15 named the son whom Hagar *b* him Ishmael.
16:16 years old when Hagar *b* him Ishmael.
21: 2 and *b* Abraham a son in his old age,
21: 3 Isaac to this son of his whom Sarah *b* him.
22:23 eight Milcah *b* to Abraham's brother Nahor.
22:24 whose name was Reumah, also *b* children:
24:24 the son of Milcah, whom she *b* to Nahor.
24:36 Sarah *b* a son to my master in her old age,
25: 2 She *b* him Zimran,
25:12 the Egyptian, Sarah's slave, *b* to Abraham.
27:41 Esau *b* Jacob a grudge because of the
29:32 Leah conceived and *b* a son,
29:33 She conceived again and *b* a son,
29:34 Again she conceived and *b* a son,
29:35 Once more she conceived and *b* a son,
30: 5 When Bilhah conceived and *b* a son,
30: 7 Bilhah conceived again and *b* a second son,
30:10 with Zilpah, and she conceived and *b* a son.
30:12 maidservant Zilpah *b* a second son to Jacob;
30:17 she conceived and *b* a fifth son to Jacob.
30:19 conceived again and *b* a sixth son to Jacob;
30:23 She conceived and *b* a son,
36: 4 Adah *b* Eliphaz to Esau;
36: 4 Basemath *b* Reuel;
36: 5 and Oholibamah *b* Jeush,
36:12 Timna, and she *b* Amalek to Eliphaz.)
36:14 whom she *b* to Esau were Jeush,
38: 3 She conceived and *b* a son,
38: 4 Again she conceived and *b* a son,
38: 5 Then she *b* still another son,
44:27 to us, 'As you know, my wife *b* me two sons.
46:15 sons whom Leah *b* to Jacob in Paddan-aram,
46:18 these she *b* to Jacob
46:20 Potiphera, priest of Heliopolis, *b* to him.
46:22 These were the sons whom Rachel *b* to Jacob
46:25 these she *b* to Jacob
Ex 2: 2 a Levite woman, who conceived and *b* a son.
2:22 She *b* him a son,
6:20 married his aunt Jochebed, who *b* him Aaron,
6:23 she *b* him Nadab,
6:25 of Putiel's daughters, who *b* him Phinehas.
19: 4 how I *b* you up on eagle wings
Lv 18:11 daughter whom your father's wife *b* to him,
Nm 17:23 blossoms as well, and even *b* ripe almonds!
26:59 *b* Aaron and Moses and their sister Miriam.
Dt 32:11 receive them and *b* them up on his pinions.
33: 3 his feet and he *b* them up on his pinions.
Jgs 8:31 who lived in Shechem also *b* him a son,
13:24 The woman *b* a son and named him Samson.
16:31 *b* him up for burial in the grave
Ru 4:12 the house of Perez, whom Tamar *b* to Judah."
4:13 enabled her to conceive and she *b* a son.
1Sm 1:20 of her term *b* a son whom she called Samuel,
2Sm 11:27 She became his wife and *b* him a son.
12:24 and she conceived and *b* him a son,
1Kgs 11:20 Tahpenes' sister *b* Hadad a son, Genubath.
1Chr 1:32 she *b* Zimran,
2: 4 Tamar *b* him Perez and Zerah,
2:17 Abigail *b* Amasa,
2:19 died, Caleb married Ephrath, who *b* him Hur.
2:21 She *b* him Segub.
2:24 of his father Hezron, and she *b* him Ashhur,
2:29 was named Abihail, *b* him Ahban and Molid.
2:35 to his slave Jarha, and she *b* him Attai.
2:46 Ephah, Caleb's concubine, *b* Haran,
2:48 Caleb's concubine, *b* Sheber and Tirhanah.
2:49 She also *b* Shaaph,
4: 6 Naarah *b* him Ahuzzam,
4: 9 him Jabez, saying, "I *b* him with pain."
4:18 His (Mered's) Egyptian wife *b* Jered,
5:18 *b* shield and sword and who drew the bow,
7:14 of Manasseh, whom his Aramean concubine *b*:
7:14 she *b* Machir, the father of Gilead.
7:16 wife, *b* a son whom she named Peresh.
7:18 His sister Molecheth *b* Ishhod,
7:23 conceived and *b* a son whom he named Beriah,
12: 9 and spear, who *b* themselves like lions,
15:15 The Levites *b* the ark of God on their
2Chr 11:19 She *b* him sons:
11:20 daughter of Absalom, who *b* him Abijah,
Neh 6: 5 *b* an unsealed letter containing this text:
9:26 they slew your prophets who *b* witness
9:29 You *b* witness against them,
2Mc 7:20 yet *b* it courageously because of her hope
8:15 and because they themselves *b* his holy,
Prv 17:25 father, and bitter sorrow to her who *b* him.
23:25 let her who *b* you exult.
Is 8: 3 prophetess and she conceived and *b* a son.
51:18 no one to guide her of all the sons she *b*;

53: 4 Yet it was our infirmities that he *b*,
Jer 15:16 of my heart, Because I *b* your name,
22:26 cast you out, you and the mother who *b* you,
50:12 to shame, she that *b* you shall be abashed;
Lam 2:22 Those whom I *b* and reared my enemy has
Ez 23: 4 They became mine and *b* sons and daughters.
Hos 1: 3 and she conceived and *b* him a son.
1: 6 When she conceived again and *b* a daughter,
1: 8 Lo-ruhama, she conceived and *b* a son.
Mt 1:25 with her at any time before she *b* a son,
8:17 "It was our infirmities he *b*,
Lk 11:27 that *b* you and the breasts that nursed you!"
23:29 never *b* and the breasts that never nursed.'
Jn 17:24 the love you *b* me before the world began.
Acts 4:33 With power the apostles *b* witness to the
Rom 7: 5 in our members and we *b* fruit for death.
1Cor 1: 6 the witness I *b* to Christ has been so
Phil 4:10 that your concern for me *b* fruit once more.
Heb 13:13 the camp, bearing the insult which he *b*.
Rv 1: 9 God's word and *b* witness to Jesus.
6: 9 of the witness they *b* to the word of God.

BORED (1)

2Kgs 12:10 then took a chest, *b* a hole in its lid,

BORN (127)

Gn 4:18 To Enoch was *b* Irad,
4:26 To Seth, in turn, a son was *b*,
6: 1 on earth and daughters were *b* to them,
10: 1 to whom sons were *b* after the flood.
10:21 of all the children of Eber, sons were *b*.
10:25 To Eber two sons were *b*:
14:14 eighteen of his retainers, *b* in his house,
17:17 be *b* to a man who is a hundred years old?
17:23 whether *b* in his house or acquired with
17:27 including the slaves *b* in his house or
21: 5 years old when his son Isaac was *b* to him.
24:15 words when Rebekah (who was *b* to Bethuel,
25:26 Isaac was sixty years old when they were *b*.
31: 3 land of your fathers, where you were *b*,
35:26 of Jacob who were *b* to him in Paddan-aram.
36: 5 who were *b* to him in the land of Canaan.
38: 5 They were in Chezib when he was *b*.
46:27 Joseph's sons who were *b* to him in Egypt
48: 5 who were *b* to you in the land of Egypt
48: 6 *b* to you after them shall remain yours;
50:23 son Machir were also *b* on Joseph's knees.
Ex 1:22 river every boy that is *b* to the Hebrews,
Lv 18: 9 born in your own household or *b* elsewhere.
19:34 differently than the natives *b* among you;
22:11 who is *b* in his house may eat of his food.
22:27 "When an ox or a lamb or a goat is *b*,
24:10 a man *b* of an Israelite mother (Shelomith,
25:45 children who are *b* and reared in your land.
Nm 26:59 the tribe of Levi, *b* to the tribe in Egypt.
26:60 To Aaron were *b* Nadab and Abihu,
Dt 23: 9 Children *b* to them may in the third
Jos 5: 5 none of those *b* in the desert during the
Jgs 11: 1 Jephthah, *b* to Gilead of a harlot.
13: 8 us what to do for the boy who will be *b*."
Ru 4:17 news that a grandson had been *b* to Naomi.
2Sm 3: 2 Sons were *b* to David in Hebron:
3: 5 These were *b* to David in Hebron.
5:13 and daughters were *b* to him in Jerusalem.
5:14 of those who were *b* to him in Jerusalem:
12:14 deed, the child *b* to you must surely die."
14:27 Absalom had three sons *b* to him,
1Kgs 13: 2 'A child shall be *b* to the house of David,
1Chr 1:19 Two sons were *b* to Eber;
2: 3 these three were *b* to him of Bathshua,
2: 9 The sons *b* to Hezron were Jerahmeel,
3: 1 sons of David who were *b* to him in Hebron:
3: 4 Six in all were *b* to him in Hebron,
3: 5 where the following were *b* to him:
7:15 but to Zelophehad only daughters were *b*.
7:21 and Ezer and Elead, who were *b* in the land,
14: 4 of those who were *b* to him in Jerusalem:
22: 9 However, a son is to be *b* to you.
26: 6 were *b* sons who ruled over their family,
Ezr 10: 3 foreign wives and the children *b* of them,
Jdt 5: 7 who were *b* in the land of the Chaldeans.
12:18 for at no time since I was *b* have I ever
1Mc 2: 7 Why was I *b* to see the ruin of my people
Jb 1: 2 sons and three daughters were *b* to him;
3: 3 Perish the day on which I was *b*,
14: 1 Man *b* of woman is short-lived and full of
15:14 one *b* of woman that he should be righteous?
38:21 You know, because you were *b* before them,
Ps(s) 22:32 yet to be *b* the justice he has shown.
51: 7 Indeed, in guilt was I *b*,
78: 6 come might know, their sons yet to be *b*,
87: 4 "This man was *b* there."
87: 5 "One and all were *b* in her;
87: 6 "This man was *b* there."
Prv 17:17 and a brother is *b* for the time of stress.
Eccl 2: 7 slaves, and slaves were *b* in my house.
3: 2 A time to be *b*,
6: 3 the child *b* dead is more fortunate than he.
Wis 2: 2 For haphazard were we *b*,
4: 6 For children *b* of lawless unions give
5:13 Even so we, once *b*,
7: 3 And I too, when *b*,
Sir 7:28 Remember, of these parents you were *b*;
10:18 man, nor stubborn anger to one *b* of woman.
14:18 one dies and another is *b*.
23:14 been *b* or cursing the day of your birth.
49:15 Was ever a man *b* like JOSEPH?
Is 9: 5 For a child is *b* to us,
48:19 and those *b* of your stock like its grains,
66: 8 day, or a nation be *b* in a single moment?
66: 9 of birth, and yet not let her child be *b*?
Jer 1: 5 you, before you were *b* I dedicated you,
16: 3 and daughters who will be *b* in this place,
20:14 Cursed be the day on which I was *b*!
20:15 "A child, a son, has been *b* to you!"
22:26 different land from the one you were *b* in;
Bar 3:26 In it were *b* the giants,
Ez 16: 4 day you were *b* your navel cord was not cut;
16: 5 as something loathsome, the day you were *b*.
Mt 1:16 that Jesus who is called the Messiah was *b*.
2: 4 of them where the Messiah was to be *b*.
11:11 *b* of woman greater than John the Baptizer.
11:11 Yet the least *b* into the kingdom of God is
26:24 Better for him if he had never been *b*."
Mk 14:21 It were better for him had he never been *b*."
Lk 1:35 to be *b* will be called Son of God.
2:11 in David's city a savior has been *b* to you,
7:28 is no man *b* of woman greater than John.
7:28 Yet the least *b* into the kingdom of God is
Jn 3: 4 "How can a man be *b* again once he is old?"
3: 4 to his mother's womb and be *b* over again?"
9: 2 his parents that caused him to be *b* blind?"
9:13 man who had been *b* blind to the Pharisees.
9:18 really been *b* blind and had begun to see,
9:24 man who had been *b* blind and said to him,
16:21 joy that a man has been *b* into the world.
18:37 The reason I was *b*,
Acts 7:20 "It was at this time that Moses was *b*.
22: 3 "I am a Jew, *b* in Tarsus in Cilicia,
23: 6 I am a Pharisee and was *b* a Pharisee.
1Cor 11:12 was made from man, so man is *b* of woman;
15: 8 by me, as one *b* out of the normal course.
Gal 1:15 set me apart before I was *b* and called
4: 4 his Son born of a woman, *b* under the law,
4:29 But just as in those days the son *b* in
4:30 terms with the son" of the one *b* free.
Eph 4:24 whose justice and holiness are *b* of truth.
Phil 2: 7 of a slave, being *b* in the likeness of men.
Jas 1:23 into a mirror at the face he was *b* with;
2Pt 2:12 brute animals *b* to be caught and destroyed.
Rv 12: 4 to devour her child when it should be *b*.

BORNE (50)

Gn 16: 1 Abram's wife Sarai had *b* him no children.
21: 7 Yet I have *b* him a son in his old age."
21: 9 *b* to Abraham playing with her son Isaac;
22:20 "Milcah too has *b* sons,
24:47 son of Nahor, *b* to Nahor by Milcah.'
29:34 to me, since I have now *b* him three sons";
30:20 now that I have *b* him six sons";
31:43 for them and for the children they have *b*.
34: 1 the daughter whom Leah had *b* to Jacob,
41:50 father of two sons, *b* to him by Asenath,
Dt 4:42 to whom he had previously *b* no malice,
19: 4 to whom he had previously *b* no malice.
19: 6 had previously *b* the slain man no malice.
Jos 4:11 the ark of the LORD, *b* by the priests,
Jgs 11: 2 Gilead's wife had also *b* him sons,
13: 2 His wife was barren and had *b* no children.
Ru 1:12 if tonight I had a husband or had *b* sons,
1Sm 6: 7 two milch cows that have not *b* the yoke;
2Sm 12:15 that the wife of Uriah had *b* to David,
21: 8 that Aiah's daughter Rizpah had *b* to Saul,
21: 8 daughter Merob that she had *b* to Adriel,
22:11 and flew, *b* on the wings of the wind.
1Kgs 3:21 I saw it was not the son whom I had *b*."
Ezr 6: 4 The costs are to be *b* by the royal palace.
Jb 30:15 My dignity is *b* off on the wind,
Ps(s) 18:11 and flew, *b* on the wings of the wind.
45:15 apparel she is *b* in to the king;
45:16 They are *b* in with gladness and joy;
55:13 an enemy had reviled me, I could have *b* it;
Wis 5:14 wicked is like thistledown *b* on the wind,
18:10 of mourning for children was *b* to them.
Sir 23:23 adultery she has *b* children by another man.
28:19 Who has not *b* its yoke nor been fettered
34: 1 and fools are *b* aloft by dreams.
Is 38:12 tent, is struck down and *b* away from me;
46: 1 They must be *b* up on shoulders,
49:21 "Who has *b* me these?
Jer 15:15 know that for you I have *b* insult.
Bar 5: 6 you *b* aloft in glory as on royal thrones.
6: 3 And now in Babylon you will see *b* upon
Ez 16:20 The sons and daughters you had *b* me you
23:37 they immolated the children they had *b* me.
36: 6 you have *b* the reproach of the nations.
Mi 5: 2 time when she who is to give birth has *b*,
Hg 2:19 the pomegranate and the olive tree yet *b*.
Jn 16:21 When she has *b* her child,
1Cor 15:15 for we have *b* witness before him that he
Col 1: 6 gospel, which has come to you, has *b* fruit,
Heb 11: 4 *b* witness to him on account of his gifts;
11:26 Moses considered the reproach *b* by God's

BORROW (5)

Dt 15: 6 will lend to many nations, and *b* from none;
28:12 will lend to many nations and *b* from none.
2Kgs 4: 3 he said, *b* vessels from all your neighbors
Jer 15:10 I neither *b* nor lend, yet all curse me.
23:31 LORD, who *b* speeches to pronounce oracles.

BORROWED (2)

2Kgs 6: 5 "O master," he cried out, "it was *b*!"
Neh 5: 4 *b* money on our fields and our vineyards.

BORROWER (4)

Prv 22: 7 poor, and the *b* is the slave of the lender.
Sir 29: 6 curses and insults the *b* pays him back,
Is 24: 2 buyer as the seller, The lender as the *b*,
Mt 5:42 Do not turn your back on the *b*.

BORROWS (3)

Ex 22:13 "When a man *b* an animal from his neighbor,
Ps(s) 37:21 The wicked man *b* and does not repay;
Sir 29: 5 When he *b*,

BOSOM (27)

Ex 4: 6 said to him, "Put your hand in your *b*."
4: 6 He put it in his *b*,
4: 7 said, "Now, put your hand back in your *b*."
4: 7 Moses put his hand back in his *b*,
Nm 11:12 that you tell me to carry them at my *b*,
2Sm 12: 3 and drank from his cup and slept in his *b*.
1Kgs 3:20 Then she laid him in her *b*,
3:20 after she had laid her dead child in my *b*.
Jb 31:33 my sins and buried my guilt in my *b*
32:19 under pressure, my *b* is ready to burst.
Ps(s) 22:15 become like wax melting away within my *b*.
35:13 and poured forth prayers within my *b*.
55:14 other self, my companion and my *b* friend!
89:51 I bear in my *b* all the accusations of the
Prv 6:27 Can a man take fire to his *b*,
14:33 but in the *b* of fools it is unknown.
16:28 and a talebearer separates *b* friends.
22:18 it will be well if you keep them in your *b*,
Eccl 7: 9 for discontent lodges in the *b* of a fool.
Sg 1:13 for me a sachet of myrrh to rest in my *b*.
Sir 9: 1 Be not jealous of the wife of your *b*,
37: 2 when your *b* companion becomes your enemy?
Is 40:11 gathers the lambs, Carrying them in his *b*,
Ez 23:21 fondled your breasts, caressing your *b*.
Mi 7: 5 in your *b* guard the portals of your mouth.
Lk 16:22 was carried by angels to the *b* of Abraham.
16:23 afar off, and Lazarus resting in his *b*.

BOSOMS (2)

Ps(s) 79:12 *b* the disgrace they have inflicted on you,
Ez 23: 3 their *b* and fondled their virginal breasts.

BOSOR (2)

1Mc 5:26 been imprisoned in Bozrah, in *B* near Alema,
5:36 he moved on and took Chaspho, Maked, *B*,

BOSSES (1)

Jb 15:26 upon him with the stout *b* of his shield,

BOTH (282)

Gn 2:25 The man and his wife were *b* naked,
3: 7 Then the eyes of *b* of them were opened,
14: 7 whole country *b* of the Amalekites
17:13 *b* the houseborn slaves and those acquired
19: 4 all the townsmen of Sodom, *b* young and old
19:34 that we may *b* have offspring by our father."
19:36 Thus *b* of Lot's daughters became pregnant
22: 5 *B* of you stay here with the donkey,
23:11 I give you *b* the field and the cave in it;
27:45 Must I lose *b* of you in a single day?"
39: 5 he owned, *b* inside the house and out.
40: 5 in the jail *b* had dreams on the same night,
41:11 Later, we *b* had dreams on the same night,
41:25 *B* of Pharaoh's dreams have the same meaning.
Ex 4:15 I will assist *b* you and him in speaking
6:13 regarding *b* the Israelites and Pharaoh,
12:12 first-born of the land, *b* man and beast,
13: 2 among the Israelites, *b* of man and beast,
13:21 Thus they could travel *b* day and night.
22: 8 *b* parties shall present their case before
26:24 *b* boards in the corners are to be made.
32:15 tablets that were written on *b* sides,
35:22 *B* the men and the women,
35:34 He has also given *b* him and Oholiab,
36:29 is how *b* boards in the corners were made.
Lv 7: 7 are alike, *b* having the same ritual,
8:30 thus consecrating *b* Aaron and his
9: 2 a ram for a holocaust, *b* without blemish,
9: 3 a calf and a lamb, *b* unblemished yearlings,
11: 9 waters has *b* fins and scales you may eat.
15:18 they shall *b* bathe in water and be unclean
16:21 Laying *b* hands on its head,
20: 5 cut off from their people *b* him and all
20:10 *b* the adulterer and the adulteress shall
20:11 *b* the man and his stepmother shall be put
20:12 *b* of them shall be put to death;

BOTH (cont.)

20:13 *b* of them shall be put to death for their
20:16 let them *b* be put to death;
20:18 *b* of them shall be cut off from their
27:10 *b* the original and its substitute shall be
27:33 *b* the original animal and its substitute
Nm 2:34 *b* in camp and on the march they were in
3:13 Israel sacred to me, *b* of man and of beast.
3:26 enclosing *b* the Dwelling and the altar,
4:26 that encloses *b* the Dwelling and the altar,
7:13 *b* filled with fine flour mixed with oil
7:19 *b* filled with fine flour mixed with oil
7:25 *b* filled with fine flour mixed with oil
7:31 *b* filled with fine flour mixed with oil
7:37 *b* filled with fine flour mixed with oil
7:43 *b* filled with fine flour mixed with oil
7:49 *b* filled with fine flour mixed with oil
7:55 *b* filled with fine flour mixed with oil
7:61 *b* filled with fine flour mixed with oil
7:67 *b* filled with fine flour mixed with oil
7:73 *b* filled with fine flour mixed with oil
7:79 *b* filled with fine flour mixed with oil
8: 4 gold in *b* its shaft and its branches,
8:17 the Israelites, *b* of man and of beast,
10: 3 When *b* are blown,
12: 5 When *b* came forward,
18: 3 or the altar, lest *b* they and you die.
19:10 *b* for the Israelites and for the aliens
20:24 because you *b* rebelled against my
27:14 you *b* rebelled against my order
31:19 This applies *b* to you and to your captives.
31:47 every fifty, *b* of persons and of beasts,
Dt 1:16 *b* parties even if one of them is an alien.
3:21 LORD, your God, has done to *b* these kings;
9:15 two tablets of the covenant in *b* my hands,
9:17 Raising the two tablets with *b* hands I
12:27 and there you must offer *b* the flesh and
14: 9 whatever has *b* fins and scales you may eat,
21:15 and if *b* bear him sons,
22: 9 *b* the crop you have sown and the yield of
22:22 *b* the man and the woman with whom he has
22:24 you shall bring them *b* out to the gate of
23:19 *b* these things are an abomination to the
28:66 and stand in dread *b* day and night,
29:18 *b* the watered soil and the parched ground,
29:28 *B* what is still hidden and what has
32:39 It is I who bring *b* death and life,
32:51 because *b* of you broke faith with me among
Jos 22:14 each one being *b* prince and military
Jgs 15: 5 *b* the shocks and the standing grain,
16:14 pulled out *b* the weaver's pin and the web.
Ru 1: 5 ten years, *b* Mahlon and Chilion died also,
1Sm 2:34 *b* shall die on the same day.
12:14 if *b* you and the king who rules you follow
12:25 do evil, *b* you and your king shall perish."
17:36 servant has killed *b* a lion and a bear,
25:43 Thus *b* of them were his wives;
2Sm 9:13 He was lame in *b* feet.
10: 9 drawn up against him, *b* front and rear,
15:27 city in peace, and *b* your sons with you,
15:36 who have there with them *b* Zadok's son
16:23 all his counsel *b* to David and to Absalom.
1Kgs 6:29 The walls on all sides of *b* the inner and
6:30 The floor of *b* the inner and the outer
7:42 in double rows on *b* pieces of network
15:16 king of Israel, a long as they *b* reigned.
2Kgs 2: 8 divided, and *b* crossed over on dry ground.
4:33 He went in, closed the door on them *b*,
11: 9 *b* those going on duty for the sabbath and
1Chr 12: 2 *b* in slinging stones and in shooting
12: 3 with Joash, *b* sons of Shemaah of Gibeah;
12:16 overflowing *b* its banks in the first month,
19:10 a battle line *b* in front of and behind him,
24: 5 descended *b* from Eleazar and from Ithamar.
2Chr 13:14 saw that they had to battle on *b* fronts,
23: 4 of your number, *b* priests and Levites,
32:26 *b* he and the inhabitants of Jerusalem;
36:22 kingdom, *b* by word of mouth and in writing:
Ezr 1: 1 kingdom, *b* by word of mouth and in writing:
3: 3 to the LORD on it, *b* morning and evening.
8:15 that *b* laymen and priests were present,
10: 9 were trembling *b* over the matter at hand
10:44 them away, *b* the women and their children.
Neh 11: 4 dwelt *b* Judahites and Benjaminites.
Tb 3:17 So Raphael was sent to heal them *b*:
6:18 with her, *b* of you first rise up to pray.
7:11 I am sure the Lord will look after you *b*."
7:11 son, may the Lord of heaven prosper you *b*.
7:12 heaven grant *b* of you peace and prosperity."
10:13 kissed them *b* and sent them away in peace.
11: 4 *b* went on ahead and Raphael said to Tobiah,
11:13 used *b* hands to peel off the cataracts.
Jdt 15: 2 *b* through the valley and in the mountains.
Est A: 5 great dragons came on, *b* poised for combat.
2: 7 for she had lost *b* father and mother.
2: 9 he transferred *b* her and her maids to the
2:23 and *b* of them were hanged on a gibbet.
E:23 so that *b* now and in the future it may be,
9:20 letters to all the Jews, *b* near and far,
9:21 He ordered them to celebrate every year *b*
1Mc 1:16 of Egypt, so as to rule over *b* kingdoms.
6: 7 surrounded with high walls *b* the sanctuary,
6:45 that they fell back from him on *b* sides.
8:12 They had conquered kings *b* far and near,
8:30 But if *b* parties hereafter decide to add
9:17 and many on *b* sides fell wounded.
10:84 and destroyed by fire *b* the temple of
12:21 *b* nations descended from Abraham.
15:25 he assaulted it continuously *b* with troops
2Mc 4:28 reason, *b* were summoned before the king.
5:15 traitor *b* to the laws and to his country,
7:23 will give you back *b* breath and life,
8:19 *b* the time of Sennacherib,
8:33 they burned *b* those who had set fire to
14:46 and flung them with *b* hands into the crowd,
Jb 9:22 *B* the innocent and the wicked he destroys.
9:33 upon us *b* and withdraw his rod from me.
21:26 down in the dust, and worms cover them *b*.
Ps(s) 104:25 number of living things *b* small and great,
113: 2 be the name of the LORD *b* now and forever.
115:13 fear the LORD, *b* the small and the great.
115:14 you more and more, *b* you and your children.
115:18 But we bless the LORD, *b* now and forever.
121: 8 coming and your going, *b* now and forever.
125: 2 round about his people, *b* now and forever.
131: 3 hope in the LORD, *b* now and forever.
135: 8 first-born in Egypt, *b* of man and of beast.
Prv 17:15 the just, are *b* an abomination to the LORD.
20:10 measures, are *b* an abomination to the LORD.
20:12 the LORD has made them *b*.
27: 3 but a fool's provocation is heavier than *b*.
29:13 the LORD gives light to the eyes of *b*.
Eccl 2:14 Yet I knew that one lot befalls *b* of them.
2:16 in days to come *b* will have been forgotten.
3:17 *b* the just and the wicked God will judge,
3:19 *B* have the same life-breath,
3:20 *B* go to the same place; both were made
3:20 the dust, and to the dust they *b* return.
4: 3 And better off than *b* is the yet unborn,
6: 6 his goods, do not *b* go to the same place?
7:14 *B* the one and the other God has made,
9: 1 *b* appear equally vain,
11: 6 or whether *b* alike will turn out well.
Sg 7:14 *B* fresh and mellowed fruits,
Wis 4: 1 because *b* by God is it acknowledged,
7:16 For *b* we and our words are in his hand,
11:11 *B* those afar off and those close by were
14:30 on *b* counts shall justice overtake them:
15: 7 *B* the vessels that serve for clean
15:19 *b* the approval of God and his blessing.
Sir 10: 7 and the sin of oppression they *b* hate.
18:16 *b* are offered by a kindly man.
20:24 liar, yet *b* will suffer disgrace;
22: 5 by *b* she is despised.
28:12 yet *b* you do with your mouth!
Is 1:31 *B* shall burn together,
8:14 stumbling stone to *b* the houses of Israel,
9: 6 By judgment and justice, *b* now and forever.
24: 4 *b* heaven and earth languish.
31: 3 fall, and *b* of them shall perish together.
47: 9 *B* these things shall come to you suddenly,
Jer 5:11 *b* the house of Israel and the house of
21: 6 inhabitants of this city, *b* man and beast;
23:11 *B* prophet and priest are godless!
23:24 Do I not fill *b* heaven and earth?
32:11 the deed of purchase, *b* the sealed copy,
32:14 *b* the sealed and the open deed of purchase,
32:20 day, *b* in Israel and among all other men,
41:16 *b* the soldiers and the women and children
46:12 trips over warrior, *b* fall together.
Lam 2: 6 scorned in fierce wrath *b* king and priest.
2: 8 grief on wall and rampart till *b* succumbed.
Ez 10: 2 fill *b* your hands with burning coals from
14:13 it and cut off from it *b* man and beast;
15: 4 *b* ends and even the middle is scorched,
18: 4 is like the life of the son, *b* are mine;
21:24 *B* roads shall lead out from the same land.
23:13 *B* had gone down the same path,
29: 8 you, and cut off from you *b* man and beast.
40:12 each of the cells on *b* sides was one cubit;
40:16 Within the gateway on *b* sides there were
40:16 vestibule on *b* sides there were windows.
40:25 and its vestibule had windows on *b* sides,
40:29 windows on *b* sides; and it was fifty cubits
40:33 and its vestibule had windows on *b* sides;
40:36 and its vestibule had windows on *b* sides;
41:15 walls on *b* sides it was one hundred cubits.
41:17 on every wall on every side in *b* the inner
41:26 on *b* side walls of the vestibule,
43:10 sins], *b* its measurements and its design;
44: 7 uncircumcised *b* in heart and flesh,
45: 7 section bordering on *b* sides
47: 7 the river I saw very many trees on *b* sides.
47:12 Along *b* banks of the river,
48:21 the land on *b* sides of the sacred tract
Dn 8: 7 blows when they met, and break *b* its horns.
13:10 Though *b* were enamored of her,
13:14 but *b* turned back,
13:59 you in two so as to make an end of you *b*."
Mal 2:12 man who does this *b* witness and advocate
Mt 9:17 wineskins, and in that way *b* are preserved."
10:28 who can destroy *b* body and soul in Gehenna.
13:52 from his storeroom *b* the new and the old."
15:14 man leads another, *b* will end in a pit."
18: 9 than be thrown with *b* into fiery Gehenna.
28:18 been given to me *b* in heaven and on earth;
Mk 2:22 skins and *b* wine and skins will be lost.
9:43 enter life maimed than to keep *b* hands
9:45 than to be thrown into Gehenna with *b* feet.
9:47 than to be thrown with *b* eyes into Gehenna,
Lk 1: 6 *B* were just in the eyes of God,
1: 7 moreover, *b* were advanced in years.
6:39 Will they not *b* fall into a ditch?
7:34 The Son of Man came and he *b* ate and drank,
7:42 was able to repay, he wrote off *b* debts.
Acts 2:36 God has made *b* Lord and Messiah
5:42 Day after day, *b* in the temple and at home,
18:24 He was *b* an authority on Scripture and
20:34 *b* my needs and those of my companions.
21:12 *b* we ourselves and the people of Caesarea
22: 4 I arrested and imprisoned *b* men and women.
25:24 Jewish community, *b* here and in Jerusalem,
Rom 3:21 *b* law and prophets bear witness to it
14: 8 *B* in life and in death we are the Lord's.
14: 9 might be Lord of *b* the dead and the living.
1Cor 6:13 God will do away with them *b* in the end"
10:28 *b* for the sake of the one who called
2Cor 1:16 *b* on my way to Macedonia and on my return,
2:15 *b* among those who are being saved and
4:14 and place *b* us and you in his presence.
Eph 2: 6 *B* with and in Christ Jesus he raised us up
2:16 reconciling *b* of us to God in one body
2:18 *b* have access in one Spirit to the Father.
Phil 1: 9 *b* in understanding and wealth of
1:23 I am strongly attracted by *b*:
Col 1:20 his person, *b* on earth and in the heavens,
1Tm 4:16 Persevere at *b* tasks.
6: 4 be recognized as *b* conceited and ignorant,
Ti 1: 9 so that he will be able *b* to encourage men
Phlm 1:11 is now useful indeed *b* to you and to me.
1:16 will know him *b* as a man and in the Lord.
Jas 2:22 There you see proof that faith was *b*
2Pt 3: 1 intending them *b* as reminders urging you
2Jn 1: 9 possesses *b* the Father and the Son.
Rv 5: 1 on *b* sides and was sealed with seven seals.
19:20 *B* were hurled down alive into the fiery

BOTHER (2)

Mk 5:35 Why *b* the Teacher further?"
Lk 8:49 do not *b* the Teacher further."

BOTHERED (1)

2Cor 10:14 be doing if we had not *b* to come to you.

BOTTLE (1)

Jb 13:28 Though he wears out like a leather *b*,

BOTTOM (18)

Gn 6:16 of the ark, which you shall make with *b*,
Ex 26:24 These two shall be double at the *b*,
28:27 fasten them to the *b* of the shoulder straps
28:33 hem at the *b* you shall make pomegranates,
36:29 These were double at the *b*,
39:20 fastened to the *b* of the two shoulder straps
1Kgs 22:35 his wound flowed to the *b* of the chariot.
Ps(s) 88: 7 You have plunged me into the *b* of the pit,
Wis 10:19 and cast them up from the *b* of the depths.
Lam 3:55 your name, O LORD, from the *b* of the pit;
Ez 32:18 thrust them down to the *b* of the earth,
32:24 down uncircumcised to the *b* of the earth,
43:14 from its base at the *b* up to the lower
Dn 6:25 Before they reached the *b* of the den,
Am 9: 3 they hide from my gaze in the *b* of the sea,
Mt 27:51 sanctuary was torn in two from top to *b*.
Mk 15:38 sanctuary was torn in two from top to *b*.
Jn 19:23 in one piece from top to *b* and had no seam.

BOUGHS (7)

Lv 23:40 and *b* of myrtles and of valley poplars,
Ps(s) 118:27 with leafy *b* up to the horns of the altar.
Is 10:33 lops off the *b* with terrible violence;
27:10 Its *b* shall be destroyed,
Ez 17:23 every winged thing in the shade of its *b*.
31: 6 In its *b* nested all the birds of the air,
31: 8 nor could the fir trees match its *b*,

BOUGHT (33)

Gn 25:10 field that Abraham had *b* from the Hittites;
33:19 he *b* for a hundred pieces of bullion
39: 1 *b* him from the Ishmaelites
49:30 the field that Abraham *b* from Ephron the
50:13 the field that Abraham had *b* for a burial
Ex 12:44 who has been *b* for money may partake of it,
Lv 27:33 sacred, without the right of being *b* back."
Jos 24:32 ground Jacob had *b* from the sons of Hamor,
2Sm 12: 3 except one little ewe lamb that he had *b*.
24:24 So David *b* the threshing floor and the
1Kgs 16:24 He then *b* the hill of Samaria from Shemer
Neh 5: 8 we *b* back our fellow Jews who had been
5: 8 own brothers, to have them *b* back by us."
Jb 28:16 It cannot be *b* with gold of Ophir,
Jer 13: 2 I *b* the loincloth,
13: 4 the loincloth which you *b* and are wearing,
32: 9 so I *b* the field in Anathoth from my
32:15 vineyards shall again be *b* in this land.
32:43 Fields shall again be *b* in this land,

32:44 Fields shall be *b* with money,
Bar 6:24 They are *b* at any price,
Hos 3: 2 So I *b* her for fifteen pieces of silver
Mt 13:44 went and sold all he had and *b* that field.
13:46 put up for sale all that he had and *b* it.
Mk 15:46 Then, having *b* a linen shroud,
16: 1 and Salome *b* perfumed oils with which they
Lk 14:18 *b* some land and must go out and inspect it.
14:19 'I have *b* five yoke of oxen and I am going
17:28 they ate and drank, they *b* and sold,
Acts 1:18 *b* a piece of land with his unjust gains,
7:16 Abraham had *b* with silver
8:20 thinking that God's gift can be *b*!
1Cor 7:23 You have been *b* at a price!

BOULDERS (1)

Mt 27:52 The earth quaked, *b* split, tombs opened.

BOUND (78)

Gn 42:24 taken from them and *b* before their eyes.
44:30 father, whose very life is *b* up with his,
Ex 39:21 Violet ribbons *b* the rings of the
Nm 5: 9 are *b* to make shall fall to the priest.
30: 5 *b* herself and says nothing to her about it,
30: 7 under a rash pledge to which she *b* herself,
30: 9 the rash pledge to which she had *b* herself,
35:28 the homicide was *b* to stay in his city of
Jgs 15:13 So they *b* him with two new ropes and
16: 6 how you may be *b* so as to be kept helpless."
16: 8 had not dried, and she *b* him with them.
16:10 Now tell me how you may be *b*."
16:12 Delilah took new ropes and *b* him with them.
16:13 Tell me how you may be *b*."
16:21 down to Gaza and *b* him with bronze fetters,
1Sm 25:29 may the life of my lord be *b* in the bundle
2Sm 3:34 Your hands were not *b* with chains,
2Kgs 25: 7 he blinded Zedekiah, *b* him with fetters,
2Chr 36: 6 *b* him with chains to take him to Babylon.
Tb 8: 3 pursued him there and *b* him hand and foot.
Jdt 6:13 where they *b* Achior and left him lying at
8: 3 field supervising those who *b* the sheaves,
10: 3 arranged her hair and *b* it with a fillet,
Jb 36: 8 Or if they are *b* with fetters and held
Ps(s) 56:13 I am *b*, O God, by vows to you;
105:18 with fetters, and he was *b* with chains,
Prv 30: 4 Who has *b* up the waters in a cloak
Wis 17:18 all were *b* by the one bond of darkness.
Sir 27:21 A wound can be *b* up,
Is 58: 6 releasing those *b* unjustly,
Jer 39: 7 *b* him in chains to bring him to Babylon.
52:11 he blinded Zedekiah, *b* him with fetters,
Ez 16:61 though I am not *b* by my covenant with you.
21:28 they are *b* by the oaths they have sworn,
30:21 it has not been *b* up with bandages and
45:16 All the people of the land shall be *b* to
Dn 3:21 They were *b* and cast into the white-hot
3:23 But these three fell, *b*,
3:91 we not cast three men *b* into the fire?"
Hos 4:19 The wind has *b* them up in its pinions;
Mt 16:19 bound on earth shall be *b* in heaven;
18:18 bound on earth shall be held *b* in heaven,
24: 6 Such things are *b* to happen,
27: 2 They *b* him and led him away to be handed
Mk 13: 7 Such things are *b* to happen,
15: 1 They *b* Jesus,
Lk 21: 9 These things are *b* to happen first,
Jn 11:44 came out *b* head and foot with linen strips,
18:12 the Jewish guards arrested Jesus and *b* him.
18:24 Annas next sent him, *b*,
19:40 Jewish burial custom *b* it up in wrappings
20:23 if you hold them bound, they are held *b*."
Acts 21: 2 When we found a ship *b* for Phoenicia,
21:33 Paul and had him *b* with double irons.
22:25 No sooner had they *b* Paul than he said to
23:12 conspiracy in which they *b* themselves
23:14 "We have *b* ourselves by oath to touch no
23:21 they have *b* themselves by oath not to eat
27: 2 *b* for ports in the province of Asia,
27: 6 an Alexandrian vessel *b* for Italy,
27:10 is *b* to meet with disaster and heavy loss,
Rom 2:12 sinners *b* by the law will be judged in
7: 2 is *b* to her husband by law while he lives,
7: 6 for we have died to what *b* us
1Cor 7:15 husband or wife is not *b* in such cases.
7:27 Are you *b* to a wife?
7:39 is *b* to her husband as long as he lives.
9:19 Although I am not *b* to anyone,
9:20 To those *b* by the law I became like one
9:20 bound (although in fact I am not *b* by it),
Gal 5: 3 that they are *b* to the law in its entirety.
Col 2:20 why should you be *b* by rules that say,
2Thes 2:13 We are *b* to thank God for you always,

BOUNDARIES (16)

Ex 23:31 I will set your *b* from the Red Sea to the
Nm 34: 2 the land of Canaan with its *b*:
34:12 be yours, with the *b* that surround it."
Dt 32: 8 He set up the *b* of the peoples after the
Jos 13: 4 to Aphek, and the *b* of the Amorites;
2Kgs 14:25 He restored the *b* of Israel from
1Chr 4:10 you may truly bless me and extend my *b*!
Jb 38:20 *b* and set them on their homeward paths?
Sir 44:23 He fixed the *b* for his tribes,
Is 10:13 I have moved the *b* of peoples,
60:18 land, or plunder and ruin within your *b*.
Ez 11:10 at the *b* of Israel I will judge you;
11:11 At the *b* of Israel I will judge you,
47:13 These are the *b* within which you shall
Mi 2: 5 out *b* by lot in the assembly of the LORD.
Acts 17:26 epochs and fixed the *b* of their regions.

BOUNDARY (81)

Nm 21:13 the Arnon forms Moab's *b* with the Amorites.
21:24 of the Ammonites, whose *b* was at Jazer.
22:36 he went out to meet him at the *b* city
34: 3 "Your southern *b* shall be at the desert
34: 6 "For your western *b* you shall have the
34: 6 this shall be your western *b*.
34: 7 following shall be your *b* on the north:
34: 8 Hamath, with the *b* extending through Zedad.
34: 9 Thence the *b* shall reach to Ziphron and
34: 9 This shall be your northern *b*.
34:10 "For your eastern *b* you shall draw a line
34:11 Shepham the *b* shall go down to Ar-Baal,
34:12 thence the *b* shall continue along the
Jos 12: 5 the *b* of the Geshurites and Maacathites,
13: 3 stream adjoining Egypt to the *b* of Ekron
13:10 in Heshbon, to the *b* of the Ammonites;
13:23 The *b* of the Reubenites was the bank of
13:26 and from Mahanaim to the *b* of Lodebar);
15: 1 in the extreme south toward the *b* of Edom,
15: 2 The *b* there ran from the bay that forms
15: 4 [This is your southern *b*
15: 5 The eastern *b* was the Salt Sea as far as
15: 6 The northern *b* climbed from the bay where
15: 8 the *b* rose to the top of the mountain at
15:10 From Baalah the *b* curved westward to Mount
15:12 western *b* was the Great Sea and its coast.
15:12 complete *b* of the clans of the Judahites.
16: 1 then the *b* went up from Jericho to the
16: 6 *b* curved eastward around Taanath-shiloh,
16: 8 From Tappuah the *b* ran westward to the
17: 7 another *b* ran southward to include the
17: 9 same *b* continued down to the Wadi Kanah.
17:10 with the sea as their common *b*,
18:12 Their northern *b* began at the Jordan and
18:14 the *b* line swung south from the
18:14 This was the western *b*.
18:15 The southern *b* began at the limits of
18:19 From there the *b* continued across the
18:19 This was the southern *b*.
19:11 Their *b* went up west . . .
19:14 the *b* ended at the valley of Iphtahel.
19:22 The *b* reached Tabor,
19:29 Then the *b* turned back to Ramah and to
19:32 The *b* of the clans of the Naphtalites
22:25 the Jordan as a *b* between you and us.
Jgs 11:18 of Moab, for the Arnon is the *b* of Moab.
Jb 26:10 of the deep as the *b* of light and darkness.
28: 3 He has set a *b* for the darkness;
Is 19:19 and a sacred pillar to the LORD near the *b*.
Ez 45: 7 boundary to the eastern *b* of the land.
47:15 is the *b* of the land on the north side:
47:17 This is the northern *b*.
47:18 The eastern *b*:
47:18 *b* down to the eastern sea as far as Tamar.
47:18 This is the eastern *b*.
47:19 The southern *b*:
47:19 This is the southern *b*.
47:20 The western *b*:
47:20 *b* up to a point parallel to Labo of Hamath.
47:20 This is the western *b*.
48: 1 reaching from the eastern to the western *b*.
48: 2 of Dan, from the eastern to the western *b*.
48: 3 Asher, from the eastern to the western *b*.
48: 4 from the eastern to the western *b*.
48: 5 from the eastern to the western *b*.
48: 6 Ephraim, from the eastern to the western *b*.
48: 7 Reuben, from the eastern to the western *b*.
48: 8 from the eastern to the western *b* there
48: 8 portions from the eastern to the western *b*.
48:21 line eastward to the eastern *b*,
48:21 line to the western *b*,
48:23 from the eastern to the western *b*.
48:24 from the eastern to the western *b*.
48:25 Simeon, from the eastern to the western *b*.
48:26 from the eastern to the western *b*.
48:27 Zebulun, from the eastern to the western *b*.
48:28 frontier of Gad shall be the southern *b*,
Hos 5:10 have become like those that move a *b* line;
Mi 7:11 on that day the *b* shall be taken away.
Mt 8:28 As he approached the Gadarene *b*,

BOUNDED (5)

Jos 18:20 The Jordan *b* it on the east.
18:20 of the Benjaminites was *b* on all sides.
Wis 18:15 word from heaven's royal throne *b*,
19: 9 about like horses, and *b* about like lambs,
Col 2:21 were still living a life *b* by this world?

BOUNDING (2)

Wis 17:19 rocks, Or the unseen gallop of *b* animals,
Na 3: 2 horses a-gallop, chariots *b*,

BOUNDS (11)

Nm 35:26 his own accord leaves the *b* of the city
35:27 finds him beyond these *b* and kills him,
Jos 15: 8 which *b* the Valley of Hinnom on the west.
Jer 48:29 heard of the pride of Moab, pride beyond *b*:
Mk 5:42 this the family's astonishment knew no *b*.
7:37 Their amazement went beyond all *b*:
12:17 Their amazement at him knew no *b*.
13:27 from the farthest *b* of earth and sky.
2Cor 7: 4 my many afflictions my joy knows no *b*.
10:13 within the *b* the God of moderation

BOUNTEOUS (1)

Ps(s) 69:17 O LORD, for *b* is your kindness;

BOUNTIFUL (6)

Est E: 2 through the *b* generosity of their patrons.
Ps(s) 51:20 Be *b*, O LORD, to Zion in your kindness
68:10 A *b* rain you showered down,
119:68 You are good and *b*;
Sir 6:19 then await her *b* crops.
2Cor 9: 5 for the *b* gift you have already promised.

BOUNTIFULLY (2)

2Cor 9: 6 and he who sows *b* will reap bountifully.

BOUNTY (7)

1Kgs 10:13 as were given her from Solomon's royal *b*.
Est 2:18 provinces and bestowing gifts with royal *b*.
Ps(s) 27:13 I believe that I shall see the *b* of the
65:12 You have crowned the year with your *b*,
Wis 16:25 serving your all-nourishing *b*
Sir 1: 8 upon every living thing according to his *b*;
Hos 3: 5 come trembling to the LORD and to his *b*,

BOUTS (1)

Eccl 10:17 time (for vigor and not in drinking *b*).

BOW (91)

Gn 9:13 I set my *b* in the clouds to serve as a
9:14 the earth, and the *b* appears in the clouds,
9:16 As the *b* appears in the clouds,
23: 7 began to *b* low before the local citizens,
27: 3 your quiver and *b*—
27:29 and may your mother's sons *b* down to you.
37:10 are to come and *b* to the ground before you?"
48:22 from the Amorites with my sword and *b*."
49: 8 sons of your father shall *b* down to you.
49:24 But each one's *b* remained stiff,
Ex 20: 5 not *b* down before them or worship them.
23:24 not *b* down in worship before their gods,
Dt 5: 9 not *b* down before them or worship them.
26:10 your God, you shall *b* down in his presence.
Jos 24:12 it was not your sword or your *b*.
1Sm 18: 4 dress, and his sword, his *b* and his belt.
2Sm 1:22 The *b* of Jonathan did not turn back,
22:35 war till my arms could bend a *b* of brass.
1Kgs 22:34 Someone, however, drew his *b* at random,
2Kgs 5:18 must *b* down in the temple of Rimmon.
6:22 have taken captive with your sword or *b*?
9:24 his *b* and shot Joram between the shoulders,
13:15 "Take a *b* and some arrows,"
13:16 king of Israel, "Put your hand on the *b*."
13:16 As the king held the *b*,
1Chr 5:18 bore shield and sword and who drew the *b*,
12: 2 stones and in shooting arrows with the *b*.
2Chr 17:17 hundred thousand armed with *b* and buckler.
18:33 drew his *b* at random and hit the king of
Neh 9: 6 and the heavenly hosts *b* down before you.
Jdt 9: 7 trusting in shield and spear, *b* and sling.
Est 3: 2 royal gate would kneel and *b* down to Haman,
3: 2 however, would not kneel and *b* down.
3: 5 Mordecai would not kneel and *b* down to him,
C: 7 I will not *b* down to anyone but you,
E:11 king,' before whom everyone was to *b* down;
Jb 9:13 the helpers of Rahab *b* beneath him.
20:24 the *b* of bronze shall pierce him through;
29:20 within me, and my *b* is renewed in my hand!"
Ps(s) 7:13 he will bend and aim his *b*,
11: 2 For, see, the wicked bend the *b*;
18:35 for war and my arms to bend a *b* of brass.
20: 9 Though they *b* down and fall,
22:28 of the nations shall *b* down before him.
22:30 shall *b* down all who sleep in the earth;
37:14 *b* to bring down the afflicted and the poor,
44: 7 For not in my *b* did I trust,
46:10 the *b* he breaks;
58: 8 when they draw the *b*,
72: 9 His foes shall *b* before him,
76: 4 he shattered the flashing shafts of the *b*,
78:57 they recoiled like a treacherous *b*.
95: 6 Come, let us *b* down in worship;
Prv 14:19 Evil men must *b* down before the good,
Wis 5:21 from a well-drawn *b* shall leap to the mark;
Sir 4: 7 before a ruler *b* your head.
43:12 this *b* bent by the mighty hand of God.
Is 7:24 Men shall go there with *b* and arrows;
21:15 From the taut *b*,

BOW (cont.)

22: 3 together, captured without the use of a *b.*
41: 2 sword he reduces them to dust, with his *b,*
46: 2 They stoop and *b* down together;
51:23 those who ordered you to *b* down,
58: 5 That a man *b* his head like a reed,
Jer 6:23 *B* and javelin they wield;
9: 2 They ready their tongues like a drawn *b;*
49:35 Behold, I will break the *b* of Elam,
50:14 encircling Babylon, you who bend the *b;*
50:29 Babylon archers, all who bend the *b;*
50:42 *B* and javelin they wield,
51: 3 Let the bowman draw his *b,*
Lam 2: 4 Like an enemy he made taut his *b;*
2:10 of Jerusalem *b* their heads to the ground.
3:12 He bent his *b,*
Ez 1:28 Like the *b* which appears in the clouds on
39: 3 I will strike the *b* from your left hand,
Hos 1: 5 the *b* of Israel in the valley of Jezreel.
1: 7 I will not save them by war, by sword or *b,*
2:20 *B* and sword and war I will destroy from
7:16 again become useless, like a treacherous *b.*
Mi 6: 6 the LORD, and *b* before God most high?
Hb 3: 6 age-old hills *b* low along his ancient ways.
3: 9 Bared and ready is your *b,*
Zec 9:10 The warrior's *b* shall be banished,
9:13 For I will bend Judah as my *b,*
10: 4 from him warrior's *b* and every officer.
Acts 27:30 to run out anchors from the *b* of the ship,
27:41 The *b* stuck fast and could not be budged,
Rom 11:10 *B* down their back forever."
1Pt 5: 6 *B* humbly under God's mighty hand,
Rv 6: 2 its rider had a *b,* and he was given a crown.

BOWED (39)

Gn 24:26 The man then *b* down in worship to the LORD,
24:48 Then I *b* down in worship to the LORD,
24:52 answer, he *b* to the ground before the LORD.
33: 6 and their children came forward and *b* low;
33: 7 and her children came forward and *b* low;
33: 7 and her children came forward and *b* low.
37: 7 a ring around my sheaf and *b* down to it."
43:26 while they *b* down before him to the ground.
43:28 they said, as they *b* respectfully.
47:31 Then Israel *b* at the head of the bed.
48:12 from his father's knees and *b* down
Ex 4:31 their affliction, they *b* down in worship.
12:27 Then the people *b* down in worship,
18: 7 meet his father-in-law, *b* down before him,
34: 8 at once *b* down to the ground in worship.
Nm 22:31 he fell on his knees and *b* to the ground.
1Sm 24: 9 *b* to the ground in homage and asked Saul:
28:14 and so he *b* face to the ground in homage.
2Sm 18:21 seen" The Cushite *b* to Joab and sped away.
1Kgs 1:16 Bathsheba *b* in homage to the king,
1Chr 21:21 threshing floor and *b* down before David,
2Chr 25:14 he *b* down before them and offered
Neh 8: 6 Then they *b* down and prostrated themselves
Jdt 10: 8 of Jerusalem"Judith *b* down to God.
13:17 They *b* down and worshiped God,
Ps(s) 35:14 a mother, I was *b* down in mourning.
38: 7 folly, I am stooped and *b* down profoundly;
44:26 For our souls are *b* down to the dust,
57: 7 they have *b* me down;
145:14 falling and raises up all who are *b* down.
146: 8 The LORD raises up those that were *b* down;
Sir 19:22 There is the wicked man who is *b* in grief,
Bar 2:18 is deeply grieved, who walks *b* and feeble,
Lk 5:12 he *b* down to the ground and said to him,
24: 5 Terrified, the women *b* to the ground.
Jn 9:38 he said, and *b* down to worship him.
19:30 Then he *b* his head,
Acts 10:25 dropped to his knees before him and *b* low.
Rom 11: 4 men who have not *b* the knee to Baal."

BOWELS (7)

2Chr 21:15 disease in your *b,* while your bowels issue
21:18 him with an incurable disease of the *b.*
21:19 his *b* issued forth because of the disease
2Mc 9: 5 pains in his *b* and sharp internal torment,
9: 6 *b* of others with many barbarous torments.
Mt 12:40 and three nights in the *b* of the earth.

BOWING (15)

Gn 18: 2 and *b* to the ground,
19: 1 and *b* down with his face to the ground,
23:12 after *b* low before the local citizens,
33: 3 ahead of them, *b* to the ground seven times,
37: 9 moon and eleven stars were *b* down to me."
1Sm 25:41 Rising and *b* to the ground,
2Sm 9: 8 *B* low, he answered,
1Kgs 1:23 the king's presence and, *b* to the floor,
1:31 *B* to the floor in homage to the king,
2Kgs 2:15 to meet him, *b* to the ground before him.
1Chr 29:20 *b* down and prostrating themselves before
Est C: 5 thus in not *b* down to the proud Haman.
Is 49:23 *B* to the ground,
60:14 oppressors shall come, *b* low before you;
Ez 8:16 they were *b* down to the sun.

BOWL (21)

Dt 28: 5 be your grain bin and your kneading *b!*
28:17 be your grain bin and your kneading *b!*
Jgs 5:25 in a princely *b* she offered curds.
2Kgs 2:20 "Bring me a new *b,*"
1Chr 28:17 *b* and the silver for each silver bowl;
Jb 41:12 issues steam, as from a seething pot or *b.*
Eccl 12: 6 and the golden *b* is broken,
Sg 7: 3 *b* that should never lack for mixed wine.
Is 51:17 drained to the dregs the *b* of staggering!
51:22 *b* of my wrath you shall no longer drink.
Dn 14:33 bread in a *b* with the stew he had boiled,
Zec 4: 2 lampstand all of gold, with a *b* at the top,"
12: 2 a *b* to stupefy all peoples round about.
Rv 16: 2 and when he poured out his *b* on the earth,
16: 3 second angel poured out his *b* on the sea.
16: 4 poured out his *b* on the rivers and springs.
16: 8 fourth angel poured out his *b* on the sun.
16:10 out his *b* on the throne of the beast.
16:12 out his *b* on the great river Euphrates.
16:17 angel poured out his *b* upon the empty air.

BOWLFUL (1)

Jgs 6:38 fleece, squeezing out of it a *b* of water.

BOWLS (30)

Ex 7:28 even into your ovens and your kneading *b.*
12:34 in their kneading *b* wrapped in their
24: 6 half of the blood and put it in large *b;*
25:29 its pitchers and *b* for pouring libations.
37:16 its pitchers and *b* for pouring libations,
Nm 4: 7 well as the *b* and pitchers for libations;
1Kgs 7:40 When Hiram made the pots, shovels, and *b,*
7:45 supporting the sea, pots, shovels, and *b.*
7:50 basins, snuffers, *b,*
2Kgs 25:14 pots, the shovels, the snuffers, the *b,*
25:15 The fire-holders and the *b* which were of
2Chr 4: 8 and he made a hundred golden *b.*
4:11 also made the pots, the shovels and the *b.*
4:22 [this was the purest gold], snuffers, *b,*
Ezr 1:10 golden *b,* thirty; silver bowls,
8:27 golden *b* valued at a thousand darics;
1Mc 1:22 the offering table, the cups and the *b,*
Is 22:24 all the little dishes, from *b* to jugs.
Jer 35: 5 I set before these Rechabite men *b* full of
52:18 pots, the shovels, the snuffers, the *b,*
52:19 The basins also, the fire holders, the *b,*
52:19 sacrificial *b* which were of gold or silver,
Am 6: 6 *b* and anoint themselves with the best oils;
Zec 9:15 they are filled with it like libation *b,*
14:20 be as the libation *b* before the altar.
Rv 15: 7 seven golden *b* filled with the wrath
16: 1 upon the earth the seven *b* of God's wrath!"
17: 1 holding the seven *b* came to me and said:
21: 9 angels who held the seven *b*

BOWMAN (4)

Gn 21:20 in the wilderness and became an expert *b,*
Jer 4:29 horseman and *b* each city takes to flight;
51: 3 Let the *b* draw his bow,
Am 2:15 save his life, nor the *b* stand his ground;

BOWMEN (1)

Ps(s) 78: 9 The sons of Ephraim, ordered ranks of *b,*

BOWS (13)

1Sm 2: 4 The *b* of the mighty are broken,
2Chr 26:14 helmets, breastplates, *b* and slingstones.
Neh 4: 7 their swords, their spears, and their *b.*
4:10 half, armed with spears, bucklers, *b,*
1Mc 6:51 *b* for shooting arrows and slingstones.
Ps(s) 37:15 own hearts, and their *b* shall be broken.
Sir 19:23 He *b* his head and feigns not to hear,
Is 5:28 arrows are sharp, and all their *b* are bent.
13: 7 *b* of the young men fall from their hands.
46: 1 Bel *b* down,
Jer 46: 9 shields, Men of Lud, stretching your *b!*"
51:56 her heroes are captured, their *b* broken;
Ez 39: 9 [shields and bucklers,] *b* and arrows,

BOWSHOT (2)

Gn 21:16 and sat down opposite him, about a *b* away;
Ps(s) 60: 6 banner to which they may flee out of *b*

BOWSTRINGS (2)

Jgs 16: 7 me with seven fresh *b* which have not dried,"
16: 8 her seven fresh *b* which had not dried,

BOX (6)

Ex 27: 8 altar itself in the form of a hollow *b,*
38: 7 altar was made in the form of a hollow *b.*
1Sm 6: 8 putting in a *b* beside it the golden
6:11 along with the *b* containing the golden
6:15 down the ark of God and the *b* beside it,
Mk 12:41 crowd putting money into the collection *b.*

BOXES (1)

Is 3:20 bangles, cinctures, perfume *b,*

BOY (86)

Gn 4:23 a man for wounding me, a *b* for bruising me.
21:12 about the *b* or about your slave woman.
21:18 lift up the *b* and hold him by the hand;
21:19 skin with water, and then let the *b* drink.
21:20 God was with the *b* as he grew up.
22: 5 while the *b* and I go on over yonder.
22:12 "Do not lay your hand on the *b,*"
37:30 "The *b* is gone!
42:22 in Reuben, "not to do wrong to the *b?*
43: 8 "Let the *b* go with me,
43:29 to him, "May God be gracious to you, my *b!*"
44:22 to my lord, 'The *b* cannot leave his father;
44:30 "If then the *b* is not with us when I go
44:30 as soon as he sees that the *b* is missing;
44:32 *b* from his father by going surety for him,
44:33 in place of the *b* as the slave of my lord,
44:33 and let the *b* go back with his brothers.
44:34 to my father if the *b* were not with me?
Ex 1:16 and see them giving birth, if it is a *b,*
1:22 river every *b* that is born to the Hebrews,
2: 6 it, she looked, and lo, there was a baby *b,*
21:31 if it is a *b* or a girl that the ox gores.
Lv 12: 2 has conceived and gives birth to a *b,*
12: 7 who gives birth to a *b* or a girl child.
27: 6 sum shall be five silver shekels for a *b,*
Nm 18:16 a *b* is to be paid when he is a month old;
Jgs 8:20 Since Jether was still a *b,*
13: 5 for this *b* is to be consecrated to God
13: 7 For the *b* shall be consecrated to God from
13: 8 us what to do for the *b* who will be born."
13:12 true, what are we expected to do for the *b?*"
13:24 The *b* grew up and the LORD blessed him;
1Sm 2:18 Meanwhile the *b* Samuel,
20:22 But if I say to the *b,*
20:35 a little *b* for his appointment with David.
20:36 There he said to the *b,*
20:36 And as the *b* ran, he shot an arrow
20:37 When the *b* made for the spot where
20:38 Jonathan's *b* picked up the arrow and
20:39 The *b* knew nothing;
20:40 weapons to this *b* of his and said to him,
20:41 When the *b* had left,
25:34 not have had a single man or *b* left alive."
1Kgs 11:17 Meanwhile, Hadad, who was only a *b,*
2Kgs 4:26 with her, with her husband, and with the *b.*"
4:29 Lay my staff upon the *b.*"
4:31 ahead and had laid the staff upon the *b,*
4:31 informed him that the *b* had not awakened.
4:32 the house, he found the *b* lying dead.
4:35 and then once more lay down upon the *b,*
Tb 4:12 My *b,* keep in mind Noah,
6: 2 When the *b* left home,
6: 3 *b* went down to wash his feet in the river,
6: 4 The *b* seized the fish and hauled it up on
6: 7 The *b* asked the angel this question:
6:11 close to Ecbatana, Raphael said to the *b,*
7:10 so he said to the *b:*
1Mc 11:40 urging Imalkue to hand over the *b* to him,
11:54 and brought with him the young *b* Antiochus,
2Mc 7:25 her to advise her *b* to save his life.
Jb 3: 3 night when they said, "The child is a *b!*"
Prv 22: 6 Train a *b* in the way he should go;
23:13 Withhold not chastisement from a *b;*
29:15 a *b* left to his whims disgraces his mother.
Wis 18: 5 a single *b* had been cast forth but saved,
Is 10:19 up for signals, that any *b* can record them.
Dn 13:45 the holy spirit of a young *b* named Daniel,
Jl 4: 3 they gave a *b* for a harlot,
Mt 8: 6 my serving *b* is at home in bed paralyzed,
8: 8 give an order and my *b* will get better.
8:13 That very moment the *b* got better.
17:18 That very moment the *b* was cured.
Mk 9:20 immediately threw the *b* into convulsions.
9:26 and throwing the *b* into convulsions,
9:26 the *b* became like a corpse,
Lk 9:42 rebuked the unclean spirit, cured the *b,*
18:21 "I have kept all these since I was a *b.*"
Jn 4:51 with the news that his *b* was going to live.
4:52 at what time the *b* had shown improvement,
Acts 20:10 himself on him, clutching the *b* to himself.
20:12 they were able to take the *b* away alive.
23:18 called me and asked me to bring you this *b,*
23:20 The *b* replied: "The Jews have agreed."
23:22 commander sent the *b* away with the order,
Rv 12: 5 a *b* destined to shepherd all the nations
12:13 the woman who had given birth to the *b.*

BOYS—BOY'S (21)

Gn 21:17 God heard the *b* cry,
21:17 has heard the *b* cry in this plight of his.
25:27 As the *b* grew up,
48:16 these *b* That in them my name be recalled,
Ex 1:17 Egypt had ordered them, but let the *b* live.
1:18 you acted thus, allowing the *b* to live?"
Lv 12: 3 of the *b* foreskin shall be circumcised,
1Sm 1:25 the *b* father had sacrificed the young bull,
2Kgs 2:23 *b* came out of the city and jeered at him.
4:30 But the *b* mother cried out:
1Mc 2:46 any uncircumcised *b* whom they found
13:17 he gave orders to get the money and the *b,*
13:18 would not send Trypho the money and the *b.*

13:19 So he sent the *b* and the hundred talents;
2Mc 7:39 since he bitterly resented the *b* contempt.
Jb 33:25 Then his flesh shall become soft as a *b;*
Ps(s) 148:12 Young men too, and maidens, old men and *b,*
Lam 5:13 *b* stagger under their loads of wood;
Zec 8: 5 with *b* and girls playing in her streets.
Mt 2:16 He ordered the massacre of all the *b* two
Mk 9:24 The *b* father immediately exclaimed,

BOZEZ (1)

1Sm 14: 4 a rocky crag on each side, one called *B,*

BOZKATH (2)

Jos 15:39 Dilean, Mizpeh, Joktheel, Lachish, *B,*
2Kgs 22: 1 name was Jedidah, daughter of Adaiah of *B.*

BOZRAH (10)

Gn 36:33 Bela died, Jobab, son of Zerah, from *B,*
1Chr 1:44 Bela died, Jobab, son of Zerah, from *B,*
1Mc 5:26 "Many of them have been imprisoned in *B,*
5:28 his army, marched across the desert to *B,*
Is 34: 6 For the LORD has a sacrifice in *B,*
63: 1 from Edom, in crimsoned garments, from *B—*
Jer 48:24 and Beth-meon, on Kerioth and on *B:*
49:13 *B* shall become an object of horror and a
49:22 soars aloft, and spreads his wings over *B;*
Am 1:12 Teman, and it will devour the castles of *B.*

BRACE (1)

Acts 27:17 made use of cables to *b* the ship itself.

BRACED (2)

Jgs 16:29 temple rested and *b* himself against them,
2Chr 18:34 and the king of Israel *b* himself up on his

BRACELET (2)

Nm 31:50 he has picked up, such as an anklet, a *b,*
Sir 21:21 to a wise man, like a *b* on his right arm.

BRACELETS (7)

Gn 24:22 nose, and two gold *b* weighing ten shekels,
24:30 As soon as he saw the ring and the *b* on
24:47 ring on her nose and the *b* on her wrists.
Jdt 10: 4 for her feet, and put on her anklets, *b,*
Is 3:19 the pendants, *b,* and veils;
Ez 16:11 I put *b* on your arms,
23:42 who put *b* on the women's arms and splendid

BRACES (2)

1Kgs 7:33 The four legs of each stand had cast *b,*
7:34 These four *b,*

BRACKISH (1)

Jas 3:12 no more can a *b* source yield fresh water.

BRAGGARTS (1)

Zep 3:11 will I remove from your midst the proud *b,*

BRAGGING (1)

2Cor 11:18 many are *b* about their human distinctions,

BRAINS (1)

Zep 1:17 out like dust, and their *b* like dung.

BRAMBLES (1)

Lk 6:44 from thornbushes, nor grapes picked from *b.*

BRANCH (29)

Ex 25:33 On one *b* there are to be three cups,
25:33 the opposite *b* there are to be three cups,
37:19 On one *b* there were three cups,
37:19 on the opposite *b* there were three cups,
Nm 13:23 a *b* with a single cluster of grapes on it,
Dt 32:32 They are a *b* of Sodom's vinestock,
1Mc 13:37 gold crown and the palm *b* that you sent.
2Mc 14: 4 him with a gold crown and a palm *b,*
Sir 35:21 Till he destroys the haughty root and *b,*
Is 4: 2 The *b* of the LORD will be luster and glory,
9:13 head and tail, palm *b* and reed in one day.
19:15 to do for head or tail, palm *b* or reed.
Jer 1:11 "I see a *b* of the watching-tree,"
Ez 8:17 now they must also put the *b* to my nose?
15: 2 That *b* among the trees of the forest!
17: 4 tearing off its topmost *b,*
19:11 strong *b* she put out as a royal scepter.
19:12 Then her strong *b* withered up,
19:14 came out of the *b* and devoured her shoots;
19:14 She is now without a strong *b,*
31: 3 [cedar] in Lebanon, beautiful of *b,*
31: 5 longer of *b* because of the abundant water.
Mal 3:19 on fire, leaving them neither root nor *b,*
3:24 on fire, leaving them neither root nor *b,*
Mt 24:32 When its *b* grows tender and sprouts leaves,
Jn 15: 2 He prunes away every barren *b,*
15: 4 No more than a *b* can bear fruit of itself
15: 6 live in me is like a withered, rejected *b,*
Rom 11:17 off and you, a *b* of the wild olive tree,

BRANCHED (1)

Gn 10:32 nations of the earth *b* out after the flood.

BRANCHES (75)

Gn 2:10 beyond there it divides and becomes four *b.*
40:10 front of me, and on the vine were three *b.*
40:12 The three *b* are three days;
Ex 25:31 its shaft and *b—*
25:32 Six *b* are to extend from the sides of the
25:32 of the lampstand, three *b* on one side,
25:33 the six *b* that extend from the lampstand.
25:35 pairs of *b* that extend from the lampstand.
25:36 Their knobs and *b* shall so spring from it
37:17 its shaft and *b* as well as its cups and
37:18 Six *b* extended from its sides,
37:18 three *b* on one side and three on the other.
37:19 the six *b* that extended from the lampstand.
37:21 of *b* that extended from the lampstand.
37:22 The knobs and *b* sprang so directly from it
Lv 23:40 *b* of palms and boughs of myrtles and of
Nm 8: 4 beaten gold in both its shaft and its *b,*
Dt 24:20 you shall not go over the *b* a second time;
2Sm 18: 9 passed under the *b* of a large terebinth,
Neh 8:15 hill country and bring in *b* of olive trees,
8:16 The people went out and brought in *b* with
Jdt 15:12 She took *b* in her hands and distributed
1Mc 13:51 shouts of jubilation, waving of palm *b,*
2Mc 10: 7 entwined with leaves, green *b* and palms,
14: 4 of the customary olive *b* from the temple.
Jb 14: 9 again and put forth *b* like a young plant.
15:32 its time, and his *b* shall be green no more.
18:16 his roots dry up, and above, his *b* wither.
29:19 the dew rests by night on my *b.*
Ps(s) 80:11 by its *b,* the cedars of God.
104:12 among the *b* they send forth their song.
Sg 7: 9 the palm tree, I will take hold of its *b.*
Wis 4: 4 even though their *b* flourish for a time,
17:18 song of birds in the spreading *b,*
Sir 1:18 her *b* are length of days.
14:26 nest in her leafage, and lodges in her *b;*
23:25 her *b* will not bring forth fruit.
24:16 I spread out my *b* like a terebinth,
24:16 terebinth, my *b* so bright and so graceful.
37:17 four *b* it shoots forth:
50: 8 Like the blossoms on the *b* in springtime,
Is 16: 8 *b* spread forth and extended over the sea.
17: 6 very top, four or five on its fruitful *b,*
18: 5 Then comes the cutting of *b* with pruning
27:11 its *b* shall wither and be broken off,
Jer 11:16 Now he sets fire to it, its *b* burn.
Ez 17: 6 Its *b* turned toward him, its roots lying
17: 6 a vine, produced *b* and put forth shoots.
17: 7 this vine bent its roots, sent out its *b,*
17: 8 waters it was planted, to grow *b,*
17:22 from its topmost *b* tear off a tender shoot,
17:23 It shall put forth *b* and bear fruit,
31: 6 its *b* all beasts of the field gave birth,
31: 8 were the plane trees like it for *b;*
31:12 its *b* lay broken in all the ravines of the
31:13 by its *b* were all the beasts of the field.
36: 8 grow *b* and bear fruit for my people Israel,
Dn 4: 9 in its *b* the birds of the air nested;
4:11 " 'Cut down the tree and lop off its *b,*
4:11 beasts flee its shade, and the birds its *b.*
4:18 and in whose *b* the birds of the air dwelt
Jl 1: 7 its *b* are made white.
Mt 13:32 sky come and build their nests in its *b.*"
21: 8 while some began to cut *b* from the trees
Mk 4:32 with *b* big enough for the birds of the sky
13:28 *b* runs high and it begins to sprout leaves,
Lk 13:19 and the birds of the air nested in its *b.*"
Jn 12:13 they got palm *b* and came out to meet him.
15: 5 I am the vine, you are the *b.*
Rom 11:16 the root is consecrated, so too are the *b.*
11:17 If some of the *b* were cut off and you,
11:17 of the olive, do not boast against the *b.*
11:19 *B* were cut off that I might be grafted in."
11:21 If God did not spare the natural *b,*
Rv 7: 9 robes and holding palm *b* in their hands.

BRANCHY (1)

Ez 19:10 *b* was she because of the abundant water.

BRAND (4)

2Mc 4: 2 He dared to *b* as a plotter against the
Am 4:11 you were like a *b* plucked from the fire;
Zec 3: 2 Is not this man a *b* snatched from the fire?"
Gal 6:17 for I bear the *b* marks of Jesus in my body.

BRANDISH (3)

Ps(s) 35: 3 *B* the lance, and block the way
Sir 46: 2 his arm, to *b* his javelin against the city!
Ez 32:10 you in horror when they see me *b* my sword,

BRANDISHED (7)

1Sm 20:33 At this Saul *b* his spear to strike him,
2Sm 23: 8 It was he who *b* his battle-ax over eight
23:18 who *b* his spear over three hundred slain.
1Chr 11:11 He *b* his spear against three hundred,
11:20 he *b* his spear against three hundred,
2Mc 5: 3 that, with *b* shields and bristling spears,
Prv 26: 9 Like a thorn stick *b* by the hand of a

BRANDISHING (2)

2Mc 11: 8 in white garments and *b* gold weapons.
Hb 1:17 *b* his sword to slay peoples without mercy?

BRANDS (1)

Is 7: 4 stumps of smoldering *b* [the blazing anger

BRASS (9)

2Sm 22:35 for war till my arms could bend a bow of *b.*
1Chr 15:19 Heman, Asaph, and Ethan, sounded *b* cymbals.
Ps(s) 18:35 for war and my arms to bend a bow of *b.*
107:16 the gates of *b* and burst the bars of iron.
Jer 1:18 city, A pillar of iron, a wall of *b,*
15:20 you toward this people a solid wall of *b.*
52:22 encircled the capital, all of *b;*
Rv 1:15 like polished *b* refined in a furnace,
2:18 fire and whose feet gleam like polished *b,*

BRAVE (18)

Dt 31: 6 Be *b* and steadfast;
31: 7 Israel said to him, "Be *b* and steadfast,
31:23 Nun, and said to him, "Be *b* and steadfast,
Jos 10: 2 the city of Ai, and all its men were *b.*
1Sm 14:52 When Saul saw any strong or *b* man,
2Sm 10:12 Be *b;* let us prove our valor
17:10 Then even the *b* man with the heart of a
17:10 and that those who are with him are *b.*
2Kgs 2:16 "Among your servants are fifty *b* men,"
1Chr 22:13 Be *b* and steadfast;
2Chr 32: 7 "Be *b* and steadfast;
Tb 7:17 "Be *b,* my daughter.
1Mc 3:58 "Arm yourselves and be *b;*
5:56 heard about the *b* deeds and the fighting
5:61 thinking that they would do *b* deeds.
8: 2 their battles and the *b* deeds
9:22 his battles, the *b* deeds he performed,
16:23 his wars and the *b* deeds he performed,

BRAVELY (8)

1Sm 14:48 he turned, he was successful and fought *b.*
1Mc 4:35 men were ready either to live or to die *b,*
6:31 sortie and burned these and they fought *b.*
9:10 let us die *b* for our kinsmen and not leave
2Mc 2:21 heroes who fought *b* for Judaism so that,
7: 5 mother encouraged one another to die *b,*
7:10 told to do so, and *b* held out his hands,
10:35 *b* stormed the wall and with savage fury

BRAVEST (1)

2Mc 13:15 picked force of the *b* young men

BRAWLS (1)

Sir 27:14 on end, their *b* make one stop one's ears.

BRAY (1)

Jb 6: 5 Does the wild ass *b* when he has grass?

BRAZEN (3)

Jb 37:18 firmament of the skies, hard as a *b* mirror?
Sir 12:11 Rub him as one polishes a *b* mirror,
23: 5 A *b* look allow me not;

BRAZENFACED (1)

Prv 21:29 The wicked man is *b,*

BRAZIER (4)

Gn 15:17 appeared a smoking *b* and a flaming torch,
Jer 36:22 and fire was burning in a *b* before him.
36:23 knife and cast it into the fire in the *b,*
Zec 12: 6 of Judah like a *b* of fire in the woodland,

BREACH (13)

Gn 38:29 "What a *b* you have made for yourself!"
Jgs 21:15 had made a *b* among the tribes of Israel.
1Kgs 11:27 up the *b* of his father's City of David.
Neh 3:35 attacked it would *b* their wall of stones!"
6: 1 there was no *b* left in it
Jb 30:14 as through a wide *b* they advance.
Ps(s) 106:23 the *b* to turn back his destructive wrath.
144:14 May there be no *b* in the walls,
Is 58:12 "Repairer of the *b,*"
Jer 32:24 have arrived at this city to *b* it;
39: 2 a *b* was made in the city's defenses.
Ez 13: 5 You did not step into the *b,*
22:30 stand in the *b* before me to keep me

BREACHED (6)

2Kgs 25: 4 had no more bread, the city walls were *b.*
Neh 1: 3 Also, the wall of Jerusalem lies *b,*
Jer 52: 7 had no more bread, the city walls were *b.*
Ez 26:10 gates, even as one enters a city that is *b.*
30:16 be *b* and its walls shall be demolished.
Am 4: 3 the *b* walls each by the most direct way,

BREACHES (3)

2Kgs 12:13 and hewn stone used in repairing the *b*,
Is 22: 9 that the *b* in the City of David were many;
Am 9:11 I will wall up its *b*,

BREAD (261)

Gn 3:19 sweat of your face shall you get *b* to eat,
14:18 king of Salem, brought out *b* and wine,
21:14 Early the next morning Abraham got some *b*
25:34 then gave him some *b* and the lentil stew;
27:17 appetizing dish and the *b* she had prepared.
28:20 me enough *b* to eat and clothing to wear,
41:55 and the people cried to Pharaoh for *b*,
45:23 and *b* and other provisions for his journey.
47:16 sell you *b* in return for your livestock."
47:17 with *b* in exchange for all their livestock.
Ex 12: 8 flesh with unleavened *b* and bitter herbs.
12:15 For seven days you must eat unleavened *b*.
12:15 Whoever eats leavened *b* from the first day
12:17 then, this custom of the unleavened *b*.
12:18 of this month you shall eat unleavened *b*.
12:20 you dwell you may eat only unleavened *b*."
13: 6 For seven days you shall eat unleavened *b*,
13: 7 *b* may be eaten during the seven days;
16: 3 sat by our fleshpots and ate our fill of *b*!
16: 4 will now rain down *b* from heaven for you.
16: 8 "and in the morning your fill of *b*,
16:12 the morning you shall have your fill of *b*,
16:15 the *b* which the LORD has given you to eat.
23:15 You shall keep the feast of Unleavened *B*.
23:15 you must eat unleavened *b* for seven days
23:18 the blood of my sacrifice with leavened *b*;
29:23 you shall take one of the loaves of *b*,
29:32 of the ram and the *b* that is in the basket.
29:34 some of the *b* remains over on the next day,
34:18 "You shall keep the feast of Unleavened *B*.
34:18 month of Abib you are to eat unleavened *b*,
34:25 me the blood of sacrifice with leavened *b*,
40:23 and arranged the *b* on it before the LORD,
Lv 7:13 loaves of leavened *b* along with the victim
8:26 cake, one loaf of *b* made with oil,
8:31 and there eat it with the *b* that is in the
8:32 flesh and *b* you shall burn up in the fire.
23: 6 month is the LORD's feast of Unleavened *B*.
23: 6 For seven days you shall eat unleavened *b*.
23:14 any *b* or roasted grain or fresh kernels.
23:17 two loaves of *b* made of two tenths
23:18 Besides the *b*, you shall offer to the LORD
23:20 The priest shall wave the *b* of the first
24: 7 to the LORD, a token offering for the *b*.
24: 8 *b* shall be set out afresh before the LORD,
26:26 And as I cut off your supply of *b*,
26:26 all the *b* they dole out to you in rations
Nm 4: 7 *b* offering shall remain on the table.
9:11 it with unleavened *b* and bitter herbs,
28:17 For seven days unleavened *b* is to be eaten.
Dt 8: 3 show you that not by *b* alone does man live,
8: 9 a land where you can eat *b* without stint
16: 3 You shall not eat leavened *b* with it.
16: 3 only unleavened *b*, the bread of affliction,
16: 8 For six days you shall eat unleavened *b*,
16:16 at the feast of Unleavened *B*,
29: 5 *b* was not your food,
Jos 9: 5 all the *b* they took was dry and crumbly.
9:12 This *b* of ours was still warm when we
Jgs 7:13 *b* was rolling into the camp of Midian.
8: 5 you give my followers some loaves of *b*?
19:19 and *b* and wine for the woman and myself
Ru 2:14 dip your *b* in the sauce."
1Sm 2: 5 The well-fed hire themselves out for *b*,
2:36 him for a piece of silver or a loaf of *b*,
2:36 that I may have a morsel of *b* to eat.'"
9: 7 There is no *b* in our bags,
10: 3 three kids, another three loaves of *b*,
10: 4 you and offer you two wave offerings of *b*,
16:20 Then Jesse took five loaves of *b*,
21: 5 no ordinary *b* on hand, only holy bread;
21: 7 priest gave him holy *b*, for no other bread
21: 7 replaced by fresh *b* when it was taken away.
25:11 Must I take my *b*, my wine, my meat
28:24 she kneaded it and baked unleavened *b*.
2Sm 3:29 falling by the sword, or one in need of *b*!"
3:35 if I eat *b* or anything else before sunset."
6:19 entire multitude of Israel, a loaf of *b*,
16: 1 asses laden with two hundred loaves of *b*,
16: 2 The *b* and summer fruits are for your
1Kgs 13: 8 nor eat *b* or drink water in this place.
13: 9 not to eat *b* or drink water
13:15 said, "Come home with me and have some *b*."
13:16 *b* or drink water with you in this place,"
13:17 LORD neither to eat *b* nor drink water here,
13:18 and to have you eat *b* and drink water."
13:19 and ate *b* and drank water in his house.
13:22 but returned and ate *b* and drank water in
13:23 After he had eaten *b* and drunk water,
17: 6 brought him *b* and meat in the morning,
17: 6 the morning, and *b* and meat in the evening,
17:11 after her, "Please bring along a bit of *b*."
22:27 of *b* and water until I return in safety.'"
2Kgs 6:22 Serve them *b* and water.
18:32 land of grain and wine, of *b* and orchards,
23: 9 with their relatives, ate the unleavened *b*.
25: 3 the city, and the people had no more *b*,
1Chr 16: 3 to every man and every woman, a loaf of *b*,
23:29 offering, of the wafers of unleavened *b*,
2Chr 8:13 on the feast of the Unleavened *B*,
18:26 of *b* and water until I return in safety!'"
30:13 feast of Unleavened *B* in the second month;
30:21 *B* with great rejoicing for seven days,
35:17 feast of the Unleavened *B* for seven days.
Ezr 6:22 the feast of Unleavened *B* for seven days,
Tb 1:17 I would give my *b* to the hungry and my
4:16 "Give to the hungry some of your *b*,
4:17 *b* and wine at the burial of the virtuous,
8:19 asked his wife to bake many loaves of *b*;
Jdt 10: 5 roasted grain, fig cakes, *b* and cheese;
2Mc 1: 8 the lamps and set out the loaves of *b*.
Jb 22: 7 and from the hungry you have withheld *b*;
27:14 His offspring shall not be filled with *b*.
28: 5 The earth, though out of it comes forth *b*,
Ps(s) 14: 4 who eat up my people just as they eat *b*?
37:25 man forsaken nor his descendants begging *b*.
41:10 who had my trust and partook of my *b*,
53: 5 who eat up my people just as they eat *b*,
78:20 give *b* and provide meat for his people?"
78:24 them for food and gave them heavenly *b*.
78:25 The *b* of the mighty was eaten by men;
80: 6 You have fed them with the *b* of tears and
102: 5 I forget to eat my *b*.
102:10 like *b* and mingle my drink with tears,
104:14 for men's use, Producing *b* from the earth,
104:15 oil, and *b* fortifies the hearts of men.
105:40 and with *b* from heaven he satisfied them.
127: 2 off your rest, You that eat hard-earned *b*,
132:15 provision, her poor I will fill with *b*.
Prv 4:17 For they eat the *b* of wickedness and drink
6:26 a loose woman may be scarcely a loaf of *b*,
9:17 sweet, and *b* gotten secretly is pleasing!"
12: 9 than one of assumed importance who lacks *b*.
20:17 The *b* of deceit is sweet to a man,
28:21 for even a morsel of *b* a man may do wrong.
Eccl 9: 7 eat your *b* with joy and drink your wine
10:19 *B* and oil call forth merriment and wine
11: 1 Cast your *b* upon the waters;
Wis 16:20 of angels and furnished them *b* from heaven,
Sir 10:26 than the boaster who is without *b*.
14:10 The miser's eye is rapacious for *b*,
15: 3 Nourish him with the *b* of understanding,
20:16 Those who eat his *b* have an evil tongue.
23:17 The rake to whom all *b* is sweet and who is
29:21 Life's prime needs are water, *b*,
34:21 *b* of charity is life itself for the needy;
48: 2 Their staff of *b* he shattered,
Is 3: 1 and prop [all supplies of *b* and water]:
3: 7 in my own house there is no *b* or clothing!
21:14 land of Tema, greet the fugitives with *b*.
30:20 The Lord will give you the *b* you need and
36:17 land of grain and wine, of *b* and vineyards.
44:15 himself, or makes a fire for baking *b*;
44:19 I baked *b* and roasted meat which I ate.
51:14 into the pit, nor shall they want for *b*.
55: 2 Why spend your money for what is not *b*;
55:10 seed to him who sows and *b* to him who eats,
58: 7 Sharing your *b* with the hungry,
58:10 *b* on the hungry and satisfy the afflicted;
Jer 5:17 They will devour your harvest and your *b*,
16: 7 They will not break *b* with the bereaved to
37:21 and given a loaf of *b* each day from the
37:21 until all the *b* in the city was eaten up.
42:14 trumpet alarm no longer, nor hunger for *b*;
52: 6 the city and the people had no more *b*,
Lam 1:11 All her people groan, searching for *b*;
5: 6 and to Assyria, to fill our need of *b*.
Ez 4: 9 in a single vessel and make *b* out of them.
4:15 bake your *b* on that.
4:16 I am breaking the staff of *b* in Jerusalem.
4:16 *b* which they have weighed out anxiously,
4:17 that, owing to the scarcity of *b* and water,
5:16 of hunger, I will break your staff of *b*;
12:18 Son of man, eat your *b* trembling,
12:19 They shall eat their *b* in anxiety and
13:19 with handfuls of barley and crumbs of *b*,
14:13 hand against it and break its staff of *b*,
24:17 your beard, and do not eat the customary *b*.
24:22 your beards nor eating the customary *b*.
45:21 for seven days unleavened *b* is to be eaten.
Dn 14:33 *b* in a bowl with the stew he had boiled,
Hos 2: 7 she said, "who give me my *b* and my water,
9: 4 Theirs will be like mourners' *b*,
Am 4: 6 have made *b* scarce in all your dwellings,
7:12 There earn your *b* by prophesying,
8:11 Not a famine of *b*,
Ob 1: 7 who eat your *b* lay snares beneath you:
Hg 2:12 of his garment and the fold touches *b*,
Mt 4: 3 God, command these stones to turn into *b*."
4: 4 'Not on *b* alone is man to live but on
6:11 Give us today our daily *b*,
12: 4 he entered God's house and ate the holy *b*,
15:33 "How could we ever get enough *b* in this
15:34 them, "How many loaves of *b* do you have?"
16: 5 they had forgotten to bring any *b* along.
16: 7 "This is because we have brought no *b*."
16: 8 do you suppose it is because you have no *b*?
16:11 I was not speaking about *b* at all
16:12 a warning against yeast [used for *b*
26:17 first day of the feast of Unleavened *B*,
26:26 During the meal Jesus took *b*,
Mk 2:26 ate the holy *b* which only the priests
6:37 two hundred days' wages for *b* to feed them?"
8: 4 people sufficient *b* in this deserted spot?"
8:14 They had forgotten to bring any *b* along;
8:16 that it was because they had no *b*.
8:17 suppose that it is because you have no *b*?
14: 1 *B* were to be observed in two days' time,
14:12 On the first day of Unleavened *B*,
14:22 During the meal he took *b*,
Lk 4: 3 of God, command this stone to turn into *b*."
4: 4 has it, 'Not on *b* alone shall man live.'"
6: 4 and ate the holy *b* and gave it to his men,
7:33 came neither eating *b* nor drinking wine,
9: 3 nor traveling bag; no *b*, no money.
11: 3 Give us each day our daily *b*.
14:15 is he who eats *b* in the kingdom of God."
22: 1 *B* known as the Passover was drawing near,
22: 7 The day of Unleavened *B* arrived on which
22:19 Then, taking *b* and giving thanks,
24:30 himself with them to eat, he took *b*,
24:30 the *b* and began to distribute it to them.
24:35 had come to know him in the breaking of *b*.
Jn 6: 5 shall we buy *b* for these people to eat?"
6:11 Jesus then took the loaves of *b*,
6:23 the *b* after the Lord had given thanks.
6:31 'He gave them *b* from the heavens to eat.'"
6:32 not Moses who gave you *b* from the heavens;
6:32 Father who gives you the real heavenly *b*.
6:33 God's *b* comes down from heaven and gives
6:34 "Sir, give us this *b* always,"
6:35 "I myself am the *b* of life.
6:41 "I am the *b* that came down from heaven."
6:48 I am the *b* of life.
6:50 This is the *b* that comes down from heaven
6:51 am the living *b* come down from heaven.
6:51 eats this *b* he shall live forever; the bread
6:58 This is the *b* that came down from heaven.
6:58 man who feeds on this *b* shall live forever."
13:18 *b* with me has raised his heel against me.'
21: 9 there with a fish laid on it and some *b*.
21:13 came over, took the *b* and gave it to them,
Acts 2:42 life, to the breaking of *b* and the prayers.
2:46 day, while in their homes they broke *b*.
12: 3 During the feast of Unleavened *B* he had
20: 6 as the festival of Unleavened *B* was over.
20: 7 when we gathered for the breaking of *b*,
20:11 Paul went upstairs again, broke *b*,
27:35 When he had said this he took some *b*,
1Cor 5: 8 the unleavened *b* of sincerity and truth.
10:16 *b* we break a sharing in the body of Christ?
10:17 Because the loaf of *b* is one,
11:23 the night in which he was betrayed took *b*,
11:26 then, you eat this *b* and drink this cup,
11:27 This means that whoever eats the *b* or
11:28 he eat of the *b* and drink of the cup.
2Cor 9:10 *b* for the eater will provide in abundance;

BREADTH (8)

Gn 13:17 in the land, through its length and *b*,
2Kgs 21:16 as to fill the length and *b* of Jerusalem.
Jdt 7: 3 out in *b* toward Dothan as far as Balbaim,
Jb 38:18 Have you comprehended the *b* of the earth?
Sir 1: 3 Heaven's height, earth's *b*,
Is 14:21 and fill the *b* of the world with tyrants.
Hb 1: 6 That marches the *b* of the land to take
Eph 3:18 the *b* and length and height and depth of

BREAK (106)

Gn 19: 9 Lot, moving in closer to *b* down the door.
32:25 man wrestled with him until the *b* of dawn.
33:12 said, "Let us *b* camp and be on our way;
Ex 12:46 You shall not *b* any of its bones.
13:13 you do not redeem it, you shall *b* its neck.
19:21 warn the people not to *b* through
19:24 must not *b* through to come up to the LORD;
34:20 you do not redeem it, you must *b* its neck.
Lv 11:33 unclean, and the vessel itself you must *b*.
26:19 sevenfold, to *b* your haughty confidence.
Nm 9:17 from the tent, the Israelites would *b* camp;
Dt 31:16 *b* the covenant which I have made with them.
33:11 *B* the backs of his adversaries and of his
Jos 3: 3 carry, you must also *b* camp and follow it,
Jgs 2: 1 that I would never *b* my covenant with you,
1Sm 2:31 the time is coming when I will *b* your
1Kgs 5:23 There I will *b* up the rafts,
13: 3 The altar shall *b* up and the ashes on it
15:19 Go, *b* your treaty with Baasha,
2Kgs 3:26 swordsmen to *b* through to the king of Aram,
1Chr 14:11 "God has used me to *b* through my enemies
2Chr 16: 3 Go, *b* your treaty with Baasha,
Tb 4: 5 desire to sin or to *b* his commandments.
Jdt 8:30 bind ourselves by an oath that we cannot *b*.
2Mc 14:28 for he hated to *b* his agreement with a man
Ps(s) 2: 3 "Let us *b* their fetters and cast their
3: 8 the teeth of the wicked you *b*.
10:15 *B* the strength of the wicked and of the
25: 3 be put to shame who heedlessly *b* faith.
46: 6 God will help it at the *b* of dawn.
52: 7 forever he shall *b* you;
58: 7 the jaw-teeth of the lions, *b*,

75:11 I will *b* off the horns of all the wicked;
98: 4 *b* into song; sing praise.
Prv 3:20 By his knowledge the depths *b* open,
25:15 persuaded, and a soft tongue will *b* a bone.
Sir 19:16 your neighbor before you *b* with him;
39:14 incense, *b* forth in blossoms like the lily.
Is 5: 5 give it to grazing, *b* through its wall,
14:25 I will *b* the Assyrian in my land and
22:25 a sure spot shall give way, *b* off and fall,
42: 3 A bruised reed he shall not *b*,
44:23 *B* forth, you mountains, into song,
49:13 and rejoice, O earth, *b* forth into song,
52: 9 *B* out together in song,
54: 1 who did not bear, *b* forth in jubilant song,
55:12 and hills shall *b* out in song before you,
58: 8 your light shall *b* forth like the dawn,
Jer 4: 4 Lest my anger *b* out like fire,
9: 9 mountains, *b* out in cries of lamentation,
14:21 your covenant with us, and *b* it not.
16: 7 They will not *b* bread with the bereaved to
19:10 And you shall *b* the flask in the sight of
21:12 Lest my fury *b* out like fire which burns
28: 2 'I will *b* the yoke of the king of Babylon.
28: 4 I will *b* the yoke of the king of Babylon.' "
28:11 years I will *b* the yoke of Nebuchadnezzar,
30: 8 "I will *b* his yoke from off your necks
33:20 If you can *b* my covenant with day,
48:12 they shall empty his flasks and *b* his jars.
49:35 Behold, I will *b* the bow of Elam,
49:37 I will *b* Elam before their foes,
Ez 5:16 of hunger, I will *b* your staff of bread;
13:11 shall fall, and a stormwind shall *b* out.
14:13 hand against it and *b* its staff of bread,
17:15 Can he *b* a covenant and still go free?
26: 9 and *b* down your towers with his weapons.
30:18 be darkened when I *b* the scepter of Egypt.
30:22 I will *b* his strong arm,
34:27 I am the LORD when I *b* the bonds
Dn 2:40 *b* in pieces and subdue all these others,
2:44 it shall *b* in pieces all these kingdoms
8: 7 blows when they met, and *b* both its horns.
Hos 1: 5 On that day I will *b* the bow of Israel in
7: 1 They practice falsehood, thieves *b* in,
10: 2 God shall *b* down their altars and destroy
10:11 was to plow, Jacob was to *b* his furrows:
10:12 *B* up for yourselves a new field,
10:14 Turmoil shall *b* out among your tribes and
13:13 not present himself where children *b* forth.
Am 1: 5 I will *b* the bar of Damascus,
9: 1 you *b* them off on the heads of them all!
9: 2 Though they *b* through to the nether world,
Mi 2:13 With a leader to *b* the path they shall
3: 3 their skin from them, and *b* their bones.
Na 1:13 Now will I *b* his yoke from off you,
2: 6 troops are called, ranks *b* at their charge;
Mal 2:10 Why then do we *b* faith with each other,
2:15 not *b* faith with the wife of your youth.
2:16 life that is your own, and not *b* faith.
Mt 6:19 thieves *b* in and steal.
6:20 rust corrode nor thieves *b* in and steal.
12: 5 *b* the sabbath rest without incurring guilt?
Lk 8:29 but he would *b* his bonds and the demon
12:39 he would not let him *b* into his house.
15:18 I will *b* away and return to my father,
Jn 8:13 This caused the Pharisees to *b* in with:
19:33 was already dead, they did not *b* his legs.
19:36 *B* none of his bones."
Rom 2:25 *b* it you might as well be uncircumcised!
2:27 your written law and circumcision, *b* it.
1Cor 10:16 bread we *b* a sharing in the body of Christ?
Gal 4:27 *b* into song,
Rv 5: 2 worthy to open the scroll and *b* its seals?"
5: 9 to receive the scroll and *b* open its seals,
6:12 When I saw the Lamb *b* open the sixth seal,

BREAKERS (6)

2Sm 22: 5 "The *b* of death surged round about me.
1Mc 1:11 in Israel men who were *b* of the law,
Ps(s) 18: 5 The *b* of death surged round about me,
42: 8 All your *b* and your billows pass over me.
93: 4 more powerful than the *b* of the sea
Jon 2: 4 All your *b* and your billows passed over me.

BREAKING (43)

Gn 19:15 As dawn was *b* the angels urged Lot on,
Lv 5: 8 the neck, yet without *b* it off completely,
13:42 it is leprosy that is *b* out there.
26:13 *b* the yoke they had laid upon you and
26:15 all my commandments and *b* my covenant,
Nm 4: 5 In *b* camp,
4:15 objects and all their utensils on *b* camp,
5: 6 and wrongs him, thus *b* faith with the LORD,
9:12 over till morning, nor *b* any of its bones,
10: 2 in assembling the community and in *b* camp.
Dt 31:20 serve them, despising me and *b* my covenant;
2Kgs 23:15 *b* up the stones and grinding them to
2Chr 14: 2 places, *b* to pieces the sacred pillars,
2Mc 13:17 Day was just *b* when this was accomplished
Ps(s) 65:11 drenching its furrows, *b* up its clods,
Sir 41:17 disloyalty, and of *b* an oath or agreement.
Is 58: 6 Setting free the oppressed, *b* every yoke;
66: 3 sacrificing a lamb, like *b* a dog's neck;
Jer 2:24 near and far, *b* away toward the desert,
28:13 By *b* a wooden yoke,
Ez 4:16 I am *b* the staff of bread in Jerusalem.
14:13 when a land sins against me by *b* faith,
16:59 you who despised your oath, *b* a covenant.
17:18 He spurned his oath, *b* his covenant.
17:20 with him there over his *b* faith with me.
20:27 fathers blasphemed me, *b* faith with me:
Dn 2:34 its iron and tile feet, *b* them in pieces.
Jon 1: 4 arose the ship was on the point of *b* up.
Zec 11:10 *b* off the covenant which I had made with
11:14 *b* off the brotherhood between Judah and
Mt 27:24 and that a riot was *b* out instead.
Mk 4:37 The waves were *b* over the boat and it
14: 3 *B* the jar,
Lk 5: 6 fish that their nets were at the *b* point.
24:35 had come to know him in the *b* of bread.
Jn 5:18 was that he not only was *b* the sabbath but,
Acts 2:42 life, to the *b* of bread and the prayers.
20: 7 week when we gathered for the *b* of bread,
21:13 are you crying and *b* my heart in this way?
Rom 2:23 the law, do you dishonor God by *b* the law?
5:14 had not sinned by *b* a precept as did Adam,
Eph 2:14 two of us one by *b* down the barrier
1Tm 5:12 them condemnation for *b* their first pledge.

BREAKS (27)

Lv 13:12 If leprosy *b* out on the skin and,
14:43 "If the infection *b* out once more after
2Kgs 7: 9 If we wait until morning *b*,
1Chr 14:11 my enemies just as water *b* through a dam."
Jb 12:14 If he *b* a thing down,
12:21 He *b* down the barriers of the streams
19:10 He *b* me down on every side,
24:16 in the dark he *b* into houses.
34:24 Without a trial he *b* the mighty,
Ps(s) 29: 5 The voice of the LORD *b* the cedars,
29: 5 cedars, the LORD *b* the cedars of Lebanon.
46:10 the bow he *b*;
141: 7 As when a plowman *b* furrows in the field,
Eccl 10: 8 and he who *b* through a wall may be bitten
Sir 10:16 He *b* down their stem to the level of the
22:20 who insults a friend *b* up the friendship.
23:16 who never stops until the fire *b* forth;
35:20 will not be still Till he *b* the backs of
43:15 storm its power and *b* off the hailstones.
Is 14: 7 whole earth rests peacefully, song *b* forth;
38:13 Like a lion he *b* all my bones;
Jer 23:19 His wrath *b* forth In a whirling storm that
30:23 His wrath *b* forth In a whirling storm that
48:45 For fire *b* forth from Heshbon,
Bar 6:54 For when fire *b* out in the temple of these
Dn 2:40 *b* in pieces and crushes everything else.
Mt 5:19 That is why whoever *b* the least

BREAST (23)

Ex 29:26 take the *b* of Aaron's ordination ram and
29:27 the *b* of whatever wave offering is waved,
Lv 7:30 is to be brought in, together with the *b*,
7:31 but the *b* belongs to Aaron and his sons.
7:34 I have taken the *b* that is waved
8:29 He then took the *b* and waved it as a wave
10:14 shall also eat the *b* of the wave offering
10:15 The leg of the raised offering and the *b*
Nm 6:20 along with the *b* of the wave offering and
18:18 just as the *b* and the right leg of the
Dt 33:12 the day while he abides securely at his *b*."
Ps(s) 22:10 first formed, my security at my mother's *b*.
Sir 19:11 a man's thigh is gossip in the *b* of a fool.
Is 16:11 Therefore for Moab my *b* moans like a lyre,
28: 9 weaned from milk, those taken from the *b*?
Jer 4:19 My *b*! my *b*! how I suffer!
31:19 I have come to myself, I strike my *b*;
Jl 2:16 the children and the infants at the *b*;
Lk 18:13 All he did was beat his *b* and say,
21:23 at the *b* will fare badly in those days!
Rv 1:13 robe, with a sash of gold about his *b*.
15: 6 each with a sash of gold about his *b*.

BREASTPIECE (23)

Ex 25: 7 gems for mounting on the ephod and the *b*.
28: 4 a *b*, an ephod, a robe
28:15 *b* of decision you shall also have made,
28:22 like cords, have been made for the *b*,
28:23 fasten them to the two upper ends of the *b*.
28:24 the two rings at the upper ends of the *b*.
28:26 put them on the two lower ends of the *b*,
28:28 rings of the *b* to the rings of the ephod,
28:28 so that the *b* will stay right above the
28:29 sons of Israel on the *b* of decision
28:30 In this *b* of decision you shall put the
29: 5 of the ephod, the ephod itself, and the *b*,
35: 9 for mounting on the ephod and on the *b*.
35:27 for mounting on the ephod and on the *b*;
39: 8 The *b* was embroidered like the ephod,
39:15 twisted like cords, were made for the *b*,
39:16 fastened to the two upper ends of the *b*.
39:17 to the two rings at the ends of the *b*.
39:19 and put on the two lower ends of the *b*,
39:21 rings of the *b* to the rings of the ephod,
39:21 so that the *b* stayed right above the
Lv 8: 8 He then set the *b* on him,
Sir 45:10 The *b* for decision,

BREASTPLATE (7)

1Kgs 22:34 king of Israel between the joints of his *b*.
2Chr 18:33 king of Israel between the joints of his *b*.
1Mc 3: 3 his people, and put on his *b* like a giant.
Wis 5:18 He shall don justice for a *b* and shall
Is 59:17 He put on justice as his *b*,
Eph 6:14 belt around your waist, justice as your *b*,
1Thes 5: 8 a *b* and the hope of salvation as a helmet.

BREASTPLATED (1)

1Mc 4: 7 the army of the Gentiles, strong and *b*,

BREASTPLATES (6)

2Chr 26:14 bucklers, lances, helmets, *b*,
Neh 4:10 armed with spears, bucklers, bows, and *b*,
1Mc 6: 2 was very rich, containing gold helmets, *b*,
Jer 46: 4 polish your spears, put on your *b*.
Rv 9: 9 teeth of lions, their chests like iron *b*.
9:17 The *b* they wore were fiery red,

BREASTS (31)

Gn 49:25 below, The blessings of *b* and womb,
Lv 9:20 top of the *b* and burned them on the altar,
9:21 having first waved the *b* and the right
2Mc 3:19 girded with sackcloth below their *b*,
6:10 with their babies hanging at their *b*
Jb 3:12 or why did I suck at the *b*?
Sg 4: 5 your *b* are like twin fawns
7: 4 Your *b* are like twin fawns,
7: 8 your *b* are like clusters.
7: 9 Now let your *b* be like clusters of the
8: 1 were my brother, nursed at my mother's *b*!
8: 8 sister is little and she has no *b* as yet.
8:10 I am a wall, and my *b* are like towers.
Is 32:12 Beat your *b* for the pleasant fields,
60:16 milk of nations, and be nursed at royal *b*;
66:11 may nurse with delight at her abundant *b*!
Lam 4: 3 bare their *b* and suckle their young;
Ez 16: 7 your *b* were formed,
23: 3 their bosoms and fondled their virginal *b*.
23: 8 *b* and pouring out their impurities on her.
23:21 when the Egyptians fondled your *b*,
23:34 of the cup, and you shall tear out your *b*;
Hos 2: 4 her, her adultery from between her *b*,
9:14 Give them an unfruitful womb, and dry *b*!
13: 8 young, and tear their hearts from their *b*;
Na 2: 8 guard, Moaning like doves, beating their *b*.
Mt 24:30 the clans of earth will strike their *b*'
Lk 11:27 that bore you and the *b* that nursed you!"
23:27 who beat their *b* and lamented over him.
23:29 never bore and the *b* that never nursed.'
23:48 happened, they went home beating their *b*.

BREATH (69)

Gn 2: 7 and blew into his nostrils the *b* of life,
6:17 creatures in which there is the *b* of life;
7:15 the *b* of life entered the ark with Noah.
7:22 *b* of life in its nostrils died out.
35:18 With her last *b*—
Ex 15: 8 At a *b* of your anger the waters piled up,
1Kgs 9: 8 passer-by shall catch his *b* in amazement,
17:21 life *b* return to the body of this child."
17:22 the life *b* returned to the child's body
2Chr 9: 4 the house of the LORD, it took her *b* away.
Tb 3: 6 and command my life *b* to be taken from me,
2Mc 7:22 it was not I who gave you the *b* of life,
7:23 mercy, will give you back both *b* and life,
Jb 4: 9 By the *b* of God they perish,
7:16 let me alone, for my days are but a *b*.
9:18 He need not suffer me to draw *b*,
12:10 thing, and the life *b* of all mankind.
19:17 My *b* is abhorred by my wife;
26: 4 whose is the *b* that comes forth from you?
26:13 With his angry *b* he scatters the waters,
27: 3 in me and the *b* of God is in my nostrils,
32: 8 is a spirit in man, the *b* of the Almighty,
33: 4 me, the *b* of the Almighty keeps me alive.
34:14 to himself, withdraw to himself his *b*,
37:10 With his *b* God brings the frost,
41:13 His *b* sets coals afire;
Ps(s) 33: 6 by the *b* of his mouth all their host.
39: 6 only a *b* is any human existence.
39:12 only a *b* is any man.
62:10 Only a *b* are mortal men;
62:10 prove lighter, all together, than a *b*.
78:39 were flesh, a passing *b* that returns not.
104:29 if you take away their *b*,
135:17 hear not, nor is there *b* in their mouths.
144: 4 Man is like a *b*;
150: 6 Let everything that has *b* praise the LORD!
Prv 20:27 A lamp from the LORD is the *b* of man;
Eccl 8: 8 of the *b* of life so as to retain it,
11: 5 Just as you know not how the *b* of life
12: 7 and the life *b* returns to God who gave it.
Sg 7: 9 and the fragrance of your *b* like apples,
Wis 2: 2 Because the *b* in our nostrils is a smoke
11:18 unknown beasts to breathe forth fiery *b*,

BREATH (cont.)

Sir 33:21 While *b* of life is still in you,
Is 2:22 man alone, in whose nostrils is but a *b*;
11: 4 the *b* of his lips he shall slay the wicked.
30:28 His *b*, like a flood in a ravine
30:33 wood in abundance, And the *b* of the LORD,
40: 7 when the *b* of the LORD blows upon it.
42: 5 Who gives *b* to its people and spirit to
59:19 river which the *b* of the LORD drives on.
Jer 10:14 He has molded a fraud, without *b* of life.
14: 6 bare heights, gasping for *b* like jackals;
19: 8 will be amazed and will catch his *b*.
38:16 the LORD lives who gave us the *b* of life,
49:17 appalled and catch his *b* at all her wounds.
50:13 Babylon will be appalled and catch his *b*,
51:17 He molded a fraud, without *b* of life.
Lam 1:11 for food, to retain the *b* of life.
4:20 anointed one of the LORD, our *b* of life,
Dn 5:23 life *b* and the whole course of your life,
10:16 now no strength or even *b* is left in me."
Hb 2:19 and silver, but there is no life *b* in it.
Lk 8:55 The *b* of life returned to her and she got
Acts 17:25 to all life and *b* and everything else.
2Cor 2:16 death, to the former a *b* bringing life.
2Thes 2: 8 destroy him with the *b* of his mouth
Jas 2:26 works is as dead as a body without *b*.
Rv 11:11 the *b* of life which comes from God

BREATHE (4)

Ps(s) 27:12 up against me, and such as *b* out violence.
Wis 11:18 unknown beasts to *b* forth fiery breath,
Lam 2:12 And *b* their last in their mothers' arms.
Ez 37: 9 and *b* into these slain that they may come

BREATHED (7)

Gn 25: 8 Then he *b* his last,
25:17 After he had *b* his last and died,
35:28 then he *b* his last.
49:33 he drew his feet into the bed, *b* his last,
Wis 15:11 him, and *b* into him a quickening soul,
Mk 15:37 Jesus, uttering a loud cry, *b* his last.
Jn 20:22 Then he *b* on them and said:

BREATHES (3)

Sg 2:17 the day *b* cool and the shadows
4: 6 the day *b* cool and the shadows lengthen,
Is 40:24 earth, When he *b* upon them and they wither,

BREATHING (7)

1Kgs 17:17 grew more severe until he stopped *b*.
Jdt 7:27 our wives and children *b* out their souls.
2Mc 7: 5 When he was completely maimed but still *b*,
9: 7 *B* fire in his rage against the Jews,
14:45 Still *b*, and inflamed with anger,
Ez 21:36 *b* my fiery wrath upon you;
Acts 9: 1 still *b* murderous threats against the

BREATHLESS (1)

1Kgs 10: 5 in the temple of the LORD, she was *b*.

BRED (1)

Ez 47:22 your midst who have *b* children among you.

BREECHES (1)

Sir 45: 8 *B* and tunic and robe with pomegranates

BREED (5)

Lv 19:19 do not *b* any of your domestic animals with
Jb 15:34 For the *b* of the impious shall be sterile,
Mt 11:16 comparison can I use to describe this *b*?
Jn 8:41 They cried, "We are no illegitimate *b*!
2Tm 2:23 As you well know, they only *b* quarrels,

BREEDING (2)

Gn 8:17 on the earth, *b* and multiplying on it."
31:10 Once, in the *b* season, I had a dream

BREEDS (1)

Sir 11:33 Avoid a wicked man, for he *b* only evil,

BREEZE (4)

Ps(s) 107:29 He hushed the storm to a gentle *b*,
147:18 he lets his *b* blow and the waters run.
Is 57:13 shall carry off, the *b* shall bear away;
Dn 3:50 a dew-laden *b* were blowing through it.

BREEZY (1)

Gn 3: 8 in the garden at the *b* time of the day,

BRETHREN (125)

1Chr 8:14 Their *b* were Elpaal,
9: 6 and six hundred and ninety of their *b*.
9:13 Their *b*, heads of their ancestral houses,
9:17 Akkub, Talmon, Ahiman, and their *b*;
9:19 and his *b* of the same ancestral house of
9:32 Benaiah the Kohathite, one of their *b*,
9:38 These, too, with their *b*,
9:38 dwelt opposite their *b* in Jerusalem.
12:30 Of the Benjaminites, the *b* of Saul:
12:33 with all their *b* under their command.
12:40 for their *b* had prepared for them.
13: 2 of our *b* from all the districts of Israel,
15: 5 and one hundred and twenty of his *b*;
15: 6 and two hundred and twenty of his *b*;
15: 7 and one hundred and thirty of his *b*;
15: 8 their chief, and two hundred of his *b*,
15: 9 Eliel, their chief, and eighty of his *b*;
15:10 chief, and one hundred and twelve of his *b*.
15:12 with your *b* and bring the ark of the LORD,
15:16 the Levites to appoint their *b* as chanters,
15:17 Heman, son of Joel, and, among his *b*,
15:17 and among the sons of Merari, their *b*,
15:18 with these, their *b* of the second rank:
16: 7 David appointed Asaph and his *b* to sing
16:37 Then David left Asaph and his *b* there
16:38 there Obed-edom and sixty-eight of his *b*,
16:39 But the priest Zadok and his priestly *b* he
23:32 and the sons of Aaron, their *b*,
25: 7 *b* who were trained in singing to the LORD,
25: 9 he and his sons and his *b* were twelve.
25: 9 he and his *b* and his sons were twelve.
25:10 The third was Zaccur, his sons, and his *b*:
25:11 fourth fell to Izri, his sons, and his *b*:
25:12 fifth was Nethaniah, his sons, and his *b*:
25:13 The sixth was Bukkiah, his sons, and his *b*:
25:14 seventh was Jesarelah, his sons, and his *b*:
25:15 eighth was Jeshaiah, his sons, and his *b*:
25:16 ninth was Mattaniah, his sons, and his *b*:
25:17 The tenth was Shimei, his sons, and his *b*:
25:18 eleventh was Uzziel, his sons, and his *b*:
25:19 fell to Hashabiah, his sons, and his *b*:
25:20 was Shubael, his sons, and his *b*:
25:21 was Mattithiah, his sons, and his *b*:
25:22 fell to Jeremoth, his sons, and his *b*:
25:23 fell to Hananiah, his sons, and his *b*:
25:24 fell to Joshbekashah, his sons, and his *b*:
25:25 fell to Hanani, his sons, and his *b*:
25:26 fell to Mallothi, his sons, and his *b*:
25:27 fell to Eliathah, his sons, and his *b*:
25:28 fell to Hothir, his sons, and his *b*:
25:29 fell to Giddalti, his sons, and his *b*:
25:30 fell to Mahazioth, his sons, and his *b*:
25:31 fell to Romamti-ezer, his sons, and his *b*:
26: 7 also his *b* who were men of might,
26: 8 who, together with their sons and their *b*,
26: 9 Of Meshelemiah, eighteen sons and *b*,
26:11 All the sons and *b* of Hosah were thirteen.
26:26 This Shelomith and his *b* superintended all
26:28 under the charge of Shelomith and his *b*.
26:30 Among the Hebronites, Hashabiah and his *b*,
26:32 His *b* were also police officers,
28: 2 "Hear me, my *b* and my people.
2Chr 19:10 your *b* living in their cities bring to you,
19:10 and his wrath come upon you and your *b*.
28:11 you have carried off from among your *b*,
28:15 to Jericho, the city of palms, to their *b*.
29:15 their *b* together and sanctified themselves;
29:34 their *b* the Levites assisted them until
30: 7 your *b* who proved faithless to the LORD,
30: 9 your *b* and your children will find mercy
31:15 to their *b* great and small alike,
35: 5 of the ancestral houses of your *b*,
35: 6 and be at the disposition of your *b*,
35:15 them to leave their stations, for their *b*,
Ezr 3: 2 Jozadak, together with his *b* the priests,
3: 2 son of Shealtiel, together with his *b*,
3: 8 together with the rest of their *b*,
3: 9 Jeshua and his sons and *b*,
3: 9 of Henadad, and their sons and their *b*,
6:20 of the exiles, for their *b* the priests,
7:18 You and your *b* may do whatever seems best
8:17 them what to say to Iddo and his *b*,
8:18 namely Sherebiah, with his sons and *b*,
8:19 sons of Merari, and their *b* and their sons,
8:24 Sherebiah, Hashabiah, and ten of their *b*,
10:18 sons of Jeshua, son of Jozadak, and his *b*:
Neh 3: 1 priestly *b* took up the task of rebuilding
3:18 their *b* carried out the work of repair:
3:34 of his *b* and the troops of Samaria:
4: 8 and to be feared, and fight for your *b*,
5:14 my *b* lived from the governor's allowance.
10:11 and their *b* Shebaniah,
10:30 join with their *b* who are their princes,
11: 8 son of Ithiel, son of Jeshaiah, and his *b*,
11:12 *b* who carried out the temple service,
11:13 of Pashhur, son of Malchijah, and his *b*,
11:14 of Meshillemoth, son of Immer, and his *b*,
11:17 Bakbukiah, second in rank among his *b*;
11:19 were Akkub, Talmon, and their *b*,
12: 7 heads and their *b* in the days of Jeshua.
12: 8 the last-mentioned, together with his *b*,
12: 9 their *b* ministered opposite them by turns.
12:24 Their *b* who stood opposite them to sing
12:36 Zaccur, son of Asaph, and his *b* Shemaiah,
13:13 duty to make the distribution to their *b*.
Est 10: 3 and was regarded with favor by his many *b*,
2Mc 1: 1 land of Judea send greetings to their *b*,
12:25 let him go for the sake of saving their *b*.
15:14 who loves his *b* and fervently prays for
Jb 6:15 My *b* are undependable as a brook,
19:13 My *b* have withdrawn from me,
42:11 all his *b* and his sisters came to him,
42:15 gave them an inheritance among their *b*.
Ps(s) 22:23 I will proclaim your name to my *b*;
133: 1 is, and how pleasant, where *b* dwell at one!
Sir 10:20 Among *b* their leader is in honor;
25: 1 Harmony among *b*,
50: 1 The greatest among his *b*,
50:12 His *b* ringed him about like a garland,
Is 66: 5 Your *b* who, because of my name,
66:20 They shall bring all your *b* from all the
Jer 7:15 away from me, as I cast away all your *b*,
29:16 your *b* who did not go with you into exile;
34:15 by proclaiming the emancipation of your *b*
Mi 5: 2 *b* shall return to the children of Israel.)

BRETHREN'S (1)

2Chr 28: 8 two hundred thousand of their *b* wives,

BREVITY (1)

2Mc 2:31 allowed to aim at *b* of expression

BRIBE (15)

Ex 23: 8 Never take a bribe, for a *b* blinds
Dt 16:19 You shall not take a *b*;
16:19 for a *b* blinds the eyes even of the wise
1Sm 12: 3 I accepted a *b* and overlooked his guilt?
Ps(s) 15: 5 and accepts no *b* against the innocent.
Prv 17: 8 has a *b* to offer rates it a magic stone;
17:23 *b* to pervert the course of justice.
Eccl 7: 7 of a wise man, and a *b* corrupts the heart.
Sir 46:19 *b* or secret gift have I taken from any man!"
Is 1:23 one of them loves a *b* and looks for gifts.
33:15 his hands free of contact with a *b*,
Mi 3:11 Her leaders render judgment for a *b*,
Mt 28:12 soldiers a large *b* with the instructions:
Acts 24:26 he hoped he would be offered a *b* by Paul,

BRIBE-TAKING (1)

2Chr 19: 7 there is no justice, no partiality, no *b*."

BRIBED (2)

Neh 6:12 because Tobiah and Sanballat had *b* him,
2Mc 10:20 be *b* by some of the men in the towers;

BRIBES (8)

Dt 10:17 who has no favorites, accepts no *b*;
1Sm 8: 3 but sought illicit gain and accepted *b*,
Ps(s) 26:10 and their right hands are full of *b*.
Prv 15:27 own house, but he who hates *b* will live.
Sir 35:11 But offer no *b*, these he does not accept!
40:12 from *b* or injustice will be wiped out,
Is 5:23 To those who acquit the guilty for *b*,
Am 5:12 Oppressing the just, accepting *b*,

BRIBING (1)

Ez 16:33 *b* them to come to you from all sides for

BRICK (2)

Ex 1:14 mortar and *b* and all kinds of field work
Na 3:14 tread the clay, take hold of the *b* mold!

BRICKMAKING (2)

Ex 5: 7 for their *b* as you have previously done.
Jdt 5:11 them, shrewdly forced them to labor at *b*,

BRICKMOLD (1)

2Sm 12:31 and iron axes, or put to work at the *b*.

BRICKS (9)

Gn 11: 3 let us mold *b* and harden them with fire."
11: 3 They used *b* for stone,
Ex 5: 8 quota of *b* as they have previously made.
5:14 prescribed amount of *b* yesterday and today,
5:16 servants, and still we are told to make *b*.
5:18 but you must still deliver your quota of *b*."
5:19 told not to reduce the daily amount of *b*.
Is 9: 9 and pride of heart, *B* have fallen,
65: 3 in the groves and burning incense on *b*,

BRICKYARD (1)

Jer 43: 9 sink them in mortar in the *b*

BRIDAL (7)

Gn 29:27 Finish the *b* week for this one,
29:28 He finished the *b* week for Leah,
34:12 No matter how high you set the *b* price,
Tb 6:14 that her husbands died in their *b* chambers.
6:17 When you go into the *b* chamber,
1Mc 1:27 she who sat in the *b* chamber mourned,
Ps(s) 19: 6 like the groom from his *b* chamber and,

BRIDE (29)

1Sm 18:25 king desires no other price for the *b*
2Sm 17: 3 to you, as a *b* returns to her husband.
Tb 6:13 girl's father to let us have her as your *b*.
1Mc 9:37 a large escort they are bringing the *b*,

Sg 4: 8 Come from Lebanon, my b,
4: 9 have ravished my heart, my sister, my b;
4:10 beautiful is your love, my sister, my b,
4:11 Your lips drip honey, my b,
4:12 are an enclosed garden, my sister, my b,
5: 1 I have come to my garden, my sister, my b;
Wis 8: 2 for my b and was enamored of her beauty.
Sir 15: 2 him, like a young b she will embrace him,
Is 49:18 like a b you shall fasten them on you.
61:10 diadem, like a b bedecked with her jewels.
62: 5 in his b so shall your God rejoice in you.
Jer 2: 2 of your youth, how you loved me as a b,
2:32 a virgin forget her jewelry, a b her sash?
7:34 of the bridegroom and the voice of the b;
16: 9 of the bridegroom and the voice of the b.
25:10 of the bridegroom and the voice of the b,
33:11 of the bridegroom, the voice of the b,
Bar 2:23 of the bridegroom and the voice of the b;
Jl 2:16 quit his room, and the b her chamber.
Jn 3:29 "It is the groom who has the b.
Rv 18:23 No voices of b and groom shall ever again
19: 7 his b has prepared herself for the wedding.
21: 2 as a b prepared to meet her husband.
21: 9 you the woman who is the b of the Lamb."
22:17 The Spirit and the B say, "Come!"

BRIDEGROOM (11)

1Mc 1:27 Every b took up lamentation,
9:39 the b and his friends and kinsmen had come
Is 61:10 of justice, Like a b adorned with a diadem,
62: 5 And as a b rejoices in his bride so shall
Jer 3: 4 father, you who are the b of my youth"?
7:34 voice of the b and the voice of the bride;
16: 9 voice of the b and the voice of the bride.
25:10 voice of the b and the voice of the bride,
33:11 the cry of gladness, the voice of the b,
Bar 2:23 voice of the b and the voice of the bride;
Jl 2:16 Let the b quit his room,

BRIDE'S (2)

1Mc 9:39 kinsmen had come out to meet the b party
Ez 22:12 are those in you take b to shed blood.

BRIDESMAIDS (2)

Mt 25: 1 likened to ten b who took their torches
25:11 Later the other b came back.

BRIDGE (1)

Ez 27: 6 Your b they made of cypress wood from the

BRIDLE (4)

Ps(s) 32: 9 with bit and b their temper must be curbed,
Prv 26: 3 The whip for the horse, the b for the ass,
Is 30:28 a b on the jaws of the peoples
Rv 14:20 around, it reached as high as a horse's b.

BRIEF (14)

2Mc 6:25 for the sake of a b moment of life,
7:36 My brothers, after enduring b pain,
Prv 10:27 life, but the years of the wicked are b.
Wis 2: 1 B and troublous is our lifetime;
15: 9 is to die nor that his span of life is b;
16: 3 While these, after a b period of privation,
Sir 32: 8 Be b, but say much in those few words
Is 10:25 For only a b moment more,
26:20 Hide yourselves for a b moment,
54: 7 For a b moment I abandoned you,
Lk 20: 5 a b conference during which someone said,
Acts 16:30 a b interval he led them out and said,
24: 4 indulgence for a b hearing of our case.
Heb 10:37 For, just a b moment,

BRIEFLY (4)

Eph 3: 3 plan as I have b described it was revealed.
Heb 13:22 for I have written to you rather b.
Jas 4:14 are a vapor that appears b and vanishes.
1Pt 5:12 I am writing b through Silvanus,

BRIER (3)

Is 9:17 burns like fire, devouring b and thorn;
Ez 28:24 a b that scratches them more than all the
Mi 7: 4 he pleases, The best of them is like a b,

BRIERS (13)

Jgs 8: 7 in with the thorns and b of the desert."
8:16 the city, and thorns and b of the desert,
Is 5: 6 or hoed, but overgrown with thorns and b;
7:23 of silver, shall be turned to b and thorns.
7:24 for all the country shall be b and thorns.
7:25 For fear of b and thorns you shall not go
10:17 his b and his thorns in a single day.
27: 4 angry, but if I were to find b and thorns,
32:13 of my people, overgrown with thorns and b;
34:13 thorns, her fortresses with thistles and b.
Mt 13:22 among b is the man who hears the message,
Lk 8: 7 Some fell among b,
8:14 The seed fallen among b are those who hear,

BRIGAND (3)

Prv 28:24 and calls it no sin, is a partner of the b.
Mt 26:55 "Am I a b,
Mk 14:48 with swords and clubs as if against a b.

BRIGANDS (3)

Sir 50: 4 He protected his people against b and
Jer 12:12 Upon every desert height b have come up.
Hos 6: 9 As b ambush a man,

BRIGHT (13)

1Sm 14:29 Look how b my eyes are from this small
Tb 13:11 A b light will shine to all parts of the
Jb 25: 5 b and the stars are not clear in his sight.
Ps(s) 37: 6 b as the noonday shall be your vindication.
Sir 24:16 my branches so b and so graceful.
Bar 6:59 The sun and moon and stars are b,
Ez 10: 4 the court was b with the glory of the LORD.
Dn 2:31 a statue, very large and exceedingly b,
7: 9 His clothing was snow b,
Mt 16: 2 say, 'Red sky at night, the day will be b';
17: 5 when suddenly a b cloud overshadowed them.
Jn 5:35 He was the lamp, set aflame and burning b,
Rv 22:16 of David, the Morning Star shining b."

BRIGHTEN (2)

2Sm 22:29 O my God, you b the darkness about me.
Ps(s) 18:29 O my God, you b the darkness about me;

BRIGHTENED (1)

Ezr 9: 8 thus our God has b our eyes and given us

BRIGHTENS (1)

Jb 18: 5 no flame b his hearth.

BRIGHTER (4)

Jb 11:17 Then your life shall be b than the noonday;
Sir 17:26 Is anything b than the sun?
23:19 LORD, ten thousand times b than the sun,
Lam 4: 7 B than snow were her princes,

BRIGHTEST (1)

Rv 1:16 and his face shone like the sun at its b.

BRIGHTLY (2)

Dn 12: 3 shine b like the splendor of the firmament,
Lk 11:36 illumined as when a lamp shines b for you."

BRIGHTNESS (11)

2Sm 22:13 From the b of his presence coals were
1Mc 6:39 their b and blazed like flaming torches.
Ps(s) 18:13 From the b of his presence coals were
Is 59: 9 darkness; for b, but we walk in gloom!
60:19 the b of the moon shine upon you at night;
Ez 1: 4 cloud with flashing fire [enveloped in b,
8: 2 to be a b like the sheen of electrum.
Jl 2:10 darkened, and the stars withhold their b.
4:15 darkened, and the stars withhold their b.
Am 5:20 and not light, gloom without any b?
1Cor 15:41 the stars, one differs from another in b.

BRILLIANCE (5)

2Mc 1:32 in the b cast from a light on the altar.
Prv 4:18 light, that grows in b till perfect day.
Wis 17: 5 nor did the flaming b of the stars succeed
Sir 43:10 high, lighting up the firmament by its b,
Acts 22:11 not see because of the b of the light,

BRILLIANT (8)

Wis 17:20 whole world shone with b light
Is 28: 5 a b diadem to the remnant of his people,
Bar 6:66 the heavens, nor are they b like the sun,
Dn 5:11 to have b knowledge and god-like wisdom.
5:14 b knowledge and extraordinary wisdom.
Acts 26:13 I saw a light more b than the sun shining
Rv 4: 3 the throne was a rainbow as b as emerald.
19: 8 to wear made of finest linen, b white."

BRIM (4)

1Kgs 7:24 Under the b, gourds encircled it,
7:26 thick, and its b resembled that of a cup,
2Chr 4: 5 and its b was made like that of a cup,
Jn 2: 7 at which they filled them to the b.

BRIMS (1)

Jer 6:11 Therefore my wrath b up within me,

BRIMSTONE (5)

Jb 18:15 over his abode b is scattered.
Ps(s) 11: 6 He rains upon the wicked fiery coals and b;
Ez 38:22 flooding rain and hailstones, fire and b,
Dn 3:46 in continued to stoke the furnace with b,
Lk 17:29 fire and b rained down from heaven and

BRING (623)

Gn 1:11 said, "Let the earth b forth vegetation:
1:24 b forth all kinds of living creatures:
3:16 in pain shall you b forth children.
3:18 and thistles shall it b forth to you,
5:29 this one shall b us relief from our work
6:17 about to b the flood [waters] on the earth,
6:19 creatures you shall b two into the ark,
7: 4 Seven days from now I will b rain down on
8:17 B out with you every living thing that is
9:14 When I b clouds over the earth,
15: 9 answered him, B me a three-year-old heifer,
15:14 b judgment on the nation they must serve,
18: 5 your servant, let me b you a little food,
19: 5 B them out to us that we may have
19: 8 Let me b them out to you,
24:46 drink, and let me b water for your camels,
27: 4 me, such as I like, and b it to me to eat,
27: 7 B me some game and with it prepare an
27:10 Then b it to your father to eat,
27:12 b on myself a curse instead of a blessing."
27:45 Then I will send for you and b you back.
28:15 you go, and b you back to this land.
29: 7 is hardly the time to b the animals home.
37:14 brothers and the flocks and b back word."
37:32 to b the long tunic to their father,
38:24 B her out," cried Judah;
41:32 by God and that God will soon b it about.
42:37 in my care, and I will b him back to you.
43: 6 "Why did you b this trouble on me by
43: 7 he would say, B your brother down here'?"
43: 9 If I fail to b him back,
44:21 B him down to me that my eyes may look on
44:32 saying, 'If I fail to b him back to you,
45:13 But hurry and b my father down here."
46: 4 I will also b you back here,
48: 9 B them to me," said his father,
50:25 b my bones up with you from this place."
Ex 3:12 when you b my people out of Egypt,
6: 8 b you into the land which I swore to give
6:13 the LORD, to b the Israelites out of Egypt,
6:27 of Egypt, to b the Israelites out of Egypt
7: 4 judgment I will b the hosts of my people,
8:14 tried to b forth gnats by their magic arts,
10: 4 I will b locusts into your country.
11: 1 will I b upon Pharaoh and upon Egypt.
14:11 had to b us out here to die in the desert?
14:11 Why did you b us out of Egypt?
16: 5 however, when they prepare what they b in,
21: 6 his master shall b him to God and there,
22:12 by a wild beast, let him b it as evidence,
23:19 soil you shall b to the house of the LORD,
23:20 way and b you to the place I have prepared.
23:23 go before you and b you to the Amorites,
26:33 ark of the commandments you shall b inside,
27:20 to b you clear oil of crushed olives,
29: 4 also b to the entrance of the meeting tent,
29: 8 B forward his sons also and clothe them
29:10 "Now b forward the bullock in front of
32: 2 they are wearing, and b them to me."
32:29 to b a blessing upon yourselves this day."
34:26 soil you shall b to the house of the LORD,
35: 5 him, shall b as a contribution to the LORD,
36: 3 to b their voluntary offerings to Moses.
40: 4 B in the table and set it.
40: 4 Then b in the lampstand and set up the
40:12 "Then b Aaron and his sons to the
40:14 B forward his sons also,
Lv 1: 2 wishes to b an animal offering to the LORD,
1: 3 he shall b it to the entrance of the
1:10 a goat, he must b a male without blemish.
2: 1 wishes to b a cereal offering to the LORD,
2: 8 any of these ways you shall b to the LORD,
3: 7 offering, he shall b it before the LORD,
3:12 a goat, he shall b it before the LORD,
4: 5 blood and b it into the meeting tent,
4:14 They shall b it before the meeting tent,
4:16 b some of its blood into the meeting tent,
4:23 b as his offering an unblemished male goat.
4:28 he shall b an unblemished she-goat as the
4:32 a lamb, he shall b an unblemished female.
5: 6 he shall b to the LORD a female animal
5: 7 he shall b to the LORD as the sin offering
5: 8 He shall b them to the priest,
5:15 he shall b to the LORD as his guilt
5:18 he shall b as a guilt offering to the
5:25 As his guilt offering he shall b to the
6:14 fried in oil on a griddle when you b it in.
7:29 peace offering to the LORD shall b a part
7:38 of Sinai to b their offerings to the LORD.
10: 6 lest you b not only death on yourselves
12: 6 she shall b to the priest at the entrance
14:23 purification he shall b them to the priest,
15:29 two pigeons and b them to the priest
16: 3 He shall b a young bullock for a sin
16: 6 "Aaron shall b in the bullock,
16: 9 shall b in and offer up as a sin offering.
16:20 altar, Aaron shall b forward the live goat.
19:21 shall b to the entrance of the meeting
22:16 they b down guilt that must be punished;
23:10 you shall b a sheaf of the first fruits of
23:14 day, when you b your God this offering,
23:15 day on which you b the wave-offering sheaf,
23:17 you shall b with you from wherever you
24: 2 "Order the Israelites to b you clear oil

BRING (cont.)

26:41 them and *b* them into their enemies' land.
Nm 5:15 he shall *b* his wife to the priest and
6:10 On the eighth day he shall *b* two
11:16 the people, and *b* them to the meeting tent.
14: 8 us, he will *b* us in and give us that land,
14:16 'The LORD was not able to *b* this people
14:24 *b* him into the land where he has just been,
14:31 said would be taken as booty, I will *b* in,
15:18 enter the land into which I will *b* you
15:27 *b* a yearling she-goat as a sin offering,
17:11 and *b* it quickly to the community to make
18: 2 *B* with you also your other kinsmen of the
18:13 that they *b* in to the LORD shall be yours;
18:32 Israelites and so *b* death on yourselves."
20: 5 only to *b* us to this wretched place which
20: 8 From the rock you shall *b* forth water for
20:10 Are we to *b* water for you out of this rock?"
20:25 his son Eleazar and *b* them up on Mount Hor.
21:16 LORD said to Moses, *B* the people together,
22:23 had to beat her to *b* her back on the road.
23:27 "Come, let me *b* you to another place;
31:50 each of us will *b* as an offering to the
32:15 will *b* about the ruin of this whole nation."
32:30 you shall *b* their wives and children and
Dt 4:38 so as to *b* you in and to make their land
7:26 not *b* any abominable thing into your house,
9:28 to *b* them into the land he promised them';
11:15 and I will *b* forth grass in your fields
12: 6 you shall *b* your holocausts and sacrifices,
12:11 shall *b* all the offerings I command you:
12:26 you shall *b* with you to the place which
14:24 you and you are not able to *b* your tithe,
14:28 third year you shall *b* out all the tithes
17: 5 you shall *b* the man (or woman) who has
22: 8 off, you will *b* bloodguilt upon your house.
22:15 and *b* it to the elders at the city gate.
22:21 they shall *b* the girl to the entrance of
22:24 you shall *b* them both out to the gate of
24: 4 *b* such guilt upon the land which the LORD,
24: 5 to *b* joy to the wife he has married.
25: 1 men have a dispute and *b* it to court,
28:21 The LORD will *b* a pestilence upon you that
28:36 "The LORD will *b* you,
28:61 will *b* upon you until you are destroyed.
30: 4 even from there will he *b* you back.
30: 5 will then *b* you into the land which your
31: 7 for you may *b* this people into the land
31:23 for it is you who must *b* the Israelites
32:39 It is I who *b* both death and life,
33: 7 you will *b* him to his people.
33:10 *b* the smoke of sacrifice to your nostrils,
Jos 6:18 else you will *b* upon the camp of Israel
6:22 house and *b* out the woman with all her kin,
7:25 "The LORD *b* upon you today the misery
10:22 the cave and *b* out those five kings to me."
18: 6 You shall *b* here to me the description of
Jgs 6:13 said 'Did not the LORD *b* us up from Egypt?'
6:18 *b* out my offering and set it before you."
6:30 to Joash, *B* out your son that he may die,
11: 5 went to *b* Jephthah from the land of Tob.
11: 9 "If you *b* me back to fight against the
19:22 man whose house it was, *B* out your guest,
19:24 *b* out my maiden daughter or his concubine.
1Sm 1:23 may the LORD *b* your resolve to fulfillment!"
2:19 which she would *b* him each time she went
9:23 *B* the portion I gave you and told you to
10:23 They ran to *b* him from there;
11: 2 that I may thus *b* ignominy on all Israel."
12: 8 Moses and Aaron to *b* them out of Egypt,
13: 9 *B* me the holocaust and peace offerings,"
14:18 Saul then said to Ahijah, *B* the ephod here."
14:34 of them to *b* his ox or his sheep to me.
15:32 Afterward Samuel commanded, *B* Agag,
16:17 me a skillful harpist and *b* him to me."
17:17 and *b* them quickly to your brothers in the
17:18 brothers and *b* home some token from them.
18:25 Saul intended in this way to *b* about
19:15 commanded them, *B* him up to me in the bed,
20:13 please my father to *b* any injury upon you,
20:31 So send for him, and *b* him to me,
21:15 Why did you *b* him to me?
21:16 *b* in this one to carry on in my presence?
23: 9 the priest Abiathar, *B* forward the ephod."
30: 7 priest, son of Ahimelech, *B* me the ephod!"
2Sm 3:13 appear before me unless you *b* back Michal,
6: 2 of Judah to *b* up from there the ark of God,
6:12 David went to *b* up the ark of God from the
9:10 You shall *b* in the produce,
12:11 will *b* evil upon you out of your own house.
12:12 *b* it about in the presence of all Israel,
12:23 Can I *b* him back again?
13:10 Tamar, *B* the nourishment into the bedroom,
14:14 Yet, though God does not *b* back life,
14:21 Go, therefore, and *b* back young Absalom."
15:25 he will *b* me back and permit me to see it
17: 3 I can *b* back the rest of the people to you,
17:13 all Israel shall *b* ropes to that city and
17:14 in order thus to *b* Absalom to ruin.
18:20 "You are not the man to *b* the news today.
19:19 They crossed over the ford to *b* the king's
23: 5 Will he not *b* to fruition all my salvation
1Kgs 1:42 are a man of worth and must *b* good news."
5:23 *b* them down from the Lebanon to the sea,
5:23 in the sea and *b* them wherever you say.
8: 1 to *b* up the ark of the LORD's covenant
8:34 and *b* them back to the land you gave their
10:10 Never again did anyone *b* such an abundance
10:11 fleet, which used to *b* gold from Ophir,
13:18 LORD to *b* you back with me to my house
17:10 *b* me a small cupful of water to drink."
17:11 after her, "Please *b* along a bit of bread."
17:13 first make me a little cake and *b* it to me.
21:29 me, I will not *b* the evil in his time.
21:29 I will *b* the evil upon his house during
2Kgs 2:20 *B* me a new bowl,"
4: 6 she said to her son, *B* me another vessel."
4:41 *B* some meal," Elisha said.
10:22 *B* out the garments for all the worshipers
11:15 *B* her outside through the ranks.
19: 3 but there is no strength to *b* them forth.
21:12 *b* such evil on Jerusalem and Judah that,
22:16 I will *b* upon this place and upon its
22:20 see all the evil I will *b* upon this place.'"
1Chr 13: 3 let us *b* the ark of our God here among us,
13: 5 to *b* the ark of God from Kiriath-jearim.
13: 6 of Judah, to *b* back the ark of God,
13:12 said, "How can I *b* the ark of God with me?"
15: 3 Jerusalem to *b* the ark of the LORD
15:12 your brethren and *b* the ark of the LORD,
15:14 themselves to *b* up the ark of the LORD,
15:25 went to *b* up the ark of the covenant
16:29 *B* gifts, and enter his presence;
17:23 *B* about what you have promised,
19:16 the Arameans sent messengers to *b* out the
21: 3 Why will he *b* guilt upon Israel?"
2Chr 1:17 and would then *b* up chariots from Egypt
5: 2 came to Jerusalem to *b* up the ark of the
6:25 and *b* them back to the land which you gave
9:24 and year out, each one would *b* his tribute
19:10 brethren living in their cities *b* to you,
24: 6 required the Levites to *b* in from Judah
28:13 "Do not *b* the captives here,
28:27 *b* him to the tombs of the kings of Israel.
29:31 and *b* forward the sacrifices and thank
31:10 *b* the offerings to the house of the LORD,
34:24 I am prepared to *b* evil upon this place
34:28 all the evil I will *b* upon this place
Ezr 7:15 and to *b* with you the silver and gold
8:30 been weighed out, to *b* them to Jerusalem,
Neh 1: 9 and *b* them back to the place which I have
8: 1 Ezra the scribe to *b* forth the book
8:15 country and *b* in branches of olive trees,
9:26 them in order to *b* them back to you,
9:29 them, in order to *b* them back to your law.
10:32 When the peoples of the land *b* in
10:36 We have agreed to *b* each year to the house
10:37 in the law, to *b* to the house of our God,
10:38 wine and of oil, we will *b* to the priests,
10:38 of our fields we will *b* to the Levites;
10:39 and the Levites shall *b* the tithe of the
10:40 and Levites *b* the offerings of grain,
11: 1 to *b* one man in ten to reside in Jerusalem,
Tb 1: 8 third year I would *b* them this offering,
2: 2 worshiper of God, *b* him back with you,
4: 6 service, your good works will *b* success,
5:17 way and *b* you back to me safe and sound;
6:13 her and *b* her back with us to your house."
6:15 I would *b* my father and mother down to
7:12 Take her and *b* her back safely
7:13 her mother and told her to *b* a scroll,
7:15 the other bedroom and *b* the girl there."
8:17 and *b* their lives to fulfillment with
8:20 *b* joy to my daughter's sorrowing spirit.
9: 2 Get the money and then *b* him along with
10:13 kinsman, may the Lord *b* you back safely,
14: 5 them and *b* them back to the land of Israel.
Jdt 9:13 Let my guileful speech *b* wound and wale on
10: 8 the God of our fathers *b* you to favor,
11:11 by which they *b* the wrath of their God
11:14 Jerusalem to *b* back to them authorization
11:22 of your people, to *b* victory to our arms,
16: 6 one struck down, nor did titans *b* him low,
Est 1:11 to *b* Queen Vashti into his presence
2: 3 to *b* together all beautiful young virgins
1Mc 6:15 son Antiochus and *b* him up to be king.
7: 2 Antiochus and Lysias to *b* them to him.
10:63 that no one is to *b* charges against him
14:35 the glory he planned to *b* to his nation,
2Mc 1:21 he ordered them to scoop some out and *b* it.
3: 6 to *b* it all under the control of the king.
4:19 to *b* there three hundred silver drachmas
6:21 urged him to *b* meat of his own providing,
6:25 I would *b* shame and dishonor on my old age.
15:37 I will *b* my own story to an end here too.
Jb 10: 9 Will you then *b* me down to dust again?
10:18 Why then did you *b* me forth from the womb?
14: 3 so as to *b* him into judgment before you,
15:35 They conceive malice and *b* forth emptiness;
33:23 for him and *b* the man back to justice,
36: 3 I will *b* my knowledge from afar,
38:26 a path To *b* rain to no man's land,
38:32 you *b* forth the Mazzaroth in their season,
40:12 *B* down the haughty with a glance;
Ps(s) 4: 9 alone, O LORD, *b* security to my dwelling.
5: 4 at dawn I *b* my plea expectantly before you.
18:28 you save but haughty eyes you *b* low;
25:17 of my heart, and *b* me out of my distress.
37:14 bow to *b* down the afflicted and the poor,
43: 3 lead me on And *b* me to your holy mountain,
55: 4 For they *b* down evil upon me,
55:24 *b* them down into the pit of destruction;
56: 8 in your wrath *b* down the peoples, O God.
59:12 shake them by your power, and *b* them down,
60:11 Who will *b* me into the fortified city?
65: 5 choose, and *b* to dwell in your courts.
66:13 I will *b* holocausts to your house;
68:30 in Jerusalem let the kings *b* you gifts.
72:10 kings of Arabia and Seba shall *b* tribute.
76:12 let all round about him *b* gifts to the
96: 8 *B* gifts, and enter his courts;
104:20 You *b* darkness, and it is night;
108:11 Who will *b* me into the fortified city?
143:12 *b* to nought all my foes,
Prv 3: 2 years of life, and peace, will they *b* you.
4: 8 she will *b* you honors if you embrace her;
18:24 Some friends *b* ruin on us,
25: 8 *b* not forth hastily against an opponent;
27: 1 for you know not what any day may *b* forth.
27:26 and the goats will *b* the price of a field,
29:17 your son, and he will *b* you comfort,
Eccl 11: 9 all this God will *b* you to judgment.
12:14 because God will *b* to judgment every work,
Sg 3: 4 I should *b* him to the home of my mother,
8: 2 you, *b* you in to the home of my mother.
Wis 6:22 search out and *b* to light knowledge of her,
16:14 can he *b* back the soul once it is confined.
Sir 1:27 lest you fall and *b* upon you dishonor;
4:18 Then she comes back to *b* him happiness and
4:20 from evil, and *b* upon yourself no shame.
11:29 *B* not every man into your house,
18:32 of a moment which *b* on poverty redoubled;
20: 8 Some misfortunes *b* success;
23:25 her branches will not *b* forth fruit.
26:19 These two *b* grief to my heart,
30: 9 you, indulge him and he will *b* you grief.
31:12 man, *b* not a greedy gullet to his table,
36: 7 Hasten the day, *b* on the time;
38:14 correct and his treatment *b* about a cure.
38:19 For grief can *b* on an extremity and
40:10 evil, and it is they who *b* on destruction.
40:19 and orchards *b* flourishing health;
40:29 His neighbor's delicacies *b* revulsion of
Is 1:13 *B* no more worthless offerings;
5: 4 crop of grapes, did it *b* forth wild grapes?
7:17 The LORD shall *b* upon you and your people
14: 2 take them and *b* them along to its place,
15: 9 blood, but I will *b* still more upon Dimon:
19: 3 them, and I will *b* to nought their counsel;
21:14 Meet the thirsty, *b* them water;
25:11 He will *b* low their pride as his hands
26:18 inhabitants of the world cannot *b* it forth.
29: 2 But I will *b* distress upon Ariel,
30:32 the LORD will *b* down on him in punishment,
31: 2 Yet he too is wise and will *b* disaster;
32:17 Justice will *b* about peace;
33:11 You conceive dry grass, *b* forth stubble;
37: 3 but there is no strength to *b* them forth.
41:21 *b* forward your reasons,
42: 1 he shall *b* forth justice to the nations,
42: 7 blind, to *b* out prisoners from confinement,
43: 5 the east I will *b* back your descendants,
43: 6 *B* back my sons from afar,
43:23 You did not *b* me sheep for your holocausts,
44:25 It is I who *b* to nought the omens of liars,
49:22 They shall *b* your sons in their arms,
56: 7 Them I will *b* to my holy mountain and make
59: 4 they conceive mischief and *b* forth malice.
60: 9 To *b* your children from afar with their
60:13 and the pine, To *b* beauty to my sanctuary,
60:17 In place of bronze I will *b* gold,
61: 1 has sent me to *b* glad tidings to the lowly,
66: 4 for them and *b* upon them what they fear.
66: 9 Shall I *b* a mother to the point of birth,
66:20 They shall *b* all your brethren from all
66:20 just as the Israelites *b* their offering to
Jer 3:14 a city, two from a clan, and *b* you to Zion.
4: 6 Evil I *b* from the north,
5:15 I will *b* against you a nation from afar,
6:19 See, I *b* evil upon this people,
6:21 this people obstacles to *b* them down;
9:23 *b* about kindness justice and uprightness
11:11 I *b* upon them misfortune which they cannot
11:23 will *b* misfortune upon the men of Anathoth,
12:15 up, I will pity them again and *b* them back,
15:19 you *b* forth the precious without the vile,
16:15 I will *b* them back to the land which I
17:18 *B* upon them the day of misfortune,
17:21 *b* them in through the gates of Jerusalem.
17:22 *B* no burden from your homes on the sabbath.
17:26 the Negeb, to *b* holocausts and sacrifices,
19: 3 I am going to *b* such evil upon this place
19:15 I will surely *b* upon this city all the
23: 3 them and *b* them back to their meadow;
23:12 Evil I will *b* upon them:
23:40 And I will *b* upon you eternal reproach,
24: 6 their good, and *b* them back to this land,
25: 6 with your handiwork, and I *b* evil upon you.
25: 9 I will *b* them against this land,

25:10 Among them I will *b* to an end the song of
26:15 it is innocent blood you *b* on yourselves,
26:23 him into Egypt to *b* Uriah back to the king,
27:22 *b* them back and restore them to this place.
28: 4 And I will *b* back to this place Jeconiah,
29:10 you my promise to *b* you back to this place.
29:14 and *b* you back to the place from which I
30: 3 and *b* them back to the land which I have
31: 8 *b* them back from the land of the north;
32:37 I will *b* them back to this place and
32:42 *b* upon them all the good I promise them.
33:11 *b* thank offerings to the house of the LORD,
34:22 the LORD, and *b* them back to this city.
35: 2 *b* them into the house of the LORD,
35:17 I will *b* upon Judah and all the citizens
36:14 "Come and *b* with you the scroll you read
39: 7 bound him in chains to *b* him to Babylon.
42:17 or escape the evil that I will *b* upon them.
43:10 king of Babylon, and *b* him here.
48:44 For I will *b* these things upon Moab in the
49: 8 For I will *b* destruction upon Esau when I
49:32 from all sides I will *b* ruin upon them,
49:36 I will *b* upon Elam the four winds from the
49:37 I will *b* evil upon them,
50:19 But I will *b* back Israel to her fold,
51: 8 *B* balm for her wounds,
51:40 *b* them down like lambs to the slaughter,
Lam 1:21 *B* on the day you have proclaimed,
5: 9 peril of our lives we *b* in our sustenance,
Bar 2:34 And I will *b* them back to the land which
4:29 in saving you, *b* you back enduring joy."
5: 6 but God will *b* them back to you borne
6: 2 I will *b* you back from there in peace.
6: 8 People *b* gold, as to a maiden in love
6:29 For women *b* the offerings to these gods of
6:40 they *b* forward Bel and ask the god to make
Ez 5:17 you, and I will *b* the sword upon you.
7: 4 I will *b* your conduct down upon you,
7:24 I will *b* in the worst of the nations,
9:10 will *b* down their conduct upon their heads.
11: 8 the sword, but the sword I will *b* upon you,
11: 9 I will *b* you out of the city,
11:21 will *b* down their conduct upon their heads,
12: 4 You shall *b* out your baggage like an exile
12:13 I will *b* him to Babylon,
12:25 house, whatever I speak I will *b* about,
13:11 I will *b* down a flooding rain;
14: 5 *b* back to their senses the house of Israel,
14:22 in it who will *b* out sons and daughters;
17:19 he broke, I swear to *b* down upon his head.
17:20 I will *b* him to Babylon and enter into
17:24 know that I, the LORD, *B* low the high tree,
20: 6 That day I swore to *b* them out of the land
20: 9 I would *b* them out of the land of Egypt.
20:13 that *b* life to those who keep them.
20:15 not to *b* them to the land I had given them,
20:21 that *b* life to those who observe them,
20:34 I will *b* you out from the nations and
20:37 the staff and *b* back but a small number.
20:38 sojourned as aliens I will *b* them out,
20:42 when I *b* you back to the land of Israel,
23:22 I will *b* them against you from every side:
24: 5 *b* to a boil these pieces and the joints
24:14 coming, for I will *b* it about without fail.
28: 7 Therefore I will *b* against you foreigners,
29: 8 I will *b* the sword against you,
30:24 which he will *b* against Egypt so as to
33: 2 When I *b* the sword against a country,
33:12 a man has done *b* about his downfall
33:15 goods, living by the statutes that *b* life,
34: 4 not *b* back the strayed nor seek the lost,
34:13 I will *b* them back to their own country
34:16 I will seek out, the strayed I will *b* back,
36:24 lands, and *b* you back to your own land.
37: 5 I will *b* spirit into you,
37:12 them, and *b* you back to the land of Israel.
37:21 all sides to *b* them back to their land.
38:16 the last days I will *b* you against my land,
38:17 those days that I would *b* you against them.
39:10 They shall not have to *b* in wood from the
39:27 When I *b* them back from among the peoples,
43:23 *b* an unblemished young bull and an
44:30 to *b* a blessing down upon your house.
Dn 1: 3 to *b* in some of the Israelites of royal
2:24 *B* me before the king,
3:43 by your wonders, and *b* glory to your name,
8:24 strong and powerful, *b* about fearful ruin,
13:17 *B* me oil and soap,"
14:14 ordered his servants to *b* some ashes,
14:33 going to *b* it to the reapers in the field,
Hos 1: 4 And *b* to an end the kingdom of the house
2:13 I will *b* an end to all her joy,
7: 1 would *b* about the restoration of my people,
7:12 like birds in the air I will *b* them down,
9:12 Even though they *b* up their children,
9:13 shall *b* out his children to the slayer.
Jl 4: 2 *b* them down to the Valley of Jehoshaphat,
4:11 *B* down, O Lord, your warriors!]
Am 4: 1 Who say to your lords, *B* drink for us!"
4: 4 Each morning *b* your sacrifices,
5:25 Did you *b* me sacrifices and offerings for
8:10 only son, and *b* their day to a bitter end.
9: 2 even from there my hand shall *b* them out;
9: 2 climb to the heavens, I will *b* them down;
9: 7 Did I not *b* the Israelites from the land
9:14 I will *b* about the restoration of my
Ob 1: 3 your heart, "Who will *b* me down to earth?"
1: 4 the stars, From there will I *b* you down,
Mi 1:15 Yet must I *b* to you the conqueror,
7: 9 He will *b* me forth to the light;
Na 2:14 preying on the land I will *b* to an end,
Zep 2: 7 visit them, and *b* about their restoration.
3:10 of the North, they shall *b* me offerings.
3:19 earth, when I *b* about their restoration.
3:20 At that time I will *b* you home,
3:20 When I *b* about your restoration before
Hg 1: 8 *b* timber, and build the house
Zec 3: 8 Yes, I will *b* my servant the Shoot.
4: 7 He shall *b* out the capstone amid
8: 8 will *b* them back to dwell within Jerusalem.
9:11 *b* forth your prisoners from the dungeon.
10: 6 I will *b* them back,
10:10 I will *b* them back from the land of Egypt,
10:10 I will *b* them into Gilead and into Lebanon,
13: 9 I will *b* the one third through fire,
Mal 1:11 And everywhere they *b* sacrifice to my name,
1:13 You *b* in what you seize,
1:13 yes, you *b* it as a sacrifice.
3:10 *B* the whole tithe into the storehouse,
Mt 5:23 If you *b* your gift to the altar and there
12:10 hoping to *b* an accusation against him:
12:45 Off it goes again to *b* back with it this
13:52 who can *b* from his storeroom
14: 8 *B* me the head of John the Baptizer on a
14:18 *B* them here," he said.
16: 5 they had forgotten to *b* any bread along.
17:17 *B* him here to me!"
21:41 "He will *b* that wicked crowd to a bad end
27:13 hear how many charges they *b* against you?"
Mk 2: 4 to *b* him to Jesus because of the crowd,
3: 2 to be able to *b* an accusation against him.
6: 9 "Do not *b* a second tunic,"
6:27 ordering him to *b* back the Baptizer's head.
6:55 began to *b* in the sick on bedrolls
8:14 They had forgotten to *b* any bread along;
9:19 *B* him to me."
11: 2 Untie it and *b* it back.
12:15 *B* me a coin and let me see it."
Lk 1:16 will he *b* back to the Lord their God.
1:19 to speak to you and *b* you this good news.
4:18 has sent me to *b* glad tidings to the poor,
5:18 to *b* him in and lay him before Jesus;
9:41 *B* your son here to me."
12:11 When they *b* you before synagogues,
14:21 town and *b* in the poor and the crippled,
15:22 *b* out the finest robe and put it on him;
19:27 *b* them in and slay them in my presence.'"
Jn 7: 7 I *b* against it that what it does is evil.
7:45 asked them, "Why did you not *b* him in?"
18:29 accusation do you *b* against this man?"
19: 4 I am going to *b* him out to you to make you
21:10 *B* some of the fish you just caught,"
Acts 3: 2 They would *b* him every day and put him at
5:31 ruler and savior is to *b* repentance
7:25 God was using him to *b* them deliverance;
7:42 'Did you *b* me sacrifices and offerings for
9: 2 and *b* to Jerusalem anyone he might find,
9:15 I have chosen to *b* my name to the Gentiles,
9:21 people and *b* them before the chief priests?"
12: 4 *b* him before the people after the Passover.
12: 6 night before Herod was to *b* him to trial,
16:16 She used to *b* substantial profit to her
17: 5 Jason in an attempt to *b* Paul and Silas
19:38 craftsmen want to *b* charges against anyone,
23:18 called me and asked me to *b* you this boy,
24:17 I had come to *b* alms to my own people and
25:11 to the charges these men *b* against me,
Rom 1: 5 and *b* to obedient faith all the Gentiles,
4:15 the law serves only to *b* down wrath,
7:13 used what was good to *b* about my death.
8:11 will *b* your mortal bodies to life also,
8:33 shall *b* a charge against God's chosen ones?
10: 6 (that is, to *b* Christ down),
10: 7 (that is, to *b* Christ up from the dead."
14:15 you eat *b* to ruin him for whom Christ died:
15:25 Jerusalem to *b* assistance to the saints.
15:31 and that the offerings I *b* to Jerusalem
1Cor 4: 5 He will *b* to light what is hidden in
6: 1 case against another dare *b* it for judgment
8: 8 Now food does not *b* us closer to God.
2Cor 4:15 abundance may *b* greater glory to God
8: 6 you, to *b* it to successful completion:
10: 5 we likewise *b* every thought into captivity
Gal 3:24 to *b* about our justification through faith.
Eph 1:10 to *b* all things in the heavens and on
5: 6 that *b* God's wrath down on the disobedient;
6: 4 *B* them up with the training and
1Thes 4:14 God will *b* forth with him from the dead
1Tm 4:16 By doing so you will *b* to salvation
5:12 This will *b* them condemnation for breaking
6:15 God will *b* to pass at his chosen time.
2Tm 4:11 Get Mark and *b* him with you,
4:13 *b* the cloak I left in Troas with Carpus,
4:18 and will *b* me safe to his heavenly kingdom.
Heb 9:28 *b* salvation to those who eagerly await him.
Jas 1:18 He wills to *b* us to birth with a word
2Jn 1:10 comes to you who does not *b* this teaching,
Jude 1:12 on the wind like clouds that *b* no rain.
Rv 15: 1 which would *b* God's wrath to a climax.
21:24 kings of the earth shall *b* their treasures.
22:12 I *b* with me the reward that will be given

BRINGING (83)

Gn 14:16 *b* back his kinsman Lot and his possessions,
27:18 *B* them to his father,
27:31 dish with his game, and *b* it to his father,
38:25 But as they were *b* her out,
Ex 18:19 God, *b* to him whatever they have to say.
36: 5 "The people are *b* much more than is
36: 6 So the people stopped *b* their offerings;
Lv 4: 4 *B* the bullock to the entrance of the
8: 6 *B* forward Aaron and his sons,
16:12 incense, and *b* them inside the veil.
16:15 goat, and *b* its blood inside the veil,
17: 4 without first *b* it to the entrance of the
17: 5 *b* them to the priest at the entrance of
17: 9 sacrifice without *b* it to the entrance
18: 3 do in the land of Canaan, where I am *b* you;
20:22 I am *b* you to dwell will vomit you out.
Nm 6:12 *b* a yearling lamb as a guilt offering.
6:14 *b* as his offering to the LORD one
14: 3 Why is the LORD *b* us into this land only
16:14 *b* us to a land flowing with milk and honey,
Dt 8: 7 your God, is *b* you into a good country,
11: 4 you, and *b* ruin upon them even to this day;
21: 4 and *b* it down to a wadi with an
26: 9 and *b* us into this country,
Jgs 15: 1 harvest, Samson visited his wife, *b* a kid.
1Sm 10: 3 one will be *b* three kids,
2Sm 3:12 I will aid you by *b* all Israel over to you."
3:22 an expedition, *b* much plunder with them.
6:15 Israelites were *b* up the ark of the LORD
14:13 for not *b* back his own banished son.
18:20 but today you would not be *b* good news,
18:26 king responded, "He, too, is *b* good news."
1Kgs 14:10 I am *b* evil upon the house of Jeroboam:
21:21 in the LORD'S sight, I am *b* evil upon you:
2Kgs 4:42 A man came from Baal-shalishah *b* the man
1Chr 12:41 Zebulun, and Naphtali came *b* food on asses,
Ezr 6: 3 offering sacrifices and *b* burnt offerings.
Neh 13:15 that they were *b* in sheaves of grain,
13:15 and *b* them to Jerusalem on the sabbath day.
Tb 1: 6 *B* with me the first fruits of the field
11:17 Blessed be your God for *b* you to us,
1Mc 3:41 *b* fetters and a large sum of silver and
7:23 and his men were *b* upon the Israelites,
9:37 with a large escort they are *b* the bride,
11:39 was *b* up Alexander's young son Antiochus.
13:12 Judah, *b* Jonathan with him as a prisoner.
Jb 33:30 *B* back his soul from the pit to the light,
39: 2 fulfill, and fix the time of their *b* forth?
Ps(s) 35:12 me evil for good, *b* bereavement to my soul.
Is 46:13 I am *b* on my justice,
63:14 you led your people, *b* glory to your name.
66: 3 *B* a cereal offering,
Jer 28: 6 prophesied by *b* the vessels of the house
32:35 and daughters to Molech, *b* sin upon Judah;
41: 5 *b* food offerings and incense for the house
45: 5 I am *b* evil on all mankind,
49: 5 I am *b* terror upon you,
51:64 rise, because of the evil I am *b* upon her.
Ez 6: 3 See, I am *b* a sword against you,
16:43 I am *b* down your conduct upon your heads,
26: 7 I am now *b* up against Tyre from the north
29: 7 broke, *b* each one of them down headlong;
29:14 *b* them back to the land of Pathros,
42: 1 *b* me to some chambers on the north that
Dn 9:12 by *b* upon us in Jerusalem the greatest
Mt 15:30 of people came to him *b* with them cripples,
25:20 came forward *b* the additional five.
Mk 2: 3 people arrived *b* a paralyzed man to him.
10:13 People were *b* their little children to him
Lk 21:12 *b* you to trial before kings and governors,
24: 1 to the tomb *b* the spices they had prepared.
Jn 4:34 me and *b* his work to completion is my food.
19:39 *b* a mixture of myrrh and aloes which
Acts 5:16 *b* their sick and those who were troubled
8:25 they went back to Jerusalem *b* the good
14:15 We are *b* you the good news that will
22: 5 I set out with the intention of *b* the
22:30 charge which the Jews were *b* against him.
2Cor 2:16 death, to the former a breath *b* life.
Gal 4:13 that first occasioned my *b* you the gospel.
Heb 2:10 fitting that when *b* many sons to glory God,
Jas 5:19 from the truth, and of another *b* him back.
2Pt 2: 1 thereby *b* on themselves swift disaster.

BRINGS (90)

Gn 49:21 hind let loose which *b* forth lovely fawns.
Lv 22:18 *b* a holocaust as a votive offering or as a
Nm 5:18 shall hold the bitter water that *b* a curse.
5:22 May this water, then, that *b* a curse,
5:27 water that *b* a curse will go into her,
Dt 6:10 *b* you into the land which he swore to your
7: 1 *b* you into the land which you are to enter
11:29 *b* you into the land which you are to enter
22:17 and now *b* monstrous charges against her,
24:11 the loan *b* his pledge outside to you.

BRINGS (cont.)

28:57 her womb and the infant she *b* forth
1Sm 14:29 “My father *b* trouble to the land.
2Sm 15: 8 ‘If the LORD ever *b* me back to Jerusalem,
1Chr 22:12 when he *b* you to rule over Israel,
Tb 13: 2 world, and he *b* up from the great abyss.
2Mc 7:23 as he *b* about the origin of everything,
12:41 who *b* to light the things that are hidden.
Jb 12:22 and *b* the gloom forth to the light.
22:29 For he *b* down the pride of the haughty.
25: 2 are his who *b* about harmony in his heavens.
28:11 the streams, and *b* hidden things to light.
34:11 and *b* home to a man his way of life.
34:20 He *b* on nobles,
37:10 With his breath God *b* the frost,
Ps(s) 7:15 pregnant with mischief, *b* forth failure.
33:10 The LORD *b* to nought the plans of nations;
45: 9 from ivory palaces string music *b* you joy.
47: 4 He *b* peoples under us;
64: 9 He *b* them down by their own tongues;
73:10 “So he *b* his people to such a pass that
75: 8 one he *b* low;
135: 7 he *b* forth the winds from his storehouse.
Prv 10:22 It is the LORD’s blessing that *b* wealth,
10:28 The hope of the just *b* them joy,
13: 3 to open wide one’s lips *b* downfall.
13: 5 hates, but the wicked *b* shame and disgrace.
13:15 Good sense *b* favor,
13:17 A wicked messenger *b* on disaster,
15:27 is greedy of gain *b* ruin on his own house,
15:30 A cheerful glance *b* joy to the heart;
16:22 but folly *b* chastisement on fools.
17: 8 at every turn it *b* him success.
21:12 there is one who *b* down the wicked to ruin.
25:23 The north wind *b* rain,
29:25 The fear of man *b* a snare,
30:33 For the stirring of milk *b* forth curds,
30:33 and the stirring of anger *b* forth blood.
31:12 She *b* him good, and not evil,
Sg 2: 4 He *b* me into the banquet hall and his
Wis 17:13 of not knowing the cause that *b* on torment.
Sir 3: 6 obeys the LORD who *b* comfort to his mother.
4:17 Fear and dread she *b* upon him and tries
10:13 afflictions and *b* men to utter ruin.
11:17 his favor *b* continued success.
11:27 *b* forgetfulness of past delights;
14: 1 Happy the man whose mouth *b* him no grief,
14: 9 refuses his neighbor and *b* ruin on himself.
22: 3 if it be a daughter she *b* him to poverty.
22:19 One who jabs the eye *b* tears:
22:26 But from him who *b* harm to his friend all
25:22 a wife who *b* no happiness to her husband.
26: 2 A worthy wife *b* joy to her husband,
30:24 one’s life, worry *b* on premature old age.
33:12 Others he curses and *b* low,
34:17 up the spirits, *b* a sparkle to the eyes,
37:29 overeating, and gluttony *b* on biliousness.
Is 26: 5 high places, and the lofty city he *b* down;
40:23 He *b* princes to nought and makes the
52: 7 are the feet of him who *b* glad tidings,
59: 4 No one *b* suit justly,
61:11 As the earth *b* forth its plants,
Jer 10:13 he *b* up clouds from the end of the earth;
50:25 and *b* forth the weapons of his wrath;
51:16 he *b* up clouds from the end of the earth;
Lam 3: 3 Against me alone he *b* back his hand again
Am 5: 9 the strong, and *b* ruin upon the fortress;
Na 1: 2 The LORD *b* vengeance on his adversaries,
Hb 1:15 He *b* them all up with his hook,
Hg 1:11 oil, and upon all that the ground *b* forth;
Mt 10:39 who seeks only himself *b* himself to ruin,
10:39 whereas he who *b* himself to nought for me
Rom 3: 7 If my falsehood *b* to light God’s truth and
1Cor 11: 4 his head covered *b* shame upon his head.
11: 5 her head uncovered *b* shame upon her head.
2Cor 7:10 salvation, whereas worldly sorrow *b* death.
Phil 1:18 That is what *b* me joy.
Col 1:27 price which this mystery *b* to the Gentiles
Heb 6: 7 and *b* forth vegetation useful to those for
12:11 but later it *b* forth the fruit of peace
Jas 5:20 the person who *b* a sinner back from his

BRISKLY (1)

Tb 11:16 people of Nineveh saw him walking along *b*,

BRISTLING (2)

2Mc 5: 3 that, with brandished shields and *b* spears,
Jer 51:27 against her, send up horses like *b* locusts.

BROAD (14)

2Sm 12:11 He shall lie with your wives in *b* daylight.
Neh 12:38 past the Oven Tower as far as the *B* Wall,
Jb 37:10 frost, and the *b* waters become congealed.
Ps(s) 119:96 *b* indeed is your command.
Eccl 1:16 has *b* experience of wisdom and knowledge”;
Is 30:33 *B* and deep it is piled with dry grass and
40: 4 a plain, the rough country, a *b* valley.
41:18 heights, and fountains in the *b* valleys;
Bar 3:24 of God, how *b* the scope of his dominion:
Ez 41: 7 There was a *b* circular passageway that led
41: 7 therefore the temple had a *b* way running
42: 4 walk ten cubits *b* and a wall of one cubit;
Hos 4:16 them *b* pastures as though they were lambs?
Am 8: 9 the earth with darkness in *b* daylight.

BROADER (1)

Jb 11: 9 the earth in measure, and *b* than the sea.

BROCADED (3)

Ex 28: 4 a breastpiece, an ephod, a robe, a *b* tunic,
28:39 “The tunic of fine linen shall be *b*.
Prv 7:16 my couch, with *b* cloths of Egyptian linen;

BROILED (1)

Tb 6: 6 Then he *b* and ate part of the fish;

BROKE (90)

Gn 39:17 slave whom you brought here *b* in on me,
42:22 “Didn’t I tell you,” *b* in Reuben,
50:17 these words to him, Joseph *b* into tears.
Ex 32:19 and *b* them on the base of the mountain.
34: 1 were on the former tablets that you *b*.
Nm 10:13 The first time that they *b* camp at the
14: 1 the whole community *b* out with loud cries,
Dt 9:17 them from me and *b* them before your eyes.
10: 2 that were on the former tablets that you *b*,
32:51 because both of you *b* faith with me among
Jos 7: 5 front of the city gate till they *b* ranks,
Jgs 7:19 the horns and *b* the jars they were holding.
7:20 companies blew horns and *b* their jars.
1Sm 5: 9 and old, and hemorrhoids *b* out on them.
11:13 But Saul *b* in to say,
13:14 people, because you *b* the LORD’S command.”
19: 8 When war *b* out again,
2Sm 23:16 So the Three warriors *b* through the
24:15 when the plague *b* out among the people.
1Kgs 13: 5 the altar *b* up and the ashes from it were
2Kgs 8:21 He arose by night and *b* through the
18:16 He *b* up the door panels and the uprights
19:36 Sennacherib, the king of Assyria, *b* camp,
23:14 He *b* to pieces the pillars,
24:13 *b* up all the gold utensils that Solomon,
25:13 of the LORD, the Chaldeans *b* into pieces;
1Chr 11:18 Thereupon the Three *b* through the
2Chr 21: 9 He arose by night and *b* through the
26:16 own destruction and *b* faith with the LORD,
26:19 of incense, leprosy *b* out on his forehead.
28:24 of God’s house and *b* them in pieces.
34: 7 *b* up the sacred poles and carved images
Jdt 7:29 All in the assembly with one accord *b* into
14:16 He *b* into a loud clamor of weeping,
Est A:10 The light of the sun *b* forth;
1Mc 4:30 who *b* the rush of the mighty one by the
6:62 he *b* the oath he had sworn and gave orders
11:12 her to Demetrius, Ptolemy *b* with Alexander;
11:53 he *b* all his promises and became estranged
13:19 but Trypho *b* his promise and would not let
15:27 he *b* all the agreements he had previously
2Mc 10:28 As soon as dawn *b*,
10:36 Still others *b* down the gates and let in
Jb 29:17 And I *b* the jaws of the wicked man;
Ps(s) 106:18 Fire *b* out against their faction;
107:14 and gloom and *b* their bonds asunder.
Is 37:37 *b* camp and went back home to Nineveh.
Jer 2:20 Long ago you *b* your yoke,
28:10 *b* it and in the presence of all the people:
31:32 for they *b* my covenant,
52:17 of the LORD, the Chaldeans *b* into pieces;
Lam 2: 3 He *b* off, in fiery wrath,
Ez 17:16 he spurned, whose covenant with him he *b*,
17:19 which he spurned, my covenant which he *b*,
29: 7 When they leaned on you, you *b*,
39:26 and all the times they *b* faith with me,
Dn 2:45 put to it, which *b* in pieces the tile,
Mt 14:19 blessed and *b* them and gave the loaves to
15:36 he *b* them and gave them to the disciples,
26:26 meal Jesus took bread, blessed it, *b* it,
Mk 6:41 pronounced a blessing, *b* the loaves,
8: 6 the seven loaves he gave thanks, *b* them,
8:19 I *b* the five loaves for the five thousand,
8:20 I *b* the seven loaves for the four thousand,
14:22 the meal he took bread, blessed and *b* it,
14:72 He *b* down and began to cry.
Lk 9:16 pronounced a blessing over them, *b* them,
15:14 a great famine *b* out in that country and
22:19 giving thanks, he *b* it and gave it to them,
24:30 then *b* the bread and began to distribute
Jn 6:66 many of his disciples *b* away and would not
19:32 *b* the legs of the men crucified with Jesus,
Acts 2:46 day, while in their homes they *b* bread.
12:18 confusion *b* out among the soldiers,
13:43 When the congregation finally *b* up,
19:23 disturbance *b* out concerning the new way.
19:40 These words of his *b* up the meeting.
20:11 Paul went upstairs again, *b* bread,
27:35 thanks to God before all of them, *b* it,
1Cor 11:24 after he had given thanks, *b* it and said,
Heb 8: 9 *b* my covenant and I grew weary of them,
11:33 they *b* the jaws of lions,
Rv 6: 1 Lamb *b* open the first of the seven seals,
6: 3 When the Lamb *b* open the second seal,
6: 5 When the Lamb *b* open the third seal,
6: 7 When the Lamb *b* open the fourth seal,
6: 9 When the Lamb *b* open the fifth seal,
8: 1 When the Lamb *b* open the seventh seal,
12: 7 Then war *b* out in heaven;
16: 2 severe and festering boils *b* out on the

BROKEN (103)

Gn 17:14 he has *b* my covenant.”
Ex 21: 8 a foreigner, since he has *b* faith with her.
Lv 2: 6 a cereal offering must be *b* into pieces,
6:14 Having *b* the offering into pieces,
6:21 it has been cooked shall thereafter be *b*;
11:35 or a jar-stand, this must be *b* to pieces;
13:20 sore of leprosy that has *b* out in the boil.
13:25 it is leprosy that has *b* out in the burn;
13:39 is only tetter that has *b* out on the skin,
15:12 touched by the afflicted man shall be *b*;
Nm 15:31 LORD and has *b* his commandment,
Dt 26:13 *b* or forgotten any of your commandments:
Jos 21:45 the LORD made to the house of Israel was *b*;
1Sm 2: 4 The bows of the mighty are *b*,
4:18 an old man and heavy, he died of a *b* neck.
5: 4 and hands *b* off and lying on the threshold,
14:33 “You have *b* faith.
2Sm 5:20 before me like waters that have *b* free.”
2Kgs 18:21 is in fact a *b* reed which pierces the hand
1Chr 13:11 the LORD’s anger had *b* out against Uzzah.
2Chr 26:18 for you have *b* faith and no longer have a
32: 5 he rebuilt the wall where it was *b* down,
Tb 1: 4 tribe of my forefather Naphtali had *b* away
2Mc 9:11 At last, *b* in spirit,
Jb 4:10 yet the teeth of the young lions are *b*;
17: 1 My spirit is *b*,
31:22 the shoulder, my forearm be *b* at the elbow!
Ps(s) 31:13 I am like a dish that is *b*.
34:21 not one of them shall be *b*.
37:15 own hearts, and their bows shall be *b*.
37:17 For the power of the wicked shall be *b*,
60: 3 you have rejected us and *b* our defenses;
69:21 Insult has *b* my heart,
80:13 Why have you *b* down its walls,
89:41 You have *b* down all his walls;
102:24 He has *b* down my strength in the way;
119:126 they have *b* your law.
124: 7 *B* was the snare,
Prv 15:13 but by mental anguish the spirit is *b*.
18:14 but a *b* spirit who can bear?
24:31 with nettles, and its stone wall *b* down.
Eccl 4:12 A three-ply cord is not easily *b*.
12: 6 and the golden bowl is *b*,
12: 6 and the *b* pulley falls into the well,
Wis 4: 5 Their twigs shall be *b* off untimely,
Sir 21:14 A fool’s mind is like a *b* jar
22: 7 Teaching a fool is like gluing a *b* pot,
22:22 But a contemptuous insult, a confidence *b*,
25:22 Depressed mind, saddened face, *b* heart
Is 5:27 belt loose, nor the thong of his sandal *b*.
8:15 many among them shall stumble and fall, *b*,
14: 5 The LORD has *b* the rod of the wicked,
14:29 of you, that the rod which smote you is *b*;
24: 5 violated statutes, *b* the ancient covenant.
24:10 *B* down is the city of chaos,
27:11 its branches shall wither and be *b* off,
28:13 when they walk, they stumble backward, *b*,
33: 8 have quit the paths, Covenants are *b*,
36: 6 is in fact a *b* reed which pierces the hand
Jer 2:13 have dug themselves cisterns, *b* cisterns,
5: 5 But, one and all, they had *b* the yoke,
8:21 *b* by the ruin of the daughter of my people.
11:10 of Israel and the house of Judah have *b*.
17:18 let them, not me, be *b*.
22:28 man Coniah a vessel despised, to be *b* up,
23: 2 My heart within me is *b*,
28:12 after the prophet Hananiah had *b* the yoke
33:21 covenant with my servant David also be *b*,
46: 5 With *b* ranks They fall back;
48:17 How the strong staff is *b*,
48:25 Moab’s strength is *b*,
50:23 of the whole earth been *b* and shattered!
51:30 Burned are their homes, and *b* their bars.
51:56 her heroes are captured, their bows *b*;
Lam 2: 9 he has removed and *b* her bars.
3: 4 my flesh and my skin, he has *b* my bones;
3:16 He has *b* my teeth with gravel,
Bar 6:15 As useless as one’s *b* tools are their gods,
6:43 as she has, and has not had her cord *b*.
Ez 6: 4 waste, your incense stands shall be *b*,
6: 6 and laid waste, your idols *b* and removed,
6: 9 after I have *b* their adulterous hearts
15: 8 land a waste, because they have *b* faith,
18:24 because he has *b* faith and committed sin;
26: 2 it is *b*, the gateway to the peoples;
30: 8 to Egypt and when all who help her are *b*.
30:21 Son of man, I have *b* the arm of Pharaoh,
31:12 lay *b* in all the ravines of the land,
44: 7 *b* my covenant by all your abominations.
Dn 3:44 and powerless, and their strength *b*;
8:22 place when it was *b* are four kingdoms
8:25 he shall be *b* without a hand being raised.
11: 4 his kingdom shall be *b* and divided
Jl 1:17 stores are destroyed, The barns are *b* down,
Am 3:14 shall be *b* off and fall to the ground.

Mi 1: 7 All her idols shall be *b* to pieces,
Zec 11:11 that day it was *b* off.
Mal 2:11 Judah has *b* faith;
2:14 have *b* faith though she is your companion,
Mt 24:43 eye and not allow his house to be *b* into.
26:38 them, "My heart is nearly *b* with sorrow.
Jn 19:31 the legs be *b* and the bodies be taken away.
1Pt 4: 1 has suffered in the flesh has *b* with sin.

BROKENHEARTED (4)

Ps(s) 34:19 The LORD is close to the *b*;
109:16 persecuted the wretched and poor and the *b*,
147: 3 He heals the *b* and binds up their wounds.
Is 61: 1 glad tidings to the lowly, to heal the *b*,

BRONZE (155)

Gn 4:22 of all who forge instruments of *b* and iron.
Ex 25: 3 gold, silver and *b*;
26:11 fifty *b* clasps and put them into the loops,
26:37 and cast five *b* pedestals for them.
27: 2 You shall then plate it with *b*.
27: 3 and fire pans, all of which shall be of *b*.
27: 4 Make a grating of *b* network for it;
27: 4 this to have four *b* rings,
27: 6 wood for the altar, and plate them with *b*.
27:10 twenty columns and twenty pedestals of *b*;
27:11 twenty columns and twenty pedestals of *b*;
27:17 and hooks of silver, and pedestals of *b*.
27:18 be used, and the pedestals must be of *b*.
27:19 the tent pegs of the court, must be of *b*.
30:18 shall make a bronze laver with a *b* base.
31: 4 in making things of gold, silver or *b*,
35: 5 to the LORD, gold, silver and *b*;
35:16 altar of holocausts, with its *b* grating,
35:24 of silver or *b* offered it to the LORD;
35:32 in making things of gold, silver or *b*,
36:18 Fifty *b* clasps were made with which the
36:38 their five pedestals were of *b*.
38: 2 The whole was plated with *b*.
38: 3 and fire pans, were likewise made of *b*.
38: 4 A grating of *b* network was made for the
38: 5 cast for the four corners of the *b* grating,
38: 6 were made of acacia wood and plated with *b*.
38: 8 The *b* laver, with its bronze base,
38: 8 The bronze laver, with its *b* base,
38:10 twenty columns and twenty pedestals of *b*,
38:11 twenty columns and twenty pedestals of *b*,
38:17 The pedestals of the columns were of *b*,
38:19 columns and four pedestals of *b* for it,
38:20 and for the court around it were of *b*.
38:29 The *b*, given as an offering,
38:30 the bronze altar with its *b* gratings and
39:39 the altar of *b* with its bronze grating,
Lv 6:21 if it is cooked in a *b* vessel,
26:19 hard as iron, and your soil as hard as *b*,
Nm 17: 4 So Eleazar the priest had the *b* censers of
21: 9 made a *b* serpent and mounted it on a pole,
21: 9 by a serpent looked at the *b* serpent,
31:22 can stand fire, such as gold, silver, *b*,
Dt 28:23 *b* and the earth under your feet like iron.
33:25 May your bolts be of iron and *b*;
Jos 6:19 and gold, and the articles of *b* or iron,
6:24 silver, gold, and articles of *b* and iron,
22: 8 livestock, with silver, gold, *b* and iron,
Jgs 16:21 down to Gaza and bound him with *b* fetters,
1Sm 17: 5 He had a *b* helmet on his head and wore a
17: 5 wore a *b* corselet of scale armor
17: 6 *b* greaves, and had a bronze scimitar
17:38 putting a *b* helmet on his head and arming
2Sm 8: 8 David removed a very large quantity of *b*.
8:10 with him articles of silver, gold, and *b*.
21:16 *b* spear weighed three hundred shekels,
1Kgs 4:13 walled cities with gates barred with *b*;
7:14 He was a *b* worker,
7:14 knowledge of how to produce any work in *b*.
7:15 Two hollow *b* columns were cast,
7:16 There were also two capitals cast in *b*,
7:27 Ten stands were also made of *b*,
7:30 stand had four *b* wheels and bronze axles.
7:38 Ten *b* basins were then made,
7:45 the temple of the LORD were of burnished *b*.
7:47 the weight of the *b*,
8:64 because the *b* altar before the LORD was
14:27 them, King Rehoboam had *b* shields made,
2Kgs 16:14 The *b* altar that stood before the LORD he
16:15 old *b* altar shall be mine for consultation."
16:17 took down the *b* sea from the bronze oxen
18: 4 smashed the *b* serpent called Nehushtan
25:13 The *b* pillars that belonged to the house
25:13 and the *b* sea in the house of the LORD,
25:13 they carried away the *b* to Babylon.
25:14 and all the *b* vessels used for service.
25:16 The weight in *b* of the two pillars,
25:16 in bronze of the two pillars, the *b* sea,
25:17 a *b* capital five cubits high surmounted
25:17 encircled the capital, all of *b*;
1Chr 18: 8 of Hadadezer, large quantities of *b*,
18: 8 which Solomon later used to make the *b* sea
18: 8 sea and the pillars and the vessels of *b*.
18:10 gold, silver and *b* utensils of every sort.
22: 3 so much *b* that it could not be weighed,
22:14 and *b* and iron in such great quantities
22:16 of craftsman skilled in gold, silver, *b*,
29: 2 *b* for what will be made of bronze,
29: 7 of silver, eighteen thousand talents of *b*,
2Chr 1: 5 The *b* altar made by Bezalel,
1: 6 on the *b* altar at the meeting tent;
2: 6 at work in gold, silver, *b* and iron,
2:13 how to work with gold, silver, *b* and iron,
4: 1 Then he made a *b* altar twenty cubits long,
4: 9 the gates he overlaid with *b*.
4:16 from polished *b* for the house of the LORD.
4:18 the weight of the *b* was not ascertained.
6:13 He had made a *b* platform five cubits long,
7: 7 since the *b* altar which Solomon had made
12:10 them, King Rehoboam made *b* bucklers,
Ezr 8:27 two vases of excellent polished *b*,
1Mc 6:35 men in coats of mail, with *b* helmets,
6:39 the sun shone on the gold and *b* shields,
8:22 on *b* tablets and sent to Jerusalem,
14:18 they sent him inscribed tablets of *b*
14:26 So they made an inscription on *b* tablets,
14:48 should be engraved on *b* tablets,
Jb 6:12 strength of stones, or is my flesh of *b*?
20:24 the bow of *b* shall pierce him through;
40:18 His bones are like tubes of *b*;
41:19 iron as straw, and *b* as rotten wood.
Wis 15: 9 silversmiths and emulates molders of *b*,
Sir 12:10 for his wickedness is like corrosion in *b*.
28:20 of iron and its chains are chains of *b*!
Is 45: 2 *B* doors I will shatter,
48: 4 neck is an iron sinew and your forehead *b*,
60:17 In place of *b* I will bring gold,
60:17 In place of wood, *b*,
Jer 27:19 of hosts concerning the pillars, the *b* sea,
52:17 The *b* pillars that belonged to the house
52:17 and the *b* sea in the house of the LORD,
52:17 they carried away all the *b* to Babylon.
52:18 and all the *b* vessels used for service.
52:20 and the twelve oxen of *b* under the sea,
52:20 The *b* of all these furnishings could not
52:22 A *b* capital five cubits high surmounted
Ez 1: 7 sparkled with a gleam like burnished *b*.
9: 2 They entered and stood beside the *b* altar.
22:18 All of them are *b* and tin,
22:20 Just as silver, *b*,
27:13 slaves and articles of *b* for your goods.
40: 3 saw a man whose appearance was that of *b*;
Dn 2:32 arms were silver, its belly and thighs *b*,
2:35 The iron, tile, *b*,
2:39 to yours, then a third kingdom, of *b*,
2:45 which broke in pieces the tile, iron, *b*,
4:12 stump and roots, fettered with iron and *b*,
4:20 with iron and *b* in the grass of the field;
5: 4 their gods of gold and silver, *b* and iron,
5:23 the gods of silver and gold, *b* and iron,
7:19 crushing with its iron teeth and *b* claws,
10: 6 his arms and feet looked like burnished *b*,
14: 7 "it is only clay inside and *b* outside;
Mi 4:13 horn I will make iron And your hoofs *b*,
Zec 6: 1 and the mountains were of *b*.
Rv 9:20 gold and silver, from *b* and stone and wood,
18:12 wooden furniture; *b*, iron and marble;

BRONZE-SMITHS (1)

2Chr 24:12 temple, and also iron- and *b* to repair it.

BRONZED (2)

Is 18: 2 swift messengers, to a nation tall and *b*,
18: 7 LORD of hosts from a people tall and *b*,

BROOCH (1)

1Mc 14:44 in royal purple or wear an official gold *b*.

BROOCHES (1)

Ex 35:22 as their heart prompted them, brought *b*,

BROOD (13)

Nm 32:14 And now here you are, a *b* of sinners,
Dt 22: 6 away the mother bird along with her *b*;
22: 7 her go, although you may take her *b* away.
32:11 nestlings forth by hovering over its *b*,
Jb 39:16 and ruthlessly makes nought of her *b*;
Wis 3:12 accursed is their *b*.
Sir 16: 1 Desire not a *b* of worthless children,
Jer 17:11 A partridge that mothers a *b* not her own
Mt 3: 7 "You *b* of vipers! Who told you to flee:
12:34 you utter anything good, you *b* of vipers,
23:33 *B* of serpents! How can you escape
Lk 3: 7 "You *b* of vipers!
1Cor 13: 5 neither does it *b* over injuries.

BROODING (1)

Sir 30:21 to sadness, torment not yourself with *b*;

BROODS (1)

Ps(s) 77: 7 I ponder, and my spirit *b*:

BROOK (7)

1Kgs 17: 7 After some time, however, the *b* ran dry,
18:40 *b* Kishon and there he slit their throats.
Jb 6:15 My brethren are undependable as a *b*,
22:24 fine gold of Ophir as pebbles from the *b*,
Ps(s) 110: 7 From the *b* by the wayside he will drink;
Prv 18: 4 but the source of wisdom is a flowing *b*.
Jer 15:18 have indeed become for me a treacherous *b*,

BROOKS (1)

Jer 31: 9 I will lead them to *b* of water,

BROOM (4)

1Kgs 19: 4 he came to a *b* tree and sat beneath it.
19: 5 lay down and fell asleep under the *b* tree,
Jb 30: 4 the roots of the *b* plant were their food.
Is 14:23 I will sweep it with the *b* of destruction,

BROTH (4)

Jgs 6:19 the meat in a basket and the *b* in a pot,
6:20 then pour out the *b*."
Is 65: 4 flesh, with carrion *b* in their dishes,
Ez 24:10 has been cooked, till the *b* has boiled.

BROTHER (382)

Gn 4: 2 Next she bore his *b* Abel.
4: 8 Cain said to his *b* Abel,
4: 8 Cain attacked his *b* Abel and killed him.
4: 9 LORD asked Cain, "Where is your *b* Abel?"
10:21 Japheth's oldest *b* and the ancestor of all
10:25 and the name of his *b* was Joktan.
20: 5 and she herself also stated, 'He is my *b*.'
20:13 place we come to, say that I am your *b*.'"
20:16 given your *b* a thousand shekels of silver.
22:20 too has borne sons, to your *b* Nahor:
22:21 Uz, his first-born, his *b* Buz,
22:23 eight Milcah bore to Abraham's *b* Nahor.
24:15 the wife of Abraham's *b* Nahor) came out
24:27 me straight to the house of my master's *b*."
24:29 Now Rebekah had a *b* named Laban.
24:53 gave costly presents to her *b* and mother.
24:55 Her *b* and mother replied,
25:26 His *b* came out next, gripping Esau's heel;
27: 6 I overheard your father tell your *b* Esau,
27:11 "But my *b* Esau is a hairy man,"
27:23 were hairy, like those of his *b* Esau;
27:30 when his *b* Esau came back from his hunt.
27:35 "Your *b* came here by a ruse and carried
27:40 you shall live, and your *b* you shall serve;
27:41 my father comes, I will kill my *b* Jacob."
27:42 Your *b* Esau intends to settle accounts
27:43 flee at once to my *b* Laban in Haran,
28: 5 of Bethuel the Aramean, and *b* of Rebekah,
32: 4 ahead to his *b* Esau in the land of Seir,
32: 7 Jacob, they said, "We reached your *b* Esau.
32:12 me, I pray, from the hand of my *b* Esau!
32:14 him the following presents for his *b* Esau:
32:18 "When my *b* Esau meets you,
32:19 shall answer, 'They belong to your *b* Jacob,
33: 3 ground seven times, until he reached his *b*.
33: 9 "you should keep what is yours, *b*."
35: 1 while you were fleeing from your *b* Esau."
35: 7 to him when he was fleeing from his *b*.
36: 6 of Seir, out of the way of his *b* Jacob.
37:26 by killing our *b* and concealing his blood?
37:27 After all, he is our *b*, our own flesh."
38: 9 to avoid contributing offspring for his *b*.
38:29 as he withdrew his hand, his *b* came out;
38:30 Afterward his *b* came out;
42: 4 It was only Joseph's full *b* Benjamin that
42:15 unless your youngest *b* comes here,
42:16 So send one of your number to get your *b*,
42:20 must come back to me with your youngest *b*.
42:21 we are being punished because of our *b*.
42:34 you come back to me with your youngest *b*,
42:34 not spies, I will restore your *b* to you,
42:38 Now that his full *b* is dead,
43: 3 in my presence unless your *b* is with you.'
43: 4 If you are willing to let our *b* go with us,
43: 5 in my presence unless your *b* is with you.'"
43: 6 by telling the man that you had another *b*?"
43: 7 Do you have another *b*?'
43: 7 he would say, 'Bring your *b* down here'?"
43:13 Take your *b*, too, and be off on your way
43:14 you, so that he may let your other *b* go,
43:29 Joseph's eye fell on his full *b* Benjamin,
43:29 he asked, "Is this your youngest *b*,
43:30 his *b* that he was on the verge of tears.
44:19 servants, 'Have you a father, or another *b*?'
44:20 'We have an aged father, and a young *b*,
44:20 This one's full *b* is dead,
44:23 your youngest *b* comes back with you,
44:26 if our youngest *b* is with us can we go,
44:26 the man if our youngest *b* is not with us.
45: 4 "I am your *b* Joseph,
45:14 on the neck of his *b* Benjamin and wept,
48:19 his younger *b* shall surpass him,
Ex 4:14 with Moses and said, "Have you not your *b*,
7: 1 and Aaron your *b* shall act as your prophet.
7: 2 your *b* Aaron shall tell Pharaoh to let the
28: 1 among the Israelites have your *b* Aaron,
28: 2 For the glorious adornment of your *b* Aaron
28: 4 vestments which your *b* Aaron and his sons
28:41 you shall clothe your *b* Aaron and his sons.

BROTHER (cont.)

Lv 16: 2 "Tell your *b* Aaron that he is not to come
18:14 father's *b* by being intimate with his wife,
18:16 for that would be a disgrace to your *b*.
19:17 not bear hatred for your *b* in your heart.
20:21 brother's wife and thus disgraces his *b*,
21: 2 or daughter, his *b* or his maiden sister,
Nm 6: 7 for his father or mother, his sister or *b*,
20: 8 the community, you and your *b* Aaron,
20:14 "Your *b* Israel has this to say:
27:13 taken to your people, as was your *b* Aaron,
Dt 3:18 over in the vanguard of your *b* Israelites.
13: 7 "If your own full *b*,
23: 8 not abhor the Edomite, since he is your *b*,
25: 5 but her husband's *b* shall go to her and
25: 6 shall continue the line of the deceased *b*,
28:54 begrudge his *b* and his beloved wife
32:50 just as your *b* Aaron died on Mount Hor and
Jos 15:17 Othniel, son of Caleb's *b* Kenaz,
Jgs 1: 3 Judah then said to his *b* Simeon,
1:13 Othniel, son of Caleb's younger *b* Kenaz,
1:17 Judah then went with his *b* Simeon,
3: 9 Othniel, son of Caleb's younger *b* Kenaz,
9:21 he remained for fear of his *b* Abimelech.
9:24 avenge their blood upon their *b* Abimelech,
20:22 I again engage my *b* Benjamin in battle?"
20:28 go out again to battle with Benjamin, my *b*,
21: 6 over their *b* Benjamin and said,
1Sm 14: 3 Ahijah, son of Ahitub, *b* of Ichabod,
17:28 When Eliab, his oldest *b*,
25: 6 Say to him, 'Peace be with you, my *b*,
26: 6 and Abishai, son of Zeruiah and *b* of Joab,
2Sm 1:26 "I grieve for you, Jonathan my *b*!
2:22 How could I face your *b* Joab?"
3:27 revenge for the killing of Joab's *b* Asahel.
3:30 [Joab and his *b* Abishai had lain in wait
3:30 killed their *b* Asahel in battle at Gibeon.]
4: 6 So Rechab and his *b* Baanah slipped past
4: 9 David replied to Rechab and his *b* Baanah,
10:10 under the command of his *b* Abishai,
13: 3 named Jonadab, son of David's *b* Shimeah,
13: 4 in love with Tamar, my *b* Absalom's sister."
13: 7 "Please go to the house of your *b* Amnon
13: 8 Tamar went to the house of her *b* Amnon,
13:10 brought them to her *b* Amnon in the bedroom.
13:12 But she answered him, "No my *b*!
13:16 She replied, "No, *b*,
13:20 Her *b* Absalom said to her:
13:20 "Has your *b* Amnon been with you?
13:20 Be still now, my sister; he is your *b*.
13:20 and forlorn in the house of her *b* Absalom.
13:26 yourself, please let my *b* Amnon come to us."
13:32 But Jonadab, son of David's *b* Shimeah,
14: 6 one of them struck his *b* and killed him.
14: 7 'Give up the one who killed his *b*.
14: 7 for the life of his *b* whom he has slain;
18: 2 of Abishai, son of Zeruiah and *b* of Joab,
20: 9 And Joab asked Amasa, "How are you, my *b*?"
20:10 Then Joab and his *b* Abishai pursued Sheba,
21:21 Israel, Jonathan, son of David's *b* Shimei,
23:18 Abishai, *b* of Joab,
23:24 Asahel, *b* of Joab. . . .
1Kgs 1:10 or the pick of the army, or his *b* Solomon.
2: 7 kindly when I was fleeing your *b* Absalom.
2:21 be given to your *b* Adonijah for his wife."
2:22 for he is my elder *b* and has with him
9:13 are these cities you have given me, my *b*?"
12:24 out to fight against your *b* Israelites.
13:30 "Alas, my *b*!"
20:32 "He is my *b*,"
20:33 his word and said, "Ben-hadad is your *b*."
2Kgs 1:17 no son, his *b* Joram succeeded him as king,
1Chr 1:19 world was divided), and his *b* was Joktan.
2:32 The sons of Jada, the *b* of Shammai,
2:42 descendants of Caleb, the *b* of Jerahmeel:
4:11 Chelub, the *b* of Shuhah,
6:24 His *b* Asaph stood at his right hand.
6:33 Their *b* Levites were appointed to all the
7:16 He had a *b* named Sheresh,
7:35 The sons of his *b* Hotham were Zophah,
8:39 The sons of Eshek, his *b*,
11:20 Abishai, the *b* of Joab.
11:26 Asahel, the *b* of Joab;
11:38 Joel, *b* of Nathan,
11:45 Jediael, son of Shimri, and Joha, his *b*,
19:11 placed under the command of his *b* Abishai,
19:15 also took to flight before his *b* Abishai,
20: 5 Jair, slew Lahmi, the *b* of Goliath of Gath,
20: 7 and Jonathan, the son of Shimea, David's *b*,
24:25 Isshiah, the *b* of Micah;
26:20 Their *b* Levites superintended the stores
26:22 of Jehiel, Zetham and his *b* Joel,
27: 7 the fourth month, was Asahel, *b* of Joab,
2Chr 31:12 and his *b* Shimei was second in charge.
31:13 Conaniah and his *b* Shimei by appointment
36: 4 *b* Eliakim king over Judah and Jerusalem,
36: 4 *b* Jehoahaz away and brought him to Egypt.
36:10 *b* Zedekiah king over Judah and Jerusalem.
Neh 7: 2 Over Jerusalem I placed Hanani, my *b*,
Tb 1:21 as king, placed Ahiqar, my *b* Anael's son,
5:10 I will of course pay you, *b*."
5:11 Tobit asked, *B*, tell me, please,
5:12 to know truthfully whose son you are, *b*,
5:14 God save you, *b*!
5:14 Do not be provoked with me, *b*,
5:17 Tobit said, "God bless you, *b*."
6: 7 *B* Azariah, what medicinal value
6:11 Raphael said to the boy, *B* Tobiah!"
6:13 the right to marry her listen to me, *b*.
6:13 So heed my words, *b*;
6:14 *B* Azariah, I have heard that this woman
6:16 So now listen to me, *b*;
7: 1 entered Ecbatana, Tobiah said, *B* Azariah,
7: 9 to eat, Tobiah said to Raphael, *B* Azariah,
7:10 to marry my daughter Sarah than you, *b*.
9: 2 *B* Azariah, take along with you four
Jdt 8:26 the flocks of Laban, his mother's *b*.
Est D: 9 "I am your *b*. Take courage!
1Mc 2:65 is your *b* Simeon who I know is a wise man;
5:17 Judas said to his *b* Simon:
5:17 I and my *b* Jonathan will go to Gilead."
5:24 Judas Maccabeus and his *b* Jonathan crossed
5:55 his *b* was in Galilee opposite Ptolemais,
9:19 Jonathan and Simon took their *b* Judas and
9:29 "Since your *b* Judas died,
9:31 and took the place of Judas his *b*.
9:33 But Jonathan and his *b* Simon and all the
9:35 Jonathan sent his *b* as leader of the
9:37 was brought to Jonathan and his *b* Simon:
9:38 Remembering the blood of John their *b*,
9:42 their revenge for the blood of their *b*,
9:65 Leaving his *b* Simon in the city,
10:18 sends greetings to his *b* Jonathan.
10:74 and Simon his *b* joined him to help him.
11:30 to his *b* Jonathan and to the Jewish nation.
11:59 he made Jonathan's *b* Simon governor of the
11:64 them, leaving his *b* Simon in the province.
13:14 that Simon had succeeded his *b* Jonathan,
13:15 "We have detained your *b* Jonathan on
13:25 sent for the remains of his *b* Jonathan,
14:17 But when the Romans heard that his *b* Simon
16: 9 was then that John's *b* Judas fell wounded;
2Mc 4: 7 Onias' *b* Jason obtained the high
4:23 Menelaus, *b* of the aforementioned Simon,
4:26 who had cheated his own *b* and now saw
4:29 Menelaus left his *b* Lysimachus as his
7: 7 When the first *b* had died in this manner,
7:13 maltreated the fourth *b* in the same way.
7:15 forward the fifth *b* and maltreated him.
7:18 After him they brought the sixth *b*.
7:24 As the youngest *b* was still alive,
9:29 His foster *b* Philip brought the body home;
10:37 they killed him, along with his *b* Chaereas,
11:22 Antiochus sends greetings to his *b* Lysias.
14:17 Judas' *b* Simon had engaged Nicanor,
Jb 1:13 wine in the house of their eldest *b*,
1:18 wine in the house of their eldest *b*,
30:29 I have become the *b* of jackals,
Ps(s) 35:14 though it were a friend of mine, or a *b*,
50:20 You sit speaking against your *b*;
Prv 17:17 and a *b* is born for the time of stress.
18: 9 is own *b* to the man who is destructive.
18:19 A *b* is a better defense than a strong city,
18:24 but a true friend is more loyal than a *b*.
27:10 a neighbor near at hand than a *b* far away.
Eccl 4: 8 with neither son nor *b*.
Sg 8: 1 Oh, that you were my *b*,
Sir 7:12 Plot no mischief against your *b*,
7:18 money, nor a dear *b* for the gold of Ophir.
29:10 Spend your money for your *b* and friend,
33:20 neither son nor wife, neither *b* nor friend,
33:32 have but one slave, deal with him as a *b*,
40:24 A *b*, a helper, for times of stress;
45: 6 also, like Moses in holiness, his *b* AARON,
Is 3: 6 a man seizes his *b* in his father's house,
9:18 No man spares his *b*,
19: 2 brother will war against *b*,
Jer 9: 3 put no trust in any *b*.
9: 3 Every *b* apes Jacob,
22:18 my *b*"; "Alas! sister."
34: 9 no one should hold a man of Judah, his *b*,
34:14 his Hebrew *b* who has sold himself to you;
Ez 38:21 Lord GOD, every man's sword against his *b*.
44:25 be their father, mother, son, daughter, *b*,
Hos 12: 4 In the womb he supplanted his *b*,
Am 1:11 Because he pursued his *b* with the sword,
Ob 1:10 Because of violence to your *b* Jacob,
1:12 Gaze not upon the day of your *b*,
Mal 1: 3 Was not Esau Jacob's *b*?
Mt 4:18 Simon now known as Peter, and his *b* Andrew,
4:21 James, Zebedee's son, and his *b* John.
5:22 with his *b* shall be liable to judgment;
5:22 his *b* shall be answerable to the Sanhedrin,
5:23 that your *b* has anything against you,
5:24 go first to be reconciled with your *b*,
7: 4 How can you say to your *b*,
10: 2 now known as Peter, and his *b* Andrew;
10: 2 James, Zebedee's son, and his *b* John;
10:21 "Brother will hand over *b* to death,
12:50 Father is *b* and sister and mother to me."
14: 3 of Herodias, the wife of his *b* Philip.
17: 1 and his *b* John and led them up on a high
18:15 *b* should commit some wrong against you,
18:15 listens to you, you have won your *b* over.
18:21 and asked him, "Lord, when my *b* wrongs me,
18:35 each of you forgives his *b* from his heart."
22:24 his *b* must take the wife and produce
22:24 the wife and produce offspring for his *b*.'
22:25 he had no children, left his wife to his *b*.
Mk 1:16 *b* Andrew casting their nets into the sea;
1:19 of James, Zebedee's son, and his *b* John.
3:17 the *b* of James (he gave these two the name
3:35 of God is *b* and sister and mother to me."
5:37 him except Peter, James, and James' *b* John.
6: 3 a *b* of James and Joses and Judas and Simon?
6:17 of Herodias, the wife of his *b* Philip,
12:19 *b* dies leaving a wife but no child,
12:19 his *b* must take the wife and produce
12:19 the wife and produce offspring for his *b*.'
13:12 Brother will hand over *b* for execution and
Lk 3: 1 Philip his *b* tetrarch of the region of
6:14 he gave the name Peter, and Andrew his *b*,
6:42 How can you say to your brother, *B*,
12:13 *b* to give me my share of our inheritance."
15:27 The servant answered, 'Your *b* is home,
15:32 This *b* of yours was dead,
17: 3 If your *b* does wrong,
20:28 a man's *b* dies leaving a wife and no child,
20:28 the *b* should marry the widow and raise
20:28 the widow and raise posterity to his *b*.
20:31 Next, the second *b* married the widow,
Jn 1:40 hearing John was Simon Peter's *b* Andrew.
1:41 did was seek out his *b* Simon and tell him,
6: 8 Jesus' disciples, Andrew, Simon Peter's *b*,
11: 2 (This Mary whose *b* Lazarus was sick was
11:19 to console Martha and Mary over their *b*.
11:21 had been here, my *b* would never have died.
11:23 "Your *b* will rise again,"
11:32 had been here my *b* would never have died."
Acts 9:17 his hands on Saul and said, "Saul, my *b*,
12: 2 He beheaded James the *b* of John,
21:20 "You see, *b*,
22: 5 received letters to our *b* Jews in Damascus.
22:13 'Saul, my *b*,' he said, 'recover your sight.'
Rom 14:10 you, how can you sit in judgment on your *b*?
14:10 Or you, how can you look down on your *b*?
14:15 *b* feels remorse for the food he has eaten,
14:21 *b* an occasion for stumbling or scandal,
16:24 our *b* Quartus wish to be remembered to you.
1Cor 1: 1 of Christ Jesus, and Sosthenes our *b*,
5:11 who bears the title *b*" if he is immoral,
6: 6 Must *b* drag brother into court,
7:12 If any *b* has a wife who is an unbeliever
8:11 one perishes, that *b* for whom Christ died.
8:13 my *b* to sin I will never eat meat again,
16:12 As for our *b* Apollos,
2Cor 1: 1 of Jesus Christ, and Timothy his *b*,
2:13 because I did not find my *b* Titus there.
8:18 We have sent along with him that *b* whom
8:22 We have sent along that *b* whose eagerness
12:18 go to you, and I sent the other *b* with him.
Gal 1:19 apostles except James, the *b* of the Lord.
2: 4 to the title of *b* were smuggled in;
Eph 6:21 dear *b* and faithful minister in the Lord,
Phil 2:25 that I must send you Epaphroditus, my *b*,
Col 1: 1 by the will of God, and Timothy our *b*,
4: 7 Tychicus, our dear *b*,
4: 9 him is Onesimus, our dear and faithful *b*,
1Thes 3: 2 He is our *b* and God's fellow worker in
4: 6 or cheating his *b* in the matter at hand;
2Thes 3: 6 to avoid any *b* who wanders from the
3:15 rather, correct him as you would a *b*.
Phlm 1: 1 of Christ Jesus, and Timothy our *b*,
1: 4 I thank God always, my *b*,
1:16 but as more than a slave, a beloved *b*,
1:20 You see, *b*, I want to make you "useful"
Heb 7: 5 tithes from the people, their *b* Israelites,
13:23 know that our *b* Timothy has been set free.
Jas 1: 9 Let the *b* in humble circumstances take
2:15 If a *b* or sister has nothing to wear and
4:11 speaks ill of his *b* or judges his brother
1Pt 5:12 whom I take to be a faithful *b* to you.
2Pt 1: 7 care for your *b*, and care for your brother,
3:15 Paul, our beloved *b*,
1Jn 2: 9 to be in light, hating his *b* all the while,
2:10 in the light is the one who loves his *b*;
2:11 But the man who hates his *b* is in darkness.
3:10 to God, nor anyone who fails to love his *b*.
3:12 belonged to the evil one and killed his *b*.
3:15 Anyone who hates his *b* is a murderer,
3:17 heart to his *b* when he sees him in need.
4:20 love is fixed on God," yet hates his *b*,
4:20 One who has no love for the *b* he has seen
4:21 whoever loves God must also love his *b*.
5:16 Anyone who sees his *b* sinning,
Jude 1: 1 a servant of Jesus Christ and *b* of James,
Rv 1: 9 I, John, your *b*,

BROTHER-IN-LAW (5)

Gn 38: 8 widow, in fulfillment of your duty as *b*,
Nm 10:29 setting out, Moses said to his *b* Hobab,
Dt 25: 5 perform the duty of a *b* by marrying her.
25: 7 'My *b* does not intend to perform his duty
Jgs 4:11 the descendants of Hobab, Moses' *b*,

BROTHERHOOD (6)

1Mc 12:10 to you for the renewal of *b* and friendship,
12:17 you our letter about the renewal of our *b*.

Am 1: 9 Edom, and did not remember the pact of b,
Zec 11:14 off the b between Judah and Israel.
1Tm 4: 6 put these instructions before the b
1Pt 5: 9 realizing that the b of believers is

BROTHERLY (1)

1Thes 4: 9 As regards b love,

BROTHERS—BROTHER'S (421)

Gn 4: 9 Am I my b keeper?"
4:10 your b blood cries out to me from the soil!
4:11 to receive your b blood from your hand.
4:21 His b name was Jubal;
9:22 and he told his two b outside about it.
9:25 The lowest of slaves shall he be to his b."
12: 5 Abram took his wife Sarai, his b son Lot,
19: 7 door behind him, he said, "I beg you my b,
27:29 Be master of your b,
27:44 until your b fury subsides
27:45 until your b anger against you subsides
34:11 too, appealed to Dinah's father and b:
34:25 in pain, Dinah's full b Simeon and Levi,
37: 2 old, he was tending the flocks with his b;
37: 4 When his b saw that their father loved him
37: 5 Joseph had a dream, which he told to his b:
37: 8 his b asked him.
37: 9 dream, and this one, too, he told to his b.
37:10 I and your mother and your b are to come
37:11 So his b were wrought up against him but
37:12 when his b had gone to pasture their
37:13 Shechem, Israel said to Joseph, "Your b,
37:14 your b and the flocks and bring back word."
37:16 "I am looking for my b," he answered.
37:17 his b and caught up with them in Dothan.
37:26 Judah said to his b:
37:27 His b agreed.
37:30 tore his clothes, and returning to his b,
38: 1 About that time Judah parted from his b
38: 8 said to Onan, "Unite with your b widow,
38: 8 and thus preserve your b line."
38: 9 whenever he had relations with his b widow,
38:11 that Shelah also might die like his b.
42: 3 So ten of Joseph's b went down to buy an
42: 6 When Joseph's b came and knelt down before
42: 8 When Joseph recognized his b,
42:13 servants," they said, "were twelve b,
42:19 of your b need be confined in this prison,
42:28 he cried out to his b.
42:32 There were twelve of us b,
42:33 leave one of your b with me,
43:32 It was served separately to him, to the b,
44:14 Judah and his b reentered Joseph's house,
44:33 lord, and let the boy go back with his b.
45: 1 about when he made himself known to his b.
45: 3 "I am Joseph," he said to his b.
45: 3 But his b could give him no answer,
45: 4 "Come closer to me," he told his b.
45:15 Joseph then kissed all his b,
45:15 only then were his b able to talk with him.
45:16 Pharaoh's palace that Joseph's b had come,
45:17 "Say to your b:
45:24 As he sent his b on their way,
46:31 said to his b and his father's household:
46:31 'My b and my father's household,
47: 1 and my b have come from the land of Canaan,
47: 2 presented to Pharaoh five of his b
47: 5 that your father and b have come to you,
47: 6 your father and b in the pick of the land."
47:11 Joseph settled his father and b and gave
47:12 And Joseph sustained his father and b and
48: 6 be recorded in the names of their two b.
48:22 I give to you, as to the one above his b,
49: 5 "Simeon and Levi, b indeed,
49: 8 "You, Judah, shall your b praise
49:26 on the brow of the prince among his b.
50: 8 well as Joseph's whole household, his b,
50:14 together with his b and all who had gone
50:15 Joseph's b became fearful and thought,
50:17 forgive the criminal wrongdoing of your b,
50:18 Then his b proceeded to fling themselves
50:24 Joseph said to his b:
Ex 1: 6 all his b and that whole generation died.
Lv 18:16 not have intercourse with your b wife,
20:21 his b wife and thus disgraces his brother,
25:48 he may be redeemed by one of his own b,
Nm 27: 9 you shall give his heritage to his b;
27:10 if he has no b, you shall give his heritage
27:10 give his heritage to his father's b;
27:11 if his father had no b,
Dt 10: 9 has no share in the heritage with his b;
18: 2 Levi shall have no heritage among his b;
25: 5 "When b live together and one of them
25: 7 a man does not care to marry his b wife,
25: 7 refuses to perpetuate his b name in Israel.'
25: 9 treated who will not build up his b family!'
33: 9 his b he would not acknowledge,
33:16 upon the brow of the prince among his b,
33:24 May he be the favorite among his b,
Jos 2:13 spare my father and mother, b and sisters,
2:18 your b and all your family into your house.
6:23 out Rahab, with her father, mother, b,
Jgs 8:19 "They were my b,
9: 5 ancestral house in Ophrah, and slew his b,
9:24 Shechem, who encouraged him to kill his b.
9:56 to his father in killing his seventy b.
11: 3 So Jephthah had fled from his b and had
19:23 went out to them and said, "No, my b;
20:13 refused to accede to the demand of their b,
21:22 When their fathers or their b come
1Sm 16:13 hand, anointed him in the midst of his b;
17:17 grain and these ten loaves for your b,
17:17 bring them quickly to your b in the camp.
17:18 your b and bring home some token from them.
17:22 to the battle line, where he greeted his b.
20:29 our city, and my b insist on my presence.
20:29 well of me, give me leave to visit my b.'
30:23 "You must not do this, my b,
2Sm 2:26 the people to stop the pursuit of their b?"
2:27 from the pursuit of their b until morning."
3: 8 your father Saul, to his b and his friends,
15:20 Return and take your b with you and,
19:13 You are my b, you are my bone and flesh.
19:42 "Why did our b the Judahites steal you
1Kgs 1: 9 near En-rogel, Adonijah invited all his b,
2:15 But the kingdom escaped me and became my b,
1Chr 2:25 then Bunah, Oren, and Ozem, his b.
4: 9 Jabez was the most distinguished of the b.
4:27 His b, however, did not have many sons,
5: 2 in fact, became powerful among his b,
5: 7 His b who belonged to his clans,
5:13 Their b, corresponding to their ancestral
6:29 Their b, the Merarites, stood at the left:
27:18 for Judah, Eliab, one of David's b;
2Chr 5:12 Heman, Jeduthun, and their sons and b,
11: 4 must not march out to fight against your b.
11:22 son of Maacah, commander among his b,
21: 2 His b, sons of Jehoshaphat,
21: 4 b and also some of the princes of Israel.
21:13 murdered your b of your father's house
35: 9 Conaniah and his b Shemaiah,
Neh 1: 2 citadel of Susa when Hanani, one of my b,
5: 8 you, however, are selling your own b,
Tb 1:10 b and relatives ate the food of heathens,
6:18 her, who will take the place of b for you.
7: 1 He said to them, "Greetings to you too, b!
7: 3 So Edna asked them, "Who are you, b?"
Jdt 7:30 But Uzziah said to them, "Courage, my b!
8:14 "No, my b, do not anger the Lord our God.
8:24 "Therefore, my b, let us set an example
14: 1 "Listen to me, my b.
1Mc 3: 2 All his b and all who had joined his
3:25 Then Judas and his b began to be feared,
3:42 Judas and his b saw that the situation had
4:36 Then Judas and his b said,
4:59 Then Judas and his b and the entire
5:10 sent a letter to Judas and his b saying:
5:61 they had not obeyed Judas and his b,
5:63 The valiant Judas and his b were greatly
5:65 Then Judas and his b went out and attacked
7: 6 "Judas and his b have destroyed all your
7:10 to Judas and his b in peaceful terms.
7:27 to Judas and his b this peaceable message:
8:20 "Judas, called Maccabeus, and his b,
10: 5 all the wrongs we have done to him, his b,
10:15 b and the troubles that they had endured.
12: 6 send greetings to their b the Spartans.
12: 7 over you, stating that you are our b,
12:11 as it is right and proper to remember b.
12:21 that the Spartans and the Jews are b;
13: 3 "You know what I, my b,
13: 4 of Israel, that all my b have perished,
13: 5 of distress, for I am not better than my b.
13: 8 in place of your b Judas and Jonathan.
13:27 his father and his b a monument of stones,
13:28 his father and his mother and his four b.
14:18 established with his b Judas and Jonathan.
14:20 and the rest of the Jewish people, our b.
14:26 He and his b and his father's house have
14:29 and his b have put themselves in danger
14:40 and b and that they had received Simon's
16: 2 "I and my b and my father's house have
16: 3 Take my place and my b,
16:21 that his father and his b had perished,
2Mc 2:19 is the story of Judas Maccabeus and his b,
7: 1 It also happened that seven b with their
7: 2 One of the b, speaking for the others,
7: 4 the rest of his b and his mother looked on.
7: 5 the b and their mother encouraged one
7:29 but be worthy of your b and accept death,
7:36 My b, after enduring brief pain,
7:37 Like my b, I offer up my body
7:38 Through me and my b,
8:22 divided his army into four, placing his b,
15:18 wives and children or their b and kinsmen;
Ps(s) 69: 9 I have become an outcast to my b,
Prv 6:19 lies, and he who sows discord among b.
17: 2 and will share the inheritance with the b.
19: 7 All the poor man's b hate him;
Sg 1: 6 My b have been angry with me;
Wis 10:10 when the just man fled from his b anger,
Sir 29:27 for my b visit I need the room!"
Jer 12: 6 For even your own b,
35: 3 son of Habazziniah, his b and all his sons,
49:10 sons, and b, and neighbors,
Hos 2: 3 Say to your b, "Ammi,"
Mt 1: 2 Jacob, Jacob the father of Judah and his b.
1:11 his b at the time of the Babylonian exile.
4:18 along the Sea of Galilee he watched two b,
4:21 farther and caught sight of two other b,
5:47 And if you greet your b only,
7: 3 b eye when you miss the plank in your own?
7: 5 clearly to take the speck from your b eye.
12:46 his b appeared outside to speak with him.
12:47 "Your mother and your b are standing out
12:48 Who are my b?"
12:50 he said, "There are my mother and my b.
13:55 and James, Joseph, Simon, and Judas his b?
19:29 who has given up home, b or sisters,
20:24 this, became indignant at the two b.
22:25 Once there were seven b.
25:40 often as you did it for one of my least b,
28:10 to my b that they are to go to Galilee,
Mk 3:31 His mother and his b arrived,
3:32 b and sisters are outside asking for you."
3:33 in reply, "Who are my mother and my b?"
3:34 continued, "These are my mother and my b.
6:18 not right for you to live with your b wife."
10:29 no one who has given up home, b or sisters,
10:30 hundred times as many homes, b and sisters,
12:20 There were these seven b.
Lk 3:19 on the subject of Herodias, his b wife,
6:41 b eye when you miss the plank in your own?
6:42 enough to remove the speck from your b eye.
8:19 His mother and b came to be with him,
8:20 "Your mother and your b are standing
8:21 "My mother and my b are those who hear
14:12 or b or relatives or wealthy neighbors.
14:26 wife and his children, his b and sisters,
16:28 to my father's house where I have five b.
18:29 is no one who has left home or wife or b,
20:29 Now there were seven b.
21:16 be delivered up even by your parents, b,
22:32 You in turn must strengthen your b."
Jn 2:12 along with his mother and b [and his
7: 3 of Booths drew near, his b had this to say:
7: 5 not even his b had much confidence in him.)
7:10 once his b had gone up to the festival he
20:17 Rather, go to my b and tell them,
21:23 b that this disciple was not going to die.
Acts 1:14 and Mary the mother of Jesus, and his b.
1:15 Peter stood up in the center of the b;
1:16 B," he said, "the saying in Scripture
2:29 B, I can speak confidently to you about
2:37 the other apostles, "What are we to do, b?"
3:17 "Yet I know, my b,
6: 3 Look around among your own number, b,
7: 2 "My b! Fathers! Listen to me.
7:13 time, Joseph made himself known to his b,
7:26 'Friends, you are blood b.
9:30 When the b learned of this,
10:23 accompanied by some of the b from Joppa.
11: 1 the apostles and the b heard that Gentiles,
11:12 These six b came along with me,
11:29 to the relief of the b who lived in Judea.
12:17 "Report this to James and the b,"
13:15 B, if you have any exhortation to address
13:26 My b, children of the family of Abraham
13:38 You must realize, my b,
14: 2 and poisoned their minds against the b.
15: 1 from Judea and began to teach the b:
15: 3 Their story caused great joy among the b.
15: 7 B, you know well enough that from the
15:13 B, listen to me.
15:23 your b, send greetings to the brothers
15:33 the b to those who had commissioned them.
15:36 see how the b are getting on
15:40 by the b to the favor of the Lord.
16: 2 Since the b in Lystra and Iconium spoke
16:40 house, where they saw and encouraged the b;
17: 6 and some of the b to the town magistrates,
17:10 the b sent Paul and Silas off to Beroea.
17:14 The b sent Paul off directly on his way to
18:18 took leave of the b and sailed for Syria,
18:27 and so the b encouraged him by writing the
21: 7 greeted the b and spent the day with them.
21:17 the b there gave us a warm welcome.
22: 1 "My b and fathers,
23: 1 Then he said, B, to this day
23: 5 "My b, I did not know that he
23: 6 B, I am a Pharisee and was born a Pharisee.
28:14 Here we found some of the b,
28:15 Certain b from Rome who heard about us
28:17 "My b, I have done nothing
28:21 nor have any of the b arrived with a
Rom 1:13 My b, I want you to know
7: 1 my b (I am speaking to men who know what
7: 4 In the same way, my b,
8:12 We are debtors, then, my b—
8:29 the Son might be the first-born of many b.
9: 3 separated from Christ for the sake of my b,
10: 1 B, my heart's desire,
11:25 B, I do not want you to be ignorant of
12: 1 And now, b, I beg you
12:10 Love one another with the affection of b.
14:13 stumbling block or hindrance in your b way.
15:14 I am convinced, my b,
15:30 I beg you, b, for the sake of our Lord
16:14 Hermas, and the b who are with them;

BROTHERS—BROTHER'S (cont.)

16:17 *B,* I beg you to be on the watch against
1Cor 1:10 I beg you, *b,* in the name of our Lord
1:11 I have been informed, my *b,*
1:26 *B,* you are among those called.
2: 1 As for myself, *b,*
3: 1 *B,* the trouble was that I could not talk
4: 6 *B,* I have applied all this to myself and
6: 8 injure and cheat your very own *b.*
7:24 *B,* each of you should continue before God
7:29 I tell you, *b,* the time is short.
8:12 your *b* and wound their weak consciences,
9: 5 apostles and the *b* of the Lord and Cephas?
10: 1 *B,* I want you to remember this:
11:33 Therefore, my *b,* when you assemble
12: 1 Now, *b,* I do not want to leave you
14: 6 Just suppose, *b,* that I should come
14:20 *B,* do not be childish in your outlook.
14:26 What do we propose, *b?*
14:39 Set your hearts on prophecy, my *b,*
15: 1 *B,* I want to remind you of the gospel I
15: 6 that he was seen by five hundred *b* at once,
15:31 I swear to you, *b,*
15:50 This is what I mean, *b:*
15:58 steadfast and persevering, my beloved *b,*
16:11 I am expecting him with the *b.*
16:12 him strongly to go to you with the *b,*
16:20 All the *b* greet you.
2Cor 1: 8 *B,* we do not wish to leave you in the dark
8: 1 *B,* I should like you to know of the grace
8:23 our *b* too are apostles of the churches,
9: 3 I nonetheless send the *b* so that our
9: 5 necessary to exhort the *b* to go to you
11: 9 for the *b* who came from Macedonia supplied
11:26 city, in the desert, at sea, by false *b;*
13:11 And now, *b,* I must say good-bye.
Gal 1: 2 I and my *b* who are with me send
1:11 I assure you, *b,* the gospel I proclaimed
3:15 *B,* let me give you an everyday example.
4: 1 *B,* as long as a designated heir is not of
4:12 I beg you, *b,* to become like me
4:28 You, my *b,* are children of the promise,
4:31 Therefore, my *b,* we are not children
5:11 As for me, *b,* I am still preaching
5:13 My *b,* remember that you have been called
6: 1 My *b,* if someone is detected in sin,
6:18 *B,* may the favor of our Lord Jesus Christ
Eph 6:23 grant the *b* peace and love and faith.
Phil 1:12 My *b,* I want you to know
1:14 most of my *b* in Christ,
3: 1 For the rest, my *b,* rejoice in the Lord.
3:13 *B,* I do not think of myself as having
3:17 Be imitators of me, my *b.*
4: 1 For these reasons, my *b,*
4: 8 Finally, my *b,* your thoughts should
4:21 My *b* here send you theirs,
Col 1: 2 ones at Colossae, faithful *b* in Christ.
4:15 Give our best wishes to the *b* at Laodicea
1Thes 1: 4 We know, too, *b,* beloved of God,
2: 1 You know well enough, *b,*
2: 9 You must recall, *b,*
2:14 *B,* you have been made like the churches of
2:17 *B,* when we were orphaned by separation
3: 6 But now, *b,* since Timothy has returned
4: 1 Now, my *b,* we beg and exhort you
4:10 respect to all the *b* throughout Macedonia.
4:10 we exhort you to even greater progress, *b.*
4:13 clear about those who sleep in death, *b;*
5: 1 As regards specific times and moments, *b,*
5: 4 You are not in the dark, *b,*
5:12 We beg you, *b,* respect those among you
5:25 *B,* pray for us too.
5:26 Greet all the *b* with a holy embrace.
2Thes 1: 3 that we thank God unceasingly for you, *b,*
2: 1 our being gathered to him, we beg you, *b,*
2:13 God for you always, beloved *b* in the Lord,
2:15 Therefore, *b,* stand firm.
3: 1 For the rest, *b,* pray for us
3: 6 We command you, *b,*
3:13 never grow weary of doing what is right, *b.*
1Tm 5: 1 You should treat younger men as *b,*
6: 2 Those slaves whose masters are *b* in the
6: 2 their work are believers and beloved *b.*
2Tm 4:21 Claudia, and all the *b* send greetings.
Heb 2:11 he is not ashamed to call them *b,*
2:12 "I will announce your name to my *b,*
2:17 he had to become like his *b* in every way,
3: 1 holy *b* who share a heavenly calling,
3:12 Take care, my *b,*
8:11 teach their fellow citizens or their *b,*
10:19 *B,* since the blood of Jesus assures our
13:22 My *b,* I beg you to bear with this word
Jas 1: 2 My *b,* count it pure joy
1:16 Make no mistake about this, my dear *b.*
1:19 Keep this in mind, dear *b.*
2: 1 My *b,* your faith in our glorious Lord
2: 5 Listen, dear *b.*
2:14 My *b,* what good is it to profess faith
3: 1 many of you should become teachers, my *b;*
3:10 This ought not to be, my *b!*
3:12 A fig tree, *b,* cannot produce olives,
4:11 Do not, my *b,* speak ill of one another.
5: 7 Be patient, therefore, my *b,*
5: 9 Do not grumble against one another, my *b,*
5:10 in suffering hardship and in patience, *b,*
5:12 Above all else, my *b,* you must not swear
5:19 My *b,* the case may arise among you
1Pt 1:22 yourselves for a genuine love of your *b;*
2:17 Foster love for the *b,*
2Pt 1:10 make your call and election permanent, *b;*
3:17 You are forewarned, beloved *b.*
1Jn 3:12 deeds were wicked while his *b* were just.
3:13 No need, then, *b,* to be surprised
3:14 to life we know because we love the *b.*
3:16 we too must lay down our lives for our *b.*
3Jn 1: 3 great joy to have the *b* bear witness
1: 5 for the *b* even though they are strangers;
1:10 Not only does he refuse to welcome the *b*
Rv 6:11 of their fellow servants and *b* to be slain,
12:10 For the accuser of our *b* is cast out,
19:10 you and your *b* who give witness to Jesus.
22: 9 servant with you and your *b* the prophets

BROUGHT (801)

Gn 1:12 the earth *b* forth every kind of plant that
2:19 and he *b* them to the man to see what he
2:22 When he *b* her to the man, the man said:
4: 3 In the course of time Cain *b* an offering
4: 4 *b* one of the best firstlings of his flock.
11:31 and *b* them out of Ur of the Chaldeans,
14:13 came and *b* the news to Abram the Hebrew,
14:18 king of Salem, *b* out bread and wine,
15: 7 "I am the LORD who *b* you from Ur of the
15:10 He *b* him all these,
18: 4 Let some water be *b,*
19:17 As soon as they had been *b* outside,
20: 9 you should have *b* such monstrous guilt
24:32 water was *b* to bathe his feet and the feet
24:53 Then he *b* out objects of silver and gold
26:10 and you would have thus *b* guilt upon us!"
26:32 That same day Isaac's servants came and *b*
27:14 went and got them and *b* them to his mother;
27:25 he *b* him wine,
27:33 asked, "that hunted game and *b* it to me?
29:13 and kissing him, he *b* him to his house.
29:23 took his daughter Leah and *b* her to Jacob,
30:14 which he *b* home to his mother Leah.
30:20 she said, "God has *b* me a precious gift.
30:39 by the rods, and so they *b* forth streaked,
31:39 never *b* you an animal torn by wild beasts;
32:24 stream and had *b* over all his possessions,
33:11 Do accept the present I have *b* you;
34:30 "You have *b* trouble upon me by making me
37: 2 and he *b* his father bad reports about them.
39: 1 from the Ishmaelites who had *b* him there.
39: 3 him and *b* him success in whatever he did,
39:14 *b* in a Hebrew slave to make sport of us!
39:17 slave whom you *b* here broke in on me,
39:23 was with him and *b* success to all he did.
41:14 and they hurriedly *b* him from the dungeon.
43: 2 up all the rations they had *b* from Egypt,
43:21 We have now *b* it back.
43:22 We have *b* other money to procure food with.
43:24 then *b* the men inside Joseph's house.
43:26 him with the gifts they had *b* inside,
43:34 were *b* to them from Joseph's table,
44: 8 We even *b* back to you from the land of
46:32 have *b* with them their flocks and herds,
47: 7 Then Joseph *b* his father Jacob and
47:17 So they *b* their livestock to Joseph,
48:10 When Joseph *b* his sons close to him,
49:10 his legs, While tribute is *b* to him,
Ex 2:10 grew, she *b* him to Pharaoh's daughter,
5:21 You have *b* us into bad odor with Pharaoh
9:19 open fields to be *b* to a place of safety.
9:19 and is not *b* to shelter shall die
10: 8 So Moses and Aaron were *b* back to Pharaoh,
10:13 At dawn the east wind *b* the locusts.
12:17 I *b* your ranks out of the land of Egypt,
12:39 they had *b* out of Egypt was not leavened,
12:51 On that same day the LORD *b* the Israelites
13: 3 a strong hand that the LORD *b* you away.
13: 5 has *b* you into the land of the Canaanites,
13: 9 a strong hand the LORD *b* you out of Egypt.
13:11 has *b* you into the land of the Canaanites,
13:14 a strong hand the LORD *b* us out of Egypt,
13:16 a strong hand the LORD *b* us out of Egypt."
15:17 And you *b* them in and planted them on the
16: 6 LORD who *b* you out of the land of Egypt;
16:32 when I *b* you out of the land of Egypt."
18: 1 how the LORD had *b* Israel out of Egypt.
18:12 *b* a holocaust and other sacrifices to God,
19: 4 up on eagle wings and *b* you here to myself.
19: 8 Then Moses *b* back to the LORD the response
20: 2 God, who *b* you out of the land of Egypt,
22: 7 the owner of the house shall be *b* to God,
28: 1 Abihu, Eleazar and Ithamar, *b* to you,
29:46 God who *b* them out of the land of Egypt,
32: 1 Moses who *b* us out of the land of Egypt,
32: 3 off their earrings and *b* them to Aaron,
32: 4 Israel, who *b* you out of the land of Egypt."
32: 6 offered holocausts and *b* peace offerings.
32: 7 whom you *b* out of the land of Egypt,
32: 8 Israel, who *b* you out of the land of Egypt!'
32:11 whom you *b* out of the land of Egypt with
32:12 say, 'With evil intent he *b* them out,
32:23 Moses who *b* us out of the land of Egypt,
33: 1 whom you have *b* up from the land of Egypt,
35:21 *b* a contribution to the LORD for the
35:22 as their heart prompted them, *b* brooches,
35:23 skins dyed red or tahash skins, *b* them.
35:24 acacia wood for any part of the work, *b* it.
35:25 were expert spinners *b* hand-spun violet,
35:27 The princes *b* onyx stones and other gems
35:29 Every Israelite man and woman *b* to the
36: 3 Israelites had *b* for establishing the service
39:33 They then *b* to Moses the Dwelling,
40:21 He *b* the ark into the Dwelling and hung
Lv 1:15 *b* it to the altar where it is to be burned,
2: 2 When he has *b* it to Aaron's sons,
4:12 shall be *b* outside the camp to a clean
4:21 must also be *b* outside the camp and burned,
5:12 When he has *b* it to the priest,
6:23 blood has been *b* into the meeting tent
7:30 The fat is to be *b* in,
8:13 Moses likewise *b* forward Aaron's sons,
8:14 *b* forward the bullock for a sin offering,
8:18 He next *b* forward the holocaust ram,
8:22 Then he *b* forward the second ram,
9: 5 So they *b* what Moses had ordered.
9:12 When his sons *b* him the blood,
9:13 They then *b* him the pieces and the head of
9:15 he had the people's offering *b* up.
9:16 Then he *b* forward the holocaust,
9:18 When his sons *b* him the blood,
10:15 shall first be *b* in with the oblations,
10:18 *b* into the inmost part of the sanctuary,
11:45 *b* you up from the land of Egypt that I
13: 2 sore of leprosy, he shall be *b* to Aaron,
13: 9 with leprosy, he shall be *b* to the priest.
14: 2 He shall be *b* to the priest,
14:42 *b* and put in the place of the old stones,
16:27 was *b* into the sanctuary to make atonement,
19:36 God, who *b* you out of the land of Egypt.
24:11 So the people *b* him to Moses,
25:38 who *b* you out of the land of Egypt to give
25:42 Since those whom I *b* out of the land of
25:55 because I *b* them out of the land of Egypt,
26:13 who *b* you out of the land of the Egyptians
26:45 whom I *b* out of the land of Egypt under
Nm 5:19 immune to the curse *b* by this bitter water.
7: 3 The offering they *b* before the LORD
7:10 the princes *b* offerings before the altar
11:31 quail from the sea and *b* them down
12:14 only then may she be *b* back."
12:15 not start out again until she was *b* back.
14:13 you *b* out this people from among them.
15:25 they have *b* their holocaust as an oblation
15:33 Those who caught him at it *b* him to Moses
15:41 God who, as God, *b* you out of Egypt that I,
17:24 Moses thereupon *b* out all the staffs from
20: 4 Why have you *b* the LORD's community into
21: 5 *b* us up from Egypt to die in this desert,
23: 7 From Aram has Balak *b* me here,
23:11 was to curse my foes that I *b* you here;
23:14 So he *b* him to the lookout field on the
23:22 It is God who *b* him out of Egypt,
24: 8 It is God who *b* him out of Egypt,
25: 6 Yet a certain Israelite came and *b* in a
31:11 they had captured, and *b* the captives,
Dt 1:25 land, they *b* it down to us and reported,
1:27 LORD, has *b* us up out of the land of Egypt,
5: 6 God, who *b* you out of the land of Egypt,
5:15 *b* you from there with his strong hand and
6:12 LORD, who *b* you out of the land of Egypt,
6:21 *b* us out of Egypt with his strong hand,
6:23 He *b* us from there to lead us into the
7: 8 that he *b* you out with his strong hand
7:19 with which the LORD, your God, *b* you out.
8:14 God, who *b* you out of the land of Egypt,
8:15 who *b* forth water for you from the flinty
9: 4 the LORD has *b* me in to possess this land';
9:12 have *b* out of Egypt have become depraved;
9:26 and *b* out of Egypt with your strong hand.
9:28 people from whose land you have *b* us say,
9:28 he *b* them out to slay them in the desert.'
9:29 whom you have *b* out by your great power
13: 6 who *b* you out of the land of Egypt and
13:11 God, who *b* you out of the land of Egypt,
16: 1 Abib that he *b* you by night out of Egypt.
20: 1 God, who *b* you up from the land of Egypt,
21:19 *b* out to the elders at the gate of his home
26: 8 He *b* us out of Egypt with his strong hand
26:10 I have now *b* you the first fruits of the
26:14 I have not *b* any of it out as one unclean;
28:51 flocks, until they have *b* about your ruin.
29:24 when he *b* them out of the land of Egypt,
29:26 *b* on it all the imprecations listed in this
31:20 For when I have *b* them into the land
31:21 before I have *b* them into the land which I
Jos 2: 2 But a report was *b* to the king of Jericho
6:23 The spies entered and *b* out Rahab,
7:23 *b* them to Joshua and all the Israelites,
8:23 king, whom they took alive and *b* to Joshua.
9:12 still warm when we *b* it from home
10:23 *b* out to him from the cave the five kings,
14: 7 and I *b* back to him a conscientious report.
21:44 LORD *b* all their enemies under their power.

24: 3 But I *b* your father Abraham from the
24: 7 whom he *b* the sea so that it engulfed them.
24: 8 I *b* you into the land of the Amorites who
24:17 who *b* us and our fathers up out of the
24:32 which the Israelites had *b* up from Egypt,
Jgs 1: 7 He was *b* to Jerusalem, and there he died.
2: 1 "It was I who *b* you up from Egypt and led
3:30 *b* under the power of Israel at that time;
5:11 his just deeds that *b* freedom to Israel.
6: 8 I *b* you out of the place of slavery.
6:19 he *b* them out to him under the terebinth
7: 2 me and say, 'My own power *b* me the victory.'
8:28 Midian *b* into subjection by the Israelites;
9:57 God also *b* all their wickedness home to
11:33 *b* into subjection by the Israelites.
11:35 have struck me down and *b* calamity upon me.
12: 9 and he *b* in as wives for his sons thirty
14: 4 that this had been *b* about by the LORD,
14:11 they *b* thirty men to be his companions.
15:13 two new ropes and *b* him up from the cliff.
16: 8 So the lords of the Philistines *b* her
16:18 came and *b* up the money with them.
16:21 Then they *b* him down to Gaza and bound him
18: 3 *b* you here and what are you doing here?"
19: 3 She *b* him into her father's house,
21:12 they *b* them to the camp at Shiloh in the
Ru 1:21 but the LORD has *b* me back destitute.
1:21 me and the Almighty has *b* evil upon me?"
2:18 Next she *b* out and gave her what she had
1Sm 1:24 Once he was weaned, she *b* him up with her,
2:14 Whatever the fork *b* up,
4: 4 *b* from there the ark of the LORD of hosts,
5: 2 of God and *b* it into the temple of Dagon,
5: 6 he *b* upon the city a great and deadly
5: 9 But after it had been *b* there,
5:10 "Why have they *b* the ark of the God of
6: 9 he has *b* this great calamity upon us;
7: 1 *b* it into the house of Abinadab
8: 8 the day I *b* them up from Egypt to this day,
9:22 and his servant and *b* them to the room,
10:18 'It was I who *b* Israel up from Egypt and
10:27 They despised him and *b* him no present.
12: 6 *b* your fathers up from the land of Egypt.
13: 4 had *b* disgrace upon the Philistines;
14:34 *b* to the LORD whatever ox he had seized,
14:45 it was he who *b* Israel this great victory?
15:15 "They were *b* from Amalek.
15:20 I have *b* back Agag,
16:12 Jesse sent and had the young man *b* to them.
17:22 David entrusted what he had *b* to the
17:54 of the Philistine and *b* it to Jerusalem;
18:27 he *b* back their foreskins and counted them
19: 5 and the LORD *b* about a great victory for
19: 7 Jonathan then *b* David to Saul,
20: 8 bond between us, into which you *b* me:
20:38 picked up the arrow and *b* it to his master.
21: 9 I *b* along neither my sword nor my weapons,
25:27 which your maidservant has *b* for my lord,
25:35 her what she had *b* him and said to her:
27: 9 On his return he *b* these to Achish,
27:11 leave a man or woman alive to be *b* to Gath,
30: 7 When Abiathar *b* him the ephod,
30:11 found in the open country and *b* to David.
30:19 David *b* back everything.
31:12 wall of Beth-shan, and *b* them to Jabesh,
2Sm 1:10 from his arm and *b* them here to my lord."
1:13 young man who had *b* him the information,
2: 3 also *b* up his men with their families,
2: 8 son of Saul, and *b* him over to Mahanaim,
3:26 who *b* him back from the cistern of Sirah.
4: 8 They *b* the head of Ishbaal to David in
5: 2 who led the Israelites out and *b* them back.
6:10 not have the ark of the Lord *b*
6:17 The ark of the LORD was *b* in and set in
7:18 my house, that you have *b* me to this point?
7:21 you have *b* about this entire magnificent
8: 6 *b* David victory in all his undertakings.
8: 7 servants and *b* them to Jerusalem.
8:10 Hadoram also *b* with him articles of silver,
8:14 *b* David victory in all his undertakings.
9: 5 him and had him *b* from the house of Machir,
11:27 sent for her and *b* her into his house.
12:30 He *b* out immense booty from the city,
13:10 *b* them to her brother Amnon in the bedroom.
13:11 But when she *b* them to him to eat,
14: 2 to Tekoa and *b* from there a gifted woman,
14:10 says a word to you, have him *b* to me,
14:23 off to Geshur and *b* Absalom to Jerusalem.
15:24 and Abiathar *b* the ark of God to a halt
17:28 the Gileadite from Rogelim, *b* couches,
21:13 When he had *b* up from there the bones of
23:10 LORD *b* about a great victory on that day;
23:12 and the LORD *b* about a great victory.
23:16 they *b* it to David he refused to drink it,
1Kgs 1: 3 the Shunamite, whom they *b* to the king.
1:53 sent to have him *b* down from the altar,
2:40 in search of his servants, whom he *b* back.
3: 1 whom he married, he *b* to the City of David,
3:24 When they *b* the sword before him,
5: 8 each *b* his quota of barley and straw to
7:13 King Solomon had Hiram *b* from Tyre.
7:51 he *b* in the dedicated offerings of his
8: 6 The priests *b* the ark of the covenant of

8:15 and by his hand has *b* it to fulfillment.
8:16 the day I *b* my people Israel out of Egypt,
8:21 when he *b* them out of the land of Egypt."
8:24 by your own power, *b* it to fulfillment.
8:51 your inheritance, whom you *b* out of Egypt,
8:53 Moses when you *b* our fathers out of Egypt,
9: 9 *b* their fathers out of the land of Egypt;
9: 9 LORD has *b* down upon them all this evil.' "
9:28 and *b* back four hundred and twenty talents
10:11 also *b* from there a large quantity of
10:12 such wood was *b* or seen to the present day.
10:25 Each one *b* his yearly tribute:
12:15 for the LORD *b* this about to fulfill the
12:24 man return home, for I have *b* this about.' "
12:28 who *b* you up from the land of Egypt."
13:20 spoke to the prophet who had *b* him back,
13:22 not be *b* to the grave of your ancestors.' "
13:26 who had *b* him back from his journey said:
13:29 and *b* it back to the city to mourn over it
15:15 He *b* into the temple of the LORD his
17: 6 Ravens *b* him bread and meat in the morning,
17:23 Elijah *b* him down into the house from the
18:37 that you have *b* them back to their senses."
18:40 and Elijah had them *b* down to the brook
20:39 someone turned and *b* me a man and said,
2Kgs 2:20 When they had *b* it to him,
5: 1 through him the LORD had *b* victory to Aram.
5: 6 To the king of Israel he *b* the letter,
5:20 Aramean Naaman, not accepting what he *b*.
6: 6 the water, and *b* the iron to the surface.
9:28 His servants *b* him in a chariot to
10: 8 "They have *b* the heads of the princes,"
10:22 he had *b* out all the garments for them,
12: 5 that are *b* to the temple of the LORD
12: 5 are freely *b* to the temple of the LORD
12:10 that were *b* to the temple of the LORD.
12:14 None of the funds *b* to the temple of the
12:17 were not *b* to the temple of the LORD;
14:20 He was *b* back on horses and buried with
16:14 the LORD he *b* from the front of the temple
17: 7 who had *b* them up from the land of Egypt,
17:24 The king of Assyria *b* people from Babylon,
17:36 who *b* you up from the land of Egypt with
19:25 Now I have *b* it to pass:
20: 7 of figs to be *b* and applied to the boil,
20:20 conduit by which water was *b* into the city,
23: 8 He *b* in all the priests from the cities of
23:30 His servants *b* his body on a chariot from
25: 6 and *b* to Riblah to the king of Babylon,
25: 7 him with fetters, and had him *b* to Babylon.
25:20 *b* them to the king of Babylon at Riblah,
1Chr 2: 7 *b* trouble upon Israel by violating the ban.
5:26 half-tribe of Manasseh and *b* them to Halah,
9:28 tallying it as it was *b* in and taken out.
10:12 of Saul and his sons, and *b* them to Jabesh.
11:14 Thus the LORD *b* about a great victory.
11:19 For at the risk of their lives they *b* it;
15:28 Thus all Israel *b* back the ark of the
16: 1 They *b* in the ark of God and set it within
17:16 you should have *b* me as far as I have come?
18: 7 attendants and *b* them to Jerusalem.
20: 2 He also *b* out a great amount of booty from
22: 2 lived in the land of Israel be *b* together,
22: 4 *b* great stores of cedar logs to David,
22:19 sacred vessels may be *b* into the house
29:16 all this wealth that we have *b* together to
2Chr 1: 4 had *b* up from Kiriath-jearim to Jerusalem,
5: 1 he *b* in the dedicated offerings of his
5: 7 The priests *b* the ark of the covenant of
6: 4 and by his own hands *b* it to fulfillment.
6: 5 day I *b* my people out of the land of Egypt,
6:15 hand you have *b* it to fulfillment this day.
7:22 who *b* them out of the land of Egypt,
7:22 why he has *b* down upon them all this evil.' "
8:11 Solomon *b* the daughter of Pharaoh up from
8:18 *b* back from there four hundred
9:10 who *b* gold from Ophir also brought cabinet
9:12 him for, more than she had *b* to the king.
9:14 from travelers and what the merchants *b*.
9:14 the country, *b* gold and silver to Solomon.
11: 4 home, for what has occurred I have *b* about.' "
15:11 thousand sheep of the booty they had *b*.
15:18 He *b* into the house of God his father's
16: 2 Asa then *b* out silver and gold from the
17:11 Some of the Philistines *b* Jehoshaphat
17:11 and the Arabs also *b* him a flock of seven
19: 4 of Ephraim and *b* them back to the LORD,
20: 2 The message was *b* to Jehoshaphat:
22: 9 he was hiding in Samaria and *b* him to Jehu,
23: 8 Each *b* his men,
23:11 Then they *b* out the king's son,
24: 9 in the desert should be *b* to the LORD.
24:10 they *b* what was asked and cast it into the
24:11 Whenever the chest was *b* to the royal
24:14 they *b* the rest of the money to the king
25:12 also *b* back another ten thousand alive,
25:14 he *b* back with him the gods
25:23 at Beth-shemesh and *b* him to Jerusalem.
25:28 They *b* him back on horses and buried him
27: 5 They *b* the same to him also in the second
28: 5 of his people, whom they *b* to Damascus.
28: 8 them much plunder, which they *b* to Samaria.
28:15 They *b* them to Jericho,

28:19 the LORD had *b* Judah low because of Ahaz,
29:16 *b* out to the court of the LORD's house,
29:21 were *b* for a sin offering for the kingdom,
29:31 " Then the assembly *b* forward the
29:32 the assembly *b* forward was seventy oxen,
30:12 the power of God *b* it about that the
30:15 *b* holocausts into the house of the LORD.
31: 5 order was promulgated, the Israelites *b*,
31: 6 cities of Judah also *b* in tithes of oxen,
31: 6 these they *b* in and set out in heaps.
32:23 Many *b* gifts for the LORD to Jerusalem and
33:11 Therefore the LORD *b* against them the army
34: 9 *b* to the house of God which the Levites,
34:14 When they *b* out the money that had been
34:16 who *b* it to the king at the same time that
34:28 They *b* back this message to the king.
35:13 *b* them quickly to all the common people.
35:24 he had in reserve, and *b* him to Jerusalem,
36: 4 brother Jehoahaz away and *b* him to Egypt.
36:10 sent for him and had him *b* to Babylon,
36:17 Then he *b* up against them the king of the
36:18 his princes, all these he *b* to Babylon.
Ezr 1: 7 LORD *b* forth which Nebuchadnezzar
1: 8 them *b* forth by the treasurer Mithredath,
1:11 were *b* back from Babylon to Jerusalem.
4: 2 king of Assyria, who had us *b* here."
6: 5 and *b* to Babylon are to be sent back:
Neh 8: 2 the priest *b* the law before the assembly,
8:16 The people went out and *b* in branches with
9: 7 who *b* him out from Ur of the Chaldees,
9:18 is your God who *b* you up out of Egypt,'
9:23 and you *b* them into the land which you had
10:35 it is to be *b* to the house of our God by
12:27 were *b* to Jerusalem to celebrate
13:11 Then I *b* the Levites together and had them
13:12 Judah once more *b* in the tithes of grain,
13:18 *b* all this evil upon us and upon this city?
Tb 7: 1 So he *b* him to the house of Raguel,
7: 1 When he *b* them into his home,
7:13 Her mother *b* the scroll,
7:16 as she was told, and *b* the girl there.
8: 1 They *b* the young man out of the dining
10:12 as the ones who *b* you into the world.
11:15 that he had *b* back the money;
12: 2 half of all the wealth he *b* back with me.
12: 3 he *b* the money back with me:
12: 4 should receive half of all that he *b* back."
12: 5 wages half of all that you have *b* back,
14:10 did to Ahiqar, the very one who *b* him up:
Jdt 6:11 and *b* him out of the camp into the plain.
6:14 city, loosed him, and *b* him into Bethulia.
6:21 Uzziah *b* him from the assembly to his home,
11: 2 not despised me and *b* this upon themselves.
12: 2 amply supplied from the things I *b* with me."
12: 9 until her food was *b* to her toward evening.
13:17 *b* to nought the enemies of your people."
14:18 A single Hebrew woman has *b* disgrace on
Est 2: 8 many maidens *b* together to the stronghold
2: 8 Esther also was *b* in to the royal palace
2:19 the time the virgins had been *b* together,
2:20 as she had when she was being *b* up by him.
B: 4 in the kingdom, *b* it to our attention that,
B: 8 him say, "when you were *b* up in my charge;
4:13 to Mordecai, he had this reply *b* to her:
C:29 From the day I was *b* here till now,
6: 1 the chronicle of notable events be *b* in.
6: 8 reward there should be *b* the royal robe
E:18 governs all, *b* just punishment upon him.
1Mc 1: 6 who had been *b* up with him from his youth,
3:29 distress he had *b* upon the land
3:49 They *b* with them the priestly vestments,
3:49 and they *b* forward the nazirites,
4:49 new sacred vessels and *b* the lampstand,
5:23 and *b* them to Judea with great rejoicing.
6: 5 a messenger *b* him news that the armies
6:53 rescued from the Gentiles and *b* to Judea.
7:47 they *b* to Jerusalem and displayed there.
9:26 friends of Judas and *b* them to Bacchides,
9:37 was *b* to Jonathan and his brother Simon:
11:24 He *b* with him silver,
11:25 of his own nation *b* charges against him,
11:54 and *b* with him the young boy Antiochus,
13:32 Thus he *b* much evil on the land.
14: 3 he captured him and *b* him to Arsaces,
14:11 He *b* peace to the land,
14:29 have thus *b* great glory to their nation.
15:18 and they *b* with them a gold shield worth a
16:21 But someone ran ahead and *b* word to John
2Mc 4:20 was in fact applied by those who *b* it,
4:43 about this affair were *b* against Menelaus.
6: 4 They also *b* into the temple things that
7: 7 they *b* the second to be made sport of.
7:15 They next *b* forward the fifth brother and
7:18 After him they *b* the sixth brother.
7:27 nursed you for three years, *b* you up,
8:34 who had *b* the thousand slave dealers to
9:29 His foster brother Philip *b* the body home;
10: 7 *b* about the purification of his own Place.
13: 6 certain other crimes is *b* up there
Jb 4:12 For a word was stealthily *b* to me,
15: 7 or were you *b* forth before the hills?
20:22 to overflowing, he shall be *b* into straits,
40:20 the produce of the mountains is *b* to him,

BROUGHT (cont.)

42:11 all the evil which the LORD had *b* upon him;
Ps(s) 22:16 to the dust of death you have *b* me down.
30: 4 O LORD, you *b* me up from the nether world;
45:15 her the virgins of her train are *b* to you.
66:11 You have *b* us into a snare;
74:15 you *b* dry land out of the primeval waters.
78:13 He cleft the sea and *b* them through,
78:16 the crag and *b* the waters forth in rivers.
78:26 and by his power *b* on the south wind.
78:29 he had *b* them what they craved.
78:54 And he *b* them to his holy land,
78:71 the ewes he *b* him to shepherd Jacob,
79: 8 quickly come to us, for we are *b* very low.
90: 2 and the earth and the world were *b* forth,
105:40 They asked, and he *b* them quail,
106:43 counsels and were *b* low by their guilt.
107:30 and he *b* them to their desired haven.
107:39 dwindled and were *b* low through oppression,
116: 6 I was *b* low,
126: 1 When the LORD *b* back the captives of Zion,
136:11 And *b* out Israel from their midst,
142: 7 Attend to my cry, for I am *b* low indeed.
Prv 8:24 When there were no depths I was *b* forth,
8:25 place, before the hills, I was *b* forth;
Wis 10:14 Until she *b* him the scepter of royalty and
10:18 Red Sea and *b* them through the deep waters
16:10 for your mercy *b* the antidote to heal them.
19:10 young of animals the land *b* forth gnats,
Sir 6:12 But if you are *b* low,
30:23 For worry has *b* death to many,
42:15 At God's word were his works *b* into being;
45:19 He *b* down upon them a miracle,
46:18 He *b* low the rulers of the enemy and
47:20 You *b* dishonor upon your reputation,
47:23 Who *b* ruin to Ephraim and caused them to
48: 3 up the heavens and three times *b* down fire.
48: 5 You *b* a dead man back to life from the
48:13 beneath him flesh was *b* back into life.
48:17 fortified his city and had water *b* into it;
Is 2: 9 But man is abased, each one *b* low.
2:12 all that is high, and it will be *b* low;
2:17 will be abased, the arrogance of men *b* low,
5:15 Men shall be abased, each one *b* low,
9: 2 *b* them abundant joy and great rejoicing,
10:12 [But when the Lord has *b* to an end all his
10:33 are felled, and the lofty ones *b* low;
14:11 Down to the nether world your pomp is *b*,
18: 7 Then will gifts be *b* to the LORD of hosts
37:26 old I planned it, now I have *b* it to pass:
48: 7 Now, not long ago, they are *b* into being,
48:15 spoken, I have called him, I have *b* him,
49: 5 That Jacob may be *b* back to him
55:12 shall depart, in peace you shall be *b* back;
57: 6 you poured out libations, and *b* offerings.
59:16 So his own arm *b* about the victory,
60: 5 the wealth of nations shall be *b* to you.
63: 5 So my own arm *b* about the victory and my
63:11 Where is he who *b* up out of the sea the
66: 8 Can a country be *b* forth in one day,
Jer 2: 6 LORD who *b* us up from the land of Egypt,
2: 7 When I *b* you into the garden land to eat
7:22 the day I *b* them out of the land of Egypt,
10: 9 Silver strips *b* from Tarshish,
11: 4 day I *b* them up out of the land of Egypt,
11: 7 from the day I *b* them up out of the land
11: 8 till I *b* upon them all the threats of this
15: 8 I *b* against the mother of youths the
16:14 lives, who *b* the Israelites out of Egypt";
16:15 who *b* the Israelites out of the land of
20: 8 has *b* me derision and reproach all the day.
20:15 be the man who *b* the news to my father,
23: 7 who *b* the Israelites out of the land of
23: 8 who *b* the descendants of the house of
23:22 They would have *b* them back from evil ways
24: 1 the skilled workers, and *b* them to Babylon.—
27:16 LORD will be *b* back from Babylon soon now,"
27:22 To Babylon they shall be *b*,
32:21 you *b* your people Israel out of the land
32:42 I *b* upon this people all this great evil,
34:13 I *b* your fathers out of the land of Egypt,
35: 3 So I went and *b* Jaazaniah,
36:21 *b* it from the room of Elishama the scribe,
37:14 in custody and *b* him to the princes.
37:17 Once King Zedekiah had him *b* to his palace
38:22 be *b* out to the princes of Babylon's king,
39: 5 He was *b* to Riblah,
39:14 of Ahikam, son of Shaphan, to be *b* home.
40: 3 he has *b* about in deed what he threatened;
41:14 *b* away from Mizpah went over to Johanan,
41:16 had *b* away from Mizpah after he killed
44: 2 You have seen all the evil I *b* on
44:21 that the LORD remembered and *b* to mind,
51:10 The LORD has *b* to light our just cause;
52: 9 therefore, was arrested and *b* to Riblah,
52:11 and had him *b* to Babylon and kept in
52:26 *b* them to the king of Babylon at Riblah,
Lam 1:14 my neck, he has *b* my strength to its knees;
2: 2 He has *b* to the ground in dishonor her
2: 8 his hand *b* ruin,
2: 8 He *b* grief on wall and rampart till both
4: 5 *b* up in purple now cling to the ash heaps.
Bar 1: 9 as captives, and *b* them to Babylon.]

2: 2 He *b* down upon us evils so great that
2: 5 We are *b* low,
2: 9 over the evils, and *b* them home to us;
2:20 have *b* your wrath and anger down upon us,
2:24 our fathers *b* out from their burial places.
3:29 taken her, or *b* her down from the clouds?
4: 9 God has *b* great mourning upon me,
4:10 God has *b* upon my sons and daughters.
4:14 daughters, *b* upon them by the Eternal God.
4:15 He has *b* against them a nation from afar,
4:18 He who has *b* this evil upon you must
4:27 He who *b* this upon you will remember you.
4:29 For he who has *b* disaster upon you will,
6:17 a man *b* to execution for a crime
Ez 8: 3 and *b* me in divine visions to Jerusalem,
8: 7 Then he *b* me to the entrance of the court,
8:14 Then he *b* me to the entrance of the north
8:16 Then he *b* me into the inner court of the
11: 1 up and *b* me to the east gate of the temple.
11:24 Spirit lifted me up and *b* me back to the
12: 7 During the day I *b* out my baggage as
14:17 Or if I *b* the sword upon this country,
14:22 brought on Jerusalem [all that I have *b*
16:54 disgraced for all the comfort you *b* them.
17: 4 branch, And *b* it to a land of tradesmen,
20:10 land of Egypt and *b* them into the desert.
20:14 nations in whose presence I had *b* them out.
20:22 nations in whose presence I *b* them out.
20:28 when I had *b* them to the land I had sworn
20:28 [there they *b* their offensive offerings],
20:41 when I have *b* you from among the nations
22: 4 you have *b* on your day,
22:31 have *b* down their conduct upon their heads,
23:30 and harlotry have *b* these things upon you,
23:42 and these were men *b* in from the desert,
27: 3 that *b* the trade of the peoples to many a
27:26 the deep waters your oarsmen *b* you home,
28:18 And I have *b* out fire from your midst
30:11 shall be *b* in to devastate the land.
31:12 Its foliage was *b* low in all the valleys,
31:18 Yet you have been *b* down with the trees of
38: 8 which has been *b* forth from among the
40: 1 *b* me in divine visions to the land
40: 3 When he had *b* me there,
40: 4 been *b* here so that I might show it to you.
40:17 Then he *b* me to the outer court,
40:28 *b* me to the inner court by the south gate,
40:32 Then he *b* me to the gate facing the east,
40:35 Then he *b* me to the north gate,
40:48 Then he *b* me into the vestibule of the
41: 1 Then he *b* me to the nave and measured the
42:15 he *b* me out by way of the gate which faces
43: 5 lifted me up and *b* me to the inner court.
44: 1 Then he *b* me back to the outer gate of the
44: 4 Then he *b* me by way of the north gate to
46:19 Then he *b* me by the entrance which is on
47: 1 he *b* me back to the entrance of the temple,
47: 6 Then he *b* me to the bank of the river,
Dn 1:18 chamberlain *b* them before Nebuchadnezzar.
2:24 quickly *b* Daniel to the king and said,
3:13 who were promptly *b* before the king.
3:28 that you have *b* upon us and upon Jerusalem,
3:31 Therefore all you have *b* upon us,
3:37 *b* low everywhere in the world this day
4: 3 wise men of Babylon should be *b* before me
5: 2 in Jerusalem, to be *b* in so that the king,
5: 3 house of God in Jerusalem had been *b* in,
5: 7 Chaldeans, and astrologers to be *b* in.
5:13 Daniel was *b* into the presence of the king.
5:13 whom my father, the king, *b* from Judah?
5:15 the wise men and enchanters were *b* in to
5:23 had the vessels of his temple *b* before you,
6:17 to be *b* and cast into the lions' den.
6:18 had been *b* to block the opening of the den.
9:14 watch over the calamity and *b* it upon us.
11: 6 be given up, together with those who *b* her,
12: 7 of the holy people was *b* to an end,
13: 6 These men, to whom all *b* their cases,
13:56 one side, he ordered the other one to be *b*.
14:39 at once *b* Habakkuk back to his own place.
Hos 12:14 a prophet the LORD *b* Israel out of Egypt,
Jl 4: 5 *b* my precious treasures into your temples!
Am 2:10 was I who *b* you up from the land of Egypt,
3: 1 family that I *b* up from the land of Egypt.
3: 5 Is a bird *b* to earth by a snare when there
4:10 your nostrils I *b* the stench of your camps;
4:11 I *b* upon you such upheaval as when God
9: 7 the land of Egypt As I *b* the Philistines
Jon 2: 7 forever, But you *b* my life up from the pit,
Mi 6: 4 For I *b* you up from the land of Egypt,
Hg 1: 6 You have sown much, but have *b* in little;
1: 9 and what you *b* home,
Mt 8:16 on, they *b* him many who were possessed.
9: 2 *b* to him a paralyzed man lying on a mat.
9:32 *b* him a mute who was possessed by a demon.
10:18 will be *b* to trial before rulers and kings,
12:22 man who was *b* to him was blind and mute.
14:11 *b* in on a platter and given to the girl,
14:35 People *b* him all the afflicted,
16: 7 only, "This is because we have *b* no bread."
17:16 I have *b* him to your disciples but they
18:24 one was *b* in who owed him a huge amount.
19:13 children were *b* to him so that he could

21: 7 they *b* the ass and the colt and laid their
25: 3 in taking their torches, *b* no oil along,
Mk 1:32 drew on, they *b* him all who were ill,
4:22 covered so as to be *b* out into the open.
5:14 off and *b* the news to field and village,
5:36 that had been *b* and said to the official:
6:28 He *b* in the head on a platter and gave it
7:32 Some people *b* him a deaf man who had a
8:22 some people *b* him a blind man and begged
9:17 "I have *b* my son to you because he is
11: 7 They *b* the colt to Jesus and threw their
12:16 When they *b* one, he said to them,
15: 3 meanwhile, *b* many accusations against him.
15:22 When they *b* Jesus to the site of Golgotha
Lk 2:22 the couple *b* him up to Jerusalem so that
2:27 and when the parents *b* in the child Jesus
5:11 With that they *b* their boats to land,
7:18 The disciples of John *b* their teacher word
7:37 She *b* in a vase of perfumed oil and stood
8:17 that will not be known and *b* to light.
8:34 they took to their heels and *b* the news to
9:42 As he was being *b*, the spirit threw him
10:34 him on his own beast and *b* him to an inn,
18:15 They even *b* babies to be touched by him.
18:40 halted and ordered that he be *b* to him.
21:13 will be *b* to give witness on account of it.
22:54 and *b* him to the house of the high priest,
22:66 Once they had *b* him before their council,
23:14 "You have *b* this man before me as one who
24:22 group have just *b* us some astonishing news.
Jn 1:42 He *b* him to Jesus,
4: 5 and his journey *b* him to a Samaritan town
4:33 that someone has *b* him something to eat?"
8:44 He *b* death to man from the beginning,
10: 4 When he has *b* out [all] those that are his,
12: 3 Mary *b* a pound of costly perfume made from
12: 5 could have *b* three hundred silver pieces,
18:16 the woman at the gate, and then *b* Peter in.
18:28 *b* Jesus from Caiaphas to the praetorium.
19:13 then *b* Jesus outside and took a seat on a
Acts 3:18 God has *b* to fulfillment by this means
4: 7 They *b* Peter and John before them and
4:28 They have *b* about the very things which in
5:21 jail that the prisoners were to be *b* in.
5:26 went off with the guard and *b* them in,
6:13 There they *b* in false witnesses, who said:
7:21 adopted him and *b* him up as her own son.
7:40 Moses who *b* us out of the land of Egypt,
7:45 they *b* it into the land during the
10:21 What *b* you here?"
11:26 he had found him, he *b* him back to Antioch.
12:17 how the Lord had *b* him out of prison.
13: 1 had been *b* up with Herod the tetrarch),
13:23 *b* forth from this man's descendants Jesus,
13:29 *b* about all that had been written of him,
14:13 *b* oxen and garlands to the gates because
18:12 against Paul and *b* him before the bench.
19:24 and *b* in no little work for his craftsmen.
19:33 Some *b* out of the crowd Alexander,
19:37 you have *b* here are not temple-robbers.
20: 1 *b* his disciples together to encourage them.
21:28 He has even *b* Greeks into the temple area
21:29 that Paul had *b* him into the temple.
22: 3 in Cilicia, but I was *b* up in this city.
22:24 Paul to be *b* inside the headquarters.
22:30 *b* Paul down and made him stand before them.
23:15 have Paul *b* down to you on the pretext
23:20 to have Paul *b* down to the Sanhedrin,
23:27 I then had him *b* before the Sanhedrin,
23:33 to the governor and *b* Paul before him.
25: 6 on the bench and ordered Paul to be *b* in.
25:17 seat on the bench and ordered the man *b* in.
25:23 At Festus' command Paul was *b* in.
25:26 That is why I have *b* him before all of you,
28:10 sail they *b* us provisions for our needs.
Rom 3: 9 We have already *b* the charge against Jews
5:16 upon one offense and *b* condemnation,
5:16 came after many offenses and *b* acquittal.
5:18 a single offense *b* condemnation to all men,
5:18 righteous act *b* all men acquittal and life.
7:10 that should have led to life *b* me death.
2Cor 5:13 and when we are *b* back to our senses,
7:11 What a measure of holy zeal it has *b* you,
Gal 4:24 Sinai, and *b* forth children to slavery;
Eph 2: 5 great love for us he *b* us to life with Christ
2:13 been *b* near through the blood of Christ.
Phil 4:12 I am experienced in being *b* low,
Col 1:13 *b* us into the kingdom of his beloved Son.
1Tm 5:10 Has she *b* up children?
6: 7 We *b* nothing into this world,
2Tm 1:10 has *b* life and immortality into clear light
Heb 7:19 for the law *b* nothing to perfection.
13:11 animals whose blood is *b* into the sanctuary
13:20 who *b* up from the dead the great Shepherd
1Pt 2:24 his own body he *b* your sins to the cross,
2Pt 2: 5 he *b* down that flood on the godless earth.
3: 5 all *b* into being by the word of God.
1Jn 4:12 us, and his love is *b* to perfection in us.
4:17 Our love is *b* to perfection in this,
Rv 7:15 was this that *b* them before God's throne:
21:26 and wealth of the nations shall be *b* there,

BROW (10)

Gn 49:26 on the *b* of the prince among his brothers.
Dt 33:16 the *b* of the prince among his brothers,
1Sm 17:49 The stone embedded itself in his *b*,
Jb 16:15 my skin, and have laid my *b* in the dust.
19: 9 my glory, and taken the diadem from my *b*.
Jer 3: 3 But because you have a harlot's *b*,
48:45 It consumes the *b* of Moab,
Ez 3: 7 is stubborn of *b* and obstinate in heart.
3: 8 theirs, and your *b* as stubborn as theirs,
Lk 4:29 leading him to the *b* of the hill on which

BROWS (1)

Nm 24:17 Israel, That shall smite the *b* of Moab,

BROWSE (4)

Sg 4: 5 young of a gazelle that *b* among the lilies.
6: 2 To *b* in the garden and to gather lilies.
Is 11: 6 calf and the young lion shall *b* together,
27:10 wilderness, where calves shall *b* and lie.

BROWSES (2)

Sg 2:16 me and I to him; he *b* among the lilies,
6: 3 he *b* among the lilies.

BRUISE (1)

Jer 30:12 Incurable is your wound, grievous your *b*;

BRUISED (4)

Lv 22:24 One that has its testicles *b* or crushed or
Is 42: 3 A *b* reed he shall not break,
Mt 12:20 The *b* reed he will not crush;
Acts 19:16 that they fled from his house naked and *b*.

BRUISES (1)

Is 30:26 he will heal the *b* left by his blows.

BRUISING (1)

Gn 4:23 a man for wounding me, a boy for *b* me.

BRUSH (2)

Ez 21:22 shall *b* one hand against the other and
Gal 4:14 you did not despise or *b* aside in disgust.

BRUSHED (1)

Is 44:22 I have *b* away your offenses like a cloud,

BRUSHES (1)

2Cor 11:23 worse beatings and frequent *b* with death.

BRUSHING (4)

Jb 34:37 rebellion to his sin by *b* off our arguments
Is 33:15 *B* his hands free of contact with a bribe,
Ez 21:19 prophesy, *b* one hand against the other:
22:13 I am *b* one hand against the other because

BRUSHWOOD (6)

Jgs 9:48 his axe in his hand, and cut down some *b*.
9:49 So all the men likewise cut down *b*,
Ps(s) 120: 4 arrows of a warrior with fiery coals of *b*.
Is 33:12 like *b* cut down for burning in the fire.
64: 1 As when *b* is set ablaze,
Acts 28: 3 fire with a bundle of *b* he had collected,

BRUTAL (1)

2Tm 3: 3 implacable, slanderous, licentious, *b*,

BRUTALLY (1)

Ez 34: 4 but you lorded it over them harshly and *b*.

BRUTE (4)

Ps(s) 73:22 I was like a *b* beast in your presence.
Sir 22:12 stupid man, be not the companion of a *b*;
2Pt 2:12 *b* animals born to be caught and destroyed.
Jude 1:10 they know by instinct, like *b* animals.

BUBBLE (1)

Prv 21: 6 tongue is chasing a *b* over deadly snares.

BUCKET (2)

Is 40:15 the nations count as a drop in the *b*,
Jn 4:11 do not have a *b* and this well is deep.

BUCKLE (2)

1Mc 10:89 He sent him a gold *b*,
11:58 in royal purple, and to wear a gold *b*.

BUCKLER (6)

1Kgs 10:17 (three minas of gold went into each *b*);
2Chr 9:16 hundred shekels of gold going into each *b*;
17:17 two hundred thousand armed with bow and *b*.
Ps(s) 35: 2 Take up the shield and *b*,
91: 4 his faithfulness is a *b* and a shield.
Jer 46: 3 Prepare shield and *b*!

BUCKLERS (13)

1Kgs 10:17 three hundred *b* of beaten gold
2Chr 9:16 shield, and three hundred *b* of beaten gold,
12: 9 including the gold *b* that Solomon had made.
12:10 replace them, King Rehoboam made bronze *b*,
14: 7 Benjamin who carried *b* and were archers,
23: 9 shields and *b* of king David which were in
26:14 for the entire army *b*,
Neh 4:10 the other half, armed with spears, *b*,
Sg 4: 4 A thousand *b* hang upon it,
Ez 23:24 Shields, *b*, and helments they shall array
27:11 they hung their *b* all around on your walls,
38: 4 a great horde with *b* and shields,
39: 9 [shields and *b* bows and arrows,

BUCKLING (1)

1Kgs 20:11 'It is not for the man who is *b* his armor

BUCKTHORN (3)

Jgs 9:14 Then all the trees said to the *b*,
9:15 But the *b* replied to the trees,
9:15 the *b* and devour the cedars of Lebanon.'

BUD (5)

Ex 9:31 the barley was in ear and the flax in *b*.
Sir 24:17 I *b* forth delights like the vine,
Is 11: 1 and from his roots a *b* shall blossom.
45: 8 Let the earth open and salvation *b* forth;
60:21 the land, They, the *b* of my planting,

BUDDED (1)

Gn 40:10 It had barely *b* when its blossoms came out,

BUDDING (1)

Lk 21:30 You observe them when they are *b*,

BUDGE (1)

Mt 23: 4 will not lift a finger to *b* them.

BUDGED (1)

Acts 27:41 The bow stuck fast and could not be *b*,

BUDS (1)

Sg 7:13 If the *b* have opened, if the pomegranates

BUFFET (1)

Jb 30:21 mercy and with your strong hand you *b* me.

BUFFETED (1)

Mt 7:25 came and the winds blew and *b* his house.

BUFFETS (1)

Is 50: 6 face I did not shield from *b* and spitting.

BUFFOON (1)

Jgs 16:25 prison, and he played the *b* before them.

BUGLES (1)

1Cor 14: 8 If the *b* sound is uncertain,

BUILD (141)

Gn 6:15 This is how you shall *b* it:
11: 4 let us *b* ourselves a city and a tower with
35: 1 Settle there and *b* an altar there to the
35: 3 and I will *b* an altar there to the God who
Ex 1:11 Thus they had to *b* for Pharaoh the supply
20:25 of stone for me, do not *b* it of cut stone,
Nm 23: 1 Balaam said to Balak, *B* me seven altars,
23:29 then said to him, "Here *b* me seven altars;
32:16 only to *b* sheepfolds here for our flocks,
32:24 *B* the towns, then, for your families,
Dt 6:10 fine, large cities that you did not *b*,
16:21 of the LORD, your God, which you will *b*;
20:20 cutting them down to *b* siegeworks with
22: 8 "When you *b* a new house,
25: 9 who will not *b* up his brother's family!'
27: 5 with plaster, you shall also *b* to the LORD,
28:30 Though you *b* a house,
Jgs 6:26 shall *b*, instead, the proper kind of altar
2Sm 7: 5 Should you *b* me a house to dwell in?
7:13 It is he who shall *b* a house for my name.
7:27 to your servant, 'I will *b* a house for you.'
24:18 "Go up and *b* an altar to the LORD on the
24:21 floor from you to *b* an altar to the LORD,
1Kgs 2:36 *B* yourself a house in Jerusalem and live
5:17 could not *b* a temple in honor of the LORD,
5:19 purpose to *b* a temple in honor of the LORD,
5:19 place who shall *b* the temple in my honor.'
6:38 Thus it took Solomon seven years to *b* it.
8:17 to *b* a temple to the honor of the LORD,
8:18 him, 'In wishing to *b* a temple to my honor,
8:19 not be you, however, who will *b* the temple;
8:19 you, he shall *b* the temple to my honor.'
9:15 in order to *b* up the temple of the LORD,
2Kgs 6: 2 apiece we can *b* ourselves a place to live."
1Chr 14: 1 and cedar wood to *b* him a house.
17: 4 who are to *b* a house for me to dwell in.
17:10 you that I, the LORD, will *b* you a house;
17:12 He it is who shall *b* me a house,
17:25 your servant that you will *b* him a house,
21:22 that I may *b* on it an altar to the LORD.
22: 6 commanded him to *b* a house for the LORD,
22: 7 *b* a house myself for the honor of the LORD,
22: 8 You may not *b* a house in my honor,
22:10 It is he who shall *b* a house in my honor;
22:19 Proceed to *b* the sanctuary of the LORD God,
28: 2 It was my purpose to *b* a house of repose
28: 2 and I was preparing to *b* it.
28: 3 to me, 'You may not *b* a house in my honor,
28: 6 Solomon who shall *b* my house and my courts,
28:10 chosen you to *b* a house as his sanctuary.
29:16 brought together to *b* you a house in honor
29:19 *b* the castle for which I have made
2Chr 2: 2 him cedars to *b* a house for his dwelling,
2: 3 to *b* a house for the honor of the LORD,
2: 4 And the house I intend to *b* must be large,
2: 5 Yet who is really able to *b* him a house,
2: 5 And who am I that I should *b* him a house,
2: 8 I intend to *b* must be lofty and wonderful.
2:11 who will *b* a house for the LORD and also a
3: 1 Then Solomon began to *b* the house of the
3: 2 He began to *b* in the second month of the
6: 7 to *b* a temple to the honor of the LORD,
6: 8 'In wishing to *b* a temple to my honor,
6: 9 However, you shall not *b* the temple;
6: 9 you will beget shall *b* the temple to my
14: 6 "Let us *b* these cities and surround them
36:23 charged me to *b* him a house in Jerusalem,
Ezr 1: 2 charged me to *b* him a house in Jerusalem,
1: 5 up to *b* the house of the LORD in Jerusalem.
4: 2 and said to them, "Let us *b* with you,
4: 3 to *b* with us a house for our God,
4: 3 God, but we alone must *b* it for the LORD,
5: 2 again to *b* the house of God in Jerusalem,
5: 3 you to *b* this house and raise this edifice?
5: 9 you to *b* this house and raise this edifice?'
Neh 3:38 We, however, continued to *b* the wall,
Tb 13:12 forever blessed are all those who *b* you up.
1Mc 1:47 to *b* pagan altars and temples and shrines,
10:10 and began to *b* and restore the city.
10:11 He ordered the workmen to *b* the walls and
Jb 19:12 they *b* up their road to attack me,
30:12 they *b* their approaches for my ruin.
39:27 fly up at your command to *b* his nest aloft?
Ps(s) 28: 5 may he tear them down and not *b* them up.
104:17 In them the birds *b* their nests;
127: 1 LORD *b* the house, they labor in vain who *b*
Eccl 3: 3 a time to tear down, and a time to *b*.
Sg 8: 9 a wall, we will *b* upon it a silver parapet;
Wis 9: 8 You have bid me *b* a temple on your holy
Sir 40:26 Wealth and vigor *b* up confidence,
49: 7 and destroy, and then to *b* and to plant.
Is 9: 9 have fallen, but we will *b* with cut stone;
27:11 and women shall come to *b* a fire with them.
57:14 *B* up, build up, prepare the way,
62:10 Build up, *b* up the highway,
65:21 They shall live in the houses they *b*,
65:22 shall not *b* houses for others to live in,
66: 1 What kind of house can you *b* for me;
Jer 1:10 destroy and to demolish, to *b* and to plant.
18: 9 to *b* up and plant a nation or a kingdom.
22:14 says, "I will *b* myself a spacious house,
24: 6 bring them back to this land, to *b* them up,
29: 5 *B* houses to dwell in;
29:28 *b* houses to live in;
31:28 I will watch over them to *b* and to plant,
35: 7 *B* no house and sow no seed;
35: 9 We *b* no houses to live in;
42:10 quietly in this land I will *b* you up,
49:16 Though you *b* your nest high as the eagle,
Ez 4: 2 *b* a tower, lay out a ramp, pitch camps
13: 5 nor did you *b* a wall about the house of
21:27 to cast up a ramp, to *b* a siege tower.
22:30 who could *b* a wall or stand in the breach
Mi 3:10 Who *b* up Zion with bloodshed,
Zep 1:13 They will *b* houses,
Hg 1: 8 and *b* the house That I may take pleasure
Zec 5:11 *b* a temple for it in the land of Shinar;
6:12 and he shall *b* the temple of the LORD.
6:13 Yes, he shall *b* the temple of the LORD,
6:15 shall come and *b* the temple of the LORD,
Mal 1: 4 They indeed may *b*, but I will tear down,
Mt 13:32 sky come and *b* their nests in its branches."
16:18 and on this rock I will *b* my church,
Mk 4:32 birds of the sky to *b* nests in its shade."
Lk 11:47 You *b* the tombs of the prophets,
12:18 pull down my grain bins and *b* larger ones.
14:28 If one of you decides to *b* a tower,
14:30 man began to *b* what he could not finish.'
Jn 2:20 "This temple took forty-six years to *b*,
Acts 7:49 What kind of house can you *b* me?
Rom 15:20 for I did not want to *b* on a foundation
1Cor 3:12 ones *b* on this foundation with gold,
14:12 to be rich in those that *b* up the church.
2Cor 12:19 Christ, I have done everything to *b* you up,
13:10 authority to *b* up rather than to destroy.
Gal 2:18 to *b* up the very things I had demolished,
Eph 4:12 the faithful to *b* up the body of Christ,
1Tm 6:19 they *b* a secure foundation for the future,

BUILDER (2)

Neh 4:12 Every *b*, while he worked
Is 62:5 marries a virgin, your *B* shall marry you;

BUILDERS (12)

1Kgs 5:32 Solomon's and Hiram's *b*,
2Kgs 12:12 and *b* working in the temple of the LORD,
22:5 then pay them out to the carpenters, *b*,
Ezr 3:10 When the *b* had laid the foundation of the
Neh 3:37 for they insulted the *b* to their face!
Ps(s) 118:22 the *b* rejected has become the cornerstone.
Ez 27:4 In the midst of the sea your *b* placed you,
Mt 21:42 'The stone which the *b* rejected has become
Mk 12:10 *b* has become the keystone of the structure.
Lk 20:17 'The stone which the *b* rejected has become
Acts 4:11 the *b* which has become the cornerstone.'
1Pt 2:7 the *b* rejected that became a cornerstone."

BUILDING (66)

Gn 11:8 the earth, and they stopped *b* the city.
Jos 22:16 against him by *b* an altar of your own!
22:19 by *b* an altar of your own in addition to
22:26 our interests by *b* this altar of our own:
22:29 from the LORD by *b* an altar for holocaust,
1Kgs 3:1 David, until he should finish *b* his palace,
5:32 the wood and stones for *b* the temple.
6:12 "As to this temple you are *b*—
6:14 When Solomon finished *b* the temple,
8:16 Israel for the *b* of a temple to my honor;
9:1 Solomon finished *b* the temple of the LORD,
11:27 King Solomon was *b* Millo,
2Kgs 10:27 the stele of Baal, tore down the *b*,
23:11 the eunuch, which was in the large *b*.
25:9 every large *b* was destroyed by fire.
1Chr 22:2 out stone blocks for *b* the house of God.
22:11 in *b* the house of the LORD your God,
26:18 as for the large *b* on the west,
26:18 four at the highway and two at the large *b*.
28:11 pattern of the portico and of the *b* itself,
2Chr 1:18 Solomon gave orders for the *b* of a house
3:3 down by Solomon for *b* the house of God:
3:6 also decorated the *b* with precious stones.
3:12 in length, extended to a wall of the *b*,
3:15 In front of the *b* he set two columns
5:13 the *b* of the LORD's temple was filled with
6:5 Israel for the *b* of a temple to my honor,
20:36 with him in *b* ships to sail to Tarshish;
36:17 their young men in their own sanctuary *b*,
Ezr 4:1 the exiles were *b* a temple for the LORD,
4:4 people of Judah so as to keep them from *b*.
5:4 names of the men who are *b* this structure?"
5:16 Since that time the *b* has been going on,
6:14 Jews continued to make progress in the *b*,
6:14 They finished the *b* according to the
Neh 2:18 They replied, "Let us be up and *b*!"
3:35 "It is a rubble heap they are *b*.
6:10 in the house of God, inside the temple *b*;
Jdt 4:11 themselves in front of the temple *b*,
1Mc 3:56 He proclaimed that those who were *b* houses,
10:45 Likewise the cost of *b* the walls of
10:45 it all around, and of *b* walls in Judea,
12:35 he made plans for *b* strongholds in Judea,
12:37 therefore worked together on *b* up the city,
Jer 43:9 the entrance to the royal *b* in Tahpanhes,
52:13 every large *b* he destroyed with fire.
Ez 11:3 we not," they say, "be *b* houses soon?
16:31 *b* your platform at every street corner and
28:26 security, *b* houses and planting vineyards.
41:12 The *b* fronting the free area on the west
41:12 of the *b* was five cubits thick all around,
41:13 area, together with the *b* and its walls,
41:15 He measured the *b* which lay the length of
42:1 area and which were also across from the *b*.
42:10 area and the *b* there were also chambers,
Mi 7:11 It is the day for *b* your walls;
Zec 8:9 of hosts was laid for the *b* of the temple.
Mt 23:35 between the temple *b* and the altar.
Lk 6:48 be likened to the man who, in *b* a house,
Acts 7:47 who constructed the *b* for that house.
Rom 15:2 so as to do him good by *b* up his spirit.
1Cor 3:9 while you are his cultivation, his *b*.
3:10 do, and now someone else is *b* upon it.
3:14 If the *b* a man has raised on this
3:15 if a man's *b* burns,
Eph 2:20 You form a *b* which rises on the foundation

BUILDINGS (8)

1Kgs 7:9 All these *b* were of fine stones,
2Chr 34:11 beams and rafters of the *b* which the kings
Ps(s) 122:7 be within your walls, prosperity in your *b*.
Mt 24:1 out to him the *b* of the temple area.
24:2 "Do you see all these *b*?
Mk 13:1 huge blocks of stone and the enormous *b*!"
13:2 Jesus said to him, "You see these great *b*?
Acts 7:48 does not dwell in *b* made by human hands,

BUILDS (12)

Jb 27:18 He *b* his house as of cobwebs,
Prv 14:1 Wisdom *b* her house,
17:19 he who *b* his gate high courts disaster.
Sir 14:26 Who *b* his nest in her leafage,
21:8 He who *b* his house with another's money
34:23 If one man *b* up and another tears down,
Jer 22:13 Woe to him who *b* his house on wrong,
Hb 2:12 Woe to him who *b* a city by bloodshed,
1Cor 3:10 however, must be careful how he *b*.
14:4 *b* up himself, but he who prophesies builds
Eph 4:16 supporting ligament, *b* itself up in love.

BUILT (208)

Gn 2:22 The LORD God then *b* up into a woman the
8:20 Then Noah *b* an altar to the LORD,
10:11 went forth to Asshur, where he *b* Nineveh,
11:5 the city and the tower that the men had *b*.
12:7 So Abram *b* an altar there to the LORD who
12:8 He *b* an altar there to the LORD and
13:4 the site where he had first *b* the altar;
13:18 There he *b* an altar to the LORD.
22:9 Abraham *b* an altar there and arranged the
26:25 So he *b* an altar there and invoked the
33:17 There he *b* a home for himself and made
35:7 he *b* an altar and named the place Bethel,
Ex 1:21 feared God, he *b* up families for them.
17:15 Moses also *b* an altar there,
32:5 *b* an altar before the calf and proclaimed,
Nm 13:22 been *b* seven years before Zoan in Egypt.]
23:14 where he *b* seven altars and offered a
32:36 and Beth-haran, and they *b* sheepfolds.
Dt 8:12 and have *b* fine houses and lived in them,
20:5 'Is there anyone who has *b* a new house and
Jos 2:15 she lived in a house *b* into the city wall.
8:30 Later Joshua *b* an altar to the LORD,
11:13 fire any of the cities *b* on raised sites,
22:10 they *b* there at the Jordan a conspicuously
22:11 half-tribe of Manasseh had *b* an altar
22:23 and if we have *b* an altar of our own to
24:13 not tilled and cities which you had not *b*,
Jgs 1:26 where he *b* a city and called it Luz,
6:24 So Gideon *b* there an altar to the LORD and
6:28 bullock offered on the altar that was *b*.
21:4 Early the next day the people *b* an altar
Ru 4:11 who between them *b* up the house of Israel.
1Sm 7:17 judged Israel and *b* an altar to the LORD.
14:35 and Saul *b* an altar to the LORD
14:35 the first time he *b* an altar to the LORD.
2Sm 5:9 he *b* up the area from Millo to the palace.
5:11 and masons, who *b* a palace for David.
7:7 Why have you not *b* me a house of cedar?'
24:25 Then David *b* an altar there to the LORD,
1Kgs 3:2 temple had been *b* to the name of the LORD.
6:2 *b* for the LORD was sixty cubits long,
6:5 an annex of several stories was *b*.
6:7 was *b* of stone dressed at the quarry,
6:9 When the temple was *b* to its full height,
6:10 was *b* all along the outside of the temple,
7:2 He *b* the hall called the Forest of Lebanon
7:7 He also *b* the vestibule of the throne
7:8 tribunal was *b* for Pharaoh's daughter,
8:13 I have truly *b* you a princely house,
8:20 and I have *b* this temple to honor the LORD,
8:27 how much less this temple which I have *b*!
8:43 which I have *b* is dedicated to your honor.
8:44 and the temple I have *b* in your honor,
8:48 and the temple I have *b* in your honor,
9:3 consecrated this temple which you have *b*;
9:10 during which Solomon *b* the two houses,
9:19 Solomon decided should be *b* in Jerusalem,
9:24 which he had built for her, Solomon *b* Millo.
9:25 on the altar which he had *b* to the LORD,
9:26 King Solomon also *b* a fleet at Ezion-geber,
10:4 great wisdom, the palace he had *b*,
11:7 Solomon then *b* a high place to Chemosh,
12:25 Jeroboam *b* up Shechem in the hill country
12:25 Then he left it and *b* up Penuel.
12:31 He also *b* temples on the high places and
12:32 Bethel priests of the high places he had *b*.
12:33 Jeroboam ascended the altar he *b* in Bethel
14:23 They, too, *b* for themselves high places,
15:22 King Asa *b* Geba of Benjamin and Mizpeh.
15:23 and accomplishments, and the cities he *b*,
16:24 for two silver talents and *b* upon the hill,
16:24 naming the city he *b* Samaria after Shemer,
16:32 the temple of Baal which he *b* in Samaria,
18:32 He *b* an altar in honor of the LORD with
22:39 the ivory palace and all the cities he *b*,
2Kgs 15:35 *b* the Upper Gate of the temple of the LORD.
16:11 Uriah the priest *b* an altar according to
16:18 had been *b* in the temple for a throne,
17:9 *b* high places in all their settlements,
21:4 He *b* altars in the temple of the LORD,
23:13 king of Israel, had *b* in honor of Astarte,
23:15 at Bethel, the high place *b* by Jeroboam,
25:1 around it, and *b* siege walls on every side.
1Chr 5:36 in the temple Solomon *b* in Jerusalem.
6:17 *b* the temple of the LORD in Jerusalem,
7:24 who *b* lower and upper Beth-horon and
8:12 who *b* Ono and Lod with its nearby towns,
15:1 David *b* houses for himself in the City of
17:6 'Why have you not *b* me a house of cedar?'
21:26 David then *b* an altar there to the LORD,
21:29 the LORD, which Moses had *b* in the desert,
22:5 but the house that is to be *b* for the LORD
22:19 into the house *b* in honor of the LORD."
2Chr 6:2 truly *b* you a princely house and dwelling,
6:10 have *b* the temple to the honor of the LORD,
6:18 how much less this temple which I have *b*!
6:33 which I have *b* is dedicated to your honor.
6:34 and of the house I have *b* to your honor,
6:38 of the house which I have *b* to your honor,
8:1 *b* the house of the LORD and his own house,
8:2 *b* up the cities which Huram had given him,
8:4 He *b* Tadmor in the desert region and all
8:4 the supply cities, which he *b* in Hamath.
8:5 He *b* Upper Beth-horon and Lower Beth-horon,
8:6 Solomon decided should be *b* in Jerusalem,
8:11 David to the palace which he had *b* for her,
8:12 LORD which he had *b* in front of the porch,
9:3 Solomon's wisdom, the palace he had *b*,
11:5 Jerusalem and *b* fortified cities in Judah.
11:6 He *b* up Bethlehem,
14:5 He *b* fortified cities in Judah,
14:6 So they *b* and prospered.
17:12 *b* strongholds and store cities in Judah.
20:8 and they *b* in it a sanctuary to your honor,
20:36 the fleet was *b* at Ezion-geber.
26:6 Jabneh and Ashdod [and *b* cities in the
26:9 *b* towers in Jerusalem at the Corner Gate,
26:10 He *b* towers in the desert and dug numerous
26:15 He also *b* machines in Jerusalem,
27:3 He *b* the upper gate of the LORD's house
27:4 he *b* cities in the hill country of Judah,
32:5 towers upon it, and *b* another wall outside.
32:29 He *b* cities for himself,
33:4 He even *b* altars in the temple of the LORD,
33:5 he *b* altars to the whole host of heaven in
33:14 Afterward he *b* an outer wall for the City
33:14 he *b* it very high.
33:15 altars he had *b* on the mount
33:19 the sites where he *b* high places and
35:3 the holy ark in the house *b* by Solomon,
Ezr 5:11 rebuilding the house *b* here long years ago,
5:11 ago, which a great king of Israel *b* and finished.
Neh 12:29 *b* themselves settlements about Jerusalem).
Tb 1:4 had been *b* and consecrated for all
13:16 shall be *b* with sapphire and emerald,
13:16 towers of Jerusalem shall be *b* with gold,
Jdt 1:2 this city he *b* a wall of blocks of stone,
1:4 gateway he *b* to a height of seventy cubits,
1Mc 1:14 Thereupon they *b* a gymnasium in Jerusalem
1:33 they *b* up the City of David with a high,
1:54 cities of Judah they *b* pagan altars.
4:47 law, and *b* a new altar like the former one.
4:60 At that time they *b* high walls and strong
6:7 which he had *b* upon the altar in Jerusalem;
9:50 Bacchides *b* strongholds in Judea:
10:12 in the strongholds that Bacchides had *b*,
12:38 Simon likewise *b* up Adida in the Shephelah,
13:30 he *b* at Modein is there to the present day.
13:33 on his part, *b* up the strongholds of Judea,
13:38 that you have *b* shall remain yours.
13:48 fortifications and *b* himself a residence.
14:36 who had *b* for themselves a citadel from
15:7 you have *b* and now occupy shall remain
16:15 stronghold called Dok which he had *b*.
Jb 3:14 earth who *b* where now there are ruins
20:19 and stolen a patrimony he had not *b* up,
Ps(s) 74:2 Remember your flock which you *b* up of old,
78:69 And he *b* his shrine like heaven,
107:36 the hungry, and they *b* a city to dwell in.
122:3 Jerusalem, *b* as a city with compact unity.
138:3 you *b* up strength within me.
Prv 9:1 Wisdom has *b* her house,
12:3 No man is *b* up by wickedness,
24:3 By wisdom is a house *b*,
Eccl 2:4 I *b* myself houses and planted vineyards;
Sir 47:13 He *b* a house to the name of God,
48:17 the rock and he *b* reservoirs for water.
49:12 In their time they *b* the house of God;
50:2 In his time also the wall was *b* with
Is 5:2 Within it he *b* a watchtower,
22:11 nor did you consider him who *b* it long ago.
Jer 7:31 In the Valley of Ben-hinnom they have *b*
12:16 shall be *b* up in the midst of my people.
19:5 They have *b* high places for Baal to
32:31 From the day it was *b* to this day,
32:35 They *b* high places to Baal in the Valley
45:4 What I have *b*, I am tearing down
52:4 around it, and *b* siege walls on every side.
Ez 13:10 was no peace, and that, as one *b* a wall,
16:25 At every street corner you *b* a dais for
17:17 are *b* for the destruction of many lives,
27:5 Senir they *b* for you all of your decks;
40:2 seemed to be a city being *b* before me.
41:6 *b* one above the other in three stories,
46:23 *b* beneath the stones all the way around.
Dn 4:27 who *b* it as a royal residence for my
Hos 8:14 has forgotten his maker and *b* palaces.
10:1 abundant his fruit, the more altars he *b*;
Am 5:11 Though you have *b* houses of hewn stone,
9:6 I have *b* heaven,
Jon 4:5 where he *b* himself a hut and waited under
Zec 1:16 my house shall be *b* in it,
9:3 Tyre *b* herself a stronghold,
Mt 7:24 like the wise man who *b* his house on rock.
7:26 man who *b* his house on sandy ground.

Lk 4:29 *b* and intending to hurl him over the edge.
6:49 man who *b* his house on the ground
7: 5 people, and even *b* our synagogue for us."
17:28 they bought and sold, they *b* and planted.
Acts 5:37 He too *b* up quite a following,
9:31 It was being *b* up and was making steady
2Cor 13: 9 is that you may be *b* up to completion.
Eph 2:22 in him you are being *b* into this temple,
Col 2: 7 Be rooted in him and *b* up in him,
Heb 11: 7 *b* an ark that his household might be saved.
1Pt 2: 5 living stones, *b* as an edifice of spirit,
3:20 God patiently waited until the ark was *b*.

BUKKI (5)

Nm 34:22 *B*, son of Jogli from the tribe of Manasseh:
1Chr 5:31 Abishua became the father of *B*.
5:31 *B* became the father of Uzzi.
6:36 whose son was Abishua, whose son was *B*,
Ezr 7: 4 son of Zerahiah, son of Uzzi, son of *B*,

BUKKIAH (2)

1Chr 25: 4 *B*, Mattaniah, Uzziel, Shubael,
25:13 The sixth was *B*,

BUL (1)

1Kgs 6:38 according to plan, in the month of *B*,

BULGING (1)

Is 30:13 descending rift *B* out in a high wall

BULL (43)

Ex 29: 1 Procure a young *b* and two unblemished rams.
Lv 1: 5 shall then slaughter the *b* before the LORD,
4: 3 unblemished *b* as a sin offering for the
4:14 shall present a young *b* as a sin offering.
23:18 unblemished yearling lambs, one young *b*,
Nm 7:15 young *b*, one ram, and one yearling lamb
7:21 weight filled with incense, one young *b*,
7:27 with incense; one young *b*, one ram,
7:33 one young *b*, one ram, and one yearling
7:39 young *b*, one ram, and one yearling lamb
7:45 young *b*, one ram, and one yearling lamb
7:51 one young *b*, one ram,
7:57 one young *b*, one ram,
7:63 *b*, one ram, and one yearling lamb
7:69 one young *b*, one ram, and one yearling
7:75 one young *b*, one ram, and one yearling
7:81 one young *b*, one ram, and one yearling
8: 8 They shall take a young *b*,
8: 8 take another young *b* for a sin offering.
15:24 one young *b* as a sweet-smelling oblation
23:22 out of Egypt, a wild *b* of towering might.
24: 8 out of Egypt, a wild *b* of towering might.
Dt 33:17 The majestic *b*, his father's first-born,
1Sm 1:24 with her, along with a three-year-old *b*,
1:25 boy's father had sacrificed the young *b*,
1Kgs 18:25 "Choose one young *b* and prepare it first,
18:26 the young *b* that was turned over to them,
18:33 cut up the young *b* and laid it on the wood.
2Chr 13: 9 consecrate himself with a young *b*
Tb 1: 5 as well as to the young *b* which Jeroboam,
Ps(s) 29: 6 leap like a calf and Sirion like a young *b*.
Prv 14: 4 crops come through the strength of the *b*.
Ez 43:19 a young *b* as a sin offering to the priests,
43:21 Then take the *b* of the sin offering,
43:22 to purify the altar as was done with the *b*.
43:23 *b* and an unblemished ram from the flock,
43:25 and a young *b* and a ram from the flock,
45:18 *b* as a sacrifice to purify the sanctuary.
45:22 people of the land, a *b* as a sin offering.
45:24 for each *b* and one ephah for each ram;
46: 6 he shall provide an unblemished young *b*,
46: 7 of one ephah for the *b* and one for the ram,
46:11 cereal offering shall be an ephah for a *b*,

BULLION (2)

Gn 33:19 pieces of *b* from the descendants of Hamor,
2Chr 34:17 have turned into *b* the metals deposited in

BULLOCK (39)

Ex 29: 3 of them along with the *b* and the two rams.
29:10 forward the *b* in front of the meeting tent.
29:11 Then slaughter the *b* before the LORD,
29:14 of the *b* you must burn up outside the camp,
29:36 sacrificing a *b* each day as a sin offering,
Lv 4: 4 the *b* to the entrance of the meeting tent,
4: 8 sin-offering *b* he shall remove all the fat:
4:11 The hide of the *b* and all its flesh,
4:12 organs, and offal, in short, the whole *b*,
4:15 the *b* has been slaughtered before the LORD,
4:20 doing with this *b* just as he did with the
4:20 as he did with the other sin-offering *b*.
4:21 This *b* must also be brought outside the
8: 2 anointing oil, the *b* for a sin offering,
8:14 brought forward the *b* for a sin offering,
8:17 The *b*, however, with its hide and flesh
16: 3 He shall bring a young *b* for a sin
16: 6 "Aaron shall bring in the *b*,
16:11 "Thus shall Aaron offer up the *b*,
16:27 The sin-offering *b* and goat whose blood
Nm 23: 2 offering a *b* and a ram on each altar.
23: 2 and have offered a *b* and a ram on each."
23:14 and offered a *b* and a ram on each of them.
23:30 offering a *b* and a ram on each altar.
28:12 oil as the cereal offering for each *b*,
28:14 shall be half a hin of wine for each *b*,
28:20 three tenths of an ephah for each *b*,
28:28 three tenths of an ephah for each *b*,
29: 2 holocaust to the LORD one *b*,
29: 3 three tenths of an ephah for the *b*,
29: 8 holocaust to the LORD one *b*,
29: 9 three tenths of an ephah for the *b*,
29:36 sweet-smelling oblation to the LORD one *b*,
Jgs 6:25 "Take the seven-year-old spare *b* and
6:26 Then take the spare *b* and offer it as a
6:28 *b* offered on the altar that was built.
Ps(s) 50: 9 I take from your house no *b*,
106:20 glory for the image of a grass-eating *b*.
Sir 38:25 Who guides the ox and urges on the *b*,

BULLOCKS (38)

Lv 4: 5 *b* blood and bring it into the meeting tent,
4: 7 The rest of the *b* blood he shall pour out
4:15 shall lay their hands on the *b* head.
16:14 Taking some of the *b* blood,
16:15 do with it as he did with the *b* blood,
16:18 Taking some of the *b* and the goat's blood,
Nm 8:12 lay their hands on the heads of the *b*,
23: 1 seven *b* and seven rams for me here."
23:29 here prepare for me seven *b* and seven rams."
28:11 offer as a holocaust to the LORD two *b*,
28:19 to the LORD, which shall consist of two *b*,
28:27 holocaust to the LORD two *b*,
29:13 holocaust to the LORD thirteen *b*,
29:14 of an ephah for each of the thirteen *b*,
29:17 the second day you shall offer twelve *b*,
29:18 and libations as prescribed for the *b*,
29:20 the third day you shall offer eleven *b*,
29:21 and libations as prescribed for the *b*,
29:23 "On the fourth day you shall offer ten *b*,
29:24 and libations as prescribed for the *b*,
29:26 "On the fifth day you shall offer nine *b*,
29:27 and libations as prescribed for the *b*,
29:29 the sixth day you shall offer eight *b*,
29:30 and libations as prescribed for the *b*,
29:32 the seventh day you shall offer seven *b*,
29:33 as prescribed for the *b*, rams and lambs
29:37 for the *b*, rams and lambs in proportion
Jb 42: 8 therefore, take seven *b* and seven rams,
Ps(s) 22:13 Many *b* surround me; the strong bulls
51:21 then shall they offer up *b* on your altar.
68:31 reeds, the herd of strong bulls and the *b*,
69:32 oxen or *b* with horns and divided hooves:
Is 34: 7 down with fatlings, and *b* with bulls;
Ez 39:18 of the land [rams, lambs, and goats, *b*,
Dn 3:40 though it were holocausts of rams and *b*,
Hos 12:12 to nought, in Gilgal they sacrifice to *b*;
14: 3 render as offerings the *b* from our stalls.
Mt 22: 4 My *b* and corn-fed cattle are killed;

BULLS (25)

Gn 32:16 forty cows and ten *b*;
Ex 24: 5 young *b* as peace offerings to the LORD,
Nm 7:87 holocausts were, in all, twelve young *b*,
Dt 32:14 Its Bashan *b* and its goats,
1Kgs 18:23 Give us two young *b*.
1Chr 15:26 seven *b* and seven rams were sacrificed.
29:21 and holocausts to the LORD, a thousand *b*,
2Chr 29:21 Seven *b*, seven rams, seven lambs
29:22 They slaughtered the *b*,
30:24 *b* and seven thousand sheep to the assembly,
30:24 a thousand *b* and ten thousand sheep.
Ezr 6: 9 young *b*, rams, and lambs for holocausts
6:17 house of God, they offered one hundred *b*,
7:17 therefore, to use this money to buy *b*,
8:35 the God of Israel twelve *b* for all Israel,
Jb 21:10 Their *b* gender without fail;
Ps(s) 22:13 the strong *b* of Bashan encircle me.
22:22 from the horns of the wild *b*,
50:13 Do I eat the flesh of strong *b*,
68:31 the herd of strong *b* and the bullocks,
92:11 You have exalted my horn like the wild *b*;
Is 34: 7 down with fatlings, and bullocks with *b*;
Ez 45:23 seven *b* and seven rams without blemish,
Heb 9:13 For if the blood of goats and *b* and the
10: 4 the blood of *b* and goats to take sins away.

BULLY (1)

Lk 3:14 He told them, "Don't *b* anyone.

BULRUSHES (1)

Is 19: 7 away, and *b* on the bank of the Nile;

BULWARK (3)

Ez 24:25 on the day I take away from them their *b*,
Dn 11: 1 as a reinforcement and a *b* for me.
1Tm 3:15 the living God, the pillar and *b* of truth.

BUNAH (1)

1Chr 2:25 Hezron, were Ram, the first-born, then *B*,

BUNCH (1)

Ex 12:22 Then take a *b* of hyssop,

BUNDLE (6)

Ru 3:15 measures of barley, helped her lift the *b*,
1Sm 25:29 be bound in the *b* of the living
Sir 21: 9 A band of criminals is like a *b* of tow;
Jer 10:17 Lift your *b* and leave the land,
Mt 13:30 collect the weeds and *b* them up to burn,
Acts 28: 3 with a *b* of brushwood he had collected,

BUNNI (3)

Neh 9: 4 Jeshua, Binnui, Kadmiel, Shebaniah, *B*,
10:16 Parosh, Pahath-moab, Elam, Zattu, Bani, *B*,
11:15 son of Azrikam, son of Hashabiah, son of *B*:

BUOYS (1)

Sir 34:17 He *b* up the spirits,

BURDEN (48)

Gn 49:15 to the *b* and became a toiling serf.
Ex 18:22 Thus, your *b* will be lightened,
23: 5 who hates you lying prostrate under its *b*,
Nm 11:11 me that you *b* me with all this people?
11:17 may share the *b* of the people with you.
Dt 1:12 I alone bear the crushing *b* that you are,
1Sm 25:31 this as a qualm or *b* on your conscience,
2Sm 13:25 of us should not go lest we be a *b* to you."
15:33 you come with me, you will be a *b* to me.
19:36 be any further *b* to my lord the king
2Chr 35: 3 shall no longer be a *b* on your shoulders.
Neh 5:15 had laid a heavy *b* on the people,
13:15 grapes, figs, and every other kind of *b*,
13:19 that no *b* might enter on the sabbath day.
Ps(s) 38: 5 they are like a heavy *b*,
66:11 you laid a heavy *b* on our backs.
81: 7 "I relieved his shoulder of the *b*;
88:16 I am dazed with the *b* of your dread.
Prv 27: 3 Stone is heavy, and sand a *b*,
Sir 13: 2 Bear no *b* too heavy for you;
Is 10:27 His *b* shall be taken from your shoulder,
14:25 from them, and his *b* from their shoulder.
46: 3 the house of Israel, My *b* since your birth,
Jer 17:22 Bring no *b* from your homes on the sabbath.
17:24 and carry no *b* through the gates of this
23:33 asks you, "What is the *b* of the LORD?"
23:33 you shall answer, "You are the *b*,
23:34 anyone else mentions "the *b* of the LORD,"
23:36 *b* of the LORD you shall mention no more.
23:36 For each man his own word becomes the *b* so
23:38 But if you ask about "the *b* of the LORD,"
23:38 you use this phrase, "the *b* of the LORD,"
Ez 12: 6 shoulder the *b* and set out in the darkness;
12: 7 set out in the darkness, shouldering my *b*.
12:12 shoulder his *b* and set out in darkness,
Hos 8:10 princes shall shortly succumb under the *b*.
Mal 1:13 You also say, "What a *b*!"
Mt 11:30 rest, for my yoke is easy and my *b* light."
21: 5 astride a colt, the foal of a beast of *b*."
Acts 15:28 *b* beyond that which is strictly necessary,
2Cor 4:17 The present *b* of our trial is light enough,
11: 9 you and in want I was a *b* to none of you,
12:13 except in this, that I was no *b* to you?
12:14 to visit you, and I am not going to *b* you;
12:16 Granted that I did not *b* you
Phil 3: 1 I find writing you these things no *b*,
1Tm 5:16 not let them become a *b* to the church,
Rv 2:24 on you I place no further *b*.

BURDENED (5)

Prv 28:17 Though a man *b* with human blood were to
Sir 3:26 A stubborn man will be *b* with sorrow;
Is 9: 3 For the yoke that *b* them,
43:24 Instead, you *b* me with your sins,
2Tm 3: 6 make captives of silly women *b* with sins

BURDENS (12)

2Chr 34:13 in charge of the men who carried the *b*,
Ps(s) 68:20 day by day be the Lord, who bears our *b*;
73: 5 They are free from the *b* of mortals,
94:20 you, which creates *b* in the guise of law?
Prv 31: 7 their misery, and think no more of their *b*.
Wis 9:15 For the corruptible body *b* the soul and
Sir 29: 4 a loan adds to the *b* of those who help him;
Is 46: 1 up on shoulders, carried as *b* by the weary.
Jer 17:21 care not to carry *b* on the sabbath day,
17:27 if you carry *b* and come through the gates
Lk 11:46 You lay impossible *b* on men but will not
Gal 6: 2 Help carry one another's *b*;

BURDENSOME (5)

Wis 17:21 to themselves more *b* than the darkness.
Sir 6:22 She will be like a *b* stone to test him,
Mt 11:28 me, all you who are weary and find life *b*,
2Cor 11: 9 possible I kept myself from being *b* to you,
1Jn 5: 3 and his commandments are not *b*.

BURGLARY (1)

Jer 2:34 innocent, whom you found committing no *b*;

BURIAL (42)

Gn 23: 4 a piece of property for a *b* ground,
23: 6 your dead in the choicest of our *b* sites.
23: 6 his burial ground for the *b* of your dead."
23: 8 you will allow me room for *b* of my dead,
23: 9 presence, at its full price, for a *b* place."
23:20 from the Hittites to Abraham as a *b* place.
47:30 out of Egypt and buried in their *b* place."
49:30 from Ephron the Hittite for a *b* ground.
50:13 for a *b* ground from Ephron the Hittite.
50:14 gone up with him for the *b* of his father.
Ex 14:11 "Were there no *b* places in Egypt that you
Dt 34: 6 this day no one knows the place of his *b*.
Jgs 16:31 bore him up for *b* in the grave of his father
Tb 4: 3 "My son, when I die, give me a decent *b*.
4:17 bread and wine at the *b* of the virtuous,
14: 1 and received an honorable *b* in Nineveh.
Jdt 16:22 the time of the death and *b* of her husband,
2Mc 4:49 crime and provided sumptuously for their *b*.
9:15 whom he had judged not even worthy of *b*,
13: 7 he was deprived even of decent *b*.
Jb 17: 1 my *b* is at hand.
27:15 survivors, when they die, shall have no *b*,
Eccl 6: 3 of his goods, or if he is deprived of *b*,
Wis 18:12 living were not even sufficient for the *b*,
Sir 38:16 the body, absent not yourself from his *b*:
Is 14:19 But you are cast forth without *b*,
53: 9 the wicked and a *b* place with evildoers,
Jer 7:32 lack of space, Topheth will be a *b* place.
8: 2 They will not be gathered up for *b*,
19:11 And Topheth shall be a *b* place,
22:19 The *b* of an ass shall he be given,
25:33 mourn them, none will gather them for *b*;
34: 5 for your *b* as they did for your fathers,
Bar 2:24 fathers brought out from their *b* places.
Mt 26:12 has contributed toward my *b* preparation.
Mk 14: 8 she is anticipating its preparation for *b*.
Jn 12: 7 it against the day they prepare me for *b*.
19:40 and in accordance with Jewish *b* custom
Acts 5: 6 up the body, and carried it out for *b*.
5:10 carried her out for *b* beside her husband.
Heb 11:22 and gave instructions about his *b*.

BURIALS (1)

Wis 19: 3 and were mourning at the *b* of the dead,

BURIED (120)

Gn 15:15 you shall be *b* at a contented old age.
23:19 Abraham *b* his wife Sarah in the cave of
25: 9 and Ishmael *b* him in the cave of Machpelah,
25:10 there he was *b* next to his wife Sarah.
35: 8 she was *b* under the oak below Bethel,
35:19 she was *b* on the road to Ephrath [that is,
35:29 His sons Esau and Jacob *b* him.
47:29 do not let me be *b* in Egypt.
47:30 out of Egypt and *b* in their burial place."
48: 7 *b* her there on the way to Ephrath [that is,
49:31 There Abraham and his wife Sarah are *b*,
49:31 his wife Rebekah, and there, too, I *b* Leah
50:13 *b* him in the cave in the field
50:14 had *b* his father he returned to Egypt,
Nm 11:34 it was there that the greedy people were *b*.
20: 1 that Miriam died, and here that she was *b*.
33: 4 While the Egyptians *b* their first-born all
Dt 10: 6 for Moserah, where Aaron died and was *b*,
34: 6 and he was *b* in the ravine opposite
Jos 24:30 He was *b* within the limits of his heritage
24:32 were *b* in Shechem in the plot of ground
24:33 he was *b* on the hill which had been given
Jgs 2: 9 and they *b* him within the borders of his
8:32 died and was *b* in the tomb of his father
10: 2 years, he died and was *b* in Shamir.
10: 5 Jair died and was *b* in Kamon.
12: 7 died and was *b* in his city in Gilead.
12:10 years, Ibzan died and was *b* in Bethlehem.
12:12 and was *b* in Elon in the land of Zebulun.
12:15 died and was *b* in Pirathon in the land of
Ru 1:17 you die I will die, and there be *b*.
1Sm 25: 1 they *b* him at his home in Ramah.
28: 3 mourned by all Israel, was *b* in his city,
31:13 *b* them under the tamarisk tree in Jabesh,
2Sm 2: 4 that the men of Jabesh-gilead had *b* Saul.
2:32 *b* him in his father's tomb in Bethlehem.
3:32 When they had *b* Abner in Hebron,
4:12 and *b* it in Abner's grave in Hebron.
17:23 so he died and was *b* in his father's tomb.
21:14 his son Jonathan were *b* in the tomb
1Kgs 2:10 ancestors and was *b* in the City of David.
2:34 he was *b* in his house in the desert.
11:43 he was *b* in his father's City of David,
13:31 After he had *b* him,
13:31 me in the grave where the man of God is *b*.
14:18 He was *b* with all Israel mourning him,
14:31 he was *b* with them in the City of David.
15: 8 he was *b* in the City of David,
15:24 he was *b* in his forefather's City of David,
16: 6 he was *b* in Tirzah,
16:28 he was *b* in Samaria,
22:37 went to Samaria, where they *b* the king.
22:51 he was *b* in his forefathers' City of David.
2Kgs 8:24 and was *b* with them in the City of David.
9:28 *b* him in the tomb of his ancestors
10:35 with his ancestors and was *b* in Samaria.
12:22 He was *b* in his forefathers' City of David,
13: 9 with his ancestors and was *b* in Samaria.
13:13 was *b* with the kings of Israel in Samaria.]
13:20 Elisha died and was *b*.
14:16 was *b* in Samaria with the kings of Israel.
14:20 He was brought back on horses and *b* with
15: 7 and was *b* with them in the City of David.
15:38 with his ancestors and was *b* with them
16:20 and was *b* with them in the City of David.
21:18 ancestors and was *b* in his palace garden,
21:26 *b* in his own grave in the garden of Uzza,
23:30 where they *b* him in his own grave.
1Chr 10:12 They *b* their bones under the oak of Jabesh,
2Chr 9:31 he was *b* in his father's City of David,
12:16 he was *b* in the City of David.
13:23 they *b* him in the City of David.
16:14 They *b* him in the tomb he had hewn for
21: 1 he was *b* with them in the City of David.
21:20 unloved and was *b* in the City of David,
22: 9 They *b* him,
24:16 was *b* in the City of David with the kings,
24:25 He was *b* in the City of David,
25:28 They brought him back on horses and *b* him
26:23 he was *b* with them in the field adjoining
27: 9 ancestors and was *b* in the City of David,
28:27 with his ancestors and was *b* in Jerusalem
32:33 he was *b* at the approach to the tombs of
33:20 his ancestors and was *b* in his own palace.
35:24 He was *b* in the tombs of his ancestors,
Neh 2: 3 where my ancestors are *b* lies in ruins,
Tb 1:18 I also *b* anyone whom Sennacherib slew when
1:19 the king that it was I who *b* the dead.
2: 7 sunset I went out, dug a grave, and *b* him.
14:12 mother died, he *b* her next to his father.
14:13 and he *b* them at Ecbatana in Media.
Jdt 8: 3 He was *b* with his forefathers in the field
16:23 they *b* her in the tomb of her husband,
1Mc 2:70 *b* in the tombs of his fathers in Modein,
9:19 Judas and *b* him in the tomb of their fathers
13:23 he had Jonathan killed and *b* there.
13:25 his brother Jonathan, and *b* him in Modein,
Jb 3:16 was I not *b* away like an untimely birth,
31:33 hidden my sins and *b* my guilt in my bosom
Sir 46:20 Even when he lay *b*,
Jer 13: 5 I went to the Parath and *b* the loincloth.
20: 6 there you shall die and be *b*,
41: 8 we have stores *b* in the field:
Ez 29: 5 field, you shall not be taken up or *b*;
39:11 Gog shall be *b* there with all his horde,
39:15 have *b* it in the Valley of Hamon-gog.
Mt 13:44 a *b* treasure which a man found in a field.
25:18 the ground, where he *b* his master's money.
25:25 so out of fear I went off and *b* your
Lk 16:22 The rich man likewise died and was *b*.
23:53 the rock, in which no one had yet been *b*.
23:55 They saw the tomb and how his body was *b*.
Jn 19:41 a new tomb in which no one had ever been *b*.
19:42 Jewish Preparation Day they *b* Jesus there,
Acts 2:29 He died and was *b*,
5: 9 *b* your husband can be heard at the door.
8: 2 Devout men *b* Stephen,
Rom 6: 4 baptism into his death we were *b* with him,
1Cor 15: 4 that he was *b* and,
Col 2:12 In baptism you were not only *b* with him

BURN (103)

Ex 21:25 hand for hand, foot for foot, *b* for burn,
21:25 hand for hand, foot for foot, burn for *b*,
29:13 on them, you shall take and *b* on the altar.
29:14 the bullock you must *b* up outside the camp,
29:25 you shall *b* them on top of the holocaust
30: 7 "On it Aaron shall *b* fragrant incense.
30: 8 he lights the lamps, he shall *b* incense.
Lv 1: 9 The priest shall then *b* the whole offering
1:13 The priest shall offer them up and then *b*
1:17 halves, the priest shall *b* it on the altar,
2: 2 shall *b* on the altar as a token offering,
2: 9 *b* on the altar as a sweet-smelling oblation
2:11 for you shall not *b* any leaven or honey as
2:16 shall then *b* some of the grits and oil,
3: 5 then *b* on the altar with the holocaust,
3:11 All this the priest shall *b* on the altar
3:16 All this the priest shall *b* on the altar
4:10 shall *b* it on the altar of holocausts.
4:19 he shall take from it and *b* on the altar,
4:26 All of the fat he shall *b* on the altar
4:31 and the priest shall *b* it on the altar for
4:35 and the priest shall *b* it on the altar
5:12 and this he shall *b* as a sin offering on
6: 5 and *b* the fat of the peace offerings.
6: 8 shall *b* on the altar as its token offering,
7: 5 *b* on the altar as an oblation to the LORD.
7:31 The priest shall *b* the fat on the altar,
8:32 flesh and bread you shall *b* up in the fire.
13:24 "If a man had a *b* on his skin,
13:24 the *b* now becomes a pink or a white blotch,
13:25 is leprosy that has broken out in the *b*;
13:28 dying out, it is merely the scab of the *b*;
13:28 clean, since it is only the scar of the *b*.
13:52 He shall therefore *b* up the garment,
16:25 *b* the fat of the sin offering on the altar.
17: 6 *b* the fat for an odor pleasing to the LORD.
24: 3 the lamps to *b* before the LORD regularly,
24: 4 lampstand, to *b* regularly before the LORD.
Nm 5:26 its token offering and *b* it on the altar.
18:17 *b* as a sweet-smelling oblation to the LORD,
Dt 13:17 you shall *b* the city with all its spoils
Jos 11: 6 their horses and *b* their chariots."
Jgs 12: 1 We will *b* your house over you."
14:15 for us, or we will *b* you and your family.
1Sm 2:28 to go up to my altar, to *b* incense,
1Kgs 9:25 the LORD, and to *b* incense before the LORD;
13: 2 you, and he shall *b* human bones upon you.'"
14:10 will *b* up the house of Jeroboam completely,
22:44 and to *b* incense on the high places.
2Kgs 8:12 You will *b* their fortresses,
12: 4 to sacrifice and to *b* incense there.
14: 4 to sacrifice and to *b* incense on them.
15: 4 to sacrifice and to *b* incense on them.
15:35 to sacrifice and to *b* incense on them.
16:15 *b* the morning holocaust and the evening
23: 5 appointed to *b* incense on the high places
2Chr 4:20 which were to *b* according to prescription
13:11 They *b* holocausts to the LORD and fragrant
13:11 golden lampstand *b* evening after evening;
26:18 for you, Uzziah, to *b* incense to the LORD,
29: 7 and refused to *b* incense and offer
Tb 6: 8 if you *b* them so that the smoke surrounds
Jdt 16: 4 He threatened to *b* my land,
16:17 flesh, and they shall *b* and suffer forever."
1Mc 7:35 victorious I will *b* this temple down."
Jb 31:12 A fire that should *b* down to the abyss
Ps(s) 21:10 Make them *b* as though in a fiery furnace,
74: 8 *b* all the shrines of God in the land."
79: 5 Will your jealousy *b* like fire?
80: 5 you *b* with anger while your people pray?
80:17 Let those who would *b* it with fire or
89:47 Will your wrath *b* like fire?
102: 4 like smoke, and my bones *b* like fire.
Sir 45:16 *b* sacrifices of sweet odor for a memorial,
Is 1:31 Both shall *b* together,
27: 4 I should *b* them all.
Jer 4: 4 like fire, and *b* till none can quench it,
7: 9 adultery and perjury, *b* incense to Baal,
7:20 it will *b* without being quenched.
11:16 Now he sets fire to it, its branches *b*.
17: 4 kindled by my wrath that will *b* forever.
18:15 *b* incense to a thing that does not exist.
21:10 king of Babylon who shall *b* it with fire.
33:18 before me, to *b* cereal offerings,
34: 5 and *b* spices for your burial as they did
36:25 urged the king not to *b* the scroll,
43:12 gods, and *b* the gods or carry them off.
44:17 we will *b* incense to the queen of heaven
44:25 we have made to *b* incense to the queen
48:35 high place, or to *b* incense to his gods.
Bar 6:62 high to *b* up the mountains and the forests,
Ez 5: 2 *B* a third in the fire,
5: 4 them in the midst of the fire and *b* them.]
16:41 They shall *b* your apartments with fire and
23:47 daughters, and *b* their houses with fire.
39: 9 the cities of Israel go out and *b* weapons:
Hos 4:13 sacrifice and on the hills they *b* incense,
Am 4: 5 *B* leavened food as a thanksgiving
Mt 3:12 the chaff he will *b* in unquenchable fire."
13:30 collect the weeds and bundle them up to *b*,
22: 7 destroy those murderers and *b* their city.
Lk 3:17 the chaff he will *b* in unquenchable fire."
Rv 16: 8 He was commissioned to *b* men with fire.

BURNED (115)

Gn 38:24 "she shall be *b*."
Ex 3: 3 sight, and see why the bush is not *b*."
12:10 is left over in the morning shall be *b* up.
22: 5 standing grain or the field itself is *b* up,
29:18 entire ram shall then be *b* on the altar,
29:34 on the next day, this remnant must be *b* up;
40:27 the veil, and on it he *b* fragrant incense,
40:38 and on it he *b* fragrant incense,
Lv 1:15 it to the altar where it is to be *b*,
4:12 deposited and there be *b* up in a wood fire.
4:12 place of the ash heap, there it must be *b*.
4:21 also be brought outside the camp and *b*,
6:15 for the LORD the whole offering shall be *b*.
6:23 such an offering must be *b* up in the fire.
7:17 the third day, it must be *b* up in the fire.
7:19 be eaten, but shall be *b* up in the fire.
8:16 with their fat, Moses *b* them on the altar.
8:17 offal he *b* in the fire outside the camp,
8:20 up the ram into pieces, he *b* the head,
8:21 he also *b* these remaining parts of the ram
8:28 Moses *b* them with the holocaust on the
9:10 He then *b* on the altar the fat,
9:11 hide he *b* up in the fire outside the camp.
9:13 the holocaust, and he *b* them on the altar.
9:14 he *b* these also with the holocaust on the
9:17 a handful of it, he *b* it on the altar.
9:20 top of the breasts and *b* them on the altar,
10:16 he discovered that it had all been *b*.
16:27 flesh and offal shall be *b* up in the fire.
19: 6 the third day shall be *b* up in the fire.
20:14 be *b* to death for their shameful conduct,

21: 9 her father also, shall be *b* to death.
Nm 11: 1 fire of the LORD *b* among them
11: 3 there the fire of the LORD *b* among them.
17: 4 censers of those *b* during the offering
19: 5 Then the heifer shall be *b* in his sight,
19: 6 the fire in which the heifer is being *b*.
19: 8 who *b* the heifer shall wash his garments,
Jos 6:24 city itself they *b* with all that was in it,
11: 9 their horses and *b* their chariots.
11:11 Hazor itself he *b*.
11:13 raised sites, except Hazor, which Joshua *b*.
1Sm 2:15 In fact, even before the fat was *b*,
2:16 "Let the fat be *b* first as is the custom,
30: 3 to find it *b* to the ground and their wives,
1Kgs 3: 3 sacrifice and *b* incense on the high places.
11: 8 who *b* incense and sacrificed to their gods.
14:10 completely, as though dung were being *b*.
15:13 this object and *b* it in the Kidron Valley.
16:18 palace and *b* down the palace over him.
2Kgs 10:26 out the stele of Baal, and *b* the shrine.
16: 4 and *b* incense on the high places,
17:11 they *b* incense like the nations whom the
22:17 me and have *b* incense to other gods,
23: 4 He had these *b* outside Jerusalem on the
23: 5 as well as those who *b* incense to Baal,
23: 6 there he had it *b* and beaten to dust,
23:16 taken from the graves and *b* on the altar,
23:20 the shrines, and *b* human bones upon them.
25: 9 He *b* the house of the LORD,
2Chr 16:14 also *b* a very great funeral pyre for him.
34: 5 of the priests he *b* upon their altars.
Jdt 2:26 all the Midianites, *b* their tents, .
9: 4 your favored sons, who *b* with zeal for you,
Est 1:12 king's wrath flared up, and he *b* with fury.
1Mc 4:20 put to flight and their camp was being *b*.
4:50 Then they *b* incense on the altar and
5: 5 annihilation and *b* down the towers
5:35 plundered the place, and *b* it down.
5:65 its strongholds and *b* the towers around it.
5:68 altars and *b* the statues of their gods;
6:31 sortie and *b* these and they fought bravely.
10:84 But Jonathan *b* and plundered Azotus with
10:85 together with those who were *b* alive,
11: 4 and the charred bodies of those *b* by
11:61 it and *b* and plundered its suburbs.
2Mc 1:23 While the sacrifice was being *b*,
1:31 After the sacrifice was *b*,
1:33 and his people had *b* the sacrifices,
2:10 and fire came down and *b* up the holocausts.
2:11 not been eaten, the sin offering was *b* up."
6:11 were betrayed to Philip and all *b* to death.
8:33 they *b* both those who had set fire to the
10: 3 for the first time in two years, *b* incense,
10:36 the fire and *b* the blasphemers alive.
Prv 6:27 to his bosom, and his garments not be *b?*
Sg 1: 6 I am swarthy, because the sun has *b* me.
Sir 49: 6 foolish foreign nation Who *b* the holy city
51:19 I *b* with desire for her,
Is 9: 4 in blood, will be *b* as fuel for flames.
42:25 them, yet they did not realize, it *b* them,
43: 2 you walk through fire, you shall not be *b;*
44:19 to say, "Half of the wood I *b* in the fire,
64:10 fathers praised you Has been *b* with fire;
65: 7 Since they *b* incense on the mountains,
Jer 32:29 incense was *b* to Baal and libations
36:27 after the king *b* the scroll with the text
36:28 which Jehoiakim, king of Judah, *b* up.
36:29 You *b* that scroll,
36:32 king of Judah, had *b* in the fire,
44:19 And when we *b* incense to the queen of
44:21 that you *b* incense in the cities of Judah
44:23 you *b* incense and sinned against the LORD,
51:30 *B* are their homes, and broken their bars.
52:13 He *b* the house of the LORD,
Am 2: 1 he *b* to ashes the bones of Edom's king,
Mi 1: 7 all her wages shall be *b* in the fire,
Mt 13:40 Just as weeds are collected and *b*,
Acts 19:19 collected their books and *b* them in public.
Rom 1:27 with women and *b* with lust for one another.
1Cor 13: 3 the poor and hand over my body to be *b*,
Heb 6: 8 it is soon cursed, and finally is *b*.
13:11 as a sin offering are *b* outside the camp.
Rv 4: 5 before it *b* seven flaming torches,
18:18 smoke go up as the city *b* to the ground:

BURNING (75)

Ex 22: 4 a man is *b* over a field or a vineyard,
27:20 so that you may keep lamps *b* regularly.
30: 1 "For *b* incense you shall make an altar of
Lv 1: 7 have put some *b* embers on the altar and
6: 2 and the fire is to be kept *b* on the altar.
6: 5 The fire on the altar is to be kept *b;*
6: 6 is to be kept *b* continuously on the altar;
24: 2 so that you may keep lamps *b* regularly.
Nm 24:22 Yet destined for *b*—
Dt 12:31 *b* their sons and daughters to their gods.
Jgs 15: 5 *b* both the shocks and the standing grain,
2Kgs 16:13 on it, *b* his holocaust and cereal-offering,
18: 4 time the Israelites were *b* incense to it.
23:15 grinding them to powder, and *b* the Asherah.
23:26 from his fiercely *b* anger against Judah.
2Chr 2: 3 the *b* of fragrant incense in his presence,
26:19 who was holding a censer for *b* the incense,
28:11 for the *b* anger of the LORD is upon you."
28:13 great, and there is a *b* anger upon Israel."
29:10 that his *b* anger may withdraw from us.
30: 8 that he may turn away his *b* anger from you.
Ezr 10:14 from us our God's *b* anger over this affair."
Jdt 12:16 He was *b* with the desire to possess her,
1Mc 2:54 Phinehas our father, for his *b* zeal,
2:58 Elijah, for his *b* zeal for the law,
12:29 and his men were watching the lights *b*,
Ps(s) 11: 6 a *b* blast is their allotted cup.
38: 8 For my loins are filled with *b* pains;
85: 4 you have revoked your *b* anger.
140:11 May he rain *b* coals upon them;
Sir 18:15 Like dew that abates a *b* wind,
23:16 For *b* passion is a blazing fire,
45:19 angry, he destroyed them in his *b* wrath.
Is 13: 9 LORD comes cruel, with wrath and *b* anger;
13:13 LORD of hosts on the day of his *b* anger.
30:27 of the LORD coming from afar in *b* wrath,
33:12 like brushwood cut down for *b* in the fire.
34: 9 sulphur, and her land shall become *b* pitch;
35: 7 The *b* sands will become pools,
54:16 the *b* coals and forges weapons as his work;
62: 1 the dawn and her victory like a *b* torch.
65: 3 in the groves and *b* incense on bricks,
66: 3 like offering swine's blood; *b* incense,
66:15 To wreak his wrath with *b* heat and his
Jer 1:16 And in *b* incense to strange gods and
19: 4 alienated this place by *b* in it incense
20: 9 then it becomes like fire *b* in my heart,
25:38 sweeping sword, by the *b* wrath of the LORD.
32:29 and set fire to it, *b* it and its houses,
36:22 and fire was *b* in a brazier before him.
44:15 their wives were *b* incense to strange gods,
44:18 But since we stopped *b* incense to the
49:37 I will bring evil upon them, my *b* wrath,
51:45 save himself from the *b* wrath of the LORD.
Bar 6:42 sit by the roads, *b* chaff for incense;
Ez 1:13 like *b* coals of fire could be seen;
10: 2 hands with *b* coals from among the cherubim,
36: 5 with *b* jealousy I speak against the rest
Dn 3:48 and spread out, *b* the Chaldeans nearby.
7: 9 was flames of fire, with wheels of *b* fire.
Hos 11: 2 to the Baals and *b* incense to idols.
Jon 4: 8 when the sun arose, God sent a *b* east wind;
Zec 12: 6 woodland, and like a *b* torch among sheaves,
Mk 12:26 of Moses, in the passage about the *b* bush,
Lk 12:35 your waists and your lamps be *b* ready.
24:32 "Were not our hearts *b* inside us as he
Jn 5:35 He was the lamp, set aflame and *b* bright,
Acts 7:30 Mount Sinai in the flame of a *b* thornbush.
Rom 12:20 this you will heap *b* coals upon his head."
Rv 8:10 *b* like a torch crashed down from the sky.
14:10 He will be tormented in *b* sulphur before
18:23 a *b* lamp shall ever again be seen in you!
19:20 alive into the fiery pool of *b* sulphur.
20:10 was hurled into the pool of *b* sulphur,
21: 8 their lot is the fiery pool of *b* sulphur,

BURNISHED (8)

1Kgs 7:45 in the temple of the LORD were of *b* bronze.
Ez 1: 7 They sparkled with a gleam like *b* bronze.
21:14 sharpened, a sword, a sword has been *b:*
21:15 to flash lightning has it been *b*.
21:16 and *b* to be put in the hand of a slayer.
21:20 to flash lightning, *b* for slaughter.
21:33 *b* to consume and to flash lightning,
Dn 10: 6 his arms and feet looked like *b* bronze,

BURNISHER (1)

Ez 21:16 to the *b* that he might hold it in his hand,

BURNS (15)

Ex 22: 4 spread so that it *b* in another's field,
Lv 16:28 The one who *b* them shall wash his garments
Ps(s) 46:10 he *b* the shields with fire.
Sir 9: 8 many perish, for lust for it *b* like fire.
23:16 not to be quenched till it *b* itself out:
28:23 to it, as it *b* among them unquenchably!
40:30 is sweet, but within him it *b* like fire.
Is 9:17 For wickedness *b* like fire,
10:17 That *b* and consumes his briers and his
44:16 Half of it he *b* in the fire,
65: 5 my wrath, a fire that *b* all the day.
Jer 21:12 like fire which *b* without being quenched,
Hb 1:16 to his net, and *b* incense to his seine;
1Cor 3:15 if a man's building *b*, he will suffer loss.
Rv 18: 9 her when they see the smoke arise as she *b*.

BURNT (31)

Lv 6:16 of a priest shall be a whole *b* offering;
Dt 13:17 spoils as a whole *b* offering to the LORD,
33:10 nostrils, and *b* offerings to your altar.
1Chr 6:34 his descendants who *b* the offerings
14:12 gods there, and David ordered them to be *b*.
2Chr 15:16 smashed it, and *b* it in the Kidron Valley.
36:19 They *b* the house of God,
Ezr 6: 3 sacrifices and bringing *b* offerings.
Neh 3:34 they recover these stones, *b* as they are,
10:35 year, to be *b* on the altar of the LORD,
Tb 14: 4 God's temple there shall be *b* to the
1Mc 1:55 They also *b* incense at the doors of houses
1:56 law which they found they tore up and *b*.
4:38 the altar desecrated, the gates *b*,
5:44 *b* the enclosure with all who were in it.
2Mc 12: 6 he set the harbor on fire, *b* the boats,
Ps(s) 51:21 due sacrifices, *b* offerings and holocausts;
66:15 will offer you, with *b* offerings of rams;
Wis 16:18 not be *b* up that were sent upon the wicked,
Sir 45:14 His cereal offering is wholly *b* with the
Is 1: 7 country is waste, your cities *b* with fire;
50:11 your own fire and by the flares you have *b!*
Jer 19:13 upon whose roofs they *b* incense
51:25 over the cliffs, and make you a *b* mountain:
Bar 1: 2 took Jerusalem and *b* it with fire].
6:54 themselves are *b* up in the fire like beams.
Ez 43:21 to be *b* in a designated part of the temple,
Dn 7:11 its body thrown into the fire to be *b* up.
Hos 2:15 for whom she *b* incense While she decked
Mk 12:33 more than any *b* offering or sacrifice."
Jn 15: 6 picked up to be thrown in the fire and *b*.

BURNT-OUT (1)

Dt 29:22 nothing but sulphur and salt, a *b* waste,

BURST (21)

Gn 7:11 the fountains of the great abyss *b* forth,
27:34 his father's words, Esau *b* into loud,
29:11 Then Jacob kissed Rachel and *b* into tears.
2Sm 20:10 so that his entrails *b* forth to the ground,
1Chr 15:13 the wrath of the LORD our God *b* upon us,
Jb 32:19 under pressure, my bosom is ready to *b*.
38: 8 the sea, when it *b* forth from the womb;
Ps(s) 107:16 the gates of brass and *b* the bars of iron.
Eccl 10: 4 Should the anger of the ruler *b* upon you,
Sir 19: 9 be assured it will not make you *b*.
22:24 Before flames *b* forth and oven smokes;
Is 24:19 The earth will *b* asunder,
35: 6 Streams will *b* forth in the desert,
Dn 14:27 and when the dragon ate them, he *b* asunder.
Mi 2:13 *b* open the gate and go out through it;
Na 1:13 from off you, and *b* asunder your bonds.
Mt 9:17 If they do, the skins *b*,
Mk 2:22 the wine will *b* the skins and both wine
Lk 5:37 do so, the new wine will *b* the old skins,
Acts 1:18 His body *b* wide open,
Jas 5:18 the sky *b* forth with rain and the land

BURSTS (2)

Jer 23:19 storm that *b* upon the heads of the wicked.
30:23 storm that *b* upon the heads of the wicked.

BURY (43)

Gn 23: 4 a burial ground, that I may *b* my dead wife."
23: 6 *B* your dead in the choicest of our burial
23:11 *B* your dead!"
23:13 it from me, that I may *b* my dead there."
23:15 you and me, as long as you can *b* your dead?"
49:29 *b* me with my fathers in the cave that lies
50: 5 made me promise on oath to *b* him in the
50: 5 up there to *b* my father and then come back?"
50: 6 Pharaoh replied, "Go and *b* your father,
50: 7 So Joseph left to *b* his father;
Dt 21:23 You shall *b* it the same day;
1Kgs 2:31 as he has said, Strike him down and *b* him,
11:15 of the army, while going to *b* the slain,
13:29 to the city to mourn over it and to *b* it.
13:31 *b* me in the grave where the man of God is
14:13 and all Israel will mourn him and *b* him,
2Kgs 9:10 of Jezreel, so that no one can *b* her.'"
9:34 "Attend to that accursed woman and *b* her;
9:35 But when they went to *b* her,
Tb 1:17 the walls of Nineveh, I would *b* him.
1:18 to take their bodies by stealth and *b* them;
2: 4 rooms, so that I might *b* him after sunset.
4: 4 she dies, *b* her in the same grave with me.
6:15 And they have no other son to *b* them!"
8:12 *b* him without anyone's knowing about it."
12:12 the same thing when you used to *b* the dead.
12:13 your dinner in order to go and *b* the dead,
14:10 The day you *b* your mother next to me,
1Mc 7:17 Jerusalem, and there was no one to *b* them."
2Mc 12:39 gather up the bodies of the slain and *b* them
Jb 40:13 *b* them in the dust together;
Ps(s) 79: 3 Jerusalem, and there is no one to *b* them.
Jer 14:16 No one shall *b* them,
19:11 place, for lack of place to *b* elsewhere.
Ez 39:12 Israel shall need seven months to *b* them.
39:13 land shall *b* them and gain renown for it,
Hos 9: 6 shall gather them in, Memphis shall *b* them.
Mt 8:21 "Lord, let me go and *b* my father first."
8:22 "Follow me, and let the dead *b* their dead."
14:12 themselves to carry his body away and *b* it.
Lk 9:59 man replied, "Let me *b* my father first."
9:60 said to him, "Let the dead *b* their dead;
Rv 11: 9 three and a half days but refuse to *b* them.

BURYING (4)

2Sm 2: 5 this kindness to your lord Saul in *b* him.
2Kgs 13:21 Once some people were *b* a man,

BURYING (cont.)

Tb 2: 8 has escaped, here he is again *b* the dead!"
Ez 39:14 through the land *b* those who lie unburied,

BUSH (8)

Ex 3: 2 appeared to him in fire flaming out of a *b*.
3: 2 on, he was surprised to see that the *b*,
3: 3 sight, and see why the *b* is not burned."
3: 4 closely, God called out to him from the *b*,
Dt 33:16 and the favor of him who dwells in the *b*.
Jer 17: 6 He is like a barren *b* in the desert that
Mk 12:26 Moses, in the passage about the burning *b*,
Lk 20:37 Moses in the passage about the *b* showed

BUSHEL (9)

Zec 5: 6 answered, "This is a *b* container coming.
5: 7 and there was a woman sitting inside the *b*.
5: 8 and he thrust her inside the *b*,
5: 9 As they lifted up the *b* into the air,
5:10 with me, "Where are they taking the *b*?"
Mt 5:15 a lamp and then put it under a *b* basket.
Mk 4:21 under a *b* basket or hidden under a bed?
Lk 8:16 puts it under a *b* basket or under a bed;
11:33 put it in the cellar or under a *b* basket,

BUSHES (2)

Ex 22: 5 further, and catches on to thorn *b*,
Jb 30: 7 Among the *b* they raised their raucous cry;

BUSIED (3)

Eccl 1:13 God has appointed for men to be *b* about.
3:10 God has appointed for men to be *b* about.
Sir 39: 3 is *b* with the hidden meanings of the sages.

BUSILY (1)

Wis 13: 7 For they search *b* among his works,

BUSINESS (17)

1Sm 21: 3 let no one know anything about the *b*
21: 9 weapons, because the king's *b* was urgent."
2Sm 16:10 "What *b* is it of mine or of yours,
Tb 10: 6 to take care of some unexpected *b* there.
Jdt 10: 9 I may go to carry out the *b* we discussed."
Est 1:13 because the king's *b* was conducted in
2Mc 11:26 but may contentedly go about their own *b*."
15: 5 take up arms and carry out the king's *b*."
Wis 13:19 And for profit in *b* and success with his
Sir 37:11 a coward about war, to a merchant about *b*,
42: 3 sharing the expenses of a *b* or a journey,
Ez 28:16 violence was your *b*,
Jon 1: 8 "Tell us," they said, "what is your *b*?
Mt 22: 5 way, one to his farm, another to his *b*.
Jn 21:22 Your *b* is to follow me."
1Cor 5:12 What *b* is it of mine to judge outsiders?
Rv 18:15 goods, who grew rich from *b* with the city,

BUSY (15)

Dt 6: 7 and abroad, whether you are *b* or at rest.
11:19 and abroad, whether you are *b* or at rest.
2Chr 35:14 were *b* offering holocausts and the fatty
Ps(s) 131: 1 I *b* not myself with great things,
Eccl 5:19 him *b* himself with the joy of his heart.
Sir 11:20 hold fast to your duty, *b* yourself with it,
Mt 26:59 were *b* trying to obtain false testimony
Mk 14:55 whole Sanhedrin were *b* soliciting testimony
Lk 10:40 was *b* with all the details of hospitality,
12:43 whom his master finds *b* when he returns.
1Cor 7:32 unmarried man is *b* with the Lord's affairs,
7:33 but the married man is *b* with this world's
Phil 2:21 Everyone is *b* seeking his own interests
2Thes 3:11 not keeping *b* but acting like busybodies.
Ti 2: 5 to be sensible, chaste, *b* at home,

BUSYBODIES (2)

2Thes 3:11 unruly, not keeping busy but acting like *b*.
1Tm 5:13 time-wasters but gossips and *b* as well,

BUSYING (1)

1Tm 1: 4 teaching false doctrines and *b* themselves

BUTCHER (2)

2Mc 5: 8 as the *b* of his country and his countrymen.
Is 22:13 celebrate, you slaughter oxen and *b* sheep,

BUTT (2)

Ps(s) 69:13 and drunkards make me the *b* of their songs.
Ez 34:21 and *b* all the weak sheep with your horns

BUTTER (3)

Dt 32:14 *B* from its cows and milk from its sheep,
2Sm 17:29 *b* and cheese from the flocks and herds,
Ps(s) 55:22 Softer than *b* is his speech,

BUTTING (1)

Dn 8: 4 I saw the ram *b* toward the west,

BUTTOCKS (2)

2Sm 10: 4 lower halves of their garments at the *b*,
Is 20: 4 with *b* uncovered [the shame of Egypt].

BUY (47)

Gn 42: 2 Go down there and *b* some for us,
42: 3 *b* an emergency supply of grain from Egypt.
44:25 come back and *b* some food for the family.
Lv 25:14 land to your neighbor or *b* any from him,
25:25 go and *b* back what his kinsman has sold.
25:26 means to *b* it back in his own name,
25:28 sufficient means to *b* back his land,
25:29 he has the right to *b* it back during the
25:44 *b* them from among the neighboring nations.
25:45 You may also *b* them from among the aliens
27:31 someone wishes to *b* back any of his tithes,
2Sm 24:21 "To *b* the threshing floor from you to
1Chr 21:24 I will *b* it from you properly,
2Chr 34:11 masons to *b* hewn stone and timber
Ezr 7:17 therefore, to use this money to *b* bulls,
Neh 10:32 we will not *b* from them on the sabbath or
Tb 1:14 I would go to Media to *b* goods for him.
1Mc 3:41 and gold, to *b* the Israelites as slaves.
2Mc 8:11 inviting them to *b* Jewish slaves and
8:25 of those who had come to *b* them as slaves.
8:34 the thousand slave dealers to *b* the Jews,
Prv 17:16 the fool's hand are the means to *b* wisdom,
Sir 20:11 A man may *b* much for little,
Is 43:24 You did not *b* me sweet cane for money,
Jer 13: 1 Go *b* yourself a linen loincloth;
19: 1 Go, *b* a potter's earthen flask.
32: 7 *B* for yourself my field in Anathoth,
32: 8 and said, "Please *b* my field in Anathoth,
32:25 *B* the field with money,
Lam 5: 4 The water we drink we must *b*,
Am 8: 6 We will *b* the lowly man for silver,
Zec 11: 5 they who *b* them slay them with impunity;
Mt 14:15 villages and *b* some food for themselves."
25: 9 go to the dealers and *b* yourselves some.'
25:10 they went off to *b* it the groom arrived,
27: 7 they used it to *b* the potter's field as a
Mk 6:36 here and *b* themselves something to eat?"
Lk 9:13 go and *b* food for all these people?"
22:36 a sword must sell his coat and *b* one.
Jn 4: 8 had gone off to the town to *b* provisions.)
6: 5 shall we *b* bread for these people to eat?"
6: 7 two hundred days' wages could we *b* loaves
13:29 him to *b* what was needed for the feast,
Rv 3:18 *B* from me gold refined by fire if you
3:18 *B* white garments in which to be clothed,
3:18 *B* ointment to smear on your eyes,
13:16 it did not allow a man to *b* or sell

BUYER (5)

Dt 28:68 and female slaves, but there will be no *b*."
Prv 20:14 says the *b*; but once he has gone his way
Sir 37:11 about business, to a *b* about value,
Is 24: 2 maid as her mistress, the *b* as the seller,
Ez 7:12 Let not the *b* rejoice nor the seller mourn,

BUYERS (1)

1Cor 7:30 *b* should conduct themselves as though they

BUYING (3)

Sir 27: 2 between *b* and selling sin is wedged in.
Mt 21:12 all those engaged there in *b* and selling.
Mk 11:15 those who were engaged in *b* and selling.

BUZ (3)

Gn 22:21 Uz, his first-born, his brother *B*,
1Chr 5:14 son of Jeshishai, son of Jahdo, son of *B*.
Jer 25:23 Dedan and Tema and *B*,

BUZI (1)

Ez 1: 3 came to the priest Ezekiel, the son of *B*,

BUZITE (2)

Jb 32: 2 the anger of Elihu, son of Barachel the *B*,
32: 6 So Elihu, son of Barachel the *B*,

BUZZARD (2)

Lv 11:18 owl, the barn owl, the desert owl, the *b*,
Dt 14:17 owl, the ibis, the desert owl, the *b*,

BUZZING (2)

Dt 28:42 *B* insects will infest all your trees and
Is 18: 1 Ah, land of *b* insects,

BY-PASS (1)

Nm 21: 4 on the Red Sea road, to *b* the land of Edom.

BY-PASSING (1)

Jgs 11:18 *b* the land of Edom and the land of Moab,

BYGONE (2)

Ez 26:20 descend into the pit, those of the *b* age;
Acts 17:30 *b* periods when men did not know him;

BYPATHS (1)

Jer 18:15 ways, the paths of old, To travel on *b*,

BYROADS (2)

Mt 22: 9 That is why you must go out into the *b* and
22:10 the *b* and rounded up everyone they met,

BYSSUS (2)

Est 1: 6 *b* from silver rings on marble pillars.
8:15 crown of gold and a cloak of crimson *b*.

BYSTANDERS (8)

Mt 26:73 later some *b* came over to Peter and said,
27:47 made some of the *b* who heard it remark,
Mk 11: 5 Some of the *b* said to them,
14:47 One of the *b* drew his sword and struck the
14:69 an eye on him, started again to tell the *b*,
14:70 little later the *b* said to Peter once more,
15:35 A few of the *b* who heard it remarked,
Jn 12:29 When the crowd of *b* heard the voice,

BYWORD (12)

1Kgs 9: 7 become a proverb and a *b* among all nations,
2Chr 7:20 it a proverb and a *b* among all peoples.
Tb 3: 4 death, till we were an object lesson, a *b*,
Jb 17: 6 as evil, and I am made a *b* of the people;
30: 9 I am become a *b* among them.
Ps(s) 44:15 You made us a *b* among the nations,
69:12 my garment, and I became a *b* for them.
Sir 42:11 the sport of your enemies, A *b* in the city,
Jer 24: 9 kingdoms of the earth, a reproach and a *b*,
Ez 14: 8 man, and make of him an example and a *b*.
23:10 Thus she became a *b* for women,
36: 3 and have become a *b* and a popular jeer;

C

CAANAN (1)

Gn 9:25 "Cursed be *C*!

CABBON (1)

Jos 15:40 Joktheel, Lachish, Bozkath, Eglon, *C*,

CABIN (1)

Ez 27: 7 from the coasts of Elishah covered your *c*.

CABINET (4)

1Kgs 10:11 quantity of *c* wood and precious stones.
2Chr 2: 7 of cedar, cypress and *c* wood from Lebanon,
9:10 also brought *c* wood and precious stones.
9:11 With the *c* wood the king made stairs for

CABLES (2)

Jb 40:17 the sinews of his thighs are like *c*.
Acts 27:17 made use of *c* to brace the ship itself.

CABUL (2)

Jos 19:27 of Beth-emek and Neiel, it extended to *C*,
1Kgs 9:13 And he called them the land of *C*,

CAESAR (8)

Mt 22:21 to them, "Then give to *C* what is Caesar's,
Mk 12:17 said to them, "Give to *C* what is Caesar's,
Lk 2: 1 In those days *C* Augustus published a
3: 1 fifteenth year of the rule of Tiberius *C*,
20:25 he said, "Then give to *C* what is Caesar's,
23: 2 opposing the payment of taxes to *C*,
Jn 19:12 you free this man you are no 'Friend of *C*.'"
19:15 priests replied, "We have no king but *C*."

CAESAREA (19)

Mt 16:13 came to the neighborhood of *C* Philippi,
Mk 8:27 set out for the villages around *C* Philippi.
Acts 8:40 news in all the towns until he reached *C*.
9:30 him down to *C* and sent him off to Tarsus.
10: 1 in *C* there was a centurion named Cornelius,
10:24 The following day, he arrived in *C*.
11:11 *C* came to the house where we were staying.
12:19 Herod left Judea to spend some time in *C*.
18:22 On landing at *C*,
21: 8 The next day we pushed on and came to *C*.
21:12 *C* urged Paul not to proceed to Jerusalem.
21:16 Some of the disciples from *C* came along to
23:23 to leave for *C* by nine o'clock tonight,
23:33 When the cavalrymen arrived in *C*,
24: 1 the high priest Ananias came down to *C*
25: 1 province, he went up from *C* to Jerusalem.
25: 4 that Paul was being kept in custody at *C*,
25: 6 days in Jerusalem, Festus went down to *C*.
25:13 in *C* and paid Festus a courtesy call.

CAESAR'S (8)

Mt 22:21 *C*," they replied.
22:21 to them, "Then give to Caesar what is *C*,
Mk 12:16 *C*," they told him.

12:17 said to them, "Give to Caesar what is C,
Lk 20:24 C," they replied,
20:25 he said, "Then give to Caesar what is C,
Jn 19:12 who makes himself a king becomes C rival."
Phil 4:22 believe, particularly those in C service.

CAGE (4)

Sir 11:30 he seem like a bird confined in a c,
Ez 19: 9 c and took him away to the king of Babylon,
Rv 18: 2 is a c for every unclean spirit, a cage

CAIAPHAS (9)

Mt 26: 3 of the high priest, whose name was C.
26:57 Jesus led him off to C the high priest,
Lk 3: 2 during the high-priesthood of Annas and C,
Jn 11:49 One of their number named C,
18:13 of C who was high priest that year.
18:14 (It was C who had proposed to the Jews the
18:24 next sent him, bound, to the high priest C.
18:28 brought Jesus from C to the praetorium.
Acts 4: 6 in Jerusalem, Annas the high priest, C,

CAIN (20)

Gn 4: 1 wife Eve, and she conceived and bore C,
4: 2 of flocks, and C a tiller of the soil.
4: 3 In the course of time C brought an
4: 5 but on C and his offering he did not.
4: 5 C greatly resented this and was crestfallen.
4: 6 So the LORD said to C:
4: 8 C said to his brother Abel,
4: 8 C attacked his brother Abel and killed him.
4: 9 Then the LORD asked C,
4:13 C said to the LORD:
4:15 kills Cain, C shall be avenged sevenfold."
4:15 So the LORD put a mark on C,
4:16 C then left the LORD's presence and
4:17 C had relations with his wife,
4:17 C also became the founder of a city,
4:24 If C is avenged sevenfold,
4:25 of Abel," she said, "because C slew him."
1Jn 3:12 We should not follow the example of C who
Jude 1:11 They have taken the road C took.

CAINAN (2)

Lk 3:36 son of Eber, son of Shelah, son of C,
3:37 son of Jared, son of Mahalaleel, son of C,

CAIN'S (1)

Heb 11: 4 offered God a sacrifice greater than C.

CAJOLE (1)

Sir 13: 6 he needs something from you he will c you,

CAKE (10)

Lv 8:26 before the LORD he took one unleavened c,
24: 5 two tenths of an ephah of flour for each c.
Nm 6:19 c and one unleavened wafer from the basket,
15:20 of a c of your first batch of dough.
1Sm 30:12 a c of pressed figs and two cakes of
2Sm 6:19 bread, a cut of roast meat, and a raisin c.
1Kgs 17:13 make me a little c and bring it to me.
19: 6 his head was a hearth c and a jug of water.
1Chr 16: 3 of bread, a piece of meat, and a raisin c.
Hos 7: 8 nations, Ephraim is a hearth c unturned.

CAKES (35)

Gn 19: 3 a meal for them, baking c without leaven,
Ex 29: 2 flour make unleavened c mixed with oil,
29:23 of bread, one of the c made with oil,
Lv 2: 4 c made of fine flour mixed with oil,
6: 9 of unleavened c and in a sacred place:
7:12 he shall offer unleavened c mixed with oil,
7:12 and c made of fine flour mixed with oil
10:12 the altar in the form of unleavened c.
24: 5 take fine flour and bake it into twelve c,
Nm 6:15 and a basket of unleavened c of fine flour
6:17 libation, and the basket of unleavened c.
11: 8 loaves, which tasted like c made with oil.
Jos 5:11 the form of unleavened c and parched grain.
Jgs 6:19 ephah of flour in the form of unleavened c.
6:20 and unleavened c and lay them on this rock;
6:21 and touched the meat and unleavened c.
6:21 which consumed the meat and unleavened c,
1Sm 25:18 grain, a hundred c of pressed raisins,
25:18 raisins, and two hundred c of pressed figs,
30:12 a cake of pressed figs and two c of
2Sm 13: 6 and prepare some fried c before my eyes,
13: 8 into cakes before his eyes and fried the c.
13: 9 took the pan and set out the c before him.
13:10 So Tamar picked up the c she had prepared
16: 1 of bread, an ephah of c of pressed raisins,
1Kgs 14: 3 Take along ten loaves, some c,
1Chr 9:31 was entrusted with preparing the c.
Jdt 10: 5 filled a bag with roasted grain, fig c,
Sg 2: 5 Strengthen me with raisin c,
Is 16: 7 For the raisin c of Kir-hareseth they sigh,
Jer 7:18 dough to make c for the queen of heaven,
44:19 we baked for her c in her image
Dn 14:27 these he boiled together and made into c.

Hos 3: 1 to other gods and are fond of raisin c.

CALAH (2)

Gn 10:11 he built Nineveh, Rehoboth-Ir, and C,
10:12 as well as Resen, between Nineveh and C,

CALAMITIES (4)

Dt 29:21 when they see the c of this land and the
1Sm 10:19 delivers you from all your evils and c,
Est E: 5 has involved them in irreparable c
2Mc 14:14 the misfortunes and c of the Jews

CALAMITY (29)

Dt 28:61 or c not mentioned in this book of the law,
Jgs 11:35 have struck me down and brought c upon me.
1Sm 6: 9 he has brought this great c upon us;
6:19 c with which the LORD had afflicted them.
2Sm 22:19 They attacked me on my day of c,
24:16 the LORD regretted the c and said to the
1Chr 21:15 the LORD saw and decided against the c,
Jb 6: 2 and my c laid with it in the scales,
21:20 he feels it, Let his own eyes see the c,
21:30 the evil man is spared c when it comes;
27: 9 attend to his cry when c comes upon him?
30:24 held out to help a wretched man in his c?
31: 3 Is it not c for the unrighteous,
Ps(s) 18:19 They attacked me in the day of my c,
Prv 17: 5 he who is glad at c will not go unpunished.
22: 8 He who sows iniquity reaps c,
Eccl 9:11 for a time of c comes to all alike.
Wis 18:21 the wrath and put a stop to the c,
Sir 8:15 man, lest he weigh you down with c;
41: 9 If you have children, c will seize them;
Jer 17:16 Yet I did not press you to send c;
25:32 c stalks from nation to nation;
Ez 6:10 threatened to inflict this c upon them.
Dn 9:12 c that has ever occurred under heaven.
9:13 the law of Moses, this c came full upon us.
9:14 watch over the c and brought it upon us.
Ob 1:13 gate of my people on the day of their c;
1:13 upon his misfortune on the day of his c;
1:13 upon his possessions on the day of his c!

CALAMUS (1)

Sg 4:14 Nard and saffron, c and cinnamon,

CALCOL (1)

1Chr 2: 6 sons of Zerah were Zimri, Ethan, Heman, C,

CALCULATE (2)

Lk 14:28 will he not first sit down and c the
Rv 13:18 anyone can c the number of the beast,

CALCULATED (1)

2Kgs 25:16 for the house of the LORD, was never c.

CALCULATIONS (2)

Eccl 7:29 but men have had recourse to many c.
Mt 2:16 making his c on the basis of the date he

CALDRON (2)

1Sm 2:14 would thrust it into the basin, kettle, c,
Mi 3: 3 flesh in a kettle, and like meat in a c.

CALDRONS (2)

2Chr 35:13 the sacred meals in pots, c and pans,
2Mc 7: 3 gave orders to have pans and c heated.

CALEB (34)

Nm 13:30 C, however, to quiet the people
14: 6 while Joshua, son of Nun, and C,
14:24 But because my servant C has a different
14:30 I solemnly swore to settle you, except C,
14:38 the land, only Joshua, son of Nun, and C,
26:65 and not one of them was left except C,
32:12 except the Kenizzite C,
34:19 C, son of Jephunneh, from
Dt 1:36 I swore to give to your fathers, except C,
Jos 14: 6 up to Joshua in Gilgal, the Kenizzite C,
14:13 Joshua blessed C,
14:14 remains the heritage of the Kenizzite C,
15:13 As the LORD had commanded, Joshua gave C,
15:14 C drove out from there the three Anakim,
15:16 C said, "I will give my daughter
15:17 C gave him his daughter Achsah in marriage.
15:18 as she alighted from the ass, C asked her,
21:12 belonging to the city had been given to C,
Jgs 1:12 And C said,
1:13 C gave him his daughter Achsah in marriage.
1:14 as she alighted from the ass, C asked her,
1:15 So C gave her the upper and the lower pool.
1:20 had commanded, Hebron was given to C,
1Sm 30:14 the territory of Judah, and the Negeb of C;
1Chr 2:18 By his wife Azubah, C,
2:19 When Azubah died, C married Ephrath,
2:24 of Hezron, C had relations with Ephrathah,
2:42 The descendants of C,
2:50 These were descendants of C,

4:15 The sons of C,
6:41 belonging to the city had been given to C,
1Mc 2:56 C, for bearing witness before the assembly,
Sir 46: 7 lifetime showed himself loyal, He and C,
46: 9 And the strength he gave to C remained

CALEBITE (1)

1Sm 25: 3 and attractive, but Nabal himself, a C,

CALEB'S (6)

Jos 15:17 Othniel, son of C brother Kenaz,
Jgs 1:13 Othniel, son of C younger brother Kenaz,
3: 9 Othniel, son of C younger brother Kenaz,
1Chr 2:46 Ephah, C concubine, bore Haran,
2:48 Maacah, C concubine, bore Sheber
2:49 Achsah was C daughter.

CALENDAR (1)

Ex 12: 2 month shall stand at the head of your c;

CALF (27)

Ex 32: 4 gold with a graving tool, made a molten c.
32: 5 built an altar before the c and proclaimed,
32: 8 themselves a molten c and worshiping it,
32:19 the camp, he saw the c and the dancing.
32:20 Taking the c they had made,
32:24 it into the fire, and this c came out."
32:35 for having had Aaron make the c for them.
Lv 9: 2 "Take a c for a sin offering and a ram
9: 3 he-goat for a sin offering, a c and a lamb,
9: 8 the c that was his own sin offering.
Dt 9:16 to you by making for yourselves a molten c!
9:21 Then, taking the c,
1Sm 28:24 The woman had a stall-fed c in the house,
Neh 9:18 they made for themselves a molten c,
Ps(s) 29: 6 leap like a c and Sirion like a young bull.
106:19 a c in Horeb and adored a molten image;
Is 11: 6 c and the young lion shall browse together,
Jer 31:18 I was an untamed c.
34:18 will make like the c which they cut in two,
34:19 who passed between the parts of the c,
Hos 8: 5 Cast away your c, O Samaria!
8: 6 such is the c of Samaria!
10: 5 of Samaria fear for the c of Beth-aven;
Lk 15:23 Take the fatted c and kill it.
15:27 c because he has him back in good health.'
15:30 loose women, you kill the fatted c for him.'
Acts 7:41 the c and offered sacrifice to the idol,

CALL (198)

Gn 2:19 to the man to see what he would c them;
17:15 for your wife Sarai, do not c her Sarai;
17:19 bear you a son, and you shall c him Isaac.
24:57 "Let us c the girl and see what she
30:13 "Women c me fortunate."
Ex 2: 7 "Shall I go and c one of the Hebrew women
Dt 4: 7 our God, is to us whenever we c upon him?
4:26 I c heaven and earth this day to witness
7:18 Rather, c to mind what the LORD,
28:37 wood and stone, and will c forth amazement,
30:19 I c heaven and earth today to witness
31:28 c heaven and earth to witness against them.
Jos 7: 3 not c for an effort from all the people."
Jgs 16:25 they said, C Samson that he may amuse us."
21: 9 A roll c of the army established that none
Ru 1:20 "Do not c me Naomi. C me Mara
1:21 Why should you c me Naomi,
1Sm 3: 5 "I did not c you," Eli said.
3: 6 But he answered, "I did not c you,
12:17 Yet I shall c to the LORD,
2Sm 15: 2 the king, Absalom would c to him and say,
17: 5 said, "Now c Hushai the Archite also;
1Kgs 1:28 King David answered, C Bathsheba here."
8:52 Hear them whenever they c upon you,
17:18 c attention to my guilt and to kill my son?"
18:24 You shall c on your gods, and I will call
18:25 C upon your gods,
18:27 C louder, for he is a god
22:13 who had gone to c Micaiah said to him,
2Kgs 4:12 servant Gehazi, C this Shunammite woman."
4:15 C her," said Elisha.
4:36 summoned Gehazi and said, C the Shunammite.
4:36 She came at his c,
8: 8 a gift with you and go c on the man of God.
2Chr 18:12 who had gone to c Micaiah said to him:
Tb 4: 2 why should I not c my son Tobiah and let
5: 9 Tobit said, C the man,
8: 7 C down your mercy on me and on her,
13:11 in you, and shall c you the chosen one,
Jdt 8:17 from him, let us c upon him to help us,
2Mc 13:10 people to c upon the LORD night and day,
Jb 3: 4 let not God above c for it,
5: 1 C now! Will anyone respond to you?
9:16 If I appealed to him and he answered my c,
9:19 if of judgment, who will c him to account?
11:10 If he seize and imprison or c to judgment,
13:22 Then c me, and I will respond;
14:15 You would c, and I would answer you;
17:14 If I must c corruption "my father,"
19:16 I c my servant, but he gives no answer,

CALL (cont.)

27:10 in the Almighty and *c* upon him constantly?
35: 9 they *c* for help because of the power of
Ps(s) 3: 5 When I *c* out to the LORD,
4: 2 When I *c*, answer me, O my just God,
4: 4 the LORD will hear me when I *c* upon him.
5: 3 Heed my *c* for help, my king and my God!
17: 6 I *c* upon you, for you will answer me,
20:10 the king, and answer us when we *c* upon you.
27: 7 Hear, O LORD, the sound of my *c*;
28: 1 To you, O LORD, I *c*;
31:18 me not be put to shame, for I *c* upon you;
50:15 Then *c* upon me in time of distress;
53: 5 just as they eat bread, who *c* not upon God?
55:17 But I will *c* upon God,
56:10 do my enemies turn back, when I *c* upon you;
57: 3 I *c* to God the Most High,
61: 3 end I *c* to you as my heart grows faint.
63: 5 up my hands, I will *c* upon your name.
79: 6 the kingdoms that *c* not upon your name;
80:19 us new life, and we will *c* upon your name.
86: 3 on me, O Lord, for to you I *c* all the day.
86: 5 in kindness to all who *c* upon you.
86: 7 In the day of my distress I *c* upon you,
88: 3 incline your ear to my *c* for help,
88:10 daily I *c* upon you,
91:15 He shall *c* upon me,
102: 3 in the day when I *c*,
116:13 up, and I will *c* upon the name of the LORD;
116:17 and I will *c* upon the name of the LORD.
119:145 *c* out with all my heart;
119:146 I *c* upon you;
141: 1 LORD, to you I *c*; hasten to me;
141: 1 hearken to my voice when I *c* upon you.
145:18 The LORD is near to all who *c* upon him,
145:18 upon him, to all who *c* upon him in truth.
Prv 1:28 "Then they *c* me, but I answer not;
2: 3 Yes, if you *c* to intelligence,
7: 4 *c* Understanding, "Friend!"
8: 1 Does not Wisdom *c*,
8: 4 "To you, O men, I *c*;
21:13 poor will himself also *c* and not be heard.
24: 8 men *c* him an intriguer.
Eccl 10:19 Bread and oil *c* forth merriment and wine
Wis 14:22 war of ignorance, they *c* such evils peace.
Sir 11:28 *C* no man happy before his death,
Is 5:20 Woe to those who *c* evil good,
8: 4 how to *c* his father or mother by name,
8:12 *C* not alliance what this people calls
21:11 They *c* to me from Seir,
26:13 from you only that we can *c* upon your name.
30: 7 Therefore I *c* her "Rahab quelled."
34:14 beasts, satyrs shall *c* to one another;
43:22 Yet you did not *c* upon me,
46:11 I *c* from the east a bird of prey,
48:13 When I *c* them, they stand forth at once.
55: 6 he may be found, *c* him while he is near.
58: 5 Do you *c* this a fast,
58: 9 Then you shall *c*,
58:12 of the breach," they shall *c* you,
58:13 If you *c* the sabbath a delight,
60:14 They shall *c* you "City of the LORD,"
60:18 You shall *c* your walls "Salvation" and
62: 4 No more shall men *c* you "Forsaken,"
65: 1 To a nation that did not *c* upon my name.
65:24 Before they *c*, I will answer;
Jer 3: 4 Even now do you not *c* me,
3:17 they will *c* Jerusalem the LORD's throne;
3:19 You would *c* me,
7:27 when you *c* to them,
10:25 on the tribes that *c* not upon your name;
11:14 *c* to me at the time of their misfortune.
25:29 I will *c* down the sword upon all who
29:12 When you *c* me,
31: 6 the watchmen will *c* out on Mount Ephraim:
32:25 Buy the field with money, *c* in witnesses.
32:43 bought in this land, which you *c* a desert,
33: 3 *C* to me, and I will answer you;
33:16 this is what they shall *c* her:
46:17 *C* Pharaoh, king of Egypt,
48:34 they *c* from Zoar to Horonaim,
49:19 who can *c* me to account?
50:29 *C* up against Babylon archers,
Lam 3:21 But I will *c* this to mind,
3:56 You heard me *c*,
Bar 3: 1 souls and dismayed spirits *c* to you.
3: 7 that we may *c* upon your name,
4:21 *c* upon God,
4:27 Fear not, my children; *c* out to God!
Ez 20:29 *c* it a high place even to the present day.
Dn 11:25 He shall *c* on his strength and cleverness
Hos 2:18 She shall *c* me "My husband,"
7:11 They *c* upon Egypt,
Jl 1:14 Proclaim a fast, *c* an assembly;
2:15 proclaim a fast, *c* an assembly;
3: 5 Jerusalem survivors whom the LORD shall *c*.
Jon 1: 6 Rise up, *c* upon your God!
3: 8 covered with sackcloth and *c* loudly to God;
Zep 2:14 Their *c* shall resound from the window,
3: 9 they all may *c* upon the name of the LORD,
Zec 13: 9 They shall *c* upon my name,
Mal 3:12 Then all nations will *c* you blessed,
3:15 Rather must we *c* the proud blessed;
Mt 1:23 to a son, and they shall *c* him Emmanuel,"
9:13 I have come to *c*, not the self-righteous,
10:25 If they *c* the head of the house Beelzebul,
20: 8 *C* the workmen and give them their pay,
23: 9 Do not *c* anyone on earth your father.
26:53 Do you not suppose I can *c* on my Father to
Mk 2:17 I have come to *c* sinners,
10:18 Jesus answered, "Why do you *c* me good?
10:47 was Jesus of Nazareth, he began to *c* out,
10:49 Then Jesus stopped and said, *C* him over."
15:12 do with the man you *c* the king of the Jews?"
Lk 1:48 all ages to come shall *c* me blessed.
6:46 Why do you *c* me 'Lord,
9:54 us *c* down fire from heaven to destroy them?"
18: 7 his chosen who *c* out to him day and night?
18:19 Jesus said to him, "Why *c* me 'good'?
Jn 4:16 He said to her, "Go, *c* your husband,
9:11 *c* Jesus made mud and smeared it on my eyes,
15:15 Instead, I *c* you friends,
Acts 9:41 The next thing he did was to *c* in those
10:15 God has purified you are not to *c* unclean."
10:28 no one should *c* any man unclean or impure.
11: 9 God has purified you are not to *c* unclean.'
22:16 wash away your sins as you *c* upon his name.'
24:14 which they *c* a sect
25:13 in Caesarea and paid Festus a courtesy *c*.
Rom 9:25 who were not my people I will *c* 'my people,'
9:25 who were not loved I will *c* 'Beloved';
10:12 rich in mercy toward all who *c* upon him.
10:14 *c* on him in whom they have not believed?
11:29 God's gifts and his *c* are irrevocable.
1Cor 1: 2 be, *c* on the name of our Lord Jesus Christ,
7:18 Did the *c* come to another who had never
7:21 Were you a slave when your *c* came?
2Cor 1:23 I *c* on God as my witness that it was out
Eph 2:11 their flesh, *c* themselves "circumcised"
4: 4 is but one hope given all of you by your *c*.
2Thes 1:11 that our God may make you worthy of his *c*,
2Tm 2:22 those who *c* on the Lord in purity of heart.
Heb 2:11 he is not ashamed to *c* them brothers,
Jas 5:11 Those who have endured we *c* blessed.
1Pt 1:17 In prayer you *c* upon a Father who judges
2Pt 1:10 to make your *c* and election permanent,
Rv 3: 3 *C* to mind how you accepted what you heard;

CALLED (470)

Gn 1: 5 *c* the light "day," and the darkness he called
1: 8 God *c* the dome "the sky."
1:10 God *c* the dry land "the earth,"
1:10 and the basin of the water he *c* "the sea."
2:19 the man *c* each of them would be its name.
2:23 This one shall be *c* 'woman,'
3: 9 LORD God then *c* to the man and asked him,
3:20 The man *c* his wife Eve,
4:25 she gave birth to a son whom she *c* Seth.
11: 9 That is why it was *c* Babel,
16:14 That is why the well is *c* Beer-lahai-roi.
17: 5 No longer shall you be *c* Abram;
19: 5 They *c* to Lot and said to him,
19:22 That is why the town is *c* Zoar.
20: 8 Early the next morning Abimelech *c* all his
21:17 and God's messenger *c* to Hagar from heaven:
21:31 This is why the place is *c* Beer-sheba;
22: 1 He *c* to him, "Abraham!"
22:11 the LORD's messenger *c* to him from heaven,
22:15 *c* to Abraham from heaven and said:
24:58 So they *c* Rebekah and asked her,
25:30 I'm starving" (That is why he was *c* Edom.)
26: 7 He was afraid, if he *c* her his wife,
26: 9 He *c* for Isaac and said:
26:20 So the well was *c* Esek,
26:21 so it was *c* Sitnah.
26:22 It was *c* Rehoboth,
26:33 He *c* it Shibah;
27: 1 he *c* his older son Esau and said to him,
27:42 *c* her younger son Jacob and said to him:
28: 1 Isaac therefore *c* Jacob,
28:19 He *c* that site Bethel,
29:16 the older was *c* Leah,
31:11 In the dream God's messenger *c* to me,
31:47 Laban *c* it Jegar-sahadutha,
33:17 That is why the place was *c* Succoth.
35: 8 below Bethel, and so it was *c* Allon-bacuth.
35:10 name is Jacob shall no longer be *c* Jacob,
35:18 she *c* him Ben-oni;
38:29 So he was *c* Perez.
38:30 he was *c* Zerah.
46: 2 speaking to Israel in a vision by night, *c*,
47:29 die, he *c* his son Joseph and said to him:
49: 1 Jacob *c* his sons and said:
Ex 1:15 of whom was *c* Shiphrah and the other Puah,
2: 8 maiden went and *c* the child's own mother.
2:10 who adopted him as her son and *c* him Moses;
3: 4 closely, God *c* out to him from the bush,
12:21 Moses *c* all the elders of Israel and said
15:23 Hence this place was *c* Marah.
16:31 The Israelites *c* this food manna.
17: 7 The place was *c* Massah and Meribah,
17:15 an altar there, which he *c* Yahweh-nissi;
18: 3 One of these was *c* Gershom;
18: 4 The other was *c* Eliezer;
19: 3 Then the LORD *c* to him and said,
24:16 he *c* to Moses from the midst of the cloud.
33: 7 The tent, which was *c* the meeting tent,
34:31 Only after Moses *c* to them did Aaron and
36: 2 Moses then *c* Bezalel and Oholiab and all
Lv 1: 1 The LORD *c* Moses,
7:35 he *c* them to be the priests of the LORD;
Nm 11: 3 Hence that place was *c* Taberah,
12: 5 entrance of the tent, *c* Aaron and Miriam.
13:16 But Hoshea, son of Nun, Moses *c* Joshua.
13:24 there that they *c* the place Wadi Eshcol.
32:38 they rebuilt, they *c* by their old names.
32:41 captured them and *c* them Havvoth-jair.
32:42 and *c* it Nobah after his own name.
Dt 2:11 It was the Moabites who *c* them Emim.
2:20 whom the Ammonites *c* Zamzummim,
3: 9 Mount Hermon [which is *c* Sirion
3:13 of Bashan was once *c* a land of the Rephaim.
3:14 *c* it after his own name Bashan Havvothjair,
Jos 5: 9 the place is *c* Gilgal to the present day.
7:26 place is *c* the Valley of Achor to this day.
8:16 in the city had been *c* out to pursue them.
14:15 Hebron was formerly *c* Kiriath-arba,
15:15 Debir, which was formerly *c* Kiriath-sepher.
Jgs 1:10 Hebron, which was formerly *c* Kiriath-arba,
1:11 Debir, which was formerly *c* Kiriath-sepher.
1:23 made of Bethel, which formerly was *c* Luz.
1:26 a city and *c* it Luz, as it is still called.
2: 5 and so that place came to be *c* Bochim.
6:24 altar to the LORD and *c* it Yahweh-shalom.
6:32 So on that day Gideon was *c* Jerubbaal,
7:23 Israelites were *c* to arms from Naphtali,
7:24 So all the Ephraimites were *c* to arms,
9:54 *c* his armor-bearer and said to him,
10: 4 are *c* Havvoth-jair to the present day.
12: 4 Then Jephthah *c* together all the men of
15:19 spring in Lehi is *c* En-hakkore to this day.
16:19 and *c* for a man who shaved off his seven
16:25 So they *c* Samson from the prison,
18:12 west of Kiriath-jearim, is *c* Mahaneh-dan.
18:23 They *c* to the Danites,
Ru 4: 1 had spoken come along, he *c* to him by name,
4:17 They *c* him Obed.
1Sm 1:20 of her term bore a son whom she *c* Samuel,
3: 4 The LORD *c* to Samuel,
3: 5 "Here I am. You *c* me."
3: 6 Again the LORD *c* Samuel,
3: 6 "You *c* me."
3: 8 The LORD *c* Samuel again,
3: 8 You *c* me."
3: 9 Samuel, "Go to sleep, and if you are *c*,
3:16 to tell Eli the vision, but Eli *c* to him,
9: 9 is now called prophet was formerly *c* seer.)
9:26 At daybreak Samuel *c* to Saul on the roof,
10:17 Samuel *c* the people together to the LORD
12:18 Samuel then *c* to the LORD,
13: 4 the soldiers were *c* up to Saul in Gilgal.
14: 4 was a rocky crag on each side, one *c* Bozez,
14:12 outpost *c* to Jonathan and his armor-bearer.
16: 8 *c* Abinadab and presented him before Samuel,
20:37 had shot the arrow Jonathan *c* after him,
20:38 Again he *c* to his lad,
23: 8 Saul then *c* all the people to war,
23:28 place came to be *c* the Gorge of Divisions.
28:15 I have *c* you to tell me what I should do."
2Sm 1: 7 turned around and, seeing me, *c* me to him.
1:15 *c* one of the attendants and said to him,
2:26 Then Abner *c* to Joab and said:
5: 9 stronghold, which was *c* the City of David;
5:20 That is why the place is *c* Baal-perazim.
6: 8 been *c* Perez-uzzah down to the present day.)
9: 9 The king then *c* Ziba,
13:17 *c* the youth who was his attendant and said,
14:33 The king then *c* Absalom,
17:11 the sands by the sea, be *c* up for combat;
18:16 Israelites, because Joab *c* on them to halt.
18:18 is *c* Yadabshalom to the present day.
18:28 Then Ahimaaz *c* out and greeted the king.
20:16 the city stood on the outworks and *c* out,
21: 2 king *c* the Gibeonites and spoke to them.
22: 7 I *c* upon the LORD and cried out to my God;
1Kgs 7: 2 He built the hall *c* the Forest of Lebanon
7:21 of the temple, one to the right, *c* Jachin,
7:21 Jachin, and the other to the left, *c* Boaz.
9:13 *c* them the land of Cabul, as they are called
17:10 he *c* out to her,
17:11 She left to get it, and he *c* out after her,
17:20 He *c* out to the LORD:
17:21 child three times and *c* out to the LORD:
18:26 it and *c* on Baal from morning to noon,
18:28 They *c* out louder and slashed themselves
20:15 So Ahab *c* up the retainers of the
20:27 *c* to arms and supplied with provisions;
20:39 was passing, he *c* out to the king and said:
22: 9 of Israel *c* an official and said to him,
2Kgs 1:11 "Man of God," he *c* out to Elijah,
3:10 "The LORD has *c* together these three
3:13 "The LORD has *c* these three kings
3:21 arms was *c* up and stationed at the border.
4:15 When she had been *c*,
4:22 on him, she went out and *c* to her husband,
6:11 the king of Aram *c* together his officers.
9: 1 The prophet Elisha *c* one of the guild
18: 4 smashed the bronze serpent *c* Nehushtan

18:18 They *c* for the king,
1Chr 4:14 so *c* because they were craftsmen.
5:20 For during the battle they *c* on God,
11: 4 the natives of the land were *c* Jebusites.
11: 7 which thenceforth was *c* the City of David.
13:11 has been *c* Perez-uzza even to this day.
14:11 Therefore that place was *c* Baal-perazim.
15: 4 David also *c* together the sons of Aaron
21:26 When he *c* upon the LORD,
22: 6 Then he *c* for his son Solomon and
2Chr 3:17 and he *c* the one to the right Jachin and
14:10 Asa *c* upon the LORD, his God, praying:
18: 8 So the king of Israel *c* an official,
20:26 ever since been *c* the Valley of Beracah.
24: 5 He *c* together the priests and Levites and
32:20 son of Amos, prayed and *c* out to heaven.
Ezr 10:23 Jozabad, Shimei, Kelaiah (also *c* Kelita),
Neh 5: 7 I *c* the nobles and magistrates to account,
5:12 Then I *c* for the priests and had them
8: 1 and they *c* upon Ezra the scribe to bring
Tb 2:13 I *c* to my wife and said:
4: 3 So he *c* his son Tobiah;
5:17 Then he *c* his son and said to him:
7:12 Then Raguel *c* his daughter Sarah,
7:13 He then *c* her mother and told her to bring
7:15 Later Raguel *c* his wife Edna and said,
8:11 went back into the house and *c* his wife,
9: 1 Then Tobiah *c* Raphael and said to him:
12: 1 Tobit *c* his son Tobiah and said to him,
12: 5 So Tobiah *c* Raphael and said,
12: 6 Raphael *c* the two men aside privately and
14: 3 *c* his son Tobiah and Tobiah's seven sons,
Jdt 6:21 they *c* upon the God of Israel for help.
9: 4 of their kinswoman, *c* on you for help.
10: 2 She *c* her maid and they went down into the
14: 6 So they *c* Achior from the house of Uzziah.
1Mc 2: 2 John, who was *c* Gaddi;
2: 3 Simon, who was *c* Thassi;
2: 4 Judas, who was *c* Maccabeus;
2: 5 Eleazar, who was *c* Avaran;
2: 5 and Jonathan, who was *c* Apphus.
3: 1 Then his son Judas, who was *c* Maccabeus,
6: 1 that in Persia there was a city *c* Elymais,
6:10 he *c* in all his Friends and said to them:
6:19 *c* all the people together to beseige them.
6:28 angry, and he *c* together all his Friends,
6:43 Eleazar *c* Avaran,
8:20 "Judas, *c* Maccabeus,
10: 1 and sixty, Alexander, who was *c* Epiphanes,
10:20 you are to be *c* the King's Friend,
11: 7 river *c* Eleutherus and then returned
11:47 So the king *c* the Jews to his aid.
12:31 against the Arabs who are *c* Zabadeans,
12:37 quarter *c* Chaphenatha was also repaired.
16: 2 Simon *c* his two oldest sons,
16:15 little stronghold *c* Dok which he had built.
2Mc 1:36 and his companions *c* the liquid nephthar,
5: 8 *C* to account before Aretas,
9: 2 He had entered the city *c* Persepolis and
10:13 *c* a traitor for having abandoned Cyprus,
10:32 to a well-fortified stronghold *c* Gazara,
11:18 referred to the king I *c* to his attention,
12:13 He also attacked a certain city *c* Caspin,
12:21 well as the baggage, to a place *c* Karnion,
12:32 After this feast *c* Pentecost,
12:35 A man *c* Dositheus,
12:36 Judas *c* upon the Lord to show himself
14: 6 "Those Jews *c* Hasideans,
14:37 he was *c* a father of the Jews because of
15:21 and *c* upon the LORD who works miracles;
15:36 of the twelfth month, *c* Adar in Aramaic,
Jb 31:24 trust in gold or *c* fine gold my security;
42:14 daughters, of whom he *c* the first Jemimah,
Ps(s) 14: 4 They have not *c* upon the LORD;
18: 7 I *c* upon the LORD and cried out to my God;
34: 7 When the afflicted man *c* out,
49:12 though they have *c* lands by their names.
81: 8 In distress you *c*,
99: 6 who called upon his name; they *c* upon
105:16 When he *c* down a famine on the land
116: 2 he has inclined his ear to me the day I *c*.
116: 4 sorrow, And I *c* upon the name of the LORD,
118: 5 In my straits I *c* upon the LORD;
120: 1 In my distress I *c* to the LORD,
138: 3 When I *c*, you answered me;
Prv 1:24 "Because I *c* and you refused,
Sg 5: 6 I *c* to him but he did not answer me.
Wis 11: 4 When they thirsted, they *c* upon you,
11:25 preserved, had it not been *c* forth by you?
18: 1 they themselves had suffered, *c* them blest;
Sir 2:10 has anyone *c* upon him and been rebuffed?
5:15 Be not *c* a detractor;
36:11 Show mercy to the people *c* by your name;
46: 5 He *c* upon the Most High God when his
46:16 He, too, *c* upon God,
47: 5 Since he *c* upon the Most High God,
47:18 You were *c* by that glorious name which was
48:20 But they *c* upon the Most High God and
51:10 I *c* out: O Lord, you are my father,
Is 1:26 After that you shall be *c* city of justice,
4: 3 that is left in Jerusalem Will be *c* holy:
19:18 one shall be *c* "City of the Sun."
22:12 GOD of hosts, *c* on you To weep and mourn,
32: 5 No more will the fool be *c* noble,
35: 8 A highway will be there, *c* the holy way;
41: 4 He who has *c* forth the generations since
41: 9 places, You whom I have *c* my servant,
42: 6 have *c* you for the victory of justice,
43: 1 I have *c* you by name:
45: 4 my chosen one, I have *c* you by your name,
47: 1 longer shall you be *c* dainty and delicate.
47: 5 you be *c* sovereign mistress of kingdoms.
48: 1 O house of Jacob *c* by the name of Israel,
48: 8 treacherous, a rebel you were *c* from birth.
48:15 I myself have spoken, I have *c* him,
49: 1 The LORD *c* me from birth,
50: 2 Why did no one answer when I *c*?
51: 2 When he was but one I *c* him,
54: 5 Holy One of Israel, *c* God of all the earth.
56: 7 be *c* a house of prayer for all peoples.
61: 3 They will be *c* oaks of justice,
61: 6 LORD, ministers of our God you shall be *c*.
62: 2 You shall be *c* by a new name pronounced by
62: 4 But you shall be *c* "My Delight,"
62:12 They shall be *c* the holy people,
62:12 the LORD, And you shall be *c* "Frequented,"
65:12 Since I *c* and you did not answer,
65:15 but my servants shall be *c* by another name
66: 4 Because, when I *c*,
Jer 6:30 "Silver rejected" they shall be *c*,
7:13 because you did not answer, though I *c* you,
7:32 of Ben-hinnom will no longer be *c* such,
19: 6 this place will no longer be *c* Topheth,
25:29 with this city, which is *c* by my name,
30:17 "The outcast" they have *c* you,
32:10 *c* witnesses and weighed out the silver on
35:17 did not obey, when I *c* they did not answer.
36: 4 So Jeremiah *c* Baruch,
42: 8 Then he *c* Johanan,
Lam 3:55 I *c* upon your name,
3:57 You came to my aid when I *c* to you;
Bar 6:29 How can they be *c* gods?
Ez 9: 3 Then he *c* to the man dressed in linen with
Dn 3:93 of the white-hot furnace and *c* to Shadrach,
13:52 from the other, he *c* one of them and said:
14: 3 The Babylonians had an idol *c* Bel,
14: 8 the king *c* his priests and said to them,
Hos 2: 1 were *c*, "Lo-ammi," They shall be called,
5: 1 It is you who are *c* to judgment.
11: 1 child I loved him, out of Egypt I *c* my son.
11: 2 The more I *c* them,
Am 7: 4 he *c* for a judgment by fire.
Jon 2: 3 Out of my distress I *c* to the LORD,
Na 2: 6 His picked troops are *c*,
Hg 1:11 And I *c* for a drought upon the land and
Zec 6: 8 the earth, he *c* out to me and said,
7:13 *c*, so he would not listen when they called,
8: 3 Jerusalem shall be *c* the faithful city,
11: 7 took two staffs, one of which I *c* "Favor,"
Mal 1: 4 And they shall be *c* the land of guilt,
Mt 1:16 that Jesus who is *c* the Messiah was born.
2: 7 Herod *c* the astrologers aside and found
2:15 "Out of Egypt I have *c* my son."
2:23 There he settled in a town *c* Nazareth.
2:23 "He shall be *c* a Nazorean."
4:22 He *c* them,
5: 9 they shall be *c* sons of God.
5:19 so shall be *c* least in the kingdom of God.
15:32 Jesus *c* his disciples to him and said:
18: 2 He *c* a little child over and stood him in
20:25 Jesus then *c* them together and said:
20:32 Jesus then stopped and *c* out to them,
21:13 it, 'My house shall be *c* a house of prayer,'
23: 7 of respect in public and of being *c* 'Rabbi.'
23:10 Avoid being *c* teachers.
25:14 He *c* in his servants and handed his funds
26:36 went with them to a place *c* Gethsemane.
27: 8 that field, even today, is *c* Blood Field.
27:24 He *c* for water and washed his hands in
27:33 Upon arriving at a site *c* Golgotha (a name
27:62 and the Pharisees *c* at Pilate's residence.
Mk 8: 1 He *c* the disciples over to him and said:
9:35 down and *c* the Twelve around him and said,
10:42 Jesus *c* them together and said to them:
10:49 So they *c* the blind man over,
11:17 be *c* a house of prayer for all peoples'
12:43 He *c* his disciples over and told them:
Lk 1:32 and he will be *c* Son of the Most High.
1:35 offspring to be born will be *c* Son of God.
1:60 saying, "No, he is to be *c* John."
1:62 the father what he wished him to be *c*.
1:76 child, shall be *c* prophet of the Most High;
6:13 At daybreak he *c* his disciples and
6:15 son of Alphaeus, and Simon *c* the Zealot,
6:35 will rightly be *c* sons of the Most High,
7:11 Soon afterward he went to a town *c* Naim,
8: 2 Mary *c* the Magdalene,
9: 1 Jesus now *c* the Twelve together and gave
9:10 with him, he retired to a town *c* Bethsaida,
11:27 saying this a woman from the crowd *c* out,
13:12 Jesus saw her, he *c* her to him and said,
15:18 I no longer deserve to be *c* your son.
15:21 I no longer deserve to be *c* your son.'
15:26 He *c* one of the servants and asked him the
16: 5 "So he *c* in each of his master's debtors,
16:24 "He *c* out, "Father Abraham, have pity
18:16 but Jesus *c* for the children,
19:29 and Bethany on the mount *c* Olivet,
20:37 when he *c* the Lord the God of Abraham,
22: 3 possession of Judas, the one *c* Iscariot,
22:25 over them are *c* their benefactors.
23:13 Pilate then *c* together the chief priests,
23:33 they came to Skull Place, as it was *c*,
Jn 1:48 "Before Philip *c* you,"
2: 9 *c* the groom over and remarked to him:
11:28 this she went back and *c* her sister Mary.
11:43 Having said this, he *c* loudly,
11:47 the Pharisees *c* a meeting of the Sanhedrin.
11:54 *c* Ephraim in the region near the desert,
12:17 The crowd that was present when he *c*
19:13 bench at the place *c* the Stone Pavement
19:17 is *c* the Place of the Skull (in Hebrew,
Acts 1:12 from the mount *c* Olivet near Jerusalem
1:23 they nominated two, Joseph *c* Barsabbas,
3: 2 put him at the temple gate *c* "the Beautiful"
4:18 So they *c* them back and made it clear that
5:40 *c* in the apostles and had them whipped.
10: 7 he *c* two servants and a devout soldier
10:18 They *c* out to inquire whether Simon Peter
10:24 had *c* in his relatives and close friends.
11:26 were *c* Christians for the first time.
13: 2 me to do the work for which I have *c* them."
14:10 He *c* out to him in a loud voice,
14:12 Paul they *c* Hermes,
14:27 they *c* the congregation together and
15:30 upon their arrival there they *c* the assembly
15:37 wanted to take along John, *c* Mark.
16:29 The jailer *c* for a light,
19:25 He *c* a meeting of these men and other
23:17 Paul then *c* for one of the centurions,
23:18 *c* me and asked me to bring you this boy,
24:21 what I *c* out as I stood in their presence:
27: 8 along the coast to a place *c* Fair Havens,
27:14 struck, the kind *c* a "northeaster."
28: 1 we learned that the island was *c* Malta.
Rom 1: 1 *c* to be an apostle and set apart to
1: 6 who have been *c* to belong to Jesus Christ.
1: 7 in Rome, beloved of God and *c* to holiness,
7: 3 She will be *c* an adulteress if,
8:28 who have been *c* according to his decree.
8:30 predestined he likewise *c*; those he called
9: 7 Isaac shall your descendants be *c*."
9:24 I am speaking about us whom he *c*,
9:26 they shall be *c* sons of the living God."
1Cor 1: 1 *c* by God's will to be an apostle of Christ
1: 2 in Christ Jesus and *c* to be a holy people,
1: 9 he who *c* you to fellowship with his Son,
1:24 but to those who are *c*,
1:26 Brothers, you are among those *c*.
7:15 God has *c* you to live in peace.
7:17 continuing as he was when the Lord *c* him.
7:18 someone *c* after he had been circumcised?
7:20 ought to continue as he was when he was *c*.
7:22 *c* in the Lord is a freedman of the Lord,
7:22 who has been *c* is a slave of Christ.
7:24 of life that was his when he was *c*.
10:28 both for the sake of the one who *c*
14:24 to task by all and *c* to account by all,
2Cor 4: 3 gospel can be *c* "veiled" in any sense,
6: 8 We are *c* imposters,
Gal 1: 6 soon deserting him who *c* you in accord
1:15 before I was born and *c* me by his favor
5:13 that you have been *c* to live in freedom
Eph 1:18 know the great hope to which he has *c* you,
2:11 stock *c* "uncircumcised" by those who,
Col 3:15 the one body you have been *c* to that peace.
1Thes 4: 7 has not *c* us to immorality but to holiness;
2Thes 2:14 He *c* you through our preaching of the good
1Tm 6:12 everlasting life to which you were *c* when,
6:20 of what is falsely *c* knowledge.
2Tm 1: 9 has saved us and has *c* us to a holy life,
Heb 5: 4 but only when *c* by God as Aaron was.
9: 2 this was *c* the holy place.
9: 3 was the tabernacle *c* the holy of holies,
9:15 those who are *c* may receive the promised
9:23 themselves *c* for better sacrifices.
11: 8 By faith Abraham obeyed when he was *c*,
11:16 God is not ashamed to be *c* their God,
11:18 Isaac shall your descendants be *c*."
Jas 3: 1 do so will be *c* to the stricter account.
1Pt 1:15 the likeness of the holy One who *c* you;
2: 9 the glorious works" of the One who *c* you
2:21 It was for this you were *c*,
3: 6 subject to Abraham and *c* him her master.
3: 9 This you have been *c* to do,
5:10 *c* you to his everlasting glory in Christ,
2Pt 1: 3 of him who *c* us by his own glory and power.
1Jn 3: 1 on us in letting us be *c* children of God!
Jude 1: 1 of James, to those who have been *c* by God;
Rv 1: 9 found myself on the island *c* Patmos
16:16 kings in a place *c* in Hebrew "Armageddon."
17:14 the ones who were *c*:
19:11 its rider was *c* "The Faithful and True."

CALLING (24)

Nm 10: 7 But in *c* forth an assembly you are to blow
Jgs 8: 1 not *c* us when you went to fight against
12: 1 the Ammonites without *c* us to go with you?

CALLING (cont.)

1Sm 3: 8 understood that the LORD was *c* the youth.
3:10 and revealed his presence, *c* out as before,
24: 9 also stepped out of the cave, *c* to Saul,
2Mc 12: 6 and after *c* upon God,
14:34 *c* upon the unfailing defender of our
14:41 gate and *c* for fire to set the door ablaze,
14:46 *c* upon the LORD of life and of spirit to
Ps(s) 69: 4 I am wearied with *c*,
Prv 9:15 *C* to passers-by as they go on their
Is 1:13 New moon and sabbath, *c* of assemblies,
40:26 army and numbers them, *c* them all by name.
Mt 11:16 in the town squares, *c* to their playmates:
Mk 10:49 He is *c* you!"
15:35 He is *c* on Elijah!"
Lk 7:32 the city squares and *c* to their playmates,
23: 2 taxes to Caesar, and *c* himself the Messiah,
Jn 9:40 this up, saying, "You are not *c* us blind,
Acts 10: 3 a messenger of God coming toward him and *c*,
Eph 4: 1 a life worthy of the *c* you have received,
Heb 3: 1 holy brothers who share a heavenly *c*,
Rv 3:20 If anyone hears me *c* and opens the door,

CALLISTHENES (1)

2Mc 8:33 had set fire to the sacred gates and *C*,

CALLS (36)

1Sm 26:14 And Abner answered, "Who is it that *c* me?"
Jb 12: 4 one whom God answers when he *c* upon him,
Ps(s) 42: 8 *c* unto deep in the roar of your cataracts;
147: 4 he *c* each by name.
Prv 1:21 Down the crowded ways she *c* out,
9: 3 she *c* from the heights out over the city:
28:24 defrauds father or mother and *c* it no sin,
Eccl 10: 3 of understanding he *c* everything foolish.
Wis 2:16 He *c* blest the destiny of the just and
Is 8:12 not alliance what this people *c* alliance,
21: 9 He *c* out and says,
45: 3 the God of Israel, who *c* you by your name.
54: 6 The LORD *c* you back,
64: 6 There is none who *c* upon your name,
Jer 50:44 who *c* me to account?
Bar 3:33 dismisses the light, and it departs, *c* it,
3:35 When he *c* them they answer,
Hos 7: 7 none of them *c* upon me.
Jl 3: 5 be rescued who *c* on the name of the LORD;
Mt 22:43 under the Spirit's influence *c* him 'lord,'
22:45 If David *c* him 'lord,'
Lk 15: 9 she *c* in her friends and neighbors to say,
23:15 this man has done nothing that *c* for death.
23:22 about him that *c* for the death penalty.
Jn 10: 3 as he *c* his own by name and leads them out.
10:35 If it *c* those men gods to whom God's word
Acts 2:21 be saved who *c* on the name of the Lord.'
2:39 still far off whom the Lord our God *c*."
17:30 but now he *c* on all men everywhere to
Rom 4:17 restores the dead to life and *c* into being
9:12 by works but by the favor of him who *c*—
10:13 *c* on the name of the Lord will be saved."
Gal 5: 8 does not come from him who *c* you.
Phil 3:14 I run toward the prize to which God *c* me
1Thes 2:12 God who *c* you to his kingship and glory.
5:24 He who *c* us is trustworthy,

CALM (11)

Jgs 6:23 The LORD answered him, "Be *c*,
Jb 37:17 a *c* from the south comes over the land,
Prv 29: 8 the city ablaze, but wise men *c* the fury.
Is 30:15 By waiting and by *c* you shall be saved,
32:17 right will produce *c* and security.
Mt 8:26 Complete *c* ensued;
Mk 4:39 The wind fell off and everything grew *c*.
Lk 8:24 The waves subsided and it grew *c*.
Acts 19:36 must *c* yourselves and not do anything rash.
1Pt 3: 4 beauty of a *c* and gentle disposition.
4: 7 remain *c* so that you will be able to pray.

CALMED (2)

Ps(s) 107:30 They rejoiced that they were *c*,
Is 57:20 are like the tossing sea which cannot be *c*,

CALMING (1)

2Mc 13:26 After *c* them and gaining their good will,

CALMS (3)

Prv 15: 1 A mild answer *c* wrath,
29:11 but by biding his time, the wise man *c* it.
Sir 43:24 His is the plan that *c* the deep,

CALNEH (1)

Am 6: 2 Pass over to *C* and see,

CALNO (1)

Is 10: 9 he says, "Is not *C* like Carchemish,

CALUMNIES (3)

Tb 3: 6 to live, because I have heard insulting *c*,
2Mc 3:11 Contrary to the *c* of the impious Simon,
14:27 Stirred up by the villain's *c*,

CALUMNY (2)

Wis 1:11 and from *c* withhold your tongues;
Sir 5:16 use not your tongue for *c*;

CALVE (1)

Jb 21:10 their cows *c* and do not miscarry.

CALVES (20)

1Sm 6: 7 but drive their *c* indoors away from them.
6:10 to the cart but shut up their *c* indoors.
14:32 upon the spoil and took sheep, oxen and *c*,
1Kgs 12:28 made two *c* of gold and said to the people:
12:30 frequented these *c* in Bethel and in Dan.
12:32 with sacrifices to the *c* he had made;
2Kgs 10:29 regards the golden *c* at Bethel and at Dan.
17:16 God, and made for themselves two molten *c*;
2Chr 11:15 high places and satyrs and *c* he had made.
13: 8 golden *c* which Jeroboam made you for gods?
Is 1:11 In the blood of *c*,
27:10 wilderness, where *c* shall browse and lie.
Jer 46:21 in her ranks are like fatted *c*;
50:11 Frisk like *c* on the green,
Hos 13: 2 "offer sacrifice. Men kiss *c*
Am 6: 4 taken from the flock, and *c* from the stall!
Mi 6: 6 him with holocausts, with *c* a year old?
Mal 3:20 And you will gambol like *c* out of the
Heb 9:12 not with the blood of goats and *c*,
9:19 people, he took the blood of goats and *c*,

CAME (1261)

Gn 1: 5 Thus evening *c*,
1: 8 Evening *c*, and morning followed—
1:13 Evening *c*, and morning followed—
1:19 Evening *c*, and morning followed—
1:23 Evening *c*, and morning followed—
1:31 Evening *c*, and morning followed—
7: 6 old when the flood waters *c* upon the earth.
7:10 the waters of the flood *c* upon the earth.
7:16 male and female, and of all species they *c*,
8: 4 ark *c* to rest on the mountains of Ararat.
8:11 In the evening the dove *c* back to him,
8:18 So Noah *c* out,
9:10 that were with you and *c* out of the ark.
9:18 of Noah who *c* out of the ark were Shem,
11: 2 they *c* upon a valley in the land of Shinar
11: 5 The LORD *c* down to see the city and the
12: 5 When they *c* to the land of Canaan,
12:14 When Abram *c* to Egypt,
14: 5 kings allied with him *c* and defeated
14: 7 turned back and *c* to Enmishpat (that is,
14:13 *c* and brought the news to Abram the Hebrew,
15: 1 word of the LORD *c* to Abram in a vision:
15: 4 Then the word of the LORD *c* to him:
19: 5 are the men who *c* to your house tonight?
19: 9 they sneered, *c* here as an immigrant,
19:29 Thus it *c* to pass:
20: 3 But God *c* to Abimelech in a dream one
22: 9 *c* to the place of which God had told him,
22:20 Some time afterward, the news *c* to Abraham:
24:15 Nahor) *c* out with a jug on her shoulder.
24:16 As she *c* up, the servant ran toward her
24:42 "When I *c* to the spring today, I prayed:
24:45 Rebekah *c* out with a jug on her shoulder.
25:24 When the time of her delivery *c*,
25:26 His brother *c* out next,
25:29 cooking a stew, Esau *c* in from the open,
26:32 That same day Isaac's servants *c* and
27:30 when his brother Esau *c* back from his hunt.
27:33 I finished eating it just before you *c*,
27:35 "Your brother *c* here by a ruse and
28:11 When he *c* upon a certain shrine,
29: 1 journey he *c* to the land of the Easterners.
30:14 he *c* upon some mandrakes which he brought
30:16 evening, when Jacob *c* home from the fields,
30:30 had before I *c* has grown into very much,
30:30 LORD's blessings *c* upon you in my company.
30:38 animals were in heat as they *c* to drink,
30:43 increasingly prosperous, and he *c* to own,
31:22 day, word *c* to Laban that Jacob had fled.
33: 6 and their children *c* forward and bowed low;
33: 7 and her children *c* forward and bowed low;
33: 7 and her children *c* forward and bowed low.
34: 5 he held his peace until they *c* home.
35: 8 Death *c* to Rebekah's nurse Deborah;
37:18 a distance, and before he *c* up to them,
37:23 So when Joseph *c* up to them,
38:27 When the time of her delivery *c*,
38:28 hand, to note that this one *c* out first.
38:29 as he withdrew his hand, his brother *c* out;
38:30 Afterward his brother *c* out;
39:11 Joseph *c* into the house to do his work,
39:14 He *c* in here to lie with me,
39:16 the cloak with her until his master *c* home.
40: 6 When Joseph *c* to them in the morning,
40:10 had barely budded when its blossoms *c* out,
41: 2 Nile, when up out of the Nile *c* seven cows,
41: 3 cows, ugly and gaunt, *c* up out of the Nile;
41:14 his clothes, he *c* into Pharaoh's presence.
41:18 Nile, when up from the Nile *c* seven cows,
41:19 Behind them *c* seven other cows,
41:27 cows that *c* up after them are seven years,
41:53 enjoyed by the land of Egypt *c* to an end,
41:55 When hunger *c* to be felt throughout the
41:57 *c* to Joseph to obtain rations of grain,
42: 5 were among those who *c* to procure rations.
42: 6 When Joseph's brothers *c* and knelt down
43:20 *c* down here once before to procure food.
43:26 When Joseph *c* home,
47: 5 Jacob and his sons *c* to Joseph in Egypt,
47:15 was spent, all the Egyptians *c* to Joseph,
47:18 *c* to him in the following one and said:
47:28 life *c* to a hundred and forty-seven years.
Ex 1: 8 nothing of Joseph, *c* to power in Egypt.
2: 5 daughter *c* down to the river to bathe,
2:16 *c* to draw water and fill the troughs
2:17 But some shepherds *c* and drove them away.
3: 1 the flock across the desert, he *c* to Horeb,
4:24 *c* upon Moses and would have killed him.
5:15 foremen *c* and made this appeal to Pharaoh:
5:20 left Pharaoh and *c* upon Moses and Aaron,
8: 2 frogs *c* up and covered the land of Egypt.
8:13 the earth and gnats *c* upon man and beast.
13: 3 this day on which you *c* out of Egypt,
13: 8 the LORD did for me when I *c* out of Egypt.'
14:20 so that it *c* between the camp of the
15:27 Then they *c* to Elim,
16: 1 community *c* into the desert of Sin,
16:13 evening quail *c* up and covered the camp.
16:22 the community *c* and reported this to Moses,
16:35 forty years, until they *c* to settled land;
17: 8 Amalek *c* and waged war against Israel.
18: 5 his father-in-law Jethro *c* to him in the
18:12 and Aaron *c* with all the elders of Israel
19: 1 the Israelites *c* to the desert of Sinai.
19:14 Then Moses *c* down from the mountain to the
19:18 smoke, for the LORD *c* down upon it in fire.
19:20 the LORD *c* down to the top of Mount Sinai,
23:15 for it was then that you *c* out of Egypt.
24: 3 When Moses *c* to the people and related all
32:15 Moses then turned and *c* down the mountain
32:24 it into the fire, and this calf *c* out."
34:18 in the month of Abib you *c* out of Egypt.
34:29 As Moses *c* down from Mount Sinai with the
34:32 Later on, all the Israelites *c* up to him,
34:34 he removed the veil until he *c* out again.
Lv 9:22 When he *c* down from offering the sin
9:24 Fire *c* forth from the LORD's presence and
10: 2 Fire therefore *c* forth from the LORD's
Nm 3:38 layman who *c* near was to be put to death.
9: 6 These men *c* up to Moses and Aaron that
9:17 wherever the cloud *c* to rest,
10:12 the cloud *c* to rest in the desert of Paran.
10:36 And when it *c* to rest,
11:25 then *c* down in the cloud and spoke to him.
11:25 and as the spirit *c* to rest on them,
11:26 yet the spirit *c* to rest on them also,
12: 5 the LORD *c* down in the column of cloud,
12: 5 When both *c* forward,
14:45 that hill country *c* down and defeated them,
16:35 And fire from the LORD *c* forth which
17: 8 Aaron *c* to the front of the meeting tent,
20:22 whole Israelite community *c* to Mount Hor.
20:28 Moses and Eleazar *c* down from the mountain,
21: 7 Then the people *c* to Moses and said,
22: 9 Then God *c* to Balaam and said,
22:11 'This people that *c* here from Egypt now
22:20 That night God *c* to Balaam and said to him,
22:39 with Balak, and they *c* to Kiriath-huzoth.
24: 2 by tribe, the spirit of God *c* upon him,
25: 6 Yet a certain Israelite *c* and brought in a
26: 4 *c* out of the land of Egypt were as follows:
27: 1 They *c* forward,
31:48 of the army *c* up to Moses and said to him,
32: 2 they *c* to Moses and the priest Eleazar and
33: 9 Setting out from Marah, they *c* to Elim,
36: 1 one of the Josephite clans *c* up and laid
Dt 1:22 Then all of you *c* up to me and said,
1:44 living there *c* out against you and,
4:11 You *c* near and stood at the foot of the
5:23 you *c* to me in the person of all your
10: 5 to me, I turned and *c* down the mountain,
22:27 was in the open fields that he *c* upon her,
29: 6 When we *c* to this place,
29: 6 of Bashan, *c* out to engage us in battle,
33: 2 "The LORD *c* from Sinai and dawned on his
33: 5 assembled and the tribes of Israel *c* together
Jos 2: 4 *c* to me, but I did not know where they *c*
2: 8 Rahab *c* to them on the roof and said:
2:10 Red Sea before you when you *c* out of Egypt,
2:23 Then the two *c* back down from the hills,
4:19 The people *c* up from the Jordan on the
5: 4 Of all the people who *c* out of Egypt,
5: 5 all the men who *c* out were circumcised,
5: 6 people that *c* forth from Egypt
8:14 and he and all his army *c* out very early
8:22 those in the city *c* out to intercept them,
9:17 the Israelites *c* to their cities of Gibeon,
10:24 They *c* forward and put their feet upon
10:33 Horam, king of Gezer, *c* up to help Lachish,
11: 4 They *c* out with all their troops,
11: 7 Joshua with his whole army *c* upon them at
14: 6 the Judahites *c* up to Joshua in Gilgal,
15:11 Jabneel, before it *c* out at the sea.
21: 1 Levite families *c* up to Eleazar the priest,

22:10 and the half-tribe of Manasseh *c* to the
22:15 When these *c* to the Reubenites,
22:17 a plague *c* upon the community of the LORD.
24:11 you crossed the Jordan and *c* to Jericho,
Jgs 1: 5 *c* upon Adonibezek and fought against him.
1:16 *c* up with the Judahites from the city of
2: 5 and so that place *c* to be called Bochim.
3:10 The spirit of the LORD *c* upon him,
3:24 When Ehud had left and the servants *c*,
4: 5 the Israelites *c* up to her for judgment.
4:22 Then when Barak *c* in pursuit of Sisera,
5:13 Then down *c* the fugitives with the mighty,
5:13 of the LORD *c* down for me as warriors.
5:14 From Machir *c* down commanders,
5:19 The kings *c* and fought;
5:23 For they *c* not to my help,
6: 5 when they *c* into the land to lay it waste.
6:11 Then the angel of the LORD *c* and sat under
6:21 Thereupon a fire *c* up from the rock which
7:13 It *c* to our tent and struck it,
7:19 who were with him *c* to the edge of the camp
9: 6 all Beth-millo *c* together and proceeded
9:26 Ebed, *c* over to Shechem with his kinsmen.
9:52 *c* up to the tower and fought against it,
10: 3 Jair the Gileadite *c* after him and judged
11:13 and the Jordan when they *c* up from Egypt.
11:16 For when they *c* up from Egypt,
11:16 the desert to the Red Sea and *c* to Kadesh.
11:29 The spirit of the LORD *c* upon Jephthah.
11:34 in Mizpah, it was his daughter who *c* forth,
13: 6 told her husband, "A man of God *c* to me;
13: 6 I did not ask him where he *c* from,
13: 9 and the angel of God *c* again to the woman
13:10 *c* to me the other day has appeared to me,"
14: 5 Timnah, a young lion *c* roaring to meet him.
14: 6 But the spirit of the LORD *c* upon Samson,
14: 9 When he *c* to his father and mother,
14:14 *c* forth food, and out of the strong *c*
14:19 The spirit of the LORD *c* upon him,
15:14 and the Philistines *c* shouting to meet him,
15:14 him, the spirit of the LORD *c* upon him:
16: 5 lords of the Philistines *c* to her and said,
16:18 *c* and brought up the money with them.
17: 8 On his journey he *c* to the house of Micah
18: 7 So the five men went on and *c* to Laish.
18:13 of Ephraim and *c* to the house of Micah.
18:28 No one *c* to their aid,
19:10 and traveled till they *c* opposite Jebus,
19:16 an old man *c* from his work in the field;
19:26 Then at daybreak the woman *c* and collapsed
19:30 *c* up from the land of Egypt to this day.
20: 1 So all the Israelites *c* out as one man:
20:21 the Benjaminites *c* out of the city and
20:25 once again the Benjaminites who *c* out of
20:48 by fire all the cities they *c* upon.
Ru 2: 4 Boaz himself *c* from Bethlehem and said to
2: 7 and ever since she *c* this morning she has
2:17 gleaned it *c* to about an ephah of barley,
3:14 that this woman *c* to the threshing floor."
4:13 When they *c* together as man and wife,
1Sm 1: 4 the day *c* for Elkanah to offer sacrifice,
2:14 treated who *c* to the sanctuary at Shiloh.
2:27 A man of God *c* to Eli and said to him:
3:10 the LORD *c* and revealed his presence,
3:20 Thus all Israel from Dan to Beer-sheba *c*
4:16 The man quickly *c* up to Eli and said,
6:14 The cart *c* to the field of Joshua the
7: 1 So the inhabitants of Kiriath-jearim *c* for
7: 2 *c* to rest in Kiriath-jearim a long time
8: 4 Therefore all the elders of Israel *c* in a
9: 5 When they *c* to the land of Zuph,
9:12 just today he *c* to the city,
9:25 *c* down from the high place into the city,
10: 9 That very day all these signs *c* to pass. . . .
10:13 When he *c* out of the prophetic state,
11: 5 Just then Saul *c* in from the field,
11: 9 The messengers *c* and reported this to the
14:26 *c* to the comb the swarm had left it;
14:30 their enemy's booty when they *c* across it,
15: 6 the Israelites when they *c* up from Egypt."
15:13 When Samuel *c* to him, Saul greeted him:
15:32 Agag *c* to him struggling and saying,
16: 4 city *c* trembling to meet him and inquired,
16: 6 As they *c*, he looked at Eliab and thought.
16:21 David *c* to Saul and entered his service.
17: 4 of Gath *c* out from the Philistine camp;
17:16 [Meanwhile the Philistine *c* forward and
17:23 *c* up from the ranks of the Philistines and
17:28 You *c* down to enjoy the battle!"
17:34 bear *c* to carry off a sheep from the flock,
18: 6 women *c* out from each of the cities of
18:10 day an evil spirit from God *c* over Saul,
18:28 Saul thus *c* to recognize that the LORD was
19: 9 Then an evil spirit from the LORD *c* upon
19:23 sheds, the spirit of God *c* upon him also,
21: 2 Nob, who *c* trembling to meet him and asked,
22:11 and they all *c* to the king.
23:16 *c* down there to David and strengthened his
23:25 When Saul and his men *c* looking for him,
23:27 capture them, when a messenger *c* to Saul,
23:28 *c* to be called the Gorge of Divisions.
24: 4 When he *c* to the sheepfolds along the way,
25:20 As she *c* down through a mountain defile
25:36 When Abigail *c* to Nabal,
25:40 David's servants *c* to Abigail in Carmel,
26: 1 Men from Ziph *c* to Saul in Gibeah
28: 8 They *c* to the woman by night,
28:21 Then the woman *c* to Saul,
29: 3 the day he *c* over to me until the present."
29:10 and your lord's servants who *c* with you,
30: 9 hundred men and *c* as far as the Wadi Besor,
30:21 When David *c* to the two hundred men who
30:21 *c* out to meet David and the men with him.
30:23 into our grip the band that *c* against us.
30:26 When David *c* to Ziklag,
31: 7 Philistines *c* and lived in those cities.
31: 8 the Philistines *c* to strip the slain,
2Sm 1: 2 On the third day a man *c* from Saul's camp,
2: 4 Then the men of Judah *c* there and anointed
2:23 And all who *c* to the place where Asahel
2:23 Asahel had fallen and died, *c* to a halt.
2:24 The sun had gone down when they *c* to the
2:28 horn, and all the soldiers *c* to a halt,
2:29 through the morning, and *c* to Mahanaim.
3:20 by twenty men, *c* to David in Hebron,
3:23 informed, "Abner, son of Ner, *c* to David;
3:24 Abner *c* to you.
3:25 Are you not aware that Abner *c* to deceive
3:37 all the people and all Israel *c* to know
4: 4 about Saul and Jonathan *c* from Jezreel,
4: 5 *c* into the house of Ishbaal during the
5: 1 of Israel *c* to David in Hebron and said:
5: 3 the elders of Israel *c* to David in Hebron,
5:18 *c* and overran the valley of Rephaim.
5:22 But the Philistines *c* up again and overran
6: 6 they *c* to the threshing floor of Nodan,
6:14 *c* dancing before the LORD with abandon,
6:20 daughter Michal *c* out to meet him and said,
8: 5 of Damascus *c* to the aid of Hadadezer,
8: 7 he *c* to Jerusalem in the days of Rehoboam,
9: 6 son of Jonathan, son of Saul, *c* to David,
10: 8 The Ammonites *c* out and drew up in battle
10:16 They *c* to Helam,
11: 4 When she *c* to him,
11: 7 When he *c*, David questioned him
11:23 and *c* out into the open against us,
12: 1 sent Nathan to David, and when he *c* to him,
13: 6 When the king *c* to visit him,
13:34 He *c* in and reported this,
13:36 finished speaking than the princes *c* in,
14:30 Joab's farmhands *c* to him with torn
14:33 who *c* to him and in homage fell on his
15: 6 Israelites who *c* to the king for judgment,
15:13 An informant *c* to David with the report,
15:20 You *c* only yesterday,
16: 5 coming out of the place, cursing as he *c*.
16:11 "If my own son, who *c* forth from my loins,
16:16 friend Hushai the Archite *c* to Absalom,
17: 6 When Hushai *c* to Absalom,
17:20 servants *c* to the woman at the house,
17:21 Ahimaaz and Jonathan *c* up out of the
17:27 When David *c* to Mahanaim,
18: 9 unexpectedly *c* up against David's servants.
18:31 When the Cushite *c* in,
19: 9 at the gate, they *c* into his presence.
19:26 When he *c* from Jerusalem to meet the king,
19:32 Barzillai the Gileadite also *c* down from
20: 3 King David *c* to his palace in Jerusalem,
20:12 because all who *c* up to him were stopping.
20:15 *c* and besieged him in Abel Beth-maacah.
21:10 until rain *c* down on them from the sky,
21:17 *c* to his assistance and struck and killed
22:10 He inclined the heavens and *c* down,
22:19 of calamity, but the LORD *c* to my support.
1Kgs 1:22 to the king, the prophet Nathan *c* in.
1:53 he *c* and paid homage to the king.
2: 8 Because he *c* down to meet me at the Jordan,
2:28 When the news *c* to Joab,
3:16 harlots *c* to the king and stood before him.
5:14 Men *c* to hear Solomon's wisdom from all
6:11 This word of the LORD *c* to Solomon:
7:14 He *c* to King Solomon and did all his metal
8: 1 Israelites, *c* to King Solomon in Jerusalem,
10: 1 fame, *c* to test him with subtle questions.
10: 2 She *c* to Solomon and questioned him on
10: 7 report until I *c* and saw with my own eyes,
10:15 addition to what *c* from the Tarshish fleet,
12:12 day all Israel *c* back to King Rehoboam,
13: 1 A man of God *c* from Judah to Bethel by the
13: 9 water and not to return by the way I *c*."
13:11 whose sons *c* and told him all that the man
13:14 "Are you the man of God who *c* from Judah?"
13:17 here, and not to go back the way I *c*,"
18:16 Ahab *c* to meet Elijah,
18:36 the prophet Elijah *c* forward and said,
18:38 fire *c* down and consumed the holocaust,
19: 4 he *c* to a broom tree and sat beneath it.
19: 7 the angel of the LORD *c* back a second time,
19: 9 There he *c* to a cave,
19: 9 But the word of the LORD *c* to him,
19:19 Elijah set out, and *c* upon Elisha,
20: 5 But the couriers *c* again and said,
20:13 Then a prophet *c* up to Ahab,
20:28 of God *c* up and said to the king of Israel:
20:33 When Ben-hadad *c* out to him,
20:36 company, a lion *c* upon him and killed him.
21: 5 His wife Jezebel *c* to him and said to him.
21:13 Two scoundrels *c* in and confronted him
22: 2 of Judah *c* down to the king of Israel,
22:15 When he *c* to the king,
22:21 *c* forth and presented himself to the LORD,
22:24 *c* up and slapped Micaiah on the cheek
2Kgs 1: 6 "A man *c* up to us,"
1: 7 *c* up to you and said these things to you?"
1:10 And fire *c* down from heaven and consumed
1:12 And divine fire *c* down from heaven,
2:11 chariot and flaming horses *c* between them,
2:23 boys *c* out of the city and jeered at him.
2:24 Then two she-bears *c* out of the woods and
3:15 of the LORD *c* upon Elisha and he announced:
3:20 water *c* from the direction of Edom and
4: 8 One day Elisha *c* to Shunem,
4:18 The day *c* when the child was old enough to
4:27 Gehazi *c* near to push her away,
4:36 She *c* at his call,
4:37 She *c* in and fell at his feet in gratitude;
4:42 A man *c* from Baal-shalishah bringing the
5: 9 Naaman *c* with his horses and chariots and
5:13 his servants *c* up and reasoned with him.
6:18 When the Arameans *c* down to get him,
6:23 Aramean raiders *c* into the land of Israel.
6:33 speaking, the king *c* down to him and said,
7: 8 Back they *c* into another tent,
7:10 *c* and summoned the city gatekeepers.
8: 5 *c* to the king to claim her house and field.
8: 7 *c* to Damascus at a time when Ben-hadad,
9:31 As Jehu *c* through the gate,
10: 8 princes," a messenger *c* in and told him.
10:13 on the way, he *c* across kinsmen of Ahaziah,
10:21 exception *c* into the temple of Baal,
11: 9 duty that week, *c* to Jehoiada the priest.
13:21 *c* in contact with the bones of Elisha, he came
15:14 son of Gadi, *c* up from Tirzah to Samaria,
15:29 king of Assyria, *c* and took Ijon,
16: 5 of Israel, *c* up to Jerusalem to attack it.
17: 7 This *c* about because the Israelites sinned
18:12 This *c* about because they had not heeded
18:37 *c* to Hezekiah with their garments torn,
19:28 mouth, and make you return the way you *c*.
19:33 He shall return by the same way he *c*,
20: 1 Isaiah, son of Amoz, *c* and said to him:
20: 4 courtyard, the word of the LORD *c* to him.
20:14 prophet *c* to King Hezekiah and asked him:
20:14 "They *c* from a distant land,
21:15 fathers *c* forth from Egypt until today.'"
23:17 man of God who *c* from Judah
24:10 Jerusalem, and the city *c* under siege.
25: 8 *c* to Jerusalem as the representative of
25:23 with their men *c* to him at Mizpah:
25:25 of royal descent, *c* with ten men,
1Chr 2:55 who *c* from Hammath the ancestor of
4:31 Until David *c* to reign,
5: 2 his brothers, so that the ruler *c* from him,
9:36 then *c* Zur,
10: 7 the Philistines *c* and occupied them.
10: 8 when the Philistines *c* to strip the slain,
11: 3 elders of Israel *c* to the king at Hebron,
11:23 but he *c* against him with a staff,
12: 1 The following men *c* to David in Ziklag
12:17 also *c* to David at the stronghold.
12:20 David when he *c* with the Philistines
12:24 armed troops that *c* to David at Hebron
12:39 *c* to Hebron with the resolute intention of
12:41 and Naphtali *c* bringing food on asses,
17: 3 same night the word of God *c* to Nathan:
17:16 David *c* in and sat in the LORD's presence,
18: 5 of Damascus *c* to the aid of Hadadezer,
19: 7 his army, who *c* and encamped before Medeba.
19: 7 from their cities and *c* out for war.
21:21 But as David *c* on toward him,
22: 8 But this word of the LORD *c* to me:
27: 1 that *c* and went month by month throughout
27:34 After Ahithophel *c* Jehoiada,
29: 6 overseers of the king's affairs *c* forward
2Chr 5: 2 *c* to Jerusalem to bring up the ark of the
5:11 When the priests *c* out of the holy place
7: 1 fire *c* down from heaven and consumed the
7: 3 the Israelites looked on while the fire *c* down
9: 1 she *c* to Jerusalem to test him with subtle
9: 1 She *c* to Solomon and questioned him on
9: 6 report until I *c* and saw with my own eyes.
10:12 Jeroboam and all the people *c* back to King
11: 2 the word of the LORD *c* to Shemaiah,
11:14 holdings and *c* to Judah and Jerusalem,
11:16 *c* to Jerusalem to sacrifice to the LORD,
12: 3 He *c* up with twelve hundred chariots and
12: 3 the army that *c* with him from Egypt
12: 4 cities of Judah and *c* as far as Jerusalem.
12: 5 Then Shemaiah the prophet *c* to Rehoboam
12: 7 the word of the LORD *c* to Shemaiah:
14: 8 chariots, and he *c* as far as Mareshah.
15: 1 Azariah, son of Oded, *c* the spirit of God.
16: 7 At that time Hanani the seer *c* to Asa,
18:14 When he *c* to the king,
18:20 until a spirit *c* forward and presented
18:23 *c* up and slapped Micaiah on the cheek
20: 1 Meunites *c* to fight against Jehoshaphat.
20: 4 cities of Judah they *c* to seek the LORD.
20:10 invade when they *c* from the land of Egypt,

CAME (cont.)

20:14 And the spirit of the LORD *c* upon Jahaziel,
20:24 When Judah *c* to the watchtower of the
20:25 and his people *c* to take plunder,
20:28 They *c* to Jerusalem,
20:29 And the fear of God *c* upon all the
21:17 They *c* up against Judah,
24:11 and an overseer for the high priest *c*,
24:17 of Judah *c* and paid homage to the king,
24:18 theirs, wrath *c* upon Judah and Jerusalem.
24:23 a force of Arameans *c* up against Joash.
24:24 Though the Aramean force *c* with few men,
25: 7 But a man of God *c* to him and said:
29:15 then they *c* as the king had ordered,
30:11 humbled themselves and *c* to Jerusalem.
32: 1 deeds, Sennacherib, king of Assyria, *c*.
34: 9 They *c* to Hilkiah the high priest and
35:20 *c* up to fight at Carchemish on the
35:22 words of Neco that *c* from the mouth of God,
36: 6 *c* up against him and bound him with chains
36:20 the kingdom of the Persians *c* to power.
Ezr 2: 1 and who *c* back to Jerusalem and Judah,
2:64 The entire assembly taken together *c* to
3: 1 Now when the seventh month *c*,
4:12 king that the Jews who *c* up from you
5: 3 At that time there *c* to them Tattenai,
5:16 Then this same Sheshbazzar *c* and laid the
7: 6 this Ezra *c* up from Babylon.
7: 7 and temple slaves also *c* up to Jerusalem
7: 8 Ezra *c* to Jerusalem in the fifth month of
9: 8 ago, mercy *c* to us from the LORD our God,
Neh 1: 2 my brothers, *c* with other men from Judah.
2:13 the Dragon Spring, and *c* to the Dung Gate,
4:15 ready, from daybreak till the stars *c* out.
5:17 who *c* to us from the nations round about,
7: 5 I *c* upon the family list of those who had
7: 6 and who *c* back to Jerusalem and Judah,
7:66 The entire assembly taken together *c* to
8: 1 Now when the seventh month *c*,
9:13 On Mount Sinai you *c* down,
12:37 until they *c* to the Water Gate on the east.
12:39 [and they *c* to a halt at the Prison Gate].
12:46 praise and thanksgiving to God *c* down
Tb 3:17 daughter Sarah *c* downstairs from her room.
4: 3 and when he *c*,
7:12 his daughter Sarah, and she *c* to him.
11:18 nephew Nadab also *c* to rejoice with Tobit.
12: 1 When the wedding celebration *c* to an end,
12:18 when I *c* to you it was not out of any
14:10 Ahiqar *c* out again into the light,
Jdt 1: 6 Thus many nations *c* together to resist the
6:14 Israelites *c* down to him from their city,
7: 8 of the seacoast, *c* to Holofernes and said:
8:11 When they *c*, she said to them:
10:18 They *c* and stood around her as she waited
10:20 *c* out and ushered her into the tent.
10:22 her to him, he *c* out to the antechamber,
11: 3 tell me why you fled from them and *c* to us.
12:13 of Holofernes, and *c* to Judith and said,
12:16 Then Judith *c* in and reclined on it.
13: 9 she *c* out and handed over the head of
14: 6 When he *c* and saw the head of Holofernes
14:13 They *c* to the tent of Holofernes and said
15: 8 *c* to see for themselves the good things
16: 3 Assyrian *c* from the mountains of the north,
16: 3 with the myriads of his forces he *c*;
Est A: 5 Two great dragons *c* on,
2:15 Modecai, when her turn *c* to visit the king,
B: 2 When I *c* to rule many peoples and to hold
4: 2 till he *c* before the royal gate,
4: 4 Esther's maids and eunuchs *c* and told her.
5: 2 She *c* up to him,
1Mc 1: 1 son, who *c* from the land of Kittim,
1:29 and he *c* to Jerusalem with a strong force.
2:15 enforcing the apostasy *c* to the city
2:23 a certain Jew *c* forward in the sight of
2:41 On that day they *c* to this decision:
2:49 When the time *c* for Mattathias to die,
3:40 they *c* and pitched their camp near Emmaus
3:41 heard of their fame, they *c* to the camp,
3:45 not one of her children entered or *c* out.
4: 5 the night Gorgias *c* into the camp of Judas,
4:13 them, they *c* out of their camp for battle,
4:29 They *c* into Idumea and camped at Beth-zur,
4:45 happy thought *c* to them to tear it down,
5:30 When morning *c*,
5:33 He *c* up behind them with three columns
5:59 *c* out of the city to meet them in battle.
6:29 Mercenary forces also *c* to him from other
7: 5 and impious men of Israel *c* to him.
7:18 and dread of them *c* upon all the people,
7:27 Nicanor *c* to Jerusalem with a large force
7:29 So he *c* to Judas,
7:33 elders of the people *c* out to greet him
7:46 Judea people *c* out and closed in on them.
9:11 and the archers *c* on ahead of the army,
9:28 of Judas *c* together and said to Jonathan:
9:43 he *c* on the sabbath to the banks of the
9:64 He *c* and pitched his camp before Bethbasi,
9:68 the enterprise he had planned *c* to nought,
9:72 and never *c* into their territory again.
10: 1 son of Antiochus, *c* up and took Ptolemais.
10:57 set out from Egypt and *c* to Ptolemais
10:67 *c* from Crete to the land of his fathers.
10:85 alive, *c* to about eight thousand men.
10:86 city *c* out to meet him with great pomp.
11:15 news, he *c* to challenge Ptolemy in battle.
11:44 When they *c* to the king,
12:26 The spies he had sent into their camp *c*
12:41 picked fighting men and *c* to Beth-shan.
12:45 That is why I *c* here."
12:52 Jonathan *c* safely into the land of Judah.
13:47 So Simon *c* to terms with them and did not
14:21 and fame, and we were happy that they *c*.
15:32 *c* to Jerusalem and on seeing the splendor
15:40 When Cendebeus *c* to Jamnia,
16:22 When the men *c* to kill him,
2Mc 1:15 a few attendants *c* to the temple precincts.
2: 6 him *c* up intending to mark the path,
2:10 fire *c* down and burned up the holocausts.
4:10 the king's approval and *c* into office,
4:44 When the king *c* to Tyre,
5:26 All those who *c* out to watch,
7:22 know how you *c* into existence in my womb;
7:28 same way the human race *c* into existence.
9:24 happened or any unwelcome news *c*,
11:13 and *c* to realize that the Hebrews were
13:25 When he *c* to Ptolemais,
14:14 have banished Judas, *c* flocking to Nicanor,
14:16 *c* upon the enemy at the village of Adasa.
14:21 *c* forward and thrones were set in place.
Jb 1: 6 *c* to present themselves before the LORD,
1: 6 before the LORD, Satan also *c* among them.
1:14 brother, a messenger *c* to Job and said,
1:16 he was yet speaking, another *c* and said,
1:17 he was yet speaking, another *c* and said,
1:18 he was yet speaking, another *c* and said,
1:19 when suddenly a great wind *c* across the
1:21 "Naked I *c* forth from my mother's womb,
2: 1 *c* to present themselves before the LORD,
2: 1 the LORD, and Satan also *c* with them.
4:14 deep sleep falls on men, Fear *c* upon me,
29:13 blessing of those in extremity *c* upon me,
30:26 evil came; when I expected light, then *c*
40:19 He *c* at the beginning of God's ways,
42: 7 And it *c* to pass after the LORD had spoken
42:11 Then all his brethren and sisters *c* to him,
Ps(s) 18:10 And he inclined the heavens and *c* down,
18:19 my calamity, but the LORD *c* to my support.
51: 2 *c* to him after his sin with Bathsheba.
76: 5 Resplendent you *c*, O powerful One,
81: 6 when he *c* forth from the land of Egypt.
105:19 Till his prediction *c* to pass and the word
105:23 Then Israel *c* to Egypt,
105:31 He spoke, and there *c* swarms of flies;
105:34 *c* locusts and grasshoppers without number;
114: 1 When Israel *c* forth from Egypt,
Prv 7:15 So I *c* out to meet you,
Eccl 5:14 As he *c* forth from his mother's womb,
5:14 so again shall he depart, naked as he *c*,
5:15 a grievous evil, that he goes just as he *c*.
6: 4 Though it *c* in vain and goes into darkness
Sg 3: 3 The watchmen *c* upon me as they made their
5: 7 The watchmen *c* upon me as they made their
6:11 I *c* down to the nut garden to look at
Wis 5:13 abruptly *c* to nought and held no sign of
6:22 is, and how she *c* to be I shall relate;
7: 7 I pleaded and the spirit of Wisdom *c* to me.
7:11 things together *c* to me in her company,
8:19 child, and I *c* by a noble nature;
12:27 this, their final condemnation *c* upon them.
14:14 by the vanity of men they *c* into the world,
16: 5 For when the dire venom of beasts *c* upon
17:15 for fear *c* upon them,
19:12 appease them quail *c* to them from the sea.
19:13 And the punishments *c* upon the sinners
Sir 24: 3 the mouth of the Most High I *c* forth,
27:27 in it without knowing how it *c* upon him.
47: 1 After him *c* NATHAN who served in the
47:16 coasts, and their peoples *c* to hear you;
47:21 Thus two governments *c* into being,
50: 5 the tent, as he *c* from within the veil!
51:14 She *c* to me in her beauty,
51:19 her gate and I *c* to know her secrets.
Is 7: 2 When word *c* to the house of David that
11:16 Israel when he *c* up from the land of Egypt.
14:28 that King Ahaz died, there *c* this oracle:
36: 3 *c* out to him the master of the palace,
36:22 *c* to Hezekiah with their garments torn,
37:29 mouth, and make you return the way you *c*.
37:34 He shall return by the same way he *c*,
38: 1 Isaiah, son of Amoz, *c* and said to him:
38: 4 Then the word of the LORD *c* to Isaiah:
38: 8 sun *c* back the ten steps it had advanced.
39: 3 prophet *c* to King Hezekiah and asked him,
39: 3 "They *c* to me from a distant land,
48: 3 suddenly I took action and they *c* to be.
50: 2 Why was no one there when I *c*?
66: 2 all these things when all of them *c* to be,
Jer 1: 2 LORD first *c* to him in the days of Josiah,
1: 4 The word of the LORD *c* to me thus:
1:11 word of the LORD *c* to me with the question:
1:13 word of the LORD *c* to me with the question:
2: 1 This word of the LORD *c* to me:
7: 1 message *c* to Jeremiah from the LORD:
11: 1 message *c* to Jeremiah from the LORD:
13: 3 time the word of the LORD *c* to me thus:
13: 8 Then the message *c* to me from the LORD:
14: 1 that *c* to Jeremiah concerning the drought:
16: 1 This message *c* to me from the LORD:
18: 1 This word *c* to Jeremiah from the LORD:
18: 5 Then the word of the LORD *c* to me.
21: 1 The message which *c* to Jeremiah from the
24: 4 Thereupon this word of the LORD *c* to me:
25: 1 The word that *c* to Jeremiah concerning all
26: 1 of Judah, this message *c* from the LORD:
26:10 they *c* up from the king's palace to the
26:17 some of the elders of the land *c* forward
27: 1 this message *c* to Jeremiah from the LORD:
28:12 the word of the LORD *c* to Jeremiah:
29:30 the word of the LORD *c* to Jeremiah:
30: 1 message *c* to Jeremiah from the LORD:
32: 1 This message *c* to Jeremiah from the LORD
32: 6 This message *c* to me from the LORD,
32: 8 *c* to me to the quarters of the guard and
32:26 Then this word of the LORD *c* to Jeremiah:
33: 1 The word of the LORD *c* to Jeremiah a
33:18 This word of the LORD also *c* to Jeremiah:
33:23 This word of the LORD *c* to Jeremiah:
34: 1 This word *c* to Jeremiah from the LORD
34: 8 This is the word that *c* to Jeremiah from
34:12 Then this word of the LORD *c* to Jeremiah:
35: 1 This word *c* to Jeremiah from the LORD in
35:12 Then this word of the LORD *c* to Jeremiah:
36: 1 this word *c* to Jeremiah from the LORD.
36: 9 all who *c* from Judah's cities to Jerusalem.
36:17 how you *c* to write down all these words."
36:27 This word of the LORD *c* to Jeremiah,
37: 4 still *c* and went freely among the people.
37: 6 of the LORD then *c* to the prophet Jeremiah:
38:27 When all the princes *c* to Jeremiah,
39: 3 of Babylon *c* and occupied the middle gate:
39:15 the guard, the word of the LORD *c* to him:
40: 1 This word *c* to Jeremiah from the LORD,
40: 8 *c* with their men to Gedaliah in Mizpah:
40:13 the leaders of the armies in the field *c*
41: 1 king's nobles, *c* with ten men to Gedaliah,
41: 5 with gashes on their bodies *c* from Shechem,
42: 7 before the word of the LORD *c* to Jeremiah.
43: 8 of the LORD *c* to Jeremiah in Tahpanhes:
44: 1 This word *c* to Jeremiah for all the people
44:28 The whole remnant of Judah who *c* to settle
46: 1 This is the word of the LORD that *c* to the
47: 1 This is the word that *c* from the LORD to
49: 9 If vintagers *c* upon you,
49:34 LORD against Elam *c* to the prophet
50: 7 Whoever *c* upon them devoured them,
52:12 *c* to Jerusalem as the representative of
Lam 3:57 You *c* to my aid when I called to you;
4:18 Our end drew near, and *c*;
Bar 1: 3 as all the people who *c* to the reading:
Ez 1: 3 word of the LORD *c* to the priest Ezekiel,
1: 3 the hand of the LORD *c* upon me.
1: 4 As I looked, a stormwind *c* from the North,
1:13 and from it *c* forth flashes of lightning.
3:15 Thus I *c* to the exiles who lived at
3:17 Thus the word of the LORD *c* to me:
3:22 The hand of the LORD *c* upon me,
6: 1 Thus the word of the LORD *c* to me:
7: 1 Thus the word of the LORD *c* to me:
10: 7 dressed in linen, who took it and *c* out.
11:14 Thus the word of the LORD *c* to me:
12: 1 Thus the word of the LORD *c* to me:
12: 8 the morning, the word of the LORD *c* to me:
12:17 Thus the word of the LORD *c* to me:
12:21 Thus the word of the LORD *c* to me:
12:26 Thus the word of the LORD *c* to me:
13: 1 Thus the word of the LORD *c* to me:
14: 1 elders of Israel *c* and sat down before me,
14: 2 before me, the word of the LORD *c* to me:
14:12 Thus the word of the LORD *c* to me:
15: 1 Thus the word of the LORD *c* to me:
16: 1 Thus the word of the LORD *c* to me:
16: 7 and developed, you *c* to the age of puberty;
17: 1 Thus the word of the LORD *c* to me:
17: 3 thick plumage, many-hued, *c* to Lebanon.
17:11 Thus the word of the LORD *c* to me:
17:12 The king of Babylon *c* to Jerusalem and
18: 1 Thus the word of the LORD *c* to me:
19:14 For fire *c* out of the branch and devoured
20: 1 some of the elders of Israel *c* to consult
20: 2 Then the word of the LORD *c* to me:
21: 1 Thus the word of the LORD *c* to me:
21: 6 Then the word of the LORD *c* to me:
21:13 Thus the word of the LORD *c* to me:
21:23 Thus the word of the LORD *c* to me:
22: 1 Thus the word of the LORD *c* to me:
22:17 Thus the word of the LORD *c* to me:
22:23 Thus the word of the LORD *c* to me;
23: 1 Thus the word of the LORD *c* to me:
23:17 Then the Babylonians *c* to her,
23:40 And so they *c*— and for them you bathed
23:44 Thus they *c* to Oholah and Oholibah,
24: 1 ninth year, the word of the LORD *c* to me:
24:15 Thus the word of the LORD *c* to me:
24:20 Thus the word of the LORD *c* to me:
25: 1 Thus the word of the LORD *c* to me:
26: 1 year, the word of the LORD *c* to me:
27: 1 Thus the word of the LORD *c* to me:

27: 9 sailor on the sea *c* to you to carry trade.
28: 1 Thus the word of the LORD *c* to me:
28:11 Thus the word of the LORD *c* to me:
28:20 Thus the word of the LORD *c* to me:
29: 1 tenth year, the word of the LORD *c* to me:
29:17 year, the word of the LORD *c* to me:
30: 1 Thus the word of the LORD *c* to me:
30:20 year, the word of the LORD *c* to me:
31: 1 year, the word of the LORD *c* to me:
32: 1 twelfth year, the word of the LORD *c* to me:
32:17 twelfth year, the word of the LORD *c* to me:
33: 1 Thus the word of the LORD *c* to me:
33:21 fugitive *c* to me from Jerusalem and said,
33:23 Thus the word of the LORD *c* to me:
34: 1 Thus the word of the LORD *c* to me:
35: 1 Thus the word of the LORD *c* to me:
35: 5 trouble, when their crimes *c* to an end,
36:16 Thus the word of the LORD *c* to me:
36:20 *c* among the nations [wherever they came],
36:20 came among the nations [wherever they *c*,
36:21 profaned among the nations where they *c*.
36:22 profaned among the nations to which you *c*.
37: 1 The hand of the LORD *c* upon me,
37: 7 it was a rattling as the bones *c* together,
37:10 the spirit came into them; they *c* alive
37:15 Thus the word of the LORD *c* to me:
38: 1 Thus the word of the LORD *c* to me:
40: 1 the hand of the LORD *c* upon me
43: 3 I had seen when he *c* to destroy the city,
Dn 1: 1 of Babylon *c* and laid siege to Jerusalem.
2: 2 *c* and presented themselves to the king,
2:29 To you in your bed there *c* thoughts about
3: 3 all these *c* together for the dedication
3: 8 some of the Chaldeans *c* and accused the
3:93 Then Nebuchadnezzar *c* to the opening of
3:93 Meshach, and Abednego *c* out of the fire.
3:94 and nobles of the king *c* together,
4: 5 Finally there *c* before me Daniel,
4:10 in bed, a holy sentinel *c* down from heaven,
4:20 that *c* down from heaven and proclaimed:
5: 8 But though all the king's wise men *c* in,
7:22 *c* when the holy ones possessed the kingdom.
8: 5 forehead suddenly *c* from the west
8: 8 and in its place *c* up four others,
8: 9 Out of one of them *c* a little horn which
8:17 When he *c* near where I was standing,
9:13 law of Moses, this calamity *c* full upon us.
9:21 *c* to me in rapid flight at the time of the
10:13 one of the chief princes, *c* to help me.
10:14 and *c* to make you understand what shall
13:28 *c* to her husband Joakim the next day,
13:28 next day, the two wicked elders also *c*,
13:37 who was hidden there, *c* and lay with her.
13:39 she was sent for, she *c* with her parents,
14:13 which they always *c* in to consume the food.
14:16 the next morning, the king *c* with Daniel.
14:40 seventh day the king *c* to mourn for Daniel.
14:40 As he *c* to the den and looked in,
Hos 1: 1 The word of the Lord that *c* to Hosea,
2:17 when she *c* up from the land of Egypt.
9:10 When they *c* to Baal-peor and consecrated
10:10 the wanton people I *c* and I chastised them;
Jl 1: 1 The word of the LORD which *c* to Joel,
Ob 1: 5 If thieves *c* to you, robbers by night
1: 5 If vintagers *c* to you,
Jon 1: 1 is the word of the LORD that *c* to Jonah,
1: 6 The captain *c* to him and said,
3: 1 word of the LORD *c* to Jonah a second time:
4:10 it *c* up in one night and in one night it
Mi 1: 1 The word of the LORD which *c* to Micah of
7:15 the days when you *c* from the land of Egypt,
Na 1:11 you he *c* who devised evil against the LORD,
Zep 1: 1 The word of the LORD which *c* to Zephaniah,
Hg 1: 1 the word of the LORD *c* through the prophet
1: 3 this word of the LORD *c* through Haggai,
1: 9 You expected much, but it *c* to little;
1:14 so that they *c* and set to work on the
2: 1 of the LORD *c* through the prophet Haggai:
2: 5 I made with you when you *c* out of Egypt,
2:10 word of the LORD *c* to the prophet Haggai:
2:20 The message of the LORD *c* a second time to
Zec 1: 1 of the LORD *c* to the prophet Zechariah,
1: 7 of the LORD *c* to the prophet Zechariah,
2: 7 and another angel *c* out to meet him,
4: 8 The word of the LORD then *c* to me:
5: 5 who spoke with me *c* forward and said to me,
6: 9 This word of the LORD then *c* to me:
7: 1 king [the word of the LORD *c* to Zechariah],
7: 4 this word of the LORD of hosts *c* to me:
7: 8 [This word of the LORD *c* to Zechariah:
8: 1 This word of the LORD of hosts *c*:
8:10 *c* and went had no security from the enemy,
8:18 This word of the Lord of hosts *c* to me:
14:16 of all the nations that *c* against Jerusalem
Mt 1:18 is how the birth of Jesus Christ *c* about.
2: 9 until it *c* to a standstill over the place
3:16 baptized, he *c* directly out of the water.
4:11 left him, and angels *c* and waited on him.
4:25 crowds that followed him *c* from Galilee,
7:25 the torrents *c* and the winds blew and
7:27 The rains fell, the torrents *c*,
8: 1 When he *c* down from the mountain,
8: 2 a leper *c* forward and did him homage,
8:24 warning a violent storm *c* up on the lake,
8:32 At that they *c* forth and entered the swine.
8:34 that the entire town *c* out to meet Jesus.
9: 1 the crossing, and *c* back to his own town.
9: 8 sight, a feeling of awe *c* over the crowd,
9:10 those known as sinners *c* to join Jesus
9:14 disciples *c* to him with the objection,
9:18 speaking to them, a synagogue leader *c* up,
9:20 hemorrhages for twelve years *c* up behind
9:27 two blind men *c* after him crying out,
12:42 She *c* from the farthest corner of the
12:44 it says, 'I will go back where I *c* from,'
13: 4 on a footpath, where birds *c* and ate it up.
13:25 enemy *c* and sowed weeds through his wheat,
13:27 The owner's slaves *c* to him and said,
13:36 His disciples *c* to him with the request,
14:12 Afterward, they *c* and informed Jesus.
14:15 his disciples *c* to him with the suggestion:
14:25 he *c* walking toward them on the lake.
15:23 disciples *c* up and began to entreat him,
15:25 She *c* forward then and did him homage with
15:30 *c* to him bringing with them cripples,
16: 1 The Pharisees and Sadducees *c* along,
16:13 *c* to the neighborhood of Caesarea Philippi,
17: 5 Out of the cloud *c* a voice which said,
17: 7 Jesus *c* toward them and laying his hand
17:14 a man *c* up to him and knelt before him.
17:18 him, and the demon *c* out of him.
18: 1 disciples *c* up to Jesus with the question,
18:21 Then Peter *c* up and asked him,
19: 1 he left Galilee and *c* to the district of
19: 3 Some Pharisees *c* up to him and said,
19:16 Another time a man *c* up to him and said,
20: 3 He *c* out about midmorning and saw other
20: 5 He *c* out again around noon and
20: 8 When evening *c* the owner of the vineyard
20: 9 *c* up they received a full day's pay,
20:20 sons *c* up to him accompanied by her sons,
21: 4 This *c* about to fulfill what was said
21:14 The blind and the lame *c* to him inside the
21:23 elders of the people *c* up to him and said:
21:30 Then the man *c* to his second son and said
21:32 When John *c* preaching a way of holiness,
22:11 "When the king *c* in to meet the guests,
22:12 is it you *c* in here not properly dressed?'
22:23 no resurrection, *c* to him with a question:
24: 1 and his disciples *c* up and pointed out to
24: 3 disciples *c* up to him privately and said:
24:39 until the flood *c* and destroyed them.
25:11 Later the other bridesmaids *c* back.
25:19 *c* home and settled accounts with them.
25:20 *c* forward bringing the additional five.
25:36 me, in prison and you *c* to visit me.'
26: 7 jar of costly perfume *c* up to him at table
26:17 the disciples *c* up to Jesus and said,
26:60 Finally two *c* forward who stated:
26:69 the serving girls *c* over to him and said,
26:73 some bystanders *c* over to Peter and said,
27:53 After Jesus' resurrection they *c* forth
28: 1 *c* with the other Mary to inspect the tomb.
28: 2 He *c* to the stone,
28: 9 The women *c* up and embraced his feet and
28:13 'His disciples *c* during the night and
28:18 Jesus *c* forward and addressed them in
Mk 1: 9 Jesus *c* from Nazareth in Galilee and was
1:11 Then a voice *c* from the heavens:
1:21 Shortly afterward they *c* to Capernaum,
1:26 and with a loud shriek *c* out of him.
2: 1 He *c* back to Capernaum after a lapse of
2:18 People *c* to Jesus with the objection,
3: 8 great multitude *c* to him from Judea,
3:13 had decided on, who *c* and joined him.
3:21 heard of this they *c* to take charge of him,
4: 4 where the birds *c* along and ate it.
5: 1 They *c* to Gerasene territory on the other
5:13 spirits *c* out and entered the swine.
5:14 and the people *c* to see what had happened.
5:22 the synagogue, a man named Jairus, *c* near.
5:27 She had heard about Jesus and *c* up behind
5:33 the woman *c* and fell in front of him and
6: 2 When the sabbath *c* he began to teach in
6:14 King Herod *c* to hear of Jesus,
6:22 Herodias' own daughter *c* in at one point
6:29 they *c* and carried his body away and laid
6:35 his disciples *c* to him with a suggestion:
6:48 he *c* walking toward them on the water;
6:53 the crossing they *c* ashore at Gennesaret,
8:11 *c* forward and began to argue with him.
9: 7 A cloud *c*, overshadowing them,
9:26 the boy into convulsions, it *c* out of him;
10: 2 Then some Pharisees *c* up and as a test
10:17 out on a journey a man *c* running up,
10:46 They *c* to Jericho next,
10:50 aside his cloak, jumped up and *c* to Jesus.
12:14 The two groups *c* and said to him:
12:18 no resurrection *c* to him with a question:
12:28 One of the scribes *c* up,
12:42 but one poor widow *c* and put in two small
14:53 the elders and the scribes *c* together.
14:66 servant girls of the high priest *c* along.
15: 8 When the crowd *c* up to press their demand
15:33 When noon *c*, darkness fell on the whole
16: 2 first day of the week they *c* to the tomb.
Lk 1:22 *c* out he was unable to speak to them,
2:22 When the day *c* to purify them according to
2:24 They *c* to offer in sacrifice "a pair of
2:27 He *c* to the temple now,
2:46 On the third day they *c* upon him in the
2:51 down with them then, and *c* to Nazareth,
3: 7 crowds that *c* out to be baptized by him:
3:12 Tax collectors also *c* to be baptized,
4:16 He *c* to Nazareth where he had been reared,
4:22 appealing discourse which *c* from his lips.
4:35 *c* out of him without doing him any harm.
5: 7 These *c*, and together they filled
5:12 town, a man full of leprosy *c* to him.
5:18 men *c* along carrying a paralytic on a mat.
6: 6 On another sabbath he *c* to teach in a
6:18 people who *c* to hear him and be healed of
6:48 *c* the torrent rushed in on that house,
7:20 When the men *c* to him they said,
7:33 *c* neither eating bread nor drinking wine,
7:34 The Son of Man *c* and he both ate and drank,
7:44 I *c* to your home and you provided me with
8:19 His mother and brothers *c* to be with him,
8:24 They *c* to awaken him,
8:27 When he *c* to land,
8:33 *c* out of the man and entered the swine,
8:41 synagogue, *c* up and fell at Jesus' feet,
8:44 *c* up behind him and touched the tassel on
8:47 gone unnoticed, she *c* forward trembling.
8:49 He was still speaking when a man *c* from
9:12 approached the Twelve *c* and said to him,
9:34 speaking, a cloud *c* and overshadowed them,
9:35 Then from the cloud *c* a voice which said,
9:37 The following day they *c* down from the
10:32 there was a Levite who *c* the same way;
10:33 *c* on him and was moved to pity
10:37 The answer *c*, "The one who treated him
10:40 details of hospitality, *c* to him and said,
11:24 it says, 'I will go back to where I *c* from.'
11:31 She *c* from the farthest corner of the
13: 6 and he *c* out looking for fruit on it but
13:31 was then that certain Pharisees *c* to him.
14: 1 When Jesus *c* on a sabbath to eat a meal in
15:28 father *c* out and began to plead with him.
16: 7 The answer *c*, 'A hundred measures
16:21 The dogs even *c* and licked his sores.
17: 7 herding sheep and he *c* in from the fields,
17:15 cured, *c* back praising God in a loud voice.
17:27 and when the flood *c*,
18:37 *c* that Jesus of Nazareth was passing by.
19: 5 Jesus *c* to the spot he looked up and said,
19:18 The second *c* and said,
19:20 The third *c* in and said:
20: 7 replying they did not know where it *c* from.
20:27 Some Sadducees *c* forward (the ones who
21:38 all the people *c* to hear him in the temple.
22:45 he rose from prayer and *c* to his disciples,
22:47 While he was still speaking a crowd *c*,
23:33 When they *c* to Skull Place,
23:44 and darkness *c* over the whole land until
24: 1 the women *c* to the tomb bringing the
24: 8 this reminder, his words *c* back to them.
Jn 1: 3 Through him all things *c* into being,
1: 3 being, and apart from him nothing *c* to be.
1: 4 Whatever *c* to be in him,
1: 7 who *c* as a witness to testify to the light,
1:11 To his own he *c*,
1:17 this enduring love *c* through Jesus Christ.
1:31 though the very reason I *c* baptizing with
1:32 dove from the sky, and it *c* to rest on him.
1:43 for Galilee, but first he *c* upon Philip.
2:14 he *c* upon people engaged in selling oxen,
3: 2 of the Jewish Sanhedrin, *c* to him at night.
3:13 except the One who *c* down from there
3:19 the light *c* into the world,
3:22 and his disciples *c* into Judean territory,
3:26 So they *c* to John,
4: 7 When a Samaritan woman *c* to draw water,
4:40 was that, when these Samaritans *c* to him,
4:41 his own spoken word many more *c* to faith.
6:16 drew on, his disciples *c* down to the lake.
6:21 but suddenly it *c* aground on the shore
6:23 Then some boats *c* out from Tiberias near
6:41 "I am the bread that *c* down from heaven."
6:58 This is the bread that *c* down from heaven.
7:31 Many in the crowd *c* to believe in him.
7:39 that *c* to believe in him were to receive.
7:45 When the temple guards *c* back,
8:14 I know where I *c* from and where I am going;
8:30 spoke this way, many *c* to believe in him.
8:42 you would love me, for I *c* forth from God,
8:58 before Abraham *c* to be, I AM."
9: 7 off and washed, and *c* back able to see.
9:30 He *c* back at them:
9:39 "I *c* into this world to divide it,
10: 8 All who *c* before me were thieves and
10:10 I *c* that they might have life and have it
10:22 and the time *c* for the feast of the
10:41 while he stayed there many people *c* to him.
10:42 In that place, many *c* to believe in him.
11:32 When Mary *c* to the place where Jesus was,
11:44 The dead man *c* out bound head and foot
12: 1 days before Passover Jesus *c* to Bethany,
12: 9 of Jews discovered he was there and *c* out,

CAME (cont.)

12:13 got palm branches and *c* out to meet him.
12:18 The crowd *c* out to meet him because they
12:22 and Andrew in turn *c* to inform Jesus.
12:27 But it was for this that I *c* to this hour.
12:28 Then a voice *c* from the sky:
13: 6 Thus he *c* to Simon Peter,
16:27 me and have believed that I *c* from God.
16:28 I *c* into the world.
16:30 We do indeed believe you *c* from God."
17: 8 They have known that in truth I *c* from you,
18: 3 the Pharisees, and *c* there with lanterns,
18:16 *c* out and spoke to the woman at the gate,
18:29 Pilate *c* out to them.
18:37 born, the reason why I *c* into the world,
19: 3 Repeatedly they *c* up to him and said,
19: 5 When Jesus *c* out wearing the crown of
19:32 the soldiers *c* and broke the legs of the
19:33 When they *c* to Jesus and saw that he was
19:38 it, so they *c* and took the body away.
19:39 first come to Jesus at night) likewise *c*,
20: 1 still dark, Mary Magdalene *c* to the tomb.
20: 6 *c* along behind him and entered the tomb.
20:19 of the Jews, Jesus *c* and stood before them.
20:24 means "Twin"), was absent when Jesus *c*.
20:26 doors, Jesus *c* and stood before them.
21: 8 the other disciples *c* in the boat,
21:13 Jesus *c* over, took the bread
Acts 1:19 This event *c* to be known by the
2: 1 *c* it found them gathered in one place.
2: 2 in the sky there *c* a noise like a strong,
2: 3 which parted and *c* to rest on each of them.
4: 1 guard, and the Sadducees *c* up to them,
4: 4 number of the men *c* to about five thousand.
5: 5 fear *c* upon all who later heard of it.
5: 6 Some of the young men *c* forward,
5: 7 Three hours later Ananias' wife *c* in,
5:10 The young men *c* in,
5:11 Great fear *c* on the whole church and on
5:25 Someone then *c* up to them,
5:36 Not long ago a certain Theudas *c* on the
5:36 In the end it *c* to nothing.
5:37 Next *c* Judas the Galilean at the time of
7:11 and great trial *c* upon Egypt and Canaan,
7:18 until a new king *c* to power in Egypt,
8: 7 spirits, which *c* out shrieking loudly.
8:36 moved along the road they *c* to some water,
8:39 When they *c* out of the water,
9:10 "Here I am, Lord," *c* the answer.
9:24 Saul, but their plot *c* to his attention.
9:39 All the widows *c* to him in tears and
9:42 of it, many *c* to believe in the Lord.
10: 4 The answer *c*: "Your prayers and your
11: 5 An object like a big canvas *c* down;
11:11 *c* to the house where we were staying.
11:12 These six brothers *c* along with me,
11:15 address them the Holy Spirit *c* upon them,
11:27 prophets *c* down from Jerusalem to Antioch.
12:10 *c* to the iron gate leading out to the city,
12:13 door and a maid named Rhoda *c* to answer it.
12:20 common consent *c* before him in his court.
13: 6 where they *c* across a Jewish magician
13:11 At once a misty darkness *c* over him,
13:14 on from Perga and *c* to Antioch in Pisidia.
14:24 passed through Pisidia and *c* to Pamphylia.
15: 1 Some men *c* down to Antioch from Judea and
16: 1 next he *c* to Lystra,
16: 7 When they *c* to Mysia they tried to go on
16: 8 Mysia instead, they *c* down to Troas.
16:39 They *c* along and tried to quiet them;
17: 1 and Apollonia and *c* to Thessalonica,
17:12 Many of them *c* to believe,
18: 5 Silas and Timothy *c* down from Macedonia,
19: 1 interior of the country and *c* to Ephesus.
19: 6 the Holy Spirit *c* down on them and they
19:17 Lord Jesus *c* to be held in great reverence.
19:18 Many who had become believers *c* forward
19:19 it *c* to fifty thousand silver pieces.
20:18 they *c* to him he delivered this address:
20:19 sorrows and trials that *c* my way
21: 1 On the following day we *c* to Rhodes and
21: 5 included *c* out of the city to see us off,
21: 8 next day we pushed on and *c* to Caesarea.
21:11 He *c* up to us, and taking Paul's belt,
21:16 Some of the disciples from Caesarea *c*
21:30 People *c* running from all sides.
22:13 Jews who lived there, *c* and stood by me.
23:16 and when he did so he *c* to headquarters.
23:30 When I later *c* to be informed of a plot
23:34 letter, asked Paul what province he *c* from,
24: 1 the high priest Ananias *c* down to Caesarea
24:24 days later Felix *c* with his Jewish wife,
25:17 When they *c* here with me,
25:23 So the next day Agrippa and Bernice *c* with
27: 5 and Pamphylia, and *c* to Myra in Lycia.
27:44 In this way all *c* safely ashore.
28:14 This is how we finally *c* to Rome.
28:15 *c* out as far as the Forum of Appius
28:23 him and *c* to his lodgings in great numbers.
28:30 lodgings, welcoming all who *c* to him.
Rom 5:16 the gift *c* after many offenses and brought
5:20 The law *c* in order to increase offenses;
7: 7 only through the law that I *c* to know sin.
7: 9 commandment came; with it sin *c* to life,
9: 5 and from them *c* the Messiah (I speak of
14: 9 is why Christ died and *c* to life again,
1Cor 2: 1 when I *c* to you I did not come proclaiming
2: 3 *c* among you it was in weakness and in fear,
7:21 Were you a slave when your call *c*?
15:21 Death *c* through a man;
15:46 *c* the natural and after that the spiritual.
2Cor 2:12 *c* to Troas to preach the gospel of Christ,
7: 9 were filled with a sorrow that *c* from God;
11: 9 who *c* from Macedonia supplied my needs.
Gal 1:12 It *c* by revelation from Jesus Christ.
1:15 But the time *c* when he who had set me
2:11 *c* to Antioch I directly withstood him,
2:12 before others *c* who were from James.
3:17 invalid by any law that *c* into being
3:19 *c* to whom the promise had been given.
3:23 *c* we were under the constraint of the law,
3:24 until Christ *c* to bring about our justification
Eph 2:17 He *c* and "announced the good news of
Phil 2:30 for he *c* near to death for the sake of
3: 6 when it *c* to justice based on the law.
1Tm 1:15 Jesus *c* into the world to save sinners.
Heb 7:28 *c* after the law appoints as priest the Son,
9:11 But when Christ *c* as high priest of the
10: 3 there *c* only a yearly recalling of sins,
11: 3 visible *c* into being through the invisible.
11:12 of this faith, there *c* forth from one man,
2Pt 1:17 *c* to him out of the majestic splendor:
1Jn 3:16 The way we *c* to understand love was that
5: 6 Christ it is who *c* through water and blood
Rv 1:16 sharp, two-edged sword *c* out of his mouth,
4: 5 From the throne *c* flashes of lightning and
4:11 by your will they *c* to be and were made."
5: 7 The Lamb *c* and received the scroll from
6: 4 Another horse *c* forth, a red one.
8: 3 angel *c* in holding a censer of gold.
8: 7 *c* hail and then fire mixed with blood,
9: 3 *c* locusts as powerful as scorpions in
9:17 their mouths *c* fire and sulphur and smoke.
11:18 but then *c* your day of wrath and the
12:16 The earth then *c* to the woman's rescue by
14:15 Another angel *c* out of the temple and in a
14:17 of the temple in heaven *c* another angel,
15: 6 and out of it *c* the seven angels holding
16:17 in the sanctuary *c* a loud voice which said,
16:21 *c* crashing down on mankind from the sky,
17: 1 holding the seven bowls *c* to me and said:
19:15 Out of his mouth *c* a sharp sword for
19:21 The rest were slain by the sword which *c*
20: 4 They *c* to life again and reigned with
20: 9 fire *c* down from heaven and devoured them.
21: 9 the seven last plagues *c* and said to me,

CAMEL (10)

Gn 24:64 alighted from her *c* and asked the servant,
31:34 the idols, put them inside a *c* cushion,
Lv 11: 4 the *c*, which indeed chews the cud,
Dt 14: 7 the *c*, the hare and the rock badger,
2Kgs 8: 9 *c* loads of the best goods of Damascus.
Is 21: 7 Someone riding an ass, someone riding a *c*,
Mt 19:24 it is easier for a *c* to pass through a
23:24 You strain out the gnat and swallow the *c*!
Mk 10:25 It is easier for a *c* to pass through a
Lk 18:25 it is easier for a *c* to go through a

CAMELS—CAMEL'S (53)

Gn 12:16 slaves, male and female asses, and *c*.
24:10 servant then took ten of his master's *c*,
24:11 the *c* kneel by the well outside the city.
24:14 a drink, and let me give water to your *c*,
24:19 she said, "I will draw water for your *c*,
24:20 until she had drawn enough for all the *c*.
24:22 When the *c* had finished drinking,
24:30 was still standing by the *c* at the spring.
24:31 for you, as well as a place for the *c*?"
24:32 and while the *c* were being unloaded and
24:35 male and female slaves, and *c* and asses.
24:44 a drink, but I will give water to your *c*,
24:46 a drink, and let me bring water for your *c*,
24:46 So I drank, and she watered the *c* also.
24:61 they mounted their *c* and followed the man.
24:63 around, he noticed that *c* were approaching.
30:43 male and female servants and *c* and asses.
31:17 to put his children and wives on *c*,
32: 8 him, as well as his flocks, herds and *c*,
32:16 thirty milch *c* and their young;
37:25 coming from Gilead, their *c* laden with gum,
Ex 9: 3 your horses, asses, *c*,
Jgs 6: 5 neither they nor their *c* could be numbered,
7:12 Nor could their *c* be counted,
8:21 that were on the necks of their *c*.
8:26 that were on the necks of their *c*.
1Sm 15: 3 and infants, oxen and sheep, *c* and asses.'"
27: 9 but would carry off sheep, oxen, asses, *c*,
30:17 young men, who mounted their *c* and fled.
1Kgs 10: 2 retinue, and with *c* bearing spices,
1Chr 5:21 fifty thousand *c*,
12:41 Naphtali came bringing food on asses, *c*,
27:30 over the *c* was Obil the Ishmaelite;
2Chr 9: 1 numerous retinue and by *c* bearing spices,
14:14 carried off a great number of sheep and *c*.
Ezr 2:67 their *c* four hundred and thirty-five,
Neh 7:68 their *c* four hundred and thirty-five,
Tb 9: 2 servants and two *c* and travel to Rages.
9: 5 together with the four servants and two *c*,
9: 5 moneybags, and they placed them on the *c*.
10:10 female slaves, oxen and sheep, asses and *c*,
Jdt 2:17 He took along a very large number of *c*,
Jb 1: 3 seven thousand sheep, three thousand *c*,
1:17 formed three columns, seized the *c*,
42:12 fourteen thousand sheep, six thousand *c*,
Is 30: 6 humps of *c* To a people good for nothing,
60: 6 Caravans of *c* shall fill you,
Jer 49:29 *c* they shall carry off for themselves,
49:32 Their *c* shall be your booty,
Ez 25: 5 I will make Rabbah a pasture for *c*,
Zec 14:15 be the plague upon the horses, mules, *c*,
Mt 3: 4 John was clothed in a garment of *c* hair,
Mk 1: 6 John was clothed in *c* hair,

CAMP (237)

Gn 25:18 *c* in opposition to his various kinsmen.
26: 2 to *c* wherever in this land I tell you.
32: 9 Esau should attack and overwhelm one *c*,"
32: 9 "the remaining *c* may still survive."
32:22 him, while he stayed that night in the *c*.
33:12 said, "Let us break *c* and be on our way;
Ex 14: 2 to turn about and *c* before Pi-hahiroth,
14: 2 You shall *c* in front of Baal-zephon,
14:19 of God, who had been leading Israel's *c*,
14:20 the *c* of the Egyptians and that of Israel.
16:13 evening quail came up and covered the *c*.
16:13 In the morning a dew lay all about the *c*,
19: 2 to the desert of Sinai, they pitched *c*.
19:16 so that all the people in the *c* trembled.
19:17 led the people out of the *c* to meet God,
29:14 the bullock you must burn up outside the *c*,
32:17 to Moses, "That sounds like a battle in *c*."
32:19 As he drew near the *c*,
32:26 he stood at the gate of the *c* and cried,
32:27 Now go up and down the *c*,
33: 7 pitch at some distance away, outside the *c*.
33: 7 go to this meeting tent outside the *c*.
33:11 Moses would then return to the *c*,
36: 6 a proclamation to be made throughout the *c*:
Lv 4:12 shall be brought outside the *c* to a clean
4:21 also be brought outside the *c* and burned,
6: 4 the ashes to a clean place outside the *c*.
8:17 offal he burned in the fire outside the *c*,
9:11 he burned up in the fire outside the *c*.
10: 4 and carry them to a place outside the *c*."
10: 5 took them, in their tunics, outside the *c*,
13:46 apart, making his abode outside the *c*.
14: 3 who is to go outside the *c* to examine him.
14: 8 thus made clean may he come inside the *c*;
16:26 only then may he enter the *c*.
16:27 atonement, shall be taken outside the *c*,
16:28 only then may he enter the *c*.
17: 3 or goat, whether in the *c* or outside of it,
24:14 "Take the blasphemer outside the *c*,
24:23 blasphemer outside the *c* and stoned him;
Nm 1:50 They shall therefore *c* around the Dwelling.
1:52 the other Israelites shall *c* by companies,
1:52 each in his own division of the *c*,
1:53 *c* around the Dwelling of the commandments.
2: 2 "The Israelites shall *c*,
2: 2 They shall *c* around the meeting tent,
2: 3 shall be the divisional *c* of Judah,
2: 5 With Judah shall *c* the tribe of Issachar
2: 9 registered by companies in the *c* of Judah
2:10 side shall be the divisional *c* of Reuben,
2:12 Beside them shall *c* the tribe of Simeon
2:16 registered by companies in the *c* of Reuben
2:17 "Then the meeting tent and the *c* of the
2:17 As in *c*, so also on the march,
2:18 side shall be the divisional *c* of Ephraim,
2:20 Beside them shall *c* the tribe of Manasseh
2:24 registered by companies in the *c* of Ephraim
2:25 side shall be the divisional *c* of Dan,
2:27 Beside them shall *c* the tribe of Asher
2:31 registered by companies in the *c* of Dan
2:34 both in *c* and on the march they were in
4: 5 In breaking *c*, Aaron and his sons
4:15 and all their utensils on breaking *c*,
5: 2 the Israelites to expel from *c* every leper,
5: 3 of the *c*; they are not to defile the camp
5: 4 they expelled them from the *c*.
9:17 the tent, the Israelites would break *c*;
9:17 the cloud came to rest, they would pitch *c*.
9:18 over the Dwelling, they remained in *c*.
9:20 bidding of the LORD that they stayed in *c*,
9:22 remained in *c* and did not depart;
10: 2 assembling the community and in breaking *c*.
10:13 *c* at the bidding of the LORD through Moses,
10:14 LORD through Moses, the *c* of the Judahites,
10:18 The *c* of the Reubenites,
10:22 The *c* of the Ephraimites next set out,
10:25 the camps, the *c* of the Danites set out,
10:31 you know where we can *c* in the desert,
10:34 And when they set out from *c*,
11: 1 them and consumed the outskirts of the *c*.
11: 9 At night, when the dew fell upon the *c*,
11:26 the gathering but had been left in the *c*.

11:26 on them also, and they prophesied in the *c*.
11:27 and Medad are prophesying in the *c*,"
11:30 Then Moses retired to the *c*,
11:31 brought them down over the *c* site
11:31 of a day's journey all around the *c*.
11:32 Then they spread them out all around the *c*.
12:14 be confined outside the *c* for seven days,
12:15 was confined outside the *c* for seven days;
14:44 covenant of the LORD nor Moses left the *c*.
15:35 whole community stone him outside the *c*."
15:36 him outside the *c* and stoned him to death,
19: 3 the *c* and slaughtered in his presence.
19: 7 and only afterward may he return to the *c*.
19: 9 them in a clean place outside the *c*.
31:12 community at their *c* on the plains of Moab,
31:13 community, went outside the *c* to meet them,
31:19 shall stay outside the *c* for seven days,
31:24 After that you may enter the *c*."
33:49 Their *c* along the Jordan on the plains of
Dt 2:14 of soldiers had perished from the *c*,
2:15 till he wiped them out of the *c* completely.
23:10 "When you are in *c* during an expedition
23:11 emission, he shall go outside the *c*,
23:12 sun has set, he may come back into the *c*.
23:13 Outside the *c* you shall have a place set
23:15 journeys along within your *c* to defend you
23:15 enemies at your mercy, your *c* must be holy;
29:10 and the aliens who live in your *c*,
Jos 1:11 "Go through the *c* and instruct the people,
3: 2 officers went through the *c*
3: 3 carry, you must also break *c* and follow it,
4: 8 and carried them along to the *c* site,
5: 8 whole nation remained in *c* where they were,
6:11 which they returned to *c* for the night.
6:14 the city once before returning to *c*;
6:18 *c* of Israel this ban and the misery of it.
6:23 and placed them outside the *c* of Israel.
8:11 the city, they pitched *c* north of Ai,
9: 6 journeyed to Joshua in the *c* at Gilgal,
10: 6 an appeal to Joshua in his *c* at Gilgal:
10:15 and all Israel returned to the *c* at Gilgal.]
10:21 safely to Joshua and the *c* at Makkedah,
10:31 where they set up a *c* during the attack.
10:43 all Israel returned to the *c* at Gilgal.
18: 9 and returned to Joshua in the *c* at Shiloh.
Jgs 7: 1 The *c* of Midian was in the valley north of
7: 8 *c* of Midian was beneath him in the valley.
7: 9 said to Gideon, "Go, descend on the *c*,
7:10 go down to the *c* with your aide Purah.
7:11 will have the courage to descend on the *c*."
7:11 his aide Purah to the outposts of the *c*.
7:13 bread was rolling into the *c* of Midian.
7:14 Midian and all the *c* into his power."
7:15 Then returning to the *c* of Israel,
7:15 delivered the *c* of Midian into your power."
7:17 "I shall go to the edge of the *c*,
7:18 blow horns all around the *c* and cry out,
7:19 the *c* at the beginning of the middle watch,
7:21 around the *c*, while the whole camp fell
7:22 and throughout the *c* the LORD set the
8:11 and attacked the *c* when it felt secure.
15: 9 Philistines went up and, from a *c* in Judah,
21:12 to the *c* at Shiloh in the land of Canaan.
1Sm 4: 3 When the troops retired to the *c*,
4: 5 When the ark of the LORD arrived in the *c*,
4: 6 loud shouting in the *c* of the Hebrews mean?"
4: 6 the ark of the LORD had come into the *c*,
4: 7 They said, "Gods have come to their *c*."
11:11 and invaded the *c* during the dawn watch.
13:17 the *c* of the Philistines in three bands.
14:16 enemy *c* had scattered and were running
14:19 tumult in the Philistine *c* kept increasing.
14:21 and had gone up with them to the *c*,
17: 4 of Gath came out from the Philistine *c*;
17:17 them quickly to your brothers in the *c*.
17:20 the barricade of the *c* just as the army,
17:53 Philistines, the Israelites looted their *c*.
26: 6 will go down into the *c* with me to Saul?"
28: 5 When Saul saw the *c* of the Philistines,
29: 6 to have you active with me in the *c*,
2Sm 1: 2 On the third day a man came from Saul's *c*,
1: 3 "I have escaped from the Israelite *c*."
5:24 you to attack the *c* of the Philistines."
23:16 Philistine *c* and drew water from the cistern
1Kgs 16:16 day in the *c* all Israel proclaimed Omri,
2Kgs 3:24 But when they reached the *c* of Israel,
7: 4 let us desert to the *c* of the Arameans.
7: 5 but when they reached the edge of the *c*,
7: 7 their asses, the whole *c* just as it was,
7: 8 the lepers reached the edge of the *c*,
7:10 "We went to the *c* of the Arameans,"
7:12 have left their *c* to hide in the field,
7:16 out and plundered the *c* of the Arameans;
19:35 and eighty-five thousand men in Assyrian *c*.
19:36 Sennacherib, the king of Assyria, broke *c*,
2Chr 32:21 commander in the *c* of the Assyrian king,
Ezr 8:15 Ahava, where we made *c* for three days.
Tb 6: 2 and made *c* beside the Tigris River.
Jdt 3:10 set up his *c* between Geba and Scythopolis,
6:11 brought him out of the *c* into the plain.
7:12 Stay in your *c*, and spare all your soldiers.
7:17 Thereupon the Moabites moved *c*,
7:20 The whole Assyrian *c*,
10:18 among the tents, a crowd gathered in the *c*.
12: 7 Thus she stayed in the *c* three days.
12: 7 she washed herself at the spring of the *c*.
13:10 They passed through the *c*,
14: 3 hurry to their *c* to awaken the generals
14:10 Consternation in the *C*.
14:19 Loud screaming and howling arose in the *c*.
15: 5 the happenings in the *c* of their enemies.
15: 6 swept down on the *c* of the Assyrians,
15:11 days the whole populace plundered the *c*,
1Mc 3: 3 battles and protected the *c* with his sword.
3:40 pitched their *c* near Emmaus in the plain.
3:41 heard of their fame, they came to the *c*,
4: 2 *c* of the Jews and take them by surprise.
4: 4 forces were still scattered away from the *c*.
4: 5 the night Gorgias came into the *c* of Judas,
4:13 them, they came out of their *c* for battle,
4:20 put to flight and their *c* was being burned.
4:23 Then Judas went back to plunder the *c*,
4:30 David and delivered the *c* of the Philistines
5:38 Judas sent men to spy on the *c*,
5:49 a proclamation to be made in the *c*
6:32 citadel and moved his *c* to Beth-zechariah,
6:32 Beth-zechariah, on the way to the king's *c*.
7:19 Jerusalem and pitched his *c* in Beth-zaith.
7:39 Jerusalem and pitched his *c* at Beth-horon,
9: 6 afraid, and many slipped away from the *c*,
9:11 out of *c* and took its position for combat.
9:64 He came and pitched his *c* before Bethbasi,
10:69 army, Apollonius pitched his *c* at Jamnia.
10:75 He pitched *c* near Joppa,
10:86 left there and pitched his *c* at Ashkalon,
11:67 their *c* near the waters of Gennesaret,
11:73 the enemy as far as their *c* in Kadesh,
11:73 in Kadesh, where they pitched their own *c*.
12:26 The spies he had sent into their *c* came
12:27 He also set outposts all around the *c*.
13:13 But Simon pitched his *c* at Adida,
2Mc 13:14 government, he pitched his *c* near Modein.
13:15 men and killed about two thousand in the *c*.
13:16 filled the *c* with terror and confusion.
Ps(s) 78:28 midst of their *c* round about their tents.
106:16 They envied Moses in the *c*, and Aaron,
Wis 19: 7 The cloud overshadowed their *c*;
Sir 48:21 God struck the *c* of the Assyrians and
Is 37:36 and eighty-five thousand in the Assyrian *c*.
37:37 broke *c* and went back home to Nineveh.
Jl 2:11 For immense indeed is his *c*,
Heb 13:11 as a sin offering are burned outside the *c*.
13:13 Let us go to him outside the *c*,

CAMPAIGN (12)

Nm 31: 6 Moses sent them out on the *c*,
31: 6 son of Eleazar, the priest for the *c*,
Jos 10:42 their lands Joshua captured in a single *c*,
1Sm 24:15 Against whom are you on *c*,
28: 1 men must go out on *c* with me to Jezreel."
2Sm 11: 1 turn of the year, when kings go out on *c*,
20: 7 from Jerusalem to *c* in pursuit of Sheba,
2Kgs 3: 6 and when he set out on a *c* from Samaria,
Jdt 1:13 King Arphaxad, and was victorious in his *c*.
2Mc 12:10 a mile from there in the *c* against Timothy,
Ez 29:18 his army in an exhausting *c* against Tyre.
29:18 from Tyre for the *c* he led against it.

CAMPAIGNED (2)

Nm 32:41 clan, *c* against the tent villages,
32:42 Nobah also *c* against Kenath,

CAMPAIGNS (5)

1Chr 18: 6 LORD made David victorious in all his *c*.
18:13 LORD made David victorious in all his *c*.
1Mc 1: 2 He fought many *c*,
2Mc 2:20 the *c* against Antiochus Epiphanes and his
9:23 whenever he went on *c* in the hinterland,

CAMPED (63)

Ex 13:20 *c* at Etham near the edge of the desert.
15:27 trees, and they *c* there near the water.
Nm 3:23 of the Gershonites *c* behind the Dwelling,
3:29 *c* at the south side of the Dwelling.
3:35 They *c* at the north side of the Dwelling.
3:38 *c* Moses and Aaron and the latter's sons.
33: 5 from Rameses, the Israelites *c* at Succoth.
33: 6 *c* at Etham near the edge of the desert.
33: 7 Baal-zephon, and they *c* opposite Migdol.
33: 8 in the desert of Etham, they *c* at Marah.
33: 9 and seventy palm trees, and they *c* there.
33:10 out from Elim, they *c* beside the Red Sea.
33:11 the Red Sea, they *c* in the desert of Sin.
33:12 from the desert of Sin, they *c* at Dophkah.
33:13 Setting out from Dophkah, they *c* at Alush.
33:14 Setting out from Alush, they *c* at Rephidim,
33:15 Rephidim, they *c* in the desert of Sinai.
33:16 of Sinai, they *c* at Kibroth-hattaavah.
33:17 from Kibroth-hattaavah, they *c* at Hazeroth.
33:18 out from Hazeroth, they *c* at Rithmah.
33:19 out from Rithmah, they *c* at Rimmon-perez.
33:20 out from Rimmon-perez, they *c* at Libnah.
33:21 Setting out from Libnah, they *c* at Rissah.
33:22 out from Rissah, they *c* at Kehelathah.
33:23 from Kehelathah, they *c* at Mount Shepher.
33:24 out from Mount Shepher, they *c* at Haradah.
33:25 out from Haradah, they *c* at Makheloth.
33:26 out from Makheloth, they *c* at Tahath.
33:27 Setting out from Tahath, they *c* at Terah.
33:28 Setting out from Terah, they *c* at Mithkah.
33:29 out from Mithkah, they *c* at Hashmonah.
33:31 out from Moseroth, they *c* at Bene-jaakan.
33:32 from Bene-jaakan, they *c* at Mount Gidgad.
33:33 out from Mount Gidgad, they *c* at Jotbathah.
33:34 out from Jotbathah, they *c* at Abronah.
33:35 out from Abronah, they *c* at Ezion-geber.
33:37 they *c* at Mount Hor on the border of the
33:41 They *c* at Zalmonah.
33:42 Setting out from Zalmonah, they *c* at Punon.
33:43 Setting out from Punon, they *c* at Oboth.
33:44 they *c* at Iye-abarim on the border of Moab.
33:45 out from Iye-abarim, they *c* at Dibon-gad.
33:46 from Dibon-gad, they *c* at Almon-diblathaim.
33:47 *c* in the Abarim Mountains opposite Nebo.
33:48 they *c* on the plains of Moab along the
Jos 4:19 and *c* in Gilgal on the eastern limits of
Jgs 18:12 were in Zorrah and Eshtaol, and *c* in Judah,
1Sm 4: 1 camped at Ebenezer, while the Philistines *c*
17: 1 *c* between Socoh and Azekah at Ephes-dammim.
17: 2 and *c* in the Vale of the Terebinth,
26: 3 *c* beside the road on the hill of Hachilah,
26: 5 and all his soldiers were *c* around him.
28: 4 they *c* on Gilboa.
1Mc 2:32 *c* opposite and prepared to attack them on
3:57 off, and they *c* to the south of Emmaus.
4:29 They came into Idumea and *c* at Beth-zur,
5:37 another army and *c* opposite Raphon,
5:39 to help them, and have *c* beyond the stream,
6:31 through Idumea and *c* before Beth-zur.
7:40 Judas *c* in Adasa with three thousand men.
9: 5 three thousand picked men, had *c* at Elasa.
9:33 and *c* by the waters of the pool of Asphar.

CAMPING (3)

Gn 14:13 *c* at the terebinth of Mamre the Amorite,
1Mc 9: 2 and *c* opposite the ascent at Arbela,
Wis 5:14 memory of the nomad *c* for a single day.

CAMPS (10)

Gn 32: 8 his flocks, herds and camels, into two *c*.
Ex 14:20 night passed without the rival *c* coming
Nm 2:32 of those registered by companies in the *c*
10:25 Finally, as rear guard for all the *c*,
1Mc 5:41 and *c* on the other side of the river,
6:48 established *c* in Judea and at Mount Zion.
Sg 1: 8 the young ones near the shepherds' *c*.
Ez 4: 2 build a tower, lay out a ramp, pitch *c*,
Am 4:10 nostrils I brought the stench of your *c*;
Zec 14:15 upon all the beasts that are in those *c*.

CAMPSITE (1)

Gn 26:17 and made the Wadi Gerar his regular *c*.

CANA (4)

Jn 2: 1 day there was a wedding at *C* in Galilee,
2:11 this first of his signs at *C* in Galilee.
4:46 He went to *C* in Galilee once more,
21: 2 "Twin"), Nathanael (from *C* in Galilee),

CANAAN (87)

Gn 9:18 (Ham was the father of *C*.)
9:22 Ham, the father of *C*,
9:26 Let *C* be his slave.
9:27 and let *C* be his slave."
10: 6 Cush, Mizraim, Put, and *C*.
10:15 *C* became the father of Sidon
11:31 of the Chaldeans, to go to the land of *C*.
12: 5 Haran, and they set out for the land of *C*.
12: 5 When they came to the land of *C*,
13:12 Abram stayed in the land of *C*,
16: 3 had lived ten years in the land of *C*,
17: 8 you are now staying, the whole land of *C*,
23: 2 (that is, Hebron) in the land of *C*,
23:19 Mamre (that is, Hebron) in the land of *C*.
31:18 to go to his father Isaac in the land of *C*.
33:18 city of Shechem, which is in the land of *C*,
35: 6 in Luz [that is, Bethel] in the land of *C*.
36: 5 Esau who were born to him in the land of *C*.
36: 6 property he had acquired in the land of *C*,
37: 1 his father had stayed, the land of *C*.
42: 5 there was famine in the land of *C* also,
42: 7 They answered, "From the land of *C*,
42:13 brothers, sons of a certain man in *C*;
42:29 to their father Jacob in the land of *C*,
42:32 present with our father in the land of *C*.'
44: 8 back to you from the land of *C* the money
45:17 and go without delay to the land of *C*.
45:25 way to their father Jacob in the land of *C*.
46: 6 they had acquired in the land of *C*,
46:12 Er and Onan died in the land of *C*;
46:31 household, whose home is in the land of *C*,
47: 1 my brothers have come from the land of *C*,
47: 4 for your servants' flocks in the land of *C*,
47:13 Egypt and *C* were languishing from hunger,

CANAAN (cont.)

47:14 money that was to be found in Egypt and C,
47:15 all the money in Egypt and C was spent,
48: 3 appeared to me at Luz in the land of C,
48: 7 to my sorrow, during the journey in C,
49:30 facing on Mamre, in the land of C,
50: 5 had prepared for himself in the land of C,
50:13 They carried him to the land of C and
Ex 6: 4 with them, to give them the land of C,
15:15 All the dwellers in C melted away;
16:35 manna until they reached the borders of C.
Lv 14:34 Aaron, "When you come into the land of C,
18: 3 shall you do as they do in the land of C,
25:38 give you the land of C and to be your God.
Nm 13: 2 "Send men to reconnoiter the land of C,
13:17 sending them to reconnoiter the land of C,
26:19 who died in the land of C were Er and Onan.
32:30 and livestock across before you into C,
32:30 their property with you in the land of C."
32:32 the land of C as troops before the LORD,
33:40 who lived in the Negeb in the land of C,
33:51 go across the Jordan into the land of C,
34: 2 When you enter the land of C,
34: 2 the land of C with its boundaries:
34:29 Israelites their heritage in the land of C.
35:10 go across the Jordan into the land of C,
35:14 the Jordan, and three in the land of C.
Dt 32:49 and view the land of C,
Jos 5:12 year ate of the yield of the land of C.
14: 1 the Israelites received in the land of C.
21: 2 the Israelites at Shiloh in the land of C,
22: 9 of C and returned to the land of Gilead,
22:10 the region of the Jordan in the land of C,
22:11 region of the Jordan facing the land of C,
22:32 Gilead to the Israelites in the land of C,
24: 3 and led him through the entire land of C.
Jgs 3: 1 of the battles with C [just to instruct,
5:19 then they fought, those kings of C,
21:12 to the camp at Shiloh in the land of C.
1Chr 1: 8 of Ham were Cush, Mesraim, Put, and C.
1:13 C became the father of Sidon,
16:18 the land of C as your allotted inheritance."
Jdt 5: 9 their abode and proceed to the land of C.
5:10 famine had gripped the whole land of C,
1Mc 9:37 daughter of one of the great princes of C,
Ps(s) 105:11 the land of C as your allotted inheritance."
106:38 Whom they sacrificed to the idols of C,
135:11 king of Bashan, and all the kings of C;
Is 19:18 of C and swearing by the LORD of hosts;
Bar 3:22 She has not been heard of in C,
Ez 16: 3 origin and birth you are of the land of C;
Dn 13:56 "Offspring of C,
Acts 7:11 and great trial came upon Egypt and C,
13:19 destroyed seven nations in the land of C

CANAANITE (20)

Gn 10:19 so that the C borders extended from Sidon
28: 1 "You shall not marry a C woman!
28: 6 him his blessing, not to marry a C woman,
28: 8 the C women were to his father Isaac,
36: 2 Esau took his wives from among the C women:
38: 2 he met the daughter of a C named Shua,
46:10 Jachin, Zohar, and Shaul, son of a C woman.
Ex 6:15 and Shaul, who was the son of a C woman;
Nm 21: 1 When the C king of Arad,
33:40 Now, when the C king of Arad,
Jos 13: 3 Ekron in the north is reckoned C territory,
Jgs 1:32 live among the C natives of the land,
1:33 they live among the C natives of the land.
4: 2 them to fall into the power of the C king,
4:23 Thus on that day God humbled the C king,
4:24 till at length they destroyed the C king,
1Chr 2: 3 were born to him of Bathshua, a C woman.
Neh 9:24 and you humbled before them the C
Ob 1:20 occupy the C land as far as Zarephath,
Mt 15:22 It happened that a C woman living in that

CANAANITES (58)

Gn 10:18 Afterward, the clans of the C spread out,
12: 6 (The C were then in the land.)
13: 7 (At this time the C and the Perizzites
15:21 the Rephaim, the Amorites, the C,
24: 3 the daughters of the C among whom I live,
24:37 daughters of the C in whose land I live;
34:30 of the land, the C and the Perizzites.
50:11 When the C who inhabited the land saw the
Ex 3: 8 with milk and honey, the country of the C,
3:17 misery of Egypt into the land of the C,
13: 5 land of the C, Hittites, Amorites, Hivites
13:11 has brought you into the land of the C,
23:23 to the Amorites, Hittites, Perizzites, C,
23:28 Hivites, C and Hittites out of your way.
33: 2 Driving out the C, Amorites, Hittites,
34:11 will drive out before you the Amorites, C,
Nm 13:29 and C along the seacoast and the banks of
14:25 Amalekites and C are living in the valleys,
14:43 For there the Amalekites and C face you,
14:45 And the Amalekites and C who dwelt in that
21: 3 Israel's prayer and delivered up the C,
Dt 1: 7 regions, the land of the C in the Arabah,
7: 1 the Hittites, Girgashites, Amorites, C,
11:30 country of the C who live in the Arabah,
20:17 the Hittites, Amorites, C,
Jos 3:10 at your approach will dispossess the C,
5: 1 the kings of the C by the sea heard
7: 9 When the C and the other inhabitants of
9: 1 Hittites, Amorites, C,
11: 3 These were C to the east and west,
12: 8 belonging to the Hittites, Amorites, C,
13: 4 C from Mearah of the Sidonians to Aphek,
16:10 did not drive out the C living in Gezer,
17:12 cities, the C persisted in this region.
17:13 stronger they impressed the C as laborers,
17:16 the C living in the valley region all have
17:18 and iron chariots, you drive out the C."
24:12 drove them [the Amorites, Perizzites, C,
Jgs 1: 1 to attack the C and to do battle with them?"
1: 3 to me, and let us engage the C in battle.
1: 4 the C and Perizzites into their power,
1: 5 When they defeated the C and Perizzites,
1: 9 the C who lived in the mountain region,
1:10 marched against the C who dwelt in Hebron,
1:17 they defeated the C who dwelt in Zephath.
1:27 The C kept their hold in this district.
1:28 stronger, they impressed the C as laborers,
1:29 did not drive out the C living in Gezer,
1:29 and so the C live in Gezer in their midst.
1:30 the C live among them,
3: 3 and all the C, the Sidonians,
3: 5 the Israelites were living among the C,
2Sm 24: 7 to all the cities of the Hivites and C,
1Kgs 9:16 and slaying all the C living in the city,
Ezr 9: 1 of the land and their abominations C,
Neh 9: 8 him and his posterity the land of the C,
Jdt 5: 3 "Now tell me, you C,
5:16 They expelled the C,

CANAAN'S (1)

Is 23:11 ordered the destruction of C strongholds.

CANALS (3)

Ex 7:19 their streams and c and pools,
8: 1 staff over the streams and c and pools,
Is 19: 6 the c of Egypt shall dwindle and dry up.

CANCEL (1)

Jas 5:20 soul from death and c a multitude of sins.

CANCELED (6)

1Mc 10:33 taxes, even those on their cattle, be c.
10:42 of the sanctuary every year shall be c,
15: 8 to the royal treasury shall be c for you,
Is 28:18 Your covenant with death shall be c and
Mt 18:32 I c your entire debt when you pleaded with
Col 2:14 He c the bond that stood against us with

CANDACE (1)

Acts 8:27 C (a name meaning queen) of the Ethiopians,

CANDOR (1)

2Cor 1:12 acted from God-given holiness and c;

CANE (4)

Ex 30:23 hundred and fifty shekels of fragrant c;
Is 43:24 You did not buy me sweet c for money,
Jer 6:20 from Sheba, or sweet c from far-off lands?
Ez 27:19 and aromatic c from Uzal for your wares.

CANNEH (1)

Ez 27:23 Haran, C, and Eden,

CANNIBAL (1)

Wis 12: 5 a c feast of human flesh and of blood,

CANNOT (276)

Gn 19:19 But I c flee to the hills to keep the
19:22 I c do anything until you arrive there."
29: 8 "We c," they replied,
31:35 offended that I c rise in your presence;
44:22 to my lord, 'The boy c leave his father;
44:26 So we reminded him, 'We c go down there;
47:18 "We c hide from my lord that,
Ex 18:18 you c do it alone.
19:23 LORD, "The people c go up to Mount Sinai,
33:20 But my face you c see,
Lv 5: 7 he c afford an animal of the flock,
12: 8 If, however, she c afford a lamb,
14:21 "If a man is poor and c afford so much,
Nm 11:14 I c carry all this people by myself,
13:31 with him said, "We c attack these people;
14:41 This c succeed.
23:20 a blessing which I c restrain.
23:25 "Even though you c curse them,"
31:23 c stand fire you shall put into the water.
Dt 7:22 You c exterminate them all at once,
28:27 eczema and the itch, until you c be cured.
28:35 malignant boils of which you c be cured,
Jos 7:12 the Israelites c stand up to their enemies,
7:13 You c stand up to your enemies until you
9:19 the God of Israel, and so we c harm them.
22:27 future your children c say to our children,
Jgs 11:35 made a vow to the LORD and I c retract."
14:13 But if you c answer it for me,
15: 3 the Philistines c blame me if I harm them."
21:18 Yet we c give them any of our daughters in
Ru 4: 6 "I c exercise my claim lest I depreciate
4: 6 in my stead, for I c exercise my claim."
1Sm 17:33 "You c go up against this Philistine and
17:39 He said to Saul, "I c go in these,
20: 2 This c be so!"
20:31 you c make good your claim to the kingship!
29: 8 that I c go to fight against the enemies
2Sm 5: 6 David was told, "You c enter here:
5: 6 their way of saying, "David c enter here."
14:14 out on the ground and c be gathered up.
23: 6 they c be taken up by hand.
24:24 for I c offer to the LORD my God
1Kgs 3: 8 so vast that it c be numbered or counted.
8:27 and the highest heavens c contain you,
13:16 "I c go back with you, and I cannot eat
20: 9 But this I c do.'"
2Kgs 18:29 you, since he c deliver you out of my hand.
22:17 this place and it c be extinguished.'
1Chr 22:14 great quantities that they c be weighed.
2Chr 2: 5 and even the highest heavens c contain him?
6:18 and the highest heavens c contain you,
24:20 the LORD's commands, so that you c prosper?
34:25 against this place and c be extinguished.'
Ezr 10:13 season, so that we c remain out-of-doors;
Tb 5:10 I am, a blind man who c see God's sunlight,
5:10 I can hear a man's voice, but I c see him."
6:13 I know that Raguel c keep her from you or
9: 3 I c violate his oath."
Jdt 8:14 You c plumb the depths of the human heart
8:30 bind ourselves by an oath that we c break.
Est B: 4 blamlessly designed by us c be established.
B: 5 that stability of government c be obtained,
8: 8 with the royal signet ring c be revoked.
1Mc 9: 9 "We certainly c. Let us save
10:72 Men say that you c make a stand against us
Jb 6:30 my tongue, or c my taste discern falsehood?
7:16 I c live forever;
9:21 Though I am innocent, I myself c know it;
14: 5 you have fixed the limit which he c pass.
19: 8 He has barred my way and I c pass;
22:11 dismay, Or darkness, in which you c see;
22:14 Clouds hide him so that he c see;
23: 8 or to the west, I c perceive him;
28:15 Solid gold c purchase it,
28:16 It c be bought with gold of Ophir,
28:17 God or crystal c equal it,
33:21 His flesh is wasted so that it c be seen,
34:12 God cannot act wickedly, the Almighty c
36: 4 For indeed, my theme c fail me:
37:19 we c, for the darkness, make our plea.
37:23 we c discover him,
39:22 He laughs at fear and c be deterred;
41: 9 that they hold fast and c be parted.
42: 3 too wonderful for me, which I c know.
Ps(s) 21:12 you, devising plots, they c succeed,
33:17 though its strength, it c provide escape.
36:13 they are thrust down and c rise.
40:13 my sins so overcome me that I c see;
69:24 Let their eyes grow dim so that they c see,
77: 5 I am troubled and c speak.
88: 9 I am imprisoned, and I c escape.
Prv 4:16 For they c rest unless they have done evil;
7:11 and unruly, in her home her feet c rest;
27:16 he c tell north from south.
30:18 wonderful for me, yes, four I c understand:
30:21 trembles, yes, under four it c bear up:
Eccl 1:15 c be made straight, and what is missing c
6:10 and that he c contend in judgment with one
7:14 that man c find fault with him in anything.
9: 1 Love from hatred man c tell;
Sg 8: 7 Deep waters c quench love,
Wis 2: 5 and our dying c be deferred because it is
13:16 for it, knowing that it c help itself;
13:18 about travel, something that c even walk.
Sir 1:19 One c justify unjust anger;
6:21 The fool c abide her.
9:10 an old friend, for the new one c equal him.
12: 8 In our prosperity we c know our friends;
12:15 but if you slip, he c hold back.
16:15 Among so many people I c be known;
17:13 to him, they c be hidden from his eyes.
17:16 Their wickedness c be hidden from him;
17:25 The like c be found in men,
18: 4 One c lessen,
20:20 to sin, yet in this tranquility he c rest.
23:11 swears without reason he c be found just,
27:16 He who betrays a secret c be trusted,
27:19 let your friend go and c recapture him;
30:18 Dainties set before one who c eat are
43:29 praise him the more, since we c fathom him,
43:32 and weary not, though you c reach the end;
Is 1:13 these I c bear.
24: 9 They c sing and drink wine;
26:14 they have no life, shades that c rise;
26:18 inhabitants of the world c bring it forth.
29:11 request, "Read this," he replies, "I c;
29:12 When it is handed to one who c read,
29:12 "Read this," he replies, "I c read."

30:14 And among its fragments *c* be found a sherd
33:23 it *c* hold the mast in place,
36:14 deceive you, since he *c* deliver you.
44:18 cannot see, and their hearts so that they *c*
44:20 *c* save itself when the flame consumes it;
45:20 wooden idols and pray to gods that *c* save.
46: 7 Although they cry out to it, it *c* answer;
47:11 shall befall you which you *c* allay.
47:14 They *c* save themselves from the spreading
48: 7 so that you *c* claim to have known them;
54:14 where destruction *c* come near you.
56:10 They are all dumb dogs, they *c* bark;
57:20 are like the tossing sea which *c* be calmed,
59: 6 Their webs *c* serve as clothing,
59:14 in the public square, uprightness *c* enter.
Jer 4:19 My heart beats wildly, I *c* be still;
5:15 know not, whose speech you *c* understand.
5:22 though its billows roar, they *c* pass.
6:10 ears are uncircumcised, they *c* give heed;
9: 4 to lying, and are perverse, and *c* repent.
10: 5 in a cucumber field are they, they *c* speak;
10: 5 must be carried about, for they *c* walk.
10:10 quakes, whose wrath the nations *c* endure:
11:11 upon them misfortune which they *c* escape.
14: 9 a man dumbfounded, a champion who *c* save?
14:19 have you struck us a blow that *c* be healed?
19:11 a clay pot so that it *c* be repaired.
20: 9 I grow weary holding it in, I *c* endure it.
24: 3 bad ones very bad, so bad they *c* be eaten."
24: 8 figs that are bad, so bad they *c* be eaten
32: 5 in fighting the Chaldeans, you *c* win!"
33:22 the host of heaven which *c* be numbered,
33:22 the sands of the sea which *c* be counted,
36: 5 I *c* go to the house of the LORD;
46: 6 The swift *c* flee, nor the hero escape:
46:23 numerous than locusts, they *c* be counted.
49:10 uncover his retreats so that he *c* hide.
49:23 they toss like the sea which *c* rest.
51: 9 tried to heal Babylon, but she *c* be healed.
Bar 6: 7 but they are a fraud, and *c* speak.
6:14 but it *c* save itself from war or pillage.
6:33 well or ill by anyone, they *c* requite it;
6:34 they *c* give anyone riches or coppers;
6:34 a vow to them, they *c* exact it of him.
6:55 They *c* resist a king, or enemy forces.
6:57 was on them, and they *c* help themselves.
6:63 that it is unthinkable, and *c* be claimed,
Ez 3: 6 language] whose words you *c* understand.
3:25 with them, so that you *c* go out among them.]
4: 8 I will bind you with cords so that you *c* turn
7:19 *c* save them on the day of the LORD's wrath.
8:12 "The LORD *c* see us;
Dn 3:33 Now we *c* open our mouths;
3:40 those who trust in you *c* be put to shame.
11:18 conduct, so that he *c* renew it against him.
13:22 if I refuse, I *c* escape your power.
14:24 "you *c* deny that this is a living god,
Hos 2: 8 against her, so that she *c* find her paths.
5:13 But he *c* heal you nor take away your sore.
9: 4 it *c* enter the house of the LORD.
Am 7:10 the country *c* endure all his words.
Jon 4:11 persons who *c* distinguish their right hand
Mi 6:14 What you acquire, you *c* save;
Hb 1:13 evil, and the sight of misery you *c* endure.
Mt 5:14 A city set on a hill *c* be hidden.
5:36 (you *c* make a single hair white or black).
6:24 You *c* give yourself to God and money.
7:18 A sound tree *c* bear bad fruit any more
10:28 the body of life but *c* destroy the soul.
12:25 split into factions *c* last for long.
20:26 It *c* be like that with you.
24:42 You *c* know the day your Lord is coming.
26:42 this *c* pass me by without my drinking it,
27:42 "He saved others but he *c* save himself!
Mk 2:19 as the groom stays with them, they *c* fast.
3:24 torn by civil strife, that kingdom *c* last.
3:26 and is torn by dissension, he *c* endure;
10:43 It *c* be like that with you.
15:31 "He saved others but he *c* save himself!
Lk 11: 7 I *c* get up to look after your needs'
14:14 should be pleased that they *c* repay you,
14:20 said, 'I am newly married and so I *c* come.'
14:26 indeed his very self, he *c* be my follower.
14:27 his cross and follow me *c* be my disciple.
14:32 If he *c*, he will send a delegation
16: 3 I *c* dig ditches.
16:11 If you *c* be trusted with elusive wealth,
16:13 You *c* give yourself to God and money."
16:26 wish to cross from here to you *c* do so,
17:20 "You *c* tell by careful watching when the
22:26 Yet it *c* be that way with you.
Jn 5:19 you, the Son *c* do anything by himself
5:30 I *c* do anything of myself.
5:31 my own behalf, you *c* verify my testimony;
7:34 where I am you *c* come."
7:36 not find me,' and, 'Where I am you *c* come'?"
8:13 Such testimony *c* be valid."
8:21 Where I am going you *c* come."
8:22 he claims, 'Where I am going you *c* come'?"
8:23 a world which *c* hold me.
8:43 It is because you *c* bear to hear my word.
9:16 "This man *c* be from God because he does
10:21 a devil *c* open the eyes of the blind!"
10:35 and Scripture *c* lose its force
13:33 'Where I am going, you *c* come.'
13:36 "I am going where you *c* follow me now;
14:17 Spirit of truth, whom the world *c* accept,
15:22 now, however, their sin *c* be excused.
16:12 more to tell you, but you *c* bear it now.
Acts 4:16 We *c* deny it.
4:20 Surely we *c* help speaking of what we have
15: 1 to Mosaic practice, you *c* be saved."
24:13 They *c* substantiate the charges they are
Rom 7:15 I *c* even understand my own actions.
8: 7 Indeed, it *c* be;
8: 8 those who are in the flesh *c* please God.
8:25 And hoping for what we *c* see means
8:26 groanings that *c* be expressed in speech.
1Cor 2:14 He *c* come to know such teaching because it
7: 9 but if they *c* exercise self-control,
10:21 You *c* drink the cup of the Lord and also
10:21 You *c* partake of the table of the Lord and
12:21 The eye *c* say to the hand,
15:50 and blood *c* inherit the kingdom of God;
2Cor 1:13 anything that you *c* read and understand.
12: 2 he was in or outside his body I *c* say,
12: 4 Paradise to hear words which *c* be uttered,
13: 8 We *c* do anything against the truth,
Gal 3:15 You *c* add anything to a man's will or set
1Tm 5:25 inconspicuous ones *c* be hidden forever.
2Tm 2: 5 he *c* receive the winner's crown unless he
2:13 remain faithful, for he *c* deny himself.
Ti 1: 2 of that eternal life which God, who *c* lie,
Heb 7:16 the power of a life which *c* be destroyed.
9: 5 We *c* speak now of each of these in detail.
Jas 1:17 *c* change and who is never shadowed over.
3:12 A fig tree, brothers, *c* produce olives,
4: 2 You envy and you *c* acquire,
1Jn 3: 9 he *c* sin because he is begotten of God.
4:20 he has seen *c* love the God he has not seen.
5:18 by him, and so the evil one *c* touch him.
Rv 2: 2 I know you *c* tolerate wicked men;
3: 3 you like a thief, at a time you *c* know.
9:20 and wood, which *c* see or hear or walk.

CANOPY (8)

Dt 33:27 he extended the ancient *c*.
1Kgs 7: 6 columned hall, and there was a *c* in front.
Jdt 10:21 a *c* with a netting of crimson and gold,
13: 9 the bed and took the *c* from its supports.
13:15 *c* under which he lay in his drunkenness.
16:19 as well as the *c* that she herself had
Sir 40:27 its *c*,
Jer 43:10 have sunk, and stretch his *c* over them.

CANTICLE (1)

2Mc 7: 6 on us, as Moses declared in his *c*,

CANTICLES (1)

1Mc 13:51 and lyres, and the singing of hymns and *c*,

CANVAS (3)

Acts 10:11 object come down that looked like a big *c*.
11: 5 An object like a big *c* came down;
11:10 then the *c* with everything in it was drawn

CAPABLE (6)

2Kgs 3:21 every man *c* of bearing arms was called up
1Chr 21: 5 of men *c* of wielding a sword,
2Chr 25: 5 for war, *c* of handling lance and shield.
1Mc 3:38 Gorgias, *c* men among the King's Friends,
Is 32: 4 The flighty will become wise and *c*,
Lk 19:17 'You showed yourself *c* in a small matter.

CAPACITY (5)

Lv 19:35 in using measures of length or weight or *c*.
1Kgs 7:26 Its *c* was two thousand measures.
7:38 in diameter with a *c* of forty measures,
2Kgs 10:21 the temple of Baal, which was filled to *c*.
2Chr 4: 5 It had a *c* of three thousand measures.

CAPARISONED (1)

2Mc 3:25 There appeared to them a richly *c* horse,

CAPER (1)

Eccl 12: 5 sluggish and the *c* berry is without effect,

CAPERNAUM (16)

Mt 4:13 went down to live in *C* by the sea
8: 5 As Jesus entered *C*,
11:23 As for you, *C*, 'Are you to be exalted
17:24 When they entered *C*,
Mk 1:21 Shortly afterward they came to *C*,
2: 1 He came back to *C* after a lapse of several
9:33 They returned to *C* and Jesus, once inside
Lk 4:23 things we have heard you have done in *C*.'
4:31 He then went down to *C*,
7: 1 in the hearing of the people, he entered *C*.
10:15 And as for you, *C*,
Jn 2:12 After this he went down to *C*,
4:46 At *C* there happened to be a royal official
6:17 intending to cross the lake toward *C*.
6:24 the boats and went to *C* looking for Jesus.
6:59 said this in a synagogue instruction at *C*.

CAPHAR-SALAMA (1)

1Mc 7:31 he went out to fight Judas near *C*.

CAPHIRIM (1)

Neh 6: 2 council together at *C* in the plain of Ono."

CAPHTOR (3)

Dt 2:23 So also the Caphtorim, migrating from *C*,
Jer 47: 4 the remnant from the coasts of *C*.
Am 9: 7 from *C* and the Arameans from Kir?

CAPHTORIM (3)

Gn 10:14 and the *C* from whom the Philistines sprang.
Dt 2:23 So also the *C*,
1Chr 1:12 Naphtuhim, Pathrusim, Casluhim, and *C*,

CAPITAL (18)

Nm 21:26 Now Heshbon was the *c* of Sihon,
21:27 let Sihon's *c* be firmly constructed.
Dt 21:22 "If a man guilty of a *c* offense is put to
22:26 since she is not guilty of a *c* offense.
1Kgs 7:17 on top of the columns, one for each *c*.
2Kgs 25:17 *c* five cubits high; a bronze *c* five
25:17 network with pomegranates encircled the *c*,
2Chr 3:15 the *c* topping each was of five cubits.
Tb 6:13 that would be a *c* crime according to the
1Mc 3:37 the army and set out from Antioch, his *c*,
Is 7: 8 Damascus is the *c* of Aram,
7: 8 Samaria is the *c* of Ephraim,
Jer 46:19 baggage for exile, *c* of daughter Egypt;
52:22 A bronze *c* five cubits high surmounted the
52:22 network with pomegranates encircled the *c*,
Ez 21:25 to Rabbah of the Ammonites or to Judah's *c*,
44:24 In *c* cases they shall stand as judges,

CAPITALS (15)

Ex 36:38 their hooks as well as their *c* and bands,
38:17 the *c* were silver-plated,
38:28 hooks on the columns, for plating the *c*,
1Kgs 7: 2 columns, with cedar *c* upon the columns.
7:16 There were also two *c* cast in bronze,
7:17 the (nodes of the) *c* on top of the columns,
7:18 the piece of network on each of the two *c*.
7:19 The *c* on top of the columns were finished
7:41 two nodes for the *c* on top of the columns,
7:41 the nodes for the *c* on top of the columns,
7:42 nodes of the *c* where they met the columns,
2Chr 3:16 which he encircled the *c* of the columns,
4:12 nodes for the *c* topping these two columns,
4:12 the nodes of the *c* topping the columns;
4:13 the two nodes of the *c* topping the columns.

CAPPADOCIA (2)

Acts 2: 9 We live in Mesopotamia, Judea and *C*
1Pt 1: 1 scattered throughout Pontus, Galatia, *C*,

CAPSTONE (2)

Zec 4: 7 bring out the *c* amid exclamations of 'Hail,
Eph 2:20 with Christ Jesus himself as the *c*.

CAPTAIN (38)

Jos 5:14 I am the *c* of the host of the LORD and I
5:15 The *c* of the host of the LORD replied to
1Sm 12: 9 of Sisera, the *c* of the army of Jabin,
22:14 the king's son-in-law, *c* of your bodyguard,
2Kgs 1: 9 Then the king sent a *c* with his company of
1:10 am a man of God," Elijah answered the *c*,
1:11 Ahaziah sent another *c* with his company of
1:13 sent a *c* with his company of fifty men.
1:13 When the third *c* arrived,
25: 8 Babylon), Nebuzaradan, *c* of the bodyguard,
25:10 Chaldean troops who were with the *c*
25:11 Then Nebuzaradan, *c* of the guard,
25:12 poor, Nebuzaradan, *c* of the guard,
25:15 silver the *c* of the guard also carried off.
25:18 The *c* of the guard also took Seraiah the
25:20 The *c* of the guard,
Jdt 14: 2 rush out of the city under command of a *c*,
Is 3: 3 and elder, The *c* of fifty and the nobleman,
Jer 37:13 of Benjamin, he met the *c* of the guard,
40: 1 after Nebuzaradan, *c* of the bodyguard,
40: 2 *c* of the bodyguard took charge of Jeremiah,
40: 5 The *c* of the bodyguard gave him food and
41:10 whom Nebuzaradan, *c* of the bodyguard,
43: 6 whom Nebuzaradan, *c* of the bodyguard,
52:12 Babylon), Nebuzaradan, *c* of the bodyguard,
52:14 Chaldean troops who were with the *c*
52:15 Then Nebuzaradan, *c* of the guard,
52:16 poor, Nebuzaradan, *c* of the guard,
52:19 these too the *c* of the guard carried off,
52:24 The *c* of the guard also took Seraiah,
52:26 The *c* of the guard,
52:30 Nebuzaradan, *c* of the guard,
Dn 2:14 with Arioch, the *c* of the king's guard,
Jon 1: 6 The *c* came to him and said,
Acts 4: 1 the priests, the *c* of the temple guard,

CAPTAIN (cont.)
5:24 the *c* of the temple guard and the high
5:26 the *c* went off with the guard and brought
Rv 18:17 Every *c* and navigator,

CAPTAINS (15)

2Kgs 1:14 two *c* with their companies of fifty men.
11: 4 the *c* of the Carians and of the guards.
11: 9 The *c* did just as Jehoiada the priest
11:10 gave the *c* King David's spears and shields,
11:14 custom, and the *c* and trumpeters near him,
11:15 instructed the *c* in command of the force:
11:19 temple of the LORD, Jehoiada with the *c*,
1Chr 12:35 one thousand *c*,
2Chr 23: 1 and entered a conspiracy with certain *c*:
23: 9 Jehoiada the priest gave the *c* the spears,
23:14 out the *c* who were in command of the army;
23:20 Then he took the *c*, the nobles, the rulers
Jdt 14:12 Assyrians saw them, they notified their *c*;
2Mc 12:19 and Sosipater, two of Maccabeus' *c*,
Jer 49: 3 into exile along with his priests and *c*.

CAPTIVATE (2)

Jdt 10: 4 to *c* the eyes of all the men who should
Prv 6:25 beauty, let her not *c* you with her glance!

CAPTIVATED (2)

Jdt 16: 9 caught his eyes, and her beauty *c* his mind.
Ez 16:15 But you were *c* by your own beauty,

CAPTIVE (48)

Nm 21: 1 them in battle and took some of them *c*.
21:29 be taken *c* by the Amorite king Sihon.
Jgs 8:12 two kings of Midian, Zebah and Zalmunna, *c*,
1Sm 30: 2 *c* the women and all who were in the city,
30: 3 their wives, sons and daughters taken *c*.
2Sm 21:16 hundred shekels, was about to take him *c*.
1Kgs 8:48 the land of the enemies who took them *c*,
2Kgs 6:13 is," he said, "so that I may take him *c*."
6:22 you have taken *c* with your sword or bow?
24:12 the eighth year of his reign, took him *c*.
24:15 and also led *c* from Jerusalem to Babylon
24:16 The king of Babylon also led *c* to Babylon
1Chr 3:17 The sons of Jeconiah the *c* were:
2Chr 6:37 land where they are *c* and are converted,
6:38 you in the land of those who hold them *c*,
28: 5 away *c* a large number of his people,
29: 9 wives have been taken *c* because of this.
36:20 escaped the sword he carried *c* to Babylon,
Ezr 5:12 this house and led the people *c* to Babylon.
Tb 1: 2 king of Assyria, was taken *c* from Thisbe,
14:15 king of Media, led them *c* into Media.
Jdt 4:12 to be seized, their wives to be taken *c*,
1Mc 1:32 walls, took *c* the women and children,
8:10 the Romans took their wives and children *c*.
15:40 where he took people *c* or massacred them.
Jb 38:30 stone that holds *c* the surface of the deep?
Ps(s) 106:46 them compassion from all who held them *c*.
Sg 7: 6 a king is held *c* in its tresses.
Is 10: 4 beneath the *c* or fall beneath the slain?
52: 2 bonds from your neck, O *c* daughter Zion!
Jer 20: 4 *c* to Babylon or slay them with the sword.
40: 7 poor who had not been led *c* to Babylon,
51:41 How has she been seized, made *c*,
52:28 the people whom Nebuchadnezzar led away *c*:
Lam 1: 5 ones have gone away, *c* before the foe.
Bar 4:24 Zion's neighbors lately saw you taken *c*,
6: 1 sent to those who were being led *c*
6: 1 being led *c* to Babylon by Nebuchadnezzar,
Ez 32: 9 when I lead you *c* among the nations,
Hos 7:12 instant I will send them *c* from their land.
Am 1: 6 took *c* whole groups to hand over to Edom,
1: 9 they delivered whole groups *c* to Edom,
Na 2: 8 shudders, Its mistress is led forth *c*,
3:10 Yet even she went *c* into exile,
Lk 21:24 will be led *c* in the midst of the Gentiles.
Col 2:15 show of them, and leading them off *c*,
2Tm 2:26 Thus, taken *c* by God to do his will,
2Pt 2: 4 He held them *c* in Tartarus

CAPTIVES (42)

Gn 14:16 along with the women and the other *c*.
31:26 and carrying off my daughters like war *c*?
Nm 31: 9 Midianites with their little ones as *c*,
31:11 they had captured, and brought the *c*,
31:19 This applies both to you and to your *c*.
31:26 *c* and the beasts that have been taken;
Dt 21:10 them into your hand, so that you take *c*,
21:11 if you see a comely woman among the *c*
21:13 pare her nails and lay aside her *c* garb.
2Chr 28: 8 The Israelites took away as *c* two hundred
28:11 send back the *c* you have carried off from
28:13 "Do not bring the *c* here,
28:14 Therefore the soldiers left their *c* and
28:15 the men just named proceeded to help the *c*.
28:17 attacked Judah, and carried off *c*.
Tb 13:10 May he gladden within you all who were *c*;
Jdt 5:18 and finally taken as *c* into foreign lands.
Est A: 3 and one of the *c* whom Nebuchadnezzar,
2: 6 Jerusalem with the *c* taken with Jeconiah,
Jb 3:18 There the *c* are at ease together,
Ps(s) 68:19 You have ascended on high, taken *c*,
126: 1 When the LORD brought back the *c* of Zion,
146: 7 The LORD sets *c* free;
Is 14: 2 making *c* of its captors and ruling over
14:17 its cities, and gave his *c* no release?
20: 4 the king of Assyria lead away *c* from Egypt,
49:24 or *c* be rescued from a tyrant?
49:25 Yes, *c* can be taken from a warrior,
61: 1 to the *c* and release to the prisoners,
Jer 40: 1 among the *c* of Jerusalem and Judah who
41:10 With these *c*, Ishmael, son of Nethaniah,
41:13 the people who were Ishmael's *c* rejoiced.
Bar 1: 9 people of the land from Jerusalem, as *c*,
Ez 12:11 as *c* they shall go into exile.
Dn 2:25 "I have found a man among the Judean *c*
Ob 1:20 The *c* of the host of the children of
1:20 And the *c* of Jerusalem who are in Sepharad
Hb 1: 9 of a stormwind that heaps up *c* like sand.
Zec 6:10 Take from the returned *c* Heldai,
Lk 4:18 to the poor, to proclaim liberty to *c*,
Eph 4: 8 he took a host of *c* and gave gifts to men."
2Tm 3: 6 who worm their way into homes and make *c*

CAPTIVITY (37)

Dt 28:41 not remain with you, but will go into *c*.
Jgs 18:30 until the time of the *c* of the land.
1Kgs 8:47 in the land of their *c* and be converted.
1Chr 9: 1 in *c* to Babylon because of its rebellion.
2Chr 6:37 entreat you in the land of their *c* and say,
Ezr 2: 1 who returned from the *c* of the exiles,
3: 8 all who had come from the *c* to Jerusalem,
8:35 time, those who had returned from the *c*,
9: 7 of foreign lands, to the sword, to *c*,
Neh 1: 2 Jews, the remnant preserved after the *c*,
1: 3 "The survivors of the *c* there in the
3:36 let them be carried away to a land of *c*!
7: 6 the *c* of the exiles whom Nebuchadnezzar,
Jdt 9: 4 over to plunder, and their daughters to *c*;
1Mc 10:33 of the Jews who has been carried into *c*
Ps(s) 78:61 And he surrendered his strength into *c*,
Is 46: 2 those who bear them, they too go into *c*.
Jer 15: 2 whoever is marked for captivity, to *c*.
48:46 taken into exile, your daughters into *c*.
Lam 1:18 My maidens and my youths have gone into *c*.
Bar 2:30 their *c* they shall have a change of heart;
2:32 shall praise me in the land of their *c*,
3: 7 upon your name, and praise you in our *c*,
3: 8 Behold us today in our *c*,
4:10 For I have seen the *c* that the Eternal God
4:14 note of the *c* of my sons and daughters,
Ez 30:17 and the cities themselves shall go into *c*.
30:18 her, and her daughters shall go into *c*.
Hos 10: 6 Ephraim shall be taken into *c*,
Am 1:15 Their king shall go into *c*,
9: 4 they are led into *c* by their enemies,
Mt 1:17 from David to the Babylonian *c*,
1:17 from the Babylonian *c* to the Messiah,
2Cor 10: 5 into *c* to make it obedient to Christ.
Rv 13:10 is destined for captivity, into *c* he goes!

CAPTORS (11)

1Kgs 8:46 that their *c* deport them to a hostile land,
8:47 entreat you in the land of their *c* and say,
8:50 you, and grant them mercy before their *c*,
2Chr 6:36 that their *c* deport them to another land,
30: 9 mercy with their *c* and return to this land;
Ps(s) 137: 3 our *c* asked of us the lyrics of our songs,
Is 14: 2 of its *c* and ruling over its oppressors.
Jer 50:33 *c* hold them fast and refuse to let them go.
Lam 1: 6 gone off without strength before their *c*.
Bar 2:14 grant us favor in the presence of our *c*,
Mi 2: 4 our fields are portioned out among our *c*,

CAPTURE (19)

Dt 20:19 to it for a long time before you *c* it,
Jos 10: 1 heard that, in the *c* and destruction of Ai,
1Sm 4:19 When she heard the news concerning the *c*
4:21 with reference to the *c* of the ark of God
23:26 David and his men in order to *c* them,
2Sm 12:28 *c* it, lest it be I that capture the city
2Chr 32:18 them so that they might *c* their city.
1Mc 6: 3 and tried to *c* and pillage the city.
6:26 the citadel in Jerusalem in order to *c* it,
9:58 he will *c* all of them in a single night."
2Mc 8:36 provide tribute for the Romans by the *c*
12:35 intending to *c* the vile wretch alive,
Jb 40:24 Who can *c* him by his eyes,
Jer 18:22 For they have dug a pit to *c* me,
32: 3 city to the king of Babylon, who will *c* it.
34:22 They shall attack and *c* it,
37: 8 they shall *c* it and destroy it with fire.
38: 3 he shall *c* it.

CAPTURED (78)

Gn 14:14 Abram heard that his nephew had been *c*,
48:22 *c* from the Amorites with my sword and bow."
Nm 21:32 Israel then *c* it with its dependencies and
31:11 with the people and beasts they had *c*,
32:39 son of Manasseh, invaded Gilead and *c* it,
32:41 *c* them and called them Havvoth-jair.
32:42 *c* it with its dependencies and called it
Dt 2:35 the livestock and the loot of the *c* cities.
3: 4 At that time we *c* all his cities,
32:42 With the blood of the slain and the *c*,
Jos 8:19 from their post, rushed in, *c* the city,
10:28 Joshua *c* and put to the sword at that time.
10:32 so that on the second day Joshua *c* it
10:35 it, they attacked it and *c* it the same day,
10:37 to Hebron, which they attacked and *c*.
10:42 their lands Joshua *c* in a single campaign,
11:10 *c* Hazor and slew its king with the sword;
11:12 Joshua thus *c* all those kings with their
11:16 So Joshua *c* all this land:
11:17 All their kings he *c* and put to death.
11:23 Thus Joshua *c* the whole country,
15:17 son of Caleb's brother Kenaz, *c* it,
19:47 Leshem, which they *c* and put to the sword.
Jgs 1: 8 fought against Jerusalem and *c* it,
1:13 son of Caleb's younger brother Kenaz, *c* it;
7:25 They *c* the two princes of Midian,
8:14 He *c* a young man of Succoth,
9:45 fought against the city, and *c* it.
9:50 to Thebez, which he invested and *c*.
1Sm 4:11 The ark of God was *c*,
4:17 the dead, and the ark of God has been *c*."
4:22 because the ark of God had been *c*.
5: 1 The Philistines, having *c* the ark of God,
2Sm 8: 4 David *c* from him one thousand seven
12:26 of the Ammonites and *c* this royal city.
12:29 When he had fought against it and *c* it,
1Kgs 16:18 When Zimri saw the city was *c*,
2Kgs 5: 2 Now the Arameans had *c* from the land of
14:13 King Jehoash of Israel *c* Amaziah,
16: 9 him and moved against Damascus, which he *c*.
18:10 siege to it, and after three years *c* it.
18:13 the fortified cities of Judah and *c* them.
1Chr 5:21 thousand men they also *c* their livestock:
11: 5 David nevertheless *c* the fortress of Zion,
2Chr 12: 4 They *c* the fortified cities of Judah and
25:23 King Joash of Israel *c* Amaziah,
28:18 they *c* Beth-shemesh,
Neh 9:25 They *c* fortified cities and fertile land;
1Mc 1: 2 He fought many campaigns, *c* fortresses,
1:19 cities in the land of Egypt were *c*,
5:28 the desert to Bozrah, and *c* the city.
5:35 turned toward Alema and attacked and *c* it;
5:44 The Jews *c* that city and burnt the
9: 2 Arbela, they *c* it and killed many people.
11:56 *c* the elephants and occupied Antioch.
12:50 had been *c* and his companions killed,
13:43 city, and attacked and *c* one of the towers.
14: 3 he *c* him and brought him to Arsaces,
14: 5 As his crowning glory he *c* the port of
2Mc 8: 6 He *c* strategic positions,
8:10 the Romans by selling *c* Jews into slavery.
8:30 of them, and *c* some very high fortresses.
10:22 and without delay *c* the two towers.
Is 8:15 stumble and fall, broken, snared, and *c*.
20: 1 of Assyria, fought against Ashdod and *c* it,
22: 3 were *c* together, captured without the use
28:13 stumble backward, broken, ensnared, and *c*.
36: 1 the fortified cities of Judah and *c* them.
Jer 34: 3 you will be *c* and fall into his hands.
39: 5 and *c* Zedekiah in the desert near Jericho.
48: 1 Kiriathaim is disgraced and *c*,
48: 7 and your treasures, you also shall be *c*.
50:46 At the cry "Babylon is *c*!"
51:56 upon her, [Babylon,] her heroes are *c*,
Am 4:10 Your horses I let be *c*,
1Tm 6: 9 They are letting themselves be *c* by
Rv 19:20 The beast was *c* along with the false

CAPTURES (2)

Jos 15:16 one who attacks Kiriath-sepher and *c* it."
Jgs 1:12 one who attacks Kiriath-sepher and *c* it."

CAPTURING (4)

Jos 10:39 it, *c* it with its king and all its towns.
1Mc 5:30 ladders and devices for *c* the stronghold,
2Mc 12:16 *C* the city by the will of God,
14:41 these troops, on the point of *c* the tower,

CARAVAN (1)

Gn 37:25 saw a *c* of Ishmaelites coming from Gilead,

CARAVANS (5)

Jgs 5: 6 of Anath, in the days of slavery *c* ceased:
Jb 6:18 *C* turn aside from their routes;
6:19 The *c* of Tema search,
Is 21:13 country spend the night, O *c* of Dedanites.
60: 6 *C* of camels shall fill you,

CARBUNCLES (1)

Is 54:12 battlements of rubies, your gates of *c*,

CARCASS (6)

Lv 5: 2 thing, as the *c* of an unclean wild animal,
Jgs 14: 8 a swarm of bees and honey in the lion's *c*.
14: 9 he had scooped the honey from the lion's *c*.
Ez 32: 5 and fill the valleys with your *c*.

Mt 24:28 Where the *c* lies,
Lk 17:37 him, and he answered, "Wherever the *c* is,

CARCASSES (3)

Gn 15:11 Birds of prey swooped down on the *c*,
Dt 28:26 Your *c* will become food for all the birds
Dn 14:32 and two *c* and two sheep had been given to

CARCHEMISH (3)

2Chr 35:20 came up to fight at *C* on the Euphrates,
Is 10: 9 he says, "Is not Calno like *C*,
Jer 46: 2 at *C* on the Euphrates by Nebuchadnezzar,

CARE (119)

Gn 2:15 garden of Eden, to cultivate and *c* for it.
30:29 how well your livestock fared under my *c*;
31:24 *c* not to threaten Jacob with any harm!"
31:29 *c* not to threaten Jacob with any harm!'
42:37 "Put him in my *c*,
50:24 God will surely take *c* of you and lead you
50:25 continued, "When God thus takes *c* of you,
Ex 19:12 Take *c* not to go up the mountain,
31:13 Take *c* to keep my sabbaths,
34:12 Take *c*, therefore, not to make a covenant
Lv 18: 4 and my statutes you shall take *c* to follow.
Nm 3:36 The Merarites were charged with the *c* of
23:12 puts in my mouth that I must repeat with *c*?"
Dt 4: 9 take *c* and be earnestly on your guard not
5: 1 may learn them and take *c* to observe them.
5:12 *c* to keep holy the sabbath day as the LORD,
6:12 your fill, take *c* not to forget the LORD,
12:13 Take *c* not to offer up your holocausts in
12:19 Take *c*, also, that you do not neglect
24: 8 Take *c* to act in accordance with the
25: 7 man does not *c* to marry his brother's wife,
Jos 1: 7 taking *c* to observe the entire law which
23:11 Take great *c*, however, to love the LORD
1Sm 25:29 the living in the *c* of the LORD your God;
2Sm 7: 8 took you from the pasture and from the *c*
15:16 he left behind to take *c* of the palace.
16:21 he left behind to take *c* of the palace.
20: 3 he had left behind to take *c* of the palace
2Kgs 4:13 her, 'You have lavished all this *c* on us;
10: 6 were in the *c* of prominent men of the city,
1Chr 9:29 Others were appointed to take *c* of the
2Chr 19: 6 "Take *c* what you do,
Ezr 4:22 Take *c* that you do not neglect this matter,
7:17 You must take *c*,
Tb 2:10 however, took *c* of me for two years,
10: 6 take *c* of some unexpected business there.
10:13 the Lord, I entrust my daughter to your *c*.
14:13 He took respectful *c* of his aging
Jdt 12:11 *c* to come and to eat and drink with us.
Est 2: 3 Under the *c* of the royal eunuch Hegai,
2: 8 stronghold of Susa under the *c* of Hegai,
2: 8 to the royal palace under the *c* of Hegai,
2:14 under the *c* of the royal eunuch Shaashgaz,
1Mc 3:33 and commissioned him to take *c* of his son
6:57 to take *c* of the affairs of the kingdom.
2Mc 3:10 money was a *c* fund for widows and orphans,
Ps(s) 8: 5 the son of man that you should *c* for him?
55:23 Cast your *c* upon the LORD,
77:21 a flock under the *c* of Moses and Aaron.
80:15 Take *c* of this vine,
88: 6 no longer and who are cut off from your *c*.
90:17 the gracious *c* of the Lord our God be ours;
Prv 12:10 The just man takes *c* of his beast,
13:24 he who loves him takes *c* to chastise him.
27:23 Take good *c* of your flocks,
29: 7 man has a *c* for the rights of the poor;
Sg 1: 6 charged me with the *c* of the vineyards:
Wis 2:20 to his own words, God will take *c* of him."
3: 9 his holy ones, and his *c* is with the elect.
6:15 keeps vigil shall quickly be free from *c*;
6:17 then, *c* for discipline is love of her;
7: 4 clothes and with constant *c* I was nurtured.
8: 9 was well, and my comfort in *c* and grief.
12:13 any god besides you who have the *c* of all,
Sir 3:12 son, take *c* of your father when he is old;
12:11 take *c* to be on your guard against him.
13:13 take *c* never to accompany men of violence.
21:17 and his words are considered with *c*.
27: 6 The fruit of a tree shows the *c* it has had;
28:26 Take *c* not to slip by your tongue and fall
29:20 means, but take *c* lest you fall thereby.
31: 1 and the *c* of wealth drives away rest.
32: 1 Take *c* of them first before you sit down;
38:26 His *c* is for plowing furrows,
38:27 His *c* is to produce a vivid impression,
38:28 His *c* is to finish his work,
38:30 His *c* is for proper coloring,
39: 6 His *c* is to seek the LORD,
41:12 Have a *c* for your name,
Is 1:11 What *c* I for the number of your sacrifices?
7: 4 Take *c* you remain tranquil and do not fear;
40:11 in his bosom, and leading the ewes with *c*.
63:15 Where is your zealous *c* and your might,
Jer 17:21 *c* not to carry burdens on the sabbath day,
18:11 Take *c*!
23: 2 I will take *c* to punish your evil deeds.
Bar 6: 4 Take *c* that you yourselves do not imitate
Dn 8:27 I arose and took *c* of the king's affairs.
Na 1: 7 takes *c* of those who have recourse to him,
Mt 4: 6 'He will bid his angels take *c* of you;
6:34 Let tomorrow take *c* of itself.
Lk 11: 8 take *c* of the man because of friendship,
11:35 Take *c*,
15:15 sent him to his farm to take *c* of the pigs.
18: 4 he thought, 'I *c* little for God or man,
21: 8 He said, "Take *c* not to be misled.
Jn 19:27 onward, the disciple took her into his *c*.
Acts 11:30 presbyters in the *c* of Barnabas and Saul.
13:40 Have a *c*, then, lest what was said
24: 2 in this nation through your provident *c*.
Rom 12: 8 should exercise his authority with *c*;
13: 6 to his service with unremitting *c*.
13:11 Take *c* to do all these things,
14:20 Take *c* not to destroy God's work
1Cor 8: 9 Take *c*, however, lest in exercising
12:23 honorable by clothing them with greater *c*,
Gal 5:15 and tearing one another to pieces, take *c*!
Eph 5:29 *c* of it as Christ cares for the church
Phil 2:25 arms, whom you sent to take *c* of my needs.
Col 4:17 "Take *c* to discharge the ministry you
1Tm 3: 5 how can he take *c* of the church of God?
Ti 3:14 work in order to take *c* of their needs,
Heb 2: 6 the son of man that you should *c* for him?
3:12 Take *c*, my brothers, lest any of you
1Pt 5: 2 give it a shepherd's *c*.
2Pt 1: 7 care for your brother, and *c* for your brother,
Rv 12: 6 *c* of for twelve hundred and sixty days.
12:14 she could be taken *c* of for a year and for

CARED (9)

Gn 25:34 Esau *c* little for his birthright.
Dt 32:10 He shielded them and *c* for them,
1Kgs 1: 4 beautiful, nursed the king and *c* for him,
2Mc 4:14 no longer *c* about the service of the altar.
Sg 1: 6 my own vineyard I have not *c* for.
Jer 23: 2 You have not *c* for them,
Ez 44:15 the Zadokites who *c* for my sanctuary when
Lk 10:34 brought him to an inn, where he *c* for him.
Acts 27: 3 to visit some friends who *c* for his needs.

CAREER (2)

Wis 4:13 he reached the fullness of a long *c*;
Acts 13:25 As John's *c* was coming to an end,

CAREFREE (2)

Ps(s) 73:12 always *c*, while they increase in wealth
Ez 23:42 was heard the shout of a *c* mob in the city,

CAREFUL (48)

Lv 19:37 Be *c*, then, to observe all my statutes
20: 8 Be *c*, therefore, to observe what I,
20:22 "Be *c* to observe all my statutes and all
22:31 "Be *c* to observe the commandments which I,
25:18 precepts and be *c* to keep my regulations,
26: 3 and are *c* to observe my commandments,
Nm 28: 2 you shall be *c* to present to me the food
Dt 2: 4 very *c* not to come in conflict with them,
5:32 "Be *c*, therefore, to do as the LORD,
6: 3 then, Israel, and be *c* to observe them,
8: 1 "Be *c* to observe all the commandments I
8:11 Be *c* not to forget the LORD,
11:16 But be *c* lest your heart be so lured away
11:22 "For if you are *c* to observe all these
11:32 be *c* to observe all the statutes and
12: 1 be *c* to observe in the land which the LORD,
12:28 Be *c* to heed all these commandments I
13: 1 I enjoin on you, you shall be *c* to observe,
17: 4 you find by *c* investigation that it is
17:10 act, being *c* to do exactly as they direct.
24: 8 "In an attack of leprosy you shall be *c*
26:16 Be *c*, then, to observe them
28: 1 and are *c* to observe all his commandments
28:15 and are not *c* to observe all his
28:58 "If you are not *c* to observe every word
Jos 6:18 But be *c* not to take,
22: 5 But be very *c* to observe the precept and
Jgs 13: 4 be *c* to take no wine or strong drink and
2Kgs 6: 9 send word to the king of Israel, "Be *c*!
10:31 But Jehu was not *c* to observe
17:37 You must be *c* to observe forever the
21: 8 are *c* to observe all I have commanded them,
1Chr 22:13 if you are *c* to observe the precepts and
2Chr 33: 8 are *c* to observe all that I commanded them,
Jb 13:17 Pay *c* heed to my speech,
Ps(s) 19:12 Though your servant is *c* of them,
Prv 27:23 flocks, give *c* attention to your herds;
Sir 22:16 *c* deliberation shaken in a moment of fear.
32:22 of smooth roads, be *c* on all your paths.
Ez 18: 9 statutes and is *c* to observe my ordinances,
18:19 and has been *c* to observe all my statutes,
20:19 my statutes and be *c* to keep my ordinances;
36:27 by my statutes, *c* to observe my decrees.
Lk 17:20 *c* watching when the reign of God will come.
Jn 17:12 I kept *c* watch,
1Cor 3:10 Everyone, however, must be *c* how he builds.
Eph 5:15 Keep *c* watch over your conduct.
Ti 3: 8 to God may be *c* to do what is right.

CAREFULLY (40)

Gn 27: 8 Now, son, listen *c* to what I tell you.
Dt 4: 6 Observe them *c*, for thus will you give
6:25 is to consist in *c* observing all these
7:11 shall therefore *c* observe the commandments,
7:12 these decrees and observing them *c*,
13:15 you must inquire *c* into the matter and
15: 5 and *c* observe all these commandments which
16:12 in Egypt, and carry out these statutes *c*.
19: 9 in the event that you *c* observe all these
28:13 God, which I order you today to observe *c*,
31:12 and *c* observe all the words of this law.
32:46 you may carry out *c* every word of this law.
Jos 1: 8 may observe *c* all that is written in it;
2Chr 19: 7 Act *c*, for with the LORD, our God
Ezr 6:12 let it be *c* executed."
Neh 1: 9 return to me and *c* keep my commandments,
10:30 observe *c* all the commandments of the LORD,
2Mc 8:31 and *c* stored them in suitable places;
Sir 21:25 but the words of the prudent are *c* weighed.
Is 6: 9 Listen *c*, but you shall not understand!
Jer 2:10 and see, send to Kedar and *c* inquire:
12:16 And if they *c* learn my people's custom of
18:18 let us *c* note his every word."
Ez 37:24 by my statutes and *c* observe my decrees.
40: 4 "Son of man, look *c* and listen intently,
43:11 may *c* observe all its laws and statutes.
44: 5 Son of man, pay strict attention, look *c*,
44:20 but they shall keep their hair *c* trimmed.
Zec 6:15 you heed *c* the voice of the LORD your God.
Mt 11:15 Heed *c* what you hear!
Mk 4: 3 "Listen *c* to this.
4:12 and not see, listen *c* and not understand,
4:24 "Listen *c* to what you hear.
Lk 1: 3 I too have *c* traced the whole sequence of
Acts 7:31 As he drew near to observe it *c*,
22:30 intending to look *c* into the charge which
23:15 you would like to examine his case more *c*.
23:20 that they want to question him more *c*.
28:26 may listen *c* yet you will never understand;
1Pt 1:10 the prophets *c* searched out and examined.

CARES (12)

Ps(s) 94:19 When *c* abound within me,
142: 5 there is no one who *c* for my life.
Eccl 5: 2 For nightmares come with many *c*,
Sir 11:10 My son, why increase your *c*,
40: 5 to rest, his *c* at night disturb his sleep.
Lk 8:14 their progress is stifled by the *c* and riches
21:34 indulgence and drunkenness and worldly *c*.
1Cor 7:34 has the *c* of this world to absorb her and
Eph 5:29 care of it as Christ *c* for the church
1Pt 3:10 "He who *c* for life and wants to see
5: 7 all your cares on him because he *c* for you.

CARESSED (1)

Ez 23: 3 There the Egyptians *c* their bosoms and

CARESSING (1)

Ez 23:21 fondled your breasts, *c* your bosom.

CARETAKERS (2)

Sg 8:11 he gave over the vineyard to *c*.
8:12 and two hundred for the *c* of its fruit.

CARGO (6)

1Kgs 10:22 Tarshish ships would come with a *c* of gold,
2Chr 9:21 would return with a *c* of gold and silver,
Jon 1: 5 themselves, they threw its *c* into the sea.
Acts 21: 3 in at Tyre, where the ship had to unload *c*.
27:10 and heavy loss, not only to ship and *c*,
27:18 day some of the *c* was thrown over the side.

CARGOES (1)

Rv 18:12 their *c* of gold and silver,

CARIA (1)

1Mc 15:23 Sparta, Delos, Myndos, Sicyon, *C*,

CARIANS (2)

2Kgs 11: 4 the captains of the *C* and of the guards.
11:19 LORD, Jehoiada with the captains, the *C*,

CARING (1)

Ez 44: 8 Instead of *c* for the service of my temple,

CARKAS (1)

Est 1:10 Harbona, Bigtha, Abagtha, Zethar, and *C*,

CARMEL (31)

Jos 12:22 Taanach, Megiddo, Kedesh, Jokneam (at *C*),
15:55 Maon, *C*,
19:26 Amad and Mishal, and reached *C* on the west,
1Sm 15:12 but was informed that Saul had gone to *C*,
25: 2 was a man of Maon who had property in *C*;
25: 2 present for the shearing of his flock in *C*.
25: 5 "Go up to *C*.

CARMEL (cont.)

25: 7 miss anything all the while they were in *C*.
25:40 David's servants came to Abigail in *C*,
27: 3 and Abigail, the widow of Nabal from *C*.
30: 5 and Abigail, the widow of Nabal from *C*,
2Sm 2: 2 and Abigail, the widow of Nabal of *C*.
3: 3 of Abigail the widow of Nabal of *C*;
23:35 Hezrai from *C*;
1Kgs 18:19 Now summon all Israel to me on Mount *C*,
18:20 and had the prophets assemble on Mount *C*.
18:42 while Elijah climbed to the top of *C*,
2Kgs 2:25 From there he went to Mount *C*,
4:25 till she reached the man of God on Mount *C*.
1Chr 3: 1 the second, Daniel, by Abigail of *C*;
11:37 Hezro, from *C*;
Jdt 1: 8 along the seacoast, to the peoples of *C*,
Sg 7: 6 You head rises like *C*;
Is 33: 9 the steppe, Bashan and *C* are stripped bare.
35: 2 to them, the splendor of *C* and Sharon;
Jer 46:18 he shall come, like *C* above the sea.
50:19 to her fold, to feed on *C* and Bashan,
Am 1: 2 will languish, and the summit of *C* wither.
9: 3 Though they hide on the summit of *C*,
Mi 7:14 apart in a woodland, in the midst of *C*.
Na 1: 4 Withered are Bashan and *C*,

CARMI (9)

Gn 46: 9 Hanoch, Pallu, Hezron, and *C*.
Ex 6:14 Israel, were Hanoch, Pallu, Hezron and *C*;
Nm 26: 6 through *C* the clan of the Carmites.
Jos 7: 1 Achan, son of *C*,
7:18 forward one by one, and Achan, son of *C*,
1Chr 2: 7 The sons of Zimri: *C*.
2: 7 The sons of *C*: Achan who brought trouble
4: 1 Perez, Hezron, *C*, Hur, and Shobal.
5: 3 Israel, were Hanoch, Pallu, Hezron, and *C*.

CARMITES (1)

Nm 26: 6 through Carmi the clan of the *C*.

CARNAGE (1)

Jer 12: 3 slaughter, set them apart for the day of *c*.

CARNAIM (3)

1Mc 5:26 near Alema, in Chaspho, Maked, and *C*—
5:43 arms and fled to the temple enclosure at *C*.
5:44 So *C* was subdued,

CARNAL (8)

Lv 18:20 have *c* relations with your neighbor's wife,
18:23 shall not have *c* relations with an animal,
19:20 "If a man has *c* relations with a female
20:15 If a man has *c* relations with an animal,
Jn 1:13 begotten not by blood, nor by *c* desire,
Col 2:11 which strips off the *c* body completely.
1Pt 2:11 I urge you not to indulge your *c* desires.
1Jn 2:16 *C* allurements, enticements for the eye,

CARNALLY (1)

Lv 15:18 "If a man lies *c* with a woman,

CARNELIAN (7)

Ex 28:17 in the first row, a *c*,
39:10 in the first row a *c*,
1Chr 29: 2 and settings for them, *c* and mosaic stones,
Sir 32: 5 Like a seal of *c* in a setting of gold is
Ez 28:13 every precious stone was your covering *c*,
Rv 4: 3 had a gemlike sparkle as of jasper and *c*.
21:20 emerald, the fifth sardonyx, the sixth *c*,

CARNELIANS (1)

Is 54:11 and unconsoled, I lay your pavements in *c*,

CAROUSAL (1)

Jb 36:21 for you have preferred *c* to affliction.

CAROUSALS (1)

Wis 14:23 or frenzied *c* in unheard-of rites,

CAROUSE (1)

Is 56:12 let us *c* with strong drink,

CAROUSING (3)

Hos 4:18 When their *c* is over,
Rom 13:13 not in *c* and drunkenness,
1Pt 4: 3 evil desires, drunkenness, orgies, *c*,

CARPENTER (3)

Wis 13:11 A *c* may saw out a suitable tree and
Is 44:13 The *c* stretches a line and marks with a
Mk 6: 3 Is this not the *c*,

CARPENTERS (9)

2Sm 5:11 cedar wood, as well as *c* and masons,
2Kgs 12:12 They in turn would give it to the *c* and
22: 5 who should then pay them out to the *c*,
1Chr 14: 1 envoys to David along with masons and *c*,
22:15 of workmen, stonecutters, masons, *c*,
2Chr 24:12 hired masons and *c* to restore the temple,
34:11 They also gave it to the *c* and the masons
Ezr 3: 7 They then hired stonecutters and *c*,
Mt 13:55 Isn't this the *c* son?

CARPETING (1)

Jb 36:29 the clouds in layers as the *c* of his tent.

CARPETS (1)

Ez 27:24 mantles, embroidered cloth, varicolored *c*,

CARPUS (1)

2Tm 4:13 bring the cloak I left in Troas with *C*,

CARRIAGE (5)

Prv 30:29 stride, yes, four are stately in their *c*:
Sg 3: 9 made himself a *c* of wood from Lebanon.
Acts 8:28 in his *c* reading the prophet Isaiah.
8:29 to Philip, "Go and catch up with that *c*."
8:38 He ordered the *c* stopped,

CARRIAGES (1)

Rv 18:13 cattle and sheep, horses and *c*;

CARRIED (160)

Gn 6:22 *c* out all the commands that God gave him.
22: 6 while he himself *c* the fire and the knife.
27:35 here by a ruse and *c* off your blessing,"
34:29 They *c* off all their wealth,
44: 2 The steward *c* out Joseph's instructions.
50:13 They *c* him to the land of Canaan and
Ex 4:20 The staff of God he *c* with him.
27: 7 on either side of the altar when it is *c*.
32:28 The Levites *c* out the command of Moses,
39:42 The Israelites had *c* out all the work just
Lv 24:23 they *c* out the command that the LORD had
Nm 8:22 Moses concerning the Levites was *c* out.
13:23 on it, which two of them *c* on a pole,
Dt 1:31 you saw how the LORD, your God, *c* you,
33:21 He *c* out the justice of the LORD and his
Jos 4: 8 and *c* them along to the camp site,
6: 8 with the seven priests who *c* the ram's
22: 3 faithfully *c* out the commands of the LORD,
Jgs 7:25 Then they pursued Midian and *c* the heads
16: 3 He hoisted them on his shoulders and *c*
21:23 they *c* off a wife for each of them from
1Sm 15:15 but we have *c* out the ban on the rest."
18: 5 David then *c* out successfully every
30: 2 they had *c* them off when they left.
30: 5 Carmel, had also been *c* off with the rest.
2Sm 5:21 there, and David and his men *c* them away.
21:12 who had *c* them off secretly from the
21:14 all that the king commanded had been *c* out.
1Kgs 2:26 because you *c* the ark of the Lord GOD
8: 4 they *c* the ark of the LORD and the meeting
8: 4 (The priests and Levites *c* them.)
13:25 and *c* the news to the city where the old
15:22 and they *c* away the stones and beams with
16:20 of Zimri, with the conspiracy he *c* out,
17:19 he *c* him to the upper room where he was
2Kgs 2:16 *c* him away to some mountain or some valley."
4:20 picked him up and *c* him to his mother;
5:23 of his servants, who *c* them before Gehazi.
5:24 took what they had, *c* it into the house,
20:17 until this day, shall be *c* off to Babylon;
23: 4 their ashes *c* to Bethel
24:13 He *c* off all the treasures of the temple
25:13 they *c* away the bronze to Babylon.
25:15 silver the captain of the guard also *c* off.
1Chr 9: 1 Now Judah had been *c* in captivity to
11:18 gate at Bethlehem, and *c* it back to David.
11:23 The Egyptian *c* a spear that was like a
15:27 as were all the Levites who *c* the ark,
18: 7 David took the golden shields that were *c*
2Chr 5: 5 and they *c* the ark and the meeting tent
5: 5 it was the levitical priests who *c* them.
8:16 All of Solomon's work was *c* out
12: 9 attacked Jerusalem and *c* off the treasures
14: 7 Benjamin who *c* bucklers and were archers,
14:12 and his army, which *c* away enormous spoils.
14:14 *c* off a great number of sheep and camels.
17:13 He *c* out many works in the cities of Judah,
21:17 and *c* away all the wealth found in the
28: 5 The Arameans defeated him and *c* away
28:11 you have *c* off from among your brethren,
28:17 attacked Judah, and *c* off captives.
29:16 them and *c* it out to the Kidron Valley.
34:13 in charge of the men who *c* the burdens,
35: 6 that all may be *c* out according to the
36: 7 Nebuchadnezzar also *c* away to Babylon some
36:20 escaped the sword he *c* captive to Babylon,
Ezr 2: 1 king of Babylon, had *c* away to Babylon,
5: 8 the work is being *c* on diligently and is
5:14 and *c* off to the temple in Babylon,
6:13 and their fellow officials *c* out fully
7:23 that is ordered by the God of heaven be *c*
Neh 3: 4 son of Hakkoz, *c* out the work of repair;
3: 5 him the Tekoites *c* out the work of repair;
3: 8 the work of repair was *c* out by Uzziel,
3: 9 the work of repair was *c* out by Rephaiah,
3:10 of Hashabneiah, *c* out the work of repair.
3:12 the work of repair was *c* out by Shallum,
3:16 the work of repair was *c* out by Nehemiah,
3:17 him, the Levites *c* out the work of repair:
3:18 their brethren *c* out the work of repair:
3:22 work of repair was *c* out by the priests,
3:23 *c* out the repair in front of their houses;
3:25 *c* out the work of repair opposite the
3:25 *c* out the work of repair to a point
3:28 Gate the priests *c* out the work of repair,
3:29 Immer, *c* out the repair before his house,
3:29 after him the repair was *c* out by Shemaiah,
3:31 *c* out the work of repair as far as the
3:32 and the merchants *c* out the work of repair.
3:36 let them be *c* away to a land of captivity!
7: 6 king of Babylon, had *c* away,
11:12 brethren who *c* out the temple service,
12:45 its appointed priests and Levites who *c* out
Tb 2: 4 and I *c* the dead man from the street and
Jdt 4: 8 *c* out the orders given them by Joakim,
7:16 and he ordered their proposal to be *c* out.
Est B: 2 not to be *c* away with the sense of power,
9: 1 order decreed by the king was to be *c* out,
1Mc 2: 9 ornaments have been *c* off as spoils,
3: 2 him, and they *c* on Israel's war joyfully.
4:43 these purified the sanctuary and *c* away
5:13 the Gentiles have *c* away their wives and
6:12 when I *c* away all the vessels of gold and
9:36 and *c* off John and everything he had.
10:33 Every one of the Jews who has been *c* into
2Mc 3:28 his whole bodyguard was *c* away helpless,
5:21 Antiochus *c* off eighteen hundred talents
5:21 on foot, so *c* away was he with pride.
7:27 me, who *c* you in my womb for nine months,
8:31 the rest of the spoils they *c* to Jerusalem.
9: 8 to the ground and had to be *c* on a litter,
Jb 1:15 them, and the Sabeans *c* them off in a raid.
1:17 columns, seized the camels, *c* them off,
21:32 and on the day he is *c* to the grave Who
Wis 18: 5 As a reproof you *c* off their multitude of
Is 8: 4 shall be *c* off by the king of Assyria.
8:10 make a resolve, and it shall not be *c* out,
39: 6 until this day, shall be *c* off to Babylon;
46: 1 up on shoulders, *c* as burdens by the weary.
46: 3 birth, whom I have *c* from your infancy.
49:22 daughters shall be *c* on their shoulders.
66:12 As nurslings, you shall be *c* in her arms,
Jer 5:13 their threats be *c* out against themselves!"
10: 5 They must be *c* about,
51:29 the LORD's plan against Babylon is *c* out,
52:17 they *c* away all the bronze to Babylon.
52:19 these too the captain of the guard *c* off,
Bar 1: 9 king of Babylon, *c* off Jeconiah,
4:26 *c* off by their enemies like sheep in a
6:17 and bolts, lest they be *c* off by robbers.
6:25 no feet, they are *c* on men's shoulders,
Ez 34:29 no longer be *c* off by famine in the land,
Dn 1: 2 God, which he *c* off to the land of Shinar,
9:12 You *c* out the threats you spoke against us
11:11 shall be given into his hand and be *c* off.
14:36 crown of his head and *c* him by the hair;
Hos 10: 6 It too shall be *c* to Assyria,
Ob 1:11 the day when aliens *c* off his possessions,
Mal 2: 3 your feasts, and you will be *c* off with it.
Mt 4:24 They *c* to him all those afflicted with
Mk 2: 3 The four who *c* him were unable to bring
6:29 and *c* his body away and laid it in a tomb.
Lk 7:12 of the town a dead man was being *c* out,
14:22 some time, 'Your orders have been *c* out,
16:22 He was *c* by angels to the bosom of Abraham.
Jn 20:15 "Sir, if you are the one who *c* him off,
Acts 3: 2 a man crippled from birth was being *c* in.
5: 6 up the body, and *c* it out for burial.
5:10 *c* her out for burial beside her husband.
5:15 The people *c* the sick into the streets and
8:13 as they occurred, and was quite *c* away.
13:49 of the Lord was *c* throughout that area.
21:35 he actually had to be *c* up by the soldiers
27:17 moving the ship and the ship was *c* along.
Eph 1:10 to be *c* out in the fullness of time:
3:11 purpose, *c* out in Christ Jesus our Lord.
4:14 *c* about by every wind of doctrine that
1Thes 1: 5 it was *c* on in the Holy Spirit and out of
Heb 13: 9 be *c* away by all kinds of strange teaching.
Rv 17: 3 The angel then *c* me away in spirit to a
21:10 He *c* me away in spirit to the top of a

CARRIERS (3)

1Kgs 5:29 Solomon had seventy thousand *c* and eighty
2Chr 2:17 Of these he made seventy thousand *c* and
Neh 4:11 The load *c*,

CARRIES (13)

Lv 18: 5 who *c* them out will find life through them.
Dt 1:31 God, carried you, as a man *c* his child,
1Sm 25:30 And when the LORD *c* out for my lord the
Jb 27:20 at night the tempest *c* him off.
40:17 He *c* his tail like a cedar;
Is 40:24 and the stormwind *c* them away like straw.
64: 5 and our guilt *c* us away like the wind.
Hos 12: 2 to terms with Assyria, and *c* oil to Egypt.

Hg 2:12 If a man *c* sanctified flesh in the fold of
Mk 3:29 He *c* the guilt of his sin without end."
Lk 11:22 such a one *c* off the arms on which he was
Rom 13: 4 without purpose that the ruler *c* the sword;
Jas 1:25 but one who *c* out the law in practice.

CARRION (2)

Is 65: 4 flesh, with *c* broth in their dishes,
Ez 4:14 eaten *c* flesh or that torn by wild beasts;

CARRY (153)

Gn 18:19 so that the LORD may *c* into effect for
38:18 "Your seal and cord, and the staff you *c*."
44: 1 bags with as much food as they can *c*,
Ex 13:19 they would *c* his bones away with them.
23:22 heed his voice and *c* out all I tell you,
25:27 as holders for the poles to *c* the table.
29:35 *C* out all these orders in regard to Aaron
33:17 which you have just made, I will *c* out,
36: 5 much more than is needed to *c* out the work
37:14 as holders for the poles to *c* the table.
37:27 side, as holders for the poles to *c* it.
Lv 6: 4 he shall *c* the ashes to a clean place
10: 4 and *c* them to a place outside the camp."
16:22 Since the goat is to *c* off their
18: 4 My decrees you shall *c* out,
26: 9 numerous, as I *c* out my covenant with you.
Nm 1:50 It is they who shall *c* the Dwelling with
4:15 camp, shall the Kohathites enter to *c* them.
4:15 meeting tent that the Kohathites shall *c*.
4:19 each of them his task and what he must *c*;
4:24 what they must do and what they must *c*:
4:25 they shall *c* the sheets of the Dwelling,
4:27 to what they must do and what they must *c*;
4:27 of them responsible for what he is to *c*.
6:21 Thus shall he *c* out the law of his
7: 9 because they had to *c* on their shoulders
11:12 that you tell me to *c* them at my bosom,
11:14 I cannot *c* all this people by myself,
15:22 "When through inadvertence you fail to *c*
Dt 1: 9 said to you, 'Alone, I am unable to *c* you.
10: 8 to *c* the ark of the covenant of the LORD,
16:12 Egypt, and *c* out these statutes carefully.
17:11 You shall *c* out the directions they give
24: 8 be careful to observe exactly and to *c* out all
29:28 we may *c* out all the words of this law.]
30: 8 must again heed the LORD'S voice and *c* out
30:12 us and tell us of it, that we may *c* it out?'
30:13 us and tell us of it, that we may *c* it out?'
30:14 you have only to *c* it out.
31: 9 who *c* the ark of the covenant of the LORD,
31:25 he gave the Levites who *c* the ark of the
32:46 may *c* out carefully every word of this law.
Jos 3: 3 God, which the levitical priests will *c*,
4: 3 *C* them over with you,
14: 5 did the Israelites *c* out the instructions
23: 6 Therefore strive hard to observe and *c* out
1Sm 3:12 On that day I will *c* out in full against
15: 9 They refused to *c* out the doom on anything
17:34 bear came to *c* off a sheep from the flock,
21:16 bring in this one to *c* on in my presence?
27: 9 man or woman alive, but would *c* off sheep,
28:18 not *c* out his fierce anger against Amalek,
2Sm 3: 9 *c* out for David what the LORD swore to him
13: 2 impossible to *c* out his designs toward her.
1Kgs 6:12 observe my statutes, *c* out my ordinances,
10: 9 you king to *c* out judgment and justice."
14:28 LORD, those on duty would *c* the shields,
18:12 will *c* you to some place I do not know,
2Kgs 4:19 *C* him to his mother,"
23:24 so that he might *c* out the stipulations of
1Chr 15: 2 may *c* the ark of God except the Levites,
15: 2 for the LORD chose them to *c* the ark of
23:26 Henceforth the Levites need not *c* the
28: 8 to *c* out all the commandments of the LORD,
29:19 that he may *c* out all these plans and
2Chr 2: 1 He conscripted seventy thousand men to *c*
16: 6 King Asa commandeered all of Judah to *c*
20:25 so much that they were unable to *c* it all;
30:12 that the people were of one mind to *c* out
Jdt 7:13 Then thirst will begin to *c* them off,
10: 5 she wrapped up and gave to the maid to *c*.
10: 9 may go to *c* out the business we discussed."
2Mc 3: 8 but in reality to *c* out the king's purpose.
7: 5 them to *c* him to the fire and fry him.
14:22 might suddenly *c* out some treacherous plan.
14:29 to *c* out this order by a stratagem.
15: 5 take up arms and *c* out the king's business."
Jb 13:14 I will *c* my flesh between my teeth,
15:12 Why do your notions *c* you away,
23:14 For he will *c* out what is appointed for me;
24:10 and famished are those who *c* the sheaves.
Ps(s) 28: 9 feed them, and *c* them forever!
58:10 thistles, let the whirlwind *c* them away.
Eccl 5:14 from his labor that he can *c* in his hand.
10:20 the birds of the air may *c* your voice,
Sir 6:26 Stoop your shoulders and *c* her;
Is 5:29 they *c* it off and none will rescue it.
10: 6 I order him To seize plunder, *c* off loot,
10:23 of hosts, will *c* out within the whole land.
13: 3 warriors, eager and bold to *c* out my anger.
15: 7 they *c* across the Gorge of the Poplars,
28:21 in the Valley of Gibeon, To *c* out his work,
30: 1 LORD, Who *c* out plans that are not mine,
30: 6 They *c* their riches on the backs of asses
33:23 spoils and the lame will *c* off the loot.
41:16 the wind shall *c* them off and the storm
44:26 *c* out the plan announced by my messengers;
46: 4 continue, and I who will *c* you to safety.
46: 7 They lift it to their shoulders to *c*;
46:11 from a distant land, one to *c* out my plan.
50:11 kindle flames and *c* about you fiery darts;
52:11 you who *c* the vessels of the LORD.
57:13 All these the wind shall *c* off,
58: 3 your fast day you *c* out your own pursuits,
Jer 17:21 care not to *c* burdens on the sabbath day,
17:24 and *c* no burden through the gates of this
17:27 if you *c* burdens and come through the
20: 5 shall seize it and *c* it away to Babylon.
22: 4 If you *c* out these commands,
43:12 gods, and burn the gods or *c* them off.
44:25 keep your vows, *c* out your resolutions!
49:29 camels they shall *c* off for themselves,
51:12 For the LORD has planned and he will *c* out
Lam 5:13 The youths *c* the millstones,
Ez 11:20 and observe and *c* out my ordinances;
27: 9 sailor on the sea came to you to *c* trade.
29:19 He shall *c* off its riches,
38:13 your horde, to *c* off silver and gold,
44:16 to me, and they who shall *c* out my service.
Dn 11: 8 gold, he shall *c* away as booty into Egypt.
Hos 5:14 I *c* it away and no one can save it from me.
Am 5:26 You will *c* away Sakkuth,
6:10 be left to *c* the dead out of the houses;
Jon 3:10 he did not *c* it out.
Mt 3:11 I am not even fit to *c* his sandals.
14:12 themselves to *c* his body away and bury it.
23: 4 They bind up heavy loads, hard to *c*,
27:32 they pressed into service to *c* the cross.
28: 8 ran to *c* the good news to his disciples.
28:10 Go and *c* the news to my brothers that they
28:20 to *c* out everything I have commanded you.
Mk 4:15 Satan comes to *c* off what was sown in them.
11:16 anyone to *c* things through the temple area.
15:21 pressed him into service to *c* the cross.
Lk 10: 4 Do not *c* a walking staff or traveling bag;
22:36 however, the man who has a purse must *c* it;
23:26 shoulder for him to *c* along behind Jesus.
Jn 5:10 you are not allowed to *c* that mat around."
6:15 would come and *c* him off to make him king,
8:44 devil, and willingly you *c* out his wishes.
21:18 you fast and *c* you off against your will."
Acts 5: 9 They stand ready to *c* you out too."
1Cor 7:37 without constraint and free to *c* out his will
2Cor 4:10 *c* about in our bodies the dying of Jesus,
8:10 work last year, not only to *c* it through,
8:11 *C* it through now to a successful completion,
8:19 as we willingly *c* on this work of charity
Gal 3:10 in the book of the law and *c* it out."
6: 2 Help *c* one another's burdens;
Eph 6: 2 first commandment to *c* a promise with it
Phil 1: 6 in you will *c* it through to completion,
Heb 13:21 *c* out in you all that is pleasing to him.
Rv 17:17 put it into their minds to *c* out his plan,

CARRYING (51)

Gn 24:46 quickly lowered the jug she was *c* and said,
31:26 and *c* off my daughters like war captives?
Ex 25:14 rings on the sides of the ark, for *c* it;
25:28 These poles for *c* the table you shall make
30: 4 as holders for the poles used in *c* it.
37: 5 rings on the sides of the ark, for *c* it.
38: 7 rings on the sides of the altar for *c* it.
Lv 7:30 *c* in with his own hands the oblations to
8:35 days, *c* out the prescriptions of the LORD;
Nm 4:31 is what they shall be responsible for *c*,
4:32 which he shall be responsible for *c*.
8:20 *c* out exactly the command which the LORD
10:17 Gershon and Merari set out, *c* the Dwelling.
10:21 out, *c* the sacred objects for the Dwelling,
11:12 my bosom, like a foster father *c* an infant,
Dt 10: 3 and went up the mountain *c* the two tablets.
34: 9 thus *c* out the LORD'S command to Moses.
Jos 3: 8 Now command the priests *c* the ark of the
3:13 feet of the priests *c* the ark of the LORD,
3:14 *c* the ark of the covenant ahead of them.
3:17 the priests *c* the ark of the covenant of
4: 9 stood who were *c* the ark of the covenant.
4:10 The priests *c* the ark remained in the bed
4:16 "Command the priests *c* the ark of the
4:18 and when the priests *c* the ark of the
6: 4 priests *c* ram's horns ahead of the ark.
6: 6 seven of the priests *c* ram's horns in front
8:33 were *c* the ark of the covenant of the LORD.
8:33 Ebal, thus *c* out the instructions of Moses,
2Kgs 8: 9 Hazael went to visit him, *c* a present,
Neh 13:10 have been *c* out the services had deserted,
Jdt 13: 5 time for aiding your heritage and for *c* out
2Mc 10: 7 *C* rods entwined with leaves,
15: 5 he did not succeed in *c* out his cruel plan.
Ps(s) 126: 6 go forth weeping, *c* the seed to be sown,
126: 6 shall come back rejoicing, *c* their sheaves.
Is 27: 8 *c* them off with my cruel wind in time of
40:11 he gathers the lambs, *C* them in his bosom,
63: 9 them and *c* them all the days of old.
Jer 31: 4 *C* your festive tambourines,
Ez 38: 4 bucklers and shields, all of them *c* swords:
Hos 9:11 no birth, no *c* in the womb, no conception.
Mt 26: 7 a woman *c* a jar of costly perfume came up
Mk 14: 3 a woman entered *c* an alabaster jar of
14:13 and you will come upon a man *c* a water jar.
Lk 5:18 Some men came along *c* a paralytic on a mat.
17: 9 the servant who was only *c* out his orders?
22:10 you will come upon a man *c* a water jar.
Jn 19:17 was led away, and *c* the cross by himself,
Acts 13:36 had spent a lifetime in *c* out God's will,
Rv 17: 7 seven-headed and ten-horned beast *c* her.

CARSHENA (1)

Est 1:14 He summoned *C*,

CART (13)

1Sm 6: 7 So now set to work and make a new *c*.
6: 7 hitch them to the *c*,
6: 8 the ark of the LORD and place it on the *c*,
6:10 to the *c* but shut up their calves indoors.
6:11 they placed the ark of the LORD on the *c*,
6:14 The *c* came to the field of Joshua the
6:14 the wood of the *c* was split up and the
2Sm 6: 3 The ark of God was placed on a new *c* and
6: 3 and Ahio, sons of Abinadab, guided the *c*,
1Chr 13: 7 God on a new *c* from the house of Abinadab;
13: 7 Uzzah and Ahio were guiding the *c*,
Sir 33: 5 the wheel of a *c* is the mind of a fool;
Is 5:18 perversity, and at sin as if with *c* ropes!

CARTS (5)

2Kgs 25:13 and the wheeled *c* and the bronze sea in
25:16 the bronze sea, and the wheeled *c*,
Is 66:20 the LORD, on horses and in chariots, in *c*,
Jer 52:17 and the wheeled *c* and the bronze sea in
52:20 and the wheeled *c* which King Solomon had

CARTWHEEL (2)

Prv 20:26 the wicked, and threshes them under the *c*.
Is 28:27 a sledge, nor does a *c* roll over cumin.

CARTWHEELS (1)

Is 28:28 he crush it with his noisy *c* and horses.

CARVE (4)

Ex 20: 4 You shall not *c* idols for yourselves in
Dt 5: 8 You shall not *c* idols for yourselves in
Is 45:16 Those go in disgrace who *c* images.
Hb 2:18 carved image, that its maker should *c* it?

CARVED (34)

Dt 27:15 be the man who makes a *c* or molten idol
Jgs 17: 3 made of them a *c* idol overlaid with silver.
17: 4 by making a *c* idol overlaid with silver."
18:14 idols, and a *c* idol overlaid with silver?
18:18 idols, and the *c* idol overlaid with silver,
18:20 and *c* idol and went off in the midst of
18:30 Danites set up the *c* idol for themselves,
18:31 They maintained the *c* idol Micah had made
1Kgs 6:18 *c* in the form of gourds and open flowers;
6:29 the outer rooms had *c* figures of cherubim,
6:32 of olive wood, with *c* figures of cherubim,
6:35 strap, front and back, and had *c* cherubim,
7:31 There was *c* work at the opening,
7:36 cherubim, lions, and palm trees were *c*,
2Chr 3:10 he made two cherubim of *c* workmanship,
33: 7 an idol that he had *c* in the house of God,
33:19 and *c* images before he humbled himself,
34: 3 sacred poles and the *c* and molten images.
34: 4 the sacred poles and the *c* and molten
34: 7 poles and *c* images and beat them into dust,
1Mc 13:29 *c* suits of armor as a perpetual memorial,
13:29 and next to the armor he placed *c* ships,
Wis 18:24 were *c* in four rows upon the stones,
Sir 38:27 laboring night and day, Fashions *c* seals,
Is 22:16 on a height and *c* his tomb in the rock:
57: 8 you *c* the symbol and gazed upon it
Ez 41:17 *c* the figures of cherubim and palmtrees:
41:20 cherubim and palmtrees were *c* on the walls.
41:25 *C* upon them [on the doors of the nave]
41:25 and palmtrees, like those *c* on the walls.
Mi 5:12 I will abolish your *c* images and the
Na 1:14 I will abolish the *c* and the molten image;
Hb 2:18 Of what avail is the *c* image,
2Cor 3: 7 ministry of death, *c* in writing on stone,

CARVES (1)

Wis 13:13 he takes and *c* to occupy his spare time.

CARVING (2)

Ex 31: 5 and mounting precious stones, in *c* wood,
35:33 and mounting precious stones, in *c* wood,

CASE (91)

Ex 22: 8 parties shall present their *c* before God;
Lv 24:12 from the LORD should settle the *c* for them.

CASE (cont.)

Nm 27: 5 When Moses laid their c before the LORD,
35:24 deciding the c between the slayer and the
Dt 1:17 Refer to me any c that is too hard for you
17: 8 "If in your own community there is a c at
17: 9 c and then hand down to you their decision.
19: 4 "It is in the following c that a homicide
21: 5 and every c of dispute or violence must be
22:26 This c is like that of a man who rises up
Jos 20: 4 he shall plead his c before the elders,
Jgs 11: 8 of Gilead said to Jephthah, "In any c,
1Sm 17:26 is this uncircumcised Philistine in any c,
22: 8 be an enemy against me, as is the c today."
22:13 me and become my enemy, as is the c today?"
24:13 LORD will exact justice from you in my c.
2Sm 12: 1 "Judge this c for me!
20:21 That is not the c at all.
1Kgs 15: 5 except in the c of Uriah the Hittite.
20:18 peace or for war, in any c take them alive."
Ezr 9: 7 and to disgrace, as is the c today.
Jdt 11: 3 In any c, you have come to safety.
2Mc 3:13 Heliodorus said that in any c the money
4:47 they had pleaded their c before Scythians.
4:48 who had prosecuted the c for the city,
Jb 9:35 Since this is not the c with me,
13:18 Behold, I have prepared my c,
13:19 If anyone can make a c against me,
31:35 Oh, that I had one to hear my c,
35:14 that you see him not, the c is before him;
Prv 18:17 his c first seems to be in the right;
25: 9 Discuss your c with your neighbor,
Is 32: 7 and the needy when they plead their c.
41:21 Present your c, says the LORD;
Jer 12: 1 even so, I must discuss the c with you.
51: 8 for her wounds, in c she can be healed.
52:31 of his reign, took up the c of Jehoiachin,
Ez 9: 2 in linen, with a writer's c at his waist.
9: 3 in linen with the writer's c at his waist,
9:11 the writing c at his waist make his report:
Mt 5:32 lewd conduct is a separate c—
18:16 so that every c may stand on the word of
19: 9 c) and marries another commits adultery,
19:10 "If that is the c between man and wife,
20: 1 "The reign of God is like the c of the
20:28 is the c with the Son of Man who has come,
21:28 "What do you think of this c?
22:17 Give us your opinion, then, in this c.
25:14 "The c of a man who was going on a
27:19 not interfere in the c of that holy man.
Lk 5:24 In any c, to make it clear to you
11:19 In such c, let them act as your judges.
14: 8 c some greater dignitary has been invited.
20: 8 Jesus said to them, "In that c,
23: 4 "I do not find a c against this man."
Jn 8: 5 What do you have to say about the c?"
18:38 for myself, I find no c against this man.
19: 4 you realize that I find no c [against him]."
19: 6 I find no c against him."
Acts 5:38 The present c is similar.
19:38 Let the parties argue their c.
23:15 would like to examine his c more carefully.
23:35 "I shall hear your c,"
24: 1 their c against Paul to the governor.
24: 4 indulgence for a brief hearing of our c.
24:22 the c when Lysias the commander arrives."
25: 2 presented him with their c against Paul,
25:14 Festus referred Paul's c to the king.
25:15 elders of the Jews presented their c
25:20 Not knowing how to decide the c,
25:21 be an imperial investigation of his c,
26: 1 "You have permission to state your c."
28:18 The Romans tried my c and wanted to
28:23 to evening he laid the c before them,
Rom 5:16 In the first c, the sentence followed
1Cor 6: 1 How can anyone with a c against another
6: 5 one among you wise enough to settle a c
9:24 In that c, run so as to win!
14: 7 c of lifeless things which produce a sound,
15:11 In any c, whether it be I or they,
Gal 3: 6 Consider the c of Abraham:
3:19 is the relevance of the law, in such c?
Eph 5:33 In any c, each oné should love his wife
Col 1: 6 This has been the c from the day you first
1Tm 1:16 so that in me, as an extreme c,
2Tm 2:17 This is the c with Hymenaeus and Philetus,
4:16 At the first hearing of my c in court,
Heb 9:17 comes into force only in the c of death;
Jas 2: 4 a c like this discriminated in your hearts?
5:19 the c may arise among you of someone
Jude 1: 9 when his c with the devil was being judged
Rv 2:25 In any c, hold fast to what you have

CASES (13)

Ex 18:22 decisions for the people in all ordinary c.
18:22 More important c they should refer to you,
18:22 the lesser c they can settle themselves.
18:26 for the people in all ordinary c.
18:26 more difficult c they referred to Moses,
18:26 all the lesser c they settled themselves.
Lv 5: 5 guilty in any of these c shall confess the sin
5:13 the man committed in any of the above c,
5:22 the sinful oaths that men make in such c,
2Mc 12:22 that in many c they wounded one another,
Ez 44:24 In capital c they shall stand as judges,
Dn 13: 6 These men, to whom all brought their c,
1Cor 7:15 husband or wife is not bound in such c.

CASIPHIA (2)

Ezr 8:17 for Iddo, the leader in the place C,
8:17 brethren, and to the temple slaves in C,

CASLUHIM (2)

Gn 10:14 the Naphtuhim, the Pathrusim, the C,
1Chr 1:12 Anamim, Lehabim, Naphtuhim, Pathrusim, C,

CASPIN (1)

2Mc 12:13 He also attacked a certain city called C,

CASSIA (3)

Ex 30:24 five hundred shekels of c—
Ps(s) 45: 9 and aloes and c your robes are fragrant;
Ez 27:19 Javan exchanged wrought iron, c,

CAST (206)

Gn 2:21 So the LORD God c a deep sleep on the man,
Ex 14:24 just before dawn the LORD c through
15: 1 horse and chariot he has c into the sea.
15:21 horse and chariot he has c into the sea.
25:12 C four gold rings and fasten them on the
26:37 and c five bronze pedestals for them.
36:36 and four silver pedestals were c for them.
37: 3 rings were c and put on its four supports,
37:13 rings of gold were c for it and fastened,
38: 5 Four rings were c for the four corners of
Lv 14:40 and c in an unclean place outside the city.
16: 8 he shall c lots to determine which one is
26:30 and c your corpses on those of your idols.
Dt 29:27 soil and c them out into a strange land,
Jos 8:29 and c at the entrance of the city gate,
10:27 and c into the cave where they had hidden;
18: 6 then c lots for you here before the LORD,
18: 8 then he would c lots for them there before
24:14 C out the gods your fathers served beyond
Jgs 9:53 But a certain woman c the upper part of a
10:16 And they c out the foreign gods from their
1Sm 14:42 C lots between me and my son Jonathan."
2Sm 18:17 up and c into a deep pit in the forest,
23: 6 wicked are all like thorns to be c away;
1Kgs 7:15 Two hollow bronze columns were c,
7:16 There were also two capitals c in bronze,
7:18 Four hundred pomegranates were also c;
7:23 The sea was then c;
7:24 rows and were c in one mold with the sea.
7:33 fellies, spokes, and hubs were all c.
7:33 The four legs of each stand had c braces,
7:46 them c in the neighborhood of the Jordan,
8:57 and may he not forsake us nor c us off.
14: 9 but me you have c behind your back.
2Kgs 3:25 each of them c stones onto every fertile
10:25 put them to the sword and c them out.
13:21 c the dead man into the grave of Elisha,
13:23 them or to c them out from his presence.
19:18 lands, and c their gods into the fire;
19:32 a shield, nor c up siege-works against it.
21:14 I will c off the survivors of my
24:20 Judah till he c them out from his presence.
1Chr 24:31 c lots in the presence of King David,
25: 8 They c lots for their functions equally,
26:13 They c lots for each gate,
26:14 When the lot was c for the east side,
26:14 Then they c lots for his son Zechariah,
28: 9 you abandon him, he will c you off forever:
2Chr 4: 3 of these c in the same mold with the sea.
4:17 The king had them c in the Jordan region,
7:20 I will c from my sight this house which I
24:10 c it into the chest until it was filled.
25:12 to the summit of the Rock and then c down,
26:15 walls to shoot arrows and c large stones.
29:22 priests collected the blood and c it
29:22 slaughtered the rams and c the blood
29:22 the lambs and c the blood on the altar
30:14 incense and c them into the Kidron Valley.
33:15 Jerusalem, and he c them outside the city.
Neh 9:26 they c your law behind their backs,
11: 1 and the rest of the people c lots to bring
Est 3: 7 was c in Haman's presence to determine the
9:24 planned to destroy them and had c the pur,
2Mc 1:32 the brilliance c from a light on the altar.
5:10 and he who had c out so many to lie
Jb 1:20 He c himself prostrate upon the ground,
6:27 You would even c lots for the orphan,
8:20 Behold, God will not c away the upright;
14: 3 Upon such a one will you c your eyes so as
16:11 the clutches of the wicked he has c me.
19: 5 against me and c up to me any reproach,
30:19 He has c me into the mire;
Ps(s) 2: 3 their fetters and c their bonds from us!"
5:11 c them out because they have rebelled
17:13 O LORD, confront them and c them down;
22:19 among them, and for my vesture they c lots.
27: 9 c me not off;
44:10 you have c us off and put us in disgrace,
44:24 C us not off forever!
50:17 hate discipline and c my words behind you?
51:13 C me not out from your presence,
55:23 C your care upon the LORD,
71: 9 C me not off in my old age;
74: 1 Why, O God, have you c us off forever?
78:66 and c them into everlasting disgrace.
94:14 For the LORD will not c off his people,
102:11 for you lifted me up only to c me down.
109:10 they be c out of the ruins of their homes.
140:11 may he c them into the depths,
141: 6 Their judges were c down over the crag,
Prv 1:14 C in your lot with us,
16:33 When the lot is c into the lap,
Eccl 3: 6 a time to keep, and a time to c away.
11: 1 C your bread upon the waters;
Wis 10:19 c them up from the bottom of the depths.
11:14 Him who of old had been c out in exposure
18: 5 a single boy had been c forth but saved,
18:18 And c half-dead,
Sir 1:28 your secrets and publicly c you down,
13:22 If he slips they c him down.
21:23 but a cultured man keeps his glance c down.
Is 14:19 But you are c forth without burial,
19: 8 and lament, all who c hook in the Nile;
34: 3 Their slain shall be c out,
37:19 lands, and c their gods into the fire;
37:33 a shield, nor c up siegeworks against it.
38: 8 I will make the shadow c by the sun on the
38:17 When you c behind your back all my sins.
40:19 An idol, c by a craftsman,
41: 9 whom I have chosen and will not c off
54: 6 A wife married in youth and then c off,
57:20 calmed, And its waters c up mud and filth.
Jer 7:15 I will cast you away from me, as I c away
7:29 For the LORD has rejected and c off the
12: 7 I abandon my house, c off my heritage;
14:16 people to whom they prophesy shall be c out
14:19 Have you c Judah off completely?
16:13 I will c you out of this land into a land
22: 7 choice cedars, and c them into the fire.
22:19 and c out beyond the gates of Jerusalem.
22:26 I will c you out,
22:28 Why are he and his descendants c out,
23:33 "You are the burden, and I c you off,
23:39 you on high and c you from my presence,
26:23 and his corpse c into the common grave.
31:37 Then will I c off the whole race of Israel
36:23 and c it into the fire in the brazier,
36:30 his corpse shall be c out,
51:34 his belly with my delights, and c me out.
52: 3 LORD that he c them out from his presence.
Lam 1:15 ones in my midst the LORD has c away;
2: 1 He has c down from heaven to earth the
Bar 6: 3 and wood, which c fear upon the pagans.
Ez 6: 4 c down your slain ones before your idols;
17:17 When ramps are c up and siege towers are
18:31 C away from you all the crimes you have
21:27 at the gates, to c up a ramp,
23:35 forgotten me and c me behind your back,
26: 8 tower against you, c up a ramp about you,
26:12 and your clay shall be c into the sea.
28:17 I c you to the earth,
29: 5 I will c you into the desert,
30:13 I will c fear into the land of Egypt,
31:15 I c gloom over Lebanon because of him,
31:16 when I c him down to the nether world with
32: 4 on the open field I will c you.
Dn 3: 6 be instantly c into a white-hot furnace."
3:11 not was to be c into a white-hot furnace.
3:15 be instantly c into the white-hot furnace;
3:20 and c them into the white-hot furnace.
3:21 They were bound and c into the white-hot
3:91 we not c three men bound into the fire?"
4:22 You shall be c out from among men and
4:29 You shall be c out from among men,
4:30 Nebuchadnezzar was c out from among men,
5:21 he was c out from among men and was made
6: 8 he shall be c into a den of lions.
6:13 he shall be c into a den of lions?"
6:17 to be brought and c into the lions' den.
6:25 their wives, to be c into the lions' den.
8:10 so that it c down to earth some of the
8:11 sacrifice, and whose sanctuary it c down,
8:12 It c truth to the ground,
Hos 8: 5 C away your calf, O Samaria!
12:15 therefore he shall c his bloodguilt upon
Jl 4: 3 Over my people they have c lots;
Am 4: 3 way, And you shall be c into the mire,
5: 7 to wormwood and c justice to the ground!
Ob 1:11 his gates and c lots over Jerusalem,
Jon 1: 7 let us c lots to find out on whose account
1: 7 So they c lots,
2: 4 For you c me into the deep,
Mi 7:19 c into the depths of the sea all our sins;
Na 3: 6 I will c filth upon you,
3:10 For her nobles they c lots,
Zec 2: 4 to c down the horns of the nations that
10: 6 shall be as though I had never c them off,
10:11 The pride of Assyria shall be c down,
Mt 5:29 body than to have it all c into Gehenna.
5:30 body than to have it all c into Gehenna.
18: 9 downfall, gouge it out and c it from you!

Mk 16: 9 out of whom he had *c* seven demons.
Lk 9:40 to *c* out the spirit but they could not."
11:14 the devil was *c* out the dumb man spoke.
11:18 say it is by Beelzebul that I *c* out devils.
11:19 If I *c* out devils by Beelzebul,
11:19 by whom do your people *c* them out?
11:20 by the finger of God that I *c* out devils,
12: 5 to *c* into Gehenna after he has killed.
13:32 tomorrow I *c* out devils and perform cures,
Jn 8: 7 no sin be the first to *c* a stone at her."
19:24 for my clothing they *c* lots.")
21: 6 *C* your net off to the starboard side,"
21: 6 So they made a *c*,
Acts 26:10 be put to death I *c* my vote against them.
Rom 13:12 Let us *c* off deeds of darkness and put on
Gal 3: 1 Who has *c* a spell over you
4:30 *C* out slave girl and son together;
1Pt 5: 7 *C* all your cares on him because he cares
Rv 2:10 The devil will indeed *c* some of you into
2:22 I mean to *c* her down on a bed of pain;
8: 8 mountain all in flames was *c* into the sea.
12:10 For the accuser of our brothers is *c* out,
12:13 saw that he had been *c* down to the earth,
18:21 the great city shall be *c* down like this,

CASTER (1)

Dt 18:11 charmer, diviner, or *c* of spells,

CASTING (14)

Ex 38:27 hundred talents of silver were used for *c*
Jos 18:10 *c* lots for them before the LORD in Shiloh.
Ru 2:10 *C* herself prostrate upon the ground,
1Kgs 7:37 ten stands were made, all of the same *c*,
2Kgs 17:20 finally *c* them out from before him.
Jb 15:33 and like an olive tree *c* off its bloom.
Ps(s) 58: 6 the voice of enchanters *c* cunning spells.
Sir 6:22 him, and he will not delay in *c* her aside.
Jer 38: 9 prophet Jeremiah, *c* him into the cistern.
Ez 24: 6 pieces, one by one, without *c* lots for it.
Mt 4:18 his brother Andrew, *c* a net into the sea.
27:35 divided his clothes among them by *c* lots;
Mk 1:16 brother Andrew *c* their nets into the sea;
Lk 11:14 Jesus was *c* out a devil which was mute,

CASTLE (5)

1Chr 29: 1 great, for this *c* is not intended for man,
29:19 the *c* for which I have made preparation."
Prv 18:19 city, and a friend is like the bars of a *c*.
Is 25: 2 The *c* of the insolent is a city no more,
32:14 Yes, the *c* will be forsaken,

CASTLES (19)

Ps(s) 48: 4 God is with her *c*;
48:14 Consider her ramparts, examine her *c*,
Is 13:22 Desert beasts shall howl in her *c*,
23:13 up towers for her, Has had her *c* destroyed,
34:13 Her *c* shall be overgrown with thorns,
Lam 2: 5 all her *c* and destroyed her fortresses;
Hos 8:14 fire upon his cities, to devour their *c*.
Am 1: 4 of Hazael, to devour the *c* of Ben-hadad.
1: 7 upon the wall of Gaza, to devour her *c*;
1:10 upon the wall of Tyre, to devour her *c*.
1:12 Teman, and it will devour the *c* of Bozrah.
1:14 and it will devour her *c* Amid clamor on
2: 2 fire upon Moab, to devour the *c* of Kerioth;
2: 5 upon Judah, to devour the *c* of Jerusalem.
3: 9 *c* of Ashdod, in the castles of the land
3:10 their *c* what they have extorted and robbed.
3:11 you of your strength, and pillage your *c*,
6: 8 I abhor the pride of Jacob, I hate his *c*,

CASTRATE (1)

Gal 5:12 might go the whole way, and *c* themselves!

CASTS (11)

1Sm 2: 6 he *c* down to the nether world;
Tb 4:19 he *c* him down to the deepest recesses of
13: 2 *c* down to the depths of the nether world,
Jb 18: 7 hemmed in, and his own counsel *c* him down.
Ps(s) 147: 6 the wicked he *c* to the ground.
Sir 21:15 them with scorn and *c* them behind his back.
Is 34:17 It is he who *c* the lot for them,
44:10 forms a god, or *c* an idol to no purpose,
Mt 9:34 *c* out demons through the prince of demons."
Lk 11:15 the prince of devils, that he *c* out devils."
1Jn 4:18 rather, perfect love *c* out all fear.

CASUALTIES (2)

2Sm 18: 7 and the *c* there that day were heavy
1Mc 1:18 at his presence and fled, leaving many *c*.

CATAPULTS (2)

1Mc 6:20 purpose he constructed *c* and other devices.
6:51 *c* and mechanical bows for shooting arrows

CATARACTS (8)

Tb 2:10 droppings settled in my eyes, causing *c*.
2:10 various salves, the worse the *c* became,
3:17 to remove the *c* from Tobit's eyes,
6: 9 you rub it on the eyes of a man who has *c*,
6: 9 blowing into his eyes right on the *c*,
11: 8 the *c* shrink and peel off from his eyes;
11:13 Tobiah used both hands to peel off the *c*.
Ps(s) 42: 8 calls unto deep in the roar of your *c*;

CATCH (23)

Gn 27: 4 your *c* prepare an appetizing dish for me,
1Kgs 9: 8 passer-by shall *c* his breath in amazement,
2Kgs 3:16 LORD, 'Provide many *c* basins in this wadi.'
Est E:14 For by such measures he hoped to *c* us
Ps(s) 10: 9 he lies in wait to *c* the afflicted;
35: 8 and let the snare they have set *c* them;
Prv 30:28 you can *c* them with your hands,
Sg 2:15 *C* us the foxes, the little foxes
Jer 5:26 they set traps, but it is men they *c*.
16:16 many fishermen, says the LORD, to *c* them.
19: 8 will be amazed and will *c* his breath.
49:17 and *c* his breath at all her wounds.
50:13 Babylon will be appalled and *c* his breath,
Mt 17:27 a line, and take out the first fish you *c*.
Mk 3:11 Unclean spirits would *c* sight of him,
12:13 Herodians after him to *c* him in his speech.
13:36 not let him come suddenly and *c* you asleep.
Lk 5: 4 deep water and lower your nets for a *c*."
5: 9 amazement at the *c* they had made seized
11:54 setting traps to *c* him in his speech.
Acts 8:29 Philip, "Go and *c* up with that carriage."
1Thes 5: 4 that the day should *c* you off guard,
1Pt 4:12 for you, but it should not *c* you off guard.
2Pt 2:18 to *c* those who have just come free of a

CATCHES (8)

Ex 22: 5 spreads further, and *c* on to thorn bushes,
Lv 17:13 *c* an animal or a bird that may be eaten,
Jb 5:13 He *c* the wise in their own ruses,
Ps(s) 10: 9 he *c* the afflicted and drags them off in
Prv 12:27 The slothful man *c* not his prey,
Sir 34: 2 a man who *c* at shadows or chases the wind,
Jn 10:12 *c* sight of the wolf coming and runs away,
1Cor 3:19 "He *c* the wise in their craftiness";

CATCHING (4)

Am 3: 5 up from the ground without *c* anything?
Mk 5: 6 *C* sight of Jesus at a distance,
9:15 Immediately on *c* sight of Jesus,
Lk 5:10 From now on you will be *c* men."

CATERPILLAR (1)

Ps(s) 78:46 He gave their harvest to the *c*,

CATERPILLARS (2)

2Chr 6:28 or blight, or mildew, or locusts, or *c*;
Is 33: 4 Men gather spoil as *c* are gathered up;

CATS (1)

Bar 6:21 and *c* as well as birds.

CATTLE (58)

Gn 1:24 *c*, creeping things, and wild animals
1:25 all kinds of wild animals, all kinds of *c*,
1:26 the sea, the birds of the air, and the *c*,
2:20 The man gave names to all the *c*,
4:20 of all who dwell in tents and keep *c*.
7:21 birds, *c*, wild animals,
7:23 man and *c*, the creeping things
21:27 Then Abraham took sheep and *c* and gave
32: 6 I own *c*, asses and sheep,
47:17 their flocks of sheep and herds of *c*,
Nm 3:41 *c* in place of all the first-born among the *c*
3:45 the Levites' cattle in place of their *c*,
11:22 enough sheep and *c* be slaughtered for them?
18:17 But the first-born of *c*,
Dt 13:16 and all life that is in it, even its *c*,
15:19 shall not work the firstlings of your *c*,
Jos 14: 4 their pasture lands for the *c* and flocks.
1Sm 23: 5 *c* and inflicted a severe defeat on them,
2Kgs 5:26 olive orchards or vineyards, sheep or *c*,
1Chr 27:29 Over the *c* that grazed in Sharon was
27:29 and over the *c* in the valleys was Shaphat,
2Chr 20:25 an abundance of *c* and personal property,
26:10 dug numerous cisterns, for he had many *c*.
32:28 the various kinds of *c* and for the flocks.
Ezr 1: 4 place with silver, gold, goods, and *c*,
1: 6 way, with silver, gold, goods, and *c*,
Neh 9:37 over our bodies and our *c* as they please.
Jdt 2:17 innumerable sheep, *c*, and goats
11: 7 beasts and the *c* and the birds of the air,
1Mc 1:32 the women and children, and seized the *c*.
2:30 and their sons, their wives and their *c*,
2:38 their wives, their children and their *c*,
10:33 let all their taxes, even those on their *c*,
12:23 that your *c* and your possessions are ours,
2Mc 12:11 with *c* and to help them in every other way.
Ps(s) 104:14 You raise grass for the *c*,
107:38 nor did he suffer their *c* to decrease.
147: 9 Who gives food to the *c*,
Eccl 2: 7 had growing herds of *c* and flocks of sheep,
Sir 38:25 bullock, and whose every concern is for *c*?
Is 7:25 for *c* and shall be trampled upon by sheep.
30:23 day your *c* will graze in spacious meadows;
46: 1 stoops, their idols are upon beasts and *c*;
63:14 country, Like *c* going down into the plain,
65:10 for the *c* of my people who have sought me.
Jer 3:24 from our youth, Their sheep and their *c*,
5:17 your daughters, Devour your sheep and *c*,
10:21 Yes, the shepherds were stupid as *c*,
Ez 38:12 a people concerned with *c* and goods,
38:13 silver and gold, to take away *c* and goods,
45: 4 their homes and pasture land for their *c*.
Jl 1:18 The herds of *c* are bewildered!
Jon 3: 7 man nor beast, neither *c* nor sheep,
4:11 from their left, not to mention the many *c*?"
Mt 22: 4 My bullocks and corn-fed *c* are killed;
Rv 18:13 *c* and sheep, horses and carriages;

CATTLE-HERDERS (1)

2Chr 14:14 They attacked also the tents of the *c* and

CAUDA (1)

Acts 27:16 under the lee of a small island named *C*

CAUGHT (78)

Gn 8: 9 he *c* the dove and drew it back to him
22:13 spied a ram *c* by its horns in the thicket.
31:23 he pursued him for seven days until he *c* up
37:17 his brothers and *c* up with them in Dothan.
Ex 14: 9 *c* up with them as they lay encamped by the
21:16 sells his victim or still has him when *c*,
22: 1 "[If a thief is *c* in the act of
22: 6 from the latter's house, the thief, if *c*,
22: 7 If the thief is not *c*,
Nm 5:13 a witness who might have *c* her in the act;
11:22 If all the fish of the sea were *c* for them,
15:33 Those who *c* him at it brought him to Moses
Dt 24: 7 "If any man is *c* kidnaping a fellow
Jgs 1: 6 set out in pursuit, and when they *c* him,
15: 4 So Samson left and *c* three hundred foxes.
1Sm 9:17 When Samuel *c* sight of Saul,
2Sm 18: 9 terebinth, his hair *c* fast in the tree.
2Chr 22: 9 They *c* him where he was hiding in Samaria
Jdt 11:11 But now their guilt has *c* up with them,
16: 9 Her sandals *c* his eyes,
1Mc 1:58 against Israel, against those who were *c*,
2:32 out after them, and having *c* up with them,
2Mc 12:35 one of Bacenor's men, *c* hold of Gorgias,
14:41 the door ablaze, Razis, now *c* on all sides,
Jb 4:12 to me, and my ear *c* a whisper of it.
Ps(s) 9:16 in the snare they set, their foot is *c*;
10: 2 *c* in the devices the wicked have contrived.
59:13 lips let them be *c* in their arrogance,
Prv 5:22 own iniquities the wicked man will be *c*,
6: 2 of your lips, *c* by the words of your mouth;
6:31 Yet if he be *c* he must pay back sevenfold;
11: 6 the faithless are *c* in their own intrigue.
Eccl 9:12 children of men are *c* when the evil time
Sir 9: 4 not familiar, lest you be *c* in her wiles.
27:26 it, and he who lays a snare is *c* in it,
Is 13:15 Everyone who is *c* shall be run through;
24:18 out of the pit will be *c* in the trap.
Jer 2:26 As the thief is shamed when *c*,
48:27 Was she *c* among thieves,
48:44 who climbs from the pit is *c* in the trap;
50:24 You ensnared yourself, and were *c*,
Lam 4:20 our breath of life, was *c* in their snares,
Ez 13:20 their arms and set free those you have *c*.
19: 4 cries against him in their pit he was *c*;
19: 8 net to take him, in their pit he was *c*.
Mt 4:21 farther and *c* sight of two other brothers,
8:34 When they *c* sight of him,
9:28 to the house, the blind men *c* up with him.
14:31 at once stretched out his hand and *c* him.
22:11 he *c* sight of a man not properly dressed
Mk 1:19 little farther along, he *c* sight of James,
5:15 they *c* sight of the man who had been
9:20 When they did so the spirit *c* sight of
Lk 5: 5 at it all night long and have *c* nothing;
5: 6 Upon doing this they *c* such a great number
15:20 father *c* sight of him and was deeply moved.
Jn 1:29 John *c* sight of Jesus coming toward him,
6: 5 *c* sight of a vast crowd coming toward him,
8: 3 a woman forward who had been *c* in adultery.
8: 4 woman has been *c* in the act of adultery.
20:14 around and *c* sight of Jesus standing there.
21: 3 All through the night they *c* nothing.
21: 5 "Children, have you *c* anything to eat?"
21:10 "Bring some of the fish you just *c*."
Acts 8:23 with gall and *c* in the grip of sin."
21: 3 We *c* sight of Cyprus but passed it by on
21:32 the crowd *c* sight of him and the soldiers,
27:15 Since the ship was *c* up in it and could
2Cor 5:13 if we are ever *c* up out of ourselves,
12:16 being crafty, you say, I *c* you by guile.
Phil 1:30 saw me engaged and now hear that I am *c* up.
1Thes 4:17 will be *c* up with them in the clouds to
2Pt 2:12 brute animals born to be *c* and destroyed.
2:20 *c* up and overcome in pollution once more,
Rv 1:10 On the Lord's day I was *c* up in ecstasy,
1:17 When I *c* sight of him I fell down at his
4: 2 At once I was *c* up in ecstasy.
12: 5 child was *c* up to God and to his throne.

CAULDRON (2)

Sir 13: 2 can the earthen pot go with the metal *c*?
Jer 1:13 "I see a boiling *c*,"

CAULK (1)

Ez 27: 9 of Gebal were in you to *c* your seams.

CAULKERS (1)

Ez 27:27 [the *c* of your seams,

CAUSE (83)

Gn 21: 6 then said, "God has given me *c* to laugh,
Ex 9: 9 *c* festering boils on man and beast
Lv 15:31 their uncleanness be the *c* of their death.
Dt 33: 7 His own hands defend his *c* and you will be
1Sm 3:11 do something in Israel that will *c* the ears
19: 5 innocent blood by killing David without *c*?"
2Sm 14:15 because the people have given me *c* to fear.
17: 2 weary and discouraged, I shall *c* him panic.
1Kgs 8:45 prayer and petition, and defend their *c*.
8:59 that he may uphold the *c* of his servant
2Kgs 19: 7 there I will *c* him to fall by the sword.' "
2Chr 6:35 prayer and petition, and defend their *c*.
6:39 prayer and petitions, and uphold their *c*.
Tb 3:10 And thus would I *c* my father in his old
9: 4 a single day, I would *c* him intense grief.
10:13 Never *c* her grief at any time in your life.
1Mc 6:12 and for no *c* gave orders that the
11:60 forces of Syria espoused his *c* as allies.
2Mc 4:44 presented to him the justice of their *c*.
4:47 Menelaus, who was the *c* of all the trouble,
Jb 2: 3 me against him to ruin him without *c*."
9:17 me, and multiply my wounds without *c*;
23: 4 I would set out my *c* before him,
Ps(s) 7: 5 spared those who without *c* were my foes
9: 5 For you upheld my right and my *c*,
35: 7 *c* they set their snare for me, without cause
35:23 in my *c*,
35:27 for joy and be glad who favor my just *c*;
38:20 many are my foes without *c*.
45: 5 the *c* of truth and for the sake of justice;
54: 3 save me, and by your might defend my *c*.
69: 5 the hairs of my head who hate me without *c*.
74:22 defend your *c*;
82: 2 unjustly and favor the *c* of the wicked?
109: 3 encompassed me and attacked me without *c*.
119:154 Plead my *c*, and redeem me;
119:161 *c* but my heart stands in awe of your word.
Prv 3:30 Quarrel not with a man without *c*.
22:23 For the LORD will defend their *c*,
23:11 he will defend their *c* against you.
24:28 against your neighbor without just *c*,
29:22 and a hotheaded man is the *c* of many sins.
Wis 11:13 For when they heard that the *c* of their
17:13 not knowing the *c* that brings on torment.
Sir 31:13 therefore it weeps for any *c*.
35:23 Till he defends the *c* of his people,
39:21 No *c* then to say:
39:34 No *c* then to say: "This is not good
Is 37: 7 there I will *c* him to fall by the sword.' "
Jer 5:28 fatherless or judging the *c* of the poor.
11:20 on them, for to you I have entrusted my *c*!
20:12 on them, for to you I have entrusted my *c*.
30:13 There is none to plead your *c*,
36:24 ministers or *c* them to rend their garments.
50:34 He will defend their *c* with success,
51:10 The LORD has brought to light our just *c*;
51:36 Surely I will defend your *c*,
Lam 3:52 without *c* hunted me down like a bird;
Ez 14:15 I were to *c* wild beasts to prowl the land,
18:30 that they may be no *c* of guilt for you.
22: 9 those in you who slander to *c* bloodshed;
29:21 I will *c* you to speak out in their midst;
Mi 7: 9 sinned against him, Until he takes up my *c*,
Hg 1: 9 For what *c*? says the LORD of hosts.
Jn 15:25 'They hated me without *c*.'
Acts 1:25 *c* and went the way he was destined to go."
15:19 *c* God's Gentile converts any difficulties.
15:26 to the *c* of our Lord Jesus Christ.
17:13 to *c* a commotion and stir up the crowds.
28:19 though I had no *c* to make accusations
Rom 13: 3 Rulers *c* no fear when a man does what is
16:17 against those who *c* dissension and scandal,
2Cor 2: 2 For if I *c* you pain,
Phil 1:13 My imprisonment in Christ's *c* has become
1:16 an opportunity to defend the gospel's *c*;
2:16 you give me *c* to boast that I did not run
2Tm 2:15 a workman who has no *c* to be ashamed,
Heb 12:11 seems a *c* for grief and not for joy,
1Pt 1: 6 There is *c* for rejoicing here.
1Jn 2:10 there is nothing in him to *c* a fall.
Rv 2: 3 are patient and endure hardship for my *c*.
6:10 before you judge our *c* and avenge our

CAUSED (47)

Ex 9:10 and it *c* festering boils on man and beast.
21:13 man down, but *c* his death by an act of God,
Jgs 8:27 and *c* the ruin of Gideon and his family.
1Kgs 14:16 has committed and *c* Israel to commit."
15:26 the sin which he had *c* Israel to commit.
15:30 Jeroboam committed and *c* Israel to commit,
15:34 and the sin he had *c* Israel to commit.
16: 2 and have *c* my people Israel to sin,
16:13 son Elah committed and *c* Israel to commit,
22:53 son of Nebat, who *c* Israel to sin.
2Kgs 7: 6 The LORD had *c* the army of the Arameans to
10:29 son of Nebat, had *c* Israel to commit,
10:31 the sins which Jeroboam *c* Israel to commit.
13: 2 the sin he had *c* Israel to commit.
13: 6 house of Jeroboam had *c* Israel to commit,
13:11 son of Nebat, had *c* Israel to commit,
14:24 son of Nebat, had *c* Israel to commit.
15: 9 son of Nebat, had *c* Israel to commit.
15:18 son of Nebat, had *c* Israel to commit.
15:24 son of Nebat, had *c* Israel to commit.
15:28 son of Nebat, had *c* Israel to commit.
21:16 to the sin which he *c* Judah to commit,
23:15 son of Nebat, who *c* Israel to sin
2Chr 28:23 they only *c* further disaster to him and to
1Mc 7:22 of Judah and *c* great distress in Israel.
9:68 This *c* him great distress.
11:53 received from him, he *c* him much trouble.
13:44 into the city and *c* a great tumult there.
15:31 of silver for the devastation you have *c*
2Mc 10:10 a summary of the chief evils *c* by the wars.
Jb 34:28 But *c* the cries of the poor to reach him,
Sir 47:24 and *c* them to be exiled from their land.
Ez 32:27 men *c* terror in the land of the living.
Dn 3:50 no way touched them or *c* them pain or harm.
Hos 13: 1 Ephraim's word *c* fear,
Am 3: 6 evil befalls a city, has not the LORD *c* it?
Mal 2: 8 have *c* many to falter by your instruction;
Mk 9:26 became like a corpse, which *c* many to say,
Jn 7:35 *c* the Jews to exclaim among themselves:
8:13 This *c* the Pharisees to break in with:
9: 2 of his parents that *c* him to be born blind?"
11:36 began to weep, which *c* the Jews to remark,
11:45 This *c* many of the Jews who had come to
Acts 14: 3 message with his grace and *c* signs
15: 3 Their story *c* great joy among the brothers.
21:38 "Aren't you that Egyptian who *c* the riot
2Cor 7: 8 that the letter *c* you grief for a time),

CAUSES (15)

Nm 35:16 with an iron instrument and *c* his death,
35:17 stone in his hand and *c* his death,
35:18 club in his hand and *c* his death,
35:20 throws something at him, and *c* his death,
35:21 another out of enmity and *c* his death,
35:23 stone which strikes him and *c* his death,
Ezr 6:12 And may the God who *c* his name to dwell
Jb 22:10 you, and a sudden terror *c* you dismay,
Prv 10:10 He who winks at a fault *c* trouble,
29:23 Man's pride *c* his humiliation,
Sir 35:15 cry out against him that *c* them to fall?
36:20 A deceitful character *c* grief,
Ez 44:18 gird themselves with anything that *c* sweat.
Dn 2:21 He *c* the changes of the times and seasons,
1Cor 8:13 if food *c* my brother to sin I will never

CAUSING (9)

Nm 5:21 imprecation among your people by *c*
2Sm 24:16 angel *c* the destruction among the people,
1Kgs 16:19 conduct of Jeroboam, thus *c* Israel to sin.
16:26 *c* Israel to sin and to provoke to the LORD,
2Kgs 17:21 the LORD, *c* them to commit a great sin.
Tb 2:10 droppings settled in my eyes, *c* cataracts.
1Mc 1: 9 many years, *c* much distress over the earth.
Lk 23:19 in prison for *c* an uprising in the city,
Jude 1:19 of the Spirit, are *c* divisions among you.

CAUTION (1)

Eccl 4:13 but foolish king who no longer knows *c*;

CAUTIOUS (2)

Prv 14:16 The wise man is *c* and shuns evil;
Sir 42: 8 *c* and recognized by all men as discreet.

CAVALRY (34)

Neh 2: 9 king also sent with me army officers and *c*.
Jdt 1:13 his entire *c* and all his chariots,
2: 5 thousand infantry and twelve thousand *c*,
2:19 their chariots and *c* and regular infantry.
2:22 took his whole force, the infantry, *c*,
6: 3 be unable to withstand the force of our *c*.
7: 6 second day Holofernes led out all his *c*
7:20 Assyrian camp, infantry, chariots, and *c*,
1Mc 3:39 forty thousand men and seven thousand *c*
4: 1 thousand infantry and a thousand picked *c*,
4: 7 strong and breastplated, flanked with *c*,
4:28 thousand picked men and five thousand *c*,
4:31 them ashamed of their troops and their *c*.
6:28 of his army, and the commanders of the *c*,
6:30 thousand foot-soldiers, twenty thousand *c*,
6:35 bronze helmets, and five hundred picked *c*.
6:38 The remaining *c* were stationed on one or
8: 6 with *c* and chariots and a very great army,
9: 4 twenty thousand men and two thousand *c*.
9:11 The *c* were divided into two squadrons,
10:73 *c* and such a force as this in the plain,
10:79 left a thousand *c* in hiding behind them.
12:49 Trypho sent soldiers and *c* to Galilee and
13:22 Although Trypho got all his *c* ready to go,
15:38 and gave him infantry and *c* forces.
16: 7 into two corps and put his *c* between them,
2Mc 5: 3 squadrons of *c* in battle array,
10:24 collected a large number of *c* from Asia;
11: 2 and all his *c* and marched against the Jews.
15:20 and their *c* stationed on the flanks.
Ez 26: 7 with *c* and a great and mighty army.
Na 3: 3 a-gallop, chariots bounding, *C* charging,
Acts 23:32 leaving it to the *c* to go on with him.
Rv 9:16 Their *c* troops, whose count I heard,

CAVALRYMEN (2)

Acts 23:23 with two hundred infantrymen, seventy *c*,
23:33 When the *c* arrived in Caesarea,

CAVE (30)

Gn 19:30 he lived with his two daughters in a *c*.
23: 9 to sell me the *c* of Machpelah that he owns;
23:11 I give you both the field and the *c* in it;
23:17 together with its *c* and all the trees
23:19 Sarah in the *c* of the field of Machpelah,
23:20 Thus the field with its *c* was
25: 9 Ishmael buried him in the *c* of Machpelah,
49:29 bury me with my fathers in the *c* that lies
49:30 Hittite, the *c* in the field of Machpelah,
49:32 the field and the *c* in it that had been
50:13 him in the *c* in the field of Machpelah,
Jos 10:16 who had fled, hid in a *c* at Makkedah.
10:17 been discovered hiding in a *c* at Makkedah,
10:18 the *c* and post men over it to guard them.
10:22 the *c* and bring out those five kings to me."
10:23 out to him from the *c* the five kings,
10:27 and cast into the *c* where they had hidden;
10:27 mouth of the *c* large stones were placed,
1Sm 24: 4 the sheepfolds along the way, he found a *c*,
24: 4 occupying the inmost recesses of the *c*.
24: 8 Saul then left the *c* and went on his way.
24: 9 David also stepped out of the *c*,
24:11 now delivered you into my grasp in the *c*.
2Sm 23:13 went down to David in the *c* of Adullam,
1Kgs 19: 9 There he came to a *c*,
19:13 went and stood at the entrance of the *c*.
1Chr 11:15 who was in the *c* of Adullam while the
2Mc 2: 5 a room in a *c* in which he put the tent,
Na 2:12 Where is the lions' *c*,
Jn 11:38 It was a *c* with a stone laid across it.

CAVERN (2)

Jgs 15: 8 and remained in a *c* of the cliff of Etam.
15:11 *c* in the cliff of Etam and said to Samson,

CAVERNS (3)

1Sm 13: 6 in caves, in thickets, among rocks, in *c*,
Is 2:21 They go into *c* in the rocks and into
65: 4 the graves and spending the night in *c*,

CAVES (13)

Jgs 6: 2 signals on the mountains, the *c* for refuge,
1Sm 13: 6 difficult situation, hid themselves in *c*,
2Sm 17: 9 in one of the *c* or in some other place.
1Kgs 18: 4 hid them away fifty each in two *c*,
18:13 prophets of the LORD, fifty each in two *c*,
2Mc 6:11 nearby *c* to observe the sabbath in secret,
10: 6 like wild animals in *c* on the mountains.
Jb 30: 6 of the wadies, in *c* of sand and stone;
Is 2:19 *c* in the rocks and into holes in the earth,
Ez 33:27 and in *c* shall die by the plague.
Na 2:13 his dens with prey, and his *c* with plunder.
Heb 11:38 they dwelt in *c* and in holes of the earth.
Rv 6:15 all hid themselves in *c* and mountain crags.

CAVITY (1)

Jgs 15:19 Then God split the *c* in Lehi,

CEASE (36)

Gn 8:22 and winter, and day and night shall not *c*."
Ex 9:29 the thunder will *c*,
Nm 17:25 so that their grumbling may *c* before me;
Jos 3:13 the water of the Jordan, it will *c* to flow;
1Sm 6: 5 Perhaps then he will *c* to afflict you,
Neh 9:19 not *c* to lead them by day on their journey,
9:19 nor did the column of fire by night *c* to light
Jb 3:17 There the wicked *c* from troubling,
6:17 them, Yet once they flow, they *c* to be;
14: 7 and that its tender shoots will not *c*.
Ps(s) 77: 9 Will his kindness utterly *c*,
104:35 May sinners *c* from the earth,
Prv 22:10 strife and insult *c*.
23: 4 to gain wealth, *c* to be concerned about it;
25:10 he reproach you, and your ill repute *c* not.
Sir 16:25 grow weary, nor ever *c* from their tasks.
24: 9 and through all ages I shall not *c* to be.
28: 6 remember death and decay, and *c* from sin!
38: 8 God's creative work continues without *c*
38:20 *c* to recall him;
39:11 and when he dies his renown will not *c*.
Is 1:16 *c* doing evil;

17: 1 shall *c* to be a city and become a ruin;
Jer 3:19 I thought, and never *c* following me.
31:16 *C* your cries of mourning,
31:36 of Israel *c* as a nation before me forever.
32:40 covenant, never to *c* doing good to them;
Bar 2:23 I will make to *c* from the cities of Judah
Ez 16:42 upon you I will *c* to be jealous of you.
30:18 Her haughty pride shall *c* from her,
Am 7: 5 *C*, O Lord GOD!
Mal 3: 6 change, nor do you *c* to be sons of Jacob.
1Cor 13: 8 Prophecies will *c*, tongues will be silent,
2Cor 1:10 hope in him who will never *c* to deliver us.
11:10 mine will not *c* in the regions of Achaia!
1Thes 5:17 Rejoice always, never *c* praying,

CEASED (24)

Gn 30: 9 Leah saw that she had *c* to bear children,
Ex 9:33 Then the thunder and the hail *c*,
9:34 that the rain and hail and thunder had *c*,
Jos 4: 7 'The waters of the Jordan *c* to flow before
5:12 of the produce of the land, the manna *c*.
Jgs 5: 6 Anath, in the days of slavery caravans *c*:
Ru 1:18 Naomi then *c* to urge her,
2Sm 4: 1 he *c* to resist and all Israel was alarmed.
10:14 Joab then *c* his attack on the Ammonites
2Chr 25:27 the time that Amaziah *c* to follow the LORD,
Jdt 10: 1 and *c* her invocation to the God of Israel,
1Mc 9:27 time prophets *c* to appear among the people.
9:73 Then the sword *c* in Israel.
12:11 have never *c* to remember you in the
Jb 32: 1 Then the three men *c* to answer Job,
32:16 speak no more, and have *c* to make reply,
Ps(s) 36: 4 he has *c* to understand how to do good.
Sir 44: 9 is no memory, for when they *c*, they *c*.
Jer 51:30 Babylon's warriors have *c* to fight,
Lam 5:15 The joy of our hearts has *c*,
Lk 7:45 has not *c* kissing my feet since I entered.
Acts 20:31 I never *c* warning you individually even to
Rom 14:15 you have *c* to follow the rule of love.

CEASES (1)

Prv 19:27 If a son *c* to hear instruction,

CEASING (6)

1Sm 12:23 sin against the LORD by *c* to pray for you
2Sm 15:30 up the Mount of Olives, he wept without *c*.
Ps(s) 30:13 soul might sing praise to you without *c*;
35:15 They tore at me without *c*;
Is 59:11 like bears, like doves we moan without *c*.
Lam 3:49 My eyes flow without *c*,

CEDAR (47)

Lv 14: 4 live, clean birds, as well as some *c* wood,
14: 6 Taking the living bird with the *c* wood,
14:49 he shall take two birds, as well as *c* wood,
14:52 along with the living bird, the *c* wood,
Nm 19: 6 and the priest shall take some *c* wood,
2Sm 5:11 he furnished *c* wood,
7: 2 "Here I am living in a house of *c*,
7: 7 Why have you not built me a house of *c*?'
1Kgs 5:13 from the *c* on Lebanon to the hyssop
6: 9 was roofed in with rafters and boards of *c*.
6:10 temple, to which it was joined by *c* beams.
6:15 floor to ceiling beams with *c* paneling,
6:16 twenty cubits was set off by *c* partitions
6:18 The *c* in the interior of the temple was
6:18 all was of *c*,
6:21 made in front of the sanctuary a *c* altar,
6:36 of hewn stones and one course of *c* beams.
7: 2 four rows of *c* columns, with cedar capitals
7: 3 *c* above the beams resting on the columns;
7: 7 paneled with *c* from floor to ceiling beams.
7:11 were fine stones hewn to size, and *c* wood.)
7:12 stones and a bonding course of *c* beams.
9:11 supplying Solomon with all the *c* wood,
2Kgs 14: 9 of Lebanon sent word to the *c* of Lebanon,
1Chr 14: 1 and *c* wood to build him a house.
17: 1 "See, I am living in a house of *c*,
17: 6 'Why have you not built me a house of *c*?'
22: 4 not be weighed, and *c* trees without number.
22: 4 brought great stores of *c* logs to David,
2Chr 2: 7 Also send me boards of *c*,
25:18 sent a message to the *c* of the Lebanon,
Ezr 3: 7 they might ship *c* trees from the Lebanon
Jb 40:17 He carries his tail like a *c*;
Ps(s) 92:13 tree, like a *c* of Lebanon shall he grow.
Sg 8: 9 door, we will reinforce it with a *c* plank."
Sir 24:13 "Like a *c* on Lebanon I am raised aloft,
Is 41:19 water, I will plant in the desert the *c*,
Jer 22:14 cuts out windows for it, panels it with *c*,
22:15 among kings by competing with them in *c*?
Ez 17: 3 He took the crest of the *c*.
17:22 I, too, will take from the crest of the *c*,
17:23 and bear fruit, and become a majestic *c*.
27: 5 *C* from Lebanon they took to make you a
31: 3 Behold, a cypress *c* in Lebanon,
Hos 14: 6 He shall strike root like the Lebanon *c*,
14: 7 tree and his fragrance like the Lebanon *c*.

CEDARS (29)

Nm 24: 6 a stream, like the *c* planted by the LORD.
Jgs 9:15 the buckthorn and devour the *c* of Lebanon.'
1Kgs 5:20 to have *c* from the Lebanon cut down for me.
5:22 provide all the *c* and fir trees you wish.
5:24 with all the *c* and fir trees he wished;
10:27 and *c* as numerous as the sycamores of the
2Kgs 19:23 I cut down its lofty *c*,
2Chr 1:15 while *c* became as numerous as the
2: 2 him *c* to build a house for his dwelling,
9:27 while *c* became as numerous as the
Ps(s) 29: 5 breaks the *c*, the LORD breaks the cedars
80:11 by its branches, the *c* of God.
104:16 the trees of the LORD, the *c* of Lebanon,
148: 9 you hills, you fruit trees and all you *c*;
Sg 1:17 the beams of our house are *c*,
5:15 the trees on Lebanon, imposing as the *c*.
Sir 50:12 a garland, like a stand of *c* on Lebanon;
Is 2:13 *c* of Lebanon and all the oaks of Bashan,
9: 9 felled, but we will replace them with *c*."
14: 8 rejoice over you, and the *c* of Lebanon:
37:24 I cut down its lofty *c*,
44:14 He cuts down *c*,
Jer 22: 7 They shall cut down your choice *c*,
22:23 who dwell on Lebanon, who nest in the *c*,
Ez 31: 8 *c* in the garden of God were not its equal,
Am 2: 9 before them, who were as tall as the *c*,
Zec 11: 1 O Lebanon, that the fire may devour your *c*!
11: 2 you cypress trees, for the *c* are fallen,

CEDARWOOD (1)

Lv 14:51 Then, taking the *c*,

CEDE (1)

Nm 35: 8 so that each group will *c* cities to the

CEDED (1)

Lv 27:26 ox or a sheep, it shall be *c* to the LORD;

CEDEMITES (1)

1Kgs 5:10 all the *C* and all the Egyptians in wisdom.

CEDING (1)

Lv 27:32 flock shall be determined by *c* to the LORD

CEILING (4)

1Kgs 6:15 from floor to *c* beams with cedar paneling,
7: 3 it had a *c* of cedar above the beams
7: 7 paneled with cedar from floor to *c* beams.
2Mc 1:16 they opened a hidden trapdoor in the *c*,

CELEBRATE (47)

Ex 5: 1 they may *c* a feast to me in the desert."
12:14 shall *c* with pilgrimage to the LORD,
12:17 you must *c* this day throughout your
12:48 you wish to *c* the Passover of the LORD,
13: 5 is in this month that you must *c* this rite,
23:14 a year you shall *c* a pilgrim feast to me.
Lv 23: 2 which you shall *c* with a sacred assembly.
23: 4 festivals of the LORD which you shall *c*
23:39 you shall *c* a pilgrim feast of the LORD
Nm 9: 2 to *c* the Passover at the prescribed time.
9: 3 is the prescribed time when you shall *c* it,
9: 4 told the Israelites to *c* the Passover.
29:12 you shall *c* a pilgrimage feast to the LORD.
36: 4 When the Israelites *c* the jubilee year,
Dt 16:13 shall *c* the feast of Booths for seven days,
16:15 *c* this pilgrim feast in honor of the LORD,
1Chr 16: 4 minister before the ark of the LORD, to *c*,
2Chr 30: 1 to *c* the Passover in honor of the LORD,
30: 2 to *c* the Passover during the second month,
30: 3 not *c* it at the time of the restoration:
30: 5 to *c* the Passover in honor of the LORD,
30:13 many people gathered in Jerusalem to *c*
30:23 assembly agreed to *c* another seven days.
Neh 8:12 portions, and to *c* with great joy,
12:27 brought to Jerusalem to *c* a joyful dedication
Est E:22 you too must *c* this memorable day among
9:19 *c* the fourteenth of the month of Adar as a
9:21 He ordered them to *c* every year both the
F:10 they shall *c* these days on the fourteenth
2Mc 1: 9 We are now reminding you to *c* the feast of
1:18 that you too may *c* the feast of Booths and
2:16 As we are about to *c* the feast of the
2:16 requesting you also to please *c* the feast.
6: 6 the sabbath or *c* the traditional feasts,
10: 8 nation should *c* these days every year.
15:36 but to *c* it on the thirteenth day of the
Wis 14:23 For while they *c* either child-slaying
Is 22:13 you feast and *c*,
Na 2: 1 *C* your feasts,
Zec 14:16 of hosts, and to *c* the feast of Booths.
14:18 do not come up to *c* the feast of Booths.
14:19 do not come up to *c* the feast of Booths.
Mt 26:18 I am to *c* the Passover with my disciples
Lk 15:23 Let us eat and *c* because this son of mine
15:29 so much as a kid goat to *c* with my friends.
15:32 But we had to *c* and rejoice!
1Cor 5: 8 Let us *c* the feast not with the old yeast,

CELEBRATED (18)

Jos 5:10 they *c* the Passover on the evening of the
1Sm 11:15 Israelites *c* the occasion with great joy.
1Kgs 8:65 of Egypt, *c* the festival before the LORD,
2Chr 7: 8 of Egypt, *c* the festival for seven days.
7: 9 for they had *c* the dedication of the altar
30:21 Israelites who were in Jerusalem *c* the feast
35: 1 Josiah *c* in Jerusalem a Passover to honor
35:16 that day so that the Passover could be *c*
Ezr 6:16 and the other returned exiles *c* the
Tb 11:18 They *c* Tobiah's wedding feast for seven
1Mc 4:56 For eight days they *c* the dedication of
10:58 Their wedding was *c* at Ptolemais with
13:52 day should be *c* every year with rejoicing,
2Mc 2:12 *c* the feast in the same way for eight days.
6: 7 and when the festival of Dionysus was *c*,
10: 6 The Jews *c* joyfully for eight days as on
Acts 16:34 and joyfully *c* with his whole family his
1Thes 1: 8 every region your faith in God is *c*,

CELEBRATING (8)

Nm 9: 5 *c* the Passover in the desert of Sinai
2Chr 20:27 turned back toward Jerusalem *c* the joyful
Est 9:27 the inviolable obligation of *c* these two
1Mc 9:37 "The sons of Jambri are *c* a great wedding,
2Mc 1:18 We shall be *c* the purification of the
8:33 *c* the victory in their ancestral city,
Jer 15:17 did not sit *c* in the circle of merrymakers;
16: 8 Enter not a house where people are *c*,

CELEBRATION (14)

Nm 10:10 On your days of *c*,
1Sm 6:19 Jeconiah did not join in the *c*
Tb 9: 2 bring him along with you to the wedding *c*.
9: 5 and was inviting him to the wedding *c*.
9: 6 early start and traveled to the wedding *c*.
10: 7 at the end of the fourteen-day wedding *c*
12: 1 When the wedding *c* came to an end.
Jdt 16:20 their *c* in Jerusalem before the sanctuary,
Est E:23 us and for loyal Persians, a *c* of victory,
2Mc 6: 7 *c* of the king's birthday the Jews had,
Lk 2:42 they went up for the *c* as was their custom.
15:24 Then the *c* began.
Jn 2: 2 had likewise been invited to the *c*.
Acts 7:41 *c* over the product of their own hands.

CELESTIAL (1)

2Pt 2:10 no qualms whatever about reviling *c* beings,

CELL (3)

Ez 40:13 wall of one cell to the back wall of the *c*
Acts 12: 7 Lord stood nearby and light shone in the *c*.

CELLAR (2)

Lk 11:33 put it in the *c* or under a bushel basket,
12:24 do not reap, they have neither *c* nor barn

CELLARS (2)

1Chr 27:27 for the wine *c* was Zabdi the Shiphmite.
Ps(s) 33: 7 in *c* he confines the deep.

CELLS (11)

Ez 40: 7 The *c* were a rod long and a rod wide,
40: 7 between the *c* measured five cubits.
40:10 The *c* of the east gate were three on
40:12 cells on both sides was one cubit; the *c*
40:16 let into the *c* [and into their pilasters];
40:21 Its *c*,
40:24 where there was a southern gate, whose *c*,
40:29 its *c*, its pilasters, and its vestibule
40:33 Its *c*, its pilasters, and its vestibule
40:36 where he measured the dimensions of its *c*,

CEMETERY (2)

2Chr 26:23 them in the field adjoining the royal *c*,
Mt 27: 7 the potter's field as a *c* for foreigners.

CENCHREAE (2)

Acts 18:18 At the port of *C* he shaved his head
Rom 16: 1 who is a deaconess of the church of *C*.

CENDEBEUS (6)

1Mc 15:38 *C* commander-in-chief of the seacoast,
15:40 When *C* came to Jamnia,
16: 1 and told his father Simon what *C* was doing.
16: 4 Setting out against *C*,
16: 8 and *C* and his army were put to flight;
16: 9 John pursued them until *C* reached Kedron,

CENSER (9)

Lv 16:12 he shall take a *c* full of glowing embers
Nm 16:17 and fifty followers shall take his own *c*,
16:17 and you and Aaron, each with his own *c*,
17:11 Then Moses said to Aaron, "Take your *c*,
17:12 took his *c* and ran in among the community,
2Chr 26:19 was holding a *c* for burning the incense,
Ez 8:11 each of them with his *c* in his hand,

CENSER (cont.)
Rv 8: 3 Another angel came in holding a *c* of gold.
8: 5 Then the angel took the *c*,

CENSERS (7)

Lv 10: 1 sons Nadab and Abihu took their *c* and,
Nm 16: 6 take your *c* [Korah and all his band] and
16:18 So they all took their *c*,
17: 2 priest, to remove the *c* from the embers;
17: 3 the *c* at the cost of their lives.
17: 4 So Eleazar the priest had the bronze *c* of
1Mc 1:22 the cups and the bowls, the golden *c*,

CENSURE (2)

Wis 2:14 To us he is the *c* of our thoughts;
1Tm 5: 1 Never *c* an older man,

CENSURED (1)

Lk 3:19 was *c* by John on the subject of Herodias,

CENSUS (42)

Ex 30:12 "When you take a *c* of the Israelites who
Nm 1: 2 *c* of the whole community of the Israelites,
1:44 in the *c* taken by Moses and Aaron and the
1:49 in the *c* along with the other Israelites.
2: 4 the *c* to seventy-four thousand six hundred.]
2: 6 the *c* to fifty-four thousand four hundred.]
2: 8 the *c* to fifty-seven thousand four hundred.
2:11 the *c* to forty-six thousand five hundred.]
2:13 the *c* to fifty-nine thousand three hundred.]
2:15 and his soldiers amounted in the *c* to
2:19 in the *c* to forty thousand five hundred.]
2:21 the *c* to thirty-two thousand two hundred.]
2:23 the *c* to thirty-five thousand four hundred.
2:26 the *c* to sixty-two thousand seven hundred.]
2:28 the *c* to forty-one thousand five hundred.]
2:30 the *c* to fifty-three thousand four hundred.
2:32 This was the *c* of the Israelites taken by
3:15 "Take a *c* of the Levites by ancestral
3:16 took their *c* in accordance with the
3:40 "Take a *c* of all the first-born males of
3:42 *c* of all the first-born of the Israelites,
4:37 *c* of all the men of the Kohathite clans
4:41 *c* of all the men of the Gershonite clans
4:45 *c* of the men of the Merarite clans
7: 2 princes of the tribes who supervised the *c*.
14:29 twenty years or more, registered in the *c*,
26: 2 "Take a *c*, by ancestral houses
26:63 in the *c* of the Israelites taken on the plains
26:64 in the *c* of the Israelites taken in the desert
2Kgs 12: 5 the *c* tax,
1Chr 21: 1 he enticed David into taking a *c* of Israel.
21: 5 Joab reported the result of the *c* to David:
21: 6 however, he did not include in the *c*,
21:17 it not I who ordered the *c* of the people?
27:24 son of Zeruiah, began to take the *c*,
2Chr 2:16 Thereupon Solomon took a *c* of all the
2:16 the *c* David his father had taken of them),
Ezr 2: 2 The *c* of the men of Israel:
Neh 7: 7 The *c* of the men of Israel:
Lk 2: 1 a decree ordering a *c* of the whole world.
2: 2 This first *c* took place while Quirinius
Acts 5:37 Judas the Galilean at the time of the *c*.

CENTER (17)

Ex 26:28 The *c* bar,
28:32 have an opening for the head in the *c*,
36:33 The *c* bar,
39:23 in its *c* like the opening of a shirt,
Nm 35: 5 with the city lying in the *c*.
1Kgs 7:25 east, with their haunches all toward the *c*,
2Chr 4: 4 east, with their haunches all toward the *c*;
Jdt 6:16 They placed Achior in the *c* of the throng,
1Mc 10:63 "Go with him to the *c* of the city and
11:45 *c* of the city in an attempt to kill him.
Ez 37: 1 the LORD and set me in the *c* of the plain,
48: 8 the *c* of the tract shall be the sanctuary.
48:10 sanctuary of the LORD shall be in its *c*.
48:15 the City shall be at their *c*.
Dn 4: 7 tree of great height at the *c* of the world.
Acts 1:15 Peter stood up in the *c* of the brothers;
Rv 4: 6 At the very *c*,

CENTERED (1)

1Pt 1:21 Your faith and hope, then, are *c* in God.

CENTRAL (1)

2Kgs 20: 4 Before Isaiah had left the *c* courtyard,

CENTS (1)

Mk 12:42 in two small copper coins worth a few *c*.

CENTURIES (1)

Ex 17:16 LORD will war against Amalek through the *c*."

CENTURION (20)

Mt 8: 5 a *c* approached him with this request:
8: 8 "Sir," the *c* said in reply,
8:13 To the *c* Jesus said, "Go home.
27:54 The *c* and his men who were keeping watch
Mk 15:39 The *c* who stood guard over him,
15:44 He summoned the *c* and inquired whether
Lk 7: 2 A *c* had a servant he held in high regard,
7: 6 the house, the *c* sent friends to tell him:
23:47 The *c*,
Acts 10: 1 in Caesarea there was a *c* named Cornelius,
10:22 "The *c* Cornelius, who is an upright
22:25 than he said to the *c* who was standing by,
22:26 the *c* ran to the commander and demanded,
23:18 The *c* took him in charge and led him to
24:23 He gave orders to the *c* that Paul was to
27: 1 were handed over to a *c* named Julius
27: 6 There the *c* discovered an Alexandrian
27:11 the *c* preferred listening to the pilot and
27:31 alerted the *c* and the soldiers to this:
27:43 but because the *c* was anxious to save Paul,

CENTURIONS (3)

Acts 21:32 and *c* and charged down on the rioters.
23:17 Paul then called for one of the *c*,
23:23 summoned two of his *c* and said to them,

CEPHAS (9)

Jn 1:42 name shall be *C* (which is rendered Peter)."
1Cor 1:12 still another, *C* has my allegiance,"
3:22 whether it be Paul, or Apollos, or *C*,
9: 5 and the brothers of the Lord and *C*?
15: 5 that he was seen by *C*,
Gal 1:18 I went up to Jerusalem to get to know *C*,
2: 9 were the acknowledged pillars, James, *C*,
2:11 *C* came to Antioch I directly withstood him,
2:14 this to say to *C* in the presence of all:

CEREAL (126)

Ex 29:41 *c* offering and libation as in the morning.
30: 9 incense, or any holocaust or *c* offering;
40:29 offered holocausts and *c* offerings on it,
Lv 2: 1 wishes to bring a *c* offering to the LORD,
2: 3 *c* offering belongs to Aaron and his sons.
2: 4 *c* offering you present is baked in an oven,
2: 5 a *c* offering that is fried on a griddle,
2: 6 a *c* offering must be broken into pieces,
2: 7 a *c* offering that is prepared in a pot,
2: 8 A *c* offering that is made in any of these
2: 9 the priest shall then lift from the *c* offering
2:10 *c* offering belongs to Aaron and his sons.
2:11 "Every *c* offering that you present to the
2:13 every *c* offering that you present to the
2:13 your God be lacking from your *c* offering.
2:14 a *c* offering of first fruits to the LORD,
2:15 On this *c* offering you shall put oil and
5:13 rest of the flour, like the *c* offerings,
6: 7 "This is the ritual of the *c* offering.
6:13 fine flour for the established *c* offering,
6:16 Every *c* offering of a priest shall be a
7: 9 every *c* offering that is baked in an oven
7:10 whereas all *c* offerings that are offered
7:37 is the ritual for holocausts, *c* offerings,
9: 4 along with a *c* offering mixed with oil;
9:17 He then presented the *c* offering;
10:12 "Take the *c* offering left over from the
14:10 fine flour mixed with oil for a *c* offering,
14:20 and offer it, together with the *c* offering,
14:21 fine flour mixed with oil for a *c* offering,
14:31 as a holocaust, along with the *c* offering.
23:13 Its *c* offering shall be two tenths of an
23:16 present the new *c* offering to the LORD.
23:18 along with their *c* offering and libations,
23:37 to the LORD holocausts and *c* offerings,
Nm 4:16 incense, the established *c* offering,
5:15 cereal offering of jealousy, a *c* offering
5:18 *c* offering of her appeal, that is, the cereal
5:25 But first he shall take the *c* offering of
5:26 he shall take a handful of the *c* offering
6:14 along with their *c* offerings and libations,
6:17 the LORD, with its *c* offering and libation,
7:13 fine flour mixed with oil for a *c* offering;
7:19 fine flour mixed with oil for *c* offering;
7:25 fine flour mixed with oil for a *c* offering;
7:31 fine flour mixed with oil for a *c* offering;
7:37 fine flour mixed with oil for a *c* offering;
7:43 fine flour mixed with oil for a *c* offering;
7:49 fine flour mixed with oil for a *c* offering;
7:55 fine flour mixed with oil for a *c* offering;
7:61 fine flour mixed with oil for a *c* offering;
7:67 fine flour mixed with oil for a *c* offering;
7:73 fine flour mixed with oil for a *c* offering;
7:79 fine flour mixed with oil for a *c* offering;
7:87 yearling lambs, with their *c* offerings;
8: 8 *c* offering of fine flour mixed with oil;
15: 4 so shall also present to the LORD a *c* offering
15: 6 you shall present a *c* offering of two tenths
15: 9 with it you shall present a *c* offering of
15:24 its prescribed *c* offering and libation,
18: 9 in whatever they offer me as *c* offerings
28: 5 each with a *c* offering of one tenth of an
28: 8 you shall offer with the same *c* offering
28: 9 yearling lambs, with their *c* offering,
28:12 oil as the *c* offering for each bullock,
28:12 with oil as the *c* offering for the ram,
28:13 with oil as the *c* offering for each lamb,
28:20 *c* offerings of fine flour mixed with oil;
28:26 you present to the LORD the new *c* offering,
28:28 with their *c* offerings of fine flour mixed
28:31 established holocaust with its *c* offering.
29: 3 *c* offerings of fine flour mixed with oil;
29: 6 new moon holocaust with its *c* offering,
29: 6 established holocaust with its *c* offering,
29: 9 *c* offerings of fine flour mixed with oil;
29:11 established holocaust with its *c* offering,
29:14 *c* offerings of fine flour mixed with oil;
29:16 holocaust with its *c* offering and libation.
29:18 with their *c* offerings and libations as
29:19 holocaust with its *c* offering and libation.
29:21 with their *c* offerings and libations as
29:22 holocaust with its *c* offering and libation.
29:24 with their *c* offerings and libations as
29:25 holocaust with its *c* offering and libation.
29:27 with their *c* offerings and libations as
29:28 holocaust with its *c* offering and libation.
29:30 with their *c* offerings and libations as
29:31 holocaust with its *c* offering and libation.
29:33 with their *c* offerings and libations as
29:34 holocaust with its *c* offering and libation.
29:37 with their *c* offerings and libations as
29:38 holocaust with its *c* offering and libation.
29:39 besides whatever holocausts, *c* offerings,
Jgs 13:19 Then Manoah took the kid with a *c* offering
13:23 a holocaust and *c* offering from our hands!
1Kgs 8:64 there the holocausts, the *c* offerings,
1Chr 21:23 the wood, and the wheat for the *c* offering.
23:29 of the fine flour for the *c* offering,
2Chr 7: 7 holocausts, the *c* offerings and the fat.
Ezr 7:17 *c* offerings and libations proper to these,
Neh 10:34 the showbread, for the daily *c* offering,
13: 5 had previously been stored the *c* offerings,
13: 9 of the house of God, the *c* offerings,
Sir 45:14 His *c* offering is wholly burnt with the
Is 66: 3 Bringing a *c* offering,
Jer 14:12 If they offer holocausts or *c* offerings,
17:26 *c* offerings and incense and thank
33:18 holocausts before me, to burn *c* offerings,
Lam 2:12 They ask their mothers, "Where is the *c*—
Bar 1:10 frankincense, and to prepare *c* offerings;
Ez 42:13 *c* offerings,
44:29 They shall eat the *c* offering,
45:17 to provide the holocausts, *c* offerings,
45:17 shall offer the sin offerings, *c* offerings,
45:24 As a *c* offering he shall offer one ephah
45:25 the same *c* offerings and offerings of oil.
46: 5 with a *c* offering of one ephah for the ram,
46: 7 with a *c* offering of one ephah for the
46:11 *c* offering shall be an ephah for a bull,
46:14 as a *c* offering one sixth of an ephah,
46:14 This *c* offering to the LORD is mandatory
46:15 The lamb, the *c* offering,
46:20 sin offerings, and bake the *c* offerings,
Am 5:22 Your *c* offerings I will not accept,

CEREAL-OFFERING (3)

2Kgs 16:13 on it, burning his holocaust and *c*,
16:15 the morning holocaust and the evening *c*,
16:15 the royal holocaust and *c*,

CEREAL-OFFERINGS (1)

2Kgs 16:15 as well as the holocausts, *c*,

CEREMONIAL (2)

Jn 2: 6 As prescribed for Jewish *c* washings,
Gal 4:10 keep the *c* observance of days and months,

CEREMONY (1)

Lv 14:11 priest who performs the purification *c*

CERTAIN (116)

Gn 15:13 "Know for *c* that your descendants shall
28:11 When he came upon a *c* shrine,
38: 1 his tent near a *c* Adullamite named Hirah.
39: 1 down to Egypt, a *c* Egyptian (Potiphar,
41:15 "I had *c* dreams that no one can interpret.
42:13 twelve brothers, sons of a *c* man in Canaan;
Ex 2: 1 Now a *c* man of the house of Levi married a
15:25 who pointed out to him a *c* piece of wood.
17: 9 said to Joshua, "Pick out *c* men,
24: 5 having sent *c* young men of the Israelites
Nm 25: 6 Yet a *c* Israelite came and brought in a
Dt 13:14 you hear it said that *c* scoundrels have
Jos 23:13 with them, know for *c* that the LORD,
Jgs 7: 4 I tell you that a *c* man is to go with you,
9:53 But a *c* woman cast the upper part of a
13: 2 There was a *c* man from Zorah,
15: 2 thought it *c* you wished to repudiate her;
1Sm 1: 1 There was a *c* man from Ramathaim,
10:27 But *c* worthless men said,
2Sm 12: 1 In a *c* town there were two men,
19: 7 Indeed I am now *c* that if Absalom were
1Kgs 2:37 Valley, be *c* you shall die without fail.
2Kgs 4: 1 A *c* woman, the widow of one of the guild
12:21 *C* of his officials entered into a plot

19: 7 a spirit that, when he hears a *c* report,
1Chr 9: 2 and dwell there were *c* lay Israelites,
16: 4 He now appointed *c* Levites to minister
2Chr 23: 1 and entered a conspiracy with *c* captains:
Ezr 5:14 Babylon and consigned to a *c* Sheshbazzar,
Neh 5: 1 their wives against *c* of their fellow Jews.
7:69 *C* of the family heads contributed to the
Tb 1:19 But a *c* citizen of Nineveh informed the
11: 7 "I am *c* that his eyes will be opened.
Est 2: 5 stronghold of Susa a *c* Jew named Mordecai,
3: 8 kingdom, there is a *c* people living apart,
1Mc 2:23 a *c* Jew came forward in the sight of all
2:31 that *c* men who had flouted the king's
11:39 When a *c* Trypho,
15: 3 Whereas *c* villains have gained control of
15:17 *C* envoys of the Jews,
2Mc 3: 4 But a *c* Simon, of the priestly course
10:11 he put a *c* Lysias in charge of the
12:13 He also attacked a *c* city called Caspin,
12:17 where there were *c* Jews known as Toubiani.
13: 6 notorious for *c* other crimes is brought up
14: 3 A *c* Alcimus, a former high priest,
14:37 A *c* Razis, one of the elders
Wis 7:22 subtle, agile, clear, unstained, *c*,
Is 37: 7 a spirit that, when he hears a *c* report,
Jer 39:18 I will make *c* that you escape and do not
Ez 14: 1 When *c* elders of Israel came and sat down
Dn 2: 8 for *c* that you are bargaining for time,
3:12 There are *c* Jews whom you have made
7:19 I wished to make *c* about the fourth beast,
10: 1 The revelation was *c*:
Hos 6: 3 as *c* as the dawn is his coming,
Mt 11:14 he is Elijah, the one who was *c* to come.
Mk 7:24 *c* house and wanted no one to recognize him;
Lk 2:25 Jerusalem at the time a *c* man named Simeon.
2:36 There was also a *c* prophetess,
5:12 On one occasion in a *c* town,
7:36 There was a *c* Pharisee who invited Jesus
7:41 "Two men owed money to a *c* money-lender;
8:53 They laughed at him, being *c* she was dead.
11: 1 One day he was praying in a *c* place.
13:31 It was then that *c* Pharisees came to him.
18: 2 a *c* city who respected neither God nor man.
Jn 2: 3 At a *c* point the wine ran out,
3: 1 A *c* Pharisee named Nicodemus,
3:25 arose between John's disciples and a *c* Jew.
11: 1 was a *c* man named Lazarus who was sick.
Acts 4:36 was a *c* Levite from Cyprus named Joseph,
5:36 Not long ago a *c* Theudas came on the scene
6: 9 *C* members of the so-called "Synagogue of
8: 9 A *c* man named Simon had been practicing
9:11 house of Judas ask for a *c* Saul of Tarsus.
9:23 has passed, *c* Jews conspired to kill Saul,
9:36 Now in Joppa there was a *c* woman convert
10: 5 some men to Joppa and summon a *c* Simon,
11:27 *c* prophets came down from Jerusalem to
12: 3 he saw that this pleased *c* of the Jews,
12:11 "Now I know for *c* that the Lord has sent
13: 1 church at Antioch *c* prophets and teachers:
15:36 After a *c* time Paul said to Barnabas,
17: 7 and claim instead that a *c* Jesus is king."
18: 4 in which he persuaded *c* Jews and Greeks.
20: 3 a plot was hatched against him by *c* Jews;
20: 9 and a *c* young lad named Eutychus who was
20:19 came my way from the plottings of *c* Jews.
22:12 "A *c* Ananias, a devout observer of the law
23:12 *c* Jews formed a conspiracy in which they
24:19 *C* Jews from the province of Asia are the
25:19 and about a *c* Jesus who had died but who
28:15 *C* brothers from Rome who heard about us
Rom 2:19 You feel *c* that you can guide the blind
5: 9 it is all the more *c* that we shall be
5:10 it is all the more *c* that we who have been
8:38 For I am *c* that neither death nor life,
14: 3 not ridicule him who abstains from *c* foods;
14: 5 Each should be *c* of his own conscience.
15:29 I am *c* that when I do visit you,
1Cor 1:11 by *c* members of Chloe's household that you
2: 6 a *c* wisdom which we express among the
2Cor 1:13 just as you know us to a *c* degree already,
8:13 there should be a *c* equality.
10: 2 dare to use courageously against *c* ones
10:12 with *c* people who recommend themselves.
Gal 2: 4 *C* false claimants to the title of brother
Col 2:23 a *c* show of wisdom in their affected piety,
1Tm 1: 3 stay on in Ephesus in order to warn *c*
2Pt 3:16 are *c* passages in them hard to understand.
1Jn 2:18 This makes us *c* that it is the final hour.
Jude 1: 4 *C* individuals have recently wormed their
1: 5 I wish to remind you of *c* things,
Rv 13:18 A *c* wisdom is needed here;
13:18 for it is a number that stands for a *c* man.

CERTAINLY (44)

Gn 3: 4 "You *c* will not die!
20: 7 that you and all who are yours will *c* die."
26: 9 "She must *c* be your wife!
27:24 really my son Esau? "*C*, he replied.
Ex 2:14 and thought, "The affair must *c* be known."
Lv 10:18 *c* have eaten the offering in the sanctuary,
13:11 quarantining him, since he is *c* unclean.
Nm 13:30 up and seize the land, for we can *c* do so."
Dt 30:18 I tell you now that you will *c* perish;
Jgs 4: 9 "I will *c* go with you,"
13:22 LORD, said to his wife, "We will *c* die,
15:13 "we will *c* not kill you but will only
1Sm 20: 9 injury upon you, I will *c* let you know."
25:28 *c* establish a lasting dynasty for my lord,
26:25 shall *c* succeed in whatever you undertake."
27:12 must *c* be detested by his people Israel.
1Kgs 13:32 the cities of Samaria shall *c* come to pass."
Tb 5:14 You are *c* of good lineage, and welcome!"
5:20 has given us to live on is *c* enough for us."
Est E:10 a Macedonian, *c* not of Persian blood,
1Mc 5:40 he will *c* defeat us.
9: 9 "We *c* cannot.
2Mc 3:38 for there is *c* some special divine power
Prv 21: 5 but all rash haste leads *c* to poverty.
Jer 36:16 "We must *c* tell the king all these things."
38: 3 This city shall *c* be handed over to the
Ez 18:13 this son *c* shall not live.
Mt 26:73 to Peter and said, "You are *c* one of them!
Mk 14:70 Peter once more, "You are *c* one of them!
Lk 9:12 for this is *c* an out-of-the-way place."
13: 5 *C* not! But I tell you, you will all
22:59 "This man was *c* with him,
Jn 18:30 would *c* not have handed him over to you."
Rom 1:21 They *c* had knowledge of God,
4: 2 *C* if Abraham was justified by his deeds he
4:13 *C* the promise made to Abraham and his
6: 2 *C* not! How can we who died to sin
7: 7 *C* not! Yet it was only through the law
10:18 *C* they have,
11:21 natural branches, he will *c* not spare you.
1Cor 9: 2 an apostle for others, I *c* am one for you.
11:22 *C* not in this matter!
15:15 but he *c* did not raise him up if the dead
Col 4:13 I can *c* testify how solicitous he is for

CERTAINTY (1)

Rom 14:14 I know with *c* on the authority of the Lord

CERTIFIES (1)

Jn 3:33 this testimony *c* that God is truthful.

CERTIFY (1)

Est 8:12 *c* that the Jews may follow their own laws,

CHABRIS (3)

Jdt 6:15 son of Micah of the tribe of Simeon, *C*,
8:10 charge of all her things to ask Uzziah, *C*,
10:6 elders of the city, *C* and Charmis

CHAEREAS (2)

2Mc 10:32 called Gazara, where *C* was in command.
10:37 they killed him, along with his brother *C*,

CHAFF (14)

Jb 21:18 and like *c* which the storm snatches away!
Ps(s) 1: 4 they are like *c* which the wind drives away.
35: 5 Let them be like *c* before the wind,
83:14 in a whirlwind, like *c* before the wind.
Is 17:13 Windswept, like *c* on the mountains,
29: 5 the horde of the tyrants like flying *c*.
41:15 and crush them, to make the hills like *c*.
Jer 13:24 *c* that flies when the desert wind blows.
Bar 6:42 sit by the roads, burning *c* for incense;
Dn 2:35 as the *c* on the threshing floor in summer,
Hos 13: 3 Like *c* storm-driven from the threshing
Zep 2: 2 you are driven away, like *c* that passes on;
Mt 3:12 the *c* he will burn in unquenchable fire."
Lk 3:17 the *c* he will burn in unquenchable fire."

CHAFING (1)

Sir 26: 7 A bad wife is a *c* yoke;

CHAGRINED (1)

2Sm 11:25 'Do not be *c* at this,

CHAIN (6)

Gn 41:42 fine linen and put a gold *c* about his neck.
Sir 21:21 Like a *c* of gold is learning to a wise man,
28:19 its yoke nor been fettered with its *c*;
Mk 5: 3 no longer be restrained even with a *c*.
Acts 16:24 going so far as to *c* their feet to a stake.
Rv 20: 1 key to the abyss and a huge *c* in his hand.

CHAINED (2)

Mk 6:17 the one who had ordered John arrested, *c*,
Rv 20: 2 Satan, and *c* him up for a thousand years.

CHAINING (1)

2Tm 2: 9 but there is no *c* the word of God!

CHAINLIKE (1)

1Kgs 7:17 Two pieces of network with a *c* mesh were

CHAINS (42)

Ex 28:14 of gold, as well as two *c* of pure gold,
28:14 the cordlike *c* to the filigree rosettes.
28:22 "when the *c* of pure gold,
39:15 *C* of pure gold,
39:17 The two gold *c* were then fastened to the
39:18 The other two ends of the two *c* were
2Sm 3:34 Your hands were not bound with *c*,
1Kgs 6:21 it with gold, and looped it with golden *c*.
2Chr 3: 5 fine gold, embossing on it palms and *c*.
3:16 He worked out *c* in the form of a collar
3:16 hundred pomegranates which he set on the *c*.
33:11 Manasseh with hooks, shackled him with *c*,
36: 6 bound him with *c* to take him to Babylon.
Ps(s) 105:18 with fetters, and he was bound with *c*,
107:10 and gloom, bondsmen in want and in *c*,
149: 8 To bind their kings with *c*,
Sir 13:12 and will not refrain from injury or *c*.
28:20 of iron and its chains are *c* of bronze!
33:29 if he becomes unruly, load him with *c*.
Is 40:19 plates with gold and fits with silver *c*?
45:14 they shall follow you, coming in *c*.
Jer 39: 7 and bound him in *c* to bring him to Babylon.
40: 1 where he had found him a prisoner in *c*,
Lam 3: 7 with no escape and weighed me down with *c*;
Na 3:10 and all her great men were put into *c*.
Mt 14: 3 Herod had had John arrested, put in *c*,
Mk 5: 4 handcuffs and *c*, but has pulled the chains
Lk 8:29 The man used to be tied with *c* and fetters,
Acts 12: 6 two soldiers, fastened with double *c*,
12: 7 that, the *c* dropped from Peter's wrists.
16:26 open and everyone's *c* were pulled loose.
20:23 city to city that *c* and hardships await me.
26:29 without these *c*!"
28:20 I wear these *c* solely because I share the
Eph 6:20 mystery for which I am an ambassador in *c*.
Phil 1:14 in Christ, taking courage from my *c*,
Col 4:18 Remember my *c*.
2Tm 1:16 has not been ashamed of me, even in my *c*.
2: 9 even to the point of being thrown into *c*—
Heb 11:36 scourging, even *c* and imprisonment.

CHAIR (5)

Jgs 3:20 So the king rose from his *c*,
1Sm 1: 9 a *c* near the doorpost of the LORD's temple.
4:13 Eli was sitting in his *c* beside the gate,
4:18 fell backward from his *c* into the gateway;
2Kgs 4:10 furnish it for him with a bed, table, *c*,

CHALCEDONY (1)

Rv 21:19 jasper, the second sapphire, the third *c*,

CHALCOL (1)

1Kgs 5:11 than Ethan the Ezrahite, or Heman, *C*,

CHALDEA (14)

Jdt 2:23 border of the desert toward the south of *C*.
Is 48:14 will against Babylon and the progeny of *C*.
48:20 Go forth from Babylon, flee from *C*!
Jer 50:10 *C* shall be their plunder,
51: 1 Babylon, and against those who live in *C*,
51: 4 The slain shall fall in the land of *C*,
51:24 live in *C* All the evil they did to Zion,
51:35 My blood upon the people of *C*,
Ez 11:24 me back to the exiles in *C* [in a vision,
16:29 you played the harlot, now going to *C*,
23:15 portraits of Babylonians, natives of *C*,
23:16 them than she sent messengers to them in *C*.
23:23 the men of Babylon and all of *C*,
Hb 1: 6 For see, I am raising up *C*,

CHALDEAN (13)

2Kgs 25: 5 But the *C* army pursued the king and
25:10 Then the *C* troops who were with the
25:24 "Do not be afraid of the *C* officials,"
Ezr 5:12 he delivered them into the power of the *C*,
Jer 37:10 defeat the whole *C* army now attacking you,
37:11 When the *C* army lifted the siege of
39: 5 of the Arabah, but the *C* army pursued them,
41: 3 Gedaliah and the *C* soldiers who were there.
51: 5 And the *C* land is full of guilt to be
52: 8 But the *C* army pursued the king and
52:14 And the *C* troops who were with the captain
Dn 2:10 a thing of any magician, enchanter, or *C*.
5:30 the *C* king, was slain

CHALDEANS (70)

Gn 11:28 Terah, in his native land, in Ur of the *C*.
11:31 Abram, and brought them out of Ur of the *C*,
15: 7 *C* to give you this land as a possession."
2Kgs 24: 2 The LORD loosed against him bands of *C*,
25: 4 Since the *C* had the city surrounded,
25:13 house of the LORD, the *C* broke into pieces;
25:25 the Jews and *C* who were in Mizpah with him.
25:26 and went to Egypt for fear of the *C*.
2Chr 36:17 brought up against them the king of the *C*,
Jdt 5: 6 "These people are descendants of the *C*.
5: 7 who were born in the land of the *C*.
Jb 1:17 and said, "The *C* formed three columns,
Is 13:19 of kingdoms, the glory and pride of the *C*,
23:13 [This people is the land of the *C*,
43:14 and the *C* shall cry out in lamentation.

CHALDEANS (cont.)

47: 1 the ground, dethroned, O daughter of the C.
47: 5 and sit in silence, O daughter of the C,
Jer 21: 4 the C who besiege you outside the walls.
21: 9 C shall live and have his life as booty.
22:25 Nebuchadnezzar, king of Babylon, and the C.
24: 5 from this place into the land of the C.
25:12 and the land of the C for their guilt,
32: 4 king of Judah, escape the hands of the C;
32: 5 in fighting the C, you cannot win!"
32:24 handed over to the C who are attacking it,
32:25 city has already been handed over to the C!
32:28 I will hand over this city to the C,
32:29 The C who are attacking it shall enter
32:43 without man or beast, handed over to the C.
33: 5 men come to battle the C,
35:11 the army of the C and the army of Aram;
37: 5 and when the C who were besieging
37: 8 The C shall return to the fight against
37: 9 thought that the C will leave you for good,
37:13 saying, "You are deserting to the C!"
37:14 answered, "I am not deserting to the C."
38: 2 but he who goes out to the C shall live;
38:18 city shall fall into the hands of the C,
38:19 men of Judah who have deserted to the C;
38:23 and sons shall be led forth to the C,
39: 8 The C set fire to the king's palace and
40: 9 their men not to be afraid to serve the C:
40:10 with the C who should come to them.
41:18 They were afraid of the C,
43: 3 to the C to be killed or exiled to Babylon."
50: 1 against Babylon, against the land of the C,
50: 8 from Babylon, leave the land of the C,
50:25 hosts has work to do in the land of the C.
50:35 A sword upon the C,
50:45 he has made against the land of the C:
51:54 dire destruction from the land of the C;
52: 7 With the C surrounding the city,
52:17 house of the LORD, the C broke into pieces;
Bar 1: 2 C took Jerusalem and burnt it with fire].
6:40 the C themselves have no respect for them;
Ez 1: 3 in the land of the C by the river Chebar
12:13 him to Babylon, into the land of the C—
23:14 the images of C drawn with vermillion,
Dn 1: 4 the language and literature of the C;
2: 2 and C be summoned to interpret the dream
2: 4 The C answered the king [Aramaic]:
2: 5 The king answered the C,
2:10 The C answered the king:
3: 8 some of the C came and accused the Jews to
3:48 and spread out, burning the C nearby.
4: 4 When the magicians, enchanters, C,
5: 7 The king shouted for the enchanters, C,
5:11 him chief of the magicians, enchanters, C,
9: 1 Medes, reigned over the kingdom of the C;
Acts 7: 4 the land of the C and settled in Haran.

CHALDEES (1)

Neh 9: 7 who brought him out from Ur of the C,

CHALK (1)

Is 27: 9 the stones of the altars like pieces of c;

CHALLENGE (6)

1Sm 17:11 when they heard this c of the Philistine,
2Kgs 14: 8 son of Jehu, king of Israel, with this c,
1Mc 11:15 the news, he came to c Ptolemy in battle.
Wis 12:12 Or when peoples perish, who can c you,
2Cor 13: 5 unless, of course, you have failed the c.
Gal 4:14 My physical condition was a c which you

CHALLENGED (4)

Gn 26:20 called Esek, because they had c him there.
2Mc 8:30 also c the forces of Timothy and Bacchides,
Jer 50:24 and seized, because you c the LORD.
Jn 4:11 "Sir," she c him,

CHALLENGING (1)

Gal 5:26 Let us never be boastful, or c,

CHALPHI (1)

1Mc 11:70 son of Absalom, and Judas, son of C.

CHAMBER (27)

Jgs 3:24 "He must be easing himself in the cool c."
16: 9 in wait in the c and so she said to him,
16:12 For there were men lying in wait in the c.
2Kgs 9: 2 away from his companions into an inner c.
23:11 near the c of Nathan-melech the eunuch,
2Chr 18:24 day when you enter an innermost c to hide."
Ezr 10: 6 house of God and entered the c of Johanan,
Neh 3:31 and as far as the upper c of the Angle.
3:32 upper c of the Angle and the Sheep Gate,
13: 5 set aside for the latter's use a large c
13: 7 him a c in the courts of the house of God.
13: 8 household goods thrown outside the c.
Tb 6:17 When you go into the bridal c,
Est 5: 1 on his royal throne in the audience c,
1Mc 1:27 she who sat in the bridal c mourned,
12: 3 the men entered the senate c and said,
Jb 37: 9 Out of its c comes forth the tempest;
Ps(s) 19: 6 forth like the groom from his bridal c and,
Jer 36:12 to the king's palace, into the scribe's c,
Ez 40:38 a c opening off the vestibule of the gate,
40:45 "This c which faces south is for the
40:46 and the c which faces north is for the
Dn 6:11 his God in the upper c three times a day,
Jl 2:16 quit his room, and the bride her c.
Am 9: 6 I have built heaven, my upper c,
Acts 25:23 great pomp and entered the audience c
26:31 After they had left the c,

CHAMBERLAIN (9)

2Kgs 18:17 of Assyria sent the general, the lord c,
2Chr 34: 8 the city, and Joah, son of Joahaz, the c,
Dn 1: 3 The king told Ashpenaz, his chief c,
1: 7 The chief c changed their names:
1: 8 the chief c to spare him this defilement.
1: 9 the favor and sympathy of the chief c,
1:11 the chief c had put in charge of Daniel,
1:18 chief c brought them before Nebuchadnezzar.
Acts 12:20 c Blastus and attempted to placate him,

CHAMBERS (53)

1Chr 9:26 of the c and treasures of the house of God.
9:33 They stayed in the c when free of duty,
23:28 LORD, having charge of the courts, the c,
28:11 storerooms, its upper rooms and inner c,
2Chr 3: 9 The upper c he likewise covered with gold.
31:11 c be constructed in the house of the LORD.
Ezr 8:29 Israel, in the c of the house of the LORD.
Neh 10:38 priests, to the c of the house of our God.
10:39 house of our God, to the c of the treasury.
10:40 For to these c the Israelites and Levites
12:44 appointed over the c set aside for stores,
13: 4 who had been placed in charge of the c
13: 9 Then I gave orders to purify the c,
Tb 6:14 that her husbands died in their bridal c.
1Mc 4:38 mountain, and the priests' c demolished.
4:57 priests' c and furnished them with doors.
Ps(s) 105:30 with frogs, even in the c of their kings.
Prv 7:27 world, leading down into the c of death.
Wis 17: 4 not even their inner c kept them fearless,
Sir 4:15 who hearkens to her dwells in her inmost c.
Is 26:20 Go, my people, enter your c,
Jer 10:13 rain, and releases stormwinds from their c.
51:16 rain, and releases stormwinds from their c.
Ez 40:17 court, where there were c and a pavement.
40:17 was laid all around the court, and the c,
40:44 to the inner court where there were two c,
41: 5 the side c,
41: 6 There were thirty side c built one above
41: 6 of the temple that enclosed the side c;
41: 7 passageway that led upward to the side c,
41: 8 the foundations of the side c—
41: 8 Between the side c of the temple and the
41: 9 enclosed the side c was five cubits.
41:10 c of the court was an open space
41:11 The side c had entrances to the open space,
41:26 vestibule, and the side c of the temple.
42: 1 bringing me to some c on the north that
42: 4 In front of the c, to the inside, was a walk
42: 4 the entrances of the c were on the north.
42: 5 The outermost c were the lowest,
42: 5 than the closest c and those in between;
42: 6 ground than the closest and the middle c.
42: 7 parallel to the c along the outer court;
42: 7 its length before these c was fifty cubits,
42: 8 for the length of the c belonging to the
42: 9 these c there was the way in from the east,
42:10 area and the building there were also c,
42:11 These looked like the c to the north,
42:12 Below the c to the south there was an
42:13 "The north and south c which border on
42:13 on the free area are the sanctuary c;
44:19 and leave them in the c of the sanctuary,
46:19 of the gate to the c [of the sanctuary,

CHAMELEON (1)

Lv 11:30 various kinds of lizards, the gecko, the c,

CHAMPION (14)

Jgs 6:12 him and said, "The LORD is with you, O c!"
6:31 intend to act in Baal's stead, or be his c?
1Sm 17: 4 A c named Goliath of Gath came out from
17:23 was talking with them, the Philistine c,
18:17 my c and fight the battles of the LORD.
2Mc 8:36 Jerusalem testified that the Jews had a c,
Ps(s) 52: 3 Why do you glory in evil, you c of infamy?
78:65 as wakes from sleep a c overcome with wine;
89:20 "On a c I have placed a crown;
Wis 18:21 the blameless man hastened to be their c,
Sir 51:10 are my father, you are my c and my savior;
Is 41: 2 stirred up from the East the c of justice,
Jer 14: 9 a man dumbfounded, a c who cannot save?
20:11 But the LORD is with me, like a mighty c:

CHAMPIONS (2)

Is 3:25 men will fall by the sword, and your c,
5:22 Woe to the c at drinking wine,

CHANCE (13)

Dt 22: 6 you c upon a bird's nest with young birds
2Sm 1: 6 "It was by c that I found myself on Mount
Sir 12:16 has tears in his eyes, if given the c,
Mk 6:21 Herodias had her c one day when Herod held
Lk 20:20 Waiting their c,
Jn 7: 1 the Jews were looking for a c to kill him.
7:19 Why do you look for a c to kill me?"
Acts 25:16 c to defend himself against their charges.
27:31 with the ship, you have no c to survive."
2Cor 11:12 at every turn those who look for a c to say
Eph 4:27 do not give the devil a c to work on you.
Heb 4: 1 be judged to have lost his c of entering.
Rv 2:21 I have given her a c to repent but she

CHANCED (1)

Jgs 20:48 cities, the livestock, and all they c upon.

CHANCELLOR (3)

2Sm 8:16 Jehoshaphat, son of Ahilud, was c.
20:24 Jehoshaphat, son of Ahilud, was the c.
1Kgs 4: 3 Jehoshaphat, son of Ahilud, c;

CHANGE (40)

Ex 13:17 might c their minds and return to Egypt.
Nm 23:19 nor human, that he should c his mind.
Dt 30: 3 you, the LORD, your God, will c your lot;
1Mc 1:49 the law ancd c all their observances.
2Mc 4:46 fresh air, and persuaded him to c his mind.
Jb 17:12 Such men c the night into day;
Ps(s) 102:27 Like clothing you c them,
Wis 12:10 And that their dispositions would never c;
Sir 43: 8 how wondrous in this c!
Is 5:20 and good evil, who c darkness into light,
5:20 into darkness, who c bitter into sweet,
Jer 2:11 Does any other nation c its gods?—
13:23 Can the Ethiopian c his skin?
17: 6 in the desert that enjoys no c of season,
29:14 you, says the LORD, and I will c your lot;
30: 3 when I will c the lot of my people (of
31:23 When I c their lot in the land of Judah
32:44 and of the Negeb, when I c their lot,
33: 7 c the lot of Judah and the lot of Israel,
33:26 For I will c their lot and show them mercy.
48:47 will c the lot of Moab in the days to come,
49: 6 I will c the lot of the Ammonites,
49:39 the days to come I will c the lot of Elam,
Bar 2:30 captivity they shall have a c of heart;
Dn 7:25 thinking to c the feast days and the law.
Zep 3: 9 will c and purify the lips of the peoples,
Mal 3: 6 of hosts, Surely I, the LORD, do not c,
Mt 6:16 They c the appearance of their faces so
10:10 no traveling bag, no c of shirt,
18: 3 you c and become like little children,
Lk 5:32 invite the self-righteous to a c of heart,
Jn 12:40 see or comprehend, or have a c of heart
Acts 6:14 Nazorean will destroy this place and c
19:26 numbers of people to c their religion.
26:20 to act in conformity with their c of heart.
2Cor 1:17 I c my mind from one minute to the next?
Heb 6:17 evidence that his purpose would not c,
7:12 c of priesthood, there is necessarily a c
Jas 1:17 cannot c and who is never shadowed over.

CHANGED (48)

Gn 31: 7 cheated me and c my wages time after time.
31:41 while you c my wages time after time.
41:14 After he shaved and c his clothes,
Ex 4: 3 it on the ground it was c into a serpent,
7: 9 Pharaoh, and it will be c into a snake."
7:10 his servants, and it was c into a snake.
7:12 down his staff, and it was c into a snake.
7:17 staff I hold, and it shall be c into blood.
7:20 the water of the river was c into blood.
10:19 LORD c the wind to a very strong west wind,
14: 5 and his servants c their minds about them.
Lv 13:55 If the infection has not c its appearance,
Nm 32:38 Kiriathaim, Nebo, Baal-meon [names to be c,
1Sm 10: 6 state and will be c into another man.
2Sm 12:20 and anointed himself, and c his clothes.
2Kgs 23:34 he c his name to Jehoiakim.
24:17 Mattaniah king, and c his name to Zedekiah.
2Chr 36: 4 and Jerusalem, and c his name to Jehoiakim.
Est D: 7 anger, the queen staggered, c color,
D: 8 But God c the king's anger to gentleness.
1Mc 5:28 Judas suddenly c direction with his army,
2Mc 3:16 for the c color of his face manifested the
8: 5 for the Lord's wrath had now c to mercy.
Jb 14:20 with c appearance you send him away.
38:14 The earth is c as is clay by the seal,
Ps(s) 30:12 You c my mourning into dancing;
66: 6 He has c the sea into dry land;
77:11 that the right hand of the Most High is c."
78:44 of Zoan, And c into blood their streams
102:27 clothing you change them, and they are c,
105:25 Whose hearts he c, so that they hated
107:33 He c rivers into desert,
107:35 He c the desert into pools of water,
Wis 19:19 land creatures were c into water creatures,
Is 29:17 and Lebanon shall be c into an orchard,

34: 9 be *c* into pitch and her earth into sulphur,
Jer 2:11 have *c* their glory for useless things.
8: 8 that has been *c* into falsehood by the
34:16 But then you *c* your mind and profaned my
Lam 4: 1 is the gold, how *c* the noble metal;
Dn 1: 7 The chief chamberlain *c* their names:
4:13 Let his mind be *c* from the human;
Mk 16:12 to them completely *c* in appearance.
Lk 9:29 his face *c* in appearance and his clothes
Acts 28: 6 they *c* their minds and began to say that
1Cor 15:51 fall asleep, but all of us are to be *c*—
15:52 be raised incorruptible, and we shall be *c*.
Heb 1:12 like a garment they will be *c*.

CHANGES (9)

Jb 37:12 He it is who *c* their rounds,
Ps(s) 15: 4 it be to his loss, *c* not his pledged word;
Wis 7:18 the *c* in the sun's course and the
Sir 13:24 The heart of a man *c* his countenance,
18:26 morning and evening the weather *c*;
25:16 Wickedness *c* a woman's looks,
27:23 But later he *c* his tone and twists your
Jer 13:16 for turns to darkness, *c* into black clouds.
Dn 2:21 He causes the *c* of the times and seasons,

CHANGING (5)

Est E: 9 taking advantage of *c* conditions and
Ps(s) 90: 5 the next morning they are like the *c* grass,
Sir 43: 6 The moon, too, that marks the *c* times,
Jer 2:36 very base you have become in *c* your course!
Jn 2:14 sheep and doves, and others seated *c* coins.

CHANNEL (1)

Jb 38:25 Who has laid out a *c* for the downpour and

CHANNELING (1)

Sir 24:28 her stream, *c* the waters into a garden,

CHANNELS (4)

Jb 28:10 He splits *c* in the rocks;
Is 8: 7 It shall rise above all its *c*,
Jl 4:18 And the *c* of Judah shall flow with water:
Zec 4:12 out fresh oil through the two golden *c*?"

CHANT (18)

1Chr 15:21 led the *c* on lyres set to "the eighth."
15:27 and Chenaniah, the leader of the *c*;
16:42 and instruments for the sacred *c*.
Jdt 16: 1 with timbrels, *c* to the Lord with cymbals;
Ps(s) 21:14 We will sing, *c* the praise of your might.
27: 6 I will sing and *c* praise to the LORD.
33: 2 with the ten-stringed lyre *c* his praises.
57: 8 I will sing and *c* praise.
57:10 I will *c* your praise among the nations,
68: 5 Sing to God, *c* praise to his name,
68:33 earth, sing to God, *c* praise to the Lord.
108: 2 I will sing and *c* praise.
108: 4 I will *c* your praise among the nations,
144: 9 a ten-stringed lyre I will *c* your praise,
Ez 32:16 the daughters of the nations shall *c* it;
32:16 Egypt and all its hordes shall they *c* it,
Mi 2: 4 over you, and there shall be a plaintive *c*:
Acts 19:34 he was a Jew, they started to *c* in unison,

CHANTED (1)

2Sm 1:17 *c* this elegy for Saul and his son Jonathan,

CHANTER (1)

1Chr 6:18 Heman, the *c*, son of Joel, son of Samuel,

CHANTERS (5)

1Kgs 10:12 of the king, and harps and lyres for the *c*.
1Chr 9:33 These were the *c* and the gatekeepers,
15:16 Levites to appoint their brethren as *c*,
15:19 The *c*, Heman, Asaph, and Ethan,
2Chr 9:11 also lyres and harps for the *c*.

CHANTING (2)

1Chr 15:22 Levites in the *c*; he directed the chanting,

CHAOS (3)

Is 22: 2 the housetops, O city full of noise and *c*,
24:10 Broken down is the city of *c*,
Acts 19:32 with the whole assembly in *c* and the

CHAPHENATHA (1)

1Mc 12:37 The quarter called *C* was also repaired.

CHARACTER (7)

Tb 2:14 Your true *c* is finally showing itself!"
2Mc 5:22 and in *c* more cruel than the man who
Sir 8: 2 many, and perverts the *c* of princes.
23:15 will never mature in *c* as long as he lives.
36:20 A deceitful *c* causes grief,
1Tm 5:10 *c* will be attested to by her good deeds.
1Pt 3: 4 is rather the hidden *c* of the heart,

CHARAX (1)

2Mc 12:17 gone on some ninety miles, they reached *C*,

CHARCOAL (2)

Jn 18:18 had made a *c* fire to warm themselves by.
21: 9 they saw a *c* fire there with a fish laid

CHARGE (147)

Gn 24: 2 who had *c* of all his possessions:
30:35 in *c* of his sons.
32:17 He put these animals in *c* of his servants,
39: 4 he put him in *c* of his household and
39: 5 *c* of his household and all his possessions,
39: 6 left everything he owned in Joseph's *c*,
39:22 in *c* of all the prisoners in the jail,
39:23 anything at all that was in Joseph's *c*,
41:33 man and put him in *c* of the land of Egypt.
41:40 You shall be in *c* of my palace,
41:41 place you in *c* of the whole land of Egypt."
47: 5 you may put them in *c* of my own livestock."
49:29 message, Then he gave them this *c*:
Ex 18:25 put them in *c* of the people as officers
Lv 18:30 Heed my *c*, then, not to defile yourselves
22: 9 keep my *c* and not do wrong in this matter;
Nm 1:50 You are to give the Levites *c* of the
1:53 have *c* of the Dwelling of the commandments."
3:10 to have *c* of the priestly functions.
3:25 *c* of whatever pertained to the Dwelling,
3:28 They had *c* of the sanctuary.
3:31 had *c* of whatever pertained to the ark,
3:32 over those who had *c* of the sanctuary.
4:16 shall be in *c* of the oil for the light,
4:16 He shall be in *c* of the whole Dwelling
7: 9 the sacred objects which were their *c*.
9:23 ever heeding the *c* of the LORD,
12:11 "please do not *c* us with the sin that we
18: 4 As your associates they shall have *c* of
18: 5 have *c* of the sanctuary and of the altar,
18: 7 But only you and your sons are to have *c*
18: 8 "I myself have given you *c* of the
31:30 Levites, who have *c* of the LORD's Dwelling."
31:47 Levites, who had *c* of the LORD's Dwelling.
Dt 11: 1 your God, therefore, and always heed his *c*:
22:20 "But if this *c* is true,
1Sm 18: 5 So Saul put him in *c* of his soldiers,
2Sm 3: 8 you *c* me with a crime involving a woman!
20:24 Adoram was in *c* of the forced labor.
1Kgs 4:13 having *c* of the villages of Jair,
5:28 Adoniram was in *c* of the draft.
11:28 he put him in *c* of the entire labor force
2Kgs 7:17 The king put in *c* of the gate the officer
1Chr 6:34 they alone had *c* of the holy of holies and
9:26 These were the Levites who also had *c* of
9:27 for it was in their *c* and they had the
9:28 of them had *c* of the liturgical equipment,
9:32 was in *c* of setting out the showbread each
11:25 David put him in *c* of his bodyguard.
12:22 helped David by taking *c* of his troops,
23:28 house of the LORD, having *c* of the courts,
23:29 They shall also have *c* of the showbread,
26:28 under the *c* of Shelomith and his brethren.
26:29 his sons were in *c* of Israel's civil affairs
2Chr 8:10 fifty overseers who had *c* of the people.
23:18 Then Jehoiada gave the *c* of the LORD's
24: 6 the king summoned Jehoiada, who was in *c*,
24:12 in *c* of the labor on the LORD's temple,
30:17 and the Levites were in *c* of slaughtering
31:12 and his brother Shimei was second in *c*.
31:14 in *c* of the freewill gifts made to God;
34:13 in *c* of the men who carried the burdens,
Neh 2: 1 Artaxerxes, when the wine was in my *c*,
5:10 lent the people money and grain without *c*.
7: 1 and the Levites] were put in *c* of them.
11: 9 of Hassenuah, was second in *c* of the city.
11:21 and Gishpa were in *c* of the temple slaves.
12: 8 with his brethren, was in *c* of the hymns,
13: 4 who had been placed in *c* of the chambers
13:13 and in *c* of the storerooms I appointed the
Tb 1:21 in *c* of all the accounts of his kingdom,
Jdt 8:10 was in *c* of all her things to ask Uzziah,
12:11 Bagoas, the eunuch in *c* of his household:
13:15 general in *c* of the Assyrian army,
14:13 and said to the one in *c* of all his things,
Est B: 6 who is in *c* of the administration and is a
B: 8 say, "when you were brought up in my *c*;
8: 2 put Mordecai in *c* of the house of Haman.
1Mc 2:15 The officers of the king in *c* of enforcing
3:32 in *c* of the king's affairs from the
5:19 "Take *c* of these people,"
6:14 and put him in *c* of his whole kingdom.
14:42 over them, and shall have *c* of the temple,
2Mc 6:21 Those in *c* of that unlawful ritual meal
8:23 he himself took *c* of the first division
10:11 he put a certain Lysias in *c* of the
13: 2 guardian, who was in *c* of the government.
13:23 who was left in *c* of the government in
15:17 but to *c* gallantly and decide the issue by
Jb 15:26 his shield, like a king prepared for the *c*.
21:31 will *c* him with his conduct to his face,
Ps(s) 35:11 things I knew not of, they lay to my *c*.
Prv 27:14 early morning a curse can be laid to his *c*.
Sir 29: 6 and acquires an enemy at no extra *c*;
Jer 27: 4 Zedekiah, king of Judah, and *c* them thus:
32:13 In their presence I gave Baruch this *c*:
40: 2 of the bodyguard took *c* of Jeremiah,
40: 7 Gedaliah, son of Ahikam, *c* of the land,
41:16 took *c* of the remnant of the people,
Ez 40:45 for the priests who have *c* of the temple,
40:46 is for the priests who have *c* of the altar.
Dn 1:11 chief chamberlain had put in *c* of Daniel,
Jon 1:14 do not *c* us with shedding innocent blood,
Na 2: 6 troops are called, ranks break at their *c*;
Zec 3: 7 If you walk in my ways and heed my *c*,
Mt 24:45 servant whom the master has put in *c*
24:47 he will put him in *c* of all his property.
25:21 I will put you in *c* of larger affairs.
25:23 I will put you in *c* of larger affairs.
27:37 they had put the *c* against him in writing:
Mk 3:21 heard of this they came to take *c* of him,
13:34 leaves home and places his servants in *c*,
Lk 6: 7 so that they could find a *c* against him.
12:44 will put him in *c* of all his property.
23:14 have no *c* against him arising
Jn 2: 8 some out and take it to the waiter in *c*."
2: 9 The waiter in *c* tasted the water made wine,
2: 9 Then the waiter in *c* called the groom over
Acts 6:11 They persuaded some men to make the *c* that
8:27 a court official in *c* of the entire
9:27 in *c* and introduced him to the apostles.
13:28 no *c* against him which deserved death,
22:30 *c* which the Jews were bringing against him.
23:18 took him in *c* and led him to the commander,
23:28 to determine what their *c* against him was.
24:19 to make whatever *c* they have against me.
25:18 *c* him with any of the crimes I expected.
Rom 3: 9 We have already brought the *c* against Jews
8:33 shall bring a *c* against God's chosen ones?
1Cor 9:17 I am nonetheless entrusted with a *c*.
9:18 I offer the gospel free of *c*
2Cor 11: 7 the gospel of God to you free of *c*,
Gal 3:25 here, we are no longer in the monitor's *c*.
1Tm 1:18 I have a solemn *c* to give you,
1:18 This *c* is in accordance with the
5:21 I *c* you before God,
6:14 I *c* you to keep God's command without
6:18 *C* them to do good,
2Tm 2:14 reminding people of these things and *c* them
4: 2 kingly power, I *c* you to preach the word,
Phlm 1:18 an injury or owes you anything, *c* it to me.
1Jn 3:20 matter what our consciences may *c* us with;
3:21 our consciences have nothing to *c* us with,
Jude 1: 9 did not venture to *c* him with blasphemy.
Rv 9:11 their king was the angel in *c* of the abyss,
14:18 in *c* of the fire at the altar of incense,
16: 5 heard the angel in *c* of the waters cry out:

CHARGED (22)

Gn 28: 1 greeted him with a blessing, and *c* him:
Nm 3:36 The Merarites were *c* with the care of
Dt 1:16 I *c* your judges at that time,
3:18 "At that time I *c* them as follows:
4:14 The LORD *c* me at that time to teach you
2Sm 7: 7 judges whom I *c* to tend my people Israel,
18:12 for the king *c* you and Abishai and Ittai
2Chr 36:23 *c* me to build him a house in Jerusalem,
Ezr 1: 2 *c* me to build him a house in Jerusalem,
2Mc 3:30 *c* so shortly before with fear and
12:37 he *c* Gorgias' men when they were not
Sg 1: 6 they *c* me with the care of the vineyards:
Jer 36: 5 Then Jeremiah *c* Baruch:
Ez 18:19 not the son *c* with the guilt of his father?"
18:20 not be *c* with the guilt of his father,
18:20 the father be *c* with the guilt of his son.
Dn 13:43 with which these wicked men have *c* me."
Mt 12:24 When the Pharisees heard this, they *c*.
Lk 8:33 the herd *c* down the bluff into the lake,
Acts 18:13 "This fellow," they *c*, "is influencing people
21:32 and centurions and *c* down on the rioters.
Heb 3: 5 as a servant *c* with the task of witnessing

CHARGES (22)

Dt 22:14 *c* against her and defames her by saying,
22:17 and now brings monstrous *c* against her,
1Mc 10:63 no one is to bring *c* against him
11:25 of his own nation brought *c* against him,
2Mc 4:43 *C* about this affair were brought against
4:47 the trouble, the king acquitted of the *c*,
5: 3 *c* and countercharges on this side and that,
Prv 31:21 all her *c* are doubly clothed.
Wis 2:12 and *c* us with violations of our training.
Sir 26: 5 Though false *c* in public,
Mt 27:13 you hear how many *c* they bring against you?"
Acts 7: 1 high priest asked whether the *c* were true.
13:38 including the remission of all those *c*
19:38 craftsmen want to bring *c* against anyone,
24:13 the *c* they are making against me.
25: 7 him and leveled many serious *c* against him,
25: 9 and stand trial before me there on these *c*?"
25:11 to the *c* these men bring against me,
25:16 a chance to defend himself against their *c*.
25:20 Jerusalem and stand trial there on these *c*.
25:27 without indicating the *c* against him."
26: 2 *c* have been leveled against me by the Jews,

CHARGING (5)

Gn 28: 6 to get himself a wife there, *c* him,
2Mc 3:25 *C* furiously, the horse attacked Heliodorus
5: 2 days, there appeared horsemen *c* in midair,
Na 3: 3 a-gallop, chariots bounding, Cavalry *c*,
Rv 9: 9 of many chariots and horses *c* into battle.

CHARIOT (67)

Gn 41:43 then had him ride in the *c* of his vizier,
46:29 Joseph hitched the horses to his *c*
Ex 14:25 *c* wheels that they could hardly drive.
15: 1 horse and *c* he has cast into the sea.
15:21 horse and *c* he has cast into the sea.
Jgs 4:15 dismounted from his *c* and fled on foot.
5:28 "Why is his *c* so long in coming?
1Sm 8:11 and horses, and they will run before his *c*.
2Sm 8: 4 And he hamstrung all the *c* horses,
1Kgs 5: 6 stalls for his twelve thousand *c* horses.
5: 8 For the *c* horses and draft animals also,
7:33 The wheels were constructed like *c* wheels;
9:22 commanders, adjutants, *c* officers,
10:26 these he allocated among the *c* cities and
10:29 A *c* imported from Egypt cost six hundred
12:18 to mount his *c* to flee to Jerusalem,
18:45 Ahab mounted his *c* and made for Jezreel.
20:20 king of Aram, escaped on a *c* steed.
20:25 you, horse for horse, *c* for chariot.
20:33 out to him, the king had him mount his *c*.
22:31 his thirty-two *c* commanders the order,
22:32 When the *c* commanders saw Jehoshaphat,
22:33 his battle cry, and the *c* commanders,
22:35 propped up in his *c* facing the Arameans,
22:35 his wound flowed to the bottom of the *c*.
22:38 the *c* was washed at the pool of Samaria,
2Kgs 2:11 *c* and flaming horses came between them,
5:21 Naaman alighted from his *c* to wait for him.
5:26 man alighted from his *c* to wait for you?
9:16 Jehu mounted his *c* and drove to Jezreel,
9:21 "Prepare my *c*," said Joram.
9:21 king of Judah, set out, each in his own *c*,
9:24 his heart and he collapsed in his *c*.
9:28 His servants brought him in a *c* to
10:15 his hand, and Jehu drew him up into his *c*.
10:16 And he took him along in his own *c*.
23:30 his body on a *c* from Megiddo to Jerusalem,
1Chr 18: 4 Of the *c* horses,
19:18 David slew seven thousand of their *c* fighters
28:18 gold for what would suggest a *c* throne:
2Chr 1:14 *c* cities and with the king in Jerusalem.
9:25 the *c* cities and to the king in Jerusalem.
10:18 to mount his *c* and flee to Jerusalem.
18:30 Aram had given his *c* commanders the order,
18:32 The *c* commanders became aware that he was
18:34 on his *c* facing the Arameans until evening.
35:24 His servants removed him from his own *c*,
Jdt 1: 4 cubits wide for the passage of his *c* forces
2Mc 9: 7 As a result he hurtled from the dashing *c*,
14:21 From each side a *c* came forward and
Ps(s) 104: 3 You make the clouds your *c*;
Sir 48: 9 in a whirlwind, in a *c* with fiery horses.
49: 8 the different creatures of the *c*;
Is 5:28 and their *c* wheels like the hurricane.
21: 7 If he sees a *c*,
21: 9 a single *c*, a pair of horses;
Jer 47: 3 hooves of his steeds, the rattling *c*,
51:21 and rider, with you I shatter *c* and driver.
Ez 23:15 their heads, all looking like *c* warriors,
Hb 3: 8 you drive the steeds of your victorious *c*?
Zec 6: 2 first *c* had red horses, the second chariot
6: 3 third *c* white horses, and the fourth chariot
6: 6 The *c* with the black horses was turning
9:10 He shall banish the *c* from Ephraim,

CHARIOTEER (3)

1Kgs 22:34 He ordered his *c*,
2Chr 18:33 He ordered his *c*,
2Mc 9: 4 Therefore he ordered his *c* to drive

CHARIOTEERS (12)

Gn 50: 9 Chariots, too, and *c* went up with him;
Ex 14: 9 whole army, his horses, chariots and *c*,
14:17 and all his army, his chariots and *c*.
14:18 through Pharaoh and his chariots and *c*."
14:23 chariots and *c* went after them right
14:26 Egyptians, upon their chariots and their *c*."
14:28 it covered the chariots and the *c* of
15:19 and chariots and *c* had gone into the sea,
2Sm 10:18 David's men killed seven hundred *c*
1Kgs 9:22 adjutants, chariot officers, and *c*.
Jer 46: 4 Harness the horses, mount, *c*!
Ez 23:23 governors and officers, *c* and warriors,

CHARIOTRY (1)

1Kgs 20: 1 by thirty-two kings with horses and *c*,

CHARIOTS (108)

Gn 50: 9 *C*, too, and charioteers went up with him;
Ex 14: 6 made his *c* ready and mustered his soldiers
14: 7 chariots and all the other *c* of Egypt,
14: 9 whole army, his horses, *c* and charioteers,
14:17 and all his army, his *c* and charioteers.
14:18 through Pharaoh and his *c* and charioteers."
14:23 all Pharaoh's horses and *c* and charioteers
14:26 upon their *c* and their charioteers."
14:28 it covered the *c* and the charioteers of
15: 4 *c* and army he hurled into the sea;
15:19 *c* and charioteers had gone into the sea,and
Dt 11: 4 Egyptian army and to their horses and *c*,
20: 1 and *c* and an army greater than your own,
Jos 11: 4 and with a multitude of horses and *c*.
11: 6 hamstring their horses and burn their *c*."
11: 9 hamstrung their horses and burned their *c*.
17:16 in the valley region all have iron *c*,
17:18 if, despite their strength and iron *c*,
24: 6 fathers to the Red Sea with *c* and horsemen.
Jgs 1:19 on the plain, because they had iron *c*.
4: 3 for with his nine hundred iron *c* he sorely
4: 7 Kishon, together with his *c* and troops,
4:13 hundred of his iron *c* and all his forces.
4:15 *c* and all his forces to rout before Barak.
4:16 pursued the *c* and the army as far as
5:28 why are the hoofbeats of his *c* delayed?"
1Sm 8:11 sons and assign them to his *c* and horses,
8:12 of war and the equipment of his *c*.
13: 5 for battle, with three thousand *c*,
2Sm 1: 6 with *c* and horsemen closing in on him.
8: 4 preserving only enough for a hundred *c*.
15: 1 After this Absalom provided himself with *c*,
1Kgs 1: 5 He acquired *c*,
9:19 for supplies, cities for *c* and for horses,
10:26 Solomon collected *c* and drivers;
10:26 four hundred *c* and twelve thousand drivers;
16: 9 His servant Zimri, commander of half his *c*,
20:21 of Israel went out, took the horses and *c*,
2Kgs 2:12 Israel's *c* and drivers!"
5: 9 Naaman came with his horses and *c* and
6:14 there a strong force with horses and *c*.
6:15 with its horses and *c* surrounding the city.
6:17 with horses and fiery *c* around Elisha.
7: 6 Arameans to hear the sound of *c* and horses,
7:14 They took two *c*,
8:21 with all his *c* crossed over to Zair.
8:21 surrounded him and the commanders of his *c*.
9:17 of Jehu coming and reported, "I see *c*."
10: 2 you," he wrote, "and you have the *c*,
13: 7 with ten *c* and ten thousand foot soldiers,
13:14 "Israel's *c* and horsemen!"
18:24 as you do on Egypt for *c* and horsemen?
19:23 my many *c* I climbed the mountain heights,
23:11 The *c* of the sun he destroyed by fire.
1Chr 18: 4 thousand foot soldiers, one thousand *c*,
19: 6 to hire *c* and horsemen from Aram Naharaim,
19: 7 They hired thirty-two thousand *c* along
2Chr 1:14 He gathered together *c* and drivers,
1:14 that he had one thousand four hundred *c*
1:17 and would then bring up *c* from Egypt and
8: 6 to Solomon, and all the cities for the *c*,
8: 9 and commanders of his *c* and his horsemen.
9:25 had four thousand stalls of horses, *c*,
12: 3 hundred *c* and sixty thousand horsemen,
14: 8 of one million men and three hundred *c*,
16: 8 army, with great numbers of *c* and drivers?
21: 9 with his officers and all the *c* he had.
21: 9 surrounded him and the commanders of his *c*.
Jdt 1:13 Arphaxad, his entire cavalry and all his *c*,
2:19 their *c* and cavalry and regular infantry.
2:22 whole force, the infantry, cavalry, and *c*,
7:20 The whole Assyrian camp, infantry, *c*,
1Mc 1:17 with a strong force, with *c* and elephants,
8: 6 with cavalry and *c* and a very great army,
2Mc 13: 2 and three hundred *c* armed with scythes.
Ps(s) 20: 8 Some are strong in *c*;
68:18 The *c* of God are myriad,
76: 7 O God of Jacob, *c* and steeds lay stilled.
Sg 1: 9 steeds of Pharaoh's *c* would I liken you,
Is 2: 7 of horses, and there is no end to their *c*.
22: 7 Your choice valleys are filled with *c*,
22:18 perish there, you and the *c* you glory in,
31: 1 their trust in *c* because of their number,
36: 9 yet you rely on Egypt for *c* and horsemen!
37:24 my many *c* I climbed the mountain heights,
43:17 waters, Who leads out *c* and horsemen,
66:15 come in fire, his *c* like the whirlwind,
66:20 offering to the LORD, on horses and in *c*,
Jer 4:13 clouds he advances, like a hurricane his *c*;
17:25 riding in their *c* or upon their horses,
22: 4 palace, riding in *c* or mounted on horses,
46: 9 drive madly, *c*!
Ez 23:24 north with *c* and wagons and many peoples.
26: 7 the king of kings, with horses and *c*,
26:10 the noise of steeds, of wheels and of *c*.
Dn 11:40 him with *c* and horsemen and a great fleet,
Hos 10:13 Because you have trusted in your *c*,
Jl 2: 5 rumble of *c* they leap on the mountaintops;
Mi 1:13 Harness steeds to the *c*,
5: 9 horses from your midst and ruin your *c*;
Na 2: 4 are the *c* on the day of his mustering.
2: 5 the *c* dash madly through the streets And
2:14 I will consume in smoke your *c*,
3: 2 horses a-gallop, *c* bounding,
Hg 2:22 I will overthrow the *c* and their riders,
Zec 6: 1 *c* coming out from between two mountains;
Rv 9: 9 of many *c* and horses charging into battle.

CHARITABLE (5)

Tb 1: 3 I performed many *c* works for my kinsmen
1:16 many *c* works for my kinsmen and my people.
2:14 "Where are your *c* deeds now?
7: 7 *c* man should be afflicted with blindness!"
9: 6 son of a noble and good, upright and *c* man,

CHARITY (9)

Sir 18:14 My son, to your *c* add no reproach,
34:21 bread of *c* is life itself for the needy;
35: 2 In works of *c* one offers fine flour,
40:24 but better than either, *c* that rescues.
Acts 9:36 by constant good deeds and acts of *c*.
2Cor 8: 6 had already begun this work of *c* among you,
8: 7 we bear you, so may you abound in this *c*.
8:19 this work of *c* for the glory of the Lord.
Eph 3:17 *c* be the root and foundation of your life.

CHARLATANS (1)

2Tm 3:13 evil men and *c* will go from bad to worse,

CHARM (5)

Prv 31:30 *C* is deceptive and beauty fleeting;
Wis 14:20 masses drawn by the *c* of the workmanship,
Sir 21:16 is *c* to be found upon the lips of the wise.
40:22 *C* and beauty delight the eye,
Jer 8:17 which no *c* will work when they bite you,

CHARMED (2)

Jdt 12:20 Holofernes, *c* by her,
Eccl 10:11 serpent bites because it has not been *c*,

CHARMER (4)

Dt 18:10 fire, nor a fortuneteller, soothsayer, *c*,
Eccl 10:11 then there is no advantage for the *c*.
Sir 12:13 Who pities a snake *c* when he is bitten,
Is 3: 3 counselor, skilled magician, and expert *c*.

CHARMERS (1)

Is 19: 3 They shall consult idols and *c*,

CHARMING (1)

Na 3: 4 debaucheries of the harlot, fair and *c*,

CHARMIS (3)

Jdt 6:15 Simeon, Chabris, son of Gothoniel, and *C*,
8:10 her things to ask Uzziah, Chabris, and *C*,
10: 6 and the elders of the city, Chabris and *C*,

CHARMS (2)

Sir 36:22 for it surpasses all else that *c* the eye;
42:12 Let her not parade her *c* before men,

CHARRED (2)

1Mc 11: 4 and the *c* bodies of those burned by
Jer 2:15 his cities are *c* ruins,

CHARY (1)

Prv 17:27 is *c* of speech is a man of intelligence.

CHASE (10)

Lv 26: 8 hundred of you will *c* ten thousand of them,
Eccl 1:14 behold, all is vanity and a *c* after wind.
1:17 I learned that this also is a *c* after wind.
2:11 all was vanity and a *c* after wind,
2:17 for all is vanity and a *c* after wind.
2:26 This also is vanity and a *c* after wind.
4: 4 This also is vanity and a *c* after wind.
4: 6 than two with toil and a *c* after wind!
4:16 This also is vanity and a *c* after wind.
6: 9 This also is vanity and a *c* after wind.

CHASED (1)

Dt 1:44 came out against you and, like bees, *c* you,

CHASES (2)

Sir 34: 2 a man who catches at shadows or *c* the wind,
Hos 12: 2 Ephraim *c* the wind,

CHASING (3)

Jgs 20:45 men among them, and *c* them up to Gidom,
Prv 21: 6 tongue is *c* a bubble over deadly snares.
Is 44:20 He is *c* ashes

CHASM (1)

Jer 48:28 that nests out of reach on the edge of a *c*.

CHASPHO (2)

1Mc 5:26 in Bozrah, in Bosor near Alema, in *C*,
5:36 From there he moved on and took *C*,

CHASTE (4)

Sir 7:24 If you have daughters, keep them *c*,
26:15 is a modest wife, priceless her *c* person.

2Cor 11: 2 presenting you as a *c* virgin to Christ.
Ti 2: 5 husbands and children, to be sensible, *c*,

CHASTEN (1)

Ps(s) 39:12 With rebukes for guilt you *c* man;

CHASTENED (3)

Lv 26:23 to be *c* by me and continue to defy me,
Jb 33:19 Or a man is *c* on his bed by pain and
Jer 31:18 You chastised me, and I am *c*;

CHASTENING (1)

Jb 5:17 The Almighty's *c* do not reject.

CHASTENS (1)

1Cor 11:32 he *c* us to keep us from being condemned

CHASTISE (15)

Lv 26:28 will *c* you with sevenfold fiercer punishment
Dt 21:18 will not obey them even though they *c* him,
22:18 city elders shall take the man and *c* him,
2Mc 10: 4 he might *c* them with moderation and not
Ps(s) 6: 2 not in your anger, nor *c* me in your wrath.
38: 2 punish me not, in your wrath *c* me not;
94:10 Shall he who instructs nations not *c*,
Prv 13:24 but he who loves him takes care to *c* him.
19:18 *C* your son, for in this there is hope;
Wis 12:22 you *c* and our enemies with a thousand
Sir 7:23 If you have sons, *c* them;
Jer 30:11 I will *c* you as you deserve,
46:28 I will *c* you as you deserve,
Lk 23:22 I will therefore *c* him and release him."
Rv 3:19 Whoever is dear to me I reprove and *c*.

CHASTISED (6)

Ps(s) 118:18 Though the LORD has indeed *c* me,
Wis 3: 5 *C* a little, they shall be greatly blessed,
11: 9 they had been tried, though only mildly *c*,
Jer 31:18 You *c* me,
Hos 10:10 the wanton people I came and I *c* them;
10:10 them when I *c* them for their two crimes.

CHASTISEMENT (9)

Lv 26:18 increase the *c* for your sins sevenfold,
Ps(s) 73:14 day after day and *c* with each new dawn.
Prv 16:22 its possessor, but folly brings *c* on fools.
23:13 Withhold not *c* from a boy;
Wis 1: 9 the Lord, for the *c* of his transgressions;
Sir 42: 8 Of *c* of the silly and the foolish,
Is 53: 5 Upon him was the *c* that makes us whole,
Lam 4:22 Your *c* is completed, O daughter Zion,
Hos 5: 9 shall become a waste on the day of *c*:

CHASTISEMENTS (5)

2Sm 7:14 him with the rod of men and with human *c*;
Tb 13:14 shall grieve over you, over all your *c*,
2Mc 6:12 but to consider that these *c* were meant
7:33 for a little while to correct us with *c*,
Ez 5:15 you in anger and fury and with furious *c*,

CHASTISES (4)

Jdt 8:27 that he *c* those who are close to him."
Prv 3:12 he reproves, and he *c* the son he favors.
Sir 30: 1 He who loves his son *c* him often,
Jer 2:19 Your own wickedness *c* you,

CHASTISING (2)

Wis 1: 8 nor will *c* condemnation pass him by.
Is 26:16 we cried out in anguish under your *c*.

CHASTITY (2)

Gal 5:23 generosity, faith, mildness, and *c*.
1Tm 2:15 her *c* being taken for granted.

CHATTELS (1)

Lv 25:45 Such slaves you may own as *c*,

CHATTER (1)

Sir 21:16 A fool's *c* is like a load on a journey,

CHEAP (1)

Mt 27:48 He soaked it in *c* wine,

CHEAT (2)

Mi 2: 2 They *c* an owner of his house,
1Cor 6: 8 injure and *c* your very own brothers.

CHEATED (9)

Gn 31: 7 *c* me and changed my wages time after time.
1Sm 12: 3 Whom have I *c*?
12: 4 They replied, "You have neither *c* us,
2Mc 4:26 *c* his own brother and now saw himself *c*
Sir 29: 6 he is *c* of his wealth and acquires an
29: 7 out of meanness, but from fear of being *c*.
1Cor 6: 7 up with injustice, and let yourselves be *c*?
2Cor 7: 2 we have corrupted no one, we have *c* no one.

CHEATING (3)

Lv 5:15 inadvertently *c* in the LORD's sacred dues,
Am 8: 5 to the shekel, and fix our scales for *c*!
1Thes 4: 6 or *c* his brother in the matter at hand;

CHEBAR (8)

Ez 1: 1 I was among the exiles by the river *C*,
1: 3 the land of the Chaldeans by the river *C*—
3:15 who lived at Tel-abib by the river *C*,
3:23 like the glory I had seen by the river *C*.
10:15 living creatures I had seen by the river *C*.
10:20 beneath the God of Israel by the river *C*,
10:22 just like those I had seen by the river *C*;
43: 3 like that which I had seen by the river *C*.

CHECK (6)

Gn 30:33 whenever you *c* on these wages of mine,
Jb 36:27 He holds in *c* the waterdrops that filter
Prv 17:14 therefore, *c* a quarrel before it begins!
25:28 is the man with no *c* on his feelings.
Sir 18:30 your lusts, but keep your desires in *c*.
Rv 7: 1 they held in *c* the earth's four winds so

CHECKED (11)

Nm 17:13 the living and the dead, the scourge was *c*.
17:15 When the scourge had been *c*,
25: 8 Thus the slaughter of Israelites was *c*;
2Sm 24:21 that the plague may be *c* among the people."
24:25 country, and the plague was *c* in Israel.
Tb 9: 5 promptly *c* over the sealed moneybags,
2Mc 13:19 but he was driven back, *c*,
Jb 16: 6 I speak, this pain I have will not be *c*;
Ps(s) 106:30 forth in judgment and the plague was *c*;
Wis 18:23 he stood in the midst and *c* the anger,
Jl 2: 8 they fall into the ditches, they are not *c*.

CHECKS (1)

Ps(s) 76:13 terrible Lord Who *c* the pride of princes,

CHEDORLAOMER (5)

Gn 14: 1 Arioch king of Ellasar, *C* king of Elam,
14: 4 twelve years they had been subject to *C*,
14: 5 In the fourteenth year *C* and the kings
14: 9 against *C* king of Elam,
14:17 *C* and the kings who were allied with him,

CHEEK (14)

Lv 13:29 or a woman has a sore on the head or *c*,
13:30 scall, a leprous disease of the head or *c*.
1Kgs 22:24 up and slapped Micaiah on the *c* saying,
2Chr 18:23 up and slapped Micaiah on the *c* saying,
Jb 16:10 They smite me on the *c* insultingly;
40:26 nose, or pierce through his *c* with a gaff?
Ps(s) 3: 8 For you strike all my enemies on the *c*;
Sg 4: 3 Your *c* is like a half-pomegranate behind
6: 7 Your *c* is like a half-pomegranate behind
Sir 35:15 Do not the tears that stream down her *c*
Lam 3:30 Let him offer his *c* to be struck,
Mi 4:14 they strike on the *c* the ruler of Israel.
Mt 5:39 When a person strikes you on the right *c*,
Lk 6:29 When someone slaps you on one *c*,

CHEEKS (6)

Sg 1:10 Your *c* lovely in pendants,
5:13 His *c* are like beds of spice with
Is 50: 6 me, my *c* to those who plucked my beard;
Jer 9:17 be wet with weeping, our *c* run with tears.
Lam 1: 2 she weeps at night, tears upon her *c*,
Hos 11: 4 like one who raises an infant to his *c*;

CHEER (6)

Tb 8:21 Be of good *c*, my son!
Est 5:14 go to the banquet with the king in good *c*."
Jb 9:27 lay aside my sadness and be of good *c*,
Sir 31:28 good *c* and merriment are wine drunk
Is 24:11 has disappeared and *c* has left the land.
1Thes 5:14 *c* the fainthearted;

CHEERED (3)

Jdt 14: 9 finished her account, the people *c* loudly,
2Mc 15:11 words, he *c* them all by relating a dream,
Zec 10: 7 and their hearts shall be *c* as by wine.

CHEERFUL (10)

1Kgs 21: 7 Eat and be *c*.
Jb 29:25 mourners took comfort from my *c* glance.
Prv 15:30 A *c* glance brings joy to the heart;
Sir 13:25 sign of a good heart is a *c* countenance;
30:25 One who is *c* and gay while at table
35: 8 each contribution show a *c* countenance,
Is 24: 8 Stilled are the *c* timbrels,
24: 8 of the jubilant, stilled is the *c* harp.
Zec 8:19 *c* festivals for the house of Judah;
2Cor 9: 7 not grudgingly, for God loves a *c* giver.

CHEERFULLY (1)

Rom 12: 8 who performs works of mercy should do so *c*.

CHEERFULNESS (1)

Sir 30:22 the very life of man, *c* prolongs his days.

CHEERS (1)

Jgs 9:13 I give up my wine that *c* gods and men,

CHEESE (3)

2Sm 17:29 butter and *c* from the flocks and herds,
Jdt 10: 5 roasted grain, fig cakes, bread and *c*;
Jb 10:10 me out as milk, and thicken me like *c*?

CHEESES (1)

1Sm 17:18 take these ten *c* for the field officer.

CHELAL (1)

Ezr 10:30 Adna, *C*, Benaiah, Maaseiah,

CHELEOUD (1)

Jdt 1: 6 came together to resist the people of *C*.

CHELOUS (1)

Jdt 1: 9 Jordan as far as Jerusalem, Bethany, *C*,

CHELUB (2)

1Chr 4:11 *C*, the brother of Shuhah,
27:26 who tilled the soil was Ezri, son of *C*.

CHELUBAI (1)

1Chr 2: 9 born to Hezron were Jerahmeel, Ram, and *C*.

CHELUHI (1)

Ezr 10:35 Maadai, Amram, Uel, Benaiah, Bedeiah, *C*,

CHEMOSH (8)

Nm 21:29 You are ruined, O people of *C*!
Jgs 11:24 that which your god *C* gave you to possess,
1Kgs 11: 7 Solomon then built a high place to *C*,
11:33 Astarte, goddess of the Sidonians, *C*,
2Kgs 23:13 of Astarte, the Sidonian horror, of *C*,
Jer 48: 7 *C* shall go into exile,
48:13 *C* shall disappoint Moab,
48:46 you, O Moab, you are ruined, O people of *C*!

CHENAANAH (5)

1Kgs 22:11 Zedekiah, son of *C*,
22:24 Thereupon Zedekiah, son of *C*,
1Chr 7:10 of Bilhan were Jeush, Benjamin, Ehud, *C*,
2Chr 18:10 Zedekiah, son of *C*,
18:23 Thereupon Zedekiah, son of *C*,

CHENANI (1)

Neh 9: 4 Shebaniah, Bunni, Sherebiah, Bani, and *C*,

CHENANIAH (3)

1Chr 15:22 *C* was the chief of the Levites in the
15:27 who carried the ark, the singers, and *C*,
26:29 *C* and his sons were in charge of Israel's

CHEPHAR-AMMONI (1)

Jos 18:24 Avvim, Parah, Ophra, *C*

CHEPHIRAH (4)

Jos 9:17 came to their cities of Gibeon, *C*,
18:26 Ramah, Beeroth, Mizpeh, *C*,
Ezr 2:25 men of Kiriath-jearim, *C*,
Neh 7:29 men of Kiriath-jearim, *C*,

CHERAN (2)

Gn 36:26 Dishon were Hemdan, Eshban, Ithran, and *C*.
1Chr 1:41 Dishon were Hemdan, Eshban, Ithran, and *C*.

CHERETHITES (9)

1Sm 30:14 We raided the Negeb of the *C*,
2Sm 8:18 was in command of the *C* and Pelethites.
15:18 As all the *C* and Pelethites,
20: 7 So Joab and the *C* and Pelethites and all
20:23 was in command of the *C* and Pelethites.
1Kgs 1:38 and the *C* and Pelethites went down,
1:44 son of Jehoiada, and the *C* and Pelethites,
1Chr 18:17 was in command of the *C* and the Pelethites;
Ez 25:16 *C* and wipe out the remnant on the seacoast.

CHERISH (10)

Lv 19:18 *c* no grudge against your fellow countrymen.
Tb 13:10 *c* within you for all generations to come.
Jdt 6: 9 *c* the hope that they will not be taken,
Ps(s) 9:11 They trust in you who *c* your name,
16: 3 me *c* the holy ones who are in his land!
66:18 Were I to *c* wickedness in my heart,
Sir 27:17 *C* your friend,
Mi 1:16 your hair, for the children whom you *c*;
Rom 15:23 and I continue to *c* the desire to visit
1Cor 15:31 in me, which I *c* in Christ Jesus our Lord,

CHERISHED (4)

2Sm 1:23 Saul and Jonathan, beloved and *c*,
Jb 17:11 are at an end, the *c* purposes of my heart.
Is 5:7 and the men of Judah are his *c* plant;
Bar 4:16 They have led away this widow's *c* sons,

CHERISHES (2)

Sir 17:17 A man's goodness God *c* like a signet ring,
28:5 If he who is but flesh *c* wrath,

CHERITH (2)

1Kgs 17:3 here, go east and hide in the Wadi *C*,
17:5 He went and remained by the Wadi *C*,

CHERUB (16)

Ex 25:19 so that one *c* springs direct from each end.
37:8 propitiatory, one *c* fastened at one end,
2Sm 22:11 He mounted a *c* and flew,
1Kgs 6:24 Each wing of a *c* measured five cubits so
6:27 *c* touched a side wall while the other wing,
6:27 the corresponding wing of the second *c*.
2Chr 3:12 one wing of each *c*,
3:12 the corresponding wing of the second *c*.
Ezr 2:59 returned from Tel-melah, Tel-harsha, *C*,
Neh 7:61 who returned from Tel-melah, Tel-harsha, *C*,
Ps(s) 18:11 He mounted a *c* and flew,
Ez 10:7 Thereupon its *c* stretched out his hand
10:9 beside them, one wheel beside each *c*;
28:14 With the *C* I placed you;
28:16 *C* drove you from among the fiery stones.
41:18 Each *c* had two faces:

CHERUBIM (59)

Gn 3:24 the *c* and the fiery revolving sword,
Ex 25:18 Make two *c* of beaten gold for the two ends
25:20 *c* shall have their wings spread out above,
25:22 the two *c* on the ark of the commandments.
26:1 scarlet yarn, with *c* embroidered on them.
26:31 linen twined, with *c* embroidered on it.
36:8 having *c* embroidered on them with violet,
36:35 linen twined, with *c* embroidered on it.
37:7 Two *c* of beaten gold were made for the two
37:9 The *c* had their wings spread out above,
Nm 7:89 the commandments, from between the two *c*;
1Sm 4:4 LORD of hosts, who is enthroned upon the *c*.
2Sm 6:2 of the LORD of hosts enthroned above the *c*.
1Kgs 6:23 In the sanctuary were two *c*,
6:25 The *c* were identical in size and shape,
6:27 The *c* were placed in the inmost part of
6:28 The *c*, too, were overlaid with gold.
6:29 the outer rooms had carved figures of *c*,
6:32 of olive wood, with carved figures of *c*,
6:32 also molded to the *c* and the palm trees.
6:35 strap, front and back, and had carved *c*,
7:29 the frames there were lions, oxen, and *c*;
7:36 wherever there was a clear space, *c*,
8:6 the wings of the *c* in the sanctuary,
8:7 The *c* had their wings spread out over the
2Kgs 19:15 LORD, God of Israel, enthroned upon the *c*!
1Chr 13:6 by the name "LORD enthroned upon the *c*."
28:18 the *c* that spread their wings and covered
2Chr 3:7 gold, and he engraved *c* upon the walls.
3:10 holies he made two *c* of carved workmanship,
3:11 The wings of the *c* spanned twenty cubits:
3:13 of the two *c* was thus twenty cubits.
3:14 fine linen, and had *c* embroidered upon it.
5:7 the wings of the *c* in the sanctuary,
5:8 The *c* had their wings spread out over the
Ps(s) 80:2 From your throne upon the *c*,
99:1 he is throned upon the *c*;
Is 37:16 hosts, God of Israel, enthroned upon the *c*!
Ez 8:4 The *c* were stationed to the right
10:1 the *c* what appeared to be a sapphire stone;
10:2 Go within the wheelwork under the *c*;
10:2 hands with burning coals from among the *c*,
10:2 the God of Israel had gone up from the *c*,
10:4 over the *c* to the threshold of the temple;
10:5 *c* could be heard as far as the outer court;
10:6 from within the wheelwork, among the *c*,
10:7 hand toward the fire that was among the *c*.
10:8 could be seen under the wings of the *c*
10:16 When the *c* moved, the wheels went
10:16 when the *c* lifted their wings to rise from
10:18 of the temple and rested upon the *c*.
10:20 Chebar, whom I now recognized to be *c*.
11:22 Then the *c* lifted their wings,
41:18 were carved the figures of *c* and palmtrees:
41:18 a palmtree between every two *c*.
41:20 *c* and palmtrees were carved on the walls.
41:25 doors of the nave] were *c* and palmtrees,
Dn 3:55 the depths from your throne upon the *c*,
Heb 9:5 Above the ark were the *c* of glory

CHESALON (1)

Jos 15:10 of the ridge of Mount Jearim (that is, *C*);

CHESED (1)

Gn 22:22 Buz, Kemuel (the father of Aram), *C*,

CHESIL (1)

Jos 15:30 Baalah, Iim, Ezem, Eltolad, *C*,

CHEST (10)

2Kgs 12:10 The priest Jehoiada then took a *c*,
12:11 was a large amount of silver in the *c*,
2Chr 24:8 king's command, therefore, they made a *c*,
24:10 and cast it into the *c* until it was filled.
24:11 Whenever the *c* was brought to the royal
24:11 for the high priest came, emptied the *c*,
Dn 2:32 was pure gold, its *c* and arms were silver,
Zec 13:6 him, "What are these wounds on your *c*?"
Jn 13:25 back against Jesus' *c* and said to him,
21:20 Jesus' *c* during the supper and said,

CHESTS (2)

1Mc 3:28 He opened his treasure *c*,
Rv 9:9 of lions, their *c* like iron breastplates.

CHESULLOTH (1)

Jos 19:18 of the Issacharites included Jezreel, *C*,

CHEW (6)

Lv 11:4 that only *c* the cud or only have hoofs:
11:7 *c* the cud and is therefore unclean for you.
11:26 or do not *c* the cud are unclean for you;
Dt 14:7 only *c* the cud or only have cloven hoofs:
14:7 the rock badger, which indeed *c* the cud,
14:8 *c* the cud and is therefore unclean for you.

CHEWS (5)

Lv 11:3 provided it is cloven-footed and *c* the cud.
11:4 the camel, which indeed *c* the cud,
11:5 the rock badger, which indeed *c* the cud,
11:6 the hare, which indeed *c* the cud,
Dt 14:6 provided it is cloven-footed and *c* the cud.

CHEZIB (1)

Gn 38:5 They were in *C* when he was born.

CHIDE (1)

Ps(s) 103:9 He will not always *c*,

CHIDON (1)

1Chr 13:9 As they reached the threshing floor of *C*,

CHIEF (175)

Gn 10:10 The *c* cities of his kingdom were Babylon,
34:2 Hamor the Hivite, who was *c* of the region,
37:36 a courtier of Pharaoh and his *c* steward.
39:1 a courtier of Pharaoh and his *c* steward)
39:21 the *c* jailer well-disposed toward him.
39:22 The *c* jailer put Joseph in charge of all
39:23 The *c* jailer did not concern himself with
40:2 the *c* cupbearer and the chief baker,
40:3 in the house of the *c* steward (the same jail
40:4 The *c* steward assigned Joseph to them,
40:9 Then the *c* cupbearer told Joseph his dream.
40:16 When the *c* baker saw that Joseph had given
40:20 heads of the chief cupbearer and *c* baker.
40:21 He restored the *c* cupbearer to his office,
40:22 but the *c* baker he impaled
40:23 the *c* cupbearer gave no thought to Joseph;
41:9 *c* cupbearer spoke up and said to Pharaoh:
41:10 *c* baker in custody in the house of the *c*
41:12 a Hebrew youth, a slave of the *c* steward;
Nm 3:32 The *c* prince of the Levites,
Jos 11:10 formerly was the *c* of all those kingdoms.
1Sm 21:8 the Edomite, and he was Saul's *c* henchman.
1Kgs 4:5 son of Nathan, *c* of the commissaries;
2Kgs 24:15 functionaries, and the *c* men of the land.
1Chr 5:7 Jeiel, the *c*, and Zechariah,
5:12 Joel was *c*, Shapham was second
9:17 Shallum was the *c*.
9:20 of Eleazar, had been their *c* in times past
9:26 four *c* gatekeepers were on constant duty.
11:6 first shall be made the *c* commander."
11:6 and so he became *c*.
11:10 These were David's *c* warriors who,
11:11 the son of Hachamoni, *c* of the Three.
11:20 He was the *c* of the Thirty;
11:42 the Reubenite, *c* of the tribe of Reuben;
12:3 Ahiezer was their *c*,
12:10 Ezer was their *c*,
12:19 enveloped Amasai, the *c* of the Thirty,
15:5 of the sons of Kohath, Uriel, their *c*,
15:6 of the sons of Merari, Asaiah, their *c*,
15:7 of the sons of Gershon, Joel, their *c*,
15:8 the sons of Elizaphan, Shemaiah, their *c*,
15:9 of the sons of Hebron, Eliel, their *c*,
15:10 of the sons of Uzziel, Amminadab, their *c*,
15:22 was the *c* of the Levites in the chanting;
16:5 Asaph was their *c*,
18:17 sons were the *c* assistants to the king.
23:8 Jehiel the *c*, then Zetham and Joel;
23:11 was the *c* and Zizah was second to him;
23:16 Shubael the *c*.
23:17 The sons of Eliezer were Rehabiah the *c*—
23:18 Shelomith the *c*.
23:19 Jeriah, the *c*, Amariah, the second,
23:20 Micah, the *c*, and Isshiah, the second.
24:21 Isshiah, the *c*,
24:23 descendants of Hebron were Jeriah, the *c*,
26:10 the *c* (for though he was not the
26:10 not the first-born his father made him *c*),
26:12 classes of gatekeepers, under their *c* men,
26:24 was *c* superintendent over the treasures.
26:31 their *c* according to their family records.
27:3 he was *c* over all the commanders of the
27:5 army commander, *c* for the third month,
2Chr 26:20 Azariah the *c* priest and all the other
Ezr 8:29 in Jerusalem in the presence of the *c* priests
Tb 1:22 of Assyria, Ahiqar had been *c* cupbearer,
5:19 I hope more money is not your *c* concern!
Jdt 2:4 Holofernes, general in *c* of his forces,
4:1 commander in *c* of Nebuchadnezzar,
5:1 commander in *c* of the Assyrian army,
6:1 commander in *c* of the Assyrian army,
10:13 the general in *c* of your forces,
13:18 blow at the head of the *c* of our enemies.
Est C:22 them and make an example of our *c* enemy.
1Mc 10:65 numbering him among his *C* Friends
11:27 and had him enrolled among his *C* Friends.
11:62 He took the sons of their *c* men as
2Mc 4:50 the *c* plotter against his fellow citizens.
8:9 son of Patroclus, one of the *C* Friends,
10:10 summary of the *c* evils caused by the wars.
15:30 soul the *c* defender of his fellow citizens,
Jb 29:9 The *c* men refrained from speaking and
Ps(s) 119:160 Permanence is your word's *c* trait;
Prv 6:7 For though she has no *c*,
Sir 39:26 *C* of all needs for human life are water
Jer 20:1 Immer, *c* officer in the house of the LORD.
39:3 of Simmagir, the *c* officer,
39:9 Nebuzaradan, *c* of the bodyguard,
39:10 Judah by Nebuzaradan, *c* of the bodyguard,
39:11 through Nebuzaradan, *c* of the bodyguard:
39:13 Thereupon Nebuzaradan, *c* of the bodyguard,
39:13 and Nergal-sharezer, the *c* officer,
51:59 Seraiah was *c* quartermaster.
Ez 38:2 Magog], the *c* prince of Meshech and Tubal,
38:3 at you, Gog, *c* prince of Meshech and Tubal.
39:1 at you, Gog, *c* prince of Meshech and Tubal.
Dn 1:3 The king told Ashpenaz, his *c* chamberlain,
1:7 The *c* chamberlain changed their names:
1:8 *c* chamberlain to spare him this defilement.
1:9 favor and sympathy of the *c* chamberlain,
1:11 *c* chamberlain had put in charge of Daniel,
1:18 the *c* chamberlain brought them before
2:48 *c* prefect over all the wise men of Babylon.
4:6 "Belteshazzar, *c* of the magicians,
5:11 your father, made him *c* of the magicians,
10:13 finally Michael, one of the *c* princes,
11:41 except Edom, Moab, and the *c* part of Ammon,
Zec 10:4 From him shall come leader and *c*,
Mt 2:4 of the *c* priests and scribes of the people,
16:21 at the hands of the elders, the *c* priests,
20:18 handed over to the *c* priests and scribes,
21:15 The *c* priests and the scribes became
21:23 the *c* priests and elders of the people
21:45 When the *c* priests and the Pharisees heard
26:3 At that time the *c* priests and elders of
26:14 went off to the *c* priests and said,
26:47 by the *c* priests and elders of the people.
26:59 The *c* priests,
27:1 At daybreak all the *c* priests and the
27:3 back to the *c* priests and elders and said,
27:6 The *c* priests picked up the silver,
27:12 he was accused by the *c* priests and elders,
27:20 the *c* priests and elders convinced the
27:41 The *c* priests, the scribes,
27:62 the *c* priests and the Pharisees called at
28:11 to the *c* priests all that had happened.
Mk 8:31 be rejected by the elders, the *c* priests,
10:33 over to the *c* priests and the scribes.
11:18 The *c* priests and the scribes heard of
11:27 in the temple precincts the *c* priests,
14:1 and therefore the *c* priests and scribes
14:10 the *c* priests to hand Jesus over to them.
14:43 people had been sent by the *c* priests,
14:53 to the high priest, and all the *c* priests,
14:55 The *c* priests with the whole Sanhedrin
15:1 As soon as it was daybreak the *c* priests,
15:3 The *c* priests,
15:10 that the *c* priests had handed him over.
15:11 the *c* priests incited the crowd to have
15:31 The *c* priests and the scribes also joined
Lk 8:41 named Jairus, who was *c* of the synagogue,
13:14 The *c* of the synagogue,
19:2 the *c* tax collector and a wealthy man.
19:47 The *c* priests and scribes meanwhile were
22:4 He went off to confer with the *c* priests
22:52 the *c* priests,
22:66 the elders of the people, the *c* priests,
23:4 reported to the *c* priests and the crowds,
23:10 The *c* priests and scribes were at hand to
23:13 Pilate then called together the *c* priests,
24:20 how our *c* priests and leaders delivered
Jn 7:32 and the *c* priests and Pharisees together
7:45 the *c* priests and Pharisees asked them,
11:47 The result was that the *c* priests and the

11:57 (The *c* priests and the Pharisees had given
12:10 the *c* priests planned to kill Lazarus too,
18: 3 by the *c* priests and the Pharisees,
18:35 *c* priests who have handed you over to me.
19: 6 As soon as the *c* priests and the temple
19:15 The *c* priests replied,
19:21 *c* priests of the Jews tried to tell Pilate,
Acts 9:14 authorization from the *c* priests to arrest
9:21 people and bring them before the *c* priests?"
22:30 He summoned the *c* priests and the whole
23:14 to the *c* priests and the elders and said:
25: 2 There the Jewish *c* priests and the leaders
25:15 While I was in Jerusalem the *c* priests and
26:10 authority I received from the *c* priests,
26:12 authority and commission of the *c* priests.
28: 7 of Publius, the *c* figure on the island.
Col 2:23 *c* effect is that they indulge men's pride.
1Pt 5: 4 so that when the *c* Shepherd appears you

CHIEFLY (1)

2Chr 30:18 of the people, in fact, *c* from Ephraim,

CHIEFS (27)

Nm 1:16 tribes, *c* of the troops of Israel.
10: 4 the princes, the *c* of the troops of Israel,
Dt 29: 9 your *c* and judges,
33: 5 When the *c* of the people assembled and the
Jgs 5: 2 Of *c* who took the lead in Israel,
1Sm 18:30 [The Philistine *c* continued to make forays,
29: 3 The Philistine *c* asked,
29: 4 *c* were angered at this and said to him:
29: 9 But the Philistine *c* have determined you
1Chr 1:51 These were the *c* of Edom:
1:51 the *c* of Timna,
1:54 Magdiel, and Iram were the *c* of Edom.
7: 3 All five of these were *c*.
7:40 men, warriors, and *c* among the princes.
8:28 their kindred, *c* who dwelt in Jerusalem.
9:34 their kindred, *c* who dwelt in Jerusalem.
11:15 of the Thirty *c* went down to the rock,
12:21 and Zillethai, *c* of thousands of Manasseh.
12:33 their *c* who were endowed with an
12:33 two hundred *c*,
15:16 David commanded the *c* of the Levites to
Ezr 10: 5 demanded an oath from the *c* of the priests,
Neh 11:16 levitical *c* who were placed over the
Jb 39:25 battle, the roar of the *c* and the shouting.
Ps(s) 83:12 all their *c* like Zebah and Zalmunna,
Is 19:13 The *c* of her tribes have led Egypt astray,
Lk 22:52 chief priests, the *c* of the temple guard,

CHIEFTAIN (1)

Jgs 11: 1 There was a *c*,

CHIEFTAINS (3)

Gn 17:20 He shall become the father of twelve *c*,
25:16 twelve *c* of as many tribal groups.
Ex 15:15 trembling seized the *c* of Moab;

CHILD (178)

Gn 11:30 Sarai was barren; she had no *c*.
17:17 "Can a *c* be born to a man who is a
18:13 laugh and say, 'Shall I really bear a *c*,
21:14 Then, placing the *c* on her back,
21:15 So she put the *c* down under a shrub,
21:16 to herself, "Let me not watch the *c* die."
37: 3 his sons, for he was the *c* of his old age;
38:24 and was then with *c* from her harlotry.
38:25 whom these things belong that I am with *c*.
44:20 and a young brother, the *c* of his old age.
Ex 2: 2 Seeing that he was a goodly *c*,
2: 3 bitumen and pitch, and putting the *c* in it,
2: 7 of the Hebrew women to nurse the *c* for you?"
2: 9 to her, "Take this *c* and nurse it for me,
2: 9 woman therefore took the *c* and nursed it.
2:10 When the *c* grew,
Lv 12: 7 woman who gives birth to a boy or a girl *c*.
Nm 31:17 every male *c* and every woman who has had
Dt 1:31 God, carried you, as a man carries his *c*,
23: 3 No *c* of an incestuous union may be
Jgs 11:34 She was an only *c*:
13: 7 'You will be with *c* and will bear a son.
Ru 4:16 Naomi took the *c*,
1Sm 1:11 me, if you give your handmaid a male *c*,
1:22 to her husband, "Once the *c* is weaned,
1:27 I prayed for this *c*,
2:11 the *c* remained in the service of the LORD
4:19 with *c* and at the point of giving birth.
4:21 [She named the *c* Ichabod,
2Sm 11: 5 to David, "I am with *c*."
12:14 deed, the *c* born to you must surely die."
12:15 The LORD struck the *c* that the wife of
12:16 David besought God for the *c*.
12:18 On the seventh day, the *c* died.
12:18 afraid to tell him that the *c* was dead,
12:18 "When the *c* was alive,
12:18 How can we tell him the *c* is dead?
12:19 and realized that the *c* was dead.
12:19 He asked his servants, "Is the *c* dead?"
12:21 While the *c* was living,
12:21 now that the *c* is dead,
12:22 "While the *c* was living,
1Kgs 3:20 after she had laid her dead *c* in my bosom.
3:21 I rose in the morning to nurse my *c*,
3:22 kept saying, "No, the dead one is your *c*,
3:23 claims, 'This, the living one, is my *c*,
3:23 The dead one is your *c*;
3:25 him, he said, "Cut the living *c* in two,
3:26 "Please, my lord, give her the living *c*—
3:27 "Give the first one the living *c*!
13: 2 'A *c* shall be born to the house of David,
14: 3 He will tell you what will happen to the *c*."
14:12 you step inside the city, the *c* will die,
14:17 the threshold of her house, the *c* died.
17:21 *c* three times and called out to the LORD:
17:21 life breath return to the body of this *c*."
17:23 Taking the *c*, Elijah brought him down
2Kgs 4:18 The day came when the *c* was old enough to
4:34 Then he lay upon the *c* on the bed,
4:34 As Elisha stretched himself over the *c*,
5:14 became again like the flesh of a little *c*,
2Chr 22:11 priest, hid the *c* from Athaliah's sight,
Tb 3:15 and he has no other *c* to make his heir,
4:21 Do not be discouraged, my *c*,
5:18 "Why have you decided to send my *c* away?
6:12 has a daughter named Sarah, but no other *c*.
6:15 I am my father's only *c*.
7: 7 "My *c*, God bless you!
9: 6 "O noble and good *c*,
10: 5 "Alas, my *c*,
10: 7 My *c* has perished!"
10: 8 "Stay, my *c*, stay with me.
10:13 "My *c* and beloved kinsman,
10:13 Go in peace, my *c*.
Est C:16 As a *c* I was wont to hear from the people
1Mc 6:17 son Antiochus, whom he had reared as a *c*,
2Mc 7:28 I beg you, *c*, to look at the heavens
Jb 3: 3 the night when they said, "The *c* is a boy!"
25: 4 or how can any woman's *c* be innocent?
Ps(s) 131: 2 and quieted my soul like a weaned *c*.
131: 2 Like a weaned *c* on its mother's lap,
Prv 4: 3 When I was my father's *c*,
20:11 Even by his manners the *c* betrays whether
22:15 Folly is close to the heart of a *c*,
Eccl 6: 3 the *c* born dead is more fortunate than he.
6: 5 dead *c* is at rest rather than such a man.
Wis 2:13 of God and styles himself a *c* of the Lord.
8:19 Now, I was a well-favored *c*,
10: 5 him resolute against pity for his *c*.
14:15 image of the *c* so quickly taken from him,
Sir 19:10 in labor, like a woman giving birth to a *c*.
22: 3 An unruly *c* is a disgrace to its father;
30: 9 your *c* and he will be a terror for you,
40:18 A *c* or a city will preserve one's name,
Is 3: 5 The *c* shall be bold toward the elder,
7:14 the virgin shall be with *c*,
7:16 For before the *c* learns to reject the bad
8: 4 for before the *c* knows how to call his
9: 5 For a *c* is born to us,
11: 6 together, with a little *c* to guide them.
11: 8 and the *c* lay his hand on the adder's lair.
49:15 without tenderness for the *c* of her womb?
66: 7 upon her, she safely delivers a male *c*.
66: 9 of birth, and yet not let her *c* be born?
Jer 4:31 the anguish of a mother with her first *c*—
6:11 will pour it out upon the *c* in the street,
6:26 Mourn as for an only *c* with bitter wailing,
20:15 the news to my father, saying, "A *c*,
31: 8 their midst, The mothers and those with *c*;
31:20 my favored son, the *c* in whom I delight?
44: 7 from Judah man and wife, *c* and nursling,
Lam 2:11 As a *c* and infant faint away in the open
Hos 11: 1 When Israel was a *c* I loved him,
11: 4 Yet, though I stooped to feed my *c*,
13:13 come for him, but he shall be an unwise *c*;
Mt 1:18 *c* through the power of the Holy Spirit.
1:20 Holy Spirit that she has conceived this *c*.
1:23 shall be with *c* and give birth to a son,
2: 8 and get detailed information about the *c*.
2: 9 standstill over the place where the *c* was.
2:11 house, found the *c* with Mary his mother.
2:13 "Get up, take the *c* and his mother,
2:13 is searching for the *c* to destroy him."
2:14 Joseph got up and took the *c* and his
2:20 "Get up, take the *c* and his mother,
2:20 had designs on the life of the *c* are dead."
2:21 He got up, took the *c* and his mother,
10:21 brother to death, and the father his *c*;
18: 2 He called a little *c* over and stood him in
18: 4 makes himself lowly, becoming like this *c*,
18: 5 one such *c* for my sake welcomes me.
Mk 5:39 The *c* is not dead.
5:40 and entered the room where the *c* lay.
5:42 The girl, a *c* of twelve,
7:30 the *c* lying in bed and the demon gone.
9:36 Then he took a little *c*,
9:37 a *c* such as this for my sake welcomes me.
10:15 like a little *c* shall not take part in it."
12:19 brother dies leaving a wife but no *c*,
13:12 execution and likewise the father his *c*;
Lk 1:59 circumcision of the *c* on the eighth day,
1:66 hearts, saying, "What will this *c* be?"
1:76 And you, O *c*, shall be called prophet
1:80 The *c* grew up and matured in spirit.
2: 5 Mary, his espoused wife, who was with *c*.
2:17 what had been told them concerning this *c*.
2:21 the name Jesus was given the *c*,
2:27 when the parents brought in the *c* Jesus
2:34 "This *c* is destined to be the downfall
2:38 gave thanks to God and talked about the *c*
2:40 The *c* grew in size and strength,
2:43 the *c* Jesus remained behind unknown to his
8:54 "Get up, *c*."
9:38 he is my only *c*.
9:47 took a little *c* and placed it beside him,
9:48 this little *c* on my account welcomes me,
16:25 'My *c*,' replied Abraham, 'remember
18:17 of God as a *c* will not enter into it."
20:28 brother dies leaving a wife and no *c*,
Jn 4:49 with him, "come down before my *c* dies."
16:21 When she has borne her *c*,
Acts 7: 5 although he had no *c*.
7:20 He proved to be an exceedingly handsome *c*.
1Cor 13:11 When I was a *c* I used to talk like a child,
13:11 child, think like a child, reason like a *c*.
1Tm 1: 2 hope, to Timothy, my own true *c* in faith.
1:18 a solemn charge to give you, Timothy, my *c*.
2Tm 1: 2 life in him, to Timothy, my *c* whom I love.
Ti 1: 4 Titus, my own true *c* in our common faith:
Phlm 1:10 prisoner for him, appeal to you for my *c*,
Heb 5:13 of the word that sanctifies, for he is a *c*.
11:23 because they saw that he was a beautiful *c*.
1Jn 5: 1 the father loves the *c* he has begotten.
Rv 12: 2 Because she was with *c*,
12: 4 to devour her *c* when it should be born.
12: 5 *c* was caught up to God and to his throne.

CHILD-SLAYING (1)

Wis 14:23 *c* sacrifices or clandestine mysteries,

CHILDBEARING (2)

Gn 3:16 "I will intensify the pangs of your *c*;
1Tm 2:15 She will be saved through *c*,

CHILDBED (1)

Bar 6:28 and women in *c* handle their sacrifices.

CHILDBIRTH (5)

Sir 48:19 and they were in anguish like that of *c*.
Jer 6:24 hold of us, throes like a mother's in *c*.
30: 6 hands on their loins like women in *c*?
50:43 seizes him, throes like a mother's in *c*.
Gal 4:27 into song, you stranger to the pains of *c*!

CHILDHOOD (7)

2Mc 6:23 of the admirable life he had lived from *c*;
15:12 trained from *c* in every virtuous practice,
Prv 29:21 If a man pampers his servant from *c*,
Sir 7:23 bend their necks from *c*.
Bar 4:15 reverence for age nor tenderness for *c*;
Mk 9:21 "From *c*," the father replied.
10:20 I have kept all these since my *c*."

CHILDISH (3)

Wis 15:14 quite senseless, and worse than *c* in mind,
1Cor 13:11 When I became a man I put *c* ways aside.
14:20 Brothers, do not be *c* in your outlook.

CHILDLESS (17)

Gn 15: 2 if I keep on being *c* and have as my heir
42:36 "Must you make me *c*?
Lv 20:20 his aunt shall pay the penalty by dying *c*.
20:21 they shall be *c* because of this incest.
Dt 7:14 be *c* nor shall your livestock be barren.
1Sm 1: 2 Peninnah had children, but Hannah was *c*.
15:33 made women *c*, so shall your mother be *c*
2Sm 6:23 Michal was *c* to the day of her death.
Wis 3:13 Yes, blessed is she who, *c* and undefiled,
Sir 16: 3 rather die *c* than have godless children!
Jer 18:21 Let their wives be made *c* and widows;
22:30 Write this man down as one *c*,
Hos 9:12 up their children, I will make them *c*,
Mk 12:21 second took the woman, and he too died *c*.
Lk 1: 7 They were *c*, for Elizabeth was sterile;
20:30 The first one married and died *c*.

CHILDLESSNESS (1)

Wis 4: 1 Better is *c* with virtue;

CHILDREN (493)

Gn 3:16 in pain shall you bring forth *c*.
10:21 and the ancestor of all the *c* of Eber,
16: 1 Abram's wife Sarai had borne him no *c*.
16: 2 "The LORD has kept me from bearing *c*.
20:17 maidservants, so that they could bear *c*;
21: 7 she added, "that Sarah would nurse *c*!
22:24 whose name was Reumah, also bore *c*:
25:22 But the *c* in her womb jostled each other
29:35 Then she stopped bearing *c*.
30: 1 saw that she failed to bear *c* to Jacob,
30: 1 said to Jacob, "Give me *c* or I shall die!"
30: 9 Leah saw that she had ceased to bear *c*,

CHILDREN (cont.)

30:26 my wives, for whom I served you, and my c,
31:16 our father really belongs to us and our c.
31:17 proceeded to put his c and wives on camels,
31:43 "The women are mine, their c are mine,
31:43 for them and for the c they have borne.
32:12 strike me down and slay the mothers and c.
32:23 with the two maidservants and his eleven c,
33: 1 So he divided his c among Leah,
33: 2 their children first, Leah and her c next,
33: 5 Esau looked about, he saw the women and c.
33: 5 "They are the c whom God has graciously
33: 6 and their c came forward and bowed low;
33: 7 Leah and her c came forward and bowed low;
33: 7 and her c came forward and bowed low.
33:13 "As my lord can see, the c are frail.
33:14 before me and at the pace of my c,
34:29 their wealth, their women, and their c,
43: 8 our c are to keep from starving to death.
45:10 you and your c and grandchildren,
45:19 wagons from the land of Egypt for your c
46: 5 father and their wives and c on the wagons
47:24 and your families [and as food for your c."
50: 8 only their c and their flocks and herds
50:21 I will provide for you and for your c."
50:23 He saw Ephraim's c to the third generation,
50:23 and the c of Manasseh's son Machir were
Ex 2: 6 and said, "It is one of the Hebrews' c."
12:26 When your c ask you,
12:37 thousand men on foot, not counting the c.
17: 3 of thirst with our c and our livestock?"
20: 5 wickedness on the c of those who hate me,
20: 6 on the c of those who love me and keep my
21: 4 the woman and her c shall remain the
21: 5 am devoted to my master and my wife and c;
22:23 wives will be widows, and your c orphans.
34: 7 but punishing c and grandchildren to the
Lv 10:14 have been assigned to you and your c
10:15 to you and your c by a perpetual ordinance,
22:13 is widowed or divorced and, having no c,
25:41 year, when he, together with his c,
25:45 c who are born and reared in your land.
25:54 be released, together with his c,
26:22 you of your c and wipe out your livestock,
Nm 5:28 be immune and will still be able to bear c.
14:18 but punishing c to the third and fourth
14:33 where your c must wander for forty years,
32:26 While our wives and c,
32:30 you shall bring their wives and c and
Dt 1:39 you said would become booty, and your c,
2:34 them all, with their men, women and c;
3: 6 the cities, with their men, women and c;
3:19 Only your wives and c,
4: 9 to your c and to your children's children.
4:10 live in the land and may so teach their c.'
4:25 "When you have c and grandchildren,
4:40 that you and your c after you may prosper,
5: 9 wickedness on the c of those who hate me,
5:10 on the c of those who love me and keep my
6: 7 Drill them into your c.
11: 2 It is not your c,
11:19 Teach them to your c,
11:21 you and your c may live on in the land
12:25 that you and your c after you may prosper
14: 1 "You are c of the LORD, your God.
20:14 but the women and c and livestock and all
23: 9 C born to them may in the third generation
24:16 their children, nor c for their fathers;
28:54 and his beloved wife and his surviving c,
28:55 any share in the flesh of his c that he
29:10 and c and the aliens who live in your camp,
30: 2 that you and your c return to the LORD,
31:12 men, women and c,
31:13 Their c also,
32: 5 has he been treated by his degenerate c,
32:46 you and which you must impress on your c,
33: 9 and his own c he refused to recognize.
Jos 1:14 Your wives, your c,
4: 6 c ask you what these stones mean to you,
4:21 when the c among you ask their fathers
5: 7 It was the c whom he raised up in their
8:35 community, including the women and c,
17: 2 and Shemida, the other male c of Manasseh,
22:24 future your c should say to our children:
22:25 Thus your c would prevent ours from
22:27 future your children cannot say to our c,
24: 4 while Jacob and his c went down to Egypt.
Jgs 13: 2 His wife was barren and had borne no c.
13: 3 "Though you are barren and have had no c,
21:10 to the sword, including the women and c.
1Sm 1: 2 Peninnah had c,
2:20 "May the LORD repay you with c from this
15: 3 him, but kill men and women, c and infants,
22:19 including men and women, c and infants,
30:22 booty, except to each man his wife and c.
2Sm 12: 3 her, and she grew up with him and his c.
2Kgs 2:24 and tore forty-two of the c to pieces.
4: 1 has come to take my two c as his slaves."
4: 4 and close the door on yourself and your c;
4: 5 so, closing the door on herself and her c.
4: 7 with what remains, you and your c can live."
8:12 you will dash their little c to pieces,
14: 6 c of the murderers he did not put to death,
14: 6 their children, nor shall c be put to death
17:31 their c by fire to their city gods,
19: 3 C are at the point of birth,
1Chr 5:29 The c of Amram were Aaron,
28: 8 it as an inheritance to your c forever.
2Chr 21:14 the LORD will strike your people, your c,
25: 4 but he did not put their c to death,
25: 4 their children, nor c for their fathers;
28:10 And now you are planning to make the c of
30: 9 your brethren and your c will find mercy
Ezr 8:21 him a safe journey for ourselves, our c,
9:12 it as an inheritance to your c forever.
10: 1 gathered about him, men, women, and c;
10: 3 our foreign wives and the c born of them,
10:44 sent them away, both the women and their c.
Neh 5: 5 kinsmen and our c are as good as theirs,
8: 2 and those c old enough to understand.
8: 3 and those c old enough to understand;
9:23 c as numerous as the stars of the heavens,
10:37 the first-born of our c and our animals,
12:43 The women and the c joined in,
13:24 Of their c,
Tb 4:12 own kinsmen and were blessed in their c.
6:18 And I suppose that you will have c by her,
8:17 for you were merciful toward two only c.
10:11 And may I see c of yours before I die!"
10:13 may I live long enough to see c of you
13: 9 but will again pity the c of the righteous.
13:13 then, rejoice over the c of the righteous,
14: 3 take your c and flee into Media for I
14: 9 "Now, c, I give you this command:
14: 9 c to do what is upright and to give alms,
14:11 So, my c,
14:12 departed with his wife and c for Media,
Jdt 4:10 they, along with their wives, and c,
4:11 women and c who lived in Jerusalem
4:12 Israel not to allow their c to be seized,
7:14 wives and c will languish with hunger,
7:22 Their c fainted away,
7:23 therefore, including youths, women, and c,
7:27 our wives and c breathing out their souls.
7:32 the women and c he sent to their homes.
9:13 Zion, and the homes your c have inherited.
16: 4 my babes to the ground, make my c a prey,
Est 3:13 young and old, including women and c,
B: 6 shall, together with their wives and c,
8:11 wipe out, along with their wives and c,
E:15 are the c of the Most High,
1Mc 1:32 walls, took captive the women and c,
1:38 her own offspring, and her c forsook her.
1:60 had their c circumcised were put to death,
2:38 with their wives, their c and their cattle,
2:64 C! be courageous
3:20 us and our wives and c and to despoil us;
3:45 not one of her c entered or came out.
5:13 away their wives and c and their goods,
5:23 their wives and c and all that they had,
5:45 with their wives and c and their goods,
8:10 the Romans took their wives and c captive.
13: 6 sanctuary, as well as your wives and c,
13:45 of the city, joined by their wives and c,
2Mc 5:13 of young and old, a killing of women and c,
6:10 arrested for having circumcised their c
7:34 raise your hand against the c of Heaven.
8: 4 the criminal slaughter of innocent c
8:28 they divided among themselves and their c.
9:15 c to be eaten by vultures and wild animals;
9:20 If you and your c are well and your
12: 3 them, together with their wives and c,
12:21 he sent on ahead of him the women and c,
14:25 He urged him to marry and have c;
15:18 wives and c or their brothers and kinsmen;
Jb 5: 4 His c shall be far from safety;
8: 4 If your c have sinned against him and he
19:18 The young c, too, despise me;
21:11 numerous as lambs, and their c dance.
21:19 not store up the man's misery for his c;
27:14 Though his c be many,
29: 5 yet with me, and my c were round about me;
42:16 and he saw his c,
Ps(s) 14: 2 looks down from heaven upon the c of men,
34:12 Come, c, hear me; I will teach you
36: 8 The c of men take refuge in the shadow of
53: 3 God looks down from heaven upon the c of
72: 4 among the people, save the c of the poor,
73:15 had been false to the fellowship of your c.
89:48 how frail you created all the c of men!
90: 3 back to dust, saying, "Return, O c of men."
90:16 your servants and your glory by their c;
102:29 The c of your servants shall abide,
103: 7 Moses, and his deeds to the c of Israel.
103:13 As a father has compassion on his c,
103:17 And his justice toward children's c
107: 8 and his wondrous deeds to the c of men,
107:15 and his wondrous deeds to the c of men,
107:21 and his wondrous deeds to the c of men.
107:31 and his wondrous deeds to the c of men.
109: 9 May his c be fatherless,
109:10 May his c be roaming vagrants and beggars;
113: 9 the barren wife as the joyful mother of c.
115:14 you more and more, both you and your c.
115:16 but the earth he has given to the c of men.
128: 3 Your c like olive plants around your table.
128: 6 May you see your children's c.
137: 7 Remember, O LORD, against the c of Edom,
147:13 he has blessed your c within you.
148:14 his faithful ones, from the c of Israel,
149: 2 let the c of Zion rejoice in their king.
Prv 4: 1 Hear, O c, a father's instruction,
5: 7 So now, O c,
7:24 So now, O c, listen to me,
8: 4 my appeal is to the c of men.
8:32 "So now, O c, listen to me;
13:22 leaves an inheritance to his children's c,
14:26 even for one's c he will be a refuge.
17: 6 men, and the glory of c is their parentage.
20: 7 and justice, happy are his c after him!
31:28 Her c rise up and praise her;
Eccl 3:18 As for the c of men,
3:21 Who knows if the life-breath of the c of
6: 3 a man have a hundred c and live many years,
9:12 like these the c of men are caught when
Wis 3:12 Their wives are foolish and their c wicked;
3:16 c of adulterers will remain without issue,
4: 6 For c born of lawless unions give evidence
9: 4 and reject me not from among your c;
12: 5 These merciless murderers of c,
12: 7 might receive a worthy colony of God's c.
12:25 Therefore as though upon unreasoning c,
13:17 he prays about his goods or marriage or c,
16:21 revealed your sweetness toward your c,
18: 9 For in secret the holy c of the good were
18:10 wail of mourning for c was borne to them.
19: 6 that your c might be preserved unharmed.
Sir 1:13 and with their c her beneficence abides.
3: 1 C, pay heed to a father's right;
3: 2 LORD sets a father in honor over his c;
3: 5 He who honors his father is gladdened by c,
3:11 disgrace for her c,
4:11 her c and admonishes those who seek her.
16: 1 Desire not a brood of worthless c,
16: 3 rather die childless than have godless c!
23: 7 Give heed, my c,
23:23 adultery she has borne c by another man.
23:24 and her punishment will extend to her c;
23:25 Her c will not take root;
25: 7 The man who finds joy in his c,
33:22 Far better that your c plead with you
39:13 Listen, my faithful c:
41: 5 A reprobate line are the c of sinners,
41: 6 Their dominion is lost to sinners' c,
41: 7 C curse their wicked father,
41: 9 If you have c, calamity will seize them;
41:14 My c, heed my instruction about shame;
42: 5 Of constant training of c,
44: 9 had not lived, they and their c after them.
45: 9 and the c of his race would be remembered;
45:23 noble heart, atoned for the c of Israel.
46:12 names receive fresh luster in their c!
Is 1: 4 with wickedness, evil race, corrupt c!
8:18 at me and the c whom the LORD has given me:
13:18 nor shall they have eyes of pity for c.
17: 9 Amorites When faced with the c of Israel:
29:23 c see the work of my hands in his midst,
30: 1 Woe to the rebellious c,
30: 9 deceitful children, C who refuse to obey
31: 6 Return, O c of Israel,
37: 3 C are at the point of birth,
45:11 You question me about my c,
47: 8 be a widow, or suffer the loss of my c—
49:20 c whom you had lost shall yet say to you,
54: 1 are the c of the deserted wife than the c
54:13 and great shall be the peace of your c.
57: 4 Are you not rebellious c,
57: 5 You who immolate c in the wadies,
59:21 c Nor the mouths of your children's c
60: 9 c from afar with their silver and gold,
60:14 The c of your oppressors shall come,
63: 8 indeed my people, c who are not disloyal;
65:23 vain, nor beget c for sudden destruction;
66: 8 in labor when she gives birth to her c.
Jer 2: 9 and even your children's c I will accuse.
2:30 In vain I struck your c;
3:14 Return, rebellious c,
3:21 the plaintive weeping of Israel's c,
3:22 Return, rebellious c,
4:22 Senseless c they are,
7:18 The c gather wood,
9:20 It cuts down the c in the street,
18:21 So now, deliver their c to famine,
30: 6 since when do men bear c?
31:15 c, she refuses to be consoled because of her c
32:39 own good and that of their c after them.
35: 6 you nor your c shall ever drink wine.
35:14 by which he forbade his c to drink wine,
35:16 Yes, the c of Jonadab,
40: 7 charge of the land, of men, women, and c,
41:16 and the women and c with their guardians,
43: 6 men, women, and c,
47: 3 Fathers turn not to save their c;
Lam 2:20 eat their offspring, their well-formed c?
4:10 of compassionate women boiled their own c,
Bar 4:12 For the sins of my c I am left desolate,
4:19 Farewell, my c, farewell:
4:21 "Fear not, my c;
4:25 "My c, bear patiently the anger

4:26 My pampered c have trodden rough roads,
4:27 Fear not, my c; call out to God!
4:32 are the cities where your c were enslaved,
5: 5 look to the east and see your c Gathered
6:32 clothing and put it on their wives and c
Ez 5:17 wild beasts that shall rob you of your c.
9: 6 Old men, youths and maidens, women and c—
16:21 You slaughtered and immolated my c to them,
16:36 sacrificed the lifeblood of your c to them,
16:45 the mother who spurned her husband and c,
16:45 to those who spurned their husbands and c—
20:18 Then I said to their c in the desert:
20:21 But their c rebelled against me:
20:31 by making your c pass through the fire,
23:37 they immolated the c they had borne me.
23:39 very day they slew their c for their idols,
36:12 Never again shall you rob them of their c
36:13 men, and you rob your people of their c";
36:14 devour men or rob your people of their c,
36:15 peoples, or rob your people of their c,
37:25 their c, and their children's children,
47:22 in your midst who have bred c among you.
Dn 6:25 Daniel, along with their c and their wives,
13:39 with her parents, c and all her relatives.
14:10 priests of Bel, besides their wives and c.
14:15 night as usual, with their wives and c,
14:20 see the footprints of men, women, and c!"
14:21 the priests, their wives, and their c.
Hos 1: 2 Go, take a harlot wife and harlot's c,
2: 1 They shall be called, C of the living God."
2: 6 children, for they are the c of harlotry.
5: 7 for they have begotten illegitimate c;
9:11 Were they to bear c,
9:12 Even though they bring up their c,
9:13 shall bring out his c to the slayer.
10:14 time of war, smashing mothers and their c.
13:13 not present himself where c break forth.
Jl 1: 3 c, and your c to their c, and their c
2:16 gather the c and the infants at the breast;
2:23 And do you, O c of Zion,
Ob 1:12 the c of Judah on the day of their ruin;
1:20 The captives of the host of the c of
Mi 1:16 out your hair, for the c whom you cherish;
2: 9 From their c you take away forever the
5: 2 brethren shall return to the c of Israel.)
Zec 10: 7 Their c shall see it
10: 9 they shall rear their c and return.
Mal 3:24 fathers to their c, and the hearts of the c
Mt 2:18 Rachel bewailing her c;
3: 9 up c to Abraham from these very stones.
7:11 sins, know how to give your c what is good,
10:21 c will turn against parents and have them
11:16 are like c squatting in the town squares,
11:25 clever you have revealed to the merest c.
14:21 five thousand, not counting women and c.
15:38 four thousand, apart from women and c.
18: 3 unless you change and become like little c,
18:25 to be sold, along with his wife, his c,
19:13 c were brought to him so that he could
19:14 but Jesus said, "Let the c come to me.
19:29 wife or c or property for my sake will
21:15 and how the c were shouting out in the
21:16 and c you have framed a hymn of praise'?"
22:24 Moses declared, 'If a man dies without c,
22:25 died after marrying, and since he had no c,
23:37 How often have I yearned to gather your c,
27:25 "Let his blood be on us and on our c."
Mk 7:27 the food of the c and throw it to the dogs."
10:13 little c to him to have him touch them,
10:14 the c come to me and do not hinder them.
10:29 sisters, mother or father, c or property,
10:30 and sisters, mothers, c and property
12:20 eldest took a wife and died, leaving no c.
12:22 fact none of the seven left any c behind.
13:12 c will turn against their parents and have
Lk 1:17 to turn the hearts of fathers to their c
3: 8 raise up c to Abraham from these stones.
7:32 They are like c squatting in the city
10:21 clever you have revealed to the merest c.
11: 7 is shut now and my c and I are in bed.
11:13 sins, know how to give your c good things,
13:34 How often have I wanted to gather your c
14:26 his father and mother, his wife and his c,
18:16 but Jesus called for the c,
18:16 "Let the little c come to me.
18:29 home or wife or brothers, parents or c,
19:44 you out, you and your c within your walls,
20:31 All seven died without leaving her any c.
20:34 "The c of this age marry and are given in
23:28 Weep for yourselves and for your c.
Jn 1:12 accept him he empowered to become c of God.
8:39 "If you were Abraham's c,
11:52 gather into one all the dispersed c of God.)
13:33 My c, I am not to be with you much longer.
21: 5 He said to them, C,
Acts 2:39 you and your c that the promise was made,
3:25 You are the c of those prophets,
13:26 c of the family of Abraham and you others
13:33 fathers he has fulfilled for us, their c,
21: 5 wives and c included
21:21 to give up the circumcision of their c,
Rom 8:16 with our spirit that we are c of God.
8:17 But if we are c, we are heirs as well:
8:21 in the glorious freedom of the c of God.
9: 7 nor are all Abraham's descendants his c,
9: 8 children of the flesh who are the c of God;
9: 8 it is the c of the promise who are to be
9:10 Rebekah had conceived twin c by one man,
1Cor 4:14 you but to admonish you as my beloved c.
7:14 were otherwise, your c should be unclean;
14:20 Be like c as far as evil is concerned,
2Cor 6:13 then (I speak as a father to his c),
12:14 C should not save up for their parents,
12:14 up for their parents, but parents for c.
Gal 4:19 You are my c, and you put me back
4:24 Sinai, and brought forth c to slavery;
4:25 which is likewise in slavery with her c.
4:27 "Rejoice, you barren one who bears no c;
4:27 For many are the c of the wife deserted
4:28 You, my brothers, are c of the promise,
4:31 we are not c of a slave girl but of a
Eph 4:14 Let us, then, be c no longer,
5: 1 Be imitators of God as his dear c.
5: 8 Well, then, live as c of light.
6: 1 C, obey your parents in the Lord,
6: 4 Fathers, do not anger your c.
Phil 2:11 Innocence of the C of God.
2:15 c of God beyond reproach in the midst of a
Col 3:20 You c, obey your parents in everything
3:21 do not nag your c lest they lose heart.
1Thes 2:11 every one of you, as a father does his c—
5: 5 all of you are c of light and of the day.
1Tm 3: 4 keeping his c under control without
3:12 managers of their c and their households.
5: 4 If a widow has any c or grandchildren,
5:10 Has she brought up c?
5:14 to see the younger ones marry, have c,
Ti 1: 6 the father of c who are believers and are
2: 4 women to love their husbands and c,
Heb 2:13 "Here am I, and the c God has given me!"
2:14 since the c are men of blood and flesh,
2:16 help angels, but rather the c of Abraham;
1Pt 3: 6 You are her c when you do what is right
1Jn 2:14 I address you, c,
2:18 C, it is the final hour;
3: 1 on us in letting us be called c of God!
3: 2 Dearly beloved, we are God's c now;
3:10 That is the way to see who are God's c,
3:18 Little c, let us love in deed
5: 2 We can be sure that we love God's c when
5:21 My little c, be on your guard
2Jn 1: 1 elder to a Lady who is elect and to her c.
1: 4 of your c walking in the path of truth,
1:13 The c of your elect sister send you their
3Jn 1: 4 to hear that my c are walking in this path.
Rv 2:23 with her, and her c I will put to death.

CHILDREN'S (9)

Dt 4: 9 to your children and to your c children.
Ps(s) 103:17 And his justice toward c children among
128: 6 May you see your c children.
Prv 13:22 leaves an inheritance to his c children,
Is 59:21 children Nor the mouths of your c children,
Jer 2: 9 and even your c children I will accuse.
31:29 grapes, and the c teeth are set on edge,"
Ez 18: 2 grapes, thus their c teeth are on edge"?
37:25 and their children, and their c children,

CHILD'S (9)

Gn 21: 8 grew, and on the day of the c weaning,
Ex 2: 8 maiden went and called the c own mother.
2Sm 12:22 'Perhaps the LORD will grant me the c life.'
1Kgs 17:22 returned to the c body and he revived.
2Kgs 4:34 bed, placing his mouth upon the c mouth,
Wis 12:26 no heed of punishment which was but c play
Mk 5:40 Jesus took the c father and mother and his
Lk 2:33 The c father and mother were marveling at
8:51 Peter, John, James, and the c parents.

CHILEAB (1)

2Sm 3: 3 the second, C, of Abigail the widow

CHILION (3)

Ru 1: 2 his wife Naomi, and his sons Mahlon and C;
1: 5 ten years, both Mahlon and C died also,
4: 9 the holdings of Elimelech, C and Mahlon.

CHILL (2)

Dn 3:67 [Cold and c, bless the Lord;
3:69 Frost and c, bless the Lord;

CHILMAD (1)

Ez 27:23 of Sheba, Asshur, and C traded with you,

CHIMHAM (4)

2Sm 19:38 Here is your servant C.
19:39 said to him, C shall come over with me,
19:41 crossed over to Gilgal, accompanied by C.
Jer 41:17 to the lodging place of C near Bethlehem,

CHINNERETH (6)

Nm 34:11 the ridge on the east side of Sea of C;
Dt 3:17 banks from C to the Salt Sea of the Arabah,
Jos 12: 3 from the eastern side of the Sea of C,
13:27 to the southeastern tip of the sea of C.
19:35 were Ziddim, Zer, Hammath, Rakkath, C,
1Kgs 15:20 Ijon, Dan, Abel-beth-maacah, and all C,

CHINNEROTH (1)

Jos 11: 2 mountain regions and in the Arabah near C,

CHIOS (1)

Acts 20:15 next day, and reached a point opposite C;

CHIRP (2)

Eccl 12: 4 When one waits for the c of a bird,
Is 8:19 fortunetellers (who c and mutter!);

CHIRPED (1)

Is 10:14 fluttered a wing, or opened a mouth, or c!"

CHIRPING (1)

Is 29: 4 earth, and your words like c from the dust.

CHISEL (2)

Jb 19:24 That with an iron c and with lead they
Ps(s) 74: 6 c and hammer they hack at all its paneling.

CHISLEV (8)

Neh 1: 1 In the month C of the twentieth year,
1Mc 1:54 On the fifteenth day of the month C,
4:52 the ninth month, that is, the month of C,
4:59 from the twenty-fifth day of the month C
2Mc 1: 9 the feast of Booths in the month of C.
1:18 on the twenty-fifth day of the month C,
10: 5 is, the twenty-fifth of the same month C,
Zec 7: 1 to Zechariah], on the fourth day of C,

CHISLON (1)

Nm 34:21 Elidad, son of C from the tribe of Dan:

CHISLOTH-TABOR (1)

Jos 19:12 Sarid eastward it ran to the district of C,

CHITLISH (1)

Jos 15:40 Bozkath, Eglon, Cabbon, Lahmam, C,

CHLOE'S (1)

1Cor 1:11 by certain members of C household that you

CHOBA (3)

Jdt 4: 4 Belmain, and Jericho, to C and Aesora,
15: 4 messengers to Betomasthaim, to C and Kona,
15: 5 them and cut them down as far as C.

CHOICE (47)

Gn 18: 7 to the herd, picked out a tender, c steer,
27: 9 Go to the flock and get me two c kids.
Nm 17:20 the staff of the man of my c shall sprout.
Jos 9:27 of the LORD, in the place of the LORD's c.
Jgs 5: 8 a mother in Israel, New gods were their c;
1Sm 27: 1 I have no c but to escape to the land of
2Kgs 19:23 cut down its lofty cedars, its c cypresses;
Neh 5:18 one beef, six c muttons,
2Mc 7:14 "It is my c to die at the hands of men
Prv 3:15 your c possessions can compare with her.
8:10 silver, and knowledge rather than c gold.
8:11 and no c possessions can compare with her.]
8:19 pure gold, and my revenue than c silver.
10:20 Like c silver is the just man's tongue;
Sg 4:13 forth pomegranates, with all c fruits;
4:16 come to his garden and eat its c fruits.
5: 5 c myrrh upon the fittings of the lock.
5:13 they drip c myrrh.
7:14 and at our doors are all c fruits;
Wis 3:14 For he shall be given fidelity's c reward
Sir 1:15 Her entire house she fills with c foods,
14:14 good things, let no c portion escape you.
15:14 man, he made him subject to his own free c.
37:28 neither become a glutton for c foods,
45:16 to offer holocausts and c offerings,
47: 2 Like the c fat of the sacred offerings,
Is 22: 7 Your c valleys are filled with chariots,
23:18 fill and clothe themselves in c attire.
25: 6 choice wines, juicy, rich food and pure, c
37:24 cut down its lofty cedars, its c cypresses;
40:20 the c portion which a skilled craftsman
Jer 2:21 you, a c vine of fully tested stock;
10:23 Man's course is not within his c,
21: 8 I am giving you a c between life and death.
22: 7 They shall cut down your c cedars,
25:34 like c rams you shall fall.
31:14 I will lavish c portions upon the priests,
Bar 3:30 her, bearing her away rather than c gold?
Ez 31:16 trees were consoled, Lebanon's c and best,
Am 5:11 Though you have planted c vineyards,
Jn 2:10 "People usually serve the c wine first;
2:10 you have done is keep the c wine until now."
Acts 1:26 The c fell to Matthias who was added to

CHOICE (cont.)

Rom 11: 6 But if the *c* is by grace,
1Cor 9:16 I am under compulsion and have no *c*.
Heb 12:17 he had no opportunity to alter his *c*,

CHOICEST (14)

Gn 23: 6 your dead in the *c* of our burial sites.
49:11 the vine, his purebred ass to the *c* stem.
Ex 23:19 The *c* first fruits of your soil you shall
34:26 "The *c* first fruits of your soil you
Dt 33:14 the year, and the *c* sheaves of the months;
1Sm 2:29 fattening yourselves with the *c* part of
Jb 33:20 and his senses reject the *c* nourishment.
Sir 11: 3 but she reaps the *c* of all harvests.
11:32 and plots against your *c* possessions.
26:15 *C* of blessings is a modest wife,
Is 5: 2 it of stones, and planted the *c* vines;
Ez 24: 4 *c* joints taken from the pick of the flock.
27:22 for your wares the very *c* spices,
44:30 All the *c* first fruits of every kind,

CHOIR (2)

1Chr 6:16 were entrusted by David with the *c* services
Neh 12:38 The second *c* proceeded to the left,

CHOIRS (3)

Neh 12:31 mount the wall, and I arranged two great *c*.
12:40 *c* took up a position in the house of God;
Ps(s) 68:27 In your *c* bless God;

CHOKE (2)

Mt 13:22 anxiety and the lure of money *c* it off.
Mk 4:19 cravings of other sorts come to *c* it off;

CHOKED (3)

Jdt 2: 8 torrent shall be *c* with their dead;
Mt 13: 7 fell among thorns, which grew up and *c* it.
Mk 4: 7 among thorns, which grew up and *c* it off,

CHOKING (2)

Jb 7:15 prefer *c* and death rather than my pains.
Am 1:11 his brother with the sword, *c* up all pity;

CHOOSE (49)

Gn 28: 2 and there *c* a wife for yourself from among
Ex 20:24 In whatever place I *c* for the remembrance
Lv 1:14 *c* a turtledove or a pigeon as his offering.
Dt 1:13 *C* wise, intelligent and experienced men
10:15 LORD was so attached to them as to *c* you,
30:19 *C* life, then, that you and your descendants
Jos 3:12 [Now *c* twelve men,
4: 2 to Joshua, *C* twelve men from the people,
18: 4 *C* three men from each of your tribes;
1Sm 2:35 I will *c* a faithful priest who shall do
17: 8 *C* one of your men,
2Sm 17: 1 "Please let me *c* twelve thousand men,
24:12 *c* one of them, and I will inflict it on you.
1Kgs 8:16 but I *c* David to rule my people Israel.'
11:36 the city in which I *c* to be honored.
18:23 Let them *c* one, cut it into pieces,
18:25 *C* one young bull and prepare it first,
2Kgs 18:32 *C* life, not death.
1Chr 21:10 *c* one of them,
21:12 Therefore *c*: What answer am I to give him?
2Chr 6: 6 but now I *c* Jerusalem,
6: 6 and I *c* David to rule my people Israel.'
1Mc 5:17 *C* men for yourself,
8:30 away anything, they shall do as they *c*,
10:32 in it such men as he shall *c* to guard it.
Jb 9:14 answer, or *c* out arguments against him!
15: 5 mouth, and you *c* to speak like the crafty.
34:33 It is you who must *c*,
Ps(s) 25:12 the LORD, he shows him the way he should *c*.
65: 5 Happy the man you *c*,
Prv 3:31 not the lawless man and *c* none of his ways:
Sir 15:15 If you *c* you can keep the commandments;
15:16 to whichever you *c*,
Is 7:15 he learns to reject the bad and *c* the good.
7:16 learns to reject the bad and *c* the good,
41:24 To *c* you is an abomination.
56: 4 eunuchs who observe my sabbaths and *c*
66: 4 I in turn will *c* ruthless treatment for
Jer 49:19 and whom I *c* I will establish there!
50:44 off, and whom I *c* I will establish there;
Bar 3:27 Not these did God *c*,
Zec 1:17 again comfort Zion, and again *c* Jerusalem.
2:16 holy land, and he will again *c* Jerusalem.
Mt 7:13 the road is clear, and many *c* to travel it.
Jn 6:70 "Did I not *c* the Twelve of you myself?
Acts 1:24 two you *c* for this apostolic ministry,
15:25 to *c* representatives and send them to you,
Rom 9:15 Moses, "I will show mercy to whomever I *c*;
Jas 2: 5 Did not God *c* those who are poor in the

CHOOSES (32)

Nm 16: 5 Whom he *c*, he will have draw near him.
16: 7 He whom the LORD then *c* is the holy one.
Dt 12: 5 *c* out of all your tribes and designates as
12:11 *c* as the dwelling place for his name you
12:14 which the LORD *c* from among your tribes;
12:18 the LORD, your God, in the place he *c*,
12:21 *c* for the abode of his name is too far,
12:26 with you to the place which the LORD *c*,
14:23 *c* as the dwelling place of his name you
14:24 *c* for the abode of his name is too far for
14:25 to the place which the LORD, your God, *c*.
15:20 the LORD, your God, in the place he *c*.
16: 2 he *c* as the dwelling place of his name.
16: 6 he *c* as the dwelling place of his name,
16: 7 eat it at the place the LORD, your God, *c*;
16:11 God, *c* as the dwelling place of his name,
16:15 LORD, your God, in the place which he *c*;
16:16 LORD, your God, in the place which he *c*:
17: 8 to the place which the LORD, your God, *c*,
17:10 give you in the place which the LORD *c*,
17:15 as your king whom the LORD, your God, *c*.
18: 6 may desire, the place which the LORD *c*,
23:17 Let him live with you wherever he *c*,
26: 2 God, *c* for the dwelling place of his name.
31:11 LORD, your God, in the place which he *c*,
2Sm 15:15 ready, whatever our lord the king *c* to do."
Tb 4:19 If the Lord *c*, he raises a man up
Ps(s) 47: 5 He *c* for us our inheritance,
Sir 15:17 death, whichever he *c* shall be given him.
Is 14: 1 LORD has pity on Jacob and again *c* Israel
Jn 7:17 Any man who *c* to do his will will know
Jas 4: 4 enemy if he *c* to be the world's friend.

CHOOSING (5)

Gn 8:20 and *c* from every clean animal and every
2Kgs 17:32 *c* from their number priests for the high
1Mc 10:74 *C* ten thousand men,
Is 40:20 for himself, *C* timber that will not rot,
Heb 7:11 *c* a priest according to the order of Aaron?

CHOP (3)

Dt 7: 5 sacred pillars, *c* down their sacred poles,
25:12 you shall *c* off her hand without pity.
Mi 3: 3 *c* them in pieces like flesh in a kettle,

CHOPS (1)

Eccl 10: 9 and he who *c* wood is in danger from it.

CHORAZIN (2)

Mt 11:21 "It will go ill with you, *C!*
Lk 10:13 ill with you, *C!* and just as ill with you

CHORUS (3)

2Chr 20:19 LORD, the God of Israel, in a resounding *c*.
Jb 38: 7 *c* and all the sons of God shouted for joy?
Lk 22:70 they asked in *c*.

CHOSE (57)

Gn 6: 2 for their wives as many of them as they *c*.
13:11 *c* for himself the whole Jordan Plain and
Dt 1:23 proposal, I *c* twelve men from your number,
4:37 For love of your fathers he *c* their
7: 7 the LORD set his heart on you and *c* you,
Jos 9: 4 They *c* provisions for a journey,
1Sm 2:28 I *c* them out of all the tribes of Israel
12:22 the LORD himself *c* to make you his people.
13: 2 Saul *c* three thousand men of Israel,
2Sm 24:15 Thus David *c* the pestilence.
1Kgs 11:34 for the sake of my servant David, whom I *c*,
12:33 *c* to establish a feast for the Israelites;
14:21 tribes of Israel, the LORD *c* to be honored.
2Kgs 8:20 of Judah and *c* a king of its own.
23:27 reject this city, Jerusalem, which I *c*,
1Chr 15: 2 for the LORD *c* them to carry the ark of
19:10 he *c* some of the best fighters among the
28: 4 *c* me from all my father's family to be
28: 4 For he *c* Judah as leader,
2Chr 12:13 tribes of Israel, the LORD *c* to be honored.
21: 8 they *c* a king of their own.
26: 1 All the people of Judah *c* Uzziah,
Neh 9: 7 "You, O LORD, are the God who *c* Abram,
Jdt 10: 4 She *c* sandals for her feet,
11: 1 anyone who *c* to serve Nebuchadnezzar,
Est 2:13 harem to the royal palace whatever she *c*.
C:16 O Lord, *c* Israel from among all peoples,
1Mc 3:38 Lysias *c* Ptolemy,
4:42 He *c* blameless priests,
7: 8 Then the king *c* Bacchides,
8:17 So Judas *c* Eupolemus,
9:25 Bacchides *c* impious men and made them
2Mc 1:25 who *c* our forefathers and sanctified them:
3: 7 The king *c* his minister Heliodorus and
14:12 The king immediately *c* Nicanor,
Jb 29:25 I *c* out their way and presided;
Ps(s) 78:67 Joseph, and the tribe of Ephraim he *c* not;
78:68 But he *c* the tribe of Judah,
78:70 And he *c* David, his servant,
Prv 1:29 knowledge, and *c* not the fear of the LORD;
Wis 7:10 And I *c* to have her rather than the light,
Sir 24: 8 he who formed me *c* the spot for my tent,
45:16 He *c* him from all mankind to offer
Is 1:29 and blush for the groves which you *c*.
66: 4 my sight, and *c* what gave me displeasure,
Ez 20: 5 The day I *c* Israel,
Jn 13:18 of all, for I know the kind of men I *c*.
15:16 not you who chose me, it was I who *c* you
15:19 But I *c* you out of the world.
Acts 13:17 of the people Israel once *c* our fathers.
15:40 *c* Silas to accompany him on his journey,
19: 9 but *c* to speak ill of the new way in the
1Cor 1:27 God *c* those whom the world considers
1:28 He *c* the world's lowborn and despised,
Gal 1:16 me by his favor *c* to reveal his Son to me,
Eph 1: 4 God *c* us in him before the world began,

CHOSEN (123)

Ex 24:11 Yet he did not smite these *c* Israelites.
31: 2 said to Moses, "See, I have *c* Bezalel,
35:30 Israelites, "See, the LORD has *c* Bezalel,
Lv 27:33 whether good ones or bad ones are thus *c*,
Nm 3:12 "It is I who have *c* the Levites from the
Dt 7: 6 he has *c* you from all the nations on the
14: 2 who has *c* you from all the nations on the
18: 5 has *c* him and his sons out of all your
21: 5 has *c* them to minister to him and to give
Jos 24:22 that you have *c* to serve the LORD."
Jgs 10:14 Go and cry out to the gods you have *c*;
1Sm 8:18 complain against the king whom you have *c*,
10:20 forward, and the tribe of Benjamin was *c*.
10:21 was *c*, and finally Saul, son of Kish, was *c*.
10:24 "Do you see the man whom the LORD has *c*?
16: 1 for I have *c* my king from among his sons."
16: 8 Samuel, who said, "The Lord has not *c* him."
16: 9 said, "The LORD has not *c* this one either."
16:10 "The LORD has not *c* any one of these."
2Sm 16:18 and all this people and all Israel have *c*,
1Kgs 3: 8 the midst of the people whom you have *c*,
8:16 I have not *c* a city out of any tribe of
8:44 toward the city you have *c* and the temple
8:48 gave their fathers, the city you have *c*,
11:13 David and of Jerusalem, which I have *c*."
11:32 I have *c* out of all the tribes of Israel.
2Kgs 21: 7 I have *c* out of all the tribes of Israel,
1Chr 9:22 those who were *c* for gatekeepers at the
16:13 his servants, sons of Jacob, his *c* ones!
16:41 Jeduthun and the others who were *c*
28: 5 he has *c* my son Solomon to sit on the
28: 6 and my courts, for I have *c* him for my son,
28:10 *c* you to build a house as his sanctuary.
29: 1 "My son Solomon, whom alone God has *c*,
2Chr 6: 5 I have not *c* any city from among all the
6: 5 nor have I *c* any man to be commander of my
6:38 their fathers, and of the city you have *c*,
7:12 *c* this place for my house of sacrifice.
7:16 And now I have *c* and consecrated this
29:11 whom the LORD has *c* to stand before him,
33: 7 Jerusalem which I have *c* from all the tribes
Neh 1: 9 I have *c* as the dwelling place for my name.'
Tb 8:15 Let all your *c* ones praise you;
13:11 in you, and shall call you the *c* one,
Est E:21 destruction of the *c* race into one of joy.
1Mc 7:37 "You have *c* this house to bear your name,
9:30 Now therefore we have *c* you today to be
12:16 So we have *c* Numenius,
13:34 Simon also sent *c* men to King Demetrius
2Mc 5:19 not *c* the people for the sake of the Place,
Ps(s) 33:12 people he has *c* for his own inheritance.
68:17 at the mountain God has *c* for his throne,
89: 4 "I have made a covenant with my *c* one,
105: 6 his servants, sons of Jacob, his *c* ones!
105:26 Aaron, whom he had *c*.
105:43 with shouts of joy, his *c* ones.
106: 5 I may see the prosperity of your *c* ones,
106:23 exterminating them, but Moses, his *c* one,
119:30 The way of truth I have *c*;
119:173 to help me, for I have *c* your precepts.
132:13 For the LORD has *c* Zion;
135: 4 For the LORD has *c* Jacob for himself,
Sg 6: 9 my dove, my perfect one, her mother's *c*,
Wis 9: 7 You have *c* me king over your people and
Sir 24:11 Thus in the *c* city he has given me rest,
32: 1 If you are *c* to preside at dinner,
39:21 Everything is *c* to satisfy a need.
46: 1 implies, the great savior of God's *c* ones,
47:22 does not uproot the posterity of his *c* one,
Is 41: 8 Israel, my servant, Jacob, whom I have *c*.
41: 9 whom I have *c* and will not cast off
42: 1 I uphold, my *c* one with whom I am pleased,
43:10 my servants whom I have *c* To know and
43:20 in the wasteland for my *c* people to drink,
44: 1 O Jacob, my servant, Israel, whom I have *c*.
44: 2 my servant, the darling whom I have *c*.
45: 4 of Jacob, my servant, of Israel my *c* one,
49: 7 the Holy One of Israel who has *c* you.
65: 9 My *c* ones shall inherit the land,
65:15 Shall be used by my *c* ones for cursing;
65:22 and my *c* ones shall long enjoy the produce
66: 3 Since these have *c* their own ways and
Jer 33:24 rejected the two tribes which he had *c*"?
Hg 2:23 for I have *c* you,
Zec 3: 2 the LORD who has *c* Jerusalem rebuke you!
Mt 12:18 "Here is my servant whom I have *c*,
24:22 For the sake of the *c*,
24:24 mislead even the *c* if that were possible.
24:31 will assemble his *c* from the four winds,
Mk 13:20 But for the sake of those he has *c*,

13:22 mislead, if it were possible, even the *c.*
13:27 and assemble his *c* from the four winds,
Lk 9:35 which said, "This is my Son, my *C* One.
10:42 Mary has *c* the better portion and she
18: 7 to his *c* who call out to him day and night?
23:35 if he is the Messiah of God, the *c* one."
Jn 1:34 and have testified, 'This is God's *c* One.' "
Acts 1: 2 apostles he had *c* through the Holy Spirit.
9:15 I have *c* to bring my name to the Gentiles,
10:41 witnesses as had been *c* beforehand by God
15:22 that representatives be *c* from among their
15:22 Those *c* were leading men of the community,
Rom 8:33 shall bring a charge against God's *c* ones?
11: 5 there is a remnant *c* by the grace of God.
11: 7 she was seeking, but those who were *c* did.
14:22 does not condemn what he has *c* to do!
16:13 to Rufus, a *c* servant of the Lord,
1Cor 16: 3 you have *c* to take your gift to Jerusalem.
Eph 1:11 In him we were *c;*
1:13 In him you too were *c;*
Col 3:12 Because you are God's *c* ones,
1Thes 1: 4 brothers beloved of God, how you were *c.*
2Thes 2:13 of those whom God has *c* for salvation,
1Tm 5:21 before God, Christ Jesus, and the *c* angels:
6:15 God will bring to pass at his *c* time.
2Tm 2:10 for the sake of those whom God has *c,*
Ti 1: 1 sake of the faith of those whom God has *c,*
1Pt 1: 1 to men *c* according to the foreknowledge of
1:20 unblemished lamb *c* before the world's
2: 9 You, however, are "a *c* race,
5:13 that is in Babylon, *c* together with you,
Rv 17:14 the *c* and the faithful."

CHRIST (460)

Mt 1: 1 A family record of Jesus *C,*
1:18 is how the birth of Jesus *C* came about.
11: 2 heard about the works *C* was performing,
Mk 1: 1 Here begins the gospel of Jesus *C,*
9:41 of water because you belong to *C* will not,
Jn 1:17 this enduring love came through Jesus *C.*
17: 3 God, and him whom you have sent, Jesus *C.)*
Acts 2:38 each one of you, in the name of Jesus *C,*
3: 6 In the name of Jesus *C,*
4:10 it was done in the name of Jesus *C*
8:12 the kingdom of God and the name of Jesus *C,*
9:34 said to him, "Aeneas, Jesus *C* cures you!
10:36 through Jesus *C* who is Lord of all.
10:48 they be baptized in the name of Jesus *C.*
11:17 when we first believed in the Lord Jesus *C,*
15:26 to the cause of our Lord Jesus *C.*
16:18 "In the name of Jesus *C* I command you,
24:24 to hear him speak about faith in *C* Jesus.
28:31 of God and taught about the Lord Jesus *C.*
Rom 1: 1 Greetings from Paul, a servant of *C* Jesus,
1: 4 Jesus *C* our Lord.
1: 6 who have been called to belong to Jesus *C.*
1: 7 from God our Father and the Lord Jesus *C.*
1: 8 I give thanks to God through Jesus *C* for
2:16 on the secrets of men through *C* Jesus.
3:22 faith in Jesus *C* for all who believe.
3:24 through the redemption wrought in *C* Jesus.
5: 1 at peace with God through our Lord Jesus *C.*
5: 6 still powerless, *C* died for us godless men.
5: 8 while we were still sinners, *C* died for us.
5:11 God our boast through our Lord Jesus *C,*
5:15 the gracious gift of the one man, Jesus *C,*
5:17 and reign through the one man, Jesus *C.*
5:21 to eternal life, through Jesus *C* our Lord.
6: 3 into *C* Jesus were baptized into his death?
6: 4 just as *C* was raised from the dead by the
6: 8 If we have died with *C,*
6: 9 know that *C,* once raised from the dead
6:11 dead to sin but alive for God in *C* Jesus.
6:23 of God is eternal life in *C* Jesus our Lord.
7: 4 you died to the law through the body of *C,*
7:25 praise to God, through Jesus *C* our Lord!
8: 1 now for those who are in *C* Jesus.
8: 2 the spirit, the spirit of life in *C* Jesus,
8: 9 Spirit of Christ, he does not belong to *C.*
8:10 If *C* is in you, the body is dead
8:11 then he who raised *C* from the dead will
8:17 heirs of God, heirs with *C,*
8:34 *C* Jesus, who died or rather was raised up
8:35 Who will separate us from the love of *C?*
8:39 love of God that comes to us in *C* Jesus,
9: 1 I speak the truth in *C:*
9: 3 from *C* for the sake of my brothers,
10: 4 *C* is the end of the law.
10: 6 (that is, to bring *C* down),
10: 7 (that is, to bring *C* up from the dead."
10:17 and what is heard is the word of *C.*
12: 5 *C* and individually members one of another.
13:14 put on the Lord Jesus *C* and make no
14: 9 That is why *C* died and came to life again,
14:15 you eat bring to ruin him for whom *C* died:
14:18 Whoever serves *C* in this way pleases God
15: 3 with Scripture, *C* did not please himself:
15: 5 another according to the spirit of *C* Jesus,
15: 6 God, the Father of our Lord Jesus *C.*
15: 7 one another, then, as *C* accepted you,
15: 8 I affirm that *C* became the servant of the
15:16 a minister of *C* Jesus among the Gentiles,
15:17 *C* Jesus for the work I have done for God.
15:18 speak of anything except what *C* has done
15:19 preaching the gospel of *C* from Jerusalem
15:30 Lord Jesus *C* and the love of the Spirit,
16: 3 my fellow workers in the service of *C* Jesus
16: 5 is the first offering that Asia made to *C.*
16: 7 and they were in *C* even before I was.
16: 9 our fellow worker in the service of *C;*
16:16 All the churches of *C* send you greetings.
16:18 Such men serve, not *C* our Lord,
16:20 the grace of our Lord Jesus *C* be with you.
16:25 which I proclaim when I preach Jesus *C,*
16:27 be given through Jesus *C* unto endless ages.
1Cor 1: 1 by God's will to be an apostle of *C* Jesus,
1: 2 in *C* Jesus and called to be a holy people,
1: 2 be, call on the name of our Lord Jesus *C,*
1: 3 from God our Father and the Lord Jesus *C.*
1: 4 favor he has bestowed on you in *C* Jesus,
1: 6 the witness I bore to *C* has been so
1: 7 for the revelation of our Lord Jesus *C.*
1: 8 blameless on the day of our Lord Jesus *C.*
1: 9 fellowship with his Son, Jesus *C* our Lord.
1:10 brothers, in the name of our Lord Jesus *C,*
1:12 and the fourth, "I belong to *C.*"
1:13 Has *C,* then, been divided into parts?
1:17 For *C* did not send me to baptize,
1:17 cross of *C* be rendered void of its meaning!
1:23 for "wisdom," but we preach *C* crucified
1:24 *C* the power of God and the wisdom of God.
1:30 it is who has given you life in *C* Jesus.
2: 2 of nothing but Jesus *C* and him crucified.
2:16 But we have the mind of *C.*
3: 1 but only as men of flesh, as infants in *C.*
3:11 the one that has been laid, namely Jesus *C.*
3:23 and you are Christ's, and *C* is God's.
4: 1 Men should regard us as servants of *C* and
4:10 Ah, but in *C* you are wise!
4:15 you have ten thousand guardians in *C,*
4:15 *C* Jesus through my preaching of the gospel.
4:17 He will remind you of my ways in *C,*
5: 3 Lord Jesus *C* on the man who did this deed.
5: 7 *C* our Passover has been sacrificed.
6:11 Lord Jesus *C* and in the Spirit of our God.
6:15 not see that your bodies are members of *C?*
7:22 who has been called is a slave of *C.*
8: 6 and one Lord Jesus *C* through whom
8:11 one perishes, that brother for whom *C* died.
8:12 consciences, you are sinning against *C.*
9:12 any obstacle in the way of the gospel of *C.*
9:21 of God, for I am subject to the law of *C),*
10: 4 was following them, and the rock was *C),*
10:16 we bless a sharing in the blood of *C?*
10:16 bread we break a sharing in the body of *C?*
11: 1 Imitate me as I imitate *C.*
11: 3 head of every man is *C;*
11: 3 and the head of *C* is the Father.
12:12 and so it is with *C.*
12:27 You, then, are the body of *C.*
15: 3 that *C* died for our sins in accordance
15:12 if *C* is preached as raised from the dead,
15:13 of the dead, *C* himself has not been raised.
15:14 And if *C* has not been raised,
15:15 witness before him that he raised up *C;*
15:16 dead are not raised, then *C* was not raised;
15:17 and if *C* was not raised,
15:18 asleep in *C* are the deadest of the dead.
15:19 hopes in *C* are limited to this life only,
15:20 as it is, *C* is now raised from the dead,
15:22 die, so in *C* all will come to life again,
15:23 *C* the first fruits and then,
15:25 *C* must reign until God has put all enemies
15:27 made everything subject to *C* is excluded.
15:31 in me, which I cherish in *C* Jesus our Lord,
15:57 us the victory through our Lord Jesus *C.*
16:24 My love to all of you in *C* Jesus.
2Cor 1: 1 Paul, by God's will an apostle of Jesus *C,*
1: 2 from God our Father and the Lord Jesus *C.*
1: 3 be God, the Father of our Lord Jesus *C,*
1: 5 we have shared much in the suffering of *C,*
1: 5 so through *C* do we share abundantly in his
1:19 Jesus *C,* whom Silvanus, Timothy
1:21 firmly establishes us along with you in *C;*
2:10 has been for your sakes and, before *C,*
2:12 I came to Troas to preach the gospel of *C,*
2:15 We are an aroma of *C* for God's sake,
3: 3 are a letter of *C* which I have delivered,
3: 4 great confidence in God is ours, through *C.*
3:14 it is only in *C* that it is taken away.
4: 4 of the gospel showing forth the glory of *C,*
4: 5 ourselves we preach but *C* Jesus as Lord,
4: 6 the glory of God shining on the face of *C.*
5:10 to be revealed before the tribunal of *C*
5:14 The love of *C* impels us who have reached
5:16 If at one time we so regarded *C,*
5:17 This means that if anyone is in *C,*
5:18 has reconciled us to himself through *C*
5:19 I mean that God, in *C,*
5:20 This makes us ambassadors for *C,*
6:15 What accord is there between *C* and Belial,
8: 9 the favor shown you by our Lord Jesus *C;*
8:23 apostles of the churches, the glory of *C.*
9:13 your obedient faith in the gospel of *C,*
10: 1 you by the meekness and kindness of *C,*
10: 5 into captivity to make it obedient to *C.*
10: 7 anyone is convinced that he belongs to *C,*
10: 7 he may belong to *C* but just as much do we.
10:14 did get as far as you with the gospel of *C.*
11: 2 presenting you as a chaste virgin to *C.*
11: 3 your sincere and complete devotion to *C.*
11:10 I swear by the *C* who is in me that this
11:13 deceit in their disguise as apostles of *C.*
11:23 Are they ministers of *C*—
12: 2 I know a man in *C* who,
12: 9 that the power of *C* may rest upon me.
12:10 and difficulties for the sake of *C;*
12:19 Before God I tell you, in *C,*
13: 3 for a proof of the *C* who speaks in me.
13: 5 do not realize that *C* Jesus is in you
13:13 The grace of the Lord Jesus *C,*
Gal 1: 1 but by Jesus *C* and God his Father who
1: 3 of God our Father and of the Lord Jesus *C,*
1: 6 in accord with his gracious design in *C,*
1: 7 the gospel of *C* must have confused you.
1:10 approval, I would surely not be serving *C!*
1:12 It came by revelation from Jesus *C.*
1:22 *C* in Judea had no idea what I looked like;
2: 4 *C* Jesus and thereby to make slaves of us,
2:16 legal observance but by faith in Jesus *C,*
2:16 in order to be justified by faith in *C,*
2:17 But if, in seeking to be justified in *C,*
2:17 does that mean that *C* is encouraging sin?
2:19 I have been crucified with *C,*
2:20 *C* is living in me.
2:21 through the law, then *C* died to no purpose!
3: 1 *C* was displayed to view upon his cross?
3:13 *C* has delivered us from the power of the
3:14 This has happened so that through *C* Jesus
3:14 might descend on the Gentiles in *C* Jesus,
3:16 that is, to *C.*
3:22 in consequence of faith in Jesus *C.*
3:24 the law was our monitor until *C* came to
3:26 of God because of your faith in *C* Jesus.
3:27 into *C* have clothed yourselves with him.
3:28 All are one in *C* Jesus.
3:29 to *C* you are the descendants of Abraham,
4:14 of God, even as if I had been *C* Jesus!
4:19 in labor pains until *C* is formed in you.
5: 1 It was for liberty that *C* freed us.
5: 2 circumcised, *C* will be of no use to you!
5: 4 from *C* and fallen from God's favor!
5: 6 In *C* Jesus neither circumcision nor the
5:24 Those who belong to *C* Jesus have crucified
6: 2 in that way you will fulfill the law of *C.*
6:12 to escaping persecution for the cross of *C.*
6:14 anything but the cross of our Lord Jesus *C!*
6:18 of our Lord Jesus *C* be with your spirit.
Eph 1: 1 by the will of God an apostle of Jesus *C,*
1: 1 ones [at Ephesus], believers in *C* Jesus.
1: 2 from God our Father and the Lord Jesus *C.*
1: 3 Lord Jesus *C,* who has bestowed on us in *C*
1: 5 us through *C* Jesus to be his adopted sons
1: 7 It is in *C* and through his blood that we
1: 9 the plan he was pleased to decree in *C,*
1:12 his glory by being the first to hope in *C.*
1:17 May the God of our Lord Jesus *C,*
1:20 like the strength he showed in raising *C*
2: 5 us to life with *C* when we were dead in sin.
2: 6 Both with and in *C* Jesus he raised us up
2: 7 by his kindness to us in *C* Jesus.
2:10 created in *C* Jesus to lead the life of
2:12 you had no part in *C* and were excluded
2:13 But now in *C* Jesus you who once were far
2:13 been brought near through the blood of *C.*
2:20 with *C* Jesus himself as the capstone.
3: 1 for *C* Jesus on behalf of you Gentiles,
3: 4 about in speaking of the mystery of *C,*
3: 6 in *C* Jesus the Gentiles are now co-heirs
3: 8 the unfathomable riches of *C*
3:11 purpose, carried out in *C* Jesus our Lord.
3:12 In *C* and through faith in him we can speak
3:17 May *C* dwell in your hearts through faith,
3:21 and in *C* Jesus through all generations,
4: 7 favor in the measure in which *C* bestows it.
4:12 the faithful to build up the body of *C,*
4:13 perfect man who is *C* come to full stature.
4:15 and the full maturity of *C* the head.
4:20 is not what you learned when you learned *C!*
4:32 just as God has forgiven you in *C.*
5: 2 the way of love, even as *C* loved you.
5: 5 inheritance in the kingdom of *C* and of God.
5:14 from the dead, and *C* will give you light."
5:20 everything in the name of our Lord Jesus *C.*
5:21 to one another out of reverence for *C.*
5:23 just as *C* is head of his body the church,
5:24 As the church submits to *C,*
5:25 love your wives, as *C* loved the church.
5:29 takes care of it as *C* cares for the church
5:32 I mean that it refers to *C* and the church.
6: 5 the awe, and the sincerity you owe to *C.*
6: 6 will with your whole heart as slaves of *C.*
6:23 May God the Father and the Lord Jesus *C*
6:24 love our Lord Jesus *C* with unfailing love.
Phil 1: 1 Paul and Timothy, servants of *C* Jesus,
1: 1 with their bishops and deacons in *C* Jesus.
1: 2 God our Father and from the Lord Jesus *C!*
1: 6 completion, right up to the day of *C* Jesus.

CHRIST (cont.)

1: 8 each of you with the affection of C Jesus!
1:10 really matter, up to the very day of C.
1:11 justice which Jesus C has ripened in you,
1:14 most of my brothers in C,
1:15 preach C from motives of envy and rivalry,
1:17 others promote C,
1:18 or genuine ones, C is being proclaimed!
1:19 I receive from the Spirit of Jesus C.
1:20 now as always C will be exalted through me,
1:21 For, to me, "life" means C;
1:23 be freed from this life and to be with C,
1:26 should make you even prouder of me in C.
1:27 then, in a way worthy of the gospel of C.
2: 1 name of the encouragement you owe me in C,
2: 5 Your attitude must be that of C:
2:11 JESUS C IS LORD!
2:16 As I look to the Day of C,
2:21 own interests rather than those of C Jesus.
3: 3 in the spirit of God and glory in C Jesus
3: 7 now reappraised as loss in the light of C.
3: 8 surpassing knowledge of my Lord Jesus C.
3: 8 C may be my wealth and I may be in him,
3: 9 is that which comes through faith in C.
3:10 I wish to know C and the power flowing
3:12 since I have been grasped by C [Jesus].
3:14 life on high in C Jesus.
3:18 shows them to be enemies of the cross of C.
3:20 the coming of our Savior, the Lord Jesus C.
4: 7 over your hearts and minds, in C Jesus.
4:19 of his magnificent riches in C Jesus.
4:21 in C Jesus to every member of the church.
4:23 of the Lord Jesus C be with your spirit.
Col 1: 1 an apostle of C Jesus by the will of God,
1: 2 ones at Colossae, faithful brothers in C.
1: 3 to God, the Father of our Lord Jesus C,
1: 4 we have heard of your faith in C Jesus
1: 7 represents us as a faithful minister of C.
1:22 But now C has achieved reconciliation for
1:24 sufferings of C for the sake of his body,
1:27 the mystery of C in you,
1:28 This is the C we proclaim while we
1:28 hoping to make every man complete in C.
2: 2 namely C— in whom every treasure
2: 5 you and the firmness of your faith in C.
2: 6 therefore, to live in C Jesus the Lord,
2: 8 based on cosmic powers rather than on C.
2: 9 In C the fullness of deity resides in
2:13 God gave you new life in company with C.
2:15 off captive, triumphed in the person of C.
2:17 the reality is the body of C.
2:20 If with C you have died to cosmic forces,
3: 1 you have been raised up in company with C,
3: 1 where C is seated at God's right hand.
3: 3 Your life is hidden now with C in God.
3: 4 When C our life appears,
3:11 Rather, C is everything in all of you.
3:16 Let the word of C,
3:24 Be slaves of C the Lord.
4: 3 an opening to proclaim the mystery of C,
4:12 He is a servant of C Jesus who is always
1Thes 1: 1 to God the Father and the Lord Jesus C.
1: 3 constancy of hope in our Lord Jesus C.
2: 7 on our own importance as apostles of C.
2:14 of God in Judea which are in C Jesus.
2:19 in, before our Lord Jesus C at his coming?
3: 2 worker in preaching the gospel of C,
4:16 those who have died in C will rise first.
5: 9 salvation through our Lord Jesus C.
5:18 such is God's will for you in C Jesus.
5:23 at the coming of our Lord Jesus C.
5:28 the grace of our Lord Jesus C be with you.
2Thes 1: 1 to God our Father and the Lord Jesus C.
1: 2 from God the Father and the Lord Jesus C.
1:12 gift of our God and of the Lord Jesus C.
2: 1 Lord Jesus C and our being gathered to him,
2:14 achieve the glory of our Lord Jesus C.
2:16 May our Lord Jesus C himself,
3: 5 in the love of God and the constancy of C.
3: 6 brothers, in the name of the Lord Jesus C,
3:12 we urge them strongly in the Lord Jesus C,
3:18 grace of our Lord Jesus C be with you all.
1Tm 1: 1 C Jesus by command of God our savior and C
1: 2 from God the Father and C Jesus our Lord.
1:12 I thank C Jesus our Lord,
1:14 the faith and love which are in C Jesus.
1:15 that C Jesus came into the world to save
1:16 Jesus C might display all his patience,
2: 5 between God and men, the man C Jesus,
3:13 much assurance in their faith in C Jesus.
4: 6 you will be a good servant of C Jesus,
5:11 them from C they will want to marry.
5:21 I charge you before God, C Jesus,
6: 3 C and the teaching proper to true religion,
6:13 who gives life to all, and before C Jesus,
6:14 until our Lord Jesus C shall appear.
2Tm 1: 1 by the will of God an apostle of C Jesus
1: 2 and from C Jesus our Lord be with you.
1: 9 the grace held out to us in C Jesus before
1:13 heard me say, in faith and love in C Jesus.
1:18 C in Ephesus you know even better than I.
2: 1 in the grace which is ours in C Jesus.
2: 3 along with me as a good soldier of C Jesus.
2: 8 Remember that Jesus C,
2:10 found in C Jesus and with it eternal glory.
3:12 in C Jesus can expect to be persecuted.
3:15 faith in Jesus C leads to salvation.
4: 1 In the presence of God and of C Jesus,
Ti 1: 1 sent as an apostle of Jesus C for the sake
1: 4 God our Father, and C Jesus our Savior,
2:13 of the great God and of our Savior C Jesus.
3: 6 lavished on us through Jesus C our Savior,
Phlm 1: 1 Paul, a prisoner of C Jesus,
1: 3 God our Father and from the Lord Jesus C.
1: 6 to know all the good which is ours in C.
1: 9 ambassador of C and now a prisoner for him,
1:20 Refresh this heart of mine in C.
1:23 Epaphras, my fellow prisoner in C Jesus,
1:25 of our Lord Jesus C be with your spirit.
Heb 3: 6 but C was faithful as the Son placed over
3:14 We have become partners of C if only we
5: 5 Even C did not glorify himself with the
6: 1 teaching about C and advance to maturity,
9:11 But when C came as high priest of the good
9:14 how much more will the blood of C,
9:24 For C did not enter into a sanctuary made
9:28 so C was offered up once to take away the
10:10 of the body of Jesus C once for all.
13: 8 Jesus C is the same yesterday,
13:21 Through Jesus C may he carry out in you
13:21 To C be glory forever!
Jas 1: 1 a servant of God and of the Lord Jesus C,
2: 1 Lord Jesus C must not allow of favoritism.
1Pt 1: 1 Peter, an apostle of Jesus C,
1: 2 to Jesus C and purification with his blood.
1: 3 be the God and Father of our Lord Jesus C,
1: 3 the resurrection of Jesus C from the dead;
1: 7 glory, and honor when Jesus C appears.
1:11 Spirit of C within them was pointing to,
1:11 for C and the glories that would follow.
1:13 be conferred on you when Jesus C appears.
2: 5 acceptable to God through Jesus C.
2:21 since C suffered for you in just this way
3:15 Venerate the Lord, that is, C,
3:16 libel your way of life in C may be shamed.
3:18 reason why C died for sins once for all,
3:21 through the resurrection of Jesus C.
4: 1 C suffered in the flesh;
4:11 God is to be glorified through Jesus C:
4:14 when you are insulted for the sake of C,
5:10 called you to his everlasting glory in C,
5:14 Peace to all of you who are in C.
2Pt 1: 1 Peter, servant and apostle of Jesus C,
1: 1 power of our God and Savior Jesus C:
1: 8 in true knowledge of our Lord Jesus C.
1:11 Savior Jesus C will be richly provided for.
1:14 indications our Lord Jesus C has given me,
1:16 the coming in power of our Lord Jesus C,
2:20 recognizing the Lord and Savior Jesus C,
3:18 knowledge of our Lord and Savior Jesus C.
1Jn 1: 3 with the Father and with his Son, Jesus C.
2: 1 in the presence of the Father, Jesus C,
2:22 He who denies that Jesus is the C.
3:23 believe in the name of his Son, Jesus C,
4: 2 Jesus C come in the flesh belongs to God,
5: 1 Jesus is the C has been begotten of God.
5: 6 C it is who came through water and blood
5:20 who is true, for we are in his Son Jesus C.
2Jn 1: 3 peace from God the Father and from Jesus C,
1: 7 acknowledge Jesus C as coming in the flesh.
1: 9 in the teaching of C does not possess God,
Jude 1: 1 a servant of Jesus C and brother of James,
1: 1 and have been guarded safely in Jesus C.
1: 4 our God to sexual excess and deny Jesus C,
1:17 words of the apostles of our Lord Jesus C;
1:21 Lord Jesus C which leads to life eternal.
1:25 God our savior, through Jesus C our Lord.
Rv 1: 1 is the revelation God gave to Jesus C,
1: 2 word of God and the testimony of Jesus C.
1: 5 and from Jesus C the faithful witness,
20: 4 and reigned with C for a thousand years.
20: 6 they shall serve God and C as priests,

CHRISTIAN (4)

Acts 26:28 Paul, and you will make a C out of me!"
1Tm 5:10 Has she washed the feet of C visitors?
1Pt 4:16 If anyone suffers for being a C,
Jude 1:12 These men are blotches on your C banquets.

CHRISTIANS (3)

Acts 11:26 disciples were called C for the first time.
20: 2 words of encouragement for the C there.
Heb 13: 1 Love your fellow C always.

CHRIST'S (20)

Rom 15:20 in places where C name was already known,
15:29 you, I shall come with C full blessing.
16:10 Apelles, who proved himself in C service,
1Cor 3:23 all these are yours, and you are C,
4:10 We are fools on C account.
6:15 Would you have me take C members and make
2Cor 2:14 leads us on in C triumphal train,
2:17 We speak in C name, pure in motivation,
5:20 We implore you, in C name:
Eph 1:10 and on earth into one under C headship.
1:22 all things under C feet and has made him,
3:18 and length and height and depth of C love,
Phil 1:13 My imprisonment in C cause has become well
1:29 is your special privilege to take C part
2:30 came near to death for the sake of C work.
Col 2:11 but with C circumcision which strips off
3:15 C peace must reign in your hearts,
1Pt 1:19 or gold, but by C blood beyond all price:
4:13 in the measure that you share C sufferings.
5: 1 a witness of C sufferings and sharer in

CHRONIC (4)

Lv 15: 2 Every man who is afflicted with a c flow
15:32 for the man who is afflicted with a c flow,
15:33 period, or who is afflicted with a c flow;
Acts 28: 8 in bed, laid up with c fever and dysentery.

CHRONICLE (4)

2Chr 20:34 can be found written in the c of Jehu,
35:26 The rest of the c of Josiah,
Est 6: 1 that the c of notable events be brought in.
1Mc 16:24 are recorded in the c of his pontificate,

CHRONICLES (39)

1Kgs 11:41 recorded in the book of the c of Solomon.
14:19 the book of the c of the kings of Israel.
14:29 in the book of the c of the kings of Judah.
15: 7 in the book of the c of the kings of Judah.
15:23 in the book of the c of the kings of Judah.
15:31 the book of the c of the kings of Israel.
16: 5 the book of the c of the kings of Israel.
16:14 the book of the c of the kings of Israel.
16:20 the book of the c of the kings of Israel.
16:27 the book of the c of the kings of Israel.
22:39 the book of the c of the kings of Israel.
22:46 in the book of the c of the kings of Judah.
2Kgs 1:18 in the book of c of the kings of Israel.
8:23 in the book of the c of the kings of Judah.
10:34 the book of the c of the kings of Israel.
12:20 in the book of the c of the kings of Judah.
13: 8 the book of the c of the kings of Israel.
13:12 the book of the c of the kings of Israel.
14:15 the book of the c of the kings of Israel.
14:18 in the book of the c of the kings of Judah.
14:28 the book of the c of the kings of Israel.
15: 6 in the book of the c of the kings of Judah.
15:11 the book of the c of the kings of Israel.
15:15 the book of the c of the kings of Israel.
15:21 the book of the c of the kings of Israel.
15:26 the book of the c of the kings of Israel.
15:31 the book of the c of the kings of Israel.
15:36 in the book of the c of the kings of Judah.
16:19 in the book of the c of the kings of Judah.
20:20 in the book of the c of the kings of Judah.
21:17 in the book of the c of the kings of Judah.
21:25 in the book of the c of the kings of Judah.
23:28 in the book of the c of the kings of Judah.
24: 5 in the book of the c of the kings of Judah.
1Chr 27:24 not enter into the book of c of King David.
2Chr 33:18 written in the c of the kings of Israel.
Neh 12:22 were written down in the Book of C,
12:23 heads were written down in the Book of C,
Est 10: 2 in the c of the kings of Media and Persia.

CHRYSOLITE (7)

Ex 28:20 in the fourth row, a c,
39:13 in the fourth row a c, an onyx
Ez 1:16 wheels had the sparkling appearance of c,
10: 9 appeared to have the luster of c stone.
28:13 covering [carnelian, topaz, and beryl, c,
Dn 10: 6 His body was like c,
Rv 21:20 the sixth carnelian, the seventh c,

CHRYSOLITES (1)

Sg 5:14 His arms are rods of gold adorned with c.

CHRYSOPRASE (1)

Rv 21:20 beryl, the ninth topaz, the tenth c,

CHURCH (75)

Mt 16:18 and on this rock I will build my c,
18:17 If he ignores them, refer it to the c.
18:17 If he ignores even the c,
Acts 5:11 on the whole c and on all who heard of it.
8: 1 a great persecution of the c in Jerusalem.
8: 3 so, After that, Saul began to harass the c.
8: 4 The members of the c who had been
9:31 Galilee, and Samaria the c was at peace.
11:22 reached the ears of the c in Jerusalem,
11:26 with the c and instructed great numbers.
12: 1 to harass some of the members of the c.
12: 5 c prayed fervently to God on his behalf.
13: 1 c at Antioch certain prophets and teachers:
14:23 In each c they installed presbyters and,
15: 3 The c saw them off and they made their way
15: 4 in Jerusalem they were welcomed by that c,
15:22 in agreement with the whole Jerusalem c,
20:17 summoning the presbyters of that c.
20:28 Shepherd the c of God,

Rom 16: 1 who is a deaconess of the *c* of Cenchreae.
16:23 who is host to me and to the whole *c*.
1Cor 1: 2 to the *c* of God which is in Corinth;
6: 4 judges those who have no standing in the *c*?
6: 5 between one member of the *c* and another?
10:32 offense to Jew or Greek or to the *c* of God,
11:22 Would you show contempt for the *c* of God,
12:28 God has set up in the *c* first apostles,
14: 4 but he who prophesies builds up the *c*.
14: 5 also interpret for the upbuilding of the *c*.
14:12 to be rich in those that build up the *c*.
14:19 but in the *c* I would rather say five
14:23 come in when the whole *c* is assembled
15: 9 in fact, because I persecuted the *c* of God,
2Cor 1: 1 to the *c* of God that is at Corinth and to
1: 1 the holy ones of the *c* who live in Achaia.
8: 4 in this service to members of the *c*.
9: 1 this collection for the members of the *c*.
9:12 the needs of the members of the *c*
Gal 1:13 the *c* of God and tried to destroy it;
Eph 1:15 your love for all the members of the *c*,
1:18 be distributed among the members of the *c*,
1:22 has made him, thus exalted, head of the *c*,
3:10 through the *c*, God's manifold wisdom
3:21 to him be glory in the *c* and in Christ
5:23 just as Christ is head of his body the *c*,
5:24 As the *c* submits to Christ,
5:25 love your wives, as Christ loved the *c*.
5:27 word, to present to himself a glorious *c*,
5:29 takes care of it as Christ cares for the *c*—
5:32 I mean that it refers to Christ and the *c*.
Phil 3: 6 and so zealous that I persecuted the *c*.
4:21 in Christ Jesus to every member of the *c*.
Col 1:18 It is he who is head of the body, the *c*;
1:24 of Christ for the sake of his body, the *c*.
1:25 I became a minister of this *c* through the
1Thes 1: 1 to the *c* of the Thessalonians who belong
2Thes 1: 1 to the *c* of the Thessalonians who belong
1Tm 3: 5 how can he take care of the *c* of God?
3: 7 be well thought of by those outside the *c*,
3:15 God's household, the *c* of the living God,
5:16 *c* member has relatives who are widows,
5:16 not let them become a burden to the *c*,
Phlm 1: 2 and to the *c* that meets in your house.
Jas 5:14 He should ask for the presbyters of the *c*.
1Pt 5:13 The *c* that is in Babylon,
3Jn 1: 6 have testified to your love before the *c*.
1: 9 I did write to the *c*;
1:10 wish to do so and expels them from the *c*!
Rv 2: 1 the presiding spirit of the *c* in Ephesus,
2: 8 the presiding spirit of the *c* in Smyrna,
2:12 the presiding spirit of the *c* in Pergamum,
2:18 the presiding spirit of the *c* in Thyatira,
3: 1 the presiding spirit of the *c* in Sardis,
3: 7 presiding spirit of the *c* in Philadelphia,
3:14 the presiding spirit of the *c* in Laodicea,

CHURCHES (31)

Acts 15:41 giving the *c* there renewed assurance.
Rom 16: 4 the *c* of the Gentiles are grateful to them.
16:16 All the *c* of Christ send you greetings.
1Cor 4:17 Christ, just as I teach them in all the *c*.
7:17 This is the rule I give in all the *c*.
11:16 nor the *c* of God recognize any other usage.
16: 1 the instructions I gave the *c* of Galatia.
16:19 The *c* of Asia send you greetings.
2Cor 8: 1 of God conferred on the *c* of Macedonia.
8:18 *c* praise for his preaching of the gospel.
8:19 our traveling companion by the *c*,
8:23 our brothers too are apostles of the *c*,
8:24 we boast about you, for all the *c* to see.
11: 8 I robbed other *c*,
11:28 pressing on me, my anxiety for all the *c*.
12:13 you inferior to the other *c* except in this,
Gal 1: 2 with me send greetings to the *c* in Galatia.
1Thes 2:14 you have been made like the *c* of God in
Rv 1: 4 To the seven *c* in the province of Asia;
1:11 you now see and send it to the seven *c*:
1:20 *c*, and the seven lampstands are the seven *c*.
2: 7 has ears heed the Spirit's word to the *c*!
2:11 has ears heed the Spirit's word to the *c*!
2:17 has ears heed the Spirit's word to the *c*!
2:23 Thus shall all the *c* come to know that I
2:29 has ears heed the Spirit's word to the *c*!'
3: 6 has ears heed the Spirit's word to the *c*!'
3:13 has ears heed the Spirit's word to the *c*!
3:22 has ears heed the Spirit's word to the *c*.'"
22:16 to give you this testimony about the *c*.

CHURCH'S (2)

1Tm 5: 9 To be on the *c* roll of widows,
6: 1 of God and the *c* teaching suffer abuse.

CHURN (2)

Ez 26: 3 I will *c* up against you many nations,
26:19 when I *c* up the abyss against you,

CHURNING (2)

Ez 32: 2 the water with your feet and *c* its streams.
Hb 3:15 your steeds amid the *c* of the deep waters.

CHURNS (2)

Jb 41:23 the sea he *c* like perfume in a kettle.
Ez 26: 3 nations, even as the sea *c* up its waves;

CHUSI (1)

Jdt 7:18 and to the east opposite Egrebel, near *C*,

CHUZA (1)

Lk 8: 3 Joanna, the wife of Herod's steward *C*,

CILICIA (17)

1Kgs 10:28 Solomon's horses were imported from *C*,
2Chr 1:16 also imported horses from Egypt and *C*.
1:16 would acquire them by purchase from *C*,
Jdt 1: 7 to the inhabitants of *C* and Damascus,
1:12 territories of *C* and Damascus and Syria,
2:21 near the mountains to the north of Upper *C*.
2:25 He seized the territory of *C*,
1Mc 11:14 King Alexander was in *C* at that time,
2Mc 4:36 the king returned from the region of *C*,
Acts 6: 9 *C* and Asia) would undertake to engage
15:23 of Gentile origin in Antioch, Syria, and *C*.
15:41 He traveled throughout Syria and *C*,
21:39 "I am a Jew, a citizen of Tarsus in *C*—
22: 3 "I am a Jew, born in Tarsus in *C*,
23:34 he came from, only to learn he was from *C*.
27: 5 open sea off the coast of *C* and Pamphylia,
Gal 1:21 I entered the regions of Syria and *C*.

CINCTURE (1)

Sir 45:10 the ephod and *c* with scarlet yarn,

CINCTURES (1)

Is 3:20 the headdresses, bangles, *c*,

CINNAMON (5)

Ex 30:23 hundred and fifty shekels, of fragrant *c*;
Prv 7:17 my bed with myrrh, with aloes, and with *c*.
Sg 4:14 Nard and saffron, calamus and *c*,
Sir 24:15 Like *c*, or fragrant balm,
Rv 18:13 *c* and amomum,

CIRCLE (10)

Jos 6: 3 Have all the soldiers *c* the city,
6: 7 people to proceed in a *c* around the city,
6:11 So he had the ark of the LORD *c* the city,
2Sm 5:23 but *c* their rear and meet them before the
Jb 26:10 He has marked out a *c* on the surface of
Ps(s) 49:20 He shall join the *c* of his forebears who
Jer 15:17 sit celebrating in the *c* of merrymakers;
Mk 3:34 him at those seated in the *c* he continued,
6:21 held a birthday dinner for his court *c*,
Acts 14:20 His disciples quickly formed a *c* about him,

CIRCLED (1)

Dt 2: 1 we *c* around the highlands of Seir for a

CIRCLES (2)

Sir 33: 5 his thoughts revolve in *c*.
Jn 11:54 no longer moved about freely in Jewish *c*.

CIRCUIT (3)

Dt 34: 3 the *c* of the Jordan with the lowlands at
34:12 the *c* of the Jordan with the lowlands at
Wis 13: 2 or the swift air, or the *c* of the stars,

CIRCULAR (3)

1Kgs 7:23 it was made with a *c* rim,
2Mc 13: 5 with a *c* rim sloping down steeply on all
Ez 41: 7 There was a broad *c* passageway that led

CIRCULATED (2)

2Mc 5: 5 a false rumor *c* that Antiochus was dead.
Mt 9:26 News of this *c* throughout the district.

CIRCULATES (1)

Mt 28:15 that *c* among the Jews to this very day.

CIRCUMCISE (5)

Gn 17:11 *C* the flesh of your foreskin,
Dt 10:16 *C* your hearts,
30: 6 will *c* your hearts and the hearts of your
Jos 5: 2 "Make flint knives and *c* the Israelite
Jn 7:22 And so, even on a sabbath you *c* a man.

CIRCUMCISED (52)

Gn 17:10 every male among you shall be *c*.
17:12 when he is eight days old, shall be *c*,
17:13 and those acquired with money must be *c*.
17:23 and he *c* the flesh of their foreskins on
17:24 old when the flesh of his foreskin was *c*,
17:25 old when the flesh of his foreskin was *c*.
17:26 day Abraham and his son Ishmael were *c*;
17:27 his money from foreigners, were *c* with him.
21: 4 Isaac was eight days old, Abraham *c* him,
34:15 like us by having every male among you *c*.
34:22 male among us be *c* as they themselves are.
34:24 able-bodied man in the community, were *c*.
Ex 12:44 of it, provided you have first *c* him.
12:48 all the males among them must first be *c*,
Lv 12: 3 flesh of the boy's foreskin shall be *c*,
Jos 5: 3 and *c* the Israelites at Gibeath-haaraloth,
5: 5 Though all the men who came out were *c*,
5: 5 after the departure from Egypt were *c*.
5: 7 he raised up in their stead whom Joshua *c*,
5: 7 not having been *c* on the journey.
Jdt 14:10 He had the flesh of his foreskin *c*,
1Mc 1:60 had had their children *c* were put to death,
1:61 also and those who had *c* them were killed.
2Mc 6:10 *c* their children were publicly paraded
Jer 4: 4 For the sake of the LORD, be *c*,
9:24 an account of all those *c* in their flesh:
Jn 7:23 If a man can be *c* on the sabbath to
Acts 7: 8 father of Isaac, *c* him on the eighth day.
10:45 The *c* believers who had accompanied Peter
11: 2 some among the *c* took issue with him,
15: 1 you are *c* according to Mosaic practice,
15: 5 be *c* and told to keep the Mosaic law.
16: 3 him *c* because of the Jews of that region,
Rom 2:26 of the law, will he not be considered *c*?
3:30 It is the same God who justifies the *c*
4: 9 Does this blessedness apply only to the *c*,
4:10 Was it after he was *c* or before?
4:12 as well as the father of those *c* who are
1Cor 7:18 Was someone called after he had been *c*?
7:18 come to another who had never been *c*
7:18 He is not to be *c*.
Gal 2: 7 just as Peter was for the *c*
2:12 to avoid trouble with those who were *c*.
5: 2 I tell you that if you have yourselves *c*,
6:12 Those who are trying to force you to be *c*
6:13 They want you to be *c* only that they may
6:15 It means nothing whether one is *c* or not.
Eph 2:11 call themselves "*c*" —remember
Phil 3: 5 I was *c* on the eighth day,
Col 2:11 You were also *c* in him,
3:11 no Greek or Jew here, *c* or uncircumcised,
4:11 These are the only *c* ones among those who

CIRCUMCISION (25)

Gn 34:17 do not comply with our terms regarding *c*,
Ex 4:26 "A spouse of blood," in regard to the *c*.
1Mc 1:15 of their *c* and abandoned the holy covenant;
2:46 they also enforced *c* for any uncircumcised
Lk 1:59 for the *c* of the child on the eighth day,
2:21 When the eighth day arrived for his *c*,
Jn 7:22 Moses gave you *c* (though it did not
Acts 7: 8 then made a covenant of *c* with him,
21:21 Moses, to give up the *c* of their children,
Rom 2:25 *C*, to be sure, has value
2:27 on you who, with your written law and *c*,
2:28 True *c* is not a sign in the flesh.
2:29 one inwardly, and true *c* is of the heart;
3: 1 being a Jew, and what value is there in *c*?
4:11 he received the sign of *c* as a seal
1Cor 7:18 He should not try to hide his *c*.
7:19 *C* counts for nothing,
Gal 2: 3 who was with me, was ordered to undergo *c*,
5: 3 to all who receive *c* that they are bound
5: 6 *c* nor the lack of it counts for anything;
5:11 me, brothers, if I am still preaching *c*,
6:13 accept *c* do not follow the law themselves.
Phil 3: 3 It is we who are the *c*,
Col 2:11 not with the *c* administered by hand but
2:11 Christ's *c* which strips off the carnal body

CIRCUMFERENCE (3)

1Kgs 7:15 cubits high and twelve cubits in *c*;
7:23 across, five in height, and thirty in *c*.
2Chr 4: 2 diameter, five in depth, and thirty in *c*;

CIRCUMSPECT (1)

Sir 18:27 A wise man is *c* in all things;

CIRCUMSTANCE (2)

Wis 19:22 you stood by them in every time and *c*.
Phil 4:12 I have learned how to cope with every *c*—

CIRCUMSTANCES (9)

Jos 5: 4 at Gileath-haaraloth, under these *c*:
Acts 4:18 no *c* were they to speak the name of Jesus
Rom 4:10 What were the *c* in which it was credited?
1Cor 16:12 He will go when *c* are more favorable.
2Cor 2: 1 not to visit you again in painful *c*.
Eph 6:16 *c* hold faith up before you as your shield;
Phil 1:16 aware that my *c* provide an opportunity to
Jas 1: 9 Let the brother in humble *c* take pride in
1Pt 1:11 They investigated the times and the *c*

CIRCUMVENT (1)

Hb 1: 4 Because the wicked *c* the just;

CISTERN (34)

Gn 37:22 throw him into that *c* there in the desert;
37:24 they took him and threw him into the *c*,
37:28 up out of the *c* and took him to Egypt.

CISTERN (cont.)

37:29 to the c and saw that Joseph was not in it,
Ex 21:33 digs a c and does not cover it over again,
21:34 the owner of the c must make good by
Lv 11:36 or a c for collecting water remains clean;
1Sm 19:22 Arriving at the c of the threshing floor
2Sm 3:26 who brought him back from the c of Sirah.
17:18 in Bahurim who had a c in his courtyard.
17:19 took the cover and spread it over the c,
17:21 of the c and went on to inform King David.
23:15 the c that is by the gate of Bethlehem!"
23:16 the c that is by the gate of Bethlehem.
23:20 the lion in the c at the time of the snow.
2Kgs 18:31 and drink the water of his own c,
1Chr 11:17 the c that is by the gate at Bethlehem!"
11:18 water from the c by the gate at Bethlehem,
11:22 he went down and killed the lion in the c.
2Mc 1:19 hid it secretly in the hollow of a dry c,
10:37 Timothy had hidden in a c,
Prv 5:15 Drink water from your own c,
Is 30:14 from the hearth or dip water from the c.
36:16 tree, and drink the water of his own c,
Jer 38: 6 threw him into the c of Prince Malchiah,
38: 6 There was no water in the c,
38: 7 that they had put Jeremiah into the c.
38: 9 prophet Jeremiah, casting him into the c.
38:10 Jeremiah out of the c before he should die.
38:11 these he sent down to Jeremiah in the c,
38:13 drew him up with the ropes out of the c.
41: 7 men slew them and threw them into the c.
41: 9 The c into which Ishmael threw all the
41: 9 this c Ishmael, son of Nethaniah, filled

CISTERNS (10)

Gn 37:20 him and throw him into one of the c here;
Dt 6:11 not garner, with c that you did not dig,
1Sm 13: 6 among rocks, in caverns, and in c,
2Chr 26:10 towers in the desert and dug numerous c,
Neh 9:25 filled with all good things, c already dug,
Jdt 7:21 inhabitants of Bethulia, and the c ran dry,
8:31 the Lord may send rain to fill up our c,
Jer 2:13 They have dug themselves c,
2:13 have dug themselves cisterns, broken c,
14: 3 but when they come to the c They find no

CITADEL (36)

1Kgs 16:18 he entered the c of the royal palace and
Neh 1: 1 year, I was in the c of Susa when Hanani,
7: 2 and Hananiah, the commander of the c,
1Mc 1:33 and strong towers, and it became their c.
1:36 c became an ambush against the sanctuary,
3:45 trampled on, and foreigners were in the c;
4: 2 Some men from the c were their guides.
4:41 appointed men to attack those in the c,
6:18 The men in the c were hemming in Israel
6:20 fifty they assembled and stormed the c,
6:26 the c in Jerusalem in order to capture it,
6:32 the c and moved his camp to Beth-zechariah,
9:52 the city of Beth-zur, Gazara and the c,
9:53 put them in custody in the c at Jerusalem.
10: 6 the hostages in the c be released to him.
10: 7 The men in the c were struck with fear
10:32 yield my authority over the c in Jerusalem,
11:20 men of Judea to attack the c in Jerusalem,
11:21 him that Jonathan was besieging the c.
11:41 withdraw his troops from the c of Jerusalem
12:36 a high barrier between the c and the city,
12:36 that would isolate the c and so prevent
13:21 The men in the c sent messengers to Trypho,
13:49 The men in the c in Jerusalem were
13:50 from the c and cleansed it of impurities.
13:51 entered the c with shouts of jubilation,
13:52 of the temple hill alongside the c,
14: 7 master of Gazara, Beth-zur, and the c.
14: 7 He cleansed the c of its impurities;
14:36 who had built for themselves a c
14:37 In this c he stationed Jewish soldiers,
15:28 Joppa and Gazara and the c of Jerusalem;
2Mc 4:28 of Sostratus, the commandant of the c,
5: 5 being taken, Menelaus took refuge in the c.
15:31 the altar, and sent for those in the c.
15:35 up Nicanor's head on the wall of the c,

CITHARAS (1)

2Sm 6: 5 their strength, with singing and with c,

CITIES (428)

Gn 10:10 The chief c of his kingdom were Babylon,
13:12 while Lot settled among the c of the Plain,
19:25 He overthrew those c and the whole Plain,
19:25 of the c and the produce of the soil.
19:29 when God destroyed the C of the Plain,
19:29 overthrew the c where Lot had been living.
41:56 Joseph opened all the c that had grain and
Ex 1:11 Pharaoh the supply c of Pithom and Raamses.
Lv 25:32 "In levitical c the Levites shall always
25:33 c that had been sold and not redeemed,
25:34 to their c shall not be sold at all;
26:25 you then huddle together in your walled c,
26:31 your c and devastate your sanctuaries,
26:33 countryside desolate and your c deserted.
Nm 21: 2 people into my hand, I will doom their c."
21: 3 Canaanites, they doomed them and their c.
21:28 It consumed the c of Moab and swallowed up
35: 2 they shall give the Levites c for homes,
35: 2 as well as pasture lands around the c.
35: 3 The c shall serve them to dwell in,
35: 4 The pasture lands of the c to be assigned
35: 5 serve them as the pasture lands of their c.
35: 6 are the c you shall give to the Levites:
35: 6 the six c of asylum which you must
35: 6 refuge, and in addition forty-two other c—
35: 7 a total of forty-eight c with their
35: 8 the c from the property of the Israelites,
35: 8 so that each group will cede c to the
35:11 yourselves cities to serve as c of asylum,
35:12 These c shall serve you as places of
35:13 Six c of asylum shall you assign:
35:15 These six c of asylum shall serve not only
Dt 1:22 road we must follow and the c we must take.'
1:28 their c are large and fortified to the sky;
2:34 we seized all his c and doomed them all,
2:35 livestock and the loot of the captured c.
2:37 Wadi Jabbok, nor the c of the highlands.
3: 4 At that time we captured all his c,
3: 4 sixty c in all,
3: 5 All the c were fortified with high walls
3: 6 Heshbon, so also here we doomed all the c,
3:10 comprising all the c of the plateau and
3:10 plateau and all Gilead and all the c
3:12 highlands of Gilead, with the c therein.
4:41 three c in the region east of the Jordan,
4:42 save his life by fleeing to one of these c:
6:10 with fine, large c that you did not build,
9: 1 having large c fortified to the sky,
13:13 "If, in any of the c which the LORD,
19: 1 and are settled in their c and houses,
19: 2 apart three c in the land which the LORD,
19: 5 refuge in one of these c to save his life.
19: 7 is why I order you to set apart three c.
19: 9 then add three c to these three.
19:11 and then takes refuge in one of these c,
20:16 in the c of those nations which the LORD,
21: 2 go out and measure the distances to the c
Jos 9:17 the Israelites came to their c of Gibeon,
10:19 Do not allow them to escape to their c,
10:20 escaped from them into the fortified c,
11:12 with their c and put them to the sword,
11:13 by fire any of the c built on raised sites,
11:14 and livestock of these c as their booty;
11:21 fulfilled the doom on them and on their c,
13:10 and Dibon, with the rest of the c of Sihon,
13:21 and the other c of the tableland and,
13:23 These c and their villages were the
13:25 included Jazer, all the c of Gilead,
13:28 These c and their villages were the
13:30 of Jair, which are sixty c in Bashan.
13:31 Edrei, once the royal c of Og in Bashan,
14: 4 no share of the land except c to live in,
14:12 Anakim are there, with large fortified c,
15: 9 extended to the c of Mount Ephron,
15:21 The c of the tribe of the Judahites in the
15:32 total of twenty-nine c with their villages.
15:36 fourteen c and their villages.
15:41 sixteen c and their villages,
15:44 nine c and their villages.
15:51 eleven c and their villages.
15:54 nine c and their villages.
15:57 ten c and their villages.
15:59 six c and their villages.
15:59 eleven c and their villages.
15:60 two c and their villages.
15:62 six c and their villages.
17: 9 The c that belonged to Ephraim from among
17: 9 belonged to Ephraim from among the c
17:12 Manassehites could not conquer these c,
18: 9 listed its c in writing in seven sections
18:21 Now the c belonging to the clans of the
18:24 twelve c and their villages.
18:28 fourteen c and their villages.
19: 6 thirteen c and their villages.
19: 7 four c and their villages,
19: 8 these c as far as Baalath-beer (that is,
19:15 there were twelve c and their villages to
19:22 These sixteen c and their villages were
19:30 there were twenty-two c and their villages
19:35 The fortified c were Ziddim,
19:38 nineteen c and their villages,
19:48 These c and their villages were the
20: 2 c of which I spoke to them through Moses,
20: 4 To one of these c the killer shall flee,
20: 9 These were the designated c to which any
21: 2 Moses, that c be given us to dwell in,
21: 3 the following c with their pasture lands.
21: 4 thirteen c by lot from the tribes of Judah,
21: 5 The rest of the Kohathites obtained ten c
21: 6 The Gershonites obtained thirteen c by lot
21: 7 twelve c from the tribes of Reuben,
21: 8 These c with their pasture lands the
21: 9 they designated the following c,
21:16 nine c from the two tribes mentioned.
21:17 four c of Gibeon with its pasture lands,
21:19 These c which with their pasture lands
21:20 by lot, from the tribe of Ephraim, four c.
21:23 four c of Elteke with its pasture lands,
21:25 two c of Taanach with its pasture lands
21:26 These c which with their pasture lands
21:27 from the half-tribe of Manasseh two c:
21:28 four c of Kishion with its pasture lands,
21:30 four c of Mishal with its pasture lands,
21:32 and from the tribe of Naphtali, three c:
21:33 These c which with their pasture lands
21:34 four c of Jokneam with its pasture lands,
21:36 Jordan, from the tribe of Reuben, four c:
21:38 from the tribe of Gad a total of four c:
21:40 The c which were allotted to the Merarite
21:41 Thus the total number of c within the
21:42 c went the pasture lands round about it.
24:13 not tilled and c which you had not built,
Jgs 10: 4 possessed thirty c in the land of Gilead;
11:26 and all the c on the banks of the Arnon?
11:33 c in all) and as far as Abel-Keramin.
20:14 assembled from their other c to Gibeah,
20:15 c on that occasion was twenty-six thousand,
20:48 to the sword the inhabitants of the c,
20:48 destroyed by fire all the c they came upon.
21:23 where they rebuilt and occupied the c.
1Sm 6:18 corresponded to the number of all the c
6:18 including fortified c and open villages.
7:14 The c from Ekron to Gath which the
7:14 c from the dominion of the Philistines.
18: 6 each of the c of Israel to meet King Saul,
30:29 cities, to those in the Kenite c,
31: 7 dead, they too abandoned their c and fled.
31: 7 the Philistines came and lived in those c.
2Sm 2: 1 "Shall I go up into one of the c of Judah?"
2: 3 and they dwelt in the c near Hebron.
10:12 sake of our people and the c of our God;
12:31 This is what he did to all the Ammonite c.
20: 6 c and take shelter while we look on."
24: 7 to all the c of the Hivites and Canaanites,
1Kgs 4:13 walled c with gates barred with bronze;
8:37 people besieges them in one of their c;
9:11 gave Hiram twenty c in the land of Galilee.
9:12 Tyre to see the c Solomon had given him,
9:13 said, "What are these c you have given me,
9:19 desert of Judah, all his c for supplies,
9:19 c supplies, c for chariots and for horses,
10:26 c and to the king's service in Jerusalem.
12:17 the Israelites who lived in the c of Judah.
13:32 c of Samaria shall certainly come to pass."
15:20 of his troops against the c of Israel.
15:23 and accomplishments, and the c he built,
20:34 c which my father took from your father,
22:39 the ivory palace and all the c he built,
2Kgs 3:25 down the Moabites, and destroying the c;
13:25 the c which Hazael had taken in battle
13:25 times, and thus recovered the c of Israel.
17: 6 river of Gozan, and in the c of the Medes.
17: 9 the watchtowers as well as the walled c.
17:24 and settled them in the c of Samaria in
17:24 possession of Samaria and dwelt in its c.
17:26 deported and settled in the c of Samaria
17:29 in the various c in which they were living;
18: 8 and walled c of the Philistines,
18:11 river of Gozan, and in the c of the Medes.
18:13 the fortified c of Judah and captured them.
19:13 of Arpad, or the kings of the c Sepharvaim,
19:25 reduce fortified c into heaps of ruins,
23: 5 high places in the c of Judah
23: 8 in all the priests from the c of Judah,
23:19 high places near the c of Samaria
1Chr 2:22 twenty-three c in the land of Gilead.
2:23 is, Kenath and its towns, sixty c in all,
4:31 these were their c and their villages.
4:32 five c,
6:45 had thirteen c with their pasture lands.
6:46 The other Kohathites obtained ten c by lot
6:47 thirteen c from the tribes of Issachar,
6:48 twelve c by lot from the tribes of Reuben,
6:49 c with their pasture lands to the Levites,
6:51 c by lot from the tribe of Ephraim.
9: 2 The first to settle again in their c and
10: 7 in the rout, they left their c and fled;
13: 2 Levites from their c with pasture lands,
18: 8 away from Tibhath and Cun, c of Hadadezer,
19: 7 from their c and came out for war.
19:13 the sake of our people and the c of our God;
20: 3 dealt with all the c of the Ammonites.
27:25 Over the stores in the country, the c,
2Chr 1:14 chariot c and with the king in Jerusalem.
8: 2 built up the c which Huram had given him,
8: 4 in the desert region and all the supply c,
8: 5 Lower Beth-horon, fortified c with walls,
8: 6 all the supply c belonging to Solomon,
8: 6 c for the chariots, the c for the horsemen,
9:25 the chariot c and to the king in Jerusalem.
10:17 Israelites who lived in the c of Judah.
11: 5 Jerusalem and built fortified c in Judah.
11:10 were fortified c in Judah and Benjamin.
11:23 and Benjamin, in all the fortified c;
12: 4 c of Judah and came as far as Jerusalem.
13:19 pursued Jeroboam and took c from him:
14: 4 and incense stands from all the c of Judah,
14: 5 He built fortified c in Judah,
14: 6 build these c and surround them with walls,
14:13 Judahites conquered all the c around Gerar,

14:13 they despoiled all the c,
15: 8 from the c he had taken in the highlands
16: 4 of his troops against the c of Israel.
16: 4 Abel-maim, and all the store c of Naphtali.
17: 2 forces in all the fortified c of Judah,
17: 2 in the c of Ephraim which his father Asa
17: 7 and Micaiah, to teach in the c of Judah.
17: 9 the c of Judah and taught among the people.
17:12 He built strongholds and store c in Judah.
17:13 carried out many works in the c of Judah,
17:19 in the fortified c throughout all Judah.
19: 5 the land, in all the fortified c of Judah,
19:10 brethren living in their c bring to you,
20: 4 the c of Judah they came to seek the LORD.
21: 3 together with fortified c in Judah,
23: 2 Levites from all the c of Judah
24: 5 "Go out to all the c of Judah and collect
25:13 the c of Judah from Samaria to Beth-horon.
26: 6 Jabneh and Ashdod [and built c in the
27: 4 he built c in the hill country of Judah,
28:18 c of the foothills and the Negeb of Judah;
31: 1 c of Judah and smashed the sacred pillars,
31: 1 Israelites returned to their various c,
31: 6 c of Judah also brought in tithes of oxen,
31:15 Under him in the priestly c were Eden,
31:19 lived on the lands attached to their c,
32: 1 He invaded Judah, besieged the fortified c,
32:29 He built c for himself,
33:14 officers in all the fortified c of Judah.
34: 6 He did likewise in the c of Manasseh,
Ezr 2:70 and the temple slaves dwelt in their c.
2:70 Thus all the Israelites dwelt in their c.
3: 1 the Israelites had settled in their c,
10:14 then let all those in our c who have taken
Neh 7:72 all Israel took up residence in their c.
8:15 made throughout their c and in Jerusalem:
9:25 They captured fortified c and fertile land;
10:38 take the tithe in all the c of our service.
11: 1 the other nine would remain in the other c.
11: 3 (In the c of Judah dwelt lay Israelites,
11:20 Levites, were in all the other c of Judah,
12:44 collect from the fields of the various c
Jdt 1: 9 to all those in Samaria and its c,
1:14 his chariots, and took possession of his c.
2:27 their flocks and herds, despoiled their c,
3: 4 Our c and their inhabitants are also at
3: 6 stationed garrisons in the fortified c;
3: 7 The people of these c and all the
4:12 the c of their inheritance to be ruined,
5: 3 Which c do they inhabit?
5:18 and their c were occupied by their enemies.
Est 9: 2 The Jews mustered in their c throughout
1Mc 1:19 c in the land of Egypt were captured,
1:29 the Mysian commander to the c of Judah,
1:44 letters to Jerusalem and to the c of Judah,
1:51 ordered the c of Judah to offer sacrifices,
1:54 c of Judah they built pagan altars.
1:58 who were caught, each month, in the c.
3: 8 c of Judah destroying the impious there.
5:26 of these are large, fortified c—
5:27 have been imprisoned in other c of Gilead.
5:36 Maked, Bosor, and the other c of Gilead.
5:68 their c he returned to the land of Judah.
11: 2 in the c opened their gates to welcome him,
11: 3 But when Ptolemy entered the c,
11: 8 King Ptolemy took possession of the c
11:18 and his men in the fortified c were killed
11:60 through West-of-Euphrates and its c,
14:10 He supplied the c with food and equipped
14:17 and was master of the country and the c,
14:33 He fortified the c of Judea,
14:34 these c he resettled with Jews,
15: 4 it and laid waste many c in my realm.
15:19 against them or their c or their country,
15:28 these are c of my kingdom.
15:30 give up the c you have seized and the
15:31 more for the tribute money of the c.
15:35 the men of these c were doing great harm
15:35 to pay you a hundred talents for these c."
16:14 As Simon was inspecting the c of the
2Mc 3: 8 to visit the c of Coelesyria and Phoenicia,
4:30 c had been given as a gift to Antiochis,
4:32 vessels in Tyre and in the neighboring c.
6: 8 c to act in the same way against the Jews:
8:11 he immediately sent word to the coastal c,
Jb 15:28 with fat, He shall dwell in ruinous c,
Ps(s) 9: 7 of the c you uprooted has perished.
48:12 Zion be glad, Let the c of Judah rejoice,
69:36 will save Zion and rebuild the c of Judah.
97: 8 and the c of Judah rejoice because of your
Sir 28:14 It destroys walled c,
Is 1: 7 country is waste, your c burnt with fire;
6:11 Until the c are desolate,
14:17 Who made the world a desert, razed its c,
17: 2 Her c shall be forever abandoned,
17: 9 On that day his strong c shall be like
19:18 On that day there shall be five c in the
36: 1 the fortified c of Judah and captured them.
37:13 of Arpad, or a king of the c of Sepharvaim,
37:26 reduce fortified c into heaps of ruins,
40: 9 not to cry out and say to the c of Judah:
42:11 Let the steppe and its c cry out,
44:26 Be inhabited; to the c of Judah:
54: 3 nations and shall people the desolate c.
61: 4 shall raise up And restore the ruined c,
64: 9 Your holy c have become a desert,
Jer 1:15 all around and opposite all the c of Judah.
2:15 his c are charred ruins,
2:28 For as numerous as your c are your gods,
4: 5 "Fall in, let us march to the fortified c."
4: 7 till your c lie waste and empty.
4:16 their war cry against the c of Judah."
4:26 with all its c destroyed before the LORD,
4:29 All the c are abandoned,
5: 6 them, Leopards keep watch round their c:
7:17 see what they are doing in the c of Judah,
7:34 In the c of Judah and in the streets of
8:14 Let us form ranks and enter the walled c,
9:10 The c of Judah I will make into a waste,
10:22 c of Judah into a desert haunt of jackals.
11: 6 c of Judah and in the streets of Jerusalem:
11:12 Then the c of Judah and the citizens of
11:13 For as numerous as your c are your gods,
13:19 The c of the Negeb are besieged,
17:26 To it people will come from the c of Judah
20:16 c which the LORD relentlessly overthrew;
25:18 [Jerusalem, the c of Judah,
26: 2 speak to the people of all the c of Judah
31:21 O virgin Israel, turn back to these your c.
31:23 their lot in the land of Judah and her c,
31:24 Judah and all her c,
32:44 in the c of Judah and of the hill country,
32:44 in the c of the foothills and of the Negeb,
33:10 and in the c of Judah,
33:12 and in all its c there shall again be
33:13 In the c of the hill country,
33:13 of Jerusalem, and in the c of Judah,
34: 1 were all attacking Jerusalem and all her c:
34: 7 Jerusalem and the remaining c of Judah,
34: 7 were left of the fortified c of Judah.
34:22 the c of Judah I will turn into a desert
36: 6 the men of Judah who come up from their c.
36: 9 all who came from Judah's c to Jerusalem.
40: 5 has appointed ruler over the c of Judah;
40:10 jars, and to settle in the c they occupied.
44: 2 on Jerusalem and the other c of Judah.
44: 6 c of Judah and the streets of Jerusalem,
44:17 c of Judah and the streets of Jerusalem.
44:21 c of Judah and the streets of Jerusalem:
47: 2 all that is in it, the c and their people.
48: 9 Its c are turned into ruins where no one
48:15 The ravager of Moab and his c advances,
48:24 on all the c of Moab, far and near.
48:28 Leave the c, dwell in the crags,
48:41 C are taken, strongholds seized:
49: 1 why have his people settled in Gad's c?
49: 2 her daughter c shall be destroyed by fire.
49:13 and all her c shall become ruins forever.
50:32 I will kindle in his c a fire that shall
51:43 Her c have become a desert,
Lam 5:11 the enemy, the maidens in the c of Judah;
Bar 2:23 I will make to cease from the c of Judah
4:32 the c where your children were enslaved,
Ez 6: 6 In all your dwelling places c shall be
12:20 Inhabited c shall be in ruins,
19: 7 their strongholds, their c he wasted.
25: 9 the shoulder of Moab totally of its c,
26:19 like c that are no longer inhabited,
29:12 its c shall be the most deserted of cities
30: 7 her c shall be the most desolate of all.
30:17 the c themselves shall go into captivity.
35: 4 Your c I will turn into ruins,
35: 9 and leave your c without inhabitants;
36: 4 the desolate ruins and abandoned c,
36:10 c shall be repeopled,
36:33 all your crimes, I will repeople the c,
36:35 "The c that were in ruins,
36:38 the c which were in ruins shall be filled
39: 9 in the c of Israel go out and burn weapons:
45: 5 temple, that they may have c to live in.
Hos 8:14 many c, but I will send fire upon his cities,
11: 6 his c and end by consuming his solitudes.
13:10 king, that he may rescue you in all your c?
Am 4: 6 your teeth clean of food in all your c,
4: 8 Though two or three c staggered to one
9:14 shall rebuild and inhabit their ruined c,
Ob 1:20 Sepharad shall occupy the c of the Negeb.
Mi 5:10 I will demolish the c of your land and
5:13 poles from your midst, and destroy your c.
Zep 1:16 and battle alarm Against fortified c,
3: 6 Their c are devastated,
Zec 1:12 mercy for Jerusalem and the c of Judah
1:17 My c shall again overflow with prosperity;
7: 7 surrounding c were inhabited and at peace,
8:20 come peoples, the inhabitants of many c;
9: 1 place, For the c of Aram are the LORD's,
Mt 4:25 followed him came from Galilee, the Ten C,
Mk 5:20 the Ten C what Jesus had done for him.
7:31 of Galilee, into the district of the Ten C.
Lk 13:22 He went through c and towns teaching
Acts 26:11 them that I pursued them even to foreign c.
2Pt 2: 6 He blanketed the c of Sodom and Gomorrah
Rv 16:19 parts, and the other Gentile c also fell.

CITIZEN (9)

Tb 1:19 But a certain c of Nineveh informed the
Jer 33:10 are now deserted, without man, without c,
Acts 21:39 "I am a Jew, a c of Tarsus in Cilicia
22:25 it legal to flog a Roman c without a trial?"
22:26 This man is a Roman c!"
22:27 Are you a Roman c?"
22:28 "Ah," said Paul, "but I am a c by birth!"
22:29 Paul he had restrained a c of Rome.
23:27 When I learned that he was a Roman c,

CITIZENS (69)

Gn 23: 7 began to bow low before the local c,
23:12 after bowing low before the local c,
Lv 20: 2 Let his fellow c stone him.
20: 4 Even if his fellow c connive at such a
Dt 21:21 all his fellow c shall stone him to death.
Jgs 9: 2 this question to all the c of Shechem:
9: 3 c of Shechem sympathized with Abimelech,
9: 6 Then all the c of Shechem and all
9: 7 "Hear me, c of Shechem,
9:18 his handmaid, king over the c of Shechem,
9:20 to devour the c of Shechem and Beth-millo,
9:20 from the c and from Beth-millo
9:23 between Abimelech and the c of Shechem,
9:24 who killed them, and upon the c of Shechem,
9:24 from the c and from Beth-millo
9:25 The c of Shechem then set men in ambush
9:26 The c of Shechem put their trust in him,
9:39 c of Shechem and fought against Abimelech.
9:46 all the c of Migdal-shechem went into the
9:47 c of Migdal-shechem were gathered together.
9:49 that every one of the c of Migdal-shechem,
9:51 and women, in a word all the c of the city,
20: 5 But the c of Gibeah rose up against me by
Ru 4:10 not perish among his kinsmen and fellow c.
1Sm 23:12 "Will the c of Keilah deliver me and my
2Sm 21:12 son Jonathan from the c of Jabesh-gilead,
1Kgs 21:11 His fellow c— the elders and the nobles
Tb 14:15 done against the c of Nineveh and Assyria.
Jdt 13:12 When the c heard her voice,
1Mc 11:60 at Ashkalon, the c welcomed him with pomp.
14:20 "The rulers and the c of Sparta send
2Mc 4:50 the chief plotter against his fellow c.
5: 6 slaughtered his fellow c without mercy,
5:23 his fellow c worse than the others did.
5:23 Out of hatred for the Jewish c,
6: 8 At the suggestion of the c of Ptolemais,
9:19 "To my esteemed Jewish c,
15:30 soul the chief defender of his fellow c,
Jer 4: 4 hearts, O men of Judah and c of Jerusalem;
8: 1 and the bones of the c of Jerusalem will
11: 2 the men of Judah and to the c of Jerusalem,
11: 9 the men of Judah and the c of Jerusalem.
11:12 Then the cities of Judah and the c of
13:13 and prophets, and all the c of Jerusalem.
17:20 you c of Jerusalem who enter these gates!
17:25 the men of Judah, and the c of Jerusalem.
18:11 to the men of Judah and the c of Jerusalem:
19: 3 LORD, kings of Judah and c of Jerusalem:
23:14 are all like Sodom, its c like Gomorrah.
25: 2 people of Judah and all the c of Jerusalem:
26:15 on yourselves, on this city and its c.
32:32 the men of Judah and the c of Jerusalem,
35:13 the men of Judah and to the c of Jerusalem:
35:17 I will bring upon Judah and all the c of
36:31 against them and the c of Jerusalem and
42:18 was poured out upon the c of Jerusalem,
Bar 1:15 shame, we men of Judah and c of Jerusalem,
Ez 27: 8 C of Sidon and Arvad served as your oarsmen;
Mi 6:16 you up to ruin, and your c to derision;
7:13 the land shall be a waste because of its c,
Mt 12:41 the c of Nineveh will rise with the
13:38 world, the good seed the c of the kingdom.
Lk 11:32 the c of Nineveh will rise along with the
19:14 But his fellow c despised him,
Acts 16:37 us into jail, although we are Roman c!
16:38 alarmed at hearing they were Roman c.
17:21 (Indeed, all Athenian c,
19:35 C of Ephesus,"
Eph 2:19 you are fellow c of the saints and members
Heb 8:11 not teach their fellow c or their brothers,

CITIZENSHIP (2)

Acts 22:28 "It cost me quite a sum to get my c."
Phil 3:20 As you well know, we have our c in heaven;

CITY (948)

Gn 4:17 Cain also became the founder of a c,
10:12 Calah, the latter being the principal c.
11: 4 a c and a tower with its top in the sky,
11: 5 the c and the tower that the men had built.
11: 8 the earth, and they stopped building the c.
18:24 there were fifty innocent people in the c;
18:26 fifty innocent people in the c of Sodom,
18:28 destroy the whole c because of its five?"
19:12 and all who belong to you in the c—
19:13 reaching the LORD against those in the c
19:14 "the LORD is about to destroy the c."
19:15 be swept away in the punishment of the c."
19:16 and led them to safety outside the c.

CITY (cont.)
24:10 his way to the c of Nahor in Aram Naharaim.
24:11 the camels kneel by the well outside the c.
26:33 hence the name of the c,
33:18 Jacob arrived safely at the c of Shechem,
33:18 Canaan, and he encamped in sight of the c.
34:25 advanced against the c without any trouble,
34:27 up the slaughter and sacked the c
34:28 was in the c and in the country around.
36:32 the name of his c was Dinhabah.
36:34 the name of his c was Avith.
36:39 the name of his c was Pau.
44: 4 c when Joseph said to his head steward:
44:13 his donkey, they returned to the c.
Ex 9:29 the c I will extend my hands to the LORD;
9:33 presence and had gone out of the c,
Lv 14:40 and cast in an unclean place outside the c.
14:41 dumped in an unclean place outside the c.
14:45 away to an unclean place outside the c.
14:53 away over the countryside outside the c.
Nm 21:28 Heshbon and a blaze from the c of Sihon;
22:36 meet him at the boundary c Ir-Moab
35: 4 cubits from the c walls in each direction.
35: 5 cubits outside the c along each side
35: 5 with the c lying in the center.
35:25 to the c of asylum where he took refuge;
35:26 the c of asylum where he has taken refuge,
35:28 the homicide was bound to stay in his c
35:32 to allow a refugee to leave his c
Dt 2:36 Arnon and from the c in the wadi itself,
2:36 no c was too well fortified for us to whom
3: 7 of each c we took as booty for ourselves.
13:14 led astray the inhabitants of their c
13:16 that c to the sword, dooming the city
13:17 you shall burn the c with all its spoils
17: 5 out to your c gates and stone him to death.
19:12 the elders of his own c shall send for him
20:10 "When you march up to attack a c,
20:15 any c at a considerable distance from you,
20:19 "When you are at war with a c and have to
20:20 to reduce the c that is resisting you.
21: 3 established which c is nearest the corpse,
21: 3 the elders of that c shall take a heifer
21: 6 Then all the elders of that c nearest the
21:19 to the elders at the gate of his home c,
21:20 where they shall say to those c elders,
22:15 and bring it to the elders at the c gate.
22:17 out the cloth before the elders of the c.
22:18 Then these c elders shall take the man and
22:23 "If within the c a man comes upon a
22:24 of the c and there stone them to death:
22:24 cry out for help though she was in the c,
25: 8 of his c shall summon him and admonish him.
28: 3 "May you be blessed in the c,
28:16 "May you be cursed in the c,
34: 3 with the lowlands at Jericho, c of palms,
34:12 with the lowlands at Jericho, c of palms,
Jos 2:15 she lived in a house built into the c wall.
3:16 Adam, a c in the direction of Zarethan;
6: 3 Have all the soldiers circle the c,
6: 4 seventh day march around the c seven times,
6: 5 The wall of the c will collapse,
6: 7 to proceed in a circle around the c,
6:11 he had the ark of the LORD circle the c,
6:14 around the c once before returning to camp;
6:15 the c seven times in the same manner;
6:15 did they march around the c seven times.
6:16 has given you the c and everything in it.
6:20 the c in a frontal attack and took it.
6:21 to the sword all living creatures in the c:
6:24 The c itself they burned with all that was
6:26 be the man who attempts to rebuild this c,
7: 5 front of the c gate till they broke ranks,
8: 1 of Ai into your power, with his people, c,
8: 2 Set an ambush behind the c."
8: 4 "See that you ambush the c from the rear,
8: 5 of the people and I will come up to the c,
8: 6 until we have drawn them away from the c,
8: 7 from ambush and take possession of the c,
8: 8 When you have taken the c,
8:11 were drawn up in position before the c,
8:12 between Bethel and Ai, west of the c
8:13 north of the c and the ambush west of it,
8:14 that there was an ambush behind the c.
8:16 the c had been called out to pursue them.
8:17 Since they were drawn away from the c,
8:17 and the c was open and unprotected.
8:18 out the javelin in his hand toward the c,
8:19 from their post, rushed in, captured the c,
8:20 the smoke from the c was already sky-high.
8:21 Israelites saw that the c had been taken
8:22 those in the c came out to intercept them,
8:24 and put to the sword those inside the c.
8:27 the livestock and the spoil of that c,
8:29 and cast at the entrance of the c gate,
10: 1 Joshua had done to that c and its king as
10: 2 a royal c, larger even than the city of Ai,
10:28 He fulfilled the doom on the c,
11:19 no c made peace with the Israelites;
13: 9 Wadi Arnon and the c in the wadi itself,
13:16 Wadi Arnon, and the c in the wadi itself,
16: 9 the villages that belonged to each c
17: 8 an Ephraimite c on the border of Manasseh.
18:14 which c belonged to the Judahites.
18:28 Zela, Haeleph, the Jebusite c (that is,
19:29 to Ramah and to the fortress c of Tyre;
19:50 they gave him the c which he requested,
19:50 He rebuilt the c and made it his home.
20: 4 and standing at the entrance of the c gate,
20: 6 he shall live on in that c till the death
20: 6 back home to his own c from which he fled."
21:12 belonging to the c had been given to Caleb,
21:13 the c of asylum for homicides at Hebron,
21:21 the c of asylum for homicides at Shechem
21:27 the c of asylum for homicides at Golan,
21:32 the c of asylum for homicides at Kedesh in
21:36 the c of asylum for homicides at Bezer
21:38 the c of asylum for homicides at Ramoth in
Jgs 1: 8 then they destroyed the c by fire.]
1:16 came up with the Judahites from the c
1:17 After having doomed the c to destruction,
1:24 a man coming out of the c and said to him,
1:24 said to him, "Show us a way into the c,
1:25 He showed them a way into the c,
1:26 where he built a c and called it Luz,
3:13 taking possession of the c of palms.
8:16 He took the elders of the c,
8:17 tower of Penuel and slew the men of the c.
8:27 of the gold and placed it in his c Ophrah.
9:30 Ebed, had said, Zebul, the ruler of the c,
9:31 and are stirring up the c against you.
9:33 tomorrow morning, make a raid on the c.
9:35 and stood at the entrance of the c gate.
9:43 till he saw the people leave the c,
9:44 in and stood by the entrance of the c gate,
9:45 entire day Abimelech fought against the c,
9:45 its inhabitants and demolished the c,
9:51 was a strong tower in the middle of the c,
9:51 in a word all the citizens of the c,
12: 7 died and was buried in his c in Gilead.
14:18 the sun set, the men of the c said to him,
16: 2 an ambush at the c gate all night long.
16: 3 doors of the c gate and the two gateposts,
17: 8 From that c he set out to find another
18:27 to the sword and destroyed their c by fire.
18:28 since the c was far from Sidon and they
18:28 The Danites then rebuilt the c,
18:29 the name of the c was formerly Laish.
19:11 let us turn off to this c of the Jebusites
19:12 will not turn off to a c of foreigners,
19:15 the public square of the c he had entered,
19:17 traveler in the public square of the c,
19:22 enjoying themselves, the men of the c,
20:11 were leagued together against the c,
20:21 Benjaminites came out of the c and felled
20:32 them away from the c onto the highways.
20:32 drawn away from the c onto the highways,
20:34 Israel, and advanced against the c itself.
20:37 it, and put the whole c to the sword.
20:38 signal they were to send up from the c.
20:40 signal column began to rise up from the c.
20:40 Benjamin looked back and saw the whole c
20:42 been in the c were spreading destruction.
21: 9 of the inhabitants of that c were present.
Ru 1:19 there, the whole c was astir over them,
2:18 into the c and showed to her mother-in-law.
3:15 her lift the bundle, and left for the c.
4: 2 of the c and asked them to sit nearby.
1Sm 1: 3 regularly went on pilgrimage from his c
4:13 c to divulge his news, which put the whole c
5: 6 the c and its vicinity with hemorrhoids;
5: 6 he brought upon the c a great and deadly
5: 9 the LORD threw the c into utter turmoil:
5:10 but as it entered that c,
5:11 A deadly panic had seized the whole c,
5:12 out-cry from the c went up to the heavens.
8:22 of Israel, "Each of you go to his own c."
9: 6 There is a man of God in this c,
9:10 went to the c where the man of God lived.
9:11 As they were going up the ascent to the c,
9:12 just today he came to the c,
9:13 When you enter the c,
9:14 So they went up to the c.
9:25 came down from the high place into the c,
9:26 he and Samuel went outside the c together.
10: 5 As you enter that c, you will meet a band
15: 5 Saul went to the c of Amalek,
16: 4 c came trembling to meet him and inquired,
20: 6 him go on short notice to his c Bethlehem,
20:28 urgently asked me to let him go to his c,
20:29 we are to have a clan sacrifice in our c,
20:36 arrow beyond him in the direction of the c.
20:40 and said to him, "Go, take them to the c."
21: 1 way, while Jonathan went back into the c.
22:19 put the priestly c of Nob to the sword,
23: 7 for he has entered a c with gates and bars."
23:10 to Keilah, to destroy the c on my account.
27: 5 your servant live with you in the royal c?"
28: 3 by all Israel, was buried in his c,
30: 1 the Negeb and Ziklag, had stormed the c,
30: 2 the women and all who were in the c,
30: 3 David and his men arrived at the c to find
30:26 spoil to the elders of Judah, city by c,
2Sm 3:27 Joab took him aside within the c gate as
5: 7 of Zion, which is the C of David.
5: 9 which was called the C of David;
6:10 the LORD brought to him in the C of David,
6:12 into the C of David amid festivities.
6:16 of the LORD was entering the C of David,
10: 3 Is it not rather to explore the c,
10: 8 formation at the entrance of their c gate,
10:14 fled from Abishai and withdrew into the c.
11:16 So while Joab was besieging the c,
11:17 men of the c made a sortie against Joab,
11:20 'Why did you go near the c to fight?
11:23 them back to the entrance of the c gate.
11:25 your attack on the c and destroy it.'
12:26 of the Ammonites and captured this royal c.
12:28 the siege against the c and capture it,
12:28 capture the c and it be credited to me."
12:30 He brought out immense booty from the c,
15: 2 call to him and say, "From what c are you?"
15:14 upon us and put the c to the sword."
15:17 As the king left the c,
15:18 Gath who had accompanied him from that c,
15:24 the soldiers had marched out of the c.
15:25 "Take the ark of God back to the c.
15:27 you and Abiathar return to the c in peace,
15:34 if you return to the c and say to Absalom,
15:37 So David's friend Hushai went into the c
17:13 And if he retires into a c,
17:13 that c and we can drag it into the gorge,
17:17 could not risk being seen entering the c.
17:23 departed, going to his home in his own c.
18: 3 that we have you to help us from the c."
18:24 to the roof of the gate above the c wall,
19: 1 up to the room over the c gate to weep.
19: 4 The soldiers stole into the c that day
19:38 own c by the tomb of his father and mother.
20:14 and they too entered the c after him.
20:15 They threw up a mound against the c,
20:16 the c stood on the outworks and called out,
20:19 beat down a c that is a mother in Israel.
20:21 him alone, and I will withdraw from the c."
20:22 scattered from the c to their own tents,
24: 5 near Aroer, south of the c in the wadi,
1Kgs 1:41 "What does this uproar in the c mean?"
1:45 rejoicing, so that the c is in an uproar.
2:10 ancestors and was buried in the C of David.
3: 1 he married, he brought to the C of David,
8: 1 from the c of David [which is Zion].
8:16 I have not chosen a c out of any tribe of
8:44 toward the c you have chosen and the
8:48 gave their fathers, the c you have chosen,
9:16 all the Canaanites living in the c,
9:24 went up from the C of David to her palace,
11:27 up the breach of his father's C of David.
11:32 the c I have chosen out of all the tribes
11:36 the c in which I choose to be honored.
11:43 he was buried in his father's C of David,
13:11 There was an old prophet living in the c,
13:25 news to the c where the old prophet lived.
13:29 to the c to mourn over it and to bury it.
14:11 When one of Jeroboam's line dies in the c,
14:12 As you step inside the c,
14:21 years in Jerusalem, the c in which,
14:31 he was buried with them in the C of David.
15: 8 he was buried in the C of David,
15:24 was buried in his forefather's C of David,
16: 4 If anyone of Baasha's line dies in the c,
16:18 When Zimri saw the c was captured,
16:24 naming the c he built Samaria after Shemer,
17:10 As he arrived at the entrance of the c,
20: 2 to Ahab, king of Israel, within the c,
20:12 and they made ready to storm the c.
20:19 But when these had come out of the c—
20:30 thousand of them, fled into the c of Aphek,
20:30 too, fled, and took refuge within the c,
21: 8 nobles who lived in the same c with Naboth.
21:11 elders and the nobles who dwelt in his c—
21:13 him out of the c and stoned him to death.
21:24 "When one of Ahab's line dies in the c,
22:26 take him back to Amon, prefect of the c,
22:36 through the army, "Every man to his c,
22:51 was buried in his forefathers' C of David.
2Kgs 2:19 inhabitants of the c complained to Elisha,
2:19 Elisha, "The site of the c is fine indeed,
2:23 boys came out of the c and jeered at him.
3:19 You shall destroy every fortified c,
6:14 They arrived by night and surrounded the c.
6:15 its horses and chariots surrounding the c.
6:19 is the wrong road, and this is the wrong c.
6:26 king of Israel was walking on the c wall,
7: 3 At the c gate were four lepers who were
7: 4 c, we shall die there, for there is famine in the c
7:10 came and summoned the c gatekeepers.
7:12 us alive and enter our c when we leave it."
7:13 "Since those who are left in the c are no
8:24 and was buried with them in the C of David.
9:15 escapes from the c to report in Jezreel."
9:28 tomb of his ancestors in the C of David.
10: 1 letters and sent them to the c rulers,
10: 2 the chariots, the horses, a fortified c,
10: 5 So the vizier and the ruler of the c,
10: 6 were in the care of prominent men of the c,
10: 8 at the entrance of the c until morning,"
11:20 of the land rejoiced and the c was quiet,
12:22 was buried in his forefathers' C of David,
14:13 down four hundred cubits of the c wall,

14:20 ancestors in the C of David in Jerusalem.
15: 7 and was buried with them in the C of David.
15:38 with them in his forefather's C of David.
16:20 and was buried with them in the C of David.
17:31 their children by fire to their c gods,
18:30 this c will not be handed over to the king
19:32 'He shall not reach this c,
19:33 same way he came, without entering the c,
19:34 shield and save this c for my own sake,
20: 6 c from the hand of the king of Assyria;
20: 6 will be a shield to this c for my own sake,
20:20 by which water was brought into the c,
23: 8 of the Gate of Joshua, governor of the c,
23: 8 city, to the left as one enters the c gate.
23:17 The men of the c replied,
23:27 I will reject this c, Jerusalem,
24:10 Jerusalem, and the c came under siege.
24:11 the c while his servants were besieging it.
25: 2 The siege of the c continued until the
25: 3 month, when famine had gripped the c,
25: 4 no more bread, the c walls were breached.
25: 4 the king and all the soldiers left the c
25: 4 Since the Chaldeans had the c surrounded,
25:11 the last of the people remaining in the c,
25:19 And from the c he took one courtier,
25:19 of the king who were still in the c,
25:19 the common people still remaining in the c.
1Chr 1:43 of Beor, the name of whose c was Dinhabah.
1:46 plateau, and the name of his c was Avith.
1:50 The name of his c was Pai,
4:12 Tehinnah, the father of the c of Nahash.
6:41 belonging to the c had been given to Caleb,
6:42 Hebron a c of asylum,
6:52 mountain region of Ephraim, a c of asylum,
11: 5 fortress of Zion, which is the C of David.
11: 7 thenceforth was called the C of David.
11: 8 He rebuilt the c on all sides,
11: 8 while Joab restored the rest of the c.
13:13 the ark back with him to the C of David,
15: 1 David built houses for himself in the C of
15:29 of the LORD was entering the C of David,
19: 9 up for a battle at the gate of the c,
19:15 his brother Abishai, and reentered the c.
20: 2 out a great amount of booty from the c.
20: 3 of the c and set them to work with saws,
2Chr 5: 2 from the C of David (which is Zion).
6: 5 I have not chosen any c from among all the
6:34 pray to you in the direction of this c
6:38 fathers, and of the c you have chosen,
8:11 up from the C of David to the palace
9:31 he was buried in his father's C of David,
11:12 In every c were shields and spears,
12:13 years in Jerusalem, the c in which,
12:16 he was buried in the C of David.
13:23 they buried him in the C of David.
15: 6 Nation crushed nation and c crushed city,
15: 6 Nation crushed nation and city crushed c,
16:14 he had hewn for himself in the C of David,
18:25 take him back to Amon, prefect of the c,
19: 5 the fortified cities of Judah, c by city,
19: 5 the fortified cities of Judah, city by c,
21: 1 he was buried with them in the C of David.
21:20 unloved and was buried in the C of David,
23:21 of the land rejoiced and the c was quiet,
24:16 buried in the C of David with the kings,
24:25 He was buried in the C of David,
25:28 him with his ancestors in the C of Judah.
27: 9 ancestors and was buried in the C of David,
28:15 brought them to Jericho, the c of palms,
28:25 In every c throughout Judah he set up high
28:27 and was buried in Jerusalem—in the c,
29:20 of the c and went up to the LORD's house.
30:10 So the couriers passed from city to c in
30:26 there had not been the like in the c.
31:19 had in every c men designated by name to
32: 3 the waters of the springs outside the c.
32: 5 He strengthened the Millo of the C of
32: 6 the c and encouraged them with these words:
32:18 them so that they might capture their c.
32:30 it underground westward to the C of David.
33:14 he built an outer wall for the C of David
33:15 Jerusalem, and he cast them outside the c.
34: 8 of Azaliah, Maaseiah, the ruler of the c,
Ezr 2: 1 own c (those who returned with Zerubbabel,
4:10 transported and settled in the c of Samaria
4:12 now rebuilding this rebellious and evil c.
4:13 if this c is rebuilt and its walls are raised up
4:15 verify that this c is a rebellious city
4:15 For that reason this c was destroyed.
4:16 that if this c is rebuilt and its walls
4:19 from ancient times this c has risen up
4:21 This c may not be rebuilt until further
10:14 and magistrates of each c in question,
Neh 2: 3 How could I not look sad when the c where
2: 5 to Judah, to the c of my ancestors' graves,
2: 8 c wall and the house that I shall occupy."
3: 6 New C Gate was repaired by Joiada,
3:15 steps that lead down from the C of David.
7: 4 Now the c was quite wide and spacious but
7: 6 own c (those who returned with Zerubbabel,
11: 1 in ten to reside in Jerusalem, the holy c,
11: 3 man on the property he owned in his own c.)
11: 9 Hassenuah, was second in charge of the c.

11:18 the holy c was two hundred and eighty-four.
12:37 straight up by the steps of the C of David
12:39 past the Ephraim Gate [the New C Gate],
13:18 all this evil upon us and upon this c?
Tb 1: 4 This c had been singled out of all
13: 9 O Jerusalem, holy c,
14:10 overnight within the confines of the c.
Jdt 1: 1 of the Assyrians in the great c of Nineveh.
1: 2 this c he built a wall of blocks of stone,
2:24 every fortified c along the Wadi Abron,
6:12 When the men of the c saw them,
6:12 ran out of the c to the crest of the ridge;
6:14 Israelites came down to him from their c,
6:14 They haled him before the rulers of the c,
6:16 then convened all the elders of the c;
7: 7 their c and located their sources of water;
7:13 them off, and they will surrender their c.
7:13 to guard against anyone's leaving the c.
7:14 will be laid low in the streets of their c.
7:22 in the streets and gateways of the c,
7:23 a crowd to Uzziah and the rulers of the c.
7:26 deliver the whole c as booty to the troops
7:32 returned to the walls and towers of the c;
7:32 Throughout the c they were in great misery.
8: 3 of this illness in Bethulia, his native c.
8: 9 c to the Assyrians at the end of five days,
8:10 Chabris, and Charmis, the elders of the c,
8:11 When you promised to hand over the c to
8:18 c of ours that worships gods made by hands,
8:33 you will surrender the c to our enemies,
10: 6 Then they went out to the gate of the c of
10: 6 and found Uzziah and the elders of the c,
10: 9 "Order the gate of the c opened for me,
10:10 The men of the c kept her in view as she
13:12 their c gate and summoned the city elders.
14: 2 out of the c under command of a captain,
14: 9 and their c resounded with shouts of joy.
Est A: 2 He was a Jew residing in the c of Susa,
3:15 the c of Susa was thrown into confusion.
4: 1 the c crying out loudly and bitterly.
6: 9 the horse in the public square of the c,
6:11 him ride in the public square of the c,
8:11 c to group together and defend their lives,
E:24 "Every c and province,
8:15 The c of Susa shouted with joy,
8:17 every province and in each and every c,
9:28 clan, in every province, and in every c.
1Mc 1:30 Then he attacked the c suddenly,
1:31 He plundered the c and set fire to it,
1:33 they built up the C of David with a high,
1:51 Judah to offer sacrifices, each c in turn.
2: 7 of my people and the ruin of the holy c,
2:15 the c of Modein to organize the sacrifices.
2:17 an honorable and great man in this c,
2:27 Mattathias went through the c shouting,
2:28 behind in the c all their possessions.
2:31 of the king who were in the C of David,
5:28 the desert to Bozrah, and captured the c.
5:28 their possessions, and set fire to the c.
5:44 The Jews captured that c and burnt the
5:46 and strongly fortified c along the way,
5:47 But the men in the c shut them out and
5:50 he assaulted the c all that day and night,
5:51 every male, razed and plundered the c,
5:59 came out of the c to meet them in battle.
6: 1 in Persia there was a c called Elymais,
6: 3 and tried to capture and pillage the c.
6: 3 of the c who rose up in battle against him.
6: 7 it had been before, and his c of Beth-zur.
6:49 men of Beth-zur, and they evacuated the c,
6:63 he found Philip in possession of the c.
6:63 fought against him and took the c by force.
7: 1 with a few men in a c on the seacoast,
7:32 the rest fled to the C of David.
9:52 He fortified the c of Beth-zur,
9:65 Leaving his brother Simon in the c,
9:67 from the c and set fire to the machines.
10:10 and began to build and restore the c.
10:63 "Go with him to the center of the c and
10:71 the c forces are on my side.
10:75 but the men in the c shut him out because
10:76 the c became afraid and opened the gates,
10:86 c came out to meet him with great pomp.
11:45 center of the c in an attempt to kill him.
11:47 around him and spread out through the c.
11:47 about a hundred thousand men in the c,
11:49 that the Jews held the c at their mercy,
11:50 let the Jews stop attacking us and our c."
11:66 He expelled them from the c,
12:36 barrier between the citadel and the c,
12:36 its garrison from commerce with the c.
12:37 worked together on building up the c,
12:48 of the c closed the gates and seized him;
13:25 buried him in Modein, the c of his fathers.
13:43 siege machine, pushed it up against the c,
13:44 into the c and caused a great tumult there.
13:45 The men of the c,
13:47 He made them leave the c,
13:47 the c with hymns and songs of praise.
14:33 especially the frontier c of Beth-zur,
14:36 those in the C of David in Jerusalem,
14:37 for the defense of the land and the c,
15:14 While he invested the c,

2Mc 1:12 out those who fought against the holy c.
2:22 the world-famous temple, liberated the c,
3: 1 While the holy c lived in perfect peace
3: 4 about the supervision of the c market.
3: 9 received by the high priest of the c,
3:14 There was great distress throughout the c.
4: 2 the man who was a benefactor of the c,
4:22 pomp by Jason and the people of the c,
4:36 the region of Cilicia, the Jews of the c,
4:38 had him led through the whole c
4:39 in the c with the connivance of Menelaus.
4:48 who had prosecuted the case for the c,
5: 2 It then happened that all over the c,
5: 5 a thousand men and suddenly attacked the c.
5: 5 back and the c was finally being taken,
5: 8 king of the Arabs, he fled from city to c,
5:26 and running through the c with armed men,
6:10 paraded about the c with their babies
6:10 thrown down from the top of the c wall.
8: 3 to have mercy on the c,
8:17 and the affliction of the humiliated c,
8:33 the victory in their ancestral c,
9: 2 He had entered the c called Persepolis and
9: 2 rob the temple and gain control of the c.
9:14 on him, that he would set free the holy c,
10: 1 had recovered the temple and the c,
10:27 a considerable distance from the c,
10:36 the troops, who took possession of the c.
12: 4 this was done by public vote of the c.
12:13 He also attacked a certain c called Caspin,
12:16 Capturing the c by the will of God,
12:27 a fortified c inhabited by people of many
12:28 got possession of the c and slaughtered
12:38 his army and went to the c of Adullam.
13:13 invade Judea and take possession of the c,
13:14 to death for the laws, the temple, the c,
13:25 of that c were angered by the peace treaty;
15:14 prays for his people and their holy c."
15:17 since their c and its temple with the
15:19 remained in the c suffered a like agony,
15:37 with the c remaining in possession of the
Jb 29: 7 of the c and set up my seat in the square
39: 7 He scoffs at the uproar of the c,
Ps(s) 31:22 kindness he has shown me in a fortified c.
45:13 And the c of Tyre is here with gifts;
46: 5 stream whose runlets gladden the c of God,
48: 2 wholly to be praised in the c of our God.
48: 3 of the North," is the c of the great King.
48: 9 have we seen in the c of the LORD of hosts,
48: 9 of the LORD of hosts, In the c of our God;
55:10 for in the c I see violence and strife;
59: 7 snarl like dogs and prowl about the c.
59:15 snarl like dogs and prowl about the c;
60:11 Who will bring me into the fortified c?
72:16 the c dwellers shall flourish like the
87: 3 things are said of you, O c of God!
101: 8 from the c of the LORD all evildoers.
107: 4 way to an inhabited c they did not find.
107: 7 by a direct way to reach an inhabited c.
107:36 the hungry, and they built a c to dwell in.
108:11 Who will bring me into the fortified c?
122: 3 Jerusalem, built as a c with compact unity.
127: 1 Unless the LORD guard the c,
Prv 1:21 out, at the c gates she utters her words:
8: 3 By the gates at the approaches of the c,
9: 3 she calls from the heights out over the c:
9:14 of her house upon a seat on the c heights,
10:15 The rich man's wealth is his strong c;
11:10 When the just prosper, the c rejoices;
11:11 blessing of the righteous the c is exalted,
16:32 rules his temper, than he who takes a c.
18:11 The rich man's wealth is his strong c;
18:19 is a better defense than a strong c,
21:22 The wise man storms a c of the mighty,
25:28 Like an open c with no defenses is the man
29: 8 Arrogant men set the c ablaze,
31:23 Her husband is prominent at the c gates as
31:31 let her works praise her at the c gates.
Eccl 7:19 man than would be ten princes in the c,
8:10 praised in the c for what they had done.
9:14 Against a small c with few men in it
9:15 But in the c lived a man who,
10:15 labor, he who knows not the way to the c?
Sg 3: 2 I will rise then and go about the c;
3: 3 me as they made their rounds of the c:
5: 7 their rounds of the c; They struck me,
Wis 9: 8 altar in the c that is your dwelling place.
Sir 9: 7 the c and wander not through its squares;
9:18 in the c is the man of railing speech,
10: 2 as the head of a c,
10: 3 c grows through the wisdom of its princes.
16: 4 Through one wise man can a c be peopled;
23:21 will be punished in the streets of the c;
24:11 Thus in the chosen c he has given me rest,
36:12 Take pity on your holy c,
36:26 an armed band that shifts from c to city?
36:26 an armed band that shifts from city to c?
38:32 Without them no c could be lived in,
40:18 A child or a c will preserve one's name,
42:11 sport of your enemies, A byword in the c,
46: 2 arm, to brandish his javelin against the c!
48:17 his c and had water brought into it;
49: 6 the holy c and left its streets desolate,

CITY (cont.)

50: 4 and strengthened his c against the enemy.
Is 1: 8 shed in a melon patch, like a c blockaded.
1:21 has she turned adulteress, the faithful c,
1:26 shall be called c of justice, faithful city.
3:26 as the c sits desolate on the ground.
12: 6 Shout with exultation, O c of Zion,
14:31 Howl, O gate; cry out, O c!
17: 1 shall cease to be a c and become a ruin;
19: 2 Neighbor against neighbor, c against city,
19:18 one shall be called C of the Sun."
22: 2 the housetops, O c full of noise and chaos,
22: 9 the breaches in the C of David were many;
23: 7 Is this your wanton c,
23:16 Take a harp, go about the c,
24:10 Broken down is the c of chaos,
24:12 In the c nothing remains but ruin;
25: 2 made the c a heap, the fortified city
25: 2 The castle of the insolent is a c no more,
26: 1 "A strong c have we;
26: 5 places, and the lofty c he brings down;
27:10 For the fortified c shall be desolate,
29: 1 Ariel, Ariel, the c where David encamped!
32:13 For all the joyful houses, the wanton c.
32:14 will be forsaken, the noisy c deserted;
32:19 The c will be utterly laid low.
33:20 Look to Zion, the c of our festivals;
36:15 this c will not be handed over to the
37:33 He shall not reach this c,
37:34 same way he came, without entering the c,
37:35 shield and save this c for my own sake,
38: 6 c from the hand of the king of Assyria;
38: 6 I will be a shield to this c."
45:13 He shall rebuild my c and let my exiles go
48: 2 the holy c and rely on the God of Israel,
52: 1 glorious garments, O Jerusalem, holy c.
60:14 They shall call you C of the LORD,"
62:12 "Frequented," a c that is not forsaken.
66: 6 A sound of roaring from the c,
Jer 1:18 this day who have made you a fortified c,
3:14 I will take you, one from a c,
4:29 horseman and bowman each c takes to flight;
5:17 sword the fortified c in which you trust.
6: 6 Woe to the c marked for punishment;
8:16 contains, the c and those who dwell in it.
10:17 the land, O c living in a state of siege!
14:18 If I enter the c, look!
15: 7 winnowed them with the fan in every c gate.
17:24 through the gates of this c on the sabbath,
17:25 on it, then, through the gates of this c,
17:25 This c will remain inhabited forever.
19: 8 this c an object of amazement and derision.
19:11 Thus will I smash this people and this c,
19:12 I will make this c like Topheth.
19:15 c all the evil with which I threatened it,
20: 5 All the wealth of this c,
21: 4 I will pile up in the midst of this c,
21: 6 I will strike the inhabitants of this c,
21: 7 people in this c who survive pestilence,
21: 9 Whoever remains in this c shall die by the
21:10 For I have turned against this c,
22: 6 turn you into a waste, a c uninhabited.
22: 8 will pass by this c and ask one another:
22: 8 has the LORD done this to so great a c?"
23:39 the c which I gave to you and your fathers.
25:29 For since with this c,
26: 6 and make this the c which all the nations
26: 9 'This c shall be desolate and deserted'?"
26:11 he has prophesied against this c,
26:12 this house and c all that you have heard.
26:15 on yourselves, on this c and its citizens.
26:20 against this c and land as Jeremiah did.
27:17 else this c will become a heap of ruins.
27:19 rest of the vessels that remain in this c,
29: 7 of the c to which I have exiled you;
29:16 and all the people who remain in this c,
30:18 C shall be rebuilt upon hill,
31:38 when the c shall be rebuilt as the LORD's,
31:40 shall the c be rooted up or thrown down.
32: 3 handing over this c to the king of Babylon,
32:24 have arrived at this c to breach it;
32:24 the c will be handed over to the Chaldeans
32:25 But the c has already been handed over to
32:28 I will hand over this c to the Chaldeans,
32:29 it shall enter this c and set fire to it,
32:31 day, this c has excited my anger and wrath,
32:36 the God of Israel, concerning this c,
33: 4 of this c and the palaces of Judah's kings,
33: 5 face from this c for all their wickedness.
34: 2 handing this c over to the king of Babylon;
34:22 the LORD, and bring them back to this c.
37: 5 this report they marched away from the c.
37: 8 shall return to the fight against this c;
37:10 would rise up and destroy the c with fire.
37:21 until all the bread in the c was eaten up.
38: 2 who remains in this c shall die by sword,
38: 3 This c shall certainly be handed over to
38: 4 the soldiers who are left in this c,
38: 9 spot, for there is no more food in the c."
38:17 this c shall not be destroyed with fire,
38:18 this c shall fall into the hands of the
38:23 and this c shall be destroyed with fire.
39: 4 leaving the c on the Royal Garden Road
39: 9 the rest of the people left in the c,
39:16 the words I spoke against this c,
41: 7 When they were once inside the c,
46: 8 the earth, destroying the c and its people.
48: 8 comes upon every city, not a c escapes;
49:25 How can the c of glory be forsaken,
51:31 king of Babylon that all his c is taken.
51:35 flesh be upon Babylon, says the c on Zion;
52: 5 The siege of the c continued until the
52: 6 the c and the people had no more bread,
52: 7 the c walls were breached
52: 7 soldiers took to flight and left the c by night
52: 7 With the Chaldeans surrounding the c,
52:15 the rest of the people left in the c,
52:25 And from the c he took one courtier,
52:25 of the king who were present in the c,
52:25 of the common people who were in the c.
Lam 1: 1 How lonely she is now, the once crowded c!
1:19 priests and my elders perished in the c;
2:12 like the wounded in the streets of the c,
2:15 "Is this the all-beautiful c,
3:51 at the sight of all the daughters of my c.
Bar 4:32 fearful the c that took your sons.
4:33 As that c rejoiced at your collapse,
Ez 4: 1 of you, and draw on it a c [Jerusalem].
4: 3 up as an iron wall between you and the c.
5: 2 Burn a third in the fire, within the c,
5: 2 around the c and strike it with the sword;
7:15 and famine shall devour those in the c.
7:23 with bloodshed and the c full of violence.
9: 1 Come, you scourges of the c!
9: 4 Pass through the c [through Jerusalem] and
9: 5 Pass through the c after him and strike!
9: 7 then go out and strike in the c.
9: 9 with bloodshed, the c with lawlessness.
10: 2 the cherubim, then scatter them over the c.
11: 2 evil and giving wicked counsel in this c.
11: 3 The c is the kettle,
11: 6 You have slain many in this c and have
11: 7 they are the meat, and the c is the kettle;
11: 9 I will bring you out of the c,
11:11 The c shall not be a kettle for you,
11:23 And the glory of the LORD rose from the c
11:23 the mountain which is to the east of the c.
17: 4 of tradesmen, set it in a c of merchants.
21:32 he comes who has the claim against the c;
22: 2 you judge, would you judge the bloody c?
22: 3 Woe to the c which sheds blood within
23:42 the shout of a carefree mob in the c,
24: 6 Woe to the bloody c,
26:10 even as one enters a c that is breached.
26:17 gone from the seas, c most prized!
26:19 When I make you a c desolate like cities
33:21 from Jerusalem and said, "The c is taken!"
39:16 [Also the name of the c shall be Hamonah.]
40: 1 fourteen years after the c was taken,
40: 2 seemed to be a c being built before me.
43: 3 I had seen when he came to destroy the c,
45: 6 As property of the C you shall designate a
45: 7 the combined sacred tract and C property,
48:15 C for dwellings and pasture; the City
48:16 These are the dimensions of the C:
48:17 The pasture lands of the C shall extend
48:18 provide food for the workers of the C.
48:19 The workers in the C shall be taken from
48:20 sacred tract together with the C property.
48:21 of the sacred tract and the C property,
48:22 property of the Levites and the C property,
48:30 These are the exits of the C,
48:35 of the C is eighteen thousand cubits.
48:35 C shall henceforth be "The LORD is here."
Dn 3:28 upon Jerusalem, the holy c of our fathers.
9:16 wrath be turned away from your c Jerusalem,
9:18 our ruins and the c which bears your name.
9:19 this c and your people bear your name!"
9:24 for your people and for your holy c:
9:26 cut down when he does not possess the c;
11:15 and take the fortified c by storm.
Hos 6: 8 Gilead is a c of evildoers,
Jl 2: 9 They assault the c,
Am 3: 6 If a trumpet sounds in a c,
3: 6 If evil befalls a c,
4: 7 sent rain upon one c but not upon another;
4: 8 two or three cities staggered to one c
5: 3 The c that marched out with a thousand
6: 8 I give over the c with everything in it;
7:17 Your wife shall be made a harlot in the c,
Jon 1: 2 "Set out for the great c of Nineveh,
3: 2 "Set out for the great c of Nineveh,
3: 3 Now Nineveh was an enormously large c;
3: 4 Jonah began his journey through the c,
4: 5 left the c for a place to the east of it,
4: 5 shade, to see what would happen to the c.
4:11 be concerned over Nineveh, the great c,
Mi 1:11 of Zaanan come not forth from their c.
4:10 forth from the c and dwell in the fields;
6: 9 the LORD cries to the c.
6: 9 Hear, O tribe and c council,
Na 3: 1 Woe to the bloody c,
Hb 2: 8 land, to the c and to all who dwell in it.
2:12 Woe to him who builds a c by bloodshed,
2:17 land, to the c and to all who dwell in it.
Zep 2:15 Is this the exultant c that dwelt secure;
3: 1 Woe to the c, rebellious and polluted,
3: 1 and polluted, to the tyrannical c!
Zec 8: 3 Jerusalem shall be called the faithful c,
8: 5 The c shall be filled with boys and girls
8:21 of one c shall approach those of another,
14: 2 the c shall be taken,
14: 2 half of the c shall go into exile,
14: 2 the people shall not be removed from the c.
Mt 4: 5 Next the devil took him to the holy c,
5:14 A c set on a hill cannot be hidden.
5:35 Jerusalem (it is the c of the great King);
21:10 the whole c was stirred to its depths,
21:17 left them and went out of the c to Bethany,
21:18 At dawn, as Jesus was returning to the c,
22: 7 destroy those murderers and burn their c.
23:34 synagogues and hunt down from city to c;
26:18 "Go to this man in the c and tell him,
27:53 entered the holy c and appeared to many.
28:11 some of the guard went into the c
Mk 11:19 Jesus and his disciples went out of the c.
14:13 "Go into the c and you will come upon a
14:16 c they found it just as he had told them,
Lk 2:11 in David's c a savior has been born to you,
7:32 c squares and calling to their playmates,
10: 8 "Into whatever c you go,
18: 2 c who respected neither God nor man.
18: 3 widow in that c kept coming to him saying,
19: 1 Entering Jericho, he passed through the c.
19:41 Coming within sight of the c,
21:21 those in the heart of the c must escape it;
21:37 and leave the c to spend the night on the
22:10 "Just as you enter the c,
23:19 in prison for causing an uprising in the c,
24:49 Remain here in the c until you are clothed
Jn 19:20 where Jesus was crucified was near the c.
Acts 1:13 Entering the c,
4:27 in this very c against your holy Servant,
7:58 him as one man, dragged him out of the c,
9: 6 Get up and go into the c,
9:24 so far as to keep close watch on the c gates
10: 9 traveling along and approaching the c,
11: 5 "I was at prayer in the c of Joppa when,
12:10 came to the iron gate leading out to the c,
13:44 entire c gathered to hear the word of God.
16:12 a leading c in the district of Macedonia
16:13 We spent some time in that c.
16:13 the c gate to the bank of the river,
16:20 agitators disturbing the peace of our c!
16:39 out with the request that they leave the c.
17:16 at the sight of idols everywhere in the c,
18:10 There are many of my people in this c."
19:29 long, confusion spread throughout the c.
20:23 Holy Spirit has been warning me from c to c
21: 5 came out of the c to see us off,
21:29 an Ephesian, with him in the c earlier,
21:30 Before long the whole c was in turmoil.
21:39 citizen of Tarsus in Cilicia—no mean c;
22: 3 in Cilicia, but I was brought up in this c.
24:12 the synagogue, nor anywhere else in the c,
25:23 officers and prominent men of the c.
Rom 16:24 Erastus, the c treasurer,
2Cor 11:26 imperiled in the c,
11:32 close watch on the c in order to arrest me,
Heb 11:10 looking forward to the c with foundations,
11:16 God, for he has prepared a c for them.
12:22 to Mount Zion and the c of the living God,
13:14 For here we have no lasting c;
Rv 2:13 in your c where Satan has his home.
3:12 of my God and the name of the c of my God,
11: 2 will crush the holy c for forty-two months.
11: 8 will lie in the streets of the great c,
11:13 and a tenth of the c fell in ruins.
14:20 The winepress was trodden outside the c,
16:19 The great c was split into three parts,
17:18 The woman you saw is the great c which has
18:10 "Alas, alas, great c that you are,
18:15 who grew rich from business with the c,
18:16 "Alas, alas, the great c,
18:18 smoke go up as the c burned to the ground:
18:18 c could have compared with this great one!"
18:19 "Alas, alas, the great c,
18:21 the great c shall be cast down like this,
20: 9 beloved c where God's people were encamped;
21: 2 I also saw a new Jerusalem, the holy c,
21:10 holy c Jerusalem coming down out
21:11 The c had the radiance of a precious jewel
21:14 The wall of the c had twelve courses of
21:15 me held a rod of gold for measuring the c,
21:16 The c is perfectly square,
21:16 He measured the c with the rod and found
21:18 the c was of pure gold,
21:19 The foundation of the c wall was ornate
21:21 and the streets of the c were of pure gold,
21:22 I saw no temple in the c.
21:23 The c had no need of sun or moon,
22:14 of life and enter the c through its gates!
22:19 tree of life and the holy c described here!

CITY'S (6)

Tb 14:15 exile of the c inhabitants when Cyaxares,
2Mc 5:17 was because of the sins of the c inhabitants
Sir 7: 7 Be guilty of no evil before the c populace,

Is 22:11 But you did not look to the *c* Maker,
Jer 33: 6 I will treat and assuage the *c* wounds;
39: 2 a breach was made in the *c* defenses.

CIVIL (5)

Dt 17: 8 or of *c* rights or of personal injury,
1Chr 26:29 Israel's *c* affairs as officials and judges.
2Mc 13:24 left him as military and *c* governor
Ps(s) 35:20 For *c* words they speak not,
Mk 3:24 If a kingdom is torn by *c* strife,

CIVILIAN (1)

2Tm 2: 4 becomes entangled in the affairs of *c* life;

CIVILLY (1)

Ps(s) 28: 3 Who speak *c* to their neighbors though evil

CLAD (3)

2Mc 5: 2 midair, *c* in garments interwoven with gold
Zec 3: 3 before the angel, *c* in filthy garments.
1Cor 4:11 hour we go hungry and thirsty, poorly *c*,

CLAIM (66)

Nm 32:19 and will not *c* any heritage with them once
Dt 15: 2 his *c* on what he has loaned his neighbor;
15: 3 the *c* on your kinsman for what is yours.
Ru 3:13 and tomorrow, if he wishes to *c* you,
3:13 claim you, as the LORD lives, I will *c*
4: 4 to put in your *c* for it if you wish to
4: 4 But if you do not wish to *c* it,
4: 4 for no one has a prior *c* to yours,
4: 4 He answered, "I will put in my *c*."
4: 6 my *c* lest I depreciate my own estate.
4: 6 Put in a *c* yourself in my stead,
4: 6 in my stead, for I cannot exercise my *c*."
1Sm 18: 2 Saul laid *c* to David that day and did not
20:31 cannot make good your *c* to the kingship!
2Sm 21: 4 "We have no *c* against Saul and his house
2Kgs 8: 3 to the king to *c* her house and her field.
8: 5 came to the king to *c* her house and field.
2Chr 32:11 famine and thirst, by his *c* that 'the LORD,
Neh 2:20 share nor *c* nor memorial in Jerusalem."
5:18 this I did not *c* the governor's allowance,
Tb 3:17 For Tobiah had the right to *c* her before
Jb 3: 5 May darkness and gloom *c* it,
31:13 to my maid, when they had a *c* against me,
Prv 3:27 he has a *c* when it is in your power to do it
18: 5 the guilty, and so to reject a rightful *c*.
25: 6 *C* no honor in the king's presence,
Sir 29: 5 him and says he is helpless to meet the *c*.
41: 4 in the nether world he has no *c* on life.
Is 29:21 and leave the just man with an empty *c*.
48: 7 so that you cannot *c* to have known them;
Jer 5:28 they do not defend By advancing the *c*
32: 8 you have the first *c* to possess it;
Lam 3:36 the Most High, When he presses a crooked *c*,
Ez 20:40 and there I will *c* your tributes and the
21:32 he comes who has the *c* against the city;
34:10 I will *c* my sheep from them and put a stop
Am 5:14 the God of hosts, be with you as you *c*!
Mi 2:11 on impulse, should make the futile *c*:
Mt 3: 9 Do not pride yourselves on the *c*,
17:10 the scribes *c* that Elijah must come first?"
24: 5 they will *c*, and they will deceive many.
27:63 while he was still alive made the *c*,
Mk 9:11 the scribes *c* that Elijah must come first?"
12:35 "How can the scribes *c*,
13: 6 'I am he,' they will *c*,
Lk 6:33 do good to you, how can you *c* any credit?
9:19 while others *c* that one of the prophets of
20:27 (the ones who *c* there is no resurrection)
Jn 4:20 but you people *c* that Jerusalem is the
6:42 How can he *c* to have come down from heaven
8:52 Yet you *c*, 'A man shall never know death
8:54 Father, the very one you *c* for your God,
10:36 do you *c* that I blasphemed when,
12:34 *c* that the Son of Man must be lifted up?
16: 2 puts you to death will *c* to be serving God!
Acts 6:14 We have heard him *c* that Jesus the
17: 7 and *c* instead that a certain Jesus is king."
2Cor 11:21 But what anyone else dares to *c*—
2Thes 3: 9 Not that we had no *c* on you,
1Tm 6:21 In laying *c* to such knowledge,
Ti 1:16 They *c* to "know God,"
1Pt 2:20 get beaten for it, what credit can you *c*?
1Jn 2:23 who denies the Son has no *c* on the Father,
2:23 the Son can *c* the Father as well.
Rv 20: 6 The second death will have no *c* on them;

CLAIMANTS (1)

Gal 2: 4 *c* to the title of brother were smuggled in;

CLAIMED (9)

Bar 6:39 can it be thought or *c* that they are gods?
6:44 can it be thought or *c* that they are gods?
6:63 that it is unthinkable, and cannot be *c*,
Mt 27:43 After all, he *c*, 'I am God's Son.'"
Jn 6:41 started to murmur in protest because he *c*,
19:21 'This man *c* to be King of the Jews'"
Acts 4:32 None of them ever *c* anything as his own;
25:19 Jesus who had died but who Paul *c* is alive.
Rom 1:22 They *c* to be wise,

CLAIMING (3)

Jn 7:41 Others were *c*, "He is the Messiah."
9: 9 Some were *c* it was he;
10:20 Many were *c*: "He is possessed by a devil

CLAIMS (15)

Ex 22: 8 where another *c* that the thing is his,
Dt 22: 2 place and keep it with you until he *c* it;
1Kgs 3:23 "One woman *c*,
Jn 8:22 he mean he will kill himself when he *c*,
2Cor 9: 3 send the brothers so that our *c* for you
10: 8 If I find I must make a few further *c*
10:13 When we make *c* we will not go over the
Col 2:14 bond that stood against us with all its *c*,
1Tm 5: 3 Honor the *c* of widows who are real widows
Jas 3:14 arrogant and false *c* against the truth.
4:16 can do is make arrogant and pretentious *c*.
1Pt 2: 9 a people he *c* for his own to proclaim the
1Jn 2: 4 The man who *c*, "I have known him
2: 6 the man who *c* to abide in him
2: 9 The man who *c* to be in light,

CLAIRVOYANT (1)

Acts 16:16 we met a slave girl who had a *c* spirit.

CLAMBERED (1)

1Sm 14:13 *c* up with his armor-bearer behind him;

CLAMOR (7)

Ezr 3:13 raised a mighty *c* which was heard afar off.
Jdt 7:23 up a great *c* and said before the elders:
14:16 He broke into a loud *c* of weeping,
Ps(s) 55: 4 voice of the enemy and the *c* of the wicked.
88: 2 at night I *c* in your presence.
Jer 51:55 mighty waters, and their *c* was heard afar.
Am 1:14 it will devour her castles Amid *c* on the day

CLAMORING (1)

Acts 25:24 about him, *c* that he should live no more.

CLAMOROUS (1)

Hb 1: 3 there is strife, and *c* discord.

CLAMPS (1)

1Chr 22: 3 nails for the doors of the gates, and *c*,

CLAN (119)

Gn 34:19 highly respected than anyone else in his *c*.
36:30 were the clans of the Horites, clan by *c*,
Nm 1:18 lineage according to *c* and ancestral house,
2:34 according to his *c* and his ancestral house.
3:21 the clan of the Libnites and the *c* of the
10:21 The *c* of Kohath then set out,
25:15 daughter of Zur, who was head of a *c*,
26: 5 *c* of the Hanochites, through Pallu the clan
26: 6 through Hezron the *c* of the Hezronites,
26: 6 *c* of the Hezronites, through Carmi the *c*
26:12 through Nemuel the *c* of the Nemuelites,
26:12 *c* of the Jaminites, through Jachin the clan
26:13 through Sohar the *c* of the Soharites,
26:13 through Shaul the *c* of the Shaulites.
26:15 *c* of the Zephonites, through Haggi the clan
26:15 through Shuni the *c* of the Shunites,
26:16 clan of the Oznites, through Eri the *c*
26:17 clan of the Arodites, through Areli the *c*
26:20 *c* of the Shelahites, through Perez the clan
26:20 through Zerah the *c* of the Zerahites.
26:21 *c* of the Hezronites, through Hamul the clan
26:23 clan of the Tolaites, through Puvah the *c*
26:24 *c* of the Jashubites, through Shimron the *c*
26:26 *c* of the Seredites, through Elon the clan
26:26 through Jahleel the *c* of the Jahleelites.
26:29 through Machir the *c* of the Machirites,
26:29 of Machir, the *c* of the Gileadites.
26:30 *c* of the Helekites, through Asriel the clan
26:31 *c* of the Asrielites, through Shechem the *c*
26:32 through Shemida the *c* of the Shemidaites,
26:32 through Hepher the *c* of the Hepherites.
26:35 Shuthelah the *c* of the Shuthelahites,
26:35 clan of the Bechrites, through Tahan the *c*
26:36 through Eran the *c* of the Eranites.
26:38 through Bela the *c* of the Belaites,
26:38 *c* of the Ashbelites, through Ahiram the *c*
26:39 through Shupham the *c* of the Shuphamites,
26:39 through Hupham the *c* of the Huphamites.
26:40 *c* of the Aradites, through Naaman the *c*
26:42 through Shuham the *c* of the Shuhamites.
26:44 *c* of the Imnites, through Ishvi the clan
26:44 through Beriah the *c* of the Beriites,
26:45 *c* of the Heberites, through Malchiel the *c*
26:48 *c* of the Jahzeelites, through Guni the clan
26:49 clan of the Jezerites, through Shillem the *c*
26:57 through Gershon the *c* of the Gershonites,
26:57 *c* of the Kohathites, through Merari the *c*
26:58 *c* of the Libnites, the clan of the
26:58 the *c* of the Mahlites, the clan of the
26:58 the clan of the Mushites, the *c* of the
27: 4 from his *c* merely because he had no son?
27:11 heritage to his nearest relative in his *c*,
31:14 of the army, the *c* and company commande
31:48 Then the officers who had been *c* and
31:52 This was from the *c* and company comma
31:54 the gold from the *c* and company comma
32:41 Jair, a Manassehite *c*,
33:54 land among yourselves by lot, clan by *c*,
36: 1 houses in the *c* of descendants of Gilead,
36: 6 marry into a *c* of their ancestral tribe,
36: 8 to a *c* of her own ancestral tribe,
36:12 remained in the tribe of their father's *c*.
Dt 3:14 Jair, a Manassehite *c*,
29:17 no man or woman, no *c* or tribe among you,
Jos 7:14 the *c* which the LORD designates shall come
7:17 forward, and the *c* of Zerah was designated.
7:17 the *c* of Zerah come forward by families,
21:10 of Aaron in the Kohathite *c* of the Levites,
21:27 The Gershonite *c* of the Levites received
Jgs 1:25 they let the man and his whole *c* go free.
9: 1 *c* to which his mother's family belonged,
13: 2 man from Zorah, of the *c* of the Danites,
18: 2 So the Danites sent from their *c* a detail
18:11 So six hundred men of the *c* of the Danites,
18:19 to be priest for a tribe and a *c* in Israel?"
21:24 his own heritage in his own *c* and tribe.
Ru 2: 1 Boaz, of the *c* of her husband Elimelech.
2: 3 belonging to Boaz of the *c* of Elimelech.
1Sm 9:21 and is not my *c* the least among the clans
10:21 in clans, and the *c* of Matri was chosen,
18:18 And who are my kin or my father's *c* in
20: 6 *c* is holding its seasonal sacrifice there.'
20:29 we are to have a *c* sacrifice in our city,
2Sm 14: 7 *c* confronted your servant and demanded:
16: 5 son of Gera of the same *c* as Saul's family,
23:13 *c* was encamped in the Vale of Rephaim.
1Chr 6:39 Aaron who belonged to *c* of the Kohathites,
6:55 belonged to the rest of the Kohathite *c*.
2Chr 20:14 of Mattaniah, a Levite of the *c* of Asaph,
Jdt 8: 2 husband, Manasseh, of her own tribe and *c*,
8:18 does there exist today, any tribe, or *c*,
Est 9:28 and kept in every generation, by every *c*,
Sir 16: 4 through a *c* of rebels it becomes desolate.
Jer 3:14 take you, one from a city, two from a *c*,

CLANDESTINE (1)

Wis 14:23 child-slaying sacrifices or *c* mysteries,

CLANG (1)

Sir 38:28 The *c* of the hammer deafens his ears,

CLANGING (2)

Ps(s) 150: 5 cymbals, praise him with *c* cymbals.
1Cor 13: 1 have love, I am a noisy gong, a *c* cymbal.

CLANS (162)

Gn 10: 5 by their *c* within their nations.
10:18 the *c* of the Canaanites spread out,
10:20 of Ham, according to their *c* and languages,
10:31 *c* and languages by their lands and nations.
36:15 following are the *c* of Esau's descendants.
36:15 the *c* of Teman,
36:16 are the *c* of Eliphaz in the land of Edom;
36:17 the *c* of Nahath,
36:17 are the *c* of Reuel in the land of Edom;
36:18 the *c* of Jeush, Jalam, and Korah.
36:18 These are the *c* of Esau's wife Oholibamah,
36:19 Esau [that is, Edom] according to their *c*.
36:21 they are the Horite *c* descended from Seir,
36:29 These are the Horite *c*:
36:29 the *c* of Lotan, Shobal, Zibeon, Anah
36:30 they were the *c* of the Horites,
36:40 The following are the names of the *c* of
36:40 the *c* of Timna, Alvah, Jetheth,
36:43 These are the *c* of the Edomites,
Ex 6:14 these are the *c* of Reuben.
6:15 these are the *c* of Simeon.
6:17 The sons of Gershon, as heads of *c*,
6:19 the *c* of Levi in their genealogical order.
6:24 These are the *c* of the Korahites.
6:25 heads of the ancestral *c* of the Levites.
Nm 1: 2 the Israelites, by *c* and ancestral houses,
1:20 by lineage in *c* and ancestral houses:
1:22 by lineage in *c* and ancestral houses:
1:24 by lineage in *c* and ancestral houses:
1:26 by lineage in *c* and ancestral houses:
1:28 by lineage in *c* and ancestral houses:
1:30 Zebulun, registered by lineage in *c*
1:32 Ephraim, registered by lineage in *c*
1:34 Manasseh, registered by lineage in *c*
1:36 Benjamin, registered by lineage in *c*
1:38 Dan, registered by lineage in *c*
1:40 Asher, registered by lineage in *c*
1:42 Naphtali, registered by lineage in *c*
3:15 of the Levites by ancestral houses and *c*,
3:18 The descendants of Gershon, by *c*,
3:19 The descendants of Kohath, by *c*,
3:20 The descendants of Merari, by *c*,
3:20 the *c* of the Levites by ancestral houses.
3:21 these were the *c* of the Gershonites.

CLANS (cont.)

3:23 The *c* of the Gershonites camped behind the
3:27 To Kohath belonged the *c* of the Amramites,
3:27 these were the *c* of the Kohathites.
3:29 The *c* of the Kohathites camped at the
3:33 the *c* of the Mahlites and the Mushites;
3:33 these were the *c* of Merari.
3:35 house of the *c* of Merari was Zuriel,
3:39 by *c* in keeping with the LORD's command,
4: 2 the Kohathites, by *c* and ancestral houses,
4:18 *c* perish from the body of the Levites.
4:22 also, by ancestral houses and *c*,
4:24 is the task of the *c* of the Gershonites,
4:29 you shall enroll by *c* and ancestral houses
4:33 is the task of the *c* of the Merarites
4:34 the Kohathites, by *c* and ancestral houses,
4:36 in the meeting tent, as registered by *c*,
4:37 *c* who were to serve in the meeting tent,
4:38 the Gershonites, by *c* and ancestral houses,
4:40 as registered by *c* and ancestral houses,
4:41 *c* who were to serve in the meeting tent,
4:42 the Merarites, by *c* and ancestral houses,
4:44 in the meeting tent, as registered by *c*,
4:45 the men of the Merarite *c* which Moses took,
4:46 the Levites, by *c* and ancestral houses,
10:17 the *c* of Gershon and Merari set out,
22:41 and from there he saw some of the *c*.
26: 5 of Israel, the Reubenites by *c* were:
26: 7 These were the *c* of the Reubenites,
26:12 The Simeonites by *c* were:
26:14 These were the *c* of the Simeonites,
26:15 The Gadites by *c* were:
26:18 These were the *c* of the Gadites,
26:20 The Judahites by *c* were:
26:22 These were the *c* of Judah,
26:23 The Issacharites by *c* were:
26:25 These were the *c* of Issachar,
26:26 The Zebulunites by *c* were:
26:27 These were the *c* of the Zebulunites,
26:29 The Manassehites by *c* were:
26:34 These were the *c* of Manasseh,
26:35 The Ephraimites by *c* were:
26:37 These were the *c* of the Ephraimites,
26:37 These were the descendants of Joseph by *c*.
26:38 The Benjaminites by *c* were:
26:41 These were the Benjaminites by *c*,
26:42 The Danites by *c* were:
26:42 These were the *c* of Dan,
26:44 The Asherites by *c* were:
26:47 These were the *c* of Asher,
26:48 The Naphtalites by *c* were:
26:50 These were the *c* of Naphtali,
26:57 The Levites registered by *c* were:
26:58 These also were *c* of Levi:
31: 5 From the *c* of Israel,
36: 1 one of the Josephite *c*—
36:12 the *c* of the descendants of Manasseh,
Jos 7:14 LORD designates shall come forward by *c*;
7:17 Then he had the *c* of Judah come forward,
13:15 What Moses gave to the Reubenite *c*:
13:23 the heritage of the *c* of the Reubenites.
13:24 What Moses gave to the Gadite *c*:
13:28 were the heritage of the *c* of the Gadites.
13:29 to the *c* of the half-tribe of Manasseh.
13:31 for half the *c* descended from Machir.
15: 1 The lot for the *c* of the Judahite tribe
15:12 boundary of the *c* of the Judahites.
15:20 of the *c* of the tribe of Judahites:
16: 5 heritage of the *c* of the Ephraimites ran
16: 8 the heritage of the *c* of the Ephraimites,
17: 2 descendants of Manasseh, the *c* of Abiezer,
18:11 fell to the *c* of the tribe of Benjaminites.
18:20 This was how the heritage of the *c* of the
18:21 *c* of the tribe of the Benjaminites were:
18:28 was the heritage of the *c* of Benjaminites.
19: 1 The heritage of the *c* of the tribe of
19: 8 of the *c* of the tribe of the Simeonites.
19:10 third lot fell to the *c* of the Zebulunites.
19:16 the heritage of the *c* of the Zebulunites.
19:17 the *c* of the Issacharites included Jezreel,
19:23 the heritage of the *c* of the Issacharites.
19:24 to the *c* of the tribe of the Asherites.
19:31 of the *c* of the tribe of the Asherites.
19:32 *c* of the Naphtalites extended from Heleph,
19:39 of the *c* of the tribe of the Naphtalites.
19:40 lot fell to the *c* of the tribe of Danites.
19:48 of the *c* of the tribe of the Danites.
21: 4 Levites fell to the *c* of the Kohathites,
21: 5 by lot from the *c* of the tribe of Ephraim,
21: 6 by lot from the *c* of the tribe of Issachar,
21: 7 The *c* of the Merarites obtained twelve
21:20 *c* among the Levites obtained by lot,
21:26 rest of the Kohathite *c* were ten in all.
21:33 to the Gershonite *c* were thirteen in all.
21:34 The Merarite *c*,
21:40 which were allotted to the Merarite *c*,
Jgs 5:15 Among the *c* of Reuben great were the
5:16 Among the *c* of Reuben great were the
1Sm 9:21 among the *c* of the tribe of Benjamin?
10:21 the tribe of Benjamin come forward in *c*,
2Sm 1:12 soldiers of the LORD of the *c* of Israel,
1Chr 2:53 Manahathites, and the *c* of Kiriath-jearim:
2:55 The *c* of the Sopherim dwelling in Jabez
4: 2 These were the *c* of the Zorathites.
4: 8 Zobebah, as well as of the *c* of Aharhel,
4:21 the *c* of the linen weavers' guild in
4:27 and as a result all their *c* did not equal
4:38 just named were princes in their *c*,
5: 7 His brothers who belonged to his *c*,
6: 4 The following were the *c* of Levi,
6:46 lot for their *c* from the tribe of Ephraim,
6:47 The *c* of the Gershonites obtained thirteen
6:48 The *c* of the Merarites obtained twelve
6:51 The *c* of the Kohathites obtained cities by
6:56 The *c* of the Gershonites received from the
7: 5 In all the *c* of Issachar there was a total
Jer 2: 4 All you *c* of the house of Israel,
Mi 5: 1 too small to be among the *c* of Judah,
Mt 24:30 and 'all the *c* of earth will strike their

CLANSMAN (1)

Lv 25:49 or by some other relative or fellow *c*;

CLANSMEN (1)

Nm 25: 6 brought in a Midianite woman to his *c*

CLAP (7)

Ps(s) 47: 2 All you peoples, *c* your hands,
98: 8 Let the rivers *c* their hands,
Sir 12:18 head and *c* his hands and hiss repeatedly,
Is 55:12 of the countryside shall *c* their hands.
Lam 2:15 All who pass by *c* their hands at you;
Ez 6:11 *C* your hands,
Na 3:19 this news of you *c* their hands over you;

CLAPPED (1)

Ez 25: 6 you *c* your hands and stamped your feet,

CLAPPING (1)

2Kgs 11:12 anointed him, *c* their hands and shouting,

CLARIFY (1)

Phil 3:15 way, God will *c* the difficulty for you.

CLASHING (1)

1Mc 6:41 of their marching, and the *c* of the arms,

CLASPED (1)

2Kgs 4:27 man of God on the mountain, she *c* his feet.

CLASPS (7)

Ex 26: 6 Then make fifty *c* of gold,
26:11 fifty bronze *c* and put them into the loops,
26:33 Hang the veil from *c*.
35:11 with its tent, its covering, its *c*,
36:13 Then fifty *c* of gold were made,
36:18 Fifty bronze *c* were made with which the
39:33 tent with all its appurtenances, the *c*,

CLASS (8)

Wis 15: 7 either *c* the worker in clay is the judge.
Mk 4:18 Those sown among thorns are another *c*.
Lk 1: 5 Zechariah of the priestly *c* of Abijah;
1: 8 when it was the turn of Zechariah's *c*
15:15 to one of the propertied *c* of the place,
18:18 One of the ruling *c* asked him then,
23:13 together the chief priests, the ruling *c*,
Acts 4: 6 who were of the high-priestly *c* were there.

CLASSED (1)

1Chr 23:11 therefore they were *c* as a single family,

CLASSES (16)

1Chr 23: 6 them into *c* according to the sons of Levi:
24: 1 of Aaron also were divided into *c*.
26: 1 As for the *c* of gatekeepers.
26:12 To these *c* of gatekeepers,
26:19 These were the *c* of the gatekeepers,
28:21 The *c* of the priests and Levites are ready
2Chr 5:11 to the rotation of their various *c*),
8:14 various *c* of the priests for their service,
8:14 of the various *c* stood guard at each gate,
31: 2 Hezekiah reestablished the *c* of the
31:15 and small alike, according to their *c*.
31:16 their service in the order of their *c*.
31:17 according to their various offices and *c*.
35: 4 in your ancestral houses and your *c*
35:10 in their *c* according to the king's command.
Ezr 6:18 they set up the priests in their *c*

CLASSIFICATION (1)

2Chr 31: 2 the Levites according to their former *c*,

CLASSIFY (1)

2Cor 10:12 as to *c* or compare ourselves with certain

CLAUDIA (1)

2Tm 4:21 Eubulus, Pudens, Linus, *C*,

CLAUDIUS (3)

Acts 11:28 (It did in fact occur while *C* was emperor.)
18: 2 of *C* had ordered all Jews to leave Rome.
23:26 *C* Lysias sends greetings to His Excellency

CLAW (1)

Is 58: 4 and fighting, striking with wicked *c*.

CLAWS (3)

1Sm 17:37 me from the *c* of the lion and the bear,
Dn 4:30 eagle, and his nails like the *c* of a bird.
7:19 crushing with its iron teeth and bronze *c*,

CLAY (33)

Gn 2: 7 LORD God formed man out of the *c*
Lv 6:21 A *c* vessel in which it has been cooked
11:33 of these creatures fall into a *c* vessel,
Jb 4:19 more with those that dwell in houses of *c*,
10: 9 Oh, remember that you fashioned me from *c*!
13:12 maxims, your fabrications are mounds of *c*.
15:28 That are crumbling into *c* with no shadow
33: 6 have been taken from the same *c* by God.
38:14 The earth is changed as is *c* by the seal,
Ps(s) 22:16 My throat is dried up like baked *c*,
Wis 15: 7 either class the worker in *c* is the judge.
15: 8 a meaningless god from the selfsame *c*;
15:10 his hope, and more ignoble than *c* his life;
Sir 33:10 So too, all men are of *c*,
33:13 Like *c* in the hands of a potter,
38:30 With his hands he molds the *c*,
Is 29:16 though the potter were taken to be the *c*:
41:25 like red earth, as the potter treads the *c*.
45: 9 Dare the *c* say to its modeler,
64: 7 we are the *c* and you the potter:
Jer 18: 4 Whenever the object of *c* which he was
18: 4 making of the *c* another object of whatever
18: 6 Indeed, like *c* in the hand of the potter,
19:11 a *c* pot so that it cannot be repaired.
Ez 4: 1 As for you, son of man, take a *c* tablet;
26:12 and your *c* shall be cast into the sea.
Dn 2:41 As you saw the iron mixed with *c* tile,
2:43 The iron mixed with *c* tile means that they
2:43 united, any more than iron mixes with *c*.
14: 7 "it is only *c* inside and bronze outside;
Na 3:14 Go down into the mud and tread the *c*,
Rom 9:21 make from the same lump of *c* one vessel
2Tm 2:20 of gold and silver but also of wood and *c*,

CLAYEY (2)

1Kgs 7:46 the *c* ground between Succoth and Zarethan.
2Chr 4:17 in the Jordan region, in the *c* ground

CLEAN (108)

Gn 7: 2 Of every *c* animal,
7: 3 likewise, of every *c* bird of the air,
7: 8 Of the *c* animals and the unclean,
8:20 from every clean animal and every *c* bird,
20: 5 I did it in good faith and with *c* hands."
Lv 4:12 brought outside the camp to a *c* place
6: 4 the ashes to a *c* place outside the camp.
7:19 "All who are *c* may partake of this flesh.
10:10 between what is *c* and what is unclean;
10:14 leg of the raised offering, in a *c* place;
11:32 until evening, when it again becomes *c*.
11:36 a cistern for collecting water remains *c*;
11:37 Any sort of cultivated grain remains *c*
11:47 distinguish between the *c* and the unclean,
12: 7 will be *c* again after her flow of blood.
12: 8 for her, and thus she will again be *c*."
13: 6 skin, the priest shall declare the man *c*;
13: 6 shall wash his garments and so become *c*.
13: 7 himself to the priest to be declared *c*,
13:13 body, he shall declare the stricken man *c*;
13:13 it has all turned white, the man is *c*.
13:17 stricken man clean, and thus he will be *c*.
13:23 the priest shall therefore declare him *c*.
13:28 priest shall therefore declare the man *c*,
13:34 the skin, he shall declare the man *c*;
13:34 wash his garments, and thus he will be *c*.
13:35 on his skin after he has been declared *c*,
13:37 *c*, and the priest shall declare him clean.
13:39 on the skin, and the person therefore is *c*.
13:58 a second time, and thus it will be *c*.
13:59 to determine whether it is *c* or unclean."
14: 4 to be purified, to get two live, *c* birds,
14: 8 is thus made *c* may he come inside the camp;
14: 9 and so he will be *c*.
14:20 made atonement for him, the man will be *c*.
14:48 plastering, he shall declare the house *c*,
14:53 made atonement for it, the house will be *c*.
15: 8 If the afflicted man spits on a *c* man,
15:13 body in fresh water, and so he will be *c*.
16:19 Thus he shall render it *c* and holy,
16:30 atonement is made for you to make you *c*,
17:15 until evening, and then he will be *c*.
20:25 *c* animals from the unclean, and the clean
22: 4 offerings, unless he again becomes *c*.
22: 7 then when the sun sets, he again becomes *c*.
Nm 9:13 anyone who is *c* and not away on a journey,
18:11 in your family who are *c* may partake of it.

18:13 your family who are c may partake of them.
19: 9 a man who is c shall gather up the ashes
19: 9 deposit them in a c place outside the camp.
19:12 seventh day, and then he will be c again.
19:12 on the seventh day, he will not become c.
19:18 Then a man who is c shall take some hyssop,
19:19 The c man shall sprinkle the unclean on
19:19 and in the evening he will be c again.
31:23 put into the fire, that it may become c;
31:24 your clothes, and then you will again be c.
Dt 12:15 the unclean as well as the c may eat it,
12:22 the unclean and the c eating it alike.
14:11 "You may eat all c birds.
14:20 But you may eat any c winged creatures.
15:22 it, the unclean and the c eating it alike,
28:39 wine, for the grubs will eat the vines c.
2Kgs 5:10 your flesh will heal, and you will be c."
5:13 now, since he said to you, 'Wash and be c,'
5:14 the flesh of a little child, and he was c.
21:13 will wipe Jerusalem c as one wipes a dish,
2Chr 29: 5 and c out the filth from the sanctuary.
30:19 though he be not c as holiness requires."
Jb 11: 4 is pure, and I am c in your sight"?
14: 4 Can a man be found who is c of defilement?
15:15 and if the heavens are not c in his sight,
17: 9 he who has c hands increase in strength.
33: 9 "I am c and without transgression;
Ps(s) 24: 4 whose hands are sinless, whose heart is c.
51:12 A c heart create for me, O God,
73: 1 the LORD, to those who are c of heart!
73:13 c and washed my hands as an innocent man?
Prv 20: 9 Who can say, "I have made my heart c,
Eccl 9: 2 and the bad, for the c and the unclean,
Wis 15: 7 serve for c purposes and their opposites,
Sir 34: 4 Can the unclean produce the c?
Is 1:16 Wash yourselves c!
28: 8 with filthy vomit, with no place left c.
66:20 to the house of the LORD in c vessels.
Jer 13:27 long will it yet be before you become c!
Bar 6:12 They wipe their faces c of the house dust
Ez 22:26 difference between the unclean and the c;
36:25 I will sprinkle c water upon you to
44:23 difference between the c and the unclean.
Am 4: 6 your teeth c of food in all your cities,
Zec 3: 5 He also said, "Put a c miter on his head."
3: 5 And they put a c miter on his head and
Mt 23:26 of the cup so that its outside may be c.
Mk 7:19 Thus did he render all foods c.
Lk 11:41 have as alms, all will be wiped c for you.
Jn 13:11 reason he said, "Not all are washed c,"
15: 2 ones he trims c to increase their yield.
15: 3 You are c already,
Rom 14:20 True, all foods are c;
Ti 1:15 To the c all things are clean,
1:15 to those defiled unbelievers nothing is c.
Heb 10:22 our hearts sprinkled c from the evil which

CLEANNESS (6)

Lv 14:57 state of uncleanness and when a state of c.
2Sm 22:21 to the c of my hands he requited me.
Jb 22:30 you shall be delivered through c of hands.
Ps(s) 18:21 to the c of my hands he requited me;
18:25 to the c of my hands in his sight.
Sir 51:20 I purified my hands in c I attained to her.

CLEANSE (25)

1Sm 16: 5 So c yourselves and join me today for the
16: 5 He also had Jesse and his sons c
2Chr 29:15 to c the LORD's house in keeping with his
29:16 the interior of the LORD's house to c it;
34: 8 order to c the temple as well as the land,
Jb 9:30 myself with snow and c my hands with lye,
Ps(s) 19:13 C me from my unknown faults!
51: 4 wash me from my guilt and of my sin c me.
51: 9 C me of sin with hyssop,
Sir 38:10 hands be just, c your heart of every sin;
Jer 4:11 Not to winnow, not to c,
4:14 C your heart of evil,
33: 8 I will c them of all the guilt they
Ez 36:25 upon you to c you from all your impurities,
36:25 and from all your idols I will c you.
37:23 and c them so that they may be my people
Mt 23:25 You c the outside of cup and dish,
23:26 First c the inside of the cup so that its
Lk 11:39 You c the outside of cup and dish,
2Tm 2:21 The lesson is that if a person will but c
Ti 2:14 and to c for himself a people of his own,
Heb 9:10 but can only c in matters of food and
9:14 c our consciences from dead works to
Jas 4: 8 C your hands,
1Jn 1: 9 forgive our sins and c us from every wrong.

CLEANSED (17)

Lv 16:30 may be c of all your sins before the LORD,
Nm 8:21 When the Levites had c themselves of sin
1Sm 20:26 by accident, and not yet have been c."
2Kgs 5:12 Could I not wash in them and be c?"
2Chr 4: 6 Here were c the victims for the holocausts;
29:18 "We have c the entire house of the LORD,
30:18 Issachar and Zebulun, had not c themselves.
Neh 13:30 Thus I c them of all foreign contamination.
1Mc 13:50 from the citadel and c it of impurities.
14: 7 He c the citadel of its impurities;
Prv 20: 9 made my heart clean, I am c of my sin"?
20:30 Evil is c away by bloody lashes,
Ez 44:26 After a priest has been c,
Jn 13:10 he is entirely c,
Heb 1: 3 When he had c us from our sins,
9:13 who are defiled so that their flesh is c,
10: 2 offering them, for the worshipers, once c,

CLEANSES (1)

1Jn 1: 7 blood of his Son Jesus c us from all sin.

CLEANSING (2)

Nm 4:13 After c the altar of its ashes,
2Pt 1: 9 He forgets the c of his long-past sins.

CLEAR (64)

Ex 12:15 you shall have your houses c of all leaven.
24:10 sapphire tilework, as c as the sky itself.
27:20 to bring you c oil of crushed olives,
Lv 24: 2 you c oil of crushed olives for the light,
Nm 13:20 Is the soil fertile or barren, wooded or c?
15:34 for there was no c decision as to what
Jos 17:15 go up to the forest and c out a place for
17:18 is now forest shall be yours when you c it.
Jgs 2: 3 you, I will not c them out of your way;
2:21 I for my part will not c away for them any
1Kgs 2:42 to your c understanding of my warning that,
7:36 the panels, wherever there was a c space,
2Mc 4:33 When Onias had c evidence of the facts,
12:40 So it was c to all that this was why these
15:35 a c and evident proof to all of the LORD's
Jb 25: 5 and the stars are not c in his sight.
Ps(s) 19: 9 The command of the LORD is c,
30: 2 for you drew me c and did not let my
Wis 7:22 holy, unique, Manifold, subtle, agile, c,
Sir 17:15 All their actions are c as the sun to him,
31:20 slumber and a c mind next day on rising.
32:16 out of obscurity he draws forth a c plan.
42:16 As the rising sun is c to all,
43: 1 The c vault of the sky shines forth like
Is 62:10 up, build up the highway, c it of stones,
Bar 6:50 kings it will be c that they are not gods,
6:68 in no way is it c to us that they are gods;
Ez 25: 9 therefore I will c the shoulder of Moab
32:14 Then will I make their waters c,
Dn 13:48 without examination and without c evidence?
Mt 3:12 He will c the threshing floor and gather
7:13 leads to damnation is wide, the road is c,
Mk 1: 3 the way of the Lord, c him a straight path.'"
5:19 "Go home to your family and make it c to
Lk 3: 4 the way of the Lord, C him a straight path.
3:17 His winnowing-fan is in his hand to c his
5:24 to make it c to you that the Son of Man
Jn 3:21 to make c that his deeds are done in God."
Acts 4:18 So they called them back and made it c
10:28 But God has made it c to me that no one
12: 9 but with no c realization that this was
23: 1 my life with a c conscience before God."
24:16 to keep my conscience c before God and man.
Rom 1:10 I may at last find my way c to visit you.
1:19 can be known about God is c to them;
2:20 at hand a c pattern of knowledge and truth.
1Cor 3: 4 c that you are still at the human level?
3:13 or straw, the work of each will be made c.
5:11 is c that you must not eat with such a man.
11: 6 it is c that she ought to wear a veil.
15:27 it is c that he who has made everything
2Cor 4: 7 to make it c that its surpassing power
Phil 1:10 so that with a c conscience and blameless
1:27 it will be c that you are standing firm in
1Thes 4:13 you be c about those who sleep in death,
1Tm 3: 9 revealed faith with a c conscience.
6:20 Stay c of worldly,
2Tm 1: 3 whom I worship with a c conscience,
1:10 into c light through the gospel.
2: 7 for the Lord will make my meaning fully c.
3: 5 Stay c of them.
Heb 7:14 It is c that our Lord rose from the tribe
1Pt 3:16 Keep your conscience c,
Rv 22: 1 river of life-giving water, c as crystal,

CLEAR-SIGHTED (1)

Ex 23: 8 c and twists the words even of the just.

CLEARED (16)

Lv 14:36 priest shall then order the house to be c
Dt 2:21 LORD c out of the way for the Ammonites,
2:23 migrating from Caphtor, c away the Avvim,
Jgs 11:23 has c the Amorites out of the way of his
11:24 that the LORD, our God, has c out for us?
2Sm 7:23 doing awe-inspiring things as you c nations
1Kgs 14:24 the LORD had c out of the Israelites' way.
2Kgs 16: 3 had c out of the way of the Israelites.
17: 8 rites of the nations whom the LORD had c
21: 2 had c out of the way of the Israelites.
1Chr 5:25 the land, whom God had c out of their way.
2Chr 28: 3 the LORD had c out before the Israelites.
33: 2 had c out of the way of the Israelites.
Ps(s) 80:10 You c the ground for it,
Is 5: 2 He spaded it, c it of stones,
35: 5 be opened, the ears of the deaf be c;

CLEARER (2)

Heb 6:17 give the heirs of his promise even c evidence
7:15 The matter is c still if another priest is

CLEAREST (1)

Ez 34:18 it not enough for you to drink the c water,

CLEARING (3)

Dt 2:12 c them out of the way and taking their
2:22 in Seir, by c the Horites out of their way,
Jos 7: 5 They pressed them back across the c in

CLEARLY (26)

Ex 10:10 C, you have some evil in mind.
Dt 27: 8 inscribe all the words of this law very c."
1Kgs 20: 7 c that this man wants to ruin us.
Jdt 9:14 all the tribes know c that you are the god
1Mc 12: 8 c referred to alliance and friendship.
2Mc 3:17 the man c showed those who saw him
3:28 c experienced the sovereign power of God.
9: 8 c manifesting to all the power of God.
Is 32: 4 the stutterers will speak fluently and c.
Hb 2: 2 Write down the vision C upon the tablets,
Mt 7: 5 then you will see c to take the speck from
12:12 C, good deeds may be performed on the
27:54 and said, C this was the Son of God!"
Mk 8:25 restored and he could see everything c.
15:39 declared, C this man was the Son of God!"
Lk 6:42 then you will see c enough to remove the
Acts 10: 3 he had a vision in which he c saw
Rom 7:13 Rather, sin, in order to be seen c as sin,
1Cor 11:19 you for the tried and true to stand out c.
2Cor 3: 3 C you are a letter of Christ which I have
Gal 2:11 him, because he was c in the wrong.
3:18 C, if one's inheritance comes through the
Eph 1:17 spirit of wisdom and insight to know him c.
Col 4: 4 Pray that I may speak it c, as I must.
1Tm 5:25 some good deeds stand out c as such;
Rv 15: 4 Your mighty deeds are c seen."

CLEARS (1)

Prv 18:16 A man's gift c the way for him,

CLEAVE (3)

Jb 19:20 My bones c to my skin,
Ps(s) 137: 6 c to my palate if I remember you not,
Ez 21:21 C to the right!

CLEAVES (2)

Ps(s) 22:16 up like baked clay, my tongue c to my jaws;
Lam 4: 4 c to the roof of its mouth in thirst;

CLEFT (8)

Nm 21:20 from Bamoth to the c in the plateau of
Ps(s) 78:13 He c the sea and brought them through,
78:15 He c the rocks in the desert and gave them
105:41 He c the rock, and the water gushed forth;
Wis 5:11 c by the rushing force Of speeding wings,
Is 48:21 he c the rock,
Jer 13: 4 there hide it in a c of the rock.
Zec 14: 4 The Mount of Olives shall be c in two from

CLEFTS (4)

Sg 2:14 "O my dove in the c of the rock,
Is 7:19 in the steep ravines and in the rocky c,
Jer 16:16 and hill and from the c of the rocks.
Ob 1: 3 you who dwell in the c of the rock,

CLEMENCY (5)

Est B: 2 but always to deal fairly and with c;
Wis 12:18 you are master of might, you judge with c,
Bar 2:27 in all your c and in all your great mercy.
Jon 4: 2 and merciful God, slow to anger, rich in c,
Mi 7:18 anger forever, but delights rather in c,

CLEMENT (1)

Phil 4: 3 C and the others who have labored with me,

CLENCHED (2)

Sir 4:31 to receive and c when it is time to give.
30:10 when finally your teeth are c in remorse.

CLEOPAS (1)

Lk 24:18 in distress, and one of them, C by name,

CLEOPATRA (2)

1Mc 10:57 So Ptolemy with his daughter C set out
10:58 gave him his daughter C in marriage.

CLERK (1)

Acts 19:35 Finally the town c quieted the mob.

CLEVER (6)

2Sm 13: 3 of David's brother Shimeah, who was very *c.*
Ez 33:32 with a pleasant voice and a *c* touch.
Mt 10:16 must be *c* as snakes and innocent as doves.
11:25 *c* you have revealed to the merest children.
Lk 10:21 *c* you have revealed to the merest children.
1Cor 1:19 wise, and thwart the cleverness of the *c.*"

CLEVERLY (2)

Mt 25:23 His master said to him, *C* done!
2Pt 1:16 It was not by way of *c* concocted myths

CLEVERNESS (2)

Dn 11:25 He shall call on his strength and *c* to
1Cor 1:19 the wise, and thwart the *c* of the clever."

CLIENTS (2)

2Kgs 12: 6 take for themselves, each from his own *c.*
12: 8 must no longer take funds from your *c,*

CLIFF (8)

Nm 24:21 O smith, and your nest is set on a *c;*
Jgs 15: 8 and remained in a cavern of the *c* of Etam.
15:11 cavern in the *c* of Etam and said to Samson,
15:13 new ropes and brought him up from the *c.*
Jb 39:28 On the *c* he dwells and spends the night,
39:28 on the spur of the *c* or the fortress.
Sg 2:14 rock, in the secret recesses of the *c,*
Am 6:12 Can horses run across a *c?*

CLIFFS (5)

Ps(s) 104:18 the *c* are a refuge for rock-badgers.
Is 2:21 in the rocks and into crevices in the *c,*
57: 5 the wadies, behind the crevices in the *c?*
Jer 51:25 hand against you, roll you down over the *c,*
Ez 38:20 shall be overturned, and *c* shall tumble,

CLIMAX (3)

Ez 7: 7 *c* has come for you who dwell in the land!
Lk 22:37 that has to do with me approaches its *c.*"
Rv 15: 1 which would bring God's wrath to a *c.*

CLIMB (10)

1Sm 14:12 said to his armor-bearer, *C* up after me,
1Kgs 18:43 *C* up and look out to sea,"
Sg 7: 9 I will *c* the palm tree,
Is 2: 3 "Come, let us *c* the LORD's mountain,
15: 5 The ascent of Luhith they *c* weeping;
Jer 5:10 *C* to her terraces,
48: 5 The ascent of Luhith they *c* weeping;
Jl 2: 9 run upon the wall, they *c* into the houses;
Am 9: 2 Though they *c* to the heavens,
Mi 4: 2 "Come, let us *c* the mount of the LORD,

CLIMBED (14)

Gn 49: 4 for you *c* into your father's bed and
Ex 17:10 after Moses had *c* to the top of the hill
Nm 20:27 *c* Mount Hor in view of the whole community,
Dt 32:50 you shall die on the mountain you have *c,*
Jos 15: 6 The northern boundary *c* from the bay where
15: 7 Thence it *c* to Debir,
1Kgs 18:42 drink, while Elijah *c* to the top of Carmel,
2Kgs 19:23 my many chariots I *c* the mountain heights,
2Mc 2: 4 which Moses *c* to see God's inheritance.
10:36 Others who *c* up the same way swung around
Is 37:24 my many chariots I *c* the mountain heights,
Ez 40: 6 the gate which faced the east, *c* its steps,
Mt 14:32 Once they had *c* into the boat,
Lk 19: 4 then *c* a sycamore tree which was along

CLIMBING (1)

Jos 15: 8 *C* again to the Valley of Ben-hinnom on the

CLIMBS (3)

Is 24:18 He who *c* out of the pit will be caught in
Jer 48:44 who *c* from the pit is caught in the trap;
Jn 10: 1 *c* in some other way is a thief

CLING (21)

2Kgs 5:27 *c* to you and your descendants forever."
Tb 5:18 Is he not the staff to which we *c,*
Jb 8:15 he shall *c* to it,
24: 8 and for want of shelter they *c* to the rock.
Ps(s) 119:31 I *c* to your decrees;
Sir 2: 3 *C* to him,
Is 27: 5 Or shall he *c* to me for refuge?
64: 6 your name, who rouses himself to *c* to you;
Jer 8: 5 Why do they *c* to deceptive idols,
13:11 and the whole house of Judah *c* to me,
42:16 you dread shall *c* to you no less in Egypt,
Lam 4: 5 up in purple now *c* to the ash heaps.
Bar 1:20 with milk and honey, *c* to us even today.
3: 4 the Lord, their God, and the evils *c* to us.
4: 1 All who *c* to her will live,
Mt 19: 5 his father and mother and *c* to his wife,
Mk 7: 3 *c* to the custom of their ancestors and
7: 8 and *c* to what is human tradition."
Jn 20:17 "Do not *c* to me,
Rom 12: 9 Detest what is evil, *c* to what is good.
Eph 5:31 father and mother, and shall *c* to his wife,

CLINGING (1)

Acts 3:11 As the man stood there *c* to Peter and John,

CLINGS (7)

Gn 2:24 his father and mother and *c* to his wife,
Nm 19:13 his uncleanness still *c* to him.
Jb 31: 7 my eyes, or any stain *c* to my hands,
Ps(s) 63: 9 My soul *c* fast to you;
91:14 Because he *c* to me, I will deliver him
Jer 13:11 close as the loincloth *c* to a man's loins,
Heb 12: 1 every encumbrance of sin which *c* to us

CLIP (1)

Lv 19:27 Do not *c* your hair at the temples,

CLOAK (53)

Gn 39:12 the house, she laid hold of him by his *c,*
39:12 But leaving the *c* in her hand,
39:13 left his *c* in her hand as he fled outside,
39:15 left his *c* beside me and ran away outside."
39:16 the *c* with her until his master came home.
39:18 he left his *c* beside me and fled outside."
Ex 22:25 If you take your neighbor's *c* as a pledge,
22:26 for this *c* of his is the only covering he
Dt 22:12 corners of the *c* that you wrap around you."
Jgs 8:25 and spread out a *c* into which everyone
Ru 3: 9 Spread the corner of your *c* over me,
3:15 to her, "Take off your *c* and hold it out."
1Kgs 11:29 area, and the prophet was wearing a new *c.*
11:30 Ahijah took off his new *c,*
19:13 Elijah hid his face in his *c* and went and
19:19 went over to him and threw his *c* over him.
Ezr 9: 3 this thing, I tore my *c* and my mantle,
9: 5 with *c* and mantle torn I fell on my knees,
Est 8:15 crown of gold and a *c* of crimson byssus.
2Mc 12:35 *c* and dragged him along by main strength,
Jb 1:20 began to tear his *c* and cut off his hair.
Ps(s) 18:12 And he made darkness the *c* about him;
74:11 keep your right hand idle beneath your *c?*
104: 2 and glory, robed in light as with a *c.*
Prv 30: 4 Who has bound up the waters in a *c*—
Sir 11: 4 the worn *c* and jibe at no man's bitter day:
Is 9: 4 in battle, every *c* rolled in blood,
Jer 43:12 As a shepherd delouses his *c,*
Bar 5: 2 Wrapped in the *c* of justice from God,
Ez 16: 8 of my *c* over you to cover your nakedness;
Mt 9:16 a piece of unshrunken cloth on an old *c;*
9:20 behind him and touched the tassel on his *c.*
9:21 "If only I can touch his *c,*"
14:36 do no more than touch the tassel of his *c.*
24:18 he must not turn back to pick up his *c.*
27:28 and wrapped him in a scarlet military *c.*
27:31 a fool of him, they stripped him of the *c,*
Mk 2:21 a patch of unshrunken cloth on an old *c.*
5:27 him in the crowd and put her hand to his *c.*
6:56 to let them touch just the tassel of his *c.*
10:50 He threw aside his *c,*
13:16 he must not turn back to pick up his *c.*
Lk 8:44 behind him and touched the tassel on his *c.*
Jn 13: 4 rose from the meal and took off his *c.*
13:12 *c* back on and reclined at table once more.
19: 2 around his shoulders a *c* of royal purple.
19: 5 the crown of thorns and the purple *c,*
Acts 12: 8 him, "Now put on your *c* and follow me."
2Tm 4:13 bring the *c* I left in Troas with Carpus,
Heb 1:12 You will roll them up like a *c;*
1Pt 2:16 do not use your freedom as a *c* for vice.
Rv 19:13 He wore a *c* that had been dipped in blood,
19:16 the part of the *c* that covered his thigh:

CLOAKS (13)

Ex 12:34 wrapped in their *c* on their shoulders.
Jb 2:12 their *c* and threw dust upon their heads.
Sir 40: 4 crown or is wrapped in the coarsest of *c*—
Is 3:22 the court dresses, wraps, *c,*
Mt 21: 7 ass and the colt and laid their *c* on them,
21: 8 The huge crowd spread their *c* on the road,
Mk 11: 7 to Jesus and threw their *c* across its back,
11: 8 Many people spread their *c* on the road,
Lk 19:35 animal to Jesus, and laying their *c* on it,
19:36 their *c* on the roadway as he moved along;
Acts 7:58 *c* at the feet of a young man named Saul.
22:20 guarded the *c* of those who killed him!'
22:23 their *c* and flung dirt through the air.

CLODS (5)

Jb 21:33 Sweet to him are the *c* of the valley,
38:38 is fused into a mass and its *c* made solid?
Ps(s) 65:11 drenching its furrows, breaking up its *c,*
Prv 8:26 not made, nor the first *c* of the world.
Jl 1:17 The seed lies shriveled under its *c;*

CLOGGED (1)

Ex 14:25 and he so *c* their chariot wheels that they

CLOPAS (1)

Jn 19:25 his mother's sister, Mary the wife of *C,*

CLOSE (74)

Gn 14: 6 as far as El-paran, *c* by the wilderness.
18: 5 that you have come this *c* to your servant,
48:10 When Joseph brought his sons *c* to him,
Ex 24: 2 but Moses alone is to come *c* to the LORD;
34:22 at the fruit harvest at the *c* of the year.
Lv 3: 9 tail, which he must sever *c* to the spine,
14:38 he shall *c* the door of the house behind
18: 6 "None of you shall approach a *c* relative
Dt 4: 7 there that has gods so *c* to it as the LORD,
11:17 against you and he will *c* up the heavens,
15: 7 heart nor *c* your hand to him in his need.
32:35 *C* at hand is the day of their disaster and
Jos 7: 9 they will *c* in around us and efface our
1Sm 17:48 then moved to meet David at *c* quarters,
1Kgs 21: 2 be my vegetable garden, since it is *c* by,
2Kgs 4: 4 *c* the door on yourself and your children;
6:32 *c* the door and hold it fast against him.
2Chr 7:13 If I *c* heaven so that there is no rain,
Tb 1:22 He was a *c* relative—in fact, my nephew.
3:15 Nor does he have a *c* kinsman or other
4:14 Keep a *c* watch on yourself,
6:10 Media and were getting *c* to Ecbatana,
6:15 slay any man who wishes to come *c* to her.
Jdt 8:27 that he chastises those who are *c* to him."
13: 7 his sword from it, drew *c* to the bed,
Est C:20 to *c* the mouths of those who praise you,
2Mc 7:27 she leaned over *c* to her son and said in
10:27 halting when they were *c* to the enemy.
Jb 41: 6 of his mouth, *c* to his terrible teeth?
41: 8 so *c* to the next that no space intervenes;
Ps(s) 34:19 The LORD is *c* to the brokenhearted;
69:16 me up, nor the pit *c* its mouth over me.
88:18 on all sides they *c* in upon me.
148:14 children of Israel, the people *c* to him.
Prv 22:15 Folly is *c* to the heart of a child,
Wis 6:19 and incorruptibility makes one *c* to God;
11:11 afar off and those *c* by were afflicted:
Sir 6:19 though plowing and sowing, draw *c* to her;
6:27 With all your soul draw *c* to her;
6:34 whoever is wise, stay *c* to him.
26:11 Follow *c* if her eyes are bold,
30:11 youth, and *c* not your eyes to his follies.
42:11 Keep a *c* watch on your daughter,
51:26 For she is *c* to those who seek her,
Is 1:15 spread out your hands, I *c* my eyes to you;
6:10 to dull their ears and *c* their eyes;
21: 7 camel, Then let him pay heed, very *c* heed.
26:20 your chambers, and *c* your doors behind you;
66: 9 who allow her to conceive, yet *c* her womb?
Jer 13:11 *c* as the loincloth clings to a man's loins,
Ez 31:15 world I made the abyss *c* up over him;
Mt 6: 6 you pray, go to your room, *c* your door,
Mk 5:21 around him and he stayed *c* to the lake.
11: 1 on the Mount of Olives, *c* to Jerusalem,
Lk 5:17 Sitting *c* by were Pharisees and teachers
9:44 "Pay *c* attention to what I tell you:
18:40 When he had come *c,*
21:34 day will suddenly *c* in on you like a trap.
Jn 13:23 Jesus loved, reclined *c* to him as they ate.
19:42 Jesus there, for the tomb was *c* at hand.
Acts 9:24 They went so far as to keep *c* watch on the
10:24 had called in his relatives and *c* friends.
2Cor 11:32 *c* watch on the city in order to arrest me,
Gal 5: 2 Pay *c* attention to me,
Col 2:19 when he should be in *c* touch with the head.
Ti 1:13 an attempt to keep them *c* to sound faith,
Heb 8:13 and has grown old is *c* to disappearing.
Jas 4: 8 Draw *c* to God, and he will draw close
1Pt 4: 7 The consummation of all is *c* at hand.
2Pt 1:14 how *c* is the day when I must fold my tent.
Rv 3: 7 David's key, who opens and no one can *c,*
3: 8 an open door before you which no one can *c.*
11: 6 These witnesses have power to *c* up the sky

CLOSED (42)

Gn 2:21 of his ribs and *c* up its place with flesh.
8: 2 and the floodgates of the sky were *c,*
19: 4 people to the last man *c* in on the house.
19:10 Lot inside with them, and *c* the door;
20:18 for God had tightly *c* every womb in
46: 4 back here, after Joseph has *c* your eyes."
Ex 14: 3 The desert has *c* in on them.'
Nm 16:33 the earth *c* over them,
Jgs 3:22 and the fat *c* over the blade because he
2Sm 18:15 Joab's young armor-bearers *c* in on Absalom,
1Kgs 8:35 "If the sky is *c,*
2Kgs 4:33 He went in, *c* the door on them both,
2Chr 6:26 When the sky is *c* so that there is no rain,
28:24 He *c* the doors of the LORD's house and had
29: 7 They also *c* the doors of the vestibule,
Neh 4: 1 for the gaps were beginning to be *c* up
13:19 I ordered the doors to be *c* and forbade
Tb 8: 4 the bedroom and *c* the door behind them,
Jdt 13: 1 Bagoas *c* the tent from the outside and
1Mc 7:46 of Judea people came out and *c* in on them.
9:55 his mouth was *c* and he was paralyzed,
12:48 men of the city *c* the gates and seized him;

15:14 the city, his ships c in along the coast,
Jb 16: 7 and stunned, all my company has c in on me.
Is 32: 3 The eyes of those who see will not be c;
60:11 day and night they shall not be c
Ez 44: 1 but it was c.
44: 2 This gate is to remain c;
44: 2 has entered by it, it shall remain c.
46: 1 remain c throughout the six working days,
46: 2 the gate shall not be c until evening.
46:12 the gate shall be c after his departure.
Dn 6:23 My God has sent his angel and c the lions'
14:14 sealed the c door with the king's ring,
Hos 13:14 My eyes are c to compassion.
Mt 13:15 their ears, they have firmly c their eyes;
Mk 3: 5 that they had c their minds against him.
6:52 completely c to the meaning of the events.
Lk 4:25 remained c for three and a half years
Acts 21:30 the temple, and immediately c its gates.
28:27 their eyes they have c,
Rv 20: 3 the abyss, which he c and sealed over him.

CLOSELY (14)

Ex 3: 4 saw him coming over to look at it more c,
Ru 3:12 Now, though indeed I am c related to you,
1Sm 31: 2 Philistines pursued Saul and his sons c,
1Kgs 16:26 c imitated the sinful conduct of Jeroboam,
Neh 8:13 and examined the words of the law more c.
Jer 8: 6 I listen c:
48:19 Stand by the wayside, watch c,
Mk 14:67 himself, she looked at him more c and said,
Lk 14: 1 the leading Pharisees, they observed him c.
Jn 18:15 another disciple, kept following Jesus c.
Acts 8: 6 performed attended c to what he had to say.
Col 2: 2 and themselves to be c united in love,
2Tm 3:10 have followed c my teaching and my conduct.
2Pt 1:19 Keep your attention c fixed on it,

CLOSER (15)

Gn 19: 9 Lot, moving in c to break down the door.
27:21 Isaac then said to Jacob, "Come c,
27:22 So Jacob moved up c to his father.
27:26 his father Isaac said to him, "Come c,
45: 4 "Come c to me," he told his brothers.
Ex 14:20 camps coming any c together all night long.
Dt 5:27 Go c, you, and hear all that the LORD,
Ru 3:12 to you, you have another relative still c.
4: 1 and when he saw the c relative of whom he
1Sm 17:41 also advanced c and c to David.
Prv 25: 7 it is better that you be told, "Come up c!"
Jer 10:22 it comes c,
Rom 13:11 is c than when we first accepted the faith.
1Cor 8: 8 Now food does not bring us c to God.

CLOSES (6)

Jb 5:16 have hope, and iniquity c her mouth.
Ps(s) 22:17 me, a pack of evildoers c in upon me;
107:42 rejoice, and all wickedness c its mouth.
Prv 17:28 if he c his lips,
1Jn 3:17 enough of this world's goods yet c his heart
Rv 3: 7 one can close, who c and no one can open,

CLOSEST (6)

Lv 25:25 sell some of his property, his c relative,
Tb 6:12 Since you are Sarah's c relative,
7:10 but you, because you are my c relative.
Prv 4:23 With c custody,
Ez 42: 5 than the c chambers and those in between;
42: 6 ground than the c and the middle chambers.

CLOSET (1)

Jer 38:11 went first to the linen c in the palace,

CLOSING (7)

Lv 23:36 that solemn c you shall do no sort of work.
2Sm 1: 6 with chariots and horsemen c in on him.
1Kgs 11:27 c up the breach of his father's City of
2Kgs 4: 5 so, c the door on herself and her children.
4:21 C the door on him,
Is 33:15 bloodshed, c his eyes lest he look on evil
Jon 2: 7 the nether world were c behind me forever,

CLOTH (38)

Ex 28: 6 embroidered on c of fine linen twined.
28:15 and scarlet yarn on c of fine linen twined.
35:35 the making of variegated c of violet,
38:23 and a weaver of variegated c of violet,
39: 8 and scarlet yarn on c of fine linen twined.
Lv 11:32 use, whether it be an article of wood, c,
15:17 Any piece of c or leather with seed on it
Nm 4: 6 and on top of this spread an all-violet c.
4: 7 violet c and put on it the plates and cups,
4: 8 c and cover all this with tahash skin.
4: 9 c to cover the lampstand with its lamps,
4:11 golden altar they shall spread a violet c,
4:12 violet c and cover them with tahash skin.
4:13 they shall spread a purple c over it.
31:20 You shall also purify every article of c,
Dt 22:11 wear c of two different kinds of thread,
22:17 out the c before the elders of the city.
Jgs 5:30 man, Spoils of dyed c as Sisera's spoil,
2Sm 7: 6 I have been going about in a tent under c.
2Kgs 8:15 The next day, however, Hazael took a c,
Tb 2:11 my wife Anna worked for hire at weaving c,
2:12 the c and sent it back to the owners.
1Mc 4:23 much gold and silver, violet and crimson c,
Prv 31:13 and flax and makes c with skillful hands.
Sg 3:10 its roof of gold, Its seat of purple c.
Sir 39:26 the blood of the grape, and oil, and c;
Is 50: 9 Lo, they will all wear out like c,
Ez 16:13 of fine linen, silk, and embroidered c.
27:16 exchanging garnets, purple, embroidered c,
27:24 garments, violet mantles, embroidered c,
Mt 9:16 a piece of unshrunken c on an old cloak;
Mk 2:21 a patch of unshrunken c on an old cloak.
14:51 who was covered by nothing but a linen c.
14:52 him he left the c behind and ran off naked.
Jn 11:44 with linen strips, his face wrapped in a c.
19:40 it up in wrappings of c with perfumed oils.
20: 7 piece of c which had covered the head
Rv 18:12 and purple garments, silk and scarlet c;

CLOTHE (16)

Ex 28:41 shall c your brother Aaron and his sons.
29: 5 the vestments and c Aaron with the tunic,
29: 8 his sons also and c them with the tunics,
40:13 C Aaron with the sacred vestments and
40:14 his sons also, and c them with the tunics.
Est 6: 9 must c the man the king wishes to reward,
Ps(s) 132:16 Her priests I will c with salvation,
132:18 His enemies I will c with shame,
Is 22:21 I will c him with your robe,
23:18 fill and c themselves in choice attire.
50: 3 I c the heavens in mourning,
Zec 3: 4 garments, and c him in festal garments."
Mt 6:30 c in such splendor the grass of the field,
25:38 away from home or c you in your nakedness?
Col 3:12 beloved, c yourselves with heartfelt mercy,
1Pt 5: 5 one another, c yourselves with humility,

CLOTHED (66)

Gn 3:21 leather garments, with which he c them.
Ex 29:30 shall be c with them for seven days.
Lv 6: 3 c in his linen robe and wearing linen
8: 7 him with the sash, c him with the robe,
8:13 forward Aaron's sons, c them with tunics,
1Sm 17:38 Then Saul c David in his own tunic,
28:14 is an old man who is rising, c in a mantle."
2Sm 1:24 Saul, who c you in scarlet and in finery,
12:16 night to lie on the ground c in sackcloth.
13:19 and tore the long tunic in which she was c.
1Kgs 22:10 c in their robes of state on a threshing
1Chr 15:27 David was c in a robe of fine linen,
21:16 David and the elders, c in sackcloth,
2Chr 5:12 their sons and brothers, c in fine linen,
6:41 priests, LORD God, be c with salvation,
18: 9 c in their robes of state on a threshing
28:15 them who were naked they c from the booty;
28:15 they c them, put sandals on their feet,
Est 4: 2 which no one c in sackcloth might enter.
D: 6 his royal throne, c in full robes of state,
6:11 Haman took the robe and horse, c Mordecai,
8:15 Mordecai left the king's presence c in a
1Mc 10:62 garments and to be c in royal purple;
10:64 and the purple with which he was c,
14:44 to be c in royal purple or wear an
2Mc 11: 8 c in white garments and brandishing gold
Jb 7: 5 My flesh is c with worms and scabs;
8:22 They that hate you shall be c with shame,
10:11 With skin and flesh you c me,
Ps(s) 30:12 off my sackcloth and c me with gladness,
35:26 Let those be c with shame and disgrace who
104: 1 You are c with majesty and glory,
109:18 may he be c with cursing as with a robe;
109:29 Let my accusers be c with disgrace and let
132: 9 May your priests be c with justice;
Prv 31:21 all her charges are doubly c.
31:25 She is c with strength and dignity,
Sir 45: 8 He c him with splendid apparel,
Is 14:19 corrupt, C as those slain at sword-point,
59:17 He c himself with garments of vengeance,
61:10 For he has c me with a robe of salvation,
Jer 10: 9 of the smelter, C with violet and purple
48:37 and the loins of all are c in sackcloth.
Ez 16:10 I c you with an embroidered gown,
23:12 and officers, warriors impeccably c,
26:16 They shall be c in mourning and,
Dn 5: 7 men of Babylon, "shall be c in purple,
5:16 me what it means, you shall be c in purple,
5:29 of Belshazzar they c Daniel in purple,
12: 6 One of them said to the man c in linen,
12: 7 The man c in linen,
Hg 1: 6 have c yourselves,
Zec 3: 5 on his head and c him with the garments.
Mt 3: 4 John was c in a garment of camel's hair,
25:36 and you welcomed me, naked and you c me.
Mk 1: 6 John was c in camel's hair,
5:15 Legion sitting fully c and perfectly sane,
Lk 24:49 until you are c with power from on high."
1Cor 15:53 body must be c with incorruptibility,
2Cor 5: 3 provided we are found c and not naked.
Gal 3:27 into Christ have c yourselves with him.
Rv 3: 5 " 'The victor shall go c in white.
3:18 Buy white garments in which to be c,
4: 4 they were c in white garments and had
12: 1 in the sky, a woman c with the sun,
16:15 awake and fully c for fear of going naked

CLOTHES (52)

Gn 27:15 Rebekah then took the best c of her older
27:27 Isaac smelled the fragrance of his c.
35: 2 then purify yourselves and put on fresh c.
37:29 that Joseph was not in it, he tore his c,
37:34 Then Jacob rent his c,
41:14 After he shaved and changed his c,
44:13 At this, they tore their c.
Nm 8: 7 shave their whole bodies and wash their c,
8:21 themselves of sin and washed their c,
31:24 On the seventh day you shall wash your c,
Dt 29: 4 Your c did not fall from you in tatters
Jgs 3:16 wore it under his c over his right thigh.
1Sm 4:12 his c torn and his head covered with dirt.
27: 9 off sheep, oxen, asses, camels, and c.
28: 8 he disguised himself, putting on other c,
2Sm 1: 2 camp, with his c torn and dirt on his head.
12:20 and anointed himself, and changed his c.
19:25 nor washed his c from the day the king left
1Kgs 22:30 go into battle, but you put on your own c,"
2Chr 18:29 disguised, but you put on your own c."
Neh 4:17 that accompanied me took off his c;
1Mc 3:47 ashes on their heads and tore their c.
4:39 tore their c and made great lamentation;
5:14 suddenly other messengers, in torn c,
11:71 Jonathan tore his c,
2Mc 8:35 laid aside his fine c and fled alone
Ps(s) 65:13 with it, and rejoicing c the hills.
84: 7 the early rain c it with generous growth.
Prv 23:21 to poverty, and torpor c a man in rags.
Wis 7: 4 c and with constant care I was nurtured.
Sir 43:21 water, and c each pool with a coat of mail.
Is 3: 6 his father's house, saying, "You have c!
Jer 41: 5 men with beards shaved off, c in rags,
Ez 16: 4 with salt, nor swathed in swaddling c.
18: 7 gives food to the hungry and c the naked;
18:16 his food to the hungry and c the naked;
23:26 your c and seize your splendid ornaments.
Mt 6:25 Is not the body more valuable than c?
6:28 As for c, why be concerned?
17: 2 as the sun, his c as radiant as light.
27:28 They stripped off his c and wrapped him in
27:31 him of the cloak, dressed him in his own c,
27:35 divided his c among them by casting lots;
Mk 9: 3 eyes and his c became dazzlingly white
15:20 of the purple, dressed him in his own c,
Lk 2: 7 in swaddling c and laid him in a manger,
2:12 will find an infant wrapped in swaddling c."
8:27 For a long time he had not worn any c;
9:29 and his c became dazzlingly white.
12:28 c in such splendor the grass of the field,
Jn 21: 7 was the Lord, Simon Peter threw on some c—
Jas 2: 2 at the same time a poor man in shabby c.

CLOTHFUL (1)

2Kgs 4:39 from which he picked a c of wild gourds.

CLOTHING (48)

Gn 24:53 of c and presented them to Rebekah;
28:20 give me enough bread to eat and c to wear,
45:22 He also gave to each of them fresh c,
Ex 3:22 for c to put on your sons and daughters.
11: 2 for silver and gold articles and for c."
12:35 for articles of silver and gold and for c.
21:10 he shall not withhold her food, her c,
Dt 8: 4 The c did not fall from you in tatters,
10:18 and befriends the alien, feeding and c him.
24:17 nor take the c of a widow as a pledge.
Jos 22: 8 iron, and with a very large supply of c,
1Kgs 18:46 who girded up his c and ran before Ahab as
2Kgs 7: 8 and took silver, gold, and c from it,
Tb 1:17 bread to the hungry and my c to the naked.
4:16 bread, and to the naked some of your c.
10:10 oxen and sheep, asses and camels, c,
2Mc 3:33 young men in the same c again appeared
Jb 22: 6 pawn, left them stripped naked of their c.
24: 7 They pass the night naked, without c,
27:16 silver like dust and store away mounds of c,
30:18 One with great power lays hold of my c;
31:19 If I have seen a wanderer without c,
Ps(s) 102:27 Like c you change them,
Prv 25:20 Like a moth in c,
27:26 in, The lambs will provide you with c,
31:22 fine linen and purple are her c.
Sir 29:21 Life's prime needs are water, bread, and c,
Is 3: 7 in my own house there is no bread or c!
4: 1 will eat our own food and wear our own c;
58: 7 C the naked when you see them,
59: 6 Their webs cannot serve as c,
Jer 2:34 c there is the life-blood of the innocent,
Bar 6:11 but though they are wrapped in purple c,
6:32 c and put it on their wives and children.
6:57 and go away with the c that was on them,
Ez 42:14 left here the c in which they ministered,
Dn 7: 9 His c was snow bright,
Mt 6:25 what you are to eat or drink or use for c.

CLOTHING (cont.)

7:15 c but underneath are wolves on the prowl.
25:43 me no welcome, naked and you gave me no c.
Mk 5:28 "If I just touch his c,"
5:30 crowd, he began to ask, "Who touched my c?"
Lk 12:23 than food and the body more than c.
Jn 19:24 for my c they cast lots.")
1Cor 12:23 less honorable by c them with greater care,
1Tm 2: 9 gold ornaments, pearls, or costly c;
6: 8 have food and c we have all that we need.
Jude 1:23 abhor so much as their flesh-stained c.

CLOTHS (7)

Ex 31:10 the laver with its base, the service c,
35:19 the service c for use in the sanctuary;
39: 1 the service c for use in the sanctuary,
39:41 the service c for use in the sanctuary,
Prv 7:16 couch, with brocaded c of Egyptian linen;
Is 54: 2 tent, spread out your tent c unsparingly;
Acts 19:12 When handkerchiefs or c which had touched

CLOUD (100)

Ex 13:21 of a column of c to show them the way,
13:22 Neither the column of c by day nor the
14:19 The column of c also,
14:20 But the c now became dark,
14:24 cast through the column of the fiery c
16:10 the glory of the LORD appeared in the c!
19: 9 him, "I am coming to you in a dense c,
19:16 lightning, and a heavy c over the mountain,
20:21 while Moses approached the c where God was.
24:15 had gone up, a c covered the mountain.
24:16 The c covered it for six days,
24:16 he called to Moses from the midst of the c.
24:18 of the c as he went up on the mountain;
33: 9 the column of c would come down and stand
33:10 of c stand at the entrance of the tent,
34: 5 Having come down in a c,
40:34 Then the c covered the meeting tent,
40:35 because the c settled down upon it and the
40:36 Whenever the c rose from the Dwelling,
40:37 But if the c did not lift,
40:38 c of the LORD was seen over the Dwelling;
40:38 fire was seen in the c by the whole house
Lv 16: 2 myself in a c above the propitiatory,
16:13 so that a c of incense may cover the
Nm 9:15 was erected, the c covered the Dwelling,
9:16 the day the Dwelling was covered by the c,
9:17 Whenever the c rose from the tent,
9:17 wherever the c came to rest,
9:18 As long as the c stayed over the Dwelling,
9:19 Even when the c tarried many days over the
9:20 yet sometimes the c was over the Dwelling
9:21 Sometimes the c remained there only from
9:21 Or if the c lifted during the day,
9:22 Whether the c tarried over the Dwelling
10:11 the c rose from the Dwelling of the
10:12 the c came to rest in the desert of Paran.
10:34 the c of the LORD was over them
11:25 then came down in the c and spoke to him.
12: 5 the LORD came down in the column of c,
12:10 departed, and the c withdrew from the tent,
14:14 Your c stands over them,
14:14 of c and by night in a column of fire.
17: 7 and the c now covered it and the glory of
Dt 1:33 by day in the c, and by night in the fire,
4:11 fire and was enveloped in a dense black c.
5:22 from the midst of the fire and the dense c.
31:15 appeared at the tent in a column of c,
1Kgs 8:10 the c filled the temple of the LORD so
8:11 could no longer minister because of the c,
8:12 "The LORD intends to dwell in the dark c;
18:44 "There is a c as small as a man's hand
2Chr 5:13 of the LORD's temple was filled with a c.
5:14 not continue to minister because of the c,
6: 1 "The LORD intends to dwell in the dark c.
Neh 9:12 With a column of c you led them by day,
9:19 The column of c did not cease to lead them
2Mc 2: 8 glory of the Lord will be seen in the c,
7: 5 As a c of smoke spread from the pan,
Jb 7: 9 As a c dissolves and vanishes,
26: 8 yet the c is not rent by their weight;
30:15 the wind, and my welfare vanishes like a c.
Ps(s) 78:14 He led them with a c by day,
99: 7 From the pillar of c he spoke to them;
105:39 He spread a c to cover them and fire
Prv 16:15 and his favor is like a rain c in spring.
Wis 2: 4 will pass away like the traces of a c,
19: 7 The c overshadowed their camp;
Sir 24: 4 did I dwell, my throne on a pillar of c.
45: 5 to hear his voice, and led him into the c,
Is 4: 5 A smoking c by day and a light of flaming
18: 4 sunshine, like a c of dew at harvest time.
19: 1 is riding on a swift c on his way to Egypt;
44:22 have brushed away your offenses like a c,
Lam 3:44 in a c which prayer could not pierce.
Ez 1: 4 a huge c with flashing fire [enveloped in
10: 3 man entered, the c filled the inner court,
10: 4 the temple was filled with the c,
38: 9 advancing like a c to cover the earth,
38:16 people Israel like a c covering the land.
Hos 6: 4 Your piety is like a morning c,
13: 3 c or like the dew that early passes away,
Mt 17: 5 when suddenly a bright c overshadowed them.
17: 5 Out of the c came a voice which said,
Mk 9: 7 A c came, overshadowing them
9: 7 them, and out of the c a voice:
Lk 9:34 speaking, a c came and overshadowed them,
9:35 Then from the c came a voice which said,
12:54 "When you see a c rising in the west,
21:27 coming on a c with great power and glory.
Acts 1: 9 in a c which took him from their sight.
2:19 blood, fire, and a c of smoke.
1Cor 10: 1 under the c and all passed through the sea;
10: 2 by the c and the sea all of them were
Heb 12: 1 part are surrounded by this c of witnesses,
Rv 10: 1 come down from heaven wrapped in a c,
11:12 heaven in a c as their enemies looked on.
14:14 white cloud appeared, and on the c sat
14:15 voice cried out to him who sat on the c,
14:16 So the one sitting on the c wielded his

CLOUDED (1)

2Mc 1:22 in time the sun, which had been c over,

CLOUDLESS (1)

2Sm 23: 4 morning light at sunrise on a c morning,

CLOUDS (77)

Gn 9:13 I set my bow in the c to serve as a sign
9:14 When I bring c over the earth,
9:14 the earth, and the bow appears in the c,
9:16 As the bow appears in the c,
Nm 10:36 "Return, O LORD, you who ride upon the c,
Jgs 5: 4 were shaken, while the c sent down showers.
2Sm 22:10 and came down, with dark c under his feet.
22:12 with spattering rain and thickening c,
1Kgs 18:45 a trice, the sky grew dark with c and wind,
Jb 3: 5 and gloom claim it, c settle upon it,
20: 6 the heavens and his head reach to the c,
22:14 C hide him so that he cannot see;
26: 8 He binds up the waters in his c,
26: 9 the full moon by spreading his c before it.
36:29 c in layers as the carpeting of his tent.
37:11 With hail, also, the c are laden,
37:15 and makes the light shine forth from his c?
37:16 Do you know how the c are banked,
37:21 see not while it is obscured among the c,
37:21 the wind comes by and sweeps the c away.
38: 9 When I made the c its garment and thick
38:34 Can you raise your voice among the c,
38:37 Who counts the c in his wisdom?
Ps(s) 18:10 and came down, with dark c under his feet.
36: 6 your faithfulness, to the c.
68: 5 his name, extol him who rides upon the c,
77:18 The c poured down water;
97: 2 C and darkness are round about him,
104: 3 You make the c your chariot;
135: 7 raises storm c from the end of the earth;
147: 8 to our God, Who covers the heavens with c,
Prv 3:20 depths break open, and the c drop down dew.
25:14 Like c and wind when no rain follows is
Eccl 11: 3 When the c are full,
11: 4 and one who watches the c will never reap.
12: 2 stars, while the c return after the rain;
Wis 5:21 lightnings shall go forth and from the c
Sir 13:22 are silent, his wisdom they extol to the c.
35:17 The prayer of the lowly pierces the c;
35:24 of distress as rain c in time of drought.
43:14 and like vultures the c hurry forth.
43:23 by flames, The dripping c restore them all,
50: 6 Like a star shining among the c,
50:10 like a cypress standing against the c;
Is 5: 6 command the c not to send rain upon it.
8:22 with the light blacked out by its c.
14:14 I will ascend above the tops of the c;
30:27 afar in burning wrath, with lowering c!
60: 2 the earth, and thick c cover the peoples;
60: 8 What are these that fly along like c,
Jer 4:13 like storm c he advances,
10:13 he brings up c from the end of the earth;
13:16 turns to darkness, changes into black c.
51: 9 judgment reaches heaven, it touches the c.
51:16 he brings up c from the end of the earth;
Bar 3:29 taken her, or brought her down from the c?
6:61 The c, too, when commanded by God
Ez 1:28 Like the bow which appears in the c on a
30: 3 a day of c, doomsday for the nations
30:18 shall cease from her, c shall cover her,
31: 3 stature, amid the very c lifted its crest.
31:10 in stature, raising its crest among the c,
31:14 in stature or raise its crest among the c;
32: 7 The sun I will cover with c,
Dn 3:73 Lightnings and c, bless the Lord;
7:13 a son of man coming, on the c of heaven;
Jl 2: 2 and of gloom, a day of c and somberness!
Na 1: 3 his path, and c are the dust at his feet;
Zep 1:15 and gloom, A day of thick black c,
Zec 10: 1 It is the LORD who makes storm c.
Mt 24:30 c of heaven' with power and great glory.
26:64 of the Power and coming on the c of heaven."
Mk 13:26 coming in the c with great power and glory.
14:62 the Power and coming with the c of heaven."
1Thes 4:17 them in the c to meet the Lord in the air.
Jude 1:12 on the wind like c that bring no rain.
Rv 1: 7 See, he comes amid the c!

CLOUDY (2)

Sir 50: 7 like the rainbow appearing in the c sky;
Ez 34:12 they were scattered when it was c and dark.

CLOVEN (1)

Dt 14: 7 only chew the cud or only have c hoofs:

CLOVEN-FOOTED (5)

Lv 11: 3 eat, provided it is c and chews the cud.
11: 7 which does indeed have hoofs and is c,
11:26 All hoofed animals that are not c or do
Dt 14: 6 eat, provided it is c and chews the cud.
14: 8 the pig, which indeed has hoofs and is c,

CLUB (5)

Nm 35:18 c in his hand and causes his death,
2Sm 23:21 he went against him with a c and wrested
2Mc 4: 9 to establish a gymnasium and a youth c
Prv 25:18 Like a c, or a sword, or a sharp arrow
Dn 14:26 will kill this dragon without sword or c."

CLUBS (7)

Jb 41:21 C he esteems as splinters;
Ez 39: 9 bucklers,] bows and arrows, c and lances;
Mt 26:47 by a great crowd with swords and c.
26:55 come armed with swords and c to arrest me?
Mk 14:43 accompanied by a crowd with swords and c;
14:48 with swords and c as if against a brigand.
Lk 22:52 come out after me armed with swords and c?

CLUE (2)

Acts 14:17 not hidden himself completely, without a c.
Rv 17: 9 Here is the c for one who possesses wisdom!

CLUMP (1)

Ps(s) 74: 5 men coming up with axes to a c of trees;

CLUNG (3)

Dt 4: 4 but you, who c to the LORD,
2Kgs 3: 3 he still c to the sin to which Jeroboam,
Jon 2: 6 seaweed c about my head.

CLUSTER (4)

Nm 13:23 a branch with a single c of grapes on it,
13:24 It was because of the c the Israelites cut
Sg 1:14 a c of henna from the vineyards of Engedi.
Mi 7: 1 There is no c to eat,

CLUSTERED (1)

Sir 50:13 in their dignity c around him like poplars,

CLUSTERS (7)

Gn 40:10 came out, and its c ripened into grapes.
Dt 32:32 are their grapes and bitter their c.
Sg 7: 8 your breasts are like c.
7: 9 Now let your breasts be like c of the vine
Is 16: 8 Whose c overpowered the lords of nations,
Ez 19:11 Notably tall was she with her many c.
Rv 14:18 the vines of the earth, for the c are ripe."

CLUTCHES (13)

1Sm 7: 8 to save us from the c of the Philistines."
9:16 my people from the c of the Philistines,
12: 9 allowed them to fall into the c of Sisera,
17:37 keep me safe from the c of this Philistine."
28:19 you as well, into the c of the Philistines.
2Sm 3: 8 friends, by keeping you out of David's c;
19:10 delivered us from the c of our enemies,
2Kgs 16: 7 Come up and rescue me from the c of the
Jb 16:11 into the c of the wicked he has cast me.
Ps(s) 31:16 the c of my enemies and my persecutors.
Sir 51: 2 From the c of the nether world you have
Mk 14:41 is to be handed over to the c of evil men.
Acts 12:11 c and from all that the Jews hoped for."

CLUTCHING (1)

Acts 20:10 threw himself on him, c the boy to himself.

CLUTTER (1)

Lk 13: 7 Why should it c up the ground?'

CNIDUS (2)

1Mc 15:23 Phaselis, Cos, Side, Aradus, Gortyna, C,
Acts 27: 7 arriving at C only with difficulty.

CO-HEIRS (1)

Eph 3: 6 Jesus the Gentiles are now c with the Jews,

CO-WORKER (1)

Phil 2:25 must send you Epaphroditus, my brother, c,

CO-WORKERS (1)

1Cor 3: 9 We are God's *c*,

COALS (20)

2Sm 22: 9 he kindled *c* into flame.
22:13 of his presence *c* were kindled to flame.
Jb 41:13 His breath sets *c* afire;
Ps(s) 11: 6 upon the wicked fiery *c* and brimstone;
18: 9 from his mouth that kindled *c* into flame.
18:13 of his presence *c* were kindled to flame.
120: 4 of a warrior with fiery *c* of brushwood.
140:11 May he rain burning *c* upon them;
Prv 6:28 Or can a man walk on live *c*,
25:22 For live *c* you will heap on his head,
26:21 What a bellows is to live *c*,
Sir 8:10 time of need, Kindle not the *c* of a sinner,
11:31 with a spark he sets many *c* afire.
Is 44:12 an iron image, works it over the *c*,
54:16 burning *c* and forges weapons as his work;
Ez 1:13 like burning *c* of fire could be seen;
10: 2 with burning *c* from among the cherubim,
24:11 on the *c* till its metal glows red hot,
Rom 12:20 this you will heap burning *c* upon his head."
Rv 8: 5 filled it with live *c* from the altar,

COARSE (1)

Sir 23:13 Let not your mouth become used to *c* talk,

COARSEST (1)

Sir 40: 4 crown or is wrapped in the *c* of cloaks

COAST (15)

Nm 34: 6 you shall have the Great Sea with its *c*;
Jos 9: 1 the *c* of the Great Sea as far as Lebanon:
15:12 boundary was the Great Sea and its *c*.
15:47 Wadi of Egypt and the *c* of the Great Sea.
19:46 Me-jarkon and Rakkon, with the *c* at Joppa.
1Kgs 4:16 of Hushai, in Asher and along the rocky *c*;
1Mc 15:14 the city, his ships closed in along the *c*,
Is 23: 2 you who dwell on the *c*,
23: 6 Tarshish, wailing, you who dwell on the *c*!
Zep 2: 7 The *c* shall belong to the remnant of the
Lk 6:17 and Jerusalem and the *c* of Tyre and Sidon,
Acts 27: 5 sea off the *c* of Cilicia and Pamphylia,
27: 8 along the *c* to a place called Fair Havens,
27:13 and proceeded, hugging the *c* of Crete.
27:29 we should be dashed against some rocky *c*,

COASTAL (1)

2Mc 8:11 he immediately sent word to the *c* cities,

COASTLAND (6)

Jdt 2:28 fell upon all the inhabitants of the *c*,
6: 1 presence of the whole throng of *c* peoples,
Is 20: 6 of this *c* shall say on that day,
Ez 27: 3 the trade of the peoples to many a *c*:
Dn 11:18 He shall turn to the *c* and take many,
Zep 2: 6 The *c* of the Cretans shall become fields

COASTLANDS (15)

Is 24:15 "For this, in the *c*,
24:15 In the *c* of the sea,
40:15 the *c* weigh no more than powder.
41: 1 Keep silence before me, O *c*;
41: 5 The *c* see, and fear; the ends of the earth
42: 4 the *c* will wait for his teaching.
42:10 the sea and what fills it resound, the *c*,
42:12 to the LORD, and utter his praise in the *c*.
49: 1 Hear me, O *c*, listen, O distant peoples.
51: 5 In me shall the *c* hope,
66:19 *c* that have never heard of my fame,
Ez 27:15 many *c* traded with you;
27:35 All who dwell on the *c* are aghast over you,
39: 6 upon those who live securely in the *c*;
Zep 2:11 all the *c* of the nations shall adore him.

COASTS (6)

Sir 47:16 Your fame reached distant *c*,
Jer 2:10 Pass over to the *c* of the Kittim and see,
31:10 LORD, O nations, proclaim it on distant *c*,
47: 4 the remnant from the *c* of Caphtor.
Ez 27: 6 made of cypress wood from the *c* of Kittim.
27: 7 from the *c* of Elishah covered your cabin.

COAT (9)

Dt 27: 2 some large stones and *c* them with plaster.
1Sm 17:38 his head and arming him with a *c* of mail.
Sir 43:21 and clothes each pool with a *c* of mail.
Jer 51: 3 draw his bow, and flaunt his *c* of mail;
Mt 5:40 over your shirt, hand him your *c* as well.
Lk 5:36 a piece from a new *c* to patch an old one.
5:36 If he does, he will only tear the new *c*,
6:29 when someone takes your *c*,
22:36 a sword must sell his *c* and buy one.

COATED (1)

Is 44:18 their eyes are *c* so that they cannot see,

COATING (1)

Dt 27: 4 command you today, and *c* them with plaster,

COATS (4)

1Mc 6:35 assigned to it a thousand men in *c* of mail,
Dn 3:21 into the white-hot furnace with their *c*,
Lk 3:11 man with two *c* give to him who has none.
9: 3 No one is to have two *c*.

COAX (1)

Jgs 14:15 *C* your husband to answer the riddle for us,

COBRAS (2)

Dt 32:33 venom of dragons and the cruel poison of *c*.
Is 11: 8 The baby shall play by the *c* den,

COBWEB (1)

Ps(s) 39:12 dissolve like a *c* all that is dear to him;

COBWEBS (1)

Jb 27:18 He builds his house as of *c*,

COCK (15)

Jb 38:36 heart, and gives the *c* its understanding?
Prv 30:31 The strutting *c*,
Mt 26:34 before the *c* crows tonight you will deny
26:74 Just then a *c* began to crow and Peter
26:75 "Before the *c* crows,
Mk 13:35 at dusk, at midnight, when the *c* crows,
14:30 this very night before the *c* crows twice,
14:68 [At that moment a *c* crowed.]
14:72 Just then a second *c* crow was heard and
14:72 *c* crows twice you will deny me three times."
Lk 22:34 the *c* will not crow today until you have
22:60 very moment he was saying this, a *c* crowed.
22:61 *c* crows today you will deny me three times."
Jn 13:38 the *c* will not crow before you have three
18:27 At that moment a *c* began to crow.

COELESYRIA (6)

1Mc 10:69 appointed Apollonius governor of *C*.
2Mc 3: 5 that time was governor of *C* and Phoenicia,
3: 8 to visit the cities of *C* and Phoenicia,
4: 4 the governor of *C* and Phoenicia,
8: 8 to Ptolemy, governor of *C* and Phoenicia,
10:11 as commander-in-chief of *C* and Phoenicia.

COERCE (2)

Ez 22:10 who *c* women in their menstrual period.
22:11 by incest, men who *c* their sisters,

COFFERS (1)

Mt 2:11 *c* and presented him with gifts of gold,

COFFIN (1)

Gn 50:26 embalmed and laid to rest in a *c* in Egypt.

COHABIT (1)

Jb 31:10 for another, and may others *c* with her!

COHORT (9)

2Mc 12:20 cohorts, with a commander over each *c*,
12:22 But when Judas' first *c* appeared,
Mt 27:27 and collected the whole *c* around him.
Mk 15:16 the same time they assembled the whole *c*.
Jn 18: 3 Judas took the *c* as well as guards
18:12 Then the soldiers of the *c*,
Acts 10: 1 named Cornelius, of the Roman *c* Italica,
21:31 of the *c* that all Jerusalem was rioting.
27: 1 named Julius from the *c* known as Augusta.

COHORTS (1)

2Mc 12:20 Maccabeus divided his army into *c*,

COIFFURE (1)

Is 3:24 of the girdle, a rope, And for the *c*,

COILED (1)

Is 27: 1 fleeing serpent, Leviathan the *c* serpent;

COIN (7)

1Mc 15: 6 I authorize you to *c* your own money,
Mt 17:27 there a *c* worth twice the temple tax.
22:19 Show me the *c* used for the tax."
22:19 When they handed him a small Roman *c*,
Mk 6: 8 bag, not a *c* in the purses in their belts.
12:15 Bring me a *c* and let me see it."
Lk 20:24 their duplicity he said, "Show me a *c*.

COINS (5)

Mk 12:42 in two small copper *c* worth a few cents.
Lk 7:41 one owed a total of five hundred *c*,
21: 2 also a poor widow putting in two copper *c*.
Jn 2:14 and doves, and others seated changing *c*.
2:15 money-changers' tables, spilling their *c*.

COLD (18)

Gn 8:22 As long as the earth lasts *c* and heat,
Jb 24: 7 for they have no covering against the *c*;
37: 9 from the north winds, the *c*.
Ps(s) 147:17 before his *c* the waters freeze.
Sir 43:21 *C* northern blasts he sends that turn the
Is 25: 4 As with the *c* rain,
Jer 36:30 to the heat of day, to the *c* of night.
Dn 3:67 *C* and chill,
Na 3:17 gathered on the rubble fences on a *c* day!
Zec 14: 6 day there shall no longer be *c* or frost.
Mt 10:42 whoever gives a cup of *c* water
24:12 of evil, the love of most will grow *c*.
Jn 18:18 Now the night was *c*,
Acts 28: 2 for it had begun to rain and was growing *c*.
2Cor 11:27 in *c* and nakedness.
Rv 3:15 I know you are neither hot nor *c*.
3:15 hot or *c*!
3:16 you are lukewarm, neither hot nor *c*,

COLDNESS (1)

2Mc 14:30 he concluded that this *c* betokened no good.

COLHOZEH (2)

Neh 3:15 Gate was repaired by Shallum, son of *C*,
11: 5 Maaseiah, son of Baruch, son of *C*,

COLLAPSE (7)

Jos 6: 5 The wall of the city will *c*,
Bar 4:33 As that city rejoiced at your *c*,
Am 6: 6 they are not made ill by the *c* of Joseph!
Hb 3: 7 I see the tents of Cushan *c*;
Mt 7:25 It did not *c*;
15:32 hungry, for fear they may *c* on the way."
Mk 8: 3 them home hungry, they will *c* on the way.

COLLAPSED (7)

Jos 6:20 The wall *c*,
Jgs 19:26 Then at daybreak the woman came and *c* at
1Kgs 20:30 the city of Aphek, and there the wall *c*.
2Kgs 9:24 through his heart and he *c* in his chariot.
1Mc 12:37 of the east wall above the ravine had *c*.
Hos 14: 2 you have *c* through your guilt.
Mt 7:27 *c* under all this and was completely ruined."

COLLAPSING (1)

Jdt 7:22 *c* in the streets and gateways of the city,

COLLAR (7)

1Kgs 7:35 there was a raised *c* half a cubit high,
2Chr 3:16 He worked out chains in the form of a *c*
Jb 30:18 by the *c* of my tunic he seizes me:
Ps(s) 133: 2 till it runs down upon the *c* of his robe.
Dn 5: 7 in purple, wear a golden *c* about his neck,
5:16 in purple, wear a gold *c* about your neck,
5:29 in purple, with a gold *c* about his neck,

COLLECT (9)

Nm 6:18 shall shave his dedicated head, *c* the hair,
2Chr 24: 5 "Go out to all the cities of Judah and *c*
Neh 12:44 in them they were to *c* from the fields of
1Mc 10:30 Neither now nor in the future will I *c*
2Mc 4:28 citadel, whose duty it was to *c* the taxes.
Jer 40:10 They were to *c* the wine,
Mt 13:30 *c* the weeds and bundle them up to burn,
13:41 Son of Man will dispatch his angels to *c*
Mk 8:20 many full hampers of fragments did you *c*?"

COLLECTED (26)

1Kgs 10:26 Solomon *c* chariots and drivers;
2Kgs 22: 4 the doorkeepers had *c* from the people.
2Chr 9:14 in addition to what was *c* from travelers
24:11 day until they had *c* a large sum of money.
29:22 *c* the blood and cast it on the altar.
34: 9 of the threshold, had *c* from Manasseh,
1Mc 1: 4 He *c* a very strong army and conquered
1:35 the plunder they had *c* from Jerusalem.
4:23 camp, and his men *c* much gold and silver,
7:47 Then the Jews *c* the spoils and the booty;
13:39 *c* in Jerusalem shall no longer be collected
2Mc 2:13 Memoirs how he *c* the books about the kings,
2:14 like manner Judas also *c* for us the books
8:27 They *c* the enemy's arms and stripped them
8:31 They *c* the enemies' weapons and carefully
10:24 and *c* a large number of cavalry from Asia;
Is 22: 9 you *c* the water of the lower pool.
Bar 1: 6 and *c* such funds as each could furnish.
Mt 9: 9 Matthew at his post where taxes were *c*.
13:40 Just as weeds are *c* and burned,
13:47 into the lake, which *c* all sorts of things.
27:27 and *c* the whole cohort around him.
Lk 15:13 Some days later this younger son *c* all his
Acts 19:19 *c* their books and burned them in public.
28: 3 fire with a bundle of brushwood he had *c*,

COLLECTING (5)

Gn 41:35 *c* the grain under Pharaoh's authority,
Lv 11:36 or a cistern for *c* water remains clean;

COLLECTING (cont.)

1Kgs 17:12 Just now I was *c* a couple of sticks,
1Mc 10:30 Instead of *c* the third of the grain and
Sir 21: 8 money is *c* stones for his funeral mound.

COLLECTION (8)

Ex 25: 2 the Israelites to take up a *c* for me.
35: 5 Take up among you a *c* for the LORD.
2Mc 12:43 He then took up a *c* among all his soldiers,
Mk 12:41 the crowd putting money into the *c* box.
1Cor 16: 1 About the *c* for the saints,
16: 2 so that the *c* will not have to be taken up
2Cor 8:20 blame over my handling of this generous *c*.
9: 1 about this *c* for the members of the church.

COLLECTOR (8)

Eccl 12:11 fixed spikes are the topics given by one *c*.
Dn 11:20 send a tax *c* through the glorious kingdom,
Mt 10: 3 Bartholomew, Thomas and Matthew the tax *c*;
18:17 him as you would a Gentile or a tax *c*.
Lk 5:27 *c* named Levi sitting at his customs post.
18:10 one was a Pharisee, the other a tax *c*.
18:11 or even like this tax *c*.
19: 2 the chief tax *c* and a wealthy man.

COLLECTORS (16)

Mt 5:46 Do not tax *c* do as much?
9:10 many tax *c* and those known as sinners
9:11 with tax *c* and those who disregard the law?"
11:19 a lover of tax *c* and those outside the law!'
17:24 the *c* of the temple tax approached Peter
21:31 "I assure you that tax *c* and prostitutes
21:32 *c* and the prostitutes did believe in him.
Mk 2:14 Levi the son of Alphaeus at his tax *c* post,
2:15 many tax *c* and those known as sinners
2:16 with tax *c* and offenders against the law,
Lk 3:12 Tax *c* also came to be baptized,
5:29 large crowd of tax *c* and others at dinner.
5:30 with tax *c* and non-observers of the law?"
7:29 that had heard Jesus, even the tax *c*,
7:34 a drunkard, a friend of tax *c* and sinners!'
15: 1 The tax *c* and sinners were all gathering

COLLECTS (3)

Sir 14: 4 What he denies himself he *c* for others,
Lk 13:34 a mother bird *c* her young under her wings,
Jn 4:36 The reaper already *c* his wages and gathers

COLONNADE (1)

2Mc 4:46 Ptolemy retired with the king under a *c*,

COLONY (2)

Wis 12: 7 might receive a worthy *c* of God's children.
Acts 16:12 in the district of Macedonia and a Roman *c*.

COLOR (4)

Est D: 7 anger, the queen staggered, changed *c*,
2Mc 3:16 for the changed *c* of his face manifested
Dn 10: 8 I turned the *c* of death and was powerless.
Rv 6: 8 Now I saw a horse sickly green in *c*.

COLORED (2)

Est 1: 6 marble, mother-of-pearl, and *c* stones.
Na 2: 4 are crimsoned, the soldiers *c* in scarlet;

COLORING (1)

Sir 38:30 His care is for proper *c*,

COLORS (1)

Wis 15: 4 of painters, A form smeared with varied *c*,

COLOSSAE (1)

Col 1: 2 Timothy our brother, to the holy ones at *C*,

COLT (12)

Gn 49:22 is a wild colt, a wild *c* by a spring,
Sir 30: 8 A *c* untamed turns out stubborn;
Zec 9: 9 is he, Meek, and riding on an ass, on a *c*,
Mt 21: 2 find an ass tethered and her *c* with her.
21: 5 display astride an ass, astride a *c*,
21: 7 and the *c* and laid their cloaks on them,
Mk 11: 2 there a *c* on which no one has ridden.
11: 4 a *c* tethered out on the street near a gate,
11: 5 them, "What do you mean by untying that *c*?"
11: 7 They brought the *c* to Jesus and threw
Jn 12:15 Your king approaches you on a donkey's *c*."

COLUMN (21)

Ex 13:21 means of a *c* of cloud to show them the way,
13:21 by means of a *c* of fire to give them light.
13:22 *c* of cloud by day nor the *c* of fire
13:22 column of cloud by day nor the *c* of fire
14:19 The *c* of cloud also,
14:24 LORD cast through the *c* of the fiery cloud
33: 9 the *c* of cloud would come down and stand
33:10 On seeing the *c* of cloud stand at the
Nm 12: 5 Then the LORD came down in the *c* of cloud,
14:14 column of cloud and by night in a *c* of
Dt 31:15 LORD appeared at the tent in a *c* of cloud,
Jgs 18:21 and their goods at the head of the *c*.
20:40 signal *c* began to rise up from the city.
2Kgs 23: 3 Standing by the *c*,
Neh 9:12 With a *c* of cloud you led them by day,
9:12 them by day, and by night with a *c* of fire,
9:19 The *c* of cloud did not cease to lead them
9:19 nor did the *c* of fire by night cease to
Sg 3: 6 like a *c* of smoke Laden with myrrh,
Sir 36:24 treasure, a helpmate, a steadying *c*.

COLUMNED (2)

1Kgs 7: 6 The porch of the *c* hall he made fifty
7: 6 The porch extended the width of the *c* hall,

COLUMNS (71)

Ex 26:32 hung on four gold-plated *c* of acacia wood,
26:37 five *c* of acacia wood for this curtain;
27:10 twenty *c* and twenty pedestals of bronze;
27:10 and bands on the *c* shall be of silver.
27:11 twenty *c* and twenty pedestals of bronze;
27:11 and bands on the *c* shall be of silver.
27:12 cubits long, with ten *c* and ten pedestals.
27:14 cubits, with three *c* and three pedestals;
27:15 cubits, with three *c* and three pedestals.
27:16 It shall have four *c* and four pedestals.
27:17 "All the *c* around the court shall have
35:11 boards, its bars, its *c* and its pedestals;
35:17 of the court, with their *c* and pedestals;
36:36 Four gold-plated *c* of acacia wood,
36:38 Its five *c*,
38:10 twenty *c* and twenty pedestals of bronze,
38:10 hooks and bands of the *c* being of silver.
38:11 twenty *c* and twenty pedestals of bronze,
38:11 hooks and bands of the *c* being of silver.
38:12 cubits long, with ten *c* and ten pedestals,
38:12 hooks and bands of the *c* being of silver.
38:14 cubits, with three *c* and three pedestals;
38:15 cubits, with three *c* and three pedestals.
38:17 The pedestals of the *c* were of bronze,
38:17 hooks and bands of the *c* were of silver;
38:17 the *c* of the court were banded with silver.
38:19 four *c* and four pedestals of bronze for it,
38:28 were used for making the hooks on the *c*,
39:33 the clasps, the boards, the bars, the *c*,
39:40 of the court with their *c* and pedestals,
40:18 boards, put in its bars, and set up its *c*.
Nm 3:36 the boards of the Dwelling, its bars, *c*,
3:37 as well as the *c* of the surrounding court
4:31 Dwelling with its bars, *c* and pedestals,
4:32 and the *c* of the surrounding court with
Jgs 16:24 Then they stationed him between the *c*.
16:26 "Put me where I may touch the *c* that
16:29 Samson grasped the two middle *c* on which
1Kgs 7: 2 columns, with cedar capitals upon the *c*.
7: 3 of cedar above the beams resting on the *c*;
7:15 Two hollow bronze *c* were cast,
7:16 cast in bronze, to place on top of the *c*,
7:17 (nodes of the) capitals on top of the *c*,
7:19 The capitals on top of the *c* were finished
7:21 The *c* were then erected adjacent to the
7:22 Thus the work on the *c* was completed.
7:41 two *c*, two nodes for the capitals
7:41 nodes for the capitals on top of the *c*,
7:41 nodes for the capitals on top of the *c*,
7:42 of the capitals where they met the *c*,
2Chr 3:15 he set two *c* thirty-five cubits high;
3:16 which he encircled the capitals of the *c*,
3:17 set up the *c* to correspond with the nave,
4:12 two *c*, two nodes for the capitals
4:12 for the capitals topping these two *c*,
4:12 the nodes of the capitals topping the *c*;
4:13 two nodes of the capitals topping the *c*.
1Mc 5:33 He came up behind them with three *c*
13:29 pyramids he devised a setting of big *c*,
Jb 1:17 and said, "The Chaldeans formed three *c*,
Ps(s) 144:12 Our daughters like wrought *c* such as stand
Prv 9: 1 her house, she has set up her seven *c*;
Sg 3:10 He made its *c* of silver,
5:15 are *c* of marble resting on golden bases.
Sir 26:18 Golden *c* on silver bases are her shapely
Is 9:17 forest thickets, which go up in *c* of smoke.
Jer 36:23 Jehudi finished reading three or four *c*
Ez 40:49 to it, and there were *c* by the pilasters,
Jl 3: 3 on the earth, blood, fire, and *c* of smoke;
Zep 2:14 and the desert owl shall roost in her *c*;

COMB (2)

1Sm 14:26 came to the *c* the swarm had left it;
Ps(s) 19:11 also than syrup or honey from the *c*.

COMBAT (20)

Nm 31:14 commanders, who were returning from *c*.
31:21 told the soldiers who had returned from *c*:
31:27 active part in the war by going out to *c*,
31:28 the LORD on the warriors who went out to *c*:
31:36 fell to those who had gone out to *c* was:
32:29 with you as *c* troops before the LORD,
32:30 with you as *c* troops before the LORD,
Jgs 20:20 array at Gibeah for the *c* with Benjamin,
20:23 *c* in the same place as on the previous day,
1Sm 17: 9 If he beats me in *c* and kills me,
2Sm 17:11 the sands by the sea, be called up for *c*;
1Chr 8:40 The sons of Ulam were *c* archers,
Jdt 2:16 and grouped them into a complete *c* force.
Est A: 5 great dragons came on, both poised for *c*.
1Mc 9:11 out of camp and took its position for *c*.
10: 2 army and marched out to engage him in *c*.
11:72 Then he went back to the *c* and so
12:27 on guard and to remain armed, ready for *c*,
2Mc 15:17 by hand-to-hand *c* with the utmost courage,
Sir 12: 5 No arms for *c* should you give him,

COMBATANTS (2)

1Sm 14:24 the whole people, about ten thousand *c*,
2Sm 18: 8 more *c* that day than did the sword.

COMBERS (1)

Is 19: 9 the *c* and weavers shall turn pale;

COMBINED (5)

2Chr 3:13 The *c* wingspread of the two cherubim was
1Mc 5:10 around us have *c* against us to destroy us,
Is 31: 1 and in horsemen because of their *c* power,
Ez 45: 7 of the *c* sacred tract and City property,
Hb 1: 9 Their *c* onset is that of a stormwind that

COME (1450)

Gn 6:20 two of each shall *c* into the ark with you,
8:12 and this time it did not *c* back.
9: 2 Dread fear of you shall *c* upon all the
9:12 sign that I am giving for all ages to *c*,
11: 3 They said to one another, *C*,
11: 4 Then they said, *C*,
15:16 time-span the others shall *c* back here;
16: 8 have you *c* from and where are you going?"
18: 5 that you have *c* this close to your servant,
19: 2 *c* aside into your servant's house for the
19: 8 they have *c* under the shelter of my roof."
19:32 *C*, let us ply our father with wine and
20:13 In whatever place we *c* to,
22: 5 We will worship and then *c* back to you."
24:31 *C*, blessed of the LORD!
26:26 had meanwhile *c* to him from Gerar,
26:27 Isaac asked them, "Why have you *c* to me,
27:21 Isaac then said to Jacob, *C* closer,
27:26 his father Isaac said to him, *C* closer,
28:21 and I *c* back safe to my father's house,
30:16 "You are now to *c* in with me,"
31:44 *C*, then, we will make a pact
33:10 since to *c* into your presence is for me
33:18 Having thus *c* from Paddan-aram,
37:10 are to *c* and bow to the ground before you?"
37:20 *C* on, let us kill him and throw him
38:16 she was his daughter-in-law, he said, *C*,
40: 8 them, "Surely, interpretations *c* from God.
42: 7 "Where do you *c* from?"
42: 9 have *c* to see the nakedness of the land."
42:10 your servants have *c* to procure food.
42:12 have *c* to see the nakedness of the land."
42:20 *c* back to me with your youngest brother.
42:21 that is why this anguish has now *c* upon us."
42:34 *c* back to me with your youngest brother,
44:23 you shall not *c* into my presence again.'
44:25 to *c* back and buy some food for the family.
45: 4 *C* closer to me," he told his brothers.
45: 8 not really you but God who had me *c* here;
45: 9 *c* to me without delay.
45:16 palace that Joseph's brothers had *c*,
45:18 your families, and then *c* back here to me;
46:27 Jacob's family who had *c* to Egypt
46:31 is in the land of Canaan, have *c* to me.
47: 1 my brothers have *c* from the land of Canaan,
47: 4 We have *c*,"
47: 5 your father and brothers have *c* to you,
48: 2 was told, "Your son Joseph has *c* to you,"
49: 1 you what is to happen to you in days to *c*.
50: 5 up there to bury my father and then *c* back?"
Ex 1:10 *C*, let us deal shrewdly with them to stop
3: 5 God said, *C* no nearer!
3: 8 Therefore I have *c* down to rescue them
3:10 *C* now! I will send you to Pharaoh
7:28 They will *c* up into your palace and into
11: 8 servants of yours shall then *c* down to me,
12:13 Egypt, no destructive blow will *c* upon you.
12:23 *c* into your houses to strike you down.
13:19 solemnly that, when God should *c* to them,
18: 8 and how the LORD had *c* to their rescue.
18:15 "The people *c* to me to consult God.
18:16 they *c* to me to have me settle the matter
19:11 for on the third day the LORD will *c* down
19:24 Then *c* up again along with Aaron.
19:24 must not break through to *c* up to the LORD;
20:20 for God has *c* to you only to test you and
20:24 of my name I will *c* to you and bless you.
23: 4 *c* upon your enemy's ox or ass going astray,
24: 1 Moses himself was told, *C* up to the LORD,
24: 2 but Moses alone is to *c* close to the LORD;
24: 2 *c* too near, and the people shall not come
24:12 to Moses, *C* up to me on the mountain and,
30:12 may *c* upon them for being registered.

32: 1 gathered around Aaron and said to him, C,
32:26 "Whoever is for the LORD, let him c to me!"
33: 9 the column of cloud would c down and stand
34: 3 No one shall c up with you,
34: 5 Having c down in a cloud,
34: 9 you, O Lord, do c along in our company.
34:30 had become, they were afraid to c near him.
34:31 the rulers of the community c back to him.
35:10 c and make all that the LORD has commanded:
36: 2 moved them to c and take part in the work.
Lv 8:24 Moses had the sons of Aaron also c forward,
9: 5 had c forward and stood before the LORD,
9: 7 C up to the altar,"
10: 4 Aaron's uncle Uzziel, with the order, C,
14: 8 thus made clean may he c inside the camp;
14:34 "When you c into the land of Canaan,
14:35 the house shall c and report to the priest,
14:44 and replastered, the priest shall c again;
16: 2 c whenever he pleases into the sanctuary,
16:18 he shall c out to the altar before the
16:24 and then c out and offer his own and the
19:23 "When you c into the land and plant any
21:17 c forward to offer up the food of his God.
21:18 of the following defects may not c forward:
23:10 you c into the land which I am giving you,
26:32 very enemies who c to live there will stand
Nm 5:16 woman c forward and stand before the LORD.
8: 9 c forward in front of the meeting tent,
8:19 should they c near the sanctuary."
10:29 C with us,
10:30 But he answered, "No, I will not c.
10:32 If you c with us,
11:17 I will c down and speak with you there.
12: 4 said to Moses and Aaron and Miriam, C out,
16:27 When Dathan and Abiram had c out and were
17:11 for wrath has c forth from the LORD and
18: 3 not c near the sacred vessels or the altar,
18: 4 But no layman shall c near you.
21:27 C to Heshbon,
22: 5 "A people has c here from Egypt who now
22: 6 Please c and curse this people for us;
22:11 Please c and lay a curse on them for us;
22:14 the report, "Balaam refused to c with us."
22:16 Please do not refuse to c to me.
22:17 c and lay a curse on this people for me."
22:20 him, "If these men have c to summon you,
22:32 It is I who have c armed to hinder you
22:37 Why did you not c to me?
22:38 him, "Well, I have c to you after all.
23: 7 C and lay a curse for me on Jacob, come
23:13 "Please c with me to another place from
23:27 Then Balak said to Balaam, C,
24:14 will do to your people in the days to c."
32:11 men of twenty years or more who have c up
Dt 1:20 have c to the hill country of the Amorites,
2: 5 careful not to c in conflict with them,
2:19 As you c opposite the Ammonites,
2:19 show hostility or c in conflict with them,
4:30 all these things shall have c upon you,
4:45 he proclaimed to them when they had c out
9:15 "When I had c down again from the blazing,
10: 1 then c up the mountain to me.
11:10 the land of Egypt from which you have c,
14:29 your community, may c and eat their fill;
17:14 you have c into the land which the LORD,
18: 9 "When you c into the land which the LORD,
20: 2 shall c forward and say to the soldiers:
22:16 in marriage, but he has c to dislike her,
22:27 for help, there was no one to c to her aid.
23:12 sun has set, he may c back into the camp.
26: 1 you have c into the land which the LORD,
26: 3 that I have indeed c into the land which
28: 2 will c upon you and overwhelm you:
28: 7 c out against you from but one direction,
28:15 curses shall c upon you and overwhelm you:
28:24 which will c down upon you from the sky
28:29 continually, with no one to c to your aid.
28:31 your enemies, with no one to c to your aid.
28:45 "All these curses will c upon you,
28:52 in c tumbling down all over your land.
29:21 who will c here from far-off lands,
33:16 These shall c upon the head of Joseph and
Jos 2: 2 had c there that night to spy out the land.
2: 3 for they have c to spy out the entire land."
2: 9 land, that a dread of you has c upon us,
2:18 When we c into the land,
3: 4 Do not c nearer to it."
3: 8 to c to a halt in the Jordan
3: 9 C here and listen to the words of the LORD,
4:16 the commandments to c up from the Jordan."
4:18 LORD had c up from the bed of the Jordan,
7:14 LORD designates shall c forward by clans;
7:14 designates shall c forward by families;
7:14 LORD designates shall c forward one by one.
7:16 Joshua had Israel c forward by tribes,
7:17 Then he had the clans of Judah c forward,
7:17 the clan of Zerah c forward by families,
7:18 he had that family c forward one by one,
8: 5 of the people and I will c up to the city,
9: 6 "We have c from a distant land to propose
9: 8 Where do you c from?"
9: 9 "Your servants have c from a faroff land,
9:12 as provisions the day we left to c to you,
10: 4 to c to his aid for an attack on Gibeon,
10: 6 C up here quickly and save us.
10:24 C forward and put your feet on the necks
Jgs 1: 3 C up with me into the territory allotted
4: 8 c with me, I will go; if you do not come
4:18 to him, "Come in, my lord, c in with me;
4:22 went out to meet him and said to him, C,
6: 3 Amalek and the Kedemites would c up,
6: 5 For they would c up with their livestock,
6:18 until I c back to you and bring out my
8:21 Zebah and Zalmunna said, C,
9:10 Then the trees said to the fig tree, C;
9:12 Then the trees said to the vine, C you,
9:14 all the trees said to the buckthorn, C;
9:15 good faith, c and take refuge in my shadow.
9:15 let fire c from the buckthorn and devour
9:20 let fire c forth from Abimelech to devour
9:29 to Abimelech, 'Get a larger army and c out!'"
9:31 and his kinsmen have c to Shechem and are
9:33 he and his followers c out against you,
11: 6 C," they said to Jephthah,
11: 7 "Why do you c to me now,
11: 8 "In any case, we have now c back to you;
11:12 me that you c to fight with me in my land?"
12: 3 c up against me this day to fight with me?"
13:17 we may honor you when your words c true?"
14: 5 When they had c to the vineyards of Timnah,
15:10 asked, "Why have you c up against us?"
15:12 to him, "We have c to take you prisoner,
16: 2 Informed that Samson had c there,
16:18 of the Philistines, saying, C up this time,
17: 9 Micah said to him, "Where do you c from?"
18: 9 were asked for a report, they replied, C,
18:19 C with us and be our father and priest.
19:11 gone, the servant said to his master, C,
19:13 C," he said to his servant,
19:17 where he was going, and whence he had c.
19:28 He said to her, C,
21: 3 why has it c to pass in Israel that today
21: 5 who did not c up to the LORD for assembly?"
21: 8 Israel had not c up to the LORD in Mizpah,
21: 8 had c to the encampment for the assembly.
21:21 girls of Shiloh c out to do their dancing,
21:22 or their brothers c to complain to us,
Ru 1:11 "Why should you c with me?
2:11 and have c to a people whom you did not
2:12 under whose wings you have c for refuge."
2:14 said to her, C here and have some food;
3:17 to c back to my mother-in-law empty-handed!"
4: 1 come along, he called to him by name, C
4: 3 who has c back from the Moabite plateau,
4:11 c into your house like Rachel and Leah,
1Sm 2:13 servant would c with a three-pronged fork,
2:15 the priest's servant would c and say to
2:36 is left of your family will c to grovel
4: 6 the ark of the LORD had c into the camp,
4: 7 They said, "Gods have c to their camp."
4:16 "It is I who have c from the battlefield;
6:21 c down and get it."
9: 5 said to the servant who was with him, C,
9: 6 all that he says is sure to c true.
9: 9 who went to consult God used to say, C,
9:10 C on, let us go!" And they went to the city
10: 5 After that you will c to Gibeath-elohim,
10: 8 of me to Gilgal, for I shall c down to you,
10: 8 Wait seven days until I c to you;
10:20 had all the tribes of Israel c forward,
10:21 the tribe of Benjamin c forward in clans,
10:22 they consulted the LORD, "Has he c here?"
11: 7 does not c out to follow Saul [and Samuel],
11: 9 To the messengers who had c he said,
11:14 Samuel said to the people, C,
13:11 since you had not c by the specified time,
13:12 will c down against me at Gilgal,
14: 1 C let us go over to the Philistine outpost
14: 6 C let us go over to that outpost of the
14: 9 to us, 'Stay there until we can c to you,'
14:10 But if they say, C up to us,'
14:12 C up here," they said, "and we will teach
14:38 Saul then said, C here,
15: 6 C! Leave Amalek and withdraw
16: 2 say, 'I have c to sacrifice to the LORD.
16: 5 I have c to sacrifice to the LORD.
17: 8 "Why c out in battle formation?
17: 8 one of your men, and have him c down to me.
17:15 David would go and c from Saul to tend his
17:28 "Why did you c down?
17:43 I a dog that you c against me with a staff?"
17:44 by his gods and said to him, C here to me,
17:45 "You c against me with sword and spear
17:45 but I c against you in the name of the
20:11 Jonathan[Jonathan replied to David, C,
20:21 pick it up,' c, for you are safe.
20:27 of Jesse not c to table yesterday or today?"
20:29 is why he has not c to the king's table."
21:16 Should this fellow c into my house?"
22: 9 "I saw the son of Jesse c to Ahimelech,
23:10 a report that Saul plans to c to Keilah,
23:11 will Saul c down as your servant has heard?
23:11 The LORD answered, "He will c down."
23:15 because Saul had c out to seek his life;
23:20 whenever the king wishes to c down,
23:23 Then c back to me with sure information,
23:27 messenger came to Saul, saying, C quickly,
24:21 over Israel shall c into your possession,
25: 8 young men, since we c at a festival time.
25:11 them to men who c from I know not where?"
25:34 if you had not c so promptly to meet me,
26: 3 saw that Saul had c into the desert after
26:20 For the king of Israel has c out to seek a
26:21 C back, my son David, I will not harm
26:22 Let an attendant c over to get it.
30:13 do you belong, and where do you c from?"
31: 4 these uncircumcised c and make sport of me."
2Sm 1: 3 David asked him, "Where do you c from?"
1:15 one of the attendants and said to him, C,
3:13 when you c to present yourself to me."
5:13 in Jerusalem after he had c from Hebron,
6: 9 "How can the ark of the LORD c to me?"
7:19 house of your Servant for a long time to c:
10: 5 beards grow," he said, "and then c back."
10:11 stronger than you, I will c to help you.
11:10 to Uriah, "Have you not c from a journey?
12: 4 a meal for the wayfarer who had c to him.
13: 5 Tamar c and encourage me to take food.
13: 6 "Please let my sister Tamar c and prepare
13:11 to eat, he seized her and said to her, C!
13:24 c with all your retainers to your servant."
13:26 c yourself, please let my brother Amnon c
13:35 The princes have c.
14:20 this to c at the issue in a roundabout way.
14:29 to the king, but Joab would not c to him.
14:29 him a second time, Joab refused to c.
14:32 "I was summoning you to c here,
14:32 'Why did I c back from Geshur?
15: 4 c to me and I would render him justice."
15:12 an invitation to c from his town,
15:33 "If you c with me,
17: 2 If I c upon him when he is weary and
17:17 was to c with information for them,
18: 3 "You must not c out with us.
18:13 would have c to the attention of the king,
18:22 of Zadok, said to Joab again, C what may,
18:23 But he insisted, C what may,
19:16 Judah had c to Gilgal to meet him and to
19:21 to c down today to meet my lord the king."
19:23 "What has c between you and me,
19:39 to him, "Chimham shall c over with me,
20:16 Tell Joab to c here,
20:17 When Joab had c near her,
24:13 a three years' famine to c upon your land,
24:21 does my lord the king c to his servant?"
1Kgs 1:12 C now, let me advise you
1:14 I will c in after you and confirm what you
1:35 When you c back in his train,
1:42 C," said Adonijah, "you are a man
2:13 "Do you c as a friend?"
2:30 and said to him, "The king says, C out.'"
3:12 after you there will c no one to equal you.
9:16 of Egypt, had c up and taken Gezer and,
10:22 ships would c with a cargo of gold,
12: 1 all Israel had c to proclaim him king.
12: 5 C back to me in three days,"
13: 7 C home with me for some refreshment,"
13:10 did not go back the way he had c to Bethel.
13:12 by the man of God who had c from Judah.
13:15 said, C home with me and have some bread."
13:21 out to the man of God who had c from Judah:
13:32 of Samaria shall certainly c to pass."
14: 6 as she entered the door, said, C in,
17:18 Have you c to me to call attention to my
18: 5 Ahab said to Obadiah, C,
18:30 said to all the people, C here to me."
20:18 they have c out for peace or for war,
20:19 But when these had c out of the city
21:18 of which he has c to take possession.
22: 4 c with me to fight against Ramoth-gilead?"
2Kgs 1: 9 ordered, "the king commands you to c down."
1:10 "may fire c down from heaven and consume
1:11 king commands you to c down immediately."
1:12 "may fire c down from heaven and consume
1:14 Already fire has c down from heaven,
3:21 that the kings had c to give them battle;
4: 1 c to take my two children as his slaves."
4: 4 Then c back and close the door on yourself
5: 8 Let him c to me and find out that there is
5:11 "I thought that he would surely c out
5:22 to say, 'Two young men have just c to me,
6: 3 "Yes, I will c," he replied.
6:32 ahead before he himself should c to him.
7: 4 C, let us desert to the camp of the
7: 9 C, let us go and inform the palace."
8: 7 was told that the man of God had c there,
9:11 Why did that madman c to you?"
9:12 C, tell us." So he told them
9:16 Ahaziah, king of Judah, had c to visit him.
10: 6 c to me in Jezreel at this time tomorrow."
10:16 C with me," he said, "and see my zeal
11: 4 them c to him in the temple of the LORD,
11: 5 the third of you who c on duty on the
12:11 royal scribe [and the priest] would c up,
14: 8 this challenge, C let us meet face to face."
16: 7 C up and rescue me from the clutches of
18:25 that I have c up to destroy this place?
18:32 I c to take you to a land like your own,
19: 5 servants of King Hezekiah had c to Isaiah,

COME (cont.)

19: 9 Ethiopia, had *c* out to fight against him.
19:27 I know whether you *c* or go,
19:31 For out of Jerusalem shall *c* a remnant,
19:32 arrow at it, nor *c* before it with a shield,
20:14 Where did they *c* from?"
23:18 of the prophet who had *c* from Samaria.
1Chr 7:22 after his kinsmen had *c* and comforted him,
10: 4 uncircumcised may not *c* and maltreat me."
12:18 "If you *c* peacefully,
12:18 But if you have *c* to betray me to my
12:32 by name to *c* and make David king.
14: 9 had *c* and raided the valley of Rephaim.
14:14 but go around them and *c* upon them from
17:16 should have brought me as far as I have *c*?
19: 3 rather *c* to you to explore the land,
19: 5 and then you may *c* back here."
19: 9 while the kings who had *c* to their help
19:12 too strong for me, you must *c* to my help;
19:19 refused to *c* to the aid of the Ammonites.
2Chr 1:12 nor will those have them who *c* after you."
6:32 arm, when they *c* in prayer to this temple,
8:11 where the ark of the LORD has *c* are holy."
10: 1 had *c* to Shechem to proclaim him king.
10: 5 days," he answered them, *c* back to me."
12:11 the LORD, the troops would *c* bearing them,
13:13 go around them to *c* at them from the rear;
14:10 your name we have *c* against this multitude.
15: 5 there was no peace for anyone to go or *c*,
18: 3 "Will you *c* with me to Ramoth-gilead?"
19:10 and his wrath *c* upon you and your brethren.
20:16 and you will *c* upon them at the end of the
21: 4 When Jehoram had *c* into his father's
22: 1 that had *c* into the fort with the Arabs.
23: 2 When they had *c* to Jerusalem,
23: 4 who *c* in on the sabbath must guard the
23: 8 those who were to *c* in on the sabbath as
23:20 When they had *c* within the upper gate of
25:10 the troops that had *c* to him from Ephraim,
25:17 son of Jehu, the king of Israel, saying, *C*,
28:20 king of Assyria, did indeed *c* to him,
29: 8 of the LORD has *c* upon Judah and Jerusalem;
30: 1 they should *c* to the house of the LORD
30: 5 that everyone should *c* to Jerusalem to
30: 8 extend your hands to the LORD and *c* to his
30:25 of the assembly that had *c* from Israel,
31: 8 and the princes had *c* and seen the heaps,
32: 4 Assyria *c* and find an abundance of water?"
35:21 I have not *c* against you this day,
Ezr 3: 8 who had *c* from the captivity to Jerusalem,
7:23 *c* upon the realm of the king and his sons.
9:13 "After all that has *c* upon us for our
Neh 2:10 *c* to seek the welfare of the Israelites.
2:17 *C*, let us rebuild the wall of Jerusalem,
4: 2 Thereupon they all plotted together to *c*
4: 5 it or see us, we shall *c* into their midst,
4: 6 had *c* to us from one place after another,
6: 2 *C*, let us hold council together at
6: 3 a great enterprise and am unable to *c* down;
6: 3 stop, while I leave it to *c* down to you?"
6: 7 these must reach the ear of the king, *c*,
9:33 all that has *c* upon us you have been just,
Tb 1: 4 and consecrated for all generations to *c*.
2: 2 son, I shall wait for you to *c* back."
2:13 "Where did this goat *c* from?
5: 5 I have *c* here to work."
5:21 health and *c* back to us in good health.
6:15 slay any man who wishes to *c* close to her.
11: 5 the road by which her son was to *c*.
11:17 *C* in daughter!"
13:10 within you for all generations to *c*.
13:11 many nations shall *c* to you from afar,
14: 5 will be rebuilt for all generations to *c*,
Jdt 2: 7 for I will *c* against them in my wrath;
3: 4 *c* and deal with them as you see fit."
5: 4 Why have they refused to *c* out to meet me
5:19 they have *c* back from the Dispersion
7: 1 allied troops that had *c* to his support,
8:15 wish to *c* to our aid within the five days,
9: 6 the things you decide on *c* forward and say,
10:12 Where do you *c* from,
10:13 I have *c* to see Holofernes,
11: 3 In any case, you have *c* to safety.
11:18 Then I will *c* and let you know,
11:19 you through Judea, till you *c* to Jerusalem,
12:11 care to *c* and to eat and drink with us.
12:13 to *c* to my lord to be honored by him,
13: 3 as on the other days, for her to *c* out;
14:13 slaves have dared *c* down to give us battle,
Est A: 8 with fear of the evils to *c* upon them,
A: 9 there appeared to *c* forth a great river,
1:12 But Queen Vashti refused to *c* at the royal
1:17 into his presence, but she would not *c*.'
1:19 forbidding Vashti to *c* into the presence
4:14 will *c* to the Jews from another source;
D:11 *C* near!"
5: 4 *c* today with Haman to a banquet I have
5: 8 *c* with Haman tomorrow to a banquet which I
6: 5 "Let him *c* in," the king said.
1Mc 1:11 from them, many evils have *c* upon us."
2:18 *C* now, be the first to obey
2:33 *C* out and obey the king's command,
2:34 But they replied, "We will not *c* out,
3:20 they *c* against us to destroy us and our wives
4:46 should *c* and decide what to do with them.
5:11 and they are preparing to *c* and seize this
5:12 *C* at once and rescue us from them,
6:11 'Into what tribulation have I *c*,
6:58 Therefore let us now *c* to terms with these
7:11 seeing that they had *c* with a great army.
7:14 of the line of Aaron has *c* with the army,
7:28 *c* with a few men to meet you peaceably."
7:30 had *c* to him with treachery in mind,
8: 4 They had crushed the kings who had *c*
8: 9 Greece had planned to *c* and destroy them,
9: 9 our lives now, and *c* back with our kinsmen,
9:10 If our time has *c*, let us die bravely
9:39 kinsmen had *c* out to meet the bride's party
10:59 also wrote to Jonathan to *c* and meet him.
10:71 your forces, *c* down now to us in the plain,
11: 9 *C*, let us make a pact with each other;
11:63 *c* with a strong force to Kadesh in Galilee,
12:17 ordered them to *c* to you and greet you,
12:45 back home, and then *c* with me to Ptolemais.
13:21 him to *c* to them by way of the desert,
14:22 *c* to us to renew their friendship with us,
15:12 what a mass of troubles had *c* upon him
15:17 have *c* to us to renew their earlier
15:31 not do this, we will *c* and make war on you."
16: 3 mercy of Heaven, have *c* to man's estate.
16:19 he sent letters inviting them to *c* to him
2Mc 1:14 Antiochus with his Friends had *c* to the
3:17 bodily trembling that had *c* over the man
3:39 down and destroys those who *c* to harm it."
8: 8 to *c* to the aid of the king's government.
8:25 of those who had *c* to buy them as slaves.
9:18 God's punishment had justly *c* upon him,
12: 7 intending to *c* back later and wipe out the
13:23 Having *c* to this agreement,
14: 7 to say, the high priesthood, I have *c* here
15:24 blasphemously *c* against your holy people!"
Jb 1: 7 the LORD said to Satan, "Whence do you *c*?"
2: 2 the LORD said to Satan, "Whence do you *c*?"
2:11 of all the misfortune that had *c* upon him,
3:11 at birth, *c* forth from the womb and expire?
6:20 they *c* there and are frustrated.
6:28 *C* now, give me your attention;
7: 6 they *c* to an end without hope.
7: 9 to the nether world shall *c* up no more.
8: 7 for in time to *c* you will flourish indeed.
9:11 Should he *c* near me,
9:32 that we should *c* together in judgment.
10:17 in waves your troops *c* against me.
13:16 no impious man can *c* into his presence.
14:14 I would wait, until my relief should *c*.
16:18 not my blood, nor let my outcry *c* to rest!
17:10 But turn now, and *c* on again;
18:20 who *c* after shall be appalled at his fate;
20:25 The dart shall *c* out of his back;
21:17 How often does destruction *c* upon them,
22:21 *C* to terms with him to be at peace.
22:21 In this shall good *c* to you:
23: 3 him, that I might *c* to his judgment seat!
23:10 if he proved me, I should *c* forth as gold.
30:14 Amid the uproar they *c* on in waves;
31:34 remained silent, and not *c* out of doors!
34:23 of his time to *c* before God in judgment.
38:11 Thus far shall you *c* but no farther,
41: 3 Who has assailed him and *c* off safe
Ps(s) 7:10 Let the malice of the wicked *c* to an end,
14: 7 of Zion would *c* the salvation of Israel!
17: 2 From you let my judgment *c*;
23: 6 in the house of the LORD for years to *c*.
24: 7 portals, that the king of glory may *c* in!
24: 9 portals, that the king of glory may *c* in!
27: 2 When evildoers *c* at me to devour my flesh,
32: 9 be curbed, else they will not *c* near you.
34:12 *C*, children, hear me; I will teach you
35: 8 Let ruin *c* upon them unawares,
38: 3 in me, and your hand has *c* down upon me.
40: 8 then said I, "Behold I *c*;
44:18 All this has *c* upon us,
45:10 The daughters of kings *c* to meet you;
46: 9 *C*! behold the deeds of the LORD
48: 5 the kings assemble, they *c* on together;
50: 3 May our God *c* and not be deaf to us!
53: 7 of Zion would *c* the salvation of Israel!
55: 6 Fear and trembling *c* upon me.
59: 4 mighty men *c* together against me.
59:11 May God *c* to my aid;
65: 3 To you all flesh must *c*
66: 5 *C* and see the works of God,
68:32 Let nobles *c* from Egypt;
69:19 *C* and ransom my life;
71:18 strength to every generation that is to *c*.
78: 4 we will declare to the generation to *c*
78: 6 So that the generation to *c* might know,
79: 1 the nations have *c* into your inheritance;
79: 8 may your compassion quickly *c* to us,
79:11 Let the prisoners' sighing *c* before you;
80: 3 Rouse your power, and *c* to save us.
83: 5 They say, *C*, let us destroy their nation
86: 9 you have made shall *c* and worship you,
88: 3 Let my prayer *c* before you;
91: 7 your right side, near you it shall not *c*.
91:10 you, nor shall affliction *c* near your tent,
95: 1 *C*, let us sing joyfully to the LORD;
95: 6 *C*, let us bow down in worship;
100: 2 *c* before him with joyful song.
101: 2 when will you *c* to me?
102: 2 hear my prayer, and let my cry *c* to you.
102:14 to pity her, for the appointed time has *c*.
102:19 this be written for the generation to *c*,
109:17 may it *c* upon him;
119:41 Let your kindness *c* to me, O LORD
119:77 your compassion *c* to me that I may live,
119:143 Though distress and anguish have *c* upon me,
119:147 Before dawn I *c* and cry out;
119:169 Let my cry *c* before you, O LORD
121: 1 whence shall help *c* to me?
126: 6 to be sown, They shall *c* back rejoicing,
133: 3 which *c* down upon the mountains of Zion;
134: 1 *C*, bless the LORD,
141: 2 Let my prayer *c* like incense before you;
144: 5 Incline your heavens, O LORD, and *c* down;
Prv 1:11 entice you, and say, *C* along with us!
2: 6 his mouth *c* knowledge and understanding;
2:19 None who enter thereon *c* back again,
3:28 not to your neighbor, "Go, and *c* again,
5:14 I have all but *c* to utter ruin,
6:11 will poverty *c* upon you like a highway man,
7:18 *C*, let us drink our fill of love,
9: 5 *C*, eat of my food, and drink of the wine
14: 4 crops *c* through the strength of the bull.
23:21 the drunkard and the glutton *c* to poverty,
24:25 on them will *c* the blessing of prosperity.
24:34 will poverty *c* upon you like a highwayman,
25: 7 it is better that you be told, *C* up closer!"
28:22 and he knows not when want will *c* upon him.
30: 4 Who has gone up to heaven and *c* down again
31:25 dignity, and she laughs at the days to *c*.
Eccl 1:11 nor of those to *c* will there be any
1:11 remembrance among those who *c* after them.
2: 1 I said to myself, *C*,
2:12 will the man do who is to *c* after the king?
2:16 in days to *c* both will have been forgotten.
2:18 leave them to a man who is to *c* after me.
3:22 will let him see what is to *c* after him?
5: 2 For nightmares *c* with many cares,
6:12 a man what will *c* after him under the sun?
7:28 One man out of a thousand have I *c* upon,
8: 7 man that he is ignorant of what is to *c*;
10:14 to *c*, for who can tell him what is to come
11: 2 not what misfortune may *c* upon the earth.
11: 8 All that is to *c* is vanity.
12: 1 before the evil days *c* And the years
Sg 2:10 my beloved, my beautiful one, and *c*!
2:12 the time of pruning the vines has *c*,
2:13 my beloved, my beautiful one, and *c*!
3:11 *c* forth and look upon King Solomon In the
4: 2 to be shorn, which *c* up from the washing,
4: 8 *C* from Lebanon, my bride, *c*
4:16 *C*, south wind! blow upon my garden
4:16 *c* to his garden and eat its choice fruits.
5: 1 I have *c* to my garden,
6: 2 My lover has *c* down to his garden,
6: 6 flock of ewes which *c* up from the washing,
7:12 *C*, my lover, let us go forth to the fields
Wis 2: 1 known to have *c* back from the nether world.
2: 6 *C*, therefore, let us enjoy the good things
4:20 Fearful shall they *c*,
6: 5 and swiftly shall he *c* against you,
8: 8 things of old, and infers those yet to *c*.
11:22 drop of morning dew *c* down upon the earth.
12:12 or who can *c* into your presence
14:11 idols of the nations shall a visitation *c*,
16: 4 oppressors, inexorable want had to *c*;
16:14 his malice, but when the spirit has *c* away,
17:12 surrender of the helps that *c* from reason;
17:14 that had *c* upon them from the recesses of
17:21 the darkness that next should *c* upon them;
Sir 2: 1 My son, when you *c* to serve the LORD,
3: 8 father that his blessing may *c* upon you;
11:24 What harm can *c* to me now?"
15: 1 is practiced in the law will *c* to wisdom.
22:24 so does abuse *c* before bloodshed.
24:18 *C* to me, all you that yearn for me
24:31 prophecy and bestow it on generations to *c*.
25: 7 There are nine who *c* to my mind as blessed,
29: 3 him and you will always *c* by what you need.
29:26 *C* here, stranger, set the table,
31:10 he has been tested by gold and *c* off safe,
33: 8 him the seasons and feasts *c* and go.
33:15 they *c* in pairs,
36: 1 *C* to our aid, O God of the universe
42:13 For just as moths *c* from garments,
42:18 sees from of old the things that are to *c*:
48:10 in time to *c* to put an end to wrath before
51:23 *C* aside to me, you untutored
Is 1:12 When you *c* in to visit me,
1:18 *C* now, let us set things right,
2: 2 In days to *c*,
2: 3 many peoples shall *c* and say:
2: 3 *C*, let us climb the LORD's mountain,
2: 5 O house of Jacob, *c*,
5:19 let it *c* to pass, that we may know it!"
5:26 speedily and promptly will they *c*.
7:19 All of them shall *c* and settle in the
13: 5 They *c* from a far-off country,

14:29 out of the serpent's root shall c an adder,
21:12 The watchman replies, "Morning has c,
21:12 If you will ask, ask; c back again."
21:16 all the glory of Kedar shall c to an end.
27: 6 In days to c Jacob shall take root,
27:11 women shall c to build a fire with them.
27:13 the outcasts in the land of Egypt Shall c
29: 1 Add year to year, let the feasts c round.
29: 4 and from the base dust your words shall c.
30: 8 Now c, write it on a tablet they can keep
31: 4 So shall the LORD of hosts c down to wage
32:19 it comes, as trees c down in the forest!
34: 1 C near, O nations, and hear, be attentive,
34: 5 lo, it shall c down in judgment upon Edom,
36:10 will that I have c up to destroy this land?
36:17 I c to take you to a land like your own,
37: 5 servants of King Hezekiah had c to Isaiah,
37: 9 Ethiopia, had c out to fight against him.
37:28 I know whether you c or go,
37:32 For out of Jerusalem shall c a remnant,
37:33 arrow at it, nor c before it with a shield,
39: 3 Where did they c from?"
39: 6 shall c when all that is in your house,
41: 1 let us c together for judgment.
41: 5 these things are near, they c to pass.
41:11 and c to nought who offer resistance.
41:22 Let them c near and foretell to us what it
41:22 or declare to us the things to c!
41:23 Foretell the things that shall c afterward,
42: 9 See, the earlier things have c to pass,
42:23 listens and pays heed for the time to c?
43:26 you have me remember, have us c to trial?
44: 7 Let them foretell to us the things to c.
45:14 Shall c over to you and belong to you;
45:20 C and assemble,
45:21 C here and declare in counsel together:
45:24 c all who vent their anger against him.
47: 1 C down, sit in the dust, O virgin daughter
47: 9 Both these things shall c to you suddenly,
47: 9 bereavement and widowhood shall c
47:11 c evil you will not know how to predict:
47:11 c upon you ruin which you will not expect.
48:16 C near to me and hear this!
49: 9 C out!
49:12 See, some shall c from afar,
49:21 where then do these c from?"
51: 5 I will make my justice c speedily;
52:11 Depart, depart, c forth from there,
52:12 Yet not in fearful haste will you c out,
54:14 where destruction cannot c near you.
55: 1 All you who are thirsty, c to the water!
55: 1 come, receive grain and eat; C, without
55: 3 C to me heedfully,
55:10 heavens the rain and snow c down
56: 1 for my salvation is about to c,
56: 9 you wild beasts of the field, c and eat,
56:12 C, I will fetch some wine;
59: 6 and deeds of violence c from their hands.
59:19 For it shall c like a pent-up river which
59:20 He shall c to Zion a redeemer to those of
60: 1 Your light has c,
60: 4 they all gather and c to you; Your sons c
60: 6 shall c bearing gold and frankincense,
60:13 The glory of Lebanon shall c to you:
60:14 The children of your oppressors shall c,
63:19 and c down, with the mountains
65:17 past shall not be remembered or c to mind.
66: 7 Before the pains c upon her,
66:15 Lo, the LORD shall c in fire,
66:18 I c to gather nations of every language;
66:18 they shall c and see my glory.
66:23 All mankind shall c to worship before me,
66:24 they shall c and see my glory.
Jer 1:15 Each king shall c and set up his throne at
2:31 We will c to you no more"?
3: 1 man, Does the first husband c back to her?
3:18 together they will c from the land of the
3:22 we now c to you because you are the LORD,
4:12 this wind from the heights c at my bidding;
5: 6 all who c out are torn to pieces For their
6: 3 Against her, shepherds c with their flocks;
7:10 and yet c to stand before me in this house
7:32 days will c,
8:16 c devouring the land and all it contains,
9:16 tell the wailing women to c,
9:17 them c quickly and intone a dirge for us,
9:20 Death has c up through our windows,
12: 9 C, gather together, all you beasts
12: 9 all you beasts of the field, c and eat!
12:12 every desert height brigands have c up.
13:18 c down from your throne;
14: 3 but when they c to the cisterns They find
16:14 However, days will surely c,
16:19 the nations c from the ends of the earth,
17:15 Let it c to pass!"
17:26 To it people will c from the cities of
17:27 if you carry burdens and c through the
18:18 C," they said, "let us contrive a plot
19: 6 Therefore, days will c, says the LORD,
20:18 Why did I c forth from the womb,
22:23 How you shall groan when pains c upon you,
22:27 c back to the land for which they yearn.
23: 7 Therefore, the days will c,
25: 3 has c to me and I spoke to you untiringly,
25:34 The time for your slaughter has c;
26: 2 who c to worship in the house of the LORD;
27: 3 who have c to Jerusalem to Zedekiah,
27: 7 until the time of his land, too, shall c.
30: 3 For behold, the days will c,
30:21 own, and his rulers shall c from his kin.
31: 6 a day will c when the watchmen will call
31:12 shall c streaming to the LORD's blessings:
31:19 I have c to myself,
32: 7 Shallum, will c to you with the offer:
33: 5 men c to battle the Chaldeans,
35:11 we decided to c into Jerusalem to escape
36: 6 men of Judah who c up from their cities.
36:14 C and bring with you the scroll you read
36:29 Babylon's king shall surely c and lay
38:14 summoned the prophet Jeremiah to c
38:25 hear I spoke to you, if they c and ask you,
40: 4 you to come with me to Babylon, you may c:
40: 4 you to come to Babylon, you need not c.
40:10 with the Chaldeans who should c to them.
41: 7 C to Gedaliah, son of Ahikam," he said
43:11 He shall c and strike the land of Egypt:
44: 8 the land of Egypt where you have c to live?
44:13 None of the remnant of Judah that have c
46:18 Like Tabor among the mountains he shall c,
46:22 Yes, they c in force;
47: 4 which has c to ruin all the Philistines,
48: 2 C, let us put an end to her as a people."
48:12 Hence, the days shall c,
48:18 C down from glory,
48:18 Moab's ravager has c up against you,
48:21 judgment has c on the land of the plateau:
48:47 change the lot of Moab in the days to c,
49: 4 treasures, saying, "Who can c against me?"
49: 8 upon Esau when I c to punish him.
49:36 to which the outcasts of Elam shall not c.
49:39 days to c I will change the lot of Elam,
50: 4 of Judah shall come, Weeping as they c,
50: 5 C, let us join ourselves to the LORD with
50:26 C upon her from every side,
50:27 their day has c,
50:31 For your day has c,
51:10 c, let us tell in Zion what the LORD
51:13 waters, rich in treasure, Your end has c,
51:33 while, and the harvest time will c for her.
51:48 destroyers c against her from the north,
51:50 from afar, let Jerusalem c to your minds.
Lam 1: 3 c upon her where she is narrowly confined.
1:10 Whom you forbade to c into your assembly.
1:12 C, all you who pass by the way,
1:22 "Let all their evil c before you;
Bar 2: 7 the Lord has warned us have c upon us:
4:14 "Let Zion's neighbors c,
4:22 and joy has c to me from the Holy One
4:24 they soon see God's salvation c to you,
4:25 the anger that has c from God upon you;
4:35 fire shall c upon her from the Eternal God,
4:37 Here c your sons whom you once let go,
6:26 them upright, nor c upright if they fall;
Ez 7: 2 has c upon the four corners of the land!
7: 7 climax has c for you who dwell in the land!
7: 7 The time has c, near is the day:
7:12 The time has c, the day dawns.
9: 1 C, you scourges of the city!
12:16 among the nations to which they will c;
14:22 when they c out to you,
16:33 c to you from all sides for your harlotry.
20: 3 Have you c to consult me?
20:39 C, each one of you, destroy your idols!
21:24 the sword of the king of Babylon can c.
21:25 so that the sword can c to Rabbah of the
21:34 day has c when their crimes are at an end.
22: 3 within herself so that her time has c,
22: 4 day, so that the end of your years has c.
23:24 They shall c against you from the north
23:40 they sent for men who had to c from afar,
23:44 they did c to her as men come to a harlot.
24:26 that day the fugitive will c to you,
27:29 from their ships c all who ply the oar;
30: 4 Then a sword shall c upon Egypt,
30: 6 fall, and down shall c her proud strength;
31:17 have c down with him to the nether world,
32:11 of the king of Babylon shall c upon you.
32:21 C down, you and your allies
33:22 The hand of the LORD had c upon me the
33:28 that its proud strength will c to an end,
33:30 C and hear the latest word that comes from
33:31 My people c to you as people always do;
36: 9 See, I c to you,
37: 3 Son of man, can these bones c to life?
37: 5 spirit into you, that you may c to life.
37: 6 may c to life and know that I am the LORD.
37: 8 I saw the sinews and the flesh c upon them,
37: 9 From the four winds c,
37: 9 into these slain that they may c to life.
37:21 among the nations to which they have c,
38: 8 in the last years you will c against a nation
38: 9 You shall c up like a sudden storm,
38:13 "Is it for plunder that you have c?
38:15 bestir yourself and c from your home
38:16 You shall c up against my people Israel
39: 2 you c up from the recesses of the north;
39:17 C together, from all sides gather
40:46 who may c near to minister to the LORD.
Dn 2:28 what is to happen in days to c;
3:93 "Servants of the most high God, c out."
4: 4 Chaldeans, and astrologers had c in,
9:22 I have now c to give you understanding.
9:23 was given which I have c to announce,
9:26 who will c shall destroy the sanctuary.
9:26 Then the end shall c like a torrent;
10:14 happen to your people in the days to c;
10:20 know," he asked, "why I have c to you?
10:20 When I leave, the prince of Greece will c;
11: 2 "Three kings of Persia are yet to c;
11: 6 daughter of the king of the south shall c
11: 7 and shall c against the rampart and enter
11:29 appointed he shall c again to the south,
11:35 the end time which is still appointed to c.
11:40 of the south shall c to grips with him,
11:45 shall c to his end with none to help him.
13: 5 said, "Wickedness has c out of Babylon:
13:42 aware of all things before they c to be:
13:50 To Daniel the elders said, C,
13:52 Now have your past sins c to term:
Hos 2: 2 one head and c up from other lands,
3: 5 c trembling to the LORD and to his bounty,
4:14 a people without understanding c to ruin.
4:15 C not to Gilgal,
6: 1 C, let us return to the LORD,
6: 3 He will c to us like the rain,
9: 7 They have c, the days of punishment!
9: 7 they have c, the days of recompense!
10:12 till he c and rain down justice upon you."
11:10 his sons shall c frightened from the west,
11:11 west, Out of Egypt they shall c trembling,
12:12 Gilead is falsehood, they have c to nought,
13:13 The birth pangs shall c for him,
13:15 among his fellows, an east wind shall c,
Jl 1:13 C, spend the night in sackcloth,
2: 9 In at the windows they c like thieves.
2:23 he has made the rain c down for you,
4:11 Hasten and c, all your neighboring peoples
4:12 and c up to the Valley of Jehoshaphat;
4:13 C and tread, for the wine press is full
Am 4: 4 C to Bethel, and sin
5: 5 Do not c to Gilgal,
5: 6 lest he c upon the house of Joseph like a
7: 1 when the late growth began to c up
Ob 1:15 deed shall c back upon your own head;
Jon 1: 2 their wickedness has c up before me."
1: 7 Then they said to one another, C,
1: 8 Where do you c from?
1:12 me that this violent storm has c upon you."
Mi 1: 9 rather, it has c even to Judah,
1:11 of Zaanan c not forth from their city.
1:12 For evil has c down from the LORD to the
3:11 No evil can c upon us!"
4: 1 In days to c the mount of the LORD's house
4: 2 Many nations shall come, and say, C,
4: 8 Unto you shall it c:
5: 1 From you shall c forth for me one who is
6: 6 With what shall I c before the LORD,
6: 6 Shall I c before him with holocausts,
7: 4 your punishment has c;
7:12 shall c to you from Assyria and from Egypt,
7:17 They shall c quaking from their fastnesses,
Na 1:14 no descendant shall c to bear your name;
2:14 I c against you, says the LORD of hosts;
3: 5 I am c against you,
Hb 1: 8 horses prance, his horsemen c from afar:
2: 3 it delays, wait for it, it will surely c,
3:13 You c forth to save your people,
3:16 that will c upon the people who attack us.
Hg 1: 2 time c to rebuild the house of the LORD.
2: 7 the treasures of all the nations will c in,
Zec 2: 4 but these have c to terrify them:
5: 4 and it shall c into the house of the thief,
6:10 of Zephaniah (these had c from Babylon).
6:15 shall c and build the temple of the LORD,
8:20 There shall yet c peoples,
8:21 approach those of another, and say, C!
8:22 Many people and strong nations shall c to
9: 5 Ekron, too, for her hope shall c to nought.
9: 9 See, your king shall c to you;
9:14 trumpet, and c in a storm from the south.
10: 4 From him shall c leader and chief,
10: 8 I will whistle for them to c together,
12: 9 of all nations that c against Jerusalem.
14: 1 a day shall c for the LORD when the spoils
14: 5 Then the LORD, my God, shall c,
14:16 c up year after year to worship the King,
14:17 not c up to Jerusalem to worship the King,
14:18 And if the family of Egypt does not c up,
14:18 not c up to celebrate the feast of Booths.
14:19 not c up to celebrate the feast of Booths.
14:21 and all who c to sacrifice shall take them
Mal 3: 1 c to the temple the LORD whom you seek,
3:24 Lest I c and strike the land with doom.
Mt 2: 2 at its rising and have c to pay him homage."
2: 6 since from you shall c a ruler who is to
3: 7 Who told you to flee from the wrath to c?
3:14 should be baptized by you, yet you c to me!"
4:19 C after me and I will make you fishers of
5:17 have c to abolish the law and the prophets.

COME (cont.)

5:17 I have c, not to abolish them,
5:24 brother, and then c and offer your gift.
6:10 hallowed be your name, your kingdom c,
7:15 who c to you in sheep's clothing but
8: 7 He said to him, "I will c and cure him."
8: 9 If I say to another, C here,' he comes.
8:11 Many will c from the east and the west and
8:19 wherever you go I will c after you."
8:29 c to torture us before the appointed time?"
9:13 I have c to call,
9:18 Please c and lay your hand on her and she
9:18 hand on her and she will c back to life."
10:11 you c to and stay with him until you leave.
10:35 c to set a man at odds with his father,
10:38 cross and c after me is not worthy of me.
11: 3 'He who is to c' or do we look for another?"
11:14 he is Elijah, the one who was certain to c.
11:28 C to me, all you who are weary
12:32 either in this age or in the age to c.
13:32 c and build their nests in its branches."
14:28 you, tell me to c to you across the water."
14:29 C!" he said
15:28 Your wish will c to pass."
16:24 "If a man wishes to c after me,
16:27 The Son of Man will c with his Father's
16:28 they see the Son of Man c in his kingship."
17:10 the scribes claim that Elijah must c first?"
17:12 you, though, that Elijah has already c,
18: 7 things will c on the world through scandal!
18:14 of these little ones shall ever c to grief.
19:14 but Jesus said, "Let the children c to me.
19:21 Afterward, c back and follow me."
19:30 shall c last, and the last shall come first
20:28 is the case with the Son of Man who has c,
22: 3 to the wedding, but they refused to c.
22: 4 C to the feast.'
22: 8 but those who were invited were unfit to c.
22: 9 invite to the wedding anyone you c upon.'
24: 5 Many will c attempting to impersonate me.
24:14 Only after that will the end c.
24:17 c down to get anything out of his house.
24:21 of the world until now or in all ages to c.
25: 6 C out and greet him!'
25:21 C, share your master's joy!'
25:23 C, share your master's joy!'
25:34 to those on his right: C
25:43 in prison and you did not c to comfort me.'
26:55 c armed with swords and clubs to arrest me?
27:40 C down off that cross if you are God's Son!"
27:42 Let's see him c down from that cross and
28: 6 C and see the place where he was laid.
Mk 1: 7 more powerful than I is to c after me.
1:17 Jesus said to them, C after me;
1:24 Have you c to destroy us?
1:25 C out of the man!"
1:38 That is what I have c to do."
2:17 I have c to call sinners,
2:20 The day will c,
3:31 outside they sent word to him to c out.
4:19 cravings of other sorts c to choke it off;
5: 8 to him, "Unclean spirit, c out of the man!")
5:23 Please c and lay your hands on her so that
6:31 C by yourselves to an out-of-the-way place
7: 1 had c from Jerusalem gathered around him.
7:21 c from the deep recesses of the heart;
7:23 c from within and render a man impure."
8: 3 Some of them have c a great distance."
8:34 "If a man wishes to c after me,
9:11 the scribes claim that Elijah must c first?"
9:12 will indeed c first and restore everything.
9:13 Let me assure you, Elijah has already c.
10:14 children c to me and do not hinder them.
10:21 After that, c and follow me."
10:30 and in the age to c,
10:31 come last, and the last shall c first."
10:37 at your left, when you c into your glory."
10:45 of Man has not c to be served but to serve
11:10 is the reign of our father David to c!
12: 7 C, let us kill him,
12: 9 He will c and destroy those tenants and
12:23 resurrection, when they all c back to life,
13: 6 number will c attempting to impersonate me.
13:13 the end is the one who will c through safe.
13:15 he must not c down or enter his house to
13:19 of creation and now, and for all time to c.
13:33 do not know when the appointed time will c.
13:36 let him c suddenly and catch you asleep.
14:13 you will c upon a man carrying a water jar.
14:42 Rouse yourselves and c along.
14:48 "You have c out to arrest me armed with
15:32 c down from that cross here and now so
15:41 others who had c up with him to Jerusalem.
Lk 1:20 They will all c true in due season."
1:35 "The Holy Spirit will c upon you and the
1:43 that the mother of my Lord should c to me?
1:48 all ages to c shall call me blessed.
2:10 I c to proclaim good news to you
3: 7 Who told you to flee from the wrath to c?
3:16 there is one to c who is mightier than I.
4:34 Have you c to destroy us?
4:35 C out of him."
5: 7 mates in the other boat to c and help them.
5:17 teachers of the law who had c
5:32 I have not c to invite the self-righteous
5:35 But when the days c that the groom is
6:47 Any man who desires to c to me will hear
7: 3 him to c and save the life of his servant.
7: 7 why I did not presume to c to you myself.
7: 8 to another, C here,'
7:19 is to c' or are we to expect someone else?"
7:20 is to c" or do we look for someone else?' "
8:29 the unclean spirit to c out of the man.
8:38 devils had departed asked to c with him,
8:41 he c to his home because his only daughter,
9:59 To another he said, C after me."
9:60 c away and proclaim the kingdom of God."
10: 6 if not, it will c back to you.
11: 2 your kingdom c.
11: 6 for a friend of mine has c in from a
11:33 so that they who c in may see the light.
12:19 have blessings in reserve for years to c.
12:38 Should he happen to c at midnight or
12:40 of Man will c when you least expect him."
12:46 that servant's master will c back on a day
12:49 "I have c to light a fire on the earth.
12:51 I have c to establish peace on the earth?
12:51 I have c for division.
13: 3 all c to the same end unless you reform.
13: 5 all c to the same end unless you reform."
13: 7 For three years now I have c in search of
13:14 C on those days to be cured,
13:24 "Try to c in through the narrow door.
13:25 in reply, 'I do not know where you c from.'
13:27 tell you, I do not know where you c from.
13:29 People will c from the east and the west,
14: 9 Then the host might c and say to you,
14:10 you he will say, 'My friend, c up higher.'
14:17 servant to say to those invited, C along,
14:20 'I am newly married and so I cannot c.'
14:23 along the hedgerows and force them to c in.
15:24 of mine was dead and has c back to life.
15:32 of yours was dead, and has c back to life.
16: 2 service, for it is about to c to an end.'
17: 1 arise, but woe to him through whom they c.
17: 7 you say to him, C and sit down at table'?
17:20 Pharisees when the reign of God would c,
17:20 watching when the reign of God will c.
17:22 "A time will c when you will long to see
18:16 "Let the little children c to me.
18:22 Then c and follow me."
18:30 age and life everlasting in the age to c."
18:40 When he had c close,
19: 9 "Today salvation has c to this house,
19:10 has c to search out and save what is lost."
19:43 Days will c upon you when your enemies
20: 4 the baptism of John c from God or from men?"
20:35 c and of resurrection from the dead do not.
21: 6 the day will c when not one stone will be
21: 8 Many will c in my name saying,
21:35 The day I speak of will c upon all who
22:10 you will c upon a man carrying a water jar.
22:37 I tell you, must c to be fulfilled in me.
22:52 But to those who had c out against him
22:52 c out after me armed with swords and clubs?
23:55 The women who had c with him from Galilee
24:35 had c to know him in the breaking of bread.
Jn 1:27 the one who is to c after me
1:30 me is to c a man who ranks ahead of me,
1:39 C and see," he answered.
1:46 was, "Can anything good c from Nazareth?"
1:46 and Philip replied, C,
2: 4 My hour has not yet c."
2: 9 wine, without knowing where it had c from;
2:22 and c to believe the Scripture and the
3: 2 "we know you are a teacher c from God,
3:20 he does not c near it for fear his deeds
4:16 call your husband, and then c back here."
4:29 C and see someone who told me everything I
4:38 the labor, and you have c into their gain."
4:47 Jesus had c back from Judea to Galilee,
4:47 to c down and restore health to his son,
4:49 with him, c down before my child dies."
5:24 He does not c under condemnation,
5:25 you, an hour is coming, has indeed c,
5:28 tombs shall hear his voice and c forth.
5:40 unwilling to c to me to possess that life.
5:43 I have c in my Father's name,
5:43 But let someone c in his own name,
6:14 the Prophet who is to c into the world."
6:15 would c and carry him off to make him king,
6:25 said to him, "Rabbi, when did you c here?"
6:37 All that the Father gives me shall c to me;
6:38 my own will that I have c down from heaven,
6:42 can he claim to have c down from heaven?"
6:44 "No one can c to me unless the Father who
6:51 am the living bread c down from heaven.
6:65 I have told you that no one can c to me
6:69 We have c to believe;
7:28 The truth is, I have not c of myself.
7:29 I know him because it is from him I c:
7:30 on him because his hour had not yet c.
7:34 where I am you cannot c."
7:36 find me,' and, 'Where I am you cannot c'?"
7:37 "If anyone thirsts, let him c to me;
7:41 the Messiah is not to c from Galilee?
7:42 of David's family, is to c from Bethlehem,
7:50 Nicodemus (the man who had c to him),
8:20 because his hour had not yet c.
8:21 Where I am going you cannot c."
8:22 he claims, 'Where I am going you cannot c'?"
8:24 sins unless you c to believe that I AM."
8:28 you will c to realize that I AM and that I
8:42 I did not c of my own will;
11:15 I was not there, that you may c to believe.
11:19 and many Jewish people had c out to
11:26 me, though he should die, will c to life;
11:27 have c to believe that you are the Messiah,
11:27 he who is to c into the world."
11:30 (Actually Jesus had not yet c into the
11:34 "Lord, c and see," they said.
11:43 this, he called loudly, "Lazarus, c out!"
11:45 many of the Jews who had c to visit Mary,
11:48 Then the Romans will c in and sweep away
11:56 Is he likely to c for the feast?"
12:12 The next day the great crowd that had c
12:20 Among those who had c up to worship at the
12:23 has c for the Son of Man to be glorified.
12:30 "That voice did not c for my sake,
12:31 "Now has judgment c upon this world,
12:35 still have it or darkness will c over you.
12:46 I have c to the world as its light,
12:47 not c to condemn the world but to save it.
13: 1 Jesus realized that the hour had c for him
13: 3 he had c from God and was going to God,
13:33 'Where I am going, you cannot c.'
13:36 later on you shall c after me."
14: 3 then I shall c back to take you with me,
14:18 I will c back to you.
14:23 we will c to him and make our dwelling
14:28 go away for a while, and I c back to you.'
14:31 C, then! Let us be on our way.
15:22 If I had not c to them and spoken to them,
16: 2 a time will c when anyone who puts you to
16: 7 to go, the Paraclete will never c to you,
16:13 and will announce to you the things to c.
16:21 is in labor she is sad that her time has c.
16:25 A time will c when I shall no longer do so,
16:28 [I did indeed c from the Father;]
16:32 has indeed already c—
17: 1 "Father, the hour has c!
17:11 but these are in the world as I c to you.
17:13 Now, however, I c to you;
18:20 temple area where all the Jews c together.
19: 9 he said to Jesus, "Where do you c from?"
19:39 first c to Jesus at night) likewise came,
21:12 C and eat your meal," Jesus told them.
21:22 "Suppose I want him to stay until I c,"
21:23 stay until I c [how does that concern you]?"
Acts 2:11 Jews, or those who have c over to Judaism;
2:17 'It shall c to pass in the last days,
7:34 groaning, and I have c down to rescue them.
7:34 C now, I will send you into Egypt.'
8:16 It had not as yet c down upon any of them
8:27 had c on a pilgrimage to Jerusalem and was
9:21 Did he not c here purposely to apprehend
9:38 "Please c over to us without delay."
10:11 c down that looked like a big canvas.
10:29 That is why I have c in response to your
10:32 to invite Simon known as Peter to c here.
10:33 and you have been kind enough to c.
11:20 among them who had c to Antioch
13:31 c up with him from Galilee to Jerusalem.
14:11 "Gods have c to us in the form of men!"
16: 3 anxious to have him c along on the journey.
16: 9 him, C over to Macedonia and help us."
16:15 in the Lord, c and stay at my house."
16:18 Jesus Christ I command you, c out of her!"
16:37 them c into the prison and escort us out."
17: 6 they c here and Jason has taken them in.
18:21 "God willing, I will c back to you again."
19: 4 tell the people about the one who would c
19:32 not even knowing why they had c together.
20:29 c among you who will not spare the flock.
21:20 many thousands of Jews have c to believe,
24:17 I had c to bring alms to my own people and
25: 5 "Your leading men can c down with me,"
25: 7 the Jews who had c down from Jerusalem
28: 9 to c to Paul and they too were healed.
Rom 2: 9 will c upon every man who has done evil,
3: 8 may we not do evil that good may c of it?
5:14 as did Adam, that type of the man to c.
6:13 men who have c back from the dead to life,
9:31 seeking a law from which justice would c,
11:11 c to the Gentiles to stir Israel to envy.
11:17 c to share in the rich root of the olive,
11:25 blindness has c upon part of Israel until
11:26 "Out of Zion will c the deliverer who
15:29 you, I shall c with Christ's full blessing.
15:32 I may c to you with joy and be refreshed
1Cor 1:21 did not c to know him through "wisdom,"
2: 1 when I came to you I did not c proclaiming
2:14 He cannot c to know such teaching because
4:18 thinking that I will not c to you.
4:19 But I shall c to you soon,
4:21 do you prefer, that I c to you with a rod,
7:18 Did the call c to another who had never
7:36 virgin because a critical moment has c
8: 6 whom all things c and for whom we live;

10:11 to us, upon whom the end of the ages has *c*.
10:13 been sent you that does not *c* to all men.
11:34 I shall give instructions when I *c*.
14: 6 that I should *c* to you speaking in tongues.
14:23 the uninitiated or unbelievers should *c*
14:36 Are you the only ones to whom it has *c*?
15:22 die, so in Christ all will *c* to life again,
15:24 After that will *c* the end,
16: 3 When I *c* I shall give letters of
16: 5 I shall *c* to you after I have passed
16:10 If Timothy should *c*,
16:11 help him *c* to me by sending him on his way
16:22 O Lord, *c*!
2Cor 1:13 you will in time *c* to know us well,
1:23 for you that I did not *c* to Corinth again.
2: 3 I wrote as I did so that when I *c* I may
6:17 *C* out from among them and separate
9: 4 Macedonians *c* with me and find you unready;
10:14 doing if we had not bothered to *c* to you.
12:20 when I *c* I may not find you to my liking,
12:21 *c* again my God may humiliate me before you,
13: 2 that if I *c* again I shall not spare you.
Gal 4: 4 but when the designated time had *c*,
4: 9 Now that you have *c* to know God
5: 8 does not *c* from him who calls you.
Eph 1:21 be given in this age or in the age to *c*.
2: 7 that in the ages to *c* he might display the
4:13 man who is Christ *c* to full stature.
Phil 1:27 whether I *c* and see you myself or hear
3: 8 I have *c* to rate all as loss in the light
4: 2 *c* to some mutual understanding in the Lord.
Col 1: 6 of truth, the gospel, which has *c* to you,
1:11 even to endure joyfully whatever may *c*,
2:17 All these were but a shadow of things to *c*;
1Thes 1:10 Jesus, who delivers us from the wrath to *c*.
2:18 So we tried to *c* to you
4:16 *c* down from heaven at the word of command,
1Tm 2: 4 men to be saved and *c* to know the truth.
6: 4 From these *c* envy,
6:10 faith, and have *c* to grief amid great pain.
2Tm 4: 3 For the time will *c* when people will not
4:13 When you *c*, bring the cloak I left
Heb 2: 5 For he did not make the world to *c*—
2:16 Surely he did not *c* to help angels,
6: 5 of God and the powers of the age to *c*,
9:11 of the good things which have *c* to be,
10: 1 had only a shadow of the good things to *c*,
10: 7 me in the book, I have *c* to do your will,
10: 9 "I have *c* to do your will."
10:37 brief moment, and he who is to *c* will *c*;
11:15 back to the place from which they had *c*,
13:14 we are seeking one which is to *c*.
Jas 1: 4 Let endurance *c* to its perfection so that
2: 2 Suppose there should *c* into your assembly
3:10 Blessing and curse *c* out of the same mouth.
3:15 Wisdom like this does not *c* from above.
4:13 *C* now, you who say, "Today or tomorrow
4:13 year there, trade, and *c* off with a profit!"
1Pt 1:23 Your rebirth has *c*,
2: 4 *C* to him, a living stone, rejected by men
4:14 Spirit in its glory has *c* to rest on you.
2Pt 2:18 who have just *c* free of a life of errors.
3: 9 none to perish but all to *c* to repentance.
3:10 The day of the Lord will *c* like a thief,
1Jn 3: 2 we shall later be has not yet *c* to light.
4: 2 Jesus Christ *c* in the flesh belongs to God,
4: 3 which, as you have heard, is to *c*;
4:16 We have *c* to know and to believe in the
5:20 that the Son of God has *c* and has given us
2Jn 1: 1 all those who have *c* to know the truth.
3Jn 1:10 if I *c* I will speak publicly of what he is
Jude 1:14 the Lord has *c* with his countless holy
1:25 from ages past, now and for ages to *c*.
Rv 1: 4 him who is and who was and who is to *c*,
1: 8 the One who is and who was and who is to *c*,
1:19 what you see now and will see in time to *c*.
2: 5 If you do not repent I will *c* to you and
2:10 Have no fear of the sufferings to *c*.
2:16 I will *c* to you soon and fight against
2:23 Thus shall all the churches *c* to know that
2:25 case, hold fast to what you have until I *c*.
3: 3 yourselves I will *c* upon you like a thief,
3: 9 but frauds, *c* and fall down at your feet;
4: 1 *C* up here and I will show you what must
4: 1 show you what must take place in time to *c*."
4: 8 He who was, and who is, and who is to *c*!"
6: 1 cry out in a voice like thunder, *C* forward!"
6: 3 second living creature cry out, *C* forward!"
6: 5 third living creature cry out, *C* forward!"
6: 7 fourth living creature cry out, *C* forward!"
6:17 The great day of vengeance has *c*.
7: 2 I saw another angel *c* up from the east
7:13 And where have they *c* from?"
9:12 There are two more to *c*.
10: 1 *c* down from heaven wrapped in a cloud,
11: 1 *C* and take the measurements of God's
11: 5 fire will *c* out of the mouths of these
11:12 voice from heaven say to them, *C* up here!"
12:10 "Now have salvation and power *c*,
12:12 and sea, for the devil has *c* down upon you!
13: 1 Then I saw a wild beast *c* out of the sea
13: 4 beast, or *c* forward to fight against it?"
13:11 another wild beast *c* up out of the earth;
13:13 it could even make fire *c* down from heaven
14: 7 for his time has *c* to sit in judgment.
15: 4 shall *c* and worship in your presence.
15: 8 of the seven angels had *c* to an end.
16:13 like frogs *c* from the mouth of the dragon,
16:15 I *c* like a thief.
17: 1 *C*, I will show you the judgment in store
17: 8 It will *c* up from the abyss once more
17:10 yet come; but when he does *c* he will
17:13 Then they will *c* to agreement and bestow
18: 8 Therefore her plagues will *c* all at once,
18:10 In a single hour your doom has *c*!"
18:19 a single hour her destruction has *c* about!"
19: 9 they *c* from God."
19:17 *C*! Gather together for the great feast
20: 1 Then I saw an angel *c* down from heaven,
20: 5 The others who were dead did not *c* to life
21: 9 seven last plagues came and said to me, *C*,
22:17 The Spirit and the Bride say, *C*!"
22:17 Let him who hears answer, *C*!"
22:17 Let him who is thirsty *c* forward;
22:20 *C*, Lord Jesus!

COMELINESS (1)

Wis 7:10 Beyond health and *c* I loved her,

COMELY (2)

Dt 21:11 if you see a *c* woman among the captives
Sir 9: 8 Avert your eyes from a *c* woman;

COMES (310)

Gn 18:21 to the cry against them that *c* to me.
24:43 to a young woman who *c* out to draw water,
24:50 "This thing *c* from the LORD;
27:41 the time of mourning for my father *c*,
29: 6 here *c* his daughter Rachel with his flock."
32:12 Otherwise I fear that when he *c* he will
37:19 "Here *c* that master dreamer!
37:20 We shall then see what *c* of his dreams."
42:15 unless your youngest brother *c* here,
42:22 Now *c* the reckoning for his blood."
44:23 your youngest brother *c* back with you,
Ex 9:19 shall die when the hail *c* upon them."
21: 3 If he *c* into service alone,
21: 3 if he *c* with a wife,
Lv 14:48 finds, when he *c* to examine the house,
25:22 into the ninth year, when the crop *c* in,
Nm 1:51 layman who *c* near it shall be put to death.
3:10 layman who *c* near shall be put to death."
5:30 when such a feeling of jealousy *c* over a man
11:20 until it *c* out of your very nostrils and
12:12 thus be like the stillborn babe that *c* forth
19:21 and anyone who *c* in contact with this
Dt 8: 3 that *c* forth from the mouth of the LORD.
13: 3 or wonder he has foretold you *c* to pass,
21:16 when he *c* to bequeath his property to his
22:13 relations with her, *c* to dislike her,
22:23 a man *c* upon a maiden who is betrothed,
22:25 that a man *c* upon such a betrothed maiden,
22:28 man *c* upon a maiden that is not betrothed,
24: 3 *c* to dislike her and dismisses her from
31:10 *c* at the end of every seven-year period,
Jgs 4:20 "If anyone *c* and asks,
6:37 If dew *c* on the fleece alone,
11:31 "whoever *c* out of the doors of my house
13:12 "Now, when that which you say *c* true,
13:14 must not eat anything that *c* from the vine,
1Sm 15:14 this bleating of sheep that *c* to my ears,
16:16 When the evil spirit from God *c* over you,
17:25 He *c* up to insult Israel.
24:14 says, 'From the wicked *c* forth wickedness.'
26:10 him, whether the time *c* for him to die,
2Sm 7:12 time *c* and you rest with your ancestors,
13: 5 When your father *c* to visit you,
18:27 he *c* with good news."
1Kgs 8:31 when he *c* and takes the oath before your
8:37 or if blight *c*,
8:41 but *c* from a distant land to honor you
8:42 when he *c* and prays toward this temple,
14: 5 When she *c*, she will be in disguise."
17:24 word of the LORD *c* truly from your mouth."
2Kgs 4:10 so that when he *c* to us he can stay there."
6:32 When the messenger *c*,
1Chr 16:33 the forest exult before the LORD, for he *c*:
16:33 he *c* to rule the earth.
29:16 holy name *c* from you and is entirely yours.
2Chr 6:22 and when he *c* for the oath before your
6:32 when he *c* from a distant land to honor
13: 9 Everyone who *c* to consecrate himself with
20: 9 your honor, saying, 'When evil *c* upon us,
20:12 this vast multitude that *c* against us.
26:18 part in the glory that *c* from the LORD God."
Tb 5: 9 find out what family and tribe he *c* from,
Jdt 8:11 within that time the Lord *c* to our aid,
8:17 we wait for the salvation that *c* from him,
9: 5 Whatever you devise *c* into being;
1Mc 3:19 army, but on strength that *c* from Heaven.
2Mc 14:15 who always *c* to the aid of his heritage.
Jb 3:21 They wait for death and it *c* not;
3:24 For sighing *c* more readily to me than food,
3:25 me, and what I shrink from *c* upon me.
3:26 I have no rest, for trouble *c*!
4: 5 But now that it *c* to you,
5: 6 For mischief *c* not out of the earth,
5:26 as a shock of grain *c* in at its season.
15:21 all is prosperous, the spoiler *c* upon him.
21:30 the evil man is spared calamity when it *c*;
26: 4 whose is the breath that *c* forth from you?
27: 9 attend to his cry when calamity *c* upon him?
28: 5 The earth, though out of it *c* forth bread,
28:20 Whence, then, *c* wisdom,
37: 9 Out of its chamber *c* forth the tempest;
37:17 when a calm from the south *c* over the land,
37:21 the wind *c* by and sweeps the clouds away.
37:22 From the North the splendor *c*,
38:29 Out of whose womb *c* the ice,
Ps(s) 19: 6 which *c* forth like the groom from his
19: 7 At one end of the heavens it *c* forth,
41: 7 When one *c* to see me,
62: 2 from him *c* my salvation.
62: 6 at rest, my soul, for from him *c* my hope.
73: 7 Out of their crassness *c* iniquity;
96:13 forest exult before the LORD, for he *c*;
96:13 for he *c* to rule the earth.
98: 9 for he comes, for he *c* to rule the earth;
118:26 is he who *c* in the name of the LORD;
Prv 1:27 When terror *c* upon you like a storm,
3:25 of the ruin of the wicked when it *c*;
6:15 Therefore suddenly ruin *c* upon him;
7:10 the woman *c* to meet him,
10:28 the expectation of the wicked *c* to nought.
11: 2 When pride comes, disgrace *c*;
11: 7 what is expected from strength *c* to nought.
12:13 ensnared, but the just *c* free of trouble.
12:14 the work of his hands *c* back to reward him.
18: 3 comes contempt, and with disgrace *c* scorn.
18:17 his opponent *c* and puts him to the test.
19:22 From a man's greed *c* his shame;
25: 4 silver, and it *c* forth perfectly purified;
26:27 and a stone *c* back upon him who rolls it.
Eccl 1: 4 One generation passes and another *c*,
2:22 For what profit *c* to a man from all the
4: 1 the hand of their oppressors *c* violence,
4:14 from a prison house one *c* forth to rule,
9:11 for a time of calamity *c* to all alike.
Sg 2: 8 here he *c* springing across the mountains,
6:10 Who is this that *c* forth like the dawn,
Wis 4: 8 honorable *c* not with the passing of time,
9: 6 the sons of men, if Wisdom, who *c* from you,
14: 7 is the wood through which justice *c* about;
Sir 1: 1 All wisdom *c* from the LORD and with him it
1:20 a time, and then contentment *c* back to him.
4:18 Then she *c* back to bring him happiness and
6:10 who will not be with you when sorrow *c*.
12: 3 *c* to him who gives comfort to the wicked,
12:17 If evil *c* upon you,
20: 6 wise man is silent till the right time *c*,
20:17 the downfall of the wicked *c* so quickly.
22:23 as to share in his inheritance when it *c*.
27: 9 and fidelity *c* to those who live by it.
29:19 The sinner through surety *c* to grief,
37:29 foods, For sickness *c* with overeating,
39:33 every need when it *c* he fills.
40:12 All that *c* from bribes or injustice will
40:14 suddenly, once and for all, *c* to an end.
42:13 garments, so harm to women *c* from women:
42:25 made in vain, For each in turn, as it *c*,
43:18 it *c* to settle like swarms of locusts.
Is 10: 3 day of punishment, when ruin *c* from afar?
13: 6 as destruction from the Almighty it *c*.
13: 9 Lo, the day of the LORD *c* cruel,
14:31 For there *c* a smoke from the north,
18: 5 Then *c* the cutting of branches with
21: 1 through the Negeb, there *c* from the desert,
21: 9 Here he *c* now:
28:29 This too *c* from the LORD of hosts;
30:13 out in a high wall whose crash *c* suddenly,
32:19 Down it *c*, as trees come down
35: 4 Here is your God, he *c* with vindication;
35: 4 With divine recompense he *c* to save you.
40:10 Here *c* with power the Lord GOD,
41:25 stirred up one from the north, and he *c*;
48:16 At the time it *c* to pass,
52:12 headlong flight, For the LORD *c* before you,
60:22 accomplish these things when their time *c*.
62:11 Say to daughter Zion, your savior *c*!
63: 1 Who is this that *c* from Edom,
66: 7 Before she *c* to labor,
Jer 4: 7 Up *c* the lion from his lair,
4:11 a wind *c* toward the daughter of my people."
5:31 what will you do when the end *c*?
6:20 what use to me incense that *c* from Sheba,
6:22 See, a people *c* from the land of the north,
6:26 For sudden upon us *c* the destroyer.
8:15 a time of healing, but terror *c* instead.
10:22 it *c* closer,
14:19 a time of healing, but terror *c* instead.
17: 8 It fears not the heat when it *c*,
23:20 When the time *c*,
30:24 When the time *c*,
31: 2 As Israel *c* forward to be given his rest,
46:21 When the day of their ruin *c* upon them,
48: 8 The destroyer *c* upon every city,
49:19 As when a lion *c* up from the thicket of

COMES (cont.)

50:41 a people *c* from the north,
50:44 As when a lion *c* up from the Jordan's
51:46 this year the rumor *c*,
51:56 For the destroyer *c* upon her,
Lam 3:37 Who commands so that it *c* to pass,
Bar 4:36 behold the joy that *c* to you from God.
6:48 For when war or disaster *c* upon them,
Ez 7:25 When anguish *c* they shall seek peace,
12:22 on, and no vision ever *c* to anything"?
21:12 when it *c* every heart shall fail,
21:32 he *c* who has the claim against the city;
28:23 sword that *c* against it from every side.
33: 4 slain by the sword that *c* against him,
33: 6 so that the sword *c* and takes anyone,
33:30 hear the latest word that *c* from the LORD."
33:33 But when it *c*—
47: 9 this water *c* the sea shall be made fresh.
Dn 11:15 When the king of the north *c*,
Hos 12: 2 he *c* to terms with Assyria,
Jl 1:15 LORD, and it *c* as ruin from the Almighty.
Mi 1: 3 For see, the LORD *c* forth from his place,
1: 5 For the crime of Jacob all this *c* to pass,
Na 2: 2 The hammer *c* up against you;
Hb 1: 4 this is why judgment *c* forth perverted.
1: 9 each *c* for the rapine,
3: 3 God *c* from Teman,
Zep 2: 2 *c* upon you the blazing anger of the LORD:
2: 2 *c* upon you the day of the LORD's anger.
Zec 5: 5 eyes and see what this is that *c* forth."
Mal 3:23 the prophet, Before the day of the LORD *c*,
3:24 the prophet, Before the day of the LORD *c*,
Mt 4: 4 utterance that *c* from the mouth of God.' "
5:18 be done away with until it all *c* true.
7:22 When that day *c*, many will plead with me,
8: 9 If I say to another, 'Come here,' he *c*.
9:15 the day *c* that the groom is taken away,
10:19 When the hour *c*, you will be given
10:23 towns of Israel before the Son of Man *c*.
15:11 it is what *c* out of his mouth."
15:18 *c* out of the mouth originates in the mind?
18: 7 woe to that man through whom scandal *c*!
21: 5 *c* to you without display astride an ass,
21: 9 is he who *c* in the name of the Lord!
21:40 will do to those tenants when he *c*?"
23:39 is he who *c* in the name of the Lord!' "
25:31 "When the Son of Man *c* in his glory,
27:49 Let's see whether Elijah *c* to his rescue."
Mk 4:15 Satan *c* to carry off what was sown in them.
7:15 that which *c* out of him,
8:38 Man will be ashamed of him when he *c*
11: 9 is he who *c* in the name of the Lord!
15:36 see whether Elijah *c* to take him down."
Lk 7: 8 to another, 'Come here,' and he *c*;
8:12 but the devil *c* and takes the word out of
8:16 lampstand so that whoever *c* in can see it.
9:26 he *c* in his glory and that of his Father
11: 5 "If one of you knows someone who *c* to him
11:22 stronger than he *c* and overpowers him,
12:33 no thief *c* near nor any moth destroys.
13:35 not see me until the time *c* when you say,
13:35 is he who *c* in the name of the Lord.' "
14:26 "If anyone *c* to me without turning his
16: 8 when it *c* to dealing with their own kind.
18: 8 But when the Son of Man *c*,
19:38 he who *c* as king in the name of the Lord!
Jn 1:15 'The one who *c* after me ranks ahead of me,
3: 8 makes but you do not know where it *c* from,
3:21 But he who acts in truth *c* into the light,
3:31 "The One who *c* from above is above all;
4:25 "When he *c*, he will tell us everything."
5:44 seek the glory that *c* from the One [God]?
6:33 God's bread *c* down from heaven and gives
6:35 No one who *c* to me shall ever be hungry,
6:37 no one who *c* will I ever reject,
6:45 the Father and learned from him *c* to me.
6:50 This is the bread that *c* down from heaven
7:16 it *c* from him who sent me.
7:17 *c* from God or is simply spoken on my own.
7:27 When the Messiah *c*,
7:31 They kept saying, "When the Messiah *c*,
8:54 I glorify myself, that glory *c* to nothing.
9: 4 The night *c* on when no one can work.
9:29 but we have no idea where this man *c* from."
9:30 You do not know where he *c* from,
10:10 *c* only to steal and slaughter and destroy,
12:13 is he who *c* in the name of the Lord!
14: 6 no one *c* to the Father but through me.
14:24 it *c* from the Father who sent me.
15:26 Paraclete *c*, the Spirit of truth who comes
16: 4 *c* you may remember my telling you of them.
16: 8 When he *c*, he will prove the world
16:13 When he *c*, however, being the Spirit
17: 7 that all that you gave me *c* from you.
Acts 1: 8 power when the Holy Spirit *c* down on you;
5:39 If, on the other hand, it *c* from God,
13:25 Rather, look for the one who *c* after me.
Rom 4:13 in view of the justice that *c* from faith.
8:39 love of God that *c* to us in Christ Jesus,
9:30 the justice which *c* from faith
9:32 Because justice *c* from faith,
10: 4 him, justice *c* to everyone who believes.
10: 5 writes of the justice that *c* from the law,
10: 6 of the justice that *c* from faith he says,
10:17 Faith, then, *c* through hearing,
1Cor 4:12 Persecution *c* our way;
11:26 proclaim the death of the Lord until he *c*!
13:10 When the perfect *c*,
15:21 of the dead *c* through a man also.
15:44 body is put down and a spiritual body *c* up.
2Cor 4: 7 power *c* from God and not from us.
11: 4 when someone *c* preaching another Jesus
11:15 It *c* as no surprise that his ministers
Gal 3:18 if one's inheritance *c* through the law,
Phil 3: 9 is that which *c* through faith in Christ.
Col 2:19 a growth from this source which *c* from God.
4:10 if he *c* to you, make him welcome.
1Thes 1: 6 with the joy that *c* from the Holy Spirit.
2Thes 1:10 glory of his might on the Day when he *c*,
2Tm 1: 8 but with the strength which *c* from God
Heb 9:17 *c* into force only in the case of death;
11: 6 who *c* to God must believe that he exists,
11: 7 the justice which *c* through faith.
Jas 1:11 When the sun *c* up with its scorching heat
1:17 gift, every genuine benefit *c* from above,
1Jn 2:16 that the world affords *c* from the Father.
2:20 the anointing that *c* from the Holy One,
3: 2 when it *c* to light we shall be like him,
2Jn 1:10 *c* to you who does not bring this teaching,
Rv 1: 7 See, he *c* amid the clouds!
10: 7 When the time *c* for the seventh angel to
11: 7 the wild beast that *c* up from the abyss
11:11 of life which *c* from God returned to them.

COMFORT (43)

Ru 4:15 be your *c* and the support of your old age,
1Chr 19: 2 him to *c* him over the death of his father.
19: 2 the land of the Ammonites to *c* Hanun,
Jb 2:11 together to give him sympathy and *c*.
7:13 When I say, "My bed shall *c* me,
21:34 How then can you offer me vain *c*,
29:25 mourners took *c* from my cheerful glance.
Ps(s) 71:21 benefits toward me, and *c* me over and over.
77: 3 my soul refuses *c*.
94:19 abound within me, your *c* gladdens my soul.
119:50 My *c* in my affliction is that your promise
119:76 Let your kindness *c* me according to your
119:82 when will you *c* me?
Prv 29:17 Correct your son, and he will bring you *c*,
Eccl 4: 1 tears of the victims with none to *c* them!
4: 1 violence, and there is none to *c* them!
Wis 3:18 have no hope nor *c* in the day of scrutiny;
8: 9 all was well, and my *c* in care and grief.
Sir 3: 6 obeys the LORD who brings *c* to his mother.
12: 3 comes to him who gives *c* to the wicked,
Is 22: 4 Do not try to *c* me for the ruin of the
40: 1 Comfort, give *c* to my people,
51: 3 *c* Zion and have pity on all her ruins;
51:12 I, it is I who *c* you.
51:19 Who is there to *c* you?
57:18 *c* to them and to those who mourn for them,
61: 2 vindication by our God, to *c* all who mourn;
66:11 you may suck fully of the milk of her *c*,
66:13 *c* you; in Jerusalem you shall find your *c*.
Lam 2:13 What example can I show you for your *c*,
Ez 16:54 disgraced for all the *c* you brought them.
Zec 1:17 the LORD will again *c* Zion,
10: 2 dreams they tell, empty *c* they offer.
Mt 2:18 no *c* for her,
25:43 and in prison and you did not come to *c* me.'
Acts 20:12 To the great *c* of the people,
2Cor 1: 4 enables us to *c* those who are in trouble,
Col 4: 8 you for this purpose, and to *c* your hearts.
4:11 They have been a great *c* to me.
1Thes 5:11 Therefore, *c* and upbuild one another,
Phlm 1: 7 I find great joy and *c* in your love,

COMFORTABLY (1)

Am 6: 4 of ivory, stretched *c* on their couches,

COMFORTED (10)

Ru 2:13 you have *c* me,
2Sm 12:24 Then David *c* his wife Bathsheba.
1Chr 7:22 but after his kinsmen had come and *c* him,
Est D: 8 recovered, and *c* her with reassuring words.
Jb 42:11 They condoled with him and *c* him for all
Ps(s) 86:17 that you, O LORD, have helped and *c* me.
119:52 your ordinances of old, O LORD, and I am *c*.
Ez 32:31 he shall be *c* for all his hordes slain by
Mt 25:36 I was ill and you *c* me,
2Cor 7:13 This done, we are *c*.

COMFORTERS (2)

Jb 16: 2 Wearisome *c* are you all!
Ps(s) 69:21 for *c*, and I found none.

COMFORTING (1)

Zec 1:13 with me, the LORD replied with *c* words.

COMFORTS (4)

Is 49:13 For the LORD *c* his people and shows mercy
52: 9 For the Lord *c* his people,
66:13 As a mother *c* her son,
2Cor 1: 4 He *c* us in all our afflictions and thus

COMING (257)

Gn 24:13 of the townsmen are *c* out to draw water,
32: 7 He is now *c* to meet you,
33: 1 Jacob looked up and saw Esau *c*,
33:10 is for me like *c* into the presence of God,
34: 7 as Jacob's sons were *c* in from the fields.
37:25 saw a caravan of Ishmaelites *c* from Gilead,
41:29 are now *c* throughout the land of Egypt;
41:35 husband all the food of the *c* good years,
Ex 3: 4 saw him *c* over to look at it more closely,
14:20 camps *c* any closer together all night long.
18: 6 Jethro, your father-in-law, am *c* to you,
19: 9 told him, "I am *c* to you in a dense cloud,
32: 1 Moses' delay in *c* down from the mountain,
34:34 On *c* out,
Lv 9:23 On *c* out they again blessed the people.
Nm 21: 1 Israelites were *c* along the way of Atharim,
22:16 On *c* to Balaam they told him,
22:36 When Balak heard that Balaam was *c*,
33:40 Canaan, heard that the Israelites were *c*.
Dt 4:46 Israelites defeated after *c* out of Egypt.
28: 6 "May you be blessed in your *c* in,
28:19 "May you be cursed in your *c* in,
Jos 8: 6 They will keep *c* out after us until we
15: 4 the Wadi of Egypt before *c* out at the sea.
Jgs 1:24 a man *c* out of the city and said to him,
5:28 "Why is his chariot so long in *c*?
9:36 "There are men *c* down from the hilltops!"
9:37 *c* down from the region of Tabbur-Haares,
9:37 one company is *c* by way of Elon-Meonenim."
19: 9 See, the day is *c* to an end.
1Sm 2:31 the time is *c* when I will break your
9:11 *c* out to draw water and inquired of them,
9:14 *c* toward them on his way to the high place.
10: 5 *c* down from the high place preceded by
14:11 some Hebrews are *c* out of the holes where
15: 2 barred his way as he was *c* up from Egypt.
17:25 "Do you see this man *c* up?
25:20 also *c* down from the opposite direction.
2Sm 3:22 and Joab were *c* in from an expedition,
13:34 saw a large group *c* down the slope
13:34 seen some men *c* down the mountainside
16: 5 as Saul's family, was *c* out of the place,
18:25 As he kept *c* nearer,
19:42 Israelites began *c* to the king and saying,
24:20 *c* toward him while he was threshing wheat.
1Kgs 14: 5 wife is *c* to consult you about her son,
2Kgs 8: 1 seven-year famine which is *c* upon the land."
9:17 saw the troop of Jehu *c* and reported,
17:11 the LORD had sent into exile at their *c*.
20:17 time is *c* when all that is in your house,
21: 9 had destroyed at the *c* of the Israelites.
1Chr 12:23 And from day to day men kept *c* to David's
2Chr 20: 2 is *c* against you from across the sea,
20:11 See how they are now repaying us by *c* to
20:16 will see them *c* up by the ascent of Ziz,
20:22 of Mount Seir who were *c* against Judah,
32: 2 When Hezekiah saw that Sennacherib was *c*
32: 7 and all the throng that is *c* with him,
33: 9 had destroyed at the *c* of the Israelites.
Ezr 3: 8 their *c* to the house of God in Jerusalem,
Neh 6:10 coming to kill you; by night they are *c*
Tb 11: 6 When she saw him *c*,
11: 6 to his father, "Tobit, your son is *c*,
Jdt 7:31 if those days pass without help *c* to us,
10:15 *c* down thus promptly to see our master,
Est E: 9 treatment matters *c* to our attention.
1Mc 3:17 But when they saw the army *c* against them,
4:60 to prevent the Gentiles from *c* and
2Mc 8: 6 *C* unexpectedly upon towns and villages,
14:15 When the Jews heard of Nicanor's *c*,
Ps(s) 22:31 Let the *c* generation be told of the LORD
37:13 at him, for he sees that his day is *c*.
60: 2 and Joab, *c* back,
72: 6 He shall be like rain *c* down on the meadow,
74: 5 men *c* up with axes to a clump of trees;
121: 8 The LORD will guard your *c* and your going,
Prv 20:20 his lamp will go out at the *c* of darkness.
Sg 3: 6 What is this *c* up from the desert,
8: 5 Who is this *c* up from the desert,
Sir 50:20 Then *c* down he would raise his hands over
Is 14: 9 below is all astir preparing for your *c*;
30:27 of the LORD *c* from afar in burning wrath,
41:27 they are *c* now,"
45:14 they shall follow you, *c* in chains.
49:18 see, they are all gathering and *c* to you.
Jer 4:16 The besiegers are *c* from the distant land,
9:24 See, days are *c*,
13:20 up your eyes and see men *c* from the north.
23: 5 Behold, the days are *c*,
31:27 The days are *c*,
31:31 The days are *c*,
31:38 The days are *c*,
33:14 The days are *c*,
44:12 Judah who insisted on *c* to dwell in Egypt,
49: 2 But the days are *c*,
51:47 *c* when I will punish the idols of Babylon;
51:52 But behold, the days are *c*,
Bar 4: 9 She indeed saw *c* upon you the anger of God;
Ez 5: 8 See, I am *c* at you!

7: 5 Disaster upon disaster. See it *c!*
7: 6 end is *c,* the end is *c* upon you! See it *c!*
7:10 See, the end is *c!*
7:11 It shall not be long in *c,*
9: 2 With that I saw six men *c* from the
13: 8 I am *c* at you, says the Lord GOD.
13:20 I am *c* at those bands of yours in which
21: 8 I am *c* at you;
21:12 See, it is *c,* it is here!
21:30 *c* when your life of crime will be ended,
24:14 it is *c,* for I will bring it about
26: 3 I am *c* at you, Tyre;
28:22 I am *c* at you, Sidon;
29: 3 I am *c* at you, Pharaoh,
29:10 I am *c* at you and against your Niles;
30: 9 on the day of Egypt, which is surely *c.*
30:22 I am *c* at Pharaoh, the king of Egypt.
33: 3 seeing the sword *c* against the country,
33: 6 *c* and fails to blow the warning trumpet,
33:33 But when it comes—and it is surely *c*— they
34:10 I swear I am *c* against these shepherds.
35: 3 I am *c* at you, Mount Seir.
38: 3 I am *c* at you, Gog, chief prince
39: 1 I am *c* at you, Gog, chief prince
39: 8 Yes, it is *c* and shall be fulfilled,
43: 2 glory of the God of Israel *c* from the east.
44:25 unclean by *c* near any dead person,
Dn 7:13 continued, I saw One like a son of man *c,*
Hos 6: 3 as certain as the dawn is his *c,*
Jl 2: 1 tremble, for the day of the LORD is *c;*
3: 4 At the *c* of the Day of the LORD,
Am 4: 2 Truly the days are *c* upon you When they
8:11 Yes, days are *c,*
9:13 Yes, days are *c,*
Mi 5: 6 of many peoples, Like dew *c* from the LORD,
Zep 1:14 day of the LORD, near and very swiftly *c,*
Zec 2: 3 And I asked, "What are these *c* to do?"
2:14 See, I am *c* to dwell among you,
5: 6 answered, "This is a bushel container *c.*
5: 9 *c* forth with a wind ruffling their wings,
6: 1 chariots *c* out from between two mountains;
6: 5 which are *c* forth after being reviewed by
Mal 3: 1 Yes, he is *c,* says the LORD of hosts.
3: 2 But who will endure the day of his *c?*
3:19 For lo, the day is *c,*
3:19 the day that is *c* will set them on fire,
3:24 the day that is *c* will set them on fire,
Mt 3:13 Later Jesus, *c* from Galilee,
8:28 he encountered two men *c* out of the tombs.
13:27 Where are the weeds *c* from?'
17: 9 As they were *c* down the mountainside Jesus
17:11 "Elijah is indeed *c,*
24: 3 sign of your *c* and the end of the world?"
24:27 west, so will the *c* of the Son of Man be.
24:30 as they see 'the Son of Man *c* on the clouds
24:37 The *c* of the Son of Man will repeat what
24:39 So will it be at the *c* of the Son of Man.
24:42 You cannot know the day your Lord is *c.*
24:43 thief was *c* he would keep a watchful eye
24:44 of Man is *c* at the time you least expect.
24:48 himself, 'My master is a long time in *c,*'
25: 5 The groom delayed his *c,*
26:64 of the Power and *c* on the clouds of heaven."
Mk 1:10 Immediately on *c* up out of the water he
1:45 yet people kept *c* to him from all sides.
2:13 kept *c* to him in crowds and he taught them.
6:31 People were *c* and going in great numbers,
9: 9 As they were *c* down the mountain,
13: 4 be the sign that all this is *c* to an end?"
13:26 *c* in the clouds with great power and glory.
13:35 know when the master of the house is *c,*
14:62 the Power and *c* with the clouds of heaven."
15:21 and Rufus, was *c* in from the fields,
15:30 yourself now by *c* down from that cross!"
Lk 2:38 *C* on the scene at this moment,
6:17 *C* down the mountain with them,
8:35 *C* on Jesus,
12:39 when the thief was *c* he would not let him
12:45 'My master is taking his time about *c,*'
12:54 west, you say immediately that rain is *c*—
14:31 enemy *c* against him with twenty thousand?
15:12 me the share of the estate that is *c* to me.'
15:17 *C* to his senses at last, he said:
18: 3 A widow in that city kept *c* to him saying,
19:41 *C* within sight of the city,
21:26 anticipation of what is *c* upon the earth.
21:27 *c* on a cloud with great power and glory.
22:18 the vine until the *c* of the reign of God."
23:26 the Cyrenean who was *c* in from the fields.
23:29 The days are *c* when they will say,
23:36 *c* forward to offer him their sour wine and
Jn 1: 9 light to every man was *c* into the world.
1:14 the glory of an only Son *c* from the Father,
1:29 John caught sight of Jesus *c* toward him,
1:47 When Jesus saw Nathanael *c* toward him,
3:23 and people kept *c* to be baptized.
4:15 and have to keep *c* here to draw water."
4:21 an hour is *c* when you will worship the
4:23 Yet an hour is *c,*
4:25 "I know there is a Messiah *c.*"
5:25 I solemnly assure you, an hour is *c,*
5:28 for an hour is *c* in which all those in
6: 5 caught sight of a vast crowd *c* toward him,
7:52 will not find the Prophet *c* from Galilee."
8: 2 and when the people started *c* to him,
10:12 catches sight of the wolf *c* and runs away,
11:20 that Jesus was *c* she went to meet him,
16:32 An hour is *c*—
Acts 2:20 before the *c* of that great and glorious day
7:52 those who foretold the *c* of the Just One;
9:12 vision a man named Ananias *c* to him
10: 3 messenger of God *c* toward him and calling,
12:12 After *c* to realize this,
13:24 John heralded the *c* of Jesus by
13:25 As John's career was *c* to an end,
21:22 What are we to do about your *c,*
24:25 continence, and the *c* judgment,
27:39 With the *c* of daylight,
Rom 5:12 thus *c* to all men inasmuch as all sinned
1Cor 15:23 Christ the first fruits and then, at his *c,*
2Cor 13: 1 This is the third time I shall be *c* to you.
Gal 3:23 the faith that was *c* should be revealed.
Phil 2:24 in the Lord that I myself will be *c* soon.
3:20 that we eagerly await the *c* of our Savior,
Col 4:16 read the letter that is *c* from Laodicea.
1Thes 2: 1 our *c* among you was not without effect.
2:19 in, before our Lord Jesus Christ at his *c?*
3:13 *c* of our Lord Jesus with all his holy ones.
4:15 that we who live, who survive until his *c,*
5: 2 of the Lord is *c* like a thief in the night.
5:23 at the *c* of our Lord Jesus Christ.
2Thes 2: 1 On the question of the *c* of our Lord Jesus
2Tm 4: 1 who is *c* to judge the living and the dead,
Heb 8: 8 "Days are *c,* says the Lord,
10: 5 Wherefore, on *c* into the world,
Jas 5: 7 my brothers, until the *c* of the Lord.
5: 8 because the *c* of the Lord is at hand.
2Pt 1:16 the *c* in power of our Lord Jesus Christ,
3: 4 "Where is that promised *c* of his?
3:12 looking for the *c* of the day of God and
1Jn 2:18 as you heard that the antichrist was *c,*
2:28 and not retreat in shame at his *c.*
2Jn 1: 7 acknowledge Jesus Christ as *c* in the flesh.
Rv 3:10 of trial which is *c* on the whole world,
3:11 I am *c* soon.
6: 6 *c* from in among the four living creatures.
9:13 and I heard a voice *c* from between the
11:14 The third is *c* very soon.
18: 1 I saw another angel *c* down from heaven.
19: 5 A voice *c* from the throne cried out:
21: 2 holy city, *c* down out of heaven from God,
21:10 Jerusalem *c* down out of heaven from God.
22: 7 "Remember, I am *c* soon!
22:12 "Remember, I am *c* soon!
22:20 this testimony says, "Yes, I am *c* soon!"

COMMAND (233)

Gn 22:18 all this because you obeyed my *c.*"
41:40 and all my people shall dart at your *c.*
Ex 7: 2 You shall tell him all that I *c* you.
32:28 The Levites carried out the *c* of Moses,
38:21 drawn up at the *c* of Moses by the Levites
Lv 4: 2 commits a sin against some *c* of the LORD
6: 2 "Give Aaron and his sons the following *c:*
8:29 was in keeping with the LORD's *c* to Moses.
8:31 in keeping with the *c* I have received:
8:35 for this is the *c* I have received."
9:21 in keeping with the LORD's *c* to Moses.
10:13 such is the *c* I have received.
10:18 in keeping with the *c* I had received."
24:23 out the *c* that the LORD had given Moses.
Nm 3:16 with the *c* the LORD had given him.
3:39 by clans in keeping with the LORD's *c,*
5: 4 obeyed the *c* that the LORD had given Moses;
8: 2 to Moses, and said, "Give Aaron this *c:*
8:20 carrying out exactly the *c* which the LORD
8:22 The *c* which the LORD had given Moses
9: 8 learn what the LORD will *c* in your regard."
22:18 great, contrary to the *c* of the LORD
24:13 or evil, contrary to the *c* of the LORD"?
31:49 have counted up the soldiers under our *c,*
32:25 Moses, "Your servants will do as you *c,*
33: 2 By the LORD's *c* Moses recorded the
33:38 priest ascended Mount Hor at the LORD's *c,*
36:10 the *c* which the LORD had given to Moses.
Dt 1:19 "Then, in obedience to the *c* of the LORD,
1:26 go up, and after defying the *c* of the LORD,
1:43 In defiance of the LORD's *c* you arrogantly
2:37 However, in obedience to the *c* of the LORD,
4: 2 add to what I *c* you nor subtract from it.
4:23 his *c* an idol in any form whatsoever.
9:23 you rebelled against this *c* of the LORD,
10: 5 in keeping with the *c* the LORD gave me.
12:11 you shall bring all the offerings I *c* you:
13: 1 "Every *c* that I enjoin on you,
15:11 that is why I *c* you to open your hand to
15:15 That is why I am giving you this *c* today.
17: 3 any of the host of the sky, against my *c;*
18:18 he shall tell them all that I *c* him.
24:18 that is why I *c* you to observe this rule.
24:22 that is why I *c* you to observe this rule.
27: 4 stones concerning which I *c* you today,
30: 2 and all your soul, just as I now *c* you,
30:11 "For this *c* which I enjoin on you today
34: 9 thus carrying out the LORD's *c* to Moses.
Jos 1: 9 I *c* you: be firm
1:18 and does not obey every *c* you give him,
3: 8 Now *c* the priests carrying the ark of the
4:16 *C* the priests carrying the ark of the
5: 6 they had not obeyed the *c* of the LORD.
8: 8 set it afire in obedience to the LORD's *c.*
8:27 to the *c* of the LORD issued to Joshua.
8:31 with the *c* to the Israelites of Moses,
10:27 they were removed from the trees at the *c*
17: 4 So in obedience to the *c* of the LORD a
19:50 In obedience to the *c* of the LORD,
21: 3 in obedience to this *c* of the LORD,
21: 8 in obedience to the LORD's *c* through Moses.
22: 2 you, and have obeyed every *c* I gave you.
22: 9 according to the LORD's *c* through Moses.
Jgs 9:29 that this people were entrusted to my *c!*
1Sm 12:14 him and do not rebel against the LORD's *c,*
12:15 the LORD and if you rebel against his *c,*
13:13 you kept the *c* the LORD your God gave you,
13:14 his people, because you broke the LORD's *c.*"
14: 2 (Saul's *c* post was under the pomegranate
15:11 has turned from me and has not kept my *c.*"
15:13 I have kept the *c* of the LORD."
15:22 as in obedience to the *c* of the LORD?
15:23 you have rejected the *c* of the LORD,
15:24 the *c* of the LORD and your instructions.
15:26 because you rejected the *c* of the LORD and
2Sm 4:12 So at a *c* from David,
5:25 David obeyed the LORD's *c* and routed the
8:16 Joab, son of Zeruiah, was in *c* of the army.
8:18 was in *c* of the Cherethites and Pelethites.
10:10 under the *c* of his brother Abishai,
14: 8 I will issue a *c* on your behalf."
17:25 put Amasa in *c* of the army in Joab's place.
18: 1 David placed officers in *c* of groups of a
18: 2 Joab's command, a third under *c* of Abishai,
18: 2 and a third under *c* of Ittai the Gittite.
18: 5 But the king gave this *c* to Joab,
20:23 Joab was in *c* of the whole army of Israel.
20:23 was in *c* of the Cherethites and Pelethites.
23:23 David put him in *c* of his bodyguard.
1Kgs 2:43 oath of the LORD and the *c* that I gave you?"
11:38 If, then, you heed all that I *c* you,
13:21 'Because you rebelled against the *c* of the
13:21 LORD and did not keep the *c* which the LORD,
13:26 God who rebelled against the *c* of the LORD.
18:36 and have done all these things by your *c.*
2Kgs 11:15 instructed the captains in *c* of the force:
14: 6 *c* written in the book of the law of Moses,
22:12 and issued this *c* to Hilkiah the priest,
23:21 The king issued a *c* to all the people to
1Chr 5:12 Joel was chief, Shapham was second in *c,*
10:13 against the LORD in disobeying his *c*
12:33 with all their brethren under their *c.*
18:15 Joab, son of Zeruiah, was in *c* of the army;
18:17 in *c* of the Cherethites and the Pelethites;
19:11 placed under the *c* of his brother Abishai,
21: 4 However, the king's *c* prevailed over Joab,
21: 6 for the king's *c* was repugnant to Joab.
21: 7 This *c* displeased God,
21:19 David went up at Gad's *c,*
28:21 the people will do everything that you *c.*"
2Chr 7:13 rain, if I *c* the locust to devour the land,
8:13 day by day according to the *c* of Moses,
8:14 each gate, since such was the *c* of David,
8:15 There was no deviation from the king's *c*
19: 9 He gave them this *c:*
19:10 bloodguilt or questions of law, *c,*
23:14 out the captains who were in *c* of the army;
24: 8 At the king's *c,*
25:11 Amaziah now assumed *c* of his army.
26:11 the recorder, under the *c* of Hananiah,
29:31 Hezekiah now spoke out this *c:*
30: 6 and Judah, and at the king's *c* they said:
30:12 one mind to carry out the *c* of the king
34:20 his garments and issued this *c* to Hilkiah,
35:10 in their classes according to the king's *c.*
Ezr 4:19 When at my *c* inquiry was made,
6:14 finished the building according to the *c*
8:17 Meshullam, wise leaders, with a *c* for Iddo,
Neh 12:24 in fulfillment of the *c* of David,
Tb 3: 6 and *c* my life breath to be taken from me,
3: 6 *c* me to be delivered from such anguish;
14: 3 Tobiah's seven sons, and gave him this *c:*
14: 9 "Now, children, I give you this *c:*
Jdt 2: 4 of his forces, second to himself in *c,*
14: 2 rush out of the city under *c* of a captain,
Est 3:15 couriers set out in haste at the king's *c;*
9:32 The *c* of Esther confirmed these
1Mc 1:42 Gentiles conformed to the *c* of the king,
1:50 the *c* of the king should be put to death.
2:18 now, be the first to obey the king's *c,*
2:33 "Come out and obey the king's *c,*
2:34 obey the king's *c* to profane the sabbath."
3:14 followers, who have despised the king's *c.*"
2Mc 7:30 I will not obey the king's *c.*
7:30 I obey the *c* of the law given to our
9: 8 thought he could *c* the waves of the sea,
10:13 not *c* the respect due to his high office,
10:32 called Gazara, where Chaereas was in *c.*
14:12 who had been in *c* of the elephants,
14:16 At their leader's *c,*
Jb 39:27 fly up at your *c* to build his nest aloft?

COMMAND (cont.)

Ps(s) 19: 9 The *c* of the LORD is clear,
91:11 For to his angels he has given *c* about you,
107:25 His *c* raised up a storm wind which tossed
119:96 broad indeed is your *c*.
119:98 Your *c* has made me wiser than my enemies,
119:127 For I love your *c* more than gold,
147:15 He sends forth his *c* to the earth;
Prv 8:29 the waters should not transgress his *c*;
Sir 15:20 No man does he *c* to sin,
24: 8 "Then the Creator of all gave me his *c*,
39:18 He has but to *c* and his will is done;
39:31 their assignments they disobey not his *c*.
43:10 At whose *c* they keep their place and never
Is 5: 6 will *c* the clouds not to send rain upon it.
28:10 says, 'Command on command, command on *c*,
28:13 "Command on command, command on *c*,
Jer 1: 7 whatever I *c* you,
1:17 stand up and tell them all that I *c* you.
7:22 no *c* concerning holocaust or sacrifice.
7:23 Walk in all the ways that I *c* you,
11: 4 Listen to my voice and do all that I *c* you.
13: 5 Obedient to the LORD's *c*,
14:14 I gave them no *c* nor did I speak to them.
23:32 From me they have no mission or *c*,
26: 2 whatever I *c* you,
29:23 and alleging in my name things I did not *c*.
34:22 I will give the *c*,
35:14 they obeyed their father's *c*.
35:16 the *c* which their father laid on them;
35:18 Since you have obeyed the *c* of Jonadab,
42: 6 difficult, we will obey the *c* of the LORD,
42: 6 well with us for obeying the *c* of the LORD,
43: 4 the LORD's *c* to stay in the land of Judah.
43: 7 Against the LORD's *c* they went to Egypt,
Lam 1:18 "The LORD is just; I had defied his *c*.
Bar 5: 8 tree have overshadowed Israel at God's *c*;
Ez 30: 9 at my *c* to terrify unsuspecting Ethiopia;
Dn 3:95 they disobeyed the royal *c* and yielded
4:23 The *c* that the stump and roots of the tree
9:10 against you and paid no heed to your *c*,
11:31 his *c* and defile the sanctuary stronghold,
Am 6:11 the *c* to shatter the great house to bits,
9: 3 I will *c* the serpent there to bite them;
9: 4 there will I *c* the sword to slay them.
9: 9 I have given the *c* to sift the house of
Mal 3:14 and what do we profit by keeping his *c*,
Mt 2:13 appeared in a dream to Joseph with the *c*:
2:20 in a dream to Joseph in Egypt with the *c*:
4: 3 of God, *c* these stones to turn into bread."
5:44 My *c* to you is:
8:16 simple *c* and cured all who were afflicted,
19: 7 "Then why did Moses *c* divorce and the
Mk 2:11 (he said to the paralyzed man), "I *c* you:
9:25 to him, "Mute and deaf spirit, I *c* you:
10: 3 reply he said, "What *c* did Moses give you?"
Lk 4: 3 of God, *c* this stone to turn into bread."
7: 8 of an order, having soldiers under my *c*.
Jn 10:18 This *c* I received from my Father."
15:14 You are my friends if you do what I *c* you.
15:17 The *c* I give you is this,
Acts 16:18 "In the name of Jesus Christ I *c* you,
25:23 At Festus' *c* Paul was brought in.
Rom 16:26 prophets, and, at the *c* of the eternal God,
1Cor 7: 6 say this by way of concession, not as a *c*.
7:10 I give this *c* (though it is not mine;
1Thes 4:16 come down from heaven at the word of *c*,
2Thes 3: 6 We *c* you,
1Tm 1: 1 an apostle of Christ Jesus by *c* of God our
6:14 I charge you to keep God's *c* without blame
Ti 1: 3 to me by the *c* of God our Savior.
2:15 and corrections with the authority of *c*.
Phlm 1: 8 right to *c* you to do what ought to be done,
Heb 12:20 for they could not bear to hear the *c*:
2Pt 3: 2 as well as the new *c* of the Lord and
Rv 6:15 of the earth, the nobles and those in *c*,

COMMANDANT (1)

2Mc 4:28 demand of Sostratus, the *c* of the citadel,

COMMANDED (228)

Gn 7: 5 Noah did just as the LORD had *c* him.
7: 9 ark with Noah, just as the LORD had *c* him.
7:16 all species they came, as God had *c* Noah.
21: 4 old, Abraham circumcised him, as God had *c*.
Ex 1:22 Pharaoh then *c* all his subjects,
7: 6 Moses and Aaron did as the LORD had *c*
7:10 went to Pharaoh and did as the LORD had *c*.
7:20 Moses and Aaron did as the LORD had *c*.
12:28 and did as the LORD had *c* Moses and Aaron.
12:35 The Israelites did as Moses had *c*:
12:50 did just as the LORD had *c* Moses and Aaron.
16:16 "Now, this is what the LORD has *c*.
16:24 put it away for the morrow, as Moses *c*,
16:32 Moses said, "This is what the LORD has *c*.
16:34 for safekeeping, as the LORD had *c* Moses.
23:15 As I have *c* you,
31:11 they shall make just as I have *c* you."
34: 4 went up Mount Sinai as the LORD had *c* him,
34:18 are to eat unleavened bread, as I *c* you;
34:34 tell the Israelites all that had been *c*.
35: 1 "This is what the LORD has *c* to be done.
35: 4 community, "This is what the LORD has *c*:
35:10 you come and make all that the LORD has *c*:
35:29 which the LORD had *c* Moses to have done.
36: 1 of the sanctuary, just as the LORD has *c*."
36: 5 out the work which the LORD has *c* us to do."
38:22 Judah, who made all that the LORD *c* Moses,
39: 1 for Aaron, as the LORD had *c* Moses.
39: 5 fine linen twined, as the LORD had *c* Moses.
39: 7 of Israel, just as the LORD had *c* Moses.
39:21 All this was just as the LORD had *c* Moses.
39:26 all this, just as the LORD had *c* Moses.
39:29 and scarlet yarn, as the LORD had *c* Moses.
39:31 a violet ribbon, as the LORD had *c* Moses.
39:32 did the work just as the LORD had *c* Moses.
39:42 all the work just as the LORD had *c* Moses.
39:43 the work was done just as the Lord had *c*,
40:16 Moses did exactly as the LORD had *c* him.
40:19 on top of the tent, as the LORD had *c* him.
40:21 of the commandments, as the LORD had *c* him.
40:23 it before the LORD, as the LORD had *c* him.
40:25 before the LORD as the LORD had *c* him.
40:27 fragrant incense, as the LORD had *c* him.
40:29 offerings on it, as the LORD had *c* him.
40:32 the altar, as the LORD had *c* Moses.
40:38 fragrant incense, as the LORD had *c* him.
Lv 7:38 he *c* the Israelites in the wilderness of Sinai
8: 4 And Moses did as the LORD had *c*.
8: 9 his forehead, as the LORD had *c* him to do.
8:13 on them, as the LORD had *c* him to do.
8:17 the camp, as the LORD had *c* him to do.
8:21 to the LORD, as the LORD had *c* him to do.
8:34 The LORD has *c* that what has been done
8:36 did all that the LORD had *c* through Moses.
9: 7 in atonement for them, as the LORD has *c*."
9:10 the sin offering, as the LORD had *c* Moses;
10: 5 tunics, outside the camp, as Moses had *c*.
10:15 a perpetual ordinance, as the LORD has *c*."
16:34 Thus was it done, as the LORD had *c* Moses.
17: 2 This is what the LORD has *c*.
Nm 1:19 ancestral house, as the LORD had *c* Moses.
1:54 fulfilled as the LORD had *c* Moses.
2:33 Israelites, for so the LORD had *c* Moses.
2:34 did just as the LORD had *c* Moses;
3:42 of the Israelites, as the LORD had *c* him.
3:51 Aaron and his sons, as the LORD had *c* him.
4:49 so the LORD had *c* Moses.
8: 3 lampstand, just as the LORD had *c* Moses.
9: 5 first month, just as the LORD had *c* Moses.
15:36 him to death, as the LORD had *c* Moses.
17:26 And Moses did as the LORD had *c* him.
20:27 Moses did as the LORD *c*.
26: 4 years or more, as the LORD had *c* Moses.
27:11 for the Israelites, as the LORD *c* Moses.
27:22 Moses did as the LORD had *c* him.
30: 2 tribes, "This is what the LORD has *c*:
31: 7 the Midianites, as the LORD had *c* Moses,
31:31 Eleazar did this, as the LORD had *c* Moses.
31:41 the priest Eleazar, as the LORD had *c* him.
32:31 "We will do what the LORD has *c* us,
34:13 which the LORD has *c* to be given to the
34:29 These are they whom the LORD *c* to assign
36: 2 "The LORD *c* you,
36: 2 were also *c* by the LORD to give the
Dt 1:41 and fight, just as the LORD, our God, *c* us.'
2: 1 on the Red Sea road, as the LORD had *c* me,
4: 5 and decrees as the LORD, my God, has *c* me,
4:13 you his covenant, which he *c* you to keep:
5:12 sabbath day as the LORD, your God, *c* you.
5:15 God, has *c* you to observe the sabbath day.
5:16 mother, as the LORD, your God, has *c* you,
5:32 to do as the LORD, your God, has *c* you,
6:24 the LORD *c* us to observe all these
18:20 an oracle that I have not *c* him to speak,
20:17 as the LORD, your God, has *c* you,
26:13 and the widow, just as you have *c* me.
26:14 LORD, my God, doing just as you have *c* me.
Jos 1:10 So Joshua *c* the officers of the people:
1:13 servant of the LORD, *c* you when he said,
1:16 "We will do all you have *c* us,"
4: 8 The twelve Israelites did as Joshua had *c*:
4:10 the LORD had *c* Joshua to tell the people.
6:10 But the people had been *c* by Joshua not to
8:35 Every single word that Moses had *c*,
9:24 *c* his servant Moses that you be given the
10:40 just as the LORD, the God of Israel, had *c*.
11: 9 Joshua did to them as the LORD had *c*:
11:12 as Moses, the servant of the LORD, had *c*.
11:15 commanded his servant Moses, so Moses *c*
11:15 that the LORD had *c* Moses should be done.
11:20 be exterminated, as the LORD had *c* Moses.
13: 6 Israelite heritage, just as I have *c* you.
15:13 As the LORD had *c*,
17: 4 "The LORD *c* Moses to give us a heritage
21: 2 of Canaan, and said to them, "The LORD *c*,
22: 2 that Moses, the servant of the LORD, *c* you,
Jgs 1:20 As Moses had *c*, Hebron was given
6:27 his servants and did as the LORD had *c* him.
13:14 Let her observe all that I have *c* her."
Ru 2: 9 I have *c* the young men to do you no harm.
1Sm 15:32 Afterward Samuel *c*, "Bring Agag,
16: 4 Samuel did as the LORD had *c* him.
17:20 set out on his errand, as Jesse had *c* him.
18:25 answer, Saul *c* them to say this to David:
19:15 messengers back to see David and *c* them,
22:17 The king then *c* his henchmen standing by:
22:18 The king therefore *c* Doeg,
2Sm 9:11 do just as my lord the king has *c* him."
13:29 servants did to Amnon as Absalom had *c*,
21:14 all that the king *c* had been carried out.
23:19 and *c* greater respect than the Thirty,
23:23 and *c* greater respect than the Thirty.
24:19 bidding, David went up as the LORD had *c*.
1Kgs 9: 4 and uprightly, doing just as I have *c* you,
17: 4 and I have *c* ravens to feed you there."
17: 5 So he left and did as the LORD had *c*.
20:12 "Prepare the assault," he *c* his servants;
2Kgs 11: 9 captains did just as Jehoiada the priest *c*.
16:15 altar," King Ahaz *c* Uriah the priest,
16:16 the priest did just as King Ahaz had *c*.
17:15 whom the LORD had *c* them not to imitate.
17:35 he made a covenant with them, he *c* them:
21: 8 are careful to observe all I have *c* them,
23: 4 Then the king *c* the high priest Hilkiah,
1Chr 11:10 even as the LORD had *c* concerning Israel.
14:16 David did as God *c* him,
15:16 David *c* the chiefs of the Levites to
17: 6 of Israel whom I *c* to guide my people,
21:18 Then the angel of the LORD *c* Gad to tell
22: 6 and *c* him to build a house for the LORD,
22:17 David also *c* all of Israel's leaders to
24:19 as the LORD, the God of Israel, had *c* him.
2Chr 7:17 doing all that I have *c* you and keeping my
13: 8 of the LORD *c* by the sons of David,
14: 3 He *c* Judah to seek the LORD,
23: 8 Judah did just as Jehoiada the priest *c*.
25: 4 law, in the Book of Moses, as the LORD *c*:
29:30 King Hezekiah and the princes then *c* the
31: 4 He also *c* the people living in Jerusalem
32:12 and altars and *c* Judah and Jerusalem,
33: 8 are careful to observe all that I *c* them,
33:16 offerings, and *c* Judah to serve the LORD,
35:16 altar of the LORD, as King Josiah had *c*.
Ezr 4: 3 Israel, as King Cyrus of Persia has *c* us."
5:15 And he *c* him:
Neh 9:23 had *c* their fathers to enter and possess.
Tb 5: 1 "Everything that you have *c* me,
6:16 He *c* you to marry a woman from your own
Jdt 2:13 fulfill them exactly as I have *c* you,
2:15 thousand picked troops, as his lord had *c*,
Est 1:17 'King Ahasuerus *c* that Queen Vashti be
2:10 for Mordecai had *c* her not to do so.
4: 5 and *c* him to find out what this action of
C: 1 went away and did exactly as Esther had *c*.
1Mc 3:28 and *c* them to be prepared for anything.
5:19 "Take charge of these people," he *c* them,
10:37 as the king has *c* in the land of Judah.
10:81 men held their ground, as Jonathan had *c*,
2Mc 7: 4 he *c* his executioners to cut out the
15: 4 who *c* the observance of the sabbath day,
Jb 38:12 Have you ever in your lifetime *c* the
42: 9 went and did as the LORD had *c* them.
Ps(s) 33: 9 he *c*, and it stood forth.
78: 5 That what he *c* our fathers they should
78:23 Yet he *c* the skies above and the doors of
106:34 the peoples, as the LORD had *c* them,
119: 4 *c* that your precepts be deligently kept.
148: 5 the LORD, for he *c* and they were created;
Sir 7:31 give him his portion as you have been *c*:
24:22 the law which Moses *c* us as an inheritance
Is 13: 3 I have *c* my dedicated soldiers,
48: 5 them, my statue, my molten image *c* them."
Jer 7:23 This rather is what I *c* them:
7:31 such a thing as I never *c* or had in mind.
11: 8 they had failed to observe as I *c* them.
13: 2 I bought the loincloth, as the LORD *c*,
17:22 keep holy the sabbath, as I *c* your fathers,
19: 5 such a thing as I neither *c* nor spoke of,
32:23 not live, and what you *c* they failed to do.
32:35 this I never *c* them,
35:10 do everything our father Jonadab *c* us.
35:18 his commands and done everything he *c* you,
36: 8 did everything the prophet Jeremiah *c*;
36:26 would not listen to them, but *c* Jerahmeel,
38:27 them in the very words the king had *c*.
47: 7 can it find rest when the LORD has *c* it?
50:21 them, says the LORD, do all I have *c* you.
Bar 2: 9 is just in all the works he *c* us to do,
5: 7 *c* that every lofty mountain be made low,
6: 1 to convey to them what God had *c* him.
6:61 when *c* by God to proceed across the whole
6:62 and the forests, does what has been *c*.
Ez 10: 6 When he *c* the man dressed in linen to take
24:18 and the next morning I did as I had been *c*.
Am 2:12 drink, and *c* the prophets not to prophesy.
Jon 2:11 *c* the fish to spew Jonah upon the shore.
Na 1:14 The LORD has *c* regarding you:
Mt 17: 9 coming down the mountainside Jesus *c* them,
27:10 potter's field just as the Lord had *c* me."
28:20 them to carry out everything I have *c* you.
Lk 17:10 you have done all you have been *c* to do,
Jn 12:49 me has *c* me what to say and how to speak.
14:31 the Father and do as the Father has *c* me.
1Jn 3:23 and we are to love one another as he *c* us.
5: 2 when we love God and do what he has *c*.
2Jn 1: 4 of truth, just as we were *c* by the Father.
Rv 9: 4 The locusts were *c* to do no harm to the

COMMANDEERED (1)

2Chr 16: 6 Then King Asa *c* all of Judah to carry away

COMMANDER (86)

Gn 21:22 accompanied by Phicol, the *c* of his army,
21:32 along with Phicol, the *c* of his army,
Jgs 11: 6 "be our *c* that we may be able to fight
11:11 and the people made him their leader and *c*.
1Sm 9:16 you are to anoint as *c* of my people Israel.
10: 1 "The LORD anoints you *c* over his heritage.
10: 1 LORD has anointed you *c* over his heritage:
13:14 and has appointed him *c* of his people,
25:30 you, and appoints you as *c* over Israel,
2Sm 5: 2 my people Israel and shall be *c* of Israel.' "
6:21 he appointed me *c* of the LORD's people,
7: 8 of the flock to be *c* of my people Israel.
1Kgs 4: 4 [Benaiah, son of Jehoiada, *c* of the army;
16: 9 His servant Zimri, *c* of half his chariots,
2Kgs 4:13 you to the king or to the *c* of the army?' "
5: 1 Naaman, the army *c* of the king of Aram,
9: 5 "I have a message for you, *c*," he said.
9: 5 "For you, *c*," he answered.
18:17 and the *c* from Lachish with a great army
18:19 The *c* said to them,
18:26 and Shebnah and Joah said to the *c*:
18:27 But the *c* replied: Was it to your master
18:28 Then the *c* stepped forward and cried out
18:37 and reported to him what the *c* had said.
19: 4 God, will hear all the words of the *c*,
19: 8 When the *c*, on his return, heard
25:19 city he took one courtier, a *c* of soldiers,
25:19 in the city, the scribe of the army *c*;
1Chr 11: 6 Jebusites first shall be made the chief *c*."
11:21 as any of the Thirty and became their *c*,
27: 5 The third army *c*,
27: 8 for the fifth month, was the *c* Shamhuth,
27:34 The *c* of the king's army was Joab.
2Chr 6: 5 chosen any man to be *c* of my people Israel;
11:22 son of Maacah, *c* among his brothers,
17:14 Adnah the *c*,
17:15 Next to him, Jehohanan the *c*,
32:21 and *c* in the camp of the Assyrian king,
Neh 7: 2 and Hananiah, the *c* of the citadel,
11: 9 Joel son of Zichri, was their *c*,
11:14 Their *c* was Zabdiel, son of Haggadol.
Jdt 4: 1 Holofernes, *c* in chief of Nebuchadnezzar,
5: 1 *c* in chief of the Assyrian army,
6: 1 *c* in chief of the Assyrian army,
1Mc 1:29 sent the Mysian *c* to the cities of Judah,
3:13 But Seron, *c* of the Syrian army,
10:63 military *c* and governor of the province.
13:53 man, Simon made him *c* of all his soldiers,
2Mc 4:29 Crates, *c* of the Cypriots
5:24 king sent Appollonius, *c* of the Mysians,
8: 9 Gorgias, a professional military *c*,
8:32 They also killed the *c* of Timothy's forces,
12: 2 nothing of Nicanor, the *c* of the Cyprians,
12:20 into cohorts, with a *c* over each cohort,
Prv 6: 7 For though she has no chief, no *c* or ruler,
Is 36: 2 Lachish the king of Assyria sent his *c*
36: 4 The *c* said to them, "Tell King Hezekiah:
36:11 Eliakim and Shebna and Joah said to the *c*,
36:12 But the *c* replied, "Was it to you
36:13 Then the *c* stepped forward and cried out
36:22 and reported to him what the *c* had said.
37: 4 your God, will hear the words of the *c*,
37: 8 When the *c* returned to Lachish and heard
55: 4 to the peoples, a leader and *c* of nations,
Jer 52:25 city he took one courtier, a *c* of soldiers,
52:25 army *c* who mustered the people of the land,
Acts 21:31 a report reached the *c* of the cohort
21:32 Immediately the *c* took his soldiers and
21:33 Then, when the *c* arrived on the scene,
21:34 The *c* could not get at the truth because
21:37 into the headquarters, he said to the *c*,
21:37 "So you know Greek!" the *c* exclaimed
22:24 the *c* directed Paul to be brought inside
22:26 the centurion ran to the *c* and demanded,
22:27 The *c* rushed in and asked Paul,
22:28 *c* then observed, "It cost me quite a sum
22:29 The *c* became alarmed because he realized
22:30 next day the *c* released Paul from prison,
23:10 *c* feared they would tear Paul to pieces.
23:15 you must suggest to the *c* that he have
23:17 he said, "Take this young man to the *c*;
23:18 took him in charge and led him to the *c*,
23:19 The *c* took him by the hand and drew him
23:22 The *c* sent the boy away with the order,
23:23 Then the *c* summoned two of his centurions
24:22 decide the case when Lysias the *c* arrives."

COMMANDER-IN-CHIEF (2)

1Mc 15:38 king appointed Cendebeus *c* of the seacoast,
2Mc 10:11 as *c* of Coelesyria and Phoenicia.

COMMANDERS (49)

Nm 31:14 of the army, the clan and company *c*,
31:48 officers who had been clan and company *c*
31:52 This was from the clan and company *c*;
31:54 the gold from the clan and company *c*,
Jos 10:24 *c* of the soldiers who had marched with him,
Jgs 5:14 From Machir came down *c*,
1Sm 8:12 will also appoint from among them his *c*
1Kgs 1:25 all the king's sons, the *c* of the army,
9:22 were his fighting force, his ministers, *c*,
22:31 given his thirty-two chariot *c* the order,
22:32 When the chariot *c* saw Jehoshaphat,
22:33 shouted his battle cry, and the chariot *c*,
2Kgs 8:21 surrounded him and the *c* of his chariots.
9: 5 arrived, the *c* of the army were in session.
25:23 *c* with their men came to him at Mizpah:
25:24 Gedaliah gave the *c* and their men his oath.
25:26 left with the army *c* and went to Egypt for
1Chr 12:15 These Gadites were army *c*,
12:22 were all warriors and became *c* of his army.
13: 1 with his *c* of thousands and of hundreds,
15:25 and the *c* of thousands went to bring up
26:26 the *c* of thousands and of hundreds,
26:26 and of hundreds, and the *c* of the army,
27: 1 heads, *c* of thousands and of hundreds,
27: 3 all the *c* of the army for the first month.
27:22 These were the *c* of the tribes of Israel.
28: 1 the *c* of the divisions who were in the
28: 1 king, the *c* of thousands and of hundreds,
29: 6 Israel, the *c* of thousands and of hundreds,
2Chr 1: 2 to the *c* of thousands and of hundreds,
8: 9 *c* of his warriors, and commanders of his
11:11 the fortifications and put *c* in them,
12: 5 prophet came to Rehoboam and the *c*
12: 6 the *c* of Israel and the king humbled
17:14 Of Judah, the *c* of thousands:
18:30 of Aram had given his chariot *c* the order,
18:31 When the *c* saw Jehoshaphat,
18:32 The chariot *c* became aware that he was not
21: 9 surrounded him and the *c* of his chariots.
32: 6 Then he appointed army *c* over the people.
33:11 them the army *c* of the Assyrian king;
Jdt 7: 8 All the *c* of the Edomites and all the
14:12 and division leaders and all their other *c*.
14:19 *c* of the Assyrian army heard these words,
1Mc 6:28 of his army, and the *c* of the cavalry.
11:70 no one stayed except the army *c* Mattathias,
Is 10: 8 "Are not my *c* all kings?"
Rv 19:18 eat the flesh of kings, of *c* and warriors,

COMMANDING (4)

2Kgs 18:22 *c* Judah and Jerusalem to worship before
Is 36: 7 *c* Judah and Jerusalem to worship before
Ez 14:17 *c* the sword to pass through the land
2Tm 2: 4 this in order to please his *c* officer.

COMMANDMENT (47)

Lv 4:22 which are forbidden by some *c* of the LORD,
5:17 which are forbidden by some *c* of the LORD,
Nm 15:23 issues the *c* down through your generations:
15:31 the word of the LORD and has broken his *c*,
20:24 against my *c* at the waters of Meribah.
28: 2 to Moses, "Give the Israelites this *c*:
Dt 13: 5 his *c* shall you observe,
2Kgs 17:37 statutes and regulations, the law and *c*,
1Mc 2:53 Joseph, when in distress, kept the *c*,
Prv 13:13 but he who reveres the *c* will be rewarded.
Eccl 8: 5 "He who keeps the *c* experiences no evil,
Mal 2: 1 And now, O priests, this *c* is for you:
2: 4 this *c* because I have a covenant with Levi,
Mt 5:21 heard the *c* imposed on your forefathers,
5:27 "You have heard the *c*,
5:33 heard the *c* imposed on your forefathers,
5:38 "You have heard the *c*, 'An eye for an eye,
5:43 "You have heard the *c*, 'You shall love
22:36 which *c* of the law is the greatest?"
22:38 This is the greatest and first *c*.
Mk 7: 8 *c* and cling to what is human tradition."
7: 9 made a fine art of setting aside God's *c*
10: 5 *c* for you because of your stubbornness.
12:31 There is no other *c* greater than these."
Jn 12:50 Since I know that his *c* means eternal life,
13:34 I give you a new *c*:
15:12 This is my *c*:
Rom 7: 8 *c* to rouse in me every kind of evil desire.
7: 9 Then the *c* came;
7:10 The *c* that should have led to life brought
7:11 Sin found its opportunity and used the *c*:
7:12 holy and the *c* is holy and just and good.
7:13 It did so that, by misusing the *c*,
13: 9 *c* there may be are all summed up in this,
1Cor 7:25 I have not received any *c* from the Lord,
14:37 what I have written you is the Lord's *c*.
Eph 6: 2 is the first *c* to carry a promise with it
Heb 7:16 in a *c* concerning physical descent,
7:18 The former *c* has been annulled because of
1Jn 2: 7 it is no new *c* that I write to you,
2: 7 The *c*, now old, is the word
2: 8 thought, the *c* that I write you is new,
3:23 His *c* is this:
4:21 The *c* we have from him is this:
2Jn 1: 5 writing you some new *c*; rather, it is a *c*
1: 6 the *c* is the way in which you should walk.

COMMANDMENTS (181)

Gn 26: 5 obeyed me, keeping my mandate (my *c*,
Ex 15:26 you heed his *c* and keep all his precepts,
16:28 long will you refuse to keep my *c* and laws?
16:34 it in front of the *c* for safekeeping,
20: 1 Then God delivered all these *c*:
20: 6 of those who love me and keep my *c*.
24:12 the *c* intended for their instruction."
25:16 you are to put the *c* which I will give you.
25:21 you are to put the *c* which I will give you.
25:22 the two cherubim on the ark of the *c*.
26:33 The ark of the *c* you shall bring inside,
26:34 on the ark of the *c* in the holy of holies.
27:21 the veil which hangs in front of the *c*.
30: 6 before the ark of *c* where I will meet you.
30:26 the meeting tent and the ark of the *c*,
30:36 put this before the *c* in the meeting tent
31: 7 the *c* with the propitiatory on top of it,
31:18 he gave him the two tablets of the *c*,
32:15 with the two tablets of the *c* in his hands,
34: 1 that I may write on them the *c* which were
34:11 must keep the *c* I am giving you today.
34:28 the words of the covenant, the ten *c*.
34:29 with the two tablets of the *c* in his hands,
38:21 on the Dwelling, the Dwelling of the *c*,
39:35 the ark of the *c* with its poles,
40: 3 Put the ark of the *c* in it,
40: 5 of incense in front of the ark of the *c*,
40:20 He took the *c* and put them in the ark;
40:21 veil, thus screening off the ark of the *c*,
Lv 4:27 which are forbidden by the *c* of the LORD,
16:13 may cover the propitiatory over the *c*;
22:31 "Be careful to observe the *c* which I,
24: 3 the veil that hangs in front of the *c*,
26: 3 precepts and are careful to observe my *c*,
26:14 not heed me and do not keep all these *c*,
26:15 to obey all my *c* and breaking my covenant,
27:34 These are the *c* which the LORD gave Moses
Nm 1:50 Dwelling of the *c* with all its equipment
1:53 shall camp around the Dwelling of the *c*.
1:53 shall have charge of the Dwelling of the *c*."
4: 5 curtain and cover the ark of the *c* with it.
7:89 the propitiatory on the ark of the *c*,
9:15 covered the Dwelling, the tent of the *c*;
10:11 the cloud rose from the Dwelling of the *c*.
15:22 of these *c* which the LORD gives to Moses,
15:39 remind you to keep all the *c* of the LORD,
15:40 to keep all my *c* and be holy to your God.
17:19 in the meeting tent, in front of the *c*,
17:22 down before the LORD in the tent of the *c*.
17:25 back Aaron's staff in front of the *c*,
18: 2 sons are in front of the tent of the *c*.
36:13 These are the *c* and decisions which the
Dt 4: 2 In your observance of the *c* of the LORD,
4:13 the ten *c*,
4:40 statutes and *c* which I enjoin on you today,
5:10 of those who love me and keep my *c*.
5:29 a mind, to fear me and to keep all my *c*!
5:31 near me and I will give you all the *c*,
6: 1 "These then are the *c*,
6: 2 his statutes and *c* which I enjoin on you,
6:17 But keep the *c* of the LORD,
6:25 all these *c* he has enjoined on us.'
7: 9 toward those who love him and keep his *c*,
7:11 shall therefore carefully observe the *c*,
8: 1 to observe all the *c* I enjoin on you today,
8: 2 or not it was your intention to keep his *c*.
8: 6 "Therefore, keep the *c* of the LORD,
8:11 by neglecting his *c* and decrees and
10: 2 I will write upon the tablets the *c* that
10: 4 the ten *c* which he spoke to you on the
10:13 to keep the *c* and statutes of the LORD
11: 1 his statutes, decrees and *c*.
11: 8 Keep all the *c*,
11:13 heed my *c* which I enjoin on you today,
11:22 to observe all these *c* I enjoin on you,
11:27 a blessing for obeying the *c* of the LORD,
11:28 curse if you do not obey the *c* of the LORD,
12:28 to heed all these *c* I enjoin on you,
13:19 all his *c* which I enjoin on you today,
15: 5 all these *c* which I enjoin on you today,
17:20 to the right or to the left from these *c*.
19: 9 all these *c* which I enjoin on you today,
26:13 have not broken or forgotten any of your *c*:
26:17 and observe his statutes, *c* and decrees,
26:18 and provided you keep all his *c*,
27: 1 all these *c* which I enjoin on you today.
27:10 *c* and statutes which I enjoin on you today."
28: 1 all his *c* which I enjoin on you today,
28: 9 Provided that you keep the *c* of the LORD,
28:13 as long as you obey the *c* of the LORD,
28:14 from any of the *c* which I now give you,
28:15 all his *c* which I enjoin on you today,
28:45 nor keep the *c* and statutes he gave you.
30: 8 out all his *c* which I now enjoin on you.
30:10 and keep his *c* and statutes that are
30:16 If you obey the *c* of the LORD,
30:16 walking in his ways, and keeping his *c*,
Jos 4:16 ark of the *c* to come up from the Jordan."
22: 5 keep his *c*;
Jgs 2:17 example of obedience to the *c* of the LORD.
3: 4 determine whether they would obey the *c*
1Kgs 3:14 follow me by keeping my statutes and *c*,
8:61 observing his statutes and keeping his *c*,
9: 6 the *c* and statutes which I set before you,
11:34 whom I chose, who kept my *c* and statutes.

COMMANDMENTS (cont.)

11:38 my statutes and my *c* like my servant David,
14: 8 my *c* and followed me with his whole heart,
2Kgs 17:13 your evil ways and keep my *c* and statutes,
17:16 They disregarded all the *c* of the LORD,
17:19 however, did not keep the *c* of the LORD,
17:34 statutes and regulations, the law and *c*,
18: 6 the *c* which the LORD had given Moses.
18:12 heeding and not fulfilling the *c* of Moses,
1Chr 28: 7 my *c* and decrees as he keeps them now.'
28: 8 and to carry out all the *c* of the LORD,
29:19 a wholehearted desire to keep your *c*,
2Chr 31:21 the house of God or for the law and the *c*,
34:31 LORD to follow the LORD and to keep his *c*,
Ezr 7:11 of the LORD's *c* and statutes for Israel:
9:10 For we have abandoned your *c*,
9:14 shall we again violate your *c* by
10: 3 and those who fear the *c* of our God.
Neh 1: 5 toward those who love you and keep your *c*,
1: 7 have we offended you, not keeping the *c*,
1: 9 you return to me and carefully keep my *c*,
9:13 firm laws, good statutes, and *c*;
9:14 holy sabbath you made known to them, *c*,
9:16 necks stiff and would not obey your *c*.
9:29 were insolent and would not obey your *c*;
9:34 they paid no attention to your *c* and the
10:30 to observe carefully all the *c* of the LORD,
10:33 We impose these *c* on ourselves:
Tb 3: 4 sinned against you, and disobeyed your *c*.
3: 5 For we have not kept your *c*,
4: 5 every desire to sin or to break his *c*.
4:19 So now, my son, keep in mind my *c*,
1Mc 2:21 that we should forsake the law and the *c*.
10:14 those who had abandoned the law and the *c*,
2Mc 1: 4 to his law and his *c* and grant you peace.
2: 2 admonished them not to forget the *c* of the
Eccl 12:13 Fear God and keep his *c*,
Sir 1:23 If you desire wisdom, keep the *c*,
6:37 let his *c* be your constant meditation;
10:19 Those who transgress the *c*.
15:15 If you choose you can keep the *c*;
17:10 with them, his *c* he has revealed to them.
23:27 nothing more salutary than to obey his *c*.
28: 7 Think of the *c*,
32:23 guard, for in this way you will keep the *c*.
35: 1 observes the *c* sacrifices a peace offering.
37:12 man, who you are sure keeps the *c*;
45: 3 He gave him the *c* for his people,
45: 5 Where, face to face, he gave him the *c*,
Is 48:18 If you would hearken to my *c*,
Bar 3: 9 Hear, O Israel, the *c* of life:
4:13 In the ways of God's *c* they did not walk,
Dn 3:30 Your *c* we have not heeded or observed,
9: 4 those who love you and observe your *c*!
9: 5 and departed from your *c* and your laws.
Mt 15: 3 *c* of God for the sake of your 'tradition'?
19:17 If you wish to enter into life, keep the *c*."
22:40 On these two *c* the whole law is based,
Mk 10:19 You know the *c*:
12:28 ask him, "Which is the first of all the *c*?"
Lk 1: 6 all the *c* and ordinances of the Lord.
18:20 You know the *c*:
Jn 14:21 *c* he has from me is the man who loves me;
15:10 *c* even as I have kept my Father's *c*,
Rom 13: 9 The *c*, "You shall not commit adultery;
1Cor 7:19 What matters is keeping God's *c*.
Heb 9:19 read all the *c* of the law to the people,
1Jn 2: 3 of our knowledge of him is to keep his *c*.
2: 4 have known him," without keeping his *c*,
3:22 *c* and doing what is pleasing in his sight.
3:24 keep his *c* remain in him and he in them.
5: 3 his commandments—and his *c* are not
2Jn 1: 6 involves our walking according to the *c*,
Rv 12:17 who keep God's *c* and give witness to Jesus.
14:12 keep the *c* of God and their faith in Jesus.

COMMANDS (69)

Gn 6:22 he carried out all the *c* that God gave him.
Ex 8:23 sacrifice to the LORD, our God, as he *c* us."
25:22 *c* that I wish you to give the Israelites.
Nm 36: 6 This is what the LORD *c* with regard to the
Dt 1: 3 Moses spoke to the Israelites all the *c*
1:18 I gave you all the *c* you were to fulfill.
1:21 the LORD, the God of your fathers, *c* you.
26:16 *c* you to observe these statutes and
Jos 22: 3 faithfully carried out the *c* of the LORD,
Jgs 4: 6 is what the LORD, the God of Israel, *c*,"
1Kgs 2: 3 his ways and observing his statutes, *c*,
6:12 out my ordinances, keep and obey all my *c*,
8:58 follow him in everything and keep the *c*,
15: 5 disobey any of his *c* as long as he lived,
18:18 the *c* of the LORD and following the Baals.
2Kgs 1: 9 he ordered, "the king *c* you to come down."
1:11 "the king *c* you to come down immediately."
2Chr 7:19 statutes and *c* which I placed before you,
14: 3 fathers, and to observe the law and its *c*.
17: 4 the God of his father and observed his *c*,
24:20 'why are you transgressing the LORD's *c*,
Tb 1: 8 of the Mosaic law and the *c* of Deborah,
Jb 6:10 not transgressed the *c* of the Holy One.
9: 7 He *c* the sun,
23:12 From the *c* of his lips I have not departed;
36:32 lightning, and he *c* it to strike the mark.
37:13 whether for punishment or mercy, as he *c*.
37:15 Do you know how God lays his *c* upon them,
Ps(s) 78: 7 forget the deeds of God but keep his *c*,
89:32 violate my statutes and keep not my *c*,
112: 1 the LORD, who greatly delights in his *c*.
119: 6 be put to shame when I beheld all your *c*.
119:10 let me not stray from your *c*.
119:19 hide not your *c* from me.
119:21 accursed proud, who turn away from your *c*.
119:32 of your *c* when you give me a docile heart.
119:35 Lead me in the path of your *c*,
119:47 And I will delight in your *c*,
119:48 to your *c* and meditate on your statutes.
119:60 and did not hesitate in keeping your *c*.
119:66 and knowledge, for in your *c* I trust.
119:73 me discernment that I may learn your *c*.
119:86 All your *c* are steadfast;
119:115 and I will observe the *c* of my God.
119:131 with open mouth in my yearning for your *c*.
119:143 have come upon me, your *c* are my delight.
119:151 are near, and all your *c* are permanent.
119:166 salvation, O LORD, and your *c* I fulfill.
119:172 of your promise, for all your *c* are just.
119:176 servant, because your *c* I do not forget.
Prv 2: 1 if you receive my words and treasure my *c*,
3: 1 forget not my teaching, keep in mind my *c*;
4: 4 keep my *c*, that you may live!
7: 1 My son, keep my words, and treasure my *c*.
7: 2 Keep my *c* and live,
10: 8 A wise man heeds *c*,
11:27 He who seeks the good *c* favor,
Wis 9: 9 eyes and what is conformable with your *c*.
Sir 29:11 of your treasure as the Most High *c*,
Jer 22: 4 If you carry out these *c*,
22: 5 But if you do not obey these *c*,
35:18 his *c* and done everything he commanded you,
Lam 3:37 Who *c* so that it comes to pass,
Mt 5:19 breaks the least significant of these *c*
5:19 *c* shall be great in the kingdom of God.
Lk 4:36 He *c* the unclean spirits with authority
8:25 man can this be who *c* even the winds
Jn 14:15 If you love me and obey the *c* I give you,
Eph 2:15 abolished the law with its *c* and precepts,

COMMEMORATE (1)

Sir 45:11 To *c* in incised letters each of the tribes

COMMEMORATED (1)

Est 9:28 were to be *c* and kept in every generation,

COMMEND (7)

Ps(s) 31: 6 Into your hands I *c* my spirit;
Eccl 8:15 Therefore I *c* mirth,
Wis 7:14 the gifts they have from discipline *c* them.
Acts 20:32 I *c* you now to the Lord,
Rom 16: 1 I *c* to you our sister Phoebe,
2Cor 4: 2 We proclaim the truth openly and *c*
Phlm 1: 4 my brother, as I *c* you in my prayers,

COMMENDED (5)

2Mc 9:25 before entrusted and *c* to most of you,
Jb 29:11 those who saw me *c* me.
Acts 14:23 *c* them to the Lord in whom they had put
14:26 where they had first been *c* to the favor
15:40 *c* by the brothers to the favor of the Lord.

COMMENDING (1)

2Cor 12:11 You are the ones who should have been *c* me.

COMMENT (1)

Mt 24: 2 His *c* was: Do you see

COMMENTED (2)

Jn 10:41 may never have performed a sign," they *c*,
Acts 17:18 Others *c*, "He sounds like a promoter

COMMERCE (1)

1Mc 12:36 prevent its garrison from *c* with the city.

COMMISSARIES (4)

1Kgs 4: 5 Azariah, son of Nathan, chief of the *c*;
4: 7 Solomon had twelve *c* for all Israel who
5: 7 These *c*, one for each month, provided food
Est 2: 3 Let the king appoint *c* in all the

COMMISSION (12)

Nm 27:19 community, and *c* him before their eyes.
27:23 laid his hands on him and gave him his *c*,
Dt 3:28 *C* Joshua, and encourage and strengthen
31:14 the meeting tent that I may give him his *c*."
Jos 18: 4 will *c* them to begin a survey of the land,
1Sm 21: 3 "The king gave me a *c* and told me to let
21: 3 on which he sent me or the *c* he gave me.
1Mc 2:55 Joshua, for executing his *c*,
2Mc 4:25 He returned with the royal *c*,
Acts 26:12 the authority and *c* of the chief priests.
Col 1:25 minister of this church through the *c* God
Rv 11: 3 I will *c* my two witnesses to prophesy for

COMMISSIONED (11)

Dt 31:23 Then the LORD *c* Joshua,
1Kgs 14: 6 I have been *c* to give you bitter news.
Tb 12:14 *c* me to heal you and your daughter-in-law,
14: 4 was said by Israel's prophets, whom God *c*,
Jdt 3: 8 *c* to destroy all the gods of the earth,
1Mc 3:33 and *c* him to take care of his son
2Mc 1:20 God, Nehemiah, *c* by the king of Persia,
Jer 42:21 that he has *c* me to make known to you.
Acts 10:42 He *c* us to preach to the people and to
15:33 from the brothers to those who had *c* them.
Rv 16: 8 He was *c* to burn men with fire.

COMMISSIONS (1)

1Pt 2:14 to the governors he *c* for the punishment

COMMIT (56)

Gn 39: 9 could I *c* so great a wrong and thus stand
Ex 20:14 "You shall not *c* adultery.
Lv 4:22 "Should a prince *c* a sin inadvertently by
Dt 5:18 'You shall not *c* adultery.
Jgs 19:23 this man is my guest, do not *c* this crime.
19:24 the man you must not *c* this wanton crime."
2Sm 13:12 Do not *c* this insensate deed.
1Kgs 14:16 has committed and caused Israel to *c*."
15:26 the sin which he had caused Israel to *c*.
15:30 Jeroboam committed and caused Israel to *c*,
15:34 and the sin he had caused Israel to *c*.
16:13 son Elah committed and caused Israel to *c*,
2Kgs 10:29 son of Nebat, had caused Israel to *c*,
10:31 the sins which Jeroboam caused Israel to *c*.
13: 2 the sin he had caused Israel to *c*.
13: 6 house of Jeroboam had caused Israel to *c*,
13:11 son of Nebat, had caused Israel to *c*,
14:24 son of Nebat, had caused Israel to *c*.
15: 9 son of Nebat, had caused Israel to *c*.
15:18 son of Nebat, had caused Israel to *c*.
15:24 son of Nebat, had caused Israel to *c*.
15:28 son of Nebat, had caused Israel to *c*.
17:21 the LORD, causing them to *c* a great sin.
21:16 to the sin which he caused Judah to *c*,
Neh 6:13 act on it of fear and *c* this sin
Tb 14:10 *c* all sorts of wickedness and treachery.
2Mc 2:25 studious who wish to *c* things to memory,
Ps(s) 37: 5 *C* to the LORD your way;
58: 3 Nay, you willingly *c* crimes;
Eccl 8:11 men are filled with the desire to *c* evil
Sir 23:14 *c* a blunder and disgrace your upbringing,
Jer 7: 9 steal and murder, *c* adultery and perjury,
7:10 we can *c* all these abominations again"?
44: 4 not to *c* this horrible deed which I hate,
Ez 16:51 Samaria did not *c* half your sins!
18:16 anyone, or exact a pledge, or *c* robbery;
18:26 man turns away from virtue to *c* iniquity,
22:29 the land practice extortion and *c* robbery;
23:43 Now they will *c* whoredom with her,
Hos 4:12 they *c* harlotry,
Mt 5:21 your forefathers, 'You shall not *c* murder;
5:27 the commandment, 'You shall not *c* adultery.'
5:32 forces her to *c* adultery.
18:15 brother should *c* some wrong against you,
19:18 'You shall not *c* adultery';
Mk 10:19 You shall not *c* adultery;
Lk 18:20 "You shall not *c* adultery.
Rom 2:22 You who forbid adultery, do you *c* adultery?
7: 3 *c* adultery by consorting with another man.
13: 9 commandments, "You shall not *c* adultery;
1Cor 7:28 Neither does a virgin *c* sin if she marries.
1Tm 5:20 The ones who do *c* sin,
Jas 2: 9 you *c* sin and are convicted by the law as
2:11 he who said, "You shall not *c* adultery,"
2:11 you do not *c* adultery but do commit murder,

COMMITING (1)

1Cor 7:28 you marry, however, you will not be *c* sin.

COMMITMENT (2)

2Kgs 11: 4 of the LORD, exacted from them a sworn *c*,
Acts 11:23 all to remain firm in their *c* to the Lord,

COMMITS (26)

Lv 4: 2 When a person inadvertently *c* a sin
4:27 "If a private person *c* a sin inadvertently
5: 1 and thus *c* a sin and has guilt to bear;
5:15 "If someone *c* a sin by inadvertently
5:17 *c* such a sin by doing one of the things
5:21 "If someone *c* a sin of dishonesty against
20:10 a man *c* adultery with his neighbor's wife,
Nm 5: 6 If a man (or a woman) *c* a fault against
Est B: 5 to our interests, and *c* the worst crimes,
Prv 6:32 But he who *c* adultery is a fool;
Sir 28: 9 *C* the sin of disrupting friendship and
34:26 his sins, but then goes and *c* them again:
Ez 18: 7 pledge received for a debt, *c* no robbery;
18:12 oppresses the poor and needy, *c* robbery,
18:14 son who, seeing all the sins his father *c*,
Mt 5:32 a divorced woman likewise *c* adultery.
19: 9 case) and marries another *c* adultery,

19: 9 who marries a divorced woman *c* adultery."
Mk 2: 7 He *c* blasphemy!
10:11 and marries another *c* adultery against her;
10:12 her husband and marries another *c* adultery."
Lk 16:18 his wife and marries another *c* adultery.
16:18 from her husband likewise *c* adultery.
1Cor 6:18 other sin a man *c* is outside his body,
7:36 He *c* no sin if there is a marriage.
1Jn 5:18 We know that no one begotten of God *c* sin;

COMMITTED (93)

Gn 13:13 wicked in the sins they *c* against the LORD.
31:36 "What crime or offense have I *c*,"
50:17 we, the servants of your father's God, *c*."
Ex 32:30 to the people, "You have *c* a grave sin.
32:31 this people has indeed *c* a grave sin in
Lv 4: 3 bull as a sin offering for the sin he *c*.
4:14 later on become known that the sin was *c*,
4:23 if later on he learns of the sin he *c*,
4:28 should he later on learn of the sin he *c*,
5: 6 as his sin offering for the sin he has *c*,
5:10 shall make atonement for the sin the man *c*,
5:13 that the man *c* in any of the above cases,
5:18 for the fault which was unwittingly *c*,
19:22 before the LORD for the sin he has *c*,
20:12 since they have *c* an abhorrent deed,
Nm 6:11 sin he has *c* by reason of the dead person.
12:11 us with the sin that we have foolishly *c*!
Dt 9:18 because of all the sin you had *c*
13:15 this abomination has been *c* in your midst,
17: 4 that this abomination has been *c* in Israel,
22:21 because she *c* a crime against Israel by
Jos 7:15 LORD and has *c* a shameful crime in Israel."
22:16 this you have *c* against the God of Israel?
22:31 *c* this act of treachery against the LORD,
Jgs 20: 6 the monstrous crime they had *c* in Israel.
20:10 of Benjamin for the crime it *c* in Israel."
1Sm 12:20 "It is true you have *c* all this evil;
14:38 and find out how this sin was *c* today.
14:39 Israel, even if my son Jonathan has *c* it,
19: 4 David, for he has *c* no offense against you,
1Kgs 8:50 all the offenses they have *c* against you,
14:16 Jeroboam has *c* and caused Israel to commit."
15: 3 all the sins his father had *c* before him,
15:30 Jeroboam *c* and caused Israel to commit,
16:13 his son Elah *c* and caused Israel to commit,
16:19 He died because of the sins he had *c*,
18: 9 But Obadiah said, "What sin have I *c*,
2Kgs 17:22 imitated Jeroboam in all the sins he *c*,
21:17 Manasseh, the sin he *c* and all that he did,
24: 3 the sins Manasseh had *c* in all that he did;
1Chr 28:19 He had successfully *c* to writing the exact
2Chr 34:32 *c* all who were of Jerusalem and Benjamin,
Neh 1: 6 sins which we of Israel have *c* against you,
1: 7 which you *c* to your servant Moses.
Jdt 11:17 me when the Israelites have *c* their crimes.
1Mc 1:52 law, joined them and *c* evil in the land.
2: 6 were being *c* in Judah and in Jerusalem,
2Mc 4: 3 were being *c* by one of his henchmen,
4:38 where he had *c* the outrage against Onias;
4:39 Many sacrilegious thefts had been *c* by
11:31 in any way for faults *c* through ignorance.
12: 3 Some people of Joppa also *c* this outrage:
13: 8 It was altogether just that he who had *c*
Ps(s) 22:11 To you I was *c* at birth,
106: 6 we have *c* crimes;
Sir 3:21 What is *c* to you, attend to;
Jer 3: 8 the adulteries rebellious Israel had *c*,
5: 7 I fed them, but they *c* adultery;
7:13 now, because you have *c* all these misdeeds,
16:10 What sin have we *c* against the LORD,
41:11 crimes Ishmael, son of Nethaniah, had *c*,
Bar 6: 1 For the sins you *c* before God,
Ez 16:50 and *c* abominable crimes in my presence;
18:21 man turns away from all the sins he *c*,
18:22 he *c* shall be remembered against him;
18:24 because he has broken faith and *c* sin;
18:26 of the iniquity he *c* that he must die.
18:27 man, turning from the wickedness he has *c*,
18:28 turned away from all the sins which he *c*,
18:31 away from you all the crimes you have *c*,
23:37 For they *c* adultery,
23:37 They *c* adultery with their idols;
23:45 and murderesses, for they have *c* adultery,
33:16 of the sins he *c* shall be held against him;
Mt 5:28 *c* adultery with her in his thoughts.
27:23 He said, "Why, what crime has he *c*?"
Mk 15: 7 rebels who had *c* murder in the uprising.
15:14 What crime has he *c*?"
Lk 11:48 they *c* the murders and you erect the tombs.
Jn 18:37 Anyone *c* to the truth hears my voice."
Acts 25: 8 "I have *c* no crime either against the law
25:11 if I have *c* a crime deserving death,
Rom 3:25 the sake of remitting sins *c* in the past
5:16 different from the sin *c* by the one man.
1Tm 6:20 O Timothy, guard what has been *c* to you.
Ti 3: 8 so that those who have *c* themselves to God
Heb 9:15 transgressions *c* under the first covenant,
Jas 5:15 If he has *c* any sins,
1Pt 3:13 if you are *c* deeply to doing what is right?
1Jn 3:19 This is our way of knowing we are *c* to
Rv 17: 2 of the earth have *c* fornication with her,
18: 3 kings of the earth *c* fornication with her,
18: 9 The kings of the earth who *c* fornication

COMMITTING (8)

Lv 21: 9 who loses her honor by *c* fornication
Prv 24:28 just cause, thus *c* folly with your lips.
Wis 12: 2 and remind them of the sins they are *c*,
Jer 2:34 the innocent, whom you found *c* no burglary;
3: 9 the land, *c* adultery with stone and wood.
26:19 of *c* this great evil to our own undoing."
29:23 *c* adultery with their neighbors' wives,
Hos 6: 9 on the way to Shechem, *c* monstrous crime.

COMMON (45)

Nm 16:29 merely suffering the fate *c* to all mankind,
31:53 what the *c* soldiers had looted each one
Jos 9: 2 a *c* attack against Joshua and Israel.
17:10 with the sea as their *c* boundary,
1Kgs 10:27 made silver as *c* in Jerusalem as stones,
13:33 the high places from among the *c* people.
2Kgs 23: 6 was then scattered over the *c* graveyard.
25:19 the *c* people still remaining in the city.
2Chr 1:15 and gold as *c* in Jerusalem as stones,
9:27 made silver as *c* in Jerusalem as stones,
35: 5 houses of your brethren, the *c* people,
35: 7 to the *c* people a flock of lambs and kids,
35:12 of the *c* people to offer to the LORD,
35:13 brought them quickly to all the *c* people.
Ezr 2:70 *c* people took up residence in Jerusalem;
Neh 5: 1 Then there rose a great outcry of the *c*
7: 5 the nobles, the magistrates, and the *c* people,
2Mc 8:29 was done, they made supplication in *c*,
9: 4 "I will make Jerusalem the *c* graveyard of
9:14 to the ground and making it a *c* graveyard;
11:15 Maccabeus, solicitous for the *c* good,
14:25 settled down, and shared the *c* life.
Prv 22: 2 Rich and poor have a *c* bond:
29:13 The poor and the oppressor have a *c* bond:
Wis 7: 3 And I too, when born, inhaled the *c* air,
7: 3 I uttered that first sound *c* to all.
Jer 26:23 sword and his corpse cast into the *c* grave.
34:19 courtiers, the priests, and the *c* people,
52:25 sixty of the *c* people who were in the city.
Ez 7:27 the hands of the *c* people shall tremble.
Jn 13:29 idea that, since Judas held the *c* purse,
19:29 There was a jar there, full of *c* wine.
Acts 2:44 Those who believed shared all things in *c*;
2:46 sincere hearts they took their meals in *c*,
4:32 rather, everything was held in *c*.
12:20 by *c* consent came before him in his court.
18: 3 pair, whose trade he had in *c* with them.
Rom 1:12 may be mutually encouraged by our *c* faith.
1Cor 12: 7 of the Spirit is given for the *c* good.
2Cor 6:14 righteousness and lawlessness have in *c*,
6:15 what *c* lot between believer and unbeliever?
1Thes 3: 3 well enough that such trials are our *c* lot.
2Tm 2:20 for distinguished and others for *c* use.
Ti 1: 4 to Titus, my own true child in our *c* faith:
1Jn 2:21 no lie has anything in *c* with the truth.

COMMONER (1)

2Sm 6:20 girls of his followers, as a *c* might do!"

COMMOTION (3)

1Sm 4:14 him, Eli inquired, "What does this *c* mean?"
2Mc 3:30 charged so shortly before with fear and *c*,
Acts 17:13 there to cause a *c* and stir up the crowds.

COMMUNAL (1)

Acts 2:42 the apostles' instruction and the *c* life,

COMMUNICATED (2)

Ezr 5:17 king's pleasure in this matter be *c* to us."
2Mc 14:20 terms, each leader *c* them to his troops;

COMMUNICATION (4)

1Kgs 15:17 and fortified Ramah to prevent *c* with Asa,
2Chr 16: 1 fortified Ramah to prevent any *c* with Asa,
Ezr 4:18 The *c* which you sent us has been read
2Mc 11:17 have presented your signed *c* and asked

COMMUNION (1)

Lk 6:12 to pray, spending the night in *c* with God.

COMMUNITIES (16)

Gn 12: 3 *c* of the earth shall find blessing in you,"
Dt 12:15 in any of your *c* you may slaughter and eat
12:17 Moreover, you shall not, in your own *c*,
15:22 your God, but in your own *c* you may eat it,
16: 5 Passover in any of the *c* which the LORD,
16:18 for the people in all the *c* which the LORD,
17: 2 you, in any one of the *c* which the LORD,
18: 6 "When a Levite goes from one of your *c*
23:17 in any one of your *c* that pleases him.
24:14 or one of the aliens who live in your *c*.
28:52 They will besiege you in each of your *c*,
28:55 your enemy will subject you in all your *c*.
28:57 your enemy will subject you in your *c*.
31:12 as well as the aliens who live in your *c*—
Gal 1:22 The *c* of Christ in Judea had no idea what
2Thes 1: 4 so much so that in God's *c* we can boast of

COMMUNITY (163)

Gn 34:24 including every able-bodied man in the *c*,
Ex 12: 3 Tell the whole *c* of Israel:
12:19 food shall be cut off from the *c* of Israel.
12:47 The whole *c* of Israel must keep this feast.
16: 1 Israelite *c* came into the desert of Sin,
16: 2 *c* grumbled against Moses and Aaron.
16: 3 desert to make the whole *c* die of famine!"
16: 9 to Aaron, "Tell the whole Israelite *c*:
16:10 announced this to the whole Israelite *c*,
16:22 of the *c* came and reported this to Moses,
17: 1 the whole Israelite *c* journeyed by stages,
34:31 all the rulers of the *c* come back to him.
35: 1 the whole Israelite *c* and said to them,
35: 4 Moses told the whole Israelite *c*,
35:20 the whole Israelite *c* left Moses' presence,
38:25 silver received from the *c* was one hundred
Lv 4:13 If the whole *c* of Israel inadvertently
4:14 the *c* shall present a young bull as a sin
4:15 the elders of the *c* shall lay their hands
4:21 This is the sin offering for the *c*.
8: 3 *c* at the entrance of the meeting tent."
8: 4 When the *c* had assembled at the entrance
9: 5 When the whole *c* had come forward and
10: 6 but God's wrath also on the whole *c*.
10:17 that you might bear the guilt of the *c*
16: 5 From the Israelite *c* he shall receive two
16:17 as well as for the whole Israelite *c*,
16:33 the priests and all the people of the *c*.
19: 2 to the whole Israelite *c* and tell them:
24:14 on his head, let the whole *c* stone him.
24:16 The whole *c* shall stone him;
Nm 1: 2 a census of the whole *c* of the Israelites,
1:16 These were councilors of the *c*,
1:18 *c* on the first day of the second month.
1:53 God's wrath will strike the Israelite *c*.
3: 7 his obligations and those of the whole *c*
4:34 *c* made a registration among the Kohathites,
8: 9 also the whole *c* of the Israelites.
8:20 *c* of the Israelites deal with the Levites,
10: 2 in assembling the *c* and in breaking camp.
10: 3 the whole *c* shall gather round you at the
13:26 whole *c* of the Israelites in the desert
14: 1 the whole *c* broke out with loud cries,
14: 2 and Aaron, the whole *c* saying to them,
14: 5 the whole assembled *c* of the Israelites;
14: 7 and said to the whole *c* of the Israelites,
14:10 the whole *c* threatened to stone them.
14:27 long will this wicked *c* grumble against me?
14:35 this wicked *c* that conspired against me:
14:36 on returning had set the whole *c* grumbling
15:24 if the *c* itself unwittingly becomes guilty
15:24 the whole *c* shall offer the holocaust of
15:25 make atonement for the whole Israelite *c*;
15:26 Not only the whole Israelite *c*,
15:35 let the whole *c* stone him outside the camp."
15:36 So the whole *c* led him outside the camp
16: 2 Israelites who were leaders in the *c*,
16: 3 The whole *c*, all of them, are holy
16: 9 has singled you out from the *c* of Israel,
16: 9 to stand before the *c* to minister for them?
16:19 of the LORD appeared to the entire *c*,
16:22 man's sin make you angry with the whole *c*?"
16:24 Moses, "Speak to the *c* and tell them:
16:26 Then he warned the *c*,
16:33 over them, and they perished from the *c*.
17: 6 *c* grumbled against Moses and Aaron,
17: 7 while the *c* was deliberating against them,
17:10 to Moses and Aaron, "Depart from this *c*,
17:11 to the *c* to make atonement for them;
17:12 took his censer and ran in among the *c*,
19: 9 lustral water for the Israelite *c*.
19:20 purified shall be cut off from the *c*,
20: 1 The whole Israelite *c* arrived in the
20: 2 As the *c* had no water,
20: 4 Why have you brought the LORD's *c* into
20: 8 "Take the staff and assemble the *c*,
20: 8 for the *c* and their livestock to drink."
20:10 Aaron assembled the *c* in front of the rock,
20:11 for the *c* and their livestock to drink.
20:12 lead this *c* into the land I will give them."
20:22 the whole Israelite *c* came to Mount Hor.
20:27 climbed Mount Hor in view of the whole *c*,
20:29 *c* understood that Aaron had passed away;
25: 6 of Moses and of the whole Israelite *c*,
26: 2 throughout the *c* of the Israelites of all
26: 9 Dathan and Abiram, councilors of the *c*,
27: 2 *c* at the entrance of the meeting tent,
27:14 because in the rebellion of the *c* in the
27:16 set over the *c* a man who shall act as
27:17 that the LORD'S *c* may not be like sheep
27:19 of the priest Eleazar and of the whole *c*,
27:20 that the whole Israelite *c* may obey him.
27:21 and the *c* as a whole shall perform all
27:22 of the priest Eleazar and of the whole *c*,
31:12 *c* at their camp on the plains of Moab,
31:13 Eleazar, with all the princes of the *c*,
31:16 which began the slaughter of the LORD's *c*.
31:27 to combat, and half to the rest of the *c*.

COMMUNITY (cont.)

31:42 which fell to the *c* when Moses had taken
32: 2 and to the princes of the *c* and said,
32: 4 LORD has laid low before the *c* of Israel,
35:12 unless he is first tried before the *c*.
35:24 *c*, deciding the case between the slayer
Dt 12:12 as with the Levite who belongs to your *c*
12:18 and the Levite who belongs to your *c*;
12:21 it to your heart's desire in your own *c*.
14:21 give it to an alien who belongs to your *c*,
14:27 neglect the Levite who belongs to your *c*,
14:28 for that year and deposit them in *c* stores,
14:29 orphan and the widow who belong to your *c*,
15: 7 *c* is in need in the land which the LORD,
16:11 and the Levite who belongs to your *c*,
16:14 orphan and the widow who belong to your *c*.
17: 8 "If in your own *c* there is a case at
23: 2 off may be admitted into the *c* of the LORD.
23: 3 may be admitted into the *c* of the LORD,
23: 4 ever be admitted into the *c* of the LORD,
23: 9 be admitted into the *c* of the LORD.
26:12 they may eat their fill in your own *c*,
28:52 They will so besiege you in every *c*
33: 4 he made the *c* of Jacob his domain,
Jos 8:35 Joshua read aloud to the entire *c*,
9:15 the princes of the *c* sealed with an oath.
9:18 of the *c* had sworn to them by the LORD,
9:18 the entire *c* grumbled against the princes,
9:21 and drawers of water for the entire *c*;
9:21 and the *c* did as the princes advised them.
9:27 for the *c* and for the altar of the LORD,
18: 1 *c* of the Israelites assembled at Shiloh,
20: 6 Once he has stood judgment before the *c*,
20: 9 blood, until he could appear before the *c*.
22:12 whole *c* at Shiloh to declare war on them.
22:16 whole *c* of the LORD sends this message:
22:17 Peor, a plague came upon the *c* of the LORD.
22:18 will be angry with the whole *c* of Israel!
22:20 not wrath fall upon the entire *c* of Israel?
22:30 the priest and the princes of the *c*,
Jgs 20: 1 the *c* was gathered to the LORD at Mizpah.
21:10 *c*, therefore, sent twelve thousand warriors
21:13 Then the whole *c* sent a message to the
21:16 And the elders of the *c* said,
1Kgs 8: 5 King Solomon and the entire *c* of Israel
8:14 the whole *c* of Israel as they stood.
8:22 in the presence of the whole *c* of Israel,
8:55 He stood and blessed the whole *c* of Israel,
2Chr 5: 6 King Solomon and the entire *c* of Israel
6: 3 the whole *c* of Israel as they stood.
6:12 *c* of Israel and stretched forth his hands.
2Mc 15:12 outstretched arms for the whole Jewish *c*.
Sir 24:22 us as an inheritance for the *c* of Jacob.
Ez 13: 9 shall not belong to the *c* of my people,
Acts 4:32 The *c* of believers were of one heart and
6: 2 assembled the *c* of the disciples and said,
6: 5 proposal was unanimously accepted by the *c*.
9:22 and reduced the Jewish *c*
10:22 well thought of in the whole Jewish *c*,
11:19 Those in the *c* who had been dispersed by
15:22 Those chosen were leading men of the *c*,
15:32 strengthened the *c* and gave them
25:24 The whole Jewish *c*,
28:17 prominent men of the Jewish *c* to visit him.
1Cor 5:12 it not those inside the *c* you must judge?
Eph 2:12 and were excluded from the *c* of Israel.

COMPACT (3)

1Mc 12:50 and went out in *c* body ready to fight.
Ps(s) 122: 3 Jerusalem, built as a city with *c* unity.
Dn 9:27 week he shall make a firm *c* with the many;

COMPANIES (27)

Gn 32:11 but my staff, I have now grown into two *c*.
Nm 1: 3 You and Aaron shall enroll in *c* all the
1:52 the other Israelites shall camp by *c*,
2: 3 divisional camp of Judah, arranged in *c*.
2: 9 The total number of those registered by *c*
2:10 divisional camp of Reuben, arranged in *c*.
2:16 The total number of those registered by *c*
2:18 divisional camp of Ephraim, arranged in *c*.
2:24 The total number of those registered by *c*
2:25 the divisional camp of Dan, arranged in *c*.
2:31 The total number of those registered by *c*
2:32 The total number of those registered by *c*
10:14 under its own standard and arranged in *c*,
10:18 under its own standard and arranged in *c*,
10:22 arranged in *c*, with Elishama,
10:25 arranged in *c*, with Ahiezer,
33: 1 Israelites journeyed up by *c* from the land
Jgs 7:16 the three hundred men into three *c*,
7:20 three *c* blew horns and broke their jars.
9:34 and set up an ambush for Shechem in four *c*.
9:43 who divided the men he had into three *c*,
9:44 while the other two *c* rushed upon all who
1Sm 11:11 Saul arranged his troops in three *c* and
2Kgs 1:14 two captains with their *c* of fifty men.
2Mc 5: 2 *c* fully armed with lances and drawn swords;
Jb 6:19 of Tema search, the *c* of Sheba have hopes;
Sg 7: 1 Shulammite as at the dance of the two *c*?

COMPANION (25)

1Sm 20:30 shame, you are the *c* of Jesse's son?
1Kgs 4: 5 son of Nathan, *c* to the king
20:35 was prompted by the LORD to say to his *c*,
Jb 30:29 the brother of jackals, *c* to the ostrich.
Ps(s) 55:14 my other self, my *c* and my bosom friend!
88:19 *C* and neighbor you have taken away from me;
119:63 I am the *c* of all who fear you and keep
Prv 2:17 Who forsakes the *c* of her youth and
13:20 wise, but the *c* of fools will fare badly.
22:24 hotheaded man, nor the *c* of a wrathful man,
28: 7 but the gluttons' *c* disgraces his father.
Eccl 4: 8 a solitary man with no *c*;
4:10 one falls, the other will lift up his *c*.
Sir 6:10 Another is a friend, a boon *c*,
7:12 brother, nor against your friend and *c*.
12:14 So is it with the *c* of the proud man,
19: 2 and the *c* of harlots becomes reckless.
22:12 the stupid man, be not the *c* of a brute;
37: 2 death when your bosom *c* becomes your enemy?
37: 3 "Alas, my *c*!
41:17 Before friend and *c*,
Mi 7: 5 in a friend, have no confidence in a *c*;
Mal 2:14 you have broken faith though she is your *c*,
2Cor 8:19 appointed our traveling *c* by the churches,
8:23 is my *c* and fellow worker in your behalf;

COMPANIONS (46)

Jgs 11:37 mountains to mourn my virginity with my *c*."
11:38 So she departed with her *c* and mourned her
14:11 him, they brought thirty men to be his *c*.
1Sm 28: 8 on other clothes, and set out with two *c*.
1Kgs 1: 8 Nathan the prophet, and Shimei and his *c*,
2Kgs 9: 2 him away from his *c* into an inner chamber.
1Mc 9:44 Then Jonathan said to his *c*,
9:58 and his *c* are living in peace and security.
9:60 telling them to seize Jonathan and his *c*.
9:62 their *c* withdrew to Bethbasi in the desert;
12:50 had been captured and his *c* killed,
13:52 the citadel, and he and his *c* dwelt there.
15:15 Numenius and his *c* left Rome with letters
2Mc 1:16 the leader and his *c* and struck them down.
1:36 and his *c* called the liquid nephthar,
3:31 Soon some of the *c* of Heliodorus begged
5:27 his *c* lived like wild animals in the hills,
8: 1 and his *c* entered the village secretly,
8:12 his *c* about the approach of the army,
10: 1 and his *c* under the Lord's leadership,
10:16 Maccabeus and his *c*,
12:11 After a hard fight, Judas and his *c*,
15: 1 and his *c* were in the territory of Samaria,
Jb 19:14 My kinsfolk and *c* neglect me,
35: 4 a reply to you and your three *c* as well.
Ps(s) 38:12 my *c* stand back because of my affliction;
Sg 1: 7 found wandering after the flocks of your *c*.
Sir 9:16 Have just men for your table *c*;
Jer 41: 8 not kill them, as he had killed their *c*.
Dn 2:13 Daniel and his *c* were also sought out.
2:17 went home and informed his *c* Hananiah,
2:18 so that Daniel and his *c* might not perish
3:49 into the furnace with Azariah and his *c*,
11:26 Even his table *c* shall seek to destroy him,
Mk 1:36 Simon and his *c* managed to track him down,
3:14 He named twelve as his *c* whom he would
5:40 *c* and entered the room where the child lay.
16:20 his *c* all that had been announced to them.
Lk 22:49 *c* of Jesus saw what was going to happen,
Acts 13:13 Paul and his *c* put out to sea and sailed
19:29 Gaius and Aristarchus, Paul's traveling *c*
20: 5 *c* went on ahead and waited for us in Troas.
20:34 served both my needs and those of my *c*.
22: 9 My *c* saw the light but did not hear the
22:11 by the hand and led into Damascus by my *c*.
Rv 2:22 her *c* in sin I will plunge into intense

COMPANIONSHIP (1)

Wis 8: 3 to nobility the splendor of *c* with God;

COMPANY (67)

Gn 30:30 the LORD's blessings came upon you in my *c*.
38:12 in *c* with his friend Hirah the Adullamite.
49: 6 or my spirit be joined with their *c*;
Ex 6:26 from the land of Egypt, *c* by company."
12:51 the Israelites out of Egypt *c* by company.
33: 3 But I myself will not go up in your *c*,
33: 5 I to go up in your *c* even for a moment,
34: 9 with you, O Lord, do come along in our *c*.
Nm 10:28 departure for the Israelites, *c* by *c*.
31:14 of the army, the clan and *c* commanders,
31:48 Then the officers who had been clan and *c*
31:52 This was from the clan and *c* commanders;
31:54 the gold from the clan and *c* commanders,
Dt 23:15 in your midst, he will leave your *c*.
Jgs 9:37 one *c* is coming by way of Elon-Meonenim."
9:44 Abimelech and the *c* with him dashed in and
11: 3 A rabble had joined *c* with him,
2Sm 4: 2 had two *c* leaders named Baanah and Rechab,
1Kgs 1:25 eating and drinking in his *c* and saying,
20:36 When they parted *c*,
2Kgs 1: 9 with his *c* of fifty men after Elijah.
1:11 with his *c* of fifty men after Elijah.
1:13 sent a captain with his *c* of fifty men.
Jdt 12:12 a woman with us without enjoying her *c*.
1Mc 3:15 And again a large *c* of renegades advanced
2Mc 14:24 but he always kept Judas in his *c*,
Jb 16: 7 and stunned, all my *c* has closed in on me.
34: 8 Keeps *c* with evildoers and goes along with
Ps(s) 1: 1 sinners, nor sits in the *c* of the insolent,
86:14 me, and the *c* of fierce men seeks my life,
111: 1 my heart in the *c* and assembly of the just.
Wis 6:23 shall I admit consuming jealousy to my *c*,
7:11 good things together came to me in her *c*,
Sir 6:34 Frequent the *c* of the elders;
27:12 but frequent the *c* of thoughtful men.
Jer 35: 3 his sons, the whole *c* of the Rechabites,
35:18 to the *c* of the Rechabites Jeremiah said:
Bar 5: 9 his glory with his mercy and justice for *c*.
Ez 31:14 for the land below, For the *c* of mortals,
32:22 There is Assyria with all her *c*,
32:23 her *c* is around Egypt's grave,
Am 7:14 nor have I belonged to a *c* of prophets;
Mk 1:20 with the hired men, and went off in his *c*.
9:38 to stop him because he is not of our *c*."
Lk 9:49 to stop him because he is not of our *c*."
13:26 begin to say, 'We ate and drank in your *c*.
24:33 the Eleven and the rest of the *c* assembled.
Jn 6:66 and would not remain in his *c* any longer.
17:24 gave me I would have in my *c* where I am,
18:15 Simon Peter, in *c* with another disciple,
Acts 1:14 There were some women in their *c*,
1:21 our *c* while the Lord Jesus moved among us,
18:18 Syria, in the *c* of Priscilla and Aquila.
19: 7 were in the *c* about twelve men in all.
25:23 entered the audience chamber in the *c*
26:30 governor and Bernice and the rest of the *c*.
Rom 15:32 joy and be refreshed in spirit by your *c*.
16:17 Avoid their *c*.
1Cor 15:33 "Bad *c* corrupts good morals."
Eph 2: 3 All of us were once of their *c*;
6:18 and attentively for all in the holy *c*.
Col 2:13 God gave you new life in *c* with Christ.
3: 1 you have been raised up in *c* with Christ,
2Pt 1:18 we were in his *c* on the holy mountain.

COMPARE (11)

Gn 47: 9 and they do not *c* with the years that my
2Kgs 23:25 nor could any after him *c* with him.
Prv 3:15 of your choice possessions can *c* with her.
8:11 and no choice possessions can *c* with her.]
Sir 25:11 its possessor is beyond *c*.
Is 46: 5 Whom would you *c* me with,
Lam 2:13 To what can I liken or *c* you,
Lk 13:20 "To what shall I *c* the reign of God?
2Cor 3:10 when you *c* that limited glory with this
10:12 as to classify or *c* ourselves with certain
Rv 13: 4 beast and said, "Who can *c* with the beast,

COMPARED (7)

Wis 7:29 *C* to light, she takes precedence
15:18 for *c* as to folly,
Bar 3:36 no other is to be *c* to him:
Lk 6:47 I will show you with whom he is to be *c*.
Acts 6: 1 as *c* with the widows of those who spoke
Rom 8:18 *c* with the glory to be revealed in us.
Rv 18:18 city could have *c* with this great one!"

COMPARING (1)

2Cor 10:12 appraisers, *c* themselves with one another,

COMPARISON (10)

Jgs 8: 2 have I accomplished now in *c* with you?"
8: 3 What have I been able to do in *c* with you?"
Wis 7: 8 And deemed riches nothing in *c* with her,
Ez 16:52 theirs, they appear just in *c* with you.
Dn 1:10 by *c* with the other young men of your age,
1:13 Then see how we look in *c* with the other
Mt 11:16 "What *c* can I use to describe this breed?
Mk 4:30 "What *c* shall we use for the reign of God?
Lk 7:31 "What *c* can I use for the men of today?
2Cor 4:17 us an eternal weight of glory beyond all *c*.

COMPARTMENTS (2)

Gn 6:14 an ark of gopherwood, put various *c* in it,
1Chr 28:12 with the surrounding *c* for the stores for

COMPASS (1)

Is 44:13 with a plane and measures it off with a *c*,

COMPASSED (3)

Jb 19: 6 with me, and *c* me round with his net.
Wis 18:14 For when peaceful stillness *c* everything
Sir 24: 5 The vault of heaven I *c* alone,

COMPASSION (30)

2Kgs 13:23 *c* because of his covenant with Abraham,
2Chr 36:15 had *c* on his people and his dwelling place.
1Mc 3:44 battle and to pray and implore mercy and *c*.
2Mc 7: 6 is looking on, and he truly has *c* on us,
Ps(s) 25: 6 Remember that your *c*, O LORD,
40:12 Withhold not, O LORD, your *c* from me;

51: 3 greatness of your *c* wipe out my offense.
77:10 Does he in anger withhold his *c*?"
79: 8 may your *c* quickly come to us,
103: 4 he crowns you with kindness and *c*,
103:13 *c* on his children, so the LORD has *c*
106:46 for them *c* from all who held them captive.
119:77 Let your *c* come to me that I may live,
119:156 Your *c* is great,
Prv 19:17 He who has *c* on the poor lends to the LORD,
Jer 13:14 I will show no *c*,
Ez 16: 5 or *c* to do any of these things for you.
Dn 9: 9 O LORD, our God, are *c* and forgiveness!
Hos 13:14 My eyes are closed to *c*.
14: 4 for in you the orphan finds *c*."
Mi 7:19 in clemency, And will again have *c* on us,
Hb 3: 2 in your wrath remember *c*!
Zec 7: 9 and show kindness and *c* toward each other.
Mal 3: 7 as a man has *c* on
3:17 I will have *c* on them
3:17 as a man has *c* on his son
Mt 20:34 Moved with *c*,
Lk 10:37 came, "The one who treated him with *c*."
Phil 2: 1 love can give, of fellowship in spirit, *c*,

COMPASSIONATE (10)

Ex 22:26 for I am *c*.
2Chr 30: 9 for merciful and *c* is the LORD,
Neh 9:17 you are a God of pardons, gracious and *c*,
Ps(s) 145: 9 is good to all and *c* toward all his works.
Sir 2:11 *C* and merciful is the LORD;
Lam 4:10 hands of *c* women boiled their own children,
Lk 6:36 "Be compassionate, as your Father is *c*.
Eph 4:32 place of these, be kind to one another, *c*,
Jas 5:11 seen what the Lord, who is *c* and merciful,

COMPATRIOTS (1)

2Mc 4: 2 of the city, a protector of his *c*,

COMPEL (2)

Nm 5: 3 you shall *c* them to go out of the camp;
Jb 20:15 God shall *c* his belly to disown them.

COMPELLED (4)

Ex 6: 1 *c* by my outstretched arm,
2Mc 6: 7 they were *c* to march in his procession,
Acts 20:22 *c* by the Spirit and not knowing what will
26:11 synagogue, I *c* them by force to blaspheme.

COMPELS (1)

Jb 32:18 the spirit within me *c* me.

COMPENSATE (2)

Ex 21:19 he must *c* him for his enforced idleness
Est 7: 4 unable to *c* for the harm done to the king."

COMPENSATION (2)

Ex 21:26 let the slave go free in *c* for the eye
21:27 let the slave go free in *c* for the tooth.

COMPETENT (2)

Jdt 11: 8 throughout the kingdom you alone are *c*,
2Tm 3:17 fully *c* and equipped for every good work.

COMPETING (1)

Jer 22:15 rank among kings by *c* with them in cedar?

COMPILE (1)

Lk 1: 1 Many have undertaken to *c* a narrative of

COMPLACENT (5)

Is 32: 9 O *c* ladies,
32:11 Tremble, you who are *c*!
Ez 16:49 sated with food, *c* in their prosperity,
Am 6: 1 Woe to the *c* in Zion,
Zec 1:15 I am exceedingly angry with the *c* nations;

COMPLAIN (7)

Jgs 21:22 fathers or their brothers come to *c* to us,
1Sm 8:18 *c* against the king whom you have chosen,
1Mc 8:32 If they *c* about you again,
Jb 7:11 I will *c* in the bitterness of my soul.
Sir 10:24 a prudent slave, the wise man does not *c*.
Lam 3:39 Why should any living man *c*,
Hos 4: 4 But let no one protest, let no one *c*;

COMPLAINED (12)

Ex 14:11 And they *c* to Moses,
Nm 11: 1 the people *c* in the hearing of the LORD;
12: 2 They *c*, "Is it through Moses alone
21: 5 the people *c* against God and Moses,
2Kgs 2:19 the inhabitants of the city *c* to Elisha,
4: 1 of one of the guild prophets, *c* to Elisha:
4:19 he *c* to his father.
Jb 31:38 out against me till its very furrows *c*;
Mt 9:11 Pharisees saw this and *c* to his disciples,
20:11 Thereupon they *c* to the owner.
Mk 2:16 against the law, they *c* to his disciples,
Acts 6: 1 the ones who spoke Greek *c* that their

COMPLAINING (3)

Nm 21: 7 have sinned in *c* against the LORD and you.
Jb 9:27 I will forget my *c*,
1Pt 4: 9 Be mutually hospitable without *c*.

COMPLAINT (13)

Ex 3: 7 their cry of *c* against their slave drivers,
24:14 If anyone has a *c*,
Neh 5: 6 when I heard the reasons they had for *c*.
Jb 7:13 comfort me, my couch shall ease my *c*,"
10: 1 I will give myself up to *c*;
21: 4 Is my *c* toward man?
23: 2 Though I know my *c* is bitter,
33:13 do you make *c* against him that he gives no
Ps(s) 142: 3 My *c* I pour out before him;
Sir 35:14 nor to the widow when she pours out her *c*;
46: 7 the people and suppressed the wicked *c*—
Hb 2: 1 me, and what answer he will give to my *c*.
Acts 16:20 them over to the magistrates with this *c*:

COMPLAINTS (2)

Dt 1:16 that time, 'Listen to *c* among your kinsmen,
Jgs 16:16 her *c* till he was deathly weary of them.

COMPLETE (48)

Ex 16:23 Tomorrow is a day of *c* rest,
21:19 idleness and provide for his *c* cure.
31:15 the seventh day is the sabbath of *c* rest,
35: 2 you as the sabbath of *c* rest to the LORD.
36: 7 more than enough, to *c* the work to be done.
Lv 23:32 a sabbath of *c* rest and mortify yourselves.
23:39 and the eighth day shall be days of *c* rest.
25: 4 seventh year the land shall have *c* rest,
Jos 15:12 *c* boundary of the clans of the Judahites.
Ru 2:11 "I have had a *c* account of what you have
2:21 servants until they *c* his entire harvest."
1Chr 27:24 to take the census, but he did not *c* it,
2Chr 15:15 whole heart and sought him with *c* desire,
Neh 3:34 they *c* their restoration in a single day?
Jdt 2:16 and grouped them into a *c* combat force.
11: 6 your handmaid, God will give you *c* success,
Est B: 2 for my subjects a life of *c* tranquillity;
1Mc 11:16 King Ptolemy's triumph was *c* when the Arab
Jb 20:26 *C* darkness is in store for him;
Ps(s) 138: 8 The LORD will *c* what he has done for me;
Prv 24:27 *C* your outdoor tasks,
Wis 15: 3 For to know you well is *c* justice,
Sir 7:32 your hand, that your blessing may be *c*;
Is 16: 4 When the struggle is ended, the ruin *c*,
47: 9 *C* bereavement and widowhood shall come
Ez 28:12 perfection, of *c* wisdom and perfect beauty,
Mi 2: 4 "Our ruin is *c*,
Mt 8:26 *C* calm ensued; the men were dumbfounded.
Lk 14:28 if he has enough money to *c* the project?
14:29 and then not being able to *c* the work;
Jn 3:29 That is my joy, and it is *c*.
15:11 my joy may be yours and your joy may be *c*.
17:23 that their unity may be *c*.
Acts 4:29 *c* assurance by stretching forth your hand
14: 3 out fearlessly, in *c* reliance on the Lord.
20:24 I can finish my race and *c* the service
Rom 15:14 with goodness, that you have *c* knowledge,
1Cor 1:18 The message of the cross is *c* absurdity to
2Cor 11: 3 your sincere and *c* devotion to Christ.
Gal 4:20 You have me at a *c* loss!
Phil 2: 2 make my joy *c* by your unanimity,
Col 1:28 hoping to make every man *c* in Christ.
1Thes 1: 5 in the Holy Spirit and out of *c* conviction.
1Tm 4: 9 depend on this as worthy of *c* acceptance.
5:21 without prejudice, act with *c* impartiality!
2Tm 1: 4 That would make my happiness *c*.
1Jn 1: 4 writing you this is that our joy may be *c*.
Rv 3: 2 is less than *c* in the sight of my God.

COMPLETED (47)

Gn 2: 1 and the earth and all their array were *c*.
29:21 my marriage with her, for my term is now *c*."
38:12 After Judah *c* the period of mourning,
Ex 5:14 "Why have you not *c* your prescribed
39:32 of the Dwelling of the meeting tent was *c*.
Lv 8:33 until the days of your ordination are *c*;
16:20 has *c* the atonement rite for the sanctuary,
Nm 4:46 had *c* the registration among the Levites,
7: 1 when Moses had *c* the erection of the
Dt 34: 8 till they had *c* the period of grief and
Jos 3:17 until the whole nation had *c* the passage.
Jgs 6: 3 when the Israelites had *c* their sowing,
1Kgs 6:38 year, and it was *c* in all particulars,
7: 1 *c* after thirteen years of construction.
7:22 Thus the work on the columns was *c*.
7:40 he therewith *c* all his work for King
7:51 Solomon in the temple of the LORD was *c*,
2Kgs 16:11 it *c* by the time the king returned home.
1Chr 17:11 have been *c* and you must join your fathers,
28:20 abandon you before you have *c* all the work
2Chr 4:11 Huram thus *c* the work he had to do for
5: 1 for the temple of the LORD had been *c*,
7:11 Solomon *c* the house of the LORD and the
8:16 of the LORD had been *c* in every detail.
29:28 trumpets until the holocaust had been *c*.
29:29 As the holocaust was *c*,
29:34 assisted them until the task was *c*
30:22 when they had *c* the seven days of festival,
31: 7 and they *c* them in the seventh month.
Ezr 5:16 has been going on, and it is not yet *c*.'
6:15 They *c* this house on the third day of the
Neh 3:38 soon filled in and *c* up to half its height.
6: 9 in the work, and it will never be *c*."
6:16 our God's help that this work had been *c*.
Tb 14: 5 era when the appointed times shall be *c*.
Jdt 2: 4 When he had *c* his plan,
1Mc 3:49 who had *c* the time of their vows.
Wis 4:16 and youth swiftly *c* condemns the many
Sir 50:14 Once he had *c* the services at the altar
50:19 As the high priest *c* the services at the
Lam 4:22 Your chastisement is *c*,
Ez 4: 8 until you have *c* the days of your siege.
5: 2 city, when the days of your siege are *c*;
Lk 2: 6 there the days of her confinement were *c*.
Acts 14:26 favor of God for the task they had now *c*.
Rom 15:19 I have *c* preaching the gospel of Christ
2Tm 4:17 through me the preaching task might be *c*

COMPLETELY (57)

Ex 17:14 I will *c* blot out the memory of Amalek
Lv 5: 8 the neck, yet without breaking it off *c*,
Dt 2:15 them, till he wiped them out of the camp *c*.
3: 3 him so *c* that we left him no survivor.
Jos 1:16 We will obey you as *c* as we obeyed Moses.
14: 8 the people, but I was *c* loyal to the LORD,
14: 9 because you have been *c* loyal to the LORD,
14:14 day, because he was *c* loyal to the LORD,
24:14 the LORD and serve him *c* and sincerely.
Jgs 16:17 her *c* into his confidence and told her,
16:18 he had taken her *c* into his confidence,
1Sm 14:31 to Aijalon, the people were *c* exhausted.
28: 5 he was dismayed and lost heart *c*.
1Kgs 6:22 with gold so that it was *c* covered with it;
14:10 and will burn up the house of Jeroboam *c*,
21:26 He became *c* abominable by following idols,
2Kgs 10:17 doing away with them *c* and thus fulfilling
11:18 They shattered its altars and images *c*,
13:17 You will *c* conquer Aram at Aphec."
13:19 you would have defeated Aram *c*.
2Chr 12:12 from him so that it did not destroy him *c*;
20:23 of Mount Seir and *c* exterminated them.
Neh 9:31 Yet in your great mercy you did not *c*
Tb 6: 8 spirit, the affliction will leave him *c*,
14: 7 of sin shall *c* disappear from the land.
2Mc 7: 5 When he was *c* maimed but still breathing,
8:29 Lord to be *c* reconciled with his servants.
Ps(s) 9: 7 The enemies are ruined *c* forever;
73:19 They are *c* wasted away amid horrors.
Wis 11:19 only could these attack and *c* destroy them;
13:19 facility of a thing with hands *c* inert.
Jer 9:15 pursue them until I have *c* destroyed them.
14:19 Have you cast Judah off *c*?
49:37 them until I have *c* made an end of them;
Ez 40: 5 an outer wall that *c* surrounded the temple.
41: 8 was a raised pavement *c* enclosing it
Dn 11:22 shall be *c* overwhelmed by him and crushed,
13:22 "I am *c* trapped," Susanna groaned.
Na 2: 1 invaded by the scoundrel; he is *c* destroyed
Zep 1: 2 I will *c* sweep away all things from the
Mt 7:27 collapsed under all this and was *c* ruined."
19:25 heard this they were *c* overwhelmed,
Mk 1:27 A *c* new teaching in a spirit of authority!
6:52 were *c* closed to the meaning of the events.
8:17 Are your minds *c* blinded?
10:26 They were *c* overwhelmed at this,
16:12 revealed to them *c* changed in appearance.
Lk 6:49 it immediately fell in and was *c* destroyed."
19:42 but you have *c* lost it from view!
20:21 words and your doctrine are *c* forthright,
20:26 His answer *c* disconcerted them and reduced
Jn 17:13 in the world that they may share my joy *c*.
Acts 14:17 his benefits, he has not hidden himself *c*,
1Cor 4: 8 At the moment you are *c* satisfied.
Col 2:11 which strips off the carnal body *c*.
1Tm 2:11 must listen in silence and be *c* submissive.
Ti 2: 6 men to keep themselves *c* under control

COMPLETES (2)

Nm 6:13 On the day he *c* the period of his
Jb 14: 6 be, while, like a hireling, he *c* his day.

COMPLETING (4)

1Mc 13:10 and quickly *c* the walls of Jerusalem,
2Mc 10:38 On *c* these exploits,
Acts 12:25 to Jerusalem upon *c* the relief mission,
24:18 found me in the temple court *c* the rites

COMPLETION (7)

2Mc 2: 9 at the dedication and the *c* of the temple.
Jn 4:34 me and bringing his work to *c* is my food.
Acts 21:27 seven-day period was nearing *c*
2Cor 8: 6 among you, to bring it to successful *c*:
8:11 Carry it through now to a successful *c*,
13: 9 prayer is that you may be built up to *c*.
Phil 1: 6 work in you will carry it through to *c*,

COMPLIANCE (1)

Phlm 1:21 Confident of your c,

COMPLICATED (1)

Dt 17: 8 issue which proves too c for you to decide,

COMPLY (4)

Gn 34:17 c with our terms regarding circumcision,
Jdt 2: 3 refused to c with the order he had issued.
2: 6 they did not c with the order I issued.
Est 1: 8 to c with the good pleasure of everyone.

COMPOSE (1)

Sir 38:18 then c yourself after your grief,

COMPOSED (5)

2Chr 35:25 Jeremiah also c a lamentation over Josiah,
Tb 13: 1 Then Tobit c this joyful prayer:
Est E:18 for he who c it has been hanged,
2Mc 7:22 the elements of which each of you is c.
15:38 so a skillfully c story delights the ears

COMPOSERS (1)

Sir 44: 5 C of melodious psalms,

COMPOSITION (1)

Sir 44: 4 Authors skilled in c,

COMPOUNDED (1)

2Chr 16:14 kinds of aromatics c into an ointment.

COMPREHEND (5)

Mk 8:17 Do you still not see or c?
Prv 1: 6 That he may c proverb and parable,
Jn 12:40 numbed their hearts, lest they see or c,
1Cor 13: 2 and, with full knowledge, c all mysteries,
14:16 how will the one who does not c be able to

COMPREHENDED (2)

Jb 38:18 Have you c the breadth of the earth?
Col 1: 6 day you first heard it and c God's gracious

COMPREHENDING (1)

Sir 24:26 The first man never finished c wisdom,

COMPREHENSION (1)

Wis 9: 5 and lacking in c of judgment and of laws.

COMPRESSES (1)

Prv 16:30 he who c his lips has mischief ready.

COMPRISE (4)

Gn 6: 3 days shall c one hundred and twenty years."
Jos 19:16 their villages to c the heritage of the clans
19:31 villages to c the heritage of the clans
19:39 to c the heritage of the clans of the

COMPRISING (3)

Gn 36: 6 as well as his livestock c various animals
46:27 all the people c Jacob's family who had
Dt 3:10 c all the cities of the plateau and all

COMPULSION (4)

Dt 21:14 her, since she was married to you under c.
Wis 19: 4 For a c suited to this ending drew them on,
Sir 20: 3 with a maiden is he who does right under c.
1Cor 9:16 I am under c and have no choice.

COMPUTE (3)

Lv 25:50 c the years from the sale to the jubilee,
27:23 the priest shall c its value in proportion
Nm 3:40 old or more, and c their total number.

COMPUTED (1)

Ez 45:14 c by the kor of ten liquid measures [or a

COMPUTING (1)

Dt 16: 9 c them from the day when the sickle is

COMRADE (2)

Sir 37: 6 Forget not your c during the battle,
Phil 2:25 my brother, co-worker, and c in arms,

COMRADES (1)

Is 1:23 Your princes are rebels and c of thieves;

COMRADESHIP (1)

Ps(s) 55:15 You, whose c I enjoyed;

COMSUMED (1)

Bar 6:71 they themselves will in the end be c,

CONANIAH (3)

2Chr 31:12 overseer of these things was C the Levite,
31:13 Benaiah were supervisors subject to C
35: 9 C and his brothers Shemaiah,

CONCEAL (11)

1Sm 20: 2 Why, then, should my father c this from me?
2Sm 14:18 do not c from me anything I may ask you!"
Tb 12:11 I will c nothing at all from you.
Jb 23:17 that thick gloom were before me to c me.
27:11 and the way of the Almighty I will not c.
Ps(s) 27: 5 He will c me in the shelter of his tent,
64: 7 and c the scheme they have devised;
Prv 10:18 is the lips of the liar that c hostility;
26:26 A man may c hatred under dissimulation,
Is 16: 3 To hide the outcasts, to c the fugitives.
26:21 blood upon her, and no longer c her slain.

CONCEALED (14)

Gn 42: 7 But he c his own identity from them and
2Kgs 11: 2 She c him from Athaliah,
Jb 28:21 from the birds of the air it is c.
Prv 17:23 a c bribe to pervert the course of justice.
21:14 secret gift allays anger, and a c present,
Sir 12: 8 in adversity an enemy will not remain c.
Is 49: 2 sword and c me in the shadow of his arm.
Jer 36:26 But the LORD kept them c.
Hb 3: 4 from beside him, where his power is c.
Mt 10:26 Nothing is c that will not be revealed,
Lk 8:17 nothing c that will not be known and
9:45 c from them they did not grasp it at all,
12: 2 is nothing c that will not be revealed,
Heb 4:13 Nothing is c from him;

CONCEALING (1)

Gn 37:26 by killing our brother and c his blood?

CONCEALS (5)

Prv 10:11 but the mouth of the wicked c violence.
10:13 [but the mouth of the wicked c violence].
12:23 A shrewd man c his knowledge,
25: 2 God has glory in what he c,
28:13 He who c his sins prospers not,

CONCEIT (1)

Phil 2: 3 Never act out of rivalry or c;

CONCEITED (4)

Rom 11:25 be ignorant of this mystery lest you be c;
2Cor 12: 7 become c I was given a thorn in the flesh,
1Tm 3: 6 lest he become c and thus incur the
6: 4 be recognized as both c and ignorant,

CONCEIVABLE (1)

2Cor 11: 6 made this evident to you in every c way.

CONCEIVE (11)

Jgs 13: 3 no children, yet you will c and bear a son.
13: 5 As for the son you will c and bear,
Ru 4:13 LORD enabled her to c and she bore a son.
Jb 15:35 They c malice and bring forth emptiness;
Wis 9:13 or who can c what our Lord intends?
Sir 42:10 Lest she c in her father's home,
Is 33:11 You c dry grass,
59: 4 they c mischief and bring forth malice.
66: 9 Or shall I who allow her to c,
Lk 1:31 You shall c and bear a son and give him
Heb 11:11 power to c though she was past the age,

CONCEIVED (44)

Gn 4: 1 with his wife Eve, and she c and bore Cain,
4:17 with his wife, and she c and bore Enoch.
6: 5 his heart c was ever anything but evil,
29:32 Leah c and bore a son,
29:33 She c again and bore a son,
29:34 Again she c and bore a son,
29:35 Once more she c and bore a son,
30: 5 When Bilhah c and bore a son,
30: 7 Bilhah c again and bore a second son,
30:10 with Zilpah, and she c and bore a son.
30:17 she c and bore a fifth son to Jacob.
30:19 Leah c again and bore a sixth son to Jacob;
30:23 She c and bore a son,
38: 3 She c and bore a son, whom she named Er.
38: 4 c and bore a son, whom she named Onan
38:18 had intercourse with her, and she c by him.
Ex 2: 2 a Levite woman, who c and bore a son.
Lv 12: 2 a woman has c and gives birth to a boy,
Nm 11:12 Was it I who c all this people?
1Sm 1:20 She c, and at the end of her term bore
2:21 The LORD favored Hannah so that she c and
18:15 successful he was, Saul c a fear of David:
2Sm 11: 5 But the woman had c,
12:24 and she c and bore him a son,
13:15 Then Amnon c an intense hatred for her,
2Kgs 4:17 Yet the woman c,
1Chr 7:23 who c and bore a son whom he named Beriah,
Ps(s) 7:15 c iniquity and was pregnant with mischief,
51: 7 was I born, and in sin my mother c me;
Sg 8: 5 c you, it was there that your parent c.
Is 8: 3 to the prophetess and she c and bore a son.
26:18 We c and writhed in pain,
59:13 words of falsehood the heart has c.
Hos 1: 3 and she c and bore him a son.
1: 6 When she c again and bore a daughter,
1: 8 she weaned Lo-ruhama, she c and bore a son.
2: 7 she that c them has acted shamefully.
Mt 1:20 the Holy Spirit that she has c this child.
Lk 1:24 Afterward, his wife Elizabeth c.
1:36 your kinswoman has c a son in her old age;
2:21 the angel had given him before he was c.
Rom 9:10 Rebekah had c twin children by one man,
Jas 1:15 Once passion has c,

CONCENTRATE (1)

Acts 6: 4 c on prayer and the ministry of the word."

CONCEPTION (1)

Hos 9:11 no birth, no carrying in the womb, no c.

CONCERN (37)

Gn 39: 8 not c himself with anything in the house,
39:23 The chief jailer did not c himself with
Ex 7:23 into his house, with no c even for this.
Dt 22: 1 driven astray without showing c about it;
22: 4 on the road without showing c about it;
29:28 revealed c us and our descendants forever,
Jos 22:24 We did it rather out of our anxious c lest
2Chr 9:29 visions of Iddo the seer which c Jeroboam,
Tb 5:19 I hope more money is not your chief c!
2Mc 2:29 has only to c himself with what is needed
7:34 insolence, c yourself with unfounded hopes,
14: 8 of my genuine c for the king's interests,
Jb 35:15 nor does he show c that a man will die.
Prv 16:11 all the weights used with them are his c.
29: 7 the wicked man has no such c.
29:10 man, but the upright show c for his life.
Wis 15: 9 But his c is not that he is to die nor
Sir 3:21 for what is hidden is not your c.
11: 9 Dispute not about what is not your c;
16:18 with my ways who will c himself?
21:25 the impious talk of what is not their c,
31: 2 C for one's livelihood banishes slumber;
38:25 bullock, and whose every c is for cattle?
38:27 seals, and whose c is to vary the pattern.
38:34 and their c is for exercise of their skill.
Jl 2:18 c for his land and took pity on his people.
Jn 2: 4 how does this c of yours involve me?
10:13 he has no c for the sheep.
12: 6 (He did not say this out of c for the poor,
21:22 Jesus replied, "how does that c you?
21:23 to stay until I come [how does that c you]?"
2Cor 7: 7 your grief, and your ardent c for me,
8: 7 and discourse, in knowledge, in total c,
8: 8 love against the c which others show.
Phil 2:12 with anxious c to achieve your salvation,
4:10 that your c for me bore fruit once more.
4:17 my c is for the ever-growing balance in

CONCERNED (26)

Gn 45:20 Do not be c about your belongings,
Ex 3:16 I am c about you and about the way you are
4:31 c about them and had seen their affliction,
Dt 2: 7 he has been c about your journey through
Neh 2:16 the others who would be c about the matter.
11:24 deputy in all affairs that c the people.
1Mc 8:15 all that c the people and their well-being.
2Mc 15:18 They were not so much c about their wives
Prv 23: 4 not to gain wealth, cease to be c about it;
Eccl 2: 3 wine, though my mind was c with wisdom,
Sir 38:29 He is always c for his products,
Ez 38:12 nations, a people c with cattle and goods,
Jon 4:10 "You are c over the plant which cost you
4:11 And should I not be c over Nineveh,
Mt 6:28 As for clothes, why be c?
Lk 10:40 are you not c that my sister has left me
12:22 why I warn you, Do not be c for your life,
Acts 15:14 Symeon has told you how God first c
1Cor 7:32 Lord's affairs, c with pleasing the Lord;
7:34 is c with things of the Lord,
7:34 her and is c with pleasing her husband.
9: 9 Is God c here for oxen,
12:25 all the members may be c for one another.
14:20 Be like children as far as evil is c,
2Cor 8:21 We are c not only for God's approval but
Phil 4:10 You had been c all along,

CONCERNING (81)

Gn 12:20 Then Pharaoh gave men orders c him,
Nm 8:20 which the LORD had given Moses c them.
8:22 given Moses c the Levites was carried out.
30:17 prescribed through Moses c the relationship
Dt 27: 4 these stones c which I command you today,
Jos 14: 2 c the remaining nine and a half tribes.
1Sm 4:19 When she heard the news c the capture of
25:30 the promise of success he has made c you,
2Sm 3:19 his own report to David in Hebron c all
7:25 you have made c your servant and his house,

17:23 Then, having left orders c his family,
2Kgs 19:21 This is the word the LORD has spoken c him:
19:32 thus says the LORD c the king of Assyria:
1Chr 11:10 even as the LORD had commanded c Israel.
17:23 promise that you have uttered c your servant
23:32 is prescribed for them c the meeting tent,
2Chr 23: 3 as the LORD promised c the sons of David.
31: 9 the priests and the Levites c the heaps,
34:21 consult the LORD c the words of the book
34:26 of Israel, c the threats you have heard:
Ezr 5: 5 a written order be sent back c this matter.
6: 8 I also issue this decree c your dealing
Neh 6:12 he voiced this prophecy c me that I might
10:35 by lot c the procurement of wood:
Est 8: 8 you see fit c the Jews and seal the letter
9:30 when Mordecai sent documents c peace and
1Mc 3:34 instructions c everything he wanted done.
8:31 c the wrongs that King Demetrius has done
9:55 utter a word to give orders c his house.
11:31 we wrote to Lasthenes our kinsman c you.
14:42 concerning its functions and c the country,
2Mc 3:40 This was how the matter c Heliodorus and
11:24 our father's policy c Greek customs
Jb 42: 7 for you have not spoken rightly c me,
42: 8 For you have not spoken rightly c me,
Is 1: 1 had c Judah and Jerusalem in the days of
2: 1 son of Amoz, saw c Judah and Jerusalem.
5: 1 my friend, my friend's song c his vineyard.
13: 1 An oracle c Babylon;
37:22 this is the word the LORD has spoken c him:
37:33 thus says the LORD c the king of Assyria:
Jer 7:22 them no command c holocaust or sacrifice.
11:21 c the men of Anathoth who seek your life,
14: 1 LORD that came to Jeremiah c the drought:
14:15 C the prophets who prophesy in my name,
16: 3 for thus says the LORD c the sons and
22: 6 the LORD c the palace of the king of Judah:
22:11 Thus says the LORD c Shallum,
22:18 Therefore, thus says the LORD c Jehoiakim,
25: 1 came to Jeremiah c all the people of Judah,
27:19 thus says the LORD of hosts c the pillars,
27:21 c the vessels that remain in the house of
29:16 LORD c the king who sits on David's throne,
29:31 Thus says the LORD c Shemaiah,
32:36 the LORD, the God of Israel, c this city,
33: 4 c the houses of this city and the palaces
39:11 C Jeremiah, Nebuchadnezzar, king
46: 2 C Egypt. Against the army of Pharaoh Neco,
46:13 Jeremiah c the advance of Nebuchadnezzar,
47: 1 to the prophet Jeremiah c the Philistines,
48: 1 C Moab, thus says the LORD of hosts,
49: 1 C the Ammonites, thus says the LORD:
49: 7 C Edom, thus says the LORD of hosts:
49:22 C Damascus.
Ez 36: 6 [Therefore, prophesy c the land of Israel,
46:20 end, I saw a place, c which he said to me,
Dn 8:13 of this vision last c the daily sacrifice,
10:14 for there is yet a vision c those days."
Am 1: 1 which he received in vision c Israel,
Mi 1: 1 vision he received c Samaria and Jerusalem.
Zec 2:12 me) c the nations that have plundered you:
12: 1 the word of the LORD c Israel.
Lk 2:17 what had been told them c this child.
18:31 c the Son of Man may be accomplished.
Acts 19:23 disturbance broke out c the new way.
Rom 1: 3 the gospel c his Son,
Gal 1:16 among the Gentiles the good tidings c him.
Heb 7:16 in a commandment c physical descent,
9:10 regulations c the flesh,
11: 1 is confident assurance c what we hope for,

CONCERNS (8)

Nm 4: 4 the meeting tent c the most sacred objects.
18: 7 c the altar and the room within the veil.
2Chr 19:10 it c bloodguilt or questions of law,
Neh 11:25 As c their villages in the country:
Prv 6:22 and when you wake, she will share your c;
Wis 9:15 weighs down the mind that has many c
Ez 12:10 This oracle c Jerusalem and the whole
Phil 2:20 him for genuine interest in whatever c you.

CONCERT (2)

Ezr 4: 7 Mithredath wrote in c with Tabeel and the
Sir 32: 5 of gold is a c when wine is served.

CONCESSION (1)

1Cor 7: 6 I say this by way of c, not as a command.

CONCESSIONS (1)

2Mc 4:11 He set aside the royal c granted to the

CONCILIATION (1)

1Cor 4:13 We are slandered, and we try c.

CONCILIATORY (1)

1Mc 10:24 them c words and offer dignities and gifts,

CONCLUDE (2)

Gn 44:28 and I had to c that he must have been torn
Dn 11:17 He shall c an agreement with him and give

CONCLUDED (13)

Dt 29:11 which he c with you today under this
Jos 10: 4 had c peace with Joshua and the Israelites.
Ru 3:17 her all the man had done for her, and c,
2Sm 14:17 And the woman c:
Ezr 9: 1 When these matters had been c,
Jdt 5:22 Now when Achior had c his recommendation,
10: 1 As soon as Judith had thus c,
2Mc 14:30 he c that this coldness betokened no good.
Eccl 2:15 I c in my heart that this too is vanity.
Dn 7:28 The report c: I, Daniel, was greatly terrified
Mk 8:16 they c among themselves that it was
Acts 15:13 When they c their presentation,
19:21 When all this was c,

CONCLUDING (1)

Acts 16:10 c that God had summoned us to proclaim the

CONCLUSION (2)

Jgs 6:29 inquiry led them to the c that Gideon,
Acts 21:15 At the c of our stay,

CONCOCT (1)

Acts 5: 4 How could you ever c such a scheme?

CONCOCTED (2)

2Pt 1:16 It was not by way of cleverly c myths that
Rv 18: 6 Pour into her cup twice the amount she c!

CONCUBINAGE (1)

Gn 25: 6 To his sons by c,

CONCUBINE (23)

Gn 16: 3 gave her to her husband Abram to be his c.
22:24 His c, whose name was Reumah,
35:22 went and lay with Bilhah, his father's c.
36:12 (Esau's son Eliphaz had a c Timna,
Jgs 8:31 c who lived in Shechem also bore him a son,
19: 1 for himself a c from Bethlehem of Judah.
19: 2 His c was unfaithful to him and left him
19: 9 was ready to go with his c and servant,
19:10 his c set out with a pair of saddled asses,
19:24 me bring out my maiden daughter or his c.
19:25 his c and thrust her outside to them.
19:27 his journey, there lay the woman, his c,
19:29 he took a knife to the body of his c,
20: 4 "My c and I went into Gibeah of Benjamin
20: 5 and my c they abused so that she died.
20: 6 So I took my c and cut her up and sent her
2Sm 3: 7 Now Saul had had a c,
3: 7 have you been intimate with my father's c?"
21:11 Rizpah, Aiah's daughter, the c of Saul,
1Chr 1:32 The descendants of Keturah, Abraham's c:
2:46 Ephah, Caleb's c, bore Haran, Moza,
2:48 Maacah, Caleb's c,
7:14 of Manasseh, whom his Aramean c bore:

CONCUBINES (13)

2Sm 5:13 David took more c and wives in Jerusalem
15:16 except for ten c whom he left behind to
16:21 "Have relations with your father's c,
16:22 his father's c in view of all Israel.
19: 6 lives of your wives and those of your c,
20: 3 he took the ten c whom he had left behind
1Kgs 11: 3 wives of princely rank and three hundred c,
1Chr 3: 9 of David, in addition to other sons by c;
2Chr 11:21 more than all his other wives and sixty c;
11:21 he had taken eighteen wives and c,
Est 2:14 royal eunuch Shaashgaz, custodian of the c.
Sg 6: 8 There are sixty queens, eighty c,
6: 9 declared her fortunate, the queens and c,

CONCURRED (2)

Mk 14:64 They all c in the verdict "guilty,"
Acts 8: 1 for his part, c in the act of killing.

CONDEMN (29)

1Kgs 8:32 C the wicked and punish him for his conduct,
Jb 9:20 I were right, my own mouth might c me;
34:17 or will you c the supreme Just One,
34:29 If he remains tranquil, who then can c?
40: 8 Would you c me that you may be justified?
Ps(s) 51: 6 in your sentence, vindicated when you c.
94:21 the life of the just and c innocent blood,
109:31 to save him from those who would c him.
Wis 2:20 Let us c him to a shameful death;
Jer 26:19 of Judah, and all Judah c him to death?
Dn 13:48 To c a woman of Israel without examination
Mt 12:41 present generation and be the ones to c it.
12:42 present generation and be the one to c it.
20:18 and scribes, who will c him to death.
Mk 10:34 They will c him to death and hand him over
Lk 6:37 Do not c, and you will not be condemned.
11:31 of this generation, and she will c them.
11:32 the present generation, and they will c it.
Jn 3:17 send the Son into the world to c the world,
7:51 "Since when does our law c any man
8:11 Jesus said, "Nor do I c you.
12:47 c him, for I did not come to condemn
12:48 is that which will c him on the last day.
Rom 2: 3 you who c these things in others yet do
8:34 Who shall c them?
14:22 does not c what he has chosen to do!
2Cor 7: 3 I do not c you.
Eph 5:11 rather, c them.

CONDEMNATION (24)

Dt 32:31 like our Rock, and our foes are under c.
2Mc 9: 4 Yet the c of Heaven rode with him,
Jb 31:28 This too would be a crime for c,
Wis 1: 8 nor will chastising c pass him by.
12:26 play were to experience a c worthy of God.
12:27 with this, their final c came upon them.
17:11 nature cowardly, testifies in its own c,
Mt 23:33 How can you escape c to Gehenna?
Jn 3:18 Whoever believes in him avoids c,
3:19 The judgment of c is this:
5:24 He does not come under c,
8:26 I could say much about you in c,
16: 8 wrong about sin, about justice, about c.
16:11 about c—
Acts 25:15 case against this man and demanded his c.
Rom 5:16 followed upon one offense and brought c,
5:18 as a single offense brought c to all men,
8: 1 no c now for those who are in Christ Jesus.
13: 2 thus shall draw c down upon themselves.
1Cor 11:34 so that your assembly may not deserve c
Gal 5:10 May c fall on whoever it is that is
1Tm 5:12 them c for breaking their first pledge.
Jas 5:12 In this way you will not incur c.
2Pt 2: 3 Their c has not lain idle all this time,
Jude 1: 4 ago destined for the c I shall describe.

CONDEMNED (37)

Gn 39: 9 great a wrong and thus stand c before God
1Mc 1:57 the law, was c to death by royal decree.
2Mc 4:47 while he c to death those poor men who
Jb 31:11 that would be heinous, a crime to be c;
32: 3 not found a good answer and had not c Job.
Ps(s) 37:33 power nor let him be c when he is on trial.
109: 7 When he is judged, let him go forth c,
Prv 5:14 to utter ruin, c by the public assembly!"
12: 2 from the LORD, but the schemer is c by him.
Wis 11: 9 they recognized how the wicked, c in anger,
11:10 former as a stern king you probed and c.
12:13 you need show you have not unjustly c;
Is 53: 8 Oppressed and c,
Dn 13:41 of the people, and they c her to death.
Mt 12: 7 you would not have c these innocent men.
12:37 acquitted, and by your words you will be c."
25:41 'Out of my sight, you c,
27: 3 him over, seeing that Jesus had been c,
Mk 16:16 man who refuses to believe in it will be c.
Lk 6:37 Do not condemn, and you will not be c.
24:20 leaders delivered him up to be c to death,
Jn 3:18 whoever does not believe is already c
8:10 Has no one c you?"
16:11 for the prince of this world has been c.
Rom 3: 7 his glory, why must I be c as a sinner?
14:23 misgivings about eating, he is already c,
1Cor 11:32 us from being c with the rest of the world.
2Cor 1: 9 men c to death so that we might trust,
3: 9 ministry of the covenant that c had glory,
Eph 5:13 are c they are seen in the light of day,
2Thes 2:12 but have delighted in evildoing will be c.
Heb 11: 7 He thereby c the world and inherited the
Jas 5: 6 You c, even killed, the just man;
5: 9 one another, my brothers, lest you be c.
1Pt 4: 6 c in the flesh in the eyes of men,
2Pt 2: 6 in ashes and c them to destruction,
Rv 19: 2 He has c the great harlot who corrupted

CONDEMNING (6)

Dt 25: 1 the innocent party and c the guilty party,
1Sm 3:13 that I am c his family once and for all,
Wis 12:10 But c them bit by bit,
Dn 13:53 passing unjust sentences, c the innocent,
Acts 13:27 and in c him they fulfilled the words of
Rom 8: 3 a sin offering, thereby c sin in the flesh,

CONDEMNS (7)

Jb 15: 6 Your own mouth c you,
Prv 17:15 who condones the wicked, he who c the just,
Wis 4:16 the just man dead c the sinful who live,
4:16 and youth swiftly completed c the many
Sir 10:28 Who will acquit him who c himself?
Is 29:21 be cut off, those whose mere word c a man,
Rv 18: 8 for mighty is the Lord God who c her."

CONDENSE (1)

2Mc 2:23 we will try to c into a single book.

CONDITION (15)

Gn 34:15 We will agree with you only on this c,
34:22 one kindred people with us only on this c,
Nm 22:20 on the c that you do exactly as I tell you."
1Sm 11: 2 "This is my c for a treaty with you:
19:23 in a prophetic c until he reached the spot.

CONDITION (cont.)

Tb 2:10 and all my kinsmen were grieved at my *c*.
Est E:16 flourishing *c* for us and for our forebears.
Mt 17:15 my son, who is demented and in a serious *c*.
Lk 9:39 then abandons him in his shattered *c*.
1Cor 3: 3 now, being still very much in a natural *c*.
7:24 *c* of life that was his when he was called.
7:39 dies she is free to marry, but on one *c*,
Gal 4: 1 his *c* is no different from that of a slave,
4:14 My physical *c* was a challenge which you
2Pt 2:20 their last *c* is worse than their first.

CONDITIONS (3)

Jdt 8:13 Almighty for whom you are laying down *c*;
Est E: 9 taking advantage of changing *c* and
Jer 32:11 the sealed copy, containing title and *c*,

CONDOLE (1)

Is 51:19 who is there to *c* with you?

CONDOLED (1)

Jb 42:11 They *c* with him and comforted him for all

CONDOLENCES (2)

2Sm 10: 2 with *c* to Hanun for the loss of his father.
10: 3 honoring your father by sending men with *c*?

CONDONES (1)

Prv 17:15 He who *c* the wicked,

CONDUCT (105)

Lv 20:14 be burned to death for their shameful *c*,
Jgs 2:19 none of their evil practices or stubborn *c*.
1Kgs 2: 4 'If your sons so *c* themselves that they
8:25 their *c* so that they live in my presence,
8:32 the wicked and punish him for his *c*,
8:39 to each one of them according to his *c*;
15:26 imitating his father's *c* and the sin which
15:34 imitating the *c* of Jeroboam and the sin he
16: 2 but you have imitated the *c* of Jeroboam
16:19 LORD by imitating the sinful *c* of Jeroboam,
16:26 closely imitated the sinful *c* of Jeroboam,
2Chr 6:16 *c* so as always to live according to my law,
6:23 man and holding him responsible for his *c*,
6:30 render to everyone according to his *c*,
Tb 4:14 do, and discipline yourself in all your *c*.
Jdt 6: 7 will now *c* you to the mountain region,
6:10 tent to seize Achior, *c* him to Bethulia,
8:19 It was for such *c* that our forefathers
Est 1:17 *c* will become known to all the women,
1:18 Median ladies who hear of the queen's *c*
1Mc 12: 4 envoys with save *c* to the land of Judah.
2Mc 4:37 the prudence and noble *c* of the deceased.
14: 8 *c* of the people just mentioned.
Jb 11:14 If you remove all iniquity from your *c*,
13:15 I will defend my *c* before him.
21:31 Who will charge him with his *c* to his face,
34:11 Rather, he requites men for their *c*,
36:23 Who prescribes for him his *c*,
Prv 1: 3 May receive training in wise *c*,
20:11 whether his *c* is innocent and right.
21: 8 but the *c* of the innocent is right.
31:27 She watches the *c* of her household,
Eccl 6: 8 man in knowing how to *c* himself in life?
Sir 3:17 My son, *c* your affairs with humility,
37:17 The root of all *c* is the mind;
42: 8 the aged and infirm answering for wanton *c*.
Jer 2:23 Consider your *c* in the Valley,
4:18 Your *c*, your misdeeds, have done this
35:15 to reform your *c*,
Ez 3:18 him from his wicked *c* so that he may live:
3:19 away from his evil nor from his wicked *c*,
7: 3 judge you according to your *c*
7: 4 I will bring your *c* down upon you,
7: 8 I will judge you according to your *c* and
7: 9 I will deal with you according to your *c*,
7:27 will deal with them according to their *c*,
9:10 I will bring down their *c* upon their heads.
11:21 I will bring down their *c* upon their heads,
13:22 to turn from his evil *c* and save his life;
14:22 you shall see their *c* and their actions
14:23 you when you see their *c* and actions,
16:27 Philistines, who revolted at your lewd *c*.
16:43 I am bringing down your *c* upon your head,
16:61 *c* and be ashamed when I take your sisters,
20:43 There you shall recall your *c* and all the
20:44 to your evil *c* and corrupt actions,
22:31 have brought down their *c* upon their heads,
24:14 your *c* and your deeds you shall be judged,
28:15 in your *c* from the day you were created,
36:17 land, they defiled it by their *c* and deeds.
36:17 In my sight their *c* was like the
36:19 to their *c* and deeds I judged them.
36:31 Then you shall remember your evil *c*,
36:32 Be ashamed and abashed because of your *c*,
Dn 8:25 holy ones, his treacherous *c* shall succeed.
11:18 leader shall put an end to his shameful *c*,
Hos 12: 3 he shall punish Jacob for his *c*,
Mt 5:32 lewd *c* is a separate case
15:19 murder, adulterous *c*,
16:27 he will repay each man according to his *c*.
19: 9 whoever divorces his wife (lewd *c* is a
Mk 7:22 fornication, theft, murder, adulterous *c*,
Acts 19:40 accused of rioting because of today's *c*.
23:24 may give him safe *c* to Felix the governor."
Rom 12:17 your *c* is honorable in the eyes of all.
13: 3 what is right but only when his *c* is evil.
1Cor 5: 1 reported that there is lewd *c* among you
6:18 Shun lewd *c*.
7:30 *c* themselves as though they owned nothing,
Gal 5:19 lewd *c*,
6: 4 Each man should look to his *c*;
Eph 4:19 and the indulgence of every sort of lewd *c*.
5: 3 *c* or promiscuousness or lust of any sort,
5:15 Keep careful watch over your *c*.
Phil 1:10 with a clear conscience and blameless *c*
1:27 *C* yourselves,
Col 3: 7 Your own *c* was once of this sort,
1Thes 2:10 our *c* was toward you who are believers.
4: 1 as you learned from us how to *c* yourselves
2Thes 3:14 ostracized that he may be ashamed of his *c*.
1Tm 3:15 of *c* befits a member of God's household,
2Tm 3:10 have followed closely my teaching and my *c*.
Ti 2:10 expressing a constant fidelity by their *c*,
1Pt 1:15 holy yourselves in every aspect of your *c*,
1:17 *c* yourselves reverently during your
2:12 *c* yourselves blamelessly among them.
3: 1 from preaching, through their wives' *c*.
2Pt 2: 7 the *c* of men unprincipled in their lusts.
3:11 How holy in your *c* and devotion,
1Jn 2: 6 abide in him to *c* himself just as he did.
Rv 2:23 will give each of you what your *c* deserves.
3: 1 I know your *c*;
20:12 to their *c* as recorded on the scrolls.
20:13 Each person was judged according to his *c*.
22:12 be given to each man as his *c* deserves.

CONDUCTED (14)

Gn 43:17 the steward *c* the men to Joseph's house.
2Kgs 8:18 He *c* himself like the kings of Israel of
8:27 He *c* himself like the house of Ahab,
16: 3 but *c* himself like the kings of Israel,
20: 3 wholeheartedly I *c* myself in your presence,
22: 2 He pleased the LORD and *c* himself
2Chr 21: 6 He *c* himself like the kings of Israel of
28: 2 but *c* himself like the kings of Israel and
Jdt 10:17 and these *c* them to the tent of Holofernes.
Est 1:13 because the king's business was *c* in
Wis 10:17 of their labors, *C* them by a wondrous road,
Is 38: 3 wholeheartedly I *c* myself in your presence,
Lk 4: 1 was *c* by the Spirit into the desert for forty
Acts 17: 2 joined the people there and *c* discussions

CONDUCTING (3)

2Kgs 13: 2 the LORD's sight, *c* himself like Jeroboam,
2Mc 11:23 to be undisturbed in *c* their own affairs.
2Cor 6: 6 *c* ourselves with innocence,

CONDUCTS (1)

Ps(s) 112: 5 and lends, who *c* his affairs with justice;

CONDUIT (4)

2Kgs 18:17 stopped at the *c* of the upper pool on the
20:20 *c* by which water was brought into the city,
Is 7: 3 at the end of the *c* of the upper pool,
36: 2 When he stopped at the *c* of the upper pool,

CONFER (4)

1Kgs 9: 3 I *c* my name upon it forever,
1Mc 15:28 of his Friends, to *c* with Simon and say:
2Mc 11:20 as well as your envoys, to *c* with you.
Lk 22: 4 He went off to *c* with the chief priests

CONFERENCE (5)

2Kgs 6:32 sitting in his house in *c* with the elders.
1Mc 11:22 for a *c* at Ptolemais as soon as possible.
2Mc 14:22 But the *c* was held in the proper way.
Lk 20: 5 held a brief *c* during which someone said,
Gal 2: 2 all this in private *c* with the leaders,

CONFERRED (14)

1Kgs 1: 7 He *c* with Joab,
Est 1:13 He *c* with the wise men versed in the law,
1Mc 14:39 Friends, and *c* the highest honors on him.
15: 5 whatever other privileges they *c* on you.
Ps(s) 21: 6 majesty and splendor you *c* upon him.
Wis 14:21 tyranny *c* the incommunicable Name
Sir 45:24 Therefore on him again God *c* the right,
47:11 He *c* on him the rights of royalty and
47:18 that glorious name which was *c* upon Israel.
Acts 8:18 on of hands that the apostles *c* the Spirit,
25:12 *c* with his council and finally declared:
2Cor 8: 1 of God *c* on the churches of Macedonia.
Gal 3:18 it is no longer *c* in virtue of the promise.
1Pt 1:13 to be *c* on you when Jesus Christ appears.

CONFERS (3)

1Sm 25:31 the LORD *c* this benefit on your lordship,
Prv 11:25 He who *c* benefits will be amply enriched,
1Cor 4: 7 Who *c* any distinction on you?

CONFESS (11)

Lv 5: 5 guilty in any of these cases shall *c* the sin
16:21 he shall *c* over it all the sinful faults
26:40 "Thus they will have to *c* that they and
Nm 5: 7 the LORD, he shall *c* the wrong he has done,
2Mc 7:37 blows to make you *c* that he alone is God.
Ps(s) 32: 5 I said, "I *c* my faults to the LORD,"
46:11 and *c* that I am God,
68:35 *C* the power of God!"
Jn 1:31 I *c* I did not recognize him,
Rom 10: 9 if you *c* with your lips that Jesus is Lord,
2Cor 11:21 To my shame I must *c* that we have been too

CONFESSED (5)

Neh 9: 2 then stood forward and *c* their sins and
Dn 9: 4 I prayed to the LORD, my God, and *c*,
Mt 3: 6 in the Jordan River as they *c* their sins.
Mk 1: 5 in the Jordan River as they *c* their sins.
Acts 19:18 and openly *c* their former practices.

CONFESSES (1)

Prv 28:13 he who *c* and forsakes them obtains mercy.

CONFESSING (3)

1Sm 7: 6 the LORD, and they fasted that day, *c*,
Neh 1: 6 *c* the sins which we of Israel have
Dn 9:20 *c* my sin and the sin of my people Israel,

CONFESSION (3)

Neh 9: 3 they made their *c* and prostrated themselves
Est A:14 two eunuchs questioned and, upon their *c*,
Rom 10:10 justification, *c* on the lips to salvation.

CONFIDANT (2)

1Chr 27:33 and Hushai the Archite was the king's *c*.
Sir 6: 6 be many, but one in a thousand your *c*.

CONFIDE (1)

Jgs 16:15 that you love me when you do not *c* in me?

CONFIDED (3)

Jer 41:10 of the bodyguard, had *c* to Gedaliah,
Mk 4:11 the mystery of the reign of God has been *c*.
Lk 8:10 mysteries of the reign of God have been *c*,

CONFIDENCE (38)

Lv 26:19 sins sevenfold, to break your haughty *c*.
Jos 7: 5 the *c* of the people melted away like water.
Jgs 16:17 her completely into his *c* and told her,
16:18 he had taken her completely into his *c*,
2Kgs 18:19 On what do you base this *c* of yours?
2Chr 32: 8 *c* from the words of King Hezekiah of Judah.
1Mc 10:71 If you have *c* in your forces,
2Mc 11: 4 exultant *c* in his myriads of foot soldiers,
Jb 4: 6 Is not your piety a source of *c*,
8:14 His *c* is but a gossamer thread and his
15:15 If in his holy one God places no *c*,
Ps(s) 16: 9 rejoices, my body, too, abides in *c*;
Prv 3:26 For the LORD will be your *c*,
11:13 secrets, but a trustworthy man keeps a *c*.
Sir 13: 5 you, and with smiles he will win your *c*;
22:22 But a contemptuous insult, a *c* broken,
27:17 but if you betray his *c*,
40:26 Wealth and vigor build up *c*,
Is 36: 4 'On what do you base this *c* of yours?
Jer 28:15 and you have raised false *c* in this people.
29:31 a mission from me, and raises false *c*,
Mi 2: 8 the tunic Of those who go their way in *c*,
7: 5 in a friend, have no *c* in a companion;
Jn 7: 5 not even his brothers had much *c* in him.)
Acts 4:31 and continued to speak God's word with *c*.
2Cor 3: 4 This great *c* in God is ours,
3:12 Our hope being such, we speak with full *c*.
5: 8 we are full of *c* and would much rather be
Eph 3:12 freely to God, drawing near him with *c*.
Phil 1:20 I have full *c* that now as always Christ
1:25 fills me with *c* that I will stay with you,
Heb 3: 6 to our *c* and the hope of which we boast.
3:14 to the end that *c* with which we began.
10:22 near in utter sincerity and absolute *c*,
10:35 Do not, then, surrender your *c*;
13: 6 Thus we may say with *c*:
1Jn 4:17 we should have *c* on the day of judgment;
5:14 We have this *c* in God:

CONFIDENT (16)

2Mc 9:27 I am *c* that,
15: 7 But Maccabeus remained *c*,
Jb 6:20 They are disappointed, though they were *c*;
Is 12: 2 I am *c* and unafraid.
Mt 9:28 said to them, "Are you *c* I can do this?"
2Cor 11:15 *C* as I am about this,
5: 6 Therefore, we continue to be *c*.
Phil 2:24 I am *c* in the Lord that I myself will be
3: 4 though I can be *c* even there.
2Thes 3: 4 In the Lord we are *c* that you are doing

2Tm 1: 5 Eunice, and which (I am *c)* you also have.
1:12 and I am *c* that he is able to guard what
Phlm 1:21 *C* of your compliance,
Heb 11: 1 is *c* assurance concerning what we hope for,
13:18 we are *c* that we have a good conscience,
1Jn 2:28 *c* and not retreat in shame at his coming.

CONFIDENTLY (2)

Acts 2:29 can speak *c* to you about our father David.
Heb 4:16 So let us *c* approach the throne of grace

CONFINE (2)

2Mc 2:28 and *c* our efforts to giving only a summary
Jer 19: 9 and those who seek their lives will *c* them.

CONFINED (13)

Gn 39:20 the jail where the royal prisoners were *c.*
40: 3 steward (the same jail where Joseph was *c).*
40: 5 king of Egypt who were *c* in the jail
42:19 of your brothers need be *c* in this prison,
Nm 12:14 her be *c* outside the camp for seven days;
12:15 was *c* outside the camp for seven days,
Wis 16:14 can he bring back the soul once it is *c.*
17: 2 they lay *c* beneath their own roofs as
17:16 into that unbarred prison and was kept *c.*
18: 4 who had kept your sons *c* through whom the
Sir 11:30 Though he seem like a bird *c* in a cage,
Jer 37:21 Jeremiah be *c* in the quarters of the guard,
Lam 1: 3 come upon her where she is narrowly *c.*

CONFINEMENT (4)

2Sm 20: 3 care of the palace and placed them in *c.*
20: 3 remained in *c* to the day of their death,
Is 42: 7 the blind, to bring out prisoners from *c,*
Lk 2: 6 there the days of her *c* were completed.

CONFINES (9)

Ex 10:19 locust remained within the *c* of Egypt,
Jos 19: 9 was within the *c* of the Judahites;
2Kgs 9:10 shall devour Jezebel at the *c* of Jezreel,
9:36 'In the *c* of Jezreel dogs shall eat the
9:37 like dung in the field in the *c* of Jezreel,
Tb 14:10 stay overnight within the *c* of the city.
1Mc 10:39 Ptolemais and its *c* I give as a present to
Jb 28: 3 to the farthest *c* he penetrates.
Ps(s) 33: 7 in cellars he *c* the deep.

CONFINING (1)

Jer 20:17 have been my grave, her womb *c* me forever.

CONFIRM (12)

2Sm 7:25 *c* for all time the prophecy you have made
1Kgs 1:14 come in after you and *c* what you have said."
Est 9:29 wrote to *c* with full authority this second
1Mc 11:34 Therefore we *c* their possession,
11:57 "I *c* you in the high priesthood and
12: 1 *c* and renew his friendship with the Romans.
14:24 minas, to *c* the alliance with the Romans.
15: 5 I *c* to you all the tax exemptions that the
Ps(s) 89: 5 Forever will I *c* your posterity and
Is 44:26 It is I who *c* the words of my servants,
Mk 16:20 *c* the message through the signs
1Pt 5:10 glory in Christ, will himself restore, *c,*

CONFIRMED (16)

Gn 24: 7 *c* by oath the promise he then made to me,
1Sm 26: 4 who *c* Saul's arrival David himself then
1Kgs 8:26 to my father David, your servant, be *c.*
1Chr 14: 2 LORD had truly *c* him as king over Israel,
2Chr 6:17 which you made to your servant David be *c.*
Est 9:32 The command of Esther *c* these
1Mc 11:27 He *c* him in the high priesthood and in all
14:38 Demetrius *c* him in the high priesthood,
2Mc 12:25 When he had fully *c* his solemn pledge to
Ps(s) 89: 3 in heaven you have *c* your faithfulness:
Sir 44:22 The covenant with all his forebears was *c,*
Acts 14: 3 He for his part *c* the message with his
1Cor 1: 6 I bore to Christ has been so *c* among you
Heb 2: 3 it was *c* to us by those who had heard him.
7:20 This has been *c* by an oath.
9:16 that the death of the testator be *c.*

CONFIRMING (1)

Rom 3:31 On the contrary, we are *c* the law.

CONFIRMS (2)

Sir 3: 2 a mother's authority he *c* over her sons.
Is 9: 6 he *c* and sustains By judgment and justice,

CONFISCATED (2)

Tb 1:20 Afterward, all my property was *c;*
2Mc 3:13 the money must be *c* for the royal treasury.

CONFISCATION (2)

Ezr 10: 8 suffer the *c* of all his possessions,
Heb 10:34 joyfully assented to the *c* of your goods,

CONFLICT (6)

Dt 2: 5 be very careful not to come in *c* with them,
2:19 not show hostility or come in *c* with them,
2Chr 25: 8 on your own, strongly prepared for the *c;*
Jb 40:32 upon him, no need to recall any other *c!*
Ez 17:17 he shall not be saved in the *c* by Pharaoh
Dn 11:20 be destroyed, though not in *c* or in battle.

CONFLICTS (1)

Jas 4: 1 do the *c* and disputes among you originate?

CONFORM (4)

Lv 18: 3 do not *c* to their customs.
20:23 Do not *c,*
Ez 42: 6 to *c* with the foundations of the courts,
Rom 12: 2 Do not *c* yourselves to this age but be

CONFORMABLE (1)

Wis 9: 9 your eyes and what is *c* with your commands.

CONFORMABLY (1)

Ezr 7:18 silver and gold, *c* to the will of your God.

CONFORMED (2)

2Chr 34:32 *c* themselves to the covenant of God,
1Mc 1:42 the Gentiles *c* to the command of the king,

CONFORMING (1)

Wis 16:20 with all delights and *c* to every taste.

CONFORMITY (1)

Acts 26:20 to act in *c* with their change of heart.

CONFOUND (1)

Ps(s) 14: 6 You would *c* the plans of the afflicted,

CONFOUNDED (11)

Ezr 9: 6 too ashamed and *c* to raise my face to you,
Jdt 16: 5 thwarted them, by a woman's hand he *c* them.
Ps(s) 35: 4 turned back and *c* who plot evil against me.
35:26 shame and *c* who are glad at my misfortune.
70: 3 be put to shame and *c* who seek my life.
83:18 let them be *c* and perish,
Jer 8: 9 The wise are *c,*
17:18 Let my persecutors, not me, be *c;*
22:22 and *c* because of all your wickedness.
50: 2 Babylon is taken, Bel *c,*
Mi 3: 7 seers be put to shame, and the diviners *c;*

CONFRONT (10)

Jgs 7:24 of Ephraim to say, "Go down to *c* Midian,
2Kgs 23:29 King Josiah set out to *c* him,
Ps(s) 17:13 Rise, O LORD, *c* them and cast them down;
Wis 5: 1 one with great assurance *c* his oppressors
5:23 shall *c* them and a tempest winnow them out;
12:14 *c* you on behalf of those you have punished.
Is 40:18 With what equal can you *c* him?
44: 7 speak, make it evident, and *c* me with it.
50: 8 Let him *c* me.
Dn 11:30 When ships of the Kittim *c* him,

CONFRONTED (4)

2Sm 14: 7 the whole clan *c* your servant and demanded:
1Kgs 21:13 came in and *c* him with the accusation,
Acts 6:12 All together they *c* him,
25:16 he had been *c* with his accusers

CONFRONTS (1)

Ps(s) 34:17 The LORD *c* the evildoers,

CONFUSE (1)

Gn 11: 7 us then go down and there *c* their language,

CONFUSED (7)

Gn 11: 9 the LORD *c* the speech of all the world.
1Sm 14:20 the fight, where the Philistines, wholly *c,*
Lk 1:51 has *c* the proud in their inmost thoughts.
Acts 2: 6 They were much *c* because each one heard
Gal 1: 7 alter the gospel of Christ must have *c* you.
2Thes 3: 2 we may be delivered from *c* and evil men.
Jude 1:22 Correct those who are *c;*

CONFUSION (25)

Jgs 20:41 the men of Benjamin were thrown into *c,*
1Sm 7:10 such *c* that they were defeated by Israel.
Neh 4: 2 Jerusalem and thus to throw us into *c.*
Est A: 4 thunder and earthquake *c* upon the earth.
A: 7 Tribulation and distress, evil and great *c,*
3:15 but the city of Susa was thrown into *c.*
2Mc 4:41 them in wild *c* at Lysimachus and his men.
10:30 and blinded, thrown into *c* and routed.
13:16 having filled the camp with terror and *c.*
Ps(s) 40:15 and *c* who seek to snatch away my life.
74:21 May the humble not retire in *c;*
86:17 that my enemies may see, to their *c,*
Wis 14:25 And all is *c*— blood and murder,
Is 22: 5 It is a day of panic, rout and *c,*
Jer 7:19 it not rather themselves, to their own *c?*
20:11 utter shame, to lasting, unforgettable *c.*
51:51 we have heard taunts, *c* covers our faces;
Bar 6:25 who worship them are put to *c* because,
Ez 16:63 you may remember and be covered with *c,*
Dn 5: 9 ashen, and his lords were thrown into *c.*
Mi 7: 4 now is the time of your *c.*
Lk 13:17 words, his opponents were covered with *c;*
Acts 12:18 daybreak, *c* broke out among the soldiers,
19:29 Before long, *c* spread throughout the city.
1Cor 14:33 control, since God is a God, not of *c,*

CONFUTE (1)

Jb 24:25 If this be not so, who will *c* me,

CONGEALED (2)

Ex 15: 8 the flood waters *c* in the midst of the sea.
Jb 37:10 the frost, and the broad waters become *c.*

CONGRATULATE (3)

2Sm 8:10 greet him and to *c* him for his victory
1Chr 18:10 to *c* him on having waged a victorious war
Jdt 15: 8 done for Israel, and to meet and *c* Judith.

CONGRATULATES (1)

Rom 4: 6 Thus David *c* the man to whom God credits

CONGREGATION (10)

Nm 16: 3 you set yourselves over the LORD's *c?"*
1Mc 4:59 brothers and the entire *c* of Israel decreed
Sir 50:20 raise his hands over all the *c* of Israel.
Jl 2:16 Gather the people, notify the *c;*
Lk 13:14 have healed on the sabbath, said to the *c.*
Acts 13:43 When the *c* finally broke up,
14:27 they called the *c* together and related all
18:22 he went up and paid his respects to the *c,*
Rom 16: 5 me also to the *c* that meets in their house.
Phil 4:15 not a single *c* except yourselves shared

CONGREGATIONS (1)

Acts 16: 5 the *c* grew stronger in faith and daily

CONIAH (3)

Jer 22:24 As I live, says the LORD, if you, *C,*
22:28 Is this man *C* a vessel despised,
37: 1 *C,* son of Jehoiakim,

CONJUGAL (3)

Ex 21:10 her food, her clothing, or her *c* rights.
Sir 40:20 the soul, but better than either, *c* love.
1Cor 7: 3 fulfill his *c* obligations toward his wife,

CONJURE (3)

1Sm 28: 8 *c* up for me the one I ask you to."
28:11 asked him, "Whom do you want me to *c* up?"
Is 30:10 speak flatteries to us, *c* up illusions.

CONJURING (1)

1Sm 28:15 Saul, "Why do you disturb me by *c* me up?"

CONNECT (1)

Is 5: 8 join house to house who *c* field with field,

CONNECTED (2)

Nm 4:32 of them all the objects *c* with his service,
18: 4 of all the work *c* with the meeting tent.

CONNECTION (1)

1Mc 13:15 in *c* with the offices that he held.

CONNIVANCE (2)

2Mc 4:39 in the city with the *c* of Menelaus.
Acts 5: 2 With the *c* of his wife he put aside a part

CONNIVE (1)

Lv 20: 4 Even if his fellow citizens *c* at such a

CONQUER (14)

Jos 17:12 the Manassehites could not *c* these cities,
2Kgs 13:17 You will completely *c* Aram at Aphec."
16: 5 besieged Ahaz, they were unable to *c* him.
Jdt 5:20 then we shall be able to go up and *c* them.
2Mc 10:24 appeared in Judea, ready to *c* it by force.
Ps(s) 44: 4 with their own sword did they *c* the land,
Is 7: 1 Jerusalem, but they were not able to *c* it.
Dn 11: 7 of the king of the north, and *c* them.
Am 9:12 That they may *c* what is left of Edom and
Rom 12:21 be conquered by evil but *c* evil with good.
Rv 6: 2 He rode forth victorious, to *c* yet again.
11: 7 wage war against them and *c* and kill them.
13: 7 wage war against God's people and *c* them.
17:14 against the Lamb but the Lamb will *c* them,

CONQUERED (26)

Nm 24:24 When they have *c* Asshur and conquered Eber,
Jos 10:40 Joshua *c* the entire country;
10:41 Joshua *c* from Kadesh-barnea to Gaza,
12: 1 Israelites *c* and whose lands they occupied,
12: 6 of the LORD, and the Israelites *c* them,
12: 7 *c* west of the Jordan and whose land,
13: 1 part of the land still remains to be *c*.
13:12 Moses *c* and occupied these territories,
21:43 Once they had *c* and occupied it,
2Sm 8: 1 David attacked the Philistines and *c* them,
8:11 he had taken from every nation he had *c*;
1Kgs 11:15 Earlier, when David had *c* Edom,
2Kgs 14:10 You have indeed *c* Edom,
2Chr 8: 3 Solomon went to Hamath of Zoba and *c* it.
14:13 Judahites *c* all the cities around Gerar,
27: 5 with the king of the Ammonites and *c* them.
1Mc 1: 4 a very strong army and *c* provinces,
8: 4 and persistence had *c* the whole country,
8:12 They had *c* kings both far and near,
Rom 12:21 be *c* by evil but conquer evil with good.
Heb 11:33 and the prophets, who by faith *c* kingdoms,
1Jn 2:13 I address you, for you have *c* the evil one.
2:14 in you, and you have *c* the evil one.
4: 4 and thus you have *c* the false prophets.
5: 4 that has *c* the world is the faith of ours.

CONQUERING (4)

1Mc 8: 2 *c* them and forcing them to pay tribute.
Wis 10:20 name and praised in unison your *c* hand
Is 18: 2 near and far, a nation strong and *c*,
18: 7 near and far, a nation strong and *c*,

CONQUEROR (4)

1Chr 1:10 who was the first to be a *c* on the earth.
Jer 31:11 he shall redeem him from the hand of his *c*.
Mi 1:15 Yet must I bring to you the *c*,
1Jn 5: 5 Who, then, is *c* of the world?

CONQUERORS (1)

Rom 8:37 than *c* because of him who has loved us.

CONQUERS (2)

Hb 1:10 at any fortress, heaps up a ramp, and *c* it.
1Jn 5: 4 Everyone begotten of God *c* the world,

CONQUEST (4)

Dt 6: 1 land into which you are crossing for *c*,
11:11 land into which you are crossing for *c*
2Chr 25:14 When Amaziah returned from his *c* of the
Acts 7:45 brought it into the land during the *c*

CONSCIENCE (39)

1Sm 25:31 have this as a qualm or burden on your *c*,
1Kgs 8:38 of *c* and offers some prayer or petition,
Wis 17:11 and because of a distressed *c*,
Sir 14: 2 the man whose *c* does not reproach him,
37:14 A man's *c* can tell him his situation
Dn 13:56 has seduced you, lust has subverted your *c*.
Acts 20:26 day that I take the blame for no man's *c*,
23: 1 lived my life with a clear *c* before God."
24:16 to keep my *c* clear before God and man.
Rom 1:31 One sees in them men without *c*,
2:15 *c* bears witness together with that law,
9: 1 My *c* bears me witness in the Holy Spirit
13: 5 to escape punishment but also for *c*' sake.
14: 5 Each should be certain of his own *c*.
14:20 a man to eat when the food offends his *c*.
14:22 Happy the man whose *c* does not condemn
14:23 when his *c* has misgivings about eating,
1Cor 4: 4 Mind you, I have nothing on my *c*.
8: 7 sacrificed, and because their *c* is weak,
8:10 may not his *c* in its weak state be
10:25 market without raising any question of *c*.
10:27 you, without raising any question of *c*.
10:28 to it and on account of the *c* issue
10:29 not your own *c* but your neighbor's.
10:29 liberty be restricted by another man's *c*?
2Cor 1:12 *C* gives testimony to the boast that in our
4: 2 ourselves to every man's *c* before God.
Phil 1:10 so that with a clear *c* and blameless
1Tm 1: 5 that springs from a pure heart, a good *c*,
1:19 fight and hold fast to faith and a good *c*.
1:19 Some men, by rejecting the guidance of *c*,
3: 9 the divinely revealed faith with a clear *c*.
2Tm 1: 3 forefathers whom I worship with a clear *c*,
Heb 9: 9 never make perfect the *c* of the worshiper,
10: 2 cleansed, would have had no sin on their *c*.
10:22 our *c* and our bodies washed in pure water.
13:18 we are confident that we have a good *c*,
1Pt 3:16 Keep your *c* clear,
3:21 *c* through the resurrection of Jesus Christ.

CONSCIENCES (8)

Dn 13: 9 They suppressed their *c*;
1Cor 8:12 your brothers and wound their weak *c*,
2Cor 5:11 that it is also known to you in your *c*.
1Tm 4: 2 men with seared *c* who forbid marriage and
Ti 1:15 Their very minds and *c* are tainted.
Heb 9:14 cleanse our *c* from dead works to worship
1Jn 3:20 no matter what our *c* may charge us with;
3:21 if our *c* have nothing to charge us with,

CONSCIENTIOUS (1)

Jos 14: 7 and I brought back to him a *c* report.

CONSCIOUS (2)

Mk 5:30 Jesus was *c* at once that healing power had
2Cor 2:17 *c* of having been sent by God and of

CONSCRIPTED (3)

1Kgs 5:27 *c* thirty thousand workmen from all Israel.
9:21 accomplish, Solomon *c* as forced laborers,
2Chr 2: 1 He *c* seventy thousand men to carry stone

CONSECRATE (15)

Ex 13: 2 *C* to me every first-born that opens the
29:36 you shall anoint it in order to *c* it.
29:44 I will *c* the meeting tent and the altar,
29:44 also *c* Aaron and his sons to be my priests.
30:30 you shall also anoint and *c* as my priests.
40:11 the laver with its base, and thus *c* it.
Lv 22: 2 offerings which the Israelites *c* to me;
22: 3 which the Israelites *c* to the LORD,
Nm 18:29 *c* to the LORD your own full contribution.
Dt 15:19 "You shall *c* to the LORD,
2Chr 2: 3 of the LORD, my God, and to *c* it to him,
13: 9 Everyone who comes to *c* himself with a
30:17 and therefore could not *c* them to the LORD.
Jn 17:17 *C* them by means of truth
17:19 I *c* myself for their sakes now,

CONSECRATED (62)

Ex 30:29 When you have *c* them,
Lv 8:10 oil, Moses anointed and *c* the Dwelling,
8:15 out the blood at its base when he *c* it.
21: 8 because I, the LORD, who have *c* him,
22: 9 I am the LORD who have *c* them.
Nm 7: 1 anointed and *c* it with all its equipment
8:17 I *c* them to myself on the day I slew all
17: 3 *c* the censers at the cost of their lives.
Jgs 13: 5 this boy is to be *c* to God from the womb.
13: 7 the boy shall be *c* to God from the womb,
16:17 I have been *c* to God from my mother's womb.
17: 4 I have *c* the silver to the LORD as my gift
17: 5 and household idols, and *c* one of his sons,
17:12 Micah *c* the young Levite,
1Sm 21: 6 I go on a journey, all the young men are *c*—
21: 6 the more so today, when they are *c* at arms!"
2Sm 8:11 These, too, King David *c* to the LORD,
1Kgs 8:64 On that day the king *c* the middle of the
9: 3 I have *c* this temple which you have built;
9: 7 repudiate the temple I have *c* to my honor.
13:33 *c* and became a priest of the high places.
1Chr 18:11 These also King David *c* to the LORD along
23:13 Aaron was set apart to be *c* as most holy,
26:28 son of Zeruiah, and all others had *c*,
2Chr 7: 7 Then Solomon *c* the middle part of the
7:16 And now I have chosen and *c* this house
7:20 this house which I have *c* to my honor,
26:18 of Aaron, who have been *c* for this purpose.
29:17 they *c* the LORD's house during eight days,
29:19 of his apostasy, we have restored and *c*,
29:33 As *c* gifts there were six hundred oxen and
30: 8 to his sanctuary that he has *c* forever,
31: 6 and things that had been *c* to the LORD,
31:12 tithes and *c* things were deposited there
31:14 the LORD and the most holy of the *c* things.
31:18 by sharing faithfully in the *c* things.
35: 3 all Israel, and who were *c* to the LORD:
36:14 LORD's temple which he had *c* in Jerusalem.
Ezr 8:28 *c* to the LORD, and the utensils are also *c*;
Neh 12:47 They made their *c* offering to the Levites,
Tb 1: 4 built and *c* for all generations to come.
Jdt 6:19 this day on those who are *c* to you."
1Mc 5: 1 been rebuilt and the sanctuary *c* as before,
2Mc 15:18 and foremost fear was for the *c* sanctuary.
Sir 46:13 mother's womb, *C* to the LORD as a prophet,
Ez 48:11 The *c* priests,
Hos 9:10 to Baal-peor and *c* themselves to the Shame,
Zep 1: 7 a slaughter feast, he has *c* his guests.
Lk 2:23 first-born male shall be *c* to the Lord."
Jn 10:36 whom the Father *c* and sent into the world,
17:19 sakes now, that they may be *c* in truth.
Acts 20:32 you a share among all who are *c* to him.
Rom 11:16 If the first fruits are *c*,
11:16 whole mass of dough, and if the root is *c*,
15:16 a pleasing sacrifice, *c* by the Holy Spirit.
1Cor 1: 2 to you who have been *c* in Christ Jesus and
6:11 but you have been washed, *c*,
7:14 husband is *c* by his believing wife;
7:14 wife is *c* by her believing husband.
Heb 2:11 who are *c* have one and the same Father.
1Pt 1: 2 *c* by the Spirit to a life of obedience to

CONSECRATES (1)

Heb 2:11 He who *c* and those who are consecrated

CONSECRATING (10)

Ex 28:38 may incur in *c* any of their sacred gifts,
28:41 and ordain them, *c* them as my priests.
29: 1 you shall perform in *c* them as my priests.
29:37 making atonement for the altar and in *c* it.
40: 9 in it, *c* it and all its furnishings,
40:10 holocausts and all its appurtenances, *c* it,
40:13 and anoint him, thus *c* him as my priest.
Lv 8:11 and the laver, with its base, thus *c* them.
8:12 anointing oil on Aaron's head, thus *c* him.
8:30 thus *c* both Aaron and his vestments and

CONSECRATION (3)

Ex 29:33 was made at their ordination and *c*;
2Chr 29:17 of *c* on the first day of the first month,
2Cor 7: 1 of God strive to fulfill our *c* perfectly.

CONSENT (12)

Dt 29:19 the LORD will never *c* to pardon him.
Jgs 11:17 But the king of Edom did not give *c*.
2Sm 14:16 For the king must surely *c* to free his
1Mc 14:44 an assembly in the country without his *c*,
2Mc 6: 9 not *c* to adopt the customs of the Greeks.
Jb 39: 9 Will the wild ox *c* to serve you,
Jer 44:19 was it without our husband's *c* that we
Mt 10:29 to the ground without your Father's *c*.
Acts 12:20 by common *c* came before him in his court.
23:21 are all ready now, waiting only for your *c*."
1Cor 7: 5 unless perhaps by mutual *c* for a time,
Phlm 1:14 not want to do anything without your *c*,

CONSENTED (1)

Jer 34:10 who entered the agreement *c* to set free

CONSENTS (1)

1Mc 2:19 of his fathers and *c* to the king's orders,

CONSEQUENCE (7)

Mt 4:24 As a *c* of this,
Jn 11:54 In *c*, Jesus no longer moved about freely
Rom 1:24 In *c*, God delivered them up in their lusts
13: 2 As a *c*, the man who opposes authority
1Cor 2: 5 As a *c*, your faith rests not on the wisdom
Gal 3:21 life, then justice would be a *c* of the law.
3:22 who believe, in *c* of faith in Jesus Christ.

CONSEQUENCES (9)

Nm 9:13 That man shall bear the *c* of his sin.
32:23 that you will not escape the *c* of your sin.
Prv 14:14 The scoundrel suffers the *c* of his ways,
Ez 7: 3 upon you the *c* of all your abominations.
7: 4 and the *c* of your abominations shall be in
7: 8 upon you the *c* of all your abominations.
7: 9 and the *c* of your abominations shall be in
44:10 idols, they shall bear the *c* of their sin.
44:12 they shall bear the *c* of their sin.

CONSEQUENTLY (3)

1Mc 14:38 *C*, King Demetrius confirmed him in the
Jn 5:10 *C*, some of the Jews began telling the man
Acts 23: 6 *C* he spoke out before the Sanhedrin:

CONSIDER (51)

Dt 1:17 judgment, do not *c* who a person is;
21:16 he may not *c* as his first-born
Jos 22:19 If you *c* the land you now possess unclean,
2Sm 24:13 Now *c* and decide what I must reply to him
1Kgs 20: 6 and take away whatever they *c* valuable.'"
2Kgs 3:18 And since the LORD does not *c* this enough,
1Chr 17:17 And yet, even this you now *c* too little,
Tb 13: 6 So now *c* what he has done for you,
1Mc 2:61 so, *c* this from generation to generation,
5:16 a great assembly convened to *c* what they
2Mc 6:12 but to *c* that these chastisements were
Jb 6:26 Do you *c* your words as proof,
13:24 do you hide your face and *c* me your enemy?
37:14 Stand and *c* the wondrous works of God!
Ps(s) 28: 5 Because they *c* not the deeds of the LORD
48:14 *C* her ramparts, examine her castles,
50:22 *C* this, you who forget God,
77: 6 I *c* the days of old;
119:15 meditate on your precepts and *c* your ways.
119:18 eyes, that I may *c* the wonders of your law.
Prv 6:35 He will not *c* any restitution,
Eccl 7:13 *C* the work of God.
7:14 enjoy good things, and on an evil day *c*:
Sir 11: 5 and some that none would *c* wear a crown.
Is 22:11 nor did you *c* him who built it long ago.
30:22 And you shall *c* unclean your silver-plated
43:18 of the past, the things of long ago *c* not;
Jer 2:23 *C* your conduct in the Valley,
Lam 2:20 "Look, O LORD, and *c*:
Am 5:22 nor *c* your stall-fed peace offerings.
Hg 1: 5 Thus says the LORD of hosts: *C* your ways!
1: 7 *C* your ways!
2:15 now, *c* from this day forward.
2:18 *C* from this day forward:
2:18 the temple of the LORD was founded, *c*
Lk 12:24 *C* the ravens:

14:31 will he not sit down first and *c* whether,
Rom 6:11 you must *c* yourselves dead to sin but
8:18 I *c* the sufferings of the present to be as
11:22 *C* the kindness and the severity of God
1Cor 1:26 *C* your situation.
12:23 We honor the members we *c* less honorable
2Cor 11: 5 I *c* myself inferior to the
Gal 3: 6 *C* the case of Abraham:
Phil 3: 7 But those things I used to *c* gain I have
Heb 10:24 We must *c* how to rouse
13: 7 *c* how their lives ended,
2Pt 1:13 I *c* it my duty,
3: 9 though some *c* it "delay."
3:15 *C* that our Lord's patience is directed
1Jn 2:29 If you *c* the holiness that is his,

CONSIDERABLE (6)

Dt 20:15 with any city at a *c* distance from you,
2Mc 10:27 and advanced a *c* distance from the city,
Lk 7:12 A *c* crowd of townsfolk were with her.
23: 9 He questioned Jesus at *c* length,
Acts 9:43 Joppa for a *c* time at the house of Simon,
14: 3 *c* time there and spoke out fearlessly,

CONSIDERATE (1)

Sir 3:13 Even if his mind fail, be *c* with him;

CONSIDERATION (6)

Neh 6:12 For on *c* it was plain to me that God had
2Mc 14: 8 secondly, out of *c* for my own countrymen,
14: 9 same gracious *c* that you show toward all.
Eccl 2:12 I went on to the *c* of wisdom,
2Cor 1:23 it was out of *c* for you that I did not come
1Pt 3: 7 must show *c* for those who share your lives.

CONSIDERED (26)

Lv 7:18 rather, it shall be *c* as refuse
25:31 *c* as belonging to the surrounding farm land;
Dt 2:11 like them they were *c* Rephaim.
2:20 [This also was *c* a country of the Rephaim
1Kgs 1:21 I and my son Solomon will be *c* criminals."
10:21 for in Solomon's time it was *c* worthless.
2Chr 9:20 was not *c* of value in Solomon's time.
2Mc 11:36 As soon as you have *c* them,
Ps(s) 73:17 sanctuary of God and *c* their final destiny.
106: 7 Our fathers in Egypt *c* not your wonders;
119:59 I *c* my ways and turned my feet to your
Prv 17:28 Even a fool, if he keeps silent, is *c* wise;
Eccl 3:10 I have *c* the task which God has appointed
4: 1 Again I *c* all the oppressions that take
8: 9 All these things I *c* and I applied my mind
Wis 1:16 and words invited death, *c* it a friend,
13: 2 the governors of the world, they *c* gods.
Sir 21:17 an assembly, and his words are *c* with care.
Is 32: 5 noble, nor the trickster be *c* honorable.
Ez 7:19 streets, and their gold shall be *c* refuse.
36: 5 joy and utter contempt have *c* my land
Hos 8:12 ordinances, they are *c* as a stranger's.
9:10 fig tree in its prime, I *c* your fathers.
Rom 2:26 of the law, will he not be *c* circumcised?
9: 8 of the promise who are to be *c* descendants.
Heb 11:26 Moses *c* the reproach borne by God's

CONSIDERING (3)

Dt 14:24 for you, *c* how the LORD has blessed you,
Jb 32: 2 He was angry with Job for *c* himself rather
Dn 7: 8 I was *c* the ten horns it had,

CONSIDERS (4)

Est E: 7 but more fully when one *c* the wicked deeds
Sir 29: 6 barely half, he *c* this an achievement;
Rom 14: 5 someone else *c* all days alike.
1Cor 1:27 whom the world *c* absurd to shame the wise;

CONSIGNED (10)

2Kgs 22: 5 They were to be *c* to the master workmen in
22: 7 of them regarding the funds *c* to them,
22: 9 have *c* them to the master workmen
Ezr 5:14 in Babylon and *c* to a certain Sheshbazzar,
7:19 The utensils *c* to you for the service of
8:26 I *c* it to them in these amounts:
8:33 of our God and *c* to the priest Meremoth,
Est 6: 9 The robe and the horse should be *c* to one
Is 38:10 I shall be *c* for the rest of my years."
2Pt 2: 4 in Tartarus *c* them to pits of darkness,

CONSIST (7)

Lv 2: 1 LORD, his offering must *c* of fine flour.
Nm 8:26 Levites shall *c* in sharing their responsibilities
28:19 to the LORD, which shall *c* of two bullocks,
Dt 6:25 is to *c* in carefully observing all these
Jdt 5: 3 In what does their power and strength *c*?
Ez 46: 4 shall *c* of six unblemished lambs
1Cor 4:20 of God does not *c* in talk but in power.

CONSISTED (13)

Nm 7: 3 *c* of six baggage wagons and twelve oxen,
7:13 His offering *c* of one silver plate
7:25 His offering *c* of one silver plate
7:31 His offering *c* of one silver plate
7:37 His offering *c* of one silver plate
7:43 His offering *c* of one silver plate
7:49 His offering *c* of one silver plate
7:55 His offering *c* of one silver plate
7:61 His offering *c* of one silver plate
7:67 His offering *c* of one silver plate
7:73 His offering *c* of one silver plate
7:79 His offering *c* of one silver plate
Neh 8: 2 law before the assembly, which *c* of men,

CONSISTENT (2)

Sir 5:12 Be *c* in your thoughts;
Ti 2: 1 your speech be *c* with your sound doctrine.

CONSISTING (3)

Nm 15: 4 *c* of a tenth of an ephah of fine flour mixed
15:20 *c* of a cake of your first batch of dough.
Jos 22:13 land of Gilead an embassy *c* of Phinehas,

CONSISTS (3)

Lv 14:37 *c* of greenish or reddish depressions
1Jn 4:10 Love, then, *c* in this:
5: 3 The love of God *c* in this:

CONSOLATION (18)

Gn 37:35 tried to console him, he refused all *c*,
Jb 6:10 *c* and could exult through unremitting pain,
21: 2 my words, and let that be the *c* you offer.
Jer 16: 7 they will not give them the cup of *c* to drink
Lk 2:25 and pious, and awaited the *c* of Israel,
6:24 "But woe to you rich, for your *c* is now.
16:25 Now he has found *c* here,
Acts 9:31 enjoyed the increased *c* of the Holy Spirit.
1Cor 14: 3 upbuilding, their encouragement, their *c*.
2Cor 1: 3 Father of mercies, and the God of all *c*!
1: 4 with the same *c* we have received from him.
1: 5 Christ do we share abundantly in his *c*.
1: 6 and when we are consoled it is for your *c*,
1: 7 sufferings, so you will share in the *c*.
7: 4 I am filled with *c*,
7:13 Beyond this *c*,
Eph 6:22 you news about me for your hearts' *c*.
2Thes 2:16 in his mercy gave us eternal *c* and hope,

CONSOLATIONS (1)

Jb 15:11 Are the *c* of God not enough for you,

CONSOLE (16)

Gn 37:35 his sons and daughters tried to *c* him,
2Sm 3:35 *c* David with food while it was still day.
Jer 15: 5 will pity you, Jerusalem, who will *c* you?
16: 7 bereaved to *c* them in their bereavement;
31: 9 in tears, but I will *c* them and guide them;
31:13 *c* and gladden them after their sorrows.
Lam 1: 2 With not one to *c* her of all her dear ones;
1: 9 is her downfall, with no one to *c* her.
1:16 Far from me are all who could *c* me,
1:17 her hands, but there was no one to *c* her;
1:21 there is no one to *c* me.
Ez 14:23 They shall *c* you when you see their
Na 3: 7 Where can one find any to *c* her?"
Jn 11:19 to *c* Martha and Mary over their brother.
1Thes 4:17 *C* one another with this message.
2Thes 2:17 *c* your hearts and strengthen them for

CONSOLED (8)

Sir 48:24 into the future and *c* the mourners of Zion;
Is 12: 1 your anger has abated, and you have *c* me.
Jer 31:15 to be *c* because her children are no more.
Ez 14:22 be *c* regarding the evil I have brought on
31:16 the land below, all Eden's trees were *c*,
Mt 5: 4 they shall be *c*.
2Cor 1: 6 when we are *c* it is for your consolation,
1Thes 3: 7 we have been much *c* by your faith

CONSOLERS (1)

1Chr 19: 3 sending you these *c*—

CONSOLIDATED (3)

2Chr 12: 1 had *c* his rule and had become powerful,
12:13 King Rehoboam *c* his power in Jerusalem and
21: 4 his father's kingdom and had *c* his power,

CONSOLING (2)

Ru 2:13 me, your servant, with your *c* words;
Jn 11:31 *c* her saw her get up quickly and go out,

CONSORT (8)

Gn 30: 4 she gave him her maidservant Bilhah as a *c*,
30: 9 her maidservant Zilpah to Jacob as a *c*.
2Kgs 17:30 the Babylonians made Marduk and his *c*;
17:31 city gods, King Hadad and his *c* Anath.
Est E:13 and of Esther, our blameless royal *c*,
Ps(s) 26: 4 worthless men, nor do I *c* with hypocrites.
Prv 23:20 *C* not with winebibbers,
Hos 4:14 You yourselves *c* with harlots,

CONSORTING (1)

Rom 7: 3 not commit adultery by *c* with another man.

CONSORTS (1)

Prv 29: 3 he who *c* with harlots squanders his wealth.

CONSPICUOUS (2)

1Mc 11:37 be displayed in a *c* place on the holy hill.'"
14:48 a *c* place in the precincts of the temple,

CONSPICUOUSLY (1)

Jos 22:10 built there at the Jordan a *c* large altar.

CONSPIRACY (11)

2Sm 15:12 So the *c* gained strength,
1Kgs 16:16 had formed a *c* and had killed the king.
16:20 acts of Zimri, with the *c* he carried out,
2Kgs 9:14 son of Nimshi, formed a *c* against Joram.
14:19 a *c* was formed against him in Jerusalem,
15:15 acts of Shallum, and the fact of his *c*,
17: 4 king of Assyria found Hoshea guilty of *c*
2Chr 23: 1 and entered a *c* with certain captains:
25:27 a *c* was formed against him in Jerusalem;
Jer 11: 9 A *c* has been found,
Acts 23:12 certain Jews formed a *c* in which they

CONSPIRATOR (1)

2Mc 14:26 appointed Judas, the *c* against the kingdom,

CONSPIRATORS (1)

2Sm 15:31 Ahithophel was among the *c* with Absalom,

CONSPIRE (5)

1Sm 22:13 "Why did you *c* against me with the son of
Ps(s) 2: 2 and the princes *c* together against the
64: 6 they *c* to set snares,
83: 4 they *c* against those whom you protect.
Acts 4:25 the Gentiles rage, the peoples *c* in folly?

CONSPIRED (15)

Nm 14:35 this wicked community that *c* against me:
1Sm 22: 8 that you have all *c* against me and no one
2Kgs 10: 9 although I *c* against my lord and slew him,
15:10 son of Jabesh, *c* against Zechariah,
15:25 him fifty men from Gilead, *c* against him,
15:30 Hoshea, son of Elah, *c* against Pekah,
21:23 Subjects of Amon *c* against him and slew
21:24 then slew all who had *c* against king Amon,
2Chr 24:21 But they *c* against him,
24:25 his servants *c* against him because of the
24:26 These *c* against him:
33:24 His servants *c* against him and put him to
33:25 slew all those who had *c* against King Amon,
Am 7:10 has *c* against you here within Israel;
Acts 9:23 has passed, certain Jews *c* to kill Saul,

CONSPIRING (1)

Nm 16:11 the LORD that you and all your band are *c*.

CONSTANCY (7)

Ps(s) 25:10 paths of the LORD are kindness and *c*
96:13 with justice and the peoples with his *c*.
Prv 14:22 those intent on good gain kindness and *c*.
Dn 9:13 from our wickedness and recognizing his *c*,
1Thes 1: 3 showing *c* of hope in our Lord Jesus Christ.
2Thes 1: 4 *c* and your faith in persecution and trial.
3: 5 in the love of God and the *c* of Christ.

CONSTANT (27)

Gn 24:27 let his *c* kindness toward my master fail.
47:29 my thigh as a sign of your *c* loyalty to me;
Ex 28:29 his heart as a *c* reminder before the LORD.
Dt 28:32 on and grieve for them in *c* helplessness.
28:59 your descendants with severe and *c* blows,
28:66 You will live in *c* suspense and stand in
1Sm 1: 6 turned it into a *c* reproach to her that
1Kgs 14:30 *c* warfare between Rehoboam and Jeroboam.
1Chr 9:26 the four chief gatekeepers were on *c* duty.
Est B: 3 for *c* devotion and steadfast loyalty,
E:13 of Mordecai, our savior and *c* benefactor,
Ps(s) 31:24 The LORD keeps those who are *c*,
69:14 great kindness answer me with your *c* help.
71: 6 *c* has been my hope in you.
Wis 7: 4 clothes and with *c* care I was nurtured.
Sir 6:37 let his commandments be your *c* meditation;
30:17 bitter life, unending sleep to *c* illness.
42: 5 Of *c* training of children,
51:11 your name and be *c* in my prayers to you.
Is 51:13 in *c* dread of the fury of the oppressor;
Acts 1:14 they devoted themselves to *c* prayer.
9:36 marked by *c* good deeds and acts of charity.
27:33 fourteen days you have been in *c* suspense;
Rom 9: 2 is great grief and *c* pain in my heart.
1Thes 5:18 never cease praying, render *c* thanks;
Ti 2:10 expressing a *c* fidelity by their conduct,
1Pt 4: 8 all, let your love for one another be *c*,

CONSTANTLY (38)

Ex 9:24 and lightning c flashed through the hail,
1Sm 8: 8 As they have treated me c from the day I
1Chr 16:11 seek to serve him c.
2Chr 1: 1 was with him, c making him more renowned.
1Mc 11:41 for they were c hostile to Israel.
Jb 27:10 in the Almighty and call upon him c?
Ps(s) 105: 4 seek to serve him c.
119:109 Though c I take my life in my hands,
Sir 20:23 man, yet it is c on the lips of the unruly.
23:10 c under scrutiny will not be without welts,
Is 21: 8 watchtower, O my Lord, I stand c by day;
52: 5 all the day my name is c reviled.
60:11 Your gates shall stand open c;
Jer 11: 7 c I warned your fathers to obey my voice,
26: 5 I send you c though you do not obey them,
Dn 6:17 said, "May your God, whom you serve so c,
6:21 so c been able to save you from the lions?"
Mt 18:10 heaven c behold my heavenly Father's face.
Mk 13: 9 Be c on your guard.
13:23 So be c on guard!
13:33 Be c on the watch!
Lk 2:37 She was c in the temple,
21:36 Pray c for the strength to escape whatever
24:53 they were to be found in the temple c,
Acts 10: 2 to the people and he c prayed to God.
Rom 1: 9 witness that I c mention you in prayer,
2Cor 4:11 c being delivered to death for Jesus' sake,
Eph 6:18 Pray c and attentively for all in the holy
Phil 1: 4 which is c,
1Thes 1: 3 for we c are mindful before our God and
2:13 That is why we thank God c that in
3: 6 and telling us that you c remember us and
2Tm 1: 3 as indeed I do c,
4: 2 c teaching and never losing patience.
Heb 9: 6 used to go into the outer tabernacle c,
1Pt 1:22 love one another c from the heart.
2Pt 1:12 I intend to recall these things to you c,
2:14 C on the lookout for a woman,

CONSTELLATION (1)

Wis 7:29 the sun and surpasses every c of the stars.

CONSTELLATIONS (2)

Jb 9: 9 Orion, the Pleiades and the c of the south;
Is 13:10 and c of the heavens send forth no light;

CONSTERNATION (2)

Jdt 14:19 rent their tunics and were seized with c.
Ez 7: 7 a time of c, not of rejoicing.

CONSTITUTED (1)

2Chr 11:22 Rehoboam c Abijah,

CONSTITUTES (1)

Mk 7:15 out of him, and only that, c impurity.

CONSTRAINT (5)

Est C:27 You know that I am under c,
1Cor 7:37 who while without c and free to carry out
Gal 3:22 locked all things in under the c of sin.
3:23 faith came we were under the c of the law,
1Pt 5: 2 as God would have you do, not under c;

CONSTRUCT (1)

Mk 14:58 I will c another not made by human hands.' "

CONSTRUCTED (14)

Nm 21:27 rebuilt, let Sihon's capital be firmly c.
1Kgs 7:28 When these stands were c,
7:33 The wheels were c like chariot wheels;
2Chr 31:11 chambers be c in the house of the LORD.
1Mc 6:20 purpose he c catapults and other devices.
6:31 they c siege-devices,
Ps(s) 104: 3 you have c your palace upon the waters.
Eccl 2: 6 And I c for myself reservoirs to water a
Sir 22:16 Neither is a resolve c with careful
Ez 1:16 c as though one wheel were within another.
Acts 7:47 however, who c the building for that house.
1Cor 12:24 God has so c the body as to give greater
Heb 9: 2 For a tabernacle was c,
Rv 21:18 The wall was c of jasper;

CONSTRUCTING (1)

1Mc 9:64 camp before Bethbasi, and c siege-machines,

CONSTRUCTION (10)

Ex 35:21 to the LORD for the c of the meeting tent,
38:24 gold used in the entire c of the sanctuary,
1Kgs 6: 1 the c of the temple of the LORD was begun.
6: 7 was to be heard in the temple during its c.)
7: 1 completed after thirteen years of c.
7: 8 deeper than the tribunal and of the same c.
2Kgs 16:10 the altar and a detailed design of its c.
20:20 and his c of the pool and conduit by which
2Chr 27: 3 and had much c done on the wall of Ophel.
2Mc 4:20 those who brought it, to the c of triremes.

CONSTRUCTIVE (2)

1Cor 10:23 which does not mean that everything is c.
14:26 as as everything is done with a c purpose.

CONSUL (2)

1Mc 15:16 "Lucius, C of the Romans,
15:22 c sent similar letters to Kings Demetrius,

CONSULT (28)

Gn 25:22 She went to c the LORD,
Ex 18:15 "The people come to me to c God.
33: 7 Anyone who wished to c the LORD would go
Lv 19:31 not go to the mediums or c fortune tellers,
Jgs 18: 5 They said to him, C God,
1Sm 9: 9 anyone who went to c God used to say,
14:36 But the priest said, "Let us c God."
1Kgs 14: 5 wife is coming to c you about her son,
22: 7 prophet of the LORD here whom we may c?"
22: 8 one other through whom we might c the LORD,
2Kgs 8: 8 Have him c the LORD as to whether I shall
22:13 "Go, c the LORD for me,
22:18 king of Judah who sent you to c the LORD,
2Chr 17: 3 the beginning, and he did not c the Baals.
18: 6 prophet of the LORD here whom we may c?"
18: 7 another through whom we may c the LORD,
20: 3 frightened, and he hastened to c the LORD.
34:21 c the LORD concerning the words of the
34:26 king of Judah who sent you to c the LORD,
Ps(s) 31:14 every side, as they c together against me,
83: 6 Yes, they c together with one mind,
Is 19: 3 They shall c idols and charmers,
40:14 Whom did he c to gain knowledge?
Jer 37: 7 king of Judah who sent you to me to c me:
Ez 14: 7 him, yet asks a prophet to c me for him,
20: 1 came to c the LORD and sat down before me.
20: 3 Have you come to c me?
Hos 4:12 They c their piece of wood,

CONSULTATION (5)

2Kgs 16:15 the old bronze altar shall be mine for c."
23:24 did away with the c of ghosts and spirits,
Est 1:13 in general c with lawyers and jurists.
Mt 27: 7 After c, they used it to buy the potter's
Acts 4:15 them out of the court while they held a c.

CONSULTATIONS (1)

Is 47:13 You wearied yourself with many c,

CONSULTED (21)

Jgs 1: 1 death of Joshua the Israelites c the LORD,
20:18 for battle, moved on to Bethel and c God.
20:27 When the Israelites c the LORD (for the
1Sm 10:22 Again they c the LORD,
22:10 c the LORD for him and gave him supplies,
22:15 this the first time I have c God for him?
23: 2 So he c the LORD,
23: 4 Again David c the LORD,
28: 6 He therefore c the LORD;
1Kgs 12: 6 King Rehoboam c the elders who had been in
12: 8 and c the young men who had grown up with
2Chr 1: 5 There Solomon and the assembly c the LORD,
10: 6 King Rehoboam c the elders who had been in
10: 8 c the young men who had grown up
Est B: 3 When I c my counselors as to how this
1Mc 3:48 the Gentiles c the images of their idols.
Jer 8: 2 loved and served, which they followed, c,
Ez 14: 3 Why should I allow myself to be c by them?
20: 3 I will not allow myself to be c by you,
20:31 Shall I let myself be c by you,
20:31 I swear I will not let myself be c by you.

CONSULTING (3)

1Sm 22:13 him food and a sword and by c God for him,
2Kgs 21: 6 reintroduced the c of ghosts and spirits.
2Chr 20:21 After c with the people,

CONSULTS (2)

Dt 18:11 nor one who c ghosts and spirits or seeks
1Sm 20:10 David C Jonathan[Jonathan replied to David,

CONSUME (38)

Ex 15: 7 you loosed your wrath to c them like
32:10 wrath may blaze up against them to c them.
Lv 26:16 in vain, for your enemies will c the crop.
Nm 16:21 from this band, that I may c them at once."
17:10 this community, that I may c them at once."
Dt 5:25 Surely this great fire will c us.
7:16 shall c all the nations which the LORD,
12:23 not c this seat of life with the flesh.
28:33 A people whom you do not know will c the
28:51 They will c the offspring of your
2Kgs 1:10 from heaven and c you and your fifty men."
1:12 from heaven and c you and your fifty men."
Jdt 11:12 and determined to c all the things which
Jb 15:34 and fire shall c the tents of extortioners.
20:26 which shall c him needs not to be fanned.
Ps(s) 21:10 May the LORD c them in his anger;
59:14 C them in wrath; consume,
Eccl 10:12 mouth win favor, but the fool's lips c him.
Wis 16:19 so as to c the produce of the wicked land.
Sir 6: 2 lest, like fire, it c your strength;
27:29 and pain will c them before they die;
36: 8 Let raging fire c the fugitive,
Is 1:20 refuse and resist, the sword shall c you:
26:11 the fire prepared for your enemies c them.
33:11 my spirit shall c you like fire.
43: 2 the flames shall not c you.
Jer 17:27 which will c the palaces of Jerusalem.
Bar 6:19 of the ground c them and their garments,
Ez 21:33 burnished to c and to flash lightning,
Dn 14:13 which they always came in to c the food.
14:21 used to enter to c what was on the table.
Hos 7: 7 all heated like ovens, and c their rulers.
11: 9 I will not let the flames c you.
Am 5: 6 house of Joseph like a fire That shall c,
Na 2:14 I will c in smoke your chariots,
3:15 There the fire shall c you,
Heb 10:27 a flaming fire to c the adversaries of God.

CONSUMED (62)

Gn 41:21 But when they had c them,
Ex 3: 2 that the bush, though on fire, was not c.
Lv 9:24 LORD's presence and c the holocaust
10: 2 forth from the LORD's presence and c them,
Nm 11: 1 among them and c the outskirts of the camp.
11:33 between their teeth, before it could be c,
12:12 its mother's womb with its flesh half c."
16:35 And fire from the LORD came forth which c
21:28 It c the cities of Moab and swallowed up
26:10 when the fire c two hundred and fifty men.
Jgs 6:21 rock which c the meat and unleavened cakes,
15:14 became as flax that is c by fire
2Sm 18: 8 and the thickets c more combatants that
23: 7 of a spear, and they must be c by fire."
1Kgs 18:38 LORD's fire came down and c the holocaust,
2Kgs 1:10 from heaven and c him and his fifty men.
2Chr 7: 1 and c the holocaust and the sacrifices,
Jdt 7:22 the women and youths were c with thirst
2Mc 2:10 from the sky and c the sacrifices,
Jb 1:16 the sheep and their shepherds and c them;
4: 9 and by the blast of his wrath they are c.
11:20 wicked, looking on, shall be c with envy.
13:28 bottle, like a garment that the moth has c?
19:26 my inmost being is c with longing.
22:20 stood, and such as were left, fire has c!"
31:12 till it c all my possessions to the roots.
Ps(s) 31:10 with sorrow my eye is c;
31:11 through affliction, and my bones are c.
49:15 Quickly their form is c;
71:13 be put to shame and c who attack my life;
78:63 Fire c their young men,
90: 7 Truly we are c by your anger,
106:18 a flame c the wicked.
119:20 My soul is c with longing for your
Prv 5:11 end, when your flesh and your body are c;
21:26 Some are c with avarice all the day,
Wis 5:13 to display, but were c in our wickedness."
16:16 and unremitting downpours, and c by fire.
16:22 their enemies' fruits Were c by a fire
19:21 neither c the flesh of the perishable
Sir 8:10 sinner, lest you be c in his flaming fire.
43: 4 By its fiery darts the land is c;
45:19 miracle, and c them with his flaming fire.
Is 1:28 those who desert the LORD shall be c.
10:18 will be c, soul and body;
51: 8 eaten by moths, like wool c by grubs;
Jer 6:29 bellows roars, the lead is c by the fire;
14:18 those c by hunger.
36:23 until the entire roll was c in the fire.
44:12 shall fall by the sword or be c by hunger.
51:34 He has c me,
Lam 2: 2 c without pity all the dwellings of Jacob;
2: 5 c Israel: c all her castles
4:11 a fire in Zion that has c her foundations.
Ez 22:31 with my fiery wrath I have c them;
43: 8 therefore I c them in my wrath.
Na 1:10 like dry stubble, they shall be utterly c.
3:13 land are open wide, fire has c their bars.
Zep 1:18 of his jealousy all the earth shall be c.
3: 8 of my jealousy shall all the earth be c.
Rv 18: 8 She shall be c by fire,

CONSUMES (15)

Nm 13:32 is a country that c its inhabitants.
Jb 18:13 side, the first-born of death c his limbs.
Ps(s) 69:10 sons, Because zeal for your house c me,
97: 3 goes before him and c his foes round about.
119:139 My zeal c me,
Prv 21:20 the house of the wise, but the fool c it.
Eccl 4: 5 fool folds his arms and c his own flesh"
Is 10:17 That burns and c his briers and his thorns
44:20 cannot save itself when the flame c it;
47:14 Lo, they are like stubble, fire c them;
Jer 12:12 The LORD has a sword which c the land,
48:45 It c the brow of Moab,
Dn 14: 8 tell me who it is that c these provisions,
14: 9 But if you can show that Bel c them,
Jn 2:17 "Zeal for your house c me."

CONSUMING (17)

Ex 24:17 was seen as a *c* fire on the mountaintop.
Dt 4:24 For the LORD, your God, is a *c* fire,
9: 3 who will cross over before you as a *c* fire;
32:22 nether world, *C* the earth with its yield,
32:24 hunger and *c* fever and bitter prestilence,
1Sm 2:33 altar, to wear out their eyes in *c* greed;
2Kgs 1:12 down from heaven, *c* him and his fifty men.
1:14 *c* two captains with their companies of
Wis 6:23 shall I admit *c* jealousy to my company,
Is 29: 6 whirlwind, storm, and the flame of *c* fire.
30:27 with fury, his tongue is like a *c* fire;
30:30 In raging fury and flame of *c* fire,
33:14 "Who of us can live with the *c* fire?
Hos 11: 6 with his cities and end by *c* his solitudes.
Am 7: 4 the great abyss, and was *c* the land,
Zec 5: 4 it shall lodge within his house, *c* it,
Heb 12:29 For our God is a *c* fire.

CONSUMMATE (1)

Gn 29:21 my wife, that I may *c* my marriage with her,

CONSUMMATED (2)

Gn 29:23 Jacob, and Jacob *c* the marriage with her.
29:30 Jacob then *c* his marriage with Rachel also,

CONSUMMATES (1)

Lv 20:17 If a man *c* marriage with her sister of his

CONSUMMATION (1)

1Pt 4: 7 The *c* of all is close at hand.

CONTACT (9)

Lv 11:34 Any solid food that was in *c* with water,
22: 4 who has become unclean by *c* with a corpse,
Nm 5: 2 who has become unclean by *c* with a corpse.
19:21 and anyone who comes in *c* with this water
Jgs 18: 7 Sidonians and had no *c* with other people.
18:28 Sidon and they had no *c* with other people.
2Kgs 13:21 the man came in *c* with the bones of Elisha,
Is 33:15 Brushing his hands free of *c* with a bribe,
Hg 2:13 from *c* with a corpse touches any of these,

CONTAGIOUS (1)

Lv 22: 5 of whatever kind it may be, is *c*,

CONTAIN (4)

Dt 8: 9 a land whose stones *c* iron and in whose
1Kgs 8:27 and the highest heavens cannot *c* you,
2Chr 2: 5 and even the highest heavens cannot *c* him?
6:18 and the highest heavens cannot *c* you,

CONTAINED (9)

1Chr 20: 2 and it *c* precious stones,
2Chr 24:11 Levites and they saw that it *c* much money,
Est 9:26 because of all that was *c* in this letter,
2Mc 11:17 and asked about the matters *c* in it.
Jer 24: 2 One basket *c* excellent figs,
24: 2 But the other basket *c* very bad figs,
36:28 on it everything that the first scroll *c*,
36:32 the words *c* in the book which Jehoiakim,
2Pt 1:20 there is no prophecy *c* in Scripture which

CONTAINER (1)

Zec 5: 6 he answered, "This is a bushel *c* coming.

CONTAINERS (3)

Gn 42:25 orders to have their *c* filled with grain,
Nm 4: 9 various *c* of oil from which it is supplied.
Mt 13:48 sat down to put what was worthwhile into *c*.

CONTAINING (10)

1Sm 6:11 along with the box *c* the golden mice and
2Chr 17: 9 with them the book *c* the law of the LORD;
Ezr 6: 2 a scroll was found *c* the following text:
Neh 6: 6 who bore an unsealed letter *c* this text:
Tb 1:14 I also deposited several pouches *c* a great
1Mc 6: 2 its temple was very rich, *c* gold helmets,
2Mc 10:18 *c* everything necessary to sustain a siege,
Jer 32:11 the sealed copy, *c* title and conditions,
Ez 24: 6 Woe to the bloody city, a pot *c* rust,
Heb 9: 4 In the ark were the golden jar *c* the manna,

CONTAINS (1)

Jer 8:16 They come devouring the land and all it *c*,

CONTAMINATED (3)

Lv 11:43 swarming creature through being *c* by them.
20:25 so that you may not be *c* with the
Acts 15:20 them to abstain from anything *c* by idols,

CONTAMINATION (1)

Neh 13:30 Thus I cleansed them of all foreign *c*.

CONTEMPLATE (2)

Jb 36:25 All men *c* it; man beholds it from afar.
Ps(s) 27: 4 loveliness of the LORD and *c* his temple.

CONTEMPLATING (2)

2Mc 15:21 Maccabeus, *c* the hosts before him,
Lk 21: 6 He said, "These things you are *c*—

CONTEMPORARIES (1)

Gal 1:14 Jewish observance far beyond most of my *c*,

CONTEMPT (22)

Jgs 9:38 these not the men for whom you expressed *c*?
1Sm 17:42 handsome in appearance, he held him in *c*.
1Mc 1:39 Her sabbaths to shame, her honor to *c*.
2Mc 7:39 since he bitterly resented the boy's *c*.
12:14 besieged treated Judas and his men with *c*,
Ps(s) 107:40 But he who pours out *c* upon princes,
119:22 Take away from me reproach and *c*,
123: 3 on us, for we are more than sated with *c*;
123: 4 of the arrogant, with the *c* of the proud.
Prv 18: 3 With wickedness comes *c*,
Wis 4:18 They see, and hold him in *c*;
Sir 26:19 illustrious men held in *c*;
Ez 36: 5 with wholehearted joy and utter *c*
Ob 1: 2 you are held in dire *c*.
Mt 5:22 him in *c* he risks the fires of Gehenna.
Lk 16:15 What man thinks important, God holds in *c*.
18: 9 while holding everyone else in *c*:
23:11 guards then treated him with *c* and insult,
Rom 2:24 of God is held in *c* among the Gentiles."
1Cor 11:22 Would you show *c* for the church of God,
Heb 6: 6 God for themselves and holding him up to *c*.
2Pt 2: 2 the true way will be made subject to *c*.

CONTEMPTIBLE (2)

Ps(s) 119:141 I am mean and *c*,
Mal 2: 9 made you *c* and base before all the people,

CONTEMPTUOUS (3)

Neh 9:26 "But they were *c* and rebellious:
Sir 22:22 But a *c* insult,
Ez 35:12 I have heard all the *c* things you have

CONTEND (7)

Jb 9: 3 Should one wish to *c* with him,
23: 6 he *c* against me with his great power,
Ps(s) 127: 5 shame when they *c* with enemies at the gate.
Eccl 6:10 and that he cannot *c* in judgment with one
Sir 8: 1 *C* not with an influential man,
8:14 *C* not at law with a judge,
Mt 12:19 He will not *c* or cry out,

CONTENDED (6)

Gn 32:29 because you have *c* with divine and human
Nm 20: 3 The people *c* with Moses,
20:13 where the Israelites *c* against the LORD,
Dt 33: 8 you *c* with him at the waters of Meribah.
Hos 12: 4 his brother, and as a man he *c* with God;
12: 5 He *c* with the angel and triumphed,

CONTENDS (1)

Is 45: 9 Woe to him who *c* with his Maker;

CONTENT (12)

Jos 7: 7 *c* to dwell on the other side of the Jordan.
Ru 3: 7 Boaz ate and drank to his heart's *c*.
Jb 21:23 in his full vigor, wholly at ease and *c*;
Ps(s) 17:15 on waking, I shall be *c* in your presence.
Sir 26: 4 Be he rich or poor, his heart is *c*,
29:23 it little or much be *c* with what you have,
Dn 4: 1 was at home in my palace, *c* and prosperous.
Lk 3:14 Be *c* with your pay."
1Cor 15:14 is void of *c* and your faith is empty too.
2Cor 12:10 Therefore I am *c* with weakness,
1Tm 6: 6 provided one is *c* with a sufficiency.
Heb 13: 5 not love money but be *c* with what you have,

CONTENTED (2)

Gn 15:15 you shall be buried at a *c* old age.
Ps(s) 49:14 folly, the end of those *c* with their lot:

CONTENTEDLY (1)

2Mc 11:26 but may *c* go about their own business."

CONTENTION (1)

Jer 15:10 a man of strife and *c* to all the land!

CONTENTIOUS (3)

Prv 26:21 fire, such is a *c* man in enkindling strife.
Rom 10:21 my hands to an unbelieving and *c* people."
1Tm 3: 3 He ought not to be *c* but,

CONTENTMENT (3)

Sir 1:20 for a time, and then *c* comes back to him.
30:15 and well-being, *c* of spirit than coral.
Jer 12: 1 prosper, why live all the treacherous in *c*?

CONTENTS (4)

2Kgs 22:11 had heard the *c* of the book of the law,
23: 2 He had the entire *c* of the book of the
Jer 29: 1 This is the *c* of the letter which the
Rv 5: 3 found to open the scroll or examine its *c*.

CONTEST (3)

Jgs 12: 2 engaged in a critical *c* with the Ammonites.
2Tm 2: 5 if one takes part in an athletic *c*,
Heb 10:32 you endured a great *c* of suffering.

CONTINENCE (1)

Acts 24:25 As Paul talked on about uprightness, *c*,

CONTINUAL (2)

1Sm 27: 1 then Saul will give up his *c* search for me
Prv 15:15 but a lighthearted man has a *c* feast.

CONTINUALLY (30)

Dt 11:12 his eyes are upon it *c* from the beginning
28:29 "You will be oppressed and robbed *c*,
Jos 6: 9 of horns was kept up *c* as they marched.
6:13 and the blowing of horns was kept up *c*.
Jgs 16:16 She importuned him *c* and vexed him with
1Sm 23:14 Though Saul sought him *c*,
2Chr 12:15 was war *c* between Rehoboam and Jeroboam.
24:14 *c* throughout the lifetime of Jehoiada.
Tb 14: 2 giving alms and *c* blessing God and
Est B: 4 and *c* disregards the decrees of kings,
B: 5 people is *c* at variance with all men,
9: 4 provinces that he was *c* growing in power.
1Mc 6:18 *c* trying to harm them and to strengthen
Ps(s) 72:15 the gold of Arabia, and to be prayed for *c*;
84: 5 *c* they praise you.
109:15 May they be *c* before the LORD,
119:44 And I will keep your law *c*,
Prv 5:19 through her love you will flourish *c*.
Sir 23:10 So one who swears *c* by the Holy Name will
Is 65: 3 own thoughts, People who provoke me *c*,
Ob 1:16 mountain, so shall all the nations drink *c*.
Mk 15:19 *C* striking Jesus on the head with a reed
Acts 5:14 in great numbers, were *c* added to the Lord.
1Cor 1: 4 I *c* thank my God for you because of the
15:30 why are we *c* putting ourselves in danger?
2Cor 4:10 *C* we carry about in our bodies the dying
11:26 I traveled *c*, endangered by floods,
Phil 1: 5 at the way you have all *c* helped promote
Heb 10: 1 same sacrifices offered *c* year after year.
13:15 let us *c* offer God a sacrifice of praise,

CONTINUE (75)

Gn 19: 2 you can get up early to *c* your journey."
26: 2 *c* to camp wherever in this land I tell you.
29: 7 the flocks now, and then *c* pasturing them?"
Ex 33:13 you, I may *c* to find favor with you.
Lv 19:25 Thus it will *c* its yield for you.
23:34 of Booths, which shall *c* for seven days.
25:22 year, you will *c* to eat from the old crop;
25:35 tenant, so that he may *c* to live with you.
26:23 to be chastened by me and *c* to defy me,
Nm 34: 8 and shall *c* it from Mount Hor to Labo in
34:12 thence the boundary shall *c* along the
Dt 25: 6 shall *c* the line of the deceased brother,
28: 1 if you *c* to heed the voice of the LORD,
Jos 6:25 who *c* in the midst of Israel to this day.
Jgs 2:22 LORD and *c* in it as their fathers had done;
1Sm 12:25 If instead you *c* to do evil,
2Sm 7:10 *c* to afflict them as they did of old,
15: 4 And he would *c*:
2Kgs 6: 1 room for us to *c* to live here with you.
9:22 and witchcrafts of your mother Jezebel *c*?"
1Chr 28: 8 that you may *c* to possess this good land
2Chr 5:14 not *c* to minister because of the cloud,
8: 8 to forced labor, as they *c* to this day.
Ezr 6: 7 of the Jews *c* to work on that house of God;
6:10 that they may *c* to offer sacrifices of
Tb 12:18 So *c* to thank him every day;
Est 5:13 as long as I *c* to see the Jew Mordecai
1Mc 7:38 their blasphemies, and do not let them *c*."
10:27 *C*, therefore, to keep faith with us,
11:23 this, Jonathan ordered the siege to *c*.
2Mc 8:26 that reason they could not *c* the pursuit.
9:26 *c* to show good will toward me and my son.
10:15 from Jerusalem and endeavored to *c* the war.
Ps(s) 89:37 His posterity shall *c* forever,
102:29 their posterity shall *c* in your presence.
Prv 22: 3 simpletons *c* on and suffer the penalty.
27:12 simpletons *c* on and suffer the penalty.
Wis 14:13 they were not, nor shall they *c* forever;
Is 46: 4 It is I who have done this, I who will *c*,
Jer 3:12 the LORD, I will not *c* my wrath forever.
17:25 upon the throne of David will *c* to enter,
22: 4 will *c* to enter the gates of this palace,
23:26 How long will this *c*?
31:22 How long will you *c* to stray,
32:18 You *c* your kindness through a thousand
44:17 will we *c* doing what we had proposed;
44:25 "We will *c* to fulfill the vows we have
Bar 2:21 you may *c* in the land I gave your fathers:
Hos 13: 2 Now they *c* to sin,

CONTINUE (cont.)

Jn 17:26 and I will *c* to reveal it so that your
Acts 19:20 Lord *c* to spread with influence and power.
27: 7 winds would not permit us to *c* our course,
Rom 6: 1 "Let us *c* in sin that grace may abound"?
15:23 and I *c* to cherish the desire to visit you
1Cor 5: 2 Still you *c* to be self-satisfied,
7:20 ought to *c* as he was when he was called.
7:24 each of you should *c* before God in the
7:26 good to me for a person to *c* as he is.
2Cor 1:10 that danger of death and will *c* to do so.
5: 6 Therefore, we *c* to be confident.
11: 9 burdensome to you, and I shall *c* to do so.
11:12 What I am doing I shall *c* to do,
Gal 5:11 circumcision, why do the attacks on me *c?*
Eph 5:17 Do not *c* in ignorance,
Phil 1:18 Indeed, I shall *c* to rejoice,
3:16 It is important that we *c* on our course,
4: 1 for, you who are my joy and my crown, *c,*
Col 2: 6 *C,* therefore, to live in Christ Jesus
1Thes 3: 8 so much so that we shall *c* to flourish
2Thes 3: 4 doing and will *c* to do whatever we enjoin.
2Tm 4:18 The Lord will *c* to rescue me from all
1Pt 4:19 as God's will requires *c* in good deeds,
2Pt 2: 9 and how to *c* the punishment of the wicked
3Jn 1: 6 God, you help them to *c* their journey.
Rv 22:11 Let the wicked *c* in their wicked ways,

CONTINUED (126)

Gn 7:17 The flood *c* upon the earth for forty days.
8: 5 waters *c* to diminish until the tenth month,
15: 3 Abram *c,* "See, you have given me
17: 3 prostrated himself, God *c* to speak to him:
22: 7 Isaac *c,* "Here are the fire and the wood,
22: 8 Then the two *c* going forward.
30:28 So," he *c,* "state what wages you want
30:36 *c* to pasture the rest of Laban's flock.
32: 2 back home, while Jacob *c* on his own way.
37:22 Instead of shedding blood," he *c,*
47: 4 We have come," they *c,*
50:25 the sons of Israel under oath, he *c,*
Ex 3: 6 I am the God of your father," he *c,*
4: 5 place so that they may believe," he *c,*
5: 5 of the land are already," *c* Pharaoh,
16: 8 you flesh to eat in the evening," *c* Moses,
32: 9 this people is," *c* the LORD to Moses.
33:21 Here," *c* the LORD,
36: 3 morning after morning the people *c* to
Nm 32: 5 your servants have livestock," they *c,*
Jos 3:10 He *c:* "This is how
15: 9 cities of Mount Ephron, and *c* to Baalah,
15:11 flank of Ekron, *c* through Shikkeron,
16: 6 Taanath-shiloh, and *c* east of it to Janoah;
17: 9 same boundary *c* down to the Wadi Kanah.
18:19 From there the boundary *c* across the
19:13 *c* eastward to Gath-hepher and to Eth-kazin,
Jgs 19:14 So they *c* on their way till the sun set on
Ru 2:20 and she *c,* "He is a relative of ours,
4: 5 Boaz *c,* "Once you acquire the field
1Sm 6:12 to Beth-shemesh and *c* along this road,
9: 4 they *c* through the land of Shaalim without
14: 8 Jonathan *c:* "We shall go over
14:23 The battle *c* past Beth-horon;
14:34 He *c:* "Mingle with the people
17:10 The Philistine *c:* "I defy the ranks
17:37 David *c:* "The Lord, who delivered me
18:30 [The Philistine chiefs *c* to make forays,
19:23 and he *c* on in a prophetic condition until
26:10 As the LORD lives," David *c,*
26:18 He *c:* "Why does my lord
30:10 David *c* the pursuit with four hundred men,
2Sm 2:24 Abishai, however, *c* the pursuit of Abner.
3:34 And all the people *c* to weep for him.
13:39 The king *c* during all that time to mourn
14:12 The woman *c,* "Please let your servant
16:13 David and his men *c* on the road,
24: 6 They *c* on to Gilead and to the district
1Kgs 3: 6 and you have *c* this great favor toward him,
3:24 The king *c,* "Get me a sword."
5:24 So Hiram *c* to provide Solomon with all the
22:19 Micaiah *c:* "Therefore hear the word
22:44 and the people *c* to sacrifice and to burn
2Kgs 9:27 He *c* his flight as far as Megiddo and died
10:15 "if you are," *c* Jehu,
12: 4 *c* to sacrifice and to burn incense there.
14: 4 *c* to sacrifice and to burn incense on them.
15: 4 *c* to sacrifice and to burn incense on them.
15:35 *c* to sacrifice and to burn incense on them.
17:40 however, but *c* in their earlier manner.]
25: 2 city *c* until the eleventh year of Zedekiah.
1Chr 21:28 Jebusite, he *c* to offer sacrifices there.
2Chr 12:13 his power in Jerusalem and *c* to rule;
13:21 he died, while Abijah *c* to grow stronger.
18:18 But Micaiah *c:* "Therefore hear the word
21:10 Edom has *c* in revolt against the
23:14 For," the priest *c,*
27: 2 the people, however, *c* to act sinfully.
27: 6 Thus Jotham *c* to grow strong because he
29:28 and they *c* to sing the song and to sound
30:23 they *c* the festivity seven days longer.
33:17 people *c* to sacrifice on the high places,
Ezr 6:14 Jews *c* to make progress in the building,
Neh 1: 4 to weep and *c* mourning for several days;
2:15 astride, I *c* on foot up the wadi by night,
3: 1 *c* the rebuilding to the Tower of Hananel.
3:38 We, however, *c* to build the wall,
5: 9 I *c:* "What you are doing
12:37 *c* along the top of the wall above the house
Tb 6:11 Raphael *c:* "Tonight we must stay
6:13 He *c:* "Since you have the right
7: 7 He *c* to weep in the arms of his kinsman
12:22 and they *c* to acknowledge these marvelous
Jdt 16:20 For three months the people *c* their
Est 2:20 Esther *c* to follow Mordecai's instructions,
1Mc 10:26 kept the treaty with us and *c* in our friendship
Jb 34: 1 Then Elihu *c* and said:
Wis 17:20 light and *c* its works without interruption;
Sir 11:17 his favor brings *c* success.
Jer 1: 3 and *c* through the reign of Jehoiakim,
16: 5 not into a house of mourning, the LORD *c:*
52: 5 *c* until the eleventh year of King Zedekiah.
Ez 8:13 He *c:* "You shall see still
Dn 1:16 So the steward *c* to take away the food and
3:46 in *c* to stoke the furnace with brimstone,
6:11 he *c* his custom of going home to kneel in
7:13 As the visions during the night *c,*
10:12 "Fear not, Daniel," he *c;*
13:48 He stood in their midst and *c,*
14: 6 Then the king *c,*
Hg 2:14 Then Haggai *c:*
Mt 9:35 *c* his tour of all the towns and villages.
Mk 3:34 him at those seated in the circle he *c,*
9:10 though they *c* to discuss what "to rise
16:20 The Lord *c* to work with them throughout
Lk 2:44 the party, they *c* their journey for a day,
4:44 he *c* to preach in the synagogues of Judea.
5: 3 he *c* to teach the crowds from the boat.
10:31 he saw him but *c* on.
Jn 8: 9 the woman, who *c* to stand there before him.
8:28 Jesus *c:*
Acts 4:31 and *c* to speak God's word with confidence.
6: 7 The word of God *c* to spread,
9: 9 For three days he *c* blind,
12:24 word of the Lord *c* to spread and increase.
13:14 They *c* to travel on from Perga and came to
14: 7 where they *c* to proclaim the good news.
15:35 Paul and Barnabas *c* in Antioch,
19:10 This *c* for two years,
21: 3 it by on our left as we *c* on toward Syria.
21: 5 when our time was up, we *c* our journey.
Col 1: 6 fruit, and has *c* to grow in your midst,
2Thes 3:16 give you *c* peace in every possible way.
Rv 5:11 As my vision *c,* I heard the voices
8:13 As my vision *c,* I heard an eagle flying
19: 9 The angel *c,* "These words are true;

CONTINUES (8)

Lv 15:25 when her flow *c* beyond the ordinary period,
1Sm 6: 3 and will learn why he *c* to afflict you."
Sir 38: 8 Thus God's creative work *c* without cease
Hg 2: 5 of Egypt, And my spirit *c* in your midst;
Col 1:17 In him everything *c* in being.
1Tm 2:15 she *c* in faith and love and holiness
5: 5 *c* night and day in supplications
1Jn 2:10 The man who *c* in the light is the one who

CONTINUING (8)

Ex 34: 7 *c* his kindness for a thousand generations,
Jos 18:16 and *c* down the Valley of Hinnom along the
1Sm 12: 6 *C,* Samuel said to the people:
2Mc 5:27 *c* to eat what grew wild to avoid sharing
Acts 21: 7 *C* our voyage from Tyre we put in at
1Cor 7:17 him, *c* as he was when the Lord called him.
1Tm 4:12 of your youth, but be a *c* example of love,
1Jn 1: 6 with him," while *c* to walk in darkness,

CONTINUOUS (2)

Jer 15:18 Why is my pain *c,*
Zec 14: 7 There shall be one *c* day,

CONTINUOUSLY (4)

Lv 6: 6 fire is to be kept burning *c* on the altar;
1Mc 15:25 he assaulted it *c* both with troops and
2Mc 13:12 merciful LORD *c* with weeping and fasting
Ez 32:10 of them shall *c* tremble for his own life.

CONTRACT (4)

Lv 11:24 "Such is the uncleanness that you *c,*
Ru 4: 7 make binding a *c* of redemption or exchange,
Tb 7:13 draw up a marriage *c* stating that he gave
7:13 brought the scroll, and he drew up the *c,*

CONTRACTED (3)

Gn 19:14 who had *c* marriage with his daughters.
Nm 12: 1 the marriage he had *c* with a Cushite woman.
2Chr 16:12 reign, Asa *c* a serious disease in his feet.

CONTRACTS (3)

Lv 15:24 he *c* her impurity and shall be unclean for
1Mc 13:42 began to write in their records and *c,*
14:43 All *c* made in the country shall be dated

CONTRADICT (5)

1Mc 14:44 decisions, or to *c* the orders given by him,
Ez 2: 6 their words when they *c* you and reject you,
Lk 21:15 adversaries can take exception to or *c.*
2Tm 2:25 and gently correcting those who *c* him,
Ti 1: 9 doctrine and to refute those who *c* it.

CONTRADICTED (1)

Jb 15:18 have not *c* since the days of their fathers,

CONTRADICTING (1)

Ti 2: 9 way, not *c* them nor stealing from them,

CONTRADICTIONS (1)

1Tm 6:20 the *c* of what is falsely called knowledge.

CONTRARY (29)

Gn 42:10 "On the *c,* your servants have come
Nm 22:18 or great, *c* to the command of the LORD,
24:13 or evil, *c* to the command of the LORD"?
Dt 21:17 On the *c,* he shall recognize
Jos 24:10 On the *c,* he had to bless you,
Jgs 11:20 On the *c,* he gathered all his soldiers,
2Sm 16:18 "On the *c,* I am his whom the LORD
1Kgs 1:43 "On the *c!*"
2Chr 30:18 ate the Passover, *c* to the prescription;
33:23 on the *c,* Amon only increased his guilt.
Est 4:16 I will go to the king, *c* to the law.
2Mc 3:11 *C* to the calumnies of the impious Simon,
4:11 and introduced customs *c* to the law.
Mt 15: 2 act *c* to the tradition of our ancestors?
15: 3 "Why do you for your part act *c* to the
Mk 5:26 on the *c,* she only grew worse.
6:52 On the *c,* their minds were completely
Lk 5:33 Yours, on the *c,* eat and drink freely."
12:51 I assure you, the *c* is true;
Rom 3:31 On the *c,* we are confirming the law.
11:24 the natural wild olive and, *c* to nature,
16:17 *c* to the teaching you have received.
1Cor 9:12 On the *c,* we put up with all sorts
2Cor 6: 4 On the *c,* in all that we do we strive
Gal 2: 7 On the *c,* recognizing that I had been
4:14 On the *c,* you took me to yourselves
1Thes 2: 7 On the *c,* when we were among you
Ti 1: 8 He should, on the *c,*
2Pt 1:11 On the *c,* your entry into the everlasting

CONTRAST (4)

Wis 19:21 Flames, by *c,* neither consumed the flesh
Sir 33:14 life, so are sinners in *c* with the just;
Gal 5:22 In *c,* the fruit of the spirit is love,
Jas 3:17 Wisdom from above, by *c,*

CONTRASTS (1)

Sir 33:14 As evil *c* with good,

CONTRIBUTE (5)

Lv 22:15 offerings which the Israelites *c* to the LORD
1Chr 29: 5 to *c* generously this day to the LORD?"
29:14 we should have the means to *c* so freely?
Ezr 7:16 *c* for the house of their God in Jerusalem.
Rom 15:27 to *c* to their temporal needs in return.

CONTRIBUTED (14)

Nm 18:28 the priest the part to be *c* to the LORD.
31:41 tax to the LORD, The taxes *c* to the LORD,
1Chr 29: 7 came forward willingly and *c* for the service
29: 9 had been *c* to the LORD wholeheartedly.
2Chr 30:24 King Hezekiah of Judah had *c* a thousand
30:24 and the princes had *c* to the assembly a
35: 7 Josiah *c* to the common people a flock of
35: 9 *c* to the Levites five thousand Passover
Ezr 2:69 *c* to the treasury for the temple service:
7:15 have freely *c* to the God of Israel,
Neh 7:69 of the family heads *c* to the service.
7:70 *c* to the treasury for the temple service:
Mt 26:12 she has *c* toward my burial preparation.
Mk 12:43 poor widow *c* more than all the others

CONTRIBUTES (1)

1Cor 14:14 spirit is at prayer but my mind *c* nothing.

CONTRIBUTING (1)

Gn 38: 9 to avoid *c* offspring for his brother.

CONTRIBUTION (29)

Ex 25: 2 the *c* that his heart prompts him to give.
29:28 Israelites by a perpetual ordinance as a *c.*
29:28 make a contribution, their *c* to the LORD.
30:13 of a half-shekel is a *c* to the LORD.
30:14 group must give this *c* to the LORD.
30:15 than a half-shekel in this *c* to the LORD
35: 5 him, shall bring as a *c* to the LORD,
35:21 brought a *c* to the LORD for the
35:24 Whoever could make a *c* of silver or bronze
Lv 7:14 present one portion as a *c* to the LORD;
7:34 ordinance as a *c* from the Israelites."

Nm 5: 9 every sacred *c* that the Israelites are
15:19 you shall offer the LORD a *c* consisting of
15:20 as you offer a *c* from the threshing floor.
15:21 give a *c* to the LORD from your first batch
18:24 the Israelites give as a *c* to the LORD.
18:26 you are to make a *c* from them to the LORD,
18:27 and your *c* will be credited to you as if
18:28 Thus you too shall make a *c* from all the
18:29 to consecrate to the LORD your own full *c*.
18:30 you have made your *c* from the best part,
18:32 so long as you make a *c* of the best part.
31:29 to the priest Eleazar as a *c* to the LORD.
31:52 The gold that they gave as a *c* to the LORD
2Mc 4:20 So the *c* destined by the sender for the
Sir 35: 8 With each *c* show a cheerful countenance,
Rom 15:26 decided to make a *c* for those in need
15:28 and have safely handed over this *c* to them,

CONTRIBUTIONS (13)

Ex 25: 3 These are the *c* you shall accept from them:
36: 3 They received from Moses all the *c* which
36: 6 woman make any more *c* for the sanctuary."
Lv 22:12 to a layman may not eat of the sacred *c*.
Nm 5:10 man may dispose of his own sacred *c*;
18: 8 "I myself have given you charge of the *c*
18:19 all the *c* from the sacred gifts
Dt 12: 6 sacrifices, your tithes and personal *c*,
12:11 sacrifices, your tithes and personal *c*,
12:17 freewill offerings, or of your personal *c*.
Neh 7:71 The *c* of the rest of the people amounted
Sir 7:31 First fruits and *c*,
Lk 21: 4 They make *c* out of their surplus,

CONTRITE (3)

Ps(s) 51:19 is a contrite spirit; a heart *c* and humbled,
Dn 3:39 But with *c* heart and humble spirit let us

CONTRIVE (1)

Jer 18:18 said, "let us *c* a plot against Jeremiah.

CONTRIVED (3)

2Chr 26:15 devices *c* to stand on the towers and at
2Mc 7:31 *c* every kind of affliction for the Hebrews,
Ps(s) 10: 2 caught in the devices the wicked have *c*.

CONTRIVER (1)

Wis 14:10 thing made shall be punished with its *c*.

CONTROL (25)

Gn 43:31 he reappeared and, now in *c* of himself,
45: 1 Joseph could no longer *c* himself in the
1Chr 18: 1 towns away from the *c* of the Philistines.
Tb 1:21 he took *c* over the entire administration.
Jdt 7:12 Have some of your servants keep *c* of the
1Mc 10:52 Demetrius and gaining *c* of my country
11:46 *c* of the main streets and began to fight.
14: 6 of his nation and gained *c* of the country.
15: 3 gained *c* of the kingdom of my ancestors,
16:13 and sought to get *c* of the country.
2Mc 3: 6 to bring it all under the *c* of the king.
5: 7 so, he did not gain *c* of the government,
9: 2 to rob the temple and gain *c* of the city.
10:17 vigorously, they gained *c* of the places,
Jb 34:17 Can an enemy of justice indeed be in *c*,
Eccl 2:19 Yet he will have *c* over all the fruits of
Sir 23: 4 of my life, abandon me not into their *c*!
33:23 Keep *c* over all your affairs;
Dn 11:43 He shall *c* the riches of gold and silver
Acts 27:16 were we able to gain *c* of the ship's boat.
1Cor 14:32 of the prophets are under the prophets' *c*,
1Tm 3: 4 under *c* without sacrificing his dignity;
Ti 2: 6 men to keep themselves completely under *c*—
Jas 1:26 *c* his tongue imagines that he is devout,
3: 2 sense, because he can *c* his entire body.

CONTROLS (2)

Ps(s) 68:21 LORD, my Lord, *c* the passageways of death.
Sir 21:11 He who keeps the law *c* his impulses;

CONTROVERSIES (1)

Ti 3: 9 and from all *c* and quarrels about the law.

CONTROVERSY (4)

Prv 18:18 and is decisive in a *c* between the mighty.
Jn 3:25 A *c* about purification arose between
Acts 15: 2 much *c* between them and Paul and Barnabas.
1Tm 6: 4 sick man in his passion for polemics and *c*.

CONTUMACIOUS (2)

Sir 6: 4 For *c* desire destroys its owner and makes
19: 3 him, for *c* desire destroys its owner.

CONVENE (1)

1Mc 14:44 or to *c* an assembly in the country without

CONVENED (9)

2Chr 15: 9 Then he *c* all Judah and Benjamin,
34:29 *c* all the elders of Judah and Jerusalem.
Jdt 6:16 They then *c* all the elders of the city;
1Mc 5:16 a great assembly *c* to consider what they
Dn 7:11 The court was *c*,
7:26 But when the court is *c*,
Mt 26:57 where the scribes and elders were *c*.
28:12 *c* with the elders and worked out their
Acts 15: 6 accordingly *c* to look into the matter.

CONVENIENT (1)

2Tm 4: 2 with this task whether *c* or inconvenient

CONVERSATION (8)

1Sm 19: 7 David and repeated the whole *c* to him.
Sir 9:15 all your *c* be about the law of the LORD.
27: 5 furnace, so in his *c* is the test of a man.
27:13 The *c* of the wicked is offensive,
Jer 38:24 Jeremiah, "Let no one know about this *c*,
38:27 nothing had been heard of the earlier *c*.
Mk 9: 4 the two were in *c* with Jesus.
Acts 7:38 it was he who was in *c* with the angel on

CONVERSE (3)

Ex 34:34 the presence of the LORD to *c* with him,
34:35 face until he went in to *c* with the LORD.
Acts 24:26 to send for him frequently to *c* with him.

CONVERSED (2)

Ex 34:29 become radiant while he *c* with the LORD.
Acts 9:27 had seen the Lord, who had *c* with him,

CONVERSING (2)

2Kgs 2:11 As they walked on *c*,
Mt 17: 3 and Elijah appeared to them *c* with him.

CONVERSION (4)

Sir 5: 8 Delay not your *c* to the LORD,
Ez 33:11 wicked man, but rather the wicked man's *c*,
Acts 15: 3 about the *c* of the Gentiles as they went.
26:20 a message of reform and of *c* to God,

CONVERT (6)

2Chr 24:19 were sent to them to *c* them to the LORD,
Mt 23:15 over sea and land to make a single *c*,
Acts 6: 5 of Antioch, who had been a *c* to Judaism.
9:36 woman *c* named Tabitha (in Greek Dorcas,
14:15 bringing you the good news that will *c* you
1Tm 3: 6 He should not be a new *c*,

CONVERTED (10)

1Kgs 8:47 in the land of their captivity and be *c*.
2Chr 6:37 the land where they are captive and are *c*,
Tb 14: 6 be *c* and shall offer God true worship;
Ps(s) 7:13 Unless they be *c*,
Ez 14: 6 Return and be *c* from your idols;
18:30 Turn and be *c* from all your crimes,
Mt 23:15 but once he is *c* you make a devil of him
Acts 9:35 upon seeing him, were *c* to the Lord.
11:21 of them believed and were *c* to the Lord.
15: 5 Some of the *c* Pharisees then got up and

CONVERTS (6)

Tb 1: 8 to *c* who were living with the Israelites.
Acts 13:43 devout Jewish *c* followed Paul and Barnabas,
15:10 place on the shoulders of these *c* a yoke
15:19 to cause God's Gentile *c* any difficulties.
21:25 As for the Gentile *c*,
Ti 1:10 especially from among the Jewish *c*—

CONVEY (7)

Gn 50: 4 "and *c* to Pharaoh this request of mine.
2Sm 11:25 "This is what you shall *c* to Joab:
1Chr 10: 9 Philistines to *c* the good news to their idols
Is 28: 9 To whom would he *c* the message?
28:19 terror alone shall *c* the message.
Bar 6: 1 to *c* to them what God had commanded him.
Acts 15:27 who will *c* this message by word of mouth:

CONVEYED (2)

Gn 23:17 was *c* to Abraham by purchase in the
Acts 16:36 The jailer *c* this information to Paul:

CONVICT (5)

Prv 24:25 those who *c* the evildoer will fare well,
Wis 4:20 lawless deeds shall *c* them to their face.
Jn 8:46 Can any one of you *c* me of sin?
Acts 13:46 but since you reject it and thus *c*
Rom 2: 1 By your judgment you *c* yourself,

CONVICTED (5)

2Mc 14:38 of the revolt, he had been *c* of Judaism,
Jb 32:12 And behold, there is none who has *c* Job,
Dn 13:61 own words Daniel had *c* them of perjury.
Rom 3:19 and the whole world stands *c* before God,
Jas 2: 9 sin and are *c* by the law as transgressors.

CONVICTING (1)

Jude 1:15 and *c* those godless sinners of every harsh

CONVICTION (5)

2Cor 5:14 reached the *c* that since one died for all,
Phil 1:19 *c* that this will turn out to my salvation,
Col 4:12 *c* about whatever pertains to God's will.
1Thes 1: 5 in the Holy Spirit and out of complete *c*.
Heb 11: 1 hope for, and *c* about things we do not see.

CONVICTS (1)

Ex 22: 8 the one whom God *c* must make twofold

CONVINCE (2)

Acts 14: 1 as to *c* a good number of Jews and Greeks.
28:23 He sought to *c* them about Jesus by

CONVINCED (17)

Gn 26:28 "We are *c* that the LORD is with you,
1Sm 24:12 be *c* that I plan no harm and no rebellion.
2Mc 15: 7 *c* that he would receive help from the LORD.
Wis 16: 8 And by this also you *c* our foes that you
Mt 27:20 the chief priests and elders *c* the crowds
Lk 16:31 be *c* even if one should rise from the dead.' "
20: 6 us, so *c* are they that John was a prophet."
Jn 6:69 we are *c* that you are God's holy one."
16:30 We are *c* that you know everything.
Acts 5:36 had been so easily *c* by him were disbanded.
16:15 "If you are *c* that I believe in the Lord,
17: 4 Some of the Jews were *c* and threw in their
26:26 I am *c* that none of this escapes him
28:24 Some, indeed, were *c* by what he said;
Rom 15:14 I am *c*, my brothers,
2Cor 2: 3 enough to be *c* that my happiness is yours.
10: 7 If anyone is *c* that he belongs to Christ,

CONVINCING (2)

Acts 1: 3 them in many *c* ways that he was alive,
1Cor 2: 4 but the *c* power of the Spirit.

CONVOKE (1)

2Chr 29:20 Then King Hezekiah hastened to *c* the

CONVOKED (1)

Acts 5:21 supporters arrived they *c* the Sanhedrin,

CONVOY (1)

1Mc 9:35 of the *c* to ask permission of his friends,

CONVULSED (4)

Is 24:19 will be shaken apart, the earth will be *c*.
Jer 25:16 They shall drink, and be *c*,
Ez 27:35 Their kings are terrified, their faces *c*.
Mk 1:26 At that the unclean spirit *c* the man

CONVULSION (1)

Lk 9:39 into a *c* and makes him foam at the mouth,

CONVULSIONS (3)

Mk 9:20 Jesus and immediately threw the boy into *c*.
9:26 Shouting, and throwing the boy into *c*,
Lk 9:42 the spirit threw him into *c* on the ground.

COOK (7)

Nm 11: 8 then *c* it in a pot and make it into loaves,
Dt 16: 7 shall *c* and eat it at the place the LORD,
1Sm 9:23 He said to the *c*,
9:24 *c* took up the leg and what went with it,
Ez 46:20 "Here the priests *c* the guilt offerings
46:24 ministers *c* the sacrifices of the people."
Zec 14:21 to sacrifice shall take them and *c* in them.

COOKED (6)

Lv 6:21 *c* shall thereafter be broken; if it is cooked
2Chr 35:13 *c* the Passover on the fire as prescribed,
35:13 and also *c* the sacred meals in pots,
Ez 24:10 the fire, Till the meat has been *c*,
Lk 24:42 They gave him a piece of *c* fish,

COOKING (1)

Gn 25:29 Once, when Jacob was *c* a stew,

COOKS (1)

1Sm 8:13 your daughters as ointment-makers, as *c*,

COOL (6)

Jgs 3:20 him where he sat alone in his *c* upper room,
3:24 must be easing himself in the *c* chamber."
2Mc 14:30 was becoming *c* in his dealings with him,
Prv 25:25 Like *c* water to one faint from thirst is
Sg 2:17 day breathes *c* and the shadows
4: 6 day breathes *c* and the shadows lengthen,

COOLED (1)

Est 2: 1 this, when King Ahasuerus' wrath had *c*,

COOLNESS (1)

Prv 25:13 Like the *c* of snow in the heat of the

COOPERATES (1)

1Cor 16:16 under everyone who *c* and toils with them.

COOPERS (1)

Jer 48:12 when I will send him *c* to turn him over;

COPE (2)

Sir 50:29 them into practice, he can *c* with anything,
Phil 4:12 learned how to *c* with every circumstance

COPIED (2)

2Mc 9:25 I have written to him the letter *c* below.
Wis 14:17 *c* the appearance of the distant king

COPIES (2)

1Mc 14:49 and that *c* of it should be deposited in
Heb 9:23 It was necessary that the *c* of the

COPIOUS (4)

2Chr 11:23 and he furnished them with *c* provisions
Ps(s) 78:15 the desert and gave them water in *c* floods.
Wis 8: 8 Or again, if one yearns for *c* learning,
2Cor 2: 4 in great sorrow and anguish, with *c* tears

COPIOUSLY (1)

1Sm 1:10 she prayed to the LORD, weeping *c*,

COPPER (5)

Dt 8: 9 iron and in whose hills you can mine *c*.
Jb 28: 2 the earth, and *c* is melted out of stone.
Mt 10: 9 gold nor silver nor *c* in your belts;
Mk 12:42 put in two small *c* coins worth a few cents.
Lk 21: 2 also a poor widow putting in two *c* coins.

COPPERS (1)

Bar 6:34 they cannot give anyone riches or *c*;

COPPERSMITH (1)

2Tm 4:14 the *c* did me a great deal of harm;

COPY (30)

Dt 9:10 with a *c* of all the words that the LORD
17:18 he shall have a *c* of this law made from
Jos 8:32 the stones a *c* of the law written by Moses.
Ezr 4:11 is a *c* of the letter that they sent to him:
4:23 As soon as a *c* of King Artaxerxes' letter
5: 6 A *c* of the letter sent to King Darius by
7:11 This is a *c* of the rescript which King
Tb 5: 3 his *c* I put with the money.
Est B: 1 This is a *c* of the letter:
3:14 A *c* of the decree to be promulgated as law
4: 8 He also gave him a *c* of the written decree
E: 1 The following is a *c* of the letter:
E:19 a *c* of this letter publicly in every place,
8:13 A *c* of the letter to be promulgated as
1Mc 8:22 and this is a *c* of the reply they
11:31 for your information a *c* of the letter
11:37 to have a *c* of these instructions made and
12: 5 This is a *c* of the letter that Jonathan
12: 7 are our brothers, as the attached *c* shows.
12:19 a *c* of the letter that was sent to Onias:
14:20 a *c* of the letter that the Spartans sent:
14:23 a *c* of their words in the public archives,
14:23 A *c* of this decree has been made for Simon
14:27 The following is a *c* of the inscription:
15:24 A *c* of the letter was also sent to Simon
Wis 9: 8 a *c* of the holy tabernacle which you had
Jer 32:11 the deed of purchase, both the sealed *c*,
Bar 6: 1 A *c* of the letter which Jeremiah sent to
Heb 8: 5 is only a *c* and shadow of the heavenly one,
9:24 made by hands, a mere *c* of the true one;

CORAL (4)

Jb 28:18 Neither *c* nor jasper should be thought of;
Sir 30:15 well-being, contentment of spirit than *c*.
Lam 4: 7 whiter than milk, More ruddy than *c*,
Ez 27:16 purple, embroidered cloth, fine linen, *c*,

CORALS (4)

Prv 3:15 She is more precious than *c*,
8:11 [For Wisdom is better than *c*,
20:15 Like gold or a wealth of *c*,
Sir 7:19 a gracious wife is more precious than *c*.

CORD (13)

Gn 38:18 She answered, "Your seal and *c*,
38:25 seal and *c* and whose staff these are."
Nm 15:38 each corner tassel with a violet *c*.
Jos 2:18 tie this scarlet *c* in the window through
2:21 gone, she tied the scarlet *c* in the window.
2Kgs 21:13 Jerusalem with the same *c* as I did Samaria,
Eccl 4:12 A three-ply *c* is not easily broken.
12: 6 Before the silver *c* is snapped.
Sir 6:30 her bonds, your purple *c*.
Bar 6:43 as she has, and has not had her *c* broken.
Ez 16: 4 day you were born your navel *c* was not cut;
40: 3 holding a linen *c* and a measuring rod.
47: 3 to the east with a measuring *c* in his hand,

CORDIAL (3)

Tb 7: 9 from the flock and gave them a *c* reception.
2Mc 14:24 for he had a *c* affection for the man.
1Cor 16:19 house, send you *c* greetings in the Lord.

CORDIALLY (1)

Jer 9: 7 He speaks *c* with his friends,

CORDLIKE (1)

Ex 28:14 the *c* chains to the filigree rosettes.

CORDON (1)

2Kgs 11: 8 and if anyone tries to approach the *c*,

CORDS (22)

Ex 28:14 two chains of pure gold, twisted like *c*,
28:22 the chains of pure gold, twisted like *c*,
28:24 The gold *c* are then to be fastened to the
28:25 the other two ends of the *c* being fastened
39:15 Chains of pure gold, twisted like *c*,
Dt 22:12 "You shall put twisted *c* on the four
2Sm 22: 6 The *c* of the nether world enmeshed me,
1Kgs 20:31 in sackcloth, with *c* around our heads,
20:32 waist, and wearing *c* around their heads,
Est 1: 6 held by *c* of crimson byssus from silver
Ps(s) 18: 6 The *c* of the nether world enmeshed me,
116: 3 The *c* of death encompassed me;
129: 4 just LORD has severed the *c* of the wicked.
140: 6 They have spread *c* for a net;
Is 5:18 who tug at guilt with *c* of perversity,
Jer 10:20 My tent is ruined, all its *c* are severed.
Bar 6:42 And their women, girt with *c*,
Ez 3:25 will put *c* upon you and bind you with them,
4: 8 I will bind you with *c* so that you cannot
27:24 varicolored carpets, and firmly woven *c*.
Hos 11: 4 I drew them with human *c*,
Jn 2:15 He made a [kind of] whip of *c* and drove

CORE (1)

Gn 30:37 the bark down to the white *c* of the shoots.

CORIANDER (2)

Ex 16:31 It was like *c* seed,
Nm 11: 7 *c* seed and had the appearance of bdellium.

CORINTH (8)

Acts 18: 1 After that, Paul left Athens and went to *C*.
18:18 Paul stayed on in *C* for quite a while;
19: 1 While Apollos was in *C*,
1Cor 1: 2 to the church of God which is in *C*;
2Cor 1: 1 church of God that is at *C* and to all
1:23 for you that I did not come to *C* again.
6:11 Men of *C*, we have spoken to you frankly,
2Tm 4:20 Erastus has stayed in *C*,

CORINTHIANS (1)

Acts 18: 8 Many of the *C*, too, who heard Paul

CORMORANT (2)

Lv 11:17 various species of hawks, the owl, the *c*,
Dt 14:17 ibis, the desert owl, the buzzard, the *c*,

CORN-FED (1)

Mt 22: 4 My bullocks and *c* cattle are killed;

CORNELIUS (8)

Acts 10: 1 in Caesarea there was a centurion named *C*,
10: 3 of God coming toward him and calling, *C*!"
10:17 the men sent by *C* arrived at the gate
10:22 "The centurion *C*,
10:24 *C*, who was expecting them,
10:25 As Peter entered, *C* went to meet him,
10:30 *C* replied:
10:31 *C*,' he said, 'your prayer has been heard

CORNER (32)

Nm 15:38 fastening each *c* tassel with a violet cord.
Dt 30: 4 been driven to the farthest *c* of the world,
Ru 3: 9 Spread the *c* of your cloak over me,
2Kgs 14:13 from the Gate of Ephraim to the *C* Gate.
2Chr 25:23 from the Ephraim Gate to the *C* Gate,
26: 9 built towers in Jerusalem at the *C* Gate,
28:24 made for himself in every *c* of Jerusalem.
Neh 1: 9 been driven to the farthest *c* of the world,
3:19 who repaired the adjoining sector, the *C*,
3:20 *C* to the entrance of the house of Eliashib,
3:24 the house of Azariah to the *C* [that is,
3:25 opposite the *C* and the tower projecting
Prv 7: 8 sense, Going along the street near the *c*,
7:12 and at every *c* she lurks in ambush
21: 9 It is better to dwell in a *c* of the
25:24 It is better to dwell in a *c* of the
Is 51:20 at every street *c* like antelopes in a net.
Jer 31:38 from the Tower of Hananel to the *C* Gate.
31:40 far as the *c* of the Horse Gate at the east,
Lam 2:19 from hunger at the *c* of every street].
4: 1 sacred stones lie strewn at every street *c*!
Ez 16: 8 So I spread the *c* of my cloak over you to
16:25 At every street *c* you built a dais for
16:31 at every street *c* and erecting your dais
46:21 saw that in each *c* there was another court:
Dn 13:38 When we, in a *c* of the garden,
Am 3:12 with the *c* of a couch or a piece of a cot.
Na 3:10 dashed to pieces at the *c* of every street;
Zec 14:10 the place of the First Gate, to the *C* Gate;
Mt 12:42 She came from the farthest *c* of the earth
Lk 11:31 She came from the farthest *c* of the world
Acts 26:26 all, it did not take place in a dark *c*!

CORNERS (31)

Ex 25:26 gold for it and fasten them at the four *c*,
26:23 for the *c* at the rear of the Dwelling.
26:24 how both boards in the *c* are to be made.
27: 2 At the four *c* there are to be horns,
27: 4 bronze rings, one at each of its four *c*.
36:28 at the *c* in the rear of the Dwelling.
36:29 That is how both boards in the *c* were made.
37:13 it and fastened, one at each of the four *c*.
38: 2 At the four *c* horns were made that sprang
38: 5 cast for the four *c* of the bronze grating,
Nm 15:38 put tassels on the *c* of their garments,
Dt 22:12 *c* of the cloak that you wrap around you."
1Kgs 7:34 braces, extending to the *c* of each stand,
Tb 11:13 Then, beginning at the *c* of Tobit's eyes,
1Mc 8: 4 against them from the far *c* of the earth
Jb 1:19 desert and smote the four *c* of the house.
Ps(s) 144:12 such as stand at the *c* of the temple.
Sir 23:19 step a man takes and peer into hidden *c*.
Is 11:12 assemble from the four *c* of the earth.
Ez 7: 2 end has come upon the four *c* of the land!
41:22 It had *c*, and its base and sides
43:20 the altar, and on the four *c* of the ledge,
45:19 on the four *c* of the ledge of the altar,
46:21 had me pass around the four *c* of the court,
46:22 in the four *c* of the court,
Zec 9:15 libation bowls, like the *c* of the altar.
Mt 6: 5 or on street *c* in order to be noticed.
Acts 10:11 It was lowered to the ground by its four *c*.
11: 5 down to me from the sky by its four *c*.
Rv 7: 1 standing at the four *c* of the earth;
20: 8 the nations in all four *c* of the earth,

CORNERSTONE (7)

Jb 38: 6 its pedestals sunk, and who laid the *c*,
Ps(s) 118:22 the builders rejected has become the *c*.
Is 28:16 tested, A precious *c* as a sure foundation;
Jer 51:26 They will not take from you a *c*,
Acts 4:11 you the builders which has become the *c*.'
1Pt 2: 6 "See, I am laying a *c* in Zion,
2: 7 the builders rejected that became a *c*."

CORONATION (1)

2Mc 4:21 sent to Egypt for the *c* of King Philometor,

CORPORAL (1)

Ezr 7:26 upon him, whether death or *c* punishment,

CORPS (1)

1Mc 16: 7 two *c* and put his cavalry between them,

CORPSE (25)

Lv 22: 4 has become unclean by contact with a *c*,
Nm 5: 2 who has become unclean by contact with a *c*.
9: 6 who were unclean because of a human *c*
9: 7 "Although we are unclean because of a *c*,
9:10 descendants is unclean because of a *c*,
Dt 21: 1 "If the *c* of a slain man is found lying
21: 2 that are in the neighborhood of the *c*.
21: 3 established which city is nearest the *c*,
21: 6 nearest the *c* shall wash their hands
21:22 is put to death and his *c* hung on a tree,
1Sm 17:46 This very day I will leave your *c* and the
1Kgs 13:22 your *c* shall not be brought to the grave
13:24 His *c* lay sprawled on the road,
2Kgs 9:37 The *c* of Jezebel shall be like dung in the
Jdt 14:15 found him lying on the floor, a headless *c*.
Sir 34:25 man again touches a *c* after he has bathed,
Is 14:19 those slain at sword-point, a trampled *c*.
Jer 26:23 sword and his *c* cast into the common grave.
36:30 his *c* shall be cast out,
Bar 6:70 of bird, or like a *c* hurled into darkness,
Ez 28: 8 down to the pit, there to die a bloodied *c*,
Hg 2:13 from contact with a *c* touches any of these,
Mk 9:26 the boy became like a *c*,
15:45 was dead, Pilate released the *c* to Joseph.
Rv 16: 3 The sea turned to blood like that of a *c*,

CORPSES (31)

Lv 26:30 and cast your *c* on those of your idols.
1Sm 17:46 *c* of the Philistine army for the birds
2Kgs 19:35 there they were, all the *c* of the dead.

2Chr 20:24 they saw only *c* fallen on the ground,
Jdt 6: 4 and their plains filled with their *c.*
1Mc 11: 4 and its suburbs demolished, *c* lying about,
Ps(s) 79: 2 They have given the *c* of your servants as
110: 6 do judgment on the nations, heaping up *c;*
Wis 4:19 *c* and an unceasing mockery among the dead.
18:23 For when *c* had already fallen one on
Is 5:25 *c* shall be like refuse in the streets.
26:19 your dead shall live, their *c* shall rise;
34: 3 cast out, their *c* shall send up a stench;
37:36 there they were, all the *c* of the dead.
66:24 the *c* of the men who rebelled against me;
Jer 7:33 The *c* of this people will be food for the
9:21 *c* of the slain lie like dung on a field,
16: 4 and their *c* will become food for the birds
16:18 my land with their detestable *c* of idols,
19: 7 Their *c* I will give as food to the birds
31:40 The whole valley of *c* and ashes,
33: 5 be filled with the *c* of those whom I slay
34:20 their *c* shall be food for the birds of the
41: 9 Ishmael threw all the *c* of the men
Ez 43: 7 the *c* of their kings [their high places].
43: 9 me their harlotry and the *c* of their kings,
Am 8: 3 Many shall be the *c,*
Na 3: 3 the spear, the many slain, the heaping *c,*
Heb 3:17 who had sinned, whose *c* fell in the desert?
Rv 11: 8 Their *c* will lie in the streets of the
11: 9 stare at their *c* for three and a half days

CORRAL (1)

Mi 2:12 fold, like a herd in the midst of its *c;*

CORRECT (11)

2Sm 7:14 I will *c* him with the rod of men and with
2Mc 7:33 a little while to *c* us with chastisements,
Jb 40: 2 Let him who would *c* God give answer!
Ps(s) 50:21 *c* you by drawing them up before your eyes.
Prv 29:17 *C* your son,
Sir 38:14 be *c* and his treatment bring about a cure.
Dn 2: 9 you can also give its *c* interpretation."
Lk 17: 3 If your brother does wrong, *c* him;
Eph 5:10 Be *c* in your judgment of what pleases the
2Thes 3:15 rather, *c* him as you would a brother.
Jude 1:22 *C* those who are confused;

CORRECTED (1)

Heb 12: 9 we respected our earthly fathers who *c* us,

CORRECTING (2)

2Tm 2:25 and gently *c* those who contradict him,
4: 2 task whether convenient or inconvenient *c,*

CORRECTION (17)

2Mc 6:12 for the ruin but for the *c* of our nation.
Jb 36:10 *c* and exhorts them to turn back from evil.
Prv 12: 1 He who loves *c* loves knowledge,
13: 1 A wise son loves *c,*
13:18 and shame befall the man who disregards *c,*
29:15 The rod of *c* gives wisdom,
Sir 21: 6 He who hates *c* walks the sinner's path,
33:27 Food, *c* and work for a slave;
Jer 2:30 the *c* they did not take.
5: 3 you laid them low, but they refused *c;*
7:27 the voice of the LORD, its God, or take *c.*
17:23 their necks so as not to hear or take *c.*
32:33 them, they would not listen to my *c.*
35:13 Will you not take *c* and obey my words?
Zep 3: 2 She hears no voice, accepts no *c;*
3: 7 now you will fear me, you will accept *c";*
2Tm 3:16 for reproof, *c,* and training in holiness

CORRECTIONS (1)

Ti 2:15 and *c* with the authority of command.

CORRECTLY (1)

Lk 10:28 Jesus said, "You have answered *c.*

CORRECTS (1)

Prv 9: 7 He who *c* an arrogant man earns insult;

CORRESPOND (4)

Gn 18:21 *c* to the cry against them that comes to me.
1Sm 6: 4 to *c* to the number of Philistine lords,
2Chr 3:17 He set up the columns to *c* with the nave,
2Cor 11:15 But their end will *c* to their deeds.

CORRESPONDED (2)

1Sm 6:18 *c* to the number of all the cities of the
2Chr 3: 8 Its length *c* to the width of the house,

CORRESPONDING (9)

Ex 26: 5 the edge of the *c* sheet in the second set,
36:17 the edge of the *c* sheet in the other set.
Lv 27:18 year, with a *c* rebate on the valuation.
1Kgs 6:27 touched the *c* wing of the second cherub.
1Chr 5:13 brothers, *c* to their ancestral houses,
2Chr 3:12 touched the *c* wing of the second cherub.
Est 1:18 royal officials, with *c* disdain and rancor.
Ez 45: 7 *c* in length to one of the tribal portions
48:13 have a territory *c* to that of the priests,

CORRESPONDS (3)

Jdt 8:29 *c* to the worthy dispositions of your heart.
Gal 4:25 Arabia and *c* to the Jerusalem of our time,
1Pt 3:21 a baptismal bath which *c* to this exactly.

CORRODE (2)

Mt 6:19 Moths and rust *c;*
6:20 nor rust *c* nor thieves break in and steal.

CORRODED (1)

Jas 5: 3 moth-eaten, your gold and silver have *c,*

CORROSION (5)

Sir 12:10 for his wickedness is like *c* in bronze.
12:11 and you will find that there is still *c.*
Bar 6:11 they are not safe from *c* or insects.
6:23 unless someone wipes away the *c,*
Jas 5: 3 their *c* shall be a testimony against you;

CORROSIVE (1)

Lv 14:44 has spread in the house, it is *c* leprosy,

CORRUPT (20)

Gn 6:11 the earth was *c* and full of lawlessness.
6:12 When God saw how *c* the earth had become,
Lv 19:29 land will become *c* and full of lewdness.
Dt 31:29 after my death you are sure to become *c*
Jgs 19:22 the men of the city, who were *c,*
20:13 Now give up these *c* men of Gibeah,
2Mc 4: 7 obtained the high priesthood by *c* means:
Jb 15:16 How much less so is the abominable, the *c:*
Ps(s) 14: 1 Such are *c;* they do abominable deeds,
53: 2 Such are *c;* they do abominable deeds;
Is 1: 4 with wickedness, evil race, *c* children!
14:19 forth without burial, loathsome and *c,*
Jer 6:28 all, dealers in slander, all of them *c.*
49: 7 the prudent, has their wisdom become *c?*
Ez 16:47 became more *c* in all your ways than they.
20:44 to your evil conduct and *c* actions,
Zep 3: 7 eagerly have they done all their *c* deeds.
Mk 8:38 and *c* age is ashamed of me and my doctrine,
Lk 18: 6 "Listen to what the *c* judge has to say.
Jas 2: 4 up as judges handing down *c* decisions?

CORRUPTED (5)

2Cor 7: 2 We have injured no one, we have *c* no one,
11: 3 your thoughts may be *c* and you may fall
2Pt 1: 4 you who have fled a world *c* by lust
Jude 1:10 are *c* through the very things they know
Rv 19: 2 harlot who *c* the earth with her harlotry.

CORRUPTIBLE (4)

Wis 9:15 For the *c* body burdens the soul and the
14: 8 produced it, and it, because though *c,*
1Cor 15:53 This *c* body must be clothed with
15:54 When the *c* frame takes on incorruptibility

CORRUPTION (18)

1Mc 2:62 man, for his glory ends in *c* and worms.
2Mc 9: 9 army was sickened by the stench of his *c.*
Jb 17:14 the darkness, If I must call *c* "my father,"
Ps(s) 16:10 you suffer your faithful one to undergo *c.*
Wis 14:12 and their invention was a *c* of life.
14:25 and murder, theft and guile, *c,*
Sir 10:11 When a man dies, he inherits *c;*
Hos 9: 9 They have sunk to the depths of *c,*
Acts 2:27 you suffer your faithful one to undergo *c.*
2:31 nether world, nor did his body undergo *c,*
13:35 not suffer your faithful one to undergo *c.'*
13:36 joined his fathers, thereby undergoing *c.*
13:37 whom God has raised up did not undergo *c.*
Rom 8:21 will be freed from its slavery to *c*
1Cor 5: 8 the old yeast, that of *c* and wickedness,
15:50 no more can *c* inherit incorruption.
Gal 6: 8 of the flesh, he will reap a harvest of *c;*
2Pt 2:19 though they themselves are slaves of *c*—

CORRUPTS (3)

Eccl 7: 7 of a wise man, and a bribe *c* the heart.
1Cor 15:33 "Bad company *c* good morals."
2Pt 2:10 the flesh in their desire for whatever *c,*

CORSELET (2)

1Sm 17: 5 wore a bronze *c* of scale
Jb 41: 5 outer garment, or penetrate his double *c?*

COS (2)

1Mc 15:23 Lycia, Halicarnassus, Rhodes, Phaselis, *C,*
Acts 21: 1 we put out to sea and sailed straight to *C.*

COSAM (1)

Lk 3:28 son of Melchi, son of Addi, son of *C,*

COSMETICS (4)

Est 2: 3 of the women, let *c* be given them.
2: 9 furnished her with *c* and provisions.
2:12 the other six months with perfumes and *c.*
Jer 4:30 with gold, Shading your eyes with *c,*

COSMIC (2)

Col 2: 8 based on *c* powers rather than on Christ.
2:20 If with Christ you have died to *c* forces,

COST (21)

Ex 21: 2 he shall be given his freedom without *c.*
21:11 her freedom absolutely, without *c* to her.
Nm 11: 5 the fish we used to eat without *c* in Egypt,
17: 3 the censers at the *c* of their lives.
2Sm 24:24 the LORD my God holocausts that *c* nothing."
1Kgs 2:23 has not proposed this at the *c* of his life.
10:29 imported from Egypt *c* six hundred shekels,
1Chr 12:20 "At the *c* of our heads he will desert to
21:24 nor offer up holocausts that *c* me nothing."
1Mc 10:44 The *c* of rebuilding and restoring the
10:45 Likewise the *c* of building the walls of
2Mc 3: 6 all proportion to the *c* of the sacrifices,
Prv 4: 7 at the *c* of all you have,
Sir 51:25 gain, at no *c,* wisdom for yourselves.
Is 55: 1 Come, without paying and without *c,*
Jer 42:20 the *c* of your lives you have deceived me,
Dn 13:55 "Your fine lie has *c* you your head,"
13:59 "Your fine lie has *c* you also your head,"
Jon 4:10 *c* you no labor and which you did not raise;
Acts 22:28 *c* me quite a sum to get my citizenship."
Rv 21: 6 *c* from the spring of life-giving water.

COSTLY (6)

Gn 24:53 gave *c* presents to her brother and mother.
2Chr 32:23 and *c* objects for King Hezekiah of Judah,
Wis 2: 7 us have our fill of *c* wine and perfumes,
Mt 26: 7 a woman carrying a jar of *c* perfume came
Jn 12: 3 *c* perfume made from genuine aromatic nard,
1Tm 2: 9 gold ornaments, pearls, or *c* clothing;

COSTS (1)

Ezr 6: 4 The *c* are to be borne by the royal palace.

COT (1)

Am 3:12 the corner of a couch or a piece of a *c.*

COTES (1)

Is 60: 8 along like clouds, like doves to their *c?*

COTS (1)

Acts 5:15 streets and laid them on *c* and mattresses,

COTTON (2)

Est 1: 6 were white *c* draperies and violet hangings,
8:15 in a royal robe of violet and of white *c,*

COUCH (24)

Gn 49: 4 father's bed and defiled my *c* to my sorrow.
1Sm 28:23 got up from the ground, and sat on a *c.*
1Chr 5: 1 he disgraced the *c* of his father his birthright
2Chr 16:14 having laid him upon a *c* which was filled
Est 7: 8 on the *c* on which Esther was reclining;
Jb 7:13 comfort me, my *c* shall ease my complaint,"
17:13 dwelling, if I spread my *c* in the darkness,
Ps(s) 6: 7 I drench my *c* with my tears.
63: 7 I will remember you upon my *c,*
88: 6 My *c* is among the dead,
104:22 rises, they withdraw and *c* in their dens.
132: 3 I live in, nor lie on the *c* where I sleep;
Prv 7:16 With coverlets I have spread my *c,*
Sg 1:16 Our *c,* too, is verdant;
Sir 41:21 girl you have, and of violating her *c;*
Is 13:20 tent there, nor shepherds *c* their flocks.
14:11 The *c* beneath you is the maggot,
57: 2 There is rest on his *c* for the sincere,
Jer 33:12 for the shepherds to *c* their flocks.
Ez 23:17 Babylonians came to her, to the love *c,*
23:41 You sat on a *c* prepared for them,
Am 3:12 with the corner of a *c* or a piece of a cot.
Zep 2: 7 at evening they shall *c* their flocks,
3:13 *c* their flocks with none to disturb them.

COUCHED (1)

Ez 19: 2 Among young lions she *c* to rear her whelps.

COUCHES (6)

2Sm 17:28 the Gileadite from Rogelim, brought *c,*
Jdt 15:11 of Holofernes, with all his silver, his *c,*
Est 1: 6 Gold and silver *c* were on the pavement,
Ps(s) 149: 5 let them sing for joy upon their *c;*
Am 6: 4 ivory, stretched comfortably on their *c,*
Mi 2: 1 iniquity, and work out evil on their *c;*

COUNCIL (24)

Gn 23:10 of the Hittites who sat on his town *c:*
23:18 the Hittites who sat on Ephron's town *c.*

COUNCIL (cont.)

34:20 his son Shechem went to their town c
49: 6 Let not my soul enter their c,
Nm 16: 2 members of the c and men of note.
20: 2 they held a c against Moses and Aaron.
Neh 6: 2 let us hold c together at Caphirim in the
6: 7 of the king, come, let us hold c together."
Jdt 6: 1 the crowd surrounding the c had subsided,
6:17 of what was said in the c of Holofernes,
11: 9 "As for Achior's speech in your c,
11:14 authorization from the c of the elders;
1Mc 9:58 transgressors of the law held a c and said:
2Mc 14: 5 he was invited to the c by Demetrius
Ps(s) 64: 3 Shelter me against the c of malefactors,
89: 8 God is terrible in the c of the holy ones;
107:32 and praise him in the c of the elders.
Jer 23:18 Now, who has stood in the c of the LORD,
23:22 Had they stood in my c,
Mi 6: 9 Hear, O tribe and city c,
Lk 22:66 Once they had brought him before their c,
Acts 5:21 the full c of the elders of Israel.
22: 5 the whole c of elders can bear me witness,
25:12 conferred with his c and finally declared:

COUNCILOR (1)

Gn 26:26 from Gerar, accompanied by Ahuzzath, his c,

COUNCILORS (2)

Nm 1:16 These were c of the community,
26: 9 same Dathan and Abiram, c of the community,

COUNSEL (80)

1Sm 28: 7 to whom I can go to seek c through her."
2Sm 15:31 LORD, turn the c of Ahithophel to folly!"
15:34 you will undo for me the c of Ahithophel.
16:20 "Offer your c on what we should do."
16:23 Now the c given by Ahithophel at that time
16:23 was all his c both to David and to Absalom.
17: 7 time Ahithophel has not given good c."
17:11 "This is what I c:
17:14 Israelites pronounced the c of Hushai
17:14 had decided to undo Ahithophel's good c,
17:15 "This is the c Ahithophel gave Absalom
17:21 has given the following c in regard to you."
17:23 saw that his c was not acted upon,
1Kgs 12:28 After taking c,
1Chr 10:13 because he had sought c of a necromancer,
12:20 for their lords took c and sent him home,
13: 1 After David had taken c with his
2Chr 22: 5 their c when he accompanied Jehoram,
25:16 has let you take c to your own destruction,
25:16 this thing and have refused to hear my c."
25:17 Having taken c,
32: 3 he decided in c with his princes and
Tb 4:18 "Seek c from every wise man,
4:19 For no pagan nation possesses good c,
Est C:22 but turn their own c against them and make
1Mc 8:15 day three hundred and twenty men took c,
9:59 So they went and took c with him.
Jb 12:13 his are c and understanding.
18: 7 hemmed in, and his own c casts him down.
21:16 if the c of the wicked is repulsive to God,
26: 3 How you c, as though he had no wisdom;
29:21 they were silent for my c.
Ps(s) 1: 1 Happy the man who follows not the c of the
32: 8 I will c you,
71:10 keep watch against my life take c together.
73:24 With your c you guide me,
106:13 they waited not for his c.
107:11 of God and scorned the c of the Most High.
Prv 1:25 Because you disdained all my c,
1:30 They ignored my c,
2: 7 He has c in store for the upright,
3:21 keep advice and c in view;
8:14 Mine are c and advice;
12:20 plot evil, but those who c peace have joy.
13:10 but with those who take c is wisdom.
15:22 Plans fail when there is no c,
19:20 Listen to c and receive instruction,
21:30 There is no wisdom, no understanding, no c,
31:26 in wisdom, and on her tongue is kindly c.
Wis 9:13 For what man knows God's c,
9:17 Or who ever knew your c,
Sir 6:24 refuse not my c.
8:17 Take no c with a fool,
19:18 nor is there prudence in the c of sinners.
21:13 knowledge wells up in a flood, and his c,
25: 4 and a knowledge of c to those on in years!
32:19 Do nothing without c,
37: 7 out a way, but some c ways of their own;
37:13 Then, too, heed your own heart's c;
39: 7 Who will direct his knowledge and his c,
Is 11: 2 A spirit of c and of strength
16: 3 Offer c, take their part:
19: 3 them, and I will bring to nought their c;
19:11 wisest of Pharaoh's advisers give stupid c.
28:29 wonderful is his c and great his wisdom.
30: 2 down to Egypt, but my c they do not seek.
41:28 is not one, no one of them to give c,
45:21 Come here and declare in c together:
Jer 18:18 from the priests, nor of c from the wise,
32:19 whose name is LORD of hosts, great in c,
38:15 If I c you, you will not listen to me!
49: 7 in Teman, has c perished from the prudent,
49:20 Therefore, hear the c of the LORD.
49:30 For c has been taken against you,
50:45 Therefore hear the c of the LORD which he
Ez 7:26 lacking to the priest, and c to the elders,
11: 2 evil and giving wicked c in this city.
Dn 2:14 Then Daniel prudently took c with Arioch,
Mi 4:12 of the LORD, nor understand his c,
Eph 1:11 everything according to his will and c,

COUNSELED (2)

2Sm 17:15 the elders of Israel, and this is what I c.
2Chr 22: 3 because his mother c him to act sinfully.

COUNSELOR (13)

2Sm 15:12 to Ahithophel the Gilonite, David's c,
1Chr 26:14 lots for his son Zechariah, a prudent c,
27:32 a man of intelligence, was c and scribe;
27:33 Ahithophel was also the king's c,
2Chr 25:16 "Have you been made the king's c?
2Mc 1:10 c of King Ptolemy and member of the family
Wis 8: 9 that she would be my c while all was well,
Sir 37: 7 Every c points out a way,
42:22 no need of a c for him!
Is 3: 3 The captain of fifty and the nobleman, c,
40:13 the LORD, or has instructed him as his c?
Mi 4: 9 Or has your c perished,
Rom 11:34 Or who has been his c?

COUNSELORS (17)

2Chr 22:4 they were his c after the death
Ezr 4: 5 They also suborned c to work against them
7:14 king and his seven c to supervise Judah
7:15 king and his c have freely contributed
7:28 me find favor with the king, with his c,
8:25 the house of our God by the king, his c,
Est B: 3 my c as to how this might be accomplished,
Jb 3:14 With kings and c of the earth who built
12:17 He sends c away barefoot,
Ps(s) 119:24 they are my c.
Prv 11:14 security lies in many c.
15:22 counsel, but they succeed when c are many.
24: 6 and the victory is due to a wealth of c.
Sir 44: 3 for their might, Or c in their prudence,
Is 1:26 at first, and your c as in the beginning;
Dn 3: 2 satraps, prefects, and governors, the c,
3: 3 satraps, prefects, and governors, the c,

COUNSELS (13)

Jb 15: 8 Are you privy to the c of God,
Ps(s) 16: 7 I bless the LORD who c me;
55:10 divide their c,
81:13 they walked according to their own c.
106:43 c and were brought low by their guilt.
Prv 22:20 you the "Thirty," with c and knowledge,
Wis 1: 3 For perverse c separate a man from God,
1: 5 deceit and withdraws from senseless c;
2:22 And they knew not the hidden c of God;
6: 3 probe your works and scrutinize your c!
Sir 24:27 deeper than the sea are her thoughts; her c,
Hos 11: 6 to repent, their own c shall devour them.
Mi 6:16 of Ahab, and you have walked in their c;

COUNT (35)

Gn 13:16 if anyone could c the dust of the earth,
15: 5 "Look up at the sky and c the stars,
16:10 "that they will be too many to c.
32:13 of the sea, which are too numerous to c.'"
Lv 23:15 sheaf, you shall c seven full weeks,
25: 8 "Seven weeks of years shall you c—
Nm 31:26 c up all the human captives and the beasts
Dt 16: 9 "You shall c off seven weeks,
1Sm 14:17 C the troops and find out if any of us are
2Sm 12: 8 enough, I could c up for you still more.
18: 3 c; even if half of us should die, we shall not c.
1Kgs 8: 5 ark sheep and oxen too many to number or c.
2Kgs 1:13 servants, c for something in your sight!
10: 6 c the heads of your master's sons and come
1Chr 27:23 David did not c those who were twenty
Jdt 2:20 A huge, irregular force, too many to c,
Jb 3: 6 year, nor enter into the c of the months!
14:16 Surely then you would c my steps,
Ps(s) 22:18 I can c all my bones.
48:13 make the round; c her towers.
Wis 2:22 neither did they c on recompense of
Sir 8:12 and whatever you lend, c it as lost.
16: 3 C not on their length of life,
Is 40:15 the nations c as a drop in the bucket,
Ez 20:37 I will c you with the staff and bring back
Mt 27:14 He did not answer him on a single c,
Acts 19:27 great goddess Artemis will c for nothing.
26: 2 I c myself fortunate to be able to make my
1Cor 1:28 and despised, those who c for nothing,
Jas 1: 2 c it pure joy when you are involved in
Rv 7: 9 no one could c from every nation and race,
9:16 Their cavalry troops, whose c I heard,
11: 1 and altar, and c those who worship there.
18: 5 as heaven, and God keeps c of her crimes.

COUNTED (29)

Gn 13:16 the earth, your descendants too might be c.
38: 9 that the descendants would not be c as his;
Lv 27:32 animal as they are c by the herdsman's rod.
Nm 23:10 Who has ever c the dust of Jacob,
31:49 have c up the soldiers under our command,
Jgs 7:12 Nor could their camels be c,
1Sm 18:27 foreskins and c them out before the king,
2Sm 2:15 So they rose and were c off:
1Kgs 3: 8 so vast that it cannot be numbered or c.
1Chr 23: 3 Levites thirty years old and above were c,
23:14 sons were c as part of the tribe of Levi.
2Chr 5: 6 that they could not be c or numbered.
25: 5 he had c those of twenty years and over,
Ezr 1: 8 Mithredath, and c out to Sheshbazzar,
Jdt 5:10 the number of their race could not be c.
Ps(s) 49:19 in his lifetime he c himself blessed.
56: 9 My wanderings you have c;
Is 14: 1 join them and be c with the house of Jacob.
33:18 "Where is he who c,
33:18 Where is he who c the towers?"
53:12 to death and was c among the wicked;
Jer 33:22 the sands of the sea which cannot be c,
46:23 numerous than locusts, they cannot be c.
Dn 4:32 All who live on the earth are c as nothing;
Hos 2: 1 sea, which can be neither measured nor c.
Zec 11:12 And they c out my wages,
Mt 10:30 you, every hair of your head has been c;
Lk 12: 7 truth, even the hairs of your head are c!
22:37 in Scripture, 'He was c among the wicked,'

COUNTENANCE (12)

Gn 39: 6 was strikingly handsome in c and body.
Jdt 16: 6 by the beauty of her c disabled him.
Est D: 5 and her c was as joyous as it was lovely,
Ps(s) 4: 7 let the light of your c shine upon us!
44: 4 your right hand and the light of your c,
89:16 in the light of your c,
119:135 Let your c shine upon your servant,
Prv 16:15 In the light of the king's c is life,
25:23 rain, and a backbiting tongue an angry c.
Sir 13:24 The heart of a man changes his c,
13:25 The sign of a good heart is a cheerful c;
35: 8 With each contribution show a cheerful c,

COUNTER (1)

1Pt 2:23 made to suffer, he did not c with threats.

COUNTERCHARGES (1)

2Mc 5: 3 array, charges and c on this side and that,

COUNTERED (3)

2Sm 19:22 But Abishai, son of Zeruiah, c:
1Mc 6:52 Jews c by setting up machines of their own,
Acts 13:45 c with violent abuse whatever Paul said.

COUNTERFEITS (1)

Wis 15: 9 of bronze, and takes pride in modeling c.

COUNTERMAND (1)

Is 43:13 who can c what I do?

COUNTERMANDS (1)

Nm 30:16 he c them some time after he first learned

COUNTERPART (1)

Lam 4: 2 Zion's precious sons, fine gold their c,

COUNTING (12)

Gn 46:26 not c the wives of Jacob's sons
Ex 12:37 thousand men on foot, not c the children.
1Kgs 5: 3 oxen, and a hundred sheep, not c harts,
2Chr 12: 3 and there was no c the army that came with
Ezr 2:65 sixty, not c their male and female slaves,
Neh 7:67 sixty, not c their male and female slaves,
Tb 9: 4 For you know that my father is c the days.
Jdt 7: 2 not c the baggage train or the men who
Wis 4:20 shall they come, at the c up of their sins,
Dn 9: 2 c of the years of which the LORD spoke
Mt 14:21 five thousand, not c women and children.
2Cor 5:19 not c men's transgressions against them,

COUNTLESS (9)

Gn 22:17 make your descendants as c as the stars
1Mc 5:30 ahead and saw a c multitude of people,
Jb 21:33 him, and the c others who have gone before.
Wis 7:11 in her company, and c riches at her hands;
18:12 And all alike by a single death had c dead;
19:10 of fishes the river swarmed with c frogs.
Ez 16:25 passer-by, playing the harlot c times.
Jude 1:14 the Lord has come with his c holy ones
Rv 5:11 They were c in number,

COUNTRIES (20)

Gn 41:54 there was famine in all the other c,
2Kgs 19:11 kings of Assyria have done to all other c:
1Chr 22: 5 it will be renowned and glorious in all c.

2Chr 17:10 the kingdoms of the *c* surrounding Judah,
Jdt 2: 2 urged the total destruction of those *c*
1Mc 15:15 as this addressed to various kings and *c*:
15:19 decided to write to various kings and *c*,
15:23 to all the *c*— Sampsames, Sparta,
Is 37:11 the kings of Assyria have done to all the *c*:
Jer 16:15 of all the *c* to which he had banished them."
Ez 5: 5 I placed her, surrounded by foreign *c*.
5: 6 more than the foreign *c* surrounding her;
11:16 nations and scattered them over foreign *c*—
11:16 sanctuary in the *c* to which they had gone
11:17 the *c* over which you have been scattered,
20:34 from the *c* over which you are scattered;
20:41 out of the *c* over which you are scattered;
Dn 9: 7 in all the *c* to which you have scattered
11:40 fleet, passing through the *c* like a flood.
11:42 He shall extend his power over the *c*,

COUNTRY (232)

Gn 10:30 all the way to Sephar, the eastern hill *c*.
12: 8 he moved on to the hill *c* east of Bethel,
14: 6 and the Horites in the hill *c* of Seir,
14: 7 and they subdued the whole *c* both of the
19:30 up from Zoar and settled in the hill *c*,
27: 3 go out into the *c* to hunt some game for me.
27: 5 the *c* to hunt some game for his father,
29: 2 about, he saw a well in the open *c*,
29:26 "It is not the custom in our *c*,"
31:23 caught up with him in the hill *c* of Gilead.
32: 4 Esau in the land of Seir, the *c* of Edom,
34:21 there is ample room in the *c* for them.
34:28 was in the city and in the *c* around.
36:34 defeated the Midianites in the *c* of Moab;
41:36 a reserve for the *c* against the seven years
42: 6 It was Joseph, as governor of the *c*,
42:30 "The man who is lord of the *c*,"
42:33 the man who is lord of the *c* said to us:
47: 4 continued, "in order to stay in this *c*,
47:13 Since there was no food in any *c* because
49:15 settled life was, and how pleasant the *c*,
Ex 1:10 to fight against us, and so leave our *c*."
3: 8 milk and honey, the *c* of the Canaanites,
10: 4 tomorrow I will bring locusts into your *c*.
18:27 father-in-law, who went off to his own *c*.
Lv 25:24 in every part of the *c* that you occupy,
26: 6 I will rid the *c* of ravenous beasts,
26:38 Gentiles, swallowed up in your enemies' *c*.
Nm 10:30 instead to my own *c* and to my own kindred."
13:19 Is the *c* in which they live good or bad?
13:26 all, and showed them the fruit of the *c*.
13:32 is a *c* that consumes its inhabitants.
14: 7 "The *c* which we went through and explored
14:45 in that hill *c* came down and defeated them,
19:16 who in the open *c* touches a dead person,
20:17 Kindly let us pass through your *c*.
21:22 the message, "Let us pass through your *c*.
21:24 and as far as the *c* of the Ammonites,
22: 4 horde will devour all the *c* around us
22: 6 to defeat them and drive them out of the *c*.
22:13 of Balak, "Go back to your own *c*,
32: 1 land of Jazer and of Gilead was grazing *c*,
32: 4 the community of Israel, is grazing *c*.
32:11 see this *c* I promised under oath
33:55 will harass you in the *c* where you live,
Dt 1: 7 Leave here and go to the hill *c* of the
1:19 direction of the hill *c* of the Amorites.
1:20 have come to the hill *c* of the Amorites,
1:24 into the hill *c* as far as the Wadi Eshcol,
1:41 making light of going up into the hill *c*.
1:43 you arrogantly marched off into the hill *c*.
2:20 [This also was considered a *c* of the
2:27 'Let me pass through your *c* by the highway;
3:25 land beyond the Jordan, this fine hill *c*,
4:22 die in this *c* without crossing the Jordan;
8: 7 your God, is bringing you into a good *c*,
8:10 your God, for the good *c* he has given you.
11:30 *c* of the Canaanites who live in the Arabah,
15:11 to your poor and needy kinsman in your *c*.
23: 8 Egyptian, since you were an alien in his *c*.
26: 9 and bringing us into this *c*,
28: 3 blessed in the city, and blessed in the *c*!
28:16 be cursed in the city, and cursed in the *c*!
28:40 you have olive trees throughout your *c*,
31: 4 whom he destroyed, and with their *c*.
Jos 2:16 "Go up into the hill *c*,"
9:11 all the inhabitants of our *c* said to us,
10: 6 mountain *c* have joined forces against us."
10:40 Joshua conquered the entire *c*;
11:23 Thus Joshua captured the whole *c*,
21:12 although the open *c* and villages belonging
24:15 the Amorites in whose *c* you are dwelling.
1Sm 1: 1 name, a Zuphite from the hill *c* of Ephraim.
9: 4 they went through the hill *c* of Ephraim,
13: 2 in Michmash and in the hill *c* of Bethel,
14:22 who were hiding in the hill *c* of Ephraim,
14:24 in every town in the hill *c* of Ephraim.
20: 5 me go and hide in the open *c* until evening.
20:11 When they were out in the open *c* together,
20:24 So David hid in the open *c*.
23:14 desert, or in the barren hill *c* near Ziph.
25:15 among them during our stay in the open *c*.
27: 5 have a place to live in one of the *c* towns.
27: 7 four months in the *c* of the Philistines.
27:11 as he lived in the *c* of the Philistines.
30:11 found in the open *c* and brought to David.
2Sm 10: 2 servants entered the *c* of the Ammonites,
10: 8 and Maacah remained apart in the open *c*.
15:19 and you, too, are an exile from your own *c*.
19:10 now he has fled from the *c* before Absalom,
20:21 from the hill *c* of Ephraim has rebelled
24: 8 Thus they toured the whole *c*,
24:25 The LORD granted relief to the *c*,
1Kgs 4: 8 the son of Hur in the hill *c* of Ephraim;
4:12 and in the *c* around Zarethan below Jezreel
10: 6 *c* about your deeds and your wisdom is true,"
10:13 returned with her servants to her own *c*.
10:15 kings of Arabia and the governors of the *c*.
11:21 "Give me leave to return to my own *c*."
11:22 you are seeking to return to your own *c*?"
12:25 in the hill *c* of Ephraim and lived there.
2Kgs 5:22 guild prophets from the hill *c* of Ephraim.
15:20 it from all the men of substance in the *c*,
15:20 did not remain in the *c* but withdrew.
25:24 in the *c* and serve the king of Babylon,
1Chr 6:41 although the open *c* and the villages
27:25 Over the stores in the *c*,
2Chr 9: 5 *c* about your deeds and your wisdom is true,"
9:12 returned to her own *c* with her servants.
9:14 of Arabia also, and the governors of the *c*,
27: 4 he built cities in the hill *c* of Judah,
32:21 he had to return shamefaced to his own *c*.
34: 6 of the surrounding *c* as far as Naphtali;
Neh 3:22 by the priests, men of the surrounding *c*.
8:15 *c* and bring in branches of olive trees,
11:25 As concerns their villages in the *c*:
Tb 1: 4 When I lived as a young man in my own *c*,
14: 4 entire *c* of Israel shall become desolate;
Jdt 2:11 slaughter and plunder in each *c* you occupy.
7: 4 "Soon they will devour the whole *c*.
15: 4 *c* of Israel to report what had happened,
1Mc 1:24 all this, he went back to his own *c*,
3:24 the rest fled to the *c* of the Philistines.
3:41 the merchants of the *c* heard of their fame,
5:65 the sons of Esau in the *c* toward the south;
7: 6 friends and have driven us out of our *c*.
7:24 preventing them from going out into the *c*.
8: 4 and persistence had conquered the whole *c*,
8:16 every year, to rule over their entire *c*,
9:24 great famine, and the *c* deserted to them.
9:25 impious men and made them masters of the *c*.
9:53 leaders of the *c* and put them in custody
9:61 men of the *c* who were ringleaders
9:69 them and resolved to return to his own *c*.
9:72 He returned to his own *c* and never came
10:13 left his place and returned to his own *c*.
10:52 Demetrius and gaining control of my *c*—
10:77 as though he were going on through the *c*,
12:25 and went into the *c* of Hamath to meet them,
13:20 Next he began to invade and ravage the *c*.
13:24 Then Trypho returned to his own *c*.
13:49 the *c* and back for the purchase of food;
14: 6 of his nation and gained control of the *c*.
14:17 and was master of the *c* and the cities,
14:28 rulers of the nation, and elders of the *c*,
14:29 there have often been wars in our *c*,
14:31 their *c* and to lay hands on their temple,
14:36 in driving the Gentiles out of their *c*,
14:42 its functions and concerning the *c*,
14:43 made in the *c* shall be dated by his name.
14:44 an assembly in the *c* without his consent,
15: 4 make a landing in my *c* and take revenge
15: 6 your own money, as legal tender in your *c*.
15:19 against them or their cities or their *c*,
15:21 from their *c* take refuge with you,
15:35 harm to our people and laying waste our *c*;
16:13 and sought to get control of the *c*.
16:14 of the *c* and providing for their needs,
16:18 him and that the *c* be turned over to him.
2Mc 4: 1 about the funds against his own *c*,
4:26 as a fugitive to the *c* of the Ammonites.
5: 7 took refuge in the *c* of the Ammonites.
5: 8 as the butcher of his *c* and his countrymen.
5: 9 so many from their *c* perished in exile;
5:15 that traitor both to the laws and to his *c*,
8:21 ready to die for their laws and their *c*.
8:35 fled alone across *c* like a runaway slave,
13: 3 on, not for the welfare of his *c*,
13:11 to be deprived of their law, their *c*,
13:14 for the laws, the temple, the city, the *c*,
14: 2 a fleet, and that he had occupied the *c*,
14: 9 act in the interest of our *c* and its
14:18 with which they fought for their *c*,
15:19 they were worried about the battle in the open *c*.
Ps(s) 60: 4 You have rocked the *c* and split it open;
Prv 25:25 from thirst is good news from a far *c*.
Eccl 5: 8 Yet an advantage for a *c* in every respect
Is 1: 7 Your *c* is waste,
7:24 for all the *c* shall be briers and thorns.
13: 5 They come from a far-off *c*,
21:13 the thicket in the nomad *c* spend the night,
32: 2 will be like streams of water in a dry *c*,
32:18 My people will live in peaceful *c*,
33: 9 The *c* languishes in mourning,
40: 4 land shall be made a plain, the rough *c*,
63:13 the depths like horses in the open *c*,
66: 8 Can a *c* be brought forth in one day,
Jer 17:26 foothills, from the hill *c* and the Negeb,
32:44 in the cities of Judah and of the hill *c*,
33:11 For I will restore this *c* as of old,
33:13 In the cities of the hill *c*,
Ez 7:15 He that is in the *c* shall die by the sword;
14:17 Or if I brought the sword upon this *c*,
33: 2 sword against a *c*, and the people of this *c*
33: 3 seeing the sword coming against the *c*,
34:13 back to their own *c* and pasture them
34:25 them, and rid the *c* of ravenous beasts,
Dn 8: 9 the south, the east, and the glorious *c*.
11: 9 king of the south, and return to his own *c*.
Jl 4: 6 Greeks, removing them far from their own *c*!
Am 7:10 the *c* cannot endure all his words.
Jon 1: 8 What is your *c*,
4: 2 what I said while I was still in my own *c*?
Mi 5: 4 invades our *c* and treads upon our land,
Hg 1: 8 Go up into the hill *c*;
Zec 2: 8 live in Jerusalem as though in open *c*,
Mt 2:12 went back to their own *c* by another route.
Mk 6: 1 part of the *c* followed by his disciples.
16:12 were walking along on their way to the *c*,
Lk 1:39 haste into the hill *c* to a town of Judah,
1:65 throughout the hill *c* of Judea these
4:23 'Do here in your own *c* the things we have
4:37 kept spreading through the surrounding *c*.
4:42 left the town and set out into the open *c*.
7:17 him throughout Judea and the surrounding *c*.
8:26 They sailed to the *c* of the Gerasenes,
8:34 the news to the town and *c* roundabout.
15:14 out in that *c* and he was in dire need.
19:12 went to a faraway *c* to become its king,
21:21 those in the *c* must not return.
Jn 4:44 that no one esteems a prophet in his own *c*.)
11:55 people from the *c* went up to Jerusalem
Acts 7: 3 to him, Leave your *c* and your kinsfolk,
12:20 because their *c* was supplied with food
13:19 to give them that *c* as their heritage
14: 6 Lystra and Derbe and to the surrounding *c*,
18:23 through the Galatian *c* and Phrygia
19: 1 the interior of the *c* and came to Ephesus.
26:20 people of Jerusalem and all the *c* of Judea;
Heb 11: 9 in the promised land as in a foreign *c*,
Rv 20: 9 They invaded the whole *c* and surrounded

COUNTRYMAN (4)

Lv 25:36 from your *c* either in money or in kind,
25:39 your *c* becomes so impoverished beside you
Dt 23:21 but not from your *c* so that the LORD,
Mt 5:43 'You shall love your *c* but hate your enemy.'

COUNTRYMEN (24)

Lv 19:18 cherish no grudge against your fellow *c*.
25:25 When one of your *c* is reduced to poverty
25:35 "When one of your fellow *c* is reduced to
25:47 "When one of your *c* is reduced to such
Dt 17:20 become estranged from his *c* through pride,
23:20 interest from your *c* on a loan of money
24:14 whether he be one of your own *c* or one of
Jgs 14:16 me, for you have proposed a riddle to my *c*,
14:17 and she explained the riddle to her *c*.
2Mc 4: 5 to the king, not as an accuser of his *c*,
4:10 initiated his *c* into the Greek way of life.
5: 6 victory over his enemies, not his fellow *c*.
5: 8 as the butcher of his country and his *c*.
12: 5 barbarous deed perpetrated against his *c*,
14: 8 out of consideration for my own *c*,
15:30 from youth his affection for his *c*,
15:31 When he arrived there, he assembled his *c*,
Ez 3:11 Now go to the exiles, to your *c*,
33: 2 Son of man, speak thus to your *c*:
33:12 As for you, son of man, tell your *c*:
33:17 Yet your *c* say,
33:30 your *c* are talking about you along the
37:18 When your *c* ask you,
1Thes 2:14 treatment from your fellow *c* as they did

COUNTRY'S (2)

2Kgs 25:12 But some of the *c* poor,
Jer 52:16 But some of the *c* poor,

COUNTRYSIDE (16)

Lv 14: 7 let the living bird fly away over the *c*.
14:53 bird fly away over the *c* outside the city.
26:33 your *c* desolate and your cities deserted.
1Sm 14:15 panic spread to the army and to the *c*,
19: 3 beside my father in the *c* where you are,
2Sm 15:23 Everyone in the *c* wept aloud as the last
1Kgs 20:27 flocks of goats, while Aram covered the *c*—
2Kgs 3:24 through the *c* striking down the Moabites,
Neh 11:30 and their villages, Lachish and its *c*,
Jdt 3: 7 all the inhabitants of the *c* received him
7:18 in the plain, covering the whole *c*.
Is 55:12 the trees of the *c* shall clap their hands.
Jer 12: 4 mourn, the green of the whole *c* wither?
Mk 1: 5 All the Judean *c* and the people of
15:33 the whole *c* and lasted until midafternoon.
Acts 8: 1 throughout the *c* of Judea and Samaria.

COUNTS (7)

Jb 19:11 he *c* me among his enemies.
38:37 Who *c* the clouds in his wisdom?
Wis 14:30 But on both *c* shall justice overtake them:
Jer 33:13 pass under the hands of the one who *c* them,
1Cor 7:19 Circumcision *c* for nothing,
Gal 5: 6 nor the lack of it *c* for anything;
Jas 2:10 remainder, has become guilty on all *c*.

COUPLE (6)

1Kgs 17:12 Just now I was collecting a *c* of sticks,
20:27 seemed like a *c* of small flocks of goats,
Is 7:21 a man shall keep a heifer or a *c* of sheep,
Mt 14:17 replied, "but five loaves and a *c* of fish."
Lk 2:22 the *c* brought him up to Jerusalem so that
Jn 6: 9 five barley loaves and a *c* of dried fish,

COURAGE (67)

Ex 15: 2 My strength and my *c* is the LORD,
Jos 5: 1 disheartened and lost *c* at their approach.
Jgs 7:11 you will have the *c* to descend on the camp."
20:23 But though the Israelite soldiers took *c*
1Sm 4: 9 Take *c* and be manly, Philistines;
17:32 "Let your majesty not lose *c*.
25:37 At this his *c* died within him,
2Sm 2: 7 Take *c*, therefore, and prove yourselves
7:27 now finds the *c* to make this prayer to you.
16:21 father, all your partisans will take *c*."
17:10 man with the heart of a lion will lose *c*.
1Kgs 2: 2 Take *c* and be a man.
1Chr 28:10 Take *c* and set to work."
2Chr 23: 1 Jehoiada took *c* and entered a conspiracy
Ezr 7:28 I therefore took *c*,
10: 4 stand by you, so have *c* and take action!"
Tb 5:10 Raphael said, "Take *c*!
5:10 healing in store for you; so take *c*!"
7:17 *C*, my daughter."
11:11 *C*, father," he said.
Jdt 7:30 But Uzziah said to them, *C*, my brothers!
11: 1 "Take *c*, lady; have no fear in your heart!
11: 3 Take *c*!
Est C:23 in the time of our distress and give me *c*.
D: 9 Take *c*!
1Mc 11:49 they lost *c* and cried out to the king in
2Mc 6:20 who have the *c* to reject the food
6:31 leaving in his death a model of *c* and an
7:12 attendants marveled at the young man's *c*,
7:21 stirred her womanly heart with manly *c*,
11: 9 their hearts were filled with such *c*
14:18 *c* with which they fought for their country,
14:43 manly *c* threw himself down into the crowd.
15:10 Having stirred up their *c*,
15:17 instill valor and stir young hearts to *c*,
15:17 by hand-to-hand combat with the utmost *c*,
Jb 23:16 Indeed God has made my *c* fail;
Ps(s) 23: 4 your rod and your staff that give me *c*.
27:14 of the living Wait for the LORD with *c*;
31:25 who act proudly Take *c* and be stouthearted,
118:14 My strength and my *c* is the LORD,
Wis 18: 6 they put their faith, they might have *c*.
Sir 30:23 Distract yourself, renew your *c*,
34:13 Lively is the *c* of those who fear the LORD,
38:23 let memory fade; rally your *c*,
Is 7: 4 let not your *c* fail before these two
12: 2 My strength and my *c* is the LORD,
19: 3 *c* of the Egyptians ebbs away within them,
Dn 10:19 take *c* and be strong."
Hg 2: 4 take *c*, Zerubbabel, says the LORD, and take *c*,
2: 4 high priest, son of Jedak, And take *c*,
Mt 8:26 "Where is your *c*?
9: 2 faith he said to the paralytic, "Have *c*,
9:22 turned around and saw her and said, *C*,
Mk 12:34 had the *c* to ask him any more questions.
Jn 16:33 But take *c*! I have overcome the world.
Acts 23:11 "Keep up your *c*!
27:22 I urge you now to keep up your *c*.
27:25 So keep up your *c*, men.
27:36 This gave them new *c*,
28:15 saw them, he thanked God and took fresh *c*.
Rom 5: 7 a good man someone may have the *c* to die.
Eph 6:20 I may have *c* to proclaim it as I ought.
Phil 1:14 in Christ, taking *c* from my chains,
2:19 *c* from learning how things go with you.
1Thes 2: 2 we drew *c* from our God to preach his good

COURAGEOUS (6)

1Chr 19:13 show ourselves *c* for the sake of our people
2Chr 26:17 eighty other priests of the LORD, *c* men,
Tb 6:12 Now the girl is sensible, *c*,
1Mc 2:64 be *c* and strong in keeping the law,
Wis 8:15 I should appear noble, and in war *c*.
Sir 45:23 Eleazar, was the *c* third of his line When,

COURAGEOUSLY (4)

2Mc 7:20 bore it *c* because of her hope in the Lord.
8:16 attacking them unjustly, but to fight *c*,
2Cor 10: 2 I might dare to use *c* against certain ones
Eph 6:19 that I may *c* make known the mystery of the

COURIERS (12)

1Sm 11: 7 territory of Israel by *c* with the message,
1Kgs 20: 2 He sent *c* to Ahab,
20: 5 But the *c* came again and said,
20: 9 Accordingly he directed the *c* of Ben-hadad,
20: 9 The *c* left and reported this.
2Chr 30: 6 Accordingly the *c*,
30:10 So the *c* passed from city to city in the
Est 3:13 were sent by *c* to all the royal provinces,
3:15 *c* set out in haste at the king's command;
8:10 mounted *c* riding thoroughbred royal steeds.
8:14 *C* mounted on royal steeds sped forth in
Na 3:16 Make your *c* more numerous than the stars,

COURSE (74)

Gn 4: 3 In the *c* of time Cain brought an offering
31:32 Jacob, of *c*, had no idea that Rachel
32:23 In the *c* of that night,
42:23 They did not know, of *c*,
Jos 4:18 *c* and as before overflowed all its banks.
10:13 for a whole day did it resume its swift *c*.
Jgs 5:15 too, was in the valley, his *c* unchecked.
1Sm 28: 1 Achish said to David, "You realize, of *c*,
1Kgs 6:36 of hewn stones and one *c* of cedar beams.
7: 9 saw, from the foundation to the bonding *c*.
7:12 hewn stones and a bonding *c* of cedar beams.
Tb 5: 3 We will, of *c*, give him a salary
5: 7 I will, of *c*, pay you."
5:10 I will of *c* pay you, brother."
2Mc 3: 4 certain Simon, of the priestly *c* of Bilgah,
Jb 1: 5 And when each feast had run its *c*,
Ps(s) 19: 6 and, like a giant, joyfully runs its *c*.
19: 7 forth, and its *c* is to their other end;
78:50 When he measured the *c* of his anger he
Prv 16: 9 In his mind a man plans his *c*,
17:23 bribe to pervert the *c* of justice.
Wis 5:11 no evidence of its *c* is to be found
7:18 sun's *c* and the variations of the seasons.
18:14 the night in its swift *c* was half spent,
Sir 11:34 with you, and he will subvert your *c*,
43: 7 this light-giver which wanes in its *c*:
Jer 2:36 base you have become in changing your *c*!
8: 6 Everyone keeps on running his *c*,
10:23 Man's *c* is not within his choice,
23:10 Theirs is an evil *c*,
Dn 5:23 life breath and the whole *c* of your life,
Hb 3: 2 In the *c* of the years revive it, in the course
Mt 17:25 "Of *c* he does," Peter replied.
21:16 Jesus said to them, "Of *c* I do!
26:21 In the *c* of the meal he said,
27:18 He knew, of *c*, that it was out of jealousy
Mk 4: 2 and in the *c* of his teaching said:
12:38 the *c* of his teaching he said:
14:18 table, and in the *c* of the meal Jesus said,
15:10 He was aware, of *c*,
Lk 13:33 For all that, I must proceed on *c* today,
22:22 of Man is following out his appointed *c*,
24:15 In the *c* of their lively exchange,
Jn 3:24 (John, of *c*, had not yet been thrown
6:64 (Jesus knew from the start, of *c*,
7:39 There was, of *c*, no Spirit as yet,
Acts 1: 3 appearing to them over the *c* of forty days
10:29 I should, of *c*, like to know why
16:11 Troas and set a *c* straight for Samothrace,
23: 8 (The Sadducees, of *c*,
27: 7 would not permit us to continue our *c*,
Rom 3: 4 Of *c* not!
3:12 All have taken the wrong *c*,
3:16 ruin and misery strew their *c*,
11: 1 Of *c* not! I myself am an Israelite.
1Cor 8: 1 Of *c* we all "know" about that.
8: 7 Not all, of *c*, possess this "knowledge."
15: 8 by me, as one born out of the normal *c*.
2Cor 3:14 Their minds, of *c*, were dulled.
10:12 We are not so bold, of *c*,
13: 5 unless, of *c*, you have failed the challenge
Gal 2: 2 leaders, to make sure the *c* I was pursuing,
4:23 girl had been begotten in the *c* of nature,
4:29 son born in nature's *c* persecuted the one
Eph 4:21 supposing, of *c*, that he has been preached
Phil 3:12 it yet, or have already finished my *c*;
3:16 It is important that we continue on our *c*,
4:10 You had been concerned all along, of *c*,
1Tm 6: 6 There is, of *c*, great gain in religion
2Tm 2:15 a straight *c* in preaching the truth.
Jas 3: 4 *c* the steerman's impulse may select.
3: 6 Its flames encircle our *c* from birth,
Rv 21:19 the first *c* of stones was jasper,

COURSES (7)

Jgs 5:20 from their *c* they fought against Sisera.
7:24 water *c* against them as far as Beth-barah,
7:24 seized the water *c* as far as Beth-barah,
1Kgs 6:36 by means of three *c* of hewn stones
7:12 The great court was enclosed by three *c* of
Ezr 6: 4 *c* of cut stone for each one of timber.
Rv 21:14 had twelve *c* of stones as its foundation,

COURSING (1)

Jer 2:23 A frenzied she-camel, *c* near and far,

COURT (140)

Gn 20: 8 Abimelech called all his *c* officials
50: 7 *c* and all the other dignitaries of Egypt,
Ex 27: 9 "You shall also make a *c* for the Dwelling.
27: 9 On the south side the *c* shall have
27:12 the width of the *c* there shall be hangings,
27:13 *c* on the east side shall be fifty cubits.
27:16 the *c* there shall be a variegated curtain,
27:17 the *c* shall have bands and hooks of silver,
27:18 of the *c* is to be one hundred cubits long,
27:19 tent pegs and all the tent pegs of the *c*,
35:17 the hangings of the *c*,
35:17 the curtain for the entrance of the *c*;
35:18 tent pegs for the Dwelling and for the *c*,
38: 9 The *c* was made as follows.
38: 9 south side of the *c* there were hangings,
38:13 the east side the *c* was fifty cubits long.
38:15 other side, beyond the entrance of the *c*,
38:16 of the *c* were woven of fine linen twined.
38:17 columns of the *c* were banded with silver.
38:18 of the *c* there was a variegated curtain,
38:18 in keeping with the hangings of the *c*.
38:20 and for the *c* around it were of bronze.
38:31 of the altar, the pedestals around the *c*,
38:31 the pedestals at the entrance of the *c*,
38:31 for the Dwelling and for the *c* around it.
39:40 of the *c* with their columns and pedestals,
39:40 of the *c* with its ropes and tent pegs,
40: 8 Set up the *c* round about,
40: 8 put the curtain at the entrance of the *c*.
40:33 he set up the *c* around the Dwelling and
40:33 hung the curtain at the entrance of the *c*.
Lv 6: 9 *c* of the meeting tent they shall eat it.
6:19 sacred place, in the *c* of the meeting tent.
Nm 3:26 the meeting tent, the hangings of the *c*,
3:26 curtain at the entrance of the *c* enclosing
3:37 of the surrounding *c* with their pedestals,
4:26 the meeting tent, the hangings of the *c*,
4:26 entrance of the *c* that encloses
4:32 of the surrounding *c* with their pedestals,
Dt 25: 1 men have a dispute and bring it to *c*,
1Kgs 6:36 The inner *c* was walled off by means of
7: 8 His living quarters were in another *c*,
7:12 The great *c* was enclosed by three courses
7:12 So also were the inner *c* of the temple of
8:64 of the *c* facing the temple of the LORD;
2Chr 4: 9 He made the *c* of the priests and the great
7: 7 *c* which lay before the house of the LORD;
20: 5 in the house of the LORD before the new *c*,
24:21 him to death in the *c* of the LORD's temple.
29:16 brought out to the *c* of the LORD's house,
Est A: 2 prominent man who served at the king's *c*,
A:12 lodged at the *c* with Bagathan and Thares,
A:12 two eunuchs of the king who were *c* guards.
A:16 also appointed Mordecai to serve at the *c*,
1: 5 *c* of the royal palace for all the people,
2:11 walk about in front of the *c* of the harem,
4:11 king in the inner *c* without being summoned,
6: 4 "Who is in the *c*?"
6: 4 Now Haman had entered the outer *c* of the
6: 5 answered him, "Haman is waiting in the *c*."
1Mc 9:54 inner *c* of the sanctuary to be torn down,
15:32 and on seeing the splendor of Simon's *c*,
2Mc 6: 4 with women even in the sacred *c*.
Ps(s) 16: 4 multiply their sorrows who *c* other gods.
Prv 13:23 but some men perish for lack of a law *c*.
Wis 1:12 *C* not death by your erring way of life,
Sir 50:11 and lent majesty to the *c* of the sanctuary.
Is 3:22 the *c* dresses, wraps, cloaks, and purses;
Jer 19:14 he stood in the *c* of the house of God and
26: 2 Stand in the *c* of the house of the LORD
26:10 *c* at the New Gate of the house of the LORD.
36:10 in the upper *c* of the LORD's house,
Ez 8: 7 he brought me to the entrance of the *c*,
8:16 me into the inner *c* of the LORD's house,
10: 3 man entered, the cloud filled the inner *c*,
10: 4 *c* was bright with the glory of the LORD.
10: 5 could be heard as far as the outer *c*;
40:14 the *c* on either side were six cubits.
40:17 Then he brought me to the outer *c*,
40:17 The pavement was laid all around the *c*,
40:19 He measured the width of the *c* from the
40:20 he proceeded north, where, on the outer *c*,
40:23 *c* had a gate opposite the north gate,
40:27 The inner *c* also had a southern gate;
40:28 me to the inner *c* by the south gate,
40:31 But its vestibule was toward the outer *c*;
40:34 But its vestibule was toward the outer *c*;
40:37 Its vestibule was toward the outer *c*;
40:44 the inner *c* where there were two chambers,
40:47 Then he measured the *c*,
41:10 chambers of the *c* was an open space
42: 1 Then he led me north to the outer *c*,
42: 3 *c* and the pavement of the outer court,
42: 7 to the chambers along the outer *c*;
42: 8 belonging to the outer *c* was fifty cubits,
42: 9 outer *c* where the wall of the court began.
42:10 outer court where the wall of the *c* began.
42:14 place for the outer *c* until they have left
42:15 east and measured all the limits of the *c*.
43: 5 lifted me up and brought me to the inner *c*.
44:17 they enter the gates of the inner *c*,

44:17 gates of the inner *c* or within the temple.
44:19 to go out to the people in the outer *c*,
44:21 drink wine when he is to enter the inner *c*.
44:27 the inner *c* to minister in the sanctuary,
45:19 the doorposts of the gates of the inner *c*.
46: 1 The gate toward the east of the inner *c*
46:20 take them into the outer *c* at the risk
46:21 Then he led me into the outer *c* and had me
46:21 me pass around the four corners of the *c*,
46:21 that in each corner there was another *c*:
46:22 in the four corners of the *c*,
Dn 2:49 Daniel himself remained at the king's *c*.
7:11 The *c* was convened, and the books
7:26 But when the *c* is convened,
13:49 Return to *c*, for they have testified falsely
Mt 5:25 opponent while on your way to *c* with him.
10:17 They will hale you into *c*,
14: 6 dance before the *c* which delighted Herod
22:16 You *c* no one's favor and do not act out of
Mk 6:21 held a birthday dinner for his *c* circle,
14:60 the *c* and began to interrogate Jesus:
Acts 4:15 of the *c* while they held a consultation.
4:21 The *c* could find no way to punish them
5:34 accused ordered out of *c* for a few minutes,
7:10 favor and wisdom in the *c* of the Pharaoh,
8:27 a *c* official in charge of the entire
12:20 by common consent came before him in his *c*.
13: 7 He was attached to the *c* of the
17:34 a member of the *c* of the Areopagus,
18:16 With that, he dismissed them from the *c*.
22:17 I was praying in the *c* of the temple,
24:18 in the temple *c* completing the rites
26:21 me in the temple *c* and tried to murder me.
1Cor 4: 3 you or any human *c* pass judgment on me.
6: 6 Must brother drag brother into *c*,
Gal 4:17 exclude you so that you may *c* their favor.
2Tm 4:16 At the first hearing of my case in *c*,
Rv 11: 2 Exclude the outer *c* of the temple,

COURTED (1)

Gal 4:18 to be *c* for the right reasons at all times,

COURTESY (3)

Sir 4: 8 poor man, and return his greeting with *c*;
Acts 25:13 in Caesarea and paid Festus a *c* call.
Ti 3: 2 and display a perfect *c* toward all men.

COURTIER (5)

Gn 37:36 a *c* of Pharaoh and his chief steward.
39: 1 a *c* of Pharaoh and his chief steward)
2Kgs 25:19 And from the city he took one *c*,
Jer 38: 7 a Cushite, a *c* in the king's palace,
52:25 And from the city he took one *c*,

COURTIERS (10)

Gn 12:14 and when Pharaoh's *c* saw her,
40: 2 Pharaoh was angry with his two *c*,
40: 7 So he asked Pharaoh's *c* who were with him
40:20 to all his staff, with his *c* around him,
45:16 had come, Pharaoh and his *c* were pleased.
50: 4 was over, Joseph spoke to Pharaoh's *c*.
1Chr 28: 1 and his sons, together with the *c*,
Jer 29: 2 King Jeconiah and the queen mother, the *c*,
34:19 princes of Judah and of Jerusalem, the *c*,
Mt 14: 2 of Jesus' reputation, exclaimed to his *c*,

COURTING (1)

Gal 4:17 not *c* your favor in any generous spirit.

COURTS (29)

2Kgs 21: 5 host of heaven, in the two *c* of the temple.
23:12 in the two *c* of the temple of the LORD.
1Chr 23:28 house of the LORD, having charge of the *c*,
28: 6 Solomon who shall build my house and my *c*,
28:12 mind by way of *c* for the house of the LORD,
2Chr 23: 5 will be in the *c* of the LORD's temple.
33: 5 of heaven in the two *c* of the LORD's house.
Neh 8:16 courtyards, in the *c* of the house of God,
13: 7 him a chamber in the *c* of the house of God.
1Mc 4:38 the *c* as in a forest or on some mountain,
4:48 interior of the temple and purified the *c*.
Ps(s) 65: 5 you choose, and bring to dwell in your *c*.
84: 3 yearns and pines for the *c* of the LORD.
84:11 day in your *c* than a thousand elsewhere;
92:14 LORD shall flourish in the *c* of our God.
96: 8 Bring gifts, and enter his *c*;
100: 4 gates with thanksgiving, his *c* with praise;
116:19 people, In the *c* of the house of the LORD,
135: 2 the LORD, in the *c* of the house of our God.
Prv 17:19 he who builds his gate high *c* disaster.
Is 1:13 Trample my *c* no more!
62: 9 drink the wine in the *c* of my sanctuary.
Ez 9: 7 to them, and fill the *c* with the slain;
42: 6 to conform with the foundations of the *c*,
46:22 in the four corners of the court, minor *c*,
Zec 3: 7 you shall judge my house and keep my *c*,
Mk 13: 9 They will hand you over to the *c*.
Acts 19:38 anyone, there are *c* in session for that.
Jas 2: 6 They are the ones who hale you into the *c*

COURTSHIP (1)

Sg 8: 8 we do for our sister when her *c* begins?

COURTYARD (17)

2Sm 17:18 man in Bahurim who had a cistern in his *c*.
2Kgs 20: 4 Before Isaiah had left the central *c*,
2Chr 4: 9 the great courtyard and the gates of the *c*;
6:13 which he had placed in the middle of the *c*.
Tb 2: 9 and went to sleep next to the wall of my *c*.
3:17 Tobit returned from the *c* to his house,
7: 1 whom they found seated by his *c* gate.
11:10 got up and stumbled out through the *c* gate.
Est 5: 1 royal garments and stood in the inner *c*,
5: 2 He saw Queen Esther standing in the *c*,
Mt 26:69 Peter was sitting in the *c* when one of the
Mk 14:54 a distance right into the high priest's *c*,
14:66 While Peter was down in the *c*,
Lk 11:21 a strong man fully armed guards his *c*,
22:55 middle of the *c* and were sitting beside it,
Jn 18:15 with Jesus as far as the high priests' *c*,

COURTYARDS (3)

Ex 8: 9 in the houses and *c* and fields died off.
Neh 8:16 on the roof of their houses, in their *c*,
Bar 6:17 Their *c* are walled in like those of a man

COUSIN (6)

Lv 25:49 of his own brothers, or by his uncle or *c*,
Tb 9: 6 I have seen the very image of my *c* Tobit!"
Est 2: 7 to Hadassah, that is, Esther, his *c*;
Jer 32: 9 the field in Anathoth from my *c* Hanamel,
32:12 in the presence of my *c* Hanamel and of
Col 4:10 So does Mark, the *c* of Barnabas.

COVENANT (289)

Gn 6:18 But with you I will establish my *c*;
9: 9 I am now establishing my *c* with you and
9:11 I will establish my *c* with you,
9:12 of the *c* between me and you and every
9:13 a sign of the *c* between me and the earth.
9:15 I will recall the *c* I have made between me
9:16 everlasting *c* that I have established
9:17 "This is the sign of the *c* I have
15:18 occasion that the LORD made a *c* with Abram,
17: 2 Between you and me I will establish my *c*,
17: 4 "My *c* with you is this:
17: 7 I will maintain my *c* with you and your
17: 9 you must keep my *c* throughout the ages.
17:10 This is my *c* with you and your descendants
17:11 be the mark of the *c* between you and me.
17:13 Thus my *c* shall be in your flesh as an
17:14 he has broken my *c*."
17:19 my *c* with him as an everlasting pact,
17:21 But my *c* I will maintain with Isaac,
Ex 2:24 and was mindful of his *c* with Abraham,
6: 4 I also established my *c* with them,
6: 5 treating as slaves, I am mindful of my *c*.
19: 5 if you hearken to my voice and keep my *c*,
23:32 shall not make a *c* with them or their gods.
24: 7 Taking the book of the *c*,
24: 8 "This is the blood of the *c* which the
31:16 their generations as a perpetual *c*.
34:10 said the LORD, "is the *c* I will make.
34:12 not to make a *c* with these inhabitants of
34:15 make a *c* with the inhabitants of that land;
34:27 I have made a *c* with you and with Israel."
34:28 he wrote on the tablets the words of the *c*,
Lv 2:13 Do not let the salt of the *c* of your God
26: 9 and numerous, as I carry out my *c* with you.
26:15 all my commandments and breaking my *c*,
26:25 I will make the sword, the avenger of my *c*,
26:42 my *c* with Jacob, my *c* with Isaac, and my *c*
26:44 them out, I make void my *c* with them;
26:45 of the *c* I made with their forefathers,
Nm 10:33 and the ark of the *c* of the LORD which was
14:44 the *c* of the LORD nor Moses left the camp.
18:19 *c* to last forever before the LORD,
Dt 4:13 He proclaimed to you his *c*,
4:23 lest, forgetting the *c* which the LORD,
4:31 nor forget the *c* which under oath he made
5: 2 LORD, our God, made a *c* with us at Horeb;
5: 3 not with our fathers did he make this *c*,
7: 2 no *c* with them and show them no mercy.
7: 9 faithful God who keeps his merciful *c*
7:12 will keep with you the merciful *c* which he
8:18 done, the *c* which he swore to your fathers.
9: 9 of the *c* which the LORD made with you.
9:11 given me the two stone tablets of the *c*,
9:15 the two tablets of the *c* in both my hands,
10: 8 Levi to carry the ark of the *c* of the LORD,
17: 2 LORD, your God, and transgresses his *c*,
28:69 These are the words of the *c* which the
28:69 to the *c* which he made with them at Horeb.
29: 8 Keep the terms of this *c*,
29:11 that you may enter into the *c* of the LORD,
29:13 with you alone that I am making this *c*,
29:20 of the *c* inscribed in this book of the law.
29:24 'Because they forsook the *c* which the LORD,
31: 9 who carry the ark of the *c* of the LORD,
31:16 break the *c* which I have made with them.
31:20 them, despising me and breaking my *c*;
31:25 the ark of the *c* of the LORD this order:
31:26 put it beside the ark of the *c* of the LORD,
33: 9 keep your words, and your *c* they uphold.
Jos 3: 3 you see the ark of the *c* of the LORD,
3: 6 ark of the *c* and go on ahead of the people;
3: 8 carrying the ark of the *c* to come to a halt
3:11 The ark of the *c* of the Lord of the whole
3:14 carrying the ark of the *c* ahead of them.
3:17 carrying the ark of the *c* of the LORD
4: 7 *c* of the LORD when it crossed the Jordan.'
4: 9 stood who were carrying the ark of the *c*.
4:18 priests carrying the ark of the *c*
6: 6 ark of the *c* with seven of the priests
6: 8 ark of the *c* of the LORD following them.
7:11 violated the *c* which I enjoined on them.
7:15 because he has violated the *c* of the LORD
8:33 were carrying the ark of the *c* of the LORD.
23:16 If you transgress the *c* of the LORD,
24:25 So Joshua made a *c* with the people that
Jgs 2: 1 that I would never break my *c* with you,
2:20 my *c* which I enjoined on their fathers,
20:27 of the *c* of God was there in those days,
2Sm 15:24 Levite bearers of the ark of the *c* of God],
23: 5 He has made an eternal *c* with me,
1Kgs 3:15 stood before the ark of the *c* of the Lord,
6:19 to house the ark of the LORD's *c*,
8: 1 *c* from the city of David [which is Zion].
8: 6 The priests brought the ark of the *c* of
8: 9 when the LORD made a *c* with the Israelites
8:21 for the ark in which is the *c* of the LORD,
8:23 you keep your *c* of kindness with your
11:11 *c* and my statutes which I enjoined on you,
19:10 but the Israelites have forsaken your *c*,
19:14 But the Israelites have forsaken your *c*,
2Kgs 11:17 Then Jehoiada made a *c* between the LORD as
11:17 and another *c*, between the king
13:23 compassion because of his *c* with Abraham,
17:15 the *c* which he had made with their fathers,
17:35 When he made a *c* with them,
17:38 The *c* which I made with you,
18:12 the LORD, their God, but violated his *c*,
23: 2 book of the *c* that had been found
23: 3 the king made a *c* before the LORD that
23: 3 of the *c* which were written in this book.
23: 3 the people stood as participants in the *c*.
23:21 as it was prescribed in that book of the *c*.
1Chr 11: 3 a *c* with them in the presence of the LORD;
15:25 ark of the *c* of the LORD with joy
15:26 were bearing the ark of the *c* of the LORD,
15:28 of the *c* of the LORD with joyful shouting,
15:29 But as the ark of the *c* of the LORD was
16: 6 trumpeters before the ark of the *c* of God.
16:15 He remembers forever his *c* which he made
16:17 statute, for Israel as an everlasting *c*,
16:37 ark of the *c* of the LORD to minister
17: 1 the *c* of the LORD dwells under tentcloth."
22:19 that the ark of the *c* of the LORD and
28: 2 myself for the ark of the *c* of the LORD,
28:18 and covered the ark of the *c* of the LORD.
2Chr 5: 2 *c* from the City of David (which is Zion).
5: 7 The priests brought the ark of the *c* of
5:10 the tablets of the *c* which the LORD made
6:11 in which abides the *c* of the LORD which he
6:14 you keep your *c* and show kindness to your
13: 5 him and to his sons, by a *c* made in salt?
15:12 They entered into a *c* to seek the LORD,
21: 7 the *c* he had made with David
23: 3 made a *c* with the king in the house of God.
23:16 Then Jehoiada made a *c* between himself and
29:10 Now, I intend to make a *c* with the LORD,
34:30 book of the *c* that had been found
34:31 the king made a *c* before the LORD to
34:31 the terms of the *c* written in this book.
34:32 conformed themselves to the *c* of God,
Ezr 10: 3 Let us therefore enter into a *c* before our
Neh 1: 5 you who preserve your *c* of mercy toward
9: 8 you made the *c* with him to give to him and
9:32 God, you who in your mercy preserve the *c*,
13:29 the *c* of the priesthood and the Levites!
Jdt 9:13 have planned dire things against your *c*,
1Mc 1:15 circumcision and abandoned the holy *c*;
1:57 Whoever was found with a scroll of the *c*
1:63 with unclean food or to profane the holy *c*;
2:20 kinsmen will keep to the *c* of our fathers.
2:27 and who stands by the *c* follow after me!
2:50 give your lives for the *c* of our fathers.
2:54 the *c* of an everlasting priesthood.
4:10 favor us, remember his *c* with our fathers,
2Mc 1: 2 remember his *c* with his faithful servants,
7:36 of never-failing life, under God's *c*,
Ps(s) 25:10 those who keep his *c* and his decrees.
25:14 LORD is with those who fear him, and his *c*,
44:18 you, nor have we been disloyal to your *c*;
50: 5 who have made a *c* with me by sacrifice."
50:16 statutes, and profess my *c* with your mouth,
74:20 Look to your *c*, for the hiding places
78:10 They kept not the *c* with God;
78:37 him, nor were they faithful to his *c*.
89: 4 "I have made a *c* with my chosen one,
89:29 toward him, and my *c* with him stands firm.
89:35 "I will not violate my *c*;
89:40 You have renounced the *c* with your servant,

COVENANT (cont.)

103:18 his *c* and remember to fulfill his precepts.
105: 8 He remembers forever his *c* which he
105:10 statute, for Israel as an everlasting *c*,
106:45 sake he was mindful of his *c* and relented,
111: 5 he will forever be mindful of his *c*.
111: 9 he has ratified his *c* forever;
132:12 *c* and the decrees which I shall teach them,
Wis 1:16 and pined for it, and made a *c* with it,
Sir 17:10 An everlasting *c* he has made with them,
24:22 is true of the book of the Most High's *c*,
28: 7 not your neighbor, of the Most High's *c*,
39: 8 and glory in the law of the LORD's *c*.
44:12 God's *c* with them their family endures,
44:22 The *c* with all his forebears was confirmed,
45:15 a lasting *c* with him and with his family,
45:24 conferred the right, in a *c* of friendship,
45:25 For even his *c* with David,
Is 2: 6 they *c* with strangers.
24: 5 violated statutes, broken the ancient *c*.
28:15 you say, "We have made a *c* with death,
28:18 Your *c* with death shall be canceled and
42: 6 you, and set you as a *c* of the people,
54:10 leave you nor my *c* of peace be shaken,
55: 3 I will renew with you the everlasting *c*,
56: 4 what pleases me and hold fast to my *c*,
56: 6 free from profanation and hold to my *c*,
59:21 the *c* with them which I myself have made,
61: 8 a lasting *c* I will make with them.
Jer 3:16 longer say, "The ark of the *c* of the LORD!"
11: 3 who does not observe the terms of this *c*,
11: 6 Hear the words of this *c* and obey them.
11: 8 threats of this *c* which they had failed
11:10 the *c* which I had made with their fathers,
14:21 remember your *c* with us,
22: 9 they have deserted their *c* with the LORD,
31:31 when I will make a new *c* with the house of
31:32 It will not be like the *c* I made with
31:32 for they broke my *c*,
31:33 But this is the *c* which I will make with
32:40 I will make with them an eternal *c*,
33:20 my covenant with day, and my *c* with night,
33:21 my *c* with my servant David also be broken,
33:21 and my *c* with the priests of Levi who
33:25 When I have no *c* with day and night,
34:13 they were slaves, I made this *c* with them:
34:18 The men who violated my *c* and did not
50: 5 ourselves to the LORD with *c* everlasting,
Bar 2:35 will establish for them, as an eternal *c*,
Ez 16: 8 oath to you and entered into a *c* with you;
16:59 you who despised your oath, breaking a *c*.
16:60 the *c* I made with you when you were a girl,
16:60 I will set up an everlasting *c* with you.
16:61 though I am not bound by my *c* with you.
16:62 For I will reestablish my *c* with you,
17:13 of the royal line with whom he made a *c*,
17:14 and would keep his *c* and obey him.
17:15 Can he break a *c* and still go free?
17:16 oath he spurned, whose *c* with him he broke,
17:18 He spurned his oath, breaking his *c*.
17:19 oath which he spurned, my *c* which he broke,
34:25 I will make a *c* of peace with them,
37:26 a *c* of peace; it shall be an everlasting *c*
44: 7 have broken my *c* by all your abominations.
Dn 3:34 deliver us up forever, or make void your *c*.
9: 4 you who keep your merciful *c* toward those
11:22 and crushed, and even the prince of the *c*.
11:28 riches, his mind set against the holy *c*;
11:30 his rage and energy against the holy *c*;
11:32 some who were disloyal to the *c* apostatize;
Hos 2:20 I will make a *c* for them on that day,
6: 7 But they, in their land, violated the *c*;
8: 1 Since they have violated my *c*,
Zec 9:11 for you, for the blood of your *c* with me,
11:10 the *c* which I had made with all peoples;
Mal 2: 4 commandment because I have a *c* with Levi,
2: 5 My *c* with him was one of life and peace;
2: 8 You have made void the *c* of Levi,
2:10 each other, violating the *c* of our fathers?
3: 1 And the messenger of the *c* whom you desire.
Mt 26:28 this is my blood, the blood of the *c*,
Mk 14:24 "This is my blood, the blood of the *c*,
Lk 1:72 fathers and remembered the holy *c* he made,
22:20 "This cup is the new *c* in my blood,
Acts 3:25 you are the heirs of the *c* God made with
7: 8 then made a *c* of circumcision with him,
13:34 the benefits assured to David under the *c*.'
Rom 11:27 and this is the *c* I will make with them
1Cor 11:25 "This cup is the new *c* in my blood.
2Cor 3: 6 ministers of a new *c*, a *c* not of a written
3: 9 ministry of the *c* that condemned had glory,
3:14 old *c* is read the veil remains unlifted;
Gal 3:17 a *c* formally ratified by God is not set
Eph 2:12 were strangers to the *c* and its promise;
Heb 7:20 the old *c* became priests without an oath,
7:22 Jesus become the guarantee of a better *c*.
7:23 Under the old *c* there were many priests
8: 6 now, just as he is mediator of a better *c*,
8: 7 If that first *c* had been faultless,
8: 8 when I will make a new *c* with the house of
8: 9 It will not be like the *c* I made with
8: 9 they broke my *c* and I grew weary of them,
8:10 But this is the *c* I will make with the
8:13 When he says, "a new *c*,"
9: 1 The first *c* has regulations for worship
9: 4 ark of the *c* entirely covered with gold.
9: 4 had blossomed, and the tablets of the *c*.
9:15 This is why he is mediator of a new *c*:
9:15 committed under the first *c*,
9:18 the first *c* was inaugurated without blood.
9:20 of the *c* which God has enjoined upon you."
10: 9 away the first *c* to establish the second.
10:16 *c* I will make with them after those days,
12:24 to Jesus, the mediator of a new *c*,
13:20 the sheep by the blood of the eternal *c*,
Rv 11:19 the temple could be seen the ark of the *c*.

COVENANT-BLOOD (1)

Heb 10:29 thinks the *c* by which he was sanctified

COVENANTED (1)

2Chr 7:18 as I *c* with your father David when I said,

COVENANTS (6)

2Mc 8:15 sake of the *c* made with their forefathers,
Wis 12:21 you gave the sworn *c* of goodly promises!
18:22 recalling the sworn *c* with their fathers.
Is 33: 8 have quit the paths, *C* are broken,
Rom 9: 4 were the adoption, the glory, the *c*,
Gal 4:24 the two women stand for two *c*.

COVER (74)

Gn 6:14 in it, and *c* it inside and out with pitch.
Ex 10: 5 They shall *c* the ground,
21:33 a cistern and does not *c* it over again,
28:42 to *c* their naked flesh from their loins to
33:22 *c* you with my hand until I have passed by.
Lv 13:13 that the leprosy does *c* his whole body,
16:13 *c* the propitiatory over the commandments;
17:13 pour out its blood and *c* it with earth.
Nm 4: 5 and *c* the ark of the commandments with it.
4: 6 these they shall put a *c* of tahash skin,
4: 8 cloth and *c* all this with tahash skin.
4: 9 cloth to *c* the lampstand with its lamps,
4:11 *c* this also with a covering of tahash skin.
4:12 violet cloth and *c* them with tahash skin.
17: 3 them hammered into plates to *c* the altar,
17: 5 This *c* was to be a reminder to the
22: 5 from Egypt who now *c* the face of the earth
22:11 from Egypt now *c* the face of the earth.
Dt 23:14 a hole and afterward *c* up your excrement.
2Sm 17:19 took the *c* and spread it over the cistern,
17:19 on the *c* so that nothing could be noticed.
1Kgs 7:17 were made to *c* the (nodes of the) capitals
2Chr 4:13 to *c* the two nodes of the capitals topping
Jdt 2: 7 I will *c* all the land with the feet of my
2:19 to *c* all the western region with their
6:13 So they took *c* below the mountain,
1Mc 9:38 and hid themselves under *c* of the mountain.
Jb 14:17 in a pouch, and you would *c* over my guilt.
16:18 O earth, *c* not my blood,
21:26 down in the dust, and worms *c* them both.
37: 8 take to *c* and remain quietly in their dens.
40:22 The lotus trees *c* him with their shade;
Ps(s) 91: 4 With his pinions he will *c* you,
104: 9 not pass, nor shall they *c* the earth again.
105:39 He spread a cloud to *c* them and fire
Is 3:17 The Lord shall *c* the scalps of Zion's
4: 6 of day, refuge and *c* from storm and rain.
28:20 out in, and the *c* too narrow to wrap in.
32:11 bare, with only a loincloth to *c* you.
59: 6 nor can they *c* themselves with their works.
60: 2 the earth, and thick clouds *c* the peoples;
Jer 3:25 down in our shame, let our disgrace *c* us,
14: 3 despairing, they *c* their heads
14: 4 farmers are ashamed, they *c* their heads.
46: 8 forward," he says, "and *c* the earth,
Ez 7:18 put on sackcloth, and horror shall *c* them;
12: 6 *c* your face that you may not see the land,
13:10 a wall, they would *c* it with whitewash,
16: 8 of my cloak over you to *c* your nakedness;
16:18 You took your embroidered gowns to *c* them;
22:28 Her prophets *c* them with whitewash,
24:17 sandals on your feet, do not *c* your beard,
26:10 surge of his horses shall *c* you with dust,
26:19 against you, and its mighty waters *c* you,
30:18 shall cease from her, clouds shall *c* her,
32: 7 When I snuff you out I will *c* the heavens,
32: 7 The sun I will *c* with clouds,
37: 6 make flesh grow over you, *c* you with skin,
37: 8 flesh come upon them, and the skin *c* them,
38: 9 advancing like a cloud to *c* the earth,
Hos 10: 8 they shall cry out to the mountains, *C* us!"
Am 8: 9 set at midday and *c* the earth with darkness
8:10 I will *c* the loins of all with sackcloth
Ob 1:10 *c* you and you shall be destroyed forever.
Mi 3: 7 They shall *c* their lips,
7:10 When my enemy sees this, shame shall *c* her:
Hb 2:17 the violence done to Lebanon shall *c* you,
Zec 5: 7 Then a leaden *c* was lifted,
5: 8 pushing the leaden *c* into the opening.
Mal 2:13 the altar of the LORD you *c* with tears,
Mt 9:16 thing he has used to *c* the hole will pull,
Mk 2:21 he has used to *c* the hole would pull away
Lk 23:30 'Fall on us,' and to the hills, *C* us.'
1Cor 11: 7 on the other hand, ought not to *c* his head,

COVERED (89)

Gn 1: 2 wasteland, and darkness *c* the abyss,
9:23 backward and *c* their father's nakedness;
24:65 Then she *c* herself with her veil.
27:16 skins of the kids she *c* up his hands
29: 2 A large stone *c* the mouth of the well.
38:15 her for a harlot, since she had *c* her face.
Ex 8: 2 the frogs came up and *c* the land of Egypt.
10:15 They *c* the surface of the whole land,
14:28 it *c* the chariots and the charioteers of
15: 5 The flood waters *c* them.
15:10 When your wind blew, the sea *c* them;
16:13 the evening quail came up and *c* the camp.
22:14 hired, this was *c* by the price of its hire.
24:15 Moses had gone up, a cloud *c* the mountain.
24:16 The cloud *c* it for six days,
40:34 Then the cloud *c* the meeting tent,
Nm 9:15 was erected, the cloud *c* the Dwelling,
9:16 the day the Dwelling was *c* by the cloud,
17: 7 *c* it and the glory of the LORD appeared.
Jgs 4:18 into her tent, and she *c* him with a rug.
4:19 milk for him to drink, and then *c* him over.
1Sm 4:12 his clothes torn and his head *c* with dirt.
2Sm 15:30 His head was *c*,
15:30 heads *c* and were weeping as they went.
19: 5 *c* his face and cried out in a loud voice,
20:12 Amasa lay *c* with blood in the middle
1Kgs 6:22 gold so that it was completely *c* with it;
7:42 pieces of network that *c* the two nodes
20:27 of goats, while Aram *c* the countryside.
1Chr 28:18 and *c* the ark of the covenant of the LORD.
2Chr 3: 5 cypress wood which he *c* with fine gold,
3: 9 The upper chambers he likewise *c* with gold.
Neh 9: 1 and in sackcloth, their heads *c* with dust.
Jdt 9: 3 and you *c* with their blood the bed in
16: 3 the torrents, their horses *c* the hills.
Est C:13 she *c* her head with dirt and ashes.
D: 6 state, and *c* with gold and precious stones,
6:12 Haman hurried home, his head *c* in grief.
7: 8 spoken when the face of Haman was *c* over.
1Mc 1:15 They *c* over the mark of their circumcision
1:28 all the house of Jacob was *c* with shame.
6:43 any of the others and *c* with royal armor,
10:44 shall be *c* out of the royal revenue.
2Mc 6: 5 so that the altar was *c* with abominable
Jb 29: 9 and *c* their mouths with their hands;
38:30 When the waters lie *c* as though with stone
Ps(s) 32: 1 whose fault is taken away, whose sin is *c*.
32: 5 my sin to you, my guilt I *c* not.
44:20 of misery and *c* us over with darkness.
78:53 while he *c* their enemies with the sea.
85: 3 you have *c* all their sins.
89:46 you have *c* him with shame.
104: 6 the ocean, as with a garment, you *c* it;
106:11 The waters *c* their foes;
106:17 up Dathan, and *c* the faction of Abiram.
Prv 11:16 but she who hates virtue is *c* with shame.
24:31 its surface was *c* with nettles,
Sg 5:14 body is a work of ivory *c* with sapphires.
Sir 16:28 Its surface he *c* with all manner of life
24: 3 I came forth, and mistlike *c* the earth.
47:15 Your understanding *c* the whole earth,
Is 28: 8 all the tables are *c* with filthy vomit,
29:10 prophets] and *c* your heads [the seers].
Jer 49:23 Hamath and Arpad are *c* with shame,
Bar 6: 7 they are *c* with gold and silver
Ez 1:11 the other two wings of each *c* his body.
2:10 It was *c* with writing front and back,
16:63 you may remember and be *c* with confusion,
24: 7 it out on the earth, to be *c* with dust.
24: 8 her blood on the bare rock, not to be *c*.
27: 7 from the coasts of Elishah *c* your cabin.
41:16 around, *c* from the ground to the windows.
Jon 3: 6 aside his robe, *c* himself with sackcloth,
3: 8 be *c* with sackcloth and call loudly to God;
Hb 3: 3 *C* are the heavens with his glory,
Mt 10:23 you will not have *c* the towns of Israel
Mk 4:22 *c* so as to be brought out into the open.
11:13 fig tree some distance off, *c* with foliage,
14:51 him who was *c* by nothing but a linen cloth.
Lk 13:17 words, his opponents were *c* with confusion;
16:20 beggar named Lazarus who was *c* with sores.
Jn 20: 7 *c* the head not lying with the wrappings,
Rom 4: 7 are forgiven, whose sins are *c* over.
1Cor 11: 4 with his head *c* brings shame upon his head.
Heb 9: 4 ark of the covenant entirely *c* with gold.
Rv 3:18 if the shame of your nakedness is to be *c*.
4: 6 creatures *c* with eyes front and back.
17: 3 beast which was *c* with blasphemous names.
19:16 on the part of the cloak that *c* his thigh:

COVERING (41)

Gn 8:13 Noah then removed the *c* of the ark and saw
38:14 veiled her face by *c* herself with a shawl,
Ex 22:26 of his is the only *c* he has for his body.
25:20 out above, *c* the propitiatory with them;
26: 7 to be used as a tent *c* over the Dwelling.
26:12 will be an extra half sheet of tent *c*,
26:14 *c* of rams' skins dyed red, and above that, a *c*

35:11 the Dwelling, with its tent, its *c*,
36:19 A *c* for the tent was made of rams' skins
36:19 red, and above that, a *c* of tahash skins.
37: 9 out above, *c* the propitiatory with them.
39:34 *c* of rams' skins dyed red, the *c* of tahash
40:19 Dwelling and put the *c* on top of the tent,
Nm 3:25 to the Dwelling, the tent and its *c*,
4:10 shall then enclose in a *c* of tahash skin,
4:11 cover this also with a *c* of tahash skin.
4:14 then spread a *c* of tahash skin over this,
4:15 his sons have finished *c* the sacred objects
4:25 *c* and the outer wrapping of tahash skin,
17: 4 offering hammered into a *c* for the altar,
1Sm 19:13 hair at its head and *c* it with a spread.
1Kgs 7:41 two pieces of network *c* the nodes for the
2Chr 4:12 and two networks *c* the nodes of the
Jdt 4:11 their sackcloth *c* before the Lord.
7:18 in the plain, *c* the whole countryside.
1Mc 6:37 A strong wooden tower *c* each elephant,
Jb 24: 7 for they have no *c* against the cold;
26: 6 is the nether world, and Abaddon has no *c*.
31:19 without clothing, or a poor man without *c*,
Is 14:11 couch beneath you is the maggot, your *c*,
27: 6 and blossom, *c* all the world with fruit.
Ez 1:23 [Each of them had two *c* his body.]
12:12 and *c* his face lest he be seen by anyone.
24:22 not *c* your beards nor eating the customary
28:13 every precious stone was your *c* [carnelian,
38:16 my people Israel like a cloud *c* the land.
Mi 2: 8 you have stripped off the mantle *c* the
Mal 2:16 And *c* one's garment with injustice,
1Cor 11:15 Her hair has been given her for a *c*.

COVERLETS (3)

2Sm 17:28 from Rogelim, brought couches, *c*,
Prv 7:16 With *c* I have spread my couch,
31:22 She makes her own *c*;

COVERS (20)

Ex 29:13 All the fat that *c* its inner organs,
29:22 tail, the fat that *c* its inner organs,
Lv 13:12 *c* all the skin of the stricken man from
1Kgs 1: 1 spread *c* over him he could not keep warm.
Jb 9:24 he *c* the faces of its judges.
22:11 a deluge of waters *c* you.
Ps(s) 44:16 and shame *c* my face At the voice of him
69: 8 sake I bear insult, and shame *c* my face.
109:19 it be for him like a garment which *c* him,
147: 8 to our God, Who *c* the heavens with clouds,
Prv 10:12 stirs up disputes, but love *c* all offenses.
17: 9 He who *c* up a misdeed fosters friendship,
Is 11: 9 knowledge of the LORD, as water *c* the sea.
60: 2 See, darkness *c* the earth,
Jer 51:51 have heard taunts, confusion *c* our faces;
Bar 6:23 Despite the gold that *c* them for adornment,
Hos 2:11 my flax, with which she *c* her nakedness.
Hb 2:14 of the LORD's glory as water *c* the sea.
2Cor 3:15 Moses is read a veil *c* their understanding.
1Pt 4: 8 constant, for love *c* a multitude of sins.

COVERTS (1)

Jb 40:21 trees he lies, in *c* of the reedy swamp.

COVES (1)

Jgs 5:17 along the shore, is resting in his *c*.

COVET (8)

Ex 20:17 "You shall not *c* your neighbor's house.
20:17 You shall not *c* your neighbor's wife,
34:24 there will be no one to *c* your land when
Dt 5:21 'You shall not *c* your neighbor's wife.
7:25 Do not *c* the silver or gold on them,
Mi 2: 2 They *c* fields, and seize them;
Rom 7: 7 unless the law had said, "You shall not *c*."
13: 9 you shall not *c*,"

COVETED (1)

1Mc 11:11 however, was that he *c* Alexander's kingdom.

COVETOUS (4)

Ps(s) 10: 3 glories in his greed, and the *c* blasphemes,
Eccl 5: 9 The *c* man is never satisfied with money,
1Cor 5:10 world, or the *c* or thieves or idolaters.
5:11 the title "brother" if he is immoral, *c*,

COVETOUSNESS (1)

2Mc 4:50 thanks to the *c* of the men in power,

COW (1)

Is 11: 7 The *c* and the bear shall be neighbors,

COWARD (1)

Sir 37:11 about her rival, nor to a *c* about war,

COWARDLY (3)

2Mc 8:13 the *c* and those who lacked faith in God's
Wis 17:11 For wickedness, of its nature *c*,
2Tm 1: 7 The Spirit God has given us is no *c* spirit,

COWARDS (1)

Rv 21: 8 As for the *c* and traitors to the faith,

COWED (1)

1Mc 3: 6 The lawbreakers were *c* by fear of him,

COWERED (1)

Nm 22:27 of the LORD there, she *c* under Balaam.

COWS—COW'S (19)

Gn 32:16 forty *c* and ten bulls;
41: 2 when up out of the Nile came seven *c*,
41: 3 Behind them seven other *c*,
41: 4 cows ate up the seven handsome, fat *c*.
41:18 Nile, when up from the Nile came seven *c*,
41:19 Behind them came seven other *c*,
41:20 ugly *c* ate up the first seven fat cows.
41:26 The seven healthy *c* are seven years,
41:27 *c* that came up after them are seven years,
Dt 32:14 Butter from its *c* and milk from its sheep,
1Sm 6: 7 two milch *c* that have not borne the yoke;
6:10 Taking two milch *c*,
6:12 The *c* went straight for the route to
6:14 *c* were offered as a holocaust to the LORD.
Jb 21:10 their *c* calve and do not miscarry.
Ez 4:15 *c* dung in place of human excrement;
Am 4: 1 the mountain of Samaria, you *c* of Bashan,

COZBI (2)

Nm 25:15 The slain Midianite woman was *C*,
25:18 Peor and as regards their kinswoman *C*,

COZEBA (1)

1Chr 4:22 the men of *C*;

CRACK (2)

Ez 17:21 All the *c* troops among his forces shall
Na 3: 2 The *c* of the whip,

CRACKLING (2)

Eccl 7: 6 For as the *c* of thorns under a pot,
Jl 2: 5 the *c* of a fiery flame devouring stubble;

CRACKS (2)

Jb 7: 5 my skin *c* and festers;
Ps(s) 60: 4 repair the *c* in it,

CRAFT (5)

Ex 31: 3 and understanding and knowledge in every *c*:
31: 5 stones, in carving wood, and in every *c*.
35:31 and understanding and knowledge in every *c*:
35:33 in carving wood, and in every other *c*.
Acts 19:25 these men and other workers in the same *c*.

CRAFTILY (2)

Ps(s) 83: 4 Against your people they plot *c*;
Acts 7:19 dealt *c* with our people and oppressed them.

CRAFTINESS (2)

Rom 1:29 will, envy, murder, bickering, deceit, *c*.
1Cor 3:19 says, "He catches the wise in their *c*";

CRAFTS (2)

Ex 35:35 thread, weaving, and all other arts and *c*.
Wis 7:16 as well as all prudence and knowledge of *c*.

CRAFTSMAN (11)

1Chr 22:15 and every kind of *c* skilled in gold,
2Chr 2:12 I am now sending you a *c* of great skill,
Prv 8:30 Then was I beside him as his *c*,
Eccl 10:10 but the *c* has the advantage of his skill.
Wis 8: 6 who in the world is a better *c* than she?
Is 40:19 An idol, cast by a *c*,
40:20 which a skilled *c* picks out for himself,
41: 7 The *c* encourages the goldsmith,
54:16 I have created the *c* who blows on the
Jer 10: 9 of the *c* and the handiwork of the smelter,
Rv 18:22 No *c* in any trade shall ever again be

CRAFTSMAN'S (1)

Dt 27:15 to the LORD, the product of a *c* hands

CRAFTSMANSHIP (1)

1Chr 28:21 to show their skill in every kind of *c*.

CRAFTSMEN (10)

2Kgs 24:14 in number, and all the *c* and smiths.
24:16 of the army, and a thousand *c* and smiths,
1Chr 4:14 Geharashim, so called because they were *c*.
2Chr 2: 6 *c* who are with me in Judah and Jerusalem,
2:13 your *c* and the *c* of my lord David
Jer 10: 3 the forest, Wrought by *c* with the adze,
Bar 6:45 else than what these *c* wish them to be.
Acts 19:24 and brought in no little work for his *c*.
19:38 *c* want to bring charges against anyone,

CRAFTY (4)

Jb 5:13 ruses, and the designs of the *c* are routed.
15: 5 mouth, and you choose to speak like the *c*.
Sir 11:29 for many are the snares of the *c* one;
2Cor 12:16 being *c*, you say, I caught you by guile.

CRAG (6)

1Sm 14: 4 outpost there was a rocky *c* on each side,
14: 5 One *c* was to the north,
Ps(s) 40: 3 He set my feet upon a *c*;
78:16 *c* and brought the waters forth in rivers.
141: 6 Their judges were cast down over the *c*,
Is 31: 9 He shall rush past his *c* in panic,

CRAGS (6)

Nm 23: 9 For from the top of the *c* I see him,
1Sm 24: 3 men in the direction of the wild goat *c*.
Prv 30:26 mighty, yet they make their home in the *c*;
Jer 48:28 Leave the cities, dwell in the *c*,
49:16 You that live in rocky *c*,
Rv 6:15 all hid themselves in caves and mountain *c*.

CRAMMED (1)

Jdt 15: 7 plain were *c* with the enormous quantity

CRAMPED (1)

2Sm 23:10 until his hand grew tired and became *c*,

CRASH (5)

Jb 41:21 he laughs at the *c* of the spear.
Wis 17:19 water, or the rude *c* of overthrown rocks,
Is 22: 5 Walls *c*; they cry for help
30:13 out in a high wall whose *c* comes suddenly,
Ez 31:16 the *c* of his fall I made the nations rock,

CRASHED (1)

Rv 8:10 burning like a torch *c* down from the sky.

CRASHES (1)

Is 30:14 It *c* like a potter's jar smashed beyond

CRASHING (4)

Wis 17: 4 for *c* sounds on all sides terrified them,
Zep 1:10 the New Quarter, loud *c* from the hills.
Rv 6:13 The stars in the sky fell *c* to earth like
16:21 came *c* down on mankind from the sky,

CRASSNESS (2)

Jb 15:27 Because he has blinded himself with his *c*,
Ps(s) 73: 7 Out of their *c* comes iniquity;

CRATES (1)

2Mc 4:29 high priesthood, while Sostratus left *C*,

CRAVE (1)

Mi 7: 1 no cluster to eat, no early fig that I *c*.

CRAVED (4)

Ps(s) 78:18 their hearts by demanding the food they *c*.
78:29 he had brought them what they *c*.
Wis 16: 2 with a novel dish, the delight they *c*,
Rv 18:14 fruit your appetite *c* has deserted you.

CRAVEN (1)

Sir 2:12 Woe to *c* hearts and drooping hands,

CRAVES (3)

Prv 13: 2 things, but the treacherous one *c* violence.
13: 4 The soul of the sluggard *c* in vain,
Eccl 6: 2 that he lacks none of all the things he *c*;

CRAVING (6)

2Sm 23:15 Now David had a strong *c* and said,
Ps(s) 78:30 They had not given over their *c*,
106:14 They gave way to *c* in the desert and
Prv 10: 3 hunger, but the *c* of the wicked he thwarts.
Wis 16: 3 be turned from even the *c* of necessities,
Ez 7:19 to satisfy their *c* or fill their bellies,

CRAVINGS (4)

Sir 23: 6 not the lustful *c* of the flesh master me,
Mk 4:19 and *c* of other sorts come to choke it off;
Gal 5:16 you will not yield to the *c* of the flesh.
Jas 4: 1 inner *c* that make war within your members?

CRAWL (6)

Gn 1:26 and all the creatures that *c* on the ground."
1:30 the living creatures that *c* on the ground,
3:14 On your belly shall you *c*,
Lv 11:10 creatures that *c* or swim in the water,
Ez 38:20 all the reptiles that *c* upon the ground,
Hos 2:20 and with the things that *c* on the ground.

CRAWLING (2)
Lv 7:21 origin or from some loathsome *c* creature,
Jas 3: 7 life, four-footed or winged, *c* or swimming,

CRAWLS (3)
Lv 11:42 Whether it *c* on its belly,
11:44 any swarming creature that *c* on the ground.
Dt 4:18 of anything that *c* on the ground or of any

CRAZE (1)
2Mc 4:13 The *c* for Hellenism and foreign customs

CRAZED (1)
Prv 26:18 Like a *c* archer scattering firebrands and

CREAM (1)
Dt 32:14 its goats, with the *c* of its finest wheat;

CREATE (9)
2Sm 19:23 that you would *c* enmity for me this day?
Ps(s) 51:12 A clean heart *c* for me, O God,
Is 4: 5 of searing judgment, Then will the LORD *c*,
45: 7 *c* the darkness, I make well-being and *c* woe:
65:17 am about to *c* new heavens and a new earth;
65:18 what I *c*; For I *c* Jerusalem to be a joy
Eph 2:15 to *c* in himself one new man from us who

CREATED (64)
Gn 1: 1 when God *c* the heavens and the earth,
1:21 God *c* the great sea monsters and all kinds
1:27 *c* man in his image; in the divine image he *c*
1:27 male and female he *c* them.
5: 1 When God *c* man,
5: 2 he *c* them male and female.
5: 2 When they were *c*,
6: 7 out from the earth the men whom I have *c*,
Dt 4:32 time, ever since God *c* man upon the earth;
32: 6 Is he not your father who *c* you?
Jdt 9:12 of the waters, King of all you have *c*,
16:14 sent forth your spirit, and they were *c*;
Ps(s) 89:13 North and south you *c*;
89:48 how frail you *c* all the children of men!
104:30 you send forth your spirit, they are *c*,
148: 5 LORD, for he commanded and they were *c*;
Wis 10: 1 of the world when he alone had been *c*;
13: 5 beauty of *c* things their original author,
Sir 1: 4 Before all things else wisdom was *c*;
1: 7 he *c* her,
1:13 With devoted men was she *c* from of old,
5:17 For shame has been *c* for the thief,
15:14 When God, in the beginning, *c* man,
16:24 When at the first God *c* his works and,
17: 1 The LORD from the earth *c* man,
24: 9 Before all ages, in the beginning, he *c* me,
31:27 who lacks the wine which was *c* for his joy?
37: 3 you *c* to blanket the earth with deceit?"
39:28 There are storm winds *c* to punish,
40:10 For the wicked, these were *c* evil,
Is 40:26 your eyes on high and see who has *c* these:
41:20 done this, the Holy One of Israel has *c* it.
42: 5 who *c* the heavens and stretched them out,
43: 1 But now, thus says the LORD, who *c* you,
43: 7 is named as mine, whom I *c* for my glory,
45: 8 I, the LORD, have *c* this.
45:12 I who made the earth and *c* mankind upon it;
54:16 I have *c* the craftsman who blows on the
54:16 who have *c* the destroyer to work havoc.
Jer 31:22 The LORD has *c* a new thing upon the earth:
Ez 21:35 In the place where you were *c*,
28:13 jewels were made, on the day you were *c*.
28:15 in your conduct from the day you were *c*,
Am 4:13 who formed the mountains, and *c* the wind,
Mal 2:10 Has not the one God *c* us?
Acts 15: 2 This *c* dissension and much controversy
Rom 8:19 the whole *c* world eagerly awaits the
1Cor 11: 9 was man *c* for woman but woman for man.
Gal 6:15 All that matters is that one is *c* anew.
Eph 2:10 *c* in Christ Jesus to lead the life of good
4:24 must put on that new man *c* in God's image,
Col 1:16 everything in heaven and on earth was *c*,
1:16 all were *c* through him,
1Tm 2:13 For Adam was *c* first,
4: 3 from foods which God *c* to be received
4: 4 Everything God *c* is good;
Heb 1: 2 whom he first *c* the universe.
4: 3 work was finished when he *c* the world,
11: 3 that the worlds were *c* by the word of God,
12:27 shows that shaken, *c* things will pass away,
2Pt 3: 4 stays just as it was when the world was *c*."
Rv 4:11 For you have *c* all things;
10: 6 who *c* heaven and earth and sea along with

CREATES (2)
Ps(s) 94:20 you, which *c* burdens in the guise of law?
Wis 15:13 stuff he *c* fragile vessels and idols alike.

CREATING (3)
Is 45:18 Not *c* it to be a waste,
Lk 22: 6 to hand him over without *c* a disturbance.
Acts 17: 6 been *c* a disturbance all over the place.

CREATION (21)
Gn 2: 3 rested from all the work he had done in *c*.
2: 4 of the heavens and the earth at their *c*.
Tb 8: 5 heavens and all your *c* praise you forever.
Wis 2: 6 real, and use the freshness of *c* avidly.
5:17 and he shall arm *c* to requite the enemy;
15: 4 did the evil *c* of men's fancy deceive us,
16:24 For your *c*, serving you, its maker,
19: 6 For all *c*, in its several kinds,
Mt 13:35 has lain hidden since the *c* of the world."
25:34 prepared for you from the *c* of the world.
Mk 10: 6 of *c* God made them male and female;
13:19 than any between God's work of *c* and now,
16:15 world and proclaim the good news to all *c*.
Rom 1:20 Since the *c* of the world,
8:20 *C* was made subject to futility,
8:22 *c* groans and is in agony even until now.
2Cor 5:17 that if anyone is in Christ, he is a new *c*.
Heb 9:11 by hands, that is, not belonging to this *c*.
9:26 over and over from the *c* of the world.
Rv 3:14 Witness and true, the Source of God's *c*,
17: 8 book of the living from the *c* of the world

CREATIVE (1)
Sir 38: 8 Thus God's *c* work continues without cease

CREATOR (28)
Gn 14:19 God Most High, the *c* of heaven and earth;
14:22 God Most High, the *c* of heaven and earth,
Jdt 9:12 Lord of heaven and earth, *C* of the waters,
13:18 be the Lord God, the *c* of heaven and earth,
2Mc 1:24 "Lord, Lord God, *c* of all things,
7:23 since it is the *C* of the universe who
13:14 Leaving the outcome to the *C* of the world,
Eccl 12: 1 Remember your *C* in the days of your youth,
Sir 3:16 accursed of his *C*,
4: 6 he curse you, his *C* will hear his prayer.
7:30 With all your strength, love your *C*,
24: 8 "Then the *C* of all gave me his command,
32:13 Above all, give praise to your *C*,
33:13 So are men in the hands of their *C*,
Is 40:14 Power of the *C* Behold,
40:28 eternal God, *c* of the ends of the earth.
43:15 the LORD, your Holy One, the *c* of Israel,
45:18 thus says the LORD, The *c* of the heavens,
57:19 and to those who mourn for them, I, the *C*,
Jer 10:16 he is the *c* of all things;
51:19 of Jacob, he is the *c* of all things;
Mt 19: 4 *C* made them male and female and declared,
Rom 1:25 and served the creature rather than the *C*—
Eph 3: 9 for ages was hidden in God, the *C* of all.
Col 3:10 as he is formed anew in the image of his *C*.
1Pt 4:19 and entrust their lives to a faithful *C*.
Rv 14: 7 Worship the *C* of heaven and earth, the *C*

CREATURE (26)
Gn 7: 4 the earth every moving *c* that I have made."
9: 3 *c* that is alive shall be yours to eat;
9:10 and with every living *c* that was with you:
9:12 me and you and every living *c* with you:
Lv 5: 2 animal, or that of an unclean swarming *c*,
7:21 origin or from some loathsome crawling *c*,
11:12 Every water *c* that lacks fins or scales is
11:42 has many legs, you shall eat no swarming *c*:
11:43 *c* through being contaminated by them.
11:44 any swarming *c* that crawls on the ground.
20:25 of any swarming *c* in the land
22: 5 swarming *c* or any man whose uncleanness,
Jdt 16:14 Let your every *c* serve you;
Eccl 10:20 voice, a winged *c* may tell what you say.
Sir 31:13 No *c* is greedier than the eye:
42:24 to meet each need, each *c* is preserved.
Ez 47: 9 of living *c* that can multiply shall live,
Rom 1:25 and served the *c* rather than the Creator
8:39 neither height nor depth nor any other *c*,
Col 1:23 has been announced to every *c* under heaven,
Rv 4: 7 The first *c* resembled a lion,
5:13 Then I heard the voices of every *c* in
6: 3 seal, I heard the second living *c* cry out,
6: 5 seal, I heard the third living *c* cry out,
6: 7 the voice of the fourth living *c* cry out,
16: 3 corpse, and every *c* living in the sea died.

CREATURES (73)
Gn 1:20 water teem with an abundance of living *c*,
1:21 of swimming *c* with which the water teems,
1:24 earth bring forth all kinds of living *c*:
1:26 and all the *c* that crawl on the ground."
1:30 all the living *c* that crawl on the ground,
3:14 all the animals and from all the wild *c*;
6:17 all *c* in which there is the breath of life;
6:19 living *c* you shall bring two into the ark,
7:15 Pairs of all *c* in which there was the
7:21 All *c* that stirred on earth perished:
8:17 all bodily *c*, be they birds or animals
8:19 the creeping *c* of the earth left the ark,
9: 2 upon all the *c* that move about on the
9:11 *c* be destroyed by the waters of a flood;
9:16 all mortal *c* that are on earth."
9:17 me and all mortal *c* that are on earth."
Lv 11: 9 "Of the various *c* that live in the water,
11:10 various *c* that crawl or swim in the water,
11:29 "Of the *c* that swarm on the ground,
11:31 Among the various swarming *c*,
11:33 any of these *c* fall into a clay vessel,
11:41 "All the *c* that swarm on the ground are
11:46 birds and for all the *c* that move about
11:47 between *c* that may be eaten and those that
Dt 14: 9 "Of the various *c* that live in the water,
14:20 But you may eat any clean winged *c*.
Jos 6:21 to the sword all living *c* in the city:
Jdt 11: 7 him who has sent you to set all *c* aright!
Ps(s) 102:19 and let his future *c* praise the LORD:
104:24 the earth is full of your *c*;
Wis 1:14 and the *c* of the world are wholesome,
9: 2 man to rule the *c* produced by you,
11:15 upon them swarms of dumb *c* for vengeance;
16: 1 they were fittingly punished by similar *c*,
16: 3 *c* sent to plague them were so loathsome,
19:19 land *c* were changed into water creatures,
Sir 43:26 In it are his *c*, stupendous, amazing,
49: 8 described the different *c* of the chariot;
Ez 1: 5 four living *c* that looked like this:
1:13 In among the living *c* something like
1:13 moving to and fro among the living *c*.
1:15 As I looked at the living *c*,
1:15 one beside each of the four living *c*.
1:19 When the living *c* moved,
1:19 the living *c* were raised from the ground,
1:20 with the living *c*; for the spirit of the living *c*
1:22 Over the heads of the living *c*,
3:13 wings of the living *c* striking one another,
10:15 living *c* I had seen by the river Chebar.
10:17 for the living *c*' spirit was in them.
10:20 these were the living *c* I had seen beneath
Dn 3:79 You dolphins and all water *c*,
Acts 10:12 *c* and reptiles and birds of the sky.
11: 6 could make out four-legged *c* of the earth,
Col 1:15 the invisible God, the first-born of all *c*.
Jas 1:18 we may be a kind of first fruits of his *c*.
2Pt 2:12 They act like *c* of instinct,
Rv 4: 6 living *c* covered with eyes front and back.
4: 8 living *c* had six wings and eyes all over,
4: 9 Whenever these *c* give glory and honor and
5: 6 with the four living *c* and the elders,
5: 8 the four living *c* and the twenty-four
5:11 the throne and the living *c* and the elders.
5:14 The four living *c* answered,
6: 1 living *c* cry out in a voice like thunder,
6: 6 coming from in among the four living *c*.
7:11 four living *c* fell down before the throne
8: 9 a third of the *c* living in the sea died,
14: 3 of the four living *c* and the elders.
15: 7 One of the four living *c* gave to the seven
19: 4 four living *c* fell down and worshiped God

CREDENCE (2)
Jn 8:45 I deal in the truth, you give me no *c*.
2Thes 2:11 which leads them to give *c* to falsehood,

CREDENTIALS (1)
Acts 2:22 with miracles, wonders, and signs as his *c*.

CREDIT (10)
Lv 7:18 him nor shall it be reckoned to his *c*;
25:52 jubilee year, the more he has to his *c*;
Neh 13:14 Remember this to my *c*, O my God!
Prv 10: 5 who fills the granaries in summer is a *c*;
Lk 6:32 those who love you, what *c* is that to you?
6:33 do good to you, how can you claim any *c*?
16: 8 devious employee *c* for being enterprising!
2Cor 3: 5 of ourselves to take *c* for anything.
3: 5 Our sole *c* is from God,
1Pt 2:20 get beaten for it, what *c* can you claim?

CREDITABLE (1)
1Sm 26:16 This is no *c* service you have performed.

CREDITED (14)
Gn 15: 6 who *c* it to him as an act of righteousness.
Nm 18:27 and your contribution will be *c* to you as
18:30 the rest of the tithes will be *c* to you
2Sm 12:28 I that capture the city and it be *c* to me."
Rom 4: 3 God, and it was *c* to him as justice."
4: 5 the sinful, his faith is *c* as justice.
4: 9 say that Abraham's faith was *c* as justice."
4:10 were the circumstances in which it was *c*?
4:11 for them too faith might be *c* as justice,
4:22 Thus his faith was *c* to him as justice.
4:23 The words, "It was *c* to him,"
4:24 For our faith will be *c* to us also if we
Gal 3: 6 God, and it was *c* to him as justice."
Jas 2:23 God, and it was *c* to him as justice";

CREDITOR (4)
Dt 15: 2 Every *c* shall relax his claim on what he
2Kgs 4: 1 yet now his *c* has come to take my two
4: 7 "Go and sell the oil to pay off your *c*;

Is 24: 2 as the borrower, the *c* as the debtor.

CREDITORS (4)

Sir 29: 5 and speaks with respect of his *c* wealth;
29:28 are abuse at home and insults from his *c*.
Is 50: 1 Or to which of my *c* have I sold you?
Hb 2: 7 Shall not your *c* rise suddenly?

CREDITS (1)

Rom 4: 6 whom God *c* justice without requiring deeds:

CREEPING (11)

Gn 1:24 cattle, *c* things, and wild animals
1:25 and all kinds of *c* things of the earth.
6: 7 and the *c* things and the birds of the air,
6:20 of beasts, and of all kinds of *c* things,
7:14 animal, every kind of *c* thing of the earth,
7:23 the *c* things and the birds of the air;
8:17 birds or animals or *c* things of the earth
8:19 the *c* creatures of the earth left the ark,
Ps(s) 148:10 animals, you *c* things and you winged fowl.
Ez 8:10 kinds of *c* things and loathsome beasts
Hb 1:14 of the sea, like *c* things without a ruler.

CREEPS (1)

Gn 7: 8 and of everything that *c* on the ground,

CREMATED (1)

1Sm 31:12 brought them to Jabesh, where they *c* them.

CRESCENS (1)

2Tm 4:10 *C* has gone to Galatia and Titus to Dalmatia.

CRESCENTS (3)

Jgs 8:21 *c* that were on the necks of their camels.
8:26 shekels, in addition to the *c* and pendants,
Is 3:18 finery of the anklets, sunbursts, and *c*;

CREST (8)

Gn 7:20 the *c* rising fifteen cubits higher than
7:24 The waters maintained their *c* over the
Jdt 6:12 ran out of the city to the *c* of the ridge;
Ez 17: 3 He took the *c* of the cedar.
17:22 I, too, will take from the *c* of the cedar,
31: 3 stature, amid the very clouds lifted its *c*.
31:10 in stature, raising its *c* among the clouds,
31:14 in stature or raise its *c* among the clouds;

CRESTFALLEN (2)

Gn 4: 5 Cain greatly resented this and was *c*.
4: 6 "Why are you so resentful and *c*?

CRESTS (1)

Jb 9: 8 heavens and treads upon the *c* of the sea.

CRETAN (2)

Zep 2: 5 who dwell by the seacoast, to the *C* folk!
Acts 27:12 This was a *C* port exposed on the southwest

CRETANS (3)

Zep 2: 6 of the *C* shall become fields for shepherds,
Acts 2:11 *C* and Arabs too.
Ti 1:12 has testified, *C* have ever been liars,

CRETE (6)

1Mc 10:67 came from *C* to the land of his fathers.
Acts 27: 7 we sailed for Salmone and the shelter of *C*.
27:13 and proceeded, hugging the coast of *C*.
27:21 taken my advice and not set sail from *C*.
Ti 1: 5 My purpose in leaving you in *C* was that
1:12 A man of *C*, one of their own prophets,

CREVICES (2)

Is 2:21 in the rocks and into *c* in the cliffs,
57: 5 in the wadies, behind the *c* in the cliffs?

CREW (2)

Ez 27:27 your wares, your sailors, and your *c*.
27:34 and all your *c* have gone down with you.

CREWMEN (1)

2Chr 8:18 him ships and *c* acquainted with the sea,

CRIB (1)

Prv 14: 4 there are no oxen, the *c* remains empty;

CRICKETS (1)

Lv 11:22 of katydids, and the various kinds of *c*.

CRIED (153)

Gn 28:17 In solemn wonder he *c* out:
29:25 So he *c* out to Laban:
38:24 "Bring her out," *c* Judah;
39:14 with me, but I *c* out as loud as I could.
41:55 and the people *c* to Pharaoh for bread,
42:28 he *c* out to his brothers.
45: 1 of all his attendants, so he *c* out,
Ex 2:23 groaned and *c* out because of their slavery.
14:10 In great fright they *c* out to the LORD.
17: 4 So Moses *c* out to the LORD,
32: 4 Then they *c* out, "This is your God,
32:26 he stood at the gate of the camp and *c*,
34: 6 Thus the LORD passed before him and *c* out,
Lv 9:24 all the people *c* out and fell prostrate.
Nm 11: 2 But when the people *c* out to Moses,
11:18 For in the hearing of the LORD you have *c*,
12:13 Then Moses *c* to the LORD,
16:22 But they fell prostrate and *c* out,
17:27 Then the Israelites *c* out to Moses,
20:16 fathers, and how, when we *c* to the LORD,
23:11 "What have you done to me?" *c* Balak
Dt 22:27 betrothed maiden may have *c* out for help,
26: 7 hard labor upon us, we *c* to the LORD,
Jos 24: 7 Because they *c* out to the LORD,
Jgs 3: 9 But when the Israelites *c* out to the LORD,
3:15 But when the Israelites *c* out to the LORD,
4: 3 But the Israelites *c* out to the LORD;
6: 6 and so the Israelites *c* out to the LORD.
6: 7 Israel *c* out to the LORD because of Midian,
7:20 the horns they were blowing, and *c* out,
9: 7 there, *c* out to them in a loud voice:
10:10 Then the Israelites *c* out to the LORD,
10:12 Yet when you *c* out to me,
15:18 very thirsty, he *c* to the LORD and said,
16:28 Samson *c* out to the LORD and said,
1Sm 5:10 entered that city, the people there *c* out,
15:11 grew angry and *c* out to the LORD all night.
2Sm 18:26 From his place atop the gate he *c* out,
19: 5 covered his face and *c* out in a loud voice,
20: 1 He sounded the horn and *c* out,
22: 7 I called upon the LORD and *c* out to my God;
22:42 They *c* for help—but no one saved them,
1Kgs 13: 2 He *c* out against the altar the word of the
13:21 and he *c* out to the man of God who had
22:32 commanders saw Jehoshaphat, they *c* out,
2Kgs 2:12 When Elisha saw it happen he *c* out,
4:28 she *c* out. "Did I not beg
4:30 But the boy's mother *c* out
6: 5 "O master," he *c* out,
6:26 on the city wall, a woman *c* out to him,
9:13 bare steps, blew the trumpet, and *c* out,
9:31 As Jehu came through the gate, she *c* out,
11:14 trumpets, she tore her garments and *c* out,
18:28 and *c* out in a loud voice in Judean,
2Chr 13:14 they *c* out to the LORD and the priests
18:31 Jehoshaphat *c* out and the LORD helped him;
23:11 and his sons anointed him, and they *c*,
23:13 Athaliah tore her garments and *c* out,
Ezr 3:12 *c* out in sorrow as they watched the
10:12 the whole assembly *c* out with a loud voice:
Neh 9: 4 Chenani, who *c* out to the LORD their God,
9:28 Then they *c* out to you,
Tb 7:16 After she had *c* over her,
Jdt 4: 9 *c* to God with great fervor and did penance
4:12 and with one accord they *c* out fervently
4:15 they *c* to the Lord with all their strength
5:12 But they *c* to their God,
6:18 worshipped God; and they *c* out:
7:19 The Israelites *c* to the Lord,
14:17 her, he rushed out to the troops and *c*:
16:11 when my weaklings *c* out,
Est A: 9 they *c* out to God, and as they *c*,
C:11 Israel, too, *c* out with all their strength,
6:11 square of the city, and *c* out before him,
F: 6 is Israel, who *c* to God and was saved.
1Mc 3:50 And they *c* aloud to Heaven:
3:54 they blew the trumpets and *c* out loudly.
4:40 given with trumpets, they *c* out to Heaven.
11:49 and *c* out to the king in supplication,
13:45 garments rent, and *c* out in loud voices,
13:50 They finally *c* out to Simon for peace,
2Mc 8: 3 to hearken to the blood that *c* out to him;
Jb 29:12 For I rescued the poor who *c* out for help,
31:38 If my land has *c* out against me till its
Ps(s) 18: 7 I called upon the LORD and *c* out to my God;
18:42 They *c* for help—but no one saved
22: 6 To you they *c* and they escaped;
22:25 away from him, but when he *c* out to him,
30: 3 my God, I *c* out to you and you healed me.
30: 9 To you, O LORD, I *c* out;
31:23 sound of my pleading when I *c* out to you.
107: 6 They *c* to the LORD in their distress;
107:13 They *c* to the LORD in their distress;
107:19 They *c* to the LORD in their distress;
107:28 They *c* to the LORD in their distress;
Is 6: 3 they *c* one to the other.
21: 8 Then the watchman *c*,
26:16 we *c* out in anguish under your chastising.
36:13 and *c* out in a loud voice in Judean,
Lam 1:19 "I *c* out to my lovers,
4:15 they *c* to them, "Away, away,
Ez 9: 1 he *c* loud for me to hear:
11:13 I fell prone and *c* out in a loud voice;
25: 3 Because you *c* out your joy over the
Dn 3: 4 A herald *c* out:
4:11 sentinel came down from heaven, and *c* out:
6:21 drew near, he *c* out to Daniel sorrowfully,
8:16 I heard a human voice that *c* out
13:42 But Susanna *c* aloud:
13:46 a young boy named Daniel, and he *c* aloud:
13:60 The whole assembly *c* aloud,
14:18 the king looked at the table and *c* aloud,
14:37 "Daniel, Daniel," *c* Habakkuk,
14:41 The king *c* aloud,
Hos 7:14 They have not *c* to me from their hearts
Jon 1: 5 frightened and each one *c* to his god.
1:14 Then they *c* to the LORD:
2: 3 the midst of the nether world I *c* for help,
Mt 8:29 With a sudden shriek they *c*:
14:30 frightened, he began to sink and *c* out,
25:11 they *c*. 'Open the door for us.'
27:22 "Crucify him!" they all *c*.
27:46 midafternoon Jesus *c* out in a loud tone,
27:50 Once again Jesus *c* out in a loud voice,
Mk 11: 9 him as well as those who followed *c* out:
15:34 At that time Jesus *c* in a loud voice,
Lk 1:42 the Holy Spirit and *c* out in a loud voice:
18:39 him to be quiet, but he *c* out all the more,
23:18 The whole crowd *c* out,
Jn 7:28 who was teaching in the temple area, *c* out:
7:37 of the festival, Jesus stood and *c* out:
8:41 They *c*, "We are no illegitimate breed!
21: 7 the disciple Jesus loved *c* out to Peter,
Acts 7:60 to his knees and *c* out in a loud voice,
14:11 Paul had done, they *c* out in Lycaonian,
Rv 5:12 and tens of thousands and they all *c* out:
5:13 everything in the universe *c* aloud:
6:10 They *c* out at the top of their voices:
6:16 They *c* out to the mountains and rocks,
7: 2 He *c* out at the top of his voice to the
7:10 They *c* out in a loud voice, "Salvation
10: 3 When he *c* out, the seven thunders
11:15 Loud voices in heaven *c* out,
14: 8 A second angel followed and *c* out:
14:15 voice *c* out to him who sat on the cloud,
14:18 *c* out in a loud voice to the one who held
18: 2 He *c* out in a strong voice:
18:18 then stood at a distance and *c* out when
18:19 They poured dust on their heads and *c* out,
19: 5 A voice coming from the throne *c* out:
19: 6 or mighty peals of thunder, as they *c*:
19:17 He *c* out in a loud voice to all the birds

CRIER (1)

Sir 20:14 often, and like a *c* he shouts aloud.

CRIES (39)

Gn 4:10 brother's blood *c* out to me from the soil!
Ex 22:26 If he *c* out to me,
32:18 like *c* of victory, nor does it sound like *c*
32:18 the sounds that I hear are *c* of revelry."
Nm 14: 1 whole community broke out with loud *c*,
Jgs 2:18 *c* of affliction under their oppressors.
Jdt 7:29 wailing and loud *c* to the Lord their God.
Jb 4:10 roars, though the king of beasts *c* out,
34:28 But caused the *c* of the poor to reach him,
39:25 of the trumpet, but at each blast he *c*,
Ps(s) 32: 7 glad *c* of freedom you will ring me round.
42: 5 God, Amid loud *c* of joy and thanksgiving,
47: 2 hands, shout to God with *c* of gladness,
72:12 he shall rescue the poor man when he *c* out,
Prv 1:20 Wisdom *c* aloud in the street,
8: 3 of the city, in the entryways she *c* aloud:
Wis 14: 1 traverse the wild waves *c* out to wood
Is 15: 5 The heart of Moab *c* out,
15: 5 the way to Horonaim they utter rending *c*.
26:17 give birth writhes and *c* out in her pains,
38:14 Like a swallow I utter shrill *c*;
40: 3 A voice *c* out: In the desert prepare
Jer 2:15 Against him lions roar full-throated *c*.
9: 9 mountains, break out in *c* of lamentation,
18:22 May *c* be heard from their homes,
20:16 Let him hear war *c* in the morning,
31:16 Cease your *c* of mourning,
46:12 hear of your shame, your *c* fill the earth
51:54 loud *c* from Babylon,
Ez 19: 4 *c* against him in their pit he was caught;
27:30 heard on your behalf, shouting bitter *c*,
Dn 13:26 in the house heard the *c* from the garden,
Mi 6: 9 the LORD *c* to the city.
Lk 23:23 demanded with loud *c* that he be crucified,
Rom 9:27 Isaiah *c* out, referring to Israel,
Gal 4: 6 the spirit of his Son which *c* out "Abba!"
Heb 5: 7 supplications with loud *c* and tears to God,
Jas 5: 4 The *c* of the harvesters have reached the

CRIME (51)

Gn 31:36 "What *c* or offense have I committed,"
50:17 Please therefore, forgive the *c* that we,
Ex 34: 7 and forgiving wickedness and *c* and sin;
Lv 20: 4 man's *c* of giving his offspring to Molech,
Nm 14:18 in kindness, forgiving wickedness and *c*;
Dt 19:15 *c* or any offense of which he may be guilty;
22:21 because she committed a *c* against Israel
Jos 7:15 and has committed a shameful *c* in Israel."
Jgs 19:23 this man is my guest, do not commit this *c*.
19:24 the man you must not commit this wanton *c*."
20: 3 asked to be told how the *c* had taken place,

CRIME (cont.)

20: 6 monstrous *c* they had committed in Israel.
20:10 Benjamin for the *c* it committed in Israel."
1Sm 3:13 family once and for all, because of this *c*:
3:14 or offering will ever expiate its *c*."
15:23 and presumption is the *c* of idolatry.
20: 1 "What *c* or what offense does your father
2Sm 3: 8 you charge me with a *c* involving a woman!
13:12 That is an intolerable *c* in Israel.
1Kgs 1:52 But if he is found guilty of *c*,
2Chr 24:18 and because of this *c* of theirs,
28:10 therefore, guilty of a *c* against the LORD,
Neh 3:37 Hide not their *c* and let not their sin be
Tb 6:13 that would be a capital *c* according to the
14:10 Nadab's disgraceful *c* rebound against him.
2Mc 4:36 with the Greeks who detested the *c*,
4:49 Tyrians were indignant over the *c*
Jb 31:11 that would be heinous, a *c* to be condemned;
31:28 This too would be a *c* for condemnation,
Ps(s) 89:33 *c* with a rod and their guilt with stripes.
Prv 10:23 *C* is the entertainment of the fool;
29:16 When the wicked prevail, *c* increases;
Sir 7: 6 if you have not strength to root out *c*,
41:16 before the public assembly, of *c*;
Jer 16:10 What is our *c*?
16:18 repay them double for their *c* and their sin
18:23 Forgive not their *c*,
Bar 6:17 to execution for a *c* against the king;
Ez 21:30 coming when your life of *c* will be ended,
Dn 13:38 we, in a corner of the garden, saw this *c*,
Hos 6: 9 the way to Shechem, committing monstrous *c*.
Mi 1: 5 For the *c* of Jacob all this comes to pass,
1: 5 What is the *c* of Jacob?
6: 7 Shall I give my first-born for my *c*,
Mt 27:23 He said, "Why, what *c* has he committed?"
Mk 15:14 What *c* has he committed?"
Acts 18:14 "If it were a *c* or a serious fraud,
23: 9 "We do not find this man guilty of any *c*.
24:20 Let those who are here declare what *c* they
25: 8 "I have committed no *c* either against the
25:11 if I have committed a *c* deserving death,

CRIMES (53)

Nm 14:34 forty years shall you suffer for your *c*:
Jdt 11:17 when the Israelites have committed their *c*.
Est B: 5 to our interests, and commits the worst *c*,
1Mc 7:25 to the king and accused them of grave *c*.
2Mc 13: 6 notorious for certain other *c* is brought up
Jb 19:29 yourselves, for these *c* deserve the sword;
Ps(s) 26:10 On their hands are *c*,
58: 3 Nay, you willingly commit *c*;
103:10 nor does he requite us according to our *c*.
106: 6 we have committed *c*;
106:39 by their works, and wanton in their *c*.
Is 32: 7 trickster uses wicked trickery, planning *c*:
43:24 with your sins, and wearied me with your *c*.
50: 1 for your *c* that your mother was dismissed.
59: 2 is your *c* that separate you from your God,
59:12 are present to us, and our *c* we know:
65: 7 *c* and the crimes of your fathers as well,
65: 7 crimes and the *c* of your fathers as well,
Jer 5: 6 their many *c* and their numerous rebellions.
5:25 Your *c* have prevented these things,
11:10 They have returned to the *c* of their
13:27 highlands I see these horrible *c* of yours.
14: 7 Even though our *c* bear witness against us,
41:11 leaders with him heard of the *c* Ishmael,
Lam 4:13 of her prophets and the *c* of her priests,
Ez 16:50 and committed abominable *c* in my presence;
18:22 None of the *c* he committed shall be
18:30 Turn and be converted from all your *c*,
18:31 away from you all the *c* you have committed,
21:29 with your *c* laid bare and your sinfulness
21:34 day has come when their *c* are at an end.
33:10 say, "Our *c* and our sins weigh us down;
35: 5 their trouble, when their *c* came to an end,
36:33 When I purify you from all your *c*,
Dn 9:16 of our sins and the *c* of our fathers,
Hos 7: 2 Even now their *c* surround them,
10:10 them when I chastised them for their two *c*.
Am 1: 3 For three *c* of Damascus,
1: 6 For three *c* of Gaza,
1: 9 says the Lord: For three *c* of Tyre
1:11 For three *c* of Edom,
1:13 For three *c* of the Ammonites,
2: 1 For three *c* of Moab,
2: 4 For three *c* of Judah,
2: 6 For three *c* of Israel,
3: 2 Therefore I will punish you for all your *c*.
3:14 On the day when I punish Israel for his *c*,
5:12 Yes, I know how many are your *c*,
Mi 1:13 Because there were in you the *c* of Israel.
3: 8 to Jacob his *c* and to Israel his sins.
Lk 3:19 brother's wife, and for all his other *c*.
Acts 25:18 charge him with any of the *c* I expected.
Rv 18: 5 as heaven, and God keeps count of her *c*.

CRIMINAL (9)

Gn 50:17 forgive the *c* wrongdoing of your brothers,
2Mc 8: 4 to remember the *c* slaughter of innocent
Ps(s) 71: 4 from the grasp of the *c* and the violent.
Sir 16:13 A *c* does not escape with his plunder;
Mi 6:10 Am I to bear any longer *c* hoarding and the
6:11 Shall I acquit *c* balances,
Lk 22:52 "Am I a *c* that you come out after me
Jn 18:30 "If he were not a *c*,"
2Tm 2: 9 in preaching it I suffer as a *c*,

CRIMINALS (9)

1Kgs 1:21 I and my son Solomon will be considered *c*."
Ps(s) 37:28 *C* are destroyed,
Sir 21: 9 A band of *c* is like a bundle of tow;
Jer 5:26 For there are among my people *c*;
29:23 For they are *c* in Israel,
Lk 23:32 *c* were led along with him to be crucified.
23:33 they crucified him there and the *c* as well,
23:39 *c* hanging in crucifixion blasphemed him:
1Pt 2:14 of *c* and the recognition of the upright.

CRIMSON (11)

Gn 38:28 and the midwife, taking a *c* thread,
2Chr 2: 6 silver, bronze and iron, in purple, *c*,
2:13 with purple, violet, fine linen and *c*,
3:14 veil of violet, purple, *c* and fine linen,
Jdt 10:21 a canopy with a netting of *c* and gold,
Est 1: 6 held by cords of *c* byssus from silver
8:15 crown of gold and a cloak of *c* byssus.
1Mc 4:23 much gold and silver, violet and *c* cloth,
Sir 45:10 vestments of gold, of violet, and of *c*,
Is 1:18 Though they be *c* red,
Heb 9:19 together with water and *c* wool and hyssop,

CRIMSONED (3)

Wis 13:14 with red and *c* its surface with red stain,
Is 63: 1 this that comes from Edom, in *c* garments,
Na 2: 4 The shields of his warriors are *c*,

CRINGE (1)

Jer 5: 3 You struck them, but they did not *c*;

CRINGED (2)

2Sm 22:46 The foreigners fawned and *c* before me;
Ps(s) 18:45 The foreigners fawned and *c* before me;

CRIPPLE (2)

Acts 3: 5 The *c* gave them his whole attention,
4: 9 answer today for a good deed done to a *c*

CRIPPLED (11)

Lv 21:19 or malformation, or a *c* foot or hand,
22:22 One that is blind or *c* or maimed,
2Sm 4: 4 had a son named Meribbaal with *c* feet.
9: 3 is still Jonathan's son, whose feet are *c*."
Prv 26: 7 mouth of a fool hangs limp, like *c* legs.
Mt 18: 8 Better to enter life maimed or *c* than be
Mk 9:45 Better for you to enter life *c* than to be
Lk 14:13 a reception, invite beggars and the *c*,
14:21 the town and bring in the poor and the *c*,
Acts 3: 2 a man *c* from birth was being carried in.
14: 8 he used to sit *c*, never having walked

CRIPPLES (5)

Mt 11: 5 the blind recover their sight, *c* walk,
15:30 people came to him bringing with them *c*,
15:31 the deformed made sound, *c* walking about,
Lk 7:22 The blind recover their sight, *c* walk,
Acts 8: 7 Many others were paralytics or *c*,

CRIPPLING (1)

Mi 2:10 For any trifle you exact a *c* pledge.

CRISIS (2)

Sir 45:23 God of all, he met the *c* of his people And,
Dn 2: 9 to present me with till the *c* is past.

CRISPUS (2)

Acts 18: 8 A leading man of the synagogue, *C*,
1Cor 1:14 I baptized none of you except *C* and Gaius,

CRITIC (1)

Jb 40: 2 we have arguing with the Almighty by the *c*?

CRITICAL (3)

Jgs 12: 2 engaged in a *c* contest with the Ammonites.
1Mc 3:42 situation had become *c* now that armies
1Cor 7:36 toward his virgin because a *c* moment

CRITICALLY (1)

Mk 5:23 "My little daughter is *c* ill.

CRITICIZE (4)

Sir 11: 7 examine first, then *c*.
Mt 26:10 "Why do you *c* the woman?
Mk 14: 6 Why do you *c* her?
1Cor 9: 3 My defense against those who *c* me is this:

CRITICIZES (1)

Sir 20:14 He gives little and *c* often,

CROAK (1)

Zep 2:14 the window, the raven's *c* from the doorway.

CROCKERY (1)

Rv 2:27 with a rod of iron and shatter them like *c*;

CROOKED (25)

Dt 32: 5 degenerate children, a perverse and *c* race!
2Sm 22:27 but toward the *c* you are astute.
Ps(s) 18:27 sincere, but toward the *c* you are astute;
101: 4 A *c* heart shall be far from me;
125: 5 But such as turn aside to *c* ways may the
139:24 See if my way is *c*,
Prv 2:15 Whose ways are *c*,
6:12 a villain, is he who deals in *c* talk.
8: 8 of my mouth, no one of them is wily or *c*;
10: 9 but he whose ways are *c* will fare badly.
19: 1 than he who is *c* in his ways and rich.
21: 8 The way of the culprit is *c*,
22: 5 and snares are on the path of the *c*;
28: 6 than he who is *c* in his ways and rich.
28:18 but he whose ways are *c* falls into the pit.
Eccl 1:15 What is *c* cannot be made straight,
7:13 Who can make straight what he has made *c*?
Wis 13:13 these remnants, *c* wood grown full of knots,
16: 5 were dying from the bite of *c* serpents,
Is 30:12 put your trust in what is *c* and devious,
42:16 before them, and make *c* ways straight.
59: 8 Their ways they have made *c*,
Lam 3:36 the Most High, When he presses a *c* claim,
Lk 18:11 grasping, *c*, adulterous
Acts 13:10 to make *c* the straight paths of the Lord?

CROP (17)

Gn 26:12 Isaac sowed a *c* in that region and reaped
Ex 23:16 of the *c* that you have sown in the field;
Lv 1:16 Its *c* and feathers shall be removed and
25:20 year, if we do not then sow or reap our *c*?'
25:21 will then be *c* enough for three years.
25:22 you will continue to eat from the old *c*;
25:22 into the ninth year, when the *c* comes in,
26:16 vain, for your enemies will consume the *c*.
Dt 22: 9 both the *c* you have sown and the yield of
Ps(s) 105:16 land and ruined the *c* that sustained them,
Is 5: 2 Then he looked for the *c* of grapes,
5: 4 Why, when I looked for the *c* of grapes,
Mt 13:26 When the *c* began to mature and yield grain,
Mk 4:29 When the *c* is ready he 'wields the sickle,
Lk 20:10 to receive his share of the *c* from them;
2Tm 2: 6 who should have the first share of the *c*.
Jas 5:18 with rain and the land produced its *c*.

CROPS (24)

Gn 41:47 plenty, when the land produced abundant *c*,
41:48 in each town the *c* of the fields around it.
Lv 25:15 on the basis of the number of years for *c*,
25:16 really the number of *c* that he sells you.
26: 4 season, so that the land will bear its *c*,
26:10 So much of the old *c* will you have stored
26:20 your land will bear no *c*,
Dt 11:17 fall, and the soil will not yield its *c*,
16:15 in all your *c* and in all your undertakings,
28:38 little, for the locusts will devour the *c*.
28:42 all your trees and the *c* of your soil.
32: 2 upon the grass, like a shower upon the *c*.
1Sm 8:15 He will tithe your *c* and your vineyards,
Ps(s) 72:16 mountains the *c* shall rustle like Lebanon;
Prv 14: 4 *c* come through the strength of the bull.
Sir 6:19 then await her bountiful *c*.
20:27 He who works his land has abundant *c*,
Is 42: 5 out, who spreads out the earth with its *c*,
Jer 35: 9 we own no vineyards or fields or *c*,
Ez 34:27 bear their fruits, and the land its *c*,
36:30 on your trees and the *c* in your fields;
Hg 1:10 from you their dew, and the earth her *c*.
Zec 8:12 its fruit, the land shall bear its *c*,
Mal 3:11 will forbid the locust to destroy your *c*;

CROSS (86)

Nm 20:17 We will not *c* any fields or vineyards,
32: 5 Do not make us *c* the Jordan."
32:19 heritage with them once we *c* the Jordan,
32:21 vanguard and to *c* the Jordan in full force
32:29 If all the Gadites and Reubenites *c* the
34: 4 south of the Akrabbim Pass, it shall *c* Zin,
34: 4 thence it shall *c* to Azmon,
Dt 2:13 Get ready, then, to *c* the Wadi Zered.'
2:29 *c* the Jordan into the land which the LORD,
3:18 troops equipped for battle must *c* over
3:25 let me *c* over and see this good land
3:27 Look well, for you shall not *c* this Jordan.
3:28 for he shall *c* at the head of this people
4:21 swore that I should not *c* the Jordan
4:22 but you will *c* over and take possession of
4:26 you will occupy when you *c* the Jordan.
9: 1 You are now about to *c* the Jordan to enter
9: 3 will *c* over before you as a consuming fire;
11:31 For you are about to *c* the Jordan to enter
27: 2 *c* the Jordan into the land which the LORD,
27: 3 Also write on them, at the time you *c*,

27:12 "When you *c* the Jordan,
30:13 'Who will *c* the sea to get it for us and
31: 2 has told me that I shall not *c* this Jordan.
31: 3 the LORD, your God, who will *c* before you;
31: 3 It is Joshua who will *c* before you,
31:13 land which you will *c* the Jordan to occupy."
32:47 land which you will *c* the Jordan to occupy."
34: 4 eyes upon it, but you shall not *c* over."
Jos 1: 2 So prepare to *c* the Jordan here,
1:11 days from now you shall *c* the Jordan here,
1:14 But all the warriors among you must *c* over
3:14 people struck their tents to *c* the Jordan,
22:19 *c* over to the land the LORD possesses,
Jgs 3:28 leading to Moab, permitting no one to *c*.
1Sm 30:10 to *c* the Wadi Besor and remained behind.
2Sm 17:16 the desert, but to *c* over without fail.
17:21 *C* the water at once,
19:34 The king said to Barzillai, *C* over with me,
19:38 Let him *c* over with my lord the king.
1Kgs 2:37 For if you leave, and *c* the Kidron Valley,
1Mc 5:41 we will *c* over to him and defeat him."
5:43 He was the first to *c* to the attack,
5:48 *c* your territory in order to reach our own;
16: 6 that his men were afraid to *c* the stream,
Prv 4:15 Shun it, *c* it not,
Is 10:29 They *c* the ravine:
23:10 *C* to your own land,
Ez 33:28 be so desolate that no one will *c* them.
Am 5: 5 come to Gilgal, and do not *c* to Beer-sheba.
Zec 10:11 I will *c* over to Egypt and smite the waves
Mt 8:18 Jesus gave orders to *c* to the other shore.
10:38 *c* and come after me is not worthy of me.
16:24 he must deny his very self, take up his *c*,
27:32 they pressed into service to carry the *c*.
27:40 Come down off that *c* if you are God's Son!"
27:42 come down from that *c* and then
Mk 4:35 them, "Let us *c* over to the farther shore."
8:34 he must deny his very self, take up his *c*,
15:21 pressed him into service to carry the *c*.
15:30 yourself now by coming down from that *c*!"
15:32 come down from that *c* here and now so that
Lk 8:22 us *c* over to the far side of the lake."
9:23 deny his very self, take up his *c* each day,
14:27 his *c* and follow me cannot be my disciple.
16:26 wish to *c* from here to you cannot do so,
16:26 so, nor can anyone *c* from your side to us.'
24:38 Why do such ideas *c* your mind?
Jn 6:17 intending to *c* the lake toward Capernaum.
19:17 led away, and carrying the *c* by himself,
19:19 an inscription placed on the *c* which read,
19:25 Near the *c* of Jesus there stood his mother,
19:31 bodies left on the *c* during the sabbath,
1Cor 1:17 lest the *c* of Christ be rendered void of
1:18 The message of the *c* is complete absurdity
Gal 3: 1 Christ was displayed to view upon his *c*?
5:11 the *c* would be a stumbling block no more.
6:12 escaping persecution for the *c* of Christ.
6:14 but the *c* of our Lord Jesus Christ!
Eph 2:16 of us to God in one body through his *c*,
Phil 2: 8 accepting even death, death on a *c*!
3:18 them to be enemies of the *c* of Christ.
Col 1:20 making peace through the blood of his *c*.
2:14 snatching it up and nailing it to the *c*.
Heb 12: 2 joy which lay before him he endured the *c*,
1Pt 2:24 own body he brought your sins to the *c*,

CROSSBEAM (1)

Lk 23:26 They put a *c* on Simon's shoulder for him

CROSSED (65)

Gn 32:11 although I *c* the Jordan here with nothing
32:23 children, and *c* the ford of the Jabbok.
Nm 33: 8 *c* over through the sea into the desert,
Dt 2:13 So we *c* it.
12:10 But after you have *c* the Jordan and dwell
27: 4 When, moreover, you have *c* the Jordan,
Jos 2:23 from the hills, *c* the Jordan to Joshua,
3:16 Thus the people *c* over opposite Jericho.
3:17 While all Israel *c* over on dry ground,
4: 1 After the entire nation had *c* the Jordan,
4: 7 covenant of the LORD when it *c* the Jordan.'
4:10 The people *c* over quickly,
4:11 also *c* to its place in front of them.
4:22 'Israel *c* the Jordan here on dry ground.'
4:23 Jordan in front of you until you *c* over,
4:23 he dried up in front of us until we *c* over;
5: 1 before the Israelites until they *c* over,
15: 4 it *c* to Azmon and then joined the Wadi of
15: 7 from there it *c* to the waters of
16: 2 it *c* the ridge to the border of the
18:13 From there it *c* over to the southern flank
24:11 Once you *c* the Jordan and came to Jericho,
Jgs 6:33 and *c* over into the valley of Jezreel,
8: 4 Jordan and *c* it with his three hundred men,
10: 9 also *c* the Jordan to fight against Judah,
12: 1 gathered together and *c* over to Zaphon.
2Sm 2:29 through the Arabah, *c* the Jordan
10:17 David assembled all Israel, *c* the Jordan,
15:23 and the king *c* the Kidron Valley with all
17:22 all his people moved on and *c* the Jordan.
17:22 there was no one left who had not *c*.
17:24 Mahanaim when Absalom *c* the Jordan
19:19 They *c* over the ford to bring the king's
19:19 When Shimei, son of Gera, *c* the Jordan,
19:40 *c* over the Jordan but the king remained;
19:41 Finally the king *c* over to Gilgal,
1Kgs 14:17 Tirzah and *c* the threshold of her house,
2Kgs 2: 8 divided, and both *c* over on dry ground.
2: 9 When they had *c* over,
2:14 struck the water it divided and he *c* over.
8:21 with all his chariots *c* over to Zair.
1Chr 12:16 It was they who *c* over the Jordan when it
19:17 gathered all Israel together, *c* the Jordan,
2Chr 21: 9 Thereupon Jehoram *c* over with his officers
Tb 5:10 Media and *c* all its plains and mountains;
Jdt 5:15 Heshbonites by main force, *c* the Jordan,
10:10 went down the mountain and *c* the valley;
1Mc 3:37 *c* the Euphrates River and advanced inland.
5: 6 Then he *c* over to the Ammonites,
5:24 his brother Jonathan *c* the Jordan
5:52 Then they *c* the Jordan to the great plain
12:30 them, for they had *c* the river Eleutherus.
16: 6 afraid to cross the stream, John *c* first.
16: 6 his men saw this, they *c* over after him.
2Mc 5: 9 into Egypt, he *c* the sea to the Spartans,
Wis 19: 8 *c* the whole nation sheltered by your hand,
Is 11:15 streamlets, so that it can be *c* in sandals.
23: 2 Whose messengers *c* the sea
Bar 3:30 Who has *c* the sea and found her,
Ez 47: 5 that could not be *c* except by swimming.
Mk 5:21 *c* back to the other side again in the boat,
Jn 6: 1 Jesus *c* the Sea of Galilee [to the shore]
Acts 20:15 on the second day we *c* to Samos,
27: 5 We *c* the open sea off the coast of Cilicia
Heb 11:29 *c* the Red Sea as if it were dry land,

CROSSES (3)

1Mc 5:40 "If he *c* over to us first,
Jer 2: 6 darkness, through a land which no one *c*,
9: 9 They are scorched, and no man *c* them,

CROSSING (16)

Gn 48:14 But Israel, *c* his hands,
Nm 32: 7 from *c* to the land the LORD has given them?
Dt 2:14 departure from Kadesh-barnea and that *c*;
4:22 die in this country without *c* the Jordan;
6: 1 the land into which you are *c* for conquest,
11: 8 of the land into which you are *c*,
11:11 the land into which you are *c* for conquest
30:18 you are *c* the Jordan to enter and occupy.
Jos 3: 1 Jordan, where they lodged before *c* over.
2Sm 19:32 escorted the king to the Jordan for his *c*,
24: 5 *C* the Jordan, they began near Aroer,
Wis 14: 5 and have been safe *c* the surge on a raft.
Mt 9: 1 Then he reentered the boat, made the *c*,
14:34 the *c* they reached the shore at Gennesaret;
Mk 6:53 the *c* they came ashore at Gennesaret,
Acts 16: 8 *C* through Mysia instead,

CROSSINGS (1)

Sg 3: 2 and *c* I will seek Him whom my heart loves.

CROSSROADS (4)

Prv 8: 2 the road, at the *c* she takes her stand;
Ob 1:14 Stand not at the *c* to slay his refugees;
Mk 6:36 they can go to the *c* and villages
6:56 in villages, in towns, or at *c*,

CROUCH (2)

Jb 38:40 of her cubs, While they *c* in their dens,
39: 3 They *c* down and bear their young;

CROUCHED (2)

1Kgs 18:42 to the top of Carmel, *c* down to the earth,
Mk 7:25 She approached him and *c* at his feet.

CROUCHES (3)

Gn 49: 9 He *c* like a lion recumbent,
49:25 the blessings of the abyss that *c* below,
Sir 27:10 As a lion *c* in wait for prey,

CROUCHING (5)

Gn 49:14 a rawboned ass, *c* between the saddlebags.
Nm 24: 9 He lies *c* like a lion,
Dt 33:13 the skies above and of the abyss *c* beneath;
Ps(s) 17:11 *c* to the ground, they fix their gaze,
Ez 29: 3 Egypt, Great *c* monster amidst your Niles:

CROW (5)

Mt 26:74 Just then a cock began to *c* and Peter
Mk 14:72 Just then a second cock *c* was heard and
Lk 22:34 the cock will not *c* today until you have
Jn 13:38 *c* before you have three times disowned me!
18:27 At that moment a cock began to *c*.

CROWD (142)

Ex 12:38 *c* of mixed ancestry also went up with them,
1Sm 10:23 he was head and shoulders above all the *c*.
2Chr 32: 4 a large *c* was gathered which stopped all
Jdt 6: 1 the *c* surrounding the council had subsided,
7:23 a *c* to Uzziah and the rulers of the city.
10:18 among the tents, a *c* gathered in the camp.
1Mc 5:45 and their goods, a great *c* of people, the
9:39 and suddenly saw a noisy *c* with baggage;
2Mc 14:43 courage threw himself down into the *c*.
14:45 anger, he got up and ran through the *c*,
14:46 and flung them with both hands into the *c*,
Ps(s) 31:14 I hear the whispers of the *c*,
Sir 16:26 Not one should ever *c* its neighbor,
Jer 44:15 women who were present in the immense *c*,
Bar 6: 5 *c* before them and behind worshiping them.
Ez 27:27 and all the great *c* within you] Sank into
Jl 4:14 Crowd upon *c* in the valley of decision;
Mt 8:18 Seeing the people *c* around him,
9: 8 sight, a feeling of awe came over the *c*,
9:23 players and the *c* who were making a din,
9:25 When the *c* had been put out he entered and
12:23 All in the *c* were astonished.
13: 2 a boat while the *c* stood along the shore.
15:10 He summoned the *c* and said to them:
15:32 "My heart is moved with pity for the *c*.
15:33 in this deserted spot to satisfy such a *c*?"
15:35 the *c* to seat themselves on the ground.
17:14 As they approached the *c*,
20:29 leaving Jericho a large *c* followed him,
20:31 The *c* began to scold them in an effort to
21: 8 The huge *c* spread their cloaks on the road,
21:11 And the *c* kept answering,
21:41 "He will bring that wicked *c* to a bad end
26:47 by a great *c* with swords and clubs.
26:55 At that very time Jesus said to the *c*:
27:15 one prisoner, whom the *c* would designate.
27:24 and washed his hands in front of the *c*,
Mk 2: 4 to bring him to Jesus because of the *c*,
3: 7 A great *c* followed him from Galilee,
3: 9 could avoid the press of the *c* against him.
3:20 house with them and again the *c* assembled,
3:32 The *c* seated around him told him,
4: 1 Such a huge *c* gathered around him that he
4: 1 while the *c* remained on the shore nearby.
4:10 Now when he was away from the *c*,
4:36 Leaving the *c*, they took him away
5:21 a large *c* gathered around him and he
5:24 went off together and a large *c* followed,
5:27 him in the *c* and put her hand to his cloak.
5:30 Wheeling about in the *c*,
5:31 him, "You can see how this *c* hems you in,
6:34 Upon disembarking Jesus saw a vast *c*.
6:45 toward Bethsaida, while he dismissed the *c*.
7:14 He summoned the *c* again and said to them:
7:17 When he got home, away from the *c*,
7:33 took him off by himself away from the *c*.
8: 1 about that time another large *c* assembled,
8: 2 "My heart is moved with pity for the *c*.
8: 6 the *c* to take their places on the ground.
8: 6 and they handed them out to the *c*.
8: 8 in the *c* ate until they had their fill;
8:34 the *c* with his disciples and said to them:
9:14 they saw a large *c* standing around,
9:15 Jesus, the whole *c* was overcome with awe.
9:17 "Teacher," a man in the *c* replied,
9:19 He replied by saying to the *c*,
9:25 Jesus, on seeing a *c* rapidly gathering,
10:46 place with his disciples and a sizable *c*,
11:18 *c* was under the spell of his teaching.
12:12 at this, yet they had reason to fear the *c*.
12:37 majority of the *c* heard this with delight.
12:41 *c* putting money into the collection box.
14:43 accompanied by a *c* with swords and clubs;
15: 8 When the *c* came up to press their demand
15:11 the *c* to have him release Barabbas instead.
15:15 So Pilate, who wished to satisfy the *c*,
Lk 5: 1 and the *c* pressed in on him to hear the
5:19 of getting him through because of the *c*,
5:19 into the middle of the *c* before Jesus.
5:29 *c* of tax collectors and others at dinner.
6:17 a large *c* of people was with them from all
6:19 the whole *c* was trying to touch him
7: 9 to the *c* which was following him to say,
7:11 disciples and a large *c* accompanied him.
7:12 considerable *c* of townsfolk were with her.
8: 4 A large *c* was gathering,
8:19 they could not reach him because of the *c*.
8:40 his return, Jesus was welcomed by the *c*;
9:12 "Dismiss the *c* so that they can go into
9:16 to his disciples for distribution to the *c*.
9:37 from the mountain and a large *c* met them.
9:38 Suddenly a man from the *c* exclaimed:
11:27 saying this a woman from the *c* called out,
12: 1 Meanwhile a *c* of thousands had gathered,
12:13 Someone in the *c* said to him,
12:15 Then he said to the *c*,
14:25 one occasion when a great *c* was with him,
18:36 Hearing a *c* go by the man asked,
19: 3 was unable to do so because of the *c*.
19:37 the entire *c* of disciples began to rejoice
19:39 Some of the Pharisees in the *c* said to him,
22:47 While he was still speaking a *c* came,
23:18 The whole *c* cried out,
23:27 A great *c* of people followed him,
23:48 When the *c* which had assembled for this
Jn 5:13 The *c* in that place was so great that
6: 2 a vast *c* kept following him because they

CROWD (cont.)

6: 5 caught sight of a vast *c* coming toward him,
6:22 *c* remained on the other side of the lake.
6:24 Once the *c* saw that neither Jesus nor his
7:12 he is only misleading the *c*!"
7:20 the *c* retorted.
7:31 Many in the *c* came to believe in him.
7:32 this debate about him among the *c*,
7:40 the *c* who heard these words began to say,
7:43 fashion the *c* was sharply divided over him.
11:42 I have said this for the sake of the *c*,
12: 9 The great *c* of Jews discovered he was
12:12 The next day the great *c* that had come for
12:17 The *c* that was present when he called
12:18 The *c* came out to meet him because they
12:29 When the *c* of bystanders heard the voice,
12:34 The *c* objected to his words:
19: 4 went out a second time and said to the *c*:
Acts 2: 6 the sound, and assembled in a large *c*.
3:11 the whole *c* rushed over to them excitedly
4: 1 and John were still addressing the *c*,
5:26 force, for fear of being stoned by the *c*.
12:22 The assembled *c* shouted back,
14:14 their garments and rushed out into the *c*.
16:22 The *c* joined in the attack on them,
17: 8 In this way they stirred up the *c*.
19:33 Some brought out of the *c* Alexander,
21:27 and began to stir up the whole *c* there.
21:32 the *c* caught sight of him and the soldiers,
21:34 in the *c* shouted out different answers.
21:36 A *c* of people was following along shouting,
22:22 speech the *c* had been listening to Paul,
24:18 without any *c* around me or any disturbance.
Rv 7: 9 After this I saw before me a huge *c* which
19: 6 what sounded like the shouts of a great *c*,

CROWDED (3)

Prv 1:21 Down the *c* ways she calls out,
Lam 1: 1 How lonely she is now, the once *c* city!
Jn 5: 3 were *c* with sick people lying there blind,

CROWDS (55)

2Mc 3:18 houses in *c* to make public supplication,
4:40 As the *c*, now thoroughly enraged,
Ez 30:15 stronghold, and cut down the *c* in Memphis.
36:10 sown, and I will settle *c* of men upon you,
36:11 I will settle *c* of men and beasts upon you,
Jl 2: 8 No one *c* another,
Mt 4:25 *c* that followed him came from Galilee,
5: 1 saw the *c* he went up on the mountainside.
7:28 and left the *c* spellbound at his teaching.
8: 1 from the mountain, great *c* followed him.
9:33 to speak, to the great surprise of the *c*.
9:36 At the sight of the *c*,
11: 7 Jesus began to speak to the *c* about John:
12:46 He was still addressing the *c* when his
13: 2 Such great *c* gathered around him that he
13:34 Jesus taught the *c* in the form of parables.
13:36 Then, dismissing the *c*, he went home.
14:13 The *c* heard of it and followed him on foot
14:15 Dismiss the *c* so that they may go to the
14:19 he ordered the *c* to sit down on the grass.
14:22 afterward, while dismissing the *c*,
15:30 Large *c* of people came to him bringing
15:31 in the *c* as they beheld the mute speaking,
15:36 disciples, who in turn gave them to the *c*.
15:39 Then, after he had dismissed the *c*,
19: 2 *c* followed him and he cured them there.
21:46 fear the *c* who regarded him as a prophet.
22:33 The *c* who listened were spellbound by his
23: 1 Then Jesus told the *c* and his disciples:
27:20 elders convinced the *c* that they should ask
Mk 2:13 kept coming to him in *c* and he taught them.
6:55 The *c* scurried about the adjacent area and
10: 1 Once more *c* gathered around him,
Lk 3: 7 the *c* that came out to be baptized by him:
3:10 The *c* asked him, "What ought we to do?"
4:42 The *c* went in search of him,
5: 3 he continued to teach the *c* from the boat.
5:15 and great *c* gathered to hear him and to be
7:24 Jesus began to speak about him to the *c*.
8:42 As Jesus went, the *c* almost crushed him.
8:45 the *c* are milling and pressing around you!"
9:11 but the *c* found this out and followed him.
9:18 to them, "Who do the *c* say that I am?"
11:14 The *c* were amazed at this.
11:29 While the *c* pressed around him he began to
12:54 He said to the *c*:
23: 4 reported to the chief priests and the *c*,
Jn 7:12 *c* there was much guarded debate about him.
Acts 5:16 *C* from the towns around Jerusalem would
8: 6 the *c* that heard Philip and saw the
13:45 When the Jews saw the *c*,
14:11 When the *c* saw what Paul had done,
14:13 to offer sacrifice to them with the *c*.
14:18 stop the *c* from offering sacrifice to them.
17:13 to cause a commotion and stir up the *c*.

CROWED (2)

Mk 14:68 [At that moment a cock *c*
Lk 22:60 very moment he was saying this, a cock *c*.

CROWN (75)

Lv 13:40 not unclean merely because of his bald *c*.
13:42 a pink sore on his bald *c* or bald forehead,
21: 5 shall not make bare the *c* of the head,
Dt 28:35 soles of your feet to the *c* of your head.
2Sm 1:10 I removed the *c* from his head and the
12:30 it, he took the *c* from Milcom's head.
14:25 the sole of his foot to the *c* of his head.
1Kgs 7:31 This was surmounted by a *c* one cubit high
2Kgs 11:12 and put the *c* and the insignia upon him.
1Chr 20: 2 took the *c* of Milcom from the idol's head.
2Chr 23:11 son, set the *c* and the insignia upon him,
Est 1:11 into his presence wearing the royal *c*,
6: 8 when the royal *c* was placed on his head.
8:15 *c* of gold and a cloak of crimson byssus.
1Mc 6:15 He gave him his *c*, his robe,
8:14 *c* or wore purple as a display of grandeur.
10:20 sent him a purple robe and a *c* of gold.
10:29 tribute, the salt tax, and the *c* levies.
11:13 entered Antioch and assumed the *c* of Asia;
11:35 of the tax on the salt pans and the *c* tax.
11:54 who became king and wore the royal *c*.
12:39 to become king of Asia, assume the *c*,
13:32 in his place, putting on the *c* of Asia.
13:37 gold *c* and the palm branch that you sent.
13:39 to now, as well as the *c* tax that you owe.
2Mc 14: 4 him with a gold *c* and a palm branch,
Jb 2: 7 the soles of his feet to the *c* of his head.
Ps(s) 7:17 *c* of his head his violence shall rebound.
21: 4 you placed on his head a *c* of pure gold.
89:20 "On a champion I have placed a *c*;
89:40 servant, and defiled his *c* in the dust.
132:18 with shame, but upon him my *c* shall shine."
Prv 4: 9 a glorious *c* will she bestow on you."
12: 4 A worthy wife is the *c* of her husband,
14:18 but shrewd men gain the *c* of knowledge.
14:24 The *c* of the wise is resourcefulness;
16:31 Gray hair is a *c* of glory;
17: 6 Grandchildren are the *c* of old men,
27:24 not forever, nor even a *c* from age to age.
Sg 3:11 In the *c* with which his mother has crowned
Wis 2: 8 *c* ourselves with rosebuds ere they wither.
4: 9 understanding is the hoary *c* for men,
5:16 shall they receive the splendid *c*,
18:24 your grandeur was on the *c* upon his head.
Sir 1: 9 and splendor, gladness and a festive *c*.
6:31 robe of glory, bear her as your splendid *c*.
11: 5 and some that none would consider wear a *c*.
25: 6 The *c* of old men is wide experience;
40: 4 *c* or is wrapped in the coarsest of cloaks
47: 6 When he assumed the royal *c*,
Is 28: 5 the LORD of hosts will be a glorious *c*
62: 3 be a glorious *c* in the hand of the LORD,
Jer 2:16 and Tahpanhes shave the *c* of your head.
Ez 21:31 Off with the turban and away with the *c*!
Dn 14:36 *c* of his head and carried him by the hair;
Zec 6:11 and gold you shall take, and make a *c*;
6:14 The *c* itself shall be a memorial offering
9:16 jewels in a *c* raised aloft over his land.
Mt 27:29 *c* out of thorns they fixed it on his head,
Mk 15:17 then wove a *c* of thorns and put it on him,
Jn 19: 2 a *c* of thorns and fixed it on his head,
19: 5 the *c* of thorns and the purple cloak,
1Cor 9:25 win a *c* of leaves that withers, but we a *c*
Phil 4: 1 and long for, you who are my joy and my *c*,
1Thes 2:19 be our hope or joy, or the *c* we exult in,
2Tm 2: 5 winner's *c* unless he has kept the rules.
4: 8 From now on a merited *c* awaits me;
Jas 1:12 he will receive the *c* of life the Lord has
1Pt 5: 4 win for yourselves the unfading *c* of glory.
Rv 2:10 death and I will give you the *c* of life.
3:11 you have lest someone rob you of your *c*.
6: 2 its rider had a bow, and he was given a *c*.
12: 1 feet, and on her head a *c* of twelve stars.
14:14 One like a Son of Man wearing a gold *c*

CROWNED (13)

Jdt 15:13 *c* themselves with garlands of olive leaves.
Ps(s) 8: 6 the angels, and *c* him with glory and honor.
65:12 You have *c* the year with your bounty,
Sg 3:11 has *c* him on the day of his marriage,
Wis 4: 2 And forever it marches *c* in triumph,
Sir 45: 7 him in honor and *c* him with lofty majesty;
45:26 bless the LORD who has *c* you with glory!
Is 35:10 enter Zion singing, *c* with everlasting joy;
51:11 enter Zion singing, *c* with everlasting joy;
Lk 19:15 He returned, however, *c* as king.
Heb 2: 7 you *c* him with glory and honor,
2: 9 but we do see Jesus *c* with glory and honor
Rv 17:12 ten kings who have not yet been *c*;

CROWNING (1)

1Mc 14: 5 As his *c* glory he captured the port of

CROWNS (12)

1Mc 1: 9 after his death they all put on royal *c*,
1:22 the golden censers, the curtain, the *c*,
4:57 of the temple with gold *c* and shields;
11:13 he thus wore two *c* on his head,
Ps(s) 68:22 *c* of those who stalk about in their guilt.
103: 4 he *c* you with kindness and compassion,
Is 23: 8 a thing against Tyre, the bestower of *c*,
Jer 13:18 From your heads fall your magnificent *c*.
Bar 6: 9 and furnish *c* for the heads of their gods.
Rv 4: 4 garments and had *c* of gold on their heads.
4:10 down their *c* before the throne and sing:
9: 7 heads they wore something like gold *c*;

CROWS (9)

Lv 11:15 of falcons, the various species of *c*,
Dt 14:14 and falcons, all the various species of *c*,
Bar 6:54 they are like *c* between heaven and earth.
Mt 26:34 *c* tonight you will deny me three times."
26:75 "Before the cock *c*,
Mk 13:35 at dusk, at midnight, when the cock *c*,
14:30 this very night before the cock *c* twice,
14:72 cock *c* twice you will deny me three times."
Lk 22:61 cock *c* today you will deny me three times."

CRUCIBLE (4)

Jdt 8:27 Lord put them in the *c* to try their hearts,
Prv 17: 3 The *c* for silver,
27:21 As the *c* tests silver and the furnace gold,
Sir 2: 5 and worthy men in the *c* of humiliation.

CRUCIFIED (36)

Mt 20:19 to be made sport of and flogged and *c*.
26: 2 Son of Man is to be handed over to be *c*."
27:26 then he handed him over to be *c*.
27:35 When they had *c* him,
27:38 Two insurgents were *c* along with him,
27:44 The insurgents who had been *c* with him
28: 5 I know you are looking for Jesus the *c*,
Mk 15:15 Jesus scourged, he handed him over to be *c*.
15:24 Then they *c* him and divided up his
15:25 about nine in the morning when they *c* him.
15:27 "With him they *c* two insurgents,
15:32 been *c* with him likewise kept taunting him.
16: 6 for Jesus of Nazareth, the one who was *c*.
Lk 23:23 demanded with loud cries that he be *c*,
23:32 criminals were led along with him to be *c*.
23:33 they *c* him there and the criminals as well,
24: 7 into the hands of sinful men, and be *c*,
24:20 him up to be condemned to death, and *c* him.
Jn 19:16 the end, Pilate handed Jesus over to be *c*.
19:18 There they *c* him,
19:20 place where Jesus was *c* was near the city.
19:23 After the soldiers had *c* Jesus they took
19:32 and broke the legs of the men *c* with Jesus,
19:41 where he had been *c* there was a garden,
Acts 2:36 Lord and Messiah this Jesus whom you *c*."
4:10 you *c* and whom God raised from the dead.
Rom 6: 6 our old self was *c* with him so that the
1Cor 1:13 Was it Paul who was *c* for you?
1:23 for "wisdom," but we preach Christ *c*—
2: 2 of nothing but Jesus Christ and him *c*.
2: 8 they would never have *c* the Lord of glory.
2Cor 13: 4 It is true he was *c* out of weakness,
Gal 2:19 I have been *c* with Christ,
5:24 Those who belong to Christ Jesus have *c*
6:14 world has been *c* to me and I to the world.
Rv 11: 8 or "Egypt," where also their Lord was *c*.

CRUCIFIXION (2)

Mt 27:31 in his own clothes, and led him off to *c*.
Lk 23:39 the criminals hanging in *c* blasphemed him:

CRUCIFY (15)

Mt 23:34 Some you will kill and *c*,
27:22 *C* him!"
27:23 But they only shouted the louder, "*C* him!"
Mk 15:13 They shouted back, "*C* him!"
15:14 They only shouted the louder, "*C* him!"
15:20 his own clothes, and led him out to *c* him.
Lk 23:21 they shouted back, "Crucify him, *c* him!"
Jn 19: 6 they shouted, "*C* him! *C* him!"
19: 6 said, "Take him and *c* him yourselves;
19:10 to release you and the power to *c* you?"
19:15 *C* him!"
19:15 "Shall I *c* your king?"
Acts 2:23 even made use of pagans to *c* and kill him.

CRUCIFYING (1)

Heb 6: 6 since they are *c* the Son of God for

CRUDE (1)

Sir 38:28 standing near his anvil, forging *c* iron.

CRUEL (22)

Gn 49: 7 their fury so fierce, and their rage so *c*!
Ex 1:13 Israelites and reduced them to *c* slavery,
1:14 the whole *c* fate of slaves.
Dt 32:33 of dragons and the *c* poison of cobras.
2Mc 4:25 of a *c* tyrant and the rage of a wild beast.
5:22 more *c* than the man who appointed him;
7:10 After him the third suffered their *c* sport.
7:27 In derision of the *c* tyrant,
15: 5 did not succeed in carrying out his *c* plan.
Ps(s) 17:10 they shut up their *c* hearts,
Sir 37:11 about generosity, to a *c* man about mercy,

Is 13: 9 Lo, the day of the LORD comes *c*,
19: 4 deliver Egypt into the power of a *c* master,
21: 2 desert, from the fearful land, A *c* sight,
27: 1 LORD will punish with his sword that is *c*,
27: 8 them off with my *c* wind in time of storm.
Jer 6:23 *c* and pitiless are they.
50:42 they wield, *c* and pitiless are they;
Lam 1: 3 into exile from oppression and *c* slavery;
4: 3 become as *c* as the ostrich in the desert.
Ez 5:16 When I loose against you the *c*,
14:21 I send Jerusalem my four *c* punishments,

CRUELLY (3)

Gn 50:17 of your brothers, who treated you so *c*.'
Jb 39:16 She *c* disowns her young and ruthlessly
Jer 30:14 as an enemy would strike, punished you *c*;

CRUELTIES (1)

2Mc 7:42 the sacrificial meals and the excessive *c*.

CRUMBLED (2)

Jos 9:12 to come to you, but now it is dry and *c*.
Dn 2:35 bronze, silver, and gold all *c* at once,

CRUMBLING (3)

Jb 15:28 That are *c* into clay with no shadow to
Is 3: 8 Jerusalem is *c*, Judah is falling;
Jer 4:24 were trembling, and all the hills were *c*!

CRUMBLY (1)

Jos 9: 5 and all the bread they took was dry and *c*.

CRUMBS (2)

Ps(s) 147:17 He scatters his hail like *c*;
Ez 13:19 with handfuls of barley and *c* of bread,

CRUSE (1)

Jdt 10: 5 a leather flask of wine and a *c* of oil.

CRUSH (29)

Nm 25:17 the Midianites as enemies and *c* them,
Jdt 9: 8 not know that " 'You, the Lord, *c* warfare;
9: 8 might, and *c* their force in your wrath;
9:10 *c* their pride by the hand of a woman.
1Mc 3:22 He himself will *c* them before us;
3:35 army against them to *c* and destroy
7:42 the same way, *c* this army before us today,
2Mc 15:16 with it you shall *c* your adversaries."
Jb 6: 9 Even that God would decide to *c* me,
39:15 the sand, Unmindful that a foot may *c* them,
Ps(s) 72: 4 children of the poor, and *c* the oppressor.
89:24 But I will *c* his foes before him and those
110: 5 he will *c* kings on the day of his wrath.
110: 6 he will *c* heads over the wide earth.
Prv 22:22 they are poor, nor *c* the needy at the gate;
Sir 36: 9 *c* the heads of the hostile rulers.
Is 28:28 *c* it with his noisy cartwheels and horses.
41:15 To thresh the mountains and *c* them,
53:10 the LORD was pleased to *c* him in infirmity.]
Jer 17:18 *c* them with repeated destruction.
Lam 1:15 an army against me to *c* my young men;
Dn 7:23 the whole earth, beat it down, and *c* it.
Am 2:13 I will *c* you into the ground as a wagon
Mi 4:13 hoofs bronze, that you may *c* many peoples;
Hb 3:13 You *c* the heads of the wicked,
Zec 11: 6 they shall *c* the earth,
Mt 12:20 The bruised reed he will not *c*;
Rom 16:20 peace will quickly *c* Satan under your feet.
Rv 11: 2 will *c* the holy city for forty-two months.

CRUSHED (62)

Ex 27:20 to bring you clear oil of *c* olives,
29:40 a fourth of a hin of oil of *c* olives and,
Lv 22:24 One that has its testicles bruised or *c* or
24: 2 you clear oil of *c* olives for the light,
Nm 28: 5 with a fourth of a hin of oil of *c* olives.
Dt 23: 2 "No one whose testicles have been *c* or
28:33 and *c* at all times without surcease,
Jgs 5:26 She hammered Sisera, *c* his head;
2Chr 14:12 they were *c* before the LORD and his army,
15: 6 Nation *c* nation and city *c* city,
25:12 then cast down, so that they were all *c*.
Neh 9:28 to the power of their enemies, who *c* them.
1Mc 3:23 Seron and his army, who were *c* before him.
4:36 said, "Now that our enemies have been *c*,
5:21 They were *c* before him,
5:43 him, and the Gentiles were *c* before them;
7:43 Nicanor's army was *c*,
8: 4 They had *c* the kings who had come against
14:13 the kings in those days were *c*.
Jb 4:19 dust, who are *c* more easily than the moth!
5: 4 shall be *c* at the gate without a rescuer.
Ps(s) 34:19 and those who are *c* in spirit he saves.
38: 9 I am numbed and severely *c*;
51:10 the bones you have *c* shall rejoice.
74:14 You *c* the heads of Leviathan,
89:11 You have *c* Rahab with a mortal blow;
118:10 in the name of the LORD I *c* them.
118:11 in the name of the LORD I *c* them.
118:12 in the name of the LORD I *c* them.
143: 3 he has *c* my life to the ground;
Prv 6:15 in an instant he is *c* beyond cure.
29: 1 rebuke will be *c* suddenly beyond cure.
Sir 47: 4 the slingstone that *c* the pride of Goliath.
Is 1:28 Rebels and sinners alike shall be *c*,
7: 9 sixty years and five, Ephraim shall be *c*,
8: 9 Arm, but be *c*! Arm, but be *c*!
19:10 The spinners shall be *c*,
28:27 a staff, and cumin *c* for food with a rod.
51: 9 Was it not you who *c* Rahab,
53: 5 pierced for our offenses, *c* for our sins;
57:15 and with the *c* and dejected in spirit,
57:15 dejected, to revive the hearts of the *c*.
63: 6 peoples in my anger, I *c* them in my wrath,
Jer 1:17 Be not *c* on their account,
1:17 as though I would leave you *c* before them;
22:20 out from Abarim, for all your lovers are *c*.
44:10 To this day they have not been *c*;
48: 4 Moab is *c*, their outcry is heard in Zoar.
51: 8 Babylon suddenly falls and is *c*:
Ez 13:14 When it falls, you shall be *c* beneath it;
Dn 6:25 overpowered them and *c* all their bones.
7: 7 iron teeth with which it devoured and *c*,
11:22 be completely overwhelmed by him and *c*,
Ob 1: 9 Your warriors, O Teman, shall be *c*,
Mal 1: 4 have been *c* but we will rebuild the ruins,"
Mt 21:44 and he on whom it falls will be *c*"
Lk 8:42 As Jesus went, the crowds almost *c* him.
2Cor 1: 8 we were *c* beyond our strength,
2: 7 not be *c* by too great a weight of sorrow.
4: 8 in every way possible, but we are not *c*;

CRUSHES (8)

Jdt 16: 2 For the Lord is God; he *c* warfare,
Jb 26:12 up the sea, and by his might he *c* Rahab;
34:25 he turns at night and *c* them.
Ps(s) 42:11 It *c* my bones that my foes mock me,
68:22 Surely God *c* the heads of his enemies,
Prv 15: 4 of life, but a perverse one *c* the spirit.
Dn 2:40 breaks in pieces and *c* everything else.
Am 2:13 as a wagon *c* when laden with sheaves.

CRUSHING (7)

Dt 1:12 can I alone bear the *c* burden that you are,
1Kgs 19:11 the mountains and *c* rocks before the LORD
1Mc 5:34 him, and he inflicted on them a *c* defeat.
10:52 and established my rule by *c* Demetrius and
Sir 2: 4 befalls you, in *c* misfortune be patient;
Is 3:15 What do you mean by *c* my people,
Dn 7:19 and *c* with its iron teeth and bronze claws,

CRUST (1)

Prv 17: 1 Better a dry *c* with peace than a house

CRUSTS (1)

Jn 6:12 "Gather up the *c* that are left over so

CRY (190)

Gn 18:21 to the *c* against them that comes to me.
21:16 As she sat opposite him, he began to *c*.
21:17 God heard the boy's *c*,
21:17 heard the boy's *c* in this plight of his.
Ex 2:23 As their *c* for release went up to God,
3: 7 have heard their *c* of complaint
3: 9 the *c* of the Israelites has reached me,
22:22 cry out to me, I will surely hear their *c*.
Lv 13:45 he shall *c* out,
Nm 20:16 he heard our *c* and sent an angel who led
Dt 1:45 not listen to your *c* or give ear to you.
15: 9 else he will *c* to the LORD against you and
22:24 *c* out for help though she was in the city,
24:15 he will *c* to the LORD against you,
26: 7 and he heard our *c* and saw our affliction,
33: 7 "The LORD hears the *c* of Judah;
Jgs 7:18 blow horns all around the camp and *c* out,
10:14 Go and *c* out to the gods you have chosen;
1Sm 9:16 their misery and accept their *c* for help."
17:20 battleground, were shouting their battle *c*.
2Sm 22: 7 heard my voice, and my *c* reached his ears.
1Kgs 1:34 Israel, and you shall blow the horn and *c*,
8:28 listen to the *c* of supplication which I,
22:32 But Jehoshaphat shouted his battle *c*,
22:36 At sunset a *c* went through the army,
2Chr 6:19 and listen to the *c* of supplication your
20: 9 and we will *c* out to you in our affliction,
Neh 9: 9 in Egypt, you heard their *c* by the Red Sea;
9:27 their oppression they would *c* out to you,
Tb 10: 7 home to wail and *c* the whole night through,
13:18 gladness, and all her houses shall *c* out,
Jdt 4:13 their *c* and had regard for their distress.
8:17 will hear our *c* if it is his good pleasure.
16:11 at the sound of their war *c*,
Est A: 5 They uttered a mighty *c*,
A: 6 at their *c* every nation prepared for war,
6: 9 square of the city, and *c* out before him,
1Mc 4:10 So now let us *c* to Heaven in the hope that
9:46 *C* out now to Heaven for deliverance from
2Mc 12:37 a battle *c* in his ancestral language,
13:15 his men the battle *c* "God's Victory,"
Jb 19: 7 If I *c* out "Injustice!"
19: 7 I *c* for help, but there is no redress.
24:12 and the souls of the wounded *c* out [yet
27: 9 to his *c* when calamity comes upon him?
30: 7 the bushes they raised their raucous *c*;
30:20 I *c* to you, but you do not answer me;
35: 9 In great oppression men *c* out;
35:12 Though thus they *c* out,
36:13 they *c* not for help when he enchains them;
38:41 ravens when their young ones *c* out to God,
Ps(s) 9:13 has not forgotten the *c* of the afflicted.
18: 7 voice, and my *c* to him reached his ears.
22: 2 far from my prayer, from the words of my *c*?
22: 3 O my God, I *c* out by day,
28: 2 the sound of my pleading, when I *c* to you,
34:16 eyes for the just, and ears for their *c*.
34:18 When the just *c* out,
39:13 to my *c* give ear;
40: 2 and he stooped toward me and heard my *c*.
61: 2 Hear, O God, my *c*; listen to my prayer!
77: 2 Aloud to God I *c*; aloud to God,
84: 3 and my flesh *c* out for the living God.
88: 2 O LORD, my God, by day I *c* out;
88:14 But I, O LORD, *c* out to you;
102: 2 hear my prayer, and let my *c* come to you.
106:44 their affliction when he heard their *c*;
119:147 Before dawn I come and *c* out;
119:169 Let my *c* come before you, O LORD;
130: 1 Out of the depths I *c* to you, O LORD;
142: 2 With a loud voice I *c* out to the LORD;
142: 6 I *c* out to you, O LORD; I say,
142: 7 Attend to my *c*,
145:19 fear him, he hears their *c* and saves them.
147: 9 and to the young ravens when they *c* to him.
Prv 21:13 He who shuts his ear to the *c* of the poor
Wis 17:19 or the roaring *c* of the fiercest beasts,
18:10 discordant *c* of their enemies responded,
Sir 31:12 a greedy gullet to his table, Nor *c* out,
35:13 weak, yet he hears the *c* of the oppressed.
35:15 *c* out against him that causes them to fall?
51: 9 from the gates of the nether world, my *c*.
Is 6: 4 At the sound of that *c*,
10:30 *C* and shriek, O daughter of Gallim!
13: 2 *c* out to them,
14:31 Howl, O gate; *c* out, O city!
15: 4 Heshbon and Elealeh *c* out,
15: 8 For the *c* has gone round the land of Moab;
16: 9 and harvests the battle *c* has fallen.
19:20 *c* out to the LORD against their oppressors,
22: 5 they *c* for help to the mountains.
24:11 In the streets they *c* out for lack of wine;
30:19 He will be gracious to you when you *c* out,
33: 7 See, the men of Ariel *c* out in the streets,
38:13 I *c* out until the dawn.
40: 6 A voice says, *C* out!"
40: 6 I answer, "What shall I *c* out?"
40: 9 *C* out at the top of your voice,
40: 9 to *c* out and say to the cities of Judah:
42:11 Let the steppe and its cities *c* out,
42:13 He shouts out his battle *c*,
42:14 But now, I *c* out as a woman in labor,
43:14 the Chaldeans shall *c* out in lamentation.
44:23 Raise a glad *c*, you heavens:
46: 7 Although they *c* out to it,
52: 8 Your watchmen raise a *c*,
54: 1 Raise a glad *c*,
57:13 They shall not help you when you *c* out,
58: 1 *C* out full-throated and unsparingly,
58: 9 the LORD will answer, you shall *c* for help,
65:14 But you shall *c* out for grief of heart and
Jer 2: 2 *c* out this message for Jerusalem to hear!
2:27 yet, in their time of trouble they *c* out,
3:21 A *c* is heard on the heights!
4:16 their war *c* against the cities of Judah."
4:31 The *c* of daughter Zion gasping,
7:34 silence the cry of joy, the *c* of gladness,
8:19 the *c* of the daughter of my people,
11:11 Though they *c* out to me,
11:12 citizens of Jerusalem will go and *c* out
14: 2 from Jerusalem ascends a *c* of anguish.
16: 9 place the cry of joy and the *c* of gladness,
20: 8 Whenever I speak, I must *c* out,
22:20 *c* out, in Bashan lift up your voice; *C* out
30: 5 A *c* of dismay we hear;
30:15 Why *c* out over your wound?
33:11 *c* of joy, the *c* of gladness,
47: 2 the people of the land set up a wailing *c*.
48: 3 a *c* from Horonaim of ruin and great
48: 5 to Horonaim the *c* of destruction is heard.
48:20 disgraced, yes, destroyed, howl and *c* out;
48:31 And so I wail over Moab, over all Moab I *c*,
48:34 The *c* of Heshbon and Elealeh is heard as
50:15 raise the war *c* against her on all sides,
50:46 At the *c* "Babylon is captured!"
51:55 lays Babylon waste, stills her loud *c*,
Lam 2:18 *C* out to the LORD; moan, O daughter Zion!
3: 8 Even when I *c* out for help,
3:56 not your ear be deaf to my *c* for help!"
4: 4 The babes *c* for food,
Bar 4:20 I live I will *c* out to the Eternal God.
Ez 6:11 your hands, stamp your feet, and *c* "Alas!"
21:17 *C* out and wail,
21:27 to raise his voice in the battle *c*,

CRY (cont.)

30: 2 *C*, Oh, the day!
Hos 8: 2 against my law, While to me they *c* out,
10: 8 Then they shall *c* out to the mountains,
11: 7 God, though in unison they *c* out to him,
Jl 1:14 of the LORD, your God, and *c* to the LORD!
1:19 To you, O LORD, I *c*!
1:20 Even the beasts of the field *c* out to you;
Am 3: 4 Does a young lion *c* out from its den
5:16 and in every street they shall *c*,
Mi 3: 4 When they *c* to the LORD,
4: 9 Now why do you *c* out so?
Na 2:14 *c* of your lionesses shall be heard no more.
Hb 1: 2 I *c* for help but you do not listen!
1: 2 I *c* out to you, "Violence!"
2:11 For the stone in the wall shall *c* out,
Zep 1:10 LORD, A *c* will be heard from the Fish Gate,
1:14 bitter, then, the warrior's *c*.
Mt 2:18 "A *c* was heard at Ramah,
7:21 None of those who *c* out,
12:19 He will not contend or *c* out,
14:26 and in their fear they began to *c* out.
Mk 6:49 it was a ghost and they began to *c* out.
14:72 He broke down and began to *c*.
15:37 Then Jesus, uttering a loud *c*,
Lk 7:13 seeing her and said to her, "Do not *c*."
9:39 sudden *c* throws him into a convulsion
19:40 I tell you the very stones would *c* out."
23:46 Jesus uttered a loud *c* and said,
Rom 8:15 spirit of adoption through which we *c* out,
1Tm 5:24 are flagrant and *c* out for judgment now,
1Pt 3:12 eyes for the just and ears for their *c*;
Rv 6: 1 creatures *c* out in a voice like thunder,
6: 3 I heard the second living creature *c* out,
6: 5 I heard the third living creature *c* out,
6: 7 voice of the fourth living creature *c* out,
8:13 flying in midheaven *c* out in a loud voice,
10: 3 then gave a loud *c* like the roar of a lion.
16: 5 the angel in charge of the waters *c* out:
16: 7 Then I heard the altar *c* out:
18:16 Weeping and mourning, they *c* out:
21: 3 I heard a loud voice from the throne *c* out:

CRYING (29)

Gn 45:15 all his brothers, *c* over each of them;
Ex 2: 6 looked, and lo, there was a baby boy, *c*!
5: 8 They are lazy; that is why they are *c*,
14:15 said to Moses, "Why are you *c* out to me?
32: 8 worshiping it, sacrificing to it and *c* out,
Nm 11:10 family, *c* at the entrance of their tents,
11:13 For they are *c* to me,
2Sm 13:19 hands to her head, she went away *c* loudly.
1Kgs 13: 4 the man of God was *c* out against the altar,
2Kgs 9:23 Joram reigned about and fled, *c* to Ahaziah,
Est 4: 1 through the city *c* out loudly and bitterly.
Is 42: 2 forth justice to the nations, Not *c* out,
65: 5 with carrion broth in their dishes, *C* out,
65:19 weeping be heard there, or the sound of *c*;
Jer 26: 8 priests and prophets laid hold of him, *c*,
Ez 9: 8 I fell prone, *c* out, Alas, Lord GOD!
Mt 9:27 there, two blind men came after him *c* out,
15:22 locality presented herself, *c* out to him,
21: 9 him as well as those following kept *c* out:
Mk 1: 3 a herald's voice in the desert, *c*,
5:38 people wailing and *c* loudly on all sides.
Lk 3: 4 "A herald's voice in the desert, *c*,
4:41 departed from many, *c* out as they did so,
8:52 "Stop *c* for she is not dead but asleep."
Jn 1:23 "I am 'a voice in the desert, *c* out:
Acts 21:13 you *c* and breaking my heart in this way?
1Cor 14:25 prostrate, he will worship God, *c* out,
Jas 5: 4 Here, *c* aloud, are the wages
Rv 21: 4 no more death or mourning, *c* out or pain,

CRYPT (3)

Jgs 9:46 went into the *c* of the temple of El-berith.
9:49 Abimelech, placed it against the *c*.
9:49 they set the *c* on fire over their heads,

CRYSTAL (3)

Jb 28:17 Gold or *c* cannot equal it,
Ez 1:22 could be seen, seeming like glittering *c*,
Rv 22: 1 river of life-giving water, clear as *c*,

CRYSTAL-CLEAR (2)

Rv 4: 6 throne was like a sea of glass that was *c*.
21:18 the city was of pure gold, *c*.

CUB (2)

Is 31: 4 a lion or a lion *c* growling over its prey,
Na 2:12 Where the lion went in and out, and the *c*,

CUBIT (25)

Gn 6:16 the ark, and finish the ark a *c* above it.
Ex 25:23 a cubit wide, and a *c* and a half high.
30: 2 a square surface, a cubit long, a *c* wide,
37:10 wood, two cubits long, and one *c* wide,
37:25 wood, on a square, a cubit long, a *c* wide,
1Kgs 7:24 it, ten to the *c* all the way around;
7:31 This was surmounted by a crown one *c* high
7:31 a receptacle a *c* and a half in depth.
7:32 Each wheel was a *c* and a half high.
7:35 there was a raised collar half a *c* high,
2Chr 4: 3 of oxen encircled the sea, ten to the *c*,
Ez 40: 5 each *c* being a cubit and a handbreadth;
40:12 each of the cells on both sides was one *c*;
40:42 one and a half cubits wide, and one *c* high.
42: 4 walk ten cubits broad and a wall of one *c*;
43:13 in cubits of one *c* plus a handbreadth.
43:13 Its base was one *c* high and one cubit deep,
43:14 cubits high, and this ledge was one *c* deep;
43:14 high, and this ledge also was one *c* deep;
43:17 And there was a base of one *c* all around.

CUBITS (241)

Gn 6:15 *c*, its width fifty *c*, and its height thirty *c*.
7:20 *c* higher than the submerged mountains.
Ex 25:10 ark of acacia wood, two and a half *c* long,
25:10 cubits wide, and one and a half *c* high.
25:17 *c* and a half long, and one and a half *c* wide.
25:23 make a table of acacia wood, two *c* long,
26: 2 twenty-eight cubits, and the width four *c*;
26: 8 be thirty cubits, and the width four *c*:
26:13 tent will have an extra *c* length
26:16 ten cubits, and its width one and a half *c*.
27: 1 *c* long and five *c* wide; it shall be three *c*
27: 9 court shall have hangings a hundred *c* long,
27:11 be similar hangings, a hundred *c* long,
27:12 there shall be hangings, fifty *c* long,
27:13 court on the east side shall be fifty *c*.
27:14 be hangings to the extent of fifteen *c*,
27:15 be hangings to the extent of fifteen *c*,
27:16 be a variegated curtain, twenty *c* long,
27:18 hundred *c* long, fifty *c* wide, and five *c*
30: 2 a cubit long, a cubit wide, and two *c* high,
36: 9 twenty-eight cubits and the width four *c*;
36:15 was thirty cubits and the width four *c*;
36:21 ten cubits, and the width one and a half *c*.
37: 1 a half cubits long, one and a half *c* wide,
37: 1 cubits wide, and one and a half *c* high.
37: 6 half cubits long and one and a half *c* wide.
37:10 table was made of acacia wood, two *c* long,
37:10 one cubit wide, and one and a half *c* high.
37:25 a cubit long, a cubit wide, and two *c* high,
38: 1 a square, five *c* long and five *c* wide;
38: 9 of fine linen twined, a hundred *c* long,
38:11 were similar hangings, one hundred *c* long,
38:12 side there were hangings, fifty *c* long,
38:13 the east side the court was fifty *c* long.
38:14 were hangings to the extent of fifteen *c*,
38:15 hangings to the extent of fifteen *c*,
38:18 twined, twenty cubits long and five *c* wide,
Nm 11:31 at a height of two *c* from the ground
35: 4 *c* from the city walls in each direction.
35: 5 *c* outside the city along each side
Dt 3:11 of iron, nine regular *c* long and four wide,
Jos 3: 4 of two thousand *c* between you and the ark.
1Sm 17: 4 he was six *c* and one span.
1Kgs 6: 2 built for the LORD was sixty *c* long,
6: 3 the temple was twenty *c* from side to side,
6: 3 and ten *c* deep in front of the temple.
6: 6 six cubits wide, the third seven *c* wide,
6: 6 five *c* wide, the middle one six cubits wide,
6:10 annex, with its lowest story five *c* high,
6:16 twenty *c* was set off by cedar partitions
6:17 front of the sanctuary, was forty *c* long.
6:20 ark of the LORD's covenant, twenty *c* long,
6:23 were two cherubim, each ten *c* high,
6:24 Each wing of a cherub measured five *c* so
6:24 wing tip to wing tip of each was ten *c*.
6:26 and shape, and each was exactly ten *c* high.
7: 2 the Forest of Lebanon one hundred *c* long,
7: 6 hall he made fifty *c* long and thirty wide.
7:10 blocks, some ten *c* and some eight cubits.
7:15 *c* high and twelve cubits in circumference;
7:16 of the columns, each of them five *c* high.
7:23 a circular rim, and measured ten *c* across,
7:27 were also made of bronze, each four *c* long,
7:38 each four *c* in diameter with a capacity
2Kgs 14:13 tore down four hundred *c* of the city wall,
25:17 eighteen *c* high; a bronze capital five *c*
25:17 capital five *c* high surmounted each pillar,
1Chr 11:23 slew the Egyptian, a huge man five *c* tall.
2Chr 3: 3 was sixty *c* according to the old measure,
3: 3 old measure, and the width was twenty *c*;
3: 4 twenty cubits, and it was twenty *c* high.
3: 8 cubits, and its width was also twenty *c*.
3:11 The wings of the cherubim spanned twenty *c*:
3:12 one wing of each cherub, five *c* in length,
3:12 the other wing, also five *c* in length,
3:13 of the two cherubim was thus twenty *c*.
3:15 he set two columns thirty-five *c* high;
3:15 the capital topping each was of five *c*.
4: 1 twenty *c* long, twenty *c* wide and ten *c*
4: 2 It was perfectly round, ten *c* in diameter,
6:13 five *c* long, five *c* wide, and three *c*
25:23 Corner Gate, a distance of four hundred *c*.
Ezr 6: 3 to be sixty cubits and its width sixty *c*.
Neh 3:13 thousand *c* of the wall up to the Dung Gate.
Jdt 1: 2 each three *c* in height and six in length.
1: 2 the wall seventy *c* high and fifty thick.
1: 3 of a hundred *c*, with a thickness of sixty *c*
1: 4 height of seventy *c*, with an opening forty *c*
Est 5:14 "Have a gibbet set up, fifty *c* in height,
7: 9 of Haman stands a gibbet fifty *c* high.
Jer 52:21 *c* high and twelve cubits in diameter;
52:22 five *c* high surmounted the one pillar,
Ez 40: 5 man was holding a measuring rod six *c* long,
40: 7 between the cells measured five *c*.
40: 9 eight *c*, and its pilasters, which were two *c*.
40:11 the gate's entrance, which was ten *c* wide,
40:11 the gate's passage itself was thirteen *c*.
40:12 cells themselves were six *c* on either side,
40:13 the width was twenty-five *c*.
40:14 the vestibule, which was twenty-five *c*.
40:14 the court on either side were six *c*.
40:15 of the vestibule on the inside was fifty *c*.
40:19 it was one hundred *c* between them.
40:21 fifty *c* long and twenty-five cubits wide.
40:23 one hundred *c* from one gate to the other.
40:25 fifty cubits long and twenty-five *c* wide.
40:27 gate to gate he measured one hundred *c*.
40:29 fifty cubits long and twenty-five *c* wide.
40:33 fifty cubits long and twenty-five *c* wide.
40:36 fifty *c* long and twenty-five cubits wide.
40:42 a half cubits long, one and a half *c* wide,
40:47 a hundred cubits long and a hundred *c* wide,
40:48 pilasters on each side, which were five *c*.
40:48 The width of the doorway was fourteen *c*,
40:48 either side of the door measured three *c*.
40:49 was twenty *c* wide and twelve cubits deep;
41: 1 which were six *c* thick on either side.
41: 2 The width of the entrance was ten *c*,
41: 2 at either side of it measured five *c* each.
41: 2 of the nave, which was found to be forty *c*,
41: 3 flanking that entrance, which were two *c*;
41: 3 the width of the entrance was six *c*,
41: 3 at either side of it extended seven *c* each.
41: 4 nave, twenty *c* long and twenty cubits wide,
41: 5 wall of the temple, which was six *c* thick;
41: 5 around the temple, had a width of four *c*.
41: 8 a full rod of six *c* in extent.
41: 9 enclosed the side chambers was five *c*.
41:10 twenty *c* wide going all around the temple.
41:11 wall surrounding the open space was five *c*.
41:12 the west side was seventy *c* front to back;
41:12 the building was five *c* thick all around,
41:12 and it measured ninety *c* from side to side.
41:13 the temple, which was one hundred *c* long.
41:13 and its walls, was a hundred *c* in length.
41:14 on the east side, was one hundred *c* wide.
41:15 walls on both sides it was one hundred *c*.
41:22 three *c* in height, two *c* long, and two *c*
42: 2 *c* on the north side, and they were fifty *c*
42: 3 Across the twenty *c* of the inner court and
42: 4 a walk ten *c* broad and a wall of one cubit;
42: 7 length before these chambers was fifty *c*,
42: 8 belonging to the outer court was fifty *c*,
42: 8 length the wall measured one hundred *c*.
42:16 five hundred *c* by his measuring rod.
42:17 five hundred *c* by the measuring rod.
42:18 five hundred *c* by the measuring rod
42:19 five hundred *c* by the measuring rod.
42:20 cubits long and five hundred *c* wide.
43:13 altar in *c* of one cubit plus a handbreadth.
43:14 up to the lower edge it was two *c* high,
43:14 to the upper ledge it was four *c* high,
43:15 the hearth of the altar was four *c* high,
43:16 twelve cubits long and twelve *c* wide.
43:17 fourteen *c* long and fourteen cubits wide.
43:17 was sixteen cubits long and sixteen *c* wide,
45: 1 thousand *c* long and twenty thousand wide;
45: 2 plot, five hundred by five hundred *c*,
45: 2 surrounded by a free space of fifty *c*,
45: 3 thousand *c* long and ten thousand wide,
45: 5 strip twenty-five thousand *c* long
45: 6 *c* wide and twenty-five thousand long,
46:22 minor courts, forty *c* long and thirty wide,
47: 3 *c* and had me wade through the water,
48: 8 twenty-five thousand *c* from north to south,
48: 9 LORD shall be twenty-five thousand *c* across
48:10 have twenty-five thousand *c* on the north,
48:13 twenty-five thousand *c* by ten thousand.
48:13 tract shall be twenty-five thousand *c* across
48:15 The remaining five thousand *c* along the
48:16 the north side, forty-five hundred *c*;
48:16 the south side, forty-five hundred *c*;
48:16 the east side, forty-five hundred *c*;
48:16 and the west side, forty-five hundred *c*.
48:17 extend north two hundred and fifty *c*,
48:17 cubits, south two hundred and fifty *c*,
48:17 fifty cubits, east two hundred and fifty *c*,
48:17 cubits, and west two hundred and fifty *c*.
48:18 *c* to the east and ten thousand to the west,
48:20 thousand by twenty-five thousand *c*;
48:30 north side, measuring forty-five hundred *c*,
48:32 east side, measuring forty-five hundred *c*,
48:33 south side, measuring forty-five hundred *c*,
48:34 west side, measuring forty-five hundred *c*,
48:35 of the City is eighteen thousand *c*.
Dn 3: 1 made, sixty cubits high and six *c* wide,
3:47 flames rose forty-nine *c* above the furnace,
Zec 5: 2 it is twenty cubits long and ten *c* wide."
Rv 21:17 hundred and forty-four *c* in height

CUBS (6)

2Sm 17: 8 as a bear in the wild robbed of her *c*.
Jb 4:11 and the *c* of the lioness are scattered.
38:39 lioness or appease the hunger of her *c*,
Prv 17:12 Face a bear robbed of her *c*,
Jer 51:38 all roar like lions, growl like lion *c*.
Na 2:13 The lion snatched enough for his *c*,

CUCUMBER (2)

Jer 10: 5 Like a scarecrow in a *c* field are they,
Bar 6:69 For like a scarecrow in a *c* patch,

CUCUMBERS (1)

Nm 11: 5 to eat without cost in Egypt, and the *c*,

CUD (11)

Lv 11: 3 it is cloven-footed and chews the *c*.
11: 4 that only chew the *c* or only have hoofs:
11: 4 the camel, which indeed chews the *c*,
11: 5 the rock badger, which indeed chews the *c*,
11: 6 the hare, which indeed chews the *c*,
11: 7 the *c* and is therefore unclean for you.
11:26 or do not chew the *c* are unclean for you;
Dt 14: 6 it is cloven-footed and chews the *c*.
14: 7 only chew the *c* or only have cloven hoofs:
14: 7 the rock badger, which indeed chew the *c*,
14: 8 the *c* and is therefore unclean for you.

CULPRIT (3)

Ex 2:13 So he asked the *c*,
Prv 21: 8 The way of the *c* is crooked,
Hb 1:11 this *c* who makes his own strength his god!

CULT (6)

1Kgs 14:24 There were also *c* prostitutes in the land.
22:47 rest of the *c* prostitutes who had remained
2Kgs 23: 7 He tore down the apartments of the *c*
1Chr 25: 1 David and the leaders of the liturgical *c*
Jer 10: 3 For the *c* idols of the nations are nothing,
Acts 7:43 Rephan, the images you had made for your *c*.

CULTIVATE (4)

Gn 2:15 the garden of Eden, to *c* and care for it.
Dt 28:39 Though you plant and *c* vineyards,
Sir 51:14 her beauty, and until the end I will *c* her.
Jas 3:18 is sown in peace for those who *c* peace.

CULTIVATED (5)

Lv 11:37 Any sort of *c* grain remains clean even
1Mc 14: 8 The people *c* their land in peace;
Hos 10:13 But you have *c* wickedness,
Rom 11:24 to nature, were grafted into the *c* olive,
Heb 6: 7 useful to those for whom it is *c*,

CULTIVATES (1)

Prv 28:19 He who *c* his land will have plenty of food,

CULTIVATING (1)

Sir 6:20 For in *c* her you will labor but little,

CULTIVATION (1)

1Cor 3: 9 are God's co-workers, while you are his *c*,

CULTURE (1)

Sir 1:24 For fear of the LORD is wisdom and *c*;

CULTURED (2)

Sir 21:23 but a *c* man keeps his glance cast down.
21:24 a *c* man would be overwhelmed by the

CUMIN (3)

Is 28:25 does he not scatter gith and sow *c*,
28:27 a sledge, nor does a cartwheel roll over *c*.
28:27 a staff, and *c* crushed for food with a rod.

CUN (1)

1Chr 18: 8 He likewise took away from Tibhath and *C*,

CUNNING (7)

Gn 3: 1 Now the serpent was the most *c* of all the
2Mc 12:24 but with great *c*,
Jb 5:12 He frustrates the plans of the *c*,
Ps(s) 58: 6 the voice of enchanters casting *c* spells.
Dn 8:25 his *c* shall be against the holy ones,
2Cor 11: 3 just as the serpent seduced Eve by his *c*,
Jas 3:15 a kind of animal, even devilish, *c*.

CUP (70)

Gn 40:11 Pharaoh's *c* was in my hand;
40:11 the grapes, pressed them out into his *c*,
40:13 You will be handing Pharaoh his *c* as you
40:21 so that he again handed the *c* to Pharaoh;
Nm 7:14 one gold *c* of ten shekels' weight filled
7:20 one gold *c* of ten shekels' weight filled
7:26 one gold *c* of ten shekels' weight filled
7:32 one gold *c* of ten shekels' weight filled
7:38 one gold *c* of ten shekels' weight filled
7:44 one gold *c* of ten shekels' weight filled
7:50 one gold *c* of ten shekels' weight filled
7:56 one gold *c* of ten shekels' weight filled
7:62 one gold *c* of ten shekels' weight filled
7:68 one gold *c* of ten shekels' weight filled
7:74 one gold *c* of ten shekels' weight filled
7:80 one gold *c* of ten shekels' weight filled
2Sm 12: 3 drank from his *c* and slept in his bosom.
1Kgs 7:26 thick, and its brim resembled that of a *c*,
2Chr 4: 5 and its brim was made like that of a *c*,
Ps(s) 11: 6 a burning blast is their alloted *c*.
16: 5 O LORD, my alloted portion and my *c*,
23: 5 my *c* overflows.
75: 9 For a *c* is in the LORD's hand,
116:13 The *c* of salvation I will take up,
Sir 50:15 had stretched forth his hand for the *c*,
Is 51:17 at the LORD's hand the *c* of his wrath;
51:22 taking from your hand the *c* of staggering;
Jer 16: 7 not give them the *c* of consolation to drink
25:15 Take this *c* of foaming wine from my hand,
25:17 I took the *c* from the hand of the LORD and
25:28 to take the *c* from your hand and drink,
25:29 The *C* of JudgmentProphesy against them all
49:12 not sentenced to drink the *c* must drink it!
51: 7 Babylon was a golden *c* in the hand of the
Lam 4:21 of Uz, To you also shall the *c* be passed;
Ez 23:31 path of your sister, I will hand you her *c*.
23:32 The *c* of your sister you shall drink,
23:33 a cup of dismay, the *c* of your sister.
23:34 dry, and gnaw at the very sherds of the *c*,
Hb 2:16 revert the *c* from the LORD's right hand,
Mt 10:42 And I promise you that whoever gives a *c*
20:22 Can you drink of the *c* I am to drink of?"
20:23 "From the *c* I drink of, you shall drink.
23:25 You cleanse the outside of *c* and dish,
23:26 of the *c* so that its outside may be clean.
26:27 Then he took a *c*,
26:39 if it is possible, let this *c* pass me by.
Mk 10:38 Can you drink the *c* I shall drink or be
10:39 "From the *c* I drink of you shall drink;
14:23 He likewise took a *c*,
14:36 Take this *c* away from me.
Lk 11:39 You cleanse the outside of *c* and dish,
22:17 *c* he offered a blessing in thanks and said:
22:20 He did the same with the *c* after eating,
22:20 "This *c* is the new covenant in my blood,
22:42 if it is your will, take this *c* from me;
Jn 18:11 not to drink the *c* the Father has given me?"
1Cor 10:16 Is not the *c* of blessing we bless a
10:21 *c* of the Lord and also the cup of demons.
11:25 he took the *c*, saying, "This cup is
11:26 then, you eat this bread and drink this *c*,
11:27 drinks the *c* of the Lord unworthily sins
11:28 he eat of the bread and drink of the *c*.
Rv 14:10 full strength into the *c* of his anger.
16:19 giving her the *c* filled with the blazing
17: 4 In her hand she held a gold *c* that was
18: 6 into her *c* twice the amount she concocted!

CUPBEARER (11)

Gn 40: 1 *c* and baker gave offense to their lord,
40: 2 courtiers, the chief *c* and the chief baker,
40: 5 the *c* and the baker of the king of Egypt
40: 9 Then the chief *c* told Joseph his dream.
40:13 formerly used to do when you were his *c*.
40:20 the heads of the chief *c* and chief baker.
40:21 He restored the chief *c* to his office,
40:23 Yet the chief *c* gave no thought to Joseph;
41: 9 the chief *c* spoke up and said to Pharaoh:
Neh 1:11 for I was *c* to the king.
Tb 1:22 king of Assyria, Ahiqar had been chief *c*,

CUPBEARERS (1)

2Chr 9: 4 and their dress, his *c* and their dress,

CUPFUL (1)

1Kgs 17:10 bring me a small *c* of water to drink."

CUPPED (2)

Prv 30: 4 who has *c* the wind in his hands?
Is 40:12 has *c* in his hand the waters of the sea,

CUPS (24)

Ex 25:29 pure gold you shall make its plates and *c*,
25:31 with its *c* and knobs and petals springing
25:33 On one branch there are to be three *c*,
25:33 three *c*, shaped like almond blossoms,
25:34 On the shaft there are to be four *c*,
37:16 were set on the table, its plates and *c*,
37:17 shaft and branches as well as its *c* and knobs
37:19 On one branch there were three *c*,
37:19 on the opposite branch there were three *c*,
37:20 On the shaft there were four *c*,
Nm 4: 7 cloth and put on it the plates and *c*,
7:84 twelve silver basins, and twelve gold *c*.
7:86 The twelve gold *c* that were filled with
7:86 so that all the gold of the *c* amounted to
1Kgs 7:50 basins, snuffers, bowls, *c*,
2Kgs 12:14 the LORD were used there to make silver *c*,
2Chr 4:22 bowls, *c* and firepans of pure gold.
Est 1: 7 was served in a variety of golden *c*,
1Mc 1:22 the offering table, the *c* and the bowls,
11:58 gave him the right to drink from gold *c*,
Sir 29:25 visitor has no thanks for filling the *c*;
Is 65:11 and fill *c* of blended wine for Destiny,
Jer 35: 5 wine and offered them *c* to drink the wine.
Mk 7: 4 the washing of *c* and jugs and kettles.

CURB (3)

Jb 38:31 Have you fitted a *c* to the Pleiades,
40:25 with a hook, or *c* his tongue with a bit?
Ps(s) 39: 2 I will set a *c* on my mouth."

CURBED (1)

Ps(s) 32: 9 with bit and bridle their temper must be *c*,

CURDS (6)

Gn 18: 8 Then he got some *c* and milk,
Jgs 5:25 in a princely bowl she offered *c*.
Prv 30:33 For the stirring of milk brings forth *c*,
Is 7:15 He shall be living on *c* and honey by the
7:22 he shall live on *c*: *c* and honey

CURE (27)

Ex 21:19 idleness and provide for his complete *c*.
2Kgs 5: 3 mistress, "he would *c* him of his leprosy."
5: 6 to you, that you may *c* him of his leprosy."
5:11 hand over the spot, and thus *c* the leprosy.
Tb 2:10 I went to see some doctors for a *c*,
Prv 6:15 in an instant he is crushed beyond *c*.
29: 1 rebuke will be crushed suddenly beyond *c*.
Sir 3:27 affliction of the proud man there is no *c*;
18:18 before sickness prepare the *c*.
38:14 correct and his treatment bring about a *c*.
Is 3: 7 "I will not undertake to *c* this,
Jer 3:22 and I will *c* you of your rebelling.
46:11 for you there is no *c*.
Bar 6:27 Even their wives *c* parts of the meat,
Mt 8: 2 "Sir, if you will to do so, you can *c* me."
8: 7 He said to him, "I will come and *c* him."
10: 1 to *c* sickness and disease of every kind.
10: 8 *C* the sick, raise the dead,
12:10 "Is it lawful to work a *c* on the sabbath?"
17:16 to your disciples but they could not *c* him."
Mk 1:40 "If you will to do so, you can *c* me."
1:44 and offer for your *c* what Moses prescribed.
Lk 5:12 "Lord, if you will to do so, you can *c* me."
6: 7 he would perform a *c* on the sabbath
9: 1 to overcome all demons and to *c* diseases.
10: 9 they set before you, and *c* the sick there.
14: 3 "Is it lawful to *c* on the sabbath or not?"

CURED (52)

Dt 28:27 eczema and the itch, until you cannot be *c*.
28:35 malignant boils of which you cannot be *c*,
2Kgs 5: 7 send someone to me to be *c* of leprosy?
Tb 12: 3 he *c* my wife;
12: 3 and he *c* you. How much of a bonus
Wis 16:12 neither herb nor application *c* them,
Mt 4:23 *c* the people of every disease and illness.
4:24 He *c* them all.
8: 3 "I do will it. Be cured."
8:16 command and *c* all who were afflicted,
9:35 reign, and he *c* every sickness and disease.
11: 5 their sight, cripples walk, lepers are *c*,
12:15 Many people followed him and he *c* them all,
12:22 *c* the man so that he could speak and see.
14:14 was moved with pity, and he *c* their sick.
15:30 They laid them at his feet and he *c* them.
17:18 That very moment the boy was *c*.
19: 2 crowds followed him and he *c* them there.
21:14 him inside the temple area and he *c* them.
Mk 1:34 Those whom he *c*,
1:41 "I do will it. Be cured."
1:42 left him then and there, and he was *c*.
3:10 Because he had *c* many,
5:29 feeling that she was *c* of her affliction
5:34 it is your faith that has *c* you.
Lk 4:27 yet not one was *c* except Naaman the Syrian."
4:40 he laid hands on each of them and *c* them.
5:13 "I do will it. Be cured."
5:15 to hear him and to be *c* of their maladies.
6:18 were troubled with unclean spirits were *c*;
6:19 power went out from him which *c* all.
7: 7 give the order and my servant will be *c*.
7:22 their sight, cripples walk, lepers are *c*,
8: 2 had been *c* of evil spirits and maladies;
8:36 witnesses how the possessed man had been *c*.
8:47 him and how she had been instantly *c*.
8:48 it is your faith that has *c* you.
9:42 then rebuked the unclean spirit, *c* the boy,
13:14 Come on those days to be *c*,
17:14 On their way there they were *c*.
17:15 One of them, realizing that he had been *c*,
Jn 5: 9 The man was immediately *c*;
5:10 Jews began telling the man who had been *c*,
5:11 "It was the man who *c* me who told me,
5:14 "Remember, now, you have been *c*.

CURED (cont.)

5:15 Jews that Jesus was the one who had *c* him.
Acts 4:14 who had been *c* standing there with them,
4:22 *c* was more than forty years of age.
5:16 by unclean spirits, all of whom were *c.*
8: 7 paralytics or cripples, and these were *c.*
19:12 were *c* and evil spirits departed from them.
28: 8 praying, laid his hands on him and *c* him.

CURES (4)

Mk 6:13 the sick with oil, and worked many *c.*
Lk 13:32 tomorrow I cast out devils and perform *c,*
Acts 4:30 forth your hand in *c* and signs and wonders
9:34 said to him, "Aeneas, Jesus Christ *c* you!

CURING (4)

Mk 6: 5 apart from *c* a few who were sick by laying
Lk 7:21 that time he was *c* many of their diseases,
9: 6 the good news everywhere and *c* diseases.
Jn 7:23 with me for *c* a whole man on the sabbath?

CURIOUS (2)

Lk 9: 9 He was very *c* to see him.
Acts 17:19 "We are *c* to know what this new teaching

CURRENT (2)

Gn 23:16 shekels of silver at the *c* market value.
Est B: 6 of the twelfth month, Adar, of the *c* year;

CURRY (2)

Prv 19: 6 Many *c* favor with a noble;
29:26 Many *c* favor with the ruler,

CURSE (99)

Gn 5:29 ground that the LORD has put under a *c,*
12: 3 who bless you and *c* those who curse you.
27:12 bring on myself a *c* instead of a blessing."
27:13 "Let any *c* against you, son, fall on me!
27:29 Cursed be those who *c* you,
Ex 22:27 revile God, nor *c* a prince of your people.
Lv 19:14 You shall not *c* the deaf,
Nm 5:18 hold the bitter water that brings a *c.*
5:19 to the *c* brought by this bitter water.
5:22 May this water, then, that brings a *c,*
5:24 it may go into her with all its bitter *c.*
5:27 water that brings a *c* will go into her,
22: 6 Please come and *c* this people for us;
22: 6 is blessed and whoever you *c* is cursed."
22:11 Please come and lay a *c* on them for us;
22:12 not go with them and do not *c* this people,
22:17 come and lay a *c* on this people for me."
23: 7 "Come and lay a *c* for me on Jacob,
23: 8 How can I *c* whom God has not cursed?
23:11 was to *c* my foes that I brought you here;
23:13 all of them, and from there *c* them for me."
23:25 "Even though you cannot *c* them,"
24:10 was to *c* my foes that I summoned you here;
Dt 11:26 you here, this day, a blessing and a *c:*
11:28 a *c* if you do not obey the commandments of
11:29 on Mount Gerizim, the *c* on Mount Ebal.
21:23 God's *c* rests on him who hangs on a tree,
23: 5 from Pethor in Aram Naharaim, to *c* you;
23: 6 and turned his *c* into a blessing for you,
28:20 "The LORD will put a *c* on you,
29:11 with you today under this sanction of a *c,*
29:13 this covenant, under this sanction of a *c;*
29:18 person, upon hearing the words of this *c,*
29:19 and every *c* mentioned in this book will
30:19 you life and death, the blessing and the *c.*
Jos 24: 9 He summoned Balaam, son of Beor, to *c* you;
Jgs 5:23 *C* Meroz," says the LORD,
5:23 the LORD, "hurl a *c* at its inhabitants!
9:57 to the Shechemites, for the *c* of Jotham,
17: 2 which you pronounced a *c* in my hearing
2Sm 16: 9 should this dead dog *c* my lord the king?
16:10 Suppose the LORD has told him to *c* David;
16:11 Let him alone and let him *c,*
1Kgs 8:31 to take an oath sanctioned by a *c,*
2Kgs 22:19 would become a desolation and a *c;*
Neh 10:30 and with the sanction of a *c* take this
13: 2 and water, but they hired Balaam to *c* them,
13: 2 our God turned the *c* into a blessing."
Jb 2: 9 *C* God and die."
3: 8 Let them *c* it who curse the sea,
3: 8 Let them curse it who *c* the sea,
31:30 to sin by uttering a *c* against his life
Ps(s) 62: 5 with their mouths, but inwardly they *c.*
102: 9 their rage against me they make a *c* of me.
109:28 Let them *c,* but do you bless;
Prv 3:33 The *c* of the LORD is on the house of the
11:26 Him who monopolizes grain, the people *c*—
24:24 men will *c* him, people will denounce him;
26: 2 flight, a *c* uncalled-for arrives nowhere.
27:14 morning a *c* can be laid to his charge.
28:27 but he who ignores them gets many a *c.*
29:24 he hears himself put under a *c,*
30:10 not a servant to his master, lest he *c* you,
Sir 3: 9 but a mother's *c* uproots the growing plant.
4: 5 not your eyes, give no man reason to *c* you;
4: 6 if in the bitterness of his soul he *c* you,
41: 7 Children *c* their wicked father,
41: 9 at death, you become a *c.*
Is 8:21 enraged, and *c* his king and his gods.
24: 6 Therefore a *c* devours the earth,
Jer 15:10 I neither borrow nor lend, yet all *c* me.
24: 9 a reproach and a byword, a taunt and a *c,*
29:22 in Babylon will pattern a *c* after them:
42:18 malediction and horror, a *c* and a reproach,
44: 8 Will you be rooted out and become a *c* and
44:12 malediction, a horror, a *c* and a reproach.
49:13 and a disgrace, a desolation and a *c;*
Lam 3:65 hardness of heart, as your *c* upon them;
Bar 1:20 the *c* which the Lord enjoined upon Moses,
3: 8 where you scattered us, a reproach, a *c,*
6:65 Kings they neither *c* nor bless.
Zec 5: 3 "This is the *c* which is to go forth over
8:13 Just as you were a *c* among the nations,
Mal 2: 2 I will send a *c* upon you and of your
2: 2 you and of your blessing I will make a *c.*
Mk 14:71 He began to *c,*
Lk 6:28 *c* you and pray for those who maltreat you.
Acts 23: 5 'You shall not *c* a prince of your people!'"
Rom 12:14 bless and do not *c* them.
1Cor 16:22 not love the Lord, let a *c* be upon him.
Gal 1: 8 we delivered to you, let a *c* be upon him!
1: 9 the one you received, let a *c* be upon him!
3:10 the law, on the other hand, are under a *c.*
3:13 law's curse by himself becoming a *c* for us,
Jas 3: 9 then we use it to *c* men,
3:10 Blessing and *c* come out of the same mouth.
Rv 22: 3 Nothing deserving a *c* shall be found there.

CURSED (55)

Gn 3:17 you to eat, *C* be the ground because of you!
9:25 *C* be Caanan!
27:29 *C* be those who curse you,
49: 7 *C* be their fury so fierce,
Lv 20: 9 since he has *c* his father or mother,
24:11 and *c* and blasphemed the LORD's name.
Nm 22: 6 is blessed and whoever you curse is *c.*"
23: 8 How can I curse whom God has not *c?*
24: 9 blesses you, and *c* is he who curses you!
Dt 27:15 *C* be the man who makes a carved or molten
27:16 *C* be he who dishonors his father or his
27:17 *C* be he who moves his neighbor's landmarks!'
27:18 *C* be he who misleads a blind man on his way!'
27:19 *C* be he who violates the rights of the
27:20 *C* be he who has relations with his
27:21 *C* be he who has relations with any animal!'
27:22 *C* be he who has relations with his sister
27:23 *C* be he who has relations with his
27:24 *C* be he who slays his neighbor in secret!'
27:25 *C* be he who accepts payment for slaying an
27:26 *C* be he who fails to fulfill any of the
28:16 cursed in the city, and *c* in the country!
28:17 *C* be your grain bin and your kneading bowl!
28:18 *C* be the fruit of your womb,
28:19 "May you be *c* in your coming in,
28:19 in your coming in, and *c* in your going out!
Jos 6:26 *C* before the LORD be the man who attempts
Jgs 9:27 where they ate and drank and *c* Abimelech.
21:18 *C* be he who gives a woman to Benjamin!'"
1Sm 14:24 *C* be the man who takes food before evening,
14:28 *C* be the man who takes food this day!'
17:43 *c* David by his gods and said to him,
26:19 but if men, may they be *c* before the LORD,
2Sm 16: 7 Shimei was saying as he *c:*
19:22 He *c* the LORD's anointed."
1Kgs 2: 8 who *c* me balefully when I was going to
21:10 and accuse him of having *c* God and king.
21:13 accusation, "Naboth has *c* God and king."
2Kgs 2:24 and he *c* them in the name of the LORD.
Neh 13:25 I took them to task and *c* them;
Jb 3: 1 this, Job opened his mouth and *c* his day.
Sir 28:13 *C* be gossips and the double-tongued,
Jer 11: 3 *C* be the man who does not observe the
17: 5 *C* is the man who trusts in human beings,
20:14 *C* be the day on which I was born!
20:15 *C* be the man who brought the news to my
48:10 *C* be he who does the LORD's work remissly,
48:10 *c* he who holds back his sword from blood.]
Mal 1:14 *C* is the deceiver,
2: 2 Yes, I have already *c* it,
Mk 11:21 The fig tree you *c* has withered up."
1Cor 12: 3 in the Spirit of God ever says, *C* be Jesus."
Gal 3:10 *C* is he who does not abide by everything
Heb 6: 8 it is soon *c,* and finally is burned.

CURSES (25)

Ex 21:17 "Whoever *c* his father or mother shall be
Lv 20: 9 "Anyone who *c* his father or mother shall
24:15 Anyone who *c* his God shall bear the
Nm 24: 9 blesses you, and cursed is he who *c* you!
Dt 27:13 shall stand on Mount Ebal to pronounce *c.*
28:15 *c* shall come upon you and overwhelm you:
28:45 "All these *c* will come upon you,
29:20 in keeping with all the *c* of the covenant
30: 1 set before you, the blessings and the *c,*
30: 7 But all those *c* the LORD,
Jos 8:34 words of the law, the blessings and the *c,*
2Sm 16:10 or of yours, sons of Zeruiah, that he *c?*
16:12 benefits for the *c* he is uttering this day."
2Chr 34:24 all the *c* written in the book that has
Ps(s) 37:22 land, while those he *c* shall be cut off.
Prv 20:20 If one *c* his father or mother,
30:11 is a group of people that *c* its father,
Sir 21:27 *c* his adversary he really curses himself.
21:27 curses his adversary he really *c* himself.
29: 6 *c* and insults the borrower pays him back,
33:12 Others he *c* and brings low,
34:24 If one man prays and another *c,*
Mt 15: 4 *c* father or mother shall be put to death.'
Mk 7:10 *c* father or mother shall be put to death.'
Rom 3:14 Their mouths are full of *c* and bitterness.

CURSING (12)

Nm 23:27 approve of your *c* them for me from there."
2Sm 16: 5 was coming out of the place, *c* as he came.
16:13 *c* and throwing stones and dirt as he went.
Ps(s) 10: 7 His mouth is full of *c,*
109:17 He loved *c;* may it come upon him;
109:18 may he be clothed with *c* as with a robe;
Sir 23:14 never been born or *c* the day of your birth.
27:15 in bloodshed, their *c* is painful to hear.
Is 65:15 Shall be used by my chosen ones for *c;*
Jer 25:18 and a desert, an object of ridicule and *c,*
26: 6 of the earth shall refer to when *c* another.
Mt 26:74 At that he began *c,*

CURTAIN (25)

Ex 26:36 of the tent make a variegated *c* of violet,
26:37 five columns of acacia wood for this *c;*
27:16 the court there shall be a variegated *c,*
35:12 poles, the propitiatory, and the *c* veil;
35:15 *c* for the entrance of the Dwelling;
35:17 the *c* for the entrance of the court;
36:37 The *c* for the entrance of the tent was
38:18 of the court there was a variegated *c,*
39:34 the covering of tahash skins, the *c* veil;
39:38 the *c* for the entrance of the tent,
39:40 the *c* for the entrance of the court with
40: 5 hang the *c* at the entrance of the Dwelling.
40: 8 and put the *c* at the entrance of the court.
40:21 ark into the Dwelling and hung the *c* veil,
40:28 hung the *c* at the entrance of the Dwelling.
40:33 hung the *c* at the entrance of the court.
Nm 3:25 the *c* at the entrance of the meeting tent,
3:26 the *c* at the entrance of the court
4: 5 take down the screening *c* and cover
4:25 the *c* at the entrance of the meeting tent,
4:26 the *c* at the entrance of the court that
1Mc 1:22 and the bowls, the golden censers, the *c,*
Mt 27:51 Suddenly the *c* of the sanctuary was torn
Mk 15:38 At that moment the *c* in the sanctuary was
Lk 23:45 The *c* in the sanctuary was torn in two.

CURTAINS (5)

Jdt 14:15 As no one answered, he parted the *c,*
1Mc 4:51 on the table and hung up *c*
Sg 1: 5 As the tents of Kedar, as the *c* of Salma.
Jer 10:20 to pitch my tent, no one to raise its *c.*
49:29 away, their tent *c* and all their goods;

CURVED (3)

Jos 15:10 From Baalah the boundary *c* westward to
16: 6 boundary *c* eastward around Taanath-shiloh,
1Kgs 7:31 on panels that were angular, not *c.*

CUSH (9)

Gn 2:13 one that winds all through the land of *C.*
10: 6 *C,* Mizraim, Put, and Canaan.
10: 7 The descendants of *C:* Seboh, Havilah
10: 8 *C* became the father of Nimrod,
1Chr 1: 8 The descendants of Ham were *C,*
1: 9 The descendants of *C* were Seba,
1:10 *C* became the father of Nimrod,
Jer 46: 9 Set out, warriors, *C* and Put,
Ez 38: 5 Persia, *C,* and Put with them

CUSHAN (1)

Hb 3: 7 I see the tents of *C* collapse;

CUSHAN-RISHATHAIM (2)

Jgs 3: 8 allowed them to fall into the power of *C,*
3:10 he went out to war, the LORD delivered *C,*

CUSHI (2)

Jer 36:14 of Nethaniah, son of Shelemiah, son of *C,*
Zep 1: 1 which came to Zephaniah, the son of *C,*

CUSHION (2)

Gn 31:34 taken the idols, put them inside a camel *c,*
Mk 4:38 stern through it all, sound asleep on a *c.*

CUSHITE (11)

Nm 12: 1 marriage he had contracted with a *C* woman.
2Sm 18:21 Then Joab said to a *C,*
18:21 seen" The *C* bowed to Joab and sped away.
18:22 may, permit me also to run after the *C.*"
18:23 way of the Jordan plain and outran the *C.*

18:31 When the *C* came in,
18:32 But the king asked the *C*,
18:32 The *C* replied, "May the enemies
Jer 38: 7 Now Ebed-melech, a *C*,
38:10 the *C* to take three men along with him,
39:16 Go, tell this to Ebed-melech the *C*:

CUSHITES (1)

Zep 2:12 You too, O *C*, shall be slain by the sword

CUSTODIAN (9)

Ex 22:10 the *c* shall swear by the LORD that he did
22:11 But if the *c* is really guilty of theft,
2Kgs 10:22 Then Jehu said to the *c* of the wardrobe,
Est 2: 3 of the royal eunuch Hegai, *c* of the women,
2: 8 under the care of Hegai, *c* of the women.
2:14 eunuch Shaashgaz, *c* of the concubines.
2:15 the royal eunuch Hegai, *c* of the women,
Bar 6: 6 is with you, and he is the *c* of your lives.
Acts 19:35 the *c* of the temple of the great Artemis,

CUSTODY (21)

Gn 40: 3 and he put them in *c* in the house of the
40: 4 After they had been in *c* for some time,
40: 7 were with him in *c* in his master's house,
41:10 in *c* in the house of the chief steward.
42:30 us in *c* as if we were spying on the land.
Lv 24:12 who kept him in *c* till a decision from the
Nm 3: 8 They shall have *c* of all the furnishings
15:34 But they kept him in *c*,
Dt 17:18 that is in the *c* of the levitical priests.
Jdt 6:11 So the servants took him in *c* and brought
10:12 The men took her in *c* and asked her,
1Mc 9:53 put them in *c* in the citadel at Jerusalem.
Prv 4:23 With closest *c*, guard your heart,
Jer 37:14 in *c* and brought him to the princes.
Mk 6:20 an upright and holy man, and kept him in *c*.
13:11 When men take you off into *c*,
Acts 12: 3 of the Jews, he took Peter into *c* too.
24:23 to be kept in *c* but allowed some freedom,
25: 4 that Paul was being kept in *c* at Caesarea,
25:14 he said, "whom Felix left behind in *c*.
25:21 in *c* until I could send him to the emperor."

CUSTOM (23)

Gn 19:31 to unite with us as was the *c* everywhere.
29:26 "It is not the *c* in our country,"
Ex 12:17 then, this *c* of the unleavened bread.
Jgs 11:39 It then became a *c* in Israel for Israelite
Ru 4: 7 Now it used to be the *c* in Israel that,
1Sm 2:16 "Let the fat be burned first as is the *c*,
27:11 This was his *c* as long as he lived in the
30:25 forward he made it a law and a *c* in Israel,
1Kgs 18:28 with swords and spears, as was their *c*,
2Kgs 11:14 king standing by the pillar, as was the *c*,
1Mc 1:14 in Jerusalem according to the Gentile *c*.
2:29 *c* went out into the desert to settle there,
10:58 great splendor according to the *c* of kings.
2Mc 12:38 according to *c* and kept the sabbath there.
Jer 12:16 learn my people's *c* of swearing by my name,
Dn 6:11 he continued his *c* of going home to kneel
Mk 7: 3 cling to the *c* of their ancestors and
15: 8 to press their demand that he honor the *c*,
Lk 2:42 went up for the celebration as was their *c*.
22:39 went out and made his way, as was his *c*,
Jn 18:39 Recall your *c* whereby I release someone to
19:40 in accordance with Jewish burial *c* bound it
Acts 17: 2 Following his usual *c*, Paul joined

CUSTOMARY (12)

Gn 23: 2 performed the *c* mourning rites for her.
Ex 22:16 pay him the *c* marriage price for virgins.
Jgs 14:10 it was *c* for the young men to do this.
1Sm 1:21 to offer the *c* sacrifice to the LORD
2:19 with her husband to offer the *c* sacrifice.
2Mc 13: 4 and executed there in the *c* local method.
14: 4 of the *c* olive branches from the temple.
14:31 the priests were offering the *c* sacrifices,
Ez 24:17 your beard, and do not eat the *c* bread.
24:22 your beards nor eating the *c* bread.
Mk 14:12 it was *c* to sacrifice the paschal lamb,
Lk 2:27 to perform for him the *c* ritual of the law,

CUSTOMS (20)

Lv 18: 3 do not conform to their *c*.
18:30 *c* that have been observed before you.
20:23 to the *c* of the nations whom I am driving
1Mc 1:42 people, each abandoning his particular *c*.
1:44 them to follow *c* foreign to their land;
2Mc 4:11 and introduced *c* contrary to the law.
4:13 and foreign *c* reached such a pitch,
6: 1 Jews to abandon the *c* of their ancestors
6: 9 not consent to adopt the *c* of the Greeks.
7:24 happy if he would abandon his ancestral *c*:
11:24 Greek *c* but prefer their own way of life.
11:24 us to let them retain their own *c*.
11:25 in keeping with the *c* of their ancestors.
Jer 10: 2 Learn not the *c* of the nations,
Lk 5:27 collector named Levi sitting at his *c* post.
Acts 6:14 change the *c* which Moses handed down to us."

16:21 which means they advocate *c* which are not
21:21 of their children, and to renounce their *c*.
26: 3 in all the various Jewish *c* and disputes.
28:17 against our people or our ancestral *c*;

CUT (228)

Gn 15:10 but the birds he did not *c* up.
17:14 flesh of his foreskin has not been *c* away,
17:14 such a one shall be *c* off from his people;
22: 3 the wood that he had *c* for the holocaust,
Ex 4:25 of flint and *c* off her son's foreskin and,
12:15 to the seventh shall be *c* off from Israel.
12:19 be *c* off from the community of Israel.
20:25 stone for me, do not build it of *c* stone,
29:17 *C* the ram into pieces;
30:33 a layman, shall be *c* off from his kinsmen."
30:38 fragrance, shall be *c* off from his kinsmen."
34: 1 Moses, *C* two stone tablets like the former,
34: 4 then *c* two stone tablets like the former,
34:13 pillars, and *c* down their sacred poles.
39: 3 into gold leaf and then *c* up into threads,
Lv 1: 6 skin the holocaust and *c* it up into pieces.
1:12 When the offerer has *c* it up into pieces,
7:20 the person shall be *c* off from his people.
7:21 too, shall be *c* off from his people."
7:25 such a one shall be *c* off from his people.
7:27 any blood shall be *c* off from his people."
17: 4 a man shall be *c* off from among his people.
17: 9 the LORD, shall be *c* off from his kinsmen.
17:10 and will *c* him off from among his people.
17:14 anyone who partakes of it shall be *c* off.
18:29 shall be *c* off from among his people.
19: 8 Such a one shall be *c* off from his people.
20: 3 and *c* him off from the body of his people;
20: 5 his family and will *c* off from their people
20: 6 such a one and *c* him off from his people.
20:17 they shall be publicly *c* off from their
20:18 of them shall be *c* off from their people,
22: 3 such a one shall be *c* off from my presence.
22:24 or *c* off you shall not offer to the LORD.
23:29 on this day shall be *c* off from his people,
26: 8 them, till they are *c* down by your sword.
26:26 And as I *c* off your supply of bread,
Nm 9:13 Passover, shall be *c* off from his people,
13:23 where they *c* down a branch with a single
13:24 because of the cluster the Israelites *c* there
15:30 and shall be *c* off from among his people.
15:31 broken his commandment, he must be *c* off.
19:13 of the LORD and shall be *c* off from Israel.
19:20 purified shall be *c* off from the community,
Dt 10: 1 me, *C* two tablets of stone like the former;
10: 3 and *c* two tablets of stone like the former,
19: 5 with his neighbor to a forest to *c* wood,
20:19 fruit, but you must not *c* down the trees.
21: 4 *c* the heifer's throat there in the wadi.
21: 6 the heifer whose throat was *c* in the wadi,
23: 2 been crushed or whose penis has been *c* off
25:18 and *c* off at the rear all those who lagged
Jos 8:22 who *c* them down without any fugitives or
19:29 it *c* back to Hosah and ended at the sea.
Jgs 1: 6 him, *c* off his thumbs and his big toes.
1: 7 with their thumbs and big toes *c* off,
6:16 you will *c* down Midian to the last man."
6:25 and *c* down the sacred pole that is by it.
6:26 wood from the sacred pole you have *c* down."
6:28 destroyed, the sacred pole near it *c* down,
6:30 *c* down the sacred pole that was near it."
9:48 axe in his hand, and *c* down some brushwood.
9:49 So all the men likewise *c* down brushwood,
19:29 of his concubine, *c* her into twelve pieces,
20: 6 So I took my concubine and *c* her up and
21: 6 one of the tribes of Israel has been *c* off.
1Sm 11: 7 a yoke of oxen, he *c* them into pieces,
14:13 turned to flee him, he *c* them down,
15:33 he *c* Agag down before the LORD in Gilgal.
17:46 I will strike you down and *c* off your head.
17:51 he dispatched him and *c* off his head.
24: 5 stealthily *c* off an end of Saul's mantle.
24: 6 that he had *c* off an end of Saul's mantle.
24:12 Since I *c* off an end of your mantle and
31: 9 They *c* off Saul's head and stripped him of
2Sm 4: 7 struck and killed him, and *c* off his head.
4:12 killed them and *c* off their hands and feet,
6:19 Israel, a loaf of bread, a *c* of roast meat,
12: 9 *c* down Uriah the Hittite with the sword;
20:22 advice, and they *c* off the head of Sheba,
1Kgs 3:25 him, he said, *C* the living child in two,
5:20 have cedars from the Lebanon *c* down for me.
9: 7 I will *c* off Israel from the land I gave
13:34 to be *c* off and destroyed from the earth.
14:10 I will *c* off every male in Jeroboam's line,
15:13 Asa *c* down this object and burned it in
18:23 Let them choose one, *c* it into pieces,
18:33 he *c* up the young bull and laid it on the
21:21 and will *c* off every male in Ahab's line,
2Kgs 4:39 On his return he *c* them up into the pot of
6: 6 out to the spot, Elisha *c* off a stick,
6:32 is sending someone to *c* off my head?
9: 8 I will *c* off every male in Ahab's line,
18: 4 pillars, and *c* down the sacred poles.
19:23 I *c* down its lofty cedars,
23:14 the pillars, *c* down the sacred poles,

1Chr 10: 9 They stripped him, *c* off his head,
11:14 kept it safe, and *c* down the Philistines.
17: 8 and I *c* down all your enemies before you.
19: 4 their garments *c* off half-way at the hips.
2Chr 2: 1 thousand to *c* the stone in the mountains,
2: 7 know how to *c* the wood of the Lebanon.
2: 9 your servants, the hewers who *c* the wood,
2:15 For our part, we will *c* trees on Lebanon,
15:16 Asa *c* this down,
22: 7 had anointed to *c* down the house of Ahab.
31: 1 sacred pillars, *c* down the sacred poles,
Ezr 5: 8 it is being rebuilt of *c* stone and the
6: 4 courses of *c* stone for each one of timber.
Tb 6: 5 *C* the fish open and take out its gall,
6: 6 After the lad had *c* the fish open,
Jdt 2:25 and *c* down everyone who resisted him.
3: 8 territory and *c* down their sacred groves,
5:22 Moab alike said he should be *c* to pieces.
13: 8 him twice in the neck and *c* off his head.
15: 5 them and *c* them down as far as Choba.
16: 9 The sword *c* through his neck.
16:12 supposed sons of rebel mothers *c* them down;
1Mc 7:47 *c* off Nicanor's head and his right arm,
11:17 Arab Zabdiel *c* off Alexander's head
2Mc 1:13 they were *c* to pieces in the temple of the
1:16 *c* off their heads and tossed them to the
5:12 He ordered his soldiers to *c* down without
5:26 men, he *c* down a large number of people.
7: 4 his executioners to *c* out the tongue
7: 4 to scalp him and *c* off his hands and feet,
10:17 walls, and *c* down those who opposed them,
10:35 fury *c* down everyone they encountered.
12:35 and *c* off his arm at the shoulder.
15:30 arm to be *c* off and taken to Jerusalem.
15:33 He *c* out the tongue of the godless Nicanor,
Jb 1:20 began to tear his cloak and *c* off his hair.
6: 9 he would put forth his hand and *c* me off!
11:20 Escape shall be *c* off from them,
14: 7 For a tree there is hope, if it be *c* down,
19:24 with lead they were *c* in the rock forever!
27: 8 the impious man expect when he is *c* off,
Ps(s) 31:23 my anguish, "I am *c* off from your sight";
37: 9 For evildoers shall be *c* off,
37:22 land, while those he curses shall be *c* off.
37:28 and the posterity of the wicked is *c* off.
37:38 the future of the wicked shall be *c* off.
80:17 *c* it down perish before you at your rebuke.
88: 6 no longer and who are *c* off from your care.
88:17 your terrors have *c* me off.
102:24 he has *c* short my days.
Prv 2:22 But the wicked will be *c* off from the land,
10:31 but the perverse tongue will be *c* off.
23:18 a future, and your hope will not be *c* off.
24:14 a future, and your hope will not be *c* off.
Wis 18:23 the anger, and *c* off the way to the living.
Sir 25:25 not by your side, *c* her away from you.
40:17 But goodness will never be *c* off,
48:17 With iron tools he *c* through the rock and
Is 9: 9 fallen, but we will build with *c* stone;
14: 8 to rest, there will be none to *c* us down."
14:12 How are you *c* down to the ground,
14:22 and *c* off from Babylon name and remnant,
29:20 All who are alert to do evil will be *c* off,
33:12 brushwood *c* down for burning in the fire.
37:24 I *c* down its lofty cedars,
48:19 *c* off or blotted out from my presence.
49:11 I will *c* a road through all my mountains,
53: 8 he was *c* off from the land of the living,
Jer 7:29 *C* off your dedicated hair and throw it away!
10: 3 are nothing, wood *c* from the forest,
11:19 us *c* him off from the land of the living,
22: 7 They shall *c* down your choice cedars,
34:18 make like the calf which they *c* in two,
36:23 columns the king would *c* off the piece
46:23 They *c* down her forest,
47: 4 And *c* off from Tyre and Sidon the last of
50:16 *C* off from Babylon the sower and him who
51:13 come, the term at which you shall be *c* off!
Ez 5: 1 of scales and divide the hair you have *c*.
5:11 abominations, I swear to *c* you down.
14: 8 will *c* him off from the midst of my people.
14:13 it and *c* off from it both man and beast;
14:21 pestilence, to *c* off from it man and beast,
16: 4 you were born your navel cord was not *c*;
21: 8 *c* off from you the virtuous and the wicked.
25: 7 nations, I will *c* you off from the peoples,
25:13 Edom and *c* off from it man and beast.
25:16 I will *c* off the Cherethites and wipe out
29: 8 you, and *c* off from you both man and beast.
30:15 and *c* down the crowds in Memphis.
31:12 *c* it down and left it on the mountains.
32:12 I will *c* down your horde with the blades
35: 7 waste, and *c* off from it any traveler.
37:11 up, our hope is lost, and we are *c* off."
39:10 the fields or *c* it down in the forests,
40:42 tables for holocausts, made of *c* stone,
Dn 2: 5 be *c* to pieces and your houses destroyed.
3:96 be *c* to pieces and his house destroyed.
4:11 *C* down the tree and lop off its branches,
4:20 *C* down the tree and destroy it,
9:26 *c* down when he does not possess the city;
13:59 waits with a sword to *c* you in two
Jl 1:16 our very eyes has not the food been *c* off;

CUT (cont.)

Na 3:15 consume you, the sword shall *c* you down.
Zec 11: 2 for the impenetrable forest is *c* down!
13: 8 two thirds of them shall be *c* off and
Mal 2:12 May the LORD *c* off from the man who does
Mt 3:10 will be *c* down and thrown into the fire.
5:30 your trouble, *c* it off and throw it away!
7:19 fruit is *c* down and thrown into the fire.
18: 8 undoing, *c* it off and throw it from you!
21: 8 while some began to *c* branches from the
Mk 6:16 exclaimed, "John, whose head I had *c* off,
9:43 your hand is your difficulty, *c* it off!
9:45 If your foot is your undoing, *c* it off!
11: 8 reeds which they had *c* in the fields.
15:46 him in a tomb which had been *c* out of rock.
Lk 3: 9 will be *c* down and thrown into the fire."
13: 7 *C* it down.
13: 9 If not, it shall be *c* down.'"
22:50 priest's servant and *c* off his right ear.
Acts 3:23 shall be ruthlessly *c* off from the people.'
27:32 *c* the ropes and let the boat drift.
27:40 They *c* loose the anchors and abandoned
Rom 11:17 If some of the branches were *c* off and you,
11:19 were *c* off that I might be grafted in."
11:20 They were *c* off because of unbelief and
11:22 if you do not, you too will be *c* off.
11:24 were *c* off from the natural wild olive and,
1Cor 11: 6 wear a veil, she ought to *c* off her hair.
11: 6 to have her hair *c* off or her head shaved,
Rv 14:15 "Use your sickle and *c* down the harvest,

CUT-UP (1)

Lv 8:20 burned the head, the *c* pieces and the suet,

CUTH (1)

2Kgs 17:30 the men of *C* made Nergal;

CUTHAH (1)

2Kgs 17:24 of Assyria brought people from Babylon, *C*,

CUTS (5)

Prv 26: 6 He *c* off his feet,
Sir 21: 3 when it *c*,
Is 44:14 He *c* down cedars,
Jer 9:20 It *c* down the children in the street,
22:14 airy rooms," Who *c* out windows for it,

CUTTER (2)

Jl 1: 4 What the *c* left,
2:25 The grasshopper, the devourer, and the *c*,

CUTTERS (2)

2Kgs 12:13 LORD, and to the lumbermen and stone *c*,
2Chr 2:17 and eighty thousand *c* in the mountains,

CUTTHROATS (1)

Acts 21:38 of four thousand *c* out into the desert?"

CUTTING (15)

Ex 31: 5 bronze, in *c* and mounting precious stones,
35:33 bronze, in *c* and mounting precious stones,
Lv 8:20 After *c* up the ram into pieces,
Dt 1:44 you, *c* you down in Seir as far as Hormah.
20:20 *c* them down to build siegeworks with which
2Sm 10: 4 *c* away the lower halves of their garments
1Kgs 5:20 is skilled in *c* timber like the Sidonians,
2Chr 14: 2 pillars, and *c* down the sacred poles.
Is 18: 5 Then comes the *c* of branches with pruning
Ez 14:17 the land *c* off from it man and beast,
14:19 fury, *c* off from it man and beast,
23:25 with you in fury, *c* off your nose and ears;
Hb 2:10 for your household, *c* off many peoples,
Mt 26:51 the high priest's servant, *c* off his ear.
Mk 14:47 the high priest's slave, *c* off his ear.

CYAMON (1)

Jdt 7: 3 Balbaim, and in length from Bethulia to *C*,

CYAXARES (1)

Tb 14:15 exile of the city's inhabitants when *C*,

CYCLES (2)

Lv 25: 8 the seven *c* amount to forty-nine years.
Wis 7:19 *C* of years, positions of the stars,

CYLINDER-SEAL (1)

Is 8: 1 Take a large *c*,

CYMBAL (1)

1Cor 13: 1 have love, I am a noisy gong, a clanging *c*.

CYMBALS (18)

2Sm 6: 5 harps, tambourines, sistrums and *c*.
1Chr 13: 8 and music on lyres, harps, tambourines, *c*,
15:16 musical instruments, harps, lyres, and *c*,
15:19 Heman, Asaph, and Ethan, sounded brass *c*.
15:28 to the sound of horns, trumpets, and *c*,
16: 5 and lyres, while Asaph was to sound the *c*,
16:42 with trumpets and *c* for accompaniment,
25: 1 the accompaniment of lyres and harps and *c*.
25: 6 of the LORD to the accompaniment of *c*,
2Chr 5:12 brothers, clothed in fine linen, with *c*,
5:13 *c* and other musical instruments to "give
29:25 the Levites in the LORD's house with *c*,
Ezr 3:10 were stationed there with the *c* to praise
Neh 12:27 with thanksgiving hymns and the music of *c*,
Jdt 16: 1 with timbrels, chant to the Lord with *c*;
1Mc 4:54 with songs, harps, flutes and *c*.
13:51 the music of harps and *c* and lyres,
Ps(s) 150: 5 sounding *c*, praise him with clanging *c*.

CYNICS (1)

Acts 13:41 'Look on in amazement, you *c*,

CYPRESS (12)

2Chr 2: 7 of cedar, *c* and cabinet wood from Lebanon,
3: 5 *c* wood which he covered with fine gold,
Sir 24:13 am raised aloft, like a *c* on Mount Hermon,
50:10 like a *c* standing against the clouds;
Is 41:19 I will set in the wasteland the *c*,
55:13 place of the thornbush, the *c* shall grow,
60:13 the *c*, the plane and the pine,
Ez 27: 5 With *c* from Senir they built for you all
27: 6 made of *c* wood from the coasts of Kittim.
31: 3 Behold, a *c* [cedar] in Lebanon,
Hos 14: 9 "I am like a verdant *c* tree"
Zec 11: 2 Wail, you *c* trees,

CYPRESSES (4)

2Kgs 19:23 I cut down its lofty cedars, its choice *c*;
Sg 1:17 of our house are cedars, our rafters, *c*.
Is 14: 8 The very *c* rejoice over you,
37:24 I cut down its lofty cedars, its choice *c*;

CYPRIANS (1)

2Mc 12: 2 nothing of Nicanor, the commander of the *C*,

CYPRIOT (1)

Acts 21:16 house of Mnason, a *C* and an early disciple,

CYPRIOTS (1)

2Mc 4:29 Sostratus left Crates, commander of the *C*,

CYPRUS (9)

1Mc 15:23 Cos, Side, Aradus, Gortyna, Cnidus, *C*,
2Mc 10:13 called a traitor for having abandoned *C*,
Acts 4:36 was a certain Levite from *C* named Joseph,
11:19 went as far as Phoenicia, *C* and Antioch,
11:20 some men of *C* and Cyrene among them who
13: 4 of Seleucia and set sail from there for *C*.
15:39 took Mark along with him and sailed for *C*.
21: 3 We caught sight of *C* but passed it by on
27: 4 side of *C* because of strong headwinds.

CYRENE (7)

1Mc 15:23 Aradus, Gortyna, Cnidus, Cyprus, and *C*.
2Mc 2:23 of *C* set forth in detail in five volumes,
Mk 15:21 A man named Simon of *C*,
Acts 2:10 Egypt, and the regions of Libya around *C*.
6: 9 Freedmen" (that is, the Jews from *C*,
11:20 some men of Cyprus and *C* among them who
13: 1 Symeon known as Niger, Lucius of *C*,

CYRENEAN (1)

Lk 23:26 the *C* who was coming in from the fields.

CYRENIAN (1)

Mt 27:32 On their way out they met a *C* named Simon.

CYRUS (24)

2Chr 36:22 In the first year of *C*,
36:22 the LORD inspired King *C* of Persia to
36:23 "Thus says *C*, king of Persia:
Ezr 1: 1 In the first year of *C*,
1: 1 the LORD inspired King *C* of Persia to
1: 2 "Thus says *C*, king of Persia:
1: 7 King *C*, too, had the utensils of the house
1: 8 *C*, king of Persia, had them brought forth
3: 7 the Lebanon to the port of Joppa, as *C*,
4: 3 as King *C* of Persia has commanded us."
4: 5 plans during the remaining years of *C*,
5:13 However, in the first year of *C*,
5:13 King *C* issued a decree for the rebuilding
5:14 King *C* ordered to be removed from the
5:17 a decree really was issued by King *C*
6: 3 year of King Cyrus, King *C* issued a decree:
6:14 decrees of *C* and Darius [and of Artaxerxes,
Is 44:28 I say of *C*:
45: 1 Thus says the LORD to his anointed, *C*,
Dn 1:21 there until the first year of King *C*.
6:29 of Darius and the reign of *C* the Persian.
10: 1 In the third year of *C*,
14: 1 *C* the Persian succeeded to his kingdom.

D

DABBESHETH (1)

Jos 19:11 *D* and the wadi that is near Jokneam.

DABERATH (3)

Jos 19:12 to the district of Chisloth-tabor, on to *D*,
21:28 pasture lands, *D* with its pasture lands,
1Chr 6:57 pasture lands, *D* with its pasture lands,

DADU (2)

2Sm 21:16 *D*, one of the Rephaim,
21:16 *D* was girt with a new sword and planned to

DAGGER (4)

Jgs 3:16 made himself a two-edged *d* a foot long,
3:21 left hand drew the *d* from his right thigh,
3:22 he did not withdraw the *d* from his body.
Bar 6:14 has in its right hand an axe or *d*,

DAGON (13)

Jgs 16:23 sacrifice to their god *D* and to make merry.
1Sm 5: 2 the temple of Dagon, placing it beside *D*.
5: 3 *D* was lying prone on the ground before the
5: 3 So they picked *D* up and replaced him.
5: 4 *D* lay prone on the ground before the ark
5: 5 neither the priests of *D* nor any others
5: 5 others who enter the temple of *D* tread on
5: 5 threshold of *D* in Ashdod to this very day;
5: 7 he is handling us and our god *D* severely."
1Chr 10:10 his skull they impaled on the temple of *D*.
1Mc 10:84 *D* and the men who had taken refuge in it.
11: 4 shown the temple of *D* destroyed by fire,

DAILY (39)

Ex 5:13 *d* amount as when your straw was supplied."
5:19 told not to reduce the *d* amount of bricks.
16: 4 are to go out and gather their *d* portion;
2Kgs 25:30 a perpetual allowance, in fixed *d* amounts,
1Chr 16:37 ark regularly according to the *d* ritual;
2Chr 8:14 the priests, as the *d* duty required.
31:16 according to the *d* rule to fulfill their service
Ezr 3: 4 and they offered the *d* holocausts in the
Neh 5:18 the *d* preparations were made at my expense
10:34 daily cereal offering, for the *d* holocaust,
11:23 the singers assigning them their *d* duties.
12:47 their portions, according to their *d* needs.
Jdt 4:14 sackcloth as they offered the *d* holocaust,
12:15 for her *d* use in reclining at her dinner.
Ps(s) 88:10 *d* I call upon you,
Prv 8:34 ways, Happy the man watching *d* at my gates,
Wis 13:11 his art, produce something fit for *d* use,
Sir 47: 8 loved his Maker and *d* had his praises sung;
Jer 52:34 a perpetual allowance, in fixed *d* amounts,
Ez 43:25 *D* for seven days you shall offer a he-goat
46:13 He shall offer as a *d* holocaust to the
Dn 1: 5 The king allotted them a *d* portion of food
8:11 host, from whom it removed the *d* sacrifice,
8:12 host, while sin replaced the *d* sacrifice.
8:13 vision last concerning the *d* sacrifice,
11:31 abolishing the *d* sacrifice and setting up
12:11 From the time that the *d* sacrifice is
14:32 and two sheep had been given to them *d*.
Mt 6:11 Give us today our *d* bread,
20: 2 agreement with them for the usual *d* wage,
20:11 yet they received the same *d* wage.
Mk 14:49 I was within your reach *d*,
Lk 11: 3 Give us each day our *d* bread.
Acts 6: 1 neglected in the *d* distribution of food,
16: 5 in faith and *d* increased in numbers.
17:17 as well as *d* debates in the public square
2Cor 11:28 there is that *d* tension pressing on me,
Heb 3:13 one another *d* while it is still "today,"

DAINTIES (4)

Gn 49:20 is rich, and he shall furnish *d* for kings.
Ps(s) 141: 4 and let me not partake of their *d*.
Prv 23: 6 a grudging man, and do not desire his *d*;
Sir 30:18 *D* set before one who cannot eat are like

DAINTY (4)

Prv 18: 8 The words of a talebearer are like *d*
26:22 The words of a talebearer are like *d*
Is 47: 1 longer shall you be called *d* and delicate.
Lam 4: 5 accustomed to *d* food perish in the streets;

DAIS (4)

Ez 16:24 a platform and a *d* in every public place.
16:25 At every street corner you built a *d* for
16:31 and erecting your *d* in every public place!
16:39 down your platform and demolish your *d*;

DALLY (1)

Dt 7:10 he does not *d* with such a one,

DALMANUTHA (1)

Mk 8:10 disciples to go to the neighborhood of *D*.

DALMATIA (1)

2Tm 4:10 has gone to Galatia and Titus to *D.*

DALPHON (1)

Est 9: 7 They also killed Parshandatha, *D,*

DAM (2)

1Chr 14:11 enemies just as water breaks through a *d.*"
Prv 17:14 of strife is like the opening of a *d;*

DAMAGE (3)

Ps(s) 74: 3 the *d* the enemy has done in the sanctuary.
Sg 2:15 the little foxes that *d* the vineyards;
Sir 27:21 but he who betrays secrets does hopeless *d.*

DAMAGED (1)

2Chr 24: 7 her sons had *d* the house of God

DAMAGES (1)

Sir 9: 5 virgin, lest you be enmeshed in *d* for her.

DAMARIS (1)

Acts 17:34 court of the Areopagus, a woman named *D,*

DAMASCUS (64)

Gn 14:15 them as far as Hobah, which is north of *D.*
2Sm 8: 5 Arameans of *D* came to the aid of Hadadezer,
8: 6 David then placed garrisons in Aram of *D,*
1Kgs 11:24 and became leader of a band, went to *D,*
11:24 settled there, and became king in *D.*
15:18 son of Hezion, king of Aram, resident in *D.*
19:15 take the road back to the desert near *D,*"
20:34 and you may make yourself bazaars in *D,*
2Kgs 5:12 Are not the rivers of *D,*
8: 7 Elisha came to *D* at a time when Ben-hadad,
8: 9 forty camel loads of the best goods of *D.*
14:28 with *D* and turned back Hamath from Israel,
16: 9 who listened to him and moved against *D,*
16:10 Ahaz went to *D* to meet Tiglath-pileser,
16:10 When he saw the altar in *D,*
16:11 the plans which King Ahaz sent him from *D,*
16:12 On his arrival from *D,*
1Chr 18: 5 Arameans of *D* came to the aid of Hadadezer,
18: 6 set up garrisons in the *D* region of Aram,
2Chr 16: 2 to Ben-hadad, king of Aram, who lived in *D,*
24:23 and sent all their spoil to the king of *D.*
28: 5 of his people, whom they brought to *D.*
28:23 to the gods of *D* who had defeated him,
Jdt 1: 7 to the inhabitants of Cilicia and *D,*
1:12 the territories of Cilicia and *D* and Syria,
2:27 of *D* at the time of the wheat harvest,
15: 5 slaughter, even beyond *D* and its territory.
1Mc 11:62 traveled on through the province as far as *D.*
12:32 on to *D* and traversed that whole region.
Sg 7: 5 the tower on Lebanon that looks toward *D.*
Is 7: 8 *D* is the capital of Aram,
7: 8 capital of Aram, and Rezin the head of *D;*
8: 4 the wealth of *D* and the spoil of Samaria
10: 9 Or Hamath like Arpad, or Samaria like *D?*
17: 1 Oracle on *D:*
17: 1 *D* shall cease to be a city and become a
17: 3 be lost to Ephraim and the kingdom to *D;*
Jer 49:22 Concerning *D.*
49:24 *D* is weakened,
49:27 hosts, I will set fire to the wall of *D,*
Ez 27:18 *D* traded with you,
47:16 along the frontiers of Hamath and *D,*
47:17 the frontier of Hamath and *D* to the north.
47:18 toward *D*— and Gilead on the one side,
48: 1 on the northerly border with *D,*
Am 1: 3 For three crimes of *D,*
1: 5 I will break the bar of *D,*
5:27 For I will exile you beyond *D,*
Zec 9: 1 of Hadrach, and *D* is its resting place,
Acts 9: 2 for letters to the synagogues in *D*
9: 3 he traveled along and was approaching *D,*
9: 8 take him by the hand and lead him into *D.*
9:10 There was a disciple in *D* named Ananias to
9:22 reduced the Jewish community of *D* to silence
9:27 out fearlessly in the name of Jesus at *D.*
22: 5 received letters to our brother Jews in *D.*
22: 6 traveling along, approaching *D* around noon,
22:10 the Lord replied, 'Get up and go into *D.*
22:11 the hand and led into *D* by my companions.
26:12 traveling toward *D* armed with the authority
26:20 to God, first to the people of *D,*
2Cor 11:32 In *D* the ethnarch of King Aretas was
Gal 1:17 later I returned to *D.*

DAMNATION (1)

Mt 7:13 The gate that leads to *d* is wide,

DAMNED (1)

Jn 5:29 the evildoers shall rise to be *d.*

DAMSEL (1)

Jgs 5:30 there must be a *d* or two for each man,

DAN (56)

Gn 14:14 his house, and went in pursuit as far as *D.*
30: 6 Therefore she named him *D.*
35:25 *D* and Naphtali; the sons of Leah's maid
46:23 The sons of *D:* Hushim
49:16 *D* shall achieve justice for his kindred
49:17 Let *D* be a serpent by the roadside,
Ex 1: 4 *D* and Naphtali; Gad and Asher.
31: 6 son of Ahisamach, of the tribe of *D.*
35:34 son of Ahisamach, of the tribe of *D,*
38:23 son of Ahisamach, of the tribe of *D,*
Lv 24:10 of the tribe of *D)* and an Egyptian father.
Nm 1:12 Abidan, son of Gideoni from *D:*
1:38 Of the descendants of *D,*
1:39 hundred were enrolled in the tribe of *D.*
2:25 side shall be the divisional camp of *D,*
2:31 registered by companies in the camp of *D*
13:12 Gemalli, of the tribe of *D*
26:42 These were the clans of *D,*
34:22 the tribe of *D:*
Dt 27:13 *D* and Naphtali shall stand on Mount Ebal
33:22 Of *D* he said: Dan is a lion's whelp.
34: 1 Gilead, and as far as *D,*
Jos 19:47 the settlement after their ancestor *D.*
21: 5 the tribe of Ephraim, from the tribe of *D,*
21:23 From the tribe of *D* they obtained the four
Jgs 5:17 why does *D* spend his time in ships?
18:29 They named it *D* after their ancestor Dan,
18:29 They named it Dan after their ancestor *D,*
20: 1 from *D* to Beer-sheba,
1Sm 3:20 Thus all Israel from *D* to Beer-sheba came
2Sm 3:10 Israel and over Judah from *D* to Beer-sheba."
17:11 Let all Israel from *D* to Beer-sheba,
20:19 if they will in Abel or in *D* whether loyalty
24: 2 *D* to Beer-sheba and register the people,
24: 6 Then they proceeded to *D;*
24:15 of the people from *D* to Beer-sheba died.]
1Kgs 5: 5 or under his fig tree from *D* to Beer-sheba,
12:29 And he put one in Bethel, the other in *D.*
12:30 frequented these calves in Bethel and in *D.*
15:20 They attacked Ijon, *D,*
2Kgs 10:29 the golden calves at Bethel and at *D.*
1Chr 2: 2 Simeon, Levi, Judah, Issachar, Zebulun, *D,*
6:46 the tribe of Ephraim, from the tribe of *D,*
6:54 From the tribe of *D:* Elteke
7:12 The sons of *D:* Hushim
21: 2 of the Israelites from Beer-sheba to *D,*
27:22 for *D,* Azarel, son of Jeroham.
2Chr 16: 4 They attacked Ijon, *D,*
30: 5 all Israel from Beer-sheba to *D,*
Tb 1: 5 Jeroboam, king of Israel, had made in *D.*
Jer 4:15 They proclaim it from *D,*
8:16 From *D* is heard the snorting of his steeds;
Ez 48: 1 *D:* at the northern extremity,
48: 2 on the frontier of *D,*
48:32 the gate of Benjamin, and the gate of *D.*
Am 8:14 of Samaria, "By the life of your god, O *D!*"

DANCE (15)

Jdt 15:12 blessed her and performed a *d* in her honor.
15:13 the people, she led the women in the *d,*
Jb 21:11 numerous as lambs, and their children *d.*
Ps(s) 87: 7 And all shall sing, in their festive *d:*
149: 3 Let them praise his name in the festive *d,*
150: 4 and harp, Praise him with timbrel and *d,*
Eccl 3: 4 a time to mourn, and a time to *d.*
Sg 7: 1 as at the *d* of the two companies?
Is 13:21 ostriches shall dwell, and satyrs shall *d.*
Jer 31:13 Then the virgins shall make merry and *d,*
Lam 5:15 has ceased, our *d* has turned into mourning;
Mt 11:17 'We piped you a tune but you did not *d!*
14: 6 Herodias' daughter performed a *d*
Mk 6:22 a *d* which delighted Herod and his guests.
Lk 7:32 'We piped you a tune but you did not *d,*

DANCED (1)

1Chr 13: 8 Israel *d* before God with great enthusiasm,

DANCERS (1)

Jgs 21:23 for each of them from their raid on the *d,*

DANCES (2)

1Sm 21:12 During their *d* do they not sing,
29: 5 David of whom they sing during their *d,*

DANCING (14)

Ex 15:20 went out after her with tambourines, *d,*
32:19 near the camp, he saw the calf and the *d.*
Jgs 11:34 came forth, playing the tambourines and *d.*
21:21 girls of Shiloh come out to do their *d,*
1Sm 18: 6 Israel to meet King Saul, singing and *d,*
2Sm 6:14 apron, came *d* before the LORD with abandon,
6:16 King David leaping and *d* before the LORD,
6:21 "I was *d* before the LORD.
1Chr 15:29 and when she saw King David leaping and *d,*
Jdt 3: 7 garlands and *d* to the sound of timbrels.
Ps(s) 30:12 You changed my mourning into *d;*
Jer 31: 4 you shall go forth *d* with the merrymakers.
Lk 15:25 home, he heard the sound of music and *d.*
15:26 him the reason for the *d* and the music.

DANGER (19)

1Sm 13: 6 of the *d* and of the difficult situation,
1Kgs 5:18 There is no enemy or threat of *d.*
1Mc 11:23 to *d* by going to the king at Ptolemais.
14:29 his brothers have put themselves in *d*
2Mc 2:22 the laws that were in *d* of being abolished,
3:18 the Place was in *d* of being profaned.
15:17 temple with the sacred vessels were in *d.*
Eccl 10: 9 and he who chops wood is in *d* from it.
Sg 3: 8 side against *d* in the watches of the night.
Wis 14: 4 Showing that you can save from any *d,*
Sir 3:25 end, and he who loves *d* will perish in it.
34:12 Often I was in *d* of death,
51: 3 From many a *d* you have saved me,
Lam 3:58 You defended me in mortal *d,*
Lk 8:23 they began to ship water and to be in *d.*
Acts 19:27 The *d* grows, not only that our trade
Rom 8:35 persecution, or hunger, or nakedness, or *d,*
1Cor 15:30 are we continually putting ourselves in *d?*
2Cor 1:10 that *d* of death and will continue to do so.

DANGERS (3)

2Mc 1:11 we have been saved by God from grave *d,*
Wis 18: 9 share alike the same good things and *d,*
Sir 51:10 of trouble, in the midst of storms and *d.*

DANIEL (111)

1Chr 3: 1 the second, *D,* by Abigail of Carmel;
Ezr 8: 2 of the sons of Ithamar, *D;*
Neh 10: 7 Malluch, Harim, Meremoth, Obadiah, *D,*
1Mc 2:60 *D,* for his innocence, was delivered
Ez 14:14 if these three men were in it, Noah, *D,*
14:20 from it man and beast, even if Noah, *D,*
28: 3 Oh yes, you are wiser than *D,*
Dn 1: 6 *D,* Hananiah, Mishael, and Azariah.
1: 7 *D* to Belteshazzar, Hananiah to Shadrach,
1: 8 But *D* was resolved not to defile himself
1: 9 Though God had given *D* the favor and
1:10 chamberlain, he nevertheless said to *D,*
1:11 Then *D* said to the steward whom the chief
1:11 chief chamberlain had put in charge of *D,*
1:17 and to *D* the understanding of all visions
1:19 all of them, none was found equal to *D,*
1:21 *D* remained there until the first year of
2:13 *D* and his companions were also sought out.
2:14 Then *D* prudently took counsel with Arioch,
2:16 *D* went and asked for time from the king,
2:17 *D* went home and informed his companions
2:18 so that *D* and his companions might not
2:19 the mystery was revealed to *D* in a vision,
2:24 So *D* went to Arioch,
2:24 quickly brought *D* to the king and said,
2:26 The king asked *D,*
2:27 In the king's presence *D* made this reply:
2:46 Nebuchadnezzar fell down and worshiped *D*
2:47 To *D* the king said, "Truly your God
2:48 He advanced *D* to a high post,
2:49 *D* himself remained at the king's court.
4: 5 Finally there came before me *D,*
4:16 Then *D,* whose name was Belteshazzar,
5:12 the extraordinary mind possessed by this *D,*
5:12 summon *D* to tell you what this means."
5:13 Then *D* was brought into the presence of
5:13 The king asked him, "Are you the *D,*
5:17 *D* answered the king:
5:29 of Belshazzar they clothed *D* in purple,
6: 3 to three supervisors, one of whom was *D.*
6: 4 *D* outshone all the supervisors and satraps
6: 5 against *D* as regards the administration.
6: 6 this *D* unless by way of the law of his God."
6:11 *D* heard that this law had been signed,
6:12 *D* praying and pleading before his God.
6:14 To this they replied, *D,*
6:15 news and he made up his mind to save *D;*
6:17 So the king ordered *D* to be brought and
6:17 To *D* he said, "May your God, whom
6:21 drew near, he cried out to *D* sorrowfully,
6:21 he cried out to Daniel sorrowfully, "O *D,*
6:22 *D* answered the king: O king, live forever!
6:24 At his order *D* was removed from the den,
6:25 then ordered the men who had accused *D,*
6:27 God of *D* is to be reverenced and feared:
6:28 and he delivered *D* from the lions' power."
6:29 So *D* fared well during the reign of Darius
7: 1 of Babylon, *D* had a dream as he lay in bed,
7:15 I, *D,* found my spirit anguished
7:28 I, *D,* was greatly terrified by my thoughts,
8: 1 After this first vision, I, *D,*
8:15 While I, *D,* sought the meaning
8:27 I, *D,* was weak and ill for some days;
9: 2 in the first year of his reign I, *D,*
9:22 *D,* I have now come to give you
10: 1 of Persia, a revelation was given to *D,*
10: 2 In those days, I, *D,*
10: 7 I alone, *D,* saw the vision;
10:11 *D,* beloved," he said to me,
10:12 "Fear not, *D,*" he continued;
12: 4 "As for you, *D,* keep secret the message
12: 5 I, *D,* looked and saw two others
12: 9 "Go, *D,*" he said, "because the words
13:45 up the holy spirit of a young boy named *D,*

DANIEL (cont.)

13:50 To *D* the elders said,
13:55 fine lie has cost you your head," said *D;*
13:56 of Canaan, not of Judah," *D* said to him,
13:59 lie has cost you also your head," said *D;*
13:61 own words *D* had convicted them of perjury.
13:64 *D* was greatly esteemed by the people.
14: 2 *D* was the king's favorite and was held in
14: 4 but *D* adored only his God.
14: 5 *D* replied, "Because I worship not idols
14: 7 *D* began to laugh.
14: 9 them, *D* shall die for blaspheming Bel."
14: 9 *D* said to the king,
14:10 king went with *D* into the temple of Bel,
14:12 *D* shall die for his lies against us."
14:14 while *D* ordered his servants to bring some
14:16 the next morning, the king came with *D.*
14:17 "Are the seals unbroken, *D?"*
14:17 And *D* answered, "They are unbroken,
14:19 *D* laughed and kept the king from entering.
14:22 them to death, and handed Bel over to *D,*
14:24 said the king to *D,* "you cannot deny
14:25 But *D* answered, "I adore the Lord,
14:27 Then *D* took some pitch,
14:29 "Hand *D* over to us,
14:30 the king was forced to hand *D* over to them.
14:31 They threw *D* into a lions' den,
14:32 given nothing, so that they would devour *D.*
14:34 you have to *D* in the lions' den at Babylon."
14:37 "Daniel, *D,"* cried Habakkuk,
14:38 "You have remembered me, O God," said *D;*
14:39 While *D* began to eat,
14:40 seventh day the king came to mourn for *D.*
14:40 came to the den and looked in, there was *D,*
14:41 "You are great, O Lord, the God of *D,*
14:42 *D* he took out,
Mt 24:15 thing which the prophet *D* foretold

DANIEL'S (1)

Dn 2:49 At *D* request the king made Shadrach,

DANITE (1)

2Chr 2:13 son of a *D* woman and of a father from Tyre;

DANITES (21)

Nm 7:66 son of Ammishaddai, prince of the *D.*
10:25 all the camps, the camp of the *D* set out,
26:42 The *D* by clans were:
Jos 19:40 lot fell to the clans of the tribe of *D.*
19:47 territory of the *D* was too small for them;
19:47 so the *D* marched up and attacked Leshem,
19:48 of the clans of the tribe of the *D.*
Jgs 1:34 hemmed in the *D* in the mountain region,
13: 2 man from Zorah, of the clan of the *D,*
18: 1 *D* were in search of a district to dwell in,
18: 2 So the *D* sent from their clan a detail of
18:11 So six hundred men of the clan of the *D,*
18:16 men girt with weapons of war, who were *D,*
18:22 The *D* had already gone some distance,
18:23 They called to the *D,*
18:25 *D* said to him, "Let us hear no further
18:26 The *D* then went on their way,
18:28 The *D* then rebuilt the city,
18:30 *D* set up the carved idol for themselves,
18:30 priests for the tribe of the *D* until the time
1Chr 12:36 Of the *D,* set in battle array:

DANNAH (1)

Jos 15:49 Shamir, Jattir, Socoh, *D,*

DAPHNE (1)

2Mc 4:33 to the inviolable sanctuary at *D,*

DARDA (2)

1Kgs 5:11 the Ezrahite, or Heman, Chalcol, and *D,*
1Chr 2: 6 were Zimri, Ethan, Heman, Calcol, and *D—*

DARE (16)

Gn 49: 9 who would *d* rouse him?
2Sm 16:10 who then will *d* to say,
Jb 10:15 if righteous, I *d* not hold up my head,
11: 7 *D* you vie with the perfection of the
Sir 29:24 for as a guest you *d* not open your mouth.
Is 45: 9 *D* the clay say to its modeler,
Jer 2:29 How *d* you still plead with me?
32: 3 "How *d* you prophesy:
Mal 3: 8 *D* a man rob God?
Lk 20:40 They did not *d* ask him anything else.
Acts 23: 4 "How *d* you insult God's high priest?"
Rom 15:18 I will not *d* to speak of anything except
1Cor 6: 1 anyone with a case against another *d* bring it
2Cor 10: 2 with that assurance I might *d* to use
11:21 I, too, will *d.*
Rv 15: 4 Who would *d* refuse you honor,

DARED (12)

Gn 18:31 "Since I have thus *d* to speak to my Lord,
Nm 14:44 Yet they *d* to go up into the foothills,
Jdt 14:13 slaves have *d* come down to give us battle,
Est 7: 5 Esther, "is the man who has *d* to do this?"
2Mc 4: 2 He *d* to brand as a plotter against the
5:15 *d* to enter the holiest temple in the world;
7:19 for having *d* to fight against God."
Sir 46:19 and no one *d* gainsay him.
Mt 22:46 therefore no one *d,*
Jn 7:13 No one *d* talk openly about him,
Acts 5:13 No one else *d* to join them,
7:32 Moses began to tremble and *d* look no more.

DARES (5)

Gn 19: 9 an immigrant, and now he *d* to give orders!
Lv 15:24 If a man *d* to lie with her,
22: 3 descendants in any future generation, *d,*
Jb 41: 2 who then *d* stand before him?
2Cor 11:21 But what anyone else *d* to claim

DARICS (2)

1Chr 29: 7 talents and ten thousand *d* of gold,
Ezr 8:27 golden bowls valued at a thousand *d;*

DARING (4)

Jdt 16:10 "The Persians were dismayed at her *d,*
2Mc 8:18 "They trust in weapons and acts of *d,"*
13:18 king, having had a taste of the Jews' *d,*
Lk 18:13 not even *d* to raise his eyes to heaven.

DARIUS (23)

Ezr 4: 5 king of Persia, and until the reign of *D,*
4:24 until the second year of the reign of *D,*
5: 5 until a report could go to *D* and then a
5: 6 of the letter sent to King *D* by Tattenai,
5: 7 "To King *D* all good wishes!
6: 1 Thereupon King *D* issued an order to search
6:12 I, *D,* have issued this decree;
6:13 the instructions King *D* had sent them.
6:14 decrees of Cyrus and *D* [and of Artaxerxes,
6:15 in the sixth year of the reign of King *D.*
Neh 12:22 up until the reign of *D* the Persian.
1Mc 1: 1 from the land of Kittim, had defeated *D,*
Dn 6: 1 and *D* the Mede succeeded to the kingdom at
6: 7 to the king and said to him, "King *D,*
6:10 *D* signed the prohibition and made it law.
6:26 Then King *D* wrote to the nations and
6:29 of *D* and the reign of Cyrus the Persian.
9: 1 It was the first year that *D,*
Hg 1: 1 sixth month in the second year of King *D,*
2:10 ninth month, in the second year of King *D,*
Zec 1: 1 In the second year of *D,*
1: 7 In the second year of *D,*
7: 1 In the fourth year of *D* the king [the word

DARK (46)

Gn 15:17 When the sun had set and it was *d,*
30:32 remove from it every *d* animal among
30:33 a speckled or spotted goat, or a *d* sheep,
Ex 14:20 But the cloud now became *d,*
Dt 28:29 you will grope like a blind man in the *d,*
Jos 2: 5 At *d,* when it was time for the gate
2Sm 22:10 came down, with *d* clouds under his feet.
1Kgs 8:12 "The LORD intends to dwell in the *d* cloud;
18:45 trice, the sky grew *d* with clouds and wind,
2Chr 6: 1 "The LORD intends to dwell in the *d* cloud.
Tb 4:10 and keeps one from going into the *d* abode.
Est A: 7 It was a *d* and gloomy day.
Jb 24:16 in the *d* he breaks into houses.
Ps(s) 11: 2 to shoot in the *d* at the upright of heart.
18:10 came down, with *d* clouds under his feet.
18:12 *d,* misty rain-clouds his wrap.
23: 4 I walk in the *d* valley I fear no evil;
35: 6 Let their way be *d* and slippery,
88: 7 the bottom of the pit, into the *d* abyss.
105:28 He sent the darkness; it grew *d,*
139:12 For you darkness itself is not *d,*
143: 3 he has left me dwelling in the *d,*
Prv 7: 9 dusk of day, at the time of the *d* of night.
Sg 1: 5 I am as *d—* but lovely,
Wis 17: 3 sins were hid under the *d* veil of oblivion
Is 13:10 The sun is *d* when it rises,
29:15 Who work in the *d,*
45:19 hiding nor from some *d* place of the earth,
Jer 13:16 to the LORD, your God, before it grows *d;*
Lam 3: 6 me to dwell in the *d* like those long dead.
Ez 34:12 were scattered when it was cloudy and *d.*
Mi 3: 6 prophets, and the day shall be *d* for them.
Mt 8:12 the kingdom will be driven out into the *d.*
26:20 When it grew *d* he reclined at table
Mk 14:17 As it grew *d* he arrived with the Twelve.
15:42 As it grew *d* (it was Preparation Day,
Lk 12: 3 in the *d* will be heard in the daylight;
Jn 6:17 By this time it was *d,*
12:35 in the *d* does not know where he is going.
12:46 who believes in me from remaining in the *d.*
20: 1 day of the week, while it was still *d,*
Acts 26:26 all, it did not take place in a *d* corner!
2Cor 1: 8 in the *d* about the trouble we had in Asia;
1Thes 5: 4 You are not in the *d,*
2Pt 1:19 as you would on a lamp shining in a *d*
1Jn 2:11 is going, since the *d* has blinded his eyes.

DARK-COLORED (2)

Gn 30:35 on them, as well as the fully *d* sheep;
30:40 the streaked or fully *d* animals of Laban.

DARKEN (5)

Jb 17: 4 You *d* their minds to knowledge;
Ps(s) 83:17 *D* their faces with disgrace,
Jer 4:28 shall mourn, the heavens above shall *d;*
Ez 32: 7 the heavens, and all their stars I will *d;*
32: 8 in the heavens I will *d* on your account,

DARKENED (12)

Jb 3: 9 May the stars of its twilight be *d;*
18: 6 The light is *d* in his tent;
Eccl 12: 2 Before the sun is *d.*
Ez 30:18 be *d* when I break the scepter of Egypt.
Jl 2:10 The sun and the moon are *d,*
4:15 Sun and moon are *d,*
Mt 24:29 stress of that period, 'the sun will be *d,*
Mk 13:24 trials of every sort the sun will be *d,*
Rom 1:21 purpose, and their senseless hearts were *d.*
11:10 their eyes be *d* so that they may not see.
Eph 4:18 their minds empty, their understanding *d.*
Rv 9: 2 the air were *d* by the smoke from the shaft.

DARKENING (1)

Jer 13:16 Before your feet stumble on *d* mountains;

DARKENS (1)

Am 5: 8 darkness into dawn, and *d* day into night;

DARKER (1)

Gn 49:12 His eyes are *d* than wine,

DARKEST (1)

2Pt 2:17 The *d* gloom has been reserved for them.

DARKNESS (160)

Gn 1: 2 wasteland, and *d* covered the abyss,
1: 4 God then separated the light from the *d.*
1: 5 light "day," and the *d* he called "night."
1:18 and to separate the light from the *d.*
15:12 and a deep, terrifying *d* enveloped him.
Ex 10:21 may be such intense *d* that one can feel it."
10:22 and there was dense *d* throughout the land
Dt 5:23 heard the voice from the midst of the *d,*
Jos 24: 7 *d* between your people and the Egyptians,
1Sm 2: 9 ones, but the wicked shall perish in the *d.*
2Sm 22:12 He made *d* the shelter about him,
22:29 O my God, you brighten the *d* about me.
Tb 5:10 see God's sunlight, but must remain in *d,*
14:10 but Nadab went into the everlasting *d,*
2Mc 3:27 fell to the ground, enveloped in great *d.*
Jb 3: 4 May that day be *d:*
3: 5 May *d* and gloom claim it,
5:14 They meet with *d* in the daytime,
10:21 not return, to the land of *d* and of gloom,
10:22 disordered land where *d* is the only light.
12:22 The recesses of the *d* he discloses,
12:25 till they grope in the *d* without light;
15:22 He despairs of escaping the *d,*
15:24 By day the *d* fills him with dread;
16:16 with weeping and there is *d* over my eyes,
17:12 there is *d* they talk of approaching light.
17:13 dwelling, if I spread my couch in the *d,*
18:18 He is driven from light into *d,*
19: 8 he has veiled my path in *d;*
20:26 Complete *d* is in store for him;
22:11 a sudden terror causes you dismay, Or *d,*
22:13 Can he judge through the thick *d?*
23:17 Yes, would that I had vanished in *d,*
24:17 the light, for daylight they regard as *d.*
26:10 of the deep as the boundary of light and *d.*
28: 3 He has set a boundary for the *d;*
29: 3 head, and by his light I walked through *d;*
30:26 when I expected light, then came *d.*
34:22 *d* so dense that evildoers can hide in it.
37:19 we cannot, for the *d,*
38: 9 garment and thick *d* its swaddling bands?
38:17 to you, or have you seen the gates of *d?*
38:19 of light, and where is the abode of *d,*
Ps(s) 18:12 And he made *d* the cloak about him;
18:29 O my God, you brighten the *d* about me;
44:20 place of misery and covered us over with *d.*
82: 5 they go about in *d;*
88:13 Are your wonders made known in the *d,*
88:19 my only friend is *d.*
91: 6 in *d* nor the devastating plague at noon.
97: 2 Clouds and *d* are round about him,
104:20 You bring *d,* and it is night;
105:28 He sent the *d;* it grew dark,
107:10 They dwelt in *d* and gloom,
107:14 *d* and gloom and broke their bonds asunder.
112: 4 He dawns through the *d,*
139:11 If I say, "Surely the *d* shall hide me,
139:12 For you *d* itself is not dark,
139:12 *D* and light are the same.]
Prv 2:13 straight paths to walk in the way of *d,*
4:19 The way of the wicked is like *d;*

20:20 his lamp will go out at the coming of *d*.
Eccl 2:13 as much as light has the advantage over *d*.
2:14 eyes in his head, but the fool walks in *d*.
6: 4 *d* and its name is enveloped in *d*;
11: 8 remember that the days of *d* will be many.
Wis 17: 2 enslave the holy nation, shackled with *d*,
17:18 for all were bound by the one bond of *d*.
17:21 of the *d* that next should come upon them;
17:21 to themselves more burdensome than the *d*.
18: 4 be deprived of light and imprisoned by *d*,
19:17 When, surrounded by yawning *d*,
Sir 11:16 Error and *d* were formed with sinners from
23:18 *D* surrounds me, walls hide me;
Is 5:20 and good evil, who change *d* into light,
5:20 darkness into light, and light into *d*,
8:21 there shall be strict *d* without any dawn
8:22 but there shall be distress and *d*
8:23 Anguish has taken wing, dispelled is *d*:
9: 1 who walked in *d* have seen a great light;
29:18 And out of gloom and *d*,
42: 7 and from the dungeon, those who live in *d*.
42:16 I will turn *d* into light before them,
45: 3 I will give you treasures out of the *d*,
45: 7 I form the light, and create the *d*,
47: 5 Go into *d* and sit in silence,
49: 9 To those in *d*: Show yourselves.
50:10 voice, And walks in *d* without any light,
58:10 Then light shall rise for you in the *d*,
59: 9 We look for light, and lo, *d*;
59:10 stumble at midday as at dusk, in Stygian *d*,
60: 2 See, *d* covers the earth,
Jer 2: 6 gullies, Through a land of drought and *d*,
2:31 I been a desert to Israel, a land of *d*?
13:16 Before the light you look for turns to *d*,
23:12 In the *d* they shall lose their footing,
Lam 3: 2 whom he has led and forced to walk in *d*,
Bar 6:70 of bird, or like a corpse hurled into *d*,
Ez 12: 6 shoulder the burden and set out in the *d*;
12: 7 while they looked on, set out in the *d*,
12:12 shoulder his burden and set out in *d*,
32: 8 And I will spread *d* over your land,
Dn 2:22 hidden things and knows what is in the *d*,
3:72 Light and *d*, bless the Lord;
Jl 2: 2 Yes, it is near, a day of *d* and of gloom,
3: 4 The sun will be turned to *d*,
Am 4:13 Who made the dawn and the *d*,
5: 8 Pleiades and Orion, who turns *d* into dawn,
5:18 *D* and not light!
5:20 not the day of the LORD be *d* and not light,
8: 9 cover the earth with *d* in broad daylight.
Mi 3: 6 you shall have night, not vision *d*,
7: 8 though I sit in *d*, the LORD is my light.
Na 1: 8 and his enemies he pursues with *d*.
Zep 1:15 and desolation, a day of *d* and gloom,
Mt 4:16 people living in *d* has seen a great light.
6:23 your eyes are bad, your body will be in *d*.
6:23 light is darkness, how deep will the *d* be!
10:27 What I tell you in *d*, speak in the light.
25:30 this worthless servant into the *d* outside,
27:45 *d* over the whole land until midafternoon.
Mk 15:33 *d* fell on the whole countryside and lasted
Lk 1:79 who sit in *d* and in the shadow of death,
11:34 your eyesight is bad, your body is in *d*.
11:35 Take care, then, that your light is not *d*.
11:36 body is lighted up and not partly in *d*,
22:53 But this is your hour—the triumph of *d*!"
23:44 and *d* came over the whole land until
Jn 1: 5 in darkness, a *d* that did not overcome it.
3:19 but men loved *d* rather than light because
8:12 No follower of mine shall ever walk in *d*;
12:35 you still have it or *d* will come over you.
Acts 2:20 The sun shall be turned to *d* and the moon
13:11 At once a misty *d* came over him,
26:18 to turn them from *d* to light and from the
Rom 2:19 guide the blind and enlighten those in *d*,
13:12 deeds of *d* and put on the armor of light.
1Cor 4: 5 in *d* and manifest the intentions of hearts.
2Cor 4: 6 God, who said, "Let light shine out of *d*,"
6:14 or what fellowship can light have with *d*?
Eph 5: 8 There was a time when you were *d*,
5:11 Take no part in vain deeds done in *d*;
6:12 and powers, the rulers of this world of *d*,
Col 1:13 He rescued us from the power of *d* and
1Thes 5: 5 We belong neither to *d* nor to night;
Heb 12:18 nor gloomy *d* and storm and trumpet blast,
1Pt 2: 9 called you from *d* into his marvelous light.
2Pt 2: 4 consigned them to pits of *d*,
1Jn 1: 5 that God is light; in him there is no *d*.
1: 6 with him," while continuing to walk in *d*,
2: 8 for the *d* is over and the real light
2: 9 brother all the while, is in *d* even now.
2:11 But the man who hates his brother is in *d*.
Jude 1: 6 *d* against the judgment of the great day.
1:13 thick gloom of *d* has been reserved forever.
Rv 8:12 were hit hard enough to be plunged into *d*.
16:10 Its kingdom was plunged into *d*;

DARKON (2)

Ezr 2:56 sons of Peruda, sons of Jaalah, sons of *D*,
Neh 7:58 sons of Perida, sons of Jaala, sons of *D*,

DARLING (5)

Dt 32:15 ate his fill, the *d* grew fat and frisky;
33: 5 his domain, and he became king of his *d*.
33:26 "There is no god like the God of the *d*,
Prv 4: 3 child, frail, yet the *d* of my mother,
Is 44: 2 my servant, the *d* whom I have chosen.

DARLINGS (1)

Hos 9:11 children, I would slay the *d* of their womb.

DART (4)

Gn 41:40 and all my people shall *d* at your command.
Jb 20:25 The *d* shall come out of his back;
41:18 nor will the spear, nor the *d*,
Wis 3: 7 shall *d* about as sparks through stubble;

DARTS (4)

Ps(s) 7:14 against them, and use fiery *d* for arrows.
Sir 43: 4 By its fiery *d* the land is consumed;
Is 50:11 kindle flames and carry about you fiery *d*;
Eph 6:16 you extinguish the fiery *d* of the evil one.

DASH (6)

Jgs 20:37 men in ambush made a sudden *d* into Gibeah,
2Kgs 8:12 you will *d* their little children to pieces,
Jdt 16: 4 to the sword, *D* my babes to the ground,
Ps(s) 91:12 up, lest you *d* your foot against a stone.
Jer 13:14 I will *d* them against each other,
Na 2: 5 the chariots *d* madly through the streets

DASHED (7)

Jgs 9:44 Abimelech and the company with him *d* in
1Mc 6:45 He *d* up to it in the middle of the phalanx,
Jb 16:12 seized me by the neck and *d* me to pieces.
Is 13:16 shall be *d* to pieces in their sight;
Hos 14: 1 their little ones shall be *d* to pieces,
Na 3:10 *d* to pieces at the corner of every street;
Acts 27:29 we should be *d* against some rocky coast,

DASHING (4)

Jgs 5:22 hoofs of the horses pounded, with the *d*,
5:22 pounded, with the dashing, *d* of his steeds.
2Mc 9: 7 As a result he hurtled from the *d* chariot,
Jer 8: 6 his course, like a steed *d* into battle.

DATE (5)

Ex 12:41 LORD left the land of Egypt on this very *d*.
Neh 2: 6 I set a *d* that was acceptable to him,
Ez 24: 2 Son of man, write down this *d* today,
Jl 1:12 The pomegranate, the *d* palm also,
Mt 2:16 the *d* he had learned from the astrologers.

DATED (2)

1Mc 14:43 made in the country shall be *d* by his name.
2Mc 1:10 *D* in the year one hundred and eighty-eight.

DATES (1)

Sir 43: 7 which we know the feast days and fixed *d*,

DATHAN (11)

Nm 16: 1 of Kohath, son of Levi, [and *D* and Abiram,
16:12 Moses summoned *D* and Abiram,
16:24 the Dwelling" [of Korah, *D* and Abiram].
16:25 of Israel, arose and went to *D* and Abiram.
16:27 When *D* and Abiram had come out and were
16:35 the Dwelling [of Korah, *D* and Abiram].
26: 9 the descendants of Eliab were *D* and Abiram
26: 9 the same *D* and Abiram,
Dt 11: 6 what he did to the Reubenites *D* and Abiram,
Ps(s) 106:17 The earth opened and swallowed up *D*,
Sir 45:18 the desert, The followers of *D* and Abiram,

DATHEMA (2)

1Mc 5: 9 these then fled to the stronghold of *D*.
5:29 they marched toward the stronghold of *D*.

DAUBED (3)

Ex 2: 3 basket, *d* it with bitumen and pitch,
Wis 13:14 When he had *d* it with red and crimsoned
13:14 red stain, and *d* over every blemish in it,

DAUGHTER (324)

Gn 11:29 of Nahor's wife was Milcah, *d* of Haran,
20:12 truth my sister, but only my father's *d*,
24:23 "Whose *d* are you?
24:24 "I am the *d* of Bethuel the son of Milcah,
24:47 When I asked her, 'Whose *d* are you?'
24:47 she answered, 'The *d* of Bethuel,
24:48 the *d* of my master's kinsman for his son.
25:20 the *d* of Bethuel the Aramean of
26:34 he married Judith, *d* of Beeri the Hittite,
26:34 and Basemath, *d* of Elon the Hivite.
28: 9 the *d* of Abraham's son Ishmael and sister
29: 6 here comes his *d* Rachel with his flock."
29:10 Jacob saw Rachel, the *d* of his uncle Laban,
29:18 you seven years for your younger *d* Rachel."
29:23 took his *d* Leah and brought her to Jacob,
29:24 Zilpah to his *d* Leah as her maidservant.)
29:26 marry off a younger *d* before an older one.
29:28 Laban gave him his *d* Rachel in marriage.
29:29 Bilhah to his *d* Rachel as her maidservant.)
30:21 Finally, she gave birth to a *d*,
34: 1 Dinah, the *d* whom Leah had borne to Jacob,
34: 3 strongly attracted to Dinah, *d* of Jacob,
34: 5 heard that Shechem had defiled his *d* Dinah;
34: 8 son Shechem has his heart set on your *d*.
34:17 we will take our *d* and go away."
34:19 since he was deeply in love with Jacob's *d*.
36: 2 Adah, *d* of Elon the Hittite;
36: 3 *d* of Ishmael and sister of Nebaioth.
36:18 clans of Esau's wife Oholibamah, *d* of Anah.
36:25 were Dishon and Oholibamah, *d* of Anah.
36:39 she was the *d* of Matred,
38: 2 he met the *d* of a Canaanite named Shua,
38:12 passed, and Judah's wife, the *d* of Shua,
41:45 in marriage Asenath, the *d* of Potiphera,
41:50 borne to him by Asenath, *d* of Potiphera,
46:15 in Paddan-aram, along with his *d* Dinah
46:18 Zilpah, whom Laban had given to his *d* Leah;
46:20 and Ephraim, whom Asenath, *d* of Potiphera,
46:25 whom Laban had given to his *d* Rachel;
Ex 2: 5 *d* came down to the river to bathe,
2: 7 Then his sister asked Pharaoh's *d*,
2: 9 Pharaoh's *d* said to her,
2:10 grew, she brought him to Pharaoh's *d*,
2:21 man gave him his *d* Zipporah in marriage.
6:23 Aaron married Amminadab's *d*,
20:10 done then either by you, or your son or *d*,
21: 7 "When a man sells his *d* as a slave,
21: 9 for his son, he shall treat her like a *d*.
Lv 12: 6 for a son or for a *d* are fulfilled,
18: 9 your father's *d* or your mother's daughter,
18: 9 your father's daughter or your mother's *d*,
18:10 son's *d* or with your daughter's daughter,
18:11 the *d* whom your father's wife bore to him,
18:17 with a woman and also with her *d*,
18:17 her son's daughter or her daughter's *d*;
19:29 your *d* by making a prostitute of her;
21: 2 his mother or father, his son or *d*,
21: 9 "A priest's *d* who loses her honor by
22:12 A priest's *d* who is married to a layman
22:13 if a priest's *d* is widowed or divorced and,
24:10 an Israelite mother (Shelomith, *d* of Dibri,
Nm 25:15 slain Midianite woman was Cozbi, *d* of Zur,
25:18 Cozbi, the *d* of a Midianite prince,
26:46 The name of Asher's *d* was Serah.
27: 8 shall let his heritage pass on to his *d*;
27: 9 if he has no *d*,
30:17 father and his *d* while she is still a maiden
36: 8 every *d* who inherits property in any of
Dt 5:14 then, whether by you, or your son or *d*,
12:18 he chooses, along with your son and *d*,
13: 7 your own full brother, or your son or *d*,
16:11 his presence together with your son and *d*,
16:14 your feast, together with your son and *d*,
18:10 who immolates his son or *d* in the fire,
22:16 'I gave my *d* to this man in marriage,
22:17 I did not find your *d* a virgin.
28:56 her son and *d* the afterbirth that issues
Jos 15:16 "I will give my *d* Achsah in marriage to
15:17 so Caleb gave him his *d* Achsah in marriage.
Jgs 1:12 "I will give my *d* Achsah in marriage to
1:13 so Caleb gave him his *d* Achsah in marriage.
11:34 in Mizpah, it was his *d* who came forth,
11:34 he had neither son nor *d* besides her.
11:35 he rent his garments and said, "Alas, *d*,
11:40 to mourn the *d* of Jephthah the Gileadite
19:24 me bring out my maiden *d* or his concubine.
21: 1 his *d* in marriage to anyone from Benjamin.
Ru 2: 2 Naomi said to her, "Go, my *d*,"
2: 8 Boaz said to Ruth, "Listen, my *d*!
3: 1 mother-in-law, Naomi said to her, "My *d*,
3:10 He said, "May the LORD bless you, my *d*!
3:11 So be assured, *d*. I will do for you
3:16 who asked, "How have you fared my *d*?"
3:18 Naomi then said, "Wait here, my *d*,
1Sm 14:50 was named Ahinoam, was the *d* of Ahimaaz.
17:25 give him great wealth, and his *d* as well,
18:17 said to David, "There is my older *d*
18:19 for Saul's *d* Merob to be given to David,
18:20 Now Saul's *d* Michal loved David,
18:27 So Saul gave him his *d* Michal in marriage.
18:28 besides, his own *d* Michal loved David.
25:43 gave David's wife Michal, Saul's own *d*,
2Sm 3: 3 Absalom, son of Maacah the *d* of Talmai,
3: 7 had had a concubine, Rizpah, the *d* of Aiah.
3:13 me unless you bring back Michal, Saul's *d*,
6:16 Saul's *d* Michal looked down through the
6:20 *d* Michal came out to meet him and said,
6:23 And so Saul's *d* Michal was childless to
11: 3 was told, "She is Bathsheba, *d* of Eliam,
12: 3 She was like a *d* to him.
14:27 sons born to him, besides a *d* named Tamar,
17:25 *d* of Jesse and sister of Joab's mother
21: 8 that Aiah's *d* Rizpah had borne to Saul,
21: 8 *d* Merob that she had borne to Adriel,
21:10 Then Rizpah, Aiah's *d*,
21:11 was informed of what Rizpah, Aiah's *d*,
1Kgs 3: 1 The *d* of Pharaoh, whom he married

DAUGHTER (cont.)

4:11 who was married to Solomon's *d* Taphath,
4:15 married to Basemath, another *d* of Solomon,
7: 8 this tribunal was built for Pharaoh's *d*,
9:16 the city, had given it as dowry to his *d*,
9:24 As soon as Pharaoh's *d* went up from the
11: 1 women besides the *d* of Pharaoh (Moabites,
15: 2 mother's name was Maacah, *d* of Abishalom.
15:10 name was Maacah, *d* of Abishalom.
16:31 He even married Jezebel, *d* of Ethbaal,
22:42 His mother's name was Azubah, *d* of Shilhi.
2Kgs 8:26 she was *d* of Omri,
9:34 after all, she was a king's *d*."
11: 2 *d* of King Jehoram and sister of Ahaziah,
14: 9 'Give your *d* to my son in marriage,'
15:33 His mother's name was Jerusha, *d* of Zadok.
18: 2 His mother's name was Abi, *d* of Zechariah.
19:21 laughs you to scorn, the virgin *d* Zion!
19:21 Behind you she wags her head, *d* Jerusalem.
21:19 was Meshullemeth, *d* of Haruz of Jotbah.
22: 1 name was Jedidah, *d* of Adaiah of Bozkath.
23:31 whose name was Hamutal, *d* of Jeremiah,
23:36 mother's name was Zebidah, *d* of Pedaiah,
24: 8 was Nehushta, *d* of Elnathan of Jerusalem.
24:18 name was Hamutal, *d* of Jeremiah of Libnah.
1Chr 1:50 She was the *d* of Matred,
1:50 of Matred, who was the *d* of Mezahab.
2:18 son of Hezron, became the father of a *d*,
2:21 Hezron had relations with the *d* of Machir,
2:35 gave his *d* in marriage to his slave Jarha,
2:49 Achsah was Caleb's *d*.
3: 2 son of Maacah, who was the *d* of Talmai,
3: 5 four by Bathsheba, the *d* of Ammiel;
4:18 were the sons of Bithiah, the *d* of Pharaoh,
7:24 He had a *d*, Sheerah, who built lower
15:29 the City of David, Michal, *d* of Saul,
2Chr 8:11 Solomon brought the *d* of Pharaoh up from
11:18 to himself as wife Mahalath, *d* of Jerimoth,
11:18 son of David and of Abihail, *d* of Eliab,
11:20 After her, he married Maacah, *d* of Absalom,
11:21 Rehoboam loved Maacah, *d* of Absalom,
13: 2 was named Michaiah, *d* of Uriel of Gibeah.
20:31 His mother was named Azubah, *d* of Shilhi.
22: 2 His mother was named Athaliah, *d* of Omri.
22:11 Jehosheba, who was the *d* of King Jehoram,
25:18 'Give your *d* to my son for his wife.'
27: 1 His mother was named Jerusa, *d* of Zadok.
29: 1 His mother was named Abia, *d* of Zechariah.
Neh 6:18 Jehohanan had married the *d* of Meshullam,
Tb 3: 7 *d* Sarah also had to listen to abuse,
3: 9 May we never see a son or *d* of yours!"
3:10 'You had only one beloved *d*,
3:15 "I am my father's only *d*,
3:17 Raguel's *d* Sarah to Tobit's son Tobiah,
3:17 *d* Sarah came downstairs from her room.
6:11 He has a *d* named Sarah,
6:13 before all other men, to marry his *d*.
7: 8 and even their *d* Sarah began to weep.
7:10 more entitled to marry my *d* Sarah than you,
7:12 Then Raguel called his *d* Sarah,
7:17 "Be brave, my *d*.
7:17 Courage, my *d*."
10: 7 which Raguel had sworn to hold for his *d*,
10:12 Then he kissed his *d* Sarah and said to her:
10:12 "My *d*, honor your father-in-law
10:12 Go in peace, my *d*;
10:13 of you and of my *d* Sarah before I die.
10:13 the Lord, I entrust my *d* to your care.
11:15 and that he had married Raguel's *d* Sarah,
11:17 "Welcome, my *d*!
11:17 be your God for bringing you to us, *d*!
11:17 is my son Tobiah, and blessed are you, *d*!
11:17 Come in *d*!"
Jdt 8: 1 Now in those days Judith, *d* of Merari,
10:12 "I am a *d* of the Hebrews,
13:18 "Blessed are you, *d*,
16: 6 But Judith, the *d* of Merari,
Est 2: 7 Mordecai had taken her as his own *d*.
2:15 *d* of Abihail and adopted daughter of his
9:29 *d* of Abihail and of Mordecai the Jew,
1Mc 9:37 *d* of one of the great princes of Canaan,
10:54 Give me your *d* for my wife;
10:57 So Ptolemy with his *d* Cleopatra set out
10:58 gave him his *d* Cleopatra in marriage.
11: 9 give you my *d* whom Alexander has married,
11:10 I regret that I gave him my *d*,
11:12 his *d* away and giving her to Demetrius,
Ps(s) 9:15 praises and, in the gates of the *d* of Zion,
45:11 Hear, O *d*, and see; turn your ear,
45:14 All glorious is the king's *d* as she enters;
73:28 your works in the gates of the *d* of Zion.
137: 8 O *d* of Babylon, you destroyer,
Sg 7: 2 are your feet in sandals, O prince's *d*!
Sir 7:25 your *d* in marriage ends a great task;
22: 3 if it be a *d* she brings him to poverty.
22: 4 *d* becomes a treasure to her husband,
42: 9 A *d* is a treasure that keeps her father
42:11 Keep a close watch on your *d*,
42:14 and a frightened *d* than any disgrace.
Is 1: 8 *d* Zion is left like a hut in a vineyard,
10:30 Cry and shriek, O *d* of Gallim!
10:32 will shake his fist at the mount of *d* Zion,
15: 2 Up goes *d* Dibon to the high places to weep;
16: 1 across the desert, to the mount of *d* Zion.
22: 4 me for the ruin of the *d* of my people.
23:12 you who are now oppressed, virgin *d* Sidon.
37:22 laughs you to scorn, the virgin *d* Zion;
37:22 Behind you she wags her head, *d* Jerusalem.
47: 1 down, sit in the dust, O virgin *d* Babylon;
47: 1 ground, dethroned, O *d* of the Chaldeans.
47: 5 and sit in silence, O *d* of the Chaldeans,
52: 2 the bonds from your neck, O captive *d* Zion!
62:11 Say to *d* Zion, your savior comes!
Jer 4:11 a wind comes toward the *d* of my people."
4:31 The cry of *d* Zion gasping,
6: 2 O lovely and delicate *d* Zion,
6:23 his place, for battle against you, *d* Zion.
6:26 O *d* of my people,
8:11 nought, the injury to the *d* of my people:
8:19 the cry of the *d* of my people,
8:21 broken by the ruin of the *d* of my people.
8:22 flesh over the wound of the *d* of my people?
8:23 night over the slain of the *d* of my people!
14:17 which overwhelms the virgin *d* of my people,
31:22 will you continue to stray, rebellious *d*?
46:11 to Gilead, and take balm, O virgin *d* Egypt!
46:19 your baggage for exile, capital of *d* Egypt;
46:24 Disgraced is *d* Egypt,
49: 2 her *d* cities shall be destroyed by fire.
49: 4 your ebbing strength, rebellious *d*?
50:42 place for battle against you, *d* Babylon.
51:33 *D* Babylon is like a threshing floor at the
52: 1 name was Hamutal, *d* of Jeremiah of Libnah.
Lam 1: 6 Gone from *d* Zion is all her glory:
1:15 trodden in the wine press virgin *d* Judah.
2: 1 the Lord in his wrath has detested *d* Zion!
2: 2 in his anger the fortresses of *d* Judah;
2: 4 *d* Zion he poured out his wrath like fire.
2: 5 For *d* Judah he has multiplied moaning and
2: 8 marked for destruction the wall of *d* Zion:
2:10 in silence sit the old men of *d* Zion
2:11 of the downfall of the *d* of my people,
2:13 can I liken or compare you, O *d* Jerusalem?
2:13 I show you for your comfort, virgin *d* Zion?
2:15 hiss and wag their heads over *d* Jerusalem:
2:18 Cry out to the LORD; moan, O *d* Zion!
3:48 over the downfall of the *d* of my people.
4: 3 The *d* of my people has become as cruel as
4: 6 The punishment of the *d* of my people is
4:10 food in the downfall of the *d* of my people.
4:21 Though you rejoice and are glad, O *d* Edom,
4:22 Your chastisement is completed, O *d* Zion,
4:22 But your wickedness, O *d* Edom,
Bar 2: 3 eat the flesh of his son or of his *d*.
Ez 14:20 that they could save neither son nor *d*;
16:44 will say of you, 'Like mother, like *d*.'
16:45 you are the true *d* of the mother who
44:25 unless it be their father, mother, son, *d*,
Dn 11: 6 the *d* of the king of the south shall come
11:17 give him a *d* in marriage in order to destroy
13: 2 woman, Susanna, the *d* of Hilkiah;
13: 3 their *d* according to the law of Moses.
13:29 "Send for Susanna, the *d* of Hilkiah,
13:57 but a *d* of Judah did not tolerate your
13:63 his wife praised God for their *d* Susanna,
Hos 1: 3 he went and took Gomer, the *d* of Diblaim;
1: 6 When she conceived again and bore a *d*,
Mi 1:13 Lachish, the beginning of sin for *d* Zion,
4: 8 And you, O Magdal-eder, hillock of *d* Zion!
4: 8 be restored, the kingdom of *d* Jerusalem.
4:10 Writhe in pain, grow faint, O *d* Zion,
4:13 Arise and thresh, O *d* Zion;
7: 6 the *d* rises up against her mother,
Zep 3:14 Shout for joy, O *d* Zion!
3:14 exult with all your heart, O *d* Jerusalem!
Zec 2:11 you who dwell in *d* Babylon.
2:14 Sing and rejoice, O *d* Zion!
9: 9 Rejoice heartily, O *d* Zion,
9: 9 Zion, shout for joy, O *d* Jerusalem!
Mt 9:18 "My *d* has just died.
9:22 around and saw her and said, "Courage, *d*!
10:35 odds with his father, a *d* with her mother,
10:37 Whoever loves father or mother, son or *d*,
14: 6 Then on Herod's birthday Herodias' *d*
15:22 My *d* is terribly troubled by a demon."
15:28 That very moment her *d* got better.
21: 5 "Tell the *d* of Zion,
Mk 5:23 "My little *d* is critically ill.
5:34 He said to her, *D*, it is your faith
5:35 house arrived saying, "Your *d* is dead.
6:22 Herodias' own *d* came in at one point and
7:25 woman, whose small *d* had an unclean spirit,
7:26 to beg him to expel the demon from her *d*.
7:29 The demon has already left your *d*."
Lk 1:28 "Rejoice, O highly favored *d*!
2:36 name, *d* of Phanuel of the tribe of Asher.
8:42 he come to his home because his only *d*,
8:48 Jesus said to her, *D*,
8:49 with the announcement, "Your *d* is dead;
12:53 against *d* and daughter against mother,
12:53 against daughter and *d* against mother,
13:16 Should not this *d* of Abraham here who has
Jn 12:15 "Fear not, O *d* of Zion!
Acts 7:21 and Pharaoh's *d* adopted him and brought
Heb 11:24 to be known as the son of Pharaoh's *d*;

DAUGHTER-IN-LAW (17)

Gn 11:31 Lot, son of Haran, and his *d* Sarai,
38:11 Thereupon Judah said to his *d* Tamar,
38:16 and not realizing that she was his *d*,
38:24 Judah was told that his *d* Tamar had played
Lv 18:15 shall not have intercourse with your *d*;
20:12 If a man lies with his *d*,
Ru 1:22 that Naomi returned with the Moabite *d*,
2:20 to the dead," Naomi exclaimed to her *d*;
4:15 age, for his mother is the *d* who loves you.
1Sm 4:19 His *d*, the wife of Phinehas,
1Chr 2: 4 Judah's *d* Tamar bore him Perez and Zerah,
Tb 11:16 out to the gate of Nineveh to meet his *d*.
12:14 God commissioned me to heal you and your *d*,
Mi 7: 6 mother, The *d* against her mother-in-law,
Mt 10:35 her mother, a *d* with her mother-in-law:
Lk 12:53 against mother, mother-in-law against *d*,
12:53 daughter-in-law, *d* against mother-in-law."

DAUGHTERS (222)

Gn 5: 4 birth of Seth, and he had other sons and *d*.
5: 7 of Enosh, and he had other sons and *d*.
5:10 of Kenan, and he had other sons and *d*.
5:13 of Mahalalel, and he had other sons and *d*.
5:16 of Jared, and he had other sons and *d*.
5:19 of Enoch, and he had other sons and *d*.
5:22 of Methuselah, and he had other sons and *d*.
5:26 of Lamech, and he had other sons and *d*.
5:30 birth of Noah, and he had other sons and *d*.
6: 1 multiply on earth and *d* were born to them,
6: 2 saw how beautiful the *d* of man were
6: 4 heaven had intercourse with the *d* of man,
11:11 of Arpachshad, and he had other sons and *d*.
11:13 of Shelah, and he had other sons and *d*.
11:15 birth of Eber, and he had other sons and *d*.
11:17 of Peleg, and he had other sons and *d*.
11:19 birth of Reu, and he had other sons and *d*.
11:21 of Serug, and he had other sons and *d*.
11:23 of Nahor, and he had other sons and *d*.
11:25 of Terah, and he had other sons and *d*.
19: 8 *d* who have never had intercourse with men.
19:12 *d* and all who belong to you in the city
19:14 who had contracted marriage with his *d*.
19:15 you your wife and your two *d* who are here,
19:16 *d* and led them to safety outside the city.
19:30 he and his two *d* went up from Zoar and
19:30 where he lived with his two *d* in a cave.
19:36 of Lot's *d* became pregnant by their father.
24: 3 the *d* of the Canaanites among whom I live,
24:13 *d* of the townsmen are coming out to draw
24:37 *d* of the Canaanites in whose land I live;
28: 2 from among the *d* of your uncle Laban.
29:16 Now Laban had two *d*;
31:26 me and carrying off my *d* like war captives?
31:28 a parting kiss to my *d* and grandchildren!
31:31 might take your *d* away from me by force.
31:41 your two *d* and six years for your flock,
31:43 But since these women are my *d*,
31:50 If you mistreat my *d*,
31:50 or take other wives besides my *d*,
32: 1 kissed his grandchildren and his *d* good-bye;
34: 9 give your *d* to us,
34: 9 to us, and take our *d* for yourselves.
34:16 give you our *d* and take yours in marriage;
34:21 We can marry their *d* and give our
34:21 and give our *d* to them in marriage.
36: 6 Esau took his wives, his sons, his *d*,
37:35 Though his sons and *d* tried to console him,
46: 7 grandsons, his *d* and his granddaughters
Ex 2:16 seven *d* of a priest of Midian came to draw
2:20 "Where is the man, he asked his *d*.
3:22 and for clothing to put on your sons and *d*.
6:25 son, Eleazar, married one of Putiel's *d*,
10: 9 "our sons and *d* as well as our flocks and
21: 4 him a wife and she bears him sons or *d*,
32: 2 "Have your wives and sons and *d* take off
34:16 you take their *d* as wives for your sons;
34:16 when their *d* render their wanton worship
Lv 10:14 With your sons and *d* you shall also eat
8:10 son's daughter or with your *d* daughter,
18:17 with her son's daughter or her *d* daughter;
26:29 to eat the flesh of your own sons and *d*.
Nm 18:11 assigned it to you and to your sons and *d*.
18:19 assigned to you and to your sons and *d*
21:29 become fugitives and his *d* be taken captive
26:33 sons, but only *d* whose names were Mahlah,
27: 1 son of Joseph, and *d* named Mahlah,
27: 7 him, "The plea of Zelophehad's *d* is just;
36: 2 of our kinsman Zelophehad to his *d*.
36: 6 with regard to the *d* of Zelophehad:
36:10 The *d* of Zelophehad obeyed the command
36:11 Hoglah, Milcah and Noah, Zelophehad's *d*,
Dt 7: 3 neither giving your *d* to their sons nor
7: 3 sons nor taking their *d* for your sons.
12:12 the LORD, your God, with your sons and *d*,
12:31 burning their sons and *d* to their gods.
22:17 But here is the evidence of my *d* virginity!'
28:32 Your sons and *d* will be given to a foreign
28:41 Though you beget sons and *d*,
28:53 flesh of your own sons and *d* whom the LORD,
32:19 loathing and anger toward his sons and *d*.
Jos 7:24 the bar of gold, and with his sons and *d*,

17: 3 of Manasseh, had had no sons, but only d,
Jgs 3: 6 gave their own d to their sons in marriage,
3: 6 In fact, they took their d in marriage,
12: 9 had thirty d married outside the family,
21: 7 not to give them any of our d in marriage?"
21:18 cannot give them any of our d in marriage,
Ru 1:11 "Go back, my d!" said Naomi
1:12 Go back, my d!
1:13 No, my d! my lot is too bitter for you.
1Sm 1: 4 wife Peninnah and to all her sons and d,
2:21 gave birth to three more sons and two d,
8:13 He will use your d as ointment-makers,
14:49 his two d were named,
30: 3 and their wives, sons and d taken captive.
30: 6 they over the fate of their sons and d.
30:19 small or great, booty or sons or d,
2Sm 1:20 rejoice, lest the d of the strangers exult!
5:13 sons and d were born to him in Jerusalem.
19: 6 your life and your sons' and d' lives,
2Kgs 17:17 They immolated their sons and d by fire,
23:10 of sons or d by fire in honor of Molech.
1Chr 2:34 Sheshan, who had no sons, only d,
4:27 Shimei had sixteen sons and six d.
7:15 but to Zelophehad only d were born.
14: 3 and became the father of more sons and d.
23:22 Eleazar died leaving no sons, only d;
25: 5 God gave Heman fourteen sons and three d.
2Chr 11:21 he fathered twenty-eight sons and sixty d.
13:21 and fathered twenty-two sons and sixteen d.
21: 6 Ahab, because one of Ahab's d was his wife.
24: 3 and he became the father of sons and d.
28: 8 of their brethren's wives, sons and d;
29: 9 our d and our wives have been taken
31:18 for their little ones, wives, sons and d—
Ezr 2:61 married one of the d of Barzillai
9: 2 d as wives for themselves and their sons,
9:12 give your d to their sons in marriage,
9:12 and do not take their d for your sons.
Neh 3:12 of Jerusalem, by himself and his d.
4: 8 fight for your brethren, your sons and d,
5: 2 "We are forced to pawn our sons and d in
5: 5 had to reduce our sons and d to slavery,
5: 5 violence has been done to some of our d!
7:63 married one of the d of Barzillai
10:29 with their wives, their sons, their d,
10:31 not marry our d to the peoples of the land,
10:31 that we will not take their d for our sons.
13:25 "You shall not marry your d to their sons
13:25 of their d for your sons or for yourselves!
Tb 4:13 your kinsmen the sons and d of your people,
8:20 shall bring joy to my d sorrowing spirit.
Jdt 9: 4 over to plunder, and their d to captivity;
Jb 1: 2 Seven sons and three d were born to him;
1:13 while his sons and his d were eating and
1:18 "Your sons and d were eating and drinking
42:13 And he had seven sons and three d,
42:15 women were as beautiful as the d of Job;
Ps(s) 45:10 The d of kings come to meet you;
106:37 their sons and their d to demons,
106:38 the blood of their sons and their d,
144:12 Our d like wrought columns such as stand
Prv 30:15 The two d of the leech are,
Eccl 12: 4 bird, but all the d of song are suppressed;
Sg 1: 5 but lovely, O d of Jerusalem
2: 7 I adjure you, d of Jerusalem,
3: 5 I adjure you, d of Jerusalem,
3:11 D of Jerusalem, come forth and look
5: 8 I adjure you, d of Jerusalem,
5:16 and such my friend, O d of Jerusalem.
6: 9 The d saw her and declared her fortunate,
8: 4 I adjure you, d of Jerusalem,
Wis 9: 7 people and magistrate for your sons and d.
Sir 7:24 If you have d, keep them chaste,
Is 3:16 Because the d of Zion are haughty,
3:17 cover the scalps of Zion's d with scabs,
4: 4 washes away the filth of the d of Zion,
16: 2 the d of Moab at the fords of the Arnon.
43: 6 afar, and my d from the ends of the earth:
49:22 your d shall be carried on their shoulders.
56: 5 and a name Better than sons and d;
60: 4 and your d in the arms of their nurses.
Jer 3:24 and their cattle, their sons and their d.
5:17 your bread, devour your sons and your d,
7:31 immolate in fire their sons and their d,
9:19 Teach your d this dirge,
11:22 their sons and d shall die by famine.
14:16 them, their wives, their sons, or their d,
16: 2 you shall not have sons or d in this place,
16: 3 sons and d who will be born in this place,
19: 9 them eat the flesh of their sons and d;
29: 6 Take wives and beget sons and d;
29: 6 that they bear sons and d
29: 6 for your sons and give your d husbands.
32:35 and immolated their sons and d to Molech,
35: 8 we, nor our wives, nor our sons, nor our d.
48:46 taken into exile, your d into captivity.
49: 3 ravager approaches, shriek, d of Rabbah!
Lam 3:51 soul at the sight of all the d of my city.
Bar 4:10 God has brought upon my sons and d.
4:14 note of the captivity of my sons and d,
4:16 sons, have left me solitary, without d.
Ez 13:17 turn toward the d of your people who
14:16 swear they could save neither sons nor d;
14:18 would be unable to save either sons or d;
14:22 left in it who will bring out sons and d;
16:20 The sons and d you had borne me you took
16:46 Your elder sister was Samaria with her d,
16:46 to the south of you, was Sodom with her d.
16:48 swear that your sister Sodom, with her d,
16:48 has not done as you and your d have done!
16:49 she and her d were proud,
16:53 the fortune of Sodom and her d and of
16:53 of Samaria and her d [and I will restore
16:55 Yes, your sisters, Sodom and her d,
16:55 and her daughters, Samaria and her d,
16:55 your d shall return to your former state].
16:61 than you, and give them to you as d,
22:11 their sisters, the d of their own fathers.
23: 2 there were two women, d of the same mother,
23: 4 They became mine and bore sons and d.
23:10 nakedness, her sons and d they took away,
23:25 They shall take away your sons and d,
23:47 They shall slay their sons and d,
24:21 d you left behind shall fall by the sword.
24:25 pride of their hearts, their sons and d,
26: 6 And her d on the mainland shall be
26: 8 Your d on the mainland he shall slay with
30:18 her, and her d shall go into captivity.
32:16 the d of the nations shall chant it;
Dn 13:57 This is how you acted with the d of Israel,
Hos 4:13 That is why your d play the harlot,
4:14 Am I then to punish your d for harlotry,
Jl 3: 1 Your sons and d shall prophesy,
4: 8 sons and your d to the people of Judah,
Am 7:17 your sons and d shall fall by the sword;
Mt 15:26 of sons and d and throw it to the dogs."
Lk 23:28 D of Jerusalem, do not weep for me.
Acts 2:17 Your sons and d shall prophesy,
21: 9 had four unmarried d gifted with prophecy.
2Cor 6:18 to you and you will be my sons and d,'

DAUGHTERS-IN-LAW (5)

Ru 1: 7 She and her two d left the place where
1: 8 land of Judah, Naomi said to her two d,
Ez 22:11 men who defile their d by incest,
Hos 4:13 the harlot, and your d are adulteresses.
4:14 for harlotry, your d for their adultery?

DAUNTED (1)

Ez 21:12 fall helpless, every spirit shall be d,

DAVID (926)

Ru 4:17 was the father of Jesse, the father of D.
4:22 of Jesse, and Jesse became the father of D.
1Sm 16:13 on, the spirit of the LORD rushed upon D.
16:19 to ask Jesse to send him his son D,
16:20 a kid, and sent them to Saul by his son D.
16:21 D came to Saul and entered his service.
16:22 message, "Allow D to remain in my service,
16:23 Saul, D would take the harp and play,
17:12 D was the son of an Ephrathite named Jesse,
17:14 D was the youngest.
17:15 D would go and come from Saul to tend his
17:17 [Now Jesse said to his son D:
17:20 with a shepherd, D set out on his errand,
17:22 D entrusted what he had brought to the
17:23 and spoke as before and D listened.
17:26 D now said to the men standing by:
17:28 the men, he grew angry with D and said:
17:29 D replied, "What have I done now?—I
17:31 The words that D had spoken were overheard
17:32 Then D spoke to Saul:
17:33 But Saul answered D, "You cannot go up
17:34 Then D told Saul:
17:37 D continued: The LORD who delivered me
17:37 Saul answered D, "Go!
17:38 Then Saul clothed D in his own tunic,
17:39 D also girded himself with Saul's sword
17:40 D selected five smooth stones from the
17:41 also advanced closer and closer to D.
17:42 When he had sized D up,
17:43 The Philistine said to D,
17:43 cursed D by his gods and said to him,
17:45 D answered him: "You come against me
17:48 then moved to meet D at close quarters,
17:48 while D ran quickly toward the battle line
17:49 D put his hand into the bag and took out a
17:50 [Thus D overcame the Philistine with sling
17:51 Then D ran and stood over him;
17:54 D took the head of the Philistine and
17:55 Saul saw D go out to meet the Philistine,
17:57 D returned from slaying the Philistine,
17:57 D was still holding the Philistine's head.
17:58 D replied, "I am the son of your servant
18: 1 [By the time D finished speaking with Saul,
18: 1 fond of D as if his life depended on him;
18: 2 Saul laid claim to D that day and did not
18: 3 And Jonathan entered into a bond with D,
18: 4 mantle he was wearing and gave it to D,
18: 5 D then carried out successfully every
18: 6 At the approach of Saul and D (on David's
18: 7 his thousands, and D his ten thousands."
18: 8 "They give D ten thousands,
18: 9 from that day on, Saul was jealous of D.
18:10 D was in attendance,
18:11 David to the wall, but twice D escaped him.]
18:12 Saul then began to fear D,
18:13 So D led the people on their military
18:15 he was, Saul conceived a fear of D:
18:17 [Saul said to D, "There is my older daughter
18:18 But D answered Saul:
18:19 Saul's daughter Merob to be given to D,
18:20 Now Saul's daughter Michal loved D,
18:21 [Thus for the second time Saul said to D,
18:22 to speak to D privately and to say:
18:23 when Saul's servants mentioned this to D,
18:25 Saul commanded them to say this to D:
18:26 the servants reported this offer to D,
18:27 D made preparations and sallied forth with
18:28 to recognize that the LORD was with D;
18:28 besides, his own daughter Michal loved D.
18:29 Therefore Saul feared D all the more [and
18:30 D was more successful against them than
19: 1 Saul discussed his intention of killing D
19: 1 son Jonathan, who was very fond of D,
19: 4 then spoke well of D to his father Saul,
19: 4 your majesty sin against his servant D,
19: 5 innocent blood by killing D without cause?"
19: 7 So Jonathan summoned D and repeated the
19: 7 Jonathan then brought D to Saul,
19: 7 David to Saul, and D served him as before.
19: 8 D went out to fight against the
19: 9 in hand and D was playing the harp nearby.
19:10 tried to nail D to the wall with the spear,
19:10 the wall with the spear, but D eluded Saul,
19:10 struck only the wall, and D got away safe.
19:12 Then Michal let D down through a window,
19:14 When Saul sent messengers to arrest D,
19:15 back to see D and commanded them,
19:18 Thus D got safely away;
19:19 told that D was in the sheds near Ramah,
19:20 near Ramah, he sent messengers to arrest D.
19:22 he inquired, "Where are Samuel and D?",
20: 1 D fled from the sheds near Ramah,
20: 3 But D replied: "Your father is well aware
20: 4 Jonathan then said to D,
20: 5 D answered: "Tomorrow is the new moon
20: 6 D urged me to let him go on short notice
20:10 D then asked Jonathan,
20:11 Jonathan replied to D, "Come, let us go
20:12 open country together, Jonathan said to D:
20:12 he is well disposed toward D or not,
20:15 enemies of D from the surface of the earth.
20:16 the family of D to die out from among you,
20:17 And in his love for D,
20:24 So D hid in the open country.
20:28 D urgently asked me to let him go to his
20:33 that his father was resolved to kill D.
20:35 a little boy for his appointment with D.
20:39 only Jonathan and D knew what was meant.
20:41 D rose from beside the mound and
20:42 At length Jonathan said to D,
21: 1 Then D departed on his way,
21: 2 D went to Ahimelech,
21: 3 D answered the priest:
21: 5 But the priest replied to D,
21: 6 D answered the priest:
21: 9 D then asked Ahimelech:
21:10 D said: "There is none to match it.
21:11 That same day D took to flight from Saul,
21:12 servants of Achish said, "Is this not D,
21:12 his thousands, but D his ten thousands'?"
21:13 D took note of these remarks and became
22: 3 From there D went to Mizpeh of Moab and
22: 4 him as long as D remained in the refuge.
22: 5 But the prophet Gad said to D:
22: 5 so D left and went to the forest of Hereth.
22: 6 heard that D and his men had been located.
22:14 among all your servants is as loyal as D,
22:17 priests of the LORD, for they assisted D.
22:20 named Abiathar, escaped and fled to D.
22:21 When Abiathar told D that Saul had slain
22:22 D said to him: I knew that day,
23: 1 D received information that the
23: 4 Again D consulted the LORD,
23: 5 D then went with his men to Keilah and
23: 6 fled to David, went down with D to Keilah,
23: 7 Saul was told that D had entered Keilah,
23: 8 down to Keilah and besiege D and his men.
23: 9 When D found out that Saul was planning to
23:10 D then said: "O LORD God of Israel
23:12 D then asked, "Will the citizens of Keilah
23:13 So D and his men, about six hundred
23:13 informed that D had escaped from Keilah,
23:14 D now lived in the refuges in the desert,
23:14 the LORD did not deliver D into his grasp.
23:15 D was apprehensive because Saul had come
23:16 D and strengthened his resolve in the LORD.
23:18 the LORD in Horesh, where D remained,
23:19 in Gibeah and said, D is hiding among us,
23:24 At this time D and his men were in the
23:25 D got word of it and went down to the
23:25 and pursued D into the desert below Maon.
23:26 the gorge, D and his men took to the other.
23:26 D was in anxious flight to escape Saul,
23:26 D and his men in order to capture them,
23:28 of D and went to meet the Philistines.

DAVID (cont.)

24: 1 D then went up from there and stayed in
24: 2 told that D was in the desert near Engedi.
24: 3 Israel and went in search of D and his men
24: 4 D and his men were occupying the inmost
24: 5 So D moved up and stealthily cut off an
24: 6 D regretted that he had cut off an end of
24: 8 With these words D restrained his men and
24: 9 D also stepped out of the cave,
24: 9 D bowed to the ground in homage
24:10 to those who say, D is trying to harm you'?
24:17 D finished saying these things to Saul,
24:17 answered, "Is that your voice, my son D?"
24:18 Saul then said to D: "You are in the right
24:23 D gave Saul his oath and Saul returned home,
24:23 while D and his men went up to the refuge.
25: 1 Then D went down to the desert of Maon.
25: 4 When D heard in the desert that Nabal was
25: 8 and your son D whatever you can manage.'"
25:10 But Nabal answered the servants of D:
25:10 "Who is D?
25:13 Thereupon D said to his men,
25:13 And so everyone, D included,
25:13 About four hundred men went up after D,
25:14 D sent messengers from the desert to greet
25:20 D and his men were also coming down from
25:21 When she met them, D had just been saying:
25:22 May God do thus and so to D,
25:23 As soon as Abigail saw D,
25:23 falling prostrate on the ground before D,
25:32 D said to Abigail: "Blessed be the LORD"
25:35 D then took from her what she had brought
25:39 On hearing that Nabal was dead, D said:
25:39 D then sent a proposal of marriage to
25:40 D has sent us to you that he may take you
25:43 and D also married Ahinoam of Jezreel.
26: 1 reporting that D was hiding on the hill
26: 2 to search for D in the desert of Ziph.
26: 3 D, who was living in the desert,
26: 5 who confirmed Saul's arrival D himself
26: 6 D asked Ahimelech the Hittite,
26: 7 So D and Abishai went among Saul's
26: 8 Abishai whispered to D:
26: 9 But D said to Abishai,
26:10 As the LORD lives," D continued,
26:12 So D took the spear and the water jug from
26:13 D stood on a remote hilltop at a great
26:15 D said to Abner: "Are you not a man
26:17 and asked, "Is that your voice, my son D?"
26:17 D answered, "Yes, my lord the king."
26:21 Come back, my son D,
26:22 But D answered: "Here is the king's spear.
26:25 Then Saul said to D: "Blessed are you,
26:25 "Blessed are you, my son D!
26:25 D went his way,
27: 1 But D said to himself:
27: 2 D departed with his six hundred men and
27: 3 D and his men lived in Gath with Achish;
27: 3 had his family, and D had his two wives,
27: 4 When Saul was told that D had fled to Gath,
27: 5 D said to Achish:
27: 7 D lived a year and four months in the
27: 8 D and his men went up and made raids on
27: 9 D would not leave a man or woman alive,
27:10 And D answered, "The Negeb of Judah,"
27:11 But D would not leave a man or woman alive
27:11 betray him by saying, "This is what D did."
27:12 And Achish trusted D,
28: 1 So Achish said to D,
28: 2 D answered Achish, "Good!
28: 2 Then Achish said to D,
28:17 grasp and has given it to your neighbor D.
29: 2 D and his men were marching in the rear
29: 3 "Why, that is D, the officer of Saul,
29: 5 D of whom they sing during their dances,
29: 5 his thousands, but D his ten thousands"?"
29: 6 So Achish summoned D and said to him:
29: 8 But D said to Achish: "What have I done?
29: 9 "You know," Achish answered D,
29:11 So D and his men left early in the morning
30: 1 Before D and his men reached Ziklag on the
30: 3 D and his men arrived at the city to find
30: 4 Then D and those who were with him wept
30: 6 Now D found himself in great difficulty,
30: 7 in the LORD his God, D said to Abiathar,
30: 8 him the ephod, D inquired of the LORD,
30: 9 So D went off with his six hundred men and
30:10 D continued the pursuit with four hundred
30:11 found in the open country and brought to D.
30:13 Then D asked him, "To whom do you
30:15 D then asked him, "Will you lead me
30:17 From dawn to sundown D attacked them,
30:18 D recovered everything the Amalekites had
30:19 D brought back everything.
30:20 Moreover, D took all the sheep and oxen,
30:21 When D came to the two hundred men who
30:21 came out to meet D and the men with him.
30:21 On nearing them D greeted them.
30:22 who had accompanied D spoke up to say,
30:23 But D said: "You must not do this."
30:26 When D came to Ziklag,
30:31 all the places frequented by D and his men.
2Sm 1: 1 D returned from his defeat of the
1: 2 Going to D, he fell to the ground
1: 3 D asked him, "Where do you come from?"
1: 4 "Tell me what happened," D bade him.
1: 5 Then D said to the youth who was reporting
1:11 D seized his garments and rent them,
1:13 Then D said to the young man who had
1:14 D said to him, "How is it that you were
1:15 D then called one of the attendants and
1:16 Meanwhile D said to him,
1:17 Then D chanted this elegy for Saul and his
2: 1 After this D inquired of the LORD,
2: 1 Then D asked, "Where shall I go?"
2: 2 So D went up there accompanied by his two
2: 3 D also brought up his men with their
2: 4 there and anointed D king of the Judahites.
2: 4 A report reached D that the men of
2: 5 So D sent messengers to the men of
2:10 The Judahites alone followed D.
2:11 D spent seven years and six months in
2:30 nineteen other servants of D were missing.
3: 1 between the house of Saul and that of D,
3: 1 that of David, in which D grew stronger,
3: 2 Sons were born to D in Hebron:
3: 5 These were born to D in Hebron.
3: 6 between the house of Saul and that of D,
3: 9 carry out for D what the LORD swore to him
3:10 establish the throne of D over Israel
3:12 Then Abner sent messengers to D in Telam,
3:14 the same time D sent messengers to Ishbaal,
3:17 time you have been seeking D as your king.
3:18 take action, for the LORD has said of D,
3:18 'By my servant D I will save my people
3:19 to make his own report to D in Hebron
3:20 by twenty men, came to D in Hebron,
3:20 D prepared a feast for Abner and for the
3:21 Then Abner said to D, "I will now go
3:21 So D bade Abner farewell,
3:22 Abner, having been dismissed by D,
3:23 informed, "Abner, son of Ner, came to D;
3:26 Joab then left D, and without David's
3:28 Later D heard of it and said:
3:31 Then D said to Joab and to all the people
3:31 King D himself followed the bier.
3:35 console D with food while it was still day.
3:35 But D swore, "May God do thus and so
4: 8 to D in Hebron and said to the king:
4: 9 D replied to Rechab and his brother Baanah,
4:12 So at a command from D,
5: 1 of Israel came to D in Hebron and said:
5: 3 the elders of Israel came to D in Hebron,
5: 3 King D made an agreement with them there
5: 4 D was thirty years old when he became king,
5: 6 D was told, "You cannot enter here:
5: 6 their way of saying, D cannot enter here."
5: 7 But D did take the stronghold of Zion,
5: 7 stronghold of Zion, which is the City of D.
5: 8 On that day D said:
5: 8 blind shall be the personal enemies of D."
5: 9 D then dwelt in the stronghold,
5: 9 which was called the City of D;
5:10 D grew steadily more powerful,
5:11 king of Tyre, sent ambassadors to D;
5:11 and masons, who built a palace for D.
5:12 And D knew that the LORD had established
5:13 D took more concubines and wives in
5:17 that D had been anointed king of Israel,
5:17 On hearing this, D went down to the refuge.
5:19 D inquired of the LORD,
5:19 The LORD replied to D, "Attack,
5:20 D then went to Baal-perazim,
5:21 there, and D and his men carried them away.
5:23 So D inquired of the LORD, who replied:
5:25 D obeyed the LORD's command and routed the
6: 1 D again assembled all the picked men of
6: 2 Then D and all the people who were with
6: 5 while D and all the Israelites made merry
6: 8 D was disturbed because the LORD had
6: 9 D feared the LORD that day and said,
6:10 So D would not have the ark of the
6:10 the LORD brought to him in the City of D,
6:12 When it was reported to King D that the
6:12 D went to bring up the ark of God from the
6:12 into the City of D amid festivities.
6:14 Then D, girt with a linen apron,
6:16 of the LORD was entering the City of D,
6:16 King D leaping and dancing before the LORD,
6:17 place within the tent D had pitched for it.
6:17 Then D offered holocausts and peace
6:20 When D returned to bless his own family,
6:21 But D replied to Michal:
7: 1 King D was settled in his palace,
7: 5 "Go, tell my servant D,
7: 8 "Now then, speak thus to my servant D,
7:17 these words and this entire vision to D.
7:18 D went in and sat before the LORD and said,
7:20 What more can D say to you?
7:26 of your servant D stands firm before you.
8: 1 After this D attacked the Philistines and
8: 2 Thus the Moabites became tributary to D.
8: 3 D defeated Hadadezer,
8: 4 D captured from him one thousand seven
8: 5 Zobah, D slew twenty-two thousand of them.
8: 6 D then placed garrisons in Aram of Damascus,
8: 6 Arameans became subjects, tributary to D.
8: 6 brought D victory in all his undertakings.
8: 7 D also took away the golden shields used
8: 8 D removed a very large quantity of bronze.
8: 9 D had defeated all the forces of Hadadezer,
8:10 sent his son Hadoram to King D to greet
8:11 These, too, King D consecrated to the LORD,
8:13 D became famous for having slain eighteen
8:14 brought D victory in all his undertakings.
8:15 D reigned over all Israel,
9: 1 D asked, "Is there any survivor
9: 2 He was summoned to D,
9: 5 So King D sent for him and had him brought
9: 6 son of Jonathan, son of Saul, came to D,
9: 6 D said, "Meribbaal," and he answered,
9: 7 "Fear not," D said to him,
10: 2 D thought, "I will be kind to Hanun,
10: 2 So D sent his servants with condolences to
10: 3 "Do you think that D is honoring your
10: 3 it, that D has sent his messengers to you?"
10: 5 King D sent out word to them
10: 6 view of the offense they had given to D,
10: 7 D sent out Joab with the entire levy of
10:17 this news, D assembled all Israel,
10:17 in formation against D and fought with him.
11: 1 D sent out Joab along with his officers
11: 1 D, however, remained in Jerusalem.
11: 2 One evening D rose from his siesta and
11: 3 D had inquiries made about the woman and
11: 4 Then D sent messengers and took her.
11: 5 conceived, and sent the information to D,
11: 6 D therefore sent a message to Joab
11: 6 So Joab sent Uriah to D.
11: 7 When he came, D questioned him about Joab,
11: 8 D then said to Uriah,
11:10 D was told that Uriah had not gone home.
11:11 Uriah answered D, "The ark and Israel
11:12 Then D said to Uriah, "Stay here today
11:13 On the day following, D summoned him,
11:13 summoned him, and he ate and drank with D,
11:14 The next morning D wrote a letter to Joab
11:18 Then Joab sent D a report of all the
11:22 and on his arrival he relayed to D all the
11:23 He told D: "The men had us at a disadvantage
11:25 D said to the messenger:
11:27 D sent for her and brought her into his
11:27 LORD was displeased with what D had done.
12: 1 The LORD sent Nathan to D,
12: 5 D grew very angry with that man and said
12: 7 Then Nathan said to D: "You are the man."
12:13 Then D said to Nathan, "I have sinned
12:13 Nathan answered D:
12:15 that the wife of Uriah had borne to D,
12:16 D besought God for the child.
12:19 But D noticed his servants whispering
12:20 the ground, D washed and anointed himself,
12:24 Then D comforted his wife Bathsheba.
12:27 He sent messengers to D with the word:
12:29 So D assembled the rest of the soldiers
12:31 D and all the soldiers then returned to
13: 7 D then sent home a message to Tamar,
13:21 King D, who got word of the whole affair,
13:30 a report reached D that Absalom had killed
15:13 An informant came to D with the report,
15:14 D said to all his servants who were with
15:30 As D went up the Mount of Olives,
15:31 When D was informed that Ahithophel was
15:32 When D reached the top,
15:33 D said to him: "If you come with me,
16: 1 D had gone a little beyond the top when
16: 5 As D was approaching Bahurim,
16: 6 stones at D and at all the king's officers,
16:10 Suppose the LORD has told him to curse D;
16:13 D and his men continued on the road,
16:23 all his counsel both to D and to Absalom.
17: 1 men, and be off in pursuit of D tonight.
17:16 So send a warning to D immediately,
17:17 in turn were to go and report to King D.
17:21 the cistern and went on to inform King D.
17:22 So D and all his people moved on and
17:24 Now D had gone to Mahanaim when Absalom
17:27 When D came to Mahanaim,
17:29 for D and those who were with him to eat;
18: 1 D placed officers in command of groups of
18: 2 D then put a third part of the soldiers
18:24 Now D was sitting between the two gates,
19:12 D sent word to the priests Zadok and
19:17 down with the Judahites to meet King D,
19:23 D replied: "What has come between you
20: 1 and cried out, "We have no portion in D,
20: 2 So all the Israelites left D for Sheba,
20: 3 King D came to his palace in Jerusalem,
20: 5 delayed beyond the time set for him by D.
20: 6 Then D said to Abishai:
20:11 who favors Joab and is for D follow Joab."
20:21 of Ephraim has rebelled against King D.
21: 1 D had recourse to the LORD,
21: 3 D said to the Gibeonites,
21: 7 a bond between D and Saul's son Jonathan.
21:11 When D was informed of what Rizpah,
21:15 D went down with his servants and fought
21:15 fought the Philistines, but D grew tired.
21:16 with a new sword and planned to kill D,

21:22 fell at the hands of *D* and his servants.
22: 1 *D* sang the words of this song to the LORD
22:51 to *D* and his posterity forever."
23: 1 These are the last words of *D:*
23: 1 "The utterance of *D,* son of Jesse;
23: 9 He was with *D* at Ephes-dammim when the
23:13 went down to *D* in the cave of Adullam,
23:14 At that time *D* was in the refuge,
23:15 Now *D* had a strong craving and said,
23:16 brought it to *D* he refused to drink it,
23:23 *D* put him in command of his bodyguard.
24: 1 and he incited *D* against the Israelites by
24:10 *D* regretted having numbered the people,
24:11 When *D* rose in the morning,
24:12 say to *D,* 'This is what the LORD says:
24:13 Gad then went to *D* to inform him.
24:14 *D* answered Gad:
24:15 Thus *D* chose the pestilence.
24:17 When *D* saw the angel who was striking the
24:18 the same day Gad went to *D* and said to him,
24:19 *D* went up as the LORD had commanded.
24:21 *D* replied, "To buy the threshing floor
24:22 But Araunah said to *D:*
24:24 So *D* bought the threshing floor and the
24:25 Then *D* built an altar there to the LORD,
1Kgs 1: 1 When King *D* was old and advanced in years,
1:11 king without the knowledge of our lord *D?*
1:13 Go, visit King *D,*
1:28 King *D* answered, "Call Bathsheba here."
1:31 Bathsheba said, "May the lord, King *D,*
1:32 Then King *D* summoned Zadok the priest,
1:37 even more than that of my lord, King *D!*"
1:43 "Our lord, King *D,* has made Solomon king.
1:47 paid their respects to our lord, King *D,*
2:10 *D* rested with his ancestors and was buried
2:10 ancestors and was buried in the City of *D.*
2:12 was seated on the throne of his father *D,*
2:24 *D* and made of me a dynasty as he promised,
2:26 my father *D* and shared in all the hardships
2:33 be the peace of the LORD forever for *D,*
2:44 heart the evil that you did to my father *D.*
3: 1 he married, he brought to the City of *D,*
3: 3 and obeyed the statutes of his father *D;*
3: 6 great favor to your servant, my father *D,*
3: 7 your servant, king to succeed my father *D;*
3:14 and commandments, as your father *D* did,
5:17 "You know that my father *D,*
5:19 LORD predicted to my father *D* when he said:
5:21 *D* a wise son to rule this numerous people."
6:12 you the promise I made to your father *D.*
7:51 the dedicated offerings of his father *D,*
8: 1 from the city of *D* [which is Zion].
8:15 own mouth made a promise to my father *D*
8:16 but I choose *D* to rule my people Israel.'
8:17 When my father *D* wished to build a temple
8:20 father *D* and sit on the throne of Israel,
8:24 kept the promise you made to my father *D,*
8:25 further promise you made to my father *D,*
8:26 this promise which you made to my father *D,*
8:66 to his servant *D* and to his people Israel.
9: 4 live in my presence as your father *D* lived,
9: 5 as I promised your father *D* when I said,
9:24 went up from the City of *D* to her palace,
11: 4 God, as the heart of his father *D* had been.
11: 6 him unreservedly as his father *D* had done.
11:12 however, for the sake of your father *D;*
11:13 the sake of my servant *D* and of Jerusalem,
11:15 Earlier, when *D* had conquered Edom,
11:21 *D* rested with his ancestors and that Joab,
11:24 Zobah, when *D* defeated them with slaughter.
11:27 up the breach of his father's City of *D.*
11:32 remain to him for the sake of *D* my servant,
11:33 and my decrees, as his father *D* did.
11:34 as he lives for the sake of my servant *D,*
11:36 that my servant *D* may always have a lamp
11:38 and my commandments like my servant *D,*
11:38 I will establish for you, as I did for *D,*
11:43 he was buried in his father's City of *D,*
12:16 "What share have we in *D?*
12:16 Now look to your own house, *D.*"
13: 2 'A child shall be born to the house of *D,*
14: 8 of *D* of the kingdom and gave it to you.
14: 8 Yet you have not been like my servant *D,*
14:31 he was buried with them in the City of *D.*
15: 3 God, like the heart of his grandfather *D.*
15: 5 because *D* had pleased the LORD and did not
15: 8 he was buried in the City of *D,*
15:11 pleased the LORD like his forefather *D,*
15:24 was buried in his forefather's City of *D,*
22:51 was buried in his forefathers' City of *D.*
2Kgs 8:19 to destroy Judah, because of his servant *D.*
8:19 For he had promised *D* that he would leave
8:24 and was buried with them in the City of *D.*
9:28 the tomb of his ancestors in the City of *D.*
12:22 was buried in his forefathers' City of *D,*
14: 3 the LORD, yet not like his forefather *D,*
14:20 ancestors in the City of *D* in Jerusalem.
15: 7 and was buried with them in the City of *D.*
15:38 with them in his forefather's City of *D.*
16: 2 the LORD, his God, like his forefather *D,*
16:20 and was buried with them in the City of *D.*
17:21 he tore Israel away from the house of *D,*
18: 3 LORD, just as his forefather *D* had done.
19:34 own sake, and for the sake of my servant *D.*'"
20: 5 says the LORD the God of your forefather *D:*
20: 6 own sake, and for the sake of my servant *D.*'"
21: 7 LORD had said to *D* and to his son Solomon:
22: 2 just as his ancestor *D* had done.
1Chr 2:15 Raddai, the fifth, Ozem, the sixth, and *D,*
3: 1 sons of *D* who were born to him in Hebron:
3: 9 All these were sons of *D,*
4:31 Until *D* came to reign,
6:16 The following were entrusted by *D* with the
7: 2 thousand six hundred in the time of *D.*
9:22 *D* and Samuel the seer had established them
10:14 slew him, and transferred his kingdom to *D,*
11: 1 Then all Israel gathered about *D* in Hebron,
11: 3 and there *D* made a covenant with them in
11: 4 Then *D* and all Israel went to Jerusalem,
11: 5 The inhabitants of Jebus said to *D,*
11: 5 *D* nevertheless captured the fortress of
11: 5 fortress of Zion, which is the City of *D.*
11: 6 *D* said, "Whoever strikes the Jebusites
11: 7 *D* took up his residence in the fortress,
11: 7 which thenceforth was called the City of *D.*
11: 9 *D* became more and more powerful,
11:13 He was with *D* at Pas-dammim,
11:15 Thirty chiefs went down to the rock, to *D,*
11:16 *D* was then in the stronghold,
11:17 *D* expressed a desire:
11:18 at Bethlehem, and carried it back to *D.*
11:18 But *D* refused to drink it.
11:25 *D* put him in charge of his bodyguard.
12: 1 The following men came to *D* in Ziklag
12: 9 Some of the Gadites also went over to *D*
12:17 Judahites also came to *D* at the stronghold.
12:18 *D* went out to meet them and addressed them
12:19 "We are yours, O *D,*
12:19 So *D* received them and placed them among
12:20 Men from Manasseh also deserted to *D* when
12:22 helped *D* by taking charge of his troops,
12:24 armed troops that came to *D* at Hebron
12:32 designated by name to come and make *D* king.
12:39 intention of making *D* king over all Israel.
12:39 was likewise of one mind to make *D* king.
12:40 They remained with *D* for three days,
13: 1 After *D* had taken counsel with his
13: 5 Then *D* assembled all Israel,
13: 6 *D* and all Israel went up to Baalah,
13: 8 while *D* and all Israel danced before God
13:11 *D* was disturbed because the LORD's anger
13:12 *D* was now afraid of God,
13:13 the ark back with him to the City of *D,*
14: 1 to *D* along with masons and carpenters,
14: 2 *D* now understood that the LORD had truly
14: 3 *D* took other wives in Jerusalem and became
14: 8 that *D* was anointed king over all Israel,
14: 8 But when *D* heard of this,
14:10 *D* inquired of God, "Shall I advance
14:11 to Baal-perazim, and *D* defeated them there.
14:11 Then *D* said, "God has used me
14:12 gods there, and *D* ordered them to be burnt.
14:14 and again *D* inquired of God.
14:16 *D* did as God commanded him,
15: 1 *D* built houses for himself in the City of
15: 1 *D* and prepared a place for the ark of God,
15: 3 Then *D* assembled all Israel in Jerusalem
15: 4 *D* also called together the sons of Aaron
15:11 *D* summoned the priests Zadok and Abiathar,
15:16 *D* commanded the chiefs of the Levites to
15:25 Thus *D,* the elders of Israel
15:27 *D* was clothed in a robe of fine linen,
15:27 *D* was also wearing a linen ephod.
15:29 of the LORD was entering the City of *D,*
15:29 when she saw King *D* leaping and dancing,
16: 1 within the tent which *D* had pitched for it.
16: 2 When *D* had finished offering up the
16: 7 *D* appointed Asaph and his brethren to sing
16:37 Then *D* left Asaph and his brethren there
16:43 home, and *D* returned to bless his household.
17: 1 *D* had taken up residence in his house,
17: 2 *D,* "Do, therefore, whatever you desire,
17: 4 "Go and tell my servant *D,*
17: 7 Therefore, tell my servant *D,*
17:15 whole vision Nathan related exactly to *D.*
17:16 *D* came in and sat in the LORD's presence,
17:18 What more can *D* say to you?
17:24 and abide forever, while the house of *D,*
18: 1 *D* defeated the Philistines and subdued
18: 3 *D* then defeated Hadadezer,
18: 4 *D* took from him twenty thousand foot
18: 4 horses, *D* hamstrung all but one hundred.
18: 5 but *D* also slew twenty-two thousand of
18: 6 Then *D* set up garrisons in the Damascus
18: 6 made *D* victorious in all his campaigns.
18: 7 *D* took the golden shields that were
18: 9 heard that *D* had defeated the entire army
18:10 sent his son Hadoram to wish King *D* well
18:10 He also sent *D* gold,
18:11 These also King *D* consecrated to the LORD
18:13 made *D* victorious in all his campaigns.
18:14 *D* reigned over all Israel and dispensed
19: 2 *D* said, "I will show kindness to Hanun,
19: 3 to Hanun, "Do you think *D* is doing this
19: 5 When *D* was informed of what had happened
19: 6 had put themselves in bad odor with *D,*
19: 8 When *D* heard of this, he sent Joab
19:17 When this was reported to *D,*
19:17 army of *D* drawn up to fight the Arameans,
19:18 and *D* slew seven thousand of their chariot
19:19 made peace with *D* and became his subjects.
20: 1 while *D* himself remained in Jerusalem.
20: 2 *D* took the crown of Milcom from the idol's
20: 2 stones, which *D* wore on his own head.
20: 3 Thus *D* dealt with all the cities of the
20: 8 died at the hands of *D* and his servants.
21: 1 enticed *D* into taking a census of Israel.
21: 2 *D* therefore said to Joab and to the other
21: 5 reported the result of the census to *D:*
21: 8 Then *D* said to God,
21:10 "Go, tell *D:* "Thus says the LORD"
21:11 Accordingly, Gad went to *D* and said to him;
21:13 Then *D* said to Gad: "I am in dire straits
21:16 When *D* raised his eyes,
21:16 *D* and the elders, clothed in sackcloth,
21:17 face to the ground, and *D* prayed to God:
21:18 angel of the LORD commanded Gad to tell *D*
21:19 *D* went up at Gad's command,
21:21 But as *D* came on toward him,
21:21 him, he looked up and saw that it was *D.*
21:21 threshing floor and bowed down before *D,*
21:22 *D* said to Ornan: "Sell me the ground
21:23 But Ornan said to *D:* Take it as your own
21:24 But King *D* replied to Ornan:
21:25 So *D* paid Ornan six hundred shekels of
21:26 *D* then built an altar there to the LORD,
21:28 Once *D* saw that the LORD had heard him on
21:30 But *D* could not go there to worship God,
22: 1 Therefore *D* said, "This is the house
22: 2 *D* then ordered that all the aliens who
22: 4 brought great stores of cedar logs to *D,*
22: 5 his death *D* laid up materials in abundance.
22: 7 *D* said to Solomon:
22:17 *D* also commanded all of Israel's leaders
23: 1 When *D* had grown old and was near the end
23: 5 instruments which *D* had devised for praise.
23: 6 *D* divided them into classes according to
23:25 *D* said: "The LORD, the God of Israel
24: 3 *D,* with Zadok,
24:31 cast lots in the presence of King *D,*
25: 1 *D* and the leaders of the liturgical cult
26:26 the votive offerings dedicated by King *D,*
26:32 King *D* appointed them to the
27:23 *D* did not count those who were twenty
27:24 into the book of chronicles of King *D.*
28: 1 *D* assembled at Jerusalem all the leaders
28: 2 King *D* rose to his feet and said:
28:11 Then *D* gave to his son Solomon the pattern
28:20 Then *D* said to his son Solomon:
29: 1 King *D* then said to the whole assembly:
29: 9 King *D* also rejoiced greatly.
29:10 Then *D* blessed the LORD in the presence of
29:20 Then *D* besought the whole assembly,
29:23 LORD as king in place of his father *D;*
29:24 and also all the other sons of King *D,*
29:26 Thus *D,* the son of Jesse, had reigned
29:29 Now the deeds of King *D,*
2Chr 1: 1 Solomon, son of *D,*
1: 4 *D* had brought up from Kiriath-jearim to
1: 8 have shown great favor to my father *D,*
1: 9 your promise to my father *D* be fulfilled,
2: 2 "As you dealt with my father *D,*
2: 6 and Jerusalem, whom my father *D* appointed.
2:11 for having given King *D* a wise son of
2:13 and the craftsmen of my lord *D* your father.
2:16 the census *D* his father had taken of them),
3: 1 had been pointed out to his father *D,*
3: 1 David, on the spot which *D* had selected,
5: 1 the dedicated offerings of his father *D,*
5: 2 from the City of *D* (which is Zion).
6: 4 own mouth made a promise to my father *D*
6: 6 and I choose *D* to rule my people Israel.'
6: 7 My father *D* wished to build a temple to
6:10 I have succeeded my father *D* and have
6:15 kept the promise you made to my father *D,*
6:16 further promise you made to my father *D,*
6:17 you made to your servant *D* be confirmed.
6:42 your anointed, remember the devotion of *D,*
7: 6 King *D* had made for "praising the LORD,
7: 6 when *D* used them to accompany the hymns.
7:10 the good things the LORD had done for *D,*
7:17 live in my presence as your father *D* did,
7:18 covenanted with your father *D* when I said,
8:11 daughter of Pharaoh up from the City of *D*
8:11 of mine shall dwell in the house of *D,*
8:14 to the ordinance of his father *D* he appointed
8:14 each gate, since such was the command of *D,*
9:31 he was buried in his father's City of *D,*
10:16 "What share have we in *D?*
10:16 Now look to your own house, *D!*"
11:17 in the way of *D* and Solomon three years.
11:18 of Jerimoth, son of *D* and of Abihail,
12:16 he was buried in the City of *D.*
13: 5 given the kingdom of Israel to *D* forever,
13: 6 Nebat, the servant of Solomon, son of *D,*
13: 8 of the LORD commanded by the sons of *D,*
13:23 they buried him in the City of *D.*
16:14 he had hewn for himself in the City of *D,*
21: 1 he was buried with them in the City of *D.*

DAVID (cont.)

21: 7 the LORD would not destroy the house of *D*
21: 7 the covenant he had made with *D*
21:12 says the LORD, the God of your ancestor *D*:
21:20 unloved and was buried in the City of *D*,
23: 3 the LORD promised concerning the sons of *D*.
23: 9 of king *D* which were in the house of God.
23:18 to whom *D* had assigned turns in the temple
23:18 with rejoicing and song, as *D* had provided.
24:16 was buried in the City of *D* with the kings,
24:25 He was buried in the City of *D*,
27: 9 ancestors and was buried in the City of *D*,
28: 1 the LORD as his forefather *D* had done,
29: 2 the LORD just as his forefather *D* had done.
29:25 lyres according to the prescriptions of *D*,
29:26 were stationed with the instruments of *D*,
29:27 of the trumpets and the instruments of *D*,
29:30 in the words of *D* and of Asaph the seer.
30:26 for since the days of Solomon, son of *D*,
32: 5 strengthened the Millo of the City of *D*
32:30 it underground westward to the City of *D*.
32:33 to the tombs of the descendants of *D*.
33: 7 God had said to *D* and his son Solomon:
33:14 of *D* to the west of Gihon in the valley,
34: 2 LORD, following the path of his ancestor *D*.
34: 3 to seek after the God of his forefather *D*,
35: 3 in the house built by Solomon, son of *D*,
35: 4 of King *D* of Israel and his son Solomon.
35:15 were at their posts as prescribed by *D*:
Ezr 3:10 the LORD in the manner laid down by *D*,
8: 2 of the sons of *D*,
8:20 Of the temple slaves (those whom *D* and the
Neh 3:15 steps that lead down from the City of *D*.
3:16 to a place opposite the tombs of *D*,
12:24 in fulfillment of the command of *D*,
12:36 Hanani, with the musical instruments of *D*,
12:37 straight up by the steps of the City of *D*
12:37 top of the wall above the house of *D*
12:45 with the prescriptions of *D* and of Solomon,
12:46 the days of *D* and Asaph in times of old.
Tb 1: 4 from the house of *D* and from Jerusalem.
1Mc 1:33 they built up the City of *D* with a high,
2:31 of the king who were in the City of *D*,
2:57 *D*, for his piety,
4:30 by the hand of your servant *D* and delivered
7:32 the rest fled to the City of *D*.
14:36 those in the City of *D* in Jerusalem,
2Mc 2:13 the writings of the prophets and of *D*,
Ps(s) 18:51 anointed, to *D* and his posterity forever.
72:20 prayers of *D* the son of Jesse are ended.
78:70 And he chose *D*, his servant,
89: 4 chosen one, I have sworn to *D* my servant:
89:21 I have found *D*, my servant;
89:36 I will not be false to *D*.
89:50 you pledged to *D* by your faithfulness?
122: 5 judgment seats, seats for the house of *D*.
132:10 For the sake of *D* your servant,
132:11 The LORD swore to *D* a firm promise from
132:17 will I make a horn to sprout forth for *D*;
144:10 who give victory to kings, and deliver *D*,
Prv 1: 1 The Proverbs of Solomon, the son of *D*,
Sir 45:25 For even his covenant with *D*,
47: 1 NATHAN who served in the presence of *D*.
47: 2 the sacred offerings, so was *D* in Israel.
47:22 a remnant, to *D* a root from his own family.
48:15 with its rulers from the house of *D*.
48:22 was right and held fast to the paths of *D*,
49: 4 Except for *D*, Hezekiah and Josiah
Is 7: 2 of *D* that Aram was encamped in Ephraim,
7:13 Listen, O house of *D*!
22: 9 the breaches in the City of *D* were many;
22:22 the key of the House of *D* on his shoulder;
29: 1 to Ariel, Ariel, the city where *D* encamped!
29: 3 Ariel, I will encamp like *D* against you;
37:35 own sake, and for the sake of my servant *D*.
38: 5 says the LORD, the God of your father *D*:
55: 3 covenant, the benefits assured to *D*.
Jer 17:25 the throne of *D* will continue to enter,
21:12 Hear the word of the LORD, O house of *D*!
22: 2 king of Judah, who sit on the throne of *D*,
22: 4 who succeed to the throne of *D* will continue
22:30 the throne of *D* as ruler again over Judah.
23: 5 I will raise up a righteous shoot to *D*;
30: 9 shall serve the LORD, their God, and *D*,
33:15 time, I will raise up for *D* a just shoot;
33:17 Never shall *D* lack a successor on the
33:21 covenant with my servant *D* also be broken,
33:22 *D* and the Levites who minister to me.
33:26 descendants of Jacob and of my servant *D*
Ez 34:23 over them to pasture them, my servant *D*;
34:24 my servant *D* shall be prince among them.
37:24 My servant *D* shall be prince over them,
37:25 with my servant *D* their prince forever.
Hos 3: 5 back and seek the LORD, their God, and *D*,
Am 6: 5 to the music of the harp, like *D*,
9:11 day I will raise up the fallen hut of *D*;
Zec 12: 7 that the glory of the house of *D* and the
12: 8 among them shall be like *D* on that day,
12: 8 on that day, and the house of *D* godlike,
12:10 I will pour out on the house of *D* and on
12:12 the family of the house of *D*,
13: 1 of *D* and to the inhabitants of Jerusalem,
Mt 1: 1 A family record of Jesus Christ, son of *D*,
1: 6 of Jesse, Jesse the father of King *D*.
1: 6 *D* was the father of Solomon,
1:17 from Abraham to *D*,
1:17 from *D* to the Babylonian captivity,
1:20 "Joseph, son of *D*,
9:27 men came after him crying out, "Son of *D*,
12: 3 what *D* did when he and his men were hungry,
15:22 crying out to him, "Lord, Son of *D*,
20:30 by, began to shout, "Lord, Son of *D*,
20:31 only shouted the louder, "Lord, Son of *D*,
21: 9 "Hosanna to the Son of *D*!
21:15 precincts, "Hosanna to the Son of *D*!"
22:43 "Then how is it that *D* under the Spirit's
22:45 If *D* calls him 'lord,'
Mk 2:25 "Have you never read what *D* did when he
10:47 he began to call out, "Jesus, Son of *D*,
10:48 but he shouted all the louder, "Son of *D*,
11:10 is the reign of our father *D* to come!
12:36 *D* himself, inspired by the Holy Spirit
12:37 If *D* himself addresses him as 'Lord,'
Lk 1:27 to a man named Joseph, of the house of *D*.
1:32 will give him the throne of *D* his father.
1:69 for us in the house of *D* his servant,
2: 4 he was of the house and lineage of *D*—
3:31 son of Mattatha, son of Nathan, son of *D*,
6: 3 what *D* did when he and his men were hungry
18:38 He shouted out, "Jesus, Son of *D*,
18:39 but he cried out all the more, "Son of *D*,
20:41 they say that the Messiah is the son of *D*?
20:42 Does not *D* himself say in the psalms,
20:44 Now if *D* accords him the title 'lord,'
Jn 7:42 from Bethlehem, the village where *D* lived?"
Acts 1:16 of *D* was destined to be fulfilled in Judas,
2:25 should keep its hold on him, *D* says of him:
2:29 confidently to you about our father *D*.
2:34 David did not go up to heaven, yet *D* says,
4:25 the lips of our father *D* your servant:
7:45 So it was until the time of *D*,
13:22 removed him and raised up *D* as their king;
13:22 'I have found *D* son of Jesse to be a man
13:34 benefits assured to *D* under the covenant.'
13:36 Now *D*, after he had spent a lifetime
15:16 return and rebuild the fallen hut of *D*:
Rom 1: 3 who was descended from *D* according to the
4: 6 Thus *D* congratulates the man to whom God
11: 9 *D* says: "Let their table
2Tm 2: 8 that Jesus Christ, a descendant of *D*,
Heb 4: 7 spoke through *D* the words we have quoted:
11:32 Jephthah, of *D* and Samuel and the prophets,
Rv 5: 5 Lion of the tribe of Judah, the Root of *D*,
22:16 I am the Root and Offspring of *D*,

DAVID'S (99)

1Sm 18: 6 (on *D* return after slaying the Philistine),
18:24 reported to him the nature of *D* answer,
18:25 about *D* death through the Philistines.
19:11 sent messengers to *D* house to guard it,
19:11 *D* wife Michal informed him,
20:25 at the king's side, and *D* place was vacant.
20:27 day of the month, *D* place was vacant.
20:34 the month, for he was grieved on *D* account,
23: 3 But *D* men said to him:
24: 5 *D* servants said to him,
25: 9 When *D* young men arrived,
25: 9 this message fully to Nabal in *D* name,
25:12 So *D* young men retraced their steps and on
25:40 When *D* servants came to Abigail in Carmel,
25:42 mounted an ass, and followed *D* messengers,
25:43 but Saul gave *D* wife Michal,
26:17 Saul recognized *D* voice and asked,
30: 5 *D* two wives,
30:20 him, they shouted, "This is *D* spoil!"
2Sm 2:13 and *D* servants also set out and met them
2:15 son of Saul, and twelve of *D* servants.
2:17 men of Israel were defeated by *D* servants.
2:31 But *D* servants had fatally wounded three
3: 5 and the sixth, Ithream, of *D* wife Eglah.
3: 8 friends, by keeping you out of *D* clutches;
3:22 Just then *D* servants and Joab were coming
3:26 *D* knowledge sent messengers after Abner,
8:14 Thus all the Edomites became *D* subjects,
8:18 And *D* sons were priests.
9:11 ate at *D* table like one of the king's sons.
10: 2 But when *D* servants entered the country of
10: 4 Hanun, therefore, seized *D* servants and,
10:18 and *D* men killed seven hundred charioteers
11:17 against Joab, some officers of *D* army fell,
12:18 *D* servants, however, were afraid
12:30 it was placed on *D* head.
13: 1 *D* son Absalom had a beautiful sister named
13: 1 named Tamar, and *D* son Amnon loved her.
13: 3 named Jonadab, son of *D* brother Shimeah,
13:32 But Jonadab, son of *D* brother Shimeah,
15:12 to Ahithophel the Gilonite, *D* counselor,
15:37 So *D* friend Hushai went into the city of
16: 6 guard, were on *D* right and on his left.
16:16 When *D* friend Hushai the Archite came to
18: 6 *D* army then took the field against Israel,
18: 7 of Israel were defeated by *D* servants,
18: 9 unexpectedly came up against *D* servants.
19:42 across the Jordan, along with all *D* men?"
20:15 So *D* servants came and besieged him in
20:26 Ira the Jairite was also *D* priest.
21: 1 During *D* reign there was a famine for
21:17 Then *D* men swore to him,
21:21 Israel, Jonathan, son of *D* brother Shimei,
23: 8 These are the names of *D* warriors.
24:11 LORD had spoken to the prophet Gad, *D* seer,
1Kgs 1: 8 and his companions, the pick of *D* army,
1:38 down, and mounting Solomon on King *D* mule,
2: 1 When the time of *D* death drew near,
2:11 of *D* reign over Israel was forty years:
2:32 the sword without my father *D* knowledge:
2:45 and *D* throne shall endure before the LORD
5:15 for Hiram had always been *D* friend.
11:39 I will punish *D* line for this,
12:19 into rebellion against *D* house to this day.
12:20 to *D* house except the tribe of Judah alone.
12:26 "The kingdom will return to *D* house.
15: 4 Yet for *D* sake the LORD,
2Kgs 11:10 the captains King *D* spears and shields,
1Chr 11:10 These were *D* chief warriors who,
11:11 Here is the list of *D* warriors:
12:23 *D* help until there was a vast encampment,
14:17 Thus *D* fame was spread abroad through
18:13 and all the Edomites became *D* subjects.
18:17 and *D* sons were the chief assistants to
19: 2 But when *D* servants had entered the land
19: 4 Thereupon Hanun seized *D* servants and had
20: 7 and Jonathan, the son of Shimea, *D* brother,
21: 9 Then the LORD spoke to Gad, *D* seer,
23:27 for *D* final orders were to enlist the
26:31 fortieth year of *D* reign search was made,
27:18 for Judah, Eliab, one of *D* brothers;
27:31 were the overseers of King *D* possessions.
27:32 *D* uncle and a man of intelligence,
29:22 time they proclaimed *D* son Solomon king,
2Chr 10:19 in rebellion against *D* house to this day.
Eccl 1: 1 The words of *D* son, Qoheleth, king
Sg 4: 4 is like *D* tower girt with battlements;
Is 9: 6 vast and forever peaceful, From *D* throne,
16: 5 and on it shall sit in fidelity [in *D* tent]
Jer 13:13 land, the kings who succeed to *D* throne,
29:16 concerning the king who sits on *D* throne,
36:30 of his shall succeed to *D* throne;
Mt 12:23 "Might this not be *D* son?"
22:42 Whose son is he? "*D*," they answered:
Mk 12:35 the scribes claim, 'The Messiah is *D* son'?
Lk 2: 4 Galilee to Judea, to *D* town of Bethlehem
2:11 in *D* city a savior has been born to you,
Jn 7:42 say that the Messiah, being of *D* family,
Rv 3: 7 holy One, the true, who wields *D* key,

DAWN (60)

Gn 19:15 As *d* was breaking the angels urged Lot on,
32:25 man wrestled with him until the break of *d*.
Ex 10:13 At *d* the east wind brought the locusts.
14:24 In the night watch just before *d* the LORD
14:27 *d* the sea flowed back to its normal depth.
Jgs 19:25 abused her all night until the following *d*,
1Sm 11:11 and invaded the camp during the *d* watch.
25:34 by *d* Nabal would not have had a single man
30:17 From *d* to sundown David attacked them,
2Sm 2:32 march, and *d* found them in Hebron.
Tb 8:18 his servants to fill in the grave before *d*.
Jdt 12: 5 In the night watch just before *d*,
1Mc 6:33 The king, rising before *d*,
2Mc 10:28 soon as *d* broke, the armies joined battle,
Jb 3: 9 have none, nor gaze on the eyes of the *d*,
7: 4 I am filled with restlessness until the *d*.
38:12 morning and shown the *d* its place
41:10 his eyes are like those of the *d*.
Ps(s) 5: 4 at *d* you hear my voice;
5: 4 *d* I bring my plea expectantly before you.
30: 6 weeping enters in, but with the *d*,
37: 6 will make justice *d* for you like the light;
46: 6 God will help it at the break of *d*.
55:18 In the evening, and at *d*,
57: 9 I will wake the *d*.
59:17 strength and revel at *d* in your kindness;
73:14 after day and chastisement with each new *d*.
90: 6 changing grass, Which at *d* springs up anew,
92: 3 To proclaim your kindness at *d* and your
108: 3 I will wake the *d*.
119:147 Before *d* I come and cry out;
130: 6 LORD more than sentinels wait for the *d*.
139: 9 If I take the wings of the *d*,
143: 8 At *d* let me hear of your kindness,
Eccl 11:10 though the *d* of youth is fleeting.
Sg 6:10 Who is this that comes forth like the *d*,
Wis 6:14 for her at *d* shall not be disappointed,
Sir 24:30 send my teachings forth shining like the *d*,
Is 8:21 shall be strict darkness without any *d*;
14:12 the heavens, O morning star, son of the *d*!
38:13 I cry out until the *d*.
58: 8 your light shall break forth like the *d*,
62: 1 the *d* and her victory like a burning torch.
Hos 6: 3 as certain as the *d* is his coming,
10:15 *d* the king of Israel shall perish utterly.
Jl 2: 2 Like *d* spreading over the mountains,
Am 4:13 Who made the *d* and the darkness,
5: 8 and Orion, who turns darkness into *d*,
Jon 4: 7 *d* God sent a worm which attacked the plant,
Zep 3: 5 he renders judgment unfailingly, at *d*.

Mt 20: 1 out at *d* to hire workmen for his vineyard.
21:18 At *d,* as Jesus was returning to the city,
Mk 13:35 when the cock crows, or at early *d.*
Lk 24: 1 On the first day of the week, at *d,*
24:22 tomb before *d* and failed to find his body,
Acts 5:21 the temple at *d* and resumed their teaching.
20:11 until his departure at *d.*
27:33 At *d* Paul urged all on board to take some
2Pt 1:19 dark place until the first streaks of *d* appear

DAWNED (3)

Dt 33: 2 from Sinai and *d* on his people from Seir;
2Mc 10:35 When the fifth day *d,*
1Cor 2: 9 nor has it so much as *d* on man what God

DAWNING (1)

Mt 28: 1 as the first day of the week was *d,*

DAWNS (4)

Ps(s) 97:11 Light *d* for the just;
112: 4 He *d* through the darkness,
Is 26: 9 When your judgment *d* upon the earth,
Ez 7:12 The time has come, the day *d.*

DAY (1581)

Gn 1: 5 God called the light *d,*"
1: 5 the first *d.*
1: 8 the second *d.*
1:13 the third *d.*
1:14 dome of the sky, to separate *d* from night.
1:16 lights, the greater one to govern the *d,*
1:18 the earth, to govern the *d* and the night,
1:19 the fourth *d.*
1:23 the fifth *d.*
1:31 the sixth *d.*
2: 2 Since on the seventh *d* God was finished
2: 2 *d* from all the work he had undertaken.
2: 3 God blessed the seventh *d* and made it holy,
3: 8 in the garden at the breezy time of the *d,*
7:11 month, on the seventeenth *d* of the month:
7:11 it was on that *d* that All the fountains of
7:13 On the precise *d* named,
8: 4 month, on the seventeenth *d* of the month,
8: 5 and on the first *d* of the tenth month the
8:13 first month, on the first *d* of the month,
8:14 on the twenty-seventh *d* of the month,
8:22 winter, and *d* and night shall not cease."
17:23 flesh of their foreskins on that same *d,*
17:26 on that same *d* Abraham and his son Ishmael
18: 1 of his tent, while the *d* was growing hot.
19:34 Next *d* the older one said to the younger:
21: 8 grew, and on the *d* of the child's weaning,
22: 4 *d* Abraham got sight of the place from afar.
24:63 One *d* toward evening he went out . . .
26:32 That same *d* Isaac's servants came and
26:33 name of the city, Beer-sheba, to this *d.*
27:45 Must I lose both of you in a single *d?*"
30:14 One *d,* during the wheat harvest,
30:35 That same *d* Laban removed the streaked
31:22 On the third *d,* word came to Laban
31:39 for anything stolen by *d* or night.
31:40 often the scorching heat ravaged me by *d,*
32:33 That is why, to this *d,* the Israelites
33:13 if overdriven for a single *d,*
33:16 *d* that Esau began his journey back to Seir,
34:25 On the third *d,*
35:20 monument marks Rachel's grave to this *d.*
37:12 One *d,* when his brothers had gone
39:10 she tried to entice him *d* after day,
39:10 she tried to entice him day after *d,*
39:11 One such *d,* when Joseph came
40:20 the third *d,* which was Pharaoh's birthday,
42:18 On the third *d* Joseph said to them:
48:15 been my shepherd from my birth to this *d,*
48:20 So when he blessed them that *d* and said,
Ex 2:13 The next *d* he went out again,
5: 6 That very *d* Pharaoh gave the taskmasters
6:28 *d* the LORD spoke to Moses in Egypt he said,
8:18 But on that *d* I will make an exception of
9: 6 And on the next *d* the LORD did so.
9:18 never been in Egypt from the *d* the nation
10: 6 have not seen from the *d* they first settled
10: 6 settled on this soil up to the present *d.*"
10:13 the land all that *d* and all that night.
10:28 The *d* you appear before me you shall die!"
12: 6 it until the fourteenth *d* of this month,
12:14 "This *d* shall be a memorial feast for you,
12:15 From the very first *d* you shall have your
12:15 bread from the first *d* to the seventh
12:16 first *d* you shall hold a sacred assembly,
12:17 Since it was on this very *d* that I brought
12:17 you must celebrate this *d* throughout your
12:18 From the evening of the fourteenth *d* of
12:18 evening of the twenty-first *d* of this month
12:51 On that same *d* the LORD brought the
13: 3 this *d* on which you came out of Egypt,
13: 4 This *d* of your departure is in the month
13: 6 *d* shall also be a festival to the LORD.
13: 8 On this *d* you shall explain to your son,
13:21 Thus they could travel both *d* and night.
13:22 Neither the column of cloud by *d* nor the
14:30 on that *d* from the power of the Egyptians.
16: 1 on the fifteenth *d* of the second month
16: 4 Each *d* the people are to go out and gather
16: 5 On the sixth *d,*
16:22 sixth *d* they gathered twice as much food,
16:23 Tomorrow is a *d* of complete rest,
16:25 On this *d* you will not find any of it on
16:26 you can gather it, but on the seventh *d,*
16:27 *d* some of the people went out to gather it,
16:29 the sixth *d* he gives you food for two days.
16:29 On the seventh *d* everyone is to stay home
16:30 that the people rested on the seventh *d.*
18:13 *d* Moses sat in judgment for the people,
19: 1 from the land of Egypt, on its first *d,*
19:11 garments and be ready for the third *d;*
19:11 for on the third *d* the LORD will come down
19:15 He warned them, "Be ready for the third *d.*
19:16 On the morning of the third *d* there were
20: 8 "Remember to keep holy the sabbath *d.*
20:10 the seventh *d* is the sabbath of the LORD,
20:11 but on the seventh *d* he rested.
20:11 has blessed the sabbath *d* and made it holy.
21:21 however, the slave survives for a *d* or two,
22:29 but on the eighth *d* you must give it to me.
23:12 work, but on the seventh *d* you must rest,
23:18 my feast be kept overnight till the next *d.*
24: 4 of the LORD and, rising early the next *d,*
24:16 and on the seventh *d* he called to Moses
29:34 of the bread remains over on the next *d,*
29:36 a bullock each *d* as a sin offering,
29:38 as the sacrifice established for each *d;*
31:14 If anyone does work on that *d,*
31:15 seventh *d* is the sabbath of complete rest,
31:15 on the sabbath *d* shall be put to death.
31:17 but on the seventh *d* he rested at his ease."
32: 6 Early the next *d* the people offered
32:28 and that *d* there fell about three thousand
32:29 to bring a blessing upon yourselves this *d.*"
32:30 On the next *d* Moses said to the people,
34:21 work, but on the seventh *d* you shall rest;
34:21 on that *d* you must rest even during the
34:25 feast be kept overnight for the next *d.*
35: 2 but the seventh *d* shall be sacred to you
35: 2 does work on that *d* shall be put to death.
35: 3 in any of your dwellings on the sabbath *d.*"
40: 2 "On the first *d* of the first month you
40:17 On the first *d* of the first month of the
Lv 5:24 on the *d* of his guilt offering he shall
6:13 to the LORD [on the *d* he is anointed]:
7:15 shall be eaten on the *d* it is offered;
7:15 none of it may be kept till the next *d.*
7:16 be eaten on the *d* the sacrifice is offered,
7:16 is left over may be eaten on the next *d.*
7:17 the sacrifice be left over on the third *d,*
7:18 peace offering is eaten on the third *d,*
7:35 Aaron and his sons on the *d* he called
7:36 on the *d* he anointed them the LORD ordered
8:35 meeting tent *d* and night for seven days,
9: 1 eighth *d* Moses summoned Aaron and his sons,
12: 3 eighth *d,* the flesh of the boy's foreskin
13: 5 *d* the priest shall again examine him.
13: 6 and once more examine him on the seventh *d.*
13:27 when examining it on the seventh *d,*
13:32 on the seventh *d* again examine the sore.
13:34 when examining the scall on the seventh *d,*
13:51 "On the seventh *d* the priest shall again
14: 9 On the seventh *d* he shall again shave off
14:10 *d* he shall take two unblemished male lambs,
14:23 On the eighth *d* of his purification he
14:39 On the seventh *d* the priest shall return
15:14 On the eighth *d* he shall take two
15:29 On the eighth *d* she shall take two
16:29 *d* of the seventh month everyone of you,
16:30 Since on this *d* atonement is made for you
19: 6 eaten on the very *d* of your sacrifice
19: 6 of your sacrifice or on the following *d.*
19: 6 the third *d* shall be burned up in the fire.
19: 7 If any of it is eaten on the third *d,*
19:13 overnight the wages of your *d* laborer.
22:27 the eighth *d* onward will it be acceptable,
22:28 sheep on one and the same *d* with its young.
22:30 must, therefore, be eaten on the same *d;*
22:30 of it shall be left over until the next *d.*
23: 3 but the seventh *d* is the sabbath rest,
23: 3 the sabbath rest, a *d* for sacred assembly,
23: 5 on the fourteenth *d* of the first month,
23: 6 The fifteenth *d* of this month is the
23: 8 Then on the seventh *d* you shall again hold
23:11 On the *d* after the sabbath the priest
23:12 On this *d,* when your sheaf is waved,
23:14 Until this *d,* when you bring your God
23:15 "Beginning with the *d* after the sabbath,
23:15 the *d* on which you bring the wave-offering
23:16 and then on the *d* after the seventh week,
23:16 after the seventh week, the fiftieth *d,*
23:21 On this same *d* you shall by proclamation
23:24 On the first *d* of the seventh month you
23:27 this seventh month is the *D* of Atonement,
23:28 On this *d* you shall not do any work,
23:28 any work, because it is the *D* of Atonement,
23:29 on this *d* shall be cut off from his people,
23:30 and if anyone does any work on this *d,*
23:34 The fifteenth *d* of this seventh month is
23:35 first *d* there shall be a sacred assembly,
23:36 and on the eighth *d* you shall again hold a
23:37 and libations, as prescribed for each *d,*
23:39 "On the fifteenth *d,*
23:39 eighth *d* shall be days of complete rest.
23:40 On the first *d* you shall gather foliage
24: 8 Regularly on each sabbath *d* this bread
25: 9 on the tenth *d* of the seventh month let
25: 9 on this, the *D* of Atonement,
25:50 as though he had been hired as a *d* laborer.
27:23 and on the same *d* the price thus
Nm 1: 1 Egypt, on the first *d* of the second month,
1:18 on the first *d* of the second month.
6: 9 his head on the *d* of his purification,
6: 9 purification, that is, on the seventh *d.*
6:10 On the eighth *d* he shall bring two
6:11 On the same *d* he shall reconsecrate his
6:13 On the *d* he completes the period of his
7:10 before the altar on the *d* it was anointed.
7:11 "Let one prince a *d* present his offering
7:12 his offering on the first *d* was Nahshon,
7:18 On the second *d* Nethanel,
7:24 On the third *d* it was the turn of Eliab,
7:30 On the fourth *d* it was the turn of Elizur,
7:36 the fifth *d* it was the turn of Shelumiel,
7:42 On the sixth *d* it was the turn of Eliasaph,
7:48 the seventh *d* it was the turn of Elishama,
7:54 the eighth *d* it was the turn of Gamaliel,
7:60 On the ninth *d* it was the turn of Abidon,
7:66 On the tenth *d* it was the turn of Ahiezer,
7:72 the eleventh *d* it was the turn of Pagiel,
7:78 On the twelfth *d* it was the turn of Ahira,
8:17 I consecrated them to myself on the *d* I
9: 3 The evening twilight of the fourteenth *d*
9: 5 of the fourteenth *d* of the first month,
9: 6 and so could not keep the Passover that *d.*
9: 6 up to Moses and Aaron that same *d* and said,
9:11 twilight of the fourteenth *d* of that month,
9:15 On the *d* when the Dwelling was erected,
9:16 *d* the Dwelling was covered by the cloud,
9:21 Or if the cloud lifted during the *d,*
10:11 on the twentieth *d* of the second month,
10:34 cloud of the LORD was over them by *d*
11:19 food, and you will eat it, not for one *d,*
11:32 All that *d,* all night, and all the next day
14:14 and you go before them by *d* in a column of
14:34 one year for each *d,*
15:32 discovered gathering wood on the sabbath *d.*
17: 6 The next *d* the whole Israelite community
17:23 The next *d,* when Moses entered the tent,
19:12 water on the third and on the seventh *d,*
19:12 himself on the third and on the seventh *d,*
19:19 unclean on the third and on the seventh *d;*
19:19 thus purified on the seventh *d,*
28: 3 lambs each *d* as the established holocaust,
28: 9 "On the sabbath *d* you shall offer two
28:16 "On the fourteenth *d* of the first month
28:17 *d* of this month is the pilgrimage feast.
28:24 each *d* for seven days as food offerings,
28:25 seventh *d* you shall hold a sacred assembly,
28:26 "On the *d* of first fruits,
29: 1 "On the first *d* of the seventh month you
29: 1 be a *d* on which you sound the trumpet.
29: 7 "On the tenth *d* of this seventh month you
29:12 "On the fifteenth *d* of the seventh month
29:17 second *d* you shall offer twelve bullocks,
29:20 third *d* you shall offer eleven bullocks,
29:23 the fourth *d* you shall offer ten bullocks,
29:26 the fifth *d* you shall offer nine bullocks,
29:29 the sixth *d* you shall offer eight bullocks,
29:32 seventh *d* you shall offer seven bullocks,
29:35 eighth *d* you shall hold a solemn meeting,
30: 6 But if on the *d* he learns of it her father
30: 8 yet says nothing to her that *d* about it,
30: 9 But if on the *d* he learns of it her
30:13 But if on the *d* he learns of them her
30:15 But if her husband, day after *d,*
30:15 because on the *d* he learned of them he
31:19 on the third and on the seventh *d.*
31:24 the seventh *d* you shall wash your clothes,
33: 3 on the fifteenth *d* of the first month.
33:38 Egypt, on the first *d* of the fifth month.
Dt 1: 3 year, on the first *d* of the eleventh month,
1:33 by *d* in the cloud,
2:25 This *d* I will begin to put a fear and
4:10 the *d* on which you stood before the LORD,
4:15 "You saw no form at all on the *d* the LORD
4:26 and earth this *d* to witness against you,
5: 1 which I proclaim in your hearing this *d,*
5: 3 us, all of us who are alive here this *d.*
5:12 to keep holy the sabbath *d* as the LORD,
5:14 the seventh *d* is the sabbath of the LORD,
5:15 has commanded you to observe the sabbath *d.*
8:19 you this *d* that you will perish utterly.
9: 7 From the *d* you left the land of Egypt
9:10 midst of the fire on the *d* of the assembly.
10: 4 midst of the fire on the *d* of the assembly.
10: 8 in his name, as they have done to this *d.*
11: 4 bringing ruin upon them even to this *d;*
11:26 "I set before you here, this *d,*
16: 3 *d* of your departure from the land of Egypt;
16: 4 day shall be kept overnight for the next *d.*

DAY (cont.)
16: 8 that *d* you shall not do any sort of work.
16: 9 computing them from the *d* when the sickle
18:16 God, at Horeb on the *d* of the assembly,
21:23 You shall bury it the same *d*;
24:15 day's wages before sundown on the *d* itself,
26:16 "This *d* the LORD,
27: 2 On the *d* you cross the Jordan into the
27: 9 *d* you have become the people of the LORD,
27:11 same *d* Moses gave the people this order:
28:66 and stand in dread both *d* and night,
29: 3 But not even at the present *d* has the LORD
31:22 So Moses wrote this song that same *d*,
32:35 Against the *d* of vengeance and requital,
32:35 Close at hand is the *d* of their disaster
32:48 On that very *d* the LORD said to Moses,
33:12 *d* while he abides securely at his breast."
34: 6 *d* no one knows the place of his burial.
Jos 1: 8 Recite it by *d* and by night,
4: 9 They are there to this *d*.
4:14 That *d* the LORD exalted Joshua in the
4:19 Jordan on the tenth *d* of the first month,
5: 9 place is called Gilgal to the present *d*.
5:11 On the *d* after the Passover they ate of
5:11 On that same *d* after the Passover on which
6: 4 *d* march around the city seven times,
6:14 On this second *d* they again marched around
6:15 On the seventh *d*, beginning at day-break,
6:15 on that *d* only did they march around the
6:25 continue in the midst of Israel to this *d*.
7:26 over him, which remains to the present *d*.
7:26 is called the Valley of Achor to this *d*.
8:25 *d* a total of twelve thousand men and women,
8:29 up over it, which remains to the present *d*.
9:12 as provisions the *d* we left to come to you,
9:17 The third *d* on the road, the Israelites
10:12 On this *d*, when the LORD delivered
10:13 a whole *d* did it resume its swift course.
10:14 before or since was there a *d* like this,
10:27 placed, which remain until this very *d*.
10:32 so that on the second *d* Joshua captured
10:35 attacked it and captured it the same *d*,
10:35 the doom that *d* on every person in it,
13:13 survive in the midst of Israel to this *d*.
14:11 today as I was the *d* Moses sent me forth,
14:12 region which the LORD promised me that *d*,
14:14 Caleb, son of Jephunneh, to the present *d*,
15:18 On the *d* of her marriage to Othniel,
15:63 beside the Judahites to the present *d*
16:10 live on within Ephraim to the present *d*,
22:16 You have seceded from the LORD this *d*,
23: 8 LORD, your God, as you have been to this *d*.
23: 9 and to this *d* no one has withstood you.
24:25 made a covenant with the people that *d*
Jgs 1:14 On the *d* of her marriage to Othniel she
1:21 beside the Benjaminites to the present *d*.
4:14 for this is the *d* on which the LORD has
4:23 on that *d* God humbled the Canaanite king,
5: 1 On that *d* Deborah [and Barak,
6:24 *d* it is still in Ophrah of the Abiezrites.
6:27 the townspeople, he would not do it by *d*,
6:32 So on that *d* Gideon was called Jerubbaal,
9:18 against his family this *d* and have killed
9:19 toward Jerubbaal and his family this *d*,
9:42 The next *d*, when the people were taking
9:45 entire *d* Abimelech fought against the city,
10: 4 are called Havvoth-jair to the present *d*.
10:15 Only save us this *d*."
11:27 decide this *d* between the Israelites and
12: 3 come up against me this *d* to fight with me?"
13: 7 from the womb, until the *d* of his death.'"
13:10 came to me the other *d* has appeared to me,"
14:15 they said on the fourth *d* to Samson's wife,
14:17 On the seventh *d*, since she importuned
14:18 On the seventh *d*, before the sun set,
15:19 in Lehi is called En-hakkore to this *d*.
18:12 hence to this *d* the place,
19: 5 On the fourth *d* they rose early in the
19: 9 See, the *d* is coming to an end.
19:11 they were near Jebus with the *d* far gone,
19:27 When her husband rose that *d* and opened
19:30 or seen from the *d* the Israelites came up
19:30 came up from the land of Egypt to this *d*.
20:19 The next *d* the Israelites advanced on
20:20 On the *d* the Israelites drew up in battle
20:23 in the same place as on the previous *d*,
20:26 before the LORD until evening of that *d*,
20:35 and on that *d* the Israelites killed
20:46 Those of Benjamin who fell on that *d* were
21: 4 Early the next *d* the people built an altar
1Sm 1: 4 the *d* came for Elkanah to offer sacrifice,
2:34 both shall die on the same *d*.
3: 2 One *d* Eli was asleep in his usual place.
3:12 On that *d* I will carry out in full against
4:12 and reached Shiloh that same *d*,
5: 5 of Dagon in Ashdod to this very *d*;
6:15 and sacrifices to the LORD that *d*.
6:16 lords returned to Ekron the same *d*.
7: 2 From the *d* the ark came to rest in
7: 6 before the LORD, and they fasted that *d*,
7:10 That *d*, however, the LORD thundered
8: 8 *d* I brought them up from Egypt to this day,
8: 8 I brought them up from Egypt to this *d*,
8:18 but on that *d* the LORD will not answer you."
9:15 The *d* before Saul's arrival,
9:24 Thus Saul dined with Samuel that *d*.
10: 9 That very *d* all these signs came to pass. . . .
11:11 On the appointed *d*, Saul arranged
11:11 Ammonites until the heat of the *d*;
11:13 say, "No man is to be put to death this *d*,
12: 2 with you from my youth to the present *d*.
12: 5 "The LORD is witness against you this *d*,
12:18 and the LORD sent thunder and rain that *d*.
13:22 And so on the *d* of battle neither sword
14: 1 One *d* Jonathan, son of Saul,
14:23 Thus the LORD saved Israel that *d*.
14:24 And Saul swore a very rash oath that *d*,
14:28 'Cursed be the man who takes food this *d*!'
14:31 routed that *d* from Michmash to Aijalon,
15:28 the kingdom of Israel from you this *d*,
16:13 from that *d* on, the spirit of the LORD
17:46 This very *d* I will leave your corpse and
18: 2 Saul laid claim to David that *d* and did
18: 9 [And from that *d* on, Saul was jealous
18:10 *d* an evil spirit from God came over Saul,
19:24 all that *d* and night he lay naked.
20:19 *d* you will be missed all the more.
20:20 third *d* of the month I will shoot arrows,
20:24 On the *d* of the new moon,
20:26 Saul, however, said nothing that *d*,
20:27 the next *d*, the second day of the month,
20:34 took no food that second *d* of the month,
21: 8 One of Saul's servants was there that *d*,
21:11 That same *d* David took to flight from Saul,
22:18 *d* eighty-five who wore the linen ephod.
22:21 "I knew that *d*, when Doeg the Edomite
24: 5 is the *d* of which the LORD said to you,
24:20 generously for what you have done this *d*.
25:16 like a rampart night and *d* the whole time
25:33 who this *d* have prevented me from shedding
26: 8 your enemy into your grasp this *d*.
26:19 exiled me so that this *d* I have no share
27: 1 shall perish some *d* at the hand of Saul.
27: 6 That same *d* Achish gave him Ziklag,
28:20 he had eaten nothing all that *d* and night.
29: 3 the *d* he came over to me until the present."
29: 6 you from the day of your arrival to this *d*.
29: 8 first *d* I have been with you to this day,
30: 1 and his men reached Ziklag on the third *d*,
30:25 And from that *d* forward he made it a law
31: 6 armor-bearer died together on that same *d*.
31: 8 The *d* after the battle the Philistines
2Sm 1: 2 On the third *d* a man came from Saul's camp,
2:17 After a very fierce battle that *d*,
3: 8 yet this *d* you charge me with a crime
3:35 David with food while it was still *d*.
3:37 So on that *d* all the people and all Israel
3:39 I am the anointed king, I am weak this *d*,
4: 3 they have been resident aliens to this *d*.
4: 5 house of Ishbaal during the heat of the *d*,
4: 8 Thus has the LORD this *d* avenged my lord
5: 8 On that *d* David said:
6: 8 called Perez-uzzah down to the present *d*.)
6: 9 David feared the LORD that *d* and said,
6:23 Michal was childless to the *d* of her death.
7: 6 I have not dwelt in a house from the *d* on
11:12 So Uriah remained in Jerusalem that *d*.
11:12 On the *d* following, David summoned
12:18 On the seventh *d*, the child died.
14:22 *d* I know that I am in good favor with you,
16:12 for the curses he is uttering this *d*."
18: 7 the casualties there that *d* were heavy
18: 8 more combatants that *d* than did the sword.
18:18 is called Yadabshalom to the present *d*.
18:20 On some other *d* you may take the good news,
18:31 that this *d* the LORD has taken your part,
19: 4 that *d* like men shamed by flight in battle.
19:20 did the *d* my lord the king left Jerusalem.
19:23 that you would create enmity for me this *d*?
19:25 *d* the king left until he returned safely.
20: 3 in confinement to the *d* of their death,
21:10 of the sky from settling on them by *d*,
22:19 They attacked me on my *d* of calamity,
23:10 brought about a great victory on that *d*;
24:18 same *d* Gad went to David and said to him,
1Kgs 1:30 this very *d* I will fulfill the oath I
1:48 *d* seated one of my sons upon my throne,
2:24 this *d* shall Adonijah be put to death."
3:18 On the third *d* after I gave birth this
5: 2 for each *d* were thirty kors of fine flour,
5:21 and said, "Blessed be the LORD this *d*,
8: 8 (They have remained there to this *d*.)
8:16 *d* I brought my people Israel out of Egypt,
8:24 You who spoke that promise, have this *d*,
8:28 I, your servant, utter before you this *d*.
8:29 eyes watch night and *d* over this temple,
8:59 our God, be present to him *d* and night,
8:59 of his people Israel as each *d* requires,
8:61 and keeping his commandments, as on this *d*."
8:64 On that *d* the king consecrated the middle
8:66 On the eighth *d* he dismissed the people,
9:13 of Cabul, as they are called to this *d*.
9:21 as forced laborers, as they are to this *d*.
10:12 wood was brought or seen to the present *d*.
12:12 *d* all Israel came back to King Rehoboam,
12:19 rebellion against David's house to this *d*.
12:32 eighth month of the fifteenth *d* of the month
12:33 on the fifteenth *d* of the eighth month,
13: 3 He gave a sign that same *d* and said:
13:11 the man of God had done that *d* in Bethel.
16:16 *d* in the camp all Israel proclaimed Omri,
17:14 until the *d* when the LORD sends rain upon
18:36 let it be known this *d* that you are God in
20:29 On the seventh *d* battle was joined,
20:29 thousand foot soldiers of Aram in one *d*.
22:25 "on that *d* when you retreat into an
22:35 The battle grew fierce during the *d*,
2Kgs 2:22 the water has stayed pure even to this *d*,
4: 8 One *d* Elisha came to Shunem,
4:18 The *d* came when the child was old enough
6:26 One *d*, as the king of Israel was walking
6:29 The next *d* I said to her,
7: 9 This is a *d* of good news,
8: 6 from the *d* she left the land until now."
8:15 The next *d*, however, Hazael took a cloth,
8:22 To this *d* Edom has been in revolt against
14: 7 it Joktheel, the name it has to this *d*.
15: 5 and he was a leper to the *d* of his death.
17:34 To this *d* they worship according to their
17:41 And their sons and grandsons, to this *d*,
19: 3 'This is a *d* of distress,
20: 8 to the temple of the LORD on the third *d*?"
20:17 your fathers have stored up until this *d*,
21:15 provoked me from the *d* their fathers came
23:16 was standing by the altar on the feast *d*.
25: 1 reign, on the tenth *d* of the month,
25: 3 On the ninth *d* of the fourth month,
25: 8 On the seventh *d* of the fifth month (this
25:27 the twenty-seventh *d* of the twelfth month,
1Chr 4:43 and have resided there to the present *d*.
5:26 Gozan, where they have remained to this *d*.
9:33 for *d* and night they had to be ready for
10: 8 On the following *d*, when the Philistines
11:22 of Ariel of Moab, and also, on a snowy *d*,
12:23 And from *d* to day men kept coming to
13:11 has been called Perez-uzza even to this *d*.
16: 7 Then, on that same *d*, David appointed
16:23 *d* after day Tell his glory among the
17: 5 when I led Israel onward, even to this *d*,
26:17 On the east, six watched each *d*,
26:17 four each day, on the south, four each *d*,
29: 5 contribute generously this *d* to the LORD?"
29:21 On the following *d* they offered sacrifices
29:22 and on that *d* they ate and drank in the
2Chr 5: 9 The ark has remained there to this *d*.
6: 5 'Since the *d* I brought my people out of
6:15 you have brought it to fulfillment this *d*.
6:20 eyes watch *d* and night over this temple,
7: 9 the eighth *d* they held a special meeting,
7:10 On the twenty-third *d* of the seventh month
8: 8 forced labor, as they continue to this *d*.
8:13 day by *d* according to the command of Moses,
8:16 from the *d* the foundation of the house
10:12 the third *d*, Jeroboam and all the people
10:19 rebellion against David's house to this *d*.
18:24 "on that *d* when you enter an innermost
18:34 The battle grew fierce during the *d*,
20:26 On the fourth *d* they held an assembly in
21:15 forth because of the disease, day after *d*.'"
24:11 This they did day after *d* until they had
26:21 remained a leper to the *d* of his death.
28: 6 twenty thousand of Judah in a single *d*,
29:17 on the first *d* of the first month,
29:17 and on the eighth *d* of the month they
29:17 and on the sixteenth *d* of the first month,
30:15 on the fourteenth *d* of the second month.
30:21 LORD *d* after *d* with all their strength.
35: 1 on the fourteenth *d* of the first month.
35:16 was arranged that *d* so that the Passover
35:21 I have not come against you this *d*,
35:25 which is recited to this *d* by all the male
Ezr 3: 4 in the proper number required for each *d*.
3: 6 From the first *d* of the seventh month they
6: 9 be delivered to them *d* by *d* without fail,
6:15 house on the third *d* of the month Adar,
6:19 on the fourteenth *d* of the first month.
7: 9 On the first *d* of the first month he
7: 9 and on the first *d* of the fifth month he
8:31 Ahava on the twelfth *d* of the first month.
8:33 On the fourth *d*, the silver, the gold,
9: 7 even to this *d* great has been our guilt,
10: 9 month, on the twentieth *d* of the month.
10:13 can be performed in a single *d* or even two,
10:16 with the first *d* of the tenth month.
10:17 By the first *d* of the first month they had
Neh 1: 6 now offer in your presence *d* and night for
1:11 Grant success to your servant this *d*,
3:34 complete their restoration in a single *d*?
4: 3 *d* and night for fear of what they might do.
4:16 a guard by night and a working force by *d*.
5:11 return to them this very *d* their fields,
5:15 each *d* forty silver shekels for their food;
6:15 was finished on the twenty-fifth *d* of Elul;
8: 2 On the first *d* of the seventh month,
8:10 Do not be saddened this *d*,
8:13 On the second *d*, the family heads
8:18 the book of the law of God *d* after *d*,
8:18 after day, from the first *d* to the last.
8:18 and the solemn assembly on the eighth *d*,

9: 1 On the twenty-fourth d of this month,
9: 3 their God, for a fourth part of the d,
9:10 made for yourself a name even to this d.
9:12 With a column of cloud you led them by d,
9:19 cease to lead them by d on their journey,
9:32 time of the kings of Assyria until this d!
10:32 kind of grain for sale on the sabbath d,
12:43 Great sacrifices were offered on that d,
13:15 them to Jerusalem on the sabbath d.
13:17 you are doing, profaning the sabbath d?
13:19 no burden might enter on the sabbath d.
13:22 so that the sabbath d might be kept holy.
Tb 3: 7 On the same d, at Ecbatana in Media,
3:10 That d she was deeply grieved in spirit.
4: 1 That same d Tobit remembered the money he
4: 9 for yourself against the d of adversity.
5:15 "For each d you are away I will give you
5:21 d when he returns to you safe and sound.
9: 4 If I should delay my return by a single d,
10: 1 Meanwhile, d by day,
10: 7 watch all d at the road her son had taken,
11: 8 will again be able to see the light of d."
11:17 That d there was joy for all the Jews who
12:18 So continue to thank him every d;
14:10 The d you bury your mother next to me,
Jdt 2: 1 on the twenty-second d of the first month,
2:10 them for me till the d of their punishment.
6:19 this d on those who are consecrated to you."
7: 1 d Holofernes ordered his whole army,
7: 2 d all their fighting men went into action.
7: 6 On the second d Holofernes led out all his
7:21 that on no d did they have enough to drink,
7:28 to do as we have proposed, this very d."
8:12 should have put God to the test this d,
11:15 On the very d when the response reaches
11:17 serving the God of heaven night and d.
12:10 On the fourth d Holofernes gave a banquet
12:14 be a joy for me till the d of my death."
12:16 time to seduce her from the d he saw her.
12:20 had ever drunk on one single d in his life.
13: 7 his head, and said, "Strengthen me this d,
13:11 he has done it this very d."
14: 8 she had been doing from the d she left
14:10 with the house of Israel to the present d.
16:17 in the d of judgment he will punish them:
Est A: 1 King Ahasuerus, on the first d of Nisan,
A: 7 It was a dark and gloomy d.
1:10 On the seventh d,
1:18 This very d the Persian and Median ladies
2:11 Day by d Mordecai would walk about in
3: 4 d after d and he would not listen to them,
3: 7 presence to determine the d and the month
3: 7 of Mordecai's people on a single d,
3: 7 on the thirteenth d of the twelfth month,
3:12 thirteenth d of the first month they wrote,
3:13 be killed, destroyed, wiped out in one d,
3:13 one d, the thirteenth d of the twelfth
B: 6 on the fourteenth d of the twelfth month,
B: 7 world by a violent death on one same d,
3:14 that they might be prepared for that d.
4:16 of you, not eating or drinking, night or d,
C:29 From the d I was brought here till now,
D: 1 the third d, putting an end to her prayers,
5: 1 [Now on the third d,
5: 9 d Haman left happy and in good spirits.
7: 2 Again, on this second d,
8: 1 d King Ahasuerus gave the house of Haman,
8: 9 on the twenty-third d of the third month,
8:12 King Ahasuerus; on a single d,
E:20 the thirteenth d of the twelfth month,
E:20 may help them on the d set for their ruin,
E:21 has turned that d for them from one of
E:22 you too must celebrate this memorable d
8:13 d to avenge themselves on their enemies.
9: 1 When the d arrived on which the order
9: 1 out, the thirteenth d of the twelfth month,
9:11 On the same d, when the number
9:17 and made it a d of feasting and rejoicing.
9:17 on the thirteenth d of the month of Adar.
9:18 and made it a d of feasting and rejoicing.)
9:19 of Adar as a d of rejoicing and feasting,
F: 8 and the d of judgment before God and among
1Mc 1:54 On the fifteenth d of the month Chislev,
1:59 On the twenty-fifth d of each month they
2:41 On that d they came to this decision:
3:47 That d they fasted and wore sackcloth;
4:25 Thus Israel had a great deliverance that d.
4:52 on the twenty-fifth d of the ninth month,
4:54 the d on which the Gentiles had defiled it,
4:54 very d it was reconsecrated with songs,
4:59 the twenty-fifth d of the month Chislev.
5:27 and destroy all these people in one d."
5:34 eight thousand of their men fell that d.
5:50 he assaulted the city all that d and night,
5:60 about two thousand Israelites fell that d.
6:57 "We are growing weaker every d,
7:16 in one d, according to the text
7:43 on the thirteenth d of the month Adar.
7:48 and observed that d as a great festival.
8:10 and reduced them to slavery even to this d.
8:15 and every d three hundred and twenty men
9:44 is not like yesterday and the d before.
9:49 men on Bacchides' side fell that d.
10:30 I renounce the right from this d forward:
10:34 the three days that precede each feast d,
10:50 until sunset, and Demetrius fell that d.
10:55 "Happy the d on which you returned to the
11:35 From this d on we grant them release from
11:47 On that d they killed about a hundred
11:74 of the foreign troops fell on that d.
13:30 built at Modein is there to the present d.
13:51 On the twenty-third d of the second month,
13:52 Simon decreed that this d should be
14:27 "On the eighteenth d of Elul,
2Mc 1:18 on the twenty-fifth d of the month Chislev,
3:14 So on the d he had set he went in to take
5:25 and waited until the holy d of the sabbath;
6:11 their respect for the holiness of that d,
7:20 saw her seven sons perish in a single d,
8:26 late hour, it was the d before the sabbath,
8:27 Lord who kept them safe for that d
10: 5 On the anniversary of the d on which the
10:35 When the fifth d dawned,
12:15 of the world, who, in the d of Joshua,
12:39 On the following d, since the task
13:10 people to call upon the LORD night and d,
13:17 D was just breaking when this was
14:21 A d was set on which the leaders would
15: 1 attack them in all safety on the d of rest.
15: 2 but show respect for the d which the
15: 3 prescribed the keeping of the sabbath d.
15: 4 commanded the observance of the sabbath d,
15:36 never to let this d pass unobserved,
15:36 on the thirteenth d of the twelfth month,
15:36 Adar in Aramaic, the eve of Mordecai's D.
Jb 1: 6 One d, when the sons of God
1:13 And so one d, while his sons
3: 1 Job opened his mouth and cursed his d.
3: 3 Perish the d on which I was born,
3: 4 May that d be darkness:
3: 6 May obscurity seize that d;
7:18 each new d and try him at every moment!
14: 6 while, like a hireling, he completes his d.
15:24 By d the darkness fills him with dread;
17:12 Such men change the night into d;
20:28 that run off in the d of God's anger.
21:32 and on the d he is carried to the grave
24:16 By d they shut themselves in;
27:20 Terrors rush upon him by d;
Ps(s) 1: 2 LORD and meditates on his law d and night.
2: 7 this d I have begotten you.
7:12 judge is God, a God who punishes d by day.
7:12 judge is God, a God who punishes day by d.
13: 3 in my soul, grief in my heart d after day?
18:19 They attacked me in the d of my calamity,
19: 3 Day pours out the word to d,
22: 3 O my God, I cry out by d,
25: 5 my savior, and for you I wait all the d.
27: 5 hide me in his abode in the d of trouble;
32: 3 wasted away with my groaning all the d,
32: 4 d and night your hand was heavy upon me;
35:28 your justice, your praise, all the d.
37:13 at him, for he sees that his d is coming.
37:26 All the d he is kindly and lends,
38: 7 all the d I go in mourning,
38:13 of ruin, treachery they talk of all the d.
41: 2 d of misfortune the LORD will deliver him.
42: 4 My tears are my food d and night,
42: 4 and night, as they say to me day after d,
42: 9 By d the LORD bestows his grace,
42:11 mock me, as they say to me d after day,
44: 9 In God we gloried d by d;
44:16 All the d my disgrace is before me,
44:23 your sake we are being slain all the d;
52: 3 All the d you plot harm;
55:11 d and night they prowl about upon its
56: 2 the d they press their attack against me.
56: 3 My adversaries trample upon me all the d;
56: 6 All the d they molest me in my efforts;
59:17 my refuge in the d of distress.
61: 9 name forever, fulfilling my vows d by d.
68:20 blessed d by d be the Lord,
71: 8 with your praise, with your glory d by d.
71:15 your justice, d by d your salvation,
71:24 d by d shall discourse on your justice.
72:15 d by d shall they bless him.
73:14 For I suffer affliction d after d and
74:16 Yours is the d, and yours the night;
74:22 how the fool blasphemes you d after d.
77: 3 on the d of my distress I seek the Lord.
78: 9 of bowmen, retreated in the d of battle.
78:14 He led them with a cloud by d,
78:42 nor the d he delivered them from the foe,
84:11 d in your courts than a thousand elsewhere;
86: 3 on me, O Lord, for to you I call all the d.
86: 7 In the d of my distress I call upon you,
88: 2 O LORD, my God, by d I cry out;
88:18 They encompass me like water all the d;
89:17 At your name they rejoice all the d,
91: 5 the night nor the arrow that flies by d;
95: 8 as in the d of Massah in the desert,
96: 2 announce his salvation, d after d.
102: 3 your face from me in the d of my distress.
102: 3 in the d when I call,
102: 9 All the d my enemies revile me;
110: 3 is princely power in the d of your birth,
110: 5 he will crush kings on the d of his wrath.
116: 2 has inclined his ear to me the d I called.
118:24 This is the d the LORD has made;
119:97 It is my meditation all the d.
119:164 a d I praise you for your just ordinances.
121: 6 The sun shall not harm you by d,
136: 8 The sun to rule over the d,
137: 7 the children of Edom, the d of Jerusalem,
139:12 is not dark, and night shines as the d.
140: 3 in their hearts, and stir up wars every d.
140: 8 you are my helmet in the d of battle!
145: 2 Every d will I bless you,
146: 4 on that d his plans perish.
Prv 4:18 that grows in brilliance till perfect d.
6:34 he will have no pity on the d of vengeance;
7: 9 In the twilight, at dusk of d,
8:30 craftsman, and I was his delight d by day,
8:30 craftsman, and I was his delight day by d,
11: 4 Wealth is useless on the d of wrath,
15:15 Every d is miserable for the depressed,
16: 4 own ends, even the wicked for the evil d.
21:26 Some are consumed with avarice all the d,
21:31 The horse is equipped for the d of battle,
27: 1 you know not what any d may bring forth.
27:15 a rainy d the match is a quarrelsome woman.
Eccl 7: 1 and the d of death than the day of birth.
7:14 On a good d enjoy good things,
7:14 good things, and on an evil d consider:
8: 8 it, and none has mastery of the d of death.
8:17 even though neither by d nor by night do
Sg 2:17 d breathes cool and the shadows lenghten,
3:11 has crowned him on the d of his marriage,
3:11 d of his marriage, on the d of the joy
4: 6 d breathes cool and the shadows lengthen,
Wis 3:18 no hope nor comfort in the d of scrutiny;
5:14 memory of the nomad camping for a single d.
10:17 for them by d and a starry flame by night.
Sir 1:11 on the d of his death he will be blessed.
5: 8 to the LORD, put it not off from d to day;
5:10 for it will be no help on the d of wrath.
11: 4 worn cloak and jibe at no man's bitter d:
11:25 d of prosperity makes one forget adversity;
11:25 d of adversity makes one forget prosperity.
11:26 For it is easy with the LORD on the d of
18:24 Think of wrath and the d of death,
18:25 poverty and want in the d of wealth.
23:14 been born or cursing the d of your birth.
31:20 slumber and a clear mind next d on rising.
33: 7 Why is one d more important than another,
33: 7 when it is the sun that lights up every d?
36: 7 Hasten the d, bring on the time;
38:27 and designer who, laboring night and d,
40: 1 d one leaves his mother's womb to the d
40: 2 troubled forebodings till the d he dies
40: 6 in his dreams he struggles as he did by d,
44: 7 in their time, each illustrious in his d.
45:14 the established sacrifice twice each d;
46: 4 stop the sun, so that one d became two?
47: 7 and shattered their power till our own d.
48:10 an end to wrath before the d of the LORD,
Is 2:11 the LORD alone will be exalted, on that d.
2:12 d against all that is proud and arrogant,
2:17 the LORD alone will be exalted, on that d.
2:20 On that d men will throw to the moles and
3: 7 Then shall he answer in that d:
3:18 On that d the Lord will do away with the
4: 1 women will take hold of one man on that d,
4: 2 On that d, The branch of the LORD
4: 5 by d and a light of flaming fire by night.
4: 6 shade from the parching heat of d,
5:30 [They will roar over it, on that d,
7:18 On that d The LORD shall whistle for the
7:20 On that d the Lord shall shave with the
7:21 On that d a man shall keep a heifer or a
7:23 On that d every place where there used to
9: 3 you have smashed, as on the d of Midian.
9:13 and tail, palm branch and reed in one d.
10: 3 What will you do on the d of punishment,
10:17 his briers and his thorns in a single d.
10:20 On that d The remnant of Israel,
10:27 On that d, His burden shall be taken
11:10 On that d, The root of Jesse,
11:11 On that d, The LORD shall again take
12: 1 On that d, you will say:
12: 4 fountain of salvation, and say on that d:
13: 6 Howl, for the d of the LORD is near;
13: 9 Lo, the d of the LORD comes cruel,
13:13 of hosts on the d of his burning anger.
14: 3 On the d the LORD relieves you of sorrow
17: 4 On that d The glory of Jacob shall fade,
17: 7 On that d man shall look to his maker,
17: 9 On that d his strong cities shall be like
17:11 Though you make them grow the d you plant
17:11 disappear on the d of the grievous blow,
19:16 that d the Egyptians shall be like women,
19:18 On that d there shall be five cities in
19:19 On that d there shall be an altar to the
19:21 Egyptians shall know the LORD in that d:
19:23 On that d there shall be a highway from
19:24 On that d Israel shall be a third party
20: 6 of this coastland shall say on that d,
21: 8 O my Lord, I stand constantly by d;
22: 5 It is a d of panic,

DAY (cont.)

22: 8 On that *d* you looked to the weapons in the
22:12 On that *d* the Lord, the GOD of hosts,
22:20 On that *d* I will summon my servant Eliakim,
22:25 On that *d,* says the LORD of hosts,
23:15 On that *d,* Tyre shall be forgotten
24:21 On that *d* the LORD will punish the host of
25: 9 On that *d* it will be said:
26: 1 On that *d* they will sing this song in the
27: 1 On that *d,* The LORD will punish
27: 2 On that *d*— The pleasant vineyard
27: 3 anyone harm it, night and *d* I guard it.
27:12 On that *d,* The LORD shall beat out
27:13 On that *d,* A great trumpet shall blow,
28: 5 On that *d* the LORD of hosts will be a
28:19 morning it shall pass, By *d* and by night;
29:18 *d* the deaf shall hear the words of a book;
30:23 On that *d* your cattle will graze in
30:25 On the *d* of the great slaughter,
30:26 On the *d* the LORD binds up the wounds of
31: 7 On that *d* each one of you shall spurn his
34: 8 For the LORD has a *d* of vengeance,
34:10 Night and *d* it shall not be quenched,
37: 3 'This is a *d* of distress,
38:12 *D* and night you give me over to torment;
38:13 *d* and night you give me over to torment].
39: 6 your fathers have stored up until this *d,*
47: 9 shall come to you suddenly, in a single *d:*
49: 8 you, on the *d* of salvation I help you,
51:13 All the *d* you are in constant dread of the
52: 5 all the *d* my name is constantly reviled.
52: 6 on that *d* my people shall know my renown,
58: 2 They seek me *d* after *d,*
58: 3 fast *d* you carry out your own pursuits,
58: 5 fasting I wish, of keeping a *d* of penance:
58: 5 this a fast, a *d* acceptable to the LORD?
58:13 following your own pursuits on my holy *d;*
58:13 a delight, and the LORD's holy *d* honorable;
60:11 *d* and night they shall not be closed But
60:19 longer shall the sun be your light by *d,*
61: 2 the LORD and a *d* of vindication by our God,
62: 6 Never, by *d* or by night,
63: 4 For the *d* of vengeance was in my heart,
65: 2 my hands all the *d* to a rebellious people,
65: 5 my wrath, a fire that burns all the *d.*
66: 8 Can a country be brought forth in one *d,*
Jer 1:10 *d* I set you over nations and over kingdoms.
1:18 this *d* who have made you a fortified city,
3:25 LORD, our God, From our youth to this *d,*
4: 9 In that *d,* says the LORD, The king will
6: 4 the *d* is waning,
7:22 *d* I brought them out of the land of Egypt,
7:25 From the *d* that your fathers left the land
7:25 left the land of Egypt even to this *d,*
8:23 That I might weep *d* and night over the
11: 4 upon your fathers the *d* I brought them
11: 7 from the *d* I brought them up out of the
11: 7 up out of the land of Egypt even to this *d.*
12: 3 set them apart for the *d* of carnage.
14:17 Let my eyes stream with tears *d* and night,
15: 9 Her sun sets in full *d,*
16:13 you can serve strange gods *d* and night,
16:19 fortress, my refuge in the *d* of distress!
17:16 the *d* without remedy I have not desired.
17:17 you, my refuge in the *d* of misfortune.
17:18 Bring upon them the *d* of misfortune,
17:21 not to carry burdens on the sabbath *d,*
18:17 back, not my face, in their *d* of disaster.
20: 7 All the *d* I am an object of laughter;
20: 8 brought me derision and reproach all the *d.*
20:14 Cursed be the *d* on which I was born!
20:14 *d* my mother gave me birth never be blessed!
25: 3 son of Amon, king of Judah, to this *d*—
25:33 that *d,* those whom the LORD has slain
27:22 shall remain, until the *d* I look for them,
30: 7 How mighty is that *d*— none like it!
30: 8 On that *d,* says the LORD of hosts,
31: 6 a *d* will come when the watchmen will call
31:32 made with their fathers the *d* I took them
31:35 LORD, He who gives the sun to light the *d,*
32:20 in the land of Egypt and to this *d,*
32:31 From the day it was built to this *d,*
33:20 If you can break my covenant with *d,*
33:20 so that *d* and night no longer alternate in
33:25 When I have no covenant with *d* and night,
34:13 The *d* I brought your fathers out of the
35:14 to this *d* they have not drunk it;
36: 2 nations, from the *d* I first spoke to you,
36: 6 Do you go on the fast *d* and read publicly
36:30 be cast out, exposed to the heat of *d,*
37:21 and given a loaf of bread each *d* from the
38:28 the guard till the *d* Jerusalem was taken.
39: 2 On the ninth *d* of the fourth month,
39:17 But on that *d* I will rescue you,
41: 4 The second *d* after the murder of Gedaliah,
42:19 never say that I did not warn you this *d.*
44:10 To this *d* they have not been crushed;
44:23 evil has befallen you at the present *d.*
46:10 the *d* of the Lord GOD of hosts, a *d*
46:21 When the *d* of their ruin comes upon them,
47: 4 Because of the *d* which has come to ruin
48:41 On that *d* the hearts of Moab's heroes are
49:22 On that *d* the hearts of Edom's heroes
49:26 On that *d,* says the LORD of hosts,
50:27 their *d* has come,
50:30 all her warriors shall perish on that *d,*
50:31 For your *d* has come,
51: 2 her from all sides on the *d* of affliction.
52: 4 of his reign, on the tenth *d* of the month,
52: 6 On the ninth *d* of the fourth month,
52:11 kept in prison until the *d* of his death.
52:12 On the tenth *d* of the fifth month (this
52:31 on the twenty-fifth *d* of the twelfth month,
52:34 days of his life until the *d* of his death.
Lam 1:12 afflicted me on the *d* of his blazing wrath.
1:13 He left me desolate, in pain all the *d.*
1:21 Bring on the *d* you have proclaimed,
2: 1 of his footstool on the *d* of his wrath.
2: 7 in the house of the LORD as on a feast *d.*
2:16 This at last is the *d* we hoped for;
2:18 your tears flow like a torrent *d* and night;
2:21 You have slain on the *d* of your wrath,
2:22 feast *d* terrors against me from all sides;
2:22 There was not, on the *d* of your wrath,
3: 3 back his hand again and again all the *d.*
3:14 all nations, their taunt all the *d* long;
3:62 of my foes, against me all the *d;*
Bar 1: 2 fifth year [on the seventh *d* of the month,
1:13 been withdrawn from us at the present *d.*
1:14 feast *d* and during the days of assembly:
1:19 of the land of Egypt until the present *d,*
2:11 for yourself a name till the present *d:*
2:25 to the heat of *d* and the frost of night.
2:28 the *d* you ordered him to write down your
Ez 1: 1 year, on the fifth *d* of the fourth month,
1: 2 On the fifth *d* of the month,
1:28 *d* was the splendor that surrounded him.
2: 3 have revolted against me to this very *d.*
4: 6 one *d* for each year I have allotted you.
4:10 shekels a day by weight; each *d* the same.
4:11 hin by measure; each *d* the same.
7: 7 The time has come, near is the *d:*
7:10 See, the *d* of the LORD!
7:12 The time has come, the *d* dawns.
7:19 save them on the *d* of the LORD's wrath.
8: 1 On the fifth *d* of the sixth month,
12: 3 during the *d* while they are looking on,
12: 7 During the *d* I brought out my baggage as
13: 5 firm against attack on the *d* of the LORD.
16: 4 the *d* you were born your navel cord was
16: 5 something loathsome, the *d* you were born.
20: 1 year, on the tenth *d* of the fifth month,
20: 5 The *d* I chose Israel,
20: 6 That *d* I swore to bring them out of the
20:29 call it a high place even to the present *d.*
20:31 with all your idols even to this *d.*
21:30 whose *d* is coming when your life of crime
21:34 *d* has come when their crimes are at an end.
22: 4 you have brought on your *d,*
23:39 *d* they slew their children for their idols,
24: 1 On the tenth *d* of the tenth month,
24: 2 for this very *d* the king of Babylon has
24:25 the *d* I take away from them their bulwark,
24:26 that *d* the fugitive will come to you,
24:27 that *d* your mouth shall be opened and you
26: 1 On the first *d* of the . . .
26:18 On this, the *d* of your fall,
27:27 of the sea on the *d* of your shipwreck.
28:13 were made, on the *d* you were created.
28:15 your conduct from the *d* you were created,
29: 1 *d* of the tenth month in the tenth year,
29:17 On the first *d* of the first month in the
29:21 On that *d* I will make a horn sprout for
30: 2 Cry, Oh, the *d!*
30: 3 *d,* near is the *d* of the LORD; a *d* of
30: 3 near is the *d* of the LORD; a *d* of
30: 9 On that *d* messengers shall hasten forth at
30: 9 they shall be in anguish on the *d* of Egypt,
30:18 In Tehaphnehes the *d* shall be darkened
30:20 On the seventh *d* of the first month in the
31: 1 *d* of the third month in the eleventh year,
31:15 On the *d* he went down to the nether world
32: 1 *d* of the twelfth month in the twelfth year,
32:10 and on the *d* of your downfall every one of
32:17 *d* of the first month in the twelfth year,
33:12 will not save him on the *d* that he sins;
33:12 on the *d* that he turns from his wickedness
33:21 On the fifth *d* of the tenth month,
38:18 But on that *d,* the *d* when Gog invades
38:19 On that *d* there shall be a great shaking
39: 8 This is the *d* I have decreed.
39:11 On that *d* I will give Gog for his tomb a
39:22 From that *d* forward the house of Israel
40: 1 On the tenth *d* of the month beginning the
40: 1 that very *d* the hand of the LORD came upon
43:22 On the second *d* present an unblemished
43:27 these days are over, from the eighth *d* on,
44:27 and on the *d* he enters the inner court to
45:18 On the first *d* of the first month you
45:20 You shall repeat this on the first *d* of
45:21 On the fourteenth *d* of the first month you
45:22 *d* the prince shall offer on his own behalf,
45:23 he shall offer one male goat each *d.*
45:25 *d* of the seventh month, the feast *d,*
46: 1 on the *d* of the new moon it shall be open.
46: 6 On the *d* of the new moon he shall provide
Dn 3:37 in the world this *d* because of our sins.
3:38 We have in our *d* no prince,
6:11 God in the upper chamber three times a *d,*
6:14 three times a *d* he offers his prayer."
9: 7 we are shamefaced even to this *d:*
9:15 made a name for yourself even to this *d,*
10: 4 On the twenty-fourth *d* of the first month
10:12 "from the first *d* you made up your mind
13: 8 old men saw her enter every *d* for her walk,
13:12 *D* by *d* they watched eagerly for her.
13:13 One *d* they said to each other,
13:15 One *d,* while they were waiting
13:28 came to her husband Joakim the next *d,*
13:62 Thus was innocent blood spared that *d.*
13:64 And from that *d* onward Daniel was greatly
14: 3 and every *d* they provided for it six
14: 4 worshiped it and went every *d* to adore it;
14: 6 see how much he eats and drinks every *d?*"
14:40 *d* the king came to mourn for Daniel.
Hos 1: 5 On that *d* I will break the bow of Israel
2: 2 for great shall be the *d* of Jezreel
2: 5 leaving her as on the *d* of her birth;
2:18 On that *d,* says the LORD.
2:20 I will make a covenant for them on that *d,*
2:23 On that *d* I will respond,
4: 5 You shall stumble in the *d,*
5: 9 become a waste on the *d* of chastisement:
6: 2 on the third *d* he will raise us up,
6: 3 judgment shines forth like the light of *d!*
7: 5 On the *d* of our king,
9: 5 the festival *d,* the *d* of the LORD's feast?
Jl 1:15 Alas, the *d!*
1:15 for near is the *d* of the LORD,
2: 1 tremble, for the *d* of the LORD is coming;
2: 2 a *d* of darkness and of gloom, a day
2:11 For great is the *d* of the LORD,
3: 4 At the coming of the *D* of the LORD,
3: 4 Day of the Lord, the great and terrible *d*
4:14 *d* of the LORD in the valley of decision.
4:18 that *d,* the mountains shall drip new wine
Am 1:14 Amid clamor on the *d* of battle
2:16 of warriors shall flee naked on that *d,*
3:14 the *d* when I punish Israel for his crimes,
4: 4 bring your sacrifices, every third *d,*
5: 8 into dawn, and darkens *d* into night;
5:18 to those who yearn for the *d* of the LORD!
5:18 What will this *d* of the LORD mean for you?
5:20 *d* of the LORD be darkness and not light,
6: 3 You would put off the evil *d,*
8: 3 songs shall become wailings on that *d,*
8: 9 On that *d,* says the LORD GOD,
8:10 son, and bring their *d* to a bitter end.
8:13 On that *d,* fair virgins and young men
9:11 *d* I will raise up the fallen hut of David;
Ob 1: 8 *d* make the wise men disappear from Edom,
1:11 On the *d* when you stood by, on the *d*
1:12 day of your brother, the *d* of his disaster;
1:12 children of Judah on the *d* of their ruin;
1:12 Speak not haughtily on the *d* of distress!
1:13 of my people on the *d* of their calamity;
1:13 his misfortune on the *d* of his calamity;
1:13 his possessions on the *d* of his calamity!
1:14 not his fugitives on the *d* of distress!
1:15 is the *d* of the LORD for all the nations!
Mi 2: 4 On that *d* a satire shall be sung over you,
3: 6 prophets, and the *d* shall be dark for them.
4: 6 On that *d,* says the LORD, I will gather
5: 9 On that *d,* says the LORD, I will destroy
7: 4 The *d* announced by your watchmen!
7:11 It is the *d* for building your walls; on that *d*
7:12 It is the *d;* and they shall come to you
Na 1: 7 is good, a refuge on the *d* of distress;
2: 4 are the chariots on the *d* of his mustering.
3:17 gathered on the rubble fences on a cold *d!*
Hb 3:16 I await the *d* of distress that will come
Zep 1: 7 for near is the *d* of the LORD,
1: 8 On the *d* of the LORD's slaughter feast I
1: 9 I will punish, on that *d,*
1:10 that *d,* says the LORD, A cry will be heard
1:14 wine, Near is the great *d* of the LORD,
1:14 swiftly coming, Hark, the *d* of the LORD!
1:15 is that day a *d* of anguish and distress,
1:15 *d* of destruction and desolation, a *d* of
1:16 a *d* of trumpet blasts and battle alarm
1:18 to save them on the *d* of the LORD's wrath,
2: 2 comes upon you the *d* of the LORD's anger.
2: 3 be sheltered on the *d* of the LORD's anger.
3: 8 against the *d* when I arise as accuser;
3:11 On that *d* You need not be ashamed of all
3:16 On that *d,* it shall be said to Jerusalem:
Hg 1: 1 On the first *d* of the sixth month in the
1:15 on the twenty-fourth *d* of the sixth month.
2: 1 on the twenty-first *d* of the seventh month,
2:10 On the twenty-fourth *d* of the ninth month,
2:15 now, consider from this *d* forward.
2:18 [Consider from this *d* forward:
2:18 the twenty-fourth *d* of the ninth month.
2:18 From the *d* on which the temple of the LORD
2:19 From this *d,* I will bless!
2:20 Haggai on the twenty-fourth *d* of the month:
2:23 On that *d,* says the LORD of hosts,
Zec 1: 7 of Darius, on the twenty-fourth *d* of Shebat,
2:15 join themselves to the LORD on that *d,*

3: 9 take away the guilt of the land in one *d.*
3:10 On that *d,* says the LORD of hosts,
4:10 For even they who were scornful on that *d*
6:10 and go the same *d* to the house of Josiah,
7: 1 to Zechariah], on the fourth *d* of Chislev,
8: 9 prophets on the *d* when the foundation
9:12 of the waiting prisoners, This very *d,*
9:16 LORD, their God, shall save them on that *d,*
11:11 that *d* it was broken off.
12: 3 On that *d* I will make Jerusalem a weighty
12: 4 On that *d,* says the LORD, I will strike
12: 6 On that *d* I will make the princes of Judah
12: 8 On that *d,* the LORD will shield
12: 8 among them shall be like David on that *d,*
12: 9 On that *d* I will seek the destruction of
12:11 On that *d* the mourning in Jerusalem shall
13: 1 On that *d* there shall be open to the house
13: 2 On that *d,* says the LORD of hosts,
13: 4 On that *d,* every prophet shall be ashamed
14: 1 a *d* shall come for the LORD when the
14: 3 nations, fighting as on a *d* of battle.
14: 4 That *d* his feet shall rest upon the Mount
14: 6 *d* there shall no longer be cold or frost.
14: 7 *d,* known to the LORD, not *d* and night,
14: 8 On that *d,* living waters shall flow
14: 9 on that *d* the LORD shall be the only one,
14:13 On that *d* there shall be among them a
14:20 On that *d* there shall be upon the bells of
14:21 On that *d* there shall no longer be any
Mal 3: 2 But who will endure the *d* of his coming?
3:17 special possession, on the *d* I take action.
3:19 For lo, the *d* is coming,
3:19 the *d* that is coming will set them on fire,
3:21 of your feet, on the *d* I take action,
3:23 prophet, Before the *d* of the LORD comes,
3:23 the LORD comes, the great and terrible *d.*
3:24 prophet, Before the *d* of the LORD comes,
3:24 the LORD comes, the great and terrible *d.*
Mt 2: 1 east arrived one *d* in Jerusalem inquiring,
7:22 When that *d* comes,
9:15 the *d* comes that the groom is taken away,
10:15 *d* of judgment than it will for that town.
11:22 Sidon than for you on the *d* of judgment.
11:24 Sodom than for you on the *d* of judgment."
12:36 on judgment *d* people will be held
13: 1 That same *d,* on leaving the house,
13: 4 "One *d* a farmer went out sowing.
16: 2 'Red sky at night, the *d* will be bright';
16: 3 'Sky red and gloomy, the *d* will be stormy.'
16:21 put to death, and raised up on the third *d.*
17:23 and he will be raised up on the third *d.*"
20: 6 have you been standing here idle all *d?*'
20:12 have worked a full *d* in the scorching heat.'
20:19 But on the third *d* he will be raised up."
22:23 That same *d* some Sadducees,
22:46 therefore no one dared, from that *d* on,
23:16 It is an evil *d* for you, blind guides!
24:36 "As for the exact *d* or hour,
24:38 right up to the *d* Noah entered the ark.
24:42 You cannot know the *d* your Lord is coming.
25:13 open, for you know not the *d* or the hour.
26:17 first *d* of the feast of Unleavened Bread,
26:29 until the *d* when I drink it new with you
26:55 From *d* to day I sat teaching in the temple
27:62 The next *d,* the one following the Day
27:64 kept under surveillance until the third *d.*
28: 1 as the first *d* of the week was dawning,
28:15 circulates among the Jews to this very *d.*
Mk 2:20 *d* will come, however, when the groom
2:20 on that *d* they will fast.
4:27 He goes to bed and gets up *d* after *d.*
4:35 That *d* as evening drew on he said to them,
5: 5 Uninterruptedly night and *d,*
6:21 Herodias had her chance one *d* when Herod
11:12 The next *d* when they were leaving Bethany
13:32 "As to the exact *d* or hour,
14:12 On the first *d* of Unleavened Bread,
14:25 *d* when I drink it new in the reign of God."
15:42 As it grew dark (it was Preparation *D,*
16: 2 first *d* of the week they came to the tomb.
16: 9 the dead early on the first *d* of the week.
Lk 1:20 until the *d* these things take place,
1:59 circumcision of the child on the eighth *d,*
1:80 He lived in the desert until the *d* when he
2:11 This *d* in David's city a savior has been
2:21 the eighth *d* arrived for his circumcision,
2:22 When the *d* came to purify them according
2:37 *d* and night in fasting and prayer.
2:44 they continued their journey for a *d,*
2:46 On the third *d* they came upon him in the
4:31 he began instructing them on the sabbath *d.*
5:17 One *d* Jesus was teaching,
6:23 On the *d* they do so,
8:22 One *d* he got into a boat with his
9:18 One *d* when Jesus was praying in seclusion
9:22 and then be raised up on the third *d.*"
9:23 his very self, take up his cross each *d,*
9:37 The following *d* they came down from the
10:12 on that *d* the fate of Sodom will be less
10:14 It will go easier on the *d* of judgment for
10:35 The next *d* he took out two silver pieces
11: 1 One *d* he was praying in a certain place.
11: 3 Give us each *d* our daily bread.
12:46 back on a *d* when he does not expect him,
13:10 *d* he was teaching in one of the synagogues.
13:32 on the third *d* my purpose is accomplished.
13:33 on course today, tomorrow, and the *d* after,
14: 5 immediately rescue him on the sabbath *d?*"
16:19 and linen and feasted splendidly every *d.*
17: 4 seven times a *d,* and seven times a *d* turns
17:22 *d* of the Son of Man but will not see it.
17:24 The Son of Man in his *d* will be like the
17:27 right up to the *d* Noah entered the ark
17:29 But on the *d* Lot left Sodom,
17:30 that on the *d* the Son of Man is revealed.
17:31 On that *d,* if a man is on the rooftop
18: 7 his chosen who call out to him *d* and night?
18:33 and on the third *d* he will rise again."
19:42 you had known the path to peace this *d;*
19:47 teaching in the temple area from *d* to *d.*
20: 1 One *d* when he was teaching the people in
21: 6 the *d* will come when not one stone will be
21:34 The great *d* will suddenly close in on you
21:35 The *d* I speak of will come upon all who
21:37 He would teach in the temple by *d,*
22: 7 The *d* of Unleavened Bread arrived on which
22:53 When I was with you day after *d* in the
23:12 each other, became friends from that *d.*
23:43 this *d* you will be with me in paradise."
23:54 That was the *D* of Preparation,
23:56 They observed the sabbath as a *d* of rest,
24: 1 On the first *d* of the week,
24: 7 crucified, and on the third *d* rise again."
24:13 Two of them that same *d* were making their
24:21 the third *d* since these things happened,
24:29 the *d* is practically over."
24:46 and rise from the dead on the third *d.*
Jn 1:29 next *d,* when John caught sight of Jesus
1:35 The next *d* John was there again
1:39 he was lodged, and stayed with him that *d.*
1:43 next *d* he wanted to set out for Galilee,
2: 1 *d* there was a wedding at Cana in Galilee,
5: 9 The *d* was a sabbath.
6:22 The next *d* they realized that there had
6:39 that I should raise it up on the last *d.*
6:40 Him I will raise up on the last *d.*"
6:44 I will raise him up on the last *d.*
6:54 and I will raise him up on the last *d.*
7:37 On the last and greatest *d* of the festival,
8:56 Abraham rejoiced that he might see my *d.*
9: 4 the deeds of him who sent me while it is *d.*
11: 9 If a man goes walking by *d* he does not
11:24 "in the resurrection on the last *d.*"
11:53 From that *d* onward there was a plan afoot
12: 7 against the *d* they prepare me for burial.
12:12 The next *d* the great crowd that had come
12:48 that which will condemn him on the last *d.*
14:20 *d* you will know that I am in my Father,
16:23 *d* you will have no questions to ask me.
16:26 On that *d* you will ask in my name and I do
19:14 (It was the Preparation *D* for Passover,
19:31 Since it was the Preparation *D* the Jews
19:31 for that sabbath was a solemn feast *d.*
19:42 Preparation *D* they buried Jesus there,
20: 1 in the morning on the first *d* of the week,
20:19 On the evening of that first *d* of the week,
Acts 1: 2 until the *d* he was taken up to heaven,
1:22 John until the *d* he was taken up from us,
2: 1 When the *d* of Pentecost came it found them
2:20 of that great and glorious *d* of the Lord.
2:29 and his grave is in our midst to this *d.*
2:41 some three thousand were added that *d.*
2:46 went to the temple area together every *d,*
2:47 Day by *d* the Lord added to their number
3: 2 They would bring him every *d* and put him
4: 5 scribes assembled the next *d* in Jerusalem,
5:42 Day after *d,* both in the temple
7: 8 of Isaac, circumcised him on the eighth *d.*
7:26 next *d* while some of them were fighting,
7:52 In their *d,* they put to death
8: 1 That *d* saw the beginning of a great
9:24 close watch on the city gates *d* and night
10: 9 About noontime the next *d,*
10:23 The next *d* he went off with them,
10:24 The following *d,* he arrived in Caesarea.
10:40 on the third *d* and grant that he be seen,
12:21 On an appointed *d* Herod,
13:14 *d* they entered the synagogue and sat down.
13:33 this *d* I have begotten you.'
14:20 The next *d* he left with Barnabas for Derbe.
16:11 Samothrace, and the next *d* on to Neapolis;
16:35 When it was *d,* the magistrates dispatched
17:11 Each *d* they studied the Scriptures to see
17:31 He has set the *d* on which he is going to
19: 9 day to *d* in the lecture hall of Tyrannus.
20: 7 On the first *d* of the week when we
20: 7 Because he intended to leave the next *d,*
20:15 From there we took off the next *d,*
20:15 on the second *d* we crossed to Samos,
20:15 on the *d* after that we put in at Miletus.
20:18 first *d* I set foot in the province of Asia
20:26 Therefore I solemnly declare this *d* that I
20:31 forget that for three years, night and *d,*
21: 1 On the following *d* we came to Rhodes and
21: 7 the brothers and spent the *d* with them.
21: 8 next *d* we pushed on and came to Caesarea.
21:18 The next *d,* Paul and the rest of us paid
21:26 rite of purification with them the next *d.*
21:26 give notice of the *d* when the period
22:30 *d* the commander released Paul from prison,
23: 1 to this *d* I have lived my life with a
23:12 When it was *d,* certain Jews formed
23:32 The next *d* they returned to headquarters,
25: 6 On the following *d* he took his seat on the
25:17 The very next *d* I took my seat on the
25:23 So the next *d* Agrippa and Bernice came
26: 7 people fervently worship God *d* and night
26:22 But I have had God's help to this very *d,*
27: 3 The following *d* we put in at Sidon,
27:18 next *d* some of the cargo was thrown over
27:19 On the third *d* they deliberately threw
28:13 A *d* later a south wind began to blow which
28:23 they arranged a *d* with him and came to his
Rom 2: 5 storing up retribution for that *d* of wrath
2:16 will accuse or defend them on the *d* when,
8:36 sake we are being slain all the *d* long;
10:21 "All *d* long I stretched out my hands to
11: 8 eyes and deaf ears, and it is so to this *d.*"
13:12 The night is far spent; the *d* draws near.
14: 5 One man regards this *d* as better than that;
14: 6 observes the *d* does so to honor the Lord.
1Cor 1: 8 on the *d* of our Lord Jesus [Christ].
3:13 The *D* will disclose it.
3:13 That *d* will make its appearance with fire,
5: 5 spirit may be saved on the *d* of the Lord.
10: 8 in one *d* twenty-three thousand perished.
15: 4 with the Scriptures, rose on the third *d;*
15:31 Jesus our Lord, that I face death every *d.*
16: 2 On the first *d* of each week everyone
2Cor 1:14 and you ours, on the *d* of our Lord Jesus.
3:14 To this very *d,* when the old covenant
4:16 renewed each *d* even though our body
6: 2 on a *d* of salvation I have helped you."
6: 2 Now is the *d* of salvation!
8:14 their surplus may one *d* supply your need,
11:25 I passed a *d* and night on the sea.
Eph 4:30 were sealed against the *d* of redemption.
5:13 condemned they are seen in the light of *d,*
6:13 of God if you are to resist on the evil *d;*
Phil 1: 5 promote the gospel from the very first *d.*
1: 6 right up to the *d* of Christ Jesus.
1:10 really matter, up to the very *d* of Christ.
2:16 As I look to the *D* of Christ,
3: 5 I was circumcised on the eighth *d,*
Col 1: 6 This has been the case from the *d* you
1Thes 2: 9 how we worked *d* and night all the time we
3:10 as we ask him fervently night and *d* that
5: 2 you know very well that the *d* of the Lord
5: 4 that the *d* should catch you off guard,
5: 5 of you are children of light and of the *d.*
5: 8 We who live by *d* must be alert,
2Thes 1:10 glory of his might on the *D* when he comes,
2: 2 believing that the *d* of the Lord is here.
3: 8 Rather, we worked *d* and night,
1Tm 5: 5 night and *d* in supplications and prayers.
2Tm 1: 3 as indeed I do constantly, night and *d.*
1:12 what has been entrusted to me until that *D.*
1:18 he stands before the Lord on the great *D,*
4: 8 on that *D* the Lord,
Heb 3: 8 revolt in the *d* of testing in the desert,
4: 4 to the seventh *d* Scripture somewhere says,
4: 4 from all his work on the seventh *d*";
4: 7 of unbelief, God once more set a *d,*
4: 8 not have spoken afterward of another *d.*
7:27 has no need to offer sacrifice *d* after *d,*
8: 9 their fathers the *d* I took them by the hand
10:11 other priest stands ministering *d* by *d,*
10:25 more because you see that the *D* draws near.
Jas 2:15 has nothing to wear and no food for the *d,*
5: 5 fattened yourselves for the *d* of slaughter.
1Pt 2:12 give glory to God on the *d* of visitation.
3:20 had disobeyed as long ago as Noah's *d,*
2Pt 1:14 close is the *d* when I must fold my tent.
2: 8 *D* after *d* that just one,
2: 9 of the wicked up to the *d* of judgment.
3: 7 they are kept for the *d* of judgment,
3: 7 the *d* when godless men will be destroyed.
3: 8 one *d* is as a thousand years and a
3: 8 years and a thousand years are as a *d.*
3:10 The *d* of the Lord will come like a thief,
3:10 that *d* the heavens will vanish with a roar;
3:12 of the *d* of God and trying to hasten it!
3:18 be to him now and to the *d* of eternity!
1Jn 4:17 have confidence on the *d* of judgment;
Jude 1: 6 against the judgment of the great *d.*
Rv 1:10 On the Lord's *d* I was caught up in ecstasy,
4: 8 *D* and night, without pause, they sang:
6:17 The great *d* of vengeance has come.
7:15 *d* and night they minister to him in his
8:12 The *d* lost a third of its light,
9:15 this was precisely the hour, the *d,*
11:18 but then came your *d* of wrath and the
12:10 night and *d* accused them before our God.
14:11 There shall be no relief *d* or night for
16:14 battle on the great *d* of God the Almighty.
19: 7 For this is the wedding *d* of the Lamb;
20:10 There they will be tortured *d* and night,
21:25 During the *d* its gates shall never be shut,

DAYBREAK (26)

Gn 32:27 man then said, "Let me go, for it is *d*."
44: 3 *d* the men and their donkeys were sent off.
Jos 6:15 On the seventh day, beginning at *d*
Jgs 19:26 Then at *d* the woman came and collapsed at
1Sm 9:26 At *d* Samuel called to Saul on the roof,
14:36 them until *d* and to kill them all off."
25:36 nothing at all before *d* the next morning.
2Sm 17:22 By *d*, there was no one left
Neh 4:15 the ready, from *d* till the stars came out.
8: 3 he read out of the book from *d* till midday,
Jdt 14: 2 At *d*, when the sun rises on the earth
14:11 At *d* they hung the head of Holofernes on
1Mc 4: 6 But at *d* Judas appeared in the plain with
11:67 and at *d* they went to the plain of Hazor.
Ps(s) 90:14 Fill us at *d* with your kindness,
Wis 16:28 before the sunrise, and turn to you at *d*.
Sir 47:10 before *d* the sanctuary would resound,
Mt 27: 1 At *d* all the chief priests and the elders
Mk 15: 1 As soon as it was *d* the chief priests,
Lk 6:13 At *d* he called his disciples and selected
21:38 At *d* all the people came to hear him in
22:66 At *d*, the elders of the people,
Jn 8: 2 At *d* he reappeared in the temple area;
18:28 At *d* they brought Jesus from Caiaphas to
21: 4 after *d* Jesus was standing on the shore,
Acts 12:18 At *d*, confusion broke out

DAYLIGHT (11)

Gn 6:16 Make an opening for *d* in the ark,
29: 7 "There is still much *d* left;
2Sm 12:11 He shall lie with your wives in broad *d*.
Jb 3: 9 may it look for *d*, but have none,
24:17 the light, for *d* they regard as darkness.
Am 8: 9 cover the earth with darkness in broad *d*.
Lk 12: 3 said in the dark will be heard in the *d*;
Jn 11: 9 "Are there not twelve hours of *d*?
Acts 27:29 anchors from the stern and prayed for *d*.
27:39 With the coming of *d*,
Rom 13:13 Let us live honorably as in *d*;

DAYS (684)

Gn 1:14 mark the fixed times, the *d* and the years,
3:14 dirt shall you eat all the *d* of your life.
3:17 you eat its yield all the *d* of your life.
6: 3 His *d* shall comprise one hundred and
7: 4 Seven *d* from now I will bring rain down on
7: 4 on the earth for forty *d* and forty nights,
7:10 As soon as the seven *d* were over,
7:12 For forty *d* and forty nights heavy rain
7:17 flood continued upon the earth for forty *d*.
7:24 over the earth for one hundred and fifty *d*
8: 3 At the end of one hundred and fifty *d*,
8: 6 At the end of forty *d* Noah opened the
8:10 He waited seven *d* more and again sent the
8:12 *d* and then released the dove once more;
14: 1 In the *d* of . . . , Amraphel King of Shinar
17:12 male among you, when he is eight *d* old,
21: 4 When his son Isaac was eight *d* old,
24:55 girl stay with us a short while, say ten *d*;
26: 1 one that had occurred in the *d* of Abraham),
26:15 dug back in the *d* of his father Abraham.)
26:18 dug back in the *d* of his father Abraham
29:20 but a few *d* because of his love for her.
30:36 three *d'* journey between himself and Jacob,
31:23 he pursued him for seven *d* until he caught
37:34 on his loins, and mourned his son many *d*.
40:12 The three branches are three *d*;
40:13 within three *d* Pharaoh will lift up your
40:18 The three baskets are three *d*;
40:19 within three *d* Pharaoh will lift up your
42:17 them up in the guardhouse for three *d*.
49: 1 you what is to happen to you in *d* to come.
50: 3 embalmed Israel, they spent forty *d* at it,
50: 3 the Egyptians mourned him for seventy *d*.
50:10 seven *d* of mourning for his father.
Ex 3:18 to go a three *d'* journey in the desert,
5: 3 Let us go a three *d'* journey in the desert,
7:25 Seven *d* passed after the LORD had struck
8:23 We must go a three *d'* journey in the
10:22 throughout the land of Egypt for three *d*.
10:23 move from where they were, for three *d*.
12:15 For seven *d* you must eat unleavened bread.
12:16 these *d* you shall not do any sort of work,
12:19 *d* no leaven may be found in your houses.
13: 6 For seven *d* you shall eat unleavened bread,
13: 7 bread may be eaten during the seven *d*;
15:22 *d* through the desert without finding water,
16: 5 as much as they gather on the other *d*."
16:26 On the other six *d* you can gather it,
16:29 the sixth day he gives you food for two *d*.
20: 9 Six *d* you may labor and do all your work,
20:11 *d* the LORD made the heavens and the earth,
22:29 *d* the firstling may stay with its mother,
23:12 "For six *d* you may do your work,
23:15 bread for seven *d* at the prescribed time
24:16 The cloud covered it for six *d*,
24:18 he stayed for forty *d* and forty nights.
29:30 shall be clothed with them for seven *d*.
29:35 *d* you shall spend in ordaining them,
29:37 Seven *d* you shall spend in making
31:15 Six *d* there are for doing work,
31:17 *d* the LORD made the heavens and the earth,
34:18 For seven *d* at the prescribed time in the
34:21 "For six *d* you may work,
34:28 with the LORD for forty *d* and forty nights,
35: 2 On six *d* work may be done,
Lv 8:33 seven *d*, until the *d* of your ordination
8:33 for your ordination is to last for seven *d*.
8:35 meeting tent day and night for seven *d*,
12: 2 a boy, she shall be unclean for seven *d*,
12: 4 *d* more in becoming purified of her blood;
12: 4 the *d* of her purification are fulfilled.
12: 5 for fourteen *d* she shall be as unclean as
12: 5 *d* in becoming purified of her blood.
12: 6 "When the *d* of her purification for a son
13: 4 quarantine the stricken man for seven *d*.
13: 5 shall quarantine him for another seven *d*,
13:21 priest shall quarantine him for seven *d*.
13:26 priest shall quarantine him for seven *d*.
13:31 the person with scall sore for seven *d*,
13:33 shall quarantine him for another seven *d*.
13:50 the infected article for seven *d*.
13:54 and then quarantined for another seven *d*.
14: 8 still remain outside his tent for seven *d*.
14:38 him and quarantine the house for seven *d*.
15:13 he shall wait seven *d* for his purification.
15:19 be in a state of impurity for seven *d*.
15:24 impurity and shall be unclean for seven *d*;
15:25 for several *d* outside her menstrual period,
15:28 her affliction, she shall wait seven *d*,
22:27 shall remain with its mother for seven *d*;
23: 2 are the festivals of the LORD, my feast *d*,
23: 3 "For six *d* work may be done;
23: 6 For seven *d* you shall eat unleavened bread.
23: 7 On the first of these *d* you shall hold a
23: 8 *d* you shall offer an oblation to the LORD.
23:34 Booths, which shall continue for seven *d*.
23:36 *d* you shall offer an oblation to the LORD,
23:39 the eighth day shall be *d* of complete rest.
Nm 9:19 Even when the cloud tarried many *d* over
9:20 was over the Dwelling only for a few *d*.
9:22 for two *d* or for a month or longer,
10:10 On your *d* of celebration,
10:33 mountain of the LORD, a three *d'* journey,
10:33 place went the three *d'* journey with them.
11:19 will eat it, not for one day, or two *d*,
11:19 or two days, or five, or ten, or twenty *d*,
11:31 of a *d* journey all around the camp.
12:14 would she not hide in shame for seven *d*?
12:14 be confined outside the camp for seven *d*;
12:15 was confined outside the camp for seven *d*,
13:25 the land for forty *d* they returned,
14:34 Forty *d* you spent in scouting the land;
19:11 human being shall be unclean for seven *d*;
19:14 in it, shall be unclean for seven *d*;
19:16 or a grave, shall be unclean for seven *d*.
20:29 *d* the whole house of Israel mourned him.
24:14 will do to your people in the *d* to come."
28:17 seven *d* unleavened bread is to be eaten.
28:18 these *d* you shall hold a sacred assembly,
28:24 each day for seven *d* as food offerings,
29:12 then, for seven *d* following,
31:19 shall stay outside the camp for seven *d*,
33: 8 a three *d'* journey in the desert of Etham,
Dt 1: 2 it is a journey of eleven *d* from Horeb to
4:32 "Ask now of the *d* of old,
5:13 Six *d* you may labor and do all your work;
6: 2 and keep, throughout the *d* of your lives,
9: 9 stayed on the mountain forty *d* and forty
9:11 at the end of the forty *d* and forty nights,
9:18 lay prostrate before the LORD for forty *d*
9:25 Those forty *d*, then, and forty nights,
10:10 forty *d* and forty nights on the mountain,
16: 3 For seven *d* you shall eat with it only
16: 4 found in all your territory for seven *d*,
16: 8 For six *d* you shall eat unleavened bread,
16:13 celebrate the feast of Booths for seven *d*,
16:15 For seven *d* you shall celebrate this
17:19 all the *d* of his life that he may learn
24:15 *d* wages before sundown on the day itself,
32: 7 Think back on the *d* of old,
33:25 your strength endure through all your *d*!"
34: 8 For thirty *d* the Israelites wept for Moses
Jos 1:11 *d* from now you shall cross the Jordan here,
2:16 Hide there for three *d*,
2:22 they stayed three *d* until their pursuers,
3: 2 Three *d* later the officers went through
6: 3 Do this for six *d*,
6:14 and for six *d* in all they did the same.
9:16 *d* after the agreement was entered into,
Jgs 5: 6 In the *d* of Shamgar,
5: 6 Anath, in the *d* of slavery caravans ceased:
11:40 the Gileadite for four *d* of the year.
14:12 If within the seven *d* of the feast you
14:15 three *d'* failure to answer the riddle,
14:17 him during the seven *d* the feast lasted.
15:20 twenty years in the *d* of the Philistines.
17: 6 In those *d* there was no king in Israel;
19: 4 three *d* with this father-in-law of his,
20:27 the covenant of God was there in those *d*,
20:28 Aaron, was ministering to him in those *d*),
21:25 In those *d* there was no king in Israel;
1Sm 9:20 As for the asses you lost three *d* ago,
10: 8 Wait seven *d* until I come to you;
11: 3 "Give us seven *d* to send messengers
13: 8 He waited seven *d*—
17:12 the *d* of Saul was old and well on in years.
17:16 his stand morning and evening for forty *d*.
25:38 *d* later the LORD struck him and he died.
28: 1 In those *d* the Philistines mustered their
30:12 drunk water for three *d* and three nights.
30:13 me because I fell sick three *d* ago today.
31:13 tree in Jabesh, and fasted for seven *d*.
2Sm 1: 1 the Amalekites and spent two *d* in Ziklag.
5: 2 In *d* past, when Saul was our king,
8: 7 he came to Jerusalem in the *d* of Rehoboam,
13:18 how maiden princesses dressed in olden *d*.
19: 3 and that *d* victory was turned into
20: 4 the Judahites for me within three *d*.
21: 9 to death during the first *d* of the harvest
24: 8 again after nine months and twenty *d*.
24:13 to have a three *d'* pestilence in your land?
1Kgs 8:65 before the LORD, our God, for seven *d*.
12: 5 "Come back to me in three *d*,"
16:15 of Judah, Zimri reigned seven *d* in Tirzah.
19: 4 there and went a *d* journey into the desert,
19: 8 *d* and forty nights to the mountain of God,
20:29 encamped opposite each other for seven *d*.
2Kgs 2:17 searched for three *d* without finding him.
3: 9 After their roundabout journey of seven *d*
19:25 I prepared it, From *d* of old I planned it.
20: 1 In those *d*, when Hezekiah was mortally
20: 5 *d* you shall go up to the LORD's temple;
1Chr 10:12 the oak of Jabesh, and fasted seven *d*.
12:40 They remained with David for three *d*,
13: 3 for in the *d* of Saul we did not visit it."
17:11 so that when your *d* have been completed
21:12 or three *d* of the LORD'S own sword,
23: 1 grown old and was near the end of his *d*,
23:31 LORD on sabbaths, new moons, and feast *d*,
2Chr 7: 8 Egypt, celebrated the festival for seven *d*.
7: 9 for seven *d* and the feast for seven days.
10: 5 "In three *d*," he answered them,
20:25 they were three *d* taking the spoil,
29:17 the LORD's house during eight *d*,
30:21 Bread with great rejoicing for seven *d*,
30:22 they had completed the seven *d* of festival,
30:23 agreed to celebrate another seven *d*.
30:23 continued the festivity seven *d* longer.
30:26 in Jerusalem, for since the *d* of Solomon,
32:24 In those *d* Hezekiah became mortally ill.
35:17 feast of the Unleavened Bread for seven *d*.
36: 9 three months [and ten *d* in Jerusalem.
Ezr 4: 2 to him since the *d* of Esarhaddon,
6:22 the feast of Unleavened Bread for seven *d*,
8:15 Ahava, where we made camp for three *d*.
8:32 where we first rested for three *d*.
10: 8 failed to appear within three *d* would,
Neh 1: 4 and continued mourning for several *d*;
2:11 I first rested there for three *d*.
5:18 kinds of wine in abundance every ten *d*,
6:15 it had taken fifty-two *d*.
8:17 nothing of this sort from the *d* of Jeshua,
8:18 They kept the feast for seven *d*,
12: 7 and their brethren in the *d* of Jeshua.
12:12 In the *d* of Joiakim these were the
12:46 the *d* of David and Asaph in times of old.
12:47 in the *d* of Zerubbabel [and in the days of
12:47 of Zerubbabel [and in the *d* of Nehemiah],
13:15 In those *d* I perceived that men in Judah
13:23 *d* I saw Jews who had married Ashdodite,
Tb 1: 3 have walked all the *d* of my life on the
1:18 from Judea during the *d* of judgment
1:21 But less than forty *d* later the king was
4: 5 "Through all your *d*,
4: 5 Perform good works all the *d* of your life,
5: 6 good two *d'* travel from Ecbatana to Rages,
8:20 fourteen *d* you shall not stir from here,
9: 4 you know that my father is counting the *d*.
10: 1 *d* was reached and his son did not appear,
10:13 of us be prosperous all the *d* of our lives."
10:14 "May I honor you all the *d* of my life!"
11:18 Tobiah's wedding feast for seven happy *d*,
14: 7 in those *d* will truly be mindful of God,
Jdt 1:16 and feasted for a hundred and twenty *d*.
4: 6 was high priest in Jerusalem in those *d*,
4:13 fast of many *d'* duration throughout Judea,
6:15 of the city, who in those *d* were Uzziah,
7:20 them thus surrounded for thirty-four *d*.
7:30 us wait five *d* more for the Lord our God,
7:31 if those *d* pass without help coming to us,
8: 1 those *d* Judith, daughter of Merari,
8: 6 She fasted all the *d* of her widowhood,
8: 9 to the Assyrians at the end of five *d*,
8:11 at the end of five *d* unless within that time
8:15 wish to come to our aid within the five *d*,
8:18 made by hands, as happened in former *d*.
8:33 and within the *d* you have specified before
10: 2 she used only on sabbaths and feast *d*.
12: 7 Thus she stayed in the camp three *d*.
13: 3 the bedroom and wait, as on the other *d*,
14: 8 tell me all that you did during these *d*."
15:11 *d* the whole populace plundered the camp,
16:21 When those *d* were over,
16:22 gave herself to no man all the *d* of her life
16:24 house of Israel mourned her for seven *d*.

Est 1: 4 For as many as a hundred and eighty d,
1: 5 king gave a feast of seven d in the garden
B: 8 "Remember the d of your lowly estate."
4:11 not been summoned to the king for thirty d."
4:16 or drinking, night or day, for three d.
9:22 month of Adar as the d on which the Jews
9:22 observe these d with feasting and gladness,
9:26 d have been named Purim after the word pur.
9:27 obligation of celebrating these two d every year
9:28 These d were to be commemorated and kept
9:28 These d of Purim were never to fall into
9:31 these d of Purim which Mordecai the Jew
F:10 they shall celebrate these d on the
1Mc 1:11 In those d there appeared in Israel men
1:45 to profane the sabbaths and feast d,
2: 1 In those d Mattathias, son of John,
4:56 For eight d they celebrated the dedication
4:59 decreed that the d of the dedication
4:59 on the anniversary every year for eight d,
5:24 and marched for three d through the desert.
6: 9 There he remained many d,
6:31 For many d they attacked it;
6:51 For many d he besieged the sanctuary,
7:45 The Jews pursued them a d journey,
9:20 They mourned for him many d,
9:24 In those d there was a very great famine,
9:64 he fought against it for many d.
10:34 all feast d, sabbaths, new moon festivals,
10:34 the three d that precede each feast day,
10:34 and the three d that follow, be days
11:18 three d later King Ptolemy himself died,
11:40 During his stay there of many d,
11:65 besieged Beth-zur, attacked it for many d,
12:11 on our feasts and other appropriate d,
13:26 lamentation, mourning over him for many d.
13:43 In those d Simon besieged Gazara and
14: 4 The land was at rest all the d of Simon,
14:13 the kings in those d were crushed.
2Mc 2:12 the feast in the same way for eight d.
5: 2 all over the city, for nearly forty d,
5:14 In the space of three d,
10: 6 for eight d as on the feast of Booths,
10: 8 nation should celebrate these d every year.
10:33 For four d Maccabeus and his men eagerly
13:12 and fasting and prostrations for three d,
14:38 In the early d of the revolt,
15: 2 exalted with holiness above all other d."
15:22 angel in the d of King Hezekiah of Judea,
Jb 2:13 ground with him seven d and seven nights,
3: 6 let it not occur among the d of the year,
7: 1 Are not his d those of a hireling?
7: 6 My d are swifter than a weaver's shuttle;
7:16 let me alone, for my d are but a breath.
8: 9 because our d on earth are but a shadow),
9:25 My d are swifter than a runner,
10: 5 Are your d as the days of a mortal,
10:20 Are not the d of my life few?
12:12 wisdom, and with length of d understanding.
14: 5 There is none, however short his d.
14:14 all the d of my drudgery I would wait,
15:18 contradicted since the d of their fathers,
15:20 The wicked man is in torment all his d,
17:11 My d are passed away,
21:13 They live out their d in prosperity,
24: 1 and why do his friends not see his d?
27: 6 heart does not reproach me for any of my d.
29: 2 as in the d when God watched over me,
29: 4 As I was in my flourishing d,
30:27 d of affliction have overtaken me.
32: 7 D should speak,
32: 9 It is not those of many d who are wise,
33:25 he shall be again as in the d of his youth.
36:11 him, they spend their d in prosperity,
38:23 of stress, for the d of war and of battle?
42:12 latter d of Job more than his earlier ones.
Ps(s) 21: 5 you gave him length of d forever and ever.
23: 6 kindness follow me all the d of my life;
27: 4 the house of the LORD all the d of my life,
34:13 life, and takes delight in prosperous d?
37:19 in d of famine they have plenty.
39: 5 my end and what is the number of my d,
39: 6 A short span you have made my d,
44: 2 deeds you did in their days, in d of old:
49: 6 d when my wicked ensnarers ring me round?
55:24 and deceit shall not live out half their d.
61: 7 Add to the d of the king's life;
72: 7 Justice shall flower in his d,
77: 6 I consider the d of old;
78:33 d and their years with sudden destruction.
89:30 forever and his throne as the d of heaven.
89:46 You have shortened the d of his youth;
90: 9 our d have passed away in your indignation;
90:12 Teach us to number our d aright,
90:14 may shout for joy and gladness all our d.
90:15 us glad, for the d when you afflicted us,
91:16 with length of d I will gratify him and
93: 5 befits your house, O LORD, for length of d.
94:13 law you teach, Giving him rest from evil d,
102: 4 For my d vanish like smoke,
102:12 My d are like a lengthening shadow,
102:24 he has cut short my d.
102:25 Take me not hence in the midst of my d;
103:15 Man's d are like those of grass;
109: 8 May his d be few;
119:84 How many are the d of your servant?
128: 5 of Jerusalem all the d of your life;
139:16 d were limited before one of them existed.
143: 5 I remember the d of old;
144: 4 breath; his d, like a passing shadow
Prv 3: 2 For many d, and years of life, and peace,
9:11 For by me your d will be multiplied and
28:16 who hates ill-gotten gain prolongs his d.
31:12 good, and not evil, all the d of her life.
31:25 dignity, and she laughs at the d to come.
Eccl 2: 3 heavens during the limited d of their life.
2:16 in d to come both will have been forgotten.
2:23 his d sorrow and grief are his occupation;
5:16 All the d of his life are passed in gloom
5:17 limited d of the life which God gives him;
6:12 the limited d of his vain life (which God
7:15 seen all manner of things in my vain d:
8:13 and he shall not prolong his shadowy d,
8:15 his toil during the limited d of the life
9: 9 all the d of the fleeting life that is
11: 8 that the d of darkness will be many.
11: 9 your heart be glad in the d of your youth.
12: 1 your Creator in the d of your youth,
12: 1 before the evil d come And the years
Sir 1: 2 the drops of rain, the d of eternity:
1:10 giving gladness and joy and length of d.
1:18 her branches are length of d.
7:36 In whatever you do, remember your last d,
17: 2 Limited d of life he gives him and makes
18: 7 d is great if it reaches a hundred years:
18: 8 these few years among the d of eternity.
22:11 Seven d of mourning for the dead,
24:23 like the Tigris in the d of the new fruits.
26: 1 a good wife, twice-lengthened are his d;
28: 6 Remember your last d,
30:22 life of man, cheerfulness prolongs his d.
33: 9 and others he lists as ordinary d.
33:24 When your few d reach their limit,
37:23 Limited are the d of one man's life,
37:23 but the life of Israel is d without number.
38:18 of sorrow, as he deserves, One or two d,
41:13 The boon of life is for limited d,
41:13 but a good name, for d without number.
43: 7 which we know the feast d and fixed dates,
44: 2 portion, his own part, since the d of old.
50: 1 in whose d the temple was reinforced.
Is 1: 1 Judah and Jerusalem in the d of Uzziah,
2: 2 In d to come,
7: 1 In the d of Ahaz,
7:17 your father's house d worse than any since
13:22 at hand and her d shall not be prolonged.
23:15 With the d of another king,
24:22 and after many d they will be punished.
27: 6 In d to come Jacob shall take root,
30: 8 it may be in future d an eternal witness:
30:26 times greater [like the light of seven d.
37:26 I prepared it, From d of old I planned it,
38: 1 those d, when Hezekiah was mortally ill,
38: 5 d you shall go up to the LORD's temple;
38:20 house of the LORD all the d of our life.
39: 6 the d shall come when all that is in your
51: 9 Awake as in the d of old,
53:11 he shall see the light in fullness of d;
54: 9 This is for me like the d of Noah,
60:20 the d of your mourning shall be at an end.
63: 9 them and carrying them all the d of old.
63:11 they remembered the d of old and Moses,
65:20 be in it an infant who lives but a few d,
Jer 1: 2 LORD first came to him in the d of Josiah,
2:32 people have forgotten me d without number.
3: 6 LORD said to me in the d of King Josiah:
3:16 LORD, They will in those d no longer say,
3:18 In those d the house of Judah will join
5:18 Yet even in those d,
7:32 d will come, says the LORD,
9:24 See, d are coming,
16:14 However, d will surely come,
19: 6 Therefore, d will come,
20:18 see sorrow and pain, to end my d in shame?
23: 5 Behold, the d are coming,
23: 6 In his d Judah shall be saved,
23: 7 Therefore, the d will come,
26:18 used to prophesy in the d of Hezekiah,
30: 3 For behold, the d will come,
31:27 The d are coming, says the LORD,
31:29 In those d they shall no longer say,
31:31 The d are coming, says the LORD,
31:33 with the house of Israel after those d,
31:38 The d are coming, says the LORD,
33:14 The d are coming,
33:15 In those d, in that time, I will raise up
33:16 In those d Judah shall be safe and
35: 1 from the LORD in the d of Jehoiakim,
36: 2 I first spoke to you, in the d of Josiah,
42: 7 Ten d passed before the word of the LORD
48:12 Hence, the d shall come,
48:47 change the lot of Moab in the d to come,
49: 2 But the d are coming,
49:39 d to come I will change the lot of Elam,
50: 4 In those d,
50:20 In those d, at that time, says the LORD:
51:47 the d are coming when I will punish the
51:52 But behold, the d are coming,
52:34 d of his life until the day of his death.
Lam 1: 7 of the d of her wretched homelessness,
2:17 the threat He set forth from d of old;
5:21 give us anew such d as we had of old.
Bar 1:14 the feast day and during the d of assembly:
3:14 you may know also where are length of d,
Ez 3:15 for seven d I sat among them distraught.
3:16 At the end of seven d. . . .
4: 4 As many d as you lie thus,
4: 5 sins I allot you the same number of d,
4: 6 the sins of the house of Judah forty d;
4: 8 you have completed the d of your siege.
4: 9 it for as many d as you lie upon your side,
5: 2 when the d of your siege are completed;
12:22 "The d drag on, and no vision ever comes
12:23 The d are at hand, and also the fulfillment
12:25 In your d, rebellious house,
22:14 be strong, in the d when I deal with you?
23:19 the more, recalling the d of her girlhood,
36:38 the sheep of Jerusalem on its feast d,
38: 8 After many d you will be mustered [in the
38:16 last d I will bring you against my land,
38:17 d that I would bring you against them.
43:25 Daily for seven d you shall offer a
43:26 unblemished, shall be offered for seven d.
43:27 And when these d are over,
44:26 he must wait an additional seven d,
45:21 seven d unleavened bread is to be eaten.
45:23 On each of the seven d of the feast he
45:25 month, the feast day, and for seven d,
46: 1 closed throughout the six working d,
Dn 1:12 "Please test your servants for ten d.
1:14 this request, and tested them for ten d;
1:15 after ten d they looked healthier and
2:28 what is to happen in d to come;
3:71 Nights and d, bless the Lord;
6: 8 any petition to god or man for thirty d,
6:13 a petition to god or man for thirty d,
7:25 thinking to change the feast d and the law.
8:26 undisclosed, because the d are to be many."
8:27 I, Daniel, was weak and ill for some d;
10: 2 In those d, I, Daniel, mourned three
10:13 Persia stood in my way for twenty-one d,
10:14 happen to your people in the d to come;
10:14 there is yet a vision concerning those d."
12:11 be one thousand two hundred and ninety d.
12:12 thousand three hundred and thirty-five d.
12:13 shall rise for your reward at the end of d."
14:31 into a lions' den, where he remained six d.
Hos 1: 1 the son of Beeri, in the d of Uzziah,
1: 1 kings of Judah, and in the d of Jeroboam,
2:15 I will punish her for the d of the Baals,
2:17 respond there as in the d of her youth,
3: 3 "Many d you shall wait for me;
3: 4 shall remain many d without king or prince,
3: 5 the LORD and to his bounty, in the last d.
6: 2 He will revive us after two d;
9: 7 They have come, the d of punishment!
9: 7 they have come, the d of recompense!
9: 9 of corruption, as in the d of Gibeah;
10: 9 Since the d of Gibeah you have sinned,
Jl 1: 2 in your days or in the d of your fathers?
3: 1 the servants and the handmaids, in those d,
4: 1 Yes, in those d, and at that time,
Am 1: 1 concerning Israel, in the d of Uzziah,
1: 1 king of Judah, and in the d of Jeroboam,
4: 2 Truly the d are coming upon you When they
8:11 Yes, d are coming, says the LORD GOD
9:11 ruins, and rebuild it as in the d of old,
9:13 Yes, d are coming,
Jon 2: 1 belly of the fish three d and three nights.
3: 3 it took three d to go through it.
3: 4 had gone but a single d walk announcing,
3: 4 d more and Nineveh shall be destroyed,"
Mi 1: 1 to Micah of Moresheth in the d of Jotham,
4: 1 In d to come the mount of the LORD's house
7:14 in Bashan and Gilead, as in the d of old;
7:15 the d when you came from the land of Egypt,
7:20 have sworn to our fathers from d of old.
Hb 1: 5 in your d that you would not have believed,
Zep 1: 1 the son of Hezekiah, in the d of Josiah,
Zec 8: 6 in those d be impossible in my eyes also,
8: 9 you who in these d hear these words spoken
8:10 before those d there were no wages for men,
8:11 the remnant of this people as in former d,
8:15 so again in these d I have determined to
8:19 The fast d of the fourth,
8:23 In those d ten men of every nationality,
14: 5 in the d of King Uzziah of Judah.
Mal 3: 7 Since the d of your fathers you have
Mt 4: 2 He fasted forty d and forty nights,
12:40 Just as Jonah spent three d and three
12:40 Son of Man spend three d and three nights
15:32 By now they have been with me three d,
17: 1 Six d later Jesus took Peter,
20: 9 came up they received a full d pay,
24:19 on pregnant or nursing mothers in those d.
24:21 for those d will be more filled with
24:22 chosen, however, the d will be shortened.
24:38 In the d before the flood people were
26: 2 that in two d' time it will be Passover,
26:61 God's sanctuary and rebuild it in three d.'"

DAYS (cont.)

27:40 the temple and rebuild it in three *d!*
27:63 made the claim, 'After three *d* I will rise.'
Mk 1:13 He stayed in the wasteland forty *d,*
2: 1 *d* and word got around that he was at home.
2:26 How he entered God's house in the *d* of
6:37 hundred *d'* wages for bread to feed them?"
8: 2 with me three *d* and have nothing to eat.
8:31 be put to death, and rise three *d* later.
9: 2 Six *d* later, Jesus took Peter,
9:31 three *d* after his death he will rise."
10:34 But three *d* later he will rise."
13:17 with pregnant and nursing women in those *d.*
13:20 he has chosen, he has shortened the *d.*
14: 1 Bread were to be observed in two *d'* time,
14:58 and 'In three *d* I will construct another
15:29 the temple and rebuild it in three *d!*
Lk 1: 5 In the *d* of Herod, king of Judea,
1:25 these *d* the Lord is acting on my behalf;
1:75 and through all our *d* be holy in his sight.
2: 1 In those *d* Caesar Augustus published a
2: 6 the *d* of her confinement were completed.
2:36 She had seen many *d,*
4: 2 by the Spirit into the desert for forty *d,*
4:25 many widows in Israel in the *d* of Elijah
5:35 But when the *d* come that the groom is
5:35 midst, they will surely fast in those *d."*
9:28 eight *d* after saying this he took Peter,
13:14 "There are six *d* for working.
13:14 Come on those *d* to be cured,
15:13 Some *d* later this younger son collected
17:26 in the *d* of Noah, so will it be in the days
17:28 It was much the same in the *d* of Lot:
19:43 *D* will come upon you when your enemies
21:22 These indeed will be *d* of retribution,
21:23 at the breast will fare badly in those *d!*
23:29 The *d* are coming when they will say,
24:18 things that went on there these past few *d?"*
Jn 2:12 but they stayed there only a few *d.*
2:19 "and in three *d* I will raise it up."
2:20 you are going to 'raise it up in three *d'!"*
4:40 So he stayed there two *d,*
4:43 When the two *d* were over,
6: 7 "Not even with two hundred *d'* wages could
11: 6 he stayed on where he was for two *d* more.
11:17 had already been in the tomb four *d.*
11:39 to him, "Lord, it has been four *d* now;
12: 1 *d* before Passover Jesus came to Bethany,
Acts 1: 3 the course of forty *d* and speaking to them
1: 5 but within a few *d* you will be baptized
1:15 At one point during those *d,*
2:17 'It shall come to pass in the last *d,*
2:18 pour out a portion of my spirit in those *d,*
3:24 have announced the events of these *d.*
6: 1 In those *d,* as the number of disciples grew,
9: 9 For three *d* he continued blind,
10:30 "Just three *d* ago at this very hour,
10:48 asked him to stay with them for a few *d.*
13:31 and for many *d* thereafter Jesus appeared
13:41 For I am doing a deed in your *d* which you
15: 7 from the early *d* God selected me
16:18 *d* until finally Paul became annoyed,
20: 6 Five *d* later we joined them in Troas,
21:10 During our few *d'* stay,
24: 1 Five *d* later, the high priest Ananias
24:11 Not more than twelve *d* have passed since I
24:24 *d* later Felix came with his Jewish wife,
25: 1 *d* after Festus had arrived in the province,
25: 6 After spending eight or ten *d* in Jerusalem,
25:13 A few *d* later King Agrippa and Bernice
25:14 Since they were to spend several *d* there,
27: 7 For many *d* we made little headway,
27:20 For many *d* neither the sun nor the stars
27:33 *d* you have been in constant suspense;
28: 7 and gave us kind hospitality for three *d.*
28:12 put in at Syracuse and spent three *d* there.
28:13 which enabled us to reach Puteoli in two *d.*
28:17 Three *d* later Paul invited the prominent
Rom 14: 5 someone else considers all *d* alike.
Gal 1:18 know Cephas, with whom I stayed fifteen *d.*
4:10 the ceremonial observance of *d* and months,
4:29 But just as in those *d* the son born in
Eph 5:16 present opportunity, for these are evil *d.*
2Tm 3: 1 there will be terrible times in the last *d.*
Heb 5: 7 In the *d* when he was in the flesh,
7: 3 without beginning of *d* or end of life,
8: 8 *D* are coming, says the Lord,
8:10 with the house of Israel after those *d,*
10:16 I will make with them after those *d,*
10:32 Recall the *d* gone by when,
11:30 fell after being encircled for seven *d.*
Jas 5: 3 up for yourselves against the last *d.*
1Pt 1: 5 stands ready to be revealed in the last *d.*
1:20 and revealed for your sake in these last *d.*
3:10 see prosperous *d* must keep his tongue
2Pt 3: 3 in the last *d,* mocking, sneering men
Jude 1:18 "In the last *d* there will be impostors
Rv 2:10 you will be tried over a period of ten *d.*
6: 6 "A *d* pay for a ration of wheat and the
11: 3 for those twelve hundred and sixty *d,*
11: 9 three and a half *d* but refuse to bury them.
11:11 But after the three and a half *d,*
12: 6 care of for twelve hundred and sixty *d.*

DAYSPRING (1)

Lk 1:78 he, the *D,* shall visit us in his mercy

DAYSTAR (1)

Ps(s) 110: 3 before the *d,* like the dew,

DAYTIME (5)

Ex 13:21 in the *d* by means of a column of cloud to
40:38 In the *d* the cloud of the LORD was seen
Jb 5:14 They meet with darkness in the *d,*
Ez 12: 4 exile in the *d* while they are looking on;
2Pt 2:13 Thinking *d* revelry a delight,

DAZED (1)

Ps(s) 88:16 I am *d* with the burden of your dread.

DAZZLED (2)

Sir 8: 2 For gold has *d* many,
43: 4 the eyes are *d* by its light.

DAZZLING (5)

Mt 17: 2 His face became as *d* as the sun,
28: 3 while his garments were as *d* as snow.
Lk 24: 4 two men in *d* garments stood beside them.
Jn 20:12 and there she saw two angels in *d* robes.
Acts 10:30 home when a man in *d* robes stood before me.

DAZZLINGLY (2)

Mk 9: 3 their eyes and his clothes became *d* white
Lk 9:29 appearance and his clothes became *d* white.

DEACONESS (1)

Rom 16: 1 who is a *d* of the church of Cenchreae.

DEACONS (5)

Phil 1: 1 with their bishops and *d* in Christ Jesus.
1Tm 3: 8 In the same way, *d* must be serious,
3:10 nothing against them, they may serve as *d.*
3:12 *D* may be married but once and must be good
3:13 Those who serve well as *d* gain a worthy

DEAD (335)

Gn 23: 3 of his *d* one and addressed the Hittites:
23: 4 a burial ground, that I may bury my *d* wife."
23: 6 your *d* in the choicest of our burial sites.
23: 6 his burial ground for the burial of your *d."*
23: 8 you will allow me room for burial of my *d,*
23:11 Bury your *d!"*
23:13 it from me, that I may bury my *d* there."
23:15 you and me, as long as you can bury your *d?"*
42:38 Now that his full brother is *d,*
44:20 This one's full brother is *d,*
50:15 Now that their father was *d,*
Ex 4:19 for all the men who sought your life are *d."*
12:30 for there was not a house without its *d.*
14:30 When Israel saw the Egyptians lying *d* on
21:34 the *d* animal, however, he may keep.
21:35 well as the *d* animal equally between them.
21:36 but the *d* animal he may keep.
Lv 11: 8 and their *d* bodies you shall not touch;
11:11 eat, and their *d* bodies you shall loathe.
11:24 *d* bodies shall be unclean until evening,
11:25 who picks up any part of their *d* bodies
11:27 *d* bodies shall be unclean until evening,
11:28 who picks up their *d* bodies shall wash
11:31 they are *d* shall be unclean until evening.
11:32 one of them falls when *d* becomes unclean.
11:35 on which one of their *d* bodies falls,
11:36 whoever touches the *d* body becomes unclean.
11:37 though one of their *d* bodies falls on it;
11:39 its *d* body shall be unclean until evening.
11:40 and anyone who eats of its *d* body shall
11:40 anyone who removes its *d* body shall wash
19:28 Do not lacerate your bodies for the *d,*
21: 1 unclean for any *d* person among his people,
21:11 nor shall he go near any *d* person.
Nm 6: 6 he shall not enter where a *d* person is.
6:11 he has committed by reason of the *d* person.
14: 2 or that here in the desert we were *d!*
14:29 in the desert shall your *d* bodies fall.
14:33 till the last of you lies *d* in the desert.
17:13 there between the living and the *d,*
19:11 "Whoever touches the *d* body of any human
19:16 who in the open country touches a *d* person,
19:18 a bone, a slain person or other *d* body,
Dt 14: 1 the hair above your foreheads for the *d.*
14: 8 and their *d* bodies you shall not touch.
18:11 and spirits or seeks oracles from the *d.*
19: 6 and overtake him and strike him *d,*
26:14 I have not offered any of it to the *d.*
31:27 How much more, then after I am *d!*
Jos 1: 2 "My servant Moses is *d.*
Jgs 3:25 There on the floor, *d,* lay their lord!
4:22 went in with her, and there lay Sisera *d,*
8:33 But after Gideon was *d,*
9:55 the Israelites saw that Abimelech was *d,*
Ru 2:20 ever merciful to the living and to the *d,"*
1Sm 4:11 Hophni and Phinehas, were among the *d.*
4:17 Hophni and Phinehas, are among the *d,*
17:51 When they saw that their hero was *d,*
24:15 A *d* dog, or a single flea!
25:39 On hearing that Nabal was *d,* David said:
31: 5 When the armor-bearer saw that Saul was *d,*
31: 7 fled and that Saul and his sons were *d,*
2Sm 1: 4 that many of them had fallen and were *d,*
1: 5 know that Saul and his son Jonathan are *d?"*
2: 7 men, for though your lord Saul is *d,*
9: 8 should pay attention to a *d* dog like me?"
11:15 back and leave him to be struck down *d."*
11:21 'Your servant Uriah the Hittite is also *d.'"*
12:18 afraid to tell him that the child was *d,*
12:18 How can we tell him the child is *d?*
12:19 and realized that the child was *d.*
12:19 He asked his servants, "Is the child *d?"*
12:21 now that the child is *d,*
12:23 But now he is *d.*
13:32 Amnon alone is *d,* for Absalom
13:33 in the report that all the princes are *d.*
13:33 Amnon alone is *d."*
14: 5 "Alas, I am a widow; my husband is *d.*
16: 9 should this *d* dog curse my lord the king?
18:20 good news, for in fact the king's son is *d."*
19: 7 Absalom were alive today and all of us *d,*
1Kgs 2:25 Benaiah, son of Jehoiada, who struck him *d.*
2:46 of Jehoiada, who struck him *d* as he left.
3:20 after she had laid her *d* child in my bosom.
3:21 to nurse my child, and I found him *d.*
3:22 living one is my son, the *d* one is yours."
3:22 kept saying, "No, the *d* one is your child,
3:23 one, is my child, and the *d* one is yours.'
3:23 The *d* one is your child;
11:21 that Joab, the general of the army, was *d,*
21:15 you, because Naboth is not alive, but *d."*
21:16 On hearing that Naboth was *d,*
22:37 every man to his land, for the king is *d!"*
2Kgs 4: 1 "My husband, your servant, is *d.*
4:32 the house, he found the boy lying *d.*
8: 5 his master had restored a *d* person to life,
11: 1 mother of Ahaziah, saw that her son was *d,*
13:21 cast the *d* man into the grave of Elisha,
19:35 there they were, all the corpses of the *d.*
1Chr 10: 5 and seeing him *d,* the armor-bearer
2Chr 22:10 of Ahaziah, learned that her son was *d,*
Tb 1:19 the king that it was I who buried the *d.*
2: 4 and I carried the *d* man from the street
2: 8 escaped, here he is again burying the *d!"*
3: 9 Because your husbands are *d?*
5:10 like the *d* who no longer see the light!
5:10 Though alive, I am among the *d.*
6:14 night they approached her, they dropped *d.*
8:12 in to see whether Tobiah is alive or *d,*
10: 2 or perhaps Gabael is *d,*
12:12 the same thing when you used to bury the *d.*
12:13 your dinner in order to go and bury the *d,*
Jdt 2: 8 torrent shall be choked with their *d;*
1Mc 6:17 When Lysias learned that the king was *d,*
7:44 When his army saw that Nicanor was *d,*
9:57 Seeing that Alcimus was *d,*
2Mc 5: 5 rumor circulated that Antiochus was *d.*
6:23 to send him at once to the abode of the *d,*
6:26 of men, I shall never, whether alive or *d,*
12:40 But under the tunic of each of the *d* they
12:43 he had the resurrection of the *d* in view;
12:46 *d* that they might be freed from this sin.
Jb 1:19 fell upon the young people and they are *d;*
33:22 to the pit, his life to the place of the *d.*
Ps(s) 6: 6 For among the *d* no one remembers you;
31:13 I am forgotten like the unremembered *d;*
88: 6 My couch is among the *d,*
88:11 Will you work wonders for the *d?*
106:28 of Peor and ate the sacrifices of *d* gods.
115:17 It is not the *d* who praise the LORD,
143: 3 me dwelling in the dark, like those long *d.*
Prv 7:26 For many are those she has struck down *d,*
Eccl 4: 2 And those now *d,*
6: 3 the child born *d* is more fortunate than he.
6: 5 *d* child is at rest rather than such a man.
9: 3 and afterward they go to the *d.*
9: 4 a live dog is better off than a *d* lion.
9: 5 to die, but the *d* no longer know anything.
Wis 3: 2 in the view of the foolish, to be *d;*
4:16 just man *d* condemns the sinful who live,
4:19 and an unceasing mockery among the *d.*
13:10 are they, and in *d* things are their hopes,
13:18 and for life he entreats the *d;*
14:15 honored as a god what was formerly a *d* man
15: 5 longs for the inanimate form of a *d* image.
15:17 he makes a *d* thing with his lawless hands.
18:12 alike by a single death had countless *d;*
19: 3 and were mourning at the burials of the *d,*
Sir 7:33 and withhold not your kindness from the *d.*
10:10 a king today—tomorrow he is *d.*
17:23 No more can the *d* give praise than those
22: 9 Weep over the *d* man,
22:10 Weep but a little over the *d* man,
22:11 Seven days of mourning for the *d,*
30: 4 At the father's death, he will seem not *d,*
38:16 who is *d* with wailing and bitter lament;
38:23 With the departed *d,* let memory fade;
48: 5 a *d* man back to life from the nether world.
49:15 Even his *d* body was provided for.

Is 8:19 apply to the *d* on behalf of the living?"
26:14 *D* they are, they have no life,
26:19 But your *d* shall live,
37:36 there they were, all the corpses of the *d*.
59:10 at dusk, in Stygian darkness, like the *d*.
Jer 22:10 Weep not for him who is *d*,
Lam 2:21 *D* in the dust of the streets lie young and
3: 6 me to dwell in the dark like those long *d*.
Bar 2:17 it is not the *d* in the nether world,
3:10 old in a foreign land, Defiled with the *d*,
6:26 one puts gifts beside them as beside the *d*.
Ez 24:17 in silence, make no lament for the *d*,
44:25 unclean by coming near any *d* person,
Am 6:10 be left to carry the *d* out of the houses;
Jon 4: 8 "I would be better off *d* than alive."
Mt 2:20 had designs on the life of the child are *d*."
8:22 "Follow me, and let the *d* bury their dead."
9:24 The little girl is not *d*.
10: 8 Cure the sick, raise the *d*,
11: 5 the deaf hear, *d* men are raised to life,
14: 2 is he in person, raised from the *d*;
17: 9 until the Son of Man rises from the *d*."
22:30 When people rise from the *d*,
22:31 As to the fact that the *d* are raised,
22:32 He is the God of the living, not of the *d*."
23:27 but inside full of filth and *d* men's bones.
27:64 the people, 'He has been raised from the *d*!'
28: 4 with fear of him and fell down like *d* men.
28: 7 the *d* and now goes ahead of you to Galilee,
Mk 5:35 house arrived saying, "Your daughter is *d*.
5:39 The child is not *d*.
6:14 the Baptizer has been raised from the *d*;
9: 9 before the Son of Man had risen from the *d*.
9:10 discuss what "to rise from the *d*" meant.
9:26 which caused many to say, "He is *d*."
12:25 When people rise from the *d*,
12:26 As to the raising of the *d*,
12:27 He is the God of the living, not of the *d*.
15:44 and inquired whether Jesus was already *d*.
15:45 Learning from him that he was *d*,
16: 9 the *d* early on the first day of the week.
Lk 7:12 of the town a *d* man was being carried out,
7:15 The *d* man sat up and began to speak.
7:22 the deaf hear, *d* men are raised to life,
8:49 the announcement, "Your daughter is *d*;
8:52 "Stop crying for she is not *d* but asleep."
8:53 laughed at him, being certain she was *d*.
9: 7 "John has been raised from the *d*";
9:19 prophets of old has returned from the *d*."
9:60 said to him, "Let the dead bury their *d*;
15:24 of mine was *d* and has come back to life.
15:32 This brother of yours was *d*,
16:23 the abode of the *d* where he was in torment,
16:30 someone would only go to them from the *d*,
16:31 even if one should rise from the *d*.'"
20:35 come and of resurrection from the *d* do not.
20:37 passage about the bush showed that the *d* rise
20:38 is not the God of the *d* but of the living.
24: 5 you search for the Living One among the *d*?
24:46 and rise from the *d* on the third day.
Jn 2:22 after Jesus had been raised from the *d*
5:21 as the Father raises the *d* and grants life,
5:25 *d* shall hear the voice of the Son of God,
8:52 "Abraham is *d*.
8:52 The prophets are *d*.
11:14 "Lazarus is *d*.
11:39 Martha, the *d* man's sister,
11:44 The *d* man came out bound head and foot
12: 1 Lazarus whom Jesus had raised from the *d*.
12: 9 see Lazarus, whom he had raised from the *d*.
12:17 him from the *d* kept testifying to it.
19:33 to Jesus and saw that he was already *d*,
20: 9 that Jesus had to rise from the *d*.)
21:14 disciples after being raised from the *d*.
Acts 3:15 But God raised him from the *d*,
4: 2 of the *d* in the person of Jesus.
4:10 crucified and whom God raised from the *d*.
5: 5 the sound of these words, Ananias fell *d*.
5:10 With that, she fell *d* at his feet.
5:10 The young men came in, found her *d*,
9:40 Turning to the *d* body,
10:41 drank with him after he rose from the *d*.
10:42 by God as judge of the living and the *d*.
13:30 Yet God raised him from the *d*,
13:34 *d* would never again see the decay of death,
14:19 out of the town, leaving him there for *d*.
17: 3 Messiah had to suffer and rise from the *d*:
17:31 the sight of all by raising him from the *d*."
17:32 they heard about the raising of the *d*,
20: 9 When they picked him up he was *d*.
23: 6 of my hope in the resurrection of the *d*."
24:21 today because of the resurrection of the *d*.'"
26: 8 to believe that God raises *d* men to life.
26:23 and that, as the first to rise from the *d*,
28: 6 to see him swell up or suddenly fall *d*.
Rom 1: 4 holiness, by his resurrection from the *d*:
4:17 the God who restores the *d* to life and
4:19 *d* (for he was nearly a hundred years old),
4:19 years old), and of the *d* womb of Sarah.
4:24 him who raised Jesus our Lord from the *d*,
6: 4 from the *d* by the glory of the Father,
6: 7 A man who is *d* has been freed from sin.
6: 9 know that Christ, once raised from the *d*,
6:11 *d* to sin but alive for God in Christ Jesus.
6:13 men who have come back from the *d* to life,
7: 4 to that Other who was raised from the *d*,
7: 8 Without law sin is *d*,
8:10 is in you, the body is *d* because of sin,
8:11 who raised Jesus from the *d* dwells in you,
8:11 then he who raised Christ from the *d* will
10: 7 (that is, to bring Christ up from the *d*."
10: 9 your heart that God raised him from the *d*,
11:15 Nothing less than life from the *d*!
14: 9 might be Lord of both the *d* and the living.
1Cor 15:12 Christ is preached as raised from the *d*,
15:12 you say there is no resurrection of the *d*?
15:13 If there is no resurrection of the *d*,
15:15 not raise him up if the *d* are not raised.
15:16 Because if the *d* are not raised,
15:18 asleep in Christ are the deadest of the *d*.
15:20 as it is, Christ is now raised from the *d*,
15:21 of the *d* comes through a man also.
15:29 If the *d* are not raised, what about
15:29 themselves baptized on behalf of the *d*?
15:29 If the raising of the *d* is not a reality,
15:32 If the *d* are not raised, "Let us eat
15:35 will say, "How are the *d* to be raised up?
15:42 So is it with the resurrection of the *d*.
15:52 and the *d* will be raised incorruptible,
2Cor 1: 9 in ourselves, but in God who raises the *d*.
6: 9 *d*,
Gal 1: 1 God his Father who raised him from the *d*—
Eph 1:20 raising Christ from the *d* and seating him
2: 1 were *d* because of your sins and offenses,
2: 5 to life with Christ when we were *d* in sin.
5:14 "Awake, O sleeper, arise from the *d*,
Phil 3:11 I may arrive at resurrection from the *d*.
Col 1:18 is the beginning, the first-born of the *d*,
2:12 the power of God who raised him from the *d*.
2:13 *d* in sin and your flesh was uncircumcised,
1Thes 1:10 from heaven the Son he raised from the *d*—
4:14 God will bring forth with him from the *d*
2Tm 2: 8 descendant of David, was raised from the *d*.
4: 1 is coming to judge the living and the *d*,
Heb 6: 1 repentance from *d* works,
6: 2 laying-on of hands, resurrection of the *d*,
9:14 from *d* works to worship the living God!
11: 4 therefore, although Abel is *d*,
11:12 one man, who was himself as good as *d*,
11:19 that God was able to raise from the *d*,
11:35 received back their *d* through resurrection.
13:20 who brought up from the *d* the great
Jas 2:26 works is as *d* as a body without breath.
1Pt 1: 3 resurrection of Jesus Christ from the *d*;
1:21 raised him from the *d* and gave him glory.
2:24 to the cross, so that all of us, *d* to sin,
4: 5 stands ready to judge the living and the *d*.
4: 6 gospel was preached even to the *d* was that,
1Jn 3:14 who does not love is among the living *d*.
Jude 1:12 they bear no fruit, being *d* and uprooted.
Rv 1: 5 from the *d* and ruler of the kings of earth.
1:17 of him I fell down at his feet as though *d*.
1:18 Once I was *d* but now I live
3: 1 of being alive, when in fact you are *d*!
11:18 day of wrath and the moment to judge the *d*:
14:13 Happy now are the *d* who die in the Lord!"
20: 5 The others who were *d* did not come to life
20:12 I saw the *d*, the great and the lowly,
20:12 The *d* were judged according to their
20:13 sea gave up its *d*; then death and the nether

DEADEST (1)

1Cor 15:18 asleep in Christ are the *d* of the dead.

DEADLY (20)

Ex 10:17 God, to take at least this *d* pest from me."
1Sm 5: 6 brought upon the city a great and *d* plague
5:11 A *d* panic had seized the whole city,
Tb 14:10 from the *d* trap Nadab had set for him.
14:10 But Nadab himself fell into the *d* trap,
Ps(s) 7:14 bow, Prepare his *d* weapons against them,
139:22 God With a *d* hatred I hate them;
Prv 12: 6 The words of the wicked are a *d* ambush,
21: 6 tongue is chasing a bubble over *d* snares.
26:18 archer scattering firebrands and *d* arrows
Jer 16: 4 Of *d* disease they shall die.
30:21 one take the *d* risk of approaching me?
Mk 16:18 be able to drink *d* poison without harm,
16:20 be able to drink *d* poison without harm,
Jas 3: 8 It is a restless evil, full of *d* poison.
1Jn 5:16 his brother sinning, if the sin is not *d*,
5:16 This is only for those whose sin is not *d*.
5:16 There is such a thing as a *d* sin;
5:17 wrong doing is sin, but not all sin is *d*.
Rv 9:19 The *d* power of the horses was not only in

DEAF (24)

Ex 4:11 man speech and makes another *d* and dumb?
Lv 19:14 You shall not curse the *d*,
Ps(s) 28: 1 O my Rock be not *d* to me,
38:14 But I am like a *d* man,
39:13 to my weeping be not *d*!
50: 3 May our God come and not be *d* to us!
50:21 you do these things, shall I be *d* to it?
Sir 35:14 He is not *d* to the wail of the orphan,
Is 29:18 day the *d* shall hear the words of a book;
35: 5 be opened, the ears of the *d* be cleared;
42:18 You who are *d*, listen,
42:19 servant, or *d* like the messenger I send?
43: 8 have eyes, who are *d* though they have ears.
44: 9 and they are more *d* than men are.
Lam 3:56 "Let not your ear be *d* to my cry for help!"
Bar 6:40 for when they see a *d* mute,
Mi 7:16 their ears shall become *d*.
Mt 11: 5 walk, lepers are cured, the *d* hear,
Mk 7:32 Some people brought him a *d* man who had a
7:37 He makes the *d* hear and the mute speak!"
9:25 by saying to him, "Mute and *d* spirit,
Lk 7:22 walk, lepers are cured, the *d* hear,
Rom 11: 8 blind eyes and *d* ears,
Heb 5:11 to explain, for you have become *d*.

DEAFENS (1)

Sir 38:28 The clang of the hammer *d* his ears,

DEAL (55)

Gn 21:23 you will not *d* falsely with me
24:12 thus *d* graciously with my master Abraham.
Ex 1:10 let us *d* shrewdly with them to stop their
Lv 25:14 or buy any from him, do not *d* unfairly.
25:17 Do not *d* unfairly,
Nm 8:20 of the Israelites *d* with the Levites,
11:15 If this is the way you will *d* with me,
Dt 7: 5 "But this is how you must *d* with them:
20:15 "That is how you shall *d* with any city at
31: 4 The LORD will *d* with them just as he dealt
31: 5 *d* with them exactly as I have ordered you.
Jos 9:20 spare their lives and so *d* with them
Jgs 9:33 against you, *d* with him as best you can."
20:10 soldiers who will go to *d* fully and suitably
1Sm 12:15 will *d* severely with you and your king,
15: 3 and *d* with him and all that he has under
1Kgs 2: 9 prudent man and will know how to *d* with
2Kgs 9: 9 I will *d* with the house of Ahab as I dealt
2Chr 2: 2 a house for his dwelling, so *d* with me.
10: 7 "If you will *d* kindly with this people
Tb 3: 6 "So now, *d* with me as you please,
Jdt 3: 4 come and *d* with them as you see fit."
Est B: 2 but always to *d* fairly and with clemency;
2Mc 6:14 with us he has decided to *d* differently,
14:40 such a man he would *d* the Jews a hard blow.
Ps(s) 83:10 *D* with them as with Midian;
103:10 according to our sins does he *d* with us,
109:21 *d* kindly with me for your name's sake;
Sir 33:32 but one slave, *d* with him as a brother,
Is 3: 9 they *d* out evil to themselves.
23:17 She shall return to her hire and *d* with
29:14 Therefore I will again *d* with this people
Jer 9: 6 how else should I *d* with their wickedness?
21: 2 Perhaps the LORD will *d* with us according
Lam 1:22 *d* with them As you have dealt with me for
Ez 7: 9 will *d* with you according to your conduct,
7:27 *d* with them according to their conduct,
16:59 *d* with you according to what you have done,
20:44 that I am the LORD when I *d* with you thus,
22:14 be strong, in the days when I *d* with you?
23:25 you, so that they shall *d* with you in fury,
23:29 They shall *d* with you in hatred,
25:14 who will *d* with Edom in accordance with my
35:11 I will *d* with you according to your anger
Dn 3:42 *d* with us in your kindness and great mercy.
Am 4:12 So now I will *d* with you in my own way,
4:12 and since I will *d* thus with you,
Zep 3:19 time I will *d* with all who oppress you;
Zec 8:11 But now I will not *d* with the remnant of
Jn 8:45 But because I *d* in the truth,
Col 2:22 *d* with things that perish in their use.
4: 1 *d* justly and fairly with your slaves,
2Tm 4:14 the coppersmith did me a great *d* of harm;
Heb 5: 2 is able to *d* patiently with erring sinners,
Rv 18:15 The merchants who *d* in these goods,

DEALER (1)

Acts 16:14 a *d* in purple goods from the town of

DEALERS (3)

2Mc 8:34 the thousand slave *d* to buy the Jews,
Jer 6:28 Arch-rebels are they all, *d* in slander,
Mt 25: 9 better go to the *d* and buy yourselves some.'

DEALING (12)

Ezr 6: 8 decree concerning your *d* with these elders
Tb 3: 5 judgments are many and true in *d* with me
2Mc 6:14 Thus, in *d* with other nations,
Prv 3:34 When he is *d* with the arrogant,
Sir 42: 5 or of bargaining in *d* with a merchant;
Dn 11:16 stop in the glorious land, *d* destruction.
Lk 16: 8 when it comes to *d* with their own kind.
Acts 19:19 A number who had been *d* in magic even
2Cor 2:16 to the latter an odor of *d* death,
13: 3 He is not weak in *d* with you,
Col 4: 5 Be prudent in *d* with outsiders;
2Pt 3:16 *d* with these matters as he does in all his

DEALINGS (5)

Nm 25:18 been your enemies by their wily *d* with you
2Mc 14:30 was becoming cool in his *d* with him,
Jb 27:11 I will teach you the manner of God's *d*,
Prv 31:18 She enjoys the success of her *d*;
Acts 10:28 with a Gentile or to have *d* with him.

DEALS (4)

Jb 15:11 for you, and speech that *d* gently with you?
Prv 6:12 a villain, is he who *d* in crooked talk.
Jer 7: 5 if each of you *d* justly with his neighbor;
Heb 12: 7 discipline of God, who *d* with you as sons.

DEALT (35)

Gn 24:14 that you have *d* graciously with my master."
Ex 1:20 Therefore God *d* well with the midwives.
10: 2 how ruthlessly I *d* with the Egyptians
18:11 occasion of their being *d* with insolently
Dt 29:23 'Why has the LORD *d* thus with this land?
31: 4 with them just as he *d* with Sihon and Og,
Jos 2:10 of Egypt, and how you *d* with Sihon and Og,
Jgs 9:16 *d* well with Jerubbaal and with his family,
1Sm 5: 6 LORD *d* severely with the people of Ashdod.
6: 6 Was it not after he had *d* ruthlessly with
2Kgs 9: 9 of Ahab as I *d* with the house of Jeroboam,
1Chr 20: 3 *d* with all the cities of the Ammonites.
2Chr 2: 2 "As you *d* with my father David,
Tb 8:16 *d* with us according to your great mercy.
Jdt 8:26 Recall how he *d* with Abraham,
1Mc 13:31 Trypho *d* treacherously with the young King
Jb 19: 6 Know then that God has *d* unfairly with me,
42: 3 I have *d* with great things that I do not
Ps(s) 105:25 and *d* deceitfully with his servants.
Jer 2: 8 Those who *d* with the law knew me not;
Lam 1:12 which has been *d* me When the LORD
1:22 them As you have *d* with me for all my sins;
Bar 2:27 you have *d* in all your clemency and in all
Ez 27:21 they *d* in lambs, rams, and goats.
31:11 *d* with it in keeping with its wickedness.
39:24 and their transgressions I *d* with them,
Jl 2:26 God, Because he has *d* wondrously with you;
Mt 18:33 have *d* mercifully with your fellow servant,
18:33 with your fellow servant, as I *d* with you?'
Lk 1:72 He has *d* mercifully with our fathers and
Acts 1: 1 I *d* with all that Jesus did and taught
7:19 This one *d* craftily with our people and
19:16 He *d* with them so violently that they fled
1Tm 1:16 that very account I was *d* with mercifully,
Heb 10:33 with those who were being so *d* with.

DEAR (33)

Ru 2:22 "You would do well, my *d*,"
2Sm 1:26 most *d* have you been to me;
Ps(s) 39:12 like a cobweb all that is *d* to him;
102:15 For her stones are *d* to your servants,
Sg 6: 9 mother's chosen, the *d* one of her parent.
Sir 7:18 nor a *d* brother for the gold of Ophir.
7:21 wise servant be *d* to you as your own self;
45: 1 *D* to God and men,
46:13 Beloved of his people, *d* to his Maker,
Is 64:10 all that was *d* to us is laid waste.
Jer 20: 5 city, all it has toiled for and holds *d*,
Lam 1: 2 not one to console her of all her *d* ones;
Zec 13: 6 I was wounded in the house of my *d* ones."
Rom 16: 8 to Ampliatus, who is *d* to me in the Lord;
16:12 and also to *d* Persis, who has labored
2Cor 12:19 done everything to build you up, my *d* ones.
Eph 5: 1 Be imitators of God as his *d* children.
6:21 my *d* brother and faithful minister in the
Phil 1: 7 in your regard since I hold all of you *d*—
4: 1 my joy and my crown, continue, my *d* ones,
4:15 You yourselves know, my *d* Philippians,
Col 1: 7 of Epaphras, our *d* fellow slave,
4: 7 Tychicus, our *d* brother,
4: 9 is Onesimus, our *d* and faithful brother,
4:14 Luke, our *d* physician,
1Thes 2: 8 our very lives, so *d* had you become to us.
Phlm 1:16 a beloved brother, especially *d* to me;
Jas 1:16 Make no mistake about this, my *d* brothers.
1:19 Keep this in mind, *d* brothers.
2: 5 Listen, *d* brothers.
2Pt 3: 1 writing you this second letter, *d* friends,
3: 8 point must not be overlooked, *d* friends.
Rv 3:19 Whoever is *d* to me I reprove and chastise.

DEARER (1)

Ex 19: 5 possession, *d* to me than all other people,

DEAREST (1)

Wis 12: 7 that the land that is *d* of all to you

DEARLY (4)

Tb 6:12 and her father loves her *d*."
Phil 2:12 So then, my *d* beloved, obedient as always
1Jn 2: 7 *D* beloved, it is no new commandment
3: 2 *D* beloved, we are God's children now;

DEATH (557)

Gn 24:67 solace after the *d* of his mother Sarah.
25:11 After the *d* of Abraham,
26:11 or his wife shall forthwith be put to *d*."
26:18 had stopped up after Abraham's *d*;
35: 8 *D* came to Rebekah's nurse Deborah;
35:18 for she was at the point of *d*—
43: 8 children are to keep from starving to *d*.
50: 5 Since my father, at the point of *d*,
Ex 2:15 of the affair and sought to put him to *d*.
19:12 touches the mountain, he must be put to *d*.
19:13 must be stoned to *d* or killed with arrows.
21:12 a man a mortal blow must be put to *d*.
21:13 down, but caused his *d* by an act of God,
21:14 him even from my altar and put him to *d*.
21:15 his father or mother shall be put to *d*.
21:16 has him when caught, shall be put to *d*.
21:17 his father or mother shall be put to *d*.
21:28 "When an ox gores a man or a woman to *d*,
21:29 but its owner also must be put to *d*.
22: 1 the act of housebreaking and beaten to *d*,
22:18 who lies with an animal shall be put to *d*.
23: 7 and the just you shall not put to *d*,
31:14 Whoever desecrates it shall be put to *d*.
31:15 work on the sabbath day shall be put to *d*.
35: 2 does work on that day shall be put to *d*.
Lv 7:24 has died a natural *d* or has been killed
10: 6 lest you bring not only *d* on yourselves
10: 9 your sons are forbidden under pain of *d*,
15:31 their uncleanness be the cause of their *d*.
16: 1 After the *d* of Aaron's two sons,
19:20 they shall be punished but not put to *d*,
20: 2 his offspring to Molech shall be put to *d*.
20: 4 to Molech, and fail to put him to *d*,
20: 9 his father or mother shall be put to *d*;
20:10 and the adulteress shall be put to *d*.
20:11 man and his stepmother shall be put to *d*;
20:12 both of them shall be put to *d*;
20:13 be put to *d* for their abominable deed;
20:14 be burned to *d* for their shameful conduct,
20:15 with an animal, the man shall be put to *d*,
20:16 let them both be put to *d*;
20:27 fortune-teller shall be put to *d* by stoning;
20:27 no one but themselves to blame for their *d*."
21: 9 her father also, shall be burned to *d*.
24:16 the name of the LORD shall be put to *d*.
24:16 put to *d* for blaspheming the LORD's name.
24:17 life of any human being shall be put to *d*;
24:21 but whoever slays a man shall be put to *d*.
27:29 they must be put to *d*.
Nm 1:51 layman who comes near it shall be put to *d*.
3: 4 they met *d* in the presence of the LORD,
3:10 layman who comes near shall be put to *d*."
3:38 layman who came near was to be put to *d*.
15:35 to Moses, "This man shall be put to *d*;
15:36 him outside the camp and stoned him to *d*,
16:29 if these men die an ordinary *d*,
18: 7 layman who draws near shall be put to *d*."
18:22 else they will incur guilt deserving *d*.
18:32 Israelites and so bring *d* on yourselves."
20:26 for there Aaron shall be taken in *d*."
23:10 May I die the *d* of the just,
35:12 shall not be put to *d* unless he is first tried
35:16 *d*, he is a murderer and shall be put to *d*
35:17 *d*, he is a murderer and shall be put to *d*.
35:18 *d*, he is a murderer and shal be put to *d*.
35:19 the murderer, putting him to *d* on sight.
35:20 throws something at him, and causes his *d*,
35:21 death, he shall be put to *d* as a murderer.
35:23 stone which strikes him and causes his *d*,
35:25 stay there until the *d* of the high priest
35:28 of asylum until the *d* of the high priest.
35:28 Only after the *d* of the high priest may
35:30 not sufficient for putting a person to *d*.
35:31 deserves the *d* penalty; he must be put to *d*.
35:32 the land before the *d* of the high priest.
Dt 2:16 "When at length *d* had put an end to all
13: 6 prophet or that dreamer shall be put to *d*,
13:11 You shall stone him to *d*,
17: 5 out to your city gates and stone him to *d*.
17: 6 person to *d*; no one shall be put to death
19: 6 even though he does not merit *d* since he
21:21 his fellow citizens shall stone him to *d*.
21:22 is put to *d* and his corpse hung on a tree,
22:21 there her townsmen shall stone her to *d*,
22:24 gate of the city and there stone them to *d*:
24: 7 sell him, the kidnaper shall be put to *d*.
24:16 shall not be put to *d* for their children,
24:16 for his own guilt shall a man be put to *d*.
30:15 before you life and prosperity, *d* and doom.
30:19 I have set before you life and *d*,
31:29 For I know that after my *d* you are sure to
32:39 It is I who bring both *d* and life,
Jos 1:18 command you give him, he shall be put to *d*.
2:13 and all their kin, and save us from *d*."
2:19 he will be responsible for his own *d*,
7:25 And all Israel stoned him to *d* and piled a
11:17 All their kings he captured and put to *d*.
20: 6 till the *d* of the high priest who is in office
20: 9 *d* at the hand of the avenger of blood,
Jgs 1: 1 After the *d* of Joshua the Israelites
4: 1 After Ehud's *d*, however, the Israelites
4:21 into the ground, so that he perished in *d*.
5:18 Zebulun is the people defying *d*;
6:31 for him, he shall be put to *d* by morning.
13: 7 God from the womb, until the day of his *d*.'"
16:30 Those he killed at his *d* were more than
20:13 to *d* and thus purge the evil from Israel."
21: 5 at Mizpah should be put to *d* without fail.
21:16 every woman in Benjamin has been put to *d*."
Ru 1:17 if aught but *d* separates me from you!"
2:11 your mother-in-law after your husband's *d*;
1Sm 2: 6 "The LORD puts to *d* and gives life;
2:25 since the LORD had decided on their *d*.
5:12 escaped *d* were afflicted with hemorrhoids,
11:12 over the men and we will put them to *d*."
11:13 say, "No man is to be put to *d* this day,
14:45 were able to rescue Jonathan from *d*.
15:32 struggling and saying, "So it is bitter *d*!"
18:25 about David's *d* through the Philistines.
20: 3 live, there is but a step between me and *d*."
22:21 responsible for the *d* of all your family.
26:16 *d* because you have not guarded your lord,
2Sm 1: 1 After the *d* of Saul,
1:16 him, "You are responsible for your own *d*,
1:23 separated neither in life nor in *d*,
3:29 the full responsibility for the *d* of Abner,
4:10 *d* the man who informed me of Saul's death,
4:11 for his *d* and destroy you from the earth!"
6:23 Michal was childless to the day of her *d*.
12: 5 lives, the man who has done this merits *d*!
13:28 I say to you, 'Kill Amnon,' put him to *d*.
13:39 as he became reconciled to the *d* of Amnon.
14: 7 We must put him to *d* for the life of his
14:32 If I am guilty, let him put me to *d*."
15:21 the king may be, whether for *d* or for life."
17: 3 is the *d* of only one man you are seeking;
19:22 "Shimei must be put to *d* for this.
19:29 deserved only *d* from my lord the king,
20: 3 in confinement to the day of their *d*,
21: 1 family because he put the Gibeonites to *d*."
21: 4 it our place to put any man to *d* in Israel."
21: 9 to *d* during the first days of the harvest
22: 5 "The breakers of *d* surged round about me.
22: 6 enmeshed me, the snares of *d* overtook me.
1Kgs 2: 1 When the time of David's *d* drew near,
2:24 this day shall Adonijah be put to *d*."
2:26 to die, I will not put you to *d* this time,
11:15 the slain, put to *d* every male in Edom.
11:40 Egypt, where he remained until Solomon's *d*.
12:18 labor, but all Israel stoned him to *d*.
19: 4 He prayed for *d*:
21:10 Then take him out and stone him to *d*."
21:13 him out of the city and stoned him to *d*.
21:14 Jezebel that Naboth had been stoned to *d*.
21:15 learned that Naboth had been stoned to *d*,
2Kgs 1: 1 After Ahab's *d*, Moab rebelled
2:21 shall *d* or miscarriage spring from it.'"
5: 7 "Am I a god with power over life and *d*,
7:17 the people trampled him to *d* at the gate,
7:20 the people trampled him to *d* at the gate.
11:16 the royal palace, where she was put to *d*.
14: 6 of the murderers he did not put to *d*,
14: 6 shall not be put to *d* for their children,
14: 6 children be put to *d* for their fathers;
15: 5 and he was a leper to the day of his *d*.
16: 9 its inhabitants to Kir and put Rezin to *d*.
18:32 Choose life, not *d*.
25:21 them struck down and put to *d* in Riblah,
1Chr 2:24 After the *d* of Hezron,
19: 2 to comfort him over the *d* of his father.
22: 5 his *d* David laid up materials in abundance.
2Chr 10:18 labor, but the Israelites stoned him to *d*.
15:13 the God of Israel, was to be put to *d*,
22: 4 his counselors after the *d* of his father.
22: 9 and brought him to Jehu, who put him to *d*.
22:11 sight, so that she did not put him to *d*.
23:14 must not put her to *d* in the LORD's temple."
23:15 of the palace, they put her to *d* there.
23:21 Athaliah had been put to *d* by the sword.
24:17 After the *d* of Jehoiada,
24:21 him to *d* in the court of the LORD's temple.
25: 4 but he did not put their children to *d*,
25: 4 shall not be put to *d* for their children,
25: 4 for his own guilt shall a man be put to *d*."
25:27 him to Lachish and put him to *d* there.
26:21 remained a leper to the day of his *d*.
32:11 you over to a *d* of famine and thirst,
32:33 of Jerusalem paid him honor at his *d*.
33:24 him and put him to *d* in his own house.
Ezr 7:26 upon him, whether *d* or corporal punishment,
Tb 1:14 *d* I would go to Media to buy goods for him.
1:19 all about me and wanted to put me to *d*,
3: 4 us over to plundering, exile, and *d*,
4: 2 he thought, "Now that I have asked for *d*,
4:10 Almsgiving frees one from *d*,
12: 9 saves one from *d* and expiates every sin.
Jdt 11:11 and fail, but *d* will overtake them.
12:14 will be a joy for me till the day of my *d*."
14: 5 of Israel and sent him here to meet his *d*."
16:22 time of the *d* and burial of her husband,
16:25 of Judith and for a long time after her *d*,
Est A:14 and, upon their confession, put to *d*.
2: 7 On the *d* of her father and mother,
B: 7 world by a violent *d* on one same day,
B: 8 is second to the king, has asked for our *d*.
B: 9 save us from *d*."
4:11 suffers the automatic penalty of *d*,

C:11 for *d* was staring them in the face.
1Mc 1: 2 captured fortresses, and put kings to *d.*
1: 9 after his *d* they all put on royal crowns,
1:50 the command of the king should be put to *d.*
1:57 law, was condemned to *d* by royal decree.
1:60 their children circumcised were put to *d,*
6:24 they have put to *d* as many of us as they
6:55 Philip, whom King Antiochus, before his *d,*
9:23 After the *d* of Judas,
9:61 in the mischief and put them to *d.*
16:22 him, he had them arrested and put to *d,*
2Mc 4:34 for justice, he immediately put him to *d.*
4:38 and there he put the murderer to *d.*
4:47 while he condemned to *d* those poor men who
5:14 lost, forty thousand meeting a violent *d,*
6: 9 and put to *d* those who would not consent
6:11 betrayed to Philip and all burned to *d.*
6:19 a glorious *d* to a life of defilement,
6:22 in this way he would escape the *d* penalty,
6:30 that, although I could have escaped *d,*
6:31 leaving in his *d* a model of courage and an
7: 9 At the point of *d* he said:
7:14 When he was near *d,*
7:29 be worthy of your brothers and accept *d,*
9:28 *d* in the mountains of a foreign land.
10:22 So he put them to *d* as traitors,
12:44 useless and foolish to pray for them in *d.*
13: 8 fire and ashes should meet his *d* in ashes.
13:14 followers to fight nobly to *d* for the laws,
14:13 him off with orders to put Judas to *d,*
14:46 Such was the manner of his *d.*
Jb 3:21 They wait for *d* and it comes not;
5:20 In famine he will deliver you from *d,*
7:15 prefer choking and *d* rather than my pains.
18:13 the first-born of *d* consumes his limbs.
28:22 Abaddon and *D* say,
30:23 *d* to the destined place of everyone alive.
38:17 Have the gates of *d* been shown to you,
Ps(s) 9:14 who have raised me up from the gates of *d,*
13: 4 I may not sleep in *d* lest my enemy say,
18: 5 The breakers of *d* surged round about me,
18: 6 enmeshed me, the snares of *d* overtook me.
22:16 to the dust of *d* you have brought me down.
33:19 *d* and preserve them in spite of famine.
49:15 *d* is their shepherd,
55: 5 the terror of *d* has fallen upon me.
55:16 Let *d* surprise them;
56:14 For you have rescued me from *d,*
68:21 my Lord, controls the passageways of *d.*
78:50 of his anger he spared them not from *d,*
79:11 your great power free those doomed to *d.*
89:49 What man shall live, and not see *d,*
107:18 so that they were near the gates of *d.*
109:16 and the brokenhearted, to do them to *d.*
116: 3 The cords of *d* encompassed me;
116: 8 For he has freed my soul from *d,*
116:15 of the LORD is the *d* of his faithful ones.
118:18 me, yet he has not delivered me to *d.*
Prv 2:18 For her path sinks down to *d,*
5: 5 Her feet go down to *d,*
7:27 world, leading down into the chambers of *d.*
8:36 all who hate me love *d.*"
10: 2 profit nothing, but virtue saves from *d.*
11: 4 the day of wrath, but virtue saves from *d.*
11:19 but he who pursues evil does so to his *d.*
12:28 is life, but the abominable way leads to *d.*
13:14 life, that a man may avoid the snares of *d.*
14:12 to a man, but the end of it leads to *d!*
14:27 life, that a man may avoid the snares of *d.*
16:14 The king's wrath is like messengers of *d,*
16:25 to a man, but the end of it leads to *d!*
18:21 *D* and life are in the power of the tongue;
19:18 but do not desire his *d.*
24:11 Rescue those who are being dragged to *d,*
Eccl 4: 2 in *d* than are the living to be still alive.
7: 1 and the day of *d* than the day of birth.
7:26 *d* I find the woman who is a hunter's trap,
8: 8 it, and none has mastery of the day of *d.*
Sg 8: 6 For stern as *d* is love,
Wis 1:12 Court not *d* by your erring way of life,
1:13 Because God did not make *d,*
1:16 wicked who with hands and words invited *d,*
2:20 Let us condemn him to a shameful *d;*
2:24 envy of the devil, *d* entered the world,
4:17 For they see the *d* of the wise man and do
5: 4 we accounted madness, and his *d* dishonored.
12:20 enemies of your servants, doomed to *d;*
16:13 For you have dominion over life and *d;*
18: 5 to put to *d* the infants of the holy ones,
18:12 all alike by a single *d* had countless dead;
18:16 he alighted, he filled every place with *d;*
18:20 of *d* touched at one time even the just,
19: 5 while those others met an extraordinary *d.*
Sir 1:11 on the day of his *d* he will be blessed.
4:28 Even to the *d* fight for truth,
9:12 remember he will not reach *d* unpunished.
9:13 you will not be filled with the dread of *d.*
11:14 Good and evil, life and *d,*
11:26 of *d* to repay man according to his deeds.
11:28 Call no man happy before his *d,*
14:12 Remember that *d* does not tarry,
15:17 Before man are life and *d,*
18:10 and understands that their *d* is grievous,
18:24 Think of wrath and the day of *d,*
22:10 but worse than *d* is the life of a fool.
23:12 There are words which merit *d;*
26: 5 lying testimony are harder to bear than *d,*
28: 6 remember *d* and decay,
28:21 Dire is the *d* it inflicts,
30: 4 At the father's *d,* he will seem not dead,
30: 5 upon through life with joy, and even in *d,*
30:17 Preferable is *d* to a bitter life,
30:23 For worry has brought *d* to many,
33:14 evil contrasts with good, and *d* with life,
33:24 the time of *d* distribute your inheritance.
34:12 Often I was in danger of *d,*
37: 2 Is it not a sorrow unto *d* when your bosom
37:18 Good and evil, *d* and life,
40: 5 and envy, trouble and dread, terror of *d,*
40: 9 the sword, plunder and ruin, famine and *d:*
41: 1 O *d!* how bitter
41: 2 O *d!* how welcome
41: 9 at *d,* you become a curse.
48:14 In life he performed wonders, and after *d,*
51: 2 You have saved me from *d,*
51: 6 I was at the point of *d,*
Is 25: 8 he will destroy *d* forever.
28:15 you say, "We have made a covenant with *d,*
28:18 Your covenant with *d* shall be canceled and
38:18 gives you thanks, nor *d* that praises you;
53:12 to *d* and was counted among the wicked;
Jer 8: 3 *D* will be preferred to life by all the
9:20 *D* has come up through our windows,
15: 2 Whoever is marked for death, to *d;*
16: 7 to drink over the *d* of father or mother.
21: 8 am giving you a choice between life and *d.*
26: 8 of him, crying, "You must be put to *d!*
26:11 to all the people, "This man deserves *d;*
26:15 if you put me to *d,* it is innocent blood
26:16 prophets, "This man does not deserve *d;*
26:19 of Judah, and all Judah condemn him to *d?*
26:24 handed over to the people to be put to *d.*
38: 4 "This man ought to be put to *d,*"
43:11 with *d,* whoever is marked for *d;*
52:11 and kept in prison until the day of his *d.*
52:27 them struck down and put to *d* in Riblah,
52:34 days of his life until the day of his *d.*
Lam 1:20 the sword bereaves, at home *d* stalks.
Bar 6:35 They neither save a man from *d,*
Ez 3:18 but I will hold you responsible for his *d.*
3:20 for his *d* if you did not warn him.
7:16 I will put them all to *d,*
18:13 his *d* shall be his own fault.
18:23 any pleasure from the *d* of the wicked?
18:32 no pleasure in the *d* of anyone who dies,
28:10 You shall die the *d* of the uncircumcised
31:14 For all of them are destined for *d,*
33: 4 him, shall be responsible for his own *d.*
33: 5 he is responsible for his own *d,*
33: 6 watchman responsible for that person's *d,*
33: 8 but I will hold you responsible for his *d.*
33:11 no pleasure in the *d* of the wicked man,
Dn 2:12 all the wise men of Babylon to be put to *d.*
2:24 "Do not put the wise men of Babylon to *d.*
3:88 world, and saved us from the power of *d;*
10: 8 I turned the color of *d* and was powerless.
13:22 "If I yield, it will be my *d;*
13:28 came, fully determined to put Susanna to *d.*
13:41 of the people, and they condemned her to *d.*
13:46 will have no part in the *d* of this woman."
13:53 and the just you shall not put to *d.'*
13:62 they put them to *d.*
14:22 He put them to *d,*
14:28 the dragon, and put the priests to *d.*"
Hos 13:14 shall I redeem them from *d?*
13:14 Where are your plagues, O *d!*
Am 2: 2 *d* amid uproar and shouts and trumpet blasts.
Jon 4: 8 Then he asked for *d,*
Hb 2: 5 the nether world, and is insatiable as *d,*
Mt 2:15 He stayed there until the *d* of Herod,
2:19 But after Herod's *d,*
4:16 those who inhabit a land overshadowed by *d,*
10:21 "Brother will hand over brother to *d,*
10:21 against parents and have them put to *d.*
10:22 holds out till the end will escape *d.*
11:23 You shall go down to the realm of *d!'*
15: 4 curses father or mother shall be put to *d.'*
16:18 the jaws of *d* shall not prevail against it.
16:21 and the scribes, and to be put to *d,*
16:28 will not experience *d* before they see the Son
17:23 the hands of men, who will put him to *d,*
20:18 and scribes, who will condemn him to *d.*
26:59 Jesus so that they might put him to *d.*
26:66 They answered, "He deserves *d!*"
27: 1 action against Jesus to put him to *d.*
27:20 ask for Barabbas and have Jesus put to *d.*
Mk 7:10 curses father or mother shall be put to *d.'*
8:31 priests, and the scribes, be put to *d,*
9: 1 not taste *d* until they see the reign of God
9:31 death; three days after his *d* he will rise."
10:34 him to *d* and hand him over to the Gentiles,
13:12 their parents and have them put to *d.*
14:34 is filled with sorrow to the point of *d.*
14:55 against Jesus that would lead to his *d,*
14:64 verdict "guilty," with its sentence of *d.*
15:39 over him, on seeing the manner of his *d,*
16:20 of sinners that I was handed over to *d,*
Lk 1:79 sit in darkness and in the shadow of *d,*
2:26 experience *d* until he had seen the Anointed
7: 2 was at that moment sick to the point of *d.*
9:22 priests and the scribes, and be put to *d,*
9:27 taste *d* until they see the reign of God."
10:15 You shall be hurled down to the realm of *d!'*
11:51 his *d* between the altar and the sanctuary!
18:33 They will scourge him and put him to *d,*
20:36 like angels and are no longer liable to *d.*
21:16 friends, and some of you will be put to *d.*
22:33 prepared to face imprisonment and *d* itself."
23:15 this man has done nothing that calls for *d.*
23:22 about him that calls for the *d* penalty.
24:20 delivered him up to be condemned to *d,*
Jn 4:47 restore health to his son, who was near *d.*
5:24 but has passed from *d* to life.
8:44 He brought *d* to man from the beginning,
8:51 is true to my word he shall never see *d.*"
8:52 man shall never know *d* if he keeps my word.'
11: 4 "This sickness is not to end in *d;*
11:13 Jesus had been speaking about his *d,*
12:33 indicated the sort of *d* he had to die.)
16: 2 puts you to *d* will claim to be serving God!
18:31 "We may not put anyone to *d,*"
18:32 indicating the sort of *d* he had to die.)
21:19 of *d* by which Peter was to glorify God.)
Acts 2:24 that *d* should keep its hold on him,
3:15 You put to *d* the Author of life.
5:30 has raised up Jesus whom you put to *d,*
7:52 they put to *d* those who foretold the
13:28 no charge against him which deserved *d,*
13:34 dead would never again see the decay of *d,*
21:13 not only for imprisonment, but for *d,*
22: 4 persecuted this new way to the point of *d.*
23:29 of anything deserving *d* or imprisonment.
25:11 if I have committed a crime deserving *d,*
25:25 that he had done anything deserving of *d,*
26:10 to be put to *d* I cast my vote against them.
26:31 nothing that deserves *d* or imprisonment."
28:18 found nothing against me deserving of *d.*
Rom 1:32 that all who do such things deserve *d;*
4:25 the Jesus who was handed over to *d* for our
5:10 were reconciled to him by the *d* of his Son,
5:12 with sin *d,* death thus coming to all men
5:14 I say, from Adam to Moses *d* reigned,
5:17 If *d* began its reign through one man
5:21 it, so that, as sin reigned through *d,*
6: 3 into Christ Jesus were baptized into his *d?*
6: 4 baptism into his *d* we were buried with him,
6: 5 united with him through likeness to his *d,*
6: 9 *d* has no more power over him.
6:10 His death was *d* to sin,
6:16 is the slavery of sin, which leads to *d,*
6:21 ashamed of, all of them tending toward *d.*
6:23 The wages of sin is *d,*
7: 5 in our members and we bore fruit for *d.*
7:10 that should have led to life brought me *d.*
7:13 Did this good thing then become *d* for me?
7:13 used what was good to bring about my *d.*
7:24 me from this body under the power of *d?*
8: 2 has freed you from the law of sin and *d.*
8: 6 The tendency of the flesh is toward *d* but
8:13 you put to *d* the evil deeds of the body,
8:38 For I am certain that neither *d* nor life,
14: 8 Both in life and in *d* we are the Lord's.
1Cor 3:22 or Cephas, or the world, or life, or *d,*
11:26 proclaim the *d* of the Lord until he comes!
15:21 *D* came through a man;
15:26 and the last enemy to be destroyed is *d.*
15:31 Jesus our Lord, that I face *d* every day.
15:54 *D* is swallowed up in victory."
15:55 "O *d,* where is your victory?
15:55 O *d,* where is your sting?"
15:56 The sting of *d* is sin,
2Cor 1: 9 men condemned to *d* so that we might trust,
1:10 that danger of *d* and will continue to do so.
2:16 to the latter an odor dealing *d,*
3: 7 If the ministry of *d,* carved in writing
4:11 being delivered to *d* for Jesus' sake,
4:12 *D* is at work in us, but life in you.
6: 9 punished, but not put to *d;*
7: 3 even to the sharing of *d* and life together.
7:10 salvation, whereas worldly sorrow brings *d.*
11:23 worse beatings and frequent brushes with *d.*
Eph 2:16 his cross, which put that enmity to *d.*
Phil 2: 8 accepting even death, *d* on a cross!
2:27 He was, in fact, sick to the point of *d,*
2:30 near to *d* for the sake of Christ's work.
3:10 by being formed into the pattern of his *d.*
Col 3: 5 Put to *d* whatever in your nature is rooted
1Thes 4:13 you be clear about those who sleep in *d,*
1Tm 5: 6 however, leads a life of living *d.*
2Tm 1:10 He has robbed *d* of its power and has
Heb 2: 9 with glory and honor because he suffered *d:*
2: 9 he might taste *d* for the sake of all men.
2:14 his *d* he might rob the devil, the prince of *d,*
2:15 who through fear of *d* had been slaves
5: 7 to God, who was able to save him from *d,*
7: 8 whereas men subject to *d* receive tithes,
7:23 prevented by *d* from remaining in office;
9:15 since his *d* has taken place for
9:16 that the *d* of the testator be confirmed.

DEATH (cont.)

9:17 comes into force only in the case of *d;*
9:26 he would have had to suffer *d* over and
9:27 that men die once, and after *d* be judged,
10:28 rejects the law of Moses is put to *d*
11:37 sawed in two, put to *d* at sword's point;
12:20 the mountain, it must be stoned to *d.*"
Jas 1:15 and when sin reaches maturity it begets *d.*
5:20 soul from *d* and cancel a multitude of sins.
1Pt 3:18 put to *d* insofar as fleshly existence goes,
1Jn 3:14 That we have passed from *d* to life we know
Rv 1:18 I hold the keys of *d* and the nether world.
2:10 *d* and I will give you the crown of life.
2:11 shall never be harmed by the second *d.*'
2:23 with her, and her children I will put to *d.*
6: 8 Its rider was named *D,*
9: 6 these men will seek *d* but will not find it;
9: 6 will yearn to die but *d* will escape them.
12:11 love for life did not deter them from *d.*
13:15 to *d* anyone who refused to worship it.
18: 8 all at once, *d* and mourning and famine.
20: 6 The second *d* will have no claim on them;
20:13 *d* and the nether world gave up their dead.
20:14 Then *d* and the nether world were hurled
20:14 the pool of fire, which is the second *d;*
21: 4 and there shall be no more *d* or mourning,
21: 8 pool of burning sulphur, the second *d!*"

DEATH-DEALING (3)

Nm 35:17 a *d* stone in his hand and causes his death,
35:18 a *d* club in his hand and causes his death,
35:23 or without seeing him throws a *d* stone

DEATHLY (2)

Jgs 16:16 her complaints till he was *d* weary of them.
Jer 30: 6 Why have all their faces turned *d* pale?

DEATHS (3)

1Sm 4:19 the *d* of her father-in-law and her husband,
Sir 41: 3 Fear not *d* decree for you;
Acts 2:24 God freed him from *d* bitter pangs,

DEBASED (3)

Wis 2:16 He judges us *d;* he holds aloof
Ez 28:17 for the sake of splendor you *d* your wisdom.
2Cor 1:12 has been prompted, not by *d* human wisdom,

DEBATE (3)

Jn 7:12 crowds there was much guarded *d* about him.
7:32 overheard this *d* about him among the crowd,
Acts 6: 9 would undertake to engage Stephen in *d,*

DEBATED (2)

Acts 9:29 the Greek-speaking Jews and *d* with them.
19: 8 a period of three months, *d* fearlessly,

DEBATES (1)

Acts 17:17 as well as daily *d* in the public square

DEBATING (1)

Acts 24:12 find me *d* with anyone or inciting a mob.

DEBAUCHERIES (1)

Na 3: 4 For the many *d* of the harlot,

DEBAUCHERY (3)

2Mc 6: 4 filled the temple with *d* and revelry;
Eph 5:18 getting drunk on wine; that leads to *d.*
1Pt 4: 3 what the pagans enjoy, living lives of *d,*

DEBIR (11)

Jos 10: 3 Jarmuth, Japhia, king of Lachish, and *D,*
10:38 Israel turned back to *D* and attacked it,
10:39 Thus was done to *D* and its king what had
11:21 and exterminated the Anakim in Hebron, *D,*
12:13 Hebron, Jarmuth, Lachish, Eglon, Gezer, *D,*
15: 7 Thence it climbed to *D,*
15:15 marched up against the inhabitants of *D,*
15:49 Socoh, Dannah, Kiriath-sannah (that is, *D),*
21:15 pasture lands, *D* with its pasture lands,
Jgs 1:11 marched against the inhabitants of *D,*
1Chr 6:43 pasture lands, *D* with its pasture lands,

DEBORAH (10)

Gn 35: 8 Death came to Rebekah's nurse *D;*
Jgs 4: 4 At this time the prophetess *D,*
4: 9 So *D* joined Barak and journeyed with him
4:10 *D* also went up with him.
4:14 *D* then said to Barak,
5: 1 On that day *D* [and Barak,
5: 7 When I, *D,* rose, when I rose, a mother
5:12 Awake, awake, *D!*
5:15 With *D* were the princes of Issachar;
Tb 1: 8 of the Mosaic law and the commands of *D,*

DEBORAH'S (1)

Jgs 4: 5 She used to sit under *D* palm tree,

DEBRIS (1)

Acts 27:44 on planks, or on other *d* from the ship.

DEBT (14)

Lv 26:43 may make good the *d* of their guilt for
Dt 24: 6 or even its upper stone as a pledge for *d,*
1Sm 22: 2 those who were in difficulties or in *d,*
2Chr 32:25 did not then discharge his *d* of gratitude,
Neh 10:32 seventh year, as well as every kind of *d.*
1Mc 10:43 owes the king, or because of any other *d,*
Wis 1: 4 nor dwells she in a body under *d* of sin.
Sir 8:13 think any pledge a *d* you must pay.
Ez 18: 7 gives back the pledge received for a *d,*
Mt 18:25 and all his property, in payment of the *d.*
18:27 let the official go and wrote off the *d.*
18:32 your entire *d* when you pleaded with me.
Rom 13: 8 Owe no *d* to anyone except the debt that
13: 8 the *d* that binds us to love one another.

DEBTOR (1)

Is 24: 2 as the borrower, the creditor as the *d.*

DEBTORS (3)

Dt 24: 6 be taking the *d* sustenance as a pledge.
Lk 16: 5 "So he called in each of his master's *d,*
Rom 8:12 We are *d,* then, my brothers—but not

DEBTS (5)

Dt 15: 1 period you shall have a relaxation of *d,*
1Mc 15: 8 All *d,* present or future, due
Prv 22:26 pledge, of those who become surety for *d;*
Hb 2: 6 he loads himself down with *d.*
Lk 7:42 was able to repay, he wrote off both *d.*

DECADENCE (1)

2Pt 2:12 of their *d* they too will be destroyed,

DECAY (6)

Tb 4:13 worthlessness there is *d* and dire poverty,
Sir 14:19 All man's works will perish in *d,*
28: 6 remember death and *d,*
Hb 3:16 *D* invades my bones,
Acts 13:34 dead would never again see the *d* of death,
1Cor 15:42 What is sown in the earth is subject to *d,*

DECAYED (5)

Jb 5: 3 his roots, but his household suddenly *d.*
Mt 7:17 good fruit, while a *d* tree bears bad fruit.
7:18 any more than a *d* tree can bear good fruit.
Lk 6:43 "A good tree does not produce *d* fruit any
6:43 any more than a *d* tree produces good fruit.

DECAYS (1)

Sir 10: 9 even during life man's body *d;*

DECEASED (4)

Nm 19:13 after touching the body of any *d* person,
Dt 25: 5 the widow of the *d* shall not marry anyone
25: 6 shall continue the line of the *d* brother,
2Mc 4:37 the prudence and noble conduct of the *d.*

DECEIT (31)

Dt 32: 4 A faithful God, without *d,*
Est E:13 and by weaving intricate webs of *d,*
1Mc 11: 1 and he sought by *d* to take Alexander's
Jb 13: 7 Is it for him that you utter *d?*
27: 4 not speak falsehood, nor my tongue utter *d!*
31: 5 falsehood and my foot has hastened to *d;*
Ps(s) 10: 7 His mouth is full of cursing, guile and *d;*
17: 1 hearken to my prayer from lips without *d.*
50:19 for evil, you harness your tongue to *d.*
55:24 and *d* shall not live out half their days.
101: 7 not dwell within my house who practices *d.*
Prv 12:20 *D* is in the hands of those who plot evil,
20:17 The bread of *d* is sweet to a man,
26:24 but in his inmost being he maintains *d;*
Wis 1: 5 *d* and withdraws from senseless counsels;
4:11 pervert his mind or *d* beguile his soul;
Sir 37: 3 you created to blanket the earth with *d?*"
Is 59: 3 speak falsehood, and your tongue utters *d.*
Jer 9: 5 Violence upon violence, deceit upon *d:*
9: 7 arrow is his tongue, his mouth utters *d;*
Dn 11:32 By his *d* he shall make some who were
Hos 12: 1 me with lies, the house of Israel, with *d;*
Zep 1: 9 house of their master with violence and *d.*
Mk 7:22 conduct, greed, maliciousness, *d,*
Rom 1:29 ill will, envy, murder, bickering, *d,*
2Cor 11:13 *d* in their disguise as apostles of Christ.
1Thes 2: 3 does not spring from *d* or impure motives
Heb 3:13 that no one grows hardened by the *d*
1Pt 2:22 no *d* was found in his mouth.
3:10 from evil and his lips from uttering *d.*
Rv 14: 5 On their lips no *d* has been found;

DECEITFUL (24)

1Mc 16:15 The son of Abubus gave them a *d* welcome in
2Mc 1:13 a *d* stratagem employed by Nanea's priests.
Ps(s) 5: 7 The bloodthirsty and the *d* the LORD abhors.
43: 1 from the *d* and impious man rescue me.
52: 6 all that means ruin, you of the *d* tongue!
Prv 4:24 dishonest talk, *d* speech put far from you.
12: 5 the designs of the wicked are *d.*
13: 5 Anything *d* the just man hates,
23: 3 they are *d* food.
Sir 5:10 Rely not upon *d* wealth,
36:20 A *d* character causes grief,
Is 30: 9 This is a rebellious people, *d* children,
Jer 7: 4 Put not your trust in the *d* words:
7: 8 your trust in *d* words to your own loss!
23:26 who prophesy lies and their own *d* fancies?
Ez 12:24 *d* divinations within the house of Israel,
Dn 2: 9 You have framed a false and *d*
Mi 6:12 falsehood with *d* tongues in their heads!
Zep 3:13 there be found in their mouths a *d* tongue;
Zec 10: 2 *D* dreams they tell,
1Tm 4: 1 away from the faith and will heed *d* spirits
1Pt 2: 1 away everything vicious, everything *d;*
2Jn 1: 7 Many *d* men have gone out into the world,
1: 7 Such is the *d* one!

DECEITFULLY (9)

Jos 7:11 ban, and have *d* put them in their baggage.
Tb 14: 6 idols which have *d* led them into error,
1Mc 1:30 He spoke to them *d* in peaceful terms,
7:10 sent messengers who spoke *d* to Judas and
7:27 with a large force and *d* sent to Judas
13:17 knew that they were speaking *d* to him,
Ps(s) 24: 4 what is vain, nor swears *d* to his neighbor.
105:25 his people, and dealt *d* with his servants.
Prv 12:17 is sure of, but a lying witness speaks *d.*

DECEITFULNESS (1)

Ps(s) 119:118 from your statutes, for their *d* is in vain.

DECEITS (1)

Hos 7: 3 the king, the princes too, with their *d.*

DECEIVE (26)

2Sm 3:25 Are you not aware that Abner came to *d* you
1Kgs 22:20 The LORD asked, 'Who will *d* Ahab,
22:21 himself to the LORD, saying, 'I will *d* him.'
2Kgs 4:16 do not *d* your servant."
4:28 "Did I not beg you not to *d* me?"
18:29 'Do not let Hezekiah *d* you,
19:10 'Do not let your God on whom you rely *d*
2Chr 18:19 The LORD asked, 'Who will *d* Ahab,
18:20 himself to the LORD, saying, 'I will *d* him.'
32:15 you further and *d* you in any such way.
Ps(s) 89:23 "No enemy shall *d* him,
Wis 15: 4 did the evil creation of men's fancy *d* us,
Is 36:14 'Do not let Hezekiah *d* you,
37:10 'Do not let your God on whom you rely *d*
Jer 37: 9 Do not *d* yourselves with the thought that
Ob 1: 7 They *d* you, they overpower you
Mt 24: 5 they will claim, and they will *d* many.
Rom 3:13 they use their tongues to *d;*
7:11 first to *d* me, then to kill me.
16:18 and they *d* the simpleminded with smooth
1Cor 6: 9 Do not *d* yourselves:
Eph 5: 6 Let no one *d* you with worthless arguments.
2Pt 2: 3 They will *d* you with fabricated tales,
1Jn 1: 8 free of the guilt of sin," we *d* ourselves;
2:26 these things about those who try to *d* you.
3: 7 Little ones, let no one *d* you;

DECEIVED (14)

1Sm 28:12 and said to Saul, "Why have you *d* me?
2Chr 32:11 Has not Hezekiah *d* you,
Jdt 9: 3 their blood the bed in which they lay *d,*
Wis 12:24 among beasts, *d* like senseless infants.
Sir 46:11 each one of them, whose hearts were not *d,*
Is 19:13 fools, the princes of Memphis have been *d.*
Jer 4:10 will say, "You only *d* us When you said:
29: 8 Do not let yourselves be *d* by the prophets
42:20 At the cost of your lives you have *d* me,
Dn 14: 7 "Do not be *d,* O king," he said;
Ob 1: 3 The pride of your heart has *d* you;
Mt 2:16 he had been *d* by the astrologers,
1Tm 2:14 it was not Adam who was *d* but the woman.
2Tm 3:13 to worse, deceiving others, themselves *d.*

DECEIVER (3)

Ps(s) 52: 4 like a sharpened razor, you practiced *d!*
Prv 30: 6 he reprove you, and you be exposed as a *d.*
Mal 1:14 Cursed is the *d,* who has in his flock

DECEIVERS (2)

Ti 1:10 men who are empty talkers and *d.*
Rv 21: 8 the idol-worshipers and *d* of every sort

DECEIVES (3)

Prv 26:19 arrows Is the man who *d* his neighbor,
Jer 9: 4 Each one *d* the other,
Col 2: 8 to it that no one *d* you through any empty,

DECEIVING (8)

1Kgs 22:22 LORD replied, 'You shall succeed in *d* him.
2Chr 18:21 'You shall succeed in *d* him.
Jdt 9: 3 bed that had felt the shame of their own *d.*
Est E: 6 by *d* with malicious slander
Sir 51: 5 From *d* lips and painters of lies,
Gal 6: 3 fact he is nothing, he is only *d* himself.
2Tm 3:13 will go from bad to worse, *d* others,
Jas 1:22 do is listen to it, you are *d* yourselves.

DECENT (5)

Tb 4: 3 "My son, when I die, give me a *d* burial.
2Mc 13: 7 he was deprived even of *d* burial.
Sir 29:21 and clothing, a house, too, for *d* privacy.
Phil 4: 8 all that is honest, pure, admirable, *d,*
Ti 1:16 and thoroughly incapable of any *d* action.

DECEPTION (4)

1Mc 8:28 shall fulfill their obligations without *d.*
Prv 14: 8 his way, but the folly of fools is their *d.*
Mi 1:14 Beth-achzib is a *d* to the kings of Israel.
1Jn 4: 6 the spirit of truth from the spirit of *d.*

DECEPTIVE (3)

Prv 31:30 Charm is *d* and beauty fleeting;
Jer 3:23 *D* indeed are the hills,
8: 5 Why do they cling to *d* idols,

DECIDE (29)

Gn 16: 5 May the LORD *d* between you and me!"
31:37 and mine, and let them *d* between us two.
Dt 17: 8 which proves too complicated for you to *d,*
17:14 should you then *d* to have a king over you
Jos 24:15 the LORD, *d* today whom you will serve,
Jgs 11:27 *d* this day between the Israelites and the
18:14 Now *d* what you must do!"
19: 6 "Why not *d* to spend the night here and
1Sm 24:16 he will *d* between me and you.
29:10 Do not *d* to take umbrage at this;
2Sm 24:13 and *d* what I must reply to him who sent me."
2Kgs 7: 4 If we *d* to go into the city,
10: 3 when this letter reaches you *d* which is
1Chr 21:11 *D* now—will it be three years of famine;
Tb 4:19 but if he should *d* otherwise,
Jdt 9: 6 the things you *d* on come forward and say,
1Mc 4:46 should come and *d* what to do with them.
8:30 hereafter *d* to add or take away anything,
2Mc 15:17 but to charge gallantly and *d* the issue by
Jb 6: 9 Even that God would *d* to crush me,
16:21 and *d* between a man and his neighbor.
Is 11: 3 shall he judge, nor by hearsay shall he *d,*
11: 4 and *d* aright for the land's afflicted.
57: 6 Should I *d* not to punish these things?
Jer 42:13 your God, and *d* not to remain in this land,
Acts 24:22 "I will *d* the case when Lysias the
25:20 Not knowing how to *d* the case,
1Cor 6: 4 If you have such matters to *d,*
2Cor 2: 1 I did *d,* however, not to visit you again

DECIDED (65)

Gn 6:13 *d* to put an end to all mortals on earth;
24:14 you have *d* upon for your servant Isaac.
24:44 the LORD has *d* upon for my master's son.'
Ex 3: 3 So Moses *d,* "I must go over to look
3:17 so I have *d* to lead you up out of the
Dt 10:10 again heard me and *d* not to destroy you,
Jos 9:26 Joshua did what he had *d:*
22:26 So we *d* to guard our interests by building
22:33 who blessed God and *d* against declaring
Jgs 17:11 So the young Levite *d* to stay with the man,
1Sm 2:25 since the LORD had *d* on their death.
5: 7 how matters stood, the men of Ashdod *d,*
20: 3 favored with your friendship, so he has *d,*
24:11 I *d,* 'I will not raise a hand
2Sm 15: 2 someone had a lawsuit to be *d* by the king,
15: 4 Then everyone who has a lawsuit to be *d*
17:14 had *d* to undo Ahithophel's good counsel,
1Kgs 1:24 "Have you *d,* my lord king,
9:19 Solomon *d* should be built in Jerusalem,
20:40 You have *d* it yourself."
2Kgs 12:18 it, Hazael *d* to go on to attack Jerusalem.
1Chr 21:15 the LORD saw and *d* against the calamity,
2Chr 8: 6 Solomon *d* should be built in Jerusalem,
24: 4 time, Joash *d* to restore the LORD's temple.
32: 3 he *d* in counsel with his princes and
Tb 5:18 "Why have you *d* to send my child away?
7:11 Your marriage to her has been *d* in heaven!
Jdt 2: 3 They *d* to do away with all those who had
11:12 ran low, they *d* to kill their animals,
Est 7: 7 he saw that the king had *d* on his doom.
1Mc 3:31 he *d* to go to Persia and levy tribute on
5: 2 So they *d* to destroy the descendants of
10:47 They therefore *d* in favor of Alexander,
11:33 *d* to bestow benefits on the Jewish nation,
15:19 *d* to write to various kings and countries,
15:20 have also *d* to accept the shield from them.
2Mc 4:19 But the bearers themselves *d* that the
6:14 but with us he has *d* to deal differently,
13:13 private meeting with the elders, he *d* that,
15: 1 he *d* to attack them in all safety on the
Jb 23:13 But he had *d,* and who can say him nay?
Jer 35:11 we *d* to come into Jerusalem to escape the
Dn 2: 5 the Chaldeans, "This is what I have *d:*
2: 8 for time, since you know what I have *d.*
4:14 By decree of the sentinels is this *d,*
6: 2 Darius *d* to appoint over his entire
13:15 She *d* to bathe, for the weather was warm.
Mt 1:19 her to the law, *d* to divorce her quietly.
18:23 *d* to settle accounts with his officials.
Mk 3:13 and summoned the men he himself had *d* on,
12:28 He *d* to ask him, "Which is the first
Lk 1: 3 and have *d* to set it in writing for you,
Jn 7: 1 He had *d* not to travel in Judea because
7:26 have *d* that this is the Messiah.
Acts 7:23 he was forty, he *d* to visit his kinsmen,
15: 2 Finally it was *d* that Paul,
20: 3 so he *d* to return by way of Macedonia.
20:16 Paul had *d* to sail past Ephesus so as not
23:30 man's life, I *d* at once to send him to you.
27: 1 it was *d* that we were to sail for Italy,
Rom 15:26 Macedonia and Achaia have kindly *d* to make
2Cor 9: 7 give according to what he has inwardly *d;*
Phil 2:25 I have *d,* too, that I must send you
1Thes 3: 1 we *d* to remain alone at Athens and send
Ti 3:12 I have *d* to spend the winter there.

DECIDES (1)

Lk 14:28 If one of you *d* to build a tower,

DECIDING (4)

Nm 35:24 *d* the case between the slayer and the
Est E: 9 *d* always with equitable treatment
2Mc 14:18 he shrank from *d* the issue by bloodshed.
1Cor 6: 3 then, we are up to *d* everyday affairs.

DECISION (27)

Ex 28:15 breastpiece of *d* you shall also have made,
28:29 on the breastpiece of *d* over his heart
28:30 of *d* you shall put the Urim and Thummim,
Lv 24:12 who kept him in custody till a *d* from the
Nm 15:34 clear *d* as to what should be done with him.
Dt 17: 9 the case and then hand down to you their *d.*
17:10 According to this *d* that they give you in
17:11 the left from the *d* they hand down to you.
21: 5 or violence must be settled by their *d.*
25: 1 and a *d* is handed down to them acquitting
1Mc 2:41 On that day they came to this *d:*
8:26 this is Rome's *d.*
8:28 this is Rome's *d.*
2Mc 11:25 our *d* is that their temple be restored to
11:26 so that, when they learn of our *d,*
15:21 through the LORD's *d* that victory is won
Jb 22:28 When you make a *d,*
Prv 16:33 lap, its *d* depends entirely on the LORD.
19:21 but it is the *d* of the LORD that endures.
Sir 45:10 The breastpiece for *d,*
Jl 4:14 Crowd upon crowd in the valley of *d;*
4:14 is the day of the LORD in the valley of *d.*
Zep 3: 8 it is my *d* to gather together the nations,
Hg 2:11 Ask the priests for a *d:*
Mk 15: 1 is, the whole Sanhedrin), reached a *d.*
Acts 15:28 'It is the *d* of the Holy Spirit,
21:25 we sent them a letter with our *d*

DECISIONS (18)

Ex 18:16 make known to them God's *d* and regulations."
18:20 them in regard to the *d* and regulations,
18:22 *d* for the people in all ordinary cases.
18:26 *d* for the people in all ordinary cases.
28:30 Thus he shall always bear the *d* for the
Nm 27:21 the *d* of the Urim in the LORD's presence;
36:13 These are the commandments and *d* which the
Dt 33:10 your *d* to Jacob and your law to Israel.
1Mc 14:41 have, therefore, made the following *d.*
14:44 or priests to nullify any of these *d,*
14:46 the right to act in accord with these *d,*
2Mc 4:23 and to obtain *d* on some important matters.
11:36 send someone to us with your *d* so that we
Sir 38:33 They set forth no *d* or judgments,
Mi 3:11 a bribe, her priests give *d* for a salary,
Mal 2: 9 my ways, but show partiality in your *d.*
Acts 16: 4 for observance the *d* which the apostles
Jas 2: 4 up as judges handing down corrupt *d?*

DECISIVE (3)

2Mc 15:20 Everyone now awaited the *d* moment.
Prv 18:18 is *d* in a controversy between the mighty.
Wis 12: 9 once by terrible beasts or by one *d* word;

DECISIVELY (2)

2Sm 5:24 in the tops of the mastic trees, act *d,*
Rom 9:28 for quickly and *d* will the Lord execute

DECKED (3)

2Sm 1:24 who *d* your attire with ornaments of gold.
Hos 2:15 While she *d* herself out with her rings
1Tm 2: 9 and not be *d* out in fancy hair styles,

DECKS (2)

Gn 6:16 shall make with bottom, second and third *d.*
Ez 27: 5 Senir they built for you all of your *d;*

DECLAIM (1)

Jb 16: 4 I could *d* over you,

DECLARATION (1)

2Pt 1:17 *d* came to him out of the majestic splendor:

DECLARE (74)

Lv 13: 3 on seeing this, shall *d* the man unclean.
13: 6 the skin, the priest shall *d* the man clean;
13: 8 on the skin, he shall *d* the man unclean;
13:11 The priest shall *d* the man unclean without
13:13 body, he shall *d* the stricken man clean;
13:15 raw flesh, the priest shall *d* him unclean,
13:17 white, he shall *d* the stricken man clean,
13:20 turned white, he shall *d* the man unclean;
13:22 the skin, the priest shall *d* him unclean;
13:23 the priest shall therefore *d* him clean.
13:25 *d* him unclean and stricken with leprosy.
13:27 he shall *d* the man unclean and stricken
13:28 the priest shall therefore *d* the man clean,
13:30 it, the priest shall *d* the person unclean,
13:34 below the skin, he shall *d* the man clean;
13:37 is clean, and the priest shall *d* him clean.
13:44 and the priest shall *d* him unclean by
13:46 sore is on him he shall *d* himself unclean,
14:48 the plastering, he shall *d* the house clean,
Dt 21: 7 throat was cut in the wadi, and shall *d,*
25: 7 go up to the elders at the gate and *d,*
26: 5 Then you shall *d* before the LORD,
26:13 own community, you shall *d* before the LORD,
Jos 22:12 whole community at Shiloh to *d* war on them.
2Sm 15:10 of the horn, *d* Absalom king in Hebron."
1Chr 17:10 Moreover, I *d* to you that I,
Jb 32: 6 and was afraid to *d* to you my knowledge.
Ps(s) 9: 2 I will *d* all your wondrous deeds.
9:15 death, That I may *d* all your praises and,
19: 2 The heavens *d* the glory of God,
40: 6 Should I wish to *d* or to tell them,
66:16 God, while I *d* what he has done for me.
71:15 My mouth shall *d* your justice,
73:28 I shall *d* all your works in the gates of
75: 2 we *d* your wondrous deeds.
78: 4 we will *d* to the generation to come The
78: 6 That they too may rise and *d* to their sons
79:13 all generations we will *d* your praise.
88:12 Do they *d* your kindness in the grave,
107:22 and *d* his works with shouts of joy.
118:17 die, but live, and *d* the works of the LORD.
119:13 lips I *d* all the ordinances of your mouth.
145: 6 your terrible deeds and *d* your greatness.
Sir 18:28 he who attains to her should *d* her praise;
51:22 a reward, and my tongue will *d* his praises.
Is 38:19 Fathers *d* to their sons,
40:27 Why, O Jacob, do you say, and *d,*
41:22 or *d* to us the things to come!
45:21 Come here and *d* in counsel together:
58: 2 They ask me to *d* what is due them,
Bar 2:18 soul, will *d* your glory and justice,
Jl 4: 9 *D* this among the nations:
Mi 3: 8 To *d* to Jacob his crimes and to Israel his
Mt 7:23 Then I will *d* to them solemnly,
12:33 *D* a tree good and its fruit good or declare
15: 5 Yet you *d,* 'Whoever says to his father
16:18 I for my part *d* to you,
16:19 *d* bound on earth shall be bound in heaven;
16:19 whatever you *d* loosed on earth shall be
18:18 whatever you *d* bound on earth shall be
18:18 and whatever you *d* loosed on earth shall
23:16 You *d,* 'If a man swears by the temple
23:18 you *d,* 'If a man swears by the altar
23:39 not see me from this time on until you *d,*
Mk 7:11 Yet you *d,* 'If a person says to his father
14:58 falsely by alleging, "We heard him *d,*
Jn 8:58 "I solemnly *d* it:
Acts 20:26 Therefore I solemnly *d* this day that I
24:20 Let those who are here *d* what crime they
2Cor 1:18 I *d* that my word to you is not "yes" one
Gal 1:20 I *d* before God that what I have just
Eph 4:17 I *d* and solemnly attest in the Lord that
Jas 5:16 Hence, *d* your sins to one another,

DECLARED (30)

Lv 13: 7 shown himself to the priest to be *d* clean,
13:35 all on his skin after he has been *d* clean,
Nm 1:18 Every man of twenty years or more then *d*
1Kgs 8:53 as you *d* through your servant Moses when
21:23 (Against Jezebel, too, the LORD *d.*
Tb 12: 7 works of God are to be *d* and made known.
2Mc 1:34 fact, fenced the place off and *d* it sacred.
4:47 poor men who would have been *d* innocent
6:23 and so he *d* that above all he would be
7: 6 on us, as Moses *d* in his canticle,
14:32 As they *d* under oath that they did not
Ps(s) 44: 2 ears have heard, our fathers have *d* to us,
78: 3 know, and what our fathers have *d* to us,
102:22 That the name of the LORD may be *d* in Zion;

DECLARED (cont.)

119:26 I *d* my ways, and you answered me;
Prv 20: 6 Many are *d* to be men of virtue:
Eccl 4: 2 I *d* more fortunate in death than are the
Sg 6: 9 The daughters saw her and *d* her fortunate,
Mt 19: 5 Creator made them male and female and *d*,
22:24 "Teacher, Moses *d*,
26: 1 these discourses, he *d* to his disciples,
26:61 "This man has *d*,
Mk 15:39 on seeing the manner of his death, *d*,
Lk 24:23 seen a vision of angels who *d* he was alive.
Acts 13:34 never again see the decay of death, God *d*,
13:46 of God has to be *d* to you first of all;
23: 9 Pharisee party arose and *d* emphatically:
25:12 conferred with his council and finally *d*:
Rom 2:13 it is those who keep it who will be *d* just.
2Cor 3:10 the former should be *d* no glory at all.

DECLARES (11)

Gn 22:16 "I swear by myself, *d* the LORD,
Ex 21: 5 If, however, the slave *d*,
1Sm 2:30 But now,' the LORD *d*, 'away with this!
2Chr 34:27 so *d* the LORD.
2Mc 10:26 and a foe to their foes, as the law *d*.
Jb 28:14 The abyss *d*,
Sir 24: 2 the presence of his hosts she *d* her worth:
37: 1 Every friend *d* his friendship,
Am 4:13 the wind, and *d* to man his thoughts;
2Thes 2: 4 God's temple and even *d* himself to be God
Heb 8:13 covenant," he *d* the first one obsolete.

DECLARING (7)

Ex 34: 7 yet not *d* the guilty guiltless,
Nm 14:18 yet not *d* the guilty guiltless,
Jos 22:33 blessed God and decided against *d* war
Ps(s) 92:16 shall they be, *D* how just is the LORD,
Mt 14:33 were in the boat showed him reverence, *d*,
27:24 in front of the crowd, *d* as he did so,
1Cor 4: 4 does not mean that I am *d* myself innocent.

DECLINE (2)

Dt 28:13 you will always mount higher and not *d*,
Est 6:13 before whom you are beginning to *d*,

DECLINED (1)

Acts 18:20 They asked him to stay on longer but he *d*.

DECORATE (1)

Mt 23:29 prophets and *d* the monuments of the saints.

DECORATED (3)

2Chr 3: 6 also *d* the building with precious stones.
Ez 40:16 The pilasters were *d* with palms.
40:26 and it was *d* with palms here and there on

DECORATION (1)

2Mc 2:29 man who undertakes the *d* and the frescoes

DECORATIONS (1)

Ez 40:22 and its palm *d* were of the same

DECREASE (3)

Ps(s) 107:38 nor did he suffer their cattle to *d*.
Jer 29: 6 There you must increase in number, not *d*.
Jn 3:30 He must increase, while I must *d*.

DECREE (74)

Nm 23:19 to speak and not act, to *d* and not fulfill?
1Kgs 1:36 LORD, the God of my lord the king, so *d*!
2Chr 30: 5 they issued a *d* to be proclaimed
Ezr 4:21 until a further *d* has been issued by me.
5: 3 "Who issued the *d* for you to build this
5: 9 'Who issued the *d* for you to build this
5:13 *d* for the rebuilding of this house of God.
5:17 to discover whether a *d* really was issued
6: 3 year of King Cyrus, King Cyrus issued a *d*:
6: 8 I also issue this *d* concerning your
6:11 I also issue this *d*:
6:12 I, Darius, have issued this *d*;
7:13 I have issued this *d*,
7:21 issue this *d* to all the treasurers of
Neh 11:23 they had been appointed by royal *d*,
Tb 1: 6 prescribed for all Israel by perpetual *d*.
1: 8 in keeping with the *d* of the Mosaic law
6:13 according to the *d* in the Book of Moses,
7:11 according to the *d* of the Book of Moses.
7:12 According to the *d* written in the Book of
7:13 wife according to the *d* of the Mosaic law.
Est 1:19 let an irrevocable royal *d* be issued by
1:20 when the *d* which the king will issue is
2: 8 When the king's order and *d* had been
3: 9 king, let a *d* be issued to destroy them;
B: 6 we hereby *d* that all those who are
3:14 A copy of the *d* to be promulgated as law
3:15 the *d* was promulgated in the stronghold of
4: 8 He also gave him a copy of the written *d*
C:20 to do away with the *d* you have pronounced,
D:10 not die because of this general *d* of ours.
E:24 that does not observe this *d* shall be
8:14 and the *d* was promulgated in the
9:13 tomorrow to act according to today's *d*,
9:14 effect, and the *d* was published in Susa.
1Mc 1:57 the law, was condemned to death by royal *d*.
1:60 were put to death, in keeping with the *d*,
14:23 *d* has been made for Simon the high priest."
2Mc 6: 8 a *d* was issued ordering the neighboring
10: 8 By public edict and *d* they prescribed
Ps(s) 2: 7 I will proclaim the *d* of the LORD:
19: 8 The *d* of the LORD is trustworthy,
78: 5 He set it up as a *d* in Jacob,
81: 6 Who made it a *d* for Joseph when he came
122: 4 of the LORD, According to the *d* for Israel,
Prv 31: 9 Open your mouth, *d* what is just,
Wis 11: 7 rebuke to the *d* for the slaying of infants,
12:12 or who can oppose your *d*?
18:16 the sharp sword of your inexorable *d*.
Sir 41: 3 Fear not death's *d* for you;
Is 45:23 uttering my just *d* and my unalterable word:
Jer 5:22 which by eternal *d* it may not overstep.
Dn 2: 9 the dream, there can be but one *d* for you.
2:13 When the *d* was issued that the wise men
3:10 you issued a *d* that everyone who heard the
3:96 Therefore I *d* for nations and peoples of
4: 3 So I issued a *d* that all the wise men of
4:14 By *d* of the sentinels is this decided,
6: 8 ought to be put in force by royal *d*:
6:13 "Did you not *d*,
6:13 king answered them, "The *d* is absolute,
6:14 to you, O king, or to the *d* you issued;
6:16 royal prohibition or *d* is irrevocable."
6:27 I *d* that throughout my royal domain the
Jon 3: 7 Nineveh, by *d* of the king and his nobles:
Mt 5:31 his wife, he must give her a *d* of divorce.'
19: 7 and the promulgation of a divorce *d*?"
Mk 10: 4 divorce and the writing of a *d* of divorce."
Lk 2: 1 a *d* ordering a census of the whole world.
Rom 1:32 They know God's just *d* that all who do
8:28 who have been called according to his *d*.
9:11 in order that God's *d* might stand fast
Eph 1: 9 the plan he was pleased to *d* in Christ,
1:11 for in the *d* of God,

DECREED (32)

1Kgs 8:29 where you have *d* you shall be honored;
22:23 the LORD himself has *d* evil against you."
2Kgs 8: 1 because the LORD has *d* a seven-year famine
1Chr 13: 2 to you, and is so *d* by the LORD our God,
16:40 law of the LORD which he has *d* for Israel.
2Chr 6:20 where you have *d* you shall be honored;
18:22 the LORD himself has *d* evil against you."
Tb 1:18 during the days of judgment *d* against him
Jdt 11:13 They *d* that they would use up the first
Est 2: 1 had done and what had been *d* against her.
2:12 twelve months' preparation *d* for the women.
9: 1 order *d* by the king was to be carried out,
1Mc 4:59 Israel *d* that the days of the dedication
7:49 They *d* that it should be observed every
13:52 Simon *d* that this day should be celebrated
14:48 It was *d* that this inscription should be
2Mc 15:36 *d* never to let this day pass unobserved,
Ps(s) 7: 7 wake to the judgment you have *d*.
Is 10:22 is *d* as overwhelming justice demands.
10:23 Yes, the destruction he has *d*,
24: 3 stripped, for the LORD has *d* this thing.
28:22 the destruction *d* for the whole earth.
Jer 11:17 The LORD of hosts who planted you has *d*
15: 3 kinds of scourge I have *d* against them,
Lam 2:17 The LORD has done as he *d*:
Ez 39: 5 open field you shall fall, for I have *d* it,
39: 8 This is the day I have *d*.
Dn 4:28 spoke from heaven, "It has been *d* for you,
9:24 *d* for your people and for your holy city:
9:26 shall be war, the desolation that is *d*.
9:27 that is *d* is poured out upon the horror."
Lk 23:24 *d* that what they demanded should be done.

DECREES (76)

Lv 18: 4 My *d* you shall carry out,
18: 5 Keep, then, my statutes and *d*,
18:26 must keep my statutes and *d* forbidding all
19:37 then, to observe all my statutes and *d*.
20:22 to observe all my statutes and all my *d*;
26:15 if you reject my precepts and spurn my *d*,
26:46 *d* and laws which the LORD had Moses
Dt 4: 1 and *d* which I am teaching you to observe,
4: 5 I teach you the statutes and *d* as the LORD,
4: 8 Or what great nation has statutes and *d*
4:14 statutes and *d* which you are to observe
4:45 statutes and *d* which he proclaimed to them
5: 1 the statutes and *d* which I proclaim in
5:31 the statutes and *d* you must teach them,
6: 1 the statutes and *d* which the LORD,
6:20 statutes and *d* mean which the LORD,
7:11 and the *d* which I enjoin on you today.
7:12 these *d* and observing them carefully,
8:11 *d* and statutes which I enjoin on you today:
11: 1 his statutes, *d* and commandments.
11:32 statutes and *d* that I set before you today.
12: 1 "These are the statutes and *d* which you
26:16 you to observe these statutes and *d*.
26:17 observe his statutes, commandments and *d*,
30:16 keeping his commandments, statutes and *d*,
33:21 of the LORD and his *d* respecting Israel."
1Kgs 2: 3 *d* as they are written in the law of Moses,
9: 4 commanded you, keeping my statutes and *d*,
11:33 to me according to my statutes and my *d*,
2Kgs 23: 3 and *d* with their whole hearts and souls,
1Chr 22:13 and *d* which the LORD gave Moses for Israel.
28: 7 my commandments and *d* as he keeps them
2Chr 34:31 the LORD and to keep his commandments, *d*,
Ezr 6:14 *d* of Cyrus and Darius [and of Artaxerxes,
Est B: 4 and continually disregards the *d* of kings,
1Mc 14:22 recorded the following in the public *d*:
Ps(s) 25:10 those who keep his covenant and his *d*.
78:56 God the Most High, and kept not his *d*.
93: 5 Your *d* are worthy of trust indeed:
99: 7 they heard his *d* and the law he gave them.
119: 2 Happy are they who observe his *d*,
119:14 In the way of your *d* I rejoice,
119:22 and contempt, for I observe your *d*.
119:24 Yes, your *d* are my delight;
119:31 I cling to your *d*;
119:36 Incline my heart to your *d* and not to gain.
119:46 your *d* before kings without being ashamed.
119:59 my ways and turned my feet to your *d*.
119:79 to me who fear you and acknowledge your *d*.
119:88 life, that I may keep the *d* of your mouth.
119:95 to destroy me, but I pay heed to your *d*.
119:99 my teachers when your *d* are my meditation.
119:108 homage of my mouth, and teach me your *d*.
119:111 Your *d* are my inheritance forever;
119:119 therefore I love your *d*.
119:125 give me discernment that I may know your *d*.
119:129 Wonderful are your *d*; therefore I observe
119:138 *d* in justice and in perfect faithfulness.
119:144 Your *d* are forever just;
119:146 save me, and I will keep your *d*.
119:152 Of old I know from your *d*,
119:157 foes are many, I turn not away from your *d*.
119:167 I keep your *d* and love them deeply.
119:168 I keep your precepts and your *d*,
132:12 and the *d* which I shall teach them,
Prv 31: 5 in drinking they forget what the law *d*,
Wis 14:16 graven things were worshiped by princely *d*.
Sir 45: 5 to Jacob, his judgments and *d* to Israel.
Is 10: 1 statutes and who write oppressive *d*,
Jer 44:23 by his law, his statutes, and his *d*,
Ez 36:27 by my statutes, careful to observe my *d*.
37:24 my statutes and carefully observe my *d*.
44:24 as judges, judging them according to my *d*.
Mi 6:16 You have kept the *d* of Omri,
Zec 1: 6 But my words and my *d*,
Acts 17: 7 they disregard the Emperor's *d* and claim

DECREPIT (1)

2Chr 36:17 nor maiden, neither the aged nor the *d*;

DEDAN (10)

Gn 10: 7 Sheba and *D*.
25: 3 Jokshan became the father of Sheba and *D*.
25: 3 The descendants of *D* were the Asshurim,
1Chr 1: 9 The descendants of Raama were Sheba and *D*.
1:32 The sons of Jokshan were Sheba and *D*.
Jer 25:23 *D* and Tema and Buz,
49: 8 hide in deep holes, you who live in *D*:
Ez 25:13 I will make it a waste from Teman to *D*;
27:20 *D* traded with you for riding gear.
38:13 Sheba and *D*,

DEDANITES (1)

Is 21:13 country spend the night, O caravans of *D*.

DEDICATE (8)

Ex 13:12 you shall *d* to the LORD every son that
Nm 6: 2 the nazirite vow to *d* himself to the LORD,
Dt 20: 5 lest he die in battle and another *d* it.
2Mc 6: 2 in Jerusalem and *d* it to Olympian Zeus,
Jer 51:27 *D* peoples to war against her,
51:28 *D* peoples to war against her:
Ez 20:40 of your offerings, and all that you *d*.
Col 3:15 *D* yourselves to thankfulness.

DEDICATED (35)

Ex 32:29 said, "Today you have been *d* to the LORD,
Lv 21:12 anointing oil upon him, he is *d* to his God,
27:15 one who *d* his house wishes to redeem it,
27:19 one who *d* his field wishes to redeem it,
27:26 to the LORD, may not be *d* by vow to him.
Nm 3: 9 aside from among the Israelites as *d* to me.
6: 6 As long as he is *d* to the LORD,
6: 9 so that his *d* head becomes unclean,
6:12 valid, because his *d* head became unclean.
6:18 tent the nazirite shall shave his *d* head,
6:19 the nazirite has shaved off his *d* hair,
8:16 among the Israelites, are strictly *d* to me;
8:19 and I have given these *d* Israelites to
18: 6 *d* to the LORD for the service of the
1Sm 1:28 as he lives, he shall be *d* to the LORD."
1Kgs 7:51 in the *d* offerings of his father David,
8:43 which I have built is *d* to your honor.

8:63 the Israelites *d* the temple of the LORD.
2Kgs 12:19 the *d* offerings presented by his forebears,
23:11 which the kings of Judah had *d* to the sun;
1Chr 26:26 of the votive offerings *d* by King David,
2Chr 5: 1 in the *d* offerings of his father David,
6:33 which I have built is *d* to your honor.
7: 6 king and all the people *d* the house of God.
24: 7 Baals the *d* resources of the LORD's temple.
Jdt 16:19 Judith *d*, as a votive offering to God,
Sir 46:13 to his Maker, *d* from his mother's womb,
Is 13: 3 I have commanded my *d* soldiers,
Jer 1: 5 I knew you, before you were born I *d* you,
7:29 Cut off your *d* hair and throw it away!
Ez 43:26 the altar, and it shall be purified and *d*.
Mt 15: 5 you might have had from me is *d* to God,
Mk 7:11 had from me is korban' (that is, *d* to God),
Acts 15:26 who have *d* themselves to the cause of our
2Tm 2:21 *d* and useful to the master of the house

DEDICATES (3)

Lv 27:14 someone *d* his house as sacred to the LORD,
27:16 "If the object which someone *d* to the
27:22 "If the field that some man *d* to the LORD

DEDICATION (23)

Lv 27:17 If the *d* of a field is made at the
Nm 6: 5 the period of his *d* to the LORD is over,
6: 7 unclean, since his head bears his *d* to God.
6:12 period of his *d* to the LORD as a nazirite,
6:13 completes the period of his *d* he shall go
6:21 included in his vow of *d* apart from
6:21 his *d* in keeping with the vow he has taken."
7:10 For the *d* of the altar also,
7:11 his offering for the *d* of the altar."
7:84 were the offerings for the *d* of the altar,
7:88 the *d* of the altar after it was anointed.
2Chr 7: 9 for they had celebrated the *d* of the altar
Ezr 6:16 the *d* of this house of God with joy.
6:17 For the *d* of this house of God,
Neh 12:27 At the *d* of the wall of Jerusalem,
12:27 to celebrate a joyful *d* with thanksgiving
1Mc 4:56 For eight days they celebrated the *d* of
4:59 decreed that the days of the *d* of the altar
2Mc 2: 9 at the *d* and the completion of the temple.
2:19 of the great temple, the *d* of the altar,
Dn 3: 2 to the *d* of the statue which he had set up.
3: 3 for the *d* and stood before the statue
Jn 10:22 came for the feast of the *D* in Jerusalem.

DEDUCTION (1)

Lv 25:27 he shall make a *d* from the price in

DEED (53)

Lv 20:12 since they have committed an abhorrent *d*,
20:13 be put to death for their abominable *d*;
20:17 off from their people for this shameful *d*;
Dt 17: 5 done the evil *d* out to your city gates
21: 7 this blood, and our eyes did not see the *d*.
22:28 with her, and their *d* is discovered,
24:13 will be a good *d* of yours before the LORD,
2Sm 3:39 the evildoer in accordance with his evil *d*."
7:23 renowned by doing this magnificent *d*,
12:12 You have done this *d* in secret,
12:14 have utterly spurned the LORD by this *d*,
13:12 Do not commit this insensate *d*.
2Chr 34:25 me by every *d* that they have performed,
Jdt 13:19 Your *d* of hope will never be forgotten by
2Mc 12: 5 *d* perpetrated against his countrymen,
12:42 the sinful *d* might be fully blotted out.
Prv 19:17 LORD, and he will repay him for his good *d*.
Eccl 9:13 other hand I saw this wise *d* under the sun,
Wis 14: 9 to God are the evildoer and his evil *d*;
Sir 3: 8 In word and *d* honor your father that his
12: 6 will meet for every good *d* you do for him.
15:19 he understands man's every *d*.
37:16 A word is the source of every *d*;
47: 8 every *d* he offered thanks to God Most High,
Is 28:21 work, his singular work, to perform his *d*,
28:21 work, to perform his deed, his strange *d*.
Jer 32:10 When I had written and sealed the *d*,
32:11 the scales, I accepted the *d* of purchase,
32:12 This *d* of purchase I gave to Baruch,
32:12 of the witnesses who had signed the *d*,
32:14 both the sealed and the open *d* of purchase,
32:16 After giving the *d* of purchase to Baruch,
32:19 of hosts, great in counsel, mighty in *d*,
40: 3 has brought about in *d* what he threatened;
44: 4 not to commit this horrible *d* which I hate,
48:30 liar in boast, liar in *d*.
Dn 13:63 she was found innocent of any shameful *d*.
Jl 4: 4 I will return your *d* upon your own head.
4: 7 I will return your *d* upon your own head.
Ob 1:15 *d* shall come back upon your own head;
Mt 26:10 It is a good *d* she has done for me.
Mk 3: 4 it permitted to do a good *d* on the sabbath
Lk 2:30 *d* displayed for all the peoples to see:
22:23 as to which of them would do such a *d*.
24:19 *d* in the eyes of God and all the people;
Jn 10:33 for any 'good *d*' that we are stoning you,"
Acts 4: 9 If we must answer today for a good *d* done
7:22 He was a man powerful in word and *d*.
13:41 For I am doing a *d* in your days which you
Rom 15:18 the Gentiles to obedience by word and *d*,
1Cor 5: 3 Jesus Christ on the man who did this *d*.
1Jn 3:18 let us love in *d* and in truth and not
Jude 1:15 godless for every evil *d* they have done,

DEEDED (1)

Gn 25: 5 Abraham *d* everything that he owned to his

DEEDS (239)

Ex 3:20 by doing all kinds of wondrous *d* there.
34:10 see how awe-inspiring are the *d* which I,
Dt 3:24 on earth can perform *d* as mighty as yours?
11: 3 signs and *d* he wrought among the Egyptians,
11: 7 all these great *d* that the LORD has done.
31:29 LORD's sight, and provoked him by your *d*."
32: 4 The Rock—how faultless are his *d*.
Jgs 5: 2 noble *d* by the people who bless the LORD,
5:11 *d* of the LORD, his just deeds that brought
6:13 Where are his wondrous *d* of which our
1Sm 2: 3 God is the LORD, a God who judges *d*.
19: 4 you, but has helped you very much by his *d*.
25:39 but has punished Nabal for his own evil *d*."
2Sm 23:12 Such were the *d* of the Three warriors.
23:22 Such were the *d* performed by Benaiah,
1Kgs 10: 6 about your *d* and your wisdom is true,"
11:41 of Solomon, with all his *d* and his wisdom,
16: 7 provoking him to anger by his evil *d*,
1Chr 11:19 *d* as these the Three warriors performed.
11:22 son of Jehoiada, a valiant man of mighty *d*,
11:24 Such *d* as these of Benaiah,
16: 8 make known among the nations his *d*.
16: 9 his praise, proclaim all his wondrous *d*.
16:12 Recall the wondrous *d* that he has wrought,
16:24 among all peoples, his wondrous *d*.
17:21 for great and awesome *d* by driving out
29:29 Now the *d* of King David,
2Chr 9: 5 about your *d* and your wisdom is true,"
12:12 and in Judah moreover, good *d* were found.
13:22 rest of Abijah's acts, his *d* and his words,
28:26 The rest of his *d* and his activities,
32: 1 after he had proved his fidelity by such *d*,
35:26 his pious *d* in regard to what is written
Ezr 9: 6 for our wicked *d* are heaped up above our
9: 7 our wicked *d* we have been delivered over,
9:13 upon us for our evil *d* and our great guilt
Neh 6:19 Thus they would praise his good *d* in my
9: 2 sins and the guilty *d* of their fathers.
9:35 nor did they turn away from their evil *d*.
Tb 2:14 "Where are your charitable *d* now?
3: 2 righteous, O Lord, and all your *d* are just;
12: 6 Before all men, honor and proclaim God's *d*,
12:22 these marvelous *d* which he had done
Jdt 11:16 perform with you such *d* that people
Est E: 7 one considers the wicked *d* perpetrated
1Mc 2:51 the *d* that our fathers did in their times,
3: 7 He made Jacob glad by his *d*,
5:56 *d* and the fighting that they were doing.
5:61 thinking that they would do brave *d*.
8: 2 brave *d* that they had performed
9:22 his battles, the brave *d* he performed,
10:15 battles and valiant *d* of Jonathan
13:46 "Do not treat us according to our evil *d*,"
16:23 his wars and the brave *d* he performed,
2Mc 3:36 Before all men he gave witness to the *d* of
8:33 received the reward his wicked *d* deserved.
Ps(s) 9: 2 I will declare all your wondrous *d*.
9:12 proclaim among the nations his *d*;
11: 7 For the LORD is just, he loves just *d*;
14: 1 they do abominable *d*;
26: 7 thanks, and recounting all your wondrous *d*.
28: 4 Repay them for their *d*,
28: 5 *d* of the LORD nor the work of his hands,
37: 7 path of the man who does malicious *d*.
40: 6 you made, O LORD, my God, your wondrous *d*!
44: 2 to us, The *d* you did in their days,
45: 5 may your right hand show you wondrous *d*.
46: 9 behold the *d* of the LORD,
53: 2 they do abominable *d*;
62:13 you render to everyone according to his *d*.
65: 4 all flesh must come because of wicked *d*.
65: 6 awe-inspiring *d* of justice you answer us,
66: 3 Say to God, "How tremendous are your *d*!
66: 5 works of God, his tremendous *d* among men.
71:17 the present I proclaim your wondrous *d*;
72:18 God of Israel, who alone does wondrous *d*.
74: 9 *D* on our behalf we do not see;
74:12 from of old, you doer of saving *d* on earth,
75: 2 we declare your wondrous *d*.
77:12 I remember the *d* of the LORD:
78: 4 glorious *d* of the LORD and his strength
78: 7 forget the *d* of God but keep his commands,
78:11 And they forgot his *d*,
86:10 For you are great, and you do wondrous *d*;
92: 5 For you make me glad, O LORD, by your *d*;
96: 3 among all peoples, his wondrous *d*.
98: 1 a new song, for he has done wondrous *d*;
103: 7 and his *d* to the children of Israel.
105: 1 make known among the nations his *d*.
105: 2 his praise, proclaim all his wondrous *d*.
105: 5 Recall the wondrous *d* that he has wrought,
106: 2 Who can tell the mighty *d* of the LORD,
106:21 saved them, who had done great *d* in Egypt,
106:22 in Egypt, Wondrous *d* in the land of Ham,
106:29 They provoked him by their *d*,
107: 8 and his wondrous *d* to the children of men,
107:15 and his wondrous *d* to the children of men,
107:21 and his wondrous *d* to the children of men.
107:31 and his wondrous *d* to the children of men.
111: 4 He has won renown for his wondrous *d*;
119:27 and I will meditate on your wondrous *d*.
141: 4 *d* of wickedness With men who are evildoers;
145: 6 your terrible *d* and declare your greatness.
150: 2 Praise him for his mighty *d*,
Prv 24:12 he will repay each one according to his *d*.
24:29 I will repay the man according to his *d*."
28:16 prudent the prince, the more his *d* oppress.
Eccl 9: 1 wise, and their *d* are in the hand of God.
Wis 2: 4 in time, and no one will recall our *d*.
4: 2 victorious in unsullied *d* of valor.
4:20 *d* shall convict them to their face.
9:12 Thus my *d* will be acceptable,
12: 4 land, whom you hated for *d* most odious
12:19 And you taught your people, by these *d*,
Sir 4:29 your speech, nor lazy and slack in your *d*.
11: 4 works of the LORD, hidden from men his *d*.
11:26 of death to repay man according to his *d*.
16:12 he judges men, each according to his *d*.
16:14 which each receives according to his *d*.
16:20 Who tells him of just *d* and what could I
17: 8 wonders of his *d* and praise his holy name.
18: 2 his works, and who can probe his mighty *d*?
35:22 he requites mankind according to its *d*,
36:14 Give evidence of your *d* of old;
44: 8 name and men recount their praiseworthy *d*;
48:14 wonders, and after death, marvelous *d*.
Is 3: 8 speech and their *d* are before the LORD,
12: 4 among the nations make known his *d*,
41: 4 Who has performed these *d*?
45:24 "Only in the LORD are just *d* and power.
59: 6 and *d* of violence come from their hands.
63: 7 I will recall, the glorious *d* of the LORD,
64: 2 wrought awesome *d* we could not hope for,
64: 3 doing such *d* for those who wait for him.
64: 5 men, all our good *d* are like polluted rags;
66:17 all perish with their *d* and their thoughts,
Jer 4: 4 none can quench it, because of your evil *d*.
7: 3 Reform your ways and your *d*,
7: 5 thoroughly reform your ways and your *d*;
17:10 his ways, according to the merit of his *d*.
18:11 reform your ways and your *d*.
21:12 quenched, because of the evil of your *d*.
21:14 you, says the LORD, as your *d* deserve!
23: 2 but I will take care to punish your evil *d*.
23:13 Among Samaria's prophets I saw unseemly *d*:
23:14 prophets I saw *d* still more shocking:
23:22 from evil ways and from their wicked *d*.
25: 5 from your evil way and from your evil *d*;
25:14 own *d* and according to their own handiwork.
26: 3 to inflict upon them for their evil *d*.
26:13 therefore, reform your ways and your *d*;
32:14 Take these *d*, both the sealed
32:19 his ways, according to the fruit of his *d*:
32:44 bought with money, *d* written and sealed
44: 9 forgotten the evil *d* which your fathers,
44:22 The LORD could no longer bear your evil *d*,
50:29 Repay her for her *d*;
Lam 3:64 deserve, O LORD, according to their *d*;
Bar 2:19 "Not on the just *d* of our fathers and our
2:33 stubbornness, and from their evil *d*,
Ez 3:20 and his virtuous *d* shall not be remembered;
6: 9 loathe themselves because of their evil *d*,
16:43 lewdness to the rest of your abominable *d*?
16:51 with all the abominable *d* you have done.
16:52 In view of your sinful *d*,
18:24 None of his virtuous *d* shall be remembered,
20:43 all the *d* by which you defiled yourselves;
21:29 sinfulness in all your wicked *d* revealed
24:14 conduct and your *d* you shall be judged,
33:13 none of his virtuous *d* shall be remembered;
36:17 they defiled it by their conduct and *d*.
36:19 to their conduct and *d* I judged them.
36:31 conduct, and that your *d* were not good;
43: 8 my holy name by their abominable *d*;
44:13 disgrace because of all their abominable *d*.
Dn 3:27 all your *d* are faultless,
4:24 atone for your sins by good *d*,
9:16 O Lord, in keeping with all your just *d*,
9:18 before you, we rely not on our just *d*,
Hos 4: 9 for their ways, and repay them for their *d*.
5: 4 *d* do not allow them to return to their God;
9:15 wicked *d* I will drive them out of my house.
12: 3 his conduct, for his *d* he shall repay him.
Mi 2: 7 LORD short of patience, or are such his *d*?"
6: 5 that you may know the just *d* of the LORD.
7:13 of its citizens, as a result of their *d*.
Zep 3: 7 eagerly have they done all their corrupt *d*.
3:11 day You need not be ashamed of all your *d*,
Zec 1: 4 from your evil ways and from your wicked *d*.
1: 6 has treated us according to our ways and *d*,
Mt 6: 4 Keep your *d* of mercy secret,
7:16 You will know them by their *d*.
12:12 good *d* may be performed on the sabbath."
23: 4 Their words are bold but their *d* are few.
Mk 6: 2 miraculous *d* are accomplished by his hands?

DEEDS (cont.)

Lk 11:48 you stand behind the *d* of your fathers:
Jn 3:19 than light because their *d* were wicked.
3:20 near it for fear his *d* will be exposed.
3:21 to make clear that his *d* are done in God."
9: 4 the *d* of him who sent me while it is day.
10:32 good *d* have I shown you from the Father.
Acts 9:36 by constant good *d* and acts of charity.
Rom 4: 2 by his *d* he has grounds for boasting,
4: 6 God credits justice without requiring *d*:
8:13 you put to death the evil *d* of the body,
13:12 Let us cast off *d* of darkness and put on
2Cor 11:15 But their end will correspond to their *d*.
12:12 apostle, signs and wonders and *d* of power.
Eph 2:10 *d* which God prepared for us in advance.
5:11 Take no part in vain *d* done in darkness;
5:13 but when such *d* are condemned they are
Col 1:21 in your hearts because of your evil *d*.
3: 9 self with its past *d* and put on a new man,
1Tm 2:10 their adornment should be good *d*.
5:10 will be attested to by her good *d*.
5:25 some good *d* stand out clearly as such;
2Tm 4:14 the Lord will repay him according to his *d*.
Ti 3: 5 not because of any righteous *d* we had done,
Heb 10:23 each other to love and good *d*.
13:16 Do not neglect good *d* and generosity;
Jas 3:17 and the kindly *d* that are its fruits,
1Pt 3:17 to do so for good *d* than for evil ones.
4:19 as God's will requires continue in good *d*,
2Pt 2: 8 the lawless *d* of those among whom he lived.)
3:10 earth and all its *d* will be made manifest.
1Jn 3:12 Because his own *d* were wicked while his
Jude 1:13 their shameless *d* abroad like foam,
Rv 2: 2 I know your *d*, your labors,
2: 5 Repent, and return to your former *d*.
2:19 I know your *d*— your love and faith
3: 2 I find that the sum of your *d* is less than
3: 8 " 'I know your *d*;
3:15 I know your *d*; I know you are neither
15: 4 Your mighty *d* are clearly seen."
16:11 they did not turn away from their wicked *d*.
17: 4 abominable and sordid *d* of her lewdness.
18: 6 pay her double for her *d*!
19: 8 dress is the virtuous *d* of God's saints.)

DEEM (2)

2Kgs 10:30 you have done well what I *d* right,
Phil 2: 6 he did not *d* equality with God something

DEEMED (2)

Wis 7: 8 *d* riches nothing in comparison with her,
12:27 tortured by the very things they *d* gods,

DEEP (77)

Gn 2:21 So the LORD God cast a *d* sleep on the man,
15:12 to set, a trance fell upon Abram, and a *d*,
1Sm 1:16 been prompted by my *d* sorrow and misery."
26:12 the LORD had put them into a *d* slumber.
2Sm 18:17 up and cast into a *d* pit in the forest,
22:17 he drew me out of the *d* waters.
1Kgs 6: 3 and ten cubits *d* in front of the temple.
Est 4: 3 reached, the Jews went into *d* mourning,
1Mc 12:52 fear, and all Israel fell into *d* mourning.
Jb 4:13 of the night, when *d* sleep falls on men,
7:12 Am I the sea, or a monster of the *d*,
26:10 *d* as the boundary of light and darkness.
33:15 [when *d* sleep falls upon men] as they
38:30 that holds captive the surface of the *d*?
41:24 think the *d* had the hoary head of age.
Ps(s) 7:16 He has opened a hole, he has dug it *d*,
18:17 he drew me out of the *d* waters.
32: 6 Though *d* waters overflow,
33: 7 in cellars he confines the *d*.
36: 7 your judgments, like the mighty *d*;
38: 3 For your arrows have sunk *d* in me,
42: 8 *D* calls unto deep in the roar of your
64: 7 *d* are the thoughts of each heart.
77:20 way, and your path through the *d* waters,
92: 6 How very *d* are your thoughts!
106: 9 led them through the *d* as through a desert.
107:23 the sea in ships, trading on the *d* waters,
Prv 8:27 out the vault over the face of the *d*;
18: 4 The words from a man's mouth are *d* waters,
19:15 Laziness plunges a man into *d* sleep,
22:14 The mouth of the adulteress is a *d* pit;
23:27 For the harlot is a *d* ditch,
Eccl 7:24 exists is far-reaching; it is *d*, very *d*:
Sg 8: 7 *D* waters cannot quench love,
Wis 4: 3 shall not strike *d* root nor take firm hold.
10:18 Sea and brought them through the *d* waters
16:11 Lest they should fall into *d* forgetfulness
Sir 24: 5 alone, through the *d* abyss I wandered.
43:24 His is the plan that calms the *d*,
43:26 kinds of life, and the monsters of the *d*.
51: 5 from the *d* belly of the nether world;
Is 7:11 let it be *d* as the nether world,
23: 3 crossed the sea over the *d* waters.
29:10 has poured out on you a spirit of *d* sleep.
29:15 would hide their plans too *d* for the LORD!
30:33 Broad and *d* it is piled with dry grass and
44:27 It is I who said to the *d*:
51:10 up the sea, the waters of the great *d*,
Jer 49: 8 Flee, retreat, hide in *d* holes,
49:30 leave your homes, hide in *d* holes,
Ez 23:32 sister you shall drink, so wide and *d*,
27:26 the *d* waters your oarsmen brought you home,
31:15 so that the *d* waters were held back.
40:49 twenty cubits wide and twelve cubits *d*;
43:13 base was one cubit high and one cubit *d*,
43:14 high, and this ledge was one cubit *d*;
43:14 high, and this ledge also was one cubit *d*;
Dn 2:22 He reveals *d* and hidden things and knows
Jon 2: 4 For you cast me into the *d*,
Hb 3:15 steeds amid the churning of the *d* waters.
Zec 14: 4 two from east to west by a very *d* valley,
Mt 6:23 is darkness, how *d* will the darkness be!
Mk 7:21 come from the *d* recesses of the heart;
Lk 5: 4 *d* water and lower your nets for a catch."
9:32 those with him had fallen into a *d* sleep;
Jn 4:11 do not have a bucket and this well is *d*.
Acts 24: 3 acknowledge our *d* gratitude to you.
Rom 11:33 How *d* are the riches and the wisdom and
1Cor 2:10 all matters, even the *d* things of God.
2Cor 8: 2 their overflowing joy and *d* poverty
Rv 2:24 of the so-called *d* secrets" of Satan;
9:17 they wore were fiery red, *d* blue,
14: 2 which resembled the roaring of the *d*,
17: 1 harlot who sits by the waters of the *d*.
19: 6 of a great crowd, or the roaring of the *d*,

DEEP-FRIED (2)

Lv 2: 7 a pot, it must be of fine flour, *d* in oil.
7: 9 offering that is baked in an oven or *d*

DEEPER (7)

Lv 13:20 sees that it is *d* than the skin and that
13:21 *d* than the skin and is already dying out,
13:26 *d* than the skin and is already dying out,
14:37 seem to go *d* than the surface of the wall,
1Kgs 7: 8 set in *d* than the tribunal and of the same
Jb 11: 8 It is *d* than the nether world;
Sir 24:27 For *d* than the sea are her thoughts;

DEEPEST (3)

Tb 4:19 down to the *d* recesses of the nether world.
Sir 42:19 and the future, and reveals the *d* secrets.
Jn 11:33 in spirit, moved by the *d* emotions.

DEEPLY (22)

Gn 34:19 he was *d* in love with Jacob's daughter.
Dt 9:20 With Aaron, too, the LORD was *d* angry,
Tb 3:10 That day she was *d* grieved in spirit.
6:18 lineage, he fell *d* in love with her,
1Mc 2:39 heard of it, they mourned *d* for them.
14:16 Jonathan had died, they were *d* grieved.
2Mc 4:37 Antiochus was *d* grieved and full of pity;
Ps(s) 119:167 I keep your decrees and love them *d*.
Bar 2:18 He whose soul is *d* grieved,
Dn 6:15 The king was *d* grieved at this news and he
Zec 1:14 *d* moved for the sake of Jerusalem and Zion,
Mt 27: 3 condemned, began to regret his action *d*.
Mk 3: 5 for he was *d* grieved that they had closed
Lk 1:12 Zechariah was *d* disturbed upon seeing him,
1:29 She was *d* troubled by his words,
6:48 dug *d* and laid the foundation on a rock.
15:20 father caught sight of him and was *d* moved.
Jn 13:21 After saying this, Jesus grew *d* troubled.
Acts 2:37 When they heard this, they were *d* shaken.
6: 3 acknowledged to be *d* spiritual and prudent,
20:38 for they were *d* distressed to hear that
1Pt 3:13 you are committed *d* to doing what is right?

DEEPS (2)

2Sm 1:21 nor rain upon you, nor upsurgings of the *d*!
Ps(s) 135: 6 and on earth, in the seas and in all the *d*.

DEER (5)

Dt 12:15 eat it, as they do the gazelle or the *d*.
12:22 eat it as you would the gazelle or the *d*:
14: 5 the red deer, the gazelle, the roe *d*,
15:22 it alike, as you would a gazelle or a *d*.

DEFAMED (3)

Dt 22:19 because the man *d* a virgin in Israel.
Wis 10:14 Showed those who had *d* him false,
1Pt 3:16 clear, so that, whenever you are *d*,

DEFAMES (1)

Dt 22:14 charges against her and *d* her by saying,

DEFAULTS (1)

1Mc 13:39 any oversights and *d* incurred up to now,

DEFEAT (32)

Ex 32:18 nor does it sound like cries of *d*;
Nm 22: 6 *d* them and drive them out of the country.
Dt 7: 2 delivers them up to you and you *d* them,
28:20 *d* and frustration in every enterprise you
Jos 8:15 fled in seeming *d* toward the desert,
Jgs 11:33 so that he inflicted a severe *d* on them,
1Sm 4:10 It was a disastrous *d*,
19: 8 and inflicted a great *d* upon them,
23: 2 "Shall I go and *d* these Philistines?"
23: 2 will *d* the Philistines and rescue Keilah."
23: 5 cattle and inflicted a severe *d* on them,
2Sm 1: 1 David returned from his *d* of the
10:15 Then the Arameans responded to their *d* by
10:19 vassal kings, in view of their *d* by Israel,
1Kgs 20:21 chariots, and inflicted a severe *d* on Aram.
20:23 level ground, we shall be sure to *d* them.
20:25 level ground, and we shall surely *d* them."
2Kgs 13:19 Now, you will *d* Aram only three times."
2Chr 13:17 his people inflicted a severe *d* upon them;
25: 8 LORD will *d* you in the face of the enemy.
25: 8 God who has the power to reinforce or to *d*."
Est 9:24 for the time of their *d* and destruction.
1Mc 5:34 him, and he inflicted on them a crushing *d*.
5:40 he will certainly *d* us.
5:41 river, we will cross over to him and *d* him."
5:61 It was a bad *d* for the people,
8: 4 earth and had inflicted on them severe *d*,
2Mc 11:13 He reflected on the *d* he had suffered,
12:27 After the *d* and destruction of these,
Sir 47: 5 his right arm To *d* the skilled warrior
Jer 37:10 Even if you were to *d* the whole Chaldean
Heb 7: 1 from his *d* of the kings and blessed him.

DEFEATED (70)

Gn 14: 5 and *d* the Rephaim in Ashteroth-karnaim,
14:15 deployed against them at night, *d* them,
36:34 He *d* the Midianites in the country of Moab;
Nm 14:45 in that hill country came down and *d* them,
21:24 But Israel *d* him at the point of the sword,
Dt 1: 4 After he had *d* Sihon,
2:33 we *d* him and his sons and all his people.
3: 3 We *d* him so completely that we left him no
4:46 the Israelites *d* after coming out of Egypt.
29: 6 but we *d* them and took over their land,
Jos 7: 4 the attack, but they were *d* by those at Ai,
7: 5 ranks, and *d* them finally on the descent,
10:33 Lachish, but Joshua *d* him and his people,
11: 8 *d* them and pursued them to Greater Sidon,
Jgs 1: 5 When they *d* the Canaanites and Perizzites,
1:10 called Kiriath-arba, and *d* Sheshai,
1:17 they *d* the Canaanites who dwelt in Zephath.
3:13 and Amalekites, he attacked and *d* Israel,
11:21 who *d* them and occupied all the land of
12: 4 and fought against Ephraim, whom they *d*;
20:35 battle, the LORD *d* Benjamin before Israel;
20:36 it had looked as though the enemy were *d*,
1Sm 4: 2 struggle Israel was *d* by the Philistines,
4: 3 us to be *d* today by the Philistines?
4:10 The Philistines fought and Israel was *d*;
7:10 such confusion that they were *d* by Israel.
14:48 He *d* Amalek and delivered Israel from the
2Sm 2:17 men of Israel were *d* by David's servants.
5:20 then went to Baal-perazim, where he *d* them.
8: 2 *d* Moab and then measured them with a line,
8: 3 David *d* Hadadezer,
8: 9 David had *d* all the forces of Hadadezer,
18: 7 of Israel were *d* by David's servants,
1Kgs 8:33 sin against you and are *d* by an enemy,
11:24 of Zobah, when David *d* them with slaughter.
20:23 That is why they *d* us.
2Kgs 10:32 Hazael *d* the Israelites throughout their
13:19 you would have *d* Aram completely.
13:25 Joash *d* Ben-hadad three times,
14:12 Judah was *d* by Israel,
1Chr 5:10 and when they had *d* them they occupied
14:11 to Baal-perazim, and David *d* them there.
18: 1 David *d* the Philistines and subdued them;
18: 2 He also *d* Moab,
18: 3 David then *d* Hadadezer,
18: 9 David had *d* the entire army of Hadadezer,
2Chr 6:24 sinned against you and are *d* by the enemy,
13:15 God *d* Jeroboam and all Israel before
14:11 LORD *d* the Ethiopians before Asa and Judah,
25:22 There Judah was *d* by Israel,
28: 5 The Arameans *d* him and carried away
28: 5 of Israel, who *d* him with great slaughter.
28:23 to the gods of Damascus who had *d* him,
Est 6:13 against him, but will surely be *d* by him."
1Mc 1: 1 came from the land of Kittim, had *d* Darius,
1:20 After Antiochus had *d* Egypt in the year
3:11 went out to meet him and *d* and killed him.
4:14 Gentiles were *d* and fled toward the plain.
5: 3 he *d* them heavily,
8: 6 and a very great army, had been *d* by them.
10:53 engaged him in battle, *d* him and his army,
14: 3 went forth and *d* the army of Demetrius;
2Mc 10:24 who had previously been *d* by the Jews,
12:11 The *d* nomads begged Judas to make friends
13:19 but he was driven back, checked, and *d*.
13:23 attacked Judas and his men. But he was *d*.
Jer 46: 2 which was *d* at Carchemish on the Euphrates
49:28 the kingdoms of Hazor, *d* by Nebuchadnezzar,
Lk 7:30 his baptism *d* God's plan in their regard.
Rv 12:11 They *d* him by the blood of the Lamb and by

DEFEATING (3)

Jgs 20:32 thought, "We are *d* them as before";

20:39 impression that they were *d* them as surely
1Mc 3:14 the kingdom by *d* Judas and his followers,

DEFEATS (1)

Prv 22:12 but he *d* the projects of the faithless.

DEFECT (10)

Lv 21:17 who has any *d* shall come forward to offer
21:21 priest who has any such *d* may draw near
21:21 on account of his *d* he may not draw near
21:23 go up to the altar on account of his *d;*
22:20 You shall not offer one that has any *d,*
22:21 it shall not have any *d.*
Nm 19: 2 *d* and on which no yoke has ever been laid.
Dt 15:21 lame or blind or has any other serious *d,*
17: 1 the flock an animal with any serious *d;*
Dn 1: 4 of the nobility, young men without any *d,*

DEFECTION (2)

Dt 19:16 a man to accuse him of a *d* from the law,
Hos 14: 5 I will heal their *d,* I will love them freely;

DEFECTIVE (1)

Lv 22:25 since they are deformed or *d,*

DEFECTS (1)

Lv 21:18 of the following *d* may not come forward:

DEFEND (32)

Dt 23:15 journeys along within your camp to *d* you
33: 7 His own hands *d* his cause and you will be
1Kgs 8:45 prayer and petition, and *d* their cause.
2Chr 6:35 prayer and petition, and *d* their cause.
Est 8:11 city to group together and *d* their lives,
E:20 *d* themselves against those who attack them.
Jb 13:15 I will *d* my conduct before him.
Ps(s) 20: 2 the name of the God of Jacob *d* you!
54: 3 name save me, and by your might *d* my cause.
59: 2 from my adversaries *d* me.
72: 4 He shall *d* the afflicted among the people,
74:22 *d* your cause; remember how the fool
82: 3 *D* the lowly and the fatherless;
Prv 22:23 For the LORD will *d* their cause,
23:11 he will *d* their cause against you.
31: 9 what is just, *d* the needy and the poor!
Wis 2:18 he will *d* him and deliver him from the
Is 1:17 hear the orphan's plea, *d* the widow.
1:23 The fatherless they *d* not,
19:20 sends them a savior to *d* and deliver them.
Jer 5:28 justice they do not *d* By advancing the
41: 9 by King Asa to *d* himself against Baasha,
50:34 He will *d* their cause with success,
51:36 Surely I will *d* your cause,
Dn 3:16 to *d* ourselves before you in this matter.
11:39 To *d* the strongholds he shall station a
Lk 12:11 about how to *d* yourselves or what to say.
Acts 25:16 chance to *d* himself against their charges.
Rom 2:15 will accuse or *d* them on the day when,
2Cor 7:11 not to speak of readiness to *d* yourselves!
Phil 1: 7 am summoned to *d* the solid grounds
1:16 an opportunity to *d* the gospel's cause;

DEFENDED (5)

Ex 2:17 got up and *d* them and watered their flocks.
2Sm 23:12 stand in the middle of the plot and *d* it.
Est 9:16 provinces, also mustered and *d* themselves,
2Mc 13:26 *d* the treaty as well as he could and won
Lam 3:58 You *d* me in mortal danger,

DEFENDER (7)

2Mc 4: 2 compatriots, and a zealous *d* of the laws.
14:34 unfailing *d* of our nation in these words:
15:30 soul the chief *d* of his fellow citizens,
Ps(s) 68: 6 *d* of widows is God in his holy dwelling.
Is 29:21 a man, Who ensnare his *d* at the gate,
34: 8 vengeance, a year of requital by Zion's *d.*
Acts 22: 3 I was a staunch *d* of God,

DEFENDERS (5)

2Sm 11:16 to a place where he knew the *d* were strong.
1Chr 11:13 *d* were retreating before the Philistines.
2Mc 5: 5 As the *d* on the walls were forced back and
10:36 up the same way swung around on the *d,*
Acts 21:20 believe, all of them staunch *d* of the law.

DEFENDING (3)

2Mc 6:11 day, they had scruples about *d* themselves.
Acts 26:24 As Paul went on *d* himself in this way,
2Cor 12:19 this recital that I am *d* myself to you?

DEFENDS (3)

Ps(s) 135:14 all generations, For the LORD *d* his people,
Sir 35:23 Till he *d* the cause of his people,
Is 51:22 your Master, your God, who *d* his people:

DEFENSE (20)

Nm 14: 9 Their *d* has left them,
Jdt 5:23 powerless people, incapable of a strong *d.*
8:24 depend on us, and the *d* of the sanctuary,
1Mc 14:10 food and equipped them with means of *d,*
14:37 for the *d* of the land and the city,
2Mc 12:27 men took up their posts in *d* of the walls,
Ps(s) 10:18 the *d* of the fatherless and the oppressed,
35: 2 shield and buckler, and rise up in my *d.*
35:23 Awake, and be vigilant in my *d;*
36:11 your just *d* of the upright of heart.
Prv 14:26 In the fear of the LORD is a strong *d;*
18:19 A brother is a better *d* than a strong city,
Eccl 7:19 Wisdom is a better *d* for the wise man than
Lk 21:14 not to worry about your *d* beforehand,
Acts 22: 1 to what I have to say to you in my *d.*"
24:10 am thus encouraged to make my *d* before you,
25: 8 Paul's *d* was,
26: 1 stretched out his hand and began his *d.*
26: 2 able to make my *d* today in your presence,
1Cor 9: 3 *d* against those who criticize me is this:

DEFENSELESS (2)

Est E:14 he hoped to catch us *d* and to transfer
Wis 12: 6 who took with their own hands *d* lives,

DEFENSES (5)

2Chr 32: 5 He then looked to his *d:*
Ps(s) 60: 3 God, you have rejected us and broken our *d;*
Prv 25:28 *d* is the man with no check on his feelings.
Sir 49:13 our ruined walls, Restored our shattered *d,*
Jer 39: 2 a breach was made in the city's *d.*

DEFER (1)

Eph 5:21 *D* to one another out of reverence for

DEFERENCE (3)

Lv 19:15 partiality to the weak nor *d* to the mighty,
2Kgs 16:18 In *d* to the king of Assyria he removed
1Pt 2:18 slaves, obey your masters with all *d,*

DEFERRED (2)

Prv 13:12 Hope *d* makes the heart sick,
Wis 2: 5 be *d* because it is fixed with a seal;

DEFIANCE (4)

Lv 26:28 will meet you with fiery *d* and will
Dt 1:43 In *d* of the LORD's command you arrogantly
Jb 15:25 against God and bade *d* to the Almighty,
Sir 45:18 Abiram, and the band of Korah in their *d.*

DEFIANT (2)

Lv 26:21 become *d* in your unwillingness to obey me,
Sir 38:15 his Maker will be *d* toward the doctor.

DEFIANTLY (1)

Nm 15:30 "But anyone who sins *d,*

DEFIED (5)

Lv 26:40 rebelled against me and of having *d* me,
Nm 16:30 will know that these men have *d* the LORD.
1Chr 20: 7 He *d* Israel, and Jonathan,
Lam 1:18 "The LORD is just; I had *d* his command.
Mal 3:13 You have *d* me in word,

DEFILE (20)

Lv 18:24 "Do not *d* yourselves by any of these
18:30 not to *d* yourselves by observing the
Nm 5: 3 are not to *d* the camp in which I dwell."
35:34 Do not *d* the land in which you live and in
Dt 21:23 a tree, you will *d* the land which the LORD,
1Sm 25:20 down through a mountain *d* riding on an ass,
Jdt 4: 7 the *d* was only wide enough for two abreast.
9: 8 to *d* the tent where your glorious name
1Mc 14:36 sally forth to *d* the environs of the temple
Ez 9: 7 *D* the temple,
18: 6 if he does not *d* his neighbor's wife,
18:15 house of Israel, or *d* his neighbor's wife;
20: 7 not *d* yourselves with the idols of Egypt:
20:18 do not *d* yourselves with their idols.
20:30 will you *d* yourselves like your fathers?
20:31 you *d* yourselves with all your idols even
22:11 men who *d* their daughters-in-law by incest,
37:23 shall they *d* themselves with their idols,
Dn 1: 8 to *d* himself with the king's food or wine;
11:31 his command and *d* the sanctuary stronghold,

DEFILED (56)

Gn 34: 5 that Shechem had *d* his daughter Dinah;
34:13 did because their sister Dinah had been *d.*
49: 4 father's bed and *d* my couch to my sorrow.
Lv 18:24 driving out of your way have *d* themselves.
18:25 Because their land has become *d,*
18:27 which the previous inhabitants *d* the land;
18:28 will vomit you out also for having *d* it,
19:31 fortune tellers, for you will be *d* by them.
20: 3 *d* my sanctuary and profaned my holy name.
Nm 5:28 If however, the woman has not *d* herself,
Dt 24: 4 her as his wife after she has become *d.*
2Kgs 23: 8 from the cities of Judah, and then *d,*
23:10 also *d* Topheth in the Valley of Ben-hinnom,
23:13 king *d* the high places east of Jerusalem,
23:16 and thus *d* it in fulfillment of the word
Neh 13:29 how they *d* the priesthood and the covenant
Tb 3:15 And that I have never *d* my own name or my
1Mc 1:37 they *d* the sanctuary.
1:48 and to let themselves be *d* with every kind
1:63 die rather than to be *d* with unclean food
2:12 laid waste, And the Gentiles have *d* them!
4:45 shame to them that the Gentiles had *d* it;
4:54 of the day on which the Gentiles had *d* it,
7:34 But he mocked and ridiculed them, *d* them,
Ps(s) 79: 1 they have *d* your holy temple,
89:40 your servant, and *d* his crown in the dust.
106:39 They became *d* by their works,
Jer 2: 7 goodly fruits, You entered and *d* my land,
2:23 How can you say, "I am not *d,*
3: 1 Would not the land be wholly *d?*
3: 2 You *d* the land by your wicked harlotry.
7:30 They have *d* the house which bears my name
19:13 Judah shall be *d* like the place of Topheth,
32:34 They *d* the house named after me by the
Lam 1: 8 of which she is guilty, Jerusalem is *d;*
Bar 3:10 old in a foreign land, *D* with the dead,
Ez 5:11 because you have *d* my sanctuary with all
7:21 spoiled and *d* by the wicked of the earth.
14:11 and may no longer be *d* by all their sins.
20:26 I let them become *d* by their gifts,
20:43 all the deeds by which you *d* yourselves;
22: 4 with the idols you made you have become *d;*
23: 7 and she *d* herself with all those for whom
23:13 I saw that she had *d* herself.
23:17 couch, and *d* her with their intercourse.
23:17 As soon as she was *d* by them,
23:38 *d* my sanctuary and desecrated my sabbaths.
36:17 land, they *d* it by their conduct and deeds.
36:18 ground, and because they *d* it with idols].
Hos 5: 3 Ephraim has played the harlot, Israel is *d.*
6:10 harlotry is found in Ephraim, Israel is *d.*
1Cor 8: 7 conscience is weak, it is *d* by the eating.
Ti 1:15 to those *d* unbelievers nothing is clean.
Heb 9:13 who are *d* so that their flesh is cleansed,
12:15 up through which many may become *d;*
Rv 14: 4 have never been *d* by immorality with women.

DEFILEMENT (14)

Gn 34:27 in reprisal for their sister Dinah's *d.*
Jdt 9: 4 abhorrence of the *d* of their kinswoman,
13:16 he did not sin with me to my *d* or disgrace."
2Mc 5:27 eat what grew wild to avoid sharing the *d.*
6:19 a glorious death to a life of *d,*
14: 3 incurred *d* at the time of the revolt,
Jb 14: 4 Can a man be found who is clean of *d?*
Ez 22: 3 and which has made idols for her own *d.*
36:17 was like the *d* of a menstruous woman.
Dn 1: 8 the chief chamberlain to spare him this *d.*
2Cor 7: 1 ourselves from every *d* of flesh and spirit,
1Pt 1: 4 inheritance, incapable of fading or *d,*
2Pt 2:13 they are stain and *d* as they share your
3:14 effort to be found without stain or *d,*

DEFILEMENTS (2)

Lv 16:16 the sinful *d* and faults of the Israelites.
16:19 holy, purged of the *d* of the Israelites.

DEFILES (5)

Nm 19:13 *d* the Dwelling of the LORD and shall be
19:20 because he *d* the sanctuary of the LORD.
Ez 18:11 the mountains, *d* the wife of his neighbor,
33:26 each one of you *d* his neighbor's wife
Jas 3: 6 The tongue *d* the entire body.

DEFILING (4)

Lv 15:31 their uncleanness, lest by *d* my Dwelling,
18:20 your neighbor's wife, *d* yourself with her.
18:23 with an animal, *d* yourself with it;
Ez 23:30 the nations by *d* yourself with their idols.

DEFINITE (2)

Ex 9: 5 And setting a *d* time,
Acts 25:26 *d* to write about him to our sovereign.

DEFLOWERED (1)

Dt 22:29 take her as his wife, because he has *d* her.

DEFORMED (3)

Lv 22:25 since they are *d* or defective,
Mt 15:30 to him bringing with them cripples, the *d,*
15:31 beheld the mute speaking, the *d* made sound,

DEFRAUD (7)

Lv 19:13 "You shall not *d* or rob your neighbor.
Dt 24:14 shall not *d* a poor and needy hired servant,
2Mc 3:12 to *d* those who had placed their trust
Hos 12: 8 who holds a false balance, who loves to *d!*
Mal 3: 5 those who *d* the hired man of his wages,
3: 5 Against those who *d* widows and orphans;
Mk 10:19 You shall not *d;*

DEFRAUDED (1)

Lk 19: 8 If I have *d* anyone in the least,

DEFRAUDERS (1)

Wis 10:11 Stood by him against the greed of his *d*,

DEFRAUDING (1)

Sir 41:19 asked, of *d* another of his appointed share,

DEFRAUDS (1)

Prv 28:24 who *d* father or mother and calls it no sin,

DEFRAYED (1)

2Mc 3: 3 *d* from his own revenues all the expenses

DEFTLY (1)

Wis 13:11 off all its bark, And *d* plying his art,

DEFTNESS (1)

Sir 9:17 Skilled artisans are esteemed for their *d*;

DEFY (4)

Lv 26:23 to be chastened by me and continue to *d* me,
26:24 will *d* you and will smite you for your
26:41 had to *d* them and bring them into their
1Sm 17:10 "I *d* the ranks of Israel today.

DEFYING (3)

Lv 26:27 you still persist in disobeying and *d* me,
Dt 1:26 go up, and after *d* the command of the LORD,
Jgs 5:18 Zebulun is the people *d* death;

DEGENERATE (2)

Dt 32: 5 has he been treated by his *d* children,
Sir 50:26 and the *d* folk who dwell in Shechem.

DEGRADATION (2)

Rom 1:24 engaged in the mutual *d* of their bodies,
6:19 impurity and licentiousness for their *d*,

DEGRADE (4)

Lv 19:29 "You shall not *d* your daughter by making
Dt 4:16 not to *d* yourselves by fashioning an idol
4:25 should you then *d* yourselves by fashioning
Is 23: 9 majesty, to *d* all the earth's honored men.

DEGRADED (5)

Nm 25: 1 the people *d* themselves by having illicit
Ezr 2:62 hence they were *d* from the priesthood,
Neh 7:64 hence they were *d* from the priesthood,
Is 8:23 First he *d* the land of Zebulun and the
16:14 shall be *d* despite all its great multitude;

DEGRADING (1)

Prv 6:33 A *d* beating will he get,

DEGREE (3)

1Mc 2:22 from our religion in the slightest *d*."
Ps(s) 49: 3 in the world, Of lowly birth or high *d*,
2Cor 1:13 just as you know us to a certain *d* already,

DEGREES (1)

Wis 12: 8 army they they might exterminate them by *d*.

DEIGN (2)

Ps(s) 40:14 *D*, O LORD, rescue me; O LORD,
70: 2 *D*, O God, to rescue me; O LORD,

DEIGNED (1)

1Chr 17:27 have *d* to bless the house of your servant,

DEITIES (1)

Gn 31:53 ancestral *d* maintain justice between us!"

DEITY (2)

Ex 18:11 the LORD is a *d* great beyond any other;
Col 2: 9 the fullness of *d* resides in bodily form.

DEJECTED (3)

2Sm 13: 4 why are you so *d* morning after morning?
Is 57:15 and with the crushed and *d* in spirit,
57:15 in spirit, To revive the spirits of the *d*,

DEJECTION (1)

Ex 6: 9 to him because of their *d* and hard slavery.

DEKER (1)

1Kgs 4: 9 the son of *D* in Makaz,

DELAIAH (7)

1Chr 3:24 Eliashib, Pelaiah, Akkub, Johanan, *D*,
24:18 to Gamul, the twenty-third to *D*,
Ezr 2:60 sons of *D*, sons of Tobiah, sons of Nekoda,
Neh 6:10 I went to the house of Shemaiah, son of *D*,
7:62 sons of *D*, sons of Tobiah, sons of Nekoda,
Jer 36:12 Elishama, the scribe, *D*, son of Shemaiah,
36:25 And though Elnathan, *D*,

DELAY (36)

Gn 45: 9 come to me without *d*.
45:17 and go without *d* to the land of Canaan.
Ex 22:28 "You shall not *d* the offering of your
32: 1 Moses' *d* in coming down from the mountain,
Dt 23:22 your God, you shall not *d* in fulfilling it;
Jgs 3:26 their *d* Ehud made good his escape and,
1Sm 20:38 to his lad, "Hurry, be quick, don't *d*!"
2Kgs 9: 3 Then open the door and flee without *d*."
Ezr 6: 8 for their expenses, in full and without *d*.
Tb 9: 4 If I should *d* my return by a single day,
Jdt 2:13 I have commanded you, and do it without *d*."
2Mc 10:22 and without *d* captured the two towers.
14:27 as a prisoner to Antioch without *d*.
15:17 to courage, the Jews determined not to *d*,
Eccl 5: 3 make a vow to God, *d* not its fulfillment.
Sir 4: 3 *d* not to give to the needy.
5: 8 *D* not your conversion to the LORD,
6:22 and he will not *d* in casting her aside.
7:16 remember, his wrath will not *d*.
18:21 *D* not to forsake sins,
35:19 God indeed will not *d*,
38: 9 My son, when you are ill, *d* not,
Jer 4: 6 standard to Zion, seek refuge without *d*!
Ez 7:11 not be long in coming, nor shall it *d*.
12:25 and it shall be done without further *d*.
Dn 9:19 O Lord, be attentive and act without *d*,
Lk 1:21 wondering at his *d* in the temple.
12:36 knocks, you will open for him without *d*.
18: 7 Will he *d* long over them, do you suppose?
Acts 9:38 "Please come over to us without *d*."
22:16 Why *d*, then? Be baptized.
25:17 came here with me, I did not *d* the matter.
Heb 10:37 he will not *d*.
2Pt 3: 9 The Lord does not *d* in keeping his promise
3: 9 though some consider it *d*."
Rv 10: 6 "There shall be no more *d*.

DELAYED (5)

Jgs 5:28 why are the hoofbeats of his chariots *d*?"
2Sm 20: 5 but *d* beyond the time set for him by David.
Ez 12:28 None of my words shall be *d* any longer;
Mt 25: 5 The groom *d* his coming,
1Tm 3:15 if I should be *d* you will know what kind

DELAYS (1)

Hb 2: 3 If it *d*, wait for it, it will surely come,

DELEGATION (1)

Lk 14:32 a *d* while the enemy is still at a distance,

DELIBERATE (1)

Bar 6:48 the priests *d* among themselves where they

DELIBERATED (1)

1Mc 4:44 They *d* what ought to be done with the

DELIBERATELY (3)

Wis 14:30 they *d* swore false oaths despising piety.
Mt 19:12 some have been *d* made so;
Acts 27:19 *d* threw even the ship's gear overboard.

DELIBERATING (3)

Nm 17: 7 But while the community was *d* against them,
2Kgs 7: 3 the city gate were four lepers who were *d*,
1Mc 8:15 *d* on all that concerned the people and

DELIBERATION (2)

Neh 5: 7 After some *d*, I called the nobles
Sir 22:16 with careful *d* shaken in a moment of fear.

DELIBERATIONS (2)

Wis 9:14 For the *d* of mortals are timid,
Sir 7:14 Thrust not yourself into the *d* of princes,

DELICACIES (3)

Jdt 12: 1 his own *d* to eat and his own wine to drink.
Prv 23: 3 Do not desire his *d*;
Sir 40:29 His neighbor's *d* bring revulsion of spirit

DELICATE (5)

Dt 28:56 *d* woman among you, so *d* and refined
Is 47: 1 No longer shall you be called dainty and *d*.
Jer 6: 2 O lovely and *d* daughter Zion,
Dn 13:31 Susanna, very *d* and beautiful,

DELICIOUS (1)

Sir 32: 6 emerald seal is string music with *d* wine.

DELIGENTLY (1)

Ps(s) 119: 4 commanded that your precepts be *d* kept.

DELIGHT (70)

Dt 28:63 once took *d* in making you grow and prosper,
28:63 now take *d* in ruining and destroying you,
30: 9 God, will again take *d* in your prosperity,
30: 9 even as he took *d* in your fathers',
1Sm 15:22 "Does the LORD so *d* in holocausts and
1Chr 29: 3 of the *d* I take in the house of my God,
2Mc 15:38 a more pleasant drink that increases *d*,
Jb 22:26 For then you shall *d* in the Almighty and
27:10 Will he then *d* in the Almighty and call
Ps(s) 5: 5 For you, O God, *d* not in wickedness;
34:13 life, and takes *d* in prosperous days?
37: 4 Take *d* in the LORD,
37:11 the land, they shall *d* in abounding peace.
40: 9 me, To do your will, O my God, is my *d*,
62: 5 they *d* in lies;
68:31 scatter the peoples who *d* in war.
109:17 he took no *d* in blessing;
119:16 In your statutes I will *d*;
119:24 Yes, your decrees are my *d*;
119:35 the path of your commands, for in it I *d*.
119:47 And I will *d* in your commands,
119:70 as for me, your law is my *d*.
119:77 me that I may live, for your law is my *d*.
119:92 Had not your law been my *d*,
119:117 I may be safe and ever *d* in your statutes.
119:143 have come upon me, your commands are my *d*.
119:174 salvation, O LORD, and your law is my *d*.
Prv 2:14 the way of darkness, Who *d* in doing evil,
8:30 his craftsman, and I was his *d* day by day,
8:31 and I found *d* in the sons of men.
11: 1 to the LORD, but a full weight is his *d*.
11:20 but those who walk blamelessly are his *d*.
12:22 LORD, but those who are truthful are his *d*.
15: 8 but the prayer of the upright is his *d*.
16:13 The king takes *d* in honest lips,
18: 2 The fool takes no *d* in understanding,
29:17 bring you comfort, and give *d* to your soul.
Sg 2: 3 I *d* to rest in his shadow,
5:16 he is all *d*.
7: 7 you are, how pleasing, my love, my *d*!
Wis 16: 2 with a novel dish, the *d* they craved,
Sir 1:24 loyal humility is his *d*.
7:13 *D* not in telling lie after lie,
30: 3 and shows his *d* in him among his friends.
40:20 Wine and music *d* the soul,
40:22 Charm and beauty *d* the eye,
45:12 renowned for splendor, a *d* to the eyes,
Is 11: 3 and his *d* shall be the fear of the LORD.
13:17 nothing of silver and take no *d* in gold.
55: 2 shall eat well, you shall *d* in rich fare.
58:13 If you call the sabbath a *d*,
58:14 Then you shall *d* in the LORD,
62: 4 But you shall be called "My *D*,"
65:18 to be a joy and its people to be a *d*;
66:11 may nurse with *d* at her abundant breasts!
Jer 31:20 not my favored son, the child in whom I *d*?
32:41 I will take *d* in doing good to them:
49:25 city of glory be forsaken, the town of *d*!
Ez 24:16 am taking away from you the *d* of your eyes,
24:21 of your pride, the *d* of your eyes,
24:25 their glorious joy, the *d* of their eyes,
Dn 11:37 ancestors or for the one in whom women *d*;
Mt 12:18 I have chosen, my loved one in whom I *d*.
Mk 12:37 majority of the crowd heard this with *d*.
Lk 19: 6 quickly descended, and welcomed him with *d*.
Acts 14:17 your spirits he fills with food and *d*."
15:31 was great *d* at the encouragement it gave.
1Thes 2:20 You are our boast and our *d*.
Heb 10: 6 and sin offerings you took no *d* in.
2Pt 2:13 Thinking daytime revelry a *d*,

DELIGHTED (11)

1Mc 11:44 to the king, he was *d* over their arrival,
14: 4 His people were *d* with his power and his
Sir 25: 1 With three things I am *d*,
Jer 12:10 *d* me they have turned into a desert waste,
Mt 14: 6 dance before the court which *d* Herod
Mk 6:22 a dance which *d* Herod and his guests.
Lk 22: 5 They were *d*, and agreed to give him money.
Acts 13:48 The Gentiles were *d* when they heard this
Rom 16:19 is known to all, and so I am *d* with you.
2Thes 2:12 but have *d* in evildoing will be condemned.
Heb 10: 8 offerings, you neither desired nor *d* in."

DELIGHTFUL (5)

Gn 2: 9 that were *d* to look at and good for food,
Ps(s) 36: 9 from your *d* stream you give them to drink.
Sg 1: 2 More *d* is your love than wine!
4:10 how much more *d* is your love than wine,
Mal 3:12 call you blessed, for you will be a *d* land,

DELIGHTS (16)

Gn 49:26 mountains, the *d* of the eternal hills.
2Mc 15:38 *d* the ears of those who read the work.
Ps(s) 1: 2 But *d* in the law of the LORD and
16:11 presence, the *d* at your right hand forever.
73:25 And when I am with you, the earth *d* me not.
111: 2 of the LORD, exquisite in all their *d*.
112: 1 the LORD, who greatly *d* in his commands.
147:10 In the strength of the steed he *d* not,

Wis 16:20 with all *d* and conforming to every taste.
Sir 11:27 affliction brings forgetfulness of past *d;*
24:17 I bud forth *d* like the vine,
26:13 A gracious wife *d* her husband,
Is 62: 4 For the LORD *d* in you,
Jer 51:34 filled his belly with my *d,*
Mi 7:18 in anger forever, but *d* rather in clemency,
3Jn 1: 4 Nothing *d* me more than to hear that my

DELILAH (7)

Jgs 16: 4 a woman in the Wadi Sorek whose name was *D.*
16: 6 So *D* said to Samson,
16:10 *D* said to Samson,
16:12 *D* took new ropes and bound him with them.
16:13 *D* said to Samson again,
16:14 *D* wove his seven locks of hair into the
16:18 When *D* saw that he had taken her

DELIVER (141)

Ex 5:18 but you must still *d* your quota of bricks."
6: 6 and will *d* you from their slavery.
18:11 insolently to *d* the people from the power
Nm 21: 2 "If you *d* this people into my hand,
21:34 *d* him with all his people and his land.
24:24 *d* his people from the hands of the Kittim?
Dt 1:27 to *d* us into the hands of the Amorites and
2:24 I now *d* into your hands Sihon,
2:30 in heart that he might *d* him up to you,
7:16 which the LORD, your God, will *d* up to you.
7:23 will *d* them up to you and will rout them
7:24 He will *d* their kings into your hand,
Jos 1: 3 *d* to you every place where you set foot.
8: 7 the LORD, your God, will *d* into your power.
8:18 toward Ai, for I will *d* it into your power."
20: 5 they are not to *d* up the homicide who slew
Jgs 2:16 *d* them from the power of their despoilers,
4: 7 troops, and will *d* them into your power."
7: 2 you for me to *d* Midian into their power,
7: 7 save you and will *d* Midian into your power.
11:30 "If you *d* the Ammonites into my power,"
15:12 to *d* you over to the Philistines."
15:13 will only bind you and *d* you over to them."
20:28 for tomorrow I will *d* him into your power."
1Sm 4: 8 *d* us from the power of these mighty gods?
7: 3 *d* you from the power of the Philistines."
12:10 but *d* us now from the power of our enemies,
14:37 Will you *d* them into the power of Israel?"
17:46 Today the LORD shall *d* you into my hand;
17:47 LORD's and he shall *d* you into our hands."
23: 4 I will *d* the Philistines into your power."
23:12 *d* me and my men into the grasp of Saul?"
23:14 the LORD did not *d* David into his grasp.
23:20 be our task to *d* him into the king's grasp."
24: 5 you, 'I will *d* your enemy into your grasp;
26:24 highly and *d* me from all difficulties."
28:19 Moreover, the LORD will *d* Israel,
30:15 you will not kill me or *d* me to my master,
2Sm 5:19 will you *d* them into my grip?"
5:19 surely *d* the Philistines into your grip."
1Kgs 8:46 anger against them you *d* them to the enemy,
20:13 When I *d* it up to you today,
20:28 I will *d* up to you all this large army,
22: 7 "The LORD will *d* it over to the king."
22:12 The LORD will *d* it over to the king."
22:15 The LORD will *d* it over to the king."
2Kgs 3:18 he will also *d* Moab into your grasp.
10:24 of those whom I shall *d* into your hands,
17:39 *d* you from the power of all your enemies."
18:29 you, since he cannot *d* you out of my hand.
21:14 my inheritance and *d* them into enemy hands,
1Chr 14:10 and will you *d* them into my power?"
14:10 for I will *d* them into your power."
16:35 gather us and *d* us from the nations,
2Chr 6:36 anger against them you *d* them to the enemy,
18: 5 "God will *d* it over to the king."
18:11 the LORD will *d* it over to the king."
20:17 see how the LORD will be with you to *d* you,
Neh 9:27 to *d* them from the power of their enemies.
Jdt 2: 7 soldiers, to whom I will *d* them as spoils.
2:11 but *d* them up to slaughter and plunder in
7:26 summon them and *d* the whole city as booty
Est 3: 9 and I will *d* to the procurators ten
C:30 power of the wicked, and *d* me from my fear."
1Mc 5:14 from Galilee to *d* a similar message:
12:17 and to *d* to you our letter about the
2Mc 4:23 Simon, to *d* the money to the king,
8:11 promising to *d* ninety slaves for a talent
8:14 time besought the Lord to *d* those whom
Jb 5:19 Out of six troubles he will *d* you,
5:20 In famine he will *d* you from death,
6:23 possessions, Or to *d* me from the enemy,
10: 7 and that none can *d* me out of your hand?
33:24 and say, *D* him from going down to the pit;
39: 3 they *d* their progeny in the desert.
Ps(s) 22: 9 let him *d* him, let him rescue him,
31: 3 your ear to me, make haste to *d* me!
33:19 To *d* them from death and preserve them in
39: 9 From all my sins *d* me;
41: 2 the day of misfortune the LORD will *d* him.
71: 2 In your justice rescue me, and *d* me;
79: 9 *D* us and pardon our sins for your name's
82: 4 from the hand of the wicked *d* them.
89:49 but *d* himself from the power of the nether
91:14 Because he clings to me, I will *d* him;
91:15 I will *d* him and glorify him;
120: 2 O LORD, *d* me from lying lip,
140: 2 *D* me, O LORD, from evil men;
144: 7 *D* me and rescue me from many waters,
144:10 You who give victory to kings, and *d* David,
144:11 From the evil sword *d* me;
Wis 2:18 him and *d* him from the hand of his foes.
Sir 4: 9 *D* the oppressed from the hand of the
4:19 him and *d* him into the hands of despoilers.
Is 19: 4 *d* Egypt into the power of a cruel master,
19:20 sends them a savior to defend and *d* them.
31: 5 shall shield Jerusalem, To protect and *d,*
36:14 deceive you, since he cannot *d* you.
43:13 There is none who can *d* from my hand.
50: 2 Have I not the strength to *d?*
Jer 1: 8 them, because I am with you to *d* you,
1:19 over you, for I am with you to *d* you,
12: 7 of my soul I *d* into the hand of her foes.
15:20 For I am with you, to *d* and rescue you,
18:21 So now, *d* their children to famine,
20: 4 Indeed, I will *d* you to terror,
20: 4 All Judah I will *d* to the king of Babylon,
22: 1 the king of Judah and there *d* this message:
22:25 I will *d* you into the hands of those who
30:10 Behold, I will *d* you from the far-off land,
30:11 I am with you, says the LORD, to *d* you.
46:27 Behold, I will *d* you from the far-off land,
Bar 2:14 supplication, and *d* us for your own sake:
4:18 himself *d* you from your enemies' hands.
4:21 will *d* you from oppression at enemy hands.
6:35 from death, nor *d* the weak from the strong.
Ez 23:46 and *d* them over to terror and plunder.
25: 4 therefore I will *d* you into the possession
37:23 *d* them from all their sins of apostasy,
Dn 3:15 is the God that can *d* you out of my hands?"
3:34 your name's sake, do not *d* us up forever,
3:43 *D* us by your wonders,
3:95 to *d* the servants that trusted in him;
Hos 2:12 and no one can *d* her out of my hand.
11: 8 I give you up, O Ephraim, or *d* you up,
13:14 *d* them from the power of the nether world?
Mi 5: 7 tramples and tears, and there is none to *d.*
6:14 what you do save, I will *d* up to the sword.
6:16 Therefore I will *d* you up to ruin,
Zec 11: 6 I will *d* each of them into the power of
11: 6 and I will not *d* it out of their power.)
Mt 6:13 to the trial but *d* us from the evil one.'
27: 4 "I did wrong to *d* up an innocent man!"
Lk 12:58 and the judge *d* you up to the jailer,
Acts 15:23 They were to *d* this letter:
15:30 the assembly together to *d* the letter.
2Cor 1:10 hope in him who will never cease to *d* us.
Gal 4: 5 to *d* from the law those who were subjected
1Thes 2: 3 The exhortation we *d* does not spring from
1Pt 4:11 The one who speaks is to *d* God's message.
2Pt 2: 7 He did *d* Lot,

DELIVERANCE (21)

Gn 45: 7 to save your lives in an extraordinary *d.*
49:18 "[I long for your *d,* O LORD!]
Jgs 13: 5 It is he who will begin the *d* of Israel
2Chr 12: 7 I will give them some *d,*
Tb 6:18 heaven to show you mercy and grant you *d.*
8: 4 LORD to have mercy on us and to grant us *d.*"
8: 5 to pray and beg that *d* might be theirs.
8:17 Grant them, Master, mercy and *d,*
Est 4:14 relief and *d* will come to the Jews from
1Mc 3:18 no difference between *d* by many or by few,
4:25 Thus Israel had a great *d* that day.
4:56 holocausts and sacrifices of *d* and praise.
9:46 out now to Heaven for *d* from our enemies."
Ps(s) 111: 9 He has sent *d* to his people;
Is 20: 6 for help and *d* from the king of Assyria;
Jon 2:10 *d* is from the LORD.
Lk 2:38 who looked forward to the *d* of Jerusalem.
21:28 heads high, for your *d* is near at hand."
Acts 7:25 that God was using him to bring them *d;*
Heb 9:15 since his death has taken place for *d* from
11:35 were tortured and would not receive *d,*

DELIVERED (143)

Gn 9: 2 into your power they are *d.*
14:20 Most High, who *d* your foes into your hand."
48:16 day, The Angel who has *d* me from all harm,
Ex 20: 1 Then God *d* all these commandments:
Nm 21: 3 Israel's prayer and *d* up the Canaanites,
Dt 2:33 since the LORD, our God, had *d* him to us,
2:36 for us to whom the LORD had *d* them up.
3: 2 for I have *d* him into your hand with all
3: 3 the LORD, our God, *d* into our hands Og,
32:30 Rock sold them and the LORD *d* them up?"
Jos 2:24 LORD has *d* all this land into our power;
6: 2 *d* Jericho and its king into your power.
8: 1 I have *d* the king of Ai into your power,
10: 8 them, for I have *d* them into your power.
10:12 LORD *d* up the Amorites to the Israelites,
10:19 LORD, your God, has *d* them into your power
10:30 king, the LORD *d* into the power of Israel.
10:32 LORD *d* Lachish into the power of Israel,
11: 8 *d* them into the power of the Israelites,
24: 8 against you, but I *d* them into your power.
24:11 you, but I *d* them also into your power.
Jgs 1: 2 I have *d* the land into his power."
1: 4 the LORD *d* the Canaanites and Perizzites
2:14 and he *d* them over to plunderers who
3:10 out to war, the LORD *d* Cushan-rishathaim,
3:28 "for the LORD has *d* your enemies the
4:14 the LORD has *d* Sisera into your power.
6: 1 who therefore *d* them into the power of
6:13 us and has *d* us into the power of Midian."
7: 9 on the camp, for I have *d* it up to you.
7:14 *d* Midian and all the camp into his power."
7:15 has *d* the camp of Midian into your power."
8: 3 your power God *d* the princes of Midian,
8: 7 has *d* Zebah and Zalmunna into my power,
8:34 who had *d* them from the power of their
11:21 *d* Sihon and all his men into the power of
11:32 them, and the LORD *d* them into his power,
12: 3 and the LORD *d* them into my power.
13: 1 who therefore *d* them into the power of the
16:23 god has *d* into our power Samson our enemy."
16:24 "Our god has *d* into our power our enemy,
1Sm 8:10 Samuel *d* the message of the LORD in full
10:18 *d* you from the power of the Egyptians
12:11 he *d* you from the power of your enemies on
14:10 because the LORD has *d* them into our grasp.
14:12 LORD has *d* them into the grasp of Israel."
14:48 He defeated Amalek and *d* Israel from the
17:37 who *d* me from the claws of the lion and
24:11 just now *d* you into my grasp in the cave.
24:19 when the LORD *d* me into your grasp and you
25: 9 they *d* this message fully to Nabal in
26: 8 has *d* your enemy into your grasp this day.
26:23 Today, though the LORD *d* you into my grasp,
28:19 and the LORD will have *d* the army of
30:23 He has protected us and *d* into our grip
2Sm 18:28 who has *d* up the men who rebelled against
19:10 king *d* us from the clutches of our enemies,
1Kgs 1:29 LORD lives, who has *d* me from all distress,
13:26 He has *d* him to a lion,
20:14 asked, "Through whom will it be *d* up?"
2Kgs 9:25 Ahab, the LORD *d* this oracle against him:
17:20 them and *d* them over to plunderers,
1Chr 22:18 *d* the occupants of the land into my power,
2Chr 13:16 Judah, and God *d* them into their hands.
16: 8 on the LORD, he *d* them into your power.
18:14 they will be *d* into your power."
28: 5 *d* him into the power of the king of Aram.
28: 5 *d* into the power of the king of Israel,
28: 9 with Judah that he *d* them into your hands.
30: 7 so that he *d* them over to desolation,
36:17 he *d* all of them over into his grip.
Ezr 5:12 he *d* them into the power of the Chaldean,
6: 9 is to be *d* to them day by day without fail,
9: 7 for our wicked deeds we have been *d* over,
Neh 9:24 the land and *d* them over into their power,
9:27 *d* them into the power of their enemies,
9:28 heaven and *d* them according to your mercy,
9:30 Thus you *d* them over into the power of the
Tb 3: 6 command me to be *d* from such anguish;
Jdt 10:12 they are about to be *d* up to you as prey.
Est C:17 have *d* us into the hands of our enemies,
7: 4 my people and I have been *d* to destruction,
11: 6 his people and *d* us from all these evils.
1Mc 2:60 innocence, was *d* from the jaws of lions.
4:30 David and *d* the camp of the Philistines
5:50 that day and night, and it was *d* to him.
7:35 Judas and his army are not *d* to me at once,
Jb 22:30 you shall be *d* through cleanness of hands.
33:28 He *d* my soul from passing to the pit,
Ps(s) 22: 5 they trusted, and you *d* them.
33:16 army, nor is a warrior *d* by great strength.
34: 5 he answered me and *d* me from all my fears.
63:11 They shall be *d* over to the sword,
78:42 hand nor the day he *d* them from the foe,
78:50 death, and *d* their beasts to the plague.
118:18 chastised me, yet he has not *d* me to death.
Eccl 9:15 was wise, and he *d* it through his wisdom.
Wis 10: 6 She *d* the just man from among the wicked
10: 9 *d* from tribulations those who served her.
10:13 man when he was sold, but *d* him from sin.
10:15 *d* them from the nation that oppressed them.
Sir 51: 3 you have *d* me,
Is 64: 6 face from us and have *d* us up to our guilt.
Jer 29: 3 *D* in Babylon by Elasah,
31: 7 The LORD has *d* his people,
Lam 1:14 The LORD has *d* me into their grip,
Ez 16:27 and *d* you over to the will of your enemies,
35: 5 whom you *d* over to the power of the sword
36: 5 their possession to be *d* over to plunder.
Dn 2:44 be destroyed or *d* up to another people;
3:88 For he has *d* us from the nether world,
3:88 the raging flame and *d* us from the fire.
6:28 and he *d* Daniel from the lions' power."
Am 1: 9 they *d* whole groups captive to Edom,
Mi 5: 5 And we shall be *d* from Assryia,
Mt 17:22 Man is going to be *d* into the hands of men,
Mk 9:31 "The Son of Man is going to be *d* into the
Lk 1:74 that, rid of fear and *d* from the enemy,
9:44 Son of Man must be *d* into the hands of men."
18:32 He will be *d* up to the Gentiles.
21:16 You will be *d* up even by your parents,
23:25 and murder, and *d* Jesus up to their wishes.

DELIVERED (cont.)
24: 7 Man must be *d* into the hands of sinful men,
24:20 leaders *d* him up to be condemned to death,
Jn 19:30 he bowed his head, and *d* over his spirit.
Acts 2:23 *d* up by the set purpose and plan of God;
17:22 up in the Areopagus and *d* this address:
20:18 When they came to him he *d* this address:
23:33 they *d* the letter to the governor and
26:17 I have *d* you from this people and from the
Rom 1:24 God *d* them up in their lusts to unclean
1:26 *d* them up to disgraceful passions.
1:28 so God *d* them up to their own depraved
2Cor 3: 3 you are a letter of Christ which I have *d*,
4:11 being *d* to death for Jesus' sake,
Gal 1: 8 not in accord with the one we *d* to you,
3:13 Christ has *d* us from the power of the
2Thes 3: 2 we may be *d* from confused and evil men.
3:14 obey our injunction, *d* through this letter,
1Pt 1:18 Realize that you were *d* from the futile
2:23 *d* himself up to the One who judges justly.
2Pt 3: 2 teaching *d* long ago by the holy prophets,
Jude 1: 3 for the faith *d* once for all to the saints.

DELIVERER (8)
Ps(s) 18: 3 O LORD, my rock, my fortress, my *d*.
40:18 You are my help and my *d*;
70: 6 my help and my *d*; O LORD, hold not back!
144: 2 and my fortress, my stronghold, my *d*,
Wis 19: 9 praising you, O Lord! their *d*.
Dn 6:28 He is a *d* and savior,
Acts 7:35 thornbush, sent to be their ruler and *d*.
Rom 11:26 *d* who shall remove all impiety from Jacob;

DELIVERING (4)
Jos 7: 7 *d* us into the power of the Amorites,
Jgs 2:23 or *d* them into the power of Israel.
2Chr 32:11 *d* you over to a death of famine and thirst,
Mk 2: 3 While he was *d* God's word to them,

DELIVERS (18)
Dt 7: 2 God, *d* them up to you and you defeat them,
20:13 the LORD, your God, *d* it into your hand,
21:10 the LORD, your God, *d* them into your hand,
31: 5 When, therefore, the LORD *d* them up to you,
Jgs 11: 9 the Ammonites and the LORD *d* them up to me,
1Sm 10:19 *d* you from all your evils and calamities,
1Mc 4:11 that there is One who redeems and *d* Israel."
Jb 22:30 God *d* him who is innocent;
Ps(s) 34: 8 around those who fear him, and *d* them.
34:20 man, but out of them all the LORD *d* him;
37:40 LORD helps them and *d* them; he delivers
97:10 from the hand of the wicked he *d* them.
Wis 16: 8 foes that you are he who *d* from all evil.
Is 41: 2 him he *d* the nations and subdues the kings;
46: 7 it *d* no one from distress.
66: 7 come upon her, she safely *d* a male child.
1Thes 1:10 Jesus, who *d* us from the wrath to come.

DELIVERY (3)
Gn 25:24 When the time of her *d* came,
38:27 When the time of her *d* came,
Lk 1:57 When Elizabeth's time for *d* arrived,

DELOS (1)
1Mc 15:23 Sampsames, Sparta, *D*,

DELOUSE (1)
Jer 43:12 *d* the land of Egypt and depart victorious.

DELOUSES (1)
Jer 43:12 As a shepherd *d* his cloak,

DELUDE (2)
1Cor 3:18 Let no one *d* himself.
Col 2: 4 no one may *d* you with specious arguments.

DELUGE (4)
Jb 22:11 a *d* of waters covers you.
Sir 44:17 and with a sign to him the *d* ended;
Is 54: 9 of Noah should never again *d* the earth;
2Pt 3: 6 it was overwhelmed by the *d*.

DEMAND (19)
Gn 9: 5 own lifeblood, too, I will *d* an accounting:
9: 5 from every animal I will *d* it,
9: 5 man I will *d* an accounting for human life.
34:11 favor, and I will pay whatever you *d* of me.
Dt 23:20 "You shall not *d* interest from your
23:21 You may *d* interest from a foreigner,
Jgs 20:13 to accede to the *d* of their brothers,
1Mc 8:25 wholeheartedly, as the occasion shall *d*;
8:27 them willingly, as the occasion shall *d*,
15:35 As for Joppa and Gazara, which you *d*,
2Mc 4:28 the king, in spite of the *d* of Sostratus,
Sir 12:12 your right hand, lest he then *d* your seat,
Is 5:11 Woe to those who *d* strong drink as soon as
42:22 as spoil, with no one to *d* their return.
Jer 9:24 when I will *d* an account of all those
Dn 2:11 What you *d*, O king, is too difficult;
Mk 15: 8 to press their *d* that he honor the custom,
Lk 6:30 man takes what is yours, do not *d* it back.
1Cor 1:22 *d* "signs" and Greeks look for "wisdom,"

DEMANDED (23)
Gn 21:10 so she *d* of Abraham:
31:26 "What do you mean," Laban *d* of Jacob,
31:36 crime or offense have I committed," he *d*,
43: 6 Israel *d*, "Why did you bring this trouble
47:31 But his father *d*, "Swear it to me!"
Ex 12:32 flocks, too, and your herds, as you *d*,
Dt 23:20 else on which interest is usually *d*.
2Sm 14: 7 whole clan confronted your servant and *d*:
1Kgs 20: 9 that you *d* of your servant the first time.
2Kgs 23:35 the land to raise the amount Pharaoh *d*.
Ezr 10: 5 *d* an oath from the chiefs of the priests,
Est E:13 deceit, he *d* the destruction of Mordecai,
Jb 31:14 what could I answer when he *d* an account?
Wis 15: 8 when the life that was lent him is *d* back.
Dn 14:29 They went to the king and *d*:
Mt 18:28 'Pay back what you owe,' he *d*.
Lk 8:30 "What is your name?" Jesus *d*.
23:23 *d* with loud cries that he be crucified,
23:24 decreed that what they *d* should be done.
Jn 18:29 do you bring against this man?" he *d*.
Acts 15: 5 Pharisees then got up and *d* that such Gentiles
22:26 the centurion ran to the commander and *d*,
25:15 against this man and *d* his condemnation.

DEMANDING (6)
Ex 22:24 toward him by *d* interest from him.
Neh 13:11 I took the magistrates to task, *d*,
13:17 the nobles of Judah to task, *d* of them:
Ps(s) 78:18 in their hearts by *d* the food they craved.
Mt 21:10 whole city was stirred to its depths, *d*,
Lk 11:16 test him, were *d* of him a sign from heaven.

DEMANDS (10)
Gn 21:12 Heed the *d* of Sarah,
Ex 7: 9 Pharaoh *d* that you work a sign or wonder,
21:22 as much as the woman's husband *d* of him,
Is 10:22 is decreed as overwhelming justice *d*.
Mi 7: 3 the prince makes *d*,
Mt 3:15 do this if we would fulfill all of God's *d*."
Mk 4:19 to the word, but anxieties over life's *d*,
Rom 2:15 *d* of the law are written in their hearts.
8: 4 so that the just *d* of the law might be
1Cor 7:33 *d* and occupied with pleasing his wife.

DEMAS (3)
Col 4:14 physician sends you greetings. So does *D*.
2Tm 4:10 Do your best to join me soon, for *D*,
Phlm 1:24 greets you, as do Mark, Aristarchus, *D*,

DEMEAN (1)
2Sm 6:22 the LORD, but I will *d* myself even more.

DEMENTED (1)
Mt 17:15 son, who is *d* and in a serious condition.

DEMETRIUS (53)
1Mc 7: 1 In the year one hundred and fifty-one, *D*,
7: 4 killed them, and *D* sat on the royal throne.
8:31 the wrongs that King *D* has done to them,
9: 1 When *D* heard that Nicanor and his army had
10: 2 When King *D* heard of it,
10: 3 *D* sent a letter to Jonathan written in
10: 6 So *D* authorized him to gather an army and
10:15 the promises that *D* had made to Jonathan;
10:22 When *D* heard of these things,
10:25 *D* sends greetings to the Jewish nation.
10:46 the great evil that *D* had done in Israel,
10:48 a large army and encamped opposite *D*.
10:49 joined battle, and when the army of *D* fled,
10:50 hard until sunset, and *D* fell that day.
10:52 *D* and gaining control of my country
10:67 and sixty-five, Demetrius, son of *D*,
10:69 *D* appointed Apollonius governor of
11: 9 He sent ambassadors to King *D*, saying:
11:12 his daughter away and giving her to *D*,
11:19 Thus *D* became king in the year one hundred
11:22 When *D* heard this, he was furious,
11:30 "King *D* sends greetings to his brother
11:32 *D* sends greetings to his father Lasthenes.
11:38 When King *D* saw that the land was peaceful
11:39 that all the troops were grumbling at *D*,
11:40 he told him of all that *D* had done and of
11:41 request to King *D* to withdraw his troops
11:42 *D*, in turn, sent this word to Jonathan:
11:52 when King *D* was sure of his royal throne,
11:55 All the soldiers whom *D* had discharged
11:55 around Antiochus and fought against *D*,
11:63 Jonathan heard that the generals of *D* had
12:24 Jonathan heard that the generals of *D* had
12:34 this stronghold to the supporters of *D*.
13:34 Simon also sent chosen men to King *D* with
13:35 King *D* sent him the following letter:
13:36 *D* sends greetings to Simon the high priest,
14: 1 King *D* assembled his army and marched into
14: 2 heard that *D* had invaded his territory,
14: 3 went forth and defeated the army of *D*;
14:38 *D* confirmed him in the high priesthood,
15: 1 Antiochus, son of King *D*,
15:22 consul sent similar letters to Kings *D*,
2Mc 1: 7 In the reign of *D*,
14: 1 later, Judas and his men learned that *D*,
14: 4 So he went to King *D* in the year one
14: 5 invited to the council by *D* and questioned
14:11 Judas quickly added fuel to *D*' indignation.
14:26 the treaty that had been made, went to *D*,
Acts 19:24 There was a silversmith named *D* who made
19:38 If *D* and his fellow craftsmen want to
3Jn 1:12 *D* is one who gets a good testimonial from

DEMOLISH (9)
Ex 23:24 must *d* them and smash their sacred pillars.
Lv 26:30 I will *d* your high places,
Nm 33:52 molten images, and *d* all their high places.
Jgs 8: 9 I return in triumph, I will *d* this tower."
Ps(s) 52: 7 God himself shall *d* you;
Jer 1:10 up and to tear down, to destroy and to *d*,
Ez 16:39 to tear down your platform and *d* your dais;
Mi 5:10 I will *d* the cities of your land and tear
2Cor 10: 4 We *d* sophistries and every proud

DEMOLISHED (14)
Jgs 8:17 He also *d* the tower of Penuel and slew the
9:45 then killed its inhabitants and *d* the city,
2Kgs 11:18 land went to the temple of Baal and *d* it.
23:12 He also *d* the altars made by the kings of
1Mc 1:31 it, *d* its houses and its surrounding walls,
4:38 some mountain, and the priests' chambers *d*.
9:62 its fortifications that had been *d*.
11: 4 by fire, Azotus and its suburbs *d*,
Prv 12:12 The stronghold of evil men will be *d*,
Jer 39: 8 the people, and *d* the walls of Jerusalem.
Lam 2: 6 He has *d* his shelter like a garden booth,
Ez 26:12 be torn down, your precious houses *d*;
30:16 shall be breached and its walls shall be *d*.
Gal 2:18 were to build up the very things I had *d*,

DEMON (18)
Gn 4: 7 but if not, sin is a *d* lurking at the door:
Tb 3: 8 but the wicked *d* Asmodeus killed them off
3:17 then drive the wicked *d* Asmodeus from her.
6: 8 who is afflicted by a *d* or evil spirit,
6:14 it said that it was a *d* who killed them.
6:15 So now I too am afraid of this *d*.
6:16 do not give another thought to this *d*,
6:18 as the *d* smells the odor they give off,
8: 3 The *d*, repelled by the odor of the fish,
Mt 9:32 him a mute who was possessed by a *d*.
9:33 the *d* was expelled the mute began to speak,
15:22 My daughter is terribly troubled by a *d*."
17:18 reprimanded him, and the *d* came out of him.
Mk 7:26 beg him to expel the *d* from her daughter.
7:29 The *d* has already left your daughter."
7:30 the child lying in bed and the *d* gone.
Lk 4:35 the *d* threw him to the ground before
8:29 *d* would drive him into places of solitude.

DEMONS (42)
Dt 32:17 They offered sacrifice to *d*,
Tb 6: 8 and no *d* will ever return to him again.
Ps(s) 106:37 their sons and their daughters to *d*,
Bar 4: 7 provoked your Maker with sacrifices to *d*,
4:35 and *d* shall dwell in her from that time on.
Mt 7:22 Have we not exorcised *d* by its power?
8:28 They were possessed by *d* and were so
8:31 The *d* kept appealing to him,
9:34 casts out *d* through the prince of demons."
9:34 casts out demons through the prince of *d*."
10: 8 raise the dead, heal the leprous, expel *d*.
12:24 expel *d* only with the help of Beelzebul,
12:24 the help of Beelzebul, the prince of *d*."
12:27 If I expel *d* with Beelzebul's help,
12:28 is by the Spirit of God that I expel *d*,
Mk 1:32 all who were ill, and those possessed by *d*.
1:34 were many, and so were the *d* he expelled.
1:34 But he would not permit the *d* to speak,
1:39 *d* throughout the whole of Galilee.
3:15 were likewise to have authority to expel *d*.
3:22 "He expels *d* with the help of the prince of *d*
6:13 They expelled many *d*,
9:38 we saw a man using your name to expel *d*
16: 9 Magdalene, out of whom he had cast seven *d*.
16:17 they will use my name to expel *d*,
Lk 4:41 *D* departed from many,
8:27 a man from the town who was possessed by *d*.
8:30 the *d* who had entered him were many.
8:32 and the *d* asked him to permit them to
8:33 The *d* then came out of the man and entered
9: 1 to overcome all *d* and to cure diseases.
9:49 we saw a man using your name to expel *d*,
10:17 even the *d* are subject to us in your name."
1Cor 10:20 the Gentiles sacrifice to *d* and not to God,
10:20 I do not want you to become sharers with *d*.
10:21 the cup of the Lord and also the cup of *d*.
10:21 of the Lord and likewise the table of *d*.
1Tm 4: 1 things taught by *d* through plausible liars

Jas 2:19 The *d* believe that, and shudder.
Rv 9:20 They did not give up the worship of *d*,
18: 2 She has become a dwelling place for *d*.

DEMONSTRATE (2)

2Cor 10:12 one another, they only *d* their ignorance.
3Jn 1: 5 you *d* fidelity by all that you do for the

DEMONSTRATION (1)

Acts 19:40 We have no valid excuse for this wild *d*."

DEMOPHON (1)

2Mc 12: 2 son of Gennaeus, as also Hieronymus and *D*,

DEMORALIZED (1)

Prv 29:18 Without prophecy the people become *d*;

DEMORALIZES (1)

Jer 38: 4 *d* the soldiers who are left in this city,

DEN (22)

Is 11: 8 The baby shall play by the cobra's *d*,
Jer 7:11 my name become in your eyes a *d* of thieves?
Dn 6: 8 he shall be cast into a *d* of lions.
6:13 he shall be cast into a *d* of lions?"
6:17 to be brought and cast into the lions' *d*.
6:18 been brought to block the opening of the *d*.
6:20 next morning and hastened to the lions' *d*.
6:24 At his order Daniel was removed from the *d*,
6:25 their wives, to be cast into the lions' *d*.
6:25 Before they reached the bottom of the *d*,
14:31 They threw Daniel into a lions' *d*,
14:32 In the *d* were seven lions,
14:34 have to Daniel in the lions' *d* at Babylon."
14:35 I have never seen, and I do not know the *d*!"
14:36 he set him down in Babylon above the *d*.
14:40 As he came to the *d* and looked in,
14:42 tried to destroy him he threw into the *d*,
Am 3: 4 from its *d* unless it has seized something?
Na 2:12 is the lions' cave, the young lions' *d*,
Mt 21:13 but you are turning it into a *d* of thieves."
Mk 11:17 but you have turned it into a *d* of thieves."
Lk 19:46 but you have made it 'a *d* of thieves.'"

DENIED (15)

Gn 30: 2 God, who has *d* you the fruit of the womb?"
Jb 31:16 If I have *d* anything to the poor,
31:28 for I should have *d* God above.
Jer 5:12 They *d* the LORD,
Mt 26:70 He *d* it in front of everyone:
26:72 Again he *d* it with an oath:
Mk 14:68 But he *d* it:
14:70 Once again he *d* it.
Lk 22:34 you have three times *d* that you know me."
22:57 He *d* it, saying, "Woman, I do not know
Jn 18:25 He *d* it and said, "I am not!"
18:27 Peter *d* it again.
1Tm 5: 8 his immediate family, he has *d* the faith;
Rv 2:13 and have not *d* the faith you have in me,
3: 8 fast to my word and have not *d* my name.

DENIES (5)

Lv 5:22 he *d* the fact and swears falsely about it
Sir 14: 4 What he *d* himself he collects for others,
34:22 he sheds blood who *d* the laborer his wages.
1Jn 2:22 He who *d* that Jesus is the Christ.
2:23 who *d* the Son has no claim on the Father,

DENOUNCE (6)

Nm 23: 7 a curse for me on Jacob, come and *d* Israel."
23: 8 How *d* whom the LORD has not denounced?
Prv 24:24 men will curse him, people will *d* him;
Jer 20:10 *D*! let us denounce him!"
Lk 3:14 *D* no one falsely.

DENOUNCED (4)

Nm 23: 8 How denounce whom the LORD has not *d*?
2Mc 14:37 Jerusalem, was *d* to Nicanor as a patriot.
Sir 31:24 He who is miserly with food is *d* in public,
Acts 28:22 very well that this sect is *d* everywhere."

DENS (4)

Jb 37: 8 to cover and remain quietly in their *d*.
38:40 of her cubs, While they crouch in their *d*,
Ps(s) 104:22 rises, they withdraw and couch in their *d*.
Na 2:13 He filled his *d* with prey,

DENSE (9)

Gn 19:28 he saw *d* smoke over the land rising like
Ex 10:22 and there was *d* darkness throughout the
19: 9 him, "I am coming to you in a *d* cloud,
Dt 4:11 fire and was enveloped in a *d* black cloud.
5:22 from the midst of the fire and the *d* cloud.
Jb 34:22 so *d* that evildoers can hide in it.
Ez 17: 6 sprout and grow up a vine, *d* and low-lying,
19:11 Stately was her height amid the *d* foliage;
Lk 12: 1 *d* that they were treading on one another.

DENY (23)

Gn 23: 6 None of us would *d* you his burial ground
Ex 23: 6 "You shall not *d* one of your needy fellow
Jos 24:27 against you, should you wish to *d* your God."
Prv 30: 7 ask of you, *d* them not to me before I die:
30: 9 Lest, being full, I *d* you,
Eccl 2:10 Nothing that my eyes desired did I *d* them,
Dn 14:24 "you cannot *d* that this is a living god,
Mt 16:24 to come after me, he must *d* his very self,
26:34 crows tonight you will *d* me three times."
26:75 the cock crows, you will *d* me three times."
Mk 8:34 to come after me, he must *d* his very self,
14:30 crows twice, you will *d* me three times."
14:31 I have to die with you, I will not *d* you."
14:72 cock crows twice you will *d* me three times."
Lk 9:23 to be my follower must *d* his very self,
22:61 cock crows today you will *d* me three times."
Acts 4:16 We cannot *d* it.
1Cor 9:25 Athletes *d* themselves all sorts of things.
2Tm 2:12 But if we deny him he will *d* us.
2:13 remain faithful, for he cannot *d* himself.
Ti 1:16 but by their actions they *d* that he exists.
2Pt 2: 1 *d* the Master who acquired them for his own,
Jude 1: 4 God to sexual excess and *d* Jesus Christ,

DENYING (3)

Lv 5:21 by *d* his neighbor a deposit or a pledge
Is 59:13 Transgressing, and *d* the LORD,
1Jn 2:22 the antichrist, *d* the Father and the Son.

DEPART (42)

Gn 15:14 in the end they will *d* with great wealth.
26:29 toward you and have let you *d* in peace.
30:26 you, and my children, too, that I may *d*.
49:10 The scepter shall never *d* from Judah,
Ex 8:25 flies may *d* tomorrow from Pharaoh
11: 1 After that he will let you *d*.
11: 8 Only then will I *d*."
Lv 8:33 you are not to *d* from the entrance of the
Nm 9:21 when it rose in the morning, they would *d*.
9:22 Israelites remained in camp and did not *d*;
10: 6 shall the alarm be sounded for them to *d*.
17:10 to Moses and Aaron, *D* from this community,
Jgs 6:18 Do not *d* from here,
18:21 As they turned to *d*,
19: 8 On the fifth morning he rose early to *d*,
2Sm 12:10 the sword shall never *d* from your house,
2Chr 23: 8 those who were to *d* on the sabbath since
Tb 3:13 Bid me to *d* from the earth,
14: 8 "Now, as for you, my son, *d* from Nineveh;
1Mc 2:22 words of the king nor *d* from our religion
2Mc 2: 3 not to let the law *d* from their hearts.
Jb 16: 6 if I leave off, it will not *d* from me.
21:14 Yet they say to God, *D* from us,
22:17 These men said to God, *D* from us!"
Ps(s) 6: 9 *D* from me, all evildoers, for the LORD
39:14 I may find respite ere I *d* and be no more.
55:12 and fraud never *d* from its streets.
139:19 and the men of blood were to *d* from me!
Prv 17:13 for good, from his house evil will not *d*.
24:10 adversity, your strength will *d* from you.
Eccl 5:14 his mother's womb, so again shall he *d*,
Is 38:10 I said, "In the noontime of life I must *d*!
52:11 *D*, depart, come forth from there,
55:12 Yes, in joy you shall *d*,
Jer 9: 1 I might leave my people and *d* from them.
32:40 fear of me, that they may never *d* from me.
43:12 delouse the land of Egypt and *d* victorious.
Ez 8: 6 here, so that I must *d* from my sanctuary?
46: 8 enter and *d* by the vestibule of the gate.
Hos 5:14 It is I who rend the prey and *d*,
Rv 18: 4 *D* from her, my people, for fear

DEPARTED (53)

Gn 17:22 speaking with him, God *d* from Abraham.
18:33 The LORD *d* as soon as he had finished
26:31 farewell, and they *d* from him in peace.
28:10 Jacob *d* from Beer-sheba and proceeded
35:13 Then God *d* from him.
35:16 Then they *d* from Bethel;
42:26 their donkeys with the rations and *d*.
46: 5 So Jacob *d* from Beer-sheba,
Nm 9:20 and it was at his bidding that they *d*.
12: 9 was the LORD against them that when he *d*,
Jgs 11:38 So she *d* with her companions and mourned
Ru 1: 1 Bethlehem of Judah *d* with his wife
1: 8 kind to you as you were to the *d* and to me!
4: 5 raise up a family for the *d* on his estate."
4:10 so that the name of the *d* may not perish
1Sm 6: 6 that the Israelites were released and *d*?
15:34 Samuel *d* for Ramah,
16:14 The spirit of the LORD had *d* from Saul,
18:12 was with him, but had *d* from Saul himself.]
21: 1 Then David *d* on his way,
27: 2 David *d* with his six hundred men and went
2Sm 14: 2 who has been long in mourning for a *d* one.
17:23 not acted upon, he saddled his ass and *d*,
1Kgs 12: 5 When the people had *d*,
13:10 So he *d* by another road and did not go
2Kgs 1: 4 And with that, Elijah *d*.
1Chr 16:43 Then all the people *d*,
21: 4 Joab, who *d* and traversed all of Israel,
2Chr 10: 5 When the people had *d*,
21:20 He *d* unloved and was buried in the City of
24:25 After the Arameans had *d* from him,
Tb 14:12 *d* with his wife and children for Media,
Jdt 13: 4 When all had *d*,
1Mc 6:10 "Sleep has *d* from my eyes,
6:63 Then he *d* in haste and returned to Antioch,
2Mc 12:18 for he had already *d* from there without
Jb 23:12 the commands of his lips I have not *d*;
Sg 5: 6 but my lover had *d*,
Wis 11:12 at the remembrance of the ones who had *d*.
Sir 38:23 With the *d* dead,
Jer 31: 9 They *d* in tears,
Ez 44:10 But as for the Levites who *d* from me when
Dn 9: 5 *d* from your commandments and your laws.
14:14 they *d* the king set the food before Bel,
14:14 closed door with the king's ring, and *d*.
Hos 10: 5 over it, because the glory has *d* from it.
Mk 6: 1 He *d* from there and returned to his own
Lk 4:41 Demons *d* from many,
8:35 devils had *d* sitting at his feet dressed
8:38 the devils had *d* asked to come with him,
19:32 They *d* on their errand and found things
Acts 16:40 afterward they *d*.
19:12 were cured and evil spirits *d* from them.

DEPARTING (3)

2Mc 15:28 battle was over and they were joyfully *d*,
Dn 3:29 have sinned and transgressed by *d* from you,
Mt 26:24 The Son of Man is *d*,

DEPARTS (4)

Lv 16:17 the sanctuary to make atonement until he *d*.
Ps(s) 146: 4 When his spirit *d* he returns to his earth;
Bar 3:33 He who dismisses the light, and it *d*,
Mt 12:43 "When the unclean spirit *d* from a man,

DEPARTURE (19)

Ex 12:33 people on, to hasten their *d* from the land;
13: 4 This day of your *d* is in the month of Abib.
16: 1 month after their *d* from the land of Egypt.
19: 1 month after their *d* from the land of Egypt,
Nm 1: 1 the Israelites' *d* from the land of Egypt,
9: 1 following their *d* from the land of Egypt,
10:28 This was the order of *d* for the Israelites,
33:38 *d* of the Israelites from the land of Egypt,
Dt 2:14 our *d* from Kadesh-barnea and that crossing;
16: 3 the day of your *d* from the land of Egypt;
16: 6 on the anniversary of your *d* from Egypt,
Jos 5: 5 after the *d* from Egypt were circumcised.
1Kgs 6: 1 *d* of the Israelites from the land of Egypt,
8: 9 at their *d* from the land of Egypt.
2Chr 5:10 with the Israelites at their *d* from Egypt.
Wis 19: 2 *d* and had anxiously sent them on their way,
Ez 46:12 and the gate shall be closed after his *d*.
Acts 20:11 until his *d* at dawn.
2Pt 1:15 recall these things frequently after my *d*.

DEPEND (17)

Jdt 8:24 Their lives *d* on us,
9:11 nor does your power *d* upon stalwart men;
1Mc 3:19 war does not *d* upon the size of the army,
Ps(s) 71: 6 On you I *d* from birth;
Sir 37:13 for what have you that you can *d* on more?
Is 30:12 what is crooked and devious, and *d* on it,
31: 1 down to Egypt for help, who *d* upon horses;
Jn 4:42 "No longer does our faith *d* on your story.
Rom 4:13 inherit the world did not *d* on the law;
Gal 3:10 All who *d* on observance of the law,
3:12 But the law does not *d* on faith.
2Thes 3: 8 were among you, nor *d* on anyone for food.
1Tm 1:15 can *d* on this as worthy of full acceptance:
3: 1 You can *d* on this:
4: 9 *d* on this as worthy of complete acceptance.
2Tm 2:11 You can *d* on this:
Ti 3: 8 You can *d* on this to be true.

DEPENDABLE (7)

Ps(s) 116:11 I said in my alarm, "No man is *d*."
Prv 22:21 to give a *d* report to one who sends you?
Sir 7:22 if they are *d*, keep them.
33: 3 the law is *d* for him as a divine oracle.
Mt 25:21 Since you were *d* in a small matter I will
25:23 Since you were *d* in a small matter I will
Phil 4: 3 and I ask you, too, my *d* fellow worker,

DEPENDED (1)

1Sm 18: 1 as fond of David as if his life *d* on him;

DEPENDENCE (1)

Prv 25:19 unsteady foot is *d* on] a faithless man

DEPENDENCIES (16)

Nm 21:25 of the Amorites, in Heshbon and all its *d*.
21:32 Israel then captured it with its *d* and
32:42 *d* and called it Nobah after his own name.
2Chr 13:19 *d*, Jeshanah and its *d*, and Ephron and its *d*.
28:18 *d*, Timnah and its *d*, and Gimzo and its *d*

DEPENDENCIES (cont.)
Neh 11:25 Kiriath-arba and its *d,* in Dibon and its *d*
11:27 in Hazarshual, in Beer-sheba and its *d,*
11:28 in Ziklag, in Meconah and its *d,*
11:30 and its countryside, Azekah and its *d.*
11:31 in Geba, Michmash, Aija, Bethel and its *d,*
1Mc 11:34 districts, together with all their *d,*

DEPENDENTS (1)
2Sm 15:22 his men and all the *d* that were with him,

DEPENDING (1)
1Chr 28:15 *d* on the use to which each lampstand was

DEPENDS (5)
Ps(s) 10:14 On you the unfortunate man *d;*
Prv 16:33 lap, its decision *d* entirely on the LORD.
Jer 29: 7 the LORD, for upon its welfare *d* your own.
Acts 19:25 know that our prosperity *d* on this work.
Rom 4:16 Hence, all *d* on faith,

DEPICTS (1)
Sir 34: 5 what you already expect, the mind *d.*

DEPLOYED (2)
Gn 14:15 He and his party *d* against them at night,
Jgs 15: 9 and, from a camp in Judah, *d* against Lehi.

DEPOPULATING (1)
Ez 14:15 the land, *d* it so that it became a waste,

DEPORT (4)
1Kgs 8:46 their captors *d* them to a hostile land,
2Chr 6:36 that their captors *d* them to another land,
Jdt 2: 9 and I will *d* them as exiles to the very
1Tm 2: 9 the women must *d* themselves properly.

DEPORTED (16)
2Kgs 16: 9 He *d* its inhabitants to Kir and put Rezin
17: 6 Samaria, and *d* the Israelites to Assyria,
17:26 "The nations whom you *d* and settled in
17:27 "Send back one of the priests whom I *d,*
17:28 So one of the priests who had been *d* from
17:33 nations from among whom they had been *d.*
18:11 The king of Assyria then *d* the Israelites
24:14 He *d* all Jerusalem:
24:15 He *d* Jehoiachin to Babylon,
1Chr 5:26 king of Assyria, who *d* the Reubenites,
8: 6 who dwelt in Geba and were *d* to Manahath.
20: 3 He *d* the people of the city and set them
Tb 1: 3 people who had been *d* with me to Nineveh,
1:10 Now, after I had been *d* to Nineveh,
Est 2: 6 Nebuchadnezzar, king of Babylon, had *d.*
Jer 39: 9 *d* to Babylon the rest of the people left

DEPORTEES (1)
2Mc 2: 1 Jeremiah the prophet ordered the *d* to take

DEPORTING (1)
2Kgs 15:29 and Galilee, *d* the inhabitants to Assyria.

DEPOSE (2)
Jgs 9:29 I would *d* Abimelech.
1Mc 8:13 those whom they wished to *d* they deposed;

DEPOSED (6)
1Kgs 2:27 So Solomon *d* Abiathar from his office of
15:13 He also *d* his grandmother Maacah from her
2Chr 15:16 he *d* as queen mother because she had made
36: 3 The king of Egypt *d* him in Jerusalem and
1Mc 8:13 those whom they wished to depose they *d;*
Lk 1:52 He has *d* the mighty from their thrones and

DEPOSIT (15)
Lv 5:21 a *d* or a pledge or a stolen article,
5:23 retained by him or the *d* left with him
Nm 19: 9 *d* them in a clean place outside the camp.
Dt 14:28 that year and *d* them in community stores,
Ezr 5:15 and *d* them in the temple of Jerusalem,
7:19 you are to *d* before the God of Jerusalem.
Est 3: 9 silver talents for *d* in the royal treasury."
1Mc 9:35 to *d* with them their great quantity of
14:23 and to *d* a copy of their words in the
Sir 42: 7 Of numbering every *d,*
Zec 5:11 ready, they will *d* it there in its place."
Mt 25:27 more reason to *d* my money with the bankers,
27: 6 "It is not right to *d* this in the temple
2Tm 1:14 Guard the rich *d* of faith with the help of
Rv 8: 3 incense to *d* on the altar of gold in front

DEPOSITED (13)
Lv 4:12 *d* and there be burned up in a wood fire.
2Chr 31:12 things were *d* there in safekeeping.
34:14 that had been *d* in the house of the LORD,
34:17 bullion the metals *d* in the LORD's house
Ezr 6: 5 of Jerusalem and *d* in the house of God.
Tb 1:14 I also *d* several pouches containing a
4: 1 he had *d* with Gabael at Rages in Media,
4:20 I wish to inform you that I have *d* a great
5: 3 have already passed since I *d* that money!
1Mc 14:49 copies of it should be *d* in the treasury,
Lk 19:21 You withdraw what you never *d.*
19:22 was a hard man, withdrawing what I never *d,*
Jn 12: 6 used to help himself to what was *d* there.)

DEPOSITING (2)
1Mc 1:35 and *d* there the plunder they had collected
2Cor 1:22 has sealed us, thereby *d* the first payment,

DEPOSITS (4)
2Mc 3:15 given the law about *d* to keep the deposits
3:22 keep the *d* safe and secure for those
Jb 39:14 eggs on the ground and *d* them in the sand,

DEPRAVED (11)
Gn 6:12 since all mortals led *d* lives on earth,
Ex 32: 7 the land of Egypt, for they have become *d.*
Dt 9:12 have brought out of Egypt have become *d;*
Prv 11:20 *d* in heart are an abomination to the LORD,
Ez 21:30 as for you, *d* and wicked prince of Israel,
21:34 lay it on the necks of *d* and wicked men
23:11 her lust was more *d* than her sister's,
Rom 1:28 their own *d* sense to do what is unseemly.
Phil 2:15 in the midst of a twisted and *d* generation
Rv 21: 8 traitors to the faith, the *d* and murderers,
22:11 wicked ways, the *d* in their depravity!

DEPRAVITY (1)
Rv 22:11 their wicked ways, the depraved in their *d!*

DEPRECIATE (1)
Ru 4: 6 exercise my claim lest I *d* my own estate.

DEPRESSED (4)
Prv 15:15 Every day is miserable for the *d,*
17:22 body, but a *d* spirit dries up the bones.
31: 6 is perishing, and wine to the sorely *d;*
Sir 25:22 *D* mind, saddened face, broken heart

DEPRESSES (1)
Prv 12:25 Anxiety in a man's heart *d* it,

DEPRESSIONS (1)
Lv 14:37 greenish or reddish *d* which seem to go

DEPRIVE (12)
Ru 1:13 would you then wait and *d* yourselves of
1Kgs 11:11 I will *d* you of the kingdom and give it to
11:12 it is your son whom I will *d.*
Est E:12 he strove to *d* us of kingdom and of life;
Eccl 2:10 I deny them, nor did I *d* myself of any joy,
4: 8 whom do I toil and *d* myself of good things?"
Sir 14:14 *D* not yourself of present good things,
Is 5:23 bribes, and *d* the just man of his rights!
Hos 4:11 wine and new *d* my people of understanding.
Mal 2: 3 I will *d* you of the shoulder and I will
Mt 10:28 "Do not fear those who *d* the body of life
1Cor 7: 5 Do not *d* one another,

DEPRIVED (19)
Nm 9: 7 why should we be *d* of presenting the
1Kgs 14: 8 I *d* the house of David of the kingdom and
Tb 2:10 For four years I was *d* of eyesight,
2Mc 3:29 he lay speechless and *d* of all hope of aid,
13: 7 he was *d* even of decent burial.
13:11 when they were about to be *d* of their law,
14: 7 now that I am *d* of my ancestral dignity,
Ps(s) 89:45 You have *d* him of his luster and hurled
Eccl 6: 3 of his goods, or if he is *d* of burial,
Wis 18: 4 be *d* of light and imprisoned by darkness,
Sir 37:20 are rejected he will be *d* of all enjoyment.
51:24 How long will you be *d* of wisdom's food,
Lam 3:17 My soul is *d* of peace,
Dn 5:20 from his royal throne and *d* of his glory;
Jl 1:13 of your God is *d* of offering and libation.
Lk 10:42 portion and she shall not be *d* of it."
Acts 8:33 In his humiliation he was *d* of justice,
8:33 for he is *d* of his life on earth?"
Rom 3:23 have sinned and are *d* of the glory of God.

DEPRIVES (1)
Sir 34:22 slays his neighbor who *d* him of his living:

DEPRIVING (3)
2Mc 7: 9 fiend, you are *d* us of this present life,
Is 10: 2 *D* the needy of judgment and robbing my
2Cor 11:12 *d* at every turn those who look for a

DEPTH (9)
Ex 14:27 dawn the sea flowed back to its normal *d.*
1Kgs 7:31 a receptacle a cubit and a half in *d.*
2Chr 4: 2 round, ten cubits in diameter, five in *d,*
Prv 25: 3 the heavens in height, and the earth in *d,*
Mt 13: 5 sprouted at once since the soil had no *d,*
Mk 4: 5 immediately because the soil had no *d.*
Acts 27:28 a sounding and found a *d* of twenty fathoms;
Rom 8:39 height nor *d* nor any other creature,
Eph 3:18 length and height and *d* of Christ's love,

DEPTHS (44)
Ex 15: 5 they sank into the *d* like a stone.
Dt 32:22 shall rage to the *d* of the nether world,
Neh 9:11 Their pursuers you hurled into the *d,*
Tb 13: 2 he casts down to the *d* of the nether world,
Jdt 8:14 You cannot plumb the *d* of the human heart
Jb 38:16 sea, or walked about in the *d* of the abyss?
41:23 He makes the *d* boil like a pot;
Ps(s) 46: 3 and mountains plunge into the *d* of the sea.
63:10 they shall go into the *d* of the earth;
68:23 will fetch them back from the *d* of the sea,
69: 3 I have reached the watery *d;*
69:15 from my foes, and from the watery *d.*
71:20 *d* of the earth you will once more raise me.
77:17 the very *d* were troubled.
86:13 rescued me from the *d* of the nether world.
95: 4 In his hands are the *d* of the earth,
107:26 they sank to the *d;*
130: 1 Out of the *d* I cry to you, O LORD;
139:15 when I was fashioned in the *d* of the earth.
140:11 may he cast them into the *d,*
148: 7 the earth, you sea monsters and all *d;*
Prv 3:20 By his knowledge the *d* break open,
8:24 When there were no *d* I was brought forth,
9:18 the *d* of the nether world are her guests!
23:34 are like one now lying in the *d* of the sea,
Wis 10:19 and cast them up from the bottom of the *d.*
Sir 1: 3 earth's breadth, the *d* of the abyss:
21:10 that end in the *d* of the nether world.
22: 7 or like disturbing a man in the *d* of sleep;
42:18 He plumbs the *d* and penetrates the heart;
51: 6 soul was nearing the *d* of the nether world;
Is 44:23 shout, you *d* of the earth.
51:10 Who made the *d* of the sea into a way for
63:13 the *d* like horses in the open country,
Bar 5: 7 *d* and gorges be filled to level ground,
Ez 27:34 are wrecked in the sea, in the watery *d;*
Dn 3:55 the *d* from your throne upon the cherubim,
Hos 9: 9 They have sunk to the *d* of corruption,
Mi 7:19 cast into the *d* of the sea all our sins;
Zec 10:11 all the *d* of the Nile shall be dried up.
Mt 18: 6 around his neck, in the *d* of the sea.
21:10 the whole city was stirred to its *d,*
Mk 8:12 a sigh from the *d* of his spirit he said,
1Cor 2:11 lies at the *d* of God but the Spirit of God.

DEPUTATION (2)
Lk 7:10 When the *d* returned to the house,
19:14 a *d* after him with instructions to say,

DEPUTY (2)
Neh 11:24 *d* in all affairs that concerned the people.
2Mc 4:31 Andronicus, one of his nobles, as his *d.*

DERANGED (1)
Lam 3:11 He *d* my ways,

DERBE (4)
Acts 14: 6 and *D* and to the surrounding country,
14:20 The next day he left with Barnabas for *D.*
16: 1 Paul arrived first at *D;*
20: 4 Gaius from *D;*

DERIDE (6)
2Chr 32:17 for he had written letters to *d* the LORD,
Jb 11: 3 and shall you *d* and no one give rebuke?
22:19 and are gladdened, and the innocent *d* them:
Ps(s) 59: 9 you *d* all the nations.
Ez 22: 5 Those near you and those far off shall *d*
Lk 16:14 men, heard all this and began to *d* him.

DERIDED (2)
2Chr 30:10 as Zebulun, but they were *d* and scoffed at.
1Mc 9:26 them to Bacchides, who punished and *d* them.

DERIDES (1)
Ps(s) 2: 4 the LORD *d* them.

DERISION (10)
Neh 2:17 so that we may no longer be an object of *d!"*
3:36 Turn back their *d* upon their own heads and
5: 9 put an end to the *d* of our Gentile enemies?
2Mc 7:27 In *d* of the cruel tyrant,
Jb 30: 1 me in *d* who are younger in years than I;
Ps(s) 79: 4 the scorn and *d* of those around us.
Sir 42:11 an object of *d* in public gatherings.
Jer 19: 8 this city an object of amazement and *d.*
20: 8 has brought me *d* and reproach all the day.
Mi 6:16 you up to ruin, and your citizens to *d;*

DERIVE (4)
Ez 18:23 Do I indeed *d* any pleasure from the death
Hb 1: 7 he, from himself *d* his law and his majesty.

Rom 15: 4 that we might *d* hope from the lessons of
Phil 2:19 that I may *d* courage from learning how

DERIVED (1)

1Chr 2:53 the people of Zorah and the Eshtaolites *d*.

DESCEND (12)

Jgs 7: 9 LORD said to Gideon, "Go, *d* on the camp,
7:11 you will have the courage to *d* on the camp."
2Mc 8:27 let *d* on them the first dew of his mercy.
Jb 17:16 Will they *d* with me into the nether world?
Sg 4: 8 *D* from the top of Amana,
Is 45: 8 Let justice *d*,
Ez 26:20 you down with those who *d* into the pit,
Mt 3:16 of God *d* like a dove and hover over him.
10:13 is deserving, your blessing will *d* on it.
Jn 1:32 saw the Spirit *d* like a dove from the sky,
1:33 you see the Spirit *d* and rest on someone,
Gal 3:14 might *d* on the Gentiles in Christ Jesus,

DESCENDANT (33)

Ex 29:30 The *d* who succeeds him as priest and who
Lv 6:15 Aaron's *d* who succeeds him as the anointed
7:33 The *d* of Aaron who offers up the blood and
21:21 No *d* of Aaron the priest who has any such
22: 4 *d* of Aaron who is stricken with leprosy,
Nm 17: 5 no layman, no one who was not a *d* of Aaron,
26:29 Machirites, through Gilead, a *d* of Machir,
Dt 23: 3 any *d* of his even to the tenth generation.
1Chr 9:15 son of Mica, son of Zichri, a *d* of Asaph;
9:16 of Shemaiah, son of Galal, a *d* of Jeduthun;
9:19 son of Kore, son of Ebiasaph, a *d* of Korah,
20: 6 a giant, also a *d* of the Raphaim,
24: 3 Zadok, a *d* of Eleazar, and Ahimelech, a *d*
24:25 and Zechariah, a *d* of Isshiah.
26:10 Hosah, a *d* of Merari, had these sons:
27: 3 a *d* of Perez,
27: 8 was the commander Shamhuth, a *d* of Zerah,
27:11 was Sibbecai the Hushathite, a *d* of Zerah,
27:13 was Maharai from Netophah, a *d* of Zerah,
Neh 11:24 Pethahiah, son of Meshezabel, a *d* of Zerah,
1Mc 14:29 son of the priest Mattathias, *d* of Joarib,
Wis 7: 1 and a *d* of the first man formed on earth.
Jer 22:30 No *d* of his shall achieve a seat on the
35:19 shall there fail to be a *d* of Jonadab,
36:30 *d* of his shall succeed to David's throne;
Dn 11: 7 a *d* of her line shall succeed to his rank,
Na 1:14 no *d* shall come to bear your name;
Lk 1: 5 his wife was a *d* of Aaron named Elizabeth.
Gal 3:16 promises spoken to Abraham and to his *d*."
3:16 it applied only to one, "and to your *d*";
3:19 be valid only until that *d* or offspring came
2Tm 2: 8 Remember that Jesus Christ, a *d* of David,

DESCENDANTS (341)

Gn 5: 1 This is the record of the *d* of Adam.
6: 9 These are the *d* of Noah.
9: 9 my covenant with you and your *d* after you
10: 1 These are the *d* of Noah's sons,
10: 2 The *d* of Japheth:
10: 3 The *d* of Gomer:
10: 4 The *d* of Javan:
10: 5 These are the *d* of Japheth,
10: 6 The *d* of Ham:
10: 7 The *d* of Cush:
10: 7 The *d* of Raamah:
10:20 These are the *d* of Ham,
10:22 The *d* of Shem:
10:23 The *d* of Aram:
10:29 All these were *d* of Joktan.
10:31 These are the *d* of Shem,
11:10 This is the record of the *d* of Shem.
11:27 This is the record of the *d* of Terah.
12: 7 said, "To your *d* I will give this land."
13:15 see I will give to you and your *d* forever.
13:16 make your *d* like the dust of the earth;
13:16 of the earth, your *d* too might be counted.
15: 5 Just so," he added, "shall your *d* be."
15:13 *d* shall be aliens in a land not their own,
15:18 "To your *d* I give this land,
16:10 I will make your *d* so numerous,"
17: 7 covenant with you and your *d* after you
17: 7 your God and the God of your *d* after you.
17: 8 I will give to you and to your *d* after you
17: 9 you and your *d* after you must keep my
17:10 and your *d* after you that you must keep:
17:19 be his God and the God of his *d* after him.
21:12 through Isaac that *d* shall bear your name.
22:17 make your *d* as countless as the stars
22:17 your *d* shall take possession of the gates
22:18 and in your *d* all the nations of the earth
24: 7 to me, 'I will give this land to your *d*—
24:60 And may your *d* gain possession of the
25: 3 The *d* of Dedan were the Asshurim,
25: 4 The *d* of Midian were Ephah,
25: 4 All of these were *d* of Keturah.
25:12 These are the *d* of Abraham's son Ishmael,
26: 3 you and your *d* I will give all these lands,
26: 4 I will make your *d* as numerous as the
26: 4 and in your *d* all the nations of the earth
26:24 your *d* for the sake of my servant Abraham."
28: 4 and your *d* the blessing he gave to Abraham,
28:13 are lying I will give to you and your *d*.
28:14 In you and your *d* all the nations of the
32:13 will make your *d* like the sands of the sea,
33:19 pieces of bullion from the *d* of Hamor,
35:12 to your *d* after you will I give this land."
36: 1 These are the *d* of Esau [that is, Edom].
36: 9 These are the *d* of Esau,
36:12 These were the *d* of Esau's wife Adah.
36:13 These were the *d* of Esau's wife Basemath.
36:14 The *d* of Esau's wife Oholibamah
36:15 The following are the clans of Esau's *d*.
36:15 The *d* of Eliphaz, Esau's first-born:
36:17 The *d* of Esau's son Reuel:
36:18 The *d* of Esau's wife Oholibamah:
36:19 Such are the *d* of Esau [that is,
36:20 The following are the *d* of Seir the Horite,
36:22 Lotan's *d* were Hori and Hemam,
36:23 Shobal's *d* were Alvan,
36:24 Zibeon's *d* were Aiah and Anah.
36:25 The *d* of Anah were Dishon and Oholibamah,
36:26 The *d* of Dishon were Hemdan,
36:27 The *d* of Ezer were Bilhan,
36:28 The *d* of Dishan were Uz and Aran.
38: 9 that the *d* would not be counted as his;
46: 6 Thus Jacob and all his *d* migrated to Egypt.
46: 7 all his *d*— he took with him to Egypt,
46: 8 names of the Israelites, Jacob and his *d*,
46:18 These were the *d* of Zilpah,
46:26 his direct *d*, not counting the wives
48: 4 your *d* after you as a permanent possession.'
48:11 God has allowed me to see your *d* as well!"
48:19 his *d* shall become a multitude of nations."
Ex 1: 5 of the direct *d* of Jacob was seventy.
12:24 ordinance for yourselves and your *d*.
16:32 Keep an omerful of manna for your *d*,
16:33 before the LORD in safekeeping for your *d*."
28:43 perpetual ordinance for him and for his *d*.
29:29 of Aaron shall be passed down to his *d*,
30:21 him and his *d* throughout their generations."
32:13 your *d* as numerous as the stars in the sky;
32:13 give your *d* as their perpetual heritage.'"
33: 1 Isaac and Jacob I would give to their *d*.
Lv 3:17 for your *d* wherever they may dwell.
6:11 All the male *d* of Aaron may partake of it
13: 2 or to one of the priests among his *d*,
17: 7 everlasting ordinance for them and their *d*.
21:17 None of your *d*, of whatever generation,
22: 3 you, or of your *d* in any future generation,
23:14 for you and your *d* wherever you dwell.
23:31 for you and your *d* wherever you dwell:
23:41 By perpetual statute for you and your *d*
23:43 in booths, that your *d* may realize that,
24: 3 by a perpetual statute for you and your *d*,
25:30 in perpetuity to the purchaser and his *d*;
25:47 or to one of the *d* of an immigrant family,
Nm 1:10 son of Pedahzur, for the *d* of Joseph;
1:20 Of the *d* of Reuben,
1:22 Of the *d* of Simeon, registered by lineage
1:24 Of the *d* of Gad,
1:26 Of the *d* of Judah,
1:28 Of the *d* of Issachar,
1:30 Of the *d* of Zebulun,
1:32 Of the *d* of Joseph
1:32 Of the *d* of Ephraim,
1:34 Of the *d* of Manasseh,
1:36 Of the *d* of Benjamin,
1:38 Of the *d* of Dan,
1:40 Of the *d* of Asher,
1:42 Of the *d* of Naphtali,
3: 1 The following were the *d* of Aaron and
3:10 But only Aaron and his *d* shall you appoint
3:18 The *d* of Gershon, by clans,
3:19 The *d* of Kohath,
3:20 The *d* of Merari,
9:10 of your *d* is unclean because of a corpse,
10: 8 by perpetual statute for you and your *d*.
13:22 Sheshai and Talmai, *d* of the Anakim,
13:28 Besides, we saw *d* of the Anakim there.
14:24 has just been, and his *d* shall possess it.
15:15 alien, a perpetual rule for all your *d*.
15:38 they and their *d* must put tassels on
16:10 you and your kinsmen, the *d* of Levi,
18:19 before the LORD, for you and for your *d*."
23:10 the just, may my *d* be as many as theirs!
25:13 for him and for his *d* after him the pledge
26: 9 and the *d* of Eliab were Dathan and Abiram
26:11 The *d* of Korah, however, did not die out
26:37 These were the *d* of Joseph by clans.
26:40 The *d* of Bela were Arad and Naaman:
26:58 Among the *d* of Kohath was Amram,
32:39 The *d* of Machir, son of Manasseh,
34:24 son of Shiphtan, for the *d* of Joseph;
35:29 shall be norms for you and all your *d*,
36: 1 houses in the clan of *d* of Gilead,
36:12 side within the clans of the *d* of Manasseh,
Dt 1: 8 Jacob, I would give to them and their *d*.'
2: 4 territory of your kinsmen, the *d* of Esau,
2: 8 and Seir, where our kinsmen, the *d* of Esau,
2: 9 have given Ar to the *d* of lot as their own.
2:12 the *d* of Esau dispossessed them,
2:19 have given it to the *d* of Lot as their own.
2:22 He had done the same for the *d* of Esau,
2:22 so that the *d* of Esau have taken their
2:29 as the *d* of Esau who dwell in Seir and the
4:37 For love of your fathers he chose their *d*
5:29 they and their *d* would prosper forever.
10:15 to them as to choose you, their *d*,
11: 9 fathers he would give to them and their *d*,
12:28 that you and your *d* may always prosper for
17:20 his *d* will enjoy a long reign in Israel.
21: 5 The priests, the *d* of Levi,
23: 4 *d* of theirs even to the tenth generation,
28:46 your *d* as a sign and a wonder for all time.
28:59 and your *d* with severe and constant blows,
29:21 your own *d* who will rise up after you,
29:28 been revealed concern us and our *d* forever,
30: 6 your hearts and the hearts of your *d*,
30:19 life, then, that you and your *d* may live,
31:21 their *d* will not have forgotten to recite,
32: 8 when he parceled out the *d* of Adam,
34: 4 and Jacob that I would give to their *d*.
Jos 13:31 of Og in Bashan, fell to the *d* of Machir,
14: 4 tribes, the *d* of Joseph formed two tribes,
14: 9 your heritage and that of your *d* forever,
15:14 from there the three Anakim, the *d* of Anak:
17: 2 was now made to the other *d* of Manasseh,
17: 6 since these female *d* of Manasseh received
17:14 The *d* of Joseph said to Joshua,
18:11 between the *d* of Judah and those of Joseph.
21: 4 the *d* of Aaron the priest obtained
21:10 and assigned them to the *d* of Aaron in the
21:13 Thus to the *d* of Aaron the priest were
21:19 lands belonged to the priestly *d* of Aaron,
22:25 You *d* of Reuben and Gad have no share in
22:27 for you on behalf of ourselves and our *d*,
22:28 they should speak thus to us or to our *d*,
24: 3 I made his *d* numerous, and gave him Isaac.
24:32 This was a heritage of the *d* of Joseph.
Jgs 1:16 The *d* of the Kenite,
4:11 from his own people, the *d* of Hobab,
8:30 Now Gideon had seventy sons, his direct *d*,
18:30 and his *d* were priests for the tribe of
Ru 4:18 These are the *d* of Perez:
1Sm 6:19 The *d* of Jeconiah did not join in the
24:22 LORD that you will not destroy my *d*
2Sm 21: 6 seven men from among his *d* be given to us,
1Kgs 2:33 Joab and his *d* shall be responsible
2:33 of the LORD forever for David, and his *d*,
8:25 provided only that your *d* look to their
9: 6 if you and your *d* ever withdraw from me,
9:20 remained in the land, *d* of the Amorites,
2Kgs 5:27 shall cling to you and your *d* forever."
10: 1 Ahab had seventy *d* in Samaria.
10: 1 to the guardians of Ahab's *d* in Samaria.
15:12 "Your *d* to the fourth generation shall
17:34 which the LORD enjoined on the *d* of Jacob,
20:18 Some of your own bodily *d* shall be taken
1Chr 1: 5 The *d* of Japheth were Gomer,
1: 6 The *d* of Gomer were Ashkenaz,
1: 7 The *d* of Javan were Elishah,
1: 8 The *d* of Ham were Cush,
1: 9 The *d* of Cush were Seba,
1: 9 The *d* of Raama were Sheba and Dedan.
1:17 The *d* of Shem were Elam,
1:17 The *d* of Aram were Uz,
1:29 These were their *d*:
1:31 These were the *d* of Ishmael.
1:32 The *d* of Keturah, Abraham's concubine:
1:33 The *d* of Midian were Ephah,
1:33 All these were the *d* of Keturah.
1:38 The *d* of Seir were Lotan,
2:33 These were the *d* of Jerahmeel.
2:42 The *d* of Caleb, the brother of Jerahmeel:
2:50 These were *d* of Caleb,
2:54 The *d* of Salma were Bethlehem,
4: 1 The *d* of Judah were:
4: 3 These were the *d* of Hareph,
4: 4 These were the *d* of Hur,
4: 6 These were the *d* of Naarah.
4:21 The *d* of Shelah, son of Judah, were:
4:26 The *d* of Mishma were his son Hammuel,
5: 7 in the family records according to their *d*,
6: 7 The *d* of Kohath were:
6:14 The *d* of Merari were Mahli,
6:18 are the following, together with their *d*.
6:34 it was Aaron and his *d* who burnt the
6:35 These were the *d* of Aaron:
6:39 To the *d* of Aaron who belonged to clan of
6:42 There were assigned to the *d* of Aaron:
7:11 All these were *d* of Jediael,
7:13 These were *d* of Bilhah.
7:17 These were the *d* of Gilead,
7:29 In these dwelt the *d* of Joseph,
7:40 All these were *d* of Asher,
8:40 All these were the *d* of Benjamin.
9: 4 Imri, son of Bani, one of the *d* of Perez,
9:14 son of Hashabiah, one of the *d* of Merari;
16:13 judgments he has uttered, You *d* of Israel,
20: 4 slew Sippai, one of the *d* of the Raphaim,
20: 8 These were the *d* of the Raphaim of Gath
24: 1 *d* of Aaron also were divided into classes.
24: 4 But since the *d* of Eleazar were found to
24:20 there were Shubael, of the *d* of Amram,
24:20 Amram, and Jehdeiah, of the *d* of Shubael;
24:21 Isshiah, the chief, of the *d* of Rehabiah;

DESCENDANTS (cont.)

24:22 and Jahath of the *d* of Shelomoth
24:23 The *d* of Hebron were Jeriah,
24:24 *d* of Uzziel were Micah; Shamir, of the *d*
24:26 *d* of Merari were Mahli, Mushi, and the *d*
24:27 The *d* of Merari through his son Uzziah:
24:28 *D* of Mahli were Eleazar,
24:29 no sons, and Jerahmeel, of the *d* of Kish.
24:30 The *d* of Mushi were Mahli,
24:30 These were the *d* of the Levites according
24:31 manner as their relatives, the *d* of Aaron,
25: 1 cult set apart for service the *d* of Asaph,
26:19 of the gatekeepers, *d* of Kore and Merari.
26:21 Among the *d* of Ladan the Gershonite,
26:21 the family heads were *d* of Jehiel:
26:21 the *d* of Jehiel,
2Chr 6:16 provided only that your *d* look to their
8: 8 that is, their *d* remaining in the land,
20: 7 and gave it forever to the *d* of Abraham,
29:12 Joel, son of Azariah, *d* of the Kohathites;
32:33 approach to the tombs of the *d* of David.
Ezr 2:55 *D* of the slaves of Solomon:
2:58 The total of the temple slaves and the *d*
Neh 7:57 *D* of the slaves of Solomon:
7:60 The total of the temple slaves and the *d*
11: 3 slaves, and the *d* of the slaves of Solomon,
Jdt 5: 6 "These people are *d* of the Chaldeans.
8:32 to generation among the *d* of our race.
Est 9:27 and took upon themselves, their *d*,
9:28 the Jews, nor into oblivion among their *d*.
1Mc 5: 2 the *d* of Jacob who were among them,
2Mc 1:20 sent the *d* of the priests who had hidden
7:17 great power will torment you and your *d*."
Jb 5:25 You shall know that your *d* are many,
Ps(s) 22:24 all you *d* of Jacob,
22:24 revere him, all you *d* of Israel!
22:31 my *d* shall serve him.
25:13 in prosperity, and his *d* inherit the land.
37:25 just man forsaken nor his *d* begging bread.
37:26 and lends, and his *d* shall be blessed.
69:37 the *d* of his servants shall inherit it,
105: 6 he has uttered, You *d* of Abraham,
106:27 To scatter their *d* among the nations,
Sir 4:16 his *d* too will inherit her.
41: 6 children, and reproach abides with their *d*.
44:11 families, their heritage with their *d*;
44:21 that in his *d* the nations would be blessed,
45:17 people, and the ritual to the *d* of Israel.
45:21 LORD are his food, a gift to him and his *d*.
45:24 So that he and his *d* should possess the
45:25 but the heritage of Aaron is for all his *d*.
47:20 upon your marriage, Wrath upon your *d*,
Is 22:24 *d* and offspring,
39: 7 Some of your own bodily *d* shall be taken
43: 5 from the east I will bring back your *d*,
44: 3 offspring, and my blessing upon your *d*.
45:19 And I have not said to the *d* of Jacob,
45:25 and the glory of all the *d* of Israel."
48:19 Your *d* would be like the sand,
53:10 for sin, he shall see his *d* in a long life,
54: 3 Your *d* shall dispossess the nations and
61: 9 *d* shall be renowned among the nations,
Jer 22:28 Why are he and his *d* cast out,
23: 8 who brought the *d* of the house of Israel
30:10 deliver you from the far-off land, your *d*,
33:22 I will multiply the *d* of my servant David
33:26 the *d* of Jacob and of my servant David,
33:26 from his *d* rulers for the race of Abraham,
36:31 *d* and his ministers for their wickedness;
46:27 deliver you from the far-off land, your *d*,
Bar 2:15 and that Israel and his *d* bear your name.
Ez 20: 5 I swore to the *d* of the house of Jacob;
Dn 11: 4 his *d* or in keeping with his mighty rule,
Lk 1:55 promised Abraham and his *d* forever."
Jn 8:33 "We are *d* of Abraham," was their answer.
Acts 2:30 one of his *d* would sit upon his throne.
7: 5 to him and his *d* after him as a possession
13:23 has brought forth from this man's *d* Jesus,
Rom 4:13 promise made to Abraham and his *d*
4:16 promise holds true for all Abraham's *d*,
4:18 "Numerous as this shall your *d* be
9: 7 nor are all Abraham's *d* his children,
9: 7 "Through Isaac shall your *d* be called."
9: 8 of the promise who are to be considered *d*.
Gal 3:16 Scripture does not say "and to your *d*,"
3:29 belong to Christ you are the *d* of Abraham,
Heb 7: 5 even though all of them are *d* of Abraham;
11:12 *d* as numerous as the stars in the the sky
11:18 "Through Isaac shall your *d* be called."

DESCENDED (29)

Gn 36:16 they are *d* from Adah.
36:17 they are *d* from Esau's wife Basemath.
36:21 they are the Horite clans *d* from Seir,
Nm 26: 8 From Pallu *d* Eliab.
Jos 13:31 Manasseh, for half the clans *d* from Machir.
15:10 thence it *d* to Beth-shemesh,
16: 3 and *d* westward to the border of the
16: 7 from there it *d* to Ataroth and Naarah,
2Kgs 20:11 *d* on the staircase to the terrace of Ahaz.
1Chr 10: 3 Saul, the whole fury of the battle *d* upon Saul.
24: 5 *d* both from Eleazar and from Ithamar.
2Chr 32:25 *d* upon him and upon Judah and Jerusalem.
Tb 8: 6 and from these two the human race *d*.
Jdt 13:12 they quickly *d* to their city gate and
1Mc 12:21 both nations *d* from Abraham.
2Mc 2:10 *d* from the sky and consumed the sacrifices,
Wis 10: 6 when he fled as fire *d* upon Pentapolis
Mt 28: 2 as the angel of the Lord *d* from heaven.
Lk 1:65 Fear *d* on all in the neighborhood;
3:22 *d* on him in visible form like a dove.
8:23 A windstorm *d* on the lake,
19: 6 He quickly *d*,
Acts 10:44 Holy Spirit *d* upon all who were listening
Rom 1: 3 who was *d* from David according to the
11: 1 I myself am an Israelite, *d* from Abraham,
Eph 4: 9 *d* into the lower regions of the earth?
4:10 He who *d* is the very one who ascended high
1Thes 2:16 but the wrath has *d* upon them at last.
Jude 1:14 was of the seventh generation *d* from Adam,

DESCENDING (6)

Nm 34:11 to Ar-Baal, east of Ain, and *d* further,
Jdt 2:27 *D* to the plain of Damascus at the time of
Is 30:13 This guilt of yours shall be like a *d* rift
Mk 1:10 in two and the Spirit *d* on him like a dove.
Jn 1:51 of God ascending and *d* on the Son of Man."
Jas 1:17 *d* from the Father of the heavenly

DESCENDS (3)

Is 30:30 and let it be seen how his arm *d* In raging
Mi 1: 3 *d* and treads upon the heights of the earth.
Hb 3:10 A torrent of rain *d*;

DESCENT (12)

Jos 7: 5 ranks, and defeated them finally on the *d*,
8:14 in battle at the *d* toward the Arabah,
10:11 before Israel along the *d* from Beth-horon,
2Kgs 25:25 Nethaniah, son of Elishama, of royal *d*,
Ezr 2:59 houses and their *d* were Israelite:
Neh 7:61 houses and their *d* were Israelite:
9: 2 Those of Israelite *d* separated themselves
1Mc 3:24 down the *d* of Beth-horon into the plain.
Jer 41: 1 of Nethaniah, son of Elishama, of royal *d*,
48: 5 On the *d* to Horonaim the cry of
Lk 19:37 on his approach to the *d* from Mount Olivet,
Heb 7:16 in a commandment concerning physical *d*,

DESCERNMENT (1)

Ps(s) 119:100 I have more *d* than the elders,

DESCRIBE (7)

Jos 18: 4 they shall *d* for purposes of inheritance.
Sir 17: 8 That they may *d* the wonders of his deeds
42:15 what I have seen, I will *d*.
43:33 For who can see him and *d* him?
Ez 43:10 *d* the temple to the house of Israel [that
Mt 11:16 comparison can I use to *d* this breed?
Jude 1: 4 destined for the condemnation I shall *d*.

DESCRIBED (8)

Jb 17: 5 My lot is *d* as evil,
Wis 17: 1 are your judgments, and hardly to be *d*;
Sir 49: 8 *d* the different creatures of the chariot;
Acts 15:12 Paul as the two *d* all the signs and wonders
21:19 and then *d* in detail all that God had
Eph 3: 3 plan as I have briefly *d* it was revealed.
Rv 22:18 visit him with all the plagues *d* herein!
22:19 the tree of life and the holy city *d* here!

DESCRIBING (1)

Sir 18: 2 Whom has he made equal to *d* his works,

DESCRIPTION (3)

Jos 18: 6 to me the *d* of the land in seven sections.
18: 8 them to survey the land, prepare a *d* of it,
Jgs 7:15 heard the *d* and explanation of the dream,

DESCRY (1)

Is 30:10 prophets, "Do not *d* for us what is right;

DESECRATE (7)

Ex 20:25 for by putting a tool to it you *d* it.
Nm 35:33 You shall not *d* the land where you live.
2Sm 1:14 forth your hand to *d* the LORD's anointed?"
1Mc 1:46 *d* the sanctuary and the sacred ministers,
Ez 23:39 idols, they entered my sanctuary to *d* it.
24:21 I will now *d* my sanctuary,
Acts 24: 6 He even tried to *d* our temple,

DESECRATED (9)

Ezr 9: 2 and thus they have *d* the holy race with
1Mc 4:38 found the sanctuary desolate, the altar *d*,
4:44 the altar of holocausts that had been *d*.
Ez 20:13 My sabbaths, too, they *d* grievously.
20:16 despised my ordinances and *d* my sabbaths.
20:21 who observe them, and my sabbaths they *d*.
20:24 but despised my statutes and *d* my sabbaths,
22: 8 have spurned, and my sabbaths you have *d*.
23:38 defiled my sanctuary and *d* my sabbaths.

DESECRATES (2)

Ex 31:14 Whoever *d* it shall be put to death.
Nm 35:33 Since bloodshed *d* the land,

DESECRATING (1)

Ps(s) 106:38 idols of Canaan, *d* the land with bloodshed;

DESECRATION (1)

Ez 25: 3 out your joy over the *d* of my sanctuary,

DESERT (325)

Gn 36:24 (He is the Anah who found water in the *d*
37:22 throw him into that cistern there in the *d*;
Ex 3: 1 Leading the flock across the *d*,
3:18 to go a three days' journey in the *d*,
4:27 to Aaron, "Go into the *d* to meet Moses."
5: 1 they may celebrate a feast to me in the *d*."
5: 3 Let us go a three days' journey in the *d*,
7:16 Let my people go to worship me in the *d*.
8:23 in the *d* to offer sacrifice to the LORD,
8:24 sacrifice to the LORD your God, in the *d*,
13:18 toward the Red Sea by way of the *d* road.
13:20 camped at Etham near the edge of the *d*.
14: 3 The *d* has closed in on them.'
14:11 had to bring us out here to die in the *d*?
14:12 of the Egyptians than to die in the *d*."
15:22 Sea, and they marched out to the *d* of Shur.
15:22 days through the *d* without finding water,
16: 1 community came into the *d* of Sin,
16: 2 Here in the *d* the whole Israelite
16: 3 But you had to lead us into this *d* to make
16:10 community, they turned toward the *d*,
16:14 there on the surface of the *d* were fine
16:32 see what food I gave you to eat in the *d*
17: 1 From the *d* of Sin the whole Israelite
18: 5 Jethro came to him in the *d* where he was
19: 1 day, the Israelites came to the *d* of Sinai.
19: 2 journey from Rephidim to the *d* of Sinai,
23: 5 under its burden, by no means *d* him;
23:31 Philistines, and from the *d* to the River;
Lv 11:18 the screech owl, the barn owl, the *d* owl,
16:10 by sending it off to Azazel in the *d*.
16:21 have it led into the *d* by an attendant.
16:22 region, it must be sent away into the *d*.
Nm 1: 1 in the meeting tent in the *d* of Sinai:
3: 4 fire before the LORD in the *d* of Sinai,
3:14 The LORD said to Moses in the *d* of Sinai,
9: 1 the LORD said to Moses in the *d* of Sinai,
9: 5 celebrating the Passover in the *d* of Sinai
10:12 moved on from the *d* of Sinai by stages,
10:12 the cloud came to rest in the *d* of Paran.
10:31 you know where we can camp in the *d*,
12:16 Hazeroth and encamped in the *d* of Paran.
13: 3 Moses dispatched them from the *d* of Paran,
13:21 from the *d* of Zin as far as where Rehob
13:26 the Israelites in the *d* of Paran at Kadesh,
14: 2 Egypt, or that here in the *d* we were dead!
14:16 that is why he slaughtered them in the *d*.'
14:22 the signs I worked in Egypt and in the *d*,
14:25 and set out in the *d* on the Red Sea road."
14:29 Here in the *d* shall your dead bodies fall.
14:32 you, your bodies shall fall here in the *d*,
14:33 till the last of you lies dead in the *d*.
14:35 in the *d* they shall die to the last man."
15:32 While the Israelites were in the *d*,
16:13 milk and honey, to make us perish in the *d*,
20: 1 arrived in the *d* of Zin in the first month,
20: 4 *d* where we and our livestock are dying?
21: 5 brought us up from Egypt to die in this *d*,
21:11 in the *d* fronting Moab on the east.
21:13 in the *d* that extends from the territory
21:23 and advanced into the *d* against Israel.
24: 1 omens, but turned his gaze toward the *d*.
26:64 of the Israelites taken in the *d* of Sinai.
26:65 them that they would surely die in the *d*,
27: 3 "Our father died in the *d*.
27:14 in the *d* of Zin you both rebelled against
27:14 water of Meribah of Kadesh in the *d* of Zin.]
32:13 LORD made them wander in the *d* forty years,
32:15 will make them stay still longer in the *d*,
33: 6 camped at Etham near the edge of the *d*.
33: 8 crossed over through the sea into the *d*,
33: 8 a three days' journey in the *d* of Etham,
33:11 the Red Sea, they camped in the *d* of Sin.
33:12 Setting out from the *d* of Sin,
33:15 Rephidim, they camped in the *d* of Sinai.
33:16 Setting out from the *d* of Sinai,
34: 3 at the *d* of Zin along the border of Edom;
Dt 1: 1 to all Israel beyond the Jordan [in the *d*,
1:19 Horeb and journeyed through the whole *d*,
1:31 very eyes in Egypt, as well as in the *d*,
1:40 and proceed into the *d* on the Red Sea road.'
2: 1 and proceed into the *d* on the Red Sea road,
2: 7 about your journey through this vast *d*.
2: 8 and we went on toward the *d* of Moab.
2:26 messengers from the *d* of Kedemoth to Sihon,
4:43 Bezer in the *d*,
8: 2 has directed all your journeying in the *d*,
8:15 *d* with its saraph serpents and scorpions,
8:16 rock and fed you in the *d* with manna,
9: 7 you angered the LORD, your God, in the *d*.

9:28 he brought them out to slay them in the *d.*'
11: 5 in the *d* until you arrived in this place;
11:24 from the *d* and from Lebanon,
14:17 owl, the screech owl, the ibis, the *d* owl,
29: 4 'I led you for forty years in the *d.*
32:10 in a wilderness, a wasteland of howling *d.*
32:51 waters of Meribath-kadesh in the *d* of Zin
Jos 1: 4 from the *d* and from Lebanon east to the
5: 4 *d* during the journey after they left Egypt.
5: 5 none of those born in the *d* during the
5: 6 had wandered forty years in the *d,*
8:15 fled in seeming defeat toward the *d,*
8:20 toward the *d* now turned on their pursuers;
8:24 Israelites into the *d* were slain by the sword
12: 8 foothills, the Arabah, the slopes, the *d,*
14:10 while Israel was journeying through the *d,*
15: 1 of Edom, the *d* of Zin in the Negeb.
15:61 In the *d:* Beth-araboh
16: 1 to the waters of Jericho east of the *d;*
18:12 till it reached the *d* of Beth-aven.
24: 7 to Egypt, and dwelt a long time in the *d,*
Jgs 1:16 to the *d* at Arad [which is in the Negeb].
8: 7 in with the thorns and briers of the *d.*"
8:16 the city, and thorns and briers of the *d,*
11:16 the *d* to the Red Sea and came to Kadesh.
11:18 Then they went through the *d,*
11:22 to the Jabbok, from the *d* to the Jordan.
20:42 men of Israel in the direction of the *d,*
20:45 and fled through the *d* to the rock Rimmon.
20:47 fled through the *d* reached the rock Rimmon,
1Sm 13:18 the Valley of the Hyenas toward the *d.*
17:28 you left those sheep in the *d* meanwhile?
23:14 David now lived in the refuges in the *d,*
23:24 David and his men were in the *d* below Maon,
23:25 went down to the gorge in the *d* below Maon.
23:25 and pursued David into the *d* below Maon.
24: 2 told that David was in the *d* near Engedi.
25: 1 Then David went down to the *d* of Maon.
25: 4 in the *d* that Nabal was shearing his flock,
25:14 messengers from the *d* to greet our master,
25:21 in the *d* so that he missed nothing.
26: 2 So Saul went off down to the *d* of Ziph
26: 2 to search for David in the *d* of Ziph.
26: 3 *d,* saw that Saul had come into the desert
2Sm 2:24 east of the valley toward the *d* near Geba.
15:23 way of the Mount of Olives, toward the *d.*
15:28 the *d* until I receive information from you."
16: 2 for those to drink who are weary in the *d.*"
17:16 to spend the night at the fords near the *d,*
17:29 been hungry and tired and thirsty in the *d.*"
1Kgs 2:34 he was buried in his house in the *d.*
9:18 Baalath, Tamar in the *d* of Judah,
19: 4 there and went a day's journey into the *d,*
19:15 take the road back to the *d* near Damascus,"
2Kgs 3: 8 upon the route through the *d* of Edom.
7: 4 Come, let us *d* to the camp of the Arameans.
25: 5 and overtook him in the *d* near Jericho,
1Chr 5: 9 *d* which extends from the Euphrates River,
6:63 Bezer in the *d* with its pasture lands,
12:20 of our heads he will *d* to his master Saul."
21:29 the LORD, which Moses had built in the *d,*
2Chr 1: 3 tent of God, made in the *d* by Moses,
8: 4 in the *d* region and all the supply cities,
20:24 of the *d* and looked toward the throng,
24: 9 in the *d* should be brought to the LORD.
26:10 towers in the *d* and dug numerous cisterns,
34:33 his lifetime they did not *d* the LORD,
Neh 9:19 mercy you did not forsake them in the *d.*
9:21 Forty years in the *d* you sustained them:
Jdt 2:23 of the *d* toward the south of Chaldea.
5:14 drove out all the inhabitants of the *d;*
1Mc 2:29 custom went out into the *d* to settle there,
2:31 had gone out to the hiding places in the *d.*
3:45 Jerusalem was uninhabited, like a *d;*
5:24 and marched for three days through the *d.*
5:28 his army, marched across the *d* to Bozrah,
9:33 and they fled to the *d* of Tekoa and camped
9:62 companions withdrew to Bethbasi in the *d;*
13:21 urging him to come to them by way of the *d,*
Jb 1:19 *d* and smote the four corners of the house.
6:18 they go into the *d* and perish.
24: 5 Like wild asses in the *d,*
38:27 ground till the *d* blooms with verdure?
39: 3 they deliver their progeny in the *d.*
Ps(s) 29: 8 the voice of the LORD shakes the *d,*
75: 7 neither from the *d* nor from the mountains
78:15 *d* and gave them water in copious floods.
78:19 saying, "Can God spread a table in the *d?*
78:40 in the *d* and grieved him in the wilderness!
78:52 sheep and guided them like a herd in the *d.*
95: 8 Meribah, as in the day of Massah in the *d,*
102: 7 I am like a *d* owl;
106: 9 led them through the deep as through a *d.*
106:14 in the *d* and tempted God in the wilderness.
106:26 against them to let them perish in the *d,*
107: 4 They went astray in the *d* wilderness;
107:33 He changed rivers into *d,*
107:35 He changed the *d* into pools of water,
126: 4 LORD, like the torrents in the southern *d.*
Sg 3: 6 What is this coming up from the *d,*
8: 5 Who is this coming up from the *d,*
Wis 10: 7 wickedness, there yet remain a smoking *d,*
10:14 dungeon, and did not *d* him in his bonds,
11: 2 They journeyed through the uninhabited *d,*
18:20 and in the *d* a plague struck the multitude;
Sir 8:16 man, nor ride with him through the *d;*
13:18 Lion's prey are the wild asses of the *d;*
45:18 against him, were jealous of him in the *d,*
Is 1:28 those who *d* the LORD shall be consumed.
13:22 *D* beasts shall howl in her castles,
14:17 Who made the world a *d,*
16: 1 like reptiles, from Sela across the *d,*
16: 8 as far as Jazer and scattered over the *d,*
21: 1 through the Negeb, there comes from the *d,*
25: 5 As with the cold rain, as with the *d* heat,
32:15 Then will the *d* become an orchard and the
32:16 in the *d* and justice abide in the orchard.
34:11 the *d* owl and hoot owl shall possess her,
34:14 Wildcats shall meet with *d* beasts,
35: 1 The *d* and the parched land will exult;
35: 6 Streams will burst forth in the *d,*
40: 3 In the *d* prepare the way of the LORD!
41:18 I will turn the *d* into a marshland,
41:19 of water, I will plant in the *d* the cedar,
43:19 In the *d* I make a way,
43:20 For I put water in the *d* and rivers in the
50: 2 I dry up the sea, I turn rivers into a *d;*
64: 9 Your holy cities have become a *d,*
64: 9 cities have become a desert, Zion is a *d,*
Jer 2: 2 loved me as a bride, Following me in the *d,*
2: 6 land of Egypt, Who led us through the *d,*
2:24 near and far, breaking away toward the *d,*
2:31 Have I been a *d* to Israel,
3: 2 you waited for them like an Arab in the *d.*
4:11 glaring heights through the *d* a wind comes
4:26 and behold, the garden land was a *d,*
5: 6 slay them, wolves of the *d* ravage them,
6: 8 Lest I turn you into a *d,*
9: 1 that I had in the *d* a travelers' lodge!
9:25 and the *d* dwellers who shave their temples.
10:22 cities of Judah into a *d* haunt of jackals.
12:10 me they have turned into a *d* waste,
12:12 Upon every *d* height brigands have come up.
13:24 chaff that flies when the *d* wind blows.
17: 6 in the *d* that enjoys no change of season,
17:11 In midlife it will *d* him;
18:14 the snow of Lebanon *d* the rocky heights?
18:16 Their land shall be turned into a *d,*
25:11 This whole land shall be a ruin and a *d.*
25:12 Their land I will turn into everlasting *d.*
25:18 her princes, to make them a ruin and a *d,*
25:23 all the *d* dwellers who shave their temples;
31: 2 the sword have found favor in the *d.*
32:43 bought in this land, which you call a *d,*
34:22 I will turn into a *d* where no man dwells.
39: 5 captured Zedekiah in the *d* near Jericho.
44:22 and so your land became a waste, a *d,*
46:19 Memphis shall become a *d,*
48: 6 to survive like the wild ass in the *d!*"
48:34 even the waters of Nimrim turn into a *d.*
49:33 become a haunt of jackals, a *d* forever,
50: 3 against her to turn her land into a *d,*
50:12 See, the last of the nations, a *d,*
50:13 she shall be empty, and become a total *d;*
50:39 wildcats and *d* beasts shall dwell there,
51:29 of Babylon into a *d* where no one lives.
51:43 Her cities have become a *d,*
51:62 it, since it would remain an everlasting *d.*"
52: 8 overtook Zedekiah in the *d* near Jericho,
Lam 4: 3 become as cruel as the ostrich in the *d.*
4:19 on the mountains and waylaid us in the *d.*
5: 9 our sustenance, in the face of the *d* heat;
Ez 6:14 a desolate waste, from the *d* to Riblah;
19:13 So now she is planted in the *d,*
20:10 land of Egypt and brought them into the *d.*
20:13 of Israel rebelled against me in the *d.*
20:13 on them in the *d* to put an end to them,
20:15 Nevertheless I swore to them in the *d* not
20:17 so I did not put an end to them in the *d.*
20:18 Then I said to their children in the *d:*
20:21 of spending my anger on them in the *d;*
20:23 Nevertheless I swore to them in the *d* that
20:35 I will lead you to the *d* of the peoples,
20:36 your fathers in the *d* of the land of Egypt,
23:42 and these were men brought in from the *d,*
29: 5 I will cast you into the *d,*
34:25 securely in the *d* and sleep in the forests.
Hos 2: 5 I will make her like the *d,*
2:16 lead her into the *d* and speak to her heart.
9:10 Like grapes in the *d,*
13: 5 I fed you in the *d,* in the torrid land.
13:15 a wind from the LORD, rising from the *d,*
Jl 2: 3 land before them, and after them a *d* waste;
4:19 Egypt shall be a waste, and Edom a *d* waste,
Am 2:10 who led you through the *d* for forty years,
5:25 and offerings for forty years in the *d,*
Zep 2:13 He will make Nineveh a waste, dry as the *d.*
2:14 and the *d* owl shall roost in her columns;
Zec 7:14 they made the pleasant land into a *d.*
Mal 1: 3 a waste, his heritage a *d* for jackals.
Mt 3: 1 appearance as a preacher in the *d* of Judea,
3: 3 "A herald's voice in the *d;*
4: 1 *d* by the Spirit to be tempted by the devil.
24:26 if they tell you, 'Look, he is in the *d,*'
Mk 1: 3 a herald's voice in the *d,*
1: 4 that John the Baptizer appeared in the *d,*
1:12 point the Spirit sent him out toward the *d.*
1:35 he went off to a lonely place in the *d;*
1:45 He stayed in *d* places;
Lk 1:80 He lived in the *d* until the day when he
3: 2 spoken to John son of Zechariah in the *d.*
3: 4 "A herald's voice in the *d,*
4: 1 by the Spirit into the *d* for forty days,
7:24 "What did you go out to see in the *d*—
Jn 1:23 prophet Isaiah, "I am 'a voice in the *d,*
3:14 as Moses lifted up the serpent in the *d,*
6:31 Our ancestors had manna to eat in the *d;*
6:49 Your ancestors ate manna in the *d,*
11:54 called Ephraim in the region near the *d,*
Acts 7:30 appeared to him in the *d* near Mount Sinai
7:36 the Red Sea, and for forty years in the *d.*
7:38 In that *d* assembly,
7:42 and offerings for forty years in the *d,*
7:44 "Our fathers in the *d* had the meeting
8:26 goes from Jerusalem to Gaza, the *d* route."
13:18 forty years he put up with them in the *d:*
21:38 of four thousand cutthroats out into the *d?*"
1Cor 10: 5 them, for "they were struck down in the *d.*"
2Cor 11:26 imperiled in the city, in the *d,*
Heb 3: 8 the revolt in the day of testing in the *d,*
3:17 had sinned, whose corpses fell in the *d?*
13: 5 for God has said, "I will never *d* you,
Rv 12: 6 The woman herself fled into the *d,*
12:14 she could fly off to her place in the *d,*

DESERTED (44)

Lv 26:22 dwindles away and your roads become *d.*
26:33 countryside desolate and your cities *d.*
1Kgs 20:25 army as large as the army that has *d* you,
2Kgs 25:11 and those who had *d* to the king of Babylon,
1Chr 12:20 Men from Manasseh also *d* to David when he
12:21 therefore, these *d* to him from Manasseh:
Neh 13:10 have been carrying out the services had *d,*
1Mc 7:19 had many of the men arrested who *d* to him,
7:24 and took revenge on the men who had *d,*
9:24 great famine, and the country *d* to them.
15:12 upon him now that his soldiers had *d* him.
2Mc 8:13 faith in God's justice *d* and got away.
Jb 6:13 Have I no helper, and has advice *d* me?
15:28 in ruinous cities, in houses that are *d,*
Is 7:16 those two kings whom you dread shall be *d.*
31: 6 of Israel, to him whom you have utterly *d.*
32:14 castle will be forsaken, the noisy city *d;*
54: 1 numerous are the children of the *d* wife
Jer 22: 9 they have *d* their covenant with the LORD,
26: 9 and 'This city shall be desolate and *d*'?"
33:10 the streets of Jerusalem that are now *d,*
38:19 men of Judah who have *d* to the Chaldeans;
39: 9 left in the city, those who had *d* to him,
52:15 and those who had *d* to the king of Babylon,
Lam 1: 4 All her gateways are *d,*
Bar 2:23 And all the land shall be *d,*
Ez 29:12 be the most *d* of cities for forty years;
Zep 3: 6 I have made their streets *d,*
Mt 14:13 by boat from there to a *d* place by himself.
14:15 "This is a *d* place and it is already late.
15:33 in this *d* spot to satisfy such a crowd?"
23:38 'You will find your temple *d.*'
26:56 Then all the disciples *d* him and fled.
Mk 6:32 off in the boat by themselves to a *d* place.
6:35 "This is a *d* place and it is already late.
8: 4 people sufficient bread in this *d* spot?"
14:50 With that, all *d* him and fled.
Lk 5:16 He often retired to *d* places and prayed.
Jn 8:29 *d* me since I always do what pleases him."
Acts 1:25 who *d* the cause and went the way he was
15:38 that, as he had *d* them at Pamphylia,
Gal 4:27 For many are the children of the wife *d*—
Jude 1: 6 own domain, who *d* their dwelling place.
Rv 18:14 "The fruit your appetite craved has *d* you.

DESERTING (5)

1Sm 8: 8 this day, *d* me and worshiping strange gods,
Is 57: 8 *D* me, you spread out your high, wide bed;
Jer 37:13 saying, "You are *d* to the Chaldeans!"
37:14 answered, "I am not *d* to the Chaldeans."
Gal 1: 6 I am amazed that you are so soon *d* him who

DESERTS (11)

Lv 26:16 then I, in turn, will give you your *d.*
Jb 27: 2 As God lives, who withholds my *d,*
Ps(s) 28: 4 give them their *d.*
94: 2 render their *d* to the proud.
Prv 19: 4 but the friend of the poor man *d* him.
Wis 5: 7 we journeyed through impassable *d,*
Is 51: 3 Her *d* he shall make like Eden,
59:18 He repays his enemies their *d,*
66: 6 of the LORD repaying his enemies their *d!*
Jer 14: 5 *d* her offspring because there is no grass.
Heb 11:38 They wandered about in *d* and on mountains,

DESERVE (25)

Lv 26:21 my blows another sevenfold, as your sins *d.*
1Sm 26:16 you people *d* death because you have not
1Kgs 2:26 Though you *d* to die,
Tb 3: 5 me as my sins and those of my fathers *d.*
1Mc 2:68 Pay back the Gentiles what they *d,*

DESERVE (cont.)

2Mc 15:21 that victory is won by those who *d* it.
Jb 19:29 yourselves, for these crimes *d* the sword;
Wis 1:16 it, Because they *d* to be in its possession.
Sir 10:27 prize yourself as you *d*.
17:18 and requite each one of them as they *d*.
Jer 21:14 punish you, says the LORD, as your deeds *d!*
26:16 the prophets, "This man does not *d* death;
30:11 I will chastise you as you *d*,
46:28 I will chastise you as you *d*,
Lam 3:64 Requite them as they *d*,
Lk 15:18 I no longer *d* to be called your son.
15:21 I no longer *d* to be called your son.'
23:41 We *d* it, after all.
Rom 1:32 decree that all who do such things *d* death;
3: 8 but they will get what they *d*.
11:35 has given him anything so as to *d* return?"
1Cor 11:34 your assembly may not *d* condemnation.
15: 9 church of God, I do not even *d* the name.
1Tm 5:17 who do well as leaders *d* to be paid double,
Rv 16: 6 they *d* it."

DESERVED (10)

Jgs 9:16 treated him as he *d* for my father fought
2Sm 19:29 house *d* only death from my lord the king,
Ezr 9:13 made less of our sinfulness than it *d*
2Mc 4:38 the Lord rendered him the punishment he *d*.
8:33 he received the reward his wicked deeds *d*.
Wis 16: 9 they *d* to be punished by such means;
18: 4 For those *d* to be deprived of light and
Lk 12:48 nonetheless *d* to be flogged will get off
Acts 13:28 found no charge against him which *d* death,
Eph 2: 3 so by nature *d* God's wrath like the rest.

DESERVES (14)

Nm 35:31 life of a murderer who *d* the death penalty;
Dt 25: 2 the guilty party, if the latter *d* stripes,
25: 2 receive the number of stripes his guilt *d*.
Sir 38:17 pay your tribute of sorrow, as he *d*,
Jer 26:11 and to all the people, "This man *d* death;
Mt 26:66 They answered, "He *d* death!"
Lk 7: 5 "He *d* this favor from you,"
Acts 26:31 doing nothing that *d* death or imprisonment."
Rom 13: 7 respect and honor to everyone who *d* them.
Phil 4: 8 to all that is true, all that *d* respect,
1Tm 5:18 and also, "The worker *d* his wages."
Heb 10:23 for he who made the promise *d* our trust
Rv 2:23 will give each of you what your conduct *d*.
22:12 will be given to each man as his conduct *d*.

DESERVING (8)

Nm 18:22 else they will incur guilt *d* death.
Neh 2: 5 and if your servant is *d* of your favor,
Mt 10:13 If the home is *d*,
Acts 23:29 guilty of anything *d* death or imprisonment.
25:11 if I have committed a crime *d* death,
25:25 find that he had done anything *d* of death,
28:18 they found nothing against me *d* of death.
Rv 22: 3 Nothing *d* a curse shall be found there.

DESIGN (12)

Jos 11:20 For it was the *d* of the LORD to encourage
2Kgs 16:10 altar and a detailed *d* of its construction.
Jdt 13: 5 carrying out my *d* to shatter the enemies
Ps(s) 33:11 the *d* of his heart,
Sir 38:27 and he keeps watch till he finishes his *d*.
Ez 43:10 sins], both its measurements and its *d;*
43:11 known to them the form and *d* of the temple,
Acts 20:27 announcing to you God's *d* in its entirety.
Gal 1: 6 in accord with his gracious *d* in Christ,
4: 7 are a son makes you an heir, by God's *d*.
Eph 3: 9 *d* which for ages was hidden in God,
2Tm 1: 9 merit of ours but according to his own *d*—

DESIGNATE (7)

Nm 4:32 You shall *d* for each man of them all the
34:18 the tribes whom you shall *d* for this task.
Jos 20: 2 "Tell the Israelites to *d* the cities of
1Kgs 1:35 I *d* him ruler of Israel and of Judah."
Ez 45: 6 As property of the City you shall *d* a
Mt 27:15 one prisoner, whom the crowd would *d*.
Acts 26:16 I have appeared to you to *d* you as my

DESIGNATED (24)

Nm 1:17 and Aaron took these men who had been *d*,
Jos 7:15 He who is *d* as having incurred the ban
7:16 by tribes, and the tribe of Judah was *d*.
7:17 come forward, and the clan of Zerah was *d*.
7:17 come forward by families, and Zabdi was *d*.
7:18 son of Zerah of the tribe of Judah, was *d*.
20: 8 they *d* Bezer on the open tableland
20: 9 These were the *d* cities to which any
21: 9 and Simeonites they *d* the following cities,
1Sm 14:41 Jonathan and Saul were *d*,
14:42 And Jonathan was *d*.
1Kgs 17: 9 I have *d* a widow there to provide for you."
1Chr 12:32 *d* by name to come and make David king.
16:41 and *d* by name to give thanks to the LORD,
2Chr 31:19 had in every city men *d* by name to
Ezr 10:16 one for each family, all of them *d* by name.
Est E:22 day among your *d* feasts with all rejoicing,
9:31 Jew and Queen Esther had *d* for the Jews,
Ez 43:21 is to be burnt in a *d* part of the temple,
Acts 3:20 sends you Jesus, already *d* as your Messiah.
22:14 fathers long ago *d* you to know his will,
Gal 4: 1 as long as a *d* heir is not of age his
4: 4 but when the *d* time had come,
Heb 5:10 *d* by God as high priest according to the

DESIGNATES (4)

Dt 12: 5 chooses out of all your tribes and *d* as
Jos 7:14 the LORD *d* shall come forward by clans;
7:14 the LORD *d* shall come forward by families;
7:14 the LORD *d* shall come forward one by one.

DESIGNATING (1)

1Chr 6:50 *d* them by name and assigning them by lot

DESIGNED (1)

Est B: 4 blamelessly *d* by us cannot be established.

DESIGNER (3)

Sir 38:27 So with every engraver and *d* who,
Is 45:18 The *d* and maker of the earth who
Heb 11:10 with foundations, whose *d* and maker is God.

DESIGNING (1)

Is 45:18 it to be a waste, but *d* it to be lived in:

DESIGNS (11)

2Sm 13: 2 impossible to carry out his *d* toward her.
1Mc 6: 8 Sick with grief because his *d* had failed,
Jb 5:13 ruses, and the *d* of the crafty are routed.
11: 7 Can you penetrate the *d* of God?
Ps(s) 33:10 he foils the *d* of peoples.
139:17 How weighty are your *d*,
Prv 7:10 him, robed like a harlot, with secret *d*—
12: 5 the *d* of the wicked are deceitful.
Mt 2:20 had *d* on the life of the child are dead."
15:19 From the mind stem evil *d*—
Mk 7:21 *d* come from the deep recesses of the heart;

DESIRABLE (6)

Gn 3: 6 to the eyes, and *d* for gaining wisdom.
Ps(s) 106:24 Yet they despised the *d* land;
Prv 16:16 understanding is more *d* than silver.
22: 1 A good name is more *d* than great riches,
Wis 8: 5 And if riches be a *d* possession in life,
15:19 for their looks are they good or *d* beasts,

DESIRE (82)

Gn 6: 5 and how no *d* that his heart conceived was
Dt 5:21 shall not *d* your neighbor's house or field,
12:15 to your heart's *d* as much meat as the LORD,
12:20 you may eat it at will, to your heart's *d;*
12:21 it to your heart's *d* in your own community.
14:26 exchange the money for whatever you *d*,
18: 6 resides, to visit, as his heart may *d*,
1Sm 9:20 Whom does Israel *d* ardently if not you and
2Sm 23: 5 fruition all my salvation and my every *d?*
1Kgs 5:23 the provisions I *d* for my household."
11:37 that you *d* and shall become king of Israel.
2Kgs 10:30 and have treated the house of Ahab as I *d*,
1Chr 11:17 David expressed a *d:*
17: 2 to David, "Do, therefore, whatever you *d*,
29:19 a wholehearted *d* to keep your commandments,
2Chr 15:15 whole heart and sought him with complete *d*,
Tb 4: 5 *d* to sin or to break his commandments.
Jdt 12:16 He was burning with the *d* to possess her,
Est C: 5 out of insolence or pride or *d* for fame
1Mc 5:67 fight in their *d* to distinguish themselves.
2Mc 11:25 Since we *d* that this people too should be
11:28 If you are well, it is what we *d*.
Ps(s) 10:17 The *d* of the afflicted you hear,
21: 3 You have granted him his heart's *d;*
38:10 O LORD, all my *d* is before you;
40:15 be turned back in disgrace who *d* my ruin.
45:12 So shall the king *d* your beauty;
70: 3 be turned back in disgrace who *d* my ruin.
112:10 the *d* of the wicked shall perish.
145:16 and satisfy the *d* of every living thing.
145:19 He fulfills the *d* of those who fear him,
Prv 10:24 him, but the *d* of the just will be granted.
11:23 The *d* of the just ends only in good;
19:18 but do not *d* his death.
23: 3 Do not *d* his delicacies;
23: 6 a grudging man, and do not *d* his dainties;
24: 1 of evil men, and *d* not to be with them;
Eccl 6: 7 for his mouth, yet his *d* is not fulfilled.
8:11 men are filled with the *d* to commit evil
Wis 4:12 whirl of *d* transforms the innocent mind.
6:11 *D* therefore my words;
6:13 herself known in anticipation of men's *d;*
6:17 discipline is a very earnest *d* for her;
6:20 the *d* for Wisdom leads up to a kingdom.
16:21 and serving the *d* of him who received it,
19:11 a new kind of bird when, prompted by *d*,
Sir 1:23 If you *d* wisdom,
6: 2 Fall not into the grip of *d*,
6: 4 For contumacious *d* destroys its owner and
6:37 mind, and the wisdom you *d* he will grant.
16: 1 *D* not a brood of worthless children,
19: 3 him, for contumacious *d* destroys its owner.
51:19 I burned with *d* for her,
Is 26: 8 name and your title are the *d* of our souls.
58: 2 me day after day, and *d* to know my ways,
Jer 42: 4 will pray to the LORD, your God, as you *d;*
Ez 24:21 delight of your eyes, the *d* of your soul.
24:25 delight of their eyes, the *d* of their soul,
Dn 13:11 to reveal their lustful *d* to have her.
13:20 give in to our *d*,
Hos 6: 6 For it is love that I *d*,
Mal 3: 1 the messenger of the covenant whom you *d*.
Mt 9:13 words, 'It is mercy I *d* and not sacrifice.'
12: 7 text, 'It is mercy I *d* and not sacrifice,'
Mk 4:19 over life's demands, and the *d* for wealth,
Jn 1:13 begotten not by blood, nor by carnal *d*,
Rom 7: 7 what evil *d* was unless the law had said,
7: 8 to rouse in me every kind of evil *d*.
7:18 *d* to do right is there but not the power.
10: 1 Brothers, my heart's *d*,
15:23 and I continue to cherish the *d* to visit
1Cor 7:35 I have no *d* to place restrictions on you,
2Cor 7:11 ardent *d* to restore the balance of justice!
Eph 4:22 which deteriorates through illusion and *d*,
Phil 2:13 in you any measure of *d* or achievement.
1Thes 4: 5 *d* as do the Gentiles who know not God;
Heb 6:11 Our *d* is that each of you show the same
10: 5 "Sacrifice and offering you did not *d*,
Jas 4: 2 What you *d* you do not obtain,
2Pt 2:10 the flesh in their *d* for whatever corrupts,
Rv 22:17 *d* it accept the gift of life-giving water.

DESIRED (15)

1Kgs 10:13 of Sheba everything she *d* and asked for,
13:33 Whoever *d* it was consecrated and became a
2Chr 9:12 Sheba everything she *d* and asked him for,
11:16 tribes who firmly *d* to seek the LORD,
Est B: 2 borders, to restore the peace *d* by all men.
1Mc 7: 5 led by Alcimus, who *d* to be high priest.
8:13 they *d* to help to a kingdom became kings,
2Mc 4:16 and whom they *d* to imitate in every thing,
Ps(s) 107:30 and he brought them to their *d* haven.
Eccl 2:10 Nothing that my eyes *d* did I deny them,
Wis 16: 3 That those others, when they *d* food,
16:25 according to what they needed and *d;*
Jer 17:16 the day without remedy I have not *d*.
Lk 22:15 "I have greatly *d* to eat this Passover
Heb 10: 8 offerings, you neither *d* nor delighted in."

DESIRES (27)

Gn 8:21 *d* of man's heart are evil from the start;
Nm 15:39 astray after the *d* of your hearts and eyes.
1Sm 18:25 "The king *d* no other price for the bride
Jb 23:13 What he *d*, that he does.
Ps(s) 24: 4 who *d* not what is vain,
34:13 Which of you *d* life,
140: 9 Grant not, O LORD, the *d* of the wicked;
Prv 21:10 The soul of the wicked man *d* evil;
Eccl 6: 9 see is better than what the *d* wander after."
Sir 5: 2 strength in following the *d* of your heart.
18:30 after your lusts, but keep your *d* in check.
23: 6 master me, surrender me not to shameless *d*.
Ez 33:31 and their *d* are fixed on dishonest gain.
Lk 6:47 Any man who *d* to come to me will hear my
Rom 13:14 make no provision for the *d* of the flesh.
1Cor 10: 6 to keep us from wicked *d* such as theirs.
2Cor 11:17 the Lord *d* but after the manner of a fool.
Gal 5:24 their flesh with its passions and *d*.
Col 3: 5 fornication, uncleanness, passion, evil *d*,
1Tm 6: 9 foolish and harmful *d* which drag men down
2Tm 3: 6 with sins and driven by *d* of many kinds,
4: 3 doctrine, but, following their own *d*,
Ti 2:12 us to reject godless ways and worldly *d*,
1Pt 1:14 *d* that once shaped you in your ignorance.
2:11 I urge you not to indulge your carnal *d*.
4: 2 life on human *d* but on the will of God.
4: 3 enjoy, living lives of debauchery, evil *d*,

DESIROUS (1)

1Thes 3: 6 are as *d* to see us as we are to see you,

DESIST (12)

Jgs 20:28 with Benjamin, my brother, or shall I *d?*"
2Sm 2:21 But Asahel would not *d* from his pursuit.
2Kgs 10:29 he did not *d* from the sins which Jeroboam,
10:31 since he did not *d* from the sins which
13: 6 they did not *d* from the sins which the
13:11 not *d* from any of the sins which Jeroboam,
14:24 not *d* from any of the sins which Jeroboam,
15: 9 and did not *d* from the sins which Jeroboam,
17:22 he committed, nor would they *d* from them.
23:26 the LORD did not *d* from his fiercely
2Mc 4: 6 and that Simon would not *d* from his folly.
Ps(s) 46:11 *D!* and confess that I am God

DESISTED (1)

2Chr 25:16 Therefore the prophet *d*.

DESISTING (3)

2Kgs 15:18 LORD, not *d* from the sins which Jeroboam,
15:24 LORD, not *d* from the sins which Jeroboam,
15:28 LORD, not *d* from the sins which Jeroboam,

DESISTS (1)

Hos 7: 4 Whose fire the baker *d* from stirring once

DESOLATE (60)

Ex 23:29 else the land will become so *d* that the
Lv 26:33 countryside *d* and your cities deserted.
26:35 during all the time that it lies *d,*
Tb 14: 4 entire country of Israel shall become *d;*
14: 4 even Samaria and Jerusalem shall become *d!*
14: 4 to the ground and shall be *d* for a while.
1Mc 1:39 Her sanctuary was as *d* as a wilderness;
4:38 They found the sanctuary *d,*
Jb 38:27 To enrich the waste and *d* ground till the
Ps(s) 69:26 Let their encampment become *d;*
73:19 How suddenly they are made *d!*
Sir 16: 4 through a clan of rebels it becomes *d.*
49: 6 the holy city and left its streets *d,*
Is 3:26 mourn, as the city sits *d* on the ground.
6:11 Until the cities are *d,*
6:11 without a man, and the earth is a *d* waste.
24:12 its gates are battered and *d.*
27:10 For the fortified city shall be *d,*
33: 8 The highways are *d,*
49: 8 restore the land and allot the *d* heritages,
49:19 Though you were waste and *d,*
54: 3 the nations and shall people the *d* cities.
61: 4 the ruined cities, *d* now for generations.
62: 4 men call you "Forsaken," or your land *D,"*
Jer 12:11 *d* it lies before me, Desolate, all the land,
12:11 waste, desolate it lies before me, *D,*
25:37 grazing place, *d* lie the peaceful pastures;
25:38 their land is made *d* By the sweeping sword,
26: 9 and 'This city shall be *d* and deserted'?"
33:10 this place of which you say, "How *d* it is,
33:12 In this place, now *d,*
Lam 1:13 He left me *d,* in pain all the day.
3:11 deranged my ways, set me astray, left me *d.*
5:18 That Mount Zion should be *d,*
Bar 4:12 For the sins of my children I am left *d,*
4:19 I am left *d.*
Ez 6: 6 shall be made *d* and high places laid waste,
6: 6 your altars will be made *d* and laid waste,
6:14 they live I will make the land a *d* waste,
26:19 *d* like cities that are no longer inhabited,
29: 9 The land of Egypt shall become a *d* waste;
29:12 make the land of Egypt the most *d* of lands,
30: 7 and her cities shall be the most *d* of all.
33:28 I will make the land a *d* waste,
33:28 shall be so *d* that no one will cross them.
33:29 when I make the land a *d* waste because of
35: 3 my hand against you and make you a *d* waste.
35: 7 I will make Mount Seir a *d* waste,
35: 9 *d* will I make you forever,
35:12 "They are *d,* they have been given
35:14 you rejoiced over my land because it was *d,*
36: 4 valleys, the *d* ruins and abandoned cities,
36:34 the *d* land shall be tilled,
36:35 *d* land has been made into a garden of Eden,"
36:36 was destroyed and replanted what was *d.*
Dn 9:17 let your face shine upon your *d* sanctuary.
Am 7: 9 and the sanctuaries of Israel made *d;*
Zec 7:14 Thus the land was left *d* after them with
Acts 1:20 'Let his encampment be *d*
Rv 17: 3 carried me away in spirit to a *d* place

DESOLATING (1)

Dn 8:13 sacrifice, the *d* sin which is placed there,

DESOLATION (12)

Lv 26:43 in its *d* it may make up its lost sabbaths,
2Kgs 22:19 inhabitants would become a *d* and a curse;
2Chr 30: 7 so that he delivered them over to *d,*
Is 51:19 *D* and destruction, famine and sword!
Jer 4: 7 left his place, To turn your land into *d,*
49:13 of horror and a disgrace, a *d* and a curse;
Lam 3:47 *d* and destruction; My eyes run
Bar 4:33 so shall she grieve over her own *d.*
Ez 29:10 Egypt a waste and a *d* from Migdol to Syene,
Dn 9:26 there shall be war, the *d* that is decreed.
Na 2:11 Emptiness, *d,* waste; melting hearts
Zep 1:15 and distress, A day of destruction and *d,*

DESPAIR (7)

Est C:30 than all, hear the voice of those in *d.*
2Mc 9:22 I do not *d* about my health since I have
Jb 6:14 A friend owes kindness to one in *d,*
9:23 he laughs at the *d* of the innocent.
Eccl 2:20 So my feelings turned to *d* of all the
Sir 22:21 you draw a sword against a friend, *d* not,
2Cor 4: 8 full of doubts, we never *d.*

DESPAIRING (3)

Jer 14: 3 Ashamed, *d,* they cover their heads
15: 9 sun sets in full day, she is disgraced, *d.*
2Cor 1: 8 strength, even to the point of *d* of life.

DESPAIRS (1)

Jb 15:22 He *d* of escaping the darkness,

DESPERATE (1)

Jb 6:26 proof, but the sayings of a *d* man as wind?

DESPERATELY (3)

Gn 31:30 were *d* homesick for your father's house,
2Sm 12:15 had borne to David, and it became *d* ill.
1Mc 9:17 The battle was fought *d,*

DESPICABLE (1)

Dn 11:21 "There shall rise in his place a *d* person,

DESPISE (20)

Jdt 10:19 "Who can *d* this people that has such
Jb 9:21 I *d* my life.
19:18 The young children, too, *d* me;
Ps(s) 10:13 Why should the wicked man *d* God,
119:118 You *d* all who stray from your statutes,
Prv 1: 7 wisdom and instruction fools *d.*
6:30 Men *d* not the thief if he steals to
23: 9 he will *d* the wisdom of your words.
23:22 you, and *d* not your mother when she is old.
Sir 10:22 not just to *d* a man who is wise but poor,
11: 2 *d* not a man for his appearance
Jer 23:17 say to those who *d* the word of the LORD,
Ez 28:24 than all the others about them who *d* them;
Mal 1: 6 of hosts to you, O priests, who *d* his name.
Mt 6:24 or be attentive to one and *d* the other.
18:10 that you never *d* one of these little ones.
Lk 16:13 or be attentive to the one and *d* the other.
Gal 4:14 you did not *d* or brush aside in disgust.
1Thes 5:20 Do not *d* prophecies.
2Pt 2:10 for whatever corrupts, and who *d* authority.

DESPISED (37)

Nm 15:31 Since he has *d* the word of the LORD and
1Sm 10:27 They *d* him and brought him no present.
2Sm 6:16 the LORD, and she *d* him in her heart.
12:10 because you have *d* me and have taken the
1Chr 15:29 and dancing, she *d* him in her heart.
2Chr 36:16 the messengers of God, *d* his warnings,
Jdt 11: 2 not *d* me and brought this upon themselves.
11:22 destruction to those who have *d* my lord.
14: 5 recognize the one who *d* the house of Israel
1Mc 3:14 followers, who have *d* the king's command."
2Mc 1:27 kindly on those who are *d* and detested,
4:15 They *d* what their ancestors had regarded
Ps(s) 15: 4 By whom the reprobate is *d,*
22: 7 the scorn of men, *d* by the people.
102:18 of the destitute, and not *d* their prayer.
106:24 Yet they *d* the desirable land;
Prv 12: 8 praised, but one with a warped mind is *d.*
Eccl 9:16 poor man is *d* and his words go unheeded.
Sir 22: 5 by both she is *d.*
31:16 guest, and be not greedy, lest you be *d.*
Is 49: 7 and the Holy One of Israel, To the one *d,*
60:14 *d* you shall fall prostrate at your feet.
Jer 6:19 heeded not my words, because they *d* my law.
22:28 Is this man Coniah a vessel *d,*
49:15 among the nations *d* among men!
Ez 16:57 *d* on all sides by the Philistines.
16:59 to what you have done, you who *d* your oath,
20:13 and they *d* my ordinances that bring life
20:16 *d* my ordinances and desecrated my sabbaths.
20:24 *d* my statutes and desecrated my sabbaths,
22: 7 Within you, father and mother are *d;*
28:26 on all their neighbors who *d* them;
36: 3 because you have been ridiculed and *d* on
Mal 1: 6 But you ask, "How have we *d* your name?"
Mk 9:12 of Man that he must suffer much and be *d?*
Lk 19:14 But his fellow citizens *d* him,
1Cor 1:28 He chose the world's lowborn and *d,*

DESPISER (1)

Prv 19:16 his life, but the *d* of the word will die.

DESPISES (8)

2Kgs 19:21 " 'She *d* you, laughs you to scorn,
Prv 13:13 He who *d* the word must pay for it,
14:21 He sins who *d* the hungry;
15:20 glad, but a fool of a man *d* his mother.
15:32 He who rejects admonition *d* his own soul,
Wis 3:11 he who *d* wisdom and instruction is doomed.
Sir 3:16 A blasphemer is he who *d* his father;
Is 37:22 She *d* you, laughs you to scorn,

DESPISING (2)

Dt 31:20 serve them, *d* me and breaking my covenant;
Wis 14:30 deliberately swore false oaths *d* piety.

DESPITE (27)

Gn 31:35 So, *d* his search, he did not find his idols.
Ex 7: 3 *d* the many signs and wonders that I will
Lv 26:27 "If, *d* all this, you still persist
Nm 14:11 *d* all the signs I have performed among
Dt 1:32 *D* this, you would not trust the LORD,
Jos 17:18 if, *d* their strength and iron chariots,
2Kgs 5:16 and *d* Naaman's urging,
Ezr 3: 3 *D* their fear of the peoples of the land,
Neh 5:18 *d* this I did not claim the governor's
Sir 48:15 *D* all this the people did not repent,
Is 16:14 be degraded *d* all its great multitude;
38:15 all my years *d* the bitterness of my soul.
Bar 6:23 *D* the gold that covers them for adornment,
Ez 16:29 but *d* this, you were still not satisfied.
32:29 who *d* their might have been placed with
Mt 26:60 *d* the many false witnesses who took the
Mk 5:32 *D* this, he kept looking around
Jn 12:37 *D* his many signs performed in their
20:26 *D* the locked doors, Jesus came
Acts 4: 4 *D* this, many of those who had heard
5:13 *d* the fact that the people held them in
Rom 5:20 but *d* the increase of sin,
2Cor 7: 4 and *d* my many afflictions my joy knows no
Gal 2: 3 undergo circumcision, *d* his being a Greek.
1Thes 1: 6 Lord, receiving the word *d* great trials,
Heb 11:39 Yet *d* the fact that all of these were
Jas 3: 4 and *d* the fact that they are driven by

DESPOIL (8)

Ex 3:22 Thus you will *d* the Egyptians."
12:36 Thus did they *d* the Egyptians.
15: 9 my hand shall *d* them!"
1Mc 3:20 us and our wives and children and to *d* us;
Is 17:14 Such is the portion of those who *d* us,
Ez 22:12 you *d* your neighbors violently;
Hb 2: 8 all the rest of the nations shall *d* you;
Mk 3:27 a strong man's house and *d* his property

DESPOILED (15)

Jgs 2:14 them over to plunderers who *d* them.
14:19 he killed thirty of their men and *d* them;
2Chr 14:13 they *d* all the cities,
Jdt 2:27 their flocks and herds, *d* their cities,
4: 1 had *d* all their temples and destroyed them,
1Mc 5: 3 defeated them heavily, overcame and *d* them.
2Mc 9:16 the holy temple which he had previously *d;*
Ps(s) 76: 6 *D* are the stouthearted;
Wis 10:20 Therefore the just *d* the wicked;
Is 42:22 This is a people *d* and plundered,
59:15 and the man who turns from evil is *d.*
Ez 34:22 my sheep so that they may no longer be *d,*
34:28 They shall no longer be *d* by the nations
Hb 2: 8 Because you *d* many peoples all the rest
Zec 11: 2 cedars are fallen, the mighty have been *d.*

DESPOILER (1)

Is 21: 2 the traitor betrays, the *d* spoils.

DESPOILERS (6)

Jgs 2:16 to deliver them from the power of their *d,*
5:12 arise, Barak, make *d* your spoil,
Ps(s) 35:10 the afflicted and the needy from their *d?"*
137: 3 our songs, And our *d* urged us to be joyous:
Sir 4:19 him and deliver him into the hands of *d.*
Is 42:24 Jacob to be plundered, Israel to the *d?*

DESPONDENT (2)

Is 19:10 crushed, all the hired laborers shall be *d.*
Heb 12: 3 do not grow *d* or abandon the struggle.

DESTINATION (1)

Nm 32:17 until we have led them to their *d.*

DESTINE (1)

Is 65:12 for Destiny, You I will *d* for the sword;

DESTINED (32)

Ex 21: 8 if her master, who had *d* her for himself,
Nm 24:22 Yet *d* for burning —even as I watch
2Chr 35:12 They separated what was *d* for the
2Mc 4:20 So the contribution *d* by the sender for
Jb 30:23 in death to the *d* place of everyone alive.
Ps(s) 92: 9 thrive, They are *d* for eternal destruction;
Sir 48:10 You are *d,* it is written,
49:12 the holy temple, *d* for everlasting glory.
Jer 43:11 with exile, everyone *d* for exile;
Bar 3:11 with those *d* for the nether world?
Ez 15: 6 which I have *d* as fuel for the fire,
21:17 son of man, for it is *d* for my people;
31:14 For all of them are *d* for death,
42:14 then approach the place *d* for the people."
Hos 8: 6 an artisan no god at all, *D* for the flames
Lk 2:34 "This child is *d* to be the downfall and
Jn 17:12 lost, none but him who was *d* to be lost
Acts 1:16 of David was *d* to be fulfilled in Judas,
1:25 the cause and went the way he was *d* to go."
13:48 *d* for life everlasting believed in it.
22:10 be told about everything you are *d* to do.'
27:24 'You are *d* to appear before the emperor.
2Cor 3:11 what was *d* to pass away was given in glory,
1Thes 5: 9 God has not *d* us for wrath but for
2Thes 2:10 wicked can devise for those *d* to ruin because

DESTINED (cont.)

Jas 2:12 *d* for judgment under the law of freedom.
1Pt 1:10 the divine favor that was *d* to be yours.
1:11 for he predicted the sufferings *d* for
Jude 1: 4 *d* for the condemnation I shall describe.
Rv 12: 5 a boy *d* to shepherd all the nations with
13:10 If one is *d* for captivity,
13:10 If one is *d* to be slain by the sword,

DESTINES (1)

Ex 21: 9 If he *d* her for his son,

DESTINY (7)

Jb 27:14 his children be many, the sword is their *d.*
Ps(s) 31:16 In your hands is my *d;*
73:17 of God and considered their final *d.*
Wis 2:16 He calls blest the *d* of the just and
Is 53: 8 who would have thought any more of his *d?*
65:11 and fill cups of blended wine for *D,*
1Pt 2: 8 it belongs to their *d* to do so.

DESTITUTE (7)

Ru 1:21 but the LORD has brought me back *d.*
Jb 30: 2 they were utterly *d.*
30:25 was not my soul grieved for the *d?*
Ps(s) 82: 3 render justice to the afflicted and the *d.*
102:18 When he has regarded the prayer of the *d,*
Prv 31: 8 of the dumb, and for the rights of the *d;*
1Tm 5: 5 The real widow, left *d,*

DESTROY (235)

Gn 6:13 So I will *d* them and all life on earth.
6:17 to *d* everywhere all creatures in which
9:15 become a flood to *d* all mortal beings.
18:28 you *d* the whole city because of those five?"
18:28 "I will not *d* it,"
18:31 "I will not *d* it,"
18:32 those ten," he replied, "I will not *d* it."
19:13 We are about to *d* this place,
19:13 is so great that he has sent us to *d* it."
19:14 "the LORD is about to *d* the city."
Nm 33:52 *d* all their stone figures and molten
Dt 1:27 us into the hands of the Amorites and *d* us.
4:31 God, he will not abandon and *d* you,
6:15 you and he *d* you from the face of the land;
7: 4 flare up against you and quickly *d* you.
7: 5 sacred poles, and *d* their idols by fire.
7:25 images of their gods you shall *d* by fire.
9: 3 you can drive them out and *d* them quickly,
9: 8 the LORD that he was angry enough to *d* you,
9:14 that I may *d* them and blot out their name
9:19 his wrath would *d* you.
9:25 LORD, because he had threatened to *d* you.
9:26 O Lord GOD, *d* not your people,
10:10 again heard me and decided not to *d* you,
12: 2 *D* without fail every place on the high
12: 3 pillars, *d* by fire their sacred poles,
20:19 not *d* its trees by putting an ax to them.
20:20 you know are not fruit trees you may *d,*
31: 3 he will *d* these nations before you,
Jos 7: 7 of the Amorites, that they might *d* us?
11:13 Israel did not *d* by fire any of the cities
24:20 gods, he will do evil to you and *d* you."
Jgs 6: 4 and *d* the produce of the land as far as
6:25 bullock and *d* your father's altar to Baal
1Sm 12:15 severely with you and your king, and *d* you.
15: 6 that I may not have to *d* you with them,
23:10 to Keilah, to *d* the city on my account.
24:22 LORD that you will not *d* my descendants
2Sm 2:26 "Must the sword *d* to the utmost?
4:11 for his death and *d* you from the earth!"
11:25 your attack on the city and *d* it.'
14:16 who would seek to *d* me and my son
20:19 you wish to *d* the inheritance of the LORD?"
20:20 I do not wish to *d* or to ruin anything.
21: 5 who intended to *d* us that we might have no
24:16 forth his hand toward Jerusalem to *d* it,
1Kgs 14:14 of Israel who will *d* the house of Jeroboam.
16: 3 me to anger by their sins, I will *d* you,
21:21 I will *d* you and will cut off every male
2Kgs 3:19 You shall *d* every fortified city,
8:19 Even so, the LORD was unwilling to *d* Judah,
9: 7 You shall *d* the house of Ahab your master;
10:19 so that he might *d* the worshipers of Baal.
13:23 He was unwilling to *d* them or to cast them
18:25 will that I have come up to *d* this place?
18:25 LORD said to me, 'Go up and *d* that land!' "
24: 2 he loosed them against Judah to *d* it,
1Chr 21:15 God also sent an angel to *d* Jerusalem;
2Chr 12: 7 have humbled themselves, I will not *d* them;
12:12 him so that it did not *d* him completely;
20:10 they passed them by and did not *d* them.
20:23 of Seir, they began to *d* each other.
21: 7 but the LORD would not *d* the house of
35:21 who is with me, as otherwise he will *d* you."
Ezr 6:12 or to *d* this house of God in Jerusalem.
9:14 us as to *d* us without remnant or survivor?
Neh 9:31 *d* them and you did not forsake them,
Tb 13:12 are all who *d* you and pull down your walls,
Jdt 1:12 and also *d* with his sword all the
3: 8 to *d* all the gods of the earth,
6: 2 and *d* them from the face of the earth.
8:15 or to *d* us in the face of our enemies.
15: 4 all might fall upon the enemy and *d* them.
Est 3: 6 nationality, he sought to *d* all the Jews,
3: 9 the king, let a decree be issued to *d* them;
4:20 have pronounced, and to *d* your heritage;
8:11 and defend their lives, and to kill, *d,*
9:24 had planned to *d* them and had cast the pur,
F: 5 who assembled to *d* the name of the Jews,
1Mc 2:37 are our witnesses that you *d* us unjustly."
2:40 they will soon *d* us from the earth."
3:20 they come against us to *d* us and our wives
3:35 to crush and *d* the power of Israel
3:42 given to *d* and utterly wipe out the people.
3:52 are gathered together against us to *d* us.
3:58 against us to *d* us and our sanctuary.
4:10 fathers, and *d* this army before us today.
5: 2 to *d* the descendants of Jacob among them,
5: 9 assembled to attack and *d* the Israelites
5:10 around us have combined against us to *d* us,
5:15 Galilee had joined forces to *d* them.
5:27 to seize and *d* all these people in one day."
6:19 But Judas planned to *d* them,
7:26 of Israel, with orders to *d* the people.
8: 9 of Greece had planned to come and *d* them,
12:49 the Great Plain to *d* all Jonathan's men.
12:53 the nations round about sought to *d* them.
13: 6 nations out of hatred have united to *d* us."
13:47 came to terms with them and did not *d* them.
2Mc 8:18 a mere nod *d* not only those who attack us,
Jb 10: 8 will you then turn and *d* me?
14:19 soil of the land, so you *d* the hope of man.
30:13 To *d* me, they attack
Ps(s) 5: 7 you *d* all who speak falsehood;
12: 4 LORD *d* all smooth lips,
21:11 *D* their fruit from the earth and their
34:17 to *d* remembrance of them from the earth.
54: 7 in your faithfulness *d* them.
73:27 you *d* everyone who is unfaithful to you.
74: 8 They said in their hearts, "Let us *d* them;
83: 5 They say, "Come, let us *d* their nation;
94:23 destroy them; the LORD, our God, will *d*
101: 5 his neighbor in secret, him will I *d.*
101: 8 I will *d* all the wicked of the land,
119:95 Sinners wait to *d* me,
139:19 If only you would *d* the wicked,
143:12 And in your kindness *d* my enemies;
145:20 who love him, but all the wicked he will *d.*
Prv 6:32 he who would *d* himself does it.
Eccl 5: 5 such words and *d* the works of your hands.
Wis 11:19 could these attack and completely *d* them;
12: 6 willed to *d* by the hands of our fathers,
Sir 6: 3 Your leaves it will eat, your fruits *d,*
8:16 is no one to help you, he will *d* you.
22:27 through them, that my tongue may not *d* me?
28:13 for they *d* the peace of many.
38:19 an extremity and heartache *d* one's health.
47:22 one, nor *d* the offspring of his friend.
49: 7 a prophet, To root out, pull down, and *d,*
Is 3:12 they *d* the paths you should follow.
10: 7 Rather, it is in his heart to *d,*
10:25 but them I will *d* in wrath.
13: 5 of his wrath, to *d* all the land.
13: 9 waste the land and *d* the sinners within it!
25: 7 he will *d* the veil that veils all peoples,
25: 8 he will *d* death forever.
36:10 will that I have come up to *d* this land?
36:10 LORD said to me, "Go up and *d* that land!" ' "
48: 9 hold it back from you, lest I should *d* you.
51:13 But when he sets himself to *d,*
65:25 shall hurt or *d* on all my holy mountain,
Jer 1:10 up and to tear down, to *d* and to demolish,
4:27 I will [not] wholly *d* it.
5:10 and ravage them, *d* them [not] wholly.
5:18 says the LORD, I will not wholly *d* you.
6: 5 us rush upon her by night, *d* her palaces!"
11:19 "Let us *d* the tree in its vigor;
12:17 I will uproot and *d* that nation entirely,
13:14 I will not spare or pity, but will *d* them.
14:12 Rather, I will *d* them with the sword,
15: 3 beasts of the earth to devour and *d* them.
15: 6 And so I stretched out my hand to *d* you,
18: 7 and tear down and *d* a nation or a kingdom.
18:18 And so, let us *d* him by his own tongue;
31:28 over them to uproot and pull down, to *d,*
34: 2 he will *d* it with fire.
34:22 attack and capture it, and *d* it with fire;
37: 8 they shall capture it and *d* it with fire.
37:10 would rise up and *d* the city with fire.
38:18 of the Chaldeans, who shall *d* it with fire,
43:13 *d* with fire the temples of the Egyptian gods.
49: 9 by night, they would *d* as they pleased.
49:38 in Elam and *d* from there king and princes,
51:11 Babylon he is resolved to *d.*
51:20 I shatter nations, with you I *d* kingdoms.
51:62 you yourself threatened to *d* this place,
Lam 3:66 wrath and *d* them from under your heavens!
Ez 6: 3 against you, and I will *d* your high places.
9: 8 Will you *d* all that is left of Israel when
20:17 on them with pity, not wanting to *d* them,
20:39 Come, each one of you, *d* your idols!
21:21 *d!* to the left!
25: 7 I will *d* you, and thus you shall know
26: 4 *d* the walls of Tyre and raze her towers.
34:16 [but the sleek and the strong I will *d,*
43: 3 I had seen when he came to *d* the city,
Dn 2:24 had appointed to *d* the wise men of Babylon,
4:20 'Cut down the tree and *d* it,
8:24 He shall *d* powerful peoples;
8:25 be proud of heart and *d* many by stealth.
9:26 leader who will come shall *d* the sanctuary.
11:17 in marriage in order to *d* the kingdom,
11:26 his table companions shall seek to *d* him,
14:42 had tried to *d* him he threw into the den,
Hos 2:20 and sword and war I will *d* from the land,
4: 5 I will *d* your mother.
10: 2 their altars and *d* their sacred pillars.
11: 9 blazing anger, I will not *d* Ephraim again;
Am 8: 4 upon the needy and *d* the poor of the land!
9: 8 *d* it from off the face of the earth.
Mi 1: 7 in the fire, and all her statues I will *d.*
5: 9 I will *d* the horses from your midst and
5:13 poles from your midst, and *d* your cities.
Zep 1: 3 will *d* mankind from the face of the earth,
1: 4 *d* from this place the last vestige of Baal,
2:13 his hand against the north, to *d* Assyria;
Hg 2:22 *d* the power of the kingdoms of the nations.
Zec 9: 6 I will *d* the pride of the Philistine
13: 2 *d* the names of the idols from the land,
Mal 3:11 I will forbid the locust to *d* your crops;
Mt 2:13 Herod is searching for the child to *d* him."
10:28 the body of life but cannot *d* the soul.
10:28 who can *d* both body and soul in Gehenna.
12:14 to plot against him to find a way to *d* him.
16:26 whole world and *d* himself in the process?
22: 7 to *d* those murderers and burn their city.
26:61 'I can *d* God's sanctuary and rebuild it in
27:40 *d* the temple and rebuild it in three days!
Mk 1:24 Have you come to *d* us?
3: 4 To preserve life—or *d* it?"
3: 6 with the Herodians how they might *d* him.
11:18 this and began to look for a way to *d* him.
12: 9 He will come and *d* those tenants and turn
14:58 'I will *d* this temple made by human hands,'
15:29 *d* the temple and rebuild it in three days!
Lk 4:34 Have you come to *d* us?
6: 9 To preserve life—or *d* it?"
9:54 us call down fire from heaven to *d* them?"
19:47 meanwhile were looking for a way to *d* him,
Jn 2:19 *D* this temple," was Jesus' answer,
10:10 comes only to steal and slaughter and *d,*
Acts 5:38 is human in its origins, it will *d* itself.
5:39 to *d* them without fighting God himself."
6:14 Jesus the Nazorean will *d* this place
Rom 14:20 Take care not to *d* God's work
1Cor 1:19 says, "I will *d* the wisdom of the wise,
3:17 destroys God's temple, God will *d* him.
2Cor 13:10 authority to build up rather than to *d.*
Gal 1:13 the church of God and tried to *d* it;
1:23 is now preaching the faith he tried to *d,*"
2Thes 2: 8 and the Lord Jesus will *d* him with the
Jas 4:12 Lawgiver and Judge, one who can save and *d.*
1Jn 3: 8 It was to *d* the devil's works that the Son
Rv 11:18 time to *d* those who lay the earth waste."

DESTROYED (198)

Gn 9:11 creatures be *d* by the waters of a flood;
13:10 before the LORD had *d* Sodom and Gomorrah
19:29 when God *d* the Cities of the Plain,
Ex 10: 7 you not yet realize that Egypt is being *d?*"
Lv 13:52 malignant leprosy, it must be *d* by fire.
13:55 article is unclean and shall be *d* by fire.
13:57 and the thing infected shall be *d* by fire.
Dt 4: 3 *d* from your midst everyone that followed
7:20 survivors who have hidden from you are *d.*
28:20 until you are speedily *d* and perish for
28:24 down upon you from the sky until you are *d.*
28:45 you and overwhelming you, until you are *d,*
28:51 the produce of your soil, until you are *d;*
28:61 LORD will bring upon you until you are *d.*
29:22 blade of grass, *d* like Sodom and Gomorrah,
31: 4 Og, the kings of the Amorites whom he *d,*
33:27 enemy out of your way and the Amorite he *d.*
Jos 7:15 having incurred the ban shall be *d* by fire,
8:28 Then Joshua *d* the place by fire,
9:24 that all its inhabitants be *d* before you.
23: 4 [as well as those I *d* between the Jordan
24: 8 and I *d* them [the two kings of Amorites]
Jgs 1: 8 then they *d* the city by fire.]
4:24 till at length they *d* the Canaanite king,
6:28 found that the altar of Baal had been *d,*
6:30 for he has *d* the altar of Baal and has cut
6:31 If he whose altar has been *d* is a god,
6:32 action against him, since he *d* his altar."
15: 6 went up and *d* her and her family by fire.
18:27 them to the sword and *d* their city by fire.
20:48 *d* by fire all the cities they came upon.
1Sm 15:20 Agag, and I have *d* Amalek under the ban.
2Sm 7: 9 and I have *d* all your enemies before you.
17:16 king and all the people with him will be *d.*"
22:38 I pursued my enemies and *d* them,
22:41 before me and those who hated me I *d.*
1Kgs 13:34 it was to be cut off and *d* from the earth.
16:12 Zimri *d* the entire house of Baasha,
18:30 the altar of the LORD which had been *d.*

22:11 you shall gore Aram until you have *d* them.' "
2Kgs 13: 7 had *d* them and trampled them like dust.
19:12 of the nations whom my fathers *d* save them?
19:18 they *d* them because they were not gods,
21: 3 places which his father Hezekiah had *d.*
21: 9 LORD had *d* at the coming of the Israelites.
23:11 The chariots of the sun he *d* by fire.
25: 9 every large building was *d* by fire.
1Chr 20: 1 When Joab had attacked Rabbah and *d* it,
2Chr 8: 8 the land, whom the Israelites had not *d*—
15: 6 for God *d* them by every kind of adversity.
18:10 you shall gore Aram until you have *d* them.' "
31: 1 Ephraim and Manasseh, until all were *d.*
32:21 sent an angel, who *d* every valiant warrior,
33: 9 LORD had *d* at the coming of the Israelites.
34: 4 presence, the altars of the Baals were *d;*
34: 7 he *d* the altars, broke up the sacred poles
36:19 afire, and *d* all its precious objects.
36:23 , and *d* all its precious objects.
Ezr 4:15 For that reason this city was *d.*
5:12 who *d* this house and led the people
Tb 14:10 fell into the deadly trap, and it *d* him.
Jdt 1:15 him through with spears, and utterly *d* him.
2:27 all their fields, *d* their flocks and herds,
4: 1 had despoiled all their temples and *d* them,
5:15 *d* all the Heshbonites by main force,
6: 8 not die till you are *d* together with them.
Est 3:13 women and children, should be killed, *d,*
B: 6 utterly *d* by the swords of their enemies,
E:24 shall be ruthlessly *d* with fire and sword,
9: 6 the Jews killed and *d* five hundred men.
9:12 Jews have killed and *d* five hundred men,
1Mc 1:30 and *d* many of the people in Israel.
3: 5 those who troubled his people he *d* by fire.
5:65 and he *d* its strongholds and burned the
5:68 He *d* their altars and burned the statues
6: 6 taken from the armies they had *d;*
6:12 orders that the inhabitants of Judah be *d.*
6:62 orders for the encircling wall to be *d.*
7: 6 "Judas and his brothers have *d* all your
8:11 had ever opposed them they *d* and enslaved;
9:73 the people and he *d* the impious in Israel.
10:84 and *d* by fire both the temple of Dagon and
11: 4 he was shown the temple of Dagon *d* by fire,
13:51 because a great enemy of Israel had been *d.*
2Mc 8: 3 *d* and about to be leveled to the ground;
8:19 eighty-five thousand of his men were *d,*
10: 2 they *d* the altars erected by the Gentiles
10:23 he *d* more than twenty thousand men in the
12:19 marched out and *d* the force of more than
Jb 4: 7 Since when are the upright *d?*
22: 9 and the resources of orphans you have *d.*
22:20 "Truly these have been *d* where they stood,
37:20 I speak, or when a man says he is being *d?*
Ps(s) 9: 4 turned back, overthrown and *d* before you.
9: 6 You rebuked the nations and *d* the wicked;
18:41 before me, and those who hated me you *d.*
37:28 Criminals are *d,*
37:34 when the wicked are *d,*
37:38 Sinners shall all alike be *d;*
63:10 But they shall be *d* who seek my life,
78:38 merciful, forgave their sin and *d* them not;
78:45 that devoured them and frogs that *d* them.
Prv 14:11 The house of the wicked will be *d,*
Wis 10: 6 from among the wicked who were being *d,*
14: 6 old, when the proud giants were being *d,*
16:27 For what was not *d* by fire,
18:12 instant their nobler offspring were *d.*
Sir 5: 9 at the time of vengeance, you will be *d.*
21: 4 so too a proud man's home is *d.*
44:18 with him, that never should all flesh be *d.*
45:19 angry, he *d* them in his burning wrath.
46: 6 army till on the slope he *d* the foe;
46:18 and *d* all the lords of the Philistines.
47: 7 He *d* the hostile Philistines and shattered
49: 2 our betrayals, and *d* the abominable idols.
Is 15: 1 Laid waste in a night, Ar of Moab is *d;*
15: 1 Laid waste in a night, Kir of Moab is *d.*
23: 1 O ships of Tarshish, for your port is *d;*
23:13 up towers for her, Has had her castles *d,*
23:14 O ships of Tarshish, for your haven is *d.*
26:14 For you have punished and *d* them,
27:10 Its boughs shall be *d,*
33: 1 Woe, O destroyer never *d,*
33: 1 When you finish destroying, you will be *d;*
37:12 of the nations whom my fathers *d* save them?
37:19 they *d* them because they were not gods but
60:12 those nations shall be utterly *d.*
Jer 4:26 with all its cities *d* before the LORD,
9:15 pursue them until I have completely *d* them.
15: 7 I *d* my people through bereavement;
33: 4 *d* in the face of siegeworks and the sword:
38:17 this city shall not be *d* with fire,
38:23 and this city shall be *d* with fire.
44:12 in Egypt, so that they shall be wholly *d.*
44:18 and are being *d* by the sword and by hunger.
44:27 sword or famine until they are utterly *d.*
48:20 Moab is disgraced, yes, *d,*
48:42 Moab shall be *d,*
49: 2 and her daughter cities shall be *d* by fire.
51:58 her lofty gates shall be *d* by fire.
52:13 every large building he *d* with fire.
Lam 2: 5 all her castles and *d* her fortresses;
2: 6 like a garden booth, he has *d* his dwelling;
2:17 he has *d* and had no pity,
2:22 I bore and reared my enemy has utterly *d.*"
Ez 19: 5 in vain she had waited, her hope was *d.*
27:32 ever *d* like Tyre in the midst of the sea?
32: 2 Lion of the nations, you are *d.*
32:12 of Egypt, and all her hordes shall be *d.*
36:35 and *d* are now repeopled and fortified."
36:36 what was *d* and replanted what was desolate.
Dn 2: 5 shall be cut to pieces and your houses *d.*
2:44 be *d* or delivered up to another people;
3:96 shall be cut to pieces and his house *d.*
6:27 his kingdom shall not be *d,*
7:14 be taken away, his kingship shall not be *d.*
11:20 glorious kingdom, but he shall soon be *d,*
14:22 over to Daniel, who *d* it and its temple.
14:28 "he has *d* Bel, killed the dragon,
Hos 10: 8 The high places of Aven shall be *d,*
Jl 1:17 the stores are *d,*
Am 2: 9 it was I who *d* the Amorites before them,
2: 9 I *d* their fruit above,
Ob 1: 5 robbers by night, how could you be thus *d:*
1: 9 be crushed, till all on Mount Esau are *d.*
1:10 shall cover you and you shall be *d* forever.
Jon 3: 4 "Forty days more and Nineveh shall be *d,*"
Mi 5: 8 your foes, and all your enemies shall be *d.*
Na 2: 1 by the scoundrel; he is completely *d*
3: 7 you runs from you, saying, "Nineveh is *d;*
Zep 1:11 for all the merchants will be *d,*
3: 6 I have *d* nations,
Mt 24:39 until the flood came and *d* them.
26:52 use the sword are sooner or later *d* by it.
Lk 6:49 immediately fell in and was completely *d.*"
17:27 and when the flood came, it *d* them all.
17:29 rained down from heaven and *d* them all.
Jn 11:50 people] than to have the whole nation *d?*"
Acts 13:19 then he *d* seven nations in the land of
Rom 6: 6 *d* and we might be slaves to sin no longer.
9:22 vessels fit for wrath, ready to be *d,*
1Cor 10: 9 some of them did, only to be *d* by snakes.
15:24 when, after having *d* every sovereignty,
15:26 feet, and the last enemy to be *d* is death.
2Cor 4: 9 we are struck down but never *d.*
4:16 our body is being *d* at the same time.
5: 1 the earthly tent in which we dwell is *d*
Heb 7:16 of the power of a life which cannot be *d.*
11:31 escaped from being *d* with the unbelievers,
2Pt 2:12 brute animals born to be caught and *d.*
2:12 of their decadence they too will be *d,*
3: 6 By water that world was then *d;*
3: 7 the day when godless men will be *d.*
3:10 the elements will be *d* by fire,
3:11 Since everything is to be *d* in this way,
3:12 the heavens will be *d* in flames and the
Jude 1: 5 but later *d* those who refused to believe.
Rv 18:17 a single hour this great wealth has been *d!*"

DESTROYER (13)

Ex 12:23 *d* come into your houses to strike you down.
Ps(s) 137: 8 O daughter of Babylon, you *d,*
Wis 18:25 To these names the *d* yielded,
Is 16: 4 live with you, be their shelter from the *d.*
33: 1 Woe, O *d* never destroyed,
54:16 also who have created the *d* to work havoc.
Jer 4: 7 his lair, the *d* of nations has set out,
6:26 wailing, For sudden upon us comes the *d.*
48: 8 The *d* comes upon every city,
51:25 destroying mountain, *d* of the entire earth,
51:56 For the *d* comes upon her,
Dn 12: 7 *d* of the holy people was brought to an end,
1Pt 4:15 a malefactor, or a *d* of another's rights.

DESTROYERS (3)

Jer 22: 7 Against you I will send *d,*
51:48 when the *d* come against her from the north,
51:53 inaccessible, *d* from me shall reach her,

DESTROYING (28)

Dt 28:63 he now take delight in ruining and *d* you,
1Kgs 9:16 after *d* it by fire and slaying all the
15:29 single soul to Jeroboam but *d* him utterly,
2Kgs 3:25 down the Moabites, and *d* the cities;
1Chr 21:12 the LORD's *d* angel in every part of Israel?
21:15 but as he was on the point of *d* it,
21:15 the calamity, and said to the *d* angel,
Est C: 8 ruin and are bent upon *d* the inheritance
9: 5 enemies with the sword, killing and *d* them;
1Mc 3: 8 the cities of Judah *d* the impious there.
9:54 torn down, thus *d* the work of the prophets.
2Mc 8:35 was eminently successful in *d* his own army.
12:23 sword and *d* as many as thirty thousand men.
Ps(s) 18: 5 about me, the *d* floods overwhelmed me;
91: 3 snare of the fowler, from the *d* pestilence.
Sir 21: 2 teeth are lion's teeth, *d* the souls of men.
Is 33: 1 When you finish *d,* you will be destroyed;
Jer 46: 8 cover the earth, *d* the city and its people.
46:16 land of our birth, away from the *d* sword."
47: 4 Yes, the LORD is *d* the Philistines,
50:16 Before the *d* sword, each of them turns
51: 1 those who live in Chaldea, a *d* wind.
51:25 I am against you, *d* mountain,
Ez 9: 2 north, each with a *d* weapon in his hand.
22:27 blood and *d* lives to get unjust gain.
22:30 before me to keep me from *d* the land;
1Cor 10:10 of them did, to be killed by the *d* angel.
Heb 11:28 that the *d* angel might not touch the

DESTROYS (17)

Ex 21:26 slave in the eye and *d* the use of the eye,
Dt 8:20 the nations which the LORD *d* before you,
28:48 an iron yoke on your neck, until he *d* you.
2Mc 3:39 down and *d* those who come to harm it."
Jb 9:22 Both the innocent and the wicked he *d.*
12:23 He makes nations great and he *d* them;
Prv 1:32 kills them, the smugness of fools *d* them.
22: 8 reaps calamity, and the rod *d* his labors.
Sir 6: 4 For contumacious desire *d* its owner and
10: 3 A wanton king *d* his people,
19: 3 him, for contumacious desire *d* its owner.
28:14 It *d* walled cities,
35:21 Till he *d* the haughty root and branch,
Mk 8:36 whole world and *d* himself in the process?
Lk 9:25 whole world and *d* himself in the process?
12:33 which no thief comes near nor any moth *d.*
1Cor 3:17 If anyone *d* God's temple,

DESTRUCTIBLE (1)

1Pt 1:23 from a *d* but from an indestructible seed,

DESTRUCTION (108)

Dt 7:10 who repays with *d* the person who hates him;
Jos 2:10 beyond the Jordan, whom you doomed to *d.*
10: 1 heard that, in the capture and *d* of Ai,
11:20 be doomed to *d* and thus receive no mercy,
Jgs 1:17 After having doomed the city to *d,*
20:42 who had been in the city were spreading *d.*
1Sm 15: 8 put into effect the ban of *d* by the sword.
15:18 put the sinful Amalekites under a ban of *d.*
2Sm 14:11 avenger of blood may not go too far in *d*
24:16 the angel causing the *d* among the people,
1Kgs 20:42 you have set free the man I doomed to *d,*
2Chr 22: 4 To his own *d,* he did evil
25:16 has let you take counsel to your own *d,*
26:16 to his own *d* and broke faith with the LORD,
Tb 14:15 of the *d* of Nineveh and saw its effects.
14:15 Before dying he rejoiced over Nineveh's *d,*
Jdt 2: 2 and urged the total *d* of those countries.
8:19 and fell with great *d* before our enemies.
11:15 it, they will be handed over to you for *d.*
11:22 and *d* to those who have despised my lord.
14:13 down to give us battle, to their utter *d.*"
Est A: 8 come upon them, and were at the point of *d.*
3: 7 the *d* of Mordecai's people on a single day,
4: 8 their *d* which had been promulgated in Susa,
7: 4 my people and I have been delivered to *d,*
8: 5 *d* of the Jews in all the royal provinces.
8: 6 and how can I behold the *d* of my race?"
E:13 of deceit, he demanded the *d* of Mordecai,
E:21 of *d* of the chosen race into one of joy.
E:23 those who plot against us a reminder of *d.*
9:24 or lot, for the time of their defeat and *d.*
1Mc 4:32 and let them tremble at their own *d.*
2Mc 12:27 After the defeat and *d* of these,
13: 6 brought up there and then hurled down to *d.*
Jb 5:22 At *d* and want you shall laugh;
15:23 vultures, he knows that his *d* is imminent.
18:14 Fiery *d* lodges in his tent,
21:17 How often does *d* come upon them,
31:29 Had I rejoiced at the *d* of my enemy or
Ps(s) 40: 3 He drew me out of the pit of *d,*
49:10 to remain alive always and not see *d.*
55:24 will bring them down into the pit of *d;*
78:33 their days and their years with sudden *d.*
92: 9 thrive, They are destined for eternal *d;*
103: 4 He redeems your life from *d,*
107:20 to heal them and to snatch them from *d.*
109:13 May his posterity meet with *d;*
Prv 24:22 For suddenly arises the *d* they send,
Wis 1:12 to yourselves *d* by the works of your hands.
1:13 nor does he rejoice in the *d* of the living.
3: 3 and their going forth from us, utter *d.*
18: 7 of the just and the *d* of their foes.
18:13 at the *d* of the first-born they
Sir 31: 6 by gold, though *d* lay before their eyes;
36: 8 and your people's oppressors meet *d.*
39:28 When *d* must be, they hurl all their force
40:10 evil, and it is they who bring on *d.*
48: 6 You sent kings down to *d,*
Is 10:22 their *d* is decreed as overwhelming
10:23 Yes, the *d* he has decreed,
13: 6 as *d* from the Almighty it comes.
14:23 I will sweep it with the broom of *d,*
23:11 has ordered the *d* of Canaan's strongholds.
28:22 hosts, the *d* decreed for the whole earth.
38:17 have preserved my life from the pit of *d,*
51:19 Desolation and *d,* famine and sword!
54:14 oppression, where *d* cannot come near you.
65:23 in vain, nor beget children for sudden *d;*
Jer 4: 6 Evil I bring from the north, and great *d.*
4:15 Dan, from Mount Ephraim they announce *d:*
6: 1 threatens from the north, and mighty *d.*
6: 7 Violence and *d* resound in her;

DESTRUCTION (cont.)
8:14 For the LORD has wrought our *d*,
14:17 Over the great *d* which overwhelms the
17:18 of misfortune, crush them with repeated *d*.
48: 3 a cry from Horonaim of ruin and great *d*!
48: 5 descent to Horonaim the cry of *d* is heard.
49: 8 *d* upon Esau when I come to punish him.
50:22 Battle alarm in the land, dire *d*!
51:54 dire *d* from the land of the Chaldeans;
Lam 2: 8 marked for *d* the wall of daughter Zion:
3:47 desolation and *d*; My eyes run
Bar 4: 6 were sold to the nations not for your *d*;
4:25 see their *d* and trample upon their necks.
Ez 17:17 towers are built for the *d* of many lives,
21:36 you over to ravaging men, artisans of *d*.
23:33 holds so much, Filled with *d* and grief,
Dn 7:26 is taken away by final and absolute *d*,
11:16 shall stop in the glorious land, dealing *d*.
Hos 8: 4 made idols for themselves, to their own *d*.
13: 9 Your *d*, O Israel!
Am 5: 9 Who flashes *d* upon the strong,
Hb 1: 3 *D* and violence are before me;
2:17 and the *d* of the beasts shall terrify you;
Zep 1:15 and distress, A day of *d* and desolation,
Zec 12: 9 On that day I will seek the *d* of all
1Cor 2: 6 of this age, who are men headed for *d*.
5: 5 him over to Satan for the *d* of his flesh,
2Cor 2:15 are being saved and those on the way to *d*;
4: 3 only for those who are headed toward *d*.
10: 4 God's power for the *d* of strongholds.
10: 8 for your upbuilding and not for your *d*,
Gal 5:15 You will end up in mutual *d*!
1Tm 6: 9 desires which drag men down to ruin and *d*.
2Pt 2: 3 their *d* is not asleep.
2: 6 Gomorrah in ashes and condemned them to *d*,
Rv 18:19 In a single hour her *d* has come about!"

DESTRUCTIVE (12)
Ex 12:13 of Egypt, no *d* blow will come upon you.
Ps(s) 106:23 him in the breach to turn back his *d* wrath.
Prv 18: 9 work is own brother to the man who is *d*.
Wis 1:14 And there is not a *d* drug among them nor
Is 28: 2 who, like a downpour of hail, a *d* storm,
30:28 Will winnow the nations with a *d* winnowing,
59: 7 Their thoughts are *d* thoughts,
Ez 5:16 against you the cruel, *d* arrows of hunger,
13:13 and hailstones shall fall with *d* wrath.
25:15 vengeance with *d* malice in their hearts,
Mt 24:15 "When you see the abominable and *d* thing
Mk 13:14 *d* presence standing where it should not be

DETACHED (3)
Jgs 4:11 Heber had *d* himself from his own people,
2Kgs 16:17 King Ahaz *d* the frames from the bases and
1Mc 11:68 *d* an ambush against him in the mountains.

DETACHMENT (4)
2Kgs 11:18 appointing a *d* for the temple of the LORD,
1Mc 4: 1 and this *d* set out at night in order to
4:19 was finishing this speech, a *d* appeared,
Ps(s) 78:49 fury and strife, a *d* of messengers of doom.

DETACHMENTS (2)
1Chr 12:24 This is the muster of the *d* of armed
Jdt 7: 7 he seized, stationing armed *d* around them,

DETAIL (13)
Jgs 18: 2 *d* of five valiant men of Zorah and Eshtaol,
2Sm 23: 5 with me, set forth in *d* and secured.
2Chr 8:16 of the LORD had been completed in every *d*.
Est F: 2 not a single *d* has been left unfulfilled
2Mc 2:23 of Cyrene set forth in *d* in five volumes,
14: 9 informed yourself in *d* on these matters,
Sir 28: 1 for he remembers their sins in *d*.
38:28 he keeps watch till he perfects it in *d*.
Lk 1:65 began to be recounted to the last *d*.
Jn 21:25 did, yet if they were written about in *d*,
Acts 18:26 to him God's new way in greater *d*.
21:19 and then described in *d* all that God had
Heb 9: 5 We cannot speak now of each of these in *d*.

DETAILED (5)
2Kgs 16:10 altar and a *d* design of its construction.
Jdt 10:17 So they *d* a hundred of their men as an
Est 10: 2 a *d* account of the greatness of Mordecai,
2Mc 2:31 and to omit *d* treatment of the matter.
Mt 2: 8 "Go and get *d* information about the child.

DETAILS (6)
2Sm 11:18 David a report of all the *d* of the battle,
11:19 giving the king all the *d* of the battle,
11:22 David all the *d* as Joab had instructed him.
2Mc 2:28 for exact *d* to the original author,
11:20 On the *d* of these matters I have
Lk 10:40 who was busy with all the *d* of hospitality,

DETAIN (1)
Gn 24:56 But he said to them, "Do not *d* me,

DETAINED (6)
Gn 32: 5 with Laban and have been *d* there until now.
Jgs 19: 4 He was *d* by the girl's father,
1Sm 21: 8 was there that day, *d* before the LORD;
Tb 10: 2 Perhaps he has been *d* there;
1Mc 13:15 "We have *d* your brother Jonathan on
Acts 12: 5 Peter was thus *d* in prison,

DETECT (1)
Ps(s) 19:13 in keeping them, Yet who can *d* failings?

DETECTED (1)
Gal 6: 1 My brothers, if someone is *d* in sin,

DETER (1)
Rv 12:11 love for life did not *d* them from death.

DETERIORATES (1)
Eph 4:22 self which *d* through illusion and desire,

DETERMINATION (1)
Wis 14:19 he, mayhap in his *d* to please the ruler,

DETERMINE (10)
Lv 13:59 to *d* whether it is clean or unclean."
16: 8 he shall cast lots to *d* which one is for
27: 8 who shall *d* the sum for his ransom in
27:12 who shall *d* its value in keeping with its
27:14 the priest shall *d* its value in keeping
Jgs 3: 4 to *d* whether they would obey the
Est 3: 7 was cast in Haman's presence to *d* the day
Jer 42:17 All those men who *d* to go to Egypt to stay,
Acts 11:29 the disciples *d* to set something aside,
23:28 to *d* what their charge against him was.

DETERMINED (39)
Lv 16: 9 The goat that is *d* by lot for the LORD,
16:10 But the goat *d* by lot for Azazel he shall
27:32 shall be *d* by ceding to the LORD as sacred
Jos 14: 1 of the Israelites *d* their heritage by lot,
Ru 1:18 her, for she saw she was *d* to go with her.
1Sm 13: 8 the time Samuel had *d*.
20: 9 my father is *d* to inflict injury upon you,
29: 9 *d* you are not to go up with us to battle.
2Sm 13:32 for Absalom was *d* on this ever since Amnon
1Kgs 7:47 weight of the bronze, therefore, was not *d*.
2Kgs 14:27 Since the LORD had not *d* to blot out the
2Chr 19: 3 from the land and have been *d* to seek God."
25:20 for God had *d* to hand them over because
Neh 10:35 have *d* by lot concerning the procurement
Jdt 11:12 and *d* to consume all the things which God
12: 4 Lord accomplishes by my hand what he has *d*."
Est B: 2 I *d* not to be carried away with the sense
1Mc 1:62 But many in Israel were *d* and resolved in
12:39 Trypho was *d* to become king of Asia,
2Mc 15: 6 Nicanor had *d* to erect a public monument
15:17 hearts to courage, the Jews *d* not to delay,
Jb 38: 5 Who *d* its size; do you know?
Wis 8: 9 So I *d* to take her to live with me,
18: 5 When they *d* to put to death the infants of
Jer 23:20 and fulfilled what he has *d* in his heart.
30:24 and fulfilled what he has *d* in his heart.
42:15 If you are *d* to go to Egypt,
44:11 I have *d* evil against you;
Ez 45:11 by the homer they shall be *d*.
Dn 11:36 is ready, for what is *d* must take place.
13:28 also came, fully *d* to put Susanna to death.
Zec 1: 6 ways and deeds, just as he had *d* he would."
8:14 As I *d* to harm you when your fathers
8:15 so again in these days I have *d* to favor
Jn 5:18 The reason why the Jews were even more *d*
Acts 5:28 are *d* to make us responsible for that man's
25:25 Majesty the Emperor, I *d* to send him on.
1Cor 2: 2 I *d* that while I was with you I would
2Cor 1:17 Or that my plans are so *d* by self-interest

DETERRED (2)
Jb 39:22 He laughs at fear and cannot be *d*;
Sir 32:18 the proud and insolent man is *d* by nothing.

DETEST (3)
Is 1:14 Your new moons and festivals I *d*;
Rom 12: 9 *D* what is evil, cling to what is good.
Rv 2: 6 you *d* the practices of the Nicolaitans,

DETESTABLE (11)
2Chr 15: 8 he was encouraged to remove the *d* idols
Sir 19:19 There is a shrewdness that is *d*,
Jer 4: 1 If you put your *d* things out of my sight,
16:18 my land with their *d* corpses of idols,
Ez 5:11 my sanctuary with all your *d* abominations,
11:18 and remove from it all its *d* abominations.
11:21 hearts are devoted to their *d* abominations,
20: 7 you, the *d* things that have held your eyes;
20: 8 away the *d* things that had held their eyes,
20:30 Will you lust after their *d* idols?
Rv 21:27 anyone who is a liar or has done a *d* act.

DETESTATION (1)
2Mc 14:39 Nicanor, to show his *d* of the Jews,

DETESTED (8)
Nm 22: 3 because of their numbers, and *d* them.
1Sm 27:12 must certainly be *d* by his people Israel.
2Mc 1:27 kindly on those who are despised and *d*,
4:36 together with the Greeks who *d* the crime,
Eccl 2:18 *d* all the fruits of my labor under the sun,
Sir 16: 8 neighbors of Lot whom he *d* for their pride;
20: 7 He who talks too much is *d*;
Lam 2: 1 the Lord in his wrath has *d* daughter Zion!

DETESTS (2)
Dt 12:31 gods every abomination that the LORD *d*,
16:22 pillar, such as the LORD, your God, *d*.

DETHRONED (1)
Is 47: 1 daughter Babylon; Sit on the ground, *d*,

DETOURED (1)
Nm 20:21 their territory, Israel *d* around them.

DETRACTOR (1)
Sir 5:16 Be not called a *d*;

DETRIMENT (1)
Ezr 4:22 lest the evil grow to the *d* of the throne."

DEVASTATE (6)
Gn 9:11 shall not be another flood to *d* the earth."
Lv 26:31 waste your cities and *d* your sanctuaries,
1Mc 14:31 Jews sought to invade and *d* their country
Ez 30:11 nations, shall be brought in to *d* the land.
30:12 in it I will hand over to foreigners to *d*.
30:13 fear into the land of Egypt, and *d* Pathros.

DEVASTATED (8)
Lv 26:32 So *d* will I leave the land that your very
Dt 33: 2 blazed forth and his wrath *d* the nations.
Jdt 2:23 He *d* Put and Lud,
2:27 despoiled their cities, *d* their plains,
3: 8 he *d* their whole territory and cut down
Ez 30: 7 She shall be the most *d* of lands,
32:15 the land shall be *d* of all that is in it;
Zep 3: 6 Their cities are *d*,

DEVASTATING (2)
Ps(s) 91: 6 roams in darkness nor the *d* plague at noon.
Prv 28: 3 poor is like a *d* rain that leaves no food.

DEVASTATION (9)
Jdt 8:22 the land, and for the *d* of our inheritance,
1Mc 15:31 talents of silver for the *d* you have caused
Sir 44:17 perfect, renewed the race in the time of *d*.
Ez 25: 3 my sanctuary, the *d* of the land of Israel,
26:21 I will make you a *d*,
35:15 In keeping with your glee over the *d* of
Mi 6:13 to strike you with *d* because of your sins.
Zep 1:13 be given to pillage and their houses to *d*;
Lk 21:20 by soldiers, know that its *d* is near.

DEVELOPED (2)
Lv 13:11 in it, it is skin leprosy that has long *d*.
Ez 16: 7 You grew and *d*, you came to the age

DEVIATED (1)
Jdt 5:18 they *d* from the way he prescribed for them,

DEVIATION (1)
2Chr 8:15 There was no *d* from the king's command in

DEVICE (1)
Jos 9: 4 of Gibeon put into effect a *d* of their own.

DEVICES (9)
2Chr 26:15 *d* contrived to stand on the towers and at
1Mc 5:30 ladders and *d* for capturing the stronghold,
6:20 he constructed catapults and other *d*.
Ps(s) 5:11 let them fall by their own *d*;
10: 2 caught in the *d* the wicked have contrived.
Prv 1:31 own way, and with their own *d* be glutted.
Wis 1: 9 *d* of the wicked man shall be scrutinized,
Jer 18:12 We will follow our own *d*;
Bar 1:22 off after the *d* of our own wicked hearts,

DEVIL (36)
Wis 2:24 But by the envy of the *d*,
Mt 4: 1 by the Spirit to be tempted by the *d*.
4: 5 Next the *d* took him to the holy city,
4: 8 The *d* then took him up a very high
4:11 At that the *d* left him,
13:39 one and the enemy who sowed them is the *d*.
23:15 a *d* of him twice as wicked as yourselves.
25:41 fire prepared for the *d* and his angels!

Lk 4: 2 forty days, where he was tempted by the *d.*
4: 3 The *d* said to him, "If you are the Son
4: 5 Then the *d* took him up higher and showed
4: 9 Then the *d* led him to Jerusalem,
4:13 When the *d* had finished all the tempting
8:12 but the *d* comes and takes the word out of
11:14 a *d* which was mute, and when the devil
Jn 6:70 Yet one of you is a *d.*"
8:44 The father you spring from is the *d,*
10:20 "He is possessed by a *d*— out of his mind!
10:21 a *d* cannot open the eyes of the blind!"
13: 2 The *d* had already induced Judas,
Acts 10:38 healing all who were in the grip of the *d,*
Eph 4:27 do not give the *d* a chance to work on you.
6:11 to stand firm against the tactics of the *d.*
1Tm 3: 6 the punishment once meted out to the *d.*
Heb 2:14 that by his death he might rob the *d,*
Jas 4: 7 God, resist the *d* and he will take flight.
1Pt 5: 8 Your opponent the *d* is prowling like a
1Jn 3: 8 sins belongs to the *d,* because the devil
Jude 1: 9 when his case with the *d* was being judged
Rv 2:10 The *d* will indeed cast some of you into
12: 9 ancient serpent known as the *d* or Satan,
12:12 and sea, for the *d* has come down upon you!
20: 2 the ancient serpent, who is the *d* or Satan,
20:10 The *d* who led them astray was hurled into

DEVILISH (1)

Jas 3:15 It is earthbound, a kind of animal, even *d,*

DEVILS—DEVIL'S (16)

Lk 8: 2 Magdalene, from whom seven *d* had gone out,
8:35 they found the man from whom the *d* had
8:38 the *d* had departed asked to come with him,
10:20 in the fact that the *d* are subject to you
11:15 "It is by Beelzebul, the prince of *d,*
11:15 the prince of devils, that he casts out *d.*"
11:18 say it is by Beelzebul that I cast out *d.*
11:19 If I cast out *d* by Beelzebul,
11:20 is by the finger of God that I cast out *d,*
13:32 tomorrow I cast out *d* and perform cures,
1Tm 3: 7 does not fall into disgrace and the *d* trap.
2Tm 2:26 do his will, they shall escape the *d* trap.
1Jn 3: 8 It was to destroy the *d* works that the Son
3:10 who are God's children, and who are the *d.*
Rv 16:14 these spirits were *d* who worked prodigies.
16:16 The *d* then assembled the kings in a place

DEVIOUS (5)

Prv 2:15 Whose ways are crooked, and *d* their paths;
14: 2 but he who is *d* in his ways spurns him.
Is 30:12 put your trust in what is crooked and *d,*
Lk 16: 8 *d* employee credit for being enterprising!
Jas 1: 8 sort, *d* and erratic in all that he does,

DEVISE (8)

2Chr 2:13 to *d* every type of artistic work
Jdt 9: 5 Whatever you *d* comes into being;
Ps(s) 64: 7 They *d* a wicked scheme,
140: 3 men, From those who *d* evil in their hearts,
Ez 38:10 your mind, and you shall *d* an evil scheme:
Dn 11:24 and *d* plots against their strongholds;
Am 6: 5 like David, they *d* their own accompaniment.
2Thes 2:10 every seduction the wicked can *d*

DEVISED (11)

1Chr 23: 5 instruments which David had *d* for praise.
Est 8: 3 and the plan he had *d* against the Jews.
9:25 wicked plan Haman had *d* against the Jews
1Mc 13:29 the pyramids he *d* a setting of big columns,
Ps(s) 64: 7 and conceal the scheme they have *d;*
Wis 14: 2 For the urge for profits *d* this latter,
14:14 and therefore a sudden end is *d* for them.
Dn 11:25 succeed because of the plots *d* against him.
Hos 7:15 their arms, yet they *d* evil against me.
Na 1:11 you he came who *d* evil against the LORD,
Hb 2:10 You have *d* shame for your household,

DEVISING (2)

Ps(s) 21:12 they intend evil against you, *d* plots,
Wis 14:12 the source of wantonness is the *d* of idols;

DEVOID (2)

Dt 32:28 For they are a people *d* of reason,
Jude 1:19 These sensualists, *d* of the Spirit,

DEVOLVED (1)

Sir 45: 2 God's honor *d* upon him,

DEVOTE (9)

1Sm 7: 3 your Ashtaroth, *d* yourselves to the LORD,
1Chr 22:19 *d* your hearts and souls to seeking the
2Chr 31: 4 that they might *d* themselves entirely to
Mi 4:13 You shall *d* their spoils to the LORD,
Rom 13: 6 ministers who *d* themselves to his service
1Cor 7: 5 for a time, to *d* yourselves to prayer.
7:35 you to *d* yourselves entirely to the Lord.
1Tm 4:13 *d* yourself to the reading of Scripture,
Ti 3:14 Let our people *d* themselves to honest work

DEVOTED (21)

Gn 22:12 I know now how *d* you are to God,
Ex 21: 5 am *d* to my master and my wife and children;
Dt 15:16 because he is *d* to you and your household,
1Kgs 8:61 You must be wholly *d* to the LORD,
2Chr 16: 9 those who are *d* to him wholeheartedly.
1Mc 4:42 He chose blameless priests, *d* to the law;
Ps(s) 86: 2 Keep my life, for I am *d* to you;
Wis 14:30 ill of God and *d* themselves to idols,
Sir 1:13 With *d* men was she created from of old,
40:19 but better than either, a *d* wife;
46: 6 And because he was a *d* follower of God
46:10 good it is to be a *d* follower of the LORD.
51:18 I became resolutely *d* to her
Ez 11:21 are *d* to their detestable abominations,
20:16 So much were their hearts *d* to their idols,
Acts 1:14 they *d* themselves to constant prayer.
2:42 They *d* themselves to the apostles'
8:13 the rest and became a *d* follower of Philip.
1Cor 8: 7 Because some were so recently *d* to idols,
16:15 and is *d* to the service of the saints.
1Pt 4: 3 *d* enough time to what the pagans enjoy,

DEVOTES (2)

Sir 7:20 nor a laborer who *d* himself to his task.
39: 1 How different the man who *d* himself to the

DEVOTING (1)

Nm 8:11 thus *d* them to the service of the LORD.

DEVOTION (14)

2Sm 16:17 "Is this your *d* to your friend?
2Chr 6:42 of your anointed, remember the *d* of David,
24:22 unmindful of the *d* shown him by Jehoiada,
Neh 13:14 Let not the *d* which I showed for the house
Est B: 3 for constant *d* and steadfast loyalty,
2Mc 6:30 with joy in my soul because of my *d* to him."
Jb 15: 4 with piety, and you lessen *d* toward God,
Sg 8: 6 love, relentless as the nether world is *d;*
Wis 10:12 that *d* to God is mightier than all else.
Jer 2: 2 I remember the *d* of your youth,
31:22 the woman must encompass the man with *d.*
2Cor 7:12 in the sight of God the *d* you have for us.
11: 3 your sincere and complete *d* to Christ.
2Pt 3:11 How holy in your conduct and *d,*

DEVOUR (66)

Nm 22: 4 "Soon this horde will *d* all the country
24: 8 He shall *d* the nations like grass,
Dt 28:38 little, for the locusts will *d* the crops.
Jgs 9:15 the buckthorn and *d* the cedars of Lebanon.'
9:20 *d* the citizens of Shechem and Beth-millo,
9:20 of Shechem and Beth-millo, to *d* Abimelech."
1Kgs 14:11 line dies in the city, dogs will *d* him;
16: 4 line dies in the city, dogs shall *d* him;
21:23 shall *d* Jezebel in the district of Jezreel.")
21:24 line dies in the city, dogs will *d* him;
21:24 the field, the birds of the sky will *d* him."
2Kgs 9:10 shall *d* Jezebel at the confines of Jezreel,
2Chr 7:13 if I command the locust to *d* the land,
Jdt 7: 4 "Soon they will *d* the whole country.
Ps(s) 21:10 consume them in his anger; let fire *d* them.
27: 2 When evildoers come at me to *d* my flesh,
57: 5 in the midst of lions which *d* men;
Prv 30:17 the young eagles will *d* it.
Eccl 5:10 riches, there are also many to *d* them.
Is 1: 7 land before your eyes strangers *d* [a waste,
9:11 on the west *d* Israel with open mouth.
31: 8 by man, no mortal sword shall *d* him;
Jer 5:14 this people is the wood that it shall *d*—
5:17 *d* your harvest and your bread, devour
5:17 Devour your sheep and cattle, *d* your
15: 3 beasts of the earth to *d* and destroy them.
21:14 forest that shall *d* all its surroundings.
30:16 Yet all who *d* you shall be devoured,
49:27 and it shall *d* the palaces of Ben-hadad.
50:32 a fire that shall *d* everything around him.
Ez 7:15 and famine shall *d* those in the city.
15: 7 from the fire, but the fire shall *d* them.
21: 3 a fire in you that shall *d* all trees,
22:25 they *d* people, seizing their wealth
28:18 out fire from your midst which will *d* you.
35:12 are desolate, they have been given us to *d.*"
36:14 *d* men or rob your people of their children,
Dn 7: 5 It was given the order, "Up, *d* much flesh."
7:23 It shall *d* the whole earth,
14:32 given nothing, so that they would *d* Daniel.
Hos 2:14 rank growth and wild beasts shall *d* them.
5: 7 new moon *d* them together with their fields.
8:14 fire upon his cities, to *d* their castles.
11: 6 to repent, their own counsels shall *d* them.
13: 8 I will *d* them on the spot like a lion,
Am 1: 4 of Hazael, to *d* the castles of Ben-hadad.
1: 7 upon the wall of Gaza, to *d* her castles;
1:10 upon the wall of Tyre, to *d* her castles.
1:12 Teman, and it will *d* the castles of Bozrah.
1:14 and it will *d* her castles Amid clamor on
2: 2 upon Moab, to *d* the castles of Kerioth;
2: 5 upon Judah, to *d* the castles of Jerusalem.
Ob 1:18 and they shall set them ablaze and *d* them;
Na 2:14 and the sword shall *d* your young lions;
Hb 1: 8 They fly like the eagle hastening to *d;*
Zec 11: 1 O Lebanon, that the fire may *d* your cedars!
11: 9 those that are left *d* one another's flesh."
12: 6 and they shall *d* right and left all the
Mk 12:40 These men *d* the savings of widows and
Jas 5: 3 it will *d* your flesh like a fire.
1Pt 5: 8 a roaring lion looking for someone to *d.*
Rv 11: 5 of these witnesses to *d* their enemies.
12: 4 to *d* her child when it should be born.
17:16 they will *d* her flesh and set her on fire.

DEVOURED (38)

Gn 37:20 we could say that a wild beast *d* him.
37:33 A wild beast has *d* him!
Nm 23:24 It rests not till it has *d* its prey and
Dt 31:17 so that they will become a prey to be *d,*
1Kgs 14:11 he will be *d* by the birds of the sky.
16: 4 he shall be *d* by the birds of the sky."
Est A:10 lowly were exalted and they *d* the nobles.
Ps(s) 78:45 that *d* them and frogs that destroyed them.
79: 7 have *d* Jacob and laid waste his dwelling.
105:35 *d* every plant throughout the land; they *d*
Is 3:14 It is you who have *d* the vineyard;
Jer 2:30 sword *d* your prophets like a ravening lion.
3:24 has *d* our fathers' toil from our youth,
10:25 For they have *d* Jacob utterly,
15:16 When I found your words, I *d* them;
30:16 Yet all who devour you shall be *d,*
46:14 the sword has already *d* your neighbors.
50: 7 Whoever came upon them *d* them,
50:17 Formerly the king of Assyria *d* her,
Lam 2:16 They say, "We have *d* her.
Ez 15: 5 less, when the fire has *d* and scorched it,
16:20 and offered as sacrifices to be *d* by them!
19: 3 He learned to seize prey, men he *d,*
19: 6 He learned to seize prey, men he *d;*
19:12 her strong branch withered up, fire *d* it.
19:14 came out of the branch and *d* her shoots;
23:25 and what is left of you shall be *d* by fire.
34:28 by the nations or *d* by beasts of the earth,
Dn 3:22 the flames *d* the men who threw Shadrach,
7: 7 iron teeth with which it *d* and crushed,
14:42 they were *d* in a moment before his eyes.
Jl 1:19 for fire has *d* the pastures of the plain,
1:20 and fire has *d* the pastures of the plain.
Am 4: 9 fig trees and olive trees the locust *d;*
7: 4 It had *d* the great abyss,
Zec 9: 4 on the sea, and she shall be *d* by fire.
Rv 20: 9 but fire came down from heaven and *d* them.

DEVOURER (2)

Jl 1: 4 what the grasshopper left, the *d* has eaten.
2:25 locust has eaten, The grasshopper, the *d,*

DEVOURING (12)

2Sm 22: 9 his nostrils, and a *d* fire from his mouth;
1Kgs 8:37 or mildew, or a locust swarm, or *d* insects;
Ps(s) 18: 9 and a *d* fire from his mouth that kindled
50: 3 Before him is a *d* fire;
Prv 30:14 are knives, *D* the needy from the earth,
Is 9:17 burns like fire, *d* brier and thorn;
Jer 8:16 They come *d* the land and all it contains,
Lam 2: 3 Jacob like a flaming fire *d* all about it.
Dn 7:19 *d* and crushing with its iron teeth and
Jl 2: 5 the crackling of a fiery flame *d* stubble;
Hb 3:14 would be of *d* the wretched in their lair.
Heb 11:34 put out raging fires, escaped the *d* sword;

DEVOURS (14)

Gn 49:27 mornings he *d* the prey,
Nm 22: 4 us as an ox *d* the grass of the field."
2Sm 11:25 for the sword *d* now here and now there.
Jb 39:24 Frenzied and trembling he *d* the ground;
Prv 13:23 A lawsuit *d* the tillage of the poor,
Eccl 6: 2 to partake of them, but a stranger *d* them.
Is 9:18 brother, each *d* the flesh of his neighbor.
9:20 Manasseh *d* Ephraim,
24: 6 Therefore a curse *d* the earth,
Jer 46:10 The sword *d,*
Ez 15: 4 fire as fuel and the fire *d* both ends
36:13 said of you, "You are a land that *d* men,
Jl 2: 3 Before them a fire *d,*
Hb 1:13 wicked man *d* one more just than himself?

DEVOUT (13)

1Mc 2:42 all of them *d* followers of the law.
2Mc 1:19 *d* priests of the time took some of the
Sir 23:12 For all such words are foreign to the *d,*
27:11 Ever wise are the discourses of the *d,*
Is 57: 1 *D* men are swept away,
Jn 9:31 that if someone is *d* and obeys his will,
Acts 2: 5 were *d* Jews of every nation under heaven.
8: 2 *D* men buried Stephen,
10: 7 he called two servants and a *d* soldier from
13:43 many Jews and *d* Jewish converts followed
22:12 a *d* observer of the law and well spoken of
Jas 1:26 control his tongue imagines that he is *d,*
2Pt 2: 9 knows how to rescue *d* men from trial,

DEVOUTLY (2)

Lk 1:75 We should serve him *d* and through all our
Ti 2:12 *d* in this age as we await our blessed hope,

DEW (42)

Gn 27:28 "May God give to you of the *d* of the
27:39 far from the *d* of the heavens above!
Ex 16:13 In the morning a *d* lay all about the camp,
16:14 about the camp, and when the *d* evaporated,
Nm 11: 9 At night, when the *d* fell upon the camp,
Dt 32: 2 and my discourse permeate like the *d*,
33:28 and wine, where the heavens drip with *d*.
Jgs 6:37 If *d* comes on the fleece alone,
6:38 morning he wrung the *d* from the fleece,
6:39 dry, but let there be *d* on all the ground."
6:40 was dry, but there was *d* on all the ground.
2Sm 1:21 may there be neither *d* nor rain upon you,
17:12 down upon him as *d* alights on the ground.
1Kgs 17: 1 shall be no *d* or rain except at my word."
2Mc 8:27 descend on them the first *d* of his mercy.
Jb 29:19 the *d* rests by night on my branches.
38:28 or who has begotten the drops of *d*?
Ps(s) 110: 3 before the daystar, like the *d*,
133: 3 It is a *d* like that of Hermon,
Prv 3:20 break open, and the clouds drop down *d*.
19:12 a lion, but his favor, like *d* on the grass.
Sg 5: 2 For my head is wet with *d*,
Wis 11:22 drop of morning *d* come down upon the earth.
Sir 18:15 Like *d* that abates a burning wind,
43:23 the scattered *d* enriches the parched land.
Is 18: 4 like a cloud of *d* at harvest time.
26:19 For your dew is a *d* of light,
45: 8 descend, O heavens, like *d* from above,
Dn 3:64 Every shower and *d*, bless the Lord;
3:68 *D* and rain, bless the Lord;
4:12 Let him be bathed with the *d* of heaven;
4:20 let him be bathed with the *d* of heaven,
4:22 an ox and be bathed with the *d* of heaven;
4:30 his body was bathed with the *d* of heaven,
5:21 his body was bathed with the *d* of heaven,
Hos 6: 4 cloud, like the *d* that early passes away.
13: 3 cloud or like the *d* that early passes away,
14: 6 I will be like the *d* for Israel:
Mi 5: 6 many peoples, Like *d* coming from the LORD,
Hg 1:10 the heavens withheld from you their *d*,
Zec 8:12 crops, and the heavens shall give their *d*;

DEW-LADEN (1)

Dn 3:50 though a *d* breeze were blowing through it.

DIADEM (16)

Ex 29: 6 on his head, the sacred *d* on the miter.
39:30 *d* was made of pure gold and inscribed,
Lv 8: 9 attaching the gold plate, the sacred *d*,
Est 2:17 So he placed the royal *d* on her head and
Jb 19: 9 of my glory, and taken the *d* from my brow.
31:36 on my shoulder or put it on me like a *d*;
Prv 1: 9 A graceful *d* will they be for your head;
4: 9 She will put on your head a graceful *d*;
14:24 the *d* of fools is folly.
Wis 5:16 the splendid crown, the beauteous *d*,
Sir 45:12 On his turban the *d* of gold,
Is 28: 5 a brilliant *d* to the remnant of his people,
61: 3 who mourn in Zion a *d* instead of ashes,
61:10 Like a bridegroom adorned with a *d*,
62: 3 of the LORD, a royal *d* held by your God.
Ez 16:12 your ears, and a glorious *d* upon your head.

DIADEMS (4)

Ez 23:42 women's arms and splendid *d* on their heads.
Rv 12: 3 on his heads were seven *d*.
13: 1 ten *d* and on its heads blasphemous names.
19:12 like fire, and on his head were many *d*.

DIAGNOSIS (1)

Sir 38:14 beseeches God That his *d* may be correct

DIAMETER (3)

1Kgs 7:38 in *d* with a capacity of forty measures,
2Chr 4: 2 It was perfectly round, ten cubits in *d*,
Jer 52:21 cubits high and twelve cubits in *d*;

DIAMOND (3)

Jer 17: 1 Engraved with a *d* point
Ez 3: 9 your brow as stubborn as theirs, like *d*,
Rv 21:11 of a precious jewel that sparkled like a *d*.

DIAMOND-HARD (1)

Zec 7:12 And they made their hearts *d* so as not to

DIASPORA (1)

Jn 7:35 is not going off to the *D* among the Greeks,

DIBLAIM (1)

Hos 1: 3 he went and took Gomer, the daughter of *D*;

DIBON (9)

Nm 21:30 plowland is ruined from Heshbon to *D*;
32: 3 and said, "The region of Ataroth, *D*,
32:34 Gadites rebuilt the fortified towns of *D*,
Jos 13: 9 through the tableland of Medeba and *D*,
13:17 its towns which are on the tableland, *D*,
Neh 11:25 dependencies, in *D* and its dependencies,
Is 15: 2 goes daughter *D* to the high places to weep;
Jer 48:18 sit on the ground, you that dwell in *D*;
48:22 on Holon, Jahzah, and Mephaath, on *D*,

DIBON-GAD (2)

Nm 33:45 out from Iye-abarim, they camped at *D*.
33:46 Setting out from *D*,

DIBRI (1)

Lv 24:10 mother (Shelomith, daughter of *D*,

DICE (3)

Mk 15:24 *d* for them to see what each should take.
Lk 23:34 divided his garments, rolling *d* for them.
Jn 19:24 Let us throw *d* to see who gets it."

DICTATE (1)

Lk 2:24 accord with the *d* in the law of the Lord.

DICTATED (5)

Est 8: 9 Exactly as Mordecai *d*,
Jer 36: 4 who wrote down on a scroll, as Jeremiah *d*,
36:18 "Jeremiah *d* all these words to me,"
36:27 with the text Jeremiah had *d* to Baruch:
45: 1 Jeremiah *d* in the fourth year of Jehoiakim,

DICTATION (3)

Est 3:12 first month they wrote, at the *d* of Haman,
Jer 36: 6 words from the scroll you wrote at my *d*;
36:32 he wrote on it at Jeremiah's *d* all the

DIDN'T (3)

Gn 12:18 Why *d* you tell me she was your wife?
18:15 Sarah dissembled, saying, "I *d* laugh."
42:22 *D* I tell you," broke in Reuben,

DIE (306)

Gn 2:17 you eat from it you are surely doomed to *d*."
3: 3 not eat it or even touch it, lest you *d*.'"
3: 4 "You certainly will not *d*!
18:25 to make the innocent *d* with the guilty,
19:19 from overtaking me, and so I shall *d*.
20: 3 to *d* because of the woman you have taken,
20: 7 you and all who are yours will certainly *d*."
21:16 to herself, "Let me not watch the child *d*."
27: 2 I am so old that I may now *d* at any time.
27: 4 give you my special blessing before I *d*."
27: 7 with the LORD's approval before I *d*.'
30: 1 to Jacob, "Give me children or I shall *d*!"
33:13 for a single day, the whole flock will *d*.
38:11 that Shelah also might *d* like his brothers.
42: 2 we may stay alive rather than *d* of hunger."
42:20 will thus be verified, and you will not *d*."
44: 9 is found to have the goblet, he shall *d*,
44:22 his father would *d* if he were to leave him.'
44:30 he will *d* as soon as he sees that the boy
45:28 I must go and see him before I *d*."
46:30 Israel said to Joseph, "At last I can *d*,
47:29 When the time approached for Israel to *d*,
48:21 Israel said to Joseph: "I am about to *d*.
50:24 "I am about to *d*.
Ex 7:18 The fish in the river shall *d*,
9: 4 none belonging to the Israelites will *d*."
9:19 shall *d* when the hail comes upon them."
10:28 The day you appear before me you shall *d*!"
11: 5 Every first-born in this land shall *d*,
12:33 thought that otherwise they would all *d*.
14:11 to bring us out here to *d* in the desert?
14:12 of the Egyptians than to *d* in the desert."
16: 3 to make the whole community *d* of famine!"
17: 3 Was it just to have us *d* here of thirst
20:19 but let not God speak to us, or we shall *d*."
28:35 presence in the sanctuary; else he will *d*.
28:43 the sanctuary, lest they incur guilt and *d*.
30:20 they must wash with water, lest they *d*.
30:21 wash their hands and feet, lest they *d*.
32:12 Let your blazing wrath *d* down;
Lv 8:35 otherwise, you shall *d*;
10: 7 of the meeting tent, else you shall *d*;
16: 2 a cloud above the propitiatory, he will *d*.
16:13 over the commandments; else he will *d*.
22: 9 else they will *d* for their profanation.
Nm 4:15 if they do they will *d*.
4:19 That they may live and not *d* when they
4:20 if they do, they will *d*."
6: 7 his sister or brother, should they *d*,
14:35 in the desert they shall *d* to the last man."
16:29 if these men *d* an ordinary death,
17:25 if it does not, they will *d*."
18: 3 or the altar, lest both they and you *d*.
21: 5 us up from Egypt to *d* in this desert,
23:10 May I *d* the death of the just,
26:11 of Korah, however, did not *d* out].
26:65 that they would surely *d* in the desert,
Dt 4:22 I myself shall *d* in this country without
5:25 But why should we *d* now?
5:25 of the LORD, our God, any more, we shall *d*.
13:18 the blazing wrath of the LORD may *d* down
17:12 LORD, your God, or to the judge, shall *d*.
18:16 see this great fire any more, lest we *d*.'
18:20 in the name of other gods, he shall *d*.'
20: 5 he *d* in battle and another dedicate it.
20: 6 lest he *d* in battle and another enjoy its
20: 7 *d* in battle and another take her to wife.'
22:22 with whom he has had relations shall *d*.
22:25 relations with her, the man alone shall *d*.
31:14 "The time is now approaching for you to *d*.
32:50 shall *d* on the mountain you have climbed,
33: 6 together "May Reuben live and not *d* out,
Jgs 6:23 You shall not *d*."
6:30 Joash, "Bring out your son that he may *d*,
13:22 said to his wife, "We will certainly *d*,
15:18 Must I now *d* of thirst or fall into the
16:30 said, "Let me *d* with the Philistines!"
Ru 1:17 Wherever you die I will *d*,
1Sm 2:33 men of your family shall *d* by the sword.
2:34 both shall *d* on the same day.
4:20 She was about to *d* when the women standing
12:19 that we may not *d* for having added to all
14:39 has committed it, he shall surely *d*!"
14:43 Am I to *d* for this?"
14:44 thus and so to me if you do not indeed *d*,
14:45 "Is Jonathan to *d*,
20: 2 "Heaven forbid that you should *d*!
20:14 But if I *d*, never withdraw
20:16 family of David to *d* out from among you,
20:32 "Why should he *d*?
22:16 But the king said, "You shall *d*,
26:10 him, whether the time comes for him to *d*,
2Sm 12:13 you shall not *d*.
12:14 deed, the child born to you must surely *d*."
14:14 We must indeed *d*;
18: 3 even if half of us should *d*,
19:23 Should anyone *d* today in Israel?
19:24 the king said to Shimei, "You shall not *d*."
19:38 Please let your servant go back to *d* in
1Kgs 1:52 if he is found guilty of crime, he shall *d*."
2:26 Though you deserve to *d*,
2:30 I will *d* here."
2:37 be certain you shall *d* without fail.
2:42 anywhere else, you should *d* without fail?
13:31 him, he said to his sons, "When I *d*,
14:12 step inside the city, the child will *d*,
17:12 when we have eaten it, we shall *d*."
2Kgs 1: 4 instead, you shall *d*.'"
1: 6 instead, you shall *d*.'"
1:16 instead you shall *d*.'"
7: 3 "Why should we sit here until we *d*?
7: 4 to go into the city, we shall *d* there,
7: 4 If we remain here, we shall *d* too.
7: 4 if they kill us, we *d*."
8:10 LORD has showed me that he will in fact *d*."
11: 2 him from Athaliah, and so he did not *d*.
11:15 her," he added, "Let him *d* by the sword,"
13:14 from the sickness of which he was to *d*,
14: 6 each one shall *d* for his own sin."
20: 1 house in order, for you are about to *d*;
2Chr 23:14 to follow her, let him *d* by the sword.
Tb 3: 6 It is better for me to *d* than to live,
3: 6 to *d* than to endure so much misery in life,
3:10 myself, but to beg the Lord to have me *d*,
4: 2 let him know about this money before I *d*?"
4: 3 "My son, when I *d*, give me a decent burial
6:15 If I should *d*, I would bring my father
8:10 must do this, because if Tobiah should *d*,
8:21 half will be yours when I and my wife *d*.
10:11 And may I see children of yours before I *d*!"
10:13 of you and of my daughter Sarah before I *d*.
11: 9 have seen you again, son, I am ready to *d*!"
Jdt 6: 8 You shall not *d* till you are destroyed
Est D:10 *d* because of this general decree of ours.
1Mc 1: 5 his bed, realizing that he was going to *d*.
1:63 they preferred to *d* rather than to be
1:63 profane the holy covenant; and they did *d*.
2:37 said, "Let us all *d* without reproach;
2:41 so that we may not all *d* as our kinsmen
2:49 When the time came for Mattathias to *d*,
3:59 It is better for us to *d* in battle than to
4:35 were ready either to live or to *d* bravely,
6: 9 with sorrow, for he knew he was going to *d*.
9:10 let us *d* bravely for our kinsmen and not
2Mc 6:28 noble example of how to *d* willingly
6:30 When he was about to *d* under the blows,
7: 2 We are ready to *d* rather than transgress
7: 5 mother encouraged one another to *d* bravely,
7:14 "It is my choice to *d* at the hands of men
7:18 When he was about to *d*, he said:
7:41 The mother was last to *d* after her sons.
8:21 to *d* for their laws and their country.
13: 7 the transgressor of the law, fated to *d*;
14:42 preferring to *d* nobly rather than fall
Jb 2: 9 Curse God and *d*."
4:21 they *d* without knowing wisdom."
12: 2 folk, and with you wisdom shall *d*!
13:19 against me, then I shall be silent and *d*.

14: 8 in the earth, and its stump *d* in the dust,
27: 5 till I *d* I will not renounce my innocence.
27:15 His survivors, when they *d*,
34:20 in a moment they *d*, even at midnight.
35:15 nor does he show concern that a man will *d*.
36:12 they *d* for lack of knowledge.
Ps(s) 41: 6 'When will he *d* and his name perish?'
49:11 For he can see that wise men *d*,
82: 7 Yet like men you shall *d*,
102:21 prisoners, to release those doomed to *d*—
118:17 I shall not *d*, but live,
Prv 5:23 He will *d* from lack of discipline,
10:21 many, but fools *d* for want of sense.
15:10 he who hates reproof will *d*.
19:16 life, but the despiser of the word will *d*.
23:13 you beat him with the rod, he will not *d*.
30: 7 ask of you, deny them not to me before I *d*:
Eccl 3: 2 A time to be born, and a time to *d*;
7:17 Why should you *d* before your time?"
9: 5 For the living know that they are to *d*,
Wis 3:18 While should they *d* abruptly,
4: 7 But the just man, though he *d* early,
15: 9 is to *d* nor that his span of life is brief;
Sir 8: 7 remember, we are all to *d*.
14:13 Before you *d*, be good to your friend,
14:17 The age-old law is: All must *d*.
16: 3 *d* childless than have godless children!
19: 9 Let anything you hear *d* within you;
25:23 beginning, and because of her we all *d*.
27:29 and pain will consume them before they *d*;
40:28 life of a beggar, better to *d* than to beg;
Is 5:13 Their nobles *d* of hunger,
22:13 "Eat and drink, for tomorrow we *d*!"
22:14 not be pardoned this wickedness till you *d*,
38: 1 house in order, for you are about to *d*;
50: 2 rot for lack of water, and *d* of thirst.
51: 6 a garment and its inhabitants *d* like flies,
51:14 they shall not *d* and go down into the pit,
59: 5 Whoever eats their eggs will *d*,
66:24 Their worm shall not *d*,
Jer 11:21 else you shall *d* by our hand."
11:22 The young men shall *d* by the sword;
11:22 their sons and daughters shall *d* by famine.
16: 4 Of deadly disease they shall *d*.
16: 6 They shall *d*, the great and the lowly
18:21 let their men *d* of pestilence,
20: 6 there you shall *d* and be buried,
21: 6 they shall *d* in a great pestilence.
21: 9 *d* by the sword or famine or pestilence.
22:12 shall *d* in the place where they exiled him;
22:26 and there you shall *d*.
27:13 should you and your people *d* by the sword,
28:16 this very year you shall *d*,
31:30 through his own fault only shall anyone *d*:
34: 4 LORD to you, you shall not *d* by the sword.
34: 5 You shall *d* in peace,
37:20 of Jonathan the scribe, or I shall *d* there.
38: 2 who remains in this city shall *d* by sword,
38: 9 He will *d* of famine on the spot,
38:10 out of the cistern before he should *d*.
38:24 about this conversation, or you shall *d*.
38:26 me back to Jonathan's house to *d* there.' "
42:16 no less in Egypt, and there you shall *d*.
42:17 go to Egypt to stay, shall *d* by the sword,
42:22 no doubt of this, you shall *d* by the sword,
44:12 High and low, they shall *d* by the sword,
Lam 4: 9 the sword than for those who *d* of hunger,
Bar 4: 1 live, but those will *d* who forsake her.
Ez 3:18 say to the wicked man, You shall surely *d*;
3:18 that wicked man shall *d* for his sin,
3:19 conduct, then he shall *d* for his sin,
3:20 a stumbling block before him, he shall *d*.
3:20 He shall *d* for his sin,
5:12 A third of your people shall *d* of
6:12 He that is far off shall *d* of pestilence,
7:15 is in the country shall *d* by the sword;
12:13 and there he shall *d*.
13:19 killing those who should not *d* and keeping
17:16 broke, there in Babylon I swear he shall *d*!
18: 4 only the one who sins shall *d*.
18:13 all these abominations, he shall surely *d*;
18:17 one shall not *d* for the sins of his father,
18:18 his people, shall in truth *d* for his sins.
18:20 Only the one who sins shall *d*.
18:21 just, he shall surely live, he shall not *d*.
18:24 because of this, he shall *d*.
18:26 the iniquity he committed that he must *d*.
18:28 he shall surely live, he shall not *d*.
18:31 Why should you *d*, O house of Israel?
28: 8 to the pit, there to *d* a bloodied corpse,
28:10 You shall *d* the death of the uncircumcised
33: 8 the wicked man that he shall surely *d*,
33: 8 he [the wicked man] shall *d* for his guilt,
33: 9 from his way, he shall *d* for his guilt,
33:11 Why should you *d*, O house of Israel?
33:13 of the wrong he has done, he shall *d*.
33:14 to the wicked man that he shall surely *d*,
33:15 he shall surely live, he shall not *d*.
33:18 is right and does wrong, he shall *d* for it.
33:27 and in caves shall *d* by the plague.
35: 5 never let *d* your hatred for the Israelites,
Dn 13:43 Here I am about to *d*,
14: 8 consumes these provisions, you shall *d*.
14: 9 them, Daniel shall *d* for blaspheming Bel."
14:12 we are to die; otherwise Daniel shall *d*
Am 6: 9 ten men in a single house, these shall *d*.
7:11 Jeroboam shall *d* by the sword,
7:17 you yourself shall *d* in an unclean land;
9:10 sword shall all sinners among my people *d*,
Jon 4: 3 for it is better for me to *d* than to live."
4: 9 Jonah answered, "angry enough to *d*."
Zec 11: 9 "What is to *d*, let it die;
11: 9 "What is to die, let it *d*;
Mt 26:35 "Even though I have to *d* with you,
Mk 14:31 vehemently, "Even if I have to *d* with you,
Lk 13:33 allowed to *d* anywhere except in Jerusalem.'
21:26 Men will *d* of fright in anticipation of
Jn 3:16 in him may not *d* but may have eternal life.
6:50 from heaven for a man to eat and never *d*.
8:21 look for me but you will *d* in your sins.
8:24 is why I said you would *d* in your sins.
8:24 You will surely *d* in your sins unless you
11:16 "Let us go along, to *d* with him."
11:26 believes in me, though he should *d*,
11:26 is alive and believes in me will never *d*.
11:50 to have one man *d* [for the people]
11:51 that Jesus would *d* for the nation
12:33 indicated the sort of death he had to *d*.)
18:14 of having one man *d* for the people.)
18:32 indicating the sort of death he had to *d*.)
19: 7 must *d* because he made himself God's Son."
21:23 that this disciple was not going to *d*.
21:23 that the disciple was not going to *d*;
Rom 5: 7 good man someone may have the courage to *d*.
6: 9 raised from the dead, will never *d* again;
8:13 live according to the flesh, you will *d*;
14: 8 Lord, and when we die we *d* as his servants.
1Cor 4: 9 line, like men doomed to *d* in the arena.
9:15 *d* than let anyone rob me of my boast!
15:22 Just as in Adam all *d*,
15:32 "Let us eat and drink, for tomorrow we *d*!"
Phil 1:20 be exalted through me, whether I live or *d*.
Heb 9:27 Just as it is appointed that men *d* once,
Rv 9: 6 will yearn to *d* but death will escape them.
14:13 Happy now are the dead who *d* in the Lord!"

DIED (255)

Gn 5: 5 nine hundred and thirty years; then he *d*.
5: 8 nine hundred and twelve years; then he *d*.
5:11 nine hundred and five years; then he *d*.
5:14 nine hundred and ten years; then he *d*.
5:17 hundred and ninety-five years; then he *d*.
5:20 hundred and sixty-two years; then he *d*.
5:27 hundred and sixty-nine years; then he *d*.
5:31 seventy-seven years; then he *d*.
7:22 breath of life in its nostrils *d* out.
9:29 nine hundred and fifty years; then he *d*.
11:28 Haran *d* before his father Terah,
11:32 then Terah *d* in Haran.
23: 2 She *d* in Kiriath-arba (that is,
25:17 After he had breathed his last and *d*,
35:19 Thus Rachel *d*; and she was buried
35:29 he *d* as an old man and was taken to his
36:33 When Bela *d*, Jobab, son of Zerah,
36:34 When Jobab *d*, Husham, from the land
36:35 When Husham *d*, Hadad, son of Bedad,
36:36 When Hadad *d*, Samlah, from Masrekah
36:37 When Samlah *d*, Shaul,
36:38 When Shaul *d*, Baal-hanan,
36:39 When Baal-hanan *d*, Hadar succeeded him
38:12 and Judah's wife, the daughter of Shua, *d*.
46:12 but Er and Onan *d* in the land of Canaan;
48: 7 from Paddan, your mother Rachel *d*,
50:16 "Before your father *d*, he gave us these
50:26 Joseph *d* at the age of a hundred and ten.
Ex 1: 6 his brothers and that whole generation *d*.
2:23 passed, during which the king of Egypt *d*.
7:21 The fish in the river *d*,
8: 9 the houses and courtyards and fields *d* off.
9: 6 All the livestock of the Egyptians *d*,
9: 7 beast belonging to the Israelites had *d*,
16: 3 *d* at the LORD's hand in the land of Egypt,
Lv 7:24 Although the fat of an animal that has *d* a
10: 2 them, so that they *d* in his presence.
16: 1 *d* when they approached the LORD's presence,
17:15 *d* of itself or was killed by a wild beast,
22: 8 by eating of any animal that has *d* of itself
Nm 11: 2 he prayed to the LORD and the fire *d* out.
14: 2 "Would that we had *d* in the land of Egypt,
14:37 land were struck down by the LORD and *d*.
17:14 thousand seven hundred *d* from the scourge,
17:14 addition to those who *d* because of Korah.
19:16 he was slain by the sword or *d* naturally,
20: 1 It was here that Miriam *d*,
20:28 Then Aaron *d* there on top of the mountain.
21: 6 bit the people so that many of them *d*.
25: 9 but only after twenty-four thousand had *d*.
26:10 the band that *d* when the fire consumed
26:19 *d* in the land of Canaan were Er and Onan.
26:61 But Nadab and Abihu *d* when they offered
27: 3 "Our father *d* in the desert.
27: 3 *d* for his own sin without leaving any sons.
32:13 evil in the sight of the LORD had *d* out.
33:38 and there he *d* in the fortieth year from
33:39 years old when he *d* on Mount Hor.
Dt 10: 6 for Moserah, where Aaron *d* and was buried,
14:21 not eat any animal that has *d* of itself,
32:50 just as your brother Aaron *d* on Mount Hor
33: 1 pronounced upon the Israelites before he *d*.
34: 5 of the LORD, *d* as the LORD had said;
34: 7 hundred and twenty years old when he *d*,
Jos 1: 1 Moses, the servant of the LORD, had *d*,
5: 4 every man of military age had *d* in the
5: 6 the people that came forth from Egypt *d*
10:11 More *d* from these hailstones than the
24:29 LORD, *d* at the age of a hundred and ten.
24:33 When Eleazar, son of Aaron, also *d*,
Jgs 1: 7 was brought to Jerusalem, and there he *d*.
2: 8 was a hundred and ten years old when he *d*;
2:19 But when the judge *d*,
2:21 of the nations which Joshua left when he *d*."
3:11 years, until Othniel, son of Kenaz, *d*.
8:32 *d* and was buried in the tomb of his father
9:54 So his attendant ran him through and he *d*.
10: 2 years, he *d* and was buried in Shamir.
10: 5 Jair *d* and was buried in Kamon.
12: 7 *d* and was buried in his city in Gilead.
12:10 years, Ibzan *d* and was buried in Bethlehem.
12:12 the Zebulunite Elon *d* and was buried in
12:15 *d* and was buried in Pirathon in the land
20: 5 and my concubine they abused so that she *d*.
Ru 1: 3 Elimelech, the husband of Naomi, *d*,
1: 5 ten years, both Mahlon and Chilion *d* also,
1Sm 4:18 old man and heavy, he *d* of a broken neck.
25: 1 Samuel *d*, and all Israel gathered
25:37 At this his courage *d* within him,
25:38 days later the LORD struck him and he *d*.
28: 3 Now Samuel had *d* and,
31: 5 he too fell upon his sword and *d* with him.
31: 6 armor-bearer *d* together on that same day.
2Sm 2:23 He fell there and *d* on the spot.
2:23 to the place where Asahel had fallen and *d*,
3:27 and he *d* in revenge for the killing of
3:33 "Would Abner have *d* like a fool?
4: 1 of Saul, heard that Abner had *d* in Hebron,
6: 7 on that spot, and he *d* there before God.
10: 1 time later the king of the Ammonites *d*,
10:18 army, was struck down and *d* on the field.
11:17 fell, and among them Uriah the Hittite *d*.
11:21 the wall above, so that he *d* in Thebez?
11:24 above, and some of the king's servants *d*,
11:26 wife of Uriah heard that her husband had *d*,
12:18 On the seventh day, the child *d*.
17:23 he *d* and was buried in his father's tomb.
19: 1 If only I had *d* instead of you,
19:11 whom we anointed over us, *d* in battle.
20:10 and he *d* without receiving a second thrust.
24:15 the people from Dan to Beer-sheba *d*
1Kgs 3:19 This woman's son *d* during the night;
14:17 the threshold of her house, the child *d*.
16:18 He *d* because of the sins he had committed,
16:22 Tibni *d* and Omri became king.
22:35 facing the Arameans, *d* in the evening.
2Kgs 1:17 Ahaziah *d* in fulfillment of the prophecy
3: 5 But when Ahab *d*, the king of Moab had
4:20 with her until noon, when he *d* in her lap.
8:15 it over the king's face, so that he *d*.
9:27 his flight as far as Megiddo and *d* there.
13:20 Elisha *d* and was buried.
13:24 So when King Hazael of Aram *d* and his son
23:34 he took away with him to Egypt, where he *d*.
1Chr 1:44 When Bela *d*, Jobab, son of Zerah,
1:45 When Jobab *d*, Husham, from the land
1:46 Husham *d* and Hadad,
1:47 *d* and Samlah of Masrekah succeeded him.
1:48 Samlah *d* and Shaul from
1:49 When Shaul *d*, Baal-hanan, son of Achbor,
1:50 Baal-hanan *d* and Hadad succeeded him.
1:51 After Hadad *d* . . .
2:19 When Azubah *d*, Caleb married Ephrath,
2:30 Seled *d* without sons.
2:32 Jether *d* without sons.
10: 5 armor-bearer also fell on his sword and *d*.
10: 6 three sons, his whole house *d* at one time.
10: 7 that Saul and his sons had *d* in the rout,
10:13 Thus Saul *d* because of his rebellion
13:10 he *d* there in God's presence,
19: 1 *d* and his son succeeded him as king.
20: 8 *d* at the hands of David and his servants.
21:14 and seventy thousand men of Israel *d*.
23:22 Eleazar *d* leaving no sons,
24: 2 Nadab and Abihu *d* before their father,
29:28 He *d* at a ripe old age,
2Chr 13:20 the LORD struck him down and he *d*,
16:13 he *d* in the forty-first year of his reign.
18:34 He *d* as the sun was setting.
21:19 of the disease and he *d* in great pain.
24:15 a hundred and thirty years old when he *d*.
35:24 and brought him to Jerusalem, where he *d*.
Tb 1: 8 for when my father *d*, he left me an orphan.
1:15 But when Shalmaneser *d* and his son
1:17 If I saw one of my people who had *d* and
6:14 her husbands *d* in their bridal chambers.
7:11 *d* on the very night they approached her.
14: 1 Tobit *d* peacefully at the age of a hundred
14: 3 Just before he *d*, he called his son Tobiah
14:12 When Tobiah's mother *d*,
14:14 He *d* at the venerable age of a hundred

DIED (cont.)

14:15 But before he *d*, he heard of the destruction
Jdt 8: 2 had *d* at the time of the barley harvest.
8: 3 and he *d* of this illness in Bethulia,
16:23 She *d* in Bethulia,
16:24 Before she *d*, she distributed her goods
1Mc 1: 7 had reigned twelve years when he *d*.
2:38 the sabbath, and they *d* with their wives,
2:41 die as our kinsmen *d* in the hiding places."
2:70 He *d* in the year one hundred and forty-six,
6:16 King Antiochus *d* in Persia in the year one
6:46 the ground on top of him, and he *d* there.
9:29 "Since your brother Judas *d*,
9:56 Finally he *d* in great agony.
11:18 three days later King Ptolemy himself *d*,
13:49 hunger, and many of them *d* of starvation.
14:16 and even in Sparta that Jonathan had *d*,
2Mc 4: 7 But Seleucus *d*, and when Antiochus
6:31 This is how he *d*,
7: 7 the first brother had *d* in this manner,
7:13 After he had *d*, they tortured
7:40 Thus he too *d* undefiled,
9:28 *d* a miserable death in the mountains of a
Jb 10:18 I should have *d* and no eye have seen me.
14:14 When a man has *d*, were he to live again
42:17 Then Job *d*, old and full of years.
Sir 37:30 Through lack of self-control many have *d*,
Is 6: 1 In the year King Uzziah *d*,
14:28 In the year that King Ahaz *d*,
Jer 28:17 the seventh month, Hananiah the prophet *d*.
Bar 2:25 They *d* in dire anguish,
Ez 11:13 Pelatiah, the son of Benaiah, *d*.
24:18 That evening my wife *d*,
44:31 that has *d* of itself or has been killed by
Hos 13: 1 but he sinned through Baal and *d*.
Mt 9:18 "My daughter has just *d*.
14:32 had climbed into the boat, the wind *d* down.
22:25 The eldest *d* after marrying,
22:27 Last of all the woman *d* too.
Mk 6:51 the boat with them and the wind *d* down.
12:20 The eldest took a wife and *d*,
12:21 took the woman, and he too *d* childless.
12:22 Last of all, the woman also *d*.
15:44 surprised that Jesus should have *d* so soon.
Lk 16:22 Eventually, the beggar *d*.
16:22 The rich man likewise *d* and was buried.
20:30 The first one married and *d* childless.
20:31 seven *d* without leaving her any children.
20:32 Finally the widow herself *d*.
Jn 6:49 ate manna in the desert, but they *d*.
6:58 your ancestors who ate and *d* nonetheless,
8:53 be greater than our father Abraham, who *d!*
8:53 Or the prophets, who *d!*
11:21 been here, my brother would never have *d*.
11:32 been here my brother would never have *d*."
Acts 2:29 He *d* and was buried,
5:37 built up quite a following, but likewise *d*,
7: 4 After his father *d*,
7:15 Jacob went down to Egypt and *d* there,
7:60 And with that he *d*.
9:37 At about that time she fell ill and *d*.
12:23 the honor to God, and he *d* eaten by worms.
25:19 who had *d* but who Paul claimed is alive.
Rom 5: 6 powerless, Christ *d* for us godless men.
5: 8 we were still sinners, Christ *d* for us.
5:15 if by the offense of the one man all *d*,
6: 2 How can we who *d* to sin go on living in it?
6: 8 If we have *d* with Christ,
7: 4 *d* to the law through the body of Christ,
7: 6 for we have *d* to what bound us
7:10 with it sin came to life, and I *d*,
8:34 Jesus, who *d* or rather was raised up,
14: 9 is why Christ *d* and came to life again,
14:15 eat bring to ruin him for whom Christ *d*:
1Cor 8:11 perishes, that brother for whom Christ *d*.
15: 3 that Christ *d* for our sins in accordance
2Cor 5:14 the conviction that since one *d* for all,
5:14 that since one died for all, all *d*.
5:15 He *d* for all so that those who live might
5:15 who for their sakes *d* and was raised up.
Gal 2:19 It was through the law that I *d* to the law,
2:21 the law, then Christ *d* to no purpose!
Col 2:20 If with Christ you have *d* to cosmic forces,
3: 3 After all, you have *d!*
1Thes 4:14 For if we believe that Jesus *d* and rose,
4:16 those who have *d* in Christ will rise first.
5:10 He *d* for us,
2Tm 2:11 *d* with him we shall also live with him;
Heb 11:13 All of these *d* in faith.
13:12 Therefore Jesus *d* outside the gate,
1Pt 3:18 reason why Christ *d* for sins once for all,
Rv 2: 8 who once *d* but now lives has this to say:
8: 9 third of the creatures living in the sea *d*,
8:11 Many people *d* from this polluted water.
16: 3 and every creature living in the sea *d*.

DIES (54)

Gn 27:10 to eat, that he may bless you before he *d*."
Ex 21:20 so hard that the slave *d* under his hand,
21:35 ox hurts another's ox so badly that it *d*,
22: 9 to another for safekeeping, if it *d*,
22:13 maimed or *d* while the owner is not present,
Lv 11:39 that you could otherwise eat, *d* of itself,
Nm 6: 9 someone *d* very suddenly in his presence,
17:28 approaches the Dwelling of the LORD, he *d!*
19:14 When a man *d* in a tent,
27: 8 If a man *d* without leaving a son,
Dt 24: 3 if this second man who has married her, *d*;
25: 5 together and one of them *d* without a son,
1Kgs 14:11 When one of Jeroboam's line *d* in the city,
14:11 when one of them *d* in the field,
16: 4 If anyone of Baasha's line *d* in the city,
16: 4 if he *d* in the field, he shall be devoured
21:24 "When one of Ahab's line *d* in the city,
21:24 when one of them *d* in the field,
Tb 4: 4 when she *d*, bury her in the same grave
Jb 14:10 But when a man *d*, all vigor leaves him;
21:23 One *d* in his full vigor,
21:25 Another *d* in bitterness of soul,
Ps(s) 49:18 of his house becomes great, For when he *d*,
Prv 11: 7 When a wicked man *d* his hope perishes,
26:20 For lack of wood, the fire *d* out;
Eccl 2:16 it that the wise man *d* as well as the fool!
3:19 the one *d* as well as the other.
9:18 that *d* can spoil the perfumer's ointment,
Sir 8: 7 Rejoice not when a man *d*;
10:11 When a man *d*, he inherits corruption;
11:19 be till he *d* and leaves them to others.
11:27 when a man *d*, his life is revealed.
14:18 one *d* and another is born.
23:17 sweet and who is never through till he *d*;
28:12 into flame, if you spit on it, it *d* out;
39:11 and when he *d* his renown will not cease.
40: 2 troubled forebodings till the day he *d*—
48:11 is he who shall have seen you before he *d*,
Is 65:20 He *d* a mere youth who reaches but a
Ez 18:26 from virtue to commit iniquity, and *d*,
18:32 no pleasure in the death of anyone who *d*,
Mt 22:24 declared, 'If a man *d* without children,
Mk 9:48 *d* not and the fire is never extinguished.'
12:19 brother *d* leaving a wife but no child,
Lk 20:28 brother *d* leaving a wife and no child,
Jn 4:49 with him, "come down before my child *d*."
12:24 grain of wheat falls to the earth and *d*,
12:24 But if it *d*, it produces much fruit.
Rom 7: 2 but if he *d* she is released from the law
7: 3 her husband *d* she is freed from that law,
14: 7 master and none of us *d* as his own master.
1Cor 7:39 If her husband *d* she is free to marry,
15:36 you sow does not germinate unless it *d*.
Rv 3: 2 and strengthen what remains before it *d*.

DIETARY (1)

2Mc 11:31 to observe their *d* laws and other laws,

DIFFER (5)

Sg 5: 9 How does your lover *d* from any other,
5: 9 How does your lover *d* from any other,
Sir 33: 8 is due to the LORD's Wisdom that they *d*;
42:25 All of them *d*, one from another,
Rom 12: 6 We have gifts that *d* according to the

DIFFERED (1)

Acts 25:19 Instead they *d* with him over issues in

DIFFERENCE (8)

Lv 15: 3 it makes no *d* whether the flow drains off
1Mc 3:18 no *d* between deliverance by many or by few,
Wis 18: 2 them, for the sake of the *d* between them.
Ez 22:26 the *d* between the unclean and the clean;
44:23 the *d* between the clean and the unclean.
Rom 10:12 Here there is no *d* between Jew and Greek;
1Cor 7:19 nothing, and its lack makes no *d* either.
Gal 2: 6 makes no *d* to me how prominent they were

DIFFERENT (39)

Lv 19:19 animals with others of a *d* species;
19:19 a field of yours with two *d* kinds of seed;
19:19 a garment woven with two *d* kinds of thread.
Nm 14:24 has a *d* spirit and follows me unreservedly,
31:30 persons, and the same from the *d* beasts,
Dt 22: 9 sow your vineyard with two *d* kinds of seed;
22:11 not wear cloth of two *d* kinds of thread,
25:14 you keep two *d* measures in your house,
Tb 2: 2 and when many *d* dishes were placed before
Est E:10 blood, and very *d* from us in generosity,
Wis 2:15 not like other men's, and *d* are his ways.
7: 5 For no king has any *d* origin or birth,
Sir 33:11 in *d* paths he has them walk.
39: 1 How *d* the man who devotes himself to the
49: 8 described the *d* creatures of the chariot;
Jer 22:26 a *d* land from the one you were born in;
Ez 16:34 harlotry you were *d* from all other women.
16:34 instead of receiving it, how *d* you were!
42: 3 three parallel rows of them on *d* levels.
Dn 7: 3 immense beasts, each *d* from the others.
7: 7 the fourth beast, *d* from all the others,
7:19 so very terrible and *d* from the others,
7:23 kingdom on earth, *d* from all the others;
7:24 up after them, *D* from those before him,
Zec 8:23 of every nationality, speaking *d* tongues,
Acts 21:34 different people in the crowd shouted out *d*
Rom 5:16 *d* from the sin committed by the one man.
1Cor 3:12 *d* ones build on this foundation with gold,
12: 4 There are *d* gifts but the same Spirit;
12: 5 there are *d* ministries but the same Lord;
12: 6 there are *d* works but the same God who
12:20 There are, indeed, many *d* members,
14:10 There are many *d* languages in the world
2Cor 11: 4 a *d* spirit than the one you have received,
Gal 4: 1 his condition is no *d* from that of a slave,
5:10 in the Lord, you will not adopt a *d* view.
Heb 7:13 these things are said was of a *d* tribe,
Jas 2:25 messengers and sent them out by a *d* route?

DIFFERENTLY (4)

Lv 19:34 you no *d* than the natives born among you;
Jdt 10: 7 Judith transformed in looks and *d* dressed,
2Mc 6:14 but with us he has decided to deal *d*,
Gal 4:20 I could be with you now and speak to you *d!*

DIFFERING (2)

Dt 25:13 shall not keep two *d* weights in your bag,
Est 3: 8 laws *d* from those of every other people.

DIFFERS (3)

Prv 27:19 As one face *d* from another,
Acts 26:22 Nothing that I say *d* from what the
1Cor 15:41 stars, one *d* from another in brightness.

DIFFICULT (11)

Ex 18:26 The more *d* cases they referred to Moses,
1Sm 13: 6 aware of the danger and of the *d* situation,
14: 6 because it is no more *d* for the LORD to
2Mc 12:21 because of the *d* terrain of that region.
Ps(s) 73:16 to understand this it seemed to me too *d*,
Jer 42: 6 Whether it is pleasant or *d*,
Ez 3: 5 Not to a people with *d* speech and
3: 6 nor to the many peoples [with *d* speech and
Dn 2:11 What you demand, O king, is too *d*;
4: 6 is in you and no mystery is too *d* for you;
Heb 5:11 have much to say, and it is *d* to explain,

DIFFICULTIES (7)

1Sm 22: 2 by all those who were in *d* or in debt,
26:24 my life highly and deliver me from all *d*."
2Mc 2:24 and the *d* encountered by those who wish to
Dn 5:12 dreams, explain enigmas, and solve *d*.
5:16 that you can interpret dreams and solve *d*;
Acts 15:19 not to cause God's Gentile converts any *d*.
2Cor 6: 4 endurance amid trials, *d*, distresses
12:10 persecutions and *d* for the sake of Christ;

DIFFICULTY (12)

1Sm 17:39 He walked with *d*,
30: 6 Now David found himself in great *d*,
2Sm 4: 9 LORD lives, who rescued me from all *d*,
24:14 "I am in very serious *d*.
Wis 9:16 what is within our grasp we find with *d*;
Mt 19:23 only with *d* will a rich man enter into the
Mk 9:43 "If your hand is your *d*, cut it off!
Acts 27: 7 headway, arriving at Cnidus only with *d*.
27: 8 Again with *d* we moved along the coast to a
27:16 only with *d* were we able to gain control
Phil 3:15 way, God will clarify the *d* for you.
1Pt 4:18 And if the just man is saved only with *d*,

DIFFUSE (1)

2Cor 2:14 and employs us to *d* the fragrance of his

DIG (9)

Gn 26:25 his servants began to *d* a well nearby.
Ex 7:24 All the Egyptians had to *d* in the
Dt 6:11 garner, with cisterns that you did not *d*,
23:14 you shall first *d* a hole and afterward
Tb 8: 9 With him they went out to *d* a grave,
Jer 18:20 that they should *d* a pit to take my life?
Ez 8: 8 Son of man, he ordered, *d* through the wall.
12: 5 *d* a hole in the wall and pass through it;
Lk 16: 3 I cannot *d* ditches.

DIGEST (1)

2Mc 2:26 upon ourselves the labor of making this *d*,

DIGGING (2)

Gn 26:32 him news about the well they had been *d*;
Tb 8:11 When they had finished *d* the grave,

DIGNIFIED (1)

Bar 6:43 her neighbor who has not been *d* as she has,

DIGNIFIES (1)

Sir 33: 9 Some he *d* and sanctifies,

DIGNITARIES (1)

Gn 50: 7 of his court and all the other *d* of Egypt,

DIGNITARY (3)

Jer 39: 3 chief officer, Nebushazban, the high *d*,

39:13 bodyguard, and Nebushazban, the high *d*,
Lk 14: 8 in case some greater *d* has been invited.

DIGNITIES (1)

1Mc 10:24 conciliatory words and offer *d* and gifts,

DIGNITY (17)

Nm 27:20 Invest him with some of your own *d*,
Est 1:19 her royal *d* to one more worthy than she.
4:14 like this that you obtained the royal *d*?"
E:12 But, unequal to this *d*,
2Mc 6:23 of his years, the *d* of his advanced age,
14: 7 now that I am deprived of my ancestral *d*,
15:13 distinguished by his white hair and *d*,
Jb 30:15 My *d* is borne off on the wind,
Prv 20:29 and the *d* of old men is gray hair.
31:25 She is clothed with strength and *d*,
Sir 9: 2 power over you to trample upon your *d*.
50:13 their *d* clustered around him like poplars,
Is 44:13 making it like a man in appearance and *d*,
Ez 16:13 beautiful, with the *d* of a queen.
Lk 1:32 Great will be his *d* and he will be called
1Tm 2: 2 and tranquil lives in perfect piety and *d*.
3: 4 under control without sacrificing his *d*;

DIGS (5)

Ex 21:33 "When a man uncovers or *d* a cistern and
Prv 26:27 He who *d* a pit falls into it;
Eccl 10: 8 He who *d* a pit may fall into it,
Sir 10:16 ground, then *d* their roots from the earth.
27:26 As he who *d* a pit falls into it,

DIKLAH (2)

Gn 10:27 Hazarmaveth, Jerah, Hadoram, Uzal, *D*,
1Chr 1:21 Hazarmaveth, Jerah, Hadoram, Uzal, *D*,

DILEAN (1)

Jos 15:38 Zenan, Hadashah, Migdal-gad, *D*,

DILIGENT (10)

Ps(s) 19:12 is careful of them, very *d* in keeping them,
Prv 10: 4 but the hand of the *d* enriches.
11:16 become impoverished, but the *d* gain wealth.]
12:24 The *d* hand will govern,
12:27 prey, but the wealth of the *d* man is great.
13: 4 vain, but the *d* soul is amply satisfied.
15:19 thorns, but the path of the *d* is a highway.
21: 5 The plans of the *d* are sure of profit,
Sir 18:13 his guidance, who are *d* in his precepts.
Lk 15: 8 sweep the house in a *d* search

DILIGENTLY (1)

Ezr 5: 8 the work is being carried on *d* and is

DILLYDALLIED (1)

Gn 43:10 Had we not *d*, we could have been there

DIM (7)

Gn 48:10 (Now Israel's eyes were *d* from age,
Lv 26:16 and fever to *d* the eyes and sap the life.
Jb 17: 2 their provocation mounts, my eyes grow *d*.
Ps(s) 69:24 their eyes grow *d* so that they cannot see,
88:10 My eyes have grown *d* through affliction;
Jer 14: 6 Their eyes grow *d*,
Lam 5:17 hearts are sick, at this our eyes grow *d*:

DIMENSIONS (4)

Ez 40:28 Its *d* were the same as the others;
40:32 gate, whose *d* were found to be the same.
40:35 gate, where he measured the *d* of its cells,
48:16 These are the *d* of the City:

DIMINISH (3)

Gn 8: 5 continued to *d* until the tenth month,
Bar 2:34 they shall not then *d*.
Am 8: 5 We will *d* the ephah,

DIMINISHABLE (1)

1Pt 1:18 to you, not by any *d* sum of silver or gold,

DIMINISHED (3)

Gn 8: 3 and fifty days, the waters had so *d* that,
Nm 36: 3 heritage that fell to us by lot will be *d*.
Ez 16:27 I *d* your allowance and delivered you over

DIMINISHING (1)

Rom 11:12 *d* have meant riches for the Gentile world,

DIMMED (2)

1Kgs 14: 4 could not see because age had *d* his sight.
Ps(s) 6: 8 My eyes are *d* with sorrow;

DIMON (2)

Is 15: 9 The waters of *D* are filled with blood,
15: 9 blood, but I will bring still more upon *D*:

DIMONAH (1)

Jos 15:22 Kabzeel, Eder, Jagur, Kinah, *D*,

DIN (5)

2Kgs 7: 6 chariots and horses, the *d* of a large army,
2Chr 23:12 When Athaliah heard the *d* of the people
Ez 1:24 of the tumult was like the *d* of an army.
Mt 9:23 players and the crowd who were making a *d*,
Mk 5:39 "Why do you make this *d* with your wailing?

DINAH (7)

Gn 30:21 birth to a daughter, and she named her *D*.
34: 1 *D*, the daughter whom Leah had borne to
34: 3 Since he was strongly attracted to *D*,
34: 5 that Shechem had defiled his daughter *D*;
34:13 because their sister *D* had been defiled.
34:26 they took *D* from Shechem's house and left.
46:15 in Paddan-aram, along with his daughter *D*—

DINAH'S (3)

Gn 34:11 too, appealed to *D* father and brothers:
34:25 in pain, *D* full brothers Simeon and Levi,
34:27 in reprisal for their sister *D* defilement.

DINE (13)

Gn 43:16 for they are to *d* with me at noon."
43:25 they had heard that they were to *d* there.
1Sm 20: 5 when I should in fact *d* with the king.
20:24 new moon, when the king sat at table to *d*,
2Kgs 4: 8 of influence, who urged him to *d* with her.
4: 8 he passed by, he used to stop there to *d*.
Prv 23: 1 When you sit down to *d* with a ruler,
Eccl 10:16 and whose princes *d* in the morning!
10:17 and whose princes *d* at the right time (for
Sir 9: 9 With a married woman *d* not,
41:18 of stretching out your elbow when you *d*;
Lk 7:36 Pharisee who invited Jesus to *d* with him.
11:37 a Pharisee invited him to *d* at his house.

DINED (3)

Gn 19: 3 baking cakes without leaven, and they *d*.
1Sm 9:24 Thus Saul *d* with Samuel that day.
Jb 42:11 and they *d* with him in his house.

DINHABAH (2)

Gn 36:32 the name of his city was *D*.
1Chr 1:43 son of Beor, the name of whose city was *D*.

DINING (3)

Tb 8: 1 of the *d* room and led him into the bedroom.
Sir 31:12 If you are *d* with a great man,
Lk 7:37 that he was *d* in the Pharisee's home.

DINNER (15)

Tb 2: 1 of Weeks, a fine *d* was prepared for me,
2: 4 sprang to my feet, leaving the *d* untouched;
12:13 your *d* in order to go and bury the dead,
Jdt 12:15 for her daily use in reclining at her *d*.
1Mc 11:58 also sent him gold dishes and a *d* service,
Sir 32: 1 If you are chosen to preside at *d*,
Mt 9:10 came to join Jesus and his disciples at *d*.
22: 4 were invited, See, I have my *d* prepared!
Mk 2:15 sinners joined him and his disciples at *d*.
6:21 held a birthday *d* for his court circle,
Lk 5:29 crowd of tax collectors and others at *d*.
14:12 "Whenever you give a lunch or *d*,
14:16 was giving a large *d* and he invited many.
14:17 At *d* time he sent his servant to say to
14:24 those invited shall taste a morsel of my *d*.'"

DIONYSIUS (1)

Acts 17:34 Among these were *D*,

DIONYSUS (2)

2Mc 6: 7 and when the festival of *D* was celebrated,
14:33 and erect here a splendid temple to *D*."

DIOSCORINTHIUS (1)

2Mc 11:21 and forty-eight, the twenty-fourth of *D*.

DIOTREPHES (1)

3Jn 1: 9 but *D*, who enjoys being their leader,

DIP (7)

Lv 14: 6 the priest shall *d* them all in the blood
14:51 he shall *d* them all in the blood of the
Nm 19:18 *d* it in this water and sprinkle it on the
Ru 2:14 *d* your bread in the sauce."
Is 30:14 the hearth or *d* water from the cistern.
Lk 16:24 Send Lazarus to *d* the tip of his finger in
Jn 13:26 I give the bit of food I *d* in the dish."

DIPPED (7)

Gn 37:31 a goat, *d* the tunic in its blood.
Lv 9: 9 he *d* his finger in the blood and put it on
1Sm 14:27 he was holding and *d* in into the honey.
2Kgs 8:15 Hazael took a cloth, *d* it in water,
Mt 26:23 "The man who has *d* his hand into the dish
Jn 13:26 He *d* the morsel, then took it and gave it
Rv 19:13 He wore a cloak that had been *d* in blood,

DIPPING (4)

Ex 12:22 and *d* it in the blood that is in the basin,
Lv 4: 6 tent, where, *d* his finger in the blood,
4:17 tent, and *d* his finger in the blood,
14:16 then, *d* his right forefinger in it,

DIPS (1)

Mk 14:20 a man who *d* into the dish with me.

DIRE (14)

Dt 6:22 our eyes signs and wonders, great and *d*,
1Chr 21:13 "I am in *d* straits.
Tb 4:13 worthlessness there is decay and *d* poverty,
Jdt 7:15 Thus you will render them *d* punishment for
9:13 planned *d* things against your covenant,
Eccl 6: 2 This is vanity and a *d* plague.
Wis 3:19 for *d* is the end of the wicked generation.
16: 5 For when the *d* venom of beasts came upon
Sir 28:21 *D* is the death it inflicts,
Jer 50:22 Battle alarm in the land, *d* destruction!
51:54 *d* destruction from the land of the
Bar 2:25 They died in *d* anguish,
Ob 1: 2 you are held in *d* contempt.
Lk 15:14 out in that country and he was in *d* need.

DIRECT (20)

Gn 18:19 that he may *d* his sons and his posterity to
46:26 his *d* descendants, not counting the wives
Ex 1: 5 of the *d* descendants of Jacob was seventy.
25:19 so that one cherub springs *d* from each end.
Dt 17:10 act, being careful to do exactly as they *d*.
Jgs 8:30 Gideon had seventy sons, his *d* descendants,
1Chr 23: 4 to *d* the service of the house of the LORD,
29:18 forever, and *d* their hearts toward you.
2Chr 6:21 Israel which they *d* toward this place.
Jdt 12: 8 to *d* her way for the triumph of his people.
1Mc 2:66 army and *d* the war against the nations.
Ps(s) 86:11 *d* my heart that it may fear your name.
107: 7 them by a *d* way to reach an inhabited city.
Prv 4:11 On the way of wisdom I *d* you,
Wis 10:10 his brother's anger, guided him in *d* ways,
Sir 39: 7 Who will *d* his knowledge and his counsel,
Jer 10:23 choice, nor is it for him to *d* his step.
Dn 11:30 Then he shall *d* his rage and energy
Am 4: 3 the breached walls each by the most *d* way,
Jn 1:20 was the *d* statement, "I am not

DIRECTED (27)

Gn 12: 4 in you," Abram went as the LORD *d* him,
41:55 Pharaoh *d* all the Egyptians to go to
Ex 17: 1 journeyed by stages, as the LORD *d*,
Nm 27:23 as the LORD had *d* through Moses.
Dt 8: 2 has *d* all your journeying in the desert,
13: 6 the LORD, your God, has *d* you to take,
31:29 aside from the way along which I *d* you,
Jos 3: 6 And he *d* the priests to take up the ark of
6:22 *d* the two men who had spied out the land,
8:18 Then the LORD *d* Joshua,
2Sm 11:15 In it he *d*: "Place Uriah up front,
1Kgs 18:43 up and look out to sea," he *d* his servant,
20: 9 Accordingly he *d* the couriers of Ben-hadad,
1Chr 15:22 he *d* the chanting, for he was skillful
2Chr 34:12 Meshullam, of the Kohathites, who *d* them.
34:13 *d* all the workers in every kind of labor.
Is 40:13 Who has *d* the spirit of the LORD,
Mt 1:24 he did as the angel of the Lord had *d* him
15:35 Then he *d* the crowd to seat themselves on
Mk 8: 6 Then he *d* the crowd to take their places
Lk 22:65 they *d* many other insulting words at him.
Jn 11:39 "Take away the stone," Jesus *d*.
Acts 22:24 the commander *d* Paul to be brought inside
Phil 4: 8 should be wholly *d* to all that is true,
1Thes 4:11 Work with your hands as we *d* you to do,
Jas 3: 4 they are *d* by very small rudders on
2Pt 3:15 our Lord's patience is *d* toward salvation.

DIRECTING (1)

1Kgs 5:30 the work, *d* the people engaged in the work.

DIRECTION (54)

Ex 38:21 by the Levites under the *d* of Ithamar,
Nm 3: 4 under the *d* of their father Aaron.
4:27 entirely under the *d* of Aaron and his sons,
35: 4 cubits from the city walls in each *d*.
Dt 1:19 the *d* of the hill country of the Amorites.
28: 7 they come out against you from but one *d*,
28:25 you advance against them from one *d*,
Jos 3:16 from Adam, a city in the *d* of Zarethan;
4: 8 placed them, according to the LORD's *d*.
8:20 Escape in any *d* was impossible,
12: 3 of the Arabah in the *d* of Beth-jeshimoth,
15: 7 in the *d* of the Gilgal that faces the pass
19:27 In the other *d*, it ran eastward
19:34 In the opposite *d*, westerly, it ran through
Jgs 7:22 far as Beth-shittah in the *d* of Zarethan,

DIRECTION (cont.)

18: 3 of the young Levite and turned in that *d.*
18:15 So turning in that *d,* they went
20:42 the men of Israel in the *d* of the desert,
1Sm 13:18 another turned in the *d* of Beth-horon;
17:48 the battle line in the *d* of the Philistine.
20:36 an arrow beyond him in the *d* of the city.
24: 3 his men in the *d* of the wild goat crags.
25:20 were also coming down from the opposite *d.*
2Sm 13:34 down the slope from the *d* of Bahurim.
13:34 the mountainside from the *d* of Bahurim.
24: 5 and went in the *d* of Gad toward Jazer.
1Kgs 8:44 "Whatever the *d* in which you may send
2Kgs 3:20 from the *d* of Edom and filled the land.
25: 4 they went in the *d* of the Arabah.
1Chr 14:14 upon them from the *d* of the mastic trees.
25: 2 under the *d* of Aspah who sang inspired
25: 3 six, under the *d* of their father Jeduthun,
25: 6 were under their fathers' *d* in the singing
2Chr 6:34 and pray to you in the *d* of this city and
6:38 when they pray in the *d* of their land
Neh 12:31 top of the wall, in the *d* of the Dung Gate,
Est 9:23 instituted at the written *d* of Mordecai.
1Mc 5:28 Judas suddenly changed *d* with his army,
2Mc 12:22 Scattering in every *d,* they rushed away
Prv 7: 8 corner, then walking in the *d* of her house
Sir 5:11 every wind, and start not off in every *d.*
32:18 The thoughtful man will not neglect *d;*
33:33 away, in what *d* will you look for him?
Jer 39: 4 He went in the *d* of the Arabah,
52: 7 the city, they went in the *d* of the Arabah.
Ez 5:10 all that remain of your people in every *d.*
5:12 and a third I will scatter in every *d,*
9: 2 *d* of the upper gate which faces the north,
10:11 for in whichever *d* they were faced,
12:14 and his troops I will scatter in every *d,*
17:21 survivors shall be scattered in every *d.*
37: 2 He made me walk among them in every *d* so
47:15 from the Great Sea in the *d* of Hethlon,
Jn 11:29 this, she got up and started out in his *d.*

DIRECTIONS (11)

Gn 43:33 seated by his *d* according to their age,
Dt 17:11 You shall carry out the *d* they give you
24: 8 out all the *d* of the levitical priests.
1Sm 14:16 scattered and were running about in all *d.*
Jdt 15: 2 they scattered in all *d,*
Jb 16:13 his arrows strike me from all *d,*
Ez 1:17 could move in any of the four *d* they faced,
10:11 their four *d* without veering as they moved;
42:20 Thus he measured it in the four *d,*
Dn 11: 4 broken and divided in four *d* under heaven;
1Tm 1: 3 I repeat the *d* I gave you

DIRECTIVE (1)

1Sm 28:18 "Because you disobeyed the LORD's *d* and

DIRECTIVES (1)

Acts 10:33 to hear whatever *d* the Lord has given you."

DIRECTLY (25)

Ex 25:31 and knobs and petals springing *d* from it.
26: 5 that the loops are *d* opposite each other.
27: 2 so made that they spring *d* from the altar.
30: 2 high, with horns that spring *d* from it.
36:12 set, with the loops *d* opposite each other.
37: 8 *d* from the propitiatory at its two ends.
37:17 and knobs and petals springing *d* from it.
37:22 The knobs and branches sprang so *d* from it
37:25 high, having horns that sprang *d* from it.
38: 2 were made that sprang *d* from the altar.
Lv 25:12 produce, except as taken *d* from the field.
Nm 22:32 rash journey of yours is *d* opposed to me.
Jdt 10:11 and her maid walked *d* across the valley,
Jb 33: 3 I will state *d* what is in my mind,
Prv 4:25 ahead and your glance be *d* forward.
Is 52: 8 they shout for joy, For they see *d,*
Bar 2:17 Look *d* at us, and behold:
Mt 3:16 was baptized, he came *d* out of the water.
Mk 14:45 He then went *d* over to him and said,
Lk 14: 2 *D* in front of him was a man who suffered
20:17 He looked *d* at them and said,
Acts 14: 9 and Paul looked *d* at him and saw that he
17:14 sent Paul off *d* on his way to the sea,
Gal 2:11 Cephas came to Antioch I *d* withstood him,
5:17 the two are *d* opposed.

DIRECTOR (2)

Neh 11:17 of Zabdi, son of Asaph, *d* of the psalms,
Wis 7:15 the guide of Wisdom and the *d* of the wise.

DIRECTS (4)

Nm 27:21 and as he *d,* Joshua, all the Israelites
Prv 11:19 Virtue *d* toward life,
16: 9 plans his course, but the LORD *d* his steps.
21: 1 wherever it pleases him, he *d* it.

DIRGE (7)

Jer 9: 9 over the pasture lands, intone a *d:*
9:17 them come quickly and intone a *d* for us,
9:18 The *d* is heard from Zion:
9:19 Teach your daughters this *d,*
Ez 32:16 This is a *d,* and it shall be sung:
Mt 11:17 We sang you a *d* but you did not wail!'
Lk 7:32 We sang you a *d* but you did not wail.'

DIRGES (1)

Ps(s) 78:64 by the sword, and their widows sang no *d.*

DIRT (10)

Gn 3:14 *d* shall you eat all the days of your life.
3:19 For you are *d,* and to dirt you shall return."
3:19 you are dirt, and to *d* you shall return."
26:15 stopped up and filled with *d* all the wells
1Sm 4:12 clothes torn and his head covered with *d.*
2Sm 1: 2 with his clothes torn and *d* on his head.
15:32 with rent garments and *d* upon his head.
16:13 and throwing stones and *d* as he went.
Est C:13 she covered her head with *d* and ashes.
Acts 22:23 their cloaks and flung *d* through the air.

DISABLED (5)

1Kgs 22:34 and take me out of the ranks, for I am *d.*"
2Chr 18:33 and take me out of the ranks, for I am *d.*"
Jdt 16: 6 by the beauty of her countenance *d* him.
2Mc 8:24 and *d* the greater part of Nicanor's army,
Jn 5: 3 sick people lying there blind, lame or *d*

DISADVANTAGE (1)

2Sm 11:23 a *d* and came out into the open against us,

DISAGREEMENT (2)

Ex 18:16 Whenever they have a *d,*
Acts 15:39 The *d* which ensued was so sharp that the

DISAPPEAR (21)

1Kgs 15:14 The high places did not *d;*
22:44 Nevertheless, the high places did not *d,*
2Kgs 12: 4 Still, the high places did not *d;*
14: 4 Thus the high places did not *d,*
15: 4 Yet the high places did not *d;*
15:35 Nevertheless the high places did not *d* and
2Chr 15:17 the high places did not *d* from Israel,
Tb 14: 7 of sin shall completely *d* from the land.
Jb 6:17 in the heat, they *d* from their place.
15:30 and with the wind his blossoms shall *d.*
Wis 3:16 will *d* For should they attain long life,
Is 17:11 shall *d* on the day of the grievous blow,
Jer 12: 4 those who dwell in it beasts and birds *d,*
Hos 10: 7 The king of Samaria shall *d,*
Ob 1: 8 on that day make the wise men *d* from Edom,
Na 1:12 still they shall be mown down and *d.*
Hb 3:17 Though the flocks *d* from the fold and
Zec 9: 5 The king shall *d* from Gaza,
Jn 8:10 to her, "Woman, where did they all *d* to?
Acts 13:41 'Look on in amazement, you cynics, then *d!*
Jas 1:10 he will *d* "like the flower of the field."

DISAPPEARED (14)

Gn 44:28 One of them, however, *d,*
Ex 22: 8 or a garment, or anything else that has *d,*
Jos 3:16 the Salt Sea of the Arabah *d* entirely.
Jgs 6:21 and the angel of the LORD *d* from sight.
1Kgs 20:40 was looking here and there, the man *d.*"
1Mc 3:45 Joy had *d* from Jacob,
2Mc 3:34 When they had said this, they *d.*
Is 24:11 all joy has *d* and cheer has left the land.
Jer 7:27 Faithfulness has *d;*
24:10 until they have *d* from the land which I
Mt 8: 3 Immediately the man's leprosy *d.*
Acts 10: 7 the messenger who spoke these words had *d,*
Rv 6:14 *d* as if it were a scroll being rolled up;
16:20 Every island fled and mountains *d.*

DISAPPEARING (2)

Dt 32:36 their protected and unprotected alike *d,*
Heb 8:13 obsolete and has grown old is close to *d.*

DISAPPEARS (3)

Jb 27:21 The storm wind seizes him and he *d;*
Sir 12: 9 in adversity even his friend *d.*
Ez 24:11 the impurities in it melt, and its rust *d.*

DISAPPOINT (3)

Ps(s) 119:116 *d* me not in my hope.
Jer 48:13 Chemosh shall *d* Moab,
Hb 2: 3 presses on to fulfillment, and will not *d;*

DISAPPOINTED (8)

1Sm 2:32 *d* rival all the benefits enjoyed by Israel,
Jb 6:20 They are *d,* though they were confident;
Wis 6:14 watches for her at dawn shall not be *d,*
Sir 2:10 has anyone hoped in the LORD and been *d?*
Is 19: 9 The linen-workers shall be *d,*
49:23 and those who hope in me shall never be *d.*
Jer 48:13 was *d* by Bethel in which they trusted.
Rom 5: 5 And this hope will not leave us *d,*

DISAPPOINTS (1)

Sir 29: 5 But when payment is due he *d* him and says

DISAPPROVAL (4)

Nm 30: 6 of it her father expresses to her his *d,*
30: 6 her father has expressed to her his *d.*
30: 9 of it her husband expresses to her his *d,*
30:12 yet says nothing to express to her his *d,*

DISARM (1)

Col 2:15 did God *d* the principalities and powers.

DISASTER (37)

Gn 19:19 the hills to keep the *d* from overtaking me,
42: 4 for he thought some *d* might befall him.
42:38 If some *d* should befall him on the journey
44:29 away from me too, and some *d* befalls him,
Dt 32:35 *d* and their doom is rushing upon them!
Jgs 2:15 undertook, the LORD turned into *d* for them,
20:32 that *d* was about to overtake them.
20:41 realized the *d* that had overtaken them.
2Sm 15:14 *d* upon us and put the city to the sword."
19: 8 greater *d* for you than any that has afflicted
2Chr 28:23 caused further *d* to him and to all Israel.
Jdt 13:20 being oppressed, and you averted our *d,*
1Mc 2:43 from the *d* joined them and supported them.
2:49 it is a time of *d* and violent anger.
2Mc 6: 9 It was obvious, therefore, that *d* impended.
Jb 18:12 *D* is ready at his side,
Prv 13:17 A wicked messenger brings on *d,*
16:18 Pride goes before *d,*
17:19 he who builds his gate high courts *d.*
Sir 9:11 fame, for you know not what *d* awaits him.
Is 31: 2 Yet he too is wise and will bring *d;*
47:11 *D* shall befall you which you cannot allay.
Jer 4:18 how bitter is this *d* of yours,
18:17 my back, not my face, in their day of *d.*
48:16 hand is Moab's ruin, his *d* hastens apace.
Bar 4:29 For he who has brought *d* upon you will,
6:48 For when war or *d* comes upon them,
6:49 save themselves either from war or from *d?*
Ez 7: 5 *D* upon *d!*
7:26 There shall be disaster after *d,*
Ob 1:12 the day of your brother, the day of his *d;*
Zep 3:18 I will remove *d* from among you,
Acts 27:10 is bound to meet with *d* and heavy loss,
Phil 3:19 Such as these will end in *d!*
2Pt 2: 1 thereby bringing on themselves swift *d.*

DISASTERS (2)

Neh 9:32 account all the *d* that have befallen us,
1Mc 13: 3 what battles and *d* we have been through.

DISASTROUS (3)

1Sm 4:10 It was a *d* defeat,
Acts 27:21 you would not have incurred this *d* loss.
1Cor 6: 7 lawsuits against one another is *d* for you.

DISBANDED (2)

2Chr 25:10 Amaziah then *d* the troops that had come to
Acts 5:36 had been so easily convinced by him were *d.*

DISBELIEF (1)

Mk 16:14 to task for their *d* and their stubbornness,

DISBELIEVE (1)

Wis 1: 2 himself to those who do not *d* him.

DISBELIEVED (2)

Wis 12:17 when the perfection of your power is *d;*
18:13 *d* at every turn on account of sorceries,

DISBELIEVERS (1)

1Pt 2: 8 stumble and fall are the *d* in God's word;

DISBELIEVING (1)

Wis 10: 7 never ripens, and the tomb of a *d* soul,

DISBURSE (1)

Tb 1: 7 each year I would go and *d* in Jerusalem.

DISBURSED (1)

Mt 25:15 To one he *d* five thousand silver pieces,

DISCARD (4)

Lv 26:10 have to *d* them to make room for the new.
Sir 9:10 *D* not an old friend,
Is 65: 8 from grapes, men say, "Do not *d* them,
65: 8 I will not *d* them all;

DISCARDING (1)

Is 18: 5 hooks and the *d* of the lopped-off shoots.

DISCERN (7)

Jdt 8:14 who has made all these things, *d* his mind,

Jb 4:16 It paused, but its likeness I could not *d;*
6:30 my tongue, or cannot my taste *d* falsehood?
34: 4 Let us *d* for ourselves what is right;
Wis 2:22 holiness nor *d* the innocent souls' reward.
13: 1 studying the works did not *d* the artisan:
Eph 5:17 but try to *d* the will of the Lord.

DISCERNING (2)

Gn 41:33 let Pharaoh seek out a wise and *d* man
41:39 no one can be as wise and *d* as you are.

DISCERNMENT (11)

1Chr 22:12 *d* when he brings you to rule over Israel,
Jb 39:26 Is it by your *d* that the hawk soars,
Ps(s) 119:34 Give me *d,* that I may observe your law
119:73 give me *d* that I may learn your commands.
119:104 Through your precepts I gain *d;*
119:125 give me *d* that I may know your decrees.
119:144 give me *d* that I may live.
119:169 in keeping with your word, give me *d.*
Prv 16:21 The wise man is esteemed for his *d,*
2Pt 1: 5 your virtue with faith, your *d* with virtue,
1: 6 and your self-control with *d*
1Jn 5:20 us *d* to recognize the One who is true.

DISCERNS (2)

Jb 34:25 Therefore he *d* their works;
Wis 5:12 so that none *d* the way it went through

DISCHARGE (7)

Nm 3: 7 They shall *d* his obligations and those of
3: 8 *d* the duties of the Israelites
5: 2 leper, and everyone suffering from a *d,*
8:19 Aaron and his sons to *d* the duties
2Sm 3:29 never be without one suffering from a *d,*
2Chr 32:25 did not then *d* his debt of gratitude,
Col 4:17 "Take care to *d* the ministry you have

DISCHARGED (3)

Nm 3:38 They *d* the obligations of the sanctuary
1Mc 11:55 All the soldiers whom Demetrius had *d*
Mt 15:17 into the stomach and is *d* into the latrine,

DISCIPLE (28)

Is 19:11 you say to Pharaoh, "I am a *d* of wise men,
Mt 8:21 Another, a *d,* said to him, "Lord, let me go
10:42 he is a *d* will not want for his reward."
Lk 14:27 up his cross and follow me cannot be my *d.*
14:33 none of you can be my *d* if he does not
Jn 9:28 "You are the one who is that man's *d.*
13:23 One of them, the *d* whom Jesus loved,
18:15 Simon Peter, in company with another *d,*
18:15 This *d,* who was known to the high priest,
18:16 The *d* known to the high priest came out
18:25 They said to him, "Are you not a *d* of his?"
19:26 his mother there with the *d* whom he loved,
19:27 In turn he said to the *d,*
19:27 hour onward, the *d* took her into his care.
19:38 a *d* of Jesus (although a secret one for
20: 2 *d* (the one Jesus loved) and told them,
20: 3 *d* started out on their way toward the tomb.
20: 4 *d* outran Peter and reached the tomb first.
20: 8 Then the *d* who had arrived first at the
21: 7 Then the *d* Jesus loved cried out to Peter,
21:20 and noticed that the *d* whom Jesus loved
21:23 brothers that this *d* was not going to die.
21:23 of fact, that the *d* was not going to die;
21:24 same *d* who is the witness to these things;
Acts 9:10 There was a *d* in Damascus named Ananias to
9:26 even refused to believe that he was a *d.*
16: 1 Lystra, where there was a *d* named Timothy,
21:16 house of Mnason, a Cypriot and an early *d,*

DISCIPLES (230)

Is 8:16 and the sealed instruction kept among my *d.*
Mt 5: 1 he had sat down his *d* gathered around him,
8:23 got into the boat and his *d* followed him.
9:10 came to join Jesus and his *d* at dinner.
9:11 saw this and complained to his *d,*
9:14 John's *d* came to him with the objection,
9:14 we and the Pharisees fast, your *d* do not?"
9:19 and followed him, and his *d* did the same.
9:37 He said to his *d:* "The harvest is good
10: 1 Then he summoned his twelve *d* and gave
11: 1 had finished instructing his twelve *d,*
11: 2 and sent a message by his *d* to ask him,
12: 1 His *d* felt hungry,
12: 2 Your *d* are doing what is not permitted on
12:49 extending his hand toward his *d*
13:10 When the *d* got near him,
13:36 His *d* came to him with the request,
14:12 Later his *d* presented themselves to carry
14:15 on, his *d* came to him with the suggestion:
14:19 broke them and gave the loaves to the *d,*
14:22 Jesus insisted that his *d* get into the
14:26 When the *d* saw him walking on the water,
15: 2 "Why do your *d* act contrary to the
15:12 His *d* approached him and said,
15:23 His *d* came up and began to entreat him,
15:32 Jesus called his *d* to him and said:
15:33 His *d* said to him,
15:36 he broke them and gave them to the *d,*
16: 5 The *d* discovered when they arrived at the
16:13 Philippi, he asked his *d* this question:
16:20 Then he strictly ordered his *d* not to tell
16:21 indicate to his *d* that he must go
16:24 Jesus then said to his *d:*
17: 6 this the *d* fell forward on the ground,
17:10 The *d* put this question to him:
17:13 The *d* then realized that he had been
17:16 him to your *d* but they could not cure him."
17:19 The *d* approached Jesus at that point and
18: 1 the *d* came up to Jesus with the question,
19:10 His *d* said to him, "If that is the case
19:13 The *d* began to scold them,
19:23 Jesus said to his *d:* "I assure you,
19:25 When the *d* heard this they were completely
21: 1 Jesus sent off two *d* with the instructions:
21: 6 *d* went off and did what Jesus had ordered;
21:20 The *d* were dumbfounded when they saw this.
22:16 They sent their *d* to him,
23: 1 Then Jesus told the crowds and his *d:*
24: 1 and his *d* came up and pointed out to him
24: 3 his *d* came up to him privately and said:
26: 1 these discourses, he declared to his *d,*
26: 8 When the *d* saw this they grew indignant,
26:17 Bread, the *d* came up to Jesus and said,
26:18 the Passover with my *d* in your house.'"
26:19 The *d* then did as Jesus had ordered,
26:26 blessed it, broke it, and gave it to his *d.*
26:35 And all the other *d* said the same.
26:36 He said to his *d,* "Stay here while I go
26:40 When he returned to his *d,*
26:45 he returned to his *d* and said to them:
26:56 Then all the *d* deserted him and fled.
27:57 He was another of Jesus' *d,*
27:64 *d* may go and steal him and tell the people,
28: 7 Then go quickly and tell the *d:*
28: 8 and ran to carry the good news to his *d.*
28:13 'His *d* came during the night and stole him
28:16 The eleven *d* made their way to Galilee,
28:19 therefore, and make *d* of all the nations.
Mk 2:15 as sinners joined him and his *d* at dinner.
2:16 against the law, they complained to his *d,*
2:18 Now John's *d* and the Pharisees were
2:18 "Why do John's *d* and those of the
2:23 and his *d* began to pull off heads of grain
3: 7 Jesus withdrew toward the lake with his *d.*
3: 9 he told his *d* to have a fishing boat ready
4:34 kept explaining things privately to his *d.*
5:31 His *d* said to him, "You can see how
6: 1 own part of the country followed by his *d.*
6:29 Later, when his *d* heard about this,
6:35 and his *d* came to him with a suggestion:
6:41 and gave them to the *d* to distribute.
6:45 he insisted that his *d* get into the boat
7: 2 his *d* eating meals without having purified
7: 5 "Why do your *d* not follow the tradition
7:17 his *d* questioned him about the proverb.
8: 1 He called the *d* over to him and said:
8: 4 His *d* replied, "How can anyone give
8: 6 them, and gave them to his *d* to distribute,
8:10 *d* to go to the neighborhood of Dalmanutha.
8:27 Then Jesus and his *d* set out for the
8:27 On the way he asked his *d* this question:
8:33 At this he turned around and, eyeing the *d,*
8:34 the crowd with his *d* and said to them:
9:14 As they approached the *d,*
9:18 Just now I asked your *d* to expel him,
9:28 the house his *d* began to ask him privately,
9:31 He was teaching his *d* in this vein:
10:10 the *d* began to question him about this.
10:13 but the *d* were scolding them for this.
10:23 Jesus looked around and said to his *d,*
10:24 The *d* could only marvel at his words.
10:32 *d* were on the road going up to Jerusalem,
10:46 that place with his *d* and a sizable crowd,
11: 1 sent off two of his *d* with the instruction:
11:14 His *d* heard all this.
11:19 on, Jesus and his *d* went out of the city.
12:43 He called his *d* over and told them:
13: 1 the temple area, one of his *d* said to him,
14:12 the paschal lamb, his *d* said to him,
14:13 sent two of his *d* with these instructions:
14:14 where I may eat the Passover with my *d?'*
14:16 The *d* went off.
14:32 here while I pray," he said to his *d;*
16: 7 Go now and tell his *d* and Peter,
Lk 5:30 the scribes of their party said to his *d,*
5:33 *d* fast frequently and offer prayers; the *d*
6: 1 His *d* were pulling off grain-heads,
6:13 At daybreak he called his *d* and selected
6:17 stretch where there were many of his *d;*
6:20 Then, raising his eyes to his *d,* he said:
7:11 his *d* and a large crowd accompanied him.
7:18 The *d* of John brought their teacher word
8: 9 His *d* began asking him what the meaning of
8:22 into a boat with his *d* and said to them,
9:14 Jesus said to his *d,* "Have them sit down
9:16 to his *d* for distribution to the crowd.
9:18 in seclusion and his *d* were with him,
9:34 *d* grew fearful as the others entered it.
9:36 The *d* kept quiet,
9:40 I asked your *d* to cast out the spirit but
9:43 all that he was doing, Jesus said to his *d:*
9:54 When his *d* James and John saw this,
10:23 Turning to his *d* he said to them privately:
11: 1 he had finished, one of his *d* asked him,
11: 1 teach us to pray, as John taught his *d.*"
12: 1 He began to speak first to his *d:*
12:22 He said to his *d:* "That is why I warn you,
16: 1 Another time he said to his *d:* "A rich man
17: 1 He said to his *d:* "Scandals will
17:22 He said to the *d:* "A time will come
18:15 When the *d* saw this, they scolded them
19:29 sent two of the *d* with these instructions:
19:37 the entire crowd of *d* began to rejoice and
19:39 said to him, "Teacher, rebuke your *d.*"
20:45 of all the people, Jesus said to his *d:*
22:11 where I may eat the Passover with my *d?'*
22:39 his *d* accompanied him.
22:45 he rose from prayer and came to his *d,*
Jn 1:35 day John was there again with two of his *d.*
1:37 The two *d* heard what he said,
2: 2 Jesus and his *d* had likewise been invited
2:11 his glory, and his *d* believed in him.
2:12 *d* but they stayed there only a few days.
2:17 His *d* recalled the words of Scripture:
2:22 did his *d* recall that he had said this,
3:22 Jesus and his *d* came into Judean territory,
3:25 arose between John's *d* and a certain Jew.
4: 1 and baptizing more *d* than John (in fact,
4: 2 not Jesus himself who baptized, but his *d),*
4: 8 (His *d* had gone off to the town to buy
4:27 His *d,* returning at this point,
4:31 Meanwhile the *d* were urging him,
4:33 At this the *d* said to one another,
6: 3 the mountain and sat down there with his *d.*
6: 8 One of Jesus' *d,* Andrew, Simon Peter's
6:12 When they had had enough, he told his *d,*
6:16 drew on, his *d* came down to the lake.
6:22 that Jesus had not left in it with his *d;*
6:24 that neither Jesus nor his *d* were there,
6:60 hearing his words, many of his *d* remarked,
6:61 Jesus was fully aware that his *d* were
6:66 many of his *d* broke away and would not
7: 3 go to Judea so that your *d* there may see
8:31 to my teaching, you are truly my *d;*
9: 2 His *d* asked him, "Rabbi, was it his sin
9:27 not tell me you want to become his *d* too?"
9:28 We are *d* of Moses.
11: 7 Finally he said to his *d,*
11: 8 "Rabbi," protested the *d,*
11:12 At this the *d* objected,
11:16 name means "Twin") said to his fellow *d,*
11:54 the desert, where he stayed with his *d.*
12: 4 of his *d* (the one about to hand him over),
12:16 first, the *d* did not understand all this,
13: 5 began to wash his *d'* feet and dry them
13:22 The *d* looked at one another,
13:35 This is how all will know you for my *d:*
15: 8 your bearing much fruit and becoming my *d.*
16:17 At this, some of his *d* asked one another:
16:29 are speaking plainly," his *d* exclaimed,
18: 1 out with his *d* across the Kidron Valley.
18: 1 garden there, and he and his *d* entered it.
18: 2 Jesus had often met there with his *d.*
18:19 priest questioned Jesus, first about his *d,*
20:10 With this, the *d* went back home.
20:18 Mary Magdalene went to the *d.*
20:19 even though the *d* had locked the doors of
20:20 At the sight of the Lord the *d* rejoiced.
20:25 The other *d* kept telling him:
20:26 later, the *d* were once more in the room,
20:30 in the presence of his *d.*
21: 1 Jesus showed himself to the *d* [once again].
21: 2 Galilee), Zebedee's sons, and two other *d.*
21: 4 though none of the *d* knew it was Jesus.
21: 8 Meanwhile the other *d* came in the boat,
21:12 Not one of the *d* presumed to inquire,
21:14 to the *d* after being raised from the dead.
Acts 6: 1 In those days, as the number of *d* grew,
6: 2 assembled the community of the *d* and said,
6: 7 of the *d* in Jerusalem enormously increased.
9: 1 murderous threats against the Lord's *d,*
9:25 Some of his *d,* therefore, took him
9:26 in Jerusalem he tried to join the *d* there;
9:38 the *d* who had heard that Peter was there
11:26 It was in Antioch that the *d* were called
11:29 the *d* determine to set something aside,
13:52 The *d* could not but be filled with joy and
14:20 His *d* quickly formed a circle about him,
14:21 news in that town and made numerous *d,*
14:22 They gave their *d* reassurances,
14:28 Then they spent some time there with the *d.*
18:23 country and Phrygia to reassure all his *d.*
18:27 him by writing the *d* there to welcome him.
19: 1 found some *d* to whom he put the question,
19: 9 He took his *d* with him,
19:30 this gathering but his *d* would not let him.
20: 1 brought his *d* together to encourage them.
21: 4 *d* there and stayed with them for a week.
21:16 Some of the *d* from Caesarea came along to

DISCIPLINE (28)

Dt 4:36 heavens he let you hear his voice to *d* you;
11: 2 who must now understand the *d* of the LORD,
Tb 4:14 you do, and *d* yourself in all your conduct.
Ps(s) 50:17 you hate *d* and cast my words behind you?
Prv 1: 2 That men may appreciate wisdom and *d*,
3:11 The *d* of the LORD, my son, disdain not;
5:23 He will die from lack of *d*,
6:23 and a way to life are the reproofs of *d*;
22:15 the rod of *d* will drive it far from him.
Wis 1: 5 For the holy spirit of *d* flees deceit and
6:17 toward *d* is a very earnest desire for her;
6:17 then, care for *d* is love of her;
7:14 the gifts they have from *d* commend them.
Sir 4:17 brings upon him and tries him with her *d*;
6:18 My son, from your youth embrace *d*;
6:23 For *d* is like her name,
22: 6 but lashes and *d* are at all times wisdom.
23: 2 to my thoughts, to my mind the rod of *d*,
30:13 *D* your son, make heavy his yoke,
32:14 He who would find God must accept *d*:
Rom 2:20 you can *d* the foolish and teach the simple,
1Cor 9:27 What I do is *d* my own body and master it,
1Tm 4: 8 the *d* of religion is incalculably more so,
Heb 12: 5 do not disdain the *d* of the Lord nor lose
12: 7 Endure your trials as the *d* of God,
12: 7 son is there whom his father does not *d*?
12: 8 If you do not know the *d* of sons,
12:11 *d* seems a cause for grief and not for joy,

DISCIPLINED (2)

Bar 4:13 did they tread the *d* paths of his justice.
Heb 12:10 They *d* us as seemed right to them,

DISCIPLINES (5)

Dt 8: 5 disciplines you even as a man *d* his son.
2Mc 6:16 Although he *d* us with misfortunes,
Sir 30: 2 He who *d* his son will benefit from him,
Heb 12: 6 For whom the Lord loves, he *d*;

DISCLAIMED (1)

Lk 8:45 Everyone *d* doing it,

DISCLOSE (4)

2Mc 2: 8 Then the Lord will *d* these things,
Prv 25: 9 but another man's secret do not *d*;
Sir 27: 6 does a man's speech *d* the bent of his mind.
1Cor 3:13 The Day will *d* it.

DISCLOSED (1)

Neh 2:16 for as yet I had *d* nothing to the Jews,

DISCLOSES (3)

1Sm 22: 8 None of you shows sympathy for me or *d* to
Jb 12:22 The recesses of the darkness he *d*,
Prv 29:24 himself put under a curse, yet *d* nothing.

DISCLOSING (1)

1Sm 20: 2 great or small, without *d* it to me.

DISCLOSURE (2)

1Sm 20:30 shame and to the *d* of your mother's shame,
2Sm 7:21 this entire magnificent *d* to your servant.

DISCOMFORT (2)

Sir 31:19 When he lies down, it is without *d*.
Jon 4: 6 giving shade that relieved him of any *d*,

DISCONCERTED (1)

Lk 20:26 *d* them and reduced them to silence.

DISCONSOLATE (4)

Jgs 21: 6 *d* over their brother Benjamin and said,
21:15 The people were still *d* over Benjamin
Sir 30:12 stubborn, disobey you, and leave you *d*.
Jer 8:21 I am *d*; horror has seized me.

DISCONTENT (1)

Eccl 7: 9 for *d* lodges in the bosom of a fool.

DISCONTENTED (1)

Eccl 7: 9 Do not in spirit become quickly *d*,

DISCONTINUE (1)

1Mc 11:22 He wrote to Jonathan to *d* the siege and to

DISCORD (9)

Prv 6:14 his heart, is always plotting evil, sows *d*.
6:19 lies, and he who sows *d* among brothers.
13:10 The stupid man sows *d* by his insolence,
15:18 up strife, but a patient man allays *d*.
16:28 An intriguer sows *d*,
22:10 Expel the arrogant man and *d* goes out;
Sir 28: 9 friendship and sows *d* among those at peace.
Hb 1: 3 there is strife, and clamorous *d*.
2Cor 12:20 I fear I may find *d*,

DISCORDANT (2)

Wis 1:10 everything, and *d* grumblings are no secret.
18:10 But the *d* cry of their enemies responded,

DISCOURAGE (1)

Nm 32: 7 Why do you wish to *d* the Israelites from

DISCOURAGED (10)

Nm 32: 9 then so *d* the Israelites that they would
Jos 2:11 everyone is *d* because of you,
14: 8 scouts who went up with me *d* the people,
2Sm 17: 2 If I come upon him when he is weary and *d*,
Tb 4:21 Do not be *d*, my child,
Jdt 8: 9 which the people, *d* by their lack of water,
1Mc 4:27 When he heard it he was disturbed and *d*,
Jer 51:46 *d* for fear of rumors spread in the land;
Zep 3:16 Fear not, O Zion, be not *d*!
Rv 2: 3 Moreover, you do not become *d*.

DISCOURAGEMENT (3)

1Chr 28:20 go to work without fear or *d*,
1Mc 9: 8 But in spite of his *d*,
2Cor 4: 1 God's mercy, we do not give in to *d*.

DISCOURAGING (2)

Nm 13:32 So they spread *d* reports among the
14:36 him by spreading *d* reports about the land;

DISCOURSE (20)

Dt 32: 2 the rain, and my *d* permeate like the dew,
Jb 33: 1 Therefore, O Job, hear my *d*,
34: 2 Hear, O wise men, my *d*,
Ps(s) 19: 4 a word nor a *d* whose voice is not heard;
71:24 tongue day by day shall *d* on your justice.
145: 6 They *d* of the power of your terrible deeds
145:11 Let them *d* of the glory of your kingdom
Sir 6:35 Be eager to hear every godly *d*;
8: 8 Spurn not the *d* of the wise,
32: 4 When wine is present, do not pour out *d*,
Mt 7:28 Jesus finished this *d* and left the crowds
19: 1 When Jesus had finished this *d*,
Mk 13: 5 Jesus began his *d*: "Be on your guard.
Lk 4:22 the appealing *d* which came from his lips.
7: 1 this *d* in the hearing of the people,
Jn 18: 1 After this *d*, Jesus went out
Acts 15:32 and gave them reassurance in a long *d*.
20:36 After this *d*, Paul knelt down with them
1Cor 12: 8 To one the Spirit gives wisdom in *d*,
2Cor 8: 7 are rich in every respect, in faith and *d*,

DISCOURSERS (1)

Sir 44: 5 of melodious psalms, or *d* on lyric themes;

DISCOURSES (5)

Jb 32:11 Behold, I have waited for your *d*,
Wis 8:18 and fair renown in sharing her *d*,
Sir 27:11 Ever wise are the *d* of the devout,
39: 2 He treasures the *d* of famous men,
Mt 26: 1 Now when Jesus had finished all these *d*,

DISCOVER (8)

Gn 44:15 as I could *d* by divination what happened."
Ezr 4:15 In the historical records you can *d* and
5:17 *d* whether a decree really was issued by King
8:15 present, but I could not *d* a single Levite.
Jb 37:23 we cannot *d* him, preeminent in power
Eccl 7:27 I might *d* the answer which my soul still
Sir 6:28 Search her out, *d* her;
Mt 17:27 *d* there a coin worth twice the temple tax.

DISCOVERED (25)

Lv 10:16 offering, he *d* that it had all been burned.
Nm 15:32 was *d* gathering wood on the sabbath day.
Dt 22:22 "If a man is *d* having relations with a
22:28 relations with her, and their deed is *d*,
Jos 10:17 had been *d* hiding in a cave at Makkedah,
1Kgs 10: 7 *d* that they were not telling me the half.
2Chr 9: 6 I have *d* that they did not tell me the
Neh 13: 7 where I *d* the evil thing that Eliashib had
Est A:13 and *d* that they were preparing to lay
1Mc 7:31 When Nicanor saw that his plan had been *d*,
8:10 to come and destroy them, the Romans *d* it,
9:33 Simon and all the men with him *d* this,
10:80 *d* that there was an ambush behind him,
2Mc 15:28 *d* Nicanor lying there in all his armor,
Ps(s) 44:22 a strange god, Would not God have *d* this?
Jer 50:24 You were *d* and seized,
Ez 23:18 harlotry was *d* and her shame was revealed,
Mt 16: 5 The disciples *d* when they arrived at the
26:60 They *d* none, despite the many false
Lk 23:22 I have not *d* anything about him that calls
Jn 12: 9 crowd of Jews *d* he was there and came out,
Acts 17:23 your shrines, I even *d* an altar inscribed,
23:29 I subsequently *d* that he was accused in
27: 6 *d* an Alexandrian vessel bound for Italy,
Rv 2: 2 of the sort, and *d* that they are impostors.

DISCOVERING (1)

Eccl 3:11 into their hearts, without men's ever *d*,

DISCOVERS (2)

Mt 10:39 himself to nought for me *d* who he is.
24:46 whom his master *d* at work on his return!

DISCREDIT (3)

Neh 6:13 had a shameful story with which to *d* me.
Sir 4:22 Show no favoritism to your own *d*;
Acts 28:21 arrived with a report or rumor to your *d*.

DISCREDITED (2)

2Sm 13:13 And you would be a *d* man in Israel.
Acts 19:27 grows, not only that our trade will be *d*,

DISCREDITS (1)

Sir 10:28 who will honor him who *d* himself?

DISCREET (1)

Sir 42: 8 cautious and recognized by all men as *d*.

DISCREETLY (1)

Wis 9:11 and will guide me *d* in my affairs and

DISCRETION (6)

Neh 10:29 daughters, all who are of the age of *d*,
Jb 12:20 trusted adviser, and takes *d* from the aged.
Prv 1: 4 simple, to the young man knowledge and *d*.
2:11 please your soul, *D* will watch over you,
5: 2 your ear, That *d* may watch over you,
Is 56:11 These are the shepherds who know no *d*;

DISCRIMINATED (1)

Jas 2: 4 not in a case like this *d* in your hearts?

DISCUS-THROWING (1)

2Mc 4:14 they hastened, at the signal for the *d*,

DISCUSS (5)

Gn 34: 6 went out to *d* the matter with Jacob,
Prv 25: 9 *D* your case with your neighbor,
Jer 12: 1 even so, I must *d* the case with you.
Mk 9:10 to *d* what "to rise from the dead" meant.
1Tm 1: 7 the matters they *d* with such assurance.

DISCUSSED (5)

1Sm 19: 1 Saul *d* his intention of killing David with
20:23 in the matter which you and I have *d*,
1Kgs 5:13 He *d* plants, from the cedar on Lebanon
2Kgs 3: 8 They *d* the route for their attack,
Jdt 10: 9 I may go to carry out the business we *d*."

DISCUSSING (4)

Mk 9:16 them, "What are you *d* among yourselves?"
9:33 them, "What were you *d* on the way home?"
Lk 24:14 *d* as they went all that had happened.
24:17 them, "What are you *d* as you go your way?"

DISCUSSION (10)

2Sm 3:17 then said in *d* with the elders of Israel:
Jdt 2: 1 was a *d* in the palace of Nebuchadnezzar,
2Mc 14:20 After a long *d* of the terms,
Jb 18: 2 Reflect, and then we can have *d*.
Sir 13:11 Engage not freely in *d* with him,
Dn 5:10 of the *d* between the king and his lords,
Mk 9:14 around, and scribes in lively *d* with them.
Lk 5:21 The scribes and the Pharisees began a *d*,
9:46 A *d* arose among them as to which of them
Acts 15: 7 After much *d*, Peter took the floor

DISCUSSIONS (6)

Acts 15:24 their *d* and disturbed your peace of mind.
17: 2 people there and conducted *d* with them
17:17 In the synagogue he used to hold *d* with
18: 4 Paul led *d* in which he persuaded certain
18:19 the synagogue to hold *d* with the Jews.
19: 9 and after that held his *d* from day to day

DISDAIN (10)

Gn 16: 4 she looked on her mistress with *d*.
16: 5 she has been looking on me with *d*.
Lv 26:11 my Dwelling among you, and will not *d* you.
1Sm 2:17 treated the offerings to the LORD with *d*.
Jdt 8:20 that he will not *d* us or any of our people.
Est 1:17 *d* upon their husbands when it is reported,
1:18 officials, with corresponding *d* and rancor.
2Mc 7:11 for the sake of his laws I *d* them;
Prv 3:11 The discipline of the LORD, my son, *d* not;
Heb 12: 5 do not *d* the discipline of the Lord nor

DISDAINED (4)

Jb 30: 1 have *d* to rank with the dogs of my flock.
Ps(s) 22:25 nor *d* the wretched man in his misery,
Prv 1:25 Because you *d* all my counsel,

Ez 16:31 unlike a prostitute, since you *d* payment.

DISDAINFULLY (2)
1Mc 7:34 ridiculed them, defiled them, and spoke *d*.
1Cor 16:11 just as I do, so let no one treat him *d*.

DISDAINING (1)
2Mc 4:14 *D* the temple and neglecting the sacrifices,

DISDAINS (1)
Heb 10:29 is due the man who *d* the Son of God,

DISEASE (14)
Lv 13:30 is scall, a leprous *d* of the head or cheek.
13:37 has grown on it, the *d* has been healed;
2Chr 16:12 Asa contracted a serious *d* in his feet.
21:15 have severe pains from a *d* in your bowels,
21:15 your bowels issue forth because of the *d*,
21:18 him with an incurable *d* of the bowels.
21:19 because of the *d* and he died in great pain.
Ps(s) 41: 9 'A malignant *d* fills his frame';
106:15 asked but sent a wasting *d* against them.
Sir 39:29 proper time, are fire and hail, famine, *d*,
Jer 16: 4 Of deadly *d* they shall die.
Mt 4:23 cured the people of every *d* and illness.
9:35 reign, and he cured every sickness and *d*.
10: 1 and to cure sickness and *d* of every kind.

DISEASED (1)
Lv 13:33 shall shave himself, but not on the *d* spot.

DISEASES (10)
Ex 15:26 the *d* with which I afflicted the Egyptians;
Dt 7:15 the malignant *d* that you know from Egypt,
28:60 with all the *d* of Egypt which you dread,
Mt 4:24 with various *d* and racked with pain:
Lk 4:40 sick with a variety of *d* took them to him,
6:18 came to hear him and be healed of their *d*.
7:21 that time he was curing many of their *d*,
9: 1 to overcome all demons and to cure *d*.
9: 6 the good news everywhere and curing *d*.
Acts 19:12 their *d* were cured and evil spirits

DISEDIFYING (1)
Mt 17:27 But for fear of *d* them go to the lake,

DISEMBARKED (2)
Mt 14:14 When he *d* and saw the vast throng,
Lk 5: 2 had *d* and were washing their nets.

DISEMBARKING (1)
Mk 6:34 Upon *d* Jesus saw a vast crowd.

DISFIGURED (1)
1Mc 1:26 and the beauty of the women was *d*.

DISFIGUREMENT (1)
Lv 21:18 or lame, or who has any *d* or malformation,

DISGORGE (2)
Jb 20:15 The riches he swallowed he shall *d*;
Jer 51:44 Babylon, and make him *d* what he swallowed;

DISGRACE (88)
Gn 30:23 son, and she said, "God has removed my *d*."
34:14 that would be a *d* for us.
Lv 18: 7 You shall not *d* your father by having
18: 8 wife, for that would be a *d* to your father.
18:10 for that would be a *d* to your own family.
18:14 You shall not *d* your father's brother by
18:15 wife, and therefore you shall not *d* her.
18:16 for that would be a *d* to your brother.
18:18 for thus you would *d* your first wife.
1Sm 13: 4 Israel had brought *d* upon the Philistines;
17:26 this Philistine and frees Israel of the *d*?
2Kgs 19: 3 is a day of distress, of rebuke, and of *d*.
Ezr 9: 7 sword, to captivity, to pillage, and to *d*,
Jdt 1:11 turned away his envoys empty-handed, in *d*.
8:23 Lord our God, will maintain it to our *d*.
12:12 It would be a *d* for us to have such a
13:16 did not sin with me to my defilement or *d*."
14:18 *d* on the house of King Nebuchadnezzar.
1Mc 4:58 now that the *d* of the Gentiles was removed.
2Mc 5: 7 the end received only *d* for his treachery,
9: 1 retreated in *d* from the region of Persia.
Jb 12: 5 downfall a *d* such as awaits unsteady feet;
14:21 if they are in *d*, he does not know
Ps(s) 35:26 clothed with shame and *d* who glory over me.
40:15 be turned back in *d* who desire my ruin.
44:10 now you have cast us off and put us in *d*,
44:16 All the day my *d* is before me,
70: 3 be turned back in *d* who desire my ruin.
71:13 in ignominy and *d* who seek to harm me.
78:66 to flight and cast them into everlasting *d*.
79:12 bosoms the *d* they have inflicted on you,
83:17 Darken their faces with *d*,
109:29 Let my accusers be clothed with *d* and let
Prv 6:33 he get, and his *d* will not be wiped away;
10: 5 a son who slumbers during harvest, a *d*.
11: 2 When pride comes, *d* comes;
13: 5 hates, but the wicked brings shame and *d*.
14:34 exalts a nation, but sin is a people's *d*.
18: 3 comes contempt, and with *d* comes scorn.
Sir 3:11 *d* for her children, a mother's shame.
6: 1 A bad name and *d* will you acquire:
7: 7 nor *d* yourself before the assembly.
10:19 Whose offspring can be in *d*?
10:19 Which offspring are in *d*?
11: 6 The exalted often fall into utter *d*;
20: 2 who admits his fault will be kept from *d*.
20:24 inveterate liar, yet both will suffer *d*;
21:24 man would be overwhelmed by the *d* of it.
22: 1 everyone hisses at his *d*.
22: 3 An unruly child is a *d* to its father;
23:14 you commit a blunder and *d* your upbringing,
23:26 her *d* will never be blotted out.
25:21 The man is a slave, in *d* and shame,
31:29 and *d* is wine drunk amid anger and strife.
41: 7 father, for they suffer *d* through him.
41:14 judge of *d* only according to my rules,
42:14 and a frightened daughter than any *d*.
47: 4 the giant and wiped out the people's *d*,
Is 4: 1 your name be given us, put an end to our *d*!"
22:18 you glory in, you *d* to your master's house!
23: 9 has planned it, to *d* all pride of majesty,
30: 3 shame, and refuge in Egypt's shadow your *d*.
37: 3 is a day of distress, of rebuke, and of *d*.
41:11 and *d* who vent their anger against you;
45:16 and *d* who vent their anger against him;
45:16 Those go in *d* who carve images.
45:17 never be put to shame or *d* in future ages."
61: 7 and *d* and spittle were their portion,
Jer 3:25 lie down in our shame, let our *d* cover us,
14:21 us not, *d* not the throne of your glory;
17:13 all who forsake you shall be in *d*;
31:19 blush with shame, I bear the *d* of my youth.
44: 8 and a *d* among all the nations of the earth?
49:13 shall become an object of horror and a *d*,
Lam 3:30 to be struck, let him be filled with *d*.
5: 1 what has befallen us, look, and see our *d*:
Bar 6:71 end be comsumed, and be a *d* in the land.
6:72 he shall be far from *d*!
Ez 32:24 *d* with those who go down into the pit;
32:30 their *d* with those who go down to the pit.
39:26 They shall forget their *d* and all the
44:13 *d* because of all their abominable deeds.
Dn 12: 2 shall be an everlasting horror and *d*.
Ob 1:10 *d* shall cover you and you shall be
Na 3: 6 filth upon you, *d* you and put you to shame;
Zep 3:18 among you, so that none may recount your *d*.
1Cor 14:35 is a *d* when a woman speaks in the assembly.
1Tm 3: 7 does not fall into *d* and the devil's trap.

DISGRACED (15)
Dt 25: 3 *d* because of the severity of the beating.
1Chr 5: 1 but because he *d* the couch of his father
19: 5 meet them, for the men had been greatly *d*.
1Mc 2: 8 "Her temple has become like a man *d*,
Ps(s) 35: 4 be put to shame and *d* who seek my life;
71:24 and how *d* are those who sought to harm me!
Is 50: 7 Lord GOD is my help, therefore I am not *d*;
54: 4 you need not blush, for you shall not be *d*.
65: 7 on the mountains, and *d* me on the hills,
Jer 15: 9 Her sun sets in full day, she is *d*,
46:24 *D* is daughter Egypt,
48: 1 *d* and captured, Disgraced and overthrown
48:20 Moab is *d*, yes, destroyed,
Ez 16:54 be *d* for all the comfort you brought them.

DISGRACEFUL (4)
Tb 14:10 made Nadab's *d* crime rebound against him.
Prv 12: 4 but a *d* one is like rot in his bones.
19:26 away his mother, is a worthless and *d* son.
Rom 1:26 therefore delivered them up to *d* passions.

DISGRACEFULLY (2)
Jdt 9: 2 her thighs, and *d* violated her body.
2Mc 14:31 that he had been *d* outwitted by the man,

DISGRACES (5)
Lv 20:11 If a man *d* his father by lying with his
20:20 If a man *d* his uncle by having intercourse
20:21 his brother's wife and thus *d* his brother,
Prv 28: 7 but the gluttons' companion *d* his father.
29:15 but a boy left to his whims *d* his mother.

DISGUISE (6)
1Kgs 14: 2 "Get ready and *d* yourself so that none
14: 5 When she comes, she will be in *d*."
14: 6 Why are you in *d*?
22:30 "I will *d* myself and go into battle,
2Cor 11:13 deceit in their *d* as apostles of Christ.
11:15 his ministers *d* themselves as ministers

DISGUISED (5)
1Sm 28: 8 So he *d* himself, putting on other clothes
1Kgs 20:38 *d* himself with a bandage over his eyes.
22:30 of Israel *d* himself and entered the fray.
2Chr 18:29 to Jehoshaphat, "I will go into battle *d*,
18:29 Israel *d* himself and they entered the fray.

DISGUISES (1)
2Cor 11:14 even Satan *d* himself as an angel of light.

DISGUST (3)
Lv 20:23 have done have filled me with *d* for them.
Ez 23:28 you hate, to those who fill you with *d*.
Gal 4:14 you did not despise or brush aside in *d*.

DISGUSTED (6)
Gn 27:46 *d* with life because of the Hittite women.
Nm 21: 5 We are *d* with this wretched food!"
Ez 23:17 defiled by them, she became *d* with them.
23:18 and I became *d* with her as I had become
23:18 disgusted with her as I had become *d*
23:22 against you, those with whom you are *d*,

DISGUSTING (4)
2Mc 6: 3 evil in an intolerable and utterly *d* way.
Wis 12:24 for gods the worthless and *d* among beasts,
Ti 1:16 They are *d*— intractable and thoroughly
Rv 18: 2 a cage for every filthy and *d* bird:

DISH (20)
Gn 27: 4 your catch prepare an appetizing *d* for me,
27: 7 it prepare an appetizing *d* for me to eat,
27: 9 prepare an appetizing *d* for your father,
27:14 and with them she prepared an appetizing *d*,
27:17 *d* and the bread she had prepared.
27:31 too prepared an appetizing *d* with his game,
2Kgs 21:13 will wipe Jerusalem clean as one wipes a *d*,
Ps(s) 2: 9 you shall shatter them like an earthen *d*."
31:13 I am like a *d* that is broken.
Prv 15:17 Better a *d* of herbs where love is than a
19:24 The sluggard loses his hand in the *d*;
26:15 The sluggard loses his hand in the *d*;
Wis 16: 2 you benefited your people with a novel *d*,
16: 3 period of privation, partook of a novel *d*,
Sir 31:14 nor reach when he does for the same *d*.
Mt 23:25 You cleanse the outside of cup and *d*,
26:23 *d* with me is the one who will hand me over.
Mk 14:20 a man who dips into the *d* with me.
Lk 11:39 You cleanse the outside of cup and *d*,
Jn 13:26 whom I give the bit of food I dip in the *d*."

DISHAN (5)
Gn 36:21 Shobal, Zibeon, Anah, Dishon, Ezer, and *D*;
36:28 The descendants of *D* were Uz and Aran.
36:30 Shobal, Zibeon, Anah, Dishon, Ezer, and *D*;
1Chr 1:38 Shobal, Zibeon, Anah, Dishon, Ezer, and *D*.
1:42 The sons of *D* were Uz and Aran.

DISHEARTEN (1)
Ezr 4: 4 to intimidate and *d* the people of Judah

DISHEARTENED (6)
Jos 2:11 At these reports, we are *d*;
5: 1 were *d* and lost courage at their approach.
Jdt 7:19 to the Lord, their God, for they were *d*,
2Mc 6:12 this book not to be *d* by these misfortunes,
Ez 13:22 Because you have *d* the upright man with
Eph 3:13 not to be *d* by the trials I endure for you;

DISHES (5)
Tb 2: 2 and when many different *d* were placed
Jdt 15:11 with all his silver, his couches, his *d*,
1Mc 11:58 also sent him gold *d* and a dinner service,
Is 22:24 and offspring, all the little *d*,
65: 4 flesh, with carrion broth in their *d*,

DISHEVELED (1)
Est C:13 were put aside, and her hair was wholly *d*.

DISHON (7)
Gn 36:21 Lotan, Shobal, Zibeon, Anah, *D*,
36:25 descendants of Anah were *D* and Oholibamah,
36:26 The descendants of *D* were Hemdan,
36:30 clans of Lotan, Shobal, Zibeon, Anah, *D*,
1Chr 1:38 Seir were Lotan, Shobal, Zibeon, Anah, *D*,
1:41 *D*. The sons of Dishon
1:41 The sons of *D* were Hemdan,

DISHONEST (11)
Ex 18:21 men, trustworthy men who hate *d* gain,
22: 8 In every question of *d* appropriation,
23: 7 You shall keep away from anything *d*.
Dt 5:20 not bear *d* witness against your neighbor.
25:16 Everyone who is *d* in any of these matters
Prv 4:24 Put away from you *d* talk,
Sir 19:21 There is a shrewdness keen but *d*,
51: 6 of lies, from the arrows of *d* tongues.
Ez 33:31 lips and their desires are fixed on *d* gain.
Lk 18:20 You shall not bear *d* witness.
2Pt 2:15 He was a man attracted to *d* gain,

DISHONESTLY (2)

Lv 19:15 shall not act *d* in rendering judgment.
19:35 "Do not act *d* in using measures of length

DISHONESTY (3)

Lv 5:21 "If someone commits a sin of *d* against
Mal 2: 6 mouth, and no *d* was found upon his lips;
Jn 7:18 there is no *d* in his heart.

DISHONOR (10)

Dt 23: 1 wife, nor shall he *d* his father's bed.
1Mc 1:40 Her *d* was as great as her glory had been,
2Mc 6:25 I would bring shame and *d* on my old age.
Sir 1:27 lest you fall and bring upon you *d;*
5:15 Honor and *d* through talking!
20:25 A liar's way leads to *d,*
47:20 You brought *d* upon your reputation,
Lam 2: 2 the ground in *d* her king and her princes.
Ez 13:19 You *d* me before my people with handfuls of
Rom 2:23 the law, do you *d* God by breaking the law?

DISHONORABLE (1)

1Cor 11:14 it is *d* for a man to wear his hair long,

DISHONORABLY (1)

1Cor 7:36 If anyone thinks he is behaving *d* toward

DISHONORED (6)

Ezr 4:14 to look on while the king is being *d.*
Wis 3:17 and *d* will their old age be at last;
4:19 And they shall afterward become *d* corpses
5: 4 life we accounted madness, and his death *d.*
Sir 10:30 *D* in wealth, in poverty how much
2Cor 6: 8 right hand and left, whether honored or *d,*

DISHONORS (5)

Lv 21: 9 fornication and thereby *d* her father also,
Dt 27:16 be he who *d* his father or his mother!'
27:20 father's wife, for he *d* his father's bed!'
Sir 23:18 And the man who *d* his marriage bed and
Mi 7: 6 For the son *d* his father,

DISINHERITED (2)

Jer 49: 1 Why then has Milcom *d* Gad,
49: 2 Israel shall inherit those who *d* her,

DISLIKE (4)

Dt 22:13 having relations with her, comes to *d* her,
22:16 man in marriage, but he has come to *d* her,
24: 3 comes to *d* her and dismisses her from his
Tb 4:15 Do to no one what you yourself *d.*

DISLIKED (2)

Sir 20: 4 wise, another is talkative and is *d.*
42: 9 or when she is married, lest she be *d;*

DISLIKES (6)

Ex 21: 8 who had destined her for himself, *d* her,
Dt 21:15 with two wives loves one and *d* the other;
21:15 but the first-born is of her whom he *d:*
21:16 first-born, the son of the wife whom he *d.*
21:17 his first-born the son of her whom he *d,*
Sir 31:15 as you do, and keep in mind your own *d:*

DISLOCATED (1)

Heb 12:13 your halting limbs may not be *d* but healed.

DISLODGE (10)

Dt 7:22 He will *d* these nations before you little
Jos 13:13 did not *d* the Geshurites and Maacathites,
23: 5 drive them out and *d* them at your approach,
Jgs 1:19 could not *d* those who lived on the plain,
1:21 not *d* the Jebusites who dwelt in Jerusalem,
1:27 he *d* the inhabitants of Dor and its towns,
1:30 Zebulun did not *d* the inhabitants of
11:23 the way of his people, are you to *d* Israel?
Ps(s) 62: 5 from my place on high they plan to *d* me;
Sir 39:28 which in their fury can *d* mountains;

DISLODGED (2)

Jgs 1:32 natives of the land, whom they have not *d.*
Jb 16:12 I was in peace, but he *d* me;

DISLODGES (1)

Dt 7: 1 and occupy, and *d* great nations before you

DISLOYAL (8)

2Sm 18:13 Had I been *d* and killed him,
22:22 ways of the LORD and was not *d* to my God.
Ps(s) 18:22 ways of the LORD and was not *d* to my God;
44:18 you, nor have we been *d* to your covenant;
Sir 16:19 if all in secret I am *d,*
42: 5 or of beating the sides of a *d* servant;
Is 63: 8 indeed my people, children who are not *d;*
Dn 11:32 some who were *d* to the covenant apostatize;

DISLOYALTY (1)

Sir 41:17 Before friend and companion, of *d,*

DISMANTLED (1)

Nm 10:17 Then, after the Dwelling was *d,*

DISMAY (7)

Jdt 7: 4 were, they said to one another in great *d:*
1Mc 6: 4 *d* withdrew from there to return to Babylon.
Jb 22:10 you, and a sudden terror causes you *d,*
23:16 the Almighty has put me in *d.*
33: 7 Therefore no fear of me should *d* you,
Jer 30: 5 A cry of *d* we hear;
Ez 23:33 with destruction and grief, a cup of *d,*

DISMAYED (34)

Gn 42:35 moneybags, they and their father were *d.*
Ex 15:15 Then were the princes of Edom *d;*
Dt 28:65 heart and wasted eyes and a *d* spirit.
31: 8 So do not fear or be *d.*"
Jos 1: 9 Do not fear nor be *d,*
8: 1 "Do not be afraid or *d.*
10:25 said to them, "Do not be afraid or *d,*
1Sm 17:11 the Philistine, were *d* and terror-stricken.
28: 5 he was *d* and lost heart completely.
2Kgs 19:26 shorn of power, are *d* and ashamed,
2Chr 32: 7 do not be afraid or *d* because of the king
Jdt 16:10 "The Persians were *d* at her daring,
Est A: 8 *d* with fear of the evils to come upon them,
1Mc 3: 6 by fear of him, and all evildoers were *d.*
2Mc 13:23 *D,* he parleyed with the Jews,
14:28 this message reached Nicanor he was *d,*
Jb 4: 5 when it touches yourself, you are *d.*
21: 6 When I think of it, I am *d,*
23:15 Therefore am I *d* before him;
32:15 They are *d,* they make no more reply;
Ps(s) 40:16 them be *d* in their shame who say to me,
104:29 If you hide your face, they are *d;*
Is 20: 5 shall be *d* and ashamed because of Ethiopia,
21: 3 I am too bewildered to hear, too *d* to look.
37:27 shorn of power, are *d* and ashamed,
41:10 be not *d;* I am your God.
51: 6 forever and my justice shall never be *d.*
51: 7 of men, be not *d* at their revilings.
Jer 8: 9 The wise are confounded, *d* and ensnared;
30:10 Jacob, fear not, says the LORD, be not *d,*
46:27 be not *d,* O Israel.
Bar 3: 1 afflicted souls and *d* spirits call to you.
Ez 2: 6 fear their words nor be *d* at their looks,
3: 9 Fear them not, nor be *d* at their looks,

DISMEMBER (2)

2Sm 21: 6 we may *d* them before the LORD in Gibeon,
2Kgs 10:32 At that time the LORD began to *d* Israel.

DISMEMBERED (3)

2Sm 21: 9 *d* them on the mountain before the LORD.
21:13 those who had been *d* were also gathered up.
2Mc 1:16 They *d* the bodies,

DISMISS (11)

Dt 15:12 year you shall *d* him from your service,
2Sm 11:12 here today also, I shall *d* you tomorrow."
Ezr 10: 3 before our God to *d* all our foreign wives
10:19 They pledged themselves to *d* their wives,
Sir 7:19 *D* not a sensible wife;
Mt 14:15 *D* the crowds so that they may go to the
Mk 6:36 Why do you not *d* them so that they can go
Lk 2:29 Master, you can *d* your servant in peace;
9:12 *D* the crowd so that they can go into the
16: 3 My employer is sure to *d* me.
Phil 4: 6 *D* all anxiety from your minds.

DISMISSED (21)

Dt 24: 4 then her former husband, who *d* her,
Jos 24:28 Then Joshua *d* the people,
Jgs 2: 6 When Joshua *d* the people,
1Sm 10:25 This done, Samuel *d* the people,
2Sm 3:22 Abner, having been *d* by David,
1Kgs 8:66 On the eighth day he *d* the people,
2Chr 23: 8 the priest had not *d* any of the divisions.
25:13 whom Amaziah had *d* from battle service
1Mc 11:38 he had no opposition, he *d* his entire army,
12:46 He *d* his troops, and they returned
Is 50: 1 bill of divorce with which I *d* your mother?
50: 1 for your crimes that your mother was *d.*
Dn 6:19 refused to eat and he *d* the entertainers.
13:21 testify against you that you *d* your maids
Mt 8: 9 If I give one man the order, *D,*'
15:39 Then, after he had *d* the crowds,
Mk 6:45 toward Bethsaida, while he *d* the crowd.
8:10 He *d* them and got into the boat with his
Acts 4:21 point they were *d* with further warnings.
5:40 the name of Jesus, and afterward *d* them.
18:16 With that, he *d* them from the court.

DISMISSES (2)

Dt 24: 3 comes to dislike her and *d* her from his
Bar 3:33 He who *d* the light, and it departs,

DISMISSING (5)

Dt 24: 1 hands it to her, thus *d* her from his house:
1Sm 9:19 In the morning, before *d* you,
Dn 13:36 shut the doors of the garden, *d* the girls.
Mt 13:36 Then, *d* the crowds, he went home.
14:22 Immediately afterward, while *d* the crowds,

DISMOUNTED (2)

Jgs 4:15 *d* from his chariot and fled on foot.
1Sm 25:23 saw David, she *d* quickly from the ass and,

DISOBEDIENCE (5)

Rom 5:19 through one man's *d* all became
11:30 now have received mercy through their *d,*
11:32 all in *d* that he might have mercy on all.
2Cor 10: 6 We are ready to punish *d* in anyone else
Heb 2: 2 and *d* received its due punishment,

DISOBEDIENT (7)

Bar 1:19 present day, we have been *d* to the Lord,
Rom 11:30 Just as you were once *d* to God and now
11:31 their disobedience, so they have become *d*—
Eph 5: 6 sins that bring God's wrath down on the *d;*
2Tm 3: 2 arrogant, abusive, *d* to their parents,
Ti 3: 3 We ourselves were once foolish, *d,*
Heb 3:18 To whom but to the *d* did he swear that

DISOBEY (11)

1Kgs 15: 5 *d* any of his commands as long as he lived,
Jdt 2:13 *d* a single one of the orders of your lord;
Est 3: 3 Mordecai, "Why do you *d* the king's order?"
Sir 2:15 Those who fear the LORD *d* not his words;
16:26 neighbor, nor should they ever *d* his word.
30:12 small, Lest he become stubborn, *d* you,
39:31 their assignments they *d* not his command.
Jer 26: 4 If you *d* me, not living according
42:13 But if you *d* the voice of the LORD,
Acts 26:19 I could not *d* that heavenly vision.
Rom 2: 8 selfishly *d* the truth and obey wickedness.

DISOBEYED (11)

Jgs 2:20 I enjoined on their fathers, and has *d* me,
1Sm 15:19 Why then have you *d* the LORD?
15:24 for I have *d* the command of the LORD and
28:18 "Because you *d* the LORD's directive and
Tb 3: 4 against you, and *d* your commandments.
Sir 23:23 First, she has *d* the law of the Most High;
Is 42:24 ways they refused to walk, his law they *d.*
Bar 1:18 have sinned in the Lord's sight and *d* him.
Dn 3:95 they *d* the royal command and yielded their
Lk 15:29 I never *d* one of your orders,
1Pt 3:20 They had *d* as long ago as Noah's day,

DISOBEYING (5)

Lv 26:27 you still persist in *d* and defying me,
Nm 14:41 "Why are you again *d* the LORD's orders?
1Chr 10:13 against the LORD in *d* his command
Est 1:15 *d* the order of King Ahasuerus issued
Heb 4: 1 we ought to be fearful of *d* lest any one

DISOBEYS (1)

Jn 3:36 Whoever *d* the Son will not see life,

DISORDER (5)

Jos 10:10 the LORD threw them into *d* before him.
Tb 4:13 such arrogance there is ruin and great *d.*
Wis 14:26 of souls, unnatural lust, *d* in marriage,
2Cor 12:20 slander and gossip, self-importance, *d.*
2Thes 3: 7 not live lives of *d* when we were among you,

DISORDERED (2)

Jb 10:22 *d* land where darkness is the only light.
Prv 23:33 sights, and your heart utters *d* thoughts;

DISORDERS (1)

Am 3: 9 of Samaria, and see the great *d* within her,

DISOWN (6)

Jb 8:18 tears him from his place, it will *d* him:
20:15 God shall compel his belly to *d* them.
42: 6 Therefore I *d* what I have said,
Hos 9:17 My God will *d* them because they have not
Mt 10:33 men I will *d* before my Father in heaven.
26:35 I have to die with you, I will never *d* you."

DISOWNED (8)

Is 1: 2 I raised and reared, but they have *d* me!
Jer 15: 6 You have *d* me, says the LORD,
Lam 2: 7 The Lord has *d* his altar,
Lk 12: 9 *d* me in the presence of men will be *d*
12: 9 be *d* in the presence of the angels of God.
Jn 13:38 not crow before you have three times *d* me!
Acts 3:13 whom you handed over and *d* in Pilate's
3:14 You *d* the Holy and Just One and preferred

DISOWNS (2)

Jb 39:16 She cruelly *d* her young and ruthlessly
Mt 10:33 Whoever *d* me before men I will disown

DISPARAGE (1)

Sir 29:23 pay no heed to him who would *d* your home;

DISPARAGING (1)

1Pt 2: 1 jealousies, and *d* remarks of any kind.

DISPATCH (7)

Jgs 9:54 said to him, "Draw your sword and *d* me,
Wis 9:10 from your glorious throne *d* her
Jer 20:17 because he did not *d* me in the womb!
28:16 I will *d* you from the face of the earth;
Mt 13:41 The Son of Man will *d* his angels to
24:31 *d* his angels 'with a mighty trumpet blast,
Mk 13:27 He will *d* his angels and assemble his

DISPATCHED (12)

Nm 13: 3 So Moses *d* them from the desert of Paran,
1Sm 16:19 Saul *d* messengers to ask Jesse to send him
17:51 its sheath] he *d* him and cut off his head.
2Sm 1:10 So I stood up to him and *d* him,
1:16 when you said, 'I *d* the LORD's anointed.' "
Mt 21:34 When vintage time arrived he *d* his slaves
21:36 time he *d* even more slaves than before,
22: 3 He *d* his servants to summon the invited
Mk 6:27 He promptly *d* an executioner,
12: 2 In due time he *d* a man in his service to
Acts 10: 8 everything to them and *d* them to Joppa.
16:35 *d* officers with orders to let these men go.

DISPATCHING (1)

Acts 11:30 *d* it to the presbyters in the care of

DISPELLED (1)

Is 8:23 Anguish has taken wing, *d* is darkness:

DISPELS (1)

Prv 20: 8 of judgment *d* all evil with his glance.

DISPENSE (4)

Ezr 7:21 requests of you, *d* to him accurately,
Jer 21:12 Each morning *d* justice,
Mt 24:45 charge of his household to *d* food at need?
Lk 12:42 to *d* their ration of grain in season?

DISPENSED (4)

Gn 42: 6 who *d* the rations to all the people.
47:14 payment for the rations that were being *d*,
1Chr 18:14 and *d* justice and right to all his people.
Jer 22:16 he *d* justice to the weak and the poor,

DISPENSING (1)

Sir 18:29 *d* sound proverbs like life-giving waters.

DISPERSE (7)

Gn 49: 7 them in Jacob, *d* them throughout Israel.
2Mc 14:13 to put Judas to death, to *d* his followers,
Ps(s) 106:27 the nations, and to *d* them over the lands.
Ez 12:15 when I *d* them among the nations and
20:23 that I would *d* them among the nations
22:15 I will *d* you among the nations and scatter
Mt 14:16 "There is no need for them to *d*.

DISPERSED (22)

Dt 30: 1 nations the LORD, your God, may have *d* you,
Jgs 21:24 Also at that time the Israelites *d*;
1Chr 12:16 and *d* all who were in the valleys to the
Jdt 7:32 Then he *d* the men to their posts,
Est 3: 8 *D* among the nations throughout the
Ps(s) 68:15 While the Almighty *d* the kings there,
147: 2 the *d* of Israel he gathers.
Prv 5:16 How may your water sources be *d* abroad,
Wis 2: 4 and will be *d* like a mist Pursued by the
Is 11:12 The *d* of Judah he shall assemble from the
56: 8 the LORD GOD, who gathers the *d* of Israel:
Jer 40:15 be *d* and the remnant of Judah will perish."
43: 5 Judah that had been *d* among the nations
Lam 4:16 The LORD himself has *d* them,
Ez 31:17 dwelt in his shade are *d* among the nations.
Zec 13: 7 the shepherd that the sheep may be *d*,
Mt 26:31 and the sheep of the flock will be *d*.'
Mk 14:27 the shepherd and the sheep will be *d*.'
Jn 11:52 gather into one all the *d* children of God.)
Acts 5:37 died, and all his followers were *d*.
8: 4 had been *d* went about preaching the word.
11:19 Those in the community who had been *d* by

DISPERSING (1)

Ez 36:19 the nations, *d* them over foreign lands;

DISPERSION (2)

Jdt 5:19 from the *D* wherein they were scattered,
Jas 1: 1 To the twelve tribes in the *d*,

DISPLACED (1)

Eccl 3:15 and God restores what would otherwise be *d*.

DISPLACES (1)

Prv 30:23 and a maidservant when she *d* her mistress.

DISPLAY (16)

1Kgs 1: 5 began to *d* his ambition to be king.
2Chr 2: 3 for the perpetual *d* of the showbread,
13:11 they *d* the showbread on the pure table,
Est 1:11 that he might *d* her beauty to the populace
1Mc 8:14 a crown or wore purple as a *d* of grandeur.
15:32 the sideboard, and the rest of his rich *d*,
Wis 5:13 to nought and held no sign of virtue to *d*,
Ez 39:21 Thus I will *d* my glory among the nations,
Am 8: 5 and the sabbath, that we may *d* the wheat?
Mt 21: 5 king comes to you without *d* astride an ass,
Lk 19:37 loudly for the *d* of power they had seen,
Jn 7: 4 as well *d* yourself to the world at large."
Acts 22:24 At that *d*, the commander directed Paul
Eph 2: 7 he might *d* the great wealth of his favor,
1Tm 1:16 Jesus Christ might *d* all his patience,
Ti 3: 2 and *d* a perfect courtesy toward all men.

DISPLAYED (10)

Nm 14:17 the power of my LORD be *d* in its greatness,
Est 1: 4 he *d* the glorious riches of his kingdom
1Mc 7:47 they brought to Jerusalem and *d* there.
11:37 that it may be *d* in a conspicuous place on
2Mc 1:15 priests of the Nanaeon had *d* the treasures,
Mt 4: 8 up a very high mountain and *d* before him
Lk 2:31 saving deed *d* for all the peoples to see:
Jn 11:40 believed you would see the glory of God *d*?"
2Cor 7:11 you have *d* your innocence in this matter.
Gal 3: 1 Jesus Christ was *d* to view upon his cross?

DISPLAYING (5)

Jdt 4:11 *d* their sackcloth covering before the Lord.
1Mc 10:70 you *d* power against us in the mountains?
Prv 18: 2 but rather in *d* what he thinks.
Bar 6:25 on men's shoulders, *d* their shame to all;
6:58 How much better to be a king *d* his valor,

DISPLAYS (3)

Prv 14:29 quick-tempered man *d* folly at its height.
Sir 14: 7 and in the end he *d* his greed.
Bar 5: 2 miter that *d* the glory of the eternal name.

DISPLEASE (2)

1Sm 29: 7 nothing that might *d* the Philistine lords."
Is 65:12 my sight and preferred things which *d* me,

DISPLEASED (13)

Ex 16:20 Therefore Moses was *d* with them.
Nm 11:11 "Why are you so *d* with me that you burden
22:34 Since it has *d* you, I will go back home."
Dt 24: 1 is later *d* with her because he finds in
1Sm 8: 6 *d* when they asked for a king to judge them.
12:17 LORD is *d* that you have asked for a king."
2Sm 11:27 the LORD was *d* with what David had done.
1Chr 21: 7 This command *d* God,
Neh 2:10 they were very much *d* that someone had
13: 8 This *d* me very much,
2Mc 11: 1 being greatly *d* at what had happened,
14:27 stating that he was *d* with the treaty,
Prv 24:18 exult, Lest the LORD see it, be *d* with you,

DISPLEASING (4)

Gn 28: 8 Esau realized how *d* the Canaanite women
1Sm 15:19 have pounced on the spoil, thus *d* the LORD."
Jon 4: 1 But this was greatly *d* to Jonah,
1Thes 2:15 *D* to God and hostile to all mankind,

DISPLEASURE (2)

Ps(s) 85: 5 our savior, and abandon your *d* against us.
Is 66: 4 in my sight, and chose what gave me *d*,

DISPOSAL (11)

Gn 13: 9 Is not the whole land at your *d*?
20:15 he said, "Here, my land lies at your *d*;
33:15 at your *d* some of the men who are with me."
47: 6 to you, the land of Egypt is at your *d*;
47:18 *d* except our bodies and our farm land.
2Kgs 8: 6 that the king placed an official at her *d*,
2Chr 26:13 and at their *d* was a mighty army of three
Jdt 3: 3 and all our encampments are at your *d*;
Sg 8:12 My vineyard is at my own *d*;
Ez 38: 7 horde assembled about you, and be at my *d*.
2Thes 2: 9 signs and wonders at the *d* of falsehood

DISPOSE (4)

Gn 43:14 *d* the man to be merciful toward you,
Nm 5:10 man may *d* of his own sacred contributions;
Sir 29:11 *D* of your treasure as the Most High
Lk 22: 2 began to look for some way to *d* of him;

DISPOSED (11)

1Sm 20:12 Whether he is well *d* toward David or not,
2Kgs 10:15 and asked, "Are you sincerely *d* toward me,
Ezr 7:27 who thus *d* the mind of the king to glorify
2Mc 5:25 he pretended to be peacefully *d* and waited
6:29 who shortly before had been kindly *d*,
12:31 be well *d* to their race in the future also.
Wis 11:20 But you have *d* all things by measure and
Bar 4:28 your hearts have been *d* to stray from God,
Acts 17:11 were better *d* than those in Thessalonica,
1Thes 2: 8 So well *d* were we to you,
1Pt 3: 8 loving toward one another, kindly *d*,

DISPOSITION (3)

2Chr 35: 6 and be at the *d* of your brethren,
Prv 11:22 is a beautiful woman with a rebellious *d*.
1Pt 3: 4 the unfading beauty of a calm and gentle *d*.

DISPOSITIONS (3)

Jdt 8:29 corresponds to the worthy *d* of your heart.
2Mc 14: 5 about the *d* and intentions of the Jews.
Wis 12:10 And that their *d* would never change;

DISPOSSESS (9)

Dt 7:17 How can we *d* them?'
9: 1 Jordan to enter in and *d* nations greater
11:23 and you will *d* nations greater and
12: 2 nations you are to *d* worship their gods.
12:29 from your way as you advance to *d* them,
18:14 Though these nations whom you are to *d*
Jos 3:10 who at your approach will *d* the Canaanites,
Is 54: 3 Your descendants shall *d* the nations and
Zep 2: 9 them, the survivors of my nation *d* them.

DISPOSSESSED (4)

Nm 21:32 and *d* the Amorites who were there.
24:18 of all the Shuthites, Till Edom is *d*,
Dt 2:12 the descendants of Esau *d* them,
Ob 1:17 shall take possession of those that *d* them.

DISPUTATIONS (1)

2Tm 2:23 nothing to do with senseless, ignorant *d*.

DISPUTE (12)

Dt 19:17 the two parties in the *d* shall appear
21: 5 and every case of *d* or violence must be
25: 1 "When men have a *d* and bring it to court,
2Chr 19:10 And in every *d* that your brethren living
Sir 8: 3 *D* not with a man of railing speech,
11: 9 *D* not about what is not your concern;
Jer 12: 1 the right, O LORD, if I should *d* with you;
Lk 22:24 A *d* arose among them about who should be
Acts 18:15 But since this is a *d* about terminology
23: 7 a *d* arose between Pharisees and Sadducees
23:10 the *d* grew worse and the commander feared
Jude 1: 9 a *d* over Moses' body

DISPUTED (2)

Acts 17:18 and Stoic philosophers *d* with him,
Rom 2:18 able to make sound judgments on *d* points.

DISPUTES (10)

Prv 10:12 Hatred stirs up *d*,
18:18 The lot puts an end to *d*,
28:25 The greedy man stirs up *d*,
29: 9 If a wise man *d* with a fool,
29:22 An ill-tempered man stirs up *d*,
Sir 28: 8 be fewer, for a quarrelsome man kindles *d*,
Is 50: 8 Who *d* my right?
Acts 26: 3 in all the various Jewish customs and *d*.
Rom 14: 1 Do not enter into *d* with them.
Jas 4: 1 do the conflicts and *d* among you originate?

DISPUTING (1)

2Tm 2:14 them before God to stop *d* about mere words.

DISQUIET (1)

Ps(s) 36:12 me nor the hand of the wicked *d* me.

DISREGARD (6)

Jdt 11:10 my lord and master, do not *d* his word,
2Mc 7:23 now *d* yourselves for the sake of his law."
Bar 1:19 our God, and only too ready to *d* his voice.
Mt 9:11 tax collectors and those who *d* the law?"
Mk 7: 8 You *d* God's commandment and cling to what
Acts 17: 7 they *d* the Emperor's decrees and claim

DISREGARDED (7)

1Sm 2:25 But they *d* their father's warning,
2Kgs 17:16 They *d* all the commandments of the LORD,
Jdt 1:11 that land *d* the summons of Nebuchadnezzar,
2Mc 5:17 a little while and hence *d* the holy Place.
Is 40:27 the LORD, and my right is *d* by my God"?
47: 7 these things to heart, you *d* their outcome.
Mk 5:36 Jesus *d* the report that had been brought

DISREGARDING (1)
Heb 11:23 his birth, thereby *d* the king's edict,

DISREGARDS (3)
Est B: 4 and continually *d* the decrees of kings,
Prv 10:17 but he who *d* reproof goes astray.
13:18 and shame befall the man who *d* correction,

DISREPUTE (1)
Ti 2: 5 Thus the word of God will not fall into *d*.

DISRESPECTFUL (1)
Jb 1:22 not sin, nor did he say anything *d* of God.

DISRUPTING (1)
Sir 28: 9 Commits the sin of *d* friendship and sows

DISSEMBLED (1)
Gn 18:15 Because she was afraid, Sarah *d*,

DISSEMBLER (1)
Sir 25: 2 A proud pauper, a rich *d*,

DISSEMBLERS (1)
Hos 7: 5 He extends his hand among *d*;

DISSEMBLING (1)
Gal 2:13 The rest of the Jews joined in his *d*,

DISSEMINATE (1)
Prv 15: 7 The lips of the wise *d* knowledge,

DISSENSION (9)
1Mc 3:29 because of the *d* and distress he had
Mt 12:26 is expelling Satan, he must be torn by *d*.
Mk 3:26 mutiny in his ranks and is torn by *d*,
Lk 11:17 Any house torn by *d* falls.
Acts 15: 2 This created *d* and much controversy
Rom 16:17 against those who cause *d* and scandal,
1Cor 12:25 that there may be no *d* in the body,
1Tm 2: 8 held aloft, and be free from anger and *d*.
6: 4 From these come envy, *d*,

DISSENSIONS (1)
Gal 5:20 outbursts of rage, selfish rivalries, *d*,

DISSIMULATE (1)
2Mc 6:25 *d* for the sake of a brief moment of life,

DISSIMULATION (1)
Prv 26:26 A man may conceal hatred under *d*,

DISSIPATING (1)
Lk 16: 1 who was reported to him for *d* his property.

DISSOLUTE (1)
Lk 15:13 where he squandered his money on *d* living.

DISSOLUTION (1)
2Tm 4: 6 The time of my *d* is near.

DISSOLVE (3)
Ps(s) 39:12 *d* like a cobweb all that is dear to him;
58: 9 Let them *d* like a melting snail,
Na 1: 5 quake before him, and the hills *d*;

DISSOLVES (1)
Jb 7: 9 As a cloud *d* and vanishes,

DISSUADE (4)
1Mc 9: 9 They tried to *d* him, saying:
Ez 3:18 speak out to *d* him from his wicked conduct
33: 8 speak out to *d* the wicked man from his way,
Jude 1: 7 They are set before us to *d* us,

DISSUADED (1)
Acts 21:14 Since he would not be *d*,

DISTAFF (1)
Prv 31:19 She puts her hands to the *d*,

DISTANCE (50)
Gn 35:16 had some *d* to go on the way to Ephrath,
37:18 They noticed him from a *d*,
48: 7 while we were still a short *d* from Ephrath;
Ex 2: 4 a *d* to find out what would happen to him.
20:21 Still the people remained at a *d*,
24: 1 You shall all worship at some *d*,
33: 7 tent, Moses used to pitch at some *d* away,
Nm 2: 2 the meeting tent, but at some *d* from it.
11:31 *d* of a day's journey all around the camp.
17: 2 and scatter the fire some *d* away,
Dt 19: 6 Should the *d* be too great,
20:15 with any city at a considerable *d* from you,
32:52 You may indeed view the land at a *d*,
Jos 3:16 in a solid mass for a very great *d* indeed,
8: 4 the city from the rear, at no great *d*;
9:22 say that you lived at a great *d* from us,
Jgs 18:22 The Danites had already gone some *d*,
1Sm 26:13 a remote hilltop at a great *d* from Abner,
2Sm 15:17 the ascent of the Mount of Olives, at a *d*,
2Kgs 2: 7 at the Jordan, stood facing them at a *d*.
3:22 saw the water at a *d* as red as blood.
4:25 When he spied her at a *d*,
5:19 Naaman had gone some *d* when Gehazi,
2Chr 25:23 Corner Gate, a *d* of four hundred cubits.
Jdt 5:21 then your lordship should keep his *d*;
13:11 Judith shouted to the guards from a *d*:
1Mc 13:27 and raised high enough to be seen at a *d*.
2Mc 10:27 advanced a considerable *d* from the city,
Jb 2:12 when, at a *d*, they lifted up their eyes
Sir 13: 9 invited by a man of influence, keep your *d*;
Mt 8:30 *d* away a large herd of swine was feeding.
26:58 a *d* as far as the high priest's residence.
27:55 women were present looking on from a *d*.
Mk 5: 6 Catching sight of Jesus at a *d*,
8: 3 Some of them have come a great *d*."
11:13 Observing a fig tree some *d* off,
14:54 a *d* right into the high priest's courtyard,
15:40 also women present looking on from a *d*.
Lk 5: 3 him to pull out a short *d* from the shore;
7: 6 When he was only a short *d* from the house,
14:32 delegation while the enemy is still at a *d*,
17:12 Keeping their *d*, they raised their voices
18:13 The other man, however, kept his *d*,
22:54 high priest, while Peter followed at a *d*.
23:49 were standing at a *d* watching everything.
Acts 27:28 after sailing on a short *d* they again took
Phil 1:27 or hear about your behavior from a *d*,
Rv 18:10 They will keep their *d* for fear of the
18:15 will keep their *d* for fear of the
18:17 then stood at a *d* and cried out when they

DISTANCES (1)
Dt 21: 2 go out and measure the *d* to the cities

DISTANT (23)
Jos 9: 6 "We have come from a *d* land to propose
Jgs 18: 7 They were *d* from the Sidonians and had no
1Kgs 8:41 but comes from a *d* land to honor you
2Kgs 20:14 "They came from a *d* land,
1Chr 17:17 family reaching into the *d* future,
2Chr 6:32 from a *d* land to honor your great name,
Ps(s) 65: 6 the ends of the earth and of the *d* seas.
Wis 14:17 copied the appearance of the *d* king
Sir 47:16 Your fame reached *d* coasts,
Is 8: 9 Give ear, all you *d* lands!
23: 7 feet have taken her to dwell in *d* lands?
39: 3 answered, "They came to me from a *d* land,
46:11 the east a bird of prey, from a *d* land,
49: 1 Hear me, O coastlands, listen, O *d* peoples.
66:19 to the *d* coastlands that have never heard
Jer 4:16 The besiegers are coming from the *d* land,
31:10 LORD, O nations, proclaim it on *d* coasts,
Ez 12:27 he prophesies of the *d* future!"
Jl 2: 2 them, even to the years of *d* generations.
Mi 4: 3 and impose terms on strong and *d* nations;
Zec 10: 9 nations, yet in *d* lands they remember me;
Lk 15:13 his belongings and went off to a *d* land,
24:13 named Emmaus seven miles *d* from Jerusalem,

DISTINCT (1)
Gn 26: 1 There was a famine in the land *d* from the

DISTINCTION (7)
Ex 8:19 this *d* between my people and your people.
Lv 7:10 belong to all of Aaron's sons without *d*.
2Mc 6:23 age, the merited *d* of his gray hair,
Mal 3:18 see the *d* between the just and the wicked;
Acts 15: 9 He made no *d* between them and us,
1Cor 4: 7 Who confers any *d* on you?
14: 7 played if there is no *d* among the notes?

DISTINCTIONS (1)
2Cor 11:18 many are bragging about their human *d*,

DISTINCTLY (1)
1Tm 4: 1 The Spirit *d* says that in later times some

DISTINGUISH (13)
Ex 9: 4 But the LORD will *d* between the livestock
Lv 10:10 You must be able to *d* between what is
11:47 may *d* between the clean and the unclean,
2Sm 19:36 Can I *d* between good and bad?
1Kgs 3: 9 your people and to *d* right from wrong.
Ezr 3:13 and no one could *d* the sound of the joyful
1Mc 5:67 to fight in their desire to *d* themselves.
Ez 22:26 not *d* between the sacred and the profane,
44:23 to *d* between the sacred and the profane,
Jon 4:11 cannot *d* their right hand from their left,
1Cor 12:10 another power to *d* one spirit from another.
Heb 5:14 trained by practice to *d* good from evil.
1Jn 4: 6 Thus do we *d* the spirit of truth from the

DISTINGUISHED (10)
Nm 22:15 more numerous and more *d* than the others.
1Chr 4: 9 Jabez was the most *d* of the brothers.
7:40 of Asher, heads of ancestral houses, *d* men,
Jdt 11: 8 in experience, and *d* in military strategy.
2Mc 15:12 appearance, gentle in manners, *d* in speech,
15:13 appeared, *d* by his white hair and dignity,
Sir 38: 2 His knowledge makes the doctor *d*,
Mk 15:43 a *d* member of the Sanhedrin.
2Tm 2:20 clay, some for *d* and others for common use.
2:21 of evil things he may be a *d* vessel,

DISTINGUISHES (2)
Ex 11: 7 *d* between the Egyptians and the Israelites.
Rv 13:10 endurance that *d* God's holy people.

DISTORT (3)
Dt 16:19 You shall not *d* justice;
Jb 8: 3 judgment, and does the Almighty *d* justice?
2Pt 3:16 The ignorant and the unstable *d* them (just

DISTORTING (1)
Acts 20:30 men will present themselves *d* the truth

DISTORTS (2)
Sir 32:17 reproof and *d* the law to suit his purpose.
Lam 3:35 When he *d* men's rights in the very sight

DISTRACT (1)
Sir 30:23 *D* yourself, renew your courage,

DISTRACTED (1)
Wis 13: 7 his works, but are *d* by what they see,

DISTRAUGHT (2)
Ez 3:15 and for seven days I sat among them *d*.
Lk 21:25 *d* at the roaring of the sea and the waves.

DISTRESS (105)
Gn 35: 3 God who answered me in my hour of *d*
35:16 began to be in labor and to suffer great *d*.
Nm 11:15 once, so that I need no longer face this *d*."
Dt 4:30 In your *d*, when all these things shall
28:53 that in the *d* of the siege to which your
Jgs 2:15 he would do, till they were in great *d*.
10: 9 of Ephraim, so that Israel was in great *d*.
10:14 let them save you now that you are in *d*."
11: 7 do you come to me now, when you are in *d*?"
2Sm 22: 7 In my *d* I called upon the LORD and cried
1Kgs 1:29 lives, who has delivered me from all *d*,
2Kgs 19: 3 'This is a day of *d*, of rebuke,
2Chr 15: 4 when in their *d* they turned to the LORD,
28:22 While he was already in *d*,
33:12 In this *d*, he began to appease
Neh 1: 3 province are in great *d* and under reproach.
9:37 We are in great *d*!"
Jdt 4:13 heard their cry and had regard for their *d*.
Est A: 7 Tribulation and *d*,
C:13 she put on garments of *d* and mourning.
C:23 in the time of our *d* and give me courage.
1Mc 1: 9 many years, causing much *d* over the earth.
2:53 Joseph, when in *d*,
3:29 because of the dissension and *d* he had
7:22 land of Judah and caused great *d* in Israel.
9:27 There had not been such great *d* in Israel
9:68 This caused him great *d*.
13: 5 then, to save my own life in any time of *d*,
2Mc 3:14 There was great *d* throughout the city.
Jb 15:24 *d* and anguish overpower him.
36:15 affliction, and instructs them through *d*.
Ps(s) 4: 2 God, you who relieve me when I am in *d*;
9:10 the oppressed, a stronghold in times of *d*.
10: 1 Why hide in times of *d*?
18: 7 In my *d* I called upon the LORD and cried
20: 2 The LORD answer you in time of *d*;
22:12 Be not far from me, for I am in *d*;
25:17 of my heart, and bring me out of my *d*.
25:22 Redeem Israel, O God, from all its *d*!
31: 8 my affliction and watched over me in my *d*,
31:10 Have pity on me, O LORD, for I am in *d*;
32: 7 from *d* you will preserve me;
34: 7 heard, and from all his *d* he saved him.
34:18 them, and from all their *d* he rescues them.
37:39 he is their refuge in time of *d*.
46: 2 our strength, an ever-present help in *d*.
50:15 Then call upon me in time of *d*;
54: 9 Because from all *d* you have rescued me,
59:17 my stronghold, my refuge in the day of *d*.
66:14 uttered and my words promised in my *d*.
69:18 in my *d*, make haste to answer me.
77: 3 on the day of my *d* I seek the Lord.
81: 8 In *d* you called, and I rescued you;
86: 7 In the day of my *d* I call upon you,
91:15 I will be with him in *d*;
102: 3 not your face from me in the day of my *d*.
107: 6 They cried to the LORD in their *d*;
107:13 They cried to the LORD in their *d*;
107:19 They cried to the LORD in their *d*;
107:28 They cried to the LORD in their *d*;

116: 3 I fell into *d* and sorrow,
119:143 Though *d* and anguish have come upon me,
120: 1 In my *d* I called to the LORD,
138: 7 Though I walk amid *d*, you preserve me;
142: 3 before him I lay bare my *d*.
143:11 in your justice free me from *d*,
Prv 1:27 when *d* and anguish befall you.
Wis 12:27 the things through which they suffered *d*,
Sir 4: 4 A beggar in *d* do not reject;
6: 8 but he will not be with you in time of *d*.
18:21 sins, neglect it not till you are in *d*.
31:20 *D* and anguish and loss of sleep,
31:31 and *d* him not in the presence of others.
35:24 of *d* as rain clouds in time of drought.
Is 8:22 earth, but there shall be *d* and darkness,
8:23 is no gloom where but now there was *d*.
25: 4 to the poor, a refuge to the needy in *d*;
29: 2 But I will bring *d* upon Ariel,
37: 3 'This is a day of *d*,
46: 7 it delivers no one from *d*.
57:13 when you cry out, nor save you in your *d*.
Jer 16:19 my fortress, my refuge in the day of *d*!
17: 8 In the year of drought it shows no *d*,
30: 7 A time of *d* for Jacob,
49:24 *D* and pangs take hold of her,
Lam 1:20 "Look, O LORD, upon my *d*:
Dn 12: 1 in *d* since nations began until that time.
Ob 1:12 Speak not haughtily on the day of *d*!
1:14 Betray not his fugitives on the day of *d*!
Jon 2: 3 Out of my *d* I called to the LORD,
Na 1: 7 LORD is good, a refuge on the day of *d*;
Hb 3:16 I await the day of *d* that will come upon
Zep 1:15 wrath is that day a day of anguish and *d*,
Mt 26:37 sons, and began to experience sorrow and *d*.
Mk 6: 6 so much did their lack of faith *d* him.
14:34 Then he began to be filled with fear and *d*.
Lk 21:23 The *d* in the land and the wrath against
24:18 They halted, in *d*, and one of them,
Rom 8:35 Trial, or *d*, or persecution, or hunger,
2Cor 12:10 with weakness, with mistreatment, with *d*,
1Thes 3: 7 by your faith throughout our *d* and trial
1Tm 5:10 Has she given help to those in *d*?
Jas 1:27 after orphans and widows in their *d*
1Pt 1: 6 a time have to suffer the *d* of many trials:
Rv 1: 9 who share with you the *d* and the kingly

DISTRESSED (10)

Gn 21:11 Abraham was greatly *d*,
21:12 *d* about the boy or about your slave woman.
45: 5 But now do not be *d*,
1Mc 10:22 heard of these things, he was *d* and said:
Wis 17:11 and because of a *d* conscience,
Is 30: 6 Through the *d* and troubled land
Mt 26:22 *D* at this, they began to say to him
Jn 14:27 Do not be *d* or fearful.
Acts 20:38 for they were deeply *d* to hear that they
Phil 2:26 and was *d* that you heard about his illness.

DISTRESSES (1)

2Cor 6: 4 endurance amid trials, difficulties, *d*,

DISTRESSFUL (2)

Jgs 2:18 LORD took pity on their *d* cries of affliction
Mk 13:19 Those times will be more *d* than any

DISTRIBUTE (13)

2Chr 31:19 men designated by name to *d* portions
Neh 8:12 went to eat and drink, to *d* portions,
Tb 4: 8 you have but little, *d* even some of that.
1Mc 3:36 their territory and *d* their land by lot.
Sir 33:24 at the time of death *d* your inheritance.
37: 6 and neglect him not when you *d* your spoils.
Ez 47:21 You shall *d* this land among yourselves
Dn 11:24 he shall *d* spoil, booty, and riches
11:39 over the many and *d* the land as a reward.
Mk 6:41 and gave them to the disciples to *d*.
8: 6 them, and gave them to his disciples to *d*,
8: 7 on the fish, he told them to *d* these also.
Lk 24:30 broke the bread and began to *d* it to them.

DISTRIBUTED (11)

2Sm 6:19 He then *d* among all the people,
1Chr 6: 4 of Levi, *d* according to their ancestors:
16: 3 name of the LORD, and *d* to every Israelite,
2Chr 31:14 he *d* the offerings made to the LORD and
Jdt 15:12 hands and *d* them to the women around her,
16:24 she *d* her goods to the relatives of her
1Mc 6:35 The beasts were *d* along the phalanxes,
2Mc 1:35 he *d* the large revenues he received there.
Ps(s) 78:55 he *d* their inheritance by lot,
Acts 4:35 to be *d* to everyone according to his need.
Eph 1:18 to be *d* among the members of the church,

DISTRIBUTES (3)

Gn 49:27 the prey, and evenings he *d* the spoils."
Prv 11:26 blessings upon the head of him who *d* it!
31:15 still night, and *d* food to her household.

DISTRIBUTING (3)

Lv 25:50 *d* the sale price over these years as
2Chr 11:23 *d* various of his sons throughout all the
1Cor 12:11 these gifts, *d* them to each as he wills.

DISTRIBUTION (7)

2Chr 31:15 *d* to their brethren great and small alike,
31:18 A *d* was also made to all who were
35: 5 so that the *d* of the Levites and the
Neh 13:13 their duty to make the *d* to their brethren.
Lk 9:16 them to his disciples for *d* to the crowd.
Acts 6: 1 being neglected in the daily *d* of food,
Heb 2: 4 and *d* of the gifts of the Holy Spirit as

DISTRIBUTORS (1)

1Pt 4:10 As generous *d* of God's manifold grace,

DISTRICT (39)

Nm 35:28 may the homicide return to his own *d*.
Jos 15:21 in the extreme southern *d* toward Edom were:
17: 8 the *d* of Tappuah belonged to Manasseh,
19:12 eastward it ran to the *d* of Chisloth-tabor,
Jgs 1:27 The Canaanites kept their hold in this *d*.
18: 1 Danites were in search of a *d* to dwell in,
1Sm 10:12 And someone from that *d* added,
13:17 took the Ophrah road toward the *d* of Shual;
2Sm 19:40 him Godspeed as he returned to his own *d*.
24: 6 to Gilead and to the *d* below Mount Hermon.
1Kgs 4:13 and of the *d* of Argob in Bashan
21:23 shall devour Jezebel in the *d* of Jezreel.")
2Kgs 15:16 of the town and of its whole *d*,
2Chr 26: 6 in the *d* of Ashdod and in Philistia].
Neh 3: 9 of Hur, leader of half the *d* of Jerusalem,
3:12 leader of half the *d* of Jerusalem,
3:14 Rechab, leader of the *d* of Beth-haccherem;
3:15 son of Colhozeh, leader of the *d* of Mizpah;
3:16 of Azbuk, leader of half the *d* of Beth-zur,
3:17 *d*, was Hashabiah, leader of half the *d*
3:18 of Henadad, leader of half the *d* of Keilah;
Jdt 1: 5 in the vast plain, in the *d* of Ragae.
10:13 take possession of the whole mountain *d*
15: 3 mountain *d* around Bethulia took to flight.
Is 8:23 west of the Jordan, the *D* of the Gentiles.
Jer 32: 8 my field in Anathoth, in the *d* of Benjamin;
37:12 out from Jerusalem for the *D* of Benjamin,
Bar 6:13 a scepter, like the human ruler of a *d*;
Ez 47: 8 into the eastern *d* down upon the Arabah,
Mt 9:26 News of this circulated throughout the *d*.
13:53 these parables, he moved on from that *d*.
15:21 and withdrew to the *d* of Tyre and Sidon.
15:39 into the boat and went to the *d* of Magadan.
19: 1 came to the *d* of Judea across the Jordan.
Mk 5:17 were begging him to go away from their *d*.
7:31 of Galilee, into the *d* of the Ten Cities.
9:30 that *d* and began a journey through Galilee,
Acts 16:12 in the *d* of Macedonia and a Roman colony.

DISTRICTS (13)

Nm 32:33 its towns and the *d* that surrounded them.
Jos 13: 2 all Geshur and all the *d* of the Philistines
1Chr 13: 2 of our brethren from all the *d* of Israel,
2Chr 11:23 throughout all the *d* of Judah and Benjamin,
1Mc 10:30 or from the three *d* annexed from Samaria.
10:38 "Let the three *d* that have been added to
11:28 and the three *d* of Samaria from tribute,
11:34 but also of the three *d* of Aphairema,
11:34 *d*, together with all their dependencies,
11:57 appoint you ruler over the four *d*
15:29 and taken possession of many *d* in my realm.
15:30 tribute money of the *d* outside the territory
Mk 10: 1 on to the *d* of Judea and across the Jordan.

DISTURB (9)

1Sm 28:15 Saul, "Why do you *d* me by conjuring me up
1Kgs 18:18 "It is not I who *d* Israel,"
1Mc 14:12 and his fig tree, with no one to *d* him.
Jb 11:19 you shall take your rest with none to *d*.
Sir 32: 3 temper your wisdom, not to *d* the singing.
40: 5 to rest, his cares at night *d* his sleep.
Ez 32:13 longer, nor shall the hoof of beast *d* them.
Na 2:12 out, and the cub, with no one to *d* them?
Zep 3:13 and couch their flocks with none to *d* them.

DISTURBANCE (8)

2Sm 7:10 may dwell in their place without further *d*.
18:29 "I saw a great *d* when the king's servant
Wis 14:26 turmoil, perjury, *D* of good men,
Lk 22: 6 to hand him over without creating a *d*.
Acts 17: 6 have been creating a *d* all over the place.
19:23 serious *d* broke out concerning the new way.
20: 1 When the *d* was over,
24:18 without any crowd around me or any *d*.

DISTURBED (29)

Gn 40: 6 the morning, he noticed that they looked *d*.
2Sm 6: 8 David was *d* because the LORD had vented
1Kgs 20:43 *D* and angry, the king of Israel went off
21: 4 Ahab went home *d* and angry at the answer
2Kgs 6:11 Greatly *d* over this,
1Chr 13:11 David was *d* because the LORD's anger had
Jdt 16:25 her death, no one again *d* the Israelites.
1Mc 4:27 When he heard it he was *d* and discouraged,
2Mc 9:24 had been entrusted, and so not be *d*.
Jb 20: 2 shame I hear, and because of this I am *d*.
40:23 If the river grows violent, he is not *d*;
Ps(s) 10: 6 He says in his heart, "I shall not be *d*;
15: 5 He who does these things shall never be *d*.
16: 8 with him at my right hand I shall not be *d*.
30: 7 my security, I said, "I shall never be *d*."
46: 6 God is in its midst; it shall not be *d*
55:23 never will he permit the just man to be *d*.
62: 3 I shall not be *d* at all.
62: 7 I shall not be *d*.
Prv 10:30 The just man will never be *d*,
12: 3 but the root of the just will never be *d*.
Wis 18:19 that *d* them had proclaimed this beforehand,
Is 31: 4 by their shouts nor *d* by their noise,
Mt 2: 3 At this news King Herod became greatly *d*,
Mk 6:20 he heard him speak he was very much *d*;
Lk 1:12 Zechariah was deeply *d* upon seeing him,
24:38 He said to them, "Why are you *d*?
Acts 2:25 with him at my right hand I shall not be *d*.
15:24 their discussions and *d* your peace of mind.

DISTURBER (1)

1Kgs 18:17 said to him, "Is it you, you *d* of Israel?"

DISTURBERS (1)

Jb 3: 8 the sea, the appointed *d* of Leviathan!

DISTURBING (3)

1Mc 7:22 who were *d* their people gathered about him.
Sir 22: 7 or like *d* a man in the depths of sleep;
Acts 16:20 men are agitators *d* the peace of our city!

DISTURBS (1)

Sir 31: 2 more than a serious illness it *d* repose.

DISUSE (1)

Est 9:28 were never to fall into *d* among the Jews,

DITCH (3)

Jb 9:31 lye, Yet you would plunge me in the *d*,
Prv 23:27 For the harlot is a deep *d*,
Lk 6:39 Will they not both fall into a *d*?

DITCHES (2)

Jl 2: 8 Though they fall into the *d*,
Lk 16: 3 I cannot dig *d*.

DIVERGE (1)

Wis 6:22 of her, nor shall I *d* from the truth.

DIVERGENT (1)

Est B: 5 with all men, lives by *d* and alien laws,

DIVERTED (2)

2Sm 6:10 *d* it to the house of Obed-edom the Gittite.
Gal 5: 7 who *d* you from the path of truth?

DIVESTED (2)

1Sm 18: 4 Jonathan *d* himself of the mantle he was
1Mc 10:62 He ordered Jonathan to be *d* of his

DIVIDE (20)

Ex 15: 9 will *d* the spoils and have my fill of them:
21:35 they shall sell the live ox and *d* this
Nm 31:27 then *d* them evenly,
Dt 19: 3 You shall thereby *d* into three regions the
Jos 18: 5 to me you shall *d* it into seven parts.
22: 8 *d* these spoils of your enemies with your
2Sm 19:30 I say, 'You and Ziba shall *d* the property.'"
1Kgs 3:26 neither mine nor yours. *D* it!"
1Mc 1: 6 to *d* his kingdom among them while he was
Jb 27:17 wear, and the innocent shall *d* the silver.
40:30 Will the merchants *d* him up?
Ps(s) 22:19 they *d* my garments among them,
55:10 *d* their counsels, for in the city
68:13 and the household shall *d* the spoils.
Is 33:23 Then the blind will *d* great spoils and the
53:12 and he shall *d* the spoils with the mighty,
Ez 5: 1 set of scales and *d* the hair you have cut.
21:26 the two roads *d* stands the king of Babylon,
Lk 22:17 "Take this and *d* it among you;
Jn 9:39 "I came into this world to *d* it,

DIVIDED (57)

Gn 10:25 Peleg, for in his time the world was *d*;
32: 8 anxiety, he *d* the people who were with him,
33: 1 So he *d* his children among Leah,
Ex 14:21 When the water was thus *d*,
Nm 26:53 groups the land shall be *d* as their heritage
26:55 But the land shall be *d* by lot,
Jos 18:10 Joshua then *d* up the land for the
19:51 tribes of the Israelites *d* the land by lot
Jgs 7:16 He *d* the three hundred men into three
9:43 who *d* the men he had into three companies,
1Kgs 16:21 At that time the people of Israel were *d*,
2Kgs 2: 8 rolled it up and struck the water, which *d*,

DIVIDED (cont.)

2:14 struck the water it *d* and he crossed over.
1Chr 1:19 Peleg (for in his time the world was *d*),
23:6 David *d* them into classes according to the
24:1 of Aaron also were *d* into classes.
24:4 the former were *d* into sixteen groups,
2Chr 26:11 standing army of fit soldiers *d* into bands
Neh 9:11 The sea you *d* before them,
9:22 which you *d* up among them as border lands.
Tb 5:3 I *d* it into two parts,
Jdt 9:4 the spoils you *d* among your favored sons,
1Mc 9:11 The cavalry were *d* into two squadrons,
16:7 Then he *d* his infantry into two corps and
2Mc 8:21 Then Judas *d* his army into four,
8:28 they *d* among themselves and their children.
8:30 They *d* the enormous plunder,
12:20 Maccabeus *d* his army into cohorts,
Ps(s) 69:32 oxen or bullocks with horns and *d* hooves:
119:113 I hate men of *d* heart, but I love your law
Sir 14:15 others, and your earnings to be *d* by lot?
Is 63:12 Who *d* the waters before them,
Ez 37:22 again shall they be *d* into two kingdoms.
Dn 2:41 of iron, mean that it shall be a *d* kingdom,
5:28 been *d* and given to the Medes and Persians."
11:4 and *d* in four directions under heaven;
Jl 4:2 them among the nations, and *d* my land.
Am 7:17 Your land shall be *d* by measuring line,
Zec 14:1 when the spoils shall be *d* in your midst.
Mt 27:35 *d* his clothes among them by casting lots;
Mk 3:25 If a household is *d* according to loyalties,
6:41 He *d* the two fish among all of them and
15:24 Then they crucified him and *d* up his
Lk 11:17 kingdom *d* against itself is laid waste.
11:18 If Satan is *d* against himself,
12:52 *d* three against two and two against three;
15:12 So the father *d* up the property.
23:34 They *d* his garments,
Jn 7:43 fashion the crowd was sharply *d* over him.
9:16 They were sharply *d* over him.
10:19 words, the Jews were sharply *d* once more.
19:23 took his garments and *d* them four ways,
19:24 "They *d* my garments among them;
Acts 14:4 Most of the townspeople were *d* over them,
23:7 and Sadducees which *d* the whole assembly.
1Cor 1:13 Has Christ, then, been *d* into parts?
7:33 This means he is *d*.

DIVIDES (4)

Gn 2:10 there it *d* and becomes four branches.
Ex 26:33 *d* the holy place from the holy of holies.
Lk 11:22 on which he was relying and *d* the spoils.
Heb 4:12 It penetrates and *d* soul and spirit,

DIVIDING (6)

Jos 16:5 the *d* line for the heritage of the clans
Jgs 5:30 "They must be *d* the spoil they took:
1Kgs 18:6 *D* the land to explore between them,
Sir 42:3 or of *d* an inheritance or property;
Is 9:2 harvest, as men make merry when *d* spoils.
Acts 2:45 *d* everything on the basis of each one's

DIVINATION (16)

Gn 30:27 "I have learned through *d* that it is
44:5 my master drinks and which he uses for *d*.
44:15 man as I could discover by *d* what happened
Lv 19:26 Do not practice *d* or soothsaying.
Nm 22:7 with the *d* fee in hand and went to Balaam.
1Sm 15:23 For a sin like *d* is rebellion,
2Kgs 17:17 by fire, practiced fortune-telling and *d*,
21:6 He practiced soothsaying and *d*,
2Chr 33:6 He practiced augury, *d* and magic,
Sir 34:5 *D*, omens and dreams all are unreal;
Jer 14:14 Lying visions, foolish *d*,
Ez 13:6 Their visions are false and their *d* lying.
13:7 the vision you saw false, and your *d* lying?
13:23 longer see false visions and practice *d*,
Mi 3:6 have night, not vision darkness, not *d*;
5:11 shall abolish the means of *d* from your use,

DIVINATIONS (3)

Ez 12:24 or deceitful *d* within the house of Israel,
21:34 planned with false visions and lying *d*
22:28 that are false and performing lying *d*,

DIVINE (34)

Gn 1:27 in the *d* image he created him;
32:29 with *d* and human beings and have prevailed."
Ex 31:3 and I have filled him with *d* spirit of
35:31 and has filled him with a *d* spirit of
2Sm 16:23 was as though one had sought *d* revelation.
2Kgs 1:12 And *d* fire came down from heaven,
1Chr 24:5 holy place, and officers of the *d* presence,
25:5 of Heman, the king's seer in *d* matters;
Tb 14:2 blessing God and praising the *d* Majesty.
Jdt 5:8 with *d* worship the God of heaven,
2Mc 2:4 how the prophet, following a *d* revelation,
3:38 some special *d* power about the Place.
9:12 God, and not to think one's mortal self *d*."
15:29 native tongue in praise of the *d* Sovereign.
15:34 praised the LORD who manifests his *d* power,
Jb 19:22 Why do you hound me as though you were *d*,
38:2 obscures *d* plans with words of ignorance?
Ps(s) 82:1 God arises in the *d* assembly;
Wis 18:9 effect with one accord the *d* institution,
Sir 33:3 law is dependable for him as a *d* oracle.
Is 35:4 With *d* recompense he comes to save you.
Ez 1:1 the heavens opened, and I saw *d* visions.
8:3 and brought me in *d* visions to Jerusalem,
40:2 me in *d* visions to the land of Israel,
Dn 11:36 shall prosper only till *d* wrath is ready,
3:11 for a salary, her prophets *d* for money,
Mt 21:25 Was it *d* or merely human?"
21:25 They thought to themselves, "If we say *d*,'
Mk 11:30 baptism of *d* origin or merely from men?"
11:31 They thought to themselves, "If we say *d*,'
Gal 4:8 as slaves to gods who are not really *d*.
1Pt 1:10 the *d* favor that was destined to be yours.
2Pt 1:3 That *d* power of his has freely bestowed on
1:4 lust might become sharers of the *d* nature.

DIVINELY (2)

2Chr 10:15 for this turn of events was *d* ordained to
1Tm 3:9 *d* revealed faith with a clear conscience.

DIVINER (1)

Dt 18:10 a fortuneteller, soothsayer, charmer, *d*,

DIVINERS (6)

2Chr 33:6 appointed necromancers and *d* of spirits,
Is 44:25 the omens of liars, who make fools of *d*;
Jer 27:9 to your prophets, to your *d* and dreamers,
29:8 by the prophets and *d* who are among you;
Mi 3:7 be put to shame, and the *d* confounded;
Zec 10:2 speak nonsense, the *d* have false visions:

DIVINING (2)

Ez 21:26 divide stands the king of Babylon, *d*;
21:27 hand is the *d* arrow marked "Jerusalem,"

DIVINITY (2)

Acts 17:29 we ought not to think of *d* as something
Rom 1:20 realities, God's eternal power and *d*,

DIVISION (26)

Nm 1:52 companies, each in his own *d* of the camp,
2:2 Israelites shall camp, each in his own *d*,
2:17 be in his proper place, with his own *d*.
Jos 13:6 areas in the *d* of the Israelite heritage,
1Chr 27:2 first *d* for the first month
27:2 and in his *d* were twenty-four thousand men;
27:4 Over the *d* of the second month was Eleazar,
27:4 and in his *d* were twenty-four thousand men.
27:5 and in his *d* were twenty-four thousand men.
27:6 His son Ammizabad was over his *d*.
27:7 and in his *d* were twenty-four thousand men.
27:8 and in his *d* were twenty-four thousand men.
27:9 and in his *d* were twenty-four thousand men.
27:10 in his *d* were twenty-four thousand men.
27:11 and in his *d* were twenty-four thousand men.
27:12 and in his *d* were twenty-four thousand men.
27:13 and in his *d* were twenty-four thousand men.
27:14 and in his *d* were twenty-four thousand men.
27:15 and in his *d* were twenty-four thousand men.
Jdt 14:12 *d* leaders and all their other commanders.
2Mc 8:22 Simon, Joseph, and Jonathan, each over a *d*,
8:23 first *d* and joined in battle with Nicanor.
Sir 44:23 for his tribes, and their *d* into twelve.
Jer 37:12 with his family in the *d* of an inheritance.
Mt 10:34 My mission is to spread, not peace, but *d*.
Lk 12:51 I have come for *d*.

DIVISIONAL (4)

Nm 2:3 the sunrise, shall be the *d* camp of Judah,
2:10 south side shall be the *d* camp of Reuben,
2:18 west side shall be the *d* camp of Ephraim,
2:25 the north side shall be the *d* camp of Dan,

DIVISIONS (12)

Nm 2:31 shall be the last of the *d* on the march."
2:34 and on the march they were in their own *d*,
1Sm 23:28 place came to be called the Gorge of *D*.
2Kgs 11:7 The two of your *d* who are going off duty
1Chr 27:1 the king in all that pertained to the *d*,
28:1 the *d* who were in the service of the king,
28:13 as for the *d* of the priests and Levites,
2Chr 23:8 the priest had not dismissed any of the *d*.
35:5 Stand in the sanctuary according to the *d*
Ezr 6:18 *d* for the service of God in Jerusalem,
1Cor 11:18 gather for a meeting there are *d* among you,
Jude 1:19 of the Spirit, are causing *d* among you.

DIVORCE (19)

Dt 22:19 and he may not *d* her as long as he lives.
22:29 he may not *d* her as long as he lives.
24:1 writes out a bill of *d* and hands it to her,
24:3 house by handing her a written bill of *d*;
Is 50:1 of *d* with which I dismissed your mother?
Jer 3:8 I put her away and gave her a bill of *d*,
Mal 2:16 For I hate *d*,
Mt 1:19 her to the law, decided to *d* her quietly.
5:31 his wife, he must give her a decree of *d*.'
19:3 a man *d* his wife for any reason whatever?"
19:7 divorce and the promulgation of a *d* decree?"
19:8 stubbornness Moses let you *d* your wives,"
Mk 10:2 permissible for a husband to *d* his wife.
10:4 *d* and the writing of a decree of divorce."
10:4 divorce and the writing of a decree of *d*."
1Cor 7:11 Similarly, a husband must not *d* his wife.
7:12 to live with him, he must not *d* her.
7:13 to live with her, she must not *d* him.

DIVORCED (8)

Lv 21:7 nor a woman who has been *d* by her husband;
21:14 Not a widow or a woman who has been *d* or a
22:13 if a priest's daughter is widowed or *d* and,
Nm 30:10 The vow of a widow or of a *d* woman,
Ez 44:22 for their wives either widows or *d* women,
Mt 5:32 a *d* woman likewise commits adultery.
19:9 man who marries a *d* woman commits adultery
Lk 16:18 The man who marries a woman *d* from her

DIVORCES (6)

Mt 5:31 was also said, 'Whenever a man *d* his wife,
5:32 everyone who *d* his wife
19:9 whoever *d* his wife (lewd conduct is a
Mk 10:11 "Whoever *d* his wife and marries another
10:12 and the woman who *d* her husband and
Lk 16:18 Everyone who *d* his wife and marries

DIVULGE (1)

1Sm 4:13 however, went into the city to *d* his news,

DIZAHAB (1)

Dt 1:1 Paran and Tophel, Laban, Hazeroth and *D*;

DIZZINESS (1)

Is 19:14 has prepared among them a spirit of *d*,

DOCILE (3)

Jb 11:12 and the wild jackass be made *d*?
Ps(s) 119:32 your commands when you give me a *d* heart.
Jas 3:17 It is also peaceable, lenient, *d*,

DOCTOR (9)

Sir 10:10 the *d* jests,
38:2 From God the *d* has his wisdom,
38:2 His knowledge makes the *d* distinguished,
38:7 Through which the *d* eases pain and the
38:12 Then give the *d* his place lest he leave;
38:15 his Maker will be defiant toward the *d*.
Mt 9:12 who are in good health do not need a *d*;
Mk 2:17 "People who are healthy do not need a *d*;
Lk 5:31 to them, "The healthy do not need a *d*;

DOCTORS (3)

Tb 2:10 I went to see some *d* for a cure,
Mk 5:26 treatment at the hands of *d* of every sort
Lk 8:43 years' duration, incurable at any *d* hands,

DOCTRINE (13)

Prv 22:17 my words, and apply your heart to my *d*;
Mal 2:6 True *d* was in his mouth,
Mk 8:38 and corrupt age is ashamed of me and my *d*,
Lk 9:26 If a man is ashamed of me and my *d*,
20:21 words and your *d* are completely forthright,
Jn 7:16 "My *d* is not my own;
7:17 to do his will will know about this *d*—
Eph 4:14 carried about by every wind of *d* that
1Tm 4:6 the sound *d* you have faithfully followed.
2Tm 4:3 when people will not tolerate sound *d*,
Ti 1:9 *d* and to refute those who contradict it.
2:1 speech be consistent with your sound *d*.
2:10 every way possible the *d* of God our Savior.

DOCTRINES (3)

Col 2:22 are based on merely human precepts and *d*.
1Tm 1:3 teaching false *d* and busying themselves
6:3 not holding to the sound *d* of our Lord

DOCUMENT (9)

Ex 17:14 down in a *d* as something to be remembered,
Ezr 4:7 The *d* was written in Aramaic and was
Neh 10:1 sealed *d* appear the names of our princes,
10:2 On the sealed *d*:
Tb 5:3 signatures on a *d* written in duplicate;
Est 8:5 let a *d* be issued to revoke the letters
1Mc 12:21 A *d* has been found stating that the
2Mc 2:4 The same *d* also tells how the prophet,
Is 8:20 then this *d* will furnish its instruction.

DOCUMENTS (1)

Est 9:30 when Mordecai sent *d* concerning peace and

DODAVAHU (1)

2Chr 20:37 But Eliezer, son of *D* from Mareshah,

DODO (6)

Jgs 10: 1 Issacharite Tola, son of Puah, son of *D*,
2Sm 23: 9 was Eleazar, son of *D* the Ahohite.
23:24 Elhanan, son of *D*,
1Chr 11:12 to him Eleazar, the son of *D* the Ahohite,
11:26 Elhanan, son of *D*,
27: 4 of the second month was Eleazar, son of *D*,

DOE (1)

Prv 5:19 youth, your lovely hind, your graceful *d*.

DOEG (5)

1Sm 21: 8 his name was *D* the Edomite,
22: 9 Then *D* the Edomite,
22:18 The king therefore commanded *D*,
22:18 So *D* the Edomite went from one to the next
22:21 that day, when *D* the Edomite was there,

DOER (1)

Ps(s) 74:12 of old, you *d* of saving deeds on earth,

DOG (16)

Ex 11: 7 and their animals not even a *d* shall growl,
Jgs 7: 5 up the water as a *d* does with its tongue;
1Sm 17:43 a *d* that you come against me with a staff?"
24:15 A dead *d*, or a single flea!
2Sm 9: 8 should pay attention to a dead *d* like me?"
16: 9 should this dead *d* curse my lord the king?
2Kgs 8:13 Hazael exclaimed, "How can a *d* like me,
Tb 6: 2 the *d* followed Tobiah out of the house and
11: 4 And the *d* ran along behind them.
Jdt 11:19 and not even a *d* will growl at you.
Ps(s) 22:21 my loneliness from the grip of the *d*.
Prv 26:11 As the *d* returns to his vomit,
26:17 Like the man who seizes a passing *d* by the
Eccl 9: 4 a live *d* is better off than a dead lion.
Sir 13:17 there be peace between the hyena and the *d*?
2Pt 2:22 "The *d* returns to its vomit,"

DOGGED (1)

Lam 4:18 Men *d* our steps so that we could not walk

DOGMAS (2)

Mt 15: 9 reverence, making *d* out of human precepts.' "
Mk 7: 7 they teach as *d* mere human precepts.'

DOGS (29)

Ex 22:30 throw it to the *d*.
Dt 23:19 You shall not offer a harlot's fee or a *d*
2Sm 3: 8 Abner said, "Am I a *d* head in Judah?
1Kgs 14:11 line dies in the city, *d* will devour him;
16: 4 line dies in the city, *d* shall devour him;
21:19 dogs licked up the blood of Naboth, the *d*
21:23 "The *d* shall devour Jezebel in the
21:24 line dies in the city, *d* will devour him;
22:38 the *d* licked up his blood and harlots
2Kgs 9:10 *D* shall devour Jezebel at the confines of
9:36 Jezreel *d* shall eat the flesh of Jezebel.
Jb 30: 1 disdained to rank with the *d* of my flock.
Ps(s) 22:17 Indeed, many *d* surround me,
59: 7 snarl like *d* and prowl about the city.
59:15 snarl like *d* and prowl about the city;
68:24 *d* will have their share of your enemies."
Is 56:10 They are all dumb *d*,
56:11 They are relentless *d*,
66: 3 sacrificing a lamb, like breaking a *d* neck;
Jer 15: 3 *d* to drag them about;
Mt 7: 6 holy to *d* or toss your pearls before swine.
15:26 sons and daughters and throw it to the *d*."
15:27 "even the *d* eat the leavings that fall
Mk 7:27 food of the children and throw it to the *d*."
7:28 "even the *d* under the table eat the
Lk 16:21 The *d* even came and licked his sores.
Phil 3: 2 Beware of unbelieving *d*.
Rv 22:15 Outside are the *d* and sorcerers,

DOINGS (6)

2Mc 15:37 Since Nicanor's *d* ended in this way,
Jb 33:13 him that he gives no account of his *d*?
Ps(s) 28: 4 for their deeds, for the evil of their *d*.
143: 5 I meditate on all your *d*,
Wis 2:12 he sets himself against our *d*,
Jer 11:18 that time you, O LORD, showed me their *d*.

DOK (1)

1Mc 16:15 stronghold called *D* which he had built.

DOLE (1)

Lv 26:26 all the bread they *d* out to you in rations

DOLPHINS (2)

Ps(s) 74:14 Leviathan, and made food of him for the *d*.
Dn 3:79 You *d* and all water creatures,

DOMAIN (15)

Dt 33: 4 he made the community of Jacob his *d*,
Jos 1: 4 *d* is to be all the land of the Hittites,
12: 2 His *d* extended from Aroer,
Jb 8: 6 awake for you and restore your rightful *d*;
Ps(s) 103:22 LORD, all his works, everywhere in his *d*.
114: 2 Judah became his sanctuary, Israel his *d*.
Wis 1:14 nor any *d* of the nether world on earth,
Sir 24:11 he has given me rest, in Jerusalem is my *d*.
47:20 descendants, and groaning upon your *d*;
Jer 10: 7 wisest of the nations, and in all their *d*,
51:28 and all its prefects, every land in his *d*.
Ez 48:12 this tract of land their own most sacred *d*,
Dn 6:27 I decree that throughout my royal *d* the
11: 5 still and govern a *d* greater than his.
Jude 1: 6 too, who did not keep to their own *d*,

DOMAINS (1)

Sir 16:25 and their *d* from generation to generation.

DOME (8)

Gn 1: 6 there be a *d* in the middle of the waters,
1: 7 *d*, and it separated the water above the *d*
1: 8 God called the *d* "the sky."
1:14 "Let there be lights in the *d* of the sky,
1:15 serve as luminaries in the *d* of the sky,
1:17 God set them in the *d* of the sky,
1:20 let birds fly beneath the *d* of the sky."

DOMESTIC (4)

Gn 7:14 kind of wild beast, every kind of *d* animal,
Lv 5: 2 animal, or that of an unclean *d* animal,
19:19 do not breed any of your *d* animals with
Jdt 4:10 their wives, and children, and *d* animals.

DOMINATE (1)

Ez 29:15 them few, that they may not *d* the nations.

DOMINATED (1)

Mk 16:20 not allow what is unclean and *d* by spirits

DOMINATION (3)

2Kgs 17: 7 land of Egypt, from under the *d* of Pharaoh,
Rom 3: 9 alike that they are under the *d* of sin.
Eph 1:21 every principality, power, virtue, and *d*,

DOMINATIONS (1)

Col 1:16 and invisible, whether thrones or *d*,

DOMINEERING (1)

2Cor 1:24 *D* over your faith is not my purpose.

DOMINION (39)

Gn 1:26 Let them have *d* over the fish of the sea,
1:28 Have *d* over the fish of the sea,
Jgs 14: 4 for at that time they had *d* over Israel.
1Sm 7:14 these cities from the *d* of the Philistines.
2Sm 8: 3 reestablish his *d* at the Euphrates River.
1Kgs 9:19 and in the entire land under his *d*.
1Chr 29:12 are from you, and you have *d* over all.
2Chr 8: 6 and in the entire land under his *d*.
Jb 25: 2 *D* and awesomeness are his who brings about
Ps(s) 22:29 For *d* is the LORD's,
145:13 and your *d* endures through all generations.
Wis 16:13 For you have *d* over life and death;
Sir 10: 8 *D* is transferred from one people to
33:21 still in you, let no man have *d* over you.
41: 6 Their *d* is lost to sinners' children,
47:19 to women and gave them *d* over your body.
Is 9: 5 upon his shoulder *d* rests.
9: 6 His *d* is vast and forever peaceful,
Bar 3:24 house of God, how broad the scope of his *d*:
Dn 2:37 the God of heaven has given *d* and strength,
3:100 and his *d* endures through all generations.
4:31 His *d* is an everlasting *d*,
6:27 destroyed, and his *d* shall be without end.
7: 6 To this beast *d* was given.
7:12 other beasts, which also lost their *d*,
7:14 He received *d*, glory, and kingship;
7:14 His *d* is an everlasting *d*
7:27 Then the kingship and *d* and majesty of all
14: 5 and earth and has *d* over all mankind."
Mi 4: 8 the former *d* shall be restored,
Zec 9:10 His *d* shall be from sea to sea,
Mt 12:26 How, then, can his *d* last?
Lk 22:29 to you the *d* my Father has assigned to me.
Acts 26:18 to light and from the *d* of Satan to God;
1Pt 4:11 to him be glory and *d* throughout the ages.
5:11 *D* be his throughout the ages!
Jude 1: 8 God's *d* and revile the angelic beings.

DOMINIONS (2)

1Mc 8:24 or any of its allies in any of their *d*,
Dn 7:27 all *d* shall serve and obey him."

DON (1)

Wis 5:18 He shall *d* justice for a breastplate and

DONATE (1)

Ex 30:16 *d* it to the service of the meeting tent,

DONATED (4)

2Kgs 22: 4 that had been *d* to the temple of the LORD,
1Mc 10:45 Judea, shall be *d* from the royal revenue."
Mk 12:43 than all the others who *d* to the treasury.
Acts 4:34 or houses sold them and *d* the proceeds.

DONATION (2)

2Mc 13:23 and honored the temple with a generous *d*.
Acts 4:37 that he owned and made a *d* of the money,

DONATIONS (1)

Lv 23:38 to those of the LORD's sabbaths, your *d*,

DONKEY (10)

Gn 22: 3 the next morning Abraham saddled his *d*,
22: 5 "Both of you stay here with the *d*,
42:27 opened his bag to give his *d* some fodder,
44:13 Then, when each man had reloaded his *d*,
49:11 He tethers his *d* to the vine,
2Kgs 4:22 husband, "Let me have a servant and a *d*.
4:24 him good-bye, and when the *d* was saddled,
4:24 Do not stop my *d* unless I tell you to."
Sir 25: 8 he who plows not like a *d* yoked with an ox.
Jn 12:14 Jesus found a *d* and mounted it;

DONKEYS (6)

Gn 42:26 their *d* with the rations and departed.
43:18 us and take our *d* and seize us as slaves."
43:24 their feet, and got fodder for their *d*.
44: 3 daybreak the men and their *d* were sent off.
47:17 of sheep and herds of cattle, and their *d*.
Jn 12:15 Your king approaches you on a *d* colt."

DONNING (1)

1Pt 3: 3 or the *d* of rich robes is not for you.

DON'T (14)

Gn 19: 8 But *d* do anything to these men,
19:17 *D* look back or stop anywhere on the Plain.
21:17 *D* be afraid;
29: 7 Why *d* you water the flocks now,
37:22 but *d* kill him outright."
1Sm 20:38 to his lad, "Hurry, be quick, *d* delay!"
Tb 6: 4 hold of the fish and *d* let it get away!"
Mt 27:40 Save yourself, why *d* you?
Lk 3:14 He told them, *D* bully anyone.
Jn 7:26 in public and they *d* say a word to him!
20: 2 We *d* know where they have put him!"
Acts 20:10 *D* be alarmed!" he said to them.
23:21 But *d* be fooled by them.
23:22 *D* tell anyone that you gave me this

DOOM (29)

Gn 8:21 again will I *d* the earth because of man,
Nm 21: 2 people into my hand, I will *d* their cities."
Dt 7: 2 you and you defeat them, you shall *d* them.
20:17 You must *d* them all
29:20 out from all the tribes of Israel for *d*,
30:15 you life and prosperity, death and *d*.
32:35 disaster and their *d* is rushing upon them!
Jos 8:26 the *d* on all the inhabitants of Ai.
10:28 He fulfilled the *d* on the city,
10:35 the *d* that day on every person in it,
10:37 the *d* on it and on every person there.
10:39 and fulfilled the *d* on every person there,
10:40 but fulfilled the *d* on all who lived there,
11:11 He also fulfilled the *d* by putting every
11:12 to the sword, fulfilling the *d* on them,
11:21 the *d* on them and on their cities,
1Sm 15: 9 out the *d* on anything that was worthwhile,
1Kgs 9:21 and Jebusites whose *d* the Israelites had
Est 7: 7 he saw that the king had decided on his *d*.
Ps(s) 78:49 strife, a detachment of messengers of *d*.
Prv 1:26 I, in my turn, will laugh at your *d*;
1:27 and your *d* approaches like a whirlwind;
Jer 25: 9 I will *d* them,
50:21 Slaughter and *d* them,
50:26 Pile up her goods in heaps and *d* it,
51: 3 Spare not her young men, *d* her entire army.
Dn 11:44 out with great fury to slay and to *d* many.
Mal 3:24 Lest I come and strike the land with *d*.
Rv 18:10 In a single hour your *d* has come!"

DOOMED (35)

Gn 2:17 you eat from it you are surely *d* to die."
Ex 22:19 god, except to the LORD alone, shall be *d*.
Lv 27:21 like a field that is *d*,
27:28 which a man vows as *d* to the LORD,
27:28 is thus *d* becomes most sacred to the LORD.
27:29 that are *d* lose the right to be redeemed;
Nm 18:14 Whatever is *d* in Israel shall be yours.
21: 3 Canaanites, they *d* them and their cities.
Dt 2:34 we seized all his cities and *d* them all,
3: 6 Heshbon, so also here we *d* all the cities,
7:26 into your house, lest you be *d* with it;
7:26 and abhor it utterly as a thing that is *d*.
13:18 You shall not retain anything that is *d*,
Jos 2:10 the Jordan, whom you *d* to destruction.
11:20 *d* to destruction and thus receive no mercy,

DOOMED (cont.)

Jgs 1:17 After having *d* the city to destruction,
1Sm 20:31 for him, and bring him to me, for he is *d.*"
1Kgs 20:42 have set free the man I *d* to destruction,
2Kgs 19:11 they *d* them!
Est E:15 were *d* to extinction by this archcriminal,
Ps(s) 79:11 your great power free those *d* to death.
102:21 prisoners, to release those *d* to die"
Wis 3:11 who despises wisdom and instruction is *d.*
12:20 were enemies of your servants, *d* to death;
13:10 But *d* are they,
18:15 bounded, a fierce warrior, into the *d* land,
Sir 16: 9 Nor did he spare the *d* people who were
46: 6 That all the *d* nations might know that the
Is 6: 5 Then I said, "Woe is me, I am *d!*
34: 2 *d* them and given them over to slaughter.
34: 5 in judgment upon Edom, a people I have *d.*
37:11 They *d* them!
Jer 4:30 You now who are *d,*
Zec 14:11 Never again shall she be *d;*
1Cor 4: 9 the line, like men *d* to die in the arena.

DOOMING (2)

Dt 13:16 *d* the city and all life that is in it,
1Sm 15: 9 *d* only what was worthless and of no

DOOMSDAY (1)

Ez 30: 3 of clouds, *d* for the nations shall it be.

DOOR (77)

Gn 4: 7 if not, sin is a demon lurking at the *d:*
19: 6 When he had shut the *d* behind him,
19: 9 Lot, moving in closer to break down the *d.*
19:10 Lot inside with them, and closed the *d;*
Ex 12:23 the LORD will pass over that *d* and not let
21: 6 him to God and there, at the *d* or doorpost,
Lv 14:38 he shall close the *d* of the house behind
Dt 15:17 and thrust it through his ear into the *d,*
Jos 19:51 at the *d* of the meeting tent in Shiloh.
Jgs 19:22 surrounded the house and beat on the *d.*
19:27 opened the *d* of the house to start out again
2Sm 13:17 away from me, and bar the *d* after her."
13:18 put her out and barred the *d* after her,
1Kgs 6:34 each *d* was banded by a metal strap,
14: 6 of her footsteps as she entered the *d,*
2Kgs 4: 4 close the *d* on yourself and your children;
4: 5 closing the *d* on herself and her children.
4:15 she had been called, and stood at the *d.*
4:21 Closing the *d* on him,
4:33 He went in, closed the *d* on them both,
5: 9 and stopped at the *d* of Elisha's house.
6:32 close the *d* and hold it fast against him.
9: 3 Then open the *d* and flee without delay."
9:10 Then he opened the *d* and fled.
18:16 He broke up the *d* panels and the uprights
Tb 8: 4 the bedroom and closed the *d* behind them,
8:13 who lit a lamp, opened the bedroom *d,*
2Mc 14:41 and calling for fire to set the *d* ablaze,
Jb 31: 9 I have lain in wait at my neighbor's *d;*
31:32 the street, but I opened my *d* to wayfarers
38:10 for it and fastened the bar of its *d,*
Ps(s) 141: 3 my mouth, a guard at the *d* of my lips.
Prv 5: 8 from her, approach not the *d* of her house,
9:14 She sits at the *d* of her house upon a seat
26:14 The *d* turns on its hinges,
Sg 8: 9 If she is a *d,*
Sir 21:24 It is rude for one to listen at a *d;*
Is 6: 4 the frame of the *d* shook and the house was
57: 8 Behind the *d* and the doorpost you placed
Bar 6:58 or the *d* of a house, that keeps safe
Ez 8: 8 I dug through the wall and saw a *d.*
8:16 and there at the *d* of the LORD's temple,
40:48 either side of the *d* measured three cubits.
41:17 As high as the lintel of the *d,*
41:20 From the ground to the lintel of the *d* the
41:23 " The nave had a double *d,*
41:24 and also the holy place had a double *d.*
41:24 Each *d* had two movable leaves;
46: 3 before the LORD at the *d* of this gate
Dn 14:11 then shut the *d* and seal it with your ring.
14:14 sealed the closed *d* with the king's ring,
14:18 As soon as he had opened the *d,*
14:21 They showed him the secret *d* by which they
Hos 2:17 and the valley of Achor as a *d* of hope.
Mt 6: 6 you pray, go to your room, close your *d,*
24:33 know that he is near, standing at your *d.*
25:10 Then the *d* was barred.
25:11 'Open the *d* for us.'
Mk 1:33 the whole town was gathered outside the *d.*
2: 2 any room for them, even around the *d.*
13:29 will know that he is near, even at the *d.*
Lk 11: 7 The *d* is shut now and my children and I
13:24 "Try to come in through the narrow *d.*
13:25 risen to lock the *d* and you stand outside
Acts 5: 9 buried your husband can be heard at the *d.*
12: 6 chains, while guards kept watch at the *d.*
12:13 *d* and a maid named Rhoda came to answer it.
12:14 that she did not stop to open the *d,*
12:16 the *d* and were astonished to see him.
14:27 had opened the *d* of faith to the Gentiles.
18: 7 his house was next *d* to the synagogue.
1Cor 16: 9 A *d* has been opened wide for my work,
2Cor 2:12 the *d* of opportunity was opened wide for
Rv 3: 8 open *d* before you which no one can close.
3:20 " 'Here I stand, knocking at the *d.*
3:20 anyone hears me calling and opens the *d,*
4: 1 above me there was an open *d* to heaven,

DOORFRAME (1)

Ez 41:21 The way into the nave was a square *d.*

DOORFRAMES (1)

1Kgs 6:31 the *d* had beveled posts.

DOORJAMB (1)

Ez 41:24 leaves were on one *d* and two on the other.

DOORJAMBS (1)

Am 9: 1 so that the *d* totter till you break them

DOORKEEPERS (2)

2Kgs 22: 4 which the *d* had collected from the people.
23: 4 and the *d* to remove from the temple of the

DOORPOST (5)

Ex 21: 6 him to God and there, at the door or *d,*
1Sm 1: 9 on a chair near the *d* of the LORD's temple.
Is 57: 8 and the *d* you placed your indecent symbol.
Ez 43: 8 my threshold and their *d* next to mine,
46: 2 and remain standing at the *d* of the gate;

DOORPOSTS (9)

Ex 12: 7 apply it to the two *d* and the lintel
12:22 the lintel and the two *d* with this blood.
12:23 the blood on the lintel and the two *d,*
Dt 6: 9 on the *d* of your houses and on your gates.
11:20 on the *d* of your houses and on your gates,
1Kgs 6:33 where the *d* of olive wood were rectangular.
Prv 8:34 daily at my gates, waiting at my *d;*
Ez 45:19 offering and put it on the *d* of the temple,
45:19 on the *d* of the gates of the inner court.

DOORS (61)

Jos 2:19 of them pass outside the *d* of your house,
Jgs 3:23 shutting the *d* of the upper room on him
3:24 that the *d* of the upper room were locked,
3:25 he did not open the *d* of the upper room,
11:31 "whoever comes out of the *d* of my house
16: 3 *d* of the city gate and the two gateposts,
1Sm 3:15 and opened the *d* of the temple of the LORD.
21:14 *d* of the gate and drooling onto his beard.
1Kgs 6:31 the sanctuary, *d* of olive wood were made;
6:32 The two *d* were of olive wood,
6:32 The *d* were overlaid with gold,
6:34 The two *d* were of fir wood;
7:50 hinges of gold for the *d* of the inner room,
7:50 of holies, and for the *d* of the outer room,
1Chr 22: 3 iron to make nails for the *d* of the gates,
2Chr 3: 7 as well as its walls and its *d,*
4:22 house, its inner *d* to the holy of holies,
4:22 *d* to the holy of holies, as well as the *d*
28:24 He closed the *d* of the LORD's house and
29: 3 *d* of the LORD's house and repaired them.
29: 7 They also closed the *d* of the vestibule,
Neh 3: 1 They timbered it and set up its *d,*
3: 3 they timbered it and set up its *d,*
3: 6 they timbered it and set up its *d,*
3:13 they rebuilt it and set up its *d,*
3:14 he rebuilt it and set up its *d,*
3:15 it, roofed it over, and set up its *d,*
6: 1 I had not yet set up the *d* in the gates),
6:10 let us lock the *d* of the temple.
7: 1 wall had been rebuilt, I had the *d* set up,
7: 3 shining they shall shut and bar the *d.*
13:19 I ordered the *d* to be closed and forbade
1Mc 1:55 at the *d* of houses and in the streets.
4:57 chambers and furnished them with *d.*
2Mc 1:15 the temple, the priests locked the *d.*
14:43 while the troops rushed in through the *d,*
Jb 3:10 Because it kept not shut the *d* of the womb
31:34 remained silent, and not come out of *d!*
38: 8 And who shut within *d* the sea,
41: 6 Who can force open the *d* of his mouth,
Ps(s) 78:23 skies above and the *d* of heaven he opened;
Eccl 12: 4 When the *d* to the street are shut,
Sg 7:14 and at our *d* are all choice fruits;
8: 1 If I met you out of *d,*
Sir 14:23 through her windows, and listens at her *d;*
28:24 with thorns, set barred *d* over your mouth;
Is 26:20 your chambers, and close your *d* behind you;
45: 1 Opening *d* before him and leaving the gates
45: 2 Bronze *d* I will shatter,
Ez 41:25 *d* of the nave] were cherubim and palmtrees,
Dn 13:17 "and shut the garden *d* while I bathe."
13:18 they shut the garden *d* and left by the
13:20 They said, "the garden *d* are shut,
13:25 as one of them ran to open the garden *d.*
13:36 two girls and shut the *d* of the garden,
13:39 he opened the *d* and ran off.
Zec 11: 1 Open your *d,* O Lebanon,
Mt 23:13 the *d* of the kingdom of God in men's faces,
Jn 20:19 though the disciples had locked the *d*
20:26 Despite the locked *d,*
Acts 16:26 Immediately all the *d* flew open and

DOORSTEP (1)

Sir 6:36 let your feet wear away his *d!*

DOORWAY (6)

Gn 19:11 they were utterly unable to reach the *d.*
Est 5: 1 the audience chamber, facing the palace *d.*
Sir 21:23 A boor peeps through the *d* of a house,
Jer 35: 4 Maaseiah, son of Shallum, keeper of the *d.*
Ez 40:48 The width of the *d* was fourteen cubits,
Zep 2:14 the window, the raven's croak from the *d.*

DOORWAYS (3)

1Kgs 7: 5 *d* were rectangular, and the *d* faced
Ez 33:30 you along the walls and in the *d* of houses.

DOPHKAH (2)

Nm 33:12 from the desert of Sin, they camped at *D.*
33:13 Setting out from *D,* they camped at Alush.

DOR (7)

Jos 12:23 (at Carmel), and *D* (in Naphath-dor),
17:11 towns, *D* and its towns and natives there,
Jgs 1:27 the inhabitants of *D* and its towns,
1Chr 7:29 Megiddo and its towns, and *D* and its towns.
1Mc 15:11 Pursued by Antiochus, Trypho fled to *D,*
15:13 Antiochus encamped before *D* with a
15:25 King Antiochus was encamped before *D,*

DORCAS (2)

Acts 9:36 woman convert named Tabitha (in Greek *D,*
9:39 *D* had made when she was still with them.

DORYMENES (2)

1Mc 3:38 Lysias chose Ptolemy, son of *D,*
2Mc 4:45 losing side, promised Ptolemy, son of *D,*

DOSITHEUS (4)

2Mc 12:19 But *D* and Sosipater,
12:24 the hands of the men under *D* and Sosipater;
12:35 A man called *D,* a powerful horseman
12:35 *D* and cut off his arm at the shoulder.

DOTAGE (1)

Sir 25: 2 and an old man lecherous in his *d.*

DOTED (1)

Lam 2: 4 as a foe, and slew all on whom the eye *d;*

DOTES (1)

Gn 44:20 mother who is left, his father *d* on him.'

DOTHAN (8)

Gn 37:17 fact, I heard them say, 'Let us go on to *D.*'"
37:17 his brothers and caught up with them in *D.*
2Kgs 6:13 Informed that Elisha was in *D,*
Jdt 3: 9 Esdraelon in the neighborhood of *D,*
4: 6 way to Esdraelon, facing the plain near *D,*
7: 3 out in breadth toward *D* as far as Balbaim,
7:18 in the mountain region opposite *D;*
8: 3 in the field between *D* and Balamon.

DOUBLE (33)

Gn 43:15 took *d* the amount of money with them,
Ex 9: 8 "Take a *d* handful of soot from a furnace,
26: 9 the sixth sheet *d* at the front of the tent.
26:24 *d* at the bottom, and likewise *d* at the top,
28:16 It is to be square when folded *d,*
36:29 *d* at the bottom, and likewise *d* at the top,
39: 9 It was square and folded *d* a span high and
Lv 16:12 as well as a *d* handful of finely ground
Dt 21:17 a *d* share of whatever he happens to own,
1Sm 1: 5 a *d* portion to Hannah because he loved her,
1Kgs 7:18 two hundred of them in a *d* row encircled
7:42 four hundred pomegranates in *d* rows on
2Kgs 2: 9 "May I receive a *d* portion of your spirit."
Jb 41: 5 outer garment, or penetrate his *d* corselet?
Ps(s) 12: 3 with smooth lips they speak, and *d* heart.
Sir 2:12 hands, to the sinner who treads a *d* path!
6: 1 "That for the evil man with *d* tongue!"
20: 9 one no good, and some must be paid back *d.*
Is 40: 2 the hand of the LORD *d* for all her sins.
51:19 Your misfortunes are *d;*
61: 7 Since their shame was *d* and disgrace and
61: 7 shall have a *d* inheritance in their land,
Jer 16:18 I will at once repay them *d* for their
Ez 41:23 " The nave had a *d* door,
41:24 door, and also the holy place had a *d* door.
Zec 9:12 day, I will return you *d* for your exile.
Acts 12: 6 two soldiers, fastened with *d* chains,
21:33 Paul and had him bound with *d* irons.
2Cor 1:15 you first so that a *d* grace might be yours.
1Tm 5:17 do well as leaders deserve to be paid *d,*

Rv 18: 6 pay her *d* for her deeds!

DOUBLE-EDGED (1)

Is 41:15 you a threshing sledge, sharp, new, and *d*,

DOUBLE-TONGUED (3)

Prv 17:20 no good, and a *d* man falls into trouble.
Sir 5:17 the reproach of his neighbor for the *d*
28:13 Cursed be gossips and the *d*,

DOUBLED (2)

Ez 21:19 While the sword is *d* and tripled,
Mt 25:17 who received the two thousand *d* his figure.

DOUBLY (2)

Prv 31:21 all her charges are *d* clothed.
Sir 23:11 his obligation, his sin is *d* great.

DOUBT (6)

Jb 12: 2 No *d* you are the intelligent folk,
Jer 16:21 them in no *d* Of my strength and my power:
42:22 Have no *d* of this,
Mt 14:33 "Beyond *d* you are the Son of God!"
Jn 21:25 I *d* there would be room enough in the
Acts 2:36 know beyond any *d* that God has made

DOUBTED (1)

Rom 4:20 Yet he never questioned or *d* God's promise;

DOUBTER (1)

Jas 1: 6 for the *d* is like the surf tossed and

DOUBTING (1)

Jas 1: 6 Yet he must ask in faith, never *d*,

DOUBTLESS (1)

Lk 4:23 to them, "You will *d* quote me the proverb,

DOUBTS (3)

Mt 28:17 who had entertained *d* fell down in homage.
Mk 11:23 and has no inner *d* but believes that what
2Cor 4: 8 full of *d*, we never despair.

DOUGH (15)

Ex 12:34 took their *d* before it was leavened,
12:39 Since the *d* they had brought out of Egypt
Nm 15:20 of a cake of your first batch of *d*.
15:21 to the LORD from your first batch of *d*.
2Sm 13: 8 Taking *d* and kneading it,
Neh 10:38 The first batch of our *d*,
Jer 7:18 *d* to make cakes for the queen of heaven,
Ez 44:30 likewise the best of your *d* you shall give
Hos 7: 4 once the *d* is kneaded until it has risen.
Mt 13:33 the whole mass of *d* began to rise."
Lk 13:21 until the whole mass of *d* began to rise."
Rom 11:16 so too is the whole mass of *d*,
1Cor 5: 6 yeast has its effect all through the *d*?
5: 7 old yeast to make of yourselves fresh *d*,
Gal 5: 9 "A little yeast can affect the entire *d*."

DOVE (20)

Gn 8: 8 Then he sent out a *d*,
8: 9 *d* could find no place to alight and perch,
8: 9 *d* and drew it back to him inside the ark.
8:10 more and again sent the *d* out from the ark.
8:11 In the evening the *d* came back to him,
8:12 days and then released the *d* once more;
Ps(s) 55: 7 me, And I say, "Had I but wings like a *d*,
68:14 the wings of the *d* shone with silver,
74:19 not to the vulture the life of your *d*;
Sg 2:12 and the song of the *d* is heard in our land.
2:14 "O my *d* in the clefts of the rock,
5: 2 "Open to me, my sister, my beloved, my *d*,
6: 9 One alone is my *d*,
Is 38:14 I moan like a *d*.
Jer 48:28 Be like a *d* that nests out of reach on the
Hos 7:11 Ephraim is like a *d*,
Mt 3:16 of God descend like a *d* and hover over him.
Mk 1:10 and the Spirit descending on him like a *d*.
Lk 3:22 descended on him in visible form like a *d*.
Jn 1:32 the Spirit descend like a *d* from the sky,

DOVE-SELLERS (1)

Mt 21:12 tables and the stalls of the *d*,

DOVES (12)

Sg 1:15 ah, you are beautiful; your eyes are *d*!
4: 1 Your eyes are *d* behind your veil.
5:12 His eyes are like *d* beside running waters,
Is 59:11 like bears, like *d* we moan without ceasing.
60: 8 along like clouds, like *d* to their cotes?
Ez 7:16 to the mountains like the *d* of the valleys
Hos 11:11 from the land of Assyria, like *d*;
Na 2: 8 her handmaids, under guard, Moaning like *d*,
Mt 10:16 must be clever as snakes and innocent as *d*.
Mk 11:15 and the stalls of the men selling *d*;
Jn 2:14 engaged in selling oxen, sheep and *d*,
2:16 He told those who were selling *d*:

DOWNCAST (7)

1Sm 1:18 with her husband, and no longer appeared *d*.
Jdt 6: 9 then there is no need for you to be *d*.
Ps(s) 42: 6 Why are you so *d*, O my soul?
42: 7 Within me my soul is *d*;
42:12 Why are you so *d*, O my soul?
43: 5 Why are you so *d*, O my soul?
Lam 3:20 over and over leaves my soul *d* within me.

DOWNFALL (32)

2Chr 22: 7 Ahaziah's *d* that he should join Jehoram,
Jb 12: 5 *d* a disgrace such as awaits unsteady feet;
Ps(s) 13: 5 my *d* though I trusted in your kindness.
Prv 10:29 walks honestly, but to evildoers, their *d*.
13: 3 to open wide one's lips brings *d*.
13: 6 honestly, but the *d* of the wicked is sin.
18:12 Before his *d* a man's heart is haughty,
29:16 but their *d* the just will behold.
Sir 1:19 anger plunges a man to his *d*.
4:22 let no one intimidate you to your own *d*.
5:15 A man's tongue can be his *d*.
8: 2 man, lest he pay out the price of your *d*;
20:17 why the *d* of the wicked comes so quickly.
25: 7 and he who lives to see his enemies' *d*.
51: 3 the snare of those who watched for my *d*,
Jer 1: 3 and until the *d* and exile of Jerusalem in
Lam 1: 9 Astounding is her *d*,
2:11 of the *d* of the daughter of my people,
2:13 For great as the sea is your *d*;
3:48 over the *d* of the daughter of my people.
4:10 food in the *d* of the daughter of my people.
Bar 4:31 who harmed you, who rejoiced at your *d*;
4:33 your collapse, and made merry at your *d*,
Ez 32:10 and on the day of your *d* every one of them
33:12 bring about his *d* on the day that he turns
Mi 4:11 her be profaned, let our eyes see Zion's *d*!"
7:10 My eyes shall see her *d*;
Mt 12:25 kingdom torn by strife is headed for its *d*.
18: 9 If your eye is your *d*, gouge it out
Mk 9:47 If your eye is your *d*, tear it out!
Lk 2:34 to be the *d* and the rise of many in Israel,
Phil 1:28 Their opposition foreshadows *d* for them,

DOWNPOUR (4)

Gn 8: 2 and the *d* from the sky was held back.
Dt 32: 2 like the dew, Like a *d* upon the grass,
Jb 38:25 Who has laid out a channel for the *d* and
Is 28: 2 one and a mighty, who, like a *d* of hail,

DOWNPOURS (1)

Wis 16:16 rains and hailstorms and unremitting *d*,

DOWNSTAIRS (2)

Tb 3:17 daughter Sarah came *d* from her room.
Acts 10:20 Go *d* and set out with them unhesitatingly,

DOWNSTREAM (1)

Jos 3:16 while those flowing *d* toward the Salt Sea

DOWNTRODDEN (2)

Sir 4: 3 Do not exasperate the *d*;
12: 4 refresh the *d*,

DOWNWARD (3)

2Sm 20: 8 that could be drawn with a *d* movement.
Ez 1:27 *d* from what resembled his waist I saw what
8: 2 *D* from what seemed to be his waist,

DOWRY (2)

1Kgs 9:16 city, had given it as *d* to his daughter,
2Mc 1:14 to get its great treasures by way of *d*.

DOZED (1)

2Sm 4: 6 of the house had *d* off while sifting wheat,

DOZEN (1)

Mk 5:25 afflicted with a hemorrhage for a *d* years.

DRACHMAS (7)

Ezr 2:69 sixty-one thousand *d* of gold,
Neh 7:69 into the treasury one thousand *d* of gold,
7:70 twenty thousand *d* of gold and two thousand
7:71 amounted to twenty thousand *d* of gold,
2Mc 4:19 silver *d* for the sacrifice to Hercules.
10:20 on receiving seventy thousand *d*,
12:43 amounting to two thousand silver *d*,

DRAFT (3)

Dt 21: 3 put to work as a *d* animal under a yoke,
1Kgs 5: 8 For the chariot horses and *d* animals also,
5:28 Adoniram was in charge of the *d*.

DRAG (8)

2Sm 17:13 that city and we can *d* it into the gorge,
Ps(s) 28: 3 *D* me not away with the wicked,
Jer 15: 3 dogs to *d* them about;
49:16 as the eagle, from there I will *d* you down,
Ez 12:22 "The days *d* on,
Am 4: 2 When they shall *d* you away with hooks,
1Cor 6: 6 Must brother *d* brother into court,
1Tm 6: 9 which *d* men down to ruin and destruction.

DRAGGED (16)

2Mc 12:35 cloak and *d* him along by main strength,
Prv 24:11 Rescue those who are being *d* to death,
Sir 23:24 Such a woman will be *d* before the assembly,
Jer 22:19 *d* forth and cast out beyond the gates of
49:20 They shall be *d* away,
50:45 They shall be *d* away,
Mt 21:39 seized him, *d* him outside the vineyard,
Mk 12: 8 killed him and *d* him outside the vineyard.
Lk 20:15 *d* him outside the vineyard and killed him.
Acts 7:58 at him as one man, *d* him out of the city,
8: 3 house after house, *d* men and women out,
14:19 They stoned Paul and *d* him out of the town,
16:19 they seized Paul and Silas and *d* them into
17: 6 they *d* Jason himself and some of the
19:29 theater and *d* in Gaius and Aristarchus,
21:30 They seized Paul, *d* him outside the temple,

DRAGNET (1)

Mt 13:47 God is also like a *d* thrown into the lake,

DRAGON (27)

Neh 2:13 by the Valley Gate, passed by the *D* Spring,
Jb 27:22 *d* as from his hand it strives to flee.
Ps(s) 91:13 you shall trample down the lion and the *d*.
Sir 25:15 With a *d* or a lion I would rather dwell
Is 27: 1 and he will slay the *d* that is in the sea.
51: 9 who crushed Rahab, you who pierced the *d*?
Jer 51:34 He has swallowed me like a *d*:
Dn 14:23 a great *d* which the Babylonians worshiped.
14:26 I will kill this *d* without sword or club."
14:27 of the dragon, and when the *d* ate them,
14:28 "he has destroyed Bel, killed the *d*,
Rv 12: 3 it was a huge *d*, flaming red,
12: 4 Then the *d* stood before the woman about to
12: 7 and his angels battled against the *d*.
12: 7 Although the *d* and his angels fought back,
12: 9 The huge *d*, the ancient serpent
12:13 When the *d* saw that he had been cast down
12:16 flood which the *d* spewed out of his mouth.
12:17 the *d* went off to make war on the rest of
13: 2 The *d* gave it his own power and throne,
13: 4 *d* for giving his authority to the beast;
13:11 two horns like a ram and it spoke like a *d*.
16:13 like frogs come from the mouth of the *d*,
20: 2 He seized the *d*, the ancient serpent,
20: 3 He did this so that the *d* might not lead
20: 3 the *d* is to be released for a short time.

DRAGONS (4)

Dt 32:33 venom of *d* and the cruel poison of cobras.
Est A: 5 Two great *d* came on,
F: 4 The two *d* are myself and Haman.
Ps(s) 74:13 smashed the heads of the *d* in the waters.

DRAGS (2)

Jb 7: 4 then the night *d* on;
Ps(s) 10: 9 the afflicted and *d* them off in his net.

DRAIN (4)

Ps(s) 75: 9 even to the dregs they shall *d* it;
Jer 48:33 I *d* the wine from the wine vats,
51:36 I will dry up her sea, and *d* her fountain.
Ez 23:34 You shall *d* it dry,

DRAINED (4)

Is 1: 6 Wound and welt and gaping gash, not *d*,
19: 5 The waters shall be *d* from the sea,
51:17 Who *d* to the dregs the bowl of staggering!
Lk 13:11 possessed by a spirit which *d* her strength.

DRAINS (1)

Lv 15: 3 whether the flow *d* off or is blocked up;

DRANK (46)

Gn 9:21 When he *d* some of the wine,
24:46 So I *d*, and she watered the camels also.
25:34 and Esau ate, *d*, got up, and went his way.
26:30 made a feast for them, and they ate and *d*.
27:25 he brought him wine, and he *d*.
30:38 of the animals that *d* from the troughs.
43:34 So they *d* freely and made merry with him.
Dt 32:14 and the foaming blood of its grapes you *d*.
32:38 sacrifices and *d* the wine of your libations
Jgs 9:27 where they ate and *d* and cursed Abimelech.
15:19 *d* till his spirit returned and he revived.
19: 6 stayed and the two men ate and *d* together.
19:21 Then they washed their feet, and ate and *d*.
Ru 3: 7 Boaz ate and *d* to his heart's content.
1Sm 1:18 her quarters, ate and *d* with her husband,
2Sm 11:13 summoned him, and he ate and *d* with David,
12: 3 and *d* from his cup and slept in his bosom.

DRANK (cont.)

1Kgs 4:20 they ate and *d* and made merry.
13:19 and ate bread and *d* water in his house.
13:22 but returned and ate bread and *d* water in
17: 6 in the evening, and he *d* from the stream.
19: 6 After he ate and *d*, he lay down again,
19: 8 He got up, ate and *d*;
2Kgs 7: 8 they went first into one tent, ate and *d*,
19:24 I dug wells and *d* water in foreign lands;
1Chr 29:22 and on that day they ate and *d* in the
Jdt 12:19 prepared, and ate and *d* in his presence.
12:20 charmed by her, *d* a great quantity of wine,
Jb 29:23 they *d* in my words like the spring rains.
Is 37:25 I dug wells and *d* water in foreign lands;
51:17 *d* at the LORD's hand the cup of his wrath;
Jer 51: 7 The nations *d* its wine,
Dn 5: 1 a thousand of his lords, with whom he *d*.
14:15 children, and they ate and *d* everything.
Jl 4: 3 and sold a girl for the wine they *d*.
Zec 7: 6 you ate, and for yourselves that you *d*?
Mk 14:23 passed it to them, and they all *d* from it.
Lk 7:34 The Son of Man came and he both ate and *d*,
13:26 to say, 'We ate and *d* in your company.
17:27 ate and *d*, they took husbands and wives,
17:28 they ate and *d*, they bought and sold,
Jn 4:12 and *d* from it with his sons and his flocks?"
Acts 9: 9 during which time he neither ate nor *d*.
10:41 and *d* with him after he rose from the dead.
1Cor 10: 4 All *d* the same spiritual drink (they drank

DRAPED (1)

Jdt 4:12 The altar, too, they *d* in sackcloth;

DRAPERIES (2)

Est 1: 6 were white cotton *d* and violet hangings,
Sg 7: 6 your hair is like *d* of purple;

DRAW (71)

Gn 24:11 at the time when women go out to *d* water,
24:13 of the townsmen are coming out to *d* water,
24:19 she said, "I will *d* water for your camels,
24:20 and ran back to the well to *d* more water,
24:43 to a young woman who comes out to *d* water,
Ex 2:16 a priest of Midian came to *d* water
15: 9 I will *d* my sword;
Lv 21:21 defect may *d* near to offer up to oblations
21:21 not *d* near to offer up the food of his God.
22: 3 to *d* near the sacred offerings which the
Nm 16: 5 one and whom he will have *d* near to him!
16: 5 Whom he chooses, he will have *d* near him.
16: 9 to have you *d* near him for the service of
34: 7 Great Sea you shall *d* a line to Mount Hor,
34:10 shall *d* a line from Hazar-enan to Shepham.
Dt 29:10 down to those who hew wood and *d* water for
Jgs 8:20 boy, he was afraid and did not *d* his sword.
9:54 said to him, *D* your sword and dispatch me,
20:32 flight so as to *d* them away from the city
1Sm 9:11 coming out to *d* water and inquired of them,
31: 4 *D* your sword and run me through,
1Kgs 8:58 May he *d* our hearts to himself,
13: 4 withered, so that he could not *d* it back.
1Chr 10: 4 *D* your sword and thrust me through with it,
Ezr 7:20 God, you may *d* from the royal treasury.
Neh 9:29 which men *d* life when they practice them.
Tb 7:13 so that he might *d* up a marriage contract
Jb 9:18 He need not suffer me to *d* breath,
13:26 For you *d* up bitter indictments against me,
33: 5 *d* up your arguments and stand forth.
Ps(s) 37:14 A sword the wicked *d*;
58: 8 when they *d* the bow,
74:11 Why *d* back your hand and keep your right
Sg 1: 4 *D* me!—We will follow you
Wis 1:12 nor *d* to yourselves destruction by the
Sir 6:19 though plowing and sowing, *d* close to her;
6:27 With all your soul *d* close to her;
22:21 Should you *d* a sword against a friend,
33: 4 *d* upon your training,
Is 12: 3 will *d* water at the fountain of salvation,
41: 1 Let them *d* near and speak;
57: 3 But you, *d* near, you sons of a sorceress,
Jer 38:10 and *d* the prophet Jeremiah out of the
51: 3 Let the bowman *d* his bow,
Lam 4:15 cried to them, "Away, away, do not *d* near!"
Ez 4: 1 of you, and *d* on it a city [Jerusalem].
21: 8 I will *d* my sword from its sheath and cut
28: 7 They shall *d* their swords against your
29: 4 then *d* you up from the midst of your Niles
30:11 They shall *d* their swords against Egypt,
32: 3 of many nations], and *d* you up in my seine.
42:13 here the priests who *d* near to the LORD
43:19 of Zadok, who *d* near me to minister to me,
44:13 no longer *d* near me to serve as my priests,
44:15 me, they shall *d* near me to minister to me,
45: 4 who *d* near to minister to the LORD;
Na 3:14 *D* water for the siege,
Hg 2:16 went to the vat to *d* fifty measures,
Mal 3: 5 I will *d* near to you for judgment,
Mt 13:41 his kingdom all who *d* others to apostasy,
Jn 2: 8 *d* some out and take it to the waiter in
4: 7 When a Samaritan woman came to *d* water,
4:15 and have to keep coming here to *d* water."
12:32 will *d* all men to myself."
Rom 13: 2 shall *d* condemnation down upon themselves.
Eph 6:10 *d* your strength from the Lord and his
Heb 7:19 and through it we *d* near to God.
10:22 let us *d* near in utter sincerity and
10:39 are not among those who *d* back and perish,
Jas 4: 8 *D* close to God, and he will *d* close

DRAWERS (8)

Ex 28:42 You must also make linen *d* for them,
39:28 *d* of linen [of fine linen twined];
Lv 6: 3 linen robe and wearing linen *d* on his body,
16: 4 tunic, with the linen *d* next his flesh,
Jos 9:21 and *d* of water for the entire community;
9:23 and *d* of water] for the house of my God."
9:27 hewers of wood and *d* of water for the
Ez 44:18 on their heads and linen *d* on their loins;

DRAWING (5)

1Sm 17: 2 *d* up their battle line to meet the
2Mc 15:20 The enemy were already *d* near with their
Ps(s) 50:21 correct you by *d* them up before your eyes.
Lk 22: 1 Bread known as the Passover was *d* near,
Eph 3:12 freely to God, *d* near him with confidence.

DRAWN (41)

Gn 24:20 until she had *d* enough for all the camels.
Ex 38:21 *d* up at the command of Moses by the
Lv 26:33 the nations at the point of my *d* sword,
Nm 22:23 LORD standing on the road with sword *d*,
22:31 LORD standing on the road with sword *d*;
Jos 5:13 one who stood facing him, *d* sword in hand.
8: 6 us until we have *d* them away from the city,
8:11 led were *d* up in position before the city,
8:17 Since they were *d* away from the city,
Jgs 20:32 *d* away from the city onto the highways,
2Sm 10: 9 Joab saw the battle lines *d* up against him,
20: 8 that could be *d* with a downward movement.
2Kgs 11: 8 surround the king, each with *d* weapons,
11:11 And the guards, with *d* weapons,
1Chr 12:39 All these soldiers, *d* up in battle order,
19:17 army of David *d* up to fight the Arameans,
2Chr 23: 7 king on all sides, each with his weapon *d*.
Tb 13:11 *d* to you by the name of the Lord God,
2Mc 5: 3 fully armed with lances and *d* swords;
15:20 near with their troops *d* up in battle line,
Ps(s) 55:22 smoother than oil, but they are *d* swords.
Wis 14:20 masses *d* by the charm of the workmanship,
Sir 9: 9 Lest your heart be *d* to her and you go
13:15 Every being is *d* to its own kind;
37:28 Be not *d* after every enjoyment,
Jer 6:29 smelter refined, the wicked are not *d* off.
9: 2 They ready their tongues like a *d* bow;
Bar 6:43 *d* aside by some passer-by who lies with her,
Ez 21:10 the LORD, have *d* my sword from its sheath,
21:29 Because you have *d* attention to your guilt,
21:29 (because attention has been *d* to you),
21:33 A sword, a sword is *d* for slaughter,
23:14 *d* on the wall, the images of Chaldeans *d*
Mi 5: 5 and the land of Nimrod with the *d* sword;
Zep 3: 2 not trusted, to her God she has not *d* near.
Jn 2: 9 waiters knew, since they had *d* the water.
Acts 11:10 in it was *d* up again into the sky.
Heb 12:18 You have not *d* near to an untouchable
12:22 you have *d* near to Mount Zion and the city
2Pt 3: 5 heavens and an earth *d* out of the waters

DRAWS (15)

Nm 18: 7 layman who *d* near shall be put to death."
Jb 33:22 His soul *d* near to the pit,
Ps(s) 88: 4 and my life *d* near to the nether world.
Prv 20: 5 but the man of intelligence *d* it forth.
Sir 23:16 of men multiply sins, a third *d* down wrath;
32:16 out of obscurity he *d* forth a clear plan.
33:12 great, some he sanctifies and *d* to himself.
Is 29:13 Since this people *d* near with words only
Jer 7:29 off the generation that *d* down his wrath.
Mt 26:18 Teacher says, My appointed time *d* near.
Jn 6:44 to me unless the Father who sent me *d* him;
Rom 13:12 The night is far spent; the day *d* near.
Heb 10:25 more because you see that the Day *d* near.
10:38 and if he *d* back I take no pleasure in him.
1Pt 1: 3 a birth unto hope which *d* its life from

DREAD (45)

Gn 9: 2 *D* fear of you shall come upon all the
Ex 15:16 terror and *d* fell upon them.
Dt 1:29 I said to you, 'Have no *d* or fear of them.
2:25 This day I will begin to put a fear and *d*
11:25 will spread the fear and *d* of you through
28:60 with all the diseases of Egypt which you *d*,
28:66 suspense and stand in *d* both day and night,
28:67 for *d* that your heart must feel and the
31: 6 have no fear or *d* of them,
Jos 2: 9 the land, that a *d* of you has come upon us,
1Sm 11: 7 In *d* of the LORD,
Ezr 9: 4 Around me gathered all who were in *d* of
Jdt 2:28 The fear and *d* of him fell upon all the
4: 2 them, they were in extreme *d* of him,
Est 7: 6 was seized with *d* of the king and queen.
1Mc 3:25 and *d* fell upon the Gentiles about them.
4: 8 afraid of their numbers or *d* their attack.
7:18 and *d* of them came upon all the people,
12:28 battle, their hearts sank with fear and *d*.
13: 2 saw that the people were in *d* and terror,
2Mc 3:21 and the high priest full of *d* and anguish.
15:23 angel now to spread fear and *d* before us.
Jb 5:22 the beasts of the earth you need not *d*.
9:28 cheer, Then I am in *d* of all my pains;
13:11 you and the *d* of him fall upon you.
15:24 By day the darkness fills him with *d*;
31:23 For the *d* of God will be upon me,
Ps(s) 31:12 to my neighbors, and a *d* to my friends;
36: 2 there is no *d* of God before his eyes,
64: 2 from the *d* enemy preserve my life.
88:16 I am dazed with the burden of your *d*.
105:38 for the *d* of them had fallen upon it.
119:39 Turn away from me the reproach which I *d*,
119:120 My flesh shudders with *d* of you,
Prv 20: 2 The *d* of the king is as when a lion roars;
Sir 4:17 Fear and *d* she brings upon him and tries
9:13 you will not be filled with the *d* of death.
36: 1 and put all the nations in *d* of you!
40: 5 Are of wrath and envy, trouble and *d*,
Is 7:16 two kings whom you *d* shall be deserted.
19:17 they shall stand in *d* because of the plan
21: 4 My yearning for twilight has turned into *d*.
33:14 On Zion sinners are in *d*,
51:13 in constant *d* of the fury of the oppressor;
Jer 42:16 you *d* shall cling to you no less in Egypt,

DREADED (6)

Ex 1:12 *d* the Israelites and reduced them to cruel
Dt 9:19 *d* the fierce anger of the LORD against you:
1Sm 12:18 all the people *d* the LORD and Samuel.
Is 18: 2 and bronzed, To a people *d* near and far,
18: 7 and bronzed, from a people *d* near and far,
Dn 5:19 peoples of every language *d* and feared him.

DREADFUL (4)

2Mc 3:25 caparisoned horse, mounted by a *d* rider.
Wis 5: 2 this, they shall be shaken with *d* fear,
Dn 11:36 *d* blasphemies against the God of gods.
Hb 1: 7 Terrible and *d* is he,

DREAM (77)

Gn 20: 3 Abimelech in a *d* one night and said to him,
20: 6 God answered him in the *d*:
28:12 Then he had a *d*:
31:10 I had a *d* in which I saw mating he-goats
31:11 In the *d* God's messenger called to me,
31:24 to Laban the Aramean in a *d* and warned him,
37: 5 Once Joseph had a *d*,
37: 6 "Listen to this *d* I had.
37: 9 Then he had another *d*,
37: 9 "I had another *d*,"
37:10 "What is the meaning of this *d* of yours?"
40: 5 same night, each *d* with its own meaning.
40: 9 Then the chief cupbearer told Joseph his *d*.
40: 9 "In my *d*," he said, "I saw a vine
40:16 "I too had a *d*.
41: 1 a lapse of two years, Pharaoh had a *d*.
41: 5 He fell asleep again and had another *d*.
41: 7 Pharaoh woke up, to find it was only a *d*.
41:12 for each of us the meaning of his *d*.
41:15 you are told a *d* you can interpret it."
41:17 "In my *d*, I was standing on the bank
41:22 In another *d* I saw seven ears of grain,
41:26 the same in each *d*.
41:32 That Pharaoh had the same *d* twice means
Jgs 7:13 one man was telling another about a *d*.
7:13 "I had a *d*,"
7:15 the description and explanation of the *d*,
1Kgs 3: 5 LORD appeared to Solomon in a *d* at night.
3:15 When Solomon awoke from his *d*,
Est A: 1 of Kish, of the tribe of Benjamin, had a *d*.
A: 4 This was his *d*.
A:11 seen this *d* and what God intended to do,
F: 2 recall the *d* I had about these very things,
2Mc 8:11 little did he *d* of the punishment that was
15:11 words, he cheered them all by relating a *d*,
Jb 20: 8 a *d* he takes flight and is not found again;
33:15 In a *d*, in a vision of the night,
Ps(s) 73:20 they were the *d* of one who had awakened,
Is 29: 7 Then like a *d*, a vision in the night,
Jer 23:25 prophesy lies in my name say, "I had a *d*!
23:28 the prophet who has a *d* recount his dream;
29: 8 not listen to those among you who *d* dreams.
Dn 2: 1 King Nebuchadnezzar had a *d* which left his
2: 2 be summoned to interpret the *d* for him.
2: 3 "I had a *d* which will allow my spirit no
2: 4 the *d* and we will give its meaning."
2: 5 unless you tell me the *d* and its meaning,
2: 6 But if you tell me the *d* and its meaning,
2: 6 Now tell me the *d* and its meaning."
2: 7 the *d* and we will give its meaning."
2: 9 If you do not tell me the *d*,
2: 9 Tell me the *d*, therefore, that I may be
2:23 you have made known to us the king's *d*."
2:24 will tell him the interpretation of the *d*."
2:26 "Can you tell me the *d* that I had,

2:28 this was the *d* you saw as you lay in bed.
2:36 "This was the *d;* the interpretation
4: 2 I had a terrifying *d* as I lay in bed,
4: 3 me to give the interpretation of the *d.*
4: 4 had come in, I related the *d* before them;
4: 5 I repeated the *d* to him:
4: 6 meaning of the visions that I saw in my *d.*
4:15 "This is the *d* that I,
4:16 "let not the *d* or its meaning terrify you."
4:17 "this *d* should be for your enemies,
7: 1 Babylon, Daniel had a *d* as he lay in bed,
7: 1 Then he wrote down the *d;*
Jl 3: 1 prophesy, your old men shall *d* dreams,
Mt 1:20 the Lord appeared in a *d* and said to him:
2:12 a message in a *d* not to return to Herod,
2:13 appeared in a *d* to Joseph with the command:
2:19 in a *d* to Joseph in Egypt with the command:
2:22 because of a warning received in a *d,*
27:19 I had a *d* about him today which has
Acts 2:17 visions and your old men shall *d* dreams.

DREAMED (1)

Dn 2:45 this is exactly what you *d,*

DREAMER (4)

Gn 37:19 "Here comes that master *d!*
Dt 13: 2 or a *d* who promises you a sign or wonder,
13: 4 to the words of that prophet or that *d;*
13: 6 prophet or that *d* shall be put to death,

DREAMERS (1)

Jer 27: 9 to your prophets, to your diviners and *d,*

DREAMING (2)

Ps(s) 126: 1 the captives of Zion, we were like men *d.*
Is 56:10 *D* as they lie there,

DREAMS (37)

Gn 37: 8 the more because of his talk about his *d.*
37:20 We shall then see what comes of his *d.*"
40: 5 in the jail both had *d* on the same night,
40: 8 They answered him, "We have had *d,*
40: 8 Please tell the *d* to me."
41: 8 *d* to them; but no one could interpret his *d*
41:11 had *d* on the same night, and each of our *d*
41:12 and when we told him our *d,*
41:15 had certain *d* that no one can interpret.
41:25 of Pharaoh's *d* have the same meaning.
42: 9 he was reminded of the *d* he had about them.
Nm 12: 6 myself to him, in *d* will I speak to him;
1Sm 28: 6 in *d* or by the Urim or through prophets.
28:15 answers me through prophets or in *d,*
Jb 7:14 me with *d* and with visions terrify me,
Wis 18:17 visions in horrible *d* perturbed them and
18:19 For the *d* that disturbed them had
Sir 34: 1 senseless, and fools are borne aloft by *d.*
34: 2 the wind, is the one who believes in *d.*
34: 3 What is seen in *d* is to reality what the
34: 5 Divination, omens and *d* all are unreal;
34: 7 For *d* have led many astray,
40: 6 in his *d* he struggles as he did by day,
Is 29: 8 As when a hungry man *d* he is eating and
29: 8 Or when a thirsty man *d* he is drinking and
Jer 14:14 divination, *d* of their own imagination,
23:27 their *d* which they recount to each other,
23:32 against the prophets who prophesy lying *d,*
29: 8 not listen to those among you who dream *d.*
Dn 1:17 the understanding of all visions and *d.*
5:12 He knew and understood how to interpret *d,*
5:16 you can interpret *d* and solve difficulties;
Jl 3: 1 prophesy, your old men shall dream *d,*
Zec 10: 2 Deceitful *d* they tell,
Acts 2:17 see visions and your old men shall dream *d.*

DREGS (2)

Ps(s) 75: 9 even to the *d* they shall drain it;
Is 51:17 drained to the *d* the bowl of staggering!

DRENCH (2)

Ps(s) 6: 7 I *d* my couch with my tears.
Sir 24:29 water my plants, my flower bed I will *d*";

DRENCHED (1)

Jb 24: 8 They are *d* with the rain of the mountains,

DRENCHING (2)

Jb 37: 6 likewise to his heavy, *d* rain.
Ps(s) 65:11 *d* its furrows, breaking up its clods,

DRESS (12)

Dt 22: 5 a man, nor shall a man put on a woman's *d;*
1Sm 18: 4 it to David, along with his military *d,*
2Chr 9: 4 their *d,* his cupbearers and their *d*
1Mc 11:58 drink from gold cups, to *d* in royal purple,
Zep 1: 8 sons, and all that *d* in foreign apparel.
Mal 3:14 penitential *d* in awe of the LORD of hosts?
Mt 11: 8 those who *d* luxuriously are to be found in
Lk 7:25 those who *d* in luxury and eat in splendor
1Tm 2: 9 They should *d* modestly and quietly,
Rv 19: 8 given a *d* to wear made of finest linen,
19: 8 *d* is the virtuous deeds of God's saints.)

DRESSED (36)

Gn 41:42 He had him *d* in robes of fine linen and
1Sm 25:18 loaves, two skins of wine, five *d* sheep,
2Sm 13:18 is how maiden princesses *d* in olden days.
1Kgs 6: 7 temple was built of stone *d* at the quarry,
20:32 So they *d* in sackcloth girded at the waist,
Jdt 10: 7 transformed in looks and differently *d,*
Prv 9: 2 She has *d* her meat,
Ez 9: 2 In their midst was a man *d* in linen,
9: 3 Then he called to the man *d* in linen with
9:11 Then I saw the man *d* in linen with the
10: 2 He said to the man *d* in linen:
10: 6 When he commanded the man *d* in linen to
10: 7 put it in the hands of the one *d* in linen,
23: 6 the Assyrians, warriors *d* in purple,
Dn 10: 5 I saw a man *d* in linen with a belt of fine
Mt 11: 8 someone luxuriously *d?*
22:11 a man not properly *d* for a wedding feast.
22:12 'how is it you came in here not properly *d?*'
27:31 him of the cloak, *d* him in his own clothes,
Mk 15:17 They *d* him in royal purple,
15:20 of the purple, *d* him in his own clothes,
16: 5 sitting at the right, *d* in a white robe.
Lk 7:25 someone *d* luxuriously?
8:35 at his feet *d* and in his full senses;
10:34 He approached him and *d* his wounds,
16:19 "Once there was a rich man who *d* in
Acts 1:10 when two men *d* in white stood beside them.
20:33 silver or gold or envy the way he *d.*
Jas 2: 2 into your assembly a man fashionably *d,*
Rv 7: 9 *d* in long white robes and holding palm
7:13 me, "Who are these people all *d* in white?
11: 3 hundred and sixty days, *d* in sackcloth."
15: 6 The angels were *d* in pure white linen,
17: 4 The woman was *d* in purple and scarlet and
18:16 *d* in fine linen and purple and scarlet,
19:14 riding white horses and *d* in fine linen,

DRESSER (1)

Am 7:14 I was a shepherd and a *d* of sycamores.

DRESSES (1)

Is 3:22 the court *d,* wraps, cloaks, and purses;

DREW (60)

Gn 8: 9 dove and *d* it back to him inside the ark.
18:23 Then Abraham *d* nearer to him and said:
24:45 she went down to the spring and *d* water,
49:33 to his sons, he *d* his feet into the bed,
Ex 2:10 for she said, "I *d* him out of the water."
2:19 even *d* water for us and watered the flock!"
32:19 As he *d* near the camp,
Jgs 3:21 hand *d* the dagger from his right thigh,
20:20 On the day the Israelites *d* up in battle
20:23 took courage and again *d* up for combat
Ru 4: 8 it for yourself," *d* off his sandal.
1Sm 4: 2 *d* up in battle formation against Israel.
7: 6 they *d* water and poured it out on the
17:21 *d* up opposite each other in battle array.
17:51 own sword [which he *d* from its sheath]
2Sm 10: 8 The Ammonites came out and *d* up in battle
10:17 The Arameans *d* up in formation against
22:17 he *d* me out of the deep waters.
23:16 through the Philistine camp and *d* water
1Kgs 2: 1 When the time of David's death *d* near,
22:34 Someone, however, *d* his bow at random,
2Kgs 9:24 But Jehu *d* his bow and shot Joram between
10:15 hand, and Jehu *d* him up into his chariot.
1Chr 5:18 bore shield and sword and who *d* the bow,
11:18 *d* water from the cistern by the gate at
2Chr 18:33 *d* his bow at random and hit the king of
Tb 7:13 the scroll, and he *d* up the contract,
Jdt 13: 7 his sword from it, *d* close to the bed,
1Mc 10:77 he *d* up three thousand horsemen and an
2Mc 14:44 as they quickly *d* back and left an opening,
Ps(s) 18:17 he *d* me out of the deep waters.
30: 2 for you *d* me clear and did not let my
40: 3 He *d* me out of the pit of destruction,
Wis 19: 4 compulsion suited to this ending *d* them on,
Jer 38:13 *d* him up with the ropes out of the cistern.
Lam 4:18 Our end *d* near,
Ez 27:33 *d* from the seas you filled many peoples;
Dn 6:21 As he *d* near, he cried out to Daniel
Hos 11: 4 I *d* them with human cords,
Mt 8:16 As evening *d* on, they brought him many
14:15 As evening *d* on, his disciples came to him
14:24 remaining there alone as evening *d* on.
21: 1 As they *d* near Jerusalem,
26:51 Jesus put his hand to his sword, *d* it,
Mk 1:32 After sunset, as evening *d* on,
4:35 That day as evening *d* on he said to them,
6:47 As evening *d* on,
11:19 When evening *d* on,
14:47 One of the bystanders *d* his sword and
Lk 18:35 As he *d* near Jericho a blind man sat at
Jn 6:16 As evening *d* on,
7: 2 as the Jewish feast of Booths *d* near,
18:10 *d* it and struck the slave of the high
Acts 1:26 Then they *d* lots between the two men.
7:17 "When the time *d* near for the fulfillment
7:31 As he *d* near to observe it carefully,
16:27 escaped, he *d* his sword to kill himself;
23:19 the hand and *d* him aside to ask privately,
Gal 2:12 But when they arrived he *d* back to avoid
1Thes 2: 2 we *d* courage from our God to preach his

DRIED (30)

Gn 8: 7 until the waters *d* off from the earth.
Nm 6: 3 juice, nor eat either fresh or *d* grapes.
Jos 2:10 For we have heard how the LORD *d* up the
4:23 *d* up the waters of the Jordan in front of
4:23 *d* up in front of us until we crossed over;
5: 1 heard that the LORD had *d* up the waters
Jgs 16: 7 seven fresh bowstrings which have not *d,*"
16: 8 her seven fresh bowstrings which had not *d,*
2Kgs 19:24 I *d* up with the soles of my feet all the
Jdt 5:13 them, God *d* up the Red Sea before them,
Ps(s) 22:16 My throat is *d* up like baked clay,
32: 4 strength was *d* up as by the heat of summer.
102: 5 Withered and *d* up like grass is my heart;
106: 9 He rebuked the Red Sea, and it was *d* up,
Is 37:25 I *d* up with the soles of my feet all the
51:10 Was it not you who *d* up the sea,
Jer 51:30 *D* up is their strength,
Ez 37:11 have been saying, "Our bones are *d* up,
Hos 9:16 Ephraim is stricken, their root is *d* up;
Jl 1:12 The vine has *d* up,
1:12 apple, all the trees of the field are *d* up;
1:20 For the streams of water are *d* up,
Am 4: 7 by rain, but another without rain *d* up;
Zec 10:11 all the depths of the Nile shall be *d* up.
Mk 5:29 Immediately her flow of blood *d* up and the
Jn 6: 9 five barley loaves and a couple of *d* fish,
6:11 he did the same with the *d* fish,
11: 2 with perfume and *d* his feet with her hair.)
12: 3 Then she *d* his feet with her hair,
Rv 16:12 Its water was *d* up to prepare the way for

DRIES (2)

Prv 17:22 but a depressed spirit *d* up the bones.
Na 1: 4 leaves it dry, and all the rivers he *d* up.

DRIFT (3)

Ps(s) 90:10 toil, for they pass quickly and we *d* away.
Acts 27:32 soldiers cut the ropes and let the boat *d.*
Heb 2: 1 more to what we have heard, lest we *d* away.

DRIFTED (1)

Jn 8: 9 Then the audience *d* away one by one,

DRILL (1)

Dt 6: 7 *D* them into your children.

DRINK (282)

Gn 21:19 skin with water, and then let the boy *d.*
24:14 I may drink,' and she answers, 'Take a *d,*
24:18 "Take a *d,*
24:18 the jug onto her hand, she gave him a *d.*
24:19 When she had let him *d* his fill,
24:44 she answers, Not only may you have a *d,*
24:45 I said to her, 'Please let me have a *d.*'
24:46 jug she was carrying and said, 'Take a *d,*
30:38 animals were in heat as they came to *d,*
Ex 7:18 Egyptians will be unable to *d* its water."
7:21 that the Egyptians could not *d* its water.
7:24 they could not *d* from the river water.
15:23 at Marah, where they could not *d* the water,
15:24 against Moses, saying, "What are we to *d?*"
17: 1 there was no water for the people to *d.*
17: 2 with Moses and said, "Give us water to *d.*"
17: 6 will flow from it for the people to *d.*"
23:25 then I will bless your food and *d,*
24:11 gazing on God, they could still eat and *d.*
32: 6 Then they sat down to eat and *d,*
32:20 on the water and made the Israelites *d.*
Lv 10: 9 generations, to *d* any wine or strong drink.
11:34 with water, and any liquid that men *d,*
Nm 5:24 water, which he is to have the woman *d,*
5:26 then shall he have the woman *d* the water.
6: 3 strong *d;* he may neither drink wine vinegar,
6:20 Only after this may the nazirite *d* wine.
20: 5 Here there is not even water to *d!*"
20: 8 for the community and their livestock to *d.*"
20:11 for the community and their livestock to *d.*
20:17 or vineyards, nor *d* of any well water,
20:19 If we or our livestock *d* any of your water,
21:22 or vineyard, nor will we *d* any well water,
33:14 there was no water for the people to *d.*
Dt 2: 6 the food you eat and the well water you *d.*
2:28 supply, and for the water you give me to *d,*
14:26 desire, oxen or sheep, wine or strong *d,*
28:39 you will not *d* or store up the wine,
29: 5 was not your food, nor wine or beer your *d.*
Jgs 4:19 her, "Please give me a little water to *d.*
4:19 But she opened a jug of milk for him to *d,*
7: 5 the other, everyone who kneels down to *d.*"
7: 6 of the soldiers knelt down to *d* the water.

DRINK (cont.)
13: 4 or strong *d* and to eat nothing unclean.
13: 7 So take neither wine nor strong *d*,
13:14 from the vine, nor take wine or strong *d*,
Ru 2: 9 you may go and *d* from the vessels the
1Sm 1:11 neither wine nor liquor shall he *d*,
30:11 food, which he ate, and given water to *d*;
2Sm 11:11 to eat and to *d* and to sleep with my wife?
16: 2 for those to *d* who are weary in the desert."
23:15 that someone would give me a *d* of water
23:16 brought it to David he refused to *d* it,
23:17 Can I *d* the blood of these men who went at
23:17 So he refused to *d* it.
1Kgs 13: 8 nor eat bread or *d* water in this place.
13: 9 eat bread or *d* water and not to return
13:16 bread or *d* water with you in this place,"
13:17 LORD neither to eat bread nor *d* water here,
13:18 and to have you eat bread and *d* water."
17: 4 You shall *d* of the stream,
17:10 bring me a small cupful of water to *d*."
18: 4 caves, and supplied them with food and *d*.
18:13 caves, and supplied them with food and *d*?
18:41 then said to Ahab, "Go up, eat and *d*,
18:42 So Ahab went up to eat and *d*,
2Kgs 3:17 your livestock and your pack animals to *d*.'
6:22 Let them eat and *d*,
18:27 eat their own excrement and *d* their urine?"
18:31 and *d* the water of his own cistern,
1Chr 11:17 that someone would give me a *d* from the
11:18 But David refused to *d* it.
11:19 could I *d* the blood of these men who
11:19 and so he refused to *d* it.
2Chr 28:15 on their feet, gave them food and *d*,
Ezr 3: 7 and sent food and *d* and oil to the
Neh 8:10 "Go eat rich foods and *d* sweet drinks,
8:12 Then all the people went to eat and *d*,
Tb 4:15 Do not *d* wine till you become drunk,
7:10 "Eat and *d* and be merry tonight,
7:11 But now, son, eat and *d*.
7:11 "I will eat or *d* nothing until you set
7:14 Afterward they began to eat and *d*.
12:19 Even though you watched me eat and *d*.
Jdt 7:21 that on no day did they have enough to *d*,
12: 1 delicacies to eat and his own wine to *d*.
12:11 your care to come and to eat and *d* with us.
12:17 said to her, *D* and be merry with us!"
12:18 Judith replied, "I will gladly *d*,
1Mc 11:58 gave him the right to *d* from gold cups,
2Mc 15:38 is harmful to *d* wine alone or water alone,
15:38 a more pleasant *d* that increases delight,
Jb 1: 4 their three sisters to eat and *d* with them.
20:16 The poison of asps he shall *d* in;
21:20 And the wrath of the Almighty let him *d*!
22: 7 the thirsty you have given no water to *d*,
39:30 His young ones greedily *d* blood;
Ps(s) 36: 9 your delightful stream you give them to *d*.
50:13 bulls, or is the blood of goats my *d*?
69:22 and in my thirst they gave me vinegar to *d*.
75: 9 all the wicked of the earth shall *d*.
78:44 running water, so that they could not *d*;
80: 6 and given them tears to *d* in ample measure.
102:10 like bread and mingle my *d* with tears,
104:11 And give *d* to every beast of the field,
110: 7 From the brook by the wayside he will *d*;
Prv 4:17 of wickedness and *d* the wine of violence.
5:15 *D* water from your own cistern,
7:18 "Come, let us *d* our fill of love,
9: 5 of my food, and *d* of the wine I have mixed!
20: 1 Wine is arrogant, strong *d* is riotous;
23: 7 "Eat and *d*,"
25:21 to eat, if he be thirsty, give him to *d*;
31: 4 kings to *d* wine; strong *d* is not for princes!
31: 6 Give strong *d* to one who is perishing,
31: 7 When they *d*,
Eccl 2:24 than to eat and *d* and provide himself
2:25 For who can eat or *d* apart from him?
3:13 to eat and *d* and enjoy the fruit of all
5:17 it is well for a man to eat and *d* and
9: 7 joy and *d* your wine with a merry heart,
Sg 5: 1 my sweetmeats, I *d* my wine and my milk.
5: 1 Eat, friends; *d*! *D* freely of love!
8: 2 you spiced wine to *d* and pomegranate juice.
Sir 9: 9 not, recline not at table to *d* by her side,
9:10 you *d* with pleasure only when it has aged.
15: 3 and give him the water of learning to *d*.
Is 5:11 *d* as soon as they rise in the morning,
5:22 wine, the valiant at mixing strong *d*!
21: 5 they eat, they *d*.
22:13 and butcher sheep, You eat meat and *d* wine:
22:13 "Eat and *d*, for tomorrow we die!"
24: 9 They cannot sing and *d* wine; strong drink
28: 7 from wine and stumble from strong *d*:
28: 7 Priest and prophet stagger from strong *d*,
28: 7 Led astray by strong *d*,
29: 9 from wine, stagger, but not from strong *d*!
32: 6 go empty and the thirsty be without *d*.
33:16 fastness, his food and *d* in steady supply.
36:12 their own excrement and *d* their own urine?"
36:16 tree, and *d* the water of his own cistern,
43:20 the wasteland for my chosen people to *d*,
51:22 The bowl of my wrath you shall no longer *d*.
55: 1 paying and without cost, *d* wine and milk!
56:12 let us carouse with strong *d*,
62: 8 Nor shall foreigners *d* your wine,
62: 9 *d* the wine in the courts of my sanctuary.
65:13 My servants shall *d*,
Jer 2:18 go to Egypt, to *d* the waters of the Nile?
2:18 Assyria, to *d* the waters of the Euphrates?
8:14 destruction, he has given us poison to *d*,
9:14 give them wormwood to eat and poison to *d*.
16: 7 to *d* over the death of father or mother.
22:15 Did not your father eat and *d*?
23:15 them wormwood to eat, and poison to *d*;
25:15 the nations to whom I will send you *d* it.
25:16 They shall *d*, and be convulsed,
25:17 hand of the LORD and gave *d* to all
25:26 after them the king of Sheshach shall *d*.
25:27 *D*! become drunk and vomit;
25:28 to take the cup from your hand and *d*,
25:28 You must *d*!
35: 2 one of the rooms, and give them wine to *d*.
35: 5 wine and offered them cups to *d* the wine.
35: 6 "We do not *d* wine," they said to me:
35: 6 you nor your children shall ever *d* wine.
35:14 by which he forbade his children to *d* wine,
49:12 not sentenced to drink the cup must *d* it!
49:12 you shall surely *d* it.
51:39 set a *d* before them to make them drunk,
Lam 3:15 bitter food, made me *d* my fill of wormwood.
5: 4 The water we *d* we must buy,
Ez 4:11 *d* shall be the sixth of a hin by measure;
4:16 and they shall *d* water which they have
12:18 and *d* your water shaking with anxiety.
12:19 in anxiety and *d* their water in horror,
23:32 The cup of your sister you shall *d*,
25: 4 they shall eat your fruits and *d* your milk.
34:18 not enough for you to *d* the clearest water,
34:19 trampled and *d* what your feet had fouled.
39:17 you shall have flesh to eat and blood to *d*.
39:18 You shall eat the flesh of warriors and *d*
39:19 are filled and *d* blood until you are drunk.
44:21 *d* wine when he is to enter the inner court.
Dn 1:10 it is he who allotted your food and *d*.
1:12 Give us vegetables to eat and water to *d*.
5: 2 and his entertainers might *d* from them.
5:23 your entertainers, might *d* wine from them;
14: 7 it has never taken any food or *d*."
Hos 2: 7 my wool and my flax, my oil and my *d*."
Am 2: 8 fined they *d* in the house of their god.
2:12 But you gave the nazirites wine to *d*,
4: 1 Who say to your lords, "Bring *d* for us!"
5:11 vineyards, you shall not *d* their wine!
6: 6 They *d* wine from bowls and anoint
9:14 cities, Plant vineyards and *d* the wine,
Ob 1:16 so shall all the nations *d* continually.
1:16 Yes, they shall *d* and swallow,
Jon 3: 7 they shall not eat, nor shall they *d* water.
Mi 2:11 pour you wine and strong *d* as my prophecy,"
6:15 pour no oil, and the grapes, yet *d* no wine.
Na 3:11 too, shall *d* of this till you faint away;
Hb 2:15 your neighbors a flood of your wrath to *d*,
2:16 *d*, you too, and stagger!
Zep 1:13 plant vineyards, but not *d* their wine,
Zec 9:15 They shall *d* blood like wine,
Mt 6:25 you are to eat or *d* or use for clothing.
6:31 'What are we to eat, or what are we to *d*,
20:22 Can you *d* of the cup I am to drink of?"
20:23 "From the cup I *d* of, you shall drink.
24:49 servants, to eat and *d* with drunkards,
25:35 me food, I was thirsty and you gave me *d*.
25:37 feed you or see you thirsty and give you *d*?
25:42 food, I was thirsty and you gave me no *d*.
26:27 "All of you must *d* from it,"
26:29 I will not *d* this fruit of the vine from
26:29 I *d* it new with you in my Father's reign."
27:34 gave him a *d* of wine flavored with gall,
27:34 gall, which he tasted but refused to *d*.
27:48 sticking it on a reed, tried to make him *d*.
Mk 9:41 Any man who gives you a *d* of water because
10:38 Can you drink the cup I shall *d* or be
10:39 "From the cup I drink of you shall *d*;
14:25 I will never again *d* of the fruit of the
14:25 day when I *d* it new in the reign of God."
15:36 stuck it on a reed to try to make him *d*.
16:18 be able to *d* deadly poison without harm,
16:20 be able to *d* deadly poison without harm,
Lk 1:15 He will never *d* wine or strong drink,
5:30 "Why do you eat and *d* with tax collectors
5:33 Yours, on the contrary, eat and *d* freely."
12:19 Eat heartily, *d* well.
12:29 be in search of what you are to eat or *d*.
12:45 servant girls, to eat and *d* and get drunk,
17: 8 apron and wait on me while I eat and *d*.
17: 8 You can eat and *d* afterward"?
22:18 from now on I will not *d* of the fruit of
22:30 my kingdom you will eat and *d* at my table,
Jn 4: 7 water, Jesus said to her, "Give me a *d*."
4: 9 ask me, a Samaritan and a woman, for a *d*?"
4:10 and who it is that is asking you for a *d*,
6:53 flesh of the Son of Man and *d* his blood,
6:55 my flesh is real food and my blood real *d*.
7:37 let him *d* who believes in me.
18:11 I not to *d* the cup the Father has given me?"
Acts 23:12 not to eat or *d* until they had killed Paul.
23:21 oath not to eat or *d* until they kill him.
Rom 12:20 if he is thirsty, give him something to *d*;
1Cor 9: 4 Do we not have the right to eat and *d*?
10: 4 All drank the same spiritual *d* (they drank
10: 7 says, "The people sat down to eat and *d*,
10:21 You cannot *d* the cup of the Lord and also
10:31 The fact is that whether you eat or *d*—
11:22 you not have homes where you can eat and *d*?
11:25 Do this, whenever you *d* it,
11:26 then, you eat this bread and *d* this cup,
11:28 he eat of the bread and *d* of the cup.
12:13 us have been given to *d* of the one Spirit.
15:32 dead are not raised, "Let us eat and *d*,
Col 2:16 you eat or *d* or what you do on yearly
1Thes 5: 7 sleep by night and drunkards *d* by night.
1Tm 3: 3 He must not be addicted to *d*.
3: 8 not overindulge in *d* or give in to greed.
Ti 2: 3 not be slanderous gossips or slaves to *d*.
Heb 9:10 of food and *d* and various ritual washings:
Rv 14: 8 *d* the poisoned wine of her lewdness!"
14:10 he too will *d* the wine of God's wrath,
16: 6 and prophets, you have given blood to *d*;
18: 3 *d* the poisoned wine of her lewdness.
21: 6 To anyone who thirsts I will give to *d*

DRINKERS (1)

Jl 1: 5 wail, all you *d* of wine,

DRINKING (48)

Gn 24:20 quickly emptied her jug into the *d* trough
24:22 When the camels had finished *d*,
Ex 7:24 the neighborhood of the river for *d* water,
34:28 without eating any food or *d* any water,
Dt 9: 9 days and forty nights without eating or *d*,
9:18 days and forty nights without eating or *d*,
Jgs 19: 4 eating and *d* and passing the night there.
Ru 3: 3 man before he has finished eating and *d*.
1Sm 25:36 a *d* party in his house like that of a king,
30:16 scattered all over the ground, eating, *d*,
1Kgs 1:25 are eating and *d* in his company and saying,
10:21 all King Solomon's *d* vessels were of gold,
16: 9 Tirzah, *d* to excess in the house of Arza,
20:12 Ben-hadad was *d* in the pavilions with the
20:16 while Ben-hadad was *d* heavily in the
2Kgs 9:34 in over her body and, after eating and *d*,
1Chr 12:40 with David for three days, feasting and *d*,
2Chr 9:20 of King Solomon's *d* vessels were of gold,
Ezr 10: 6 the night neither eating food nor *d* water,
Tb 8: 1 When they had finished eating and *d*,
8:20 but shall remain here eating and *d* with me;
Jdt 7:21 to drink, but their *d* water was rationed.
12:13 be honored by him, to enjoy *d* wine with us,
Est 1: 8 ordinance of the king the *d* was unstinted,
4:16 on my behalf, all of you, not eating or *d*,
5: 6 During the *d* of the wine,
7: 2 this second day, during the *d* of the wine,
Jb 1:13 his daughters were eating and *d* wine
1:18 *d* wine in the house of their eldest brother,
Prv 31: 5 Lest in *d* they forget what the law decrees,
Eccl 8:15 the sun except eating and *d* and mirth:
10:17 right time (for vigor and not in *d* bouts).
Is 5:22 Woe to the champions at *d* wine,
29: 8 dreams he is *d* and awakens faint and dry,
Jer 16: 8 to sit with them eating and *d*.
Dn 5: 3 and his entertainers were *d* wine from them.
Zec 7: 6 And when you were eating and *d*,
Mt 11:18 words, John appeared neither eating nor *d*,
11:19 The Son of Man appeared eating and *d*,
24:38 before the flood people were eating and *d*,
26:42 if this cannot pass me by without my *d* it,
Lk 5:39 No one, after *d* old wine, wants new.
7:33 came neither eating bread nor *d* wine,
10: 7 the one house eating and *d* what they have,
Jn 2:10 then when the guests have been *d* awhile,
Rom 14:17 of God is not a matter of eating or *d*,
14:21 you abstained from eating meat, or *d* wine,
1Tm 5:23 Stop *d* water only.

DRINKS (20)

Gn 44: 5 master *d* and which he uses for divination.
Dt 11:11 valleys that *d* in rain from the heavens,
2Sm 19:36 Can your servant taste what he eats and *d*,
Neh 8:10 "Go eat rich foods and drink sweet *d*,
Jb 6: 4 pierce me, and my spirit *d* in their poison;
15:16 man, who *d* in iniquity like water!
34: 7 He *d* in blasphemies like water,
Prv 26: 6 He cuts off his feet, he *d* down violence,
Sir 24:20 still, he who *d* of me will thirst for more;
26:12 eager mouth *d* from any water that he finds,
Is 44:12 and weak, *d* no water and becomes exhausted.
Dn 14: 6 not see how much he eats and *d* every day?"
Jn 4:13 who *d* this water will be thirsty again.
4:14 But whoever *d* the water I give him will
6:54 He who feeds on my flesh and *d* my blood
6:56 on my flesh and *d* my blood remains in me,
1Cor 11:27 bread or *d* the cup of the Lord unworthily
11:29 He who eats and *d* without recognizing the
11:29 the body eats and *d* a judgment on himself.
Heb 6: 7 Ground which *d* in the rain falling on it

DRIP (6)

Dt 33:28 and wine, where the heavens *d* with dew.
Prv 5: 3 The lips of an adulteress *d* with honey,

Sg 4:11 Your lips *d* honey,
5:13 they *d* choice myrrh.
Jl 4:18 that day, the mountains shall *d* new wine,
Am 9:13 juice of grapes shall *d* down the mountains,

DRIPPING (3)

Sg 5: 5 open to my lover, with my hands *d* myrrh:
5: 5 With my fingers *d* choice myrrh upon the
Sir 43:23 by flames, The *d* clouds restore them all,

DRIVE (61)

Gn 21:10 *D* out that slave and her son!
Ex 6: 1 arm, he will *d* them from his land."
11: 1 he will *d* you away.
14:25 chariot wheels that they could hardly *d*.
23:28 you I will send hornets to *d* the Hivites,
23:29 one year will I *d* them all out before you;
23:30 *d* them out little by little before you,
34:11 "I will *d* out before you the Amorites,
34:24 Since I will *d* out the nations before you
Nm 22: 6 defeat them and *d* them out of the country.
22:11 be able to give them battle and *d* them out.' "
33:52 *d* out all the inhabitants of the land
33:55 "But if you do not *d* out the inhabitants
Dt 9: 3 can *d* them out and destroy them quickly,
11:23 will *d* all these nations out of your way,
Jos 13: 6 At the advance of the Israelites I will *d*
14:12 is with me I shall be able to *d* them out,
15:63 in Jerusalem the Judahites could not *d* out;
16:10 not *d* out the Canaanites living in Gezer,
17:13 as laborers, but they did not *d* them out.
17:18 iron chariots, you *d* out the Canaanites."
23: 5 will *d* them out and dislodge them at your
23:13 no longer *d* these nations out of your way.
Jgs 1:28 as laborers, but did not *d* them out.
1:29 not *d* out the Canaanites living in Gezer,
1:31 Nor did Asher *d* out the inhabitants of
1:33 Naphtali did not *d* out the inhabitants of
1Sm 6: 7 but *d* their calves indoors away from them.
2Sm 5: 6 the blind and the lame will *d* you away!"
13:16 because to *d* me out would be far worse
2Chr 20:11 by coming to *d* us out of the possession
Tb 3:17 then *d* the wicked demon Asmodeus from her.
Jdt 11:19 *d* them like sheep that have no shepherd,
Est E: 4 do they *d* out gratitude from among men;
2Mc 9: 4 Therefore he ordered his charioteer to *d*
9: 7 the Jews, he gave orders to *d* even faster.
Jb 24: 3 The asses of orphans they *d* away;
30:22 You raise me up and *d* me before the wind;
Prv 22:15 rod of discipline will *d* it far from him.
Sir 11:11 One may toil and struggle and *d*,
22:22 treacherous attack will *d* away any friend.
28:15 A meddlesome tongue can *d* virtuous women
30:23 courage, *d* resentment far away from you;
Is 58: 3 your own pursuits, and *d* all your laborers.
Jer 7:33 of the field, which no one will *d* away.
24: 9 in all the places to which I will *d* them.
27:10 you, in order to *d* you far from your land,
46: 9 *d* madly, chariots!
49:19 So I, in an instant, will *d* men off;
50:44 So I, in one instant, will *d* them off,
Lam 5: 5 On our necks is the yoke of those who *d* us;
Hos 9:15 wicked deeds I will *d* them out of my house.
Jl 2:20 and *d* him out into a land arid and waste,
Ob 1: 7 To the border they *d* you
Mi 2: 9 you *d* out from their pleasant houses;
Hb 3: 8 *d* the steeds of your victorious chariot?
Zep 2: 4 a waste, Ashdod they shall *d* out at midday,
Mk 5:10 not to *d* them away from that neighborhood.
9:29 "This kind you can *d* out only by prayer."
11:15 began to *d* out those who were engaged in
Lk 8:29 demon would *d* him into places of solitude.

DRIVEN (43)

Gn 26:27 you hate me and have *d* me away from you?"
Ex 10:11 that they were *d* from Pharaoh's presence.
23:31 hand over to you to be *d* out of your way.
Nm 32:21 before the LORD until he has *d* his enemies
Dt 22: 1 *d* astray without showing concern about it;
28:34 are *d* mad by what your eyes must look upon.
30: 4 been *d* to the farthest corner of the world,
Jos 23: 9 LORD has *d* out large and strong nations,
Jgs 11: 2 the sons of the wife had *d* Jephthah away,
1Sm 28: 3 Meanwhile Saul had *d* mediums and
2Kgs 21: 8 to be *d* off the land I gave their fathers,
Neh 1: 9 been *d* to the farthest corner of the world,
1Mc 1:53 Israel was *d* into hiding,
6: 6 army and been *d* back by the Israelites;
7: 6 friends and have *d* us out of our country.
9:16 wing saw that the right wing was *d* back,
2Mc 4:26 was *d* out as a fugitive to the country of
5: 8 After being *d* into Egypt,
13:19 but he was *d* back,
Jb 18:18 He is *d* from light into darkness,
24: 4 all the poor of the land are *d* into hiding.
30: 8 nameless men, they were *d* out of the land.
Ps(s) 44:11 You have let us be *d* back by our foes;
68: 3 As smoke is *d* away, so are they *d*;
Sir 27: 2 Like a peg *d* between fitted stones,
Is 41: 2 them to dust, with his bow, to *d* straw.
Jer 23: 2 have scattered my sheep and *d* them away.
23: 3 *d* them and bring them back to their meadow;
46:28 of all the nations to which I have *d* you,
Ez 12: 4 go out like one of those *d* into exile;
34:21 with your horns until you have *d* them out,
46:18 of my people will be *d* from their property.
Mi 4: 7 and of those *d* far off a strong nation;
Zep 2: 2 Before you are *d* away,
Mt 8:12 of the kingdom will be *d* out into the dark.
Jn 12:31 now will this world's prince be *d* out,
Acts 27:17 that they would be *d* on the reef of Syrtis,
27:27 were still being *d* across the Ionian Sea,
2Cor 12:11 You have *d* me to it.
2Tm 3: 6 with sins and *d* by desires of many kinds,
Jas 1: 6 is like the surf tossed and *d* by the wind.
3: 4 the fact that they are *d* by fierce winds,
Rv 12: 9 the seducer of the whole world, was *d* out;

DRIVER (7)

2Kgs 9:17 "Get a *d*."
9:18 So a *d* went out to meet him and said.
9:19 Joram sent a second *d*,
Jb 3:18 and hear not the voice of the slave *d*.
39: 7 of the city, and hears no shouts of a *d*.
Jer 51:21 rider, with you I shatter chariot and *d*.
Zec 1: 8 There appeared the *d* of a red horse,

DRIVERS (8)

Ex 3: 7 cry of complaint against their slave *d*,
1Kgs 1: 5 acquired chariots, *d*, and fifty henchmen.
10:26 Solomon collected chariots and *d*;
10:26 hundred chariots and twelve thousand *d*;
2Kgs 2:12 Israel's chariots and *d*!"
2Chr 1:14 twelve thousand *d* he could station
1:14 He gathered together chariots and *d*,
16: 8 with great numbers of chariots and *d*?

DRIVES (7)

Ps(s) 1: 4 they are like chaff which the wind *d* away.
Prv 19:26 mistreats his father, or *d* away his mother,
Sir 22:20 He who throws stones at birds *d* them away,
31: 1 flesh, and the care of wealth *d* away rest.
42: 9 wakeful, and worry over her *d* away rest:
43:17 A word from him *d* on the south wind,
Is 59:19 river which the breath of the LORD *d* on.

DRIVING (20)

Ex 5:13 while the taskmasters kept *d* them on,
33: 2 *D* out the Canaanites,
Lv 18:24 *d* out of your way have defiled themselves.
20:23 of the nations whom I am *d* out of your way,
Nm 32:39 it, *d* out the Amorites who were there.
Dt 4:38 *d* out of your way nations greater and
9: 4 that the LORD is *d* them out before you.
9: 5 is *d* these nations out before you on
18:12 God, is *d* these nations out of your way.
1Sm 28: 9 in *d* the mediums and fortune-tellers out
2Kgs 9:20 The *d* is like that of Jehu,
9:25 we were *d* teams behind his father Ahab,
16: 6 Elath for Edom, *d* the Judeans out of it.
1Chr 17:21 by *d* out the nations before your people.
1Mc 14:36 in *d* the Gentiles out of their country,
Ps(s) 35: 5 wind, with the angel of the LORD *d* them on.
Is 30:30 of consuming fire, in *d* storm and hail.
Lk 20:12 they likewise maltreated before *d* him away.
Acts 2: 2 *d* wind which was heard all through the
26:24 And your great learning is *d* you mad!"

DROMEDARIES (2)

Is 60: 6 shall fill you, *d* from Midian and Ephah;
66:20 in chariots, in carts, upon mules and *d*,

DROOLING (1)

1Sm 21:14 the doors of the gate and *d* onto his beard.

DROOP (1)

Jas 1:11 parches the meadow, the field flowers *d*,

DROOPING (2)

Sir 2:12 Woe to craven hearts and *d* hands,
Heb 12:12 your *d* hands and your weak knees.

DROP (12)

Dt 28:40 for your olives will *d* off unripe.
Ru 2:16 and even to let *d* some handfuls and leave
Jb 16:20 before God my eyes *d* tears,
29:22 but received my pronouncement drop by *d*.
Prv 3:20 break open, and the clouds *d* down dew.
Wis 11:22 *d* of morning dew come down upon the earth.
Sir 18: 8 Like a *d* of sea water,
Is 40:15 the nations count as a *d* of the bucket,
45: 8 like gentle rain let the skies *d* it down.
Ez 30:25 but the arms of Pharaoh shall *d*
39: 3 and make the arrows *d* from your right.

DROPPED (7)

Jos 18:17 Then it *d* to Eben-Bohan-ben-Reuben,
Tb 6:14 night they approached her, they *d* dead.
Ez 31:15 all the trees in the land *d* on his account.
Mt 18:29 *d* to his knees and began to plead with him,
Acts 10:25 *d* to his knees before him and bowed low.
12: 7 that, the chains *d* from Peter's wrists.
27:29 they *d* four anchors from the stern and

DROPPING (1)

Mt 27:29 to mock him by *d* to their knees before him,

DROPPINGS (1)

Tb 2:10 me, till their warm *d* settled in my eyes,

DROPS (4)

Jb 38:28 or who has begotten the *d* of dew?
Sir 1: 2 The sand of the seashore, the *d* of rain,
Ez 30:22 arm, so that the sword *d* from his hand.
Lk 22:44 like *d* of blood falling to the ground.

DROPSY (1)

Lk 14: 2 front of him was a man who suffered from *d*.

DROSS (8)

Ps(s) 12: 7 are sure, like tried silver, freed from *d*,
119:119 account all the wicked of the earth as *d*;
Prv 25: 4 Remove the *d* from silver,
Is 1:22 Your silver is turned to *d*,
1:25 you, and refine your *d* in the furnace,
Ez 22:18 the house of Israel has become *d* for me.
22:18 *d* from silver have they become.
22:19 Because all of you have become *d*,

DROUGHT (7)

Dt 28:22 and fever, with scorching, fiery *d*,
Jb 12:15 He holds back the waters and there is *d*;
Sir 35:24 of distress as rain clouds in time of *d*.
Jer 2: 6 gullies, Through a land of *d* and darkness,
14: 1 that came to Jeremiah concerning the *d*:
17: 8 In the year of *d* it shows no distress,
Hg 1:11 a *d* upon the land and upon the mountains;

DROVE (34)

Gn 31:18 and he *d* off with all his livestock and
32:17 keep a space between one *d* and the next."
Ex 2:17 But some shepherds came and *d* them away.
Nm 11:31 that *d* in quail from the sea and brought
Dt 33:27 He *d* the enemy out of your way and the
Jos 15:14 Caleb *d* out from there the three Anakim,
24:12 ahead of you which *d* them [the Amorites,
24:18 approach the LORD *d* out [all the peoples,
Jgs 1:20 who then *d* from it the three sons of Anak.
4:21 *d* the peg through his temple down into
6: 9 I *d* them out before you and gave you their
9:41 Zebul *d* Gaal and his kinsmen from Shechem,
11: 7 hated me and *d* me from my father's house?"
1Sm 23: 5 He *d* off their cattle and inflicted a
30:20 and oxen, and as they *d* these before him,
1Kgs 21:26 whom the LORD *d* out before the Israelites.
2Kgs 9:16 Jehu mounted his chariot and *d* to Jezreel,
17:21 he *d* the Israelites away from the LORD,
2Chr 20: 7 who *d* out the inhabitants of this land
Neh 13:28 I *d* him from my presence.
Jdt 5:14 *d* out all the inhabitants of the desert;
1Mc 9:15 *d* back the right wing and pursued them as
13:11 *d* out the occupants and remained there.
2Mc 1:12 it was he who *d* out those who fought
10:17 places, *d* back all who manned the walls,
Ps(s) 78:55 And he *d* out nations before them;
80: 9 you *d* away the nations and planted it.
Wis 11:17 upon them a *d* of bears or fierce lions,
Ez 28:16 Cherub *d* you from among the fiery stones.
Dn 3:49 *d* the fiery flames out of the furnace,
Mt 21:12 Jesus entered the temple precincts and *d*
Jn 2:15 He made a [kind of] whip of cords and *d*
Acts 7:45 God *d* out to make room for our fathers.
1Cor 12: 2 led astray to mute idols, as impulse *d* you.

DROVES (6)

Gn 29: 2 with three *d* of sheep huddled near it, for *d*
32:17 in charge of his servants, in separate *d*,
32:20 all the others who followed behind the *d*,
33: 8 intended with all those *d* that I encountered?"
Zep 2:14 in *d* all the wild life of the hollows;

DROWN (3)

Is 43: 2 in the rivers you shall not *d*.
Mk 4:38 not matter to you that we are going to *d*?"
5:13 bluff into the lake, where they began to *d*.

DROWNED (5)

2Mc 12: 4 to sea and *d* at least two hundred of them.
Mt 8:32 down the bluff into the sea and were *d*.
18: 6 me, to be *d* by a millstone around his neck,
Lk 8:33 down the bluff into the lake, where they *d*.
Heb 11:29 attempted the same thing they were *d*.

DROWSIER (2)

Acts 20: 9 on the window-sill became *d* and *d*

DRUDGERY (2)

Jb 7: 1 Is not man's life on earth a *d?*
14:14 again, all the days of my *d* I would wait,

DRUG (1)

Wis 1:14 there is not a destructive *d* among them

DRUGGED (1)

Mk 15:23 they tried to give him wine *d* with myrrh,

DRUGGIST (1)

Sir 38: 7 pain and the *d* prepares his medicines;

DRUMMING (1)

1Sm 21:14 *d* on the doors of the gate and drooling

DRUNK (43)

Gn 9:21 he became *d* and lay naked inside his tent.
24:19 camels, too, until they have *d* their fill."
24:54 he and the men with him had eaten and *d,*
Nm 23:24 its prey and has *d* the blood of the slain.
Dt 32:42 I will make my arrows *d* with blood,
1Sm 1:13 Eli, thinking her *d,*
25:36 and Nabal was merry because he was very *d.*
30:12 *d* water for three days and three nights.
2Sm 11:13 ate and drank with David, who made him *d.*
1Kgs 13:23 After he had eaten bread and *d* water,
2Kgs 6:23 they had eaten and *d* he sent them away,
Tb 4:15 Do not drink wine till you become *d.*
Jdt 6: 4 the mountains shall be *d* with their blood,
12:20 had ever *d* on one single day in his life.
Est C:28 of the king or *d* the wine of libations.
1Mc 16:16 Then, when Simon and his sons had *d* freely,
2Mc 7:36 brief pain, have *d* of never-failing life,
Sir 31:28 are wine *d* freely at the proper time.
31:29 disgrace is wine *d* amid anger and strife.
Is 29: 9 Be *d,* but not from wine, stagger, but not
34: 5 my sword has *d* its fill in the heavens,
49:26 and they shall be *d* with their own blood
51:21 But now, hear this, O afflicted one, *d,*
Jer 23: 2 I am like a man who is *d,*
25:27 become *d* and vomit;
35: 8 All our lives we have not *d* wine,
35:14 to this day they have not *d* it;
46:10 devours, is sated, *d* with their blood:
48:26 make Moab *d* so that he retches and vomits,
51: 7 of the LORD which made the whole earth *d;*
51:39 set a drink before them to make them *d,*
51:57 will make her princes and her wise men *d,*
Lam 4:21 you shall become *d* and naked.
Ez 39:19 are filled and drink blood until you are *d.*
Ob 1:16 As you have *d* upon my holy mountain,
Hb 2:15 of your wrath to drink, and make them *d,*
Hg 1: 6 have *d,* but have not been exhilarated;
Lk 12:45 servant girls, to eat and drink and get *d,*
Acts 2:15 You must realize that these men are not *d,*
1Cor 11:21 person goes hungry while another gets *d.*
Eph 5:18 Avoid getting *d* on wine;
Rv 17: 2 have grown *d* on the wine of her lewdness."
17: 6 I saw that the woman was *d* with the blood

DRUNKARD (11)

Dt 21:20 he is a glutton and a *d.'*
Prv 23:21 For the *d* and the glutton come to poverty,
26: 9 of a *d* is a proverb in the mouth of fools.
Is 19:14 she does, as a *d* staggers in his vomit.
24:20 The earth will reel like a *d,*
28: 1 to the majestic garland of the *d* Ephraim,
28: 3 the majestic garland of the *d* Ephraim.
Mt 11:19 they say, 'This one is a glutton and *d,*
Lk 7:34 and you say, 'Here is a glutton and a *d,*
1Cor 5:11 an idolater, an abusive person, a *d,*
Ti 1: 7 He may not be self-willed or arrogant, a *d,*

DRUNKARDS (5)

Ps(s) 69:13 me, and *d* make me the butt of their songs.
Jl 1: 5 Wake up, you *d,*
Mt 24:49 fellow servants, to eat and drink with *d,*
1Cor 6:10 sodomites, thieves, misers, or *d,*
1Thes 5: 7 sleep by night and *d* drink by night.

DRUNKEN (5)

1Sm 1:14 long will you make a *d* show of yourself?
Jb 12:25 he makes them stagger like *d* men.
Ps(s) 107:27 They reeled and staggered like *d* men,
Prv 26:10 all who pass by is he who hires a *d* fool.
Sir 26: 8 A *d* wife arouses great anger,

DRUNKENNESS (8)

Gn 9:24 When Noah woke up from his *d* and learned
Tb 4:15 drunk, nor let *d* accompany you on your way.
Jdt 13:15 is the canopy under which he lay in his *d.*
Jer 13:13 with *d* all the inhabitants of this land,
Lk 21:34 with indulgence and *d* and worldly cares.
Rom 13:13 not in carousing and *d,*
Gal 5:21 rivalries, dissensions, factions, envy, *d,*
1Pt 4: 3 lives of debauchery, evil desires, *d,*

DRUSILLA (1)

Acts 24:24 later Felix came with his Jewish wife, *D,*

DRY (81)

Gn 1: 9 basin, so that the *d* land may appear."
1: 9 into its basin, and the *d* land appeared.
1:10 God called the *d* land "the earth,"
7:22 Everything on *d* land with the faintest
8:13 the water began to *d* up on the earth.
8:14 day of the month, the earth was *d.*
37:24 into the cistern, which was empty and *d.*
Ex 4: 9 from the river and pour it on the *d* land.
4: 9 the river will become blood on the *d* land."
14:16 Israelites may pass through it on *d* land.
14:21 the night and so turned it into *d* land.
14:22 into the midst of the sea on *d* land,
14:29 on *d* land through the midst of the sea,
15:19 on *d* land through the midst of the sea.
Lv 7:10 that are offered up *d* or mixed with oil
Jos 3:17 While all Israel crossed over on *d* ground,
3:17 LORD remained motionless on *d* ground
4:18 soles of their feet regained the *d* ground,
4:22 crossed the Jordan here on *d* ground.'
9: 5 all the bread they took was *d* and crumbly.
9:12 come to you, but now it is *d* and crumbled.
Jgs 6:37 fleece alone, while all the ground is *d,*
6:39 Let the fleece alone be *d,*
6:40 the fleece alone was *d,*
1Kgs 17: 7 After some time, however, the brook ran *d,*
17:14 not go empty, nor the jug of oil run *d,*
17:16 not go empty, nor the jug of oil run *d,*
2Kgs 2: 8 divided, and both crossed over on *d* ground.
Neh 9:11 on *d* ground they passed through the midst
Jdt 7:21 of Bethulia, and the cisterns ran *d,*
2Mc 1:19 it secretly in the hollow of a *d* cistern,
Jb 6:15 as watercourses that run *d* in the wadies;
14:11 lake fail, or a stream grows *d* and parches,
18:16 Below, his roots *d* up,
Ps(s) 66: 6 He has changed the sea into *d* land;
74:15 brought *d* land out of the primeval waters.
95: 5 sea, for he has made it, and the *d* land,
105:41 flowed through the *d* lands like a stream,
Prv 17: 1 Better a *d* crust with peace than a house
Wis 19: 7 been water, *d* land was seen emerging:
Sir 6: 3 destroy, and you will be left a *d* tree,
Is 5:24 stubble, as *d* grass shrivels in the flame,
11:15 shall *d* up the tongue of the Sea of Egypt,
19: 5 the sea, the river shall shrivel and *d* up;
19: 6 the canals of Egypt shall dwindle and *d* up.
19: 7 along the Nile shall *d* up and blow away,
29: 8 he is drinking and awakens faint and *d,*
30:33 piled with *d* grass and wood in abundance,
32: 2 be like streams of water in a *d* country,
33:11 You conceive *d* grass,
41:18 and the *d* ground into springs of water,
42:15 and hills, all their herbage I will *d* up;
42:15 into marshes, and the marshes I will *d* up.
44: 3 ground, and streams upon the *d* land;
44:27 Be dry; I will *d* up your wellsprings.
48:21 thirst when he led them through *d* lands;
50: 2 Lo, with my rebuke I *d* up the sea,
56: 3 let the eunuch say, "See, I am a *d* tree."
Jer 18:14 *d* up that flow fresh down the mountains?
50:12 last of the nations, a desert, *d* and waste.
50:38 sword upon her waters, that they may *d* up!
51:36 I will *d* up her sea,
Lam 4: 8 skin shrinks on their bones, as *d* as wood.
Ez 19:13 in the desert, in a land *d* and parched,
21: 3 all trees, the green as well as the *d.*
23:34 You shall drain it *d,*
30:12 I will turn the Niles into *d* land and sell
37: 2 How *d* they were!
37: 4 *D* bones, hear the word of the LORD!
Hos 9:14 them an unfruitful womb, and *d* breasts!
13:15 *d* up his spring, and leave his fountain *d*
Jon 1: 9 of heaven, who made the sea and the *d* land."
Na 1: 4 He rebukes the sea and leaves it *d,*
1:10 thornbushes is set aflame, like *d* stubble,
Zep 2:13 will make Nineveh a waste, *d* as the desert.
Hg 2: 6 and the earth, the sea and the *d* land.
Lk 23:31 the green wood, what will happen in the *d?"*
Jn 13: 5 *d* them with the towel he had around him.
Heb 11:29 crossed the Red Sea as if it were *d* land,

DRYING (3)

Gn 8:13 that the surface of the ground was *d* up.
Ez 26: 5 a *d* place for nets in the midst of the sea.
26:14 a *d* place for nets shall you be.

DUE (55)

Gn 14:24 share that is *d* to the men who joined me
Ex 29:28 Such things are *d* to Aaron and his sons
Lv 10:13 is your *d* from the oblations of the LORD,
10:14 children as your *d* from the peace offerings
26: 4 I will give you rain in *d* season,
Dt 18: 1 of the LORD and the portions *d* to him.
28:12 to give your land rain in *d* season,
1Chr 16:29 Give to the LORD the glory *d* his name!
Neh 13: 5 and the offerings *d* the priests.
13: 6 After *d* time, however, I asked leave
13:10 *d* the Levites were no longer being given,
Tb 12: 1 *d* to the man who made the journey with you;
12: 7 Praise them with *d* honor.
12:11 of God are to be made known with *d* honor.'
1Mc 10:36 them, as is *d* to all the king's soldiers.
11:35 things that would henceforth be *d* to us,
15: 8 *d* to the royal treasury shall be canceled
2Mc 3:29 hope of aid, *d* to an act of God's power,
10:13 command the respect *d* to his high office,
Jb 9:15 but should rather beg for what was *d* me.
34: 5 innocent, but God has taken what is my *d.*
Ps(s) 1: 3 water, That yields its fruit in *d* season,
29: 2 Give to the LORD the glory *d* his name;
51:21 shall you be pleased with *d* sacrifices,
96: 8 give to the LORD the glory *d* his name!
104:27 look to you to give them food in *d* time.
145:15 and you give them their food in *d* season;
Prv 24: 6 the victory is *d* to a wealth of counselors.
Sir 7:31 *d* sacrifices and holy offerings.
11:22 man, and in *d* time his hopes bear fruit.
29: 2 back your neighbor when a loan falls *d;*
29: 5 But when payment is *d* he disappoints him
33: 8 is *d* to the LORD's Wisdom that they differ;
50:19 by presenting to God the sacrifice *d;*
51:30 Work at your tasks in *d* season,
Is 58: 2 They ask me to declare what is *d* them,
Jer 10: 7 you, King of the nations, for it is your *d!*
51: 6 vengeance for the LORD, he pays her her *d.*
Ez 34:26 about my hill, sending rain in *d* season,
Mal 1: 6 I am a father, where is the honor *d* to me?
1: 6 a master, where is the reverence *d* to me?—
3: 3 they may offer *d* sacrifice to the LORD.
Mk 12: 2 In *d* time he dispatched a man in his
Lk 1:20 They will all come true in *d* season."
Acts 21:24 follow the law yourself with *d* observance.
Rom 4: 4 are not regarded as a favor but as his *d.*
13: 7 Pay each one his *d:*
13: 7 taxes to whom taxes are *d;*
13: 7 toll to whom toll is *d;*
Gal 6: 9 in *d* time we shall reap our harvest.
Heb 2: 2 and disobedience received its *d* punishment,
10:29 is *d* the man who disdains the Son of God,
1Pt 5: 6 so that in *d* time he may lift you high.
Rv 15: 4 refuse you honor, or the glory *d* your name,
16: 9 they did not repent or give him *d* honor.

DUES (2)

Lv 5:15 cheating in the LORD's sacred *d,*
1Mc 10:42 the *d* of five thousand silver shekels that

DUG (28)

Gn 21:30 acknowledgment that the well was *d* by me."
26:15 *d* back in the days of his father Abraham.)
26:18 his father's servants had *d* back in the days
26:19 But when Isaac's servants *d* in the wadi
26:21 Then they *d* another well,
26:22 on from there, he *d* still another well;
Nm 21:18 sank, that the nobles of the people *d,*
2Kgs 19:24 I *d* wells and drank water in foreign lands;
2Chr 26:10 in the desert and *d* numerous cisterns,
Neh 9:25 with all good things, cisterns already *d,*
Tb 2: 7 Then at sunset I went out, *d* a grave,
Ps(s) 7:16 He has opened a hole, he has *d* it deep,
35: 7 without cause they *d* a pit against my life.
35: 8 into the pit they have *d* let them fall.
57: 7 They have *d* a pit before me,
94:13 days, till the pit be *d* for the wicked.
119:85 The proud have *d* pits for me;
Sir 50: 3 In his time the reservoir was *d,*
Is 37:25 I *d* wells and drank water in foreign lands;
Jer 2:13 They have *d* themselves cisterns,
18:22 For they have *d* a pit to capture me,
Ez 8: 8 I *d* through the wall and saw a door.
12: 7 and at evening I *d* a hole through the wall
12:12 through a hole that he has *d* in the wall,
Mt 21:33 put a hedge around it, *d* out a vat,
25:18 off instead and *d* a hole in the ground,
Mk 12: 1 put a hedge around it, *d* out a vat,
Lk 6:48 *d* deeply and laid the foundation on a rock.

DULL (4)

Ps(s) 4: 3 of rank, how long will you be *d* of heart?
Eccl 10:10 If the iron becomes *d,*
Is 6:10 to *d* their ears and close their eyes;
59: 1 short to save, nor his ear too *d* to hear.

DULLED (1)

2Cor 3:14 Their minds, of course, were *d.*

DULY (1)

Dt 33:19 to the mountains where feasts are *d* held,

DUMAH (3)

Gn 25:14 Kedar, Adbeel, Mibsam, Mishma, *D,*
Jos 15:52 Arab, *D,* Eshan, Janim, Bethtappuah,
1Chr 1:30 then Kedar, Adbeel, Mibsam, Mishma, *D,*

DUMB (16)

Ex 4:11 man speech and makes another deaf and *d?*
Ps(s) 38:14 not, like a *d* man who opens not his mouth.
39: 3 man was before me I kept *d* and silent;

Prv 31: 8 Open your mouth in behalf of the *d*,
Wis 10:21 Because Wisdom opened the mouths of the *d*,
11:15 *d* serpents and worthless insects,
11:15 them swarms of *d* creatures for vengeance;
Is 35: 6 a stag, then the tongue of the *d* will sing.
56:10 They are all *d* dogs,
Jer 10: 8 One and all they are *d* and senseless,
Ez 3:26 you will be *d* and unable to rebuke them
24:27 be opened and you shall be *d* no longer.
33:22 mouth was opened, and I was *d* no longer.
Hb 2:18 maker should trust in it, and make *d* idols?
2:19 to *d* stone, "Arise!"
Lk 11:14 the devil was cast out the *d* man spoke.

DUMBFOUNDED (6)

Gn 45: 3 give him no answer, so *d* were they at him.
45:26 ruler of all the land of Egypt," he was *d*;
Jer 14: 9 Why are you like a man *d*,
Mt 8:27 Complete calm ensued; the men were *d*.
21:20 The disciples were *d* when they saw this.
Acts 2:12 They were *d*, and could make nothing

DUMBNESS (1)

Ps(s) 31:19 Let *d* strike their lying lips that speak

DUMPED (1)

Lv 14:41 be *d* in an unclean place outside the city.

DUNG (16)

1Kgs 14:10 completely, as though *d* were being burned.
2Kgs 9:37 *d* in the field in the confines of Jezreel,
Neh 2:13 the Dragon Spring, and came to the *D* Gate,
3:13 cubits of the wall up to the *D* Gate.
3:14 The *D* Gate was repaired by Malchijah,
12:31 the wall, in the direction of the *D* Gate,
Ps(s) 83:11 they became *d* on the ground.
Sir 22: 2 The sluggard is like a lump of *d*;
Jer 8: 2 but will lie like *d* upon the ground.
9:21 corpses of the slain lie like *d* on a field,
16: 4 they will lie like *d* on the ground.
25:33 they shall lie like *d* on the field.
Ez 4:15 cow's *d* in place of human excrement;
Zep 1:17 out like dust, and their brains like *d*.
Mal 2: 3 dung in your faces, The *d* of your feasts,

DUNGEON (8)

Gn 40:15 for which I should have been put into a *d*."
41:14 and they hurriedly brought him from the *d*.
Ex 12:29 the first-born of the prisoner in the *d*,
Wis 10:14 She went down with him into the *d*,
Is 24:22 They will be shut up in a *d*,
42: 7 prisoners from confinement, and from the *d*,
Jer 37:16 And so Jeremiah entered the vaulted *d*,
Zec 9:11 will bring forth your prisoners from the *d*.

DUNGHILL (1)

Ps(s) 113: 7 from the *d* he lifts up the poor To seat

DUPE (2)

Gn 29:25 Why did you *d* me?"
31:27 Why did you *d* me by stealing away secretly?

DUPED (3)

Jdt 14:18 "The slaves have *d* us!
Jer 20: 7 *d* me, O LORD, and I let myself be *d*;

DUPLICATE (2)

1Kgs 12:32 *d* in Bethel the pilgrimage feast of Judah,
Tb 5: 3 signatures on a document written in *d*;

DUPLICITY (5)

2Mc 13: 3 and with great *d* kept urging Antiochus on,
Prv 11: 3 the faithless are ruined by their *d*.
Sir 1:25 the LORD, nor approach it with *d* of heart.
19:21 but dishonest, which by *d* wins a judgment.
Lk 20:23 Realizing their *d* he said,

DURA (1)

Dn 3: 1 the plain of *D* in the province of Babylon.

DURATION (3)

Jdt 4:13 a fast of many days' *d* throughout Judea,
Bar 1:11 equal the *d* of the heavens above the earth;
Lk 8:43 with a hemorrhage of twelve years' *d*,

DURING (174)

Gn 30:14 One day, *d* the wheat harvest,
41:34 the land *d* the seven years of abundance.
41:47 *D* the seven years of plenty,
48: 7 to my sorrow, *d* the journey in Canaan,
Ex 2:23 passed, *d* which the king of Egypt died.
12: 6 be slaughtered *d* the evening twilight.
12:31 *D* the night Pharaoh summoned Moses and
13: 7 bread may be eaten *d* the seven days;
34:21 *d* the seasons of plowing and harvesting.
Lv 10: 1 *D* this time Aaron's sons Nadab and Abihu
15:20 or sits *d* her impurity shall be unclean.
15:25 be unclean, just as *d* her menstrual period.
15:26 she lies *d* such a flow becomes unclean,
15:26 unclean, as it would *d* her menstruation,
15:26 becomes unclean just as *d* her menstruation.
20:18 with a woman *d* her menstrual period,
23:42 *D* this week every native Israelite among
25: 4 But *d* the seventh year the land shall have
25:29 *d* the time of one full year from its sale.
26:34 lost sabbaths *d* all the time it lies waste,
26:35 *d* all the time that it lies desolate,
Nm 4:33 clans of the Merarites *d* all their service
9: 5 desert of Sinai *d* the evening twilight
9:11 *d* the evening twilight of the fourteenth
9:16 *d* the day the Dwelling was covered by the
9:21 Or if the cloud lifted *d* the day,
17: 4 censers of those burned *d* the offering
28: 4 and the other *d* the evening twilight,
28: 8 lamb, to be offered *d* the evening twilight,
Dt 23:10 camp *d* an expedition against your enemies,
Jos 3:15 banks *d* the entire season of the harvest,
4:14 and thenceforth *d* his whole life they
5: 4 desert *d* the journey after they left Egypt.
5: 5 desert *d* the journey after the departure
10:31 where they set up a camp *d* the attack.
24:31 Israel served the LORD *d* the entire
Jgs 2: 7 the LORD *d* the entire lifetime of Joshua,
3:26 *D* their delay Ehud made good his escape and,
8:28 for forty years, *d* the lifetime of Gideon.
9:34 *D* the night Abimelech advanced with all
11:26 why did you not recover them *d* that time?
14:17 him *d* the seven days the feast lasted.
16:30 than those he had killed *d* his lifetime.
1Sm 3: 1 *D* the time young Samuel was minister to
11:11 and invaded the camp *d* the dawn watch.
14:52 against the Philistines *d* Saul's lifetime.
21:12 *D* their dances do they not sing,
25:15 among them *d* our stay in the open country.
29: 4 us, lest *d* the battle he become our enemy.
29: 5 the David of whom they sing *d* their dances,
2Sm 3: 6 *D* the war between the house of Saul and
4: 5 the house of Ishbaal *d* the heat of the day,
13:39 *d* all that time to mourn over his son;
18:18 *D* his lifetime Absalom had taken a pillar
19:33 the king *d* his stay in Mahanaim.
21: 1 *D* David's reign there was a famine for
21: 9 to death *d* the first days of the harvest
23:13 *D* the harvest three of the Thirty went
1Kgs 3:19 This woman's son died *d* the night;
6: 7 be heard in the temple *d* its construction.)
8: 2 King Solomon *d* the festival in the month
9:10 years *d* which Solomon built the two houses,
11:12 I will not do this *d* your lifetime,
16:34 *D* his reign, Hiel from Bethel rebuilt
17: 1 *d* these years there shall be no dew or
21:29 evil upon his house *d* the reign of his son."
22:35 The battle grew fierce *d* the day,
2Kgs 8:20 *D* Jehoram's reign, Edom revolted
13:22 Israel *d* the entire reign of Jehoahaz.
15:18 *D* his reign, Pul, king of Assyria,
15:29 *D* the reign of Pekah, king of Israel,
23:22 *d* the period when the Judges ruled Israel,
23:22 or *d* the entire period of the kings of
24: 1 *D* his reign Nebuchadnezzar,
1Chr 4:41 by name set out *d* the reign of Hezekiah,
5:10 *D* the reign of Saul they waged war with
5:20 For *d* the battle they called on God,
17:10 and *d* all the time when I appointed judges
2Chr 5: 3 king *d* the festival of the seventh month.
7:12 to Solomon *d* the night and said to him:
8: 1 After the twenty years *d* which Solomon
10: 6 service of his father *d* Solomon's lifetime,
13:20 did not regain power *d* the time of Abijah;
13:23 *D* his time, ten years of peace
14: 5 no war was waged against him *d* these years,
18:34 The battle grew fierce *d* the day,
21: 8 *D* his time Edom revolted against the
29:17 consecrated the LORD's house *d* eight days,
29:19 All the articles which King Ahaz *d* his
30: 2 celebrate the Passover *d* the second month,
32:26 his anger on them *d* the time of Hezekiah.
34:33 *D* his lifetime they did not desert the LORD,
36:21 *d* all the time it lies waste it shall have
Ezr 4: 5 their plans *d* the remaining years of Cyrus,
7: 1 these events, *d* the reign of Artaxerxes,
8: 1 Babylon *d* the reign of King Artaxerxes:
Neh 5: 3 that we may have grain *d* the famine."
5:14 *d* these twelve years neither I nor my
8:14 in booths *d* the feast of the seventh month;
9: 3 and *d* another fourth part they made their
13: 6 *D* all this time I had not been in Jerusalem,
Tb 1: 2 Naphtali, who *d* the reign of Shalmaneser,
1:16 *D* Shalmaneser's reign I performed many
1:18 fugitive from Judea *d* the days of judgment
Jdt 14: 8 now, tell me all that you did *d* these days."
16:25 *D* the life of Judith and for a long time
Est 1: 1 *D* the reign of Ahasuerus
2:21 And *d* the time that Mordecai spent at the
5: 6 *D* the drinking of the wine,
7: 2 second day, *d* the drinking of the wine,
1Mc 4: 5 *D* the night Gorgias came into the camp of
5:55 *D* the time that Judas and Jonathan were in
11:40 *D* his stay there of many days,
2Mc 1: 7 we Jews wrote to you *d* the trouble and
Jb 4:13 In my thoughts *d* visions of the night,
Ps(s) 134: 1 the house of the LORD *d* the hours of night.
Prv 10: 5 a son who slumbers *d* harvest,
Eccl 2: 3 heavens *d* the limited days of their life.
3:12 than to be glad and to do well *d* life.
5:17 his labor under the sun *d* the limited days
8:15 accompaniment of his toil *d* the limited days
9: 3 and madness is in their hearts *d* life;
Wis 17:14 So they, *d* that night,
Sir 10: 9 even *d* life man's body decays;
37: 6 Forget not your comrade *d* the battle,
47:13 SOLOMON reigned *d* an era of peace,
48:12 *D* his lifetime he feared no one,
48:18 *D* his reign Sennacherib led an invasion
Jer 16: 9 Before your very eyes and *d* your lifetime
19: 9 eat one another's flesh *d* the strict siege
Bar 1:14 the feast day and *d* the days of assembly:
Ez 4: 5 *d* which you will bear the sins of the
12: 3 man, *d* the day while they are looking on,
12: 7 *D* the day I brought out my baggage as
Dn 2:19 *D* the night the mystery was revealed to
5:11 *d* the lifetime of your father he was
6:29 So Daniel fared well *d* the reign of Darius
7: 2 In the vision I saw *d* the night,
7:13 As the visions *d* the night continued,
9:25 *D* sixty-two weeks it shall be rebuilt,
Zec 1: 8 I had a vision *d* the night.
Mt 2: 1 of Judea *d* the reign of King Herod,
26: 5 but they said, "Not *d* the festival,
26:26 *D* the meal Jesus took bread,
28:13 'His disciples came *d* the night and stole
Mk 1: 9 *D* that time,
13:24 *D* that period after trials of every sort
14: 2 Yet they pointed out, "Not *d* the festival,
14:22 *D* the meal he took bread,
Lk 3: 2 *d* the high priesthood of Annas and
4: 2 *D* that time he ate nothing,
20: 5 a brief conference *d* which someone said,
Jn 2:23 was in Jerusalem *d* the Passover festival,
7:11 *D* the festival,
13: 2 and so, *d* the supper,
19:31 the bodies left on the cross *d* the sabbath,
21:20 against Jesus' chest *d* the supper and said,
Acts 1:15 At one point *d* those days,
5:19 *D* the night,
7:45 they brought it into the land *d* the
9: 9 *d* which time he neither ate nor drank.
12: 1 *D* that period,
12: 3 *D* the feast of Unleavened Bread he had him
12: 6 *D* the night before Herod was to bring him
13:17 great *d* their sojourn in the land of Egypt,
18:12 *D* Gallio's proconsulship in Achaia,
21:10 *D* our few days' stay,
2Cor 10:11 are by word, in the letters *d* our absence,
Phlm 1:10 whom I have begotten *d* my imprisonment.
1Pt 1:17 *d* your sojourn in a strange land.
Rv 9: 6 *D* that time these men will seek death but
11: 6 rain will fall *d* the time of their mission.
11:13 persons were killed *d* the earthquake;
21:25 *D* the day its gates shall never be shut,

DUSK (4)

Jgs 19: 9 said to him, "It is already growing *d*.
Prv 7: 9 In the twilight, at *d* of day,
Is 59:10 We stumble at midday as at *d*,
Mk 13:35 of the house is coming, whether at *d*,

DUST (115)

Gn 13:16 your descendants like the *d* of the earth;
13:16 if anyone could count the *d* of the earth,
18:27 to my Lord, though I am but *d* and ashes!
28:14 be as plentiful as the *d* of the earth,
Ex 8:12 his staff and strike the *d* of the earth,
8:13 and with his staff he struck the *d* of the
8:13 The *d* of the earth was turned into gnats
9: 9 It will then turn into fine *d* over the
30:36 Grind some of it into fine *d* and put this
Nm 5:17 as well as some *d* that he has taken from
23:10 Who has ever counted the *d* of Jacob,
Dt 9:21 I ground it down to powder as fine as *d*,
28:24 the LORD will give your land powdery *d*,
32:24 the venom of reptiles gliding in the *d*.
Jos 7: 6 and they threw *d* on their heads.
1Sm 2: 8 He raises the needy from the *d*;
2Sm 22:43 I ground them fine as the *d* of the earth;
1Kgs 16: 2 *d* and made you ruler of my people Israel,
18:38 the holocaust, wood, stones, and *d*,
20:10 is enough *d* in Samaria to make handfuls
2Kgs 13: 7 destroyed them and trampled them like *d*.
23: 6 there he had it burned and beaten to *d*,
23:12 and threw the *d* into the Kidron Valley.
2Chr 1: 9 people as numerous as the *d* of the earth.
34: 4 images were shattered and beaten into *d*,
34: 7 and carved images and beat them into *d*,
Neh 3:34 burnt as they are, from the heaps of *d*?"
9: 1 in sackcloth, their heads covered with *d*.
Tb 3: 6 I may go from the face of the earth into *d*.
Jdt 2:20 count, like locusts or the *d* of the earth,
1Mc 2:63 be found, because he has returned to his *d*,
Jb 2:12 their cloaks and threw *d* upon their heads.
4:19 of clay, whose foundation is in the *d*,
7:21 For soon I shall lie down in the *d*;

DUST (cont.)

10: 9 Will you then bring me down to *d* again?
14: 8 in the earth, and its stump die in the *d*,
16:15 my skin, and have laid my brow in the *d*.
17:16 Shall we go down together into the *d*?
19:25 he will at last stand forth upon the *d*;
20:11 vigor, this shall lie with him in the *d*.
21:26 Alike they lie down in the *d*,
22:24 from your tent, And treat raw gold like *d*,
24:12 From the *d* the dying groan,
27:16 like *d* and store away mounds of clothing,
28: 6 of sapphires, and there is gold in its *d*.
30:19 I am leveled with the *d* and ashes.
34:15 together, and man would return to the *d*.
38:38 So that the *d* of earth is fused into a mass
40:13 bury them in the *d* together;
42: 6 I have said, and repent in *d* and ashes.
Ps(s) 7: 6 to the ground, and lay my glory in the *d*.
18:43 ground them fine as the *d* before the wind;
22:16 to the *d* of death you have brought me down.
22:30 him shall bend all who go down into the *d*.
30:10 Would *d* give you thanks or proclaim your
44:26 For our souls are bowed down to the *d*,
72: 9 him, and his enemies shall lick the *d*.
78:27 And he rained meat upon them like *d*,
89:40 servant, and defiled his crown in the *d*.
90: 3 You turn man back to *d*,
102:15 servants, and her *d* moves them to pity.
103:14 he remembers that we are *d*.
104:29 breath, they perish and return to their *d*.
113: 7 III He raises up the lowly from the *d*;
119:25 DalethI lie prostrate in the *d*;
Eccl 3:20 the *d*, and to the *d* they both return.
12: 7 the *d* returns to the earth as it once was,
Sg 3: 6 and with the perfume of every exotic *d*?
Sir 10: 9 Why are *d* and ashes proud?
11:12 he raises him free of the vile *d*,
17:27 heaven, while all men are *d* and ashes.
40: 3 a lofty throne or grovels in *d* and ashes,
44:21 make him numerous as the grains of *d*,
Is 2:10 Get behind the rocks, hide in the *d*,
5:24 rotten and their blossom scatter like *d*;
25:12 down level with the earth, with the very *d*.
26: 5 it to the ground, levels it with the *d*.
26:19 awake and sing, you who lie in the *d*.
29: 4 and from the base *d* your words shall come.
29: 4 and your words like chirping from the *d*.
29: 5 of your arrogant shall be like fine *d*,
40:12 has held in a measure the *d* of the earth,
40:15 a drop in the bucket, as *d* on the scales;
41: 2 With his sword he reduces them to *d*,
47: 1 Come down, sit in the *d*,
49:23 worship you and lick the *d* at your feet.
52: 2 Shake off the *d*,
65:25 the ox [but the serpent's food shall be *d*.
Jer 25:34 roll in the *d*, leaders of the flock!
Lam 2:10 They strew *d* on their heads and gird
2:21 in the *d* of the streets lie young and old;
3:16 with gravel, pressed my face in the *d*;
3:29 Let him put his mouth to the *d*;
Bar 6:12 of the house *d* which is thick upon them.
6:16 full of *d* from the feet of those who enter.
Ez 24: 7 it out on the earth, to be covered with *d*.
26:10 of his horses shall cover you with *d*,
27:30 bitter cries, Strewing *d* on their heads,
28:18 I have reduced you to *d* on the earth in
Dn 12: 2 sleep in the *d* of the earth shall awake;
Am 2: 7 heads of the weak into the *d* of the earth,
Mi 1:10 In Beth-leaphrah roll in the *d*.
7:17 They shall lick the *d* like the serpent,
Na 1: 3 his path, and clouds are the *d* at his feet;
Zep 1:17 And their blood shall be poured out like *d*,
Zec 9: 3 a stronghold, and heaped up silver like *d*,
Mt 10:14 once outside it shake its *d* from your feet.
Mk 6:11 shake its *d* from your feet in testimony
Lk 9: 5 leave that town and shake its *d* from your
10:11 'We shake the *d* of this town from our feet
20:18 It will make *d* of anyone on whom it falls."
Acts 13:51 So the two shook the *d* from their feet in
1Cor 15:47 The first man was of earth, formed from *d*,
Rv 18:19 They poured *d* on their heads and cried out,

DUTIES (11)

Nm 3: 8 discharge the *d* of the Israelites
7: 5 to each group in proportion to its *d*."
7: 7 the Gershonites in proportion to their *d*,
7: 8 to the Merarites in proportion to their *d*,
8:19 his sons to discharge the *d* of the Israelites
8:26 you are to regulate the *d* of the Levites."
1Sm 2:13 nor for the priests' *d* toward the people.
2Chr 13:11 for we observe our *d* to the LORD,
35: 2 He reappointed the priests to their *d* and
Neh 11:23 the singers assigning them their daily *d*.
1Tm 4:15 Attend to your *d*;

DUTIFUL (1)

Ps(s) 12: 2 for no one now is *d*;

DUTY (39)

Gn 38: 8 in fulfillment of your *d* as brother-in-law,
Dt 24: 5 nor shall any public *d* be imposed on him.
25: 5 the *d* of a brother-in-law by marrying her.
25: 7 does not intend to perform his *d* toward me
2Sm 18:11 Then it would have been my *d* to give you
1Kgs 14:27 on *d* at the entrance of the royal palace.
14:28 LORD, those on *d* would carry the shields,
2Kgs 11: 5 the third of you who come on *d* on the
11: 7 divisions who are going off *d* that week
11: 9 on *d* for the sabbath and those going off *d*
1Chr 9:26 four chief gatekeepers were on constant *d*.
9:27 they had the *d* of opening it each morning.
9:33 stayed in the chambers when free of *d*,
23:28 their *d* shall be to assist the sons of
2Chr 8:14 the priests, as the daily *d* required.
12:10 on *d* at the entrance of the royal palace.
Ezr 10: 4 Rise, then, for this is your *d*!
10:12 "Yes, it is our *d* to do as you say!
Neh 13:13 It was their *d* to make the distribution to
Est 9:31 race the *d* of fasting and supplication.
1Mc 6:57 and it is our *d* to take care of the
2Mc 4:28 whose *d* it was to collect the taxes.
Ps(s) 148: 6 he gave them a *d* which shall not pass away.
Prv 8:20 On the way of *d* I walk,
Sir 11:20 My son, hold fast to your *d*,
16:20 and what could I expect for doing my *d*?"
32: 2 when you have fulfilled your *d*,
Jer 5: 4 the way of the LORD, their *d* to their God.
5: 5 the way of the LORD, their *d* to their God.
Ez 45:17 *d* of the prince to provide the holocausts,
Mi 3: 1 Is it not your *d* to know what is right,
Mt 12: 5 how the priests on temple *d* can break
Lk 17:10 We have done no more than our *d*.'"
Acts 26: 9 I once thought it my *d* to oppose the name
Rom 15:16 with the priestly *d* of preaching the
Eph 6:13 do all that your *d* requires,
Col 3:18 This is your *d* in the Lord.
2Pt 1:13 I consider it my *d*,

DWELL (206)

Gn 4:20 of all who *d* in tents and keep cattle.
13: 6 so great that they could not *d* together.
36: 7 become too great for them to *d* together,
49:13 "Zebulun shall *d* by the seashore [This
Ex 8:18 there shall be no flies where my people *d*,
12:20 you *d* you may eat only unleavened bread."
23:31 all who *d* in this land I will hand over to
25: 8 for me, that I may *d* in their midst.
29:45 I will *d* in the midst of the Israelites
29:46 I, the LORD, their God, might *d* among them.
Lv 3:17 for your descendants wherever they may *d*.
7:26 Wherever you *d*,
13:46 He shall *d* apart,
20:22 I am bringing you to *d* will vomit you out.
23: 3 shall belong to the LORD wherever you *d*.
23:14 you and your descendants wherever you *d*.
23:21 a perpetual statute for you wherever you *d*.
23:31 you and your descendants wherever you *d*:
23:42 Israelite among you shall *d* in booths,
23:43 the land of Egypt, I made them *d* in booths.
25:18 for then you will *d* securely in the land.
26: 5 so that you may *d* securely in your land.
Nm 5: 3 are not to defile the camp in which I *d*."
13:19 towns in which they *d* open or fortified?
13:29 Jebusites and Amorites *d* in the highlands,
35: 3 The cities shall serve them to *d* in,
35:32 asylum and again *d* elsewhere in the land
35:34 you live and in the midst of which I *d*;
Dt 2:22 for the descendants of Esau, who *d* in Seir,
2:29 Esau who *d* in Seir and the Moabites who *d*
12:10 Jordan and *d* in the land which the LORD,
13:13 the LORD, your God, gives you to *d* in,
Jos 7: 7 to *d* on the other side of the Jordan.
15:63 so the Jebusites *d* in Jerusalem beside the
21: 2 Moses, that cities be given us to *d* in,
24:13 cities which you had not built, to *d* in;
Jgs 3: 3 and the Hivites who *d* in the mountain
11: 8 be the leader of all of us who *d* in Gilead."
18: 1 were in search of a district to *d* in,
2Sm 7: 5 Should you build me a house to *d* in?
7:10 so that they may *d* in their place
1Kgs 6:13 I will *d* in the midst of the Israelites
8:12 "The LORD intends to *d* in the dark cloud;
1Chr 9: 2 and *d* there were certain lay Israelties,
17: 4 who are to build a house for me to *d* in.
17: 9 in it to *d* there henceforth undisturbed;
2Chr 6: 1 "The LORD intends to *d* in the dark cloud.
8:11 wife of mine shall *d* in the house of David,
Ezr 6:12 And may the God who causes his name to *d*
Neh 8:14 that the Israelites must *d* in booths during
Tb 14: 4 "As for our kinsmen who *d* in Israel,
14: 7 they *d* forever in the land of Abraham,
Jdt 7:10 the height of the mountains where they *d*;
11: 2 your people who *d* in the mountain region,
11:23 *d* in the palace of King Nebuchadnezzar,
Est 9:19 is why the rural Jews, who *d* in villages,
Jb 4:19 more with those that *d* in houses of clay,
11:14 and let not injustice *d* in your tent,
15:28 with fat, He shall *d* in ruinous cities,
22: 8 and only the privileged were to *d* in it.
30: 6 To *d* on the slopes of the wadies,
Ps(s) 15: 1 Who shall *d* on your holy mountain?
23: 6 And I shall *d* in the house of the LORD for
24: 1 the world and those who *d* in it.
26: 8 O LORD, I love the house in which you *d*,
27: 4 To *d* in the house of the LORD all the days
33: 8 let all who *d* in the world revere him.
33:14 throne he beholds all who *d* on the earth,
37: 3 you may *d* in the land and enjoy security.
37:29 shall possess the land and *d* in it forever.
49: 2 hearken, all who *d* in the world,
65: 5 choose, and bring to *d* in your courts.
68:17 where the LORD himself will *d* forever?
69:26 in their tents let there be no one to *d*.
69:36 They shall *d* in the land and own it,
75: 4 Though the earth and all who *d* in it quake,
84: 5 Happy they who *d* in your house!
84:11 my God than *d* in the shelter of the wicked.
91: 1 You who *d* in the shelter of the Most High,
94:17 help, I would soon *d* in the silent grave.
98: 7 resound, the world and those who *d* in it;
101: 6 of the land, that they may *d* with me.
101: 7 not *d* within my house who practices deceit.
104:12 Beside them the birds of heaven *d*;
107:36 the hungry, and they built a city to *d* in.
120: 5 Meshech, that I *d* amid the tents of Kedar!
132:14 in her will I *d*, for I prefer her.
133: 1 and how pleasant, where brethren *d* at one!
140:14 the upright shall *d* in your presence.
Prv 2:21 For the upright will *d* in the land,
8:12 "I, Wisdom, *d* with experience,
21: 9 It is better to *d* in a corner of the
21:19 It is better to *d* in a wilderness than
25:24 It is better to *d* in a corner of the
Eccl 5:19 will hardly *d* on the shortness of his life,
Sir 23:27 Thus all who *d* on the earth shall know,
24: 4 In the highest heavens did I *d*,
25:15 rather *d* than live with an evil woman.
28:16 it has no rest, nor can he *d* in peace.
50:26 and the degenerate folk who *d* in Shechem.
Is 5: 8 left to *d* alone in the midst of the land!
8:14 and a snare to those who *d* in Jerusalem;
9: 8 it, Ephraim and those who *d* in Samaria,
10:24 O my people, who *d* in Zion,
13:21 There ostriches shall *d*,
18: 3 you who inhabit the world, who *d* on earth,
18: 4 I will quietly look on from where I *d*,
21:14 you who *d* in the land of Tema,
23: 2 you who *d* on the coast,
23: 6 Tarshish, wailing, you who *d* on the coast!
23: 7 feet have taken her to *d* in distant lands?
23:18 those who *d* before the LORD shall eat
24: 6 Therefore they who *d* on earth turn pale,
30:19 O people of Zion, who *d* in Jerusalem,
32:16 Right will *d* in the desert and justice
33:16 He shall *d* on the heights,
33:18 Your mind will *d* on the terror:
34:11 the screech owl and raven shall *d* in her.
34:11 to be an empty waste for satyrs to *d* in.
34:17 and *d* there from generation to generation.
38:11 fellow men among those who *d* in the world."
40:22 veil, spreads them out like a tent to *d* in.
42:10 the coastlands, and those who *d* in them.
57:15 On high I *d*,
65: 9 the land, my servants shall *d* there.
Jer 1:14 will boil over upon all who *d* in the land.
6:12 my hand against those who *d* in this land,
8:16 contains, the city and those who *d* in it.
12: 4 who *d* in it beasts and birds disappear,
22:23 You who *d* on Lebanon,
23: 6 shall be saved, Israel shall *d* in security.
27:11 says the LORD, to till it and *d* in it.
29: 5 Build houses to *d* in;
31:24 who lead the flock, shall *d* there together.
33:16 shall be safe and Jerusalem shall *d* secure;
35: 7 You shall *d* in tents all your life,
43: 5 thence to *d* again in the land of Judah:
44:12 Judah who insisted on coming to *d* in Egypt,
48:18 sit on the ground, you that *d* in Dibon;
48:19 watch closely, you that *d* in Aroer;
48:28 *d* in the crags, you that *d* in Moab,
49:18 says the LORD, not a man shall *d* there:
50:39 wildcats and desert beasts shall *d* there,
50:40 says the LORD, Not a man shall *d* there,
51:13 You who *d* by mighty waters,
51:62 that neither man nor beast should *d* in it,
Lam 3: 6 me to *d* in the dark like those long dead.
4:21 daughter Edom, you who *d* in the land of Uz,
Bar 4:35 demons shall *d* in her from that time on.
Ez 7: 7 climax has come for you who *d* in the land!
17:23 Birds of every kind shall *d* beneath it,
26:20 and I will make you *d* in the nether lands,
27:35 *d* on the coastlands are aghast over you,
28:26 They shall *d* secure while I inflict
29: 6 who *d* in Egypt may know that I am the
34:25 that they may *d* securely in the desert and
34:27 they shall *d* securely on their own soil.
34:28 by beasts of the earth, but shall *d* secure,
38: 8 peoples and all of whom now *d* in security.
38:12 and goods, who *d* at the navel of the earth."
43: 7 here I will *d* among the Israelites forever.
43: 9 kings, and I will *d* in their midst forever.
Dn 2:11 except the gods who do not *d* among men."
2:38 and birds of the air, wherever they may *d*,
3:98 every language, wherever they *d* on earth:
4:22 out from among men and *d* with wild beasts;
4:29 among men, and shall *d* with wild beasts;

6:26 language, wherever they d on the earth:
Hos 9: 3 They shall not d in the LORD's land;
14: 8 they shall d in his shade and raise grain;
Jl 1: 2 Pay attention, all you who d in the land!
1:14 Gather the elders, all who d in the land,
2: 1 Let all who d in the land tremble,
Am 3:12 So the Israelites who d in Samaria shall
8: 8 because of this, and all who d in it mourn,
9: 5 my touch, so that all who d on it mourn,
Ob 1: 3 you who d in the clefts of the rock,
Mi 1:11 Pass by, you who d in Shaphir!
4:10 go forth from the city and d in the fields;
Na 1: 5 before him, the world and all who d in it.
Hb 2: 8 land, to the city and to all who d in it.
2:17 land, to the city and to all who d in it.
Zep 1:13 will build houses, but shall not d in them,
2: 5 Woe to you who d by the seacoast,
Hg 1: 4 for you to d in your own paneled houses,
Zec 2:11 you who d in daughter Babylon.
2:14 See, I am coming to d among you,
2:15 be his people, and he will d among you,
8: 3 to Zion, and I will d within Jerusalem;
8: 8 will bring them back to d within Jerusalem.
Lk 11:26 than itself, who enter in and d there.
21:35 upon all who d on the face of the earth.
Acts 1:20 May no one d on it.'
7: 4 from there to this land where you now d.
7:48 not d in buildings made by human hands,
17:24 not d in sanctuaries made by human hands;
17:26 of mankind to d on the face of the earth.
2Cor 5: 1 earthly tent in which we d is destroyed
5: 6 we d in the body we are away from the Lord.
6:16 "I will d with them and walk among them.
Eph 3:17 May Christ d in your hearts through faith,
Col 3:16 word of Christ, rich as it is, d in you.
Rv 12:12 you heavens, and you that d therein!
21: 3 He shall d with them and they shall be his

DWELLERS (7)

Ex 15:14 anguish gripped the d in Philistia.
15:15 All the d in Canaan melted away;
Ps(s) 65: 9 And the d at the earth's ends are in fear
72:16 the city d shall flourish like the verdure
Jer 9:25 and the desert d who shave their temples.
25:23 all the desert d who shave their temples;
Ez 26:17 she was mighty on the sea, she and her d,

DWELLING (198)

Gn 27:39 far from the fertile earth shall be your d;
Ex 15:13 strength you guided them to your holy d.
25: 9 This D and all its furnishings you shall
26: 1 "The D itself you shall make out of
26: 6 of sheets, so that the D forms one whole.
26: 7 to be used as a tent covering over the D.
26:12 to hang down over the rear of the D.
26:13 down on either side of the D to protect it.
26:15 boards of acacia wood as walls for the D.
26:17 way all the boards of the D are to be made.
26:18 Set up the boards of the D as follows:
26:20 twenty boards on the other side of the D,
26:22 six boards for the rear of the D,
26:23 for the corners at the rear of the D.
26:26 five for the boards on one side of the D,
26:30 You shall erect the D according to the
26:35 the latter on the south side of the D,
27: 9 "You shall also make a court for the D.
27:19 All the fittings of the D,
35:10 the D, with its tent, its covering,
35:15 curtain for the entrance of the D;
35:18 the tent pegs for the D and for the court,
36: 8 made the D with its ten sheets woven of
36:13 were joined so that the D formed one whole.
36:14 hair were also woven as a tent over the D.
36:20 acacia wood were made as walls for the D.
36:22 this way all the boards of the D were made.
36:25 twenty boards on the other side of the D,
36:27 six boards at the rear of the D,
36:28 boards at the corners in the rear of the D.
36:31 five for the boards on one side of the D,
38:20 All the tent pegs for the D and for the
38:21 on the D, the D of the commandments,
38:31 pegs for the D and for the court around it.
39:32 of the D of the meeting tent was completed.
39:33 They then brought to Moses the D,
39:40 the service of the D of the meeting tent;
40: 2 you shall erect the D of the meeting tent.
40: 5 hang the curtain at the entrance of the D.
40: 6 the entrance of the D of the meeting tent.
40: 9 oil and anoint the D and everything in it,
40:17 month of the second year the D was erected.
40:18 It was Moses who erected the D.
40:19 D and put the covering on top of the tent,
40:21 ark into the D and hung the curtain veil,
40:22 meeting tent, on the north side of the D,
40:24 the table, on the south side of the D,
40:28 hung the curtain at the entrance of the D.
40:29 the entrance of the D of the meeting tent,
40:33 he set up the court around the D and the
40:34 and the glory of the LORD filled the D.
40:35 it and the glory of the LORD filled the D.
40:36 Whenever the cloud rose from the D,
40:38 the cloud of the LORD was seen over the D;
Lv 8:10 oil, Moses anointed and consecrated the D,
15:31 their uncleanness, lest by defiling my D,
17: 4 an offering to the LORD in front of his D,
25:29 "When someone sells a d in a walled town,
26:11 I will set my D among you,
Nm 1:50 charge of the D of the commandments
1:50 It is they who shall carry the D with all
1:50 They shall therefore camp around the D.
1:51 When the D is to move on,
1:51 when the D is to be pitched,
1:53 camp around the D of the commandments.
1:53 have charge of the D of the commandments."
3: 7 the meeting tent by serving at the D.
3: 8 of the Israelites in the service of the D.
3:23 of the Gershonites camped behind the D,
3:25 had charge of whatever pertained to the D,
3:26 court enclosing both the D and the altar,
3:29 camped at the south side of the D.
3:35 They camped at the north side of the D.
3:36 whatever pertained to the boards of the D,
3:38 East of the D,
4:16 He shall be in charge of the whole D with
4:25 they shall carry the sheets of the D,
4:26 that encloses both the D and the altar,
4:31 the boards of the D with its bars,
5:17 that he has taken from the floor of the D.
7: 1 Moses had completed the erection of the D
7: 3 presented as their offering before the D.
9:15 D was erected, the cloud covered the D
9:15 took on the appearance of fire over the D.
9:16 the day the D was covered by the cloud,
9:18 As long as the cloud stayed over the D,
9:19 many days over the D the Israelites obeyed
9:20 cloud was over the D only for a few days.
9:22 D for two days or for a month or longer,
10:11 cloud rose from the D of the commandments.
10:17 Then, after the D was dismantled,
10:17 Gershon and Merari set out, carrying the D.
10:21 carrying the sacred objects for the D,
16: 9 service of the LORD's D and to stand before
16:24 from the space around the D" [of Korah,
16:35 from the space around the D [of Korah,
17:28 time anyone approaches the D of the LORD,
19:13 defiles the D of the LORD and shall be cut
31:30 Levites, who have charge of the LORD's D."
31:47 Levites, who had charge of the LORD's D.
Dt 12: 5 all your tribes and designates as his d
12:11 chooses as the d place for his name you
14:23 chooses as the d place of his name you
16: 2 he chooses as the d place of his name.
16: 6 he chooses as the d place of his name,
16:11 God, chooses as the d place of his name,
26: 2 God, chooses for the d place of his name.
Jos 22:19 possesses, where the D of the LORD stands,
22:29 LORD, our God, which stands before his D."
24:15 of the Amorites in whose country you are d.
Jgs 6:10 of the Amorites in whose land you are d.
11:21 the land of the Amorites d in that region,
18: 7 They saw that the people d there lived
1Kgs 8:13 house, a d where you may abide forever."
8:30 from your heavenly d and grant pardon.
8:39 from your heavenly d place and forgive.
8:43 this temple, listen from your heavenly d.
8:49 in your honor, listen from your heavenly d.
1Chr 2:55 Sopherim d in Jabez were the Tirathites,
5:22 their d place until the time of the exile.
6:17 They served as singers before the D of the
6:33 services of the D of the house of God.
6:39 The following were their d places to which
16:39 D of the LORD on the high place at Gibeon,
21:29 The D of the LORD,
23:25 and has taken up his d in Jerusalem.
23:26 D or any of its furnishings or equipment.
2Chr 1: 5 in front of the LORD's D on the high place.
2: 2 him cedars to build a house for his d,
6: 2 truly built you a princely house and d,
6:21 Listen from your heavenly d,
6:30 temple, listen from your heavenly d place,
6:33 temple, listen from your heavenly d place,
6:39 honor, listen from your heavenly d place,
29: 6 turned away their faces from the LORD's d,
30:27 their prayer reached heaven, God's holy d.
36:15 compassion on his people and his d place.
Ezr 7:15 the God of Israel, whose d is in Jerusalem,
Neh 1: 9 I have chosen as the d place for my name.'
3:27 Ophel [the temple slaves were d on Ophel].
Tb 1: 4 in the place where the temple, God's d,
2Mc 3:39 He who has his d in heaven watches over
14:35 of a temple for your d place among us.
15:32 out against the holy d of the Almighty.
Jb 17:13 If I look for the nether world as my d,
18:21 is it then with the d of the impious man,
20: 9 nor shall his d again behold him.
21:28 and where the d place of the wicked?"
38:19 Which is the way to the d place of light,
39: 6 his home and the salt flats his d.
Ps(s) 4: 9 you alone, O LORD, bring security to my d.
46: 5 city of God, the holy d of the Most High.
68: 6 defender of widows is God in his holy d.
68:19 the LORD God enters his d.
76: 3 In Salem is his abode; his d is in Zion.
79: 7 have devoured Jacob and laid waste his d.
83:13 us take for ourselves the d place of God."
84: 2 How lovely is your d place,
85:10 to those who fear him, glory d in our land.
87: 2 gates of Zion, more than any d of Jacob.
132: 5 the LORD, a d for the Mighty One of Jacob."
132: 7 Let us enter into his d
132:13 he prefers her for his d.
143: 3 he has left me d in the dark,
Prv 3:33 wicked, but the d of the just he blesses;
24:15 of the just man, ravage not his d place;
Wis 8:16 Within my d, I should take my repose
9: 8 an altar in the city that is your d place.
Sir 24: 8 for my tent, Saying, 'In Jacob make your d,
36:12 on your holy city, Jerusalem, your d place.
Is 11:10 seek out, for his d shall be glorious.
38:12 My d, like a shepherd's tent,
Jer 7:12 the d place of my name in the beginning.
10:25 Jacob utterly, and laid waste his d.
25:30 high, from his holy d he raises his voice;
Lam 2: 6 a garden booth, he has destroyed his d;
Bar 2:16 from your holy d and take thought of us;
Ez 6: 6 In all your d places cities shall be made
37:27 My d shall be with them;
38:14 When my people Israel are d in security,
Jl 4:17 that I, the LORD, am your God, d on Zion,
Zep 3: 6 are devastated, with no man d in them.
Zec 2:17 for he stirs forth from his holy d.
Mt 12:44 and returns to find the d unoccupied,
Jn 1:14 Word became flesh and made his d among us,
14: 2 my Father's house there are many d places;
14:23 come to him and make our d place with him.
Acts 7:46 find a d place for the house of Jacob.
Rom 8:11 to life also, through his Spirit d in you.
2Cor 5: 1 d provided for us by God, a d in the heavens,
5: 4 rather to have the heavenly d envelop us,
Eph 2:22 to become a d place for God in the Spirit.
Heb 11: 9 country, d in tents with Isaac and Jacob,
Jude 1: 6 own domain, who deserted their d place.
Rv 18: 2 She has become a d place for demons.
21: 3 "This is God's d among men.

DWELLING-PLACE (1)

Ps(s) 43: 3 bring me to your holy mountain, to your d.

DWELLINGS (11)

Ex 35: 3 a fire in any of your d on the sabbath day."
1Chr 7:28 and their d were in Bethel and its towns.
Jdt 3: 3 Our d and all our wheat fields,
Ps(s) 49:12 forever, their d through all generations,
55:16 the nether world, for evil is in their d,
Is 32:18 in secure d and quiet resting places.
Jer 30:18 the tents of Jacob, his d I will pity;
Lam 2: 2 consumed without pity all the d of Jacob;
Ez 48:15 assigned to the City for d and pasture;
Am 4: 6 and have made bread scarce in all your d,
Hb 1: 6 breadth of the land to take d not his own.

DWELLS (43)

Gn 9:27 so that he d among the tents of Shem;
Nm 35:34 LORD who d in the midst of the Israelites."
Dt 33:16 and the favor of him who d in the bush.
Jgs 5:17 Asher, who d along the shore,
2Sm 7: 2 of cedar, while the ark of God d in a tent!"
1Kgs 8:27 it indeed be that God d among men on earth?
1Chr 17: 1 the covenant of the LORD d under tentcloth."
2Chr 6:18 indeed be that God d with mankind on earth?
Jdt 5: 3 of people is this that d in the mountains?
Jb 39:28 On the cliff he d and spends the night,
Ps(s) 135:21 from Zion be the LORD, who d in Jerusalem.
Prv 1:33 But he who obeys me d in security,
Wis 1: 4 not, nor d she in a body under debt of sin.
7:28 God loves, be it not one who d with Wisdom.
Sir 4:13 wherever he d,
4:15 hearkens to her d in her inmost chambers.
14:27 with her from the heat, and d in her home.
25: 8 Happy is he who d with a sensible wife,
Is 8:18 from the LORD of hosts who d on Mount Zion.
18: 7 Zion where d the name of the LORD of hosts.
33:24 No one who d there will say,
42:11 cry out, the villages where Kedar d;
Jer 2: 6 land which no one crosses, where no man d?"
4:29 cities are abandoned, and no one d in them.
6: 8 you into a desert, a land where no man d.
9:10 I will make into a waste, where no one d.
34:22 I will turn into a desert where no man d.
48: 9 are turned into ruins where no one d.
49:31 That has no gates or bars, and d alone.
Dn 2:22 in the darkness, for the light d with him.
Hos 4: 3 and everything that d in it languishes:
Jl 4:21 The LORD d in Zion.
Mi 7:14 inheritance, That d apart in a woodland,
Mt 23:21 is swearing by it and by him who d there.
Rom 7:18 I know that no good d in me,
7:20 is not I who do it, but sin which d in me.
8: 9 spirit, since the Spirit of God d in you.
8:11 who raised Jesus from the dead d in you,
1Cor 3:16 God, and that the Spirit of God d in you?
1Tm 6:16 and who d in unapproachable light,
2Tm 1:14 help of the Holy Spirit who d within us.
1Jn 4:12 Yet if we love one another God d in us,
4:15 the Son of God, God d in him and he in God.

DWELT (74)

Gn 14: 7 and of the Amorites who *d* in Hazazon-tamar.
Ex 9:26 the land of Goshen, where the Israelites *d*,
10:23 all the Israelites had light where they *d*.
Nm 14:45 And the Amalekites and Canaanites who *d* in
Dt 2:23 who once *d* in villages as far as Gaza,
4:46 who *d* in Heshbon and whom Moses and the
33:28 Israel has *d* securely,
Jos 24: 2 *d* beyond the River and served other gods.
24: 7 to Egypt, and *d* a long time in the desert,
24:18 including] the Amorites who *d* in the land.
Jgs 1:10 against the Canaanites who *d* in Hebron,
1:17 defeated the Canaanites who *d* in Zephath.
1:21 dislodge the Jebusites who *d* in Jerusalem,
4: 2 was Sisera, who *d* in Harosheth-ha-goiim.
2Sm 2: 3 and they *d* in the cities near Hebron.
5: 9 David then *d* in the stronghold,
7: 6 I have not *d* in a house from the day on
1Kgs 21:11 elders and the nobles who *d* in his city
2Kgs 13: 5 of Aram, *d* in their own homes as formerly.
17:24 possession of Samaria and *d* in its cities.
1Chr 4:28 They *d* in Beer-sheba,
4:33 Here is where they *d*,
4:41 tents of Ham (for Hamites *d* there formerly)
4:41 that is still in force and *d* in their place
5: 9 toward the east they *d* as far as the
5:16 They *d* in Gilead,
7:29 In these *d* the descendants of Joseph,
8: 6 *d* in Geba and were deported to Manahath.
8:13 family heads of those who *d* in Aijalon,
8:28 their kindred, chiefs who *d* in Jerusalem.
8:29 In Gibeon *d* Jeiel,
8:32 too, *d* with their relatives in Jerusalem,
9:34 their kindred, chiefs who *d* in Jerusalem.
9:35 In Gibeon *d* Jeiel,
9:38 *d* opposite their brethren in Jerusalem.
17: 5 For I have never *d* in a house,
2Chr 19: 4 Jehoshaphat *d* in Jerusalem;
20: 8 They have *d* in it and they built in it a
26: 7 against the Arabs who *d* in Gurbaal,
26:21 As a leper he *d* in a segregated house,
34:22 she *d* in Jerusalem,
Ezr 1: 4 survived, in whatever place he may have *d*,
2:70 and the temple slaves *d* in their cities.
2:70 Thus all the Israelites *d* in their cities.
Neh 8:17 returned exiles made booths and *d* in them.
11: 3 (In the cities of Judah *d* lay Israelites,
11: 4 *d* both Judahites and Benjaminites.
11: 6 The total of the sons of Perez who *d* in
Jdt 1: 6 region, all who *d* along the Euphrates,
1: 7 Persia, and to all those who *d* in the West:
1: 7 to all who *d* along the seacoast,
2:28 and Tyre, and those who *d* in Sur and Ocina,
4: 1 *d* in Judea heard of all that Holofernes,
5: 7 They formerly *d* in Mesopotamia,
5: 8 to Mesopotamia and *d* there a long time.
15: 8 of the Israelites, who *d* in Jerusalem,
Est 9:16 other Jews, who *d* in the royal provinces,
1Mc 1:25 for Israel, in every place where they *d*,
10:10 Thereafter Jonathan *d* in Jerusalem,
13:52 citadel, and he and his companions *d* there.
Jb 18:19 people, nor any survivor where once he *d*.
Ps(s) 78:60 in Shiloh, the tent where he *d* among men.
107:10 They *d* in darkness and gloom,
120: 6 long have I *d* with those who hate peace.
Is 9: 1 *d* in the land of gloom a light has shone.
13:20 She shall never be inhabited, nor *d* in,
Bar 3:13 of God, you would have *d* in enduring peace.
3:20 have seen the light, have *d* in the land,
Ez 26:17 spread terror into all that *d* by the sea.
31: 6 its shade *d* numerous peoples of every race.
31:17 those who *d* in his shade are dispersed
Dn 4:18 in whose branches the birds of the air *d*—
Zep 2:15 Is this the exultant city that *d* secure;
Heb 11:38 they *d* in caves and in holes of the earth.

DWINDLE (3)

Is 19: 6 and the canals of Egypt shall *d* and dry up.
Jer 10:24 not in anger, lest you have us *d* away.
Bar 2:29 throng will *d* away among the nations

DWINDLED (1)

Ps(s) 107:39 *d* and were brought low through oppression,

DWINDLES (2)

Lv 26:22 *d* away and your roads become deserted.
Prv 13:11 Wealth quickly gotten *d* away,

DYED (8)

Ex 25: 5 rams' skins *d* red, and tahash skins;
26:14 shall make a covering of rams' skins *d* red,
35: 7 goat hair; rams' skins *d* red,
35:23 hair, rams' skins *d* red or tahash skins,
36:19 for the tent was made of rams' skins *d* red,
39:34 the covering of rams' skins *d* red,
Jgs 5:30 man, Spoils of *d* cloth as Sisera's spoil,
Jb 38:14 seal, and *d* as though it were a garment;

DYING (29)

Gn 25: 8 he breathed his last, *d* at a ripe old age,
25:32 said Esau, "I'm on the point of *d*.
Lv 13: 6 now *d* out and has not spread on the skin,
13:21 deeper than the skin and is already *d* out,
13:26 deeper than the skin and is already *d* out,
13:28 spreading on the skin and is already *d* out,
13:39 on the skin are white and already *d* out,
13:56 finds that it is *d* out after the washing,
20:20 aunt shall pay the penalty by *d* childless.
Nm 20: 4 desert where we and our livestock are *d*?
2Chr 24:22 And as he was *d*,
Tb 14:15 *d* he rejoiced over Nineveh's destruction,
Jdt 7:27 behold our little ones *d* before our eyes
1Mc 6:13 and now I am *d*, in bitter grief,
2Mc 7: 9 It is for his laws that we are *d*."
Jb 24:12 From the dust the *d* groan,
Wis 2: 1 neither is there any remedy for man's *d*,
2: 5 and our *d* cannot be deferred because it is
16: 5 were *d* from the bite of crooked serpents,
18:18 each was revealing the reason for his *d*.
Sir 18:22 wait not to fulfill them when you are *d*.
Lk 8:42 daughter, a girl of about twelve, was *d*.
Jn 11:37 done something to stop this man from *d*?"
1Cor 11:30 are sick and infirm, and why so many are *d*.
2Cor 4:10 carry about in our bodies the *d* of Jesus,
Phil 1:21 hence *d* is so much gain.
Col 1:22 for you in his mortal body by *d*,
Heb 11: 5 By faith Enoch was taken away without *d*,
11:21 By faith Jacob, when *d*,

DYNASTIES (1)

Sir 28:14 walled cities, and overthrows powerful *d*.

DYNASTY (3)

1Sm 25:28 establish a lasting *d* for my lord,
1Kgs 2:24 David and made of me a *d* as he promised,
11:38 for you, as I did for David, a lasting *d*;

DYSENTERY (1)

Acts 28: 8 in bed, laid up with chronic fever and *d*.

E

EACH (619)

Gn 2:19 the man called *e* of them would be its name.
6:20 two of *e* shall come into the ark with you,
10: 5 respective lands *e* with its own language
13:11 Thus they separated from *e* other;
15:10 two, and placed *e* half opposite the other;
25:18 and *e* of them pitched camp in opposition
25:22 jostled *e* other so much that she exclaimed,
31:49 and me when we are out of *e* other's sight.
40: 5 same night, *e* dream with its own meaning.
41:11 and *e* of our dreams had its own meaning.
41:12 for *e* of us the meaning of his dream.
41:26 the same in *e* dream.
41:48 *e* town the crops of the fields around it.
42:25 their money replaced in *e* one's sack,
42:35 there in *e* one's sack was his moneybag!
43:21 was *e* man's money in the mouth of his bag
44: 1 put *e* man's money in the mouth of his bag.
44:11 Then *e* of them eagerly lowered his bag to
44:13 Then, when *e* man had reloaded his donkey,
45:15 all his brothers, crying over *e* of them;
45:22 He also gave to *e* of them fresh clothing,
49:24 But *e* one's bow remained stiff,
49:28 gave to *e* of them an appropriate message,
Ex 7:12 *E* one threw down his staff,
12: 3 itself a lamb, one apiece for *e* household.
16: 4 *E* day the people are to go out and gather
16:16 has enough to eat, an omer for *e* person,
16:16 *e* man providing for those of his own tent."
16:21 they gathered it, till *e* had enough to eat;
16:22 twice as much food, two omers for *e* person.
18: 7 Having greeted *e* other,
22: 3 shall restore two animals for *e* one stolen.
25:19 that one cherub springs direct from *e* end.
25:20 they shall be turned toward *e* other,
25:26 them at the four corners, one at *e* leg,
25:33 blossoms, *e* with its knob and petals;
25:33 blossoms, *e* with its knob and petals;
25:35 including a knob below *e* of the three
26: 2 length of *e* shall be twenty-eight cubits,
26: 5 the loops are directly opposite *e* other.
26: 8 the length of *e* shall be thirty cubits,
26:16 The length of *e* board is to be ten cubits,
26:17 *E* board shall have two arms that shall
26:19 that there are two pedestals under *e* board,
26:21 forty silver pedestals, two under *e* board;
26:25 pedestals, two pedestals under *e* board.
27: 4 bronze rings, one at *e* of its four corners.
28:21 *e* stone engraved like a seal with the name
29:36 a bullock *e* day as a sin offering,
29:38 as the sacrifice established for *e* day;
30:12 Israelites who are to be registered, *e* one,
36: 9 The length of *e* sheet was twenty-eight
36:12 with the loops directly opposite *e* other.
36:15 The length of *e* sheet was thirty cubits
36:21 The length of *e* board was ten cubits,
36:22 *E* board had two arms,
36:24 there were two pedestals under *e* board,
36:26 forty silver pedestals, two under *e* board;
36:30 pedestals, two pedestals under *e* board.
37: 9 They were turned toward *e* other,
37:13 and fastened, one at *e* of the four corners.
37:19 blossoms, *e* with its knob and petals;
37:19 blossoms, *e* with its knob and petals;
37:21 including a knob below *e* of the three
38:27 of the veil, one talent for *e* pedestal,
39:14 and *e* stone was engraved like a seal with
Lv 7:14 From *e* of his offerings he shall present
23: 8 On *e* of the seven days you shall offer an
23:37 and libations, as prescribed for *e* day,
24: 5 two tenths of an ephah of flour for *e* cake.
24: 6 shall place in two piles, six in *e* pile,
24: 7 On *e* pile put some pure frankincense,
24: 8 Regularly on *e* sabbath day this bread
Nm 1: 2 houses, registering *e* male individually.
1: 4 you there shall be a man from *e* tribe,
1:44 *e* according to his ancestral house,
1:52 *e* in his own division of the camp,
2: 2 shall camp, *e* in his own division,
3:47 shall take five shekels for *e* individual,
4:19 *e* of them his task and what he must carry;
4:27 you shall make *e* man of them responsible
4:32 You shall designate for *e* man of them all
5:10 *E* Israelite man may dispose of his own
7: 5 to *e* group in proportion to its duties."
7:85 *E* silver plate weighed a hundred and
7:85 shekels, and *e* silver basin seventy,
8:24 *E* from his twenty-fifth year onward shall
13: 2 shall send one man from *e* ancestral tribe,
14:34 one year for *e* day.
15: 5 with *e* lamb sacrificed in holocaust or
15: 6 With *e* sacrifice of a ram you shall
15:11 The same is to be done for *e* ox,
15:12 you offer, do the same for *e* of them.
15:38 *e* corner tassel with a violet cord.
16:17 Then *e* of your two hundred and fifty
16:17 and you and Aaron, *e* with his own censer,
17:17 one staff from them for *e* ancestral house,
17:17 in all, one from *e* of their tribal princes.
17:17 Mark *e* man's name on his staff;
17:21 twelve in all, one from *e* tribal prince;
17:24 After *e* prince identified his own staff
22:24 vineyards with a stone wall on *e* side.
23: 2 offering a bullock and a ram on *e* altar.
23: 2 and have offered a bullock and a ram on *e*."
23:14 offered a bullock and a ram on *e* of them.
23:30 offering a bullock and a ram on *e* altar.
25: 5 *E* of you shall kill those of his men who
26:53 with the number of individuals in *e* group.
26:54 *e* group receiving its heritage in
26:56 As the lot falls shall *e* group,
28: 3 lambs *e* day as the established holocaust,
28: 5 *e* with a cereal offering of one tenth of
28:10 *E* sabbath there shall be the sabbath
28:11 "On the first of *e* month you shall offer
28:12 oil as the cereal offering for *e* bullock,
28:13 with oil as the cereal offering for *e* lamb,
28:14 shall be half a hin of wine for *e* bullock,
28:14 the ram, and a fourth of a hin for *e* lamb.
28:20 three tenths of an ephah for *e* bullock,
28:21 and one tenth for *e* of the seven lambs;
28:24 *e* day for seven days as food offerings,
28:28 three tenths of an ephah for *e* bullock,
28:29 and one tenth for *e* of the seven lambs.
29: 4 and one tenth for *e* of the seven lambs.
29:10 and one tenth for *e* of the seven lambs.
29:14 of an ephah for *e* of the thirteen bullocks,
29:14 bullocks, two tenths for *e* of the two rams,
29:15 and one tenth for *e* of the fourteen lambs.
31: 4 From *e* of the tribes of Israel you shall
31: 5 a thousand men of *e* tribe were levied,
31: 6 on the campaign, a thousand from *e* tribe,
31:50 *e* of us will bring as an offering to the
31:53 soldiers had looted *e* one kept for himself.
34:18 and one prince from *e* of the tribes whom
35: 4 cubits from the city walls in *e* direction.
35: 5 cubits outside the city along *e* side
35: 8 so that *e* group will cede cities to the
Dt 1:13 and experienced men from *e* of your tribes,
1:23 men from your number, one from *e* tribe.
1:41 And *e* of you girded on his weapons,
3: 7 of *e* city we took as booty for ourselves.
14:22 *E* year you shall tithe all the produce
16:17 but *e* of you with as much as he can give,
24:15 You shall pay him *e* day's wages before
28:52 will besiege you in *e* of your communities,
Jos 3:12 men, one from *e* of the tribes of Israel.]
4: 2 men from the people, one from *e* tribe,
4: 4 among the Israelites, one from *e* tribe,
16: 9 villages that belonged to *e* city set aside
17: 4 to *e* of them among their father's kinsmen.
17: 6 received *e* a portion among his sons.
18: 4 Choose three men from *e* of your tribes;
21:42 With *e* and every one of these cities went
22:14 *e* one being both prince and military
24:28 the people, *e* to his own heritage.
Jgs 2: 6 *e* Israelite went to take possession of his
5:30 there must be a damsel or two for *e* man,
8:24 *e* of you give me a ring from his booty?"
15: 4 he tied between *e* pair of tails one of the

16: 5 We will *e* give you eleven hundred shekels
21:21 leave the vineyards and *e* of you seize one
21:23 *e* of them from their raid on the dancers,
21:24 *e* of them left for his own heritage in his
Ru 1: 8 two daughters-in-law, "Go back, *e* of you,
1: 9 May the LORD grant *e* of you a husband and
1Sm 1: 4 he used to give a portion *e* to his wife
1: 7 *e* time they made their pilgrimage to the
2:19 which she would bring him *e* time she went
7:16 judging Israel at *e* of these sanctuaries.
8:22 men of Israel, *E* of you go to his own city."
10:25 dismissed the people, *e* to his own place.
12:10 *E* time they appealed to the LORD and said,
14: 4 outpost there was a rocky crag on *e* side,
14:34 "Mingle with the people and tell *e* of
17:21 drew up opposite *e* other in battle array.
18: 6 women came out from *e* of the cities of
18:30 forays, but *e* time they took the field,
20:41 kissed *e* other and wept aloud together.
22: 7 Will he make *e* of you an officer over a
26:23 *e* man for his justice and faithfulness.
27: 3 *e* one had his family,
30:22 except to *e* man his wife and children.
2Sm 2:16 Then *e* one grasped his opponent's head and
6:19 to *e* man and each woman in the entire
21:20 on *e* hand and six toes on each foot
21:20 on each hand and six toes on *e* foot
1Kgs 1:49 left in terror, *e* going his own way.
4: 7 *e* having to provide for one month in the
5: 2 for *e* day were thirty kors of fine flour,
5: 7 These commissaries, one for *e* month,
5: 8 *e* brought his quota of barley and straw to
5:28 Lebanon *e* month in relays often thousand,
6:23 were two cherubim, *e* ten cubits high,
6:24 *E* wing of a cherub measured five cubits so
6:24 wing tip to wing tip of *e* was ten cubits.
6:26 shape, and *e* was exactly ten cubits high.
6:27 so that one wing of *e* cherub touched a
6:34 *e* door was banded by a metal strap,
7: 5 and the doorways faced *e* other,
7:15 *e* eighteen cubits high and twelve cubits
7:16 of the columns, *e* of them five cubits high.
7:17 on top of the columns, one for *e* capital.
7:18 piece of network on *e* of the two capitals.
7:27 also made of bronze, *e* four cubits long,
7:30 *E* stand had four bronze wheels and bronze
7:32 *E* wheel was a cubit and a half high.
7:33 The four legs of *e* stand had cast braces,
7:33 they had wreaths on *e* side.
7:34 extending to the corners of *e* stand,
7:38 *e* four cubits in diameter with a capacity
7:38 basin for the top of *e* of the ten stands.
8:39 to *e* one of them according to his conduct;
8:59 and of his people Israel as *e* day requires,
10:16 (six hundred gold shekels went into *e* shield)
10:17 (three minas of gold went into *e* buckler);
10:19 top, and an arm on *e* side of the seat.
10:19 Next to *e* arm stood a lion;
10:20 to a step, one on either side of *e* step.
10:25 *E* one brought his yearly tribute:
18: 4 hid them away fifty *e* in two caves,
18:10 he made *e* kingdom and nation swear they
18:13 prophets of the LORD, fifty *e* in two caves,
19: 2 with your life what was done to *e* of them."
20:20 them *e* of them struck down his man.
20:29 encamped opposite *e* other for seven days.
22:10 of Judah were seated, *e* on his throne,
22:17 Let *e* of them go back home in peace.'"
2Kgs 3:25 *e* of them cast stones onto every fertile
4: 4 into all the vessels, and as *e* is filled,
9:13 At once *e* took his garment,
9:21 of Judah, set out, *e* in his own chariot,
11: 8 surround the king, *e* with drawn weapons,
11: 9 *E* one with his men,
12: 6 for themselves, *e* from his own clients.
13:20 of Moabites used to raid the land *e* year.
14: 6 *e* one shall die for his own sin."
15:20 the country, fifty silver shekels from *e*.
17:29 Samarians had made, *e* people set up gods.
18:31 Then *e* of you will eat of his own vine and
23:35 people of the land, from *e* proportionately,
25:17 *E* of the pillars was eighteen cubits high;
25:17 five cubits high surmounted *e* pillar,
1Chr 9:27 they had the duty of opening it *e* morning.
9:32 of setting out the showbread *e* sabbath.
16:43 all the people departed, *e* to his own home,
20: 6 to *e* hand and six toes to each foot;
20: 6 to each hand and six toes to *e* foot;
24: 4 into eight groups, *e* under its family head.
24: 6 from Eleazar before *e* one from Ithamar.
26:12 of the LORD, for *e* group in the same way.
26:13 They cast lots for *e* gate,
26:16 For *e* family, watches were established.
26:17 On the east, six watched *e* day,
26:17 four each day, on the south, four *e* day,
27: 1 divisions, of twenty-four thousand men *e*,
28:15 of gold for *e* lampstand and its lamps,
28:15 of silver for *e* lampstand and its lamps,
28:15 the use to which *e* lampstand was to be put.
28:16 of gold for *e* table to hold the showbread,
28:17 *e* golden bowl and the silver for *e* silver bowl;
2Chr 3:12 one wing of *e* cherub,
3:15 the capital topping *e* was of five cubits.
4:13 with two rows of pomegranates to *e* network,
8:14 the various classes stood guard at *e* gate,
9:13 The gold that Solomon received *e* year
9:15 shekels of beaten gold going into *e* shield,
9:16 shekels of gold going into *e* buckler;
9:18 and there was an arm on *e* side of the seat,
9:19 stood there, one on either side of *e* step.
9:24 year out, *e* one would bring his tribute
18: 9 of Judah were seated *e* on his throne,
18:12 the king, let your word, like *e* of theirs,
18:16 Let *e* of them go back home in peace.'"
20:23 of Seir, they began to destroy *e* other.
23: 7 king on all sides, *e* with his weapon drawn.
23: 8 *E* brought his men,
23:10 all the people, *e* with his spear in hand,
25:17 "Come, let us meet *e* other face to face."
31: 1 various cities, *e* to his own possession.
31: 2 to *e* priest and Levite his proper service,
35: 7 *e* to serve as a Passover victim for any
Ezr 2: 1 *e* man in his own city (those who returned
3: 4 in the proper number required for *e* day.
6: 4 courses of cut stone for *e* one of timber.
10:14 and magistrates of *e* city in question,
10:16 who were family heads, one for *e* family,
Neh 3:28 the work of repair, *e* before his own house.
4: 9 went back, *e* to his own task at the wall.
4:11 *e* did his work with one hand and held a
4:16 Jerusalem, *e* man with his own attendant,
5:15 *e* day forty silver shekels for their food;
6: 4 proposal, and *e* time I gave the same reply.
7: 6 *e* man to his own city (those who returned
10:33 to give a third of a shekel *e* year for the
10:35 by *e* of our family houses at stated times *e*
10:36 We have agreed to bring *e* year to the
11: 3 *e* man on the property he owned in his own
11:20 cities of Judah, *e* man in his inheritance.
13:10 had deserted, *e* man to his own field.
13:30 Levites, so that *e* had his appointed task.
Tb 1: 7 which *e* year I would go and disburse in
5: 3 it into two parts, and *e* of us kept one;
5:15 "For *e* day you are away I will give you
Jdt 1: 2 *e* three cubits in height and six in length.
2:11 and plunder in *e* country you occupy.
2:18 abundant provisions for *e* man,
11:17 but *e* night your handmaid will go out to
12: 7 *E* night she went out to the ravine of
14: 2 the earth, let *e* of you seize his weapons,
16:21 over, *e* one returned to his inheritance.
Est 1:22 *e* province in its own script and to *e* people
2:12 *E* girl went in turn to visit King
3:12 *e* province in its own script and to *e* people
4: 3 (Likewise in *e* of the provinces,
8: 9 to *e* province in its own script and to *e*
8:11 authorized the Jews in *e* and every city
8:13 law in *e* and every province was published
8:17 In *e* and every province and in *e* and
1Mc 1: 8 over his kingdom, *e* in his own territory,
1:42 *e* abandoning his particular customs.
1:51 Judah to offer sacrifices, *e* city in turn.
1:58 against those who were caught, *e* month,
1:59 On the twenty-fifth day of *e* month they
2:19 so that *e* forsakes the religion of his
3:56 were afraid, could *e* return to his home,
6:35 *e* elephant having assigned to it a
6:37 A strong wooden tower covering *e* elephant,
6:54 the rest scattered *e* to his own home,
9:51 In *e* he put a garrison to oppose Israel.
10:13 *e* one of them left his place and returned
10:34 the three days that precede *e* feast day,
10:54 us now establish friendship with *e* other.
10:56 in Ptolemais, so that we may see *e* other,
10:71 and let us test *e* other's strength there;
11: 3 he stationed garrison troops in *e* one.
11: 6 greeted *e* other and spent the night there.
11: 9 "Come, let us make a pact with *e* other;
11:34 received from them *e* year from the produce
2Mc 3:26 Standing on *e* side of him,
7:21 she exhorted *e* of them in the language of
7:22 the elements of which *e* of you is composed.
7:23 the universe who shapes *e* man's beginning,
8:22 Jonathan, *e* over a division, assigning to *e*
9:26 Therefore I beg and entreat *e* of you to
12:20 cohorts, with a commander over *e* cohort,
12:40 But under the tunic of *e* of the dead they
14:20 *e* leader communicated them to his troops;
14:21 From *e* side a chariot came forward and
14:26 Alcimus saw their friendship for *e* other,
15:11 When he had armed *e* of them,
Jb 1: 5 And when *e* feast had run its course,
2:11 him, they set out *e* one from his own place:
7:18 with *e* new day and try him at every moment!
18:11 they harry him at *e* step.
39:25 of the trumpet, but at *e* blast he cries,
41: 8 They are fitted *e* so close to the next
42:11 and *e* one gave him a piece of money and a
Ps(s) 33:15 the earth, He who fashioned the heart of *e*,
55:21 *E* one lays hands on his associates,
59: 7 *E* evening they return,
59:15 *E* evening they return,
64: 7 deep are the thoughts of *e* heart.
73:14 after day and chastisement with *e* new dawn.
101: 8 *E* morning I will destroy all the wicked of
119:160 *e* of your just ordinances is everlasting.
141:10 all the wicked fall, *e* into his own net,
147: 4 he calls *e* by name.
Prv 5:21 *e* man's ways are plain to the LORD's sight;
24:12 he will repay *e* one according to his deeds.
29:26 but the rights of *e* are from the LORD.
Eccl 4:11 two sleep together, they keep *e* other warm.
Sg 3: 8 *E* with his sword at his side against
Wis 14:24 *e* either waylays and kills his neighbor,
15: 7 molds for our service *e* several article:
15: 7 As to what shall be the use of *e* vessel of
16:21 blended to whatever flavor *e* one wished,
18:18 *e* was revealing the reason for his dying.
19:17 *e* sought the entrance of his own gate.
Sir 16:12 he judges men, *e* according to his deeds.
16:14 which *e* receives according to his deeds.
17:12 *e* of them he gives precepts about his
17:18 and requite *e* one of them as they deserve.
35: 8 *e* contribution show a cheerful countenance,
38:31 hands, *e* one an expert at his own task;
39:34 for *e* shows its worth at the proper time.
42:24 to meet each need, *e* creature is preserved.
42:25 of them has he made in vain, For *e* in turn,
43: 8 As its name says, *e* month it renews itself;
43:21 and clothes *e* pool with a coat of mail.
43:27 For him *e* messenger succeeds,
44: 1 men, our ancestors, *e* in his own time:
44: 7 in their time, *e* illustrious in his day.
45: 9 through whose pleasing sound at *e* step He
45:11 incised letters *e* of the tribes of Israel;
45:14 with the established sacrifice twice *e* day;
46:11 The JUDGES, too, *e* one of them,
47: 9 *e* year With string music before the altar,
Is 1:23 *E* one of them loves a bribe and looks for
2: 9 But man is abased, *e* one brought low.
5:15 Men shall be abased, *e* one brought low,
6: 2 *e* of them had six wings:
9:18 *e* devours the flesh of his neighbor.
13: 8 They look aghast at *e* other,
14:18 nations lie in glory, *e* in his own tomb;
31: 7 On that day *e* one of you shall spurn his
32: 2 *E* of them will be a shelter from the wind,
36:16 Then *e* of you will eat of his own vine and
47:13 at *e* new moon what would happen to you.
47:15 *E* wanders his own way,
53: 6 astray like sheep, *e* following his own way;
56:11 *E* of them goes his own way,
Jer 1:15 *E* king shall come and set up his throne at
4:29 horseman and bowman *e* city takes to flight;
5: 8 they are, *e* neighs after another's wife.
6: 3 their tents, *e* one grazes his portion.
6:23 they ride forth on steeds, *E* in his place,
7: 5 if *e* of you deals justly with his neighbor;
9: 4 *E* one deceives the other,
9:19 this dirge, and *e* other this lament.
11: 8 *E* one followed the hardness of his evil
12:15 back, each to his heritage, *e* to his land.
13:14 I will dash them against *e* other,
18:11 Return, *e* of you,
18:12 *e* one of us will behave according to the
21:12 *E* morning dispense justice,
22: 7 you I will send destroyers, *e* with his axe:
23:27 their dreams which they recount to *e* other,
23:30 the LORD, who steal my words from *e* other.
23:36 For *e* man his own word becomes the burden
25: 5 Turn back, *e* of you,
26: 3 listen and turn back, *e* from his evil way,
32:19 of men, giving to *e* according to his ways,
34:14 Every seventh year *e* of you shall set free
36: 3 they will turn back *e* from his evil way,
36:23 *E* time Jehudi finished reading three or
37:10 only the wounded remained, *e* in his tent,
37:21 and given a loaf of bread *e* day from the
49: 5 be scattered, *e* man in headlong flight,
50:16 sword, *e* of them turns to his own people,
50:42 *E* in his place for battle against you,
51: 6 let *e* one save his life,
51: 9 Leave her, let us go, *e* to his own land."
51:45 let *e* one save himself from the burning
52:21 *E* of the pillars was eighteen cubits high
52:21 *e* was four fingers thick,
Lam 3:23 They are renewed *e* morning,
Bar 1: 6 collected such funds as *e* could furnish.
1:22 but *e* one of us went off after the devices
2: 8 *e* from the figments of his evil heart.
6:13 *E* has a scepter,
6:14 *E* has in its right hand an axe or dagger,
Ez 1: 6 human, but *e* had four faces and four wings,
1: 9 but *e* went straight forward [Each went
1:10 *e* of the four had the face of a man,
1:10 ox, and finally *e* had the face of an eagle.
1:11 *E* had two wings spread out above so that
1:11 the other two wings of *e* covered his body.
1:12 straight forward *E* went straight forward;
1:15 one beside *e* of the four living creatures.
1:23 *E* of them had two covering his body.]
4: 6 one day for *e* year I have allotted you.
4:10 *e* day the same.
4:11 *e* day the same.
7:16 them all to death, *e* one for his own sins.
8:11 *e* of them with his censer in his hand,
8:12 what *e* of these elders of the house of
9: 2 *e* with a destroying weapon in his hand.
10: 9 beside them, one wheel beside *e* cherub;

EACH (cont.)

10:14 E had four faces:
10:21 E had four faces and four wings;
10:22 e one went straight forward.
14:10 E shall receive punishment for his sin,
18:30 of Israel, e one according to his ways,
20: 7 Throw away, e of you,
20:39 Come, e one of you, destroy your idols!
21:24 Then put a signpost at the head of e road,
29: 7 bringing e one of them down headlong;
33:26 e one of you defiles his neighbor's wife
40: 5 e cubit being a cubit and a handbreadth;
40: 5 e of which were found to be one rod.'
40:12 e of the cells on both sides was one cubit;
40:48 and measured the pilasters on e side,
41: 2 either side of it measured five cubits e.
41: 3 either side of it extended seven cubits e.
41:18 E cherub had two faces:
41:24 E door had two movable leaves;
45:13 sixth of an ephah from e homer of wheat,
45:13 sixth of an ephah from e homer of barley.
45:23 On e of the seven days of the feast he
45:23 he shall offer one male goat e day.
45:24 for e bull and one ephah for each ram;
45:24 he shall offer one hin of oil for e ephah.
46: 5 the lambs, and a hin of oil for e ephah.
46: 7 has at hand, and for e ephah a hin of oil.
46:11 one pleases, and a hin of oil with e ephah.
46:21 that in e corner there was another court:
46:23 A wall of stones surrounded e of the four,
Dn 7: 3 beasts, e different from the others.
13:10 they did not tell e other their trouble,
13:13 One day they said to e other,
13:14 met again, they asked e other the reason.
Jl 2: 7 They advance, e in his own lane,
2: 8 another, e advances in his own track;
Am 4: 3 breached walls e by the most direct way,
4: 4 E morning bring your sacrifices,
Jon 1: 5 frightened and e one cried to his god.
Mi 2:12 will gather you, O Jacob, e and every one,
4: 5 the peoples walk e in the name of its god,
7: 2 to shed blood, e one ensnares the other.
Hb 1: 9 e comes for the rapine,
Zep 2:11 Then, e from its own place,
Hg 1: 9 while e of you hurries to his own house.
Zec 4:11 two olive trees at e side of the lampstand?"
7: 9 kindness and compassion toward e other.
8: 4 e with staff in hand because of old age,
11: 6 e of them into the power of his neighbor,
12:12 And the land shall mourn, e family apart;
12:14 the rest of the families, e family apart,
14:13 and the hand of e shall be raised against
Mal 2:10 Why then do we break faith with e other,
Mt 16:27 will repay e man according to his conduct.
18:35 same way unless e of you forgives
25:14 to them according to e man's abilities.
Mk 13:34 servants in charge, e with his own task;
15:24 dice for them to see what e should take.
Lk 2: 3 went to register, e to his own town.
4:40 he laid hands on e of them and cured them.
6:44 E tree is known by its yield.
6:45 E man speaks from his heart's abundance.
9:23 his very self, take up his cross e day,
11: 3 Give us e day our daily bread.
16: 5 he called in e of his master's debtors,
19:13 and gave them sums of ten units e,
19:15 the money, to learn what profit e had made.
23:12 had previously been set against e other,
Jn 2: 6 e holding fifteen to twenty-five gallons.
6: 7 loaves enough to give e of them a mouthful!"
8:53 [Then e went off to his own house,
11:56 in the temple vicinity saying to e other,
13:14 then you must wash e other's feet.
13:34 for you, so must your love be for e other.
16:32 will be scattered and e will go his way,
19:23 divided them four ways, one for e soldier.
19:24 They said to e other,
Acts 2: 3 which parted and came to rest on e of them.
2: 6 They were much confused because e one
2: 8 e of us hears them in his native tongue?
2:11 Yet e of us hears them speaking in his own
2:38 must reform and be baptized, e one of you,
2:45 everything on the basis of e one's need.
7:26 Why are you trying to hurt e other?'
11:29 something aside, e according to his means,
14:23 In e church they installed presbyters and,
15:36 brothers are getting on in e of the towns
17:11 E day they studied the Scriptures to see
21:26 the offering was to be made for e of them.
Rom 12: 3 I warn e of you not to think more highly
12: 4 as e of us has one body with many members,
12: 6 according to the favor bestowed on e of us.
12:10 Anticipate e other in showing respect.
13: 7 Pay e one his due:
14: 5 E should be certain of his own conscience.
15: 2 E should please his neighbor so as to do
1Cor 3: 5 e of them doing only what the Lord
3: 8 E will receive his wages in proportion to
3:13 or straw, the work of e will be made clear.
3:13 fire will test the quality of e man's work.
7: 7 Still, e one has his own gift from God,
7:17 The general rule is that e one should lead
7:24 e of you should continue before God in the
12: 7 To e person the manifestation of the
12:11 gifts, distributing them to e as he wills.
12:18 God has set e member of the body in the
14:27 let it be at most two or three, e in turn,
14:28 e one speaking only to himself and to God.
15:23 to life again, but e one in proper order:
15:38 to e seed its own fruition.
16: 2 On the first day of e week everyone should
2Cor 4:16 our inner being is renewed e day
5:10 so that e one may receive his recompense,
Gal 3:26 E one of you is a son of God because of
6: 1 e of you trying to avoid falling into
6: 4 E man should look to his conduct;
Eph 4: 7 E of us has received God's favor in the
4:16 firmly together by e supporting ligament,
5:33 e one should love his wife as he loves
6: 8 You know that e one,
Phil 1: 8 I long for e of you with the affection
2: 4 e of you looking to others' interests
1Thes 4: 4 e of you guarding his member in sanctity
4: 6 and that e refrain from overreaching or
Heb 6:11 e of you show the same zeal till the end,
9: 5 cannot speak now of e of these in detail.
10:23 e other to love and good deeds.
11:21 dying, blessed e of the sons of Joseph,
1Pt 1:17 e one justly on the basis of his actions.
4:10 another, e in the measure he has received.
2Jn 1: 1 In truth I love e of you
3Jn 1:15 greet the beloved there, e by name.
Rv 2:23 give e of you what your conduct deserves.
4: 8 E of the four living creatures had six
6:11 E of the martyrs was given a long white
15: 6 e with a sash of gold about his breast.
20:13 E person was judged according to his
21:21 twelve pearls, e made of a single pearl;
22: 2 fruit twelve times a year, once e month;
22:12 be given to e man as his conduct deserves.

EAGER (19)

1Chr 28:21 all those who are e to show their skill
Sir 6:35 Be e to hear every godly discourse;
26:12 As a thirsty traveler with e mouth drinks
Is 13: 3 warriors, e and bold to carry out my anger.
Jer 3: 9 E to sin, she polluted the land,
Zec 6: 7 e to set about patrolling the earth,
Mt 12:39 evil and unfaithful age is e for a sign!
16: 4 An evil, faithless age is e for a sign,
Jn 19:12 After this, Pilate was e to release him,
Acts 20:16 for he was e to get to Jerusalem by the
Rom 1:15 That is why I am e to preach the gospel to
2Cor 8:17 but being very e he has gone to you freely.
8:22 He is now more e than ever for this work
Phil 2:28 I have been especially e to send him so
4:17 It is not that I am e for the gift;
1Tm 5:10 she been e to do every possible good work?
2Tm 4: 8 looked for his appearing with e longing.
Ti 2:14 a people of his own, e to do what is right.
1Pt 2: 2 Be as e for milk as newborn babies

EAGERLY (9)

Gn 44:11 Then each of them e lowered his bag to the
2Mc 10:33 and his men e besieged the fortress.
Dn 13:12 Day by day they watched e for her.
Zep 3: 7 e have they done all their corrupt deeds.
Rom 8:19 e awaits the revelation of the sons of God.
1Cor 14: 1 Seek e after love.
Gal 5: 5 we e await the justification we hope for,
Phil 3:20 that we e await the coming of our Savior,
Heb 9:28 bring salvation to those who e await him.

EAGERNESS (1)

2Cor 8:22 whose e has been proved to us in many ways.

EAGLE (22)

Ex 19: 4 on e wings and brought you here to myself.
Lv 11:13 the e, the vulture, the osprey, the kite,
Dt 14:12 the e, the vulture, the osprey, the various
28:49 of the earth, that swoops down like an e,
32:11 As an e incites its nestlings forth by
Jb 9:26 of reed, like an e swooping upon its prey.
39:27 Does the e fly up at your command to build
Prv 23: 5 wings, like the e that flies toward heaven.
30:19 The way of an e in the air,
Jer 48:40 Behold, like an e he soars,
49:16 Though you build your nest high as the e,
49:22 like an e he soars aloft,
Ez 1:10 ox, and finally each had the face of an e.
10:14 of a lion, and the fourth that of an e.
17: 3 The great e, with great wings,
17: 7 there was another great e, great of wing,
Dn 4:30 his hair grew like the feathers of an e,
Ob 1: 4 Though you go as high as the e,
Hb 1: 8 They fly like the e hastening to devour;
Rv 4: 7 the fourth looked like an e in flight.
8:13 I heard an e flying in midheaven cry out
12:14 wings of a gigantic e so that she could fly

EAGLES (8)

2Sm 1:23 in life nor in death, swifter than e,
Ps(s) 103: 5 your youth is renewed like the e.
Prv 30:17 the young e will devour it.
Is 40:31 strength, they will soar as with e' wings;
Jer 4:13 Swifter than e are his steeds:
Lam 4:19 pursuers were swifter than e in the air,
Dn 7: 4 first was like a lion, but with e wings.
Mi 1:16 Let your baldness be as the e,

EAR (79)

Ex 9:31 the barley was in e and the flax in bud.
21: 6 he shall pierce his e with an awl,
29:20 Aaron's right e and on the tips of his sons'
Lv 8:23 and put it on the tip of Aaron's right e,
14:14 put it on the tip of the man's right e,
14:17 put some on the tip of the man's right e,
14:25 of the right e of the man being purified,
14:28 also put on the tip of the man's right e,
Nm 23:18 give e to my testimony,
Dt 1:17 give e to the lowly and to the great alike,
1:45 not listen to your cry or give e to you.
15:17 and thrust it through his e into the door,
32: 1 Give e, O heavens, while I speak;
Jgs 5: 3 Give e, O princes!
2Kgs 4:42 the first fruits, and fresh grain in the e.
19:16 Incline your e, O LORD, and listen!
Neh 1: 6 your commandments, may your e be attentive,
1:11 may your e be attentive to my prayer and
6: 7 like these must reach the e of the king,
Jb 4:12 to me, and my e caught a whisper of it.
12:11 the e judge words as the mouth tastes food?
13: 1 my e has heard and perceived it.
32:11 and have given e to your arguments.
34: 3 For the e tests words,
Ps(s) 17: 6 incline your e to me;
31: 3 justice rescue me, incline your e to me,
39:13 to my cry give e;
45:11 turn your e, forget your people
49: 5 My e is intent upon a proverb;
71: 2 incline your e to me,
86: 1 Incline your e, O LORD; answer me,
88: 3 incline your e to my call for help,
94: 9 Shall he who shaped the e not hear?
102: 3 Incline your e to me;
116: 2 has inclined his e to me the day I called.
Prv 2: 2 my commands, Turning your e to wisdom,
4:20 attentive, to my sayings incline your e;
5: 1 attentive, to my knowledge incline your e,
5:13 nor to my instructors incline my e!
18:15 and the e of the wise seeks knowledge.
20:12 The e that hears,
21:13 He who shuts his e to the cry of the poor
22:17 Incline your e, and hear my words,
25:12 gold, is a wise reprover to an obedient e.
28: 9 one turns away his e from hearing the law,
Eccl 1: 8 seeing nor is the e filled with hearing.
Wis 1:10 Because a jealous e hearkens to everything,
Sir 3:28 and an attentive e is the wise man's joy.
16: 5 seen, even more than these has my e heard.
33:19 O rulers of the assembly, give e!
Is 8: 9 Give e, all you distant lands!
28:23 Give e and hear my voice,
37:17 Incline your e, O LORD, and listen!
42:23 Who of you gives e to this?
50: 4 morning he opens my e that I may hear;
51: 4 my folk, give e to me.
59: 1 short to save, nor his e too dull to hear.
64: 3 No e has ever heard,
Jer 11: 8 But they did not listen or give e.
13:15 Give e, listen humbly,
17:23 though they did not listen or give e,
Lam 3:56 not your e be deaf to my cry for help!"
Bar 2:16 turn, O Lord, your e to hear us.
Dn 9:18 Give e, O my God, and listen;
Hos 5: 1 of Israel, O household of the king, give e!
8: 7 grain that forms no e can yield no flour;
Am 3:12 of legs or the tip of an e of his sheep,
Mt 15:10 "Give e and try to understand.
26:51 high priest's servant, cutting off his e.
Mk 4:28 the ear, finally the ripe wheat in the e.
14:47 the high priest's slave, cutting off his e.
Lk 22:50 priest's servant and cut off his right e.
22:51 Then he touched the e and healed the man.
Jn 18:10 of the high priest, severing his right e.
18:26 of the man whose e Peter had severed.
1Cor 2: 9 "Eye has not seen, e has not heard,
12:16 If the e should say,
12:17 If it were all e,

EARLIER (14)

Gn 26: 1 distinct from the e one that had occurred
Jgs 20:39 them as surely as in the e fighting,
1Kgs 11:15 E, when David had conquered Edom,
2Kgs 17:40 however, but continued in their e manner.]
Neh 5:15 The e governors,
1Mc 12: 3 to renew the e friendship and alliance
15:17 us to renew their e alliance of friendship.
Jb 42:12 latter days of Job more than his e ones.
Is 42: 9 See, the e things have come to pass,
43: 9 this, or foretold to us the e things?
Jer 38:27 had been heard of the e conversation.
Jn 10:40 the place where John had been baptizing e,
Acts 21:29 an Ephesian, with him in the city e,
2Cor 12:21 e and have not repented of the uncleanness,

EARLIEST (4)

Neh 7: 5 of those who had returned in the *e* period.
Jdt 8:29 but from your *e* years all the people have
Sir 51:15 from *e* youth I was familiar with her.
Jer 6:16 Stand beside the *e* roads,

EARLY (73)

Gn 19: 2 you can get up *e* to continue your journey."
19:27 *E* the next morning Abraham went to the
20: 8 *E* the next morning Abimelech called all
21:14 *E* the next morning Abraham got some bread
22: 3 *E* the next morning Abraham saddled his
26:31 *E* the next morning they exchanged oaths.
28:18 *E* the next morning Jacob took the stone
32: 1 *E* the next morning,
Ex 8:16 *E* tomorrow morning present yourself to
9:13 *E* tomorrow morning present yourself to
24: 4 of the LORD and, rising *e* the next day,
32: 6 *E* the next day the people offered
34: 4 and *e* the next morning he went up Mount
Nm 13:20 It was then the season for *e* grapes.
14:40 *E* the next morning they started up into
Dt 11:14 to your land, the *e* rain and the late rain,
Jos 3: 1 *E* the next morning, Joshua moved
6:12 *E* the next morning, Joshua had the priests
7:16 *E* the next morning Joshua had Israel come
8:10 *E* the next morning Joshua mustered the
8:14 his army came out very *e* in the morning
Jgs 6:28 *E* the next morning the townspeople found
6:38 *E* the next morning he wrung the dew from
7: 1 *E* the next morning Jerubbaal (that is,
19: 5 *e* in the morning and he prepared to go.
19: 8 On the fifth morning he rose *e* to depart,
19: 9 *E* tomorrow you can start your journey
21: 4 *E* the next day the people built an altar
1Sm 1:19 *E* the next morning they worshiped before
3:15 when he got up *e* and opened the doors of
5: 3 people of Ashdod rose *e* the next morning,
5: 4 But the next morning *e*,
15:12 *E* in the morning he went to meet Saul,
17:20 *E* the next morning, having left the flock
29:10 But make an *e* morning start,
29:11 So David and his men left *e* in the morning
2Sm 15: 2 Absalom used to rise *e* and stand alongside
2Kgs 3:22 *E* that morning, when the sun shone
6:15 *E* the next morning, when the attendant
19:35 *E* the next morning, there they were,
2Chr 20:20 In the *e* morning they hastened out to the
36:15 *E* and often did the LORD,
Tb 9: 6 The following morning they got an *e* start
1Mc 4:52 *E* in the morning on the twenty-fifth day
16: 5 they spent the night at Modein, rose *e*,
2Mc 14:38 In the *e* days of the revolt,
Jb 1: 5 rising *e* and offering holocausts for every
15:30 flame shall wither him up in his *e* growth,
Ps(s) 84: 7 the *e* rain clothes it with generous growth.
127: 2 It is vain for you to rise *e*,
Prv 27:14 neighbor with a loud voice in the *e* morning
Sg 7:13 Let us go *e* to the vineyards,
Wis 4: 7 But the just man, though he die *e*,
Is 28: 4 valley Will be like an *e* fig before summer:
37:36 *E* the next morning,
Jer 5:24 our God, Who gives us rain *e* and late,
Dn 6:20 the king rose very *e* the next morning and
14:16 *E* the next morning, the king came
Hos 6: 4 cloud, like the dew that *e* passes away.
13: 3 cloud or like the dew that *e* passes away,
Jl 2:23 for you, the *e* and the late rain as before.
Mi 7: 1 no cluster to eat, no *e* fig that I crave.
Na 3:12 but fig trees, bearing *e* figs That fall,
Mt 24: 8 These are the *e* stages of the birth pangs.
Mk 1:35 Rising *e* the next morning, he went off
11:20 *E* next morning, as they were walking
13:35 when the cock crows, or at *e* dawn.
16: 2 Very *e*, just after sunrise, on the first day
16: 9 the dead *e* on the first day of the week.
Jn 20: 1 *E* in the morning on the first day of the
Acts 15: 7 from the *e* days God selected me
21:16 of Mnason, a Cypriot and an *e* disciple,
Rv 2: 4 you have turned aside from your *e* love.

EARLY-RIPENING (1)

Jer 24: 2 contained excellent figs, the *e* kind.

EARN (2)

Am 7:12 There *e* your bread by prophesying,
2Thes 3:12 to *e* the food they eat by working quietly.

EARNED (3)

Hg 1: 6 And he who *e* wages earned them for a bag
Lk 19:16 the sum you gave me has *e* you another ten.'

EARNEST (5)

Wis 6:17 discipline is a very *e* desire for her;
Sir 51:26 her, and the one who is in *e* finds her.
Dn 9: 3 to the Lord God, pleading in *e* prayer,
Mk 5:23 he fell at his feet and made this *e* appeal:
Rv 3:19 Be *e* about it, therefore.

EARNESTLY (9)

Gn 44:18 lord, let your servant speak *e* to my lord,
Dt 4: 9 take care and be *e* on your guard not to
Ps(s) 109:30 I will speak my thanks *e* to the
Wis 12:22 may think *e* of your goodness when we judge.
Sir 27: 3 you *e* hold fast to the fear of the LORD,
Lk 7: 4 approaching Jesus they petitioned him *e*.
Col 4:12 pleading *e* in prayer that you stand firm,
2Tm 1:17 in Rome, he sought me out *e* and found me.
Jas 5:17 yet he prayed *e* that it would not rain and

EARNINGS (5)

Prv 5:10 your hard-won *e* go to an alien's house;
15: 6 but the *e* of the wicked are in turmoil.
31:16 out of her *e* she plants a vineyard
Sir 14:15 to others, and your *e* to be divided by lot?
Is 45:14 the *e* of Egypt, the gain of

EARNS (2)

Prv 9: 7 He who corrects an arrogant man *e* insult;
2Cor 4:17 and *e* for us an eternal weight of glory

EARRING (2)

Nm 31:50 as an anklet, a bracelet, a ring, an *e*,
Prv 25:12 Like a golden *e*,

EARRINGS (4)

Ex 32: 2 take off the golden *e* they are wearing,
32: 3 took off their *e* and brought them to Aaron,
35:22 heart prompted them, brought brooches, *e*,
Jdt 10: 4 put on her anklets, bracelets, rings, *e*,

EARS (101)

Gn 35: 4 and also the rings they had in their *e*.
41: 5 He saw seven *e* of grain,
41: 6 Behind them sprouted seven *e* of grain,
41: 7 ears swallowed up the seven fat, healthy *e*.
41:22 In another dream I saw seven *e* of grain,
41:23 Behind them sprouted seven *e* of grain,
41:24 thin *e* swallowed up the seven healthy ears.
41:26 and the seven healthy *e* are seven years
41:27 as are the seven thin, wind-blasted *e*;
Ex 17:14 and recite it in the *e* of Joshua:
29:20 tips of his sons' right *e* and on the thumbs
Lv 2:14 the form of fresh grits of new *e* of grain,
8:24 of the blood on the tips of their right *e*,
19: 9 nor shall you glean the stray *e* of grain.
23:22 shall you glean the stray *e* of your grain.
Dt 23:26 you may pluck some of the *e* with your hand,
29: 3 understand, or eyes to see, or *e* to hear.
Ru 2: 2 "Let me go and glean *e* of grain in the
1Sm 3:11 the *e* of everyone who hears it to ring.
15:14 this bleating of sheep that comes to my *e*,
2Sm 22: 7 heard my voice, and my cry reached his *e*.
2Kgs 19:28 me and your fury which has reached my *e*,
21:12 anyone hears of it, his *e* shall ring.
2Chr 6:40 *e* attentive to the prayer of this place.
7:15 my *e* attentive to the prayer of this place.
2Mc 15:38 delights the *e* of those who read the work.
Jb 15:21 The sound of terrors is in his *e*;
24:24 like *e* of grain they shrivel.
33:16 the *e* of men and as a warning to them,
36:10 He opens their *e* to correction and exhorts
Ps(s) 18: 7 my voice, and my cry to him reached his *e*.
34:16 has eyes for the just, and *e* for their cry.
40: 7 not, but *e* open to obedience you gave me.
44: 2 O God, our *e* have heard,
58: 5 that of a stubborn snake that stops its *e*,
78: 1 incline your *e* to the words of my mouth.
92:12 and my *e* have heard of the fall of my
115: 6 They have *e* but hear not;
130: 2 *e* be attentive to my voice in supplication:
135:17 They have *e* but hear not,
Prv 23:12 and your *e* to words of knowledge.
26:17 a passing dog by the *e* is he who meddles
Wis 15:15 nostrils to snuff the air, Nor *e* to hear,
Sir 17: 5 He forms men's tongues and eyes and *e*,
17:11 beheld, his glorious voice their *e* heard.
25: 9 a friend and he who speaks to attentive *e*.
27:14 on end, their brawls make one stop one's *e*.
38:28 The clang of the hammer deafens his *e*,
Is 6:10 to dull their *e* and close their eyes;
6:10 Else their eyes will see, their *e* hear,
17: 5 one gleans the *e* in the Valley of Rephaim.
22:14 This reaches the *e* of the LORD of hosts
30:21 from behind, a voice shall sound in your *e*:
32: 3 the *e* of those who hear will be attentive.
33:15 stopping his *e* lest he hear of bloodshed,
35: 5 be opened, the *e* of the deaf be cleared;
37:29 me and your fury which has reached my *e*,
42:20 your *e* are open,
43: 8 have eyes, who are deaf though they have *e*.
48: 8 knew, they did not reach your *e* beforehand.
Jer 5:21 eyes and see not, who have *e* and hear not.
6:10 their *e* are uncircumcised,
9:19 the LORD, let your *e* receive his message.
19: 3 who hear of it will feel their *e* tingle.
26:11 city, as you have heard with your own *e*."
Bar 2:31 I will give them hearts, and heedful *e*:
Ez 12: 2 do not see, and *e* to hear but do not hear,
16:12 a ring in your nose, pendants in your *e*,
23:25 you in fury, cutting off your nose and *e*;
Mi 7:16 their *e* shall become deaf.
Zec 7:11 and stopped their *e* so as not to hear.
Mt 13:15 They have scarcely heard with their *e*,
13:15 with their eyes, and hear with their *e*,
13:16 see and blest are your *e* because they hear.
Mk 4: 9 "Let him who has *e* to hear me, hear!"
4:23 Let him who has *e* to hear me, hear!"
7:33 He put his fingers into the man's *e* and,
7:35 At once, the man's *e* were opened;
8:18 *E* but no hearing?
Lk 1:44 The moment your greeting sounded in my *e*,
8: 8 who has *e* attend to what he has heard."
Jn 12:38 who has believed what has reached our *e*?
Acts 7:51 people, uncircumcised in heart and *e*,
7:57 their hands over their *e* as they did so.
11:22 reached the *e* of the church in Jerusalem,
28:27 They have scarcely used their *e* to listen;
28:27 see with their eyes, hear with their *e*,
Rom 11: 8 blind eyes and deaf *e*,
2Tm 4: 3 with teachers who tickle their *e*.
Jas 5: 4 have reached the *e* of the Lord of hosts.
1Pt 3:12 has eyes for the just and *e* for their cry;
Rv 2: 7 *e* heed the Spirit's word to the churches!
2:11 *e* heed the Spirit's word to the churches!
2:17 *e* heed the Spirit's word to the churches!
2:29 *e* heed the Spirit's word to the churches!'
3: 6 *e* heed the Spirit's word to the churches!'
3:13 *e* heed the Spirit's word to the churches!
3:22 *e* heed the Spirit's word to the churches.' "
13: 9 Let him who has *e* heed these words!

EARSHOT (2)

2Kgs 18:26 within *e* of the people who are on the wall."
Is 36:11 within *e* of the people who are on the wall."

EARTH (880)

Gn 1: 1 when God created the heavens and the *e*,
1: 2 the earth, the *e* was a formless wasteland,
1:10 God called the dry land "the *e*,"
1:11 said, "Let the *e* bring forth vegetation:
1:11 on *e* that bears fruit with its seed in it."
1:12 the *e* brought forth every kind of plant
1:12 on *e* that bears fruit with its seed in it.
1:15 dome of the sky, to shed light upon the *e*."
1:17 dome of the sky, to shed light upon the *e*,
1:20 and on the *e* let birds fly beneath the
1:22 and let the birds multiply on the *e*."
1:24 "Let the *e* bring forth all kinds of
1:25 and all kinds of creeping things of the *e*.
1:28 fill the *e* and subdue it.
1:28 all the living things that move on the *e*."
1:29 every seed-bearing plant all over the *e*
2: 1 the *e* and all their array were completed.
2: 4 of the heavens and the *e* at their creation.
2: 4 the LORD God made the *e* and the heavens
2: 5 *e* and no grass of the field had sprouted,
2: 5 *e* and there was no man to till the soil,
2: 6 a stream was welling up out of the *e*
4:12 shall become a restless wanderer on the *e*."
4:14 and become a restless wanderer on the *e*,
6: 1 on *e* and daughters were born to them,
6: 4 Nephilim appeared on *e* (as well as later),
6: 5 saw how great was man's wickedness on *e*,
6: 6 he regretted that he had made man on the *e*,
6: 7 out from the *e* the men whom I have created,
6:11 the *e* was corrupt and full of lawlessness.
6:12 When God saw how corrupt the *e* had become,
6:12 since all mortals led depraved lives on *e*,
6:13 mortals on *e*; the earth is full of lawlessness
6:13 So I will destroy them and all life on *e*.
6:17 to bring the flood [waters] on the *e*,
6:17 everything on *e* shall perish.
7: 3 will keep their issue alive over all the *e*.
7: 4 on the *e* for forty days and forty nights,
7: 4 *e* every moving creature that I have made."
7: 6 old when the flood waters came upon the *e*.
7:10 the waters of the flood came upon the *e*.
7:12 nights heavy rain poured down on the *e*.
7:14 every kind of creeping thing of the *e*,
7:17 flood continued upon the *e* for forty days.
7:17 the ark, so that it rose above the *e*.
7:19 and higher above the *e* rose the waters,
7:21 All creatures that stirred on *e* perished:
7:21 animals, and all that swarmed on the *e*,
7:23 The LORD wiped out every living thing on *e*:
7:23 all were wiped out from the *e*.
7:24 over the *e* for one hundred and fifty days
8: 1 So God made a wind sweep over the *e*
8: 3 Gradually the waters receded from the *e*.
8: 7 to see if the waters had lessened on the *e*.
8: 7 until the waters dried off from the *e*.
8: 8 to see if the waters had lessened on the *e*.
8: 9 ark, for there was water all over the *e*.
8:11 knew that the waters had lessened on the *e*.
8:13 month, the water began to dry up on the *e*.
8:14 day of the month, the *e* was dry.
8:17 or animals or creeping things of the *e*—
8:17 and let them abound on the *e*,
8:19 creeping creatures of the *e* left the ark,
8:21 again will I doom the *e* because of man,

EARTH (cont.)
8:22 As long as the *e* lasts cold and heat,
9: 1 "Be fertile and multiply and fill the *e*.
9: 2 of the *e* and all the birds of the air,
9: 7 abound on *e* and subdue it."
9:11 not be another flood to devastate the *e*."
9:13 sign of the covenant between me and the *e*.
9:14 When I bring clouds over the *e*,
9:16 all mortal creatures that are on *e*."
9:17 me and all mortal creatures that are on *e*."
9:19 and from them the whole *e* was peopled.
10: 8 Nimrod, who was the first potentate on *e*.
10:32 of the *e* branched out after the flood.
11: 4 we shall be scattered all over the *e*."
11: 8 scattered them from there all over the *e*,
11: 9 that he scattered them all over the *e*.
12: 3 of the *e* shall find blessing in you,"
13:16 your descendants like the dust of the *e*;
13:16 if anyone could count the dust of the *e*,
14:19 Most High, the creator of heaven and *e*;
14:22 Most High, the creator of heaven and *e*,
18:18 of the *e* are to find blessing in him?
19:23 rising over the *e* as Lot arrived in Zoar,
19:31 and there is not a man on *e* to unite with
22:18 the nations of the *e* shall find blessing
24: 3 LORD, the God of heaven and the God of *e*,
26: 4 the nations of the *e* shall find blessing
27:28 of the *e* abundance of grain and wine.
27:39 from the fertile *e* shall be your dwelling;
28:14 be as plentiful as the dust of the *e*,
28:14 the nations of the *e* shall find blessing.
45: 7 ensure for you a remnant on *e* and to save
48:16 may become teeming multitudes upon the *e*!"
Ex 8:12 his staff and strike the dust of the *e*,
8:13 of the *e* and gnats came upon man and beast.
8:13 The dust of the *e* was turned into gnats
8:18 that I am the LORD in the midst of the *e*.
9:14 that there is none like me anywhere on *e*.
9:15 pestilence as would wipe you from the *e*.
9:16 to make my name resound throughout the *e*!
9:23 Lightning flashed toward the *e*,
9:29 you shall learn that the *e* is the LORD's.
9:33 the rain no longer poured down upon the *e*.
15:12 out your right hand, the *e* swallowed them!
19: 5 all other people, though all the *e* is mine.
20: 4 *e* below or in the waters beneath the earth;
20:11 days the LORD made the heavens and the *e*,
20:24 "An altar of *e* you shall make for me,
31:17 days the LORD made the heavens and the *e*,
32:12 exterminate them from the face of the *e*?
33:16 out from every other people on the *e*."
34:10 been wrought in any nation anywhere on *e*,
Lv 17:13 pour out its blood and cover it with *e*.
Nm 12: 3 far the meekest man on the face of the *e*.
14:21 the LORD's glory that fills the whole *e*,
16:32 and the *e* opened its mouth and swallowed
16:33 the *e* closed over them,
16:34 saying, "The *e* might swallow us too!"
22: 5 of the *e* and are settling down opposite us!
22:11 from Egypt now cover the face of the *e*.
26:10 The *e* opened its mouth and swallowed them
Dt 3:24 on *e* can perform deeds as mighty as yours?
4:17 the *e* or of any bird that flies in the sky,
4:18 or of any fish in the waters under the *e*.
4:26 and *e* this day to witness against you,
4:32 ever since God created man upon the *e*;
4:36 on *e* he let you see his great fire,
4:39 is God in the heavens above and on *e* below,
5: 8 *e* below or in the waters beneath the earth;
7: 6 of the *e* to be a people peculiarly his own.
10:14 God, as well as the *e* and everything on it.
11:21 as long as the heavens are above the *e*.
13: 8 away, from one end of the *e* to the other:
14: 2 of the *e* to be a people peculiarly his own.
28: 1 you high above all the nations of the *e*.
28:10 the *e* see you bearing the name of the LORD,
28:23 bronze and the *e* under your feet like iron.
28:25 example to all the kingdoms of the *e*.
28:49 a nation from afar, from the end of the *e*,
28:64 nations from one end of the *e* to the other,
30:19 heaven and *e* today to witness against you:
31:28 call heaven and *e* to witness against them.
32: 1 let the *e* hearken to the words of my mouth!
32:22 world, Consuming the *e* with its yield,
33:16 With the best of the *e* and its fullness,
33:17 nations, even those at the ends of the *e*."
Jos 2:11 God, is God in heaven above and on *e* below.
3:11 whole *e* will precede you into the Jordan.
3:13 ark of the LORD, the Lord of the whole *e*,
4:24 peoples of the *e* may learn that the hand
7: 9 around us and efface our name from the *e*.
Jgs 5: 4 The *e* quaked and the heavens were shaken,
1Sm 2: 8 For the pillars of the *e* are the LORD's,
2:10 the LORD judges the ends of the *e*,
4: 5 shouted so loudly that the *e* resounded.
14:15 The *e* also shook so that the panic was
20:15 enemies of David from the surface of the *e*.
20:31 long as the son of Jesse lives upon the *e*,
28:13 a preternatural being rising from the *e*."
2Sm 4:11 for his death and destroy you from the *e*!"
7: 9 you famous like the great ones of the *e*.
7:23 on *e* is there like your people Israel,
14: 7 neither name nor posterity upon the *e*."
14:20 of God, so that he knows all things on *e*."
18: 9 He hung between heaven and *e* while the
22: 8 "The *e* swayed and quaked:
22:16 the foundations of the *e* were laid bare,
22:43 I ground them fine as the dust of the *e*;
1Kgs 1:40 as to split open the *e* with their shouting.
5:14 kings of the *e* who had heard of his wisdom.
8:23 God like you in heaven above or on *e* below;
8:27 indeed be that God dwells among men on *e*?
8:43 the peoples of the *e* may know your name,
8:53 the peoples of the *e* for your inheritance,
8:60 that all the peoples of the *e* may know the
10:23 riches and wisdom all the kings of the *e*.
13:34 was to be cut off and destroyed from the *e*.
17:14 day when the LORD sends rain upon the *e*.'"
18: 1 he said, "that I may send rain upon the *e*."
18:42 the top of Carmel, crouched down to the *e*,
2Kgs 5:15 I know that there is no God in all the *e*,
5:17 your servant, have two mule-loads of *e*,
19:15 are God over all the kingdoms of the *e*.
19:15 You have made the heavens and the *e*.
19:19 kingdoms of the *e* may know that you alone,
1Chr 1:10 was the first to be a conqueror on the *e*.
16:14 throughout the *e* his judgments prevail He
16:23 Sing to the LORD, all the *e*,
16:30 Tremble before him, all the *e*;
16:31 Let the heavens be glad and the *e* rejoice;
16:33 he comes to rule the *e*.
17: 8 great like that of the greatest on the *e*.
17:21 *e* whom a god went to redeem as his people?
21:16 of the LORD standing between *e* and heaven,
22: 8 shed too much blood upon the *e* in my sight.
29:11 For all in heaven and on *e* is yours;
29:15 on *e* is like a shadow that does not abide.
2Chr 1: 9 a people as numerous as the dust of the *e*.
2:11 the God of Israel, who made heaven and *e*,
6:14 is no god like you in heaven or on *e*;
6:18 be that God dwells with mankind on *e*?
6:33 the peoples of the *e* may know your name,
7: 3 with their faces to the *e* and adored,
9:22 of the *e* in riches as well as in wisdom.
9:23 of the *e* sought audience with Solomon,
16: 9 eyes of the LORD roam over the whole *e*,
32:19 of the gods of the other peoples of the *e*,
36:23 'All the kingdoms of the *e* the LORD,
Ezr 1: 2 'All the kingdoms of the *e* the LORD,
5:11 the servants of the God of heaven and *e*,
Neh 9: 6 their host, the *e* and all that is upon it,
Tb 3: 6 I may go from the face of the *e* into dust.
3:13 Bid me to depart from the *e*,
10:14 and he blessed the Lord of heaven and *e*,
13:11 light will shine to all parts of the *e*;
13:11 inhabitants of all the limits of the *e*,
14:10 Ahiqar went down alive into the *e*!
Jdt 2: 5 says the great king, the lord of all the *e*:
2: 7 Tell them to have *e* and water ready,
2: 9 them as exiles to the very ends of the *e*.
2:20 count, like locusts or the dust of the *e*,
3: 8 to destroy all the gods of the *e*,
6: 2 and destroy them from the face of the *e*.
6: 4 King Nebuchadnezzar, lord of all the *e*;
7:28 We adjure you by heaven and *e*,
9:12 heritage of Israel, Lord of heaven and *e*,
11: 1 to serve Nebuchadnezzar, king of all the *e*.
11: 7 life of Nebuchadnezzar, king of all the *e*,
11:23 and shall be renowned throughout the *e*."
13:18 Most High God, above all the women on *e*;
13:18 the Lord God, the creator of heaven and *e*,
14: 2 At daybreak, when the sun rises on the *e*,
Est A: 4 confusion upon the *e*.
A: 7 evil and great confusion, lay upon the *e*.
C: 3 You made heaven and *e* and every wonderful
1Mc 1: 3 He advanced to the ends of the *e*,
1: 3 the *e* fell silent before him,
1: 9 years, causing much distress over the *e*.
2:37 heaven and *e* are our witnesses that you
2:40 they will soon destroy us from the *e*."
3: 9 and was renowned to the ends of the *e*;
8: 4 *e* and had inflicted on them severe defeat,
9:13 The *e* shook with the noise of the armies,
11:71 tore his clothes, threw *e* on his head,
14:10 glorious name reached the ends of the *e*.
15: 9 your glory will be manifest in all the *e*."
2Mc 7:28 and the *e* and see all that is in them;
10:25 sprinkling *e* upon their heads and girding
14:15 they sprinkled themselves with *e* and
15: 5 he said, "I, on my part, am ruler on *e*,
Jb 1: 7 "From roaming the *e* an patrolling it."
1: 8 and that there is no one on *e* like him,
2: 2 "From roaming the *e* and patrolling it."
2: 3 and that there is no one on *e* like him,
3:14 kings and counselors of the *e* who built
5: 6 For mischief comes not out of the *e*,
5:10 upon the *e* and sends water upon the fields;
5:22 the beasts of the *e* you need not dread.
5:25 and your offspring as the grass of the *e*.
7: 1 Is not man's life on *e* a drudgery?
8: 9 because our days on *e* are but a shadow),
9: 6 He shakes the *e* out of its place,
9:24 *e* is given into the hands of the wicked;
11: 9 It is longer than the *e* in measure,
12: 8 Or the reptiles on *e* to instruct you,
14: 8 Even though its root grow old in the *e*,
16:18 O *e*, cover not my blood,
18: 4 shall the *e* be neglected on your account
18:17 from the land, and he has no name on the *e*.
20: 4 time, since man was placed upon the *e*,
20:27 guilt, and the *e* shall rise up against him.
26: 7 and suspends the *e* over nothing at all;
28: 2 Iron is taken from the *e*,
28: 5 The *e*, though out of it comes forth bread,
28:24 *e* and sees all that is under the heavens.
34:13 Who gave him government over the *e*,
35:11 Taught us rather than the beasts of the *e*,
37: 3 with his lightning, to the ends of the *e*.
37: 6 For he says to the snow, "Fall to the *e*";
37:12 in their task upon the surface of the *e*,
38: 4 Where were you when I founded the *e*?
38:13 For taking hold of the ends of the *e*,
38:14 The *e* is changed as is clay by the seal,
38:18 Have you comprehended the breadth of the *e*?
38:24 whence the east wind spreads over the *e*?
38:33 you put into effect their plan on the *e*?
38:38 So that the dust of *e* is fused into a mass
41:25 Upon the *e* there is not his like,
Ps(s) 2: 2 The kings of the *e* rise up,
2: 8 and the ends of the *e* for your possession.
2:10 take warning, you rulers of the *e*.
8: 2 how glorious is your name over all the *e*!
8:10 how glorious is your name over all the *e*!
10:18 and the oppressed, that man, who is of *e*,
18: 8 The *e* swayed and quaked;
19: 5 Through all the *e* their voice resounds,
21:11 the *e* and their posterity from among men.
22:28 the *e* shall remember and turn to the LORD;
22:30 shall bow down all who sleep in the *e*;
24: 1 The LORD's are the *e* and its fullness;
33: 5 of the kindness of the LORD the *e* is full.
33: 8 Let all the *e* fear the LORD;
33:14 throne he beholds all who dwell on the *e*,
34:17 to destroy remembrance of them from the *e*.
41: 3 he will make him happy on the *e*,
44:26 the dust, our bodies are pressed to the *e*.
46: 3 though the *e* be shaken and mountains
46: 7 his voice resounds, the *e* melts away,
46: 9 the astounding things he has wrought on *e*:
46:10 He has stopped wars to the end of the *e*:
46:11 among the nations, exalted upon the *e*.
47: 3 awesome, is the great king over all the *e*.
47: 8 For the king of all the *e* is God;
47:10 For God's are the guardians of the *e*;
48: 3 of heights, is the joy of all the *e*;
48:11 your praise reaches to the ends of the *e*.
50: 1 the LORD has spoken and summoned the *e*,
50: 4 summons the heavens from above, and the *e*,
57: 6 above all the *e* be your glory!
57:12 above all the *e* be your glory!
58: 3 on *e* you look to the fruits of extortion.
58:12 truly there is a God who is judge on *e*!"
59:14 ruler of Jacob, yes, to the ends of the *e*.
63: 2 pines and my soul thirsts like the *e*,
63:10 they shall go into the depths of the *e*;
65: 6 the ends of the *e* and of the distant seas.
66: 1 Shout joyfully to God, all you on *e*,
66: 4 all on *e* worship and sing praise to you,
67: 3 So may your way be known upon *e*;
67: 5 the nations on the *e* you guide.
67: 7 The *e* has yielded its fruits;
67: 8 and may all the ends of the *e* fear him!
68: 9 through the wilderness, The *e* quaked;
68:33 You kingdoms of the *e*, sing to God,
69:35 Let the heavens and the *e* praise him,
71:20 of the *e* you will once more raise me.
72: 6 on the meadow, like showers watering the *e*.
72: 8 and from the River to the ends of the *e*.
72:16 there be an abundance of grain upon the *e*;
72:17 shall all the tribes of the *e* be blessed;
72:19 may the whole *e* be filled with his glory.
73: 9 and their pronouncements roam the *e*:
73:25 when I am with you, the *e* delights me not.
74:12 of old, you doer of saving deeds on *e*,
75: 4 Though the *e* and all who dwell in it quake,
75: 9 all the wicked of the *e* shall drink.
76: 9 the *e* feared and was silent When God arose
76:10 to save all the afflicted of the *e*.
76:13 who is terrible to the kings of the *e*.
77:19 the *e* quivered and quaked.
78:69 like the *e* which he founded forever.
79: 2 your faithful ones to the beasts of the *e*.
82: 5 all the foundations of the *e* are shaken.
82: 8 judge the *e*, for yours are all the nations.
83:19 are the LORD, the Most High over all the *e*.
85:12 Truth shall spring out of the *e*,
89:12 Yours are the heavens, and yours is the *e*;
89:28 first-born, highest of the kings of the *e*.
90: 2 and the *e* and the world were brought forth,
94: 2 Rise up, judge of the *e*;
95: 4 In his hands are the depths of the *e*,
96: 9 Tremble before him, all the *e*;
96:11 Let the heavens be glad and the *e* rejoice;
96:13 for he comes to rule the *e*.
97: 1 The LORD is king; let the *e* rejoice;
97: 4 the *e* sees and trembles.
97: 5 the LORD, before the Lord of all the *e*.
97: 9 O LORD, are the Most High over all the *e*,
98: 3 the *e* have seen the salvation by our God.

98: 9 for he comes, for he comes to rule the *e;*
99: 1 upon the cherubim; the *e* quakes.
102:16 and all the kings of the *e* your glory,
102:20 holy height, from heaven he beheld the *e,*
102:26 Of old you established the *e,*
103:11 For as the heavens are high above the *e,*
104: 5 You fixed the *e* upon its foundation,
104: 9 not pass, nor shall they cover the *e* again.
104:13 *e* is replete with the fruit of your works.
104:14 for men's use, Producing bread from the *e,*
104:24 the *e* is full of your creatures;
104:30 created, and you renew the face of the *e.*
104:32 He who looks upon the *e,*
104:35 May sinners cease from the *e,*
105: 7 throughout the *e* his judgments prevail.
106:17 The *e* opened and swallowed up Dathan,
108: 6 over all the *e* be your glory!
109:15 the memory of these parents from the *e,*
110: 6 he will crush heads over the wide *e.*
112: 2 His posterity shall be mighty upon the *e;*
113: 6 looks upon the heavens and the *e* below?
114: 7 Before the face of the Lord, tremble, O *e,*
115:15 blessed by the LORD, who made heaven and *e.*
115:16 the *e* he has given to the children of men.
119:19 I am a wayfarer of *e;*
119:64 Of your kindness, O LORD, the *e* is full;
119:87 have all but put an end to me on the *e,*
119:90 you have established the *e,*
119:119 account all the wicked of the *e* as dross;
121: 2 is from the LORD, who made heaven and *e.*
124: 8 name of the LORD, who made heaven and *e.*
134: 3 you from Zion, the maker of heaven and *e.*
135: 6 the LORD wills he does in heaven and on *e,*
135: 7 raises storm clouds from the end of the *e;*
136: 6 Who spread out the *e* upon the waters,
138: 4 kings of the *e* shall give thanks to you,
139:15 I was fashioned in the depths of the *e.*
146: 4 his spirit departs he returns to his *e;*
146: 6 the LORD, his God, Who made heaven and *e,*
147: 8 with clouds, who provides rain for the *e;*
147:15 He sends forth his command to the *e;*
148: 7 Praise the LORD from the *e,*
148:11 Let the kings of the *e* and all peoples,
148:11 the princes and all the judges of the *e,*
148:13 His majesty is above *e* and heaven,

Prv 3:19 The LORD by wisdom founded the *e,*
8:16 all the rulers of *e.*
8:23 poured forth, at the first, before the *e.*
8:26 as yet the *e* and the fields were not made,
8:28 he fixed fast the foundations of the *e;*
8:31 while, playing on the surface of his *e;*
11:31 If the just man is punished on *e,*
17:24 eyes of a fool are on the ends of the *e.*
25: 3 the heavens in height, and the *e* in depth,
30: 4 who has marked out all the ends of the *e?*
30:14 are knives, Devouring the needy from the *e,*
30:16 the *e,* that is never saturated with water,
30:21 Under three things the *e* trembles,
30:24 things are among the smallest on the *e,*

Eccl 5: 1 God is in heaven and you are on *e;*
7:20 on *e* so just as to do good and never sin.
8:14 This is a vanity which occurs on *e:*
8:16 wisdom and to observe what is done on *e,*
11: 2 not what misfortune may come upon the *e.*
11: 3 are full, they pour out rain upon the *e.*
12: 7 the dust returns to the *e* as it once was,

Sg 2:12 The flowers appear on the *e,*

Wis 1: 1 Love justice, you who judge the *e;*
1:14 nor any domain of the nether world on *e,*
5:23 lawlessness shall lay the whole *e* waste
7: 1 a descendant of the first man formed on *e.*
7: 3 common air, and fell upon the kindred *e;*
9:16 And scarce do we guess the things on *e,*
9:18 were the paths of those on *e* made straight,
10: 4 When on his account the *e* was flooded,
11:22 a drop of morning dew come down upon the *e.*
15: 7 potter, laboriously working the soft *e,*
15: 8 was made from the *e* And after a little,
15:10 more worthless than *e* is his hope,
18:16 to heaven, while he stood upon the *e.*

Sir 10: 4 over the *e* is in the hand of God,
10:16 ground, then digs their roots from the *e.*
10:17 and effaces the memory of them from the *e.*
16:16 *e* and the abyss tremble at his visitation;
16:27 Then the LORD looked upon the *e,*
17: 1 The LORD from the *e* created man,
17: 2 gives him and makes him return to *e* again.
17: 3 and with power over all things else on *e.*
23:27 Thus all who dwell on the *e* shall know,
24: 3 I came forth, and mistlike covered the *e.*
33:10 men are of clay, for from *e* man was formed;
36:17 ends of the *e* that you are the eternal God.
37: 3 you created to blanket the *e* with deceit?"
38: 4 God makes the *e* yield healing herbs which
38: 8 in its efficacy on the surface of the *e.*
39:22 Euphrates it enriches the surface of the *e.*
40:11 All that is of earth returns to *e,*
43: 3 At noon it seethes the surface of the *e,*
43:16 thunder of his voice makes the *e* writhe;
44:21 and from the River to the ends of the *e.*
47:15 Your understanding covered the whole *e,*
48:15 of their land and scattered all over the *e.*
49:14 Few on *e* have been made the equal of ENOCH,

50:22 of all, who has done wondrous things on *e;*
51: 9 So I raised my voice from the very *e,*

Is 1: 2 Hear, O heavens, and listen, O *e,*
2:19 in the rocks and into holes in the *e,*
2:19 majesty, when he arises to overawe the *e.*
2:21 majesty, when he arises to overawe the *e.*
4: 2 and the fruit of the *e* will be honor and
5:26 and whistle to them from the ends of the *e;*
6: 3 "All the *e* is filled with his glory!"
6:11 a man, and the *e* is a desolate waste.
8:22 gaze at the *e,* but there shall be distress
10:14 eggs left alone, so I took in all the *e;*
11: 9 for the *e* shall be filled with knowledge
11:12 assemble from the four corners of the *e.*
12: 5 let this be known throughout all the *e.*
13:13 and the *e* shall be shaken from its place,
14: 7 The whole *e* rests peacefully,
14: 9 to greet you, all the leaders of the *e;*
14:16 "Is this the man who made the *e* tremble,
14:21 Lest they rise and possess the *e,*
14:26 This is the plan proposed for the whole *e,*
16: 1 them forth, hugging the *e* like reptiles,
18: 3 you who inhabit the world, who dwell on *e,*
18: 6 them all the beasts of the *e* shall winter.
23:17 the world's kingdoms on the face of the *e.*
24: 3 The *e* is utterly laid waste,
24: 4 The *e* mourns and fades,
24: 4 both heaven and *e* languish.
24: 5 *e* is polluted because of its inhabitants,
24: 6 Therefore a curse devours the *e,*
24: 6 Therefore they who dwell on *e* turn pale,
24:16 From the end of the *e* we hear songs:
24:17 trap are upon you, inhabitant of the *e;*
24:18 and the foundations of the *e* will shake.
24:19 The *e* will burst asunder, the earth will
24:19 be shaken apart, the *e* will be convulsed.
24:20 The *e* will reel like a drunkard,
24:21 and the kings of the *e* on the earth.
25: 8 his people he will remove from the whole *e;*
25:12 raze, and strike it down level with the *e,*
26: 9 When your judgment dawns upon the *e,*
26:18 Salvation we have not achieved for the *e,*
26:21 The *e* will reveal the blood upon her,
28:22 the destruction decreed for the whole *e.*
29: 4 Prostrate you shall speak from the *e,*
29: 4 voice shall be like a ghost's from the *e,*
34: 1 Let the *e* and what fills it listen,
34: 7 with blood, and their *e* greasy with fat.
34: 9 changed into pitch and her *e* into sulphur,
37:16 are God over all the kingdoms of the *e.*
37:16 You have made the heavens and the *e.*
37:20 the kingdoms of the *e* may know that you,
40:12 has held in a measure the dust of the *e,*
40:21 Since the *e* was founded He sits enthroned
40:22 sits enthroned above the vault of the *e,*
40:23 and makes the rulers of the *e* as nothing.
40:24 scarcely is their stem rooted in the *e,*
40:28 eternal God, creator of the ends of the *e.*
41: 5 the ends of the *e* tremble:
41: 9 the *e* and summoned from its far-off places,
41:25 shall trample the rulers down like red *e,*
42: 4 Until he establishes justice on the *e;*
42: 5 out, who spreads out the *e* with its crops,
42:10 new song, his praise from the end of the *e:*
43: 6 and my daughters from the ends of the *e:*
44:23 shout, you depths of the *e.*
44:24 when I spread out the *e,*
45: 8 Let the *e* open and salvation bud forth;
45: 9 a potsherd among potsherds of the *e!*
45:12 who made the *e* and created mankind upon it;
45:18 and maker of the *e* who established it.
45:19 hiding nor from some dark place of the *e,*
45:22 to me and be safe, all you ends of the *e,*
48:13 Yes, my hand laid the foundations of the *e;*
48:20 Publish it to the ends of the *e,*
49: 6 salvation may reach to the ends of the *e.*
49:13 Sing out, O heavens, and rejoice, O *e,*
51: 6 to the heavens, and look at the *e* below;
51: 6 the *e* wears out like a garment and its
51:13 heavens and laid the foundations of the *e?*
51:16 heavens, who laid the foundations of the *e,*
52:10 the *e* will behold the salvation of our God.
53: 2 him, like a shoot from the parched *e;*
54: 5 One of Israel, called God of all the *e.*
54: 9 of Noah should never again deluge the *e;*
55: 9 As high as the heavens are above the *e,*
55:10 return there till they have watered the *e,*
58:14 make you ride on the heights of the *e;*
60: 2 See, darkness covers the *e,*
61:11 As the *e* brings forth its plants,
62: 7 And makes of it the pride of the *e.*
62:11 the LORD proclaims to the ends of the *e:*
65:17 about to create new heavens and a new *e;*
66: 1 are my throne, the *e* is my footstool.
66:22 *e* which I will make Shall endure before me,

Jer 4:20 the whole *e* is laid waste.
4:23 I looked at the *e,*
4:28 Because of this the *e* shall mourn,
6:18 Therefore hear, O nations, and know, O *e,*
6:22 nation, roused from the ends of the *e.*
7:20 trees of the field and the fruits of the *e;*
9:23 kindness justice and uprightness on the *e;*
10:10 King, Before whose anger the *e* quakes,

10:11 make heaven and *e* perish from the earth,
10:12 He who made the *e* by his power,
10:13 he brings up clouds from the end of the *e;*
12: 4 How long must the *e* mourn,
15: 3 beasts of the *e* to devour and destroy them.
15: 4 kingdoms of the *e* because of what Manasseh,
16:19 the nations come from the ends of the *e,*
17: 6 stands in a lava waste, a salt and empty *e.*
23:24 Do I not fill both heaven and *e?*
24: 9 of horror to all the kingdoms of the *e,*
25:26 all the kingdoms upon the face of the *e*
25:29 down the sword upon all who inhabit the *e,*
25:31 the *e* to its very ends the uproar spreads;
25:32 storm is unleashed from the ends of the *e.*
25:33 strewn from one end of the *e* to the other.
26: 6 the *e* shall refer to when cursing another.
27: 5 *e,* and man and beast on the face of the *e*
28:16 will dispatch you from the face of the *e;*
29:18 of horror to all the kingdoms of the *e,*
31:22 LORD has created a new thing upon the *e:*
31:37 or the foundations below the *e* be sounded,
32:17 have made heaven and *e* by your great might,
33: 2 made the *e* and gave it form and firmness,
33: 9 my glory, before all the nations of the *e,*
33:25 and have given no laws to heaven and *e,*
34:17 of horror to all the kingdoms of the *e.*
35: 7 live long on the *e* where you are wayfarers.'
44: 8 a disgrace among all the nations of the *e?*
46: 8 forward," he says, "and cover the *e,*
46:12 hear of your shame, your cries fill the *e.*
49:21 At the noise of their fall the *e* quakes,
50:23 of the whole *e* been broken and shattered!
50:34 with success, and give rest to the *e,*
50:41 mighty kings roused from the ends of the *e.*
50:46 the *e* quakes; the outcry is heard
51: 7 of the LORD which made the whole *e* drunk;
51:15 He has sworn who made the *e* by his power,
51:16 he brings up clouds from the end of the *e;*
51:25 mountain, destroyer of the entire *e,*
51:27 Raise a signal on the *e,*
51:29 The *e* quakes and writhes,
51:48 heaven, and *e,* and everything in them
51:49 Babylon have fallen the slain of all the *e.*

Lam 2: 1 down from heaven to *e* the glory of Israel,
2:15 all-beautiful city, the joy of the whole *e?*"
4:12 The kings of the *e* did not believe,

Bar 1:11 the duration of the heavens above the *e;*
2:15 the whole *e* may know that you are the Lord,
3:16 lorded it over the wild beasts of the *e,*
3:23 The sons of Hagar who seek knowledge on *e,*
3:32 He who established the *e* for all time,
3:38 Since then she has appeared on *e,*
5: 3 For God will show all the *e* your splendor:
6:54 they are like crows between heaven and *e.*

Ez 7:21 spoiled and defiled by the wicked of the *e.*
10:16 lifted their wings to rise from the *e,*
10:19 wings, and I saw them rise from the *e,*
24: 7 she did not pour it out on the *e,*
27:33 you enriched the kings of the *e.*
28:17 I cast you to the *e,*
28:18 *e* in the sight of all who should see you.
29: 5 To the beasts of the *e* and the birds of
32: 4 the beasts of the *e* eat their fill of you.
32:18 thrust them down to the bottom of the *e,*
32:24 down uncircumcised to the bottom of the *e,*
34: 6 my sheep were scattered over the whole *e,*
34:28 nations or devoured by beasts of the *e,*
38: 9 advancing like a cloud to cover the *e,*
38:12 and goods, who dwell at the navel of the *e.*"
43: 2 waters, and the *e* shone with his glory.

Dn 2:10 is not a man on *e* who can do what you ask,
2:35 a great mountain and filled the whole *e.*
2:39 bronze, which shall rule over the whole *e.*
3:74 Let the *e* bless the Lord,
3:76 Everything growing from the *e,*
3:98 every language, wherever they dwell on *e:*
4: 8 and it could be seen to the ends of the *e.*
4:12 But leave in the *e* its stump and roots,
4:12 to eat, among beasts, the grass of the *e.*
4:17 that could be seen by the whole *e,*
4:19 and your rule extends over the whole *e.*
4:20 it, but leave in the *e* its stump and roots,
4:32 who live on the *e* are counted as nothing;
4:32 as well as with those who live on the *e.*
6:26 language, wherever they dwell on the *e:*
6:28 signs and wonders in heaven and on *e,*
7:17 four kingdoms which shall arise on the *e.*
7:23 beast shall be a fourth kingdom on *e,*
7:23 It shall devour the whole *e,*
8: 5 the whole *e* without touching the ground.
8:10 so that it cast down to *e* some of the host
12: 2 who sleep in the dust of the *e* shall awake;
14: 5 and *e* and has dominion over all mankind."

Hos 2:23 heavens, and they shall respond to the *e;*
2:24 The *e* shall respond to the grain,
6: 3 rain, like spring rain that waters the *e.*"

Jl 1:10 The field is ravaged, the *e* mourns,
2:10 Before them the *e* trembles,
3: 3 work wonders in the heavens and on the *e,*
4:16 The heavens and the *e* quake,

Am 2: 7 heads of the weak into the dust of the *e,*
3: 2 more than all the families of the *e;*
3: 5 *e* by a snare when there is no lure for it?

EARTH (cont.)

4:13 and strides upon the heights of the *e*:
5: 8 pours them out upon the surface of the *e*;
8: 9 the *e* with darkness in broad daylight.
9: 5 GOD of hosts, I melt the *e* with my touch,
9: 6 and established my vault over the *e*;
9: 6 and pour them upon the surface of the *e*,
9: 8 destroy it from off the face of the *e*.
Ob 1: 3 your heart, "Who will bring me down to *e*?"
Mi 1: 2 O peoples, all of you, give heed, O *e*,
1: 3 and treads upon the heights of the *e*.
4:13 their riches to the Lord of the whole *e*.
5: 3 greatness shall reach to the ends of the *e*;
6: 2 pay attention, O foundations of the *e*!
7: 2 The faithful are gone from the *e*,
Na 1: 5 The *e* is laid waste before him,
Hb 2:14 But the *e* shall be filled with the
2:20 silence before him, all the *e*!
3: 3 glory, and with his praise the *e* is filled.
3: 6 He pauses to survey the *e*;
3: 9 Into streams you split the *e*;
3:12 In wrath you bestride the *e*,
Zep 1: 2 away all things from the face of the *e*,
1: 3 destroy mankind from the face of the *e*,
1:18 his jealousy all the *e* shall be consumed.
1:18 a sudden end, of all who live on the *e*.
2: 3 Seek the LORD, all you humble of the *e*,
2:11 he makes all the gods of *e* to waste away;
3: 8 of my jealousy shall all the *e* be consumed.
3:19 give them praise and renown in all the *e*,
3:20 praise, among all the peoples of the *e*,
Hg 1:10 from you their dew, and the *e* her crops.
2: 6 and I will shake the heavens and the *e*,
2:21 I will shake the heavens and the *e*;
Zec 1:10 whom the LORD has sent to patrol the *e*."
1:11 patrolled the *e*; see, the whole *e* is tranquil
4:10 of the LORD that range over the whole *e*.
4:14 who stand by the LORD of the whole *e*."
5: 3 which is to go forth over the whole *e*;
6: 5 being reviewed by the Lord of all the *e*."
6: 7 the earth, he said, "Go, patrol the *e*!"
6: 7 Then, as they patrolled the *e*,
9:10 and from the River to the ends of the *e*.
11: 6 I spare the inhabitants of the *e* any more,
11: 6 they shall crush the *e*,
12: 1 heavens, lays the foundations of the *e*,
12: 3 of the *e* shall be gathered against her.
14: 9 LORD shall become king over the whole *e*;
14:17 If any of the families of the *e* does not
Mt 5:13 "You are the salt of the *e*.
5:18 until heaven and *e* pass away,
5:35 nor by the *e* (it is his footstool),
6:10 your will be done on *e* as it is in heaven.
9: 6 Man has authority on *e* to forgive sins"
10:34 that my mission on *e* is to spread peace.
11:25 "Father, Lord of heaven and *e*,
12:40 and three nights in the bowels of the *e*.
12:42 the *e* to listen to the wisdom of Solomon;
16:19 bound on *e* shall be bound in heaven;
16:19 loosed on *e* shall be loosed in heaven."
18:18 bound on *e* shall be held bound in heaven,
18:18 loosed on *e* shall be held loosed in heaven.
18:19 voices on *e* to pray for anything whatever,
23: 9 Do not call anyone on *e* your father.
23:35 all the blood of the just ones shed on *e*,
24:30 and 'all the clans of *e* will strike their
24:35 The heavens and the *e* will pass away but
27:52 The *e* quaked,
28:18 been given to me both in heaven and on *e*;
Mk 2:10 Man has authority on *e* to forgive sins"
13:27 from the farthest bounds of *e* and sky.
13:31 The heavens and the *e* will pass away but
Lk 2:14 on *e* to those on whom his favor rests."
5:24 Man has authority on *e* to forgive sins"
10:21 praise, O Father, Lord of heaven and *e*,
12:49 "I have come to light a fire on the *e*.
12:51 I have come to establish peace on the *e*?
12:56 can interpret the portents of *e* and sky,
16:17 It is easier for the heavens and the *e* to
18: 8 Man comes, will he find any faith on the *e*?"
21:25 On the *e*, nations will be in anguish,
21:26 anticipation of what is coming upon the *e*.
21:33 The heavens and the *e* will pass away,
21:35 upon all who dwell on the face of the *e*.
Jn 3:31 the one who is of the *e* is earthly,
12:24 the grain of wheat falls to the *e* and dies,
12:32 once I am lifted up from *e*—
17: 4 *e* by finishing the work you gave me to do.
Acts 1: 8 Samaria, yes, even to the ends of the *e*."
2:19 the heavens above and signs on the *e* below:
3:25 all the families of the *e* shall be blessed.'
4:24 and *e* and sea and all that is in them,
4:26 The kings of the *e* were aligned,
7:49 are my throne, the *e* is my footstool;
8:33 for he is deprived of his life on *e*?"
11: 6 make out four-legged creatures of the *e*,
13:47 a means of salvation to the ends of the *e*.'"
14:15 and *e* and the sea and all that is in them.'
17:24 that is in it, the Lord of heaven and *e*,
17:26 of mankind to dwell on the face of the *e*.
22:22 Rid the *e* of the likes of him!
Rom 9:17 might be proclaimed throughout all the *e*."
9:28 will the Lord execute sentence upon the *e*."
10:18 voice has sounded over the whole *e*,
1Cor 8: 5 gods in the heavens and on the *e*—
10:26 "The *e* and its fullness are the Lord's."
15:42 What is sown in the *e* is subject to decay,
15:47 The first man was of *e*,
15:48 Earthly men are like the man of *e*,
15:49 Just as we resemble the man from *e*,
Eph 1:10 and on *e* into one under Christ's headship.
3:15 family in heaven and on *e* takes its name;
4: 9 descended into the lower regions of the *e*?
6: 3 and that you may have long life on the *e*."
Phil 2:10 heavens, on the earth, and under the *e*,
Col 1:16 everything in heaven and on *e* was created,
1:20 his person, both on *e* and in the heavens,
3: 2 on things above rather than on things of *e*.
3: 5 whatever in your nature is rooted in *e*;
Heb 1:10 And, "Lord, of old you established the *e*,
8: 4 If he were on *e* he would not be a priest,
11:13 to be strangers and foreigners on the *e*,
11:38 they dwelt in caves and in holes of the *e*.
12:25 to listen as God spoke to them on *e*,
12:26 His voice then shook the *e*,
12:26 will once more shake not only *e* but heaven!"
Jas 5: 5 You lived in wanton luxury on the *e*;
5:12 at all, either "by heaven" or "by *e*."
2Pt 2: 5 he brought down that flood on the godless *e*.
3: 5 there were heavens and an *e* drawn out
3: 7 and *e* are reserved by God's word for fire;
3:10 *e* and all its deeds will be made manifest.
3:13 we await are new heavens and a new *e* where,
Rv 1: 5 from the dead and ruler of the kings of *e*.
1: 7 peoples of the *e* shall lament him bitterly.
3:10 on the whole world, to test all men on *e*.
5: 3 on earth or under the *e* could be found
5:10 our God, and they shall reign on the *e*."
5:13 on earth and under the *e* and in the sea;
6: 4 Its rider was given power to rob the *e* of
6: 8 given authority over one quarter of the *e*,
6: 8 and plague and the wild beasts of the *e*.
6:10 our blood among the inhabitants of the *e*?"
6:13 *e* like figs shaken loose by a mighty wind.
6:15 The kings of the *e*,
7: 1 standing at the four corners of the *e*;
8: 5 the altar, and hurled it down to the *e*.
8: 5 of lightning followed, and the *e* trembled.
8: 7 with blood, which was hurled down to the *e*.
8:13 inhabitants of *e* from the trumpet blasts
9: 1 I saw a star fall from the sky to the *e*.
10: 6 *e* and sea along with everything in them:
11: 4 stand in the presence of the Lord of the *e*.
11: 6 the *e* at will with any kind of plague.
11:10 these two prophets harassed everyone on *e*.
11:18 time to destroy those who lay the *e* waste."
12: 4 from the sky and hurled them down to the *e*.
12: 9 hurled down to *e* and his minions with him.
12:12 But woe to you, *e* and sea,
12:13 saw that he had been cast down to the *e*,
12:16 The *e* then came to the woman's rescue by
13: 8 those inhabitants of *e* who did not have
13:11 another wild beast come up out of the *e*;
13:13 down from heaven to *e* as men looked on.
14: 7 Worship the Creator of heaven and *e*,
14:16 all the *e* and reaped the earth's harvest.
14:18 gather the grapes from the vines of the *e*,
14:19 the earth and gathered the grapes of the *e*.
16: 1 upon the *e* the seven bowls of God's wrath!"
16: 2 and when he poured out his bowl on the *e*,
16:14 assemble all the kings of the *e* for battle
16:18 it in all the time men have lived on the *e*.
17: 2 the *e* have committed fornication with her,
17: 8 All the men of the *e* whose names have not
17:18 has sovereignty over the kings of the *e*."
18: 1 that all the *e* was lighted up by his glory.
18: 3 of the *e* committed fornication with her,
18: 9 The kings of the *e* who committed
18:24 saints and of all who were slain on the *e*."
19: 2 who corrupted the *e* with her harlotry.
19:19 I saw the beast and the kings of the *e*,
20: 8 the nations in all four corners of the *e*,
20:11 The *e* and the sky fled from his presence
21: 1 Then I saw new heavens and a new *e*.
21: 1 heavens and the former *e* had passed away,
21:24 kings of the *e* shall bring their treasures.

EARTHBOUND (1)

Jas 3:15 It is *e*, a kind of animal,

EARTHEN (11)

Lv 14: 5 over an *e* vessel with spring water in it.
14:50 over an *e* vessel with spring water in it.
Nm 5:17 In an *e* vessel he shall meanwhile put some
Ps(s) 2: 9 you shall shatter them like an *e* dish."
Wis 9:15 *e* shelter weighs down the mind
15:13 when out of *e* stuff he creates fragile
Sir 13: 2 can the *e* pot go with the metal cauldron?
Jer 19: 1 Go, buy a potter's *e* flask.
32:14 deed of purchase, and put them in an *e* jar,
Lam 4: 2 than *e* jars made by the hands of a potter!
2Cor 4: 7 This treasure we possess in *e* vessels,

EARTHENWARE (3)

Lv 15:12 *E* touched by the afflicted man shall be
2Sm 17:28 brought couches, coverlets, basins and *e*,
Prv 26:23 on *e* are smooth lips with a wicked heart.

EARTHLY (14)

2Chr 12: 8 me and what it is to serve *e* kingdoms."
Est 4:21 false gods, and to extol an *e* king forever.
Mt 6:19 not lay up for yourselves an *e* treasure.
Lk 22:25 *E* kings lord it over their people.
Jn 3:12 not believe when I tell you about *e* things,
3:31 is earthly, and he speaks on an *e* plane.
1Cor 15:40 are heavenly bodies and there are *e* bodies.
15:40 bodies is one thing, that of the *e* another.
15:48 *E* men are like the man of earth,
2Cor 5: 1 we know that when the *e* tent in which we
Heb 9: 1 regulations for worship and an *e* sanctuary.
12: 9 respected our *e* fathers who corrected us,
1Pt 4: 2 not to spend what remains of your *e* life

EARTHQUAKE (16)

1Kgs 19:11 was an *e*— but the LORD was not in the *e*.
19:12 After the *e* there was fire
Est A: 4 There was noise and tumult, thunder and *e*—
Sir 22:16 with wooden beams is not loosened by an *e*;
Is 29: 6 by the LORD of hosts, With thunder, *e*,
Am 1: 1 king of Israel, two years before the *e*:
Zec 14: 5 the *e* in the days of King Uzziah of Judah.
Mt 27:54 at seeing the *e* and all that was happening,
28: 2 Suddenly there was a mighty *e* as the angel
Acts 16:26 a severe *e* suddenly shook the place,
Rv 6:12 the sixth seal, there was a violent *e*;
11:13 *e* and a tenth of the city fell in ruins.
11:13 thousand persons were killed during the *e*;
11:19 of lightning and peals of thunder, an *e*,
16:18 and peals of thunder, then a violent *e*.

EARTHQUAKES (3)

Mt 24: 7 famine and pestilence and *e* in many places.
Mk 13: 8 There will be *e* in various places and
Lk 21:11 There will be great *e*,

EARTH'S (17)

Ps(s) 61: 3 From the *e* end I call to you as my heart
65: 9 at the *e* ends are in fear at your marvels;
Wis 6: 1 learn, you magistrates of the *e* expanse!
Sir 1: 3 Heaven's height, *e* breadth,
16:17 roots of the mountains, the *e* foundations,
Is 23: 8 whose traders are the *e* honored men?
23: 9 majesty, to degrade all the *e* honored men.
26:21 punish the wickedness of the *e* inhabitants;
Jer 34: 1 armies and the *e* kingdoms subject to him,
Mk 4:31 soil, is the smallest of all the *e* seeds,
Acts 10:12 Inside it were all the *e* four-legged
Rv 7: 1 they held in check the *e* four winds so
11:10 The *e* inhabitants gloat over them and in
13:14 beast, it led astray the *e* inhabitants,
14:15 the *e* harvest is fully ripe."
14:16 all the earth and reaped the *e* harvest.
17: 2 and the *e* inhabitants have grown drunk on

EARTHWARD (1)

Eccl 3:21 and the life-breath of beasts goes *e*?

EARTHWORKS (2)

2Mc 12:13 fortified with *e* and ramparts and
Is 29: 7 Ariel with all the *e* of her besiegers.

EASE (13)

Gn 43:23 "Be at *e*," he replied;
Ex 31:17 but on the seventh day he rested at his *e*."
Dt 23:14 with it, when you go outside to *e* nature,
1Sm 24: 4 found a cave, which he entered to *e* nature.
2Kgs 8:11 him down until Hazael became ill at *e*.
Jb 3:18 There the captives are at *e* together,
3:26 I have no peace nor *e*;
7:13 comfort me, my couch shall *e* my complaint,"
21:23 in his full vigor, wholly at *e* and content;
Sir 32:11 There take your *e*, And there enjoy
Lam 1: 5 foes are uppermost, her enemies are at *e*;
Mk 14:41 Still taking your *e*?
1Cor 16:10 come, be sure to put him at *e* among you.

EASED (1)

Is 1: 6 not drained, or bandaged, or *e* with salve.

EASES (1)

Sir 38: 7 Through which the doctor *e* pain and the

EASIER (11)

Sir 22:15 iron mass are *e* to bear than a stupid man.
Mt 10:15 it will go *e* for the region of Sodom and
11:22 it will go *e* for Tyre and Sidon than for
11:24 it will go *e* for Sodom than for you on the
19:24 it is *e* for a camel to pass through a
Mk 2: 9 Which is *e*, to say to the paralytic,
10:25 It is *e* for a camel to pass through a
Lk 5:23 Which is *e*: to say your sins are forgiven

10:14 It will go *e* on the day of judgment for
16:17 It is *e* for the heavens and the earth to
18:25 it is *e* for a camel to go through a

EASILY (6)

Lv 14:22 or pigeons, which he can more *e* afford,
Jb 4:19 dust, who are crushed more *e* than the moth!
Eccl 4:12 A three-ply cord is not *e* broken.
Jer 13:23 As *e* would you be able to do good,
Acts 5:36 been so *e* convinced by him were disbanded.
2Thes 2: 2 not to be so *e* agitated or terrified,

EASING (1)

Jgs 3:24 "He must be *e* himself in the cool chamber."

EAST (145)

Gn 2: 8 God planted a garden in Eden, in the *e*,
2:14 it is the one that flows *e* of Asshur.
3:24 he settled him *e* of the garden of Eden;
4:16 and settled in the land of Nod, *e* of Eden.
11: 2 While men were migrating in the *e*,
12: 8 moved on to the hill country *e* of Bethel,
12: 8 with Bethel to the west and Ai to the *e*.
13:14 gaze to the north and south, *e* and west;
28:14 them you shall spread out *e* and west,
41: 6 of grain, thin and blasted by the *e* wind;
41:23 and thin and blasted by the *e* wind,
Ex 10:13 and the LORD set an *e* wind blowing over
10:13 At dawn the *e* wind brought the locusts.
14:21 LORD swept the sea with a strong *e* wind
27:13 court on the *e* side shall be fifty cubits.
38:13 the *e* side the court was fifty cubits long.
Lv 1:16 on the ash heap at the *e* side of the altar.
Nm 2: 3 "Encamped on the *e* side,
3:38 *E* of the Dwelling,
10: 6 those encamped on the *e* side shall set out;
21:11 in the desert fronting Moab on the *e*.
34: 3 on the *e* it shall begin at the end of the
34:11 shall go down to Ar-Baal, *e* of Ain,
34:11 ridge on the *e* side of Sea of Chinnereth;
35: 5 cubits outside the city along each side *e*,
Dt 3:27 the north, and to the south, and to the *e*.
4:41 three cities in the region *e* of the Jordan,
4:47 the Amorites in the region *e* of the Jordan:
4:49 Hermon) and all the Arabah *e* of the Jordan,
Jos 1: 4 Lebanon *e* to the great river Euphrates
1:15 of the LORD, has given you *e* of the Jordan."
11: 3 These were Canaanites to the *e* and west,
12: 1 The kings of the land *e* of the Jordan,
13: 5 and all the Lebanon on the *e*,
13: 8 the LORD, had given them *e* of the Jordan:
13:32 of Moab, beyond the Jordan *e* of Jericho.
16: 1 to the waters of Jericho *e* of the desert;
16: 5 Ephraimites ran from *e* of Ataroth-addar
16: 6 and continued *e* of it to Janoah;
17:10 Asher on the north and Issachar on the *e*.
18: 7 the heritage *e* of the Jordan which Moses,
18:20 The Jordan bounded it on the *e*.
19:34 Asher on the west, and the Jordan on the *e*.
20: 8 And beyond the Jordan *e* of Jericho they
24: 8 of the Amorites who lived *e* of the Jordan.
Jgs 8:11 of the nomads *e* of Nobah and Jogbehah,
11:18 went *e* of the land of Moab and encamped
20:43 were now pursued to a point *e* of Gibeah,
21:19 *e* of the highway that goes up from Bethel
1Sm 13: 5 they encamped in Michmash, *e* of Beth-aven.
2Sm 2:24 hill of Ammah which lies *e* of the valley
1Kgs 7:25 three facing south, and three facing *e*,
17: 3 go *e* and hide in the Wadi Cherith, east
17: 5 by the Wadi Cherith, *e* of the Jordan.
2Kgs 10:33 *e* of the Jordan (all the land of Gilead,
13:17 and said, "Open the window toward the *e*."
23:13 defiled the high places *e* of Jerusalem,
1Chr 4:39 the approaches of Gedor, *e* of the valley,
5: 9 toward the *e* they dwelt as far as the
5:10 tents throughout the region *e* of Gilead.
6:63 *e* of the Jordan] they received from the
7:28 Naaran to the *e*,
9:18 guard at the king's gate on the *e* side;
9:24 were stationed at the four sides, to the *e*,
12:16 in the valleys to the *e* and to the west.
26:14 When the lot was cast for the *e* side,
26:17 On the *e*, six watched each day,
2Chr 4: 4 three west, three south, and three *e*,
5:12 harps and lyres, stood *e* of the altar,
29: 4 gathered them in the open space to the *e*,
Neh 3:26 a point opposite the Water Gate on the *e*,
3:29 son of Shecaniah, keeper of the *E* Gate.
12:37 until they came to the Water Gate on the *e*.
Jdt 7:18 to the south and to the *e* opposite Egrebel,
1Mc 12:37 the *e* wall above the ravine had collapsed.
Jb 1: 3 was greater than any of the men of the *E*.
23: 8 But if I go to the *e*,
38:24 whence the *e* wind spreads over the earth?
Ps(s) 48: 8 the *e* were shattering ships of Tarshish.
65: 9 *e* and west you make resound with joy.
75: 7 For neither from the *e* nor from the west,
78:26 He stirred up the *e* wind in the heavens,
103:12 As far as the *e* is from the west,
107: 3 from the lands, from the *e* and the west,
Is 9:11 Aram on the *e* and the Philistines on the
41: 2 up from the *E* the champion of justice,
41:25 from the *e* I summon him by name;
43: 5 the *e* I will bring back your descendants,
46:11 I call from the *e* a bird of prey,
59:19 the name of the LORD, and those in the *e*,
Jer 18:17 Like the *e* wind, I will scatter them
31:40 as the corner of the Horse Gate at the *e*,
Bar 4:36 Look to the *e*, Jerusalem!
4:37 gathered in from the *e* and from the west
5: 5 look to the *e* and see your children
5: 5 Gathered from the *e* and the west
Ez 8:16 LORD's temple and their faces toward the *e*;
11: 1 and brought me to the *e* gate of the temple.
11:23 the mountain which is to the *e* of the city.
17:10 rather wither, when touched by the *e* wind,
19:12 The *e* wind withered her up,
27:26 *e* wind smashed you in the heart of the sea.
39:11 *e* of the sea [it is blocked to travelers].
40: 6 he went to the gate which faced the *e*,
40:10 of the *e* gate were three on either side,
40:22 as those of the gate facing the *e*.
40:23 the north gate, just as at the *e* gate;
40:32 he brought me to the gate facing the *e*,
41:14 along with the free area, on the *e* side,
42: 9 chambers there was the way in from the *e*,
42:12 wall, by which one could enter from the *e*.
42:15 *e* and measured all the limits of the court.
42:16 He measured the *e* side:
43: 1 he led me to the gate which faces the *e*,
43: 2 of the God of Israel coming from the *e*.
43: 4 by way of the gate which faces the *e*,
43:17 The steps of the altar face the *e*.
44: 1 outer gate of the sanctuary, facing the *e*;
46: 1 The gate toward the *e* of the inner court
47: 1 the threshold of the temple toward the *e*,
47: 1 the façade of the temple was toward the *e*;
47: 2 and around to the outer gate facing the *e*,
47: 3 to the *e* with a measuring cord in his hand,
48:10 on the west, ten thousand on the *e*,
48:16 the *e* side, forty-five hundred cubits;
48:17 cubits, *e* two hundred and fifty cubits,
48:18 to the *e* and ten thousand to the west,
48:32 On the *e* side, measuring forty-five hundred
Dn 8: 9 which kept growing toward the south, the *e*,
11:44 from the *e* and the north terrifies him,
Hos 13:15 among his fellows, an *e* wind shall come,
Am 8:12 to the *e* In search of the word of the LORD,
Jon 4: 5 left the city for a place to the *e* of it,
4: 8 the sun arose, God sent a burning *e* wind;
Zec 14: 4 which is opposite Jerusalem to the *e*.
14: 4 two from *e* to west by a very deep valley,
Mt 2: 1 *e* arrived one day in Jerusalem inquiring,
8:11 Many will come from the *e* and the west and
24:27 lightning from the *e* flashes to the west,
Mk 16:20 Jesus himself sent out from *e* to west
Lk 13:29 People will come from the *e* and the west,
Rv 7: 2 the *e* holding the seal of the living God.
16:12 to prepare the way for the kings of the *E*.
21:13 There were three gates facing *e*,

EASTERN (38)

Gn 10:30 all the way to Sephar, the *e* hill country.
Nm 23: 7 me here, Moab's king, from the *E* Mountains:
32:19 for ourselves on this *e* side of the Jordan."
34:10 "For your *e* boundary you shall draw a
34:15 their heritage on the *e* side of the Jericho
Dt 3:17 Jordan and its *e* banks from Chinnereth
Jos 4:19 in Gilgal on the *e* limits of Jericho.
7: 2 to Ai, which is near Bethel on its *e* side,
12: 1 including all the *e* section of the
12: 3 from the *e* side of the Sea of Chinnereth,
12: 3 as far south as the *e* side of the Salt Sea
15: 5 The *e* boundary was the Salt Sea as far as
2Chr 31:14 a Levite and the keeper of the *e* gate,
Ez 10:19 entrance of the *e* gate of the LORD's house,
45: 7 western side and eastward on the *e* side,
45: 7 boundary to the *e* boundary of the land.
46:12 the *e* gate shall be opened for him,
47: 8 into the *e* district down upon the Arabah,
47:18 The *e* boundary:
47:18 boundary down to the *e* sea as far as Tamar.
47:18 This is the *e* boundary.
48: 1 from the *e* to the western boundary.
48: 2 of Dan, from the *e* to the western boundary.
48: 3 Asher, from the *e* to the western boundary.
48: 4 from the *e* to the western boundary.
48: 5 from the *e* to the western boundary.
48: 6 from the *e* to the western boundary.
48: 7 Reuben, from the *e* to the western boundary.
48: 8 from the *e* to the western boundary there
48: 8 from the *e* to the western boundary.
48:21 line eastward to the *e* boundary,
48:23 from the *e* to the western boundary.
48:24 from the *e* to the western boundary.
48:25 Simeon, from the *e* to the western boundary.
48:26 from the *e* to the western boundary.
48:27 from the *e* to the western boundary.
Jl 2:20 and waste, With his van toward the *e* sea,
Zec 14: 8 flow from Jerusalem, half to the *e* sea,

EASTERNERS (4)

Gn 29: 1 his journey he came to the land of the *E*.
Jer 49:28 Rise up, attack Kedar, ravage the *E*.
Ez 25: 4 deliver you into the possession of the *E*.
25:10 Ammonites, into the possession of the *E*,

EASTWARD (9)

Gn 13:11 the whole Jordan Plain and set out *e*.
25: 6 was still living, as he sent them away *e*,
Jos 11: 8 and *e* to the valley of Mizpeh.
16: 6 boundary curved *e* around Taanath-shiloh,
19:12 *e* it ran to the district of Chisloth-tabor,
19:13 *e* to Gath-hepher and to Eth-kazin,
19:27 other direction, it ran *e* of Beth-dagon,
Ez 45: 7 the western side and *e* on the eastern side,
48:21 line *e* to the eastern boundary,

EASY (14)

1Sm 18:23 think it *e* to become the king's son-in-law?
2Kgs 2:10 "You have asked something that is not *e*,"
5:20 master was too *e* with this Aramean Naaman,
20:10 is *e* for the shadow to advance ten steps,"
Jdt 4: 7 be *e* to ward off the attacking forces,
7:10 *e* to reach the summit of their mountains.
1Mc 3:18 "It is *e* for many to be overcome by a few;
2Mc 2:25 as well as to make it *e* for the studious
2:26 this digest, the task, far from being *e*,
Prv 14: 6 knowledge is *e* to the man of intelligence.
Eccl 10:10 dull, though at first he made *e* progress,
Sir 11:21 For it is *e* with the LORD suddenly,
11:26 For it is *e* with the LORD on the day of
Mt 11:30 rest, for my yoke is *e* and my burden light."

EAT (449)

Gn 2:16 "You are free to *e* from any of the trees
2:17 you shall not *e*; the moment you eat from it
3: 1 to *e* from any of the trees in the garden?"
3: 2 *e* of the fruit of the trees in the garden;
3: 3 said, 'You shall not *e* it or even touch it,
3: 5 God knows well that the moment you *e* of it
3:11 the tree of which I had forbidden you to *e*!"
3:14 dirt shall you *e* all the days of your life.
3:17 the tree of which I had forbidden you to *e*,
3:17 you *e* its yield all the days of your life.
3:18 you, as you *e* of the plants of the field.
3:19 of your face shall you get bread to *e*,
3:22 also, and thus *e* of it and live forever."
9: 3 that is alive shall be yours to *e*;
9: 4 its lifeblood still in it you shall not *e*.
24:33 "I will not *e* until I have told my tale."
27: 4 such as I like, and bring it to me to *e*,
27: 7 it prepare an appetizing dish for me to *e*,
27:10 Then bring it to your father to *e*,
27:19 Please sit up and *e* some of my game,
27:25 may *e* of it and then give you my blessing."
27:31 father, *e* some of your son's game,
28:20 me enough bread to *e* and clothing to wear,
32:33 the Israelites do not *e* the sciatic muscle
43:32 (Egyptians may not *e* with Hebrews;
Ex 2:20 Invite him to have something to *e*."
10: 5 They shall *e* up the remnant you saved
10:12 locusts may swarm over it and *e* up all
12: 8 That same night they shall *e* its roasted
12:11 "This is how you are to *e* it:
12:11 you shall *e* like those who are in flight.
12:15 For seven days you must *e* unleavened bread.
12:18 of this month you shall *e* unleavened bread.
12:20 may you *e*; wherever you dwell you may *e*
13: 6 seven days you shall *e* unleavened bread,
16: 8 LORD gives you flesh to *e* in the evening,"
16:12 In the evening twilight you shall *e* flesh,
16:15 bread which the LORD has given you to *e*.
16:16 gather it that everyone has enough to *e*,
16:18 so gathered that everyone had enough to *e*.
16:21 gathered it, till each had enough to *e*;
16:25 Moses then said, *E* it today,
16:32 see what food I gave you to *e* in the desert
22:30 to pieces in the field you shall not *e*;
23:11 *e* of it and the beasts of the field may *e*
23:15 you must *e* unleavened bread for seven days
24:11 on God, they could still *e* and drink.
29:32 his sons shall *e* the flesh of the ram
29:33 They themselves are to *e* of these things
29:33 but no layman may *e* of them,
32: 6 Then they sat down to *e* and drink,
34:18 of Abib you are to *e* unleavened bread,
Lv 6: 9 The rest of it Aaron and his sons may *e*;
6: 9 court of the meeting tent they shall *e* it.
7:23 not *e* the fat of any ox or sheep or goat.
7:24 be put to any other use, you may not *e* it.
8:31 and there *e* it with the bread that is in
8:31 'Aaron and his sons shall *e* of it.'
10:12 and *e* it beside the altar in the form of
10:13 sacred, you must *e* it in a sacred place.
10:14 shall also *e* the breast of the wave offering
10:17 not *e* the sin offering in the sacred place,
11: 2 land animals these are the ones you may *e*:
11: 3 any animal that has hoofs you may *e*,
11: 4 But you shall not *e* any of the following
11: 8 Their flesh you shall not *e*,
11: 9 live in the water, you may *e* the following:
11: 9 waters has both fins and scales you may *e*.
11:11 Their flesh you shall not *e*,

EAT (cont.)

11:21 you may e those that have jointed legs
11:22 hence of these you may e the following:
11:39 of the animals that you could otherwise e,
11:42 legs, you shall e no swarming creature:
19:25 until the fifth year may you e its fruit.
19:26 "Do not e meat with the blood still in it.
22: 4 a flow, may e of these sacred offerings,
22: 6 may not e of the sacred portions until
22: 7 Only then may he e of the sacred offerings
22:10 hired servant may e of any sacred offering.
22:11 who is born in his house may e of his food.
22:12 may not e of the sacred contributions.
22:13 e of her father's food as in her youth.
22:13 No layman, however, may e of it.
23: 6 seven days you shall e unleavened bread.
23:14 you shall not e any bread or roasted grain
24: 9 his sons, who must e it in a sacred place,
25:12 for you, you may not e of its produce,
25:20 say, 'What shall we e in the seventh year,
25:22 you will continue to e from the old crop;
25:22 in, you will still have the old to e from.
26: 5 and you will have food to e in abundance,
26:29 e the flesh of your own sons and daughters.
Nm 6: 3 juice, nor e either fresh or dried grapes.
6: 4 not e anything of the produce of the vine;
11: 5 fish we used to e without cost in Egypt,
11:18 tomorrow, when you shall have meat to e.
11:19 give you meat for food, and you will e it,
11:21 will give them meat to e for a whole month.'
15:19 and begin to e of the food of that land,
18:31 as well as you, may e them anywhere,
Dt 2: 6 food you e and the well water you drink.
2:28 For the food I e which you will supply,
4:28 neither see nor hear, neither e nor smell.
6:11 and when, therefore, you e your fill,
8: 9 a land where you can e bread without stint
11:15 Thus you may e your fill.
12: 7 you and your families shall e and make
12:15 may slaughter and e to your heart's desire
12:15 the unclean as well as the clean may e it,
12:18 These you must e before the LORD,
12:20 wish meat for food, you may e it at will,
12:21 and e it to your heart's desire in your
12:22 e it as you would the gazelle or the deer:
14: 3 "You shall not e any abominable thing.
14: 4 These are the animals you may e:
14: 6 Any animal that has hoofs you may e,
14: 7 But you shall not e any of the following
14: 8 Their flesh you shall not e,
14: 9 has both fins and scales you may e,
14:10 lack either fins or scales you shall not e,
14:11 "You may e all clean birds.
14:12 But you shall not e any of the following:
14:20 But you may e any clean winged creatures.
14:21 not e any animal that has died of itself,
14:21 belongs to your community, and he may e it,
14:23 e in his presence your tithe of the grain,
14:29 your community, may come and e their fill;
15:20 your family shall e them before the LORD,
15:22 but in your own communities you may e it,
16: 3 You shall not e leavened bread with it.
16: 3 you shall e with it only unleavened bread,
16: 7 shall cook and e it at the place the LORD,
16: 8 For six days you shall e unleavened bread,
18: 8 receive the same portions to e as the rest,
20:19 You may e their fruit,
23:25 may e as many of his grapes as you wish,
26:12 may e their fill in your own community,
27: 7 sacrifice peace offerings and e them there,
28:31 your eyes, and you will not e of its flesh.
28:39 wine, for the grubs will e the vines clean.
28:53 you, you will e the fruit of your womb,
Jgs 13: 4 or strong drink and to e nothing unclean.
13: 7 nor strong drink, and e nothing unclean.
13:14 not e anything that comes from the vine,
13:14 or strong drink, nor e anything unclean.
14: 9 father and mother, he gave them some to e,
1Sm 1: 7 her, and Hannah would weep and refuse to e.
1: 8 do you weep, and why do you refuse to e?
2:36 that I may have a morsel of bread to e.'"
9:13 before he goes up to the high place to e.
9:13 The people will not e until he arrives;
9:13 the sacrifice will the invited guests e.
9:19 me to the high place and e with me today.
9:24 E, for it was kept for you until your
14:34 Slaughter it here and then e,
21: 5 from women, you may e some of that."
28:22 Let me set something before you to e,
28:23 But he refused, saying, "I will not e."
2Sm 3:35 I e bread or anything else before sunset."
9: 7 Saul, and you shall always e at my table."
9:10 shall be food for your lord's family to e.
9:10 lord's son, shall always e at my table."
11:11 e and to drink and to sleep with my wife?
13: 5 for me to see, I will e it from her hand.'"
13: 9 But Amnon would not e;
13:11 But when she brought them to him to e,
16: 2 summer fruits are for your servants to e,
17:29 David and those who were with him to e;
19:43 we had anything to e at the king's expense?
1Kgs 2: 7 Gileadite, and have them e at your table.
13: 8 nor e bread or drink water in this place.
13: 9 LORD not to e bread or drink water
13:16 and I cannot e bread or drink water with
13:17 neither to e bread nor drink water here,
13:18 and to have you e bread and drink water."
17:15 She was able to e for a year,
18:19 of Asherah who e at Jezebel's table."
18:41 then said to Ahab, "Go up, e and drink,
18:42 So Ahab went up to e and drink,
19: 5 him and ordered him to get up and e.
19: 7 touched him, and ordered, "Get up and e,
19:21 flesh, and gave it to his people to e.
21: 4 he turned away from food and would not e.
21: 5 "Why are you so angry that you will not e?"
21: 7 E and be cheerful.
2Kgs 4:40 And they could not e it.
4:40 men to eat, but when they began to e it,
4:41 and said, "Serve it to the people to e."
4:42 "Give it to the people to e,"
4:43 "Give it to the people to e,"
4:43 shall e and there shall be some left over.'"
6:22 Let them e and drink,
6:28 'Give up your son that we may e him today;
6:28 then tomorrow we will e my son.'
6:29 'Now give up your son that we may e him.'
7: 2 Elisha said, "but you shall not e of it."
7:19 your own eyes, but you shall not e of it."
9:36 Jezreel dogs shall e the flesh of Jezebel.
18:27 will have to e their own excrement and
18:31 e of his own vine and of his own fig-tree,
19:29 this year you shall e the aftergrowth,
19:29 reap, plant vineyards and e their fruit!
Neh 5: 2 order to get grain to e that we may live."
8:10 "Go e rich foods and drink sweet drinks,
8:12 Then all the people went to e and drink,
9:25 They could e and have their fill,
9:36 they might e its fruits and good things
Tb 2: 1 was prepared for me, and I reclined to e.
2:13 owners, we have no right to e stolen food!"
7: 9 When they had bathed and reclined to e,
7:10 E and drink and be merry tonight,
7:11 But now, son, e and drink.
7:11 "I will e or drink nothing until you set
7:14 Afterward they began to e and drink.
12:19 Even though you watched me e and drink,
Jdt 11:12 which God in his laws forbade them to e.
12: 1 delicacies to e and his own wine to drink.
12:11 care to come and to e and drink with us.
1Mc 1:62 in their hearts not to e anything unclean;
2Mc 5:27 continuing to e what grew wild to avoid
6:18 being forced to open his mouth to e pork.
6:21 such as he could legitimately e,
7: 1 them to e pork in violation of God's law.
7: 7 "Will you e the pork rather than have
Jb 1: 4 three sisters to e and drink with them.
5: 5 they have reaped the hungry shall e up;
31: 8 hands, Then may I sow, but another e of it,
Ps(s) 14: 4 who e up my people just as they e bread?
22:27 The lowly shall e their fill;
50:13 Do I e the flesh of strong bulls,
53: 5 who e up my people just as they eat bread,
53: 5 who eat up my people just as they e bread,
102: 5 I forget to e my bread.
102:10 For I e ashes like bread and mingle my
127: 2 your rest, You that e hard-earned bread,
128: 2 you shall e the fruit of your handiwork;
Prv 1:31 they must e the fruit of their own way,
4:17 For they e the bread of wickedness and
9: 5 understanding, I say, Come, e of my food,
18:21 who make it a friend shall e its fruit.
23: 7 E and drink," he says to you,
23:20 nor with those who e meat to excess;
24:13 If you e honey, my son,
25:16 If you find honey, e only what you need,
25:21 your enemy be hungry, give him food to e,
25:27 To e too much honey is not good;
Eccl 2:24 There is nothing better for man than to e
2:25 For who can e or drink apart from him?
3:13 to e and drink and enjoy the fruit of all
5:17 it is well for a man to e and drink and
9: 7 e your bread with joy and drink your wine
Sg 4:16 to his garden and e its choice fruits.
5: 1 my spices, I e my honey and my sweetmeats,
5: 1 E, friends; drink! Drink freely of love.
Sir 6: 3 Your leaves it will e,
6:20 little, and soon you will e of her fruits.
20:16 Those who e his bread have an evil tongue.
29:26 the table, give me to e the food you have!
30:18 Dainties set before one who cannot e are
Is 1:19 you shall e the good things of the land;
3:10 them, the fruit of their works they will e.
4: 1 e our own food and wear our own clothing;
5:17 and kids shall e in the ruins of the rich.
9:19 though they e on the left,
11: 7 the lion shall e hay like the ox.
14:30 In my pastures the poor shall e,
21: 5 they e, they drink.
22:13 butcher sheep, You e meat and drink wine:
22:13 E and drink, for tomorrow we die!"
23:18 dwell before the LORD shall e their fill
30:24 asses that till the ground will e silage
36:12 will have to e their own excrement and
36:16 e of his own vine and of his own fig tree,
37:30 this year you shall e the aftergrowth,
37:30 reap, plant vineyards and e their fruit!
49:26 make your oppressors e their own flesh,
50: 9 out like cloth, the moth will e them up.
55: 1 have no money, come, receive grain and e;
55: 2 Heed me, and you shall e well,
56: 9 you wild beasts of the field, come and e,
61: 6 You shall e the wealth of the nations and
62: 9 But you who harvest the grain shall e it,
65:13 Lo, my servants shall e,
65:21 e the fruit of the vineyards they plant;
65:22 to live in, or plant for others to e.
65:25 and the lion shall e hay like the ox [but
66:17 stands within, they who e swine's flesh,
Jer 2: 7 the garden land to e its goodly fruits,
7:21 e up the flesh!
9:14 them wormwood to e and poison to drink.
12: 9 all you beasts of the field, come and e!
19: 9 e the flesh of their sons and daughters;
19: 9 they shall e one another's flesh during
22:15 Did not your father e and drink?
23:15 Behold, I will give them wormwood to e,
29: 5 plant gardens, and e their fruits.
29:28 plant gardens and e their fruits. . . ."
44:17 had enough food to e and we were well off;
Lam 2:20 Must women e their offspring,
Bar 2: 3 e the flesh of his son or of his daughter.
Ez 2: 8 your mouth and e what I shall give you.
3: 1 Son of man, e what is before you;
3: 1 e this scroll, then go, speak to the house
3: 2 mouth and he gave me the scroll to e.
4: 9 E it for as many days as you lie upon your
4:10 e shall be twenty shekels a day by weight;
4:13 Thus the Israelites shall e their food
4:16 They shall e bread which they have weighed
5:10 means that fathers within you shall e sons,
5:10 shall eat sons, and sons shall e fathers.
12:18 Son of man, e your bread trembling,
12:19 They shall e their bread in anxiety and
18: 6 just, if he does not e on the mountains,
18:15 a son who does not e on the mountains,
24:17 beard, and do not e the customary bread.
25: 4 shall e your fruits and drink your milk.
32: 4 beasts of the earth e their fill of you.
33:25 You e on the mountains,
39:17 shall have flesh to e and blood to drink.
39:18 You shall e the flesh of warriors and
39:19 you shall e fat until you are filled and
42:13 to the LORD shall e the most sacred meals,
44: 3 to e his meal in the presence of the LORD.
44:29 They shall e the cereal offering,
44:31 The priests shall not e anything,
Dn 1:12 Give us vegetables to e and water to drink.
1:13 other young men who e from the royal table,
4:12 his lot be to e, among beasts,
4:22 you shall be given grass to e like an ox
4:29 you shall be given grass to e like an ox,
6:19 to e and he dismissed the entertainers.
14:39 While Daniel began to e,
Hos 4:10 They shall e but not be satisfied,
8:13 offer sacrifice, immolate flesh and e it,
9: 3 and in Assyria they shall e unclean food.
9: 4 bread, that makes unclean all who e of it;
Jl 2:26 You shall e and be filled,
Am 6: 4 couches, They e lambs taken from the flock,
9:14 the wine, set out gardens and e the fruits.
Ob 1: 7 who e your bread lay snares beneath you:
Jon 3: 7 they shall not e, nor shall they drink water
Mi 3: 3 They e the flesh of my people,
6:14 You shall e, without being satisfied,
7: 1 There is no cluster to e,
Zec 11:16 he will e the flesh of the fat ones and
Mt 6:25 you are to e or drink or use for clothing.
6:31 over questions like, 'What are we to e,
12: 1 to pull off the heads of grain and e them.
14:16 Give them something to e yourselves."
15:27 "even the dogs e the leavings that fall
15:32 with me three days, and have nothing to e.
24:49 servants, to e and drink with drunkards,
26:26 "Take this and e it,"
Mk 2:15 Jesus was reclining to e in Levi's house,
2:16 "Why does he e with such as these?"
2:26 which only the priests were permitted to e?
5:43 and told them to give her something to e.
6:31 it impossible for them to so much as e.
6:36 here and buy themselves something to e?"
6:37 "You give them something to e,"
7: 3 e without scrupulously washing their hands.
7: 4 they never e anything from the market
7:28 under the table e the family's leavings."
8: 1 and they were without anything to e.
8: 2 with me three days and have nothing to e.
11:14 "Never again shall anyone e of your fruit!"
14:14 I may e the Passover with my disciples?'
Lk 5:30 "Why do you e and drink with tax
5:33 Yours, on the contrary, e and drink freely."
6: 4 though only priests are allowed to e it?"
7:25 those who dress in luxury and e in
7:36 to the Pharisee's home and reclined to e.
8:55 he told them to give her something to e.
9:13 not give them something to e yourselves?"
10: 8 welcome you, e what they set before you,
12:19 E heartily, drink well.
12:22 for your life, what you are to e,

12:29 be in search of what you are to *e* or drink.
12:45 girls, to *e* and drink and get drunk,
14: 1 When Jesus came on a sabbath to *e* a meal
15:17 father's place have more than enough to *e*,
15:23 Let us *e* and celebrate because this son
16:21 Lazarus longed to *e* the scraps that fell
17: 8 apron and wait on me while I *e* and drink.
17: 8 You can *e* and drink afterward'?
22:11 I may *e* the Passover with my disciples?'
22:15 *e* this Passover with you before I suffer.
22:16 I will not *e* again until it is fulfilled
22:30 kingdom you will *e* and drink at my table,
24:30 When he had seated himself with them to *e*,
24:41 to them, "Have you anything here to *e*?"
Jn 4:31 were urging him, "Rabbi, *e* something."
4:32 have food to *e* of which you do not know."
4:33 someone has brought him something to *e*?"
6: 5 shall we buy bread for these people to *e*?"
6:31 Our ancestors had manna to *e* in the desert;
6:31 'He gave them bread from the heavens to *e*.' "
6:50 from heaven for a man to *e* and never die.
6:52 "How can he give us his flesh to *e*?"
6:53 if you do not *e* the flesh of the Son of
18:28 if they were to *e* the Passover supper.
21: 5 "Children, have you caught anything to *e*?"
21:12 "Come and *e* your meal," Jesus told them.
Acts 10:13 "Get up, Peter! Slaughter, then *e*."
11: 7 'Get up, Peter! Slaughter, then *e*.'
23:12 to *e* or drink until they had killed Paul.
23:21 oath not to *e* or drink until they kill him.
27:35 all of them, broke it, and began to *e*.
27:36 courage, and they too had something to *e*.
27:38 When they had had enough to *e*,
Rom 14: 2 man of sound faith knows he can *e* anything,
14: 3 The man who will *e* anything must not
14: 6 who does not *e* abstains to honor the Lord,
14:15 *e* bring to ruin him for whom Christ died:
14:20 God's work for the sake of something to *e*.
14:20 to *e* when the food offends his conscience.
1Cor 5:11 clear that you must not *e* with such a man.
8: 7 so recently devoted to idols, they *e* meat,
8: 8 We suffer no loss through failing to *e*,
8:13 brother to sin I will never *e* meat again,
9: 4 Do we not have the right to *e* and drink?
9: 7 a vineyard and does not *e* of its yield?
10: 7 says, "The people sat down to *e* and drink,
10:18 *e* the sacrifices do not share in the altar!
10:25 *E* whatever is sold in the market without
10:27 to go, *e* whatever is placed before you,
10:28 was offered in idol worship," do not *e* it,
10:31 The fact is that whether you *e* or drink
11:20 assemble it is not to *e* the Lord's Supper,
11:21 everyone is in haste to *e* his own supper.
11:22 not have homes where you can *e* and drink?
11:26 then, you *e* this bread and drink this cup,
11:28 he *e* of the bread and drink of the cup.
11:34 If anyone is hungry let him *e* at home,
15:32 dead are not raised, "Let us *e* and drink,
Phil 4:12 how to *e* well or go hungry,
Col 2:16 in terms of what you *e* or drink
2Thes 3:10 anyone who would not work should not *e*.
3:12 to earn the food they *e* by working quietly.
Heb 13:10 serve the tabernacle have no right to *e*.
Rv 2:14 tempting them to *e* food sacrificed to idols
2:20 lewdness and to *e* food sacrificed to idols.
10: 9 He said to me, "Here, take it and *e* it!
19:18 You are to *e* the flesh of kings,

EATEN (87)

Gn 3:11 You have *e*, then, from the tree
6:21 with all the food that is to be *e*,
24:54 he and the men with him had *e* and drunk,
31:54 When they had *e*, they passed the night
Ex 12: 9 It shall not be *e* raw or boiled,
12:46 It must be *e* in one and the same house;
13: 3 Nothing made with leaven must be *e*.
13: 7 bread may be *e* during the seven days;
21:28 its flesh may not be *e*.
29:34 it is not to be *e*, since it is sacred.
Lv 6: 9 but it must be *e* in the form of unleavened
6:16 it may not be *e*."
6:19 but it must be *e* in a sacred place,
7: 6 but it must be *e* in a sacred place,
7:15 shall be *e* on the day it is offered;
7:16 be *e* on the day the sacrifice is offered,
7:16 what is left over may be *e* on the next day.
7:18 the peace offering is *e* on the third day,
7:19 touch anything unclean, it may not be *e*,
10:18 have *e* the offering in the sanctuary,
10:19 Had I then *e* of the sin offering today,
11:13 and, as loathsome, they shall not be *e*:
11:41 ground are loathsome and shall not be *e*.
11:47 may be *e* and those that may not be eaten."
17:13 catches an animal or a bird that may be *e*,
19: 6 it must be *e* on the very day of your
19: 7 If any of it is *e* on the third day,
19:23 remains uncircumcised, it may not be *e*.
22:30 it must, therefore, be *e* on the same day;
Nm 28:17 For seven days unleavened bread is to be *e*.
Dt 8:10 But when you have *e* your fill,
8:12 lest, when you have *e* your fill,
12:27 LORD, your God, but their flesh may be *e*.
14:19 are unclean for you and shall not be *e*.
26:14 I have not *e* any of the tithe as a mourner;
31:20 and they have *e* their fill and grown fat,
Jos 24:13 you have *e* of vineyards and olive groves
Jgs 19: 8 When he and his father-in-law had *e*,
1Sm 14:30 if the people had *e* freely today of their
28:20 he had *e* nothing all that day and night.
30:12 When he had *e*, he revived;
1Kgs 13:23 After he had *e* bread and drunk water,
13:28 not *e* the body nor had it harmed the ass.
17:12 when we have *e* it, we shall die."
2Kgs 4:44 And when they had *e*,
6:23 they had *e* and drunk he sent them away,
2Chr 31:10 *e* to the full and have had much left over,
Neh 2: 3 and its gates have been *e* out by fire?"
2:13 ruins and its gates had been *e* out by fire.
Est C:28 have never *e* at the table of Haman,
1Mc 6:53 tide-over provisions had been *e* up
2Mc 2:11 had said, "Because it had not been *e*,
9:15 to be *e* by vultures and wild animals;
Jb 6: 6 Can a thing insipid be *e* without salt?
31:39 If I have *e* its produce without payment
Ps(s) 78:25 The bread of the mighty was *e* by men;
Prv 23: 8 The little you have *e* you will vomit up,
Sir 31:21 If perforce you have *e* too much,
Is 51: 8 They shall be like a garment *e* by moths,
Jer 24: 2 very bad figs, so bad they could not be *e*.
24: 3 bad ones very bad, so bad they cannot be *e*."
24: 8 that are bad, so bad they cannot be *e*—
29:17 them like rotten figs, too bad to be *e*.
37:21 until all the bread in the city was *e* up.
Bar 6:19 it is said their hearts are *e* away.
Ez 4:14 never have I *e* carrion flesh or that torn
18: 2 "Fathers have *e* green grapes,
39: 4 to the wild beasts I am giving you to be *e*.
45:21 for seven days unleavened bread is to be *e*.
Dn 14:12 *e* it all when you return in the morning,
Hos 10:13 perversity, and *e* the fruit of falsehood.
Jl 1: 4 the cutter left, the locust swarm has *e*;
1: 4 locust swarm left, the grasshopper has *e*;
1: 4 the grasshopper left, the devourer has *e*.
2:25 you for the years which the locust has *e*,
Hg 1: 6 you have *e*, but have not been satisfied;
Mk 6:44 *e* the loaves numbered five thousand men.
8: 9 who had *e* numbered about four thousand.
Jn 6:23 near the place where they had *e* the bread
6:26 because you have *e* your fill of the loaves.
13:30 had Judas *e* the morsel than he went out.
21:15 When they had *e* their meal,
Acts 10:14 *e* anything unclean or impure in my life."
12:23 the honor to God, and he died *e* by worms.
27:33 you have gone hungry *e* nothing.
Rom 14:15 feels remorse for the food he has *e*,

EATER (2)

Jgs 14:14 to them, "Out of the *e* came forth food,
2Cor 9:10 bread for the *e* will provide in abundance;

EATING (56)

Gn 27:33 I finished *e* it just before you came,
Ex 34:28 without *e* any food or drinking any water,
Lv 22: 8 He shall not make himself unclean by *e* of
22:16 profaned nor in the *e* of the sacred offering
Nm 9:11 *e* it with unleavened bread and bitter
18:10 *e* them you shall treat them as most sacred;
Dt 9: 9 and forty nights without *e* or drinking,
9:18 and forty nights without *e* or drinking,
12:22 the unclean and the clean *e* it alike.
15:22 it, the unclean and the clean *e* it alike,
Jgs 19: 4 *e* and drinking and passing the night there.
Ru 3: 3 man before he has finished *e* and drinking.
1Sm 14:32 on the ground and *e* the flesh with blood.
14:33 against the LORD by *e* the flesh with blood,
14:34 against the LORD by *e* the flesh with blood."
30:16 scattered all over the ground, *e*,
1Kgs 1:25 *e* and drinking in his company and saying,
2Kgs 9:34 in over her body and, after *e* and drinking,
Ezr 10: 6 night neither *e* food nor drinking water,
Tb 1:11 but I refrained from *e* that kind of food.
8: 1 When they had finished *e* and drinking,
8:20 shall remain here *e* and drinking with me;
Est 4:16 my behalf, all of you, not *e* or drinking,
2Mc 6:21 and to pretend to be *e* some of the meat of
Jb 1:13 his daughters were *e* and drinking wine
1:18 "Your sons and daughters were *e* and
Eccl 8:15 the sun except *e* and drinking and mirth:
Wis 4: 5 and their fruit be useless, unripe for *e*,
Sir 31:20 Moderate *e* ensures sound slumber and a
Is 29: 8 he is *e* and awakens with an empty stomach,
65: 4 the night in caverns, *E* swine's flesh,
Jer 16: 8 to sit with them *e* and drinking.
Ez 24:22 your beards nor *e* the customary bread.
Am 7: 2 they were *e* all the grass in the land,
Zec 7: 6 And when you were *e* and drinking,
Mt 9:11 Teacher have for *e* with tax collectors
11:18 John appeared neither *e* nor drinking,
11:19 The Son of Man appeared *e* and drinking,
15: 2 their hands, for example, before *e* a meal."
15:20 As for *e* with unwashed hands
24:38 the flood people were *e* and drinking,
Mk 2:16 he was *e* with tax collectors and offenders
7: 2 disciples *e* meals without having purified
14:18 to betray me, yes, one who is *e* with me."
Lk 6: 1 shelling them with their hands, and *e* them.
7:33 came neither *e* bread nor drinking wine,
10: 7 one house *e* and drinking what they have,
11:38 the ablutions prescribed before *e*.
22:20 He did the same with the cup after *e*,
Acts 15:20 of strangled animals, and from *e* blood.
Rom 14:17 of God is not a matter of *e* or drinking,
14:21 acting nobly if you abstained from *e* meat,
14:23 his conscience has misgivings about *e*,
1Cor 8: 4 of *e* meats that have been offered to idols:
8: 7 conscience is weak, it is defiled by the *e*.
8: 8 failing to eat, and we gain no favor by *e*.

EATS (38)

Ex 12:15 Whoever *e* leavened bread from the first
12:19 who *e* leavened food shall be cut off from
Lv 7:18 who *e* of it shall have his guilt to bear.
7:20 a state of uncleanness *e* any of the flesh
7:21 and then *e* of a peace offering belonging
7:25 If anyone *e* the fat of an animal from
11:40 and anyone who *e* of its dead body shall
14:47 Whoever sleeps or *e* in such a house shall
17:15 who *e* of an animal that died of itself or
19: 8 whoever *e* of it then shall pay the penalty
22:14 If such a one *e* of a sacred offering
2Sm 19:36 your servant taste what he *e* and drinks,
Prv 13: 2 the fruit of his words a man *e* good things,
13:25 When the just man *e*, his hunger
19:23 one *e* and sleeps without being visited by
27:18 He who tends a fig tree *e* its fruit,
30:20 she *e*, wipes her mouth, and says,
31:27 and *e* not her food in idleness.
Eccl 5:11 laboring man, whether he *e* little or much,
Sir 24:20 He who *e* of me will hunger still,
Is 44:16 he *e* what he has roasted until he is full,
55:10 to him who sows and bread to him who *e*,
59: 5 Whoever *e* their eggs will die,
Jer 31:30 *e* the unripe grapes shall be set on edge.
Ez 18:11 of them), a son who *e* on the mountains,
Dn 14: 6 not see how much he *e* and drinks every day
Lk 14:15 is he who *e* bread in the kingdom of God."
15: 2 man welcomes sinners and *e* with them."
Jn 6:51 anyone *e* this bread he shall live forever;
Rom 14: 2 one who is weak in faith *e* only vegetables.
14: 3 must not sit in judgment on him who *e*.
14: 6 The man who *e* does so to honor the Lord,
14:23 But if a man *e* when his conscience has
1Cor 8:10 to the point that he *e* the idol-offering?
11:27 This means that whoever *e* the bread or
11:29 He who *e* and drinks without recognizing
11:29 body *e* and drinks a judgment on himself.
Rv 2: 7 I will see to it that the victor *e* from

EBAL (8)

Gn 36:23 descendants were Alvan, Mahanath, *E*,
Dt 11:29 on Mount Gerizim, the curse on Mount *E*.
27: 4 besides setting up on Mount *E* these stones
27:13 shall stand on Mount *E* to pronounce curses.
Jos 8:30 the LORD, the God of Israel, on Mount *E*,
8:33 facing Mount Gerizim and half Mount *E*,
1Chr 1:22 Jerah, Hadoram, Uzal, Diklah, *E*,
1:40 The sons of Shobal were Alian, Manahath, *E*,

EBBED (1)

Jb 11:16 or recall it like waters that have *e* away.

EBBING (1)

Jer 49: 4 glory in your strength, your *e* strength,

EBBS (2)

Jb 30:16 My soul *e* away from me;
Is 19: 3 of the Egyptians *e* away within them,

EBED (6)

Jgs 9:26 Now Gaal, son of *E*,
9:28 Gaal, son of *E*, said, "Who is Abimelech?
9:30 At the news of what Gaal, son of *E*,
9:31 "Gaal, son of *E*, and his kinsmen
9:35 Gaal, son of *E*, went out and stood
Ezr 8: 6 of the sons of Adin, *E*,

EBED-MELECH (5)

Jer 38: 7 Now *E*, a Cushite, a courtier
38: 8 and *E* went there from the palace and said
38:10 Then the king ordered *E* the Cushite to
38:11 *E* took the men along with him,
39:16 Go, tell this to *E* the Cushite:

EBENEZER (3)

1Sm 4: 1 to engage them in battle and camped at *E*,
5: 1 of God, transferred it from *E* to Ashdod.
7:12 he named it *E*, explaining, "To this point

EBEN-BOHAN-BEN-REUBEN (1)

Jos 18:17 Then it dropped to *E*

EBER (16)

Gn 10:21 and the ancestor of all the children of *E*,
10:24 Shelah, and Shelah became the father of *E*.
10:25 To *E* two sons were born:
11:14 years old, he became the father of *E*.

EBER (cont.)

11:15 and three years after the birth of *E,*
11:16 When *E* was thirty-four years old,
11:17 *E* lived four hundred and thirty years
Nm 24:24 they have conquered Asshur and conquered *E,*
1Chr 1:18 Shelah, and Shelah became the father of *E.*
1:19 Two sons were born to *E;*
1:25 Shem, Arpachshad, Shelah, *E,*
5:13 Meshullam, Sheba, Jorai, Jacan, Zia, and *E*—
8:12 The sons of Elpaal were *E,*
8:22 were the sons of Shimei, Ishpan, *E,*
Neh 12:20 for Amok, *E;* for Hilkiah, Hashabiah;
Lk 3:35 Serug, son of Reu, son of Peleg, son of *E,*

EBEZ (1)

Jos 19:20 Shion, Anaharath, Rabbith, Kishion, *E,*

EBIASAPH (3)

1Chr 6: 8 whose son was Elkanah whose son was *E,*
6:22 son of Tahath, son of Assir, son of *E,*
9:19 Shallum, son of Kore, son of *E,*

EBONY (1)

Ez 27:15 tusks and *e* wood they gave you for payment.

ECBATANA (11)

Ezr 6: 2 and in *E,* the stronghold in the province
Tb 3: 7 On the same day, at *E* in Media,
5: 6 is a good two days' travel from *E* to Rages,
5: 6 at the mountains, *E* out on the plateau."
6:10 entered Media and were getting close to *E,*
7: 1 When they entered *E,* Tobiah said,
14:12 settled in *E* with his father-in-law Raguel.
14:13 and he buried them at *E* in Media.
Jdt 1: 1 time Arphaxad ruled over the Medes in *E.*
1:14 He pressed on to *E* and took its towers,
2Mc 9: 3 On his arrival in *E,* he learned

ECHO (1)

Wis 17:19 *e* resounding from the hollow of the hills,

ECHOED (1)

1Thes 1: 8 Lord has *e* forth from you resoundingly.

ECHOING (1)

2Kgs 6:32 His master's footsteps are *e* behind him."

ECLIPSE (1)

Lk 23:44 until midafternoon with an *e* of the sun.

ECLIPSED (1)

Sir 17:26 Yet it can be *e.*

ECSTASY (2)

Rv 1:10 On the Lord's day I was caught up in *e,*
4: 2 At once I was caught up in *e.*

ECZEMA (5)

Lv 13: 6 declare the man clean; it was merely *e.*
13: 7 clean, the *e* spreads at all on his skin,
13: 8 that the *e* has indeed spread on the skin,
21:20 or walleyed, or who is afflicted with *e,*
Dt 28:27 boils and with tumors, *e* and the itch,

EDEN (15)

Gn 2: 8 Then the LORD God planted a garden in *E,*
2:10 A river rises in *E* to water the garden;
2:15 the man and settled him in the garden of *E,*
3:23 banished him from the garden of *E,*
3:24 he settled him east of the garden of *E;*
4:16 and settled in the land of Nod, east of *E.*
2Chr 29:12 Joah, son of Zimmah, and *E,*
31:15 Under him in the priestly cities were *E,*
Is 51: 3 Her deserts he shall make like *E,*
Ez 27:23 Haran, Canneh, and *E,* the merchants
28:13 complete wisdom and perfect beauty, In *E,*
31:18 in glory or size among the trees of *E?*
31:18 down with the trees of *E* to the land below.
36:35 land has been made into a garden of *E,*"
Jl 2: 3 the garden of *E* is the land before them,

EDENITES (2)

2Kgs 19:12 Gozan, Haran, Rezeph, or the *E* in Telassar?
Is 37:12 Haran, Rezeph, and the *E* in Telassar?

EDENS (2)

Ez 31: 9 envy of all *E* trees in the garden of God.
31:16 the land below, all *E* trees were consoled,

EDER (4)

Jos 15:21 Kabzeel, *E,* Jagur, Kinah, Dimonah,
1Chr 8:15 Zebadiah, Arad, *E,* Michael, Ishpah,
23:23 Mahli, *E,* and Jeremoth; three in all.
24:30 The descendants of Mushi were Mahli, *E,*

EDGE (54)

Gn 23: 9 it is at the *e* of his field.
Ex 13:20 camped at Etham near the *e* of the desert.
17:13 and his people with the *e* of the sword.
26: 3 sheets are to be sewed together, *e* to edge;
26: 4 along the *e* of the end sheet in one set,
26: 4 the *e* of the end sheet in the other set.
26: 5 and fifty loops along the *e* of the
26: 5 the *e* of the end sheet in the first set,
26: 9 Sew five of the sheets, edge to *e,*
26:10 along the *e* of the end sheet in one set,
26:10 the *e* of the end sheet in the second set.
28:26 breastpiece, on its *e* that faces the ephod.
36:10 the sheets were sewed together, *e* to edge;
36:10 the sheets were sewed together, edge to *e;*
36:11 the *e* of the end sheet in the first set,
36:11 the *e* of the end sheet in the second set.
36:16 sheets were sewed edge to *e* into one set;
36:17 along the *e* of the end sheet in one set,
36:17 and fifty loops along the *e* of the
39:19 the breastpiece, on the *e* facing the ephod.
Lv 19: 9 that you reap the field to its very *e,*
23:22 that you reap the field to its very *e,*
Nm 20:16 town of Kadesh at the *e*
33: 6 camped at Etham near the *e* of the desert.
Dt 2:36 From Aroer on the *e* of the Wadi Arnon and
3:12 from Aroer, on the *e* of the Wadi Arnon,
4:48 from Aroer on the *e* of the Wadi Arnon to
Jos 3: 8 Jordan when they reach the *e* of the waters."
3:15 into the waters at the *e* of the Jordan,
18:16 It went down to the *e* of the mountain on
Jgs 7:17 "I shall go to the *e* of the camp,
7:19 were with him came to the *e* of the camp
Ru 3: 7 went and lay down at the *e* of the sheaves,
1Sm 9:27 As they were approaching the *e* of town,
26: 1 hill of Hachilah at the *e* of the wasteland.
26: 3 of Hachilah, at the *e* of the wasteland.
2Kgs 7: 5 but when they reached the *e* of the camp,
7: 8 After the lepers reached the *e* of the camp,
Jb 5:15 But the poor from the *e* of the sword and
Ps(s) 141: 7 are strewn by the *e* of the nether world.
Sir 28:18 Many have fallen by the *e* of the sword,
Jer 21: 7 shall strike them with the *e* of the sword,
31:29 and the children's teeth are set on *e,*"
31:30 eats the unripe grapes shall be set on *e.*
48:28 nests out of reach on the *e* of a chasm.
Ez 18: 2 thus their children's teeth are on *e*"?
21:21 wherever your *e* is turned.
43:14 up to the lower *e* it was two cubits high,
Zec 8:23 every Jew by the *e* of his garment and say,
14: 5 of those two mountains reaches its *e;*
Lk 4:30 built and intending to hurl him over the *e.*

EDGES (3)

Lv 19:27 the temples, nor trim the *e* of your beard.
21: 5 of the head, nor shave the *e* of the beard,
Ez 43:13 deep, with a rim around its *e* of one span.

EDICT (5)

Ezr 6:11 If any man violates this *e,*
2Mc 10: 8 By public *e* and decree they prescribed
Jer 34: 8 in Jerusalem to issue an *e* of emancipation.
Acts 18: 2 An *e* of Claudius had ordered all Jews to
Heb 11:23 birth, thereby disregarding the king's *e,*

EDICTS (1)

1Mc 6:23 and to follow his orders and obey his *e.*

EDIFICE (3)

Ezr 5: 3 you to build this house and raise this *e?*
5: 9 you to build this house and raise this *e?*'
1Pt 2: 5 are living stones, built as an *e* of spirit,

EDNA (7)

Tb 7: 2 them into his home, he said to his wife *E,*
7: 3 So *E* asked them,
7: 8 His wife *E* also wept for Tobit;
7:15 Later Raguel called his wife *E* and said,
8:21 I am your father, and *E* is your mother;
10:13 Then *E* said to Tobiah:
10:14 he said good-bye to Raguel and his wife *E,*

EDOM (93)

Gn 25:30 starving" (That is why he was called *E.*)
32: 4 Esau in the land of Seir, the country of *E,*
36: 1 are the descendants of Esau [that is, *E.*]
36: 8 [Esau is *E.*]
36:16 are the clans of Eliphaz in the land of *E;*
36:17 are the clans of Reuel in the land of *E;*
36:19 Esau [that is, *E* according to their clans.
36:21 descended from Seir, in the land of *E.*
36:31 reigned in the land of *E* before any king
36:32 Bela, son of Beor, became king in *E;*
Ex 15:15 Then were the princes of *E* dismayed;
Nm 20:14 sent men to the king of *E* with the message:
20:18 But *E* answered him, "You shall not pass
20:20 But *E* still said, "No, you shall not pass
20:21 since *E* refused to let them pass through
20:23 Mount Hor, on the border of the land of *E,*
21: 4 the Red Sea road, to by-pass the land of *E.*
24:18 all the Shuthites, Till *E* is dispossessed,
33:37 Mount Hor on the border of the land of *E.*
34: 3 the desert of Zin along the border of *E;*
Jos 15: 1 the extreme south toward the boundary of *E,*
15:21 extreme southern district toward *E* were:
Jgs 5: 4 when you marched from the land of *E,*
11:17 sent messengers to the king of *E* saying,
11:17 But the king of *E* did not give consent.
11:18 the land of *E* and the land of Moab,
2Sm 8:12 from *E* and Moab, from the Ammonites
8:14 after which he placed garrisons in *E.*
1Kgs 9:26 the shore of the Red Sea in the land of *E.*
11:14 Edomite, who was of the royal line in *E.*
11:15 Earlier, when David had conquered *E,*
11:15 the slain, put to death every male in *E.*
11:16 until they had killed off every male in *E.*
11:25 a rift in Israel by becoming king over *E.*
22:48 There was no king in *E,*
2Kgs 3: 8 upon the route through the desert of *E.*
3: 9 by the king of Judah and the king of *E.*
3:12 Israel, Judah, and *E* went down to Elisha.
3:20 the direction of *E* and filled the land.
8:20 *E* revolted against the sovereignty of
8:22 To this day *E* has been in revolt against
14:10 You have indeed conquered *E,*
16: 6 the king of *E* recovered Elath for Edom,
16: 6 the king of Edom recovered Elath for *E,*
1Chr 1:43 The kings who reigned in the land of *E*
1:51 These were the chiefs of *E:*
1:54 Magdiel, and Iram were the chiefs of *E.*
18:11 from *E,* Moab, the Ammonites,
18:13 He set up garrisons in *E,*
2Chr 8:17 to Elath on the seashore of the land of *E.*
20: 2 against you from across the sea, from *E;*
21: 8 During his time *E* revolted against the
21:10 *E* has continued in revolt against the
25:19 You are thinking, 'See, I have beaten *E!*',
25:20 they had had recourse to the gods of *E.*
Ps(s) 60:10 upon *E* I will set my shoe;
60:11 Who will lead me into *E?*
76:11 For wrathful *E* shall glorify you,
83: 7 The tents of *E* and the Ishmaelites,
108:10 upon *E* I will set my shoe;
108:11 Who will lead me into *E?*
137: 7 O LORD, against the children of *E,*
Is 11:14 *E* and Moab shall be their possessions,
21:11 Oracle on *E:*
34: 5 lo, it shall come down in judgment upon *E,*
34: 6 Bozrah, a great slaughter in the land of *E.*
63: 1 Who is this that comes from *E,*
Jer 9:25 Egypt and Judah, *E* and the Ammonites,
25:21 *E,* Moab, and the Ammonites
27: 3 Send to the kings of *E,*
40:11 those among the Ammonites, those in *E,*
49: 7 Concerning *E,* thus says the LORD of hosts:
49:17 *E* shall become an object of horror.
49:20 which he has taken against *E;*
Lam 4:21 you rejoice and are glad, O daughter *E,*
4:22 But your wickedness, O daughter *E,*
Ez 25:12 Because *E* has taken vengeance on the house
25:13 *E* and cut off from it man and beast,
25:14 upon *E* I will entrust to my people Israel,
25:14 *E* in accordance with my anger and my fury;
27:16 *E* traded with you,
32:29 There are *E,* her kings, and all her princes,
35:15 you be, Mount Seir, you and the whole of *E.*
36: 5 rest of the nations [and against all of *E*
Dn 11:41 land and many shall fall, except *E,*
Jl 4:19 shall be a waste, and *E* a desert waste,
Am 1: 6 captive whole groups to hand over to *E,*
1: 9 they delivered whole groups captive to *E,*
1:11 For three crimes of *E,*
9:12 *E* and all the nations shall bear my name,
Ob 1: 1 *E* we have heard a message from the LORD,
1: 8 day make the wise men disappear from *E,*
Mal 1: 4 If *E* says, "We have been crushed

EDOMITE (7)

Dt 23: 8 But do not abhor the *E,*
1Sm 21: 8 his name was Doeg the *E,*
22: 9 Then Doeg the *E,* who was standing
22:18 So Doeg the *E* went from one to the next
22:21 knew that day, when Doeg the *E* was there,
1Kgs 11:14 Hadad the *E,* who was of the royal line
11:17 Egypt with some *E* servants of his father.

EDOMITES (17)

Gn 36: 9 the descendants of Esau, ancestor of the *E,*
36:43 These are the clans of the *E,*
36:43 [Esau was the father of the *E*
2Sm 8:13 eighteen thousand *E* in the Salt Valley;
8:14 Thus all the *E* became David's subjects,
1Kgs 11: 1 of Pharaoh (Moabites, Ammonites, *E,*
2Kgs 8:21 He arose by night and broke through the *E*
14: 7 slew ten thousand *E* in the Salt Valley,
16: 6 The *E* then entered Elath,
1Chr 18:12 eighteen thousand *E* in the Valley of Salt.
18:13 and all the *E* became David's subjects.
2Chr 21: 9 He arose by night and broke through the *E*
25:14 returned from his conquest of the *E*
28:17 The *E* had returned,

Jdt 7: 8 the *E* and all the leaders of the Ammonites,
7:18 The *E* and the Ammonites went up and
Ez 16:57 reproached by the *E* and all your neighbors,

EDOMS (3)

Is 34: 9 *E* streams shall be changed into pitch and
Jer 49:22 On that day the hearts of *E* heroes shall
Am 2: 1 he burned to ashes the bones of *E* king,

EDREI (8)

Nm 21:33 with all his people to give battle at *E.*
Dt 1: 4 Bashan, who lived in Ashtaroth and in *E,*
3: 1 us with all his people to give battle at *E.*
3:10 of Og in Bashan including Salecah and *E.*
Jos 12: 4 the Rephaim, who lived at Ashtaroth and *E.*
13:12 Rephaim, who reigned at Ashtaroth and *E.*
13:31 Half of Gilead, with Ashtaroth and *E,*
19:37 Adamah, Ramah, Hazor, Kedesh, *E,*

EDUCATED (3)

2Mc 7:27 *e* and supported you to your present age.
Acts 7:22 Moses was *e* in all the lore of Egypt.
22: 3 was *e* strictly in the law of our fathers.

EDUCATES (1)

Sir 30: 3 He who *e* his son makes his enemy jealous,

EDUCATION (1)

Jn 7:15 this man get his *e* when he had no teacher?"

EFFACE (2)

Jos 7: 9 in around us and *e* our name from the earth.
1Mc 3:35 Jerusalem and *e* their memory from the land.

EFFACED (1)

Sir 39: 9 his fame can never be *e;*

EFFACES (1)

Sir 10:17 and *e* the memory of them from the earth.

EFFECT (19)

Gn 18:19 so that the LORD may carry into *e* for
Jos 9: 4 of Gibeon put into *e* a device of their own.
Jgs 12: 3 When I saw that you would not *e* a rescue,
1Sm 3:19 permitting any word of his to be without *e.*
15: 8 into *e* the ban of destruction by the sword.
30: 8 shall surely overtake them and *e* a rescue."
Est 1:22 to the *e* that every man should be lord in
9:14 The king then gave an order to this *e,*
1Mc 3:29 the laws which had been in *e* from of old.
Jb 38:33 can you put into *e* their plan on the earth?
Eccl 12: 5 sluggish and the caper berry is without *e,*
Wis 18: 9 *e* with one accord the divine institution,
Sir 12: 1 it, and your kindness will have its *e.*
Jer 50: 9 none shall return without *e.*
Acts 23:25 then wrote the governor a letter to this *e:*
1Cor 5: 6 yeast has its *e* all through the dough?
Eph 5: 5 in *e* an idolator—has any inheritance
Col 2:23 chief *e* is that they indulge men's pride.
1Thes 2: 1 our coming among you was not without *e.*

EFFECTIVE (4)

Est B: 2 humane and *e* as far as the borders,
Jb 11: 6 that the secrets of wisdom are twice as *e:*
Sir 22:27 over my mouth, and upon my lips an *e* seal,
Heb 4:12 Indeed, God's word is living and *e,*

EFFECTS (2)

Tb 14:15 the destruction of Nineveh and saw its *e.*
Acts 28: 5 fire and suffered no ill *e* from the bite.

EFFICACY (1)

Sir 38: 8 cease in its *e* on the surface of the earth.

EFFORT (10)

Gn 31: 6 know what *e* I put into serving your father;
Jos 7: 3 need not call for an *e* from all the people."
1Chr 22:14 with great *e* I have laid up for the house
Prv 10:22 wealth, and no *e* can substitute for it.
Mt 20:31 them in an *e* to reduce them to silence,
Gal 2:10 one thing that I was making every *e* to do.
Eph 4: 3 Make every *e* to preserve the unity which
Phil 2:30 He risked his life in an *e* to render me
2Pt 1: 5 *e* to undergird your virtue with faith,
3:14 *e* to be found without stain or defilement,

EFFORTS (10)

Neh 6: 9 But instead, I now redoubled my *e.*
2Mc 2:28 our *e* to giving only a summary outline.
Ps(s) 56: 6 All the day they molest me in my *e;*
Eccl 10:10 easy progress, he must increase his *e;*
Acts 16:10 made *e* to get across to Macedonia,
24: 2 through your *e* we enjoy great peace.
Gal 4:11 all my *e* with you may have been wasted.
6: 9 if we do not relax our *e,*
1Thes 2: 9 must recall, brothers, our *e* and our toil:
Rv 2:19 *e* of recent times are greater than ever.

EFFRONTERIES (2)

Neh 9:18 out of Egypt,' and were guilty of great *e,*
9:26 to you, and they were guilty of great *e.*

EFFRONTERY (1)

Prv 21:24 overbearing pride who acts with scornful *e.*

EFFUSION (1)

Wis 7:25 and a pure *e* of the glory of the Almighty:

EGG (2)

Jb 6: 6 Is there flavor in the white of an *e?*
Lk 11:12 or hand him a scorpion if he asks for an *e?*

EGGS (6)

Dt 22: 6 a bird's nest with young birds or *e* in it,
Jb 39:14 When she leaves her *e* on the ground and
Is 10:14 As one takes *e* left alone,
34:15 There the hoot owl shall nest and lay *e,*
59: 5 They hatch adders' *e,*
59: 5 Whoever eats their *e* will die,

EGLAH (2)

2Sm 3: 5 and the sixth, Ithream, of David's wife *E.*
1Chr 3: 3 the sixth, Ithream, by his wife *E.*

EGLAIM (1)

Is 15: 8 As far as *E* the wailing,

EGLATH-SHELISHIYAH (2)

Is 15: 5 Moab cries out, his fugitives reach Zoar *E.*
Jer 48:34 they call from Zoar to Horonaim, and to *E,*

EGLON (12)

Jos 10: 3 king of Lachish, and Debir, king of *E,*
10: 5 Jerusalem, Hebron, Jarmuth, Lachish and *E,*
10:23 Jerusalem, Hebron, Jarmuth, Lachish and *E.*
10:34 Joshua passed on with all Israel to *E;*
10:36 From *E,* Joshua went up
10:37 no survivors, just as Joshua had done to *E.*
12:12 Jerusalem, Hebron, Jarmuth, Lachish, *E,*
15:39 Mizpeh, Jokteel, Lachish, Bozkath, *E,*
Jgs 3:12 who because of this offense strengthened *E,*
3:14 The Israelites then served *E,*
3:15 the Israelites sent their tribute to *E,*
3:17 He presented the tribute to *E,*

EGLON'S (1)

Jgs 3:21 right thigh, and thrust it into *E* belly.

EGREBEL (1)

Jdt 7:18 to the south and to the east opposite *E,*

EGYPT (632)

Gn 12:10 so Abram went down to *E* to sojourn there,
12:11 When he was about to enter *E,*
12:14 When Abram came to *E,*
13: 1 From *E* Abram went up to the Negeb with his
13:10 like the LORD's own garden, or like *E.*
15:18 of *E* to the Great River [the Euphrates],
21:21 got a wife for him from the land of *E.*
25:18 which is on the border of *E,*
26: 2 "Do not go down to *E,*
37:25 gum, balm and resin to be taken down to *E.*
37:28 up out of the cistern and took him to *E.*
37:36 meanwhile, sold Joseph in *E* to Potiphar,
39: 1 When Joseph was taken down to *E,*
40: 1 gave offense to their lord, the king of *E.*
40: 5 the baker of the king of *E* who were confined
41: 8 of *E* and recounted his dreams to them;
41:19 specimens as these in all the land of *E!*
41:29 are now coming throughout the land of *E;*
41:30 in the land of *E* will be forgotten.
41:33 man and put him in charge of the land of *E.*
41:36 that are to follow in the land of *E,*
41:41 place you in charge of the whole land of *E.*"
41:43 Joseph installed over the whole land of *E.*
41:44 move hand or foot in all the land of *E.*"
41:46 entered the service of Pharaoh, king of *E.*
41:46 he traveled throughout the land of *E.*
41:48 *E* was enjoying and stored it in the towns,
41:53 enjoyed by the land of *E* came to an end,
41:54 was available throughout the land of *E.*
41:55 came to be felt throughout the land of *E*
41:56 since the famine had gripped the land of *E.*
42: 1 that grain rations were available in *E,*
42: 2 "that rations of grain are available in *E.*
42: 3 to buy an emergency supply of grain from *E.*
43: 2 all the rations they had brought from *E,*
43:15 down to *E* to present themselves to Joseph.
45: 4 brother Joseph, whom you once sold into *E.*
45: 8 and ruler over the whole land of *E.*
45: 9 God has made me lord of all *E;*
45:13 high position in *E* and what you have seen.
45:18 I will assign you the best land in *E,*
45:19 Take wagons from the land of *E* for your
45:20 best in the whole land of *E* shall be yours.'"
45:23 loaded with the finest products of *E*
45:25 So they left *E* and made their way to their
45:26 is he who is ruler of all the land of *E.*"
46: 3 Do not be afraid to go down to *E,*
46: 4 Not only will I go down to *E* with you;
46: 6 and all his descendants migrated to *E.*
46: 7 he took with him to *E.*
46: 8 and his descendants, who migrated to *E.*
46:20 In the land of *E* Joseph became the father
46:26 Jacob's people who migrated to *E*—
46:27 Joseph's sons who were born to him in *E*—
46:27 to *E* amounted to seventy persons in all.
47: 5 Jacob and his sons came to Joseph in *E,*
47: 5 Joseph in Egypt, and Pharaoh, king of *E,*
47: 6 to you, the land of *E* is at your disposal;
47:11 them holdings in *E* on the pick of the land,
47:13 *E* and Canaan were languishing from hunger,
47:14 money that was to be found in *E* and Canaan,
47:15 all the money in *E* and Canaan was spent,
47:20 all the farm land of *E* for Pharaoh,
47:26 Joseph made it a law for the land in *E,*
47:27 Thus Israel settled in the land of *E,*
47:28 lived in the land of *E* for seventeen years;
47:29 do not let me be buried in *E.*
47:30 out of *E* and buried in their burial place."
48: 5 in the land of *E* before I joined you here,
50: 7 court and all the other dignitaries of *E,*
50:14 had buried his father he returned to *E,*
50:22 Joseph remained in *E,*
50:26 embalmed and laid to rest in a coffin in *E.*
Ex 1: 1 households, migrated with Jacob into *E:*
1: 5 Joseph was already in *E.*
1: 8 knew nothing of Joseph, came to power in *E.*
1:15 The king of *E* told the Hebrew midwives,
1:17 not do as the king of *E* had ordered them,
2:23 passed, during which the king of *E* died.
3: 7 my people in *E* and have heard their cry
3:10 lead my people, the Israelites, out of *E.*"
3:11 Pharaoh and lead the Israelites out of *E?*"
3:12 when you bring my people out of *E,*
3:16 about the way you are being treated in *E;*
3:17 of *E* into the land of the Canaanites,
3:18 shall go to the king of *E* and say to him:
3:19 "Yet I know that the king of *E* will not
3:20 and smite *E* by doing all kinds of wondrous
4:18 me go back, please, to my kinsmen in *E,*
4:19 the LORD said to Moses, "Go back to *E,*
4:20 sons, and started back to the land of *E,*
4:21 LORD said to him, "On your return to *E,*
5: 4 The king of *E* answered them,
5:12 the land of *E* to gather stubble for straw,
6:11 Moses, "Go and tell Pharaoh, king of *E,*
6:13 LORD, to bring the Israelites out of *E,*
6:13 both the Israelites and Pharaoh, king of *E.*
6:26 the Israelites from the land of *E,*
6:27 the ones who spoke to Pharaoh, king of *E,*
6:27 of Egypt, to bring the Israelites out of *E*—
6:28 day the LORD spoke to Moses in *E* he said,
6:29 Repeat to Pharaoh, king of *E,*
7: 3 wonders that I will work in the land of *E,*
7: 4 Therefore I will lay my hand on *E* and by
7: 4 the Israelites, out of the land of *E,*
7: 5 as I stretch out my hand against *E* and
7:11 and they also, the magicians of *E,*
7:19 out your hand over the waters of *E*—
7:19 the land of *E* there shall be blood,
7:21 There was blood throughout the land of *E.*
8: 1 pools, to make frogs overrun the land of *E.*"
8: 2 out his hand over the waters of *E,*
8: 2 frogs came up and covered the land of *E.*
8: 3 too, made frogs overrun the land of *E.*
8:12 turned into gnats throughout the land of *E.*"
8:13 turned into gnats throughout the land of *E.*
8:20 *E* the land was infested with flies.
9: 4 the livestock of Israel and that of *E,*
9: 9 into fine dust over the whole land of *E*
9:18 fierce hail as there has never been in *E*
9:22 hail may fall upon the entire land of *E,*
9:22 and every growing thing in the land of *E.*"
9:23 LORD rained down hail upon the land of *E;*
9:24 seen in the land since *E* became a nation.
9:25 was in the open throughout the land of *E;*
10: 7 not yet realize that *E* is being destroyed?"
10:12 out your hand over the land of *E,*
10:13 out his staff over the land of *E,*
10:14 of *E* and settled down on every part of it.
10:15 any tree or plant throughout the land of *E.*
10:19 locust remained within the confines of *E,*
10:21 that over the land of *E* there may be such
10:22 throughout the land of *E* for three days.
11: 1 will I bring upon Pharaoh and upon *E.*
11: 3 servants and the people in the land of *E.*
11: 4 At midnight I will go forth through *E,*
11: 6 be loud wailing throughout the land of *E,*
11: 9 wonders may be multiplied in the land of *E.*"
12: 1 said to Moses and Aaron in the land of *E,*
12:12 on this same night I will go through *E,*
12:12 executing judgment on all the gods of *E*—
12:13 thus, when I strike the land of *E,*
12:17 I brought your ranks out of the land of *E,*
12:27 over the houses of the Israelites in *E;*
12:29 slew every first-born in the land of *E,*
12:30 and there was a loud wailing throughout *E,*

EGYPT (cont.)

12:39 they had brought out of *E* was not leavened,
12:39 They had been rushed out of *E* and had no
12:40 in *E* was four hundred and thirty years.
12:41 LORD left the land of *E* on this very date.
12:42 LORD, as he led them out of the land of *E;*
12:51 the Israelites out of *E* company by company.
13: 3 this day on which you came out of *E,*
13: 8 the LORD did for me when I came out of *E.'*
13: 9 strong hand the LORD brought you out of *E.*
13:14 a strong hand the LORD brought us out of *E,*
13:15 killed every first-born in the land of *E,*
13:16 a strong hand the LORD brought us out of *E."*
13:17 might change their minds and return to *E.*
13:18 array the Israelites marched out of *E.*
14: 5 to the king of *E* that the people had fled,
14: 7 chariots and all the other chariots of *E,*
14:11 "Were there no burial places in *E* that
14:11 Why did you bring us out of *E?*
14:12 Did we not tell you this in *E,*
16: 1 after their departure from the land of *E.*
16: 3 died at the LORD's hand in the land of *E,*
16: 6 LORD who brought you out of the land of *E;*
16:32 when I brought you out of the land of *E."*
17: 3 saying, "Why did you ever make us leave *E?*
18: 1 how the LORD had brought Israel out of *E.*
19: 1 after their departure from the land of *E,*
20: 2 God, who brought you out of the land of *E,*
22:20 once aliens yourselves in the land of *E.*
23: 9 once aliens yourselves in the land of *E.*
23:15 for it was then that you came out of *E.*
29:46 God who brought them out of the land of *E,*
32: 1 Moses who brought us out of the land of *E,*
32: 4 who brought you out of the land of *E."*
32: 7 whom you brought out of the land of *E,*
32: 8 who brought you out of the land of *E!'*
32:11 out of the land of *E* with such great power
32:23 Moses who brought us out of the land of *E,*
33: 1 you have brought up from the land of *E,*
34:18 for in the month of Abib you came out of *E.*
Lv 11:45 the land of *E* that I might be your God,
18: 3 shall not do as they do in the land of *E,*
19:34 you too were once aliens in the land of *E.*
19:36 God, who brought you out of the land of *E.*
22:33 sacred and led you out of the land of *E,*
23:43 I led the Israelites out of the land of *E,*
25:38 who brought you out of the land of *E* to
25:42 out of the land of *E* are servants of mine,
25:55 I brought them out of the land of *E,*
26:45 of *E* under the very eyes of the Gentiles,
Nm 1: 1 Israelites' departure from the land of *E,*
3:13 slew all the first-born in the land of *E,*
8:17 I slew all the first-born in the land of *E.*
9: 1 their departure from the land of *E,*
11: 5 the fish we used to eat without cost in *E,*
11:18 Oh, how well off we were in *E!'*
11:20 you have wailed, 'Why did we ever leave *E?'"*
13:22 had been built seven years before Zoan in *E*
14: 2 that we had died in the land of *E,*
14: 3 it not be better for us to return to *E?"*
14: 4 "Let us appoint a leader and go back to *E."*
14:19 as you have forgiven them from *E* until now."
14:22 the signs I worked in *E* and in the desert,
15:41 who, as God, brought you out of *E* that I,
20: 5 Why did you lead us out of *E,*
20:15 us, how our fathers went down to *E,*
20:16 cry and sent an angel who led us out of *E.*
21: 5 brought us up from *E* to die in this desert,
22: 5 "A people has come here from *E* who now
22:11 from *E* now cover the face of the earth.
23:22 It is God who brought him out of *E,*
24: 8 It is God who brought him out of *E,*
26: 4 came out of the land of *E* were as follows:
26:59 the tribe of Levi, born to the tribe in *E.*
32:11 who have come up from *E* shall ever see
33: 1 of *E* under the guidance of Moses and Aaron.
33: 3 went forth in triumph, in view of all *E.*
33:38 of the Israelites from the land of *E,*
34: 5 and turning from Azmon to the Wadi of *E,*
Dt 1:27 has brought us up out of the land of *E,*
1:30 took your part before your very eyes in *E,*
4:20 taken and led out of that iron foundry, *E,*
4:34 did for you in *E* before your very eyes?
4:37 led you out of *E* by his great power,
4:45 to them when they had come out of *E*
4:46 Israelites defeated after coming out of *E.*
5: 6 God, who brought you out of the land of *E,*
5:15 that you too were once slaves in *E,*
6:12 LORD, who brought you out of the land of *E,*
6:21 son, 'We were once slaves of Pharaoh in *E,*
6:21 brought us out of *E* with his strong hand,
6:22 *E* and against Pharaoh and his whole house.
7: 8 you from the hand of Pharaoh, king of *E.*
7:15 malignant diseases that you know from *E,*
7:18 your God, did to Pharaoh and to all *E:*
8:14 God, who brought you out of the land of *E,*
9: 7 land of *E* until you arrived in this place,
9:12 have brought out of *E* have become depraved;
9:26 and brought out of *E* with your strong hand.
10:19 once aliens yourselves in the land of *E.*
10:22 ancestors went down to *E* seventy strong,
11: 3 the Egyptians, on Pharaoh, king of *E,*
11:10 the land of *E* from which you have come,
13: 6 who brought you out of the land of *E* and
13:11 God, who brought you out of the land of *E,*
15:15 you too were once slaves in the land of *E,*
16: 1 Abib that he brought you by night out of *E.*
16: 3 day of your departure from the land of *E;*
16: 3 in frightened haste you left the land of *E.*
16: 6 the anniversary of your departure from *E,*
16:12 that you too were once slaves in *E,*
17:16 people go back again to *E* to acquire them,
20: 1 God, who brought you up from the land of *E,*
23: 5 water on your journey after you left *E,*
24: 9 to Miriam on the journey after you left *E.*
24:18 For, remember, you were once slaves in *E,*
24:22 remember that you were once slaves in *E;*
25:17 to you on the journey after you left *E,*
26: 5 a wandering Aramean who went down to *E*
26: 8 He brought us out of *E* with his strong
28:60 with all the diseases of *E* which you dread,
28:68 LORD will send you back in galleys to *E,*
29: 1 all that the LORD did in the land of *E*
29:15 surroundings we lived in the land of *E*
29:24 when he brought them out of the land of *E,*
34:11 to perform in the land of *E* against Pharaoh
Jos 2:10 Red Sea before you when you came out of *E,*
5: 4 Of all the people who came out of *E,*
5: 4 during the journey after they left *E.*
5: 5 the departure from *E* were circumcised.
5: 6 people that came forth from *E* died off
5: 9 I have removed the reproach of *E* from you."
9: 9 all that he did in *E* and all that he did
13: 3 the stream adjoining *E* to the boundary
15: 4 the Wadi of *E* before coming out at the sea.
15:47 Wadi of *E* and the coast of the Great Sea.
24: 4 Jacob and his children went down to *E.*
24: 5 and smote *E* with the prodigies which I
24: 6 Afterward I led you out of *E,*
24: 7 After you witnessed what I did to *E,*
24:14 fathers served beyond the River and in *E,*
24:17 us and our fathers up out of the land of *E,*
24:32 the Israelites had brought up from *E,*
Jgs 2: 1 I who brought you up from *E* and led you
2:12 who had led them out of the land of *E,*
6: 8 I led you up from *E;*
6: 9 of *E* and of all your other oppressors.
6:13 said 'Did not the LORD bring us up from *E?'*
11:13 and the Jordan when they came up from *E.*
11:16 For when they came up from *E,*
19:30 came up from the land of *E* to this day.
1Sm 2:27 in *E* as slaves to the house of Pharaoh.
8: 8 day I brought them up from *E* to this day,
10:18 'It was I who brought Israel up from *E*
12: 6 brought your fathers up from the land of *E.*
12: 8 went to *E* and the Egyptians oppressed them,
12: 8 Moses and Aaron to bring them out of *E,*
15: 2 barred his way as he was coming up from *E.*
15: 6 to the Israelites when they came up from *E."*
15: 7 approaches of Shur, on the frontier of *E.*
27: 8 on the approach to Shur, and the land of *E.*
2Sm 7: 6 led the Israelites out of *E* to the present,
7:23 which you redeemed for yourself from *E?*
8: 7 [These Shishak, king of *E,*
1Kgs 3: 1 by marriage with Pharaoh, king of *E.*
5: 1 the Philistines, down to the border of *E;*
6: 1 of the Israelites from the land of *E,*
8: 9 at their departure from the land of *E.*
8:16 day I brought my people Israel out of *E,*
8:21 when he brought them out of the land of *E."*
8:51 inheritance, whom you brought out of *E,*
8:53 when you brought our fathers out of *E,*
8:65 from Labo of Hamath to the Wadi of *E,*
9: 9 their fathers out of the land of *E;*
9:16 Hazor, Megiddo, Gezer (Pharaoh, king of *E,*
10:29 imported from *E* cost six hundred shekels,
11:17 *E* with some Edomite servants of his father.
11:18 went into Egypt to Pharaoh, king of *E,*
11:21 When Hadad in *E* heard that David rested
11:40 he escaped to King Shishak, in *E,*
12: 2 son of Nebat, who was still in *E,*
12: 2 returned from *E* as soon as he learned this.
12:28 who brought you up from the land of *E."*
14:25 year of King Rehoboam, Shishak, king of *E,*
2Kgs 17: 4 sending envoys to the king of *E* at Sais,
17: 7 had brought them up from the land of *E,*
17: 7 the domination of Pharaoh, king of *E,*
17:36 of *E* with great power and outstretched arm:
18:21 This *E,* the staff on which you rely,
18:21 king of *E* is to all who rely on him.
18:24 as you do on *E* for chariots and horsemen?
19:24 the soles of my feet all the rivers of *E.*
21:15 fathers came forth from *E* until today.'"
23:29 In his time Pharaoh Neco, king of *E,*
23:34 Jehoahaz he took away with him to *E,*
24: 7 king of *E* did not again leave his own land,
24: 7 taken all that belonged to the king of *E*
24: 7 from the Wadi of *E* to the Euphrates River.
25:26 and went to *E* for fear of the Chaldeans.
1Chr 13: 5 Israel, from Shihor of *E* to Labo of Hamath,
17:21 people Israel, whom you redeemed from *E,*
2Chr 1:16 also imported horses from *E* and Cilicia.
1:17 bring up chariots from *E* and export them
5:10 the Israelites at their departure from *E.*
6: 5 I brought my people out of the land of *E,*
7: 8 from Labo of Hamath to the Wadi of *E,*
7:22 who brought them out of the land of *E,*
9:26 Philistines and down to the border of *E.*
9:28 for Solomon from *E* and from all the lands.
10: 2 in *E* where he had fled from King Solomon,
10: 2 fled from King Solomon, he returned from *E.*
12: 2 year of King Rehoboam, Shishak, king of *E,*
12: 3 the army that came with him from *E*—
12: 9 Therefore Shishak, king of *E,*
20:10 invade when they came from the land of *E,*
26: 8 to Uzziah and his fame spread as far as *E,*
35:20 to restore the temple, Neco, king of *E,*
36: 3 The king of *E* deposed him in Jerusalem and
36: 4 Then the king of *E* made his brother
36: 4 brother Jehoahaz away and brought him to *E.*
Neh 9: 9 saw the affliction of our fathers in *E,*
9:17 heads to return to their slavery in *E.*
9:18 is your God who brought you up out of *E,'*
Tb 8: 3 the odor of the fish, fled into Upper *E;*
Jdt 1: 9 Chelous, Kadesh, and the River of *E;*
1:10 of *E* as far as the borders of Ethiopia.
1:12 in *E* as far as the borders of the two seas.
5:10 land of Canaan, they went down into *E.*
5:11 The king of *E,* however, rose up against
5:12 and he struck the land of *E* with plagues
6: 5 revenge on this race of people from *E.*
Est C: 9 which you redeemed for yourself out of *E.*
1Mc 1:16 Antiochus proposed to become king of *E,*
1:17 He invaded *E* with a strong force,
1:18 fleet, to make war on Ptolemy, king of *E.*
1:19 cities in the land of *E* were captured,
1:19 and Antiochus plundered the land of *E.*
1:20 *E* in the year one hundred and forty-three,
2:53 the commandment, and he became master of *E.*
3:32 the Euphrates River to the frontier of *E,*
10:51 sent ambassadors to Ptolemy, king of *E,*
10:57 his daughter Cleopatra set out from *E*
11: 1 The king of *E* gathered his forces,
11:13 on his head, that of *E* and that of Asia.
11:59 the Ladder of Tyre to the frontier of *E.*
2Mc 1: 1 greetings to their brethren, the Jews in *E,*
1:10 the anointed priests, and to the Jews in *E.*
4:21 to *E* for the coronation of King Philometor,
5: 1 sent his second expedition into *E.*
5: 8 After being driven into *E,*
5:11 set out from *E* and took Jerusalem by storm.
9:29 Antiochus' son, he later withdrew into *E,*
Ps(s) 68:32 Let nobles come from *E;*
78:12 he did wondrous things, in the land of *E,*
78:43 in *E* and his marvels in the plain of Zoan,
78:51 He smote every first-born in *E,*
80: 9 A vine from *E* you transplanted;
81: 6 when he came forth from the land of *E.*
81:11 God who led you forth from the land of *E;*
87: 4 tell of *E* and Babylon among those that
105:23 Then Israel came to *E,* and Jacob
105:38 *E* rejoiced at their going,
106: 7 fathers in *E* considered not your wonders;
106:21 saved them, who had done great deeds in *E,*
114: 1 When Israel came forth from *E,*
135: 8 He smote the first-born in *E,*
135: 9 signs and wonders into your midst, O *E,*
Is 7:18 fly that is in the farthest streams of *E,*
10:26 his staff over the sea as he did against *E.*
11:11 people that is left from Assyria and *E,*
11:15 shall dry up the tongue of the Sea of *E,*
11:16 Israel when he came up from the land of *E.*
19: 1 Oracle on *E:*
19: 1 riding on a swift cloud on his way to *E;*
19: 1 The idols of *E* tremble before him,
19: 2 I will rouse *E* against *E:*
19: 4 deliver *E* into the power of a cruel master,
19: 6 the canals of *E* shall dwindle and dry up.
19:12 the LORD of hosts has planned against *E.*
19:13 The chiefs of her tribes have led *E* astray,
19:14 have made *E* stagger in whatever she does,
19:15 *E* shall have no work to do for head or tail,
19:18 five cities in the land of *E* speaking
19:19 be an altar to the LORD in the land of *E,*
19:20 to the LORD of hosts in the land of *E,*
19:21 The LORD shall make himself known in *E,*
19:22 Although the LORD shall smite *E* severely,
19:23 there shall be a highway from *E* to Assyria;
19:23 the Assyrians shall enter *E,*
19:23 enter Assyria, and *E* shall serve Assyria.
19:24 shall be a third party with *E* and Assyria,
19:25 "Blessed be my people *E,*
20: 3 a sign and portent against *E* and Ethiopia,
20: 4 king of Assyria lead away captives from *E,*
20: 4 with buttocks uncovered [the shame of *E.*
20: 5 of Ethiopia, their hope, and because of *E,*
23: 5 When it is heard in *E* they shall be in
27:12 between the Euphrates and the Wadi of *E,*
27:13 Assyria and the outcasts in the land of *E*
30: 2 They go down to *E,* but my counsel
30: 7 to *E* whose help is futile and vain.
31: 1 Woe to those who go down to *E* for help,
36: 6 This *E,* the staff on which you rely,
36: 6 That is what Pharaoh, king of *E,*
36: 9 you rely on *E* for chariots and horsemen!
37:25 the soles of my feet all the rivers of *E.*
43: 3 I give *E* as your ransom,
45:14 The earnings of *E,* the gain of Ethiopia,
52: 4 To *E* in the beginning my people went down,

Jer 2: 6 LORD who brought us up from the land of E,
2:18 And now, why go to E,
2:36 By E will you be shamed,
7:22 day I brought them out of the land of E,
7:25 left the land of E even to this day,
9:25 E and Judah, Edom and the Ammonites,
11: 4 I brought them up out of the land of E,
11: 7 up out of the land of E even to this day.
16:14 who brought the Israelites out of E";
23: 7 the Israelites out of the land of E";
24: 8 those who have settled in the land of E.
25:19 Pharaoh, king of E, and his servants,
26:21 Uriah heard of it and fled in fear to E.
26:22 him into E to bring Uriah back to the king,
31:32 to lead them forth from the land of E;
32:20 wonders in the land of E and to this day,
32:21 E amid signs and wonders and great terror.
34:13 brought your fathers out of the land of E,
37: 5 Also, Pharaoh's army had set out from E,
37: 7 to help you will return to its own land, E.
41:17 they stopped, intending to flee into E.
42:14 this land, saying, "No, we will go to E,
42:15 If you are determined to go to E,
42:16 you fear shall reach you in the land of E;
42:16 you dread shall cling to you no less in E,
42:17 those men who determine to go to E to stay,
42:18 be poured out on you when you reach E.
42:19 do not go to E!
43: 2 you to tell us not to go to E to settle.
43: 7 Against the LORD's command they went to E,
43:11 He shall come and strike the land of E:
43:12 the land of E and depart victorious.
43:13 in the land of E and destroy with fire
44: 1 the people of Judah who were living in E,
44: 1 Tahpanhes, and Memphis, and in Upper E:
44: 8 the land of E where you have come to live?
44:12 who insisted on coming to dwell in E,
44:12 In the land of E they shall fall by the
44:13 Thus will I punish those who live in E,
44:13 in the land of E shall escape or survive.
44:15 the people who lived in Lower and Upper E,
44:24 the LORD, all you Judeans in the land of E:
44:26 all you people of Judah who live in E;
44:26 in the whole land of E no man of Judah
44:27 All the men of Judah in E shall perish by
44:28 the sword to return from the land of E
44:28 settle in E shall know whose word stands,
44:30 will hand over Pharaoh Hophra, king of E,
46: 2 Concerning E.
46: 2 the army of Pharaoh Neco, king of E,
46: 8 E surges like the Nile,
46:11 Gilead, and take balm, O virgin daughter E!
46:13 king of Babylon, to attack the land of E:
46:14 Announce it in E, publish it in Migdol,
46:17 Call Pharaoh, king of E,
46:19 baggage for exile, capital of daughter E;
46:20 E is a pretty heifer,
46:24 Disgraced is daughter E,
46:25 I will punish Amon of Thebes, and E,
46:26 But later on E shall be inhabited again,
Lam 5: 6 To E we submitted, and to Assyria,
Bar 1:19 out of the land of E until the present day,
1:20 led our fathers forth from the land of E
2:11 out of the land of E with your mighty hand,
Ez 17:15 to E to obtain horses and a great army.
19: 4 took him away with hooks to the land of E.
20: 5 of E I revealed myself to them and swore:
20: 6 of E to the land I had scouted for them,
20: 7 not defile yourselves with the idols of E:
20: 8 eyes, they did not abandon the idols of E.
20: 8 my anger on them there in the land of E;
20: 9 I would bring them out of the land of E.
20:10 land of E and brought them into the desert.
20:36 fathers in the desert of the land of E,
23: 3 even as young girls played the harlot in E.
23: 8 up the harlotry which she had begun in E,
23:19 she had been a harlot in the land of E.
23:20 She lusted for the lechers of E,
23:27 and to the harlotry you began in E;
23:27 toward it, nor shall you remember E again.
27: 7 Fine embroidered linen from E became your
29: 2 set your face against Pharaoh, king of E,
29: 2 and prophesy against him and against all E.
29: 3 I am coming at you, Pharaoh, king of E,
29: 6 who dwell in E may know that I am the LORD.
29: 9 land of E shall become a desolate waste;
29:10 I will make the land of E a waste and a
29:12 the land of E the most desolate of lands,
29:19 now giving the land of E to Nebuchadnezzar,
29:20 his toil I have given him the land of E,
30: 4 Then a sword shall come upon E,
30: 4 be in Ethiopia, when the slain fall in E,
30: 6 Those who support E shall fall,
30: 8 to E and when all who help her are broken.
30: 9 they shall be in anguish on the day of E,
30:10 throngs of E by the hand of Nebuchadnezzar,
30:11 They shall draw their swords against E,
30:13 Memphis and the princes of the land of E,
30:13 I will cast fear into the land of E,
30:16 I will set fire to E;
30:18 be darkened when I break the scepter of E.
30:19 Thus will I inflict punishments on E,
30:21 broken the arm of Pharaoh, the king of E,
30:22 I am coming at Pharaoh, the king of E,
30:24 against E so as to plunder and pillage it.
30:25 for him to wield against the land of E.
31: 2 Son of man, say to Pharaoh, the king of E,
32: 2 utter a lament over Pharaoh, the king of E,
32:12 They shall lay waste the glory of E,
32:15 When I turn E into a waste,
32:16 E and all its hordes shall they chant it,
32:18 Son of man, lament over the throngs of E,
32:20 the mighty warriors shall speak to E:
47:19 Meribath-kadesh, thence to the Wadi of E,
48:28 and from there to the Wadi of E,
Dn 9:15 out of the land of E with a strong hand,
11: 8 gold, he shall carry away as booty into E.
11:42 and not even the land of E shall escape.
11:43 and silver and all the treasures of E;
Hos 2:17 youth, when she came up from the land of E.
7:11 They call upon E, they go to Assyria.
7:16 thus they shall be mocked in the land of E.
8:13 they shall return to E.
9: 3 Ephraim shall return to E,
9: 6 go from the ruins, E shall gather them in,
11: 1 I loved him, out of E I called my son.
11: 5 He shall return to the land of E,
11:11 west, Out of E they shall come trembling,
12: 2 terms with Assyria, and carries oil to E.
12:10 the LORD, your God, since the land of E;
12:14 a prophet the LORD brought Israel out of E,
13: 4 the LORD, your God, since the land of E;
Jl 4:19 E shall be a waste,
Am 2:10 I who brought you up from the land of E,
3: 1 that I brought up from the land of E.
3: 9 of Ashdod, in the castles of the land of E:
4:10 sent upon you a pestilence like that of E,
8: 8 Nile, and settles back like the river of E?
9: 5 and settles back like the river of E;
9: 7 bring the Israelites from the land of E
Mi 6: 4 For I brought you up from the land of E,
7:12 shall come to you from Assyria and from E,
7:15 the days when you came from the land of E,
Na 3: 9 Ethiopia was her strength, and E,
Hg 2: 5 I made with you when you came out of E,
Zec 10:10 I will bring them back from the land of E,
10:11 I will cross over to E and smite the waves
10:11 cast down, and the scepter of E taken away.
14:18 And if the family of E does not come up,
14:19 This shall be the punishment of E,
Mt 2:13 the child and his mother, and flee to E.
2:14 and his mother and left that night for E.
2:15 "Out of E I have called my son."
2:19 in a dream to Joseph in E with the command:
Acts 2:10 of Asia, Phrygia, and Pamphylia, E,
7: 9 patriarchs sold Joseph into slavery in E,
7:10 in the court of the Pharaoh, king of E,
7:10 of E and of the Pharaoh's entire household.
7:11 and great trial came upon E and Canaan,
7:12 Hearing that there was grain in E,
7:15 Jacob went down to E and died there,
7:17 people in E grew more and more numerous,
7:18 until a new king came to power in E,
7:22 Moses was educated in all the lore of E.
7:34 people in E and have heard their groaning,
7:34 Come now, I will send you into E.'
7:36 wonders and signs in the land of E,
7:39 thrust him aside and longed to return to E.
7:40 Moses who brought us out of the land of E,
13:17 during their sojourn in the land of E,
Heb 3:16 Was it not all whom Moses had led out of E?
8: 9 hand to lead them forth from the land of E:
11:26 greater riches than the treasures of E,
11:27 By faith he left E,
Jude 1: 5 rescued his people from the land of E
Rv 11: 8 which has the symbolic name "Sodom" or E,"

EGYPTIAN (31)

Gn 16: 1 had, however, an E maidservant named Hagar.
16: 3 his wife Sarai took her maid, Hagar the E,
21: 9 Sarah noticed the son whom Hagar the E had
25:12 of Abraham's son Ishmael, whom Hagar the E,
39: 1 taken down to Egypt, a certain E (Potiphar,
39: 2 assigned to the household of his E master.
47:20 for them to bear, every E sold his field;
Ex 1:19 Hebrew women are not like the E women.
2:11 labor, he saw an E striking a Hebrew,
2:12 one, he slew the E and hid him in the sand.
2:14 thinking of killing me as you killed the E?"
2:19 "An E saved us from the interference of
7:22 But the E magicians did the same by their
14:24 column of the fiery cloud upon the E force
Lv 24:10 of the tribe of Dan) and an E father.
Dt 11: 4 E army and to their horses and chariots,
23: 8 since he is your brother, nor the E,
28:27 strike you with E boils and with tumors,
1Sm 30:11 An E was found in the open country and
30:13 "I am an E, the slave of an Amalekite.
2Sm 23:21 he, too, who slew an E of large stature.
23:21 Although the E was armed with a spear,
1Chr 2:34 only daughters, had an E slave named Jarha.
4:18 His (Mered's) E wife bore Jered,
11:23 He likewise slew the E,
11:23 The E carried a spear that was like a
Prv 7:16 my couch, with brocaded cloths of E linen;
Jer 43:13 with fire the temples of the E gods.
Acts 7:24 and avenged the victim by slaying the E.
7:28 killing me as you killed the E yesterday?'
21:38 "Aren't you that E who caused the riot

EGYPTIANS (98)

Gn 12:12 When the E see you,
12:14 the E saw how beautiful the woman was;
39: 5 LORD blessed the E house for Joseph's sake;
41:55 Pharaoh directed all the E to go to Joseph
41:56 that had grain and rationed it to the E,
43:32 and to the E who partook of his board.
43:32 E may not eat with Hebrews;
45: 2 his sobs were so loud that the E heard him,
46:34 since all shepherds are abhorrent to the E."
47:15 Canaan was spent, all the E came to Joseph,
50: 3 and the E mourned him for seventy days.
50:11 is a solemn funeral the E are having."
Ex 1:12 The E, then, dreaded the Israelites
3: 8 from the hands of the E and lead them out
3: 9 truly noted that the E are oppressing them.
3:21 E so well-disposed toward this people that,
3:22 Thus you will despoil the E."
6: 5 whom the E are treating as slaves,
6: 6 E and will deliver you from their slavery.
6: 7 when I free you from the labor of the E
7: 5 so that the E may learn that I am the LORD,
7:18 the E will be unable to drink its water."
7:21 that the E could not drink its water.
7:24 All the E had to dig in the neighborhood
8:17 The houses of the E and the very ground on
8:22 LORD, our God, are an abomination to the E.
8:22 to them, will not the E stone us?
9: 6 All the livestock of the E died,
9:11 no less than on the rest of the E.
10: 2 the E and what signs I wrought among them,
10: 6 houses of your servants and of all the E;
11: 3 made the E well-disposed toward the people;
11: 7 between the E and the Israelites.
12:23 the LORD will go by, striking down the E.
12:27 when he struck down the E,
12:30 he and all his servants and all the E;
12:33 The E likewise urged the people on,
12:35 they asked the E for articles of silver
12:36 The LORD indeed had made the E so
12:36 Thus did they despoil the E.
14: 4 and the E will know that I am the LORD."
14: 9 The E, then, pursued them;
14:10 the E were on the march in pursuit of them.
14:12 Let us serve the E'?
14:12 slaves of the E than to die in the desert."
14:13 These E whom you see today you will never
14:17 But I will make the E so obstinate that
14:18 The E shall know that I am the LORD,
14:20 the camp of the E and that of Israel.
14:23 The E followed in pursuit;
14:25 the E sounded the retreat before Israel,
14:25 LORD was fighting for them against the E.
14:26 that the water may flow back upon the E,
14:27 The E were fleeing head on toward the sea,
14:30 Israel on that day from the power of the E.
14:30 When Israel saw the E lying dead on the
14:31 that the LORD had shown against the E,
15:26 the diseases with which I afflicted the E;
18: 8 Pharaoh and the E for the sake of Israel,
18: 9 in rescuing them from the hands of the E.
18:10 people from the hands of Pharaoh and the E.
18:11 deliver the people from the power of the E."
19: 4 seen for yourselves how I treated the E
32:12 Why should the E say,
Lv 26:13 of the E and freed you from their slavery,
Nm 14:13 "Are the E to hear this?
20:15 how the E maltreated us and our fathers,
33: 4 While the E buried their first-born all of
Dt 11: 3 signs and deeds he wrought among the E,
26: 6 When the E maltreated and oppressed us,
Jos 24: 6 the E pursued your fathers to the Red Sea
24: 7 darkness between your people and the E,
Jgs 10:11 "Did not the E, the Amorites,
1Sm 4: 8 E with various plagues and with pestilence.
6: 6 as the E and Pharaoh were stubborn?
10:18 delivered you from the power of the E
12: 8 went to Egypt and the E oppressed them,
2Sm 23:21 club and wrested the spear from the E hand,
1Kgs 5:10 all the Cedemites and all the E in wisdom.
1Chr 11:23 a staff, wrested the spear from the E hand,
Ezr 9: 1 Jebusites, Ammonites, Moabites, E,
Jdt 5:12 When the E expelled them,
Ps(s) 136:10 Who smote the E in their first-born,
Is 19: 1 him, the hearts of the E melt within them.
19: 3 The courage of the E ebbs away within them,
19:16 On that day the E shall be like women,
19:17 land of Judah shall be a terror to the E.
19:21 and the E shall know the LORD in that day:
19:23 shall enter Egypt, and the E enter Assyria,
31: 3 The E are men, not God,
Ez 16:26 You played the harlot with the E,
23: 3 There the E caressed their bosoms and
23:21 girlhood, when the E fondled your breasts,
29:12 and I will scatter the E among the nations
29:13 I will gather the E from the peoples
30:23 I will scatter the E among the nations and

EGYPTIANS (cont.)
30:26 [I will scatter the *E* among the nations
Heb 11:29 but when the *E* attempted the same thing

EGYPT'S (8)
Gn 47:21 from one end of *E* territory to the other.
Is 30: 2 protection and take refuge in *E* shadow;
30: 3 and refuge in *E* shadow your disgrace.
Jer 43:12 He shall set fire to the temples of *E* gods,
Ez 29:14 scattered, and I will restore *E* fortune,
30:15 out my wrath on Pelusium, *E* stronghold,
32:23 her company is around *E* grave,
32:24 is Elam with all her throng about *E* grave,

EHUD (12)
Jgs 3:15 up for them a savior, the Benjaminite *E*,
3:16 *E* made himself a two-edged dagger a foot
3:20 and *E* went in to him where he sat alone in
3:20 sat alone in his cool upper room, *E* said,
3:21 and then *E* with his left hand drew the
3:23 Then *E* went out into the hall,
3:24 When *E* had left and the servants came,
3:26 their delay *E* made good his escape and,
1Chr 7:10 sons of Bilhan were Jeush, Benjamin, *E*,
8: 3 Bela were Addar and Gera, the father of *E*.
8: 4 The sons of *E* were Abishua,
8: 6 These were the sons of *E*,

EHUD'S (1)
Jgs 4: 1 After *E* death,

EIGHT (64)
Gn 5: 4 *e* hundred years after the birth of Seth,
5: 7 Seth lived *e* hundred and seven years after
5:10 Enosh lived *e* hundred and fifteen years
5:13 Kenan lived *e* hundred and forty years
5:16 Mahalalel lived *e* hundred and thirty years
5:17 was *e* hundred and ninety-five years;
5:19 *e* hundred years after the birth of Enoch,
17:12 male among you, when he is *e* days old,
21: 4 When his son Isaac was *e* days old,
22:23 *e* Milcah bore to Abraham's brother Nahor.
Ex 26:25 Thus, there shall be in the rear *e* boards,
36:30 Thus, there were in the rear *e* boards,
Nm 2:24 was one hundred and *e* thousand one hundred.]
3:28 they numbered *e* thousand three hundred.
4:48 was *e* thousand five hundred and eighty,
7: 8 and four wagons and *e* oxen to the
29:29 the sixth day you shall offer *e* bullocks,
Jgs 3: 8 Naharaim, whom they served for *e* years.
12:14 After having judged Israel for *e* years,
1Sm 17:12 He had *e* sons,
2Sm 23: 8 over *e* hundred slain in a single encounter.
24: 9 *e* hundred thousand men fit for military
1Kgs 7:10 blocks, some ten cubits and some *e* cubits.
2Kgs 8:17 reign, and he reigned *e* years in Jerusalem.
22: 1 was *e* years old when he began to reign,
1Chr 12:25 six thousand *e* hundred armed troops.
12:31 twenty thousand *e* hundred warriors,
24: 4 groups, and the latter into *e* groups,
2Chr 13: 3 him in battle with *e* hundred thousand
21: 5 king, and he reigned *e* years in Jerusalem.
21:20 king, and he reigned *e* years in Jerusalem.
29:17 consecrated the LORD's house during *e* days,
34: 1 Josiah was *e* years old when he became king,
34: 3 In the *e* year of his reign,
Ezr 2: 6 Joab, two thousand *e* hundred and twelve;
Neh 7:11 Joab, two thousand *e* hundred and eighteen;
7:13 sons of Zattu, *e* hundred and forty-five;
11:12 temple service, *e* hundred and twenty-two;
1Mc 3:24 About *e* hundred of their men fell,
4:56 For *e* days they celebrated the dedication
4:59 on the anniversary every year for *e* days,
5:20 into Galilee, and *e* thousand men to Judas,
5:34 *e* thousand of their men fell that day.
9: 6 camp, until only *e* hundred men remained.
10:85 burned alive, came to about *e* thousand men.
15:13 thousand infantry and *e* thousand horsemen.
2Mc 2:12 the feast in the same way for *e* days.
8:20 when only *e* thousand Jews fought along
8:20 the *e* thousand routed one hundred and
10: 6 for *e* days as on the feast of Booths,
Eccl 11: 2 Make seven or *e* portions;
Jer 41:15 and fled to the Ammonites with *e* men.
52:29 *e* hundred and thirty-two persons from
Ez 40: 9 vestibule of the gate, which was *e* cubits,
40:31 and it had a stairway of *e* steps.
40:34 there, and it had a stairway of *e* steps.
40:37 there, and it had a stairway of *e* steps.
40:41 on either side of the gate *e* tables],
Mi 5: 4 it seven shepherds, *e* men of royal rank;
Lk 9:28 *e* days after saying this he took Peter,
Acts 9:33 who had been bedridden for *e* years.
25: 6 After spending *e* or ten days in Jerusalem,
1Pt 3:20 At that time, a few persons, *e* in all,

EIGHTEEN (24)
Gn 14:14 three hundred and *e* of his retainers,
Jgs 3:14 served Eglon, king of Moab, for *e* years.
10: 8 For *e* years they afflicted and oppressed
20:25 against them felled *e* thousand Israelites,
20:44 of Gibeah, while *e* thousand of them fell,
2Sm 8:13 *e* thousand Edomites in the Salt Valley;
1Kgs 7:15 each *e* cubits high and twelve cubits in
2Kgs 24: 8 was *e* years old when he began to reign,
25:17 Each of the pillars was *e* cubits high;
1Chr 12:32 *e* thousand, designated by name
18:12 *e* thousand Edomites in the Valley of Salt.
26: 9 Of Meshelemiah, *e* sons and brethren,
29: 7 of silver, *e* thousand talents of bronze,
2Chr 11:21 he had taken *e* wives and sixty concubines,
36: 9 was *e* years old when he became king,
Ezr 8: 9 and with him two hundred and *e* males;
8:18 with his sons and brethren, *e* men.
Neh 7:11 Joab, two thousand eight hundred and *e*;
2Mc 5:21 off *e* hundred talents from the temple,
Jer 52:21 Each of the pillars was *e* cubits high and
Ez 48:35 perimeter of the City is *e* thousand cubits.
Lk 13: 4 Or take those *e* who were killed by a
13:11 There was a woman there who for *e* years
13:16 in the bondage of Satan for *e* years

EIGHTEENTH (13)
1Kgs 15: 1 In the *e* year of King Jeroboam,
2Kgs 3: 1 in Samaria [in the *e* year of Jehoshaphat,
22: 3 In his *e* year, King Josiah sent the scribe
23:23 of Judah, until the *e* year of king Josiah,
1Chr 24:15 seventeenth to Hezir, the *e* to Happizzez,
25:25 The *e* fell to Hanani,
2Chr 13: 1 In the *e* year of King Jeroboam,
34: 8 In the *e* year of his reign,
35:19 It was in the *e* year of Josiah's reign
Jdt 2: 1 In the *e* year, on the twenty-second day
1Mc 14:27 "On the *e* day of Elul,
Jer 32: 1 of Judah, the *e* year of Nebuchadnezzar.
52:29 in the *e* year of Nebuchadnezzar,

EIGHTH (37)
Ex 22:29 but on the *e* day you must give it to me.
Lv 9: 1 *e* day Moses summoned Aaron and his sons,
12: 3 On the *e* day, the flesh of the boy's
14:10 "On the *e* day he shall take two
14:23 On the *e* day of his purification he shall
15:14 On the *e* day he shall take two turtledoves
15:29 On the *e* day she shall take two
22:27 the *e* day onward will it be acceptable,
23:36 and on the *e* day you shall again hold a
23:39 the *e* day shall be days of complete rest.
25:22 When you sow in the *e* year,
Nm 6:10 On the *e* day he shall bring two
7:54 On the *e* day it was the turn of Gamaliel,
29:35 the *e* day you shall hold a solemn meeting,
1Kgs 6:38 to plan, in the month of Bul, the *e* month,
8:66 On the *e* day he dismissed the people,
12:32 Jeroboam established a feast in the *e* month
12:33 Bethel on the fifteenth day of the *e* month,
2Kgs 24:12 Babylon, who, in the *e* year of his reign,
1Chr 12:13 Attai sixth, Eliel seventh, Johanan *e*,
15:21 led the chant on lyres set to "the *e*."
24:10 the seventh to Hakkoz, the *e* to Abijah,
25:15 The *e* was Jeshaiah,
26: 5 Issachar, the seventh, Peullethai, the *e*,
27:11 *E*, for the *e* month,
2Chr 7: 9 On the *e* day they held a special meeting,
29:17 and on the *e* day of the month they arrived
Neh 8:18 days, and the solemn assembly on the *e* day,
Ez 43:27 these days are over, from the *e* day on,
Zec 1: 1 of Darius, in the *e* month
Lk 1:59 the circumcision of the child on the *e* day,
2:21 the *e* day arrived for his circumcision,
Acts 7: 8 of Isaac, circumcised him on the *e* day.
Phil 3: 5 I was circumcised on the *e* day,
Rv 17:11 no longer, even though it is an *e* king,
21:20 the seventh chrysolite, the *e* beryl,

EIGHTIETH (1)
1Kgs 6: 1 In the four hundred and *e* year from the

EIGHTY (28)
Gn 35:28 of Isaac was one hundred and *e* years;
Ex 7: 7 Moses was *e* years old and Aaron
Nm 4:48 was eight thousand five hundred and *e*,
Jgs 3:30 and the land had rest for *e* years.
2Sm 19:33 very old man of *e* and very wealthy besides,
19:36 I am now *e* years old.
1Kgs 5:29 *e* thousand stonecutters in the mountain.
12:21 hundred and *e* thousand seasoned warriors
2Kgs 6:25 an ass's head sold for *e* pieces of silver,
10:24 stationed *e* men outside with this warning,
1Chr 15: 9 Eliel, their chief, and *e* of his brethren;
2Chr 2: 1 men to carry stone and *e* thousand to cut
2:17 and *e* thousand cutters in the mountains,
11: 1 a hundred and *e* thousand seasoned warriors,
14: 7 *e* thousand from Benjamin
17:15 and with him two hundred *e* thousand.
17:18 hundred and *e* thousand equipped for war.
26:17 and with him *e* other priests of the LORD,
Ezr 8: 8 son of Michael, and with him *e* males;
Est 1: 4 For as many as a hundred and *e* days,
2Mc 4: 8 as *e* talents from another source of income.
5:14 space of three days, *e* thousand were lost,
11: 2 mustered about *e* thousand infantry and all
11: 4 thousands of horsemen, and his *e* elephants.
Ps(s) 90:10 Seventy is the sum of our years, or *e*,
Sg 6: 8 There are sixty queens, *e* concubines,
Jer 41: 5 knew of it, *e* men with beards shaved off,
Lk 16: 7 said, 'Take your invoice and make it *e*.'

EIGHTY-EIGHT (3)
1Chr 25: 7 of them skilled men, was two hundred and *e*.
Neh 7:26 Bethlehem and Netophah, one hundred and *e*;
2Mc 1:10 Dated in the year one hundred and *e*.

EIGHTY-FIVE (7)
Jos 14:10 and although I am now *e* years old,
1Sm 22:18 on that day *e* who wore the linen ephod.
2Kgs 19:35 and *e* thousand men in Assyrian camp.
1Mc 7:41 killed a hundred and *e* thousand of them.
2Mc 8:19 and *e* thousand of his men were destroyed,
15:22 and *e* thousand men of Sennacherib's army.
Is 37:36 and *e* thousand in the Assyrian camp.

EIGHTY-FOUR (2)
Neh 11:18 in the holy city was two hundred and *e*.
Lk 2:37 and then as a widow until she was *e*.

EIGHTY-SEVEN (2)
Gn 5:25 Methuselah was one hundred and *e* years old,
1Chr 7: 5 total of *e* thousand warriors in their family

EIGHTY-SIX (2)
Gn 16:16 *e* years old when Hagar bore him Ishmael.
Nm 2: 9 one hundred and *e* thousand four hundred.]

EIGHTY-THREE (1)
Ex 7: 7 old and Aaron *e* when they spoke to Pharaoh.

EIGHTY-TWO (2)
Gn 5:26 and *e* years after the birth of Lamech,
5:28 Lamech was one hundred and *e* years old,

EITHER (80)
Gn 24:50 can say nothing to you *e* for or against it.
Ex 12: 5 may take it from *e* the sheep or the goats.
16:23 You may *e* bake or boil the manna,
20:10 No work may be done then *e* by you,
26:13 on *e* side of the Dwelling to protect it.
27: 7 on *e* side of the altar when it is carried.
Lv 3: 1 the LORD *e* a male or a female animal,
3: 6 he may offer *e* a male or a female animal,
11:10 *e* fins or scales are loathsome for you,
25:36 from your countryman *e* in money or in kind,
27:10 by exchanging *e* a better for a worse one
Nm 6: 3 juice, nor eat *e* fresh or dried grapes.
22:26 room to move *e* to the right or to the left.
30:14 her husband can *e* allow to remain valid or
Dt 14:10 lack *e* fins or scales you shall not eat;
Jos 1: 7 from it *e* to the right or to the left,
8:22 Ai were hemmed in by Israelites on *e* side,
8:33 stood on *e* side of the ark facing the
Jgs 19:13 for some other place, *e* Gibeah or Ramah,
1Sm 16: 9 said, "The LORD has not chosen this one *e*."
1Kgs 7: 4 There were three window frames at *e* end,
7: 5 doorways faced each other, three at *e* end.
10:20 two to a step, one on *e* side of each step.
1Chr 12: 2 who could use *e* the right or the left hand,
2Chr 9:19 also stood there, one on *e* side of each step.
Tb 12: 8 but better than *e* is almsgiving
1Mc 4:35 men were ready *e* to live or to die bravely,
5:46 to encircle it on *e* the right or the left;
Prv 24:22 they send, and the ruin from *e* one,
Wis 13: 2 But *e* fire, or wind, or the swift air,
14:21 that men enslaved to *e* grief or tyranny
14:23 For while they celebrate *e* child-slaying
14:24 longer safeguard *e* lives or pure wedlock;
14:24 but each *e* waylays and kills his neighbor,
14:28 For they *e* go mad with enjoyment,
15: 7 of *e* class the worker in clay is the judge.
Sir 13:24 his countenance, *e* for good or for evil.
20:29 of what value is *e*?
40:17 but better than *e* is finding a treasure.
40:18 preserve one's name, but better than *e*,
40:19 but better than *e*, a devoted wife;
40:20 music delight the soul, but better than *e*,
40:21 harp offer sweet melody, but better than *e*,
40:22 beauty delight the eye, but better than *e*,
40:23 are timely guides, but better than *e*,
40:24 but better than *e*, charity that rescues.
40:25 make one's way secure, but better than *e*,
40:26 build up confidence, but better than *e*,
Jer 7:27 to them, they will not listen to you *e*;
Lam 2:22 day of your wrath, *e* fugitive or survivor;
Bar 6:49 themselves *e* from war or from disaster?
Ez 14:18 be unable to save *e* sons or daughters;
40:10 of the east gate were three on *e* side,
40:10 on *e* side were also of equal size.
40:12 cells themselves were six cubits on *e* side,
40:14 the court on *e* side were six cubits.
40:21 Its cells, three on *e* side,
40:39 the gate there were two tables on *e* side,

40:41 on *e* side of the gate [eight tables],
40:48 *e* side of the door measured three cubits.
40:49 columns by the pilasters, one on *e* side.
41: 1 which were six cubits thick on *e* side.
41: 2 at *e* side of it measured five cubits each.
41: 3 at *e* side of it extended seven cubits each.
44:22 for their wives *e* widows or divorced women,
Dn 5: 8 none of them could *e* read the writing or
12: 5 one standing on *e* bank of the river.
Mt 6:24 He will *e* hate one and love the other or
12:32 *e* in this age or in the age to come.
Lk 16:13 *E* he will hate the one and love the other
Jn 9: 3 no sin, *e* of this man or of his parents.
19:18 one on *e* side,
Acts 25: 8 "I have committed no crime *e* against the
Rom 7:13 became death for me. Not that *e!*
1Cor 7:11 she must *e* remain single or become
7:19 and its lack makes no difference *e.*
2Thes 2:15 from us, *e* by our word or by letter.
Jas 5:12 oath at all, *e* "by heaven" or "by earth."
1Pt 5: 2 and not for shameful profit *e,*
Rv 22: 2 On *e* side of the river grew the trees of

EJECTED (1)

Jn 12:42 fear they might be *e* from the synagogue.

EJECTING (1)

Lk 19:45 the temple and began *e* the traders saying:

EKER (1)

1Chr 2:27 of Jerahmeel, were Maaz, Jamin, and *E.*

EKRON (23)

Jos 13: 3 adjoining Egypt to the boundary of *E*
13: 3 in Gaza, Ashdod, Ashkelon, Gath and *E);*
15:11 extended along the northern flank of *E,*
15:45 *E* and its towns and villages,
15:46 its towns and villages, from *E* to the sea,
19:43 Aijalon, Ithlah, Elon, Timnah, *E,*
Jgs 1:18 its territory, or *E* with its territory.
1Sm 5:10 The ark of God was next sent to *E;*
6:16 lords returned to *E* the same day.
6:17 for Ashkelon, one for Gath, and one for *E.*
7:14 The cities from *E* to Gath which the
17:52 approaches of Gath and to the gates of *E,*
17:52 road from Shaaraim as far as Gath and *E.*
2Kgs 1: 2 and inquire of Baalzebub, the god of *E,*
1: 3 to inquire of Baalzebub, the god of *E?'*
1: 6 to inquire of Baalzebub, the god of *E?*
1:16 to inquire of Baalzebub, the god of *E,*
1Mc 10:89 *E* and all its territory as a possession.
Jer 25:20 Ashkelon, Gaza, *E*
Am 1: 8 I will turn my hand against *E,*
Zep 2: 4 out at midday, and *E* shall be uprooted.
Zec 9: 5 *E,* too, for her hope shall come to nought
9: 7 Judah, and *E* shall be like the Jebusites.

EL (1)

Gn 33:20 up a memorial stone there and invoked *E,*

EL-BERITH (1)

Jgs 9:46 went into the crypt of the temple of *E.*

EL-PARAN (1)

Gn 14: 6 in the hill country of Seir, as far as *E,*

ELA (1)

1Kgs 4:18 Shimei, son of *E,*

ELABORATE (2)

2Mc 15:21 the hosts before him, their *e* equipment,
1Pt 3: 3 The affectation of an *e* hairdress,

ELAH (13)

Gn 36:41 of Timna, Alvah, Jetheth, Oholibamah, *E,*
1Kgs 16: 6 and his son *E* succeeded him as king.
16: 8 year of Asa, king of Judah, *E,*
16:13 *E* committed and caused Israel to commit,
16:14 The rest of the acts of *E,*
2Kgs 15:30 Hoshea, son of *E,*
17: 1 of Ahaz, king of Judah, Hoshea, son of *E,*
18: 1 In the third year of Hoshea, son of *E,*
18: 9 was the seventh year of Hoshea, son of *E,*
1Chr 1:52 of Timna, Aliah, Jetheth, Oholibamah, *E,*
4:15 of Caleb, son of Jephunneh, were Ir, *E,*
4:15 The sons of *E* were . . .
9: 8 *E,* son of Uzzi, son of Michri;

ELAM (28)

Gn 10:22 *E,* Asshur, Arpachshad, Lud, and Aram.
14: 1 king of Ellasar, Chedorlaomer king of *E,*
14: 9 against Chedorlaomer king of *E,*
1Chr 1:17 The descendants of Shem were *E,*
8:24 Eliel, Abdon, Zichri, Hanan, Hananiah, *E,*
26: 3 the third, Jathniel, the fourth, *E,*
Ezr 2: 7 sons of *E,*
2:31 sons of the other *E,*
8: 7 of the sons of *E,*
10: 2 the son of Jehiel, one of the sons of *E,*
10:26 of the sons of *E:*
Neh 7:12 sons of *E,*
7:34 sons of another *E,*
10:15 Parosh, Pahath-moab, *E,*
12:42 Eleazar, Uzzi, Jehohanan, Malchijah, *E,*
Is 11:11 and Egypt, Pathros, Ethiopia, and *E,*
21: 2 "Go up, *E;* besiege, O Media;
22: 6 *E* takes up the quivers,
Jer 25:25 all the kings of Zimri, of *E,*
49:34 The following word of the LORD against *E*
49:35 Behold, I will break the bow of *E,*
49:36 I will bring upon *E* the four winds from
49:36 to which the outcasts of *E* shall not come.
49:37 I will break *E* before their foes,
49:38 *E* and destroy from there king and princes,
49:39 days to come I will change the lot of *E,*
Ez 32:24 *E* with all her throng about Egypt's grave,
Dn 8: 2 the fortress of Susa in the province of *E;*

ELAMITE (1)

Ezr 4: 9 Urukian, Babylonian, Susian (that is *E),*

ELAMITES (2)

Jdt 1: 6 and the Hydaspes, and King Arioch of the *E,*
Acts 2: 9 We are Parthians, Medes, and *E.*

ELAPSED (5)

Dt 2:14 Thirty-eight years had *e* between our
1Sm 7: 2 twenty years *e,*
2Chr 21:19 went on until a period of two years had *e,*
Jer 25:12 but when the seventy years have *e,*
29:10 Only after seventy years have *e* for

ELASA (1)

1Mc 9: 5 three thousand picked men, had camped at *E.*

ELASAH (2)

Ezr 10:22 Ishmael, Nethanel, Jozabad, and *E.*
Jer 29: 3 Delivered in Babylon by *E,*

ELATH (7)

Dt 2: 8 we left behind us in Arabah route, *E,*
1Kgs 9:26 which is near *E* on the shore of the shore
2Kgs 14:22 who rebuilt *E* and restored it to Judah,
16: 6 time the king of Edom recovered *E* for Edom,
16: 6 The Edomites then entered *E,*
2Chr 8:17 to *E* on the seashore of the land of Edom.
26: 2 He rebuilt *E* and restored it to Judah;

ELBOW (2)

Jb 31:22 shoulder, my forearm be broken at the *e!*
Sir 41:18 and of stretching out your *e* when you dine;

ELDAAH (2)

Gn 25: 4 were Ephah, Epher, Hanoch, Abida, and *E.*
1Chr 1:33 were Ephah, Epher, Hanoch, Abida, and *E.*

ELDAD (2)

Nm 11:26 two men, one named *E* and the other Medad,
11:27 *E* and Medad are prophesying in the camp,"

ELDER (14)

1Sm 14:49 his two daughters were named, the *e,*
1Kgs 2:22 for he is my *e* brother and has with him
Tb 5:13 "I am Azariah, son of Hananiah the *e,*
5:14 Nathaniah, the two sons of Shemaiah the *e;*
Is 3: 2 judge and prophet, fortune-tellers and *e,*
3: 5 The child shall be bold toward the *e,*
9:14 [The *e* and the noble are the head,
Ez 16:46 *e* sister was Samaria with her daughters,
23: 4 Oholah was the name of the *e,*
Mt 21:28 He approached the *e* and said,
Lk 15:25 "Meanwhile the *e* son was out on the land.
1Pt 5: 1 To the elders among you I, a fellow *e,*
2Jn 1: 1 The *e* to a Lady who is elect and to her
3Jn 1: 1 The *e* to the beloved Gaius,

ELDERS (208)

Ex 3:16 "Go and assemble the *e* of the Israelites,
3:18 Then you and the *e* of Israel shall go to
4:29 and assembled all the *e* of the Israelites.
12:21 all the *e* of Israel and said to them,
17: 5 people, along with some of the *e* of Israel,
17: 6 did, in the presence of the *e* of Israel.
18:12 and Aaron came with all the *e* of Israel to
19: 7 went and summoned the *e* of the people.
24: 1 Abihu, and seventy of the *e* of Israel.
24: 9 Nadab, Abihu, and seventy *e* of Israel,
24:14 The *e,* however, had been told by him,
Lv 4:15 the *e* of the community shall lay their
9: 1 his sons, together with the *e* of Israel,
9: 3 Tell the *e* of Israel, too:
Nm 11:16 for me seventy of the *e* of Israel,
11:16 true *e* and authorities among the people,
11:24 Gathering seventy *e* of the people,
11:25 on Moses, he bestowed it on the seventy *e;*
11:30 to the camp, along with the *e* of Israel.
16:25 Moses, followed by the *e* of Israel,
22: 4 So Moab said to the *e* of Midian,
22: 7 Then the *e* of Moab and of Midian left with
Dt 5:23 the person of all your tribal heads and *e,*
19:12 the *e* of his own city shall send for him
21: 2 your *e* and judges shall go out and measur
21: 3 the *e* of that city shall take a heifer
21: 6 Then all the *e* of that city nearest the
21:19 out to the *e* at the gate of his home city,
21:20 where they shall say to those city *e,*
22:15 and bring it to the *e* at the city gate.
22:16 the father of the girl shall say to the *e,*
22:17 out the cloth before the *e* of the city.
22:18 city *e* shall take the man and chastise him,
25: 7 go up to the *e* at the gate and declare,
25: 8 Thereupon the *e* of his city shall summon
25: 9 sister-in-law, in the presence of the *e,*
27: 1 Then Moses, with the *e* of Israel,
29: 9 chiefs and judges, your *e* and officials,
31: 9 of the LORD, and to all the *e* of Israel,
31:28 your tribal *e* and your officials before me,
32: 7 you, ask your *e* and they will tell you:
Jos 7: 6 Joshua, together with the *e* of Israel,
8:10 up to Ai at its head, with the *e* of Israel.
8:33 stranger and native alike, with their *e,*
9:11 So our *e* and all the inhabitants of our
20: 4 he shall plead his case before the *e,*
23: 2 he summoned all Israel (including their *e,*
24: 1 of Israel at Shechem, summoning their *e,*
24:31 that of the *e* who outlived Joshua
Jgs 2: 7 and of those *e* who outlived Joshua and who
8:14 the seventy-seven princes and *e* of Succoth.
8:16 He took the *e* of the city,
11: 5 When this occurred the *e* of Gilead went to
11: 7 Jephthah replied to the *e* of Gilead.
11: 8 The *e* of Gilead said to Jephthah,
11: 9 Jephthah answered the *e* of Gilead,
11:10 The *e* of Gilead said to Jephthah,
11:11 So Jephthah went with the *e* of Gilead,
21:16 And the *e* of the community said,
Ru 4: 2 *e* of the city and asked them to sit nearby.
4: 4 here present, including the *e* of my people,
4: 9 then said to the *e* and to all the people,
4:11 All those at the gate, including the *e,*
1Sm 4: 3 retired to the camp, the *e* of Israel said,
8: 4 Therefore all the *e* of Israel came in a
11: 3 The *e* of Jabesh said to him:
15:30 the *e* of my people and before Israel.
16: 4 the *e* of the city came trembling to meet
30:26 sent part of the spoil to the *e* of Judah,
2Sm 3:17 said in discussion with the *e* of Israel:
5: 3 the *e* of Israel came to David in Hebron,
12:17 The *e* of his house stood beside him urging
17: 4 to Absalom and to all the *e* of Israel.
17:15 gave Absalom and the *e* of Israel,
19:12 "Say to the *e* of Judah:
1Kgs 8: 1 the *e* of Israel and all the leaders of the
8: 3 When all the *e* of Israel had arrived,
12: 6 King Rehoboam consulted the *e* who had been
12: 8 he ignored the advice the *e* had given him,
12:13 Ignoring the advice the *e* had given him,
20: 7 summoned all the *e* of the land and said:
20: 8 All the *e* and all the people said to him,
21: 8 sent them to the *e* and to the nobles who
21:11 the *e* and the nobles who dwelt in his city
2Kgs 6:32 in his house in conference with the *e.*
6:32 Elisha had said to the *e:*
10: 1 sent them to the city rulers, to the *e,*
10: 5 city, along with the *e* and the guardians,
19: 2 the scribe, and the *e* of the priests,
23: 1 The king then had all the *e* of Judah and
1Chr 11: 3 the *e* of Israel came to the king at Hebron,
15:25 Thus David, the *e* of Israel,
21:16 David and the *e,*
2Chr 5: 2 At Solomon's order the *e* of Israel and all
5: 4 When all the *e* of Israel had arrived,
10: 6 King Rehoboam consulted the *e* who had been
10: 8 But he ignored the advice the *e* had given
10:13 Ignoring the advice the *e* had given him,
34:29 convened all the *e* of Judah and Jerusalem.
Ezr 5: 5 But their God watched over the *e* of the
5: 9 We then questioned the *e,*
6: 7 Let the governor and the *e* of the Jews
6: 8 your dealing with these *e* of the Jews
6:14 The *e* of the Jews continued to make
10: 8 to the judgment of the leaders and *e,*
10:14 *e* and magistrates of each city in question,
Jdt 6:16 They then convened all the *e* of the city;
6:21 home, where he gave a banquet for the *e.*
7:23 up a great clamor and said before the *e:*
8:10 Chabris, and Charmis, the *e* of the city,
10: 6 and found Uzziah and the *e* of the city,
11:14 authorization from the council of the *e;*
13:12 to their city gate and summoned the city *e.*
15: 8 priest Joakim and the *e* of the Israelites,
1Mc 1:26 dwelt, and the rulers and the *e* groaned.
7:33 some of the *e* of the people came out
11:23 He selected some *e* and priests of Israel
12:35 returned, he assembled the *e* of the people,
13:36 kings, and to the *e* and the Jewish people.
14:20 greetings to Simon the high priest, the *e,*
14:28 rulers of the nation, and *e* of the country,
2Mc 13:13 After a private meeting with the *e,*

ELDERS (cont.)

14:37 A certain Razis, one of the e of Jerusalem,
Jb 29: 8 withdrew, while the e rose up and stood;
Ps(s) 105:22 to be like him and teach his e wisdom.
107:32 and praise him in the council of the e.
119:100 I have more descernment than the e,
Prv 31:23 gates as he sits with the e of the land.
Wis 8:10 esteem from the e though I be but a youth.
Sir 6:34 Frequent the company of the e;
32: 9 When among your e be not forward,
Is 3:14 judgment with his people's e and princes:
24:23 Jerusalem, glorious in the sight of his e.
37: 2 the scribe, and the e of the priests,
Jer 19: 1 of the e of the people and of the priests,
26:17 some of the e of the land came forward and
29: 1 to the remaining e among the exiles,
Lam 1:19 My priests and my e perished in the city;
4:16 with favor, nor show kindness to the e.
5:12 were gibbeted by them, e shown no respect.
Bar 1: 4 the nobles, the kings' sons, the e,
Ez 7:26 to the priest, and counsel to the e,
8: 1 my house, and the e of Judah sat before me,
8:11 seventy of the e of the house of Israel,
8:12 what each of these e of the house of
9: 6 men [the e who were in front of the temple.
14: 1 e of Israel came and sat down before me,
20: 1 some of the e of Israel came to consult
20: 3 speak with the e of Israel and say to them:
27: 9 The e and experts of Gebal were in you to
Dn 13: 5 two e of the people were appointed judges,
13: 5 e who were to govern the people as judges."
13:16 Nobody else was there except the two e,
13:18 unaware that the e were hidden inside.
13:28 the next day, the two wicked e also came,
13:34 e rose up and laid their hands on her head.
13:36 The e made this accusation:
13:41 since they were e and judges of the people,
13:50 To Daniel the e said,
13:61 They rose up against the two e,
Jl 1: 2 Hear this, you e!
1:14 Gather the e,
2:16 Assemble the e,
Mt 16:21 greatly there at the hands of the e,
21:23 e of the people came up to him and said:
26: 3 At that time the chief priests and e of
26:47 by the chief priests and e of the people.
26:57 where the scribes and e were convened.
27: 1 chief priests and the e of the people
27: 3 back to the chief priests and e and said,
27:12 he was accused by the chief priests and e,
27:20 the chief priests and e convinced the
27:41 and the e also joined in the jeering:
28:12 with the e and worked out their strategy,
Mk 8:31 had to suffer much, be rejected by the e,
11:27 and the e approached him and said to him,
14:43 the chief priests, the scribes, and the e.
14:53 the e and the scribes came together.
15: 1 priests, with the e and scribes (that is,
Lk 7: 3 about Jesus he sent some Jewish e to him,
9:22 many sufferings, be rejected by the e,
20: 1 and Pharisees, accompanied by the e,
22:66 At daybreak, the e of the people,
Jn 8: 9 away one by one, beginning with the e.
Acts 4: 5 When the leaders, the e,
4: 8 "Leaders of the people! E!
4:23 told them what the priests and e had said.
5:21 the full council of the e of Israel.
6:12 in this way they incited the people, the e,
22: 5 the whole council of e can bear me witness,
23:14 to the chief priests and the e and said:
24: 1 of the e and an attorney named Tertullus.
25:15 priests and the e of the Jews presented
1Pt 5: 1 To the e among you I,
5: 5 you younger men must be obedient to your e.
Rv 4: 4 upon which were seated twenty-four e;
4:10 the twenty-four e fall down before the One
5: 5 One of the e said to me:
5: 6 with the four living creatures and the e,
5: 8 twenty-four e fell down before the Lamb.
5: 8 the e were holding vessels of gold filled
5:11 throne and the living creatures and the e.
5:14 and the e fell down and worshiped.
7:11 e and the four living creatures fell down
7:13 Then one of the e asked me,
11:16 The twenty-four e who were enthroned in
14: 3 of the four living creatures and the e.
19: 4 the four and twenty e and the four living

ELDEST (5)

Jos 17: 1 since his e son,
Jb 1:13 wine in the house of their e brother,
1:18 wine in the house of their e brother,
Mt 22:25 The e died after marrying,
Mk 12:20 The e took a wife and died,

ELEAD (1)

1Chr 7:21 Ephraim's son Shuthelah, and Ezer and E,

ELEADAH (1)

1Chr 7:20 whose son was Tahath, whose son was E,

ELEALEH (5)

Nm 32: 3 Ataroth, Dibon, Jazer, Nimrah, Heshbon, E,
32:37 The Reubenites rebuilt Heshbon, E,
Is 15: 4 Heshbon and E cry out,
16: 9 I water you with tears, Heshbon and E;
Jer 48:34 of Heshbon and E is heard as far as Jahaz;

ELEASAH (4)

1Chr 2:39 Helez became the father of E.
2:40 E became the father of Sismai.
8:37 whose son was Raphah, whose son was E,
9:43 whose son was Rephaiah, whose son was E,

ELEAZAR (84)

Ex 6:23 she bore him Nadab, Abihu, E and Ithamar.
6:25 Aaron's son, E,
28: 1 with his sons Nadab, Abihu, E and Ithamar,
Lv 10: 6 said to Aaron and his sons E and Ithamar,
10:12 and his surviving sons, E and Ithamar,
10:16 the surviving sons of Aaron, E and Ithamar,
Nm 3: 2 Aaron were Nadab his first-born, Abihu, E,
3: 4 Thereafter only E and Ithamar performed
3:32 prince of the Levites, however, was E,
4:16 E, son of Aaron the priest,
17: 2 The LORD said to Moses, "Tell E,
17: 4 So E the priest had the bronze censers of
19: 3 This is to be given to E the priest,
19: 4 E the priest shall take some of its blood
20:25 his son E and bring them up on Mount Hor.
20:26 of his garments and put them on his son E;
20:28 of his garments and put them on his son E.
20:28 Moses and E came down from the mountain,
25: 7 When Phinehas, son of E,
25:11 LORD said to Moses, "Phinehas, son of E,
26: 1 slaughter the LORD said to Moses and E,
26: 3 E registered those of twenty years or more,
26:60 were born Nadab and Abihu, E and Ithamar.
26:63 men registered by Moses and the priest E
27: 2 in the presence of Moses, the priest E,
27:19 of the priest E and of the whole community,
27:21 He shall present himself to the priest E,
27:22 of the priest E and of the whole community,
31: 6 from each tribe, with Phinehas, son of E,
31:12 to Moses and the priest E and to the
31:13 When Moses and the priest E,
31:21 E the priest told the soldiers who had
31:26 E and of the heads of the ancestral houses,
31:29 the priest E as a contribution to the LORD.
31:31 So Moses and the priest E did this,
31:41 to the LORD, Moses gave to the priest E,
31:51 the priest E accepted this gold from them,
31:54 and the priest E accepted the gold from
32: 2 they came to Moses and the priest E
32:28 order in their regard to the priest E,
34:17 E the priest, and Joshua, son of Nun,
36: 1 this plea before Moses and the priest E
Dt 10: 6 E succeeding him in the priestly office.
Jos 14: 1 E the priest, Joshua, son of Nun
17: 4 These presented themselves to E the priest,
19:51 the final portions into which E the priest,
21: 1 Levite families came up to E the priest,
22:13 of Phinehas, son of E the priest,
22:31 Phinehas, son of E the priest,
22:32 Phinehas, son of E the priest,
24:33 When E, son of Aaron, also died,
Jgs 20:28 in those days, and Phinehas, son of E,
1Sm 7: 1 son E as guardian of the ark of the LORD.
2Sm 23: 9 to him, among the Three warriors, was E,
23:10 the soldiers turned back after E,
1Chr 5:29 The sons of Aaron were Nadab, Abihu, E,
5:30 E became the father of Phinehas.
6:35 his son E, whose son was Phinehas,
9:20 Phinehas, son of E,
11:12 Next to him E,
23:21 E and Kish.
23:22 E died leaving no sons,
24: 1 The sons of Aaron were Nadab, Abihu, E,
24: 2 only E and Ithamar served as priests.
24: 3 David, with Zadok, a descendant of E,
24: 4 But since the descendants of E were found
24: 5 descended both from E and from Ithamar.
24: 6 groups from E before each one from Ithamar.
24:28 Descendants of Mahli were E,
27: 4 the division of the second month was E,
Ezr 7: 5 son of Abishua, son of Phinehas, son of E,
8:33 son of Uriah, who was assisted by E,
10:25 Ramiah, Izziah, Malchijah, Mijamin, E,
Neh 12:42 the trumpets, and Maaseiah, Shemaiah, E,
1Mc 2: 5 E, who was called Avaran;
6:43 E called Avaran,
8:17 John, son of Accos, and Jason, son of E,
2Mc 6:18 E, one of the foremost scribes,
6:24 E had gone over to an alien religion.
8:23 (There was also E.)
Sir 45:23 PHINEHAS too, the son of E,
50:27 written in this book, I, Jesus, son of E,
Mt 1:15 father of Eleazar, E the father of Matthan,

ELECT (5)

Gn 23: 6 You are an e of God among us.
Wis 3: 9 his holy ones, and his care is with the e.
Mt 22:14 The invited are many, the e are few."
2Jn 1: 1 to a Lady who is e and to her children.
1:13 of your e sister send you their greetings.

ELECTION (2)

Rom 11:28 in respect to the e,
2Pt 1:10 to make your call and e permanent,

ELECTRUM (3)

Ez 1: 4 of the fire] something gleamed like e.
1:27 his waist I saw what gleamed like e;
8: 2 to be a brightness like the sheen of e.

ELEGY (3)

2Sm 1:17 this e for Saul and his son Jonathan,
3:33 And the king sang this e over Abner:
Jer 7:29 on the heights intone an e;

ELEMENT (1)

Neh 13: 3 they separated from Israel every foreign e.

ELEMENTS (9)

Nm 11: 4 The foreign e among them were so greedy
2Mc 7:22 the e of which each of you is composed.
Wis 7:17 of the universe and the force of its e,
19:18 For the e, in variable harmony
Gal 4: 3 slaves subordinated to the e of the world;
4: 9 natural e to which you seem willing to
Heb 5:12 again the basic e of the oracles of God;
2Pt 3:10 the e will be destroyed by fire,
3:12 flames and the e will melt away in a blaze.

ELEPHANT (4)

1Mc 6:35 each e having assigned to it a thousand
6:37 A strong wooden tower covering each e,
6:46 under the e and stabbed it in the belly,
2Mc 13:15 They also slew the lead e and its rider.

ELEPHANTS (11)

1Mc 1:17 with a strong force, with chariots and e,
3:34 to him half of the army, and the e,
6:30 cavalry, and thirty-two e trained for war.
6:34 They showed the e the juice of grapes and
8: 6 hundred and twenty e and with cavalry
11:56 Trypho captured the e and occupied Antioch.
2Mc 11: 4 thousands of horsemen, and his eighty e.
13: 2 hundred horsemen, twenty-two e,
14:12 Nicanor, who had been in command of the e,
15:20 their e placed in strategic positions,
15:21 equipment, and the fierceness of their e,

ELEUTHERUS (2)

1Mc 11: 7 called E and then returned to Jerusalem.
12:30 them, for they had crossed the river E.

ELEVEN (26)

Gn 32:23 the two maidservants and his e children,
37: 9 moon and e stars were bowing down to me."
Ex 26: 8 E such sheets are to be made;
26: 8 all e sheets shall be of the same size.
36:14 E such sheets were made.
36:15 all e sheets were the same size.
Nm 29:20 the third day you shall offer e bullocks,
Dt 1: 2 it is a journey of e days from Horeb to
Jos 15:51 e cities and their villages.
15:59 e cities and their villages.
Jgs 16: 5 each give you e hundred shekels of silver."
17: 2 "The e hundred shekels of silver over
17: 3 e hundred shekels of silver to his mother,
2Kgs 23:36 reign, and he reigned e years in Jerusalem.
24:18 king, and he reigned e years in Jerusalem.
2Chr 36: 5 king, and he reigned e years in Jerusalem.
36:11 king, and he reigned e years in Jerusalem.
2Mc 11:11 they laid low e thousand foot soldiers and
Jer 52: 1 king, and he reigned e years in Jerusalem.
Mt 28:16 The e disciples made their way to Galilee,
Mk 16:14 were at table, Jesus was revealed to the E.
16:20 The E went forth and preached everywhere.
Lk 24: 9 all these things to the E and the others.
24:33 E and the rest of the company assembled.
Acts 1:26 Matthias who was added to the e apostles.
2:14 Peter stood up with the E,

ELEVENTH (19)

Nm 7:72 On the e day it was the turn of Pagiel,
Dt 1: 3 year, on the first day of the e month,
1Kgs 6:38 of Bul, the eighth month, in the e year.
2Kgs 9:29 king of Judah in the e year of Joram,
25: 2 continued until the e year of Zedekiah.
1Chr 12:14 ninth, Jeremiah tenth, and Machbannai e.
24:12 the tenth to Shecaniah, the e to Eliashib,
25:18 The e was Uzziel,
27:14 E, for the e month,
1Mc 16:14 and seventy-seven, in the e month (that is,
Jer 1: 3 the fifth month of the e year of Zedekiah,
39: 2 fourth month, in the e year of Zedekiah,
52: 5 until the e year of King Zedekiah.
Ez 26: 1 month in the e year,

30:20 day of the first month in the *e* year,
31: 1 first day of the third month in the *e* year,
Zec 1: 7 twenty-fourth day of Sabat, the *e* month,
Rv 21:20 the tenth chrysoprase, the *e* hyacinth,

ELHANAN (4)

2Sm 21:19 with the Philistines in Gob, in which *E*,
23:24 *E*, son of Dodo,
1Chr 11:26 *E*,
20: 5 there was war with the Philistines, and *E*,

ELI (34)

1Sm 1: 3 to him at Shiloh, where the two sons of *E*,
1: 9 *E* the priest was sitting on a chair near
1:12 before the LORD, *E* watched her mouth,
1:13 *E*, thinking her drunk,
1:17 *E* said, "Go in peace,
1:25 Hannah, his mother, approached *E* and said:
2:11 the service of the LORD under the priest *E*.
2:12 Now the sons of *E* were wicked;
2:20 And *E* would bless Elkanah and his wife,
2:22 When *E* was very old,
2:27 A man of God came to *E* and said to him:
3: 1 Samuel was minister to the Lord under *E*,
3: 2 One day *E* was asleep in his usual place.
3: 5 He ran to *E* and said, "Here I am.
3: 5 "I did not call you," *E* said.
3: 6 LORD called Samuel, who rose and went to *E*.
3: 8 Getting up and going to *E*,
3: 8 Then *E* understood that the LORD was
3:12 I will carry out in full against *E* everything
3:14 I swear to the family of *E* that no
3:15 He feared to tell *E* the vision,
3:16 tell Eli the vision, but *E* called to him,
3:17 Then *E* asked, "What did he say to you?
3:18 *E* answered, "He is the LORD.
4: 4 The two sons of *E*,
4:13 *E* was sitting in his chair beside the gate,
4:14 of the men standing near him, *E* inquired,
4:15 *E* was ninety-eight years old,
4:16 The man quickly came up to *E* and said,
4:18 *E* fell backward from his chair into the
14: 3 who was the son of Phinehas, son of *E*,
1Kgs 2:27 had made in Shiloh about the house of *E*.
Mt 27:46 Jesus cried out in a loud tone, "*E*, *E*,

ELIAB (22)

Nm 1: 9 *E*, son of Helon;
2: 7 [Their prince was *E*,
7:24 On the third day it was the turn of *E*,
7:29 This was the offering of *E*, son of Helon.
10:16 the host of the tribe of Issachar, and *E*,
16: 1 Levi, [and Dathan and Abiram, sons of *E*,
16:12 summoned Dathan and Abiram, sons of *E*,
26: 8 From Pallu descended *E*.
26: 9 descendants of *E* were Dathan and Abiram
Dt 11: 6 Reubenites Dathan and Abiram, sons of *E*,
1Sm 16: 6 As they came, he looked at *E* and thought.
17:13 off to war were named, the first-born *E*,
17:28 When *E*, his oldest brother,
1Chr 2:13 Jesse became the father of *E*,
6:12 whose son was Nahath, whose son was *E*,
12:10 their chief, Obadiah was second, *E* third,
15:18 Uzziel, Shemiramoth, Jehiel, Unni, *E*,
15:20 Uzziel, Shemiramoth, Jehiel, Unni, *E*,
16: 5 Uzziel, Shemiramoth, Jehiel, Mattithiah, *E*,
27:18 for Judah, *E*, one of David's brothers;
2Chr 11:18 son of David and of Abihail, daughter of *E*,
Jdt 8: 1 son of Elijah, son of Hilkiah, son of *E*,

ELIADA (3)

1Kgs 11:23 another adversary, in Rezon, the son of *E*,
1Chr 3: 8 Nogah, Nepheg, Japhia, Elishama, *E*,
2Chr 17:17 *E*, a valiant warrior,

ELIAHBA (2)

2Sm 23:32 *E* from Shaalbon;
1Chr 11:33 *E*,

ELIAKIM (15)

2Kgs 18:18 for the king, who sent out to them *E*,
18:26 Then *E*, son of Hilkiah,
18:37 Then the master of the palace, *E*,
19: 2 He sent *E*, the master of the palace,
23:34 Pharaoh Neco then appointed *E*,
2Chr 36: 4 brother *E* king over Judah and Jerusalem,
Neh 12:41 me half the magistrates, the priests *E*,
Is 22:20 On that day I will summon my servant *E*,
36: 3 out to him the master of the palace, *E*,
36:11 Then *E* and Shebna and Joah said to the
36:22 Then the master of the palace, *E*,
37: 2 He sent *E*,
Mt 1:13 father of *E*, Eliakim the father of Azor.
Lk 3:30 son of Joseph, son of Jonam, son of *E*,

ELIAM (2)

2Sm 11: 3 told, "She is Bathsheba, daughter of *E*,
23:34 *E*, son of Ahithophel, from Gilo;

ELIASAPH (6)

Nm 1:14 *E*, son of Reuel; from Naphtali:
2:14 [Their prince was *E*,
3:24 The prince of their ancestral house was *E*,
7:42 On the sixth day it was the turn of *E*,
7:47 This was the offering of *E*, son of Reuel.
10:20 the host of the tribe of Simeon, and *E*,

ELIASHIB (15)

1Chr 3:24 The sons of Elioenai were Hodaviah, *E*,
24:12 the tenth to Shecaniah, the eleventh to *E*,
Ezr 10: 6 entered the chamber of Johanan, son of *E*,
10:24 *E* and Zakkur; of the gatekeepers:
10:27 Elioenai, *E*, Mattaniah, Jeremoth,
10:36 Bedeiah, Cheluhi, Vaniah, Meremoth, *E*,
Neh 3: 1 *E* the high priest and his priestly
3:20 Corner to the entrance of the house of *E*,
12:10 father of Eliashib, and *E* became
12:22 In the time of *E*,
12:23 up until the time of Johanan, the son of *E*.
13: 4 Before this, the priest *E*,
13: 7 the evil thing that *E* had done for Tobiah,
13:28 sons of Joiada, son of *E* the high priest,

ELIASHIB'S (1)

Neh 3:21 of *E* house to the end of the house.

ELIATHAH (2)

1Chr 25: 4 Hananiah, Hanani, *E*,
25:27 The twentieth fell to *E*,

ELIDAD (1)

Nm 34:21 *E*, son of Chislon;from the tribe of Dan:

ELIEHOENAI (2)

1Chr 26: 3 Elam, the fifth, Jehohanan, the sixth, *E*,
Ezr 8: 4 of the sons of Pahath-moab, *E*,

ELIEL (10)

1Chr 5:24 Epher, Ishi, *E*,
6:19 son of Elkanah, son of Jeroham, son of *E*,
8:20 Zichri, Zabdi, Elienai, Zillethai, *E*,
8:22 were the sons of Shimei, Ishpan, Eber, *E*,
11:46 *E* the Mahavite;
11:47 *E*, Obed, and Jaasiel the Mezobian.
12:12 Jeremiah fifth, Attai sixth, *E* seventh,
15: 9 of his brethren, of the sons of Hebron, *E*,
15:11 Levites Uriel, Asaiah, Joel, Shemaiah, *E*,
2Chr 31:13 Nahath, Asahel, Jerimoth, Jozabad, *E*,

ELIENAI (1)

1Chr 8:20 Jakim, Zichri, Zabdi, *E*,

ELIEZER (15)

Gn 15: 2 have as my heir the steward of my house, *E*?"
Ex 18: 4 The other was called *E*;
1Chr 7: 8 The sons of Becher were Zemirah, Joash, *E*,
15:24 Amasai, Zechariah, Benaiah, and *E*,
23:15 The sons of Moses were Gershom and *E*.
23:17 The sons of *E* were Rehabiah the chief
23:17 Rehabiah the chief *E* had no other sons,
26:25 His associate pertained to *E*,
27:16 for the Reubenites the leader was *E*,
2Chr 20:37 But *E*, son of Dodavahu from Mareshah,
Ezr 8:16 Therefore I sent *E*,
10:18 Maaseiah, *E*, Jarib, and Gedaliah.
10:23 called Kelita), Pethahiah, Judah and *E*.
10:31 *E*, Isshijah, Malchijah, Shemaiah,
Lk 3:29 son of Er, son of Joshua, son of *E*,

ELIGIBLE (1)

2Chr 31:16 for all priests who were *e* to enter the

ELIHOREPH (1)

1Kgs 4: 3 *E* and Ahijah, sons of Shisha, scribes:

ELIHU (10)

1Sm 1: 1 He was the son of Jeroham, son of *E*,
1Chr 12:21 Jozabad, Jediael, Michael, Jozabad, *E*,
26: 7 who were men of might, *E* and Semachiah.
Jb 32: 2 But the anger of *E*,
32: 4 he, *E* bided his time before addressing Job.
32: 5 *E* saw that there was no reply in the
32: 6 So *E*, son of Barachel the Buzite,
34: 1 Then *E* continued and said:
35: 1 Then *E* proceeded and said:
36: 1 *E* proceeded further and said:

ELIJAH (113)

1Kgs 17: 1 *E* the Tishbite,
17: 2 The LORD then said to *E*:
17:13 "Do not be afraid," *E* said to her.
17:15 She left and did as *E* had said.
17:16 dry, as the LORD had foretold through *E*.
17:18 So she said to *E*,
17:19 "Give me your son," *E* said to her.
17:22 The LORD heard the prayer of *E*;
17:23 *E* brought him down into the house from the
17:23 *E* said to her, "your son is alive."
17:24 are a man of God," the woman replied to *E*.
18: 1 in the third year, the LORD spoke to *E*,
18: 2 So *E* went to present himself to Ahab.
18: 7 As Obadiah was on his way, *E* met him.
18: 7 and asked, "Is it you, my lord *E*?"
18: 8 "Go tell your master, *E* is here!' "
18:11 *E* is here!'
18:14 *E* is here!'
18:15 *E* answered,
18:16 Ahab came to meet *E*,
18:17 came to meet Elijah, and when he saw *E*,
18:21 *E* appealed to all the people and said,
18:22 So *E* said to the people,
18:25 *E* then said to the prophets of Baal,
18:27 When it was noon, *E* taunted them:
18:30 Then *E* said to all the people,
18:36 the prophet *E* came forward and said,
18:40 Then *E* said to them,
18:40 and *E* had them brought down to the brook
18:41 *E* then said to Ahab,
18:42 while *E* climbed to the top of Carmel,
18:44 *E* said, "Go and say to Ahab,
18:46 But the hand of the LORD was on *E*,
19: 1 Ahab told Jezebel all that *E* had done
19: 2 then sent a messenger to *E* and said,
19: 3 *E* was afraid and fled for his life,
19: 9 LORD came to him, "Why are you here, *E*?"
19:13 *E* hid his face in his cloak and went and
19:13 A voice said to him, *E*,
19:19 *E* set out,
19:19 *E* went over to him and threw his cloak
19:20 Elisha left the oxen, ran after *E*,
19:20 "Go back!" *E* answered.
19:21 he left and followed *E* as his attendant.
21:17 But the LORD said to *E* the Tishbite:
21:20 found me out, my enemy?" Ahab said to *E*.
21:28 Then the LORD said to *E* the Tishbite,
2Kgs 1: 3 angel of the LORD said to *E* the Tishbite:
1: 4 And with that, *E* departed.
1: 8 "It is *E* the Tishbite!"
1: 9 with his company of fifty men after *E*.
1:10 am a man of God," *E* answered the captain,
1:11 with his company of fifty men after *E*.
1:11 "Man of God," he called out to *E*,
1:12 "If I am a man of God," *E* answered him,
1:13 arrived, he fell to his knees before *E*,
1:15 Then the angel of the LORD said to *E*,
1:16 So *E* left and went down with him and
1:17 of the prophecy of the LORD spoken by *E*.
2: 1 to take *E* up to heaven in a whirlwind,
2: 2 "Stay here, please," *E* said to Elisha.
2: 4 Then *E* said to him,
2: 6 *E* said to Elisha,
2: 8 *E* took his mantle,
2: 9 they had crossed over, *E* said to Elisha,
2:11 and *E* went up to heaven in a whirlwind.
2:14 the mantle which had fallen from *E*,
2:14 said, "Where is the LORD, the God of *E*?"
2:15 said, "The spirit of *E* rests on Elisha."
3:11 who poured water on the hands of *E*,
9:36 through his servant *E* the Tishbite:
10:10 all that he foretold through his servant *E*."
10:17 prophecy which the LORD had spoken to *E*.
1Chr 8:27 Jaareshiah, *E*,
2Chr 21:12 from the prophet *E* with this message:
Ezr 10:21 Maaseiah, *E*,
10:26 Zechariah, Jehiel, Abdi, Jeremoth, and *E*:
Jdt 8: 1 son of Raphain, son of Ahitob, son of *E*,
1Mc 2:58 *E*, for his burning zeal for the law,
Sir 48: 4 How awesome are you, *E*,
48:12 shall have seen you before he dies, O *E*,
Mal 3:23 Lo, I will send you *E*,
3:24 Lo, I will send you *E*,
Mt 11:14 If you are prepared to accept it, he is *E*,
16:14 "Some say John the Baptizer, others *E*,
17: 3 and *E* appeared to them conversing with him.
17: 4 one for you, one for Moses, and one for *E*."
17:10 the scribes claim that *E* must come first?"
17:11 *E* is indeed coming,
17:12 you, though, that *E* has already come,
27:47 who heard it remark, "He is invoking *E*!"
27:49 Let's see whether *E* comes to his rescue."
Mk 6:15 Others were saying, "He is *E*";
8:28 "Some, John the Baptizer, others, *E*,
9: 4 *E* appeared to them along with Moses;
9: 5 one for you, one for Moses, and one for *E*."
9:11 the scribes claim that *E* must come first?"
9:12 *E* will indeed come first and restore
9:13 Let me assure you, *E* has already come.
15:35 He is calling on *E*!"
15:36 let's see whether *E* comes to take him down."
Lk 1:17 before him, in the spirit and power of *E*,
4:25 many widows in Israel in the days of *E*
4:26 It was to none of these that *E* was sent,
9: 8 others, *E* has appeared";
9:19 they replied, "and some say *E*,
9:30 Moses and *E*.
9:33 one for you, one for Moses, and one for *E*."
Jn 1:21 *E*?" "I am not *E*,"
1:25 "If you are not the Messiah, nor *E*,
Rom 11: 2 you not know what Scripture says about *E*,

ELIJAH (cont.)

Jas 5:17 *E* was only a man like us,

ELIJAH'S (1)

2Kgs 2:13 up *E* mantle which had fallen from him,

ELIKA (1)

2Sm 23:25 *E* from En-harod;

ELIM (5)

Ex 15:27 Then they came to *E*,
16: 1 Having set out from *E*,
16: 1 of Sin, which is between *E* and Sinai,
Nm 33: 9 Setting out from Marah, they came to *E*,
33:10 Setting out from *E*,

ELIMELECH (6)

Ru 1: 2 The man was named *E*,
1: 3 their arrival on the Moabite plateau, *E*,
2: 1 named Boaz, of the clan of her husband *E*.
2: 3 section belonging to Boaz of the clan of *E*.
4: 3 of land that belonged to our kinsman *E*,
4: 9 acquired from Naomi all the holdings of *E*,

ELIOENAI (7)

1Chr 3:23 The sons of Neariah were *E*,
3:24 The sons of *E* were Hodaviah,
4:36 son of Seraiah, son of Asiel, *E*,
7: 8 of Becher were Zemirah, Joash, Eliezer, *E*,
Ezr 10:22 *E*, Maaseiah, Ishmael, Nethanel,
10:27 *E*, Eliashib, Mattaniah, Jeremoth,
Neh 12:41 Eliakim, Maaseiah, Minjamin, Micaiah, *E*,

ELIPHAZ (15)

Gn 36: 4 Adah bore *E* to Esau;
36:10 *E*, son of Esau's wife Adah;
36:11 The sons of *E* were Teman,
36:12 (Esau's son *E* had a concubine Timna,
36:12 concubine Timna, and she bore Amalek to *E*.)
36:15 The descendants of *E*, Esau's first-born:
36:16 are the clans of *E* in the land of Edom;
1Chr 1:35 The sons of Esau were *E*,
1:36 The sons of *E* were Teman,
Jb 2:11 *E* from Teman,
4: 1 Then spoke *E* the Temanite, who said:
15: 1 Then *E* the Temanite spoke and said:
22: 1 Then *E* the Temanite answered and said:
42: 7 Job, that the LORD said to *E* the Temanite,
42: 9 Then *E* the Temanite,

ELIPHELEHU (2)

1Chr 15:18 Eliab, Benaiah, Maaseiah, Mattithiah, *E*,
15:21 But Mattithiah, *E*, Mikneiah, Obed-edom,

ELIPHELET (8)

2Sm 5:16 Nepheg, Japhia, Elishama, Baaliada, and *E*.
23:34 Ahiam, son of Sharar the Hararite, *E*,
1Chr 3: 6 Ibhar, Elishua, *E*,
3: 8 Nepheg, Japhia, Elishama, Eliada, and *E*—
8:39 first-born, Jeush, the second son, and *E*,
14: 7 Nepheg, Japhia, Elishama, Beeliada, and *E*.
Ezr 8:13 younger sons, whose names were *E*,
10:33 Mattenai, Mattattah, Zabad, *E*,

ELIPHELETH (1)

1Chr 11:35 *E*, son of Ahasabi, from Beth-maacah;

ELIS (1)

1Sm 4:11 ark of God was captured, and *E* two sons,

ELISHA (97)

1Kgs 19:16 son of Nimshi, as king of Israel, and *E*,
19:17 escapes the sword of Jehu, *E* will kill him.
19:19 Elijah set out, and came upon *E*,
19:20 *E* left the oxen,
19:21 *E* left him and,
2Kgs 2: 1 he and *E* were on their way from Gilgal.
2: 2 "Stay here, please," Elijah said to *E*.
2: 2 and as you yourself live," *E* replied,
2: 3 guild prophets went out to *E* and asked him,
2: 4 said to him, "Stay here, please, *E*,
2: 4 and as you yourself live," *E* replied,
2: 5 guild prophets approached *E* and asked him.
2: 6 Elijah said to *E*,
2: 6 and as you yourself live," *E* replied,
2: 9 they had crossed over, Elijah said to *E*,
2: 9 *E* answered, "May I receive a double
2:12 When *E* saw it happen he cried out,
2:12 *E* gripped his own garment and tore it in
2:14 When *E* struck the water it divided and he
2:15 said, "The spirit of Elijah rests on *E*."
2:18 When they returned to *E* in Jericho,
2:19 inhabitants of the city complained to *E*,
2:20 "Bring me a new bowl," *E* said,
2:22 even to this day, just as *E* prophesied.
2:23 From there *E* went up to Bethel.
3:11 officers of the king of Israel replied, *E*,
3:12 of Israel, Judah, and Edom went down to *E*.
3:13 *E* asked the king of Israel.
3:14 Then *E* said,
3:15 of the LORD came upon *E* and he announced:
4: 1 one of the guild prophets, complained to *E*:
4: 2 *E* answered her.
4: 8 One day *E* came to Shunem,
4:11 Sometime later *E* arrived and stayed in
4:12 He did so, and when she stood before *E*,
4:14 Later *E* asked,
4:15 "Call her," said *E*.
4:16 *E* promised,
4:17 given birth to a son, as *E* had promised.
4:29 "Gird your loins," *E* said to Gehazi,
4:31 He returned to meet *E* and informed him
4:32 When *E* reached the house,
4:34 As *E* stretched himself over the child,
4:36 *E* summoned Gehazi and said,
4:36 She came at his call, and *E* said to her,
4:38 When *E* returned to Gilgal,
4:41 "Bring some meal," *E* said.
4:42 "Give it to the people to eat," *E* said.
4:43 it to the people to eat," *E* insisted.
5: 8 When *E*, the man of God,
5:16 I serve, I will not take it," *E* replied;
5:19 "Go in peace," *E* said to him.
5:20 distance when Gehazi, the servant of *E*,
5:25 He went in and stood before *E* his master,
5:26 But *E* said to him:
5:27 And Gehazi left *E*, a leper white as snow.
6: 1 The guild prophets once said to *E*:
6: 2 "Go," *E* said.
6: 6 pointed out to the spot, *E* cut off a stick,
6:12 "The Israelite prophet *E* can tell the
6:13 Informed that *E* was in Dothan,
6:15 he said to *E*.
6:16 "Do not be afraid," *E* answered.
6:17 with horses and fiery chariots around *E*.
6:18 came down to get him, *E* prayed to the LORD,
6:19 Then *E* said to them:
6:20 When they entered Samaria, *E* prayed,
6:22 "You must not kill them," replied *E*.
6:31 the king exclaimed, "if the head of *E*,
6:32 *E* was sitting in his house in conference
6:32 *E* had said to the elders:
6:33 While *E* was still speaking,
7: 1 *E* said: "Hear the word
7: 2 shall see it with your own eyes," *E* said,
7:19 And *E* had replied,
8: 1 *E* once said to the woman whose son he had
8: 4 "all the great things that *E* has done."
8: 5 the very woman whose son *E* had restored to
8: 5 that son of hers whom *E* restored to life."
8: 7 *E* came to Damascus at a time when
8:10 "Go and tell him," *E* answered,
8:12 *E* replied, "Because I know the evil
8:13 you to me as king over Aram," replied *E*.
8:14 Hazael left *E* and returned to his master.
8:14 "What did *E* tell you?"
9: 1 The prophet *E* called one of the guild
13:14 When *E* was suffering from the sickness of
13:15 a bow and some arrows," *E* said to him.
13:16 had done so, *E* said to the king of Israel,
13:16 *E* placed his hands over the king's hands
13:17 *E* said, "Shoot," and he shot.
13:18 *E* said to him, "Strike the ground!"
13:20 *E* died and was buried.
13:21 they cast the dead man into the grave of *E*,
13:21 man came in contact with the bones of *E*,
Sir 48:12 Then *E*, filled with a twofold portion
Lk 4:27 in Israel in the time of *E* the prophet;

ELISHAH (3)

Gn 10: 4 *E*, Tarshish, the Kittim, and the Rodanim.
1Chr 1: 7 The descendants of Javan were *E*,
Ez 27: 7 from the coasts of *E* covered your cabin.

ELISHAMA (16)

Nm 1:10 *E*, son of Ammihud, and from Manasseh:
2:18 [Their prince was *E*,
7:48 On the seventh day it was the turn of *E*,
7:53 This was the offering of *E*,
10:22 and arranged in companies, with *E*,
2Sm 5:16 Solomon, Ibhar, Elishua, Nepheg, Japhia, *E*,
2Kgs 25:25 month Ishmael, son of Nethaniah, son of *E*,
1Chr 2:41 Jekamiah became the father of *E*.
3: 8 Eliphelet, Nogah, Nepheg, Japhia, *E*,
7:26 whose son was Ammihud, whose son was *E*,
14: 7 Elishua, Elpelet, Nogah, Nepheg, Japhia, *E*,
2Chr 17: 8 together with the priests *E* and Jehoram.
Jer 36:12 *E*, the scribe,
36:20 in safekeeping in the room of *E* the scribe,
36:21 brought it from the room of *E* the scribe,
41: 1 month Ishmael, son of Nethaniah, son of *E*,

ELISHAPHAT (1)

2Chr 23: 1 and *E*, son of Zichri.

ELISHA'S (1)

2Kgs 5: 9 and stopped at the door of *E* house.

ELISHEBA (1)

Ex 6:23 Aaron married Amminadab's daughter, *E*,

ELISHUA (3)

2Sm 5:15 Shobab, Nathan, Solomon, Ibhar, *E*,
1Chr 3: 6 Ibhar, *E*, Eliphelet, Nogah, Nepheg,
14: 5 Shobab, Nathan, Solomon, Ibhar, *E*,

ELITE (3)

Ex 15: 4 the *e* of his officers were submerged in
1Mc 15:26 Antiochus' support two thousand *e* troops,
Ez 23: 7 to them, to all the *e* of the Assyrians,

ELIUD (2)

Mt 1:14 the father of Achim, Achim the father of *E*.
1:15 *E* was the father of Eleazar,

ELIZABETH (9)

Lk 1: 5 his wife was a descendant of Aaron named *E*.
1: 7 They were childless, for *E* was sterile;
1:13 Your wife *E* shall bear a son whom you
1:24 Afterward, his wife *E* conceived.
1:36 Know that *E* your kinswoman has conceived
1:40 entered Zechariah's house and greeted *E*.
1:41 When *E* heard Mary's greeting,
1:41 *E* was filled with the Holy Spirit and
1:56 Mary remained with *E* about three months

ELIZABETH'S (1)

Lk 1:57 When *E* time for delivery arrived,

ELIZAPHAN (4)

Nm 3:30 The prince of their ancestral house was *E*,
34:25 *E*, son of Parnach; from
1Chr 15: 8 of the sons of *E*,
2Chr 29:13 of the sons of *E*:

ELIZUR (5)

Nm 1: 5 *E*, son of Shedeur; from Simeon:
2:10 [Their prince was *E*,
7:30 On the fourth day it was the turn of *E*,
7:35 This was the offering of *E*,
10:18 was the next to set out, with *E*,

ELKANAH (20)

Ex 6:24 sons of Korah were Assir, *E* and Abiasaph.
1Sm 1: 1 a certain man from Ramathaim, *E* by name,
1: 4 When the day came for *E* to offer sacrifice,
1: 8 Her husband *E* used to ask her:
1:19 When *E* had relations with his wife Hannah,
1:21 The next time her husband *E* was going up
1:23 Her husband *E* answered her:
2:11 When *E* returned home to Ramah,
2:20 And Eli would bless *E* and his wife,
1Chr 6: 8 whose son was *E* whose son was Ebiasaph,
6:10 The sons of *E* were Amasai and Ahimoth,
6:11 were Amasai and Ahimoth, whose son was *E*,
6:12 whose son was Jeroham, whose son was *E*,
6:19 son of Joel, son of Samuel, son of *E*,
6:20 Eliel, son of Toah, son of Zuth, son of *E*,
6:21 son of Mahath, son of Amasi, son of *E*,
9:16 and Berechiah, son of Asa, son of *E*,
12: 7 *E*, Isshiah, Azarel, Joezer, and Ishbaal,
15:23 and *E* were gatekeepers before the ark.
2Chr 28: 7 the master of the palace, and also *E*,

ELKIAH (1)

Jdt 8: 1 son of Joseph, son of Oziel, son of *E*,

ELKOSH (1)

Na 1: 1 The book of the vision of Nahum of *E*.

ELLASAR (2)

Gn 14: 1 Amraphel king of Shinar, Arioch king of *E*,
14: 9 king of Shinar, and Arioch king of *E*—

ELMADAM (1)

Lk 3:28 son of Addi, son of Cosam, son of *E*,

ELNAAM (1)

1Chr 11:46 Jeribai and Joshaviah, sons of *E*;

ELNATHAN (5)

2Kgs 24: 8 was Nehushta, daughter of *E* of Jerusalem.
Ezr 8:16 I sent Eliezer, Ariel, Shemaiah, Jarib, *E*,
Jer 26:22 Thereupon King Jehoiakim sent *E*,
36:12 the scribe, Delaiah, son of Shemaiah, *E*,
36:25 And though *E*,

ELOI (2)

Mk 15:34 Jesus cried in a loud voice, "*E*, *E*,

ELON (9)

Gn 26:34 and Basemath, daughter of *E* the Hivite.
36: 2 Adah, daughter of *E* the Hittite;

46:14 Sered, *E,* and Jahleel.
Nm 26:26 through *E* the clan of the Elonites,
Jos 19:43 Irshemesh, Shaalabbin, Aijalon, Ithlah, *E,*
Jgs 12:11 After him the Zebulunite *E* judged Israel.
12:12 Zebulunite *E* died and was buried in *E*
1Kgs 4: 9 Shaalbim, Beth-shemesh, *E* and Beth-hanan;

ELON-MEONENIM (1)

Jgs 9:37 and one company is coming by way of *E.*"

ELONITES (1)

Nm 26:26 Seredites, through Elon the clan of the *E,*

ELOQUENCE (2)

Acts 18:24 a native of Alexandria and a man of *e,*
1Cor 2: 1 with any particular *e* or "wisdom."

ELOQUENT (4)

Ex 4:10 you please, Lord, I have never been *e,*
4:14 I know that he is an *e* speaker.
Prv 16:23 The mind of the wise man makes him *e,*
Sir 15: 5 in the assembly she will make him *e.*

ELOQUENTLY (1)

Heb 12:24 which speaks more *e* than that of Abel.

ELPAAL (4)

1Chr 8:11 he became the father of Abitub and *E.*
8:12 The sons of *E* were Eber,
8:14 Their brethren were *E,*
8:18 Izliah, and Jobab were the sons of *E.*

ELPELET (1)

1Chr 14: 5 Nathan, Solomon, Ibhar, Elishua, *E,*

ELSE (105)

Gn 19:12 "Who *e* belongs to you here?
28:17 This is nothing *e* but an abode of God,
31:50 that even though no one *e* is about,
34:19 highly respected than anyone *e* in his clan.
45: 1 Thus no one *e* was about when he made
46:32 herds, as well as everything *e* they own.
47: 1 flocks and herds and everything *e* they own;
Ex 4:13 "If you please, Lord, send someone *e!*"
9:19 whatever *e* you have in the open fields
19:22 *e* he will vent his anger upon them."
19:24 *e* he will vent his anger upon them."
20:17 or ass, nor anything *e* that belongs to him."
22: 8 or anything *e* that has disappeared,
22:26 What *e* has he to sleep in?
23:29 *e* the land will become so desolate that
28:35 *e* he will die.
29:27 *e* belonging to Aaron or to his sons.
34:12 *e* they will become a snare among you.
34:15 *e,* when they render their wanton worship
Lv 5:24 found or whatever *e* he swore falsely about;
10: 7 entry of the meeting tent, *e* you shall die;
16:13 *e* he will die.
16:17 No one *e* may be in the meeting tent from
19:29 *e* the land will become corrupt and full of
22: 2 *e* they will profane my holy name.
22: 9 *e* they will die for their profanation.
27:20 such a field, he sells it to someone *e,*
Nm 6:21 from anything *e* which his means may allow.
18:22 *e* they will incur guilt deserving death.
22:19 till I learn what *e* the LORD may tell me."
Dt 14:26 drink, or anything *e* you would enjoy,
15: 9 *e* he will cry to the LORD against you and
20:14 all *e* in it that is worth plundering
22: 3 or anything *e* which your kinsman loses and
23:20 *e* on which interest is usually demanded.
28:55 using for food when nothing *e* is left him
28:57 uses them for food for want of anything *e,*
33:29 Where *e* is a nation victorious in the LORD?
Jos 6:18 *e* you will bring upon the camp of Israel
Jgs 19:19 there is nothing *e* we need."
21:17 *e* one of the Israelite tribes will be
1Sm 2:16 it to me now, or *e* I will take it by force."
29: 4 how *e* can he win back his master's favor,
2Sm 3:35 if I eat bread or anything *e* before sunset."
19:39 anything *e* you would like me to do for you,
1Kgs 2:36 Do not go anywhere *e.*
2:42 that, if you left and went anywhere *e,*
9: 1 and everything *e* that he had planned,
9:19 and whatever *e* Solomon decided should be
19: 7 *e* the journey will be too long for you!"
1Chr 28:12 He provided also the pattern for all *e*
29: 5 who *e* is willing to contribute generously
2Chr 8: 6 and whatever *e* Solomon decided should be
Ezr 6: 9 Whatever *e* is required
7:20 Whatever *e* you may be required to supply
Jb 34:13 or who *e* set all the land in its place?
Ps(s) 32: 9 be curbed, *e* they will not come near you.
73:25 Whom *e* have I in heaven?
Prv 14:10 bitterness, and in its joy no one *e* shares.
27: 2 Someone *e*— not your own lips.
Wis 10:12 devotion to God is mightier than all *e.*
Sir 1: 4 Before all things *e* wisdom was created;
17: 3 and with power over all things *e* on earth.
25:11 Fear of the LORD surpasses all *e.*
36:22 for it surpasses all *e* that charms the eye;
Is 6:10 *E* their eyes will see,
45:14 "With you only is God, and nowhere *e;*
47: 8 Saying to yourself, "I, and no one *e!*
47:10 you said to yourself, "I, and no one *e!*"
Jer 9: 6 how *e* should I deal with their wickedness?
11:21 *e* you shall die by our hand."
17: 9 tortuous than all *e* is the human heart,
23:34 anyone *e* mentions "the burden of the LORD,"
27:17 *e* this city will become a heap of ruins.
30:21 how *e* should one take the deadly risk of
Bar 6:45 and they are nothing *e* than what these
Dn 2:40 breaks in pieces and crushes everything *e.*
5:17 gifts, or give your presents to someone *e;*
13:16 Nobody *e* was there except the two elders,
Mal 2:17 or *e,*
Mk 7:20 and nothing *e* is what makes him impure.
Lk 7:19 is to come' or are we to expect someone *e?*"
7:20 is to come" or do we look for someone *e?*' "
13: 4 than anyone *e* who lived in Jerusalem?
13:17 everyone *e* rejoiced at the marvels Jesus
18: 9 while holding everyone *e* in contempt:
20:40 They did not dare ask him anything *e.*
22:58 while later someone *e* saw him and said,
Jn 5: 7 there, someone *e* has gone in ahead of me."
14:11 the Father and the Father is in me, or *e,*
Acts 4:12 There is no salvation in anyone *e,*
5:13 No one *e* dared to join them,
8:34 himself or someone *e?*"
17:25 to all life and breath and everything *e.*
24:12 the synagogue, nor anywhere *e* in the city,
Rom 14: 5 someone *e* considers all days alike.
14:21 or anything *e* that offers your brother an
1Cor 1:16 I am not aware of having baptized anyone *e.*
3: 4 says, "I belong to Paul," and someone *e,*
3:10 do, and now someone *e* is building upon it.
2Cor 10: 6 *e* once your own obedience is perfect.
11:21 But what anyone *e* dares to claim
Phil 3: 8 I have accounted all *e* rubbish so that
Col 1:17 He is before all *e* that is.
Jas 5:12 Above all *e,* my brothers,

ELSE'S (4)

Gn 43:34 was five times as large as anyone *e.*
Ru 2: 8 Do not go to glean in anyone *e* field;
2:22 in someone *e* field you might be insulted."
Lk 16:12 not been trustworthy with someone *e* money,

ELSEWHERE (7)

Lv 18: 9 was born in your own household or born *e.*
Nm 35:32 again dwell *e* in the land before the death
Ezr 4:10 and *e* in the province West-of-Euphrates,
4:17 and *e* in the province West-of-Euphrates,
Ps(s) 84:11 one day in your courts than a thousand *e;*
Jer 19:11 burial place, for lack of place to bury *e.*
Jn 12:39 not believe was that, as Isaiah says *e:*

ELTEKE (2)

Jos 21:23 four cities of *E* with its pasture lands,
1Chr 6:54 *E* with its pasture lands,

ELTEKOH (1)

Jos 19:44 Aijalon, Ithlah, Elon, Timnah, Ekron, *E,*

ELTEKON (1)

Jos 15:59 Beth-zur, Gedor, Maarath, Beth-anoth and *E;*

ELTOLAD (2)

Jos 15:30 Baalah, Iim, Ezem, *E,*
19: 4 Moladah, Hazar-shual, Balah, Ezem, *E,*

ELUDED (2)

1Sm 19:10 the wall with the spear, but David *e* Saul,
Jn 10:39 tried to arrest him, but he *e* their grasp.

ELUDING (1)

Dt 3: 4 all his cities, none of them *e* our grasp,

ELUL (2)

Neh 6:15 was finished on the twenty-fifth day of *E;*
1Mc 14:27 "On the eighteenth day of *E,*

ELUSIVE (1)

Lk 16:11 If you cannot be trusted with *e* wealth,

ELUZAI (1)

1Chr 12: 6 *E;* Jerimoth; Bealiah; Shemariah;

ELYMAIS (2)

Tb 2:10 of me for two years, until he left for *E.*
1Mc 6: 1 that in Persia there was a city called *E,*

ELYMAS (1)

Acts 13: 8 But *E* —"the magician," for that is what

ELZABAD (2)

1Chr 12:13 Eliel seventh, Johanan eighth, *E* ninth,
26: 7 Shemaiah were Othni, Rephael, Obed, and *E;*

ELZAPHAN (2)

Ex 6:22 sons of Uzziel were Mishael, *E* and Sithri.
Lv 10: 4 Then Moses summoned Mishael and *E,*

EMACIATING (1)

Dt 32:24 *E* hunger and consuming fever and bitter

EMANCIPATION (2)

Jer 34: 8 people in Jerusalem to issue an edict of *e.*
34:15 proclaiming the *e* of your brethren

EMBALM (1)

Gn 50: 2 physicians in his service to *e* his father.

EMBALMED (2)

Gn 50: 2 When they *e* Israel,
50:26 *e* and laid to rest in a coffin in Egypt.

EMBALMING (1)

Gn 50: 3 at it, for that is the full period of *e;*

EMBARK (2)

2Mc 12: 3 to *e* on boats which they had provided.
Wis 14: 4 so that even one without skill may *e.*

EMBARKED (2)

Jn 6:17 They *e,* intending to cross the lake
6:24 they too *e* in the boats and went to

EMBARKING (1)

Acts 20: 3 As he was on the point of *e* for Syria,

EMBARRASS (2)

1Cor 11:22 of God, and *e* those who have nothing?
2Cor 10: 8 this will not *e* me in the least.

EMBARRASSED (1)

2Kgs 2:17 kept urging him, until he was *e* and said,

EMBASSY (3)

Jos 22:13 land of Gilead an *e* consisting of Phinehas,
1Kgs 5:15 place of his father, he sent an *e* to him;
2Mc 4:11 would later go on an *e* to the Romans

EMBEDDED (1)

1Sm 17:49 The stone *e* itself in his brow,

EMBER (2)

Is 6: 6 holding an *e* which he had taken with tongs
47:14 This is no warming *e,*

EMBERS (8)

Lv 1: 7 *e* on the altar and laid some wood on them,
1: 8 on top of the wood and *e* on the altar.
16:12 glowing *e* from the altar before the LORD,
Nm 17: 2 priest, to remove the censers from the *e;*
Tb 6:17 and place them on the *e* for the incense.
8: 2 and placed them on the *e* for the incense.
Is 44:16 the fire, and on its *e* he roasts his meat;
44:19 and on its *e* I baked bread and roasted

EMBITTERED (5)

1Sm 22: 2 in difficulties or in debt, or who were *e,*
Ps(s) 73:21 my heart was *e* and my soul was pierced,
106:33 on their account, For they *e* his spirit,
106:43 but they *e* him with their counsels and
Sir 7:11 Laugh not at an *e* man;

EMBITTERMENT (1)

Gn 26:35 became a source of *e* to Isaac and Rebekah.

EMBLEM (1)

Sg 2: 4 banquet hall and his *e* over me is love.

EMBODIES (1)

Ti 1: 1 of the truth as our religion *e* it.

EMBOLDENED (1)

Phil 1:14 *e* to speak the word of God fearlessly.

EMBOSSING (1)

2Chr 3: 5 with fine gold, *e* on it palms and chains.

EMBRACE (10)

Gn 16: 5 I myself gave my maid to your *e;*
Prv 4: 8 she will bring you honors if you *e* her;
Eccl 3: 5 a time to *e,* and a time to be far from *e*
Sir 6:18 My son, from your youth *e* discipline;
15: 2 him, like a young bride she will *e* him,

EMBRACE (cont.)

Mt 26:48 saying, "The man I shall *e* is the one;
Mk 14:44 saying, "The man I shall *e* is the one;
Lk 22:47 He approached Jesus to *e* him.
1Thes 5:26 Greet all the brothers with a holy *e.*
1Pt 5:14 Greet one another with the *e* of true love.

EMBRACED (10)

Gn 33: 4 Esau ran to meet him, *e* him,
48:10 sons close to him, he kissed and *e* them.
Tb 10:11 He *e* Tobiah and said to him:
Est D:12 he touched her neck with it, *e* her,
8:17 many of the peoples of the land *e* Judaism,
Mt 26:49 said to him, "Peace, Rabbi," and *e* him.
28: 9 came up and *e* his feet and did him homage.
Mk 10:16 Then he *e* them and blessed them,
14:45 and said "Rabbi!" and *e* him.
Acts 6: 7 many priests among those who *e* the faith.

EMBRACES (7)

Prv 5:20 wife and accept the *e* of an adulteress?
Eccl 3: 5 to embrace, and a time to be far from *e.*
Sg 2: 6 is under my head and his right arm *e* me.
8: 3 is under my head and his right arm *e* me.
Sir 41: 3 remember, it *e* those before you,
Is 57: 8 And of those whose *e* you love you carved
2Cor 7:15 His heart *e* you with an expanding love as

EMBRACING (1)

Gn 29:13 After *e* and kissing him,

EMBROIDERED (25)

Ex 26: 1 and scarlet yarn, with cherubim *e* on them.
26:31 fine linen twined, with cherubim *e* on it.
28: 6 yarn, *e* on cloth of fine linen twined.
28: 8 The *e* belt of the ephod shall extend out
28:15 *e* like the ephod with gold thread and
28:27 the ephod in front, just above its *e* belt.
28:28 stay right above the *e* belt of the ephod
29: 5 the *e* belt of the ephod around him.
36: 8 having cherubim *e* on them with violet,
36:35 fine linen twined, with cherubim *e* on it.
39: 3 yarn into an *e* pattern on the fine linen.
39: 5 *e* belt on the ephod extended out from it,
39: 8 The breastpiece was *e* like the ephod,
39:20 the ephod in front, just above its *e* belt.
39:21 breastpiece stayed right above the *e* belt
Lv 8: 7 girded him with the *e* belt of the ephod,
2Chr 3:14 and fine linen, and had cherubim *e* upon it.
Ps(s) 45:15 In *e* apparel she is borne in to the king;
Ez 16:10 I clothed you with an *e* gown,
16:13 were of fine linen, silk, and *e* cloth.
16:18 You took your *e* gowns to cover them;
26:16 robes, and strip off their *e* garments.
27: 7 Fine *e* linen from Egypt became your sail
27:16 exchanging garnets, purple, *e* cloth,
27:24 you rich garments, violet mantles, *e* cloth,

EMBROIDERER (1)

Ex 38:23 tribe of Dan, who was an engraver, an *e,*

EMBROIDERING (1)

Ex 35:35 engraving, *e,* the making of variegated

EMBROIDERY (3)

Ex 31: 4 in the production of *e,*
35:32 in the production of *e,*
Sir 45:10 of violet, and of crimson, wrought with *e;*

EMEK-KEZIZ (1)

Jos 18:21 Jericho, Beth-hoglah, *E,*

EMERALD (7)

Ex 28:17 first row, a carnelian, a topaz and an *e;*
39:10 first row a carnelian, a topaz and an *e;*
Tb 13:16 shall be built with sapphire and *e,*
Sir 32: 6 *e* seal is string music with delicious wine.
Ez 28:13 onyx, and jasper, sapphire, garnet, and *e;*
Rv 4: 3 the throne was a rainbow as brilliant as *e.*
21:19 the third chalcedony, the fourth *e,*

EMERALDS (1)

Jdt 10:21 and gold, *e* and other precious stones.

EMERGE (1)

Gn 25:25 The first to *e* was reddish,

EMERGED (4)

Jos 15: 7 the waters of En-shemesh and *e* at En-rogel.
Dn 7: 3 sea, from which *e* four immense beasts,
Zec 6: 7 As these strong horses *e,*
Acts 12:10 *e* and made their way down a narrow alley,

EMERGENCY (2)

Gn 42: 3 to buy an *e* supply of grain from Egypt.
Bar 6:36 sight, nor do they save any man in an *e.*

EMERGES (1)

Mk 7:20 "What *e* from within a man,

EMERGING (1)

Wis 19: 7 had before been water, dry land was seen *e:*

EMIM (3)

Gn 14: 5 Zuzim in Ham, the *E* in Shaveh-kiriathaim,
Dt 2:10 [Formerly the *E* lived there,
2:11 It was the Moabites who called them *E.*

EMINENCE (1)

Jas 1: 9 pride in his *e* and the rich man be proud

EMINENTLY (1)

2Mc 8:35 *e* successful in destroying his own army.

EMISSION (4)

Lv 15:16 "When a man has an *e* of seed,
15:32 a chronic flow, or who has an *e* of seed,
22: 4 corpse, or if anyone has had an *e* of seed,
Dt 23:11 becomes unclean because of a nocturnal *e,*

EMITTED (1)

Mk 7:34 then he looked up to heaven and *e* a groan.

EMMANUEL (1)

Mt 1:23 to a son, and they shall call him *E,*"

EMMAUS (5)

1Mc 3:40 and pitched their camp near *E* in the plain.
3:57 off, and they camped to the south of *E.*
4: 3 soldiers to attack the king's army at *E,*
9:50 the Jericho fortress, as well as *E,*
Lk 24:13 named *E* seven miles distant from Jerusalem,

EMOTIONS (1)

Jn 11:33 troubled in spirit, moved by the deepest *e.*

EMPEROR (15)

Mt 22:17 Is it lawful to pay tax to the *e* or not?"
Mk 12:14 it lawful to pay the tax to the *e* or not?
Lk 20:22 May we pay tax to the *e* or not?"
Acts 11:28 (It did in fact occur while Claudius was *e.)*
25: 8 or against the temple or against the *e.*"
25:11 I appeal to the *e!*"
25:12 "You have appealed to the *e.*
25:12 To the *e* you shall go."
25:21 in custody until I could send him to the *e.*"
25:25 so when he appealed to His Majesty the *E,*
26:32 liberty, if he had not appealed to the *e!*"
27:24 'You are destined to appear before the *e.*
28:19 objected, I was forced to appeal to the *e,*
1Pt 2:13 whether to the *e* as sovereign or to the
2:17 reverence for God, respect for the *e.*

EMPERORS (1)

Acts 17: 7 they disregard the *E* decrees and claim

EMPHATICALLY (1)

Acts 23: 9 of the Pharisee party arose and declared *e:*

EMPIRE (1)

Est B: 4 so that the unity of *e* blamelessly designed

EMPLACEMENT (1)

2Kgs 16:18 *e* which had been built in the temple

EMPLOYED (3)

2Mc 1:13 a deceitful stratagem *e* by Nanea's priests.
10:14 he *e* foreign troops and used every
Ez 39:14 Men shall be permanently *e* to pass through

EMPLOYEE (1)

Lk 16: 8 devious *e* credit for being enterprising!

EMPLOYER (1)

Lk 16: 3 My *e* is sure to dismiss me.

EMPLOYMENT (1)

Ti 3: 1 laws, to be ready to take on any honest *e.*

EMPLOYS (1)

2Cor 2:14 and *e* us to diffuse the fragrance of his

EMPOWER (1)

Acts 9: 2 in Damascus which would *e* him to arrest

EMPOWERED (3)

Jn 1:12 accept him he *e* to become children of God.
1Cor 5: 4 in spirit with you and *e* by our Lord Jesus,
Rv 20: 4 sitting on them were *e* to pass judgment.

EMPTIED (8)

Gn 24:20 she quickly *e* her jug into the drinking
2Chr 24:11 for the high priest came, *e* the chest,
Neh 5:13 and may he thus be shaken out and *e!*"
Sir 31:21 too much, once you have *e* your stomach,
Is 60: 5 of the sea shall be *e* out before you,
Jer 8: 1 Jerusalem will be *e* out of their graves
Ez 12:19 that their land may be *e* of the violence
Phil 2: 7 he *e* himself and took the form of a slave,

EMPTIES (2)

Is 24: 2 Lo, the LORD *e* the land and lays it waste;
Ez 47: 8 down upon the Arabah, and *e* into the sea,

EMPTINESS (4)

Jb 15:35 They conceive malice and bring forth *e;*
Is 59: 4 They trust in *e* and tell lies;
Jer 23:16 of your prophets, who fill you with *e;*
Na 2:11 *E,* desolation, waste; melting hearts

EMPTY (50)

Gn 37:24 him into the cistern, which was *e* and dry.
Jgs 7:16 with *e* jars and torches inside the jars.
1Kgs 17:14 says, 'The jar of flour shall not go *e,*
17:16 The jar of flour did not go *e,*
2Kgs 4: 3 as many *e* vessels as you can.
2Mc 14:44 he fell into the middle of the *e* space.
Jb 11:12 Will *e* man then gain understanding,
26: 7 He stretches out the North over *e* space,
Ps(s) 36: 4 The words of his mouth are *e* and false;
62:11 in plunder take no *e* pride;
Prv 11:18 The wicked man makes *e* profits,
11:29 his household has *e* air for a heritage;
14: 4 there are no oxen, the crib remains *e;*
Sir 34: 1 *E* and false are the hopes of the senseless,
Is 16: 6 insolence that his *e* words do not match.
29: 8 he is eating and awakens with an *e* stomach,
29:21 and leave the just man with an *e* claim.
32: 6 go *e* and the thirsty be without drink.
34:11 to be an *e* waste for satyrs to dwell in.
41:29 works are nought, their idols are *e* wind!
45:19 of Jacob, "Look for me in an *e* waste."
Jer 2: 5 after empty idols, and became *e* themselves?
4: 7 till your cities lie waste and *e.*
14: 3 They find no water and return with *e* jars.
16:19 heritage of our fathers, *e* idols of no use."
17: 6 stands in a lava waste, a salt and *e* earth.
23:32 their lies and by their *e* boasting.
36:29 waste this land and *e* it of man and beast?"
46:19 Memphis shall become a desert, an *e* ruin.
48:12 they shall *e* his flasks and break his jars.
50:13 of the LORD's wrath she shall be *e,*
51:34 of Babylon,] he has left me as an *e* vessel;
Ez 24:11 Then I will set the pot *e* on the coals
Mi 6:14 satisfied, food that will leave you *e;*
Zec 10: 2 dreams they tell, *e* comfort they offer.
Mt 15: 9 They do me *e* reverence,
Mk 7: 7 *E* is the reverence they do me because they
Lk 1:53 thing, while the rich he has sent *e* away.
Rom 4:14 *e* word and the promise loses its meaning.
1Cor 3:20 knows how *e* are the thoughts of the wise."
15:14 is void of content and your faith is *e* too.
2Cor 9: 3 for you in this regard may not be shown *e.*
Eph 4:17 their minds *e,*
Col 2: 8 it that no one deceives you through any *e,*
2:18 he is inflated with *e* pride by his human
Ti 1:10 men who are *e* talkers and deceivers.
2Pt 2:18 They talk *e* bombast while baiting their
1Jn 2:16 for the eye, the life of *e* show
Rv 16:17 angel poured out his bowl upon the *e* air.

EMPTY-HANDED (13)

Gn 31:42 my side, you would now have sent me away *e.*
Ex 3:21 that, when you leave, you will not go *e.*
23:15 No one shall appear before me *e.*
34:20 "No one shall appear before me *e.*
Dt 15:13 you do so, you shall not send him away *e,*
16:16 No one shall appear before the LORD *e,*
Ru 3:17 wish me to come back to my mother-in-law *e*
Jdt 1:11 to them, and turned away his envoys *e,*
Jb 22: 9 You have sent widows away *e,*
Sir 29: 9 and in their want, do not send them away *e*
35: 4 Appear not before the LORD *e,*
Mk 12: 3 seized him, beat him, and sent him off *e.*
Lk 20:10 but they beat him and sent him away *e.*
20:11 Him too they sent away *e,*

EMPTYING (1)

Gn 42:35 When they were *e* their sacks,

EMULATE (1)

Prv 23:17 Let not your heart *e* sinners,

EMULATED (1)

2Mc 4:16 very people whose manner of life they *e,*

EMULATES (1)

Wis 15: 9 and silversmiths and *e* molders of bronze,

EMULOUS (1)

Prv 24: 1 Be not *e* of evil men,

EN-DURES (1)

1Chr 16:41 the LORD, "because his kindness *e* forever,"

EN-GANNIM (2)

Jos 19:21 Rabbith, Kishion, Ebez, Remeth, *E*,
21:29 lands, and *E* with its pasture lands;

EN-GEDI (7)

Jos 15:62 Middin, Secacah, Nibshan, Ir-hamelah and *E*;
1Sm 24: 1 there and stayed in the refuges behind *E*.
24: 2 told that David was in the desert near *E*.
2Chr 20: 2 already in Hazazon-tamar" (which is *E*).
Sg 1:14 cluster of henna from the vineyards of *E*.
Sir 24:14 on Mount Hermon, Like a palm tree in *E*,
Ez 47:10 be standing along it from *E* to En-eglaim,

EN-EGLAIM (1)

Ez 47:10 standing along it from En-gedi to *E*

EN-HADDAH (1)

Jos 19:21 Ebez, Remeth, En-gannim, *E* and Beth-pazzez.

EN-HAKKORE (1)

Jgs 15:19 spring in Lehi is called *E* to this day.

EN-HAROD (6)

Jgs 7: 1 encamped by *E* with all his soldiers.
2Sm 23:25 Shammah from *E*;
23:25 Elika from *E*;
1Chr 11:27 of Dodo, from Bethlehem, Shammoth, from *E*;
11:34 Jonathan, son of Shagee, from *E*;
11:35 Ahiam, son of Sachar, from *E*;

EN-HAZOR (1)

Jos 19:37 Adamah, Ramah, Hazor, Kedesh, Edrei, *E*,

EN-RIMMON (3)

Jos 15:32 Sansannah, Lebaoth, Shilhim and *E*;
19: 7 Also *E*, Ether and Ashan;
Neh 11:29 in Meconah and its dependencies, in *E*,

EN-ROGEL (4)

Jos 15: 7 the waters of En-shemesh and emerged at *E*.
18:16 southern flank of the Jebusites, reached *E*.
2Sm 17:17 Jonathan and Ahimaaz were staying at *E*,
1Kgs 1: 9 fatlings at the stone Zoheleth, near *E*,

EN-SHEMESH (2)

Jos 15: 7 to the waters of *E* and emerged at En-rogel.
18:17 Inclining to the north, it extended to *E*,

EN-TAPPUAH (1)

Jos 17: 7 ran southward to include the natives of *E*,

ENABLE (4)

1Mc 6:49 no food there to *e* them to stand a siege,
Rom 15: 5 *e* you to live in perfect harmony with one
2Tm 2:25 will *e* them to repent and know the truth.
Phlm 1: 6 with others may *e* you to know all the good

ENABLED (2)

Ru 4:13 LORD *e* her to conceive and she bore a son.
Acts 28:13 which *e* us to reach Puteoli in two days.

ENABLES (2)

Hb 3:19 of hinds and *e* me to go upon the heights.
2Cor 1: 4 *e* us to comfort those who are in trouble,

ENABLING (1)

Ps(s) 31: 9 the enemy but *e* me to move about at large.

ENACT (1)

Is 10: 1 Woe to those who *e* unjust statutes and who

ENACTMENT (1)

Est 4: 3 wherever the king's legal *e* reached,

ENAIM (2)

Gn 38:14 shawl, and sat down at the entrance to *E*,
38:21 prostitute, the one by the roadside in *E*?"

ENAM (1)

Jos 15:34 Ashnah, Zanoah, Engannim, Tappuah, *E*,

ENAMORED (4)

Dt 21:11 *e* of her that you wish to have her as wife,
Wis 8: 2 her for my bride and was *e* of her beauty.
Dn 13:10 Though both were *e* of her,
2Tm 4:10 me soon, for Demas, *e* of the present world,

ENAN (5)

Nm 1:15 Ahira, son of *E*."
2:29 [Their prince was Ahira, son of *E*,
7:78 day it was the turn of Ahira, son of *E*,
7:83 This was the offering of Ahira, son of *E*.
10:27 the tribe of Asher, and Ahira, son of *E*,

ENCAMP (8)

Gn 16:12 In opposition to all his kin shall he *e*."
Jgs 6: 4 Kedemites would come up, *e* opposite them,
Jdt 7:13 and *e* there to guard against anyone's
Jb 19:12 to attack me, and they *e* around my tent.
Ps(s) 27: 3 Though an army *e* against me,
Is 29: 3 Ariel, I will *e* like David against you;
Jer 50:29 *E* around her,
Zec 9: 8 I will *e* by my house as a guard that none

ENCAMPED (55)

Gn 33:18 of Canaan, and he *e* in sight of the city.
35:22 While Israel was *e* in that region,
Ex 14: 9 up with them as they lay *e* by the sea,
17: 1 as the LORD directed, and *e* at Rephidim.
18: 5 where he was *e* near the mountain of God,
19: 2 Israel was *e* here in front of the mountain,
Nm 2: 3 *E* on the east side,
9:18 moved on, and at his bidding they *e*.
9:23 at the bidding of the LORD that they *e*,
10: 6 those *e* on the east side shall set out;
10: 6 those *e* on the south side shall set out;
10: 6 those *e* on the north side shall set out.
10: 6 those *e* on the west side shall set out;
12:16 from Hazeroth and *e* in the desert of Paran.
21:10 The Israelites moved on and *e* in Oboth.
21:11 they *e* in Iye-abarim in the desert
21:12 out from there, they *e* in the Wadi Zered.
21:13 they *e* on the other side of the Arnon,
22: 1 Then the Israelites moved on and *e* in the
24: 2 When he raised his eyes and saw Israel *e*,
Jos 5:10 were *e* at Gilgal on the plains of Jericho,
11: 5 they *e* together to fight against Israel.
Jgs 6:33 into the valley of Jezreel, where they *e*.
7: 1 *e* by En-harod with all his soldiers.
10:17 had gathered for war and *e* in Gilead,
10:17 the Israelites assembled and *e* in Mizpah.
11:18 of the land of Moab and *e* across the Arnon.
11:20 soldiers, who *e* at Jahaz and fought Israel.
1Sm 13: 5 up against Israel, they *e* in Michmash,
13:16 and the Philistines were *e* at Michmash.
26: 5 where Saul was *e* and examined the spot
28: 4 Philistine levies advanced to Shunem and *e*.
29: 1 were *e* at the spring of Harod near Jezreel.
2Sm 11:11 majesty's servants are *e* in the open field.
17:26 and Absalom *e* in the territory of Gilead.
23:13 clan was *e* in the Vale of Rephaim.
1Kgs 20:27 The Israelites, *e* opposite them,
20:29 were *e* opposite each other for seven days.
2Kgs 25: 1 advanced against Jerusalem, *e* around it,
1Chr 11:15 were *e* in the valley of Rephaim.
19: 7 and his army, who came and *e* before Medeba.
Jdt 2:21 and from Bectileth they next *e* near the
7: 3 They *e* at the spring in the valley near
7:17 They *e* in the valley,
7:18 *e* in the mountain region opposite Dothan;
7:18 of the Assyrian army was *e* in the plain,
1Mc 3:42 that armies were *e* within their territory;
9: 3 and fifty-two, they *e* against Jerusalem.
10:48 a large army and *e* opposite Demetrius.
15:13 Antiochus *e* before Dor with a hundred and
15:25 When King Antiochus was *e* before Dor,
Is 7: 2 house of David that Aram was *e* in Ephraim,
29: 1 to Ariel, Ariel, the city where David *e*!
Jer 52: 4 advanced against Jerusalem, *e* around it,
Rv 20: 9 beloved city where God's people were *e*;

ENCAMPING (1)

Jos 10:34 *e* near it, they attacked it and captured it

ENCAMPMENT (14)

Gn 32: 3 he saw them he said, "This is God's *e*."
42:27 At the night *e*,
43:21 arrived at a night's *e* and opened our bags,
Jgs 21: 8 had come to the *e* for the assembly.
1Chr 6:39 places to which their *e* was limited.
9:19 guarded the entrance to the *e* of the LORD.
11:18 broke through the *e* of the Philistines,
12:23 was a vast encampment, like an *e* of angels.
2Chr 31: 2 in the gates of the *e* of the LORD.
Jdt 16: 2 warfare, and sets his *e* among his people;
1Mc 9:66 and the sons of Phasiron in their *e*;
Ps(s) 69:26 Let their *e* become desolate;
Acts 1:20 'Let his *e* be desolate.

ENCAMPMENTS (7)

Gn 25:16 their names by their villages and *e*;
Nm 24: 5 O Jacob; your *e*, O Israel!
31:10 where they had settled and all their *e*.
1Chr 9:18 gatekeepers for the *e* of the Levites.
Jdt 3: 3 herds, and all our *e* are at your disposal;
Sir 46:14 the nation, when he visited the *e* of Jacob.
Ez 25: 4 up their *e* among you and pitch their tents;

ENCAMPS (2)

Ps(s) 34: 8 of the LORD *e* around those who fear him,
Sir 14:24 Who *e* near her house,

ENCHAINS (1)

Jb 36:13 they cry not for help when he *e* them;

ENCHANTER (1)

Dn 2:10 asked such a thing of any magician, *e*,

ENCHANTERS (8)

Ps(s) 58: 6 the voice of *e* casting cunning spells.
Dn 1:20 all the magicians and *e* in his kingdom.
2: 2 So he ordered that the magicians, *e*,
2:27 the king has inquired, the wise men, *e*,
4: 4 When the magicians, *e*,
5: 7 The king shouted for the *e*,
5:11 made him chief of the magicians, *e*,
5:15 the wise men and *e* were brought in to me

ENCIRCLE (6)

1Mc 5:46 to *e* it on either the right or the left;
10:11 to build the walls and *e* Mount Zion
Ps(s) 22:13 the strong bulls of Bashan *e* me.
Is 29: 3 I will *e* you with outposts and set up
Lk 19:43 you when your enemies *e* you with a rampart,
Jas 3: 6 Its flames *e* our course from birth,

ENCIRCLED (10)

Lv 25:31 houses in villages that are not *e* by walls
1Kgs 7:18 a double row *e* the piece of network
7:24 Under the brim, gourds *e* it,
2Kgs 25:17 a network with pomegranates *e* the capital,
2Chr 3:16 which he *e* the capitals of the columns,
4: 3 rim a ring of figures of oxen *e* the sea,
Sg 7: 3 Your body is a heap of wheat *e* with lilies.
Jer 52:22 a network with pomegranates *e* the capital,
Lk 21:20 "When you see Jerusalem *e* by soldiers,
Heb 11:30 Jericho fell after being *e* for seven days.

ENCIRCLING (4)

2Chr 33:14 extending to the Fish Gate and *e* Ophel;
1Mc 6:62 gave orders for the *e* wall to be destroyed.
Jer 50:14 Take your posts *e* Babylon,
Zec 2: 9 But I will be for her an *e* wall of fire,

ENCLOSE (1)

Nm 4:10 shall then *e* in a covering of tahash skin,

ENCLOSED (7)

1Kgs 6: 5 temple, which *e* the nave and the sanctuary,
7:12 The great court was *e* by three courses of
Sg 4:12 You are an *e* garden, my sister,
4:12 garden, my sister, my bride, an *e* garden,
Ez 41: 6 of the temple that *e* the side chambers;
41: 7 for the temple was *e* all the way around
41: 9 which *e* the side chambers was five cubits

ENCLOSES (1)

Nm 4:26 that *e* both the Dwelling and the altar,

ENCLOSING (3)

Nm 3:26 court *e* both the Dwelling and the altar,
1Kgs 6:16 the floor to the rafters, *e* the sanctuary,
Ez 41: 8 was a raised pavement completely *e* it

ENCLOSURE (5)

Ex 27:18 The *e* of the court is to be one hundred
2Kgs 11:11 southern to the northern limit of the *e*,
2Chr 23:10 to the northern extremity of the *e*,
1Mc 5:43 arms and fled to the temple *e* at Carnaim.
5:44 and burnt the *e* with all who were in it.

ENCLOSURES (1)

2Mc 10: 2 in the marketplace and the sacred *e*.

ENCOMPASS (2)

Ps(s) 88:18 They *e* me like water all the day;
Jer 31:22 the woman must *e* the man with devotion.

ENCOMPASSED (5)

Ps(s) 109: 3 have *e* me and attacked me without cause.
116: 3 The cords of death *e* me;
118:10 All the nations *e* me; in the name
118:11 They *e* me on every side;
118:12 They *e* me like bees,

ENCOUNTER (5)

Dt 3:21 the kingdoms which you will *e* over there.
2Sm 23: 8 over eight hundred slain in a single *e*.
2Kgs 23:29 but was slain at Megiddo at the first *e*.
1Chr 11:11 three hundred, whom he slew in a single *e*.
2Chr 20:17 You will not have to fight in this *e*.

ENCOUNTERED (8)

Gn 32: 2 Then God's messengers *e* Jacob.
33: 8 you intend with all those droves that I *e?*"
1Chr 20: 6 another battle, at Gath, they *e* a giant,
2Chr 22: 8 he also *e* the princes of Judah and the
Jdt 10:11 the valley, they *e* the Assyrian outpost.
2Mc 2:24 and the difficulties *e* by those who wish
10:35 with savage fury cut down everyone they *e.*
Mt 8:28 he *e* two men coming out of the tombs.

ENCOURAGE (13)

Dt 1:38 *E* him, for he is to give Israel its heritage.
3:28 Joshua, and *e* and strengthen him,
Jos 11:20 LORD to *e* them to wage war against Israel,
2Sm 11:25 attack on the city and destroy it. *E* him."
13: 5 my sister Tamar come and *e* me to take food.
2Chr 16: 9 to *e* those who are devoted to him
Acts 20: 1 brought his disciples together to *e* them.
2Cor 13:11 *E* one another.
1Thes 3: 2 strengthen and *e* you in regard to your faith
Ti 1: 9 both to *e* men to follow sound doctrine
Heb 3:13 *E* one another daily while it is still
10:25 assembly, as some do, but *e* one another;
Jude 1: 3 But now I feel obliged to write and *e* you

ENCOURAGED (20)

Jgs 9:24 of Shechem, who *e* him to kill his brothers.
2Chr 15: 8 he was *e* to remove the detestable idols
17: 6 Thus he was *e* to follow the LORD's ways,
32: 6 of the city and *e* them with these words:
35: 2 *e* them in the service of the Lord's house.
1Mc 12:50 *e* one another and went out in compact body
2Mc 7: 5 their mother *e* one another to die bravely,
8:21 With such words he *e* them and made them
13:12 Judas *e* them and told them to stand ready.
15:17 *E* by Judas' noble words,
Ez 13:22 and have *e* the wicked man not to turn from
Acts 11:23 He *e* them all to remain firm in their
14:22 and *e* them to persevere in the faith with
16:40 house, where they saw and *e* the brothers;
18:27 and so the brothers *e* him by writing the
24:10 I am thus *e* to make my defense before you,
Rom 1:12 we may be mutually *e* by our common faith.
1Cor 14:31 one, so that all may be instructed and *e.*
1Thes 2:12 how we *e* and pleaded with you to make
Heb 6:18 might be strongly *e* to seize the hope

ENCOURAGEMENT (13)

1Mc 12: 9 since we have for our *e* the sacred books
2Mc 15:11 and spear as with the *e* of noble words,
Bar 4:30 He who gave you your name is your *e.*
Acts 4:36 the name Barnabas (meaning "son of *e*").
15:31 there was great delight at the *e* it gave.
20: 2 many words of *e* for the Christians there.
Rom 15: 4 and the words of *e* in the Scriptures.
15: 5 May God, the source of all patience and *e,*
1Cor 14: 3 to men for their upbuilding, their *e,*
2Cor 1: 6 afflicted it is for your *e* and salvation,
Phil 2: 1 In the name of the *e* you owe me in Christ,
Heb 13:22 I beg you to bear with this word of *e,*
1Pt 5:12 Herewith are expressed my *e* and my

ENCOURAGES (2)

Sir 17:19 a way back, he *e* those who are losing hope!
Is 41: 7 The craftsman *e* the goldsmith,

ENCOURAGING (4)

1Mc 5:53 stragglers and *e* the people the whole way,
2Mc 15: 9 By *e* them with words from the law and the
Gal 2:17 does that mean that Christ is *e* sin?
Heb 12: 5 the *e* words addressed to you as sons:

ENCOURAGINGLY (1)

2Chr 30:22 Hezekiah spoke *e* to all the Levites who

ENCROACH (1)

Dt 2:37 did not *e* upon any of the Ammonite land,

ENCUMBERED (1)

Gn 33:13 Besides, I am *e* with the flocks and herds,

ENCUMBRANCE (1)

Heb 12: 1 let us lay aside every *e* of sin which clings

END (314)

Gn 6:13 to put an *e* to all mortals on earth;
8: 3 At the *e* of one hundred and fifty days,
8: 6 At the *e* of forty days Noah opened the
15:14 the *e* they will depart with great wealth.
27:23 so in the *e* he gave him his blessing.)
41:53 enjoyed by the land of Egypt came to an *e,*
47:21 one *e* of Egypt's territory to the other.
50:20 it for good, to achieve his present *e,*
Ex 12:41 At the *e* of four hundred and thirty years,
23:16 at the fruit harvest at the *e* of the year,
25:19 that one cherub springs direct from each *e.*
26: 4 along the edge of the *e* sheet in one set,
26: 4 the edge of the *e* sheet in the other set.
26: 5 the edge of the *e* sheet in the first set,
26:10 the edge of the *e* sheet in the second set.
26:28 boards, shall reach across from end to *e.*
36:11 the edge of the *e* sheet in the first set,
36:17 along the edge of the *e* sheet in one set,
36:33 was made to reach across from *e* to end.
37: 8 at one end, the other at the other *e,*
Lv 25:30 not been redeemed at the *e* of a full year,
Nm 22:36 Arnon at the *e* of the Moabite territory.
24:20 Amalek, but this *e* is to perish forever.
25:11 that is why I did not put an *e* to the
34: 3 it shall begin at the *e* of the Salt Sea,
Dt 2:16 an *e* to all the soldiers among the people,
4:32 ask from one *e* of the sky to the other:
7:24 you, till you have put an *e* to them.
8:16 you, but also make you prosperous in the *e.*
9:11 the *e* of the forty days and forty nights,
11:12 from the beginning of the year to the *e.*
13: 8 away, from one *e* of the earth to the other:
14:28 "At the *e* of every third year you shall
15: 1 "At the *e* of every seven-year period you
28:49 nation from afar, from the *e* of the earth,
28:64 from one *e* of the earth to the other,
31:10 comes at the *e* of every seven-year period,
31:30 words of this song from beginning to *e,*
32:26 'I will make an *e* of them and blot out
Jos 15: 2 that forms the southern *e* of the Salt Sea,
15: 8 at the northern *e* of the Valley of Rephaim,
18:19 Salt Sea, at the southern *e* of the Jordan.
Jgs 11:39 At the *e* of the two months she returned to
19: 9 See, the day is coming to an *e.*
Ru 2:23 the *e* of the barley and wheat harvests.
1Sm 1:20 and at the *e* of her term bore a son whom
14:27 thrust out the *e* of the staff he was
14:43 from the *e* of the staff I was holding.
15:27 to go, Saul seized a loose *e* of his mantle,
24: 5 stealthily cut off an *e* of Saul's mantle.
24: 6 that he had cut off an *e* of Saul's mantle.
24:12 here at this *e* of your mantle which I hold.
24:12 an *e* of your mantle and did not kill you,
2Sm 14:26 which he used to do at the *e* of every year,
22:38 did I turn again till I made an *e* of them.
1Kgs 7: 4 There were three window frames at either *e,*
7: 5 faced each other, three at either *e.*
2Kgs 8: 3 At the *e* of the seven years,
23: 5 He also put an *e* to the pseudo-priests
1Chr 23: 1 grown old and was near the *e* of his days,
2Chr 20:16 and you will come upon them at the *e* of
Ezr 9:11 one *e* to the other in their uncleanness.
Neh 3:21 of Eliashib's house to the *e* of the house.
4: 4 strength, there is no *e* to the rubbish;
4: 5 midst, kill them, and put an *e* to the work."
5: 9 *e* to the derision of our Gentile enemies?
5:10 Let us put an *e* to this usury!
8: 3 Standing at one *e* of the open place that
Tb 10: 7 Now at the *e* of the fourteen-day wedding
12: 1 the wedding celebration came to an *e,*
13:18 The *e* of Tobit's hymn of praise.
Jdt 8: 9 to the Assyrians at the *e* of five days,
8:11 city to our enemies at the *e* of five days
11:21 "No other woman from one *e* of the world
Est 1: 5 At the *e* of this time the king gave a
D: 1 the third day, putting an *e* to her prayers,
2Mc 5: 7 *e* received only disgrace for his treachery,
5: 8 At length he met a miserable *e.*
7:38 may there be an *e* to the wrath of the
9: 2 so that in the *e* Antiochus was put to
10: 9 was the *e* of Antiochus surnamed Epiphanes.
15:37 I will bring my own story to an *e* here too.
15:38 Let this, then, be the *e.*
Jb 7: 6 they come to an *e* without hope.
8:13 So is the *e* of everyone who forgets God,
16: 3 Is there no *e* to windy words?
17:11 days are passed away, my plans are at an *e,*
18: 2 When will you put an *e* to words?
Ps(s) 7:10 Let the malice of the wicked come to an *e,*
18:38 did I turn again till I made an *e* of them.
19: 7 At one *e* of the heavens it comes forth,
19: 7 forth, and its course is to their other *e;*
25:18 Put an *e* to my affliction and my suffering,
39: 5 my *e* and what is the number of my days,
46:10 He has stopped wars to the *e* of the earth:
49:14 the *e* of those contented with their lot:
61: 3 *e* I call to you as my heart grows faint.
73:24 and in the *e* you will receive me in glory.
90: 5 You make an *e* of them in their sleep;
102:28 you are the same, and your years have no *e.*
119:87 have all but put an *e* to me on the earth,
135: 7 storm clouds from the *e* of the earth;
139:18 did I reach the *e* of them,
Prv 5: 4 But in the *e* she is as bitter as wormwood,
5:11 And you groan in the *e,*
14:12 to a man, but the *e* of it leads to death!
14:13 may be sad, and the *e* of joy may be sorrow.
16:25 to a man, but the *e* of it leads to death!
18:18 The lot puts an *e* to disputes,
20:21 at the outset will in the *e* not be blessed.
23:32 But in the *e* it bites like a serpent,
28:23 in the *e* than one with a flattering tongue.
Eccl 3:11 ever discovering, from beginning to *e,*
4: 8 Yet there is no *e* to all his toil,
4:16 There is no *e* to all these people,
7: 2 feasting, For that is the *e* of every man,
7: 8 is the *e* of speech than its beginning;
10:13 and the *e* of his talk is utter madness;
12:12 Of the making of many books there is no *e,*
Wis 3:19 dire is the *e* of the wicked generation.
7:18 and the *e* and the midpoint of times,
8: 1 she reaches from *e* to end mightily and
11:14 but in the *e* of events,
14:14 therefore a sudden *e* is devised for them.
16: 5 serpents, your anger endured not the *e.*
19: 1 merciless wrath assailed until the *e.*
Sir 1:11 He who fears the LORD will have a happy *e;*
3:25 A stubborn man will fare badly in the *e,*
12:12 And in the *e* you appreciate my advice,
14: 7 and in the *e* he displays his greed.
21: 9 they will *e* in a flaming fire.
21:10 that *e* in the depths of the nether world.
27:14 oath-filled talk makes the hair stand on *e,*
38:20 think rather of the *e.*
40:14 suddenly, once and for all, comes to an *e.*
43:32 weary not, though you cannot reach the *e;*
46:19 When Samuel approached the *e* of his life,
46:20 as a prophet, to put an *e* to wickedness.
48:10 an *e* to wrath before the day of the LORD,
48:25 foretold what should be till the *e* of time,
49: 4 these kings of Judah, right to the very *e.*
51:14 and until the *e* I will cultivate her.
Is 2: 7 gold, and there is no *e* to their treasures;
2: 7 and there is no *e* to their chariots.
4: 1 name be given us, put an *e* to our disgrace!"
7: 3 at the *e* of the conduit of the upper pool,
8:23 in the *e* he has glorified the seaward road,
10: 7 destroy, to make an *e* of nations not a few.
10:12 [But when the Lord has brought to an *e* all
13: 5 country, and from the *e* of the heavens,
13:11 will put an *e* to the pride of the arrogant,
14: 4 How the oppressor has reached his *e!*
21: 2 I will put an *e* to all groaning!"
21:16 all the glory of Kedar shall come to an *e.*
23:15 of another king, at the *e* of seventy years,
23:17 At the *e* of the seventy years the LORD
24:16 From the *e* of the earth we hear songs:
40: 2 to her that her service is at an *e,*
42:10 song, his praise from the *e* of the earth:
55:11 will, achieving the *e* for which I sent it.
60:20 the days of your mourning shall be at an *e.*
Jer 3: 5 forever, will he hold his grudge to the *e?*"
5:31 what will you do when the *e* comes?
8:20 harvest has passed, the summer is at an *e,*
10:13 brings up clouds from the *e* of the earth;
12:12 which consumes the land, from *e* to end:
14:15 famine shall these prophets meet their *e.*
16: 4 Sword and famine will make an *e* of them,
17:11 in the *e* he is only a fool.
20:18 see sorrow and pain, to *e* my days in shame?
25:10 *e* the song of joy and the song of gladness,
25:33 from one *e* of the earth to the other.
30:11 I will make an *e* of all the nations among
30:11 but of you I will not make an *e.*
46:28 I will make an *e* of all the nations to
46:28 you, But of you I will not make an *e:*
48: 2 "Come, let us put an *e* to her as a people."
48:33 *e* in the fruit gardens of the land of Moab.
49:37 until I have completely made an *e* of them;
51:13 waters, rich in treasure, Your *e* has come,
51:16 brings up clouds from the *e* of the earth;
Lam 1: 9 she gave no thought how she would *e.*
4:18 Our *e* drew near,
Bar 3:17 of whose possessions there was no *e?*
6:71 they themselves will in the *e* be comsumed,
Ez 3:16 At the *e* of seven days. . . .
7: 2 An *e!* The *e* has come upon the four corners
7: 3 Now the *e* is upon you;
7: 6 An end is coming, the *e* is coming upon you!
7:10 See, the *e* is coming!
7:24 I will put an *e* to their proud strength,
12:23 I will put an *e* to this proverb;
16:41 Thus I will put an *e* to your harlotry,
20:13 on them in the desert to put an *e* to them,
20:17 I did not put an *e* to them in the desert.
21:34 day has come when their crimes are at an *e.*
22: 4 day, so that the *e* of your years has come.
23:27 I will put an *e* to your lewdness and to
23:48 I will put an *e* to lewdness in the land,
26:13 I will put an *e* to the noise of your songs,
29:13 At the *e* of forty years I will gather the
30:10 I will put an *e* to the throngs of Egypt by
30:13 I will put an *e* to the great ones of
33:28 that its proud strength will come to an *e,*
35: 5 trouble, when their crimes came to an *e,*
46:19 There, at their west *e,*
Dn 1:18 At the *e* of the time the king had
2:44 all these kingdoms and put an *e* to them,
5:26 numbered your kingdom and put an *e* to it;
6:27 and his dominion shall be without *e.*
8:17 man, that the vision refers to the *e* time."
8:19 at the appointed time, there will be an *e.*
9:24 transgression will stop and sin will *e,*
9:26 the *e* shall come like a torrent; until the *e*
10: 3 at all until the *e* of the three weeks.
11:18 shall put an *e* to his shameful conduct,
11:27 because the appointed *e* is not yet.
11:35 *e* time which is still appointed to come.
11:45 shall come to his *e* with none to help him.

12: 4 message and seal the book until the *e* time;
12: 6 it be to the *e* of these appalling things?"
12: 7 to an *e*, all these things should *e*.
12: 9 be kept secret and sealed until the *e* time.
12:13 rise for your reward at the *e* of days."
13:59 you in two so as to make an *e* of you both."
Hos 1: 4 to an *e* the kingdom of the house of Israel;
2:13 I will bring an *e* to all her joy,
11: 6 cities and *e* by consuming his solitudes.
Am 1:11 in his anger and kept his wrath to the *e*,
8:10 son, and bring their day to a bitter *e*.
Na 1: 8 He makes an *e* of his opponents,
1: 9 It is he who will make an *e!*
2:10 There is no *e* to the treasure,
2:14 preying on the land I will bring to an *e*,
3: 9 strength, and Egypt, and others without *e;*
Zep 1:18 For he shall make an end, yes, a sudden *e*,
Mt 10:22 holds out till the *e* will escape death.
13:39 The harvest is the *e* of the world,
13:40 so will it be at the *e* of the world.
13:49 is how it will be at the *e* of the world.
15:14 man leads another, both will *e* in a pit."
20: 8 with the last group and *e* with the first.'
21:41 bring that wicked crowd to a bad *e*
24: 3 sign of your coming and the *e* of the world?"
24: 6 bound to happen, but that is not yet the *e*.
24:13 The man who holds out to the *e*,
24:14 Only after that will the *e* come.
24:31 from one *e* of the heavens to the other.'
28:20 with you always, until the *e* of the world!"
Mk 3:29 He carries the guilt of his sin without *e*."
13: 4 the sign that all this is coming to an *e?*"
13: 7 bound to happen, but this is not yet the *e*.
13:13 *e* is the one who will come through safe.
Lk 1:33 forever and his reign will be without *e*."
2:43 they were returning at the *e* of the feast,
4: 2 nothing, and at the *e* of it he was hungry.
13: 3 all come to the same *e* unless you reform.
13: 5 all come to the same *e* unless you reform."
16: 2 service, for it is about to come to an *e*.'
16:28 they may not *e* in this place of torment.'
17:24 flashes from one *e* of the sky to the other.
18: 5 favor or she will *e* by doing me violence.'"
20:16 He will make an *e* to those tenant farmers
21: 9 but the *e* does not follow immediately."
Jn 11: 4 "This sickness is not to *e* in death;
13: 1 and would show his love for them to the *e*.
19:16 In the *e*, Pilate handed Jesus over
Acts 5:36 In the *e* it came to nothing.
13:20 the *e* of some four hundred and fifty years.
13:25 As John's career was coming to an *e*,
27:20 Toward the *e*, we abandoned any hope
Rom 3: 3 unbelief put an *e* to God's faithfulness?
10: 4 Christ is the *e* of the law.
1Cor 1: 8 He will strengthen you to the *e*,
3: 8 and he who waters work to the same *e*.
4: 9 has put us apostles at the *e* of the line,
6:13 will do away with them both in the *e*"
10:11 us, upon whom the *e* of the ages has come.
13:13 There are in the *e* three things that last:
15:24 After that will come the *e*,
2Cor 11:15 But their *e* will correspond to their deeds.
Gal 3: 3 the spirit, are you now to *e* in the flesh?
5:15 You will *e* up in mutual destruction!
Eph 3:21 through all generations, world without *e*.
4:25 to it, then, that you put an *e* to lying;
Phil 3:19 Such as these will *e* in disaster!
2Tm 2:12 out to the *e* we shall also reign with him.
Heb 1:12 the same, and your years will have no *e*."
3:14 the *e* that confidence with which we began.
6:11 each of you show the same zeal till the *e*,
6:16 to a promise and puts an *e* to all argument.
7: 3 without beginning of days or *e* of life,
9:26 But now he has appeared at the *e* of the
11:22 By faith Joseph, near the *e* of his life,
Jas 1:12 man who holds out to the *e* through trial!
5:11 compassionate and merciful, did in the *e*.
1Pt 4:17 what must be the *e* for those who refuse
Jude 1:12 trees at the year's *e* they bear no fruit,
Rv 2:26 victory, who keeps to my ways till the *e*,
15: 8 of the seven angels had come to an *e*.
21: 6 and the Omega, the Beginning and the *E*.
22:13 and the Last, the Beginning and the *E!*

ENDANGER (1)

Dn 1:10 your age, you will *e* my life with the king."

ENDANGERED (1)

2Cor 11:26 I traveled continually, *e* by floods,

ENDEAR (1)

Sir 4: 7 *E* yourself to the assembly;

ENDEAVOR (1)

2Mc 11:19 *e* to further your interests in the future.

ENDEAVORED (3)

Gn 34: 3 with the girl, he *e* to win her affection.
2Mc 10:12 he *e* to have peaceful relations with them.
10:15 from Jerusalem and *e* to continue the war.

ENDEAVORS (1)

Tb 4:19 to grant success to all your *e* and plans.

ENDED (24)

Gn 47:18 When that year *e*,
Jos 16: 7 and skirting Jericho, it *e* at the Jordan.
16: 8 to the Wadi Kanah and *e* at the sea.
17: 9 ran north of the wadi and *e* at the sea.
19:14 the boundary *e* at the valley of Iphtahel.
19:29 it cut back to Hosah and *e* at the sea.
19:33 and Jabneel, and *e* at the Jordan.
2Sm 20:19 whether loyalty is finished or *e* in Israel.'
1Kgs 1:41 him heard it, just as they *e* their banquet.
2Chr 7: 1 When Solomon had *e* his prayer,
2Mc 10:13 office, he *e* his life by taking poison.
15:24 With this he *e* his prayer.
15:37 Since Nicanor's doings *e* in this way,
Jb 31:37 The words of Job are *e*.
Ps(s) 72:20 prayers of David the son of Jesse are *e*.
78:33 Therefore he quickly *e* their days and
Sir 44:17 and with a sign to him the deluge *e;*
Is 16: 4 When the struggle is *e*,
18: 5 the vintage, when the flowering is *e*,
24: 8 timbrels, *e* the shouts of the jubilant,
Ez 21:30 coming when your life of crime will be *e*,
Lk 20: 7 They *e* by replying they did not know where
Acts 18:11 *e* by settling there for a year and a half,
Heb 13: 7 consider how their lives *e*,

ENDING (7)

Gn 44:12 with the oldest and *e* with the youngest,
Jos 16: 3 and to Gezer, *e* thence at the sea.
19:22 and Beth-shemesh, *e* at the Jordan.
2Sm 24: 7 *e* up at Beer-sheba in the Negeb of Judah.
2Kgs 23:33 of Hamath, thus *e* his reign in Jerusalem.
2Mc 12:38 As the week was *e*,
Wis 19: 4 a compulsion suited to this *e* drew them on,

ENDLESS (7)

Jb 22: 5 Are not your iniquities *e?*
Bar 3:25 Vast and *e*, high and immeasurable!
Na 3: 3 corpses, the *e* bodies to stumble upon!
Mt 18: 8 with two hands or two feet into *e* fire.
Rom 16:27 be given through Jesus Christ unto *e* ages.
Gal 1: 5 to him be glory for *e* ages.
Ti 1: 2 who cannot lie, promised in *e* ages past.

ENDOR (3)

Jos 17:11 natives there, *E* and its towns and natives,
1Sm 28: 7 "There is a woman in *E* who is a medium."
Ps(s) 83:11 at the torrent Kishon, Who perished at *E;*

ENDORSED (1)

Acts 17:31 one whom he has *e* in the sight of all by

ENDOW (3)

Jb 39:19 his strength, and *e* his neck with splendor?
Ps(s) 72: 1 O God, with your judgment *e* the king,
Mt 12:18 I will *e* him with my spirit and he will

ENDOWED (13)

Gn 41:38 "a man so *e* with the spirit of God?"
Ex 28: 3 expert workmen whom I have *e* with skill,
31: 6 I have also *e* all the experts with the
35:35 He has *e* them with skill to execute all
36: 1 experts whom the LORD has *e* with skill
36: 2 experts whom the LORD had *e* with skill,
1Kgs 7:14 He was *e* with skill,
1Chr 12:33 their chiefs who were *e* with an
Ps(s) 30: 8 you had *e* me with majesty and strength:
Wis 16:20 *e* with all delights and conforming to
Mk 6: 2 What kind of wisdom is he *e* with?
1Cor 1: 5 *e* with every gift of speech and knowledge.
Col 1:11 *e* with the strength needed to stand fast,

ENDOWMENTS (1)

Wis 7:15 suitably and value these *e* at their worth:

ENDOWS (2)

Sir 17: 3 He *e* man with a strength of his own,
38: 6 He *e* men with the knowledge to glory in

ENDS (70)

Ex 25:18 gold for the two *e* of the propitiatory,
28: 7 shoulder straps joined to its two upper *e*.
28:23 them to the two upper *e* of the breastpiece.
28:24 rings at the upper *e* of the breastpiece,
28:25 the other two *e* of the cords being
28:26 them on the two lower *e* of the breastpiece,
37: 7 made for the two *e* of the propitiatory,
37: 8 from the propitiatory at its two *e*.
39: 4 made for it and joined to its two upper *e*.
39:16 to the two upper *e* of the breastpiece.
39:17 the two rings at the *e* of the breastpiece.
39:18 The other two *e* of the two chains were
39:19 put on the two lower *e* of the breastpiece,
Dt 33:17 nations, even those at the *e* of the earth."
1Sm 2:10 the LORD judges the *e* of the earth,
1Kgs 8: 8 The poles were so long that their *e* could
2Chr 5: 9 long enough so that their *e* could be seen
Jdt 2: 9 them as exiles to the very *e* of the earth.
1Mc 1: 3 He advanced to the *e* of the earth,
2:62 for his glory *e* in corruption and worms.
3: 9 and was renowned to the *e* of the earth;
14:10 glorious name reached the *e* of the earth.
Jb 28:24 For he beholds the *e* of the earth and sees
37: 3 with his lightning, to the *e* of the earth.
38:13 For taking hold of the *e* of the earth,
Ps(s) 2: 8 and the *e* of the earth for your possession.
19: 5 voice resounds, and to the *e* of the world,
22:28 All the *e* of the earth shall remember
48:11 your praise reaches to the *e* of the earth.
59:14 of Jacob, yes, to the *e* of the earth.
65: 6 *e* of the earth and of the distant seas.
65: 9 the earth's *e* are in fear at your marvels;
67: 8 and may all the *e* of the earth fear him!
72: 8 and from the River to the *e* of the earth.
98: 3 All the *e* of the earth have seen the
Prv 11:23 The desire of the just *e* only in good;
16: 4 The LORD has made everything for his own *e*,
17:24 eyes of a fool are on the *e* of the earth.
30: 4 who has marked out all the *e* of the earth?
Sir 7:25 your daughter in marriage *e* a great task;
11:28 happy before his death, for how he *e*,
18: 5 When a man *e* he is only beginning,
27:15 Wrangling among the haughty *e* in bloodshed,
36:17 will be known to the very *e* of the earth
44:21 and from the River to the *e* of the earth.
Is 5:26 whistle to them from the *e* of the earth;
40:28 eternal God, creator of the *e* of the earth.
41: 5 the *e* of the earth tremble:
41: 9 You whom I have taken from the *e* of the
43: 6 and my daughters from the *e* of the earth:
45:22 to me and be safe, all you *e* of the earth,
48:20 Publish it to the *e* of the earth,
49: 6 salvation may reach to the *e* of the earth.
52:10 All the *e* of the earth will behold the
58: 4 your fast *e* in quarreling and fighting,
62:11 the LORD proclaims to the *e* of the earth:
Jer 6:22 nation, roused from the *e* of the earth.
16:19 the nations come from the *e* of the earth,
25:31 the earth to its very *e* the uproar spreads;
25:32 storm is unleashed from the *e* of the earth.
31: 8 I will gather them from the *e* of the world,
49:36 four winds from the four *e* of the heavens:
50:41 kings roused from the *e* of the earth.
Ez 15: 4 both *e* and even the middle is scorched,
Dn 4: 8 and it could be seen to the *e* of the earth.
Mi 5: 3 shall reach to the *e* of the earth;
Zec 9:10 and from the River to the *e* of the earth.
Acts 1: 8 Samaria, yes, even to the *e* of the earth."
13:47 a means of salvation to the *e* of the earth.'"
Rom 1:17 of God which begins and *e* with faith;

ENDURANCE (14)

1Sm 14:15 shook so that the panic was beyond human *e*.
Lk 21:19 By patient *e* you will save your lives.
Rom 5: 3 We know that affliction makes for *e*,
5: 4 for endurance, and *e* for tested virtue,
8:25 see means awaiting it with patient *e*.
2Cor 6: 4 of God, acting with patient *e* amid trials,
Gal 5:22 the spirit is love, joy, peace, patient *e*,
2Tm 3:10 fidelity, patience, love, and *e*,
Jas 1: 3 when your faith is tested this makes for *e*.
1: 4 Let *e* come to its perfection so that you
Rv 1: 9 kingly reign and the *e* we have in Jesus,
2: 2 deeds, your labors, and your patient *e*.
2:19 as well as your patient *e;*
13:10 *e* that distinguishes God's holy people.

ENDURE (57)

Ex 18: 8 they had had to *e* on their journey,
Dt 33:25 may your strength *e* through all your days!"
1Sm 13:14 as things are, your kingdom shall not *e*.
2Sm 7:16 and your kingdom shall *e* forever before me;
1Kgs 2:45 throne shall *e* before the LORD forever."
15: 4 after him and permitting Jerusalem to *e;*
Tb 3: 6 me to die than to *e* so much misery in life,
2Mc 2:27 many we will gladly *e* these inconveniences,
9:10 no one could *e* to transport the man
Jb 6:11 What strength have I that I should *e?*
8:15 he shall cling to it, but it shall not *e*.
15:29 be rich, and his possessions shall not *e;*
20:21 up, Therefore his prosperity shall not *e*,
Ps(s) 72: 5 May he *e* as long as the sun,
81:16 flatter me, but their fate would *e* forever.
89:30 I will make his posterity *e* forever and
101: 5 eyes and puffed-up heart I will not *e*.
102:25 through all generations your years *e*.
104:31 May the glory of the LORD *e* forever;
112: 3 his generosity shall *e* forever.
112: 9 his generosity shall *e* forever;
Prv 12:19 Truthful lips *e* forever,
Eccl 3:14 that whatever God does will *e* forever;
Sir 44:13 And for all time their progeny will *e*,
50:24 May his goodness toward us *e* in Israel as
51:24 how long will you *e* such bitter thirst?
Is 66:22 earth which I will make Shall *e* before me,
66:22 LORD, so shall your race and your name *e*.
Jer 10:10 quakes, whose wrath the nations cannot *e:*

ENDURE (cont.)

20: 9 I grow weary holding it in, I cannot *e* it.
Am 7:10 the country cannot *e* all his words.
Mi 7: 9 I will *e* because I have sinned against him,
Hb 1:13 evil, and the sight of misery you cannot *e.*
Mal 3: 2 But who will *e* the day of his coming?
Mt 17:17 How long can I *e* you?
Mk 3:26 and is torn by dissension, he cannot *e;*
9:19 How long can I *e* you?
Lk 9:22 he said, "must first *e* many sufferings,
9:41 How long can I *e* you?
Jn 3:36 not see life, but must *e* the wrath of God."
6:60 remarked, "This sort of talk is hard to *e!*
15:16 Your fruit must *e,*
1Cor 10:13 out of it so that you may be able to *e* it.
13: 7 to its trust, its hope, its power to *e.*
2Cor 1: 6 *e* patiently the same sufferings we endure.
11: 1 You must *e* little of my folly.
11: 4 you accepted, you seem to *e* it quite well.
Eph 3:13 be disheartened by the trials I *e* for you;
Col 1:11 fast, even to *e* joyfully whatever may come,
1:24 I find my joy in the suffering I *e* for you.
1Thes 3: 1 That is why, when we could *e* it no longer,
2Thes 1: 4 You *e* these as an expression of God's
Heb 12: 7 *E* your trials as the discipline of God,
1Pt 2:19 When a man can suffer injustice and *e*
Rv 2: 3 are patient and *e* hardship for my cause.
2: 9 I know the slander you *e* from self-styled

ENDURED (13)

Gn 41:51 sufferings I *e* at the hands of my family";
1Kgs 2:26 shared in all the hardships my father *e.*"
1Mc 10:15 brothers and the troubles that they had *e.*
Wis 16: 5 crooked serpents, your anger *e* not the end.
Sir 28:19 sheltered from it, and has not *e* its wrath;
Is 53: 4 that he bore, our sufferings that he *e,*
Mt 8:17 infirmities he bore, our sufferings he *e.*"
Rom 9:22 has *e* with much patience vessels fit for
Heb 10:32 you *e* a great contest of suffering.
11:36 Still others *e* mockery,
12: 2 joy which lay before him he *e* the cross,
12: 3 how he *e* the opposition of sinners;
Jas 5:11 Those who have *e* we call blessed.

ENDURES (63)

1Chr 16:34 for he is good, for his kindness *e* forever;
16:41 because his kindness *e* forever
2Chr 5:13 for he is good, for his mercy *e* forever,"
7: 3 "for he is good, for his mercy *e* forever."
7: 6 the LORD, for his mercy *e* forever,"
20:21 to the LORD, for his mercy *e* forever."
Ezr 3:11 for his kindness to Israel *e* forever";
1Mc 4:24 "for he is good, for his mercy *e* forever."
Ps(s) 100: 5 the LORD, whose kindness *e* forever,
107: 1 for he is good, for his kindness *e* forever!"
111: 3 are his work, and his justice *e* forever.
111:10 His praise *e* forever.
117: 2 us, and the fidelity of the LORD *e* forever.
118: 2 house of Israel say, "His mercy *e* forever."
118: 3 house of Aaron say, "His mercy *e* forever."
118: 4 fear the LORD say, "His mercy *e* forever."
118:29 for his kindness *e* forever.
119:89 Your word, O LORD, *e* forever;
119:90 Through all generations your truth *e;*
135:13 Your name, O LORD, *e* forever;
136: 1 for he is good, for his mercy *e* forever;
136: 2 the God of gods, for his mercy *e* forever;
136: 3 the Lord of lords, for his mercy *e* forever;
136: 4 great wonders, for his mercy *e* forever;
136: 5 heavens in wisdom, for his mercy *e* forever;
136: 6 upon the waters, for his mercy *e* forever;
136: 7 the great lights, for his mercy *e* forever;
136: 8 rule over the day, for his mercy *e* forever;
136: 9 over the night, for his mercy *e* forever;
136:10 their first-born, for his mercy *e* forever;
136:11 from their midst, for his mercy *e* forever;
136:12 outstretched arm, for his mercy *e* forever;
136:13 Red Sea in twain, for his mercy *e* forever;
136:14 through its midst, for his mercy *e* forever;
136:15 into the Red Sea, for his mercy *e* forever;
136:16 the wilderness, for his mercy *e* forever;
136:17 smote great kings, for his mercy *e* forever;
136:18 powerful kings, for his mercy *e* forever;
136:19 of the Amorites, for his mercy *e* forever;
136:20 king of Bashan, for his mercy *e* forever;
136:21 land a heritage, for his mercy *e* forever;
136:22 his servant, for his mercy *e* forever;
136:23 in our abjection, for his mercy *e* forever;
136:24 us from our foes, for his mercy *e* forever;
136:25 food to all flesh, for his mercy *e* forever.
136:26 the God of heaven, for his mercy *e* forever.
138: 8 your kindness, O LORD, *e* forever;
145:13 your dominion *e* through all generations.
Prv 16:12 for by righteousness the throne *e.*
19:21 but it is the decision of the LORD that *e.*
Sir 37:25 heritage of glory, and his name *e* forever.
40:17 never be cut off, and justice *e* forever.
44:12 God's covenant with them their family *e,*
Jer 33:11 his mercy *e* forever."
Bar 4: 1 precepts of God, the law that *e* forever;
Dn 3:89 for he is good, for his mercy *e* forever.
3:90 him thanks, because his mercy *e* forever."
3:100 and his dominion *e* through all generations.
4:31 and his kingdom *e* through all generations.
2Cor 3:11 glory, greater by far is the glory that *e.*
9: 9 gave to the poor, his justice *e* forever."
1Pt 1:24 wilts, but the word of the Lord *e* forever."
1Jn 2:17 but the man who does God's will *e* forever.

ENDURING (17)

Nm 24:21 Your abode is *e,*
1Kgs 10: 9 In his *e* love for Israel,
2Mc 6:30 I am not only *e* terrible pain in my body
7:36 My brothers, after *e* brief pain,
Ps(s) 19:10 The fear of the LORD is pure, *e* forever;
Prv 8:18 riches and honor, *e* wealth and prosperity.
12:12 demolished, but the root of the just is *e.*
Sir 37:22 the fruits of his knowledge are *e:*
Is 54: 8 But with *e* love I take pity on you,
Bar 3:13 of God, you would have dwelt in *e* peace.
4:23 you back to me with *e* gladness and joy.
4:29 will, in saving you, bring you back *e* joy."
Dn 6:27 "For he is the living God, *e* forever;
Jn 1:14 coming from the Father, filled with *e* love.
1:17 this *e* love came through Jesus Christ.
2Cor 11:27 *e* labor, hardship, many sleepless nights;
1Pt 1:23 seed, through the living and *e* word of God.

ENEMIES (300)

Gn 22:17 take possession of the gates of their *e,*
24:60 gain possession of the gates of their *e!*"
49: 8 your hand on the neck of your *e;*
Ex 1:10 too may join our *e* to fight against us,
23:22 an enemy to your *e* and a foe to your foes.
23:27 make all your *e* turn from you in flight,
Lv 26: 7 your *e* and lay them low with your sword.
26:16 in vain, for your *e* will consume the crop.
26:17 before your *e* and lorded over by your foes.
26:32 that your very *e* who come to live there
26:34 while you are in the land of your *e;*
26:36 their *e* I will make so fainthearted that,
26:38 Gentiles, swallowed up in your *e'* country.
26:39 survive in the lands of their *e* will waste
26:41 them and bring them into their *e'* land.
26:44 so, even while they are in their *e'* land,
Nm 10:35 O LORD, that your *e* may be scattered,
14:42 go, you will be beaten down before your *e.*
25:17 "Treat the Midianites as *e* and crush them,
25:18 for they have been your *e* by their wily
32:21 until he has driven his *e* out of his way
Dt 1:42 lest you be beaten down before your *e,*
6:19 thrusting all your *e* out of your way.
7:15 Egypt, but will leave them with all your *e.*
12:10 given you rest from all your *e* round about
20: 1 "When you go out to war against your *e*
20: 3 you are going into battle against your *e.*
20: 4 you against your *e* and give you victory.'
20:14 use this plunder of your *e* which the LORD,
21:10 go out to war against your *e* and the LORD,
23:10 camp during an expedition against your *e,*
23:15 defend you and to put your *e* at your mercy,
25:19 gives you rest from all your *e* round about
28: 7 before you the *e* that rise up against you;
28:25 will let you be beaten down before your *e;*
28:31 Your flocks will be given to your *e,*
28:48 you will serve the *e* whom the Lord
28:68 sale to your *e* as male and female slaves,
30: 7 to your *e* and the foes who persecuted you.
32:27 Had I not feared the insolence of their *e,*
33:29 Your *e* fawn upon you,
Jos 5:13 asked, "Are you one of us or of our *e?*"
7: 8 that Israel has turned its back to its *e?*
7:12 the Israelites cannot stand up to their *e,*
7:13 You cannot stand up to your *e* until you
10:19 Pursue your *e,* and harry them in the rear.
10:25 do to all the *e* against whom you fight."
21:44 Not one of their *e* could withstand them;
21:44 LORD brought all their *e* under their power.
22: 8 spoils of your *e* with your kinsmen there."
23: 1 rest from all their *e* round about them,
Jgs 2:14 fall into the power of their *e* round about
2:18 of their *e* as long as the judge lived;
3:28 your *e* the Moabites into your power."
5:31 May all your *e* perish thus, O LORD!
8:34 from the power of their *e* all around them.
11:36 vengeance for you on your *e* the Ammonites."
1Sm 2: 1 I have swallowed up my *e;*
4: 3 us and save us from the grasp of our *e.*"
10: 1 them from the grasp of their *e* round about.
12:10 but deliver us now from the power of our *e,*
12:11 you from the power of your *e* on every side,
14:24 before I am able to avenge myself on my *e.*"
14:47 Saul waged war on all their surrounding *e*—
18:25 that he may thus take vengeance on his *e.*"
20:15 *e* of David from the surface of the earth.
25:26 May your *e* and those who seek to harm my
25:29 of your *e* as from the hollow of a sling.
29: 8 to fight against the *e* of my lord the king?"
30:26 you from the spoil of the *e* of the LORD":
2Sm 3:18 and from the grasp of all their *e.*'"
5: 8 the blind shall be the personal *e* of David."
5:20 "The LORD has scattered my *e* before me
7: 1 given him rest from his *e* on every side,
7: 9 and I have destroyed all your *e* before you.
7:11 I will give you rest from all your *e.*
18:19 has set him free from the grasp of his *e.*"
18:32 "May the *e* of my lord the king and all
19:10 delivered us from the clutches of our *e,*
22: 1 of all his *e* and from the hand of Saul.
22: 4 LORD,' I exclaim, and I am safe from my *e.*
22:38 I pursued my *e* and destroyed them,
22:41 My *e* you put to flight before me and those
22:49 to me and helped me escape from my *e,*
1Kgs 3:11 for riches, nor for the life of your *e,*
5:17 of the *e* surrounding him on all sides,
5:17 put these *e* under the soles of his feet.
8:44 your people forth to war against their *e,*
8:48 in the land of the *e* who took them captive,
2Kgs 17:39 deliver you from the power of all your *e.*"
21:14 become a prey and a booty for all their *e,*
1Chr 12:18 to my *e* though my hands have done no wrong,
14:11 my *e* just as water breaks through a dam."
17: 8 went, and I cut down all your *e* before you.
17:10 And I will subdue all your *e.*
21:12 or three months of fleeing your *e,*
22: 9 give him rest from all his *e* on every side.
2Chr 6:28 their *e* besiege them at any of their gates;
6:34 people go forth to war against their *e,*
20:27 the LORD had given them over their *e.*
20:29 LORD had fought against the *e* of Israel.
26:13 great valor to help the king against his *e.*
Ezr 4: 1 When the *e* of Judah and Benjamin heard
8:22 to protect us against *e* along the way,
8:31 us from *e* and bandits along the way.
Neh 4: 5 Our *e* thought, "Before they are aware
4: 9 When our *e* became aware that we had been
5: 9 an end to the derision of our Gentile *e?*
6: 1 and our other *e* that I had rebuilt the
6:16 When all our *e* had heard of this,
6:16 our *e* lost much face in the eyes of the
9:27 delivered them into the power of their *e,*
9:27 to deliver them from the power of their *e.*
9:28 you abandoned them to the power of their *e,*
Tb 12:10 guilty of sin are their own worst *e.*
Jdt 5:18 and their cities were occupied by their *e.*
7:19 since all their *e* had them surrounded,
8:11 hand over the city to our *e* at the end
8:15 or to destroy us in the face of our *e.*
8:19 fell with great destruction before our *e.*
8:33 you will surrender the city to our *e,*
8:35 go before you to take vengeance upon our *e!*"
13: 5 to shatter the *e* who have risen against us."
13:11 in Israel and his power against our *e;*
13:14 shattered our *e* by my hand this very night."
13:17 brought to nought the *e* of your people."
13:18 blow at the head of the chief of our *e.*
15: 5 of the happenings in the camp of their *e.*
Est B: 6 destroyed by the swords of their *e,*
C: 8 for our *e* plan our ruin and are bent upon
C:17 have delivered us into the hands of our *e,*
8:13 that day to avenge themselves on their *e.*
9: 1 on which the *e* of the Jews had expected to
9: 1 the Jews became masters of their *e.*
9: 5 struck down all their *e* with the sword,
9: 5 they did to their *e* as they pleased.
9:16 themselves, and obtained rest from their *e.*
9:22 Jews obtained rest from their *e*
1Mc 2: 7 while it is given into the hands of *e,*
4:18 firm against our *e* and overthrow them.
4:36 said, "Now that our *e* have been crushed,
5:16 kinsmen who were being attacked by *e.*
5:27 Tomorrow their *e* plan to attack the
6:24 the sons of our people have become our *e;*
7:29 But Judas' *e* were prepared to seize him.
7:46 them in, and all the *e* fell by the sword;
9: 8 "Let us go forward to meet our *e;*
9:29 has been no one like him to oppose our *e,*
9:46 now to Heaven for deliverance from our *e.*"
10:26 our friendship and not gone over to our *e,*
11:21 of the law, *e* of their own nation,
12:15 we have been saved from our *e*
14: 7 He took many *e* prisoners of war and made
14:26 have stood firm and repulsed Israel's *e.*
14:29 danger and resisted the *e* of their nation,
14:31 When the *e* of the Jews sought to invade
15:33 for a time had been unjustly held by our *e.*
2Mc 4:16 every thing, became their *e* and oppressors.
5: 6 that he was winning a victory over his *e,*
8:31 They collected the *e'* weapons and
10:21 setting their *e* free to fight against them.
10:26 to them, and to be an enemy to their *e,*
12:28 who forcibly shatters the might of his *e,*
Jb 16: 9 My *e* lord it over me;
19:11 he counts me among his *e.*
Ps(s) 3: 8 For you strike all my *e* on the cheek;
5: 9 Because of my *e,*
6:11 my *e* shall be put to shame in utter terror;
9: 4 Most High, Because my *e* are turned back,
9: 7 The *e* are ruined completely forever;
17: 9 My ravenous *e* beset me;
18: 4 LORD, I exclaim, and I am safe from my *e.*
18:38 I pursued my *e* and overtook them,
18:41 My *e* you put to flight before me,
18:49 subject to me and preserved me from my *e,*
21: 9 May your hand reach all your *e,*
25: 2 put to shame, let not my *e* exult over me.
25:19 Behold, my *e* are many,

27: 2 foes and my e themselves stumble and fall.
27: 6 head is held high above my e on every side.
30: 2 clear and did not let my e rejoice over me.
31:16 the clutches of my e and my persecutors.
34:22 and the e of the just pay for their guilt.
35:19 Let not my unprovoked e rejoice over me;
37:20 the wicked perish, and the e of the LORD,
38:20 But my undeserved e are strong;
41: 3 and not give him over to the will of his e.
41: 6 My e say the worst of me:
45: 6 the king's e lose heart.
54: 9 me, and my eyes look down upon my e.
56:10 Then do my e turn back,
59: 2 Rescue me from my e, O my God;
66: 3 your great strength your e fawn upon you.
68: 2 his e are scattered,
68:22 Surely God crushes the heads of his e,
68:24 your dogs will have their share of your e."
69: 5 strength are they who wrongfully are my e.
69:19 as an answer for my e,
71:10 forsake me not, For my e speak against me,
72: 9 before him, and his e shall lick the dust.
78:53 while he covered their e with the sea.
80: 7 over by our neighbors, and our e mock us.
81:15 my ways, Quickly would I humble their e;
83: 3 For behold, your e raise a tumult,
86:17 a proof of your favor, that my e may see,
89:11 your strong arm you have scattered your e.
89:43 of his foes, you have gladdened all his e.
89:52 the nations With which your e have reviled,
92:10 your e, O LORD, for behold, your e
102: 9 All the day my e revile me;
106:42 Their e oppressed them,
110: 1 hand till I make your e your footstool."
110: 2 "Rule in the midst of your e.
119:98 Your command has made me wiser than my e,
127: 5 shame when they contend with e at the gate.
132:18 His e I will clothe with shame,
138: 7 the anger of my e you raise your hand;
139:22 they are my e.
143: 9 Rescue me from my e.
143:12 And in your kindness destroy my e;
Prv 16: 7 he makes even his e be at peace with him.
Wis 10:19 But their e she overwhelmed,
11: 3 e and took vengeance on their foes.
12:20 For these were e of your servants,
12:22 and our e with a thousand blows you punish,
15:14 are the e of your people who enslaved them.
16: 4 be shown how their e were being tormented.
16:22 that they might know that their e' fruits
18:10 the discordant cry of their e responded,
Sir 6: 4 its owner and makes him the sport of his e.
6:13 Keep away from your e;
18:31 they will make you the sport of your e.
25: 7 and he who lives to see his e' downfall.
25:13 worst of all vengeance is that of one's e:
37: 5 your e he will be your shield-bearer.
42:11 lest she make you the sport of your e,
46: 5 High God when his e beset him on all sides,
Is 1:24 vengeance on my foes and fully repay my e!
9:10 them and stirs up their e to action:
26:11 the fire prepared for your e consume them.
42:13 cry, against his e he shows his might:
59:18 He repays his e their deserts,
62: 8 will I give your grain as food to your e;
63:18 why have our e trampled your sanctuary?
64: 1 e and the nations would tremble before you,
66: 6 of the LORD repaying his e their deserts!
66:14 be known to his servants, but to his e,
Jer 15: 9 I will give to the sword before their e,
17: 4 you to your e in a land that you know not:
18:17 wind, I will scatter them before their e;
19: 7 them fall by the sword before their e,
19: 9 their e and those who seek their lives
20: 4 see them fall by the sword of their e,
21: 7 of their e and those who seek their lives.
30:16 devoured, all your e shall go into exile.
34:20 I will hand over, all of them, to their e,
34:21 his princes, I will hand over to their e,
44:30 Pharaoh Hophra, king of Egypt, to his e,
50: 7 upon them devoured them, and their e said,
Lam 1: 2 have all betrayed her and become her e.
1: 5 Her foes are uppermost, her e are at ease;
1:21 All my e rejoice at my misfortune:
2:16 All your e open their mouths against you;
3:46 our e have opened their mouths against us;
3:52 e without cause hunted me down like a bird;
Bar 4:18 himself deliver you from your e' hands.
4:25 Your e have persecuted you,
4:26 off by their e like sheep in a raid.
5: 6 Led away on foot by their e they left you:
Ez 16:27 delivered you over to the will of your e,
39:27 gather them from the lands of their e,
Dn 3:32 You have handed us over to our e,
4:17 replied, "this dream should be for your e,
Am 9: 4 they are led into captivity by their e,
Mi 4:10 LORD redeem you from the hand of your e.
5: 8 foes, and all your e shall be destroyed.
7: 6 and a man's e are those of his household.
Na 1: 2 adversaries, and lays up wrath for his e;
1: 8 and his e he pursues with darkness.
Zep 3:15 against you, he has turned away your e;
Mt 5:44 love your e, pray for your persecutors.
10:36 make a man's e those of his own household.
22:44 until I humble your e beneath your feet'?
Mk 12:36 hand until I make your e your footstool.'
Lk 1:71 our e and from the hands of all our foes.
6:27 Love your e,
19:27 e of mine who do not want me to be king,
19:43 when your e encircle you with a rampart,
20:43 hand while I make your e your footstool'?
Acts 2:35 hand until I make your e your footstool.'
Rom 5:10 if, when we were God's e,
11:28 the Jews are e of God for your sake;
1Cor 15:25 until God has put all e under his feet,
Phil 3:18 shows them to be e of the cross of Christ.
1Tm 5:14 give our e no occasion to speak ill of us.
Heb 1:13 hand till I make your e your footstool"?
10:13 until his e are placed beneath his feet.
Rv 11: 5 of these witnesses to devour their e.
11:12 to heaven in a cloud as their e looked on.

ENEMY (168)

Ex 15: 6 right hand, O LORD, has shattered the e.
15: 9 The e boasted,
23:22 e to your enemies and a foe to your foes.
Lv 26:25 till you are forced to surrender to the e.
Nm 10: 9 to war against an e that is attacking you,
35:23 he was not his e nor seeking to harm him:
Dt 28:53 of the siege to which your e subjects you,
28:55 e will subject you in all your communities.
28:57 e will subject you in your communities.
32:42 Flesh from the heads of the e leaders."
33:27 He drove the e out of your way and the
Jos 7: 3 The e there are few;
Jgs 8:24 being Ishmaelites, the e had gold rings.)
16:23 has delivered into our power Samson our e."
16:24 god has delivered into our power our e,
20:36 had looked as though the e were defeated,
1Sm 14:16 saw that the e camp had scattered
18:29 all the more [and was his e ever after].
19:17 You have helped my e to get away!"
22: 8 up my servant to be an e against me,
22:13 he might rebel against me and become my e,
24: 5 'I will deliver your e into your grasp;
24:20 For if a man meets his e,
26: 8 delivered your e into your grasp this day.
29: 4 us, lest during the battle he become our e.
2Sm 4: 8 is the head of Ishbaal, son of your e Saul,
22:18 He rescued me from my mighty e,
24:13 your e three months while he pursues you,
1Kgs 5:18 There is no e or threat of danger.
8:33 sin against you and are defeated by an e,
8:37 if an e of your people besieges them in
8:46 against them you deliver them to the e,
11:25 an e of Israel as long as Solomon lived;
21:20 "Have you found me out, my e?"
2Kgs 21:14 inheritance and deliver them into e hands,
2Chr 6:24 against you and are defeated by the e,
6:36 against them you deliver them to the e,
25: 8 LORD will defeat you in the face of the e.
Jdt 15: 4 all might fall upon the e and destroy them.
Est 3:10 Hammedatha the Agagite, the e of the Jews.
C:22 them and make an example of our chief e.
C:24 and turn his heart to hatred for our e,
7: 4 the e will be unable to compensate for the
7: 6 "The e oppressing us is this wicked Haman."
8: 1 gave the house of Haman, e of the Jews,
1Mc 2: 9 her young men by the sword of the e.
2:35 Then the e attacked them at once;
6:38 e and to be protected from the phalanxes.
7:26 officers, who was a bitter e of Israel,
8:23 may sword and e be far from them.
9:48 e did not pursue them across the Jordan.
10:83 e fled to Azotus and entered Beth-dagon,
11:72 overwhelmed the e that they took to flight.
11:73 the e as far as their camp in Kadesh,
12:26 reported that the e had made ready
12:28 When the e heard that Jonathan and his men
13:51 a great e of Israel had been destroyed.
14:34 a place previously occupied by the e;
16: 6 his men took their position against the e.
16:10 and about two thousand of the e perished.
2Mc 3:38 an e or a plotter against the government,
8: 6 and put to flight a large number of the e.
8:16 them not be panic-stricken before the e,
8:24 killed more than nine thousand of the e,
8:25 When they had pursued the e for some time,
10:26 to them, and to be an e to their enemies,
10:27 halting when they were close to the e.
10:29 there appeared to the e from the heavens
10:30 arrows and hurled thunderbolts at the e,
11:11 Hurling themselves upon the e like lions,
12:22 the e was overwhelmed with fear and terror
13:21 army, betrayed military secrets to the e.
14:16 came upon the e at the village of Adasa.
14:17 of the e suffered a slight repulse.
14:22 fear that the e might suddenly carry out
15: 8 He urged his men not to fear the e,
15:20 The e were already drawing near with their
Jb 6:23 possessions, Or to deliver me from the e,
13:24 you hide your face and consider me your e?
27: 7 Let my e be as the wicked and my adversary
31:29 of my e or exulted when evil fell upon him,
33:10 against me and reckons me as his e.
34:17 Can an e of justice indeed be in control,
Ps(s) 7: 6 Let the e pursue and overtake me;
13: 3 How long will my e triumph over me?
13: 5 I may not sleep in death lest my e say,
18:18 me from my mighty e and from my foes,
31: 9 e but enabling me to move about at large.
41:12 this, that my e does not triumph over me,
42:10 in mourning, with the e oppressing me?"
43: 2 in mourning, with the e oppressing me?
44:17 in the presence of the e and the avenger.
55: 4 of the e and the clamor of the wicked.
55:13 If an e had reviled me,
61: 4 refuge, a tower of strength against the e.
64: 2 from the dread e preserve my life.
74: 3 the damage the e has done in the sanctuary.
74:10 Shall the e revile your name forever?
74:18 Remember how the e has blasphemed you,
89:23 "No e shall deceive him,
106:10 and freed them from the hands of the e.
143: 3 For the e pursues me; he has crushed
Prv 24:17 Rejoice not when your e falls,
24:18 you, and withdraw his wrath from your e.
25:21 If your e be hungry, give him food to eat,
26:24 With his lips an e pretends,
26:28 The lying tongue is its owner's e,
27: 6 the greetings of an e one prays against.
29:24 The accomplice of a thief is his own e:
Wis 5:17 he shall arm creation to requite the e;
Sir 6: 9 Another is a friend who becomes an e,
11: 6 the honored are given into e hands.
12: 8 adversity an e will not remain concealed.
12: 9 man is successful even his e is friendly;
12:10 Never trust your e,
12:16 With his lips an e speaks sweetly,
12:16 Though your e has tears in his eyes,
19: 8 it against you, and in time become your e.
20:22 of shame, and has him for his e needlessly.
23: 3 to my foes, and my e rejoice over me?
27:18 For as an e might kill a man,
29: 6 and acquires an e at no extra charge;
30: 3 who educates his son makes his e jealous,
36: 6 your anger, pour out wrath, humble the e,
37: 2 when your bosom companion becomes your e?
46: 1 e and to win the inheritance for Israel.
46:18 He brought low the rulers of the e and
47: 7 battled and subdued the e on every side.
50: 4 and strengthened his city against the e.
Is 63:10 So he turned on them like an e,
Jer 12: 8 has roared against me, I treat her as an e.
30:14 I struck you as an e would strike,
44:30 king of Judah, to his e and mortal foe,
Lam 1: 7 When her people fell into e hands,
1: 9 upon her misery, for the e has triumphed!
1:16 reduced to silence when the e prevailed."
2: 3 of his right hand when the e approached;
2: 4 Like an e he made taut his bow;
2: 5 The Lord has become an e,
2: 7 of her towers he has handed over to the e,
2:17 Letting the e gloat over you and exalting
2:22 bore and reared my e has utterly destroyed."
4:12 That e or foe could enter the gates of
5:11 The wives in Zion were ravished by the e,
Bar 4:21 deliver you from oppression at e hands.
6:55 They cannot resist a king, or e forces.
Ez 36: 2 Because the e has said of you, "Ha!
Hos 8: 3 the e shall pursue them.
Am 3:11 An e shall surround the land,
Mi 2: 8 But of late my people has risen up as an e:
7: 8 Rejoice not over me, O my e!
7:10 When my e sees this,
Na 1: 9 The e shall not rise a second time;
Zec 8:10 came and went had no security from the e,
Mt 5:43 shall love your countryman but hate your e.'
13:25 e came and sowed weeds through his wheat,
13:39 one and the e who sowed them is the devil.
Lk 1:74 rid of fear and delivered from the e,
6:35 "Love your e and do good;
10:19 and scorpions and all the forces of the e,
14:31 e coming against him with twenty thousand?
14:32 while the e is still at a distance,
Acts 13:10 son of Satan and e of all that is right!
Rom 12:20 But "if your e is hungry,
1Cor 15:26 and the last e to be destroyed is death.
Gal 4:16 your e just because I tell you the truth?
2Thes 3:15 But do not treat him like an e;
Jas 4: 4 e if he chooses to be the world's friend.

ENEMY'S (10)

Ex 23: 4 come upon your e ox or ass going astray,
1Sm 14:30 of their e booty when they came across it,
Jdt 15: 5 struck the e flanks with great slaughter,
1Mc 10:81 whereas the e horses became tired out.
14:33 previously the e arms had been stored.
16: 7 for the e horsemen were very numerous.
2Mc 8:27 They collected the e arms and stripped
Jer 6:25 not into the street, Beware of the e sword;
31:16 LORD, they shall return from the e land.
Mt 13:28 He answered, 'I see an e hand in this.'

ENERGY (3)

Wis 13: 4 if they were struck by their might and e,
Dn 11:30 his rage and e against the holy covenant;

ENERGY (cont.)
Col 1:29 impelled by that *e* of his which is so

ENFOLDS (1)
Jb 23: 9 Where the north *e* him,

ENFORCED (2)
Ex 21:19 he must compensate him for his *e* idleness
1Mc 2:46 they also *e* circumcision for any

ENFORCING (1)
1Mc 2:15 The officers of the king in charge of *e*

ENGAGE (18)
Ex 17: 9 and tomorrow go out and *e* Amalek in battle.
Nm 32: 6 "Are your kinsmen, then, to *e* in war,
Dt 2: 9 to the Moabites or *e* them in battle,
2:24 Begin the occupation; *e* him in battle.
29: 6 king of Bashan, came out to *e* us in battle,
Jos 8:14 early in the morning to *e* Israel in battle
Jgs 1: 3 me, and let us *e* the Canaanites in battle.
20:22 I again *e* my brother Benjamin in battle?"
1Sm 4: 1 to *e* them in battle and camped at Ebenezer,
1Kgs 20:27 then they went out to *e* the foe.
1Chr 19:14 with his men to *e* the Arameans in battle;
Jdt 7: 1 passes, and *e* the Israelites in battle.
Est 9:10 However, they did not *e* in plundering.
9:15 However, they did not *e* in plundering.
1Mc 10: 2 army and marched out to *e* him in combat.
Prv 23:30 those who *e* in trials of blended wine.
Sir 13:11 *E* not freely in discussion with him,
Acts 6: 9 would undertake to *e* Stephen in debate,

ENGAGED (29)
Gn 24:42 to make successful the errand I am *e* on!
30: 8 "I *e* in a fateful struggle with my sister,
Ex 17:10 he *e* Amalek in battle after Moses had
Nm 21: 1 he *e* them in battle and took some of them
21:23 he reached Jahaz, he *e* Israel in battle.
Jos 8:17 with every man *e* in this pursuit of Joshua
Jgs 12: 2 *e* in a critical contest with the Ammonites.
18: 5 the undertaking we are *e* in will succeed."
18: 6 favorable to the undertaking you are *e* in."
1Kgs 5:30 work, directing the people *e* in the work.
9:23 who policed the people *e* in the work
Ezr 3: 9 who were *e* in the work on the house of God.
Neh 6: 3 "I am *e* in a great enterprise and am
Tb 6:13 you or let her become *e* to another man;
6:13 the girl, so that we may have her *e* to you.
1Mc 4:34 Then they *e* in battle,
10:53 for I *e* him in battle,
10:78 him to Azotus, and they *e* in battle.
2Mc 14:17 Judas' brother Simon had *e* Nicanor,
Wis 19: 3 For while they were still *e* in funeral
Mt 1:18 When his mother Mary was *e* to Joseph,
21:12 all those *e* there in buying and selling.
Mk 11:15 out those who were *e* in buying and selling.
Jn 2:14 he came upon people *e* in selling oxen,
Acts 13: 2 while they were *e* in the liturgy of the
17: 5 who *e* loafers from the public square to
Rom 1:24 they *e* in the mutual degradation of their
1Cor 15:58 brothers, fully *e* in the work of the Lord.
Phil 1:30 saw me *e* and now hear that I am caught up.

ENGAGING (2)
Est 9:16 of their foes, without *e* in plunder,
Ps(s) 141: 4 to the evil of *e* in deeds of wickedness

ENGANNIM (2)
Jos 15:34 Eshtaol, Zorah, Ashnah, Zanoah, *E*,
1Chr 6:58 lands, and *E* with its pasture lands.

ENGENDER (1)
Sir 8:18 secret, for you know not what it will *e*.

ENGRAVE (3)
Ex 28: 9 *e* on them the names of the sons of Israel;
28:36 also make a plate of pure gold and *e* on it,
Zec 3: 9 I will *e* its inscription,

ENGRAVED (10)
Ex 28:11 so shall you have the two stones *e* with
28:21 each stone *e* like a seal with the name of
32:16 on them that were *e* by God himself.
39: 6 they were *e* like seal engravings with the
39:14 and each stone was *e* like a seal with the
2Chr 2: 6 fabrics, and who know how to do *e* work,
2:13 also how to do all kinds of *e* work
3: 7 gold, and he *e* cherubim upon the walls.
1Mc 14:48 inscription should be *e* on bronze tablets,
Jer 17: 1 *E* with a diamond point Judah's Sin and

ENGRAVER (2)
Ex 38:23 of the tribe of Dan, who was an *e*,
Sir 38:27 So with every *e* and designer who,

ENGRAVES (1)
Ex 28:11 As a gem-cutter *e* a seal,

ENGRAVING (3)
Ex 28:36 gold and engrave on it, as on a seal *e*,
35:35 *e*, embroidering,
39:30 of pure gold and inscribed, as on a seal *e*:

ENGRAVINGS (2)
Ex 39: 6 *e* with the names of the sons of Israel.
Sir 45:11 stones with seal *e* in golden settings,

ENGULF (1)
Ps(s) 55:10 *E* them, O Lord; divide their counsels,

ENGULFED (2)
Jos 24: 7 whom he brought the sea so that it *e* them.
Is 9:15 mislead them and those to be led are *e*.

ENGULFING (1)
Dt 11: 4 *e* them in the water of the Red Sea as they

ENHANCE (2)
1Chr 25: 5 to *e* his prestige, God gave Heman
Is 60: 7 and I will *e* the splendor of my house.

ENHANCEMENT (1)
1Chr 26:27 wars, for the *e* of the house of the LORD.

ENIGMAS (1)
Dn 5:12 how to interpret dreams, explain *e*,

ENJOIN (27)
Dt 4: 2 of the LORD, your God, which I *e* upon you,
4:40 and commandments which I *e* on you today,
6: 2 statutes and commandments which I *e* on you,
6: 6 heart these words which I *e* on you today.
7:11 and the decrees which I *e* on you today.
8: 1 all the commandments I *e* on you today,
8:11 and statutes which I *e* on you today:
10:13 which I *e* on you today for your own good?
11: 8 commandments, then, which I *e* on you today,
11:13 my commandments which I *e* on you today,
11:22 observe all these commandments I *e* on you,
11:27 the LORD, your God, which I *e* on you today;
12:14 shall make whatever offerings I *e* upon you.
12:28 to heed all these commandments I *e* on you,
13: 1 "Every command that I *e* on you,
13:19 his commandments which I *e* on you today,
15: 5 these commandments which I *e* on you today,
19: 9 these commandments which I *e* on you today,
27: 1 these commandments which I *e* on you today.
27:10 and statutes which I *e* on you today."
28: 1 his commandments which I *e* on you today,
28:15 his commandments which I *e* on you today,
30: 8 all his commandments which I now *e* on you.
30:11 "For this command which I *e* on you today
30:16 the LORD, your God, which I *e* on you today,
2Thes 3: 4 and will continue to do whatever we *e*.
3:12 We *e* all such, and we urge them strongly

ENJOINED (25)
Ex 4:28 and of the various signs he had *e* upon him.
34:32 and he *e* on them all that the LORD had
Lv 7:38 which the LORD *e* on Moses at Mount Sinai
Dt 6:17 ordinances and statutes he has *e* on you.
6:20 mean which the LORD, our God, has *e* on you,
6:25 all these commandments he has *e* on us.'
Jos 1: 7 entire law which my servant Moses *e* on you.
7:11 violated the covenant which I *e* on them.
22: 5 Moses, the servant of the LORD, *e* upon you:
23:16 of the LORD, your God, which he *e* on you,
Jgs 2:20 my covenant which I *e* on their fathers,
3: 4 LORD had *e* on their fathers through Moses.
1Kgs 8:58 and ordinances which he *e* on our fathers.
11:11 covenant and my statutes which I *e* on you,
2Kgs 17:13 entire law which I *e* on your fathers
17:34 the LORD *e* on the descendants of Jacob,
21: 8 law which my servant Moses *e* upon them."
Est 9:31 just as they had previously *e* upon
Jer 11: 4 which I *e* upon your fathers the day I
Bar 1:20 and the curse which the Lord *e* upon Moses,
Mal 3:22 Moses my servant, which I *e* him on Horeb,
Mk 5:43 He *e* them strictly not to let anyone know
7:36 Then he *e* them strictly not to tell anyone;
9: 9 he strictly *e* them not to tell anyone what
Heb 9:20 of the covenant which God has *e* upon you."

ENJOY (36)
Dt 14:26 drink, or anything else you would *e*,
17:20 descendants will *e* a long reign in Israel.
20: 6 and another *e* its fruits in his stead.
28:30 a vineyard, you will not *e* its fruits.
32:47 you are to *e* a long life on the land
Jgs 19: 6 to spend the night here and *e* yourself?"
19: 9 Spend the night here and *e* yourself.
1Sm 17:28 You came down to *e* the battle!"
2Kgs 14:10 *E* your glory, but stay at home!
Ezr 9:12 grow strong, *e* the produce of the land,
Tb 12: 9 regularly give alms shall *e* a full life;
Jdt 12:13 honored by him, to *e* drinking wine with us,
2Mc 14:10 it is impossible for the state to *e* peace."
Jb 20:18 Restoring his gains, he shall not *e* them;
Ps(s) 37: 3 you may dwell in the land and *e* security.
Eccl 3:13 to eat and drink and *e* the fruit of all
5:17 drink and *e* all the fruits of his labor
6: 6 twice a thousand years and not *e* his goods,
7:14 On a good day *e* good things,
9: 9 *E* life with the wife whom you love,
Wis 2: 6 let us *e* the good things that are real,
Sir 14: 5 himself and does not *e* what is his own?
14:11 whatever you have and *e* it as best you can;
22:23 thus will you *e* his prosperity with him.
32:12 your ease, And there *e* doing as you wish,
41: 1 who still can *e* life's pleasures.
Is 65:22 shall long *e* the produce of their hands.
Jer 31: 5 those who plant them shall *e* the fruits.
Mt 26:45 *E* your rest!
Lk 12:19 *E* yourself.'
Acts 24: 2 through your efforts we *e* great peace.
Rom 6:21 What benefit did you then *e*?
Gal 2: 4 spy on the freedom we *e* in Christ Jesus
Heb 11:25 rather than *e* the fleeting rewards of sin.
1Pt 4: 3 devoted enough time to what the pagans *e*,
2Pt 3:17 the wicked, and forfeit the security you *e*.

ENJOYED (12)
Gn 41:53 *e* by the land of Egypt came to an end,
Dt 20: 6 a vineyard and never yet *e* its fruits?
Jos 11:23 And the land *e* peace.
14:15 And the land *e* peace.
1Sm 2:32 rival all the benefits *e* by Israel,
1Chr 29:25 been *e* by any king over Israel before him
2Chr 17: 5 gifts, so that he *e* great wealth and glory.
20:30 Thereafter Jehoshaphat's kingdom *e* peace,
Jdt 12:18 have I ever *e* life as much as I do today."
Est E:11 He so far *e* the good will which we have
Ps(s) 55:15 You, whose comradeship I *e*;
Acts 9:31 at the same time it *e* the increased

ENJOYING (5)
Gn 41:48 of Egypt was *e* and stored it in the towns,
Lv 26:35 *e* the rest that you would not let it have
Jgs 19:22 While they were *e* themselves,
Jdt 12:12 such a woman with us without *e* her company.
2Mc 14: 6 keep the kingdom from *e* peace and quiet.

ENJOYMENT (7)
Ex 30:38 like this for his own *e* of its fragrance,
2Mc 2:27 for one who thus seeks to give *e* to others.
Eccl 2: 1 you with pleasure and the *e* of good things."
Wis 14:28 For they either go mad with *e*,
Sir 37:20 are rejected he will be deprived of all *e*.
37:24 One wise for himself has full *e*,
37:28 Be not drawn after every *e*,

ENJOYS (4)
Prv 31:18 She *e* the success of her dealings;
Eccl 11: 8 a man may live, let him, as he *e* them all,
Jer 17: 6 in the desert that *e* no change of season,
3Jn 1: 9 but Diotrephes, who *e* being their leader,

ENKINDLE (1)
Is 65: 5 These things *e* my wrath,

ENKINDLED (3)
Dt 32:22 "For by my wrath a fire is *e* that shall
Sir 16: 6 Against a sinful band fire is *e*,
Jl 1:19 and flame has *e* all the trees of the field.

ENKINDLES (1)
Jl 2: 3 a fire devours, and after them a flame *e*;

ENKINDLING (1)
Prv 26:21 such is a contentious man in *e* strife.

ENLARGE (2)
Is 54: 2 *E* the space for your tent,
Acts 20:32 that gracious word of his which can *e* you,

ENLARGED (2)
Dt 12:20 the LORD, your God, has *e* your territory,
1Mc 14: 6 He *e* the borders of his nation and gained

ENLARGES (2)
Dt 19: 8 if the LORD, your God, *e* your territory,
Is 5:14 Therefore the nether world *e* its throat

ENLIGHTEN (5)
Ex 18:20 *E* them in regard to the decisions and
Sir 6:37 Then he will *e* your mind,
Rom 2:19 guide the blind and *e* those in darkness,
Eph 1:18 May he *e* your innermost vision that you
3: 9 to *e* all men on the mysterious design

ENLIGHTENED (2)

Heb 6: 4 For when men have once been *e* and have
10:32 days gone by when, after you had been *e*,

ENLIGHTENING (1)

Ps(s) 19: 9 command of the LORD is clear, *e* the eye;

ENLIST (1)

1Chr 23:27 David's final orders were to *e* the Levites

ENLISTED (2)

2Sm 10:16 and *e* Arameans from beyond the Euphrates.
Jb 16:10 they are all *e* against me.

ENLISTING (1)

2Mc 8: 1 *e* others who remained faithful to Judaism,

ENMESHED (3)

2Sm 22: 6 The cords of the nether world *e* me,
Ps(s) 18: 6 The cords of the nether world *e* me,
Sir 9: 5 a virgin, lest you be *e* in damages for her.

ENMISHPAT (1)

Gn 14: 7 They turned back and came to *E* (that is,

ENMITY (11)

Gn 3:15 I will put *e* between you and the woman,
Nm 35:21 another out of *e* and causes his death,
35:22 another accidentally and not out of *e*,
2Sm 19:23 that you would create *e* for me this day?
1Mc 11:12 their *e* became open.
2Mc 12: 3 There was no hint of *e* toward them;
Sir 28: 6 Remember your last days, set *e* aside;
Ez 25:15 malice in their hearts, with an undying *e*,
Rom 8: 7 The flesh in its tendency is at *e* with God;
Eph 2:16 his cross, which put that *e* to death.
Jas 4: 4 aware that love of the world is *e* to God?

ENOCH (15)

Gn 4:17 his wife, and she conceived and bore *E*.
4:17 of a city, which he named after his son *E*.
4:18 To *E* was born Irad,
5:18 years old, he became the father of *E*.
5:19 eight hundred years after the birth of *E*,
5:21 When *E* was sixty-five years old,
5:22 *E* lived three hundred years after the
5:23 *E* was three hundred and sixty-five years.
5:24 Then *E* walked with God,
1Chr 1: 3 Seth, Enosh, Kenan, Mahalalel, Jared, *E*,
Sir 44:16 *E* walked with the LORD and was taken up,
49:14 on earth have been made the equal of *E*,
Lk 3:37 of Lamech, son of Methuselah, son of *E*,
Heb 11: 5 By faith *E* was taken away without dying,
Jude 1:14 It was about these that *E*,

ENORMOUS (6)

2Chr 14:12 and his army, which carried away *e* spoils.
Jdt 7:18 Their *e* store of tents and equipment was
15: 7 the *e* quantity of booty they had seized.
2Mc 8:30 They divided the *e* plunder,
Mk 13: 1 huge blocks of stone and the *e* buildings!"
Rv 9: 2 of the shaft like smoke from an *e* furnace.

ENORMOUSLY (2)

Jon 3: 3 Now Nineveh was an *e* large city;
Acts 6: 7 of the disciples in Jerusalem *e* increased.

ENOS (2)

Sir 49:16 Glorious, too, were SHEM and SETH and *E*;
Lk 3:38 of Mahalaleel, son of Cainan, son of *E*,

ENOSH (7)

Gn 4:26 turn, a son was born, and he named him *E*.
5: 6 five years old, he became the father of *E*.
5: 7 and seven years after the birth of *E*,
5: 9 When *E* was ninety years old,
5:10 *E* lived eight hundred and fifteen years
5:11 of *E* was nine hundred and five years;
1Chr 1: 1 Adam, Seth, *E*,

ENOUGH (124)

Gn 19:19 "You have already thought *e* of your
19:20 this town ahead is near *e* to escape to.
24:20 until she had drawn *e* for all the camels.
28:20 me *e* bread to eat and clothing to wear,
30:15 it not *e* for you to take away my husband,
45:28 "It is *e*," said Israel.
Ex 9:28 we have had *e* of God's thunder and hail.
16:16 So gather it that everyone has *e* to eat,
16:18 so gathered that everyone had *e* to eat.
16:21 they gathered it, till each had *e* to eat;
21:18 not mortally, but *e* to put him in bed,
23:30 numerous *e* to take possession of the land.
32:22 well *e* how prone the people are to evil.
36: 7 enough at hand, in fact, more than *e*,
Lv 25:21 there will then be crop *e* for three years.
26:26 not *e* food to still your hunger.
Nm 11:22 *e* sheep and cattle be slaughtered for them?
11:22 were caught for them, would they have *e*?"
16: 3 and Aaron, to whom they said, *E* from you!
16: 7 *E* from you Levites!"
Dt 1: 6 'You have stayed long *e* at this mountain.
2: 3 have wandered round these highlands long *e*;
3:26 *E*!' the LORD said to me
9: 8 LORD that he was angry *e* to destroy you,
11: 8 that you may be strong *e* to enter in and
15: 8 him and freely lend him *e* to meet his need.
Jos 10: 2 Gibeon was large *e* for a royal city,
17:16 "Our mountain regions are not *e* for us;
Jgs 21:14 but these proved to be not *e* for them.
1Sm 21:16 Do I not have *e* madmen,
2Sm 8: 4 preserving only *e* for a hundred chariots.
12: 8 And if this were not *e*,
19:37 the Jordan, your servant is doing little *e*!
24:16 the destruction among the people, *E* now!
1Kgs 12:28 have been going up to Jerusalem long *e*.
16:31 *e* for him to imitate the sins of Jeroboam,
18:32 the altar large *e* for two seahs of grain.
19: 4 "This is *e*, O LORD!
20:10 there is *e* dust in Samaria to make handfuls
2Kgs 3:18 since the LORD does not consider this *e*,
4:18 The day came when the child was old *e* to
6: 1 "There is not *e* room for us to continue
1Chr 21:15 and said to the destroying angel, *E* now!
2Chr 5: 9 The poles were long *e* so that their ends
22: 9 no one powerful *e* to wield the kingship.
Neh 8: 2 and those children old *e* to understand.
8: 3 and those children old *e* to understand;
Tb 5: 9 he is trustworthy *e* to travel with you,
5:20 given us to live on is certainly *e* for us."
10:13 and may I live long *e* to see children of
Jdt 4: 7 the defile was only wide *e* for two abreast.
7:21 so that on no day did they have *e* to drink,
Est 3: 6 was not *e* to lay hands on Mordecai alone.
1Mc 2:33 *E* of this!" the pursuers said to them
3:30 he would not have *e* for his expenses and
13:27 and raised high *e* to be seen at a distance.
2Mc 3:24 who had been bold *e* to follow Heliodorus
7:42 *E* has been said about the sacrificial
Jb 7:19 let me alone long *e* to swallow my spittle?
15:11 Are the consolations of God not *e* for you,
Ps(s) 49: 9 he would never have *e* to remain alive
107:43 Who is wise *e* to observe these things and
Prv 25:17 house, lest he have more than *e* of you,
30:15 are never satisfied, four never say, *E*!"
30:16 with water, and fire, that never says, *E*!"
Wis 14:22 Then it was not *e* for them to err in their
18:25 for the mere trial of anger was *e*.
Sir 12:16 chance, he will never have *e* of your blood.
42:25 can one ever see *e* of their splendor?
Is 1:11 *e* of whole-burnt rams and fat of fatlings;
7:13 Is it not *e* for you to weary men,
40:16 fuel, nor its animals be *e* for holocausts.
56:11 dogs, they know not when they have *e*.
Jer 44:17 we had *e* food to eat and we were well off;
Ez 16: 8 and saw that you were now old *e* for love.
16:20 Was it not *e* that you had become a harlot?
30:21 that it may be strong *e* to hold the sword.
34:18 not *e* for you to graze on the best pasture,
34:18 not *e* for you to drink the clearest water,
44: 6 *E* of all these abominations of yours,
45: 9 *E*, you princes of Israel!
Ob 1: 5 they not steal merely till they had *e*?
Jon 4: 9 angry," Jonah answered, "angry *e* to die."
Na 2:13 The lion snatched *e* for his cubs,
Mt 6:34 *E*, then, of worrying about tomorrow.
6:34 Today has troubles *e* of its own.
15:33 "How could we ever get *e* bread in this
25: 9 'No, there may not be *e* for you and us.
Mk 4:32 with branches big *e* for the birds of the
5: 4 No one had proved strong *e* to tame him.
6:43 up *e* leftovers to fill twelve baskets,
12:12 well *e* that he meant the parable for them.)
15:43 He was bold *e* to seek an audience with
Lk 6:42 then you will see clearly *e* to remove the
9:17 They all ate until they had *e*.
14:28 if he has *e* money to complete the project?
15:17 my father's place have more than *e* to eat,
22:38 He answered, *E*."
22:51 Jesus said in answer to their question, *E*!"
Jn 6: 7 loaves *e* to give each of them a mouthful!"
6:12 much as they wanted, When they had had *e*,
9:21 He is old *e* to speak for himself."
13:13 as 'Teacher' and 'Lord,' and fittingly *e*,
14: 8 us the Father and that will be *e* for us."
21:25 I doubt there would be room *e* in the
Acts 10:33 and you have been kind *e* to come.
15: 7 you know well *e* that from the early days
24:25 "That's *e* for now!
27:38 When they had had *e* to eat,
1Cor 6: 5 no one among you wise *e* to settle a case
13: 2 if I have faith great *e* to move mountains,
2Cor 2: 3 I know you all well *e* to be convinced that
2: 6 by the majority on such a one is *e*;
4:17 present burden of our trial is light *e*,
9: 8 you may always have *e* of everything
12: 9 He said to me, "My grace is *e* for you,
1Thes 2: 1 You know well *e*, brothers,
3: 3 well *e* that such trials are our common lot.
1Pt 4: 3 devoted *e* time to what the pagans enjoy,
2Pt 1: 5 This is reason *e* for you to make every
1Jn 3:17 survive in a man who has *e* of this world's
Rv 8:12 hit hard *e* to be plunged into darkness.
9:10 was *e* venom to harm men for five months.

ENRAGED (17)

Gn 31:36 Jacob, now *e*, upbraided Laban.
39:19 how his slave had treated her, he became *e*.
2Sm 3: 8 *E* at the words of Ishbaal, Abner said,
2Chr 16:10 so greatly was he *e* at him over this.
2Mc 4:40 As the crowds, now thoroughly *e*,
7:39 the king became *e* and treated him even
14:27 the villain's calumnies, the king became *e*.
Ps(s) 78:21 Then the LORD heard and was *e*;
78:59 and was *e* and utterly rejected Israel.
78:62 sword and was *e* against his inheritance.
89:39 and spurned and been *e* at your anointed.
Wis 5:22 The water of the sea shall be *e* against
Is 8:21 and in his hunger he shall become *e*,
Jer 37:15 The princes were *e*,
Ez 16:43 a girl, but *e* me with all these things,
Dn 14: 8 *E*, the king called his priests and said to
Rv 12:17 *E* at her escape, the dragon went

ENRAPTURED (2)

Nm 24: 4 Of one who sees what the Almighty sees, *e*,
24:16 Almighty sees, *e* and with eyes unveiled.

ENRICH (3)

Jb 38:27 To *e* the waste and desolate ground till
Prv 22:16 He who oppresses the poor to *e* himself
2Cor 6:10 poor, yet we *e* many.

ENRICHED (13)

Gn 27:37 besides, I have *e* him with grain and wine.
Dt 33:23 "Naphtali is *e* with favors and filled
1Mc 2:18 be *e* with silver and gold and many gifts."
14:15 the temple splendid and *e* its equipment.
Ps(s) 17:14 Their sons are *e* and bequeath their
65:10 greatly have you *e* it.
Prv 11:25 He who confers benefits will be amply *e*,
27:18 who is attentive to his master will be *e*.
Wis 10:11 the greed of his defrauders, and *e* him;
Jer 50:10 plunder, and all her plunderers shall be *e*,
Ez 27:33 merchandise you *e* the kings of the earth.
2Cor 9:11 In every way your liberality is *e*;
Col 2: 2 *e* with full assurance by their knowledge

ENRICHES (4)

Prv 10: 4 but the hand of the diligent *e*.
Sir 35: 5 The just man's offering *e* the altar and
39:22 Euphrates it *e* the surface of the earth.
43:23 and the scattered dew *e* the parched land.

ENROLL (6)

Nm 1: 3 You and Aaron shall *e* in companies all the
1:49 "The tribe of Levi alone you shall not *e*
4:29 you shall *e* by clans and ancestral houses
1Mc 8:20 *e* ourselves among your allies and friends."
2Mc 4: 9 and to *e* men in Jerusalem as Antiochians.
1Tm 5:11 Refuse to *e* the younger widows,

ENROLLED (21)

Ex 30:12 to be registered, each one, as he is *e*,
Nm 1:21 five hundred were *e* in the tribe of Reuben.
1:23 hundred were *e* in the tribe of Simeon.
1:25 and fifty were *e* in the tribe of Gad.
1:27 six hundred were *e* in the tribe of Judah.
1:29 hundred were *e* in the tribe of Issachar.
1:31 hundred were *e* in the tribe of Zebulun.
1:33 hundred were *e* in the tribe of Ephraim.
1:35 hundred were *e* in the tribe of Manasseh.
1:37 hundred were *e* in the tribe of Benjamin.
1:39 seven hundred were *e* in the tribe of Dan.
1:41 five hundred were *e* in the tribe of Asher.
1:43 hundred were *e* in the tribe of Naphtali.
1Chr 23:24 were *e* one by one according to their names.
Ezr 8: 3 him one hundred and fifty males were *e*;
8:20 All these men were *e* by name.
1Mc 10:36 "Let thirty thousand Jews be *e* in the
11:27 and had him *e* among his Chief Friends.
13:40 enrollment in our service, let them be *e*.
Ps(s) 87: 6 They shall note, when the peoples are *e*:
Heb 12:23 the assembly of the first-born *e* in heaven,

ENROLLMENT (1)

1Mc 13:40 of you are qualified for *e* in our service,

ENSIGNS (1)

Nm 2: 2 under the *e* of their ancestral houses.

ENSLAVE (9)

Dt 21:14 but you shall not sell her or *e* her,
24: 7 Israelite in order to *e* him and sell him,
2Chr 8: 9 did not *e* the Israelites for his works.
Wis 17: 2 the lawless thought to *e* the holy nation,
Sir 13: 4 as the rich man can use you he will *e* you,

ENSLAVE (cont.)
Jer 17: 4 I will *e* you to your enemies in a land
30: 8 Strangers shall no longer *e* them;
1Cor 7:23 Do not *e* yourselves to men.
Gal 4: 9 you seem willing to *e* yourselves once more?

ENSLAVED (17)

Gn 15:13 be *e* and oppressed for four hundred years.
1Kgs 9:22 But Solomon *e* none of the Israelites,
Jdt 5:11 labor at brickmaking, oppressed and *e* them.
8:22 Wherever we shall be *e* among the nations,
1Mc 8:11 ever opposed them they destroyed and *e;*
Prv 12:24 will govern, but the slothful will be *e.*
Wis 14:21 that men *e* to either grief or tyranny
15:14 are the enemies of your people who *e* them.
Sir 23: 7 for he who keeps it will not be *e.*
Is 14: 3 the hard service in which you have been *e,*
Jer 25:11 nations shall be *e* to the king of Babylon;
25:14 be *e* to great nations and mighty kings,
Bar 4:32 are the cities where your children were *e,*
Ez 34:27 them from the power of those who *e* them.
Na 3: 4 Who *e* nations with her harlotries,
Rom 6:19 Just as formerly you *e* your bodies to
1Cor 6:12 but I will not let myself be *e* by anything.

ENSLAVEMENT (1)

Jdt 8:23 Our *e* will not be turned to our benefit,

ENSLAVING (1)

Wis 19:14 but these were *e* beneficent guests.

ENSNARE (2)

Ps(s) 109:11 May the usurer *e* all his belongings,
Is 29:21 a man, Who *e* his defender at the gate,

ENSNARED (8)

Dt 7:16 lest you be *e* into serving their gods.
7:25 it for yourselves, lest you be *e* by it;
Prv 12:13 In the sin of his lips the evil man is *e,*
Sir 23: 8 Through his lips is the sinner *e;*
31: 6 Many have been *e* by gold,
Is 28:13 walk, they stumble backward, broken, *e,*
Jer 8: 9 The wise are confounded, dismayed and *e;*
50:24 You *e* yourself, and were caught,

ENSNARERS (1)

Ps(s) 49: 6 evil days when my wicked *e* ring me round?

ENSNARES (1)

Mi 7: 2 wait to shed blood, each one *e* the other.

ENSNARING (1)

Ex 23:33 me by *e* you into worshiping their gods."

ENSUED (3)

Mt 8:26 Complete calm *e;* the men were dumbfounded.
Acts 15:39 *e* was so sharp that the two separated.
23: 9 A loud uproar *e.*

ENSUES (1)

Ex 21:23 But if injury *e,* you shall give life

ENSUING (1)

2Mc 12:34 In the *e* battle, a few of the Jews

ENSURE (2)

Gn 45: 7 sent me on ahead of you to *e* for you a
1Tm 3: 7 to *e* that he does not fall into disgrace

ENSURES (1)

Sir 31:20 Moderate eating *e* sound slumber and a

ENTAILS (1)

2Tm 1: 8 share of the hardship which the gospel *e.*

ENTANGLED (2)

2Mc 5:18 If they had not become *e* in so many sins,
2Tm 2: 4 becomes *e* in the affairs of civilian life;

ENTANGLES (1)

Prv 26: 8 Like one who *e* the stone in the sling is

ENTER (210)

Gn 12:11 When he was about to *e* Egypt,
49: 6 Let not my soul *e* their council,
Ex 29:30 as priest and who is to *e* the meeting tent
30:20 When they are about to *e* the meeting tent,
34:12 of the land that you are to *e;*
40:35 Moses could not *e* the meeting tent,
Lv 12: 4 touch anything sacred nor *e* the sanctuary
16: 3 Only in this way may Aaron *e* the sanctuary.
16:26 only then may he *e* the camp.
16:28 only then may he *e* the camp.
25: 2 When you *e* the land that I am giving you,
Nm 4:15 camp, shall the Kohathites *e* to carry them.
5:22 *e* your body to make your belly swell and
6: 6 he shall not *e* where a dead person is.
8:15 *e* upon their service in the meeting tent.
8:22 Only then did they *e* upon their service in
14:30 not one shall *e* the land where I solemnly
15:18 When you *e* the land into which I will
20:24 *e* the land I am giving to the Israelites,
31:24 After that you may *e* the camp."
32: 9 not *e* the land the LORD had given them.
34: 2 When you *e* the land of Canaan,
Dt 1:37 and said, 'Not even you shall *e* there,
1:38 but your aide Joshua, son of Nun, shall *e.*
1:39 they shall *e;* to them I will give it,
4: 1 and may *e* in and take possession of the
4:21 not cross the Jordan nor *e* the good land
6:18 and may *e* in and possess the good land
7: 1 the land which you are to *e* and occupy,
8: 1 and may *e* in and possess the land which
9: 1 to *e* in and dispossess nations greater
10:11 that they may *e* in and occupy the land
11: 8 that you may be strong enough to *e* in and
11:10 "For the land which you are to *e* and
11:29 the land which you are to *e* and occupy,
11:31 to *e* and occupy the land which the LORD,
23:21 on the land you are to *e* and occupy.
24:10 *e* his house to receive a pledge from him,
27: 3 that you may thus *e* into the land flowing
29:11 you may *e* into the covenant of the LORD,
30:18 are crossing the Jordan to *e* and occupy.
31:16 will live in the land they are about to *e.*
32:52 but you shall not *e* that land which I am
Jgs 15: 1 private," her father would not let him *e,*
19:15 they turned off to *e* Gibeah for the night.
1Sm 5: 5 nor any others who *e* the temple of Dagon
7:13 never again to *e* the territory of Israel,
9:13 When you *e* the city, you may reach him
10: 5 As you *e* that city, you will meet a band
2Sm 5: 6 David was told, "You cannot *e* here:
5: 6 their way of saying, "David cannot *e* here."
5: 8 blind and the lame shall not *e* the palace."
15:37 of Jerusalem as Absalom was about to *e* it.
2Kgs 7:12 us alive and *e* our city when we leave it."
9: 2 *E* and take him away from his companions
1Chr 11: 5 said to David, "You shall not *e* here."
16:29 Bring gifts, and *e* his presence;
27:24 Therefore the number did not *e* into the
2Chr 7: 2 priests could not *e* the house of the LORD,
18:24 when you *e* an innermost chamber to hide."
23: 6 Let no one *e* the LORD's house except the
23: 6 They may *e* because they are holy;
23: 7 Whoever tries to *e* the house must be slain.
23:19 that no one unclean in any respect might *e.*
27: 2 though he did not *e* the temple of the LORD;
31:16 who were eligible to *e* the house
Ezr 10: 3 Let us therefore *e* into a covenant before
Neh 6:11 man like me *e* the temple to save his life?
9:15 You bade them *e* and occupy the land which
9:23 commanded their fathers to *e* and possess.
13:19 that no burden might *e* on the sabbath day.
Tb 12:15 *e* and serve before the Glory of the Lord."
Est 4: 2 which no one clothed in sackcloth might *e.*
1Mc 7: 2 to *e* the royal palace of his ancestors,
12:25 giving them no time to *e* his province.
2Mc 2:30 To *e* into questions and examine them
5:15 dared to *e* the holiest temple in the world;
Jb 3: 6 year, nor *e* into the count of the months!
Ps(s) 5: 8 your abundant kindness, will *e* your house;
45:16 they *e* the palace of the king.
95:11 They shall not *e* into my rest."
96: 8 Bring gifts, and *e* his courts;
100: 4 *E* his gates with thanksgiving,
118:19 I will *e* them and give thanks to the LORD.
118:20 the just shall *e* it.
132: 3 "I will not *e* the house I live in,
132: 7 Let us *e* into his dwelling.
143: 2 And *e* not into judgment with your servant,
Prv 2:10 For wisdom will *e* your heart,
2:19 None who *e* thereon come back again,
4:14 The path of the wicked *e* not,
27:10 ruin befalls you, *e* not a kinsman's house.
Eccl 8:10 Meanwhile I saw wicked men approach and *e;*
Is 13: 2 for them to *e* the gates of the volunteers.
16:12 places, he shall *e* his sanctuary to pray,
19:23 the Assyrians shall *e* Egypt,
19:23 enter Egypt, and the Egyptians *e* Assyria,
26:20 Go, my people, *e* your chambers,
35:10 ransomed will return and *e* Zion singing,
51:11 ransomed will return and *e* Zion singing,
52: 1 the uncircumcised or the unclean *e* you.
59:14 in the public square, uprightness cannot *e.*
Jer 7: 2 who *e* these gates to worship the LORD!
8:14 Let us form ranks and *e* the walled cities,
14:18 If I *e* the city, look!
16: 8 *E* not a house where people are celebrating,
17:19 where the kings of Judah *e* and leave,
17:20 citizens of Jerusalem who *e* these gates!
17:25 the throne of David will continue to *e,*
19: 5 nor spoke of, nor did it ever *e* my mind.
22: 2 and your people that *e* by these gates!
22: 4 continue to *e* the gates of this palace,
32:29 it shall *e* this city and set fire to it,
32:35 nor did it even *e* my mind that they should
Lam 1:10 She has seen those nations *e* her sanctuary
4:12 or foe could *e* the gates of Jerusalem.
Bar 6:16 full of dust from the feet of those who *e.*
Ez 7:22 robbers shall *e* and profane it.
8: 9 *E,* he said to me, and see the abominable
13: 9 house of Israel, nor *e* the land of Israel;
17:20 I will bring him to Babylon and *e* into
20:35 will *e* into judgment with you face to face.
20:36 Egypt, so will I *e* into judgment with you,
42: 9 so that one could *e* from the outer court
42:12 wall, by which one could *e* from the east.
44: 2 is not to be opened for anyone to *e* by it;
44: 3 *e* by way of the vestibule of the gate,
44: 9 and in flesh, shall ever *e* my sanctuary;
44:16 It is they who shall *e* my sanctuary,
44:17 they *e* the gates of the inner court,
44:21 drink wine when he is to *e* the inner court.
46: 2 The prince shall *e* from outside by way of
46: 8 *e* and depart by the vestibule of the gate.
46: 9 When the people of the land *e* the presence
46: 9 if they *e* by the north gate they shall
46: 9 and if they *e* by the south gate they shall
46:10 prince shall be in their midst when they *e,*
Dn 1: 5 training they were to *e* the king's service.
11: 7 *e* the stronghold of the king of the north,
11:24 By stealth he shall *e* prosperous provinces
11:41 *e* the glorious land and many shall fall,
13: 7 used to *e* her husband's garden for a walk.
13: 8 old men saw her *e* every day for her walk,
14:21 used to *e* to consume what was on the table.
Hos 9: 4 it cannot *e* the house of the LORD.
Jl 4: 2 And I will *e* into judgment with them there
Ob 1:13 *E* not the gate of my people on the day of
Zec 14:18 family of Egypt does not come up, or *e,*
Mt 5:20 you shall not *e* the kingdom of God.
7:13 *E* through the narrow gate.
7:21 will *e* the kingdom of God but only the one
10: 5 territory and do not *e* a Samaritan town.
10:12 As you *e* his home bless it.
12:29 "How can anyone *e* a strong man's house
18: 3 you will not *e* the kingdom of God.
18: 8 Better to *e* life maimed or crippled than
18: 9 Better to *e* life with one eye than be
19:17 If you wish to *e* into life,
19:23 will a rich man *e* into the kingdom of God.
19:24 for a rich man to *e* the kingdom of God."
23:13 nor admitting those who are trying to *e.*
Mk 1:45 possible for Jesus to *e* a town openly.
3:27 No one can *e* a strong man's house and
5:12 "Let us *e* them."
9:25 Get out of him and never *e* him again!"
9:43 Better for you to *e* life maimed than to
9:43 and *e* Gehenna with its unquenchable fire.
9:45 Better for you to *e* life crippled than to
9:47 Better for you to *e* the kingdom of God
10:23 it is for the rich to *e* the kingdom of God!"
10:24 how hard it is to *e* the kingdom of God!
10:25 for a rich man to *e* the kingdom of God."
11: 2 and as soon as you *e* it you will find
13:15 or *e* his house to get anything out of it.
Lk 1: 9 priestly usage to *e* the sanctuary of the Lord
7: 6 for I am not worthy to have you *e* my house.
8:32 asked him to permit them to *e* the swine.
8:51 no one to *e* with him except Peter,
9: 4 house you *e* and proceed from there.
10:10 of any town you *e* do not welcome you,
11:26 than itself, who *e* in and dwell there.
11:52 yet you have stopped those who wished to *e!"*
13:24 I tell you, will try to *e* and be unable.
18:17 of God as a child will not *e* into it."
18:25 for a rich man to *e* the kingdom of heaven."
22:10 "Just as you *e* the city,
23:42 remember me when you *e* upon your reign."
24:26 undergo all this so as to *e* into his glory?"
Jn 3: 5 no one can *e* into God's kingdom without
10: 1 Whoever does not *e* the sheepfold through
12:12 feast heard that Jesus was to *e* Jerusalem.
18:28 They did not *e* the praetorium themselves,
20: 5 He did not *e* but bent down to peer in,
Acts 14:22 if we are to *e* into the reign of God."
23:16 They allowed him to *e,*
Rom 11:25 until the full number of Gentiles *e* in,
14: 1 Do not *e* into disputes with them.
Heb 3:11 my anger, 'They shall never *e* into my rest.' "
3:18 swear that they would not *e* into his rest?
4: 3 we who have believed who *e* into that rest,
4: 3 They shall never *e* into my rest.' "
4: 5 says, "They shall never *e* into my rest."
4: 6 since it remains for some to *e,*
4:11 Let us strive to *e* into that rest,
9:24 did not *e* into a sanctuary made by hands,
Rv 3:20 will *e* his house and have supper with him,
15: 8 no one could *e* it until the seven plagues
21:27 there, but nothing profane shall *e* it,
21:27 Only those shall *e* whose names are
22:14 of life and *e* the city through its gates!

ENTERED (177)

Gn 7: 9 two] male and female *e* the ark with Noah,
7:13 three wives of Noah's sons had *e* the ark,
7:15 was the breath of life *e* the ark with Noah.
7:16 Those that *e* were male and female,
19: 3 turned aside to his place and *e* his house.

41:46 years old when he *e* the service of Pharaoh,
Ex 8:20 Thick swarms of flies *e* the house of
12:25 observe this rite when you have *e* the land
33: 8 tents, watching Moses until he *e* the tent.
33: 9 As Moses *e* the tent,
34:34 Whenever Moses *e* the presence of the LORD
38:26 years or more who *e* the registered group;
Lv 16:23 vestments he had put on when he *e* there.
Nm 7:89 Moses *e* the meeting tent to speak with him,
15: 2 When you have *e* the land I will give you
17:23 The next day, when Moses *e* the tent,
Jos 2: 3 out the visitors who have *e* your house,
6: 1 the Israelites, so that no one left or *e*.
6:23 The spies *e* and brought out Rahab,
9:15 them and *e* into an agreement to spare them,
9:16 Three days after the agreement was *e* into,
Jgs 18:17 the land went up and *e* the house of Micah.
19:15 in the public square of the city he had *e*,
Ru 2: 3 The field she *e* to glean after the
1Sm 5:10 but as it *e* that city, the people there
9:14 As they *e* it.
16: 4 When he *e* Bethlehem,
16:21 Thus David came to Saul and *e* his service.
18: 3 And Jonathan *e* into a bond with David,
19:16 But when the messengers *e*,
23: 7 When Saul was told that David had *e* Keilah,
23: 7 for he has *e* a city with gates and bars."
24: 4 he found a cave, which he *e* to ease nature.
2Sm 4: 7 Baanah slipped past and *e* the house
10: 2 servants *e* the country of the Ammonites,
16:15 *e* Jerusalem with all the Israelites.
20:14 and they too *e* the city after him.
1Kgs 1:23 the prophet *e* the king's presence and,
1:32 When they had *e* the king's presence,
14: 4 She made the journey to Shiloh and *e* the
14: 6 sound of her footsteps as she *e* the door,
16:10 of his palace in Tirzah, Zimri *e*;
16:18 he *e* the citadel of the royal palace and
20:43 of Israel went off homeward and *e* Samaria.
22:30 of Israel disguised himself and *e* the fray.
2Kgs 6:20 When they *e* Samaria, Elisha prayed,
10:23 *e* the temple of Baal and said to the
12:10 the right as one *e* the temple of the LORD.
12:21 Certain of his officials *e* into a plot
16: 6 The Edomites then *e* Elath,
1Chr 16:16 Which he *e* into with Abraham and by his
19: 2 But when David's servants had *e* the land
2Chr 15:12 They *e* into a covenant to seek the LORD,
18:29 disguised himself and they *e* the fray.
23: 1 and *e* a conspiracy with certain captains:
26:16 He *e* the temple of the LORD to make an
29:16 The priests *e* the interior of the LORD's
32:21 And when he *e* the temple of his god,
Ezr 10: 6 house of God and *e* the chamber of Johanan,
Tb 5:10 When Raphael *e* the house,
6:10 *e* Media and were getting close to Ecbatana,
7: 1 When they *e* Ecbatana,
9: 6 When they *e* Raguel's house,
Jdt 14:15 he parted the curtains, *e* the bedroom,
14:17 *e* the tent where Judith had her quarters;
Est 6: 4 Now Haman had *e* the outer court of the
6: 6 When Haman *e*, the king said to him,
9:25 Yet, when Esther *e* the royal presence,
1Mc 3:45 not one of her children *e* or came out.
6:62 But when the king *e* Mount Zion and saw how
8:19 envoys *e* the senate and spoke as follows:
10:83 The enemy fled to Azotus and *e* Beth-dagon,
11: 2 He *e* Syria with peaceful words,
11: 3 But when Ptolemy *e* the cities,
11:13 *e* Antioch and assumed the crown of Asia;
12: 3 the men *e* the senate chamber and said,
12:48 Then as soon as Jonathan had *e* Ptolemais,
12:48 all who had *e* with him,
13:47 *e* the city with hymns and songs of praise.
13:51 *e* the citadel with shouts of jubilation,
2Mc 1:15 As soon as he *e* the temple,
3:28 The man who a moment before had *e* that
8: 1 and his companions *e* the village secretly,
9: 2 He had *e* the city called Persepolis and
Jb 38:16 Have you *e* into the sources of the sea,
38:22 Have you *e* the storehouse of the snow,
Ps(s) 73:17 Till I *e* the sanctuary of God and
105: 9 Which he *e* into with Abraham and by his
Wis 2:24 the envy of the devil, death *e* the world,
10:16 She *e* the soul of the Lord's servant,
Sir 44:20 High, and *e* into an agreement with him;
Jer 2: 7 goodly fruits, You *e* and defiled my land,
9:20 up through our windows, has *e* our palaces;
32:23 They *e* and took possession of it,
34:10 All the princes and the others who *e* the
36:20 scribe, they *e* the room where the king was.
37:16 And so Jeremiah *e* the vaulted dungeon,
51:51 *e* the holy places of the house of the LORD.
Bar 3:15 of wisdom, who has *e* into her treasuries?
Ez 2: 2 spirit *e* into me and set me on my feet,
3:24 spirit *e* into me and set me on my feet,
4:14 never has any unclean meat *e* my mouth."
8:10 I *e* and saw that all around upon the wall
9: 2 They *e* and stood beside the bronze altar.
10: 2 As I looked on, he *e*.
10: 3 As the man *e*, the cloud filled the inner
10: 6 the man *e* and stood by one of the wheels.
16: 8 oath to you and *e* into a covenant with you;
20:36 Just as I *e* into judgment with your
23:39 idols, they *e* my sanctuary to desecrate it.
42:14 When the priests have once *e*,
43: 4 I fell prone as the glory of the LORD *e*
44: 2 the LORD, the God of Israel, has *e* by it,
46: 9 by the gate through which he has *e*,
Dn 1:19 and so they *e* the king's service.
5:10 his lords, she *e* the banquet hall and said,
13:15 right moment, she *e* the garden as usual,
13:36 this woman *e* with two girls and shut the
14:15 The priests *e* that night as usual,
Ob 1:11 *e* his gates cast lots of Jerusalem,
Mt 8: 5 As Jesus *e* Capernaum,
8:14 Jesus *e* Peter's house and found Peter's
8:32 At that they came forth and *e* the swine.
9:25 been put out he *e* and took her by the hand,
12: 4 he *e* God's house and ate the holy bread,
17:24 When they *e* Capernaum,
21:10 As he *e* Jerusalem the whole city was
21:12 Jesus *e* the temple precincts and drove out
21:23 After Jesus had *e* the temple precincts,
24:38 right up to the day Noah *e* the ark.
27:53 and *e* the holy city and appeared to many.
Mk 1:21 he *e* the synagogue and began to teach.
1:29 he *e* the house of Simon and Andrew with
2:26 How he *e* God's house in the days of
5:13 unclean spirits came out and *e* the swine.
5:39 He *e* and said to them:
5:40 and *e* the room where the child lay.
11:11 He *e* Jerusalem and went into the temple
11:15 When they reached Jerusalem he *e* the
14: 3 a woman *e* carrying an alabaster jar of
Lk 1:40 *e* Zechariah's house and greeted Elizabeth.
4:38 the synagogue, he *e* the house of Simon.
6: 4 how he *e* God's house and took and ate the
7: 1 the hearing of the people, he *e* Capernaum.
7:45 has not ceased kissing my feet since I *e*.
8:30 because the demons who had *e* him were many.
8:33 then came out of the man and *e* the swine,
9:34 disciples grew fearful as the others *e* it.
9:52 These *e* a Samaritan town to prepare for
10:38 On their journey Jesus *e* a village where a
11:37 He *e* and reclined at table.
17:27 wives, right up to the day Noah *e* the ark
19:45 Then he *e* the temple and began ejecting
24: 3 but when they *e* the tomb,
Jn 13:27 Immediately after, Satan *e* his heart.
18: 1 there, and he and his disciples *e* it.
20: 6 Peter came along behind him and *e* the tomb.
Acts 3: 2 to beg from the people as they *e*.
8: 3 He *e* house after house,
9:17 When he *e* the house he laid his hands on
10:25 As Peter *e*,
11: 3 "You *e* the house of uncircumcised men and
11: 8 unclean or impure has ever *e* my mouth!'
11:12 along with me, and we *e* the man's house.
13:14 day they *e* the synagogue and sat down.
14: 1 they *e* the Jewish synagogue and spoke in
18:19 and *e* the synagogue to hold discussions
19: 8 Paul *e* the synagogue,
21: 8 we *e* the home of Philip the evangelist,
21:26 Then he *e* the temple precincts to give
25:23 with great pomp and *e* the audience chamber
Rom 5:12 one man sin *e* the world and with sin death,
Gal 1:21 I *e* the regions of Syria and Cilicia.
Heb 6:20 Jesus, our forerunner, has *e* on our behalf,
9:11 be, he *e* once for all into the sanctuary,
9:12 He *e*, not with the blood of goats
9:24 he *e* heaven itself that he might appear

ENTERING (28)

Dt 4: 5 them in the land you are *e* to occupy.
28:21 you from the land you are *e* to occupy.
28:63 out of the land you are now *e* to occupy.
30:16 bless you in the land you are *e* to occupy.
2Sm 6:16 ark of the LORD was *e* the City of David,
17:17 they could not risk being seen *e* the city.
2Kgs 19:33 the same way he came, without *e* the city,
1Chr 15:29 of the LORD was *e* the City of David,
Ezr 9:11 the land which you are *e* to take as your
Neh 10: 1 of all this, we are *e* into a firm pact,
Tb 2:13 On *e* my house the goat began to bleat.
Is 37:34 the same way he came, without *e* the city,
Dn 14:19 Daniel laughed and kept the king from *e*.
Am 5:19 Or as if on *e* his house he were to rest
Mt 2:11 at seeing the star, and on *e* the house,
17:25 Then Jesus on *e* the house asked,
21: 1 *e* Bethphage on the Mount of Olives,
21:31 are *e* the kingdom of God before you.
23:13 neither *e* yourselves nor admitting those
Mk 16: 5 On *e* the tomb they saw a young man sitting
Lk 4:16 and *e* the synagogue on the sabbath as he
10: 5 On *e* any house, first say, 'Peace
17:12 As he was *e* a village, ten lepers met him.
19: 1 *E* Jericho, he passed through the city.
19:30 Upon *e* it you will find an ass tied there
Acts 1:13 *E* the city, they went to the upstairs
Heb 3:19 was their unbelief that kept them from *e*.
4: 1 you be judged to have lost his chance of *e*.

ENTERPRISE (3)

Dt 28:20 and frustration in every *e* you undertake,
Neh 6: 3 in a great *e* and am unable to come down;
1Mc 9:68 the *e* he had planned came to nought,

ENTERPRISES (1)

1Sm 18:14 expeditions, and prospered in all his *e*,

ENTERPRISING (1)

Lk 16: 8 his devious employee credit for being *e*!

ENTERS (34)

Ex 28:29 "Whenever Aaron *e* the sanctuary,
28:30 whenever he *e* the presence of the LORD.
28:35 be heard as he *e* and leaves the LORD's
30:13 Everyone who *e* the registered group must
30:14 Everyone of twenty years or more who *e* the
Lv 14:46 Whoever *e* a house while it is quarantined
16:17 from the time he *e* the sanctuary to make
Nm 19:14 dies in a tent, everyone who *e* the tent,
2Kgs 5:18 *e* the temple of Rimmon to worship there,
23: 8 city, to the left as one *e* the city gate.
Jb 22: 4 that he *e* with you into judgment?
Ps(s) 30: 6 At nightfall, weeping *e* in,
45:14 glorious is the king's daughter as she *e*;
68:19 the LORD God *e* his dwelling.
Wis 1: 4 into a soul that plots evil wisdom *e* not,
7:25 nought that is sullied *e* into her.
Is 3:14 The LORD *e* into judgment with his people's
57: 2 of evil, the just man *e* into peace;
Ez 26:10 as he *e* your gates, even as one enters
44:27 and on the day he *e* the inner court to
Mi 6: 2 people, and he *e* into trial with Israel.
Mt 7: 8 The one who knocks, *e*.
15:17 "Do you not see that everything that *e*
Mk 7:15 *e* a man from outside can make him impure;
7:18 *e* a man from outside can make him impure?
7:19 but *e* his stomach only and passes into the
14:14 Whatever house he *e*, say to the owner,
Lk 22:10 Follow him into the house he *e*,
Jn 10: 2 The one who *e* through the gate is shepherd
10: 9 Whoever *e* through me will be safe.
1Cor 14:24 *e* while all are uttering prophecy,
Heb 4:10 And he who *e* into God's rest,
9:25 as the high priest *e* year after year into

ENTERTAIN (2)

Sir 9: 5 *E* no thoughts against a virgin,
Phil 1: 7 It is only right that I should *e* such

ENTERTAINED (3)

Jb 31: 1 eyes and *e* any thoughts against a maiden;
Mt 28:17 those who had *e* doubts fell down in homage.
Heb 13: 2 some have *e* angels without knowing it.

ENTERTAINERS (4)

Dn 5: 2 his wives and his *e* might drink from them.
5: 3 and his *e* were drinking wine from them,
5:23 and your nobles, your wives and your *e*,
6:19 he refused to eat and he dismissed the *e*.

ENTERTAINING (2)

Dt 15: 9 *e* the mean thought that the seventh year,
Sir 41:21 and of *e* thoughts about another's wife;

ENTERTAINMENT (1)

Prv 10:23 Crime is the *e* of the fool;

ENTHRONED (25)

Dt 17:18 When he is *e* in his kingdom,
1Sm 4: 4 LORD of hosts, who is *e* upon the cherubim.
2Sm 6: 2 of the LORD of hosts *e* above the cherubim.
2Kgs 19:15 LORD, God of Israel, *e* upon the cherubim!
1Chr 13: 6 by the name "LORD *e* upon the cherubim."
Ps(s) 7: 8 above them on high be *e*.
9: 8 But the LORD sits *e* forever;
9:12 Sing praise to the LORD *e* in Zion;
22: 4 Yet you are *e* in the holy place,
29:10 enthroned above the flood; the LORD is *e*
61: 8 Let him sit *e* before God forever;
113: 5 who is *e* on high and looks upon the
123: 1 you I lift up my eyes who are *e* in heaven.
Is 10:13 and, like a giant, I have put down the *e*.
33: 5 The LORD is exalted, *e* on high;
37:16 hosts, God of Israel, *e* upon the cherubim!
40:22 He sits *e* above the vault of the earth,
47: 8 Now hear this voluptuous one, *e* securely,
Lam 5:19 You, O LORD, are *e* forever;
Bar 3: 3 for you are *e* forever,
Rv 11:16 The twenty-four elders who were *e* in God's
17: 9 are seven hills on which the woman sits *e*.
17:15 you saw the harlot *e* are large numbers
18: 7 she said to herself, 'I sit *e* as a queen.

ENTHUSIASM (3)

1Chr 13: 8 all Israel danced before God with great *e*,
2Mc 15: 9 already won, he filled them with fresh *e*.
Acts 17:11 and welcomed the message with great *e*.

ENTICE (3)

Gn 39:10 Although she tried to *e* him day after day,
Jdt 12:12 If we do not *e* her,
Prv 1:10 My son, should sinners *e* you,

ENTICED (3)

1Chr 21: 1 he *e* David into taking a census of Israel.
Jb 31: 9 If my heart has been *e* toward a woman,
31:27 *e* to waft them a kiss with my hand;

ENTICEMENT (1)

Gal 5: 8 *e* does not come from him who calls you.

ENTICEMENTS (1)

1Jn 2:16 Carnal allurements, *e* for the eye,

ENTICES (1)

Dt 13: 7 friend, *e* you secretly to serve other gods,

ENTIRE (113)

Gn 31: 8 the *e* flock would bear speckled young;
31: 8 the *e* flock would bear streaked young.
Ex 9:22 hail may fall upon the *e* land of Egypt,
29:18 *e* ram shall then be burned on the altar,
38:24 in the *e* construction of the sanctuary,
39:32 Thus the *e* work of the Dwelling of the
Nm 16:19 of the LORD appeared to the *e* community,
Dt 5:22 spoke with a loud voice to your *e* assembly
Jos 1: 7 taking care to observe the *e* law which my
2: 3 for they have come to spy out the *e* land."
3:15 banks during the *e* season of the harvest,
4: 1 After the *e* nation had crossed the Jordan,
6:23 Her *e* family they led forth and placed
8:25 men and women, the *e* population of Ai.
8:35 Joshua read aloud to the *e* community,
9:18 *e* community grumbled against the princes,
9:21 and drawers of water for the *e* community;
9:24 that you be given the *e* land
10:40 Joshua conquered the *e* country;
11:16 the *e* Negeb all the land of Goshen,
11:21 Anab, the *e* mountain region of Judah,
11:21 Judah, and the *e* mountain region of Israel.
13:12 as Salecah, the *e* kingdom in Bashan of Og,
13:30 all of Bashan, the *e* kingdom of Og,
22:20 wrath fall upon the *e* community of Israel?
24: 3 and led him through the *e* land of Canaan.
24:17 protected us along our *e* journey
24:31 Israel served the LORD during the *e*
Jgs 2: 7 the LORD during the *e* lifetime of Joshua,
4:16 *e* army of Sisera fell beneath the sword,
8:12 captive, throwing the *e* army into panic.
9:45 *e* day Abimelech fought against the city,
20:26 So the *e* Israelite army went up to Bethel,
Ru 2:21 servants until they complete his *e* harvest."
1Sm 7: 9 offered it *e* as a holocaust to the LORD.
2Sm 6:19 each woman in the *e* multitude of Israel,
7:17 all these words and this *e* vision to David.
7:21 *e* magnificent disclosure to your servant.
10: 7 Joab with the *e* levy of trained soldiers.
15:16 set out, accompanied by his *e* household,
18: 8 The battle spread out over that *e* region,
19:29 For though my father's *e* house deserved
1Kgs 6:22 The *e* temple was overlaid with gold so
8: 5 King Solomon and the *e* community of Israel
8:38 if then any one [of your *e* people Israel]
8:54 this *e* prayer of petition to the LORD,
8:56 gone unfulfilled of the *e* generous promise
9:19 and in the *e* land under his dominion.
11:28 the *e* labor force of the house of Joseph.
15:29 he killed off the *e* house of Jeroboam,
16:12 Zimri destroyed the *e* house of Baasha,
2Kgs 13:22 Israel during the *e* reign of Jehoahaz.
17:13 in accordance with the *e* law which I
21: 8 the *e* law which my servant Moses enjoined
23: 2 He had the *e* contents of the book of the
23:22 or during the *e* period of the kings of
23:25 in accord with the *e* law of Moses;
1Chr 18: 9 David had defeated the *e* army of Hadadezer,
2Chr 5: 6 King Solomon and the *e* community of Israel
8: 6 and in the *e* land under his dominion.
26:12 The *e* number of family heads over these
26:14 provided for them—for the *e* army
29:18 "We have cleansed the *e* house of the LORD,
29:28 The *e* assembly prostrated itself,
30: 2 and the *e* assembly in Jerusalem had agreed
30: 4 approved by the king and the *e* assembly,
31:18 thus for the *e* assembly,
34:30 read aloud to them the *e* text of the book
35:16 Thus the *e* service of the LORD was
Ezr 2:64 The *e* assembly taken together came to
Neh 7:66 The *e* assembly taken together came to
8:17 Thus the *e* assembly of the returned exiles
9:32 prophets, our fathers, and your *e* people,
Tb 1: 4 the *e* tribe of my forefather Naphtali had
1:21 he took control over the *e* administration.
14: 4 *e* country of Israel shall become desolate;
Jdt 1:13 his *e* cavalry and all his chariots,
Est E:18 been hanged, together with his *e* household,
1Mc 4:59 Then Judas and his brothers and the *e*
8:16 every year, to rule over their *e* country,
11:38 had no opposition, he dismissed his *e* army,
2Mc 8: 9 nations to wipe out the *e* Jewish race.
9: 9 so that the *e* army was sickened by the
12: 7 and wipe out the *e* population of Joppa.
14: 8 since our *e* nation is suffering great
Sir 1:15 Her *e* house she fills with choice foods,
Jer 36:23 until the *e* roll was consumed in the fire.
51: 3 Spare not her young men, doom her *e* army.
51:25 mountain, destroyer of the *e* earth,
Ez 42: 8 but along its *e* length the wall measured
48:20 The *e* tract shall be twenty-five thousand
Dn 6: 2 *e* kingdom one hundred and twenty satraps,
6: 4 of giving him authority over the *e* kingdom.
11:17 to penetrate the *e* strength of his kingdom.
Mt 8:34 was that the *e* town came out to meet Jesus.
10:31 are worth more than an *e* flock of sparrows.
18:32 your *e* debt when you pleaded with me.
Lk 3: 3 He went about the *e* region of the Jordan
7:29 The *e* populace that had heard Jesus,
8:37 the *e* population of the Gerasene territory
19:37 the *e* crowd of disciples began to rejoice
19:48 for indeed the *e* populace was listening to
23: 1 Then the *e* assembly rose up and led him
Jn 21:25 *e* world to hold the books to record them.
Acts 7:10 of Egypt and of the Pharaoh's *e* household.
8:27 a court official in charge of the *e* treasury
13:44 *e* city gathered to hear the word of God.
Gal 5: 9 "A little yeast can affect the *e* dough."
Phil 3:14 My *e* attention is on the finish line as I
1Thes 5:23 May he preserve you whole and *e*,
Jas 2:10 law, even though he keeps the *e* remainder,
3: 2 sense, because he can control his *e* body.
3: 6 The tongue defiles the *e* body.

ENTIRELY (23)

Gn 41:51 "God has made me forget *e* the sufferings
Ex 28:31 ephod you shall make *e* of violet material.
39:22 of the ephod was woven *e* of violet yarn,
Nm 4:27 The service of the Gershonites shall be *e*
16:30 But if the LORD does something *e* new,
Jos 3:16 the Salt Sea of the Arabah disappeared *e*.
1Kgs 11: 4 and his heart was not *e* with the LORD,
15: 3 him, and his heart was not *e* with the LORD,
15:14 was *e* with the LORD as long as he lived.
1Chr 29:16 holy name comes from you and is *e* yours.
2Chr 31: 4 devote themselves *e* to the law of the LORD.
Prv 16:33 lap, its decision depends *e* on the LORD.
Jer 12:17 I will uproot and destroy that nation *e*,
Zec 11:17 Let his arm wither away *e*,
Mk 9:13 They did *e* as they pleased with him,
16:17 demons, they will speak *e* new languages,
Jn 13:10 he is *e* cleansed, just as you are;
Acts 1:21 It is *e* fitting therefore, that one of those
Rom 3: 9 Not *e*. We have already
5:16 The gift is *e* different from the sin
1Cor 7:35 you to devote yourselves *e* to the Lord.
1Tm 3:11 They should be temperate and *e* trustworthy.
Heb 9: 4 ark of the covenant *e* covered with gold.

ENTIRETY (3)

Dt 31:24 a scroll the words of the law in their *e*,
Acts 20:27 announcing to you God's design in its *e*.
Gal 5: 3 that they are bound to the law in its *e*.

ENTITLED (2)

Tb 7:10 more *e* to marry my daughter Sarah than you,
2Cor 3: 5 *e* of ourselves to take credit for anything.

ENTRAILS (5)

2Sm 20:10 so that his *e* burst forth to the ground,
Tb 6: 5 but throw away the *e*.
2Mc 14:46 he tore out his *e* and flung them with both
Ps(s) 109:18 *e* like water and like oil into his bones;
Acts 1:18 burst wide open, all his *e* spilling out.

ENTRANCE (138)

Gn 6:16 Put an *e* in the side of the ark,
18: 1 of Mamre, as he sat in the *e* of his tent,
18: 2 ran from the *e* of the tent to greet them;
18:10 Sarah was listening at the *e* of the tent,
19: 6 Lot went out to meet them at the *e*.
19:11 they struck the men at the *e* of the house,
38:14 a shawl, and sat down at the *e* to Enaim,
43:19 and talked to him at the *e* of the house.
Ex 26:36 For the *e* of the tent make a variegated
27:16 "At the *e* of the court there shall be a
29: 4 also bring to the *e* of the meeting tent,
29:11 the LORD, at the *e* of the meeting tent.
29:32 At the *e* of the meeting tent Aaron and his
29:42 the LORD at the *e* of the meeting tent,
33: 8 rise and stand at the *e* of their own tents,
33: 9 at its *e* while the LORD spoke with Moses.
33:10 column of cloud stand at the *e* of the tent,
33:10 and worship at the *e* of their own tents.
35:15 entrance curtain for the *e* of the Dwelling;
35:17 the curtain for the *e* of the court;
36:37 for the *e* of the tent was made of violet,
38: 8 who served at the *e* of the meeting tent.
38:15 the other side, beyond the *e* of the court,
38:18 At the *e* of the court there was a
38:30 the pedestals at the *e* of the meeting tent,
38:31 court, the pedestals at the *e* of the court,
39:38 the curtain for the *e* of the tent,
39:40 the curtain for the *e* of the court with
40: 5 hang the curtain at the *e* of the Dwelling.
40: 6 the *e* of the Dwelling of the meeting tent.
40: 8 and put the curtain at the *e* of the court.
40:12 and his sons to the *e* of the meeting tent,
40:28 hung the curtain at the *e* of the Dwelling.
40:29 the *e* of the Dwelling of the meeting tent,
40:33 and hung the curtain at the *e* of the court.
Lv 1: 3 he shall bring it to the *e* of the meeting
1: 5 which is at the *e* of the meeting tent.
3: 2 slaughter it at the *e* of the meeting tent;
4: 4 the bullock to the *e* of the meeting tent,
4: 7 which is at the *e* of the meeting tent.
4:18 which is at the *e* of the meeting tent.
8: 3 community at the *e* of the meeting tent."
8: 4 had assembled at the *e* of the meeting tent,
8:31 the flesh at the *e* of the meeting tent,
8:33 the *e* of the meeting tent for seven days,
8:35 Hence you must remain at the *e* of the
12: 6 the priest at the *e* of the meeting tent
14:11 the LORD at the *e* of the meeting tent.
14:23 the *e* of the meeting tent before the LORD.
15:14 the LORD, to the *e* of the meeting tent,
15:29 to the priest at the *e* of the meeting tent.
16: 7 the LORD at the *e* of the meeting tent,
17: 4 without first bringing it to the *e* of the
17: 5 bringing them to the priest at the *e*
17: 6 *e* of the meeting tent and there burn the fat
17: 9 or sacrifice without bringing it to the *e*
19:21 shall bring to the *e* of the meeting tent a
Nm 3:25 the curtain at the *e* of the meeting tent,
3:26 the curtain at the *e* of the court
4:25 the curtain at the *e* of the meeting tent,
4:26 the curtain at the *e* of the court that
6:10 to the priest at the *e* of the meeting tent.
6:13 he shall go to the *e* of the meeting tent,
6:18 Then at the *e* of the meeting tent the
10: 3 round you at the *e* of the meeting tent;
11:10 family, crying at the *e* of their tents,
12: 5 cloud, and standing at the *e* of the tent,
16:18 they took their stand by the *e* of the
16:19 against them at the *e* of the meeting tent,
17:15 to Moses at the *e* of the meeting tent.
20: 6 the assembly to the *e* of the meeting tent,
25: 6 were weeping at the *e* of the meeting tent.
27: 2 community at the *e* of the meeting tent,
Dt 22:21 they shall bring the girl to the *e* of her
31:15 which stood still at the *e* of the tent.
Jos 8:29 tree and cast at the *e* of the city gate,
20: 4 and standing at the *e* of the city gate,
Jgs 3: 3 between Baal-hermon and the *e* to Hamath.
4:20 "Stand at the *e* of the tent,"
9:35 out and stood at the *e* of the city gate.
9:40 fell slain right up to the *e* of the gate.
9:44 in and stood by the *e* of the city gate,
9:52 the very *e* of the tower to set it on fire.
18:16 were Danites, stood by the *e* of the gate,
19:26 the woman came and collapsed at the *e*
19:27 at the *e* of the house with her hands on
2Sm 10: 8 formation at the *e* of their city gate,
11: 9 But Uriah slept at the *e* of the royal
11:23 pushed them back to the *e* of the city gate.
1Kgs 6: 8 The *e* to the lowest floor of the annex was
6:31 At the *e* of the sanctuary,
6:33 The same was done at the *e* to the nave,
14:27 guard on duty at the *e* of the royal palace.
17:10 As he arrived at the *e* of the city,
19:13 and went and stood at the *e* of the cave.
22:10 floor at the *e* of the gate of Samaria,
2Kgs 10: 8 heaps at the *e* of the city until morning,"
16:18 for a throne, and the outer *e* for the king.
23: 8 which was at the *e* of the Gate of Joshua,
23:11 were at the *e* of the temple of the LORD,
1Chr 9:19 the *e* to the encampment of the LORD.
2Chr 12:10 guard on duty at the *e* of the royal palace.
18: 9 floor at the *e* of the gate of Samaria,
23:13 king standing beside his pillar at the *e*,
23:15 at the *e* to the Horse Gate of the palace,
Neh 3:20 Corner to the *e* of the house of Eliashib,
3:21 sector from the *e* of Eliashib's house
Est 2:21 of the royal eunuchs who guarded the *e*,
6: 2 of the royal eunuchs who guarded the *e*,
2Mc 2: 5 then he blocked up the *e*.
Wis 19:17 each sought the *e* of his own gate.
Sir 39: 4 on the great, and has *e* to the ruler.
Jer 19: 2 Ben-hinnom, at the *e* of the Potsherd Gate;
36:10 house, at the *e* of the New Temple-Gate,
38:14 at the third *e* to the house of the LORD.
43: 9 the *e* to the royal building in Tahpanhes,
Ez 8: 3 to Jerusalem, to the *e* of the north gate,
8: 7 Then he brought me to the *e* of the court,
8:14 to the *e* of the north gate of the temple,
10:19 *e* of the eastern gate of the LORD's house,
11: 1 At the *e* of the gate I saw twenty-five men,
40:11 He measured the gate's *e*,
40:15 The length of the gate from the front *e* to
40:40 but outside, near the *e* of the north gate,
41: 2 The width of the *e* was ten cubits,
41: 3 measured the pilasters flanking that *e*,
41: 3 the width of the *e* was six cubits,

41:11 e on the north and another on the south.
42:12 south there was an e at the beginning
46:19 Then he brought me by the e which is on
47: 1 he brought me back to the e of the temple,
Dn 14:13 under the table they had made a secret e
Mt 27:60 across the e of the tomb and went away.
Mk 15:46 he rolled a stone across the e of the tomb.
16: 3 the stone for us from the e to the tomb?"
Heb 4: 1 the promise of e into his rest still holds,
10:19 since the blood of Jesus assures our e

ENTRANCES (5)

Nm 16:27 out and were standing at the e of their tents
Ez 41:11 The side chambers had e to the open space,
42: 4 the e of the chambers were on the north.
42:11 wide, with the same exits and plan and e.
43:11 design of the temple, its exits and e,

ENTRAP (5)

Ps(s) 140:12 evil shall abruptly e the violent man.
Ez 13:18 every size of head so as to e their owners.
13:18 Do you think to e the lives of my people,
13:20 bands of yours in which you e men's lives:

ENTRAPPED (1)

Eccl 7:26 her, but the sinner will be e by her.

ENTREAT (11)

1Kgs 8:33 pray to you, and e you in this temple,
8:47 e you in the land of their captors and say,
13: 6 E the LORD, your God," he said,
2Chr 6:24 they pray to you and e you in this temple,
6:37 when they e you in the land of their
2Mc 9:26 Therefore I beg and e each of you to
Jb 11:19 Many shall e your favor,
22:27 You shall e him and he will hear you,
Ps(s) 119:58 I e you with all my heart,
Jer 26:19 fear the LORD and e the favor of the LORD,
Mt 15:23 His disciples came up and began to e him,

ENTREATED (3)

Gn 25:21 Isaac e the LORD on behalf of his wife,
1Kgs 13: 6 So the man of God e the LORD,
2Kgs 13: 4 Then Jehoahaz e the LORD,

ENTREATIES (1)

1Sm 28:23 in urging him, he listened to their e,

ENTREATING (1)

Hos 12: 5 the angel and triumphed, e him with tears.

ENTREATS (2)

2Chr 6:33 place, and do whatever the foreigner e you,
Wis 13:18 and for life he e the dead;

ENTREATY (3)

Gn 25:21 The LORD heard his e,
Wis 19: 3 and those whom they had sent away with e,
Is 47: 3 will take vengeance, I will yield to no e,

ENTRUST (6)

Tb 10:13 the Lord, I e my daughter to your care.
2Mc 7:24 him his Friend and e him with high office.
Prv 16: 3 E your works to the LORD,
Ez 25:14 upon Edom I will e to my people Israel,
Mt 16:19 e to you the keys of the kingdom of heaven.
1Pt 4:19 and e their lives to a faithful Creator.

ENTRUSTED (34)

Gn 39: 4 household and e to him all his possessions.
39: 8 in the house, but has e to me all he owns.
Dt 31: 9 he e it to the levitical priests who carry
Jgs 9:29 that this people were e to my command!
1Sm 17:22 David e what he had brought to the keeper
1Kgs 14:27 which he e to the officers of the guard on
1Chr 6:16 The following were e by David with the
9:31 Koreite, was e with preparing the cakes.
2Chr 12:10 which he e to the officers of the guard on
34:16 doing everything that has been e to them;
Est E: 5 the fair speech of friends e with the
1Mc 3:34 He e to him half of the army,
8:16 e their government to one man every year,
2Mc 9:24 know to whom the government had been e,
9:25 before e and commended to most of you,
10:13 Cyprus, which Philometor had e to him,
Jer 11:20 take on them, for to you I have e my cause!
13:20 Where is the flock e to you,
20:12 take on them, for to you I have e my cause.
39:14 quarters of the guard, and e to Gedaliah,
43: 6 of the bodyguard, had e to Gedaliah,
Zec 1: 6 which I e to my servants the prophets,
Mt 25:22 you have e me with two thousand
Lk 12:48 be asked of a man to whom more has been e.
Jn 17: 8 e to them the message you entrusted to me,
Rom 3: 2 of all, the Jews were e with words of God.
1Cor 9:17 I am nonetheless e with a charge.
2Cor 5:19 has e the message of reconciliation to us.
Gal 2: 7 e with the gospel for the uncircumcised,
1Thes 2: 4 us by God, as men e with the good tidings,
1Tm 1:11 blessed be he—with which I have been e.
2Tm 1:12 guard what has been e to me until that Day.
Ti 1: 3 e to me by the command of God our Savior.

ENTRUSTING (2)

1Kgs 15:18 E them to his ministers, King Asa sent
Prv 31:11 Her husband, e his heart to her,

ENTRY (12)

Lv 10: 7 you go beyond the e of the meeting tent,
1Sm 2:22 serving at the e of the meeting tent].
2Kgs 12:10 The priests who guarded the e would put
25:18 priest, and the three keepers of the e.
2Chr 4:22 As for the e to the house,
Jdt 14:14 went in, and knocked at the e of the tent,
Wis 7: 6 birth, but one is the e into life for all;
Sir 14:22 a scout, and lies in wait at her e way;
Is 24:10 down is the city of chaos, shut against e,
Jer 52:24 priest, and the three keepers of the e.
Acts 28:16 Upon our e into Rome Paul was allowed to
2Pt 1:11 your e into the everlasting kingdom of our

ENTRYWAYS (1)

Prv 8: 3 of the city, in the e she cries aloud:

ENTWINED (2)

2Mc 10: 7 Carrying rods e with leaves,
Jb 8:17 About a heap of stones are his roots e;

ENVELOP (2)

2Cor 5: 2 yearn to have our heavenly habitation e us.
5: 4 rather to have the heavenly dwelling e us,

ENVELOPED (11)

Gn 15:12 and a deep, terrifying darkness e him.
Dt 4:11 with fire and was e in a dense black cloud.
Jgs 6:34 The spirit of the LORD e Gideon;
1Chr 12:19 Then spirit e Amasai,
2Mc 3:27 he fell to the ground, e in great darkness.
Eccl 6: 4 darkness and its name is e in darkness;
Sir 48:12 he dies, O Elijah, e in the whirlwind!
Ez 1: 4 cloud with flashing fire e in brightness],
7:27 while the prince shall be e in terror,
Jon 2: 4 the heart of the sea, and the flood e me;
2: 6 the abyss e me;

ENVELOPING (1)

1Kgs 7:20 the level of the nodes and their e network.

ENVIED (1)

Ps(s) 106:16 They e Moses in the camp,

ENVIOUS (5)

Gn 26:14 that the Philistines became e of him.
30: 1 to Jacob, she became e of her sister.
Ps(s) 73: 3 Because I was e of the arrogant when I saw
Prv 24:19 with evildoers, nor e of the wicked;
Mt 20:15 Or are you e because I am generous?'

ENVIRONS (2)

1Mc 14:36 sally forth to defile the e of the temple
Mt 2:16 old and under in Bethlehem and its e,

ENVOY (3)

Ezr 7:14 You are the e from the king and his seven
1Mc 12: 8 the e with honor and received the letter,
Prv 13:17 but a trustworthy e is a healing remedy.

ENVOYS (17)

2Kgs 17: 4 for sending e to the king of Egypt at Sais,
19: 9 he sent e to Hezekiah with this message:
1Chr 14: 1 sent e to David along with masons and
19: 2 Therefore he sent e to him to comfort him
Jdt 1:11 them, and turned away his e empty-handed,
1Mc 8:19 e entered the senate and spoke as follows:
12: 4 e with save conduct to the land of Judah.
13:14 him, he sent e to him with this message:
14:21 The e you sent to our people have informed
14:22 and Antipater, son of Jason, e of the Jews,
14:40 they had received Simon's e with honor.
15:17 Certain e of the Jews,
2Mc 4:19 the vile Jason sent e as representatives
11:17 John and Absalom, your e,
11:20 my representatives, as well as your e,
Is 37: 9 he sent e to Hezekiah with this message:
Ez 17:15 sending e to Egypt to obtain horses and a

ENVY (23)

1Mc 8:16 and there was no e or jealousy among them.
Jb 11:20 looking on, shall be consumed with e.
Prv 3:31 E not the lawless man and choose none of
Wis 2:24 But by the e of the devil,
Sir 9:11 E not a sinner's fame,
30:24 E and anger shorten one's life,
37:10 from those who e you,
40: 5 Are of wrath and e, trouble and dread,
Is 11:13 The e of Ephraim shall pass away,
Ez 31: 9 e of all Eden's trees in the garden of God.
35:11 according to your anger and your e
Mk 7:22 maliciousness, deceit, sensuality, e,
Acts 7: 9 Out of e, the patriarchs sold Joseph
20:33 silver or gold or e the way he dressed.
Rom 1:29 maliciousness, greed, ill will, e,
11:11 come to the Gentiles to stir Israel to e.
11:14 my fellow Jews to e and save some of them.
Gal 5:21 rivalries, dissensions, factions, e,
Phil 1:15 Christ from motives of e and rivalry,
1Tm 6: 4 From these come e, dissension,
Ti 3: 3 We went our way in malice and e,
Jas 4: 2 You e and you cannot acquire,

ENWRAPS (1)

Ps(s) 73: 6 as a robe violence e them.

EPAENETUS (1)

Rom 16: 5 Greetings to my beloved E;

EPAPHRAS (3)

Col 1: 7 intention through the instructions of E,
4:12 E, who is one of you, sends greetings.
Phlm 1:23 E, my fellow prisoner in Christ Jesus,

EPAPHRODITUS (2)

Phil 2:25 have decided, too, that I must send you E,
4:18 of what I received from you through E,

EPHAH (54)

Gn 25: 4 The descendants of Midian were E,
Ex 16:36 [An omer is one tenth of an e
29:40 shall be a tenth of an e of fine flour
Lv 5:11 his sin one tenth of an e of fine flour.
6:13 one tenth of an e of fine flour for the
14:10 three tenths of an e of fine flour mixed
14:21 one tenth of an e of fine flour mixed with
19:36 weights, an honest e and an honest hin.
23:13 of an e of fine flour mixed with oil,
23:17 an e of fine flour and baked with leaven.
24: 5 two tenths of an e of flour for each cake.
Nm 5:15 for her a tenth of an e of barley meal.
15: 4 consisting of a tenth of an e of fine flour
15: 6 a cereal offering of two tenths of a e
15: 9 offering of three tenths of an e of fine flour
28: 5 one tenth of an e of fine flour mixed
28: 9 of an e of fine flour mixed with oil,
28:12 with three tenths of an e of fine flour
28:12 two tenths of an e of fine flour mixed
28:13 and one tenth of an e of fine flour mixed
28:20 three tenths of an e for each bullock,
28:28 three tenths of an e for each bullock,
29: 3 three tenths of an e for the bullock,
29: 9 three tenths of an e for the bullock,
29:14 of an e for each of the thirteen bullocks,
Jgs 6:19 e of flour in the form of unleavened cakes.
Ru 2:17 gleaned it came to about an e of barley,
1Sm 1:24 bull, an e of flour and a skin of wine,
17:17 "Take this e of roasted grain and these
2Sm 16: 1 ephah of cakes of pressed raisins, an e
1Chr 1:33 The descendants of Midian were E,
2:46 E, Caleb's concubine, bore Haran,
2:47 were Regem, Jotham, Geshan, Pelet, E,
Is 5:10 And a homer of seed shall yield but an e.
60: 6 fill you, dromedaries from Midian and E;
Ez 45:10 You shall have honest scales, an honest e,
45:11 The e and the liquid measure shall be of
45:11 the e equal to a tenth of a homer
45:13 one sixth of an e from each homer of wheat,
45:13 sixth of an e from each homer of barley.
45:24 one e for each bull and one ephah for
45:24 he shall offer one hin of oil for each e.
46: 5 a cereal offering of one e for the ram,
46: 5 for the lambs, and a hin of oil for each e.
46: 7 of one e for the bull and one for the ram,
46: 7 has at hand, and for each e a hin of oil.
46:11 be an ephah for a bull, an e for a ram,
46:11 one pleases, and a hin of oil with each e.
46:14 as a cereal offering one sixth of an e,
Am 8: 5 We will diminish the e,
Mi 6:10 hoarding and the meager e that is accursed?

EPHAI (1)

Jer 40: 8 the sons of E of Netopha;

EPHER (4)

Gn 25: 4 The descendants of Midian were Ephah, E,
1Chr 1:33 The descendants of Midian were Ephah, E,
4:17 The sons of Ezrah were Jether, Mered, E,
5:24 E, Ishi, Eliel, Azriel, Jeremiah,

EPHES-DAMMIM (2)

1Sm 17: 1 and camped between Socoh and Azekah at E.
2Sm 23: 9 He was with David at E when the

EPHESIAN (1)

Acts 21:29 They had seen Trophimus, an E,

EPHESUS (20)

Acts 18:19 When they landed at E, he left Priscilla
18:21 Then he set sail from E.
18:24 a man of eloquence, arrived by ship at E.
19: 1 the interior of the country and came to E.
19:17 known to the Jews and Greeks living in E,
19:26 not only at E but throughout most of the
19:28 began to shout, "Long live Artemis of E!"
19:34 chant in unison, "Long live Artemis of E!"
19:35 "Citizens of E," he said, "what man is there
19:35 E is the custodian of the temple
20:16 sail past E so as not to lose time in Asia,
20:17 Paul sent word from Miletus to E,
1Cor 15:32 those beasts at E for purely human motives,
16: 8 I intend to stay in E until Pentecost.
Eph 1: 1 of Jesus Christ, to the holy ones [at E,
1Tm 1: 3 stay on in E in order to warn certain
2Tm 1:18 Christ in E you know even better than I
4:12 Tychicus I have sent to E.
Rv 1:11 to E, Smyrna, Pergamum, Thyatira,
2: 1 the presiding spirit of the church in E,

EPHLAL (2)

1Chr 2:37 Zabad became the father of E.
2:37 E became the father of Obed.

EPHOD (48)

Ex 25: 7 for mounting on the e and the breastpiece.
28: 4 a breastpiece, an e, a robe,
28: 6 "The e they shall make of gold thread and
28: 8 belt of the e shall extend out from it and,
28:12 e as memorial stones of the sons of Israel.
28:15 like the e with gold thread and violet,
28:25 attached to the shoulder straps of the e.
28:26 breastpiece, on its edge that faces the e.
28:27 next to where they join the e in front,
28:28 of the breastpiece to the rings of the e,
28:28 belt of the e and not swing loose from it.
28:31 "The robe of the e you shall make
29: 5 tunic, the robe of the ephod, the e itself,
29: 5 the embroidered belt of the e around him.
35: 9 mounting on the e and on the breastpiece.
35:27 mounting on the e and on the breastpiece;
39: 2 e was woven of gold thread and of violet,
39: 5 belt on the e extended out from it,
39: 7 e as memorial stones of the sons of Israel,
39: 8 breastpiece was embroidered like the e,
39:18 attached to the shoulder straps of the e.
39:19 the breastpiece, on the edge facing the e.
39:20 next to where they joined the e in front,
39:21 of the breastpiece to the rings of the e,
39:21 of the e and did not swing loose from it.
39:22 of the e was woven entirely of violet yarn,
Lv 8: 7 him with the robe, placed the e on him,
8: 7 him with the embroidered belt of the e,
Nm 34:23 Hanniel, son of E;
Jgs 8:27 Gideon made an e out of the gold and
17: 5 He also made an e and household idols,
18:14 know that in these houses there are an e,
18:18 When they had gone in and taken the e,
18:20 The priest, agreeing, took the e,
1Sm 2:28 burn incense, and to wear the e before me;
14: 3 of the LORD at Shiloh, was wearing the e.)
14:18 then said to Ahijah, "Bring the e here."
14:18 e in front of the Israelites at that time.)
21:10 is here [wrapped in a mantle] behind an e.
22:18 that day eighty-five who wore the linen e.
23: 6 David to Keilah, taking the e with him.
23: 9 the priest Abiathar, "Bring forward the e."
30: 7 pr st, son of Ahimelech, "Bring me the e!"
30: 7 When Abiathar brought him the e,
1Chr 15:27 David was also wearing a linen e.
Sir 45:10 the e and cincture with scarlet yarn,
Hos 3: 4 pillar, without e or household idols.

EPHPHATHA (1)

Mk 7:34 He said to him, E!"

EPHRAIM (157)

Gn 41:52 and the second he named E,
46:20 became the father of Manasseh and E,
48: 1 with him his two sons, Manasseh and E.
48: 5 E and Manasseh shall be mine as much as
48:13 Joseph took the two, E with his right hand,
48:14 right hand and laid it on the head of E,
48:20 E and Manasseh,'" he placed Ephraim
Nm 1:10 from E: Elishama, son of Ammihud
1:32 Of the descendants of E, registered by
1:33 hundred were enrolled in the tribe of E.
2:18 side shall be the divisional camp of E,
2:24 registered by companies in the camp of E
13: 8 son of Nun of the tribe of E
26:28 The sons of Joseph were Manasseh and E.
34:24 and from the tribe of E:
Dt 33:17 [These are the myriads of E,
34: 2 all Naphtali, the land of E and Manasseh,
Jos 14: 4 Joseph formed two tribes, Manasseh and E.
16: 4 Within the heritage of Manasseh and E,
16:10 who live on within E to the present day,
17: 9 The cities that belonged to E from among
17:10 to E and that on the north to Manasseh;
17:15 the mountain regions of E are so narrow."
17:17 Joshua therefore said to E and Manasseh,
19:50 Timnah-serah in the mountain region of E.
20: 7 Shechem in the mountain region of E,
21: 5 by lot from the clans of the tribe of E,
21:20 obtained by lot, from the tribe of E,
21:21 at Shechem in the mountain region of E;
24:30 mountain region of E north of Mount Gaash.
24:33 son Phinehas in the mountain region of E.
Jgs 2: 9 mountain region of E north of Mount Gaash.
3:27 the horn in the mountain region of E,
4: 5 and Bethel in the mountain region of E,
5:14 From E, princes were in the valley;
7:24 throughout the mountain region of E to say,
8: 2 of E better than the vintage of Abiezer?
10: 1 of Shamir in the mountain region of E.
10: 9 Judah, Benjamin, and the house of E,
12: 1 The men of E gathered together and crossed
12: 4 the men of Gilead and fought against E,
12: 4 in territory belonging to E and Manasseh."
12: 5 took the fords of the Jordan toward E.
12:15 of E on the mountain of the Amalekites.
17: 1 mountain region of E whose name was Micah.
17: 8 house of Micah in the mountain region of E.
18: 2 house of Micah in the mountain region of E,
18:13 region of E and came to the house of Micah.
19: 1 of E who had taken for himself a concubine
19:16 he was from the mountain region of E,
19:18 Judah far up into the mountain region of E,
1Sm 1: 1 name, a Zuphite from the hill country of E.
9: 4 they went through the hill country of E,
14:22 who were hiding in the hill country of E,
14:24 in every town in the hill country of E.
2Sm 2: 9 over Gilead, the Ashurites, Jezreel, E,
13:23 Absalom had shearers in Baal-hazor near E,
20:21 of E has rebelled against King David.
1Kgs 4: 8 the son of Hur in the hill country of E;
12:25 in the hill country of E and lived there.
2Kgs 5:22 guild prophets from the hill country of E.
14:13 from the Gate of E to the Corner Gate.
1Chr 6:46 lot for their clans from the tribe of E,
6:51 obtained cities by lot from the tribe of E.
6:52 Shechem in the mountain region of E,
7:20 The sons of E:
7:22 Their father E mourned a long time,
27:10 from Beth-phelet, of the sons of E,
27:14 month, was Benaiah the Pirathonite, of E,
27:20 for the sons of E, Hoshea, son of Azaziah;
2Chr 13: 4 Zemariam, which is in the highlands of E,
15: 8 cities he had taken in the highlands of E,
15: 9 and Benjamin, together with those of E,
17: 2 cities of E which his father Asa had taken.
19: 4 of E and brought them back to the LORD,
25:10 the troops that had come to him from E,
25:23 from the E Gate to the Corner Gate,
30: 1 and even wrote letters to E and Manasseh
30:10 of E and Manasseh and as far as Zebulun,
30:18 of the people, in fact, chiefly from E,
31: 1 throughout Judah, Benjamin, E and Manasseh,
34: 6 did likewise in the cities of Manasseh, E,
34: 9 threshold, had collected from Manasseh, E,
Neh 8:16 spaces of the Water Gate and the Gate of E.
12:39 then past the E Gate [the New City Gate],
Ps(s) 60: 9 E is the helmet for my head;
78: 9 The sons of E, ordered ranks of bowmen,
78:67 of Joseph, and the tribe of E he chose not;
80: 3 upon the cherubim, shine forth before E,
108: 9 Manasseh, E is the helmet for my head;
Sir 47:21 into being, when in E kingship was usurped.
47:23 Who brought ruin to E and caused them to
Is 7: 2 of David that Aram was encamped in E,
7: 5 because of the mischief that Aram E
7: 8 Samaria is the capital of E,
7: 9 sixty years and five, E shall be crushed,
7:17 worse than any since E seceded from Judah.
9: 8 know it, E and those who dwell in Samaria,
9:20 Manasseh devours Ephraim, and E Manasseh;
11:13 The envy of E shall pass away,
11:13 E shall not be jealous of Judah,
11:13 and Judah shall not be hostile to E;
17: 3 be lost to E and the kingdom to Damascus;
28: 1 to the majestic garland of the drunkard E,
28: 3 the majestic garland of the drunkard E.
Jer 4:15 from Mount E they announce destruction:
7:15 all your brethren, all the offspring of E.
31: 6 when the watchmen will call out on Mount E:
31: 9 am a father to Israel, E is my first-born.
31:18 I hear, I hear E pleading:
31:20 Is E not my favored son,
50:19 and Bashan, And on Mount E and Gilead,
Ez 37:16 Joseph [the stick of E and all the house
37:19 of Joseph, which is in the hand of E,
48: 5 E: on the frontier
48: 6 on the frontier of E, from the eastern
Hos 4:17 E is an associate of idols,
5: 3 I know E, and Israel is not hidden
5: 3 Now E has played the harlot,
5: 5 E stumbles in his guilt,
5: 9 E shall become a waste on the day of
5:11 Is E maltreated, his rights violated?
5:12 I am like a moth for E,
5:13 E saw his infirmity, and Judah his sore, E
5:14 For I am like a lion to E,
6: 4 What can I do with you, E?
6:10 there harlotry is found in E,
7: 1 heal Israel, The guilt of E stands out,
7: 8 Ephraim mingles with the nations, E
7:11 E is like a dove,
8: 9 E bargained for lovers.
8:11 When E made many altars to expiate sin,
9: 3 E shall return to Egypt,
9:11 The glory of E flies away like a bird:
9:13 E, as I saw, was like Tyre,
9:13 But E shall bring out his children to the
9:16 E is stricken, their root is dried up;
10: 6 E shall be taken into captivity,
10:11 E was a trained heifer,
10:11 E was to be harnessed,
11: 3 Yet it was I who taught E to walk,
11: 8 How could I give you up, O E,
11: 9 blazing anger, I will not destroy E again;
12: 1 E has surrounded me with lies,
12: 2 E chases the wind,
12: 9 Though E says, "How rich I have
12:15 E has exasperated his Lord;
14: 9 E! What more has he to do with idols?
Ob 1:19 the lands of E and the lands of Samaria,
Zec 9:10 He shall banish the chariot from E,
9:13 Judah as my bow, I will arm myself with E;
10: 7 Then E shall be valiant men,
Jn 11:54 called E in the region near the desert,

EPHRAIMITE (8)

Jos 17: 8 was an E city on the border of Manasseh.
Jgs 12: 4 "You of Gilead are E fugitives in
12: 5 of Gilead would say to him, "Are you an E?"
1Sm 1: 1 of Elihu, son of Tohu, son of Zuph, an E.
1Kgs 11:26 an E from Zeredah with a widowed mother,
2Chr 25: 7 the LORD is not with Israel, with any E.
28: 7 Zichri, an E warrior,
28:12 At this, some of the E leaders,

EPHRAIMITES (15)

Nm 7:48 Elishama, son of Ammihud, prince of the E.
10:22 The camp of the E next set out,
26:35 The E by clans were:
26:37 These were the clans of the E,
Jos 16: 5 heritage of the clans of the E ran from east
16: 8 was the heritage of the clans of the E,
16: 9 E within the territory of the Manassehites.
Jgs 1:29 the E did not drive out the Canaanites
7:24 So all the E were called to arms,
8: 1 But the E said to him, "What have you
12: 4 for the E had said, "You of Gilead
12: 5 When any of the fleeing E said,
12: 6 forty-two thousand E fell at that time.
1Chr 9: 3 also E and Manassehites.
12:31 Of the E: twenty thousand eight hundred

EPHRAIM'S (6)

Gn 48:17 father had laid his right hand on E head,
48:17 to remove it from E head to Manasseh's,
50:23 He saw E children to the third generation,
1Chr 7:21 E son Shuthelah, and Ezer and Elead,
Hos 9: 8 A prophet is E watchman with God,
13: 1 E word caused fear,

EPHRATH (5)

Gn 35:16 had some distance to go on the way to E,
35:19 she was buried on the road to E [that is,
48: 7 we were still a short distance from E;
48: 7 buried her there on the way to E [that is,
1Chr 2:19 When Azubah died, Caleb married E,

EPHRATHAH (6)

Jos 15:59 Tekoa, E (that is, Bethlehem),
Ru 4:11 you do well in E and win fame in Bethlehem.
1Chr 2:24 of Hezron, Caleb had relations with E,
2:50 of Caleb, sons of Hur, the first-born of E:
4: 4 descendants of Hur, the first-born of E,
Ps(s) 132: 6 Behold, we heard of it in E;

EPHRATHITE (1)

1Sm 17:12 [David was the son of an E named Jesse,

EPHRATHITES (1)

Ru 1: 2 they were E from Bethlehem of Judah.

EPHRON (14)

Gn 23: 8 Intercede for me with E,
23:10 Now E was present with the Hittites.
23:10 So E the Hittite replied to Abraham in the
23:12 addressed E in the hearing of these men:
23:14 E replied to Abraham, "Please.
23:16 out to him the silver that E had stipulated
25: 9 the cave of Machpelah, in the field of E,
49:29 that lies in the field of E the Hittite,
49:30 from E the Hittite for a burial ground.
50:13 for a burial ground from E the Hittite.
Jos 15: 9 extended to the cities of Mount E,
2Chr 13:19 dependencies, and E and its dependencies.

1Mc 5:46 When they reached E, a large and strongly
2Mc 12:27 of these, he moved his army to E,

EPHRON'S (3)

Gn 23:16 Abraham accepted E terms;
23:17 Thus E field in Machpelah,
23:18 all the Hittites who sat on E town council.

EPICUREAN (1)

Acts 17:18 E and Stoic philosophers disputed with him,

EPIGRAMS (2)

Sir 44: 4 and forgers of e with their spikes;
Hb 2: 6 against him, satire and e about him to say:

EPIPHANES (6)

1Mc 1:10 from these a sinful offshoot, Antiochus E,
10: 1 and sixty, Alexander, who was called E,
2Mc 2:20 against Antiochus E and his son Eupator,
4: 7 surnamed E succeeded him on the throne,
10: 9 Such was the end of Antiochus surnamed E.
10:13 and for having gone over to Antiochus E.

EPOCHS (1)

Acts 17:26 It is he who set limits to their e and

EQUAL (33)

Gn 44:18 your servant, for you are the e of Pharaoh.
Ex 30:34 these are pure frankincense in e parts;
Dt 34:11 He had no e in all the signs and wonders
Jos 4: 5 e in number the tribes of the Israelites.
2Sm 18: 3 You are e to ten thousand of us.
1Kgs 3:12 after you there will come no one to e you.
1Chr 4:27 did not e the number of the Judahites.
Jb 28:13 Man knows nothing to e it,
28:17 Gold or crystal cannot e it,
Ps(s) 40: 6 your plans for us there is none to e you;
Sir 2:18 For e to his majesty is the mercy that he
9:10 old friend, for the new one cannot e him.
18: 2 Whom has he made e to describing his works,
20:13 for in his eyes the one gift is e to seven
48: 4 are you, ELIJAH, Whose glory is e to yours?
49:14 Few on earth have been made the e of ENOCH,
Is 40:18 With what e can you confront him?
40:25 To whom can you liken me as an e?
46: 5 Whom would you compare me with, as an e,
Bar 1:11 that their lifetimes may e the duration of
6:62 But these false gods are not their e,
Ez 31: 8 in the garden of God were not its e,
31:18 e in glory or size among the trees of Eden?
40:10 gate were three on either side, of e size,
40:10 on either side were also of e size.
45:11 the ephah e to a tenth of a homer
45:11 the liquid measure e to a tenth of a homer;
Dn 1:19 all of them, none was found e to Daniel,
Mk 6:15 "He is a prophet e to any of the prophets."
Jn 5:18 own Father, thereby making himself God's e.
2Cor 8:16 an e zeal for you in the heart of Titus!
Gal 4:30 never be an heir on e terms with the son"

EQUALITY (4)

2Mc 9:15 perfect e with the Athenians all the Jews,
2Cor 8:13 there should be a certain e.
8:14 day supply your need, with e as the result.
Phil 2: 6 deem e with God something to be grasped at.

EQUALLY (9)

Ex 21:35 as well as the dead animal e between them.
Lv 25: 6 all its produce will be food e for you
1Chr 25: 8 They cast lots for their functions e,
Jdt 8:15 he has it e within his power to protect
Eccl 9: 1 both appear e vain,
Wis 14: 9 E odious to God are the evildoer and his
Mk 3: 8 e great multitude came to him from Judea,
1Cor 7: 4 e, a husband does not belong to himself
2Cor 7:14 boasting to Titus has been proved e true.

EQUALS (1)

Jb 18: 3 like the beasts, their e in your sight?

EQUIP (1)

1Mc 14:32 large sums of his own money to e the men

EQUIPMENT (16)

Ex 39:40 all the e for the service of the Dwelling
Nm 1:50 with all its e and with all that belongs to it.
1:50 all its e and who shall be its ministers.
7: 1 e (as well as the altar with all its equipment),
Dt 23:14 also keep a trowel in your e and with it,
1Sm 8:12 of war and the e of his chariots.
1Kgs 19:21 the plowing e for fuel to boil their flesh,
1Chr 9:28 of them had charge of the liturgical e,
23:26 Dwelling or any of its furnishings or e.
Jdt 3:10 month to refurbish all the e of his army.
7:18 e was spread out in profusion everywhere.
1Mc 9:39 with tambourines and musicians and much e.
14:15 the temple splendid and enriched its e.
15:26 together with gold and silver and much e.

2Mc 15:21 the hosts before him, their elaborate e,

EQUIPPED (10)

Dt 3:18 But all you troops e for battle must cross
Jos 4:13 About forty thousand troops e for battle
1Chr 12: 9 soldiers e with shield and spear,
12:38 men e with every kind of weapon of war:
2Chr 17:18 one hundred and eighty thousand e for war.
1Mc 14:10 with food and e them with means of defense,
15: 3 troops and e warships to make a landing
Prv 21:31 The horse is e for the day of battle,
2Tm 3:17 fully competent and e for every good work.
Rv 9: 7 the locusts were like horses e for battle.

EQUITABLE (1)

Est E: 9 deciding always with e treatment matters

EQUITY (8)

Ps(s) 9: 9 he governs the peoples with e.
67: 5 exult because you rule the peoples in e;
75: 3 the appointed time, I will judge with e.
96:10 he governs the peoples with e.
98: 9 world with justice and the peoples with e.
99: 4 you have established e;
111: 8 forever and ever, wrought in truth and e.
Jer 10:24 Punish us, O LORD, but with e,

ER (10)

Gn 38: 3 conceived and bore a son, whom she named E.
38: 6 a wife named Tamar for his first-born, E.
38: 7 But E, Judah's first-born, greatly offended
46:12 E, Onan, Shelah, Perez, and Zerah—but Er
Nm 26:19 died in the land of Canaan were E and Onan.
1Chr 2: 3 E, Onan, and Shelah;
2: 3 But Judah's first-born, E,
4:21 E, the father of Lecah;
Lk 3:28 son of Cosam, son of Elmadam, son of E,

ERA (2)

Tb 14: 5 until the e when the appointed times shall
Sir 47:13 SOLOMON reigned during an e of peace,

ERAN (1)

Nm 26:36 through E the clan of the Eranites.

ERANITES (1)

Nm 26:36 through Eran the clan of the E.

ERASE (1)

Rv 3: 5 e his name from the book of the living,

ERASED (2)

Tb 4:19 and never let them be e from your heart.
Ps(s) 69:29 May they be e from the book of the living,

ERASTUS (3)

Acts 19:22 sent two of his assistants, Timothy and E,
Rom 16:24 E, the city treasurer, and our brother
2Tm 4:20 E has stayed in Corinth,

ERE (2)

Ps(s) 39:14 may find respite e I depart and be no more.
Wis 2: 8 ourselves with rosebuds e they wither.

ERECH (1)

Gn 10:10 cities of his kingdom were Babylon, E,

ERECT (18)

Ex 26:30 You shall e the Dwelling according to the
40: 2 shall e the Dwelling of the meeting tent.
Lv 26: 1 You shall not e an idol or a sacred pillar
26:13 had laid upon you and letting you walk e.
Dt 16:22 nor shall you e a sacred pillar,
1Chr 21:18 go up and e an altar to the LORD
2Mc 14:33 and e here a splendid temple to Dionysus."
15: 6 had determined to e a public monument
Ps(s) 20: 9 bow down and fall, yet we stand e and firm.
Hos 2: 8 way with thorns and e a wall against her,
Mt 17: 4 your permission I will e three booths here,
23:29 You e tombs for the prophets and decorate
Mk 9: 5 Let us e three booths on this site,
Lk 5:25 At once the man stood e before them.
11:48 committed the murders and you e the tombs.
13:11 quite incapable of standing e.
21:28 happen, stand e and hold your heads high,
Heb 8: 5 for Moses, when about to e the tabernacle,

ERECTED (26)

Ex 24: 4 he e at the foot of the mountain an altar
40:17 of the second year the Dwelling was e.
40:18 It was Moses who e the Dwelling.
Nm 9:15 On the day when the Dwelling was e,
10:21 which was to be e before their arrival.
23: 2 said to him, "I have e the seven altars,
Dt 19:14 neighbor's landmarks e by your forefathers
1Sm 15:12 where he e a trophy in his own honor,
2Sm 18:17 very large mound of stones was e over him.
18:18 and e it for himself in the King's Valley,
1Kgs 7:21 then e adjacent to the porch of the temple,
16:32 Ahab e an altar to Baal in the temple of
2Kgs 21: 3 He e altars to Baal,
23:19 Samaria which the kings of Israel had e,
2Chr 33: 3 had torn down, e altars for the Baals,
33:19 he built high places and e sacred poles
34: 4 incense stands e above them were torn down;
Est 5:14 pleased Haman, and he had the gibbet e.
1Mc 1:54 the king e the horrible abomination upon
1:59 the altar e over the altar of holocausts.
13:27 Then Simon e over the tomb of his father
2Mc 10: 2 they destroyed the altars e by the
Sir 49:12 They e the holy temple,
Mt 21:33 around it, dug out a vat, and e a tower.
Mk 12: 1 around it, dug out a vat, and e a tower.
Rv 2:13 the very place where Satan's throne is e;

ERECTING (2)

1Mc 12:36 and for e a high barrier between the
Ez 16:31 and e your dais in every public place!

ERECTION (1)

Nm 7: 1 when Moses had completed the e of the

ERI (2)

Gn 46:16 Zephon, Haggi, Shuni, Ezbon, E,
Nm 26:16 Oznites, through E the clan of the Erites,

ERITES (1)

Nm 26:16 Oznites, through Eri the clan of the E,

ERR (2)

Wis 14:22 for them to e in their knowledge of God;
Is 29:24 e in spirit shall acquire understanding,

ERRAND (10)

Gn 24:21 or not the LORD had made his e successful.
24:40 with you and make your e successful,
24:42 to make successful the e I am engaged on!
24:56 now that the LORD has made my e successful;
Jos 2:14 "If you do not betray this e of ours,
2:20 If, however, you betray this e of ours,
1Sm 9: 6 he can tell us how to accomplish our e."
17:20 with a shepherd, David set out on his e,
Jer 51:59 e given by the prophet Jeremiah to Seraiah,
Lk 19:32 e and found things just as he had said.

ERRATIC (1)

Jas 1: 8 sort, devious and e in all that he does,

ERRED (2)

Jb 6:24 prove to me wherein I have e.
Wis 2:21 These were their thoughts, but they e;

ERRING (6)

Ps(s) 95:10 They are a people of e heart,
Wis 1:12 Court not death by your e way of life,
Sir 25:24 outlet, and be not indulgent to an e wife.
42: 6 Of a seal to keep an e wife at home,
Heb 3:10 I said, 'They have always been of e heart,
5: 2 is able to deal patiently with e sinners,

ERROR (7)

Tb 14: 6 which have deceitfully led them into e,
Wis 12:24 they went far astray in the paths of e,
Sir 11:16 E and darkness were formed with sinners
23:11 If he swears in e, he incurs guilt;
Eph 4:14 in human trickery and skill in proposing e.
2Pt 3:17 you be led astray by the e of the wicked,
Jude 1:11 abandoned themselves to Balaam's e for pay,

ERRORS (1)

2Pt 2:18 who have just come free of a life of e.

ESARHADDON (6)

2Kgs 19:37 His son E reigned in his stead.
Ezr 4: 2 sacrificed to him since the days of E,
Tb 1:21 His son E, who succeeded him as king,
1:22 and E reappointed him.
2: 1 Thus under King E I returned to my home,
Is 37:38 His son E reigned in his stead.

ESAU (89)

Gn 25:25 so they named him E.
25:27 boys grew up, E became a skillful hunter,
25:28 Isaac preferred E, because he was fond
25:29 cooking a stew, E came in from the open,
25:32 "Look," said E, "I'm on the point
25:34 and E ate, drank, got up, and went his way.
25:34 E cared little for his birthright.
26:34 When E was forty years old,
27: 1 he called his older son E and said to him,
27: 5 while Isaac was speaking to his son E.
27: 5 So when E went out into the country to
27: 6 overheard your father tell your brother E,
27:11 "But my brother E is a hairy man,"

ESAU (cont.)

27:15 her older son *E* that she had in the house,
27:19 "I am *E*, your first-born.
27:21 whether you really are my son *E* or not."
27:23 were hairy, like those of his brother *E*;
27:24 he asked him, "Are you really my son *E*?"
27:30 when his brother *E* came back from his hunt.
27:32 "I am *E*," he replied, "your first-born son."
27:34 his father's words, *E* burst into loud,
27:36 carried off your blessing," *E* exclaimed,
27:38 But *E* urged his father,
27:38 and *E* wept aloud.
27:41 *E* bore Jacob a grudge because of the
27:42 news of what her older son *E* had in mind,
27:42 Your brother *E* intends to settle accounts
28: 5 of Rebekah, the mother of Jacob and *E*.
28: 6 *E* noted that Isaac had blessed Jacob when
28: 8 *E* realized how displeasing the Canaanite
32: 4 ahead to his brother *E* in the land of Seir,
32: 5 "Thus shall you say to my lord *E*:
32: 7 they said, "We reached your brother *E*.
32: 9 *E* should attack and overwhelm one camp,"
32:12 me, I pray, from the hand of my brother *E*!
32:14 the following presents for his brother *E*:
32:18 "When my brother *E* meets you,
32:19 have been sent as a gift to my lord *E*;
32:20 "Thus and thus shall you say to *E*,
33: 1 Jacob looked up and saw *E* coming,
33: 4 *E* ran to meet him,
33: 5 When *E* looked about,
33: 8 Then *E* asked,
33: 9 "I have plenty," replied *E*;
33:11 Since he so urged him, *E* accepted.
33:12 Then *E* said,
33:15 *E* replied,
33:16 day that *E* began his journey back to Seir,
35: 1 while you were fleeing from your brother *E*."
35:29 His sons *E* and Jacob buried him.
36: 1 These are the descendants of *E* [that is,
36: 2 *E* took his wives from among the Canaanite
36: 4 Adah bore Eliphaz to *E*;
36: 5 These are the sons of *E* who were born to
36: 6 *E* took his wives,
36: 8 So *E* settled in the highlands of Seir.
36: 8 *E* is Edom.]
36: 9 These are the descendants of *E*,
36:14 whom she bore to *E* were Jeush,
36:19 Such are the descendants of *E* [that is,
36:40 are the names of the clans of *E* individually
36:43 *E* was the father of the Edomites.]
Dt 2: 4 of your kinsmen, the descendants of *E*,
2: 5 *E* possession of the highlands of Seir.
2: 8 where our kinsmen, the descendants of *E*,
2:12 the descendants of *E* dispossessed them,
2:22 done the same for the descendants of *E*,
2:22 so that the descendants of *E* have taken
2:29 as the descendants of *E* who dwell in Seir
Jos 24: 4 To Isaac I gave Jacob and *E*.
24: 4 To *E* I assigned the mountain region of
1Chr 1:34 The sons of Isaac were *E* and Israel.
1:35 The sons of *E* were Eliphaz,
1Mc 5: 3 the sons of *E* at Akrabattene in Idumea,
5:65 sons of *E* in the country toward the south;
Jer 49: 8 upon *E* when I come to punish him.
49:10 So I myself will strip *E*;
Ob 1: 6 How they search *E*,
1: 8 and understanding from the mount of *E*?
1: 9 crushed, till all on Mount *E* are destroyed.
1:18 The house of *E* shall be stubble,
1:18 Then none shall survive of the house of *E*,
1:19 shall occupy the Negeb, the mount of *E*,
1:21 ascend Mount Zion to rule the mount of *E*,
Mal 1: 3 Was not *E* Jacob's brother?
1: 3 yet I loved Jacob, but hated *E*;
Rom 9:13 says, "I have loved Jacob and hated *E*."
Heb 11:20 and *E* blessings that were still to be.
12:16 you no fornicator or godless person like *E*,

ESAU'S (15)

Gn 25:26 His brother came out next, gripping *E* heel;
27:22 the voice is Jacob's, the hands are *E*."
36:10 *E* sons; Eliphaz, son of Esau's wife
36:10 and Reuel, son of *E* wife Basemath.
36:12 *E* son Eliphaz had a concubine Timna,
36:12 These are the descendants of *E* wife Adah.
36:13 are the descendants of *E* wife Basemath.
36:14 The descendants of *E* wife Oholibamah
36:15 following are the clans of *E* descendants.
36:15 The descendants of Eliphaz, *E* first-born:
36:17 The descendants of *E* son Reuel:
36:17 they are descended from *E* wife Basemath.
36:18 The descendants of *E* wife Oholibamah:
36:18 These are the clans of *E* wife Oholibamah,

ESCAPE (92)

Gn 19:20 this town ahead is near enough to *e* to.
19:22 Hurry, *e* there!
31:21 Thus he made his *e* with all that he had.
Lv 26:37 over one another as if to *e* a weapon,
Nm 32:23 will not *e* the consequences of your sin.
Jos 8:20 *E* in any direction was impossible,
10:19 Do not allow them to *e* to their cities,
20: 9 a person accidentally might flee to *e* death
Jgs 3:26 their delay Ehud made good his *e* and,
16:20 good his *e* as he had done time and again,
1Sm 19:12 a window, and he made his *e* in safety.
23:26 David was in anxious flight to *e* Saul,
27: 1 but to *e* to the land of the Philistines;
2Sm 15:14 flight, or none of us will *e* from Absalom.
22:49 to me and helped me *e* from my enemies,
1Kgs 18:40 Let none of them *e*!"
2Kgs 10:24 "If one of you lets anyone *e* of those
10:25 Let no one *e*."
Tb 13: 2 No one can *e* his hand.
Jdt 5: 5 no lie shall *e* your servant's lips.
Est 4:13 palace, you alone of all the Jews will *e*.
E: 4 they suppose they will *e* the vindictive
1Mc 9:45 on the other, and there is no way of *e*.
2Mc 6:22 in this way he would *e* the death penalty,
6:26 alive or dead, *e* the hands of the Almighty.
7:31 for the Hebrews, will not *e* the hands of God.
10:20 they allowed a number of them to *e*.
Jb 11:20 *E* shall be cut off from them,
15:13 God and let such words *e* your mouth!
20:24 Should he *e* the iron weapon,
Ps(s) 33:17 though its strength, it cannot provide *e*.
60: 7 of bowshot That your loved ones may *e*;
88: 9 I am imprisoned, and I cannot *e*.
108: 7 That your loved ones may *e*,
141:10 fall, each into his own net, while I *e*.
142: 5 I have lost all means of *e*;
Prv 11: 9 their knowledge the just make their *e*.
11:21 unpunished, but those who are just shall *e*.
19: 5 and he who utters lies will not *e*.
Eccl 7:26 He who is pleasing to God will *e* her,
Wis 16:15 But your hand none can *e*.
17:10 even the air that they could nowhere *e*.
Sir 6:35 let no wise saying *e* you.
14:14 good things, let no choice portion *e* you.
16:13 A criminal does not *e* with his plunder;
Jer 11:11 upon them misfortune which they cannot *e*.
16:17 from me, nor does their guilt *e* my view.
25:35 no *e* for the leaders of the flock.
32: 4 of Judah, *e* the hands of the Chaldeans;
34: 3 Neither shall you *e* his hand;
35:11 come into Jerusalem to *e* the army
38:18 with fire, and you shall not *e* their hands.
38:23 Chaldeans, and you shall not *e* their hands;
39:18 that you *e* and do not fall by the sword.
42:17 or *e* the evil that I will bring upon them.
44:13 in the land of Egypt shall *e* or survive.
44:28 Those who *e* the sword to return from the
46: 6 The swift cannot flee, nor the hero *e*:
48:19 man who flees, the woman who tries to *e*:
50:29 Encamp around her, let no one *e*.
Lam 3: 7 with no *e* and weighed me down with chains;
Ez 7:16 Even those who *e* and flee to the mountains
12:16 I will leave a few of them to *e* the sword,
17:15 Can he who does such things *e*?
17:18 He shall not *e*!
Dn 11:41 of Ammon, which shall *e* from his power.
11:42 and not even the land of Egypt shall *e*.
12: 1 At that time your people shall *e*,
13:22 if I refuse, I cannot *e* your power.
Jl 2: 3 from them there is no *e*.
Am 2:15 The swift of foot shall not *e*,
3:12 Israelites who dwell in Samaria shall *e*
9: 1 not one shall flee, no survivor shall *e*.
Na 2: 9 Nineveh is like a pool whose waters *e*;
Hb 2: 9 nest on high to *e* the reach of misfortune!
Zec 2:11 Up, *e* to Zion!
Mt 10:22 holds out till the end will *e* death.
23:33 How can you *e* condemnation to Gehenna?
Mk 7:24 however, he could not *e* notice.
Lk 21:21 those in the heart of the city must *e* it;
21:36 the strength to *e* whatever is in prospect,
Acts 25:11 death, I do not seek to *e* that penalty.
27:42 so that none might swim away and *e*;
28: 4 be a murderer if, after his *e* from the sea,
Rom 2: 3 then, that you will *e* his judgment,
13: 5 *e* punishment but also for conscience' sake.
1Thes 5: 3 a woman in labor, and there will be no *e*.
2Tm 2:26 do his will, they shall *e* the devil's trap.
Heb 2: 3 how shall we *e* if we ignore a salvation as
12:25 For if the Israelites did not *e* punishment
Rv 9: 6 will yearn to die but death will *e* them.
12:17 Enraged at her *e*, the dragon went off

ESCAPED (47)

Ex 14:28 Not a single one of them *e*.
Jos 10:20 had *e* from them into the fortified cities,
Jgs 3:29 Not a man *e*.
9: 5 the youngest son of Jerubbaal, Jotham, *e*,
1Sm 5:12 *e* death were afflicted with hemorrhoids,
18:11 David to the wall, but twice David *e* him.]
22:20 named Abiathar, *e* and fled to David.
23:13 was informed that David had *e* from
30:17 that none *e* except four hundred young men,
2Sm 1: 3 "I have *e* from the Israelite camp."
1Kgs 2:15 the kingdom *e* me and became my brother's,
11:40 for his rebellion he *e* to King Shishak,
20:20 king of Aram, *e* on a chariot steed.
1Chr 4:43 the surviving Amalekites who had *e*,
2Chr 16: 7 army of the king of Aram has *e* your hand.
36:20 *e* the sword he carried captive to Babylon,
Tb 1:21 who then *e* into the mountains of Ararat.
2: 8 yet now that he has *e*,
14:10 he *e* from the deadly trap Nadab had set
1Mc 4:26 But those of the foreigners who had *e* went
6:21 Some of the besieged *e*,
7:46 not a single one *e*.
15:37 had gotten aboard a ship and *e* to Orthosia.
2Mc 6:30 well that, although I could have *e* death,
7:35 You have not yet *e* the judgment of
11:12 Lysias himself *e* only by shameful flight.
Jb 1:15 the sword, and I alone have *e* to tell you."
1:16 and I alone have *e* to tell you."
1:17 the sword, and I alone have *e* to tell you."
1:19 and I alone have *e* to tell you."
19:20 I have *e* with my flesh between my teeth.
Ps(s) 22: 6 To you they cried and they *e*;
Wis 15:19 but they have *e* both the approval of God
Jer 31: 2 *e* the sword have found favor in the desert.
41:15 *e* from Johanan and fled to the Ammonites
50:28 fugitives, the *e* from the land of Babylon:
51:50 You who have *e* the sword,
Ez 6: 8 have *e* to other nations from the sword,
6: 9 then those who have *e* will remember me
15: 7 they have *e* from the fire,
33: 5 warning he would have *e* with his life.
Acts 16:27 Thinking that the prisoners had *e*,
2Cor 11:33 a window in the wall and *e* his hands.
Heb 11:31 By faith Rahab the harlot *e* from being
11:34 out raging fires, *e* the devouring sword;
1Pt 3:20 in all, *e* in the ark through the water.
Rv 9:20 That part of mankind which *e* the plagues

ESCAPES (10)

1Kgs 19:17 If anyone *e* the sword of Hazael,
19:17 If he *e* the sword of Jehu,
2Kgs 9:15 one *e* from the city to report in Jezreel."
Ps(s) 19: 7 nothing *e* its heat.
Prv 11: 8 The just man *e* trouble,
Sir 25:17 neighbors, a bitter sigh *e* him unawares.
39:19 not a thing *e* his eye.
42:20 no single thing *e* him.
Jer 48: 8 comes upon every city, not a city *e*;
Acts 26:26 I am convinced that none of this *e* him

ESCAPING (3)

Jb 15:22 He despairs of *e* the darkness,
Acts 28: 3 when a poisonous snake, *e* from the heat,
Gal 6:12 to *e* persecution for the cross of Christ.

ESCORT (8)

2Sm 19:16 to meet him and to *e* him across the Jordan.
19:42 Judahites steal you away and *e* the king
1Kgs 1:33 upon my own mule and *e* him down to Gihon.
Jdt 10:17 of their men as an *e* for her and her maid,
1Mc 9:37 with a large *e* they are bringing the bride,
Acts 16:37 Let them come into the prison and *e* us out."
17:15 Paul was taken as far as Athens by his *e*,
21:16 came along to *e* us to the house of Mnason,

ESCORTED (8)

2Sm 19:32 *e* the king to the Jordan for his crossing,
19:41 the people of Israel had *e* the king across.
1Kgs 1:38 on King David's mule, *e* him to Gihon.
2Mc 4:22 *e* him with torchlights and acclamations;
Mt 25:31 his glory, *e* by all the angels of heaven,
Acts 16:39 then they *e* them out with the request that
20:38 Then they *e* him to the ship.
23:31 and *e* him that night as far as Antipatris.

ESCORTING (1)

2Sm 19:37 In *e* the king across the Jordan,

ESDRAELON (4)

Jdt 1: 8 Upper Galilee, and the vast plain of *E*,
3: 9 reached *E* in the neighborhood of Dothan,
4: 6 Betomesthaim], which is on the way to *E*,
7: 3 from Bethulia to Cyamon, which faces *E*.

ESDRIS (1)

2Mc 12:36 After *E* and his men had been fighting for

ESEK (1)

Gn 26:20 So the well was called *E*,

ESHAN (1)

Jos 15:52 Arab, Dumah, *E*,

ESHBAAL (2)

1Chr 8:33 of Jonathan, Malchishua, Abinadab, and *E*.
9:39 of Jonathan, Malchishua, Abinadab, and *E*.

ESHBAN (2)

Gn 36:26 The descendants of Dishon were Hemdan, *E*,
1Chr 1:41 The sons of Dishon were Hemdan, *E*,

ESHCOL (6)

Gn 14:13 Mamre the Amorite, a kinsman of *E* and
14:24 Aner, *E* and Mamre; let them take their
Nm 13:23 They also reached the Wadi *E*,
13:24 there that they called the place Wadi *E*.
32: 9 to the Wadi *E* and reconnoitered the land,
Dt 1:24 into the hill country as far as the Wadi *E*,

ESHEK (1)

1Chr 8:39 The sons of *E*, his brother,

ESHTAOL (7)

Jos 15:33 *E*, Zorah, Ashnah, Zanoah,
19:41 heritage was the territory of Zorah, *E*,
Jgs 13:25 Mahaneh-dan, which is between Zorah and *E*.
16:31 of his father Manoah between Zorah and *E*.
18: 2 detail of five valiant men of Zorah and *E*,
18: 8 in Zorah and *E* and were asked for a report,
18:11 out from where they were in Zorah and *E*,

ESHTAOLITES (1)

1Chr 2:53 the people of Zorah and the *E* derived.

ESHTEMOA (4)

Jos 21:14 pasture lands, *E* with its pasture lands,
1Sm 30:28 to those in Siphmoth, to those in *E*,
1Chr 4:17 Shammai, and Ishbah, the father of *E*.
6:42 pasture lands, *E* with its pasture lands,

ESHTEMOH (1)

Jos 15:50 Kiriath-sannah (that is, Debir), Anab, *E*,

ESHTON (2)

1Chr 4:11 father of Mehir, who was the father of *E*.
4:12 *E* became the father of Bethrapha,

ESLI (1)

Lk 3:25 son of Amos, son of Nahum, son of *E*,

ESPECIALLY (21)

Gn 21:11 *e* on account of his son Ishmael.
2Kgs 24: 4 *e* because of the innocent blood he shed,
1Mc 14:33 of Judea, *e* the frontier city of Beth-zur,
14:36 *e* those in the City of David in Jerusalem,
2Mc 8: 7 nights as being *e* helpful for such attacks.
9:25 *e* those on the borders of our kingdom,
Ps(s) 19:14 From wanton sin *e*, restrain your servant;
Acts 26: 3 *e* since you are expert in all the various
2Cor 1:12 *e* toward you we have always acted
Gal 6:10 but *e* those of the household of the faith.
Phil 2:28 I have been *e* eager to send him so that
1Tm 2: 2 men, *e* for kings and those in authority,
4:10 of all men, but *e* of those who believe.
5: 8 and *e* for members of his immediate family,
5:17 *e* those whose work is preaching and
2Tm 4:13 Carpus, and the books, *e* the parchments.
Ti 1: 5 *e* the appointment of presbyters in every
1:10 teachers, *e* from among the Jewish converts
Phlm 1:16 a slave, a beloved brother, *e* dear to me;
Heb 13:19 I *e* ask your prayers that I may be
2Pt 2:10 He knows, *e*, how to treat those who live

ESPOUSE (3)

Hos 2:21 *e* you to me forever; I will espouse you
2:22 I will *e* you in fidelity,

ESPOUSED (4)

2Sm 3:14 whom I *e* by paying a hundred Philistine
1Mc 11:60 the forces of Syria *e* his cause as allies.
Is 62: 4 be called "My Delight," and your land *E*."
Lk 2: 5 to register with Mary, his *e* wife,

ESSENTIAL (1)

Sir 38: 1 the physician in honor, for he is *e* to you,

ESTABLISH (37)

Gn 6:18 But with you I will *e* my covenant;
9:11 I will *e* my covenant with you,
17: 2 Between you and me I will *e* my covenant,
Lv 26: 6 I will *e* peace in the land,
Nm 35: 6 the six cities of asylum which you must *e*
Dt 28: 9 will *e* you as a people sacred to himself,
29:12 so that he may now *e* you as his people and
1Sm 2:35 I will *e* a lasting house for him which
13:13 now *e* your kingship in Israel as lasting;
25:28 certainly *e* a lasting dynasty for my lord,
2Sm 3:10 *e* the throne of David over Israel
7:11 to you that he will *e* a house for you.
1Kgs 8:32 but acquit the just and *e* his innocence.
9: 5 I will *e* your throne of sovereignty over
11:38 I will *e* for you, as I did for David,
12:33 chose to *e* a feast for the Israelites;
2Kgs 21: 4 said, "I will *e* my name in Jerusalem"
1Chr 17:11 of your own sons, and I will *e* his kingdom.
17:12 a house, and I will *e* his throne forever.
22:10 and I will *e* the throne of his kingship
28: 7 I will *e* his kingdom forever,
2Chr 7:18 I will *e* your royal throne as I covenanted
31: 7 month that they began to *e* these heaps,
1Mc 8:17 to *e* an alliance of friendship with them.
10:54 let us now *e* friendship with each other.
2Mc 4: 9 if he were given authority to *e* a
4:11 to *e* a treaty of friendship with them);
Ps(s) 89: 5 and *e* your throne for all generations."
Prv 8:15 By me kings reign, and lawgivers *e* justice;
24:27 afterward you can *e* your house.
Jer 49:19 and whom I choose I will *e* there!
50:44 them off, and whom I choose I will *e* there;
Bar 2:35 I will *e* for them, as an eternal covenant,
Lk 12:51 think I have come to *e* peace on the earth?
Rom 10: 3 God's justice and seeking to *e* their own,
Heb 10: 9 away the first covenant to *e* the second.
1Pt 5:10 *e* those who have suffered a little while.

ESTABLISHED (99)

Gn 9:16 I have *e* between God and all living beings
9:17 covenant I have *e* between me and all mortal
Ex 6: 4 I also *e* my covenant with them,
15:17 the sanctuary, O LORD, which your hands *e*.
29:38 lambs as the sacrifice *e* for each day;
29:42 Throughout your generations this *e*
30: 8 be the *e* incense offering before the LORD.
Lv 5:18 ram of the flock of the *e* value.
5:25 ram of the flock of the *e* value.
6:13 of fine flour for the *e* cereal offering,
27:15 pay one fifth more than the price thus *e*,
27:19 pay one fifth more than the price thus *e*,
27:23 *e* shall be given as sacred to the LORD;
Nm 4: 7 *e* bread offering shall remain on the table.
4:16 fragrant incense, the *e* cereal offering,
28: 3 yearling lambs each day as the *e* holocaust,
28: 6 This is the *e* holocaust that was offered
28:10 to the *e* holocaust and its libation.
28:15 to the *e* holocaust and its libation.
28:23 in addition to the *e* morning holocaust;
28:24 to the *e* holocaust with its libation,
28:31 the *e* holocaust with its cereal offering.
29: 6 the *e* holocaust with its cereal offering,
29:11 the *e* holocaust with its cereal offering,
29:16 offered in addition to the *e* holocaust
29:19 besides the *e* holocaust with its cereal
29:22 besides the *e* holocaust with its cereal
29:25 besides the *e* holocaust with its cereal
29:28 besides the *e* holocaust with its cereal
29:31 besides the *e* holocaust with its cereal
29:34 besides the *e* holocaust with its cereal
29:38 besides the *e* holocaust with its cereal
Dt 13:15 If you find that it is true and an *e* fact
17: 4 is true and an *e* fact that this abomination
19:15 a judicial fact shall be *e* only on the
21: 3 it is *e* which city is nearest the corpse,
32: 6 Has he not made you and *e* you?
Jgs 6: 2 *e* the fire signals on the mountains,
21: 9 A roll call of the army *e* that none of the
2Sm 5:12 And David knew that the LORD had *e* him as
7:24 You have *e* for yourself your people Israel
1Kgs 2:12 David, with his sovereignty firmly *e*,
12:32 Jeroboam *e* a feast in the eighth month
1Chr 9:22 seer had *e* them in their position of trust.
16:17 Which he *e* for Jacob by statute,
17:14 and his throne shall be firmly *e* forever."
17:24 David, your servant, is *e* in your presence.
26:16 For each family, watches were *e*.
Ezr 3: 5 Thereafter they offered the *e* holocaust,
Neh 13:30 I *e* the various functions for the priests
Est B: 4 blameleshly designed by us cannot be *e*.
9:27 the Jews *e* and took upon themselves,
9:31 Thus were *e*, for their appointed time,
1Mc 6:48 king *e* camps in Judea and at Mount Zion.
8: 1 They *e* a friendly alliance with all who
10:52 and *e* my rule by crushing Demetrius and
14:18 had *e* with his brothers Judas and Jonathan.
2Mc 4:12 He quickly *e* a gymnasium at the very foot
13: 3 but in the hope of being *e* in office.
14:15 and prayed to him who *e* his people forever,
Ps(s) 24: 2 it upon the seas and *e* it upon the rivers.
78: 5 in Jacob, and *e* it as a law in Israel,
87: 5 And he who has *e* her is the Most High LORD.
89: 3 have said, "My kindness is *e* forever";
99: 4 you have *e* equity; justice and judgment
102:26 Of old you *e* the earth,
103:19 The LORD has *e* his throne in heaven,
105:10 Which he *e* for Jacob by statute,
119:90 you have *e* the earth,
119:152 your decrees, that you have *e* them forever.
148: 6 He *e* them forever and ever;
Prv 3:19 the earth, *e* the heavens by understanding;
8:27 "When he *e* the heavens I was there,
10:25 but the just man is *e* forever.
Wis 9: 2 in your wisdom have *e* man to rule
9: 8 tabernacle which you had *e* from of old.
Sir 38: 1 you, and God it was who *e* his profession.
44: 6 *e* and at peace in their own estates
45: 7 He *e* him in honor and crowned him with
45:14 burnt with the *e* sacrifice twice each day;
46:13 At God's word he *e* the kingdom and
47:11 of royalty and *e* his throne in Israel.
47:13 the name of God, and *e* a lasting sanctuary.
Is 2: 2 mountain of the LORD's house shall be *e*
14:32 "The LORD has *e* Zion,
45:18 designer and maker of the earth who *e* it.
54:14 In justice shall you be *e*,
Jer 10:12 by his power, *e* the world by his wisdom,
51:15 his power, and *e* the world by his wisdom,
Bar 3:32 He who *e* the earth for all time,
Ez 46:14 the LORD is mandatory with the *e* holocaust.
46:15 be offered every morning as an *e* holocaust.
Hos 8: 4 they *e* princes, but without my approval.
Am 9: 6 chamber, and *e* my vault over the earth;
Mi 4: 1 house Shall be *e* higher than the mountains;
Mk 9: 1 until they see the reign of God *e* in power."
Rom 13: 1 and all authority that exists is *e* by God.
2Cor 13: 1 "A judicial fact shall be *e* only on the
Heb 1:10 And, "Lord, of old you *e* the earth,

ESTABLISHES (6)

Ps(s) 113: 9 He *e* in her home the barren wife as the
Sir 10:14 overturns and *e* the lowly in their stead.
Is 42: 4 quench, Until he *e* justice on the earth;
Mi 7: 9 Until he takes up my cause, and *e* my right.
Hb 2:12 by bloodshed, and *e* a town by wickedness!
2Cor 1:21 who firmly *e* us along with you in Christ;

ESTABLISHING (3)

Gn 9: 9 I am now *e* my covenant with you and your
Ex 36: 3 brought for *e* the service of the sanctuary.
Acts 18:28 as he went about *e* from the Scriptures

ESTATE (17)

Lv 25:10 property, every one to his own family *e*.
Ru 4: 5 up a family for the departed on his *e*."
4: 6 my claim lest I depreciate my own *e*.
4:10 up a family for her late husband on his *e*,
2Chr 1:18 and also of a house for his own royal *e*.
2:11 the LORD and also a house for his royal *e*.
Tb 6:12 father's *e* is rightfully yours to inherit.
14:13 *e* as well as that of his father Tobit.
Jdt 16:21 back to Bethulia and remained on her *e*.
Est 1: 4 and the resplendent wealth of his royal *e*.
4: 8 "Remember the days of your lowly *e*."
1Mc 3:43 us restore our people from their ruined *e*,
16: 3 the mercy of Heaven, have come to man's *e*.
Mt 20: 1 God is like the case of the owner of an *e*
Lk 15:12 me the share of the *e* that is coming to me.'
Acts 28: 7 of that place was the *e* of Publius,
Phil 2: 7 He was known to be of human *e*,

ESTATES (3)

1Chr 28: 1 of all the king's *e* and possessions,
1Mc 6:24 they could find and have plundered our *e*.
Sir 44: 6 established and at peace in their own *e*—

ESTEEM (25)

1Sm 9: 6 of God in this city, a man held in high *e*;
15:17 "Though little in your own *e*,
2Sm 6:22 lowly in your *e*, but in the esteem
2Mc 9:21 affection the *e* and good will you bear me.
Jb 12: 5 The undisturbed *e* my downfall a disgrace
14:15 you would *e* the work of your hands.
Prv 3: 4 win favor and good *e* before God and man.
11:16 A gracious woman wins *e*,
22: 1 desirable than great riches, and high *e*,
Wis 3:17 long life, they will be held in no *e*,
8:10 *e* from the elders though I be but a youth.
9: 6 be not with him, he shall be held in no *e*.
Sir 7:16 Do not *e* yourself better than your fellows;
32:10 a storm is the *e* that shines on modesty.
Is 5:21 own sight, and prudent in their own *e*!
53: 3 faces, spurned, and we held him in no *e*.
Dn 14: 2 *e* than any of the friends of the king.
Lk 14:10 will win you the *e* of your fellow guests.
Acts 5:13 fact that the people held them in great *e*.
Rom 14:18 this way pleases God and wins the *e* of men.
2Cor 8:21 approval but also for the good *e* of men.
Phil 2:29 in the Lord and hold men like him in *e*,
1Thes 5:13 *e* them with the greatest love because of
1Pt 2:17 You must *e* the person of every man.

ESTEEMED (9)

2Kgs 5: 1 was highly *e* and respected by his master,
2Mc 4:15 highly prized what the Greeks *e* as glory.
9:19 "To my *e* Jewish citizens,
Prv 16:21 The wise man is *e* for his discernment,
Wis 15:12 Instead, he *e* our life a plaything,
15:15 they *e* all the idols of the nations gods,
Sir 9:17 Skilled artisans are *e* for their deftness;
Lam 1: 8 All who *e* her think her vile now that they
Dn 13:64 onward Daniel was greatly *e* by the people.

ESTEEMS (2)

Jb 41:21 Clubs he *e* as splinters;
Jn 4:44 that no one *e* a prophet in his own country.)

ESTHER (52)

Est 2: 7 was foster father to Hadassah, that is, *E*,
2: 8 *E* also was brought in to the royal palace
2:10 *E* did not reveal her nationality or family,
2:11 *E* was faring and what was to become of her.

ESTHER (cont.)

2:15 As for *E,* daughter of Abihail
2:16 *E* was led to King Ahasuerus in his palace
2:17 The king loved *E* more than all other women,
2:18 of *E* to all his officials and ministers,
2:20 *E* had not revealed her family or
2:20 and *E* continued to follow Mordecai's
2:22 became known to Mordecai, he told Queen *E,*
4: 5 *E* then summoned Hathach,
4: 8 in Susa, to show and explain to *E.*
4: 9 to *E* and told her what Mordecai had said.
4:10 Then *E* replied to Hathach and gave him this
4:15 *E* sent back to Mordecai the response:
C: 1 away and did exactly as *E* had commanded.
C:12 Queen *E,* seized with mortal anguish,
D: 9 "What is it, *E?*"
5: 1 *E* put on her royal garments and stood in
5: 2 He saw Queen *E* standing in the courtyard,
5: 3 king said to her, "What is it, Queen *E?*
5: 4 "If it please your majesty," *E* replied,
5: 5 Haman make haste to fulfill the wish of *E.*"
5: 5 with Haman to the banquet *E* had prepared.
5: 6 drinking of the wine, the king said to *E,*
5: 7 *E* replied: This is my petition
5:12 "Queen *E* invited no one but me to the
6:14 Haman off to the banquet *E* had prepared.
7: 1 Haman went to the banquet with Queen *E.*
7: 2 to *E,* "Whatever you ask, Queen Esther,
7: 3 Queen *E* replied: "If I had found favor
7: 5 where," said King Ahasuerus to Queen *E,*
7: 6 *E* replied, "The enemy oppressing us
7: 7 Haman stayed to beg Queen *E* for his life,
7: 8 on the couch on which *E* was reclining;
8: 1 of Haman, enemy of the Jews, to Queen *E;*
8: 1 for *E* had revealed his relationship to her.
8: 2 and *E* put Mordecai in charge of the house
8: 3 *E* fell at his feet and tearfully implored
8: 4 stretched forth the golden scepter to *E.*
8: 7 said to Queen *E* and to the Jew Mordecai:
8: 7 that I have given *E* the house of Haman,
E:13 savior and constant benefactor, and of *E,*
9:12 reported to the king, he said to Queen *E:*
9:13 So *E* said, "If it pleases your majesty,
9:25 Yet, when *E* entered the royal presence,
9:29 Queen *E,* daughter of Abihail
9:31 and Queen *E* had designated for the Jews,
9:32 The command of *E* confirmed these
11: 3 The river is *E,* whom the king married

ESTHER'S (2)

Est 4: 4 *E* maids and eunuchs came and told her.
4:12 When *E* words were reported to Mordecai,

ESTIMATE (2)

Lv 27:18 the priest shall *e* its money value
Rom 12: 3 Let him *e* himself soberly,

ESTIMATION (2)

1Sm 2:26 in worth in the *e* of the LORD and of men.
Rom 12:16 Do not be wise in your own *e.*

ESTRANGE (1)

1Tm 5:11 *e* them from Christ they will want to marry.

ESTRANGED (8)

Dt 17:17 number of wives, lest his heart be *e,*
17:20 become *e* from his countrymen through pride,
1Mc 11:53 his promises and became *e* from Jonathan.
Jb 19:13 from me, and my friends are wholly *e.*
Jer 6: 8 warned, O Jerusalem, lest I be *e* from you;
Ez 14: 5 become *e* from me through all their idols.
14: 7 any alien resident in Israel is *e* from me,
Eph 4:18 They are *e* from a life in God because of

ESTRANGEMENT (1)

Prv 18: 1 In *e* one seeks pretexts:

ETAM (6)

Jos 15:59 Ephrathah (that is, Bethlehem), Peor, *E,*
Jgs 15: 8 and remained in a cavern of the cliff of *E.*
15:11 in the cliff of *E* and said to Samson,
1Chr 4: 3 the descendants of Hareph, the father of *E:*
4:32 *E,* also, and Ain, Rimmon,
2Chr 11: 6 He built up Bethlehem, *E,*

ETERNAL (81)

Gn 21:33 he invoked by name the LORD, God the *E.*
49:26 mountains, the delights of the *e* hills.
2Sm 23: 5 He has made an *e* covenant with me,
2Mc 1:25 alone are gracious, just, almighty, and *e,*
Ps(s) 55:20 me and will humble them from his *e* throne;
92: 9 They are destined for *e* destruction;
Wis 7:26 For she is the refulgence of *e* light,
10:14 defamed him false, and gave him *e* glory.
17: 2 own roofs as exiles from the *e* providence.
Sir 18: 1 The *E* is the judge of all things without
36:17 ends of the earth that you are the *e* God.
Is 26: 4 For the LORD is an *e* Rock.
30: 8 That it may be in future days an *e* witness:
40:28 The LORD is the *e* God,
56: 5 an *e,* imperishable name will I give them.
63:12 before them, winning for himself *e* renown;
Jer 5:22 which by *e* decree it may not overstep.
10:10 true God, he is the living God, the *e* King,
23:40 I will bring upon you eternal reproach, *e,*
32:40 I will make with them an *e* covenant,
51:57 warriors, so that they sleep an *e* sleep,
Bar 2:35 will establish for them, as an *e* covenant,
4: 8 You forsook the *E* God who nourished you,
4:10 the captivity that the *E* God has brought
4:14 daughters, brought upon them by the *E* God.
4:20 while I live I will cry out to the *E* God.
4:22 have trusted in the *E* God for your welfare,
4:22 will swiftly reach you from your *e* savior.
4:24 great glory and the splendor of the *E* God.
4:35 fire shall come upon her from the *E* God,
5: 2 that displays the glory of the *e* name.
Dn 13:42 "O *e* God, you know what is hidden
Hb 3: 6 The *e* mountains are shattered,
Mt 25:46 *e* punishment and the just to eternal life."
Mk 16:20 and immortal proclamation of *e* salvation.
Jn 3:15 all who believe may have *e* life in him.
3:16 in him may not die but may have *e* life.
3:36 Whoever believes in the Son has life *e.*
4:14 within him, leaping up to provide *e* life."
4:36 his wages and gathers a yield for *e* life,
5:24 faith in him who sent me possesses *e* life.
5:39 in which you think you have *e* life
6:27 but for food that remains unto life *e,*
6:40 Son and believes in him shall have *e* life.
6:47 assure you, he who believes has *e* life.
6:54 *e* and I will raise him up on the last day.
6:68 You have the words of *e* life.
10:28 I give them *e* life,
12:25 life in this world preserves it to life *e.*
12:50 I know that his commandment means *e* life,
17: 2 he may bestow *e* life on those you gave him.
17: 3 *E* life is this:
Rom 1:20 realities, God's *e* power and divinity,
2: 7 *e* life to those who strive for glory,
5:21 reign by way of justice leading to *e* life,
6:22 sanctification as you tend toward *e* life.
6:23 of God is *e* life in Christ Jesus our Lord.
16:26 prophets, and, at the command of the *e* God,
2Cor 4:17 an *e* weight of glory beyond all comparison.
2Thes 1: 9 penalty of *e* ruin apart from the presence
2:16 his mercy gave us *e* consolation and hope,
2Tm 2:10 found in Christ Jesus and with it *e* glory.
Ti 1: 2 in the hope of that *e* life which God,
3: 7 grace and become heirs, in hope, of *e* life.
Heb 5: 9 source of *e* salvation for all who obey him,
6: 2 resurrection of the dead, and *e* judgment.
9:12 his own blood, and achieved *e* redemption.
9:14 who through the *e* spirit offered himself
9:15 may receive the promised *e* inheritance.
13:20 the sheep by the blood of the *e* covenant,
1Jn 1: 1 and we proclaim to you the *e* life that was
2:25 the promise is no less than this: *e* life.
3:15 that *e* life abides in no murder's heart.
5:11 God gave us *e* life,
5:13 make you realize that you possess *e* life
5:20 He is the true God and *e* life.
Jude 1: 7 us, as they undergo a punishment of *e* fire.
1:21 Lord Jesus Christ which leads to life *e.*

ETERNALLY (1)

Is 57:15 says he who is high and exalted, living *e,*

ETERNITY (16)

1Chr 16:36 the LORD, the God of Israel, through all *e!*
29:10 of Israel our father, from *e* to eternity.
Neh 9: 5 the LORD, your God, from eternity to *e!*"
Ps(s) 41:14 the God of Israel, from all *e* and forever.
103:17 eternity to *e* toward those who fear him,
106:48 the LORD, the God of Israel, through all *e!*
Sir 1: 2 seashore, the drops of rain, the days of *e:*
1: 4 and prudent understanding, from *e.*
18: 8 so are these few years among the days of *e.*
42:21 he is from all *e* one and the same,
Is 43:13 I am God, yes, from *e* I am He;
Hb 1:12 Are you not from *e,*
2Pt 3:18 Glory be to him now and to the day of *e!*

ETH-KAZIN (1)

Jos 19:13 eastward to Gath-hepher and to *E,*

ETHAM (4)

Ex 13:20 camped at *E* near the edge of the desert.
Nm 33: 6 camped at *E* near the edge of the desert.
33: 7 Setting out from *E,* they turned back
33: 8 a three days' journey in the desert of *E,*

ETHAN (7)

1Kgs 5:11 than *E* the Ezrahite,
1Chr 2: 6 The sons of Zerah were Zimri, *E,*
2: 8 The sons of *E:*
6:27 son of Zerah, son of Adaiah, son of *E,*
6:29 *E,* son of Kishi, son of Abdi,
15:17 the sons of Merari, their brethren, *E,*
15:19 The chanters, Heman, Asaph, and *E,*

ETHANIM (1)

1Kgs 8: 2 in the month of *E* (the seventh month).

ETHBAAL (1)

1Kgs 16:31 He even married Jezebel, daughter of *E,*

ETHER (2)

Jos 15:42 cities and their villages, Libnah, *E,*
19: 7 Also En-rimmon, *E* and Ashan;

ETHIOPIA (23)

2Kgs 19: 9 heard a report that Tirhakah, king of *E,*
Jdt 1:10 of Egypt as far as the borders of *E.*
Est 1: 1 twenty-seven provinces from India to *E—*
B: 1 twenty-seven provinces from India to *E,*
8: 9 and twenty-seven provinces from India to *E:*
E: 1 twenty-seven satrapies from India to *E,*
Ps(s) 68:32 let *E* extend its hands to God.
87: 4 Of Philistia, Tyre, *E:*
Is 11:11 left from Assyria and Egypt, Pathros, *E,*
18: 1 buzzing insects, beyond the rivers of *E,*
20: 3 as a sign and portent against Egypt and *E,*
20: 4 captives from Egypt, and exiles from *E,*
20: 5 be dismayed and ashamed because of *E,*
37: 9 heard a report that Tirhakah, king of *E,*
43: 3 your ransom, *E* and Seba in return for you.
45:14 The earnings of Egypt, the gain of *E,*
Ez 29:10 to Syene, and even to the frontier of *E.*
30: 4 upon Egypt, and anguish shall be in *E,*
30: 5 *E,* Put, Lud, all Arabia, Libya, and people
30: 9 at my command to terrify unsuspecting *E:*
Dn 11:43 Libya and *E* shall be in his train.
Na 3: 9 *E* was her strength,
Zep 3:10 *E* and as far as the recesses of the North,

ETHIOPIAN (3)

2Chr 14: 8 Zerah the *E* moved against them with
Jer 13:23 Can the *E* change his skin?
Acts 8:27 It happened that an *E* eunuch,

ETHIOPIANS (7)

2Chr 12: 3 Libyans, Sukkites and *E.*
14:11 LORD defeated the *E* before Asa and Judah,
14:12 the *E* fell until there were no survivors,
16: 8 Were not the *E* and Libyans a vast army,
21:16 and of the Arabs who bordered on the *E.*
Am 9: 7 Are you not like the *E* to me,
Acts 8:27 Candace (a name meaning queen) of the *E,*

ETHNAN (1)

1Chr 4: 7 The sons of Helah were Zereth, Izhar, *E,*

ETHNARCH (4)

1Mc 14:47 and *e* of the Jewish people and priests and
15: 1 sea to Simon, the priest and *e* of the Jews,
15: 2 sends greetings to Simon, the priest and *e,*
2Cor 11:32 In Damascus the *e* of King Aretas was

ETHNI (1)

1Chr 6:26 of Baaseiah, son of Malchijah, son of *E,*

EUBULUS (1)

2Tm 4:21 *E,* Pudens, Linus, Claudia, and all

EUMENES (1)

1Mc 8: 8 these from him and gave them to King *E.*

EUNICE (1)

2Tm 1: 5 grandmother Lois and to your mother *E,*

EUNUCH (13)

2Kgs 23:11 near the chamber of Nathan-melech the *e,*
Jdt 12:11 Bagoas, the *e* in charge of his household:
Est 2: 3 Under the care of the royal *e* Hegai,
2:14 under the care of the royal *e* Shaashgaz,
2:15 for anything but what the royal *e* Hegai,
Wis 3:14 also the *e* whose hand wrought no misdeed,
Sir 20: 3 Like a *e* lusting for intimacy with a
Is 56: 3 Nor let the *e* say, "See, I am a dry tree."
Acts 8:27 It happened that an Ethiopian *e,*
8:34 The *e* said to Philip,
8:36 they came to some water, and the *e* said,
8:38 into the water with the *e* and baptized him.
8:39 Philip away and the *e* saw him no more.

EUNUCHS (15)

1Sm 8:15 give the revenue to his *e* and his slaves.
2Kgs 9:32 this two or three *e* looked down toward him.
Est A:12 two *e* of the king who were court guards.
A:14 and the king had the two *e* questioned and,
A:17 people because of the two *e* of the king.
1:10 the seven *e* who attended King Ahasuerus,
1:12 at the royal order issued through the *e.*
1:15 of King Ahasuerus issued through the *e?*"
2:21 of the royal *e* who guarded the entrance,

4: 4 Esther's maids and *e* came and told her.
4: 5 king's *e* whom he had placed at her service,
6: 2 of the royal *e* who guarded the entrance,
6:14 the king's *e* arrived and hurried Haman off
7: 9 one of the *e* who attended the king,
Is 56: 4 To the *e* who observe my sabbaths and

EUPATOR (6)

1Mc 6:17 and he gave him the title *E.*
2Mc 2:20 against Antiochus Epiphanes and his son *E,*
10:10 relate what happened under Antiochus *E,*
10:11 When *E* succeeded to the kingdom,
10:13 was accused before *E* by the King's Friends.
13: 1 *E* was invading Judea with a large force,

EUPHRATES (30)

Gn 2:14 The fourth river is the *E.*
15:18 Wadi of Egypt to the Great River [the *E,*
31:21 Once he was across the *E,*
Nm 22: 5 Balaam, son of Beor, at Pethor on the *E,*
Dt 1: 7 and as far as the Great River [the *E.*
11:24 from the *E* River to the Western Sea,
Jos 1: 4 great river *E* and west to the Great Sea.
2Sm 8: 3 to re-establish his dominion at the *E* River.
10:16 and enlisted Arameans from beyond the *E.*
1Kgs 5: 4 He ruled over all the land west of the *E,*
2Kgs 23:29 toward the river *E* to the king of Assyria.
24: 7 from the Wadi of Egypt to the *E* River.
1Chr 5: 9 the desert which extends from the *E* River,
18: 3 to set up his victory stele at the river *E.*
2Chr 35:20 came up to fight at Carchemish on the *E,*
Jdt 1: 6 region, all who dwelt along the *E,*
2:24 Then following the *E,* he went through
1Mc 3:32 from the *E* River to the frontier of Egypt,
3:37 he crossed the *E* River and advanced inland.
Sir 24:24 It runs over, like the *E,*
39:22 the *E* it enriches the surface of the earth.
Is 11:15 and wave his hand over the *E* in his fierce
27:12 grain between the *E* and the Wadi of Egypt,
Jer 2:18 to Assyria, to drink the waters of the *E?*
46: 2 at Carchemish on the *E* by Nebuchadnezzar,
46: 6 There in the north, on the *E'* bank,
46:10 slaughter feast in the northland, on the *E.*
51:63 tie a stone to it and throw it in the *E.*
Rv 9:14 tied up on the banks of the great river *E!"*
16:12 poured out his bowl on the great river *E.*

EUPOLEMUS (3)

1Mc 8:17 So Judas chose *E,* son of John,
2Mc 4:11 father of *E* (that Eupolemus who would

EUTYCHUS (1)

Acts 20: 9 and a certain young lad named *E* who was

EVACUATED (2)

1Mc 6:49 the men of Beth-zur, and they *e* the city,
6:61 on these terms they *e* the fortification.

EVALUATING (1)

2Sm 14:17 is like an angel of God, *e* good and bad.

EVANGELIST (2)

Acts 21: 8 There we entered the home of Philip the *e,*
2Tm 4: 5 with hardship, perform your work as an *e,*

EVANGELISTS (1)

Eph 4:11 It is he who gave apostles, prophets, *e,*

EVANGELIZING (1)

Phil 4:15 Philippians, that at the start of my *e,*

EVAPORATED (1)

Ex 16:14 all about the camp, and when the dew *e,*

EVE (7)

Gn 3:20 The man called his wife *E,*
4: 1 The man had relations with his wife *E,*
Tb 8: 6 him his wife *E* to be his help and support;
2Mc 15:36 Adar in Aramaic, the *e* of Mordecai's Day.
Mk 15:42 Day, that is, the *e* of the sabbath),
2Cor 11: 3 as the serpent seduced *E* by his cunning,
1Tm 2:13 For Adam was created first, *E* afterward;

EVENING (146)

Gn 1: 5 Thus *e* came,
1: 8 *E* came, and morning followed—the second
1:13 *E* came, and morning followed—the third
1:19 *E* came, and morning followed—the fourth
1:23 *E* came, and morning followed—the fifth
1:31 *E* came, and morning followed—the sixth
8:11 In the *e* the dove came back to him,
19: 1 The two angels reached Sodom in the *e,*
24:11 Near *e,* at the time when women go out
24:63 One day toward *e* he went out . . .
30:16 That *e,* when Jacob came home
Ex 12: 6 shall be slaughtered during the *e* twilight.
12:18 From the *e* of the fourteenth day of the
12:18 until the *e* of the twenty-first day
16: 6 "At *e* you will know that it was the LORD
16: 8 the LORD gives you flesh to eat in the *e,"*
16:12 In the *e* twilight you shall eat flesh,
16:13 the *e* quail came up and covered the camp.
18:13 who waited about him from morning until *e.*
18:14 to stand about you from morning till *e?"*
27:21 From *e* to morning Aaron and his sons shall
29:39 and the other lamb at the *e* twilight.
29:41 lamb you shall offer at the *e* twilight,
30: 8 the lamps, and again in the *e* twilight,
Lv 6:13 half in the morning and half in the *e.*
11:24 dead bodies shall be unclean until *e,*
11:25 wash his garments and be unclean until *e.*
11:27 dead bodies shall be unclean until *e,*
11:28 wash his garments and be unclean until *e.*
11:31 they are dead shall be unclean until *e.*
11:32 be put in water and remain unclean until *e,*
11:39 its dead body shall be unclean until *e.*
11:40 wash his garments and be unclean until *e;*
14:46 it is quarantined shall be unclean until *e.*
15: 5 bathe in water, and be unclean until *e.*
15: 6 bathe in water, and be unclean until *e.*
15: 7 bathe in water, and be unclean until *e.*
15: 8 bathe in water, and be unclean until *e.*
15:10 was under him shall be unclean until *e;*
15:10 bathe in water, and be unclean until *e.*
15:11 bathe in water, and be unclean until *e.*
15:16 whole body in water and be unclean until *e.*
15:17 washed with water and be unclean until *e.*
15:18 both bathe in water and be unclean until *e.*
15:19 who touches her shall be unclean until *e.*
15:21 bathe in water, and be unclean until *e.*
15:22 bathe in water, and be unclean until *e.*
15:23 he touches it, he shall be unclean until *e.*
15:27 bathe in water, and be unclean until *e.*
17:15 bathe in water, and be unclean until *e,*
22: 6 shall be unclean until *e* and may not eat
23: 5 day of the first month, at the *e* twilight.
23:32 on the *e* of the ninth of the month,
23:32 this sabbath of yours from evening to *e."*
24: 3 the LORD regularly, from *e* till morning.
Nm 9: 3 The *e* twilight of the fourteenth day of
9: 5 during the *e* twilight of the fourteenth day
9:11 during the *e* twilight of the fourteenth
9:15 but from *e* until morning it took on the
9:21 remained there only from *e* until morning;
19: 7 He remains unclean until the *e,*
19: 8 his body in water, and be unclean until *e.*
19:10 wash his garments and be unclean until *e.*
19:19 water, and in the *e* he will be clean again.
19:21 with this water shall be unclean until *e.*
19:22 who touches it becomes unclean until *e."*
28: 4 and the other during the *e* twilight,
28: 8 lamb, to be offered during the *e* twilight,
Dt 16: 4 meat which you sacrificed on the *e*
16: 6 place of his name, and in the *e* at sunset,
23:12 the camp, and not return until, toward *e,*
28:67 you will say, 'Would that it were *e!'*
28:67 and in the *e* you will say,
Jos 5:10 on the *e* of the fourteenth of the month.
7: 6 before the ark of the LORD until *e;*
8:29 the king of Ai hanged on a tree until *e;*
10:26 trees, where they remained hanging until *e.*
Jgs 19:16 In the *e,* however, an old man came
20:22 went up and wept before the LORD until *e.*
20:26 before the LORD until *e* of that day,
21: 2 and remained there before God until *e,*
Ru 2:17 She gleaned in the field until *e,*
3: 2 This *e* he will be winnowing barley at the
1Sm 14:24 be the man who takes food before *e,*
17:16 his stand morning and *e* for forty days.
20: 5 me go and hide in the open country until *e.*
2Sm 1:12 until *e* for Saul and his son Jonathan,
11: 2 One *e* David rose from his siesta and
11:13 But in the *e* he went out to sleep on his
1Kgs 17: 6 the morning, and bread and meat in the *e,*
22:35 chariot facing the Arameans, died in the *e.*
2Kgs 16:15 holocaust and the *e* cereal-offering,
1Chr 16:40 of holocausts regularly, morning and *e,*
23:30 to praise the LORD, and likewise in the *e;*
2Chr 2: 3 showbread, for holocausts morning and *e,*
13:11 morning after morning and *e* after evening;
13:11 the golden lampstand burn evening after *e;*
18:34 on his chariot facing the Arameans until *e.*
31: 3 of morning and *e* and those on sabbaths,
Ezr 3: 3 to the LORD on it, both morning and *e.*
9: 4 remained motionless until the *e* sacrifice.
9: 5 Then, at the time of the *e* sacrifice,
Jdt 9: 1 in the temple of God in Jerusalem that *e,*
12: 9 until her food was brought to her toward *e.*
Est 2:14 She would go in the *e* and return in the
1Mc 9:13 and the battle raged from morning until *e.*
10:80 until *e* they showered his men with arrows.
Jb 4:20 Morning or *e* they may be shattered;
Ps(s) 55:18 In the *e,* and at dawn,
59: 7 Each *e* they return, they snarl
59:15 Each *e* they return, they snarl like dogs
90: 6 springs up anew, but by *e* wilts and fades.
104:23 to his work and to his tillage till the *e.*
141: 2 up of my hands, like the *e* sacrifice.
Eccl 11: 6 seed, and at *e* let not your hand be idle:
Sir 18:26 Between morning and *e* the weather changes;
Is 17:14 In the *e,* they spread terror,
Jer 6: 4 the day is waning, *e* shadows lengthen;
Ez 12: 4 in the *e,* again while they are looking on,
12: 7 and at *e* I dug a hole through the wall
24:18 That *e* my wife died,
33:22 upon me the *e* before the fugitive arrived,
46: 2 the gate shall not be closed until *e.*
Dn 9:21 flight at the time of the *e* sacrifice.
Hb 1: 8 his horses, and keener than wolves at *e.*
Zep 2: 7 at *e* they shall couch their flocks,
Zec 14: 7 for in the *e* time there shall be light.
Mt 8:16 As *e* drew on, they brought him many
14:15 As *e* drew on, his disciples came to him
14:24 pray, remaining there alone as *e* drew on.
16: 2 ["In the *e* you say, 'Red sky at night,
20: 8 When *e* came the owner of the vineyard said
27:57 When *e* fell, a wealthy man
Mk 1:32 After sunset, as *e* drew on,
4:35 That day as *e* drew on he said to them,
6:47 As *e* drew on, the boat was far out
11:19 When *e* drew on, Jesus and his disciples
Lk 24:29 It is nearly *e*— the day is practically over."
Jn 6:16 As *e* drew on, his disciples came down
20:19 On the *e* of that first day of the week,
Acts 4: 3 It was *e* by now, so they arrested them
28:23 morning to *e* he laid the case before them,

EVENINGS (3)

Gn 49:27 the prey, and *e* he distributes the spoils."
Dn 8:14 two thousand three hundred *e* and mornings;
8:26 vision of the *e* and the mornings is true,

EVENLY (2)

Nm 31:27 then divide them *e,* giving half to those
1Kgs 6:35 flowers, over which gold was *e* applied.

EVENT (6)

Dt 19: 9 in the *e* that you carefully observe all these
1Kgs 13:33 not give up his evil ways after this *e,*
2Mc 1:33 When the *e* became known and the king of
Lk 2:15 this *e* which the Lord has made known to us."
Jn 11:15 In any *e,* let us go to him."
Acts 1:19 This *e* came to be known by the inhabitants

EVENTS (27)

Gn 15: 1 Some time after these *e,* this word
22: 1 Some time after these *e,* God put
Jos 24:29 After these *e,* Joshua, son of Nun,
1Chr 4:22 [These are *e* of old.]
29:30 and of the *e* that affected him and all
2Chr 10:15 for this turn of *e* was divinely ordained
21:18 After these *e,* the LORD afflicted him
Ezr 7: 1 After these *e,* during the reign
Jdt 9: 5 *e* and of what preceded and followed them.
Est 3: 1 After these *e* King Ahasuerus raised Haman,
6: 1 the chronicle of notable *e* be brought in.
9:20 these *e* and sent letters to all the Jews,
1Mc 3:27 When Antiochus heard about these *e,*
5:37 After these *e* Timothy assembled another
10:88 When King Alexander heard of these *e,*
Eccl 7:18 he who fears God will win through at all *e.*
Wis 11:14 but in the end of *e,* they marveled
Is 43:18 Remember not the *e* of the past,
44: 7 Who of old announced future *e?*
48: 6 to you, hidden *e* of which you knew not.
Dn 8:13 "How long shall the *e* of this vision last
Mk 6:52 completely closed to the meaning of the *e.*
Lk 1: 1 *e* which have been fulfilled in our midst,
1: 2 precisely as those *e* were transmitted to
1: 3 the whole sequence of *e* from the beginning,
Jn 19:36 These *e* took place for the fulfillment of
Acts 3:24 onward, have announced the *e* of these days.

EVENTUALLY (7)

Prv 19:20 instruction, that you may *e* become wise.
Mt 13:33 *E* the whole mass of dough began to rise."
Lk 16:22 *E,* the beggar died.
Acts 11:22 News of this *e* reached the ears of the
17:27 to grope for him and perhaps *e* to find him
18:18 but *e* he took leave of the brothers and
28:10 and when we *e* set sail they brought us

EVER (207)

Gn 6: 5 heart conceived was *e* anything but evil,
8:21 I *e* again strike down all living beings,
16: 5 *e* since she became aware of her pregnancy,
21:26 about it, nor did I *e* hear of it until now."
31:38 no ewe or she-goat of yours *e* miscarried,
Ex 5:23 *E* since I went to Pharaoh to speak in your
10:10 "if I *e* let your little ones go with you!
10:14 swarm of locusts, nor will there *e* be.
11: 6 as has never been, nor will *e* be again.
13: 9 the law of the LORD will *e* be on your lips,
13:22 *e* left its place in front of the people.
15:18 The LORD shall reign forever and *e.*
17: 3 "Why did you *e* make us leave Egypt?
22:22 If *e* you wrong them and they cry out to me,
32:21 "What did this people *e* do to you that
Lv 26:12 *E* present in your midst,
Nm 9:23 *e* heeding the charge of the LORD,

EVER (cont.)

11:20 you have wailed, 'Why did we *e* leave Egypt?'
19: 2 and on which no yoke has *e* been laid.
23:10 Who has *e* counted the dust of Jacob,
32:11 come up from Egypt shall *e* see this country
Dt 4:32 *e* since God created man upon the earth;
4:32 Did anything so great *e* happen before?
4:32 Was it *e* heard of?
4:33 Did a people *e* hear the voice of God
9:24 *E* since I have known you,
19: 9 LORD, your God, and *e* walking in his ways:
23: 4 No Ammonite or Moabite may *e* be admitted
Jos 7: 7 "why did you *e* allow this people to pass
23:12 For if you *e* abandon him and ally
Jgs 4:24 their power weighed *e* heavier upon him,
11:25 Did he *e* quarrel with Israel,
Ru 2: 7 and *e* since she came this morning she has
2:20 who is *e* merciful to the living and to the
1Sm 1:11 drink, and no razor shall *e* touch his head."
3:14 or offering will *e* expiate its crime."
18:29 all the more [and was his enemy *e* after].
20: 9 If *e* I find out that my father is
2Sm 7: 7 did I *e* utter word to any one of the
13:32 this *e* since Amnon shamed his sister Tamar.
15: 8 'If the LORD *e* brings me back to Jerusalem,
1Kgs 9: 6 and your descendants *e* withdraw from me,
22:28 Micaiah said, "If *e* you return in safety,
2Kgs 18:33 Has any of the gods of the nations *e*
18:35 lands *e* rescued his land from my hand?
1Chr 17: 6 Did I *e* say a word to any of the judges of
17: 9 nor shall wicked men *e* again oppress them,
21:12 with the sword of your foes *e* at your back;
2Chr 9:19 had *e* been produced in any other kingdom.
18:27 Micaiah said, "If *e* you return in safety,
20:26 *e* since been called the Valley of Beracah.
Neh 13: 1 may *e* be admitted into the assembly of God;
Tb 5:18 cling, *e* there with us in all that we do?
6: 8 and no demons will *e* return to him again.
7:11 She is yours today and *e* after.
8: 5 praised be your name forever and *e*.
10: 7 do not believe they will *e* see me again.
14:15 and he blessed the Lord God forever and *e*.
Jdt 12:18 I *e* enjoyed life as much as I do today."
12:20 had *e* drunk on one single day in his life.
15:10 blessed by the Lord Almighty forever and *e*!"
1Mc 8:11 that had *e* opposed them they destroyed
10:16 "Shall we *e* find another man like him?
11:36 of these provisions shall *e* be revoked.
2Mc 13:10 night and day, to help them now, if *e*,
15:30 who was *e* in body and soul the chief
Jb 15:22 the darkness, and looks *e* for the sword;
38:12 Have you *e* in your lifetime commanded the
Ps(s) 9: 6 their name you blotted out forever and *e*.
10:16 The LORD is king forever and *e*;
16: 8 I set the LORD *e* before me;
21: 5 you gave him length of days forever and *e*.
22:27 "May your hearts be *e* merry!"
25:15 My eyes are *e* toward the LORD,
34: 2 his praise shall be *e* in my mouth.
35:27 And may they *e* say, "The LORD be
40:12 your kindness and your truth *e* preserve me.
40:17 may those who love your salvation say *e*,
45: 7 Your throne, O God, stands forever and *e*;
45:18 shall nations praise you forever and *e*.
48:15 that such is God, Our God forever and *e*;
52:10 Trust in the kindness of God forever and *e*.
70: 5 may those who love your salvation say *e*,
71:14 always hope and praise you *e* more and more.
85: 6 Will you be *e* angry with us,
111: 8 all his precepts, Reliable forever and *e*,
119:44 keep your law continually, forever and *e*.
119:98 wiser than my enemies, for it is *e* with me.
119:117 may be safe and *e* delight in your statutes.
145: 1 and I will bless your name forever and *e*.
145: 2 and I will praise your name forever and *e*.
145:21 flesh bless his holy name forever and *e*.
148: 6 He established them forever and *e*;
Eccl 3:11 their hearts, without men's *e* discovering,
Wis 9:17 Or who *e* knew your counsel,
14:31 retribution of sinners *e* follows upon
Sir 13:16 Is a wolf *e* allied with a lamb?
14: 7 If *e* he is generous, it is by mistake;
16:25 grow weary, nor *e* cease from their tasks.
16:26 ever crowd its neighbor, nor should they *e*
17:13 Their ways are *e* known to him,
17:15 sun to him, his eyes are *e* upon their ways.
20:25 to dishonor, his shame remains *e* with him.
26: 4 is content, and a smile is *e* on his face.
27:11 *E* wise are the discourses of the devout,
31: 4 a meager subsistence, and if *e* he rests,
34: 4 can the liar *e* speak the truth?
34:11 travels, learned more than *e* I could say.
35: 6 most pleasing, nor will it *e* be forgotten.
36:16 for you are *e* gracious to your people;
42:25 can one *e* see enough of their splendor?
43:13 nor may they *e* be worn by any Except his
45:26 Lest their welfare should *e* be forgotten,
46:11 may their memory be *e* blessed,
49:15 Was *e* a man born like JOSEPH?
51:11 I will *e* praise your name and be constant
Is 25: 2 is a city no more, nor *e* to be rebuilt.
29:19 The lowly will *e* find joy in the LORD,
36:18 Has any of the gods of the nations *e*
36:20 lands *e* rescued his land from my hand?
49:16 your walls are *e* before me.
64: 3 No ear has *e* heard, no eye ever seen,
66: 8 Who *e* heard of such a thing,
Jer 6: 7 *e* before me are wounds and blows.
18:13 who has *e* heard the like?
19: 5 nor spoke of, nor did it *e* enter my mine.
31:36 If *e* these natural laws give way in spite
33:18 nor shall priests of Levi *e* be lacking,
35: 6 you nor your children shall *e* drink wine.
Lam 2:20 whom have you *e* treated thus?
4:17 Our eyes *e* wasted away,
Ez 12:22 on, and no vision *e* comes to anything"?
27:32 Who was *e* destroyed like Tyre in the midst
44: 9 and in flesh, shall *e* enter my sanctuary;
Dn 2:20 "Blessed be the name of God forever and *e*,
7:18 the kingship, to possess it forever and *e*."
9:12 calamity that has *e* occurred under heaven.
Hos 12: 2 chases the wind, *e* pursuing the gale.
Jon 1:13 not, for the sea grew *e* more turbulent.
Mi 4: 5 name of the LORD, our God, forever and *e*.
Na 1:12 LORD, be they *e* so many and so vigorous,
Mt 7:16 Do you *e* pick grapes from thornbushes,
9:33 like this has *e* been seen in Israel!"
15:33 "How could we *e* get enough bread in this
16:22 forbid that any such thing *e* happen to you!"
18:14 of these little ones shall *e* come to grief.
Lk 1:54 Israel his servant, *e* mindful of his mercy;
10:19 the enemy, and nothing shall *e* injure you.
Jn 1:18 No one has *e* seen God.
1:18 God the only Son, *e* at the Father's side,
4:29 see someone who told me everything I *e* did!
4:39 "He told me everything I *e* did."
6:35 No one who comes to me shall *e* be hungry,
6:35 no one who believes in me shall *e* thirst.
6:37 no one who comes will I *e* reject,
7:46 "No man *e* spoke like that before,"
8:12 follower of mine shall *e* walk in darkness;
9:32 *e* gave sight to a person blind from birth.
15:24 among them as no one has *e* done before,
19: 8 kind of talk, he was more afraid than *e*.
19:41 new tomb in which no one had *e* been buried.
Acts 2:25 'I have set the Lord *e* before me,
4:32 None of them *e* claimed anything as his own;
5: 4 How could you *e* concoct such a scheme?
7:52 Was there *e* any prophet whom your fathers
8:33 justice, Who will *e* speak of his posterity,
11: 8 unclean or impure has *e* entered my mouth!'
20:25 the kingdom will *e* see my face again.
1Cor 12: 3 who speaks in the Spirit of God *e* says,
2Cor 5:13 if we are *e* caught up out of ourselves,
7:14 as everything I *e* said to you was true,
8:22 He is now more eager than *e* for this work
12:17 Did I *e* take advantage of you through any
Eph 5:29 Observe that no one *e* hates his own flesh;
Col 1: 9 *E* since we heard this we have been praying
2: 7 up in him, growing *e* stronger in faith,
1Tm 1:17 only God, be honor and glory forever and *e*!
6:16 whom no human being has *e* seen or can see.
2Tm 4:18 To him be glory forever and *e*.
Ti 1:12 has testified, "Cretans have *e* been liars,
Heb 1: 5 To which of the angels did God *e* say,
1: 8 throne, O God, stands forever and *e*;
1:13 To which of the angels has God *e* said,
7:13 of whose members *e* officiated at the altar.
1Pt 3:15 this hope of yours, be *e* ready to reply,
1Jn 4:12 No one has *e* seen God.
Jude 1: 2 and love be yours in *e* greater measure.
Rv 1: 6 to him be glory and power forever and *e*!
1:18 was dead but now I live—forever and *e*.
2:19 efforts of recent times are greater than *e*.
4: 9 on the throne, who lives forever and *e*,
4:10 and worship him who lives forever and *e*.
5:13 and honor, glory and might, forever and *e*!"
7:12 power and might, to our God forever and *e*.
10: 6 oath by the One who lives forever and *e*,
11:15 One, and he shall reign forever and *e*."
14:10 of their torment shall rise forever and *e*.
15: 7 wrath of the God who lives forever and *e*.
18:22 trumpeters, shall *e* again be heard in you!
18:22 in any trade shall *e* again be found in you!
18:22 millstone shall *e* again be heard in you!
18:23 lamp shall *e* again be seen in you!
18:23 and groom shall *e* again be heard in you!
19: 3 began to rise from her forever and *e*,
20:10 be tortured day and night, forever and *e*.

EVER-GROWING (1)

Phil 4:17 is for the *e* balance in your account.

EVER-PRESENT (1)

Ps(s) 46: 2 and our strength, an *e* help in distress.

EVERFLOWING (1)

Dt 21: 4 bringing it down to a wadi with an *e* stream

EVERLASTING (72)

Gn 9:16 I will see it and recall the *e* covenant
17: 7 after you throughout the ages as an *e* pact,
17:13 shall be in your flesh as an *e* pact.
17:19 maintain my covenant with him as an *e* pact,
49:26 blossoms, The blessings of the *e* mountains,
Ex 31:17 and the Israelites it is to be an *e* token;
Lv 16:29 "This shall be an *e* ordinance for you:
16:31 by *e* ordinance it shall be a most solemn
16:34 then, shall be an *e* ordinance for you:
17: 7 *e* ordinance for them and their descendants.
24: 8 part of the Israelites by an *e* agreement.
Nm 25:13 after him the pledge of an *e* priesthood,
Jos 8:28 fire, reducing it to an *e* mound of ruins,
1Chr 16:17 by statute, for Israel as an *e* covenant,
Tb 3: 6 let me go to the *e* abode;
14:10 light, but Nadab went into the *e* darkness,
Jdt 13:20 May God make this redound to your *e* honor,
1Mc 2:51 you shall win great glory and an *e* name.
2:54 received the covenant of an *e* priesthood.
2:57 as a heritage a throne of *e* royalty.
6:44 his people and win an *e* name for himself.
2Mc 7:20 and worthy of *e* remembrance was the mother,
Ps(s) 76: 5 came, O powerful One, from the *e* mountains.
78:66 to flight and cast them into *e* disgrace.
90: 2 forth, from everlasting to *e* you are God.
93: 2 from *e* you are, O LORD
105:10 by statute, for Israel as an *e* covenant,
112: 6 the just man shall be in *e* remembrance.
119:142 Your justice is *e* justice,
119:160 each of your just ordinances is *e*.
Wis 8:13 and leave to those after me an *e* memory.
Sir 15: 6 gladness he will find, an *e* name inherit.
17:10 An *e* covenant he has made with them,
49:12 the holy temple, destined for *e* glory.
Is 33:14 who of us can live with the *e* flames?"
35:10 and enter Zion singing, crowned with *e* joy;
51:11 and enter Zion singing, crowned with *e* joy;
55: 3 I will renew with you the *e* covenant,
55:13 the LORD'S renown, an *e* imperishable sign.
61: 7 in their land, *e* joy shall be theirs.
Jer 25: 9 of horror, of ridicule, of *e* reproach.
25:12 Their land I will turn into *e* desert.
50: 5 join ourselves to the LORD with covenant *e*,
51:62 in it, since it would remain an *e* desert."
Ez 16:60 and I will set up an *e* covenant with you.
26:20 dwell in the nether lands, in the *e* ruins,
36: 2 the *e* heights have become our possession"
37:26 it shall be an *e* covenant with them,
Dn 3:100 his kingdom is an *e* kingdom,
4:31 His dominion is an *e* dominion,
7:14 an *e* dominion that shall not be taken away,
7:27 of the Most High, Whose kingdom shall be *e*:
9:24 be expiated, *E* justice will be introduced,
12: 2 others shall be an *e* horror and disgrace.
Mt 19:16 what good must I do to possess *e* life?"
19:29 many times as much and inherit *e* life.
25:41 into that *e* fire prepared for the devil
Mk 10:17 Teacher, what must I do to share in *e* life?"
10:30 and in the age to come, *e* life.
Lk 10:25 what must I do to inherit *e* life?"
18:18 teacher, what must I do to share in *e* life?"
18:30 in this age and life *e* in the age to come."
Acts 13:46 convict yourselves as unworthy of *e* life,
13:48 were destined for life *e* believed in it.
Gal 6: 8 is the spirit, he will reap *e* life.
1Tm 1:16 later have faith in him and gain *e* life.
6:12 the *e* life to which you were called when,
6:16 To him be honor and *e* rule!
1Pt 5:10 who called you to his *e* glory in Christ,
2Pt 1:11 your entry into the *e* kingdom of our Lord
Rv 14: 6 herald of *e* good news to the whole world,

EVERY (798)

Gn 1:11 every kind of plant that bears seed and *e*
1:12 *e* kind of plant that bears seed and *e* kind
1:29 I give you *e* seed-bearing plant all over
1:29 *e* tree that has seed-bearing fruit
7: 2 Of *e* clean animal, take with you seven
7: 3 likewise, of *e* clean bird of the air,
7: 4 earth *e* moving creature that I have made."
7:14 *e* kind of wild beast, *e* kind of domestic
7:14 *e* kind of creeping thing of the earth,
7:14 thing of the earth, *e* kind of bird.
7:23 The LORD wiped out *e* living thing on earth:
8:17 with you *e* living thing that is with you
8:20 from every clean animal and *e* clean bird,
9: 3 *E* creature that is alive shall be yours to
9: 5 from *e* animal I will demand it,
9:10 with *e* living creature that was with you:
9:12 me and you and *e* living creature with you:
17:10 *e* male among you shall be circumcised.
17:12 Throughout the ages, *e* male among you,
17:23 acquired with his money *e* male among
20:18 for God had tightly closed *e* womb in
24: 1 age, and the LORD had blessed him in *e* way.
30:32 *e* dark animal among the sheep and every
34:15 us by having *e* male among you circumcised.
34:22 that *e* male among us be circumcised as
34:24 *e* able-bodied man in the community,
47:20 them to bear, *e* Egyptian sold his field;
Ex 1:22 river *e* boy that is born to the Hebrews,
3:22 *E* woman shall ask her neighbor and her
9:22 and *e* growing thing in the land of Egypt."
9:25 It struck down *e* man and beast that was in
9:25 *e* growing thing and splintered every tree

10:14 of Egypt and settled down on *e* part of it.
11: 2 *e* man is to ask his neighbor, and *e* woman
11: 5 *E* first-born in this land shall die,
12: 3 On the tenth of this month *e* one of your
12: 7 *e* house in which they partake of the lamb.
12:12 striking down *e* first-born of the land,
12:29 slew *e* first-born in the land of Egypt,
13: 2 "Consecrate to me *e* first-born that opens
13:12 to the LORD *e* son that opens the womb;
13:13 *E* first-born of an ass you shall redeem
13:13 *E* first-born son you must redeem.
13:15 killed *e* first-born in the land of Egypt,
13:15 of Egypt, *e* first-born of man and of beast.
13:15 and why I redeem *e* first-born of my sons.'
22: 8 In *e* question of dishonest appropriation,
23:27 I will throw into panic *e* nation you reach.
25: 2 From *e* man you shall accept the
31: 3 and understanding and knowledge in *e* craft:
31: 5 stones, in carving wood, and in *e* craft.
32:27 Put your sword on your hip, *e* one of you!
33:16 out from *e* other people on the earth."
34:19 "To me belongs *e* first-born male that
35:10 "Let *e* expert among you come and make all
35:29 *E* Israelite man and woman brought to the
35:31 and understanding and knowledge in *e* craft:
35:33 in carving wood, and in *e* other craft.
38:26 was received from *e* man of twenty years or
Lv 2:11 *E* cereal offering that you present to the
2:13 *e* cereal offering that you present to the
2:13 On *e* offering you shall offer salt.
6: 5 *E* morning the priest shall put firewood on
6:16 *E* cereal offering of a priest shall be a
7: 9 *e* cereal offering that is baked in an oven
7:27 *E* person who partakes of any blood shall
11:12 *E* water creature that lacks fins or scales
14:54 law for *e* kind of human leprosy and scall,
15: 2 *E* man who is afflicted with a chronic flow
15:12 and *e* wooden article shall be rinsed with
15:24 *e* bed on which he then lies also becomes
17:14 the life of *e* living body is its blood,
23:42 During this week *e* native Israelite among
25:10 when *e* one of you shall return to his own
25:10 property, *e* one to his own family estate.
25:13 *e* one of you shall return to his own
25:24 in *e* part of the country that you occupy,
27: 9 that may be sacrificed, *e* such animal,
27:25 *E* valuation shall be made according to the
27:32 ceding to the LORD as sacred *e* tenth animal
Nm 1:18 *E* man of twenty years or more then
2:17 march, *e* man shall be in his proper place,
2:34 *e* man according to his clan and his
3:12 of *e* first-born that opens the womb
3:13 are mine, because *e* first-born is mine.
3:15 registering *e* male of a month or more."
5: 2 the Israelites to expel from camp *e* leper,
5: 9 *e* sacred contribution that the Israelites
7: 3 every two princes, and an ox for *e* prince.
8:16 taken them for myself in place of *e* first-born
17:28 *E* time anyone approaches the Dwelling of
18:10 *e* male among you may partake of them.
18:11 gift in *e* wave offering of the Israelites;
18:15 *E* living thing that opens the womb,
19: 2 heifer that is free from *e* blemish and defect
19:15 likewise, *e* vessel that is open,
28:14 moon holocaust for *e* new moon of the year.
31: 7 Moses, and killed *e* male among them.
31:17 *e* male child and every woman who has had
31:20 You shall also purify *e* article of cloth,
31:28 one out of *e* five hundred persons,
31:30 you shall take one out of *e* fifty persons,
31:47 LORD had ordered, took one out of *e* fifty,
32:18 We will not return to our homes until *e*
32:22 of *e* obligation to the LORD and to Israel,
36: 8 *e* daughter who inherits property in any of
Dt 2:25 of you into *e* nation under the heavens,
8: 3 but by *e* word that comes forth from the
11: 6 and *e* living thing that belonged to them.
11:24 *E* place where you set foot shall be yours:
12: 2 without fail *e* place on the high mountains,
12: 2 and under *e* leafy tree where the nations
12:11 and *e* special offering you have vowed to
12:31 gods *e* abomination that the LORD detests,
13: 1 *E* command that I enjoin on you,
14:28 "At the end of *e* third year you shall
15: 1 "At the end of *e* seven-year period you
15: 2 *E* creditor shall relax his claim on what
16:16 *e* male among you shall appear before the
19: 3 *e* homicide will be able to find a refuge.
20:13 your hand, put *e* male in it to the sword;
21: 5 and *e* case of dispute or violence must be
28:20 frustration in *e* enterprise you undertake,
28:47 joy and gratitude for abundance of *e* kind,
28:52 They will so besiege you in *e* community
28:58 "If you are not careful to observe *e* word
29:19 and *e* curse mentioned in this book will
31:10 comes at the end of *e* seven-year period,
32:46 may carry out carefully *e* word of this law.
Jos 1: 3 deliver to you *e* place where you set foot.
1:18 and does not obey *e* command you give him,
5: 4 *e* man of military age had died in the
8:17 with *e* man engaged in this pursuit of
8:35 *E* single word that Moses had commanded,
9:23 *e* one of you shall always be a slave

10:28 city, on its king, and on *e* person in it,
10:30 He put it to the sword with *e* person there,
10:32 put it to the sword with *e* person in it,
10:35 the doom that day on *e* person in it,
10:37 king, all its towns, and *e* person there,
10:37 the doom on it and on *e* person there.
10:39 and fulfilled the doom on *e* person there,
11:11 by putting *e* person there to the sword,
21:42 With each and *e* one of these cities went
21:44 it, the LORD gave them peace on *e* side,
21:45 Israel was broken; *e* one was fulfilled.
22: 2 you, and have obeyed *e* command I gave you.
22:14 ten princes, one from *e* tribe of Israel,
23:14 *E* promise has been fulfilled for you,
23:15 But just as *e* promise the LORD,
23:15 for you, so will he fulfill *e* threat,
Jgs 9:49 *e* one of the citizens of Migdal-shechem,
20: 6 through *e* part of the territory of Israel,
20:10 the tribes of Israel ten men for *e* hundred,
20:10 *e* thousand, a thousand for *e* ten thousand,
20:16 *e* one of them able to sling a stone at a
21:11 and *e* woman who was not still a virgin.
21:16 *e* woman in Benjamin has been put to death."
1Sm 2:29 part of *e* offering of my people Israel?'
4:10 *e* man fled to his own tent.
8: 7 "Grant the people's *e* request.
11: 2 I must gouge out *e* man's right eye,
12: 1 "I have granted your request in *e* respect,"
12:11 from the power of your enemies on *e* side,
14:24 in *e* town in the hill country of Ephraim.
18: 5 *e* mission on which Saul sent him.
2Sm 7: 1 given him rest from his enemies on *e* side,
8:11 had taken from *e* nation he had conquered;
14:26 which he used to do at the end of *e* year,
20: 1 *E* man to his tent, O Israel!"
23: 5 fruition all my salvation and my *e* desire?
1Kgs 5: 5 *e* man under his vine or under his fig tree
5:25 while Solomon *e* year gave Hiram twenty
9: 8 *E* passerby shall catch his breath in
10: 2 on *e* subject in which she was interested.
10:14 The gold that Solomon received *e* year
10:22 Once *e* three years the fleet of Tarshish
11:15 the slain, put to death *e* male in Edom.
11:16 until they had killed off *e* male in Edom.
12:24 Let *e* man return home,
14:10 I will cut off *e* male in Jeroboam's line,
14:23 *e* high hill and under every green tree.
21:21 you and will cut off *e* male in Ahab's line,
22:36 "Every man to his city, *e* man to his land,
2Kgs 3:19 You shall destroy *e* fortified city, fell *e*
3:19 and ruin *e* fertile field with stones."
3:21 *e* man capable of bearing arms was called
3:25 each of them cast stones onto *e* fertile
3:25 stopped up and *e* useful tree they felled.
9: 8 I will cut off *e* male in Ahab's line,
16: 4 places, on hills, and under *e* leafy tree.
17:10 on every high hill and under *e* leafy tree.
17:13 Israel and Judah by *e* prophet and seer,
25: 1 around it, and built siege walls on *e* side.
25: 9 *e* large building was destroyed by fire.
1Chr 12:34 battle array with *e* kind of weapon for war:
12:38 men equipped with *e* kind of weapon of war:
13: 1 that is to say, with *e* one of his leaders,
14:17 fame was spread abroad through *e* land,
16: 3 *e* Israelite, to *e* man and *e* woman,
18:10 gold, silver and bronze utensils of *e* sort.
21:12 destroying angel in *e* part of Israel?
22: 9 him rest from all his enemies on *e* side.
22:15 and *e* kind of craftsman skilled in gold,
22:18 Has he not given you rest on *e* side?
23:30 They must be present *e* morning to offer
23:31 and at *e* offering of holocausts to the
28: 1 the warriors and *e* important man.
28:21 their skill in *e* kind of craftsmanship.
29: 2 stones, *e* other kind of precious stone,
29: 5 for *e* work that is to be done by artisans.
2Chr 2:13 to devise *e* type of artistic work
8:16 of the LORD had been completed in *e* detail.
9: 1 on *e* subject in which she was interested.
9:21 Once *e* three years the fleet of Tarshish
11: 4 Let *e* man return home,
11:12 In *e* city were shields and spears,
14: 6 him, and he has given us rest on *e* side."
15: 6 God destroyed them by *e* kind of adversity.
15:15 And the LORD gave them rest on *e* side.
19:10 And in *e* dispute that your brethren living
20: 4 from *e* one of the cities of Judah they
20:30 peace, for his God gave him rest on *e* side.
28: 4 on hills, and under *e* leafy tree.
28:24 made for himself in *e* corner of Jerusalem.
28:25 In *e* city throughout Judah he set up high
31:19 had in *e* city men designated by name to
31:19 *e* male among the priests and to every
32:21 an angel, who destroyed *e* valiant warrior,
32:22 every other power; he gave them rest on *e*
34:13 all the workers in *e* kind of labor.
34:25 me by *e* deed that they have performed,
34:33 Josiah removed *e* abominable thing from all
35:15 The gatekeepers were at *e* gate;
Ezr 1: 6 their neighbors gave them help in *e* way,
6:12 dwell there overthrow *e* king or people
6:20 *e* one of whom had purified himself for the
Neh 4:12 *E* builder, while he worked,

5:13 *e* man who fails to keep this promise,
5:18 all kinds of wine in abundance *e* ten days,
10:32 seventh year, as well as *e* kind of debt.
10:34 and for *e* service of the house of our God.
10:38 and our offerings of the fruit of *e* tree,
13: 3 separated from Israel *e* foreign element.
13:15 grapes, figs, and *e* other kind of burden,
13:16 were importing fish and *e* other kind
Tb 1: 8 *E* third year I would bring them this
1:14 *E* now and then until his death I would go
4: 5 and suppress *e* desire to sin or to break
4:12 guard, son, against *e* form of immorality,
4:18 "Seek counsel from *e* wise man,
5:10 so I know *e* road well."
8:15 you, O God, with *e* holy and pure blessing!
12: 9 saves one from death and expiates *e* sin.
12:18 So continue to thank him *e* day;
13: 4 Exalt him before *e* living being,
13:11 *E* generation shall give joyful praise in
Jdt 2:24 down *e* fortified city along the Wadi Abron,
3: 8 so that *e* nation might worship
3: 8 and *e* people and tribe invoke him as a god.
14: 7 *e* tent of Judah; and in *e* foreign nation,
15: 2 in all directions, and fled along *e* road,
16:14 Let your *e* creature serve you;
16:16 the sweet odor of *e* sacrifice is a trifle,
Est A: 6 and at their cry *e* nation prepared for war,
A:11 He kept it in mind, and tried in *e* way,
1:22 that *e* man should be lord in his own home.
3: 8 differing from those of *e* other people.
3:12 *e* province, and the officials of every
B: 4 which by its laws is opposed to *e* other
3:14 promulgated as law in *e* province
C: 3 and *e* wonderful thing under the heavens.
4:23 King of gods and Ruler of *e* power.
8:11 authorized the Jews in each and *e* city
8:11 *e* armed group of any nation or province
E:19 a copy of this letter publicly in *e* place,
E:24 *E* city and province, without exception
8:13 in each and *e* province was published among
8:17 and every province and in each and *e* city,
9:21 He ordered them to celebrate *e* year both
9:27 of celebrating these two days *e* year
9:28 *e* clan, in *e* province, and in *e* city.
1Mc 1:25 for Israel, in *e* place where they dwelt,
1:27 *E* bridegroom took up lamentation,
1:48 with *e* kind of impurity and abomination,
4:59 on the anniversary *e* year for eight days,
5:51 He slaughtered *e* male,
6:57 "We are growing weaker *e* day,
7:49 observed *e* year on the thirteenth of Adar.
8: 4 and the rest paid tribute to them *e* year.
8:15 and *e* day three hundred and twenty men
8:16 their government to one man *e* year,
9:23 law raised their heads in *e* part of Israel,
10:33 *E* one of the Jews who has been carried
10:34 and exemption for *e* Jew in my kingdom.
10:42 of the sanctuary *e* year shall be canceled,
11:38 his entire army, *e* man to his home,
13:10 walls of Jerusalem, fortified it on *e* side.
13:52 should be celebrated *e* year with rejoicing,
14:12 *E* man sat under his vine and his fig tree,
14:35 In *e* way he sought to exalt his people.
2Mc 4:16 whom they desired to imitate in *e* thing,
5: 3 ornaments, together with armor of *e* sort.
7:31 *e* kind of affliction for the Hebrews,
9: 7 and *e* part of his body was racked by the
9:17 a Jew himself and visit *e* inhabited place
10: 8 nation should celebrate these days *e* year.
10:14 and used *e* opportunity to attack the Jews.
11: 3 put the high priesthood up for sale *e* year.
12:11 cattle and to help them in *e* other way.
12:22 Scattering in *e* direction, they rushed away
15:12 from childhood in *e* virtuous practice,
Jb 1: 5 and offering holocausts for *e* one of them.
7:18 with each new day and try him at *e* moment!
12:10 In his hand is the soul of *e* living thing,
13: 4 and offering vain remedies, *e* one of you!
18:11 On *e* side terrors affright him;
19:10 He breaks me down on *e* side,
34:34 say to me, *e* wise man who hears my views:
39: 8 pasture, and seeks out *e* patch of green.
Ps(s) 3: 7 of people arrayed against me on *e* side.
6: 7 *e* night I flood my bed with weeping;
12: 4 LORD destroy all smooth *e* boastful tongue,
20: 5 is in your heart and fulfill your *e* plan.
27: 6 is held high above my enemies on *e* side.
31:14 of the crowd, that frighten me from *e* side,
32: 6 For this shall *e* faithful man pray to you
56: 6 their *e* thought is of evil against me.
71:18 strength to *e* generation that is to come.
78:51 He smote *e* first-born in Egypt,
80:13 so that *e* passer-by plucks its fruit,
104:11 And give drink to *e* beast of the field,
105:35 they devoured *e* plant throughout the land;
105:36 struck *e* first-born throughout their land,
118:11 They encompassed me on *e* side;
119:101 From *e* evil way I withhold my feet,
119:104 therefore I hate *e* false way.
119:128 *e* false way I hate.
140: 3 in their hearts, and stir up wars *e* day.
144:13 garners be full, affording *e* kind of store;
145: 2 *E* day will I bless you,

EVERY (cont.)

145:16 and satisfy the desire of *e* living thing.
Prv 2: 9 and justice, honesty, *e* good path;
7:12 and at *e* corner she lurks in ambush
15: 3 The eyes of the LORD are in *e* place,
15:15 *E* day is miserable for the depressed,
16: 5 *E* proud man is an abomination to the LORD;
17: 8 at *e* turn it brings him success.
20: 3 shun strife, while *e* fool starts a quarrel.
24: 4 with *e* precious and pleasing possession.
30: 5 *E* word of God is tested;
Eccl 3: 1 and a time for *e* affair under the heavens.
3:13 For *e* man, moreover, to eat and drink
3:17 for *e* affair and on every work a judgment.
5: 8 in *e* respect is a king for the arable land.
7: 2 of feasting, For that is the end of *e* man,
7:21 Do not give heed to *e* word that is spoken
8: 9 mind to *e* work that is done under the sun,
12:14 because God will bring to judgment *e* work,
Sg 3: 6 and with the perfume of *e* exotic dust?
Wis 7:29 and surpasses *e* constellation of the stars.
13:14 red stain, and daubed over *e* blemish in it,
15:12 one must," says he, "make profit *e* way,
16:20 all delights and conforming to *e* taste.
18:13 at *e* turn on account of sorceries,
18:16 he alighted, he filled *e* place with death;
19:22 For *e* way, O Lord!
19:22 stood by them in *e* time and circumstance.
Sir 1: 8 *e* living thing according to his bounty;
5:11 Winnow not in *e* wind,
5:11 wind, and start not off in *e* direction.
6:35 Be eager to hear *e* godly discourse;
10: 5 over *e* man is in the hand of God,
11:29 Bring not *e* man into your house,
12: 6 will meet for *e* good deed you do for him.
13:14 *E* living thing loves its own kind, *e* man
13:15 *E* being is drawn to its own kind;
13:15 with his own kind *e* man associates.
15:19 he understands man's *e* deed.
17:14 Over *e* nation he places a ruler,
19:14 *e* story you must not believe.
21: 3 *E* offense is a two-edged sword;
23:19 Observe *e* step a man takes and peer into
24: 6 land, over *e* people and nation I held sway.
26:12 every tent peg and opens her quiver for *e*
27:23 uses honeyed talk, and admires your *e* word,
29:12 house, and it will save you from *e* evil;
30: 7 and will quake inwardly at *e* outcry.
31: 7 who are avid for it, a snare for *e* fool.
33: 7 when it is the sun that lights up *e* day?
33:18 I toiled, but for *e* seeker after wisdom.
37: 1 *E* friend declares his friendship,
37: 7 *E* counselor points out a way,
37:16 source of every deed; a thought, of *e* act.
37:27 For not *e* food is good for everyone,
37:27 nor is everything suited to *e* taste.
37:28 Be not drawn after *e* enjoyment,
38:10 hands be just, cleanse your heart of *e* sin;
38:25 bullock, and whose *e* concern is for cattle?
38:27 So with *e* engraver and designer who,
39:16 in its own time *e* need is supplied.
39:33 *e* need when it comes he fills.
42: 7 Of numbering *e* deposit,
43:21 He freezes over *e* body of water,
47: 7 battled and subdued the enemy on *e* side.
47: 8 *e* deed he offered thanks to God Most High,
47:25 more, and they lent themselves to *e* evil.
51: 4 from flames that hemmed me in on *e* side;
51: 7 I turned *e* way, but there was no one
51: 8 in him, and rescues them from *e* evil.
51:12 *e* kind and preserved me in time of trouble.
Is 2:15 every lofty tower and *e* fortified wall,
3: 5 one another, yes, *e* man his neighbor.
3:16 go, their anklets tinkling with *e* step,
4: 3 *e* one marked down for life in Jerusalem.
7:23 On that day *e* place where there used to be
9: 4 *e* boot that trampled in battle, every cloak
9:16 sinful, and *e* mouth gives vent to folly.
13: 7 *E* man's heart melts in terror;
13:14 *E* man shall turn to his kindred and flee
15: 2 Every head is shaved, *e* beard sheared off.
19:17 *E* time they remember Judah,
24:10 city of chaos, shut against entry, *e* house.
27: 3 LORD, am its keeper, I water it *e* moment;
30:25 Upon *e* high mountain and lofty hill there
30:32 While at *e* sweep of the rod which the LORD
32:20 Happy are you who sow beside *e* stream,
33: 2 Be our strength *e* morning,
40: 4 *E* valley shall be filled in, every mountain
44:28 My shepherd, who fulfills my *e* wish;
45:23 To me *e* knee shall bend; by me *e* tongue
46:10 shall stand, I accomplish my *e* purpose.
49: 9 on *e* bare height shall their pastures be.
51:20 at *e* street corner like antelopes in a net.
54:17 *e* tongue you shall prove false that
56:11 his own way, *e* one of them to his own gain:
57: 5 among the terebinths, under *e* green tree;
58: 6 free the oppressed, breaking *e* yoke;
63: 9 became their savior in their *e* affliction.
66:18 I come to gather nations of *e* language;
66:24 *e* language;
Jer 2:20 On every high hill, under *e* green tree,
3: 6 *e* high mountain, and under *e* green tree
3:13 to strangers [under *e* green tree] and would
6:25 of the enemy's sword; terror on *e* side!
9: 3 *E* brother apes Jacob, the supplanter, *e*
10:14 *E* man is stupid, ignorant; *e* artisan
12:12 Upon *e* desert height brigands have come up.
13:12 *E* wineflask is meant to be filled with wine.
15: 7 winnowed them with the fan in *e* city gate.
16:12 Here you are, *e* one of you,
16:16 hunters to hunt them out from *e* mountain
18:18 let us carefully note his *e* word."
19: 8 *e* passer-by will be amazed and will catch
20: 3 the LORD will name you "Terror on *e* side."
20:10 "Terror on *e* side!
31:25 *e* soul that languishes I will replenish.
34:14 *E* seventh year each of you shall set free
35:17 of Jerusalem *e* evil that I threatened;
46: 5 Terror on *e* side, says the LORD!
48: 8 The destroyer comes upon *e* city,
48:37 *E* head has been made bald,
48:37 *e* beard shaved; *e* hand is gashed,
48:38 On *e* roof of Moab and in all his squares
49:17 *E* passer-by shall be appalled and catch
49:29 shout from upon them, "Terror on *e* side!"
50:26 Come upon her from *e* side,
51:17 *E* man is stupid, ignorant; every artisan
51:28 and all its prefects, *e* land in his domain.
52: 4 around it, and built siege walls on *e* side.
52:13 *e* large building he destroyed with fire.
Lam 2:19 in the night, at the beginning of *e* watch;
2:19 from hunger at the corner of *e* street].
4: 1 stones lie strewn at *e* street corner!
Bar 5: 7 that *e* lofty mountain be made low,
5: 8 The forests and *e* fragrant kind of tree
6:70 a garden on which perches *e* kind of bird,
Ez 5:10 that remain of your people in *e* direction.
5:12 and a third I will scatter in *e* direction,
5:14 surround you, which *e* passer-by may see.
6:13 *e* high hill and mountaintop, beneath every
12:14 his troops I will scatter in *e* direction,
12:23 hand, and also the fulfillment of *e* vision.
13:18 make veils for *e* size of head
16:15 you lavished your harlotry on *e* passer-by,
16:24 a platform and a dais in *e* public place.
16:25 At *e* street corner you built a dais for
16:25 spreading your legs for *e* passer-by,
16:31 building your platform at *e* street corner
16:31 and erecting your dais in *e* public place !
17:21 shall be scattered in *e* direction.
17:23 *e* kind shall dwell beneath it, every winged
20:26 gifts, by their immolation of *e* first-born,
21: 3 to north *e* face shall be scorched by it.
21:12 every heart shall fail, *e* hand shall fall
21:12 *e* spirit shall be daunted, and every knee
21:15 You have spurned the rod and *e* judgment!
21:20 all around, That *e* heart may tremble;
23:22 I will bring them against you from *e* side:
26:16 at *e* moment and be horrified at you.
27: 9 *E* ship and sailor on the sea came to you
28:13 and *e* precious stone was your covering
28:23 sword that comes against it from *e* side.
29: 7 throwing *e* shoulder out of joint;
31: 5 grew taller than *e* other tree of the field,
31: 6 its shade dwelt numerous peoples of *e* race.
32:10 and on the day of your downfall *e* one of
33:20 judge *e* one of you according to his ways,
34: 8 my sheep have become food for *e* wild beast,
34:12 I will rescue them from *e* place where they
36:34 exposed to the gaze of *e* passer-by.
37: 2 He made me walk among them in *e* direction
38:20 and *e* wall shall fall to the ground.
38:21 *e* terror, says the LORD GOD, *e* man's sword
39: 4 To birds of prey of *e* kind and to the wild
39:17 birds of *e* kind and to all the wild beasts:
39:20 with warriors and soldiers of *e* kind,
41:17 on every wall on *e* side in both the inner
41:18 a palmtree between *e* two cherubim.
41:19 on *e* side throughout the whole temple.
44:30 All the choicest first fruits of *e* kind,
44:30 all the best of your offerings of *e* kind,
45:14 for *e* measure of oil,
45:15 *e* two hundred from the pasturage of Israel,
46:13 this he shall offer *e* morning.
46:14 With it *e* morning he shall provide as a
46:15 *e* morning as an established holocaust.
47: 9 *e* sort of living creature that can
47:12 river, fruit trees of *e* kind shall grow;
47:12 *E* month they shall bear fresh fruit,
Dn 3: 4 "Nations and peoples of *e* language,
3: 7 the nations and peoples of *e* language all
3:29 from you, and we have done *e* kind of evil.
3:64 *E* shower and dew,
3:96 decree for nations and peoples of *e* language
3:98 to the nations and peoples of *e* language,
5:19 of *e* language dreaded and feared him.
6:16 Persian law *e* royal prohibition or decree is
6:26 to the nations and peoples of *e* language,
7:14 and peoples of *e* language serve him.
13: 8 old men saw her enter *e* day for her walk,
14: 3 and *e* day they provided for it six barrels
14: 4 worshiped it and went *e* day to adore it;
14: 6 not see how much he eats and drinks *e* day?"
Hos 9: 1 a harlot's hire upon *e* threshing floor.
13:15 It shall loot his land of *e* precious thing.
Jl 2: 6 peoples are in torment, *e* face blanches.
Am 4: 4 morning bring your sacrifices, *e* third day,
5:16 In *e* square there shall be lamentation,
5:16 and in *e* street they shall cry,
5:17 And in *e* vineyard there shall be
8:10 all with sackcloth and make *e* head bald.
Jon 3: 8 *e* man shall turn from his evil way and
Mi 2:12 I will gather you, O Jacob, each and *e* one,
4: 4 *E* man shall sit under his own vine or
Na 2:10 their wealth in precious things of *e* kind!
2:11 Writhing in every frame, *e* face blanched!
3:10 dashed to pieces at the corner of *e* street;
Zec 5: 3 with it shall *e* thief be swept away,
5: 3 it shall *e* perjurer be expelled from here.
8:10 for I set *e* man against his neighbor.
8:23 In those days ten men of *e* nationality,
8:23 *e* Jew by the edge of his garment and say,
10: 4 from him warrior's bow and *e* officer.
12: 4 LORD, I will strike *e* horse with fright,
13: 4 *e* prophet shall be ashamed to prophesy his
14:13 *e* man shall seize the hand of his neighbor,
14:21 And *e* pot in Jerusalem and in Judah shall
Mal 2:17 *E* evildoer is good in the sight of the
Mt 3:10 *E* tree that is not fruitful will be cut
4: 4 but on *e* utterance that comes from
4:23 cured the people of *e* disease and illness.
5:11 persecute you and utter *e* kind of slander
5:21 *e* murderer shall be liable to judgment.'
7:19 *E* tree that does not bear good fruit is
9:35 reign, and he cured *e* sickness and disease.
10: 1 and to cure sickness and disease of *e* kind.
10:11 "Look for a worthy person in *e* town or
10:30 you, *e* hair of your head has been counted;
12:31 I assure you, is why *e* sin, every blasphemy,
12:36 for *e* unguarded word they speak.
13:52 *E* scribe who is learned in the reign of
15:13 *E* planting not put down by my heavenly
18:16 so that *e* case may stand on the word of
Mk 3:28 *e* sin will be forgiven mankind and all the
5:26 treatment at the hands of doctors of *e* sort
13:24 trials of *e* sort the sun will be darkened,
14:44 him and lead him away, taking *e* precaution."
Lk 1:53 The hungry he has given *e* good thing,
2:23 *E* first-born male shall be consecrated to
2:41 His parents used to go *e* year to Jerusalem
3: 5 *E* valley shall be filled And every
3: 9 *E* tree that is not fruitful will be cut
5:17 of the law who had come from *e* village
6:40 but *e* student when he has finished his
10: 1 to *e* town and place he intended to visit.
11:17 *E* kingdom divided against itself is laid
16:16 people of *e* sort are forcing their way in.
16:19 and linen and feasted splendidly *e* day.
19:43 hem you in, and press you hard from *e* side.
21: 4 not afford *e* penny she had to live on."
24:27 he interpreted for them *e* passage of
Jn 1: 9 light to *e* man was coming into the world.
8:47 Whoever is of God hears *e* word God speaks.
15: 2 He prunes away *e* barren branch,
Acts 2: 5 were devout Jews of *e* nation under heaven.
2:46 went to the temple area together *e* day,
3: 2 They would bring him *e* day and put him at
8:10 People from *e* rank of society were paying
13:22 my own heart who will fulfill my *e* wish.'
13:39 In him, *e* believer is acquitted.
15:21 Moses has been proclaimed in *e* town
15:21 read aloud in the synagogues on *e* sabbath."
17:22 *e* respect you are scrupulously religious.
17:26 From one stock he made *e* nation of mankind
18: 4 *E* sabbath, in the synagogue,
22:19 in you and flogged them in *e* synagogue.
26: 9 of Jesus the Nazorean in *e* way possible.
Rom 1:29 They are filled with *e* kind of wickedness:
2: 1 That is why *e* one of you who judges
2: 6 he will repay *e* man for what he has done:
2: 9 will come upon *e* man who has done evil,
3: 2 The answer is, much in *e* respect.
3: 4 true even though *e* man be proved a liar,
3:19 This means that *e* mouth is silenced and
7: 8 to rouse in me *e* kind of evil desire.
14:11 *e* knee shall bend before me and *e* tongue
14:12 *E* one of us will have to give an account
1Cor 1: 5 with *e* gift of speech and knowledge.
6:18 *E* other sin a man commits is outside his
7: 2 *e* man should have his own wife and every
11: 3 head of *e* man is Christ;
11:26 *E* time, then, you eat this bread
12:27 *E* one of you is a member of it.
15:24 when, after having destroyed *e* sovereignty,
15:31 Jesus our Lord, that I face death *e* day.
2Cor 2: 5 some measure, to say no more, *e* one of you.
4: 2 ourselves to *e* man's conscience before God.
4: 8 We are afflicted in *e* way possible,
7: 1 from *e* defilement of flesh and spirit,
7:11 In *e* way you have displayed your innocence
8: 7 that just as you are rich in *e* respect,
9:11 In *e* way your liberality is enriched;
10: 5 We demolish sophistries and *e* proud
10: 5 we likewise bring *e* thought into captivity
11: 6 this evident to you in *e* conceivable way.
11: 9 In *e* way possible I kept myself from being
11:12 depriving at *e* turn those who look for a
Gal 2:10 one thing that I was making *e* effort to do.

Eph 1: 3 Christ *e* spiritual blessing in the heavens!
1:21 hand in heaven, high above *e* principality,
1:21 and *e* name that can be given in this age
2: 3 of the flesh, following *e* whim and fancy,
3:15 before the Father from whom *e* family
4: 3 Make *e* effort to preserve the unity which
4:14 carried about by *e* wind of doctrine that
4:19 the indulgence of *e* sort of lewd conduct.
4:31 harsh words, slander, and malice of *e* kind.
5: 9 *e* kind of goodness and justice and truth.
5:24 should submit to their husbands in *e* thing.
6:18 At *e* opportunity pray in the Spirit,
6:18 using prayers and petitions of *e* sort.
Phil 1: 3 thanks to my God *e* time I think of you
1: 4 which is constantly, in *e* prayer I utter
1:18 All that matters is that in any and *e* way,
2: 9 on him the name above *e* other name,
2:10 name *e* knee must bend in the heavens,
2:11 and *e* tongue proclaim to the glory of God
4: 6 Present your needs to God in *e* form of
4:12 learned how to cope with *e* circumstance
4:21 in Christ Jesus to *e* member of the church.
Col 1:10 of the Lord and pleasing to him in *e* way.
1:10 of *e* sort and grow in the knowledge of God.
1:23 been announced to *e* creature under heaven,
1:28 hoping to make *e* man complete in Christ.
2: 3 in whom *e* treasure of wisdom and knowledge
2:10 is the head of *e* principality and power.
4: 5 make the most of *e* opportunity.
1Thes 1: 8 *e* region your faith in God is celebrated,
2:11 know how we exhorted *e* one of you,
2Thes 1:11 power *e* honest intention and work of faith.
2: 4 above *e* so-called god proposed for worship,
2:10 by *e* seduction the wicked can devise for
2:17 strengthen them for *e* good work and word.
3: 2 For not *e* man has faith,
3:16 give you continued peace in *e* possible way.
3:17 append this signature to *e* letter I write.
1Tm 2: 8 that in *e* place the men shall offer
5:10 she been eager to do *e* possible good work?
2Tm 2:20 In *e* large household there are vessels not
2:21 of the house and ready for *e* noble service.
3:17 competent and equipped for *e* good work.
Ti 1: 5 the appointment of presbyters in *e* town.
2: 9 They should try to please them in *e* way,
2:10 so as to adorn in *e* way possible the
Phlm 1: 8 although I feel that I have *e* right to
Heb 2:17 had to become like his brothers in *e* way,
3: 4 *E* house is founded by someone,
4:15 one who was tempted in *e* way that we are,
5: 1 *E* high priest is taken from among men and
8: 3 Now *e* high priest is appointed to offer
10:11 *E* other priest stands ministering day by
12: 1 let lay aside *e* encumbrance of sin which
12: 6 he scourges *e* son he receives."
13: 4 Let marriage be honored in *e* way and the
13:18 as we do, to act rightly in *e* respect.
Jas 1: 2 when you are involved in *e* sort of trial.
1:14 and lure of his own passion tempt *e* man.
1:17 *E* worthwhile gift, every genuine benefit
1:19 Let *e* man be quick to hear,
1:21 away all that is filthy, *e* vicious excess.
3: 7 *E* form of life, four-footed or winged,
1Pt 1:15 yourselves in *e* aspect of your conduct,
2:13 Lord, be obedient to *e* human institution,
2:17 You must esteem the person of *e* man.
2Pt 1: 5 This is reason enough for you to make *e*
3:14 make *e* effort to be found without stain or
1Jn 1: 9 our sins and cleanse us from *e* wrong.
4: 1 Beloved, do not trust *e* spirit,
4: 2 *e* spirit that acknowledges Jesus Christ
4: 3 while *e* spirit that fails to acknowledge
Jude 1:15 the godless for *e* evil deed they have done,
1:15 those godless sinners of *e* harsh word
Rv 1: 7 *E* eye shall see him,
5: 9 *e* race and tongue, of *e* people and nation.
5:13 Then I heard the voices of *e* creature in
6:14 *e* mountain and island was uprootted from
7: 4 forty-four thousand from *e* tribe of Israel;
7: 9 no one could count from *e* nation and race,
7:17 and God will wipe *e* tear from their eyes."
8: 7 a third of the trees and *e* green plant.
11: 9 Men from *e* people and race,
13: 7 granted authority over *e* race and people,
14: 6 to the whole world, to *e* nation and race,
16: 3 and *e* creature living in the sea died.
16:20 *E* island fled and mountains disappeared.
18: 2 *e* unclean spirit, a cage for every filthy
18:12 fragrant wood of *e* kind,
18:17 *E* captain and navigator,
21: 4 He shall wipe *e* tear from their eyes,
21: 8 idol-worshipers and deceivers of *e* sort
21:19 was ornate with precious stones of *e* sort:

EVERYBODY (1)

Mk 1:37 him, they told him, *E* is looking for you!"

EVERYDAY (2)

1Cor 6: 3 then, we are up to deciding *e* affairs.
Gal 3:15 Brothers, let me give you an *e* example.

EVERYONE (176)

Gn 16:12 a wild ass of a man, his hand against *e*,
20:16 your honor has been preserved with *e*."
45: 1 so he cried out, "Have *e* withdraw from me!"
Ex 12:16 except to prepare the food that *e* needs.
16:16 So gather it that *e* has enough to eat,
16:18 They so gathered that *e* had enough to eat.
16:29 *e* is to stay home and no one is to go out."
30:13 *E* who enters the registered group must pay
30:14 *E* of twenty years or more who enters the
35: 5 *E*, as his heart prompts him,
35:21 community left Moses' presence, *e*,
35:22 *E* who could presented an offering of gold
35:23 *E* who happened to have violet,
35:24 and *e* who happened to have acacia wood for
Lv 11:24 that *e* who touches their dead bodies shall
11:25 and *e* who picks up any part of their dead
11:26 *e* who touches them becomes unclean.
11:27 *e* who touches their dead bodies shall be
11:28 and *e* who picks up their dead bodies shall
11:31 *E* who touches them when they are dead
16:29 tenth day of the seventh month *e* of you,
17:15 *E*, whether a native or an alien,
18:29 *E* who does any of these abominations shall
Nm 5: 2 *e* suffering from a discharge, and everyone
19:13 *E* who fails to purify himself after
19:14 *e* who enters the tent, as well as everyone
19:16 *e* who in the open country touches a dead
Dt 4: 3 midst *e* that followed the Baal of Peor;
12: 8 here, *e* does what seems right to himself,
25:16 *E* who is dishonest in any of these matters
Jos 2:11 *e* is discouraged because of you,
Jgs 7: 5 "You shall set to one side *e* who laps up
7: 5 to the other, *e* who kneels down to drink."
8:25 into which *e* threw a ring from his booty.
17: 6 *e* did what he thought best.
19:30 *E* who saw this said,
21:25 *e* did what he thought best.
1Sm 3:11 cause the ears of *e* who hears it to ring.
14:34 So *e* brought to the LORD whatever ox he
17:30 and *e* gave him the same answer as before.
25:13 said to his men, "Let *e* gird on his sword."
25:13 *e*, David included, girded on his sword.
2Sm 13: 9 he said, "Have *e* leave me."
15: 4 Then *e* who has a lawsuit to be decided
15:23 *E* in the countryside wept aloud as the
20:13 *e* went on after Joab in pursuit of Sheba,
2Kgs 13:21 into the grave of Elisha, and *e* went off.
2Chr 6:30 render to *e* according to his conduct,
7:21 *e* passing by it will be amazed and ask:
10:16 *E* to your tents, O Israel!
13: 9 *E* who comes to consecrate himself with a
15:13 and *e* who would not seek the LORD,
30: 5 that *e* should come to Jerusalem to
30:19 pardon to *e* who has resolved to seek God,
Ezr 1: 4 Let *e* who has survived,
1: 5 Benjamin and the priests and Levites *e*,
Neh 4:17 *e* kept his weapon at his right hand.
Jdt 2:25 Cilicia, and cut down *e* who resisted him.
Est 1: 8 to comply with the good pleasure of *e*.
E:11 the king,' before whom *e* was to bow down;
1Mc 2:27 "Let *e* who is zealous for the law and who
5:49 that *e* make an attack from the place
2Mc 1:22 a great fire blazed up, so that *e* marveled.
10:35 savage fury cut down *e* they encountered.
15:20 *E* now awaited the decisive moment.
15:34 *e* looked toward heaven and praised the
Jb 8:13 So is the end of *e* who forgets God,
30:23 in death to the destined place of *e* alive.
Ps(s) 12: 3 *E* speaks falsehood to his neighbor;
62:13 you render to *e* according to his deeds.
63:12 *e* who swears by him shall glory,
73:27 you destroy *e* who is unfaithful to you.
115: 8 shall be like them, *e* that trusts in them.
135:18 shall be like them, *e* that trusts in them.
Prv 1:19 This is the fate of *e* greedy of loot:
Sir 22: 1 *e* hisses at his disgrace.
37:27 For not every food is good for *e*,
41:24 you would be looked upon by *e* with favor.
Is 13:15 *E* who is caught shall be run through;
15: 3 On the rooftops and in the squares *e* wails.
43: 7 *E* who is named as mine,
Jer 8: 6 *E* keeps on running his course,
9: 3 Be on your guard, *e* against his neighbor;
17:10 heart, To reward *e* according to his ways,
20: 7 *e* mocks me.
23:17 And to *e* who walks in hardness of heart,
34: 9 *E* was to free his Hebrew slaves,
43: 6 the princesses and *e* whom Nebuzaradan,
43:11 with exile, *e* destined for exile;
50:13 *E* who passes by Babylon will be appalled
50:16 to his own people, *e* flees to his own land.
Ez 4:17 *e* shall be filled with terror and waste
16:44 *e* who is fond of proverbs will say of you,
20:11 to them my ordinances, which *e* must keep,
21: 4 *E* shall see that I, the LORD
21: 9 its sheath against *e* from south to north,
21:10 south to north, and *e* shall know that I,
Dn 3:10 that *e* who heard the sound of the trumpet,
12: 1 escape, *e* who is found written in the book.
Jl 3: 5 Then *e* shall be rescued who calls on the
Na 3: 7 Till *e* who sees you runs from you,
Zec 10: 1 And sends men the pouring rain; for *e*,
Mt 5:22 *e* who grows angry with his brother shall
5:32 *e* who divorces his wife
13: 9 Let *e* heed what he hears!"
13:25 While *e* was asleep, his enemy
13:43 Let *e* heed what he hears!
19:11 He said, "Not *e* can accept this teaching,
19:29 Moreover, *e* who has given up home,
22:10 into the byroads and rounded up *e* they met,
26:70 He denied it in front of *e*:
Mk 2:12 his mat and went outside in the sight of *e*.
7:16 Let *e* heed what he hears!"
9:49 *E* will be salted with fire.
13:13 Because of my name, you will be hated by *e*.
Lk 2: 3 *E* went to register, each to his own town.
8: 8 *e* who has ears attend to what he has heard."
8:45 *E* disclaimed doing it,
8:52 While *e* wept and lamented her,
12:41 for us, Lord, or do you mean it for *e*?"
13:17 *e* else rejoiced at the marvels Jesus was
14:11 For *e* who exalts himself shall be humbled
16:18 *E* who divorces his wife and marries
18: 9 while holding *e* else in contempt:
18:14 For *e* who exalts himself shall be humbled
19: 7 When this was observed, *e* began to murmur,
Jn 3: 8 So it is with *e* begotten of the Spirit."
3:20 *E* who practices evil hates the light;
3:26 is baptizing now, and *e* is flocking to him."
4:13 *E* who drinks this water will be thirsty
6:40 that *e* who looks upon the Son and believes
6:45 *E* who has heard the Father and learned
8: 3 They made her stand there in front of *e*.
8:34 *e* who lives in sin is the slave of sin.
Acts 2:21 Then shall *e* be saved who calls on the
4:16 *E* who lives in Jerusalem knows what a
4:35 be distributed to *e* according to his need.
9:40 Peter first made *e* go outside;
10:43 saying that *e* who believes in him has
15: 3 telling *e* about the conversion of the
16:32 word of God to him and to *e* in his house.
21:24 *e* will know that there is nothing in what
Rom 1:16 leading *e* who believes in it to salvation,
2:10 honor, and peace for *e* who has done good,
10: 4 him, justice comes to *e* who believes.
10:13 *E* who calls on the name of the Lord will
12:18 If possible, live peaceably with *e*.
13: 1 *e* obey the authorities that are over him,
13: 7 respect and honor to *e* who deserves them.
1Cor 3:10 *E*, however, must be careful how he builds.
4: 5 time, *e* will receive his praise from God.
7:20 *E* ought to continue as he was when he was
11:21 for *e* is in haste to eat his own supper.
12: 6 same God who accomplishes all of them in *e*.
14:23 is assembled and *e* is speaking in tongues,
16: 2 On the first day of each week *e* should put
16:16 under *e* who cooperates and toils with them.
2Cor 9: 7 *E* must give according to what he has
Gal 6: 5 *E* should bear his own responsibility.
Eph 4:25 let *e* speak the truth to his neighbor,
Phil 2:21 *E* is busy seeking his own interests rather
4: 5 *E* should see how unselfish you are.
1Tm 4:15 you, so that *e* may see your progress.
2Tm 2:19 "Let *e* who professes the name of the Lord
4:16 In fact, *e* abandoned me.
Heb 5:13 *E* whose food is milk alone is ignorant of
1Jn 2:29 you can be sure that *e* who acts in
3: 3 *E* who has this hope based on him keeps
3: 4 *E* who sins acts lawlessly,
4: 7 *e* who loves is begotten of God and has
5: 1 *E* who believes that Jesus is the Christ
5: 1 *e* who loves the father loves the child he
5: 4 *E* begotten of God conquers the world,
Rv 11:10 these two prophets harassed *e* on earth.

EVERYONE'S (4)

Gn 16:12 against everyone, and *e* hand against him;
Ez 13:18 Woe to those who sew bands for *e* wrists
Lk 4:35 threw him to the ground before *e* eyes
Acts 16:26 flew open and *e* chains were pulled loose.

EVERYTHING (203)

Gn 1:31 God looked at *e* he had made,
6:17 *e* on earth shall perish.
7: 8 birds, and of *e* that creeps on the ground,
7:22 *E* on dry land with the faintest breath of
14:20 Then Abram gave him a tenth of *e*.
20: 8 and informed them of *e* that had happened,
21:22 "God is with you in *e* you do.
24:36 old age, and he has given him *e* he owns.
25: 5 deeded *e* that he owned to his son Isaac.
28:22 Of *e* you give me, I will faithfully return
31: 1 has taken *e* that belonged to our father,
31:43 *e* you see belongs to me.
39: 5 the LORD's blessing was on *e* he owned,
39: 6 Having left *e* he owned in Joseph's charge,
39:22 and *e* that had to be done there was done
45:10 your flocks and herds, and *e* that you own.
46:32 and herds, as well as *e* else they own.
47: 1 their flocks and herds and *e* else they own;
Ex 4:30 told them *e* the LORD had said to Moses,
13:15 LORD *e* of the male sex that opens the womb,
19: 8 all answered together, *E* the LORD has said,

EVERYTHING (cont.)

24: 3 "We will do *e* that the LORD has told us."
40: 9 oil and anoint the Dwelling and *e* in it,
Lv 11:32 *E* on which one of them falls when dead
11:33 a clay vessel, *e* in it becomes unclean,
14:36 lest *e* in the house become unclean.
27:28 *e* that is thus doomed becomes most sacred
Dt 10:14 your God, as well as the earth and *e* on it.
15:18 LORD, your God, will bless you in *e* you do.
23:10 you shall keep yourselves from *e* offensive.
Jos 4:10 bed of the Jordan until *e* had been done
6:17 LORD has given you the city and *e* in it.
1Sm 3:12 Eli *e* I threatened against his family.
3:18 So Samuel told him *e*,
30:18 recovered *e* the Amalekites had taken,
30:19 David brought back *e*.
2Sm 3:36 they were pleased with *e* that the king did.
16: 4 *E* Meribbaal had is yours."
1Kgs 8:58 may follow him in *e* and keep the commands,
9: 1 palace, and *e* else that he had planned,
10: 3 King Solomon explained *e* she asked about,
10:13 queen of Sheba *e* she desired and asked for,
14:26 He took *e*, including the treasures
2Kgs 5:21 "Is *e* all right?"
10: 5 servants, and we will do *e* you tell us.
20:15 "They saw *e* in my house,"
20:17 and *e* that your fathers have stored up
22:17 me by *e* to which they turn their hands,
1Chr 23:28 chambers, and the preservation of *e* holy:
26:32 in *e* pertaining to God and to the king.
28:21 all the people will do *e* that you command."
29:14 For *e* is from you,
2Chr 7:11 he successfully accomplished *e* he had
9: 2 Solomon explained to her *e* she asked about,
9:12 of Sheba *e* she desired and asked him for,
12: 9 He took *e*, including the gold bucklers
19:11 over you in *e* that pertains to the LORD,
31: 5 they gave a generous tithe of *e*.
31:21 *E* that he undertook, for the service
34:16 doing *e* that has been entrusted to them;
Ezr 7:23 Let *e* that is ordered by the God of heaven
8:34 *E* was in order as to number and weight,
Neh 5:12 *e* and exact nothing further from them.
Tb 4:14 watch on yourself, my son, in *e* you do,
5: 1 *E* that you have commanded me,
14: 4 but *e* shall take place in the time
Est 6:13 all his friends *e* that had happened to him,
1Mc 1:22 He stripped off *e*, and took away the gold
3:34 instructions concerning *e* he wanted done.
9:36 seized and carried off John and *e* he had.
13: 9 battles, and we will do *e* that you tell us."
13:48 After removing from it *e* that was impure,
2Mc 7:23 as he brings about the origin of *e*,
8:14 But the others sold *e* they had left,
10:18 containing *e* necessary to sustain a siege,
11:14 persuading them to settle *e* on just terms,
Ps(s) 150: 6 Let *e* that has breath praise the LORD!
Prv 13:16 The shrewd man does *e* with prudence.
14:15 The simpleton believes *e*,
16: 4 The LORD has made *e* for his own ends,
Eccl 3: 1 There is an appointed time for *e*,
3:11 He has made *e* appropriate to its time,
8: 6 for there is a time and a judgment for *e*—
10: 3 lack of understanding he calls *e* foolish.
10:19 the living glad, but money answers for *e*.
Wis 1:10 Because a jealous ear hearkens to *e*,
7:27 and renews *e* while herself perduring;
18:14 For when peaceful stillness compassed *e*
Sir 10:26 of *e* than the boaster who is without bread.
37:27 everyone, nor is *e* suited to every taste.
39:21 *E* is chosen to satisfy a need.
Is 39: 2 armory, and *e* that was in his storerooms;
39: 4 Hezekiah replied, "They saw *e* in my house;
39: 6 and *e* that your fathers have stored up
Jer 35:10 do *e* our father Jonadab commanded us.
35:18 his commands and done *e* he commanded you,
36: 8 did *e* the prophet Jeremiah commanded;
36:20 When they told him *e* that had happened,
36:28 on it *e* that the first scroll contained,
44:18 we are in need of *e* and are being
50:32 a fire that shall devour *e* around him.
51:48 and *e* in them shall shout over Babylon
Ez 7:14 shall sound the trumpet and make *e* ready,
11:25 I told the exiles *e* the LORD had shown me.
30:12 The land and *e* in it I will hand over to
44:14 work and for *e* that is to be done in it.
Dn 2:40 iron breaks in pieces and crushes *e* else.
3:76 *E* growing from the earth,
14:15 and children, and they ate and drank *e*.
Hos 4: 3 mourns, and *e* that dwells in it languishes:
Am 6: 8 and I give over the city with *e* in it;
Mt 8:33 in the town related *e* that had happened,
11:27 *E* has been given over to me by my Father.
15:17 "Do you not see that *e* that enters the
17:11 is indeed coming, and he will restore *e*.
19:27 "Here we have put *e* aside to follow you.
21:38 'Here is the one who will inherit *e*.
22: 4 and corn-fed cattle are killed; *e* is ready.
23: 3 do *e* and observe everything they tell you.
23:20 the altar is swearing by it and by *e* on it.
28:20 them to carry out *e* I have commanded you.
Mk 4:39 The wind fell off and *e* grew calm.
7:37 "He has done *e* well!
8:25 was restored and he could see *e* clearly.
9:12 will indeed come first and restore *e*.
9:23 *E* is possible to a man who trusts."
10:28 him, "We have put aside *e* to follow you!"
11:11 He inspected *e* there,
12: 7 'Here is the one who will inherit *e*.
Lk 5:11 they brought their boats to land, left *e*,
5:28 Leaving *e* behind, Levi stood up
10:22 *E* has been given over to me by my Father.
12: 3 *E* you have said in the dark will be heard
14:17 those invited, 'Come along, *e* is ready now.'
15:14 After he had spent *e*, a great famine broke
15:31 are with me always, and *e* I have is yours.
22:13 went off and found *e* just as he had said;
23:49 were standing at a distance watching *e*.
24:44 *e* written about me in the law of Moses and
Jn 3:35 loves the Son and has given *e* over to him.
4:25 "When he comes, he will tell us *e*."
4:29 and see someone who told me *e* I ever did!
4:39 "He told me *e* I ever did."
5:20 the Son and *e* the Father does he shows him.
13: 3 the Father who had handed *e* over to him
14:26 send in my name, will instruct you in *e*,
16:30 We are convinced that you know *e*.
19:28 Jesus, realizing that *e* was now finished,
21:17 "Lord, you know *e*.
Acts 2:45 dividing *e* on the basis of each one's need.
3:22 shall listen to him in *e* he says to you.
4:32 rather, *e* was held in common.
10: 8 *e* to them and dispatched them to Joppa.
11:10 *e* in it was drawn up again into the sky.
17:25 gives to all life and breath and *e* else.
22:10 be told about *e* you are destined to do.'
Rom 3:19 We know that *e* the law says is addressed
4:16 Hence, all depends on faith, *e* is grace.
15: 4 *E* written before our time was written for
1Cor 2:15 man, on the other hand, can appraise *e*,
6:12 *E* is lawful for me"—but that does not
6:12 that does not mean that *e* is good for me.
8: 6 whom *e* was made and through whom we live.
10:23 which does not mean that *e* is constructive.
13: 3 If I give *e* I have to feed the poor and
14:26 as *e* is done with a constructive purpose.
14:40 sure that *e* is done properly and in order.
15:27 when it says that *e* has been made subject,
15:27 has made *e* subject to Christ is excluded.
16:14 Do *e* with love.
2Cor 4:15 Indeed, *e* is ordered to your benefit,
6:10 We seem to have nothing, yet *e* is ours!
7:14 just as *e* I ever said to you was true,
9: 8 of *e* and even a surplus for good works,
12:19 in Christ, I have done *e* to build you up,
Gal 3:10 Cursed is he who does not abide by *e* written
Eph 1:11 *e* according to his will and counsel,
5:20 for *e* in the name of our Lord Jesus Christ.
Phil 2:14 In *e* you do, act without grumbling
3: 8 For his sake I have forfeited *e*;
3:21 body, by his power to subject *e* to himself.
4:13 of my strength I have strength for *e*.
Col 1:16 him *e* in heaven and on earth was created,
1:17 In him *e* continues in being.
1:18 the dead, so that primacy may be his in *e*.
1:20 means of him, to reconcile *e* in his person,
3:11 Rather, Christ is *e* in all of you.
3:20 in *e* as the acceptable way in the Lord.
1Thes 5:21 Test *e*; retain what is good.
1Tm 4: 4 *E* God created is good;
Ti 3:13 seen to it that they have *e* they need.
Heb 8: 5 "See that you make *e* according to the
9:22 to the law almost *e* is purified by blood,
1Pt 2: 1 strip away everything vicious, *e* deceitful;
2Pt 1: 3 us *e* necessary for a life of genuine piety,
3: 4 but *e* stays just as it was when the world
3:11 Since *e* is to be destroyed in this way,
Rv 5:13 *e* in the universe cried aloud:
10: 6 and earth and sea along with *e* in them:

EVERYWHERE (25)

Gn 6:17 to destroy *e* all creatures in which there
7:19 all the highest mountains *e* were submerged,
19:31 earth to unite with us as was the custom *e*.
2Sm 7: 7 all my wanderings *e* among the Israelites,
Jdt 7:18 equipment was spread out in profusion *e*.
1Mc 13:20 army moved along opposite him *e* he went.
2Mc 2:18 from *e* under the heavens to his holy Place,
8: 7 Soon the fame of his valor spread *e*.
Jb 37: 3 *E* under the heavens he sends it,
Ps(s) 103:22 the LORD, all his works, *e* in his domain.
Wis 2: 9 *e* let us leave tokens of our rejoicing,
Is 16: 7 Moab wails for Moab, *e* they wail;
Ez 23:24 and helmets they shall array against you *e*.
Dn 3:37 brought low *e* in the world this day
Am 8: 3 Many shall be the corpses, strewn *e*—
Mal 1:11 And *e* they bring sacrifice to my name,
Mk 16:20 The Eleven went forth and preached *e*.
Lk 9: 6 the good news *e* and curing diseases.
Acts 17:16 at the sight of idols *e* in the city.
17:30 calls on all men *e* to reform their lives.
21:28 his teaching *e* against our people,
24: 3 *e* acknowledge our deep gratitude to you.
28:22 very well that this sect is denounced *e*."
2Cor 2:14 diffuse the fragrance of his knowledge *e*!
Col 1: 6 in your midst, as it has *e* in the world.

EVES (2)

Jdt 8: 6 eves and sabbaths, new moon *e* and new

EVI (2)

Nm 31: 8 *E*, Rekem, Zur, Hur
Jos 13:21 *E*, Rekem, Zur, Hur and Reba;

EVICTING (2)

Ez 45: 9 Stop *e* my people!
46:18 the people by *e* them from their property.

EVIDENCE (24)

Ex 22:12 by a wild beast, let him bring it as *e*,
Nm 5:13 husband has not sufficient *e* of the fact,
35:30 the *e* of witnesses is required for the
35:30 The *e* of a single witness is not
Dt 4: 6 for thus will you give *e* of your wisdom
22:15 of the girl shall take the *e* of her virginity
22:17 here is the *e* of my daughter's virginity!'
22:20 and *e* of the girl's virginity is not found,
Jos 22:27 but as *e* for you on behalf of ourselves
2Mc 4:33 When Onias had clear *e* of the facts,
Wis 4: 6 give *e* of the wickedness of their parents,
5:11 no *e* of its course is to be found
Sir 36:14 Give *e* of your deeds of old;
Dn 13:48 without examination and without clear *e*?
Mt 3: 8 Give some *e* that you mean to reform.
Lk 3: 8 Give some *e* that you mean to reform.
19:22 I intend to judge you on your own *e*.
Jn 7: 7 but it does hate me because of the *e* I
8:17 law that *e* given by two persons is valid.
18:23 "If I said anything wrong produce the *e*,
Acts 11:23 he rejoiced to see the *e* of God's favor.
18: 5 *e* to the Jews that Jesus was the Messiah.
Phil 3: 4 has a right to put his trust in external *e*,
Heb 6:17 *e* that his purpose would not change,

EVIDENT (6)

Jdt 8:29 Not today only is your wisdom made *e*,
2Mc 15:35 and *e* proof to all of the LORD's help.
Is 44: 7 Let him stand up and speak, make it *e*,
Ez 16:57 yourself, before your wickedness became *e*?
Mk 12:14 It is *e* you do not act out of human
2Cor 11: 6 this *e* to you in every conceivable way.

EVIL (552)

Gn 6: 5 heart conceived was ever anything but *e*,
8:21 of man's heart are *e* from the start;
44: 4 to them, 'Why did you repay good with *e*?
Ex 10:10 Clearly, you have some *e* in mind.
32:12 say, 'With *e* intent he brought them out,
32:22 well enough how prone the people are to *e*.
Lv 5: 4 it, rashly utters an oath to do good or *e*,
Nm 24:13 of my own accord to anything, good or *e*,
32:13 *e* in the sight of the LORD had died out.
Dt 1:35 'Not one man of this *e* generation shall
4:25 this *e* done in his sight provoke the LORD,
9:18 LORD and the *e* you had done to provoke him.
13: 6 Thus shall you purge the *e* from your midst.
13:12 again do such *e* as this in your midst.
17: 2 woman who does *e* in the sight of the LORD,
17: 5 man (or woman) who has done the *e* deed
17: 7 Thus shall you purge the *e* from your midst.
17:12 Thus shall you purge the *e* from your midst.
19:19 Thus shall you purge the *e* from your midst.
19:20 and never again do a thing so *e* among you.
21:21 Thus shall you purge the *e* from your midst,
22:21 Thus shall you purge the *e* from your midst.
22:22 Thus shall you purge the *e* from your midst.
22:24 Thus shall you purge the *e* from your midst.
24: 7 Thus shall you purge the *e* from your midst.
28:20 for the *e* you have done in forsaking me.
31:18 *e* they have done in turning to other gods.
31:29 so that *e* will befall you in some future
31:29 you have done *e* in the LORD's sight,
Jos 24:20 gods, he will do *e* to you and destroy you."
Jgs 2:19 of their *e* practices or stubborn conduct.
9:56 Thus did God requite the *e* Abimelech had
20:12 is this *e* which has occurred among you?
20:13 to death and thus purge the *e* from Israel."
Ru 1:21 me and the Almighty has brought *e* upon me
1Sm 12:19 our other sins the *e* of asking for a king."
12:20 is true you have committed all this *e*;
12:25 If instead you continue to do *e*,
16:14 tormented by an *e* spirit sent by the LORD.
16:15 An *e* spirit from God is tormenting you.
16:16 When the *e* spirit from God comes over you,
16:23 better, for the *e* spirit would leave him.
17:28 I know your arrogance and your *e* intent.
18:10 day an *e* spirit from God came over Saul,
19: 9 Then an *e* spirit from the LORD came upon
25:17 for you must realize that otherwise *e* is
25:21 He has repaid good with *e*.
25:28 *e* to be found in you your whole life long.
25:39 *e*, but has punished Nabal for his own evil
26:18 What *e* do I plan?
2Sm 3:39 the evildoer in accordance with his *e* deed."
12: 9 spurned the LORD and done *e* in his sight?

12:11 bring *e* upon you out of your own house.
18:32 you with *e* intent be as that young man!"
1Kgs 2:44 the *e* that you did to my father David.
9: 9 LORD has brought down upon them all this *e.*
11: 6 Solomon did *e* in the sight of the LORD;
13:33 not give up his *e* ways after this event,
14:10 I am bringing *e* upon the house of Jeroboam:
14:22 Judah did *e* in the sight of the LORD,
15:26 He did *e* in the LORD'S sight,
15:34 He did *e* in the LORD'S sight,
16: 7 the *e* Baasha did in the sight of the LORD,
16: 7 provoking him to anger by his *e* deeds,
16:19 doing *e* in the sight of the LORD by
16:25 But Omri did *e* in the LORD'S sight beyond
16:30 did *e* in the sight of the LORD more than
21:20 yourself up to doing *e* in the LORD'S sight,
21:21 the LORD'S sight, I am bringing *e* upon you:
21:25 of *e* in the sight of the LORD as did Ahab,
21:29 me, I will not bring the *e* in his time.
21:29 I will bring the *e* upon his house during
22: 8 he prophesies not good but *e* about me."
22: 8 not your majesty speak of *e* against you."
22:18 you he prophesies not good but *e* about me?"
22:23 the LORD himself has decreed *e* against you."
22:53 He did *e* in the sight of the LORD,
2Kgs 3: 2 He did *e* in the LORD'S sight,
6:33 to him and said, "This *e* is from the LORD.
8:12 "Because I know the *e* that you will
8:18 and he did *e* in the LORD'S sight.
8:27 doing *e* in the LORD'S sight as they did,
13: 2 He did *e* in the LORD'S sight,
13:11 He did *e* in the sight of the LORD;
14:24 He did *e* in the sight of the LORD;
15: 9 He did *e* in the sight of the LORD as his
15:18 He did *e* in the sight of the LORD,
15:24 He did *e* in the sight of the LORD,
15:28 He did *e* in the sight of the LORD,
17: 2 He did *e* in the sight of the LORD,
17:11 They did *e* things that provoked the LORD,
17:13 "Give up your *e* ways and keep my
17:17 into *e* doing in the LORD'S sight,
21: 2 He did *e* in the sight of the LORD,
21: 6 He did much *e* in the LORD'S sight and
21: 9 misled them into doing even greater *e*
21:11 these abominations and has done greater *e*
21:12 bring such *e* on Jerusalem and Judah that,
21:15 because they have done *e* in my sight and
21:16 Manasseh did *e* in the sight of the LORD,
21:20 He did *e* in the sight of the LORD,
22:16 its inhabitants all the *e* that is threatened
22:20 see all the *e* I will bring upon this place.' "
23:32 He did *e* in the sight of the LORD,
23:37 He did *e* in the sight of the LORD,
24: 9 He did *e* in the sight of the LORD,
24:19 He also did *e* in the sight of the LORD,
1Chr 7:23 Beriah, since *e* had befallen his house.
2Chr 7:14 my presence and turn from their *e* ways,
7:22 he has brought down upon them all this *e.*' "
12:14 He did *e,* for he had not truly resolved
18: 7 prophesies not good but always *e* about me.
18: 7 not your Majesty speak of *e* against you."
18:17 he prophesies no good about me, but only *e?"*
18:22 the LORD himself has decreed *e* against you."
20: 9 your honor, saying, 'When *e* comes upon us,
20:35 with King Ahaziah of Israel, who did *e.*
21: 6 He did *e* in the sight of the LORD,
22: 4 he did *e* in the sight of the LORD,
29: 6 and did *e* in the eyes of the LORD,
33: 2 He did *e* in the sight of the LORD,
33: 6 with the great *e* that he did in his sight.
33: 9 into doing even greater *e* than the nations
33:22 He did *e* in the sight of the LORD,
34:24 *e* upon this place and upon its inhabitants,
34:28 Your eyes shall not see all the *e* I will
36: 5 He did *e* in the sight of the LORD,
36: 9 He did *e* in the sight of the LORD.
36:12 He did *e* in the sight of the LORD,
Ezr 4:12 now rebuilding this rebellious and *e* city.
4:22 the *e* grow to the detriment of the throne."
9:13 us for our *e* deeds and our great guilt
Neh 2:17 "You see the *e* plight in which we stand:
9:28 would go back to doing *e* in your sight.
9:33 for you kept faith while we have done *e.*
9:35 nor did they turn away from their *e* deeds.
13: 7 *e* thing that Eliashib had done for Tobiah,
13:17 "What is this *e* thing that you are doing,
13:18 all this *e* upon us and upon this city?
13:27 that you have done this same very great *e,*
Tb 6: 8 who is afflicted by a demon or *e* spirit,
12: 7 good, and *e* will not find its way to you.
Est A: 7 and distress, *e* and great confusion,
8: 6 witness the *e* that is to befall my people,
1Mc 1:52 joined them and committed *e* in the land.
10:46 great *e* that Demetrius had done in Israel,
11: 8 Plotting *e* against Alexander,
13:32 Thus he brought much *e* on the land.
13:46 "Do not treat us according to our *e* deeds,"
16:17 act of treason he repaid good with *e.*
2Mc 1:25 and eternal, Israel's savior from all *e,*
3: 1 the high priest Onias and his hatred of *e,*
6: 3 This intensified the *e* in an intolerable
8: 4 and to manifest his hatred of *e.*
Jb 1: 1 named Job, who feared God and avoided *e.*
1: 8 and upright, fearing God and avoiding *e?"*
2: 3 and upright, fearing God and avoiding *e?*
2:10 and should we not accept *e?"*
5:19 and at the seventh no *e* shall touch you.
17: 5 My lot is described as *e,*
21:30 the *e* man is spared calamity when it comes;
28:28 and avoiding *e* is understanding.
30:26 Yet when I looked for good, then *e* came;
31:29 my enemy or exulted when *e* fell upon him,
33:17 man from *e* and keeping pride away from him,
36:10 and exhorts them to turn back from *e.*
36:21 Take heed, turn not to *e;*
42:11 the *e* which the LORD had brought upon him;
Ps(s) 5: 5 no *e* man remains with you;
7: 5 hands, If I have repaid my friend with *e,*
21:12 Though they intend *e* against you,
23: 4 I walk in the dark valley I fear no *e;*
28: 3 neighbors though *e* is in their hearts.
28: 4 for their deeds, for the *e* of their doings.
34:14 from *e* and your lips from speaking guile;
34:15 Turn from *e,* and do good;
35: 4 back and confounded who plot *e* against me.
35:12 They have repaid me *e* for good,
36: 5 that is not good, with no repugnance for *e.*
37:19 They are not put to shame in an *e* time;
37:27 Turn from *e* and do good,
38:21 *e* for good harass me for pursuing good.
49: 6 Why should I fear in *e* days when my
50:19 To your mouth you give free rein for *e,*
51: 6 sinned, and done what is *e* in your sight"
52: 3 Why do you glory in *e,*
52: 5 You love *e* rather than good,
54: 7 Turn back the *e* upon my foes;
55: 4 For they bring down *e* upon me,
55:11 *E* and mischief are in its midst;
55:16 nether world, for *e* is in their dwellings,
56: 6 their every thought is of *e* against me.
73: 8 They scoff and speak *e;*
90:15 afflicted us, for the years when we saw *e.*
91:10 No *e* shall befall you,
94:13 law you teach, Giving him rest from *e* days,
97:10 The LORD loves those that hate *e;*
101: 4 *e* I will not know.
109: 5 me *e* for good and hatred for my love.
109:20 and upon those who speak *e* against me.
112: 7 An *e* report he shall not fear;
119:101 From every *e* way I withhold my feet,
121: 7 The LORD will guard you from all *e;*
137: 8 who shall repay you the *e* you have done us!
140: 2 Deliver me, O LORD, from *e* men;
140: 3 From those who devise *e* in their hearts,
140:12 *e* shall abruptly entrap the violent man.
141: 4 Let not my heart incline to the *e* of
144:11 From the *e* sword deliver me;
Prv 1:16 [For their feet run to *e,*
2:12 Saving you from the way of *e* men,
2:14 way of darkness, Who delight in doing *e,*
3: 7 fear the LORD and turn away from *e;*
3:29 Plot no *e* against your neighbor,
4:14 enter not, walk not on the way of *e* men;
4:16 they cannot rest unless they have done *e;*
4:27 nor to left, keep your foot far from *e.*
6:14 in his heart, is always plotting *e,*
6:18 schemes, feet that run swiftly to *e,*
8:13 hate evil;] Pride, arrogance, the *e* way,
11:19 but he who pursues *e* does so to his death.
11:21 Truly the *e* man shall not go unpunished,
11:27 he who pursues evil will have *e* befall him.
12:12 The stronghold of *e* men will be demolished,
12:13 the sin of his lips the *e* man is ensnared,
12:20 Deceit is in the hands of those who plot *e,*
13:19 the soul, but fools hate to turn from *e.*
14:16 The wise man is cautious and shuns *e;*
14:19 *E* men must bow down before the good,
14:22 Do not those who plot *e* go astray?
15: 3 place, keeping watch on the *e* and the good.
15:28 but the mouth of the wicked pours out *e.*
16: 4 own ends, even the wicked for the *e* day.
16: 6 and by the fear of the LORD man avoids *e.*
16:27 A scoundrel is a furnace of *e,*
17: 4 The *e* man gives heed to wicked lips,
17:13 *e* for good, from his house evil will not depart.
20: 8 of judgment dispels all *e* with his glance.
20:22 Say not, "I will repay *e!"*
20:30 *E* is cleansed away by bloody lashes,
21:10 The soul of the wicked man desires *e;*
22: 3 The shrewd man perceives *e* and hides,
24: 1 Be not emulous of *e* men,
24: 8 He who plots *e* doing
24:20 For the *e* man has no future,
27:12 The shrewd man perceives *e* and hides;
28: 5 *E* men understand nothing of justice,
28:10 *e* way will himself fall into his own pit.
28:14 he who hardens his heart will fall into *e.*
31:12 She brings him good, and not *e,*
Eccl 2:17 the work that is done under the sun is *e;*
4:17 for they know not how to keep from doing *e.*
5:12 grievous *e* which I have seen under the sun:
5:15 This too is a grievous *e,*
6: 1 another *e* which I have seen under the sun,
7:14 good things, and on an *e* day consider:
8: 5 keeps the commandment experiences no *e,*
8:11 are filled with the desire to commit *e*—
8:12 sinner does *e* a hundred times and survives.
8:14 men treated as though they had done *e*
9: 3 Hence the minds of men are filled with *e,*
9:12 when the *e* time falls suddenly upon them.
10: 5 I have seen under the sun another *e,*
12: 1 before the *e* days come And the years
Wis 1: 4 into a soul that plots *e* wisdom enters not,
14: 9 to God are the evildoer and his *e* deed;
14:27 reason and source and extremity of all *e.*
15: 4 the *e* creation of men's fancy deceive us,
15: 6 Lovers of *e* things,
15:12 profit every way, be it even out of *e."*
16: 8 that you are he who delivers from all *e.*
Sir 3:27 he is the offshoot of an *e* plant.
4:20 guard yourself from *e,*
6: 1 "That for the *e* man with double tongue!"
7: 1 Do no *e,* and evil will not overtake you;
7: 7 guilty of no *e* before the city's populace,
9: 1 lest you teach her to do *e* against you.
11:14 Good and *e,* life and death,
11:16 birth, and *e* grows old with evildoers.
11:31 The talebearer turns good into *e;*
11:32 The *e* man lies in wait for blood,
11:33 Avoid a wicked man, for he breeds only *e,*
12: 6 With twofold *e* you will meet for every
12:17 If *e* comes upon you,
13:23 poverty is *e* by the standards of the proud.
13:24 his countenance, either for good or for *e.*
17: 6 good and *e* he shows them.
17:12 He says to them, "Avoid all *e";*
18: 6 the good, the *e* in him, what are these?
19: 5 He who gloats over evil will meet with *e,*
19: 5 he who repeats an *e* report has no sense.
20:16 Those who eat his bread have an *e* tongue.
25:15 rather dwell than live with an *e* woman.
25:18 There is scarce any *e* like that in a woman;
25:22 this from an *e* wife.
29:12 house, and it will save you from every *e;*
31:10 did not, could have done *e* but would not,
31:13 Remember that gluttony is *e.*
33: 1 No *e* can harm the man who fears the LORD;
33:14 As *e* contrasts with good,
35: 3 To refrain from *e* pleases the LORD,
37:18 Good and *e,* death and life, their absolute
39: 5 to learn what is good and *e* among men.
39:27 good, but for the wicked they turn out *e.*
40:10 For the wicked, these were created *e,*
47:25 more, and they lent themselves to every *e.*
49: 3 his whole heart, and, though times were *e,*
51: 8 in him, and rescues them from every *e.*
51:12 He saved me from *e* of every kind and
Is 1: 4 people laden with wickedness, *e* race,
1:16 cease doing *e;* learn to do good.
3: 9 they deal out *e* to themselves.
5:20 Woe to those who call *e* good, and good *e,*
13:11 for its *e* and the wicked for their guilt.
14:20 be named forever, that scion of an *e* race!
29:20 All who are alert to do *e* will be cut off,
32: 6 speaks foolishly, planning *e* in his heart:
33:15 closing his eyes lest he look on *e*—
41:23 Do something, good or *e,*
47:11 come *e* you will not know how to predict:
57: 1 he is taken away from the presence of *e,*
59: 6 Their works are *e* works,
59: 7 Their feet run to *e,*
59:15 and the man who turns from *e* is despoiled.
65: 2 in *e* paths and follow their own thoughts,
65:12 But did what was *e* in my sight and
66: 4 Because they did what was *e* in my sight,
Jer 1:14 *e* will boil over upon all who dwell in the
2: 3 to partake of them, *e* would befall him,
2:19 *e* and bitter is your forsaking the LORD,
3: 5 yet you do all the *e* you can.
4: 4 can quench it, because of your *e* deeds.
4: 6 *E* I bring from the north,
4:14 Cleanse your heart of *e,*
4:22 They are wise in *e,*
5:12 No *e* shall befall us,
6: 1 For *e* threatens from the north,
6:19 See, I bring *e* upon this people,
7:24 of their *e* hearts and turned their backs,
7:30 of Judah have done what is *e* in my eyes,
9: 2 They go from *e* to evil,
11: 8 one followed the hardness of his *e* heart,
11:17 because of the *e* done by the house of Israel
12:14 Thus says the LORD against all my *e*
13:23 to do good, accustomed to *e* as you are.
15: 7 they returned not from their *e* ways.
16:12 of his *e* heart instead of listening to me.
18: 8 turns from its evil, I also repent of the *e*
18:10 if that nation does what is *e* in my eyes,
18:11 fashioning *e* against you and making a plan.
18:11 Return, each of you, from, his *e* way;
18:12 to the stubbornness of his *e* heart!"
18:20 Must good be repaid with *e* that they
19: 3 I am going to bring such *e* upon this place
19:15 city all the *e* with which I threatened it,
21:12 quenched, because of the *e* of your deeds.
23: 2 I will take care to punish your *e* deeds.
23:10 Theirs is an *e* course,
23:12 *E* I will bring upon them:
23:14 the wicked, so that no one turns from *e;*
23:17 of heart, "No *e* shall overtake you,"

EVIL (cont.)

23:22 from *e* ways and from their wicked deeds.
25: 5 from your evil way and from your *e* deeds;
25: 6 your handiwork, and I bring *e* upon you.
25:29 is called by my name, I begin to inflict *e*,
26: 3 evil way, so that I may repent of the *e* I have
26: 3 to inflict upon them for their *e* deeds.
26:13 of the *e* with which he threatens you.
26:19 of the *e* with which he had threatened them?
26:19 committing this great *e* to our own undoing."
32:30 youth have done only what is *e* in my eyes;
32:42 brought upon this people all this great *e*,
35:15 to turn back, all of you, from your *e* way;
35:17 of Jerusalem every *e* that I threatened;
36: 3 all the *e* I have in mind to do to them,
36: 3 they will turn back each from his *e* way,
36: 7 and will all turn back from their *e* way;
36:31 all the threats of *e* which went unheeded.
39:16 against this city, for *e* and not for good;
42:10 for I regret the *e* I have done you.
42:17 escape the *e* that I will bring upon them.
44: 2 You have seen all the *e* I brought on
44: 3 because of the *e* they did to provoke me,
44: 5 from the *e* of sacrificing to strange gods.
44: 7 you inflict so great an *e* upon yourselves?
44: 9 forgotten the *e* deeds which your fathers,
44:11 I have determined *e* against you;
44:22 The LORD could no longer bear your *e* deeds,
44:23 this *e* has befallen you at the present day.
44:27 I am watching over them to do *e*, not good.
45: 5 I am bringing *e* on all mankind,
48: 2 *E* they plan against Heshbon:
49:37 I will bring *e* upon them,
51:24 live in Chaldea All the *e* they did to Zion,
51:64 because of the *e* I am bringing upon her.
52: 2 He did what was *e* in the eyes of the LORD,
Lam 1:22 "Let all their *e* come before you;
Bar 1:22 gods, and did *e* in the sight of the Lord,
2: 8 each from the figments of his *e* heart.
2:33 stubbornness, and from their *e* deeds,
4:18 He who has brought this *e* upon you must
Ez 3:19 from his *e* nor from his wicked conduct,
6: 9 loathe themselves because of their *e* deeds,
11: 2 *e* and giving wicked counsel in this city.
13:22 turn from his *e* conduct and save his life;
14:22 be consoled regarding the *e* I have brought
18:23 he turns from his *e* way that he may live?
18:24 turns from the path of virtue to do *e*,
20:43 because of all the *e* things you did.
20:44 to your *e* conduct and corrupt actions,
28:15 you were created, Until *e* was found in you,
33:11 Turn, turn from your *e* ways!
36:31 Then you shall remember your *e* conduct,
38:10 mind, and you shall devise an *e* scheme:
Dn 3:29 from you, and we have done every kind of *e*.
9: 5 We have sinned, been wicked and done *e*;
11:27 The two kings, resolved on *e*,
12: 4 many shall fall away and *e* shall increase."
13:52 "How you have grown *e* with age!
Hos 7:15 their arms, yet they devised *e* against me.
Am 3: 6 If *e* befalls a city, has not the LORD
5:13 silent at this time, for it is an *e* time.
5:14 Seek good and not *e*,
5:15 Hate *e* and love good,
6: 3 You would put off the *e* day,
9: 4 I will fix my gaze upon them for *e*,
9:10 who say, *E* will not reach or overtake us."
Jon 3: 8 *e* way and from the violence he has in hand.
3:10 their *e* way, he had repented of the evil that
Mi 1:12 For *e* has come down from the LORD to the
2: 1 iniquity, and work out *e* on their couches;
2: 3 I am planning against this race an *e*
2: 3 with head high, for it will be a time of *e*.
3: 2 You who hate what is good, and love *e*?
3: 4 that time, because of the *e* they have done.
3:11 No *e* can come upon us!"
7: 3 Their hands succeed at *e*;
Na 1:11 you he came who devised *e* against the LORD,
Hb 1:13 Too pure are your eyes to look upon *e*,
2: 9 him who pursues *e* gain for his household,
Zep 1:12 "Neither good nor *e* can the LORD do."
Zec 1: 4 your *e* ways and from your wicked deeds.
7:10 plot *e* against one another in your hearts.
8:17 of you plot *e* against another in his heart,
Mal 1: 8 blind animal for sacrifice, is this not *e*?
1: 8 offer the lame or the sick, is it not *e*?
2: 6 uprightness, and turned many away from *e*.
Mt 5:37 Anything beyond that is from the *e* one.
6:13 to the trial but deliver us from the *e* one.'
9: 4 "Why do you harbor *e* thoughts?
12:34 you brood of vipers, when you are so *e*?
12:35 an *e* man produces evil from his evil store.
12:39 *e* and unfaithful age is eager for a sign!
12:45 this time seven spirits more *e* than itself.
12:45 is how it will be with this *e* generation."
13:19 The *e* one approaches him to steal away
13:38 The weeds are the followers of the *e* one
15:19 From the mind stem *e* designs
16: 4 An *e*, faithless age is eager for a sign,
23:16 It is an *e* day for you, blind guides!
23:28 while hypocrisy and *e* fill you within.
24:12 Because of the increase of *e*,
26:45 is to be handed over to the power of *e* men.
Mk 3: 4 good deed on the sabbath—or an *e* one?
14:41 to be handed over to the clutches of *e* men.
Lk 6: 9 lawful to do good on the sabbath—or *e*?
6:22 your name as *e* because of the Son of Man.
6:45 *e* man produces evil out of his store of *e*.
7:21 their diseases, afflictions, and *e* spirits;
8: 2 had been cured of *e* spirits and maladies;
11:29 "This is an *e* age.
11:39 you are filled with rapaciousness and *e*.
Jn 3:20 Everyone who practices *e* hates the light;
7: 7 I bring against it that what it does is *e*.
17:15 world, but to guard them from the *e* one.
Acts 3:26 bless you by turning you from your *e* ways."
8:22 Reform your *e* ways.
19:12 cured and *e* spirits departed from them.
19:13 over those who were possessed by *e* spirits,
19:15 were doing this, the *e* spirit answered,
19:16 Then the man with the *e* spirit sprang at
Rom 2: 9 will come upon every man who has done *e*,
3: 8 may we not do *e* that good may come of it?
6:13 of your body to sin as weapons for *e*.
7: 7 what *e* desire was unless the law had said,
7: 8 to rouse in me every kind of *e* desire.
7:19 I will to do, but the *e* I do not intend.
8:13 you put to death the *e* deeds of the body,
9:11 unborn and had done neither good nor *e*,
12: 9 Detest what is *e*, cling to what is good.
12:21 conquered by *e* but conquer evil with good.
13: 3 is right but only when his conduct is *e*.
16:19 to what is good and innocent of all *e*.
1Cor 14:20 Be like children as far as *e* is concerned,
2Cor 13: 7 We pray God that you may do no *e*—
Gal 1: 4 sins, to rescue us from the present *e* age,
Eph 4:29 Never let *e* talk pass your lips;
5:16 present opportunity, for these are *e* days.
6:12 darkness, the *e* spirits in regions above.
6:13 of God if you are to resist on the *e* day;
6:16 extinguish the fiery darts of the *e* one.
Phil 3: 2 Watch out for workers of *e*.
Col 1:21 in your hearts because of your *e* deeds.
3: 5 uncleanness, passion, *e* desires,
1Thes 5:15 See that no one returns *e* to any other;
5:22 Avoid any semblance of *e*.
2Thes 3: 2 may be delivered from confused and *e* men.
3: 3 you and guard you against the *e* one.
1Tm 6: 4 envy, dissension, slander, *e* suspicions
6:10 The love of money is the root of all *e*.
2Tm 2:19 professes the name of the Lord abandon *e*."
2:21 *e* things he may be a distinguished vessel,
3:13 But all the while *e* men and charlatans
Ti 3: 2 not to speak *e* of anyone or be quarrelsome.
Heb 3:12 lest any of you have an *e* and unfaithful
5:14 by practice to distinguish good from *e*.
10:22 our hearts sprinkled clean from the *e*
Jas 1:13 Surely God, who is beyond the grasp of *e*,
3: 8 It is a restless *e*, full of deadly poison.
1Pt 3: 9 not return evil for *e* or insult for insult.
3:10 from *e* and his lips from uttering deceit.
3:11 He must turn from *e* and do good,
3:17 to do so for good deeds than for *e* ones.
4: 3 living lives of debauchery, *e* desires,
1Jn 2:13 you, for you have conquered the *e* one.
2:14 in you, and you have conquered the *e* one.
3:12 to the *e* one and killed his brother.
5:18 by him, and so the *e* one cannot touch him.
5:19 while the whole world is under the *e* one.
2Jn 1:11 whoever greets him shares in the *e* he does.
3Jn 1:10 is doing in spreading *e* nonsense about us.
1:11 do not imitate what is *e* but what is good.
1:11 whoever does what is *e* has never seen God.
Jude 1:15 godless for every *e* deed they have done,

EVIL-MERODACH (2)

2Kgs 25:27 day of the twelfth month, *E*
Jer 52:31 twenty-fifth day of the twelfth month, *E*,

EVILDOER (6)

2Sm 3:39 the *e* in accordance with his evil deed."
Ps(s) 10:15 the strength of the wicked and of the *e*;
Prv 24:25 But those who convict the *e* will fare well,
29:27 The *e* is an abomination to the just,
Wis 14: 9 odious to God are the *e* and his evil deed;
Mal 2:17 "Every *e* is good in the sight of the LORD,

EVILDOERS (43)

Est E:15 by this archcriminal, are not *e*,
1Mc 3: 6 by fear of him, and all *e* were dismayed.
9:23 of Israel, and all kinds of *e* appeared.
Jb 31: 3 for the unrighteous, and woe for *e*?
34: 8 with *e* and goes along with wicked men,
34:22 no darkness so dense that *e* can hide in it.
Ps(s) 5: 6 You hate all *e*;
6: 9 Depart from me, all *e*,
14: 4 Will all these *e* never learn,
22:17 surround me, a pack of *e* closes in upon me;
26: 5 I hate the assembly of *e*,
27: 2 When *e* come at me to devour my flesh,
34:17 The LORD confronts the *e*,
36:13 See how the *e* have fallen;
37: 1 Be not vexed over *e*,
37: 9 For *e* shall be cut off,
53: 5 Will all these *e* never learn,
59: 3 Rescue me from *e*;
64: 3 of malefactors, against the tumult of *e*,
92: 8 flourish like grass and all *e* thrive,
92:10 all *e* shall be scattered.
94: 4 insolent speeches, boasting, all the *e*?
94:16 Who will stand by me against the *e*?
101: 8 And uproot from the city of the LORD all *e*.
125: 5 ways may the LORD lead away with the *e*!
141: 4 in deeds of wickedness With men who are *e*;
141: 9 have set for me, and from the snares of *e*.
Prv 10:29 to him who walks honestly, but to *e*,
21:15 is a joy for the just, but terror for *e*.
24:19 Be not provoked with *e*,
Eccl 8:11 against *e* is not promptly executed,
Sir 11:16 their birth, and evil grows old with *e*.
27:10 in wait for prey, so do sins for *e*.
Is 31: 2 of the wicked and against those who help *e*.
53: 9 the wicked and a burial place with *e*,
Hos 6: 8 Gilead is a city of *e*, tracked with blood.
Mal 3:15 for indeed *e* prosper,
3:19 all the proud and all *e* will be stubble,
Mt 7:23 Out of my sight, you *e*!'
13:41 all who draw others to apostasy, and all *e*.
Lk 13:27 Away from me, you *e*!'
Jn 5:29 the *e* shall rise to be damned.
1Pt 3:12 but against *e* the Lord sets his face."

EVILDOING (10)

Ps(s) 94:23 And he will requite them for their *e*,
Wis 5:23 and *e* overturn the thrones of potentates.
Is 56: 2 from profanation, and his hand from any *e*.
Jer 31:34 their *e* and remember their sin no more.
Ez 16:23 Then after all your *e*— woe, woe to you!
18: 8 if he holds off from *e*,
18:17 who holds off from *e*,
2Thes 2:12 but have delighted in *e* will be condemned.
Heb 8:12 I will forgive their *e*,
2Pt 2:16 gain, but he was rebuked for his *e*.

EVILS (25)

Dt 31:17 and many *e* and troubles will befall them.
31:17 not among us that these *e* have befallen us?'
31:21 then, when many *e* and troubles befall them,
1Sm 10:19 you from all your *e* and calamities,
Est A: 8 with fear of the *e* to come upon them,
F: 6 people and delivered us from all these *e*.
1Mc 1:11 from them, many *e* have come upon us."
6:12 But I now recall the *e* I did in Jerusalem,
6:13 that this is why these *e* have overtaken me;
7:23 When Judas saw all the *e* that Alcimus and
2Mc 10:10 summary of the chief *e* caused by the wars.
Ps(s) 40:13 For all about me are *e* beyond reckoning;
Wis 14:22 war of ignorance, they call such *e* peace.
Sir 25:12 heart, worst of all *e* is that of a woman.
Jer 2:13 Two *e* have my people done:
16:10 pronounced all these great *e* against us?
32:23 Hence you let all these *e* befall them.
Bar 1:20 And the *e* and the curse which the Lord
2: 2 He brought down upon us *e* so great that
2: 7 All the *e* of which the Lord has warned us
2: 9 And the Lord kept watch over the *e*,
3: 4 the Lord, their God, and the *e* cling to us.
Ez 8: 9 the abominable *e* which they are doing here.
Dn 3:44 be routed who inflict *e* on your servants;
Mk 7:23 *e* come from within and render a man impure

EVODIA (1)

Phil 4: 2 I plead with *E* just as I do with Syntyche:

EWE (10)

Gn 21:28 also set apart seven *e* lambs of the flock,
21:29 seven *e* lambs that you have set apart?"
21:30 "The seven *e* lambs you shall accept from
31:38 no *e* or she-goat of yours ever miscarried,
Lv 5: 6 from the flock, a *e* lamb or a she-goat.
14:10 lambs, one unblemished yearling *e* lamb,
Nm 6:14 yearling *e* lamb for a sin offering,
2Sm 12: 3 one little *e* lamb that he had bought.
12: 4 Instead he took the poor man's *e* lamb and
12: 6 He shall restore the *e* lamb fourfold

EWES (5)

Gn 32:15 two hundred *e* and twenty rams;
Ps(s) 78:71 the *e* he brought him to shepherd Jacob,
Sg 4: 2 teeth are like a flock of *e* to be shorn,
6: 6 flock of *e* which come up from the washing,
Is 40:11 in his bosom, and leading the *e* with care.

EXACT (21)

Lv 25:36 Do not *e* interest from your countryman
Jos 22:23 it, the LORD himself will *e* the penalty.
1Sm 24:13 LORD will *e* justice from you in my case.
1Chr 28:19 the *e* specifications of the pattern,
Neh 5:12 everything and *e* nothing further from them.
Est 4: 7 as well as the *e* amount of silver Haman
1Mc 10:35 Let no man have authority to *e* payment
2Mc 2:28 for *e* details to the original author,
Sir 5: 3 for the LORD will *e* the punishment.
Is 43:23 not *e* from you the service of offerings,

Bar 6:34 a vow to them, they cannot *e* it of him.
Ez 18: 8 he does not lend at interest nor *e* usury;
18:16 who does not oppress anyone, or *e* a pledge,
22:12 You *e* interest and usury;
Mi 2:10 For any trifle you *e* a crippling pledge.
Mt 2: 7 them the *e* time of the star's appearance.
24:36 "As for the *e* day or hour,
Mk 13:32 "As to the *e* day or hour,
Lk 3:13 *E* nothing over and above your fixed amount."
Acts 1: 7 "The *e* time it is not yours to know.
Heb 1: 3 the *e* representation of the Father's being,

EXACTED (5)

2Kgs 11: 4 the LORD, *e* from them a sworn commitment,
18:14 The king of Assyria *e* three hundred
23:35 He *e* the silver and gold from the people
Am 5:11 the weak and *e* of them levies of grain,
Rv 18:20 has *e* punishment from her on your account.

EXACTING (2)

2Kgs 15:20 king of Assyria by *e* it from all the men
Neh 5: 7 "You are *e* interest from your own kinsmen!"

EXACTION (1)

2Cor 9: 5 be ready as a gracious gift, not as an *e*.

EXACTITUDE (1)

Wis 12:21 With what *e* you judged your sons,

EXACTLY (29)

Ex 25: 9 you shall make *e* according to the pattern
40:16 Moses did *e* as the LORD had commanded
Nm 8:20 carrying out *e* the command which the LORD
22:20 the condition that you do *e* as I tell you."
28:24 you shall make *e* the same offerings each
30: 3 must fulfill *e* the promise he has uttered.
Dt 5:33 *e* the way prescribed for you by the LORD,
10:12 the LORD, your God, and following his ways *e*,
11:22 LORD, your God, and following his ways *e*,
17:10 act, being careful to do *e* as they direct.
18:16 This is *e* what you requested of the LORD,
24: 8 be careful to observe *e* and to carry out all
31: 5 deal with them *e* as I have ordered you.
Jos 8:34 *e* as written in the book of the law.
1Kgs 6:26 and shape, and each was *e* ten cubits high.
6:38 in all particulars, *e* according to plan,
2Kgs 21:21 He followed *e* the path his father had trod,
1Chr 17:15 whole vision Nathan related *e* to David.
Ezr 7:23 out *e* for the house of the God of heaven,
Jdt 2:13 fulfill them *e* as I have commanded you,
Est 4:16 away and did *e* as Esther had commanded.
8: 9 *E* as Mordecai dictated,
2Mc 14:43 of the struggle he failed to strike *e*.
Ps(s) 119:33 your statutes, that I may *e* observe them.
Wis 19:18 *e* from a review of what took place.
Dn 2:45 this is *e* what you dreamed,
Mt 18:35 My heavenly Father will treat you in *e* the
28: 6 He has been raised, *e* as he promised.
1Pt 3:21 bath which corresponds to this *e*.

EXACTS (1)

Ez 18:13 things, lends at interest and *e* usury

EXALATION (1)

1Mc 1:40 been, and her *e* was turned into mourning.

EXALT (51)

Jos 3: 7 begin to *e* you in the sight of all Israel,
1Sm 2:10 his king, and *e* the horn of his anointed!"
2Sm 22:49 Above my adversaries you *e* me and from the
1Kgs 1:37 and *e* his throne even more than that of my
1:47 you and *e* his throne more than your own!'
Tb 13: 4 *E* him before every living being,
13: 6 righteousness, and *e* the King of the ages.
13: 7 "As for me, I *e* my God,
Jdt 16: 1 to him a new song, *e* and acclaim his name.
1Mc 14:35 In every way he sought to *e* his people.
Ps(s) 18:49 Truly above my adversaries you *e* me and
66: 7 rebels may not *e* themselves.
Prv 4: 8 Extol her, and she will *e* you;
Sir 1:27 *E* not yourself lest you fall and bring
15: 5 She will *e* him above his fellows;
44:21 dust, and *e* his posterity like the stars;
Is 10:15 the saw *e* itself above him who wields it?
Dn 3:57 Lord, praise and *e* him above all forever.
3:58 Lord, praise and *e* him above all forever.
3:59 Lord, praise and *e* him above all forever.
3:60 Lord, praise and *e* him above all forever.
3:61 praise and *e* him above all forever.
3:62 praise and *e* him above all forever.
3:63 praise and *e* him above all forever.
3:64 praise and *e* him above all forever.
3:65 praise and *e* him above all forever.
3:66 praise and *e* him above all forever.
3:67 praise and *e* him above all forever.
3:68 rain, bless the LORD; praise and *e* him
3:69 chill, bless the LORD; praise and *e* him
3:70 snow, bless the LORD; praise and *e* him
3:71 and days, bless the LORD; praise and *e* him
3:72 darkness, bless the LORD; praise and *e* him
3:73 and clouds, bless the LORD; praise and *e* him
3:74 the earth bless the Lord, praise and *e* him
3:75 and hills, bless the Lord; praise and *e* him
3:76 the earth, bless the Lord; praise and *e* him
3:77 springs, bless the Lord; praise and *e* him
3:78 rivers, bless the Lord; praise and *e* him
3:79 creatures, bless the Lord, praise and *e* him
3:80 the air, bless the Lord, praise and *e* him
3:81 tame, bless the Lord; praise and *e* him
3:82 of men, bless the Lord; praise and *e* him
3:83 O Israel, bless the Lord; praise and *e* him
3:84 bless the Lord; praise and *e* him
3:85 Lord, bless the Lord; praise and *e* him
3:86 the just, bless the Lord; praise and *e* him
3:87 heart, bless the Lord; praise and *e* him
3:88 Mishael, bless the Lord; praise and *e* him
4:34 praise and *e* and glorify the King of heaven,
Zep 3:11 no longer *e* yourself on my holy mountain.

EXALTATION (2)

Jdt 10: 8 *e* of Jerusalem"Judith bowed down to God.
13: 4 on my undertaking for the *e* of Jerusalem;

EXALTED (66)

Lv 21:10 "The most *e* of the priests,
Nm 24: 7 and his royalty shall be *e*.
Jos 4:14 LORD *e* Joshua in the sight of all Israel,
1Sm 2: 1 exults in the LORD, my horn is *e* in my God.
2Sm 5:12 as king of Israel and had *e* his rule
1Kgs 14: 7 I *e* you from among the people and made you
1Chr 14: 2 *e* for the sake of his people Israel.
29:11 you are *e* as head over all.
29:25 And the LORD *e* Solomon greatly in the eyes
2Chr 7:21 This temple which is so *e*—
32:23 was *e* in the eyes of all the nations.
Neh 9: 5 name, and *e* above all blessing and praise."
Est A:10 lowly were *e* and they devoured the nobles.
1Mc 2:63 Today he is *e*,
8:13 and they were greatly *e*.
2Mc 15: 2 has *e* with holiness above all other days."
Jb 24:24 They are *e* for a while,
36: 7 kings upon thrones he sets them, *e* forever.
Ps(s) 8: 2 You have *e* your majesty above the heavens.
46:11 *e* among the nations, exalted upon
57: 6 Be *e* above the heavens,
57:12 Be *e* above the heavens,
89:14 strong is your hand, *e* your right hand.
89:17 day, and through your justice they are *e*.
89:18 strength, and by your favor our horn is *e*.
89:25 and through my name shall his horn be *e*.
89:43 You have *e* the right hands of his foes,
92:11 You have *e* my horn like the wild bull's;
97: 9 over all the earth, *e* far above all gods.
108: 6 Be *e* above the heavens,
112: 9 his horn shall be *e* in glory.
118:16 the right hand of the LORD is *e*;
138: 6 The LORD is *e*, yet the lowly he sees,
148:13 name of the LORD, for his name alone is *e*;
Prv 11:11 blessing of the righteous the city is *e*,
Wis 6: 5 you, because judgment is stern for the *e*—
Sir 11: 6 The *e* often fall into utter disgrace;
47:11 him his sins and *e* his strength forever;
Is 2:11 be abased, and the LORD alone will be *e*,
2:17 brought low, And the LORD alone will be *e*,
5:16 LORD of hosts shall be *e* by his judgment,
12: 4 his deeds, proclaim how *e* is his name.
33: 5 The LORD is *e*, enthroned on high;
33:10 I rise up, says the LORD, now will I be *e*,
52:13 he shall be raised high and greatly *e*.
57:15 For thus says he who is high and *e*,
Jer 17:12 A throne of glory, *e* from the beginning,
Dn 3:52 God of our fathers, praiseworthy and *e*
3:52 praiseworthy and *e* above all for all ages.
3:54 praiseworthy and *e* above all forever.
3:55 praiseworthy and *e* above all forever.
5:19 whomever he wished, he *e* or humbled.
Hos 13: 1 word caused fear, for he was *e* in Israel;
Zec 12: 7 of Jerusalem may not be *e* over Judah.
14:10 but Jerusalem shall remain *e* in its place.
Mt 11:23 Capernaum, 'Are you to be *e* to the skies?
23:12 but whoever humbles himself shall be *e*.
Lk 10:15 Capernaum, 'Are you to be *e* to the skies?
14:11 and he who humbles himself shall be *e*."
18:14 while he who humbles himself shall be *e*."
Acts 2:33 *E* at God's right hand,
5:31 He whom God has *e* at his right hand as
Eph 1:22 Christ's feet and has made him, thus *e*,
Phil 1:20 now as always Christ will be *e* through me,
2: 9 God highly *e* him and bestowed on him the

EXALTING (3)

Lam 2:17 gloat over you and *e* the horn of your foes.
Dn 11:36 *e* himself and making himself greater than
2Cor 11: 7 humbling myself with a view to *e* you?

EXALTS (9)

1Sm 2: 7 poor and makes rich, he humbles, he also *e*.
Jb 5:11 lowly, and those who mourn he *e* to safety.
Prv 14:34 Virtue *e* a nation,
Sir 7:11 be mindful of him who *e* and humbles.
11:13 and *e* him to the amazement of the many.
Mt 23:12 Whoever *e* himself shall be humbled,
Lk 14:11 For everyone who *e* himself shall be
18:14 For everyone who *e* himself shall be
2Thes 2: 4 perdition and adversary who *e* himself

EXAMINATION (3)

Lv 13:20 on *e*, sees that it is deeper than the skin
13:39 white blotches, the priest shall make an *e*.
Dn 13:48 without *e* and without clear evidence?

EXAMINE (28)

Lv 13: 3 who shall *e* the sore on his skin.
13: 5 seventh day the priest shall again *e* him.
13: 6 and once more *e* him on the seventh day.
13:25 or a white blotch, the priest shall *e* it.
13:32 and on the seventh day again *e* the sore.
13:36 clean, the priest shall again *e* it.
13:43 The priest shall *e* him;
13:51 day the priest shall again *e* the infection.
13:55 "Then the priest shall again *e* the
14: 3 who is to go outside the camp to *e* him.
14:36 out before he goes in to *e* the infection,
14:36 after this is he to go in to *e* the house.
14:39 priest shall return to *e* the house again.
14:48 priest finds, when he comes to *e* the house,
Ezr 10:16 They held sessions to *e* the matter,
Neh 7: 5 people, and to *e* their family records,
2Mc 2:30 To enter into questions and *e* them
Ps(s) 48:14 Consider her ramparts, *e* her castles,
Sir 11: 7 *e* first, then criticize.
Lam 3:40 *e* our ways that we may return to the LORD!
Dn 13:51 two far from one another that I may *e* them."
Jn 20:27 "Take your finger and *e* my hands.
Acts 23:15 would like to *e* his case more carefully.
1Cor 11:28 A man should *e* himself first;
11:31 If we were to *e* ourselves,
2Cor 13: 5 are living in faith; *e* yourselves.
Rv 5: 3 found to open the scroll or *e* its contents.
5: 4 be found worthy to open or *e* the scroll.

EXAMINED (9)

Lv 13:50 Having *e* the infection,
1Sm 26: 5 and *e* the spot where Saul and Abner,
1Kgs 3:21 But when I *e* him in the morning light,
2Chr 26:20 priest and all the other priests *e* him,
Neh 8:13 and *e* the words of the law more closely.
Wis 4: 6 of their parents, when they are *e*.
Lk 23:14 I have *e* him in your presence and have no
Acts 22:24 He issued orders that he be *e* under the
1Pt 1:10 the prophets carefully searched out and *e*.

EXAMINING (13)

Lv 13: 8 Should the priest, on *e* it,
13:10 Should the priest, on *e* him,
13:13 to foot, should the priest then, on *e* him,
13:17 should the latter, on *e* him,
13:21 But if the priest, on *e* him,
13:26 But if the priest, on *e* it,
13:27 the priest, when *e* it on the seventh day,
13:30 head or cheek, should the priest, on *e* it,
13:31 But if the priest, on *e* the scall sore,
13:34 when *e* the scall on the seventh day,
13:53 But if the priest, on *e* the infection,
13:56 But if the priest, on *e* the infection,
14:37 If the priest, on *e* it,

EXAMPLE (45)

Ex 23: 2 *e* of the many as an excuse for doing wrong,
Nm 5:21 'may the LORD make you an *e* of malediction
5:27 an *e* of imprecation among her people.
Dt 19: 5 For *e*, if he goes with his neighbor
28:25 *e* to all the kingdoms of the earth.
Jgs 2:17 and did not follow their *e* of obedience to
1Sm 8: 3 His sons did not follow his *e* but sought
8: 5 old, and your sons do not follow your *e*,
Jdt 8:24 brothers, let us set an *e* for our kinsmen.
Est C:22 them and make an *e* of our chief enemy.
2Mc 6:28 the young a noble *e* of how to die willingly
6:31 a model of courage and an unforgettable *e*
Sir 44:16 succeeding generations might learn by his *e*
Jer 42:18 become an *e* of malediction and horror,
44:12 by hunger, and become an *e* of malediction,
Lam 2:13 What *e* can I show you for your comfort,
Bar 6: 4 their alien *e* and stand in fear of them,
Ez 14: 8 man, and make of him an *e* and a byword.
Mt 6: 2 When you give alms, for *e*,
15: 2 They do not wash their hands, for *e*,
17:15 For *e*, he often falls into the fire
23: 3 But do not follow their *e*.
Mk 7: 4 for *e*, the washing of cups and jugs
7:10 For *e*, Moses said, 'Honor your father
Jn 8:39 you would be following Abraham's *e*.
13:15 What I just did was to give you an *e*:
Acts 8: 5 Philip, for *e*, went down to the town
Rom 6:19 (I use the following *e* from human affairs
7: 2 For *e*, a married woman is bound to her
1Cor 2:11 Who, for *e*, knows man's innermost
4: 6 and Apollos by way of *e* for your benefit.
10: 6 These things happened as an *e* to keep us

EXAMPLE (cont.)

10:11 things that happened to them serve as an *e.*
Gal 3:15 Brothers, let me give you an everyday *e.*
Phil 3:17 guide those who follow the *e* that we set.
1Thes 4:12 good *e* to outsiders and want for nothing.
2Thes 3: 9 ourselves as an *e* for you to imitate.
1Tm 1:16 and that I might become an *e* to those who
4:12 your youth, but be a continuing *e* of love,
Ti 2: 3 By their good *e* they must teach the
2: 7 may you yourself fail to set them good *e.*
Heb 4:11 in imitation of the *e* of Israel's unbelief.
1Pt 2:21 for you in just this way and left you an *e,*
3: 6 for *e,* Sarah, who was subject to Abraham
1Jn 3:12 We should not follow the *e* of Cain who

EXAMPLES (3)

Hos 12:11 the prophets, through whom I set forth *e.*
Mk 3:23 he then began to speak to them by way of *e:*
1Pt 5: 3 Be *e* to the flock,

EXASPERATE (1)

Sir 4: 3 Do not *e* the downtrodden;

EXASPERATED (2)

Hos 12:15 Ephraim has *e* his Lord;
Acts 17:16 he grew *e* at the sight of idols everywhere

EXCEEDINGLY (9)

Gn 17: 2 my covenant, and I will multiply you *e.*"
17: 6 I will render you *e* fertile;
17:20 make him fertile and will multiply him *e.*
Prv 30:24 smallest on the earth, and yet are *e* wise:
Ez 16:13 You were *e* beautiful,
Dn 2:31 you saw a statue, very large and *e* bright,
Jl 2:11 is the day of the LORD, and *e* terrible;
Zec 1:15 I am *e* angry with the complacent nations;
Acts 7:20 He proved to be an *e* handsome child.

EXCEL (2)

Gn 49: 4 Unruly as water, you shall no longer *e,*
Ez 32:19 "Whom do you *e* in beauty?

EXCELLED (1)

Prv 31:29 of proven worth, but you have *e* them all."

EXCELLENCY (9)

Ezr 2:63 and His *E* ordered them not to partake of
Neh 7:65 and His *E* ordered them not to partake of
7:69 His *E* put into the treasury one thousand
8: 9 Then [Nehemiah, that is, His *E,*
10: 2 His *E* Nehemiah,
Lk 1: 4 so that Your *E* may see how reliable the
Acts 23:26 Lysias sends greetings to His *E* Felix,
24: 2 "Your *E,* through your efforts
26:25 "No, Your *E,*" answered Paul,

EXCELLENT (10)

Gn 2:12 The gold of that land is *e;*
Ezr 8:27 two vases of *e* polished bronze,
2Mc 12:43 this he acted in a very *e* and noble way,
Prv 4: 2 Yes, *e* advice I give you;
Sg 7:10 apples, And your mouth like an *e* wine
Wis 13: 3 know how far more *e* is the Lord than these;
Jer 24: 2 One basket contained *e* figs,
Mk 9:50 Salt is *e* in its place;
12:32 *E,* Teacher! You are right in saying
Heb 8: 6 Jesus has obtained a more *e* ministry now,

EXCELLING (2)

Gn 49: 3 manhood, excelling in rank and *e* in power!

EXCELS (1)

Est B: 3 Haman, who *e* among us in wisdom,

EXCEPT (91)

Gn 2:17 *e* the tree of knowledge of good and bad.
14:24 Nothing for me *e* what my servants have
47:18 disposal *e* our bodies and our farm land.
Ex 12:16 *e* to prepare the food that everyone needs.
22:19 sacrifices to any god, *e* to the LORD alone,
33:16 favor with you, *e* by your going with us?
Lv 21: 2 his people, *e* for his nearest relatives,
25:12 *e* as taken directly from the field.
Nm 14:30 I solemnly swore to settle you, *e* Caleb,
26:65 and not one of them was left *e* Caleb,
32:12 *e* the Kenizzite Caleb,
35:33 it *e* through the blood of him who shed it.
Dt 1:36 I swore to give to your fathers, *e* Caleb,
Jos 6:24 with all that was in it, *e* the silver,
8: 2 *e* that you may take its spoil and
8:23 any fugitives or survivors *e* the king,
11:13 the cities built on raised sites, *e* Hazor,
14: 4 no share of the land *e* cities to live in,
1Sm 21: 7 for no other bread was on hand *e* the
21:10 there is no sword here *e* that one."
30:17 that none escaped *e* four hundred young men,
30:22 booty, *e* to each man his wife and children.
2Sm 12: 3 *e* one little ewe lamb that he had bought.
15:16 *e* for ten concubines whom he left be-hind
22:32 "For who is God *e* the LORD?
1Kgs 12:20 David's house *e* the tribe of Judah alone.
15: 5 lived, *e* in the case of Uriah the Hittite.
17: 1 there shall be no dew or rain *e* at my word."
22:31 with anyone at all *e* the king of Israel."
2Kgs 5:15 is no God in all the earth, *e* in Israel.
5:17 sacrifice to any other god *e* to the LORD.
13: 7 *e* fifty horsemen with ten chariots and ten
24:14 among the people of the land *e* the poor.
1Chr 15: 2 one may carry the ark of God *e* the Levites,
2Chr 18:30 one, small or great, *e* the king of Israel."
23: 6 Let no one enter the LORD's house *e* the
Tb 1: 7 And *e* for sabbatical years, I used to give
1:20 *e* for my wife Anna and my son Tobiah.
Jdt 8: 6 her widowhood, *e* sabbath eves and sabbaths,
11:10 them, *e* when they sin against their God.
Est C:29 now, your handmaid has had no joy *e* in you,
1Mc 11:38 *e* the foreign troops which he had hired
11:70 stayed *e* the army commanders Mattathias,
2Mc 12:18 without having done anything *e* to leave
Ps(s) 18:32 For who is God *e* the LORD?
Eccl 5:10 they to the owner *e* to feast his eyes upon?
8:15 the sun *e* eating and drinking and mirth:
Wis 8:21 not otherwise possess her *e* God gave it
9:17 *e* you had given Wisdom and sent your holy
Sir 45:13 be worn by any *E* his sons and them alone,
49: 4 *E* for David, Hezekiah and Josiah,
Jer 22:17 are set on nothing *e* on your own gain,
Lam 3:37 it comes to pass, *e* the Lord ordains it;
3:38 *E* it proceeds from the mouth of the Most
Ez 47: 5 that could not be crossed *e* by swimming.
48:22 *e* for the property of the Levites and the
Dn 2:11 king *e* the gods who do not dwell among men
3:95 serve or worship any god *e* their own God.
6: 8 to god or man for thirty days, *e* to you,
6:13 to god or man for thirty days, *e* to you,
10:21 against all these *e* Michael,
11:41 glorious land and many shall fall, *e* Edom,
13:16 Nobody else was there *e* the two elders,
Mt 13:57 is without honor *e* in his native place,
16: 4 no sign will be given it *e* that of Jonah."
21:19 to it, but found nothing there *e* leaves.
Mk 2: 7 Who can forgive sins *e* God alone?"
5:37 not permit anyone to follow him *e* Peter,
6: 4 is without honor *e* in his native place,
8:14 *e* for one loaf they had none with them in
Lk 4:27 yet not one was cured *e* Naaman the Syrian."
8:51 permitted no one to enter with him *e* Peter,
10:22 No one knows the Son *e* the Father and no
10:22 and no one knows the Father *e* the Son
11:29 sign will be given it *e* the sign of Jonah.
13:33 be allowed to die anywhere *e* in Jerusalem.'
17:18 and give thanks to God *e* this foreigner?"
Jn 3:13 heaven *e* the One who came down from there
13:10 bathed has no need to wash *e* for his feet];
Acts 8: 1 All *e* the apostles scattered throughout
20:23 *e* that the Holy Spirit has been warning me
21:14 be dissuaded, we said nothing further *e,*
Rom 13: 1 him, for there is no authority *e* from God,
13: 8 Owe no debt to anyone *e* the debt that
15:18 I will not dare to speak of anything *e*
1Cor 1:14 I baptized none of you *e* Crispus and Gaius,
12: 3 "Jesus is Lord," *e* in the Holy Spirit.
2Cor 12:13 inferior to the other churches *e* in this,
Gal 1:19 I did not meet any other apostles *e* James,
Phil 4:15 not a single congregation *e* yourselves
Rv 14: 3 This hymn no one could learn *e* the hundred

EXCEPTION (12)

Ex 8:18 will make an *e* of the very land of Goshen:
Jos 11:19 the *e* of the Hivites who lived in Gibeon,
23:14 fulfilled for you, with not one single *e.*
Jgs 20:11 *e* were leagued together against the city,
1Kgs 15:22 King Asa summoned all Judah without *e,*
2Kgs 10:21 without *e* came into the temple of Baal,
Est E:24 "Every city and province, without *e,*
Sir 18: 1 is the judge of all things without *e;*
Ez 20:40 house of Israel without *e* shall worship me;
Lk 21:15 adversaries can take *e* to or contradict.
Acts 8: 6 Without *e,* the crowds that heard Philip
Ti 2: 8 sound words to which no one can take *e.*

EXCEPTIONAL (1)

1Kgs 5: 9 wisdom and *e* understanding and knowledge,

EXCESS (9)

1Kgs 16: 9 Tirzah, drinking to *e* in the house of Arza
Prv 23:20 nor with those who eat meat to *e;*
Eccl 7:16 "Be not just to *e,* and be not overwise,
7:17 Be not wicked to *e,* and be not foolish.
Rom 13:13 and drunkenness, not in sexual *e* and lust,
2Cor 8:15 *e* and he who gathered little had no lack."
Gal 1:14 in my *e* of zeal to live out all the
Jas 1:21 away all that is filthy, every vicious *e.*
Jude 1: 4 our God to sexual *e* and deny Jesus Christ,

EXCESSIVE (2)

2Mc 7:42 the sacrificial meals and the *e* cruelties.
9:11 he began to give up his *e* arrogance,

EXCHANGE (19)

Gn 25:31 give me your birthright in *e* for it."
30:15 "In *e* for your son's mandrakes,
47:17 with bread in *e* for all their livestock.
47:19 Take us and our land in *e* for food,
Lv 27:33 ones are thus chosen, and no *e* may be made.
27:33 If any *e* is attempted,
Dt 14:25 you, you may *e* the tithe for money and,
14:26 then *e* the money for whatever you desire,
Ru 4: 7 binding a contract of redemption or *e,*
1Kgs 21: 2 I will give you a better vineyard in *e,*
21: 6 prefer, I will give you a vineyard in *e.*'
Is 43: 4 for you and peoples in *e* for your life.
Ez 48:14 They may not sell or *e* or alienate this,
Dn 11:27 shall sit at table together and *e* lies,
Mt 16:26 can a man offer in *e* for his very self?
Mk 8:37 What can a man offer in *e* for his life?
Lk 24:15 In the course of their lively *e,*
2Cor 6:13 In fair *e,* then (I speak as a father
Rv 11:10 over them and in their merriment *e* gifts,

EXCHANGED (9)

Gn 26:31 Early the next morning they *e* oaths.
Tb 5: 3 "We *e* signatures on a document written in
2Mc 12:12 pledge of friendship had been *e*
Ps(s) 106:20 They *e* their glory for the image of a
Ez 27:14 steeds, and mules were *e* for your wares.
27:19 Javan *e* wrought iron,
Rom 1:23 they *e* the glory of the immortal God for
1:25 these men who *e* the truth of God for a lie
1:26 women *e* natural intercourse for unnatural,

EXCHANGING (8)

Lv 27:10 for it by *e* either a better for a worse one
Ez 27:12 you, so great was your wealth, *e* silver,
27:13 *e* slaves and articles of bronze for your
27:16 you, so many were your products, *e* garnets,
27:17 trafficked with you, *e* Minnith wheat,
27:18 your wealth, *e* Helbon wine and Zahar wool.
27:22 *e* for your wares the very choicest spices,
Hos 4: 7 sin against me, *e* their glory for shame.

EXCITE (1)

Ez 24: 8 To work up my wrath, to *e* my vengeance,

EXCITED (1)

Jer 32:31 day, this city has *e* my anger and wrath,

EXCITEDLY (2)

Lk 17:23 Do not go running about *e.*
Acts 3:11 rushed over to them *e* in Solomon's Portico.

EXCITEMENT (1)

2Mc 14:43 In the *e* of the struggle he failed to

EXCLAIM (3)

2Sm 22: 4 'Praised be the LORD,' I *e,*
Ps(s) 18: 4 Praised be the LORD, I *e,*
Jn 7:35 This caused the Jews to *e* among themselves:

EXCLAIMED (49)

Gn 25:22 jostled each other so much that she *e,*
26:10 "How could you do this to us!" *e* Abimelech.
27:36 and carried off your blessing," Esau *e,*
28:16 When Jacob awoke from his sleep, he *e,*
37:30 and returning to his brothers, he *e:*
37:33 He recognized it and *e:*
Ex 14: 5 "What have we done!" they *e.*
Nm 31:15 spared all the women!" he *e.*
Ru 2:20 the dead," Naomi *e* to her daughter-in-law;
2Kgs 1: 8 the Tishbite!" he *e.*
3:10 *e* the king of Israel.
3:23 "This is blood!" they *e.*
4:40 but when they began to eat it, they *e,*
5: 7 the king of Israel tore his garments and *e:*
6:31 God do thus and so to me," the king *e,*
8:13 Hazael *e,* "How can a dog like me,
13:14 he *e,* weeping over him.
13:17 The prophet *e,* "The LORD's arrow
2Chr 18:31 the commanders saw Jehoshaphat, they *e,*
Tb 2: 3 When he returned he *e,* "Father!"
5:14 Tobit *e:* "Welcome! God save you
7: 5 Then Tobiah *e,* "He is my father!"
11: 6 she saw him coming, she *e* to his father,
11:14 He *e,* "I can see you, son,
Jdt 11:20 they marveled at her wisdom and *e,*
Est 7: 8 Esther was reclining; and the king *e,*
Jb 31:31 Had not the men of my tent *e,*
Dn 3:95 Nebuchadnezzar *e,* "Blessed be the God
Mt 9:33 has ever been seen in Israel!" they *e.*
14: 2 of Jesus' reputation, *e* to his courtiers,
14:31 "How little faith you have!" he *e.*
19:25 they were completely overwhelmed, and *e,*
25:26 His master *e:* You worthless lazy lout
Mk 6:16 On hearing of Jesus, Herod *e,*
9:24 The boy's father immediately *e,*
10:26 overwhelmed at this, and *e* to one another,
Lk 8: 8 As he said this *e*
8:28 at his feet and *e* at the top of his voice,

9:38 Suddenly a man from the crowd *e:*
Jn 1:29 sight of Jesus coming toward him, he *e:*
4:17 you have no husband!" Jesus *e.*
9:34 they *e,* "You are steeped in sin
16:29 are speaking plainly," his disciples *e,*
19:15 Pilate *e.*
Acts 5: 3 Peter *e:*
7:56 he *e,* "I see an opening in the sky,
13:10 he stared at him and *e:*
21:37 the commander *e.*
24:25 Before long he *e:*

EXCLAIMING (2)

Nm 20: 3 The people contended with Moses, *e,*
Tb 9: 6 Gabael, who wept an and blessed him, *e:*

EXCLAMATIONS (1)

Zec 4: 7 bring out the capstone amid *e* of 'Hail,

EXCLUDE (3)

Is 56: 3 LORD will surely *e* me from his people";
Gal 4:17 to *e* you so that you may court their favor.
Rv 11: 2 *E* the outer court of the temple,

EXCLUDED (6)

2Chr 26:21 for he was *e* from the house of the LORD.
Ezr 10: 8 be *e* from the assembly of the exiles.
Jdt 13: 1 tent from the outside and *e* the attendants
Ez 44: 5 those who are to be *e* from the sanctuary.
1Cor 15:27 has made everything subject to Christ is *e.*
Eph 2:12 and were *e* from the community of Israel.

EXCREMENT (5)

Dt 23:14 dig a hole and afterward cover up your *e.*
2Kgs 18:27 to eat their own *e* and drink their urine?"
Is 36:12 eat their own *e* and drink their own urine?"
Ez 4:12 barley loaves over human *e* in their sight,
4:15 your cow's dung in place of human *e;*

EXCRUCIATING (1)

2Mc 9: 5 he was seized with *e* pains in his bowels

EXCUSE (6)

Ex 23: 2 of the many as an *e* for doing wrong,
Mk 16:20 They offered this *e:*
Lk 14:18 But they began to *e* themselves,
14:18 I am going out to test them. Please *e* me.'
14:19 Please *e* me.'
Acts 19:40 no valid *e* for this wild demonstration."

EXCUSED (1)

Jn 15:22 now, however, their sin cannot be *e.*

EXECRATION (1)

2Chr 6:22 to take an oath of *e* against himself,

EXECUTE (13)

Ex 35:35 them with skill to *e* all types of work:
36: 1 in knowing how to *e* all the work for
Nm 31: 3 and *e* the LORD'S vengeance on them.
35:19 The avenger of blood may *e* the murderer,
35:21 of blood may *e* the murderer on sight.
Jdt 9: 9 me, a widow, the strong hand to *e* my plan.
Ps(s) 149: 7 to *e* vengeance on the nations,
149: 9 To *e* on them the written sentence.
Bar 6:63 They can neither *e* judgment,
Ez 5:15 When I *e* judgment upon you in anger and
25:11 Thus I will *e* judgment upon Moab,
25:17 I will *e* great acts of vengeance on them,
Rom 9:28 will the Lord *e* sentence upon the earth."

EXECUTED (10)

Nm 31: 8 and they also *e* Balaam,
33: 4 on their gods, too, the LORD *e* judgments.
Ezr 6:12 let it be carefully *e.*"
7:26 king, let strict judgment be *e* upon him,
2Mc 13: 4 and *e* there in the customary local method.
Eccl 8:11 against evildoers is not promptly *e,*
Ez 39:21 have *e* and the hand I have laid upon them.
Dn 3:28 You have *e* proper judgments in all that
Acts 12:19 he had the guards tried and *e.*
13:28 death, they begged Pilate to have him *e.*

EXECUTES (1)

Dt 10:18 who *e* justice for the orphan and the widow,

EXECUTING (5)

Ex 12:12 and *e* judgment on all the gods of Egypt
36: 4 Thereupon the experts who were *e* the
36: 8 The various experts who were *e* the work,
2Chr 22: 8 Jehu was *e* judgment on the house of Ahab,
1Mc 2:55 Joshua, for *e* his commission,

EXECUTION (9)

Nm 25: 4 *e* of the guilty ones before the LORD,
35:30 is required for the *e* of the murderer.
Dt 17: 7 At the *e,* the witnesses are to be the first
2Sm 8: 2 He told off two lengths of line for *e,*
Tb 2: 8 down for *e* because of this very thing;
Prv 24:11 and from those tottering to *e* withdraw not.
Bar 6:17 brought to *e* for a crime against the king;
Dn 13:45 As she was being led to *e,*
Mk 13:12 for *e* and likewise the father his child;

EXECUTIONER (2)

2Mc 7:29 Do not be afraid of this *e,*
Mk 6:27 He promptly dispatched an *e,*

EXECUTIONERS (1)

2Mc 7: 4 he commanded his *e* to cut out the tongue

EXEMPT (4)

Dt 24: 5 *e* for one year for the sake of his family,
1Mc 10:29 "I now free you, as I also *e* all the Jews,
11:28 Jonathan asked the king to *e* Judea and the
Mt 17:26 "Then their sons are *e.*

EXEMPTION (3)

1Sm 17:25 grant *e* to his father's family in Israel."
1Mc 10:34 immunity and *e* for every Jew in my kingdom.
Eccl 8: 8 There is no *e* from the struggle,

EXEMPTIONS (2)

1Mc 10:28 you many *e* and will bestow gifts on you.
15: 5 I confirm to you all the tax *e* that the

EXERCISE (13)

Nm 3: 3 who were ordained to *e* the priesthood.
Ru 4: 6 *e* my claim lest I depreciate my own estate.
4: 6 in my stead, for I cannot *e* my claim."
1Mc 14:47 and to *e* supreme authority over all.' "
Sir 38:34 and their concern is for *e* of their skill.
Mt 20:25 "You know how those who *e* authority among
Mk 10:42 who seem to *e* authority lord it over them;
Lk 22:25 Those who *e* authority over them are called
Rom 12: 8 who rules should *e* his authority with care;
1Cor 7: 9 but if they cannot *e* self-control,
2Cor 13:10 I may not have to *e* with severity the
Eph 3: 7 bestowed on me by the *e* of his power,
1Thes 5:12 *e* authority in the Lord and admonish you;

EXERCISED (2)

Nm 3:31 which the ministry of the sanctuary was *e,*
Ez 35:11 you have *e* [in your hatred] against them.

EXERCISES (1)

2Mc 4:14 in the unlawful *e* on the athletic field.

EXERCISING (1)

1Cor 8: 9 lest in *e* your right you become an

EXERTING (1)

Phil 1:27 firm in unity of spirit and *e* yourselves

EXHAUST (2)

Dt 32:23 upon woe and *e* all my arrows against them:
Sir 18: 3 power, or *e* the tale of his mercies?

EXHAUSTED (16)

Jgs 8: 4 hundred men, they were *e* and famished.
8: 5 They are *e,* and I am pursuing Zebah
1Sm 14:31 to Aijalon, the people were completely *e.*
30:10 but two hundred were too *e* to cross the
30:21 men who had been too *e* to follow him,
1Mc 3:29 that this *e* the money in his treasury;
10:82 When the horsemen were *e,*
Jb 16: 7 But now that I am *e* and stunned,
Sir 13: 4 he will enslave you, but when you are *e,*
Is 44:12 and weak, drinks no water and becomes *e.*
Jer 4:31 I sink *e* before the slayers!"
48:45 Heshbon's shadow stop short the *e* refugees;
Lam 3:22 The favors of the LORD are not *e,*
Mk 5:26 sort and *e* her savings in the process,
Lk 22:45 only to find them asleep, *e* with grief.
2Cor 7: 5 arrived in Macedonia I was restless and *e.*

EXHAUSTING (1)

Ez 29:18 led his army in an *e* campaign against Tyre.

EXHAUSTION (3)

Jdt 7:25 before them in thirst and utter *e.*
Mt 9:36 They were lying prostrate from *e,*
2Thes 3: 8 of *e* so as not to impose on any of you.

EXHIBIT (1)

Est E:19 "You shall *e* a copy of this letter

EXHIBITED (1)

Dt 34:12 that Moses *e* in the sight of all Israel.

EXHILARATED (1)

Hg 1: 6 You have drunk, but have not been *e;*

EXHORT (7)

1Chr 28: 8 I *e* you to keep and to carry out all the
Rom 12: 8 one with the power of exhortation should *e.*
2Cor 9: 5 I have thought it necessary to *e* the
10: 1 *e* you by the meekness and kindness of
1Thes 4: 1 we beg and *e* you in the Lord Jesus that
4:10 Yet we *e* you to even greater progress,
5:14 We *e* you to admonish the unruly;

EXHORTATION (3)

Acts 13:15 if you have any *e* to address to the people,
Rom 12: 8 one with the power of *e* should exhort.
1Thes 2: 3 The *e* we deliver does not spring from

EXHORTATIONS (1)

Lk 3:18 Using *e* of this sort,

EXHORTED (7)

1Mc 13: 3 the people and *e* them in these words:
2Mc 7:21 she *e* each of them in the language of
8:16 and *e* them not be panic-stricken before
11: 7 and he *e* the others to join him in risking
12:31 *e* them to be well disposed to their race
2Cor 8: 6 That is why I have *e* Titus,
1Thes 2:11 likewise know how we *e* every one of you,

EXHORTING (1)

2Mc 13:14 and *e* his followers to fight nobly to

EXHORTS (2)

Jb 36:10 and *e* them to turn back from evil.
Ps(s) 16: 7 even in the night my heart *e* me.

EXILE (65)

2Sm 15:19 you, too, are an *e* from your own country.
2Kgs 17:11 the LORD had sent into *e* at their coming.
17:23 *e* from their native soil to Assyria, an *e*
25:11 led into *e* the last of the people
25:27 thirty-seventh year of the *e* of Jehoiachin,
1Chr 5: 6 the king of Assyria, took into *e;*
5:22 dwelling place until the time of the *e.*
5:41 those who went into the *e* which the LORD
8: 7 The last, who led them into *e,*
Ezr 6:21 returned from the *e* partook of it together
Tb 3: 4 So you handed us over to plundering, *e,*
3:15 or my father's name in the land of my *e.*
13: 6 In the land of my *e* I praise him,
14: 4 and led away into *e* from the Good Land.
14: 5 all of them shall return from their *e,*
14:15 *e* of the city's inhabitants when Cyaxares,
Jdt 4: 3 Now, they had lately returned from *e,*
2Mc 5: 9 so many from their country perished in *e;*
Ps(s) 119:54 the theme of my song in the place of my *e.*
144:14 May there be no breach in the walls, no *e,*
Is 5:13 Therefore my people go into *e,*
Jer 1: 3 and until the downfall and *e* of Jerusalem
13:17 tears for the LORD's flock, led away to *e.*
13:19 All Judah is banished in universal *e.*
20: 6 members of your household shall go into *e.*
22:22 shepherds, your lovers shall go into *e.*
29:16 brethren who did not go with you into *e;*
30:10 your descendants, from their land of *e;*
30:16 devoured, all your enemies shall go into *e.*
43:11 death; with *e,* everyone destined for exile;
46:19 Pack your baggage for *e,*
46:27 your descendants, from their land of *e.*
48: 7 Chemosh shall go into *e,*
48:11 one flask to another, he went not into *e.*
48:46 Your sons are taken into *e,*
49: 3 into *e* along with his priests and captains.
52:15 *e* the rest of the people left in the city,
52:31 thirty-seventh year of the *e* of Jehoiachin,
Lam 1: 3 into *e* from oppression and cruel slavery;
4:22 daughter Zion, he will not prolong your *e;*
Ez 1: 2 year, that is, of King Jehoiachin's *e,*
12: 3 on, prepare your baggage as though for *e,*
12: 4 *e* in the daytime while they are looking on;
12: 4 go out like one of those driven into *e;*
12: 7 my baggage as though it were that of an *e,*
12:11 as captives they shall go into *e.*
25: 3 of Israel, and the *e* of the house of Judah,
33:21 tenth month, in the twelfth year of our *e,*
39:23 its sins the house of Israel went into *e;*
40: 1 beginning the twenty-fifth year of our *e,*
Dn 5:13 him, "Are you the Daniel, the Jewish *e,*
6:14 this they replied, "Daniel, the Jewish *e,*
11:33 become victims of the sword, of flames, *e,*
Am 5: 5 For Gilgal shall be led into *e,*
5:27 For I will *e* you beyond Damascus,
6: 7 now they shall be the first to go into *e,*
Na 3:10 Yet even she went captive into *e,*
Zec 9:12 day, I will return you double for your *e.*
14: 2 half of the city shall go into *e.*
Mt 1:11 brothers at the time of the Babylonian *e.*
1:12 *e* Jehoniah was the father of Shealtiel,
Acts 7:43 For that I will *e* you beyond Babylon.'
1Pt 2:11 Beloved, you are strangers and in *e;*

EXILED (27)

1Sm 26:19 because they have *e* me so that this day I
2Kgs 25:21 Thus was Judah *e* from her land.
Tb 2: 2 from among our kinsmen *e* here in Nineveh.
Est 2: 6 who had been *e* from Jerusalem with the
2Mc 1:19 When our fathers were being *e* to Persia,
1:33 where the *e* priests had hidden the fire,
5: 9 There he who had *e* so many from their
Sir 29:18 Has *e* men of prominence and sent them
47:24 and caused them to be *e* from their land.
Is 49:21 I was bereft and barren *e* and repudiated];
Jer 22:12 he shall die in the place where they *e* him;
24: 1 of Babylon, had *e* from Jerusalem Jeconiah,
27:20 Babylon, did not take when he *e* Jeconiah,
29: 1 and all the people who were *e* by
29: 4 exiles whom I *e* from Jerusalem to Babylon:
29: 7 welfare of the city to which I have *e* you;
29:14 back to the place from which I have *e* you.
40: 1 and Judah who were being *e* to Babylon.
43: 3 the Chaldeans to be killed or *e* to Babylon."
52:27 Thus was Judah *e* from her land.
52:30 *e* seven hundred and forty-five people of
Ez 6: 9 the nations to which they have been *e*,
39:28 God, since I who *e* them among the nations,
Am 1: 5 the people of Aram shall be *e* to Kir,
7:11 and Israel shall surely be *e* from its land."
7:17 Israel shall be *e* far from its land.
Mi 1:16 the eagle's, because they are *e* from you.

EXILES (34)

Ezr 1:11 when the *e* were brought back from Babylon
2: 1 who returned from the captivity of the *e*,
4: 1 the *e* were building a temple for the LORD,
6:16 Levites, and the other returned *e*—
6:19 The *e* kept the Passover on the fourteenth
6:20 the Passover for the rest of the *e*,
8:35 had returned from the captivity, the *e*,
9: 4 God of Israel on this apostasy of the *e*,
10: 6 was in mourning over the betrayal by the *e*.
10: 7 the *e* should gather together in Jerusalem,
10: 8 be excluded from the assembly of the *e*.
10:16 The *e* did as agreed.
Neh 7: 6 the captivity of the *e* whom Nebuchadnezzar,
8:17 returned *e* made booths and dwelt in them.
Tb 7: 3 "We are of the *e* from Naphtali at Nineveh."
Jdt 2: 9 them as *e* to the very ends of the earth.
8:22 kinsmen, for the taking of *e* from the land,
Wis 17: 2 own roofs as *e* from the eternal providence.
Is 20: 4 captives from Egypt, and *e* from Ethiopia,
45:13 let my *e* go free Without price or ransom,
Jer 24: 5 so will I regard with favor Judah's *e*
28: 4 and all the *e* of Judah who went to Babylon,'
28: 6 all the *e* back from Babylon to this place!
29: 1 to the remaining elders among the *e*,
29: 4 *e* whom I exiled from Jerusalem to Babylon:
29:20 all you *e* whom I sent away from Jerusalem
29:22 All the *e* of Judah in Babylon will pattern
29:31 Send the message to all the *e*:
Ez 1: 1 I was among the *e* by the river Chebar,
3:11 Now go to the *e*, to your countrymen,
3:15 Thus I came to the *e* who lived at Tel-abib
11:15 it is about your kinsmen, your fellow *e*
11:24 me back to the *e* in Chaldea [in a vision,
11:25 the *e* everything the LORD had shown me.

EXIST (7)

1Sm 26:15 not a man whose like does not *e* in Israel?
Jdt 8:18 recent generations, nor does there *e* today,
Sir 23:20 *e* still knows them all after they are made.
Jer 18:15 burn incense to a thing that does not *e*.
Gal 3:28 There does not *e* among you Jew or Greek,
Heb 2:10 for whom and through whom all things *e*,
Rv 17: 8 exists no longer, and yet it will *e* again.

EXISTED (6)

Tb 6:18 was set apart for you before the world *e*.
Ps(s) 139:16 my days were limited before one of them *e*.
Eccl 1:10 has already *e* in the ages that preceded us.
Rv 17: 8 you saw *e* once but now exists no longer.
17: 8 for it *e* once and now exists no longer,
17:11 which *e* once but now exists no longer,

EXISTENCE (5)

Dt 28:66 both day and night, never sure of your *e*.
2Mc 7:22 not know how you came into *e* in my womb;
7:28 in the same way the human race came into *e*.
Ps(s) 39: 6 only a breath is any human *e*.
1Pt 3:18 was put to death insofar as fleshly *e* goes,

EXISTING (2)

2Mc 7:28 that God did not make them out of *e* things;
Wis 7:17 For he gave me sound knowledge of *e* things,

EXISTS (8)

Eccl 7:24 What *e* is far-reaching;
Rom 13: 1 authority that *e* is established by God.
Ti 1:16 but by their actions they deny that he *e*.
Heb 11: 6 who comes to God must believe that he *e*,
Jas 3: 6 It *e* among our members as a whole universe
Rv 17: 8 you saw existed once but now *e* no longer.
17: 8 for it existed once and now *e* no longer,
17:11 which existed once but now *e* no longer,

EXITS (3)

Ez 42:11 with the same *e* and plan and entrances.
43:11 design of the temple, its *e* and entrances
48:30 These are the *e* of the City,

EXODUS (1)

Heb 11:22 his life, spoke of the *E* of the Israelites,

EXONERATED (1)

Gn 44:10 my slave, and the rest of you shall be *e*."

EXORCISED (1)

Mt 7:22 Have we not *e* demons by its power?

EXORCISTS (1)

Acts 19:13 Some itinerant Jewish *e* once tried to

EXOTIC (1)

Sg 3: 6 and with the perfume of every *e* dust?

EXPAND (1)

Gn 9:27 May God *e* Japheth,

EXPANDING (1)

2Cor 7:15 His heart embraces you with an *e* love as

EXPANSE (1)

Wis 6: 1 learn, you magistrates of the earth's *e*!

EXPANSIVE (1)

Sir 47:23 behind him one of his sons, *E* in folly,

EXPECT (20)

2Mc 7: 2 do you *e* to achieve by questioning us?
15: 8 from heaven in the past, to *e* that now,
Jb 27: 8 can the impious man *e* when he is cut off,
Wis 14:29 *e* no harm when they have sworn falsely.
Sir 16:20 deeds and what could I *e* for doing my duty?"
28: 3 his fellows and *e* healing from the LORD?
34: 5 what you already *e*, the mind depicts.
Is 47:11 come upon you ruin which you will not *e*.
Mt 6: 1 *e* no recompense from your heavenly Father.
19:27 What can we *e* from it?"
24:44 of Man is coming at the time you least *e*.
Lk 6:34 lend to those from whom you *e* repayment,
7:19 is to come' or are we to *e* someone else?"
12:40 Son of Man will come when you least *e* him."
12:46 come back on a day when he does not *e* him,
Jn 4:11 Where do you *e* to get this flowing water?
1Cor 9:10 and the harvester *e* a share in the grain.
9:11 too much to *e* a material harvest from you?
2Tm 3:12 in Christ Jesus can *e* to be persecuted.
Jas 1: 7 not *e* to receive anything from the Lord.

EXPECTANT (3)

Sir 18:17 a grudging gift wears out the *e* eyes.
Hos 14: 1 their *e* mothers shall be ripped open.
Am 1:13 they ripped open *e* mothers in Gilead,

EXPECTANTLY (2)

Ps(s) 5: 4 at dawn I bring my plea *e* before you.
Lk 23:51 town, and he looked *e* for the reign of God.

EXPECTATION (5)

Prv 10:28 but the *e* of the wicked comes to nought.
11:23 the *e* of the wicked is wrath.
Wis 16:17 For against all *e*, in water which quenches
17:13 the more one's *e* is of itself uncertain,
Heb 10:27 only a fearful *e* of judgment and a flaming

EXPECTATIONS (1)

Phil 1: 7 I should entertain such *e* in your regard

EXPECTED (11)

Gn 48:11 Joseph, "I never *e* to see your face again,
Jgs 13:12 true, what are we *e* to do for the boy?"
1Kgs 2:15 was mine, and all Israel *e* me to be king.
Est 9: 1 the Jews had *e* to become masters of them,
Jb 30:26 when I *e* light, then came darkness.
Prv 11: 7 what is *e* from strength comes to nought.
Hg 1: 9 You *e* much, but it came to little;
Jn 7:31 be *e* to perform more signs than this man?"
Acts 25:18 not charge him with any of the crimes I *e*.
28: 6 They *e* to see him swell up or suddenly
Eph 6: 1 in the Lord, for that is what is *e* of you.

EXPECTING (6)

2Mc 12:37 they were not *e* it and put them to flight.
12:44 if he were not *e* the fallen to rise again,
Lk 6:34 lend to sinners, *e* to be repaid in full.
6:35 lend without *e* repayment.
Acts 10:24 Cornelius, who was *e* them,
1Cor 16:11 I am *e* him with the brothers.

EXPECTS (2)

Sir 23:21 when he least *e* it,
Mt 24:50 when he is not ready and least *e* him.

EXPEDIENT (1)

Jude 1:16 Whenever it is *e*, they resort to flattery.

EXPEDITION (12)

Dt 23:10 in camp during an *e* against your enemies,
24: 5 wed, he need not go out on a military *e*,
Jgs 4: 9 in the *e* on which you are setting out,
18: 9 about beginning your *e* to possess the land.
1Sm 23:13 escaped from Kielah, he abandoned the *e*.
2Sm 3:22 servants and Joab were coming in from an *e*,
1Kgs 12:24 of the LORD and gave up the *e* accordingly.
2Kgs 18:13 went on an *e* against all the fortified
2Chr 11: 4 LORD and gave up the *e* against Jeroboam.
Jdt 2:19 their *e* in advance of King Nebuchadnezzar,
2Mc 5: 1 Antiochus sent his second *e* into Egypt.
Is 36: 1 went on an *e* against all the fortified

EXPEDITIONS (2)

1Sm 18:13 David led the people on their military *e*,
18:16 loved him, since he led them on their *e*.

EXPEL (20)

Nm 5: 2 the Israelites to *e* from camp every leper,
Prv 22:10 *E* the arrogant man and discord goes out;
Mt 8:31 kept appealing to him, "If you *e* us,
10: 1 gave them authority to *e* unclean spirits
10: 8 raise the dead, heal the leprous, *e* demons.
12:24 *e* demons only with the help of Beelzebul,
12:27 If I *e* demons with Beelzebul's help,
12:27 help, by whose help do your people *e* them?
12:28 it is by the Spirit of God that I *e* demons,
17:19 him privately, "Why could we not *e* it?"
Mk 3:15 likewise to have authority to *e* demons.
3:23 "How can Satan *e* Satan?
7:26 beg him to *e* the demon from her daughter.
9:18 Just now I asked your disciples to *e* him,
9:28 "Why is it that we could not *e* it?"
9:38 we saw a man using your name to *e* demons
16:17 they will use my name to *e* demons,
Lk 9:49 we saw a man using your name to *e* demons,
Jn 16: 2 Not only will they *e* you from synagogues;
1Cor 5:13 *E* the wicked man from your midst."

EXPELLED (16)

Gn 3:24 When he *e* the man, he settled him east
Nm 5: 4 they *e* them from the camp.
2Chr 13: 9 "Have you not *e* the priests of the LORD,
26:20 was leprous, they *e* him from the temple.
Jdt 5: 8 *e* them from the presence of their gods.
5:12 When the Egyptians *e* them,
5:16 They *e* the Canaanites,
1Mc 11:66 He *e* them from the city,
13:50 He *e* them from the citadel and cleansed it
Zec 5: 3 it shall every perjurer be *e* from here.
Mt 8:16 He *e* the spirits by a simple command and
9:33 the demon was *e* the mute began to speak,
Mk 1:34 were many, and so were the demons he *e*.
6:13 They *e* many demons,
Lk 4:29 They rose up and *e* him from the town,
Acts 13:50 Jews finally *e* them from their territory.

EXPELLING (4)

Jgs 2:23 to remain instead of *e* them immediately,
Is 27: 8 Expunging and *e*, I should strive against
Mt 12:26 If Satan is *e* Satan,
Mk 1:39 *e* demons throughout the whole of Galilee.

EXPELS (4)

Sir 33:12 brings low, and *e* them from their place.
39:23 his wrath *e* the nations and turns fertile
Mk 3:22 and "He *e* demons with the help of the
3Jn 1:10 wish to do so and *e* them from the church!

EXPENSE (4)

2Sm 19:43 we had anything to eat at the king's *e*?
Neh 5:18 the daily preparations were made at my *e*—
Lk 10:35 further *e* I will repay you on my way back.'
22:63 guarding Jesus amused themselves at his *e*.

EXPENSES (8)

2Kgs 12:13 *e* that were necessary to repair the temple.
Ezr 6: 8 let these men be repaid for their *e*,
Tb 5:15 wages, plus *e* for you and for my son.
1Mc 3:30 he would not have enough for his *e* and for
10:39 for the necessary *e* of the sanctuary.
2Mc 3: 3 *e* necessary for the sacrificial services.
9:16 revenues the *e* required for the sacrifices.
Sir 42: 3 sharing the *e* of a business or a journey,

EXPENSIVE (2)

Mk 14: 3 jar of perfume made from *e* aromatic nard.

Rv 18:12 of ivory pieces and *e* wooden furniture;

EXPERIENCE (19)

Dt 11: 2 children, who have not known it from *e*,
Jgs 3: 1 those Israelites who had no *e* of the battles
3: 2 who would not have had that previous *e*:
Jdt 11: 8 you alone are competent, rich in *e*,
Jb 8: 8 and give heed to the *e* of the fathers
Prv 8:12 "I, Wisdom, dwell with *e*,
Eccl 1:16 mind has broad *e* of wisdom and knowledge";
Wis 2:24 and they who are in his possession *e* it.
12:26 were to *e* a condemnation worthy of God.
19: 5 and your people might *e* a glorious
Sir 25: 6 The crown of old men is wide *e*;
34: 9 a man of *e* speaks sense.
Mt 16:28 will not *e* death before they see the Son
26:37 sons, and began to *e* sorrow and distress.
Lk 2:26 he would not *e* death until he had seen
Eph 3:19 *e* this love which surpasses all knowledge,
Phil 1: 9 both in understanding and wealth of *e*.
2:22 know from *e* what Timothy's qualities are,
Col 2:18 Such a one takes his stand on his own *e*;

EXPERIENCED (7)

Dt 1:13 and *e* men from each of your tribes,
1:15 men of your tribes, wise and *e*,
1Chr 12: 9 *e* soldiers equipped with shield and spear,
Est 9:26 they had witnessed and *e* in this affair,
2Mc 3:28 clearly *e* the sovereign power of God.
Sir 36:20 but an *e* man can turn the tables on him.
Phil 4:12 I am *e* in being brought low,

EXPERIENCES (2)

Eccl 8: 5 "He who keeps the commandment *e* no evil,
Gal 3: 4 had such remarkable *e* all to no purpose

EXPERIENCING (1)

1Cor 1:18 who are *e* salvation it is the power of God.

EXPERT (10)

Gn 21:20 in the wilderness and became an *e* bowman,
Ex 28: 3 *e* workmen whom I have endowed with skill,
35:10 "Let every *e* among you come and make all
35:25 were *e* spinners brought hand-spun violet,
1Kgs 9:27 own *e* seamen with the servants of Solomon.
1Mc 4: 7 with cavalry, and made up of *e* soldiers.
Sg 3: 8 All of them *e* with the sword,
Sir 38:31 their hands, each one an *e* at his own task;
Is 3: 3 counselor, skilled magician, and *e* charmer.
Acts 26: 3 especially since you are *e* in all the

EXPERTLY (2)

Ex 30:25 oil, perfumed ointment *e* prepared.
30:35 This fragrant powder, *e* prepared,

EXPERTS (8)

Ex 31: 6 I have also endowed all the *e* with the
36: 1 work with Oholiab and with all the *e*
36: 2 *e* whom the LORD had endowed with skill,
36: 4 Thereupon the *e* who were executing the
36: 8 The various *e* who were executing the work,
Eccl 9:11 riches by the shrewd, nor favor by the *e*;
Ez 27: 9 *e* of Gebal were in you to caulk your seams.
Mk 7: 1 The Pharisees and some of the *e* in the law

EXPIATE (4)

1Sm 3:14 or offering will ever *e* its crime."
Hos 8:11 When Ephraim made many altars to *e* sin,
14: 1 Samaria shall *e* her guilt,
Heb 2:17 their behalf, to *e* the sins of the people.

EXPIATED (3)

Prv 16: 6 By kindness and piety guilt is *e*,
Is 40: 2 her service is at an end, her guilt is *e*;
Dn 9:24 stop and sin will end, guilt will be *e*,

EXPIATES (1)

Tb 12: 9 saves one from death and *e* every sin.

EXPIATION (3)

Is 27: 9 then, shall be the *e* of Jacob's guilt,
Rom 3:25 him the means of *e* for all who believe.
Heb 9: 5 of glory overshadowing the place of *e*.

EXPIATORY (1)

2Mc 12:43 to Jerusalem to provide for an *e* sacrifice.

EXPIRE (4)

2Mc 3:31 the man who was about to *e* might be spared.
Jb 3:11 at birth, come forth from the womb and *e*?
11:20 cut off from them, they shall wait to *e*.
36:14 Therefore they *e* in youth,

EXPIRED (2)

Lam 4:18 our time had *e*.
Lk 23:46 After he said this, he *e*.

EXPIRES (1)

Jb 14:10 when man *e*, where then is he?

EXPLAIN (15)

Ex 13: 8 On this day you shall *e* to your son,
Dt 1: 5 Moses began to *e* the law in the land of
1Kgs 10: 3 hidden from him that he could not *e* to her.
2Chr 9: 2 from Solomon that he could not *e* to her.
Tb 7:10 I will *e* the situation to you very frankly.
Est 4: 8 in Susa, to show and *e* to Esther.
Dn 2:27 and astrologers could not *e* to the king.
5:12 how to interpret dreams, *e* enigmas,
8:16 out, "Gabriel, *e* the vision to this man."
Mt 13:36 *E* to us the parable of the weeds in the
15:15 Peter spoke up to say, *E* the parable to us."
Acts 4: 9 and *e* how he was restored to health,
19:33 he wanted to *e* something to the gathering.
Heb 5:11 have much to say, and it is difficult to *e*,
Rv 17: 7 I will *e* to you the symbolism of the woman

EXPLAINED (25)

Gn 27:35 When Isaac *e*, "Your brother came
41:12 *e* for each of us the meaning of his dream.
Jgs 14:17 and she *e* the riddle to her countrymen.
1Sm 9:24 I *e* that I was inviting some guests."
10:25 Samuel next *e* to the people the law of
1Kgs 10: 3 King Solomon *e* everything she asked about,
2Chr 9: 2 *e* to her everything she asked about,
Neh 2:18 Then I *e* to them how the favoring hand of
8: 7 Hanan, and Pelaiah *e* the law to the people,
2Mc 3: 9 given, and *e* the reason for his presence,
3:10 *e* that part of the money was a care fund
Mk 5:16 *e* what had happened to the possessed man,
Lk 19:34 They *e* that the Master needed it.
22:10 He *e* to them:
24:32 us on the road and *e* the Scriptures to us?"
Jn 4:34 Jesus *e* to them:
5:11 He *e*: "It was the man
6:35 Jesus *e* to them:
Acts 9:27 He *e* to them how on his journey Saul had
10: 8 He *e* everything to them and dispatched
11: 4 Peter then *e* the whole affair to them step
12:17 and *e* how the Lord had brought him out of
17: 3 He *e* many things,
18:26 *e* to him God's new way in greater detail.
19: 4 Paul then *e*, "John's baptism

EXPLAINING (4)

1Sm 1:22 vows, Hannah did not go, *e* to her husband,
7:12 he named it Ebenezer, *e*,
2Mc 6:23 him at once to the abode of the dead, *e*:
Mk 4:34 kept *e* things privately to his disciples.

EXPLAINS (2)

Acts 8:31 man replied, "unless someone *e* it to me?"
1Tm 4:10 This *e* why we work and struggle as we do;

EXPLANATION (5)

Gn 41:24 but none of them can give me an *e*."
Jgs 7:15 heard the description and *e* of the dream,
Est 3: 4 to see whether Mordecai's *e* was acceptable,
Eccl 8: 1 wise man, and who knows the *e* of things?
Acts 23:18 and led him to the commander, with the *e*,

EXPLOIT (2)

1Sm 14:14 In this first *e* Jonathan and his
2Cor 11:20 You even put up with those who *e* you,

EXPLOITING (1)

Jas 2: 6 Are not the rich *e* you?

EXPLOITS (2)

2Mc 10:38 On completing these *e*,
Ps(s) 77:13 your *e* I ponder.

EXPLORE (5)

2Sm 10: 3 Is it not rather to *e* the city,
1Kgs 18: 6 Dividing the land to *e* between them,
1Chr 19: 3 servants rather come to you to *e* the land,
Sir 1: 3 who can *e* these?
Zep 1:12 At that time I will *e* Jerusalem with lamps;

EXPLORED (4)

Nm 13:32 "The land that we *e* is a country that
14: 7 which we went through and *e* is a fine,
Dt 1:24 as far as the Wadi Eshcol, and *e* it.
Jos 7: 2 When they had *e* Ai,

EXPLORES (1)

Sir 39: 1 He *e* the wisdom of the men of old and

EXPORT (1)

2Chr 1:17 and *e* them at six hundred silver shekels,

EXPORTED (1)

1Kgs 10:29 they were *e* at these rates to all the

EXPOSE (3)

Is 57:12 I will *e* your justice and your works;
Ez 16:37 all sides and *e* you naked for them to see.
Mt 1:19 upright man unwilling to *e* her to the law,

EXPOSED (17)

Neh 4: 7 below, behind the wall, near the *e* points,
Jdt 9: 2 maiden's girdle, shamefully *e* her thighs,
1Mc 11:23 and *e* himself to danger by going to the king
Prv 30: 6 he reprove you, and you be *e* as a deceiver.
Is 43:28 Jacob under the ban, and *e* Israel to scorn.
Jer 36:30 shall be cast out, *e* to the heat of day,
Bar 2:25 they lie *e* to the heat of day and the
Ez 23:10 They *e* her nakedness,
23:29 so that your indecent nakedness is *e*.
36:34 wasteland *e* to the gaze of every passer-by.
Lk 8:17 is nothing hidden that will not be *e*,
Jn 3:20 come near it for fear his deeds will be *e*.
Acts 27:12 port *e* on the southwest and the northwest.
1Cor 15:15 should then be *e* as false witnesses of God,
Heb 4:13 all lies bare and *e* to the eyes of him to
10:33 you were publicly *e* to insult and trial;
Rv 16:15 fear of going naked and *e* for all to see!)

EXPOSING (1)

2Sm 6:20 *e* himself to the view of the slave girls

EXPOSURE (2)

Wis 11:14 out in *e* they indeed mockingly rejected;
Acts 7:19 to *e* so that the people would not survive.

EXPOUNDED (1)

Neh 8:12 the words that had been *e* to them.

EXPRESS (6)

Nm 30:12 says nothing to *e* to her his disapproval,
32:24 flocks, but also fulfill your *e* promise."
Acts 2: 4 They began to *e* themselves in foreign
18:26 to *e* himself fearlessly in the synagogue.
1Cor 2: 6 which we *e* among the spiritually mature.
12: 8 to another the power to *e* knowledge.

EXPRESSED (8)

Nm 30: 6 her father has *e* to her his disapproval.
Jgs 9:38 these not the men for whom you *e* contempt?
1Chr 11:17 David *e* a desire:
2Mc 14:20 and when general agreement was *e*,
Rom 8:26 with groanings that cannot be *e* in speech.
Heb 7:16 not in virtue of a law *e* in a commandment
1Pt 3: 4 *e* in the unfading beauty of a calm and
5:12 Herewith are *e* my encouragement and my

EXPRESSES (3)

Nm 30: 6 of it her father *e* to her his disapproval,
30: 9 of it her husband *e* to her his disapproval,
Gal 5: 6 only faith, which *e* itself through love.

EXPRESSING (2)

Acts 9:28 moving freely about Jerusalem and *e*
Ti 2:10 but *e* a constant fidelity by their conduct,

EXPRESSION (2)

2Mc 2:31 brevity of *e* and to omit detailed treatment
2Thes 1: 5 these as an *e* of God's just judgment,

EXPRESSLY (1)

Nm 30:13 then whatever she has *e* promised in her

EXPROPRIATE (1)

2Mc 3: 7 instructions to *e* the aforesaid wealth.

EXPULSION (1)

Jn 9:35 When Jesus heard of his *e*,

EXPUNGING (1)

Is 27: 8 *E* and expelling, I should strive against

EXQUISITE (1)

Ps(s) 111: 2 works of the LORD, *e* in all their delights.

EXTEND (22)

Gn 28: 4 May he *e* to you and your descendants the
Ex 9:29 the city I will *e* my hands to the LORD;
25:32 are to *e* from the sides of the lampstand,
25:33 the six branches that *e* from the lampstand.
25:35 of branches that *e* from the lampstand.
28: 8 belt of the ephod shall *e* out from it and,
Lv 25:35 *e* to him the privileges of an alien or a
Nm 34: 4 *e* south of Kadesh-barnea to Hazar-addar;
35: 4 Levites shall *e* a thousand cubits
2Sm 15: 5 him to show homage, he would *e* his hand,
1Chr 4:10 you may truly bless me and *e* my boundaries!
2Chr 30: 8 *e* your hands to the LORD and come to his
Jb 25: 3 Yet to which of them does not his light *e*?
Ps(s) 68:32 let Ethiopia *e* its hands to God.
Sir 7:32 To the poor man also *e* your hand,

EXTEND (cont.)

23:24 and her punishment will *e* to her children;
Ez 41: 8 a full rod of six cubits in *e*.
47:17 border shall *e* from the sea to Hazar-enon,
48:17 shall *e* north two hundred and fifty cubits,
48:28 which shall *e* from Tamar to the waters of
Dn 11:42 He shall *e* his power over the countries,
Rom 14: 1 *E* a kind welcome to those who are weak in

EXTENDED (33)

Gn 10:19 borders *e* from Sidon all the way to Gerar,
10:30 Their settlements *e* all the way to Sephar,
Ex 9:33 of the city, he *e* his hands to the LORD.
37:18 Six branches *e* from its sides,
37:19 the six branches that *e* from the lampstand.
37:21 of branches that *e* from the lampstand.
39: 5 belt on the ephod *e* out from it,
Nm 33:49 Moab *e* from Beth-jeshimoth to Abel-shittim.
Dt 33:27 he *e* the ancient canopy.
Jos 12: 2 His domain *e* from Aroer,
15: 9 Nephtoah, *e* to the cities of Mount Ephron,
15:11 then *e* along the northern flank of Ekron,
16: 1 The lot that fell to the Josephites *e* from
18:17 Inclining to the north, it *e* to En-shemesh,
18:19 and *e* to the northern tip of the Salt Sea,
19:13 Gath-hepher and to Eth-kazin, *e* to Rimmon,
19:27 of Beth-emek and Neiel, it *e* to Cabul,
19:33 the clans of the Naphtalites *e* from Heleph,
19:34 Aznoth-tabor and from there *e* to Hukkok;
Jgs 1:36 *e* from the Akrabim pass to Sela and beyond.
Ru 1:13 the LORD, has *e* his hand against me."
1Kgs 7: 6 The porch *e* the width of the columned hall,
2Chr 3:12 in length, *e* to a wall of the building,
1Mc 6:40 Part of the king's army *e* over the heights,
Prv 1:24 I *e* my hand and no one took notice;
Is 16: 8 branches spread forth and *e* over the sea.
26:15 and *e* far all the borders of the land.
Jer 1: 9 the LORD *e* his hand and touched my mouth,
Ez 41: 3 at either side of it *e* seven cubits each.
41: 5 which *e* all the way around the temple,
Dn 8:10 Its power *e* to the host of heaven,
Lk 1:58 that the Lord had *e* his mercy to her,
Acts 16:15 had been baptized, she *e* us an invitation:

EXTENDING (9)

Nm 34: 8 Hamath, with the boundary *e* through Zedad.
1Kgs 7:34 braces, *e* to the corners of each stand,
2Chr 33:14 *e* to the Fish Gate and encircling Ophel;
Est 5: 2 and made her welcome by *e* toward her the
Ez 43:15 and *e* from the top of the hearth were the
45: 7 *e* westward on the western side and
48:21 *e* along the twenty-five-thousand-cubit
Am 1:13 mothers in Gilead, while *e* their territory,
Mt 12:49 Then, *e* his hand toward his disciples,

EXTENDS (8)

Nm 21:13 that *e* from the territory of the Amorites;
1Chr 5: 9 desert which *e* from the Euphrates River,
Est 4:11 the king *e* to him the golden scepter,
Prv 31:20 to the poor, and *e* her arms to the needy.
Is 25:11 in Moab as a swimmer *e* his hands to swim;
Dn 4:19 and your rule *e* over the whole earth.
Hos 7: 5 He *e* his hand among dissemblers;
Heb 6:19 hope *e* beyond the veil through which Jesus,

EXTENSIVE (1)

Neh 4:13 "Our work is scattered and *e*,

EXTENT (10)

Ex 27:14 be hangings to the *e* of fifteen cubits,
27:15 be hangings to the *e* of fifteen cubits,
38:14 were hangings to the *e* of fifteen cubits,
38:15 hangings to the *e* of fifteen cubits,
Jos 17:14 because of the *e* to which the LORD has
2Kgs 10:18 "Ahab served Baal to some *e*,
17: 2 to the *e* of the kings of Israel before him.
1Chr 4:38 ancestral houses spread out to such an *e*
Ps(s) 71:15 your salvation, though I know not their *e*.
Ez 41: 8 rod of six cubits in *e*
1Tm 4: 8 physical training is to some *e* valuable,

EXTERIOR (1)

Mt 23:28 *e* while hypocrisy and evil fill you within.

EXTERMINATE (8)

Ex 32:12 and *e* them from the face of the earth'?
33: 3 otherwise I might *e* you on the way."
33: 5 company even for a moment, I would *e* you.
Dt 7:22 You cannot *e* them all at once,
Jos 23:15 *e* you from this good land which the LORD,
Ps(s) 106:34 They did not *e* the peoples,
Wis 12: 8 army they they might *e* them by degrees.
Sir 39:30 and the avenging sword to *e* the wicked;

EXTERMINATED (6)

Dt 28:21 will persist until he has *e* you from the land
Jos 11:14 sword, until they had *e* the last of them,
11:20 and thus receive no mercy, but be *e*,
11:21 regions and *e* the Anakim in Hebron,
1Sm 15:18 Fight against them until you have *e* them.'
2Chr 20:23 of Mount Seir and completely *e* them.

EXTERMINATES (1)

1Sm 20:15 And when the LORD *e* all the enemies of

EXTERMINATING (2)

2Sm 21: 5 "As for the man who was *e* us and who
Ps(s) 106:23 Then he spoke of *e* them,

EXTERNAL (3)

Neh 11:16 over the *e* affairs of the house of God;
2Cor 5:12 to those who take pride in *e* appearances,
Phil 3: 4 has a right to put his trust in *e* evidence,

EXTINCTION (2)

Est 7: 4 delivered to destruction, slaughter, and *e*.
E:15 who were doomed to *e* by this archcriminal,

EXTINGUISH (3)

2Sm 14: 7 we must *e* the heir also.'
Est C:20 *e* the glory of your temple and your altar;
Eph 6:16 help you *e* the fiery darts of the evil one.

EXTINGUISHED (8)

1Sm 3: 3 The lamp of God was not yet *e*,
2Kgs 22:17 against this place and it cannot be *e*.'
2Chr 29: 7 the doors of the vestibule, *e* the lamps,
34:25 ablaze against this place and cannot be *e*.'
Jb 17: 1 My spirit is broken, my lamp of life *e*;
18: 5 Truly, the light of the wicked is *e*;
Is 66:24 worm shall not die, nor their fire be *e*,
Mk 9:48 'the worm dies not and the fire is never *e*.'

EXTOL (15)

Ex 15: 2 the God of my father, I *e* him.
Est C:21 gods, and to *e* an earthly king forever.
Jb 36:24 Remember, you should *e* his work,
Ps(s) 30: 2 I will *e* you, O LORD,
34: 4 LORD with me, let us together *e* his name.
68: 5 his name, *e* him who rides upon the clouds,
99: 5 *E* the LORD, our God, and worship
99: 9 *E* the LORD, our God,
107:32 Let them *e* him in the assembly of the
118:28 O my God, I *e* you.
145: 1 I will *e* you, O my God and King,
Prv 4: 8 *E* her, and she will exalt you;
Sir 13:22 silent, his wisdom they *e* to the clouds.
43:32 *E* him with renewed strength,
Is 25: 1 my God, I will *e* you and praise your name;

EXTOLLED (4)

2Sm 22:47 *E* be my God, rock of my salvation,
Ps(s) 18:47 *E* be God my savior.
21:14 Be *e*, O LORD, in your strength!
Sir 49:13 *E* be the memory of NEHEMIAH!

EXTOLLING (2)

Tb 12: 6 you, by blessing and *e* his name in song.
Sir 51:19 preoccupied with her, never weary of *e* her.

EXTOLS (1)

Prv 31:28 her husband, too, *e* her:

EXTORT (1)

Ez 22: 7 your midst, they *e* from the resident alien;

EXTORTED (1)

Am 3:10 their castles what they have *e* and robbed.

EXTORTION (5)

Ps(s) 58: 3 on earth you look to the fruits of *e*.
62:11 Trust not in *e*; in plunder take no empty
Sir 35:11 Trust not in sacrifice of the fruits of *e*,
Jer 22:17 blood, on practicing oppression and *e*.
Ez 22:29 of the land practice *e* and commit robbery;

EXTORTIONER (1)

Ex 22:24 you shall not act like an *e* toward him by

EXTORTIONERS (1)

Jb 15:34 and fire shall consume the tents of *e*.

EXTRA (5)

Gn 43:12 Also take *e* money along,
Ex 26:12 will be an *e* half sheet of tent covering,
26:13 the tent will have an *e* cubit's length
Nm 3:48 and his sons as ransom for the *e* number."
Sir 29: 6 and acquires an enemy at no *e* charge;

EXTRACTION (1)

Neh 9: 2 themselves from all who were of foreign *e*,

EXTRAORDINARY (11)

Gn 45: 7 and to save your lives in an *e* deliverance.
2Kgs 5:13 the prophet had told you to do something *e*,
2Mc 15:13 dignity, and with an air about him of *e*,
Wis 19: 5 journey while those others met an *e* death.
Dn 5:12 of the *e* mind possessed by this Daniel,
5:14 possess brilliant knowledge and *e* wisdom.
6: 4 and satraps because an *e* spirit was in him,
7: 7 terrifying, horrible, and of *e* strength;
Acts 19:11 God worked *e* miracles at the hands of Paul.
28: 2 The natives showed us *e* kindness by
2Cor 12: 7 As to the *e* revelations,

EXTRAVAGANCE (1)

Mt 26: 8 "What is the point of such *e*?

EXTRAVAGANT (1)

Mk 14: 4 is the point of this *e* waste of perfume?

EXTREME (6)

Gn 47:13 because of the *e* severity of the famine,
Jos 15: 1 in the *e* south toward the boundary of Edom,
15:21 the *e* southern district toward Edom were:
Jdt 4: 2 them, they were in *e* dread of him,
2Mc 9:28 after *e* sufferings such as he had
1Tm 1:16 mercifully, so that in me, as an *e* case,

EXTREMELY (5)

1Sm 20:30 was *e* angry with Jonathan and said to him:
Neh 4: 1 they became *e* angry.
5: 6 I was *e* angry when I heard the reasons
Sir 48:16 what was right, but others were *e* sinful.
Lk 23: 8 Herod was *e* pleased to see Jesus.

EXTREMES (1)

Gal 1:13 You know that I went to *e* in persecuting

EXTREMITY (5)

2Chr 23:10 to the northern *e* of the enclosure,
Jb 29:13 The blessing of those in *e* came upon me,
Wis 14:27 is the reason and source and *e* of all evil.
Sir 38:19 on an *e* and heartache destroy one's health.
Ez 48: 1 at the northern *e*, adjoining Hamath,

EXULT (40)

Dt 32:43 *E* with him, you heavens,
2Sm 1:20 lest the daughters of the strangers *e*!
1Chr 16:33 the trees of the forest *e* before the LORD,
Jb 6:10 and could *e* through unremitting pain,
Ps(s) 5:12 take refuge in you be glad and *e* forever.
9: 3 I will be glad and *e* in you;
14: 7 then shall Jacob *e* and Israel be glad.
25: 2 put to shame, let not my enemies *e* over me.
32:11 *e*, all you upright of heart.
33: 1 *E*, you just, in the LORD,
40:17 may all who seek you *e* and be glad in you,
53: 7 then shall Jacob *e* and Israel be glad.
67: 5 *e* because you rule the peoples in equity;
68: 4 But the just rejoice and *e* before God;
68: 5 Whose name is the LORD; *e* before him.
70: 5 may all who seek you *e* and be glad in you,
75:10 But as for me, I will *e* forever;
96:12 the trees of the forest *e* before the LORD,
149: 5 Let the faithful *e* in glory;
Prv 23:16 And my inmost being will *e*,
23:24 The father of a just man will *e* with glee;
23:25 let her who bore you *e*.
24:17 when he stumbles, let not your heart *e*,
Sir 16: 2 *e* not in them if they have not the fear of
Is 23:12 You shall *e* no more,
35: 1 The desert and the parched land will *e*;
42:11 Let the inhabitants of Sela *e*,
65:19 rejoice in Jerusalem and *e* in my people.
66:10 Exult, *e* with her, all you who were
Jer 31: 7 for Jacob, *e* at the head of the nations;
50:11 Yes, rejoice and *e*,
Hos 9: 1 not, O Israel, *e* not like the nations!
Jl 2:21 *e* and rejoice!
2:23 of Zion, *e* and rejoice in the LORD,
Ob 1:12 *E* not over the children of Judah on the
Hb 3:18 rejoice in the LORD and *e* in my saving God.
Zep 3:14 Be glad and *e* with all your heart,
Lk 6:23 On the day they do so, rejoice and *e*,
1Thes 2:19 be our hope or joy, or the crown we *e* in,

EXULTANT (5)

2Mc 11: 4 but felt *e* confidence in his myriads of
Ps(s) 63: 6 and with *e* lips my mouth shall praise you.
Zep 2:15 Is this the *e* city that dwelt secure;
Acts 2:46 With *e* and sincere hearts they took their
Jude 1:24 and *e* in the presence of his glory.

EXULTANTLY (3)

Ps(s) 60: 8 *E* I will apportion Shechem,
108: 8 *E* I will apportion Shechem,
1Pt 4:13 his glory is revealed, you will rejoice *e*.

EXULTATION (4)

Est 8:16 and merriment for the Jews, *e* and triumph.
8:17 order arrived, there was merriment and *e*,
Is 12: 6 Shout with *e*, O city of Zion,

Bar 4:34 and her *e* shall be turned to mourning:

EXULTED (2)

Jb 31:29 of my enemy or *e* when evil fell upon him,
Jn 5:35 for a while you *e* willingly in his light.

EXULTINGLY (1)

Jb 3:22 for hidden treasures, Rejoice in it *e*,

EXULTS (3)

1Sm 2: 1 "My heart *e* in the LORD,
Ps(s) 28: 7 then my heart *e*, and with my song
Hb 1:15 and so he rejoices and *e*.

EYE (83)

Gn 43:29 *e* fell on his full brother Benjamin,
Ex 21:24 you shall give life for life, *e* for eye,
21:26 in the eye and destroys the use of the *e*,
21:26 slave go free in compensation for the *e*.
Lv 24:20 Limb for limb, *e* for eye, tooth for tooth!
Nm 24: 3 the utterance of the man whose *e* is true,
24:15 the utterance of the man whose *e* is true,
Dt 19:21 Life for life, *e* for eye,
32:10 them, guarding them as the apple of his *e*.
1Sm 2:29 Why do you keep a greedy *e* on my
11: 2 I must gouge out every man's right *e*,
Jb 7: 8 *e* that now sees me shall no more behold me;
10:18 I should have died and no *e* have seen me.
13: 1 Lo, all this my *e* has seen;
17: 7 My *e* has grown blind with anguish,
20: 9 The *e* which saw him does so no more;
24:15 The *e* of the adulterer watches for the
24:15 he says, "No *e* will see me."
28: 7 knows, nor has the hawk's *e* seen that path.
42: 5 word of mouth, but now my *e* has seen you.
Ps(s) 17: 8 Keep me as the apple of your *e*;
19: 9 of the LORD is clear, enlightening the *e*;
31:10 with sorrow my *e* is consumed;
32: 8 I will counsel you, keeping my *e* on you.
92:12 And my *e* has looked down upon my foes,
94: 9 or he who formed the *e* not see?
Prv 7: 2 live, my teaching as the apple of your *e*;
16:30 He who winks his *e* is plotting trickery;
20:12 The ear that hears, and the *e* that sees
30:17 The *e* that mocks a father,
Eccl 1: 8 The *e* is not satisfied with seeing nor is
Sir 3:24 Where the pupil of the *e* is missing,
14:10 The miser's *e* is rapacious for bread,
16: 5 Many such things has my *e* seen,
16:19 If I sin, no *e* will see me;
17:17 a man's virtue, like the apple of his *e*.
22:19 One who jabs the *e* brings tears:
31:13 No creature is greedier than the *e*:
36:22 it surpasses all else that charms the *e*;
39:19 not a thing escapes his *e*.
40: 6 day, Terrified by what his mind's *e* sees,
40:22 Charm and beauty delight the *e*,
Is 64: 3 No ear has ever heard, no *e* ever seen,
Lam 2: 4 as a foe, and slew all on whom the *e* doted;
Zec 2:12 touches you touches the apple of my *e*.
11:17 fall upon his arm and upon his right *e*;
11:17 entirely, and his right *e* be blind forever!
Mt 5:29 If your right *e* is your trouble,
5:38 heard the commandment, 'An eye for an *e*,
6:22 The *e* is the body's lamp.
7: 3 *e* when you miss the plank in your own?
7: 4 'Let me take that speck out of your *e*,'
7: 5 Remove the plank from your own *e* first;
7: 5 to take the speck from your brother's *e*.
18: 9 If your *e* is your downfall,
18: 9 Better to enter life with one *e* than be
19:24 for a camel to pass through a needle's *e*
24:43 he would keep a watchful *e* and not allow
Mk 3: 2 They kept an *e* on Jesus to see whether he
9:47 If your *e* is your downfall, tear it out!
9:47 to enter the kingdom of God with one *e*
10:25 through a needle's *e* than for a rich man
13:34 man at the gate to watch with a sharp *e*.
14:69 The servant girl, keeping an *e* on him,
Lk 6:41 *e* when you miss the plank in your own?
6:42 let me remove the speck from your *e*,'
6:42 remove the plank from your own *e* first;
6:42 to remove the speck from your brother's *e*.
11:34 The *e* is the lamp of your body.
18:25 a camel to go through a needle's *e* than
1Cor 2: 9 *E* has not seen, ear has not heard,
12:16 I am not an *e* I do not belong to the body,"
12:17 If the body were all *e*,
12:21 The *e* cannot say to the hand,
15:52 an instant, in the twinkling of an *e*,
Gal 6:12 with an *e* to escaping persecution for the
1Jn 2:16 Carnal allurements, enticements for the *e*,
Rv 1: 7 Every *e* shall see him,

EYEBROWS (1)

Lv 14: 9 the hair of his head, his beard, his *e*,

EYEING (1)

Mk 8:33 this he turned around and, *e* the disciples,

EYELIDS (3)

Ps(s) 132: 4 I will give my eyes no sleep my *e* no rest,
Prv 6: 4 sleep to your eyes, nor slumber to your *e*;
Sir 26: 9 By her *e* and her haughty stare an unchaste

EYES (471)

Gn 3: 5 moment you eat of it your *e* will be opened
3: 6 tree was good for food, pleasing to the *e*,
3: 7 Then the *e* of both of them were opened,
6:11 In the *e* of God the earth was corrupt and
21:19 Then God opened her *e*,
29:17 Leah had lovely *e*,
31:40 frost by night, while sleep fled from my *e*!
42:24 taken from them and bound before their *e*.
44:21 him down to me that my *e* may look on him.'
46: 4 back here, after Joseph has closed your *e*."
47:15 us food or we shall perish under your *e*;
47:19 we and our land perish before your very *e*?
48:10 (Now Israel's *e* were dim from age,
49:12 His *e* are darker than wine,
Ex 8:22 If before their very *e* we offer sacrifices
15:26 told them, "and do what is right in his *e*:
19:11 Mount Sinai before the *e* of all the people.
34:10 Before the *e* of all your people I will
Lv 25:53 lord it over him harshly under your very *e*.
26:16 and fever to dim the *e* and sap the life.
26:45 of Egypt under the very *e* of the Gentiles,
Nm 10:31 the desert, and you will serve as *e* for us.
15:39 after the desires of your hearts and *e*.
16:14 inheritance, will you also gouge out our *e*?
22:31 LORD removed the veil from Balaam's *e*
24: 2 he raised his *e* and saw Israel encamped,
24: 4 sees, enraptured, and with *e* unveiled:
24:16 sees, enraptured and with *e* unveiled.
27:19 and commission him before their *e*.
33:55 barbs in your *e* and thorns in your sides,
Dt 1:30 took your part before your very *e* in Egypt,
3:21 'Your *e* have seen all that the LORD,
4: 3 your own *e* what the LORD did at Baal-peor:
4: 9 the things which your own *e* have seen,
4:34 did for you in Egypt before your very *e*?
6:22 and wrought before our *e* signs and wonders,
7:19 great testings which your own *e* have seen,
9:17 them from me and broke them before your *e*.
10:21 terrible things which your own *e* have seen.
11: 7 With your own *e* you have seen all these
11:12 his *e* are upon it continually from the
16:19 for a bribe blinds the *e* even of the wise
21: 7 this blood, and our *e* did not see the deed.
28:31 Your ox will be slaughtered before your *e*,
28:34 driven mad by what your *e* must look upon.
28:65 heart and wasted *e* and a dismayed spirit.
28:67 feel and the sight that your *e* must see.
29: 1 before your very *e* to Pharaoh
29: 2 the great testings your own *e* have seen,
29: 3 you a mind to understand, or *e* to see,
34: 4 I have let you feast your *e* upon it,
34: 7 his *e* were undimmed and his vigor unabated.
Jos 5:13 his *e* and saw one who stood facing him,
23:13 for your sides and thorns for your *e*,
24:17 those great miracles before our very *e*
Jgs 16:21 seized him and gouged out his *e*.
16:28 this last time that for my two *e* I may
1Sm 2:33 to wear out their *e* in consuming greed;
3: 2 His *e* had lately grown so weak that he
4:15 years old, and his *e* would not focus,
12:16 LORD is about to accomplish before your *e*.
14:27 he raised it to his mouth and his *e* lit up.
14:29 Look how bright my *e* are from this small
2Sm 13: 6 and prepare some fried cakes before my *e*,
13: 8 cakes before his *e* and fried the cakes.
22:28 though on the lofty your *e* look down.
24: 3 royal majesty to see it with his own *e*.
1Kgs 1:48 my throne, so that I see it with my own *e*.'"
8:29 *e* watch night and day over this temple,
8:52 "Thus may your *e* be open to the petition
9: 3 my *e* and my heart shall be there always.
10: 7 report until I came and saw with my own *e*,
20:38 himself with a bandage over his *e*.
20:41 removed the bandage from his *e*,
2Kgs 4:34 the child's mouth, his *e* upon the eyes,
4:35 now sneezed seven times and opened his *e*.
6:17 Then he prayed, "O LORD, open his *e*,
6:17 And the LORD opened the *e* of the servant,
6:20 "O LORD, opened their *e* that they may see."
6:20 The LORD, opened their *e*,
7: 2 "You shall see it with your own *e*,"
7:19 "You shall see it with your own *e*,
9:30 arrived in Jezreel, she shadowed her *e*,
19:16 Open your *e*, O LORD, and see!
19:22 your voice And lifted up your *e* on high?
22:20 and your *e* shall not see all the evil I
25: 7 He had Zedekiah's sons slain before his *e*.
1Chr 21:16 When David raised his *e*,
29:25 Solomon greatly in the *e* of all Israel,
2Chr 6:20 *e* watch day and night over this temple,
6:40 may your *e* be open and your ears attentive
7:15 Now my *e* shall be open and my ears
7:16 *e* and my heart also shall be there always.
9: 6 report until I came and saw with my own *e*.
16: 9 *e* of the LORD roam over the whole earth,
20:12 to do, hence our *e* are turned toward you."
29: 6 and did evil in the *e* of the LORD,
29: 8 and mockery, as you see with your own *e*.
32:23 was exalted in the *e* of all the nations.
34:28 Your *e* shall not see all the evil I will
Ezr 9: 8 our *e* and given us relief in our servitude.
Neh 1: 6 may your ear be attentive, and your *e* open,
6:16 lost much face in the *e* of the nations,
Tb 2:10 till their warm droppings settled in my *e*,
2:10 they anointed my *e* with various salves,
3:12 Lord, to you I turn my face and raise my *e*.
3:17 to remove the cataracts from Tobit's *e*,
5:21 Your own *e* will see the day when he
6: 9 rub it on the *e* of a man who has cataracts,
6: 9 blowing into his *e* right on the cataracts,
10: 5 "Alas, my child, light of my *e*,
11: 7 "I am certain that his *e* will be opened.
11: 8 cataracts shrink and peel off from his *e*;
11:11 and holding him firmly, blew into his *e*.
11:12 Next he smeared the medicine on his *e*,
11:13 beginning at the corners of Tobit's *e*,
11:14 "I can see you, son, the light of my *e*!"
11:17 God had mercifully restored sight to his *e*.
Jdt 7:27 behold our little ones dying before our *e*
8:22 and a reproach in the *e* of our masters.
10: 4 the *e* of all the men who should see her.
16: 9 Her sandals caught his *e*,
1Mc 6:10 "Sleep has departed from my *e*,
11:51 in the *e* of the king and all his subjects,
2Mc 3:36 high God that he had seen with his own *e*.
8:17 keeping before their *e* the lawless outrage
12:42 for they had seen with their own *e* what
Jb 2:12 up their *e* and did not recognize him,
3: 9 have none, nor gaze on the *e* of the dawn,
3:10 of the womb to shield my *e* from trouble!
4:16 a figure was before my *e*,
10: 4 Have you *e* of flesh?
14: 3 Upon such a one will you cast your *e* so as
15:12 carry you away, and why do your *e* blink,
16:16 weeping and there is darkness over my *e*,
16:20 before God my *e* drop tears,
17: 2 as their provocation mounts, my *e* grow dim.
19:27 my own *e*, not another's, shall behold him,
21:20 feels it, Let his own *e* see the calamity,
24:23 his strength, and his *e* are on their ways.
27:19 he opens his *e* and nothing remains to him.
28:10 his *e* behold all that is precious.
28:21 It is hid from the *e* of any beast;
29:15 I was *e* to the blind,
31: 1 If I have made an agreement with my *e* and
31: 7 the way, and my heart has followed my *e*,
31:16 or allowed the *e* of the widow to languish
32: 1 Job, because he was righteous in his own *e*.
34:21 For his *e* are upon the ways of man,
39:29 his *e* behold it afar off.
40:24 Who can capture him by his *e*,
41:10 his *e* are like those of the dawn.
Ps(s) 6: 8 My *e* are dimmed with sorrow;
10: 8 his *e* spy upon the unfortunate.
11: 4 His *e* behold, his searching glance
13: 4 Give light to my *e* that I may not sleep
17: 2 your *e* behold what is right.
18:28 you save but haughty *e* you bring low;
25:15 My *e* are ever toward the LORD,
26: 3 For your kindness is before my *e*,
33:18 *e* of the LORD are upon those who fear him,
34:16 The LORD has *e* for the just,
35:21 We saw him with our own *e*!"
36: 2 there is no dread of God before his *e*,
38:11 the very light of my *e* has failed me.
50:21 you by drawing them up before your *e*.
54: 5 they set not God before their *e*.
54: 9 me, and my *e* look down upon my enemies.
66: 7 his *e* watch the nations;
69: 4 My *e* have failed with looking for my God.
69:24 their *e* grow dim so that they cannot see,
77: 5 You keep my *e* watchful;
86:14 life, nor do they set you before their *e*.
88:10 My *e* have grown dim through affliction;
91: 8 Rather with your *e* shall you behold and
101: 3 I will not set before my *e* any base thing.
101: 5 *e* and puffed-up heart I will not endure.
101: 6 My *e* are upon the faithful of the land,
101: 7 falsehood shall not stand before my *e*.
115: 5 they have *e* but see not;
116: 8 freed my soul from death, my *e* from tears,
116:15 Precious in the *e* of the LORD is the death
118:23 it is wonderful in our *e*.
119:18 Open my *e*, that I may consider
119:37 Turn away my *e* from seeing what is vain;
119:82 My *e* strain after your promise;
119:123 My *e* strain after your salvation and your
119:136 My *e* shed streams of tears because your
119:148 My *e* greet the night watches in meditation
121: 1 I lift up my *e* toward the mountains;
123: 1 I lift up my *e* who are enthroned in heaven.
123: 2 as the *e* of servants are on the hands of
123: 2 As the *e* of a maid are on the hands of her
123: 2 of her mistress, So are our *e* on the LORD,
131: 1 heart is not proud, nor are my *e* haughty;
132: 4 will give my *e* no sleep my eyelids no rest,
135:16 they have *e* but see not;
139:16 Your *e* have seen my actions;
141: 8 you, O GOD, my Lord, my *e* are turned;

EYES (cont.)
145:15 The *e* of all look hopefully to you,
Prv 1:17 a net is spread before the *e* of any bird
3: 7 Be not wise in your own *e.*
4:25 Let your *e* look straight ahead and your
6: 4 Give no sleep to your *e,*
6:13 He winks his *e,* shuffles his feet,
6:17 Haughty *e,* a lying tongue,
10:26 vinegar to the teeth, and smoke to the *e,*
12:15 way of the fool seems right in his own *e,*
15: 3 The *e* of the LORD are in every place,
16: 2 ways of a man may be pure in his own *e,*
17:24 *e* of a fool are on the ends of the earth.
20:13 *e* wide open mean abundant food.
21: 2 ways of a man may be right in his own *e,*
21: 4 Haughty *e* and a proud heart
21:10 his neighbor finds no pity in his *e.*
22:12 The *e* of the LORD safeguard knowledge,
23:26 your heart, and let your *e* keep to my ways.
23:29 Who have black *e?*
23:33 Your *e* behold strange sights,
25: 8 What your *e* have seen bring not forth
26: 5 folly, lest he become wise in his own *e.*
26:12 You see a man wise in his own *e?*
27:20 so too the *e* of men.
28:11 The rich man is wise in his own *e,*
29:13 the LORD gives light to the *e* of both.
30:12 There is a group that is pure in its own *e,*
30:13 There is a group—how haughty their *e!*
Eccl 2:10 Nothing that my *e* desired did I deny them,
2:14 The wise man has *e* in his head,
5:10 to the owner except to feast his *e* upon?
6: 9 "What the *e* see is better than what the
8:17 nor by night do his *e* find rest in sleep.
11: 7 it is pleasant for the *e* to see the sun.
11: 9 ways of your heart, the vision of your *e;*
Sg 1:15 your *e* are doves!
4: 1 Your *e* are doves behind your veil.
4: 9 my heart with one glance of your *e,*
5:12 *e* are like doves beside running waters,
6: 5 as bannered troops, Turn your *e* from me,
7: 5 Your *e* are like the pools in Heshbon by
8:10 in his *e* I have become one to be welcomed.
Wis 9: 9 understands what is pleasing in your *e*
11:18 or flash terrible sparks from their *e.*
15:15 which have no use of the *e* for vision,
Sir 4: 1 force not the *e* of the needy to turn away.
4: 5 From the needy turn not your *e,*
9: 8 Avert your *e* from a comely woman;
11:12 the *e* of the LORD look favorably upon him;
12:16 Though your enemy has tears in his *e,*
15:19 The *e* of God see all he has made;
17: 5 He forms men's tongues and *e* and ears,
17:11 His majestic glory their *e* beheld,
17:13 to him, they cannot be hidden from his *e.*
17:15 sun to him, his *e* are ever upon their ways.
18:17 a grudging gift wears out the expectant *e.*
20:13 in his *e* the one gift is equal to seven.
20:28 Favors and gifts blind the *e;*
23:19 is not mindful, fearing only the *e* of men;
23:19 does not understand that the *e* of the LORD,
26:11 Follow close if her *e* are bold,
27: 1 and the struggle for wealth blinds the *e.*
27:22 He who has shifty *e* plots mischief and no
30:11 youth, and close not your *e* to his follies.
30:20 who groans at the good things his *e* behold!
31: 6 though destruction lay before their *e;*
31:14 Toward what he *e,* do not put out a hand;
34:16 *e* of the LORD are upon those who love him;
34:17 up the spirits, brings a sparkle to the *e,*
38:28 His *e* are fixed on the tool he is shaping.
43: 4 the *e* are dazzled by its light.
43:19 Its shining whiteness blinds the *e,*
45:12 renowned for splendor, a delight to the *e,*
Is 1: 7 before your *e* strangers devour [a waste,
1:15 spread out your hands, I close my *e* to you;
1:16 Put away your misdeeds from before my *e;*
2:11 The haughty *e* of man will be lowered,
5:15 low, and the *e* of the haughty lowered,
6: 5 yet my *e* have seen the King,
6:10 close their *e;* Else their eyes will see,
10:13 and the boastfulness of his haughty *e.*
13:18 nor shall they have *e* of pity for children.
17: 7 his *e* turned toward the Holy One of Israel.
29:10 He has shut your *e* [the prophets] and
29:18 and darkness, the *e* of the blind shall see.
30:20 with your own *e* you shall see your Teacher,
32: 3 The *e* of those who see will not be closed;
33:15 closing his *e* lest he look on evil
33:17 Your *e* will see a king in his splendor,
33:20 let your *e* see Jerusalem as a quiet abode,
35: 5 Then will the *e* of the blind be opened,
37:17 Open your *e,* O LORD and see!
37:23 your voice And lifted up your *e* on high?
38:14 My *e* grow weak, gazing heavenward:
40:26 *e* on high and see who has created these:
42: 7 the nations, To open the *e* of the blind,
43: 4 you are precious in my *e* and glorious,
43: 8 people who are blind though they have *e,*
44:18 their *e* are coated so that they cannot see,
51: 6 Raise your *e* to the heavens,
52: 8 joy, For they see directly, before their *e,*
59:10 like people without *e* we feel our way.
60: 4 Raise your *e* and look about;
65:16 shall be forgotten, and hidden from my *e.*
Jer 3: 2 Lift your *e* to the heights,
4:30 with gold, Shading your *e* with cosmetics,
5: 3 O LORD, do your *e* not look for honesty?
5:21 senseless people Who have *e* and see not,
7:11 my name become in your *e* a den of thieves?
7:30 of Judah have done what is evil in my *e,*
8:23 of water, my *e* a foundation of tears,
9:17 for us, That our *e* may be wet with weeping,
13:17 *e* will run with tears for the LORD's flock,
13:20 your *e* and see men coming from the north.
14: 6 Their *e* grow dim,
14:17 Let my *e* stream with tears day and night,
16: 9 Before your very *e* and during your
16:17 For my *e* are upon all their ways;
18:10 if that nation does what is evil in my *e,*
20: 4 Your own *e* shall see them fall by the
22:17 But your *e* and heart are set on nothing
29:21 Babylon, who will slay them before your *e.*
31:16 of mourning, wipe the tears from your *e.*
31:26 Upon this I awoke and opened my *e;*
32:19 whose *e* are open to all the ways of men,
32:30 youth have done only what is evil in my *e;*
33:24 if it were no longer a nation in their *e.*
34:15 what is right in my *e* by proclaiming
39:16 and this before your very *e.*
51:24 to Zion, as you shall see with your own *e,*
52: 2 He did what was evil in the *e* of the LORD,
Lam 1:16 "At this I weep, my *e* run with tears:
2:11 Worn out from weeping are my *e,*
2:18 no respite for you, no repose for your *e.*
3:48 My *e* run with streams of water over the
3:49 My *e* flow without ceasing,
3:51 My *e* torment my soul at the sight of all
4:17 Our *e* ever wasted away,
5:17 hearts are sick, at this our *e* grow dim:
Bar 1:12 may give us strength, and light to our *e,*
2:18 feeble, with failing *e* and famished soul,
3:14 of days, and life, where light of the *e,*
6:16 their *e* are full of dust from the feet of
Ez 1:18 that their rims were full of *e* all around.
6: 9 me [and their *e* which lusted after idols].
10:12 the four wheels were full of *e* all around.
12: 2 they have *e* to see but do not see,
18: 6 his *e* to the idols of the house of Israel:
18:12 give back a pledge, raises his *e* to idols,
18:15 his *e* to the idols of the house of Israel,
20: 7 detestable things that have held your *e;*
20: 8 detestable things that had held their *e,*
20:24 with *e* only for the idols of their fathers.
21:28 In their *e* this is but a lying oracle;
22:16 to be profaned in the *e* of the nations;
23:16 no sooner had she set *e* on them than she
23:40 them you bathed yourself, painted your *e,*
24:16 away from you the delight of your *e,*
24:21 of your pride, the delight of your *e,*
24:25 glorious joy, the delight of their *e,*
33:25 mountains, you raise your *e* to your idols,
Dn 4:31 I, Nebuchadnezzar, raised my *e* to heaven;
7: 8 This horn had *e* like a man,
7:20 the *e* and the mouth that spoke arrogantly,
9:18 open your *e* and see our ruins and the city
10: 6 lightning, his *e* were like fiery torches,
13: 9 would not allow their *e* to look to heaven,
14:42 were devoured in a moment before his *e.*
Hos 2:12 bare her shame before the *e* of her lovers,
13:14 My *e* are closed to compassion.
Jl 1:16 our very *e* has not the food been cut off;
Am 9: 8 The *e* of the Lord GOD are on this sinful
Mi 4:11 be profaned, let our *e* see Zion's downfall!"
7:10 My *e* shall see her downfall;
Hb 1:13 Too pure are your *e* to look upon evil,
Zep 3:20 about your restoration before your very *e,*
Hg 2: 3 Does it not seem like nothing in your *e?*
Zec 2: 1 I raised my *e* and looked;
2: 5 Again I raised my *e* and looked:
4:10 These seven facets are the *e* of the LORD
5: 1 raised my *e* again and saw a scroll flying.
5: 5 *e* and see what this is that comes forth."
5: 9 Then I raised my *e* and saw two women
6: 1 Again I raised my *e* and saw four chariots
8: 6 in the *e* of the remnant of this people,
8: 6 in those days be impossible in my *e* also,
12: 4 upon the house of Judah I will open my *e,*
14:12 and their *e* shall rot in their sockets,
Mal 1: 5 Your own *e* shall see it,
Mt 6:22 If your *e* are good,
6:23 if your *e* are bad,
9:29 At that he touched their *e* and said,
13:15 ears, they have firmly closed their *e;*
13:15 otherwise they might see with their *e,*
13:16 "But blest are your *e* because they see
17: 2 He was transfigured before their *e.*
20:33 "Lord," they told him, "open our *e!*"
20:34 with compassion, Jesus touched their *e,*
25:13 keep your *e* open,
26:43 they could not keep their *e* open.
Mk 6:41 two fish, Jesus raised his *e* to heaven,
8:15 he instructed them, "Keep your *e* open!
8:18 Have you *e* but no sight?
8:23 his *e* he laid his hands on him and asked,
8:24 The man opened his *e* and said,
8:25 a second time Jesus laid hands on his *e,*
9: 2 *e* and his clothes became dazzlingly white
9:47 than to be thrown with both *e* into Gehenna,
14:40 They could not keep their *e* open,
Lk 1: 6 Both were just in the *e* of God,
1:15 for he will be great in the *e* of the Lord.
2:30 For my *e* have witnessed your saving deed
4:20 in the synagogue had their *e* fixed on him.
4:35 before everyone's *e* and came out of him
6:20 Then, raising his *e* to his disciples,
9:16 the two fish, Jesus raised his *e* to heaven,
10:23 "Blest are the *e* that see what you see.
16:15 "You justify yourselves in the *e* of men,
16:23 he raised his *e* and saw Abraham afar off,
18:13 not even daring to raise his *e* to heaven.
24:19 deed in the *e* of God and all the people;
24:31 *e* were opened and they recognized him;
Jn 4:35 Open your *e* and see!
9: 6 and smeared the man's *e* with the mud.
9:10 said to him then, "How were your *e* opened?"
9:11 call Jesus made mud and smeared it on my *e,*
9:14 had made the mud paste and opened his *e.)*
9:15 He told them, "He put mud on my *e.*
9:17 "Since it was your *e* he opened,
9:21 how he can see now, or who opened his *e,*
9:26 How did he open your *e?*"
9:30 where he comes from, yet he opened my *e.*
10:21 a devil cannot open the *e* of the blind!"
11:37 said, "He opened the *e* of that blind man.
12:40 "He has blinded their *e,*
Acts 1: 9 lifted up before their *e* in a cloud
9: 8 unable to see, even though his *e* were open.
9:18 fell from his *e* and he regained his sight.
9:40 She opened her *e,*
26:18 the *e* of those to whom I am sending you,
28:27 their *e* they have closed,
28:27 closed, Lest they should see with their *e,*
Rom 3:18 the fear of God is not before their *e.*"
11: 8 blind *e* and deaf ears, and it is so
11:10 *e* be darkened so that they may not see.
12:17 your conduct is honorable in the *e* of all.
Gal 3: 1 you before whose *e* Jesus Christ was
4:15 plucked out your *e* and given them to me.
Heb 3: 1 a heavenly calling, fix your *e* on Jesus,
4:13 *e* of him to whom we must render an account.
12: 2 let us keep our *e* fixed on Jesus,
Jas 2: 5 are poor in the *e* of the world to be rich
1Pt 2: 4 nonetheless, and precious in God's *e.*
2:20 is right, this is acceptable in God's *e.*
3: 4 This is precious in God's *e.*
3:12 has *e* for the just and ears for their cry;
4: 6 condemned in the flesh in the *e* of men,
4: 6 might live in the spirit in the *e* of God.
2Pt 3: 8 In the Lord's *e,* one day is as a thousand
1Jn 2:11 is going, since the dark has blinded his *e.*
Rv 1:14 snow-white wool and his *e* blazed like fire.
2:18 whose *e* blaze like fire and whose feet
3:18 Buy ointment to smear on your *e,*
4: 6 creatures covered with *e* front and back.
4: 8 creatures had six wings and *e* all over,
5: 6 seven *e;* these eyes are the seven spirits
7:17 and God will wipe every tear from their *e.*"
19:12 His *e* blazed like fire,
21: 4 He shall wipe every tear from their *e,*

EYESIGHT (6)
Gn 27: 1 Isaac was so old that his *e* had failed him,
Tb 2:10 For four years I was deprived of *e,*
7: 7 when he heard that Tobit had lost his *e,*
14: 2 sixty-two years old when he lost his *e,*
Lk 11:34 When your *e* is sound,
11:34 body is lighted up, but when your *e* is bad,

EYEWITNESS (1)
Jn 19:35 (This testimony has been given by an *e,*

EYEWITNESSES (2)
Lk 1: 2 the original *e* and ministers of the word.
2Pt 1:17 for we were *e* of his sovereign majesty.

EZBAI (1)
1Chr 11:37 Naarai, the son of *E;*

EZBON (2)
Gn 46:16 Zephon, Haggi, Shuni, *E,*
1Chr 7: 7 The sons of Bela were *E,*

EZEKIEL (3)
Sir 49: 8 *E* beheld the vision and described the
Ez 1: 3 the word of the LORD came to the priest *E,*
24:24 *E* shall be a sign for you:

EZEM (3)
Jos 15:29 Baalah, Iim, *E,*
19: 3 Shema, Moladah, Hazar-shual, Balah, *E,*
1Chr 4:29 Moladah, Hazar-shual, Bilhah, *E,*

EZER (10)
Gn 36:21 Lotan, Shobal, Zibeon, Anah, Dishon, *E,*

36:27 The descendants of *E* were Bilhan,
36:30 of Lotan, Shobal, Zibeon, Anah, Dishon, *E,*
1Chr 1:38 Lotan, Shobal, Zibeon, Anah, Dishon, *E,*
1:42 The sons of *E* were Bilhan,
4: 4 of Gedor, and *E* the father of Hushah.
7:21 Ephraim's son Shuthelah, and *E* and Elead,
12:10 *E* was their chief,
Neh 3:19 next to him *E,* son of Jeshua,
12:42 Uzzi, Jehohanan, Malchijah, Elam, and *E.*

EZION-GEBER (7)

Nm 33:35 Setting out from Abronah, they camped at *E.*
33:36 Setting out from *E*—
Dt 2: 8 left behind us in Arabah route, Elath, *E,*
1Kgs 9:26 King Solomon also built a fleet at *E,*
22:49 because they were wrecked *E*
2Chr 8:17 In those times Solomon went to *E* and to
20:36 the fleet was built at *E.*

EZRA (29)

Ezr 7: 1 reign of Artaxerxes, king of Persia, *E,*
7: 6 this *E* came up from Babylon.
7: 8 *E* came to Jerusalem in the fifth month of
7:10 *E* had set his heart on the study and
7:11 Artaxerxes gave to *E* the priest-scribe,
7:12 king of kings, to *E* the priest,
7:21 Whatever *E* the priest,
7:25 "As for you, *E,* in accordance
10: 1 *E* prayed and acknowledged their guilt,
10: 2 of the sons of Elam, made this appeal to *E:*
10: 5 *E* rose to his feet and demanded an oath
10: 6 Then *E* retired from his place before the
10:10 Then *E,* the priest, stood up
10:16 *E* appointed as his assistants men who were
Neh 8: 1 and they called upon *E* the scribe to bring
8: 2 *E* the priest brought the law before the
8: 4 *E* the scribe stood on a wooden platform
8: 5 *E* opened the scroll so that all the people
8: 6 *E* blessed the LORD,
8: 8 *E* read plainly from the book of the law of
8: 9 and] *E* the priest-scribe [and the Levites
8:13 Levites gathered around *E* the scribe
8:18 *E* read from the book of the law of God day
9: 6 Then *E* said: "It is you, O LORD"
12: 1 Seraiah, Jeremiah, *E,*
12:13 for *E,* Meshullam; for Amariah,
12:26 the governor and of *E* the priest-scribe].
12:33 princes of Judah, along with Azariah, *E,*
12:36 *E* the scribe was at their head.]

EZRAH (1)

1Chr 4:17 The sons of *E* were Jether,

EZRAHITE (1)

1Kgs 5:11 than Ethan the *E,* or Heman,

EZRI (1)

1Chr 27:26 the farm workers who tilled the soil was *E,*

F

FABLES (1)

2Tm 4: 4 to the truth and will wander off to *f.*

FABRICATED (1)

2Pt 2: 3 They will deceive you with *f* tales,

FABRICATIONS (1)

Jb 13:12 are ashy maxims, your *f* are mounds of clay.

FABRICS (1)

2Chr 2: 6 iron, in purple, crimson, and violet *f,*

FACADE (5)

1Mc 1:22 the golden ornament on the *f* of the temple.
4:57 They ornamented the *f* of the temple with
Ez 41:14 The *f* of the temple,
44: 4 of the north gate to the *f* of the temple,
47: 1 the *f* of the temple was toward the east;

FACE (248)

Gn 3:19 sweat of your *f* shall you get bread to eat,
19: 1 and bowing down with his *f* to the ground,
30:40 and he set these animals to *f* the streaked
32:21 that precede me, then later, when I *f* him,
32:31 "Because I have seen God *f* to *f,*"
38:14 her *f* by covering herself with a shawl,
38:15 for a harlot, since she had covered her *f.*
43:31 After washing his *f,* he reappeared
48:11 "I never expected to see your *f* again,
48:12 down before him with his *f* to the ground.
50: 1 *f* and wept over him as he kissed him.
Ex 3: 6 Moses hid his *f,*
32:12 exterminate them from the *f* of the earth"?
33:11 The LORD used to speak to Moses face to *f,*
33:20 But my *f* you cannot see,
33:23 but my *f* is not to be seen."
34:29 skin of his *f* had become radiant
34:30 how radiant the skin of his *f* had become,
34:33 with them, he put a veil over his *f.*
34:35 see that the skin of Moses' *f* was radiant;
34:35 would again put the veil over his *f*
Lv 20: 5 I myself will set my *f* against that man
Nm 6:25 The LORD let his *f* shine upon you,
8: 3 to *f* toward the front of the lampstand,
11:15 so that I need no longer *f* this distress."
12: 3 far the meekest man on the *f* of the earth.
12: 8 face to *f* I speak to him,
12:14 "Suppose her father had spit in her *f,*
14:43 there the Amalekites and Canaanites *f* you,
22: 5 who now cover the *f* of the earth
22:11 from Egypt now cover the *f* of the earth.
Dt 5: 4 The LORD spoke with you *f* to face on the
6:15 and he destroy you from the *f* of the land;
7: 6 from all the nations on the *f* of the earth
14: 2 on the *f* of the earth to be a people
25: 9 sandal from his foot and spit in his *f,*
31:17 will forsake them and hide my *f* from them,
31:18 Yet I will be hiding my *f* from them at
32:20 "I will hide my *f* from them,"
34:10 like Moses, whom the LORD knew *f* to face.
Jgs 6:22 have seen the angel of the LORD face to *f!*"
1Sm 28:14 and so he bowed *f* to the ground in homage.
2Sm 2:22 How could I *f* your brother Joab?"
14:33 on his *f* to the ground before the king.
18:28 With *f* to the ground he paid homage to the
19: 5 his *f* and cried out in a loud voice,
24:20 homage to the king, with *f* to the ground.
1Kgs 19:13 Elijah hid his *f* in his cloak and went and
21:10 get two scoundrels to *f* him and accuse him
2Kgs 8:15 in water and spread it over the king's *f,*
14: 8 challenge, "Come let us meet *f* to face."
20: 2 his *f* to the wall and prayed to the LORD:
1Chr 21:16 prostrated themselves *f* to the ground,
21:21 down before David, his *f* to the ground.
2Chr 20:18 knelt down with his *f* to the ground,
25: 8 LORD will defeat you in the *f* of the enemy.
25:17 "Come, let us meet each other *f* to face."
30: 9 away his *f* from you if you return to him."
Ezr 9: 6 and confounded to raise my *f* to you,
Neh 3:37 for they insulted the builders to their *f!*
6:16 lost much *f* in the eyes of the nations,
Tb 2: 9 Because of the heat I left my *f* uncovered.
3: 6 I may go from the *f* of the earth into dust.
3:12 Lord, to you I turn my *f* and raise my eyes.
4: 7 *f* away from any of the poor, and God's *f*
13: 6 to you, and no longer hide his *f* from you.
Jdt 6: 2 and destroy them from the *f* of the earth.
6: 5 you shall not see my *f* after today,
8:15 or to destroy us in the *f* of our enemies.
10:14 men heard her words and gazed upon her *f,*
10:23 they all marveled at the beauty of her *f.*
13:16 my *f* that seduced Holofernes to his ruin,
16: 7 She anointed her *f* with fragrant oil;
Est C:11 for death was staring them in the *f.*
D: 6 till she stood face to *f* with the king,
7: 8 when the *f* of Haman was covered over.
2Mc 3:16 his *f* manifested the anguish of his soul.
Jb 1:11 and surely he will blaspheme you to your *f.*"
2: 5 and surely he will blaspheme you to your *f.*"
6:28 surely I will not lie to your *f.*
11:15 then you may lift up your *f* in innocence;
13:24 you hide your *f* and consider me your enemy?
16:16 My *f* is inflamed with weeping and there is
21:31 will charge him with his conduct to his *f,*
22:26 and you shall lift up your *f* toward God.
24:15 roams about, and he puts a mask over his *f;*
30:10 me, they do not hesitate to spit in my *f!*
33:26 he shall see God's *f* with rejoicing.
34:29 If he hides his *f,*
Ps(s) 10:11 "God has forgotten; he hides his *f,*
11: 7 the upright shall see his *f.*
13: 2 How long will you hide your *f* from me?
17:15 But I in justice shall behold your *f;*
22:25 Nor did he turn his *f* away from him,
24: 6 him, that seeks the *f* of the God of Jacob.
27: 9 Hide not your *f* from me;
30: 8 but when you hid your *f* I was terrified.
31:17 Let your *f* shine upon your servant;
35: 3 and block the way in the *f* of my pursuers;
42: 3 When shall I go and behold the *f* of God?
44:16 and shame covers my *f* At the voice of him
44:25 Why do you hide your *f,*
51:11 Turn away your *f* from my sins,
67: 2 may he let his *f* shine upon us.
69: 8 sake I bear insult, and shame covers my *f.*
69:18 Hide not your *f* from your servant;
80: 4 if your *f* shine upon us,
80: 8 if your *f* shine upon us,
80:20 if your *f* shine upon us,
84:10 and look upon the *f* of your anointed.
88:15 why hide from me your *f?*
102: 3 your *f* from me in the day of my distress.
104:29 If you hide your *f,* they are dismayed;
104:30 created, and you renew the *f* of the earth.
114: 7 Before the *f* of the Lord,
114: 7 O earth, before the *f* of the God of Jacob,
143: 7 Hide not your *f* from me lest I become like
Prv 8:27 out the vault over the *f* of the deep;
15:13 A glad heart lights up the *f.*
17:12 *F* a bear robbed of her cubs,
27:19 As one *f* differs from another,
Eccl 7: 3 when the *f* is sad the heart grows wiser.
8: 1 A man's wisdom illumines his *f,*
Wis 4:20 deeds shall convict them to their *f.*
17:10 reluctant to *f* even the air that they
Sir 4: 4 avert not your *f* from the poor.
12:18 and hiss repeatedly, and show his true *f.*
18:24 time of vengeance when he will hide his *f.*
25:22 Depressed mind, saddened *f,*
26: 4 is content, and a smile is ever on his *f.*
26:17 are her beauty of *f* and graceful figure.
34: 3 reflection of a face is to the *f* itself.
36:22 beauty makes her husband's *f* light up,
45: 5 led him into the cloud, Where, *f* to face,
Is 8:17 is hiding his *f* from the house of Jacob;
23:17 the world's kingdoms on the *f* of the earth.
29:22 be ashamed of, nor shall his *f* grow pale.
38: 2 his *f* to the wall and prayed to the LORD:
50: 6 My *f* I did not shield from buffets and
50: 7 I have set my *f* like flint,
54: 8 of wrath, for a moment I hid my *f* from you;
59: 2 hide his *f* so that he will not hear you.
64: 6 For you have hidden your *f* from us and
65: 3 who provoke me continually, to my *f,*
Jer 18:17 I will show them my back, not my *f,*
25:26 all the kingdoms upon the *f* of the earth
27: 5 and man and beast on the *f* of the earth,
28:16 will dispatch you from the *f* of the earth;
32: 4 They shall meet and speak *f* to face,
33: 4 in the *f* of siegeworks and the sword:
33: 5 *f* from this city for all their wickedness.
34: 3 king of Babylon and speak to him *f* to face.
Lam 3:16 with gravel, pressed my *f* in the dust;
3:39 complain, any mortal, in the *f* of his sins?
5: 9 sustenance, in the *f* of the desert heat;
Ez 1:10 *f* of an ox, and finally each had the face
1:10 *f* of a lion, and on the left side the face
2: 4 Hard of *f* and obstinate of heart are they
3: 8 But I will make your *f* as hard as theirs,
7:22 I will turn away my *f* from them,
10:14 the first *f* was that of an ox,
12: 6 cover your *f* that you may not see the land,
12:12 covering his *f* lest he be seen by anyone.
15: 7 I will set my *f* against them;
15: 7 am the LORD, when I turn my *f* against them.
20:35 enter into judgment with you face to *f.*
21: 3 to north every *f* shall be scorched by it.
28: 9 when you *f* your murderers?
29: 2 Son of man, set your *f* against Pharaoh,
35: 2 Son of man, set your *f* against Mount Seir,
39:23 and I hid my *f* from them and handed them
39:24 I dealt with them, hiding my *f* from them.
39:29 No longer will I hide my *f* from them,
41:19 man's *f* looking at a palmtree on one side,
41:19 *f* looking at a palmtree on the other;
43:17 The steps of the altar *f* the east.
46:19 reserved to the priests] which *f* the north.
Dn 3:19 Nebuchadnezzar's *f* became livid with utter
5: 6 wrist and hand that wrote, his *f* blanched;
5: 9 his *f* went ashen,
7:28 by my thoughts, and my *f* blanched,
9:17 your *f* shine upon your desolate sanctuary.
10: 6 chrysolite, his *f* shown like lightning,
10: 9 of his voice, I fell *f* forward in a faint.
13:32 *f* so as to sate themselves with her beauty.
Jl 2: 6 peoples are in torment, every *f* blanches.
Am 9: 8 destroy it from off the *f* of the earth.
Mi 3: 4 shall he hide his *f* from them at that time,
Na 1: 6 firm, and who can *f* his blazing anger?
2:11 Writhing in every frame, every *f* blanched!
Zep 1: 2 away all things from the *f* of the earth,
1: 3 destroy mankind from the *f* of the earth,
Mt 6:17 that you groom your hair and wash your *f.*
17: 2 His *f* became as dazzling as the sun,
18:10 constantly behold my heavenly Father's *f.*
26:67 they began to spit in his *f* and hit him.
Mk 10:22 At these words the man's *f* fell.
Lk 9:29 his *f* changed in appearance and his
17:16 He threw himself on his *f* at the feet of
21:35 upon all who dwell on the *f* of the earth.
22:33 to *f* imprisonment and death itself."
Jn 11:44 linen strips, his *f* wrapped in a cloth.
18:22 nearby gave Jesus a sharp blow on the *f.*
19: 3 slapping his *f* as they did so.
Acts 6:15 Stephen's *f* seemed like that of an angel.
17:26 of mankind to dwell on the *f* of the earth.
20:25 the kingdom will ever see my *f* again.
20:38 hear that they would never see his *f* again.
27:26 still have to *f* shipwreck on some island."
1Cor 13:12 then we shall see *f* to face.
15:31 Jesus our Lord, that I *f* death every day.
2Cor 3: 7 not look on Moses' *f* because of the glory
3:13 who used to hide his *f* with a veil so that
4: 6 glory of God shining on the *f* of Christ.
11:20 put on airs, with those who slap your *f.*
1Thes 2: 2 to you in the *f* of great opposition.
3:10 we may see you *f* to face and remedy
Jas 1:23 into a mirror at the *f* he was born with;
1Pt 3:12 but against evildoers the Lord sets his *f.*"
2Jn 1:12 to visit you and talk with you face to *f,*
3Jn 1:14 see you soon, when we can talk *f* to face.

FACE (cont.)

Rv 1:16 his *f* shone like the sun at its brightest.
4: 7 the third had the *f* of a man,
6:16 Hide us from the *f* of the One who sits on
10: 1 his *f* shone like the sun and his legs like
22: 4 face to *f* and bear his name

FACED (6)

1Kgs 7: 5 rectangular, and the doorways *f* each other,
2Chr 13:13 so that while his army *f* Judah,
Is 17: 9 When *f* with the children of Israel:
Ez 1:17 move in any of the four directions they *f*,
10:11 for in whichever direction they were *f*,
40: 6 Then he went to the gate which *f* the east,

FACES (53)

Gn 9:23 since their *f* were turned the other way,
25: 9 son of Zohar the Hittite, which *f* Mamre,
42: 6 down before him with their *f* to the ground,
Ex 25:20 their *f* looking toward the propitiatory.
28:26 breastpiece, on its edge that *f* the ephod.
37: 9 their *f* looking toward the propitiatory.
Dt 34: 1 the headland of Pisgah which *f* Jericho,
Jos 15: 7 of the Gilgal that *f* the pass of Adummim,
18:16 where it *f* the Valley of Ben-hinnom;
2Chr 7: 3 with their *f* to the earth and adored,
29: 6 away their *f* from the LORD's dwelling,
Neh 8: 6 before the LORD, their *f* to the ground.
Jdt 7: 3 from Bethulia to Cyamon, which *f* Esdraelon.
1Mc 4:40 ashes and fell with their *f* to the ground.
7: 3 of this, he said, "Do not show me their *f*."
Jb 9:24 he covers the *f* of its judges.
Ps(s) 34: 6 joy, and your *f* may not blush with shame.
83:17 Darken their *f* with disgrace,
104:15 hearts, So that their *f* gleam with oil,
Is 6: 2 with two they veiled their *f*,
13: 8 look aghast at each other, their *f* aflame.
25: 8 GOD will wipe away the tears from all *f*;
53: 3 One of those from whom men hide their *f*,
Jer 2:27 They turn to me their backs, not their *f*;
5: 3 They set their *f* harder than stone,
7:24 hearts and turned their backs, not their *f*,
30: 6 Why have all their *f* turned deathly pale?
32:33 turned their backs to me, not their *f*;
51:51 have heard taunts, confusion covers our *f*;
Bar 6:12 They wipe their *f* clean of the house dust
6:20 *f* are blackened by the smoke of the house.
Ez 1: 6 human, but each had four *f* and four wings,
1: 9 Their *f* [and their wings] looked out on
1:10 Their *f* were like this:
7:18 their *f* and baldness on all their heads.
8:16 LORD's temple and their *f* toward the east;
9: 2 of the upper gate which *f* the north,
10:14 Each had four *f*:
10:21 Each had four *f* and four wings;
10:22 Their *f* looked just like those I had seen
27:35 kings are terrified, their *f* convulsed.
40:45 "This chamber which *f* south is for the
40:46 and the chamber which *f* north is for the
41:18 Each cherub had two *f*:
42:15 the gate which *f* east and measured
43: 1 he led me to the gate which *f* the east,
43: 4 temple by way of the gate which *f* the east,
Mal 2: 3 shoulder and I will strew dung in your *f*,
Mt 6:16 *f* so that others may see they are fasting.
23:13 doors of the kingdom of God in men's *f*,
2Cor 3:18 on the Lord's glory with unveiled *f*,
Rv 9: 7 their *f* were like men's faces but they had

FACETS (2)

Zec 3: 9 before Joshua, one stone with seven *f*.
4:10 These seven *f* are the eyes of the LORD

FACILITY (1)

Wis 13:19 *f* of a thing with hands completely inert.

FACING (41)

Gn 23:17 Thus Ephron's field in Machpelah, *f* Mamre,
23:19 the field of Machpelah, *f* Mamre (that is,
49:30 cave in the field of Machpelah, *f* on Mamre,
50:13 cave in the field of Machpelah, *f* on Mamre,
Ex 39:19 the breastpiece, on the edge *f* the ephod.
Dt 32:49 [it is in the land of Moab *f* Jericho];
Jos 5:13 his eyes and saw one who stood *f* him,
8:33 stood on either side of the ark *f* the
8:33 were *f* Mount Gerizim and half Mount Ebal,
22:11 region of the Jordan *f* the land of Canaan,
1Sm 20:25 place against the wall, Jonathan sat *f* him,
1Kgs 7:25 *f* north, three facing west, three *f* south,
7:25 west, three facing south, and three *f* east,
8:64 of the court *f* the temple of the LORD;
22:35 propped up in his chariot *f* the Arameans,
2Kgs 2: 7 at the Jordan, stood *f* them at a distance.
2Chr 3:13 upon their own feet, *f* toward the nave.
4: 4 It rested on twelve oxen, three *f* north,
18:34 his chariot *f* the Arameans until evening.
Tb 3:11 she spread out her hands, and *f* the window,
Jdt 4: 6 way to Esdraelon, *f* the plain near Dothan,
Est 5: 1 the audience chamber, *f* the palace doorway.
1Mc 4:61 people might have a stronghold *f* Idumea.
13:13 pitched his camp at Adida, *f* the plain.
13:28 He set up seven pyramids *f* one another for
16: 5 There, *f* them, was an immense army
Ez 40:20 the outer court, there was a gate *f* north,
40:22 as those of the gate *f* the east.
40:32 Then he brought me to the gate *f* the east,
40:44 one beside the north gate, *f* south,
40:44 the other beside the south gate, *f* north.
41:16 with trellises about them *f* the threshold].
44: 1 outer gate of the sanctuary, *f* the east;
47: 2 and around to the outer gate *f* the east,
Dn 8: 8 up four others, *f* the four winds of heaven.
10:16 I opened my mouth and said to the one *f* me,
Mt 27:61 Mary remained sitting there, *f* the tomb.
Mk 13: 3 seated on the Mount of Olives *f* the temple,
Rv 21:13 There were three gates *f* east,

FACT (89)

Gn 20: 6 In *f*, it was I who kept you from sinning
21:26 "In *f*, you never told me about it
37:17 in *f*, I heard them say,
39: 5 in *f*, the LORD's blessing
40:20 And in *f*, on the third day,
41:57 In *f*, all the world came to Joseph
45:26 in *f*, it is he who is ruler of all
Ex 11: 1 In *f*, he will not merely let you go
22: 9 away, without anyone witnessing the *f*,
36: 7 there was already enough at hand, in *f*,
Lv 5:22 he denies the *f* and swears falsely about
13:46 himself unclean, since he is in *f* unclean.
14:48 has in *f* not spread after the plastering,
Nm 5:13 has not sufficient evidence of the *f*,
Dt 13:15 find that it is true and an established *f*
17: 4 an established *f* that this abomination
19:15 a judicial *f* shall be established only on
Jgs 3: 6 In *f*, they took their daughters in marriage
1Sm 2:15 In *f*, even before the fat was burned,
4:17 in *f*, the troops suffered heavy losses.
20: 5 when I should in *f* dine with the king.
20:21 If in *f* I say to him,
2Sm 18:20 good news, for in *f* the king's son is dead."
1Kgs 22:49 but in *f* the ships did not go,
2Kgs 8:10 LORD has showed me that he will in *f* die."
15:15 of Shallum, and the *f* of his conspiracy,
18:21 is in *f* a broken reed which pierces the
1Chr 5: 2 Judah, in *f*, became powerful
2Chr 29:34 the Levites, in *f*, were more willing
30:18 The greater part of the people, in *f*,
Ezr 4:16 by that very *f* you will no longer own any
Tb 1:22 He was a close relative—in *f*, my nephew.
1Mc 9:61 In *f*, Jonathan's men seized about fifty
15:27 in *f*, he broke all the agreements
2Mc 1:34 the king, after verifying the *f*,
4:20 was in *f* applied by those who brought it,
6:13 It is, in *f*, a sign of great kindness
10:13 In *f*, on all sides he heard himself
13:25 in *f* they were so indignant that they
Jb 15: 4 You in *f* do away with piety,
Eccl 5: 7 in the realm, do not be shocked by the *f*,
Is 36: 6 is in *f* a broken reed which pierces the
Jer 44:25 stated your intentions, and kept them in *f*:
Ez 3:21 man not to sin, and he has in *f* not sinned,
Dn 5:11 In *f*, King Nebuchadnezzar,
Mt 22:31 As to the *f* that the dead are raised,
Mk 5: 4 In *f*, he had frequently been secured
7: 3 The Pharisees, and in *f* all Jews,
12:22 in *f* none of the seven left any children
Lk 4:24 But in *f*," he went on,
10:20 in the *f* that the devils are subject
22:27 Who, in *f*, is the greater
Jn 3:28 are witnesses to the *f* that I said:
4: 2 baptizing more disciples than John (in *f*,
4:18 "The *f* is, you have had five,
7: 5 (As a matter of *f*, not even his brothers
8:40 The *f* is, you are trying to kill me
9:19 you account for the *f* that now he can see?"
12:10 The *f* was, the chief priests planned
16:10 from the *f* that I go to the Father and
21:23 Jesus never told him, as a matter of *f*,
Acts 4:22 The *f* was, the man thus miraculously
5:13 despite the *f* that the people held them in
11:28 did in *f* occur while Claudius was emperor.)
17:29 If we are in *f* God's offspring,
19:27 In *f*, she whom Asia and all the world
Rom 1:19 In *f*, whatever can be known about God
4:11 In *f*, he received the sign of circumcision
7:16 that very *f* I agree that the law is good.
1Cor 6: 7 the very *f* that you have lawsuits against
9:20 bound (although in *f* I am not bound by it),
9:23 In *f*, I do all that I do for the sake
10:31 The *f* is that whether you eat or drink
12:22 seem less important are in *f* indispensable.
15: 9 in *f*, because I persecuted the church
2Cor 6: 9 nobodies who in *f* are well known;
13: 1 "A judicial *f* shall be established only
Gal 3:22 In *f*, however, Scripture has locked all
4: 6 The proof that you are sons is the *f* that
4: 7 the *f* that you are a son makes you an heir,
6: 3 to something, when in *f* he is nothing,
Phil 2:24 In *f*, I am confident in the Lord
2:27 He was, in *f*, sick to the point of death,
1Thes 2: 8 So well disposed were we to you, in *f*,
2Tm 4:16 In *f*, everyone abandoned me.
Heb 11:39 Yet despite the *f* that all of these were
Jas 3: 4 the *f* that they are driven by fierce winds,
1Jn 4: 3 in *f*, it is in the world already.
Rv 3: 1 of being alive, when in *f* you are dead!

FACTION (2)

Ps(s) 106:17 up Dathan, and covered the *f* of Abiram.
106:18 Fire broke out against their *f*;

FACTIONS (4)

Mt 12:25 split into *f* cannot last for long.
1Cor 1:10 Let there be no *f*;
11:19 There may even have to be *f* among you for
Gal 5:20 rage, selfish rivalries, dissensions, *f*,

FACTS (3)

2Mc 4:33 When Onias had clear evidence of the *f*,
Jn 7:51 first hearing him and knowing the *f*?"
Acts 24: 9 and maintained that these were the *f*.

FACULTIES (1)

Heb 5:14 for those whose *f* are trained by practice

FADE (5)

Ps(s) 1: 3 in due season, and whose leaves never *f*.
Sir 38:23 With the departed dead, let memory *f*;
Is 17: 4 On that day The glory of Jacob shall *f*,
Ez 7:26 Prophetic vision shall *f*;
47:12 their leaves shall not *f*,

FADES (6)

Jb 14: 2 Like a flower that springs up and *f*,
20: 8 he *f* away like a vision of the night.
Ps(s) 90: 6 up anew, but by evening wilts and *f*.
Is 24: 4 mourns and *f*, the world languishes and *f*;
Na 1: 4 and Carmel, and the bloom of Lebanon *f*;

FADING (5)

Is 28: 1 To the *f* blooms of his glorious beauty,
28: 4 The *f* blooms of his glorious beauty on the
2Cor 3: 7 shone on it (even though it was a *f* glory),
3:13 could not see the final *f* of that glory.
1Pt 1: 4 inheritance, incapable of *f* or defilement,

FAGGOTS (1)

Dn 3:46 furnace with brimstone, pitch, tow, and *f*.

FAIL (53)

Gn 24:27 his constant kindness toward my master *f*.
43: 9 If I *f* to bring him back,
44:32 saying, 'If I *f* to bring him back to you,
Lv 20: 4 to Molech, and *f* to put him to death,
Nm 15:22 "When through inadvertence you *f* to carry
Dt 12: 2 *f* every place on the high mountains,
31: 6 he will never *f* you or forsake you."
31: 8 you and will never *f* you or forsake you.
Jgs 21: 5 at Mizpah should be put to death without *f*.
2Sm 17:16 the desert, but to cross over without *f*.
1Kgs 2:37 Valley, be certain you shall die without *f*.
2:42 anywhere else, you should die without *f*?
9: 6 *f* to keep the commandments and statutes
1Chr 28:20 He will not *f* you or abandon you before
Ezr 6: 9 be delivered to them day by day without *f*,
Jdt 11: 6 lord will not *f* in any of his undertakings.
11:11 so that my lord will not be repulsed and *f*,
1Mc 2:61 none who hope in him shall *f* in strength.
6:22 you *f* to do justice and avenge our kinsmen?
Jb 14:11 As when the waters of a lake *f*,
21:10 Their bulls gender without *f*;
23:16 Indeed God has made my courage *f*;
32:15 they make no more reply; words *f* them.
36: 4 For indeed, my theme cannot *f* me:
37:17 whom the streams of water *f* when a calm
Ps(s) 77: 9 cease, his promise *f* for all generations?
Prv 15:22 Plans *f* when there is no counsel,
Sir 3:13 Even if his mind *f*,
22:27 seal, That I may not *f* through them,
24:21 to shame, he who serves me will never *f*."
34: 8 The law is fulfilled without *f*,
42:17 *f* in recounting the wonders of the LORD,
47:22 nor permit even one of his promises to *f*.
Is 7: 4 let not your courage *f* before these two
32:10 The vintage will *f*,
Jer 25: 4 the LORD has sent you without *f* all his
35:19 there *f* to be a descendant of Jonadab,
Ez 21:12 when it comes every heart shall *f*,
24:14 for I will bring it about without *f*.
47:12 leaves shall not fade, nor their fruit *f*.
Dn 11: 6 But her bid for power shall *f*:
11:14 in fulfillment of vision, but they shall *f*.
Hos 9: 2 nourish them, the new wine shall *f* them.
Hb 3:17 *f* and the terraces produce no nourishment,
Zep 3: 7 not *f* to see all I have visited upon her.
Mt 22:29 "You are badly misled because you *f* to
Mk 12:24 because you *f* to understand the Scriptures
Lk 6:42 yet *f* yourself to see the plank lodged in
16: 9 world's goods, so that when they *f* you,
22:32 prayed for you that your faith may never *f*.

Jn 8:49 my Father, while you *f* to respect me.
16: 7 If I *f* to go, the Paraclete will never come
Ti 2: 7 you yourself *f* to set them good example.

FAILED (33)

Gn 27: 1 was so old that his eyesight had *f* him,
27:23 (He *f* to identify him because his hands
30: 1 saw that she *f* to bear children to Jacob,
Nm 14:22 times already and have *f* to heed my voice,
Ru 4:14 not *f* to provide you today with an heir!
1Sm 9: 4 Benjamin, but they *f* to find the animals.
22:17 he was a fugitive and yet *f* to inform me."
2Kgs 3:26 through to the king of Aram, but he *f*.
Ezr 10: 8 *f* to appear within three days would,
Jdt 7:20 of water *f* the inhabitants of Bethulia,
1Mc 6: 8 Sick with grief because his designs had *f*,
2Mc 14:43 of the struggle he *f* to strike exactly.
Ps(s) 31:11 My strength has *f* through affliction,
38:11 the very light of my eyes has *f* me.
69: 4 My eyes have *f* with looking for my God.
76: 6 the hands of all the mighty ones have *f*.
Jer 3: 3 showers were withheld, the spring rain *f*.
11: 8 they had *f* to observe as I commanded them.
32:23 live, and what you commanded they *f* to do.
46:15 has Apis fled, your mighty one *f* to stand?
Lam 1:19 "I cried out to my lovers, but they *f* me.
Jl 1:10 the grain is ravaged, the must has *f*,
1:17 barns are broken down, for the grain has *f*.
Mk 9:32 Though they *f* to understand his words,
Lk 6:48 but *f* to shake it because of its solid
9:45 They *f*, however, to understand
19:44 *f* to recognize the time of your visitation."
24:23 tomb before dawn and *f* to find his body,
Acts 13:27 and their rulers *f* to recognize him,
Rom 9: 6 Not that God's word has *f*.
2Cor 13: 5 of course, you have *f* the challenge.
13: 6 you will understand that we have not *f*.
13: 7 is good, even though we may seem to have *f*.

FAILING (10)

Gn 48: 1 Joseph was informed, "Your father is *f*."
Dt 32:36 When he sees their strength *f*,
32:51 by *f* to manifest my sanctity
Sir 41: 2 sentence to the weak man of *f* strength,
41:20 appointed share, Of *f* to return a greeting,
Bar 2:18 and feeble, with *f* eyes and famished soul,
Lk 7:30 by *f* to receive his baptism defeated God's
11:24 *f* to find one, it says, 'I will go back
Rom 2:21 of others, are you *f* to teach yourself?
1Cor 8: 8 We suffer no loss through *f* to eat,

FAILINGS (3)

Ps(s) 19:13 in keeping them, Yet who can detect *f*?
Sir 23: 2 of discipline, That my *f* may not be spared,
23: 3 Lest my *f* increase, and my sins

FAILS (19)

Nm 9:13 a journey, who yet *f* to keep the Passover,
19:12 But if he *f* to purify himself on the third
19:13 Everyone who *f* to purify himself after
19:20 Any unclean man who *f* to have himself
Dt 27:26 'Cursed be he who *f* to fulfill any of the
Neh 5:13 every man who *f* to keep this promise,
Ps(s) 40:13 the hairs of my head, and my heart *f* me.
71: 9 as my strength *f*, forsake me not
143: 7 to answer me, O LORD, for my spirit *f* me.
Sir 4:19 But if he *f* her, she will abandon him
Is 55: 2 your wages for what *f* to satisfy?
58:11 garden, like a spring whose water never *f*.
65:20 *f* of a hundred shall be thought accursed.
Bar 6:34 if one *f* to fulfill a vow to them,
Ez 33: 6 coming and *f* to blow the warning trumpet,
Mi 3: 5 when one *f* to put something in their mouth,
1Cor 13: 8 Love never *f*.
1Jn 3:10 God, nor anyone who *f* to love his brother.
4: 3 while every spirit that *f* to acknowledge

FAILURE (10)

Jgs 14:15 After three days' *f* to answer the riddle,
2Kgs 14:10 and Judah with you in misfortune and *f*?"
17: 4 and for *f* to pay the annual tribute to his
2Chr 25:19 and Judah with you, in misfortune and *f*?"
2Mc 5: 6 over one's own kindred was the greatest *f*,
Jb 15:35 they give birth to *f*.
Ps(s) 7:15 was pregnant with mischief, brings forth *f*.
Sir 11:12 Another goes his way a weakling and a *f*,
Jer 20:11 In their *f* they will be put to utter shame,
Mt 11:20 had been worked, with their *f* to reform:

FAINT (27)

Jdt 14: 6 of the people, he fell forward in a *f*.
Jb 26:14 his ways, and how *f* is the word we hear!
Ps(s) 61: 3 end I call to you as my heart grows *f*.
77: 4 when I ponder, my spirit grows *f*.
142: 4 When my spirit is *f* within me,
143: 4 And my spirit is *f* within me,
Prv 25:25 Like cool water to one *f* from thirst is
Sg 2: 5 me with apples, for I am *f* with love.
5: 4 within me, and I grew *f* when he spoke.
5: 8 that I am *f* with love.
Sir 2:13 Woe to the *f* of heart who trust not,
Is 1: 5 The whole head is sick, the whole heart *f*.
29: 8 he is drinking and awakens *f* and dry,
40:28 He does not *f* nor grow weary,
40:30 Though young men *f* and grow weary,
40:31 and not grow weary, walk and not grow *f*.
57:16 For their spirits would *f* before me,
Jer 8:18 is incurable, my heart within me is *f*.
Lam 2:11 *f* away in the open spaces of the town.
2:12 As they *f* away like the wounded in the
2:19 your little ones [Who *f* from hunger
Dn 8:18 As he spoke to me, I fell forward in a *f*;
10: 9 of his voice, I fell face forward in a *f*.
Am 8:13 virgins and young men shall *f* from thirst;
Jon 4: 8 beat upon Jonah's head till he became *f*.
Mi 4:10 Writhe in pain, grow *f*,
Na 3:11 too, shall drink of this till you *f* away;

FAINTED (4)

Jdt 7:22 Their children *f* away,
Est D:15 As she said this, she *f*.
2Mc 3:24 at God's power and *f* away in terror.
Jon 2: 8 When my soul *f* within me,

FAINTEST (1)

Gn 7:22 *f* breath of life in its nostrils died out.

FAINTHEARTED (5)

Lv 26:36 of their enemies I will make so *f* that,
Dt 1:28 Our kinsmen have made us *f* by reporting
20: 8 lest he make his fellows as *f* as himself.'
Is 46:12 Listen to me, you *f*,
1Thes 5:14 cheer the *f*; support the weak;

FAINTING (1)

Is 40:29 He gives strength to the *f*;

FAIR (24)

Gn 34:18 seemed *f* to Hamor and his son Shechem.
Tb 12: 4 Tobit answered, "It is only *f*,
Jdt 11:23 You are *f* to behold,
12:13 "So *f* a maiden should not be reluctant to
Est E: 5 the *f* speech of friends entrusted with the
Ps(s) 16: 6 *f* to me indeed is my inheritance.
Wis 8:18 and *f* renown in sharing her discourses,
13: 7 they see, because the things seen are *f*.
Sir 13: 5 have anything he will speak *f* words to you,
24:14 Jericho, Like a *f* olive tree in the field,
24:17 vine, my blossoms become fruit *f* and rich.
Ez 18:25 You say, "The LORD's way is not *f*!"
18:29 of Israel says, "The LORD's way is not *f*!"
18:29 Is it my way that is not *f*,
18:29 rather, is it not that your ways are not *f*?
33:17 say, "The way of the LORD is not *f*!";
33:17 but it is their way that is not *f*.
33:20 you say, "The way of the LORD is not *f*?"
Hos 10:11 I myself laid a yoke upon her *f* neck;
Am 8:13 *f* virgins and young men shall faint from
Na 3: 4 debaucheries of the harlot, *f* and charming,
Mt 20: 4 vineyard and I will pay you whatever is *f*.'
Acts 27: 8 along the coast to a place called *F* Havens,
2Cor 6:13 In *f* exchange, then (I speak as a father

FAIRER (2)

Ps(s) 45: 3 *F* in beauty are you than the sons of men;
Wis 7:29 For she is *f* than the sun and surpasses

FAIREST (1)

Ps(s) 48: 3 His holy mountain, *f* of heights,

FAIRLY (5)

Est B: 2 but always to deal *f* and with clemency;
2Mc 10:12 taken the lead in treating the Jews *f*
Ps(s) 58: 2 like gods pronounce justice and judge *f*,
Ez 18: 8 judges *f* between a man and his opponent;
Col 4: 1 owners, deal justly and *f* with your slaves,

FAITH (329)

Gn 15: 6 Abram put his *f* in the LORD,
20: 5 I did it in good *f* and with clean hands."
20: 6 "Yes, I know you did it in good *f*.
Ex 19: 9 you, they may always have *f* in you also."
21: 8 foreigner, since he has broken *f* with her.
Nm 5: 6 wrongs him, thus breaking *f* with the LORD,
Dt 32:51 because both of you broke *f* with me among
Jgs 9:15 wish to anoint me king over you in good *f*,
9:16 if you have acted in good *f* and honorably
9:19 you have acted in good *f* and with honor
1Sm 14:33 "You have broken *f*.
2Sm 13:33 So let not my lord the king put *f* in the
15:11 They had been invited and went in good *f*,
2Chr 26:16 own destruction and broke *f* with the LORD,
26:18 for you have broken *f* and no longer have a
Neh 9:33 for you kept *f* while we have done evil.
1Mc 2:59 Azariah and Mishael, for their *f*,
10:27 Continue, therefore, to keep *f* with us,
2Mc 8:13 *f* in God's justice deserted and got away.
Ps(s) 25: 3 be put to shame who heedlessly break *f*.
146: 6 Who keeps *f* forever,
Wis 18: 6 of the oaths in which they put their *f*,
Sir 27:17 Cherish your friend, keep *f* with him;
49:10 to Jacob and saved him by their *f* and hope.
Is 7: 9 your *f* is firm you shall not be firm!
26: 2 in a nation that is just, one that keeps *f*.
28:16 who puts his *f* in it shall not be shaken.
Ez 14:13 when a land sins against me by breaking *f*,
15: 8 land a waste, because they have broken *f*,
17:20 with him there over his breaking *f* with me.
18:24 because he has broken *f* and committed sin;
20:27 fathers blasphemed me, breaking *f* with me:
39:26 and all the times they broke *f* with me,
Hb 2: 4 but the just man, because of his *f*,
Mal 2:10 Why then do we break *f* with each other,
2:11 Judah has broken *f*;
2:14 have broken *f* though she is your companion,
2:15 not break *f* with the wife of your youth.
2:16 life that is your own, and not break *f*.
Mt 6:30 not provide much more for you, O weak in *f*!
8:10 I have never found this much *f* in Israel.
8:26 How little *f* you have!"
9: 2 Jesus saw their *f* he said to the paralytic,
9:22 Your *f* has restored you to health."
9:29 of your *f* it shall be done to you";
13:58 miracles there because of their lack of *f*.
14:31 "How little *f* you have!"
15:28 said in reply, "Woman, you have great *f*!
16: 8 How weak your *f* is!
17:20 if you had *f* the size of a mustard seed,
21:22 all that you pray for, provided you have *f*."
21:25 ask us, 'Then why did you not put *f* in it?';
21:32 a way of holiness, you put no *f* in him;
22:18 recognized their bad *f* and said to them,
23:23 of the law, justice and mercy and good *f*.
26:31 "Tonight your *f* in me will be shaken,
26:33 all may have their *f* in you shaken,
Mk 2: 5 When Jesus saw their *f*,
4:40 Why are you lacking in *f*?"
5:34 it is your *f* that has cured you.
6: 6 so much did their lack of *f* distress him.
10:52 Your *f* has healed you."
11:31 ask, 'Then why did you not put *f* in it?'
13: 9 and have to testify to your *f* before them.
14:27 "Your *f* in me shall be shaken,
14:29 to him, "Even though all are shaken in *f*,
16:13 no more *f* in them than in Mary Magdalene.
16:14 since they had put no *f* in those who had
16:17 accompany those who have professed their *f*:
Lk 5:20 Seeing their *f*, Jesus said,
7: 9 never found so much *f* among the Israelites."
7:50 woman, "Your *f* has been your salvation.
8:25 Then he asked them, "Where is your *f*?"
8:48 it is your *f* that has cured you.
12:28 more will he provide for you, O weak in *f*!
17: 5 said to the Lord, "Increase our *f*."
17: 6 "If you had *f* the size of a mustard seed,
17:19 your *f* has been your salvation."
18: 8 Man comes, will he find any *f* on the earth?"
18:42 Your *f* has healed you."
22:32 prayed for you that your *f* may never fail.
Jn 4:41 his own spoken word many more came to *f*.
4:42 longer does our *f* depend on your story.
5:24 the man who hears my word and has *f* in him
6:29 have *f* in the One whom he sent."
6:30 "So that we can put *f* in you,"
6:61 "Does it shake your *f*?"
10:37 perform my Father's works, put no *f* in me.
10:38 put no faith in me, put *f* in these works,
11:45 seen what Jesus did, to put their *f* in him.
12:36 you have the light, keep *f* in the light;
12:44 "Whoever puts *f* in me believes not so
14: 1 Have *f* in God and faith in me.
14:12 man who has *f* in me will do the works I do,
16: 1 all this to keep your *f* from being shaken.
20:31 this *f* you may have life in his name.
Acts 3:16 Such *f* has given him perfect health,
6: 5 a man filled with *f* and the Holy Spirit;
6: 7 priests among those who embraced the *f*.
11:24 good man filled with the Holy Spirit and *f*.
13: 8 to turn the governor away from the *f*.
14: 9 him and saw that he had the *f* to be saved.
14:22 persevere in the *f* with this instruction:
14:23 to the Lord in whom they had put their *f*.
14:27 had opened the door of *f* to the Gentiles.
15: 9 purified their hearts by means of *f* also.
16: 5 in *f* and daily increased in numbers.
16:34 his whole family his newfound *f* in God.
18: 8 his whole household, put his *f* in the Lord.
20:21 before God and on *f* in our Lord Jesus.
24:24 to hear him speak about *f* in Christ Jesus.
26:18 that through their *f* in me they may obtain
Rom 1: 5 and bring to obedient *f* all the Gentiles,
1: 8 your *f* is heralded throughout the world.
1:12 may be mutually encouraged by our common *f*.
1:17 of God which begins and ends with *f*;
1:17 says, "The just man shall live by *f*."
3:22 *f* in Jesus Christ for all who believe.
3:27 By the law of *f*.
3:28 by *f* apart from observance of the law.
3:30 and the uncircumcised on the basis of *f*.
3:31 we then abolishing the law by means of *f*?
4: 5 the sinful, his *f* is credited as justice.
4: 9 that Abraham's *f* was "credited as justice."

FAITH (cont.)
4:11 through *f* while he was still uncircumcised.
4:11 them too *f* might be credited as justice,
4:12 follow the path of *f* which Abraham walked
4:13 in view of the justice that comes from *f*.
4:14 then *f* becomes an empty word and the
4:16 Hence, all depends on *f*,
4:16 have the law but for all who have his *f*.
4:19 weak in *f* he thought of his own body,
4:20 strengthened in *f* and gave glory to God,
4:22 Thus his *f* was credited to him as justice.
4:24 For our *f* will be credited to us also if
5: 1 Now that we have been justified by *f*,
5: 2 by *f* to the grace in which we now stand,
9:30 the justice which comes from *f*—
9:32 Because justice comes from *f*,
10: 6 of the justice that comes from *f* he says,
10: 8 (that is, the word of *f* which we preach).
10:10 *F* in the heart leads to justification,
10:17 *F*, then, comes through hearing,
11:20 of unbelief and you are there because of *f*.
12: 3 measure of *f* that God has apportioned him.
12: 6 its use should be in proportion to his *f*.
13:11 closer than when we first accepted the *f*.
14: 1 a kind welcome to those who are weak in *f*.
14: 2 A man of sound *f* knows he can eat anything,
14: 2 one who is weak in *f* eats only vegetables.
14:22 Use the *f* you have as your rule of life in
15: 1 We who are strong in *f* should be patient
15: 1 with the scruples of those whose *f* is weak;
1Cor 2: 5 your *f* rests not on the wisdom of men but
12: 9 Through the Spirit one receives *f*;
13: 2 if I have *f* great enough to move mountains,
13:13 *f*, hope, and love, and the greatest
14:22 are without faith but for those who have *f*.
15:14 is void of content and your *f* is empty too.
15:17 Christ was not raised, your *f* is worthless.
16:13 Be on your guard, stand firm in the *f*,
2Cor 1:24 Domineering over your *f* is not my purpose.
1:24 As regards *f*, you are standing firm.
4:13 spirit of *f* of which the Scripture says,
5: 7 We walk by *f*, not by sight.
8: 7 rich in every respect, in *f* and discourse,
9:13 your obedient *f* in the gospel of Christ,
10:15 we hope that as your *f* grows our influence
13: 5 to see whether you are living in *f*;
Gal 1:23 is now preaching the *f* he tried to destroy,"
2:16 legal observance but by *f* in Jesus Christ,
2:16 in order to be justified by *f* in Christ,
2:20 but it is a life of *f* in the Son of God,
3: 2 of the law or through *f* in what you heard?
3: 5 because you have *f* in what you heard
3: 8 justifying the Gentiles would be through *f*,
3: 9 blessed along with Abraham, the man of *f*.
3:11 law, for "the just man shall live by *f*."
3:12 But the law does not depend on *f*.
3:14 to receive the promised Spirit through *f*.
3:22 in consequence of *f* in Jesus Christ.
3:23 Before *f* came we were under the constraint
3:23 the *f* that was coming should be revealed.
3:24 to bring about our justification through *f*.
3:25 But now that *f* is here,
3:26 of God because of your *f* in Christ Jesus.
5: 5 we hope for, and only *f* can yield it.
5: 6 only *f*, which expresses itself through love.
5:22 patient endurance, kindness, generosity, *f*,
6:10 especially those of the household of the *f*.
Eph 1:15 first heard of your *f* in the Lord Jesus
2: 8 favor that salvation is yours through *f*.
3:12 *f* in him we can speak freely to God,
3:17 May Christ dwell in your hearts through *f*,
4: 5 There is one Lord, one *f*,
4:13 one in *f* and in the knowledge of God's Son,
6:16 hold *f* up before you as your shield;
6:23 grant the brothers peace and love and *f*.
Phil 1:25 for your joy and your progress in the *f*.
1:27 with one accord for the *f* of the gospel.
2:17 over the sacrifical service of your *f*,
3: 9 is that which comes through *f* in Christ.
3: 9 It has its origin in God and is based on *f*.
Col 1: 4 we have heard of your *f* in Christ Jesus
1:23 But you must hold fast to *f*,
2: 5 you and the firmness of your *f* in Christ.
2: 7 up in him, growing ever stronger in *f*,
1Thes 1: 3 Father of the way you are proving your *f*,
1: 8 every region your *f* in God is celebrated,
3: 2 encourage you in regard to your *f*
3: 5 I sent to find out about your *f*
3: 6 reporting the good news of your *f* and love,
3: 7 your *f* throughout our distress and trial
3:10 face and remedy any shortcomings in your *f*?
5: 8 putting on *f* and love as a breastplate and
2Thes 1: 3 because your *f* grows apace and your mutual
1: 4 and your *f* in persecution and trial.
1:11 power every honest intention and work of *f*.
3: 2 For not every man has *f*,
3: 3 every man has faith, but the Lord keeps *f*;
1Tm 1: 2 hope, to Timothy, my own true child in *f*.
1: 4 than that training in *f* which God requires.
1: 5 heart, a good conscience, and sincere *f*.
1:14 the *f* and love which are in Christ Jesus.
1:16 have *f* in him and gain everlasting life.
1:19 and hold fast to *f* and a good conscience.
1:19 have made shipwreck of their *f*,
2: 7 the teacher of the nations in the true *f*.
2:15 she continues in *f* and love and holiness
3: 9 revealed *f* with a clear conscience.
3:13 much assurance in their *f* in Christ Jesus.
3:16 Wonderful, indeed, is the mystery of our *f*,
4: 1 some will turn away from the *f*
4: 6 reared in the words of *f* and the sound
4:12 but be a continuing example of love, *f*,
5: 8 his immediate family, he has denied the *f*;
6: 2 brothers in the *f* must not take liberties
6:10 passion for it have strayed from the *f*,
6:11 Instead, seek after integrity, piety, *f*,
6:12 Fight the good fight of *f*.
6:12 you made your noble profession of *f*.
6:21 some men have missed the goal of *f*.
2Tm 1: 5 your sincere *f*—faith which first belonged
1:13 me say, in *f* and love in Christ Jesus.
1:14 Guard the rich deposit of *f* with the help
2:18 They are upsetting some people's *f*.
2:22 youthful passions and pursue integrity, *f*,
3: 8 with perverted minds they falsify the *f*.
3:15 *f* in Jesus Christ leads to salvation.
4: 7 have finished the race, I have kept the *f*.
Ti 1: 1 sake of the *f* of those whom God has chosen,
1: 4 Titus, my own true child in our common *f*:
1:13 an attempt to keep them close to sound *f*,
2: 2 likewise sound in the *f*,
3: 3 foolish, disobedient, and far from true *f*;
3:15 Greet those who love us in the *f*.
Phlm 1: 5 your love and *f* toward the Lord Jesus
1: 6 your sharing of the *f* with others
Heb 3: 1 and high priest whom we acknowledge in *f*,
4: 2 them, for they did not receive it in *f*.
4:14 let us hold fast to our profession of *f*.
6: 1 repentance from dead works, *f* in God,
6:12 imitate those who, through *f* and patience,
10:38 My just man will live by *f*,
10:39 but among those who have *f* and live.
11: 1 *F* is confident assurance concerning what
11: 2 of *f* the men of old were approved by God.
11: 3 Through *f* we perceive that the worlds were
11: 4 By *f* Abel offered God a sacrifice greater
11: 5 By *f* Enoch was taken away without dying,
11: 6 but without *f*, it is impossible to please him.
11: 7 By *f* Noah, warned about things
11: 7 the justice which comes through *f*.
11: 8 By *f* Abraham obeyed when he was called,
11: 9 By *f* he sojourned in the promised land as
11:11 By *f* Sarah received power to conceive
11:12 As a result of this *f*, there came forth
11:13 All of these died in *f*.
11:17 By *f* Abraham, when put to the test,
11:20 By *f* Isaac invoked for Jacob and Esau
11:21 By *f* Jacob, when dying, blessed each
11:22 By *f* Joseph, near the end of his life,
11:23 By *f* Moses' parents hid him for three
11:24 By *f* Moses, when he had grown up
11:27 By *f* he left Egypt,
11:28 By *f* he kept the Passover and sprinkled
11:29 By *f* the Israelites crossed the Red Sea as
11:30 Because of Israel's *f*, the walls of Jericho
11:31 By *f* Rahab the harlot escaped from being
11:33 the prophets, who by *f* conquered kingdoms,
11:39 of these were approved because of their *f*,
12: 2 on Jesus, who inspires and perfects our *f*.
13: 7 how their lives ended, and imitate their *f*.
Jas 1: 3 your *f* is tested this makes for endurance.
1: 6 Yet he must ask in *f*,
2: 1 your *f* in our glorious Lord Jesus Christ
2: 5 in the eyes of the world to be rich in *f*
2:14 is it to profess *f* without practicing it?
2:14 Such *f* has no power to save one, has it?
2:17 with the *f* that does nothing in practice.
2:18 might say, "You have *f* and I have works
2:18 Show me your *f* without works,
2:18 show you the *f* that underlies my works!
2:20 ignoramus, that without works *f* is idle?
2:22 There you see proof that *f* was both
2:24 justified by his works and not by *f* alone.
2:26 that *f* without works is as dead as a body
5:15 in *f* will reclaim the one who is ill,
1Pt 1: 5 are guarded with God's power through *f*;
1: 7 but this is so that your *f*,
1:21 Your *f* and hope, then, are centered
2: 6 who puts his *f* in it shall not be shaken."
2: 7 The stone is of value for you who have *f*.
2: 7 For those without *f*, it is rather, "A stone
5: 9 Resist him, solid in your *f*,
2Pt 1: 1 to those who have been given a *f* like ours
1: 5 effort to undergird your virtue with *f*,
1Jn 5: 4 has conquered the world is the *f* of ours.
Jude 1: 3 the *f* delivered once for all to the saints.
1:20 holy *f* through prayer in the Holy Spirit.
Rv 2:13 and have not denied the *f* you have in me,
2:19 your love and *f* and service
14:12 commandments of God and their *f* in Jesus.
17: 6 of those martyred for their *f* in Jesus.
21: 8 As for the cowards and traitors to the *f*,

FAITHFUL (95)

Nm 20:12 "Because you were not *f* to me in showing
Dt 7: 9 the *f* God who keeps his merciful covenant
32: 4 A *f* God, without deceit,
Jos 2:14 we will be *f* in showing kindness to you
1Sm 2: 9 He will guard the footsteps of his *f* ones,
2:35 I will choose a *f* priest who shall do what
2Sm 2: 6 And now may the LORD be kind and *f* to you.
15:20 and, and may the LORD be kind and *f* to you."
22:26 "Toward the *f* you are faithful;
1Kgs 2: 4 they remain *f* to me with their whole heart
8:23 who are *f* to you with their whole heart.
2Chr 6:14 servants who are wholeheartedly *f* to you.
6:41 may your *f* ones rejoice in good things.
31:20 was good, upright and *f* before the LORD,
Neh 9: 8 you had found his heart *f* in your sight,
1Mc 2:52 Was not Abraham found *f* in trial,
3:13 him, an assembly of *f* men ready for war.
7: 8 man in the kingdom, and *f* to the king.
2Mc 1: 2 remember his covenant with his *f* servants,
8: 1 enlisting others who remained *f* to Judaism,
Ps(s) 4: 4 that the LORD does wonders for his *f* one;
16:10 suffer your *f* one to undergo corruption.
18:26 Toward the *f* you are faithful,
30: 5 Sing praise to the LORD, you his *f* ones,
31: 6 you will redeem me, O LORD, O *f* God.
31:24 Love the LORD, all you his *f* ones!
32: 6 every *f* man pray to you in time of stress.
37:28 what is right, and forsakes not his *f* ones.
50: 5 "Gather my *f* ones before me,
52:11 goodness of your name before your *f* ones.
78: 8 steadfast nor its spirit *f* toward God.
78:37 him, nor were they *f* to his covenant.
79: 2 of your *f* ones to the beasts of the earth.
85: 9 peace To his people, and to his *f* ones.
89:20 in a vision, and to your *f* ones you said:
89:38 a *f* witness in the sky."
97:10 he guards the lives of his *f* ones;
101: 6 My eyes are upon the *f* of the land,
111: 7 The works of his hands are *f* and just;
116:15 of the LORD is the death of his *f* ones.
132: 9 let your *f* ones shout merrily for joy.
132:16 and her *f* ones shall shout merrily for joy.
145:10 O LORD, and let your *f* ones bless you.
145:13 The LORD is *f* in all his words and holy in
148:14 Be this his praise from all his *f* ones,
149: 1 song of praise in the assembly of the *f*.
149: 5 Let the *f* exult in glory;
149: 9 This is the glory of all his *f*.
Prv 25:13 is a *f* messenger for the one who sends him.
Wis 3: 9 and the *f* shall abide with him in love:
Sir 1:12 which is formed with the *f* in the womb.
6:14 A *f* friend is a sturdy shelter;
6:15 A *f* friend is beyond price,
6:16 A *f* friend is a life-saving remedy,
34: 8 wisdom is found in the mouth of the *f* man.
39:13 Listen, my *f* children:
Is 1:21 How has she turned adulteress, the *f* city,
1:26 shall be called city of justice, *f* city.
25: 1 your wonderful plans of old, *f* and true.
49: 7 themselves Because of the LORD who is *f*,
Jer 5: 1 one Who lives uprightly and seeks to be *f*,
Hos 12: 1 God, against the Holy One, who is *f*.
Mi 7: 2 The *f* are gone from the earth,
Zec 8: 3 Jerusalem shall be called the *f* city,
Mt 24:45 Who is the *f*, farsighted servant
Lk 12:42 said, "Who in your opinion is that *f*,
Acts 2:27 suffer your *f* one to undergo corruption.
13:35 suffer your *f* one to undergo corruption.'
1Cor 1: 9 God is *f*, and it was he who called
4:17 Timothy, my beloved and *f* son in the Lord.
Eph 4:12 for the *f* to build up the body of Christ,
6:21 my dear brother and *f* minister in the Lord,
Col 1: 2 ones at Colossae, *f* brothers in Christ.
1: 7 represents us as a *f* minister of Christ.
4: 7 *f* minister and fellow slave in the Lord,
4: 9 him is Onesimus, our dear and *f* brother,
1Tm 1:12 he has made me his servant and judged me *f*.
2Tm 2:13 we are unfaithful he will still remain *f*,
3:14 *f* to what you have learned and believed,
Heb 2:17 *f* high priest before God on their behalf,
3: 2 faith, who was *f* to him who appointed him.
3: 2 too, "was *f* in all God's household,"
3: 5 Moses "was *f* in all God's household" as
3: 6 was *f* as the Son placed over God's house.
1Pt 4:19 and entrust their lives to a *f* Creator.
5:12 whom I take to be a *f* brother to you.
Rv 1: 5 and from Jesus Christ the *f* witness,
2:10 Remain *f* until death and I will give you
2:13 at the time when Antipas, my *f* witness,
3:14 " 'The Amen, the *f* Witness and true,
13:10 Such is the *f* endurance that distinguishes
17:14 the chosen and the *f*."
19:11 its rider was called "The *F* and True."

FAITHFULLY (18)

Gn 28:22 me, I will *f* return a tenth part to you."
Jos 22: 3 *f* carried out the commands of the LORD,
22: 5 follow him *f*, keep his commandments;
1Sm 12:24 and worship him *f* with your whole heart;
1Kgs 3: 6 David, because he behaved *f* toward you,
2Kgs 20: 3 remember how *f* and wholeheartedly I
2Chr 19: 9 "You shall act *f* and wholeheartedly in
31:15 who *f* made the distribution to their

31:18 by sharing *f* in the consecrated things.
34:12 The men worked *f* at their task;
Tb 14: 9 God *f* and do what is right before him;
Sir 7:20 Mistreat not a servant who *f* serves,
Is 38: 3 remember how *f* and wholeheartedly I
61: 8 I will give them their recompense *f*,
Jer 42: 5 and *f* follow all the instructions the LORD,
1Tm 4: 6 and the sound doctrine you have *f* followed.
6: 2 They must perform their tasks even more *f*,
Rv 22: 3 there, and his servants shall serve him *f*.

FAITHFULNESS (35)

1Sm 26:23 will reward each man for his justice and *f*.
Ps(s) 12: 2 *f* has vanished from among men.
30:10 dust give you thanks or proclaim your *f*?
36: 6 your *f*, to the clouds.
40:11 your *f* and your salvation I have spoken of;
54: 7 in your *f* destroy them.
57: 4 may God send his kindness and his *f*.
57:11 to the heavens, and your *f* to the skies.
61: 8 bid kindness and *f* preserve him.
71:22 thanks with music on the lyre, for your *f*,
88:12 your *f* among those who have perished?
89: 2 generations my mouth shall proclaim your *f*.
89: 3 in heaven you have confirmed your *f*:
89: 6 proclaim your wonders, O LORD, and your *f*,
89: 9 are you, O LORD, and your *f* surrounds you.
89:25 My *f* and my kindness shall be with him,
89:34 not take from him, nor will I belie my *f*.
89:50 Lord, which you pledged to David by your *f*?
91: 4 his *f* is a buckler and a shield.
92: 3 at dawn and your *f* throughout the night,
98: 3 and his *f* toward the house of Israel.
100: 5 whose kindness endures forever, and his *f*,
108: 5 to the heavens, and your *f* to the skies.
119:75 just, and in your *f* you have afflicted me.
119:138 your decrees in justice and in perfect *f*.
143: 1 hearken to my pleading in your *f*;
Is 11: 5 his waist, and *f* a belt upon his hips.
38:19 declare to their sons, O God, your *f*.
Jer 7:27 *F* has disappeared;
Lam 3:23 renewed each morning, so great is his *f*.
Mi 7:20 You will show *f* to Jacob,
Zec 8: 8 I will be their God, with *f* and justice.
8:19 only love *f* and peace.
Rom 3: 3 not their unbelief put an end to God's *f*?
15: 8 of God's *f* in fulfilling the promises

FAITHLESS (23)

2Chr 28:19 own way and proved utterly *f* to the LORD.
30: 7 and your brethren who proved *f* to the LORD,
Neh 1: 8 'Should you prove *f*,
Ps(s) 43: 1 God, and fight my fight against a *f* people;
78:57 turned back and were *f* like their fathers;
139:20 your foes swear *f* oaths.
Prv 2:22 the land, the *f* will be rooted out of it.
11: 3 the *f* are ruined by their duplicity.
11: 6 but the *f* are caught in their own intrigue.
13:15 favor, but the way of the *f* is their ruin.
21:18 the just, and the *f* man for the righteous.
22:12 but he defeats the projects of the *f*.
23:28 a robber, and increases the *f* among men.
25:19 [dependence on] a *f* man in time of trouble.
Sir 1:25 Be not *f* to the fear of the LORD,
Jer 3:20 *f* to her lover, even so have you been *f*
9: 1 They are all adulterers, a *f* band.
Ez 23: 5 Oholah became a harlot *f* to me;
Hb 1:13 do you gaze on the *f* in silence while the
Mt 16: 4 An evil, *f* age is eager for a sign,
Mk 8:38 If anyone in this *f* and corrupt age is
16:20 "This lawless and *f* age is under Satan,

FAITHLESSLY (1)

2Chr 29: 6 *f* and did evil in the eyes of the LORD,

FAITHLESSNESS (2)

Nm 14:33 for forty years, suffering for your *f*,
Wis 14:25 murder, theft and guile, corruption, *f*,

FAITHS (1)

1Pt 1: 9 glory because you are achieving *f* goal,

FALCONS (2)

Lv 11:14 the kite, the various species of *f*,
Dt 14:13 the osprey, the various kites and *f*,

FALL (238)

Gn 27:13 "Let any curse against you, son, *f* on me!
Ex 9:22 hail may *f* upon the entire land of Egypt,
21:33 again, should an ox or an ass *f* into it,
Lv 11:33 of these creatures *f* into a clay vessel,
Nm 5: 8 be the LORD's and shall *f* to the priest;
5: 9 are bound to make shall *f* to the priest.
14: 3 this land only to have us *f* by the sword?
14:29 in the desert shall your dead bodies *f*.
14:32 your bodies shall *f* here in the desert,
14:43 face you, and you will *f* by the sword.
18: 5 wrath may not *f* again upon the Israelites.
34: 2 that shall *f* to you as your heritage
Dt 4:19 has let *f* to the lot of all other nations
8: 4 The clothing did not *f* from you in tatters,
11:17 up the heavens, so that no rain will *f*,
29: 4 Your clothes did not *f* from you in tatters
29:25 and whom he had not let *f* to their lot:
Jos 22:20 *f* upon the entire community of Israel?
Jgs 2:14 He allowed them to *f* into the power of
3: 8 to *f* into the power of Cushan-rishathaim,
4: 2 to *f* into the power of the Canaanite king,
4: 9 have Sisera *f* into the power of a woman."
10: 7 allowed them to *f* into the power
15:18 or *f* into the hands of the uncircumcised?"
18:25 lest fierce men *f* upon you and you and
1Sm 12: 9 them to *f* into the clutches of Sisera,
14:45 hair of his head shall *f* to the ground,
2Sm 3:34 as men *f* before the wicked,
14:11 a hair of your son shall *f* to the ground."
17: 9 our soldiers should *f* at the first attack,
24:14 Let us *f* by the hand of God,
24:14 but let me not *f* by the hand of man."
1Kgs 1:52 worthy, not a hair shall *f* from his head.
22:20 that he will go up and *f* at Ramoth-gilead?'
2Kgs 6: 6 "Where did it *f*?"
19: 7 there I will cause him to *f* by the sword.' "
1Chr 21:13 I prefer to *f* into the hand of the LORD,
2Chr 18:19 that he will go up and *f* at Ramoth-gilead?"
34:11 kings of Judah had allowed to *f* into ruin.
Jdt 6: 6 sides, and you shall *f* among their slain.
7:11 not a single one of your troops will *f*.
8:21 If we are taken, all Judea will *f*,
15: 4 might *f* upon the enemy and destroy them.
Est 9:28 were never to *f* into disuse among the Jews,
1Mc 7:38 and his army, and let them *f* by the sword.
7:43 himself was the first to *f* in the battle.
13:22 go, there was a heavy *f* of snow that night,
2Mc 8:11 that was to *f* upon him from the Almighty.
9: 7 of his body was racked by the violent *f*.
10: 4 might never again *f* into such misfortunes,
14:42 *f* into the hands of vile men and suffer
Jb 13: 2 I *f* not short of you.
13:11 you and the dread of him *f* upon you.
20:25 terrors shall *f* upon him.
31:22 Then may my arm *f* from the shoulder,
37: 6 For he says to the snow, *F* to the earth";
41:17 the waves of the sea *f* back.
Ps(s) 4: 9 soon as I lie down, I *f* peacefully asleep,
5:11 let them *f* by their own devices;
6:11 they shall *f* back in sudden shame.
10:10 till by his violence *f* the unfortunate.
20: 9 Though they bow down and *f*,
27: 2 and my enemies themselves stumble and *f*.
35: 8 into the pit they have dug let them *f*.
37:24 Though he *f*, he does not lie prostrate,
57: 7 dug a pit before me, but they *f* into it.
59:11 may he show me the *f* of my foes.
69:10 of those who blaspheme you *f* upon me.
82: 7 men you shall die, and *f* like any prince."
91: 7 Though a thousand *f* at your side,
92:12 heard of the *f* of my wicked adversaries.
129: 5 be put to shame and *f* back that hate Zion.
141:10 Let all the wicked *f*,
Prv 11:28 He who trusts in his riches will *f*,
16:18 disaster, and a haughty spirit before a *f*.
22:14 with whom the LORD is angry will *f* into it.
28:10 evil way will himself *f* into his own pit.
28:14 he who hardens his heart will *f* into evil.
28:28 but at their *f* the just flourish.
Eccl 4:10 For if he should *f*, he has no one to lift
10: 8 He who digs a pit may *f* into it,
Wis 10: 1 And she raised him up from his *f*,
10: 8 they could not even be hidden in their *f*.
13:16 Thus lest it *f* down he provides for it,
16:11 Lest they should *f* into deep forgetfulness
Sir 1:27 lest you *f* and bring upon you dishonor;
2: 7 for his mercy, turn not away lest you *f*.
2:18 Let us *f* into the hands of the LORD and
6: 2 *F* not into the grip of desire,
8: 1 influential man, lest you *f* into his power.
9: 3 strange woman, lest you *f* into her snares.
11: 6 The exalted often *f* into utter disgrace;
11:11 and drive, and *f* short all the more.
15: 4 He will lean upon her and not *f*,
20:17 A *f* to the ground is less sudden than a
23: 1 of my life, permit me not to *f* by them!
23: 8 the railer and the arrogant man *f* thereby.
25:18 may she *f* to the lot of the sinner!
28:23 who forsake the LORD will *f* victims to it,
28:26 and *f* victim to your foe waiting in ambush.
29:20 means, but take care lest you *f* thereby.
35:15 cry out against him that causes them to *f*?
37: 8 why should the profit *f* to him?
37:12 yourself and will feel for you if you *f*.
43:19 eyes, the mind is baffled by its steady *f*.
50:17 would quickly *f* prostrate to the ground
Is 3:25 Your men will *f* by the sword,
8:15 And many among them shall stumble and *f*,
10: 4 beneath the captive or *f* beneath the slain?
13: 7 fall helpless, the bows of the young men *f*
13:15 to a man, they shall *f* by the sword.
22:25 sure spot shall give way, break off and *f*,
24:18 at the sound of terror will *f* into the pit;
30:25 of the great slaughter, when the towers *f*,
31: 3 shall stumble, the one helped shall *f*,
31: 8 shall *f* by a sword not wielded by man,
37: 7 there I will cause him to *f* by the sword.' "
40:30 and grow weary, and youths stagger and *f*,
45:14 Before you they shall *f* prostrate,
46: 6 a god before which they *f* down in worship.
54:15 whoever attacks you shall *f* before you.
60:14 you shall *f* prostrate at your feet.
Jer 4: 5 Say, *F* in, let us march
6:12 Their houses will *f* to strangers,
6:15 Hence they shall be among those who *f*;
6:24 helpless *f* our hands, Anguish takes hold
8:12 Hence they shall be among those who *f*;
12: 5 And if in a land of peace you *f* headlong,
13:18 From your heads *f* your magnificent crowns.
19: 7 them *f* by the sword before their enemies,
20: 4 see them *f* by the sword of their enemies.
23:12 shall lose their footing, and *f* headlong;
25:27 *f*, never to rise, before the sword
25:34 like choice rams you shall *f*.
34: 3 you will be captured and *f* into his hands.
38:18 shall *f* into the hands of the Chaldeans,
39:18 that you escape and do not *f* by the sword.
44:12 *f* by the sword or be consumed by hunger.
46: 4 *F* in with your helmets;
46: 5 With broken ranks They *f* back;
46: 6 on the Euphrates' bank, they stumble and *f*.
46:12 trips over warrior, both *f* together.
47: 3 their hands *f* helpless Because of the day
49:21 At the noise of their *f* the earth quakes,
49:26 now her young men shall *f* in her streets,
50:15 all sides, She surrenders, her bastions *f*,
50:30 her young men shall *f* in her streets,
50:43 news of them, and helpless *f* his hands;
51: 4 The slain shall *f* in the land of Chaldea,
51:49 Babylon, too, must *f*,
Bar 6:26 confusion because, if they *f* to the ground,
6:26 them upright, nor come upright if they *f*;
Ez 5:12 third shall *f* by the sword all around you;
6: 7 [The slain shall *f* in your midst,
6:11 for which they shall *f* by the sword,
6:12 he that is near shall *f* by the sword,
11:10 By the sword you shall *f*;
13:11 hailstones shall *f*,
13:13 hailstones shall *f* with destructive wrath.
17:21 among his forces shall *f* by the sword,
21:12 shall fail, every hand shall *f* helpless,
23:25 what is left of you shall *f* by the sword.
24:21 you left behind shall *f* by the sword.
25:13 they shall *f* by the sword.
26:15 At the noise of your *f*,
26:18 On this, the day of your *f*,
28:23 Within it shall *f* those slain by the sword
29: 5 You shall *f* upon the open field,
30: 4 be in Ethiopia, when the slain *f* in Egypt,
30: 5 territory shall *f* by the sword with them.
30: 6 Those who support Egypt shall *f*,
30: 6 to Syene they shall *f* there by the sword,
30:17 of On and of Pibeseth shall *f* by the sword,
31:16 the crash of his *f* I made the nations rock,
32:20 of those slain by the sword shall they *f*,
33:27 in the ruins I swear shall *f* by the sword;
35: 8 [in them the slain shall *f* by the sword]:
38:20 and every wall shall *f* to the ground.
39: 4 Upon the mountains of Israel you shall *f*,
39: 5 On the open field you shall *f*,
47:14 that it might *f* to you as your inheritance.
Dn 3: 5 you are ordered to *f* down and worship the
3: 6 Whoever does not *f* down and worship shall
3:10 *f* down and worship the golden statue;
3:15 *f* down and worship the statue I had made,
11:19 of his own land, but shall stumble and *f*,
11:26 be overwhelmed, and many shall *f* slain.
11:34 When they *f*, few people shall help them,
11:35 Of the wise men, some shall *f*,
11:41 enter the glorious land and many shall *f*,
12: 4 many shall *f* away and evil shall increase."
13:23 Yet it is better for me to *f* in your power
Hos 7:16 Their princes shall *f* by the sword because
10: 8 and to the hills, *F* upon us!"
14: 1 They shall *f* by the sword,
Jl 2: 8 Though they *f* into the ditches,
Am 3:14 shall be broken off and *f* to the ground.
7:17 sons and daughters shall *f* by the sword;
8:14 those shall *f*, never to rise again.
9: 9 a sieve, letting no pebble *f* to the ground.
Na 3:12 but fig trees, bearing early figs That *f*,
Zec 11:17 *f* upon his arm and upon his right eye;
14:17 LORD of hosts, no rain shall *f* upon them.
14:18 upon them shall *f* the plague which the
Mt 15:27 leavings that *f* from their masters' tables."
16:23 You are trying to make me trip and *f*.
24:29 her light, the stars will *f* from the sky,
25: 5 so they all began to nod, then to *f* asleep.
Mk 13:25 its light, stars will *f* out of the skies,
Lk 6:39 Will they not both *f* into a ditch?
8:13 a while, but *f* away in time of temptation.
10:18 Satan *f* from the sky like lightning.
21:24 The people will *f* before the sword:
23:30 begin saying to the mountains, *F* on us,'
Acts 5:15 shadow might *f* on one or another of them.
28: 6 to see him swell up or suddenly *f* dead.
Rom 9:33 men stumble and a rock to make them *f*;
1Cor 6: 9 will not *f* heir to the kingdom of God?
10:12 he is standing upright watch out lest he *f*!

FALL (cont.)
15:51 Not all of us shall *f* asleep,
2Cor 11: 3 may *f* away from your sincere and complete
Gal 5:10 *f* on whoever it is that is unsettling you!
1Thes 5: 3 ruin will *f* on them with the suddenness of
1Tm 3: 7 not *f* into disgrace and the devil's trap.
Ti 2: 5 the word of God will not *f* into disrepute.
Heb 3:12 spirit and *f* away from the living God.
4:11 into that rest, so that no one may *f*.
10:31 to *f* into the hands of the living God.
Jas 3: 2 All of us *f* short in many respects.
1Pt 2: 8 and *f* are the disbelievers in God's word;
1Jn 2:10 there is nothing in him to cause a *f*.
Jude 1:24 There is One who can protect you from a *f*
Rv 3: 9 but frauds, come and *f* down at your feet;
4:10 *f* down before the One seated on the throne,
6:16 out to the mountains and rocks, *F* on us!
9: 1 I saw a star *f* from the sky to the earth.
11: 6 will *f* during the time of their mission.

FALLEN (75)

Gn 29:18 Since Jacob had *f* in love with Rachel,
Lv 19:10 bare, nor gather up the grapes that have *f*.
Jgs 8:10 and twenty thousand swordsmen having *f*.
2Sm 1: 4 and that many of them had *f* and were dead,
1:12 of Israel, because they had *f* by the sword.
1:19 how can the warriors have *f*!
1:25 "How can the warriors have *f*—
1:27 "How can the warriors have *f*,
2:23 to the place where Asahel had *f* and died,
3:38 that a great general has *f* today in Israel.
1Kgs 17: 7 ran dry, because no rain had *f* in the land.
2Kgs 1: 2 Ahaziah had *f* through the lattice of his
2:13 up Elijah's mantle which had *f* from him,
2:14 the mantle which had *f* from Elijah,
1Chr 5:22 Many had *f* in battle,
10: 8 his sons where they had *f* on Mount Gilboa.
2Chr 20:24 they saw only corpses *f* on the ground,
1Mc 5:12 rescue us from them, for many of us have *f*.
5:54 holocausts, because not one of them had *f*;
9: 1 that Nicanor and his army had *f* in battle,
9:21 and they said, "How the mighty one has *f*,
2Mc 7:38 that has justly *f* on our whole nation."
12:42 because of the sin of those who had *f*.
12:44 he were not expecting the *f* to rise again,
Jb 1:16 "Lightning has *f* from heaven and struck
Ps(s) 16: 6 measuring lines have *f* on pleasant sites;
36:13 See how the evildoers have *f*;
55: 5 the terror of death has *f* upon me.
105:38 going, for the dread of them had *f* upon it.
Prv 6: 3 you have *f* into your neighbor's power:
Wis 18:23 had already *f* one on another in heaps,
Sir 18:20 Before you have *f*, humble yourself;
28:18 Many have *f* by the edge of the sword,
Is 6:13 whose trunk remains when its leaves have *f*.
9: 9 and pride of heart, "Bricks have *f*,
14:12 How have you *f* from the heavens,
16: 9 fruits and harvests the battle cry has *f*.
21: 9 calls out and says, 'Fallen, *f* is Babylon,
Jer 48:32 upon your vintage, the ravager has *f*.
51:47 and all her slain shall lie *f* within her.
51:49 Babylon have *f* the slain of all the earth.
Lam 2:21 maidens and young men have *f* by the sword;
5:16 Garlands have *f* from our heads:
Ez 13:12 And when the wall has *f*,
21:20 for many will be the *f*.
31:13 *f* trunk rested all the birds of the air,
32:23 grave, all of them slain, *f* by the sword,
32:24 grave, all of them slain, *f* by the sword:
32:27 do not lie with the mighty men *f* of old,
Hos 7: 7 All their kings have *f*;
Am 5: 2 She is *f*, to rise no more, the virgin Israel;
9:11 day I will raise up the *f* hut of David;
Mi 7: 8 though I have *f*, I will arise
Zep 1: 6 And those who have *f* away from the LORD,
Zec 11: 2 you cypress trees, for the cedars are *f*,
Mt 27:53 of saints who had *f* asleep were raised.
Lk 8:14 The seed *f* among briers are those who hear,
9:32 and those with him had *f* into a deep sleep;
Jn 11:11 added, "Our beloved Lazarus has *f* asleep,
Acts 15:16 will return and rebuild the *f* hut of David:
Rom 11:11 stumbling mean that they are forever *f*?
1Cor 15: 6 still alive, although some have *f* asleep.
15:18 and those who have *f* asleep in Christ are
15:20 first fruits of those who have *f* asleep.
Gal 5: 4 from Christ and *f* from God's favor!
1Thes 4:14 also who have *f* asleep believing in him.
4:15 an advantage over those who have *f* asleep.
Heb 6: 6 of the age to come, and then have *f* away,
Rv 2: 5 in mind the heights from which you have *f*.
14: 8 *F*, fallen is Babylon the great,
17:10 five have already *f*,
18: 2 *F*, fallen is Babylon the great!

FALLING (21)

Nm 17:11 come forth from the LORD and the blow is *f*."
17:12 where the blow was already *f* on the people.
1Sm 25:23 *f* prostrate on the ground before David,
31: 1 and *f* mortally wounded on Mount Gilboa,
2Sm 3:29 leper, or one unmanly, one *f* by the sword,
14:22 *F* prostrate to the ground in homage and
Neh 13:19 When the shadows were *f* on the gates of
Ps(s) 38:18 For I am very near to *f*,
118:13 I was hard pressed and was *f*,
145:14 are *f* and raises up all who are bowed down.
Sir 34:16 guard against stumbling, a help against *f*.
Is 1:30 You shall become like a tree with *f* leaves,
3: 8 Jerusalem is crumbling, Judah is *f*;
Lk 8:47 *F* at his feet, she related before the whole
13: 4 who were killed by a *f* tower in Siloam.
22:44 became like drops of blood *f* to the ground.
1Cor 11:31 would not be *f* under judgment in this way;
14:25 *F* prostrate, he will worship God
Gal 6: 1 trying to avoid *f* into temptation himself.
1Tm 6: 9 be rich are *f* into temptation and a trap.
Heb 6: 7 drinks in the rain *f* on it again and again,

FALLS (55)

Lv 11:32 one of them *f* when dead becomes unclean.
11:35 on which one of their dead bodies *f*,
11:37 though one of their dead bodies *f* on it;
11:38 becomes unclean when one of these *f* on it.
23: 5 *f* on the fourteenth day of the first month,
Nm 26:56 As the lot *f* shall each group,
28:16 the first month *f* the Passover of the LORD,
33:54 Wherever anyone's lot *f*,
Dt 22: 8 otherwise, if someone *f* off,
Jb 4:13 of the night, when deep sleep *f* on men,
14:18 But as a mountain *f* at last and its rock
30:30 My blackened skin *f* away from me;
33:15 *f* upon men] as they slumber in their beds,
Ps(s) 7:16 but he *f* into the pit which he has made.
Prv 11: 5 but by his wickedness the wicked man *f*.
11: 8 and the wicked man *f* into it in his stead.
11:14 For lack of guidance a people *f*;
17:20 and a double-tongued man *f* into trouble.
24:16 the just man *f* seven times and rises again,
24:17 Rejoice not when your enemy *f*,
26:27 He who digs a pit *f* into it;
28:18 he whose ways are crooked *f* into the pit.
Eccl 4:10 If the one *f*, the other will lift up
9:12 when the evil time *f* suddenly upon them.
11: 3 a tree *f* to the south or to the north,
11: 3 the south or to the north, wherever it *f*,
12: 6 and the broken pulley *f* into the well,
Sir 3:30 when he *f*, he finds a support.
14:18 one *f* off and another sprouts
27:25 As a stone *f* back on him who throws it up,
27:26 As he who digs a pit *f* into it,
29: 2 pay back your neighbor when a loan *f* due;
29:19 he who undertakes too much *f* into lawsuits.
Is 9: 7 sent word against Jacob, it *f* upon Israel,
10:34 the axe, and Lebanon in its splendor *f*.
24:20 rebellion will weigh it down, until it *f*,
Jer 8: 4 When someone *f*, does he not rise again?
48:44 who flees from the terror *f* into the pit;
50:32 Insolence stumbles and *f*;
51: 8 Babylon suddenly *f* and is crushed:
51:44 The wall of Babylon *f*!
Ez 13:14 When it *f*, you shall be crushed beneath it;
Mt 10:29 Yet not a single sparrow *f* to the ground
12:11 a sheep and it *f* into a pit on the sabbath.
17:15 he often *f* into the fire and frequently
21:44 *f* upon that stone will be smashed to bits;
21:44 and he on whom it *f* will be crushed.]"
Lk 11:17 Any house torn by dissension *f*.
14: 5 you has a son or an ox and he *f* into a pit,
20:18 *f* on that stone will be smashed to pieces.
20:18 It will make dust of anyone on whom it *f*."
Jn 12:24 the grain of wheat *f* to the earth and dies,
Rom 14: 4 alone can judge whether he stands or *f*.
Heb 12:15 that no man *f* away from the grace of God;
Jas 2:10 Whoever *f* into sin on one point of the law,

FALSE (87)

Ex 8:25 must not play *f* again by refusing to let
20:16 not bear *f* witness against your neighbor.
23: 1 "You shall not repeat a *f* report.
Lv 26: 1 "Do not make *f* gods for yourselves.
Dt 19:18 a *f* witness and has accused his kinsman
Tb 14: 4 word of the prophecies shall prove *f*.
Jdt 6: 9 my words shall not prove *f* in any respect."
Est 4:21 of the heathen to acclaim their *f* gods,
2Mc 4: 1 made *f* accusation that it was Onias who
5: 5 *f* rumor circulated that Antiochus was dead.
Ps(s) 27:12 for *f* witnesses have risen up against me,
36: 4 The words of his mouth are empty and *f*;
73:15 been *f* to the fellowship of your children.
89:36 I will not be *f* to David.
119:104 therefore I hate every *f* way.
119:128 every *f* way I hate.
144: 8 Whose mouths swear *f* promises while their
144:11 Whose mouths swear *f* promises while
Prv 6:19 to evil, The *f* witness who utters lies,
11: 1 *F* scales are an abomination to the LORD,
14: 5 does not lie, but a *f* witness utters lies.
16:10 no judgment he pronounces is *f*.
19: 5 The *f* witness will not go unpunished,
19: 9 The *f* witness will not go unpunished,
20:23 to the LORD, and *f* scales are not good.
21:28 The *f* witness will perish,
25:18 who bears *f* witness against his neighbor.
Wis 10:14 Showed those who had defamed him *f*,
14:30 deliberately swore *f* oaths despising piety.
Sir 3:23 and *f* reasoning unbalanced their judgment.
26: 5 Though *f* charges in public,
29:14 and only the shameless would play him *f*;
34: 1 Empty and *f* are the hopes of the senseless,
37: 4 A *f* friend will share your joys,
Is 54:17 *f* that launches an accusation against you.
57:11 that you became *f* And did not remember me
58: 9 *f* accusation and malicious speech;
Jer 28:15 have raised *f* confidence in this people.
29:31 a mission from me, and raises *f* confidence,
Lam 2:14 had for you *f* and specious visions;
2:14 you in vision *f* and misleading portents.
Bar 6:58 the joy of its owner, than these *f* gods;
6:58 who are within, rather than these *f* gods;
6:58 post in a palace, rather than these *f* gods!
6:62 But these *f* gods are not their equal,
Ez 12:24 There shall no longer be any *f* visions or
13: 6 visions are *f* and their divination lying.
13: 7 Was not the vision you saw *f*,
13: 9 who have *f* visions and who foretell lies.
13:23 see *f* visions and practice divination,
21:34 because you planned with *f* visions and
22:28 are *f* and performing lying divinations,
Dn 2: 9 You have framed a *f* and deceitful
Hos 4: 2 *F* swearing, lying, murder, stealing
10: 2 Their heart is *f*,
10: 4 Nothing but make promises, swear *f* oaths,
12: 8 A merchant who holds a *f* balance,
Mi 6:11 criminal balances, bags of *f* weights?
Zec 8:17 another in his heart, nor love a *f* oath.
10: 2 nonsense, the diviners have *f* visions:
Mt 5:33 on your forefathers, 'Do not take a *f* oath;
7:15 "Be on your guard against *f* prophets,
15:19 conduct, fornication, stealing, *f* witness,
19:18 'You shall not bear *f* witness';
24:11 *F* prophets will rise in great numbers to
24:24 False messiahs and *f* prophets will appear,
26:59 were busy trying to obtain *f* testimony
26:60 the many *f* witnesses who took the stand.
Mk 10:19 You shall not bear *f* witness;
13:22 False messiahs and *f* prophets will appear
Lk 6:26 treated the *f* prophets in just this way.
Acts 6:13 There they brought in *f* witnesses,
1Cor 15:15 then be exposed as *f* witnesses of God,
2Cor 11:13 Such men are *f* apostles.
11:26 city, in the desert, at sea, by *f* brothers;
Gal 2: 4 Certain *f* claimants to the title of
1Tm 1: 3 teaching *f* doctrines and busying themselves
Jas 3:14 arrogant and *f* claims against the truth.
2Pt 2: 1 there were *f* prophets among God's people,
2: 1 among you also there will be *f* teachers
1Jn 4: 1 many *f* prophets have appeared in the world.
4: 4 and thus you have conquered the *f* prophets.
Rv 16:13 beast, and from the mouth of the *f* prophet;
19:20 The beast was captured along with the *f*
20:10 and the *f* prophet had also been thrown.

FALSEHOOD (30)

Jb 6:30 on my tongue, or cannot my taste discern *f*?
13: 7 Is it for God that you speak *f*?
27: 4 in my nostrils, My lips shall not speak *f*,
31: 5 in *f* and my foot has hastened to deceit;
Ps(s) 4: 3 do you love what is vain and seek after *f*?
5: 7 you destroy all who speak *f*;
12: 3 Everyone speaks *f* to his neighbor;
40: 5 to idolatry or to those who stray after *f*.
52: 5 than good, *f* rather than honest speech.
101: 7 speaks *f* shall not stand before my eyes.
119:29 Remove from me the way of *f*,
Prv 17: 4 and listens to *f* from a mischievous tongue.
30: 8 Put *f* and lying far from me,
Sir 41:15 before master and mistress, of *f*;
51: 3 tongue, and from lips that went over to *f*;
Is 9:14 the prophet who teaches *f* is the tail.]
28:15 and in *f* we have found a hiding place,"—
53: 9 he had done no wrong nor spoken any *f*.
59: 3 Your lips speak *f*,
59:13 words of *f* the heart has conceived.
Jer 8: 8 into *f* by the lying pen of the scribes!
Ez 13: 8 have spoken *f* and have seen lying visions,
Hos 7: 1 They practice *f*,
10:13 perversity, and eaten the fruit of *f*.
12:12 In Gilead is *f*,
Mi 6:12 *f* with deceitful tongues in their heads!
Rom 3: 7 If my *f* brings to light God's truth and
2Thes 2: 9 signs and wonders at the disposal of *f*—
2:11 which leads them to give credence to *f*,
Rv 22:15 the idol-worshipers and all who love *f*.

FALSEHOODS (2)

Jb 13: 4 glossing over *f* and offering vain remedies,
Hos 12: 2 His lies and *f* are many:

FALSELY (18)

Gn 21:23 *f* with me or with my progeny and posterity,
Lv 5:22 he denies the fact and swears *f* about it
5:24 he found or whatever else he swore *f* about;
19:11 shall not lie or speak *f* to one another.
19:12 You shall not swear *f* by my name,
Nm 23:19 God is not man that he should speak *f*,
Dt 19:18 witness and has accused his kinsman *f*,

Ps(s) 63:12 of those who speak *f* shall be stopped.
Wis 14:29 they expect no harm when they have sworn *f*.
Jer 5: 2 say, "As the LORD lives," they swear *f*.
5:31 The prophets prophesy *f*,
27:15 the Lord, but they prophesy *f* in my name,
Dn 13:43 know that they have testified *f* against me.
13:49 for they have testified *f* against her."
Mk 14:56 Many spoke against him *f* under oath but
14:57 taking the stand, testified *f* by alleging,
Lk 3:14 Denounce no one *f*.
1Tm 6:20 of what is *f* called knowledge.

FALSIFY (2)

2Cor 4: 2 resort to trickery or *f* the word of God.
2Tm 3: 8 with perverted minds they *f* the faith.

FALTER (6)

Ps(s) 37:31 is in his heart, and his steps do not *f*.
Mal 2: 8 have caused many to *f* by your instruction;
Mt 14:31 "Why did you *f*?"
21:21 "Believe me, if you trust and do not *f*,
24:10 Many will *f* then,
Mk 4:17 overtakes them because of the word, they *f*.

FALTERED (1)

Ps(s) 17: 5 in your paths, my feet have not *f*.

FALTERING (1)

Jb 4: 4 you have strengthened his *f* knees.

FALTERS (1)

Mt 13:21 involving the message occurs, he soon *f*.

FAME (23)

Jos 6:27 so that his *f* spread throughout the land.
9: 9 faroff land, because of the *f* of the LORD,
Ru 4:11 well in Ephrathah and win *f* in Bethlehem.
1Sm 18:30 and as a result acquired great *f*.
1Kgs 5:11 and his *f* spread throughout the
10: 1 of Sheba, having heard of Solomon's *f*,
1Chr 14:17 *f* was spread abroad through every land,
2Chr 9: 1 the queen of Sheba heard of Solomon's *f*,
26: 8 to Uzziah and his *f* spread as far as Egypt,
26:15 His *f* spread far and wide,
Est C: 5 pride or desire for *f* that I acted thus
1Mc 3:26 His *f* reached the king,
3:41 merchants of the country heard of their *f*,
8:12 who heard of their *f* were afraid of them.
14:21 have informed us of your glory and *f*,
2Mc 8: 7 Soon the *f* of his valor spread everywhere.
Ps(s) 145: 7 They publish the *f* of your abundant
Sir 9:11 Envy not a sinner's *f*,
20:10 Humiliation can follow *f*,
39: 9 his *f* can never be effaced;
47:16 Your *f* reached distant coasts,
Is 66:19 coastlands that have never heard of my *f*,
Hos 14: 8 his *f* shall be like the wine of Lebanon.

FAMILIAR (10)

1Sm 3: 7 that time Samuel was not *f* with the LORD,
Jb 28:23 it is he who is *f* with its place.
Ps(s) 139: 3 you scrutinize, with all my ways you are *f*.
Sir 8: 4 Be not too *f* with an unruly man,
9: 4 With a singing girl be not *f*,
23: 9 or becoming too *f* with the Holy Name.
51:15 from earliest youth I was *f* with her.
Mk 12:10 you not *f* with this passage of Scripture:
Jn 18: 2 The place was *f* to Judas as well (the one
2Cor 6: 5 as men *f* with hard work,

FAMILIES (46)

Gn 42:19 take home provisions for your starving *f*.
42:33 go home with rations for your starving *f*.
45:18 There get your father and your *f*,
47:24 and your *f* [and as food for your children]."
Ex 1:21 feared God, he built up *f* for them.
12: 3 of your *f* must procure for itself a lamb,
12:21 them, "Go and procure lambs for your *f*,
Nm 16:32 its mouth and swallowed them and their *f*
18:31 Your *f*, as well as you, may eat them
32:16 here for our flocks, and towns for our *f*;
32:17 *f* can remain here in the fortified towns,
32:24 Build the towns, then, for your *f*,
Dt 11: 6 with their *f* and tents and every living
12: 7 you and your *f* shall eat and make merry
Jos 7:14 LORD designates shall come forward by *f*;
7:17 He had the clan of Zerah come forward by *f*,
14: 1 and the heads of *f* in the tribes of the
19:51 and the heads of *f* in the tribes of the
21: 1 the Levite *f* came up to Eleazar the priest,
21: 1 and to the heads of *f* of the other tribes
1Sm 10:19 before the LORD according to tribes and *f*."
23:23 search him out among all the *f* of Judah."
2Sm 2: 3 also brought up his men with their *f*,
1Chr 9: 9 various *f* were nine hundred and fifty-six.
15:12 "You, the heads of the levitical *f*,
16:28 Give to the LORD, you *f* of nations,
23: 9 These were the heads of the *f* of Ladan.
24:31 the heads of the priestly and levitical *f*;
26:13 each gate, the small and the large *f* alike.
26:26 by King David, the heads of the *f*,
26:32 two thousand seven hundred heads of *f*.
29: 6 Then the heads of the *f*,
2Chr 23: 2 and also the heads of the Israelite *f*.
35: 5 of the Levites and the *f* may be the same.
Neh 12:46 For the heads of the *f* of the singers and
1Mc 1:61 their *f* also and those who had circumcised
Ps(s) 22:28 *f* of the nations shall bow down before him.
96: 7 Give to the LORD, you *f* of nations,
107:41 misery and made the *f* numerous like flocks.
Sir 44:11 Their wealth remains in their *f*,
45:18 Men of other *f* were inflamed against him,
Am 3: 2 favored, more than all the *f* of the earth;
Zec 12:14 and all the rest of the *f*,
14:17 If any of the *f* of the earth does not come
Acts 3:25 all the *f* of the earth shall be blessed.'
Ti 1:11 They are upsetting whole *f* by teaching

FAMILY (217)

Gn 25:19 This is the *f* history of Isaac,
34:30 attack me, I and my *f* will be wiped out."
35: 2 his *f* and all the others who were with him:
37: 2 This is his *f* history.
41:51 I endured at the hands of my *f*";
43: 7 man kept asking about ourselves and our *f*:
44:25 to come back and buy some food for the *f*.
45:11 so that you and your *f* and all that are
46:27 the people comprising Jacob's *f* who had
50:22 in Egypt, together with his father's *f*.
Ex 12: 4 If a *f* is too small for a whole lamb,
Lv 9: 7 in atonement for yourself and for your *f*;
16:11 to atone for himself and for his *f*.
18:10 for that would be a disgrace to your own *f*.
20: 5 set my face against that man and his *f*
21: 3 of his own *f* while she remains unmarried;
21: 4 of his *f* he shall not make himself unclean;
25:10 property, every one to his own *f* estate.
25:47 one of the descendants of an immigrant *f*,
Nm 11:10 Moses heard the people, family after *f*,
18:11 in your *f* who are clean may partake of it.
18:13 your *f* who are clean may partake of them.
Dt 14:26 partake of it and make merry with your *f*.
15:20 and your *f* shall eat them before the LORD,
24: 5 for one year for the sake of his *f*,
25: 5 shall not marry anyone outside the *f*;
25: 9 who will not build up his brother's *f*!'
25:10 'the *f* of the man stripped of his sandal.'
26:11 Then you and your *f*, together
Jos 2:12 you in turn will show kindness to my *f*;
2:18 brothers and all your *f* into your house.
6:23 Her entire *f* they led forth and placed
6:25 spared her with her *f* and all her kin,
7:14 the *f* which the LORD designates shall come
7:18 he had that *f* come forward one by one,
Jgs 4:17 and the *f* of the Kenite Heber were at
6:15 My *f* is the meanest in Manasseh,
6:27 fear of his *f* and of the townspeople,
8:27 and caused the ruin of Gideon and his *f*.
8:35 Nor were they grateful to the *f* of
9: 1 clan to which his mother's *f* belonged,
9:16 dealt well with Jerubbaal and with his *f*,
9:18 but you have risen against his *f* this day
9:19 honor toward Jerubbaal and his *f* this day,
11: 2 him, "You shall inherit nothing in our *f*,
12: 9 thirty daughters married outside the *f*,
12: 9 sons thirty young women from outside the *f*.
14:15 for us, or we will burn you and your *f*.
14:19 Then he went off to his own *f* in anger,
15: 6 up and destroyed her and her *f* by fire.
16:31 All his *f* and kinsmen went down and bore
18:19 for you to be priest for the *f* of one man
18:25 you and you and your *f* lose your lives."
Ru 4: 5 up a *f* for the departed on his estate."
4:10 up a *f* for her late husband on his estate,
1Sm 2:27 reveal myself to your father's *f*
2:28 of the Israelites to your father's *f*.
2:30 'I said in the past that your *f* and your
2:31 father's family, so that no man in your *f*
2:32 there shall never be an old man in your *f*.
2:33 some of your *f* to remain at my altar,
2:33 the men of your *f* shall die by the sword.
2:36 Then whoever is left of your *f* will come
3:12 Eli everything I threatened against his *f*.
3:13 I am condemning his *f* once and for all,
3:14 I swear to the *f* of Eli that no sacrifice
9:20 ardently if not you and your father's *f*?"
17:25 exemption to his father's *f* in Israel."
20:16 the *f* of David to die out from among you,
22:11 and to all his *f* who were priests in Nob;
22:15 servant or anyone in my *f* of such a thing.
22:16 shall die, Ahimelech, with all your *f*."
22:21 am responsible for the death of all your *f*.
24:22 that you will not blot out my name and *f*."
25: 6 be with you, my brother, and with your *f*,
25:17 store for our master and for his whole *f*.
27: 3 each one had his *f*,
2Sm 3:29 of Ner, be laid to Joab and to all his *f*.
3:29 May the men of Joab's *f* never be without
6:12 LORD had blessed the *f* of Obed-edom
6:20 When David returned to bless his own *f*,
6:21 your father and his whole *f* when he
9: 2 was a servant of the *f* of Saul named Ziba.
9: 9 all that belonged to Saul and to all his *f*.
9:10 shall be food for your lord's *f* to eat.
9:12 tenants of Ziba's *f* worked for Meribbaal.
14: 9 him, "Let me and my *f* be to blame,
16: 5 son of Gera of the same clan as Saul's *f*,
16: 8 you for all the bloodshed in the *f* of Saul,
17:23 Then, having left orders concerning his *f*,
21: 1 *f* because he put the Gibeonites to death."
1Kgs 2:31 me and from my *f* the blood which Joab
18:18 he answered, "but you and your *f*,
2Kgs 8: 1 with your *f* and settle wherever you can,
8: 2 setting out with her *f* and settling in the
9: 8 and by all the rest of the *f* of Ahab.
10:11 who were left of the *f* of Ahab in Jezreel,
10:13 the princes and the *f* of the queen mother."
11: 1 she began to kill off the whole royal *f*.
1Chr 4:33 was inscribed of them in their *f* records.
5: 1 in the *f* records according to birthright.
5: 7 *f* records according to their descendants,
5:17 in the *f* records in the time of Jotham,
7: 5 thousand warriors in their *f* records.
7: 7 Their *f* records listed twenty-two thousand
7: 9 Their *f* records listed twenty thousand two
7:40 Their *f* records numbered twenty-six
8: 6 *f* heads over those who dwelt in Geba and
8:10 These were his sons, *f* heads.
8:13 were *f* heads of those who dwelt in Aijalon,
8:28 These were *f* heads over their kindred,
9: 1 Thus all Israel was inscribed in its *f*
9:16 whose *f* lived in the villages of the
9:22 in the *f* records of their villages.
9:33 the gatekeepers, *f* heads over the Levites.
9:34 the levitical *f* heads over their kindred,
13:14 of Obed-edom with his *f* for three months,
17:16 "Who am I, O LORD God, and what is my *f*,
17:17 *f* reaching into the distant future,
21:17 LORD, my God, strike me and my father's *f*,
23:11 therefore they were classed as a single *f*,
23:24 the *f* heads as they were enrolled one by
24: 4 into eight groups, each under its *f* head.
24: 6 listing two successive *f* groups from
24:31 the more important *f* did so in the same
25: 9 first lot fell to Asaph, the *f* of Joseph;
26: 6 were born sons who ruled over their *f*,
26:16 For each *f*, watches were established.
26:21 the *f* heads were descendants of Jehiel:
26:31 their chief according to their *f* records.
27: 1 This is the list of the Israelite *f* heads,
27:15 the Netophathite, of the *f* of Othniel,
28: 4 father's *f* to be king over Israel forever.
28: 4 chose Judah as leader, then one *f* of Judah,
2Chr 1: 2 the princes of all Israel, and the *f* heads;
12:15 and of Iddo the seer [his *f* record].
19: 8 priests and some of the *f* heads of Israel
26:12 The entire number of *f* heads over these
31:17 The priests were inscribed in their *f*
31:18 to all who were inscribed in the *f* records,
31:19 to every Levite listed in the *f* records.
Ezr 1: 5 Then the *f* heads of Judah and Benjamin and
2:62 These men searched their *f* records,
2:68 some of the *f* heads made
3:12 Many of the priests, Levites, and *f* heads,
4: 2 and the *f* heads and said to them,
4: 3 of the *f* heads of Israel answered them,
7:28 *f* heads to make the return journey with me.
8: 1 This is the list of the *f* heads who
8:29 and Levites and the *f* leaders of Israel,
10:16 as his assistants men who were *f* heads,
10:16 men who were family heads, one for each *f*,
Neh 4: 7 them by *f* groups with their swords,
7: 5 their *f* records, I came upon the family
7:64 These men searched their *f* records,
7:69 of the *f* heads contributed to the service.
7:70 Some of the *f* heads contributed to the
8:13 the *f* heads of the whole people and also
10:35 of our *f* houses at stated times each year,
11:13 of Malchijah, and his brethren, *f* heads,
12:12 of Joiakim these were the priestly *f* heads:
12:22 the *f* heads of the priests were written
12:23 the *f* heads were written down in the Book
Tb 1: 1 of Aduel, son of Gabael of the *f* of Asiel,
5: 9 find out what *f* and tribe he comes from,
5:11 me, please, what *f* and tribe are you from?"
5:12 Do you need a tribe and a *f*?
5:14 wanting to learn the truth about your *f*.
6:16 you to marry a woman from your own *f*.
Est 2:10 did not reveal her nationality or *f*,
2:20 had not revealed her *f* or nationality,
1Mc 2: 1 son of Simeon, a priest of the *f* of Joarib,
5:62 But they did not belong to the *f* of those
2Mc 1:10 member of the *f* of the anointed priests,
Jb 1:10 *f* and all that he has with your protection?
8:15 He shall rely upon his *f*,
19:17 I am loathsome to the men of my *f*.
21:21 what interest has he in his *f* after him,
32: 2 of Barachel the Buzite, of the *f* of Ram,
Sir 3: 9 a father's blessing gives a *f* firm roots,
44:12 God's covenant with them their *f* endures,
45:15 lasting covenant with him and with his *f*,
46: 9 his *f* too received an inheritance,
47:22 a remnant, to David a root from his own *f*.
Is 22:23 spot, to be a place of honor for his *f*;

FAMILY (cont.)
22:24 On him shall hang all the glory of his *f*:
Jer 1: 1 of Hilkiah, of a priestly *f* in Anathoth,
37:12 his *f* in the division of an inheritance.
38:17 with fire, and you and your *f* shall live.
Ez 22: 6 the princes of Israel, family by *f*,
Dn 14:29 over to us, or we will kill you and your *f*."
Am 3: 1 *f* that I brought up from the land of Egypt.
Zec 9: 7 our God, and shall be like a *f* in Judah,
12:12 each *f* apart; the family of the house
12:12 the *f* of the house of David,
12:12 the *f* of the house of Nathan,
12:13 the *f* of the house of Levi,
12:13 the *f* of Shemei, and their wives;
12:14 all the rest of the families, each *f* apart,
14:18 And if the *f* of Egypt does not come up,
Mt 1: 1 A *f* record of Jesus Christ,
Mk 3:21 When his *f* heard of this they came to take
5:19 "Go home to your *f* and make it clear to
Jn 7:42 say that the Messiah, being of David's *f*,
8:35 (No slave has a permanent place in the *f*,
Acts 7:13 and his *f* ties became known to the Pharaoh.
13:26 children of the *f* of Abraham and you
16:34 with his whole *f* his newfound faith in God.
Eph 3:15 *f* in heaven and on earth takes its name;
1Tm 5: 8 especially for members of his immediate *f*,
2Tm 1:16 Lord have mercy on the *f* of Onesiphorus,
4:19 Prisca and Aquila and the *f* of Onesiphorus.

FAMILY'S (3)
Tb 6:18 was his kinswoman, of his own *f* lineage,
Mk 5:42 At this the *f* astonishment knew no bounds.
7:28 dogs under the table eat the *f* leavings."

FAMINE (100)
Gn 12:10 There was *f* in the land;
12:10 there, since the *f* in the land was severe.
26: 1 There was a *f* in the land (distinct from
41:27 they are seven years of *f*.
41:30 will be followed by seven years of *f*,
41:30 When the *f* has ravaged the land,
41:31 the land because of the *f* that follows it
41:31 so utterly severe will that *f* be.
41:36 *f* that are to follow in the land of Egypt,
41:36 so that the land may not perish in the *f*."
41:50 Before the *f* years set in,
41:54 to an end, the seven years of *f* set in,
41:54 there was *f* in all the other countries,
41:56 When the *f* had spread throughout the land,
41:56 since the *f* had gripped the land of Egypt.
41:57 grain, for *f* had gripped the whole world.
42: 5 there was *f* in the land of Canaan also,
43: 1 Now the *f* in the land grew more severe.
45: 6 two years now the *f* has been in the land,
45:11 Since five years of *f* still lie ahead,
47: 4 of Canaan, so severe has the *f* been there.
47:13 because of the extreme severity of the *f*,
47:20 since with the *f* too much for them to bear,
Ex 16: 3 to make the whole community die of *f*!"
Ru 1: 1 of the judges there was a *f* in the land;
2Sm 21: 1 there was a *f* for three successive years.
24:13 a three years' *f* to come upon your land,
1Kgs 8:37 "If there is *f* in the land or pestilence;
18: 3 Now the *f* in Samaria was bitter,
2Kgs 4:38 to Gilgal, there was a *f* in the land.
6:25 Because of the siege the *f* in Samaria was
7: 4 die there, for there is *f* in the city.
7:12 Knowing that we are in *f*,
8: 1 seven-year *f* which is coming upon the land."
25: 3 fourth month, when *f* had gripped the city,
1Chr 21:12 will it be three years of *f*:
2Chr 6:28 When there is *f* in the land,
20: 9 sword of judgment, or pestilence, or *f*,
32:11 you over to a death of *f* and thirst,
Neh 5: 3 that we may have grain during the *f*."
Tb 4:13 for worthlessness is the mother of *f*.
Jdt 5:10 *f* had gripped the whole land of Canaan,
1Mc 6:54 own home, for the *f* was too much for them.
9:24 In those days there was a very great *f*,
Jb 5:20 In *f* he will deliver you from death,
Ps(s) 33:19 from death and preserve them in spite of *f*.
37:19 in days of *f* they have plenty.
105:16 When he called down a *f* on the land and
Sir 39:29 for the proper time, are fire and hail, *f*,
40: 9 the sword, plunder and ruin, *f* and death:
Is 14:30 with *f* that shall slay even your remnant.
51:19 Desolation and destruction, *f* and sword!
Jer 5:12 us, neither sword nor *f* shall we see.
11:22 their sons and daughters shall die by *f*.
14:12 I will destroy them with the sword, *f*,
14:13 *f* shall not befall you.
14:15 "Sword and *f* shall not befall this land":
14:15 and *f* shall these prophets meet their end.
14:16 streets of Jerusalem by *f* and the sword.
15: 2 whoever is marked for famine, to *f*;
16: 4 Sword and *f* will make an end of them,
18:21 So now, deliver their children to *f*,
21: 7 city who survive pestilence, sword, and *f*,
21: 9 shall die by the sword or *f* or pestilence.
24:10 I will send upon them the sword, *f*,
27: 8 I will punish that nation with sword, *f*,
27:13 you and your people die by the sword, *f*,
29:17 against them sword, *f* and pestilence.
29:18 I will pursue them with sword, *f*,
32:24 who are attacking it, amid sword, *f*,
32:36 over to the king of Babylon amid sword, *f*,
34:17 you free, says the LORD, for the sword, *f*,
38: 2 in this city shall die by sword, or *f*,
38: 9 He will die of *f* on the spot,
42:17 Egypt to stay, shall die by the sword, *f*,
42:22 of this, you shall die by the sword, *f*,
44:27 or *f* until they are utterly destroyed.
52: 6 when *f* had gripped the city and the people
Lam 5:10 by a furnace, with the searing blasts of *f*.
Ez 5:17 I will send *f* against you,
6:11 which they shall fall by the sword, by *f*,
6:12 and he that is besieged shall perish by *f*;
7:15 and *f* shall devour those in the city.
12:16 them to escape the sword, *f* and pestilence,
14:13 I let *f* loose upon it and cut off from it
14:21 my four cruel punishments, the sword, *f*,
34:29 no longer be carried off by *f* in the land,
36:29 and I will not send *f* against you.
36:30 bear among the nations the reproach of *f*.
Am 8:11 Lord GOD, when I will send *f* upon the land:
8:11 Not a *f* of bread, or thirst for water,
Mt 24: 7 There will be *f* and pestilence and
Mk 13: 8 in various places and there will be *f*.
Lk 4:25 years and a great *f* spread over the land.
15:14 a great *f* broke out in that country and
Acts 7:11 When *f* and great trial came upon Egypt and
11:28 going to be a severe *f* all over the world.
Rv 6: 8 to kill with sword and *f* and plague and
18: 8 come all at once, death and mourning and *f*.

FAMINES (1)
Lk 21:11 plagues and *f* in various places

FAMISHED (5)
Gn 25:29 a stew, Esau came in from the open, *f*.
Nm 11: 6 But now we are *f*;
Jgs 8: 4 hundred men, they were exhausted and *f*.
Jb 24:10 and *f* are those who carry the sheaves.
Bar 2:18 and feeble, with failing eyes and *f* soul,

FAMOUS (10)
Ru 4:14 May he become *f* in Israel!
2Sm 7: 9 you *f* like the great ones of the earth.
8:13 David became *f* for having slain eighteen
1Kgs 1:47 'May God make Solomon more *f* than you and
1Chr 5:24 men who were warriors, *f* men,
11:21 He was twice as *f* as any of the Thirty and
11:25 He was more *f* than any of the Thirty,
1Mc 6: 1 *f* for its wealth in silver and gold,
7:26 king sent Nicanor, one of his *f* officers,
Sir 39: 2 He treasures the discourses of *f* men,

FAN (1)
Jer 15: 7 them with the *f* in every city gate.

FANCIES (3)
Ps(s) 73: 7 their *f* overflow their hearts.
Prv 18:11 he *f* it a high wall.
Jer 23:26 prophesy lies and their own deceitful *f*?

FANCY (6)
Dt 12:13 up your holocausts in any place you *f*,
Wis 15: 4 the evil creation of men's *f* deceive us,
Jer 23:16 Visions of their own *f* they speak,
Hos 13: 2 images, Silver idols according to their *f*,
Eph 2: 3 of the flesh, following every whim and *f*,
1Tm 2: 9 and not be decked out in *f* hair styles,

FANGS (2)
Jb 20:16 the viper's *f* shall slay him.
Wis 16:10 *f* of poisonous reptiles overcame your sons,

FANNED (1)
Jb 20:26 which shall consume him needs not to be *f*.

FAR (266)
Gn 12: 6 land as *f* as the sacred place at Shechem,
13:10 the whole Jordan Plain was as *f* as Zoar,
14: 6 the hill country of Seir, as *f* as El-paran,
14:14 his house, and went in pursuit as *f* as Dan.
14:15 them, and pursued them as *f* as Hobah,
18:25 *F* be it from you to do such a thing,
26:16 you have become *f* too numerous for us."
27:39 *f* from the fertile earth shall be your
27:39 *f* from the dew of the heavens above!
44: 4 They had not gone *f* out of the city when
44: 7 *F* be it from your servants to do such a
44:17 *F* be it from me to act thus!"
Ex 8:24 not go too *f* away and that you pray for me."
14:12 *F* better for us to be the slaves of the
Lv 13:12 the skin and, as *f* as the priest can see,
Nm 12: 3 *f* the meekest man on the face of the earth.
13:21 as *f* as where Rehob adjoins Labo of Hamath.
14:45 them, beating them back as *f* as Hormah.
16:14 *F* from bringing us to a land flowing with
21:24 and as *f* as the country of the Ammonites,
21:30 fires blaze as *f* as Medeba."
Dt 1: 7 as *f* as the Great River [the Euphrates].
1:24 the hill country as *f* as the Wadi Eshcol,
1:44 cutting you down in Seir as *f* as Hormah.
2:23 who once dwelt in villages as *f* as Gaza,
2:36 city in the wadi itself, as *f* as Gilead,
3:14 took all the region of Argob as *f* as the
4:49 as *f* as the Arabah Sea under the slopes of
12:21 for the abode of his name is too *f*,
13: 8 any other nations, near at hand or *f* away,
14:24 for the abode of his name is too *f* for you,
34: 1 Gilead, and as *f* as Dan,
34: 2 the land of Judah as *f* as the Western Sea,
34: 3 Jericho, city of palms, and as *f* as Zoar.
34:12 Jericho, city of palms, and as *f* as Zoar.
Jos 9: 1 the coast of the Great Sea as *f* as Lebanon:
10:10 them as *f* as Azekah and Makkedah.
11:17 that rises toward Seir as *f* as Baal-gad
12: 3 as *f* south as the eastern side of the Salt
12: 5 and all Bashan as *f* as the boundary of the
12: 5 of Gilead as *f* as the territory of Sihon,
13:11 Hermon, and all Bashan as *f* as Salecah,
13:25 the land of the Ammonites as *f* as Aroer,
15: 5 Salt Sea as *f* as the mouth of the Jordan.
15:47 as *f* as the Wadi of Egypt and the coast
19: 8 these cities as *f* as Baalath-beer (that is,
22:29 *F* be it from us to rebel against the LORD
23:15 even so *f* as to exterminate you from this
24:16 *F* be it from us to forsake the LORD for
Jgs 4:16 and the army as *f* as Haro-sheath-ha-goiim.
6: 4 of the land as *f* as the outskirts of Gaza,
7:22 The army fled as *f* as Beth-shittah in the
7:24 courses against them as *f* as Beth-barah,
7:24 the water courses as *f* as Beth-barah,
11:33 cities in all) and as *f* as Abel-Keramin.
18: 2 they traveled as *f* as the house of Micah
18:28 since the city was *f* from Sidon and they
19:11 they were near Jebus with the day *f* gone,
19:18 *f* up into the mountain region of Ephraim,
1Sm 2:27 'I went so *f* as to reveal myself to your
6:12 them as *f* as the border of Beth-shemesh.
12:23 *f* be it from me to sin against the LORD by
17:52 road from Shaaraim as *f* as Gath and Ekron.
26:20 the ground *f* from the presence of the LORD.
30: 9 men and came as *f* as the Wadi Besor,
2Sm 3:16 who followed her weeping as *f* as Bahurim.
5:25 the Philistines from Gibeon as *f* as Gezer.
13:15 *f* surpassed the love he had had for her.
13:16 drive me out would be *f* worse than the first
14:11 avenger of blood may not go too *f* in
19: 8 and this will be a *f* greater disaster for
1Kgs 8:46 deport them to a hostile land, *f* or near,
18:46 Ahab as *f* as the approaches of Jezreel.
2Kgs 7:15 followed the Arameans as *f* as the Jordan,
9:27 his flight as *f* as Megiddo and died there.
1Chr 4:33 all their outlying villages as *f* as Baal.
5: 8 in Aroer and as *f* as Nebo and Baal-meon;
5: 9 toward the east they dwelt as *f* as the desert
5:11 them in the land of Bashan as *f* as Salecah.
5:23 in the land of Bashan as *f* as Baal-hermon,
7:28 and its towns as *f* as Ayyah and its towns.
12:41 their neighbors from as *f* as Issachar,
17:16 should have brought me as *f* as I have come?
29: 2 the house of my God, as *f* as I was able,
2Chr 6:36 deport them to another land, *f* or near,
12: 4 cities of Judah and came as *f* as Jerusalem.
14: 8 chariots, and he came as *f* as Mareshah.
14:12 those with him pursued them as *f* as Gerar,
26: 8 Uzziah and his fame spread as *f* as Egypt,
26:15 His fame spread *f* and wide,
30:10 Ephraim and Manasseh and as *f* as Zebulun,
34: 6 the surrounding country as *f* as Naphtali;
Neh 3: 8 as *f* as the wall of the public square.
3:11 adjoining sector, as *f* as the Oven Tower,
3:15 near the king's garden as *f* as the steps
3:16 *f* as the artificial pool and the barracks.
3:31 of repair as *f* as the quarters of the temple
3:31 and as *f* as the upper chamber of the Angle.
5: 8 "As *f* as we were able,
12:38 past the Oven Tower as *f* as the Broad Wall,
12:39 as *f* as the Sheep Gate [and they came to a
Tb 3:10 It is *f* better for me not to hang myself,
Jdt 1: 9 and west of the Jordan as *f* as Jerusalem,
1:10 of Egypt as *f* as the borders of Ethiopia.
1:12 Egypt as *f* as the borders of the two seas.
7: 3 in breadth toward Dothan as *f* as Balbaim,
15: 5 them and cut them down as *f* as Choba.
Est B: 2 humane and effective as *f* as the borders,
E:11 He so *f* enjoyed the good will which we
9:20 letters to all the Jews, both near and *f*,
1Mc 4:15 as *f* as Gazara and the plains of Judea,
8: 4 against them from the *f* corners of the earth
8:12 They had conquered kings both *f* and near,
8:23 may sword and enemy be *f* from them.
9:10 *F* be it from me to do such a thing as to
9:15 pursued them as *f* as the mountain slopes.
11: 7 Jonathan accompanied the king as *f* as the
11: 8 the seacoast as *f* as Seleucia-by-the-Sea.
11:62 on through the province as *f* as Damascus.
11:73 the enemy as *f* as their camp in Kadesh,
12:33 Simon also set out and went as *f* as
13: 5 *F* be it from me, then, to save my own life
2Mc 2:26 this digest, the task, *f* from being easy,

9: 7 *F* from giving up his insolence,
12: 9 the flames was visible as *f* as Jerusalem,
Jb 5: 4 His children shall be *f* from safety;
13:21 Withdraw your hand *f* from me,
22:18 But *f* be from me the mind of the impious!]
22:23 if you put iniquity *f* from your tent,
27: 5 *F* be it from me to account you right;
34:10 *f* be it from God to do wickedness; far
38:11 Thus *f* shall you come but no farther,
Ps(s) 10: 5 your judgments are *f* from his mind;
22: 2 why have you forsaken me, *f* from my prayer,
22:12 Be not *f* from me, for I am in distress;
22:20 But you, O LORD, be not *f* from me;
35:22 Lord, be not *f* from me!
38:22 my God, be not *f* from me!
43: 2 Why do you keep me so *f* away?
55: 8 *F* away I would flee;
71:12 O God, be not *f* from me;
80:12 to the Sea, its shoots as *f* as the River.
97: 9 all the earth, exalted *f* above all gods.
101: 4 A crooked heart shall be *f* from me;
103:12 *f* as the east is from the west, so far has
109:17 may it be *f* from him.
119:150 persecutors who are *f* from your law.
Prv 4:24 talk, deceitful speech put *f* from you.
4:27 nor to left, keep your foot *f* from evil.
5: 8 Keep your way *f* from her,
15:29 The LORD is *f* from the wicked,
20: 5 heart is like water *f* below the surface,
22:15 rod of discipline will drive it *f* from him.
25:25 from thirst is good news from a *f* country.
27: 8 is *f* from its nest is a man who is far
27:10 near at hand than a brother *f* away.
30: 8 Put falsehood and lying *f* from me,
31:10 worthy wife, her value is *f* beyond pearls.
Eccl 3: 5 embrace, and a time to be *f* from embraces.
Wis 12:24 they went *f* astray in the paths of error,
13: 3 *f* more excellent is the Lord than these;
13: 9 For if they so *f* succeeded in knowledge
14:17 Men who lived so *f* away that they could
Sir 9:13 Keep *f* from the man who has power to kill,
13:10 keep not too *f* away lest you be forgotten.
15: 8 *F* from the impious is she,
23:11 the scourge will never be *f* from his house.
27:20 Follow him not, for he is *f* away,
30:23 courage, drive resentment *f* away from you;
33:22 *F* better that your children plead with
Is 6:12 Until the LORD removes men *f* away,
15: 4 cry out, they are heard as *f* as Jahaz.
15: 8 As *f* as Eglaim the wailing,
16: 8 *f* as Jazer and scattered over the desert,
17:13 rebuke them, and they shall flee *f* away;
18: 2 bronzed, To a people dreaded near and *f*,
18: 7 bronzed, from a people dreaded near and *f*,
26:15 and extended *f* all the borders of the land.
29:13 alone, though their hearts are *f* from me,
33:13 Hear, you who are *f* off,
46:12 you who seem *f* from the victory of justice:
46:13 am bringing on my justice, it is not *f* off,
49:19 those who swallowed you up will be *f* away.
54:14 established, *f* from the fear of oppression,
57: 9 While you sent your ambassadors *f* away,
57:19 Peace, peace to the *f* and the near,
59: 9 is *f* from us and justice does not reach us.
59:11 for salvation, and it is *f* from us.
59:14 is repelled, and justice stands *f* off;
Jer 2:23 A frenzied she-camel, coursing near and *f*,
8:19 of my people, *f* and wide in the land!
12: 2 lips, but *f* from their inmost thoughts.
23:23 only, says the LORD, and not a God *f* off?
25:26 all the kings of the north, near and *f*,
27:10 in order to drive you *f* from your land,
31:40 as *f* as the corner of the Horse Gate at
48:24 on all the cities of Moab, *f* and near.
48:32 to the sea, as *f* as Jazer they stretched.
48:34 Heshbon and Elealeh is heard as *f* as Jahaz;
48:47 Thus *f* the judgment on Moab.
Lam 1:16 *F* from me are all who could console me,
Bar 3:21 their offspring were *f* from the way to her.
6:72 he shall be *f* from disgrace!
Ez 6:12 He that is *f* off shall die of pestilence,
10: 5 could be heard as *f* as the outer court;
11:15 say, "They are *f* away from the LORD;
11:16 Though I have removed them *f* among the
22: 5 Those near you and those *f* off shall
42: 7 On the *f* side there was a wall running
43: 9 From now on they shall put *f* from me their
47:18 down to the eastern sea as *f* as Tamar.
Dn 9: 7 of Jerusalem, and all Israel, near and *f*,
13:51 *f* from one another that I may examine them."
Jl 2:20 the northerner I will remove *f* from you,
4: 6 removing them *f* from their own country!
4: 8 sell them to the Sabeans, a nation *f* off.
Am 7:17 Israel shall be exiled *f* from its land.
Ob 1:20 the Canaanite land as *f* as Zarephath,
Mi 4: 7 and of those driven *f* off a strong nation;
Zep 3:10 and as *f* as the recesses of the North,
Mt 15: 8 lip service but their heart is *f* from me.
26:58 as *f* as the high priest's residence.
Mk 6:23 He went so *f* as to swear to her:
6:47 the boat was *f* out on the lake while he
7: 6 lip service but their heart is *f* from me.
12:34 him, "You are not *f* from the reign of God."
Lk 8:22 us cross over to the *f* side of the lake."
11:26 seven other spirits *f* worse than itself,
22:50 One of them went so *f* as to strike the
Jn 11:18 The village was not *f* from Jerusalem
14:12 the works I do, and greater *f* than these.
18:15 Jesus as *f* as the high priests' courtyard,
21: 8 Actually they were not *f* from land
Acts 2:39 still *f* off whom the Lord our God calls."
9:24 They went so *f* as to keep close watch on
11:19 because of Stephen went as *f* as Phoenicia,
13: 6 over the whole island as *f* as Paphos,
16:24 so *f* as to chain their feet to a stake.
17:15 was taken as *f* as Athens by his escort,
17:27 he is not really *f* from any one of us.
22:21 I mean to send you *f* from here,
23:31 escorted him that night as *f* as Antipatris.
28:15 came out as *f* as the Forum of Appius
Rom 5:11 we go so *f* as to make God our boast
5:20 increase of sin, grace has *f* surpassed it,
13:12 The night is *f* spent; the day draws near.
1Cor 14:20 Be like children as *f* as evil is concerned,
2Cor 3: 9 greater by *f* is the glory of the ministry
3:11 greater by *f* is the glory that endures.
10:14 get as *f* as you with the gospel of Christ.
11:23 with *f* worse beatings and frequent brushes
Gal 1:14 *f* beyond most of my contemporaries,
4:10 You even go so *f* as to keep the ceremonial
4:27 *f* more than of her who has a husband!"
Eph 2:13 who once were *f* off have been brought near
2:17 good news of peace to you who were *f* off,
Phil 1:23 Christ, for that is the *f* better thing;
2Tm 2:18 who have gone *f* wide of the truth in
3: 9 But they will not get very *f*;
Ti 3: 3 disobedient, and *f* from true faith;
Heb 1: 4 as *f* superior to the angels as the name he
2Pt 2: 1 They will go so *f* as to deny the Master
Rv 12:14 in the desert, where, *f* from the serpent,

FAR-FLUNG (1)

Ez 28:16 found in you, the result of your *f* trade;

FAR-OFF (7)

Dt 29:21 foreigners who will come here from *f* lands,
Is 5:26 He will give a signal to a *f* nation,
13: 5 They come from a *f* country,
41: 9 the earth and summoned from its *f* places,
Jer 6:20 from Sheba, or sweet cane from *f* lands?
30:10 Behold, I will deliver you from the *f* land,
46:27 Behold, I will deliver you from the *f* land,

FAR-REACHING (1)

Eccl 7:24 What exists is *f*; it is deep, very deep:

FARAWAY (1)

Lk 19:12 went to a *f* country to become its king,

FARE (10)

Prv 10: 9 but he whose ways are crooked will *f* badly.
13:20 but the companion of fools will *f* badly.
24:25 those who convict the evildoer will *f* well,
Sir 3:25 A stubborn man will *f* badly in the end,
29:22 Better a poor man's *f* under the shadow of
Is 55: 2 eat well, you shall delight in rich *f*.
Hos 4: 9 priests shall *f* no better than the people:
Jon 1: 3 a ship going to Tarshish, paid the *f*,
Hg 2:16 in the temple of the LORD, how did you *f*?
Lk 21:23 at the breast will *f* badly in those days!

FARED (4)

Gn 30:29 how well your livestock *f* under my care;
Ru 3:16 who asked, "How have you *f* my daughter?"
Ps(s) 106:32 Meribah, and Moses *f* ill on their account,
Dn 6:29 So Daniel *f* well during the reign of

FARES (1)

Dt 15:16 your household, since he *f* well with you,

FAREWELL (17)

Gn 26:31 Then Isaac bade them *f*,
32:30 With that, he bade him *f*.
47:10 Pharaoh *f* and withdrew from his presence.
49:28 as he bade them *f* and gave to each of them
Ex 18:27 Then Moses bade *f* to his father-in-law,
Jos 2:21 as you say," she replied, and bade them *f*.
2Sm 3:21 So David bade Abner *f*,
1Kgs 8:66 bade the king *f* and went to their homes,
Tb 10:11 Bidding them *f*, he let them go.
2Mc 3:35 who had spared his life, he bade Onias *f*,
11:21 your envoys to confer with you. *F.*"
11:33 *F.*" In the year one hundred
11:38 *F.*" In the year one hundred
Bar 4:19 *F*, my children, farewell:
Jn 14:27 'Peace' is my *f* to you,
Acts 15:29 avoid these things. *F.*' "

FARING (1)

Est 2:11 Esther was *f* and what was to become of her.

FARM (7)

Gn 47:18 disposal except our bodies and our *f* land.
47:20 all the *f* land of Egypt for Pharaoh,
Lv 25:31 as belonging to the surrounding *f* land;
1Chr 27:26 the *f* workers who tilled the soil was Ezri,
Mt 22: 5 and went their way, one to his *f*,
Lk 15:15 sent him to his *f* to take care of the pigs.
Acts 4:37 He sold a *f* that he owned and made a

FARMER (8)

Wis 17:17 For whether one was a *f*,
Jer 51:23 with you I shatter the *f* and his team,
Mt 13: 4 "One day a *f* went out sowing.
13:37 "The *f* sowing good seed is the Son of Man;
Mk 4: 3 A *f* went out sowing.
Lk 8: 5 "A *f* went out to sow some seed.
2Tm 2: 6 The hardworking *f* is the one who should
Jas 5: 7 *f* awaits the precious yield of the soil.

FARMERS (12)

2Kgs 25:12 guard, left behind as vinedressers and *f*.
Is 61: 5 shall be your *f* and vinedressers.
Jer 14: 4 is no rain in the land the *f* are ashamed,
31:24 cities, the *f* and those who lead the flock,
52:16 guard, left behind as vinedressers and *f*.
Am 5:16 They shall summon the *f* to wail and
Mt 21:33 it out to tenant *f* and went on a journey.
Mk 12: 1 it to tenant *f* and went on a journey.
Lk 20: 9 planted a vineyard, leased it to tenant *f*,
20:10 he sent a servant to the tenant *f* to receive
20:14 "But when the tenant *f* saw the son,
20:16 tenant *f* and give the vineyard to others."

FARMHANDS (2)

2Sm 14:30 Joab's *f* came to him with torn garments
Jas 5: 4 from the *f* who harvested your fields.

FARMING (2)

2Mc 12: 1 the king, and the Jews went about their *f*.
Sir 7:15 Hate not laborious tasks, nor *f*,

FARMS (2)

Jer 39:10 given at the same time vineyards and *f*.
Lk 9:12 into the villages and *f* in the neighborhood

FAROFF (1)

Jos 9: 9 "Your servants have come from a *f* land,

FARSIGHTED (2)

Mt 24:45 *f* servant whom the master has put in
Lk 12:42 *f* steward whom the master will set over

FARTHER (12)

Gn 18:22 While the two men walked on *f* toward Sodom,
Ex 20:18 a position much *f* away and said to Moses,
1Sm 10: 3 *F* on, when you arrive at the terebinth
20:37 called after him, "The arrow is *f* on!"
2Sm 2:28 pursuing Israel no *f* and fighting no more.
Jb 38:11 Thus far shall you come but no *f*,
Wis 11:10 you tested, admonishing them as a *f*;
Hos 11: 2 I called them, the *f* they went from me,
Mt 4:21 *f* and caught sight of two other brothers,
Mk 1:19 Proceeding a little *f* along,
4:35 them, "Let us cross over to the *f* shore."
Lk 24:28 going, and he acted as if he were going *f*.

FARTHEST (9)

Dt 30: 4 been driven to the *f* corner of the world,
Neh 1: 9 been driven to the *f* corner of the world,
Jb 28: 3 to the *f* confines he penetrates.
Ps(s) 65: 9 *f* east and west you make resound with joy.
139: 9 if I settle at the *f* limits of the sea,
Is 7:18 the fly that is in the *f* streams of Egypt,
Mt 12:42 She came from the *f* corner of the earth to
Mk 13:27 winds, from the *f* bounds of earth and sky.
Lk 11:31 She came from the *f* corner of the world to

FASHION (10)

Dt 4:23 you *f* for yourselves against his command
Jb 31:15 Did not the same One *f* us before our birth?
Ps(s) 35:20 in the land they *f* treacherous speech.
Sir 44: 2 Subduers of the land in kingly *f*,
Is 29:14 this people in surprising and wondrous *f*:
Mt 13: 3 at length in parables, speaking in this *f*:
Lk 18:11 with head unbowed prayed in this *f*:
Jn 7:43 *f* the crowd was sharply divided over him.
9:22 *f* because they were afraid of the Jews,
Acts 4: 7 them and began the interrogation in this *f*:

FASHIONABLY (1)

Jas 2: 2 come into your assembly a man *f* dressed,

FASHIONED (18)

Dt 4:28 There you shall serve gods *f* by the hands
Jb 10: 8 Your hands have formed me and *f* me;
10: 9 Oh, remember that you *f* me from clay!
Ps(s) 8: 3 you have *f* praise because of your foes,

FASHIONED (cont.)

33:15 on the earth, He who *f* the heart of each,
74:16 you *f* the moon and the sun.
119:73 Your hands have made me and *f* me;
139:15 when I was *f* in the depths of the earth.
Wis 1:14 he *f* all things that they might have being;
11:17 had *f* the universe from formless matter,
11:24 for what you hated, you would not have *f*.
13: 3 for the original source of beauty *f* them.
15:11 Because he knew not the one who *f* him,
15:16 one whose spirit has been lent him *f* them.
Is 54:17 No weapon *f* against you shall prevail;
Ez 21:20 sword for slaughter, *F* to flash lightning,
Acts 7:41 It was then that they *f* the calf and
2Cor 5: 5 God has *f* us for this very thing and has

FASHIONING (5)

Ex 32: 4 and *f* this gold with a graving tool,
Dt 4:16 by *f* an idol to represent any figure,
4:25 you then degrade yourselves by *f* an idol
Wis 15:16 no man succeeds in *f* a god like himself;
Jer 18:11 I am *f* evil against you and making a plan.

FASHIONS (4)

Eccl 11: 5 *f* the human frame in the mother's womb,
Sir 38:27 laboring night and day, *F* carved seals,
50:22 womb, and *f* them according to his will!
Is 44:12 The smith *f* an iron image,

FAST (83)

Dt 10:20 hold *f* to him and swear by his name.
11:22 his ways exactly, and holding *f* to him,
13: 5 serving him and holding *f* to him alone.
30:20 heeding his voice, and holding *f* to him.
2Sm 12:16 He kept a *f*, retiring for the night
12:23 Why should I *f*?
18: 9 terebinth, his hair caught *f* in the tree.
23:10 and became cramped, holding *f* to the sword.
1Kgs 21: 9 *f* and set Naboth at the head of the people.
21:12 They proclaimed a *f* and placed Naboth at
2Kgs 6:32 close the door and hold it *f* against him.
2Chr 20: 3 He proclaimed a *f* for all Judah
Ezr 8:21 Then I proclaimed a *f*.
Jdt 4:13 *f* of many days' duration throughout Judea,
Est 4:16 *f* on my behalf, all of you,
4:16 I and my maids will also *f* in the same way.
Jb 2: 3 He still holds *f* to his innocence although
36: 8 fetters and held *f* by bonds of affliction,
41: 9 that they hold *f* and cannot be parted.
Ps(s) 16: 5 and my cup, you it is who hold *f* my lot.
63: 9 My soul clings *f* to you;
139:10 guide me, and your right hand hold me *f*.
Prv 3:18 grasp her, and he is happy who holds her *f*.
4: 4 "Let your heart hold *f* my words:
4:13 Hold *f* to instruction,
5:22 meshes of his own sin he will be held *f*;
8:28 he fixed *f* the foundations of the earth;
Sir 4:13 He who holds her *f* inherits glory;
11:20 My son, hold *f* to your duty,
22:23 Make *f* friends with a man while he is poor;
27: 3 earnestly hold *f* to the fear of the LORD,
48:22 was right and held *f* to the paths of David,
Is 56: 4 what pleases me and hold *f* to my covenant,
58: 3 "Why do we *f*, and you do not see it?
58: 3 your *f* day you carry out your own pursuits,
58: 4 your *f* ends in quarreling and fighting,
58: 4 *f* so as to make your voice heard on high!
58: 5 Do you call this a *f*,
Jer 14:12 If they *f*, I will not listen
36: 6 Do you go on the *f* day and read publicly
36: 9 king of Judah a *f* to placate the LORD was
50:33 hold them *f* and refuse to let them go.
Jl 1:14 Proclaim a *f*, call an assembly;
2:15 proclaim a *f*, call an assembly; Gather
Jon 1: 5 hold of the ship, and lay there *f* asleep.
3: 5 they proclaimed a *f* and all of them,
Zec 8:19 The *f* days of the fourth,
Mt 6:16 "When you *f*, you are not to look glum
6:17 When you *f*, see to it that you groom
9:14 is it that while we and the Pharisees *f*,
9:15 the groom is taken away, then they will *f*.
Mk 2:18 and the Pharisees were accustomed to *f*.
2:18 of the Pharisees *f* while yours do not?"
2:19 *f* as long as the groom is still among them?
2:19 the groom stays with them, they cannot *f*.
2:20 on that day they will *f*.
Lk 5:33 disciples *f* frequently and offer prayers;
5:34 groom *f* while the groom is still with them?
5:35 midst, they will surely *f* in those days."
18:12 I *f* twice a week.
Jn 21:18 you *f* and carry you off against your will."
Acts 13:43 urged them to hold *f* to the grace of God.
27: 9 The autumn *f* was over,
27:41 The bow stuck *f* and could not be budged,
Rom 9:11 in order that God's decree might stand *f*
1Cor 11: 2 always remember me and are holding *f*
15: 2 you hold *f* to it as I preached it to you.
Eph 6:14 Stand *f*, with the truth as the belt
Phil 2:16 sky while holding *f* to the word of life.
Col 1:11 with the strength needed to stand *f*.
1:23 But you must hold *f* to faith,
2Thes 2:15 *f* to the traditions you received from us,
1Tm 1:19 and hold *f* to faith and a good conscience.
3: 9 They must hold *f* to the divinely revealed
Ti 1: 9 he must hold *f* to the authentic message,
Heb 3: 6 It is we who are that house if we hold *f*
4:14 let us hold *f* to our profession of faith.
12:28 kingdom should hold *f* to God's grace,
Rv 2:13 and I know you hold *f* to my name and have
2:25 case, hold *f* to what you have until I come.
3: 8 *f* to my word and have not denied my name.
3:10 Because you have kept my plea to stand *f*,
3:11 Hold *f* to what you have lest someone rob

FASTED (16)

1Sm 7: 6 before the LORD, and they *f* that day,
31:13 tree in Jabesh, and *f* for seven days.
2Sm 1:12 They mourned and wept and *f* until evening
12:21 was living, you *f* and wept and kept vigil;
12:22 "While the child was living, I *f* and wept,
1Kgs 21:27 He *f*, slept in the sackcloth,
1Chr 10:12 under the oak of Jabesh, and *f* seven days.
Ezr 8:23 So we *f*, and prayed to our God
Neh 1: 4 I *f* and prayed before the God in heaven.
Jdt 8: 6 She *f* all the days of her widowhood,
1Mc 3:47 That day they *f* and wore sackcloth;
Bar 1: 5 They wept and *f* and prayed before the Lord,
Zec 7: 5 When you *f* and mourned in the fifth and in
7: 5 years, was it really for me that you *f*?
Mt 4: 2 He *f* forty days and forty nights,
Acts 13: 3 Then, after they had *f* and prayed,

FASTEN (8)

Ex 25:12 and *f* them on the four supports of the ark,
25:26 gold for it and *f* them at the four corners,
26:17 that shall serve to *f* the boards in line.
28:14 and *f* the cordlike chains to the filigree
28:23 make two rings of gold for it and *f* them
28:27 Then make two more rings of gold and *f*
Jgs 16:13 hair into the web and *f* them with the pin,
Is 49:18 like a bride you shall *f* them on you.

FASTENED (23)

Gn 24:22 half a shekel, which he *f* on her nose,
Ex 28:24 The gold cords are then to be *f* to the two
28:25 cords being *f* in front to the two filigree
37: 8 the propitiatory, one cherub *f* at one end,
37:13 Four rings of gold were cast for it and *f*,
39:16 *f* to the two upper ends of the breastpiece.
39:17 The two gold chains were then *f* to the two
39:18 *f* in front to the two filigree rosettes,
39:20 Two more gold rings were made and *f* to the
Jgs 16:14 into the web, and *f* them in with the pin.
1Kgs 6: 6 not be *f* into the walls of the temple.
2Chr 9:18 a footstool of gold was *f* to it,
Jdt 16: 8 with a fillet she *f* her tresses,
1Mc 6:37 each elephant, and *f* to it by a harness,
Jb 16:15 I have *f* sackcloth over my skin,
38:10 limits for it and *f* the bar of its door,
Prv 6:21 Keep them *f* over your heart always,
Jer 10: 4 With nails and hammers they are *f*,
Mk 9:42 with a great millstone *f* around his neck.
Lk 12:35 "Let your belts be *f* around your waists
Jn 21:18 *f* your belt and went about as you pleased;
Acts 12: 6 between two soldiers, *f* with double chains,
28: 3 from the heat, *f* itself on his hand.

FASTENING (6)

Ex 25:19 *f* them so that one cherub springs direct
29: 5 *f* the embroidered belt of the ephod around
36:22 Each board had two arms, *f* them in line.
Lv 8: 7 belt of the ephod, *f* it around him.
Nm 15:38 *f* each corner tassel with a violet cord.
Wis 13:15 and puts it on the wall, *f* it with a nail.

FASTENS (2)

Sir 14:24 and *f* his tent pegs next to her walls;
Is 41: 7 good, and he *f* it with nails to steady it.

FASTER (1)

2Mc 9: 7 the Jews, he gave orders to drive even *f*.

FASTIDIOUS (1)

Dt 28:54 The most refined and *f* man among you will

FASTING (20)

Jgs 20:26 where they wept and remained *f* before the
Neh 9: 1 gathered together *f* and in sackcloth,
Tb 12: 8 Prayer and *f* are good,
Est 4: 3 the Jews went into deep mourning, with *f*,
9:31 their race the duty of *f* and supplication.
1Mc 3:17 Besides, we are weak today from *f*."
2Mc 13:12 and *f* and prostrations for three days,
Ps(s) 35:13 *f* and poured forth prayers within my bosom.
69:11 I humbled myself with *f*,
109:24 My knees totter from my *f*,
Is 58: 5 Is this the manner of *f* I wish,
58: 6 This, rather, is the *f* that I wish:
Dn 9: 3 God, pleading in earnest prayer, with *f*,
Jl 2:12 to me with your whole heart, with *f*,
Mt 6:16 faces so that others may see they are *f*.
6:18 you are *f* but your Father who is hidden;
17:21 kind does not leave but by prayer and *f*."
Lk 2:37 worshiping day and night in *f* and prayer.
Acts 13: 2 in the liturgy of the Lord and were *f*,
14:23 presbyters and, with prayer and *f*,

FASTINGS (2)

2Cor 6: 5 with hard work, sleepless nights, and *f*;
11:27 in hunger and thirst and frequent *f*;

FASTNESS (1)

Is 33:16 his stronghold shall be the rocky *f*,

FASTNESSES (2)

Ez 33:27 in *f* and in caves shall die by the plague.
Mi 7:17 They shall come quaking from their *f*,

FASTS (1)

Sir 34:26 So with a man who *f* for his sins,

FAT (88)

Gn 41: 2 the Nile came seven cows, handsome and *f*;
41: 4 cows ate up the seven handsome, *f* cows.
41: 5 He saw seven ears of grain, *f* and healthy,
41: 7 seven thin ears swallowed up the seven *f*,
41:18 Nile came seven cows, *f* and well-formed;
41:20 ugly cows ate up the first seven *f* cows.
41:22 I saw seven ears of grain, *f* and healthy,
45:18 where you will live off the *f* of the land.'
Ex 23:18 nor shall the *f* of my feast be kept
29:13 All the *f* that covers its inner organs,
29:13 together with the *f* that is on them,
29:22 "Now from this ram you shall take its *f*:
29:22 tail, the *f* that covers its inner organs,
29:22 its two kidneys with the *f* that is on them,
Lv 3: 3 organs, and all the *f* that adheres to them,
3: 4 kidneys, with the *f* on them near the loins,
3: 9 shall present the *f* of the peace offering:
3: 9 organs, and all the *f* that adheres to them,
3:10 kidneys, with the *f* on them near the loins,
3:14 organs, and all the *f* that adheres to them,
3:15 kidneys, with the *f* on them near the loins,
3:16 All the *f* belongs to the LORD.
3:17 shall not partake of any *f* or any blood."
4: 8 bullock he shall remove all the *f*:
4: 8 organs, and all the *f* that adheres to them,
4: 9 kidneys, with the *f* on them near the loins,
4:19 All of its *f* he shall take from it and
4:26 *f* he shall burn on the altar like the fat
4:31 All the *f* shall be removed, just as the fat
4:35 the fat shall be removed, just as the *f*
6: 5 and burn the *f* of the peace offerings.
7: 3 *f* shall be taken from it and offered up:
7: 4 kidneys with the *f* on them near the loins,
7:23 not eat the *f* of any ox or sheep or goat.
7:24 Although the *f* of an animal that has died
7:25 If anyone eats the *f* of an animal from
7:30 The *f* is to be brought in,
7:31 The priest shall burn the *f* on the altar,
7:33 blood and *f* of the peace offering
8:16 all the *f* that was over the inner organs,
8:16 the liver and the two kidneys with their *f*,
8:25 He then took the *f*:
8:25 tail and all the *f* over the inner organs,
8:25 liver and the two kidneys with their *f*,
8:26 top of the portions of *f* and the right leg.
9:10 He then burned on the altar the *f*,
9:19 portions of *f* from the ox and from the ram,
9:19 two kidneys, with the *f* that is on them,
9:24 and the remnants of the *f* on the altar.
16:25 the *f* of the sin offering on the altar.
17: 6 the *f* for an odor pleasing to the LORD.
Nm 18:17 you must splash on the altar and their *f*
Dt 31:20 they have eaten their fill and grown *f*,
32:14 sheep, with the *f* of its lambs and rams;
32:15 grew *f* and frisky; you became fat and gross
32:38 Let those who ate the *f* of your sacrifices
Jgs 3:17 to Eglon, king of Moab, who was very *f*.
3:22 and the *f* closed over the blade because he
1Sm 2:15 In fact, even before the *f* was burned,
2:16 the *f* be burned first as is the custom,
15: 9 Agag and the best of the *f* sheep and oxen,
15:22 and submission than the *f* of rams.
1Kgs 8:64 and the *f* of the peace offerings,
2Chr 7: 7 and the *f* of the peace offerings,
7: 7 holocausts, the cereal offerings and the *f*.
29:35 along with the *f* of the peace offerings
Jdt 16:16 and the *f* of all holocausts but little in
Jb 15:27 his crassness, padding his loins with *f*,
Ps(s) 119:70 Their heart has become gross and *f*;
Sir 47: 2 Like the choice *f* of the sacred offerings,
Is 1:11 of whole-burnt rams and *f* of fatlings;
10:16 hosts, will send among his *f* ones leanness,
34: 6 a sword filled with blood, greasy with *f*,
34: 6 and goats, with the *f* of rams' kidneys;
34: 7 with blood, and their earth greasy with *f*.
43:24 nor fill me with the *f* of your sacrifices;
Jer 5:28 they grow powerful and rich, *f* and sleek.
Ez 34:20 I judge between the *f* and the lean sheep.

39:19 you shall eat *f* until you are filled and
44: 7 to profane it when you offered me food, *f*,
44:15 stand before me to offer me *f* and blood,
Dn 3:40 rams and bullocks, or thousands of *f* lambs,
14:27 Then Daniel took some pitch, *f*,
Zec 11:16 of the *f* ones and tear off their hoofs!

FATAL (2)

Ezr 4:15 which has proved *f* to kings and provinces,
Eccl 9:12 his own time than fish taken in the *f* net,

FATALLY (1)

2Sm 2:31 But David's servants had *f* wounded three

FATE (16)

Ex 1:14 the whole cruel *f* of slaves.
Nm 16:29 suffering the *f* common to all mankind,
17: 5 lest he meet the *f* of Korah and his band.
1Sm 30: 6 over the *f* of their sons and daughters.
Jb 18:20 who come after shall be appalled at his *f*;
Ps(s) 81:16 me, but their *f* would endure forever,
Prv 1:19 This is the *f* of everyone greedy of loot:
Sir 38:22 Remember that his *f* will also be yours;
46:20 he made known to the king his *f*,
Is 50:11 This is your *f* from my hand:
Jer 40: 3 obey his voice, this *f* has befallen you.
Lam 2:14 not lay bare your guilt, to avert your *f*;
Bar 2:33 because they shall remember the *f* of their
Mt 23:36 will be the *f* of the present generation.
Lk 10:12 on that day the *f* of Sodom will be less
20:15 What *f* do you suppose the owner of the

FATED (1)

2Mc 13: 7 the transgressor of the law, *f* to die;

FATEFUL (1)

Gn 30: 8 "I engaged in a *f* struggle with my sister,

FATHER (1123)

Gn 2:24 his *f* and mother and clings to his wife,
4:18 father of Mehujael; Mehujael became the *f*
4:18 and Methusael became the *f* of Lamech.
5: 6 five years old, he became the *f* of Enosh.
5: 9 ninety years old, he became the *f* of Kenan.
5:12 years old, he became the *f* of Mahalalel.
5:15 years old, he became the *f* of Jared.
5:18 years old, he became the *f* of Enoch.
5:21 years old, he became the *f* of Methuselah.
5:25 years old, he became the *f* of Lamech.
5:32 hundred years old, he became the *f* of Shem,
9:18 (Ham was the *f* of Canaan.)
9:22 Ham, the *f* of Canaan,
10: 8 Cush became the *f* of Nimrod,
10:13 Mizraim became the *f* of the Ludim,
10:15 Canaan became the *f* of Sidon,
10:24 father of Shelah, and Shelah became the *f*
10:26 Joktan became the *f* of Almodad,
11:10 years old, he became the *f* of Arpachshad,
11:12 years old, he became the *f* of Shelah.
11:14 thirty years old, he became the *f* of Eber.
11:16 years old, he became the *f* of Peleg.
11:18 thirty years old, he became the *f* of Reu.
11:20 years old, he became the *f* of Serug.
11:22 thirty years old, he became the *f* of Nahor.
11:24 years old, he became the *f* of Terah.
11:26 years old, he became the *f* of Abram,
11:27 Terah became the *f* of Abram,
11:27 and Haran, and Haran became the *f* of Lot.
11:28 Haran died before his *f* Terah,
11:29 of Haran, the *f* of Milcah and Iscah.
17: 4 are to become the *f* of a host of nations.
17: 5 I am making you the *f* of a host of nations.
17:20 He shall become the *f* of twelve chieftains,
19:31 "Our *f* is getting old,
19:32 ply our *f* with wine and then lie with him,
19:32 him, that we may have offspring by our *f*."
19:33 So that night they plied their *f* with wine,
19:33 the older one went in and lay with her *f*;
19:34 "Last night it was I who lay with my *f*.
19:34 that we may both have offspring by our *f*."
19:35 night, too, they plied their *f* with wine,
19:36 Lot's daughters became pregnant by their *f*.
19:37 whom she named Moab, saying, "From my *f*."
22: 7 on together, Isaac spoke to his *f* Abraham.
22: 7 *F*!" he said. "Yes, son,"
22:21 his brother Buz, Kemuel (the *f* of Aram),
22:23 Bethuel became the *f* of Rebekah.
25: 3 Jokshan became the *f* of Sheba and Dedan.
26: 3 of the oath that I swore to your *f* Abraham.
26:15 had dug back in the days of his *f* Abraham.)
26:18 dug back in the days of his *f* Abraham
26:18 the same names that his *f* had given them.)
26:24 "I am the God of your *f* Abraham.
27: 1 "Yes, *f*!" he replied
27: 5 the country to hunt some game for his *f*,
27: 6 I overheard your *f* tell your brother Esau,
27: 9 will prepare an appetizing dish for your *f*,
27:10 Then bring it to your *f* to eat,
27:12 Suppose my *f* feels me?
27:14 an appetizing dish, such as his *f* liked.
27:18 Bringing them to his father, Jacob said, *F*!"
27:19 Jacob answered his *f*:
27:22 So Jacob moved up closer to his *f*.
27:26 Finally his *f* Isaac said to him,
27:30 Jacob had scarcely left his *f*,
27:31 it to his father, he said, "Please, *f*,
27:32 his *f* Isaac asked him.
27:34 *F*, bless me too!"
27:38 *f*, "Have you only that one blessing, father?
27:41 of the blessing his *f* had given him.
27:41 "When the time of mourning for my *f* comes,
28: 2 to the home of your mother's *f* Bethuel,
28: 7 his *f* and mother and gone to Paddan-aram.
28: 8 the Canaanite women were to his *f* Isaac,
29:12 Rebekah's son, and she ran to tell her *f*.
31: 1 taken everything that belonged to our *f*,
31: 5 but the God of my *f* has been with me.
31: 6 what effort I put into serving your *f*;
31: 7 yet your *f* cheated me and changed my wages
31: 8 Whenever your *f* said,
31:16 *f* really belongs to us and our children.
31:18 to go to his *f* Isaac in the land of Canaan.
31:29 last night the God of your *f* said to me,
31:35 finding them, Rachel said to her *f*,
32:10 of my *f* Abraham and God of my father Isaac!
34: 4 Shechem also asked his *f* Hamor,
34: 6 Now Hamor, the *f* of Shechem,
34:11 too, appealed to Dinah's *f* and brothers:
34:13 to Shechem and his *f* Hamor with guile,
35:18 his *f*, however, named him Benjamin.
35:27 Jacob went home to his *f* Isaac at Mamre,
36:24 he was pasturing the asses of his *f* Zibeon.)
36:43 [Esau was the *f* of the Edomites.]
37: 1 in the land where his *f* had stayed,
37: 2 he brought his *f* bad reports about them.
37: 4 their *f* loved him best of all his sons,
37:10 told it to his *f*, his father reproved him.
37:11 against him but his *f* pondered the matter.
37:22 from their hands and restore him to his *f*.
37:32 someone to bring the long tunic to their *f*,
37:35 Thus did his *f* lament him.
41:50 set in, Joseph became the *f* of two sons,
42:13 the youngest one is at present with our *f*,
42:29 to their *f* Jacob in the land of Canaan,
42:32 twelve of us brothers, sons of the same *f*;
42:32 present with our *f* in the land of Canaan.'
42:35 moneybags, they and their *f* were dismayed.
42:36 Their *f* Jacob said to them:
42:37 Then Reuben told his *f*:
43: 2 brought from Egypt, their *f* said to them,
43: 7 'Is your *f* still living?
43: 8 Then Judah urged his *f* Israel:
43:11 Their *f* Israel then told them:
43:23 Your God and the God of your *f* must have
43:27 he asked them, "And how is your aged *f*,
43:28 our *f* is thriving and still in good health,"
44:17 you may go back safe and sound to your *f*."
44:19 My lord asked your servants, 'Have you a *f*,
44:20 So we said to my lord, 'We have an aged *f*,
44:20 mother who is left, his *f* dotes on him.'
44:22 cannot leave his father; his *f* would die
44:24 When we returned to your servant our *f*,
44:25 our *f* told us to come back and buy some
44:27 Then your servant our *f* said to us,
44:30 us when I go back to your servant my *f*,
44:31 of our *f* down to the nether world in grief.
44:32 the boy from his *f* by going surety for him,
44:32 'If I fail to bring him back to you, *f*,
44:34 back to my *f* if the boy were not with me?
44:34 see the anguish that would overcome my *f*."
45: 3 "Is my *f* still in good health?"
45: 8 and he has made of me a *f* to Pharaoh,
45: 9 "Hurry back, then, to my *f* and tell him:
45:13 Tell my *f* all about my high position in
45:13 But hurry and bring my *f* down here."
45:18 There get your *f* and your families,
45:19 to transport your *f* on your way back here.
45:23 what he sent to his *f* was ten jackasses
45:25 way to their *f* Jacob in the land of Canaan.
45:27 the spirit of their *f* Jacob revived.
46: 1 sacrifices to the God of his *f* Isaac.
46: 3 "I am God, the God of your *f*.
46: 5 sons of Israel put their *f* and their wives
46:20 became the *f* of Manasseh and Ephraim,
46:29 and rode to meet his *f* Israel in Goshen.
47: 1 "My *f* and my brothers have come from the
47: 5 that your *f* and brothers have come to you,
47: 6 *f* and brothers in the pick of the land."
47: 7 his *f* Jacob and presented him to Pharaoh.
47:11 Joseph settled his *f* and brothers and gave
47:12 And Joseph sustained his *f* and brothers
47:31 But his *f* demanded, "Swear it to me!"
48: 1 Joseph was informed, "Your *f* is failing."
48: 9 are my sons," Joseph answered his *f*,
48: 9 "Bring them to me," said his *f*,
48:17 When Joseph saw that his *f* had laid his
48:18 saying, "That is not right, *f*;
48:19 But his *f* resisted.
49: 2 sons of Jacob, listen to Israel, your *f*.
49: 8 the sons of your *f* shall bow down to you.
49:25 the Rock of Israel, The God of your *f*,
49:28 and this is what their *f* said about them,
50: 2 physicians in his service to embalm his *f*.
50: 5 Since my *f*, at the point of death,
50: 5 up there to bury my *f* and then come back?"
50: 6 Pharaoh replied, "Go and bury your *f*,
50: 7 So Joseph left to bury his *f*;
50:10 observed seven days of mourning for his *f*.
50:14 had buried his *f* he returned to Egypt,
50:14 gone up with him for the burial of his *f*.
50:15 Now that their *f* was dead,
50:16 "Before your *f* died,
Ex 2:18 When they returned to their *f* Reuel,
3: 6 I am the God of your *f*,"
15: 2 the God of my *f*,
20:12 "Honor your *f* and your mother,
21:15 his *f* or mother shall be put to death.
21:17 his *f* or mother shall be put to death.
22:16 If her *f* refuses to give her to him,
40:15 As you have anointed their *f*,
Lv 16:32 to the priesthood in succession to his *f*.
18: 7 *f* by having intercourse with your mother.
18: 8 for that would be a disgrace to your *f*.
19: 3 Revere your mother and *f*,
20: 9 his *f* or mother shall be put to death;
20: 9 since he has cursed his *f* or mother,
20:11 his *f* by lying with his father's wife,
21: 2 his nearest relatives, his mother or *f*,
21: 9 and thereby dishonors her *f* also,
21:11 Not even for his *f* or mother may he thus
24:10 of the tribe of Dan) and an Egyptian *f*.
Nm 3: 4 under the direction of their *f* Aaron.
6: 7 Not even for his *f* or mother,
11:12 bosom, like a foster *f* carrying an infant,
12:14 "Suppose her *f* had spit in her face,
27: 3 "Our *f* died in the desert.
27:11 if his *f* had no brothers,
30: 5 if her *f* learns of her vow or the pledge
30: 6 it her *f* expresses to her his disapproval,
30: 6 her *f* has expressed to her his disapproval.
30:17 as well as between a *f* and his daughter
Dt 5:16 'Honor your *f* and your mother,
21:13 mourned her *f* and mother for a full month,
21:18 son who will not listen to his *f* or mother,
21:19 his *f* and mother shall have him
22:15 the *f* and the mother of the girl shall
22:16 the *f* of the girl shall say to the elders,
22:19 which they shall give to the girl's *f*,
22:29 shall pay the girl's *f* fifty silver shekels
26: 5 'My *f* was a wandering Aramean who went
27:16 be he who dishonors his *f* or his mother!'
32: 6 Is he not your *f* who created you?
32: 7 Ask your *f* and he will inform you,
33: 9 He said of his *f*,
Jos 2:13 that you are to spare my *f* and mother,
2:18 and gather your *f* and mother,
6:23 entered and brought out Rahab, with her *f*,
15:13 Kiriath-arba (Arba was the *f* of Anak),
15:18 she induced him to ask her *f* for some land.
17: 1 his eldest son, Machir, the *f* of Gilead,
21:11 Kiriath-arba (Arba was the *f* of Anak),
24: 2 down to Terah, *f* of Abraham and Nahor,
24: 3 But I brought your *f* Abraham from the
24:32 from the sons of Hamor, *f* of Shechem,
Jgs 1:14 she induced him to ask her *f* for some land.
8:32 of his *f* Joash in Ophrah of the Abiezrites.
9:17 as he deserved for my *f* fought for you
9:28 subject to the men of Hamor, *f* of Shechem?
9:56 to his *f* in killing his seventy brothers.
11:36 *F*," she replied, "you have made a vow
11:37 Then she said to her *f*, "Let me have this
11:39 of the two months she returned to her *f*,
14: 2 On his return he told his *f* and mother,
14: 3 His *f* and mother said to him,
14: 3 But Samson answered his *f*,
14: 4 Now his *f* and mother did not know that
14: 5 went down to Timnah with his *f* and mother.
14: 7 to his *f* or mother what he had done.
14: 9 When he came to his *f* and mother,
14:10 His *f* also went down to the woman,
14:16 have not told it even to my *f* or my mother,
15: 1 private," her *f* would not let him enter,
16:31 of his *f* Manoah between Zorah and Eshtaol.
17:10 "Be *f* and priest to me,
18:19 Come with us and be our *f* and priest.
19: 3 the girl's *f* joyfully made him welcome.
19: 4 He was detained by the girl's *f*,
19: 5 But the girl's *f* said to his son-in-law,
19: 6 Then the girl's *f* said to the husband,
19: 8 early to depart, but the girl's *f* said,
19: 9 and servant, the girl's *f* said to him,
Ru 2:11 you have left your *f* and your mother and
4:17 He was the father of Jesse, the *f* of David.
4:18 Perez was the *f* of Hezron, Hezron was
4:19 father of Ram, Ram was the *f* of Amminadab,
4:20 *f* of Nahshon, Nahshon was the father
4:21 Salmon was the *f* of Boaz, Boaz was the father
4:22 *f* of Jesse, and Jesse became the father
1Sm 1:25 the boy's *f* had sacrificed the young bull,
9: 3 Now the asses of Saul's *f*,
9: 5 lest my *f* forget about the asses and
10: 2 *f* is no longer worried about the asses,
10:12 that district added, "And who is their *f*?"
14: 1 But he did not inform his *f*.
14:27 that his *f* had put the people under oath,
14:28 *f* put the people under a strict oath,

FATHER (cont.)

14:29 "My *f* brings trouble to the land.
14:51 Kish, Saul's *f*, and Ner, Abner's *f*,
19: 2 "My *f* Saul is trying to kill you.
19: 3 my *f* in the countryside where you are,
19: 4 then spoke well of David to his *f* Saul,
20: 1 *f* hold against me that he seeks my life?"
20: 2 My *f* does nothing,
20: 2 then, should my *f* conceal this from me?
20: 3 "Your *f* is well aware that I am favored
20: 6 If it turns out that your *f* misses me,
20: 8 Why should you give me up to your *f*?"
20: 9 *f* is determined to inflict injury upon you,
20:10 tell me if your *f* gives you a harsh answer?"
20:12 sound out my *f* about this time tomorrow.
20:13 please my *f* to bring any injury upon you,
20:13 LORD be with you even as he was with my *f*.
20:32 But Jonathan asked his *f* Saul:
20:33 that his *f* was resolved to kill David.
20:34 since his *f* had railed against him.
22: 3 Moab, "Let my *f* and mother stay with you,
23:17 my *f* Saul shall not lay a hand to you.
23:17 Even my *f* Saul knows this."
24:11 he is the LORD's anointed and a *f* to me.'
2Sm 3: 8 a kindness to the house of your *f* Saul,
6:21 who preferred me to your *f* and his whole
7:14 I will be a *f* to him,
9: 7 to you for the sake of your *f* Jonathan.
10: 2 son of Nahash, as his *f* was kind to me."
10: 2 condolences to Hanun for the loss of his *f*.
10: 3 your *f* by sending men with condolences?
13: 5 When your *f* comes to visit you,
16:19 as I was in attendance upon your *f*,
16:21 odious you have made yourself to your *f*,
17: 8 know that your *f* and his men are warriors,
17: 8 since your *f* is skilled in warfare,
17:10 For all Israel knows that your *f* is a
19:38 own city by the tomb of his *f* and mother.
21:14 buried in the tomb of his *f* Kish at Zela
1Kgs 1: 6 Yet his *f* never rebuked him or asked why
2:12 was seated on the throne of his *f* David,
2:24 firmly on the throne of my *f* David
2:26 ark of the Lord GOD before my *f* David
2:26 shared in all the hardships my *f* endured."
2:32 the sword without my *f* David's knowledge:
2:44 heart the evil that you did to my *f* David.
3: 3 and obeyed the statutes of his *f* David;
3: 6 great favor to your servant, my *f* David,
3: 7 your servant, king to succeed my *f* David;
3:14 and commandments, as your *f* David did,
5:15 had been anointed king in place of his *f*,
5:17 "You know that my *f* David,
5:19 LORD predicted to my *f* David when he said:
6:12 you the promise I made to your *f* David.
7:14 his *f* had been from Tyre.
7:51 in the dedicated offerings of his *f* David,
8:15 own mouth made a promise to my *f* David
8:17 When my *f* David wished to build a temple
8:20 my *f* David and sit on the throne of Israel,
8:24 kept the promise you made to my *f* David,
8:25 the further promise you made to my *f* David,
8:26 this promise which you made to my *f* David,
9: 4 live in my presence as your *f* David lived,
9: 5 as I promised your *f* David when I said,
11: 4 God, as the heart of his *f* David had been.
11: 6 him unreservedly as his *f* David had done.
11:12 however, for the sake of your *f* David;
11:17 Egypt with some Edomite servants of his *f*.
11:33 and my decrees, as his *f* David did.
12: 4 "Your *f* put on us a heavy yoke.
12: 4 and the heavy yoke your *f* imposed on us,
12: 9 to lighten the yoke my *f* imposed on them?"
12:10 you to lighten the yoke your *f* put on them:
12:11 Whereas my *f* put a heavy yoke on you,
12:11 My *f* beat you with whips,
12:14 "My *f* put on you a heavy yoke,
12:14 My *f* beat you with whips,
13:11 *f* the words he had spoken to the king,
13:12 had spoken to the king, the *f* asked them,
15: 3 the sins his *f* had committed before him,
15:12 and removing all the idols his *f* had made.
15:19 as there was between your *f* and my father.
19:20 let me kiss my *f* and mother good-bye,
20:34 cities which my *f* took from your father,
20:34 in Damascus, as my *f* did in Samaria."
22:43 all the ways of his *f* Asa unswervingly,
22:47 who had remained in the reign of his *f* Asa.
22:53 sight of the LORD, behaving like his *f*,
22:54 the God of Israel, just as his *f* had done.
2Kgs 2:12 Elisha saw it happen he cried out, "My *f*!
2:12 my *f*!
3: 2 though not as much as his *f* and mother.
3: 2 the pillar of Baal, which his *f* had made,
3:13 your *f* and to the prophets of your mother."
4:18 to go out to his *f* among the reapers.
4:19 he complained to his *f*.
4:19 to his mother," the *f* said to a servant.
5:13 "My *f*," they said, "if the prophet
6:21 them, he asked, "Shall I kill them, my *f*?"
9:25 we were driving teams behind his *f* Ahab,
13:14 "My *f*, my *f*!" Israel's chariots
13:25 had taken in battle from his *f* Jehoahaz.
14: 3 since he did just as his *f* Joash had done.
14: 5 officials who had murdered the king, his *f*.
14:21 him king to succeed his *f* Amaziah.
15: 3 the LORD just as his *f* Amaziah had done.
15:34 the LORD, just as his *f* Uzziah had done.
21: 3 places which his *f* Hezekiah had destroyed.
21:20 of the LORD, as his *f* Manasseh had done.
21:21 followed exactly the path his *f* had trod,
21:21 and worshiping the idols his *f* had served.
23:30 and proclaimed him king to succeed his *f*.
23:34 of Josiah, king in place of his *f* Josiah;
1Chr 1:10 Cush became the *f* of Nimrod,
1:11 Mesraim became the *f* of the Ludim,
1:13 Canaan became the *f* of Sidon,
1:18 father of Shelah, and Shelah became the *f*
1:20 Joktan became the *f* of Almodad,
1:34 Abraham became the *f* of Isaac.
2:10 Ram became the *f* of Amminadab,
2:10 and Amminadab became the *f* of Nahshon,
2:11 Nahshon became the *f* of Salma.
2:11 Salma became the *f* of Boaz.
2:12 Boaz became the *f* of Obed.
2:12 Obed became the *f* of Jesse.
2:13 Jesse became the *f* of Eliab,
2:17 Amasa, whose *f* was Jether the Ishmaelite.
2:18 son of Hezron, became the *f* of a daughter,
2:20 the father of Uri, and Uri became the *f*.
2:21 the daughter of Machir, the *f* of Gilead,
2:22 Segub became the *f* of Jair,
2:23 to the sons of Machir, the *f* of Gilead.
2:24 *f* Hezron, and she bore him Ashhur, the *f*
2:36 Attai became the *f* of Nathan.
2:36 Nathan became the *f* of Zabad.
2:37 Zabad became the *f* of Ephlal.
2:37 Ephlal became the *f* of Obed.
2:38 Obed became the *f* of Jehu.
2:38 Jehu became the *f* of Azariah.
2:39 Azariah became the *f* of Helez.
2:39 Helez became the *f* of Eleasah.
2:40 Eleasah became the *f* of Sismai.
2:40 Sismai became the *f* of Shallum.
2:41 Shallum became the *f* of Jekamiah.
2:41 Jekamiah became the *f* of Elishama.
2:42 his first-born, who was the *f* of Ziph.
2:42 sons of Mareshah, who was the *f* of Hebron.
2:44 *f* of Raham, who was the father
2:44 Rekem became the *f* of Shammai.
2:45 Maon, who was the *f* of Beth-zur.
2:46 Haran became the *f* of Gazez.
2:49 She also bore Shaaph, the *f* of Madmannah,
2:49 the father of Machbenah, and the *f* of Gibea.
2:50 Shobal, the *f* of Kiriath-jearim,
2:51 father of Bethlehem, and Hareph, the *f*
2:52 sons of Shobal, the *f* of Kiriath-jearim,
4: 2 *f* of Jahath, and Jahath became the father
4: 3 the descendants of Hareph, the *f* of Etam:
4: 4 *f* of Gedor, and Ezer the father
4: 4 of Ephrathah, the *f* of Bethlehem.
4: 5 Ashhur, the *f* of Tekoa,
4: 8 Koz became the *f* of Anub and Zobebah,
4:11 the *f* of Mehir, who was the father
4:12 Eshton became the *f* of Bethrapha,
4:12 and Tehinnah, the *f* of the city of Nahash.
4:14 Meonothai became the *f* of Ophrah.
4:14 the father of Joab, the *f* of Geharashim,
4:17 *f* of Miriam, Shammai, and Ishbah, the *f*
4:18 the father of Gedor, Heber, the *f* of Soco,
4:18 of Soco, and Jekuthiel, the *f* of Zanoah.
4:19 wife, the sister of Naham, the *f* of Keilah,
4:21 the *f* of Lecah; Laadah, the father of
5: 1 he disgraced the couch of his *f*
5:30 Eleazar became the *f* of Phinehas.
5:30 Phinehas became the *f* of Abishua.
5:31 Abishua became the *f* of Bukki.
5:31 Bukki became the *f* of Uzzi.
5:32 Uzzi became the *f* of Zerahiah.
5:32 Zerahiah became the *f* of Meraioth.
5:33 Meraioth became the *f* of Amariah.
5:33 Amariah became the *f* of Ahitub.
5:34 Ahitub became the *f* of Zadok.
5:34 Zadok became the *f* of Ahimaaz.
5:35 Ahimaaz became the *f* of Azariah.
5:35 Azariah became the *f* of Johanan.
5:36 Johanan became the *f* of Azariah,
5:37 Azariah became the *f* of Amariah.
5:37 Amariah became the *f* of Ahitub.
5:38 Ahitub became the *f* of Zadok.
5:38 Zadok became the *f* of Shallum.
5:39 Shallum became the *f* of Hilkiah.
5:39 Hilkiah became the *f* of Azariah.
5:40 Azariah became the *f* of Seraiah.
5:40 Seraiah became the *f* of Jehozadak.
7:14 she bore Machir, the *f* of Gilead.
7:22 Their *f* Ephraim mourned a long time,
7:31 and Malchiel, who was the *f* of Birzaith.
7:32 Heber became the *f* of Japhlet,
8: 1 Benjamin became the *f* of Bela,
8: 3 of Bela were Addar and Gera, the *f* of Ehud.
8: 7 exile, became the *f* of Uzza and Ahihud.
8: 8 Shaharaim became a *f* on the Moabite
8: 9 his wife Hodesh he became the *f* of Jobab,
8:11 he became the *f* of Abitub and Elpaal.
8:32 Mikloth became the *f* of Shimeah.
8:33 father of Kish, and Kish became the *f* of Saul.
8:33 Saul became the *f* of Jonathan,
8:34 and Meribbaal became the *f* of Micah.
8:36 Ahaz became the *f* of Jehoaddah,
8:36 and Jehoaddah became the *f* of Alemeth,
8:36 Zimri became the *f* of Moza.
8:37 Moza became the *f* of Binea,
9:38 Mikloth became the *f* of Shimeah.
9:39 Ner became the *f* of Kish,
9:39 of Kish, and Kish became the *f* of Saul.
9:39 Saul became the *f* of Jonathan,
9:40 and Meribbaal became the *f* of Micah.
9:42 Ahaz became the *f* of Jehoaddah,
9:42 and Jehoaddah became the *f* of Alemeth,
9:42 Zimri became the *f* of Moza.
9:43 Moza became the *f* of Binea,
14: 3 became the *f* of more sons and daughters.
17:13 I will be a *f* to him,
19: 2 Nahash, for his *f* treated me with kindness."
19: 2 to comfort him over the death of his *f*.
19: 3 you these consolers—to honor your *f*?
22:10 be a son to me, and I will be a *f* to him,
24: 2 Nadab and Abihu died before their *f*,
24:19 the precepts given them by Aaron, their *f*,
25: 3 under the direction of their *f* Jeduthun,
26:10 not the first-born his *f* made him chief),
28: 4 then one family of Judah, that of my *f*;
28: 4 and finally, among all the sons of my *f*,
28: 6 him for my son, and I will be a *f* to him.
28: 9 know the God of your *f* and serve him with
29:10 may you be, O LORD, God of Israel our *f*,
29:23 the LORD as king in place of his *f* David;
2Chr 1: 8 "You have shown great favor to my *f* David,
1: 9 your promise to my *f* David be fulfilled,
2: 2 "As you dealt with my *f* David,
2: 6 and Jerusalem, whom my *f* David appointed.
2:13 son of a Danite woman and of a *f* from Tyre;
2:13 and the craftsmen of my lord David your *f*.
2:16 the census David his *f* had taken of them),
3: 1 which had been pointed out to his *f* David,
5: 1 in the dedicated offerings of his *f* David,
6: 4 own mouth made a promise to my *f* David
6: 7 My *f* David wished to build a temple to the
6:10 I have succeeded my *f* David and have taken
6:15 kept the promise you made to my *f* David,
6:16 the further promise you made to my *f* David,
7:17 live in my presence as your *f* David did,
7:18 I covenanted with your *f* David when I said,
8:14 And according to the ordinance of his *f*
10: 4 "Your *f* laid a heavy yoke upon us.
10: 4 the heavy yoke that your *f* imposed on us,
10: 6 service of his *f* during Solomon's lifetime,
10: 9 to lighten the yoke my *f* imposed on them?"
10:10 to you, 'Your *f* laid a heavy yoke upon us,
10:11 Whereas my *f* put a heavy yoke on you,
10:11 My *f* beat you with whips,
10:14 "My *f* laid a heavy yoke on you,
10:14 My *f* beat you with whips,
16: 3 as there was between your *f* and my father.
17: 2 of Ephraim which his *f* Asa had taken.
17: 3 ways his *f* had pursued in the beginning,
17: 4 the God of his *f* and observed his commands,
20:32 the path of his *f* Asa unswervingly,
21: 3 Their *f* gave them numerous gifts of silver,
21:12 followed the path of your *f* Jehoshaphat,
22: 4 his counselors after the death of his *f*.
24: 3 and he became the *f* of sons and daughters.
24:22 shown him by Jehoiada, Zechariah's *f*,
25: 3 servants who had killed the king, his *f*.
26: 1 him king to succeed his *f* Amaziah.
26: 4 the LORD, just as his *f* Amaziah had done.
27: 2 the LORD just as his *f* Uzziah had done,
33: 3 places which his *f* Hezekiah had torn down,
33:22 the LORD, just as his *f* Manasseh had done.
33:22 the idols which his *f* Manasseh had made,
33:23 before the LORD as his *f* Manasseh had done;
Neh 12:10 *f* of Joiakim, Joiakim became the father
12:10 and Eliashib became the *f* of Joiada.
12:11 *f* of Johanan, and Johanan became the father
Tb 1: 8 my *f* Tobiel; for when my father died,
2: 3 When he returned he exclaimed, *F*!"
2: 3 He answered, *F*, one of our people
3:10 would level this insult against my *f*:
3:10 And thus would I cause my *f* in his old age
5: 1 Then Tobiah replied to his *f* Tobit:
5: 1 "Everything that you have commanded me, *f*,
5: 7 young man, till I go back and tell my *f*;
5: 9 back to tell his *f* Tobit what had happened.
5: 9 "Young man, my *f* would like to see you."
5:17 journey, Tobiah kissed his *f* and mother.
6:12 and her *f* loves her dearly."
6:13 girl's *f* to let us have her as your bride.
6:15 I would bring my *f* and mother down to
7: 5 Then Tobiah exclaimed, "He is my *f*!"
7: 7 You are the son of a noble and good *f*.
7:12 bring her back safely to your *f*.
8:21 when you go back in good health to your *f*;
8:21 I am your *f*, and Edna is your mother;
9: 4 you know that my *f* is counting the days.
9: 6 your wife, and to your wife's *f* and mother.
10: 7 for I know that my *f* and mother do not
10: 7 I beg you, father, let me go back to my *f*.
10: 8 I am sending messengers to your *f* Tobit,
10: 9 "No, I beg you to let me go back to my *f*."

11: 2 "You know how we left your *f.*
11: 6 saw him coming, she exclaimed to his *f,*
11: 7 said to Tobiah before he reached his *f:*
11: 8 then your *f* will again be able to see the
11:11 "Courage, *f,*" he said.
11:15 his *f* that his journey had been a success;
11:17 Blessed are your *f* and your mother.
12: 2 *F,* how much shall I pay him?
13: 4 is the Lord our God, our *F* and God forever.
14:12 mother died, he buried her next to his *f.*
14:13 estate as well as that of his *f* Tobit.
Est 2: 7 He was foster *f* to Hadassah,
2: 7 for she had lost both *f* and mother.
2: 7 On the death of her *f* and mother,
B: 6 the administration and is a second *f* to us,
E:11 that he was proclaimed *f* of the king,'
1Mc 2:54 Phinehas our *f,* for his burning zeal,
2:65 to him always, and he will be a *f* to you,
3: 2 and all who had joined his *f* supported him,
6:23 We agreed to serve your *f* and to follow
11:32 sends greetings to his *f* Lasthenes.
13:27 *f* and his brothers a monument of stones,
13:28 his *f* and his mother and his four brothers.
16: 1 told his *f* Simon what Cendebeus was doing.
16:21 that his *f* and his brothers had perished,
16:24 that he succeeded his *f* as high priest.
2Mc 4:11 *f* of Eupolemus (that Eupolemus who would
9:23 Nevertheless, I know that my *f,*
11:23 our *f* has taken his place among the gods,
14:37 *f* of the Jews because of his love for them.
Jb 15:10 us more advanced in years than your *f.*
17:14 If I must call corruption "my *f,*"
29:16 I was a *f* to the needy;
31:18 like a *f* God has reared me from my youth.
38:28 Has the rain a *f;*
42:15 and their *f* gave them an inheritance among
Ps(s) 27:10 Though my *f* and mother forsake me,
68: 6 The *f* of orphans and the defender of
89:27 "He shall say of me, 'You are my *f,*
103:13 As a *f* has compassion on his children,
Prv 10: 1 A wise son makes his *f* glad,
15:20 A wise son makes his *f* glad,
17:21 the *f* of a numskull has no joy.
17:25 A foolish son is vexation to his *f,*
19:13 The foolish son is ruin to his *f,*
19:26 He who mistreats his *f,*
20:20 If one curses his *f* or mother,
23:22 Listen to your *f* who begot you,
23:24 The *f* of a just man will exult with glee;
23:25 Let your *f* and mother have joy;
28: 7 the gluttons' companion disgraces his *f.*
28:24 defrauds *f* or mother and calls it no sin,
29: 3 He who loves wisdom makes his *f* glad,
30:11 is a group of people that curses its *f,*
30:17 The eye that mocks a *f,*
Wis 2:16 of the just and boasts that God is his *F.*
10: 1 She preserved the first-formed *f* of the
11:10 admonishing them as a *f*
14: 3 But your providence, O *F!*
14:15 For a *f,* afflicted with untimely mourning,
Sir 3: 2 LORD sets a *f* in honor over his children;
3: 3 He who honors his *f* atones for sins;
3: 5 who honors his *f* is gladdened by children,
3: 6 He who reveres his *f* will live a long life;
3: 7 He who fears the LORD honors his *f,*
3: 8 your *f* that his blessing may come upon you;
3:12 My son, take care of your *f* when he is old;
3:14 For kindness to a *f* will not be forgotten,
3:16 A blasphemer is he who despises his *f;*
4:10 To the fatherless be as a *f,*
7:27 With your whole heart honor your *f;*
22: 3 An unruly child is a disgrace to its *f;*
22: 5 A hussy shames her *f* and her husband;
23: 1 LORD, *F* and Master of my life,
23: 4 LORD, *F* and God of my life,
23:14 Keep your *f* and mother in mind when you
41: 7 Children curse their wicked *f,*
41:15 *f* and mother be ashamed of immorality,
42: 9 is a treasure that keeps her *f* wakeful,
44:19 ABRAHAM, *f* of many peoples,
44:22 the same promise because of Abraham, his *f.*
51: 1 I give you thanks, O God of my *f;*
51:10 O LORD, you are my *f,*
Is 8: 4 knows how to call his *f* or mother by name,
22:21 be a *f* to the inhabitants of Jerusalem,
38: 5 says the LORD, the God of your *f* David:
43:27 Your first *f* sinned;
45:10 Woe to him who asks a *f,*
51: 2 Look to Abraham, your *f,*
58:14 you with the heritage of Jacob, your *f,*
63:16 O Lord, hold not back, for you are our *f.*
63:16 to acknowledge us, You, LORD, are our *f,*
64: 7 Yet, O LORD, you are our *f;*
Jer 2:27 say to a piece of wood, "You are my *f,*"
3: 4 Even now do you not call me, "My *f,*
3:19 You would call me, "My *F,*"
16: 7 to drink over the death of *f* or mother.
20:15 be the man who brought the news to my *f,*
22:11 king of Judah, who succeeded his *f* as king.
22:15 Did not your *f* eat and drink?
23:27 just as their *f* forgot my name
31: 9 For I am a *f* to Israel,
35: 6 "Jonadab, Rechab's son, our *f,*
35: 8 have heeded Jonadab, Rechab's son, our *f,*
35:10 do everything our *f* Jonadab commanded us.
35:16 the command which their *f* laid on them;
35:18 obeyed the command of Jonadab, your *f,*
Ez 16: 3 *f* was an Amorite and your mother a Hittite.
16:45 mother was a Hittite and your *f* an Amorite.
18: 4 life of the *f* is like the life of the son,
18:11 things (though the *f* does none of them),
18:14 son who, seeing all the sins his *f* commits,
18:17 one shall not die for the sins of his *f,*
18:18 Only the *f,* since he violated rights,
18:19 the son charged with the guilt of his *f?*"
18:20 of his *f,* nor shall the father be charged
22: 7 Within you, *f* and mother are despised;
44:25 any dead person, unless it be their *f,*
Dn 5: 2 vessels which Nebuchadnezzar, his *f,*
5:11 during the lifetime of your *f* he was
5:11 In fact, King Nebuchadnezzar, your *f,*
5:13 the Daniel, the Jewish exile, whom my *f,*
5:18 The Most High God gave your *f*
Am 2: 7 Son and *f* go to the same prostitute,
Mi 7: 6 For the son dishonors his *f,*
Zec 13: 3 prophesies, his parents, *f* and mother,
13: 3 he prophesies, his parents, *f* and mother,
Mal 1: 6 A son honors his *f,*
1: 6 If then I am a *f,* where is the honor due
2:10 Have we not all the one *F?*
Mt 1: 2 Abraham was the *f* of Isaac,
1: 2 father of Jacob, Jacob the *f* of Judah
1: 3 Judah was the *f* of Perez and Zerah,
1: 3 the father of Hezron, Hezron the *f* of Ram.
1: 4 Ram was the *f* of Amminadab,
1: 4 father of Nahshon, Nahshon the *f* of Salmon.
1: 5 Salmon was the *f* of Boaz,
1: 5 mother was Rahab, Boaz was the *f* of Obed,
1: 5 Obed was the *f* of Jesse,
1: 6 father of Jesse, Jesse the *f* of King David.
1: 6 David was the *f* of Solomon,
1: 7 Solomon was the *f* of Rehoboam,
1: 7 the father of Abijah, Abijah the *f* of Asa.
1: 8 Asa was the *f* of Jehoshaphat,
1: 8 *f* of Joram, Joram the father of Uzziah.
1: 9 the father of Jotham, Jotham the *f* of Ahaz,
1: 9 the father of Ahaz, Ahaz the *f* of Hezekiah.
1:10 *f* of Manasseh, Manasseh the father
1:10 the father of Amos, Amos the *f* of Josiah,
1:11 Josiah became the *f* of Jechoniah and his
1:12 father of Shealtiel, Shealtiel the *f* of
1:13 father of Abiud, Abiud the *f* of Eliakim,
1:13 father of Eliakim, Eliakim the *f* of Azor.
1:14 the father of Zadok, Zadok the *f* of Achim,
1:14 the father of Achim, Achim the *f* of Eliud.
1:15 Eliud was the *f* of Eleazar,
1:15 father of Matthan, Matthan the *f* of Jacob.
1:16 was the *f* of Joseph the husband of Mary.
2:22 had succeeded his *f* Herod as king of Judea,
3: 9 yourselves on the claim, 'Abraham is our *f.*'
4:21 getting their nets in order with their *f,*
4:22 they abandoned boat and *f* to follow him.
5:16 acts and give praise to your heavenly *F.*
5:45 that you are sons of your heavenly *F,*
5:48 made perfect as your heavenly *F* is perfect.
6: 1 expect no recompense from your heavenly *F.*
6: 4 your *F* who sees in secret will repay you.
6: 6 your door, and pray to your *F* in private.
6: 6 Then your *F,* who sees what no man sees,
6: 8 *F* knows what you need before you ask him.
6: 9 'Our *F* in heaven, hallowed be your name,
6:14 your heavenly *F* will forgive you yours.
6:15 others, neither will your *F* forgive you.
6:18 your *F* who is hidden; and your Father
6:26 yet your heavenly *F* feeds them.
6:32 Your heavenly *F* knows all that you need.
7:11 *F* give good things to anyone who asks him!
7:21 one who does the will of my *F* in heaven.
8:21 him, "Lord, let me go and bury my *f* first."
10:20 Spirit of your *F* will be speaking in you.
10:21 over brother to death, and the *f* his child;
10:32 I will acknowledge before my *F* in heaven.
10:33 men I will disown before my *F* in heaven.
10:35 have come to set a man at odds with his *f,*
10:37 Whoever loves *f* or mother,
11:25 *F,* Lord of heaven and earth,
11:26 *F,* it is true. You have graciously willed
11:27 but the *F,* and no one knows the Father
11:17 has been given over to me by my *F.*
12:50 *F* is brother and sister and mother to me."
15: 4 has said, 'Honor your *f* and your mother,'
15: 4 curses *f* or mother shall be put to death.'
15: 5 'Whoever says to his *f* or his mother,
15: 6 to God, need not honor his *f* or his mother.'
15:13 put down by my heavenly *F* will be uprooted,"
16:17 revealed this to you, but my heavenly *F.*
18:19 it shall be granted you by my *F* in heaven.
18:35 My heavenly *F* will treat you in exactly
19: 5 his *f* and mother and cling to his wife,
19:19 'Honor your *f* and your mother';
19:29 up home, brothers or sisters, *f* or mother,
20:23 those to whom it has been reserved by my *F.*"
21:31 Which of the two did what the *f* wanted?"
23: 9 Do not call anyone on earth your *f.*
23: 9 Only one is your *f,* the One in heaven.
24:36 in heaven nor the Son, but the *F* only.
26:39 "My *F,* if it is possible, let this cup pass me
26:42 "My *F,* if this cannot pass me by
26:53 Do you not suppose I can call on my *F* to
28:19 Baptize them in the name of the *F,*
Mk 1:20 They abandoned their *f* Zebedee,
5:40 Jesus took the child's *f* and mother and
7:10 Moses said, 'Honor your *f* and your mother';
7:10 curses *f* or mother shall be put to death.'
7:11 'If a person says to his *f* or mother,
7:12 him to do nothing more for his *f* or mother.
9:21 Then Jesus questioned the *f:*
9:21 "From childhood," the *f* replied.
9:24 The boy's *f* immediately exclaimed,
10: 7 a man shall leave his *f* and mother
10:19 Honor your *f* and your mother.'"
10:29 up home, brothers or sisters, mother or *f,*
11:10 is the reign of our *f* David to come!
11:25 *F* may in turn forgive you your faults."
13:12 for execution and likewise the *f* his child;
13:32 in heaven nor even the Son, but only the *F.*
14:36 He kept saying, "Abba (O *F*),
15:21 of Cyrene, the *f* of Alexander and Rufus,
Lk 1:32 will give him the throne of David his *f.*
1:59 intended to name him after his *f* Zechariah.
1:62 the *f* what he wished him to be called.
1:67 Then Zechariah his *f,*
1:73 swore to Abraham our *f* he would grant us:
2:33 The child's *f* and mother were marveling at
2:48 You see that your *f* and I have been
3: 8 by saying to yourselves, 'Abraham is our *f.*'
6:36 compassionate, as your *F* is compassionate.
9:26 and that of his *F* and his holy angels.
9:42 cured the boy, and restored him to his *f.*
9:59 The man replied, "Let me bury my *f* first."
10:21 "I offer you praise, O *F,*
10:21 "Yes, *F,* you have graciously willed it so.
10:22 has been given over to me by my *F.*
10:22 the *F* and no one knows the Father
11: 2 *F,* hallowed be your name.
11:11 What *f* among you will give his son a snake
11:13 how much more will the heavenly *F* give the
12:30 Your *F* knows that you need such things.
12:32 has pleased your *F* to give you the kingdom.
12:53 *f* will be split against son and son
12:53 be split against son and son against *f,*
14:26 turning his back on his *f* and mother,
15:12 The younger of them said to his father, *F,*
15:12 So the *f* divided up the property.
15:18 return to my *f,* and say to him, Father,
15:20 *f* caught sight of him and was deeply moved.
15:21 The son said to him, *F,*
15:22 The *f* said to his servants:
15:27 and your *f* has killed the fatted calf
15:28 his *f* came out and began to plead with him.
15:29 "He said to his *f* in reply:
15:31 "'My son,' replied the *f,*
16:24 "He called out, *F* Abraham,
16:27 *F,* I ask you, then,' the rich man said,
16:30 'No, *F* Abraham,' replied the rich man.
18:20 Honor your *f* and your mother."
22:29 you the dominion my *F* has assigned to me.
22:42 *F,* if it is your will,
23:34 [Jesus said, *F,* forgive them;
23:46 Jesus uttered a loud cry and said, *F,*
24:49 I send down upon you the promise of my *F.*
Jn 1:14 the glory of an only Son coming from the *F,*
3:35 The *F* loves the Son and has given
4:21 will worship the *F* neither on this mountain
4:23 will worship the *F* in Spirit and truth.
4:23 it is just such worshipers the *F* seeks.
4:53 It was at that very hour, the *f* realized,
5:17 "My *F* is at work until now,
5:18 still, was speaking of God as his own *F,*
5:19 he can do only what he sees the *F* doing.
5:19 For whatever the *F* does,
5:20 *F* loves the Son and everything the Father
5:21 as the *F* raises the dead and grants life,
5:22 The *F* himself judges no one,
5:23 may honor the Son just as they honor the *F.*
5:23 Son refuses to honor the *F* who sent him.
5:26 just as the *F* possesses life in himself,
5:27 The *F* has given over to him power to pass
5:36 the works the *F* has given me to accomplish.
5:36 on my behalf that the *F* has sent me.
5:37 the *F* who sent me has himself given
5:45 that I will be your accuser before the *F;*
6:27 is on him that God the *F* has set his seal."
6:32 my *F* who gives you the real heavenly bread.
6:37 All that the *F* gives me shall come to me;
6:40 Indeed, this is the will of my *F,*
6:42 Do we not know his *f* and mother?
6:44 to me unless the *F* who sent me draws him;
6:45 the *F* and learned from him comes to me.
6:46 Not that anyone has seen the *F*—
6:46 the one who is from God has seen the *F.*
6:57 Just as the *F* who has life sent me and I
6:57 sent me and I have life because of the *F,*
6:65 to me unless it is granted him by the *F.*"
8:16 have at my side the One who sent me [the *F.*
8:18 my behalf, the *F* who sent me is the other."
8:19 "And where is this *F* of yours?"
8:19 "You know neither me nor my *F.*
8:19 If you knew me, you would know my *F* too."

FATHER (cont.)

8:27 that he was speaking to them of the F.
8:28 I say only what the F has taught me.
8:38 you do what you have heard from your f."
8:39 They retorted, "Our f is Abraham."
8:41 We have but one f and that is God himself."
8:42 "Were God your f you would love me,
8:44 The f you spring from is the devil,
8:44 he is a liar and the f of lies.
8:49 However, I revere my F,
8:53 pretend to be greater than our f Abraham,
8:54 He who gives me glory is the F,
8:56 Your f Abraham rejoiced that he might see
10:15 that the F knows me and I know the Father;
10:17 The F loves me for this:
10:18 This command I received from my F."
10:29 My F is greater than all,
10:30 The F and I are one."
10:32 good deeds have I shown you from the F.
10:36 the F consecrated and sent into the world,
10:38 it means that the F is in me and I in him."
11:41 F, I thank you for having heard me.
12:26 If anyone serves me, him the F will honor.
12:27 F, save me from this hour?
12:28 F, glorify your name!"
12:49 the F who sent me has commanded me what to
13: 1 for him to pass from this world to the F.
13: 3 the F who had handed everything over to
14: 6 no one comes to the F but through me.
14: 7 really knew me, you would know my F also.
14: 8 us the F and that will be enough for us."
14: 9 "Whoever has seen me has seen the F.
14: 9 How can you say, 'Show us the F'?
14:10 that I am in the Father and the F is in me?
14:10 F who lives in me accomplishing his works.
14:11 that I am in the Father and the F is in me,
14:12 Because I go to the F,
14:13 will do, so as to glorify the F in the Son.
14:16 F and he will give you another Paraclete
14:20 that day you will know that I am in my F,
14:21 and he who loves me will be loved by my F.
14:23 be true to my word, and my F will love him;
14:24 it comes from the F who sent me.
14:26 Spirit whom the F will send in my name,
14:28 to the Father, for the F is greater than I.
14:31 Father and do as the F has commanded me.
15: 1 the true vine and my F is the vinegrower.
15: 8 My F has been glorified in your bearing
15: 9 "As the F has loved me,
15:15 known to you all that I heard from my F.
15:16 you ask the F in my name he will give you.
15:23 To hate me is to hate my F.
15:24 seen, and they go on hating me and my F.
15:26 the Spirit of truth who comes from the F,
15:26 and whom I myself will send from the F—
16: 3 because they knew neither the F nor me.
16:10 I go to the F and you can see me no more;
16:15 All that the F has belongs to me.
16:17 he not say that he is going back to the F?"
16:23 you my assurance, whatever you ask the F,
16:25 shall tell you about the F in plain speech.
16:26 not say that I will petition the F for you.
16:27 The F already loves you,
16:28 come from the F I came into the world.
16:28 Now I am leaving the world to go to the F."
16:32 the F is with me.)
17: 1 F, the hour has come!
17: 5 Do you now, F, give me glory
17:11 O F most holy, protect them
17:21 their word, that all may be one as you, F,
17:24 F, all those you gave me I would have in
17:25 Just F, the world has not known you,
18:11 I not to drink the cup the F has given me?"
20:17 me, for I have not yet ascended to the F.
20:17 'I am ascending to my Father and your F,
20:21 "As the F has sent me, so I send you."
Acts 1: 7 The F has reserved that to himself.
2:29 speak confidently to you about our f David.
2:33 the promised Holy Spirit from the F,
4:25 the lips of our f David your servant:
7: 2 The God of glory appeared to our f Abraham
7: 4 After his f died, God made him move
7: 8 Abraham, who had become the f of Isaac,
7:14 Then Joseph sent for his f Jacob,
7:29 Midian, where he became the f of two sons.
16: 1 and a believer, and whose f was a Greek.
16: 3 knew that it was only his f who was Greek.
28: 8 happened that Publius' f was sick in bed,
Rom 1: 7 from God our F and the Lord Jesus Christ.
4:11 the f of all the uncircumcised who believe,
4:12 as well as the f of those circumcised who
4:16 He is f of us all,
4:17 f in the sight of God in whom he believed,
4:17 says, "I have made you f of many nations."
4:18 and so became the f of many nations,
6: 4 raised from the dead by the glory of the F,
8:15 "Abba!" (that is, F").
9:10 twin children by one man, our f Isaac
15: 6 God, the F of our Lord Jesus Christ.
1Cor 1: 3 from God our F and the Lord Jesus Christ.
4:15 guardians in Christ, you have only one f.
8: 6 for us there is one God, the F,
11: 3 and the head of Christ is the F.
15:24 he will hand over the kingdom to God the F.
2Cor 1: 2 from God our F and the Lord Jesus Christ.
1: 3 be God, the F of our Lord Jesus Christ, the F
6:13 then (I speak as a f to his children),
6:18 I will welcome you and be a f to you and
11:31 The God and F of the Lord Jesus knows
Gal 1: 1 and God his F who raised him from the dead
1: 3 of God our F and of the Lord Jesus Christ,
1: 4 present evil age, as our God and F willed
4: 2 administrators until the time set by his f.
4: 6 which cries out "Abba!" ("F!")
Eph 1: 2 from God our F and the Lord Jesus Christ.
1: 3 be the God and F of our Lord Jesus Christ,
1:17 of our Lord Jesus Christ, the F of glory,
2:18 we both have access in one Spirit to the F.
3:14 That is why I kneel before the F from whom
4: 6 one God and F of all,
5:20 Give thanks to God the F always and for
5:31 reason a man shall leave his f and mother,
6: 2 "Honor your f and mother" is the first
6:23 May God the F and the Lord Jesus Christ
Phil 1: 2 God our F and from the Lord Jesus Christ!
2:11 tongue proclaim to the glory of God the F:
4:20 glory to our God and F for unending ages!
Col 1: 2 May God our F give you grace and peace.
1: 3 to God, the F of our Lord Jesus Christ,
1:12 giving thanks to the F for having made you
3:17 Give thanks to God the F through him.
1Thes 1: 1 to God the F and the Lord Jesus Christ.
1: 3 F of the way you are proving your faith,
2:11 one of you, as a f does his children
3:11 May God himself, who is our F,
3:13 our God and F at the coming of our Lord
2Thes 1: 1 to God our F and the Lord Jesus Christ.
1: 2 from God the F and the Lord Jesus Christ.
2:16 may God our F who loved us and in his
1Tm 1: 2 from God the F and Christ Jesus our Lord.
5: 1 an older man, but appeal to him as to a f.
2Tm 1: 2 and peace from God the F and from Christ
Ti 1: 4 May grace and peace from God our F,
1: 6 the f of children who are believers and
Phlm 1: 3 God our F and from the Lord Jesus Christ.
Heb 1: 5 Or again, "I will be his f,
2:11 are consecrated have one and the same F.
7: 3 Without f, mother or ancestry,
7: 9 to speak, tithed in the person of his f,
12: 7 is there whom his f does not discipline?
12: 9 all the more submit to the F of spirits,
Jas 1:17 from the F of the heavenly luminaries,
1:27 worship without stain before our God and F.
2:21 Was not our f Abraham justified by his
3: 9 it to say, "Praised be the Lord and F";
1Pt 1: 2 to the foreknowledge of God the F,
1: 3 be the God and F of our Lord Jesus Christ,
1:17 In prayer you call upon a F who judges
2Pt 1:17 received glory and praise from God the F
1Jn 1: 1 present to the F and became visible to us.)
1: 3 of ours is with the F and with his Son,
2: 1 sin, we have, in the presence of the F,
2:14 you, children, for you have known the F.
2:16 that the world affords comes from the F.
2:22 the antichrist, denying the F and the Son.
2:23 who denies the Son has no claim on the F,
2:23 the Son can claim the F as well.
2:24 turn will remain in the Son and in the F,
3: 1 See what love the F has bestowed on us in
4:14 F has sent the Son as savior of the world.
5: 1 loves the f loves the child he has begotten.
2Jn 1: 3 peace from God the F and from Jesus Christ,
1: 4 truth, just as we were commanded by the F.
1: 9 teaching possesses both the F and the Son.
Jude 1: 1 who have found love in God the F and have
Rv 1: 6 priests in the service of his God and F—
2:26 the same authority I received from my F.
3: 5 him in the presence of my F and his angels.
3:21 and took my seat beside my F on his throne.
14: 1 name of his F written on their foreheads.

FATHER-FOREVER (1)

Is 9: 5 name him Wonder-Counselor, God-Hero, F,

FATHER-IN-LAW (29)

Gn 38:13 When Tamar was told that her f was on his
38:25 bringing her out, she sent word to her f,
Ex 3: 1 was tending the flock of his f Jethro,
4:18 returned to his f Jethro and said to him,
18: 1 Now Moses' f Jethro,
18: 2 So his f Jethro took along Zipporah,
18: 5 his f Jethro came to him in the desert
18: 6 sent word to Moses, "I, Jethro, your f,
18: 7 Moses went out to meet his f,
18: 8 Moses then told his f of all that the LORD
18:12 Then Jethro, the f of Moses,
18:12 with Moses' f in the meal before God.
18:14 f saw all that he was doing for the people,
18:15 Moses answered his f,
18:17 are not acting wisely," his f replied.
18:24 of his f and did all that he had suggested.
18:27 Then Moses bade farewell to his f,
Jgs 1:16 The descendants of the Kenite, Moses' f,
19: 4 so he spent three days with this f of his,
19: 7 but when his f pressed him he went back
19: 8 When he and his f had eaten,
1Sm 4:19 and the deaths of her f and her husband,
4:21 ark of God and to her f and her husband.]
Tb 10:12 honor your f and your mother-in-law,
14:12 he settled in Ecbatana with his f Raguel.
14:13 care of his aging f and mother-in-law;
1Mc 10:56 I will become your f as you have proposed."
11: 2 them to do, since Ptolemy was his f.
Jn 18:13 the f of Caiaphas who was high priest that

FATHERED (2)

2Chr 11:21 he f twenty-eight sons and sixty daughters.
13:21 f twenty-two sons and sixteen daughters.

FATHERLESS (11)

Jb 31:17 alone, with no share in it for the f,
Ps(s) 10:14 of the f you are the helper.
10:18 To the defense of the f and the oppressed,
82: 3 Defend the lowly and the f;
94: 6 and stranger they slay, the f they murder,
109: 9 May his children be f,
146: 9 the f and the widow he sustains,
Sir 4:10 To the f be as a father,
Is 1:23 The f they defend not,
Jer 5:28 of the f or judging the cause of the poor.
Lam 5: 3 We have become orphans, f;

FATHERS—FATHER'S (553)

Gn 9:22 the father of Canaan, saw his f nakedness,
9:23 backward and covered their f nakedness;
9:23 way, they did not see their f nakedness.
12: 1 f house to a land that I will show you.
20:12 in truth my sister, but only my f daughter,
20:13 God sent me wandering from my f house,
24: 7 me from my f house and the land of my kin,
24:23 in your f house for us to spend the night?"
24:38 instead, you shall go to my f house,
24:40 my son from my own kindred of my f house.
26:15 the wells that his f servants had dug back
26:18 (Isaac reopened the wells which his f
27:34 On hearing his f words,
28:21 wear, and I come back safe to my f house,
29: 9 with them, Rachel arrived with her f sheep;
29:12 He told her that he was her f relative,
31: 1 this wealth of his by using our f property."
31: 3 to Jacob, "Return to the land of your f,
31: 5 "I have noticed that your f attitude
31: 9 your f livestock and gave it to me.
31:14 we still an heir's portion in our f house?
31:19 appropriated her f household idols.
31:30 were desperately homesick for your f house,
35:22 went and lay with Bilhah, his f concubine.
37: 2 the sons of his f wives Bilhah and Zilpah,
37:12 gone to pasture their f flocks at Shechem,
38:11 f house until my son Shelah grows up"
38:11 So Tamar went to live in her f house.
46:31 said to his brothers and his f household:
46:31 'My brothers and my f household,
47:12 his f whole household down to the youngest,
48:12 Joseph removed them from his f knees and
48:15 whose ways my f Abraham and Isaac walked,
48:16 and the names of my f Abraham and Isaac,
48:17 so he took hold of his f hand,
48:21 and will restore you to the land of your f.
49: 4 f bed and defiled my couch to my sorrow.
49:29 bury me with my f in the cave that lies in
50: 1 f face and wept over him as he kissed him.
50: 8 his brothers, and his f household;
50:17 crime that we, the servants of your f God,
50:22 in Egypt, together with his f family.
Ex 2:16 fill the troughs to water their f flock.
3:13 'The God of your f has sent me to you,'
3:15 The LORD, the God of your f,
3:16 The LORD, the God of your f,
4: 5 "that the LORD, the God of their f,
10: 6 such a sight your f and grandfathers have
13: 5 which he swore to your f he would give you,
13:11 swore to you and your f he would give you,
18: 4 for he said, "My f God is my helper;
20: 5 inflicting punishment for their f'
34: 7 fourth generation for their f' wickedness!"
Lv 18: 8 not have intercourse with your f wife,
18: 9 your f daughter or your mother's daughter,
18:11 the daughter whom your f wife bore to him,
18:12 father's sister, since she is your f relative.
18:14 f brother by being intimate with his wife,
20:11 his father by lying with his f wife,
20:19 with your mother's sister or your f sister;
22:13 father's house, she may then eat of her f
26:39 away for their own and their f' guilt.
26:40 confess that they and their f were guilty
Nm 11:12 you have promised under oath to their f?
14:18 fourth generation for their f' wickedness.'
14:23 land which I promised on oath to their f.
20:15 befallen us, how our f went down to Egypt,
20:15 how the Egyptians maltreated us and our f.
27: 4 But why should our f name be withdrawn
27: 4 have property among our f kinsmen."
27: 7 hereditary property among their f kinsmen,
27: 7 letting their f heritage pass on to them.
27:10 shall give his heritage to his f brothers;

30: 4 woman, while still a maiden in her *f* house,
30:17 while she is still a maiden in her *f* house.
32: 8 That is just what your *f* did when I sent
32:14 rising up in your *f'* place to add still
36:11 married relatives on their *f* side within
36:12 remained in the tribe of their *f* clan.
Dt 1: 8 now and occupy the land I swore to your *f*,
1:11 May the LORD, the God of your *f*,
1:21 occupy it, as the LORD, the God of your *f*,
1:35 the good land I swore to give to your *f*,
4: 1 the land which the LORD, the God of your *f*,
4:31 which under oath he made with your *f*.
4:37 For love of your *f* he chose their
5: 3 not with our *f* did he make this covenant,
5: 9 inflicting punishments for their *f'*
6: 3 promise of the LORD, the God of your *f*,
6:10 into the land which he swore to your *f*,
6:18 which the LORD promised on oath to your *f*,
6:23 into the land he promised on oath to our *f*,
7: 8 to the oath he had sworn to your *f*,
7:12 which he promised on oath to your *f*.
7:13 which he swore to your *f* he would give you.
8: 1 which the LORD promised on oath to your *f*.
8: 3 manna, a food unknown to you and your *f*,
8:16 with manna, a food unknown to your *f*,
8:18 the covenant which he swore to your *f*.
9: 5 promise which he made on oath to your *f*,
10:11 which I swore to their *f* I would give them.'
10:15 Yet in his love for your *f* the LORD was so
11: 9 the LORD swore to your *f* he would give
11:21 LORD swore to your *f* he would give them.
12: 1 land which the LORD, the God of your *f*,
13: 7 gods, whom you and your *f* have not known,
13:18 multiply you as he promised your *f* on oath;
19: 8 your territory, as he swore to your *f*,
19: 8 gives you all the land he promised your *f*
22:21 bring the girl to the entrance of her *f* house
22:21 Israel by her unchasteness in her *f* house.
23: 1 *f* wife, nor shall he dishonor his father's
24:16 *F* shall not be put to death for their
24:16 their children, nor children for their *f*;
26: 3 which he swore to our *f* he would give us.'
26: 7 we cried to the LORD, the God of our *f*,
26:15 honey which you promised on oath to our *f*.'
27: 3 the LORD, your God, and the God of your *f*,
27:20 father's wife, for he dishonors his *f* bed!'
28:11 which he swore to your *f* he would give you.
28:36 nation which you and your *f* have not known,
28:64 such as you and your *f* have not known.
29:12 you and as he swore to your *f* Abraham,
29:24 which the LORD, the God of their *f*,
30: 5 into the land which your *f* once occupied,
30: 5 more prosperous and numerous than your *f*.
30: 9 even as he took delight in your *f*,
30:20 swore he would give to your *f* Abraham,
31: 7 LORD swore to their *f* he would give them;
31:16 "Soon you will be at rest with your *f*,
31:20 honey which I promised on oath to their *f*,
31:21 land which I promised on oath to their *f*."
32:17 of whom their *f* had never stood in awe.
33:17 The majestic bull, his *f* first-born,
Jos 1: 6 which I swore to their *f* I would give them.
4:21 you ask their *f* what these stones mean,
5: 6 he had promised their *f* he would give us.
17: 4 to each of them among their *f* kinsmen.
18: 3 the land which the LORD, the God of your *f*,
21:43 he had sworn to their *f* he would give them.
21:44 side, just as he had promised their *f*.
22:28 of the altar of the LORD which our *f* made,
24: 2 In times past your *f*, down to Terah,
24: 6 the Egyptians pursued your *f* to the Red
24:14 *f* served beyond the River and in Egypt,
24:15 the gods your *f* served beyond the River or
24:17 us and our *f* up out of the land of Egypt,
Jgs 2: 1 land which I promised on oath to your *f*.
2:10 that generation were gathered to their *f*,
2:12 Abandoning the LORD, the God of their *f*,
2:17 to stray from the way their *f* had taken,
2:19 would relapse and do worse than their *f*,
2:20 my covenant which I enjoined on their *f*,
2:22 and continue in it as their *f* had done;
3: 4 LORD had enjoined on their *f* through Moses.
6:13 his wondrous deeds of which our *f* told us
6:15 I am the most insignificant in my *f* house."
6:25 destroy your *f* altar to Baal and cut down
11: 7 who hated me and drove me from my *f* house?"
19: 2 him for her *f* house in Bethlehem of Judah,
19: 3 She brought him into her *f* house,
21:22 When their *f* or their brothers come to
1Sm 2:25 But they disregarded their *f* warning,
2:27 reveal myself to your *f* family
2:28 of the Israelites to your *f* family.
2:30 family and your *f* family should minister
2:31 strength and the strength of your *f* family,
9:20 ardently if not you and your *f* family?"
12: 6 brought your *f* up from the land of Egypt.
12: 7 mercy the LORD has done for you and your *f*.
12: 8 them, your *f* appealed to the LORD,
17:15 from Saul to tend his *f* sheep at Bethlehem.
17:25 grant exemption to his *f* family in Israel."
17:34 "Your servant used to tend his *f* sheep,
18: 2 did not allow him to return to his *f* house.
18:18 And who are my kin or my *f* clan in Israel

2Sm 2:32 and buried him in his *f* tomb in Bethlehem.
3: 7 have you been intimate with my *f* concubine?"
15:34 I was formerly your *f* servant,
16: 3 Israelites will restore to me my *f* kingdom.' "
16:21 "Have relations with your *f* concubines,
16:22 his *f* concubines in view of all Israel.
17:23 so he died and was buried in his *f* tomb.
19:29 For though my *f* entire house deserved only
1Kgs 1:21 when my lord the king sleeps with his *f*,
8:21 which he made with our *f* when he brought
8:34 them back to the land you gave their *f*.
8:40 as they live on the land you gave our *f*.
8:48 to you toward the land you gave their *f*,
8:53 Moses when you brought our *f* out of Egypt,
8:57 be with us as he was with our *f* and may he
8:58 and ordinances which he enjoined on our *f*.
9: 9 brought their *f* out of the land of Egypt;
11:27 up the breach of his *f* City of David.
11:43 he was buried in his *f* City of David,
12: 6 been in his *f* service while he was alive,
12:10 little finger is thicker than my *f* body.
14:15 from this good land which he gave their *f*,
14:22 him even more than their *f* had done.
15:15 *f* and his own votive offerings of silver,
15:26 imitating his *f* conduct and the sin which
19: 4 Take my life, for I am no better than my *f*."
2Kgs 10: 3 offspring, place him on his *f* throne,
14: 6 *F* shall not be put to death for their
14: 6 shall children be put to death for their *f*;
15: 9 in the sight of the LORD as his *f* had done,
17:13 entire law which I enjoined on your *f*
17:14 but were as stiff-necked as their *f*
17:15 covenant which he had made with their *f*,
17:41 to this day, are doing as their *f* did.
19:12 the nations whom my *f* destroyed save them?
20:17 that your *f* have stored up until this day,
21: 8 to be driven off the land I gave their *f*,
21:15 their *f* came forth from Egypt until today.' "
21:22 He abandoned the LORD, the God of his *f*,
22:13 because our *f* did not obey the
1Chr 5:25 they offended the God of their *f* by
9:19 just as their *f* had guarded the entrance
12:18 may the God of our *f* see and punish you."
12:29 with twenty-two princes of his *f* house.
17:11 been completed and you must join your *f*,
21:17 O LORD, my God, strike me and my *f* family,
25: 6 were under their *f'* direction in the
28: 4 my *f* family to be king over Israel forever.
29:15 we are only your guests, like all our *f*.
29:18 O LORD, God of our *f* Abraham,
29:20 blessed the LORD, the God of their *f*,
2Chr 6:25 the land which you gave them and their *f*.
6:31 as they live on the land you gave our *f*.
6:38 of their land which you gave their *f*,
7:22 forsook the LORD, the God of their *f*,
9:31 he was buried in his *f* City of David,
10:10 little finger is thicker than my *f* body.
11:16 sacrifice to the LORD, the God of their *f*.
13:12 against the LORD, the God of your *f*,
13:18 relied on the LORD, the God of their *f*.
14: 3 to seek the LORD, the God of their *f*,
15:12 to seek the LORD, the God of their *f*,
15:18 of God his *f* votive offerings and his own:
19: 4 them back to the LORD, the God of their *f*.
20: 6 "LORD, God of our *f*,
20:33 fixed their hearts on the God of their *f*.
21: 4 *f* kingdom and had consolidated his power,
21:10 he had forsaken the LORD, the God of his *f*.
21:13 of your *f* house who were better than you,
21:19 not made a pyre for him like that of his *f*.
24:18 temple of the LORD, the God of their *f*,
24:24 had abandoned the LORD, the God of their *f*.
25: 4 *F* shall not be put to death for their
25: 4 their children, nor children for their *f*:
28: 6 had abandoned the LORD, the God of their *f*.
28: 9 was because the LORD, the God of your *f*,
28:25 Thus he angered the LORD, the God of his *f*.
29: 5 the house of the LORD, the God of your *f*,
29: 6 Our *f* acted faithlessly and did evil in
29: 9 For our *f*, as you know, fell by the sword,
30: 7 Be not like your *f* and your brethren who
30: 7 faithless to the LORD, the God of their *f*,
30: 8 Be not obstinate, as your *f* were;
30:19 to seek God, the LORD, the God of his *f*,
30:22 praises to the LORD, the God of their *f*,
32:13 Do you not know what my *f* and I have done
32:14 nations which my *f* put under the ban
32:15 people from my hand or the hands of my *f*,
33: 8 leave the land which I assigned to your *f*,
33:12 before the God of his *f* and prayed to him.
34:21 since our *f* have not kept the word of the
34:32 to the covenant of God, the God of their *f*.
34:33 not desert the LORD, the God of their *f*.
36: 1 made him king in Jerusalem in his *f* stead.
36:15 often did the LORD, the God of their *f*,
Ezr 4:15 made in the historical records of your *f*.
5:12 *f* provoked the wrath of the God of heaven,
7:27 Blessed be the LORD, THE GOD of our *f*,
8:28 offering to the LORD, the God of your *f*.
9: 7 From the time of our *f* even to this day
10:11 give praise to the LORD, the God of your *f*,
Neh 1: 6 against you, I and my *f* house included.
9: 2 their sins and the guilty deeds of their *f*.

9: 9 "You saw the affliction of our *f* in Egypt,
9:16 "But they, our *f*, proved to be insolent;
9:23 had commanded their *f* to enter and possess.
9:32 princes, our priests, our prophets, our *f*,
9:34 priests, and our *f* have not kept your law;
9:36 for the land which you gave our *f*
13:18 Did not your *f* act in this same way,
Tb 3: 3 offenses, nor for those of my *f*.
3: 5 me as my sins and those of my *f* deserve.
3: 7 listen to abuse, from one of her *f* maids.
3:10 room in her *f* house with the intention
3:15 name or my *f* name in the land of my exile.
3:15 "I am my *f* only daughter,
4:12 a stranger who is not of your *f* tribe,
4:12 Isaac, and Jacob, our *f* from of old:
6:12 *f* estate is rightfully yours to inherit.
6:15 I am my *f* only child.
6:16 "Do you not remember your *f* orders?
8: 5 "Blessed are you, O God of our *f*;
Jdt 10: 8 "May the God of our *f* bring you to favor,
Est 4:14 but you and your *f* house will perish.
C:16 and our *f* from among all their ancestors,
1Mc 2:19 of his *f* and consents to the king's orders,
2:20 kinsmen will keep to the covenant of our *f*.
2:50 give your lives for the covenant of our *f*.
2:51 the deeds that our *f* did in their times,
2:69 blessed them, and he was united with his *f*.
2:70 was buried in the tombs of his *f* in Modein,
4: 9 how our *f* were saved in the Red Sea,
4:10 favor us, remember his covenant with our *f*,
9:19 him in the tomb of their *f* at Modein.
10:52 taken my seat on the throne of my *f*,
10:55 *f* and took your seat on their royal throne!
10:67 came from Crete to the land of his *f*.
10:72 because your *f* were twice put to flight
11: 9 and you shall reign over your *f* kingdom.
11:40 that he might make him king in his *f* place.
13: 3 and my *f* house have done for the laws and
13:25 buried him in Modein, the city of his *f*.
14:26 He and his brothers and his *f* house have
16: 2 "I and my brothers and my *f* house have
2Mc 1:19 When our *f* were being exiled to Persia,
11:24 the Jews do not agree with our *f* policy
13: 9 than those they suffered in his *f* time.
Jb 8: 8 give heed to the experience of the *f*
15:18 contradicted since the days of their *f*,
30: 1 Whose *f* I should have disdained to rank
Ps(s) 22: 5 In you our *f* trusted;
39:13 before you, a pilgrim like all my *f*.
44: 2 ears have heard, our *f* have declared to us,
45:11 ear, forget your people and your *f* house.
45:17 The place of your *f* your sons shall have;
78: 3 know, and what our *f* have declared to us,
78: 5 our *f* they should make known to their sons;
78: 8 his commands, And not be like their *f*,
78:12 Before their *f* he did wondrous things,
78:57 back and were faithless like their *f*;
95: 9 in the desert, Where your *f* tempted me;
106: 6 We have sinned, we and our *f*;
106: 7 Our *f* in Egypt considered not your wonders;
109:14 guilt of his *f* be remembered by the LORD;
Prv 1: 8 Hear, my son, your *f* instruction,
4: 1 Hear, O children, a *f* instruction,
4: 3 When I was my *f* child,
6:20 Observe, my son, your *f* bidding,
15: 5 The fool spurns his *f* admonition,
22:28 the ancient landmark which your *f* set up.
27:10 own friend and your *f* friend forsake not;
Wis 9: 1 God of my *f*, Lord of mercy,
9:12 people justly and be worthy of my *f* throne.
12: 6 willed to destroy by the hands of our *f*,
12:21 to whose *f* you gave the sworn covenants
18: 6 That night was known beforehand to our *f*,
18: 9 previously sung the praises of the *f*.
18:22 recalling the sworn covenants with their *f*.
18:24 and the glories of the *f* were carved in
Sir 3: 1 Children, pay heed to a *f* right;
3: 9 For a *f* blessing gives a family firm roots,
3:10 Glory not in your *f* shame,
3:11 His *f* honor is a man's glory;
8: 9 men which they have learned from their *f*;
22: 4 husband, a shameless one is her *f* grief.
30: 4 At the *f* death, he will seem not dead,
34:20 Like the man who slays a son in his *f*
42:10 Lest she conceive in her *f* home,
47:23 Solomon finally slept with his *f*
48:10 back the hearts of *f* toward their sons,
Is 3: 6 a man seizes his brother in his *f* house,
7:17 your *f* house days worse than any since
14:21 his sons for the guilt of their *f*;
37:12 the nations whom my *f* destroyed save them?
38:19 *F* declare to their sons,
39: 6 that your *f* have stored up until this day,
49:23 Kings shall be your foster *f*,
64:10 *f* praised you Has been burned with fire;
65: 7 crimes and the crimes of your *f* as well,
Jer 2: 5 *f* find in me that they withdrew from me,
3:18 land which I gave to your *f* as a heritage.
3:24 has devoured our *f* toil from our youth,
3:25 our youth to this day, we and our *f* also;
6:21 *F* and sons alike,
7: 7 which I gave your *f* long ago and forever.
7:14 this place which I gave to you and your *f*,

FATHERS—FATHER'S (cont.)
7:18 gather wood, their *f* light the fire,
7:22 In speaking to your *f* on the day I brought
7:25 *f* left the land of Egypt even to this day,
7:26 their necks and done worse than their *f*.
9:13 and the Baals, as their *f* had taught them;
9:15 whom neither they nor their *f* have known;
11: 4 which I enjoined upon your *f* the day I
11: 5 fulfill the oath which I swore to your *f*,
11: 7 I warned your *f* to obey my voice,
11:10 covenant which I had made with their *f*.
12: 6 own brothers, the members of your *f* house,
13:14 against each other, *f* and sons together,
14:20 O LORD, our wickedness, the guilt of our *f*;
16: 3 the *f* who will beget them in this land:
16:11 It is because your *f* have forsaken me,
16:12 And you have done worse than your *f*.
16:13 that neither you nor your *f* have known;
16:15 them back to the land which I gave their *f*.
16:19 "Mere frauds are the heritage of our *f*,
17:22 holy the sabbath, as I commanded your *f*,
19: 4 gods which neither they nor their *f* knew;
23:27 just as their *f* forgot my name
23:39 the city which I gave to you and your *f*
24:10 the land which I gave them and their *f*.
25: 5 land which the LORD gave you and your *f*,
30: 3 to the land which I have gave to their *f*;
31:29 no longer say, "The *f* ate unripe grapes,
31:32 covenant I made with their *f* the day I took
32:18 and you repay the *f* guilt,
32:22 as you had promised their *f* under oath,
34: 5 for your burial as they did for your *f*,
34:13 I brought your *f* out of the land of Egypt,
34:14 Your *f*, however, did not heed me
35:14 they obeyed their *f* command.
35:15 on the land which I gave you and your *f*;
44: 3 neither they, nor you, nor your *f* knew.
44: 9 you forgotten the evil deeds which your *f*,
44:10 statutes which I set before you and your *f*.
44:17 out libations to her, as we and our *f*,
44:21 you, your *f*, you kings and princes
47: 3 *F* turn not to save their children;
50: 7 against the LORD, the hope of their *f*.
Lam 5: 7 Our *f*, who sinned, are no more;
Bar 1:16 and priests and prophets, and with our *f*,
1:19 From the time the Lord led our *f* out of
1:20 at the time he led our *f* forth from the
2: 6 and we, like our *f*, are flushed with shame
2:19 "Not on the just deeds of our *f* and our
2:21 you may continue in the land I gave your *f*:
2:24 our *f* brought out from their burial places.
2:33 of their *f* who sinned against the Lord.
2:34 which with my oath I promised to their *f*,
3: 5 at this time not the misdeeds of our *f*,
3: 7 wickedness of our *f* who sinned against you.
3: 8 a requital for all the misdeeds of our *f*,
Ez 2: 3 they and their *f* have revolted against me
5:10 means that *f* within you shall eat sons,
5:10 you shall eat sons, and sons shall eat *f*.
18: 2 *F* have eaten green grapes,
20:24 with eyes only for the idols of their *f*.
20:27 In this way also your *f* blasphemed me,
20:30 will you defile yourselves like your *f*?
20:36 your *f* in the desert of the land of Egypt,
20:42 the land which I swore to give to your *f*.
22:10 who uncover the nakedness of their *f*,
22:11 sisters, the daughters of their own *f*.
36:28 You shall live in the land I gave your *f*;
37:25 Jacob, the land where their *f* lived;
47:14 this land which I swore to give to your *f*.
Dn 2:23 To you, O God of my *f*,
3:26 and praiseworthy, O Lord, the God of our *f*,
3:28 and upon Jerusalem, the holy city of our *f*.
3:52 are you, O Lord, the God of our *f*,
9: 6 your name to our kings, our princes, our *f*,
9: 8 like our kings, our princes, and our *f*,
9:16 of our sins and the crimes of our *f*,
11:24 that which his *f* or grandfathers never did;
11:38 to his *f* he shall glorify with gold,
14: 1 After King Astyages was laid with his *f*,
Hos 9:10 fig tree in its prime, I considered your *f*.
Jl 1: 2 in your days or in the days of your *f*?
Am 2: 4 their *f* followed have led them astray,
Mi 7:20 you have sworn to our *f* from days of old.
Zec 1: 2 The LORD was indeed angry with your *f* . . .
1: 4 your *f* whom the former prophets warned:
1: 5 Your *f*, where are they?
1: 6 prophets, did not these overtake your *f*?
8:14 harm you when your *f* provoked me to wrath,
Mal 2:10 other, violating the covenant of our *f*?
3: 7 *f* you have turned aside from my statutes,
3:24 turn the hearts of the *f* to their children,
3:24 and the hearts of the children to their *f*,
Mt 10:29 falls to the ground without your *F* consent.
13:43 will shine like the sun in their *F* kingdom.
16:27 with his *F* glory accompanied by his angels.
18:10 constantly behold my heavenly *F* face.
18:14 it is no part of your heavenly *F* plan that
25:34 You have my *F* blessing!
26:29 I drink it new with you in my *F* reign."
Mk 8:38 comes with the holy angels in his *F* glory."
Lk 1:17 to turn the hearts of *f* to their children
1:55 Even as he promised our *f*,
1:72 *f* and remembered the holy covenant he made,
2:49 Did you not know I had to be in my *F* house?
6:23 it was that their *f* treated the prophets.
6:26 Their *f* treated the false prophets in just
11:47 but it was your *f* who murdered them.
11:48 that you stand behind the deeds of your *f*:
15:17 at my *f* place have more than enough to eat,
15:20 With that he set off for his *f* house.
16:27 to my *f* house where I have five brothers.
Jn 1:18 It is God the only Son, ever at the *F* side,
2:16 Stop turning my *F* house into a marketplace!"
5:43 I have come in my *F* name,
8:38 you what I have seen in the *F* presence;
8:41 Indeed you are doing your *f* works!"
10:25 I do in my *F* name give witness in my favor,
10:37 If I do not perform my *F* works,
14: 2 my *F* house there are many dwelling places;
15:10 even as I have kept my *F* commandments,
Acts 1: 4 for the fulfillment of my *F* promise,
3:13 of Isaac, and of Jacob, the God of our *f*,
3:25 made with your *f* when he said to Abraham,
5:30 The God of our *f* has raised up Jesus whom
7: 2 *F*! Listen to me.
7:11 and Canaan, our *f* could find no sustenance.
7:12 Jacob sent our *f* there on a first mission.
7:15 down to Egypt and died there, as did our *f*.
7:19 He forced our *f* to abandon their infants
7:20 three months he was reared in his *f* house,
7:32 'I am the God of your *f*,
7:38 the angel on Mount Sinai and with our *f*;
7:39 He it was whom our *f* would not obey;
7:44 "Our *f* in the desert had the meeting tent
7:45 The next generation of our *f* inherited it.
7:45 whom God drove out to make room for our *f*.
7:51 Holy Spirit just as your *f* did before you.
7:52 any prophet whom your *f* did not persecute?
13:17 God of the people Israel once chose our *f*.
13:32 God promised our *f* he has fulfilled for us,
13:36 God's will, fell asleep and joined his *f*,
15:10 neither we nor our *f* were able to bear?
22: 1 "My brothers and *f*,
22: 3 was educated strictly in the law of our *f*.
22:14 'The God of our *f* long ago designated you
24:14 that I worship the God of our *f*.
26: 6 hope in the promise made by God to our *f*.
28:25 said to your *f* through the prophet Isaiah:
1Cor 5: 1 a man living with his *f* wife.
10: 1 our *f* were all under the cloud and all
Eph 6: 4 *F*, do not anger your children.
Phil 2:22 *f* side serving the gospel along with me.
Col 3:21 And *f*, do not nag your children
1Tm 1: 9 godless, men who kill their *f* or mothers,
Heb 1: 1 varied ways to our *f* through the prophets;
1: 3 This Son is the reflection of the *F* glory,
1: 3 the exact representation of the *F* being,
3: 9 desert, When your *f* tested and tried me,
7:10 his *f* loins when Melchizedek met Abraham.
8: 9 covenant I made with their *f* the day I took
12: 9 respected our earthly *f* who corrected us,
12:17 he wanted to inherit his *f* blessing,
1Pt 1:18 futile way of life your *f* handed on to you,
1Jn 2:13 *F*, I address you,
2:14 I address you, *f*,
2:15 the world, the *F* love has no place in him,
2Jn 1: 3 Father and from Jesus Christ, the *F* Son.

FATHOM (3)
Jdt 8:14 how then can you *f* God,
Prv 25: 2 conceals, kings have glory in what they *f*.
Sir 43:29 praise him the more, since we cannot *f* him,

FATHOMING (1)
Sir 24:26 wisdom, nor will the last succeed in *f* her.

FATHOMS (1)
Acts 27:28 a sounding and found a depth of twenty *f*;

FATLING (1)
2Sm 6:13 six steps, he sacrificed an ox and a *f*.

FATLINGS (8)
1Kgs 1: 9 sheep, oxen, and *f* at the stone Zoheleth,
1:19 He has slaughtered oxen, *f*,
1:25 went down today and slaughtered oxen, *f*,
Ps(s) 66:15 Holocausts of *f* I will offer you,
Is 1:11 enough of whole-burnt rams and fat of *f*;
34: 7 Wild oxen shall be struck down with *f*,
Ez 34: 3 worn their wool, and slaughtered the *f*,
39:18 lambs, and goats, bullocks, *f* of Bashan,

FATTED (7)
1Kgs 5: 3 fine flour, sixty kors of meal, ten *f* oxen,
5: 3 harts, gazelles, roebucks, and *f* fowl.
Prv 15:17 love is than a *f* ox and hatred with it.
Jer 46:21 mercenaries in her ranks are like *f* calves;
Lk 15:23 Take the *f* calf and kill it.
15:27 and your father has killed the *f* calf
15:30 loose women, you kill the *f* calf for him.'

FATTEN (1)
Neh 9:25 *f* and feast themselves on your immense

FATTENED (1)
Jas 5: 5 you *f* yourselves for the day of slaughter.

FATTENING (1)
1Sm 2:29 *f* yourselves with the choicest part of

FATTY (13)
Ex 29:22 its *f* tail, the fat that covers
Lv 3: 3 LORD the *f* membrane over the inner organs,
3: 9 the whole *f* tail, which he must sever
3: 9 the *f* membrane over the inner organs,
3:14 LORD the *f* membrane over the inner organs,
4: 8 the *f* membrane over the inner organs,
7: 3 the *f* tail, the fatty membrane over
8:25 the *f* tail and all the fat over the inner
9:19 the fatty tail, the *f* membrane
10:15 in with the oblations, the *f* portions,
2Chr 35:14 holocausts and the *f* portions until night;

FAULT (30)
Ex 5:16 It is you who are at *f*."
9:27 it is I and my subjects who are at *f*.
Lv 5:18 for the *f* which was unwittingly committed,
Nm 5: 6 a *f* against his fellow man and wrongs him,
15:24 becomes guilty of the *f* of inadvertence,
15:26 *f* of inadvertence affects all the people.
1Sm 29: 3 and I have no *f* to find with him from the
Jdt 5:20 lord and master, if these people are at *f*,
Jb 4:18 and with his angels he can find *f*.
19: 4 am at *f* and that my fault remains with me,
Ps(s) 7: 4 O LORD, my God, if I am at *f* in this,
32: 1 Happy is he whose *f* is taken away,
Prv 10:10 He who winks at a *f* causes trouble,
Eccl 7:14 man cannot find *f* with him in anything.
Sir 11: 7 Before investigating, find no *f*;
19: 7 if you have a *f*, reveal it not,
20: 2 admits his *f* will be kept from disgrace.
31: 8 Happy the rich man found without *f*,
Is 29:24 those who find *f* shall receive instruction.
Jer 2: 5 What *f* did your fathers find in me that
31:30 through his own *f* only shall anyone die:
38: 9 these men have been at *f* in all they have
Ez 18:13 his death shall be his own *f*.
Dn 6: 5 no *f* of neglect or misconduct was to be
Mt 18:15 wrong against you, go and point out his *f*,
Acts 25: 5 me," he said, "and if this man is at *f*,
Rom 9:19 say to me, "Why, then, does he find *f*?
Heb 8: 8 But God, finding *f* with them, says:
Jas 3: 2 If a person is without *f* in speech he is a

FAULTLESS (5)
Dt 32: 4 The Rock—how *f* are his deeds.
Jb 2: 3 is no one on earth like him, *f* and upright,
Ps(s) 119: 9 How shall a young man be *f* in his way?
Dn 3:27 all your deeds are *f*,
Heb 8: 7 If that first covenant had been *f*,

FAULTS (14)
Lv 16:16 defilements and *f* of the Israelites.
16:21 *f* and transgressions of the Israelites,
2Mc 11:31 any way for *f* committed through ignorance.
Jb 13:23 What are my *f* and my sins?
13:26 me, and punish in me the *f* of my youth.
Ps(s) 19:13 Cleanse me from my unknown *f*!
32: 5 I said, "I confess my *f* to the LORD,"
69: 6 my folly, and my *f* are not hid from you.
Sir 20:27 he who pleases the great is pardoned his *f*.
21: 7 speaker but the wise man knows his own *f*.
27: 4 so do a man's *f* when he speaks.
28: 7 the Most High's covenant, and overlook *f*.
Mt 6:14 "If you forgive the *f* of others,
Mk 11:25 Father may in turn forgive you your *f*."

FAVOR (185)
Gn 4: 4 looked with *f* on Abel and his offering,
6: 8 But Noah found *f* with the LORD.
17:18 God, "Let but Ishmael live on by your *f*!"
18: 3 "Sir, if I may ask you this *f*,
19:21 "I will also grant you the *f* you now ask.
20:13 'Would you do me this *f*?
32: 6 information in the hope of gaining your *f*.' "
33: 8 answered, "It was to gain my lord's *f*."
33:10 "If you will do me the *f*,
34:11 "Do me this *f*,
40:14 do me the *f* of mentioning me to Pharaoh,
50: 4 "Please do me this *f*,"
Ex 8: 5 "Do me the *f* of appointing the time when
12:32 and you will be doing me a *f*."
23: 3 You shall not *f* a poor man in his lawsuit.
28:38 so that they may find *f* with the LORD.
33:12 and also, 'You have found *f* with me.'
33:13 Now, if I have found *f* with you,
33:13 you, I may continue to find *f* with you.
33:16 your people and I, have found *f* with you,
33:17 *f* with me and you are my intimate friend."
34: 9 Then he said, "If I find *f* with you,
Lv 1: 3 To find *f* with the LORD,
7:18 it shall not win *f* for him nor shall it be
26: 9 I will look with *f* upon you,

Nm 11:15 please do me the *f* of killing me at once,
32: 5 they continued, "if we find *f* with you,
Dt 33: 8 Thummim, to the man of your *f* your Urim;
33:16 and the *f* of him who dwells in the bush.
Jgs 6:17 He answered him, "If I find *f* with you,
11:37 said to her father, "Let me have this *f*.
17: 4 to the LORD as my gift in *f* of my son,
Ru 2: 2 field of anyone who will allow me that *f*."
1Sm 25:35 have granted your request as a personal *f*."
29: 4 how else can he win back his master's *f*,
2Sm 7:15 I will not withdraw my *f* from him
14:22 day I know that I am in good *f* with you,
15:25 If I find *f* with the LORD,
16: 4 May I find *f* with you!"
1Kgs 2:16 But now there is one *f* I would ask of you.
2:20 "There is one small *f* I would ask of you,"
3: 6 "You have shown great *f* to your servant,
3: 6 you have continued this great *f* toward him,
11:19 Hadad won great *f* with Pharaoh,
1Chr 17:13 and I will not withdraw my *f* from him as I
2Chr 1: 8 have shown great *f* to my father David,
Ezr 7:28 and who let me find *f* with the king,
Neh 1:11 day, and let him find *f* with this man"
2: 5 if your servant is deserving of your *f*,
5:19 in my *f* all that I did for this people.
10:29 of the lands in *f* of the law of God,
13:22 This, too, remember in my *f*,
13:31 Remember this in my *f*, O my God!
Tb 1:13 granted me *f* and status with Shalmaneser,
3: 3 be mindful of me, and look with *f* upon me.
12:18 to you it was not out of any *f* on my part,
13: 6 look with *f* upon you and show you mercy.
Jdt 4:15 look with *f* on the whole house of Israel.
6:19 and look with *f* this day on those who
10: 8 the God of our fathers bring you to *f*,
Est 2: 9 The girl pleased him and won his *f*.
2:17 the virgins she won his *f* and benevolence.
5: 8 if I have found *f* with the king and if it
7: 3 "If I have found *f* with you,
8: 5 if I have found *f* with you and you love me,
10: 3 was regarded with *f* by his many brethren,
1Mc 1:43 many Israelites were in *f* of his religion;
4:10 to Heaven in the hope that he will *f* us,
6:60 found *f* with the king and the leaders;
10:47 They therefore decided in *f* of Alexander,
10:60 gold and many gifts and thus won their *f*.
11:24 other presents, and found *f* with the king.
11:34 to Judea in *f* of all those who offer sacrifices
11:43 Do me the *f*, therefore, of sending men
Jb 10:12 Grace and *f* you granted me,
11:19 Many shall entreat your *f*,
33:26 He shall pray and God will *f* him;
Ps(s) 19:15 the thought of my heart find *f* before you,
35:27 for joy and be glad who *f* my just cause;
45:13 the rich among the people seek your *f*.
69:14 to you, O LORD, for the time of your *f*,
82: 2 unjustly and *f* the cause of the wicked?
86:17 Grant me a proof of your *f*,
89:18 and by your *f* our horn is exalted.
106: 4 Remember me, O LORD, as you *f* your people;
119:29 way of falsehood, and *f* me with your law.
Prv 3: 4 win *f* and good esteem before God and man.
8:35 me finds life, and wins *f* from the LORD;
11:27 He who seeks the good commands *f*,
12: 2 The good man wins *f* from the LORD,
13:15 Good sense brings *f*,
14: 9 arrogant, but *f* in the house of the just.
16:15 and his *f* is like a rain cloud in spring.
18:22 it is a *f* he receives from the LORD.
19: 6 Many curry *f* with a noble;
19:12 is like the roaring of a lion, but his *f*,
29:26 Many curry *f* with the ruler,
Eccl 9:11 riches by the shrewd, nor *f* by the experts;
10:12 Words from the wise man's mouth win *f*,
Sir 3:18 you are, and you will find *f* with God.
4:12 those who seek her out win her *f*.
7: 6 show *f* to the ruler and mar your integrity.
11:17 his *f* brings continued success.
17: 7 He looks with *f* upon their hearts,
34:18 presents from the lawless win not God's *f*.
41:24 would be looked upon by everyone with *f*.
45: 1 was to spring the man who won the *f* of all:
Is 30:18 Yet the LORD is waiting to show you *f*,
49: 8 In a time of *f* I answer you,
61: 2 To announce a year of *f* from the LORD and
Jer 6:20 Your holocausts find no *f* with me,
24: 5 even so will I regard with *f* Judah's
26:19 the LORD and entreat the *f* of the LORD,
31: 2 the sword have found *f* in the desert.
31:20 threaten him, I still remember him with *f*;
Lam 4:16 He does not receive the priests with *f*,
Bar 1:12 serve them long, finding *f* in their sight.
2:14 grant us *f* in the presence of our captors,
Ez 16:52 you are an argument in *f* of your sisters!
Dn 1: 9 *f* and sympathy of the chief chamberlain,
3:38 to offer first fruits, to find *f* with you.
7:22 in *f* of the holy ones of the Most High,
11:17 but this shall not succeed in his *f*.
Zec 6:14 in the temple of the LORD in *f* of Heldai,
7: 2 his men to implore *f* of the LORD
8:15 to *f* Jerusalem and the house of Judah;
8:21 let us go to implore the *f* of the LORD";
8:22 Jerusalem and to implore the *f* of the LORD.
11: 7 took two staffs, one of which I called *F*,"
11:10 I took my staff *F*" and snapped it asunder,
Mt 3:17 My *f* rests on him."
17: 5 is my beloved Son on whom my *f* rests.
20:20 sons, to do him homage and ask of him a *f*.
22:16 *f* and do not act out of human respect.
Mk 1:11 On you my *f* rests."
7:13 in *f* of the traditions you have handed on.
Lk 1:30 You have found *f* with God.
2:14 on earth to those on whom his *f* rests."
3:22 On you my *f* rests."
4:19 To announce a year of *f* from the Lord."
7: 5 "He deserves this *f* from you,"
18: 5 her *f* or she will end by doing me violence.'"
Jn 10:25 in my Father's name give witness in my *f*,
Acts 7:10 *f* and wisdom in the court of the Pharaoh,
7:46 who found *f* with God and begged that he
11:23 he rejoiced to see the evidence of God's *f*.
14:26 first been commended to the *f* of God
15:11 the *f* of the Lord Jesus and so are they."
15:40 by the brothers to the *f* of the Lord.
18:27 who through God's *f* had become believers.
25: 3 requesting that he *f* them rather than Paul,
27:24 Therefore, as a *f* to you, God has granted
Rom 4: 4 are not regarded as a *f* but as his due.
9:12 by works but by the *f* of him who calls"
12: 3 Thus, in virtue of the *f* given to me,
12: 6 according to the *f* bestowed on each of us.
1Cor 1: 4 *f* he has bestowed on you in Christ Jesus,
3:10 Thanks to the *f* God showed me I laid a
8: 8 failing to eat, and we gain no *f* by eating.
15:10 But by God's *f* I am what I am.
15:10 *f* of his to me has not proved fruitless.
15:10 not on my own but through the *f* of God.
16:23 The *f* of the Lord Jesus be with you.
2Cor 8: 4 the *f* of sharing in this service to members
8: 9 the *f* shown you by our Lord Jesus Christ;
Gal 1: 3 We wish you the *f* and peace of God our
1:15 me by his *f* chose to reveal his Son to me,
2: 9 and recognizing, too, the *f* bestowed on me,
4:17 not courting your *f* in any generous spirit.
4:17 exclude you so that you may court their *f*.
5: 4 from Christ and fallen from God's *f*!
6:18 may the *f* of our Lord Jesus Christ be with
Eph 1: 6 *f* he has bestowed on us in his beloved.
1: 8 so immeasurably generous is God's *f* to us.
2: 5 By this *f* you were saved.
2: 7 might display the great wealth of his *f*,
2: 8 *f* that salvation is yours through faith.
4: 7 Each of us has received God's *f* in the
Phil 4:23 May the *f* of the Lord Jesus Christ be with
Heb 4:16 and *f* and to find help in time of need.
Jas 4: 6 the proud but bestows his *f* on the lowly."
1Pt 1: 2 *F* and peace be yours in abundance.
1:10 the divine *f* that was destined to be yours.
2Pt 1:17 is my beloved Son, on whom my *f* rests."
Rv 2: 6 But you have this much in your *f*:

FAVORABLE (8)

Gn 40:16 Joseph had given this *f* interpretation,
Jgs 18: 6 is *f* to the undertaking you are engaged in."
1Kgs 12: 7 and submit to them, giving them a *f* answer,
2Kgs 20:19 of the LORD which you have spoken is *f*."
Ezr 6:22 by making the king of Assyria *f* to them,
Ps(s) 77: 8 the Lord reject forever and nevermore be *f*?
Is 39: 8 of the LORD which you have spoken is *f*."
1Cor 16:12 He will go when circumstances are more *f*.

FAVORABLY (5)

Gn 24:12 let it turn out *f* for me today and thus
Tb 3:15 me, look *f* upon me and have pity on me;
Sir 11:12 Yet the eyes of the LORD look *f* upon him;
Mal 2:13 sacrifice nor accepts it *f* from your hand;
Lk 4:22 All who were present spoke *f* of him;

FAVORED (16)

Ru 2:10 I, a foreigner, be *f* with your notice?"
1Sm 2:21 The LORD *f* Hannah so that she conceived
20: 3 aware that I am *f* with your friendship,
2Sm 13:21 whom he *f* because he was his first-born.
Jdt 9: 4 the spoils you divided among your *f* sons,
1Mc 12: 1 When Jonathan saw that the times *f* him,
2Mc 2:22 *f* them with all his generous assistance.
Ps(s) 85: 2 You have *f*, O LORD, your land;
128: 2 happy shall you be, and *f*.
Sir 31:16 Behave at table like a *f* guest,
Is 63: 7 He has *f* us according to him mercy and his
Jer 31:20 Is Ephraim not my *f* son,
Am 3: 2 You alone have I *f*,
6: 1 Leaders of a nation *f* from the first,
Lk 1:28 "Rejoice, O highly *f* daughter!
Rom 1: 5 him we have been *f* with apostleship,

FAVORING (5)

Ezr 7: 9 for the *f* hand of his God was upon him.
8:18 for the *f* hand of our God was upon us
8:22 *f* hand of our God is upon all who seek him,
Neh 2: 8 for the *f* hand of my God was upon me.
2:18 the *f* hand of my God had rested upon me,

FAVORITE (3)

Dt 33:24 May he be the *f* among his brothers,
2Sm 23: 1 of Jacob, *f* of the Mighty One of Israel.
Dn 14: 2 Daniel was the king's *f* and was held in

FAVORITES (4)

Dt 10:17 God, mighty and awesome, who has no *f*,
Sir 35:12 For he is a God of justice, who knows no *f*.
Gal 2: 6 God plays no *f*),
Eph 6: 9 have a Master in heaven who plays no *f*.

FAVORITISM (5)

Sir 4:22 Show no *f* to your own discredit;
Rom 2:11 With God there is no *f*.
Col 3:25 No *f* will be shown.
Jas 2: 1 Lord Jesus Christ must not allow of *f*.
2: 9 But if you show *f*, you commit sin

FAVORS (18)

Ex 33:19 I who show *f* to whom I will,
Dt 33:23 "Naphtali is enriched with *f* and filled
2Sm 20:11 who *f* Joab and is for David follow Joab."
1Mc 10:27 *f* in return for what you do in our behalf.
11:53 for all the *f* he had received from him,
2Mc 1:35 king wished to bestow *f* he distributed
Jb 34:19 Who neither *f* the person of princes,
Ps(s) 89: 2 The *f* of the LORD I will sing forever;
89:50 Where are your ancient *f*,
107:43 things and to understand the *f* of the LORD?
Prv 3:12 he reproves, and he chastises the son he *f*.
14:35 The king *f* the intelligent servant,
Eccl 9: 7 because it is now that God *f* your works.
Sir 20:28 *F* and gifts blind the eyes;
32:13 your Creator, who showers his *f* upon you.
Is 63: 7 The *f* of the LORD I will recall,
Lam 3:22 The *f* of the LORD are not exhausted,
2Cor 9: 8 God can multiply his *f* among you so that

FAWN (2)

Dt 33:29 Your enemies *f* upon you,
Ps(s) 66: 3 great strength your enemies *f* upon you.

FAWNED (2)

2Sm 22:46 The foreigners *f* and cringed before me;
Ps(s) 18:45 The foreigners *f* and cringed before me;

FAWNS (3)

Gn 49:21 hind let loose which brings forth lovely *f*.
Sg 4: 5 Your breasts are like twin *f*,
7: 4 Your breasts are like twin *f*,

FEAR (454)

Gn 9: 2 Dread *f* of you shall come upon all the
15: 1 *F* not, Abram!
20:11 would surely be no *f* of God in this place,
26:24 You have no need to *f*,
32:12 Otherwise I *f* that when he comes he will
35:17 her midwife said to her, "Have no *f*!
43:23 "you have no need to *f*.
50:19 "Have no *f*.
50:21 Therefore have no *f*.
Ex 9:30 I know, do not yet *f* the LORD God."
14:13 But Moses answered the people, *F* not!
20:20 only to test you and put his *f* upon you,
23:27 "I will have the *f* of me precede you,
Lv 19:14 of the blind, but you shall *f* your God.
19:32 thus shall you *f* your God.
25:17 but stand in *f* of your God.
25:36 but out of *f* of God let him live with you.
25:43 them harshly, but stand in *f* of your God.
Nm 12: 8 not *f* to speak against my servant Moses?"
Dt 1:21 Do not *f* or lose heart.'
1:29 I said to you, 'Have no dread or *f* of them.
2:25 This day I will begin to put a *f* and dread
3:22 *F* them not, for the LORD, your God,
4:10 that they may learn to *f* me as long as
5:29 to *f* me and to keep all my commandments!
6: 2 your son and your grandson may *f* the LORD,
6:13 The LORD, your God, shall you *f*;
6:24 all these statutes in *f* of the LORD,
10:12 your God, ask of you but to *f* the LORD,
10:20 The LORD, your God, shall you *f*,
11:25 will spread the *f* and dread of you through
13: 5 shall you follow, and him shall you *f*;
13:12 shall *f* and never again do such evil as
14:23 that you may learn always to *f* the LORD,
17:13 all the people, on hearing of it, shall *f*,
17:19 his life that he may learn to *f* the LORD,
18:22 and you shall have no *f* of him.
19:20 The rest, on hearing of it, shall *f*,
21:21 and all Israel, on hearing of it, shall *f*.
25:18 *f* of any god he harassed you along the way,
31: 6 have no *f* or dread of them,
31: 8 So do not *f* or be dismayed."
31:12 hear it and learn it, and so *f* the LORD,
31:13 and learn it, that they too may *f* the LORD,
Jos 1: 9 Do not *f* nor be dismayed,
2: 9 of the land are overcome with *f* of you.
2:24 of the land are overcome with *f* of us."

FEAR (cont.)

4:24 is mighty, and that you may *f* the LORD,
9:24 advance, we were in great *f* for our lives,
10: 2 them and that there was great *f* abroad,
10: 8 the LORD said to Joshua, "Do not *f* them,
11: 6 The LORD said to Joshua, "Do not *f* them,
24:14 *f* the LORD and serve him completely and
Jgs 6: 2 For *f* of Midian the Israelites established
6:23 LORD answered him, "Be calm, do not *f*.
6:27 *f* of his family and of the townspeople,
9:21 he remained for *f* of his brother Abimelech.
1Sm 4:20 standing around her said to her, "Never *f*!
12:14 If you *f* the LORD and worship him,
12:20 "Do not *f*," Samuel answered them.
12:24 But you must *f* the LORD and worship him
13: 7 all his followers were seized with *f*.
15:24 In my *f* of the people,
18:12 Saul then began to *f* David,
18:15 he was, Saul conceived a *f* of David:
20:21 the LORD lives, there will be nothing to *f*.
22:23 *F* nothing; he that seeks your life
23:17 "Have no *f*,
28:13 But the king said to her, "Have no *f*.
2Sm 3:11 In his *f* of Abner,
9: 7 *F* not," David said to him,
14:15 the people have given me cause to *f*.
23: 3 men in justice, that rules in the *f* of God,
1Kgs 1:50 Adonijah, in *f* of Solomon,
1:51 that Adonijah, in his *f* of King Solomon,
8:40 so treat them that they may *f* you as long
8:43 name, may *f* you as do your people Israel,
2Kgs 25:26 and went to Egypt for *f* of the Chaldeans.
1Chr 10: 4 But the armor-bearer, in great *f*, refused.
14:17 and the LORD made all the nations *f* him.
22:13 do not *f* or lose heart.
28:20 go to work without *f* or discouragement,
2Chr 6:31 So may they *f* you and walk in your ways as
14:13 Gerar, for the *f* of the LORD was upon them;
17:10 Now the *f* of the LORD was upon all the
19: 7 And now, let the *f* of the LORD be upon you.
19: 9 and wholeheartedly in the *f* of the LORD.
20:15 'Do not *f* or lose heart at the sight of
20:17 Do not *f* or lose heart.
20:29 And the *f* of God came upon all the
26: 5 Zechariah lived, who taught him to *f* God;
Ezr 3: 3 Despite their *f* of the peoples of the land,
10: 3 those who *f* the commandments of our God.
Neh 2: 2 Though I was seized with great *f*,
4: 3 day and night for *f* of what they might do.
4: 8 "Have no *f* of them!
5: 9 Should you not walk in the *f* of our God,
6:13 act on it out of *f* and commit this sin.
Tb 1:19 then in my *f* I took to flight.
4:21 You will be a rich man if you *f* God,
5:16 "I will go with him; have no *f*.
12:16 Stricken with *f*, the two men fell
12:17 "No need to *f*; you are safe.
Jdt 2:28 The *f* and dread of him fell upon all the
10:16 stand before him, have no *f* in your heart;
11: 1 have no *f* in your heart!
15: 2 amazed, and overcome with *f* and trembling.
16:15 "But to those who *f* you,
Est A: 8 with *f* of the evils to come upon them,
C:30 of the wicked, and deliver me from my *f*."
D: 5 lovely, though her heart was shrunk with *f*.
D:13 heart was troubled with *f* of your majesty.
5: 9 gate did not rise, and showed no *f* of him,
8:17 for they were seized with a *f* of the Jews.
9: 2 all peoples were seized with a *f* of them.
9: 3 supported the Jews from *f* of Mordecai;
1Mc 2:62 Do not *f* the words of a sinful man,
3: 6 The lawbreakers were cowed by *f* of him,
4:32 Strike them with *f*,
6: 8 he was struck with *f* and very much shaken.
7:18 Then *f* and dread of them came upon all the
10: 8 The men in the citadel were struck with *f*
12:28 battle, their hearts sank with *f* and dread.
12:52 Jonathan and his men, and were in great *f*,
13:17 for *f* of provoking much hostility among
2Mc 3:30 so shortly before with *f* and commotion,
8:16 nor to *f* the large number of the Gentiles
12:22 enemy was overwhelmed with *f* and terror
14:22 for *f* that the enemy might suddenly carry
15: 8 He urged his men not to *f* the enemy,
15:18 *f* was for the consecrated sanctuary.
15:23 angel now to spread *f* and dread before us.
Jb 3:25 For what I *f* overtakes me,
4:14 deep sleep falls on men, *F* came upon me,
5:21 hidden, and shall not *f* approaching ruin.
6:14 he have forsaken the *f* of the Almighty.
21: 9 Their homes are safe and without *f*,
23:15 when I take thought, I *f* him.
28:28 Behold, the *f* of the LORD is wisdom;
33: 7 Therefore no *f* of me should dismay you,
39:22 He laughs at *f* and cannot be deterred;
41:26 All, however lofty, *f* him;
Ps(s) 2:11 Serve the LORD with *f*,
3: 7 I *f* not the myriads of people arrayed
5: 8 worship at your holy temple in *f* of you,
14: 5 then they shall be in great *f*,
15: 4 while he honors those who *f* the LORD;
19:10 The *f* of the LORD is pure,
22:24 "You who *f* the Lord,
22:26 fulfill my vows before those who *f* him.
23: 4 I walk in the dark valley I *f* no evil;
25:14 of the LORD is with those who *f* him,
27: 3 encamp against me, my heart will not *f*;
31:20 you have in store for those who *f* you,
33: 8 Let all the earth *f* the LORD;
33:18 eyes of the LORD are upon those who *f* him,
34: 8 of the LORD encamps around those who *f* him,
34:10 *F* the LORD, you his holy ones,
34:10 for nought is lacking to those who *f* him.
34:12 I will teach you the *f* of the LORD.
46: 3 Therefore we *f* not, though the earth
49: 6 Why should I *f* in evil days when my
49:17 *F* not when a man grows rich,
53: 6 they were in great *f*, where no fear was,
55: 6 *F* and trembling come upon me.
55:20 is not in them, nor do they *f* God.
56: 4 O Most High, when I begin to *f*,
56: 5 promise I glory, in God I trust without *f*;
56:12 promise I glory, in God I trust without *f*;
60: 6 You have raised for those who *f* you a
61: 6 me the heritage of those who *f* your name.
64: 5 man, suddenly shooting at him without *f*.
64:10 And all men *f* and proclaim the work of God,
65: 9 the earth's ends are in *f* at your marvels;
66:16 Hear now, all you who *f* God,
67: 8 and may all the ends of the earth *f* him!
85:10 indeed is his salvation to those who *f* him,
86:11 direct my heart that it may *f* your name.
90:11 indignation toward those who should *f* you?
91: 5 You shall not *f* the terror of the night
103:11 is his kindness toward those who *f* him.
103:13 the LORD has compassion on those who *f* him,
103:17 to eternity toward those who *f* him,
111: 5 He has given food to those who *f* him;
111:10 *f* of the LORD is the beginning of wisdom;
112: 7 An evil report he shall not *f*;
112: 8 he shall not *f* till he looks upon his foes.
115:11 Those who *f* the LORD trust in the LORD;
115:13 He will bless those who *f* the LORD,
118: 4 Let those who *f* the LORD say,
118: 6 The LORD is with me; I *f* not;
119:38 servant your promise to those who *f* you.
119:63 of all who *f* you and keep your precepts.
119:74 Those who *f* you shall see me and be glad,
119:79 me who *f* you and acknowledge your decrees.
119:120 with dread of you, and I *f* your ordinances.
128: 1 Happy are you who *f* the LORD,
135:20 you who *f* the LORD, bless the LORD.
145:19 He fulfills the desire of those who *f* him,
147:11 The LORD is pleased with those who *f* him,
Prv 1: 7 The *f* of the LORD is the beginning of
1:29 knowledge, and chose not the *f* of the LORD;
1:33 in security, in peace, without *f* of harm."
2: 5 Then will you understand the *f* of the LORD;
3: 7 *f* the LORD and turn away from evil;
8:13 [The *f* of the LORD is to hate evil;]
9:10 beginning of wisdom is the *f* of the LORD,
10:27 The *f* of the LORD prolongs life,
14:26 In the *f* of the LORD is a strong defense;
14:27 The *f* of the LORD is a fountain of life,
15:16 Better a little with *f* of the LORD than a
15:33 The *f* of the LORD is training for wisdom,
16: 6 and by the *f* of the LORD man avoids evil.
19:23 The *f* of the LORD is an aid to life;
22: 4 of humility and *f* of the LORD is riches,
23:17 be zealous for the *f* of the LORD always;
24:21 My son, *f* the LORD and the king;
29:25 The *f* of man brings a snare,
Eccl 5: 6 Rather, *f* God!
8:12 that it shall be well with those who *f* God,
12:13 *F* God and keep his commandments,
Wis 5: 2 they shall be shaken with dreadful *f*,
6: 7 no partiality, nor does he *f* greatness,
12:11 Neither out of *f* for anyone did you grant
17: 8 themselves sickened with a ridiculous *f*.
17:12 For *f* is nought but the surrender of the
17:15 for *f* came upon them,
Sir 1: 9 *F* of the LORD is glory and splendor,
1:10 *F* of the LORD warms the heart,
1:12 The beginning of wisdom is *f* of the LORD,
1:14 Fullness of wisdom is *f* of the LORD;
1:16 Wisdom's garland is *f* of the LORD,
1:18 The root of wisdom is *f* of the LORD;
1:22 but *f* of the LORD is an abomination to the
1:24 For *f* of the LORD is wisdom and culture;
1:25 Be not faithless to the *f* of the LORD,
1:29 Because you approached the *f* of the LORD
2: 7 You who *f* the LORD, wait for his mercy,
2: 8 You who *f* the LORD, trust him
2: 9 You who *f* the LORD, hope for good
2:10 persevered in his *f* and been forsaken?
2:15 Those who *f* the LORD disobey not his words;
2:16 Those who *f* the LORD seek to please him,
2:17 Those who *f* the LORD prepare their hearts
4:17 *F* and dread she brings upon him and tries
7:29 With all your soul, *f* God,
9:16 in the *f* of God be your glory.
10:19 Those who *f* God.
10:21 or pauper, his glory is the *f* of the LORD.
15:13 he does not let it befall those who *f* him.
16: 2 in them if they have not the *f* of the LORD.
17: 4 He puts the *f* of him in all flesh,
19:17 All wisdom is *f* of the LORD;
19:20 those with little understanding who *f* God,
21:11 who is perfect in *f* of the LORD has wisdom.
22:16 deliberation shaken in a moment of *f*.
22:18 on foolish plans withstand *f* of any kind.
22:22 you speak sharply to a friend, *f* not,
23:18 why should I *f* sin?"
23:27 nothing is better than the *f* of the LORD,
25: 6 their glory, the *f* of the LORD.
25:11 *F* of the LORD surpasses all else.
27: 3 earnestly hold fast to the *f* of the LORD,
29: 7 of meanness, but from *f* of being cheated.
34:13 is the courage of those who *f* the LORD,
40: 2 living, His thoughts, the *f* in his heart,
40: 7 up astonished that there was nothing to *f*.
40:26 but better than either, *f* of God.
40:26 *F* of the LORD leaves nothing wanting;
40:27 The *f* of God is a paradise of blessings;
41: 3 *F* not death's decree for you;
43:35 and to those who *f* him he gives wisdom.
50:29 for the *f* of the LORD is his lamp.
Is 7: 4 care you remain tranquil and do not *f*;
7:25 For *f* of briers and thorns you shall not
8: 6 And melts with *f* before the loftiness of
8:12 *f* not, nor stand in awe of what they fear.
8:13 for him be your *f* and your awe.
10:24 who dwell in Zion, do not *f* the Assyrian,
11: 2 spirit of knowledge and of *f* of the LORD,
11: 3 his delight shall be the *f* of the LORD.
19:16 shall be like women, trembling with *f*,
25: 3 will honor you, fierce nations will *f* you.
33: 6 the *f* of the LORD is her treasure.
35: 4 Be strong, *f* not!
40: 9 *F* not to cry out and say to the cities of
41: 5 The coastlands see, and *f*;
41:10 *F* not, I am with you;
41:13 It is I who say to you, *F* not,
41:14 *F* not, O worm Jacob,
41:23 or evil, that will put us in awe and in *f*.
43: 1 *F* not, for I have redeemed you;
43: 5 *F* not, for I am with you;
44: 2 *F* not, O Jacob, my servant,
44: 8 *F* not, be not troubled:
44:11 stand forth, to be reduced to *f* and shame.
51: 7 *F* not the reproach of men,
51:12 Can you then *f* mortal man,
54: 4 *F* not, you shall not be put to shame;
54:14 established, far from the *f* of oppression,
57:11 Whom did you *f*, that you became false
57:11 so that you would not have me to *f*?
59:19 in the west shall *f* the name of the LORD,
63:17 and harden our hearts so that we *f* you not?
66: 4 for them and bring upon them what they *f*.
Jer 1: 8 Have no *f* before them,
2:19 the LORD, your God, And showing no *f* of me,
5:22 Should you not *f* me,
5:24 not in their hearts, "Let us *f* the LORD,
10: 2 and have no *f* of the signs of the heavens,
10: 2 of the heavens, though the nations *f* them.
10: 5 *F* them not, they can do no harm,
10: 7 Who would not *f* you,
22:25 the hands of those whom you *f*;
23: 4 so that they need no longer *f* and tremble;
26:19 Did they not rather *f* the LORD and entreat
26:21 Uriah heard of it and fled in *f* to Egypt.
30: 5 *f* reigns, not peace.
30:10 But you, my servant Jacob, *f* not,
32:39 will give them, that they may *f* me always,
32:40 into their hearts I will put the *f* of me,
33: 9 They shall be in *f* and trembling over all
42:11 Do not *f* the king of Babylon,
42:11 do not *f* him, says the LORD,
42:16 you *f* shall reach you in the land of Egypt;
44:10 they do not *f* or follow the law and the
46:27 But you, my servant Jacob, *f* not;
46:28 You, my servant Jacob, never *f*,
51:46 for *f* of rumors spread in the land;
Lam 3:57 you said, "Have no *f*!"
Bar 3: 7 this, you put into our hearts the *f* of you:
4: 5 *F* not, my people!
4:21 *F* not, my children;
4:27 *F* not, my children; call out to God!
4:30 *F* not, Jerusalem!
6: 3 and wood, which cast *f* upon the pagans.
6: 4 their alien example and stand in *f* of them,
6:14 do not *f* them.
6:22 that they are not gods, and do not *f* them.
6:28 this that they are not gods, do not *f* them.
6:64 that they are not gods, and do not *f* them.
6:68 so do not *f* them.
Ez 2: 6 *f* neither them nor their words when they
2: 6 Neither *f* their words nor be dismayed at
3: 9 *F* them not, nor be dismayed
11: 8 You *f* the sword,
30:13 I will cast *f* into the land of Egypt,
Dn 3:41 whole heart, we *f* you and we pray to you.
3:90 the God of gods, all you who *f* the Lord;
10: 7 great *f* seized the men who were with me;
10:12 *F* not, Daniel," he continued;
10:19 again and strengthened me, saying, *F* not,
13:57 Israel, and in their *f* they yielded to you;
Hos 10: 3 Since they do not *f* the LORD,
10: 5 of Samaria *f* for the calf of Beth-aven;

13: 1 Ephraim's word caused *f*,
Jl 2:21 *F* not, O land!
2:22 *F* not, beasts of the field!
Jon 1:10 were seized with great *f* and said to him.
1:16 Struck with great *f* of the LORD,
Mi 6: 9 [It is wisdom to *f* your name!]
7:17 trembling in *f* of you [the LORD,
Zep 2:11 The LORD shall inspire them with *f* when he
3: 7 I said, "Surely now you will *f* me,
3:15 midst, you have no further misfortune to *f*.
3:16 *F* not, O Zion, be not discouraged!
Hg 2: 5 spirit continues in your midst; do not *f*!
Zec 8:13 do not *f*, but let your hands be strong.
8:15 the house of Judah; do not *f*!
Mal 2: 5 *f* I put in him,
3: 5 the stranger, and those who do not *f* me,
3:16 they who *f* the LORD spoke with one another,
3:16 those who *f* the LORD and trust in his name.
3:20 But for you who *f* my name,
Mt 1:20 have no *f* about taking Mary as your wife.
10:28 "Do not *f* those who deprive the body of
10:28 *f* him who can destroy both body and soul
14:26 said, and in their *f* they began to cry out.
15:32 hungry, for *f* they may collapse on the way."
17: 6 forward on the ground, overcome with *f*.
17:27 for *f* of disedifying them go to the lake,
21:26 we shall have reason to *f* the people,
21:46 *f* the crowds who regarded him as a prophet.
25:25 so out of *f* I went off and buried your
26: 5 festival, for *f* of a riot among the people."
28: 4 with *f* of him and fell down like dead men.
Mk 5:15 sane, and they were seized with *f*.
5:36 *F* is useless.
10:32 while that of those who followed was *f*.
10:49 did so, "You have nothing to *f* from him!
11:32 (They had reason to *f* the people,
12:12 this, yet they had reason to *f* the crowd.
14:34 he began to be filled with *f* and distress.
16: 8 and because of their great *f*,
Lk 1:12 upon seeing him, and overcome by *f*.
1:30 "Do not *f*, Mary.
1:50 is from age to age on those who *f* him.
1:65 *F* descended on all in the neighborhood;
1:74 rid of *f* and delivered from the enemy,
2:10 "You have nothing to *f*!
7:16 *F* seized them all and they began to praise
8:25 Filled with *f* and admiration,
8:37 for a great *f* had seized them;
8:50 *F* is useless; what is needed is trust
12: 5 I will show you whom you ought to *f*.
12: 5 *F* him who has power to cast into Gehenna
12: 5 Yes, I tell you, *f* him.
12: 7 *F* nothing, then.
12:32 "Do not live in *f*, little flock.
14:29 He will do that for *f* of laying the
23:40 "Have you no *f* of God,
Jn 3:20 near it for *f* his deeds will be exposed.
7:13 about him, however, for *f* of the Jews.
12:15 *F* not, O daughter of Zion!
12:42 *f* they might be ejected from the synagogue.
19:38 (although a secret one for *f* of the Jews),
20:19 place where they were for *f* of the Jews,
Acts 2:43 A reverent *f* overtook them all,
5: 5 *f* came upon all who later heard of it.
5:11 Great *f* came on the whole church and on
5:26 force, for *f* of being stoned by the crowd.
9:31 steady progress in the *f* of the Lord;
10: 4 He stared at the sight and said in *f*,
19:17 Greeks living in Ephesus, *f* fell upon all,
27:17 Because of their *f* that they would be
27:29 For *f* that we should be dashed against
Rom 3:18 the *f* of God is not before their eyes."
8:15 spirit of slavery leading you back into *f*,
13: 3 Rulers cause no *f* when a man does what is
13: 3 wish to be free from the *f* of authority?
1Cor 2: 3 came among you it was in weakness and in *f*,
9:27 for *f* that after having preached to others
2Cor 7: 1 and in the *f* of God strive to fulfill our
7:11 What indignation, *f*, and longing!
7:15 when you received him in *f* and trembling.
11: 3 My *f* is that, just as the serpent seduced
12:20 I *f* that when I come I may not find you to
12:20 I *f* I may find discord,
12:21 I *f* that when I come again my God may
Gal 4:11 I *f* for you;
1Tm 5:20 so that the rest may *f* to offend.
Heb 2:15 and free those who through *f* of death had
1Pt 3:14 *F* not and do not stand in awe of what this
1Jn 4:18 fear; rather, perfect love casts out all *f*.
4:18 And since *f* has to do with punishment.
Rv 1:17 "There is nothing to *f*.
2:10 Have no *f* of the sufferings to come.
16:15 for *f* of going naked and exposed
18: 4 for *f* of sinning with her and sharing the
18:10 for *f* of the punishment inflicted on her,
18:15 for *f* of the punishment inflicted on her.

FEARED (33)

Gn 38:11 for he *f* that Shelah also might die like
Ex 1:17 The midwives, however, *f* God;
1:21 And because the midwives *f* God,
9:20 Some of Pharaoh's servants *f* the warning
14:31 they *f* the LORD and believed in him and in
20:18 mountain smoking, they all *f* and trembled.
Nm 22: 3 Moab *f* the Israelites greatly because of
Dt 32:27 Had I not *f* the insolence of their enemies,
32:27 *f* that these foes would mistakenly boast,
1Sm 3:15 He *f* to tell Eli the vision,
14:26 from it, because the people *f* the oath.
18:29 Therefore Saul *f* David all the more [and
2Sm 6: 9 David *f* the LORD that day and said,
Neh 4: 8 in mind the Lord who is great and to be *f*,
5:15 But I, because I *f* God, did not act thus.
Tb 8:16 what I *f* did not happen.
Jdt 2:28 in Azotus and Ascalon also *f* him greatly.
1Mc 3:25 Then Judas and his brothers began to be *f*,
3:30 He *f* that, as had happened more than
Jb 1: 1 man named Job, who *f* God and avoided evil.
31:34 Because I *f* the noisy multitude and the scorn
Ps(s) 76: 9 the earth *f* and was silent When God arose
Wis 18:25 the destroyer yielded, and these he *f*;
Sir 9:18 *F* in the city is the man of railing speech,
48:12 During his lifetime he *f* no one,
Dn 5:19 of every language dreaded and *f* him.
6:27 God of Daniel is to be reverenced and *f*:
Hb 3: 2 O LORD, I have heard your renown, and *f*,
Hg 1:12 him, and the people *f* because of the LORD.
Mal 1:14 and my name will be *f* among the nations.
2: 5 fear I put in him, and he *f* me,
Mk 6:20 Herod *f* John,
Acts 23:10 commander *f* they would tear Paul to pieces.

FEARFUL (24)

Gn 50:15 Joseph's brothers became *f* and thought,
Dt 1:19 whole desert, vast and *f* as you have seen,
Jgs 7: 3 the soldiers, 'If anyone is afraid or *f*,
1Chr 21:30 *f* of the sword of the angel of the LORD.
Wis 4:20 *F* shall they come,
17: 3 of oblivion Were scattered in *f* trembling,
17: 6 *f* fires flashed through upon them;
Sir 45: 2 the Lord strengthened him with *f* powers;
Is 21: 1 comes from the desert, from the *f* land,
52:12 Yet not in *f* haste will you come out,
Jer 50:38 and they shall be made frantic by *f* things.
Bar 4:31 *F* are those who harmed you,
4:32 *F* are the cities where your children were
4:32 enslaved, *f* the city that took your sons.
Dn 8:24 be strong and powerful, bring about *f* ruin,
Mk 5:33 *F* and beginning to tremble now as she
Lk 9:34 disciples grew *f* as the others entered it.
21:11 and in the sky *f* omens and great signs.
Jn 14:27 Do not be distressed or *f*.
Rom 11:20 Do not be haughty on that account, but *f*.
Heb 4: 1 we ought to be *f* of disobeying lest any
10:27 only a *f* expectation of judgment and a
10:31 It is a *f* thing to fall into the hands of
12:21 so *f* was the spectacle that Moses said,

FEARFULLY (2)

Ps(s) 139:14 I give you thanks that I am *f*,
Ez 4:16 water which they have measured out *f*.

FEARING (11)

Dt 1:17 the lowly and to the great alike, *f* no man,
8: 6 your God, by walking in his ways and *f* him.
1Sm 27:11 *f* that they would betray him by saying,
2Chr 6:33 your name, *f* you as do your people Israel,
2Mc 3:32 *F* that the king might think that
9:29 but *f* Antiochus' son, he later withdrew
Jb 1: 8 and upright, *f* God and avoiding evil?"
2: 3 and upright, *f* God and avoiding evil?
Sir 23:19 he is not mindful, *f* only the eyes of men;
1Thes 3: 5 *f* that the tempter had put you to the test
Heb 11:27 he left Egypt, not *f* the king's wrath,

FEARLESS (1)

Wis 17: 4 not even their inner chambers kept them *f*,

FEARLESSLY (6)

Acts 9:27 out *f* in the name of Jesus at Damascus.
13:46 Paul and Barnabas spoke out *f*,
14: 3 considerable time there and spoke out *f*,
18:26 to express himself *f* in the synagogue.
19: 8 over a period of three months, debated *f*,
Phil 1:14 emboldened to speak the word of God *f*.

FEARS (36)

Jdt 16:16 sight, one who *f* the Lord is forever great.
Ps(s) 25:12 When a man *f* the LORD, he shows him
34: 5 answered me and delivered me from all my *f*.
112: 1 Happy the man who *f* the LORD,
128: 4 thus is the man blessed who *f* the LORD.
Prv 10:24 What the wicked man *f* will befall him,
14: 2 He who walks uprightly *f* the LORD,
31:21 She *f* not the snow for her household;
31:30 the woman who *f* the LORD is to be praised.
Eccl 7:18 who *f* God will win through at all events.
9: 2 rashly, so it is for him who *f* an oath.
12: 5 And one *f* heights, and perils in the street;
Wis 17: 8 For they who undertook to banish *f* and
18:17 them and unexpected *f* assailed them;
Sir 1:11 He who *f* the LORD will have a happy end;
3: 7 He who *f* the LORD honors his father,
6:16 remedy, such as he who *f* God finds;
6:17 For he who *f* God behaves accordingly,
10:20 he who *f* God is in honor among his people.
10:23 but none is greater than he who *f* God.
15: 1 He who *f* the LORD will do this;
21: 6 but he who *f* the LORD repents in his heart.
25:10 but not greater than he who *f* the LORD.
26: 3 gift bestowed upon him who *f* the LORD;
32:16 His judgment is sound who *f* the LORD;
33: 1 No evil can harm the man who *f* the LORD;
34:14 He who *f* the LORD is never alarmed,
34:15 Happy the soul that *f* the LORD!
Is 50:10 Who among you *f* the LORD,
Jer 17: 8 It *f* not the heat when it comes,
Ez 18:14 commits, yet *f* and does not imitate him;
Mal 1: 6 his father, and a servant *f* his master;
Acts 10:35 the man of any nation who *f* God and acts
2Cor 7: 5 quarrels with others and *f* within myself.
1Pt 3: 6 do what is right and let no *f* alarm you.
3:14 do not stand in awe of what this people *f*."

FEARSOME (2)

Wis 10:16 withstood *f* kings with signs and portents;
17:15 Were partly smitten by *f* apparitions and

FEASIBLE (1)

1Sm 10: 7 signs fulfilled, do whatever you judge *f*,

FEAST (134)

Gn 21: 8 child's weaning, Abraham held a great *f*.
26:30 Isaac then made a *f* for them,
29:22 all the local inhabitants and gave a *f*.
Ex 5: 1 they may celebrate a *f* to me in the desert."
10: 9 That is what a *f* of the LORD means to us."
12:14 "This day shall be a memorial *f* for you,
12:47 whole community of Israel must keep this *f*.
23:14 year you shall celebrate a pilgrim *f* to me.
23:15 You shall keep the *f* of Unleavened Bread.
23:16 You shall also keep the *f* of the grain
23:16 the *f* at the fruit harvest at the end of
23:18 my *f* be kept overnight till the next day.
32: 5 proclaimed, "Tomorrow is a *f* of the LORD."
34:18 "You shall keep the *f* of Unleavened Bread.
34:22 "You shall keep the *f* of Weeks with the
34:22 the *f* at the fruit harvest at the close of
34:25 *f* be kept overnight for the next day.
Lv 19:24 to the LORD as a thanksgiving *f* to him.
23: 2 are the festivals of the LORD, my *f* days,
23: 6 month is the LORD's *f* of Unleavened Bread.
23:34 seventh month is the LORD's *f* of Booths.
23:39 a pilgrim *f* of the LORD for a whole week.
23:41 shall keep this pilgrim *f* of the LORD
Nm 28:17 day of this month is the pilgrimage *f*.
28:26 day of first fruits, on your *f* of Weeks,
29:12 shall celebrate a pilgrimage *f* to the LORD.
Dt 16:10 keep the *f* of Weeks in honor of the LORD,
16:13 celebrate the *f* of Booths for seven days,
16:14 You shall make merry at your *f*,
16:15 this pilgrim *f* in honor of the LORD,
16:16 at the *f* of Unleavened Bread,
16:16 the feast of Weeks, and at the *f* of Booths.
31:10 "On the *f* of Booths,
34: 4 I have let you *f* your eyes upon it,
Jgs 14:12 of the *f* you solve it for me successfully,
14:17 him during the seven days the *f* lasted.
21:19 of the yearly *f* of the LORD at Shiloh,
2Sm 3:20 David prepared a *f* for Abner and for the
1Kgs 12:32 Jeroboam established a *f* in the eighth
12:32 in Bethel the pilgrimage *f* of Judah,
12:33 chose to establish a *f* for the Israelites;
2Kgs 6:23 The king spread a great *f* for them.
23:16 was standing by the altar on the *f* day.
1Chr 23:31 LORD on sabbaths, new moons, and *f* days,
2Chr 7: 9 for seven days and the *f* for seven days.
8:13 on the *f* of the Unleavened Bread,
8:13 the feast of Weeks and the *f* of Booths.
30:13 *f* of Unleavened Bread in the second month;
30:21 celebrated the *f* of Unleavened Bread
35:17 *f* of the Unleavened Bread for seven days.
Ezr 3: 4 the *f* of Booths in the manner prescribed,
6:22 the *f* of Unleavened Bread for seven days,
Neh 8:14 booths during the *f* of the seventh month;
8:18 They kept the *f* for seven days,
9:25 *f* themselves on your immense good gifts.
12:43 great *f* of the LORD in which they shared.
Tb 2: 1 our festival of Pentecost, the *f* of Weeks,
6:13 Rages, we will hold the wedding *f* for her.
8:19 So the servants began to prepare the *f*.
11:18 Tobiah's wedding *f* for seven happy days,
Jdt 10: 2 which she used only on sabbaths and *f* days.
Est 1: 3 a *f* for all his officers and ministers:
1: 5 At the end of this time the king gave a *f*
1: 9 Queen Vashti also gave a *f* for the women
2:18 Then the king gave a great *f* in honor of
3:15 The king and Haman then sat down to *f*,
1Mc 1:45 to profane the sabbaths and *f* days,
10:21 one hundred and sixty at the *f* of Booths,
10:34 Let all *f* days, sabbaths, new moon
10:34 and the three days that precede each *f* day,
2Mc 1: 9 the *f* of Booths in the month of Chislev.

FEAST (cont.)

1:18 that you too may celebrate the *f* of Booths
2:12 the *f* in the same way for eight days.
2:16 the *f* of the purification of the temple,
2:16 you also to please celebrate the *f*.
10: 6 for eight days as on the *f* of Booths,
10: 6 they had spent the *f* of Booths living like
12:31 Jerusalem, shortly before the *f* of Weeks.
12:32 After this *f* called Pentecost,
Jb 1: 5 And when each *f* had run its course,
Ps(s) 81: 4 moon, at the full moon, on our solemn *f*;
Prv 7:18 of love, until morning, let us *f* on love!
15:15 but a lighthearted man has a continual *f*.
Eccl 5:10 to the owner except to *f* his eyes upon?
Wis 12: 5 a cannibal *f* of human flesh and of blood,
Sir 11:19 found rest, now I will *f* on my possessions,"
43: 7 which we know the *f* days and fixed dates,
Is 5:12 lyre, timbrel and flute, they *f* on wine;
22:13 you *f* and celebrate, you slaughter oxen
25: 6 peoples A *f* of rich food and choice wines,
30:29 sing as on a night when a *f* is observed,
Jer 46:10 hosts holds a slaughter *f* in the northland,
Lam 2: 6 has made *f* and sabbath to be forgotten;
2: 7 in the house of the LORD as on a *f* day.
2:22 a *f* day terrors against me from all sides;
Bar 1:14 the *f* day and during the days of assembly:
Ez 22: 9 you are those who *f* on the mountains;
36:38 the sheep of Jerusalem on its *f* days,
45:21 you shall observe the *f* of the Passover;
45:23 On each of the seven days of the *f* he
45:25 day of the seventh month, the *f* day,
Dn 7:25 thinking to change the *f* days and the law.
Hos 9: 5 the festival day, the day of the LORD's *f*?
Zep 1: 7 Yes, the LORD has prepared a slaughter *f*,
1: 8 slaughter *f* I will punish the princes,
Zec 14:16 of hosts, and to celebrate the *f* of Booths.
14:18 not come up to celebrate the *f* of Booths.
14:19 not come up to celebrate the *f* of Booths.
Mt 22: 4 Come to the *f*.'
22:11 a man not properly dressed for a wedding *f*.
26:17 the first day of the *f* of Unleavened Bread,
Lk 2:41 to Jerusalem for the *f* of the Passover,
2:43 they were returning at the end of the *f*,
13:29 their place at the *f* in the kingdom of God.
22: 1 The *f* of Unleavened Bread known as the
Jn 4:45 They themselves had been at the *f* and had
5: 1 Later, on the occasion of a Jewish *f*,
6: 4 The Jewish *f* of Passover was near;
7: 2 as the Jewish *f* of Booths drew near,
7:14 The *f* was half over by the time Jesus went
10:22 for the *f* of the Dedication in Jerusalem.
11:56 Is he likely to come for the *f*?"
12:12 *f* heard that Jesus was to enter Jerusalem.
12:20 up to worship at the *f* were some Greeks.
13: 1 Before the *f* of Passover, Jesus realized
13:29 him to buy what was needed for the *f*,
19:31 for that sabbath was a solemn *f* day.
Acts 12: 3 During the *f* of Unleavened Bread he had
20:16 by the *f* of Pentecost if at all possible.
1Cor 5: 8 us celebrate the *f* not with the old yeast,
Rv 19: 9 been invited to the wedding *f* of the lamb."
19:17 for the great *f* God has prepared for you!

FEASTDAYS (1)

Jdt 8: 6 *f* and holidays of the house of Israel.

FEASTED (3)

Gn 31:38 and I have never *f* on a ram of your flock.
Jdt 1:16 and *f* for a hundred and twenty days.
Lk 16:19 and linen and *f* splendidly every day.

FEASTING (8)

1Chr 12:40 with David for three days, *f* and drinking,
Est 8:17 exultation, banqueting and *f* for the Jews.
9:17 and made it a day of *f* and rejoicing.
9:18 and made it a day of *f* and rejoicing.)
9:19 month of Adar as a day of rejoicing and *f*,
9:22 to observe these days with *f* and gladness,
Prv 17: 1 peace than a house full of *f* with strife.
Eccl 7: 2 house of mourning than to the house of *f*,

FEASTS (22)

Nm 10:10 your festivals, and your newmoon *f*,
Dt 33:19 to the mountains where *f* are duly held,
Est E:22 among your designated *f* with all rejoicing
1Mc 1:39 her *f* were turned into mourning,
12:11 offer on our *f* and other appropriate days,
2Mc 6: 6 the sabbath or celebrate the traditional *f*,
Jb 1: 4 His sons used to take turns giving *f*,
Sir 33: 8 through him the seasons and *f* come and go.
47: 9 He added beauty to the *f* and solemnized
Is 29: 1 Add year to year, let the *f* come round.
Lam 1: 4 mourn for lack of pilgrims going to her *f*;
Ez 45:17 cereal offerings, and libations on the *f*,
46:11 On the *f* and festivals the cereal offering
Hos 2:13 I will bring an end to all her joy, her *f*,
Am 5:21 I hate, I spurn your *f*,
8:10 I will turn your *f* into mourning and all
Na 2: 1 Celebrate your *f*, O Judah,
Mal 2: 3 dung in your faces, The dung of your *f*,
Mk 14: 1 The *f* of Passover and Unleavened Bread

Col 2:16 or what you do on yearly or monthly *f*,
2Pt 2:13 they share your *f* in a spirit of seduction.
Jude 1:12 They join your solemn *f* without shame and

FEATHERS (2)

Lv 1:16 Its crop and *f* shall be removed and thrown
Dn 4:30 until his hair grew like the *f* of an eagle,

FEATURES (1)

Est D: 7 *f* ablaze with the height of majestic anger,

FED (17)

Dt 8: 3 with hunger, and then *f* you with manna,
8:16 rock and *f* you in the desert with manna,
Jb 31:31 "Who has not been *f* with his meat!"
Ps(s) 80: 6 You have *f* them with the bread of tears
Jer 5: 7 I *f* them, but they committed adultery;
Ez 16:19 the oil, and the honey with which I *f* you,
31:14 no tree *f* by water may stand by itself in
31:16 choice and best, all that were *f* by water.
34: 3 You have *f* off their milk,
Dn 1:15 better *f* than any of the young men who ate
Hos 13: 5 I *f* you in the desert, in the torrid land.
Zec 11: 7 the other, "Bonds," and I *f* the flock.
Mt 15:38 people who were *f* numbered four thousand,
Jn 6:13 who had been *f* with the five barley loaves.
Acts 28: 3 Paul had just *f* the fire with a bundle of
1Cor 3: 2 I *f* you with milk,
Jas 2:16 Keep warm and well *f*,"

FEE (3)

Nm 22: 7 divination *f* in hand and went to Balaam.
Dt 23:19 You shall not offer a harlot's *f* or a
Acts 21:24 pay the *f* for the shaving of their heads.

FEEBLE (7)

Gn 30:42 So the *f* animals would go to Laban,
Jb 4: 3 many, and have made firm their *f* hands.
26: 2 the powerless, what strength to the *f* arm!
Ps(s) 69:24 cannot see, and keep their backs always *f*.
Sir 25:22 *F* hands and quaking knees
Is 35: 3 Strengthen the hands that are *f*,
Bar 2:18 is deeply grieved, who walks bowed and *f*,

FEED (21)

1Kgs 17: 4 and I have commanded ravens to *f* you there."
22:27 Put this man in prison and *f* him scanty
2Chr 18:26 Put this man in prison and *f* him scanty
2Mc 15:33 saying he would *f* it piecemeal to the
Ps(s) 28: 9 *f* them, and carry them forever!
80:14 and the beasts of the field *f* upon it?
81:17 Israel I would *f* with the best of wheat,
Jer 50:19 to her fold, to *f* on Carmel and Bashan,
Ez 3: 3 *f* your belly and fill your stomach with
23:37 to *f* them they immolated the children they
Hos 4: 8 They *f* on the sin of my people,
11: 4 Yet, though I stooped to *f* my child,
Mi 7:14 Let them *f* in Bashan and Gilead,
Zec 11: 9 "I will not *f* you," I said.
11:16 nor heal the injured, nor *f* what survives
Mt 25:37 when did we see you hungry and *f* you or
Mk 6:37 hundred days' wages for bread to *f* them?"
Jn 21:15 At which Jesus said, *F* my lambs."
21:17 Jesus said to him, *F* my sheep."
Rom 12:20 But "if your enemy is hungry, *f* him;
1Cor 13: 3 If I give everything I have to *f* the poor

FEEDING (7)

Dt 10:18 befriends the alien, *f* and clothing him.
Sir 13:18 so too the poor are *f* grounds for the rich.
Jer 49:19 of Jordan to the permanent *f* grounds,
50:44 thicket to the permanent *f* grounds,
Mt 8:30 distance away a large herd of swine was *f*.
Mk 5:11 was *f* there on the slope of the mountain.
Lk 8:32 herd of swine was *f* nearby on the hillside,

FEEDS (9)

Jb 40:15 made Behemoth, that *f* on grass like an ox.
Prv 15:14 but the mouth of fools *f* on folly.
Is 40:11 Like a shepherd he *f* his flock;
Mt 6:26 yet your heavenly Father *f* them.
Lk 12:24 yet God *f* them.
Jn 6:54 He who *f* on my flesh and drinks my blood
6:56 The man who *f* on my flesh and drinks my
6:57 who *f* on me will have life because of me.
6:58 man who *f* on this bread shall live forever."

FEEL (26)

Gn 27:21 "Come closer, son, that I may *f* you,
31:35 "Let not my lord *f* offended that I cannot
Ex 10:21 be such intense darkness that one can *f* it."
Dt 28:67 *f* and the sight that your eyes must see.
1Sm 16:16 you, he will play and you will *f* better."
16:23 and Saul would be relieved and *f* better,
Ps(s) 60: 5 You have made your people *f* hardships;
71:20 you have made me *f* many bitter afflictions,
115: 7 They have hands but *f* not;
Sir 37:12 yourself and will *f* for you if you fall.
Is 44:16 I am warm, I *f* the fire."

59:10 like people without eyes we *f* our way.
Jer 19: 3 who hear of it will *f* their ears tingle.
Bar 6:19 them and their garments, they do not *f* it.
6:23 did they *f* anything when they were molded.
Hos 1: 6 I no longer *f* pity for the house of Israel;
1: 7 Yet for the house of Judah I *f* pity;
Zec 11: 5 Even their own shepherds do not *f* for them.
Lk 12:50 What anguish I *f* till it is over!
Acts 24: 8 *F* free now to question him about all this
Rom 2:19 You *f* certain that you can guide the blind
2Cor 1: 9 We were left to *f* like men condemned to
7: 8 Or if I did *f* some regret (because I
1Thes 3: 9 joy we *f* in his presence because of you,
Phlm 1: 8 although I *f* that I have every right to
Jude 1: 3 But now I *f* obliged to write and encourage

FEELING (5)

Nm 5:14 or if a man is overcome by a *f* of jealousy
5:30 or when such a *f* of jealousy comes over a
Wis 15:15 to hear, nor fingers on their hands for *f*;
Mt 9: 8 the sight, a *f* of awe came over the crowd,
Mk 5:29 the *f* that she was cured of her affliction

FEELINGS (6)

Jgs 9:23 God put bad *f* between Abimelech and the
Jb 13:13 that I may speak and give vent to my *f*.
Prv 25:28 defenses is the man with no check on his *f*.
Eccl 2:20 So my *f* turned to despair of all the
Sir 22:19 he who pierces the heart bares its *f*.
40:29 of spirit to one who understands inward *f*:

FEELS (6)

Gn 27:12 Suppose my father *f* me?
Ex 23: 9 you well know how it *f* to be an alien,
Jb 21:19 requite the man himself so that he *f* it,
Prv 28: 1 just man, like a lion, *f* sure of himself.
Sir 31:15 Recognize that your neighbor *f* as you do,
Rom 14:15 *f* remorse for the food he has eaten,

FEET (239)

Gn 18: 4 be brought, that you may bathe your *f*,
19: 2 house for the night, and bathe your *f*;
24:32 bathe his *f* and the feet of the men
43:24 He gave them water to bathe their *f*,
49:33 to his sons, he drew his *f* into the bed,
Ex 3: 5 Remove the sandals from your *f*,
12:11 sandals on your *f* and your staff in hand,
24:10 *f* there appeared to be sapphire tilework,
29:20 hands and the great toes of their right *f*.
30:19 shall use it in washing their hands and *f*.
30:21 the LORD they must wash their hands and *f*,
40:31 sons used to wash their hands and *f* there,
Lv 8:24 and on the big toes of their right *f*.
Dt 8: 4 nor did your *f* swell these forty years.
28:23 and the earth under your *f* like iron.
28:35 soles of your *f* to the crown of your head.
29: 4 in tatters nor your sandals from your *f*;
33: 3 his *f* and he bore them up on his pinions.
33:24 the oil of his olive trees runs over his *f*!
Jos 3:13 When the soles of the *f* of the priests
4:18 soles of their *f* regained the dry ground,
5:15 Joshua, "Remove your sandals from your *f*,
10:24 and put your *f* on the necks of these kings."
10:24 forward and put their *f* upon their necks.
Jgs 5:27 At her *f* he sank down,
5:27 down at her *f* he sank and fell;
19:21 Then they washed their *f*,
Ru 3: 4 Then go, uncover a place at his *f*,
3: 7 she stole up, uncovered a place at his *f*,
3: 8 around to find a woman lying at his *f*.
3:14 So she lay at his *f* until morning,
1Sm 25:24 As she fell at his *f* she said:
25:41 slave to wash the *f* of my lord's servants."
2Sm 3:34 with chains, nor your *f* placed in fetters;
4: 4 had a son named Meribbaal with crippled *f*.
4:12 them and cut off their hands and *f*,
9: 3 still Jonathan's son, whose *f* are crippled."
9:13 He was lame in both *f*.
11: 8 "Go down to your house and bathe your *f*."
19:25 He had not washed his *f* nor trimmed his
22:10 came down, with dark clouds under his *f*.
22:34 Who made my *f* swift as those of hinds and
22:39 they fell beneath my *f*.
1Kgs 5:17 put these enemies under the soles of his *f*.
15:23 his old age, Asa had an infirmity in his *f*.
2Kgs 4:27 of God on the mountain, she clasped his *f*.
4:37 She came in and fell at his *f* in gratitude;
9:35 found nothing of her but the skull, the *f*,
13:21 he came back to life and rose to his *f*.
19:24 the soles of my *f* all the rivers of Egypt.
1Chr 28: 2 King David rose to his *f* and said:
28: 2 LORD, the footstool for the *f* of our God;
2Chr 3:13 They stood upon their own *f*,
16:12 Asa contracted a serious disease in his *f*.
28:15 they clothed them, put sandals on their *f*,
33: 8 I will not again allow Israel's *f* to leave
Ezr 10: 5 Ezra rose to his *f* and demanded an oath
Neh 9:21 worn, and their *f* did not become swollen.
Tb 2: 4 I sprang to my *f*,
6: 3 boy went down to wash his *f* in the river,
12:21 to their *f* and could no longer see him.

Jdt 2: 7 all the land with the *f* of my soldiers,
10: 4 She chose sandals for her *f*,
14: 7 threw himself at the *f* of Judith in homage,
Est C: 6 soles of his *f* for the salvation of Israel.
8: 3 Esther fell at his *f* and tearfully
2Mc 7: 4 to scalp him and cut off his hands and *f*,
13: 5 at that place a tower seventy-five *f* high,
Jb 2: 7 soles of his *f* to the crown of his head.
12: 5 a disgrace such as awaits unsteady *f*;
13:27 You put my *f* in the stocks;
29:15 eyes to the blind, and *f* to the lame was I;
33:11 He puts my *f* in the stocks;
Ps(s) 8: 7 your hands, putting all things under his *f*:
17: 5 in your paths, my *f* have not faltered.
18:10 came down, with dark clouds under his *f*.
18:34 Who made my *f* swift as those of hinds
18:39 they fell beneath my *f*.
22:17 They have pierced my hands and my *f*;
25:15 LORD, for he will free my *f* from the snare.
40: 3 He set my *f* upon a crag;
47: 4 peoples under us; nations under our *f*.
56:14 For you have rescued me from death, my *f*,
57: 7 They have prepared a net for my *f*;
58:11 bathe his *f* in the blood of the wicked.
66: 9 to our souls, and has not let our *f* slip.
68:24 So that you will bathe your *f* in blood;
73: 2 my *f* all but slipped,
115: 7 they have *f* but walk not;
116: 8 my eyes from tears, my *f* from stumbling.
119:59 my ways and turned my *f* to your decrees.
119:10! From every evil way I withhold my *f*,
119:105 A lamp to my *f* is your word,
140: 5 from violent men Who plan to trip up my *f*—
Prv 1:16 [For their *f* run to evil,
4:26 Survey the path for your *f*,
5: 5 Her *f* go down to death,
6:13 He winks his eyes, shuffles his *f*,
6:18 wicked schemes, *f* that run swiftly to evil,
6:28 on live coals, and his *f* not be scorched?
7:11 and unruly, in her home her *f* cannot rest;
26: 6 He cuts off his *f*,
29: 5 neighbor is spreading a net under his *f*.
Sg 5: 3 I have bathed my *f*,
7: 2 How beautiful are your *f* in sandals,
Wis 14:11 men and a trap for the *f* of the senseless.
15:15 even their *f* are useless to walk with.
Sir 6:25 Put your *f* into her fetters,
6:36 let your *f* wear away his doorstep!
25:19 to aged *f* is a railing wife to a quiet man.
26:18 bases are her shapely limbs and steady *f*.
37:15 to God to set your *f* in the path of truth.
38:29 his labor, revolving the wheel with his *f*.
38:30 molds the clay, and with his *f* softens it.
51: 2 the nether world you have snatched my *f*;
51:15 My *f* kept to the level path because from
Is 6: 2 their faces, with two they veiled their *f*,
20: 2 waist, and remove the sandals from your *f*.
23: 7 *f* have taken her to dwell in distant lands?
28: 3 With *f* that will trample the majestic
37:25 the soles of my *f* all the rivers of Egypt.
41: 3 loss, by a path his *f* do not even tread.
49:23 worship you and lick the dust at your *f*.
52: 7 are the *f* of him who brings glad tidings,
59: 7 Their *f* run to evil,
60:13 and glory to the place where I set my *f*.
60:14 you shall fall prostrate at your *f*.
Jer 13:16 your *f* stumble on darkening mountains;
14:10 to wander that they do not spare their *f*.
18:22 capture me, they have hid snares for my *f*;
38:22 Now that your *f* are stuck in the mud,
Lam 1:13 He spread a net for my *f*,
Bar 6:16 full of dust from the *f* of those who enter.
6:25 Having no *f*, they are carried on men's
Ez 1: 7 the soles of their *f* were round.
2: 2 spirit entered into me and set me on my *f*,
3:24 spirit entered into me and set me on my *f*,
6:11 Clap your hands, stamp your *f*,
16:10 put sandals of fine leather on your *f*;
24:17 your turban, put your sandals on your *f*,
24:23 on your heads, your sandals on your *f*.
25: 6 you clapped your hands and stamped your *f*,
32: 2 water with your *f* and churning its streams.
34:18 the rest of your pastures with your *f*?
34:18 you had to foul the remainder with your *f*?
34:19 feet had trampled and drink what your *f*
43: 7 is where I will set the soles of my *f*;
Dn 2:33 iron, its *f* partly iron and partly tile.
2:34 put to it, struck its iron and tile *f*,
2:41 The *f* and toes you saw,
7: 4 the ground to stand on two *f* like a man,
7: 7 and what was left it trampled with its *f*.
7:19 and trampling with its *f* what was left;
10: 6 arms and *f* looked like burnished bronze,
Na 1: 3 path, and clouds are the dust at his *f*;
Hb 3:19 he makes my *f* swift as those of hinds and
Zec 14: 4 his *f* shall rest upon the Mount of Olives,
14:12 shall rot while they stand upon their *f*,
Mal 3:21 become ashes under the soles of your *f*,
Mt 10:14 once outside it shake its dust from your *f*.
15:30 They laid them at his *f* and he cured them.
18: 8 with two hands or two *f* into endless fire.
22:44 I humble your enemies beneath your *f*'?
26:62 priest rose to his *f* and addressed him:
28: 9 up and embraced his *f* and did him homage.
Mk 3:11 of him, fling themselves down at his *f*,
5:22 fell at his *f* and made this earnest appeal:
6:11 *f* in testimony against them as you leave."
7:25 She approached him and crouched at his *f*.
9:27 him by the hand and helped him to his *f*.
9:45 than to be thrown into Gehenna with both *f*.
14:60 The high priest rose to his *f* before the
Lk 1:79 to guide our *f* into the way of peace."
7:38 *f*, weeping so that her tears fell upon his *f*
7:44 and you provided me with no water for my *f*.
7:44 She has washed my *f* with her tears and
7:45 not ceased kissing my *f* since I entered.
7:46 but she has anointed my *f* with perfume.
8:28 *f* and exclaimed at the top of his voice,
8:35 at his *f* dressed and in his full senses;
8:41 synagogue, came up and fell at Jesus' *f*,
8:47 Falling at his *f*, she related before
9: 5 from your *f* as a testimony against them."
10:11 town from our *f* as testimony against you.
10:39 at the Lord's *f* and listened to his words.
15:22 a ring on his finger and shoes on his *f*.
17:16 at the *f* of Jesus and spoke his praises.
24:39 Look at my hands and my *f*; it is really I.
24:40 said this he showed them his hands and *f*.
Jn 11: 2 with perfume and dried his *f* with her hair.)
11:32 him, she fell at his *f* and said to him,
12: 3 nard, with which she anointed Jesus' *f*.
12: 3 Then she dried his *f* with her hair,
13: 5 wash his disciples' *f* and dry them
13: 6 to him, "Lord, are you going to wash my *f*?"
13: 8 Peter replied, "You shall never wash my *f*!"
13: 9 Peter said to him, "then not only my *f*,
13:10 has no need to wash [except for his *f*;
13:12 After he had washed their *f*,
13:14 But if I washed your *f*—
13:14 then you must wash each other's *f*.
Acts 3: 7 the beggar's *f* and ankles became strong;
4:35 They used to lay them at the *f* of the
4:37 of the money, laying it at the apostles' *f*.
5: 2 he took and laid at the *f* of the apostles.
5:10 With that, she fell dead at his *f*.
7:33 'Remove the sandals from your *f*,
7:58 cloaks at the *f* of a young man named Saul.
9:41 gave her his hand and helped her to her *f*.
10:26 Peter said as he helped him to his *f*,
13:25 worthy to unfasten the sandals on his *f*.'
13:51 their *f* in protest and went on to Iconium.
14:10 On your *f*!"
16:24 so far as to chain their *f* to a stake.
16:29 fell trembling at the *f* of Paul and Silas.
21:11 belt, tied his own hands and *f* with it.
22: 3 Here I sat at the *f* of Gamaliel and was
26:16 Get up now and stand on your *f*.
Rom 3:15 Swiftly run their *f* to shed blood;
10:15 are the *f* of those who announce good news!"
16:20 will quickly crush Satan under your *f*.
1Cor 12:21 any more than the head can say to the *f*,
15:25 until God has put all enemies under his *f*,
15:27 God "has placed all things under his *f*."
Eph 1:22 things under Christ's *f* and has made him,
1Tm 5:10 Has she washed the *f* of Christian visitors?
Heb 2: 8 and honor, and put all things under his *f*."
10:13 until his enemies are placed beneath his *f*.
Rv 1:15 His *f* gleamed like polished brass refined
1:17 of him I fell down at his *f* as though dead.
2:18 fire and whose *f* gleam like polished brass,
3: 9 but frauds, come and fall down at your *f*;
11:11 *f* sheer terror gripped those who saw them.
12: 1 with the sun, with the moon under her *f*,
19:10 I fell at his *f* to worship him,
22: 8 the *f* of the angel who showed them to me.

FEIGNED (1)

1Sm 21:14 he *f* insanity and acted like a madman in

FEIGNING (1)

Sir 12:17 *f* to help, he will trip you up,

FEIGNS (1)

Sir 19:23 He bows his head and *f* not to hear,

FELIX (9)

Acts 23:24 give him safe conduct to *F* the governor."
23:26 Lysias sends greetings to His Excellency *F*,
24: 2 began his prosecution by addressing *F*:
24:22 *F* was rather well informed about the new
24:24 few days later *F* came with his Jewish wife,
24:25 the coming judgment, *F* became frightened.
24:27 which *F* was succeeded by Porcius Festus.
24:27 *F* wanted to ingratiate himself with the
25:14 he said, "whom *F* left behind in custody.

FELL (262)

Gn 14:10 Sodom and Gomorrah fled, they *f* into these,
15:12 was about to set, a trance *f* upon Abram,
35: 5 from God *f* upon the towns round about,
41: 5 He *f* asleep again and had another dream.
43:29 eye *f* on his full brother Benjamin,
Ex 15:16 terror and dread *f* upon them.
32:28 there *f* about three thousand of the people.
Lv 9:24 all the people cried out and *f* prostrate.
Nm 11: 9 dew *f* upon the camp, the manna also fell.
14: 5 But Moses and Aaron *f* prostrate before the
16: 4 When Moses heard this, he *f* prostrate.
16:22 But they *f* prostrate and cried out,
17:10 But they *f* prostrate.
20: 6 the meeting tent, where they *f* prostrate.
22:31 he *f* on his knees and bowed to the ground.
31:36 *f* to those who had gone out to combat was:
31:37 and seventy-five *f* as tax to the LORD;
31:38 of which seventy-two *f* as tax to the LORD;
31:39 of which sixty-one *f* as tax to the LORD;
31:40 of whom thirty-two *f* as tax to the LORD,
31:42 which *f* to the community when Moses had
36: 3 that *f* to us by lot will be diminished.
Dt 19: 5 wood, and as he swings his ax to *f* a tree,
Jos 2: 8 Before the spies *f* asleep,
5:14 *f* prostrate to the ground in worship,
8:25 There *f* that day a total of twelve
13:31 in Bashan, *f* to the descendants of Machir,
15: 1 Judahite tribe *f* in the extreme south
16: 1 The lot that *f* to the Josephites extended
17: 1 Now as for the lot that *f* to the tribe of
17: 5 Thus ten shares *f* to Manasseh apart from
17: 6 Gilead *f* to the rest of the Manassehites.
18:11 One lot *f* to the clans of the tribe of
19: 1 The second lot *f* to Simeon.
19:10 lot *f* to the clans of the Zebulunites.
19:17 The fourth lot *f* to Issachar.
19:24 The fifth lot *f* to the clans of the tribe
19:32 The sixth lot *f* to the Naphtalites.
19:40 lot *f* to the clans of the tribe of Danites.
21: 4 Levites *f* to the clans of the Kohathites,
21:10 the Levites, since the first lot *f* to them:
Jgs 4:16 entire army of Sisera *f* beneath the sword,
5:27 At her feet he sank down, *f*,
5:27 fell; where he sank down, there he *f*,
7:13 and as it *f* it turned the tent upside down."
7:21 camp *f* to running and shouting and fleeing.
9:40 and many *f* slain right up to the entrance
12: 6 thousand Ephraimites *f* at that time.
13:20 saw this, they *f* prostrate to the ground;
16: 4 After that he *f* in love with a woman in
16:30 and the temple *f* upon the lords and all
20:44 Gibeah, while eighteen thousand of them *f*,
20:46 Those of Benjamin who *f* on that day were
1Sm 4:18 *f* backward from his chair into the gateway;
17:49 his brow, and he *f* prostrate on the ground.
17:52 and Philistines *f* wounded along the road
19:20 they too *f* into the prophetic state.
19:21 who also *f* into the prophetic state.
19:21 but they too *f* into the prophetic state.
25:24 As she *f* at his feet she said:
28:20 Saul *f* full length on the ground,
30:13 me because I *f* sick three days ago today.
31: 4 So Saul took his own sword and *f* upon it.
31: 5 he too *f* upon his sword and died with him.
2Sm 1: 2 to David, he *f* to the ground in homage.
2:16 opponent's side, and all *f* down together.
2:23 He *f* there and died on the spot.
3:34 as men fall before the wicked, you *f*."
4: 4 their hasty flight, he *f* and became lame.]
9: 6 came to David, he *f* prostrate in homage.
11:17 Joab, some officers of David's army *f*,
14: 4 and *f* prostrate to the ground in homage,
14:33 who came to him and in homage *f* on his
19:19 he *f* down before the king and said to him:
21: 9 The seven *f* at the one time;
21:22 *f* at the hands of David and his servants.
22:39 they *f* beneath my feet.
1Kgs 11: 2 But Solomon *f* in love with them.
17:17 son of the mistress of the house *f* sick,
18: 7 him, Obadiah *f* prostrate and asked,
18:39 this, all the people *f* prostrate and said,
18:45 with clouds and wind, and a heavy rain *f*.
19: 5 lay down and *f* asleep under the broom tree,
2Kgs 1:13 arrived, he *f* to his knees before Elijah,
3:19 every fortified city, *f* every fruit tree,
4:37 She came in and *f* at his feet in gratitude;
6: 4 at the Jordan they began to *f* trees.
1Chr 6:39 Kohathites, since the first lot *f* to them,
10: 1 the Philistines, and a number of them *f*,
10: 4 So Saul took his own sword and *f* on it;
10: 5 armor-bearer also *f* on his sword and died.
24: 7 The first lot *f* to Jehoiarib,
25: 9 The first lot *f* to Asaph,
25:11 The fourth *f* to Izri,
25:19 The twelfth *f* to Hashabiah,
25:22 The fifteenth *f* to Jeremoth,
25:23 The sixteenth *f* to Hananiah,
25:24 The seventeenth *f* to Joshbekashah,
25:25 The eighteenth *f* to Hanani,
25:26 The nineteenth *f* to Mallothi,
25:27 The twentieth *f* to Eliathah,
25:28 The twenty-first *f* to Hothir,
25:29 The twenty-second *f* to Giddalti,
25:30 The twenty-third *f* to Mahazioth,
25:31 The twenty-fourth *f* to Romamti-ezer,
26:14 for the east side, it *f* to Meshelemiah.
26:14 counselor, and the north side *f* to his lot.
26:15 To Obed-edom *f* the south side,
26:16 To Hosah *f* the west side with the

FELL (cont.)

27:24 it, for because of it wrath *f* upon Israel.
2Chr 7: 3 and they *f* down upon the pavement with
13:17 thousand picked men of Israel *f* slain.
14:12 Ethiopians *f* until there were no survivors,
20:18 *f* down before the LORD in worship.
29: 9 our fathers, as you know, *f* by the sword,
29:30 then *f* down and prostrated themselves.
Ezr 9: 5 with cloak and mantle torn I *f* on my knees,
Tb 6:18 lineage, he *f* deeply in love with her,
12:16 with fear, the two men *f* to the ground.
14:10 But Nadab himself *f* into the deadly trap,
Jdt 1:12 Then Nebuchadnezzar *f* into a violent rage
2:28 The fear and dread of him *f* upon all the
6:18 the people *f* prostrate and worshiped God;
8:19 and *f* with great destruction before our
14: 6 of the people, he *f* forward in a faint.
Est 3: 7 and the lot *f* on the thirteenth day of the
8: 3 Esther *f* at his feet and tearfully
1Mc 1: 3 the earth *f* silent before him,
3:11 Many *f* wounded, and the rest fled.
3:24 About eight hundred of their men *f*.
3:25 and dread *f* upon the Gentiles about them.
4:15 Their whole rearguard *f* by the sword,
4:15 About three thousand of their men *f*.
4:34 of Lysias' men *f* in hand-to-hand fighting.
4:40 ashes and *f* with their faces to the ground.
5:22 About three thousand men of the Gentiles *f*,
5:34 it was Maccabeus, they *f* back before him,
5:34 eight thousand of their men *f* that day.
5:60 about two thousand Israelites *f* that day.
5:67 At that time some priests *f* in battle who
6:42 and six hundred men of the king's army *f*.
6:45 that they *f* back from him on both sides.
6:46 The beast *f* to the ground on top of him,
7:32 About five hundred men of Nicanor's army *f*;
7:46 in, and all the enemies *f* by the sword;
8:10 Many were wounded and *f*,
9:17 and many on both sides *f* wounded.
9:18 Then Judas *f*, and the rest fled.
9:40 Many *f* wounded,
9:49 thousand men on Bacchides' side *f* that day.
10:50 until sunset, and Demetrius *f* that day.
10:85 Those who *f* by the sword,
11:74 of the foreign troops *f* on that day.
12:52 fear, and all Israel *f* into deep mourning.
15:36 had seen, the king *f* into a violent rage.
16: 8 many of them *f* wounded,
16: 9 then that John's brother Judas *f* wounded;
2Mc 3:27 Suddenly he *f* to the ground,
9:21 I *f* victim to a troublesome illness;
12:24 Timothy himself *f* into the hands of the
14:44 he *f* into the middle of the empty space.
Jb 1:19 *f* upon the young people and they are dead;
31:29 my enemy or exulted when evil *f* upon him,
Ps(s) 18:39 they *f* beneath my feet.
68:15 the kings there, snow *f* on Zalmon."
78:28 Which *f* in the midst of their camp round
78:64 Their priests *f* by the sword,
116: 3 I *f* into distress and sorrow,
Wis 7: 3 common air, and *f* upon the kindred earth;
17:16 whoever was there *f* into that unbarred
Sir 15:11 "It was God's doing that I *f* away";
Jer 46:16 he stumbled repeatedly, and *f*.
Lam 1: 7 When her people *f* into enemy hands,
Ez 3:23 I *f* prone, but then spirit entered
8: 1 the hand of the Lord GOD *f* upon me there.
9: 8 I *f* prone, crying out, Alas, Lord GOD!
11: 5 Then the spirit of the LORD *f* upon me,
11:13 I *f* prone and cried out in a loud voice;
39:23 foes, so that all of them *f* by the sword.
43: 3 I *f* prone as the glory of the LORD entered
44: 4 filling the LORD's temple, and I *f* prone.
Dn 2:46 Then King Nebuchadnezzar *f* down and
3: 7 peoples of every language all *f* down
3:23 But these three *f*,
7:20 sprang up, before which three horns *f*;
8:17 I was standing, I *f* prostrate in terror.
8:18 As he spoke to me, I *f* forward in a faint;
10: 9 of his voice, I *f* face forward in a faint.
10:15 thus to me, I *f* forward and kept silent.
Mt 7:27 The rains *f*, the torrents came,
13: 5 Part of it *f* on rocky ground,
13: 7 Again, part of the seed *f* among thorns,
13:20 The seed that *f* on patches of rock is the
17: 6 this the disciples *f* forward on the ground,
26:39 a little and *f* prostrate in prayer.
27:57 When evening *f*, a wealthy man
28: 4 with fear of him and *f* down like dead men.
28:17 had entertained doubts *f* down in homage.
Mk 4:39 The wind *f* off and everything grew calm.
5:22 *f* at his feet and made this earnest appeal:
5:33 the woman came and *f* in front of him and
9:20 As he *f* to the ground he began to roll
9:34 At this they *f* silent,
10:22 At these words the man's face *f*.
14:35 He advanced a little and *f* to the ground,
15:33 darkness *f* on the whole countryside and
Lk 1: 9 it *f* to him by lot according to priestly
5: 8 Simon Peter *f* at the knees of Jesus saying,
6:49 *f* in and was completely destroyed."
7:38 weeping so that her tears *f* upon his feet.
8: 5 some *f* on the footpath where it was walked
8: 6 Some *f* on rocky ground,
8: 7 Some *f* among briers,
8: 8 But some *f* on good soil,
8:28 then he *f* at his feet and exclaimed at the
8:41 synagogue, came up and *f* at Jesus' feet,
9:36 When the voice *f* silent, Jesus was there
10:30 Jerusalem to Jericho who *f* prey to robbers.
10:36 to the man who *f* in with the robbers?"
16:21 scraps that *f* from the rich man's table.
24:52 They *f* down to do him reverence,
Jn 11:32 him, she *f* at his feet and said to him,
18: 6 retreated slightly and *f* to the ground.
Acts 1:18 his unjust gains, and *f* headlong upon it.
1:26 The choice *f* to Matthias who was added to
5: 5 the sound of these words, Ananias *f* dead.
5:10 With that, she *f* dead at his feet.
7:60 He *f* to his knees and cried out in a loud
9: 4 He *f* to the ground and at the same time
9:18 *f* from his eyes and he regained his sight.
9:37 At about that time she *f* ill and died.
10:10 it was being prepared he *f* into a trance.
13:36 will, *f* asleep and joined his fathers,
15:12 At that the whole assembly *f* silent.
16:29 *f* trembling at the feet of Paul and Silas.
19:17 Greeks living in Ephesus, fear *f* upon all,
19:35 and of her image which *f* from the sky?
20: 9 and *f* from the third story to the ground.
21:40 A great hush *f* on them as he began to
22: 7 I *f* to the ground and heard a voice say to
22:17 where I *f* into a trance and saw Jesus
26:14 All of us *f* to the ground and I heard a
Rom 11:22 severity toward those who *f*,
15: 3 they uttered against you *f* on me."
1Tm 2:14 was she who was led astray and *f* into sin.
Heb 3:17 had sinned, whose corpses *f* in the desert?
11:30 *f* after being encircled for seven days.
Jas 5:17 no rain *f* on the land for three years
Rv 1:17 of him I *f* down at his feet as though dead.
5: 8 twenty-four elders *f* down before the Lamb.
5:14 and the elders *f* down and worshiped.
6:13 The stars in the sky *f* crashing to earth
7:11 *f* down before the throne to worship God.
8:10 It *f* on a third of the rivers and the
11:13 and a tenth of the city *f* in ruins.
11:16 presence *f* down to worship God and said:
16:19 parts, and the other Gentile cities also *f*.
19: 4 living creatures *f* down and worshiped God
19:10 I *f* at his feet to worship him,
22: 8 and when I heard and saw them I *f* down to

FELLED (6)

Jgs 20:21 and *f* twenty-two thousand men of Israel.
20:25 them *f* eighteen thousand Israelites,
2Kgs 3:25 stopped up and every useful tree they *f*.
Is 9: 9 Sycamores are *f*,
10:33 The tall of stature are *f*,
10:34 The forest thickets are *f* with the axe,

FELLIES (1)

1Kgs 7:33 their axles, *f*, spokes, and hubs

FELLING (1)

2Kgs 6: 5 While one of them was *f* a tree trunk,

FELLOW (91)

Gn 9: 5 and from man in regard to his *f* man I
19: 9 This *f*," they sneered,
34:20 presented the matter to their *f* townsmen:
Ex 2:13 "Why are you striking your *f* Hebrew?"
23: 6 your needy *f* men his rights in his lawsuit.
Lv 19:15 to the mighty, but judge your *f* men justly.
19:17 Though you may have to reprove your *f* man,
19:18 no grudge against your *f* countrymen.
20: 2 Let his *f* citizens stone him.
20: 4 Even if his *f* citizens connive at such a
25:35 "When one of your *f* countrymen is reduced
25:49 or by some other relative or *f* clansman;
Nm 5: 6 a fault against his *f* man and wrongs him,
8:26 His service with his *f* Levites shall
Dt 18: 7 like all his *f* Levites who are in
21:20 and unruly *f* who will not listen to us;
21:21 his *f* citizens shall stone him to death.
24: 7 "If any man is caught kidnaping a *f*
Jos 14: 8 My *f* scouts who went up with me
20: 5 who slew his *f* man unintentionally
Ru 4:10 perish among his kinsmen and *f* citizens.
1Sm 10:27 men said, "How can this *f* save us?"
21:16 Should this *f* come into my house?"
1Kgs 21:11 His *f* citizens—the elders and the nobles
1Chr 7: 5 more wives and sons than their *f* tribesmen.
8:32 in Jerusalem, opposite their *f* tribesmen.
Ezr 4: 7 the rest of his *f* officials to Artaxerxes,
4: 9 Shimshai, the scribe, and their *f* judges,
4:17 and their *f* officials living in Samaria
4:23 the scribe, and their *f* officials,
5: 3 and Shethar-bozenai, and their *f* officials,
5: 6 their *f* officials from West-of-Euphrates;
6: 6 their *f* officials in West-of-Euphrates,
6:13 and their *f* officials carried out fully
Neh 5: 1 wives against certain of their *f* Jews.
5: 8 our *f* Jews who had been sold to Gentiles;
Est 3: 1 seating him above all his *f* officials.
2Mc 4:50 the chief plotter against his *f* citizens.
5: 6 slaughtered his *f* citizens without mercy,
5: 6 over his enemies, not his *f* countrymen.
5:23 his *f* citizens worse than the others did.
15:30 soul the chief defender of his *f* citizens,
Jb 35: 8 and your justice only a *f* human being.
Ps(s) 15: 3 Who harms not his *f* man,
45: 8 the oil of gladness above your *f* kings.
Prv 27:17 sharpens iron, so man sharpens his *f* man.
Sir 17:12 of them he gives precepts about his *f* men.
18:11 Man may be merciful to his *f* man,
Is 38:11 *f* men among those who dwell in the world."
Ez 11:15 it is about your kinsmen, your *f* exiles,
Mt 18:28 he met a *f* servant who owed him
18:29 His *f* servant dropped to his knees and
18:31 When his *f* servants saw what had happened
18:33 have dealt mercifully with your *f* servant,
24:49 coming,' and begins to beat his *f* servants,
Lk 7:49 his *f* guests began to ask among themselves,
14:10 will win you the esteem of your *f* guests.
19:14 But his *f* citizens despised him,
Jn 9: 8 "Isn't this the *f* who used to sit and beg?"
11:16 means "Twin") said to his *f* disciples,
Acts 3:12 *F* Israelites, why does this surprise you?
5:35 then said to the assembly, *F* Israelites,
13:16 *F* Israelites and you others who reverence
16:25 hymns to God as their *f* prisoners listened,
18:13 "This *f*," they charged, "is influencing
19:38 If Demetrius and his *f* craftsmen want to
21:28 *F* Israelites, help us!
Rom 11:14 my *f* Jews to envy and save some of them.
16: 3 they were my *f* workers in the service of
16: 7 and Junias, my kinsmen and *f* prisoners;
16: 9 our *f* worker in the service of Christ;
16:21 Timothy, my *f* worker,
2Cor 6: 1 As your *f* workers we beg you not to
8:23 my companion and *f* worker in your behalf;
Eph 2:19 you are *f* citizens of the saints and
Phil 4: 3 and I ask you, too, my dependable *f* worker,
Col 1: 7 instructions of Epaphras, our dear *f* slave,
4: 7 faithful minister and *f* slave in the Lord,
1Thes 2:14 same treatment from your *f* countrymen
3: 2 *f* worker in preaching the gospel of Christ,
Phlm 1: 1 our beloved friend and *f* worker Philemon,
1: 2 our sister, to our *f* soldier Archippus,
1:23 Epaphras, my *f* prisoner in Christ Jesus,
1:24 Aristarchus, Demas, and Luke, my *f* workers.
Heb 1: 9 the oil of gladness above your *f* kings."
8:11 teach their *f* citizens or their brothers,
13: 1 Love your *f* Christians always.
1Pt 5: 1 To the elders among you I, a *f* elder,
Rv 6:11 their *f* servants and brothers to be slain,
19:10 I am merely a *f* servant with you and your
22: 9 I am merely a *f* servant with you and your

FELLOWS (8)

Dt 20: 8 he make his *f* as fainthearted as himself.'
Jb 40:19 and was made the taskmaster of his *f*;
Sir 7:16 Do not esteem yourself better than your *f*;
15: 5 She will exalt him above his *f*;
28: 3 his *f* and expect healing from the LORD?
28: 4 Should a man refuse mercy to his *f*,
Dn 7:20 which appeared greater than its *f*.
Hos 13:15 Though he be fruitful among his *f*,

FELLOWSHIP (10)

Ps(s) 73:15 I had been false to the *f* of your children.
Wis 6:23 because that can have no *f* with Wisdom.
1Cor 1: 9 it was he who called you to *f* with his Son,
2Cor 6:14 or what *f* can light have with darkness?
13:13 the *f* of the Holy Spirit be with you all!
Gal 2: 9 gave Barnabas and me the handclasp of *f*,
Phil 2: 1 solace that love can give, of *f* in spirit,
1Jn 1: 3 This *f* of ours is with the Father and with
1: 6 If we say, "We have *f* with him,"
1: 7 in the light, we have *f* with one another,

FELT (22)

Gn 2:25 wife were both naked, yet they *f* no shame.
27:22 When Isaac *f* him, he said,
41:55 When hunger came to be *f* throughout the
Nm 13:33 we *f* like mere grasshoppers,
14:39 the Israelites, the people *f* great remorse.
Jgs 8:11 and attacked the camp when it *f* secure.
2Sm 14: 1 observed how the king *f* toward Absalom,
1Kgs 3:26 son it was, in the anguish she *f* for it,
Jdt 9: 3 had *f* the shame of their own deceiving.
2Mc 11: 4 but *f* exultant confidence in his myriads
Prv 23:35 They beat me, but I *f* it not;
Is 47:10 Because you *f* secure in your wickedness,
Ez 16:56 by you while you *f* proud of yourself,
Dn 13:27 old men, the servants *f* very much ashamed,
Zec 1:12 that have *f* your anger these seventy years?"
Mt 12: 1 His disciples *f* hungry,
20:25 their great ones make their importance *f*.
21:18 was returning to the city, he *f* hungry.
Mk 6:20 yet he *f* the attraction of his words.
10:42 their great ones make their importance *f*.
11:12 when they were leaving Bethany he *f* hungry.
2Pt 2: 8 *f* himself tormented by seeing and hearing

FEMALE (58)

Gn 1:27 male and *f* he created them.
5: 2 he created them male and *f*.
6:19 bring two into the ark, one male and one *f*,
7: 3 of the air, seven pairs, a male and a *f*,
7: 3 unclean birds, one pair, a male and a *f*,
7: 9 two] male and *f* entered the ark with Noah,
7:16 Those that entered were male and *f*,
12:16 male and female slaves, male and *f* asses,
20:14 male and *f* slaves and gave them to Abraham;
24:35 herds, silver and gold, male and *f* slaves,
30:43 male and *f* servants and camels and asses.
32: 6 and sheep, as well as male and *f* servants.
46:15 thirty-three persons in all, male and *f*.
Ex 20:10 son or daughter, or your male or *f* slave,
20:17 neighbor's wife, nor his male or *f* slave,
21:20 "When a man strikes his male or *f* slave
21:26 "When a man strikes his male or *f* slave
21:27 knocks out a tooth of his male or *f* slave,
21:32 if it is a male or a *f* slave that it gores,
Lv 3: 1 the LORD either a male or a *f* animal,
3: 6 he may offer either a male or a *f* animal,
4:32 a lamb, he shall bring an unblemished *f*.
5: 6 to the LORD a *f* animal from the flock,
15:33 the law for male and *f*;
19:20 "If a man has carnal relations with a *f*
25: 6 yourself and for your male and *f* slaves,
25:44 "Slaves, male and *f*, you may indeed
Nm 5: 3 Male and *f* alike, you shall compel them
Dt 5:14 son or daughter, or your male or *f* slave,
5:14 male and *f* slave should rest as you do.
5:21 house or field, nor his male or *f* slave,
12:12 sons and daughters, your male and *f* slaves,
12:18 son and daughter, your male and *f* slave,
15:17 Your *f* slave, also, you shall treat
16:11 son and daughter, your male and *f* slave,
16:14 son and daughter, your male and *f* slave,
28:68 sale to your enemies as male and *f* slaves,
Jos 17: 6 since these *f* descendants of Manasseh
1Sm 8:16 He will take your male and *f* servants,
2Kgs 5:26 sheep or cattle, male or *f* servants?
2Chr 35:25 the male and *f* singers in their lamentations
Ezr 2:65 not counting their male and *f* slaves,
2:65 also had two hundred male and *f* singers.
Neh 7:67 not counting their male and *f* slaves,
7:67 also had two hundred male and *f* singers.
Tb 10:10 male and *f* slaves,
Eccl 2: 7 I acquired male and *f* slaves,
2: 8 male and *f* singers and all human luxuries.
Sir 25:16 looks, and makes her sullen as a *f* bear.
Is 14: 2 as male and *f* slaves on the Lord's soil,
Jer 34: 9 was to free his Hebrew slaves, male and *f*,
34:10 to set free their male and *f* servants,
34:11 they took back their male and *f* slaves
34:16 your male and *f* slaves to whom you had
Mt 19: 4 Creator made them male and *f* and declared,
Mk 10: 6 of creation God made them male and *f*;
Gal 3:28 Jew or Greek, slave or freeman, male or *f*.

FEMININE (1)

Jdt 12:15 festive garments and all her *f* adornments.

FENCE (3)

Ezr 9: 9 has granted us a *f* in Judah and Jerusalem.
Ps(s) 62: 4 him down as though he were a sagging *f*,
Mi 4:14 Now *f* yourself in, Bat-gader!

FENCED (1)

2Mc 1:34 *f* the place off and declared it sacred.

FENCES (1)

Na 3:17 gathered on the rubble *f* on a cold day!

FENDING (1)

2Sm 21:10 *f* off the birds of the sky from settling

FERMENT (2)

Lam 1:20 all within me is in *f*,
2:11 are my eyes, within me all is in *f*;

FERTILE (21)

Gn 1:22 was, and God blessed them, saying, "Be *f*,
1:28 "Be *f* and multiply;
9: 1 "Be *f* and multiply and fill the earth.
9: 7 Be *f*, then, and multiply;
17: 6 I will render you exceedingly *f*;
17:20 him *f* and will multiply him exceedingly.
27:39 from the *f* earth shall be your dwelling;
28: 3 May God Almighty bless you and make you *f*,
47:27 There they acquired property, were *f*,
48: 4 'I will make you *f* and numerous and raise
Nm 13:20 Is the soil *f* or barren, wooded or clear?
2Kgs 3:19 and ruin every *f* field with stones."
3:25 every *f* field till they had loaded it down;
Neh 9:25 They captured fortified cities and *f* land;
9:35 *f* land that you had spread out before them,
Sir 39:23 nations and turns *f* land into a salt marsh.
Is 5: 1 My friend had a vineyard on a *f* hillside;
28: 4 glorious beauty on the head of the *f* valley
55:10 the earth, making it *f* and fruitful,
Ez 17: 8 *f* field by plentiful waters it was planted,

FERTILITY (1)

Gn 27:28 *f* of the earth abundance of grain and wine.

FERVENT (3)

2Mc 8:27 then observed the sabbath with *f* praise
Rom 12:11 Do not grow slack but be *f* in spirit;
Jas 5:16 The *f* petition of a holy man is powerful

FERVENTLY (5)

Jdt 4:12 they cried out *f* to the God of Israel
2Mc 15:14 *f* prays for his people and their holy city."
Acts 12: 5 the church prayed *f* to God on his behalf.
26: 7 The twelve tribes of our people *f* worship
1Thes 3:10 as we ask him *f* night and day that we may

FERVOR (2)

Jdt 4: 9 cried to God with great *f* and did penance
Acts 18:25 Apollos was a man full of spiritual *f*.

FESTAL (5)

2Kgs 5: 5 thousand gold pieces, and ten *f* garments.
5:22 them a talent of silver and two *f* garments.' "
5:23 and gave them, with the two *f* garments,
Zec 3: 4 garments, and clothe him in *f* garments."
Heb 12:22 to myriads of angels in *f* gathering,

FESTERING (4)

Ex 9: 9 and cause *f* boils on man and beast
9:10 and it caused *f* boils on man and beast.
Ps(s) 38: 6 and *f* are my sores because of my folly,
Rv 16: 2 severe and *f* boils broke out on the men

FESTERS (1)

Jb 7: 5 my skin cracks and *f*;

FESTIVAL (24)

Ex 13: 6 seventh day shall also be a *f* to the LORD.
Jgs 9:27 a *f* and went to the temple of their god,
1Sm 25: 8 these young men, since we come at a *f* time.
1Kgs 8: 2 during the *f* in the month of Ethanim
8:65 of Egypt, celebrated the *f* before the LORD,
2Chr 5: 3 the king during the *f* of the seventh month.
7: 8 of Egypt, celebrated the *f* for seven days.
30:22 they had completed the seven days of *f*,
Tb 2: 1 Then on our *f* of Pentecost,
1Mc 7:48 and observed that day as a great *f*.
2Mc 6: 7 and when the *f* of Dionysus was celebrated,
Ps(s) 42: 5 thanksgiving, with the multitude keeping *f*.
Hos 9: 5 What will you do on the *f* day,
Mt 26: 5 but they said, "Not during the *f*,
27:15 Now on the occasion of a *f* the procurator
Mk 14: 2 Yet they pointed out, "Not during the *f*,
15: 6 a *f* he would release for them one prisoner
Jn 2:23 he was in Jerusalem during the Passover *f*,
7: 8 Go up yourselves to the *f*.
7: 8 *f* because the time is not yet ripe for me."
7:10 had gone up to the *f* he too went up,
7:11 During the *f*, naturally, the Jews
7:37 On the last and greatest day of the *f*,
Acts 20: 6 soon as the *f* of Unleavened Bread was over.

FESTIVALS (24)

Lv 23: 2 The following are the *f* of the LORD,
23: 4 are the *f* of the LORD which you shall
23:37 are the *f* of the LORD on which you shall
23:44 to the Israelites the *f* of the LORD.
Nm 10:10 On your days of celebration, your *f*,
15: 3 a freewill offering, or for one of your *f*,
29:39 you shall make to the LORD on your *f*,
2Chr 2: 3 the sabbaths, new moons, and *f* of the LORD,
8:13 and on the fixed *f* three times a year:
31: 3 and those on sabbaths, new moons and *f*,
Ezr 3: 5 new moons and all the *f* sacred to the LORD,
Neh 10:34 for the sabbaths, new moons, and *f*,
Tb 1: 6 Jerusalem for the *f* as is prescribed for all
2: 6 "Your *f* shall be turned into mourning,
1Mc 10:34 Let all feast days, sabbaths, new moon *f*,
Ps(s) 76:11 the survivors of Hamath shall keep your *f*.
Is 1:14 Your new moons and *f* I detest;
33:20 Look to Zion, the city of our *f*;
Ez 44:24 observe my laws and statutes on all my *f*,
45:17 on all the *f* of the house of Israel.
46: 9 presence of the LORD to worship on the *f*,
46:11 On the feasts and *f* the cereal offering
Zep 3:18 because of you, as one sings at *f*.
Zec 8:19 cheerful *f* for the house of Judah;

FESTIVE (10)

1Sm 30:16 and in a *f* mood because of all the rich
Jdt 10: 3 *f* attire she had worn while her husband,
12:15 *f* garments and all her feminine adornments.
Est C:13 all her *f* adornments were put aside,
2Mc 2:27 just as the preparation of a *f* banquet is
Ps(s) 87: 7 And all shall sing, in their *f* dance:
149: 3 Let them praise his name in the *f* dance,
Sir 1: 9 glory and splendor, gladness and a *f* crown.
Jer 31: 4 Carrying your *f* tambourines,
Acts 7:41 and had a *f* celebration over the product

FESTIVITIES (2)

2Sm 6:12 of Obed-edom into the City of David amid *f*.
Wis 19:16 Yet these, after welcoming them with *f*,

FESTIVITY (2)

2Chr 30:23 they continued the *f* seven days longer.
Est 9:22 from sorrow into joy, from mourning into *f*.

FESTUS (14)

Acts 24:27 which Felix was succeeded by Porcius *F*.
25: 1 days after *F* had arrived in the province,
25: 3 and urging *F* to send him to Jerusalem.
25: 4 But *F* answered that Paul was being kept in
25: 6 days in Jerusalem, *F* went down to Caesarea.
25: 9 But *F*, wishing to please the Jewish people,
25:12 Thereupon *F* conferred with his council and
25:13 in Caesarea and paid *F* a courtesy call.
25:14 there, *F* referred Paul's case to the king.
25:22 Agrippa said to *F*,
25:22 "Tomorrow you shall hear him," replied *F*.
25:23 At *F*' command Paul was brought in.
26:24 in this way, *F* interrupted with a shout,
26:32 Agrippa further remarked to *F*,

FETCH (11)

Ex 2: 5 the reeds, she sent her handmaid to *f* it.
1Sm 4: 3 Let us *f* the ark of the LORD from Shiloh
20:36 he said to the boy, "Run and *f* the arrow."
Ps(s) 68:23 *f* them back from Bashan; I will fetch
Is 56:12 "Come, I will *f* some wine;
Jer 13: 6 Go now to the Parath and *f* the loincloth
25: 9 send for and *f* all the tribes of the north,
36:21 happened, he sent Jehudi to *f* the scroll.
Dn 13:18 by the side gate to *f* what she had ordered,
Acts 11:13 'Send someone to Joppa and *f* Simon,

FETTERED (4)

Wis 17: 2 with darkness, *f* by the long night,
Sir 28:19 borne its yoke nor been *f* with its chain;
Dn 4:12 stump and roots, *f* with iron and bronze,
4:20 *f* with iron and bronze in the grass of the

FETTERS (15)

Jgs 16:21 down to Gaza and bound him with bronze *f*,
2Sm 3:34 with chains, nor your feet placed in *f*;
2Kgs 25: 7 Then he blinded Zedekiah, bound him with *f*,
1Mc 3:41 *f* and a large sum of silver and gold,
Jb 36: 8 *f* and held fast by bonds of affliction,
Ps(s) 2: 3 their *f* and cast their bonds from us!"
105:18 They had weighed him down with *f*,
149: 8 with chains, their nobles with *f* of iron;
Sir 6:25 Put your feet into her *f*,
6:30 Her *f* will be your throne of majesty;
21:19 Like *f* on the legs is learning to a fool,
Jer 40: 4 you today from the *f* that bind your hands;
52:11 he blinded Zedekiah, bound him with *f*,
Mk 5: 4 pulled the chains apart and smashed the *f*.
Lk 8:29 The man used to be tied with chains and *f*,

FEVER (12)

Lv 26:16 and *f* to dim the eyes and sap the life.
Dt 28:22 LORD will strike you with wasting and *f*,
32:24 and consuming *f* and bitter prestilence,
Mt 8:14 Peter's mother-in-law in bed with a *f*.
8:15 He took her by the hand and the *f* left her.
Mk 1:30 Simon's mother-in-law lay ill with a *f*,
1:31 hand and helped her up, and the *f* left her.
Lk 4:38 was in the grip of a severe *f*,
4:39 over her and addressed himself to the *f*,
Jn 4:52 *f* left him yesterday afternoon about one."
Acts 8: 8 The rejoicing in that town rose to *f* pitch.
28: 8 bed, laid up with chronic *f* and dysentery.

FEW (84)

Gn 29:20 but a *f* days because of his love for her.
34:30 I have so *f* men that,
47: 9 *F* and hard have been these years of my life,
Lv 25:16 when the years are *f*,
Nm 9:20 was over the Dwelling only for a *f* days.
13:18 living there strong or weak, *f* or many?
Dt 28:62 stars in the sky, only a *f* will be left,
33: 6 live and not die out, but let his men be *f*."
Jos 7: 3 The enemy there are *f*;
1Sm 14: 6 victory through a *f* than through many."
1Chr 16:19 When they were *f* in number,
2Chr 24:24 Though the Aramean force came with *f* men,
29:34 Since the priests were too *f* in number to
Neh 2:12 Then I set out by night with only a *f*
1Mc 3:16 Judas went out to meet him with a *f* men.
3:17 "How can we, *f* as we are,
3:18 is easy for many to be overcome by a *f*;
3:18 between deliverance by many or by *f*,
6:54 *F* men remained in the sanctuary;
7: 1 with a *f* men in a city on the seacoast,
7:28 come with a *f* men to meet you peaceably."

FEW (cont.)

9: 9 Now we are too *f*."
12:45 Pick out a *f* men to stay with you,
15:10 to him, so that *f* were left with Trypho.
2Mc 1:15 *f* attendants came to the temple precincts.
2:21 for Judaism so that, *f* as they were,
4:42 wounded many of them and even killed a *f*,
12:34 ensuing battle, a *f* of the Jews were slain.
Jb 10:20 Are not the days of my life *f*?
Ps(s) 105:12 When they were *f* in number,
109: 8 May his days be *f*;
Prv 14:28 but if his people are *f*,
Eccl 5: 1 therefore let your words be *f*.
9:14 with *f* men in it advanced a mighty king,
12: 3 the grinders are idle because they are *f*,
Sir 17:20 sin, pray to him and make your offenses *f*.
18: 8 these *f* years among the days of eternity.
20:12 man makes himself popular by a *f* words,
32: 8 Be brief, but say much in those *f* words,
33:24 When your *f* days reach their limit,
43:34 only a *f* of his works have we seen.
49:14 *F* on earth have been made the equal of
Is 10: 7 destroy, to make an end of nations not a *f*.
10:19 of the trees in his forest will be so *f*,
21:17 *F* of Kedar's stalwart archers shall remain,
24: 6 on earth turn pale, and *f* men are left.
65:20 be in it an infant who lives but a *f* days,
Jer 30:19 I will make them not *f*,
42: 2 We are now *f* who once were many,
44:28 to the land of Judah shall be *f* in number.
Bar 2:13 for we are left *f* in number among the
3: 4 of Israel, hear the prayer of Israel's *f*,
Ez 12:16 will leave a *f* of them to escape the sword,
29:15 I will make them *f*,
Dn 11:34 When they fall, *f* people shall help them,
Am 6:10 Only a *f* shall be left to carry the dead
Mt 7:14 the road, and how *f* there are who find it!
15:34 they replied, "and a *f* small fish."
22:14 The invited are many, the elect are *f*."
23: 4 Their words are bold but their deeds are *f*.
Mk 6: 5 a *f* who were sick by laying hands on them,
7: 2 They had observed a *f* of his disciples
8: 7 They also had a *f* small fish;
12:42 in two small copper coins worth a *f* cents.
15:35 *f* of the bystanders who heard it remarked,
Lk 10: 2 harvest is rich but the workers are *f*;
12: 6 Are not five sparrows sold for a *f* pennies?
13:23 are they *f* in number who are to be saved?"
24:18 that went on there these past *f* days?"
Jn 2:12 but they stayed there only a *f* days.
13:29 A *f* had the idea that,
Acts 1: 5 but within a *f* days you will be baptized
2:12 another, while a *f* remarked with a sneer,
5:34 ordered out of court for a *f* minutes,
10:48 asked him to stay with them for a *f* days.
17:34 A *f* did join him,
17:34 a woman named Damaris, and a *f* others.
21:10 During our *f* days' stay,
24:24 A *f* days later Felix came with his Jewish
25:13 A *f* days later King Agrippa and Bernice
2Cor 10: 8 If I find I must make a *f* further claims
1Pt 3:20 At that time, a *f* persons,
Rv 2:14 I hold a *f* matters against you:
3: 4 I realize that you have in Sardis a *f*

FEWER (4)

Lv 25:52 the *f* years there are left before the
Nm 35: 8 a larger group and *f* from a smaller one,
Sir 28: 8 Avoid strife and your sins will be *f*,
Lk 12:48 to be flogged will get off with *f* stripes.

FICKLE (5)

Dt 32:20 What a *f* race they are,
Prv 7:11 She is *f* and unruly,
9:13 The woman Folly is *f*,
Sir 33: 6 *f* friend is like the stallion that neighs,
Is 3: 4 the *f* shall govern them,

FIDELITY (15)

Ex 34: 6 slow to anger and rich in kindness and *f*,
Dt 7: 8 *f* to the oath he had sworn to your fathers,
2Chr 32: 1 after he had proved his *f* by such deeds,
Ps(s) 43: 3 Send forth your light and your *f*;
86:15 slow to anger, abounding in kindness and *f*.
117: 2 us, and the *f* of the LORD endures forever.
Prv 3: 3 Let not kindness and *f* leave you;
Sir 27: 9 kind, and *f* comes to those who live by it.
Is 16: 5 and on it shall sit in *f* [in David's
Hos 2:22 I will espouse you in *f*,
4: 1 There is no *f*,
2Thes 2:13 in holiness of spirit and *f* to truth.
2Tm 3:10 You have observed my resolution, *f*,
Ti 2:10 expressing a constant *f* by their conduct,
3Jn 1: 5 you demonstrate *f* by all that you do for

FIDELITY'S (1)

Wis 3:14 For he shall be given *f* choice reward and

FIELD (218)

Gn 2: 5 *f* shrub on earth and no grass of the field
3:18 to you, as you eat of the plants of the *f*.
4: 8 his brother Abel, "Let us go out in the *f*."
4: 8 When they were in the *f*,
23: 9 it is at the edge of his *f*.
23:11 I give you both the *f* and the cave in it;
23:13 I will pay you the price of the *f*.
23:17 Thus Ephron's *f* in Machpelah,
23:19 Sarah in the cave of the *f* of Machpelah,
23:20 Thus the *f* with its cave was transferred
24:63 in the *f*, and as he looked around,
25: 9 the cave of Machpelah, in the *f* of Ephron,
25:10 the *f* that Abraham had bought from the
27:27 fragrance of a *f* that the LORD has blessed!
30:14 harvest, when Reuben was out in the *f*,
31: 4 him where he was in the *f* with his flock.
37: 7 There we were, binding sheaves in the *f*,
47:20 them to bear, every Egyptian sold his *f*;
49:29 that lies in the *f* of Ephron the Hittite,
49:30 Hittite, the cave in the *f* of Machpelah,
49:30 the *f* that Abraham bought from Ephron the
49:32 the *f* and the cave in it that had been
50:13 him in the cave in the *f* of Machpelah,
50:13 the *f* that Abraham had bought for a burial
Ex 1:14 mortar and brick and all kinds of *f* work
9: 3 will afflict all your livestock in the *f*—
22: 4 a man is burning over a *f* or a vineyard,
22: 4 spread so that it burns in another's *f*,
22: 4 the best produce of his own *f* or vineyard.
22: 5 grain or the *f* itself is burned up,
22:30 torn to pieces in the *f* you shall not eat;
23:11 of the *f* may eat what the poor leave.
23:16 of the crop that you have sown in the *f*;
Lv 17: 5 as they used to offer up in the open *f*
19: 9 that you reap the *f* to its very edge,
19:19 do not sow a *f* of yours with two different
23:22 that you reap the *f* to its very edge,
25: 3 For six years you may sow your *f*,
25: 4 neither sow your *f* nor prune your vineyard.
25:12 except as taken directly from the *f*.
27:17 If the dedication of a *f* is made at the
27:19 who dedicated his *f* wishes to redeem it,
27:20 If, instead of redeeming such a *f*,
27:21 like a *f* that is doomed,
27:22 "If the *f* that some man dedicates to the
27:24 the *f* shall revert to the hereditary owner
27:28 being or an animal or a hereditary *f*,
Nm 21:22 will not turn aside into any *f* or vineyard,
22: 4 us as an ox devours the grass of the *f*."
22:23 turned off the road and went into the *f*,
23:14 him to the lookout *f* on the top of Pisgah,
Dt 5:21 not desire your neighbor's house or *f*,
14:22 produce that grows in the *f* you have sown;
20:19 After all, are the trees of the *f* men,
24:19 in your *f* and overlook a sheaf there,
28:26 of the air and for the beasts of the *f*,
28:38 "Though you spend much seed on your *f*,
Jgs 9:42 day, when the people were taking the *f*,
9:44 all who were in the *f* and attacked them.
13: 9 to the woman as she was sitting in the *f*,
19:16 an old man came from his work in the *f*;
20:31 of the Israelite soldiers in the open *f*,
Ru 2: 2 *f* of anyone who will allow me that favor."
2: 3 The *f* she entered to glean after the
2: 8 Do not go to glean in anyone else's *f*;
2: 9 Watch to see which *f* is to be harvested,
2:17 She gleaned in the *f* until evening,
2:22 in someone else's *f* you might be insulted."
4: 5 "Once you acquire the *f* from Naomi,
1Sm 6:14 The cart came to the *f* of Joshua the
6:14 At a large stone in the *f*,
6:18 LORD was placed is still in the *f* of Joshua
11: 5 Just then Saul came in from the *f*,
17:18 take these ten cheeses for the *f* officer.
17:44 birds of the air and the beasts of the *f*."
17:46 birds of the air and the beasts of the *f*;
18:13 his presence by appointing him a *f* officer.
18:30 forays, but each time they took the *f*,
20:11 to David, "Come, let us go out into the *f*."
20:35 next morning Jonathan went out into the *f*
2Sm 2:16 is in Gideon, was named the *F* of the Sides.
2:18 fleet of foot as a gazelle in the open *f*,
5:17 they all took the *f* in search of him.
10:18 army, was struck down and died on the *f*.
11:11 servants are encamped in the open *f*.
14: 6 had two sons, who quarreled in the *f*.
14:30 "You see Joab's *f* that borders mine,
14:30 so Absalom's servants set the *f* on fire.
14:31 "Why have your servants set my *f* on fire?"
18: 6 army then took the *f* against Israel,
20:12 to the *f* and placed a garment over him,
1Kgs 14:11 when one of them dies in the *f*,
16: 4 if he dies in the *f*,
21:24 when one of them dies in the *f*,
2Kgs 3:19 and ruin every fertile *f* with stones."
3:25 fertile *f* till they had loaded it down;
4:39 *f* to gather herbs and found a wild vine,
7:12 have left their camp to hide in the *f*,
8: 3 to the king to claim her house and her *f*.
8: 5 came to the king to claim her house and *f*.
8: 6 with all that the *f* produced from the day
9:21 him near the *f* of Naboth the Jezreelite.
9:25 him into the *f* of Naboth the Jezreelite.
9:37 dung in the *f* in the confines of Jezreel,
18:17 pool on the highway of the fuller's *f*.
19:26 Becoming like the plants of the *f*,
1Chr 19: 9 to their help remained apart in the open *f*.
2Chr 26:23 them in the *f* adjoining the royal cemetery,
Neh 13:10 had deserted, each man to his own *f*.
Tb 1: 6 of the *f* and the firstlings of the flock,
Jdt 8: 3 *f* supervising those who bound the sheaves,
8: 3 in the *f* between Dothan and Balamon.
1Mc 9:65 a small group of men, went out into the *f*.
14: 8 produce and the trees of the *f* their fruit.
2Mc 4:14 the unlawful exercises on the athletic *f*.
Jb 5:23 be in league with the stones of the *f*,
Ps(s) 8: 8 and oxen, yes, and the beasts of the *f*,
80:14 and the beasts of the *f* feed upon it?
103:15 like a flower of the *f* he blooms;
104:11 And give drink to every beast of the *f*,
141: 7 As when a plowman breaks furrows in the *f*,
Prv 24:27 tasks, and arrange your work in the *f*;
24:30 I passed by the *f* of the sluggard,
27:26 and the goats will bring the price of a *f*,
31:16 She picks out a *f* to purchase;
Sg 2: 7 by the gazelles and hinds of the *f*,
3: 5 by the gazelles and hinds of the *f*,
8: 4 by the gazelles and hinds of the *f*,
Sir 24:14 Jericho, Like a fair olive tree in the *f*,
40:22 better than either, the flowers of the *f*.
Is 5: 8 house to house who connect *f* with field,
7: 3 pool, on the highway of the fuller's *f*,
36: 2 pool, on the highway of the fuller's *f*,
37:27 Becoming like the plants of the *f*,
40: 6 all their glory like the flower of the *f*.
56: 9 All you wild beasts of the *f*,
Jer 6:25 Go not forth into the *f*,
7:20 trees of the *f* and the fruits of the earth;
7:33 of the sky and for the beasts of the *f*,
9:21 corpses of the slain lie like dung on a *f*,
10: 5 Like a scarecrow in a cucumber *f* are they,
12: 9 gather together, all you beasts of the *f*,
14: 5 Even the hind in the *f* deserts her
14:18 If I walk out into the *f*, look!
16: 4 birds of the sky and the beasts of the *f*,
19: 7 birds of the sky and the beasts of the *f*.
25:33 they shall lie like dung on the *f*.
26:18 Zion shall become a plowed *f*,
27: 6 of the *f* I have given him for his use.
28:14 even the beasts of the *f* I give him.
32: 7 "Buy for yourself my *f* in Anathoth,
32: 8 and said, "Please buy my *f* in Anathoth,
32: 9 the *f* in Anathoth from my cousin Hanamel,
32:25 Buy the *f* with money, call in witnesses.
34:20 birds of the air and the beasts of the *f*.
40: 7 army leaders who were still in the *f*
40:13 armies in the *f* came to Gedaliah in Mizpah
41: 8 we have stores buried in the *f*:
Lam 4: 9 through, lacking the fruits of the *f*!
Ez 16: 7 your blood and grow like a plant in the *f*.
17: 8 *f* by plentiful waters it was planted,
17:24 all the trees of the *f* shall know that I,
29: 5 You shall fall upon the open *f*,
31: 4 its streams to all the trees of the *f*.
31: 5 taller than every other tree of the *f*,
31: 6 branches all beasts of the *f* gave birth,
31:13 its branches were all the beasts of the *f*.
32: 4 on the open *f* I will cast you.
33:27 those who are in the open *f* I have given
34:27 The trees of the *f* shall bear their fruits,
38:20 the beasts of the *f* and all the reptiles
39: 5 On the open *f* you shall fall,
Dn 4:12 iron and bronze, in the grass of the *f*.
4:20 iron and bronze in the grass of the *f*;
14:33 going to bring it to the reapers in the *f*,
Hos 2:20 on that day, with the beasts of the *f*,
4: 3 The beasts of the *f*,
10: 4 grows wild like wormwood in a plowed *f*!
10:12 Break up for yourselves a new *f*,
12:12 heaps of stones in the furrows of the *f*.
Jl 1:10 The *f* is ravaged,
1:11 because the harvest of the *f* has perished.
1:12 apple, all the trees of the *f* are dried up;
1:19 flame has enkindled all the trees of the *f*.
1:20 Even the beasts of the *f* cry out to you;
2:22 Fear not, beasts of the *f*!
Am 4: 7 One *f* was watered by rain,
Mi 1: 6 I will make Samaria a stone heap in the *f*,
3:12 of you, Zion shall be plowed like a *f*,
Zep 2: 9 A *f* of nettles and a salt pit and a waste
Mal 3:11 And the vine in the *f* will not be barren,
Mt 6:30 in such splendor the grass of the *f*,
13:24 to a man who sowed good seed in his *f*.
13:27 'Sir, did you not sow good seed in your *f*?
13:31 seed which someone took and sowed in his *f*.
13:36 to us the parable of the weeds in the *f*."
13:38 the *f* is the world,
13:44 a buried treasure which a man found in a *f*.
13:44 went and sold all he had and bought that *f*.
24:18 If a man is in the *f*,
24:40 Two men will be out in the *f*;
27: 7 potter's *f* as a cemetery for foreigners.
27: 8 that field, even today, is called Blood *F*.
27:10 *f* just as the Lord had commanded me."
Mk 5:14 off and brought the news to *f* and village,
13:16 If a man is in the *f*,
Lk 12:28 in such splendor the grass of the *f*,

17:31 should the man in the *f* return home.
Acts 1:19 who named the property *F* of Blood
5: 3 yourself some of the proceeds from that *f*?
1Cor 9: 6 What soldier in the *f* pays for his rations?
Gal 6: 8 If he sows in the *f* of the flesh,
Jas 1:10 will disappear "like the flower of the *f*."
1:11 parches the meadow, the *f* flowers droop,
1Pt 1:24 glory of men is like the flower of the *f*.

FIELDS (72)

Gn 24:65 out there, walking through the *f* toward us?"
30:16 evening, when Jacob came home from the *f*.
34: 5 sons were out in the *f* with his livestock,
34: 7 as Jacob's sons were coming in from the *f*.
37:15 met him as he was wandering about in the *f*.
41:48 in each town the crops of the *f* around it.
47:24 four-fifths as seed for your *f* and as food
Ex 8: 9 the houses and courtyards and *f* died off.
9:19 open *f* to be brought to a place of safety.
9:19 Whatever man or beast remains in the *f* and
9:21 left their servants and livestock in the *f*.
9:25 thing and splintered every tree in the *f*.
10: 5 foliage that has since sprouted in your *f*.
23:16 when you gather in the produce from the *f*.
Lv 27:30 from the *f* or in fruit from the trees,
Nm 16:14 us *f* and vineyards for our inheritance,
20:17 We will not cross any *f* or vineyards,
Dt 11:15 forth grass in your *f* for your animals.
22:25 it is in the open *f* that a man comes upon
22:27 it was in the open *f* that he came upon her,
32:13 land and live off the products of its *f*,
Jgs 9:27 trust in him, and went out into the *f*,
9:32 set an ambush tonight in the *f*,
9:43 companies, and set up an ambush in the *f*.
1Sm 5: 6 swarmed in their ships and overran their *f*.
8:14 He will take the best of your *f*,
22: 7 of Jesse give all of you *f* and vineyards?
2Chr 31: 5 and honey, and all the produce of the *f*;
Neh 5: 3 'We are forced to pawn our *f*,
5: 4 borrowed money on our *f* and our vineyards.
5: 5 our *f* and our vineyards belong to others."
5:11 you return to them this very day their *f*,
10:36 fruits of our *f* and of our fruit trees,
10:38 of our *f* we will bring to the Levites;
12:44 to collect from the *f* of the various cities
Jdt 2:27 wheat harvest, he set fire to all their *f*,
3: 3 Our dwellings and all our wheat *f*,
4: 5 since their *f* had recently been harvested,
8: 7 servants and maids, livestock and *f*,
Jb 5:10 upon the earth and sends water upon the *f*;
Ps(s) 65:14 The *f* are garmented with flocks and the
72:16 shall flourish like the verdure of the *f*.
107:37 They sowed *f* and planted vineyards,
132: 6 we found it in the *f* of Jaar.
Prv 8:26 as yet the earth and the *f* were not made,
23:10 landmark, nor invade the *f* of orphans;
Sg 7:12 *f* and spend the night among the villages.
Is 32:12 Beat your breasts for the pleasant *f*,
Jer 4:17 Like watchmen of the *f* they surround her,
6:12 strangers, their *f* and their wives as well;
8:10 wives to strangers, their *f* to spoilers.
32:15 Houses and *f* and vineyards shall again be
32:43 *F* shall again be bought in this land,
32:44 *F* shall be bought with money,
35: 9 we own no vineyards or *f* or crops,
Ez 34:29 prepare for them peaceful *f* for planting;
36:30 on your trees and the crops in your *f*;
39:10 from the *f* or cut it down in the forests,
Hos 5: 7 new moon devour them together with their *f*.
Mi 2: 2 They covet *f*, and seize them;
2: 4 our *f* are portioned out among our captors,
2: 4 The *f* of my people are measured out,
4:10 go forth from the city and dwell in the *f*;
Zep 2: 6 the Cretans shall become *f* for shepherds,
Zec 10: 1 for everyone, grassy *f*.
Mk 11: 8 spread reeds which they had cut in the *f*.
15:21 and Rufus, was coming in from the *f*,
Lk 2: 8 living in the *f* and keeping night watch by
17: 7 herding sheep and he came in from the *f*,
23:26 the Cyrenean who was coming in from the *f*.
Jn 4:35 The *f* are shining for harvest!
Jas 5: 4 from the farmhands who harvested your *f*.

FIEND (1)

2Mc 7: 9 "You accursed *f*,

FIERCE (28)

Gn 49: 7 Cursed be their fury so *f*,
Ex 9:18 at this hour I will rain down such *f* hail
9:24 such *f* hail as had never been seen in the
10:14 had there been such a *f* swarm of locusts,
Nm 13:28 people who are living in the land are *f*,
Dt 9:19 the *f* anger of the LORD against you:
29:23 Why this *f* outburst of wrath?'
Jgs 18:25 lest *f* men fall upon you and you and your
20:34 In a *f* battle, the LORD defeated Benjamin
1Sm 4: 2 After a *f* struggle Israel was defeated by
28:18 not carry out his *f* anger against Amalek,
2Sm 2:17 After a very *f* battle that day,
11:15 Uriah up front, where the fighting is *f*.
17: 8 *f* as a bear in the wild robbed of her cubs.
1Kgs 22:35 The battle grew *f* during the day,
2Chr 18:34 The battle grew *f* during the day,
2Mc 10:29 In the midst of the *f* battle,
Ps(s) 37:35 I saw a wicked man, *f*, and stalwart
54: 5 up against me, and *f* men seek my life;
78:49 He loosed against them his *f* anger,
86:14 me, and the company of *f* men seeks my life,
Wis 11:17 send upon them a drove of bears or *f* lions,
18:15 heaven's royal throne bounded, a *f* warrior,
Is 11:15 his hand over the Euphrates in his *f* anger
25: 3 will honor you, *f* nations will fear you.
Lam 2: 6 scorned in *f* wrath both king and priest.
Lk 11:53 Pharisees began to manifest *f* hostility
Jas 3: 4 the fact that they are driven by *f* winds,

FIERCELY (3)

Gn 31:36 demanded, "that you should hound me so *f*?
2Sm 19:44 spoke even more *f* than the Israelites.
2Kgs 23:26 from his *f* burning anger against Judah.

FIERCENESS (1)

2Mc 15:21 equipment, and the *f* of their elephants,

FIERCER (2)

Lv 26:28 with sevenfold *f* punishment for your sins,
Sir 28:10 the more underlying it, the *f* the fight;

FIERCEST (1)

Wis 17:19 or the roaring cry of the *f* beasts,

FIERY (36)

Gn 3:24 the cherubim and the *f* revolving sword,
Ex 14:24 cast through the column of the *f* cloud
Lv 26:28 will meet you with *f* defiance and will
Dt 9:15 down again from the blazing, *f* mountain,
28:22 and fever, with scorching, *f* drought,
2Kgs 6:17 with horses and *f* chariots around Elisha.
Jb 18:14 *F* destruction lodges in his tent,
28: 5 forth bread, is in *f* upheaval underneath.
Ps(s) 7:14 against them, and use *f* darts for arrows.
11: 6 upon the wicked *f* coals and brimstone;
21:10 Make them burn as though in a *f* furnace,
29: 7 The voice of the LORD strikes *f* flames;
120: 4 of a warrior with *f* coals of brushwood.
Wis 11:18 unknown beasts to breathe forth *f* breath,
Sir 43: 3 of the earth, and who can bear its *f* heat?
43: 4 By its *f* darts the land is consumed;
48: 9 in a whirlwind, in a chariot with *f* horses.
Is 50:11 kindle flames and carry about you *f* darts;
66:15 heat and his punishment with *f* flames.
Lam 2: 3 He broke off, in *f* wrath,
Ez 21:36 breathing my *f* wrath upon you;
22:31 with my *f* wrath I have consumed them;
28:14 of God, walking among the *f* stones.
28:16 Cherub drove you from among the *f* stones.
38:19 my anger and in my jealousy, in my *f* wrath,
Dn 3:49 drove the *f* flames out of the furnace,
10: 6 lightning, his eyes were like *f* torches,
Jl 2: 5 crackling of a *f* flame devouring stubble;
Na 2: 4 *F* steel are the chariots on the day of his
Mt 13:42 The angels will hurl them into the *f*
13:50 and hurl the wicked into the *f* furnace,
18: 9 than be thrown with both into *f* Gehenna.
Eph 6:16 you extinguish the *f* darts of the evil one.
Rv 9:17 The breastplates they wore were *f* red,
19:20 alive into the *f* pool of burning sulphur.
21: 8 their lot is the *f* pool of burning sulphur,

FIFTEEN (22)

Gn 5:10 and *f* years after the birth of Kenan,
7:20 the crest rising *f* cubits higher than the
Ex 27:14 be hangings to the extent of *f* cubits,
27:15 be hangings to the extent of *f* cubits,
38:14 were hangings to the extent of *f* cubits,
38:15 hangings to the extent of *f* cubits,
Lv 27: 7 fixed sum shall be *f* shekels for a man,
Jgs 8:10 with their force of about *f* thousand men;
2Sm 9:10 Ziba, who had *f* sons and twenty servants,
19:18 by his *f* sons and twenty servants,
1Kgs 7: 3 beams numbered forty-five, *f* to a row.
2Kgs 14:17 of Jehoahaz, king of Israel, by *f* years.
20: 6 I will add *f* years to your life.
2Chr 25:25 of Jehoahaz, king of Israel, by *f* years.
1Mc 10:40 I make a yearly personal grant of *f*
2Mc 8:22 division, assigning to each *f* hundred men.
Is 38: 5 I will add *f* years to your life.
Ez 45:12 shekels, plus *f* shekels shall be your mina.
Hos 3: 2 So I bought her for *f* pieces of silver and
Jn 2: 6 each holding *f* to twenty-five gallons.
Acts 27:28 again took a sounding and found it to be *f*.
Gal 1:18 to know Cephas, with whom I stayed *f* days.

FIFTEENTH (22)

Ex 16: 1 on the *f* day of the second month after
Lv 23: 6 The *f* day of this month is the LORD's
23:34 The *f* day of this seventh month is the
23:39 "On the *f* day,
Nm 28:17 and the *f* day of this month is the
29:12 "On the *f* day of the seventh month you
33: 3 month, on the *f* day of the first month.
1Kgs 12:32 the eighth month of the *f* day of the month
12:33 in Bethel on the *f* day of the eighth month,
2Kgs 14:23 In the *f* year of Amaziah,
1Chr 24:14 the fourteenth to Ishbaal, the *f* to Bilgah,
25:22 The *f* fell to Jeremoth,
2Chr 15:10 third month of the *f* year of Asa's reign,
Est 9:18 But on the *f* they rested,
9:21 fourteenth and the *f* of the month of Adar
F:10 fourteenth and *f* of the month Adar
1Mc 1:54 On the *f* day of the month Chislev,
2Mc 11:33 and forty-eight, the *f* of Xanthicus.
11:38 and forty-eight, the *f* of Xanthicus.
Ez 32:17 On the *f* day of the first month in the
45:25 On the *f* day of the seventh month,
Lk 3: 1 the *f* year of the rule of Tiberius Caesar,

FIFTH (57)

Gn 1:23 morning followed—the *f* day.
30:17 she conceived and bore a *f* son to Jacob.
47:24 is in, you must give a *f* of it to Pharaoh,
47:26 a *f* of its produce should go to Pharaoh.
Lv 5:16 sanctuary, adding to it a *f* of its value.
5:24 give the owner one *f* of its value.
19:25 Not until the *f* year may you eat its fruit.
22:14 with an increment of one *f* of the amount.
27:13 shall pay one *f* more than this valuation.
27:15 one *f* more than the price thus established,
27:19 one *f* more than the price thus established,
27:27 by paying one *f* more than its fixed value.
27:31 he shall pay one *f* more than their value.
Nm 5: 7 *f* of their value to the one he has wronged.
7:36 On the *f* day it was the turn of Shelumiel,
29:26 the *f* day you shall offer nine bullocks,
33:38 of Egypt, on the first day of the *f* month.
Jos 19:24 The *f* lot fell to the clans of the tribe
Jgs 19: 8 On the *f* morning he rose early to depart,
2Sm 3: 4 the *f*, Shephatiah, son of Abital;
1Kgs 14:25 In the *f* year of King Rehoboam,
2Kgs 8:16 In the *f* year of Joram,
25: 8 On the seventh day of the *f* month (this
1Chr 2:14 Nethanel, the fourth, Raddai, the *f*,
3: 3 the *f*, Shephatiah, by Abital;
8: 2 third, Nohah, the fourth, and Rapha, the *f*.
12:11 third, Mishmannah fourth, Jeremiah *f*,
24: 9 the fourth to Seorim, the *f* to Malchijah,
25:12 The *f* was Nethaniah,
26: 3 the *f*, Jehohanan, the sixth, Eliehoenai,
26: 4 the *f*, Ammiel, the sixth, Issachar,
27: 8 Fifth, for the *f* month,
2Chr 12: 2 that in the *f* year of King Rehoboam,
Ezr 7: 8 *f* month of that seventh year of the king.
7: 9 day of the *f* month he arrived at Jerusalem,
Neh 6: 5 Then, the *f* time,
2Mc 7:15 forward the *f* brother and maltreated him.
10:35 When the *f* day dawned,
Jer 1: 3 *f* month of the eleventh year of Zedekiah,
28: 1 Judah, in the *f* month of the fourth year,
36: 9 ninth month, in the *f* year of Jehoiakim,
52:12 On the tenth day of the *f* month (this was
Bar 1: 2 *f* year [on the seventh day of the month,
Ez 1: 1 year, on the *f* day of the fourth month,
1: 2 On the fifth day of the month, the *f* year,
8: 1 On the *f* day of the sixth month,
20: 1 year, on the tenth day of the *f* month,
33:21 On the *f* day of the tenth month,
Zec 7: 3 "Must I mourn and abstain in the *f* month
7: 5 When you fasted and mourned in the *f* and
8:19 The fast days of the fourth, the *f*,
Rv 6: 9 When the Lamb broke open the *f* seal,
9: 1 Then the *f* angel blew his trumpet,
16:10 The *f* angel poured out his bowl on the
21:20 the fourth emerald, the *f* sardonyx,

FIFTIES (5)

Ex 18:21 groups of thousands, of hundreds, of *f*,
18:25 groups of thousands, of hundreds, of *f*,
Dt 1:15 over hundreds, over *f* and over tens,
1Mc 3:55 over thousands, over hundreds, over *f*,
Mk 6:40 people took their places in hundreds and *f*.

FIFTIETH (4)

Lv 23:16 the day after the seventh week, the *f* day,
25:10 This *f* year you shall make sacred by
25:11 In this *f* year, your year of jubilee,
2Kgs 15:23 In the *f* year of Azariah,

FIFTY (122)

Gn 6:15 three hundred cubits, its width *f* cubits,
7:24 over the earth for one hundred and *f* days,
8: 3 At the end of one hundred and *f* days,
9:28 three hundred and *f* years after the flood.
9:29 of Noah was nine hundred and *f* years;
18:24 there were *f* innocent people in the city;
18:24 sake of the *f* innocent people within it?
18:26 *f* innocent people in the city of Sodom,
18:28 there are five less than *f* innocent people?
Ex 26: 5 There are to be *f* loops along the edge of
26: 5 and *f* loops along the edge of the
26: 6 Then make *f* clasps of gold,
26:10 Make *f* loops along the edge of the end
26:10 and *f* loops along the edge of the end

FIFTY (cont.)

26:11 Also make *f* bronze clasps and put them
27:12 there shall be hangings, *f* cubits long,
27:13 court on the east side shall be *f* cubits.
27:18 be one hundred cubits long, *f* cubits wide,
30:23 amount, that is, two hundred and *f* shekels,
30:23 hundred and *f* shekels of fragrant cane;
36:12 *F* loops were thus put on one inner sheet,
36:12 and *f* loops on the inner sheet in the
36:13 Then *f* clasps of gold were made,
36:17 *F* loops were made along the edge of the
36:17 and *f* loops along the edge of the
36:18 *F* bronze clasps were made with which the
38:12 side there were hangings, *f* cubits long,
38:13 the east side the court was *f* cubits long.
38:26 and three thousand five hundred and *f* men.
Lv 27: 3 shall be *f* silver shekels for a man,
27:16 seed being valued at *f* silver shekels.
Nm 1:25 and *f* were enrolled in the tribe of Gad.
1:46 and three thousand, five hundred and *f*.
2:15 to forty-five thousand six hundred and *f*.
2:16 fifty-one thousand four hundred and *f*
2:32 and three thousand five hundred and *f*.
4: 3 between thirty and *f* years of age;
4:23 the men between thirty and *f* years of age;
4:30 men between thirty and *f* years of age;
4:35 the men between thirty and *f* years of age.
4:36 numbered two thousand seven hundred and *f*.
4:39 the men between thirty and *f* years of age.
4:43 the men from thirty up to *f* years of age.
4:47 men between thirty and *f* years of age
8:25 When he is *f* years old,
16: 2 Reuben] took two hundred and *f* Israelites
16:17 and *f* followers shall take his own censer,
16:35 and *f* men who were offering the incense.
26:10 the fire consumed two hundred and *f* men.
31:30 you shall take one out of every *f* persons,
31:47 LORD had ordered, took one out of every *f*,
31:52 thousand seven hundred and *f* shekels.
Dt 22:29 *f* silver shekels and take her as his wife,
Jos 7:21 and a bar of gold *f* shekels in weight;
2Sm 15: 1 with chariots, horses, and *f* henchmen.
18:11 to give you *f* pieces of silver and a belt."
24:24 floor and the oxen for *f* silver shekels.
1Kgs 1: 5 acquired chariots, drivers, and *f* henchmen.
7: 2 of Lebanon one hundred cubits long, *f* wide,
7: 6 hall he made *f* cubits long and thirty wide.
9:23 in the work numbered five hundred and *f*.
10:29 shekels, a horse one hundred and *f* shekels;
18: 4 hid them away *f* each in two caves,
18:13 prophets of the LORD, *f* each in two caves,
18:19 as well as the four hundred and *f* prophets
18:22 are four hundred and *f* prophets of Baal.
2Kgs 1: 9 with his company of *f* men after Elijah.
1:10 from heaven and consume you and your *f* men.
1:10 from heaven and consumed him and his *f* men.
1:11 with his company of *f* men after Elijah.
1:12 from heaven and consume you and your *f* men.
1:12 from heaven, consuming him and his *f* men.
1:13 sent a captain with his company of *f* men.
1:13 "let my life and the lives of these *f* men,
1:14 two captains with their companies of *f* men.
2: 7 *F* of the guild prophets followed,
2:16 "Among your servants are *f* brave men,"
2:17 So they sent the *f* men,
13: 7 except *f* horsemen with ten chariots and
15:20 in the country, *f* silver shekels from each.
15:25 who had with him *f* men from Gilead,
1Chr 5:21 *f* thousand camels, two hundred fifty
8:40 one hundred and *f*.
12:34 *f* thousand men rallying with a single
2Chr 1:17 horses going for a hundred and *f* shekels.
3: 9 The weight of the nails was *f* gold shekels.
8:10 *f* overseers who had charge of the people.
8:18 and *f* talents of gold to King Solomon.
Ezr 8: 3 him one hundred and *f* males were enrolled;
8: 6 son of Jonathan, and with him *f* males;
8:26 silver, six hundred and *f* talents;
Neh 5:17 I set my table for a hundred and *f* persons,
7:69 one thousand drachmas of gold, *f* basins,
Jdt 1: 2 the wall seventy cubits high and *f* thick.
Est 5:14 "Have a gibbet set up, *f* cubits in height,
7: 9 of Haman stands a gibbet *f* cubits high.
1Mc 6:20 *f* they assembled and stormed the citadel,
9:61 Jonathan's men seized about *f* of the men
2Mc 4: 9 this he agreed to pay a hundred and *f* more,
Is 3: 3 elder, The captain of *f* and the nobleman,
Ez 40:15 the vestibule on the inside was *f* cubits.
40:21 *f* cubits long and twenty-five cubits wide.
40:25 *f* cubits long and twenty-five cubits wide.
40:29 *f* cubits long and twenty-five cubits wide.
40:33 *f* cubits long and twenty-five cubits wide.
40:36 *f* cubits long and twenty-five cubits wide.
42: 2 north side, and they were *f* cubits wide.
42: 7 length before these chambers was *f* cubits,
42: 8 belonging to the outer court was *f* cubits,
45: 2 surrounded by a free space of *f* cubits,
48:17 *f* cubits, south two hundred and fifty
48:17 fifty cubits, and west two hundred and *f*
Hg 2:16 another went to the vat to draw *f* measures,
Lk 7:41 a total of five hundred coins, the other *f*.
9:14 "Have them sit down in groups of *f* or so."
16: 6 invoice, sit down quickly, and make it *f*.'
Jn 8:57 "You are not yet *f*!
Acts 13:20 the end of some four hundred and *f* years.
19:19 it came to *f* thousand silver pieces.

FIFTY-FIVE (3)

2Kgs 21: 1 reign, and he reigned *f* years in Jerusalem.
2Chr 33: 1 king, and he reigned *f* years in Jerusalem.
Neh 7:20 sons of Adin, six hundred and *f*;

FIFTY-FOUR (7)

Nm 1:29 *f* thousand four hundred were enrolled in
2: 6 in the census to *f* thousand four hundred.]
Ezr 2: 7 of Elam, one thousand two hundred and *f*;
2:15 sons of Adin, four hundred and *f*;
2:31 Elam, one thousand two hundred and *f*;
Neh 7:12 of Elam, one thousand two hundred and *f*;
7:34 Elam, one thousand two hundred and *f*;

FIFTY-NINE (2)

Nm 1:23 *f* thousand three hundred were enrolled in
2:13 in the census to *f* thousand three hundred.]

FIFTY-ONE (3)

Nm 2:16 and *f* thousand four hundred and fifty.]
1Mc 7: 1 In the year one hundred and *f*,
2Mc 14: 4 Demetrius in the year one hundred and *f*

FIFTY-SECOND (1)

2Kgs 15:27 In the *f* year of Azariah,

FIFTY-SEVEN (3)

Nm 1:31 *f* thousand four hundred were enrolled in
2: 8 in the census to *f* thousand four hundred.
2:31 was one hundred and *f* thousand six hundred.]

FIFTY-SIX (4)

1Chr 9: 9 various families were nine hundred and *f*.
Ezr 2:14 sons of Bigvai, two thousand and *f*;
2:22 men of Netophah, *f*;
2:30 sons of Magbish, one hundred and *f*;

FIFTY-THREE (7)

Nm 1:43 *f* thousand four hundred were enrolled in
2:30 in the census to *f* thousand four hundred.
26:47 of whom *f* thousand four hundred men were
2Chr 2:16 number one hundred *f* thousand six hundred.
1Mc 9:54 In the year one hundred and *f*,
2Mc 13: 2 thousand foot soldiers, *f* hundred horsemen,
Jn 21:11 one hundred *f* of them!

FIFTY-TWO (11)

Nm 26:34 of whom *f* thousand seven hundred men were
2Kgs 15: 2 reign, and he reigned *f* years in Jerusalem.
2Chr 26: 3 king, and he reigned *f* years in Jerusalem.
Ezr 2:29 sons of Nebo, *f*;
2:37 sons of Immer, one thousand and *f*;
2:60 Tobiah, sons of Nekoda, six hundred and *f*.
Neh 6:15 it had taken *f* days.
7:10 sons of Arah, six hundred and *f*;
7:33 men of Nebo, *f*;
7:40 sons of Immer, one thousand and *f*
1Mc 9: 3 first month of the year one hundred and *f*,

FIG (41)

Gn 3: 7 so they sewed *f* leaves together and made
Dt 8: 8 of vines and *f* trees and pomegranates,
Jgs 9:10 Then the trees said to the *f* tree,
9:11 But the *f* tree answered them,
1Kgs 5: 5 or under his *f* tree from Dan to Beer-sheba,
2Kgs 18:31 will eat of his own vine and of his own *f*,
Jdt 10: 5 filled a bag with roasted grain, *f* cakes,
1Mc 14:12 man sat under his vine and his *f* tree,
Ps(s) 105:33 He struck down their vines and their *f*
Prv 27:18 He who tends a *f* tree eats its fruit,
Sg 2:13 The *f* tree puts forth its figs,
Is 28: 4 Will be like an early *f* before summer:
34: 4 the vine, or as the *f* withers on the tree.
36:16 eat of his own vine and of his own *f* tree,
Jer 5:17 and cattle, devour your vines and *f* trees;
8:13 grapes on the vine, No figs on the *f* trees,
Hos 2:14 I will lay waste her vines and *f* trees,
9:10 first fruits of the *f* tree in its prime,
Jl 1: 7 laid waste my vine, and blighted my *f* tree;
1:12 vine has dried up, the *f* tree is withered;
2:22 the *f* tree and the vine give their yield.
Am 4: 9 your *f* trees and olive trees the locust
Mi 4: 4 under his own vine or under his own *f* tree,
7: 1 no cluster to eat, no early *f* that I crave.
Na 3:12 All your fortresses are but *f* trees,
Hb 3:17 For though the *f* tree blossom not nor
Hg 2:19 not sprouted, nor have the vine, the *f*,
Zec 3:10 one another under your vines and *f* trees."
Mt 21:19 *f* tree by the roadside he went over to it,
21:20 "Why did the *f* tree wither up so quickly?"
21:21 only will you do what I did to the *f* tree,
24:32 From the *f* tree learn a lesson.
Mk 11:13 Observing a *f* tree some distance off,
11:20 they saw the *f* tree withered to its roots.
11:21 The *f* tree you cursed has withered up."
13:28 Learn a lesson from the *f* tree.
Lk 13: 6 man had a *f* tree growing in his vineyard,
13: 7 of fruit on this *f* tree and found none.
21:29 "Notice the *f* tree, or any other tree.
Jn 1:48 answered, "I saw you under the *f* tree."
1:50 I told you I saw you under the *f* tree?
Jas 3:12 A *f* tree, brothers, cannot produce olives,

FIGHT (133)

Ex 1:10 too may join our enemies to *f* against us,
13:17 the people see that they would have to *f*,
14:14 The LORD himself will *f* for you;
17:11 raised up, Israel had the better of the *f*,
17:11 hands rest, Amalek had the better of the *f*.
21:22 men have a *f* and hurt a pregnant woman,
Dt 1:30 goes before you, will himself *f* for you,
1:41 We will go up ourselves and *f*,
1:42 Do not go up and *f*,
3:22 for the LORD, your God, will *f* for you.'
20: 4 who goes with you to *f* for you against
Jos 10:25 do to all the enemies against whom you *f*."
11: 5 they encamped together to *f* against Israel.
Jgs 1: 9 Afterward the Judahites went down to *f*
8: 1 us when you went to *f* against Midian?"
9:38 Go out now and *f* with them."
10: 9 also crossed the Jordan to *f* against Judah,
11: 6 that we may be able to *f* the Ammonites."
11: 8 you go with us to *f* against the Ammonites,
11: 9 "If you bring me back to *f* against the
11:12 me that you come to *f* with me in my land?"
11:32 on to the Ammonites to *f* against them,
12: 1 "Why do you go on to *f* with the Ammonites
12: 3 come up against me this day to *f* with me?"
20:42 with the *f* being pressed against them.
1Sm 4: 9 So *f* manfully!"
8:20 to lead us in warfare and *f* our battles."
14:20 all his men shouted and rushed into the *f*,
15:18 *F* against them until you have exterminated
17:10 Give me a man and let us *f* together."
17:32 your service to go and *f* this Philistine."
17:33 up against this Philistine and *f* with him,
18:17 my champion and *f* the battles of the LORD.
19: 8 David went out to *f* against the
28: 1 their military forces to *f* against Israel.
29: 8 *f* against the enemies of my lord the king?"
2Sm 11:20 'Why did you go near the city to *f*?
1Kgs 12:21 to *f* against the house of Israel,
12:24 out to *f* against your brother Israelites.
20:23 But if we *f* them on level ground,
20:25 Let us *f* them on level ground,
20:26 and went up to Aphek to *f* against Israel.
22: 4 come with me to *f* against Ramoth-gilead?"
22:15 shall we go to *f* against Ramoth-gilead,
22:31 "Do not *f* with anyone at all except the
22:32 and shifted to *f* him.
2Kgs 7: 6 and the kings of the borderlands to *f* us."
10: 3 throne, and *f* for your master's house."
19: 9 of Ethiopia, had come out to *f* against him.
1Chr 19:17 army of David drawn up to *f* the Arameans,
2Chr 11: 1 to have them *f* against Israel and restore
11: 4 not march out to *f* against your brothers.
18:14 shall we go to *f* against Ramoth-gilead,
18:30 commanders the order, *F* with no one,
18:31 and shifted to *f* him.
20: 1 Meunites came to *f* against Jehoshaphat.
20:17 You will not have to *f* in this encounter.
32: 8 our God, to help us and to *f* our battles."
35:20 up to *f* at Carchemish on the Euphrates,
35:22 but went out to *f* in the plain of Megiddo.
Neh 4: 2 to come and *f* against Jerusalem
4: 8 and to be feared, and *f* for your brethren,
4:14 our God will *f* with us."
Jdt 6: 2 and to tell us not to *f* against the
Est A: 6 war, to *f* against the race of the just.
1Mc 2:40 "and do not *f* against the Gentiles for
2:41 "Let us *f* against anyone who attacks us
3:10 army from Samaria, to *f* against Israel.
3:17 as we are, *f* such a mighty host as this?
3:43 and *f* for our people and our sanctuary!"
3:58 in the morning be ready to *f* these
4:17 the plunder, for there is a *f* ahead of us,
5:19 not *f* against the Gentiles until we return."
5:32 men of his army, *F* for our kinsmen today."
5:67 out rashly to *f* in their desire to distinguish
6:34 grapes and mulberries to provoke them to *f*.
6:42 Judas with his army advanced to *f*,
6:52 their own, and kept up the *f* a long time.
7:28 "Let there be no *f* between me and you.
7:31 he went out to *f* Judas near Caphar-salama.
9: 8 we can put up a good *f* against them."
9: 9 with our kinsmen, and then *f* against them.
9:30 leader in his place, and to *f* our battle."
9:44 "Let us get up now and *f* for our lives,
11:43 therefore, of sending men to *f* for me,
11:46 control of the main streets and began to *f*.
12:40 not permit him, but would *f* against him.
12:50 and went out in compact body ready to *f*.
12:51 that they were ready to *f* for their lives,
13: 9 *F* our battles, and we will do everything

13:10 So Simon mustered all the men able to *f*,
13:14 Jonathan, and that he intended to *f* him,
14: 1 to obtain help so that he could *f* Trypho.
15:19 are not to assist those who *f* against them.
16: 3 brother's, and go out and *f* for our nation;
2Mc 7:19 for having dared to *f* against God."
8:16 them unjustly, but to *f* courageously,
10:21 their enemies free to *f* against them.
10:28 other taking fury as their leader in the *f*.
12:11 After a hard *f*,
13:14 followers to *f* nobly to death for the laws,
Ps(s) 35: 1 I Fight, O LORD, against those who *f* me;
43: 1 and fight my *f* against a faithless people;
56: 3 yes, many *f* against me.
Sir 4:28 Even to the death *f* for truth,
28:10 the more underlying it, the fiercer the *f*;
29:13 spear it will *f* for you against the foe.
37: 5 friend will *f* with you against the foe,
Is 37: 9 of Ethiopia, had come out to *f* against him.
Jer 1:19 They will *f* against you,
15:20 Though they *f* against you,
21: 4 which you intend to *f* the king of Babylon
21: 5 and I myself will *f* against you with
37: 8 shall return to the *f* against this city;
51:30 Babylon's warriors have ceased to *f*,
Dn 10:20 Soon I must *f* the prince of Persia again.
11:11 go out to *f* against the king of the north,
Zec 14: 3 shall go forth and *f* against those nations,
14:14 Judah also shall *f* against Jerusalem.
1Cor 9:26 I do not *f* as if I were shadowboxing.
1Tm 1:19 may *f* the good fight and hold fast to faith
6:12 Fight the good *f* of faith.
2Tm 4: 7 I have fought the good *f*,
Heb 12: 4 In your *f* against sin you have not yet
Jas 4: 2 you cannot acquire, so you quarrel and *f*.
Jude 1: 3 encourage you to *f* hard for the faith
Rv 2:16 *f* against them with the sword of my mouth.
13: 4 the beast, or come forward to *f* against it?"
17:14 They will *f* against the Lamb but the Lamb

FIGHTERS (3)

1Chr 19:10 he chose some of the best *f* among the
19:18 slew seven thousand of their chariot *f*
1Mc 8: 1 They were valiant *f* and acted amiably to

FIGHTING (27)

Ex 2:13 went out again, and now two Hebrews were *f*!
14:25 LORD was *f* for them against the Egyptians.
Dt 25:11 "When two men are *f* and the wife of one
Jgs 20:39 them as surely as in the earlier *f*,
1Sm 14:24 and there was scattered *f* in every town in
17:19 and all Israel are *f* against the
25:28 your lordship is *f* the battles of the LORD,
2Sm 2:28 pursuing Israel no farther and *f* no more.
11:15 Uriah up front, where the *f* is fierce.
1Kgs 9:22 the Israelites, for they were his *f* force,
2Chr 26:13 five hundred *f* men of great valor to help
35:22 for he had sought a pretext for *f* with him.
Jdt 7: 2 same day all their *f* men went into action.
1Mc 3:21 but we are *f* for our lives and our laws.
4:34 of Lysias' men fell in hand-to-hand *f*.
5:56 brave deeds and the *f* that they were doing.
5:57 out and *f* against the Gentiles around us."
11:44 thousand good *f* men to him at Antioch.
12:41 picked *f* men and came to Beth-shan.
2Mc 12:36 had been *f* for a long time and were weary,
15:27 *F* with their hands and praying to God with
Is 58: 4 Yes, your fast ends in quarreling and *f*,
Jer 32: 5 in *f* the Chaldeans,
Zec 14: 3 those nations, *f* as on a day of battle.
Jn 18:36 my subjects would be *f* to save me from
Acts 5:39 able to destroy them without *f* God himself."
7:26 the next day while some of them were *f*,

FIGHTS (2)

Jos 23:10 the LORD, your God, himself who *f* for you,
Wis 16:17 For the universe *f* on behalf of the just.

FIGMENTS (1)

Bar 2: 8 or turn, each from the *f* of his evil heart.

FIGS (25)

Nm 13:23 a pole, as well as some pomegranates and *f*.
20: 5 grain nor *f* nor vines nor pomegranates?
1Sm 25:18 and two hundred cakes of pressed *f*,
30:12 a cake of pressed *f* and two cakes of
2Kgs 20: 7 of *f* to be brought and applied to the boil,
1Chr 12:41 in great quantity of meal, pressed *f*,
Neh 13:15 asses, together with wine, grapes, *f*,
Tb 1: 7 of grain, wine, olive oil, pomegranates, *f*,
Sg 2:13 The fig tree puts forth its *f*,
Is 38:21 of *f* to be taken and applied to the boil,
Jer 8:13 grapes on the vine, No *f* on the fig trees,
24: 1 of *f* placed before the temple of the LORD.
24: 2 One basket contained excellent *f*,
24: 2 But the other basket contained very bad *f*,
24: 3 *F*," I replied; "the good ones are very good,
24: 5 Like these good *f*,
24: 8 And like the *f* that are bad,
29:17 I will make them like rotten *f*,
Ez 27:17 with you, exchanging Minnith wheat, *f*,
Na 3:12 but fig trees, bearing early *f* That fall,
Mt 7:16 from thornbushes, or *f* from prickly plants?
Mk 11:13 it was not the time for *f*.
Lk 6:44 *F* are not taken from thornbushes,
Jas 3:12 cannot produce olives, or a grapevine *f*;
Rv 6:13 earth like *f* shaken loose by a mighty wind.

FIGURE (11)

Lv 26: 1 set up a stone *f* for worship in your land;
Dt 4:16 by fashioning an idol to represent any *f*,
Jb 4:16 a *f* was before my eyes,
21:24 His *f* is full and nourished,
Sg 7: 8 Your very *f* is like a palm tree.
Sir 26:17 are her beauty of face and graceful *f*.
Dn 8:15 I had seen, a manlike *f* stood before me,
Mt 25:17 received the two thousand doubled his *f*.
Lk 5:36 He then proposed to them this *f*:
Jn 10: 6 Even though Jesus used this *f* with them,
Acts 28: 7 of Publius, the chief *f* on the island.

FIGURED (1)

Ez 41:19 thus they were *f* on every side throughout

FIGUREHEAD (1)

Acts 28:11 with the "Heavenly Twins" as its *f*.

FIGURES (8)

Nm 33:52 all their stone *f* and molten images,
1Kgs 6:29 the outer rooms had carved *f* of cherubim,
6:32 of olive wood, with carved *f* of cherubim,
2Chr 4: 3 rim a ring of *f* of oxen encircled the sea,
Ez 1: 5 Within it were *f* resembling four living
8:10 pictured the *f* of all kinds of creeping things
41:18 carved the *f* of cherubim and palmtrees:
Mk 4:13 you going to understand other *f* like it?

FILIGREE (9)

Ex 28:11 of Israel and then mounted in gold *f* work.
28:13 Make *f* rosettes of gold,
28:14 the cordlike chains to the *f* rosettes.
28:20 stones are to be mounted in gold *f* work,
28:25 fastened in front to the two *f* rosettes
39: 6 were prepared and mounted in gold *f* work;
39:13 They were mounted in gold *f* work.
39:16 two gold *f* rosettes and two gold rings.
39:18 fastened in front to the two *f* rosettes,

FILL (93)

Gn 1:22 multiply, and *f* the water of the seas;
1:28 *f* the earth and subdue it.
9: 1 "Be fertile and multiply and *f* the earth.
24:19 When she had let him drink his *f*,
24:19 camels, too, until they have drunk their *f*."
44: 1 *F* the men's bags with as much food as they
Ex 2:16 came to draw water and *f* the troughs
10: 6 They shall *f* your houses and the houses of
15: 9 divide the spoils and have my *f* of them:
16: 3 by our fleshpots and ate our *f* of bread!
16: 8 "and in the morning your *f* of bread,
16:12 the morning you shall have your *f* of bread,
Dt 6:11 and when, therefore, you eat your *f*,
8:10 But when you have eaten your *f*,
8:12 lest, when you have eaten your *f*,
11:15 Thus you may eat your *f*.
14:29 your community, may come and eat their *f*;
26:12 they may eat their *f* in your own community,
31:20 and they have eaten their *f* and grown fat,
32:15 So Jacob ate his *f*,
Ru 2:14 and she ate her *f* and had some left over.
1Sm 16: 1 *F* your horn with oil, and be on your way.
1Kgs 18:34 *F* four jars with water,"
2Kgs 21:16 to *f* the length and breadth of Jerusalem.
Neh 9:25 They could eat and have their *f*,
Tb 8:18 his servants to *f* in the grave before dawn.
Jdt 2: 8 slain shall *f* their ravines and wadies,
8:31 Lord may send rain to *f* up our cisterns,
Jb 8:21 more will he *f* your mouth with laughter,
9:18 breath, but might *f* me with bitter griefs.
23: 4 before him, and *f* my mouth with arguments;
40:31 Can you *f* his hide with barbs,
Ps(s) 17:14 with your treasures you *f* their bellies.
22:27 The lowly shall eat their *f*;
36: 9 their *f* of the prime gifts of your house;
81:11 open wide your mouth, and I will *f* it.
81:17 with honey from the rock I would *f* them."
90:14 *F* us at daybreak with your kindness,
132:15 provision, her poor I will *f* with bread.
Prv 1:13 we gain, we shall *f* our houses with booty;
5:10 Lest strangers have their *f* of your wealth,
7:18 "Come, let us drink our *f* of love,
12:14 his words a man has his *f* of good things,
18:20 the fruit of his mouth a man has his *f*;
28:19 idle pursuits a man has his *f* of poverty.
Wis 2: 7 us have our *f* of costly wine and perfumes,
5: 7 our *f* of the ways of mischief and of ruin;
13:12 in preparing his food, and have his *f*;
19: 4 *f* out the torments of their punishment,
Sir 36:13 *F* Zion with your majesty,
Is 13:21 rest there and owls shall *f* the houses;
14:21 *f* the breadth of the world with tyrants.
23:18 *f* and clothe themselves in choice attire.
34: 5 my sword has drunk its *f* in the heavens,
43:24 nor *f* me with the fat of your sacrifices;
60: 6 Caravans of camels shall *f* you,
65:11 and *f* cups of blended wine for Destiny,
Jer 23:16 of your prophets, who *f* you with emptiness;
23:24 Do I not *f* both heaven and earth?
46:12 of your shame, your cries *f* the earth.
50:19 Ephraim and Gilead, till she has her *f*.
51:11 Sharpen the arrows, *f* the quivers;
51:14 will *f* you with men as numerous as locusts,
Lam 3:15 food, made me drink my *f* of wormwood.
5: 6 and to Assyria, to *f* our need of bread.
Ez 3: 3 feed your belly and *f* your stomach with
7:19 satisfy their craving or *f* their bellies,
9: 7 to them, and *f* the courts with the slain;
10: 2 *f* both your hands with burning coals from
23:28 you hate, to those who *f* you with disgust.
24: 4 *F* it with the choicest joints taken from
30:11 Egypt, and *f* the land with the slain.
32: 4 the beasts of the earth eat their *f* of you.
32: 5 and *f* the valleys with your carcass.
35: 8 With the slain I will *f* your hills,
Hos 13: 6 They ate their *f*;
Zep 1: 9 Who *f* the house of their master with
Hg 2: 7 in, And I will *f* this house with glory,
Mt 5: 6 they shall have their *f*.
14:20 All those present ate their *f*.
23:28 while hypocrisy and evil *f* you within.
23:32 *f* up the vessel measured out by your
Mk 6:42 them and they ate until they had their *f*.
6:43 up enough leftovers to *f* twelve baskets,
8: 8 in the crowd ate until they had their *f*;
Lk 15:16 He longed to *f* his belly with the husks
Jn 2: 7 *F* those jars with water,"
6:26 you have eaten your *f* of the loaves.
Acts 2:28 you will *f* me with joy in your presence.'
5: 3 why have you let Satan *f* your heart so as
Rom 15:13 *f* you with all joy and peace in believing
Eph 4:10 that he might *f* all men with his gifts.
Col 1:24 In my own flesh I *f* up what is lacking in

FILLED (214)

Gn 21:19 She went and *f* the skin with water,
24:16 She went down to the spring and *f* her jug.
26:15 (The Philistines had stopped up and *f*
42:25 to have their containers *f* with grain,
Ex 1: 7 and strong that the land was *f* with them.
8:17 they stand shall be *f* with swarms of flies.
31: 3 and I have *f* him with divine spirit of
35:31 and has *f* him with a divine spirit of
40:34 and the glory of the LORD *f* the Dwelling.
40:35 and the glory of the LORD *f* the Dwelling.
Lv 20:23 have done have *f* me with disgust for them.
Nm 7:13 both *f* with fine flour mixed with oil for
7:14 cup of ten shekels' weight *f* with incense;
7:19 both *f* with fine flour mixed with oil for
7:20 cup of ten shekels' weight *f* with incense,
7:25 both *f* with fine flour mixed with oil for
7:26 cup of ten shekels' weight *f* with incense;
7:31 both *f* with fine flour mixed with oil for
7:32 cup of ten shekels' weight *f* with incense;
7:37 both *f* with fine flour mixed with oil for
7:38 cup of ten shekels' weight *f* with incense;
7:43 both *f* with fine flour mixed with oil for
7:44 cup of ten shekels' weight *f* with incense;
7:49 both *f* with fine flour mixed with oil for
7:50 cup of ten shekels' weight *f* with incense;
7:55 both *f* with fine flour mixed with oil for
7:56 cup of ten shekels' weight *f* with incense;
7:61 both *f* with fine flour mixed with oil for
7:62 cup of ten shekels' weight *f* with incense;
7:67 both *f* with fine flour mixed with oil for
7:68 cup of ten shekels' weight *f* with incense;
7:73 both *f* with fine flour mixed with oil for
7:74 cup of ten shekels' weight *f* with incense;
7:79 both *f* with fine flour mixed with oil for
7:80 cup of ten shekels' weight *f* with incense;
7:86 *f* with incense weighed ten shekels apiece,
Dt 32:19 he was *f* with loathing and anger toward
33:23 and *f* with the blessings of the LORD;
34: 9 of Nun, was *f* with the spirit of wisdom,
Jos 9:13 wineskins, which were new when we *f* them,
Ru 2: 9 from the vessels the young men have *f*."
1Kgs 8:10 the cloud *f* the temple of the LORD so that
8:11 LORD's glory had *f* the temple of the LORD.
18:35 altar, and the trench was *f* with the water.
2Kgs 3:17 yet this wadi will be *f* with water for you,
3:20 from the direction of Edom and *f* the land.
4: 4 oil into all the vessels, and as each is *f*,
4: 6 When all the vessels were *f*,
6:17 mountainside *f* with horses and fiery chariots
10:21 temple of Baal, which was *f* to capacity.
23:14 and *f* the places where they had been with
24: 4 blood he shed, with which he *f* Jerusalem,
2Chr 5:13 of the LORD's temple was *f* with a cloud.
5:14 since the LORD's glory *f* the house of God.
7: 1 and the glory of the LORD *f* the house.
7: 2 of the LORD had *f* the house of the LORD.
16:14 upon a couch which was *f* with spices
24:10 and cast it into the chest until it was *f*.

FILLED (cont.)

Ezr 6:22 for the LORD had *f* them with joy by making
9:11 they have *f* it from one end to the other
Neh 3:38 *f* in and completed up to half its height.
9:25 of houses *f* with all good things,
Jdt 6: 4 and their plains *f* with their corpses.
10: 5 She *f* a bag with roasted grain,
Est 3: 5 and bow down to him, he was *f* with anger.
5: 9 of him, he was *f* with anger toward him.
1Mc 2:24 Mattathias saw him, he was *f* with zeal;
14:11 the land, and Israel was *f* with happiness.
2Mc 3:19 below their breasts, *f* the streets;
3:30 and commotion, was *f* with joy and gladness,
6: 4 *f* the temple with debauchery and revelry;
7:21 *F* with a noble spirit that stirred her
9: 7 he was all the more *f* with arrogance.
11: 9 and their hearts were *f* with such courage
12:16 to be *f* with the blood that flowed into it.
13:16 *f* the camp with terror and confusion.
15: 9 won, he *f* them with fresh enthusiasm.
Jb 3:15 had gold and *f* their houses with silver.
7: 4 I am *f* with restlessness until the dawn.
10:15 *f* with ignominy and sodden with affliction!
22:18 he had *f* their houses with good things!
27:14 His offspring shall not be *f* with bread.
Ps(s) 38: 8 For my loins are *f* with burning pains;
59:16 if they are not *f*,
65: 5 we be *f* with the good things of your house,
65:10 God's watercourses are *f*;
71: 8 My mouth shall be *f* with your praise,
72:19 may the whole earth be *f* with his glory.
80:10 for it, and it took root and *f* the land.
104:28 your hand, they are *f* with good things.
107: 9 and *f* the hungry soul with good things.
126: 2 Then our mouth was *f* with laughter,
127: 5 Happy the man whose quiver is *f* with them;
Prv 3:10 Then will your barns be *f* with grain,
20:17 afterward his mouth will be *f* with gravel.
24: 4 And by knowledge are its rooms *f* with
Eccl 1: 8 with seeing nor is the ear *f* with hearing.
8:11 men are *f* with the desire to commit evil
9: 3 Hence the minds of men are *f* with evil,
Wis 18:16 he alighted, he *f* every place with death;
Sir 2:16 him, those who love him are *f* with his law.
9:13 you will not be *f* with the dread of death.
16:27 the earth, and *f* it with his blessings.
24:18 that yearn for me, and be *f* with my fruits;
33:17 till like a vintager I have *f* my winepress,
39: 6 will be *f* with the spirit of understanding;
47:15 and, like a sea, *f* it with knowledge.
48:12 *f* with a twofold portion of his spirit,
Is 2: 6 are *f* with fortune-tellers and soothsayers,
6: 3 "All the earth is *f* with his glory!"
6: 4 door shook and the house was *f* with smoke.
9:19 they eat on the left, they are not *f*.
11: 9 shall be *f* with knowledge of the LORD,
15: 9 The waters of Dimon are *f* with blood,
21: 3 Therefore my loins are *f* with anguish,
22: 7 Your choice valleys are *f* with chariots,
30:27 His lips are *f* with fury,
34: 6 The LORD has a sword *f* with blood,
40: 4 Every valley shall be *f* in,
51:20 They are *f* with the wrath of the LORD,
Jer 13:12 Every wineflask is meant to be *f* with wine.
15:17 alone because you *f* me with indignation.
19: 4 and the kings of Judah have *f* this place
23:10 With adulterers the land is *f*;
31:14 and my people shall be *f* with my blessings,
33: 5 and these houses will be *f* with the
41: 9 son of Nethaniah, *f* with the slain.
51:34 *f* his belly with my delights,
Lam 3:30 to be struck, let him be *f* with disgrace.
Bar 3:32 all time, and *f* it with four-footed beasts;
5: 7 depths and gorges be *f* to level ground,
Ez 4:17 everyone shall be *f* with terror and waste
7:23 for the land is *f* with bloodshed and the
8:17 they have *f* the land with violence,
9: 9 the land is *f* with bloodshed,
10: 3 man entered, the cloud *f* the inner court,
10: 4 the temple was *f* with the cloud,
11: 6 and have *f* its streets with your slain.
23:33 so much, *F* with destruction and grief,
27:33 you drew from the seas you *f* many peoples;
32: 6 the river beds shall be *f* with your blood.
36:38 in ruins shall be *f* with flocks of men;
37: 1 of the plain, which was now *f* with bones.
39:19 are *f* and drink blood until you are drunk.
39:20 be *f* at my table with horses and riders,
43: 5 temple was *f* with the glory of the LORD.
Dn 2:35 a great mountain and *f* the whole earth.
Hos 13: 6 when *f*, they became proud of heart
Jl 2:19 and oil, and you shall be *f* with them;
2:26 You shall eat and be *f*,
Mi 3: 8 But as for me, I am *f* with power,
Na 2:13 He *f* his dens with prey,
Hb 2:14 But the earth shall be *f* with the
2:16 You are *f* with shame instead of glory;
3: 3 glory, and with his praise the earth is *f*.
3: 9 is your bow, *f* with arrows is your quiver.
Zec 8: 5 The city shall be *f* with boys and girls
9:15 they are *f* with it like libation bowls,
14: 5 valley of the LORD's mountain shall be *f* up
14: 5 it shall be *f* up as it was filled up by
14: 5 it shall be filled up as it was *f* up by
Mt 6:22 are good, your body will be *f* with light;
13:54 They were *f* with amazement,
14:20 when gathered up, *f* twelve baskets.
15:37 fragments left over, these *f* seven hampers.
22:10 This *f* the wedding hall with banqueters.
23:25 and leave the inside *f* with loot and lust!
24:21 for those days will be more *f* with anguish
Mk 14:34 he began to be *f* with fear and distress.
14:34 is *f* with sorrow to the point of death.
Lk 1:15 and he will be *f* with the Holy Spirit from
1:41 Elizabeth was *f* with the Holy Spirit and
1:67 his father, *f* with the Holy Spirit,
2:40 grew in size and strength, *f* with wisdom,
3: 5 Every valley shall be *f* And every mountain
4:28 in the synagogue was *f* with indignation.
5: 7 *f* the two boats until they nearly sank.
6:21 Blest are you who hunger; you shall be *f*.
8:25 *F* with fear and admiration,
9:17 had left, over and above, *f* twelve baskets.
11:39 you are *f* with rapaciousness and evil.
24:52 then returned to Jerusalem *f* with joy.
Jn 1:14 from the Father, *f* with enduring love.
2: 7 ordered, at which they *f* them to the brim.
7:15 The Jews were *f* with amazement and said,
12: 3 house was *f* with the ointment's fragrance.
Acts 2: 4 All were *f* with the Holy Spirit.
4: 8 Then Peter, *f* with the Holy Spirit,
4:31 They were *f* with the Holy Spirit and
5:17 party of the Sadducees), *f* with jealousy,
5:28 yet you have *f* Jerusalem with your
6: 5 a man *f* with faith and the Holy Spirit;
6: 8 spoken of was a man *f* with grace and power,
7:55 Stephen meanwhile, *f* with the Holy Spirit,
9:17 your sight and be *f* with the Holy Spirit."
11:24 good man *f* with the Holy Spirit and faith.
13: 9 known as Paul) was *f* with the Holy Spirit;
13:52 not but be *f* with joy and the Holy Spirit.
Rom 1:29 They are *f* with every kind of wickedness:
15:14 my brothers, that you are *f* with goodness,
2Cor 7: 4 I am *f* with consolation,
7: 9 were *f* with a sorrow that came from God;
Eph 5:18 Be *f* with the Spirit,
1Tm 1:13 a persecutor, a man *f* with arrogance;
Jas 3:13 through a humility *f* with good sense.
Rv 5: 8 vessels of gold *f* with aromatic spices,
6:11 quota was *f* of their fellow servants
8: 5 *f* it with live coals from the altar,
15: 7 golden bowls *f* with the wrath of the God
15: 8 Then the sanctuary became so *f* with the
16:19 cup *f* with the blazing wine of his wrath.
17: 4 gold cup that was *f* with the abominable
21: 9 seven bowls *f* with the seven last plagues

FILLET (2)

Jdt 10: 3 arranged her hair and bound it with a *f*,
16: 8 with a *f* she fastened her tresses,

FILLING (8)

Prv 8:21 those who love me, and *f* their treasuries.
Sir 29:25 The visitor has no thanks for *f* the cups;
Is 6: 1 with the train of his garment *f* the temple.
Jer 13:13 I am *f* with drunkenness all the
16:18 and *f* my heritage with their abominations.
20:15 *f* him with great joy.
Ez 44: 4 the glory of the LORD *f* the LORD's temple,
1Thes 2:16 they have been *f* up their quota of sins,"

FILLS (24)

Nm 14:21 the LORD's glory that *f* the whole earth,
1Chr 16:32 Let the sea and what *f* it resound;
Jb 15:24 By day the darkness *f* him with dread;
Ps(s) 41: 9 'A malignant disease *f* his frame';
96:11 let the sea and what *f* it resound;
98: 7 Let the sea and what *f* it resound,
103: 5 compassion, He *f* your lifetime with good;
129: 7 With which the reaper *f* not his hand,
147:14 with the best of wheat he *f* you.
Prv 10: 5 who *f* the granaries in summer is a credit;
Wis 1: 7 For the spirit of the Lord *f* the world,
Sir 1:15 Her entire house she *f* with choice foods,
17: 6 With wisdom and knowledge he *f* them;
39:33 every need when it comes he *f*.
42:16 so the glory of the LORD *f* all his works;
Is 33: 5 he *f* Zion with right and justice.
34: 1 Let the earth and what *f* it listen,
42:10 Let the sea and what *f* it resound,
Ez 12:19 of all its inhabitants that now *f* it.
Mi 1: 2 give heed, O earth, and all that *f* you!
Mt 12:34 The mouth speaks whatever *f* the mind.
Acts 14:17 your spirits he *f* with food and delight."
Eph 1:23 of him who *f* the universe in all its parts.
Phil 1:25 This *f* me with confidence that I will stay

FILTER (1)

Jb 36:27 that *f* in rain through his mists,

FILTH (9)

2Chr 29: 5 and clean out the *f* from the sanctuary.
Ezr 9:11 with the *f* of the peoples of the land,
Prv 30:12 its own eyes, yet is not purged of its *f*.
Is 4: 4 washes away the *f* of the daughters of Zion,
57:20 calmed, And its waters cast up mud and *f*.
Lam 1: 9 Her *f* is on her skirt;
Hos 5:11 No, he has willingly gone after *f*!
Na 3: 6 I will cast *f* upon you,
Mt 23:27 but inside full of *f* and dead men's bones.

FILTHY (6)

Is 28: 8 all the tables are covered with *f* vomit,
30:22 them away like *f* rags to which you say,
Zec 3: 3 before the angel, clad in *f* garments.
3: 4 before him, "Take off his *f* garments,
Jas 1:21 Strip away all that is *f*,
Rv 18: 2 a cage for every *f* and disgusting bird:

FINAL (18)

Jos 19:51 *f* portions into which Eleazar the priest,
1Chr 23:27 for David's *f* orders were to enlist the
2Chr 23: 5 and the *f* third at the Foundation Gate,
Jb 31:37 This is my *f* plea;
Ps(s) 73:17 of God and considered their *f* destiny.
Wis 12:27 this, their *f* condemnation came upon them.
Ez 5: 2 the *f* third strew in the wind,
12:25 Whatever I speak is *f*,
12:28 whatever I speak is *f*,
Dn 7:26 taken away by *f* and absolute destruction,
Mt 27:64 *f* imposture would be worse than the first."
Acts 28:25 Then Paul added one *f* word:
2Cor 3:13 could not see the *f* fading of that glory.
Heb 1: 2 in this, the *f* age,
1Jn 2:18 Children, it is the *f* hour;
2:18 makes us certain that it is the *f* hour.
Rv 15: 1 seven angels holding the seven *f* plagues
17: 8 the abyss once more before going to *f* ruin.

FINALLY (89)

Gn 27:26 *F* his father Isaac said to him,
27:39 *F* Isaac spoke again and said to him:
30:21 *F*, she gave birth to a daughter,
Ex 23:16 and *f*, the feast at the fruit harvest
29:26 *F*, take the breast of Aaron's ordination
40:33 *F*, he set up the court around the Dwelling
Lv 8:31 *F*, Moses said to Aaron and his sons,
9:18 *F* he slaughtered the ox and the ram,
Nm 10:25 *F*, as rear guard for all the camps,
19: 9 *F*, a man who is clean shall gather up the
Dt 2: 2 *F* the LORD said to me,
4:30 upon you, you shall *f* return to the LORD,
Jos 7: 5 ranks, and defeated them *f* on the descent,
7:18 *F* he had that family come forward one by
10:20 Once Joshua and the Israelites had *f*
Jgs 3:25 They waited until they *f* grew suspicious.
1Sm 10:21 the clan of Matri was chosen, and *f* Saul,
21:15 *F* Achish said to his servants:
2Sm 19:41 *F* the king crossed over to Gilgal,
2Kgs 3:25 *F* only Kir-hareseth was left behind its
9:12 what the young man had said to him, and *f*,
17:20 *f* casting them out from before him.
17:23 *F*, the LORD put Israel away out of his
1Chr 12: 8 Joelah, *f*, and Zebadiah, sons of Jeroham
28: 4 and *f*, among all the sons of my father,
28:18 *f*, gold for what would suggest a chariot
Ezr 6:18 *F*, they set up the priests in their
8:36 *F*, the orders of the king were presented
Tb 2:14 Your true character is *f* showing itself!"
10:12 *F* he said good-bye to them and sent them
10:14 *F* he said good-bye to Raguel and his wife
Jdt 5:18 and *f* taken as captives into foreign lands.
1Mc 9:56 *F* he died in great agony.
11:51 *F* they returned to Jerusalem with much
13:50 They *f* cried out to Simon for peace,
2Mc 5: 5 forced back and the city was *f* being taken,
12:31 *F* they arrived in Jerusalem,
13:16 *F* they withdrew in triumph,
Prv 21:28 but he who listens will *f* have his say.
Sir 30:10 when *f* your teeth are clenched in remorse.
47:23 Solomon *f* slept with his fathers,
Ez 1:10 an ox, and *f* each had the face of an eagle.
Dn 4: 5 *F* there came before me Daniel,
10:13 way for twenty-one days, until *f* Michael,
Mt 13: 8 Part of it, *f*, landed on good soil
16:12 They *f* realized he was not issuing a
20: 6 *F*, going out in late afternoon he found
21:37 *F* he sent his son to them,
25:24 *F* the man who had received the thousand
26:45 *F* he returned to his disciples and said to
26:60 *F* two came forward who stated:
27:24 Pilate *f* realized that he was making no
27:31 *F*, when they had finished making a fool of
Mk 4: 8 Some seed, *f*, landed on good soil
4:28 then the ear, *f* the ripe wheat in the ear.
4:38 They *f* woke him and said to him,
9:11 *F* they put to him this question:
10:34 and spit at him, flog him, and *f* kill him.
12:12 *F* they left him and went off.
15:46 *F* he rolled a stone across the entrance of
16:14 *F*, as they were at table,
Lk 1:22 *f* came out he was unable to speak to them,
18: 4 For a time he refused, but *f* he thought,
20:32 *F* the widow herself died.

Jn 1:22 F they said to him:
6:19 F, when they had rowed three or four miles,
8:10 Jesus f straightened up and said to her,
11: 7 F he said to his disciples,
11:14 F Jesus said plainly:
Acts 10:40 They killed him, f,
12:10 and f came to the iron gate leading out to
12:16 They f opened the door and were astonished
13:43 When the congregation f broke up,
13:50 Jews f expelled them from their territory.
15: 2 F it was decided that Paul,
16:18 several days until f Paul became annoyed,
19:35 F the town clerk quieted the mob.
20: 2 F he arrived in Greece,
20: 9 He f went sound asleep,
21: 1 When we had f taken leave of them,
21: 3 F we put in at Tyre,
23: 9 F, some scribes of the Pharisee party
25:12 conferred with his council and f declared:
28:14 This is how we f came to Rome.
1Cor 15:28 When, f, all has been subjected to the Son,
Eph 6:10 F, draw your strength from the Lord and
Phil 4: 8 F, my brothers,
Heb 6: 8 it is soon cursed, and f is burned.
Rv 16:17 F, the seventh angel poured out his bowl

FIND (283)

Gn 8: 9 dove could f no place to alight and perch,
12: 3 of the earth shall f blessing in you,"
18:18 of the earth are to f blessing in him?
18:21 I mean to f out."
18:26 "If I f fifty innocent people in the city
18:28 he answered, "if I f forty-five there."
18:30 doing it if I can f but thirty there."
22:18 the nations of the earth shall f blessing
26: 4 the nations of the earth shall f blessing
28:14 the nations of the earth shall f blessing.
31:32 one you f them with shall not remain alive!
31:33 but he did not f the idols.
31:35 despite his search, he did not f his idols.
38:20 but he could not f her.
38:22 to Judah and told him, "I could not f her;
38:23 kid, even though you were unable to f her."
41: 7 Pharaoh woke up, to f it was only a dream.
41:38 "Could we f another like him,"
Ex 2: 4 distance to f out what would happen to him.
5:11 straw yourselves, wherever you can f it.
16:25 day you will not f any of it on the ground.
16:27 to gather it, although they did not f any.
28:38 so that they may f favor with the LORD.
33:13 you, I may continue to f favor with you.
34: 9 Then he said, "If I f favor with you,
Lv 1: 3 To f favor with the LORD,
13: 8 f that the eczema has indeed spread on the
13:10 f that there is a white scab on the skin
13:13 f that the leprosy does cover his whole
13:17 f that the sore has indeed turned white,
13:27 f that it has spread at all on the skin,
13:30 f that the sore has penetrated below the
18: 5 carries them out will f life through them.
22:21 offering, if it is to f acceptance,
Nm 32: 5 they continued, "if we f favor with you,
Dt 1:33 before you to f you a resting place
4:29 and you shall indeed f him when you search
8: 2 f out whether or not it was your intention
13:15 If you f that it is true and an
17: 4 you f by careful investigation that it is
19: 3 every homicide will be able to f a refuge.
19:18 judges f that the witness is a false witness
22: 3 your kinsman loses and you happen to f;
22:14 with her I did not f her a virgin,'
22:17 I did not f your daughter a virgin.
28:29 man in the dark, unable to f your way.
28:65 Among these nations you will f no repose,
Jos 2:16 them, "that your pursuers may not f you.
Jgs 6:17 He answered him, "If I f favor with you,
14: 3 "Can you f no wife among your kinsfolk or
16: 5 and f out the secret of his great strength,
17: 8 he set out to f another place of residence.
17: 9 my way to f some other place of residence."
Ru 1: 9 and a home in which you will f rest."
3: 8 around to f a woman lying at his feet.
1Sm 9: 4 Benjamin, but they failed to f the animals.
9:13 for you should f him right now."
10:14 When we could not f them,
14:17 troops and f out if any of us are missing."
14:38 and f out how this sin was committed today.
16:17 F me a skillful harpist and bring him to
17:56 the king said, F out whose son the lad is."
20: 9 If ever I f out that my father is
21: 4 Give me five loaves, or whatever you can f."
28: 7 his servants, F me a woman who is a medium,
29: 3 and I have no fault to f with him from the
30: 3 f it burned to the ground and their wives,
2Sm 15:25 If I f favor with the LORD,
16: 4 May I f favor with you!"
17:12 We can then attack him wherever we f him,
20: 6 lest he f fortified cities and take
1Kgs 14: 2 where you will f the prophet Ahijah.
18: 5 may f grass and save the horses and mules,
18:10 and nation swear they could not f you.
18:12 I go to inform Ahab and he does not f you,
22:25 "You shall f out,"
2Kgs 5: 8 f out that there is a prophet in Israel."
6:13 "Go, f out where he is,"
6:27 Where could I f help for you:
7:14 "Go and f out," he ordered.
1Chr 21: 2 f out the number of the Israelites from
2Chr 18:24 "You shall f out,"
30: 9 your children will f mercy with their captors
32: 4 Assyria come and f an abundance of water?"
Ezr 7:28 and who let me f favor with the king,
Neh 1:11 day, and let him f favor with this man"
5: 8 silent, for they could f no answer.
Tb 1:18 looked for them, he could not f them.
2: 2 go out and try to f a poor man from among
5: 3 f yourself a trustworthy man who will make
5: 9 f out what family and tribe he comes from,
12: 7 good, and evil will not f its way to you.
Jdt 14: 3 to the tent of Holofernes and do not f him,
Est 4: 5 and commanded him to f out what this
E:15 But we f that the Jews,
1Mc 1:23 took all the hidden treasures he could f.
6:24 could f and have plundered our estates.
10:16 "Shall we ever f another man like him?
11:42 and your nation when I f the opportunity.
2Mc 1:21 informed us that they could not f any fire,
2: 1 You will f in the records,
2: 6 to mark the path, but they could not f it.
5: 9 among whom he hoped to f protection
12:18 But they did not f Timothy in that region,
Jb 4:18 and with his angels he can f fault.
17:10 for I shall not f a wise man among you!
23: 3 Oh, that today I might f him,
Ps(s) 17: 3 me with fire, you shall f no malice in me.
19:15 the thought of my heart f favor before you,
28: 7 In him my heart trusts, and I f help;
39:14 may f respite ere I depart and be no more.
55: 9 I would hasten to f shelter from the
107: 4 way to an inhabited city they did not f.
132: 5 no rest, Till I f a place for the LORD,
Prv 1:28 they seek me, but f me not;
2: 5 the knowledge of God you will f;
4:22 For they are life to those who f them,
8:17 me I also love, and those who seek me f me.
20: 6 but who can f one worthy of trust?
21:21 justice and kindness will f life and honor.
24: 9 sin, it is arrogance that men f abominable.
24:14 If you f it, you will have a future,
25:16 If you f honey,
30:28 yet they f their way into king's palaces.
Eccl 7:14 man cannot f fault with him in anything.
7:24 who can f it out?
7:26 death I f the woman who is a hunter's trap,
8:17 man is unable to f out all God's work
8:17 nor by night do his eyes f rest in sleep.
8:17 toils in searching, he does not f it out;
8:17 that he knows, he is unable to f it out.
11: 1 after a long time you may f it again.
12:10 Qoheleth sought to f pleasing sayings,
Sg 3: 1 I sought him but I did not f him.
3: 2 I sought him but I did not f him.
5: 6 I sought him but I did not f him;
5: 8 daughters of Jerusalem, if you f my lover
Wis 2:17 let us f out what will happen to him.
6:14 for he shall f her sitting by his gate.
6:21 then, you f pleasure in throne and scepter,
9:16 is within our grasp we f with difficulty;
13: 6 though they seek God and wish to f him.
13: 9 how did they not more quickly f its Lord?
Sir 3:18 you are, and you will f favor with God.
6:18 thus will you f wisdom with graying hair.
6:28 seek her and you will f her.
6:29 Thus will you afterward f rest in her,
11: 7 Before investigating, f no fault;
11:10 however you seek it, you will not f it.
12:11 you will f that there is still corrosion.
12:17 comes upon you, you will f him at hand;
15: 6 Joy and gladness he will f,
22:13 you will f rest and not be wearied
27:16 he will never f an intimate friend.
31:22 later you will f my advice good.
32:14 He who would f God must accept discipline:
37: 8 advice, f out first of all what he wants.
51: 7 for one to sustain me, but could f no one.
Is 1:11 of calves, lambs and goats I f no pleasure.
14:32 her the afflicted of his people f refuge."
23:12 the Kittim, even there you shall f no rest.
27: 4 but if I were to f briers and thorns,
29:19 The lowly will ever f joy in the LORD,
29:24 who f fault shall receive instruction.
30: 2 They f their strength in Pharaoh's
34:14 repose, and f for herself a place to rest.
41:12 You shall seek out, but shall not f,
49: 9 Along the ways they shall f pasture,
66:13 in Jerusalem you shall f your comfort.
Jer 2: 5 fathers f in me that they withdrew from me,
5: 1 to f even one Who lives uprightly and
6:16 thus you will f rest for your souls.
6:20 Your holocausts f no favor with me,
14: 3 They f no water and return with empty jars.
23:11 In my very house I f their wickedness,
29: 6 f wives for your sons and give your
29:13 When you look for me, you will f me.
29:14 all your heart, you will f me with you,
30:10 Jacob shall again f rest,
45: 3 weary from groaning, and can f no rest":
46:27 Jacob shall again f rest,
47: 6 how long till you f rest?
47: 7 it f rest when the LORD has commanded it?
Lam 1: 6 Her princes, like rams that f no pasture,
Dn 3:38 to offer first fruits, to f favor with you.
6: 5 satraps tried to f grounds for accusation
6: 6 "We shall f no grounds for accusation
14:12 If you do not f that Bel has eaten it all
Hos 2: 8 her, so that she cannot f her paths.
2: 9 if she looks for them she shall not f them.
5: 6 to seek the LORD, but they shall not f him;
Am 8:12 word of the LORD, but they shall not f it.
Jon 1: 7 let us cast lots to f out on whose account
Na 3: 7 Where can one f any to console her?"
Mt 7: 7 Seek, and you will f.
7:14 the road, and how few there are who f it!
8:11 west and will f a place at the banquet
11:28 you who are weary and f life burdensome,
11:29 Your souls will f rest,
12:14 plot against him to f a way to destroy him.
12:21 In his name, the Gentiles will f hope."
12:44 and returns to f the dwelling unoccupied,
13:44 and rejoicing at his f went and sold all
16:25 loses his life for my sake will f it.
21: 2 f an ass tethered and her colt with her.
21:42 did this and we f it marvelous to behold'?
23:38 'You will f your temple deserted.'
Mk 6:10 "Whatever house you f yourself in,
11: 2 enter it you will f tethered there a colt
11:13 over to see if he could f anything on it.
12:11 did it and we f it marvelous to behold'?"
14:55 to his death, but they could not f any.
Lk 2:12 f an infant wrapped in swaddling clothes."
5:39 He says, 'I f the old wine better.' "
6: 7 so that they could f a charge against him.
9:12 and f themselves lodging and food,
11: 9 seek and you shall f;
11:24 failing to f one,
11:25 returns, to f the house swept and tidied.
12:38 or before sunrise and f them prepared,
13: 6 looking for fruit on it but did not f any.
18: 8 comes, will he f any faith on the earth?"
19:30 Upon entering it you will f an ass tied
22:45 to his disciples, only to f them asleep,
23: 4 "I do not f a case against this man."
24: 3 they did not f the body of the Lord Jesus.
24:23 tomb before dawn and failed to f his body,
Jn 6:10 grass for them to f a place on the ground.
7:34 will look for me, but you will not f me;
7:35 he intend to go that we will not f him?
7:36 will look for me, but you will not f me,'
7:52 will not f the Prophet coming from Galilee."
10: 9 He will go in and out, and f pasture.
15:18 "If you f that the world hates you know
16:33 you all this that in me you may f peace.
18:38 for myself, I f no case against this man.
19: 4 you realize that I f no case [against him]."
19: 6 I f no case against him."
21: 6 he suggested, "and you will f something."
Acts 4:21 The court could f no way to punish them
5:22 got to the jail they could not f them,
7:11 Canaan, our fathers could f no sustenance.
7:42 f it written in the Book of the Prophets:
7:46 f a dwelling place for the house of Jacob.
9: 2 and bring to Jerusalem anyone he might f,
17: 6 When they could not f them there,
17:27 for him and perhaps eventually to f him
21:33 He tried to f out who he was and what he
22:24 be examined under the lash to f out why
23: 6 I f myself on trial now because of my hope
23: 9 "We do not f this man guilty of any crime.
24:12 did my accusers f me debating with anyone
24:25 I'll send for you again when I f the time."
25:25 But I did not f that he had done anything
26: 8 should f it hard to believe that God
Rom 1:10 I may at last f my way clear to visit you.
3: 9 f ourselves in a position of superiority?
9:19 say to me, "Why, then, does he f fault?
15:12 in him the Gentiles will f hope."
1Cor 1:31 This is just as you f it written,
4:19 to you soon, the Lord willing, and f out,
2Cor 2:13 because I did not f my brother Titus there.
9: 4 Macedonians come with me and f you unready;
10: 8 If I f I must make a few further claims
12:20 f you to my liking, nor may you find
12:20 I fear I may f discord,
Gal 4:29 in the realm of spirit, so do we f it now.
Eph 4: 8 Thus you f Scripture saying:
Phil 3: 1 I f writing you these things no burden,
4:11 for whatever the situation I f myself in I
Col 1:24 f my joy in the suffering I endure for you.
1Thes 3: 5 That is why I sent to f out about your
2Tm 1: 5 I f myself thinking of your sincere faith
Ti 2: 8 be able to f anything bad to say about us,
Phlm 1: 7 I f great joy and comfort in your love,
Heb 4:16 and favor and to f help in time of need.
Jas 5:16 for one another, that you may f healing.
2Jn 1: 4 It has given me great joy to f some of
Rv 3: 2 I f that the sum of your deeds is less
9: 6 men will seek death but will not f it;
14:13 "Yes, they shall f rest from their labors,

FIND (cont.)
18:14 you shall never *f* them again!"

FINDING (17)

Gn 31:34 the rest of her tent without *f* them,
Ex 15:22 days through the desert without *f* water,
Jos 2:22 them all along the road without *f* them,
Jgs 21:12 *F* among the inhabitants of Jabesh-gilead
1Sm 9: 4 Not *f* them there,
2Kgs 2:17 who searched for three days without *f* him.
Jdt 14:17 and, not *f* her,
2Mc 5:25 then, *f* the Jews refraining from work,
Jb 9:10 He does great things past *f* out,
Sir 26:10 an unruly wife, lest, *f* an opportunity,
40:17 but better than either is *f* a treasure.
Bar 1:12 serve them long, *f* favor in their sight.
Mt 12:43 searching for a place of rest and *f* none.
18:13 If he succeeds in *f* it,
Mk 11: 4 and *f* a colt tethered out on the street
Lk 2:45 Not *f* him,
Heb 8: 8 But God, *f* fault with them, says:

FINDS (53)

Lv 13:21 *f* that there is no white hair in it and
13:26 *f* that there is no white hair on the
13:31 *f* that it has not penetrated below the
13:34 *f* that it has not spread on the skin and
13:53 *f* that it has not spread on the garment,
13:56 *f* that it is dying out after the washing,
14: 3 If the priest *f* that the sore of leprosy
14:37 *f* that the infection on the walls of the
14:39 If he *f* that the infection has spread on
14:44 and if he *f* that the infection has spread
14:48 If the priest *f*,
Nm 35:27 *f* him beyond these bounds and kills him,
Dt 24: 1 her because he *f* in her something indecent,
2Sm 7:27 *f* the courage to make this prayer to you.
Ps(s) 84: 4 Even the sparrow *f* a home,
Prv 3:13 Happy the man who *f* wisdom,
8:35 For he who finds me *f* life,
14:32 but the just man *f* a refuge in his honesty.
17:20 He who is perverse in heart *f* no good,
18:22 He who finds a wife *f* happiness;
21:10 his neighbor *f* no pity in his eyes.
31:10 When one *f* a worthy wife,
Eccl 5:18 lot and *f* joy in the fruits of his toil,
Sir 3:30 when he falls, he *f* a support.
6:14 he who *f* one finds a treasure.
6:16 remedy, such as he who fears God *f*;
19:24 from sinning, when he *f* the opportunity,
25: 7 The man who *f* joy in his children,
25: 9 Happy is he who *f* a friend and he who
25:10 He who *f* wisdom is great indeed,
26:12 mouth drinks from any water that he *f*,
31: 4 and if ever he rests, he *f* himself in want.
32:15 masters it, but the hypocrite *f* it a trap.
51:26 her, and the one who is in earnest *f* her.
Lam 1: 3 among the nations she *f* no place to rest:
Ez 34:12 he *f* himself among his scattered sheep,
Hos 14: 4 for in you the orphan *f* compassion."
Mi 1:11 of Beth-ezel *f* in you its grounds.
Mt 7: 8 The one who seeks, *f*.
11: 6 is the man who *f* no stumbling block in me."
Lk 1:47 Lord, my spirit *f* joy in God my savior,
7:23 is that man who *f* no stumbling block in me."
11:10 whoever seeks, *f*;
12:37 whom the master *f* wide awake on his return.
12:43 whom his master *f* busy when he returns.
15: 4 and follow the lost one until he *f* it?
15: 5 when he *f* it, he puts it on his shoulders
15: 9 And when she *f* it, she calls in her friends
Jn 8:37 me because my word *f* no hearing among you.
1Jn 1:10 him a liar and his word *f* no place in us.

FINE (152)

Gn 18: 6 Sarah, "Quick, three seahs of *f* flour!
41:42 He had him dressed in robes of *f* linen and
Ex 9: 9 It will then turn into *f* dust over the
16:14 were *f* flakes like hoarfrost on the ground.
21:30 If, however, a *f* is imposed on him,
25: 4 *f* linen and goat hair;
26: 1 woven of *f* linen twined and of violet,
26:31 and scarlet yarn, and of *f* linen twined,
26:36 and scarlet yarn and of *f* linen twined.
27: 9 cubits long, woven of *f* linen twined,
27:16 and scarlet yarn and of *f* linen twined.
27:18 *F* linen twined must be used,
28: 5 purple and scarlet yarn and *f* linen.
28: 6 embroidered on cloth of *f* linen twined.
28: 8 and scarlet yarn, and of *f* linen twined.
28:15 scarlet yarn on cloth of *f* linen twined.
28:33 purple and scarlet yarn and *f* linen twined,
28:39 "The tunic of *f* linen shall be brocaded.
28:39 The miter shall be made of *f* linen.
29: 2 With *f* wheat flour make unleavened cakes
29:40 ephah of *f* flour mixed with a fourth of a hin
30:36 Grind some of it into *f* dust and put this
35: 6 *f* linen and goat hair;
35:23 or scarlet yarn, *f* linen or goat hair,
35:25 purple and scarlet yarn and *f* linen thread,
35:35 purple and scarlet yarn and *f* linen thread,
36: 8 its ten sheets woven of *f* linen twined,
36:35 and scarlet yarn, and of *f* linen twined,
36:37 and scarlet yarn, and of *f* linen twined,
38: 9 were hangings, woven of *f* linen twined,
38:16 of the court were woven of *f* linen twined.
38:18 and scarlet yarn and of *f* linen twined,
38:23 purple and scarlet yarn and of *f* linen.
39: 2 and scarlet yarn and of *f* linen twined.
39: 3 into an embroidered pattern on the *f* linen.
39: 5 and scarlet yarn, and of *f* linen twined,
39: 8 scarlet yarn on cloth of *f* linen twined.
39:24 and scarlet yarn and of *f* linen twined;
39:27 there were also woven tunics of *f* linen;
39:28 *f* linen; the ornate turbans of fine linen;
39:28 the ornate turbans of *f* linen;
39:28 drawers of linen [of *f* linen twined];
39:29 work made of *f* linen twined and of violet,
Lv 2: 1 LORD, his offering must consist of *f* flour.
2: 2 take a handful of this *f* flour and oil,
2: 4 cakes made of *f* flour mixed with oil,
2: 5 of *f* flour mixed with oil and unleavened.
2: 7 prepared in a pot, it must be of *f* flour,
5:11 his sin one tenth of an ephah of *f* flour.
6: 8 from it a handful of its *f* flour and oil,
6:13 one tenth of an ephah of *f* flour for the
7:12 of *f* flour mixed with oil and well kneaded.
13:30 skin and that there is *f* yellow hair on it,
14:10 three tenths of an ephah of *f* flour mixed
14:21 one tenth of an ephah of *f* flour mixed
23:13 of an ephah of *f* flour mixed with oil,
23:17 an ephah of *f* flour and baked with leaven.
24: 5 take *f* flour and bake it into twelve cakes,
Nm 6:15 unleavened cakes of *f* flour mixed with oil
7:13 both filled with *f* flour mixed with oil
7:19 *f* flour mixed with oil for cereal offering;
7:25 both filled with *f* flour mixed with oil
7:31 both filled with *f* flour mixed with oil
7:37 both filled with *f* flour mixed with oil
7:43 both filled with *f* flour mixed with oil
7:49 both filled with *f* flour mixed with oil
7:55 both filled with *f* flour mixed with oil
7:61 both filled with *f* flour mixed with oil
7:67 both filled with *f* flour mixed with oil
7:73 both filled with *f* flour mixed with oil
7:79 both filled with *f* flour mixed with oil
8: 8 cereal offering of *f* flour mixed with oil;
14: 7 which we went through and explored is a *f*,
15: 4 tenth of an ephah of *f* flour mixed
15: 6 *f* flour mixed with a third of a hin of oil,
15: 9 of *f* flour mixed with half a hin of oil,
28: 5 offering of one tenth of an ephah of *f* flour
28: 9 of an ephah of *f* flour mixed with oil,
28:12 with three tenths of an ephah of *f* flour
28:12 two tenths of an ephah of *f* flour mixed
28:13 and one tenth of an ephah of *f* flour mixed
28:20 cereal offerings of *f* flour mixed with oil;
28:28 offerings of *f* flour mixed ed with oil;
29: 3 cereal offerings of *f* flour mixed with oil;
29: 9 cereal offerings of *f* flour mixed with oil;
29:14 cereal offerings of *f* flour mixed with oil;
Dt 3:25 beyond the Jordan, this *f* hill country,
6:10 that he would give you, a land with *f*,
8:12 and have built *f* houses and lived in them,
9:21 I ground it down to powder as *f* as dust,
20: 8 In *f*, the officials shall say to the soldiers,
2Sm 22:43 I ground them *f* as the dust of the earth;
1Kgs 5: 2 for each day were thirty kors of *f* flour,
5:31 By order of the king, *f*,
7: 9 All these buildings were of *f* stones,
7:10 (The foundation was made of *f*,
7:11 Above were *f* stones hewn to size,
21: 7 "A *f* ruler over Israel you are indeed!"
2Kgs 2:19 Elisha, "The site of the city is *f* indeed,
7: 1 a seah of *f* flour will sell for a shekel,
7:16 and then a seah of *f* flour sold for a
7:18 and one seah of *f* flour for a shekel at
20:13 his silver, gold, spices and *f* oil,
23:33 He imposed a *f* upon the land of a hundred
1Chr 9:29 the sacred vessels, as well as the *f* flour,
15:27 David was clothed in a robe of *f* linen,
23:29 of the *f* flour for the cereal offering,
2Chr 2:13 with purple, violet, *f* linen and crimson,
3: 5 cypress wood which he covered with *f* gold,
3: 8 He overlaid it with *f* gold to the amount
3:14 of violet, purple, crimson and *f* linen,
5:12 sons and brothers, clothed in *f* linen,
9:17 ivory throne which he overlaid with *f* gold.
Ezr 7:26 corporal punishment, or a *f* on his goods,
Tb 2: 1 of Weeks, a *f* dinner was prepared for me,
2Mc 1: 8 we offered sacrifices and *f* flour;
8:35 laid aside his *f* clothes and fled alone
Jb 22:24 *f* gold of Ophir as pebbles from the brook,
31:24 trust in gold or called *f* gold my security;
Ps(s) 18:43 ground them *f* as the dust before the wind;
119:127 your command more than gold, however *f*.
Prv 17: 7 *F* words are out of place in a fool;
17:26 It is wrong to *f* an innocent man,
25:12 a golden earring, or a necklace of *f* gold,
31:22 *f* linen and purple are her clothing.
Wis 5:14 thistledown borne on the wind, and like *f*,
Sir 35: 2 In works of charity one offers *f* flour,
Is 5: 9 houses shall be in ruins, large ones and *f*,
29: 5 of your arrogant shall be like *f* dust,
39: 2 the silver and gold, the spices and *f* oil,
Lam 4: 2 precious sons, *f* gold their counterpart,
Ez 16:10 fine leather on your feet; I gave you a *f*
16:13 your garments were of *f* linen,
16:13 *F* flour, honey, and oil were your food.
16:19 the food that I had given you, the *f* flour,
27: 7 *F* embroidered linen from Egypt became your
27:16 purple, embroidered cloth, *f* linen,
46:14 of a hin of oil to moisten the *f* flour.
Dn 2:35 *f* as the chaff on the threshing floor in
10: 5 with a belt of *f* gold around his waist.
13:55 "Your *f* lie has cost you your head,"
13:59 "Your *f* lie has cost you also your head,"
14: 3 provided for it six barrels of *f* flour,
Mt 13:45 is like a merchant's search for *f* pearls.
Mk 7: 9 "You have made a *f* art of setting aside
Lk 23:53 He took it down, wrapped it in *f* linen,
Jas 5: 2 your *f* wardrobe has grown moth-eaten,
Rv 18:12 *f* linen and purple garments,
18:13 wine and olive oil, *f* flour and grain;
18:16 dressed in *f* linen and purple and scarlet,
19:14 riding white horses and dressed in *f* linen,

FINED (3)

Ex 21:22 the guilty one shall be *f* as much as the
2Chr 36: 3 deposed him in Jerusalem and *f* the land
Am 2: 8 *f* they drink in the house of their god.

FINELY (1)

Lv 16:12 handful of *f* ground fragrant incense,

FINERY (3)

2Sm 1:24 Saul, who clothed you in scarlet and in *f*,
Is 3:18 will do away with the *f* of the anklets,
Rv 17:16 will strip off her *f* and leave her naked;

FINEST (8)

Gn 45:23 loaded with the *f* products of Egypt
Ex 30:23 LORD said to Moses, "Take the *f* spices:
Dt 32:14 its goats, with the cream of its *f* wheat;
33:15 With the *f* gifts of the age-old mountains
2Mc 9:16 he would adorn with the *f* offerings the
Sg 4:14 Myrrh and aloes, with all the *f* spices.
Lk 15:22 bring out the *f* robe and put it on him;
Rv 19: 8 been given a dress to wear made of *f* linen,

FINGER (27)

Gn 41:42 his signet ring and put it on Joseph's *f*.
Ex 8:15 said to Pharaoh, "This is the *f* of God."
29:12 your *f* put it on the horns of the altar.
31:18 the stone tablets inscribed by God's own *f*.
Lv 4: 6 tent, where, dipping his *f* in the blood,
4:17 tent, and dipping his *f* in the blood,
4:25 blood of the sin offering on his *f* and put it
4:30 then take some of its blood on his *f*
4:34 offering on his *f* and put it on the horns
8:15 *f* he put it on the horns around the altar,
9: 9 he dipped his *f* in the blood and put it on
16:14 he shall sprinkle it with his *f* on the
16:14 *f* seven times in front of the propitiatory.
16:19 and with his *f* sprinkle some of the blood
Nm 19: 4 blood on his *f* and sprinkle it seven times
Dt 9:10 of stone inscribed, by God's own *f*,
1Kgs 12:10 little *f* is thicker than my father's body.
2Chr 10:10 little *f* is thicker than my father's body.
Mt 23: 4 themselves will not lift a *f* to budge them.
Lk 11:20 is by the *f* of God that I cast out devils,
11:46 men but will not lift a *f* to lighten them.
15:22 put a ring on his *f* and shoes on his feet.
16:24 tip of his *f* in water to refresh my tongue,
Jn 7:30 *f* on him because his hour had not yet come.
8: 6 started tracing on the ground with his *f*.
20:25 without putting my *f* in the nailmarks and
20:27 "Take your *f* and examine my hands.

FINGERS (17)

2Sm 21:20 man of large stature with six *f* on each hand
1Kgs 7:15 their metal was of four *f*' thickness.
1Chr 20: 6 *f* to each hand and six toes to each foot;
Ps(s) 8: 4 I behold your heavens, the work of your *f*,
144: 1 trains my hands for battle, my *f* for war;
Prv 6:13 shuffles his feet, makes signs with his *f*;
7: 3 Bind them on your *f*,
31:19 to the distaff, and her *f* ply the spindle.
Sg 5: 5 With my *f* dripping choice myrrh upon the
Wis 15:15 to hear, nor *f* on their hands for feeling;
Is 2: 8 their hands, that which their *f* have made.
17: 8 nor shall he regard what his *f* have made:
59: 3 are stained with blood, your *f* with guilt;
Jer 52:21 each was four *f* thick,
Dn 5: 5 lampstand, the *f* of a human hand appeared,
Mk 7:33 He put his *f* into the man's ears and,
Jas 2: 2 dressed, with gold rings on his *f*,

FINING (1)

Dt 22:19 besides *f* him one hundred silver shekels,

FINISH (15)

Gn 6:16 in the ark, and *f* the ark a cubit above it.

29:27 *F* the bridal week for this one,
Ex 5:13 kept driving them on, saying, *F* your work,
2Sm 1: 9 me, 'Stand up to me, please, and *f* me off,
1Kgs 3: 1 until he should *f* building his palace,
Prv 26:23 Like a glazed *f* on earthenware are smooth
Sir 38:28 His care is to *f* his work,
Is 33: 1 you *f* destroying, you will be destroyed
Ez 4: 6 When you *f* this,
Zec 4: 9 of this house, and his hands shall *f* it;
Lk 14:30 man began to build what he could not *f.*'
Acts 20:24 I put no value on my life if only I can *f*
1Cor 9:26 like a man who loses sight of the *f* line.
Phil 3:13 of myself as having reached the *f* line.
3:14 My entire attention is on the *f* line as I

FINISHED (84)

Gn 2: 2 God was *f* with the work he had been doing,
17:22 When he had *f* speaking with him,
18:33 as soon as he had *f* speaking with Abraham,
24:15 He had scarcely *f* these words when Rebekah
24:22 When the camels had *f* drinking,
24:45 "I had scarcely *f* saying this prayer to
27:30 just after Isaac had *f* blessing him,
27:33 I *f* eating it just before you came,
29:28 He *f* the bridal week for Leah,
49:33 *f* giving these instructions to his sons,
Ex 31:18 had *f* speaking to Moses on Mount Sinai,
34:33 When he *f* speaking with them,
40:33 Thus Moses *f* all the work.
Nm 4:15 "Only after Aaron and his sons have *f*
16:31 No sooner had he *f* saying all this than
Dt 20: 9 officials have *f* speaking to the soldiers,
26:12 "When you have *f* setting aside all the
31: 1 had *f* speaking these words to all Israel,
31:24 When Moses had *f* writing out on a scroll
32:45 *f* speaking all these words to all Israel,
Jgs 15:17 *f* speaking he threw the jawbone from him;
Ru 3: 3 man before he has *f* eating and drinking.
1Sm 13:10 just *f* this offering when Samuel arrived.
14:13 armor-bearer followed him and *f* them off.
18: 1 [By the time David *f* speaking with Saul,
24:17 When David *f* saying these things to Saul,
2Sm 6:18 When he *f* making these offerings,
11:19 "When you have *f* giving the king all the
13:36 he *f* speaking than the princes came in,
20:19 whether loyalty is *f* or ended in Israel.'
1Kgs 6:14 When Solomon *f* building the temple,
7:19 The capitals on top of the columns were *f*
8:54 When Solomon *f* offering this entire prayer
9: 1 Solomon *f* building the temple of the LORD,
2Kgs 10:25 As soon as he *f* offering the holocaust,
1Chr 16: 2 When David had *f* offering up the
2Chr 20:23 they had *f* with the inhabitants of Seir,
24:14 After they had *f,* they brought the rest
29:17 day of the first month, they had *f.*
Ezr 5:11 ago, which a great king of Israel built and *f.*
6:14 They *f* the building according to the
Neh 6:15 wall was *f* on the twenty-fifth day of Elul;
Tb 2:12 *f* the cloth and sent it back to the owners.
8: 1 When they had *f* eating and drinking,
8:11 When they had *f* digging the grave,
Jdt 14: 9 When she *f* her account,
1Mc 2:23 As he *f* saying these words, a certain Jew
3:23 When he *f* speaking, he rushed suddenly
4:51 they *f* all the work they had undertaken.
2Mc 7:30 scarcely *f* speaking when the youth said:
9: 4 without stopping until he *f* the journey.
Jb 21:21 him, when the number of his months is *f?*
Sir 24:26 The first man never *f* comprehending wisdom,
Jer 26: 8 When Jeremiah *f* speaking all that the LORD
36:23 Each time Jehudi *f* reading three or four
43: 1 When Jeremiah *f* speaking to the people all
51:63 When you have *f* reading this book,
Ez 42:15 he had *f* measuring the inner temple area,
43:23 When you have *f* the purification,
Mt 7:28 Jesus *f* this discourse and left the crowds
9:18 Before Jesus had *f* speaking to them,
11: 1 had *f* instructing his twelve disciples,
13:53 When Jesus had *f* these parables,
19: 1 When Jesus had *f* this discourse,
26: 1 Now when Jesus had *f* all these discourses,
27:31 when they had *f* making a fool of him,
Mk 3:26 he is *f.*
5:35 He had not *f* speaking when people from the
15:20 When they had *f* mocking him,
Lk 4:13 devil had *f* all the tempting he left him,
5: 4 When he had *f* speaking he said to Simon,
6:40 but every student when he has *f* his
7: 1 When he had *f* this discourse in the
11: 1 When he had *f,*
Jn 19:28 realizing that everything was now *f,*
19:30 took the wine, he said, "Now it is *f.*"
21:19 When Jesus had *f* speaking he said to him,
Acts 10:44 Peter had not *f* these words when the Holy
Rom 15:28 When I have *f* my task and have safely
Phil 3:12 it yet, or have already *f* my course;
2Tm 4: 7 fought the good fight, I have *f* the race,
Heb 4: 3 God's work was *f* when he created the world,
Rv 11: 7 When they have *f* giving their testimony,
16:17 came a loud voice which said, "It is *f!*"

FINISHES (1)

Sir 38:27 and he keeps watch till he *f* his design.

FINISHING (2)

1Mc 4:19 As Judas was *f* this speech,
Jn 17: 4 on earth by *f* the work you gave me to do.

FINS (5)

Lv 11: 9 waters has both *f* and scales you may eat.
11:10 either *f* or scales are loathsome for you,
11:12 lacks *f* or scales is loathsome for you.
Dt 14: 9 whatever has both *f* and scales you may eat,
14:10 lack either *f* or scales you shall not eat;

FIR (7)

1Kgs 5:22 all the cedars and *f* trees you wish.
5:24 with all the cedars and *f* trees he wished;
6:15 and its floor was laid with *f* planking.
6:34 The two doors were of *f* wood;
9:11 Solomon with all the cedar wood, *f* wood,
Ps(s) 104:17 *f* trees are the home of the stork.
Ez 31: 8 nor could the *f* trees match its boughs,

FIRE (481)

Gn 11: 3 let us mold bricks and harden them with *f.*"
19:24 rained down sulphurous *f* upon Sodom
22: 6 he himself carried the *f* and the knife.
22: 7 continued, "Here are the *f* and the wood,
Ex 3: 2 appeared to him in *f* flaming out of a bush.
3: 2 to see that the bush, though on *f,*
13:21 means of a column of *f* to give them light.
13:22 column of *f* by night ever left its place
19:18 smoke, for the LORD came down upon it in *f.*
22: 4 if he lets the *f* spread so that it burns
22: 5 If the *f* spreads further,
22: 5 started the *f* must make full restitution.
24:17 seen as a consuming *f* on the mountaintop.
27: 3 well as shovels, basins, forks and *f* pans,
32:20 in the *f* and then ground it down to powder,
32:24 gave it to me, and I threw it into the *f,*
35: 3 You shall not even light a *f* in any of
38: 3 pots, shovels, basins, forks and *f* pans,
40:38 *f* was seen in the cloud by the whole house
Lv 1:12 on top of the wood and the *f* on the altar.
1:17 it on the altar, over the wood on the *f,*
2:14 grits of new ears of grain, roasted by *f.*
3: 5 the holocaust, on the wood over the *f,*
4:12 and there be burned up in a wood *f.*
6: 2 the *f* is to be kept burning on the altar.
6: 3 *f* has reduced the holocaust on the altar,
6: 5 The *f* on the altar is to be kept burning;
6: 6 The *f* is to be kept burning continuously
6:23 an offering must be burned up in the *f.*
7:17 third day, it must be burned up in the *f.*
7:19 be eaten, but shall be burned up in the *f.*
8:17 offal he burned in the *f* outside the camp,
8:32 flesh and bread you shall burn up in the *f.*
9:11 he burned up in the *f* outside the camp.
9:24 *F* came forth from the LORD's presence and
10: 1 incense on the *f* they had put in them,
10: 1 they offered up before the LORD profane *f,*
10: 2 *F* therefore came forth from the LORD's
10: 6 for those whom the LORD's *f* has smitten;
13:52 leprosy, it must be destroyed by *f.*
13:55 is unclean and shall be destroyed by *f.*
13:57 the thing infected shall be destroyed by *f.*
16:13 the LORD he shall put incense on the *f,*
16:27 and offal shall be burned up in the *f.*
19: 6 the third day shall be burned up in the *f.*
Nm 3: 4 *f* before the LORD in the desert of Sinai,
4:14 the *f* pans,
6:18 in the *f* that is under the peace offering.
9:15 on the appearance of *f* over the Dwelling.
9:16 which at night had the appearance of *f.*
11: 1 that the *f* of the LORD burned among them
11: 2 he prayed to the LORD and the *f* died out.
11: 3 there the *f* of the LORD burned among them.
14:14 of cloud and by night in a column of *f.*
16: 7 put *f* in them and place incense in them
16:18 incense on the *f* they had put in them,
16:35 And *f* from the LORD came forth which
17: 2 and scatter the *f* some distance away,
17:11 your censer, put *f* from the altar in it,
19: 6 the *f* in which the heifer is being burned.
21:28 For *f* went forth from Heshbon and a blaze
26:10 the *f* consumed two hundred and fifty men.
26:61 they offered profane *f* before the LORD.
31:10 while they set on *f* all the towns where
31:22 Whatever can stand *f,*
31:23 tin and lead, you shall put into the *f,*
31:23 stand *f* you shall put into the water.
Dt 1:33 by day in the cloud, and by night in the *f,*
4:11 *f* and was enveloped in a dense black cloud.
4:12 LORD spoke to you from the midst of the *f.*
4:15 to you at Horeb from the midst of the *f.*
4:24 For the LORD, your God, is a consuming *f,*
4:33 voice of God speaking from the midst of *f,*
4:36 on earth he let you see his great *f,*
4:36 and you heard him speaking out of the *f.*
5: 4 on the mountain from the midst of the *f.*
5: 5 of the *f* and would not go up the mountain,
5:22 the midst of the *f* and the dense cloud.
5:23 while the mountain was ablaze with *f,*
5:24 heard his voice from the midst of the *f*
5:25 Surely this great *f* will consume us.
5:26 living God speaking from the midst of *f,*
7: 5 sacred poles, and destroy their idols by *f.*
7:25 of their gods you shall destroy by *f.*
9: 3 cross over before you as a consuming *f;*
9:10 midst of the *f* on the day of the assembly.
9:21 object you had made, and fusing it with *f,*
10: 4 midst of the *f* on the day of the assembly.
12: 3 pillars, destroy by *f* their sacred poles,
18:10 immolates his son or daughter in the *f,*
18:16 our God, nor see this great *f* any more,
32:22 "For by my wrath a *f* is enkindled that
33: 2 While at his right hand a *f* blazed forth
Jos 7:15 incurred the ban shall be destroyed by *f,*
8:19 the city, and immediately set it on *f.*
8:28 Then Joshua destroyed the place by *f,*
11:13 *f* any of the cities built on raised sites,
Jgs 1: 8 then they destroyed the city by *f*
6: 2 established the *f* signals on the mountains,
6:21 Thereupon a *f* came up from the rock which
9:15 let *f* come from the buckthorn and devour
9:20 let *f* come forth from Abimelech to devour
9:20 let *f* come forth from the citizens
9:49 they set the crypt on *f* over their heads,
9:52 very entrance of the tower to set it on *f.*
15: 6 up and destroyed her and her family by *f.*
15:14 *f* and his bonds melted away from his hands.
18:27 to the sword and destroyed their city by *f.*
20:48 by *f* all the cities they came upon.
1Sm 30: 1 had stormed the city, and had set it on *f.*
30:14 and we set Ziklag on *f.*"
2Sm 14:30 Go, set it on *f.*"
14:30 so Absalom's servants set the field on *f.*
14:31 "Why have your servants set my field on *f?*"
22: 9 nostrils, and a devouring *f* from his mouth;
23: 7 of a spear, and they must be consumed by *f.*"
1Kgs 7:50 bowls, cups, and *f* pans of pure gold;
9:16 after destroying it by *f* and slaying all
18:23 and place it on the wood, but start no *f.*
18:23 place it on the wood, but shall start no *f.*
18:24 The God who answers with *f* is God."
18:25 upon your gods, but do not start the *f.*"
18:38 *f* came down and consumed the holocaust,
19:12 there was *f*—but the LORD was not in the *f.*
19:12 the *f* there was a tiny whispering sound.
2Kgs 1:10 "may *f* come down from heaven and consume
1:10 And *f* came down from heaven and consumed
1:12 "may *f* come down from heaven and consume
1:12 And divine *f* came down from heaven,
1:14 Already *f* has come down from heaven,
16: 3 Israel, and even immolated his son by *f,*
17:17 immolated their sons and daughters by *f,*
17:31 their children by *f* to their city gods,
19:18 lands, and cast their gods into the *f;*
21: 6 He immolated his son by *f*
23:10 sons or daughters by *f* in honor of Molech.
23:11 The chariots of the sun he destroyed by *f.*
25: 9 every large building was destroyed by *f.*
1Chr 21:26 *f* from heaven upon the altar of holocausts.
2Chr 7: 1 *f* came down from heaven and consumed the
7: 3 All the Israelites looked on while the *f*
28: 3 and immolated his sons by *f* according to
33: 6 his sons by *f* in the Valley of Ben-hinnom.
35:13 cooked the Passover on the *f* as prescribed,
Neh 1: 3 and its gates have been gutted with *f.*"
2: 3 and its gates have been eaten out by *f?*"
2:13 and its gates had been eaten out by *f.*
2:17 ruins and its gates have been gutted by *f.*
9:12 by day, and by night with a column of *f,*
9:19 nor did the column of *f* by night cease to
Tb 13:12 your towers and set *f* to your homes;
Jdt 2:27 harvest, he set *f* to all their fields,
13:13 They made a *f* for light;
16:17 He will send *f* and worms into their flesh,
Est E:24 be ruthlessly destroyed with *f* and sword,
1Mc 1:31 He plundered the city and set *f* to it,
2:59 for their faith, were saved from the *f.*
3: 5 who troubled his people he destroyed by *f.*
5:28 their possessions, and set *f* to the city.
9:67 from the city and set *f* to the machines.
10:84 and destroyed by *f* both the temple of
11: 4 shown the temple of Dagon destroyed by *f,*
11:48 set on *f* and plundered on a large scale.
16:10 plain of Azotus, but John set *f* to these,
2Mc 1: 8 setting *f* to the gatehouse and shedding
1:18 and of the *f* that appeared when Nehemiah,
1:19 took some of the *f* from the altar and hid it
1:20 who had hidden the *f* to look for it.
1:21 us that they could not find any *f,*
1:22 began to shine, a great *f* blazed up,
1:33 where the exiled priests had hidden the *f,*
2: 1 some of the aforementioned *f* with them,
2:10 Just as Moses prayed to the Lord and *f*
2:10 *f* came down and burned up the holocausts.
7: 5 them to carry him to the *f* and fry him.
8: 6 towns and villages, he would set them on *f.*
8:33 set *f* to the sacred gates and Callisthenes,
9: 7 Breathing *f* in his rage against the Jews,
10: 3 Then, with *f* struck from flint,
10:36 the *f* and burned the blasphemers alive.

FIRE (cont.)
12: 6 In a night attack he set the harbor on *f*,
12: 9 setting *f* to the harbor and the fleet,
13: 8 *f* and ashes should meet his death in ashes.
14:41 and calling for *f* to set the door ablaze,
Jb 15:34 *f* shall consume the tents of extortioners.
20: 7 perishes forever like the fuel of his *f*,
20:26 the *f* which shall consume him needs not to
22:20 and such as were left, *f* has consumed!"
31:12 A *f* that should burn down to the abyss
41:11 sparks of *f* leap forth.
Ps(s) 17: 3 it in the night, though you try me with *f*,
18: 9 and a devouring *f* from his mouth that
21:10 let *f* devour them.
39: 4 in my thoughts, a *f* blazed forth.
46:10 he burns the shields with *f*.
50: 3 Before him is a devouring *f*;
66:10 You have tried us as silver is tried by *f*;
66:12 we went through *f* and water,
68: 3 as wax melts before the *f*,
74: 7 They set your sanctuary on *f*;
78:14 by day, and all night with a glow of *f*.
78:21 and *f* blazed up against Jacob,
78:63 *F* consumed their young men,
79: 5 Will your jealousy burn like *f*?
80:17 Let those who would burn it with *f* or
83:15 As a *f* raging in a forest,
89:47 Will your wrath burn like *f*?
97: 3 *F* goes before him and consumes his foes
102: 4 like smoke, and my bones burn like *f*.
104: 4 messengers, and flaming *f* your ministers.
105:39 them and *f* to give them light by night.
106:18 *F* broke out against their faction;
118:12 bees, they flared up like *f* among thorns;
148: 8 *F* and hail, snow and mist,
Prv 6:27 Can a man take *f* to his bosom,
16:27 and on his lips there is a scorching *f*.
26:20 For lack of wood, the *f* dies out;
26:21 is to live coals, what wood is to *f*,
30:16 that is never saturated with water, and *f*,
Sg 8: 6 its flames are a blazing *f*.
Wis 10: 6 he fled as *f* descended upon Pentapolis
13: 2 But either *f*, or wind, or the swift air,
16:16 unremitting downpours, and consumed by *f*.
16:17 quenches anything, the *f* grew more active;
16:19 *f* blazed beyond its strength so as to
16:22 and ice withstood *f* and were not melted,
16:22 Were consumed by a *f* that blazed
16:23 *f*, again, that the just might be nourished
16:27 For what was not destroyed by *f*,
17: 5 No force, even of *f*,
19:20 *F* in water maintained its own strength,
Sir 2: 5 For in *f* gold is tested,
3:29 Water quenches a flaming *f*,
6: 2 not into the grip of desire, lest, like *f*,
8: 3 of railing speech, heap no wood upon his *f*.
8:10 lest you be consumed in his flaming *f*.
9: 8 many perish, for lust for it burns like *f*.
15:16 There are set before you *f* and water;
16: 6 Against a sinful band *f* is enkindled,
21: 9 they will end in a flaming *f*.
23:16 For burning passion is a blazing *f*,
23:16 who never stops until the *f* breaks forth;
28:10 The more wood, the greater the *f*,
28:11 Pitch and resin make *f* flare up,
36: 8 Let raging *f* consume the fugitive,
38:28 The heat from the *f* sears his flesh,
38:30 and he keeps watch on the *f* of his kiln.
39:26 all needs for human life are water and *f*,
39:29 kept for the proper time, are *f* and hail,
40:30 is sweet, but within him it burns like *f*.
45:19 and consumed them with his flaming *f*.
48: 1 Till like a *f* there appeared the prophet
48: 3 the heavens and three times brought down *f*.
50: 9 like the *f* of incense at the sacrifice;
51: 4 From the midst of unremitting *f*,
Is 1: 7 is waste, your cities burnt with *f*;
4: 5 by day and a light of flaming *f* by night.
5:24 as the tongue of *f* licks up stubble,
9:17 For wickedness burns like *f*,
9:18 and the people are like fuel for *f*;
10:16 will be kindling like the kindling of *f*.
10:17 The light of Israel will become a *f*,
26:11 *f* prepared for your enemies consume them.
27:11 women shall come to build a *f* with them.
29: 6 storm, and the flame of consuming *f*.
30:14 a sherd to scoop *f* from the hearth
30:27 fury, his tongue is like a consuming *f*;
30:30 In raging fury and flame of consuming *f*,
31: 9 has a *f* in Zion and a furnace in Jerusalem.
33:11 my spirit shall consume you like *f*.
33:12 brushwood cut down for burning in the *f*.
33:14 "Who of us can live with the consuming *f*?
37:19 lands, and cast their gods into the *f*;
43: 2 When you walk through *f*,
44:15 himself, or makes a *f* for baking bread;
44:16 Half of it he burns in the *f*,
44:16 I am warm, I feel the *f*."
44:19 say, "Half of the wood I burned in the *f*,
47:14 Lo, they are like stubble, *f* consumes them;
47:14 is no warming ember, no *f* to sit before,
50:11 own *f* and by the flares you have burnt!
64: 1 is set ablaze, or *f* makes the water boil!
64:10 fathers praised you Has been burned with *f*;
65: 5 my wrath, a *f* that burns all the day.
66:15 Lo, the LORD shall come in *f*,
66:16 shall judge all mankind by *f* and sword.
66:24 shall not die, nor their *f* be extinguished,
Jer 4: 4 Lest my anger break out like *f*,
5:14 I make my words in your mouth, a *f*,
6:29 roars, the lead is consumed by the *f*;
7:18 gather wood, their fathers light the *f*,
7:31 in *f* their sons and their daughters,
11:16 Now he sets *f* to it,
17: 4 For a *f* has been kindled by my wrath that
17:27 I will set unquenchable *f* to its gates,
19: 5 their sons in *f* as holocausts to Baal:
20: 9 then it becomes like *f* burning in my heart,
21:10 king of Babylon who shall burn it with *f*.
21:12 like *f* which burns without being quenched,
21:14 I will kindle a *f* in its forest that shall
22: 7 choice cedars, and cast them into the *f*.
23:29 Is not my word like *f*,
32:29 it shall enter this city and set *f* to it,
34: 2 he will destroy it with *f*.
34:22 and capture it, and destroy it with *f*;
36:22 and *f* was burning in a brazier before him.
36:23 and cast it into the *f* in the brazier,
36:23 the entire roll was consumed in the *f*.
36:32 king of Judah, had burned in the *f*,
37: 8 shall capture it and destroy it with *f*.
37:10 would rise up and destroy the city with *f*.
38:17 this city shall not be destroyed with *f*,
38:18 the Chaldeans, who shall destroy it with *f*,
38:23 and this city shall be destroyed with *f*.
39: 8 The Chaldeans set *f* to the king's palace
43:12 shall set *f* to the temples of Egypt's gods,
43:13 with *f* the temples of the Egyptian gods.
48:45 For *f* breaks forth from Heshbon,
49: 2 daughter cities shall be destroyed by *f*.
49:27 I will set *f* to the wall of Damascus,
50:32 *f* that shall devour everything around him.
51:32 been seized, and the fortresses set on *f*,
51:58 her lofty gates shall be destroyed by *f*.
52:13 every large building he destroyed with *f*.
52:19 The basins also, the *f* holders,
Lam 1:13 on high he sent *f* down into my very frame;
2: 3 like a flaming *f* devouring all about it.
2: 4 Zion he poured out his wrath like *f*.
4:11 He has kindled a *f* in Zion that has
Bar 1: 2 took Jerusalem and burnt it with *f*.
4:35 *f* shall come upon her from the Eternal God,
6:54 For when *f* breaks out in the temple of
6:54 are burnt up in the *f* like beams.
6:62 *f*, sent from on high to burn up
Ez 1: 4 with flashing *f* [enveloped in brightness],
1: 4 of the *f* something gleamed like electrum.
1:13 like burning coals of *f* could be seen;
1:13 The *f* gleamed,
1:27 his waist I saw what looked like *f*;
5: 2 Burn a third in the *f*,
5: 4 them in the midst of the *f* and burn them.]
8: 2 what seemed to be his waist, there was *f*;
10: 6 linen to take *f* from within the wheelwork,
10: 7 toward the *f* that was among the cherubim.
15: 4 *f* as fuel and the fire devours both ends
15: 5 when the *f* has devoured and scorched it,
15: 6 which I have destined as fuel for the *f*,
15: 7 from the fire, but the *f* shall devour them.
16:21 to them, making them pass through *f*.
16:41 They shall burn your apartments with *f* and
19:12 strong branch withered up, *f* devoured it.
19:14 For *f* came out of the branch and devoured
20:31 making your children pass through the *f*,
21: 3 a *f* in you that shall devour all trees,
21:37 You shall be fuel for the *f*,
22:21 the *f* of my anger and smelt you with it.
23:25 what is left of you shall be devoured by *f*.
23:47 daughters, and burn their houses with *f*.
24:10 piling on wood and kindling the *f*,
24:12 even with *f* will its great rust be removed.
28:18 *f* from your midst which will devour you.
30: 8 when I set *f* to Egypt and when all who
30:14 I will set *f* to Zoan,
30:16 I will set *f* to Egypt;
38:22 rain and hailstones, *f* and brimstone,
39: 6 I will send *f* upon Magog and upon those
Dn 3:22 So huge a *f* was kindled in the furnace
3:25 In the *f* Azariah stood up and prayed aloud:
3:50 The *f* in no way touched them or caused
3:66 *F* and heat,
3:88 raging flame and delivered us from the *f*.
3:91 we not cast three men bound into the *f*?"
3:92 unfettered and unhurt, walking in the *f*,
3:93 Meshach, and Abednego came out of the *f*.
3:94 they saw that the *f* had had no power over
3:94 there was not even a smell of *f* about them.
7: 9 flames of fire, with wheels of burning *f*.
7:10 stream of *f* flowed out from where he sat;
7:11 its body thrown into the *f* to be burnt up.
Hos 7: 4 Whose *f* the baker desists from stirring
7: 6 in the morning it flares like a blazing *f*.
8:14 cities, but I will send *f* upon his cities,
Jl 1:19 *f* has devoured the pastures of the plain,
1:20 *f* has devoured the pastures of the plain.
2: 3 Before them a *f* devours,
3: 3 in the heavens and on the earth, blood, *f*,
Am 1: 4 I will send *f* upon the house of Hazael,
1: 7 Edom, I will send *f* upon the wall of Gaza,
1:10 I will send *f* upon the wall of Tyre,
1:12 wrath to the end, I will send *f* upon Teman,
1:14 I will kindle a *f* upon the wall of Rabbah,
2: 2 of Edom's king, I will send *f* upon Moab,
2: 5 led them astray, I will send *f* upon Judah,
4:11 you were like a brand plucked from the *f*;
5: 6 of Joseph like a *f* That shall consume,
7: 4 he called for a judgment by *f*.
Ob 1:18 The house of Jacob shall be a *f*,
Mi 1: 4 valleys split open, Like wax before the *f*,
1: 7 all her wages shall be burned in the *f*,
Na 1: 6 His fury is poured out like *f*,
3:13 are open wide, *f* has consumed their bars.
3:15 There the *f* shall consume you,
Zep 1:18 When in the *f* of his jealousy all the
3: 8 For in the *f* of my jealousy shall all the
Zec 2: 9 I will be for her an encircling wall of *f*,
3: 2 not this man a brand snatched from the *f*?"
9: 4 on the sea, and she shall be devoured by *f*.
11: 1 Lebanon, that the *f* may devour your cedars!
12: 6 Judah like a brazier of *f* in the woodland,
13: 9 I will bring the one third through *f*,
Mal 1:10 you from kindling *f* on my altar in vain!
3: 2 For he is like the refiner's *f*,
3:19 the day that is coming will set them on *f*,
3:24 the day that is coming will set them on *f*,
Mt 3:10 will be cut down and thrown into the *f*.
3:11 will baptize you in the Holy Spirit and *f*.
3:12 the chaff he will burn in unquenchable *f*."
6:30 today and is thrown on the *f* tomorrow,
7:19 fruit is cut down and thrown into the *f*.
17:15 into the *f* and frequently into the water.
18: 8 with two hands or two feet into endless *f*.
25:41 *f* prepared for the devil and his angels!
Mk 9:22 it throws him into *f* and into water.
9:43 and enter Gehenna with its unquenchable *f*.
9:48 dies not and the *f* is never extinguished.'
9:49 Everyone will be salted with *f*.
14:54 guard and began to warm himself at the *f*.
Lk 3: 9 will be cut down and thrown into the *f*."
3:16 baptize you in the Holy Spirit and in *f*.
3:17 the chaff he will burn in unquenchable *f*."
9:54 us call down *f* from heaven to destroy them?"
12:28 today and is thrown on the *f* tomorrow,
12:49 "I have come to light a *f* on the earth.
17:29 *f* and brimstone rained down from heaven
22:55 Later they lighted a *f* in the middle of
22:56 girl saw him sitting in the light of the *f*.
Jn 15: 6 picked up to be thrown in the *f* and burnt.
18:18 made a charcoal *f* to warm themselves by.
21: 9 they saw a charcoal *f* there with a fish
Acts 2: 3 Tongues as of *f* appeared,
2:19 blood, *f*, and a cloud of smoke.
28: 2 a *f* and gathering us all around it,
28: 3 Paul had just fed the *f* with a bundle of
28: 5 But Paul shook the snake off into the *f*
1Cor 3:13 with *f*, and *f* will test the quality of each
3:15 saved, but only as one fleeing through *f*.
7: 9 It is better to marry than to be on *f*.
Heb 1: 7 winds, and his ministers flaming *f*";
10:27 *f* to consume the adversaries of God.
12:18 an untouchable mountain and a blazing *f*,
12:29 For our God is a consuming *f*.
Jas 3: 6 from birth, and its *f* is kindled by hell.
5: 3 it will devour your flesh like a *f*.
1Pt 4:12 a trial by *f* is occurring in your midst.
2Pt 3: 7 earth are reserved by God's word for *f*;
3:10 the elements will be destroyed by *f*,
Jude 1: 7 as they undergo a punishment of eternal *f*.
1:22 you must rescue, snatching them from the *f*.
Rv 1:14 snow-white wool and his eyes blazed like *f*.
2:18 *f* and whose feet gleam like polished brass,
3:18 refined by *f* if you would be truly rich.
8: 7 came hail and then *f* mixed with blood,
9:17 their mouths came *f* and sulphur and smoke.
9:18 and *f* which shot out of their mouths
10: 1 the sun and his legs like pillars of *f*.
11: 5 *f* will come out of the mouths of these
13:13 it could even make *f* come down from heaven
14:18 in charge of the *f* at the altar of incense,
15: 2 like a sea of glass mingled with *f*.
16: 8 He was commissioned to burn men with *f*.
17:16 will devour her flesh and set her on *f*.
18: 8 She shall be consumed by *f*,
19:12 His eyes blazed like *f*,
20: 9 *f* came down from heaven and devoured them.
20:14 world were hurled into the pool of *f*,
20:15 the living was hurled into this pool of *f*.

FIRE-HOLDERS (1)

2Kgs 25:15 The *f* and the bowls which were of gold or

FIRE-THROWERS (1)

1Mc 6:51 setting up artillery and machines, *f*,

FIRE-TRIED (3)

2Sm 22:31 the promise of the LORD is *f*;
Ps(s) 18:31 unerring, the promise of the LORD is *f*;

1Pt 1: 7 than the passing splendor of *f* gold,

FIREBRANDS (3)

Jb 41:11 Out of his mouth go forth *f*;
Prv 26:18 Like a crazed archer scattering *f* and
Na 2: 5 And wheel in the squares, looking like *f*.

FIREPANS (1)

2Chr 4:22 snuffers, bowls, cups and *f* of pure gold.

FIRES (9)

Nm 21:30 *f* blaze as far as Medeba."
Jdt 7: 5 their weapons, lighted *f* on their bastions,
1Mc 12:28 They lighted *f* and then withdrew.
Ps(s) 105:32 with flashing *f* throughout their land.
Wis 17: 6 fearful *f* flashed through upon them;
Ez 39: 9 seven years they shall make *f* with them.
39:10 for they shall make *f* with the weapons.
Mt 5:22 him in contempt he risks the *f* of Gehenna.
Heb 11:34 broke the jaws of lions, put out raging *f*.

FIREWOOD (1)

Lv 6: 5 Every morning the priest shall put *f* on it.

FIRM (78)

Jos 1: 6 Be *f* and steadfast, so that you may give
1: 7 Above all, be *f* and steadfast,
1: 9 I command you: be *f* and steadfast!
1:18 But be *f* and steadfast."
10:25 be afraid or dismayed, be *f* and steadfast.
Jgs 1:35 The Amorites had a *f* hold in Har-heres,
2Sm 7:12 your loins, and I will make his kingdom *f*.
7:13 And I will make his royal throne *f* forever.
7:16 your throne shall stand *f* forever.' "
7:26 of your servant David stands *f* before you.
23: 5 Is not my house *f* before God?
1Chr 16:30 he has made the world *f*,
17:23 servant and his house remain *f* forever.
28:20 *f* and steadfast; go to work without fear
2Chr 20:17 Take your places, stand *f*,
20:20 LORD, your God, and you will be found *f*.
Neh 9:13 You gave them just ordinances, *f* laws,
10: 1 of all this, we are entering into a *f* pact,
Jdt 4: 7 them to keep *f* hold of the mountain passes,
1Mc 4:18 *f* against our enemies and overthrow them.
14:26 have stood *f* and repulsed Israel's enemies.
Jb 4: 3 many, and have made *f* their feeble hands.
11:15 you may stand *f* and unafraid.
Ps(s) 20: 9 down and fall, yet we stand erect and *f*.
37:23 By the LORD are the steps of a man made *f*,
40: 3 he made *f* my steps.
48: 9 God makes it *f* forever.
75: 4 in it quake, I have set *f* its pillars.
89:29 him, and my covenant with him stands *f*.
93: 1 with strength, And he has made the world *f*,
93: 2 Your throne stands *f* from of old;
96:10 He has made the world *f*,
112: 7 his heart is *f*,
119: 5 be *f* in the ways of keeping your statutes!
119:89 it is *f* as the heavens.
119:90 established the earth, and it stands *f*.
119:91 to your ordinances they still stand *f*:
132:11 *f* promise from which he will not withdraw:
Prv 8:28 When he made *f* the skies above,
12: 7 more, but the house of the just stands *f*.
24: 3 built, by understanding is it made *f*;
25: 5 his throne is made *f* through righteousness.
29:14 of the poor, his throne stands *f* forever.
Wis 4: 3 shall not strike deep root nor take *f* hold.
7:23 unhampered, beneficent, kindly, *F*,
Sir 1:20 A patient man need stand *f* but for a time,
3: 9 a father's blessing gives a family *f* roots,
12:15 While you stand *f*,
26:14 and her *f* virtue is of surpassing worth.
42:17 the strength to stand *f* before his glory.
Is 7: 9 your faith is *f* you shall not be firm!
26: 3 A nation of *f* purpose you keep in peace;
35: 3 are feeble, make *f* the knees that are weak,
46: 8 Remember this and be *f*,
54: 2 lengthen your ropes and make *f* your stakes.
Jer 30:20 old, his assembly before me shall stand *f*;
Ez 13: 5 *f* against attack on the day of the LORD.
22:14 Can your heart remain *f*,
Dn 9:27 he shall make a *f* compact with the many;
Mi 5: 3 He shall stand *f* and shepherd his flock by
Na 1: 6 Before his wrath, who can stand *f*,
Acts 11:23 remain *f* in their commitment to the Lord,
1Cor 7:37 man, however, who stands *f* in his resolve,
15: 1 you received and in which you stand *f*.
16:13 Be on your guard, stand *f* in the faith,
2Cor 1: 7 Our hope for you is *f* because we know that
1:24 As regards faith, you are standing *f*.
Gal 5: 1 So stand *f*,
Eph 6:11 stand *f* against the tactics of the devil.
Phil 1:27 that you are standing *f* in unity of spirit
4: 1 my dear ones, to stand *f* in the Lord.
Col 4:12 earnestly in prayer that you stand *f*,
1Thes 3: 8 flourish only if you stand *f* in the Lord!
2Thes 2:15 Therefore, brothers, stand *f*.
1Tm 6:12 Take *f* hold on the everlasting life to
2Tm 2:19 But the foundation God has laid stands *f*.
Heb 6:19 Like a sure and *f* anchor,

FIRMAMENT (10)

Jb 37:18 you spread out with him the *f* of the skies,
Ps(s) 19: 2 of God, and the *f* proclaims his handiwork.
150: 1 praise him in the *f* of his strength.
Sir 43:10 high, lighting up the *f* by its brilliance,
Ez 1:22 something like a *f* could be seen,
1:23 the *f* their wings were stretched out,
1:26 Above the *f* over their heads something
10: 1 I looked and saw in the *f* above the
Dn 3:56 Blessed are you in the *f* of heaven,
12: 3 shine brightly like the splendor of the *f*,

FIRMLY (23)

Nm 21:27 let Sihon's capital be *f* constructed.
1Kgs 2:12 David, with his sovereignty *f* established,
2:24 who has seated me *f* on the throne of my
3: 1 With the royal power *f* in his grasp,
2Kgs 14: 5 When Amaziah had the kingdom *f* in hand,
1Chr 17:14 his throne shall be *f* established forever."
2Chr 11:16 tribes who *f* desired to seek the LORD,
19:11 Act *f*,
Tb 11:11 fish gall in his hand, and holding him *f*,
Jdt 14:10 God of Israel had done, believed *f* in him.
Is 22:17 He shall grip you *f* And roll you up and
Jer 32:41 I will replant them *f* in this land,
Ez 27:24 varicolored carpets, and *f* woven cords.
Mt 13:15 their ears, they have *f* closed their eyes;
Lk 9:51 he *f* resolved to proceed toward Jerusalem,
Jn 6:47 Let me *f* assure you,
Rom 2:17 *f* on the law and pride yourself on God.
2Cor 1:21 *f* establishes us along with you in Christ;
Eph 4:16 *f* together by each supporting ligament,
Phil 1:20 I *f* trust and anticipate that I shall
Col 1:23 faith, be *f* grounded and steadfast in it,
2Pt 1:12 and are *f* rooted in the truth you possess.
Rv 2: 5 Keep *f* in mind the heights from which you

FIRMNESS (3)

Jer 33: 2 who made the earth and gave it form and *f*,
Col 2: 5 you and the *f* of your faith in Christ.
Heb 6:16 an oath gives *f* to a promise and puts an

FIRST (520)

Gn 1: 5 morning followed—the *f* day.
2:11 The name of the *f* is the Pishon;
4:19 the name of the *f* was Adah,
8: 5 and on the *f* day of the tenth month the
8:13 the six hundred and *f* year of Noah's life,
8:13 the first month, on the *f* day of the month,
9:20 of the soil, was the *f* to plant a vineyard.
10: 8 Nimrod, who was the *f* potentate on earth.
10:25 the name of the *f* was Peleg,
13: 4 the site where he had *f* built the altar;
25:25 The *f* to emerge was reddish,
25:31 *F* give me your birthright in exchange for
25:33 But Jacob insisted, "Swear to me *f*!"
27:36 *F* he took away my birthright,
32:21 I *f* appease him with gifts that precede me,
33: 2 putting the maids and their children *f*,
38:28 his hand, to note that this one came out *f*.
41:20 ugly cows ate up the *f* seven fat cows.
43:18 the money put back in our bags the *f* time,
43:22 not know who put the *f* money in our bags."
49: 3 my strength and the *f* fruit of my manhood,
Ex 4: 8 you, nor heed the message of the *f* sign,
10: 6 have not seen from the day they *f* settled
12: 2 shall reckon it the *f* month of the year.
12:15 From the very *f* day you shall have your
12:15 Whoever eats leavened bread from the *f* day
12:16 the *f* day you shall hold a sacred assembly,
12:18 evening of the fourteenth day of the *f* month
12:44 of it, provided you have *f* circumcised him.
12:48 males among them must *f* be circumcised,
19: 1 from the land of Egypt, on its *f* day,
23:16 with the *f* of the crop that you have sown
23:19 The choicest *f* fruits of your soil you
26: 5 the edge of the end sheet in the *f* set,
26:24 likewise double at the top, to the *f* ring.
28:17 in the *f* row,
28:34 *f* a gold bell,
29:17 inner organs and shanks you shall *f* wash,
29:40 With the *f* lamb there shall be a tenth of
34:22 of Weeks with the *f* of the wheat harvest;
34:26 "The choicest *f* fruits of your soil you
36:11 the edge of the end sheet in the *f* set,
36:29 likewise double at the top, to the *f* ring.
39: 3 Gold was *f* hammered into gold leaf and
39:10 in the *f* row a carnelian,
39:26 *f* a bell,
40: 2 "On the first day of the *f* month you
40:17 On the first day of the *f* month of the
Lv 1: 9 the offerer shall *f* wash with water.
1:13 the offerer shall *f* wash with water.
2:12 to the LORD in the offering of *f* fruits,
2:14 a cereal offering of *f* fruits to the LORD,
5: 8 shall offer the one for the sin offering *f*.
6: 7 sons shall *f* present it before the LORD,
8: 6 and his sons, he *f* washed them with water.
9: 8 Aaron *f* slaughtered the calf that was his
9:21 having *f* waved the breasts and the right
10:15 shall *f* be brought in with the oblations,
13:11 the man unclean without *f* quarantining him,
16: 4 on until he has *f* bathed his body in water.
17: 4 without *f* bringing it to the entrance of
18:18 for thus you would disgrace your *f* wife.
19:23 *f* look upon its fruit as if it were
22: 6 until he has *f* bathed his body in water,
23: 5 falls on the fourteenth day of the *f* month,
23: 7 On the *f* of these days you shall hold a
23:10 the *f* fruits of your harvest to the priest,
23:17 wave offering of your *f* fruits to the LORD,
23:20 The priest shall wave the bread of the *f*
23:24 On the *f* day of the seventh month you
23:35 the *f* day there shall be a sacred assembly,
23:39 The *f* and the eighth day shall be days of
23:40 On the *f* day you shall gather foliage from
26:43 But the land must *f* be rid of them,
Nm 1: 1 of Egypt, on the *f* day of the second month,
1:18 community on the *f* day of the second month.
2: 9 These shall be *f* on the march.
5:16 "The priest shall *f* have the woman come
5:25 But *f* he shall take the cereal offering of
7:12 his offering on the *f* day was Nahshon,
9: 1 In the *f* month of the year following their
9: 5 of the fourteenth day of the *f* month,
10: 5 When you sound the *f* alarm,
10:13 The *f* time that they broke camp at the
10:14 in companies, was the *f* to set out.
15:20 of a cake of your *f* batch of dough.
15:21 to the LORD from your *f* batch of dough.
15:23 from the time the LORD *f* issues the
18:12 they give to the LORD as their *f* fruits;
18:13 the *f* products that they bring in to the
20: 1 in the desert of Zin in the *f* month,
24:14 let me *f* warn you what this people will do
24:20 *F* of the peoples was Amalek,
28: 7 And as the libation for the *f* lamb,
28:11 "On the *f* of each month you shall offer
28:16 the *f* month falls the Passover of the LORD,
28:18 On the *f* of these days you shall hold a
28:26 "On the day of *f* fruits,
29: 1 "On the *f* day of the seventh month you
30:16 them some time after he *f* learned of them,
33: 3 *f* month, on the fifteenth day of the *f* month.
33:38 of Egypt, on the *f* day of the fifth month.
35:12 unless he is *f* tried before the community.
Dt 1: 3 year, on the *f* day of the eleventh month,
13:10 hand shall be the *f* raised to slay him;
16: 4 you sacrificed on the evening of the *f* day
16: 9 the sickle is *f* put to the standing grain.
17: 7 be the *f* to raise their hands against him;
18: 4 *f* fruits of your grain and wine and oil,
18: 4 the *f* fruits of the shearing of your flock;
20:10 attack a city, *f* offer it terms of peace.
21:17 since he is the *f* fruits of his manhood,
22:14 but when I *f* had relations with her I did
23:14 you shall *f* dig a hole and afterward cover
26: 2 you shall take some *f* fruits
26:10 I have now brought you the *f* fruits of the
Jos 4:19 the Jordan on the tenth day of the *f* month,
8:33 of the people of Israel on this *f* occasion.
12: 2 *F*, Sihon, king of the Amorites,
21: 4 When the *f* lot among the Levites fell to
21:10 the Levites, since the *f* lot fell to them:
21:11 *f*, Kiriath-arba (Arba was the father of
22:13 *F* however, they sent to the Reubenites,
Jgs 1: 1 asking "Who shall be *f* among us to attack
13:25 of the LORD *f* stirred him in Mahaneh-dan,
20:18 go *f* in the attack on the Benjaminites,
20:18 the LORD said, "Judah shall go *f*."
1Sm 2:16 "Let the fat be burned *f* as is the custom,
14:14 In this *f* exploit Jonathan and his
14:35 the *f* time he built an altar to the LORD.
22:15 the *f* time I have consulted God for him?
29: 8 the *f* day I have been with you to this day,
29:10 So the *f* thing tomorrow,
2Sm 7:11 I *f* appointed judges over my people Israel.
13:16 worse than the *f* injury you have done me."
17: 9 our soldiers should fall at the *f* attack,
18:27 notice that the *f* one runs like Ahimaaz,
19:21 Yet realize that I have been the *f* of the
19:44 we not *f* to speak of restoring the king?"
21: 9 to death during the *f* days of the harvest
23: 8 son of Hachamoni, was the *f* of the Three.
1Kgs 1:51 Solomon *f* swear that he will not kill me,
3:22 But the *f* kept saying,
3:27 "Give the *f* one the living child!
16:23 twelve years, the *f* six of them in Tirzah.
17:13 *f* make me a little cake and bring it to me.
18:25 "Choose one young bull and prepare it *f*,
20: 9 you demanded of your servant the *f* time.
20:17 governors of the provinces marched out *f*,
2Kgs 4:42 barely loaves made from the *f* fruits,
7: 8 of the camp, they went *f* into one tent,
15:37 at that time that the LORD *f* loosed Rezin,
17:25 When they *f* settled there,
23:29 was slain at Megiddo at the *f* encounter.
1Chr 1:10 was the *f* to be a conqueror on the earth.
1:19 the *f* was named Peleg (for in his time the
6:39 Kohathites, since the *f* lot fell to them,
9: 2 The *f* to settle again in their cities
11: 6 *f* shall be made the chief commander."

FIRST (cont.)
11: 6 the son of Zeruiah, was the *f* to go up;
12:16 overflowing both its banks in the *f* month,
15:13 Because you were not with us the *f* time,
16: 7 for the *f* time these praises of the LORD:
17: 9 ever again oppress them, as they did at *f*,
24: 7 The *f* lot fell to Jehoiarib,
25: 9 The *f* lot fell to Asaph,
27: 2 Over the *f* division for the first month
27: 2 division for the *f* month was Ishabaal,
27: 3 the commanders of the army for the *f* month.
29:29 Now the deeds of King David, *f* and last,
2Chr 9:29 rest of the acts of Solomon, *f* and last,
12:15 The acts of Rehoboam, *f* and last,
16:11 Now the acts of Asa, *f* and last,
20:34 of the acts of Jehoshaphat, *f* and last,
25:26 rest of the acts of Amaziah, *f* and last,
26:22 the rest of the acts of Uzziah, *f* and last.
28:26 his deeds and his activities, *f* and last,
29: 3 the first month of the *f* year of his reign,
29:17 on the first day of the *f* month,
29:17 and on the sixteenth day of the *f* month,
35: 1 on the fourteenth day of the *f* month.
35:26 law of the LORD, and his acts, *f* and last,
36:22 In the *f* year of Cyrus,
Ezr 1: 1 In the *f* year of Cyrus,
3: 6 From the *f* day of the seventh month they
5:13 However, in the *f* year of Cyrus,
6: 3 In the *f* year of King Cyrus,
6:19 on the fourteenth day of the *f* month.
7: 9 On the first day of the *f* month he
7: 9 and on the *f* day of the fifth month he
8:31 of Ahava on the twelfth day of the *f* month.
8:32 where we *f* rested for three days
10:16 with the *f* day of the tenth month.
10:17 By the *f* day of the first month they had
Neh 2:11 Jerusalem, I *f* rested there for three days.
8: 2 On the *f* day of the seventh month,
8:18 day after day, from the *f* day to the last.
10:36 house of the LORD the *f* fruits of our fields
10:38 The *f* batch of our dough,
12:30 priests and Levites *f* purified themselves,
12:31 The *f* of these proceeded to the right,
12:44 set aside for stores, offerings, *f* fruits,
13:31 wood at stated times and for the *f* fruits.
Tb 1: 6 Bringing with me the *f* fruits of the field
1: 6 my income and the *f* shearings of the sheep,
5:10 entered the house, Tobit greeted him *f*.
6:18 with her, both of you *f* rise up to pray.
7: 1 They greeted him *f*.
14: 5 temple, but it will not be like the *f* one,
Jdt 2: 1 on the twenty-second day of the *f* month,
5:14 *F* they drove out all the inhabitants of
11:13 that they would use up the *f* fruits of grain
Est A: 1 King Ahasuerus, on the *f* day of Nisan,
1:14 service and held *f* rank in the realm,
3: 7 In the *f* month,
3:12 thirteenth day of the *f* month they wrote,
1Mc 1: 1 in his place, having *f* ruled in Greece.
2:18 now, be the *f* to obey the king's command,
3:49 them the priestly vestments, the *f* fruits,
5:40 "If he crosses over to us *f*,
5:43 He was the *f* to cross to the attack,
6: 2 king of Macedon, the *f* king of the Greeks.
6: 6 that Lysias had gone at *f* with a strong
7:13 The Hasideans were the *f* among the
7:43 he himself was the *f* to fall in the battle.
8:24 But if war is *f* made on Rome,
8:27 way, if war is made *f* on the Jewish nation,
9: 3 In the *f* month of the year one hundred and
10: 4 *f* to make peace with
10:41 hand over as they had done in the *f* years,
10:47 had been the *f* to address them peaceably,
11:68 having *f* detached an ambush against him in
13:42 and contracts, "In the *f* year of Simon,
16: 6 afraid to cross the stream, John crossed *f*.
2Mc 7: 7 When the *f* brother had died in this manner,
7: 8 turn suffered the same tortures as the *f*.
8:23 he himself took charge of the *f* division
8:27 let descend on them the *f* dew of his mercy.
10: 3 sacrifice for the *f* time in two years,
11: 7 himself was the *f* to take up arms,
12:22 But when Judas' *f* cohort appeared,
14: 8 *f*, out of my genuine concern
15:18 their *f* and foremost fear was for the
Jb 13:22 or let me speak *f*,
14: 9 Yet at the *f* whiff of water it may
42:14 daughters, of whom he called the *f* Jemimah,
Ps(s) 22:10 have been my guide since I was *f* formed,
78:51 *f* fruits of manhood in the tents of Ham;
105:36 land, the *f* fruits of all their manhood.
Prv 3: 9 wealth, with *f* fruits of all your produce;
8:23 From of old I was poured forth, at the *f*,
8:26 not made, nor the *f* clods of the world.
18:17 pleads his case *f* seems to be in the right;
Eccl 10:10 dull, though at *f* he made easy progress,
Wis 6:17 For the *f* step toward discipline is a very
7: 1 a descendant of the *f* man formed on earth.
7: 3 I uttered that *f* sound common to all.
10: 8 *f* were bereft of knowledge of the right,
Sir 4:17 and at *f* she puts him to the test;
6: 7 When you gain a friend, *f* test him,
7:31 *F* fruits and contributions,

11: 7 examine *f*,
16:24 When at the *f* God created his works and,
19:25 a wise man is known as such when *f* met.
23:23 *F*, she has disobeyed the law of the Most
24:26 *f* man never finished comprehending wisdom,
31:17 Be the *f* to stop, as befits good manners:
31:18 be not the *f* to reach out your hand.
32: 1 Take care of them *f* before you sit down;
37: 8 advice, find out *f* of all what he wants.
39:32 So from the *f* I took my stand,
51:20 At *f* acquaintance with her,
Is 1:26 I will restore your judges as at *f*,
8:23 *F* he degraded the land of Zebulun and the
41: 4 I, the LORD, am the *f*,
41:27 one heard you say, "The *f* news for Zion:
43:27 Your *f* father sinned;
44: 6 I am the *f* and I am the last;
48:12 I, it is I who am the *f*,
Jer 1: 2 LORD *f* came to him in the days of Josiah,
2: 3 was Israel, the *f* fruits of his harvest;
3: 1 man, Does the *f* husband come back to her?
4:31 the anguish of a mother with her *f* child
25: 1 of Judah (the *f* year of Nebuchadnezzar,
32: 7 relative have the *f* right of purchase
32: 8 you have the *f* claim to possess it;
34: 5 the kings who preceded you from the *f*;
36: 2 the nations, from the day I *f* spoke to you,
36:28 it everything that the *f* scroll contained,
38:11 went *f* to the linen closet in the palace,
Bar 3:26 it were born the giants, renowned at the *f*,
Ez 10:14 the *f* face was that of an ox,
20:40 and the *f* fruits of your offerings,
26: 1 On the *f* day of the . . .
29:17 On the *f* day of the first month in the
30:20 day of the *f* month in the eleventh year,
31: 1 On the *f* day of the third month in the
32: 1 On the *f* day of the twelfth month in the
32:17 day of the *f* month in the twelfth year,
40:21 same measurements as those of the *f* gate;
44:30 All the choicest *f* fruits of every kind,
45:18 On the *f* day of the first month you shall
45:20 You shall repeat this on the *f* day of the
45:21 On the fourteenth day of the *f* month you
Dn 1:21 there until the *f* year of King Cyrus.
3:38 or incense, no place to offer *f* fruits,
7: 1 the *f* year of King Belshazzar of Babylon,
7: 4 The *f* was like a lion,
7:11 from the *f* of the arrogant words which the
8: 1 After this *f* vision,
8:21 great horn on its forehead is the *f* king.
9: 1 It was the *f* year that Darius,
9: 2 in the *f* year of his reign I,
10: 4 On the twenty-fourth day of the *f* month I
10:12 "from the *f* day you made up your mind to
Hos 2: 9 say, "I will go back to my *f* husband,
9:10 the *f* fruits of the fig tree in its prime,
Am 6: 1 Leaders of a nation favored from the *f*,
6: 7 now they shall be the *f* to go into exile,
Jon 4: 2 This is why I fled at *f* to Tarshish.
Hg 1: 1 On the *f* day of the sixth month in the
Zec 6: 2 The *f* chariot had red horses,
12: 7 The LORD shall save the tents of Judah *f*,
14:10 of Benjamin to the place of the *F* Gate,
Mt 5:24 go *f* to be reconciled with your brother,
6:33 Seek *f* his kingship over you,
7: 5 Remove the plank from your own eye *f*;
8:21 "Lord, let me go and bury my father *f*."
10: 2 *f* Simon, now known as Peter,
12:29 his property unless he *f* ties him securely?
12:45 state of that man becomes worse than the *f*.
13:20 the message and at *f* receives it with joy.
13:30 *F* collect the weeds and bundle them up to
17:10 the scribes claim that Elijah must come *f*?"
17:27 a line, and take out the *f* fish you catch.
19:30 *f* shall come last, and the last shall come
20: 8 with the last group and end with the *f*.'
20:10 and when the *f* group appeared they
20:16 last shall be first and the *f* shall be last."
20:27 *f* among you must serve the needs of all.
22:38 This is the greatest and *f* commandment.
23:26 *F* cleanse the inside of the cup so that
26:17 the *f* day of the feast of Unleavened Bread,
27:26 Jesus, however, he *f* had scourged;
27:64 final imposture would be worse than the *f*."
28: 1 as the *f* day of the week was dawning,
Mk 1:30 *f* thing they did was to tell him about her.
3:27 unless he has *f* put him under restraint.
4:28 The soil produces of itself *f* the blade,
7: 4 from the market without *f* sprinkling it.
7:27 household satisfy themselves at table *f*.
9:11 the scribes claim that Elijah must come *f*?"
9:12 will indeed come *f* and restore everything.
9:35 and said, "If anyone wishes to rank *f*,
10:31 *f* shall come last, and the last shall come *f*."
10:44 *f* among you must serve the needs of all.
12:28 "Which is the *f* of all the commandments?"
12:29 "This is the *f*: "Hear, O Israel!
13:10 must *f* be proclaimed to all the Gentiles.
14:12 On the *f* day of Unleavened Bread,
16: 2 *f* day of the week they came to the tomb.
16: 9 the dead early on the *f* day of the week.
16: 9 He *f* appeared to Mary Magdalene,
Lk 2: 2 This *f* census took place while Quirinius

6:42 remove the plank from your own eye *f*;
9:22 he said, "must *f* endure many sufferings,
9:59 The man replied, "Let me bury my father *f*."
9:61 *f* let me take leave of my people at home."
10: 5 On entering any house, *f* say,
11:26 last state of the man is worse than the *f*."
11:38 that he had not *f* performed the ablutions
12: 1 He began to speak *f* to his disciples:
13:30 be *f* and some who are first will be last."
14:18 The *f* one said to the servant,
14:28 will he not *f* sit down and calculate the
14:31 he not sit down *f* and consider whether,
16: 5 of his master's debtors, and said to the *f*,
17:25 *F*, however, he must suffer much
19: 4 He *f* ran on in front,
19:16 The *f* presented himself and said,
20:30 The *f* one married and died childless.
21: 9 These things are bound to happen *f*,
22:64 They blindfolded him *f*,
24: 1 On the *f* day of the week,
Jn 1:41 The *f* thing he did was seek out his
1:43 out for Galilee, but *f* he came upon Philip.
2:10 "People usually serve the choice wine *f*;
2:11 this *f* of his signs at Cana in Galilee.
7:51 *f* hearing him and knowing the facts?"
8: 7 has no sin be the *f* to cast a stone at her."
9:24 *F* of all, we know this man is a sinner."
12:16 (At *f*, the disciples did not understand
18:13 They led him *f* to Annas,
18:19 questioned Jesus, *f* about his disciples,
19:32 the men crucified with Jesus, *f* of the one,
19:39 *f* come to Jesus at night) likewise came,
20: 1 in the morning on the *f* day of the week,
20: 4 outran Peter and reached the tomb *f*.
20: 8 who had arrived *f* at the tomb went in.
20:19 On the evening of that *f* day of the week,
Acts 1: 1 In my *f* account,
1: 2 having *f* instructed the apostles he had
2:33 he *f* received the promised Holy Spirit
3:26 he sent him to you *f* to bless you by
6: 6 who *f* prayed over them and then imposed
7:12 sent our fathers there on a *f* mission.
7:20 For the *f* three months he was reared in
9:40 Peter *f* made everyone go outside;
11:17 we *f* believed in the Lord Jesus Christ,
11:26 were called Christians for the *f* time.
12:10 They passed the *f* guard,
13:46 of God has to be declared to you *f* of all;
14:21 their steps to Lystra and Iconium *f*,
14:26 where they had *f* been commended to the
15:14 Symeon has told you how God *f* concerned
16: 1 Paul arrived *f* at Derbe;
16:40 the two *f* made their way to Lydia's house,
20: 7 On the *f* day of the week when we gathered
20:18 *f* day I set foot in the province of Asia
21:19 Paul *f* greeted them,
26:20 to God, *f* to the people of Damascus,
26:23 and that, as the *f* to rise from the dead,
27:42 The soldiers thought at *f* of killing the
27:43 swim to jump overboard *f* and make for land.
Rom 1: 8 *F* of all, I give thanks to God
1:16 who believes in it to salvation, the Jew *f*,
2: 9 every man who has done evil, the Jew *f*,
2:10 who has done good, likewise the Jew *f*,
3: 2 *F* of all, the Jews were entrusted with
5:16 In the *f* case,
7: 9 sin is dead, and at *f* I lived without law.
7:11 *f* to deceive me, then to kill me.
8:23 although we have the Spirit as *f* fruits,
10:19 *F* of all, Moses says,
11:16 If the *f* fruits are consecrated,
13:11 closer than when we *f* accepted the faith.
16: 5 is the *f* offering that Asia made to Christ.
1Cor 4: 2 The *f* requirement of an administrator is
11:18 *F* of all, I hear that when you gather
11:28 A man should examine himself *f*;
12:28 God has set up in the church *f* apostles,
14:30 the *f* ones should then keep quiet.
15: 3 on to you *f* of all what I myself received,
15:20 *f* fruits of those who have fallen asleep.
15:23 Christ the *f* fruits and then,
15:45 Scripture has it that Adam, the *f* man,
15:46 spiritual was not *f*; first came the natural
15:47 The *f* man was of earth,
16: 2 On the *f* day of each week everyone should
16:15 the household of Stephanas is the *f* fruits
2Cor 1:15 *f* so that a double grace might be yours.
1:22 us, thereby depositing the *f* payment,
8: 5 Beyond our hopes they *f* gave themselves to
Gal 4:13 *f* occasioned my bringing you the gospel.
Eph 1:12 his glory by being the *f* to hope in Christ.
1:14 the *f* payment against the full redemption
1:15 from the time I *f* heard of your faith in
4: 9 he had *f* descended into the lower regions
6: 2 "Honor your father and mother" is the *f*
Phil 1: 5 promote the gospel from the very *f* day.
Col 1: 6 This has been the case from the day you *f*
1Thes 4:16 those who have died in Christ will rise *f*.
2Thes 2:13 because you are the *f* fruits of those whom
1Tm 2: 1 *F* of all, I urge that petitions,
2:13 For Adam was created *f*,
3:10 They should be put on probation *f*;
5:12 condemnation for breaking their *f* pledge.

2Tm 1: 5 faith which *f* belonged to your grandmother
2: 6 who should have the *f* share of the crop.
4:16 At the *f* hearing of my case in court,
Ti 3:13 having *f* seen to it that they have
Heb 1: 2 whom he *f* created the universe.
2: 3 Announced *f* by the Lord,
4: 6 *f* announced did not because of unbelief,
7:27 *f* for his own sins and then for those of
8: 7 If that *f* covenant had been faultless,
8:13 covenant," he declares the *f* one obsolete.
9: 1 The *f* covenant has regulations for worship
9: 8 while the *f* tabernacle was still standing,
9:15 committed under the *f* covenant,
9:18 *f* covenant was inaugurated without blood.
10: 8 *F* he says, "Sacrifices and offerings,
10: 9 the *f* covenant to establish the second.
Jas 1:18 may be a kind of *f* fruits of his creatures.
3:17 above, by contrast, is *f* of all innocent.
2Pt 1:19 in a dark place until the *f* streaks of dawn
1:20 *F* you must understand this:
2:20 their last condition is worse than their *f*.
3: 3 Note this *f* of all: in the last days,
1Jn 4:19 for our part, love because he *f* loved us.
Jude 1: 5 The Lord *f* rescued his people from the
Rv 1:17 the *F* and the Last and the One who lives.
2: 8 " 'The *F* and the Last who once died but
4: 7 The *f* creature resembled a lion,
6: 1 Lamb broke open the *f* of the seven seals,
8: 7 When the *f* angel blew his trumpet,
9:12 The *f* woe is past, but beware!
13:12 It used the authority of the *f* beast to
13:12 all its inhabitants worship the *f* beast,
13:14 to perform by authority of the *f* beast,
13:17 was *f* marked with the name of the beast
14: 4 *f* fruits of mankind for God and the Lamb.
16: 2 The *f* angel went out,
20: 5 This is the *f* resurrection;
20: 6 are they who share in the *f* resurrection!
21:19 the *f* course of stones was jasper,
22:13 Alpha and the Omega, the *F* and the Last,

FIRST-BORN (125)

Gn 10:15 became the father of Sidon, his *f*,
22:21 Uz, his *f*, his brother Buz,
25:13 Nebaioth (Ishmael's *f*),
27:19 "I am Esau, your *f*.
27:32 "I am Esau," he replied, "your *f* son."
35:23 Reuben, Jacob's *f*,
36:15 The descendants of Eliphaz, Esau's *f*:
38: 6 Judah got a wife named Tamar for his *f*,
38: 7 Er, Judah's *f*, greatly offended the LORD;
41:51 He named his *f* Manasseh,
46: 8 Reuben, Jacob's *f*, and the sons of Reuben:
48:14 head of Manasseh, although he was the *f*.
48:18 the other one is the *f*;
49: 3 "You, Reuben, my *f*,
Ex 4:22 Israel is my son, my *f*.
4:23 I warn you, I will kill your son, your *f*.
6:14 The sons of Reuben, the *f* of Israel,
11: 5 *f* in this land shall die, from the first-born
11: 5 to the *f* of the slave-girl at the handmill,
11: 5 as well as all the *f* of the animals.
12:12 Egypt, striking down every *f* of the land,
12:29 the LORD slew every *f* in the land of Egypt,
12:29 from the *f* of Pharaoh on the throne to the
12:29 to the *f* of the prisoner in the dungeon,
12:29 as well as all the *f* of the animals.
13: 2 *f* that opens the womb among the Israelites,
13:13 *f* of an ass you shall redeem with a sheep.
13:13 Every *f* son you must redeem.
13:15 LORD killed every *f* in the land of Egypt,
13:15 land of Egypt, every *f* of man and of beast.
13:15 womb, and why I redeem every *f* of my sons.'
22:28 You shall give me the *f* of your sons.
34:19 "To me belongs every *f* male that opens
34:20 The *f* among your sons you shall redeem.
Lv 27:26 "Note that a *f* animal,
Nm 1:20 the descendants of Reuben, the *f* of Israel,
3: 2 The sons of Aaron were Nadab his *f*,
3:12 *f* that opens the womb among the Israelites.
3:13 are mine, because every *f* is mine.
3:13 I slew all the *f* in the land of Egypt,
3:13 I made all the *f* in Israel sacred to me,
3:40 "Take a census of all the *f* males of the
3:41 in place of all the *f* of the Israelites,
3:41 the *f* among the cattle of the Israelites."
3:42 a census of all the *f* of the Israelites,
3:43 *f* males of a month or more were registered,
3:45 in place of all the *f* of the Israelites,
3:46 *f* of the Israelites who outnumber
3:50 From the *f* of the Israelites he received
8:16 *f* that opens the womb among the Israelites.
8:17 Indeed, all the *f* among the Israelites,
8:17 day I slew all the *f* in the land of Egypt.
8:18 the *f* Israelites I have taken the Levites;
18:15 but you must let the *f* of man,
18:17 But the *f* of cattle,
26: 5 Of Reuben, the *f* of Israel,
33: 4 *f* all of whom the LORD had struck down;
Dt 12:17 or oil, of the *f* of your herd or flock,
21:15 sons, but the *f* is of her whom he dislikes:
21:16 as his *f* the son of the wife he loves,
21:16 wife he loves, in preference to his true *f*,
21:17 as his *f* the son of her whom he dislikes,
21:17 and to him belong the rights of the *f*.
25: 6 The *f* son she bears shall continue the
33:17 The majestic bull, his father's *f*,
Jos 6:26 lose his *f* when he lays its foundation,
17: 1 the tribe of Manasseh as the *f* of Joseph:
Jgs 8:20 Then he said to his *f*,
1Sm 8: 2 His *f* was named Joel,
17:13 gone off to war were named, the *f* Eliab,
2Sm 3: 2 his *f*, Amnon of Ahinoam
13:21 whom he favored because he was his *f*.
19:44 we are the *f* rather than you
1Kgs 16:34 He lost his *f* son, Abiram,
2Kgs 3:27 his *f*, his heir apparent, and offered him
1Chr 1:13 Canaan became the father of Sidon, his *f*,
1:29 Nebaioth, the *f* of Ishmael,
2: 3 Judah's *f*, Er, was wicked in the sight
2:13 Jesse became the father of Eliab, his *f*,
2:25 The sons of Jerahmeel, the *f* of Hezron,
2:25 the first-born of Hezron, were Ram, the *f*,
2:27 The sons of Ram, the *f* of Jerahmeel,
2:42 [Mesha] his *f*, who was the father of Ziph.
2:50 of Caleb, sons of Hur, the *f* of Ephrathah:
3: 1 the *f*, Amnon, by Ahinoam of Jezreel;
3:15 the *f* Johanan; the second, Jehoiakim;
4: 4 descendants of Hur, the *f* of Ephrathah,
5: 1 The sons of Reuben, the *f* of Israel.
5: 1 (He was indeed the *f*,
5: 3 The sons of Reuben, the *f* of Israel,
6:13 The sons of Samuel were Joel, the *f*,
8: 1 Benjamin became the father of Bela, his *f*,
8:30 also his *f* son, Abdon,
8:38 six sons, whose names were Azrikam, his *f*,
8:39 of Eshek, his brother, were Ulam, his *f*,
9: 5 Among the Shelanites were Asaiah, the *f*,
9:31 the Levites, the *f* of Shallum the Koreite,
9:36 His *f* son was Abdon;
9:44 six sons, whose names were Azrikam, his *f*,
26: 2 Zechariah, the *f*,
26: 4 Shemaiah, the *f*,
26:10 was not the *f* his father made him chief),
2Chr 21: 3 he gave to Jehoram because he was the *f*.
Neh 10:37 God, the *f* of our children and our animals,
10:37 including the *f* of our flocks and herds.
Jb 15: 7 Are you indeed the *f* of mankind,
18:13 side, the *f* of death consumes his limbs.
Ps(s) 78:51 He smote every *f* in Egypt,
89:28 And I will make him the *f*,
105:36 he struck every *f* throughout their land,
135: 8 He smote the *f* in Egypt,
136:10 Who smote the Egyptians in their *f*,
Prv 8:22 begot me, the *f* of his ways
31: 2 What, my son, my *f*!
Wis 18:13 at the destruction of the *f* they
Sir 36:11 Israel, whom you named your *f*,
44:23 God acknowledged him as the *f*,
Jer 31: 9 I am a father to Israel, Ephraim is my *f*.
Ez 20:26 gifts, by their immolation of every *f*,
Mi 6: 7 Shall I give my *f* for my crime,
Zec 12:10 grieve over him as one grieves over a *f*.
Lk 2: 7 She gave birth to her *f* son and wrapped
2:23 *f* male shall be consecrated to the Lord."
Rom 8:29 the Son might be the *f* of many brothers.
Col 1:15 the invisible God, the *f* of all creatures.
1:18 he who is the beginning, the *f* of the dead,
Heb 1: 6 again, when he leads his *f* into the world,
11:28 angel might not touch the *f* of Israel.
12:23 the assembly of the *f* enrolled in heaven,
Rv 1: 5 the *f* from the dead and ruler of the kings

FIRST-CLASS (1)

Ex 14: 7 six hundred *f* chariots and all the other

FIRST-FORMED (1)

Wis 10: 1 She preserved the *f* father of the world

FIRSTLING (3)

Ex 22:29 seven days the *f* may stay with its mother,
34:20 The *f* of an ass you shall redeem with one
Dt 15:21 a *f* is lame or blind or has any other

FIRSTLINGS (8)

Gn 4: 4 brought one of the best *f* of his flock.
Ex 13:12 *f* of your animals shall belong to the LORD.
Dt 12: 6 and the *f* of your herds and flocks.
14:23 as well as the *f* of your herd and flock,
15:19 the male *f* of your herd and of your flock.
15:19 *f* of your cattle, nor shear the *f* of your flock
Tb 1: 6 fruits of the field and the *f* of the flock,

FISH (65)

Gn 1:26 them have dominion over the *f* of the sea,
1:28 Have dominion over the *f* of the sea,
Ex 7:18 The *f* in the river shall die,
7:21 The *f* in the river died,
Nm 11: 5 the *f* we used to eat without cost in Egypt,
11:22 all the *f* of the sea were caught for them,
Dt 4:18 or of any *f* in the waters under the earth.
2Chr 33:14 to the *F* Gate and encircling Ophel;
Neh 3: 3 The *F* Gate was rebuilt by the sons of
12:39 Gate [the New City Gate], the *F* Gate,
13:16 who were resident there were importing *f*
Tb 6: 3 a large *f* suddenly leaped out of the
6: 4 hold of the *f* and don't let it get away!"
6: 4 seized the *f* and hauled it up on the shore.
6: 5 "Cut the *f* open and take out its gall,
6: 6 After the lad had cut the *f* open,
6: 6 Then he broiled and ate part of the *f*;
8: 3 The demon, repelled by the odor of the *f*,
11: 8 Smear the *f* gall on them.
11:11 went up to him with the *f* gall in his hand,
Jb 12: 8 you, and the *f* of the sea to inform you.
40:31 hide with barbs, or his head with *f* spears?
Ps(s) 105:29 their waters into blood and killed their *f*.
Eccl 9:12 his own time than *f* taken in the fatal net,
Is 50: 2 Their *f* rot for lack of water,
Ez 29: 4 the *f* of your Niles stick to your scales,
29: 4 *f* of your Niles sticking to your scales.
29: 5 desert, you and all the *f* of your Niles;
38:20 the *f* of the sea and the birds of the air,
47: 9 shall live, and there shall be abundant *f*,
47:10 of *f* shall be like those of the Great Sea,
Hos 4: 3 the air, and even the *f* of the sea perish.
Jon 2: 1 But the LORD sent a large *f*,
2: 1 belly of the *f* three days and three nights.
2: 2 the *f* Jonah said this prayer to the LORD,
2:11 the *f* to spew Jonah upon the shore.
Hb 1:14 You have made man like the *f* of the sea,
Zep 1:10 LORD, A cry will be heard from the *F* Gate,
Mt 7:10 or a poisonous snake when he asks for a *f*?
14:17 "but five loaves and a couple of *f*."
14:19 He took the five loaves and two *f*,
15:34 they replied, "and a few small *f*."
15:36 He took the seven loaves and the *f*,
17:27 a line, and take out the first *f* you catch.
Mk 6:38 number they answered, "Five, and two *f*."
6:41 taking the five loaves and the two *f*,
6:41 He divided the two *f* among all of them and
6:43 baskets, besides what remained of the *f*.
8: 7 few small *f*; asking a blessing on the *f*
Lk 5: 6 such a great number of *f* that their nets
9:13 have nothing but five loaves and two *f*.
9:16 taking the five loaves and the two *f*,
11:11 give his son a snake if he asks for a *f*,
24:42 They gave him a piece of cooked *f*,
Jn 6: 9 five barley loaves and a couple of dried *f*,
6:11 he did the same with the dried *f*,
21: 3 Peter said to them, "I am going out to *f*."
21: 6 so many *f* they could not haul the net in.
21: 8 came in the boat, towing the net full of *f*.
21: 9 there with a *f* laid on it and some bread.
21:10 "Bring some of the *f* you just caught,"
21:11 ashore the net loaded with sizable *f*—
21:13 it to them, and did the same with the *f*.
1Cor 15:39 Birds are of their kind, *f* are of theirs.

FISHERMEN (6)

Is 19: 8 The *f* shall mourn and lament,
Jer 16:16 I will send many *f*,
Ez 47:10 *F* shall be standing along it from En-gedi
Mt 4:18 They were *f*. Casting a net into the sea
Mk 1:16 they were *f*.
Lk 5: 2 the *f* had disembarked and were washing

FISHERS (2)

Mt 4:19 after me and I will make you *f* of men."
Mk 1:17 I will make you *f* of men."

FISHES (5)

Gn 9: 2 on the ground and all the *f* of the sea;
1Kgs 5:13 spoke about beasts, birds, reptiles, and *f*.
Ps(s) 8: 9 The birds of the air, the *f* of the sea,
Wis 19:10 *f* the river swarmed with countless frogs.
Zep 1: 3 the birds of the sky, and the *f* of the sea.

FISHHOOKS (1)

Am 4: 2 away with hooks, the last of you with *f*;

FISHING (1)

Mk 3: 9 he told his disciples to have a *f* boat ready

FISH'S (4)

Tb 6: 7 medicinal value is there in the *f* heart,
6: 8 "As regards the *f* heart and liver,
6:17 bridal chamber, take the *f* liver and heart,
8: 2 took the *f* liver and heart from the bag

FIST (5)

Ex 21:18 the other with a stone or with his *f*,
Sir 48:18 *f* at Zion and blasphemed God in his pride.
Is 10:32 shake his *f* at the mount of daughter Zion,
19:16 of the LORD of hosts shaking his *f* at them.
Zep 2:15 passes by her hisses, and shakes his *f*!

FIT (49)

Gn 27:33 with a *f* of uncontrollable trembling.
Nm 1: 3 or more who are *f* for military service.
1:20 were *f* for military service were polled,
1:22 were *f* for military service were polled,
1:24 were *f* for military service were polled,
1:26 were *f* for military service were polled,
1:28 were *f* for military service were polled,
1:30 were *f* for military service were polled,
1:32 were *f* for military service were polled,
1:34 were *f* for military service were polled,
1:36 were *f* for military service were polled,
1:38 were *f* for military service were polled,
1:40 were *f* for military service were polled,
1:42 were *f* for military service were polled,
1:45 or more who were *f* for military service,
26: 2 who are *f* for military service in Israel."
Jos 9:25 do with us what you think *f* and right."
1Sm 24: 5 do with him as you see *f*.' "
2Sm 13:27 Absalom prepared a banquet *f* for royalty.
15:26 let him do to me as he sees *f*."
24: 9 thousand men *f* for military service;
1Chr 5:18 and sixty men *f* for military service.
7:11 two hundred men *f* for military service . . .
7:40 thousand men *f* for military service.
12:26 Of the Simeonites, warriors *f* for battle:
12:34 From Zebulun, men *f* for military service,
12:37 *f* for military service and set in battle
26: 8 were mighty men, *f* for the service.
2Chr 25: 5 hundred thousand picked men *f* for war,
26:11 Uzziah also had a standing army of *f*
Jdt 3: 4 come and deal with them as you see *f*."
Est 8: 8 write in the king's name what you see *f*
2Mc 9: 6 a *f* punishment for him who had tortured.
9:15 but *f* only to be thrown out with their
Eccl 2:26 *f* he gives wisdom and knowledge and joy;
2:26 to be given to whatever man God sees *f*.
Wis 4: 5 unripe for eating, and *f* for nothing.
13:11 his art, produce something *f* for daily use,
Jer 27: 5 and I can give them to whomever I think *f*.
Jon 1:14 for you, LORD, have done as you saw *f*."
Mt 3:11 I am not even *f* to carry his sandals.
Mk 1: 7 *f* to stoop and untie his sandal straps.
Lk 1:25 has seen *f* to remove my reproach among men."
3:16 I am not *f* to loosen his sandal strap.
14:35 *f* for neither the soil nor the manure heap;
Acts 15:38 he was not *f* to be taken along now.
27:12 the harbor was not *f* to pass the winter in,
Rom 1:28 They did not see *f* to acknowledge God,
9:22 with much patience vessels *f* for wrath,

FITNESS (1)

Jb 41: 4 his strength, and the *f* of his armor.

FITS (2)

Is 40:19 plates with gold and *f* with silver chains?
2Pt 2:22 How well the proverb *f* them:

FITTED (5)

Jb 38:31 Have you *f* a curb to the Pleiades,
41: 8 They are *f* each so close to the next that
Sir 27: 2 Like a peg driven between *f* stones,
Lam 3: 9 He has blocked my ways with *f* stones,
Eph 2:21 Through him the whole structure is *f*

FITTEST (1)

2Kgs 10: 3 best and the *f* of your master's offspring,

FITTING (8)

Ps(s) 33: 1 in the LORD, praise from the upright is *f*.
147: 1 it is *f* to praise him.
Wis 13:15 a *f* shrine for it and puts it on the wall,
Acts 1:21 It is entirely *f* therefore,
1Cor 16: 4 If it seems *f* that I should go myself,
1Tm 2: 6 This truth was attested at the *f* time.
Heb 2:10 it was *f* that when bringing many sons to
7:26 *f* that we should have such a high priest:

FITTINGLY (5)

Wis 16: 1 they were *f* punished by similar creatures,
Sir 49:11 How can we *f* praise ZERUBBABEL,
Jn 13:13 me as 'Teacher' and 'Lord,' and *f* enough,
1Cor 7:38 the man who marries his virgin, acts *f*;
1Tm 5: 4 *f* support their parents and grandparents;

FITTINGS (3)

Ex 27:19 All the *f* of the Dwelling,
Nm 3:36 bars, columns, pedestals, and all its *f*,
Sg 5: 5 choice myrrh upon the *f* of the lock.

FIVE (264)

Gn 5: 6 When Seth was one hundred and *f* years old,
5:11 of Enosh was nine hundred and *f* years;
5:30 Lamech lived *f* hundred and ninety-five
5:32 When Noah was *f* hundred years old,
11:11 Shem lived *f* hundred years after the birth
11:32 of Terah was two hundred and *f* years;
14: 9 four kings against *f*.
18:28 are *f* less than fifty innocent people?
18:28 destroy the whole city because of those *f*?"
43:34 was *f* times as large as anyone else's.
45: 6 *f* more years tillage will yield no harvest.
45:11 Since *f* years of famine still lie ahead,
45:22 shekels of silver and *f* sets of garments.
47: 2 He then presented to Pharaoh *f* of his
Ex 21:37 it, he shall restore *f* oxen for the one ox,
26: 3 *F* of the sheets are to be sewed together,
26: 3 and the same for the other *f*.
26: 9 Sew *f* of the sheets,
26:26 *f* for the boards on one side of the
26:27 *f* for those on the other side, and *f* for
26:37 *f* columns of acacia wood for this curtain;
26:37 and cast *f* bronze pedestals for them.
27: 1 square, *f* cubits long and five cubits wide;
27:18 long, fifty cubits wide, and *f* cubits high.
30:23 *f* hundred shekels of free-flowing myrrh;
30:24 *f* hundred shekels of cassia
36:10 *F* of the sheets were sewed together,
36:10 and the same for the other *f*.
36:16 *F* of these sheets were sewed edge to edge
36:31 *f* for the boards on one side of the
36:32 Dwelling, *f* for those on the other side,
36:32 other side, and *f* for those at the rear,
36:38 Its *f* columns,
36:38 their *f* pedestals were of bronze.
38: 1 square, five cubits long and *f* cubits wide;
38:18 twenty cubits long and *f* cubits wide,
38:26 and three thousand *f* hundred and fifty men.
Lv 26: 8 *F* of you will put a hundred of your foes
27: 5 persons between the ages of *f* and twenty,
27: 6 between the ages of one month and *f* years,
27: 6 sum shall be *f* silver shekels for a boy,
Nm 1:21 forty-six thousand *f* hundred were enrolled
1:33 forty thousand *f* hundred were enrolled in
1:41 forty-one thousand *f* hundred were enrolled
1:46 and three thousand, *f* hundred and fifty.
2:11 census to forty-six thousand *f* hundred.]
2:19 in the census to forty thousand *f* hundred.]
2:28 the census to forty-one thousand *f* hundred.]
2:32 and three thousand *f* hundred and fifty.
3:22 they numbered seven thousand *f* hundred.
3:47 shall take *f* shekels for each individual,
4:48 was eight thousand *f* hundred and eighty,
7:17 *f* rams, *f* goats, and *f* yearling lambs
7:23 *f* rams, *f* goats, and *f* yearling lambs
7:29 *f* rams, *f* goats, and *f* yearling lambs
7:35 *f* rams, *f* goats, and *f* yearling lambs
7:41 *f* rams, *f* goats, and *f* yearling lambs
7:47 *f* rams, *f* goats, and *f* yearling lambs
7:53 *f* rams, *f* goats, and *f* yearling lambs
7:59 *f* rams, *f* goats, and *f* yearling lambs
7:65 *f* rams, *f* goats, and *f* yearling lambs
7:71 *f* rams, *f* goats, and *f* yearling lambs
7:77 *f* rams, *f* goats, and *f* yearling lambs
7:83 *f* rams, *f* goats, and *f* yearling lambs
11:19 it, not for one day, or two days, or *f*,
18:16 it is fixed at *f* silver shekels according
26:18 thousand *f* hundred men were registered.
26:22 thousand *f* hundred men were registered.
26:27 thousand *f* hundred men were registered.
26:37 thousand *f* hundred men were registered.
31: 8 battle, they killed the *f* Midianite kings:
31:28 one out of every *f* hundred persons,
31:36 and thirty-seven thousand *f* hundred sheep,
31:39 thirty thousand *f* hundred asses,
31:43 and thirty-seven thousand *f* hundred sheep,
31:45 oxen, thirty thousand *f* hundred asses,
Jos 8:12 [He took about *f* thousand men and set them
10: 5 The *f* Amorite kings,
10:16 Meanwhile the *f* kings who had fled,
10:17 When Joshua was told that the *f* kings had
10:22 the cave and bring out those *f* kings to me."
10:23 out to him from the cave the *f* kings,
10:26 killed them, and hanged them on *f* trees,
13: 3 by the *f* lords of the Philistines in Gaza,
Jgs 3: 3 the *f* lords of the Philistines;
18: 2 of *f* valiant men of Zorah and Eshtaol,
18: 7 So the *f* men went on and came to Laish.
18: 8 When the *f* returned to their kinsmen in
18:14 The *f* men who had gone to reconnoiter the
18:17 Meanwhile the *f* men who had gone to
20:45 picked off *f* thousand men among them,
1Sm 6: 4 *F* golden hemorrhoids and five golden mice
6:16 the *f* Philistine lords returned to Ekron
6:18 the Philistines belonging to the *f* lords,
16:20 Then Jesse took *f* loaves of bread,
17: 5 of scale armor weighing *f* thousand shekels,
17:40 David selected *f* smooth stones from the
21: 4 Give me *f* loaves,
25:18 *f* dressed sheep, five seahs of roasted
25:42 *f* maids following in attendance upon her.
2Sm 4: 4 He was *f* years old when the news about
21: 8 and the *f* sons of Saul's daughter Merob
24: 9 in Judah, *f* hundred thousand.
1Kgs 5:12 and his songs numbered a thousand and *f*.
6: 6 Its lowest story was *f* cubits wide,
6:10 annex, with its lowest story *f* cubits high,
6:24 Each wing of a cherub measured *f* cubits so
7:16 of the columns, each of them *f* cubits high.
7:23 measured ten cubits across, *f* in height,
7:39 *f* on the south side of the temple and five
7:49 *f* to the right and five to the left before
9:23 in the work numbered *f* hundred and fifty.
2Kgs 6:25 a kab of wild onion for *f* pieces of silver.
7:13 let some of us take *f* of the abandoned
13:19 "You should have struck *f* or six times;
25:17 a bronze capital *f* cubits high;
25:19 *f* men in the personal service of the king
1Chr 2: 4 and Zerah, so that he had *f* sons in all.
2: 6 Ethan, Heman, Calcol, and Darda *f* in all.
3:20 Ohel, Berechiah, Hasadiah, Jushabhesed *f*.
4:32 Ain, Rimmon, Tochen, and Ashan *f* cities,
4:42 *F* hundred of them (the Simeonites) went to
7: 3 All *f* of these were chiefs.
7: 7 Ezbon, Uzzi, Uzziel, Jerimoth, and Iri *f*.
11:23 the Egyptian, a huge man *f* cubits tall.
29: 7 of the house of God *f* thousand talents
2Chr 3:12 wing of each cherub, *f* cubits in length,
3:12 the other wing, also *f* cubits in length,
3:15 the capital topping each was of *f* cubits.
4: 2 round, ten cubits in diameter, *f* in depth,
4: 6 placing *f* of them to the right and five to
4: 7 nave, *f* to the right and five to the left.
4: 8 nave, *f* to the right and five to the left;
6:13 platform *f* cubits long, five cubits wide,
13:17 *f* hundred thousand picked men of Israel
26:13 seven thousand *f* hundred fighting men
35: 9 to the Levites *f* thousand Passover victims,
35: 9 victims, together with *f* hundred oxen.
Ezr 1:11 *f* thousand four hundred pieces.
2:69 of gold, *f* thousand minas of silver,
Neh 7:69 for priests, and *f* hundred minas of silver.
Jdt 7:17 camp, together with *f* thousand Assyrians.
7:30 us wait *f* days more for the Lord our God,
8: 9 city to the Assyrians at the end of *f* days,
8:11 at the end of *f* days unless within that time
8:15 wish to come to our aid within the *f* days,
16:23 the advanced age of a hundred and *f*.
Est 9: 6 Jews killed and destroyed *f* hundred men.
9:12 have killed and destroyed *f* hundred men,
1Mc 2: 2 He had *f* sons:
4: 1 Now Gorgias took *f* thousand infantry and a
4:28 thousand picked men and *f* thousand cavalry,
4:34 and about *f* thousand of Lysias' men fell
6:35 helmets, and *f* hundred picked cavalry.
7:32 About *f* hundred men of Nicanor's army fell;
10:42 the dues of *f* thousand silver shekels that
15:31 pay me *f* hundred talents of silver for the
15:31 *f* hundred talents more for the tribute
2Mc 2:23 of Cyrene set forth in detail in *f* volumes,
10:29 from the heavens *f* majestic men riding on
12:10 least *f* thousand foot soldiers, and *f* hundred
14:39 more than *f* hundred soldiers to arrest him.
Jb 1: 3 *f* hundred yoke of oxen, *f* hundred she-asses,
Is 7: 9 But within sixty years and *f*,
17: 6 top, four or *f* on its fruitful branches,
19:18 On that day there shall be *f* cities in the
30:17 if *f* threaten you,
Jer 52:22 *f* cubits high surmounted the one pillar,
Ez 40: 7 between the cells measured *f* cubits.
40:48 on each side, which were *f* cubits.
41: 2 either side of it measured *f* cubits each.
41: 9 enclosed the side chambers was *f* cubits.
41:11 surrounding the open space was *f* cubits.
41:12 the building was *f* cubits thick all around,
42:16 *f* hundred cubits by his measuring rod.
42:17 *f* hundred cubits by the measuring rod.
42:18 *f* hundred cubits by the measuring rod.
42:19 *f* hundred cubits by the measuring rod.
42:20 *f* hundred cubits long and five hundred
45: 2 plot, *f* hundred by five hundred cubits,
45: 6 you shall designate a strip *f* thousand cubits
48:15 The remaining *f* thousand cubits along the
Mt 14:17 "but *f* loaves and a couple of fish."
14:19 He took the *f* loaves and two fish,
14:21 Those who ate were about *f* thousand,
16: 9 remember the five loaves among *f* thousand
25: 2 *F* of them were foolish, while the other *f*
25:15 one he disbursed *f* thousand silver pieces,
25:16 Immediately the man who received the *f*
25:16 went to invest it and made another *f*.
25:20 The man who had received the *f* thousand
25:20 came forward bringing the additional *f*.
25:20 he said, 'you let me have *f* thousand.
25:20 See, I have made *f* thousand more.'
Mk 6:38 they learned the number they answered, *F*,
6:41 Then, taking the *f* loaves and the two fish,
6:44 eaten the loaves numbered *f* thousand men.
8:19 I broke the five loaves for the *f* thousand,
Lk 1:24 She went into seclusion for *f* months,
7:41 one owed a total of *f* hundred coins,
9:13 have nothing but *f* loaves and two fish.
9:14 (There were about *f* thousand men.)
9:16 Then, taking the *f* loaves and the two fish,
12: 6 Are not *f* sparrows sold for a few pennies?
12:52 a household of *f* will be divided three
14:19 'I have bought *f* yoke of oxen and I am
16:28 my father's house where I have *f* brothers.
19:18 investment, my lord, has netted you *f*.'
19:19 His word to him was, 'Take over *f* villages.'
Jn 4:18 "The fact is, you have had *f*,
5: 2 Its *f* porticoes were crowded with sick
6: 9 *f* barley loaves and a couple of dried fish,
6:10 though the men numbered about *f* thousand,
6:13 who had been fed with the *f* barley loaves.

Acts 4: 4 number of the men came to about *f* thousand.
20: 6 *F* days later we joined them in Troas,
24: 1 *F* days later, the high priest Ananias
1Cor 14:19 rather say *f* intelligible words to instruct
15: 6 he was seen by *f* hundred brothers at once,
2Cor 11:24 *F* times at the hands of the Jews I
Rv 9: 5 them but only to torture them for *f* months;
9:10 was enough venom to harm men for *f* months.
17:10 *f* have already fallen,

FIX (12)

Dt 4:39 why you must now know, and *f* in your heart,
2Sm 7:10 I will *f* a place for my people Israel;
Jb 14:13 would *f* a time for me,
39: 2 and *f* the time of their bringing forth?
Ps(s) 17:11 crouching to the ground, they *f* their gaze,
Sir 34: 6 by the Most High, *f* not your heart on it;
Is 22:23 I will *f* him like a peg in a sure spot,
Ez 4: 3 *F* your gaze on it:
Am 8: 5 the shekel, and *f* our scales for cheating!
9: 4 I will *f* my gaze upon them for evil,
2Cor 4:18 We do not *f* our gaze on what is seen but
Heb 3: 1 a heavenly calling, *f* your eyes on Jesus,

FIXED (43)

Gn 1:14 Let them mark the *f* times,
47:22 Since the priests had a *f* allowance from
Lv 27: 2 who are to be ransomed at a *f* sum of money,
27: 3 the ages of twenty and sixty, the *f* sum,
27: 5 *f* sum shall be twenty shekels for a youth,
27: 6 the *f* sum shall be five silver shekels for
27: 7 *f* sum shall be fifteen shekels for a man,
27: 8 took the vow is too poor to meet the *f* sum,
27:27 by paying one fifth more than its *f* value.
27:27 redeemed, it shall be sold at its *f* value.
Nm 18:16 it is *f* at five silver shekels according
2Kgs 25:30 a perpetual allowance, in *f* daily amounts,
2Chr 8:13 and on the *f* festivals three times a year:
20:33 *f* their hearts on the God of their fathers.
Neh 11:23 and there was a *f* schedule for the singers
Jb 14: 5 you have *f* the limit which he cannot pass.
28:25 the wind, and *f* the scope of the waters;
Ps(s) 33:14 From his *f* throne he beholds all who dwell
74:17 You *f* all the limits of the land;
104: 5 You *f* the earth upon its foundation,
104: 8 valleys to the place you had *f* for them.
Prv 8:28 he *f* fast the foundations of the earth,
Eccl 12:11 like *f* spikes are the topics given by one
Wis 2: 5 be deferred because it is *f* with a seal;
Sir 24:10 before him, and in Zion I *f* my abode.
38:28 His eyes are *f* on the tool he is shaping.
43: 7 which we know the feast days and *f* dates,
44:23 He *f* the boundaries for his tribes,
Is 22:25 the peg *f* in a sure spot shall give way,
Jer 52:34 a perpetual allowance, in *f* daily amounts,
Ez 33:31 and their desires are *f* on dishonest gain.
Mt 27:29 crown out of thorns they *f* it on his head,
Mk 10:27 Jesus *f* his gaze on them and said,
Lk 3:13 nothing over and above your *f* amount."
4:20 in the synagogue had their eyes *f* on him.
16:26 you and us there is *f* a great abyss,
Jn 19: 2 a crown of thorns and *f* it on his head,
Acts 3: 4 Peter *f* his gaze on the man; so did John.
17:26 and *f* the boundaries of their regions.
1Tm 4:10 our hopes are *f* on the living God who is
Heb 12: 2 let us keep our eyes *f* on Jesus,
2Pt 1:19 Keep your attention closely *f* on it,
1Jn 4:20 If anyone says, "My love is *f* on God,"

FIXES (1)

Prv 17:24 man of intelligence *f* his gaze on wisdom,

FIXING (2)

Ez 4: 7 *F* your gaze on the siege of Jerusalem,
Mt 27:66 of the guard, after *f* a seal to the stone.

FIXTURES (1)

1Mc 1:21 lampstand for the light with all its *f*,

FLAG (1)

Is 30:17 on the mountaintop, like a *f* on the hill.

FLAGGING (1)

Ps(s) 77: 3 night my hands are stretched out without *f*;

FLAGRANT (1)

1Tm 5:24 sins are *f* and cry out for judgment now,

FLAGSTAFF (1)

Is 30:17 you are left like a *f* on the mountaintop,

FLAKES (1)

Ex 16:14 were fine *f* like hoarfrost on the ground.

FLAME (33)

Jgs 13:20 as the *f* rose to the sky from the altar,
13:20 of the LORD ascended in the *f* of the altar.
16: 9 thread of tow is severed by a whiff of *f*;
2Sm 22: 9 he kindled coals into *f*.
22:13 of his presence coals were kindled to *f*.
2Mc 1:32 As soon as this was done, a *f* blazed up,
Jb 15:30 *f* shall wither him up in his early growth,
18: 5 no *f* brightens his hearth.
41:13 a *f* pours from his mouth.
Ps(s) 18: 9 from his mouth that kindled coals into *f*.
18:13 of his presence coals were kindled to *f*.
83:15 as a *f* setting the mountains ablaze,
106:18 a *f* consumed the wicked.
Wis 10:17 for them by day and a starry *f* by night.
16:18 For now the *f* was tempered so that the
Sir 28:12 you blow upon a spark, it quickens into *f*,
28:22 among the just nor scorch them in its *f*,
Is 5:24 stubble, as dry grass shrivels in the *f*,
10:17 will become a fire, Israel's Holy One a *f*,
29: 6 storm, and the *f* of consuming fire.
30:30 In raging fury and *f* of consuming fire,
44:20 cannot save itself when the *f* consumes it;
Jer 44: 6 my anger poured forth in *f* over the cities
Ez 21: 3 The blazing *f* shall not be quenched,
Dn 3:88 raging *f* and delivered us from the fire.
Jl 1:19 *f* has enkindled all the trees of the field.
2: 3 fire devours, and after them a *f* enkindles;
2: 5 crackling of a fiery *f* devouring stubble;
Ob 1:18 be a fire, and the house of Joseph a *f*;
Na 3: 3 Cavalry charging, The *f* of the sword,
Acts 7:30 Sinai in the *f* of a burning thornbush.
2Tm 1: 6 I remind you to stir into *f* the gift of
Jas 3: 6 The tongue is such a *f*.

FLAMES (34)

Dt 32:22 licking with *f* the roots of the mountains,
Jgs 20:40 saw the whole city in *f* against the sky
2Mc 12: 9 of the *f* was visible as far as Jerusalem,
Ps(s) 29: 7 The voice of the LORD strikes fiery *f*;
Sg 8: 6 its *f* are a blazing fire.
Wis 19:21 *F*, by contrast, neither consumed
Sir 5: 9 For suddenly his wrath *f* forth;
16: 6 upon a godless people wrath *f* out.
22:24 Before *f* burst forth an oven smokes;
43:22 and the flowering plains as though by *f*,
51: 4 from *f* that hemmed me in on every side;
Is 1:31 and there shall be none to quench the *f*.
9: 4 in blood, will be burned as fuel for *f*.
33:14 who of us can live with the everlasting *f*?"
43: 2 the *f* shall not consume you.
47:14 save themselves from the spreading *f*.
50:11 kindle *f* and carry about you fiery darts;
66:15 heat and his punishment with fiery *f*.
Jer 29:22 whom the king of Babylon roasted in the *f*."
51:58 for the *f* the peoples weary themselves.
Ez 22:20 a furnace and smelted in the roaring *f*,
Dn 3:22 the *f* devoured the men who threw Shadrach,
3:24 They walked about in the *f*,
3:47 *f* rose forty-nine cubits above the furnace,
3:49 drove the fiery *f* out of the furnace,
7: 9 His throne was *f* of fire,
11:33 will become victims of the sword, of *f*,
Hos 8: 6 artisan no god at all, Destined for the *f*—
11: 9 I will not let the *f* consume you.
Hb 2:13 peoples toil for the *f*,
Lk 16:24 my tongue, for I am tortured in these *f*.'
Jas 3: 6 Its *f* encircle our course from birth,
2Pt 3:12 the heavens will be destroyed in *f* and the
Rv 8: 8 mountain all in *f* was cast into the sea.

FLAMING (21)

Gn 15:17 appeared a smoking brazier and a *f* torch,
Ex 3: 2 appeared to him in fire *f* out of a bush.
2Kgs 2:11 a *f* chariot and flaming horses came
1Mc 6:39 their brightness and blazed like *f* torches.
Ps(s) 104: 4 your messengers, and *f* fire your ministers.
Wis 17: 5 nor did the *f* brilliance of the stars
18: 3 you furnished the *f* pillar which was a
Sir 3:29 Water quenches a *f* fire,
8:10 sinner, lest you be consumed in his *f* fire.
21: 9 they will end in a *f* fire.
45:19 miracle, and consumed them with his *f* fire.
48: 1 prophet whose words were as a *f* furnace.
Is 4: 5 by day and a light of *f* fire by night.
Jer 12:13 their harvest, the *f* anger of the LORD.
Lam 2: 3 Jacob like a *f* fire devouring all about it.
2Thes 1: 8 when "with *f* power he will inflict
Heb 1: 7 angels winds, and his ministers *f* fire";
10:27 a *f* fire to consume the adversaries of God.
Rv 4: 5 before it burned seven *f* torches,
12: 3 it was a huge dragon, *f* red,

FLANK (8)

Gn 49:13 ships], and his *f* shall be based on Sidon.
Jos 15: 8 the southern *f* of the Jebusites [that is,
15:11 extended along the northern *f* of Ekron,
18:12 and went over the northern *f* of Jericho,
18:13 over to the southern *f* of Luz (that is,
18:16 along the southern *f* of the Jebusites,
18:18 the northern *f* of the Arabah overlook,
18:19 across the northern *f* of Beth-hoglah

FLANKED (2)

1Mc 4: 7 strong and breastplated, *f* with cavalry,
9:12 *F* by the two squadrons,

FLANKING (2)

1Sm 14: 4 *F* the ravine through which Jonathan
Ez 41: 3 and measured the pilasters *f* that entrance,

FLANKS (3)

Jdt 15: 5 struck the enemy's *f* with great slaughter,
1Mc 6:38 one or the other of the two *f* of the army,
2Mc 15:20 and their cavalry stationed on the *f*.

FLARE (8)

Ex 22:23 My wrath will *f* up,
Dt 6:15 *f* up against you and he destroy you from
7: 4 *f* up against you and quickly destroy you.
11:17 For then the wrath of the LORD will *f* up
29:19 and jealousy will *f* up against that man,
31:17 that time my anger will *f* up against them;
Jos 23:16 the anger of the LORD will *f* up against
Sir 28:11 Pitch and resin make fire *f* up,

FLARED (14)

Ex 32:19 With that, Moses' wrath *f* up,
Nm 11: 1 and when he heard it his wrath *f* up so
11:33 the LORD's wrath *f* up against the people,
22:22 now the anger of God *f* up at him for going,
25: 3 Peor, the LORD's anger *f* up against Israel.
32:10 At that time the wrath of the LORD *f* up,
Jos 7: 1 of the LORD *f* up against the Israelites.
Jgs 2:14 the anger of the LORD *f* up against Israel,
3: 8 the anger of the LORD *f* up against them,
2Sm 22: 8 trembled and shook when his wrath *f* up.
24: 1 The LORD's anger against Israel *f* again,
Est 1:12 At this the king's wrath *f* up,
Ps(s) 18: 8 trembled and shook when his wrath *f* up.
118:12 bees, they *f* up like fire among thorns;

FLARES (2)

Is 50:11 your own fire and by the *f* you have burnt!
Hos 7: 6 in the morning it *f* like a blazing fire.

FLASH (10)

Ps(s) 144: 6 *F* forth lightning,
Wis 11:18 or *f* terrible sparks from their eyes.
Jer 4:20 my tents are ravaged; in a *f*,
10:13 He makes the lightning *f* in the rain,
51:16 He makes the lightning *f* in the rain,
Ez 21:15 to *f* lightning has it been burnished.
21:20 for slaughter, Fashioned to *f* lightning,
21:33 burnished to consume and to *f* lightning,
Na 3: 3 The flame of the sword, the *f* of the spear,
Mt 28: 3 In appearance he resembled a *f* of

FLASHED (7)

Ex 9:23 Lightning *f* toward the earth,
9:24 lightning constantly *f* through the hail,
2Sm 22:15 he *f* lightning and routed them.
Wis 16:22 in the hail and *f* lightning in the rain.
17: 6 fearful fires *f* through upon them;
Acts 9: 3 a light from the sky suddenly *f* about him.
22: 6 light from the sky suddenly *f* all about me.

FLASHES (14)

2Mc 5: 3 flights of arrows and *f* of gold ornaments,
Jb 37:11 laden, as they scatter their *f* of light.
39:23 *f* the spear and the javelin.
41:10 When he sneezes, light *f* forth;
Sir 32:10 Like the lightning that *f* before a storm
Bar 6:60 Likewise the lightning, when it *f*,
Ez 1:13 and from it came forth *f* of lightning.
Am 5: 9 Who *f* destruction upon the strong,
Mt 24:27 the lightning from the east *f* to the west,
Lk 17:24 *f* from one end of the sky to the other.
Rv 4: 5 came *f* of lightning and peals of thunder;
8: 5 of thunder and *f* of lightning followed,
11:19 were *f* of lightning and peals of thunder,
16:18 followed lightning *f* and peals of thunder,

FLASHING (6)

Dt 32:41 I live forever, I will sharpen my *f* sword,
Ps(s) 76: 4 There he shattered the *f* shafts of the bow,
105:32 hail, with *f* fires throughout their land.
Ez 1: 4 with *f* fire [enveloped in brightness],
Na 2: 5 like firebrands, *f* like lightning bolts.
Hb 3:11 arrows, at the gleam of your *f* spear.

FLASK (11)

1Sm 10: 1 Then, from a *f* he had with him.
2Kgs 9: 1 your loins, take this *f* of oil with you,
9: 3 From the *f* you have,
Jdt 10: 5 a leather *f* of wine and a cruse of oil.
Ps(s) 33: 7 He gathers the waters of the sea as in a *f*;
56: 9 my tears are stored in your *f*;
119:83 shriveled like a leathern *f* in the smoke,
Sir 39:17 word the waters become still as in a *f*;
Jer 19: 1 Go, buy a potter's earthen *f*.
19:10 And you shall break the *f* in the sight of
48:11 He was not poured from one *f* to another,

FLASKS (2)

Jer 48:12 they shall empty his *f* and break his jars.
Mt 25: 4 took *f* of oil as well as their torches.

FLAT (2)

Jer 5:17 They will beat *f* with the sword the
Mt 5:13 But what if salt goes *f*?

FLATS (1)

Jb 39: 6 his home and the salt *f* his dwelling.

FLATTER (3)

Ps(s) 5:10 they *f* with their tongue.
81:16 who hated the LORD would seek to *f* me,
Wis 14:17 to honor, out of zeal to *f* him when absent,

FLATTERED (2)

2Mc 4:24 he *f* him with such an air of authority
Ps(s) 78:36 But they *f* him with their mouths and lied

FLATTERIES (1)

Is 30:10 speak *f* to us,

FLATTERING (5)

Jb 32:21 to anyone, nor give *f* titles to any.
Prv 26:28 owner's enemy, and the *f* mouth works ruin.
28:23 thanks in the end than one with a *f* tongue.
Rom 16:18 simpleminded with smooth and *f* speech.
1Thes 2: 5 of *f* words or greed under any pretext,

FLATTERS (1)

Prv 29: 5 The man who *f* his neighbor is spreading a

FLATTERY (3)

Jb 32:22 For I know nought of *f*;
Sir 41:16 Before prince and ruler, of *f*;
Jude 1:16 Whenever it is expedient, they resort to *f*.

FLAUNT (4)

Sir 7: 5 and before the king *f* not your wisdom.
10:25 *F* not your wisdom in managing your affairs,
32: 4 and *f* not your wisdom at the wrong time.
Jer 51: 3 draw his bow, and *f* his coat of mail;

FLAVOR (4)

Jb 6: 6 Is there *f* in the white of an egg?
Wis 16:21 was blended to whatever *f* each one wished,
Mt 5:13 How can you restore its *f*?
Lk 14:34 loses its *f* what good is it for seasoning?

FLAVORED (1)

Mt 27:34 they gave him a drink of wine *f* with gall,

FLAW (1)

Rv 14: 5 they are indeed without *f*.

FLAX (7)

Ex 9:31 Now the *f* and the barley were ruined,
9:31 the barley was in ear and the *f* in bud.
Jos 2: 6 among her stalks of *f* spread out there.
Jgs 15:14 the ropes around his arms became as *f* that
Prv 31:13 and *f* and makes cloth with skillful hands.
Hos 2: 7 my bread and my water, my wool and my *f*,
2:11 I will snatch away my wool and my *f*,

FLAY (1)

Mi 3: 3 of my people, and *f* their skin from them,

FLEA (2)

1Sm 24:15 A dead dog, or a single *f*!
26:20 to seek a single *f* as if he were hunting

FLED (141)

Gn 14:10 and as the kings of Sodom and Gomorrah *f*,
14:10 these, while the rest *f* to the mountains.
31:22 day, word came to Laban that Jacob had *f*.
31:40 frost by night, while sleep *f* from my eyes!
39:13 left his cloak in her hand as he *f* outside,
39:18 he left his cloak beside me and *f* outside."
Ex 2:15 But Moses *f* from him and stayed in the
14: 5 the king of Egypt that the people had *f*,
Nm 16:34 Israelites near them *f* at their shrieks,
Jos 8:15 *f* in seeming defeat toward the desert,
10:11 While they *f* before Israel along the
10:16 Meanwhile the five kings who had *f*,
20: 6 back home to his own city from which he *f*."
Jgs 1: 6 Canaanites and Perizzites, Adonibezek *f*.
4:15 dismounted from his chariot and *f* on foot.
4:17 had *f* on foot to the tent of Jael,
7:22 The army *f* as far as Beth-shittah in the
8:12 Zebah and Zalmunna *f*.
9:40 Abimelech routed him, and he *f* before him;
9:51 word all the citizens of the city, *f* there,
11: 3 So Jephthah had *f* from his brothers and
20:45 *f* through the desert to the rock Rimmon.
20:47 But six hundred others who turned and *f*
1Sm 4:10 every man *f* to his own tent.
4:12 A Benjaminite *f* from the battlefield and
4:16 I *f* from there today."
4:17 "Israel *f* from the Philistines;
20: 1 David *f* from the sheds near Ramah,
22:20 named Abiathar, escaped and *f* to David.
23: 6 son of Ahimelech, who had *f* to David,
27: 4 Saul was told that David had *f* to Gath,
30:17 young men, who mounted their camels and *f*.
31: 7 had *f* and that Saul and his sons were dead,
31: 7 they too abandoned their cities and *f*.
2Sm 1: 4 He answered that the soldiers had *f* the
4: 3 the Beerothites *f* to Gittaim,
4: 4 Jezreel, and his nurse took him up and *f*.
10:13 the Arameans for battle, they *f* before him.
10:14 Arameans had *f*, also *f* from Abishai
13:29 princes rose, mounted their mules, and *f*.
18:17 all the Israelites *f* to their own tents.
19: 9 Israelites had *f* to their separate tents,
19:10 he has *f* from the country before Absalom,
23:11 When the soldiers *f* from the Philistines,
1Kgs 2:28 he *f* to the tent of the LORD and seized
2:29 King Solomon was told that Joab had *f* to
11:17 *f* toward Egypt with some Edomite servants
11:23 the son of Eliada, who had *f* from his lord,
12: 2 in Egypt, where he had *f* from King Solomon,
19: 3 Elijah was afraid and *f* for his life,
20:20 The Arameans *f* with Israel pursuing them,
20:30 thousand of them, *f* into the city of Aphek,
20:30 Ben-hadad, too, *f*, and took refuge
2Kgs 3:24 and attacked the Moabites, who *f* from them.
7: 7 Then in the twilight they *f*,
8:21 Then his army *f* homeward.
9:10 Then he opened the door and *f*.
9:23 Joram reigned about and *f*,
9:27 king of Judah, *f* toward Beth-haggan.
14:12 and all the Judean soldiery *f* homeward.
14:19 against him in Jerusalem, he *f* to Lachish.
19:37 the sword and *f* into the land of Ararat.
1Chr 10: 1 the Israelites *f* before the Philistines,
10: 7 in the rout, they left their cities and *f*;
19:14 but they *f* before him.
19:15 the Ammonites saw that the Arameans had *f*,
19:18 But the Arameans *f* before Israel,
2Chr 10: 2 in Egypt where he had *f* from King Solomon,
13:16 The Israelites *f* before Judah,
14:11 before Asa and Judah, and they *f*.
15: 9 for many had *f* to him from Israel when
25:22 and all the Judean soldiers *f* homeward.
25:27 hence he *f* to Lachish.
26:20 He himself *f* willingly,
Tb 8: 3 the odor of the fish, *f* into Upper Egypt;
Jdt 5: 8 So they *f* to Mesopotamia and dwelt there a
11: 3 tell me why you *f* from them and came to us.
11:16 handmaid, learned all this, I *f* from them.
15: 2 in all directions, and *f* along every road,
1Mc 1:18 was frightened at his presence and *f*,
1:38 them the inhabitants of Jerusalem *f* away,
2:28 he *f* to the mountains with his sons,
2:44 the survivors *f* to the Gentiles for safety.
3:11 Many fell wounded, and the rest *f*.
3:24 rest *f* to the country of the Philistines.
4:14 were defeated and *f* toward the plain.
4:22 attack, they all *f* to Philistine territory.
5: 9 these then *f* to the stronghold of Dathema.
5:11 seize this stronghold to which we have *f*.
5:43 and *f* to the temple enclosure at Carnaim.
7:32 the rest *f* to the City of David.
7:44 was dead, they threw down their arms and *f*.
9:18 Then Judas fell, and the rest *f*.
9:33 and they *f* to the desert of Tekoa and
9:40 after the survivors *f* toward the mountain,
10:49 battle, and when the army of Demetrius *f*,
10:64 with which he was clothed, they all *f*.
10:83 enemy *f* to Azotus and entered Beth-dagon,
11:16 Alexander *f* to Arabia to seek protection.
11:55 against Demetrius, who was routed and *f*.
11:70 All of Jonathan's men *f*;
15:11 Pursued by Antiochus, Trypho *f* to Dor,
16: 8 and the rest *f* toward the stronghold.
2Mc 5: 8 king of the Arabs, he *f* from city to city,
8:35 laid aside his fine clothes and *f* alone
10:32 however *f* to a well-fortified stronghold
12:35 Then Gorgias *f* to Marisa.
Jb 30: 3 lot, they who *f* to the parched wastelands:
Ps(s) 104: 7 At your rebuke they *f*,
114: 3 The sea beheld and *f*; Jordan turned back.
Wis 10: 6 he *f* as fire descended upon Pentapolis
10:10 the just man *f* from his brother's anger,
Sir 27:20 he has *f* like a gazelle from the trap.
Is 10:29 Ramah is in terror, Gibeah of Saul has *f*.
20: 6 We have *f* here for help and deliverance
22: 3 leaders fled away together, *f* afar off;
37:38 the sword and *f* into the land of Ararat.
Jer 9: 9 of the air as well as beasts, all have *f*,
26:21 Uriah heard of it and *f* in fear to Egypt.
39: 4 them, he and all his warriors *f* by night,
41:15 and *f* to the Ammonites with eight men.
46:15 Why has Apis *f*,
50: 3 there, because man and beast have *f* away.
52: 8 Jericho, while his whole army *f* from him.
Lam 1: 3 Judah has *f* into exile from oppression and
Dn 10: 7 they *f* and hid themselves,
Hos 12:13 When Jacob *f* to the land of Aram,
Jon 4: 2 This is why I *f* at first to Tarshish.
Mt 26:56 Then all the disciples deserted him and *f*.
Mk 14:50 With that, all deserted him and *f*.
16: 8 *f* from the tomb bewildered and trembling;
Jn 6:15 king, so he *f* back to the mountain alone.
Acts 7:29 On hearing this, Moses *f*.
14: 6 they *f* to the Lycaonian towns of Lystra
19:16 they *f* from his house naked and bruised.
2Pt 1: 4 you who have *f* a world corrupted by lust
2:20 When men have *f* a polluted world by
Rv 12: 6 The woman herself *f* into the desert,
16:20 Every island *f* and mountains disappeared.
20:11 The earth and the sky *f* from his presence

FLEE (82)

Gn 19:17 *F* for your life! Don't look back
19:19 But I cannot *f* to the hills to keep the
19:20 Let me *f* there
27:43 *f* at once to my brother Laban in Haran,
Ex 21:13 may *f* to a place which I will set apart
Lv 26:36 rustle behind them, they will *f* headlong,
Nm 10:35 and those who hate you may *f* before you."
Dt 28: 7 direction, they will *f* before you in seven.
28:25 direction, you will *f* before them in seven,
Jos 8: 5 did the last time, we will *f* from them.
20: 3 may *f* for asylum from the avenger of blood.
20: 4 To one of these cities the killer shall *f*,
20: 9 a person accidentally might *f* to escape
1Sm 14:13 as the Philistines turned to *f* him,
2Sm 17: 2 When all the people with him *f*,
18: 3 For if we should *f*, we shall not count;
24:13 or to *f* from your enemy three months while
1Kgs 12:18 to mount his chariot to *f* to Jerusalem,
2Kgs 9: 3 Then open the door and *f* without delay."
2Chr 10:18 to mount his chariot and *f* to Jerusalem.
Tb 6:18 *f* and never again show himself near her.
14: 4 take your children and *f* into Media for I
Jdt 14: 3 seize them, and they will *f* before you.
1Mc 9:10 me to do such a thing as to *f* from them!
10:73 is not a stone or a pebble or a place to *f*."
Jb 9:25 are swifter than a runner, they *f* away;
27:22 dragon as from his hand it strives to *f*.
Ps(s) 11: 1 say to me, *F* to the mountain like a bird!
17: 7 O savior of those who *f* from their foes
31:12 they who see me abroad *f* from me.
55: 8 Far away I would *f*;
60: 6 to which they may *f* out of bowshot
68: 2 and those who hate him *f* before him.
114: 5 Why is it, O sea, that you *f*?
139: 7 from your presence where can I *f*?
Prv 28:17 with human blood were to *f* to the grave,
Sir 21: 2 *F* from sin as from a serpent.
38:10 *F* wickedness;
Is 10: 3 To whom will you *f* for help?
13:14 turn to his kindred and *f* to his own land.
17:13 rebuke them, and they shall *f* far away;
20: 6 where can we *f* now?"
21:15 They *f* from the sword,
30:16 "No," you said, "Upon horses we will *f*."
30:16 —Very well, *f*! Upon swift steeds
30:17 if five threaten you, you shall *f*,
31: 8 He shall *f* before the sword,
31: 9 shall *f* in terror from his standard,
33: 3 At the roaring sound, peoples *f*;
35:10 and gladness, sorrow and mourning will *f*.
48:20 Go forth from Babylon, *f* from Chaldea!
51:11 and gladness, sorrow and mourning will *f*.
Jer 6: 1 *F*, sons of Benjamin, out of Jerusalem!
41:17 they stopped, intending to *f* into Egypt.
46: 5 They *f* headlong without making a stand.
46: 6 The swift cannot *f*, nor the hero escape:
46:21 They too turn and *f* together,
48: 6 *F*, save your lives,
49: 8 *F*, retreat, hide in deep holes,
49:24 Damascus is weakened, she turns to *f*,
49:30 *F*! leave your homes, hide
50: 8 *F* from Babylon,
51: 6 *F* out of Babylon;
Bar 6:54 gods, though the priests *f* and are safe,
Ez 7:16 Even those who escape and *f* to the
Dn 4:11 let the beasts *f* its shade,
Am 2:16 of warriors shall *f* naked on that day,
5:19 As if a man went to *f* from a lion,
7:12 you, visionary, *f* to the land of Judah!
9: 1 not one shall *f*,
Jon 1: 3 ready to *f* to Tarshish away from the LORD.
Zec 2:10 *F* from the land of the north,
Mt 2:13 the child and his mother, and *f* to Egypt.
3: 7 Who told you to *f* from the wrath to come?
10:23 persecute you in one town, *f* to the next.
24:16 those in Judea must *f* to the mountains.
24:20 not have to *f* in winter or on a sabbath,
Mk 13:14 in Judea must *f* to the mountains.
Lk 3: 7 Who told you to *f* from the wrath to come?
21:21 Judea at the time must *f* to the mountains;
Jn 10: 5 such a one they will *f*,
1Tm 6:11 Man of God that you are, *f* from all this.

FLEECE (8)

Jgs 6:37 this woolen *f* on the threshing floor.

6:37 If dew comes on the *f* alone,
6:38 next morning he wrung the dew from the *f.*
6:39 Let me make just one more test with the *f.*
6:39 Let the *f* alone be dry,
6:40 the *f* alone was dry,
Jdt 12:15 the *f* Bagoas had furnished for her daily use
Jb 31:20 me when warmed with the *f* of my sheep;

FLEEING (22)

Gn 35: 1 while you were *f* from your brother Esau."
35: 7 to him when he was *f* from his brother.
Ex 14:27 Egyptians were *f* head on toward the sea,
Dt 4:42 save his life by *f* to one of these cities:
Jos 8: 6 we are *f* from them as we did the last time.
Jgs 7:21 camp fell to running and shouting and *f.*
12: 5 When any of the *f* Ephraimites said,
1Sm 14:22 on hearing that the Philistines were *f,*
31: 1 with the Israelites *f* before them and
1Kgs 2: 7 kindly when I was *f* your brother Absalom.
2Kgs 7: 7 camp just as it was, and *f* for their lives.
1Chr 21:12 or three months of *f* your enemies,
Jdt 10:12 of the Hebrews, and I am *f* from them,
1Mc 2:43 And all those who were *f* from the disaster
4: 5 mountains, saying, "They are *f* from us."
Ps(s) 68:13 "Kings and their hosts are fleeing, *f,*
Is 15: 9 Lions for those who are *f* from Moab and
27: 1 great, and strong, Leviathan the *f* serpent,
Bar 6:67 by *f* to shelter are better than they are.
Jon 1:10 knew that he was *f* from the LORD,
1Cor 3:15 be saved, but only as one *f* through fire.

FLEES (6)

Prv 28: 1 wicked man *f* although no one pursues him;
Wis 1: 5 For the holy spirit of discipline *f* deceit
Is 24:18 He who *f* at the sound of terror will fall
Jer 48:19 Ask the man who *f,*
48:44 who *f* from the terror falls into the pit;
50:16 his own people, everyone *f* to his own land.

FLEET (14)

2Sm 2:18 *f* of foot as a gazelle in the open field,
1Kgs 9:26 King Solomon also built a *f* at Ezion-geber,
9:27 In this *f* Hiram placed his own expert
10:11 Hiram's *f,*
10:15 addition to what came from the Tarshish *f,*
10:22 *f* of Tarshish ships at sea with Hiram's *f.*
10:22 Once every three years the *f* of Tarshish
2Chr 9:21 Once every three years the *f* of Tarshish
20:36 the *f* was built at Ezion-geber.
1Mc 1:17 chariots and elephants, and with a large *f,*
2Mc 12: 9 setting fire to the harbor and the *f,*
14: 1 of Tripolis with a powerful army and a *f,*
Dn 11:40 with chariots and horsemen and a great *f,*

FLEETING (8)

Prv 31:30 Charm is deceptive and beauty *f;*
Eccl 9: 9 *f* life that is granted you under the sun.
11:10 presence, though the dawn of youth is *f.*
Wis 5: 9 passed like a shadow and like a *f* rumor;
Sir 18:26 before the LORD all things are *f.*
41:11 Man's body is a *f* thing,
42:23 works, even to the spark and the *f* vision!
Heb 11:25 rather than enjoy the *f* rewards of sin.

FLEETNESS (1)

Ps(s) 147:10 not, nor is he pleased with the *f* of men.

FLESH (253)

Gn 2:21 of his ribs and closed up its place with *f.*
2:23 is bone of my bones and *f* of my flesh;
6: 3 remain in man forever, since he is but *f.*
9: 4 Only *f* with its lifeblood still in it you
17:11 Circumcise the *f* of your foreskin,
17:13 shall be in your *f* as an everlasting pact.
17:14 *f* of his foreskin has not been cut away,
17:23 the *f* of their foreskins on that same day,
17:24 when the *f* of his foreskin was circumcised,
17:25 when the *f* of his foreskin was circumcised.
29:14 to him, "You are indeed my *f* and blood."
37:27 After all, he is our brother, our own *f.*"
40:19 birds will be pecking the *f* from your body."
Ex 12: 8 *f* with unleavened bread and bitter herbs.
12:46 not take any of its *f* outside the house.
16: 8 the LORD gives you *f* to eat in the evening,"
16:12 In the evening twilight you shall eat *f,*
21:28 its *f* may not be eaten.
22:30 *F* torn to pieces in the field you shall
28:42 naked *f* from their loins to their thighs.
29:14 But the *f* and hide and offal of the
29:31 "You shall take the *f* of the ordination
29:32 his sons shall eat the *f* of the ram
29:34 If some of the *f* of the ordination
Lv 4:11 The hide of the bullock and all its *f*
6:20 Whatever touches its *f* shall become sacred.
7:15 "The *f* of the thanksgiving sacrifice
7:17 Should any *f* from the sacrifice be left
7:18 any of the *f* of the peace offering is
7:19 Should the *f* touch anything unclean,
7:19 "All who are clean may partake of this *f.*
7:20 eats any of the *f* of a peace offering
8:17 with its hide and *f* and offal he burned in
8:31 the *f* at the entrance of the meeting tent,
8:32 *f* and bread you shall burn up in the fire.
9:11 but the *f* and the hide he burned up in the
11: 8 Their *f* you shall not eat,
11:11 Their *f* you shall not eat,
12: 3 the *f* of the boy's foreskin shall be
13:10 hair white and that there is raw *f* in it,
13:14 But as soon as raw *f* appears on him,
13:15 on observing the raw *f,*
13:15 him unclean, because raw *f* is unclean;
13:16 If, however, the raw *f* again turns white,
13:24 and the proud *f* of the burn now becomes a
16: 4 tunic, with the linen drawers next his *f,*
16:27 *f* and offal shall be burned up in the fire.
26:29 eat the *f* of your own sons and daughters.
Nm 12:12 its mother's womb with its *f* half consumed."
19: 5 burned in his sight, with its hide and *f,*
Dt 12:23 not consume this seat of life with the *f.*
12:27 you must offer both the *f* and the blood
12:27 LORD, your God, but their *f* may be eaten.
14: 8 Their *f* you shall not eat,
28:31 your eyes, and you will not eat of its *f.*
28:53 the *f* of your own sons and daughters whom
28:55 any share in the *f* of his children that he
32:42 and my sword shall gorge itself with *f*—
32:42 *F* from the heads of the enemy leaders."
Jgs 8: 7 I will grind your *f* in with the thorns and
9: 2 remember that I am your own *f* and bone."
1Sm 14:32 on the ground and eating the *f* with blood.
14:33 the LORD by eating the *f* with blood,
14:34 the LORD by eating the *f* with blood."
17:44 and I will leave your *f* for the birds of
2Sm 5: 1 "Here we are, your bone and your *f.*
19:13 You are my brothers, you are my bone and *f.*
19:14 'Are you not my bone and *f?*
1Kgs 19:21 plowing equipment for fuel to boil their *f,*
21:27 and put on sackcloth over his bare *f.*
2Kgs 5:10 times in the Jordan, and your *f* will heal,
5:14 His *f* became again like the flesh of a
9:36 of Jezreel dogs shall eat the *f* of Jezebel.
1Chr 11: 1 we are of the same bone and *f* as you.
2Chr 32: 8 For he has only an arm of *f,*
Jdt 14:10 He had the *f* of his foreskin circumcised,
16:17 He will send fire and worms into their *f,*
1Mc 7:17 "The *f* of your saints they have strewn,
2Mc 9: 9 in hideous torments, his *f* rotted off,
Jb 2: 5 your hand and touch his bone and his *f,*
4:15 before me, and the hair of my *f* stood up.
6:12 strength of stones, or is my *f* of bronze?
7: 5 My *f* is clothed with worms and scabs;
10: 4 Have you eyes of *f?*
10:11 With skin and *f* you clothed me,
13:14 I will carry my *f* between my teeth,
14:22 Only his own *f* pains him,
19:20 I have escaped with my *f* between my teeth.
19:26 behold him, And from my *f* I shall see God;
21: 6 am dismayed, and horror takes hold on my *f.*
33:21 His *f* is wasted so that it cannot be seen,
33:25 Then his *f* shall become soft as a boy's;
34:15 his breath, All *f* would perish together,
41:15 his *f,* as the lower millstone.
Ps(s) 27: 2 When evildoers come at me to devour my *f,*
38: 4 health in my *f* because of your indignation;
38: 8 there is no health in my *f.*
50:13 Do I eat the *f* of strong bulls,
56: 5 what can *f* do against me?
56:12 what can *f* do against me?
63: 2 for you my *f* pines and my soul thirsts
65: 3 To you all *f* must come
73:26 Though my *f* and my heart waste away,
78:39 He remembered that they were *f,*
79: 2 the *f* of your faithful ones to the beasts
84: 3 heart and my *f* cry out for the living God.
109:24 and my *f* is wasted of its substance.
119:120 My *f* shudders with dread of you,
136:25 Who gives food to all *f,*
145:21 all *f* bless his holy name forever and ever.
Prv 3: 8 health for your *f* and vigor for your bones.
5:11 when your *f* and your body are consumed;
Eccl 4: 5 folds his arms and consumes his own *f*—
12:12 in much study there is weariness for the *f.*
Wis 7: 1 mother's womb I was molded into *f*
12: 5 a cannibal feast of human *f* and of blood,
19:21 neither consumed the *f* of the perishable
Sir 14:17 All *f* grows old,
14:18 So with the generations of *f* and blood:
17: 4 He puts the fear of him in all *f,*
17:26 obscure then the thoughts of *f* and blood!
18:11 man, but the LORD's mercy reaches all *f,*
23: 6 the lustful cravings of the *f* master me,
23:16 A man given to sins of the *f,*
26:13 her thoughtfulness puts *f* on his bones;
28: 5 If he who is but *f* cherishes wrath,
31: 1 Keeping watch over riches wastes the *f,*
38:28 The heat from the fire sears his *f,*
40: 8 So it is with all *f,*
41: 4 Thus God has ordained for all *f;*
44:18 him, that never should all *f* be destroyed.
44:20 In his own *f* he incised the ordinance,
48:13 beneath him *f* was brought back into life.
Is 9:18 each devours the *f* of his neighbor.
31: 3 are men, not God, their horses are *f,*
49:26 will make your oppressors eat their own *f,*
65: 4 the night in caverns, Eating swine's *f,*
66:17 who stands within, they who eat swine's *f,*
Jer 7:21 eat up the *f!*
8:22 Why grows not new *f* over the wound of the
9:24 of all those circumcised in their *f:*
17: 5 human beings, who seeks his strength in *f,*
19: 9 them eat the *f* of their sons and daughters;
19: 9 they shall eat one another's *f* during the
51:35 My torn *f* be upon Babylon,
Lam 3: 4 He has worn away my *f* and my skin,
Bar 2: 3 eat the *f* of his son or of his daughter.
Ez 4:14 carrion *f* or that torn by wild beasts;
32: 5 I will leave your *f* on the mountains,
37: 6 put sinews upon you, make *f* grow over you,
37: 8 I saw the sinews and the *f* come upon them,
39:17 you shall have *f* to eat and blood to drink.
39:18 You shall eat the *f* of warriors and drink
40:43 On the tables themselves the *f* was laid.
44: 7 uncircumcised both in heart and *f,*
44: 9 uncircumcised in heart and in *f,*
44:31 shall not eat anything, whether *f* or fowl,
Dn 7: 5 was given the order, "Up, devour much *f.*"
7:15 spirit anguished within its sheath of *f,*
Hos 8:13 offer sacrifice, immolate *f* and eat it,
Mi 3: 2 from them, and their *f* from their bones!
3: 3 They eat the *f* of my people,
3: 3 chop them in pieces like *f* in a kettle,
Hg 2:12 If a man carries sanctified *f* in the fold
Zec 11: 9 those that are left devour one another's *f.*"
11:16 *f* of the fat ones and tear off their hoofs!
14:12 their *f* shall rot while they stand upon
Mal 2:15 he not make one being, with *f* and spirit:
Mt 19: 6 Thus they are no longer two but one *f.*
Mk 10: 8 They are no longer two but one *f.*
Lk 24:39 a ghost does not have *f* and bones as I do."
24:53 a ghost does not have *f* and bones as I do."
Jn 1:14 became *f* and made his dwelling among us,
3: 6 Flesh begets *f,* Spirit begets spirit.
6:51 the bread I will give is my *f,*
6:52 saying, "How can he give us his *f* to eat?"
6:53 *f* of the Son of Man and drink his blood,
6:54 He who feeds on my *f* and drinks my blood
6:55 my *f* is real food and my blood real drink.
6:56 on my *f* and drinks my blood remains in me,
6:63 the *f* is useless.
Acts 21:25 idols, blood, the *f* of strangled animals,
Rom 1: 3 descended from David according to the *f*
2:28 True circumcision is not a sign in the *f.*
4: 1 Abraham, our ancestor according to the *f?*
7: 5 When we were in the *f,*
7:14 I am weak *f* sold into the slavery of sin.
7:18 no good dwells in me, that is, in my *f;*
7:25 law of God but with my *f* the law of sin.
8: 3 because of its weakening by the *f.*
8: 3 the likeness of sinful *f* as a sin offering,
8: 3 offering, thereby condemning sin in the *f,*
8: 4 in us who live, not according to the *f,*
8: 5 *f* are intent on the things of the flesh,
8: 6 The tendency of the *f* is toward death but
8: 7 *f* in its tendency is at enmity with God;
8: 8 those who are in the *f* cannot please God.
8: 9 But you are not in the *f;*
8:12 *f,* so that we should live according to the *f.*
8:13 If you live according to the *f,*
9: 8 of the *f* who are the children of God;
13:14 make no provision for the desires of the *f.*
1Cor 3: 1 you as spiritual men but only as men of *f,*
3: 3 quarrels among you, are you not of the *f?*
5: 5 to Satan for the destruction of his *f,*
6:16 says, "The two shall become one *f.*"
10:18 Look at Israel according to the *f* and see
15:50 *f* and blood cannot inherit the kingdom of
2Cor 3: 3 of stone but on tablets of *f* in the heart.
4:11 of Jesus may be revealed in our mortal *f.*
7: 1 from every defilement of *f* and spirit,
12: 7 conceited I was given a thorn in the *f,*
Gal 3: 3 in the spirit, are you now to end in the *f?*
5:13 a freedom that gives free rein to the *f.*
5:16 will not yield to the cravings of the *f.*
5:17 The *f* lusts against the spirit and the
5:17 the spirit and the spirit against the *f;*
5:19 It is obvious what proceeds from the *f:*
5:24 their *f* with its passions and desires.
6: 8 If he sows in the field of the *f,*
Eph 2: 3 we lived at the level of the *f,*
2:11 virtue of a hand-executed rite on their *f,*
2:15 In his own *f* he abolished the law with its
5:29 Observe that no one ever hates his own *f;*
Phil 1:22 other hand, I am to go on living in the *f,*
3: 3 rather than putting our trust in the *f*—
Col 1:24 In my own *f* I fill up what is lacking in
2: 1 others who have never seen me in the *f.*
2:13 dead in sin and your *f* was uncircumcised,
1Tm 3:16 "He was manifested in the *f,*
Heb 2:14 since the children are men of blood and *f,*
5: 7 In the days when he was in the *f,*
9:10 regulations concerning the *f,*
9:13 are defiled so that their *f* is cleansed,
10:20 the veil (the "veil" meaning his *f*),
Jas 5: 3 it will devour your *f* like a fire.
1Pt 4: 1 Christ suffered in the *f;*
4: 1 has suffered in the *f* has broken with sin.

FLESH (cont.)
4: 6 condemned in the *f* in the eyes of men,
2Pt 2:10 *f* in their desire for whatever corrupts,
2:18 passion, with the lustful ways of the *f*.
1Jn 4: 2 Jesus Christ come in the *f* belongs to God,
2Jn 1: 7 Jesus Christ as coming in the *f*.
Jude 1: 8 these visionaries pollute the *f*;
Rv 17:16 they will devour her *f* and set her on fire.
19:18 You are to eat the *f* of kings,
19:18 the *f* of all men,
19:21 gorged themselves on the *f* of the slain.

FLESH-STAINED (1)
Jude 1:23 abhor so much as their *f* clothing.

FLESHLY (1)
1Pt 3:18 put to death insofar as *f* existence goes,

FLESHPOTS (1)
Ex 16: 3 we sat by our *f* and ate our fill of bread!

FLESHY (1)
Lv 13:43 of skin leprosy of the *f* part of the body,

FLEW (7)
Gn 8: 7 It *f* back and forth until the waters dried
1Sm 25:14 our master, but he *f* at them screaming.
2Sm 22:11 He mounted a cherub and *f*,
Ps(s) 18:11 He mounted a cherub and *f*,
Is 6: 6 Then one of the seraphim *f* to me,
Dn 3:13 *f* into a rage and sent for Shadrach,
Acts 16:26 Immediately all the doors *f* open and

FLIES (17)
Ex 8:17 I will loose swarms of *f* upon you and your
8:17 stand shall be filled with swarms of *f*.
8:18 there shall be no *f* where my people dwell,
8:20 Thick swarms of *f* entered the house of
8:20 Egypt the land was infested with *f*.
8:25 *f* may depart tomorrow from Pharaoh
8:27 He removed the *f* from Pharaoh and his
Dt 4:17 the earth or of any bird that *f* in the sky,
19: 5 its head *f* off the handle and hits his
Ps(s) 78:45 He sent among them *f* that devoured them
91: 5 of the night nor the arrow that *f* by day;
105:31 He spoke, and there came swarms of *f*;
Prv 23: 5 wings, like the eagle that *f* toward heaven.
Wis 16: 9 the bites of locusts and of *f* slew them,
Is 51: 6 a garment and its inhabitants die like *f*,
Jer 13:24 chaff that *f* when the desert wind blows.
Hos 9:11 The glory of Ephraim *f* away like a bird:

FLIGHT (65)
Gn 31:20 by not telling him of his intended *f*.
Ex 12:11 you shall eat like those who are in *f*.
23:27 make all your enemies turn from you in *f*,
Lv 26: 8 you will put a hundred of your foes to *f*,
26:17 will take to *f* though no one pursues you.
Dt 32:30 or two men put ten thousand to *f*,
Jos 23:10 One of you puts to *f* a thousand,
Jgs 9:21 Then Jotham went in *f* to Beer,
20:32 had planned the *f* so as to draw them away
1Sm 17:51 hero was dead, the Philistines took to *f*.
19: 8 great defeat upon them, putting them to *f*.
21:11 That same day David took to *f* from Saul,
23:26 David was in anxious *f* to escape Saul,
2Sm 4: 4 But in their hasty *f*,
13:34 Meanwhile, Absalom had taken *f*.
13:37 But Absalom, who had taken *f*,
15:14 Let us take *f*,
19: 4 that day like men shamed by *f* in battle.
22:15 He sent forth arrows to put them to *f*;
22:41 My enemies you put to *f* before me and
2Kgs 9:27 his *f* as far as Megiddo and died there.
1Chr 8:13 and they put the inhabitants of Gath to *f*.
19:15 also took to *f* before his brother Abishai,
Neh 6:11 "A man like me take *f*?
Tb 1:19 then in my fear I took to *f*.
Jdt 15: 3 district around Bethulia took to *f*.
16:11 the sound of their war cry, they took to *f*.
1Mc 2:47 They put to *f* the arrogant,
4:20 put to *f* and their camp was being burned.
6: 5 into the land of Judah had been put to *f*;
10:12 that Bacchides had built, took *f*,
10:72 were twice put to *f* in their own land.
10:82 phalanx, overwhelmed it and put it to *f*.
11:15 him with a strong force and put him to *f*.
11:72 overwhelmed the enemy that they took to *f*.
16: 8 and Cendebeus and his army were put to *f*;
2Mc 2:21 whole land, put to *f* the barbarian hordes,
4:42 a few, while they put all the rest to *f*.
8: 6 and put to *f* a large number of the enemy.
8:24 Nicanor's army, and put all of them to *f*.
9: 2 so that in the end Antiochus was put to *f*
9: 4 injury done by those who had put him to *f*.
11:11 horsemen, and put all the rest to *f*.
11:12 Lysias himself escaped only by shameful *f*.
12:22 they rushed away in such headlong *f*
12:37 were not expecting it and put them to *f*.
Jb 20: 8 a dream he takes *f* and is not found again;
41:20 The arrow will not put him to *f*;
Ps(s) 18:15 He sent forth his arrows to put them to *f*,
18:41 My enemies you put to *f* before me,
21:13 succeed, For you shall put them to *f*;
78:66 *f* and cast them into everlasting disgrace.
104: 7 the sound of your thunder they took to *f*;
144: 6 Flash forth lightning, and put them to *f*,
Prv 26: 2 in its flitting, like the swallow in its *f*,
Is 10:31 Madmenah is in *f*,
52:12 you come out, nor leave in headlong *f*,
Jer 4:29 horseman and bowman each city takes to *f*;
25:35 There is no *f* for the shepherds,
49: 5 shall be scattered, each man in headlong *f*,
52: 7 Then all the soldiers took to *f* and left
Dn 9:21 *f* at the time of the evening sacrifice.
Am 2:14 *F* shall perish from the swift,
Jas 4: 7 God, resist the devil and he will take *f*.
Rv 4: 7 while the fourth looked like an eagle in *f*.

FLIGHTS (1)
2Mc 5: 3 *f* of arrows and flashes of gold ornaments,

FLIGHTY (1)
Is 32: 4 The *f* will become wise and capable,

FLING (3)
Gn 50:18 to *f* themselves down before him and said,
Ez 7:19 They shall *f* their silver into the streets,
Mk 3:11 of him, *f* themselves down at his feet,

FLINGING (1)
Gn 33: 4 embraced him, and *f* himself on his neck,

FLINT (8)
Ex 4:25 of *f* and cut off her son's foreskin and,
Jos 5: 2 "Make *f* knives and circumcise the
5: 3 So Joshua made *f* knives and circumcised
2Mc 10: 3 Then, with fire struck from *f*,
Ps(s) 114: 8 pools of water, the *f* into flowing springs.
Is 5:28 The hoofs of their horses seem like *f*,
50: 7 I have set my face like *f*,
Ez 3: 9 as theirs, like diamond, harder than *f*.

FLINTY (2)
Dt 8:15 brought forth water for you from the *f* rock
Jb 28: 9 He sets his hand to the *f* rock,

FLITS (1)
Prv 23: 5 While your glance *f* to it,

FLITTING (1)
Prv 26: 2 Like the sparrow in its *f*,

FLOAT (1)
2Chr 2:15 *f* them down to you at the port of Joppa,

FLOATED (1)
Gn 7:18 but the ark *f* on the surface of the waters.

FLOCK (113)
Gn 4: 4 one of the best firstlings of his *f*.
21:28 also set apart seven ewe lambs of the *f*,
27: 9 Go to the *f* and get me two choice kids.
29: 6 here comes his daughter Rachel with his *f*."
30:31 I will again pasture and tend your *f*.
30:32 go through your whole *f* today and remove
30:36 continued to pasture the rest of Laban's *f*.
30:40 own, which he did not put with Laban's *f*.
31: 4 him where he was in the field with his *f*.
31: 8 the entire *f* would bear speckled young;
31: 8 the entire *f* would bear streaked young.
31:12 All the he-goats in the *f*,
31:38 I have never feasted on a ram of your *f*.
31:41 two daughters and six years for your *f*,
33:13 for a single day, the whole *f* will die.
38:17 "I will send you a kid from the *f*."
Ex 2:16 fill the troughs to water their father's *f*.
2:19 even drew water for us and watered the *f*!"
3: 1 tending the *f* of his father-in-law Jethro,
3: 1 Leading the *f* across the desert,
34:19 livestock, whether in the herd or in the *f*.
34:20 an ass you shall redeem with one of the *f*;
Lv 1: 2 must be from the herd or from the *f*.
1:10 "If his holocaust offering is from the *f*,
3: 6 he presents to the LORD is from the *f*,
5: 6 to the LORD a female animal from the *f*,
5: 7 he cannot afford an animal of the *f*,
5:15 offering an unblemished ram from the *f*,
5:18 ram of the *f* of the established value.
5:25 ram of the *f* of the established value.
22:21 the herd or the *f* in fulfillment of a vow,
27:32 The tithes of the herd and the *f* shall be
Nm 15: 3 oblation from the herd or from the *f*,
Dt 12:17 oil, of the first-born of your herd or *f*,
12:21 your herd or *f* that the LORD has given you,
14:23 well as the firstlings of your herd and *f*,
15:14 your *f* and threshing floor and wine press,
15:19 male firstlings of your herd and of your *f*.
15:19 cattle, nor shear the firstlings of your *f*.
16: 2 from your *f* or your herd to the LORD,
17: 1 the *f* an animal with any serious defect;
18: 3 the victim is from the herd or from the *f*,
18: 4 first fruits of the shearing of your *f*;
1Sm 16:19 send him his son David, who was with the *f*.
17:20 morning, having left the *f* with a shepherd,
17:34 bear came to carry off a sheep from the *f*,
25: 2 for the shearing of his *f* in Carmel.
25: 4 the desert that Nabal was shearing his *f*,
2Sm 7: 8 the *f* to be commander of my people Israel.
2Chr 17:11 the Arabs also brought him a *f*
35: 7 to the common people a *f* of lambs and kids,
Ezr 10:19 for their guilt they gave a ram from the *f*.
Tb 1: 6 of the field and the firstlings of the *f*,
7: 9 the *f* and gave them a cordial reception.
Jb 30: 1 disdained to rank with the dogs of my *f*.
Ps(s) 68:11 Your *f* settled in it;
74: 2 Remember your *f* which you built up of old,
77:21 like a *f* under the care of Moses and Aaron.
80: 2 hearken, O guide of the *f* of Joseph!
95: 7 the people he shepherds, the *f* he guides.
100: 3 his people, the *f* he tends.
114: 4 rams, the hills like the lambs of the *f*.
114: 6 You hills, like the lambs of the *f*?
Sg 1: 7 my heart loves, where you pasture your *f*,
1: 8 Follow the tracks of the *f* and pasture the
4: 1 Your hair is like a *f* of goats streaming
4: 2 teeth are like a *f* of ewes to be shorn,
6: 5 a *f* of goats streaming down from Gilead.
6: 6 *f* of ewes which come up from the washing,
Sir 18:12 teaching, as a shepherd guides his *f*;
47: 3 kids, and of bears, like lambs of the *f*.
Is 13:14 hunted gazelle, or a *f* that no one gathers,
40:11 Like a shepherd he feeds his *f*;
63:11 up out of the sea the shepherd of his *f*?
Jer 9: 9 them, unheard is the bleat of the *f*;
13:17 eyes will run with tears for the LORD's *f*,
13:20 Where is the *f* entrusted to you,
23: 1 mislead and scatter the *f* of my pasture,
23: 3 I myself will gather the remnant of my *f*
25:34 roll in the dust, leaders of the *f*!
25:35 no escape for the leaders of the *f*.
25:36 shepherds, howling by the leaders of the *f*!
31:10 he guards them as a shepherd his *f*.
31:24 the farmers and those who lead the *f*,
50: 8 be like the rams at the head of the *f*.
51:23 With you I shatter the shepherd and his *f*,
Ez 24: 5 joints taken from the pick of the *f*.
34:12 As a shepherd tends his *f* when he finds
43:23 bull and an unblemished ram from the *f*,
43:25 and a young bull and a ram from the *f*,
45:15 One sheep from the *f* for every two hundred
Am 6: 4 couches, They eat lambs taken from the *f*,
7:15 The LORD took me from following the *f*,
Mi 2:12 I will group them like a *f* in the fold,
5: 3 shepherd his *f* by the strength of the LORD,
7:14 with your staff, the *f* of your inheritance,
Zec 9:16 them on that day, his people, like a *f*.
10: 3 For the LORD of hosts will visit his *f*,
11: 4 Shepherd the *f* to be slaughtered.
11: 7 So I became the shepherd of the *f* to be
11: 7 and the other, "Bonds," and I fed the *f*.
11:17 to my foolish shepherd who forsakes the *f*!
Mal 1:14 is the deceiver, who has in his *f* a male,
Mt 10:31 worth more than an entire *f* of sparrows.
26:31 and the sheep of the *f* will be dispersed.'
Lk 12: 7 You are worth more than a *f* of sparrows.
12:32 "Do not live in fear, little *f*.
Jn 10:16 There shall be one *f* then, one shepherd.
Acts 20:28 *f* the Holy Spirit has given you to guard.
20:29 come among you who will not spare the *f*.
1Cor 9: 7 not nourish himself with the milk of his *f*?
1Pt 5: 2 God's *f* is in your midst;
5: 3 Be examples to the *f*,

FLOCKING (2)
2Mc 14:14 have banished Judas, came *f* to Nicanor,
Jn 3:26 is baptizing now, and everyone is *f* to him."

FLOCKS (85)
Gn 4: 2 Abel became a keeper of *f*,
12:16 with Abram, and he received *f* and herds,
13: 5 with Abram, also had *f* and herds and tents,
20:14 Then Abimelech took *f* and herds and male
24:35 he has given him *f* and herds,
26:14 He acquired such *f* and herds,
29: 3 from the mouth of the well and water the *f*.
29: 7 Why don't you water the *f* now,
29: 8 only then can we water the *f*."
30:40 Thus he produced special *f* of his own,
30:43 and he came to own, not only large *f*,
31:43 children are mine, and the *f* are mine;
32: 8 people who were with him, as well as his *f*,
33:13 I am encumbered with the *f* and herds,
34:28 They seized their *f*,
37: 2 he was tending the *f* with his brothers;
37:12 to pasture their father's *f* at Shechem,
37:13 you know, are tending our *f* at Shechem.
37:14 brothers and the *f* and bring back word."
37:16 tell me where they are tending the *f*?"
45:10 and grandchildren, your *f* and herds,

46:32 have brought with them their *f* and herds,
47: 1 *f* and herds and everything else they own;
47: 4 for your servants' *f* in the land of Canaan,
47:17 their *f* of sheep and herds of cattle,
50: 8 only their children and their *f* and herds
Ex 2:17 up and defended them and watered their *f*.
9: 3 your horses, asses, camels, herds and *f*—
10: 9 well as our *f* and herds must accompany us.
10:24 But your *f* and herds must remain."
12:32 Take your *f*,
12:38 their livestock, very numerous *f* and herds.
34: 3 even the *f* and the herds are not to go
Nm 31: 9 all their herds and *f* and wealth as spoil,
32:16 only to build sheepfolds here for our *f*,
32:24 your families, and the folds for your *f*,
35: 3 serve their herds and *f* and other animals.
Dt 7:13 of your herds and the young of your *f*,
8:13 them, and have increased your herds and *f*,
12: 6 and the firstlings of your herds and *f*.
28: 4 of your herds and the young of your *f*!
28:18 of your herds and the young of your *f*!
28:31 Your *f* will be given to your enemies,
28:51 issue of your herds or young of your *f*,
Jos 14: 4 their pasture lands for the cattle and *f*.
1Sm 8:17 He will tithe your *f* and you yourselves
2Sm 12: 2 rich man had *f* and herds in great numbers.
12: 4 he would not take from his own *f* and herds
17:29 butter and cheese from the *f* and herds,
1Kgs 20:27 seemed like a couple of small *f* of goats,
1Chr 4:39 of the valley, seeking pasture for their *f*.
4:41 they found pasture there for their *f*.
27:31 and over the *f* was Jaziz the Hagrite.
2Chr 32:28 the various kinds of cattle and for the *f*.
Neh 10:37 the first-born of our *f* and herds.
Jdt 2:27 their fields, destroyed their *f* and herds,
3: 3 and all our wheat fields, our *f* and herds,
8:26 while he was tending the *f* of Laban,
Ps(s) 65:14 *f* and the valleys blanketed with grain.
78:48 their beasts and their *f* to the lightning.
107:41 and made the families numerous like *f*.
Prv 27:23 Take good care of your *f*,
Eccl 2: 7 had growing herds of cattle and *f* of sheep,
Sg 1: 7 wandering after the *f* of your companions.
Is 13:20 tent there, nor shepherds couch their *f*.
17: 2 given over to *f* to lie in undisturbed.
32:19 wild asses to frolic in, and *f* to pasture,
60: 7 the *f* of Kedar shall be gathered for you,
61: 5 shall stand ready to pasture your *f*,
65:10 Sharon shall be a pasture for the *f* and
Jer 6: 3 Against her, shepherds come with their *f*;
10:21 no success, and all their *f* were scattered.
33:12 for the shepherds to couch their *f*.
33:13 *f* will again pass under the hands of the
Ez 25: 5 of the Ammonites a resting place for *f*.
36:38 in ruins shall be filled with *f* of men;
Hos 5: 6 With their *f* and their herds they shall go
Jl 1:18 even the *f* of sheep have perished.
Mi 5: 7 forest, like a young lion among *f* of sheep;
Hb 3:17 Though the *f* disappear from the fold and
Zep 2: 6 fields for shepherds, and folds for *f*.
2: 7 at evening they shall couch their *f*,
3:13 couch their *f* with none to disturb them.
Lk 2: 8 keeping night watch by turns over their *f*.
Jn 4:12 and drank from it with his sons and his *f*?"

FLOG (4)

Mt 10:17 court, they will *f* you in their synagogues.
23:34 others you will *f* in your synagogues and
Mk 10:34 who will mock him and spit at him, *f* him,
Acts 22:25 legal to *f* a Roman citizen without a trial?"

FLOGGED (7)

2Mc 3:26 they *f* him unceasingly until they had
5:18 would have been *f* and turned back from his
Mt 20:19 to be made sport of and *f* and crucified.
Lk 12:48 to be *f* will get off with fewer stripes.
Acts 16:22 stripped them and ordered them to be *f*.
16:37 "They *f* us in public without even a trial,
22:19 in you and *f* them in every synagogue.

FLOOD (42)

Gn 6:17 about to bring the *f* [waters] on the earth,
7: 6 old when the *f* waters came upon the earth.
7: 7 the ark because of the waters of the *f*.
7:10 the waters of the *f* came upon the earth.
7:17 *f* continued upon the earth for forty days.
9:11 water of a *f*; there shall not be another *f*
9:15 become a *f* to destroy all mortal beings.
9:28 three hundred and fifty years after the *f*.
10: 1 to whom sons were born after the *f*.
10:32 of the earth branched out after the *f*.
11:10 of Arpachshad, two years after the *f*.
Ex 15: 5 The *f* waters covered them.
15: 8 *f* waters congealed in the midst of the sea.
Est A: 9 river, a *f* of water from a little spring.
2Mc 2:24 In view of the *f* of statistics,
Jb 20:28 The *f* shall sweep away his house with the
22:16 whose foundations a *f* swept away?
Ps(s) 6: 7 every night I *f* my bed with weeping;
29:10 The LORD is enthroned above the *f*;
69: 3 the *f* overwhelms me.
Wis 19: 7 and a grassy plain out of the mighty *f*.
Sir 21:13 A wise man's knowledge wells up in a *f*,
43:10 weapon against the *f* waters stored on high,
47:14 with instruction, like the Nile in *f*!
Is 8: 8 pass into Judah, and *f* it all throughout:
28: 2 a destructive storm, Like a *f* of water,
28:17 lies, and waters shall *f* the hiding place.
30:28 like a *f* in a ravine that reaches suddenly
Jer 47: 2 a torrent in *f*; It shall flood the land
Dn 11:10 armed host, which shall advance like a *f*,
11:40 passing through the countries like a *f*.
Jon 2: 4 heart of the sea, and the *f* enveloped me;
Na 1: 8 have recourse to him, when the *f* rages;
3: 8 the *f* for her rampart and water her wall?
Hb 2:15 your neighbors a *f* of your wrath to drink,
Mt 24:38 the *f* people were eating and drinking,
24:39 until the *f* came and destroyed them.
Lk 17:27 and when the *f* came,
2Pt 2: 5 he brought down that *f* on the godless earth.
Rv 12:16 *f* which the dragon spewed out of his mouth.

FLOOD-WATERS (1)

Ps(s) 69:16 Let not the *f* overwhelm me,

FLOODED (1)

Wis 10: 4 When on his account the earth was *f*,

FLOODGATES (3)

Gn 7:11 forth, and the *f* of the sky were opened.
8: 2 the abyss and the *f* of the sky were closed,
Mal 3:10 Shall I not open for you the *f* of heaven,

FLOODING (3)

Ez 13:11 I will bring down a *f* rain;
13:13 of my anger there shall be a *f* rain,
38:22 *f* rain and hailstones,

FLOODS (11)

2Sm 22: 5 the *f* of perdition overwhelmed me;
1Mc 6:11 I come, and in what *f* of sorrow am I now.
Jb 14:19 and *f* wash away the soil of the land,
Ps(s) 18: 5 about me, the destroying *f* overwhelmed me;
78:15 desert and gave them water in copious *f*.
93: 3 The *f* lift up, O LORD, the floods lift up
93: 3 the *f* lift up their tumult.
Sg 8: 7 cannot quench love, nor *f* sweep it away.
Lk 6:48 *f* came the torrent rushed in on that house,
2Cor 11:26 I traveled continually, endangered by *f*,

FLOOR (51)

Nm 5:17 he has taken from the *f* of the Dwelling.
15:20 offer a contribution from the threshing *f*.
18:27 the threshing *f* or new wine from the press.
18:30 of the threshing *f* or of the wine press.
Dt 15:14 your flock and threshing *f* and wine press,
16:13 from your threshing *f* and wine press.
Jgs 3:25 There on the *f*, dead, lay their lord!
6:37 this woolen fleece on the threshing *f*.
Ru 3: 2 be winnowing barley at the threshing *f*.
3: 3 best attire and go down to the threshing *f*.
3: 6 So she went down to the threshing *f* and
3:14 that this woman came to the threshing *f*."
1Sm 14: 2 the threshing *f* on the outskirts of Geba;
19:22 of the threshing *f* on the bare hilltop,
2Sm 6: 6 When they came to the threshing *f* of Nodan,
24:16 at the threshing *f* of Araunah the Jebusite.
24:18 the threshing *f* of Araunah the Jebusite."
24:21 *f* from you to build an altar to the LORD,
24:24 *f* and the oxen for fifty silver shekels.
1Kgs 1:23 the king's presence and, bowing to the *f*,
1:31 Bowing to the *f* in homage to the king,
6: 8 The entrance to the lowest *f* of the annex
6:15 *f* to ceiling beams with cedar paneling,
6:15 and its *f* was laid with fir planking.
6:16 cedar partitions from the *f* to the rafters,
6:30 The *f* of both the inner and the outer
7: 7 paneled with cedar from *f* to ceiling beams.
22:10 *f* at the entrance of the gate of Samaria,
2Kgs 6:27 from the threshing *f* or the winepress?"
1Chr 13: 9 As they reached the threshing *f* of Chidon,
21:15 by the threshing *f* of Ornan the Jebusite.
21:18 on the threshing *f* of Ornan the Jebusite.
21:21 threshing *f* and bowed down before David,
21:22 "Sell me the ground of this threshing *f*,
21:28 on the threshing *f* of Ornan the Jebusite,
2Chr 3: 1 the threshing *f* of Ornan
18: 9 *f* at the entrance of the gate of Samaria,
Jdt 14:15 the bedroom, and found him lying on the *f*,
Jb 39:12 gather in the yield of your threshing *f*?
Is 21:10 been threshed, beaten on my threshing *f*!
Jer 51:33 a threshing *f* at the time it is trodden;
Dn 2:35 as the chaff on the threshing *f* in summer,
14:19 "Look at the *f*."
Hos 9: 1 a harlot's hire upon every threshing *f*.
9: 2 *f* and wine press shall not nourish them,
13: 3 *f* or like smoke out of the window.
Mi 4:12 them like sheaves on the threshing *f*.
Mt 3:12 *f* and gather his grain into the barn,
Lk 3:17 *f* and gather the wheat into his barn;
Acts 15: 7 Peter took the *f* and said to them:
Rv 4: 6 The *f* around the throne was like a sea of

FLOORS (2)

1Sm 23: 1 Keilah and plundering the threshing *f*.
Jl 2:24 The threshing *f* shall be full of grain and

FLOUR (71)

Gn 18: 6 told Sarah, "Quick, three seahs of fine *f*!
Ex 29: 2 *f* make unleavened cakes mixed with oil,
29:40 fine *f* mixed with a fourth of a hin of oil
Lv 2: 1 LORD, his offering must consist of fine *f*.
2: 2 take a handful of this fine *f* and oil,
2: 4 cakes made of fine *f* mixed with oil,
2: 5 be of fine *f* mixed with oil and unleavened.
2: 7 is prepared in a pot, it must be of fine *f*,
5:11 his sin one tenth of an ephah of fine *f*.
5:12 a handful of this *f* as a token offering,
5:13 The rest of the *f*,
6: 8 from it a handful of its fine *f* and oil,
6:13 fine *f* for the established cereal offering,
7:12 of fine *f* mixed with oil and well kneaded.
14:10 *f* mixed with oil for a cereal offering,
14:21 *f* mixed with oil for a cereal offering,
23:13 of an ephah of fine *f* mixed with oil,
23:17 an ephah of fine *f* and baked with leaven.
24: 5 take fine *f* and bake it into twelve cakes,
24: 5 two tenths of an ephah of *f* for each cake.
Nm 6:15 basket of unleavened cakes of fine *f*
7:13 *f* mixed with oil for a cereal offering;
7:19 fine *f* mixed with oil for cereal offering;
7:25 *f* mixed with oil for a cereal offering;
7:31 *f* mixed with oil for a cereal offering;
7:37 *f* mixed with oil for a cereal offering;
7:43 *f* mixed with oil for a cereal offering;
7:49 *f* mixed with oil for a cereal offering;
7:55 *f* mixed with oil for a cereal offering;
7:61 *f* mixed with oil for a cereal offering;
7:67 *f* mixed with oil for a cereal offering;
7:73 *f* mixed with oil for a cereal offering;
7:79 *f* mixed with oil for a cereal offering;
8: 8 cereal offering of fine *f* mixed with oil;
15: 4 fine *f* mixed with a fourth of a hin of oil,
15: 6 fine *f* mixed with a third of a hin of oil,
15: 9 of fine *f* mixed with half a hin of oil,
28: 5 of fine *f* mixed with a fourth of a hin of oil
28: 9 of an ephah of fine *f* mixed with oil,
28:12 ephah of fine *f* mixed with oil as the cereal
28:12 two tenths of an ephah of fine *f* mixed
28:13 and one tenth of an ephah of fine *f* mixed
28:20 cereal offerings of fine *f* mixed with oil;
28:28 offerings of fine *f* mixed ed with oil;
29: 3 cereal offerings of fine *f* mixed with oil;
29: 9 cereal offerings of fine *f* mixed with oil;
29:14 cereal offerings of fine *f* mixed with oil;
Jgs 6:19 ephah of *f* in the form of unleavened cakes.
1Sm 1:24 bull, an ephah of *f* and a skin of wine,
28:24 Then taking *f*,
2Sm 17:28 earthenware, as well as wheat, barley, *f*,
1Kgs 5: 2 for each day were thirty kors of fine *f*,
17:12 of *f* in my jar and a little oil in my jug.
17:14 says, 'The jar of *f* shall not go empty,
17:16 The jar of *f* did not go empty,
2Kgs 7: 1 a seah of fine *f* will sell for a shekel,
7:16 and then a seah of fine *f* sold for a
7:18 and one seah of fine *f* for a shekel at
1Chr 9:29 the sacred vessels, as well as the fine *f*,
23:29 of the fine *f* for the cereal offering,
2Mc 1: 8 we offered sacrifices and fine *f*,
Sir 35: 2 In works of charity one offers fine *f*,
Is 47: 2 Take the millstone and grind *f*,
Ez 16:13 Fine *f*, honey, and oil were your food.
16:19 the food that I had given you, the fine *f*,
46:14 of a hin of oil to moisten the fine *f*.
Dn 14: 3 they provided for it six barrels of fine *f*,
Hos 8: 7 of grain that forms no ear can yield no *f*;
Mt 13:33 took and kneaded into three measures of *f*.
Lk 13:21 took to knead into three measures of *f*
Rv 18:13 wine and olive oil, fine *f* and grain;

FLOURISH (18)

Gn 26:22 us ample room, and we shall *f* in the land."
Jb 8: 7 for in time to come you will *f* indeed.
8:11 Can the reed grass *f* without water?
14: 9 *f* again and put forth branches like a young
Ps(s) 72:16 shall *f* like the verdure of the fields.
92: 8 *f* like grass and all evildoers thrive,
92:13 The just man shall *f* like the palm tree,
92:14 the LORD shall *f* in the courts of our God.
Prv 5:19 through her love you will *f* continually.
11:28 fall, but like green leaves the just *f*.
14:11 but the tent of the upright will *f*.
28:28 but at their fall the just *f*.
Wis 4: 4 even though their branches *f* for a time,
Sir 40:15 The offshoot of violence will not *f*,
Is 66:14 rejoice and your bodies *f* like the grass;
Ez 31: 4 Waters made it grow, the abyss made it *f*,
Zec 9:17 grain that makes the youths *f*,
1Thes 3: 8 to *f* only if you stand firm in the Lord!

FLOURISHES (1)

Ez 7:10 Lawlessness is in full bloom, insolence *f*,

FLOURISHING (5)

Est E:16 a *f* condition for us and for our forebears.
Jb 29: 4 As I was in my *f* days,
Ps(s) 37:35 a wicked man, fierce, and stalwart as a *f*,
Eccl 2: 6 myself reservoirs to water a *f* woodland.
Sir 40:19 Sheepfolds and orchards bring *f* health;

FLOUT (2)

2Mc 4:17 It is no light matter to *f* the laws of God,
1Tm 1:10 and those who in other ways *f* the sound

FLOUTED (1)

1Mc 2:31 that certain men who had *f* the king's

FLOW (40)

Ex 14:26 the water may *f* back upon the Egyptians,
15:19 the waters of the sea *f* back upon them,
17: 6 will *f* from it for the people to drink."
Lv 12: 7 will be clean again after her *f* of blood.
15: 2 man who is afflicted with a chronic *f*
15: 3 *f* that it makes no difference whether the *f*
15: 4 on which the man afflicted with the *f* lies,
15:13 with a *f* becomes free of his affliction,
15:15 atonement before the LORD for the man's *f*.
15:19 "When a woman has her menstrual *f*,
15:25 "When a woman is afflicted with a *f* of
15:25 her *f* continues beyond the ordinary period,
15:25 this unclean *f* she shall be unclean,
15:26 she lies during such a *f* becomes unclean,
15:30 before the LORD for her unclean *f*.
15:32 the man who is afflicted with a chronic *f*,
15:33 or who is afflicted with a chronic *f*;
22: 4 with leprosy, or who suffers from a *f*,
Nm 13:27 It does indeed *f* with milk and honey,
Jos 3:13 water of the Jordan, it will cease to *f*;
4: 7 'The waters of the Jordan ceased to *f*
1Sm 26:20 Do not let my blood *f* to the ground far
Jb 6:17 snow heaped upon them, Yet once they *f*,
12:19 lets their never-failing waters *f* away.
Ps(s) 78:16 He made streams *f* from the crag and
Wis 19:18 while the *f* of music steadily persists.
Is 8: 6 the waters of Shiloah that *f* gently,
Jer 18:14 dry up that *f* fresh down the mountains?
Lam 2:18 your tears *f* like a torrent day and night;
3:49 My eyes *f* without ceasing,
Ez 21:37 your blood shall *f* throughout the land.
28:23 and blood shall *f* in its streets.
32:14 waters clear, and their streams *f* like oil,
47:12 be watered by the *f* from the sanctuary.
Jl 4:18 new wine, and the hills shall *f* with milk;
4:18 the channels of Judah shall *f* with water:
Zec 14: 8 day, living waters shall *f* from Jerusalem,
Mk 5:29 Immediately her *f* of blood dried up and
Jn 7:38 within him rivers of living water shall *f*.'"

FLOWED (13)

Ex 14:27 at dawn the sea *f* back to its normal depth.
14:28 As the water *f* back,
1Kgs 18:35 The water *f* around the altar,
22:35 his wound *f* to the bottom of the chariot.
Est 1: 7 golden cups, and the royal wine *f* freely,
2Mc 12:16 to be filled with the blood that *f* into it.
Jb 29: 6 milk, and the rock *f* with streams of oil;
Ps(s) 105:41 it *f* through the dry lands like a stream,
Lam 3:54 The waters *f* over my head,
Ez 47: 1 the water *f* down from the southern side of
Dn 7:10 stream of fire *f* out from where he sat;
Jn 19:34 and immediately blood and water *f* out.
Rv 22: 2 Lamb and *f* down the middle of the streets.

FLOWER (13)

Jb 14: 2 Like a *f* that springs up and fades,
Ps(s) 72: 7 Justice shall *f* in his days,
103:15 like a *f* of the field he blooms;
Sg 2: 1 I am a *f* of Sharon.
Sir 24:29 water my plants, my *f* bed I will drench";
Is 40: 6 all their glory like the *f* of the field.
40: 7 The grass withers, the *f* wilts,
40: 8 Though the grass withers and the *f* wilts,
Jer 48:15 *f* of his youth goes down to be slaughtered,
Mk 6:40 and fifties, neatly arranged like *f* beds.
Jas 1:10 will disappear "like the *f* of the field."
1Pt 1:24 glory of men is like the *f* of the field.
1:24 The grass withers, the *f* wilts,

FLOWERING (2)

Sir 43:22 heat, and the *f* plains as though by flames,
Is 18: 5 Before the vintage, when the *f* is ended,

FLOWERS (11)

1Kgs 6:18 carved in the form of gourds and open *f*;
6:29 of cherubim, palm trees, and open *f*.
6:32 of cherubim, palm trees, and open *f*.
6:35 carved cherubim, palm trees, and open *f*,
7:49 left before the sanctuary, with their *f*,
2Chr 4:21 to prescription before the sanctuary, *f*,
Sg 2:12 The *f* appear on the earth,
Sir 40:22 but better than either, the *f* of the field.
Is 35: 2 They will bloom with abundant *f*,

Mt 6:28 a lesson from the way the wild *f* grow.
Jas 1:11 it parches the meadow, the field *f* droop,

FLOWING (36)

Ex 3: 8 land, a land *f* with milk and honey,
3:17 Jebusites, a land *f* with milk and honey.
13: 5 give you, a land *f* with milk and honey.
15: 8 piled up, the *f* waters stood like a mound,
33: 3 you to the land *f* with milk and honey.
Lv 20:18 have laid bare the *f* fountain of her blood.
20:24 possession, a land *f* with milk and honey.
Nm 14: 8 us that land, a land *f* with milk and honey.
16:13 away from a land *f* with milk and honey,
16:14 us to a land *f* with milk and honey,
Dt 6: 3 to give you a land *f* with milk and honey.
11: 9 descendants, a land *f* with milk and honey.
26: 9 he gave us this land *f* with milk and honey.
26:15 given us in the land *f* with milk and honey
27: 3 enter into the land *f* with milk and honey,
31:20 brought them into the land *f* with milk
Jos 3:13 for the water *f* down from upstream will
3:16 than the waters *f* from upstream halted,
3:16 while those *f* downstream toward the Salt
5: 6 he would not let them see the land *f* with
Ps(s) 58: 8 Let them vanish like water *f* off;
114: 8 pools of water, the flint into *f* springs.
Prv 18: 4 but the source of wisdom is a *f* brook.
Sg 4:15 a well of water *f* fresh from Lebanon.
Sir 46: 8 the land *f* with milk and honey.
Is 44: 4 verdure like poplars beside the *f* waters.
48:21 Water from the rock he set *f* for them;
Jer 11: 5 to give them a land *f* with milk and honey:
32:22 under oath, a land *f* with milk and honey.
Bar 1:20 to give us the land *f* with milk and honey,
Ez 20: 6 for them, a land *f* with milk and honey,
20:15 given them, a land *f* with milk and honey,
23:15 their waists, *f* turbans on their heads,
47: 1 and I saw water *f* out from beneath the
Jn 4:11 Where do you expect to get this *f* water?
Phil 3:10 and the power *f* from his resurrection;

FLOWN (1)

Jer 4:25 even the birds of the air had *f* away!

FLOWS (8)

Gn 2:14 it is the one that *f* east of Asshur.
Ezr 8:15 assemble by the river that *f* toward Ahava,
Jdt 7:12 that *f* out at the base of the mountain,
Sg 7:10 that *f* smoothly for my lover,
Wis 5:12 the parted air straightway *f* together
Ez 32: 6 I will water the land with what *f* from you,
47: 8 "This water *f* into the eastern district
47: 9 Wherever the river *f*,

FLUENTLY (1)

Is 32: 4 the stutterers will speak *f* and clearly.

FLUID (1)

Wis 5:11 But the *f* air,

FLUNG (7)

Gn 44:14 they *f* themselves on the ground before him.
45:14 Thereupon he *f* himself on the neck of his
46:29 he *f* himself on his neck and wept a long
2Mc 14:46 and *f* them with both hands into the crowd,
Ez 19:12 was torn up in fury and *f* to the ground;
Mt 27: 5 Judas *f* the money into the temple and left.
Acts 22:23 their cloaks and *f* dirt through the air.

FLUSHED (3)

Is 16: 2 Like *f* birds,
Bar 1:15 and we today are *f* with shame,
2: 6 our fathers, are *f* with shame even today.

FLUTE (11)

1Mc 3:45 Jacob, and the *f* and the harp were silent.
Jb 21:12 harp, and make merry to the sound of the *f*.
Sir 40:21 The *f* and the harp offer sweet melody,
Is 5:12 With harp and lyre, timbrel and *f*,
30:29 with a *f* Toward the mountain of the LORD,
Dn 3: 4 when you hear the sound of the trumpet, *f*,
3: 7 as they heard the sound of the trumpet, *f*,
3:10 who heard the sound of the trumpet, *f*,
3:15 you hear the sound of the trumpet, *f*,
Mt 9:23 saw the *f* players and the crowd who
1Cor 14: 7 produce a sound, such as a *f* or a harp,

FLUTES (5)

1Sm 10: 5 by lyres, tambourines, *f* and harps.
1Kgs 1:40 playing *f* and rejoicing so much as to
1Mc 4:54 with songs, harps, *f* and cymbals.
Jer 48:36 the wail of *f* for Moab is in my heart;
48:36 of Kir-heres the wail of *f* is in my heart;

FLUTISTS (1)

Rv 18:22 and minstrels, of *f* and trumpeters,

FLUTTERED (1)

Is 10:14 No one *f* a wing,

FLUTTERING (1)

Sir 43:18 He sprinkles the snow like *f* birds;

FLY (13)

Gn 1:20 let birds *f* beneath the dome of the sky."
Lv 14: 7 living bird *f* away over the countryside.
14:53 He shall then let the living bird *f* away
Jb 5: 7 begets mischief, as sparks *f* upward.
39:27 Does the eagle *f* up at your command to
Ps(s) 55: 7 like a dove, I would *f* away and be at rest.
Eccl 9:18 "A *f* that dies can spoil the perfumer's
Sir 47: 4 When his hand let *f* the slingstone that
Is 7:18 that day The LORD shall whistle for the *f*
60: 8 What are these that *f* along like clouds,
Na 3:17 grasshoppers will spread their wings and *f*.
Hb 1: 8 They *f* like the eagle hastening to devour;
Rv 12:14 she could *f* off to her place in the desert,

FLYING (10)

Wis 5:11 Or like a bird *f* through the air;
Is 14:29 an adder, its fruit shall be a *f* saraph.
29: 5 the horde of the tyrants like *f* chaff.
30: 6 roaring lion, of the viper and *f* saraph,
Hb 3:11 its shelter, At the light of your *f* arrows,
Zec 5: 1 I raised my eyes again and saw a scroll *f*.
5: 2 I answered, "I see a scroll *f*;
Rv 8:13 *f* in midheaven cry out in a loud voice,
14: 6 Then I saw another angel *f* in midheaven,
19:17 loud voice to all the birds *f* in midheaven.

FOAL (2)

Zec 9: 9 on an ass, on a colt, the *f* of an ass.
Mt 21: 5 astride a colt, the *f* of a beast of burden."

FOAM (6)

Ps(s) 46: 4 *f* and the mountains quake at its surging.
Wis 5:14 the wind, and like fine, tempest-driven *f*;
Hos 10: 7 shall disappear, like *f* upon the waters.
Mk 9:20 he began to roll around and *f* at the mouth.
Lk 9:39 a convulsion and makes him *f* at the mouth,
Jude 1:13 their shameless deeds abroad like *f*,

FOAMING (3)

Dt 32:14 and the *f* blood of its grapes you drank.
Ps(s) 75: 9 the LORD's hand, full of spiced and *f* wine,
Jer 25:15 Take this cup of *f* wine from my hand,

FOAMS (1)

Mk 9:18 he *f* at the mouth and grinds his teeth and

FOCUS (1)

1Sm 4:15 years old, and his eyes would not *f*,

FODDER (9)

Gn 24:25 is plenty of straw and *f* at our place,"
24:32 unloaded and provided with straw and *f*,
42:27 opened his bag to give his donkey some *f*,
43:24 their feet, and got *f* for their donkeys.
Jgs 19:19 We have straw and *f* for our asses,
19:21 to his house and provided *f* for the asses.
Jb 6: 5 Does the ox low over his *f*?
Sir 33:25 *F* and whip and loads for an ass;
Lk 15:16 with the husks that were *f* for the pigs,

FOE (24)

Ex 23:22 enemy to your enemies and a *f* to your foes.
1Kgs 20:27 then they went out to engage the *f*.
Est 9:10 son of Hammedatha, the *f* of the Jews.
9:24 the Agagite, the *f* of all the Jews,
2Mc 10:26 to their enemies, and a *f* to their foes,
Ps(s) 60:13 Give us aid against the *f*,
74:10 How long, O God, shall the *f* blaspheme?
78:42 nor the day he delivered them from the *f*,
78:61 his glory into the hands of the *f*.
107: 2 of the *f* 3And gathered from the lands,
108:13 Give us aid against the *f*,
Sir 6: 1 be not a *f* instead of a friend;
19: 7 Tell nothing to friend or *f*;
28:26 fall victim to your *f* waiting in ambush.
29:13 spear it will fight for you against the *f*.
36: 6 out wrath, humble the enemy, scatter the *f*.
37: 5 friend will fight with you against the *f*,
46: 6 army till on the slope he destroyed the *f*;
Jer 44:30 king of Judah, to his enemy and mortal *f*,
Lam 1: 5 ones have gone away, captive before the *f*.
1:10 The *f* stretched out his hand to all her
2: 4 his right hand He took his stand as a *f*,
4:12 or *f* could enter the gates of Jerusalem.
Na 3:11 you, too, shall seek a refuge from the *f*.

FOES (96)

Gn 14:20 High, who delivered your *f* into your hand."
Ex 23:22 enemy to your enemies and a foe to your *f*.
32:25 that, to the scornful joy of their *f*,

Lv 26: 8 you will put a hundred of your *f* to flight,
26:17 your enemies and lorded over by your *f*.
26:37 will you be to take a stand against your *f*!
Nm 10: 9 will remember you and save you from your *f*.
23:11 was to curse my *f* that I brought you here;
24:10 was to curse my *f* that I summoned you here;
24:19 valiantly, and Jacob shall overcome his *f*.
Dt 30: 7 your enemies and the *f* who persecuted you.
32:27 feared that these *f* would mistakenly boast,
32:31 our Rock, and our *f* are under condemnation.
32:41 repay my *f* and requite those who hate me.
33: 7 and you will be his help against his *f*."
33:11 the backs of his adversaries and of his *f*,
Jos 10:13 while the nation took vengeance on its *f*.
1Sm 2:10 the LORD's *f* shall be shattered.
2Sm 22:18 rescued me from my mighty enemy, from my *f*,
1Chr 21:12 with the sword of your *f* ever at your back;
Est 9:16 killed seventy-five thousand of their *f*,
2Mc 10:26 to their enemies, and a foe to their *f*,
Ps(s) 6: 8 they have aged because of all my *f*.
7: 5 spared those who without cause were my *f*—
7: 7 rise against the fury of my *f*;
8: 3 have fashioned praise because of your *f*,
9:14 see how I am afflicted by my *f*,
10: 5 all his *f* he scorns.
13: 5 Lest my *f* rejoice at my downfall though
17: 7 from their *f* to refuge at your right hand.
18:18 me from my mighty enemy and from my *f*,
21: 9 enemies, may your right hand reach your *f*!
23: 5 the table before me in the sight of my *f*;
27: 2 My *f* and my enemies themselves tumble and
27:12 Give me not up to the wishes of my *f*;
31:12 For all my *f* I am an object of reproach,
35:19 let not my undeserved *f* wink knowingly.
38:20 many are my *f* without cause.
41: 8 All my *f* whisper together against me;
42:11 It crushes my bones that my *f* mock me,
44: 6 Our *f* through you we struck down;
44: 8 But you saved us from our *f*,
44:11 You have let us be driven back by our *f*;
54: 7 Turn back the evil upon my *f*;
59:11 may he show me the fall of my *f*.
60:14 it is he who will tread down our *f*.
69:15 may I be rescued from my *f*,
69:20 before you are all my *f*.
72: 9 His *f* shall bow before him,
74: 4 Your *f* roar triumphantly in your shrine;
74:23 Be not unmindful of the voice of your *f*;
78:66 And he put his *f* to flight and cast them
81:15 against their *f* I would turn my hand.
89:24 But I will crush his *f* before him and
89:43 You have exalted the right hands of his *f*,
92:12 And my eye has looked down upon my *f*,
97: 3 before him and consumes his *f* round about.
105:24 made them stronger than their *f*
106:11 The waters covered their *f*;
106:41 the nations, and their *f* ruled over them.
108:14 it is he who will tread down our *f*.
112: 8 not fear till he looks down upon his *f*.
118: 7 help me, and I shall look down upon my *f*.
119:139 me, because my *f* forget your words.
119:157 Though my persecutors and my *f* are many,
136:24 And freed us from our *f*,
139:20 your *f* swear faithless oaths.
143:12 bring to nought all my *f*,
Wis 2:18 him and deliver him from the hand of his *f*.
10:12 She preserved him from *f*,
11: 3 enemies and took vengeance on their *f*.
11: 5 For by the things through which their *f*
16: 8 And by this also you convinced our *f* that
18: 7 of the just and the destruction of their *f*.
Sir 23: 3 Lest I succumb to my *f*,
25:13 of all sufferings is that from one's *f*,
30: 6 The avenger he leaves against his *f*,
Is 1:24 on my *f* and fully repay my enemies!
9:10 But the LORD raises up their *f* against
59:18 deserts, and requites his *f* with wrath.
Jer 12: 7 my soul I deliver into the hand of her *f*.
20: 5 give as plunder into the hand of their *f*,
46:10 a day of vengeance, vengeance on his *f*!
49:37 I will break Elam before their *f*,
Lam 1: 5 Her *f* are uppermost,
1: 7 When her *f* gloated over her,
1:17 Jacob for his neighbors to be his *f*;
2:17 over you and exalting the horn of your *f*.
3:62 me], The whispered murmurings of my *f*,
Bar 3:10 that you are in the land of your *f*,
4: 6 God that you were handed over to your *f*.
Ez 39:23 from them and handed them over to their *f*,
Dn 4:17 your enemies, and its meaning for your *f*.
Mi 5: 8 Your hand shall be lifted above your *f*,
Na 3:13 *f* the gates of your land are open wide,
Lk 1:71 enemies and from the hands of all our *f*.

FOIL (1)

Jer 19: 7 I will *f* the plan of Judah and Jerusalem;

FOILS (1)

Ps(s) 33:10 he *f* the designs of peoples.

FOLD (10)

Ps(s) 50: 9 house no bullock, no goats out of your *f*.
Jer 50: 6 they wandered, losing the way to their *f*.
50:19 But I will bring back Israel to her *f*,
Mi 2:12 I will group them like a flock in the *f*,
Hb 3:17 the *f* and there be no herd in the stalls,
Hg 2:12 *f* of his garment and the *f* touches bread,
Lk 6:38 will they pour into the *f* of your garment.
Jn 10:16 other sheep that do not belong to this *f*.
2Pt 1:14 how close is the day when I must *f* my tent.

FOLDED (5)

Ex 28:16 It is to be square when *f* double,
39: 9 *f* double a span high and a span wide its *f*
Is 8:16 The record is to be *f* and the sealed
38:12 You have *f* up my life,

FOLDING (2)

Prv 6:10 slumber, a little *f* of the arms to rest
24:33 slumber, a little *f* of the arms to rest

FOLDS (4)

Nm 32:24 your families, and the *f* for your flocks,
Neh 5:13 I also shook out the *f* of my garment,
Eccl 4: 5 *f* his arms and consumes his own flesh"
Zep 2: 6 fields for shepherds, and *f* for flocks.

FOLIAGE (10)

Ex 10: 5 *f* that has since sprouted in your fields.
Lv 23:40 day you shall gather *f* from majestic trees,
Ps(s) 80:12 It put forth its *f* to the Sea,
Jer 8:13 vine, No figs on the fig trees, *f* withered!
Ez 19:11 Stately was her height amid the dense *f*;
31: 7 beautiful and stately in its spread of *f*,
31: 9 I made it beautiful, with much *f*,
31:12 Its *f* was brought low in all the valleys,
Dn 4:18 which had beautiful *f* and abundant fruit,
Mk 11:13 tree some distance off, covered with *f*,

FOLK (6)

Jb 12: 2 No doubt you are the intelligent *f*,
21:11 These *f* have infants numerous as lambs,
Sir 44: 4 Resolute princes of the *f*,
50:26 and the degenerate *f* who dwell in Shechem.
Is 51: 4 my *f*, give ear to me.
Zep 2: 5 who dwell by the seacoast, to the Cretan *f*!

FOLLIES (2)

Sir 30:11 youth, and close not your eyes to his *f*.
Acts 14:15 just such *f* as these to the living God,

FOLLOW (144)

Gn 24: 5 woman is unwilling to *f* me to this land?
24: 8 If the woman is unwilling to *f* you,
24:39 master, 'What if the woman will not *f* me?,'
41:36 famine that are to *f* in the land of Egypt,
Ex 16: 4 see whether they *f* my instructions or not.
Lv 18: 4 and my statutes you shall take care to *f*.
20: 6 and fortune-tellers and *f* their wanton ways,
Dt 1:22 road we must *f* and the cities we must take.'
6:14 You shall not *f* other gods,
8:19 the LORD, your God, and *f* other gods,
10:12 the LORD, your God, and *f* his ways exactly,
11:28 I ordain for you today, to *f* other gods,
13: 3 sign or wonder, urging you to *f* other gods,
13: 5 The LORD, your God, shall you *f*,
28:14 in order to *f* other gods and serve them.
Jos 3: 3 carry, you must also break camp and *f* it,
14: 1 Here *f* the portions which the Israelites
22: 5 *f* him faithfully; keep his commandments;
Jgs 2:17 and did not *f* their example of obedience
3:28 *F* me," he said to them,
6:34 the horn that summoned Abiezer to *f* him.
7:17 "Watch me and *f* my lead," he told them.
Ru 2: 9 which field is to be harvested, and *f* them;
1Sm 8: 3 His sons did not *f* his example but sought
8: 5 old, and your sons do not *f* your example,
11: 7 does not come out to *f* Saul [and Samuel],
12:14 the king who rules you *f* the LORD your God
25:19 I will *f* you."
25:27 it be given to the young men who *f* my lord.
30:21 men who had been too exhausted to *f* him,
2Sm 17: 6 Shall we *f* his proposal?
20:11 who favors Joab and is for David *f* Joab."
1Kgs 3:14 And if you *f* me by keeping my statutes and
8:58 *f* him in everything and keep the commands,
11: 6 he did not *f* him unreservedly as his
11:38 you heed all that I command you, *f* my ways,
18:21 LORD is God, *f* him; if Baal, *f* him."
19:20 and mother good-bye, and I will *f* you."
2Kgs 6:19 *F* me! I will take you
21:22 and did not *f* the path of the LORD.
23: 3 would *f* him and observe his ordinances,
2Chr 17: 6 he was encouraged to *f* the LORD's ways,
23:14 the ranks, and if anyone tries to *f* her,
25:27 the time that Amaziah ceased to *f* the LORD,
34:31 to *f* the LORD and to keep his commandments,
Neh 10:30 curse take this oath to *f* the law of God
Jdt 5: 7 for they did not wish to *f* the gods of
11: 6 if you *f* out the words of your handmaid,
Est 2:20 continued to *f* Mordecai's instructions,
E:19 certify that the Jews may *f* their own laws,
1Mc 1:44 them to *f* customs foreign to their land;
2:27 and who stands by the covenant *f* after me!
6:23 and to *f* his orders and obey his edicts.
10:34 each feast day, and the three days that *f*,
10:37 among them, and let them *f* their own laws,
2Mc 3:24 who had been bold enough to *f* Heliodorus
15: 2 The Jews who were forced to *f* him pleaded,
Ps(s) 23: 6 and kindness *f* me all the days of my life;
34:15 seek peace, and *f* after it.
49:18 his wealth shall not *f* him down.
68:26 The singers lead, the minstrels *f*,
94:15 and all the upright of heart shall *f* it.
Eccl 11: 9 *F* the ways of your heart,
Sg 1: 8 *F* the tracks of the flock and pasture the
Sir 14:19 decay, and his handiwork will *f* after him.
20:10 Humiliation can *f* fame,
26:11 *F* close if her eyes are bold,
27:17 if you betray his confidence, *f* him not;
27:20 *F* him not,
Is 3:12 they destroy the paths you should *f*.
45:14 they shall *f* you,
65: 2 in evil paths and *f* their own thoughts,
Jer 7: 6 place, or *f* strange gods to your own harm,
13:10 and *f* strange gods to serve and adore them,
18:12 We will *f* our own devices;
25: 6 not *f* strange gods to serve and adore them,
32:18 even into the lap of their sons who *f* them.
35:15 and not *f* strange gods or serve them,
42: 5 faithfully *f* all the instructions the LORD,
44:10 they do not fear or *f* the law and the
Bar 2:10 or *f* the precepts of the Lord which he set
Ez 13: 3 *f* their own spirit and have seen no vision.
29:16 guilt for having turned to *f* after them.
Dn 3:40 presence today as we *f* you unreservedly;
3:41 And now we *f* you with our whole heart,
Hos 11:10 They shall *f* the LORD,
Mt 3:11 one who will *f* me is more powerful than I.
4:22 they abandoned boat and father to *f* him.
8:22 But Jesus told him, *F* me,
9: 9 He said to him, *F* me."
16:24 his cross, and begin to *f* in my footsteps.
19:21 Afterward, come back and *f* me."
19:27 we have put everything aside to *f* you.
23: 3 But do not *f* their example.
Mk 2:14 collector's post, and said to him, *F* me."
5:37 not permit anyone to *f* him except Peter,
7: 5 not *f* the tradition of our ancestors,
8:34 self, take up his cross, and *f* in my steps.
10:21 After that, come and *f* me."
10:28 "We have put aside everything to *f* you!"
10:52 his sight and started to *f* him up the road.
14:13 carrying a water jar. *F* him.
Lk 5:27 He said to him, *F* me."
9:23 up his cross each day, and *f* in my steps.
12:31 over you, and the rest will *f* in turn.
14:27 his cross and *f* me cannot be my disciple.
15: 4 and *f* the lost one until he finds it?
18:22 Then come and *f* me."
18:43 he was given his sight and began to *f* him,
21: 8 Do not *f* them.
21: 9 first, but the end does not *f* immediately."
22:10 *F* him into the house he enters,
Jn 1:43 *F* me," Jesus said to him.
10: 4 *f* him because they recognize his voice.
10: 5 They will not *f* a stranger;
10:27 I know them, and they *f* me.
12:26 If anyone would serve me, let him *f* me;
13:36 "I am going where you cannot *f* me now;
13:37 said to him, "why can I not *f* you now?
21:19 had finished speaking he said to him, *F* me."
21:22 Your business is to *f* me."
Acts 12: 8 told him, "Now put on your cloak and *f* me."
16:17 to *f* Paul and the rest of us shouting,
20:30 truth and leading astray any who *f* them.
21:24 you *f* the law yourself with due observance.
27:44 The rest were to *f*,
Rom 4:12 *f* the path of faith which Abraham walked
14:15 you have ceased to *f* the rule of love.
1Cor 16: 1 *f* the instructions I gave the churches of
Gal 5:25 by the spirit, let us *f* the spirit's lead.
6:13 circumcision do not *f* the law themselves.
6:16 and mercy on all who *f* this rule of life,
Eph 5: 2 *F* the way of love,
Phil 3:17 guide those who *f* the example that we set.
2Thes 3: 6 not *f* the tradition you received from us.
1Tm 5:15 Already, some have turned away to *f* Satan.
Ti 1: 9 encourage men to *f* sound doctrine
1Pt 1:11 for Christ and the glories that would *f*.
2:21 an example, to have you *f* in his footsteps.
3:11 and do good, seek peace and *f* after it,
1Jn 3:12 We should not *f* the example of Cain who
Rv 2:14 among you who *f* the teaching of Balaam,
14: 4 are pure and *f* the Lamb wherever he goes.

FOLLOWED (111)

Gn 1: 5 evening came, and morning *f*— the first day.
1: 8 Evening came, and morning *f*— the second day.
1:13 Evening came, and morning *f*— the third day.
1:19 Evening came, and morning *f*— the fourth day.

FOLLOWED (cont.)

1:23 Evening came, and morning f— the fifth day.
1:31 Evening came, and morning f— the sixth day.
24:61 they mounted their camels and f the man.
32:20 to all the others who f behind the droves,
34:27 Then the other sons of Jacob f up the
41:30 these will be f by seven years of famine,
Ex 14:23 The Egyptians f in pursuit;
14:28 which had f the Israelites into the sea.
18:24 Moses f the advice of his father-in-law
Nm 16:25 Moses, f by the elders of Israel,
25: 8 f the Israelite into his retreat where be
32:11 'Because they have not f me unreservedly,
32:12 of Nun, who have f the LORD unreservedly.'
Dt 1:36 because he has f the LORD unreservedly.'
4: 3 midst everyone that f the Baal of Peor;
33: 3 they f at his feet and he bore them up on
Jos 6: 9 the rear guard f the ark,
6:13 while the rear guard f the ark of the LORD,
Jgs 2:12 they f the other gods of the various
3:28 So they f him down and seized the fords of
4:10 to Kedesh, and ten thousand men f him.
4:14 Mount Tabor, f by his ten thousand men.
13:11 so Manoah got up and f his wife.
1Sm 6:12 The Philistine lords f them as far as the
14:13 armor-bearer f him and finished them off.
17:13 oldest sons of Jesse had f Saul to war;
25:42 mounted an ass, and f David's messengers,
2Sm 2:10 The Judahites alone f David.
3: 1 There f a long war between the house of
3:16 Laish, who f her weeping as far as Bahurim.
3:31 King David himself f the bier.
1Kgs 11:33 he has not f my ways or done what is
13:14 it, he mounted and f the man of God,
14: 8 commandments and f me with his whole heart,
19:21 Then he left and f Elijah as his attendant.
22:43 He f all the ways of his father Asa
2Kgs 2: 7 Fifty of the guild prophets f,
7:15 They f the Arameans as far as the Jordan,
17: 8 They f the rites of the nations whom the
17:15 they f the surrounding nations whom the
17:19 God, but f the rites practiced by Israel.
21:21 He f exactly the path his father had trod,
2Chr 20:32 f the path of his father Asa unswervingly,
21:12 not f the path of your father Jehoshaphat,
22: 3 He, too, f the ways of the house of Ahab,
26:17 priests of the LORD, courageous men, f him.
Neh 12:32 f by Hoshaiah and half the princes of
12:38 f by myself and the other half of the
Tb 6: 2 the dog f Tobiah out of the house and went
Jdt 9: 5 events and of what preceded and f them.
13:16 who has protected me in the path I have f,
15:13 while the men of Israel f in their armor,
Est D: 4 gently for support, while the other f her,
1Mc 9:16 back, they turned and f Judas and his men,
10:78 Jonathan f him to Azotus,
2Mc 2: 6 f him came up intending to mark the path,
8:36 that they f the laws laid down by him.
Jb 31: 7 out of the way, and my heart has f my eyes,
32:12 I f you attentively as you searched out
Jer 8: 2 which they loved and served, which they f,
9:12 and have not f it or listened to my voice,
9:13 but f rather the hardness of their hearts
11: 8 Each one f the hardness of his evil heart,
11:10 They also have f and served strange gods;
16:11 me, says the LORD, and f strange gods,
35:14 his children to drink wine, has been f:
Bar 1:18 nor f the precepts which the Lord set
Ez 23:31 Because you f in the path of your sister,
Am 2: 4 which their fathers f have led them astray,
Mt 4:25 great crowds that f him came from Galilee,
8: 1 down from the mountain, great crowds f him.
8:23 got into the boat and his disciples f him.
9: 9 Matthew got up and f him.
9:19 Jesus stood up and f him,
12:15 Many people f him and he cured them all,
14:13 of it and f him on foot from the towns.
19: 2 Great crowds f him and he cured them there.
19:28 you who have f me shall likewise take your
20:29 were leaving Jericho a large crowd f him,
27:55 They had f Jesus from Galilee to attend to
Mk 2:15 The number of those who f him was large.
3: 7 A great crowd f him from Galilee,
5:24 two went off together and a large crowd f,
6: 1 own part of the country f by his disciples.
10:32 while that of those who f was fear.
11: 9 him as well as those who f cried out:
14:54 Peter f him at a distance right into the
15:41 These women had f Jesus when he was in
Lk 9:11 but the crowds found this out and f him.
9:15 f his instructions and got them all seated.
22:54 high priest, while Peter f at a distance.
23:27 A great crowd of people f him,
23:55 come with him from Galilee f along behind.
Jn 1:37 disciples heard what he said, and f Jesus.
1:40 One of the two who had f him after hearing
11:31 get up quickly and go out, so they f her,
Acts 8:11 Those who f him had been under the spell
12: 9 Peter f him out,
13:43 devout Jewish converts f Paul and Barnabas,
Rom 5:16 the sentence f upon one offense and
1Tm 4: 6 the sound doctrine you have faithfully f
2Tm 3:10 have f closely my teaching and my conduct.
Rv 8: 5 of thunder and flashes of lightning f,
13: 3 the whole world f after the beast.
14: 8 A second angel f and cried out:
14: 9 f the others and said in a loud voice:
16:18 f lightning flashes and peals of thunder,

FOLLOWER (11)

1Kgs 18: 4 vizier, who was a zealous f of the LORD.
Sir 46: 6 And because he was a devoted f of God
46:10 good it is to be a devoted f of the LORD.
Mk 2:14 Levi got up and became his f.
Lk 5:28 behind, Levi stood up and became his f.
9:23 wishes to be my f must deny his very self,
9:57 to him, "I will be your f wherever you go."
9:61 another said to him, "I will be your f,
14:26 indeed his very self, he cannot be my f.
Jn 8:12 No f of mine shall ever walk in darkness;
Acts 8:13 the rest and became a devoted f of Philip.

FOLLOWERS (32)

Ex 11: 8 beg me, 'Leave us, you and all your f!'
Nm 16:17 and fifty f shall take his own censer,
Jos 13:22 and among their slain f the Israelites put
Jgs 8: 5 "Will you give my f some loaves of bread?
8:15 that we should give food to your weary f?' "
9: 4 hired shiftless men and ruffians as his f.
9:33 When he and his f come out against you,
1Sm 13: 7 although all his f were seized with fear.
2Sm 2:31 and sixty men of Benjamin, f of Abner.
6:20 to the view of the slave girls of his f,
17: 9 say, 'Absalom's f have been slaughtered.'
17:12 neither he nor any of his f.
1Kgs 20:10 in Samaria to make handfuls for all my f."
1Mc 2:42 all of them devout f of the law.
3:14 the kingdom by defeating Judas and his f,
7:25 But when Alcimus saw that Judas and his f
2Mc 1: 7 after Jason and his f had revolted
13:14 his f to fight nobly to death for the laws,
14:13 to put Judas to death, to disperse his f,
Sir 45:18 in the desert, The f of Dathan and Abiram,
Is 66:17 the groves, as f of one who stands within,
Mt 4:20 abandoned their nets and became his f.
8:10 on hearing this and remarked to his f,
13:38 The weeds are the f of the evil one and
20:34 and they became his f.
Mk 1:18 abandoned their nets and became his f.
16:10 went to announce the good news to his f,
Lk 5:11 to land, left everything, and became his f.
18:28 "We have left all we own to become your f."
Jn 18:17 Peter, "Are you not one of this man's f?"
Acts 5:37 died, and all his f were dispersed.
Rv 17:14 victorious, too, will be his f—

FOLLOWING (152)

Gn 32:14 him the f presents for his brother Esau:
36:15 The f are the clans of Esau's descendants.
36:20 f are the descendants of Seir the Horite,
36:31 The f are the kings who reigned in the
36:40 The f are the names of the clans of Esau
47:18 they came to him in the f one and said:
Ex 16:20 kept a part of it over until the f morning,
38:21 The f is an account of the various amounts
Lv 6: 2 "Give Aaron and his sons the f command:
11: 4 But you shall not eat any of the f that
11: 9 that live in the water, you may eat the f:
11:22 hence of these you may eat the f:
11:29 on the ground, the f are unclean for you:
19: 6 very day of your sacrifice or on the f day.
21:18 any of the f defects may not come forward:
23: 2 The f are the festivals of the LORD,
Nm 1: 1 In the year f that of the Israelites'
3: 1 The f were the descendants of Aaron and
9: 1 f their departure from the land of Egypt,
14:43 You have turned back from f the LORD;
29:12 then, for seven days f,
32:15 If you turn away from f him,
33: 1 The f are the stages by which the
34: 7 f shall be your boundary on the north:
Dt 5:33 but f exactly the way prescribed for you
7: 4 your sons from f me to serving other gods,
11:22 the LORD, your God, and f his ways exactly,
12:30 their land, you will be lured into f them.
14: 7 But you shall not eat any of the f that
14:12 But you shall not eat any of the f:
18: 3 a right to the f things from the people:
19: 4 "It is in the f case that a homicide may
33: 7 The f is for Judah.
Jos 6: 8 the ark of the covenant of the LORD f them.
21: 3 the f cities with their pasture lands.
21: 9 Simeonites they designated the f cities,
Jgs 2:19 f other gods in service and worship,
3: 1 The f are the nations which the LORD
9:49 cut down brushwood, and f Abimelech,
19:25 and abused her all night until the f dawn,
1Sm 20:19 the f day you will be missed all the more.
25:42 her five maids f in attendance upon her.
2Sm 11:12 On the day f,
13: 1 Some time later the f incident occurred.
17:21 has given the f counsel in regard to you."
24:19 F Gad's bidding,
1Kgs 2: 3 God, f his ways and observing his statutes,
11:10 him this very act of f strange gods,
16:21 of Israel were divided, half f Tibni,
18:18 the commands of the LORD and f the Baals.
19:19 he was f the twelfth.
20:19 of the provinces with the army f them
21:26 He became completely abominable by f idols,
2Kgs 4:17 the f year she had given birth to a son,
17:33 f the worship of the nations from among
21: 2 f the abominable practices of the nations
1Chr 1:43 before they had Israelite kings were the f:
3: 1 The f were the sons of David who were born
3: 5 in Jerusalem, where the f were born to him:
5:24 f were the heads of their ancestral houses:
6: 4 The f were the clans of Levi,
6:16 The f were entrusted by David with the
6:18 Those who so performed are the f,
6:39 The f were their dwelling places to which
10: 8 On the f day,
12: 1 The f men came to David in Ziklag while he
17: 7 you from the pasture, from f the sheep,
20: 1 At the beginning of the f year,
29:21 On the f day they offered sacrifices and
2Chr 2:16 in the land of Israel f the census David
22: 5 He was also f their counsel when he accompanied
33: 2 f the abominable practices of the nations
34: 2 the LORD, f the path of his ancestor David.
Ezr 2:59 The f who returned from Tel-melah,
4: 8 wrote the f letter against Jerusalem to
4:17 West-of-Euphrates, greetings and the f:
5: 7 him a report in which was written the f:
5: 9 the elders, addressing to them the f words:
6: 2 a scroll was found containing the f text:
10:18 the f were found to have taken foreign
Neh 7: 5 There I found the f written:
7:61 The f who returned from Tel-melah,
12: 1 The f are the priests and Levites who
Tb 9: 6 The f morning they got an early start and
Jdt 2:24 Then f the Euphrates,
7: 1 f day Holofernes ordered his whole army,
Est E: 1 The f is a copy of the letter:
1Mc 4:28 So the f year he gathered together sixty
11:29 The king agreed and wrote the f letter to
13:35 King Demetrius sent him the f letter:
14:22 have recorded the f in the public decrees:
14:27 The f is a copy of the inscription:
14:28 the country, the f proclamation was made:
14:41 have, therefore, made the f decisions.
2Mc 2: 4 how the prophet, f a divine revelation,
4:17 the laws of God, as the f period will show.
4:22 f this, he led his army into Phoenicia.
9:18 wrote the f letter to the Jews
9:27 I am confident that, f my policy,
12:39 On the f day,
Ps(s) 78:71 From f the ewes he brought him to shepherd
Sir 5: 2 strength in f the desires of your heart.
41:22 and of f up your gifts with insults;
Is 53: 6 gone astray like sheep, each f his own way;
58:13 from f your own pursuits on my holy day;
58:13 If you honor it by not f your ways,
59:13 the LORD, turning back from f our God,
Jer 2: 2 loved me as a bride, F me in the desert,
3:19 Father," I thought, and never cease f me.
7: 1 f message came to Jeremiah from the LORD:
11: 1 f message came to Jeremiah from the LORD:
30: 1 f message came to Jeremiah from the LORD:
39:11 gave the f orders through Nebuzaradan,
49:34 The f word of the LORD against Elam came
Dn 6: 8 governors are agreed that the f prohibition
Am 7:15 The LORD took me from f the flock,
Zec 1: 7 of Berechiah, son of Iddo, in the f way:
Mt 10: 5 after giving them the f instructions:
21: 9 him as well as those f kept crying out:
26:58 Peter kept f him at a distance as far as
27:62 next day, the one f the Day of Preparation,
Mk 14:51 There was a young man f him who was
Lk 1: 6 blamelessly f all the commandments and
7: 9 turned to the crowd which was f him to say,
9:37 The f day they came down from the mountain
20: 9 began to tell the people the f parable:
22:22 Son of Man is f out his appointed course,
Jn 1:16 love f upon love.
1:38 Jesus turned around and noticed them f him,
6: 2 a vast crowd kept f him because they saw
8:39 children, you would be f Abraham's example.
18:15 another disciple, kept f Jesus closely.
21:20 that the disciple whom Jesus loved was f
Acts 5:37 He too built up quite a f,
6: 5 F this they selected Stephen,
10:24 The f day, he arrived in Caesarea.
13:42 on this subject again on the f sabbath.
13:44 The f sabbath,
17: 2 F his usual custom,
21: 1 On the f day we came to Rhodes and went on
21:36 A crowd of people was f along shouting,
24: 2 F Paul's summons to the bar,
24:27 f which Felix was succeeded by Porcius
25: 6 On the f day he took his seat on the bench
27: 3 The f day we put in at Sidon,
Rom 6:19 (I use the f example from human affairs
1Cor 10: 4 from the spiritual rock that was f them,
2Cor 10:16 F the rule laid down for us,
Eph 2: 3 level of the flesh, f every whim and fancy,
1Tm 5: 7 Make the f rules about widows,

2Tm 2:15 *f* a straight course in preaching the truth.
4: 3 sound doctrine, but, *f* their own desires,

FOLLOWS (38)

Gn 32: 5 'Your servant Jacob speaks as *f*:
41:31 the land because of the famine that *f* it
Ex 26:18 Set up the boards of the Dwelling as *f*:
36:23 They were set up as *f*:
38: 9 The court was made as *f*.
Nm 14:24 a different spirit and *f* me unreservedly,
26: 4 came out of the land of Egypt were as *f*:
34:19 These shall be as *f*:
Dt 1: 5 the land of Moab beyond the Jordan, as *f*:
3:18 "At that time I charged them as *f*:
15: 2 of debts, which shall be observed as *f*.
1Sm 6:17 as a guilt offering to the LORD were as *f*:
8:11 of the king who will rule you will be as *f*:
2Kgs 11:15 If anyone *f* her,"
Ezr 4:10 in the province West-of-Euphrates, as *f*.
4:11 the men of West-of-Euphrates, as *f*:
Est B: 1 the governors subordinate to them, as *f*:
1Mc 8:19 envoys entered the senate and spoke as *f*:
15: 2 and to all the nations, which read as *f*:
2Mc 1:24 The prayer was as *f*:
11:27 The king's letter to the people was as *f*:
11:34 The Romans also sent them a letter as *f*:
Jb 21:33 While all the line of mankind *f* him,
Ps(s) 1: 1 Happy the man who *f* not the counsel of the
Prv 7:22 He *f* her stupidly,
12:11 but he who *f* idle pursuits is a fool.
25:14 Like clouds and wind when no rain *f* is the
Wis 14:31 *f* upon the transgression of the wicked.
Jer 27:16 priests and to all the people I spoke as *f*:
Ez 43:13 The height of the altar itself was as *f*:
Dn 12: 8 so I asked, "My lord, what *f* this?"
Hos 4: 2 their lawlessness, bloodshed *f* bloodshed.
Hb 3: 5 pestilence, and the plague *f* in his steps.
Mk 3:16 He appointed the Twelve as *f*:
Acts 3:12 saw this, he addressed the people as *f*:
24:10 then gestured to Paul, who replied as *f*:
Rom 7: 7 What *f* from what I have said?
Col 2: 8 philosophy that *f* mere human traditions,

FOLLY (52)

2Sm 15:31 LORD, turn the counsel of Ahithophel to *f*!"
2Mc 4: 6 and that Simon would not desist from his *f*.
4:40 a man as advanced in *f* as he was in years.
15:33 other wages of his *f* opposite the temple.
Ps(s) 2: 1 the nations rage and the peoples utter *f*?
38: 6 festering are my sores because of my *f*,
49:14 This is the way of those whose trust is *f*,
69: 6 O God, you know my *f*,
Prv 5:23 the greatness of his *f* he will be lost.
9:13 The woman *F* is fickle,
12:23 but the hearts of fools gush forth *f*.
13:16 but the fool peddles *f*.
14: 1 but *F* tears hers down with her own hands.
14: 8 way, but the *f* of fools is their deception.
14:18 The adornment of simpletons is *f*,
14:24 the diadem of fools is *f*.
14:29 man displays *f* at its height.
15: 2 but the mouth of fools spurts forth *f*.
15:14 but the mouth of fools feeds on *f*.
15:21 *F* is joy to the senseless man,
16:22 but *f* brings chastisement on fools.
17:12 of her cubs, but never a fool in his *f*!
18:13 his is the *f* and the shame.
19: 3 A man's own *f* upsets his way,
22:15 *F* is close to the heart of a child,
24: 9 Beyond intrigue and *f* and sin,
24:28 cause, thus committing *f* with your lips.
26: 4 Answer not the fool according to his *f*,
26: 5 Answer the fool according to his *f*,
26:11 to his vomit, so the fool repeats his *f*.
27:22 in a mortar, his *f* would not go out of him.
Eccl 1:17 know wisdom and knowledge, madness and *f*,
2: 3 concerned with wisdom, and of taking up *f*,
2:12 the consideration of wisdom, madness and *f*.
2:13 saw that wisdom has the advantage over *f*
7:25 wickedness is foolish and *f* is madness.
10: 1 than wisdom or wealth is a little *f*!
10:13 The beginning of his words is *f*,
Wis 10: 8 they left mankind a memorial of their *f*—
12:23 those unjust also, who lived a life of *f*,
15:18 for compared as to *f*,
Sir 8:15 and through his *f* you will perish with him.
20:30 his *f* than the one who hides his wisdom.
30:13 heavy his yoke, lest his *f* humiliate you.
47:23 him one of his sons, Expansive in *f*,
Is 9:16 sinful, and every mouth gives vent to *f*.
Bar 3:28 lack of prudence, perished through their *f*.
Acts 4:25 Gentiles rage, the peoples conspire in *f*?
1Cor 1:20 God turned the wisdom of this world into *f*?
1:25 For God's *f* is wiser than men,
2Cor 11: 1 You must endure little of my *f*.
12: 6 if I were to boast it would not be *f* in me

FOND (8)

Gn 25:28 preferred Esau, because he was *f* of game;
1Sm 16:21 Saul became very *f* of him,
18: 1 *f* of David as if his life depended on him;
18:22 "The king is *f* of you,
19: 1 son Jonathan, who was very *f* of David,
Ez 16:44 who is *f* of proverbs will say of you,
Hos 3: 1 to other gods and are *f* of raisin cakes.
Mt 23: 6 They are *f* of places of honor at banquets

FONDLED (3)

Is 66:12 be carried in her arms, and *f* in her lap;
Ez 23: 3 their bosoms and *f* their virginal breasts.
23:21 when the Egyptians *f* your breasts,

FONDLING (4)

Gn 26: 8 surprised to see Isaac *f* his wife Rebekah.
2Kgs 4:16 time next year you will be *f* a baby son."
Ez 23: 8 *f* her virginal breasts and pouring out
1Thes 2: 7 as any nursing mother *f* her little ones.

FONDLY (1)

Gn 39: 7 wife began to look *f* at him and said,

FOOD (300)

Gn 1:29 has seed-bearing fruit on it to be your *f*;
1:30 ground, I give all the green plants for *f*."
2: 9 were delightful to look at and good for *f*,
3: 6 woman saw that the tree was good for *f*,
6:21 with all the *f* that is to be eaten,
14:11 seized all the possessions and *f* supplies
18: 5 your servant, let me bring you a little *f*,
39: 6 Joseph there, to anything but the *f* he ate.
41:35 husband all the *f* of the coming good years,
41:35 authority, to be stored in the towns for *f*.
41:36 This *f* will serve as a reserve for the
41:48 he husbanded all the *f* of these years of
41:54 *f* was available throughout the land of
42: 7 "From the land of Canaan, to procure *f*."
42:10 your servants have come to procure *f*.
43: 2 "Go back and procure us a little more *f*."
43: 4 us, we will go down to procure *f* for you.
43:20 came down here once before to procure *f*.
43:22 have brought other money to procure *f* with.
44: 1 bags with as much *f* as they can carry,
44:25 to come back and buy some *f* for the family.
47:12 household down to the youngest, with *f*.
47:13 Since there was no *f* in any country
47:15 us *f* or we shall perish under your eyes;
47:17 he sold them *f* in return for their horses,
47:19 Take us and our land in exchange for *f*,
47:24 *f* for yourselves and your families [and as *f*
Ex 12:16 to prepare the *f* that everyone needs.
12:19 who eats leavened *f* shall be cut off from
12:39 even to prepare *f* for the journey.
16:22 sixth day they gathered twice as much *f*,
16:29 the sixth day he gives you *f* for two days.
16:31 The Israelites called this *f* manna.
16:32 that they may see what *f* I gave you to eat
21:10 another wife, he shall not withhold her *f*,
23:25 then I will bless your *f* and drink,
29:23 *f* that you have set before the LORD,
34:28 without eating any *f* or drinking any water,
Lv 3:11 the altar as the *f* of the LORD's oblation.
3:16 as the *f* of the sweet-smelling oblation.
8: 2 two rams, and the basket of unleavened *f*.
8:26 from the basket of unleavened *f* that was
11:34 Any solid *f* that was in contact with water,
21: 6 oblations of the LORD, the *f* of their God,
21: 8 as sacred who offers up the *f* of your God;
21:17 come forward to offer up the *f* of his God.
21:21 not draw near to offer up the *f* of his God.
21:22 may, however, partake of the *f* of his God:
22: 7 of the sacred offerings which are his *f*.
22:11 who is born in his house may eat of his *f*.
22:13 then eat of her father's *f* as in her youth.
22:25 animals to offer up as the *f* of your God;
25: 6 all its produce will be *f* equally for you
25:19 its fruit and you will have *f* in abundance,
25:37 money at interest nor *f* at a profit.
26: 5 and you will have *f* to eat in abundance,
26:10 old crops will you have stored up for *f*
26:26 not enough *f* to still your hunger.
Nm 11: 4 again, "Would that we had meat for *f*!
11:13 are crying to me, 'Give us meat for our *f*.'
11:18 have cried, 'Would that we had meat for *f*!
11:18 the LORD will give you meat for *f*,
14: 9 they are but *f* for us!
15:19 you and begin to eat of the *f* of that land,
21: 5 this desert, where there is no *f* or water?
21: 5 We are disgusted with this wretched *f*!"
28: 2 be careful to present to me the *f* offerings
28:24 each day for seven days as *f* offerings,
Dt 2: 6 the *f* you eat and the well water you drink.
2:28 For the *f* I eat which you will supply,
8: 3 manna, a *f* unknown to you and your fathers,
8:16 with manna, a *f* unknown to your fathers,
12:20 he promised you, when you wish meat for *f*,
23: 5 would not succor you with *f* and water
23:20 loan of money or of *f* or of anything else
28:26 Your carcasses will become *f* for all the
28:55 he himself is using for *f* when nothing else
28:57 uses them for *f* for want of anything else,
29: 5 bread was not your *f*,
Jgs 8: 6 that we should give *f* to your army?"
8:15 we should give *f* to your weary followers?' "
13:16 you press me, I will not partake of your *f*.
14:14 to them, "Out of the eater came forth *f*,
17:10 a year, a set of garments, and your *f*."
19: 5 "Fortify yourself with a little *f*;
Ru 1: 6 had visited his people and given them *f*.
2:14 said to her, "Come here and have some *f*;
1Sm 14:24 be the man who takes *f* before evening,
14:24 So none of the people tasted *f*.
14:28 'Cursed be the man who takes *f* this day!'
20:34 and took no *f* that second day of the month,
22:13 son of Jesse by giving him *f* and a sword
30:11 He was provided with *f*,
30:12 he had not taken *f* nor drunk water for
2Sm 3:35 David with *f* while it was still day.
9:10 shall be *f* for your lord's family to eat.
12: 3 She shared the little *f* he had and drank
12:17 would not, nor would he take *f* with them.
12:20 where at his request *f* was set before him,
12:21 the child is dead, you rise and take *f*."
13: 5 Tamar come and encourage me to take *f*.
1Kgs 4: 7 supplied *f* for the king and his household,
5: 7 provided *f* for King Solomon and for all
10: 5 palace he had built, the *f* at his table,
18: 4 caves, and supplied them with *f* and drink.
18:13 caves, and supplied them with *f* and drink?
19: 8 then strengthened by that *f*,
21: 4 he turned away from *f* and would not eat.
1Chr 12:41 and Naphtali came bringing *f* on asses,
2Chr 2: 9 I will furnish as *f* for your servants,
9: 4 palace he had built, the *f* at his table,
11:11 put commanders in them, with supplies of *f*,
28:15 on their feet, gave them *f* and drink,
Ezr 3: 7 and sent *f* and drink and oil to the
10: 6 night neither eating *f* nor drinking water,
Neh 5:15 each day forty silver shekels for their *f*;
9:15 *F* from heaven you gave them in their hunger,
13: 2 not succor the Israelites with *f* and water,
Tb 1:10 and relatives ate the *f* of heathens,
1:11 but I refrained from eating that kind of *f*.
2: 5 I washed myself and ate my *f* in sorrow.
2:13 owners, we have no right to eat stolen *f*!"
Jdt 2:17 cattle, and goats for their *f* supply;
11:12 *f* gave out and all their water ran low,
12: 9 her *f* was brought to her toward evening.
13:10 to her maid, who put it into her *f* pouch;
Est 9:19 which they send gifts of *f* to one another.
9:22 *f* to one another and gifts to the poor.
1Mc 1:63 unclean *f* or to profane the holy covenant;
6:49 no *f* there to enable them to stand a siege,
13:49 country and back for the purchase of *f*;
14:10 *f* and equipped them with means of defense,
2Mc 6:20 courage to reject the *f* which it is unlawful
Jb 3:24 sighing comes more readily to me than *f*,
6: 7 they are loathsome *f* to me.
12:11 the ear judge words as the mouth tastes *f*?
15:23 A wanderer, *f* for the vultures,
20:14 Yet in his stomach the *f* shall turn;
24: 5 their task of seeking *f*; The steppe provides *f*
30: 4 the roots of the broom plant were their *f*.
33:20 that to his appetite *f* becomes repulsive,
34: 3 the ear tests words, as the taste does *f*.
36:31 the nations, and gives them *f* in abundance.
38:41 out to God, and they rove abroad without *f*?
Ps(s) 42: 4 My tears are my *f* day and night,
69:22 Rather they put gall in my *f*,
74:14 and made *f* of him for the dolphins.
78:18 hearts by demanding the *f* they craved.
78:24 them for *f* and gave them heavenly bread.
78:30 and their *f* was still in their mouths,
79: 2 your servants as *f* to the birds of heaven,
104:21 for the prey and seek their *f* from God.
104:27 all look to you to give them *f* in due time.
107:18 their sins, They loathed all manner of *f*,
111: 5 He has given *f* to those who fear him;
136:25 Who gives *f* to all flesh,
145:15 and you give them their *f* in due season;
147: 9 Who gives *f* to the cattle,
Prv 6: 8 or ruler, She procures her *f* in the summer,
9: 5 understanding, I say, Come, eat of my *f*,
12:11 He who tills his own land has *f* in plenty,
20:13 eyes wide open mean abundant *f*.
23: 3 they are deceitful *f*.
23: 6 Do not take *f* with a grudging man,
25:21 If your enemy be hungry, give him *f* to eat,
28: 3 like a devastating rain that leaves no *f*.
28:19 cultivates his land will have plenty of *f*,
30: 8 [provide me only with the *f* I need;]
30:22 and a fool when he is glutted with *f*;
30:25 yet they store up their *f* in the summer;
31:15 night, and distributes *f* to her household.
31:27 and eats not her *f* in idleness.
Wis 13:12 from his handiwork in preparing his *f*,
16: 2 craved, by providing quail for their *f*;
16: 3 That those others, when they desired *f*,
16:20 you nourished your people with *f* of angels
19:21 icelike, quick-melting kind of ambrosial *f*.
Sir 20:18 Insipid *f* is the untimely tale;
29:26 the table, give me to eat the *f* you have!
30:25 gay while at table benefits from his *f*.
31:12 Nor cry out, "How much *f* there is here!"
31:23 On a man generous with *f*,
31:24 is miserly with *f* is denounced in public,

FOOD (cont.)

33:27 *F*, correction and work for a slave;
36:18 The throat can swallow any *f*,
37:27 For not every *f* is good for everyone,
45:21 The oblations of the LORD are his *f*,
51:24 long will you be deprived of wisdom's *f*,
Is 4: 1 eat our own *f* and wear our own clothing;
7:22 be the *f* of all who remain in the land.
25: 6 rich *f* and choice wines, juicy, rich *f*
28:27 staff, and cumin crushed for *f* with a rod.
33:16 fastness, his *f* and drink in steady supply.
62: 8 I give your grain as *f* to your enemies;
65:25 the ox [but the serpent's *f* shall be dust].
Jer 7:33 The corpses of this people will be *f* for
16: 4 and their corpses will become *f* for the
19: 7 Their corpses I will give as *f* to the
34:20 their corpses shall be *f* for the birds of
38: 9 spot, for there is no more *f* in the city."
40: 5 gave him *f* and gifts and let him go.
41: 5 bringing *f* offerings and incense for the
44:17 had enough *f* to eat and we were well off;
Lam 1:11 They give their treasures for *f*,
1:19 Where they sought *f* for themselves,
3:15 He has sated me with bitter *f*,
4: 4 The babes cry for *f*,
4: 5 to dainty *f* perish in the streets;
4:10 To serve them as mourners' *f* in the
Ez 4:10 The *f* you eat shall be twenty shekels a
4:12 For your *f* you must bake barley loaves
4:13 Thus the Israelites shall eat their *f*
16:13 Fine flour, honey, and oil were your *f*.
16:19 the *f* that I had given you,
16:49 her daughters were proud, sated with *f*,
18: 7 *f* to the hungry and clothes the naked;
18:16 his *f* to the hungry and clothes the naked;
29: 5 and the birds of the air I give you as *f*,
33:27 I have given to the wild beasts for *f*;
34: 5 and became *f* for all the wild beasts.
34: 8 sheep have become *f* for every wild beast,
34:10 they may no longer be *f* for their mouths.
44: 7 to profane it when you offered me *f*,
47:12 Their fruit shall serve for *f*,
48:18 provide *f* for the workers of the City.
Dn 1: 5 portion of *f* and wine from the royal table.
1: 8 defile himself with the king's *f* or wine;
1:10 it is he who allotted your *f* and drink.
1:16 away the *f* and wine they were to receive,
4: 9 its fruit abundant, providing *f* for all
4:18 and abundant fruit, providing *f* for all,
10: 3 I ate no savory *f*,
14: 7 it has never taken any *f* or drink."
14:11 O king, set out the *f* and prepare the wine;
14:13 which they always came in to consume the *f*.
14:14 departed the king set the *f* before Bel,
Hos 9: 3 and in Assyria they shall eat unclean *f*.
9: 4 *f* as they have shall be for themselves;
Jl 1:16 our very eyes has not the *f* been cut off;
Am 4: 5 leavened *f* as a thanksgiving sacrifice,
4: 6 your teeth clean of *f* in all your cities,
Mi 6:14 satisfied, *f* that will leave you empty;
Hg 2:12 pottage, or wine, or oil, or any other *f*,
Mal 1: 7 By offering polluted *f* on my altar!
1:12 may be polluted, and its *f* slighted.
3:10 That there may be *f* in my house,
Mt 3: 4 Grasshoppers and wild honey were his *f*.
6:25 Is not life more than *f*?
14:15 the villages and buy some *f* for themselves."
15:26 "It is not right to take the *f* of sons
24:45 of his household to dispense *f* at need?
25:35 For I was hungry and you gave me *f*,
25:42 I was hungry and you gave me no *f*,
Mk 1: 6 His *f* was grasshoppers and wild honey.
3:20 impossible for them to get any *f* whatever.
6: 8 but a walking stick—no *f*,
7: 5 take *f* without purifying their hands?"
7:27 *f* of the children and throw it to the dogs."
Lk 3:11 The man who has *f* should do the same."
9:12 and find themselves lodging and *f*,
9:13 go and buy *f* for all these people?"
12:23 than *f* and the body more than clothing.
Jn 4:32 "I have *f* to eat of which you do not know."
4:34 bringing his work to completion is my *f*.
6:27 should not be working for perishable *f*
6:27 but for *f* that remains unto life eternal,
6:27 *f* which the Son of Man will give you;
6:55 my flesh is real *f* and my blood real drink.
13:26 whom I give the bit of *f* I dip in the dish."
Acts 6: 1 neglected in the daily distribution of *f*,
9:19 returned to him after he had taken *f*.
10:10 He became hungry and asked for some *f*,
12:20 supplied with *f* from the king's territory.
14:17 your spirits he fills with *f* and delight."
23:14 by oath to touch no *f* until we kill Paul.
27:21 All hands had gone without *f* for a long
27:33 Paul urged all on board to take some *f*:
27:34 Now I urge you to take some *f*,
Rom 14:15 feels remorse for the *f* he has eaten,
14:15 You must not let the *f* you eat bring to
14:20 to eat when the *f* offends his conscience.
1Cor 3: 2 solid *f* because you were not ready for it.
6:13 *F* is for the stomach and the stomach for *f*,
8: 8 Now *f* does not bring us closer to God.
8:13 if *f* causes my brother to sin I will never
10: 3 All ate the same spiritual *f*.
10:30 blamed for the *f* over which I gave thanks?
2Thes 3: 8 were among you, nor depend on anyone for *f*.
3:12 to earn the *f* they eat by working quietly.
1Tm 6: 8 *f* and clothing we have all that we need.
Heb 5:12 you need milk, not solid *f*.
5:13 Everyone whose *f* is milk alone is ignorant
5:14 Solid *f* is for the mature,
9:10 of *f* and drink and various ritual washings:
Jas 2:15 has nothing to wear and no *f* for the day,
Rv 2:14 tempting them to eat *f* sacrificed to idols
2:20 lewdness and to eat *f* sacrificed to idols.

FOODS (12)

Ezr 2:63 them not to partake of the most holy *f*
Neh 7:65 them not to partake of the most holy *f*
8:10 "Go eat rich *f* and drink sweet drinks,
Wis 19:11 by desire, they asked for pleasant *f*;
Sir 1:15 Her entire house she fills with choice *f*,
36:18 yet some *f* are more agreeable than others;
37:28 neither become a glutton for choice *f*,
Mk 7:19 Thus did he render all *f* clean.
Rom 14: 3 ridicule him who abstains from certain *f*;
14:20 True, all *f* are clean;
1Tm 4: 3 abstinence from *f* which God created
Heb 13: 9 by the grace of God and not by *f*

FOOL (95)

1Sm 25:25 Fool is his name, and he acts the *f*.
26:21 been a *f* and have made a serious mistake."
2Sm 3:33 "Would Abner have died like a *f*?
Jb 5: 2 the *f* and indignation slays the simpleton.
5: 3 I have seen a *f* spreading his roots,
Ps(s) 14: 1 The *f* says in his heart,
53: 2 The *f* says in his heart,
74:22 how the *f* blasphemes you day after day.
92: 7 knows not, nor does a *f* understand this.
Prv 6:32 But he who commits adultery is a *f*;
10: 6 the just, but a rod for the back of the *f*.
10: 8 but a prating *f* will be overthrown.
10:14 but the mouth of a *f* is imminent ruin.
10:18 but he who spreads accusations is a *f*.
10:23 Crime is the entertainment of the *f*;
11:29 the *f* will become slave to the wise man.
12:11 but he who follows idle pursuits is a *f*.
12:15 way of the *f* seems right in his own eyes,
12:16 The *f* immediately shows his anger,
13:16 but the *f* peddles folly.
14: 3 the mouth of the *f* is a rod for his back,
14:16 the *f* is reckless and sure of himself.
14:17 quick-tempered man makes a *f* of himself,
15: 5 The *f* spurns his father's admonition,
15:20 glad, but a *f* of a man despises his mother.
17: 7 Fine words are out of place in a *f*;
17:10 intelligence than a hundred lashes for a *f*.
17:12 of her cubs, but never a *f* in his folly!
17:24 eyes of a *f* are on the ends of the earth.
17:28 Even a *f*, if he keeps silent,
18: 2 The *f* takes no delight in understanding,
19:10 Luxury is not befitting a *f*;
20: 3 strife, while every *f* starts a quarrel.
21:20 house of the wise, but the *f* consumes it.
24: 7 For a *f*, to be silent is wisdom;
26: 1 in harvest, honor for a *f* is out of place.
26: 4 Answer not the *f* according to his folly,
26: 5 Answer the *f* according to his folly,
26: 6 down violence, who sends messages by a *f*.
26: 7 A proverb in the mouth of a *f* hangs limp,
26: 8 in the sling is he who gives honor to a *f*.
26:10 who pass by is he who hires a drunken *f*.
26:11 to his vomit, so the *f* repeats his folly.
26:12 There is more hope for a *f* than for him.
27:22 should pound the *f* to bits with the pestle,
28:26 He who trusts in himself is a *f*,
29: 9 If a wise man disputes with a *f*,
29:11 The *f* gives vent to all his anger;
29:20 More can be hoped for from a *f*!
30:22 king, and a *f* when he is glutted with food;
Eccl 2:14 in his head, but the *f* walks in darkness.
2:16 the *f* will there be an abiding remembrance,
2:16 it that the wise man dies as well as the *f*!
2:19 knows whether he will be a wise man or a *f*?
4: 5 "The *f* folds his arms and consumes his
6: 8 advantage has the wise man over the *f*,
7: 7 For oppression can make a *f* of a wise man,
7: 9 for discontent lodges in the bosom of a *f*.
10: 3 When the *f* walks through the street,
10: 6 a *f* put in lofty position while the rich
10:14 yet the *f* multiplies words.
10:15 When will the *f* be weary of his labor,
Sir 6:21 The *f* cannot abide her.
8:17 Take no counsel with a *f*,
18:17 Only a *f* upbraids before giving;
19:10 When a *f* hears something,
19:11 man's thigh is gossip in the breast of a *f*.
20: 6 but a boasting *f* ignores the proper time.
20:15 A *f* has no friends,
20:19 A proverb when spoken by a *f* is unwelcome,
21:18 Like a house in ruins is wisdom to a *f*;
21:19 fetters on the legs is learning to a *f*,
21:20 A *f* raises his voice in laughter,
21:22 The *f* steps boldly into a house,
22: 7 Teaching a *f* is like gluing a broken pot,
22: 8 talks with a slumberer who talks with a *f*,
22: 9 weep over the *f*,
22:10 but worse than death is the life of a *f*.
22:11 but for the wicked *f* a whole lifetime.
22:14 than lead, and what is its name but *F*"?
31: 7 who are avid for it, a snare for every *f*.
31:30 More and more wine is a snare for the *f*;
33: 5 the wheel of a cart is the mind of a *f*;
Is 32: 5 No more will the *f* be called noble,
32: 6 For the *f* speaks foolishly,
Jer 17:11 in the end he is only a *f*.
Hos 9: 7 "The prophet is a *f*,
Mt 27:31 when they had finished making a *f* of him,
Lk 12:20 But God said to him, 'You *f*!
1Cor 3:18 in a worldly way, he had better become a *f*.
2Cor 11:16 then accept me as a *f* all the way and let
11:17 Lord desires but after the manner of a *f*.
11:23 Now I am really talking like a *f*—
12:11 What a *f* I have become!
Gal 6: 7 mistake about it, no one makes a *f* of God!

FOOLED (1)

Acts 23:21 But don't be *f* by them.

FOOLHARDY (2)

Wis 1: 3 power, put to the proof, rebukes the *f*;
5:20 universe shall war with him against the *f*.

FOOLISH (35)

Dt 32: 6 thus repaid by you, O stupid and *f* people?
32:21 with a *f* nation I will anger them.
1Sm 13:13 "You have been *f*!
2Sm 24:10 of your servant, for I have been very *f*."
2Mc 12:44 useless and *f* to pray for them in death.
Prv 10: 1 glad, but a *f* son is a grief to his mother.
14: 7 To avoid the *f* man, take steps!
17:25 A *f* son is vexation to his father,
19:13 The *f* son is ruin to his father,
Eccl 4:13 old but *f* king who no longer knows caution;
7:17 Be not wicked to excess, and be not *f*.
7:25 that wickedness is *f* and folly is madness.
10: 3 of understanding he calls everything *f*.
Wis 3: 2 They seemed, in the view of the *f*,
3:12 wives are *f* and their children wicked;
13: 1 by nature *f* who were in ignorance of God,
Sir 16:21 men, which only the *f* knave will think.
22:18 on *f* plans withstand fear of any kind.
42: 8 Of chastisement of the silly and the *f*,
49: 5 their glory to a *f* foreign nation
Is 44:25 wise men back and make their knowledge *f*.
Jer 5: 4 is only the lowly, I thought, who are *f*;
5:21 *f* and senseless people Who have eyes and
14:14 Lying visions, *f* divination,
Zec 11:15 This time take the gear of a *f* shepherd.
11:17 to my *f* shepherd who forsakes the flock!
Mt 7:26 *f* man who built his house on sandy ground.
25: 2 Five of them were *f*,
25: 3 The *f* ones, in taking their torches,
25: 8 The *f* ones said to the sensible,
Rom 2:20 can discipline the *f* and teach the simple,
2Cor 11:16 let no one think me *f*.
1Tm 6: 9 are letting themselves be captured by *f*
Ti 3: 3 We ourselves were once *f*,
1Pt 2:15 talk of *f* men by your good behavior.

FOOLISHLY (5)

Nm 12:11 us with the sin that we have *f* committed!
1Chr 21: 8 servant's guilt, for I have acted very *f*."
2Chr 16: 9 You have acted *f* in this matter,
Prv 30:32 If you have *f* been proud or presumptuous
Is 32: 6 For the fool speaks *f*,

FOOLISHNESS (2)

Prv 9: 6 Forsake *f* that you may live;
2Cor 11:21 I speak with absolute *f* now

FOOLS (60)

Jb 12:17 away barefoot, and of judges he makes *f*.
Ps(s) 39: 9 a *f* taunt let me not suffer.
94: 8 and, you *f*, when will you be wise?
Prv 1: 7 wisdom and instruction *f* despise.
1:30 and like *f* they hated knowledge:
1:32 them, the smugness of *f* destroys them.
3:35 of wise men, but *f* inherit shame.
8: 5 You simple ones, gain resource, you *f*,
10:21 nourish many, but *f* die for want of sense.
12:23 but the hearts of *f* gush forth folly.
13:19 the soul, but *f* hate to turn from evil.
13:20 but the companion of *f* will fare badly.
14: 8 way, but the folly of *f* is their deception.
14:24 the diadem of *f* is folly.
14:33 but in the bosom of *f* it is unknown.
15: 2 but the mouth of *f* spurts forth folly.
15: 7 knowledge, but the heart of *f* is perverted.
15:14 but the mouth of *f* feeds on folly.
16:22 but folly brings chastisement on *f*.
17:16 in the *f* hand are the means to buy wisdom,
17:21 To be a *f* parent is grief for a man;
18: 6 The *f* lips lead him into strife,

18: 7 The *f* mouth is his ruin;
19:29 the arrogant, and blows for the backs of *f*.
23: 9 Speak not for the *f* hearing;
26: 3 for the ass, and the rod for the back of *f*.
26: 9 a drunkard is a proverb in the mouth of *f*.
27: 3 but a *f* provocation is heavier than both.
Eccl 2:15 myself, if the *f* lot is to befall me also,
4:17 rather than the *f* offering of sacrifice;
5: 2 cares, and a *f* utterance with many words.
5: 3 For God has no pleasure in *f*;
7: 4 the heart of *f* is in the house of mirth.
7: 5 rebuke than to hearken to the song of *f*;
7: 6 thorns under a pot, so is the *f* laughter.
9:17 heeded than the shout of a ruler of *f*—
10: 2 the *f* understanding turns him to his left.
10:12 win favor, but the *f* lips consume him.
Wis 5: 4 and as a type for mockery, *f* that we were!
Sir 20:12 *f* pour forth their blandishments in vain.
20:21 shame, and perish through a *f* intimidation.
21:14 A *f* mind is like a broken jar
21:16 A *f* chatter is like a load on a journey,
21:26 *F'* thoughts are in their mouths,
27:12 Limit the time you spend among *f*,
34: 1 and *f* are borne aloft by dreams.
Is 19:11 Utter *f* are the princes of Zoan!
19:13 The princes of Zoan have become *f*,
35: 8 may pass over it, nor *f* go astray on it.
44:25 the omens of liars, who make *f* of diviners;
Jer 4:22 *F* my people are,
50:36 the soothsayers, that they may become *f*!
Ez 13: 3 Woe to those prophets who are *f*,
Dn 13:48 midst and continued, "Are you such *f*,
Mt 23:17 Blind *f*!
Lk 11:40 *F*! Did not he who made the outside
Rom 1:22 to be wise, but turned into *f* instead:
1Cor 4:10 We are *f* on Christ's account.
2Cor 11:19 wise yourselves, you gladly put up with *f*.
Eph 5:15 Do not act like *f*,

FOOT (103)

Gn 41:44 move hand or *f* in all the land of Egypt."
Ex 12:37 about six hundred thousand men on *f*,
19:17 themselves at the *f* of the mountain.
21:24 tooth for tooth, hand for hand, *f* for foot,
24: 4 he erected at the *f* of the mountain an
Lv 8:23 hand, and on the big toe of his right *f*.
13:12 skin of the stricken man from head to *f*,
14:14 right hand, and the big toe of his right *f*.
14:17 right hand, and the big toe of his right *f*,
14:25 hand, and on the big toe of his right *f*.
14:28 right hand, and the big toe of his right *f*,
21:19 or malformation, or a crippled *f* or hand,
Dt 2: 5 not give you so much as a *f* of their land,
4:11 near and stood at the *f* of the mountain,
11:24 Every place where you set *f* shall be yours:
11:25 of you through any land where you set *f*,
19:21 for tooth, hand for hand, and *f* for foot!
25: 9 his sandal from his *f* and spit in his face,
28:56 to set the sole of her *f* on the ground,
28:65 no repose, not a *f* of ground to stand upon,
Jos 1: 3 deliver to you every place where you set *f*.
11: 3 at the *f* of Hermon in the land of Mizpah.
11:17 Lebanon valley at the *f* of Mount Hermon.
13: 5 from Baal-gad at the *f* of Mount Hermon to
14: 9 'The land where you have set *f* shall
Jgs 3:16 made himself a two-edged dagger a *f* long,
4:15 dismounted from his chariot and fled on *f*.
4:17 had fled on *f* to the tent of Jael,
20: 2 thousand *f* soldiers who were swordsmen,
1Sm 4:10 Israel lost thirty thousand *f* soldiers.
13: 5 and *f* soldiers as numerous as the sands of
15: 4 *f* soldiers and ten thousand men of Judah.
23:22 place where he sets *f*" (for he thought,
2Sm 2:18 fleet of *f* as a gazelle in the open field,
8: 4 horsemen and twenty thousand *f* soldiers.
10: 6 *f* soldiers from Beth-rehob and Zobah,
10:18 forty thousand of the Aramean *f* soldiers.
14:25 the sole of his *f* to the crown of his head.
21:20 on each hand and six toes on each *f*—
1Kgs 2: 5 belt about my waist and the sandal on my *f*.
20:29 thousand *f* soldiers of Aram in one day.
2Kgs 13: 7 ten chariots and ten thousand *f* soldiers,
1Chr 18: 4 took from him twenty thousand *f* soldiers,
19:18 and forty thousand of their *f* soldiers;
20: 6 to each hand and six toes to each *f*;
Neh 2:15 I continued on *f* up the wadi by night,
Tb 6: 3 of the water and tried to swallow his *f*.
8: 3 pursued him there and bound him hand and *f*.
Jdt 6:13 left him lying at the *f* of the mountain;
7: 2 train or the men who accompanied it on *f*—
1Mc 16: 5 an immense army of *f* soldiers and horsemen,
2Mc 4:12 a gymnasium at the very *f* of the acropolis,
5:21 land navigable and the sea passable on *f*,
10:26 Lying prostrate at the *f* of the altar,
10:31 Twenty-five hundred of their *f* soldiers
11: 4 confidence in his myriads of *f* soldiers,
11:11 *f* soldiers and sixteen hundred horsemen,
12:10 at least five thousand *f* soldiers,
12:20 hundred and twenty thousand *f* soldiers
12:33 *f* soldiers and four hundred horsemen.
13: 2 of one hundred and ten thousand *f* soldiers,
Jb 23:11 My *f* has always walked in his steps;
31: 5 falsehood and my *f* has hastened to deceit;
39:15 sand, Unmindful that a *f* may crush them,
39:18 *f* she makes sport of the horse and rider.
Ps(s) 9:16 in the snare they set, their *f* is caught;
26:12 My *f* stands on level ground;
36:12 Let not the *f* of the proud overtake me nor
38:17 be glad on my account who, when my *f* slips,
66: 6 through the river they passed on *f*;
91:12 up, lest you dash your *f* against a stone.
94:18 When I say, "My *f* is slipping,"
121: 3 May he not suffer your *f* to slip;
122: 2 " And now we have set *f* within your gates,
Prv 1:15 them, hold back your *f* from their path!
3:23 your *f* will never stumble;
3:26 and will keep your *f* from the snare.
4:27 nor to left, keep your *f* far from evil.
25:17 your *f* be seldom in your neighbor's house,
25:19 Like an infected tooth or an unsteady *f* is
Sir 16:10 Nor the six hundred thousand *f* soldiers
50:15 And poured it out at the *f* of the altar,
Is 1: 6 the *f* to the head there is no sound spot:
58:13 If you hold back your *f* on the sabbath
Bar 5: 6 away on *f* by their enemies they left you:
Ez 29:11 No *f* of man or beast shall pass through it;
32:13 The *f* of man shall stir them no longer,
Am 2:15 The swift of *f* shall not escape,
Mt 7: 6 They will trample them under *f*,
14:13 of it and followed him on *f* from the towns.
18: 8 If your hand or *f* is your undoing,
22:13 'Bind him hand and *f* and throw him out
Mk 6:33 all the towns hastened on *f* to the place,
9:45 If your *f* is your undoing, cut it off!
Jn 11:44 out bound head and *f* with linen strips,
20:12 *f* of the place where Jesus' body had lain.
Acts 7: 5 it as his heritage, not even a *f* of land,
20:18 first day I set *f* in the province of Asia
1Cor 12:15 If the *f* should say,
Rv 10: 2 *f* on the sea and his left foot on the land,

FOOT-SOLDIERS (1)

1Mc 6:30 His army numbered a hundred thousand *f*,

FOOTGEAR (1)

Eph 6:15 to propagate the gospel of peace as your *f*.

FOOTHILLS (23)

Nm 14:40 next morning they started up into the *f*,
14:44 Yet they dared to go up into the *f*,
Dt 1: 7 in the Arabah, the mountains, the *f*,
Jos 9: 1 in the mountain regions and in the *f*,
10:40 the mountain regions, the Negeb, the *f*,
11: 2 in the Arabah near Chinneroth, in the *f*,
11:16 Negeb all the land of Goshen, the *f*,
11:16 as the mountain regions and *f* of Israel,
12: 8 It included the mountain regions and *f*,
15:33 In the *f*: Eshtaol, Zorah
Jgs 1: 9 region, in the Negeb, and in the *f*.
1Kgs 10:27 as numerous as the sycamores of the *f*.
1Chr 27:28 of the *f* was Baalhanan the Gederite,
2Chr 1:15 as numerous as the sycamores of the *f*.
9:27 as numerous as the sycamores of the *f*.
26:10 He had plowmen in the *f* and the plains,
28:18 the cities of the *f* and the Negeb of Judah;
Is 11:14 on the *f* of the Philistines to the west,
Jer 17:26 from the land of Benjamin and from the *f*,
32:44 in the cities of the *f* and of the Negeb,
33:13 the cities of the hill country, of the *f*,
Ob 1:19 of Esau, and the *f* of the Philistines;
Zec 7: 7 when the Negeb and the *f* were inhabited?

FOOTHOLD (1)

Ps(s) 69: 3 in the abysmal swamp where there is no *f*;

FOOTING (2)

Dt 32:35 against the time they lose their *f*?"
Jer 23:12 In the darkness they shall lose their *f*,

FOOTPATH (4)

Mt 13: 4 Part of what he sowed landed on a *f*,
Mk 4: 4 Some of what he sowed landed on the *f*,
Lk 8: 5 some fell on the *f* where it was walked on
8:12 Those on the *f* are people who hear,

FOOTPRINTS (2)

Dn 14:19 "whose *f* are these?"
14:20 "I see the *f* of men,

FOOTREST (1)

Jas 2: 3 or "Sit over there by my *f*."

FOOTSTEPS (13)

1Sm 2: 9 He will guard the *f* of his faithful ones,
1Kgs 14: 6 the sound of her *f* as she entered the door,
2Kgs 6:32 His master's *f* are echoing behind him."
Jb 13:27 watch all my paths and trace out all my *f*.
29: 6 When my *f* were bathed in milk,
Ps(s) 77:20 deep waters, though your *f* were not seen.
119:133 Steady my *f* according to your promise,
Prv 2:18 to death, and her *f* lead to the shades;
Is 26: 6 by the needy, by the *f* of the poor.
Mt 16:24 up his cross, and begin to follow in my *f*.
Acts 5: 9 The *f* of the men who have just buried your
2Cor 12:18 act in the one spirit, walk in the same *f*?
1Pt 2:21 an example, to have you follow in his *f*.

FOOTSTOOL (13)

1Chr 28: 2 of the LORD, the *f* for the feet of our God;
2Chr 9:18 a *f* of gold was fastened to it,
Ps(s) 99: 5 the LORD, our God, and worship at his *f*;
110: 1 right hand till I make your enemies your *f*."
132: 7 let us worship at his *f*.
Is 66: 1 heavens are my throne, the earth is my *f*.
Lam 2: 1 Unmindful of his *f* on the day of his wrath.
Mt 5:35 throne), nor by the earth (it is his *f*),
Mk 12:36 hand until I make your enemies your *f*.'
Lk 20:43 hand while I make your enemies your *f*'?
Acts 2:35 hand until I make your enemies your *f*.'
7:49 heavens are my throne, the earth is my *f*;
Heb 1:13 hand till I make your enemies your *f*"?

FORAGE (1)

Jer 14:18 and the priest *f* in a land they know not.

FORAYS (1)

1Sm 18:30 Philistine chiefs continued to make *f*,

FORBADE (8)

Neh 13:19 *f* them to be reopened till after the sabbath.
Jdt 9: 2 This they did, though you *f* it.
11:12 things which God in his laws *f* them to eat.
Jer 23:38 of the LORD," though I *f* you to use it,
35: 6 son, our father, *f* us in these words:
35:14 by which he *f* his children to drink wine,
Lam 1:10 Whom you *f* to come into your assembly.
Lk 9:21 He strictly *f* them to tell this to anyone.

FORBEARANCE (2)

Rom 2: 4 Or do you presume on his kindness and *f*?
1Cor 13: 7 There is no limit to love's *f*,

FORBEARING (1)

Ti 3: 2 They must be *f* and display a perfect

FORBID (14)

1Sm 20: 2 "Heaven *f* that you should die!
24: 7 "The LORD *f* that I should do such a thing
26:11 But the LORD *f* that I touch his anointed!
2Sm 23:17 "The LORD *f* that I do this!
1Kgs 21: 3 "The LORD *f*."
1Chr 11:19 "God *f* that I should do such a thing!
1Mc 2:21 God *f* that we should forsake the law and
Mal 3:11 I will *f* the locust to destroy your crops;
Mt 16:22 *f* that any such thing ever happen to you!"
Lk 20:16 When they heard this they said, "God *f*!"
Rom 2:22 You who *f* adultery,
1Cor 6:15 God *f*!
14:39 and do not *f* those who speak in tongues,
1Tm 4: 3 men with seared consciences who *f* marriage

FORBIDDEN (12)

Gn 3:11 from the tree of which I had *f* you to eat!"
3:17 from the tree of which I had *f* you to eat,
Lv 4: 2 of the LORD by doing one of the *f* things,
4:13 LORD has *f* and thus makes itself guilty,
4:22 are *f* by some commandment of the LORD,
4:27 are *f* by the commandments of the LORD,
5:17 are *f* by some commandment of the LORD,
10: 9 and your sons are *f* under pain of death,
1Kgs 11: 2 LORD had *f* the Israelites to intermarry,
11:10 though the LORD had *f* him this very act
2Mc 6: 4 into the temple things that were *f*,
Mt 12: 4 a thing *f* to him and his men or anyone

FORBIDDING (2)

Lv 18:26 decrees *f* all such abominations
Est 1:19 *f* Vashti to come into the presence of King

FORBIDS (2)

2Mc 12:40 Jamnia, which the law *f* the Jews to wear.
Eph 5: 3 your holiness *f* this.

FORCE (91)

Gn 21:25 well that Abimelech's men had seized by *f*.
31:31 take your daughters away from me by *f*.
34: 2 her, he seized her and lay with her by *f*.
47:26 the land in Egypt, which is still in *f*,
Ex 14:24 *f* a glance that threw it into a panic;
Nm 20:20 them with a large and heavily armed *f*.
32:21 cross the Jordan in full *f* before the LORD
Jgs 8:10 with their *f* of about fifteen thousand men;
1Sm 2:16 it to me now, or else I will take it by *f*."
2Sm 3:23 and the whole *f* he had with him arrived,
1Kgs 9:22 Israelites, for they were his fighting *f*,
11:28 the entire labor *f* of the house of Joseph.
2Kgs 6:14 there a strong *f* with horses and chariots.
6:15 he saw the *f* with its horses and chariots
11:15 the captains in command of the *f*:

FORCE (cont.)

1Chr 4:41 against them the ban that is still in *f*
20: 1 go to war, Joab led the army out in *f*,
2Chr 13: 3 *f* of four hundred thousand picked warriors,
14: 8 the Ethiopian moved against them with a *f*
24:23 year a *f* of Arameans came up against Joash.
24:24 Though the Aramean *f* came with few men,
24:24 a very large *f* into their power,
Ezr 4:23 and stopped their work by *f* of arms.
Neh 4:16 as a guard by night and a working *f* by day.
Jdt 1:13 He routed the whole *f* of Arphaxad,
2:16 and grouped them into a complete combat *f*.
2:20 A huge, irregular *f*,
2:22 From there Holofernes took his whole *f*,
5:15 destroyed all the Heshbonites by main *f*,
6: 2 He will send his *f* and destroy them from
6: 3 unable to withstand the *f* of our cavalry.
9: 7 "Here are the Assyrians, a vast *f*,
9: 8 might, and crush their *f* in your wrath;
11:18 so that you may go out with your whole *f*,
1Mc 1:17 He invaded Egypt with a strong *f*,
1:20 to Israel and to Jerusalem with a strong *f*.
1:29 and he came to Jerusalem with a strong *f*.
3:41 A *f* from Idumea and Philistia joined with
5:38 rallied to him, making a very large *f*;
6:33 moved his *f* hastily along the road to
6:63 fought against him and took the city by *f*.
7:27 Nicanor came to Jerusalem with a large *f*
9:14 on the right, with the main *f* of his army,
9:43 to the banks of the Jordan with a large *f*.
9:60 Bacchides was setting out with a large *f*,
9:63 *f* and sent word to those who were in Judea.
10:73 cavalry and such a *f* as this in the plain,
11:15 him with a strong *f* and put him to flight.
11:63 come with a strong *f* to Kadesh in Galilee,
13:11 son of Absalom, to Joppa with a large *f*;
13:38 we have guaranteed to you remains in *f*,
2Mc 6: 1 sent an Athenian senator to *f* the Jews
7: 1 to *f* them to eat pork in violation of
10:20 But some of the men in Simon's *f* who were
10:24 gathered a tremendous *f* of foreign troops
10:24 in Judea, ready to conquer it by *f*.
12:19 marched out and destroyed the *f* of more
12:20 who had a *f* of a hundred and twenty
13: 1 Eupator was invading Judea with a large *f*,
13:15 with a picked *f* of the bravest young men
Jb 24: 4 They *f* the needy off the road;
41: 6 Who can *f* open the doors of his mouth,
Eccl 9:16 I had said, "Wisdom is better than *f*,"
Wis 5:11 cleft by the rushing *f* Of speeding wings,
7:17 of the universe and the *f* of its elements,
17: 5 No *f*, even of fire,
18:22 not by bodily strength, not by *f* of arms;
Sir 4: 1 *f* not the eyes of the needy to turn away.
33:28 *F* him to work that he be not idle,
39:28 *f* and appease the anger of their Maker.
Is 7: 6 tear Judah asunder, make it our own by *f*,
Jer 12: 6 they have recruited a *f* against you.
46:22 Yes, they come in *f*;
Dn 6: 8 ought to be put in *f* by royal decree:
8: 6 river, and rushed toward it with savage *f*.
8: 7 ram, which had not the *f* to withstand it,
Am 2: 7 the earth, and *f* the lowly out of the way.
Mt 11:12 violence, and the violent take it by *f*.
Lk 14:23 along the hedgerows and *f* them to come in.
16:16 law and the prophets were in *f* until John.
Jn 10:35 and Scripture cannot lose its *f*—
Acts 5:26 brought them in, but without any show of *f*,
26:11 I compelled them by *f* to blaspheme.
1Cor 2: 4 the persuasive *f* of "wise" argumentation,
Gal 2:14 do you *f* the Gentiles to adopt Jewish ways?"
6:12 Those who are trying to *f* you to be
Eph 4: 3 as its origin and peace as its binding *f*.
Col 1:29 of his which is so powerful a *f* within me.
2Thes 2: 7 secret *f* of lawlessness is already at work,
Heb 9:17 into *f* only in the case of death; it has no *f*

FORCED (35)

Ex 1:11 Israelites to oppress them with *f* labor.
2:11 his kinsmen and witnessed their *f* labor,
3:19 will not allow you to go unless he is *f*.
6: 1 *F* by my mighty hand,
6: 6 I will free you from the *f* labor of the
Lv 26:25 till you are *f* to surrender to the enemy.
Dt 20:11 be found in it shall serve you in *f* labor.
Jgs 1:30 among them, but have become *f* laborers.
1:33 Beth-anath have become *f* laborers for them.
2Sm 20:24 Adoram was in charge of the *f* labor.
1Kgs 4: 6 son of Abda, superintendent of the *f* labor.
9:15 This is an account of the *f* labor which
9:21 Solomon conscripted as *f* laborers,
12:18 out Adoram, superintendent of the *f* labor,
2Chr 8: 8 Solomon subjected to *f* labor,
10:18 who was superintendent of the *f* labor,
Neh 5: 2 "We are *f* to pawn our sons and daughters
5: 3 'We are *f* to pawn our fields,
Jdt 5:11 shrewdly *f* them to labor at brickmaking,
8:30 that they *f* us to speak to them as we did,
1Mc 5: 5 He *f* them to take refuge in towers,
2Mc 5: 5 As the defenders on the walls were *f* back
6:18 was being *f* to open his mouth to eat pork.
9: 2 natives and *f* to beat a shameful retreat.
15: 2 The Jews who were *f* to follow him pleaded,
Jb 29:17 from his teeth I *f* the prey.
Jer 34:11 had set free and again *f* them into service.
34:16 you *f* them once more into slavery.
Lam 3: 2 whom he has led and *f* to walk in darkness,
Dn 14:30 the king was *f* to hand Daniel over to them.
Acts 7:19 He *f* our fathers to abandon their infants
28:19 objected, I was *f* to appeal to the emperor,
1Cor 9: 6 Barnabas who are *f* to work for a living?
Phlm 1:14 be *f* on you but might be freely bestowed.
Rv 13:16 It *f* all men,

FORCEFUL (1)

2Cor 10:10 His letters, they say, are severe and *f*,

FORCES (52)

Gn 14: 3 joined *f* in the Valley of Siddim (that is,
Nm 21:23 but mustered all his *f* and advanced into
Jos 10: 5 all their *f* and marched against Gibeon,
10: 6 mountain country have joined *f* against us."
11: 5 *f* and marched to the waters of Merom,
Jgs 1: 4 When the *f* of Judah attacked,
4:13 hundred of his iron chariots and all his *f*.
4:15 and all his *f* to rout before Barak.
20:19 Israelites advanced on Gibeah with their *f*.
1Sm 17: 1 The Philistines rallied their *f* for battle
23: 3 to Keilah against the *f* of the Philistines!"
28: 1 their military *f* to fight against Israel.
29: 1 had mustered all their *f* in Aphek,
2Sm 8: 9 David had defeated all the *f* of Hadadezer,
18: 7 The *f* of Israel were defeated by David's
1Kgs 20: 1 king of Aram, gathered all his *f*,
20:22 "Go, regroup your *f*.
2Kgs 12:19 who then led his *f* away from Jerusalem.
2Chr 17: 2 *f* in all the fortified cities of Judah,
32: 9 remained at Lachish with all his *f*,
Jdt 1: 4 *f* and the marshaling of his infantry.
2: 4 Holofernes, general in chief of his *f*,
4: 7 would be easy to ward off the attacking *f*,
7: 2 Their *f* numbered a hundred and seventy
7:26 the troops of Holofernes and to all his *f*;
10:13 the general in chief of your *f*,
16: 3 north, with the myriads of his *f* he came;
1Mc 3:27 a muster of all the *f* of his kingdom,
3:40 Setting out with all their *f*,
4: 4 *f* were still scattered away from
5:15 Galilee had joined *f* to destroy them.
6:29 Mercenary *f* also came to him from other
6:47 of the royal army and the ardor of its *f*,
9:66 set out to go up to the siege with their *f*.
10:71 If you have confidence in your *f*,
10:71 the city *f* are on my side.
11: 1 The king of Egypt gathered his *f*,
11:60 *f* of Syria espoused his cause as allies.
14:32 nation's armed *f* and giving them their pay.
15:38 and gave him infantry and cavalry *f*.
2Mc 8:30 challenged the *f* of Timothy and Bacchides,
8:32 also killed the commander of Timothy's *f*,
9: 3 had happened to Nicanor and to Timothy's *f*.
Jb 29:25 I took a king's place in the armed *f*.
Ps(s) 83: 9 they are the *f* of the sons of Lot.
Bar 6:55 They cannot resist a king, or enemy *f*.
Ez 17:21 troops among his *f* shall fall by the sword,
Dn 11:31 Armed *f* shall move at his command and
Mt 5:32 a separate case *f* her to commit adultery.
Lk 10:19 and scorpions and all the *f* of the enemy,
Eph 6:12 Our battle is not against human *f* but
Col 2:20 If with Christ you have died to cosmic *f*,

FORCIBLY (3)

2Kgs 11:16 *f* to the horse gate of the royal palace,
2Mc 12:28 who *f* shatters the might of his enemies,
Jb 9:12 Should he seize me *f*,

FORCING (4)

1Mc 2:25 of the king who was *f* them to sacrifice,
8: 2 conquering them and *f* them to pay tribute.
2Mc 14:41 were *f* the outer gate and calling for fire
Lk 16:16 people of every sort are *f* their way in.

FORD (2)

Gn 32:23 children, and crossed the *f* of the Jabbok.
2Sm 19:19 They crossed over the *f* to bring the

FORDS (8)

Jos 2: 7 out along the way to the *f* of the Jordan,
Jgs 3:28 seized the *f* of the Jordan leading to Moab,
12: 5 took the *f* of the Jordan toward Ephraim.
12: 6 him and kill him at the *f* of the Jordan.
2Sm 15:28 I shall be waiting at the *f* near the
17:16 spend the night at the *f* near the desert,
Is 16: 2 daughters of Moab at the *f* of the Arnon.
Jer 51:32 The *f* have been seized,

FORE (1)

Lv 16:14 sprinkle it with his finger on the *f* part

FOREARM (1)

Jb 31:22 the shoulder, my *f* be broken at the elbow!

FOREBEAR (2)

Gn 18:29 will *f* doing it for the sake of the forty."
18:30 *f* doing it if I can find but thirty there."

FOREBEARANCE (1)

Rom 3:26 his justice in the present, by way of *f*,

FOREBEARS (8)

2Kgs 12:19 dedicated offerings presented by his *f*,
23:32 sight of the LORD, just as his *f* had done.
23:37 sight of the LORD, just as his *f* had done.
24: 9 sight of the LORD, just as his *f* had done.
Est E:16 flourishing condition for us and for our *f*.
Ps(s) 49:20 of his *f* who shall never more see light.
Sir 8: 4 an unruly man, lest he speak ill of your *f*.
44:22 The covenant with all his *f* was confirmed,

FOREBODINGS (1)

Sir 40: 2 and his troubled *f* till the day he dies

FORECAST (1)

Is 47:13 the stargazers who *f* at each new moon what

FOREFATHER (13)

Gn 28:13 God of your *f* Abraham and the God of Isaac;
1Kgs 15:11 Asa pleased the LORD like his *f* David,
2Kgs 14: 3 pleased the LORD, yet not like his *f* David,
16: 2 please the LORD, his God, like his *f* David,
18: 3 the LORD, just as his *f* David had done.
20: 5 says the LORD the God of your *f* David:
2Chr 28: 1 please the LORD as his *f* David had done,
29: 2 the LORD just as his *f* David had done.
34: 3 began to seek after the God of his *f* David,
Tb 1: 4 the entire tribe of my *f* Naphtali had
1: 5 the rest of the tribe of my *f* Naphtali,
Jdt 9: 2 "Lord, God of my *f* Simeon!
9:12 "Please, please, God of my *f*,

FOREFATHERS (28)

Gn 15:15 You, however, shall join your *f* in peace;
Lv 26:45 of the covenant I made with their *f*,
Dt 19:14 neighbor's landmarks erected by your *f*
1Kgs 15:24 he was buried in his *f* City of David,
22:51 he was buried in his *f* City of David.
2Kgs 12:22 He was buried in his *f* City of David,
15:38 buried with them in his *f* City of David.
Tb 4:12 marry a woman of the lineage of your *f*.
Jdt 5: 7 not wish to follow the gods of their *f*
5: 8 their *f* expelled them from the presence of
7:28 earth, and by our God, the Lord of our *f*,
7:28 us for our sins and those of our *f*,
8: 3 *f* in the field between Dothan and Balamon.
8:19 It was for such conduct that our *f* were
8:25 putting us to the test, as he did our *f*.
Est C:16 the people of the land of my *f* that you,
2Mc 1:25 evil, who chose our *f* and sanctified them:
7: 8 Answering in the language of his *f*,
7:21 the language of their *f* with these words:
7:30 of the law given to our *f* through Moses.
8:15 sake of the covenants made with their *f*,
Jer 11:10 of their *f* who refused to obey my words.
Mt 5:21 heard the commandment imposed on your *f*,
5:33 heard the commandment imposed on your *f*,
23:30 'Had we lived in our *f* time we would not
23:32 fill up the vessel measured out by your *f*.
2Tm 1: 3 *f* whom I worship with a clear conscience,
2Pt 3: 4 Our *f* have been laid to rest,

FOREFINGER (2)

Lv 14:16 then, dipping his right *f* in it,
14:27 *f* sprinkle it seven times before the LORD.

FOREHEAD (18)

Ex 13: 9 on your hand and as a reminder on your *f*;
13:16 on your hand and as a pendant on your *f*:
28:38 on the front of the miter, over Aaron's *f*.
28:38 this plate must always be over his *f*,
Lv 8: 9 over the front of the miter, at his *f*,
13:41 not unclean merely because of his bald *f*.
13:42 a pink sore on his bald crown or bald *f*,
Dt 6: 8 and let them be as a pendant on your *f*.
11:18 sign, and let them be a pendant on your *f*.
1Sm 17:49 sling and struck the Philistine on the *f*.
2Chr 26:19 of incense, leprosy broke out on his *f*.
26:20 and when they saw that his *f* was leprous,
Is 48: 4 neck is an iron sinew and your *f* bronze,
Dn 8: 5 he-goat with a prominent horn on its *f*
8:21 the great horn on its *f* is the first king.
Rv 13:16 image on their right hand or their *f*.
14: 9 or accepts its mark on his *f* or hand,
17: 5 On her *f* was written a symbolic name,

FOREHEADS (7)

Dt 14: 1 shave the hair above your *f* for the dead.
Ez 9: 4 mark an X on the *f* of those who moan
Rv 7: 3 seal on the *f* of the servants of our God."
9: 4 men who had not the seal of God on their *f*.
14: 1 the name of his Father written on their *f*.

20: 4 its mark on their *f* or their hands.
22: 4 face to face and bear his name on their *f*.

FOREIGN (72)

Gn 35: 2 rid of the *f* gods that you have among you;
35: 4 handed over to Jacob all the *f* gods
Ex 2:22 for he said, "I am a stranger in a *f* land."
18: 3 for he said, "I am a stranger in a *f* land."
Nm 11: 4 The *f* elements among them were so greedy
Dt 28:32 daughters will be given to a *f* nation
Jos 12:23 Dor (in Naphath-dor), the *f* king of Gilgal,
Jgs 10:16 And they cast out the *f* gods from their
1Sm 7: 3 put away your *f* gods and your Ashtaroth,
1Kgs 11: 1 King Solomon loved many *f* women besides
11: 8 He did the same for all his *f* wives who
2Kgs 19:24 I dug wells and drank water in *f* lands;
2Chr 13: 9 priests like the peoples of *f* lands?
33:15 He removed the *f* gods and the idol from
Ezr 9: 7 to the will of the kings of *f* lands,
10: 2 taking as wives *f* women of the peoples
10: 3 our *f* wives and the children born of them,
10:10 "Your unfaithfulness in taking *f* women as
10:11 peoples of the land and from these *f* women."
10:14 who have taken *f* women for wives
10:17 the men who had taken *f* women for wives.
10:18 were found to have taken *f* women for wives:
10:44 All these had taken *f* wives;
Neh 9: 2 from all who were of *f* extraction,
13: 3 they separated from Israel every *f* element.
13:26 yet even he was made to sin by *f* women.
13:27 betraying our God by marrying *f* women?"
13:30 I cleansed them of all *f* contamination.
Jdt 5:18 and finally taken as captives into *f* lands.
14: 7 and in every *f* nation,
1Mc 1:44 them to follow customs *f* to their land;
6:13 I am dying, in bitter grief, in a *f* land."
11:38 except the *f* troops which he had hired
11:74 thousand of the *f* troops fell on that day.
15:33 "We have not seized any *f* land;
2Mc 4:13 and *f* customs reached such a pitch,
9:28 death in the mountains of a *f* land.
10:14 he employed *f* troops and used every
10:24 gathered a tremendous force of *f* troops
Ps(s) 137: 4 we sing a song of the LORD in a *f* land?
Sir 23:12 For all such words are *f* to the devout,
29:18 and sent them wandering through *f* lands.
39: 5 He travels among the peoples of *f* lands to
49: 5 their glory to a foolish *f* nation
Is 17:10 pagan plants and set out your *f* vine slips,
37:25 I dug wells and drank water in *f* lands;
Jer 8:19 with their idols, with their *f* nonentities?]
25:20 all the people under him, native and *f*;
Bar 3:10 land of your foes, grown old in a *f* land,
Ez 5: 5 I placed her, surrounded by *f* countries.
5: 6 more than the *f* countries surrounding her;
6: 8 and have been scattered over the *f* lands,
11:16 and scattered them over *f* countries
12:15 the nations and scatter them over *f* lands.
20:23 the nations and scatter them over *f* lands;
20:32 the nations, like the peoples of *f* lands,
22: 4 nations and a laughingstock to all *f* lands.
22:15 the nations and scatter you over *f* lands,
29:12 the nations and strew them over *f* lands.
30:23 the nations and strew them over *f* lands.
30:26 the nations and strew them over *f* lands.]
34:13 peoples and gather them from the *f* lands;
36:19 the nations, dispersing them over *f* lands;
36:24 nations, gather you from all the *f* lands,
Dn 11:39 he shall station a people of a *f* god.
Zep 1: 8 sons, and all that dress in *f* apparel.
Acts 2: 4 They began to express themselves in *f*
7: 6 posterity will be strangers in a *f* land,
17:18 "He sounds like a promoter of *f* gods,"
26:11 them that I pursued them even to *f* cities.
Heb 11: 9 in the promised land as in a *f* country,
11:34 in battle, and turned back *f* invaders.

FOREIGNER (21)

Gn 17:12 money from any *f* who is not of your blood.
Ex 12:43 No *f* may partake of it.
21: 8 He has no right to sell her to a *f*,
Lv 22:25 nor receive from a *f* any such animals
Dt 14:21 he may eat it, or you may sell it to a *f*.
15: 3 You may press a *f*,
17:15 a *f*, who is no kin of yours,
23:21 You may demand interest from a *f*,
Ru 2:10 she said to him, "Why should I, a *f*,
2Sm 15:19 with the king, for you are a *f* and you,
1Kgs 8:41 "To the *f*, likewise, who is not of your
8:43 Do all that the *f* asks of you,
2Chr 6:32 "For the *f*, too, who is not of your people
6:33 place, and do whatever the *f* entreats you,
Est C:26 the bed of the uncircumcised or of any *f*.
Jb 15:19 land was given, when no *f* moved among them.
Is 56: 3 Let not the *f* say,
Lk 17:18 and give thanks to God except this *f*?"
1Cor 14:11 foreigner to the speaker and he a *f* to me.
Col 3:11 Jew here, circumcised or uncircumcised, *f*,

FOREIGNERS (31)

Gn 17:27 house or acquired with his money from *f*,
Dt 29:21 *f* who will come here from far-off lands,
Jgs 19:12 "We will not turn off to a city of *f*,
2Sm 22:46 The *f* fawned and cringed before me;
Jdt 9: 2 into his hand to take revenge upon the *f*
1Mc 3:36 He was to settle *f* in all their territory
3:45 was trampled on, and *f* were in the citadel;
4:12 When the *f* looked up and saw them marching
4:26 But those of the *f* who had escaped went
10:12 The *f* in the strongholds that Bacchides
11:68 of him on the plain, was the army of the *f*.
Ps(s) 18:45 The *f* fawned and cringed before me;
Is 56: 6 And the *f* who join themselves to the LORD,
60:10 *F* shall rebuild your walls,
61: 5 *f* shall be your farmers and vinedressers.
62: 8 Nor shall *f* drink your wine,
Lam 5: 2 turned over to strangers, our homes to *f*.
Ez 7:21 I will hand them over as booty to *f*,
11: 9 out of the city, and hand you over to *f*,
28: 7 god, Therefore I will bring against you *f*,
28:10 of the uncircumcised at the hands of *f*,
30:12 in it I will hand over to *f* to devastate.
31:12 *F*, the most ruthless of the nations,
44: 7 You have admitted *f*,
44: 9 No *f*, uncircumcised in heart
44: 9 of the *f* who live among the Israelites.
Mt 17:25 tax or toll from their sons, or from *f*?"
17:26 When he replied, "From *f*,"
27: 7 buy the potter's field as a cemetery for *f*.
Acts 17:21 citizens, as well as the *f* who live there,
Heb 11:13 to be strangers and *f* on the earth,

FOREKNEW (2)

Rom 8:29 Those whom he *f* he predestined to share
11: 2 God has not rejected his people whom he *f*.

FOREKNOWLEDGE (2)

Jdt 9: 6 and your judgment is made with *f*.
1Pt 1: 2 according to the *f* of God the Father,

FOREMAN (1)

Mt 20: 8 the owner of the vineyard said to his *f*,

FOREMEN (5)

Ex 5: 6 taskmasters and *f* of the people this order:
5:10 and *f* of the people went out and told them,
5:14 The *f* of the Israelites,
5:15 *f* came and made this appeal to Pharaoh:
5:19 *f* knew they were in a sorry plight,

FOREMOST (2)

2Mc 6:18 Eleazar, one of the *f* scribes,
15:18 *f* fear was for the consecrated sanctuary.

FORERUNNER (2)

Prv 8:22 ways, the *f* of his prodigies of long ago;
Heb 6:20 the veil through which Jesus, our *f*,

FORERUNNERS (1)

Wis 12: 8 and sent wasps as *f* of your army they they

FORESAIL (1)

Acts 27:40 the rudders, hoisted the *f* into the wind,

FORESHADOWING (1)

Eph 5:32 This is a great *f*:

FORESHADOWS (1)

Phil 1:28 Their opposition *f* downfall for them,

FORESKIN (7)

Gn 17:11 Circumcise the flesh of your *f*,
17:14 the flesh of his *f* has not been cut away,
17:24 when the flesh of his *f* was circumcised,
17:25 when the flesh of his *f* was circumcised.
Ex 4:25 piece of flint and cut off her son's *f* and,
Lv 12: 3 flesh of the boy's *f* shall be circumcised,
Jdt 14:10 He had the flesh of his *f* circumcised,

FORESKINS (6)

Gn 17:23 the flesh of their *f* on that same day,
Jos 5: 7 circumcised, for these were yet with *f*,
1Sm 18:25 than the *f* of one hundred Philistines,
18:27 *f* and counted them out before the king,
2Sm 3:14 espoused by paying a hundred Philistine *f*."
Jer 4: 4 circumcised, remove the *f* of your hearts,

FOREST (45)

Dt 19: 5 goes with his neighbor to a *f* to cut wood,
Jos 17:15 go up to the *f* and clear out a place for
17:18 is now *f* shall be yours when you clear it.
1Sm 22: 5 so David left and went to the *f* of Hereth.
2Sm 18: 6 a battle was fought in the *f* near Mahanaim.
18:17 up and cast into a deep pit in the *f*,
1Kgs 7: 2 the *F* of Lebanon one hundred cubits long,
10:17 put them in the hall of the *F* of Lebanon.
10:21 hall of the *F* of Lebanon were of pure gold.
2Kgs 19:23 I reached the remotest heights, its *f* park.
1Chr 16:33 the trees of the *f* exult before the LORD,
2Chr 9:16 king put in the hall of the *F* of Lebanon.
9:20 hall of the *F* of Lebanon were of pure gold;
27: 4 the *f* land he set up fortresses and towers.
1Mc 4:38 the courts as in a *f* or on some mountain,
Ps(s) 80:14 fruit, The boar from the *f* lays it waste,
83:15 As a fire raging in a *f*,
96:12 the trees of the *f* exult before the LORD,
104:20 then all the beasts of the *f* roam about;
Is 7: 2 as the trees of the *f* tremble in the wind.
9:17 It kindles the *f* thickets,
10:19 of the trees in his *f* will be so few,
10:34 The *f* thickets are felled with the axe,
22: 8 to the weapons in the House of the *F*;
29:17 and the orchard be regarded as a *f*!
32:15 orchard and the orchard be regarded as a *f*.
32:19 Down it comes, as trees come down in the *f*!
37:24 I reached the remotest heights, its *f* park.
44:14 and lays hold of other trees of the *f*,
44:23 forth, you mountains, into song, you *f*,
56: 9 come and eat, all you beasts in the *f*!
Jer 5: 6 Therefore lions from the *f* slay them,
10: 3 nations are nothing, wood cut from the *f*,
21:14 *f* that shall devour all its surroundings.
26:18 of ruins, and the temple mount a *f* ridge.
46:23 They cut down her *f*,
Ez 15: 2 That branch among the trees of the *f*!
15: 6 wood of the vine among the trees of the *f*,
21: 2 against the *f* of the southern land.
21: 3 you shall say to the southern *f*.
Am 3: 4 a lion roar in the *f* when it has no prey?
Mi 3:12 And the mount of the temple to a *f* ridge.
5: 7 Like a lion among beasts of the *f*,
Zec 11: 2 Bashan, for the impenetrable *f* is cut down!
Jas 3: 5 the spark is that sets a huge *f* ablaze!

FORESTALL (2)

1Mc 6:27 Unless you quickly *f* them,
Dn 6:18 To *f* any tampering,

FORESTS (7)

Ps(s) 29: 9 the LORD twists the oaks and strips the *f*,
50:10 For mine are all the animals of the *f*,
Is 10:18 His splendid *f* and orchards.
Bar 5: 8 The *f* and every fragrant kind of tree
6:62 on high to burn up the mountains and the *f*,
Ez 34:25 securely in the desert and sleep in the *f*.
39:10 from the fields or cut it down in the *f*,

FORETELL (8)

Is 41:22 and *f* to us what it is that shall happen!
41:23 *F* the things that shall come afterward,
42: 9 have come to pass, new ones I now *f*;
44: 7 Let them *f* to us the things to come.
44: 8 did I not announce and *f* it long ago?
45:19 LORD, promise justice, I *f* what is right.
46:10 At the beginning I *f* the outcome;
Ez 13: 9 who have false visions and who *f* lies.

FORETOLD (34)

Gn 41:25 thus *f* to Pharaoh what he is about to do.
Ex 7:13 not listen to them, just as the LORD had *f*.
7:22 to Moses and Aaron, just as the LORD had *f*.
8:11 not listen to them just as the LORD had *f*.
8:15 not listen to them, just as the LORD had *f*.
9:12 to them, just as the LORD had *f* to Moses.
9:35 go, as the LORD had *f* through Moses.
Dt 13: 3 sign or wonder he has *f* you comes to pass,
Jos 11:23 country, just as the LORD had *f* to Moses.
1Sm 28:17 LORD has done to you what he *f* through me:
1Kgs 8:20 on the throne of Israel, as the LORD *f*,
16:34 gates, as the LORD had *f* through Joshua,
17:16 run dry, as the LORD had *f* through Elijah.
2Kgs 10:10 all that he *f* through his servant Elijah."
17:23 sight as he had *f* through all his servants,
24:13 the temple of the LORD, as the LORD had *f*.
2Chr 6:10 on the throne of Israel, as the LORD *f*,
Sir 48:25 He *f* what should be till the end of time,
49: 7 its streets desolate, As JEREMIAH had *f*;
Is 40:21 Was it not *f* you from the beginning?
41:26 Not one of you *f* it,
43: 9 this, or *f* to us the earlier things?
43:12 It is I who *f*,
45:21 from the beginning and *f* it from of old?
48: 3 Things of the past I *f* long ago,
48: 5 forehead bronze, I *f* them to you of old;
48:14 Who among you *f* these things?
52: 6 know my renown, that it is I who have *f* it.
Jer 32: 8 Then, as the LORD *f*,
40: 2 LORD your God, *f* the ruin of this place.
Mt 24:15 Daniel *f* standing on holy ground
Acts 7:52 those who *f* the coming of the Just One;
26:22 differs from what the prophets and Moses *f*:
Gal 3: 8 faith, it *f* this good news to Abraham:

FOREVER (423)

Gn 3:22 life also, and thus eat of it and live *f*."
6: 3 "My spirit shall not remain in man *f*,
13:15 I will give to you and your descendants *f*.
43: 9 presence, you can hold it against me *f*.

FOREVER (cont.)

44:32 you, father, you can hold it against me *f.*'
Ex 3:15 "This is my name *f*;
15:18 The LORD shall reign *f* and ever.
21: 6 an awl, thus keeping him as his slave *f.*
Nm 18:19 covenant to last *f* before the LORD,
24:20 was Amalek, but this end is to perish *f.*
24:24 and conquered Eber, He too shall perish *f.*
Dt 4:40 which the LORD, your God, is giving you *f.*"
5:29 their descendants would prosper *f*
13:17 Let it be a heap of ruins *f,*
15:17 door, and he shall then be your slave *f.*
29:28 revealed concern us and our descendants *f,*
32:40 As surely as I live *f,*
Jos 4:24 that you may fear the LORD, your God, *f.*"
14: 9 heritage and that of your descendants *f,*
1Sm 1:22 before the LORD and to remain there *f*;
2:30 family should minister in my presence *f.*
2:35 function in the presence of my anointed *f.*
20:23 the LORD shall be between you and me *f.*"
20:42 me, and between your posterity and mine *f.*"
27:12 I shall have him as my vassal *f.*"
2Sm 3:28 I and my kingdom are *f* innocent.
7:13 And I will make his royal throne firm *f.*
7:16 *f* before me; your throne shall stand firm *f.*
7:24 for yourself your people Israel as yours *f,*
7:26 Your name will be *f* great,
7:29 your servant that it may be before you *f*;
7:29 house of your servant shall be blessed *f.*"
22:51 to David and his posterity *f.*"
1Kgs 1:31 said, "May the lord, King David, live *f!*"
2:33 shall be responsible *f* for their blood.
2:33 shall be the peace of the LORD *f* for David,
2:45 throne shall endure before the LORD *f.*"
8:13 house, a dwelling where you may abide *f.*"
9: 3 I confer my name upon it *f,*
9: 5 your throne of sovereignty over Israel *f,*
11:39 punish David's line for this, but not *f.*'"
12: 7 answer, they will be your servants *f.*"
2Kgs 5:27 shall cling to you and your descendants *f.*"
17:37 to observe *f* the statutes and regulations,
21: 7 tribes of Israel, I shall place my name *f.*
1Chr 15: 2 ark of the LORD and to minister to him *f.*"
16:15 his judgments prevail He remembers *f*
16:34 he is good, for his kindness endures *f*;
16:41 LORD, "because his kindness endures *f,*"
17:12 a house, and I will establish his throne *f.*
17:14 him in my house and in my kingdom *f,*
17:14 his throne shall be firmly established *f.*"
17:22 You made your people Israel your own *f,*
17:23 your servant and his house remain firm *f.*
17:24 God of Israel, may be great and abide *f,*
17:27 of your servant, so that it will remain *f*—
17:27 O LORD, who blessed it, it is blessed *f.*"
22:10 the throne of his kingship over Israel *f.*'
23:13 as most holy, he and his sons *f,*
23:13 minister to him, and to bless his name *f.*
28: 4 father's family to be king over Israel *f.*
28: 7 I will establish his kingdom *f,*
28: 8 it as an inheritance to your children *f.*
28: 9 if you abandon him, he will cast you off *f*:
29:18 in the hearts and minds of your people *f,*
2Chr 5:13 for he is good, for his mercy endures *f,*"
6: 2 house and dwelling, where you may abide *f.*"
7: 3 "for he is good, for his mercy endures *f.*"
7: 6 the LORD, for his mercy endures *f,*"
7:16 this house that my name may be there *f*;
9: 8 loved Israel as to will to make it last *f,*
10: 7 request, they will be your servants *f.*"
13: 5 given the kingdom of Israel to David *f,*
20: 7 gave it *f* to the descendants of Abraham,
20:21 to the LORD, for his mercy endures *f.*"
30: 8 his sanctuary that he has consecrated *f,*
33: 4 said, "In Jerusalem shall my name be *f*":
33: 7 tribes of Israel I shall place my name *f.*
Ezr 3:11 for his kindness to Israel endures *f*";
9:12 it as an inheritance to your children *f.*
Neh 2: 3 "May the king live *f!*
Tb 8: 5 praised be your name *f* and ever.
8: 5 heavens and all your creation praise you *f.*
8:15 let them bless you *f!*
8:21 to you and to your beloved now and *f.*
12:17 Thank God now and *f.*
13: 1 Blessed be God who lives *f,*
13: 4 is the Lord our God, our Father and God *f.*
13:11 you the chosen one, through all ages *f.*
13:12 *f* blessed are all those who build you up.
13:14 in you as they behold all your joy *f.*
13:16 Jerusalem shall be rebuilt as his home *f.*
13:18 in you they shall praise his holy name *f.*
14: 7 shall they dwell *f* in the land of Abraham,
14:15 and he blessed the Lord God *f* and ever.
Jdt 15:10 be blessed by the Lord Almighty *f* and ever!"
16:16 sight, one who fears the Lord is *f* great.
16:17 flesh, and they shall burn and suffer *f.*"
Est C:21 false gods, and to extol an earthly king *f.*
E:24 even shunned by wild beasts and birds *f.*"
1Mc 3: 7 by his deeds, and his memory is blessed *f.*
4:24 "for he is good, for his mercy endures *f.*"
8:23 the Jewish nation at sea and on land *f*;
2Mc 1:17 *F* blessed be our God,
7: 9 the world will raise us up to live again *f.*
14:15 to him who established his people *f,*

14:36 holiness, preserve *f* undefiled this house,
Jb 4:20 with no heed paid to it, they perish *f.*
7:16 I cannot live *f*;
19:24 and with lead they were cut in the rock *f!*
20: 7 he perishes *f* like the fuel of his fire,
36: 7 kings upon thrones he sets them, exalted *f.*
40:28 you that you may have him as a slave *f?*
Ps(s) 5:12 who take refuge in you be glad and exult *f.*
9: 6 their name you blotted out *f* and ever.
9: 7 The enemies are ruined completely *f*;
9: 8 But the LORD sits enthroned *f*;
9:19 shall the hope of the afflicted *f* perish.
10:16 The LORD is king *f* and ever;
16:11 the delights at your right hand *f.*
18:51 anointed, to David and his posterity *f.*
19:10 The fear of the LORD is pure, enduring *f*;
21: 5 you gave him length of days *f* and ever.
21: 7 For you made him a blessing *f*;
28: 9 feed them, and carry them *f!*
29:10 the LORD is enthroned as king *f.*
30:13 O LORD, my God, *f* will I give you thanks.
33:11 But the plan of the LORD stands *f*;
37:18 their inheritance lasts *f.*
37:27 evil and do good, that you may abide *f*;
37:29 shall possess the land and dwell in it *f.*
41:13 sustain me and let me stand before you *f.*
41:14 the God of Israel, from all eternity and *f.*
44:24 Cast us not off *f!*
45: 3 thus God has blessed you *f.*
45: 7 Your throne, O God, stands *f* and ever;
45:18 shall nations praise you *f* and ever.
48: 9 God makes it firm *f.*
48:15 that such is God, Our God *f* and ever;
49:12 Tombs are their homes *f,*
52: 7 *f* he shall break you;
52:10 Trust in the kindness of God *f* and ever.
61: 5 Oh, that I might lodge in your tent *f,*
61: 8 Let him sit enthroned before God *f*;
61: 9 So will I sing the praises of your name *f,*
66: 7 He rules by his might *f*;
68:17 where the LORD himself will dwell *f?*
72:17 May his name be blessed *f*;
72:19 And blessed *f* be his glorious name;
73:26 is the rock of my heart and my portion *f.*
74: 1 Why, O God, have you cast us off *f?*
74:10 Shall the enemy revile your name *f?*
74:19 be not *f* unmindful of the lives of your
75:10 But as for me, I will exult *f*;
77: 8 Lord reject *f* and nevermore be favorable?
78:69 heaven, like the earth which he founded *f.*
79: 5 Will you be angry *f?*
79:13 your pasture, will give thanks to you *f*;
81:16 flatter me, but their fate would endure *f,*
83:18 Let them be shamed and put to rout *f*;
86:12 my heart, and I will glorify your name *f.*
89: 2 The favors of the LORD I will sing *f*;
89: 3 said, "My kindness is established *f*";
89: 5 *F* will I confirm your posterity and
89:29 *F* I will maintain my kindness toward him,
89:30 *f* and his throne as the days of heaven.
89:37 His posterity shall continue *f,*
89:38 Like the moon, which remains *f*—
89:47 Will you hide yourself *f?*
89:53 Blessed be the LORD *f.*
92: 9 while you, O LORD, are the Most High *f.*
100: 5 the LORD, whose kindness endures *f,*
102:13 But you, O LORD, abide *f,*
103: 9 chide, nor does he keep his wrath *f.*
104: 5 upon its foundation, not to be moved *f*;
104:31 May the glory of the LORD endure *f*;
105: 8 He remembers *f* his covenant which he
106:31 to him for merit through all generations *f.*
107: 1 for he is good, for his kindness endures *f!*"
110: 4 "You are a priest *f,*
111: 3 are his work, and his justice endures *f.*
111: 5 he will *f* be mindful of his covenant.
111: 8 are all his precepts, Reliable *f* and ever,
111: 9 he has ratified his covenant *f*;
111:10 His praise endures *f.*
112: 3 his generosity shall endure *f.*
112: 9 his generosity shall endure *f*;
113: 2 be the name of the LORD both now and *f.*
115:18 But we bless the LORD, both now and *f.*
117: 2 us, and the fidelity of the LORD endures *f.*
118: 2 house of Israel say, "His mercy endures *f.*"
118: 3 house of Aaron say, "His mercy endures *f.*"
118: 4 fear the LORD say, "His mercy endures *f.*"
118:29 for his kindness endures *f.*
119:44 will keep your law continually, *f* and ever.
119:89 Your word, O LORD, endures *f*;
119:111 Your decrees are my inheritance *f*;
119:144 Your decrees are *f* just;
119:152 decrees, that you have established them *f.*
121: 8 your coming and your going, both now and *f.*
125: 1 which *f* stands.
125: 2 is round about his people, both now and *f.*
131: 3 Israel, hope in the LORD, both now and *f.*
132:12 sons, too, *f* shall sit upon your throne."
132:14 "Zion is my resting place *f*;
133: 3 LORD has pronounced his blessing, life *f.*
135:13 Your name, O LORD, endures *f*;
136: 1 for he is good, for his mercy endures *f*;
136: 2 the God of gods, for his mercy endures *f*;

136: 3 Lord of lords, for his mercy endures *f*;
136: 4 great wonders, for his mercy endures *f*;
136: 5 in wisdom, for his mercy endures *f*;
136: 6 upon the waters, for his mercy endures *f*;
136: 7 the great lights, for his mercy endures *f*;
136: 8 over the day, for his mercy endures *f*;
136: 9 over the night, for his mercy endures *f*;
136:10 their first-born, for his mercy endures *f*;
136:11 from their midst, for his mercy endures *f*;
136:12 outstretched arm, for his mercy endures *f*;
136:13 Red Sea in twain, for his mercy endures *f*;
136:14 its midst, for his mercy endures *f*;
136:15 into the Red Sea, for his mercy endures *f*;
136:16 the wilderness, for his mercy endures *f*;
136:17 great kings, for his mercy endures *f*;
136:18 powerful kings, for his mercy endures *f*;
136:19 of the Amorities, for his mercy endures *f*;
136:20 king of Bashan, for his mercy endures *f*;
136:21 land a heritage, for his mercy endures *f*;
136:22 his servant, for his mercy endures *f*;
136:23 in our abjection, for his mercy endures *f*;
136:24 us from our foes, for his mercy endures *f*;
136:25 food to all flesh, for his mercy endures *f.*
136:26 the God of heaven, for his mercy endures *f.*
138: 8 your kindness, O LORD, endures *f*;
145: 1 and I will bless your name *f* and ever.
145: 2 and I will praise your name *f* and ever.
145:21 all flesh bless his holy name *f* and ever.
146: 6 Who keeps faith *f,*
146:10 The LORD shall reign *f*;
148: 6 He established them *f* and ever;
Prv 10:25 but the just man is established *f.*
12:19 Truthful lips endure *f,*
27:24 For wealth lasts not *f,*
29:14 of the poor, his throne stands firm *f.*
Eccl 1: 4 and another comes, but the world *f* stays.
3:14 that whatever God does will endure *f*;
Wis 3: 8 and the Lord shall be their King *f.*
4: 2 And *f* it marches crowned in triumph,
5:15 But the just live *f,*
6:21 Wisdom, that you may reign as kings *f.*
14:13 they were not, nor shall they continue *f*;
Sir 1: 1 from the LORD and with him it remains *f.*
37:25 heritage of glory, and his name endures *f.*
40:17 never be cut off, and justice endures *f.*
42:24 The universe lives and abides *f*;
45:24 should possess the high priesthood *f.*
47:11 him his sins and exalted his strength *f*;
Is 2:18 The idols will perish *f.*
9: 6 His dominion is vast and *f* peaceful,
9: 6 By judgment and justice, both now and *f.*
14:20 Let him not be named *f,*
17: 2 Her cities shall be *f* abandoned,
25: 8 he will destroy death *f.*
26: 4 Trust in the LORD *f!*
28:24 Is the plowman *f* plowing,
32:19 wasteland *f* for wild asses to frolic in,
34:10 not be quenched, its smoke shall rise *f.*
34:17 They shall possess her *f,*
40: 8 flower wilts, the word of our God stands *f.*"
45:17 saved by the LORD, saved *f!*
47: 7 shall remain always a sovereign mistress *f!*"
51: 6 *f* and my justice shall never be dismayed.
51: 8 my justice shall remain *f* and my salvation,
57:16 I will not accuse *f,*
59:21 children's children, from now on and *f.*
60:19 The LORD shall be your light *f,*
60:20 For the LORD will be your light *f,*
63:16 our father, our redeemer you are named *f.*
64: 8 angry, LORD, keep not our guilt *f* in mind;
Jer 3: 5 "Will he keep his wrath *f,*
3:12 the LORD, I will not continue my wrath *f.*
7: 7 which I gave your fathers long ago and *f.*
17: 4 been kindled by my wrath that will burn *f.*
17:25 This city will remain inhabited *f.*
20:17 been my grave, her womb confining me *f.*
25: 5 you and your fathers, from of old and *f.*
31:36 of Israel cease as a nation before me *f.*
33:11 his mercy endures *f.*"
49:13 and all her cities shall become ruins *f.*
49:33 become a haunt of jackals, a desert *f,*
51:26 Ruins *f* shall you be,
Lam 3:31 For the Lord's rejection does not last *f*;
5:19 You, O LORD, are enthroned *f*;
Bar 3: 3 for you are enthroned *f,*
3: 3 forever, while we are perishing *f.*
4: 1 precepts of God, the law that endures *f*;
5: 1 put on the splendor of glory from God *f*:
5: 4 be named by God *f* the peace of justice,
Ez 21: 5 this the one who is *f* spinning parables?'"
35: 9 desolate will I make you *f,*
37:25 they shall live on it *f,*
37:25 with my servant David their prince *f.*
37:26 them, and put my sanctuary among them *f.*
37:28 my sanctuary shall be set up among them *f.*
43: 7 here I will dwell among the Israelites *f.*
43: 9 kings, and I will dwell in their midst *f.*
Dn 2: 4 "O king, live *f!*
2:20 "Blessed be the name of God *f* and ever,
2:44 put an end to them, and it shall stand *f.*
3: 9 "O king, live *f!*
3:26 our fathers, and glorious *f* is your name.
3:34 your name's sake, do not deliver us up *f,*

3:52 praiseworthy and exalted above all *f*;
3:53 praiseworthy and glorious above all *f*.
3:54 praiseworthy and exalted above all *f*.
3:55 praiseworthy and exalt above all *f*.
3:56 of heaven, praiseworthy and glorious *f*.
3:57 the Lord, praise and exalt him above all *f*.
3:58 the Lord, praise and exalt him above all *f*.
3:59 the Lord, praise and exalt him above all *f*.
3:60 the Lord, praise and exalt him above all *f*.
3:61 praise and exalt him above all *f*.
3:62 praise and exalt him above all *f*.
3:63 praise and exalt him above all *f*.
3:64 praise and exalt him above all *f*.
3:65 praise and exalt him above all *f*.
3:66 praise and exalt him above all *f*.
3:67 praise and exalt him above all *f*.
3:68 praise and exalt him above all *f*
3:69 praise and exalt him above all *f*.
3:70 praise and exalt him above all *f*.
3:71 praise and exalt him above all *f*.
3:72 praise and exalt him above all *f*.
3:73 praise and exalt him above all *f*.
3:74 the Lord, praise and exalt him above all *f*.
3:75 praise and exalt him above all *f*.
3:76 praise and exalt him above all *f*.
3:77 praise and exalt him above all *f*.
3:78 praise and exalt him above all *f*.
3:79 the Lord, praise and exalt him above all *f*.
3:80 praise and exalt him above all *f*.
3:81 praise and exalt him above all *f*.
3:82 praise and exalt him above all *f*.
3:83 praise and exalt him above all *f*.
3:84 praise and exalt him above all *f*.
3:85 praise and exalt him above all *f*.
3:86 praise and exalt him above all *f*.
3:87 praise and exalt him above all *f*.
3:88 praise and exalt him above all *f*.
3:89 for he is good, for his mercy endures *f*.
3:90 him thanks, because his mercy endures *f*."
4:31 I praised and glorified him who lives *f*:
5:10 banquet hall and said, "O king, live *f*!
6: 7 and said to him, "King Darius, live *f*!
6:22 "O king, live *f*!
6:27 "For he is the living God, enduring *f*;
7:18 the kingship, to possess it *f* and ever."
12: 2 some shall live *f*,
12: 3 man to justice shall be like the stars *f*.
12: 7 who lives *f* that it should be for a year,
Hos 2:21 I will espouse you to me *f*;
Jl 4:20 But Judah shall abide *f*,
Ob 1:10 cover you and you shall be destroyed *f*.
Jon 2: 7 the nether world were closing behind me *f*,
Mi 2: 9 you take away *f* the honor I gave them.
4: 5 the name of the LORD, our God, *f* and ever.
4: 7 over them on Mount Zion, from now on *f*.
7:18 Who does not persist in anger *f*,
Zep 2: 9 of nettles and a salt pit and a waste *f*.
Zec 1: 5 And the prophets, can they live *f*?
11:17 entirely, and his right eye be blind *f*!
Mal 1: 4 the people with whom the LORD is angry *f*.
Lk 1:32 Jacob *f* and his reign will be without end."
1:55 promised Abraham and his descendants *f*."
Jn 6:51 If anyone eats this bread he shall live *f*;
6:58 man who feeds on this bread shall live *f*."
8:35 family, but the son has a place there *f*.)
12:34 in the law that the Messiah is to remain *f*.
Rom 1:25 blessed be he *f*,
9: 5 Blessed *f* be God who is over all!
11:10 Bow down their back *f*."
11:11 stumbling mean that they are *f* fallen?
11:36 To him be glory *f*.
2Cor 4:18 what is unseen lasts *f*.
5: 1 heavens, not made by hands but to last *f*.
9: 9 gave to the poor, his justice endures *f*."
11:31 blessed be he *f*—
1Tm 1:17 only God, be honor and glory *f* and ever!
5:25 even inconspicuous ones cannot be hidden *f*.
2Tm 4:18 To him be glory *f* and ever.
Phlm 1:15 that you might possess him *f*,
Heb 1: 8 "Your throne, O God, stands *f* and ever;
5: 6 in another place, "You are a priest *f*,
6:20 *f* according to the order of Melchizedek.
7: 3 like the Son of God he remains a priest *f*.
7:17 "You are a priest *f* according to the order
7:21 'You are a priest *f*, according to the order
7:24 but Jesus, because he remains *f*,
7:25 he *f* lives to make intercession for them.
7:28 appoints as priest the Son, made perfect *f*.
10:12 took his seat *f* at the right hand of God;
10:14 *f* perfected those who are being sanctified.
13: 8 Christ is the same yesterday, today, and *f*.
13:21 To Christ be glory *f*!
1Pt 1:24 wilts, but the word of the Lord endures *f*."
1Jn 2:17 but the man who does God's will endures *f*.
2Jn 1: 2 that abides in us and will be with us *f*.
Jude 1:13 gloom of darkness has been reserved *f*.
Rv 1: 6 to him be glory and power *f* and ever!
1:18 Once I was dead but now I live *f* and ever.
4: 9 seated on the throne, who lives *f* and ever,
4:10 and worship him who lives *f* and ever.
5:13 and honor, glory and might, *f* and ever!"
7:12 power and might, to our God *f* and ever.
10: 6 an oath by the One who lives *f* and ever,
11:15 One, and he shall reign *f* and ever."
14:10 of their torment shall rise *f* and ever.
15: 7 the wrath of the God who lives *f* and ever.
19: 3 smoke began to rise from her *f* and ever,
20:10 will be tortured day and night, *f* and ever.
22: 5 give them light, and they shall reign *f*.

FOREWARN (1)

Dt 8:19 I *f* you this day that you will perish

FOREWARNED (1)

2Pt 3:17 You are *f*, beloved brothers.

FOREWARNINGS (1)

Wis 19:13 *f* from the violence of the thunderbolts.

FOREWARNS (1)

Jb 34:23 For he *f* no man of his time to come before

FORFEIT (7)

Ex 30:12 shall give the LORD a *f* for his life,
30:15 to the LORD to pay the *f* for their lives.
30:16 receive this *f* money from the Israelites,
30:16 the LORD, of the *f* paid for their lives."
Lv 20:16 their lives are *f*.
Dt 22: 9 if you do, its produce shall become *f*,
2Pt 3:17 the wicked, and *f* the security you enjoy.

FORFEITED (5)

Lv 20: 9 his father or mother, he has *f* his life.
20:11 they have *f* their lives.
20:12 an abhorrent deed, they have *f* their lives.
20:13 they have *f* their lives.
Phil 3: 8 For his sake I have *f* everything;

FORFEITING (1)

Hb 2:10 cutting off many peoples, *f* your own life:

FORFEITS (1)

Prv 20: 2 he who incurs his anger *f* his life.

FORGAVE (3)

Ps(s) 78:38 *f* their sin and destroyed them not;
Sir 16: 7 He *f* not the leaders of old who rebelled
47:11 The LORD *f* him his sins and exalted his

FORGE (3)

Gn 4:22 all who *f* instruments of bronze and iron.
Ps(s) 119:69 Though the proud *f* lies against me,
Jer 28:13 breaking a wooden yoke, you *f* an iron yoke!

FORGERS (1)

Sir 44: 4 and *f* of epigrams with their spikes;

FORGES (2)

Is 44:12 with hammers, and *f* it with his strong arm.
54:16 burning coals and *f* weapons as his work;

FORGET (52)

Gn 41:51 "God has made me *f* entirely the
Dt 4: 9 *f* the things which your own eyes have seen,
4:31 nor *f* the covenant which under oath he
6:12 eat your fill, take care not to *f* the LORD,
8:11 Be careful not to *f* the LORD,
8:19 But if you *f* the LORD,
9: 7 mind and do not *f* how you angered the LORD,
25:19 Amalek from under the heavens. Do not *f*!
1Sm 1:11 if you remember me and do not *f* me,
9: 5 lest my father *f* about the asses and
2Kgs 17:38 which I made with you, you must not *f*;
1Mc 1:49 so that they might *f* the law ancd change
2Mc 2: 2 admonished them not to *f* the commandments
Jb 9:27 I will *f* my complaining,
11:16 For then you shall *f* your misery,
Ps(s) 9:18 turn back, all the nations that *f* God.
10:12 *F* not the afflicted!
13: 2 Will you utterly *f* me?
42:10 "Why do you *f* me?
45:11 ear, *f* your people and your father's house.
50:22 "Consider this, you who *f* God,
78: 7 *f* the deeds of God but keep his commands,
102: 5 I *f* to eat my bread.
103: 2 O my soul, and *f* not all his benefits;
119:16 I will not *f* your words.
119:93 Never will I *f* your precepts,
119:109 my life in my hands, yet I *f* not your law.
119:139 consumes me, because my foes *f* your words.
119:176 servant, because your commands I do not *f*.
137: 5 If I *f* you,
Prv 3: 1 My son, *f* not my teaching,
4: 5 not *f* or turn aside from the words I utter.
31: 5 in drinking they *f* what the law decrees,
31: 7 When they drink, they will *f* their misery,
Sir 7:27 your mother's birthpangs *f* not.
11:25 day of prosperity makes one *f* adversity;
11:25 day of adversity makes one *f* prosperity.
29:15 *F* not the kindness of your backer,
37: 6 *F* not your comrade during the battle,
Is 49:15 Can a mother *f* her infant,
49:15 Even should she forget, I will never *f* you.
51:13 to be looked upon as grass, And *f* the LORD,
54: 4 The shame of your youth you shall *f*,
Jer 2:32 Does a virgin *f* her jewelry,
23:27 think to make my people *f* my name for Baal.
Lam 5:20 Why, then, should you *f* us,
Ez 39:26 They shall *f* their disgrace and all the
Am 8: 7 Never will I *f* a thing they have done!
Acts 20:31 Do not *f* that for three years,
2Tm 3: 1 Do not *f* this:
Heb 6:10 he will not *f* your work and the love you

FORGETFUL (2)

Wis 19: 4 and made them *f* of what had befallen them,
Jas 1:25 He is no *f* listener,

FORGETFULNESS (2)

Wis 16:11 Lest they should fall into deep *f* and
Sir 11:27 affliction brings *f* of past delights;

FORGETS (6)

Gn 27:45 subsides] and he *f* what you did to him.
Jb 8:13 So is the end of everyone who *f* God,
Prv 2:17 of her youth and *f* the pact with her God;
Hb 3:10 The sun *f* to rise,
Jas 1:24 off and promptly *f* what he looked like.
2Pt 1: 9 He *f* the cleansing of his long-past sins.

FORGETTING (5)

Dt 4:23 lest, *f* the covenant which the LORD,
Jgs 3: 7 had offended the LORD by *f* the LORD,
8:34 Baal of Berith their god and *f* the LORD,
Ps(s) 44:25 *f* our woe and our oppression?
Is 65:11 who forsake the LORD, *f* my holy mountain,

FORGING (1)

Sir 38:28 standing near his anvil, *f* crude iron.

FORGIVE (62)

Gn 32:21 when I face him, perhaps he will *f* me."
50:17 *f* the criminal wrongdoing of your brothers,
50:17 Please therefore, *f* the crime that we,
Ex 10:17 But now, do *f* me my sin once more,
23:21 against him, for he will not *f* your sin.
32:32 If you would only *f* their sin!
Jos 24:19 not *f* your transgressions or your sins.
Jgs 19: 3 went after her to *f* her and take her back.
1Sm 15:25 Now *f* my sin,
25:28 *f* the transgression of your handmaid,
2Sm 24:10 But now, LORD, *f* the guilt of your servant,
1Kgs 8:34 heaven and *f* the sin of your people Israel,
8:36 listen in heaven and *f* the sin of your
8:39 from your heavenly dwelling place and *f*.
8:50 *F* your people their sins and all the
2Kgs 5:18 I trust the LORD will *f* your servant this:
5:18 May the LORD *f* your servant this."
24: 4 he filled Jerusalem, the LORD would not *f*.
2Chr 6:25 heaven and *f* the sin of your people Israel,
6:27 listen in heaven and *f* the sin of your
6:30 from your heavenly dwelling place, and *f*.
6:39 *F* your people who have sinned against you.
Sir 5: 6 my many sins he will *f*."
28: 2 *F* your neighbor's injustice;
28: 5 flesh cherishes wrath, who will *f* his sins?
34:19 their many sacrifices does he *f* their sins.
Jer 18:23 *F* not their crime,
31:34 for I will *f* their evildoing and remember
33: 8 sinned and rebelled against me, I will *f*.
36: 3 I may *f* their wickedness and their sin.
50:20 for I will *f* the remnant I preserve.
Hos 14: 3 Say to him, *F* all iniquity,
Am 7: 2 *F*, O Lord GOD!
7: 8 I will *f* them no longer.
8: 2 I will *f* them no longer.
Jon 3: 9 Who knows, God may relent and *f*,
Mt 6:12 *f* us the wrong we have done as we *f*
6:14 "If you *f* the faults of others,
6:14 your heavenly Father will *f* you yours.
6:15 If you do not *f* others,
6:15 others, neither will your Father *f* you.
9: 6 of Man has authority on earth to *f* sins"
18:21 brother wrongs me, how often must I *f* him?
Mk 2: 7 Who can *f* sins except God alone?"
2:10 to *f* sins" (he said to the paralyzed man),
11:25 *f* anyone against whom you have a grievance
11:25 Father may in turn *f* you your faults."
Lk 5:21 Who can *f* sins but God alone?"
5:24 of Man has authority on earth to *f* sins"
11: 4 *F* us our sins for we too forgive all who
17: 3 if he repents, *f* him.
17: 4 back to you saying, 'I am sorry,' *f* him."
23:34 [Jesus said, "Father, *f* them;
Jn 20:23 If you *f* men's sins,
2Cor 2:10 If you *f* a man anything, so do I.
12:13 *F* me this injustice!
Col 3:13 *f* whatever grievances you have against one
3:13 *F* as the Lord has forgiven you.
Heb 8:12 I will *f* their evildoing,

FORGIVE (cont.)
1Jn 1: 9 *f* our sins and cleanse us from every wrong.

FORGIVEN (47)
Lv 4:20 atonement for them, and they will be *f*.
4:26 for the prince's sin, and it will be *f*.
4:31 make atonement for him, and he will be *f*.
4:35 for the man's sin, and it will be *f*.
5:10 sin the man committed, and it will be *f*.
5:13 any of the above cases, and it will be *f*.
5:16 the guilt-offering ram, and he will be *f*.
5:18 unwittingly committed, and it will be *f*.
5:26 be *f* whatever guilt he may have incurred."
19:22 sin he has committed, and it will be *f* him.
Nm 14:19 as you have *f* them from Egypt until now."
15:25 thus they will be *f* the inadvertence for
15:26 the aliens residing among you, shall be *f*,
15:28 has been made for him, he will be *f*.
2Sm 12:13 "The LORD on his part has *f* your sin:
Ps(s) 85: 3 You have *f* the guilt of your people;
Sir 21: 1 more, and for your past sins pray to be *f*.
27:21 A wound can be bound up, and an insult *f*,
28: 2 when you pray, your own sins will be *f*.
Is 33:24 who live there will be *f* their guilt.
Lam 3:42 you have not *f* us.
Mt 9: 2 "Have courage, son, your sins are *f*."
9: 5 'Your sins are *f*' or 'Stand up and walk'?
12:31 every sin, every blasphemy, will be *f* men,
12:31 blasphemy against the Spirit will not be *f*.
12:32 anything against the Son of Man will be *f*,
12:32 against the Holy Spirit will not be *f*,
Mk 2: 5 paralyzed man, "My son, your sins are *f*."
2: 9 to say to the paralytic, 'Your sins are *f*,'
3:28 every sin will be *f* mankind and all the
3:29 against the Holy Spirit will never be *f*.
4:12 lest perhaps they repent and be *f*."
Lk 5:20 said, "My friend, your sins are *f* you."
5:23 to say, 'Your sins are *f* you,'
7:47 tell you, that is why her many sins are *f*—
7:47 Little is *f* the one whose love is small."
7:48 He said to her then, "Your sins are *f*";
12:10 speaks against the Son of Man will be *f*,
12:10 blasphemes the Holy Spirit will never be *f*.
Jn 20:23 If you forgive men's sins, they are *f* them;
Acts 2:38 of Jesus Christ, that your sins may be *f*;
Rom 4: 7 "Blest are they whose iniquities are *f*,
Eph 1: 7 that we have been redeemed and our sins *f*,
4:32 forgiving, just as God has *f* you in Christ.
Col 3:13 Forgive as the Lord has *f* you.
Heb 10:18 Once these have been *f*,
1Jn 2:12 for through his Name your sins have been *f*.

FORGIVENESS (15)
Ps(s) 130: 4 But with you is *f*,
Sir 5: 5 Of *f* be not overconfident,
13: 3 of it, the poor man is wronged and begs *f*.
17:24 the LORD, his *f* of those who return to him!
Dn 9: 9 O LORD, our God, are compassion and *f*!
Mt 26:28 out in behalf of many for the *f* of sins.
Mk 1: 4 of repentance which led to the *f* of sins.
Lk 3: 3 of repentance which led to the *f* of sins,
Acts 5:31 bring repentance to Israel and *f* of sins.
10:43 in him has *f* of sins through his name."
13:38 the *f* of sins is being proclaimed to you,
26:18 they may obtain the *f* of their sins
Col 1:14 him we have redemption, the *f* of our sins.
Heb 9:22 the shedding of blood there is no *f*.
Jas 5:15 he has committed any sins, *f* will be his.

FORGIVES (5)
Sir 2:11 he *f* sins,
16:11 anger alike are with him who remits and *f*,
18:10 is grievous, and so he *f* them all the more.
Mt 18:35 each of you *f* his brother from his heart."
Lk 7:49 "Who is this that he even *f* sins?"

FORGIVING (7)
Ex 34: 7 and *f* wickedness and crime and sin;
Nm 14:18 rich in kindness, *f* wickedness and crime;
Ps(s) 86: 5 For you, O Lord, are good and *f*,
99: 8 a *f* God you were to them,
Is 55: 7 to our God, who is generous in *f*.
2Cor 2:10 *f* I have done has been for your sakes and,
Eph 4:32 another, compassionate, and mutually *f*,

FORGO (1)
Neh 10:32 We will *f* the seventh year,

FORGOT (10)
Dt 32:18 you, You *f* the God who gave you birth.
1Sm 12: 9 But they *f* the LORD their God;
Ps(s) 78:11 And they *f* his deeds,
106:13 But soon they *f* his works;
106:21 They *f* the God who had saved them,
Wis 16:23 be nourished, *f* even its proper strength;
19:20 strength, and water *f* its quenching nature;
Jer 23:27 just as their fathers *f* my name
Hos 2:15 and, in going after her lovers, *f* me,
13: 6 they became proud of heart and *f* me.

FORGOTTEN (47)
Gn 40:23 he had *f* him.
41:30 abundance in the land of Egypt will be *f*.
Dt 26:13 not broken or *f* any of your commandments:
31:21 descendants will not have *f* to recite,
Neh 13:14 the house of my God and its services be *f*!
Jdt 13:19 be *f* by those who tell of the might of God.
Jb 19:14 neglect me, and my guests have *f* me.
Ps(s) 9:13 he has not *f* the cry of the afflicted.
9:19 For the needy shall not always be *f*,
10:11 He says in his heart, "God has *f*;
31:13 I am *f* like the unremembered dead;
44:18 has come upon us, though we have not *f* you,
44:21 If we had *f* the name of our God and
77:10 Has God *f* pity?
119:61 are twined about me your law I have not *f*.
119:83 in the smoke, I have not *f* your statutes.
119:141 but your precepts I have not *f*.
119:153 and rescue me, for I have not *f* your law.
137: 5 you, Jerusalem, may my right hand be *f*!
Eccl 2:16 for in days to come both will have been *f*.
Wis 2: 4 Even our name will be *f* in time,
Sir 3:14 For kindness to a father will not be *f*,
13:10 but keep not too far away lest you be *f*.
35: 6 is most pleasing, nor will it ever be *f*.
44:10 godly men whose virtues have not been *f*;
45:26 Lest their welfare should ever be *f*,
Is 17:10 For you have *f* God,
23:15 day, Tyre shall be *f* for seventy years.
23:16 Take a harp, go about the city, O *f* harlot;
44:21 O Israel, by me you shall never be *f*:
49:14 my Lord has *f* me."
65:16 For the hardships of the past shall be *f*,
Jer 2:32 my people have *f* me days without number.
3:21 have perverted their ways and *f* the LORD,
13:25 Because you have *f* me,
18:15 Yet my people have *f* me:
30:14 All your lovers have *f* you,
44: 9 you *f* the evil deeds which your fathers,
50: 5 with covenant everlasting, never to be *f*."
Lam 2: 6 LORD has made feast and sabbath to be *f*;
3:17 of peace, I have *f* what happiness is;
Ez 22:12 and me you have *f*,
23:35 you have *f* me and cast me behind your back,
Hos 8:14 Israel has *f* his maker and built palaces.
Mt 16: 5 that they had *f* to bring any bread along.
Mk 8:14 They had *f* to bring any bread along;
Heb 12: 5 you have *f* the encouraging words addressed

FORK (3)
1Sm 2:13 servant would come with a three-pronged *f*,
2:14 Whatever the *f* brought up,
Ez 21:26 For at the *f* where the two roads divide

FORKS (5)
Ex 27: 3 well as shovels, basins, *f* and fire pans,
38: 3 the pots, shovels, basins, *f* and fire pans,
Nm 4:14 the fire pans, *f*,
1Chr 28:16 gold to be used for the *f* and pitchers,
2Chr 4:16 likewise the pots, the shovels and the *f*.

FORLORN (1)
2Sm 13:20 and *f* in the house of her brother Absalom.

FORM (53)
Gn 34:22 live with us and *f* one kindred people
Ex 25:36 *f* but a single piece of pure beaten gold.
27: 8 the altar itself in the *f* of a hollow box,
37:29 prepared in their pure *f* by a perfumer.
38: 7 altar was made in the *f* of a hollow box.
39: 9 span high and a span wide in its folded *f*.
Lv 2: 4 it must be in the *f* of unleavened cakes
2:14 the *f* of fresh grits of new ears of grain,
6: 9 but it must be eaten in the *f* of
10:12 the altar in the *f* of unleavened cakes.
Dt 4:12 heard the sound of the words, but saw no *f*;
4:15 "You saw no *f* at all on the day the LORD
4:16 whether it be in the *f* of a man or a woman,
4:23 his command an idol in any *f* whatsoever.
4:25 fashioning an idol in any *f* and by this evil
Jos 5:11 *f* of unleavened cakes and parched grain.
Jgs 6:19 of flour in the *f* of unleavened cakes.
Ru 4: 7 This was the *f* of attestation in Israel.
1Kgs 6:18 carved in the *f* of gourds and open flowers;
2Chr 3:16 He worked out chains in the *f* of a collar
24:13 house of God according to its original *f*,
Tb 4:12 guard, son, against every *f* of immorality,
2Mc 9:18 to the Jews in the *f* of a supplication.
9:21 to *f* plans for the general welfare of all.
Jb 33: 2 my tongue and my voice *f* words.
Ps(s) 49:15 Quickly their *f* is consumed;
Wis 15: 4 painters, A *f* smeared with varied colors,
15: 5 longs for the inanimate *f* of a dead image.
Sir 21:12 one *f* of shrewdness is thoroughly bitter.
23: 9 Let not your mouth *f* the habit of swearing,
Is 8:10 *F* a plan, and it shall be thwarted;
45: 7 I *f* the light,
Jer 8:14 Let us *f* ranks and enter
33: 2 made the earth and gave it *f* and firmness,
Ez 1: 5 their *f* was human,
8: 2 up and saw a *f* that looked like a man.
37:17 so that they *f* one stick in your hand.
43:11 to them the *f* and design of the temple,
47:18 the Jordan shall *f* the boundary down to
Mt 13:34 taught the crowds in the *f* of parables.
Lk 3:22 descended on him in visible *f* like a dove.
Jn 5:37 never heard, his *f* you have never seen,
Acts 14:11 "Gods have come to us in the *f* of men!"
17: 5 to *f* a mob and start a riot in the town.
Eph 2:20 You *f* a building which rises on the
4:13 and *f* that perfect man who is Christ come
Phil 2: 6 Though he was in the *f* of God,
2: 7 emptied himself and took the *f* of a slave,
3:21 He will give a new *f* to this lowly body of
4: 6 Present your needs to God in every *f* of
Col 2: 9 the fullness of deity resides in bodily *f*.
Jas 3: 7 Every *f* of life,

FORMAL (1)
Mt 27: 1 *f* action against Jesus to put him to death.

FORMALLY (1)
Gal 3:17 a covenant *f* ratified by God is not set

FORMATION (6)
1Sm 4: 2 then drew up in battle *f* against Israel.
17: 8 "Why come out in battle *f*?
2Sm 10: 8 *f* at the entrance of their city gate,
10:17 up in *f* against David and fought with him.
Jdt 7:11 sir, do not attack them in regular *f*;
Mt 27:60 tomb which had been hewn from a *f* of rock.

FORMED (53)
Gn 2: 7 the LORD God *f* man out of the clay of the
2: 8 and he placed there the man whom he had *f*.
2:19 So the LORD God *f* out of the ground
29:17 eyes, but Rachel was well *f* and beautiful.
37: 7 and your sheaves *f* a ring around my sheaf
Ex 36:13 joined so that the Dwelling *f* one whole.
36:18 the tent was joined so that it *f* one whole.
37:22 *f* but a single piece of pure beaten gold.
Jos 9: 2 they all *f* an alliance to launch a common
14: 4 the descendants of Joseph *f* two tribes,
Jgs 20:30 for the third time and *f* their line of battle
2Sm 21: 7 because of the LORD's oath that *f* a bond
1Kgs 16:16 had *f* a conspiracy and had killed the king.
2Kgs 9:14 of Nimshi, *f* a conspiracy against Joram.
14:19 conspiracy was *f* against him in Jerusalem,
2Chr 25:27 conspiracy was *f* against him in Jerusalem;
Jdt 8: 7 She was beautifully *f* and lovely to behold.
Est 2: 7 was beautifully *f* and lovely to behold.
Jb 1:17 and said, "The Chaldeans *f* three columns,
10: 8 Your hands have *f* me and fashioned me;
Ps(s) 22:10 You have been my guide since I was first *f*,
94: 9 or he who *f* the eye not see?
95: 5 and the dry land, which his hands have *f*.
103:14 who fear him, For he knows how we are *f*;
104:26 Leviathan, which you *f* to make sport of it.
139:13 Truly you have *f* my inmost being;
Wis 2:23 For God *f* man to be imperishable;
7: 1 a descendant of the first man *f* on earth.
Sir 1:12 which is *f* with the faithful in the womb.
11:16 were *f* with sinners from their birth,
24: 8 and he who *f* me chose the spot for my tent,
33:10 men are of clay, for from earth man was *f*;
46: 1 to Moses in the prophetic office, *F* to be,
Is 27:11 nor shall he who *f* them have mercy on them.
42: 6 I *f* you,
43: 1 LORD, who created you, O Jacob, and *f* you,
43: 7 I created for my glory, whom I *f* and made.
43:10 Before me no god was *f*,
43:21 to drink, The people whom I *f* for myself,
44: 2 your help who *f* you
44:21 I *f* you to be a servant to me;
44:24 your redeemer, who *f* you from the womb:
49: 5 who *f* me as his servant from the womb,
Jer 1: 5 Before I *f* you in the womb I knew you,
49:30 has been *f* against you [Nebuchadnezzar,
Ez 16: 7 your breasts were *f*,
Am 4:13 Him who *f* the mountains,
Acts 14:20 His disciples quickly *f* a circle about him,
23:12 certain Jews *f* a conspiracy in which they
1Cor 15:47 The first man was of earth, *f* from dust,
Gal 4:19 in labor pains until Christ is *f* in you.
Phil 3:10 by being *f* into the pattern of his death.
Col 3:10 he is *f* anew in the image of his Creator.

FORMER (53)
Gn 28:19 the *f* name of the town had been Luz.
Ex 34: 1 Moses, "Cut two stone tablets like the *f*,
34: 1 which were on the *f* tablets that you broke.
34: 4 then cut two stone tablets like the *f*,
Nm 21:26 who had fought against the *f* king of Moab
Dt 2:12 the *f* inhabitants were the Horites;
2:20 of the Rephaim from its *f* inhabitants,
10: 1 me, 'Cut two tablets of stone like the *f*;
10: 2 that were on the *f* tablets that you broke,
10: 3 and cut two tablets of stone like the *f*,
24: 4 then her *f* husband,
1Sm 9: 9 (In *f* times in Israel,
1Kgs 16:24 he built Samaria after Shemer, the *f* owner.

1Chr 24: 4 the *f* were divided into sixteen groups,
2Chr 15: 5 In that *f* time there was no peace for
31: 2 according to their *f* classification,
Ezr 3:12 the old men who had seen the *f* house,
5:15 the house of God be rebuilt on its *f* site.
6: 7 they are to rebuild it on its *f* site.
Jdt 8:18 gods made by hands, as happened in *f* days.
1Mc 4:47 law, and built a new altar like the *f* one.
12:16 our *f* friendship and alliance with them.
15: 3 it, that I may restore it to its *f* state.
2Mc 14: 3 A certain Alcimus, a *f* high priest,
15:12 Onias, the *f* high priest,
Jb 8: 7 Your *f* state will be of little moment,
8: 8 If you inquire of the *f* generations,
42:11 came to him, and all his *f* acquaintances,
Eccl 7:10 is it that *f* times were better than these?
Wis 11:10 *f* as a stern king you probed and condemned.
Is 46: 8 remember the *f* things,
61: 4 the *f* wastes they shall raise up And
Ez 16:55 shall return to their *f* state [you and
16:55 daughters shall return to your *f* state].
Mi 4: 8 the *f* dominion shall be restored,
Hg 2: 3 you that saw this house in its *f* glory?
2: 9 the future glory of this house than the *f*,
Zec 1: 4 your fathers whom the *f* prophets warned:
7: 7 the LORD spoke through the *f* prophets,
7:12 sent by his spirit through the *f* prophets.
8:11 the remnant of this people as in *f* days,
Acts 19:18 and openly confessed their *f* practices.
2Cor 2:16 death, to the *f* a breath bringing life.
3:10 the *f* should be declared no glory at all.
Gal 1:13 the story of my *f* way of life in Judaism.
Eph 2:12 remember that, in *f* times,
3: 5 unknown to men in *f* ages but now revealed
4:22 that you must lay aside your *f* way of life
Heb 7:18 The *f* commandment has been annulled
Rv 2: 5 Repent, and return to your *f* deeds.
21: 1 former heavens and the *f* earth had passed
21: 4 or pain, for the *f* world has passed away."

FORMERLY (28)

Gn 13: 3 Bethel and Ai where his tent had *f* stood,
40:13 *f* used to do when you were his cupbearer.
Dt 2:10 *F* the Emim lived there,
Jos 11:10 *f* was the chief of all those kingdoms.
14:15 Hebron was *f* called Kiriath-arba,
15:15 Debir, which was *f* called Kiriath-sepher.
Jgs 1:10 in Hebron, which was *f* called Kiriath-arba,
1:11 Debir, which was *f* called Kiriath-sepher.
1:23 made of Bethel, which *f* was called Luz.
18:29 However, the name of the city was *f* Laish.
1Sm 9: 9 is now called prophet was *f* called seer.)
2Sm 15:34 I was *f* your father's servant,
2Kgs 13: 5 of Aram, dwelt in their own homes as *f*.
1Chr 4:41 *f*) and also the Meunites who were there.
11: 2 Even *f*,
Jdt 5: 7 They *f* dwelt in Mesopotamia,
1Mc 3:46 *f* at Mizpah a place of prayer for Israel.
6:59 to live according to their own laws as *f*;
11:34 taxes that *f* the king received from them
Wis 14:15 And now honored as a god what was *f* a dead
18: 2 who *f* had been wronged did not harm them,
Jer 12:16 they who *f* taught my people to swear by
50:17 *F* the king of Assyria devoured her,
Ez 36:34 which was *f* a wasteland exposed to the
Rom 6:19 Just as *f* you enslaved your bodies to
Gal 1:23 who was *f* persecuting us is now preaching
Phil 1:30 the one in which you *f* saw me engaged and
Phlm 1:11 for he who was *f* useless to you is now

FORMING (2)

2Sm 2:25 rallied around Abner, *f* a single group,
Am 7: 1 He was *f* a locust swarm when the late

FORMLESS (2)

Gn 1: 2 and the earth, the earth was a *f* wasteland,
Wis 11:17 had fashioned the universe from *f* matter,

FORMS (10)

Ex 26: 6 sheets, so that the Dwelling *f* one whole.
Nm 21:13 Arnon *f* Moab's boundary with the Amorites.
Jos 15: 2 that *f* the southern end of the Salt Sea,
Wis 18: 1 their voices but did not see their *f*,
Sir 17: 5 He *f* men's tongues and eyes and ears,
Is 44:10 all the associates of anyone who *f* a god,
Ez 47:20 the Great Sea *f* the boundary up to a point
Hos 8: 7 of grain that *f* no ear can yield no flour;
Zec 12: 1 earth, and *f* the spirit of man within him:
Lk 12:15 to the crowd, "Avoid greed in all its *f*.

FORNICATION (10)

Lv 21: 9 *f* and thereby dishonors her father also,
Mt 15:19 murder, adulterous conduct, *f*,
Mk 7:21 acts of *f*,
2Cor 12:21 have not repented of the uncleanness, *f*,
Col 3: 5 your nature is rooted in earth; *f*,
Rv 2:14 food sacrificed to idols and to practice *f*.
9:21 or their sorcery, their *f* or their thefts.
17: 2 of the earth have committed *f* with her,
18: 3 kings of the earth committed *f* with her,
18: 9 The kings of the earth who committed *f*

FORNICATIONS (1)

2Kgs 9:22 "as long as the many *f* and witchcrafts of

FORNICATOR (3)

1Cor 6:18 body, but the *f* sins against his own body.
Eph 5: 5 no *f*, no unclean or lustful person
Heb 12:16 among you no *f* or godless person like Esau,

FORNICATORS (5)

1Cor 6: 9 no *f*, idolaters, or adulterers,
1Tm 1:10 their fathers or mothers, murderers, *f*,
Heb 13: 4 for God will judge *f* and adulterers.
Rv 21: 8 and murderers, the *f* and sorcerers,
22:15 dogs and sorcerers, the *f* and murderers,

FORSAKE (50)

Dt 31: 6 he will never fail you or *f* you."
31: 8 with you and will never fail you or *f* you.
31:16 They will *f* me and break the covenant
31:17 I will *f* them and hide my face from them,
Jos 1: 5 I will not leave you nor *f* you.
24:16 *f* the LORD for the service of other gods.
24:20 you, you *f* the LORD and serve strange gods,
Ru 1:16 said, "Do not ask me to abandon or *f* you!
1Kgs 6:13 Israelites and will not *f* my people Israel."
8:57 and may he not *f* us nor cast us off.
2Chr 7:19 But if you turn away and *f* my statutes and
Ezr 8:22 his mighty wrath is against all who *f* him."
Neh 9:17 you did not *f* them.
9:19 mercy you did not *f* them in the desert.
9:31 destroy them and you did not *f* them,
Jdt 7:30 he will not utterly *f* us.
1Mc 2:21 we should *f* the law and the commandments.
2Mc 1: 5 you, and never *f* you in time of adversity.
Ps(s) 9:11 name, for you *f* not those who seek you,
27: 9 *f* me not,
27:10 Though my father and mother *f* me,
37: 8 Give up your anger, and *f* wrath;
38:22 *F* me not, O LORD; my God, be not far
71: 9 as my strength fails, *f* me not,
71:18 *f* me not Till I proclaim your strength to
89:31 "If his sons *f* my law and walk not
119: 8 do not utterly *f* me.
119:53 me because of the wicked who *f* your law.
138: 8 *f* not the work of your hands.
Prv 4: 2 my teaching do not *f*.
4: 6 *F* her not, and she will preserve you
9: 6 *F* foolishness that you may live;
27:10 own friend and your father's friend *f* not;
Eccl 10: 4 the ruler burst upon you, *f* not your place;
Sir 2: 3 Cling to him, *f* him not;
7:30 love your Creator, *f* not his ministers.
18:21 Delay not to *f* sins,
28:23 who *f* the LORD will fall victims to it,
41: 8 sinful men, who *f* the law of the Most High.
51:20 understanding such that I will never *f* her.
Is 41:17 I, the God of Israel, will not *f* them.
42:16 I do for them, and I will not *f* them.
55: 7 Let the scoundrel *f* his way,
65:11 But you who *f* the LORD,
Jer 14: 9 Your name we bear! do not *f* us!
17:13 all who *f* you shall be in disgrace;
Bar 4: 1 will live, but those will die who *f* her.
Dn 11:30 who *f* it he shall once more single out.
Jon 2: 9 worship vain idols *f* their source of mercy.
Heb 13: 5 will never desert you, nor will I *f* you."

FORSAKEN (40)

Jgs 10:10 have *f* our God and have served the Baals."
1Kgs 11:33 he has *f* me and has worshiped Astarte,
19:10 but the Israelites have *f* your covenant,
19:14 But the Israelites have *f* your covenant,
2Kgs 22:17 *f* me and have burned incense to other gods,
2Chr 13:10 the LORD is our God, and we have not *f* him.
21:10 sovereignty because he had *f* the LORD,
Jdt 9:11 of the weak, the protector of the *f*,
2Mc 5:20 and what the Almighty had *f* in his anger
7:16 do not think that our nation is *f* by God.
Jb 6:14 though he have *f* the fear of the Almighty.
Ps(s) 22: 2 My God, my God, why have you *f* me,
37:25 man *f* nor his descendants begging bread.
68: 7 God gives a home to the *f*;
71:11 They say, "God has *f* him;
119:87 the earth, but I have not *f* your precepts.
Sir 2:10 anyone persevered in his fear and been *f*?
Is 1: 4 They have *f* the LORD,
27:10 an abandoned pasture, a *f* wilderness,
32:14 Yes, the castle will be *f*,
49:14 But Zion said, "The LORD has *f* me;
54: 6 back, like a wife *f* and grieved in spirit,
60:15 Once you were *f*,
62: 4 No more shall men call you *F*,"
62:12 "Frequented," a city that is not *f*.
Jer 2:13 they have *f* me,
5: 7 Your sons have *f* me,
5:19 "As you have *f* me to serve strange gods
16:11 It is because your fathers have *f* me,
16:11 but me they have *f*,
17:13 *f* the source of living waters [the LORD].
19: 4 This is because they have *f* me and
49:25 How can the city of glory be *f*,
Bar 3:12 You have *f* the fountain of wisdom!
Ez 8:12 the LORD has *f* the land."
9: 9 They think that the LORD has *f* the land,
Dn 14:38 "you have not *f* those who love you."
Zep 2: 4 For Gaza shall be *f*,
Mt 27:46 is, "My God, my God, why have you *f* me?"
Mk 15:34 "My God, my God, why have you *f* me?"

FORSAKES (6)

1Mc 2:19 so that each *f* the religion of his fathers
Ps(s) 37:28 what is right, and *f* not his faithful ones.
38:11 my strength *f* me;
Prv 2:17 Who *f* the companion of her youth and
28:13 he who confesses and *f* them obtains mercy.
Zec 11:17 Woe to my foolish shepherd who *f* the flock!

FORSAKING (7)

Dt 28:20 perish for the evil you have done in *f* me.
1Sm 12:10 'We have sinned in *f* the LORD and
1Kgs 18:18 by *f* the commands of the LORD and
Jer 1:16 them for all their wickedness in *f* me,
2:17 Has not the *f* of the LORD,
2:19 how evil and bitter is your *f* the LORD,
Hos 4:12 they commit harlotry, *f* their God.

FORSOOK (11)

Dt 29:24 they *f* the covenant which the LORD,
Jgs 10:13 you still *f* me and worshiped other gods.
1Kgs 9: 9 'They *f* the LORD,
2Chr 7:22 'They *f* the LORD,
24:18 They *f* the temple of the LORD,
32:31 in the land, God *f* him to test him,
1Mc 1:38 her own offspring, and her children *f* her.
Ps(s) 78:60 And he *f* the tabernacle in Shiloh,
Wis 3:10 they neglected justice and *f* the Lord.
10: 8 For those who *f* Wisdom first were bereft
Bar 4: 8 You *f* the Eternal God who nourished you,

FORSWEAR (1)

Wis 14:28 or live lawlessly or lightly *f* themselves.

FORT (1)

2Chr 22: 1 that had come into the *f* with the Arabs.

FORTH (349)

Gn 1:11 said, "Let the earth bring *f* vegetation:
1:12 the earth brought *f* every kind of plant
1:24 bring *f* all kinds of living creatures:
3:16 in pain shall you bring *f* children.
3:18 and thistles shall it bring *f* to you,
7:11 the fountains of the great abyss burst *f*,
8: 7 It flew back and *f* until the waters dried
10:11 From that land he went *f* to Asshur,
12: 1 "Go *f* from the land of your kinsfolk and
13:17 Set *f* and walk about in the land,
30:39 the rods, and so they brought *f* streaked,
49:21 hind let loose which brings *f* lovely fawns.
Ex 8:14 tried to bring *f* gnats by their magic arts,
8:16 to Pharaoh when he goes *f* to the water,
9:23 the LORD sent *f* hail and peals of thunder.
11: 4 At midnight I will go *f* through Egypt.
Lv 9:24 Fire came *f* from the LORD's presence and
10: 2 Fire therefore came *f* from the LORD's
Nm 10: 7 But in calling *f* an assembly you are to
12:12 babe that comes *f* from its mother's womb
16:35 And fire from the LORD came *f* which
17:11 *f* from the LORD and the blow is falling."
17:23 had sprouted and put *f* not only shoots,
20: 8 From the rock you shall bring *f* water for
20:12 *f* my sanctity before the Israelites,
21:28 For fire went *f* from Heshbon and a blaze
23:24 like a lioness, and stalks *f* like a lion;
33: 3 morrow the Israelites went *f* in triumph,
Dt 8: 3 that comes *f* from the mouth of the LORD.
8:15 who brought *f* water for you from the
11:15 *f* grass in your fields for your animals.
28:37 wood and stone, and will call *f* amazement,
28:57 she brings *f* when she secretly uses them
32:11 its nestlings *f* by hovering over its brood,
33: 2 He shone *f* from Mount Paran and advanced
33: 2 *f* and his wrath devastated the nations.
33:22 a lion's whelp, that springs *f* from Bashan!"
Jos 5: 6 people that came *f* from Egypt died off
6:23 Her entire family they led *f* and placed
14:11 today as I was the day Moses sent me *f*,
Jgs 9:20 let fire come *f* from Abimelech to devour
9:20 let fire come *f* from the citizens
11:34 in Mizpah, it was his daughter who came *f*,
14:14 *f* food, and out of the strong came forth
1Sm 7:11 *f* from Mizpah and pursued the Philistines,
18:27 *f* with his men and slew two hundred
24:14 says, 'From the wicked comes *f* wickedness.'
2Sm 1:14 not afraid to put *f* your hand to desecrate
5:24 for the LORD will have gone *f* before you
16:11 "If my own son, who came *f* from my loins,
20:10 so that his entrails burst *f* to the ground,
22:14 the Most High gave *f* his voice.

FORTH (cont.)

22:15 He sent *f* arrows to put them to flight;
22:46 they staggered *f* from their fortresses."
23: 5 with me, set *f* in detail and secured.
24:16 *f* his hand toward Jerusalem to destroy it,
1Kgs 8:22 and stretching *f* his hands toward heaven.
8:44 your people *f* to war against their enemies,
13: 4 *f* his hand from the altar and said,
13: 4 hand he stretched *f* against him withered,
22:21 came *f* and presented himself to the LORD,
22:22 'I will go *f* and become a lying spirit in
22:22 Go *f* and do this.'
2Kgs 19: 3 but there is no strength to bring them *f*.
19:35 That night the angel of the LORD went *f*
21:15 fathers came *f* from Egypt until today.'"
1Chr 14:15 of the mastic trees, then go *f* to battle,
2Chr 6:12 of Israel and stretched *f* his hands.
6:13 and stretched *f* his hands toward heaven.
6:34 people go *f* to war against their enemies,
15: 2 He went *f* to meet Asa and said to him:
18:21 'I will go *f* and become a lying spirit in
18:21 Go *f* and do this.'
20:21 as it went *f* at the head of the army.
21:15 your bowels issue *f* because of the disease,
21:19 his bowels issued *f* because of the disease
31: 1 went *f* to the cities of Judah and smashed
Ezr 1: 7 brought *f* which Nebuchadnezzar had taken
1: 8 them brought *f* by the treasurer Mithredath,
Neh 8: 1 bring *f* the book of the law of Moses
Jdt 2: 5 Go *f* from my presence,
9: 9 and send *f* your wrath upon their heads.
16:14 and they were made, You sent *f* your spirit,
Est A: 9 there appeared to come *f* a great river,
A:10 The light of the sun broke *f*;
8: 4 stretched *f* the golden scepter to Esther.
8:14 steeds sped *f* in haste at the king's order,
1Mc 9:67 Simon and his men then sallied *f* from the
14: 3 went *f* and defeated the army of Demetrius;
14:36 they used to sally *f* to defile the environs
2Mc 2:23 of Cyrene set *f* in detail in five volumes,
Jb 1:11 *f* your hand and touch anything that he has,
1:12 Satan went *f* from the presence of the LORD.
1:21 "Naked I came *f* from my mother's womb,
2: 5 But now put *f* your hand and touch his bone
2: 7 So Satan went *f* from the presence of the
3:11 at birth, come *f* from the womb and expire?
3:24 than food, and my groans well *f* like water.
6: 9 he would put *f* his hand and cut me off!
8:16 and beyond his garden his shoots go *f*;
10:18 then did you bring me *f* from the womb?
12:15 sends them *f* and they overwhelm the land.
12:22 and brings the gloom *f* to the light.
14: 9 and put *f* branches like a young plant.
15: 7 or were you brought *f* before the hills?
15:35 They conceive malice and bring *f* emptiness;
19:25 that he will at last stand *f* upon the dust;
23:10 if he proved me, I should come *f* as gold.
24: 5 these go *f* to their task of seeking food;
26: 4 whose is the breath that comes *f* from you?
28: 5 The earth, though out of it comes *f* bread,
29: 7 When I went *f* to the gate of the city and
32:10 let me too set *f* my knowledge!
33: 5 draw up your arguments and stand *f*.
37: 2 angry voice as it rumbles *f* from his mouth!
37: 9 Out of its chamber comes *f* the tempest;
37:15 makes the light shine *f* from his clouds?
38: 8 the sea, when it burst *f* from the womb;
38:32 you bring *f* the Mazzaroth in their season,
38:35 Can you send *f* the lightnings on their way.
39: 2 and fix the time of their bringing *f*?
41:10 When he sneezes, light flashes *f*;
41:11 go *f* firebrands; sparks of fire leap forth.
Ps(s) 7:15 pregnant with mischief, brings *f* failure.
18:14 heaven, the Most High gave *f* his voice;
18:15 He sent *f* his arrows to put them to flight,
18:46 they staggered *f* from their fortresses.
19: 6 which comes *f* like the groom from his
19: 7 At one end of the heavens it comes *f*,
33: 9 he commanded, and it stood *f*.
35:13 and poured *f* prayers within my bosom.
39: 4 in my thoughts, a fire blazed *f*.
43: 3 Send *f* your light and your fidelity;
44:10 disgrace, and you go not *f* with our armies.
49: 5 set *f* my riddle to the music of the harp.
50: 2 From Zion, perfect in beauty, God shines *f*.
60:12 O God, rejected us, so that you go not *f*,
68: 7 he leads *f* prisoners to prosperity;
68: 8 you went *f* at the head of your people,
68:29 Show *f*, O God, your power.
77:18 the skies gave *f* their voice;
78:16 crag and brought the waters *f* in rivers.
78:20 when he struck the rock, waters gushed *f*,
78:52 But his people he led *f* like sheep and
80: 2 the cherubim, shine *f*
80:12 It put *f* its foliage to the Sea,
81: 6 when he came *f* from the land of Egypt.
81:11 God who led you *f* from the land of Egypt;
90: 2 the earth and the world were brought *f*,
104:10 You sent *f* springs into the watercourses
104:12 among the branches they send *f* their song.
104:23 Man goes *f* to his work and to his tillage
104:30 When you send *f* your spirit,
105:37 he led them *f* laden with silver and gold,
105:41 He cleft the rock, and the water gushed *f*;
105:43 And he led *f* his people with joy;
106:30 *f* in judgment and the plague was checked;
107:14 And he led them *f* from darkness and gloom
107:20 He sent *f* his word to heal them and to
108:12 O God, rejected us, So that you go not *f*,
109: 7 When he is judged, let him go *f* condemned,
110: 2 power the LORD will stretch *f* from Zion:
114: 1 When Israel came *f* from Egypt,
119:171 My lips pour *f* your praise,
125: 3 the just put *f* to wickedness their hands.
126: 6 Although they go *f* weeping,
132:17 will I make a horn to sprout *f* for David;
135: 7 he brings *f* the winds from his storehouse.
142: 8 Lead me *f* from prison,
144: 6 Flash *f* lightning,
147:15 He sends *f* his command to the earth;
Prv 8:23 From of old I was poured *f*,
8:24 When there were no depths I was brought *f*,
8:25 place, before the hills, I was brought *f*;
12:23 but the hearts of fools gush *f* folly.
15: 2 but the mouth of fools spurts *f* folly.
20: 5 but the man of intelligence draws it *f*.
25: 4 silver, and it comes *f* perfectly purified;
25: 8 bring not *f* hastily against an opponent;
27: 1 for you know not what any day may bring *f*.
30:33 For the stirring of milk brings *f* curds,
30:33 and the stirring of anger brings *f* blood.
Eccl 4:14 from a prison house one comes *f* to rule,
5:14 As he came *f* from his mother's womb,
10:19 *f* merriment and wine makes the living glad,
Sg 1:12 banquet my nard gives *f* its fragrance.
2:13 The fig tree puts *f* its figs,
2:13 and the vines, in bloom, give *f* fragrance.
3:11 come *f* and look upon King Solomon In the
4:13 You are a park that puts *f* pomegranates,
6:10 Who is this that comes *f* like the dawn,
7:12 let us go *f* to the fields and spend the
7:14 The mandrakes give *f* fragrance,
Wis 3: 3 an affliction and their going *f* from us,
5:21 shafts of lightnings shall go *f*
9:10 Send her *f* from your holy heavens and from
11:18 unknown beasts to breathe *f* fiery breath,
11:25 preserved, had it not been called *f* by you?
18: 5 a single boy had been cast *f* but saved,
19:10 young of animals the land brought *f* gnats,
Sir 1: 8 He has poured her *f* upon all his works,
5: 9 For suddenly his wrath flames *f*;
15:16 whichever you choose, stretch *f* your hand.
20:12 fools pour *f* their blandishments in vain.
22:24 Before flames burst *f* an oven smokes;
23:16 who never stops until the fire breaks *f*;
23:25 her branches will not bring *f* fruit.
24: 3 "From the mouth of the Most High I came *f*,
24:15 balm, or precious myrrh, I give *f* perfume;
24:17 I bud *f* delights like the vine,
24:30 send my teachings *f* shining like the dawn,
32:16 out of obscurity he draws *f* a clear plan.
36: 5 *f* the splendor of your right hand and arm;
37:17 four branches it shoots *f*:
38:33 They set *f* no decisions or judgments,
39: 6 He will pour *f* his words of wisdom and in
39:12 Once more I will set *f* my theme to shine
39:14 incense, break *f* in blossoms like the lily.
43: 1 of the sky shines *f* like heaven itself,
43:14 and like vultures the clouds hurry *f*.
46:17 Then the LORD thundered *f* from heaven,
50:15 And had stretched *f* his hand for the cup,
50:27 gushed *f* from my heart's understanding.
Is 2: 3 For from Zion shall go *f* instruction,
5: 4 crop of grapes, did it bring *f* wild grapes?
13:10 of the heavens send *f* no light;
14: 7 earth rests peacefully, song breaks *f*;
14:19 But you are cast *f* without burial,
16: 1 Send them *f*, hugging the earth like reptiles,
16: 8 spread *f* and extended over the sea.
25:11 He will stretch *f* his hands in Moab as a
26:18 inhabitants of the world cannot bring it *f*.
26:21 See, the LORD goes *f* from his place,
31: 3 When the LORD stretches *f* his hand,
33:11 You conceive dry grass, bring *f* stubble;
35: 6 Streams will burst *f* in the desert,
37: 3 but there is no strength to bring them *f*.
37:36 The angel of the LORD went *f* and struck
41: 4 *f* the generations since the beginning.
42: 1 he shall bring *f* justice to the nations,
42:13 The LORD goes *f* like a hero,
43:19 Now it springs *f*, do you not perceive it?
44:11 they will all assemble and stand *f*,
44:23 Break *f*,
45: 8 Let the earth open and salvation bud *f*;
47:13 Let the astrologers stand *f* to save you,
48: 3 long ago, they went *f* from my mouth,
48:13 When I call them, they stand *f* at once.
48:20 Go *f* from Babylon, flee from Chaldea!
48:21 he cleft the rock, and waters welled *f*."
49:13 and rejoice, O earth, break *f* into song,
49:17 you down and laid you waste go *f* from you;
51: 4 For law shall go *f* from my presence,
51: 5 go *f* [and my arm shall judge the nations];
52:11 Depart, depart, come *f* from there,
54: 1 who did not bear, break *f* in jubilant song,
55:11 shall my word be that goes *f* from my mouth;
58: 8 your light shall break *f* like the dawn,
59: 4 they conceive mischief and bring *f* malice.
61:11 As the earth brings *f* its plants,
62: 1 Until her vindication shines *f* like the
66: 8 Can a country be brought *f* in one day,
Jer 4:31 Zion gasping, as she stretches *f* her hands:
6:12 For I will stretch *f* my hand against those
6:23 the roaring sea as they ride *f* on steeds,
6:25 Go not *f* into the field,
9: 2 not with truth, they hold *f* in the land.
15:19 you bring *f* the precious without the vile,
20:18 Why did I come *f* from the womb,
22:19 dragged *f* and cast out beyond the gates
23:15 ungodliness has gone *f* into the whole land.
23:19 His wrath breaks *f* In a whirling storm
30:23 His wrath breaks *f* In a whirling storm
31: 4 shall go *f* dancing with the merrymakers.
31:32 hand to lead them *f* from the land of Egypt;
38:23 and sons shall be led *f* to the Chaldeans,
44: 6 Therefore the fury of my anger poured *f* in
48:45 For fire breaks *f* from Heshbon,
50:25 and brings *f* the weapons of his wrath;
50:42 the roaring sea, as they ride *f* on steeds,
51:25 I will stretch *f* my hand against you,
Lam 2:17 the threat He set *f* from days of old;
Bar 1:20 at the time he led our fathers *f* from the
4:23 With mourning and lament I sent you *f*,
Ez 1:13 and from it came *f* flashes of lightning.
17: 6 a vine, produced branches and put *f* shoots.
17:23 It shall put *f* branches and bear fruit,
30: 9 On that day messengers shall hasten *f* at
38: 4 I will lead you *f* with all your army,
38: 8 which has been brought *f* from among the
Hos 6: 3 judgment shines *f* like the light of day!
12:11 prophets, through whom I set *f* examples.
13:13 not present himself where children break *f*.
14: 7 the Lebanon cedar, and put *f* his shoots.
Mi 1: 3 For see, the LORD comes *f* from his place,
1:11 of Zaanan come not *f* from their city.
4: 2 For from Zion shall go *f* instruction,
4:10 go *f* from the city and dwell in the fields;
5: 1 *f* for me one who is to be ruler in Israel;
7: 9 He will bring me *f* to the light;
Na 2: 8 shudders, Its mistress is led *f* captive,
Hb 1: 4 this is why judgment comes *f* perverted.
3: 4 rays shine *f* from beside him,
3:10 the ocean gives *f* its roar.
3:13 You come *f* to save your people,
Hg 1:11 and upon all that the ground brings *f*;
Zec 2:17 for he stirs *f* from his holy dwelling.
5: 3 which is to go *f* over the whole earth;
5: 4 I will send it *f*,
5: 5 eyes and see what this is that comes *f*."
5: 9 coming *f* with a wind ruffling their wings,
6: 5 which are coming *f* after being reviewed by
6: 8 they that go *f* to the land of the north
9:11 bring *f* your prisoners from the dungeon.
9:14 and his arrow shall shoot *f* as lightning;
14: 3 shall go *f* and fight against those nations,
Mt 8:32 At that they came *f* and entered the swine.
27:53 After Jesus' resurrection they came *f* from
Mk 16:20 The Eleven went *f* and preached everywhere.
Lk 8:46 I know that power has gone *f* from me."
9: 2 He sent them *f* to proclaim the reign of
Jn 5:28 tombs shall hear his voice and come *f*.
8:42 you would love me, for I came *f* from God,
9: 3 it was to let God's works show *f* in him.
15:16 was I who chose you to go *f* and bear fruit.
Acts 4:30 complete assurance by stretching *f* your
5:19 opened the gates of the jail, led them *f*,
7:36 It was he who led them *f*
13: 4 These two, sent *f* by the Holy Spirit,
13:23 *f* from this man's descendants Jesus,
13:26 that this message of salvation was sent *f*.
2Cor 4: 4 the gospel showing *f* the glory of Christ,
Gal 4: 4 come, God sent *f* his Son born of a woman,
4: 6 God has sent *f* into our hearts the spirit
4:24 Sinai, and brought *f* children to slavery;
1Thes 1: 8 Lord has echoed *f* from you resoundingly.
4:14 God will bring *f* with him from the dead
Heb 6: 7 and brings *f* vegetation useful to those
8: 9 hand to lead them *f* from the land of Egypt:
11: 8 and went *f* to the place he was to receive
11: 8 he went *f*, moreover, not knowing
11:12 of this faith, there came *f* from one man,
12:11 but later it brings *f* the fruit of peace
Jas 3:11 Does a spring gush *f* fresh water and foul
5:18 *f* with rain and the land produced its crop.
Rv 6: 2 He rode *f* victorious,
6: 4 Another horse came *f*, a red one.

FORTHRIGHT (1)

Lk 20:21 words and your doctrine are completely *f*,

FORTHWITH (2)

Gn 26:11 man or his wife shall *f* be put to death."
Wis 18:17 Then, *f*, visions in horrible dreams

FORTIETH (3)

Nm 33:38 and there he died in the *f* year from the
Dt 1: 3 In the *f* year,

1Chr 26:31 f year of David's reign search was made,

FORTIFICATION (2)

1Mc 6:61 and on these terms they evacuated the f.
10:11 Mount Zion with square stones for its f.

FORTIFICATIONS (7)

2Chr 11:11 the f and put commanders in them,
1Mc 9:62 its f that had been demolished.
12:38 f by providing them with gates and bars.
13:33 strengthening their f with high towers,
13:48 its f and built himself a residence.
13:52 f of the temple hill alongside the citadel,
14:37 f for the defense of the land and the city,

FORTIFIED (72)

Nm 13:19 the towns in which they dwell open or f?
13:28 and the towns are f and very strong.
32:17 families can remain here in the f towns,
32:34 The Gadites rebuilt the f towns of Dibon,
Dt 1:28 their cities are large and f to the sky;
2:36 no city was too well f for us to whom the
3: 5 were f with high walls and gates and bars.
9: 1 having large cities f to the sky,
Jos 10:20 had escaped from them into the f cities,
14:12 the Anakim are there, with large f cities,
19:35 The f cities were Ziddim,
1Sm 6:18 including f cities and open villages.
2Sm 20: 6 lest he find f cities and take shelter
1Kgs 15:17 f Ramah to prevent communication with Asa,
2Kgs 3:19 You shall destroy every f city,
10: 2 have the chariots, the horses, a f city,
18:13 the f cities of Judah and captured them.
19:25 should reduce f cities into heaps of ruins,
2Chr 8: 5 and Lower Beth-horon, f cities with walls,
11: 5 in Jerusalem and built f cities in Judah.
11:10 these were f cities in Judah and Benjamin.
11:23 of Judah and Benjamin, in all the f cities;
12: 4 They captured the f cities of Judah and
14: 5 He built f cities in Judah,
16: 1 attacked Judah and f Ramah to prevent any
16: 6 Ramah, and with them he f Geba and Mizpah.
17: 2 armed forces in all the f cities of Judah,
17:19 in the f cities throughout all Judah.
19: 5 in the land, in all the f cities of Judah,
21: 3 objects, together with f cities in Judah,
26: 9 Gate, and at the Angle, and he f them.
32: 1 He invaded Judah, besieged the f cities,
33:14 army officers in all the f cities of Judah.
Neh 9:25 They captured f cities and fertile land;
Jdt 2:24 down every f city along the Wadi Abron,
3: 6 and stationed garrisons in the f cities;
4: 5 of the high mountains, f their villages,
5: 1 f the summits of all the higher peaks,
1Mc 1:19 The f cities in the land of Egypt were
1:34 perverse men, who f themselves inside it,
4:61 to protect it, and likewise f Beth-zur,
5:26 all of these are large, f cities
5:46 a large and strongly f city along the way,
6:26 and they have f the sanctuary and Beth-zur.
6:62 Mount Zion and saw how the place was f,
9:52 He f the city of Beth-zur,
11:18 and his men in the f cities were killed by
13:10 the walls of Jerusalem, f it on every side.
14:33 He f the cities of Judea,
14:34 He also f Joppa by the sea and Gazara on
15:41 he f Kedron and stationed horsemen and
16: 9 Cendebeus reached Kedron, which he had f.
2Mc 11: 5 f place about twenty miles from Jerusalem,
12:13 f with earthworks and ramparts and
12:27 a f city inhabited by people of many
Ps(s) 31:22 kindness he has shown me in a f city.
60:11 Who will bring me into the f city?
108:11 Who will bring me into the f city?
Sir 48:17 f his city and had water brought into it;
Is 2:15 Against every lofty tower and every f wall,
25: 2 made the city a heap, the f city a ruin;
27:10 For the f city shall be desolate,
36: 1 the f cities of Judah and captured them.
37:26 should reduce f cities into heaps of ruins,
Jer 1:18 is I this day who have made you a f city,
4: 5 "Fall in, let us march to the f cities."
5:17 the sword the f city in which you trust.
34: 7 alone were left of the f cities of Judah.
Ez 36:35 and destroyed are now repeopled and f."
Dn 11:15 up siegeworks and take the f city by storm.
Hos 8:14 Judah, too, has f many cities,
Zep 1:16 blasts and battle alarm Against f cities,

FORTIFIES (1)

Ps(s) 104:15 with oil, and bread f the hearts of men.

FORTIFY (3)

Jgs 19: 5 son-in-law, F yourself with a little food;
19: 8 F yourself and tarry until the afternoon."
1Mc 15:39 and to f Kedron and strengthen its gates,

FORTIFYING (5)

1Kgs 15:21 Baasah heard of it, he left off f Ramah,
15:22 and beams with which Baasha was f Ramah.
2Chr 16: 5 Baasha heard of it, he left off f Ramah;
16: 6 wood with which Baasha had been f Ramah,
1Mc 10:45 the walls of Jerusalem and f it all around,

FORTITUDE (1)

Wis 8: 7 moderation and prudence, justice and f.

FORTRESS (21)

Jos 19:29 back to Ramah and to the f city of Tyre;
2Sm 24: 7 going to the f of Tyre and to all the
1Chr 11: 5 David nevertheless captured the f of Zion,
11: 7 David took up his residence in the f,
1Mc 9:50 the Jericho f, as well as Emmaus,
2Mc 10:33 and his men eagerly besieged the f
13:19 against Beth-zur, a strong f of the Jews;
Jb 39:28 night, on the spur of the cliff or the f.
Ps(s) 18: 3 LORD, my strength, O LORD, my rock, my f,
31: 4 You are my rock and my f;
71: 3 me safety, for you are my rock and my f.
91: 2 Say to the LORD, "My refuge and my f,
144: 2 My refuge and my f,
Is 17: 3 The f shall be lost to Ephraim and the
23: 4 Shame, O Sidon, f on the sea,
25:12 The high-walled f he will raze,
Jer 16:19 O LORD, my strength, my f,
Dn 8: 2 in the f of Susa in the province of Elam;
Am 5: 9 the strong, and brings ruin upon the f;
Hb 1:10 He laughs at any f,
Zec 9:12 return to the f of the waiting prisoners,

FORTRESSES (15)

2Sm 22:46 they staggered forth from their f."
2Kgs 8:12 You will burn their f,
2Chr 27: 4 in the forest land he set up f and towers.
1Mc 1: 2 He fought many campaigns, captured f,
13:33 bars, and he stored up provisions in the f.
2Mc 8:30 of them, and captured some very high f.
Ps(s) 18:46 they staggered forth from their f.
Is 34:13 thorns, her f with thistles and briers.
Jer 51:32 have been seized, and the f set on fire,
Lam 2: 2 down in his anger the f of daughter Judah;
2: 5 all her castles and destroyed her f;
Hos 10:14 your tribes and all your f shall be ravaged
Mi 5:10 of your land and tear down all your f.
Na 3:12 All your f are but fig trees,
3:14 water for the siege, strengthen your f;

FORTUNATE (7)

Gn 30:13 "Women call me f."
Dt 33:29 How f you are, O Israel!
Eccl 4: 2 I declared more f in death than are the
6: 3 that the child born dead is more f than he.
Sg 6: 9 The daughters saw her and declared her f,
Lk 12:43 That servant is f whom his master finds
Acts 26: 2 I count myself f to be able to make my

FORTUNATUS (1)

1Cor 16:17 very happy at the arrival of Stephanas, F,

FORTUNE (13)

Gn 30:13 and Leah said, "What good f—
1Sm 28: 8 said to her, "Tell my f through a ghost;
1Chr 29: 3 of my God my personal f in gold and silver:
Neh 5:13 f every man who fails to keep this promise,
Tb 3:10 but she hanged herself because of ill f!'
2Mc 5:20 afterward participated in their good f;
Prv 15:16 of the LORD than a great f with anxiety.
21: 6 He who makes a f by a lying tongue is
Is 65:11 You who spread a table for F and fill cups
Ez 16:53 the f of Sodom and her daughters and of
16:53 I will restore your f along with them],
29:14 scattered, and I will restore Egypt's f,
Hos 12: 9 I have made a f!"

FORTUNE-TELLER (3)

Lv 20:27 or f shall be put to death by stoning;
Dt 18:10 his son or daughter in the fire, nor a f,
Is 3: 2 warrior, judge and prophet, f and elder,

FORTUNE-TELLERS (8)

Lv 19:31 not go to the mediums or consult f
20: 6 mediums and f and follow their wanton ways,
Dt 18:14 listen to their soothsayers and f,
1Sm 6: 2 when they summoned priests and f to ask,
28: 3 had driven mediums and f out of the land.
28: 9 driving the mediums and f out of the land.
Is 2: 6 they are filled with f and soothsayers,
8:19 "Inquire of mediums and f

FORTUNE-TELLING (2)

2Kgs 17:17 by fire, practiced f and divination,
Acts 16:16 substantial profit to her masters by f.

FORTUNES (4)

Ps(s) 126: 4 Restore our f, O LORD, like the torrents
Ez 16:53 I will restore their f,
39:25 Now I will restore the f of Jacob and have
Jl 4: 1 would restore the f of Judah and Jerusalem

FORTY (109)

Gn 5:13 and f years after the birth of Mahalalel,
7: 4 on the earth for forty days and f nights,
7:12 For f days and forty nights heavy rain
7:17 flood continued upon the earth for f days.
8: 6 At the end of f days Noah opened the hatch
18:29 saying, "What if only f are found there?"
18:29 forebear doing it for the sake of the f."
25:20 was f years old when he married Rebekah,
26:34 When Esau was f years old,
32:16 f cows and ten bulls;
50: 3 embalmed Israel, they spent f days at it,
Ex 16:35 The Israelites ate this manna for f years,
24:18 he stayed for f days and forty nights.
26:19 f silver pedestals under the twenty boards,
26:21 north side, with their f silver pedestals,
34:28 with the LORD for f days and forty nights,
36:24 f silver pedestals under the twenty boards,
36:26 north side, with their f silver pedestals,
Nm 1:33 f thousand five hundred were enrolled in
2:19 in the census to f thousand five hundred.]
13:25 the land for f days they returned,
14:33 your children must wander for f years,
14:34 F days you spent in scouting the land; f
26:18 of whom f thousand five hundred men were
32:13 made them wander in the desert f years,
Dt 2: 7 is now f years that he has been with you,
8: 2 Remember how for f years now the LORD,
8: 4 nor did your feet swell these f years.
9: 9 forty days and f nights without eating
9:11 at the end of the forty days and f nights,
9:18 before the LORD for f days and forty nights
9:25 "Those forty days, then, and f nights,
10:10 f days and forty nights on the mountain,
25: 3 F stripes may be given him,
29: 4 'I led you for f years in the desert.
Jos 4:13 About f thousand troops equipped for
5: 6 had wandered f years in the desert,
14: 7 f years old when the servant of the LORD,
Jgs 3:11 The land then was at rest for f years,
5: 8 nor a lance, among f thousand in Israel!
5:31 And the land was at rest for f years.
8:28 And the land had rest for f years,
12:14 He had f sons and thirty grandsons who
13: 1 the power of the Philistines for f years.
1Sm 4:18 He had judged Israel for f years.
17:16 his stand morning and evening for f days.
2Sm 2:10 was f years old when he became king over
5: 4 he became king, and he reigned for f years:
10:18 f thousand of the Aramean foot soldiers.
1Kgs 2:11 of David's reign over Israel was f years:
6:17 front of the sanctuary, was f cubits long.
7:38 diameter with a capacity of f measures,
11:42 in Jerusalem over all Israel was f years.
19: 8 he walked f days and forty nights to the
2Kgs 8: 9 and with f camel loads of the best goods
12: 2 Jehu, and he reigned f years in Jerusalem.
1Chr 12:37 Set in battle array; f thousand.
19:18 and f thousand of their foot soldiers;
29:27 that he reigned over Israel was f years:
2Chr 9:30 in Jerusalem over all Israel for f years.
24: 1 king, and he reigned f years in Jerusalem.
Neh 5:15 each day f silver shekels for their food;
9:21 F years in the desert you sustained them:
Tb 1:21 But less than f days later the king was
Jdt 1: 4 with an opening f cubits wide for the
1Mc 3:39 and with them he sent f thousand men and
12:41 Jonathan marched out against him with f
2Mc 5: 2 that all over the city, for nearly f days,
5:14 lost, f thousand meeting a violent death,
Jb 42:16 this, Job lived a hundred and f years;
Ps(s) 95:10 F years I loathed that generation,
Ez 4: 6 bear the sins of the house of Judah f days;
29:11 it, and it will be uninhabited for f years.
29:12 be the most deserted of cities for f years;
29:13 At the end of f years I will gather the
41: 2 the nave, which was found to be f cubits,
46:22 courts, f cubits long and thirty wide,
Dn 14: 3 for it six barrels of fine flour, f sheep,
Am 2:10 who led you through the desert for f years,
5:25 and offerings for f years in the desert,
Jon 3: 4 F days more and Nineveh shall be destroyed,"
Mt 4: 2 He fasted f days and forty nights,
Mk 1:13 He stayed in the wasteland f days,
Lk 4: 2 by the Spirit into the desert for f days,
Acts 1: 3 appearing to them over the course of f days
4:22 cured was more than f years of age.
7:23 When he was f, he decided to visit
7:30 F years later an angel appeared to him in
7:36 the Red Sea, and for f years in the desert.
7:42 and offerings for f years in the desert,
13:18 f years he put up with them in the desert:
13:21 tribe of Benjamin, who ruled for f years.
23:13 than f of them who took the oath together.)
23:21 More than f of them are lying in wait;
2Cor 11:24 of the Jews I received f lashes less one;
Heb 3:10 and tried me, and saw my works for f years.
3:17 With whom was God angry for f years?

FORTY-EIGHT (8)

Nm 35: 7 a total of *f* cities with their pasture
Jos 21:41 lands, belonged to the Levites, was *f*.
Neh 7:15 sons of Binnui, six hundred and *f*;
7:44 sons of Asaph, one hundred and *f*.
1Mc 4:52 of Chislev, in the year one hundred and *f*,
2Mc 11:21 The year one hundred and *f*,
11:33 In the year one hundred and *f*,
11:38 In the year one hundred and *f*,

FORTY-FIRST (1)

2Chr 16:13 he died in the *f* year of his reign.

FORTY-FIVE (23)

Gn 18:28 it," he answered, "if I find *f* there."
Nm 1:25 *f* thousand six hundred and fifty were
2:15 census to *f* thousand six hundred and fifty.
26:41 *f* thousand six hundred men were registered.
26:50 of whom *f* thousand four hundred men were
Jos 14:10 *f* years since the LORD spoke thus to Moses;
1Kgs 7: 3 these beams numbered *f*.
Ezr 2: 8 sons of Zattu, nine hundred and *f*;
2:34 sons of Jericho, three hundred and *f*;
2:66 thirty-six, their mules two hundred and *f*,
Neh 7:13 sons of Zattu, eight hundred and *f*;
7:36 sons of Jericho, three hundred and *f*;
7:67 thirty-six, their mules two hundred and *f*,
1Mc 1:54 Chislev, in the year one hundred and *f*,
Jer 52:30 exiled seven hundred and *f* people of Judah:
Ez 48:16 the north side, *f* hundred cubits;
48:16 the south side, *f* hundred cubits;
48:16 the east side, *f* hundred cubits;
48:16 and the west side, *f* hundred cubits.
48:30 the north side, measuring *f* hundred cubits,
48:32 the east side, measuring *f* hundred cubits,
48:33 the south side, measuring *f* hundred cubits,
48:34 the west side, measuring *f* hundred cubits,

FORTY-FOUR (4)

Rv 7: 4 and *f* thousand from every tribe of Israel;
14: 1 and with him were the hundred and *f*
14: 3 one could learn except the hundred and *f*
21:17 Its wall measured a hundred and *f* cubits

FORTY-NINE (4)

Lv 25: 8 so that the seven cycles amount to *f* years.
1Mc 6:16 in Persia in the year one hundred and *f*.
2Mc 13: 1 In the year one hundred and *f*,
Dn 3:47 The flames rose *f* cubits above the furnace,

FORTY-ONE (5)

Nm 1:41 *f* thousand five hundred were enrolled in
2:28 in the census to *f* thousand five hundred.]
1Kgs 14:21 He was *f* years old when he became king,
15:10 he reigned *f* years in Jerusalem.
2Chr 12:13 he was *f* years old when he became king,

FORTY-ONE-YEAR (1)

2Kgs 14:23 of Israel, began his *f* reign in Samaria.

FORTY-SEVEN (4)

Gn 47:28 of his life came to a hundred and *f* years.
Ezr 2:38 Pashhur, one thousand two hundred and *f*;
Neh 7:40 Pashhur, one thousand two hundred and *f*;
1Mc 3:37 capital, in the year one hundred and *f*;

FORTY-SIX (4)

Nm 1:21 *f* thousand five hundred were enrolled in
2:11 in the census to *f* thousand five hundred.]
1Mc 2:70 He died in the year one hundred and *f*,
Jn 2:20 "This temple took *f* years to build,

FORTY-THREE (4)

Nm 26: 7 of whom *f* thousand seven hundred and
Ezr 2:25 and Beeroth, seven hundred and *f*;
Neh 7:29 and Beeroth, seven hundred and *f*;
1Mc 1:20 Egypt in the year one hundred and *f*,

FORTY-TWO (12)

Nm 35: 6 refuge, and in addition *f* other cities
Jgs 12: 6 *f* thousand Ephraimites fell at that time.
2Kgs 2:24 woods and tore *f* of the children to pieces.
10:14 They were taken alive, *f* in number,
Ezr 2:10 sons of Bani, six hundred and *f*;
2:24 men of Beth-azmaveth, *f*;
2:64 came to *f* thousand three hundred and sixty,
Neh 7:28 men of Beth-azmaveth, *f*
7:62 Tobiah, sons of Nekoda, six hundred and *f*.
7:66 came to *f* thousand three hundred and sixty,
11:13 brethren, family heads, two hundred and *f*;
Rv 11: 2 who will crush the holy city for *f* months.
13: 5 it received was to last only *f* months.

FORUM (1)

Acts 28:15 came out as far as the *F* of Appius

FORWARD (117)

Gn 22: 8 Then the two continued going *f*.
33: 6 and their children came *f* and bowed low;
33: 7 Leah and her children came *f* and bowed low;
33: 7 and her children came *f* and bowed low.
Ex 14:15 Tell the Israelites to go *f*.
15:22 Then Moses led Israel *f* from the Red Sea,
29: 8 Bring *f* his sons also and clothe them with
29:10 *f* the bullock in front of the meeting tent.
40:14 Bring *f* his sons also,
40:37 *f*; only when it lifted did they go forward.
Lv 8: 6 Bringing *f* Aaron and his sons,
8:13 Moses likewise brought *f* Aaron's sons,
8:14 brought *f* the bullock for a sin offering,
8:18 He next brought *f* the holocaust ram,
8:22 Then he brought *f* the second ram,
8:24 Moses had the sons of Aaron also come *f*,
9: 5 had come *f* and stood before the LORD,
9:16 Then he brought *f* the holocaust,
16:20 altar, Aaron shall bring *f* the live goat.
21:17 come *f* to offer up the food of his God.
21:18 of the following defects may not come *f*:
Nm 5:16 the woman come *f* and stand before the LORD.
8: 9 come *f* in front of the meeting tent,
12: 5 When both came *f*,
27: 1 They came *f*, and standing in the presence
Dt 20: 2 shall come *f* and say to the soldiers:
24:15 since he is poor and looks *f* to them.
Jos 7:14 the LORD designates shall come *f* by clans;
7:14 LORD designates shall come *f* by families;
7:14 LORD designates shall come *f* one by one.
7:16 morning Joshua had Israel come *f* by tribes,
7:17 Then he had the clans of Judah come *f*,
7:17 had the clan of Zerah come *f* by families,
7:18 he had that family come *f* one by one,
10:24 "Come *f* and put your feet on the necks of
10:24 came *f* and put their feet upon their necks.
Jgs 8:21 stepped *f* and killed Zebah and Zalmunna.
1Sm 10:20 Samuel had all the tribes of Israel come *f*,
10:21 had the tribe of Benjamin come *f* in clans,
13:23 had pushed *f* to the pass of Michmash.
17:16 [Meanwhile the Philistine came *f* and took
23: 9 the priest Abiathar, "Bring *f* the ephod."
30:25 *f* he made it a law and a custom in Israel,
1Kgs 18:36 the prophet Elijah came *f* and said,
2Kgs 18:28 *f* and cried out in a loud voice in Judean,
20: 9 Shall the shadow go *f* or back ten steps?"
1Chr 29: 6 came *f* willingly and contributed
2Chr 18:20 came *f* and presented himself to the LORD,
29:31 and bring *f* the sacrifices and thank
29:31 " Then the assembly brought *f* the
29:32 the assembly brought *f* was seventy oxen,
Neh 9: 2 then stood *f* and confessed their sins and
Jdt 9: 6 the things you decide on come *f* and say,
14: 6 of the people, he fell *f* in a faint.
1Mc 2:23 a certain Jew came *f* in the sight of all
2:24 he sprang *f* and killed him upon the altar.
3:49 and they brought *f* the nazirites,
5:39 So Judas went *f* to attack them.
6:40 they marched *f* steadily and in good order.
9: 8 "Let us go *f* to meet our enemies;
10:30 I renounce the right from this day *f*:
2Mc 6:19 and went *f* of his own accord to the
7:15 *f* the fifth brother and maltreated him.
14:21 came *f* and thrones were set in place.
Ps(s) 119:128 For in all your precepts I go *f*;
Prv 4:25 ahead and your glance be directly *f*.
Sir 32: 9 When among your elders be not *f*,
Is 36:13 *f* and cried out in a loud voice in Judean,
41:21 bring *f* your reasons,
Jer 26:17 *f* and said to all the people assembled,
31: 2 As Israel comes *f* to be given his rest,
46: 7 Who is this that surges *f* like the Nile,
46: 8 "I will surge *f*,"
46: 9 *F*, horses!
Bar 6:40 bring *f* Bel and ask the god to make noise,
Ez 1: 9 straight *f* [Each went straight forward;
1:12 straight forward [Each went straight *f*;
10:22 each one went straight *f*.
39:22 From that day *f* the house of Israel shall
Dn 8:18 As he spoke to me, I fell *f* in a faint;
10: 9 of his voice, I fell face *f* in a faint.
10:15 thus to me, I fell *f* and kept silent.
Hg 2:15 now, consider from this day *f*.
2:18 [Consider from this day *f*:
Zec 5: 5 who spoke with me came *f* and said to me,
Mt 3: 7 Sadducees were stepping *f* for this bath,
8: 2 Suddenly a leper came *f* and did him homage,
15:25 *f* then and did him homage with the plea,
17: 6 this the disciples fell *f* on the ground,
25:20 came *f* bringing the additional five.
25:22 the two thousand then stepped *f*
25:24 who had received the thousand stepped *f*.
26:50 they stepped *f* to lay hands on Jesus,
26:60 Finally two came *f* who stated:
28:18 came *f* and addressed them in these words:
Mk 8:11 came *f* and began to argue with him.
15:43 another who looked *f* to the reign of God.
Lk 2:38 looked *f* to the deliverance of Jerusalem.
7:14 Then he stepped *f* and touched the litter;
8:47 not gone unnoticed, she came *f* trembling.
20:27 Some Sadducees came *f* (the ones who claim
23:36 *f* to offer him their sour wine and saying,
Jn 8: 3 a woman *f* who had been caught in adultery.
18: 4 happen to him, stepped *f* and said to them,
Acts 5: 6 Some of the young men came *f*,
19:18 Many who had become believers came *f* and
19:33 crowd Alexander, as the Jews pushed him *f*.
Heb 11:10 was looking *f* to the city with foundations,
Jas 5: 7 He looks *f* to it patiently while the soil
2Pt 1:21 has never been put *f* by man's willing it.
Rv 6: 1 cry out in a voice like thunder, "Come *f*!"
6: 3 second living creature cry out, "Come *f*!"
6: 5 third living creature cry out, "Come *f*!"
6: 7 fourth living creature cry out, "Come *f*!"
13: 4 the beast, or come *f* to fight against it?"
22:17 Let him who is thirsty come *f*;

FOSTER (5)

Nm 11:12 bosom, like a *f* father carrying an infant,
Est 2: 7 He was *f* father to Hadassah,
2Mc 9:29 His *f* brother Philip brought the body home;
Is 49:23 Kings shall be your *f* fathers,
1Pt 2:17 *F* love for the brothers,

FOSTERED (5)

Ezr 4:15 has been *f* there since ancient times.
4:19 rebellion and sedition have been *f* there.
Bar 4: 8 you, and you grieved Jerusalem who *f* you.
4:11 With joy I *f* them;
Hos 11: 4 I *f* them like one who raises an infant to

FOSTERS (2)

Prv 17: 9 He who covers up a misdeed *f* friendship,
Sir 50:22 *f* men's growth from their mother's womb,

FOUGHT (65)

Nm 21:26 who had *f* against the former king of Moab
Jos 10:14 for the LORD *f* for Israel.
10:42 the LORD, the God of Israel, *f* for Israel.
23: 3 the LORD, your God, himself who *f* for you.
24: 8 They *f* against you,
24:11 Jericho, the men of Jericho *f* against you,
Jgs 1: 5 came upon Adonibezek and *f* against him.
1: 8 *f* against Jerusalem and captured it,
5:19 The kings came and *f*; then they fought,
5:20 fought; from their courses they *f* against
9:17 my father *f* for you at the risk of his life
9:39 of Shechem and *f* against Abimelech.
9:45 entire day Abimelech *f* against the city,
9:52 came up to the tower and *f* against it,
11:20 who encamped at Jahaz and *f* Israel.
12: 4 the men of Gilead and *f* against Ephraim,
1Sm 4:10 The Philistines *f* and Israel was defeated;
14:48 he turned, he was successful and *f* bravely.
23: 5 men to Keilah and *f* with the Philistines.
2Sm 10:17 in formation against David and *f* with him.
12:26 Joab *f* against Rabbah of the Ammonites and
12:27 "I have *f* against Rabbah and have taken
12:29 When he had *f* against it and captured it,
18: 6 a battle was *f* in the forest near Mahanaim.
21:15 with his servants and *f* the Philistines,
23:10 but he stood his ground and *f* the
1Kgs 22:46 his prowess, what he did and how he *f*,
2Kgs 3:23 *f* among themselves and killed one another.
13:12 the valor with which he *f* against Amaziah,
14:15 Jehoash, his valor, and how he *f* Amaziah,
14:28 how he *f* with Damascus and turned back
1Chr 28: 3 you are a man who *f* wars and shed blood.'
2Chr 20:29 LORD had *f* against the enemies of Israel.
26: 6 He went out and *f* the Philistines and
27: 5 He *f* with the king of the Ammonites and
1Mc 1: 2 He *f* many campaigns,
3:12 Judas, who *f* with it the rest of his life.
5: 7 He *f* many battles with them,
5:21 and *f* many battles with the Gentiles.
6:31 sortie and burned these and they *f* bravely.
6:37 mahout, three soldiers who *f* from it.
6:63 *f* against him and took the city by force.
8: 6 who had *f* against them with a hundred and
9:17 The battle was *f* desperately,
9:64 he *f* against it for many days.
9:68 They *f* against Bacchides,
11:55 around Antiochus and *f* against Demetrius,
14:32 temple, Simon rose up and *f* for his nation,
16: 2 father's house have *f* the battles of Israel
2Mc 1:11 for having *f* on our side against the king;
1:12 out those who *f* against the holy city.
2:21 heroes who *f* bravely for Judaism so that,
8:20 *f* along with four thousand Macedonians;
12:27 of the walls, from which they *f* valiantly;
14:18 with which they *f* for their country,
Ps(s) 80: 7 have left us to be *f* over by our neighbors,
Sir 46: 3 him when he *f* the battles of the LORD?
Is 20: 1 Assyria, *f* against Ashdod and captured it,
63:10 on them like an enemy, and *f* against them.
Zec 14:12 all nations that have *f* against Jerusalem:
1Cor 15:32 If I *f* those beasts at Ephesus for purely
2Tm 4: 7 I have *f* the good fight,
Rv 12: 7 Although the dragon and his angels *f* back,

FOUL (8)

2Mc 3:32 some *f* play at the hands of the Jews,
Prv 24: 2 violence, and their lips speak of *f* play.
Sir 20:23 A lie is a *f* blot in a man,
Is 19: 6 Its streams shall become *f*.
Ez 22: 5 *f* reputation and your great perversity.
34:18 you had to *f* the remainder with your feet?
Col 3: 8 the malice, the insults, the *f* language.
Jas 3:11 fresh water and *f* from the same outlet?

FOULED (1)

Ez 34:19 trampled and drink what your feet had *f*.

FOULNESS (1)

Jl 2:20 And his *f* shall go up,

FOUND (337)

Gn 1:31 he had made, and he *f* it very good.
6: 8 But Noah *f* favor with the LORD.
7: 1 in this age have I *f* to be truly just.
16: 7 *f* her by a spring in the wilderness,
18:29 saying, "What if only forty are *f* there?"
18:30 What if only thirty are *f* there?"
24:67 In his love for her Isaac *f* solace after
31:37 have you *f* a single object taken from your
36:24 (He is the Anah who *f* water in the desert
37:32 "We *f* this. See whether it is your son's
38:27 came, she was *f* to have twins in her womb.
41:31 no trace of the abundance will be *f* in the
44: 8 money that we *f* in the mouths of our bags.
44: 9 of your servants is *f* to have the goblet,
44:10 who is *f* to have it shall become my slave,
44:16 one in whose possession the goblet was *f*."
44:17 the goblet was *f* shall become my slave;
47:14 money that was to be *f* in Egypt and Canaan,
Ex 12:19 days no leaven may be *f* in your houses.
13: 7 leavened may be *f* in all your territory.
22: 3 what he stole is *f* alive in his possession,
33:12 and also, 'You have *f* favor with me.'
33:13 Now, if I have *f* favor with you,
33:16 your people and I, have *f* favor with you,
33:17 because you have *f* favor with me and you
Lv 5:22 unjustly, or if, having *f* a lost article,
5:23 *f* or whatever else he swore falsely about;
20:14 such shamefulness may not be *f* among you.
Dt 5:24 have *f* out today that man can still live
16: 4 be *f* in all your territory for seven days,
17: 2 "If there is *f* among you,
18:10 Let there not be *f* among you anyone who
20:11 be *f* in it shall serve you in forced labor.
21: 1 "If the corpse of a slain man is *f* lying
22:20 evidence of the girl's virginity is not *f*,
32:10 He *f* them in a wilderness,
Jos 7:22 to the tent and *f* them hidden there,
Jgs 6:28 Early the next morning the townspeople *f*
14: 8 *f* a swarm of bees and honey in the lion's
21: 8 they *f* that none of the men of
1Sm 9:20 not worry about them, for they have been *f*.
10: 2 asses you went to look for have been *f*.
10:16 "He assured us that the asses had been *f*."
12: 5 that you have *f* nothing in my possession."
13:19 was to be *f* in the whole land of Israel,
13:22 nor spear could be *f* in the possession
14:17 *f* Jonathan and his armor-bearer missing.
19:16 they *f* the household idol in the bed,
23: 9 *f* out that Saul was planning to harm him,
24: 4 the sheepfolds along the way, he *f* a cave,
25:28 evil to be *f* in you your whole life long.
26: 7 *f* Saul lying asleep within the barricade,
29: 6 for I have *f* nothing wrong with you from
30: 6 Now David *f* himself in great difficulty,
30:11 *f* in the open country and brought to David.
31: 8 and *f* Saul and his three sons lying on
2Sm 1: 6 "It was by chance that I *f* myself on
2:32 all-night march, and dawn *f* them in Hebron.
17:13 so that not even a pebble of it can be *f*."
17:20 They searched, but *f* no one,
1Kgs 1: 3 of Israel, and *f* Abishag the Shunamite,
1:52 But if he is *f* guilty of crime,
3:21 to nurse my child, and I *f* him dead.
13:14 of God, whom he *f* seated under a terebinth.
13:28 he went off and *f* the body lying in the
14:13 to the LORD, the God of Israel, been *f*.
21:20 "Have you *f* me out, my enemy?"
2Kgs 1: 9 was seated on a hilltop when he *f* him.
4:32 reached the house, he *f* the boy lying dead.
4:39 field to gather herbs and *f* a wild vine,
9:35 her, they *f* nothing of her but the skull,
17: 4 But the king of Assyria *f* Hoshea guilty of
19: 8 from Lachish, he *f* him besieging Libnah.
22: 8 "I have *f* the book of the law in the
22:13 stipulations of this book that has been *f*,
23: 2 that had been *f* in the temple of the LORD,
23:24 Helkiah had *f* in the temple of the LORD.
1Chr 4:40 They *f* abundant and good pastures,
4:41 they *f* pasture there for their flocks.
10: 3 Then the archers *f* him,
10: 8 they *f* Saul and his sons where they had
20: 2 It was *f* to weigh a talent of gold;
23: 3 was *f* to be thirty-eight thousand men.
24: 4 descendants of Eleazar were *f* to be more
26:31 and there were *f* among them outstanding
28: 9 seek him, he will let himself be *f* by you;
29:29 can be *f* written in the history of Samuel
2Chr 2:16 who were *f* to number one hundred
12:12 and in Judah moreover, good deeds were *f*.
16:11 can be *f* recorded in the book of the kings
19: 3 Yet some good things are to be *f* in you,
20:20 the LORD, your God, and you will be *f* firm.
20:25 and they *f* an abundance of cattle and
20:34 can be *f* written in the chronicle of Jehu,
21:17 away all the wealth *f* in the king's palace,
25: 5 he *f* them to be three hundred thousand
25:24 he *f* in the house of God with Obed-edom,
25:26 Amaziah, first and last, can be *f* written,
27: 7 can be *f* written in the book of the kings
28:26 can be *f* written in the book of the kings
29:16 and whatever they *f* in the LORD's temple
32:32 can be *f* written in the Vision of the
33:18 can be *f* written in the chronicles of the
33:19 *f* written down in the history of his seers.
34:14 Hilkiah the priest *f* the book of the law
34:15 "I have *f* the book of the law in the
34:21 the words of the book that has been *f*.
34:30 that had been *f* in the house of the LORD.
35:25 and can be *f* written in the Lamentations.
35:26 can be *f* written in the book of the kings
36: 8 can be *f* written in the book of the kings
Ezr 2:62 their names could not be *f* written there;
6: 2 scroll was *f* containing the following text:
10:18 *f* to have taken foreign women for wives:
Neh 7: 5 There I *f* the following written:
7:64 their names could not be *f* written there;
8:14 They *f* it written in the law prescribed by
9: 8 had *f* his heart faithful in your sight,
13: 1 it was *f* written there that "no Ammonite
Tb 1:19 When I *f* out that the king knew all about
5: 4 he *f* the angel Raphael standing before him,
5: 9 "I have just *f* a man who is one of our
7: 1 whom they *f* seated by his courtyard gate.
8:13 went in, and *f* them sound asleep together.
9: 6 house, they *f* Tobiath reclining at table.
Jdt 5:10 stayed there as long as they *f* sustenance,
10: 6 and *f* Uzziah and the elders of the city,
14:15 the bedroom, and *f* him lying on the floor,
Est 1:21 This proposal *f* acceptance with the king
5: 8 if I have *f* favor with the king and if it
7: 3 "If I have *f* favor with you,
8: 5 if I have *f* favor with you and you love me,
1Mc 1:53 wherever places of refuge could be *f*.
1:56 law which they *f* they tore up and burnt.
1:57 was *f* with a scroll of the covenant,
2:46 whom they *f* in the territory of Israel.
2:52 Was not Abraham *f* faithful in trial,
2:63 exalted, and tomorrow he is not to be *f*,
3:29 He then *f* that this exhausted the money in
4: 5 into the camp of Judas, and *f* no one there;
4:38 They *f* the sanctuary desolate,
5: 6 where he *f* a strong army and a large body
5:46 they *f* it impossible to encircle it on
6:60 *f* favor with the king and the leaders;
6:63 he *f* Philip in possession of the city.
11:24 other presents, and *f* favor with the king.
12:21 A document has been *f* stating that the
2Mc 1:33 a liquid was *f* with which Nehemiah and his
2: 5 he *f* a room in a cave in which he put the
4:16 this, they *f* themselves in serious trouble:
12:40 *f* amulets sacred to the idols of Jamnia,
13:21 He was *f* out, arrested, and imprisoned.
14: 5 But he *f* an opportunity to further his mad
Jb 14: 4 Can a man be *f* who is clean of defilement?
19:28 that the root of the matter is *f* in him?"
20: 8 a dream he takes flight and is not *f* again;
32: 3 *f* a good answer and had not condemned Job.
33:24 I have *f* him a ransom."
Ps(s) 36: 3 that his guilt will not be *f* out or hated.
37:36 I sought him, but he could not be *f*.
69:21 for comforters, and I *f* none.
89:21 I have *f* David, my servant;
119:162 your promise, as one who has *f* rich spoil.
132: 6 we *f* it in the fields of Jaar.
Prv 7:15 you, to look for you, and I have *f* you!
8:31 and I *f* delight in the sons of men.
10:13 On the lips of the intelligent is *f* wisdom,
Eccl 4: 7 Again I *f* this vanity under the sun:
7:27 Behold, this have I *f*,
7:28 which my soul still seeks and has not *f*:
7:28 but a woman among them all I have not *f*.
7:29 Behold, only this have I *f* out:
Sg 1: 7 Lest I be *f* wandering after the flocks of
3: 4 them when I *f* him whom my heart loves.
8:14 boasts of having *f* welcome from her lover.
Wis 1: 2 Because he is *f* by those who test him not,
3: 5 tried them and *f* them worthy of himself.
5:10 when it has passed, no trace can be *f*,
5:11 no evidence of its course is to be *f*—
5:11 no mark of passage can be *f* in it.
6:10 the holy precepts hallowed shall be *f* holy,
6:12 who love her, and *f* by those who seek her.
16: 9 and no remedy was *f* to save their lives
Sir 11:19 "I have *f* rest, now I will feast
17:25 The like cannot be *f* in men,
21:16 is charm to be *f* upon the lips of the wise.
23:11 swears without reason he cannot be *f* just,
31: 8 Happy the rich man *f* without fault,
34: 8 is *f* in the mouth of the faithful man.
38:33 judgments, nor are they *f* among the rulers;
44:17 NOAH, *f* just and perfect,
44:20 ordinance, and when tested he was *f* loyal.
51:27 labored only a little, but have *f* much.
Is 28:15 and in falsehood we have *f* a hiding place,"—
30:14 cannot be *f* a sherd to scoop fire
37: 8 had left there, he *f* him besieging Libnah.
51: 3 *f* in her thanksgiving and the sound of song.
55: 6 Seek the LORD while he may be *f*,
57:10 New strength you *f*,
65: 1 me not, to be *f* by those who sought me not.
Jer 2:34 whom you *f* committing no burglary;
11: 9 A conspiracy has been *f*.
12: 3 me, you have *f* that at heart I am with you.
15:16 When I *f* your words,
31: 2 the sword have *f* favor in the desert.
40: 1 where he had *f* him a prisoner in chains,
50:20 sins, but these shall no longer be *f*;
Lam 1:19 sought food for themselves, they *f* it not.
Bar 3:15 Who has *f* the place of wisdom,
3:30 Who has crossed the sea and *f* her,
Ez 22:30 but I *f* no one.
26:21 you shall be sought, but never again *f*,
28:15 you were created, Until evil was *f* in you,
40: 5 each of which were *f* to be one rod.'
40: 6 threshold, which was *f* to be a rod wide.
40:32 whose dimensions were *f* to be the same.
40:36 and its vestibule, and *f* them the same.
41: 2 the nave, which was *f* to be forty cubits,
Dn 1:19 all of them, none was *f* equal to Daniel,
1:20 he *f* them ten times better than all the
2:25 "I have *f* a man among the Judean captives
4: 9 Under it the wild beasts *f* shade,
5:27 been weighed on the scales and *f* wanting;
6: 5 neglect or misconduct was to be *f* in him.
6:12 So these men rushed in and *f* Daniel
6:23 For I have been *f* innocent before him;
7:15 *f* my spirit anguished within its sheath of
11:19 shall stumble and fall, to be *f* no more.
12: 1 everyone who is *f* written in the book.
13:63 she was *f* innocent of any shameful deed.
Hos 6:10 there harlotry is *f* in Ephraim,
9:10 Like grapes in the desert, I *f* Israel;
Jon 1: 3 down to Joppa, *f* a ship going to Tarshish,
Zep 3:13 be *f* in their mouths a deceitful tongue;
Mal 2: 6 and no dishonesty was *f* upon his lips;
Mt 1:18 she was *f* with child through the power of
2: 7 Herod called the astrologers aside and *f*
2: 8 When you have *f* him,
2:11 house, *f* the child with Mary his mother.
8:10 I have never *f* this much faith in Israel.
8:14 Jesus entered Peter's house and *f* Peter's
11: 8 luxuriously are to be *f* in royal palaces.
13:44 a buried treasure which a man *f* in a field.
13:46 When he *f* one really valuable pearl,
13:57 They *f* him altogether too much for them.
20: 6 he *f* still others standing around.
21:19 to it, but *f* nothing there except leaves.
26:40 to his disciples, he *f* them asleep.
26:43 Once more, on his return, he *f* them asleep;
Mk 1:37 to track him down, and when they *f* him,
6: 3 They *f* him too much for them.
7:30 she *f* the child lying in bed and the demon
11:13 When he reached it he *f* nothing but leaves;
14:16 city they *f* it just as he had told them,
14:37 When he returned he *f* them asleep.
14:40 Once again he *f* them asleep on his return.
14:54 where he *f* a seat with the temple guard
16: 4 they *f* that the stone had been rolled back.
Lk 1:30 You have *f* favor with God.
2:16 They went in haste and *f* Mary and Joseph,
4:17 and *f* the passage where it was written:
4:42 and when they *f* him they tried to keep him
5:19 but they *f* no way of getting him through
7: 9 never *f* so much faith among the Israelites."
7:10 they *f* the servant in perfect health.
7:25 in splendor are to be *f* in royal palaces.
8:35 they *f* the man from whom the devils had
9:11 but the crowds *f* this out and followed him.
13: 7 of fruit on this fig tree and *f* none.
15: 6 with me because I have *f* my lost sheep.'
15: 9 I have *f* the silver piece I lost.'
15:24 He was lost and is *f*.'
15:32 He was lost, and is *f*.'"
16:25 found consolation here, but you have *f*
17:23 you he is to be *f* in this place or that.
19:32 errand and *f* things just as he had said.
22:13 off and *f* everything just as he had said;
23: 2 "We *f* this man subverting our nation,
24: 2 *f* the stone rolled back from the tomb;
24:24 tomb and *f* it to be just as the women said;
24:33 where they *f* the Eleven and the rest of
24:53 they were to be *f* in the temple constantly,
Jn 1: 4 Whatever came to be in him, *f* life,
1:41 and tell him, "We have *f* the Messiah!"
1:45 have *f* the one Moses spoke of in the law
5:14 Jesus *f* him in the temple precincts and
6:25 they *f* him on the other side of the lake,
11:17 he *f* that Lazarus had already been in the
12:14 Jesus *f* a donkey and mounted it;
Acts 2: 1 came it *f* them gathered in one place.

FOUND (cont.)

5:10 The young men came in, *f* her dead,
5:23 "We *f* the jail securely locked and the
5:23 but when we opened it we *f* no one inside."
7:46 who *f* favor with God and begged that he
8:40 Philip *f* himself at Azotus next,
9:33 There he *f* a man named Aeneas,
10:27 He *f* many people assembled there,
11:26 once he had *f* him,
13:22 'I have *f* David son of Jesse to be a man
13:28 Even though they *f* no charge against him
18: 2 There he *f* a Jew named Aquila,
19: 1 There he *f* some disciples to whom he put
21: 2 When we *f* a ship bound for Phoenicia,
24: 5 We have *f* that this man is a troublemaker
24:18 That is what I was doing when they *f* me in
24:19 the province of Asia are the ones who *f* me.
24:20 declare what crime they *f* me guilty of
27:28 a sounding and *f* a depth of twenty fathoms;
27:28 took a sounding and *f* it to be fifteen.
28:14 Here we *f* some of the brothers,
28:18 *f* nothing against me deserving of death.
Rom 7:11 *f* its opportunity and used the commandment:
10:20 "I was *f* by those who were not seeking me;
1Cor 1:20 Where is the wise man to be *f*?
5: 1 you of a kind not even *f* among the pagans
2Cor 5: 3 provided we are *f* clothed and not naked.
Gal 5:14 has *f* its fulfillment in this one saying:
Phil 1:11 It is my wish that you may be *f* rich in
2Thes 1: 5 in order to be *f* worthy of his kingdom
2Tm 1:17 Rome, he sought me out earnestly and *f* me.
2:10 obtain the salvation to be *f* in Christ Jesus
1Pt 2:10 no mercy for you, but now you have *f* mercy.
2:22 no deceit was *f* in his mouth.
2Pt 3:14 effort to be *f* without stain or defilement,
1Jn 1: 8 the truth is not to be *f* in us.
Jude 1: 1 who have *f* love in God the Father and have
Rv 1: 9 *f* myself on the island called Patmos
5: 3 the earth could be *f* to open the scroll
5: 4 be *f* worthy to open or examine the scroll.
14: 5 On their lips no deceit has been *f*;
18:21 this, with violence, and nevermore be *f*!
18:22 in any trade shall ever again be *f* in you!
18:24 "In her was *f* the blood of prophets and
20:15 anyone whose name was not *f* inscribed in
21:16 *f* it twelve thousand furlongs in length,
22: 3 Nothing deserving a curse shall be *f* there.

FOUNDATION (39)

Jos 6:26 lose his first-born when he lays its *f*,
1Kgs 5:31 to give the temple a *f* of hewn stone.
7: 9 a saw, from the *f* to the bonding course.
7:10 (The *f* was made of fine,
16:34 son, Abiram, when he laid the *f*,
2Chr 8:16 day the *f* of the house of the LORD was laid
23: 5 palace and the final third at the *F* Gate,
Ezr 3: 6 though the *f* of the temple of the LORD had
3:10 had laid the *f* of the LORD's temple,
3:11 the *f* of the LORD's house had been laid.
3:12 the *f* of the present house being laid.
Jb 4:19 in houses of clay, whose *f* is in the dust,
Ps(s) 87: 1 His *f* upon the holy mountains
89:15 and judgment are the *f* of your throne;
97: 2 and judgment are the *f* of his throne.
104: 5 You fixed the earth upon its *f*,
Is 28:16 A precious cornerstone as a sure *f*;
Jer 51:26 take from you a cornerstone, or a *f* stone;
Zec 8: 9 *f* of the house of the LORD of hosts
Lk 6:48 house, dug deeply and laid the *f* on a rock.
6:48 failed to shake it because of its solid *f*.
6:49 his house on the ground without any *f*.
11:50 the prophets shed since the *f* of the world.
14:29 He will do that for fear of laying the *f*
Rom 15:20 for I did not want to build on a *f* laid by
1Cor 3:10 laid a *f* as a wise master-builder might do,
3:11 a *f* other than the one that has been laid,
3:12 different ones build on this *f* with gold,
3:14 a man has raised on this *f* still stands,
Eph 2:20 on the *f* of the apostles and prophets,
3:17 may charity be the root and *f* of your life.
1Tm 6:19 will they build a secure *f* for the future,
2Tm 2:19 But the *f* God has laid stands firm.
Heb 6: 1 maturity, not laying the *f* all over again:
1Pt 1:20 chosen before the world's *f* and revealed
Rv 21:14 had twelve courses of stones as its *f*,
21:19 The *f* of the city wall was ornate with

FOUNDATIONS (35)

2Sm 22: 8 the *f* of the heavens trembled and shook
22:16 the *f* of the earth were laid bare,
1Kgs 6:37 The *f* of the LORD's temple were laid in
Ezr 3: 3 *f* and offered holocausts to the LORD on it,
4:12 walls, and the *f* have already been laid.
5:16 the *f* of the house of God in Jerusalem.
Jb 22:16 whose *f* a flood swept away?
28: 9 and overturns the mountains at their *f*.
Ps(s) 18: 8 the *f* of the mountains trembled and
18:16 and the *f* of the world were laid bare,
82: 5 all the *f* of the earth are shaken.
137: 7 said, "Raze it, raze it down to its *f*!"
Prv 8:28 when he fixed fast the *f* of the earth;
Wis 4:19 and prostrate and rock them to their *f*;
Sir 16:17 The roots of the mountains, the earth's *f*,
Is 24:18 opened, and the *f* of the earth will shake.
44:28 and of the temple, "Let its *f* be laid."
48:13 Yes, my hand laid the *f* of the earth;
51:13 the heavens and laid the *f* of the earth?
51:16 the heavens, who laid the *f* of the earth,
54:11 in carnelians, and your *f* in sapphires;
58:12 the *f* from ages past you shall raise up;
Jer 31:37 or the *f* below the earth be sounded,
Lam 4:11 a fire in Zion that has consumed her *f*.
Ez 13:14 level it to the ground, laying bare its *f*.
30: 4 riches are seized and her *f* are overthrown.
41: 8 the *f* of the side chambers
42: 6 had no *f* to conform with the foundations
Mi 1: 6 the valley her stones, and lay bare her *f*.
6: 2 the LORD, pay attention, O *f* of the earth!
Zec 4: 9 Zerubbabel have laid the *f* of this house,
12: 1 out the heavens, lays the *f* of the earth,
Acts 16:26 the place, rocking the prison to its *f*.
Heb 11:10 he was looking forward to the city with *f*,

FOUNDED (11)

Ex 9:18 day the nation was *f* up to the present.
Jb 38: 4 Where were you when I *f* the earth?
Ps(s) 24: 2 For he *f* it upon the seas and established
78:69 heaven, like the earth which he *f* forever.
89:12 the world and its fullness you have *f*;
Prv 3:19 The LORD by wisdom *f* the earth,
Is 23:13 She whom the impious *f*,
40:21 Since the earth was *f* He sits enthroned
Hg 2:18 day on which the temple of the LORD was *f*,
Heb 3: 4 Every house is *f* by someone,
8: 6 a better covenant, *f* on better promises.

FOUNDER (6)

Gn 4:17 Cain also became the *f* of a city,
33:19 the descendants of Hamor, the *f* of Shechem.
1Chr 8:29 *f* of Gibeon whose wife's name was Maacah;
9:35 In Gibeon dwelt Jeiel, the *f* of Gibeon,
Heb 3: 3 as the *f* of a house is more honorable than
3: 4 by someone, but God is the *f* of all.

FOUNDERING (1)

Dt 22: 4 see your kinsman's ass or ox *f* on the road

FOUNDRY (2)

Dt 4:20 he has taken and led out of that iron *f*,
Jer 11: 4 up out of the land of Egypt, that iron *f*,

FOUNTAIN (20)

Lv 20:18 have laid bare the flowing *f* of her blood.
Dt 33:28 and the *f* of Jacob has been undisturbed In
Jos 15: 9 it ran to the *f* of waters of Nephtoah,
Ps(s) 36:10 For with you is the *f* of life,
Prv 5:17 Let your *f* be yours alone,
10:11 A *f* of life is the mouth of the just,
13:14 The teaching of the wise is a *f* of life,
14:27 The fear of the LORD is a *f* of life,
16:22 Good sense is a *f* of life to its possessor,
25:26 Like a troubled *f* or a polluted spring is
Sg 4:12 my bride, an enclosed garden, a *f* sealed.
4:15 You are a garden *f*,
Is 12: 3 you will draw water at the *f* of salvation,
Jer 8:23 spring of water, my eyes a *f* of tears
51:36 I will dry up her sea, and drain her *f*.
Bar 3:12 You have forsaken the *f* of wisdom!
Hos 13:15 dry up his spring, and leave his *f* dry.
Jl 4:18 A *f* shall issue from the house of the LORD,
Zec 13: 1 a *f* to purify from sin and uncleanness.
Jn 4:14 water I give shall become a *f* within him,

FOUNTAINS (5)

Gn 7:11 All the *f* of the great abyss burst forth,
8: 2 The *f* of the abyss and the floodgates of
Dt 8: 7 and *f* welling up in the hills and valleys,
Prv 8:24 when there were no *f* or springs of water;
Is 41:18 bare heights, and *f* in the broad valleys;

FOUR (271)

Gn 2:10 there it divides and becomes *f* branches.
11:13 Arpachshad lived *f* hundred and three years
11:15 Shelah lived *f* hundred and three years
11:17 Eber lived *f* hundred and thirty years
14: 9 king of Ellasar *f* kings against five.
15:13 enslaved and oppressed for *f* hundred years.
23:15 of land worth *f* hundred shekels of silver
23:16 *f* hundred shekels of silver at the current
32: 7 to meet you, accompanied by *f* hundred men."
33: 1 Esau coming, accompanied by *f* hundred men.
Ex 12:40 in Egypt was *f* hundred and thirty years.
12:41 At the end of *f* hundred and thirty years,
21:37 the one ox, and *f* sheep for the one sheep.
25:12 Cast *f* gold rings and fasten them on the
25:12 fasten them on the *f* supports of the ark,
25:26 You shall also make *f* rings of gold for it
25:26 for it and fasten them at the *f* corners,
25:34 On the shaft there are to be *f* cups,
26: 2 cubits, and the width *f* cubits;
26: 8 be thirty cubits, and the width *f* cubits:
26:32 on *f* gold-plated columns of acacia wood,
26:32 gold and shall rest on *f* silver pedestals.
27: 2 At the *f* corners there are to be horns,
27: 4 *f* bronze rings, one at each of its *f* corners.
27:16 It shall have *f* columns and four pedestals.
28:17 you shall mount *f* rows of precious stones:
30: 3 Its grate on top, its walls on all *f* sides,
36: 9 twenty-eight cubits and the width *f* cubits;
36:15 was thirty cubits and the width *f* cubits;
36:36 *F* gold-plated columns of acacia wood,
36:36 and *f* silver pedestals were cast for them.
37: 3 *F* gold rings were cast and put on its four
37:13 *F* rings of gold were cast for it and
37:13 and fastened, one at each of the *f* corners.
37:20 On the shaft there were *f* cups,
37:26 Its grate on top, its walls on all *f* sides,
38: 2 At the *f* corners horns were made that
38: 5 *F* rings were cast for the four corners of
38:19 There were *f* columns and four pedestals of
38:29 talents and two thousand *f* hundred shekels.
39:10 *F* rows of precious stones were mounted on
Lv 11:23 that have *f* legs are loathsome for you.
Nm 1:29 fifty-four thousand *f* hundred were
1:31 fifty-seven thousand *f* hundred were
1:37 thirty-five thousand *f* hundred were
1:43 fifty-three thousand *f* hundred were
2: 6 census to fifty-four thousand *f* hundred.]
2: 8 census to fifty-seven thousand *f* hundred.
2: 9 hundred and eighty-six thousand *f* hundred.]
2:16 and fifty-one thousand *f* hundred and fifty.]
2:23 census to thirty-five thousand *f* hundred.
2:30 census to fifty-three thousand *f* hundred.
7: 7 He gave two wagons and *f* oxen to the
7: 8 and *f* wagons and eight oxen to the
7:85 amounted to two thousand *f* hundred shekels,
26:43 thousand *f* hundred men were registered.
26:47 thousand *f* hundred men were registered.
26:50 thousand *f* hundred men were registered.
Dt 3:11 iron, nine regular cubits long and *f* wide,
22:12 "You shall put twisted cords on the *f*
Jos 19: 7 *f* cities and their villages,
21:17 *f* cities of Gibeon with its pasture lands,
21:20 lot, from the tribe of Ephraim, *f* cities.
21:23 *f* cities of Elteke with its pasture lands,
21:28 they obtained the *f* cities of Kishion
21:30 *f* cities of Mishal with its pasture lands,
21:34 *f* cities of Jokneam with its pasture lands,
21:36 Jordan, from the tribe of Reuben, *f* cities:
21:38 from the tribe of Gad a total of *f* cities:
Jgs 9:34 up an ambush for Shechem in *f* companies.
11:40 the Gileadite for *f* days of the year.
19: 2 Judah, where she stayed for some *f* months.
20: 2 *f* hundred thousand foot soldiers who were
20:17 mustered *f* hundred thousand swordsmen
20:47 Rimmon, where they remained for *f* months.
21:12 of Jabesh-gilead *f* hundred young virgins,
1Sm 4: 2 about *f* thousand men on the battlefield.
22: 2 About *f* hundred men were with him.
25:13 About *f* hundred men went up after David,
27: 7 *f* months in the country of the Philistines.
30:10 continued the pursuit with *f* hundred men,
30:17 none escaped except *f* hundred young men,
2Sm 15: 7 After a period of *f* years,
21:22 These *f* were Rephaim in Gath,
1Kgs 5: 6 Solomon had *f* thousand stalls for his
6: 1 In the *f* hundred and eightieth year from
7: 2 was supported by *f* rows of cedar columns,
7:15 their metal was of *f* fingers' thickness.
7:18 *F* hundred pomegranates were also cast;
7:27 of bronze, each four cubits long, *f* wide,
7:30 stand had *f* bronze wheels and bronze axles.
7:32 The *f* wheels were below the paneling,
7:33 The *f* legs of each stand had cast braces,
7:34 These *f* braces,
7:38 each *f* cubits in diameter with a capacity
7:42 *f* hundred pomegranates in double rows on
9:28 and brought back *f* hundred and twenty
10:26 he had one thousand *f* hundred chariots and
18:19 as well as the *f* hundred and fifty
18:19 *f* hundred prophets of Asherah who eat
18:22 are *f* hundred and fifty prophets of Baal.
18:34 "Fill *f* jars with water,"
22: 6 the prophets, about *f* hundred of them,
2Kgs 7: 3 gate were *f* lepers who were deliberating,
14:13 down *f* hundred cubits of the city wall,
1Chr 3: 5 Shobab, Nathan, Solomon *f* by Bathsheba,
7: 1 were Tola, Puah, Jashub, and Shimron: *f*.
9:24 gatekeepers were stationed at the *f* sides,
9:26 *f* chief gatekeepers were on constant duty.
12:27 *f* thousand six hundred,
21: 5 in Judah *f* hundred and seventy thousand.
21:20 the king, and his *f* sons who were with him,
23: 5 judges, *f* thousand were to be gatekeepers,
23: 5 and *f* thousand were to praise the LORD
23:10 these were the sons of Shimei, *f* in all.
23:12 Amram, Izhar, Hebron, and Uzziel; *f* in all.
26:17 four each day, on the south, *f* each day,
26:18 there were *f* at the highway and two at the
2Chr 1:14 so that he had one thousand *f* hundred
4:13 also *f* hundred pomegranates for the two
8:18 *f* hundred and fifty talents of gold to King
9:25 also had *f* thousand stalls of horses,
13: 3 of *f* hundred thousand picked warriors,

18: 5 gathered his prophets, *f* hundred in number,
25:23 Gate, a distance of *f* hundred cubits.
Ezr 1:10 silver bowls, *f* hundred and ten;
1:11 five thousand *f* hundred pieces.
2:15 sons of Adin, *f* hundred and fifty-four;
2:67 their camels *f* hundred and thirty-five,
6:17 two hundred rams, and *f* hundred lambs,
Neh 6: 4 *F* times they sent me this same proposal,
7:68 their camels *f* hundred and thirty-five,
11: 6 was *f* hundred and sixty-eight valiant men.
Tb 2:10 For *f* years I was deprived of eyesight,
8:19 *f* rams which he ordered to be slaughtered.
9: 2 take along with you *f* servants and two
9: 5 with the *f* servants and two camels,
Jdt 8: 4 remained three years and *f* months at home,
1Mc 11:57 appoint you ruler over the *f* districts
13:28 father and his mother and his *f* brothers.
2Mc 3:11 the total amounted to *f* hundred talents of
8:20 fought along with *f* thousand Macedonians;
8:21 Then Judas divided his army into *f*,
10:33 For *f* days Maccabeus and his men eagerly
12:33 foot soldiers and *f* hundred horsemen.
Jb 1:19 and smote the *f* corners of the house.
Prv 30:15 things are never satisfied, *f* never say,
30:18 for me, yes, *f* I cannot understand:
30:21 trembles, yes, under *f* it cannot bear up:
30:24 *F* things are among the smallest on the
30:29 yes, *f* are stately in their carriage:
Wis 18:24 were carved in *f* rows upon the stones,
Sir 37:17 *f* branches it shoots forth:
Is 11:12 assemble from the *f* corners of the earth.
17: 6 top, *f* or five on its fruitful branches,
Jer 15: 3 *F* kinds of scourge I have decreed against
36:23 Jehudi finished reading three or *f* columns
49:36 *f* winds from the four ends of the heavens:
52:21 each was *f* fingers thick,
52:30 *f* thousand six hundred persons in all.
Ez 1: 5 *f* living creatures that looked like this:
1: 6 human, but each had *f* faces and four wings,
1: 9 wings] looked out on all their *f* sides;
1:10 each of the *f* had the face of a man,
1:15 one beside each of the *f* living creatures.
1:16 and all *f* of them looked the same:
1:17 move in any of the *f* directions they faced,
1:18 The *f* of them had rims,
7: 2 has come upon the *f* corners of the land!
10: 9 I also saw *f* wheels beside them,
10:10 All *f* of them seemed to be made the same,
10:11 *f* directions without veering as they moved;
10:12 the *f* wheels were full of eyes all around.
10:14 Each had *f* faces:
10:21 Each had *f* faces and four wings;
14:21 I send Jerusalem my *f* cruel punishments,
37: 9 From the *f* winds come,
40:41 There were *f* tables on either side of the
40:42 There were *f* tables for holocausts,
41: 5 around the temple, had a width of *f* cubits.
42:20 Thus he measured it in the *f* directions,
43:14 to the upper ledge it was *f* cubits high,
43:15 the hearth of the altar was *f* cubits high,
43:15 the hearth were the *f* horns of the altar.
43:20 *f* horns of the altar, and on the *f* corners
45:19 on the *f* corners of the ledge of the altar,
46:21 me pass around the *f* corners of the court,
46:22 *f* corners of the court, minor courts, forty
46:23 A wall of stones surrounded each of the *f*,
Dn 1:17 To these *f* young men God gave knowledge
3:92 "I see *f* men unfettered and unhurt,
7: 2 *f* winds of heaven stirred up the great sea,
7: 3 sea, from which emerged *f* immense beasts,
7: 6 four wings like those of a bird, and it had *f*
7:17 "These *f* great beasts stand for *f* kingdoms
8: 8 four others, facing the *f* winds of heaven.
8:22 The *f* that rose in its place when it was
8:22 *f* kingdoms that will issue from his nation,
11: 4 and divided in *f* directions under heaven;
Am 1: 3 For three crimes of Damascus, and for *f*,
1: 6 For three crimes of Gaza, and for *f*,
1: 9 Tyre, and for *f* I will not revoke my word;
1:11 For three crimes of Edom, and for *f*,
1:13 three crimes of the Ammonites, and for *f*,
2: 1 For three crimes of Moab, and for *f*,
2: 4 For three crimes of Judah, and for *f*,
2: 6 For three crimes of Israel, and for *f*,
Zec 2: 1 there were *f* horns.
2: 3 Then the LORD showed me *f* blacksmiths.
2:10 for I scatter you to the *f* winds of heaven,
6: 1 Again I raised my eyes and saw *f* chariots
6: 5 "These are the *f* winds of the heavens,
Mt 15:38 people who were fed numbered *f* thousand,
16:10 Or the seven loaves among *f* thousand and
24:31 will assemble his chosen from the *f* winds,
Mk 2: 3 The *f* who carried him were unable to bring
8: 9 who had eaten numbered about *f* thousand.
8:20 broke the seven loaves for the *f* thousand,
13:27 and assemble his chosen from the *f* winds,
Jn 1:39 (It was about *f* in the afternoon.)
4:35 *F* months more and it will be harvest!"?
6:19 when they had rowed three or *f* miles,
11:17 had already been in the tomb *f* days.
11:39 to him, "Lord, it has been *f* days now;
19:23 took his garments and divided them *f* ways,
Acts 5:36 About *f* hundred men joined him.
7: 6 to slavery and oppressed *f* hundred years.
10:11 was lowered to the ground by its *f* corners.
11: 5 down to me from the sky by its *f* corners.
12: 4 with *f* squads of soldiers to guard him.
13:20 the end of some *f* hundred and fifty years.
21: 9 *f* unmarried daughters gifted with prophecy.
21:23 are *f* men among us who have made a vow.
21:38 *f* thousand cutthroats out into the desert?"
27:29 they dropped *f* anchors from the stern and
Gal 3:17 being *f* hundred and thirty years later,
Rv 4: 6 stood *f* living creatures covered with eyes
4: 8 Each of the *f* living creatures had six
5: 6 with the *f* living creatures and the elders,
5: 8 the *f* living creatures and the twenty-four
5:14 The *f* living creatures answered,
6: 1 and I heard one of the *f* living creatures
6: 6 from in among the *f* living creatures.
6: 8 These *f* were given authority over one
7: 1 I saw *f* angels standing at the *f* corners
7: 1 they held in check the earth's *f* winds so
7: 2 *f* angels who were given power to ravage
7:11 *f* living creatures fell down before
9:14 "Release the *f* angels who are tied up on
9:15 So the *f* angels were released;
14: 3 of the *f* living creatures and the elders.
15: 7 One of the *f* living creatures gave to the
19: 4 the *f* and twenty elders and the *f* living
20: 8 the nations in all *f* corners of the earth,

FOUR-FIFTHS (1)

Gn 47:24 while you keep *f* as seed for your fields

FOUR-FOOTED (2)

Bar 3:32 for all time, and filled it with *f* beasts;
Jas 3: 7 Every form of life, *f* or winged,

FOUR-LEGGED (2)

Acts 10:12 Inside it were all the earth's *f* creatures
11: 6 I could make out *f* creatures of the earth,

FOURFOLD (2)

2Sm 12: 6 He shall restore the ewe lamb *f* because he
Lk 19: 8 anyone in the least, I pay him back *f*."

FOURS (3)

Lv 11:20 that walk on all *f* are loathsome for you.
11:21 various winged insects that walk on all *f*
11:42 it crawls on its belly, goes on all *f*,

FOURTEEN (28)

Gn 31:41 I slaved *f* years for your two daughters
46:22 whom Rachel bore to Jacob *f* persons in all.
Lv 12: 5 for *f* days she shall be as unclean as at
Nm 17:14 Yet *f* thousand seven hundred died from the
29:13 and *f* yearling lambs that are unblemished,
29:15 and one tenth for each of the *f* lambs.
29:17 two rams, and *f* unblemished yearling lambs,
29:20 two rams, and *f* unblemished yearling lambs,
29:23 two rams, and *f* unblemished yearling lambs,
29:26 two rams, and *f* unblemished yearling lambs,
29:29 two rams, and *f* unblemished yearling lambs,
29:32 two rams, and *f* unblemished yearling lambs,
Jos 15:36 *f* cities and their villages.
18:28 *f* cities and their villages.
1Chr 25: 5 God gave Heman *f* sons and three daughters.
2Chr 13:21 He took to himself *f* wives and fathered
Tb 8:20 "For *f* days you shall not stir from here,
Jb 42:12 For he had *f* thousand sheep,
Ez 40: 1 exile, *f* years after the city was taken,
40:48 The width of the doorway was *f* cubits,
43:17 *f* cubits long and fourteen cubits wide.
Mt 1:17 from Abraham to David, *f* generations;
1:17 to the Babylonian captivity, *f* generations;
1:17 captivity to the Messiah, *f* generations.
Acts 27:33 *f* days you have been in constant suspense;
2Cor 12: 2 I know a man in Christ who, *f* years ago,
Gal 2: 1 Then, after *f* years,

FOURTEEN-DAY (1)

Tb 10: 7 Now at the end of the *f* wedding

FOURTEENTH (25)

Gn 14: 5 In the *f* year Chedorlaomer and the kings
Ex 12: 6 keep it until the *f* day of this month,
12:18 From the evening of the *f* day of the first
Lv 23: 5 LORD falls on the *f* day of the first month,
Nm 9: 3 The evening twilight of the *f* day of this
9: 5 twilight of the *f* day of the first month,
9:11 twilight of the *f* day of that month,
28:16 "On the *f* day of the first month falls
Jos 5:10 on the evening of the *f* of the month.
2Kgs 18:13 In the *f* year of King Hezekiah,
1Chr 24:13 the thirteenth to Huppah, the *f* to Ishbaal,
25:21 The *f* was Mattithiah,
2Chr 30:15 Passover on the *f* day of the second month.
35: 1 on the *f* day of the first month.
Ezr 6:19 Passover on the *f* day of the first month.
Est B: 6 mercy, on the *f* day of the twelfth month,
9:15 mustered again on the *f* of the month
9:17 On the *f* of the month they rested,
9:18 on the thirteenth and *f* of the month.
9:19 celebrate the *f* of the month of Adar as a
9:21 every year both the *f* and the fifteenth
F:10 they shall celebrate these days on the *f*
Is 36: 1 In the *f* year of King Hezekiah,
Ez 45:21 On the *f* day of the first month you shall
Acts 27:27 It was the *f* night of the storm,

FOURTH (83)

Gn 1:19 the *f* day.
2:14 The *f* river is the Euphrates.
15:16 In the *f* time-span the others shall come
Ex 20: 5 me, down to the third and *f* generation;
28:20 in the *f* row,
29:40 a *f* of a hin of oil of crushed olives and,
29:40 as its libation, a *f* of a hin of wine.
34: 7 *f* generation for their fathers' wickedness!"
39:13 in the *f* row a chrysolite,
Lv 19:24 In the *f* year, however, all of its fruit
23:13 its libation shall be a *f* of a hin of wine.
Nm 7:30 On the *f* day it was the turn of Elizur,
10: 6 when you sound the *f* alarm,
14:18 children to the third and *f* generation
15: 4 fine flour mixed with a *f* of a hin of oil,
15: 5 well as a libation of a *f* of a hin of wine,
28: 5 with a *f* of a hin of oil of crushed olives.
28: 7 LORD in the sanctuary a *f* of a hin of wine.
28:14 the ram, and a *f* of a hin for each lamb.
29:23 the *f* day you shall offer ten bullocks,
Dt 5: 9 third and *f* generation but bestowing mercy,
Jos 19:17 The *f* lot fell to Issachar.
Jgs 14:15 they said on the *f* day to Samson's wife,
19: 5 On the *f* day they rose early in the
2Sm 3: 4 the *f*, Adonijah, son of Haggith;
1Kgs 6: 1 the *f* year of Solomon's reign over Israel,
6:38 laid in the month of Ziv in the *f* year,
22:41 to reign over Judah in the *f* year of Ahab,
2Kgs 6:25 and a *f* of a kab of wild onion for five
10:30 your sons to the *f* generation shall sit
15:12 "Your descendants to the *f* generation
18: 9 In the *f* year of King Hezekiah,
25: 3 On the ninth day of the *f* month,
1Chr 2:14 son, Shimea, the third, Nethanel, the *f*,
3: 2 daughter of Talmai, king of Geshur, the *f*,
3:15 the *f*, Shallum.
8: 2 son, Aharah, the third, Nohah, the *f*,
12:11 was second, Eliab third, Mishmannah *f*,
23:19 Jahaziel, the third, and Jekameam, the *f*.
24: 8 the third to Harim, the *f* to Seorim,
24:23 Jahaziel, the third, Jekameam, the *f*.
25:11 The *f* fell to Izri,
26: 2 son, Zebadiah, the third, Jathniel, the *f*,
26: 4 son, Joah, the third, Sachar, the *f*,
26:11 son, Tebaliah, the third, Zechariah, the *f*.
27: 7 *F*, for the fourth month,
2Chr 3: 2 second month of the *f* year of his reign.
20:26 On the *f* day they held an assembly in the
Ezr 8:33 On the *f* day, the silver, the gold,
Neh 9: 3 LORD their God, for a *f* part of the day,
9: 3 and during another *f* part they made their
Jdt 12:10 On the *f* day Holofernes gave a banquet for
2Mc 7:13 maltreated the *f* brother in the same way.
Sir 26: 5 my heart quakes, a *f* before which I quail:
Jer 25: 1 of Judah, in the *f* year of Jehoiakim,
28: 1 of Judah, in the fifth month of the *f* year,
36: 1 In the *f* year of Jehoiakim,
39: 2 On the ninth day of the *f* month,
45: 1 dictated in the *f* year of Jehoiakim,
46: 2 of Babylon, in the *f* year of Jehoiakim,
51:59 in the *f* year of the reign of Zedekiah;
52: 6 On the ninth day of the *f* month,
Ez 1: 1 year, on the fifth day of the *f* month,
10:14 that of a lion, and the *f* that of an eagle.
Dn 2:40 There shall be a *f* kingdom,
3:92 fire, and the *f* looks like a son of God."
7: 7 the visions of the night I saw the *f* beast,
7:19 I wished to make certain about the *f* beast,
7:23 *f* beast shall be a fourth kingdom on earth,
11: 2 *f* shall acquire the greatest riches of all.
Zec 6: 3 horses, and the *f* chariot spotted horses
7: 1 In the *f* year of Darius the king [the word
7: 1 to Zechariah], on the *f* day of Chislev,
8:19 The fast days of the *f*,
1Cor 1:12 "Cephas has my allegiance," and the *f*,
Rv 4: 7 while the *f* looked like an eagle in flight.
6: 7 fourth seal, I heard the voice of the *f* living
8:12 When the *f* angel blew his trumpet,
16: 8 The *f* angel poured out his bowl on the sun.
21:19 the third chalcedony, the *f* emerald,

FOWL (4)

1Kgs 5: 3 harts, gazelles, roebucks, and fatted *f*.
Ps(s) 78:27 and, like the sand of the sea, winged *f*,
148:10 you creeping things and you winged *f*.
Ez 44:31 not eat anything, whether flesh or *f*,

FOWLER (2)

Ps(s) 91: 3 he will rescue you from the snare of the *f*,
Prv 6: 5 snare, or as a bird from the hand of the *f*.

FOWLERS (3)

Ps(s) 124: 7 were rescued like a bird from the *f* snare;
Jer 5:26 like *f* they set traps,
Hos 9: 8 with God, yet a *f* snare is on all his ways,

FOX (2)

Neh 3:35 Any *f* that attacked it would breach their
Lk 13:32 "Go tell that *f*, 'Today and tomorrow

FOXES (7)

Jgs 15: 4 So Samson left and caught three hundred *f*.
15: 5 kindled the torches and set the *f* loose
Sg 2:15 Catch us the *f*, the little foxes
Ez 13: 4 Like *f* among ruins are your prophets,
Mt 8:20 Jesus said to him, "The *f* have lairs,
Lk 9:58 Jesus said to him, "The *f* have lairs,

FRACTION (1)

Mt 18:28 owed him a mere *f* of what he himself owed.

FRACTURED (1)

Jgs 9:53 on Abimelech's head, and it *f* his skull.

FRAGILE (2)

Wis 15:13 stuff he creates *f* vessels and idols alike.
Dn 2:42 shall be partly strong and partly *f*.

FRAGMENTARY (1)

Heb 1: 1 God spoke in *f* and varied ways to our

FRAGMENTS (6)

Jb 41:22 His belly is sharp as pottery *f*;
Is 30:14 And among its *f* cannot be found a sherd to
Mt 14:20 The *f* remaining, when gathered up
15:37 When they gathered up the *f* left over,
Mk 8:19 how many baskets of *f* you gathered up?"
8:20 how many full hampers of *f* did you collect?"

FRAGRANCE (16)

Gn 27:27 Isaac smelled the *f* of his clothes.
27:27 the *f* of my son is like the fragrance of a
Ex 30:38 like this for his own enjoyment of its *f*,
Sg 1:12 king's banquet my nard gives forth its *f*.
2:13 and the vines, in bloom, give forth *f*.
4:10 the *f* of your ointments than all spices!
4:11 *f* of your garments is the *f* of Lebanon.
7: 9 vine and the *f* of your breath like apples,
7:14 The mandrakes give forth *f*,
Ez 8:11 the *f* of the incense was rising upward.
Hos 14: 7 tree and his *f* like the Lebanon cedar.
Jn 12: 3 the house was filled with the ointment's *f*.
2Cor 2:14 diffuse the *f* of his knowledge everywhere!
Eph 5: 2 an offering to God, a gift of pleasing *f*.

FRAGRANT (25)

Ex 25: 6 the anointing oil and for the *f* incense;
30: 7 "On it Aaron shall burn *f* incense.
30:23 hundred and fifty shekels, of *f* cinnamon;
30:23 two hundred and fifty shekels of *f* cane;
30:35 This *f* powder, expertly prepared,
31:11 oil, and the *f* incense for the sanctuary.
35: 8 the anointing oil and for the *f* incense;
35:15 the anointing oil, and the *f* incense;
35:28 the light, anointing oil, and *f* incense.
37:29 The sacred anointing oil and the *f* incense
39:38 altar, the anointing oil, the *f* incense;
40:27 of the veil, and on it he burned *f* incense,
40:38 and on it he burned *f* incense,
Lv 4: 7 blood on the horns of the altar of *f* incense
4:18 altar of *f* incense which is before the LORD
16:12 double handful of finely ground *f* incense,
Nm 4:16 of the oil for the light, the *f* incense,
2Chr 2: 3 the burning of *f* incense in his presence,
13:11 They burn holocausts to the LORD and *f*
Jdt 16: 7 She anointed her face with *f* oil;
Ps(s) 45: 9 and aloes and cassia your robes are *f*;
Sir 24:15 Like cinnamon, or *f* balm,
Bar 5: 8 The forests and every *f* kind of tree have
Phil 4:18 you through Epaphroditus, a *f* offering,
Rv 18:12 *f* wood of every kind,

FRAIL (4)

Gn 33:13 "As my lord can see, the children are *f*.
Ps(s) 39: 5 of my days, that I may learn how *f* I am.
89:48 how *f* you created all the children of men!
Prv 4: 3 When I was my father's child, *f*,

FRAILEST (2)

Wis 10: 4 saved it, piloting the just man on *f* wood.
14: 5 men trust their lives even to *f* wood.

FRAILTIES (1)

Ps(s) 25: 7 The sins of my youth and my *f* remember not;

FRAME (20)

Ex 25:25 Surround it with a *f*,
25:25 high, with a molding of gold around the *f*.
25:27 on two opposite sides of the *f* as holders
37:12 A *f* a handbreadth high was also put around
37:12 it, with a molding of gold around the *f*.
37:14 The rings were alongside the *f* as holders
Jb 17: 7 and all my *f* is shrunken to a shadow.
20:11 Though his *f* is full of youthful vigor,
30:17 My *f* takes no rest by night;
30:30 the heat scorches my very *f*.
33:19 pain and unceasing suffering within his *f*,
40:18 his *f* is like iron rods.
Ps(s) 41: 9 'A malignant disease fills his *f*';
139:15 *f* unknown to you When I was made in secret,
Eccl 11: 5 fashions the human *f* in the mother's womb,
Sir 30:14 and robust, than a rich man with wasted *f*.
Is 6: 4 the *f* of the door shook and the house was
Lam 1:13 on high he sent fire down into my very *f*;
Na 2:11 and trembling knees, Writhing in every *f*,
1Cor 15:54 When the corruptible *f* takes on

FRAMED (2)

Dn 2: 9 You have *f* a false and deceitful
Mt 21:16 and children you have *f* a hymn of praise'?"

FRAMES (4)

1Kgs 7: 4 There were three window *f* at either end,
7:29 the panels between the *f* there were lions,
7:29 and on the *f* likewise,
2Kgs 16:17 King Ahaz detached the *f* from the bases

FRAMEWORK (2)

1Kgs 7:28 constructed, panels were set within the *f*.
Sg 3:10 its *f* inlaid with ivory.

FRANKINCENSE (16)

Ex 30:34 galbanum, these are pure *f* in equal parts;
Lv 2: 1 He shall pour oil on it and put *f* over it.
2: 2 flour and oil, together with all the *f*,
2:15 cereal offering you shall put oil and *f*.
2:16 the grits and oil, together with all the *f*,
5:11 He shall not put oil or *f* on it,
6: 8 oil, together with all the *f* that is on it,
24: 7 On each pile put some pure *f*,
Nm 5:15 shall not pour oil on it nor put *f* over it,
1Chr 9:29 the fine flour, the wine, the oil, the *f*,
Sg 3: 6 column of smoke Laden with myrrh, with *f*,
Is 43:23 service of offerings, nor weary you for *f*.
60: 6 from Sheba shall come bearing gold and *f*,
Bar 1:10 procure holocausts, sin offerings, and *f*,
Mt 2:11 and presented him with gifts of gold, *f*,
Rv 18:13 and amomum, perfumes, myrrh and *f*;

FRANKLY (3)

Tb 7:10 I will explain the situation to you very *f*.
Prv 10:10 but he who *f* reproves promotes peace.
2Cor 6:11 Men of Corinth, we have spoken to you *f*,

FRANKNESS (1)

2Cor 7: 4 you with utter *f* and boast much about you.

FRANTIC (1)

Jer 50:38 and they shall be made *f* by fearful things.

FRANTICALLY (1)

Acts 14:15 they shouted *f*.

FRATRICIDAL (1)

Wis 10: 3 his anger, he perished through his *f* wrath.

FRAUD (12)

Ps(s) 55:12 and *f* never depart from its streets.
72:14 From *f* and violence he shall redeem them,
Is 44:20 "Is not this thing in my right hand a *f*?"
Jer 6:13 prophet and priest, all practice *f*.
8:10 gain, prophet and priest, all practice *f*.
10:14 He has molded a *f*, without breath of life.
51:17 He molded a *f*, without breath of life.
Bar 6: 7 but they are a *f*,
6:44 that takes place around these gods is a *f*:
Dn 11:21 stealth and *f* he shall seize the kingdom.
Acts 13:10 are an impostor and a thoroughgoing *f*,
18:14 "If it were a crime or a serious *f*,

FRAUDS (10)

Jer 16:19 "Mere *f* are the heritage of our fathers,
Bar 6:47 left *f* and opprobrium to their successors.
6:50 they will later be known for *f*.
Mt 23:13 you *f*! You shut the doors of the kingdom
23:15 Woe to you scribes and Pharisees, you *f*!
23:23 you *f*! You pay tithes on mint and herbs
23:25 you *f*! You cleanse the outside of the cup
23:27 Woe to you scribes and Pharisees, you *f*!
23:29 you *f*! You erect tombs for the prophets
Rv 3: 9 Jews who are not really Jews but *f*,

FRAY (2)

1Kgs 22:30 Israel disguised himself and entered the *f*.
2Chr 18:29 disguised himself and they entered the *f*.

FREE (131)

Gn 2:16 "You are *f* to eat from any of the trees
Ex 6: 6 I will *f* you from the forced labor of the
6: 7 am your God when I *f* you from the labor of
21: 5 I will not go *f*,'
21: 7 she shall not go *f* as male slaves do.
21:26 slave go *f* in compensation for the eye.
21:27 slave go *f* in compensation for the tooth.
Lv 15:13 with a flow becomes *f* of his affliction,
19:20 but not put to death, because she is not *f*.
Nm 5:31 The man shall be *f* from guilt,
19: 2 red heifer that is *f* from every blemish
35:25 shall *f* the homicide from the avenger of
Dt 15:12 dismiss him from your service, a *f* man.
15:18 not be reluctant to let your slave go *f*,
Jos 22:18 We are still not *f* of that;
22:31 Israelites *f* from punishment by the LORD."
Jgs 1:25 they let the man and his whole clan go *f*.
1Sm 14:41 were designated, and the people went *f*.
2Sm 5:20 before me like waters that have broken *f*."
14:16 For the king must surely consent to *f* his
18:19 set him *f* from the grasp of his enemies."
22:20 He set me *f* in the open.
1Kgs 20:34 terms," Ahab replied, "I will set you *f*."
20:34 an agreement with him and then set him *f*.
20:42 have set *f* the man I doomed to destruction,
1Chr 4:10 Help me and make me *f* of misfortune,
9:33 They stayed in the chambers when *f* of duty,
1Mc 2:11 From being *f*, she has become a slave.
10:29 "I now *f* you,
10:31 and her tolls, be sacred and *f* from tax.
13:16 he is set *f* he will not revolt against us,
15: 7 Jerusalem and its temple shall be *f*.
2Mc 1:27 *f* those who are the slaves of the Gentiles,
9:14 on him, that he would set *f* the holy city,
10:21 their enemies *f* to fight against them.
12:42 the soldiers to keep themselves *f* from sin,
Jb 3:19 same, and the servant is *f* from his master.
16:17 Although my hands are *f* from violence,
Ps(s) 18:20 He set me *f* in the open,
25:15 LORD, for he will *f* my feet from the snare.
31: 5 will *f* me from the snare they set for me,
50:19 To your mouth you give *f* rein for evil,
51:16 *F* me from blood guilt,
73: 5 They are *f* from the burdens of mortals,
79:11 your great power *f* those doomed to death.
105:20 him, the ruler of the peoples set him *f*.
118: 5 the LORD answered me and set me *f*.
119:108 Accept, O LORD, the *f* homage of my mouth,
143:11 in your justice *f* me from distress,
146: 7 The LORD sets captives *f*;
Prv 6: 3 So do this, my son, to *f* yourself,
6: 5 *F* yourself as a gazelle from the snare,
12:13 ensnared, but the just comes *f* of trouble.
Wis 2: 9 Let no meadow be *f* from our wantonness;
6:15 keeps vigil shall quickly be *f* from care;
Sir 10:24 When *f* men serve a prudent slave,
11:12 he raises him *f* of the vile dust,
15:14 he made him subject to his own *f* choice.
19:19 while the simple man may be *f* from sin.
23:10 the Holy Name will not remain *f* from sin.
26:20 upright, nor a shopkeeper *f* from sin:
31: 5 The lover of gold will not be *f* from sin,
33:26 his hands be idle and he will seek to be *f*.
38:24 is *f* from toil can become a wise man.
Is 33:15 his hands *f* of contact with a bribe,
45:13 let my exiles go *f* Without price or ransom,
56: 2 Who keeps the sabbath *f* from profanation,
56: 6 All who keep the sabbath *f* from
58: 6 Setting *f* the oppressed,
Jer 15:21 I will *f* you from the hand of the wicked,
34: 9 Everyone was to *f* his Hebrew slaves,
34:10 to set *f* their male and female servants,
34:11 set *f* and again forced them into service.
34:14 each of you shall set *f* his Hebrew brother
34:14 serve you, but then you shall let him go *f*.
34:17 proclaiming your neighbors and kinsmen *f*.
34:17 I now proclaim you *f*,
Ez 13:20 their arms and set *f* those you have caught.
17:15 Can he break a covenant and still go *f*?
34:27 break the bonds of their yoke and *f* them
41:12 The building fronting the *f* area on the
41:13 The *f* area, together with the building
41:14 of the temple, along with the *f* area,
41:15 lay the length of the *f* area and behind it,
42: 1 on the north that lay across the *f* area
42:10 To the south along the side of the *f* area
42:13 on the *f* area are the sanctuary chambers;
45: 2 surrounded by a *f* space of fifty cubits,
Mt 20:15 I am *f* to do as I please with my money,
Mk 5:34 Go in peace and be *f* of this illness."
Lk 13:12 said, "Woman, you are *f* of your infirmity."
24:21 that he was the one who would set Israel *f*.
Jn 8:32 the truth, and the truth will set you *f*."
8:33 do you mean by saying, 'You will be *f*'?"
8:36 if the son frees you, you will really be *f*.
11:44 him," Jesus told them, "and let him go *f*."
19:12 *f* this man you are no 'Friend of Caesar.'"
Acts 24: 8 Feel *f* now to question him about all this
Rom 6:15 the law but under grace, are we *f* to sin?

7:24 Who can *f* me from this body under the
13: 3 wish to be *f* from the fear of authority?
1Cor 7:21 Even supposing you could go *f*,
7:27 Are you *f* of a wife?
7:32 I should like you to be *f* of all worries.
7:37 while without constraint and *f* to carry out
7:39 If her husband dies she is *f* to marry,
9: 1 Am I not *f*?
9:18 preaching I offer the gospel *f* of charge
9:21 to it (not that I am *f* from the law of God,
12:13 of us, whether Jew or Greek, slave or *f*,
2Cor 11: 7 the gospel of God to you *f* of charge,
Gal 4:23 the *f* woman was the fruit of the promise.
4:30 terms with the son" of the one born *f*.
4:31 of a slave girl but of a mother who is *f*.
5:13 a freedom that gives *f* rein to the flesh.
Eph 6: 8 know that each one, whether slave or *f*,
Col 1:22 you to God holy, *f* of reproach and blame.
2:16 No one is *f*,
1Tm 2: 8 aloft, and be *f* from anger and dissension.
5:16 which ought to be *f* to give help to the
Heb 2:15 and *f* those who through fear of death had
13:23 that our brother Timothy has been set *f*.
Jas 1:13 No one who is tempted is *f* to say,
1Pt 2:16 Live as *f* men,
2Pt 2:18 who have just come *f* of a life of errors.
1Jn 1: 8 If we say, "We are *f* of the guilt of sin,"
2:27 all things and is true *f* from any lie
Rv 6:15 wealthy and powerful, the slave and the *f*—
13:16 and great, rich and poor, slave and *f*,
19:18 the flesh of all men, the *f* and the slave,
22:14 have *f* access to the tree of life and enter

FREE-FLOWING (2)

Ex 30:23 five hundred shekels of *f* myrrh;
Nm 24: 7 His wells shall yield *f* waters,

FREEBORN (2)

Gal 4:22 slave girl, and the other by his *f* wife.
4:26 But the Jerusalem on high is *f*,

FREED (25)

Lv 15:28 "If she becomes *f* from her affliction,
26:13 the Egyptians and *f* you from their slavery,
1Sm 7:14 Israel also *f* the territory of these
2Kgs 13: 5 the Israelites, *f* from the power of Aram,
Neh 1:10 *f* by your great might and your strong hand.
2Mc 12:46 dead that they might be *f* from this sin.
Ps(s) 12: 7 are sure, like tried silver, *f* from dross,
81: 7 his hands were *f* from the basket.
106:10 and *f* them from the hands of the enemy.
116: 8 For he has *f* my soul from death,
124: 7 Broken was the snare, and we were *f*.
136:24 And *f* us from our foes,
Jer 34:10 But though they agreed and *f* them,
Dn 3:88 He has *f* us from the raging flame and
Mk 7:35 he was *f* from the impediment,
Acts 2:24 God *f* him from death's bitter pangs,
Rom 6: 7 A man who is dead has been *f* from sin.
6:18 *f* from your sin,
6:22 *f* from sin and have become slaves of God,
7: 3 if her husband dies she is *f* from that law,
8: 2 has *f* you from the law of sin and death.
8:21 because the world itself will be *f* from
Gal 5: 1 It was for liberty that Christ *f* us.
Phil 1:23 be *f* from this life and to be with Christ,
Rv 1: 5 us and *f* us from our sins by his own blood,

FREEDMAN (1)

1Cor 7:22 called in the Lord is a *f* of the Lord,

FREEDMEN (1)

Acts 6: 9 "Synagogue of Roman *F*" (that is,

FREEDOM (25)

Ex 21: 2 year he shall be given his *f* without cost.
21:11 she shall be given her *f* absolutely,
Lv 19:20 has not yet been redeemed or given her *f*,
Dt 21:14 liking for her, you shall give her her *f*,
Jgs 5: 7 Gone was *f* beyond the walls,
5:11 his just deeds that brought *f* to Israel.
Jdt 16:24 and to the maid she gave her *f*.
1Mc 6:59 Let us grant them *f* to live according to
Jb 39: 5 Who has given the wild ass his *f*,
Ps(s) 32: 7 glad cries of *f* you will ring me round.
55:19 *f* and peace from those who war against me,
Sir 7:21 refuse him not his *f*.
Jer 34:16 slaves to whom you had given their *f*;
Lk 1:77 of salvation in *f* from their sins,
Acts 24:23 to be kept in custody but allowed some *f*,
Rom 6:20 were slaves of sin, you had *f* from justice.
8:21 in the glorious *f* of the children of God.
1Cor 7:27 Then do not seek your *f*.
2Cor 3:17 the Spirit of the Lord is, there is *f*.
Gal 2: 4 spy on the *f* we enjoy in Christ Jesus
5:13 in freedom—but not a *f* that gives free
Jas 2:12 destined for judgment under the law of *f*.
1Pt 2:16 but do not use your *f* as a cloak for vice.
2Pt 2:19 They promise them *f* though they themselves

FREEDOMS (1)

Jas 1:25 peers into *f* ideal law and abides by it.

FREEING (3)

2Sm 18:31 *f* you from the grasp of all who rebelled
Jer 40: 4 I am *f* you today from the fetters that
Dn 13:53 condemning the innocent, and *f* the guilty,

FREELY (38)

Gn 34:10 you can settle and move about *f* in it,
34:21 settle in the land and move about in it *f*;
42:34 you, and you may move about *f* in the land.' "
43:34 So they drank *f* and made merry with him.
Nm 6: 5 and shall let the hair of his head grow *f*.
Dt 15: 8 him and *f* lend him enough to meet his need.
15:10 give to him, give *f* and not with ill will;
23:24 offering you have *f* promised to the LORD.
31: 2 old and am no longer able to move about *f*;
1Sm 14:30 if the people had eaten *f* today of their
2Kgs 12: 5 are *f* brought to the temple of the LORD
1Chr 29:14 should have the means to contribute so *f*?
Ezr 7:15 have *f* contributed to the God of Israel,
7:16 people and priests *f* contribute
Est 1: 7 golden cups, and the royal wine flowed *f*,
1Mc 4:18 Afterward you can *f* take the plunder."
16:16 Then, when Simon and his sons had drunk *f*,
Ps(s) 54: 8 *F* will I offer you sacrifice:
Sg 5: 1 Drink *f* of love!
Sir 13:11 Engage not *f* in discussion with him,
14:11 use *f* whatever you have and enjoy it as
31:28 are wine drunk *f* at the proper time.
Is 32:20 stream, and let the ox and the ass go *f*!
Jer 37: 4 he still came and went *f* among the people.
Ez 17: 7 more *f* than the bed where it was planted.
Hos 14: 5 heal their defection, I will love them *f*;
Zec 4:12 two olive tufts which *f* pour out fresh oil
Mt 19:12 and some there are who have *f* renounced
Mk 1:45 and began to proclaim the whole matter *f*,
Lk 5:33 Yours, on the contrary, eat and drink *f*."
Jn 10:18 No one takes it from me; I lay it down *f*.
11:54 no longer moved about *f* in Jewish circles.
Acts 9:28 moving *f* about Jerusalem and expressing
26:26 Before him I can speak *f*.
2Cor 8:17 but being very eager he has gone to you *f*.
Eph 3:12 through faith in him we can speak *f* to God,
Phlm 1:14 be forced on you but might be *f* bestowed.
2Pt 1: 3 That divine power of his has *f* bestowed on

FREEMAN (7)

1Kgs 14:10 line, whether slave or *f* in Israel,
21:21 male in Ahab's line, whether slave or *f*,
2Kgs 9: 8 Ahab's line, whether slave or *f* in Israel.
14:26 where there was neither slave nor *f*,
1Cor 7:22 *f* who has been called is a slave of Christ.
Gal 3:28 exist among you Jew or Greek, slave or *f*,
Col 3:11 foreigner, Scythian, slave or *f*.

FREES (3)

1Sm 17:26 Philistine and *f* Israel of the disgrace?
Tb 4:10 Almsgiving *f* one from death,
Jn 8:36 That is why, if the son *f* you,

FREEWILL (25)

Lv 7:16 the sacrifice is a votive or a *f* offering
22:18 as a *f* offering to the LORD
22:21 fulfillment of a vow, or as a *f* offering
22:23 you may indeed present as a *f* offering
23:38 *f* offerings that you present to the LORD.
Nm 15: 3 fulfillment of a vow, or as a *f* offering,
29:39 you present as your votive or *f* offerings."
Dt 12: 6 contributions, your votive and *f* offerings,
12:17 you have vowed, of your *f* offerings,
16:10 and the measure of your own *f* offering
1Chr 29: 9 The people rejoiced over these *f* offerings
2Chr 29:31 all the holocausts which were *f* offerings
31:14 was in charge of the *f* gifts made to God
35: 8 princes also gave a *f* gift to the people
Ezr 1: 4 together with *f* offerings for the house of
1: 6 gifts besides all their *f* offerings
2:68 made *f* offerings for the house of God
3: 5 anyone might offer as a *f* gift to the LORD.
7:16 together with the *f* offerings which the
8:28 and the gold are a *f* offering to the LORD
Jdt 4:14 and the *f* offerings of the people
16:18 they offered their holocausts, *f* offerings,
Sir 35: 7 to the LORD, be not sparing of *f* gifts.
Ez 46:12 the prince makes a *f* offering to the LORD,
Am 4: 5 proclaim publicly your *f* offerings,

FREEZE (1)

Ps(s) 147:17 before his cold the waters *f*.

FREEZES (1)

Sir 43:21 He *f* over every body of water,

FRENZIED (5)

Jb 39:24 *F* and trembling he devours the ground;
Wis 14:23 or *f* carousals in unheard-of rites,
Jer 2:23 A *f* she-camel, coursing near and far

Na 2: 4 The horses are *f*;
Lk 6:11 At this they became *f* and began asking one

FRENZY (1)

1Sm 19:20 presided over by Samuel, in a prophetic *f*,

FREQUENT (8)

Jdt 5:18 down steadily, more and more, by *f* wars,
2Mc 8: 8 successful advances were becoming more *f*,
Ps(s) 18:15 flight, with *f* lightnings he routed them.
Sir 6:34 *F* the company of the elders;
27:12 fools, but *f* the company of thoughtful men.
2Cor 11:23 worse beatings and *f* brushes with death.
11:27 in hunger and thirst and *f* fastings;
1Tm 5:23 stomach, and because of your *f* illnesses.

FREQUENTED (4)

1Sm 30:31 to all the places *f* by David and his men.
1Kgs 12:30 people *f* these calves in Bethel and in Dan.
Is 62:12 of the LORD, And you shall be called *F*."
Dn 13: 6 brought their cases, *f* the house of Joakim.

FREQUENTING (1)

Wis 8:18 that in *f* her society there is prudence,

FREQUENTLY (5)

Mt 17:15 falls into the fire and *f* into the water.
Mk 5: 4 *f* been secured with handcuffs and chains,
Lk 5:33 disciples fast *f* and offer prayers;
Acts 24:26 to send for him *f* to converse with him.
2Pt 1:15 recall these things *f* after my departure.

FRESCOES (1)

2Mc 2:29 *f* has only to concern himself with what is

FRESH (36)

Gn 30:37 however, got some *f* shoots of poplar,
35: 2 purify yourselves and put on *f* clothes.
45:22 He also gave to each of them *f* clothing,
49:26 the blessings of *f* grain and blossoms,
Ex 15:25 this into the water, the water became *f*.
Lv 2:14 the form of *f* grits of new ears of grain,
15:13 garments and bathe his body in *f* water,
23:14 any bread or roasted grain or *f* kernels.
Nm 6: 3 juice, nor eat either *f* or dried grapes.
Jgs 15:15 Near him was the *f* jawbone of an ass;
16: 7 seven *f* bowstrings which have not dried,"
16: 8 her seven *f* bowstrings which had not dried,
1Sm 21: 7 replaced by *f* bread when it was taken away.
2Kgs 4:42 the first fruits, and *f* grain in the ear.
2Mc 4:46 under a colonnade, as if to get some *f* air,
15: 9 won, he filled them with *f* enthusiasm.
Jb 29:20 My glory is *f* within me,
Sg 4:15 a well of water flowing *f* from Lebanon.
6:11 to look at the *f* growth of the valley,
7:14 Both *f* and mellowed fruits,
Sir 46:12 names receive *f* luster in their children!
Jer 18:14 dry up that flow *f* down the mountains?
Ez 14: 3 memory of their idols *f* in their hearts,
47: 8 the sea, the salt waters, which it makes *f*.
47: 9 this water comes the sea shall be made *f*.
47:11 its marshes and swamps shall not be made *f*;
47:12 Every month they shall bear *f* fruit,
Zec 4:12 out *f* oil through the two golden channels?"
Mt 27:59 Joseph wrapped it in *f* linen and laid it
Lk 5:38 New wine should be poured into *f* skins.
Acts 28:15 them, he thanked God and took *f* courage.
1Cor 5: 7 old yeast to make of yourselves *f* dough,
Eph 4:23 illusion and desire, and acquire a *f*,
1Thes 2: 2 *F* from the humiliation we had suffered at
Jas 3:11 *f* water and foul from the same outlet?
3:12 more can a brackish source yield *f* water.

FRESHNESS (1)

Wis 2: 6 are real, and use the *f* of creation avidly.

FRIED (5)

Lv 2: 5 a cereal offering that is *f* on a griddle,
6:14 *f* in oil on a griddle when you bring it in.
7: 9 *f* on a griddle shall belong to the priest
2Sm 13: 6 and prepare some *f* cakes before my eyes,
13: 8 into cakes before his eyes and *f* the cakes.

FRIEND (105)

Gn 38:12 in company with his *f* Hirah the Adullamite.
38:20 Judah sent the kid by his *f* the Adullamite
Ex 33:12 Yet you have said, 'You are my intimate *f*,'
33:17 favor with me and you are my intimate *f*."
Dt 13: 7 or your beloved wife, or your intimate *f*,
2Sm 13: 3 Now Amnon had a *f* named Jonadab,
15:37 So David's *f* Hushai went into the city of
16:16 *f* Hushai the Archite came to Absalom,
16:17 "Is this your devotion to your *f*?
16:17 Why did you not go with your *f*?"
1Kgs 2:13 "Do you come as a *f*?"
5:15 for Hiram had always been David's *f*.
16:11 sparing a single male relative or *f* of his.
2Chr 20: 7 to the descendants of Abraham, your *f*?

FRIEND (cont.)

1Mc 10:16 Let us now make him our *f* and ally."
10:19 a mighty warrior and worthy to be our *f*.
10:20 you are to be called the King's *F*,
13:36 to Simon the high priest, the *f* of kings,
15:32 So Athenobius, the king's *F*,
2Mc 7:24 him his *F* and entrust him with high office.
11:14 also, and to induce him to become their *f*.
Jb 6:14 A *f* owes kindness to one in despair,
6:27 the orphan, and would barter away your *f*!
Ps(s) 7: 5 my hands, If I have repaid my *f* with evil,
35:14 As though it were a *f* of mine,
41:10 *f* who had my trust and partook of my bread,
55:14 my other self, my companion and my bosom *f*!
88:19 my only *f* is darkness.
Prv 7: 4 call Understanding, *F*!"
17:17 He who is a *f* is always a friend,
18:19 city, and a *f* is like the bars of a castle.
18:21 those who make it a *f* shall eat its fruit.
18:24 but a true *f* is more loyal than a brother.
19: 4 but the *f* of the poor man deserts him.
19: 8 who gains intelligence is his own best *f*;
22:11 of winning speech has the king for his *f*.
27: 6 from a *f* may be accepted as well meant,
27:10 own *f* and your father's friend forsake not;
Sg 5:16 Such is my lover, and such my *f*,
Wis 1:16 words invited death, considered it a *f*,
Sir 6: 1 be not a foe instead of a *f*;
6: 7 When you gain a *f*,
6: 8 sort of *f* is a friend when it suits him,
6: 9 Another is a *f* who becomes an enemy,
6:10 Another is a *f*,
6:14 A faithful *f* is a sturdy shelter;
6:15 A faithful *f* is beyond price,
6:16 A faithful *f* is a life-saving remedy,
6:17 and his *f* will be like himself.
7:12 brother, nor against your *f* and companion.
7:18 Barter not a *f* for money,
9:10 Discard not an old *f*,
9:10 A new *f* is like new wine which you drink
12: 9 in adversity even his *f* disappears.
13:20 rich man stumbles he is supported by a *f*;
13:20 a poor man trips he is pushed down by a *f*.
14:13 Before you die, be good to your *f*,
19: 7 Tell nothing to *f* or foe;
19:12 Admonish your *f*—
19:14 Admonish your *f*—
20:22 A man makes a promise to a *f* out of shame,
22:20 who insults a *f* breaks up the friendship.
22:21 Should you draw a sword against a *f*,
22:22 Should you speak sharply to a *f*,
22:22 a treacherous attack will drive away any *f*.
22:25 From a *f* in need of support no one need
22:26 his *f* all will stand aloof who hear of it.
25: 9 a *f* and he who speaks to attentive ears.
27:16 trusted, he will never find an intimate *f*.
27:17 Cherish your *f*,
27:19 let your *f* go and cannot recapture him;
29:10 Spend your money for your brother and *f*,
33: 6 fickle *f* is like the stallion that neighs,
33:20 son nor wife, neither brother nor *f*,
37: 1 Every *f* declares his friendship,
37: 4 A false *f* will share your joys,
37: 5 true *f* will fight with you against the foe,
40:23 A *f*, a neighbor, are timely guides,
41:17 Before *f* and companion,
41:20 return a greeting, and of rebuffing a *f*;
47:22 one, nor destroy the offspring of his *f*.
Is 5: 1 Let me now sing of my *f*,
5: 1 My *f* had a vineyard on a fertile hillside;
41: 8 offspring of Abraham my *f*—
48:14 The LORD's *f* shall do his will against
Jer 9: 3 supplanter, every *f* is guilty of slander.
Mi 7: 5 Put no trust in a *f*,
Mt 20:13 'My *f*,' he said to one in reply,
22:12 'My *f*,' he said, 'how is it you came in
26:50 Jesus answered, *F*,
Lk 5:20 Seeing their faith, Jesus said, "My *f*,
7:34 a *f* of tax collectors and sinners!'
11: 5 middle of the night and says to him, *F*,
11: 6 for a *f* of mine has come in from a journey
12:14 He replied, *F*, who has set me up as your
14:10 host approaches you he will say, 'My *f*,
22:60 Peter responded, "My *f*,
Jn 19:12 you free this man you are no *F* of Caesar."
Rom 9:20 *F*, who are you to answer God back?
Phlm 1: 1 our beloved *f* and fellow worker Philemon,
Jas 2:23 for this he received the title "God's *f*."
4: 4 enemy if he chooses to be the world's *f*.

FRIENDLY (8)

Gn 34:21 "These men are *f* toward us.
1Mc 8: 1 a *f* alliance with all who applied to them.
2Mc 12: 4 treachery and wishing to live on *f* terms,
Prv 22:24 Be not *f* with a hotheaded man,
Sir 6: 5 and gracious lips prompt *f* greetings.
12: 9 a man is successful even his enemy is *f*;
Jer 12: 6 even if they are *f* to you in their words.
Zec 6:13 two of them there shall be *f* understanding.

FRIENDS (110)

Gn 29: 4 Jacob said to them, *F*,
Ex 32:27 your own kinsmen, your *f* and neighbors!"
Jgs 5:31 your *f* be as the sun rising in its might!
2Sm 3: 8 father Saul, to his brothers and his *f*,
Est 5:10 he summoned his *f* and his wife Zeresh.
5:14 His wife Zeresh and all his *f* said to him,
6:13 his *f* everything that had happened to him,
E: 5 the fair speech of *f* entrusted with the
1Mc 2:18 sons shall be numbered among the King's *F*,
2:38 When Mattathias and his *f* heard of it,
2:45 Mattathias and his *f* went about and tore
3:38 Gorgias, capable men among the King's *F*,
6:10 So he called in all his *F* and said to them:
6:14 Then he summoned Philip, one of his *F*,
6:28 angry, and he called together all his *F*,
7: 6 *f* and have driven us out of our country.
7: 8 king chose Bacchides, one of the King's *F*,
7:15 "We will not try to injure you or your *f*."
8:12 with their *f*,
8:20 enroll ourselves among your allies and *f*."
8:31 yoke heavy upon our *f* and allies the Jews?
9:26 *f* of Judas and brought them to Bacchides,
9:28 Then all the *f* of Judas came together and
9:35 of the convoy to ask permission of his *f*,
9:39 the bridegroom and his *f* and kinsmen had
10:60 gave them and their *f* silver and gold
10:63 numbering him among his Chief *F*
11:26 great honor in the presence of all his *F*.
11:27 and had him enrolled among his Chief *F*.
11:33 *f* and who observe their obligations to us.
11:57 and wish you to be one of the King's *F*."
12:14 the rest of our allies and *f* in these wars;
12:43 with honor, introduced him to all his *f*,
12:43 He also ordered his *f* and soldiers to obey
14:39 high priesthood, made him one of his *F*,
14:40 the Romans had addressed the Jews as *f*,
15:17 envoys of the Jews, our *f* and allies,
15:28 He sent Athenobius, one of his *F*,
2Mc 1:14 Antiochus with his *F* had come to the place
8: 9 son of Patroclus, one of the Chief *F*,
10:13 was accused before Eupator by the King's *F*.
12:11 nomads begged Judas to make *f* with them
14:11 the other *F* who were hostile to Judas
Jb 2:11 Now when three of Job's *f* heard of all the
16:20 My *f* it is who wrong me;
19:13 from me, and my *f* are wholly estranged.
19:19 All my intimate *f* hold me in horror;
19:21 Pity me, pity me, O you my *f*,
24: 1 and why do his *f* not see his days?
32: 3 He was angry also with the three *f* because
42: 7 "I am angry with you and with your two *f*;
42:10 of Job, after he had prayed for his *f*;
Ps(s) 31:12 to my neighbors, and a dread to my *f*;
36:11 Keep up your kindness toward your *f*,
38:12 My *f* and my companions stand back because
69:23 a snare before them, and a net for their *f*.
88: 9 You have taken my *f* away from me;
122: 8 Because of my relatives and *f* I will say,
Prv 14:20 is hated, but the *f* of the rich are many.
16:28 and a talebearer separates bosom *f*.
17: 9 but he who gossips about it separates *f*.
18:24 Some *f* bring ruin on us,
19: 4 Wealth adds many *f*,
19: 6 are *f* of the man who has something to give.
19: 7 how much more do his *f* shun him!
Sg 5: 1 Eat, *f*; drink!
8:13 my *f* are listening for your voice,
Wis 7:27 to age, she produces *f* of God and prophets.
Sir 1: 8 he has lavished her upon his *f*.
6: 5 A kind mouth multiplies *f*,
6:13 be on your guard with your *f*.
12: 8 In our prosperity we cannot know our *f*;
20:15 A fool has no *f*,
22:23 Make fast *f* with a man while he is poor;
30: 3 and shows his delight in him among his *f*.
30: 6 and the one to repay his *f* with kindness.
37: 1 there are *f* who are friends in name only.
41:22 Of using harsh words with *f*,
Is 5: 1 friend, my *f* song concerning his vineyard.
Jer 6:21 sons alike, neighbors and *f* shall perish.
9: 7 He speaks cordially with his *f*,
20: 4 deliver you to terror, you and all your *f*.
20: 6 Babylon you shall go, you and all your *f*;
20:10 *f* are on the watch for any misstep of mine.
31:34 their *f* and kinsmen how to know the LORD.
38:22 betrayed you, outdid you, your good *f*!
Lam 1: 2 Her *f* have all betrayed her and become her
Dn 14: 2 esteem than any of the *f* of the king.
Lk 7: 6 house, the centurion sent *f* to tell him:
12: 4 "I say to you who are my *f*:
14:12 do not invite your *f* or brothers or
15: 6 *f* and neighbors in and says to them,
15: 9 she calls in her *f* and neighbors to say,
15:29 much as a kid goat to celebrate with my *f*.
16: 9 Make *f* for yourselves through your use of
21:16 by your parents, brothers, relatives and *f*,
23:12 against each other, became *f* from that day.
23:49 All his *f* and the women who had
Jn 15:13 to lay down one's life for one's *f*.
15:14 You are my *f* if you do what I command you.
15:15 Instead, I call you *f*,
Acts 7:26 *F*, you are blood brothers.
10:24 had called in his relatives and close *f*.
14:15 *F*, why do you do this?"
19:31 Even some of the Asiarchs who were *f* of
24:23 to prevent his *f* from seeing to his wants.
27: 3 to visit some *f* who cared for his needs.
2Pt 3: 1 am writing you this second letter, dear *f*,
3: 8 This point must not be overlooked, dear *f*.

FRIENDSHIP (33)

Nm 25:12 that I hereby give him my pledge of *f*,
1Sm 20: 3 well aware that I am favored with your *f*,
1Mc 8:12 who relied on them, they maintained *f*.
8:17 to establish an alliance of *f* with them.
10:23 get ahead of us by gaining the *f* of the Jews
10:26 in our *f* and not gone over to our enemies,
10:54 let us now establish *f* with each other.
12: 1 to confirm and renew his *f* with the Romans.
12: 3 *f* and alliance between you and them."
12: 8 which clearly referred to alliance and *f*.
12:10 you for the renewal of brotherhood and *f*,
12:16 renew our former *f* and alliance with them.
14:18 tablets of bronze to renew with him the *f*
14:22 have come to us to renew their *f* with us,
15:17 to us to renew their earlier alliance of *f*.
2Mc 4:11 to establish a treaty of *f* with them);
6:22 kindly because of their old *f* with him.
11:26 to give them our assurances of *f*,
12:12 After the pledge of *f* had been exchanged,
14:26 When Alcimus saw their *f* for each other,
Ps(s) 25:14 *f* of the LORD is with those who fear him,
Prv 3:32 abomination, but with the upright is his *f*.
17: 9 He who covers up a misdeed fosters *f*,
Wis 7:14 who gain this treasure win the *f* of God,
8:18 with Wisdom, and good pleasure in her *f*,
Sir 22:20 he who insults a friend breaks up the *f*.
25: 1 Harmony among brethren, *f* among neighbors,
27:18 a man, you have killed your neighbor's *f*.
28: 9 *f* and sows discord among those at peace.
37: 1 Every friend declares his *f*,
45:24 conferred the right, in a covenant of *f*,
Jer 16: 5 For I have withdrawn my *f* from this people,
Lk 11: 8 up and take care of the man because of *f*,

FRIGHT (5)

Ex 14:10 In great *f* they cried out to the LORD.
2Kgs 10: 4 They were overcome with *f* and said,
Zec 12: 4 the LORD, I will strike every horse with *f*,
Lk 21:26 Men will die of *f* in anticipation of what
24:37 *f* they thought they were seeing a ghost.

FRIGHTEN (11)

Dt 28:26 of the field, with no one to *f* them off.
2Chr 32:18 to *f* and terrify them so that they might
Neh 6: 9 They were all trying to *f* us,
6:14 the other prophets who were trying to *f* me.
6:19 and Tobiah sent letters trying to *f* me.
Jb 9:34 Would that his terrors did not *f* me;
13:21 me, and let not the terror of you *f* me.
Ps(s) 31:14 of the crowd, that *f* me from every side,
Jer 36:24 Hearing all these words did not *f* the king
Ez 34:28 shall dwell secure, with no one to *f* them.
39:26 on their land with no one to *f* them.

FRIGHTENED (26)

Gn 31:31 "I was *f*," Jacob replied to Laban,
32: 8 Jacob was very much *f*.
Dt 16: 3 for in *f* haste you left the land of Egypt.
20: 3 be neither alarmed nor *f* by them.
1Sm 4: 7 come into the camp, the Philistines were *f*.
31: 4 But his armor-bearer, badly *f*,
2Kgs 19: 6 Do not be *f* by the words you have heard,
2Chr 20: 3 Jehoshaphat was *f*,
1Mc 1:18 Ptolemy was *f* at his presence and fled,
Wis 17: 9 For even though no monstrous thing *f* them,
Sir 42:14 and a *f* daughter than any disgrace.
Is 31: 4 Is neither *f* by their shouts nor disturbed
35: 4 are weak, Say to those whose hearts are *f*:
37: 6 Do not be *f* by the words you have heard,
Jer 3: 8 her traitor sister Judah was not *f*;
36:16 words, they were *f* and said to one another,
Dn 4: 2 the images and the visions of my mind *f* me.
Hos 11:10 roars, his sons shall come *f* from the west,
Am 3: 6 sounds in a city, will the people not be *f*?
Jon 1: 5 became *f* and each one cried to his god.
Mt 14:30 how strong the wind was, becoming *f*,
28: 5 not be *f*. I know you are looking for Jesus
Mk 16: 6 This *f* them thoroughly,
Lk 1:13 "Do not be *f*, Zechariah;
Jn 6:19 They were *f*, but he told them, "It is I;
Acts 24:25 and the coming judgment, Felix became *f*.

FRIGHTFUL (2)

2Mc 14:45 with blood gushing from his *f* wounds.
Wis 11:19 even their *f* appearance itself could slay.

FRISK (1)

Jer 50:11 *F* like calves on the green,

FRISKY (1)

Dt 32:15 ate his fill, the darling grew fat and *f*;

FRIVOLITY (1)

Sir 30:10 not in his *f* lest you share in his sorrow,

FRO (4)

Jer 49: 3 Put on sackcloth and mourn, run to and *f*,
Ez 1:13 moving to and *f* among the living creatures.
Zec 7:14 after them with no one traveling to and *f*;
9: 8 as a guard that none may pass to and *f*;

FROGS (15)

Ex 7:27 send a plague of *f* over all your territory.
7:28 The river will teem with *f*.
7:29 The *f* will swarm all over you and your
8: 1 pools, to make *f* overrun the land of Egypt."
8: 2 *f* came up and covered the land of Egypt.
8: 3 too, made *f* overrun the land of Egypt.
8: 4 to remove the *f* from me and my subjects,
8: 5 that the *f* may be taken away from you and
8: 7 The *f* shall leave you and your houses,
8: 8 promise he had made to Pharaoh about the *f*;
8: 9 The *f* in the houses and courtyards and
Ps(s) 78:45 devoured them and *f* that destroyed them.
105:30 Their land swarmed with *f*,
Wis 19:10 fishes the river swarmed with countless *f*.
Rv 16:13 like *f* come from the mouth of the dragon,

FROLIC (1)

Is 32:19 wasteland forever for wild asses to *f* in,

FRONDS (1)

Sg 5:11 his locks are palm *f*,

FRONT (105)

Gn 30:38 so that they would be in *f* of the animals
40: 9 he said, "I saw a vine in *f* of me,
Ex 13:22 ever left its place in *f* of the people.
14: 2 You shall camp in *f* of Baal-zephon,
14: 9 sea, at Pi-hahiroth, in *f* of Baal-zephon.
14:19 The column of cloud also, leaving the *f*,
16:34 in *f* of the commandments for safekeeping,
17: 5 Moses, "Go over there in *f* of the people,
17: 6 there in *f* of you on the rock in Horeb.
19: 2 was encamped here in *f* of the mountain,
25:37 light on the space in *f* of the lampstand.
26: 9 sixth sheet double at the *f* of the tent.
27:21 veil which hangs in *f* of the commandments.
28:25 fastened in *f* to the two filigree rosettes
28:27 next to where they join the ephod in *f*,
28:37 a way that it rests on the *f* of the miter,
29:10 the bullock in *f* of the meeting tent.
30: 6 This altar you are to place in *f* of the
32:15 were written on both sides, *f* and back;
39:18 fastened in *f* to the two filigree rosettes,
39:20 next to where they joined the ephod in *f*,
40: 5 in *f* of the ark of the commandments,
40: 6 Put the altar of holocausts in *f* of the
40:26 in the meeting tent, in *f* of the veil,
40:29 He put the altar of holocausts in *f* of the
Lv 6: 7 it before the LORD, in *f* of the altar.
8: 9 the sacred diadem, over the *f* of the miter,
13:41 if he loses the hair on the *f* of his head,
16: 2 veil, in *f* of the propitiatory of the ark;
16:14 seven times in *f* of the propitiatory.
17: 4 offering to the LORD in *f* of his Dwelling,
18:23 herself in *f* of an animal to mate with it;
19:14 or put a stumbling block in *f* of the blind,
24: 3 veil that hangs in *f* of the commandments,
Nm 3:38 that is, in *f* of the meeting tent,
8: 2 their light toward the *f* of the lampstand."
8: 3 to face toward the *f* of the lampstand,
8: 9 come forward in *f* of the meeting tent,
17: 8 Aaron came to the *f* of the meeting tent,
17:19 the meeting tent, in *f* of the commandments,
17:25 Aaron's staff in *f* of the commandments,
18: 2 are in *f* of the tent of the commandments.
19: 4 times toward the *f* of the meeting tent.
20:10 assembled the community in *f* of the rock,
Dt 26: 4 shall set it in *f* of the altar of the LORD,
Jos 4: 5 of the Jordan in *f* of the ark of the LORD,
4:11 also crossed to its place in *f* of them.
4:23 Jordan in *f* of you until you crossed over,
4:23 dried up in *f* of us until we crossed over;
6: 6 ram's horns in *f* of the ark of the LORD.
6: 9 In *f* of the priests with the horns marched
6:13 horns marched in *f* of the ark of the LORD,
7: 5 *f* of the city gate till they broke ranks,
1Sm 14:18 ephod in *f* of the Israelites at that time.)
2Sm 10: 9 drawn up against him, both *f* and rear,
11:15 "Place Uriah up *f*,
1Kgs 6: 3 The porch in *f* of the temple was twenty
6: 3 and ten cubits deep in *f* of the temple.
6:17 part of the temple in *f* of the sanctuary,
6:21 made in *f* of the sanctuary a cedar altar,
6:34 was banded by a metal strap, *f* and back,
7: 6 columned hall, and there was a canopy in *f*.
7: 9 to size and trimmed *f* and back with a saw,
2Kgs 16:14 LORD he brought from the *f* of the temple
1Chr 19:10 a battle line both in *f* of and behind him,
2Chr 1: 5 *f* of the LORD's Dwelling on the high place.
3:15 In *f* of the building he set two columns
8:12 LORD which he had built in *f* of the porch,
Neh 3:23 out the repair in *f* of their houses;
Jdt 4:11 themselves in *f* of the temple building,
12:15 ground for her in *f* of Holofernes the fleece
Est 2:11 walk about in *f* of the court of the harem,
4: 6 the public square in *f* of the royal gate,
D: 7 against the head of the maid in *f* of her.
1Mc 5:52 to the great plain in *f* of Beth-shan,
9:11 and all the valiant men were in the *f* line.
11:68 There, in *f* of him on the plain,
13:27 a monument of stones, polished *f* and back,
2Mc 3:25 horse attacked Heliodorus with its *f* hoofs.
Ez 2:10 It was covered with writing *f* and back,
4: 1 lay it in *f* of you,
9: 6 [the elders] who were in *f* of the temple.
40:15 the gate from the *f* entrance to the front
40:19 court from the *f* of the lower gate to the *f*
40:47 The altar stood in *f* of the temple.
41:12 the west side was seventy cubits *f* to back;
41:21 In *f* of the holy place was something that
42: 4 In *f* of the chambers,
Mt 23: 6 at banquets and the *f* seats in synagogues,
26:70 He denied it in *f* of everyone:
27:24 and washed his hands in *f* of the crowd,
Mk 3: 3 "Stand up here in *f*!"
5:33 in *f* of him and told him the whole truth.
12:39 in public, *f* seats in the synagogues,
Lk 6: 8 was withered, "Get up and stand here in *f*."
11:43 You love the *f* seats in synagogues and
14: 2 Directly in *f* of him was a man who
19: 4 He first ran on in *f*,
20:46 respect in public, *f* seats in synagogues,
Jn 8: 3 They made her stand there in *f* of everyone.
10: 4 those that are his, he walks in *f* of them,
Rv 4: 6 creatures covered with eyes *f* and back.
8: 3 on the altar of gold in *f* of the throne,

FRONTAL (2)

Jos 6: 5 and they will be able to make a *f* attack."
6:20 stormed the city in a *f* attack and took it.

FRONTALLY (1)

2Sm 5:23 "You must not attack *f*,

FRONTIER (18)

1Sm 15: 7 the approaches of Shur, on the *f* of Egypt.
1Mc 3:32 from the Euphrates River to the *f* of Egypt,
11:59 from the Ladder of Tyre to the *f* of Egypt.
14:33 Judea, especially the *f* city of Beth-zur,
Ez 29:10 to Syene, and even to the *f* of Ethiopia.
47:17 the *f* of Hamath and Damascus to the north.
48: 2 on the *f* of Dan,
48: 3 on the *f* of Asher,
48: 4 on the *f* of Naphtali,
48: 5 on the *f* of Manasseh,
48: 6 on the *f* of Ephraim,
48: 7 on the *f* of Reuben,
48: 8 On the *f* of Judah,
48:24 on the *f* of Benjamin,
48:25 on the *f* of Simeon,
48:26 on the *f* of Issachar,
48:27 on the *f* of Zebulun,
48:28 *f* of Gad shall be the southern boundary,

FRONTIERS (2)

1Mc 5:60 beaten, and were pursued to the *f* of Judea,
Ez 47:16 along the *f* of Hamath and Damascus,

FRONTING (2)

Nm 21:11 in the desert *f* Moab on the east.
Ez 41:12 The building *f* the free area on the west

FRONTS (1)

2Chr 13:14 and saw that they had to battle on both *f*,

FROST (10)

Gn 31:40 heat ravaged me by day, and the *f* by night,
Jb 37:10 With his breath God brings the *f*,
Ps(s) 78:47 vines with hail and their sycamores with *f*.
147:16 *f* he strews like ashes.
Wis 16:29 a wintry *f* and runs off like useless water.
Sir 3:15 warmth upon *f* it will melt away your sins.
43:20 He scatters *f* like so much salt;
Bar 2:25 to the heat of day and the *f* of night.
Dn 3:69 *F* and chill, bless the Lord;
Zec 14: 6 day there shall no longer be cold or *f*.

FROZEN (1)

Ex 15:16 might of your arm they were *f* like stone,

FRUIT (171)

Gn 1:11 kind of fruit tree on earth that bears *f*
1:12 on earth that bears *f* with its seed in it.
1:29 has seed-bearing *f* on it to be your food,
3: 2 eat of the *f* of the trees in the garden;
3: 3 it is only about the *f* of the tree in the
3: 6 So she took some of its *f* and ate it;
3:12 she gave me *f* from the tree,
3:22 hand to take *f* from the tree of life also,
4: 3 to the LORD God from the *f* of the soil,
30: 2 God, who has denied you the *f* of the womb?"
49: 3 my strength and the first *f* of my manhood,
Ex 10:15 *f* of whatever trees the hail had spared.
23:16 at the *f* harvest at the end of the year,
34:22 at the *f* harvest at the close of the year.
Lv 19:23 plant any *f* tree there, first look upon its *f*
19:23 years, while its *f* remains uncircumcised,
19:24 all of its *f* shall be sacred to the LORD
19:25 Not until the fifth year may you eat its *f*.
25:19 its *f* and you will have food in abundance,
26: 4 bear its crops, and the trees their *f*;
26:20 will bear no crops, and its trees no *f*.
27:30 from the fields or in *f* from the trees,
Nm 13:20 your best to get some of the *f* of the land."
13:26 all, and showed them the *f* of the country.
13:27 with milk and honey, and here is its *f*.
Dt 1:25 taking along some of the *f* of the land,
7:13 he will bless the *f* of your womb and the
20:19 You may eat their *f*,
20:20 you know are not *f* trees you may destroy,
24:20 you knock down the *f* of your olive trees,
28: 4 "Blessed be the *f* of your womb,
28:11 than goodly measure the *f* of your womb,
28:18 "Cursed be the *f* of your womb,
28:33 the *f* of your soil and of all your labor,
28:53 you, you will eat the *f* of your womb,
30: 9 from all your labors, the *f* of your womb,
Jgs 9:11 'Must I give up my sweetness and my good *f*,
2Kgs 3:19 every fortified city, fell every *f* tree,
18:32 and orchards, of olives, oil and *f* syrup.
19:29 and reap, plant vineyards and eat their *f*!
19:30 again strike root below and bear *f* above
Neh 9:25 olive groves, and *f* trees in abundance.
10:36 fruits of our fields and of our *f* trees,
10:38 and our offerings of the *f* of every tree,
1Mc 10:30 the *f* of the trees that should be my share,
11:34 produce of the soil and the *f* of the trees.
14: 8 produce and the trees of the field their *f*.
Ps(s) 1: 3 water, That yields its *f* in due season,
21:11 Destroy their *f* from the earth and their
80:13 so that every passer-by plucks its *f*,
92:15 They shall bear *f* even in old age;
104:13 earth is replete with the *f* of your works.
105:35 they devoured the *f* of their soil.
109:11 and strangers plunder the *f* of his labors.
127: 3 the *f* of the womb is a reward.
128: 2 For you shall eat the *f* of your handiwork;
148: 9 you hills, you *f* trees and all you cedars;
Prv 1:31 "Now they must eat the *f* of their own way,
8:19 My *f* is better than gold,
11:30 The *f* of virtue is a tree of life,
12:14 From the *f* of his words a man has his fill
13: 2 the *f* of his words a man eats good things,
14:14 and the good man reaps the *f* of his paths.
18:20 From the *f* of his mouth a man has his fill;
18:21 those who make it a friend shall eat its *f*.
27:18 He who tends a fig tree eats its *f*,
Eccl 2: 5 and set out in them *f* trees of all sorts.
2:10 my heart rejoiced in the *f* of all my toil.
3:13 the *f* of all his labor is a gift of God.
5: 9 and the lover of wealth reaps no *f* from it;
Sg 2: 3 shadow, and his *f* is sweet to my mouth.
8:11 For its *f* one would have to pay a
8:12 two hundred for the caretakers of its *f*.
Wis 3:13 shall bear *f* at the visitation of souls.
3:15 the *f* of noble struggles is a glorious one;
4: 5 off untimely, and their *f* be useless,
10: 7 desert, Plants bearing *f* that never ripens,
10:10 and made abundant the *f* of his works,
Sir 11:22 just man, and in due time his hopes bear *f*.
23:25 her branches will not bring forth *f*.
24:17 vine, my blossoms become *f* fair and rich.
27: 6 The *f* of a tree shows the care it has had;
28:15 homes and rob them of the *f* of their toil;
50:10 Like a luxuriant olive tree thick with *f*,
Is 3:10 them, the *f* of their works they will eat.
4: 2 and the *f* of the earth will be honor and
13:18 The *f* of the womb they shall not spare,
14:29 an adder, its *f* shall be a flying saraph.
27: 6 and blossom, covering all the world with *f*.
27: 9 this the whole *f* of the removal of his sin:
37:30 and reap, plant vineyards and eat their *f*!
37:31 again strike root below and bear *f* above.
65:21 and eat the *f* of the vineyards they plant;
Jer 6:19 this people, the *f* of their own schemes,
12: 2 root, they keep on growing and bearing *f*.
17: 8 it shows no distress, but still bears *f*.
32:19 his ways, according to the *f* of his deeds:
40:10 to collect the wine, the *f* and the oil,
40:12 and had a rich harvest of wine and *f*.
48:33 end in the *f* gardens of the land of Moab.
Ez 17: 8 it was planted, to grow branches, bear *f*,
17: 9 it out by the roots and strip off its *f*,
17:23 It shall put forth branches and bear *f*,
19:12 wind withered her up, her *f* was torn off;
36: 8 branches and bear *f* for my people Israel,
36:30 I will increase the *f* on your trees and
47:12 river, *f* trees of every kind shall grow;
47:12 leaves shall not fade, nor their *f* fail.
47:12 Every month they shall bear fresh *f*,
47:12 Their *f* shall serve for food,
Dn 4: 9 leaves were beautiful and its *f* abundant,

FRUIT (cont.)

4:11 strip off its leaves and scatter its *f*;
4:18 had beautiful foliage and abundant *f*,
Hos 9:16 they shall bear no *f*.
10: 1 luxuriant vine whose *f* matches its growth.
10: 1 The more abundant his *f*,
10:12 yourselves justice, reap the *f* of piety;
10:13 perversity, and eaten the *f* of falsehood.
14: 9 Because of me you bear *f*!
Jl 2:22 The tree bears its *f*,
Am 2: 9 I destroyed their *f* above,
6:12 gall, and the *f* of justice into wormwood.
8: 1 Lord GOD showed me: a basket of ripe *f*.
8: 2 I answered, "A basket of ripe *f*."
Mi 6: 7 the *f* of my body for the sin of my soul?
7: 1 I am as when the *f* is gathered,
Hb 3:17 fig tree blossom not nor *f* be on the vines,
Zec 8:12 the vine shall yield its *f*,
Mt 7:17 fruit, while a decayed tree bears bad *f*.
7:18 A sound tree cannot bear bad *f* any more
7:18 more than a decayed tree can bear good *f*.
7:19 *f* is cut down and thrown into the fire.
7:20 You can tell a tree by its *f*.
12:33 Declare a tree good and its *f* good or
12:33 or declare a tree rotten and its *f* rotten,
12:33 other, for you can tell a tree by its *f*.
21:19 to it, "Never again shall you produce *f*!";
26:29 I will not drink this *f* of the vine from
Mk 11:14 "Never again shall anyone eat of your *f*!"
14:25 I will never again drink of the *f* of the
Lk 1:42 women and blest is the *f* of your womb.
6:43 "A good tree does not produce decayed *f*
6:43 more than a decayed tree produces good *f*.
8:15 retain it, and bear *f* through perseverance.
13: 6 looking for *f* on it but did not find any.
13: 7 of *f* on this fig tree and found none.
13: 9 then perhaps it will bear *f*.
22:18 I will not drink of the *f* of the vine
Jn 12:24 But if it dies, it produces much *f*.
15: 4 can bear *f* of itself apart from the vine,
15: 4 the vine, can you bear *f* apart from me.
15: 8 bearing much *f* and becoming my disciples.
15:16 was I who chose you to go forth and bear *f*.
15:16 Your *f* must endure,
Rom 7: 4 the dead, so that we might bear *f* for God.
7: 5 in our members and we bore *f* for death.
2Cor 7:11 the *f* of this sorrow which stems from God.
Gal 4:23 of the free woman was the *f* of the promise.
5:22 In contrast, the *f* of the spirit is love,
Phil 4:10 that your concern for me bore *f* once more.
Col 1: 6 which has come to you, has borne *f*,
Heb 12:11 but later it brings forth the *f* of peace
13:15 the *f* Final Exhortation of lips which
2Pt 1: 8 they bear *f* in true knowledge of our Lord
Jude 1:12 trees at the year's end they bear no *f*,
Rv 18:14 *f* your appetite craved has deserted you.
22: 2 life which produce *f* twelve times a year,

FRUITFUL (21)

Gn 29:31 saw that Leah was unloved, he made her *f*,
30:22 he heard her prayer and made her *f*.
35:11 "I am God Almighty; be *f* and multiply.
41:52 has made me *f* in the land of my affliction."
Ex 1: 7 But the Israelites were *f* and prolific.
Lv 26: 9 upon you, and make you *f* and numerous,
Ps(s) 107:34 thirsty ground, *F* land into salt marsh,
107:37 vineyards, And they obtained a *f* yield.
128: 3 like a *f* vine in the recesses of your home;
Is 17: 6 very top, four or five on its *f* branches,
32:12 for the pleasant fields, the *f* vine,
55:10 the earth, making it fertile and *f*,
Jer 3:16 When you multiply and become *f* in the land,
Ez 19:10 *F* and branchy was she because of the
36:11 and beasts upon you, to multiply and be *f*.
Hos 13:15 Though he be *f* among his fellows,
Mt 3:10 Every tree that is not *f* will be cut down
Lk 3: 9 Every tree that is not *f* will be cut down
Jn 15: 2 but the *f* ones he trims clean to increase
Rom 1:13 it) in order to do some *f* work among you,
Ti 3:14 they may be in position to live *f* lives.

FRUITION (2)

2Sm 23: 5 to *f* all my salvation and my every desire?
1Cor 15:38 to each seed its own *f*.

FRUITLESS (4)

Ps(s) 90:10 we are strong, And most of them are *f* toil,
Wis 3:11 Vain is their hope, *f* are their labors,
15: 4 deceive us, nor the *f* labor of painters,
1Cor 15:10 This favor of his to me has not proved *f*.

FRUITS (81)

Gn 31:42 But God saw my plight and the *f* of my toil,
Ex 23:19 The choicest first *f* of your soil you
34:26 "The choicest first *f* of your soil you
Lv 2:12 to the LORD in the offering of first *f*,
2:14 a cereal offering of first *f* to the LORD,
23:10 the first *f* of your harvest to the priest,
23:17 wave offering of your first *f* to the LORD,
23:20 shall wave the bread of the first *f*
Nm 18:12 they give to the LORD as their first *f*;
28:26 "On the day of first *f*,
Dt 18: 4 the first *f* of your grain and wine and oil,
18: 4 the first *f* of the shearing of your flock;
20: 6 a vineyard and never yet enjoyed its *f*?
20: 6 and another enjoy its *f* in his stead.
21:17 since he is the first *f* of his manhood,
26: 2 you shall take some first *f*
26:10 *f* of the products of the soil which you,
28:30 plant a vineyard, you will not enjoy its *f*.
2Sm 16: 1 of pressed raisins, an ephah of summer *f*,
16: 2 and summer *f* are for your servants to eat,
2Kgs 4:42 twenty barely loaves made from the first *f*,
Neh 9:36 that they might eat its *f* and good things
10:36 *f* of our fields and of our fruit trees,
12:44 set aside for stores, offerings, first *f*,
13:31 wood at stated times and for the first *f*.
Tb 1: 6 Bringing with me the first *f* of the field
1: 7 olive oil, pomegranates, figs, and other *f*.
Jdt 11:13 they would use up the first *f* of grain
1Mc 3:49 them the priestly vestments, the first *f*,
Jb 39:11 and leave to him the *f* of your toil?
Ps(s) 58: 3 on earth you look to the *f* of extortion.
67: 7 The earth has yielded its *f*;
78:46 the *f* of their toil to the locust.
78:51 the first *f* of manhood in the tents of Ham;
105:36 land, the first *f* of all their manhood.
Prv 3: 9 wealth, with first *f* of all your produce;
Eccl 2:18 all the *f* of my labor under the sun,
2:19 all the *f* of my wise labor under the sun.
2:20 of all the *f* of my labor under the sun.
5:17 enjoy all the *f* of his labor under the sun
5:18 his lot and finds joy in the *f* of his toil,
Sg 4:13 forth pomegranates, with all choice *f*;
4:16 come to his garden and eat its choice *f*.
7:14 choice *f*; Both fresh and mellowed fruits,
Wis 8: 7 justice, the *f* of her works are virtues;
16:22 they might know that their enemies' *f*
16:26 the various kinds of *f* that nourish man,
Sir 1:14 she inebriates men with her *f*.
6: 3 Your leaves it will eat, your *f* destroy,
6:20 but little, and soon you will eat of her *f*.
7:31 First *f* and contributions,
24:18 yearn for me, and be filled with my *f*;
24:23 like the Tigris in the days of the new *f*.
35:11 not in sacrifice of the *f* of extortion,
37:21 the *f* of his knowledge are seen in his own
37:22 the *f* of his knowledge are enduring:
Is 16: 9 *f* and harvests the battle cry has fallen.
Jer 2: 3 was Israel, the first *f* of his harvest;
2: 7 into the garden land to eat its goodly *f*,
7:20 trees of the field and the *f* of the earth;
29: 5 plant gardens, and eat their *f*.
29:28 plant gardens and eat their *f*. . . ."
31: 5 those who plant them shall enjoy the *f*.
Lam 4: 9 through, lacking the *f* of the field!
Ez 20:40 tributes and the first *f* of your offerings,
25: 4 they shall eat your *f* and drink your milk.
34:27 The trees of the field shall bear their *f*,
44:30 All the choicest first *f* of every kind,
Dn 3:38 or incense, no place to offer first *f*,
Hos 9:10 the first *f* of the fig tree in its prime,
Am 9:14 the wine, set out gardens and eat the *f*.
Rom 8:23 although we have the Spirit as first *f*,
11:16 If the first *f* are consecrated,
1Cor 15:20 first *f* of those who have fallen asleep.
15:23 Christ the first *f* and then,
16:15 Stephanas is the first *f* of Achaia
2Thes 2:13 because you are the first *f* of those whom
Jas 1:18 may be a kind of first *f* of his creatures.
3:17 and the kindly deeds that are its *f*,
Rv 14: 4 first *f* of mankind for God and the Lamb.

FRUSTRATED (1)

Jb 6:20 they come there and are *f*.

FRUSTRATES (1)

Jb 5:12 He *f* the plans of the cunning,

FRUSTRATION (1)

Dt 28:20 and *f* in every enterprise you undertake,

FRY (1)

2Mc 7: 5 them to carry him to the fire and *f* him.

FUEL (10)

1Kgs 19:21 equipment for *f* to boil their flesh,
2Mc 14:11 quickly added *f* to Demetrius' indignation.
Jb 20: 7 he perishes forever like the *f* of his fire,
Is 9: 4 in blood, will be burned as *f* for flames.
9:18 quakes, and the people are like *f* for fire;
40:16 Lebanon would not suffice for *f*,
44:15 and the rain made grow to serve man for *f*.
Ez 15: 4 If you throw it on the fire as *f* and the
15: 6 which I have destined as *f* for the fire,
21:37 You shall be *f* for the fire,

FUGITIVE (13)

Gn 14:13 A *f* came and brought the news to Abram the
Nm 24:18 is dispossessed, and no *f* is left in Seir.
1Sm 22:17 he was a *f* and yet failed to inform me."
Tb 1:18 slew when he returned as a *f* from Judea
2Mc 4:26 out as a *f* to the country of the Ammonites.
Jb 27:22 His hand pierces the *f* dragon as from his
Sir 36: 8 Let raging fire consume the *f*,
40: 6 mind's eye sees, like a *f* being pursued;
Lam 2:22 day of your wrath, either *f* or survivor;
Ez 24:26 daughters, that day the *f* will come to you,
33:21 the *f* came to me from Jerusalem and said,
33:22 upon me the evening before the *f* arrived
33:22 mouth when the *f* reached me in the morning.

FUGITIVES (14)

Nm 21:29 He let his sons become *f* and his daughters
Jos 8:22 without any *f* or survivors except the king,
Jgs 5:13 Then down came the *f* with the mighty,
12: 4 "You of Gilead are Ephraimite *f* in
2Mc 10:15 they welcomed *f* from Jerusalem and
Wis 19: 3 sent away with entreaty, they pursued as *f*.
Is 15: 5 out, his *f* reach Zoar [Eglath-shelishiyah].
16: 3 To hide the outcasts, to conceal the *f*.
21:14 the land of Tema, greet the *f* with bread.
45:20 together, you *f* from among the gentiles!
66:19 from them I will send *f* to the nations:
Jer 49: 5 flight, with no one to rally the *f*.
50:28 the *f*, the escaped from the land
Ob 1:14 Betray not his *f* on the day of distress!

FULFILL (84)

Ex 8: 8 Moses implored the LORD to *f* the promise
Nm 23:19 to speak and not act, to decree and not *f*?
30: 3 must *f* exactly the promise he has uttered.
32:24 flocks, but also *f* your express promise."
Dt 1:18 I gave you all the commands you were to *f*.
17:19 and to heed and *f* all the words of this
23:24 But you must keep your solemn word and *f*
27:26 to *f* any of the provisions of this law!'
29: 8 of this covenant, therefore, and *f* them,
Jos 2:17 is how we will *f* the oath you made us take:
23:15 for you, so will he *f* every threat,
1Sm 1:21 sacrifice to the LORD and to *f* his vows,
15:20 *f* the mission on which the LORD sent me.
2Sm 15: 7 to Hebron and *f* a vow I made to the LORD.
1Kgs 1:30 will *f* the oath I swore to you by the LORD,
2: 4 and the LORD may *f* the promise he made on
6:12 I will *f* toward you the promise I made to
12:15 *f* the prophecy he had uttered to Jeroboam,
2Kgs 22:13 this book, nor *f* our written obligations."
2Chr 10:15 ordained to *f* the prophecy the LORD
31:16 according to the daily rule to *f* their service
36:21 *f* the word of the LORD spoken by Jeremiah:
36:22 *f* the word of the LORD spoken by Jeremiah,
Ezr 1: 1 *f* the word of the LORD spoken by Jeremiah,
Jdt 2:13 *f* them exactly as I have commanded you,
Est 5: 5 Haman make haste to *f* the wish of Esther."
1Mc 8:26 They shall *f* their obligations without
8:28 *f* their obligations without deception.
Jb 22:27 will hear you, and your vows you shall *f*.
39: 2 hinds, Number the months that they must *f*,
Ps(s) 20: 5 is in your heart and *f* your every plan.
22:26 I will *f* my vows before those who fear him.
50:14 sacrifice and *f* your vows to the Most High;
56:13 your thank offerings I will *f*.
66:13 to you I will *f* the vows Which my lips
76:12 vows to the LORD, your God, and *f* them;
103:18 covenant and remember to *f* his precepts.
119:38 *F* for your servant your promise to those
119:112 in my heart to *f* your statutes always,
119:166 salvation, O LORD, and your commands I *f*.
148: 8 snow and mist, storm winds that *f* his word;
Eccl 5: 3 *f* what you have vowed.
5: 4 not make a vow than make it and not *f* it.
Sir 18:22 wait not to *f* them when you are dying.
18:23 Before making a vow have the means to *f* it;
19:16 thus will you *f* the law of the Most High.
36:14 *f* the prophecies spoken in your name,
Is 19:21 and *f* the vows they make to the LORD.
Jer 1:12 you seen, for I am watching to *f* my word.
11: 5 *f* the oath which I swore to your fathers,
25:13 Against that land I will *f* all the words I
28: 6 May he *f* the things you have prophesied by
29:10 I visit you and *f* for you my promise
33:14 when I will *f* the promise I made to the
36:31 men of Judah I will *f* all the threats of evil
44:25 "We will continue to *f* the vows we have
Bar 6:34 if one fails to *f* a vow to them,
6:61 across the whole world, *f* the order;
Ez 13: 6 then they wait for him to *f* their word!
Na 2: 1 your feasts, O Judah, *f* your vows!
Mt 1:22 All this happened to *f* what the Lord had
2:15 to *f* what the Lord had said through the
3:15 do this if we would *f* all of God's demands."
4:14 to *f* what had been said through Isaiah the
5:17 come, not to abolish them, but to *f* them.
12:17 This was to *f* what had been said through
13:35 *f* what had been said through the prophet:
21: 4 to *f* what was said through the prophet:
Lk 9:31 which he was about to *f* in Jerusalem.
12:47 to *f* them will get a severe beating,
Jn 12:38 was to *f* the word of the prophet Isaiah:
18: 9 (This was to *f* what he had said,
18:32 (This was to *f* what Jesus had said
19:28 was now finished, said to *f* the Scripture,
Acts 13:22 my own heart who will *f* my every wish.'

Rom 15:21 but rather to *f* the words of Scripture,
1Cor 7: 3 *f* his conjugal obligations toward his wife,
2Cor 7: 1 God strive to *f* our consecration perfectly.
Gal 6: 2 in that way you will *f* the law of Christ.
2Thes 1:11 and *f* by his power every honest intention
2Tm 4: 5 work as an evangelist, *f* your ministry.
Heb 13:17 So act that they may *f* their task with joy,
Jas 1:20 for a man's anger does not *f* God's justice.
2: 8 however, if you *f* the law of the kingdom.

FULFILLED (76)

Lv 12: 4 till the days of her purification are *f.*
12: 6 for a son or for a daughter are *f,*
Nm 1:54 *f* as the LORD had commanded Moses.
Dt 18:22 LORD, if his oracle is not *f* or verified,
30: 1 the blessings and the curses, are *f* in you,
Jos 8:26 *f* the doom on all the inhabitants of Ai.
10:28 He *f* the doom on the city,
10:35 *f* the doom that day on every person in it,
10:37 *f* the doom on it and on every person there.
10:39 sword and *f* the doom on every person there,
10:40 but *f* the doom on all who lived there,
11:11 He also *f* the doom by putting every person
11:21 *f* the doom on them and on their cities,
21:45 every one was *f.*
23:14 Every promise has been *f* for you,
23:15 your God, made to you has been *f* for you,
1Sm 10: 7 When you see these signs *f,*
28:21 my hands and *f* the request you made of me.
1Kgs 8:20 the LORD has *f* the promise that he made:
2Kgs 7:18 Thus was *f* the prophecy of the man of God
15:12 sit upon the throne of Israel," was *f.*
2Chr 1: 9 may your promise to my father David be *f,*
6:10 the LORD has *f* the promise that he made.
36:21 shall have rest while seventy years are *f.*"
Neh 9: 8 These promises of yours you *f,*
Est C:16 and that you *f* all your promises to them.
F: 8 These two lots were *f* in the hour,
Ps(s) 65: 2 To you must vows be *f,*
119:121 I have *f* just ordinances;
Prv 7:14 offerings, and today I have *f* my vows;
13:12 heart sick, but a wish *f* is a tree of life.
Eccl 6: 7 is for his mouth, yet his desire is not *f.*
Sir 32: 2 when you have *f* your duty,
34: 8 The law is *f* without fail,
48:25 the end of time, hidden things yet to be *f.*
Is 25: 1 For you have *f* your wonderful plans of old,
Jer 23:20 and *f* what he has determined in his heart.
28: 9 only when his prophetic prediction is *f.*
30:24 and *f* what he has determined in his heart.
44:29 threats of punishment for you shall be *f,*
Lam 2:17 *f* the threat He set forth from days of old;
Bar 2: 1 *f* the warning he had uttered against us:
2:24 and you *f* the threats you had made through
Ez 39: 8 Yes, it is coming and shall be *f,*
48:11 who *f* my service and did not stray along
Dn 4:30 At once this was *f.*
9: 2 ruins of Jerusalem seventy years must be *f.*
Mt 2:17 through Jeremiah the prophet was then *f:*
2:23 what was said through the prophets was *f:*
13:14 Isaiah's prophecy is *f* in them which says:
26:54 be *f* which say it must happen this way?"
27: 9 said through Jeremiah the prophet was *f:*
Mk 14:49 But now, so that the Scriptures may be *f* . . ."
16:20 of the years of Satan's power has been *f,*
Lk 1: 1 the events which have been *f* in our midst,
1:45 that the Lord's words to her would be *f.*"
2:29 you have *f* your word.
2:39 When the pair had *f* all the prescriptions
4:21 Scripture passage is *f* in your hearing."
21:22 when all that is written must be *f.*
21:24 until the times of the Gentiles are *f.*
22:16 again until it is *f* in the kingdom of God."
22:37 this, I tell you, must come to be *f* in me.
24:44 and the prophets and psalms had to be *f.*"
Jn 19:24 of this was to have the Scripture *f:*
Acts 1:16 of David was destined to be *f* in Judas,
13:27 and in condemning him they *f* the words of
13:33 God promised our fathers he has *f* for us,
26: 7 the hope that they will see that promise *f.*
Rom 8: 4 of the law might be *f* in us who live,
13: 8 He who loves his neighbor has *f* the law.
1Cor 15:54 then will the saying of Scripture be *f:*
2Cor 1:20 promises God has made have been *f* in him;
Gal 3:22 promise might be *f* in those who believe,
Jas 2:23 see how the Scripture was *f* which says,
Rv 21: 6 "These words are already *f!*

FULFILLING (13)

Dt 8:18 you the power to acquire wealth, by *f,*
23:22 your God, you shall not delay in *f* it;
Jos 11:12 put them to the sword, *f* the doom on them,
1Kgs 2:27 thus *f* the prophecy with the LORD had made
2Kgs 10:17 *f* the prophecy which the LORD had spoken
18:12 and not *f* the commandments of Moses,
1Chr 23:11 as a single family, *f* a single office.
Ps(s) 61: 9 your name forever, *f* my vows day by day.
Jer 39:16 now *f* the words I spoke against this city,
Ez 5: 7 living by my statutes nor *f* my ordinances,
Mt 8:17 thereby *f* what had been said through
Lk 1: 8 was *f* his functions as a priest before God,
Rom 15: 8 in *f* the promises to the patriarchs,

FULFILLMENT (31)

Gn 26: 3 in *f* of the oath that I swore to your
38: 8 widow, in *f* of your duty as brother-in-law,
Lv 22:21 from the herd or the flock in *f* of a vow,
Nm 15: 3 the flock, in holocaust, in *f* of a vow,
15: 8 an ox as a holocaust, or in *f* of a vow,
1Sm 1:23 Only, may the LORD bring your resolve to *f!*"
1Kgs 8:15 David and by his hand has brought it to *f.*
8:24 day, by your own power, brought it to *f.*
2Kgs 1:17 Ahaziah died in *f* of the prophecy of the
23:16 and thus defiled it in *f* of the word of
2Chr 6: 4 David and by his own hands brought it to *f.*
6:15 own hand you have brought it to *f* this day.
Neh 12:24 thanksgiving in *f* of the command of David,
Tb 8:17 their lives to *f* with happiness and mercy."
Ps(s) 119:96 I see that all *f* has its limits;
Eccl 5: 3 you make a vow to God, delay not its *f.*
Sir 19:17 perfect wisdom is the *f* of the law.
35: 4 all that you offer is in *f* of the precepts.
Ez 12:23 at hand, and also the *f* of every vision.
Dn 11:14 your people shall rise up in *f* of vision,
Hb 2: 3 still has its time, presses on to *f,*
Mt 26:56 in *f* of the writings of the prophets."
Mk 1:15 "This is the time of *f.*
Jn 13:18 my purpose here is the *f* of Scripture:
17:12 in *f* of Scripture.
19:36 events took place for the *f* of Scripture:
Acts 1: 4 rather, for the *f* of my Father's promise,
3:18 God has brought to *f* by this means what he
7:17 *f* of the promise made by God to Abraham,
Rom 13:10 neighbor, hence love is the *f* of the law.
Gal 5:14 law has found its *f* in this one saying:

FULFILLS (6)

Lv 27: 2 When anyone *f* a vow of offering one or
Ps(s) 145:19 He *f* the desire of those who fear him,
Sir 29: 1 and he *f* the precepts who holds out a
Is 44:28 My shepherd, who *f* my every wish;
Mt 5:19 Whoever *f* and teaches these commands shall
Jn 15:25 However, this only *f* the text in their law:

FULL (196)

Gn 6:11 the earth was corrupt and *f* of lawlessness.
6:13 earth is *f* of lawlessness because of them.
14:10 the Valley of Siddim was *f* of bitumen pits;
15:16 not have reached its *f* measure until then."
23: 9 it to me in your presence, at its *f* price,
25: 8 a ripe old age, grown old after a *f* life;
30:41 in the troughs in *f* view of these animals,
34:25 pain, Dinah's *f* brothers Simeon and Levi,
35:29 After a *f* life,
42: 4 It was only Joseph's *f* brother Benjamin
42:38 Now that his *f* brother is dead,
43:21 our money in the *f* amount!
43:29 eye fell on his *f* brother Benjamin,
44:20 This one's *f* brother is dead,
47: 2 whom he had selected from their *f* number.
50: 3 it, for that is the *f* period of embalming;
50:15 us back in *f* for all the wrong we did him!"
Ex 7:20 in *f* view of Pharaoh and his servants,
21:36 not keep it in, he must make *f* restitution,
22: 2 He must make *f* restitution.
22: 5 started the fire must make *f* restitution.
23:26 and I will give you a *f* span of life.
Lv 5:24 make *f* restitution of the thing itself,
16:12 he shall take a censer *f* of glowing embers
19:29 land will become corrupt and *f* of lewdness.
23:15 sheaf, you shall count seven *f* weeks,
25:29 the time of one *f* year from its sale.
25:30 not been redeemed at the end of a *f* year,
27:17 jubilee period, the *f* valuation shall hold;
Nm 5: 7 done, restore his ill-gotten goods in *f,*
5:30 priest shall apply this law in *f* to her.
18:29 to the LORD your own *f* contribution.
22:18 gave me his house *f* of silver and gold,
24:13 gave me his house *f* of silver and gold,
32:21 cross the Jordan in *f* force before the LORD
Dt 6:11 with houses *f* of goods of all sorts that
13: 7 "If your own *f* brother,
21:13 her father and mother for a *f* month,
Jgs 16:27 The temple was *f* of men and women:
Ru 2:12 May you receive a *f* reward from the LORD,
1Sm 3:12 On that day I will carry out in *f* against
8:10 *f* to those who were asking him for a king.
28:20 Saul fell *f* length on the ground,
2Sm 3:29 *f* responsibility for the death of Abner,
8: 2 for execution, and a *f* length to be spared.
10:15 by Israel with a *f* mustering of troops;
23:11 there was a plot of land *f* of lentils.
1Kgs 6: 9 When the temple was built to its *f* height,
1Chr 21:22 Sell it to me at its *f* price,
21:24 buy it from you properly, at its *f* price.
2Chr 29:30 They sang praises till their joy was *f,*
31:10 eaten to the *f* and have had much left over,
Ezr 6: 8 for their expenses, in *f* and without delay.
Tb 2:12 They paid her the *f* salary,
10:14 left Raguel, he was *f* of happiness and joy,
11:15 rejoicing and praising God with *f* voice.
12: 9 regularly give alms shall enjoy a *f* life;
13: 6 done for you, and praise him with *f* voice.
Est D: 6 royal throne, clothed in *f* robes of state,
D:14 lord, though your glance is *f* of kindness."
9:29 wrote to confirm with *f* authority this
2Mc 3: 6 Jerusalem was so *f* of untold riches
3:21 and the high priest *f* of dread and anguish.
4:37 Antiochus was deeply grieved and *f* of pity;
6:14 reach the *f* measure of their sins
6:30 in his holy knowledge knows *f* well that,
11:30 *f* permission to observe their dietary laws
13: 5 a tower seventy-five feet high, *f* of ashes,
13: 9 his mind *f* of savage plans for inflicting
Jb 5:26 You shall approach the grave in *f* vigor,
8:16 He is *f* of sap before sunrise,
14: 1 of woman is short-lived and *f* of trouble,
20:11 Though his frame is *f* of youthful vigor,
21:23 One dies in his *f* vigor,
21:24 His figure is *f* and nourished,
26: 9 *f* moon by spreading his clouds before it.
32:18 For I am *f* of matters to utter;
42:17 Then Job died, old and *f* of years.
Ps(s) 10: 7 His mouth is *f* of cursing,
26:10 and their right hands are *f* of bribes.
33: 5 of the kindness of the LORD the earth is *f.*
48:11 Of justice your right hand is *f;*
74:20 the land and the plains are *f* of violence.
75: 9 LORD's hand, *f* of spiced and foaming wine,
81: 4 the trumpet at the new moon, at the *f* moon,
104:24 the earth is *f* of your creatures;
119:64 Of your kindness, O LORD, the earth is *f;*
139:14 My soul also you knew *f* well;
144:13 May our garners be *f,*
Prv 7:20 not till the *f* moon will he return home."
11: 1 to the LORD, but a *f* weight is his delight.
17: 1 than a house *f* of feasting with strife.
27: 7 One who is *f,* tramples on virgin honey;
30: 9 Lest, being *f,* I deny you, saying,
Eccl 1: 7 the sea, yet never does the sea become *f.*
6: 3 if he has not the *f* benefit of his goods,
11: 3 When the clouds are *f,*
Wis 3: 4 yet is their hope *f* of immortality;
13:13 remnants, crooked wood grown *f* of knots,
Sir 1:17 and *f* understanding she showers down;
1:29 of the LORD with your heart *f* of guile.
19:22 bowed in grief, but is *f* of guile within;
26: 2 to her husband, peaceful and *f* is his life.
37:24 One wise for himself has *f* enjoyment,
39:35 So now with *f* joy of heart proclaim and
50: 6 like the *f* moon at the holyday season;
Is 1:15 Your hands are *f* of blood!
2: 7 Their land is *f* of silver and gold,
2: 7 Their land is *f* of horses,
2: 8 Their land is *f* of idols;
8: 8 spread its wings the *f* width of your land,
17: 4 Jacob shall fade, and his *f* body grow thin,
22: 2 the housetops, O city *f* of noise and chaos,
44:16 he eats what he has roasted until he is *f,*
57:18 I will give *f* comfort to them and to those
65: 6 will not be quiet until I have paid in *f*
65: 7 *f* measure their recompense into their laps.
65:20 man who does not round out his *f* lifetime;
Jer 5:27 *f* of treachery as a bird-cage is of birds;
15: 9 Her sun sets in *f* day,
29:11 plans to give you a future *f* of hope.
35: 5 I set before these Rechabite men bowls *f*
51: 5 And the Chaldean land is *f* of guilt to be
Lam 5:22 in *f* measure turned your wrath against us.
Bar 6:16 *f* of dust from the feet of those who enter.
Ez 1:18 that their rims were *f* of eyes all around.
7:10 Lawlessness is in *f* bloom,
7:23 with bloodshed and the city *f* of violence.
10:12 the four wheels were *f* of eyes all around.
27:25 You were *f* and heavily laden in the heart
41: 8 a *f* rod of six cubits in extent.
Dn 9:13 law of Moses, this calamity came *f* upon us.
10: 2 days, I, Daniel, mourned three *f* weeks.
Jl 2:24 The threshing floors shall be *f* of grain
4:13 Come and tread, for the wine press is *f;*
Mi 6:12 You whose rich men are *f* of violence,
Na 3: 1 to the bloody city, all lies, *f* of plunder,
Mt 13:48 When it was *f* they hauled it ashore and
15:37 All ate until they were *f.*
18:26 with me and I will pay you back in *f.*'
18:29 give me time and I will pay you back in *f.*'
20: 9 came up they received a *f* day's pay,
20:12 have worked a *f* day in the scorching heat.'
23:27 but inside *f* of filth and dead men's bones.
28:18 *F* authority has been given to me both in
Mk 8:20 *f* hampers of fragments did you collect?"
Lk 1:10 While the *f* assembly of people was praying
3:15 The people were *f* of anticipation,
4: 1 Jesus, *f* of the Holy Spirit,
5:12 town, a man *f* of leprosy came to him.
5:26 *F* of awe,
6:25 Woe to you who are *f;* you shall go hungry.
6:34 to sinners, expecting to be repaid in *f.*
8:35 at his feet dressed and in his *f* senses;
14:23 I want my house to be *f,*
24:12 away *f* of amazement at what had occurred.
Jn 6:13 they gathered twelve baskets *f* of pieces
10:10 they might have life and have it to the *f.*
16:24 you shall receive, that your joy may be *f.*
19:29 There was a jar there, *f* of common wine.
21: 8 came in the boat, towing the net *f* of fish.
Acts 5:21 the *f* council of the elders of Israel.

FULL (cont.)

5:41 for their part left the Sanhedrin *f* of joy
18:17 and beat him in *f* view of the bench;
18:25 Apollos was a man *f* of spiritual fervor.
28:30 For two *f* years Paul stayed on in his
28:31 With *f* assurance,
Rom 3:14 mouths are *f* of curses and bitterness.
11:12 world, how much more their *f* number!
11:25 until the *f* number of Gentiles enter in,
15:29 you, I shall come with Christ's *f* blessing.
1Cor 4:18 Some have grown *f* of self-importance,
9:18 *f* use of the authority the gospel gives me.
13: 2 the gift of prophecy and, with *f* knowledge,
2Cor 3:12 being such, we speak with *f* confidence.
4: 8 *f* of doubts,
5: 8 we are *f* of confidence and would much
Eph 1: 4 blameless in his sight, to be *f* of love;
1:14 first payment against the *f* redemption
4:13 man who is Christ come to *f* stature.
4:15 and the *f* maturity of Christ the head.
Phil 1:20 I have *f* confidence that now as always
4: 6 of prayer and in petitions *f* of gratitude.
Col 1: 9 you may attain *f* knowledge of his will
1:28 and teach them in the *f* measure of wisdom,
2: 2 enriched with *f* assurance by their
3:24 since you know *f* well you will receive an
4:12 that you be perfect and have *f* conviction
1Tm 1:15 depend on this as worthy of *f* acceptance:
6: 1 their masters as worthy of *f* respect;
Heb 2:14 Jesus likewise had a *f* share in ours,
Jas 3: 8 It is a restless evil, *f* of deadly poison.
2Jn 1: 8 you must receive your reward in *f*.
1:12 you face to face, so that our joy may be *f*.
Rv 10: 7 the prophets, shall be accomplished in *f*."
14:10 *f* strength into the cup of his anger.

FULL-BLOWN (1)

1Cor 15:37 When you sow, you do not sow the *f* plant,

FULL-GROWN (1)

Mt 13:32 yet when *f* it is the largest of plants.

FULL-LENGTH (1)

Wis 18:24 For on his *f* robe was the whole world,

FULL-THROATED (2)

Is 58: 1 Cry out *f* and unsparingly,
Jer 2:15 Against him lions roar *f* cries.

FULLERS (4)

2Kgs 18:17 upper pool on the highway of the *f* field.
Is 7: 3 upper pool, on the highway of the *f* field,
36: 2 upper pool, on the highway of the *f* field,
Mal 3: 2 like the refiner's fire, or like the *f* lye.

FULLEST (1)

Jas 3: 2 fault in speech he is a man in the *f* sense,

FULLNESS (20)

Dt 33:16 With the best of the earth and its *f*,
2Mc 6:15 later, when our sins have reached their *f*.
Ps(s) 16:11 path of life, *f* of joys in your presence,
24: 1 The LORD's are the earth and its *f*;
50:12 tell you, for mine are the world and its *f*.
89:12 the world and its *f* you have founded;
Wis 4:13 while, he reached the *f* of a long career;
Sir 1:14 *F* of wisdom is fear of the LORD;
3:13 revile him not in the *f* of your strength.
39:12 my theme to shine like the moon in its *f*!
Is 53:11 he shall see the light in *f* of days;
Jn 1:16 Of his *f* we have all had a share
1Cor 10:26 "The earth and its *f* are the Lord's."
Eph 1:10 Christ, to be carried out in the *f* of time:
1:23 the *f* of him who fills the universe in all
3:19 you may attain to the *f* of God himself.
Col 1:19 *f* reside in him and by means of him,
1:25 me to preach among you his word in its *f*,
2: 9 the *f* of deity resides in bodily form.
2: 9 Yours is a share of this *f*,

FULLY (46)

Gn 18:21 actions *f* correspond to the cry against them
30:35 them, as well as the *f* dark-colored sheep;
30:40 or *f* dark-colored animals of Laban.
Jos 9:24 servants were *f* informed of how the LORD,
Jgs 18:11 the Danites, *f* armed with weapons of war,
20:10 will go to deal *f* and suitably with Gibeah
1Sm 25: 9 this message *f* to Nabal in David's name,
2Sm 1: 9 for I am in great suffering, yet *f* alive.'
1Chr 11:13 The plow-land was *f* planted with barley,
Ezr 6:13 fellow officials carried out *f* the instructions
Est E: 2 but more *f* when one considers the wicked
2Mc 5: 2 *f* armed with lances and drawn swords;
5: 5 Jason gathered *f* a thousand men and
5:25 work, he ordered his men to parade *f* armed.
12:25 When he had *f* confirmed his solemn pledge
12:42 the sinful deed might be *f* blotted out.
15: 7 *f* convinced that he would receive help
Sir 4:17 the proof, until his heart is *f* with her.
38:17 Weeping bitterly, mourning *f*,
Is 1:24 on my foes and *f* repay my enemies!
66:11 you may suck *f* of the milk of her comfort,
Jer 2:21 you, a choice vine of *f* tested stock;
23:20 the time comes, you shall *f* understand.
30:24 When the time comes, you will *f* understand.
Dn 13:28 came, *f* determined to put Susanna to death.
Mt 14:36 as touched it were *f* restored to health.
Mk 5:15 sitting *f* clothed and perfectly sane,
Lk 11:21 a strong man *f* armed guards his courtyard,
11:36 it will be as *f* illumined as when a lamp
Jn 6:61 Jesus was *f* aware that his disciples were
13: 3 Jesus *f* aware that he had come from God
Rom 4:21 *f* persuaded that God could do whatever he
1Cor 8: 7 meat, *f* aware that it has been sacrificed,
15:58 *f* engaged in the work of the Lord.
Eph 1: 9 us the wisdom to understand *f* the mystery,
3:18 Thus you will be able to grasp *f*,
Phil 4:18 says that I have been *f* paid and more.
4:19 My God in turn will supply your needs *f*,
2Tm 2: 7 for the Lord will make my meaning *f* clear.
3:17 that the man of God may be *f* competent
Heb 6:11 end, *f* assured of that for which you hope.
Jas 1: 4 you may be *f* mature and lacking in nothing.
1Jn 2:28 we may be *f* confident and not retreat in
Jude 1: 3 I was already *f* intent on writing you,
Rv 14:15 the earth's harvest is *f* ripe."
16:15 Happy the man who stays wide awake and *f*

FUMES (1)

Gn 19:28 over the land rising like *f* from a furnace.

FUN (1)

Lk 23:36 The soldiers also made *f* of him,

FUNCTION (5)

1Sm 2:35 *f* in the presence of my anointed forever.
2:36 Appoint me, I beg you, to a priestly *f*,
2Kgs 23: 9 *f* at the altar of the LORD in Jerusalem;
Sir 33:13 Creator, to be assigned by him their *f*.
Rom 12: 4 and not all the members have the same *f*,

FUNCTIONARIES (2)

2Kgs 24:12 mother, his ministers, officers, and *f*,
24:15 Babylon the king's mother and wives, his *f*,

FUNCTIONED (1)

1Chr 24:19 when they *f* in the house of the LORD

FUNCTIONING (1)

Eph 4:16 and with the proper *f* of the members

FUNCTIONS (10)

Nm 3: 4 Ithamar performed the priestly *f*
3:10 appoint to have charge of the priestly *f*.
18: 7 priestly *f* in whatever concerns the altar
1Chr 24: 3 assigned the *f* for the priestly service.
24: 5 Their *f* were assigned impartially by lot,
25: 8 They cast lots for their *f* equally,
2Chr 8:14 according to their *f* of praise and ministry
Neh 13:30 the various *f* for the priests and Levites,
1Mc 14:42 its *f* and concerning the country,
Lk 1: 8 fulfilling his *f* as a priest before God,

FUND (1)

2Mc 3:10 money was a care *f* for widows and orphans,

FUNDS (18)

2Kgs 12: 5 "All the *f* for sacred purposes that are
12: 5 and whatever *f* are freely brought to the
12: 8 must no longer take *f* from your clients,
12: 9 they would neither take *f* from the people
12:10 all the *f* that were brought to the temple
12:11 the *f* that were in the temple of the LORD,
12:14 None of the *f* brought to the temple of the
12:16 provided with the *f* to give to the workmen,
12:17 The *f* from guilt-offerings and from
18:15 Hezekiah paid him all the *f* there were in
22: 7 of them regarding the *f* consigned to them,
1Mc 10:41 All the additional *f* that the officials
10:42 since these *f* belong to the priests who
2Mc 3:14 he went in to take an inventory of the *f*.
4: 1 about the *f* against his own country,
Bar 1: 6 and collected such *f* as each could furnish.
1:10 "We send you *f*, with which you are to
Mt 25:14 called in his servants and handed his *f* over

FUNERAL (7)

Gn 50:11 is a solemn *f* the Egyptians are having."
2Chr 16:14 also burned a very great *f* pyre for him.
2Mc 5:10 unmourned himself with no *f* of any kind
Jb 21:33 and over him the *f* mound keeps watch,
Wis 19: 3 For while they were still engaged in *f*
Sir 21: 8 is collecting stones for his *f* mound.
Bar 6:31 their gods as others do at a *f* banquet.

FURIES (1)

Ps(s) 88:17 Your *f* have swept over me;

FURIOUS (10)

Dt 29:22 *f* wrath they and all the nations will ask,
29:27 in his *f* wrath and tremendous anger the
1Mc 11:22 When Demetrius heard this, he was *f*,
Jer 42:18 Just as my *f* anger was poured out upon the
Ez 5:15 in anger and fury and with *f* chastisements,
22:20 I will gather you together in my *f* wrath,
Dn 8: 7 attack the ram with *f* blows when they met,
Jon 1: 4 and in the *f* tempest that arose the ship
Mt 2:16 deceived by the astrologers, he became *f*.
22: 7 At this the king grew *f* and sent his army

FURIOUSLY (7)

2Kgs 22:13 the LORD has been set *f* ablaze against us,
2Chr 25:10 They, however, became *f* angry with Judah,
34:21 the LORD has been set *f* ablaze against us,
2Mc 3:25 Charging *f*, the horse attacked Heliodorus
12:15 then they *f* stormed the ramparts.
Ez 8:18 Therefore I in turn will act *f*:
25:17 of vengeance on them, punishing them *f*.

FURLONG (1)

1Sm 14:14 slew about twenty men within half a *f*.

FURLONGS (1)

Rv 21:16 and found it twelve thousand *f* in length,

FURNACE (42)

Gn 19:28 over the land rising like fumes from a *f*.
Ex 9: 8 "Take a double handful of soot from a *f*,
9:10 a *f* and stood in the presence of Pharaoh.
19:18 The smoke rose from it as though from a *f*,
1Kgs 8:51 out of Egypt, from the midst of an iron *f*.
Ps(s) 21:10 Make them burn as though in a fiery *f*,
Prv 16:27 A scoundrel is a *f* of evil,
17: 3 crucible for silver, and the *f* for gold,
27:21 the crucible tests silver and the *f* gold,
Wis 3: 6 As gold in the *f*, he proved them,
Sir 27: 5 test of what the potter molds is in the *f*,
31:26 As the *f* probes the work of the smith,
38:28 his flesh, yet he toils away in the *f* heat.
43: 4 Like a blazing *f* of solid metal,
48: 1 prophet whose words were as a flaming *f*.
Is 1:25 you, and refine your dross in the *f*,
31: 9 has a fire in Zion and a *f* in Jerusalem.
48:10 silver, tested you in the *f* of affliction.
Lam 5:10 Our skin is shriveled up, as though by a *f*,
Ez 22:18 tin, iron and lead [in the midst of a *f*:
22:20 into a *f* and smelted in the roaring flames,
22:22 by it just as silver is smelted in a *f*.
Dn 3: 6 shall be instantly cast into a white-hot *f*."
3:11 did not was to be cast into a white-hot *f*.
3:15 be instantly cast into the white-hot *f*;
3:17 from the white-hot *f* and from your hands,
3:19 He ordered the *f* to be heated seven times
3:20 and cast them into the white-hot *f*.
3:21 cast into the white-hot *f* with their coats,
3:22 So huge a fire was kindled in the *f* that
3:23 bound, into the midst of the white-hot *f*.
3:46 in continued to stoke the *f* with brimstone,
3:47 flames rose forty-nine cubits above the *f*,
3:49 into the *f* with Azariah and his companions,
3:49 drove the fiery flames out of the *f*,
3:50 and made the inside of the *f* as though a
3:51 these three in the *f* with one voice sang,
3:93 of the white-hot *f* and called to Shadrach,
Mt 13:42 angels will hurl them into the fiery *f*
13:50 just and hurl the wicked into the fiery *f*,
Rv 1:15 like polished brass refined in a *f*,
9: 2 of the shaft like smoke from an enormous *f*.

FURNISH (8)

Gn 49:20 is rich, and he shall *f* dainties for kings.
1Kgs 5:23 *f* the provisions I desire for my household."
2Kgs 4:10 on the roof and *f* it for him with a bed,
2Chr 2: 9 I will *f* as food for your servants,
Is 8:20 then this document will *f* its instruction.
Bar 1: 6 and collected such funds as each could *f*.
6: 9 and *f* crowns for the heads of their gods.
Heb 13:21 our Lord, *f* you with all that is good,

FURNISHED (11)

2Sm 5:11 he *f* cedar wood,
2Chr 11:23 and he *f* them with copious provisions and
Jdt 12:15 Bagoas had *f* for her daily use in reclining
Est 2: 9 *f* her with cosmetics and provisions.
1Mc 4:57 priests' chambers and *f* them with doors.
14:34 and *f* them with all that was necessary for
Wis 14: 3 it, for you have *f* even in the sea a road,
16:20 of angels and *f* them bread from heaven,
18: 3 you *f* the flaming pillar which was a guide
Mk 14:15 show you an upstairs room, spacious, *f*,
Lk 22:12 show you an upstairs room, spacious and *f*.

FURNISHINGS (7)

Ex 25: 9 This Dwelling and all its *f* you shall make
31: 7 on top of it, all the *f* of the tent,
40: 9 in it, consecrating it and all its *f*,
Nm 3: 8 They shall have custody of all the *f* of

2Kgs 25:16 all of them *f* which Solomon had made for
1Chr 23:26 the Dwelling or any of its *f* or equipment.
Jer 52:20 bronze of all these *f* could not be weighed.

FURNITURE (6)

Lv 15: 4 and any piece of *f* on which he sits,
15: 6 *f* on which the afflicted man was sitting,
15:22 any article of *f* on which she was sitting,
15:26 and any article of *f* on which she sits
Jdt 15:11 his couches, his dishes, and all his *f*,
Rv 18:12 of ivory pieces and expensive wooden *f*;

FURROW (1)

Jb 39:10 Will a rope bind him in the *f*,

FURROWS (8)

Jb 31:38 out against me till its very *f* complained;
Ps(s) 65:11 drenching its *f*, breaking up its clods,
129: 3 long did they make their *f*.
141: 7 As when a plowman breaks *f* in the field,
Sir 7: 3 Sow not in the *f* of injustice,
38:26 His care is for plowing *f*,
Hos 10:11 was to plow, Jacob was to break his *f*:
12:12 like heaps of stones in the *f* of the field.

FURTHER (68)

Gn 17:15 God *f* said to Abraham:
29: 6 He inquired *f*, "Is he well?"
31:51 Laban said *f* to Jacob:
38:26 But he had no *f* relations with her.
45:19 Instruct them *f*: 'Do this. Take wagons from
Ex 3:15 God spoke *f* to Moses,
21:22 she suffers a miscarriage, but no *f* injury,
22: 5 If the fire spreads *f*,
Nm 34:11 to Ar-Baal, east of Ain, and descending *f*,
Jgs 18:25 to him, "Let us hear no *f* sound from you,
1Sm 6: 4 When asked *f*, "What guilt offering
2Sm 7:10 dwell in their place without *f* disturbance.
10:19 were afraid to give *f* aid to the Ammonites.
18:15 in on Absalom, and killed him with *f* blows.
19:29 I still have to make *f* appeal to the king?"
19:36 be any *f* burden to my lord the king?
20: 3 for them, but had no *f* relations with them.
1Kgs 8:25 the *f* promise you made to my father David,
2Kgs 10:20 Jehu said *f*, "Proclaim a solemn assembly
16: 4 *F*, he sacrificed and burned incense on the
23:24 *F*, Josiah did away with the consultation
2Chr 6:16 the *f* promise you made to my father David,
28:23 caused *f* disaster to him and to all Israel.
32:15 you *f* and deceive you in any such way.
Ezr 4:21 until a *f* decree has been issued by me.
Neh 2: 7 I asked the king *f*:
5:12 everything and exact nothing *f* from them.
8:10 He said *f*: "Go eat rich foods
Jdt 8:31 our cisterns, lest we be weakened still *f*."
2Mc 2:32 we shall begin our account without *f* ado;
6:17 Without *f* ado we must go on with our story.
11:19 endeavor to *f* your interests in the future.
14: 5 But he found an opportunity to *f* his mad
Jb 36: 1 Elihu proceeded *f* and said:
Ps(s) 140: 9 *f* not their plans.
Eccl 9: 5 There is no *f* recompense for them,
Wis 8:12 and as I spoke on *f*,
Sir 11:23 What *f* pleasure can be mine?"
Jer 44:24 Jeremiah said *f* to all the people,
Ez 12:25 and it shall be done without *f* delay.
23:14 same path, yet she went *f* in her harlotry.
Zep 3:15 midst, you have no *f* misfortune to fear.
Zec 1:17 Proclaim *f*: Thus says the Lord
Mt 19:20 what do I need to do *f*?"
26:65 What *f* need have we of witnesses?
Mk 5:35 Why bother the Teacher *f*?"
14:63 "What *f* need do we have of witnesses?
15: 5 surprise, Jesus made no *f* response.
Lk 8:49 do not bother the Teacher *f*."
10: 1 the Lord appointed a *f* seventy-two and
10:35 *f* expense I will repay you on my way back.'
18:22 "There is one thing *f* you must do.
21:10 He said to them *f*:
Jn 1:21 They questioned him *f*, "Who, then?
1:25 had sent proceeded to question him *f*:
Acts 4:17 To stop this from spreading *f* among the
4:21 point they were dismissed with *f* warnings.
19:39 is any *f* matter you want to investigate,
21:14 not be dissuaded, we said nothing *f* except,
26:32 Agrippa *f* remarked to Festus,
27:38 the ship *f* by throwing the wheat overboard.
Rom 11:11 I *f* ask, does their stumbling mean
2Cor 10: 8 If I find I must make a few *f* claims about
Phil 1:14 have been *f* emboldened to speak the word
Heb 10:18 forgiven, there is no *f* offering for sin.
10:26 remains for us no *f* sacrifice for sin
Jas 2: 3 Suppose *f* that you were to take notice of
Rv 2:24 on you I place no *f* burden.

FURTHERANCE (1)

Phil 1:12 has worked out to the *f* of the gospel.

FURTHERMORE (8)

Jos 17: 3 *F*, Zelophehad, son of Hepher
2Sm 16:19 *F*, as I was in attendance upon your father,
2Chr 9:20 *F*, all of King Solomon's drinking vessels
Ezr 9: 2 *F*, the leaders and rulers have taken a
Acts 16:20 *F*, they are Jews,
22: 4 *F*, I persecuted this new way to the point
1Cor 12:28 *F*, God has set up in the church first
Gal 3:29 *F*, if you belong to Christ you are the

FURY (69)

Gn 27:44 until your brother's *f* subsides
49: 6 For in their *f* they slew men,
49: 7 Cursed be their *f* so fierce,
2Kgs 9:20 like that of Jehu, son of Nimshi, in its *f*."
19:28 me and your *f* which has reached my ears,
1Chr 10: 3 the whole *f* of the battle descended upon Saul.
2Chr 28: 9 with a *f* that has reached up to heaven.
Est 1:12 wrath flared up, and he burned with *f*.
1Mc 2:24 heart was moved and his just *f* was aroused;
2Mc 7: 3 At that the king, in *f*,
10:28 taking *f* as their leader in the fight.
10:35 *f* cut down everyone they encountered.
Jb 20:23 God shall send against him the *f* of his
36:33 for him and incites the *f* of the storm.
40:11 Let loose the *f* of your wrath;
Ps(s) 7: 7 rise against the *f* of my foes;
55: 4 evil upon me, and with *f* they persecute me.
69:25 let the *f* of your anger overtake them.
76: 8 can withstand you for the *f* of your anger?
78:49 his fierce anger, wrath and *f* and strife,
90:11 Who knows the *f* of your anger or your
102:11 tears, Because of your *f* and your wrath;
124: 3 When their *f* was inflamed against us,
Prv 29: 8 the city ablaze, but wise men calm the *f*.
Sir 39:28 which in their *f* can dislodge mountains;
40: 5 and dread, terror of death, *f* and strife.
Is 21:15 From the taut bow, from the *f* of battle.
30:27 His lips are filled with *f*,
30:30 In raging *f* and flame of consuming fire,
37:29 me and your *f* which has reached my ears,
42:25 upon them, his anger, and the *f* of battle;
51:13 constant dread of the *f* of the oppressor;
51:13 what is there of the oppressor's *f*?
Jer 21:12 Lest my *f* break out like fire which burns
36: 7 for great is the *f* of anger with which the
44: 6 Therefore the *f* of my anger poured forth
Ez 5:13 wreak my *f* upon them till I am appeased;
5:13 in my jealousy when I spend my *f* upon them.
5:15 anger and *f* and with furious chastisements,
6:12 so will I spend my *f* upon them.
7: 8 my *f* upon you and spend my anger upon you;
9: 8 when you pour out your *f* on Jerusalem?"
13:13 In my *f* I will let loose stormwinds;
13:15 my *f* on the wall and its whitewashers,
14:19 pouring out upon it my bloodthirsty *f*,
16:38 I will wreak *f* and jealousy upon you.
16:42 When I have wreaked my *f* upon you I will
19:12 was torn up in *f* and flung to the ground;
20: 8 Then I thought of pouring out my *f* on them
20:13 Then I thought of pouring out my *f* on them
20:21 Then I thought of pouring out my *f* on them,
21:22 one hand against the other and wreak my *f*.
22:22 I, the LORD, have poured out my *f* on you.
22:24 is, not rained on] at the time of my *f*.
22:31 Therefore I have poured out my *f* upon them;
23:25 so that they shall deal with you in *f*,
24:13 not be purified until I wreak my *f* on you.
25:14 Edom in accordance with my anger and my *f*;
36: 6] With jealous *f* I speak,
36:18 Therefore I poured out my *f* upon them
38:18 says the Lord GOD, my *f* shall be aroused.
Dn 11:44 out with great *f* to slay and to doom many.
Na 1: 6 His *f* is poured out like fire,
Hb 3:12 the earth, in *f* you trample the nations.
Acts 5:33 were stung to *f* and wanted to kill them.
19:28 were overcome with *f* and began to shout,
26:11 so wild was my *f* against them that I
Rom 2: 8 wrath and *f* to those who selfishly disobey
Rv 12:12 His *f* knows no limits,

FUSED (2)

Ex 32:20 he *f* it in the fire and then ground it
Jb 38:38 is *f* into a mass and its clods made solid?

FUSING (1)

Dt 9:21 object you had made, and *f* it with fire,

FUTILE (3)

Is 30: 7 to Egypt whose help is *f* and vain.
Mi 2:11 acting on impulse, should make the *f* claim:
1Pt 1:18 you were delivered from the *f* way of life

FUTILITY (1)

Rom 8:20 Creation was made subject to *f*,

FUTURE (50)

Gn 30:33 In the *f*,
Ex 40:15 priesthood throughout all *f* generations."
Lv 22: 3 or of your descendants in any *f* generation,
Nm 15:14 Likewise, in any *f* generation,
Dt 29:21 *F* generations, your own descendants
31:29 evil will befall you in some *f* age
Jos 4: 6 In the *f*, these are to be a sign among you
4:21 saying to the Israelites, "In the *f*,
22:24 *f* your children should say to our children:
22:27 *f* your children cannot say to our children,
22:28 that if in the *f* they should speak thus to
2Kgs 21: 8 I will not in *f* allow Israel to be driven
1Chr 17:17 family reaching into the distant *f*,
Jdt 9: 5 present, also, and the *f* you have planned.
11: 3 Your life is spared tonight and for the *f*.
Est B: 7 affairs stable and undisturbed for the *f*."
E: 8 We must provide for the *f*
E:23 so that both now and in the *f* it may be,
9:23 The Jews took upon themselves for the *f*
F:10 all *f* generations of his people Israel."
1Mc 10:30 Neither now nor in the *f* will I collect
15: 8 All debts, present or *f*,
2Mc 11:19 to further your interests in the *f*.
12:31 well disposed to their race in the *f* also.
Ps(s) 37:37 for there is a *f* for the man of peace.
37:38 the *f* of the wicked shall be cut off.
48:14 may tell a *f* generation that such is God,
102:19 and let his *f* creatures praise the LORD:
Prv 23:18 For you will surely have a *f*,
24:14 If you find it, you will have a *f*,
24:20 For the evil man has no *f*,
Wis 14: 6 a raft, left to the world a *f* for his race,
Sir 2: 3 thus will your *f* be great.
16: 3 length of life, have no hope in their *f*.
42:19 He makes known the past and the *f*,
48:24 the *f* and consoled the mourners of Zion;
Is 30: 8 it may be in *f* days an eternal witness:
44: 7 Who of old announced *f* events?
45:17 be put to shame or disgrace in *f* ages."
Jer 29:11 plans to give you a *f* full of hope.
31:17 There is hope for your *f*,
Lam 3:18 I tell myself my *f* is lost,
Ez 12:27 he prophesies of the distant *f*!"
Dn 2:29 about what should happen in the *f*,
2:45 to the king what shall be in the *f*;
Hg 2: 9 the *f* glory of this house than the former,
Rom 8:38 neither the present nor the *f*,
1Cor 3:22 life, or death, or the present, or the *f*:
1Tm 6:19 they build a secure foundation for the *f*,
2Pt 2: 6 what would happen in the *f* to the godless.

G

GAAL (9)

Jgs 9:26 Now *G*, son of Ebed, came over to
9:28 *G*, son of Ebed, said, "Who is Abimelech?
9:30 At the news of what *G*,
9:31 *G*, son of Ebed, and his kinsmen have come
9:35 *G*, son of Ebed, went out and stood
9:36 of ambush, *G* saw them and said to Zebul,
9:37 But *G* went on to say,
9:39 So *G* went out at the head of the citizens
9:41 Zebul drove *G* and his kinsmen from Shechem,

GAASH (3)

Jos 24:30 region of Ephraim north of Mount *G*.
Jgs 2: 9 region of Ephraim north of Mount *G*.
1Chr 11:32 Hurai, from the valley of *G*;

GABAEL (10)

Tb 1: 1 of Aduel, son of *G* of the family of Asiel,
1:14 a great sum of money with my kinsman *G*,
4: 1 he had deposited with *G* at Rages in Media,
4:20 money with Gabri's son *G* at Rages in Media.
5: 3 but get back that money from *G*."
5: 6 I used to stay with our kinsman *G*,
9: 5 Raphael gave *G* his bond and told him about
9: 5 *G* promptly checked over the sealed
9: 6 He sprang up and greeted *G*,
10: 2 or perhaps *G* is dead,

GABAEL'S (2)

Tb 9: 2 Go to *G* house and give him this bond.
9: 5 in Media, where they stayed at *G* house.

GABBATHA (1)

Jn 19:13 called the Stone Pavement *G* in Hebrew.

GABRI (1)

Tb 1:14 of money with my kinsman Gabael, son of *G*,

GABRIEL (4)

Dn 8:16 I heard a human voice that cired out, *G*,
9:21 still occupied with this prayer, when *G*,
Lk 1:19 "I am *G*,
1:26 the angel *G* was sent from God to a town of

GABRI'S (1)

Tb 4:20 money with *G* son Gabael at Rages in Media.

GAD (43)

Gn 30:11 So she named him *G*.

GAD (cont.)

35:26 sons of Leah's maid Zilpah: *G* and Asher.
46:16 The sons of *G:* Zephon, Haggi
49:19 *G* shall be raided by raiders,
Ex 1: 4 *G* and Asher.
Nm 1:14 from *G:* Eliasaph, son Reuel
1:24 Of the descendants of *G,*
1:25 and fifty were enrolled in the tribe of *G.*
2:14 and next the tribe of *G.*
10:20 of Reuel, over the host of the tribe of *G.*
13:15 son of Machi, of the tribe of *G.*
34:14 the ancestral houses of the tribe of *G,*
Dt 3:12 gave Reuben and *G* the territory from Aroer,
3:16 and to Reuben and *G* the territory from
27:13 over the people, while Reuben, *G,*
33:20 Of *G* he said: "Blessed be he who has made *G*
Jos 18: 7 while *G,*
20: 8 Ramoth in Gilead in the tribe of *G,*
21: 7 from the tribes of Reuben, *G* and Zebulun.
21:38 from the tribe of *G* a total of four cities:
22:25 of Reuben and *G* have no share in the LORD.
1Sm 13: 7 the Jordan into the land of *G* and Gilead.
22: 5 But the prophet *G* said to David:
2Sm 24: 5 went in the direction of *G* toward Jazer.
24:11 the LORD had spoken to the prophet *G,*
24:13 *G* then went to David to inform him.
24:14 David answered *G:*
24:18 same day *G* went to David and said to him,
1Chr 2: 2 Dan, Joseph, Benjamin, Naphtali, *G,*
6:48 cities by lot from the tribes of Reuben, *G,*
6:65 From the tribe of *G:*
21: 9 Then the LORD spoke to *G,*
21:11 *G* went to David and said to him;
21:13 Then David said to *G:*
21:18 Then the angel of the LORD commanded *G* to
29:29 the prophet, and the history of *G* the seer.
2Chr 29:25 of David, of *G* the king's seer,
Jer 49: 1 Why then has Milcom disinherited *G,*
Ez 48:27 *G:* on the frontier of Zebulun,
48:28 of *G* shall be the southern boundary,
48:34 the gate of *G,*
Rv 7: 5 twelve thousand from the tribe of *G,*

GADARENE (1)

Mt 8:28 As he approached the *G* boundary,

GADDI (2)

Nm 13:11 *G,* son of Susi
1Mc 2: 2 John, who was called *G;*

GADI (2)

2Kgs 15:14 Menahem, son of *G,*
15:17 Azariah, king of Judah, Menahem, son of *G,*

GADITE (3)

Jos 13:24 What Moses gave to the *G* clans:
2Sm 23:36 Bani the *G;*
1Chr 11:38 brother of Nathan, from Rehob, the *G;*

GADITES (37)

Nm 7:42 of Eliasaph, son of Reuel, prince of the *G.*
26:15 The *G* by clans were:
26:18 These were the clans of the *G,*
32: 1 and *G* had a very large number of livestock.
32: 6 But Moses answered the *G* and Reubenites:
32:25 The *G* and Reubenites answered Moses,
32:29 If all the *G* and Reubenites cross the
32:31 To this the *G* and Reubenites replied,
32:33 So Moses gave them [the *G* and Reubenites,
32:34 The *G* rebuilt the fortified towns of Dibon,
Dt 4:43 Ramoth in Gilead for the *G;*
29: 7 gave as a heritage to the Reubenites, *G,*
Jos 1:12 Joshua reminded the Reubenites, the *G,*
4:12 The Reubenites, *G,*
12: 6 their land to the Reubenites, the *G,*
13: 8 Manasseh as well as the Reubenites and *G,*
13:28 were the heritage of the clans of the *G.*
22: 1 Joshua summoned the Reubenites, the *G,*
22: 9 So the Reubenites, the *G,*
22:10 When the Reubenites, the *G,*
22:11 the report that the Reubenites, the *G,*
22:13 they sent to the Reubenites, the *G,*
22:15 When these came to the Reubenites, the *G,*
22:21 The Reubenites, the *G,*
22:30 the *G* and the Manassehites had to say,
22:31 the Reubenites, the *G* and the Manassehites,
22:32 returned from the Reubenites and the *G*
22:33 and *G* or ravaging the land they occupied.
22:34 The Reubenites and the *G* gave the altar
2Kgs 10:33 Jordan (all the land of Gilead, of the *G,*
1Chr 5:11 The *G* lived alongside them in the land of
5:18 The Reubenites, *G,*
5:26 who deported the Reubenites, the *G,*
12: 9 Some of the *G* also went over to David when
12:15 These *G* were army commanders,
12:38 side of the Jordan, of the Reubenites, *G,*
26:32 administration of the Reubenites, the *G,*

GAD'S (3)

2Sm 24:19 Following *G* bidding,
1Chr 21:19 David went up at *G* command,
Jer 49: 1 why have his people settled in *G* cities?

GAFF (1)

Jb 40:26 nose, or pierce through his cheek with a *g?*

GAHAM (1)

Gn 22:24 Tebah, *G,* Tahash, and Maacah.

GAHAR (2)

Ezr 2:47 sons of Hanan, sons of Giddel, sons of *G,*
Neh 7:49 sons of Hanan, sons of Giddel, sons of *G,*

GAILY (1)

Prv 13: 9 The light of the just shines *g,*

GAIN (67)

Gn 24:60 *g* possession of the gates of their enemies!"
28: 4 so that you may *g* possession of the land
33: 8 answered, "It was to *g* my lord's favor."
Ex 18:21 men, trustworthy men who hate dishonest *g,*
Jgs 4: 9 "but you shall not *g* the glory in the
1Sm 8: 3 but sought illicit *g* and accepted bribes,
2Mc 5: 7 so, he did not *g* control of the government,
9: 2 rob the temple and *g* control of the city.
9:11 arrogance, and to *g* some understanding,
Jb 11:12 Will empty man then *g* understanding,
21:15 And what *g* shall we have if we pray to him?"
22: 3 a *g* to him if you make your ways perfect?
Ps(s) 30:10 "What *g* would there be from my lifeblood,
90:12 days aright, that we may *g* wisdom of heart.
119:36 my heart to your decrees and not to *g.*
119:104 Through your precepts I *g* discernment;
Prv 1: 5 an intelligent man will *g* sound guidance,
1:13 All kinds of precious wealth shall we *g,*
1:19 unlawful *g* takes away the life of him who
2:19 come back again, or *g* the paths of life.
4: 1 be attentive, that you may *g* understanding!
8: 5 You simple ones, *g* resource,
8: 5 ones, gain resource, you fools, *g* sense.
11:16 impoverished, but the diligent *g* wealth.]
14:18 but shrewd men *g* the crown of knowledge.
14:22 intent on good *g* kindness and constancy.
15:27 greedy of *g* brings ruin on his own house,
23: 4 Toil not to *g* wealth,
28:10 [And blameless men will *g* prosperity.]
28:12 but when the wicked *g* pre-eminence,
28:16 who hates ill-gotten *g* prolongs his days.
28:28 When the wicked *g* pre-eminence,
Wis 7:14 *g* this treasure win the friendship of God,
15:12 and our span of life a holiday for *g;*
Sir 6: 7 When you *g* a friend,
28:21 which even the nether world is a *g;*
31: 8 without fault, who turns not aside after *g!*
34:23 tears down, what do they *g* but trouble?
34:25 bathed, what did he *g* by the purification?
51:25 *g,* at no cost, wisdom for yourselves.
Is 30: 5 be ashamed of a people that *g* them nothing,
40:14 Whom did he consult to *g* knowledge?
45:14 The earnings of Egypt, the *g* of Ethiopia,
56:11 own way, every one of them to his own *g:*
58: 2 is due them, pleased to *g* access to God.
Jer 6:13 and great alike, all are greedy for *g;*
8:10 and great alike, all are greedy for *g,*
22:17 are set on nothing except on your own *g,*
Ez 22:27 blood and destroying lives to get unjust *g.*
33:31 and their desires are fixed on dishonest *g.*
39:13 land shall bury them and *g* renown for it,
Hos 12: 9 All his *g* shall not suffice him for the
Hb 2: 9 him who pursues evil *g* for his household,
Mt 16:26 *g* the whole world and destroy himself
Jn 4:38 the labor, and you have come into their *g."*
Acts 27:16 we able to *g* control of the ship's boat.
Rom 13: 3 what is right and you will *g* its approval,
1Cor 8: 8 to eat, and we *g* no favor by eating.
13: 3 be burned, but have not love, I *g* nothing.
Phil 1:21 hence dying is so much *g.*
3: 7 But those things I used to consider *g* I
1Tm 1:16 have faith in him and *g* everlasting life.
3:13 Those who serve well as deacons *g* a worthy
6: 5 religion only as a means of personal *g.*
6: 6 There is, of course, great *g* in religion
Ti 1:11 and all for sordid *g!*
2Pt 2:15 He was a man attracted to dishonest *g,*

GAINED (22)

Gn 37:26 "What is to be *g* by killing our brother
Jgs 1:19 he *g* possession of the mountain region.
1:35 as the house of Joseph *g* the upper hand,
2Sm 15:12 So the conspiracy *g* strength,
Est B: 3 who has *g* the second rank in the kingdom,
1Mc 11:46 while the populace *g* control of the main
11:51 The Jews thus *g* glory in the eyes of the
14: 6 of his nation and *g* control of the country.
15: 3 *g* control of the kingdom of my ancestors,
2Mc 10:17 vigorously, they *g* control of the places,
Prv 16:31 it is *g* by virtuous living.
20:21 Possessions *g* hastily at the outset will
Eccl 2:11 after wind, with nothing *g* under the sun.
Wis 14:16 *g* strength and was observed as law,
Sir 20: 8 some things *g* are a man's loss.
30:23 nor is there aught to be *g* from resentment.
34:26 and what has he *g* by his mortification?
51:20 I *g* understanding such that I will never
Is 33:15 who spurns what is *g* by oppression,
Jer 32:20 all other men, until now you have *g* renown.
Lk 11:52 You yourselves have not *g* access,
Rom 5: 2 Through him we have *g* access by faith to

GAINING (8)

Gn 3: 6 to the eyes, and desirable for *g* wisdom.
32: 6 information in the hope of *g* your favor.' "
2Sm 3: 6 Abner was *g* power in the house of Saul.
1Mc 7:25 Judas and his followers were *g* strength
10:23 *g* the friendship of the Jews
10:52 Demetrius and *g* control of my country
2Mc 8: 8 When Philip saw that Judas was *g* ground
13:26 After calming them and *g* their good will,

GAINS (15)

Jb 20:18 Restoring his *g,*
Prv 3:13 finds wisdom, the man who *g* understanding!
10:16 leads to life, the *g* of the wicked,
15:32 but he who heeds reproof *g* understanding.
18:15 The mind of the intelligent *g* knowledge,
18:16 way for him, and *g* him access to great men.
19: 8 who *g* intelligence is his own best friend;
19:25 rebuke an intelligent man, he *g* knowledge.
21:11 the wise man is instructed, he *g* knowledge.
22:16 yield up his *g* to the rich as sheer loss.
Sir 34: 9 A man with training *g* wide knowledge;
Mk 8:36 What profit does a man show who *g* the
Lk 4:24 prophet *g* acceptance in his native place.
9:25 What profit does he show who *g* the whole
Acts 1:18 bought a piece of land with his unjust *g,*

GAINSAY (3)

Jdt 8:28 good sense, and no one can *g* your words.
Sir 4:25 Never *g* the truth,
46:19 and no one dared *g* him.

GAIT (1)

Sir 19:26 attire, his hearty laughter and his *g,*

GAIUS (5)

Acts 19:29 theater and dragged in *G* and Aristarchus,
20: 4 *G* from Derbe;
Rom 16:23 Greetings also from *G,*
1Cor 1:14 baptized none of you except Crispus and *G,*
3Jn 1: 1 The elder to the beloved *G,*

GALAL (3)

1Chr 9:15 of Merari; Bakbakkar; Heresh; *G;*
9:16 Obadiah, son of Shemaiah, son of *G,*
Neh 11:17 and Abda, son of Shammua, son of *G,*

GALATIA (4)

1Cor 16: 1 the instructions I gave the churches of *G.*
Gal 1: 2 me send greetings to the churches in *G.*
2Tm 4:10 has gone to *G* and Titus to Dalmatia.
1Pt 1: 1 strangers scattered throughout Pontus, *G,*

GALATIAN (2)

Acts 16: 6 They next traveled through Phrygia and *G*
18:23 systematically through the *G* country

GALATIANS (2)

2Mc 8:20 of the battle in Babylonia against the *G,*
Gal 3: 1 You senseless *G!*

GALAXIES (1)

Acts 7:42 to the worship of the *g* in the heavens.

GALBANUM (2)

Ex 30:34 storax and onycha and *g,*
Sir 24:15 Like *g* and onycha and sweet spices,

GALE (2)

Hos 12: 2 chases the wind, ever pursuing the *g.*
2Pt 2:17 waterless springs, mists whipped by the *g.*

GALEED (2)

Gn 31:47 it Jegar-sahadutha, but Jacob named it *G.*
31:48 That is why it was named *G*—

GALILEAN (6)

Mt 26:69 and said, "You too were with Jesus the *G."*
Mk 14:70 You are a *G,* are you not?"
Lk 22:59 man was certainly with him, for he is a *G."*
23: 6 this Pilate asked if the man was a *G;*
Jn 7:52 "Do not tell us you are a *G* too,"
Acts 5:37 came Judas the *G* at the time of the census.

GALILEANS (4)

Jdt 15: 5 The Gileadites and the *G* struck the
Lk 13: 1 were present who told him about the *G*

13: 2 "Do you think that these *G* were the
Acts 2: 7 not all of these men who are speaking *G?*

GALILEE (81)

Jos 20: 7 in *G* in the mountain region of Naphtali,
21:32 of asylum for homicides at Kedesh in *G,*
1Kgs 9:11 gave Hiram twenty cities in the land of *G.*
2Kgs 15:29 the territory of Naphtali, Gilead, and *G,*
1Chr 6:61 Kedesh in *G* with its pasture lands,
Tb 1: 2 is south of Kedesh Naphtali in upper *G,*
1: 5 offer sacrifice on all the mountains of *G*
Jdt 1: 8 to the peoples of Carmel, Gilead, Upper *G,*
1Mc 5:14 from *G* to deliver a similar message:
5:15 *G* had joined forces to destroy them.
5:17 and go, rescue your kinsmen in *G;*
5:20 men were allotted to Simon, to go into *G,*
5:21 Simon went into *G* and fought many battles
5:23 him the Jews who were in *G* and in Arbatta,
5:55 his brother was in *G* opposite Ptolemais,
9: 2 They took the road to *G,*
11:63 come with a strong force to Kadesh in *G,*
12:47 to *G* while one thousand accompanied him.
12:49 Trypho sent soldiers and cavalry to *G* and
Mt 2:22 in a dream, Joseph went to the region of *G.*
3:13 Later Jesus, coming from *G,*
4:12 John had been arrested, he withdrew to *G.*
4:15 along the sea beyond the Jordan, heathen *G:*
4:18 along the Sea of *G* he watched two brothers,
4:23 Jesus toured all of *G.*
4:25 crowds that followed him came from *G,*
15:29 that place and passed along the Sea of *G.*
17:22 When they met again in *G,*
19: 1 he left *G* and came to the district of
21:11 is the prophet Jesus from Nazareth in *G.*"
26:32 am raised up, I will go to *G* ahead of you."
27:55 Jesus from *G* to attend to his needs.
28: 7 the dead and now goes ahead of you to *G,*
28:10 to my brothers that they are to go to *G,*
28:16 The eleven disciples made their way to *G,*
Mk 1: 9 *G* and was baptized in the Jordan by John.
1:14 in *G* proclaiming the good news of God:
1:16 As he made his way along the Sea of *G,*
1:28 throughout the surrounding region of *G.*
1:39 expelling demons throughout the whole of *G.*
3: 7 A great crowd followed him from *G,*
6:21 officers, and the leading men of *G.*
7:31 returned by way of Sidon to the Sea of *G,*
9:30 district and began a journey through *G,*
14:28 am raised up, I will go to *G* ahead of you."
15:41 when he was in *G* and attended to his needs.
16: 7 and Peter, 'He is going ahead of you to *G,*
Lk 1:26 from God to a town of *G* named Nazareth,
2: 4 from the town of Nazareth in *G* to Judea,
2:39 to *G* and their own town of Nazareth.
3: 1 procurator of Judea, Herod tetrarch of *G,*
4:14 returned in the power of the Spirit to *G,*
4:31 then went down to Capernaum, a town of *G,*
5:17 village of *G* and from Judea and Jerusalem.
8:26 of the Gerasenes, which is opposite *G.*
13: 2 in *G* just because they suffered this?
17:11 passed along the borders of Samaria and *G.*
23: 5 throughout the whole of Judea, from *G,*
23:49 women who had accompanied him from *G*
23:55 come with him from *G* followed along behind.
24: 6 he said to you while he was still in *G*—
Jn 1:43 The next day he wanted to set out for *G,*
2: 1 third day there was a wedding at Cana in *G,*
2:11 this first of his signs at Cana in *G.*
4: 3 he left Judea and started back for *G* again.
4:43 When the two days were over, he left for *G.*
4:45 When he arrived in *G,*
4:46 He went to Cana in *G* once more,
4:47 that Jesus had come back from Judea to *G,*
4:54 performed on returning from Judea to *G.*
6: 1 the Sea of *G* [to the shore] of Tiberias;
7: 1 After this, Jesus moved about within *G.*
7: 9 Having said this, he stayed on in *G.*
7:41 the Messiah is not to come from *G?*
7:52 will not find the Prophet coming from *G.*"
12:21 Philip, who was from Bethsaida in *G,*
21: 2 (the "Twin"), Nathanael (from Cana in *G),*
Acts 1:11 "Men of *G,*" they said, "why do you stand
9:31 Meanwhile throughout all Judea, *G,*
10:37 in *G* with the baptism John preached;
13:31 had come up with him from *G* to Jerusalem.

GALL (15)

Tb 6: 5 "Cut the fish open and take out its *g,*
6: 5 Its *g,* heart, and liver make useful
6: 6 had cut the fish open, he put aside the *g,*
6: 7 is there in the fish's heart, liver, and *g?*"
6: 9 And as for the *g,*
11: 4 said to Tobiah, "Have the *g* in your hand!"
11: 8 Smear the fish *g* on them.
11:11 went up to him with the fish *g* in his hand,
Jb 16:13 mercy, he pours out my *g* upon the ground.
Ps(s) 69:22 Rather they put *g* in my food,
Lam 2:11 My *g* is poured out on the ground because
3:19 of my homeless poverty is wormwood and *g;*
Am 6:12 Yet you have turned judgment into *g,*
Mt 27:34 gave him a drink of wine flavored with *g,*
Acts 8:23 with *g* and caught in the grip of sin."

GALLANTLY (2)

2Mc 14:43 he *g* ran up to the top of the wall and
15:17 but to charge *g* and decide the issue by

GALLED (1)

Ez 29:18 became bald and their shoulders were *g;*

GALLEYS (1)

Dt 28:68 The LORD will send you back in *g* to Egypt,

GALLIM (3)

Jos 15:59 Peor, Etam, Kulom, Tatam, Zores, Karim, *G,*
1Sm 25:43 to Palti, son of Laish, who was from *G.*
Is 10:30 Cry and shriek, O daughter of *G!*

GALLIO (2)

Acts 18:14 in self-defense when *G* said to the Jews:
18:17 but *G* paid no attention to it.

GALLIO'S (1)

Acts 18:12 During *G* proconsulship in Achaia,

GALLONS (1)

Jn 2: 6 each holding fifteen to twenty-five *g.*

GALLOP (1)

Wis 17:19 rocks, Or the unseen *g* of bounding animals,

GAMADITES (1)

Ez 27:11 your walls, and the *G* were in your towers;

GAMALIEL (7)

Nm 1:10 *G,* son of Pedahzur,
2:20 the tribe of Manasseh [Their prince was *G,*
7:54 On the eighth day it was the turn of *G,*
7:59 This was the offering of *G,*
10:23 son of Ammihud, over their host, and *G,*
Acts 5:34 Sanhedrin stood up, a Pharisee named *G,*
22: 3 Here I sat at the feet of *G* and was

GAMBOL (1)

Mal 3:20 And you will *g* like calves out of the

GAME (9)

Gn 25:28 preferred Esau, because he was fond of *g;*
27: 3 out into the country to hunt some *g* for me.
27: 5 the country to hunt some *g* for his father,
27: 7 'Bring me some *g* and with it prepare an
27:19 Please sit up and eat some of my *g,*
27:25 Then Isaac said, "Serve me your *g,*
27:31 prepared an appetizing dish with his *g,*
27:31 father, eat some of your son's *g,*
27:33 "that hunted *g* and brought it to me?

GAMES (1)

2Mc 4:18 When the quinquennial *g* were held at Tyre

GAMUL (1)

1Chr 24:17 to Jachin, the twenty-second to *G,*

GAPING (2)

Gn 42: 1 "Why do you keep *g* at one another?
Is 1: 6 Wound and welt and *g* gash,

GAPS (1)

Neh 4: 1 for the *g* were beginning to be closed up

GARB (8)

Gn 38:14 his sheep, she took off her widow's *g,*
38:19 her shawl and put on her widow's *g* again.
Dt 21:13 her nails and lay aside her captive's *g.*
1Kgs 10: 5 the attendance and *g* of his waiters,
20:31 us, therefore, to *g* ourselves in sackcloth,
2Kgs 25:29 Jehoiachin took off his prison *g* and ate
Jdt 16: 7 *g* to raise up the afflicted in Israel.
Jer 52:33 Jehoiachin took off his prison *g* and ate

GARBED (1)

Heb 11:37 about *g* in the skins of sheep or goats,

GARDEN (70)

Gn 2: 8 Then the LORD God planted a *g* in Eden,
2: 9 the tree of life in the middle of the *g*
2:10 A river rises in Eden to water the *g;*
2:15 the man and settled him in the *g* of Eden,
2:16 eat from any of the trees of the *g*
3: 1 not to eat from any of the trees in the *g?*"
3: 2 eat of the fruit of the trees in the *g;*
3: 3 tree in the middle of the *g* that God said,
3: 8 in the *g* at the breezy time of the day,
3: 8 from the LORD God among the trees of the *g.*
3:10 He answered, "I heard you in the *g;*
3:23 therefore banished him from the *g* of Eden,
3:24 man, he settled him east of the *g* of Eden;
13:10 was as far as Zoar, like the LORD's own *g,*
Dt 11:10 then water it by hand, as in a vegetable *g.*
1Kgs 21: 2 me your vineyard to be my vegetable *g,*
2Kgs 21:18 buried in his palace garden, the *g* of Uzza.
21:26 buried in his own grave in the *g* of Uzza,
25: 4 the two walls which was near the king's *g,*
2Chr 26:10 in the highlands and the *g* land.
Neh 3:15 Aqueduct Pool near the king's *g*
Est 1: 5 gave a feast of seven days in the *g* court
7: 7 in anger and went into the *g* of the palace,
7: 8 the *g* of the palace to the banquet hall,
Jb 8:16 and beyond his *g* his shoots go forth;
Sg 4:12 garden, my sister, my bride, an enclosed *g,*
4:15 You are a *g* fountain,
4:16 my *g* that its perfumes may spread abroad.
4:16 come to his *g* and eat its choice fruits.
5: 1 I have come to my *g,*
6: 2 My lover has come down to his *g,*
6: 2 To browse in the *g* and to gather lilies.
6:11 I came down to the nut *g* to look at the
Sir 24:28 stream, channeling the waters into a *g,*
Is 1:30 falling leaves, like a *g* that has no water.
51: 3 Eden, her wasteland like the *g* of the LORD;
58:11 and you shall be like a watered *g,*
61:11 plants, and a *g* makes its growth spring up,
Jer 2: 7 into the *g* land to eat its goodly fruits,
4:26 looked and behold, the *g* land was a desert,
39: 4 leaving the city on the Royal *G* Road
52: 7 the two walls which was near the king's *g.*
Lam 2: 6 has demolished his shelter like a *g* booth,
Bar 6:70 in a *g* on which perches every kind of bird,
Ez 28:13 and perfect beauty, In Eden, the *g* of God,
31: 8 cedars in the *g* of God were not its equal,
31: 8 no tree in the *g* of God matched its beauty.
31: 9 envy of all Eden's trees in the *g* of God.
36:35 land has been made into a *g* of Eden,"
Dn 13: 4 he had a *g* near his house,
13: 7 used to enter her husband's *g* for a walk.
13:15 right moment, she entered the *g* as usual,
13:17 "and shut the *g* doors while I bathe."
13:18 they shut the *g* doors and left by the side
13:20 They said, "the *g* doors are shut,
13:25 as one of them ran to open the *g* doors.
13:26 in the house heard the cries from the *g,*
13:36 "As we were walking in the *g* alone,
13:36 with two girls and shut the doors of the *g,*
13:38 When we, in a corner of the *g,*
Jl 2: 3 Like the *g* of Eden is the land before them,
Lk 11:42 on mint and rue and all the *g* plants,
13:19 seed which a man took and planted in his *g.*
Jn 18: 1 There was a *g* there,
18:26 "But did I not see you with him in the *g?*"
19:41 was a *g,* and in the garden a new tomb
Rv 2: 7 tree of life which grows in the *g* of God.'

GARDEN-DWELLER (1)

Sg 8:13 GO *g,* my friends are listening

GARDENER (1)

Jn 20:15 She supposed he was the *g,*

GARDENS (8)

Nm 24: 6 They are like *g* beside a stream,
Eccl 2: 5 I made *g* and parks,
Jer 29: 5 plant *g,* and eat their fruits.
29:28 plant *g* and eat their fruits. . . ."
31:12 They themselves shall be like watered *g,*
48:33 an end in the fruit *g* of the land of Moab.
Am 4: 9 your many *g* and vineyards,
9:14 the wine, set out *g* and eat the fruits.

GAREB (3)

2Sm 23:38 *G* from Jattir;
1Chr 11:40 *G,* from Jattir;
Jer 31:39 to the hill *G* and then turn to Goah.

GARLAND (4)

Sir 1:16 Wisdom's *g* is fear of the LORD,
50:12 His brethren ringed him about like a *g,*
Is 28: 1 to the majestic *g* of the drunkard Ephraim,
28: 3 the majestic *g* of the drunkard Ephraim.

GARLANDS (5)

Jdt 3: 7 *g* and dancing to the sound of timbrels.
15:13 crowned themselves with *g* of olive leaves.
15:13 their armor, wearing *g* and singing hymns.
Lam 5:16 *G* have fallen from our heads:
Acts 14:13 brought oxen and *g* to the gates because he

GARLIC (1)

Nm 11: 5 melons, the leeks, the onions, and the *g.*

GARMENT (43)

Ex 22: 8 an ox, or an ass, or a sheep, or a *g,*
Lv 6:20 If any of its blood is spilled on a *g,*
13:47 infection is on a *g* of wool or of linen,
13:49 leather, if the infection on the *g* or hide,
13:51 If it has spread on the *g,*
13:52 He shall therefore burn up the *g,*

GARMENT (cont.)

13:53 finds that it has not spread on the *g*,
13:56 shall tear the infected part out of the *g*,
13:57 the infection again appears on the *g*,
13:58 the washing, the infection has left the *g*,
13:59 leprous infection on a *g* of wool or linen,
19:19 *g* woven with two different kinds of thread.
Dt 22: 3 shall do the same with his ass, or his *g*,
1Sm 2:19 His mother used to make a little *g* for him,
2Sm 20:12 road to the field and placed a *g* over him,
2Kgs 1: 8 "Wearing a hairy *g*,"
2:12 gripped his own *g* and tore it in two.
9:13 At once each took his *g*,
Neh 5:13 I also shook out the folds of my *g*,
Jb 13:28 like a *g* that the moth has consumed?
29:14 I wore my honesty like a *g*;
38: 9 *g* and thick darkness its swaddling bands?
38:14 the seal, and dyed as though it were a *g*;
41: 5 Who can strip off his outer *g*,
Ps(s) 69:12 I made sackcloth my *g*,
102:27 though all of them grow old like a *g*.
104: 6 With the ocean, as with a *g*,
109:19 it be for him like a *g* which covers him,
Prv 20:16 Take his *g* who becomes surety for another,
27:13 Take his *g* who becomes surety for another,
Sir 14:17 All flesh grows old, like a *g*;
Is 6: 1 with the train of his *g* filling the temple.
51: 6 a *g* and its inhabitants die like flies,
51: 8 They shall be like a *g* eaten by moths,
Bar 4:20 I have taken off the *g* of peace,
Ez 5: 3 number and tie them in the hem of your *g*.
Hg 2:12 fold of his *g* and the fold touches bread,
Zec 8:23 of every Jew by the edge of his *g* and say,
Mal 2:16 And covering one's *g* with injustice,
Mt 3: 4 John was clothed in a *g* of camel's hair,
Lk 6:38 will they pour into the fold of your *g*.
Heb 1:11 all of them will grow old like a *g*.
1:12 like a *g* they will be changed.

GARMENTED (1)

Ps(s) 65:14 The fields are *g* with flocks and the

GARMENTS (154)

Gn 3:21 and his wife the LORD God made leather *g*,
45:22 shekels of silver and five sets of *g*.
49:11 In wine he washes his *g*,
Ex 19:10 their *g* and be ready for the third day;
19:14 them sanctify themselves and wash their *g*.
Lv 6: 4 off these *g* and put on other garments,
10: 6 "Do not bare your heads or tear your *g*,
11:25 wash his *g* and be unclean until evening.
11:28 wash his *g* and be unclean until evening.
11:40 wash his *g* and be unclean until evening;
13: 6 man shall wash his *g* and so become clean.
13:34 the latter shall wash his *g*,
13:45 shall keep his *g* rent and his head bare,
14: 8 man being purified shall then wash his *g*
14: 9 wash his *g* and bathe his body in water;
14:47 eats in such a house shall also wash his *g*,
14:55 and scall, for leprosy of *g* and houses,
15: 5 who touches his bed shall wash his *g*,
15: 6 man was sitting, shall wash his *g*,
15: 7 of the afflicted man shall wash his *g*,
15: 8 a clean man, the latter shall wash his *g*,
15:10 lifts up any such thing shall wash his *g*,
15:11 with unrinsed hands shall wash his *g*,
15:13 his *g* and bathe his body in fresh water,
15:21 who touches her bed shall wash his *g*,
15:22 which she was sitting, shall wash his *g*,
15:27 he shall wash his *g*,
16:26 wash his *g* and bathe his body in water;
16:28 wash his *g* and bathe his body in water;
16:32 He shall wear the linen *g*,
17:15 killed by a wild beast, shall wash his *g*,
21:10 shall not bare his head or rend his *g*,
Nm 14: 6 tore their *g* and said to the whole
15:38 put tassels on the corners of their *g*,
19: 7 wash his *g* and bathe his body in water.
19: 8 he who burned the heifer shall wash his *g*,
19:10 wash his *g* and be unclean until evening.
19:19 wash his *g* and bathe his body in water,
19:21 the lustral water shall wash his *g*,
20:26 of his *g* and put them on his son Eleazar;
20:28 of his *g* and put them on his son Eleazar.
Jos 7: 6 rent his *g* and lay prostrate before the
9: 5 wore old, patched sandals and shabby *g*;
9:13 Look at our *g* and sandals,
Jgs 8:26 the purple *g* worn by the kings of Midian,
11:35 When he saw her, he rent his *g* and said,
14:12 thirty linen tunics and thirty sets of *g*.
14:13 give me thirty tunics and thirty sets of *g*."
14:19 *g* to those who had answered the riddle.
17:10 you ten silver shekels a year, a set of *g*,
1Sm 19:24 he, too, stripped himself of his *g* and he,
2Sm 1:11 David seized his *g* and rent them,
3:31 people who were with him, "Rend your *g*,
10: 4 lower halves of their *g* at the buttocks,
13:31 The king stood up, rent his *g*,
13:31 servants standing by him also rent their *g*.
14:30 *g* and reported to him what had been done.
15:32 him, with rent *g* and dirt upon his head.
1Kgs 10:25 silver or gold articles, *g*,
21:27 *g* and put on sackcloth over his bare flesh.
2Kgs 5: 5 six thousand gold pieces, and ten festal *g*.
5: 7 king of Israel tore his *g* and exclaimed:
5: 8 that the king of Israel had torn his *g*,
5: 8 "Why have you torn your *g*?
5:22 them a talent of silver and two festal *g*.'"
5:23 bags and gave them, with the two festal *g*,
5:26 Is this a time to take money or to take *g*,
6:30 heard the woman's words, he tore his *g*.
7:15 whole route was strewn with *g*
10:22 out the *g* for all the worshipers of Baal."
10:22 When he had brought out all the *g* for them,
11:14 trumpets, she tore her *g* and cried out,
18:37 Asaph, came to Hezekiah with their *g* torn,
19: 1 King Hezekiah heard this, he tore his *g*,
22:11 he tore his *g* and issued this command to
22:19 because you tore your *g* and wept before me;
23: 7 in which the women wove *g* for the Asherah.
1Chr 19: 4 and their *g* cut off half-way at the hips.
2Chr 9:24 silver and gold articles, *g*,
20:25 personal property, *g* and precious vessels.
23:13 Athaliah tore her *g* and cried out,
34:19 his *g* and issued this command to Hilkiah,
34:27 yourself before me, have torn your *g*,
Ezr 2:69 silver, and one hundred *g* for the priests.
Neh 7:69 gold, fifty basins, thirty *g* for priests,
7:71 of silver, and sixty-seven *g* for priests.
9:21 their *g* did not become worn,
Jdt 10: 3 had on, laid aside the *g* of her widowhood,
12:15 festive *g* and all her feminine adornments.
14:16 groaning, and howling, and rent his *g*.
Est 4: 1 all that was happening, he tore his *g*,
4: 4 anguish, she sent *g* for Mordecai to put on,
C:13 off her splendid *g*, she put on *g* of distress
D: 1 *g* and arrayed herself in her royal attire.
5: 1 royal *g* and stood in the inner courtyard,
1Mc 2:14 Then Mattathias and his sons tore their *g*,
10:62 *g* and to be clothed in royal purple;
13:45 went up on the wall, with their *g* rent,
2Mc 4:38 of his purple robe, tore off his other *g*,
5: 2 in midair, clad in *g* interwoven with gold
11: 8 in white *g* and brandishing gold weapons.
Jb 9:31 in the ditch, so that my *g* would abhor me.
Ps(s) 22:19 they divide my *g* among them,
Prv 6:27 fire to his bosom, and his *g* not be burned?
31:24 She makes *g* and sells them,
Eccl 9: 8 At all times let your *g* be white,
Sg 4:11 of your *g* is the fragrance of Lebanon.
Sir 42:13 For just as moths come from *g*,
50:11 robes, and wearing his *g* of splendor,
Is 36:22 Asaph, came to Hezekiah with their *g* torn,
37: 1 King Hezekiah heard this, he tore his *g*,
52: 1 Put on your glorious *g*,
59:17 He clothed himself with *g* of vengeance,
63: 1 this that comes from Edom, in crimsoned *g*,
63: 2 and your *g* like those of the wine presser?
63: 3 Their blood spurted on my *g*;
Jer 36:24 ministers or cause them to rend their *g*.
Lam 4:14 that people could not touch even their *g*:
Bar 6:10 They trick them out in *g* like men,
6:19 out of the ground consume them and their *g*,
Ez 16:13 your *g* were of fine linen,
16:39 *g* and take away your splendid ornaments,
26:16 robes, and strip off their embroidered *g*.
27:24 with you, marketing with you rich *g*,
42:14 They shall put on other *g*,
44:17 the inner court, they shall wear linen *g*;
44:19 they shall take off the *g* in which they
44:19 of the sanctuary, putting on other *g*;
44:19 holiness to the people with their *g*.
Dn 3:21 with their coats, hats, shoes and other *g*,
3:94 had been singed, nor were their *g* altered;
Jl 2:13 Rend your hearts, not your *g*,
Am 2: 8 Upon *g* taken in pledge they recline beside
Zec 3: 3 before the angel, clad in filthy *g*.
3: 4 filthy *g*, and clothe him in festal garments."
3: 5 on his head and clothed him with the *g*.
14:14 be gathered together, gold, silver, and *g*,
Mt 28: 3 while his *g* were as dazzling as snow.
Mk 15:24 they crucified him and divided up his *g*
Lk 23:34 They divided his *g*, rolling dice for them.
24: 4 two men in dazzling *g* stood beside them.
Jn 19:23 they took his *g* and divided them four ways,
19:24 "They divided my *g* among them;
Acts 9:39 showed him the various *g* Dorcas had made
14:14 tore their *g* and rushed out into the crowd.
18: 6 shake out his *g* in protest and say to them:
Rv 3: 4 a few persons who have not soiled their *g*;
3:18 Buy white *g* in which to be clothed,
4: 4 *g* and had crowns of gold on their heads.
18:12 fine linen and purple *g*,

GARMITE (1)

1Chr 4:19 were Shimon the *G* and Ishi the Maacathite.

GARNER (1)

Dt 6:11 of goods of all sorts that you did not *g*,

GARNERED (1)

Gn 41:49 Joseph *g* grain in quantities like the

GARNERS (1)

Ps(s) 144:13 May our *g* be full,

GARNET (3)

Ex 28:18 in the second row, a *g*,
39:11 in the second row, a *g*,
Ez 28:13 chrysolite, onyx, and jasper, sapphire, *g*,

GARNETS (1)

Ez 27:16 so many were your products, exchanging *g*,

GARRISON (15)

1Sm 10: 5 where there is a *g* of the Philistines.
13: 3 the Philistine *g* which was in Gibeah,
13: 4 Saul had overcome the *g* of the Philistines
2Sm 23:14 there was a *g* of Philistines in Bethlehem.
1Chr 11:16 and a Philistine *g* was at Bethlehem.
1Mc 4:61 Judas also placed a *g* there to protect it,
6:50 and stationed a *g* there to hold it.
9:51 In each he put a *g* to oppose Israel.
10:75 him out because Apollonius had a *g* there.
11: 3 cities, he stationed *g* troops in each one.
11:66 took possession of it, and put a *g* there.
12:34 He left a *g* there to guard it.
12:36 prevent its *g* from commerce with the city.
14:33 where he stationed a *g* of Jewish soldiers,
2Mc 12:18 leave behind in one place a very strong *g*.

GARRISONS (8)

2Sm 8: 6 David then placed *g* in Aram of Damascus,
8:14 after which he placed *g* in Edom.
1Chr 18: 6 set up *g* in the Damascus region of Aram,
18:13 He set up *g* in Edom,
2Chr 17: 2 and put *g* in the land of Judah and in the
Jdt 3: 6 and stationed *g* in the fortified cities;
1Mc 12:45 with other strongholds and their *g*,
Na 3:17 the stars, your *g* as many as grasshoppers,

GARRULOUS (1)

Jb 11: 2 or must the *g* man necessarily be right?

GASH (4)

Dt 14: 1 You shall not *g* yourselves nor shave the
Is 1: 6 Wound and welt and gaping *g*,
Jer 16: 6 will *g* himself or shave his head for them.
47: 5 strength, how long will you *g* yourself?

GASHED (2)

Jer 48:37 every hand is *g*,
Mk 5: 5 he screamed and *g* himself with stones.

GASHES (1)

Jer 41: 5 with *g* on their bodies came from Shechem,

GASHING (1)

Jer 49: 3 and mourn, run to and fro, *g* yourselves;

GASP (1)

Ps(s) 119:131 I *g* with open mouth in my yearning for

GASPING (4)

Is 42:14 cry out as a woman in labor, *g* and panting.
Jer 4:31 The cry of daughter Zion *g*,
14: 6 bare heights, *g* for breath like jackals;
15: 9 of seven swoons away, *g* out her life;

GATAM (3)

Gn 36:11 sons of Eliphaz were Teman, Omar, Zepho, *G*,
36:16 of Teman, Omar, Zepho, Kenaz, Korah, *G*,
1Chr 1:36 sons of Eliphaz were Teman, Omar, Zephi, *G*,

GATE (277)

Gn 19: 1 as Lot was sitting at the *g* of Sodom.
Ex 32:26 he stood at the *g* of the camp and cried,
32:27 go up and down the camp, from *g* to gate,
Dt 21:19 to the elders at the *g* of his home city,
22:15 and bring it to the elders at the city *g*.
22:24 bring them both out to the *g* of the city
25: 7 go up to the elders at the *g* and declare,
Jos 2: 5 when it was time for the *g* to be shut,
2: 7 and once they had left, the *g* was shut.
7: 5 front of the city *g* till they broke ranks,
8:29 and cast at the entrance of the city *g*,
20: 4 standing at the entrance of the city *g*,
Jgs 9:35 and stood at the entrance of the city *g*.
9:40 slain right up to the entrance of the *g*.
9:44 and stood by the entrance of the city *g*,
16: 2 an ambush at the city *g* all night long.
16: 3 doors of the city *g* and the two gateposts,
18:16 Danites, stood by the entrance of the *g*,
Ru 4: 1 Boaz went and took a seat at the *g*;
4:11 at the *g*, including the elders, said, "We do
1Sm 4:13 Eli was sitting in his chair beside the *g*,
21:14 doors of the *g* and drooling onto his beard.
2Sm 3:27 *g* as though to speak with him privately.
10: 8 formation at the entrance of their city *g*,

11:23 them back to the entrance of the city *g.*
15: 2 stand alongside the road leading to the *g.*
18: 4 and he stood by the *g* as all the soldiers
18:24 to the roof of the *g* above the city wall,
18:26 From his place atop the *g* he cried out,
19: 1 up to the room over the city *g* to weep.
19: 9 So the king stepped out and sat at the *g.*
19: 9 that the king was sitting at the *g,*
23:15 the cistern that is by the *g* of Bethlehem!"
23:16 the cistern that is by the *g* of Bethlehem.
1Kgs 22:10 floor at the entrance of the *g* of Samaria,
2Kgs 7: 3 *g* were four lepers who were deliberating,
7:17 of the *g* the officer who was his adjutant;
7:17 the people trampled him to death at the *g,*
7:18 at this time tomorrow at the *g* of Samaria."
7:20 the people trampled him to death at the *g.*
9:31 As Jehu came through the *g,*
11: 6 gate Sur; and the last third shall be at the *g*
11:16 to the horse *g* of the royal palace,
11:19 LORD through the guards' *g* to the palace,
14:13 from the *G* of Ephraim to the Corner Gate.
15:35 the Upper *G* of the temple of the LORD.
23: 8 was at the entrance of the *G* of Joshua,
23: 8 city, to the left as one enters the city *g.*
25: 4 left the city by night through the *g*
1Chr 9:18 guard at the king's *g* on the east side;
9:21 guarded the *g* of the meeting tent.
11:17 the cistern that is by the *g* at Bethlehem!"
11:18 from the cistern by the *g* at Bethlehem,
16:42 The sons of Jeduthun kept the *g.*
19: 9 lined up for a battle at the *g* of the city,
26:13 They cast lots for each *g,*
26:16 the Shallecheth *g* at the ascending highway.
2Chr 8:14 the various classes stood guard at each *g,*
18: 9 floor at the entrance of the *g* of Samaria,
23: 5 and the final third at the Foundation *G,*
23:15 the entrance to the Horse *G* of the palace,
23:20 within the upper *g* of the king's house,
24: 8 put outside the *g* of the LORD's temple.
25:23 from the Ephraim Gate to the Corner *G,*
26: 9 built towers in Jerusalem at the Corner *G,*
26: 9 at the Corner Gate, at the Valley *G,*
27: 3 He built the upper *g* of the LORD's house
31:14 a Levite and the keeper of the eastern *g,*
32: 6 his presence in the open space at the *g*
33:14 to the Fish *G* and encircling Ophel;
35:15 The gatekeepers were at every *g;*
Neh 2:13 I rode out at night by the Valley *G,*
2:13 the Dragon Spring, and came to the Dung *G,*
2:14 to the Spring *G* and to the King's Pool.
2:15 till I once more reached the Valley *G,*
3: 1 took up the task of rebuilding the Sheep *G.*
3: 3 *G* was rebuilt by the sons of Hassenaah;
3: 6 New City *G* was repaired by Joiada,
3:13 The Valley *G* was repaired by Hanun and the
3:13 cubits of the wall up to the Dung *G.*
3:14 The Dung *G* was repaired by Malchijah,
3:15 The Spring *G* was repaired by Shallum,
3:26 a point opposite the Water *G* on the east,
3:28 Above the Horse *G* the priests carried out
3:29 son of Shecaniah, keeper of the East *G.*
3:31 before the *G* of Inspection and as far as
3:32 chamber of the Angle and the Sheep *G,*
8: 1 man in the open space before the Water *G,*
8: 3 open place that was before the Water *G,*
8:16 of the Water *G* and the Gate of Ephraim.
12:31 the wall, in the direction of the Dung *G,*
12:37 At the Spring *G* they went straight up by
12:37 until they came to the Water *G* on the east.
12:39 Ephraim *G* [the New City *G,* the Fish *G,*
12:39 [and they came to a halt at the Prison *G.*
12:39 as far as the Sheep *G* [and they came to a
Tb 7: 1 whom they found seated by his courtyard *g.*
11:10 and stumbled out through the courtyard *g.*
11:15 for she was approaching the *g* of Nineveh.
11:16 *g* of Nineveh to meet his daughter-in-law.
Jdt 8:33 Stand at the *g* tonight to let me pass
10: 6 Then they went out to the *g* of the city of
10: 9 "Order the *g* of the city opened for me,
10: 9 to open the *g* for her as she requested.
13:11 Open the *g!*
13:12 their city *g* and summoned the city elders.
13:13 opened the *g* and welcomed the two women.
Est 2:19 was passing his time at the king's *g,*
2:21 time that Mordecai spent at the king's *g,*
3: 2 royal *g* would kneel and bow down to Haman,
3: 3 who were at the royal *g* said to Mordecai,
4: 2 till he came before the royal *g,*
4: 6 the public square in front of the royal *g,*
5: 9 that Mordecai at the royal *g* did not rise,
5:13 the Jew Mordecai sitting at the royal *g."*
6:10 Mordecai, who is sitting at the royal *g.*
6:12 Mordecai then returned to the royal *g,*
1Mc 5:22 he pursued them to the very *g* of Ptolemais.
2Mc 14:41 were forcing the outer *g* and calling for
Jb 5: 4 be crushed at the *g* without a rescuer.
29: 7 When I went forth to the *g* of the city and
31:21 I saw that I had supporters at the *g—*
Ps(s) 69:13 They who sit at the *g* gossip about me,
118:20 This *g* is the LORD's;
127: 5 when they contend with enemies at the *g.*
Prv 17:19 he who builds his *g* high courts disaster.
22:22 are poor, nor crush the needy at the *g;*
24: 7 not to open his mouth at the *g.*
Sg 7: 5 pools in Heshbon by the *g* of Bath-rabbim.
Wis 6:14 for he shall find her sitting by his *g.*
19:17 each sought the entrance of his own *g.*
Sir 51:19 her *g* and I came to know her secrets.
Is 14:31 Howl, O *g;* cry out, O city!
28: 6 to those who turn back the battle at the *g.*
29:21 a man, Who ensnare his defender at the *g,*
Jer 7: 2 Stand at the *g* of the house of the LORD,
15: 7 winnowed them with the fan in every city *g.*
17:19 Go, stand at the *G* of Benjamin,
19: 2 at the entrance of the Potsherd *G;*
20: 2 *G* of Benjamin in the house of the LORD.
26:10 at the New *G* of the house of the LORD.
31:38 from the Tower of Hananel to the Corner *G.*
31:40 as the corner of the Horse *G* at the east,
37:13 But when he reached the *G* of Benjamin,
38: 7 just then to be at the *G* of Benjamin,
39: 3 of Babylon came and occupied the middle *g:*
39: 4 Road through the *g* between the two walls.
52: 7 left the city by night through the *g*
Lam 5:14 The old men have abandoned the *g,*
Ez 8: 3 Jerusalem, to the entrance of the north *g,*
8: 5 the *g* the altar of the statue of jealousy.
8:14 the entrance of the north *g* of the temple,
9: 2 of the upper *g* which faces the north,
10:19 of the eastern *g* of the LORD's house,
11: 1 and brought me to the east *g* of the temple.
11: 1 entrance of the *g* I saw twenty-five men,
40: 3 he was standing in the *g,*
40: 6 Then he went to the *g* which faced the east,
40: 7 *g* adjoining the vestibule of the gate
40: 8 He measured the vestibule of the *g,*
40: 9 vestibule of the *g* was toward the inside.
40:10 of the east *g* were three on either side,
40:13 He measured the *g* from the back wall of
40:15 The length of the *g* from the front
40:19 lower gate to the front of the inner *g;*
40:20 outer court, there was a *g* facing north,
40:21 same measurements as those of the first *g;*
40:22 as those of the *g* facing the east.
40:23 *g* opposite the north *g,* just as at the east *g;*
40:23 one hundred cubits from one *g* to the other.
40:24 me south, to where there was a southern *g,*
40:25 The *g* and its vestibule had windows on
40:27 had a southern gate; from *g* to gate he
40:28 south gate, where he measured the south *g.*
40:29 The *g* and its vestibule had windows on
40:32 *g* facing the east, where he measured the *g,*
40:33 the *g* and its vestibule had windows on
40:35 Then he brought me to the north *g,*
40:36 The *g* and its vestibule had windows on
40:38 chamber opening off the vestibule of the *g,*
40:39 the *g* there were two tables on either side,
40:40 outside, near the entrance of the north *g,*
40:40 vestibule of the *g* there were two tables.
40:41 on either side of the *g* [eight tables],
40:44 were two chambers, one beside the north *g,*
40:44 south, and the other beside the south *g,*
42:15 he brought me out by way of the *g* which
43: 1 he led me to the *g* which faces the east,
43: 4 by way of the *g* which faces the east.
44: 1 me back to the outer *g* of the sanctuary,
44: 2 This *g* is to remain closed;
44: 3 enter by way of the vestibule of the *g,*
44: 4 of the north *g* to the façade of the temple,
46: 1 The *g* toward the east of the inner court
46: 2 outside by way of the vestibule of the *g*
46: 2 remain standing at the doorpost of the *g;*
46: 2 the *g* and then leave; the gate shall not
46: 3 of this *g* on the sabbaths and new moons.
46: 8 enter and depart by the vestibule of the *g.*
46: 9 they shall leave by the south *g,*
46: 9 south *g* they shall leave by the north gate;
46: 9 by the *g* through which he has entered,
46: 9 but he shall leave by the opposite *g.*
46:12 the eastern *g* shall be opened for him,
46:12 the *g* shall be closed after his departure.
46:19 of the *g* to the chambers [of the sanctuary,
47: 2 north *g,* and around to the outer gate
48:31 *g* of Reuben, the *g* of Judah, and the *g*
48:32 *g* of Joseph, the *g* of Benjamin, and the *g*
48:33 *g* of Simeon, the *g* of Issachar, and the *g*
48:34 *g* of Gad, the *g* of Asher, and the *g*
Dn 13:18 the side *g* to fetch what she had ordered,
13:26 the side *g* to see what had happened to her.
Am 5:10 the *g* and abhor him who speaks the truth.
5:12 bribes, repelling the needy at the *g!*
5:15 good, and let justice prevail at the *g;*
Ob 1:13 Enter not the *g* of my people on the day of
Mi 1: 9 to Judah, It reaches to the *g* of my people,
1:12 down from the LORD to the *g* of Jerusalem.
2:13 burst open the *g* and go out through it;
Zep 1:10 LORD, A cry will be heard from the Fish *G,*
Zec 14:10 From the *G* of Benjamin to the place of the
14:10 place of the First Gate, to the Corner *G;*
Mt 7:13 "Enter through the narrow *g.*
7:13 The *g* that leads to damnation is wide,
7:14 But how narrow is the *g* that leads to life,
26:71 When he went out to the *g* another girl saw
Mk 11: 4 a colt tethered out on the street near a *g,*
13:34 the man at the *g* to watch with a sharp eye.
Lk 7:12 As he approached the *g* of the town a dead
16:20 At his *g* lay a beggar named Lazarus who
Jn 10: 1 not enter the sheepfold through the *g*
10: 2 through the *g* is shepherd of the sheep;
10: 3 the keeper opens the *g* for him.
10: 9 I am the *g.*
18:16 while Peter was left standing at the *g.*
18:16 came out and spoke to the woman at the *g,*
18:17 servant girl who kept the *g* said to Peter,
Acts 3: 2 every day and put him at the temple *g*
3:10 to sit at the Beautiful *G* of the temple.
10:17 at the *g* asking for the house of Simon.
12:10 came to the iron *g* leading out to the city,
16:13 the city *g* to the bank of the river,
Heb 13:12 Therefore Jesus died outside the *g,*
Jas 5: 9 The judge stands at the *g.*

GATEHOUSE (1)

2Mc 1: 8 fire to the *g* and shedding innocent blood.

GATEKEEPER (1)

Ezr 7:24 or tolls on any priest, Levite, singer, *g,*

GATEKEEPERS (34)

2Kgs 7:10 They came and summoned the city *g.*
7:11 The *g* announced this and it was reported
1Chr 9:17 The *g* were Shallum,
9:18 *g* for the encampments of the Levites.
9:22 those who were chosen for *g* at the
9:24 The *g* were stationed at the four sides,
9:26 the four chief *g* were on constant duty.
9:33 These were the chanters and the *g,*
15:18 the *g* Zechariah,
15:23 and Elkanah were *g* before the ark.
15:24 and Jeiel were also *g* before the ark.
16:38 son of Jeduthun, and Hosah, to be *g.*
23: 5 and judges, four thousand were to be *g,*
26: 1 As for the classes of *g.*
26:12 To these classes of *g,*
26:19 These were the classes of the *g,*
2Chr 8:14 The *g* of the various classes stood guard
34:13 Levites were scribes, officials and *g.*
35:15 The *g* were at every gate;
Ezr 2:42 The *g:* sons of Shallum,
2:70 but the singers, the *g,*
7: 7 and some priests, Levites, singers, *g,*
10:24 Eliashib and Zakkur; of the *g:*
Neh 7: 1 and the *g* [and the singers and the
7:45 The *g:* sons of Shallum, sons of Ater,
7:72 The priests, the Levites, the *g,*
10:29 rest of the people, priests, Levites, *g,*
10:40 and the ministering priests, the *g,*
11:19 The *g* were Akkub,
12:25 Meshullam, Talmon, and Akkub were *g.*
12:45 (as did the singers and the *g)*
12:47 gave the singers and the *g* their portions,
13: 5 allotted to the Levites, singers, and *g,*
Ez 44:11 in my sanctuary as *g* and temple servants;

GATEPOSTS (1)

Jgs 16: 3 the doors of the city gate and the two *g,*

GATES (143)

Gn 22:17 take possession of the *g* of their enemies,
24:60 gain possession of the *g* of their enemies!"
Dt 3: 5 fortified with high walls and *g* and bars.
6: 9 the doorposts of your houses and on your *g.*
11:20 doorposts of your houses and on your *g,*
17: 5 out to your city *g* and stone him to death.
20:11 your terms of peace and opens its *g* to you,
Jos 6:26 his youngest son when he sets up its *g.*
Jgs 5: 8 then the war was at their *g.*
1Sm 17:52 approaches of Gath and to the *g* of Ekron,
23: 7 for he has entered a city with *g* and bars."
2Sm 18:24 Now David was sitting between the two *g,*
1Kgs 4:13 walled cities with *g* barred with bronze;
16:34 youngest son, Segub, when he set up the *g,*
1Chr 9:23 guard over the *g* of the house of the LORD,
22: 3 iron to make nails for the doors of the *g,*
2Chr 4: 9 the gates of the courtyard; the *g*
6:28 enemies besiege them at any of their *g;*
8: 5 fortified cities with walls, *g* and bars;
14: 6 them with walls, towers, *g* and bars.
23:19 he stationed guards at the *g* of the LORD's
31: 2 in the *g* of the encampment of the LORD.
Neh 1: 3 and its *g* have been gutted with fire."
2: 3 and its *g* have been eaten out by fire?"
2: 8 he may give me wood for timbering the *g*
2:13 ruins and its *g* had been eaten out by fire.
2:17 ruins and its *g* have been gutted by fire.
6: 1 I had not yet set up the doors in the *g),*
7: 3 "The *g* of Jerusalem are not to be opened
11:19 their brethren, who kept watch over the *g;*
12:25 kept watch over the storerooms at the *g.*
12:30 then they purified the people, the *g,*
13:19 on the *g* of Jerusalem before the sabbath,
13:19 I posted some of my own men at the *g* so
13:22 themselves and to go and watch the *g,*
Tb 13:16 The *g* of Jerusalem shall be built with
13:18 The *g* of Jerusalem shall sing hymns of
Jdt 1: 3 the *g* he raised towers of a hundred cubits,

GATES (cont.)

13:10 As they approached its g,
Est E:18 his entire household, before the g of Susa.
1Mc 4:38 the altar desecrated, the g burnt,
4:57 they repaired the g and the priests'
5:47 them out and blocked up the g with stones.
9:50 and Tephon, with high walls and g and bars.
10:76 the city became afraid and opened the g,
11: 2 the cities opened their g to welcome him,
11:61 people of Gaza locked their g against him.
12:38 by providing them with g and bars.
12:48 of the city closed the g and seized him;
13:33 high towers, thick walls, and g with bars,
15:39 to fortify Kedron and strengthen its g,
2Mc 3:19 indoors ran together, some to the g,
8:33 set fire to the sacred g and Callisthenes,
10:36 the g and let in the rest of the troops,
12: 7 When the g of the town were shut,
Jb 38:17 Have the g of death been shown to you,
38:17 to you, or have you seen the g of darkness?
Ps(s) 9:14 who have raised me up from the g of death,
9:15 and, in the g of the daughter of Zion,
24: 7 Lift up, O g, your lintels; reach up,
24: 9 Lift, up, O g,
73:28 works in the g of the daughter of Zion.
87: 2 The g of Zion,
100: 4 Enter his g with thanksgiving,
107:16 the g of brass and burst the bars of iron.
107:18 so that they were near the g of death.
118:19 Open to me the g of justice;
122: 2 " And now we have set foot within your g,
147:13 For has strengthened the bars of your g;
Prv 1:21 out, at the city g she utters her words:
8: 3 By the g at the approaches of the city,
8:34 Happy the man watching daily at my g,
14:19 good, and the wicked, at the g of the just.
31:23 g as he sits with the elders of the land.
31:31 and let her works praise her at the city g.
Wis 16:13 you lead down to the g of the nether world,
Sir 49:13 shattered defenses, and set up g and bars.
51: 9 very earth, from the g of the nether world,
Is 3:26 Her g will lament and mourn,
13: 2 for them to enter the g of the volunteers.
22: 7 chariots, and horses are posted at the g,
24:12 its g are battered and desolate.
26: 2 up the g to let in a nation that is just,
38:10 To the g of the nether world I shall be
43:28 against me Till I repudiated the holy g,
45: 1 before him and leaving the g unbarred:
54:12 of rubies, your g of carbuncles,
60:11 Your g shall stand open constantly;
60:18 walls "Salvation" and your g "Praise."
62:10 Pass through, pass through the g,
Jer 7: 2 who enter these g to worship the LORD!
14: 2 Judah mourns, her g are lifeless;
17:19 and leave, and at the other g of Jerusalem.
17:20 citizens of Jerusalem who enter these g!
17:21 bring them in through the g of Jerusalem.
17:24 through the g of this city on the sabbath,
17:25 on it, then, through the g of this city,
17:27 through the g of Jerusalem on the sabbath,
17:27 I will set unquenchable fire to its g,
22: 2 and your people that enter by these g!
22: 4 continue to enter the g of this palace,
22:19 and cast out beyond the g of Jerusalem.
49:31 says the LORD, That has no g or bars,
51:58 her lofty g shall be destroyed by fire.
Lam 2: 9 Sunk into the ground are her g;
4:12 or foe could enter the g of Jerusalem.
Bar 6:17 their houses with g and bars and bolts,
Ez 21:20 g I have appointed the sword for slaughter,
21:27 cry, to post battering-rams at the g,
26:10 walls shall shake as he enters your g,
38:11 without walls, having neither bars nor g,
40: 6 its steps, and measured the g threshold,
40:11 He measured the g entrance,
40:11 the g passage itself was thirteen cubits.
40:18 the g, as wide as the gates were long;
44:17 g of the inner court or within the temple.
45:19 the doorposts of the g of the inner court.
48:30 the g of which are named after the tribes
48:31 hundred cubits, there shall be three g:
48:32 hundred cubits, there shall be three g:
48:33 hundred cubits, there shall be three g:
48:34 hundred cubits, there shall be three g:
Ob 1:11 his g and cast lots over Jerusalem,
Na 2: 7 The river g are opened,
3:13 your foes the g of your land are open wide,
Zec 8:16 and peace in the judgments at your g,
Mal 1:10 one among you would shut the temple g
Acts 5:19 angel of the Lord opened the g of the jail,
5:23 the guards at their posts outside the g,
9:24 keep close watch on the city g day and night
14:13 brought oxen and garlands to the g because
16:27 woke up to see the prison g wide open.
21:30 the temple, and immediately closed its g.
Rv 21:12 g at which twelve angels were stationed.
21:12 Twelve names were written on the g,
21:13 There were three g facing east,
21:15 rod of gold for measuring the city, its g,
21:21 The twelve g were twelve pearls,
21:25 During the day its g shall never be shut,
22:14 of life and enter the city through its g!

GATEWAY (8)

Gn 28:17 abode of God, and that is the g to heaven!"
1Sm 4:18 fell backward from his chair into the g;
9:18 Saul met Samuel in the g and said,
Jdt 1: 4 g he built to a height of seventy cubits,
1Mc 14: 5 and made it a g to the isles of the sea.
Ez 26: 2 it is broken, the g to the peoples;
40:16 Within the g on both sides there were
Mk 14:68 Then he went out into the g.

GATEWAYS (3)

Jdt 7:22 in the streets and g of the city,
Jer 1:15 set up his throne at the g of Jerusalem,Call
Lam 1: 4 All her g are deserted,

GATH (36)

Jos 11:22 However, some survived in Gaza, in G,
13: 3 in Gaza, Ashdod, Ashkelon, G and Ekron);
1Sm 5: 8 The men of G replied,
5: 9 moved the ark of the God of Israel to G!
6:17 one for Gaza, one for Ashkelon, one for G,
7:14 The cities from Ekron to G which the
17: 4 of G came out from the Philistine camp;
17:23 Philistine champion, by name Goliath of G,
17:52 approaches of G and to the gates of Ekron,
17:52 road from Shaaraim as far as G and Ekron.
21:11 from Saul, going to Achish, king of G.
21:13 very much afraid of Achish, king of G.
27: 2 over to Achish, son of Maoch, king of G.
27: 3 David and his men lived in G with Achish;
27: 4 Saul was told that David had fled to G,
27:11 a man or woman alive to be brought to G,
2Sm 1:20 "Tell it not in G,
15:18 G who had accompanied him from that city,
21:19 Jair from Bethlehem, killed Goliath of G,
21:20 There was another battle at G in which
21:22 These four were Rephaim in G,
1Kgs 2:39 was informed that his servants were in G,
2:39 away to Achish, son of Maacah, king of G.
2:40 to Achish in G in search of his servants,
2:41 that Shimei had gone from Jerusalem to G,
2Kgs 12:18 of Aram mounted a siege against G.
1Chr 7:21 were slain by the inhabitants of G because
8:13 they put the inhabitants of G to flight.
18: 1 and he took G and its towns away from the
20: 5 slew Lahmi, the brother of Goliath of G,
20: 6 In still another battle, at G,
20: 8 descendants of the Raphaim of G who died
2Chr 11: 8 Etam, Tekoa, Beth-zur, Soco, Adullam, G,
26: 6 the Philistines and razed the walls of G,
Am 6: 2 great, and down to G of the Philistines!
Mi 1:10 Publish it not in G,

GATH-HEPHER (2)

Jos 19:13 continued eastward to G and to Eth-kazin,
2Kgs 14:25 the prophet Jonah, son of Amittai, from G.

GATH-RIMMON (3)

Jos 19:45 Gibethon, Baalath, Jehud, Bene-berak, G,
21:24 lands, and G with its pasture lands,
1Chr 6:54 lands, and G with its pasture lands.

GATHER (121)

Gn 31:46 Jacob said to his kinsmen, G some stones."
49: 1 G around,
Ex 5: 7 Let them go and g straw themselves!
5:11 Go and g the straw yourselves,
5:12 the land of Egypt to g stubble for straw,
16: 4 are to go out and g their daily portion;
16: 5 twice as much as they g on the other days."
16:16 So g it that everyone has enough to eat,
16:26 On the other six days you can g it,
16:27 day some of the people went out to g it,
23:10 you may sow your land and g in its produce.
23:16 when you g in the produce from the fields.
Lv 19:10 bare, nor g up the grapes that have fallen.
23:40 you shall g foliage from majestic trees,
Nm 10: 3 the whole community shall g round you at
10: 4 of the troops of Israel, shall g round you.
19: 9 a man who is clean shall g up the ashes of
25: 4 to Moses, G all the leaders of the people,
Dt 11:14 may have your grain, wine and oil to g in;
30: 3 he will again g you from all the nations
30: 4 from there will the LORD, your God, g you;
Jos 2:18 and g your father and mother,
Ru 2: 7 She asked leave to g the gleanings into
1Sm 7: 5 then gave orders, G all Israel to Mizpah,
2Kgs 4:39 the field to g herbs and found a wild vine,
22:20 I will therefore g you to your ancestors;
1Chr 16:35 g us and deliver us from the nations,
2Chr 34:28 I will g you to your ancestors and you
Ezr 10: 7 the exiles should g together in Jerusalem,
Neh 1: 9 of the world, I will g them from there,
7: 5 it into my mind to g together the nobles,
Tb 13: 5 He will g you from all the Gentiles among
1Mc 2:67 also g about you all who observe the law,
9: 7 no time to g them together
10: 6 to g an army and procure arms as his ally;
10: 8 king had given him authority to g an army.
2Mc 1:27 G together our scattered people,
2:18 have mercy on us and g us together
12:39 Judas and his men went to g up the bodies
Jb 39:12 and g in the yield of your threshing floor?
Ps(s) 26: 9 G not my soul with those of sinners,
50: 5 G my faithful ones before me,
56: 7 They g together in hiding,
102:23 Jerusalem, When the peoples g together,
104:28 When you give it to them, they g it;
106:47 our God, and g us from among the nations,
142: 8 g around me when you have been good to me.
Eccl 3: 5 to scatter stones, and a time to g them;
Sg 5: 1 I g my myrrh and my spices,
6: 2 To browse in the garden and to g lilies.
Sir 36:10 G all the tribes of Jacob,
Is 11:12 the nations and g the outcasts of Israel;
33: 4 g spoil as caterpillars are gathered up;
34:15 hatch them out and g them in her shadow;
34:16 it, and his spirit shall g them there.
43: 5 descendants, from the west I will g you.
43: 9 Let all the nations g together,
45:20 Come and assemble, g together,
56: 8 I g to him besides those already gathered.
60: 4 they all g and come to you;
62: 9 You who g the grapes shall drink the wine
66:18 I come to g nations of every language;
Jer 7:18 The children g wood,
8:13 I will g them all in, says the LORD:
9:21 the harvester, with no one to g them.
12: 9 Come, g together,
23: 3 I myself will g the remnant of my flock
25:33 mourn them, none will g them for burial;
29:14 I will g you together from all the nations
31: 8 I will g them from the ends of the world,
32:37 I will g them together from all the lands
49:14 G together, move against her,
Ez 11:17 I will g you from the nations and assemble
16:37 I will now g together all your lovers whom
16:37 I will g them against you from all sides
20:34 bring you out from the nations and g you
22:19 I must g you together within Jerusalem.
22:20 I will g you together in my furious wrath,
28:25 When I g the house of Israel from the
29:13 At the end of forty years I will g the
34:13 peoples and g them from the foreign lands;
36:24 nations, g you from all the foreign lands,
37:21 and g them from all sides to bring them
39:17 from all sides g for the slaughter I am
39:27 g them from the lands of their enemies,
39:28 nations, will g them back on their land,
Hos 8:10 with the nations, I will now g an army;
9: 6 go from the ruins, Egypt shall g them in,
Jl 1:14 G the elders,
2:16 G the people,
2:16 g the children and the infants at the
Am 3: 9 G about the mountain of Samaria,
Mi 2:12 I will g you,
4: 6 that day, says the LORD, I will g the lame,
Na 3:18 upon the mountains, with none to g them.
Zep 2: 1 G, gather yourselves together,
3: 8 is my decision to g together the nations,
3:20 you home, and at that time I will g you;
Zec 10:10 the land of Egypt, and g them from Assyria.
14: 2 And I will g all the nations against
Mt 3:12 floor and g his grain into the barn,
6:26 not sow or reap, they g nothing into barns;
9:38 to send out laborers to g his harvest."
12:30 me, and he who does not g with me scatters.
13:30 up to burn, then g the wheat into my barn.' "
23:37 often have I yearned to g your children,
24:28 the carcass lies, there the vultures g.
25:24 not sow and g where you did not scatter,
25:26 did not sow and g where I did not scatter.
Mk 2: 2 At that they began to g in great numbers.
Lk 3:17 floor and g the wheat into his barn;
11:23 me, and he who does not g with me scatters.
13:34 How often have I wanted to g your children
17:37 the carcass is, there will the vultures g."
Jn 6:12 G up the crusts that are left over so that
11:52 but to g into one all the dispersed
Acts 5:16 from the towns around Jerusalem would g,
1Cor 11:18 I hear that when you g for a meeting there
Rv 14:18 g the grapes from the vines of the earth,
19:17 G together for the great feast God has

GATHERED (157)

Gn 1: 9 under the sky be g into a single basin,
1: 9 water under the sky was g into its basin,
47:14 were languishing from hunger, Joseph g in,
Ex 8:10 g up and there was a stench in the land.
16:17 Some g a large and some a small amount.
16:18 had g a large amount did not have too much,
16:18 g a small amount did not have too little.
16:18 They so g that everyone had enough to eat.
16:21 Morning after morning they g it,
16:22 On the sixth day they g twice as much food,
32: 1 they g around Aaron and said to him,
Lv 23:39 when you have g in the produce of the land,
Nm 11: 8 When they had gone about and g it up,
11:32 all the next day the people g in the quail.
11:32 one who got the least g ten homers of them.
19:10 He who has g up the ashes of the heifer
Dt 16:13 when you have g in the produce from your

33:21 while the heads of the people were *g*.
Jos 24: 1 Joshua *g* together all the tribes of Israel
Jgs 2:10 of that generation were *g* to their fathers,
9:47 citizens of Migdal-shechem were *g* together.
10:17 had *g* for war and encamped in Gilead,
11:20 On the contrary, he *g* all his soldiers,
12: 1 *g* together and crossed over to Zaphon.
20: 1 the community was *g* to the LORD at Mizpah.
1Sm 4: 1 the Philistines *g* for an attack on Israel.
7: 6 When they were *g* at Mizpah,
7: 7 heard that the Israelites had *g* at Mizpah,
17: 2 *g* and camped in the Vale of the Terebinth,
25: 1 Samuel died, and all Israel *g* to mourn him;
2Sm 14:14 out on the ground and cannot be *g* up.
21:13 who had been dismembered were also *g* up.
1Kgs 11:24 Rezon *g* men about him and became leader of
12:21 Rehoboam *g* together all the house of Judah
20: 1 Ben-hadad, king of Aram, *g* all his forces,
22: 6 The king of Israel *g* together the prophets,
2Kgs 10:18 *g* all the people together and said to them:
1Chr 11: 1 Then all Israel *g* about David in Hebron,
19:17 to David, he *g* all Israel together,
23: 2 then *g* together all the leaders of Israel,
2Chr 1:14 He *g* together chariots and drivers,
5: 6 entire community of Israel *g* about him
11: 1 *g* together the house of Judah and Benjamin,
12: 5 who had *g* at Jerusalem because of Shishak,
15:10 They *g* at Jerusalem in the third month of
18: 5 The king of Israel *g* his prophets,
20: 4 Then Judah *g* to seek help from the LORD;
28:24 Ahaz *g* up the utensils of God's house and
29: 4 *g* them in the open space to the east,
29:15 They *g* their brethren together and
30: 3 and the people were not *g* at Jerusalem.
30:13 Thus many people *g* in Jerusalem to
32: 4 a large crowd was *g* which stopped all the
32: 6 He *g* them together in his presence in the
Ezr 3: 1 the people *g* at Jerusalem as one man.
7:28 I *g* together Israelite family heads to
9: 4 Around me *g* all who were in dread of the
10: 1 large assembly of Israelites *g* about him,
10: 9 All the men of Judah and Benjamin *g*
Neh 5:16 and all my men were *g* there for the work.
8: 1 the whole people *g* as one man in the open
8:13 priests and the Levites *g* around Ezra
9: 1 *g* together fasting and in sackcloth,
12:28 *g* together from the region about Jerusalem,
Tb 13:13 who shall all be *g* together and shall
14: 7 shall be *g* together and go to Jerusalem;
Jdt 4: 3 all the people of Judea been *g* together,
6:16 women, *g* in haste at the place of assembly.
10:18 among the tents, a crowd *g* in the camp.
13:13 and when they *g* around the two,
15:12 All the women of Israel *g* to see her;
1Mc 2:16 Mattathias and his sons *g* in a group apart.
2:44 They *g* an army and struck down sinners in
3: 9 he *g* together those who were perishing.
3:10 Then Apollonius *g* the Gentiles,
3:13 heard that Judas had *g* many about him,
3:44 The assembly *g* together to prepare for
3:52 are *g* together against us to destroy us.
4:28 So the following year he *g* together sixty
5:22 the Gentiles fell, and he *g* their spoils.
5:64 and men *g* about them and praised them.
7:12 *g* about Alcimus and Bacchides to ask for a
7:22 were disturbing their people *g* about him.
9:63 he *g* together his whole force and sent
10:21 and he *g* an army and procured many arms.
10:48 King Alexander *g* together a large army and
10:69 Having *g* a large army,
11: 1 The king of Egypt *g* his forces,
11:20 At that time Jonathan *g* together the men
14:30 their high priest, he was *g* to his kinsmen.
2Mc 5: 5 Jason *g* fully a thousand men and suddenly
5:16 *g* up with profane hands the votive
10:24 *g* a tremendous force of foreign troops and
14:23 of ordinary people who *g* around him;
14:30 So he *g* together a large number of his men,
Jb 24:24 laid low and, like all others, are *g* up;
Ps(s) 35:15 I stumbled they were glad and *g* together;
35:15 they *g* together striking me unawares.
47:10 The princes of the peoples are *g* together
107: 3 the hand of the foe And *g* from the lands,
Prv 27:25 appears, and the mountain greens are *g* in,
Sir 47:18 Gold you *g* like so much iron,
Is 24:22 be *g* together like prisoners into a pit;
33: 4 Men gather spoil as caterpillars are *g* up;
49: 5 back to him and Israel *g* to him
56: 8 I gather to him besides those already *g*.
60: 7 All the flocks of Kedar shall be *g* for you,
Jer 3:17 there all nations will be *g* together to
6:11 the street, upon the young men *g* together.
8: 2 They will not be *g* up for burial,
26: 9 *g* about Jeremiah in the house of the LORD.
Bar 4:37 *g* in from the east and from the west By
5: 5 see your children *G* from the east
Ez 20:41 *g* you out of the countries over which you
22:20 and tin are *g* into a furnace and smelted
38:12 and against a people *g* from the nations,
Hos 2: 2 of Judah and of Israel shall be *g* together;
10:10 I *g* troops against them when I chastised
Mi 1: 7 As the wages of a harlot they were *g*,
4:11 How many nations are *g* against you!
4:12 *g* them like sheaves on the threshing floor.
7: 1 I am as when the fruit is *g*,
Na 3:17 *g* on the rubble fences on a cold day!
Zec 12: 3 of the earth shall be *g* against her.
14:14 surrounding nations shall be *g* together,
Mt 5: 1 he had sat down his disciples *g* around him,
13: 2 Such great crowds *g* around him that he
14:20 The fragments remaining, when *g* up,
15:37 When they *g* up the fragments left over,
18:20 Where two or three are *g* in my name,
Mk 1:33 long the whole town was *g* outside the door.
4: 1 Such a huge crowd *g* around him that he
5:21 a large crowd *g* around him and he stayed
6:43 They *g* up enough leftovers to fill twelve
7: 1 who had come from Jerusalem *g* around him.
8: 8 *g* up seven wicker baskets of leftovers.
8:19 how many baskets of fragments you *g* up?"
10: 1 Once more crowds *g* around him,
Lk 5:15 and great crowds *g* to hear him and to be
12: 1 Meanwhile a crowd of thousands had *g*,
Jn 6:13 they *g* twelve baskets full of pieces left
10:24 when the Jews *g* around him and said,
Acts 1:15 have been a hundred and twenty *g* together.
2: 1 came it found them *g* in one place.
4:26 the princes *g* together against the Lord
4:27 they *g* in this very city against your holy
4:31 where they were *g* shook as they prayed.
12:12 Mark), where many others were *g* in prayer.
13:44 the entire city *g* to hear the word of God.
16:13 and spoke to the women who were *g* there.
20: 7 week when we *g* for the breaking of bread,
21:26 Paul *g* the men together and went through
28:17 When they had *g* he said:
2Cor 8:15 *g* much had no excess and he who gathered
2Thes 2: 1 Lord Jesus Christ and our being *g* to him,
Rv 14:19 the earth and *g* the grapes of the earth.

GATHERER (1)

Ps(s) 129: 7 his hand, nor the *g* of sheaves his arms;

GATHERING (19)

Lv 25: 3 prune your vineyard, *g* in their produce.
Nm 11:24 *G* seventy elders of the people,
11:26 not in the *g* but had been left in the camp.
15:32 was discovered *g* wood on the sabbath day.
1Kgs 17:10 of the city, a widow was *g* sticks there;
2Chr 23: 2 *g* the Levites from all the cities of Judah
Est F:10 *G* together with joy and happiness before
1Mc 1: 3 of the earth, *g* plunder from many nations;
13: 1 When Simon heard that Trypho was *g* a large
Eccl 2:26 he gives the task of *g* possessions
Is 49:18 and see, they are all *g* and coming to you.
Mk 9:25 Jesus, on seeing a crowd rapidly *g*,
Lk 8: 4 A large crowd was *g*,
11:53 After he had left this *g*,
15: 1 and sinners were all *g* around to hear him,
Acts 19:30 this *g* but his disciples would not let him.
19:33 he wanted to explain something to the *g*.
28: 2 by lighting a fire and *g* us all around it,
Heb 12:22 to myriads of angels in festal *g*,

GATHERINGS (3)

Sir 42:11 people, an object of derision in public *g*.
44:15 At *g* their wisdom is retold,
1Cor 14:34 women should keep silent in such *g*.

GATHERS (13)

2Mc 2: 7 remain unknown until God *g* his people
Ps(s) 33: 7 He *g* the waters of the sea as in a flask;
147: 2 the dispersed of Israel he *g*.
Prv 28: 8 *g* it for him who is kind to the poor.
Is 13:14 hunted gazelle, or a flock that no one *g*,
17: 5 of stalks when he *g* the standing grain;
40:11 in his arms he *g* the lambs,
56: 8 LORD GOD, who *g* the dispersed of Israel:
Jer 31:10 who scattered Israel, now *g* them together,
Hb 1:15 away with his net, He *g* them in his seine;
2: 5 as death, Who *g* to himself all the nations,
Mt 23:37 a mother bird *g* her young under her wings,
Jn 4:36 his wages and *g* a yield for eternal life,

GAUDY (1)

Ez 16:16 gowns and made for yourself *g* high places,

GAULS (1)

1Mc 8: 2 that they had performed against the *G*,

GAUNT (4)

Gn 41: 3 Behind them seven other cows, ugly and *g*,
41: 4 the ugly, *g* cows ate up the seven handsome,
41:19 other cows, scrawny, most ill-formed and *g*.
41:20 The *g*, ugly cows ate up the first

GAVE (606)

Gn 2:16 The LORD God *g* man this order:
2:20 The man *g* names to all the cattle,
3: 6 and she also *g* some to her husband,
3:12 she *g* me fruit from the tree,
4:20 Adah, *g* birth to Jabal,
4:22 Zillah, on her part, *g* birth to Tubalcain,
4:25 she *g* birth to a son whom she called Seth.
6:22 out all the commands that God *g* him.
12:20 Then Pharaoh *g* men orders concerning him,
14:20 Then Abram *g* him a tenth of everything.
16: 3 and *g* her to her husband Abram to be his
16: 5 I myself *g* my maid to your embrace;
16:13 To the LORD who spoke to her she *g* a name,
18: 7 choice steer, and *g* it to a servant,
19:37 one *g* birth to a son whom she named Moab,
19:38 The younger one, too, *g* birth to a son,
20:14 and female slaves and *g* them to Abraham;
21: 3 Abraham *g* the name Isaac to this son of
21:14 and a skin of water and *g* them to Hagar.
21:27 Then Abraham took sheep and cattle and *g*
24:18 the jug onto her hand, she *g* him a drink.
24:53 he also *g* costly presents to her brother
25:34 then *g* him some bread and the lentil stew;
26:11 therefore *g* this warning to all his men:
26:18 he *g* them the same names that his father
27:15 *g* them to her younger son Jacob to wear;
27:23 so in the end he *g* him his blessing.)
28: 4 descendants the blessing he *g* to Abraham,
28: 6 charging him, as he *g* him his blessing,
29:22 all the local inhabitants and *g* a feast.
29:28 *g* him his daughter Rachel in marriage.
30: 4 *g* him her maidservant Bilhah as a consort,
30: 9 she *g* her maidservant Zilpah to Jacob as a
30:21 Finally, she *g* birth to a daughter,
30:25 After Rachel *g* birth to Joseph,
31: 9 your father's livestock and *g* it to me.
31:42 of my toil, and last night he *g* judgment."
32:18 servant in the lead he *g* this instruction:
32:20 He *g* similar instructions to the second
35:12 *g* to Abraham and Isaac I now give to you;
38:18 *g* them to her and had intercourse with her,
39: 6 owned in Joseph's charge, he *g* no thought,
40: 1 and baker *g* offense to their lord,
40:20 when he *g* a banquet to all his staff,
40:23 the chief cupbearer *g* no thought to Joseph;
41:45 Joseph, and he *g* him in marriage Asenath,
42:25 Then Joseph *g* orders to have their
43:24 He *g* them water to bathe their feet,
43:31 now in control of himself, *g* the order,
44: 1 *g* his head steward these instructions:
45:21 Joseph *g* them the wagons,
45:22 He also *g* to each of them fresh clothing,
45:22 but to Benjamin he *g* three hundred
47:11 settled his father and brothers and *g* them
49:28 *g* to each of them an appropriate message,
49:29 message, Then he *g* them this charge:
50:16 father died, he *g* us these instructions:
Ex 2:21 *g* him his daughter Zipporah in marriage.
5: 6 That very day Pharaoh *g* the taskmasters
6:13 spoke to Moses and Aaron and *g* them his
16:32 that they may see what food I *g* you to eat
31:18 *g* him the two tablets of the commandments,
32:24 They *g* it to me,
Lv 1: 1 from the meeting tent *g* him this message:
27:34 *g* Moses on Mount Sinai for the Israelites.
Nm 3:51 *g* this ransom silver to Aaron and his sons,
4:49 they *g* them their individual assignments
7: 7 He *g* two wagons and four oxen to the
7: 9 He *g* none to the Kohathites,
11:12 or was it I who *g* them birth,
17:21 and their princes *g* him staffs,
22:18 *g* me his house full of silver and gold,
23: 7 Then Balaam *g* voice to his oracle:
23:18 Balaam *g* voice to his oracle:
24: 3 upon him, and he *g* voice to his oracle:
24:13 *g* me his house full of silver and gold,
24:15 Then Balaam *g* voice to his oracle:
24:20 Amalek, Balaam *g* voice to his oracle:
24:21 the Kenites, he *g* voice to his oracle:
24:23 he *g* voice to his oracle:
27:23 his hands on him and *g* him his commission,
30: 1 then *g* the Israelites these instructions,
31:41 to the LORD, Moses *g* to the priest Eleazar,
31:47 and of beasts, and *g* them to the Levites,
31:52 The gold that they *g* as a contribution to
32:28 *g* this order in their regard to the priest
32:33 Moses *g* them [the Gadites and Reubenites,
32:40 [Moses *g* Gilead to Machir,
34:13 Moses also *g* this order to the Israelites:
35: 1 The LORD *g* these instructions to Moses on
36: 5 So Moses *g* this regulation to the
Dt 1:18 *g* you all the commands you were to fulfill.
1:43 I *g* you this warning but you would not
3:12 *g* Reuben and Gad the territory from Aroer,
3:13 region, I *g* to the half-tribe of Manasseh.
3:15 To Machir I *g* Gilead,
5:22 upon two tablets of stone and *g* them to me.
9:10 *g* me the two tablets of stone inscribed,
10: 5 in keeping with the command the LORD *g* me.
22:16 'I *g* my daughter to this man in marriage,
26: 9 *g* us this land flowing with milk and honey.
27: 1 elders of Israel, *g* the people this order:
27:11 same day Moses *g* the people this order:
28:45 the commandments and statutes he *g* you.
29: 7 we then *g* as a heritage to the Reubenites,
31:25 he *g* the Levites who carry the ark of the
32:18 you, You forgot the God who *g* you birth.
33: 4 A law he *g* to us;

GAVE (cont.)

34: 9 so the Israelites *g* him their obedience,
Jos 1:14 land Moses *g* you here beyond the Jordan.
6:10 any noise or outcry until he *g* the word:
11:23 Joshua *g* it to Israel as their heritage,
13:15 What Moses *g* to the Reubenite clans:
13:24 What Moses *g* to the Gadite clans:
13:29 What Moses *g* to the clans of the
13:32 Moses *g* when he was in the plains of Moab,
13:33 Moses *g* no heritage to the tribe of Levi,
14:13 and *g* him Hebron as his heritage.
15:13 As the LORD had commanded, Joshua *g* Caleb,
15:17 *g* him his daughter Achsah in marriage.
15:19 So he *g* her the upper and the lower pools.
18: 7 Moses, the servant of the LORD, *g* them."
19:50 they *g* him the city which he requested,
21: 3 the Israelites *g* the Levites the following
21:43 And so the LORD *g* Israel all the land he
21:44 it, the LORD *g* them peace on every side,
22: 2 you, and have obeyed every command I *g* you.
22: 4 Moses, the servant of the LORD, *g* you.
22:34 The Reubenites and the Gadites *g* the
24: 3 his descendants numerous, and *g* him Isaac.
24: 4 To Isaac I *g* Jacob and Esau.
24:13 "I *g* you a land which you had not tilled
Jgs 1:13 *g* him his daughter Achsah in marriage.
1:15 Caleb *g* her the upper and the lower pool.
3: 6 and *g* their own daughters to their sons in
5:25 He asked for water, she *g* him milk;
6: 9 them out before you and *g* you their land.
9: 4 They also *g* him seventy silver shekels
11:24 which your god Chemosh *g* you to possess,
14: 9 father and mother, he *g* them some to eat,
14:10 to the woman, and Samson *g* a banquet there,
14:19 he *g* their garments to those who had
15: 2 so I *g* her to your best man.
17: 3 of them and *g* them to the silversmith,
20:36 for the men of Israel *g* ground to Benjamin,
21:14 they *g* them as wives the women of
Ru 2:18 *g* her what she had left over from lunch.
3: 8 the man *g* a start and turned around to
3:17 "He *g* me these six measures of barley
4:17 And the neighbor women *g* him his name,
1Sm 2:21 Hannah so that she conceived and *g* birth
4:19 with the pangs of labor, and *g* birth.
7: 5 Samuel then *g* orders,
9:23 portion I *g* you and told you to put aside."
10: 9 to leave Samuel, God *g* him another heart.
12: 8 Egypt, and he *g* them this place to live in.
13:13 kept the command the LORD your God *g* you,
14:46 Saul *g* up the pursuit of the Philistines,
17:30 everyone *g* him the same answer as before.
18: 4 mantle he was wearing and *g* it to David,
18:27 Saul *g* him his daughter Michal in marriage.
20:40 Then Jonathan *g* his weapons to this boy of
21: 3 "The king *g* me a commission and told me
21: 3 which he sent me or the commission he *g* me.
21: 7 So the priest *g* him holy bread,
22:10 the LORD for him and *g* him supplies,
24:23 *g* Saul his oath and Saul returned home,
25:43 but Saul *g* David's wife Michal,
27: 6 That same day Achish *g* him Ziklag,
28: 6 but the LORD *g* no answer,
2Sm 10:18 But the Arameans *g* way before Israel,
12: 8 I *g* you your lord's house and your lord's
12: 8 I *g* you the house of Israel and of Judah.
17:15 *g* Absalom and the elders of Israel,
18: 5 But the king *g* this command to Joab,
19:24 And the king *g* him his oath.
22:14 the Most High *g* forth his voice.
22:51 You who *g* great victories to your king and
1Kgs 2: 1 *g* these instructions to his son Solomon:
2:15 my brother's, for the LORD *g* it to him.
2:43 of the LORD and the command that I *g* you?"
2:46 The king then *g* the order to Benaiah,
3:15 and *g* a banquet for all his servants.
3:17 *g* birth in the house while she was present.
3:18 after I gave birth this woman also *g* birth.
5: 9 God *g* Solomon wisdom and exceptional
5:25 while Solomon every year *g* Hiram twenty
5:26 *g* Solomon wisdom as he promised him,
7: 7 of the throne where he *g* judgment
8:34 them back to the land you *g* their fathers.
8:40 as they live on the land you *g* our fathers.
8:48 to you toward the land you *g* their fathers,
9: 7 I will cut off Israel from the land I *g* them
9:11 King Solomon *g* Hiram twenty cities in the
10:10 Then she *g* the king one hundred and twenty
10:10 as the queen of Sheba *g* to King Solomon.
10:13 King Solomon *g* the queen of Sheba
11:18 king of Egypt, who *g* Hadad a house,
11:19 so that he *g* him in marriage the sister of
12:13 him, the king *g* the people a harsh answer.
12:24 LORD and *g* up the expedition accordingly.
13: 3 He *g* a sign that same day and said:
13: 8 "If you *g* me half your kingdom,"
13:21 command which the LORD, your God, *g* you,
14: 8 of David of the kingdom and *g* it to you.
14:15 this good land which he *g* their fathers,
15: 4 LORD, his God, *g* him a lamp in Jerusalem,
17:23 the upper room and *g* him to his mother.
19:21 their flesh, and *g* it to his people to eat.
21:25 no one *g* himself up to the doing of evil
22:33 the king of Israel, *g* up pursuit of him.
2Kgs 3: 9 the water *g* out for the army
3:27 they *g* up the siege and returned
5:23 up these silver talents in bags and *g* them,
10:15 Jehonadab *g* him his hand,
11: 5 He *g* them these orders:
11:10 He *g* the captains King David's spears and
13: 5 So the LORD *g* Israel a savior,
15:19 and Menahem *g* him a thousand talents of
17:27 The king of Assyria *g* the order,
18:16 and *g* the gold to the king of Assyria.
21: 8 be driven off the land I *g* their fathers,
22: 8 Hilkiah *g* the book to Shaphan,
23:35 Jehoiakim *g* the silver and gold to Pharaoh,
25:24 *g* the commanders and their men his oath.
25:28 He spoke kindly to him and *g* him a throne
1Chr 2:35 Sheshan *g* his daughter in marriage to his
11:24 *g* him a reputation like that of the Three.
19:17 up to fight the Arameans, they *g* battle.
21:27 Then the LORD *g* orders to the angel to
22:13 decrees which the LORD *g* Moses for Israel.
25: 5 *g* Heman fourteen sons and three daughters.
28:11 Then David *g* to his son Solomon the
29: 8 Those who had precious stones *g* them into
2Chr 1:18 Solomon *g* orders for the building of a
6:25 land which you *g* them and their fathers.
6:27 which you *g* your people as their heritage.
6:31 as they live on the land you *g* our fathers.
6:38 of their land which you *g* their fathers,
7:20 uproot the people from the land I *g* them;
9: 9 Then she *g* the king one hundred and twenty
9: 9 which the queen of Sheba *g* to King Solomon.
9:12 King Solomon *g* the queen of Sheba
10:13 given him, the king *g* them a harsh answer,
11: 4 and *g* up the expedition against Jeroboam.
15:15 And the LORD *g* them rest on every side.
17: 5 secure, and all Judah *g* Jehoshaphat gifts,
18:32 of Israel and *g* up their pursuit of him.
19: 9 He *g* them this command:
20: 7 Israel and *g* it forever to the descendants
20:30 for his God *g* him rest on every side.
21: 3 father *g* them numerous gifts of silver,
21: 3 *g* to Jehoram because he was the first-born.
23: 9 the priest *g* the captains the spears,
23:18 Then Jehoiada *g* the charge of the LORD's
24:12 Then the king and Jehoiada *g* it to the
28:15 on their feet, *g* them food and drink,
31: 5 they *g* a generous tithe of everything.
31:11 Hezekiah then *g* orders that chambers be
32:22 he *g* them rest on every side.
32:29 numbers, for God *g* him very great riches.
34:11 They also *g* it to the carpenters and the
34:15 Hilkiah *g* the book to Shaphan,
35: 8 also *g* a freewill gift to the people,
35: 8 *g* to the priests two thousand six hundred
35:12 what was destined for the holocaust and *g* it
Ezr 1: 6 their neighbors *g* them help in every way,
6:22 so that he *g* them help in their work on
7:11 Artaxerxes *g* to Ezra the priest-scribe,
8:36 who *g* their support to the people
9: 8 remnant and *g* us a stake in his holy place;
9:11 you *g* through your servants the prophets:
10:19 their guilt they *g* a ram from the flock.
Neh 1: 8 the promise which you *g* through Moses,
6: 4 proposal, and each time I *g* the same reply.
9:13 You *g* them just ordinances,
9:15 from heaven you *g* them in their hunger,
9:20 and you *g* them water in their thirst.
9:22 You *g* them kingdoms and peoples,
9:36 and as for the land which you *g* our
12:47 *g* the singers and the gatekeepers their
13: 9 Then I *g* orders to purify the chambers,
Tb 1: 8 The third tithe I *g* to orphans and widows,
2:12 and also *g* her a young goat for the table.
7: 9 the flock and *g* them a cordial reception.
7:12 hand and *g* her to Tobiah with the words:
7:13 marriage contract stating that he *g* Sarah
8: 6 You made Adam and you *g* him his wife Eve
9: 5 Raphael *g* Gabael his bond and told him
14: 3 seven sons, and *g* him this command:
Jdt 6:21 home, where he *g* a banquet for the elders.
10: 5 She *g* her maid a leather flask of wine and
10: 5 she wrapped up and *g* to the maid to carry.
11:12 food *g* out and all their water ran low,
12:10 *g* a banquet for his servants alone,
16:22 but she *g* herself to no man all the days
16:24 and to the maid she *g* her freedom.
Est 1: 5 At the end of this time the king *g* a feast
1: 9 Queen Vashti also *g* a feast for the women
2:18 Then the king *g* a great feast in honor of
3:10 ring from his hand and *g* it to Haman,
4: 8 He also *g* him a copy of the written decree
4:10 Hathach and *g* him this message for Mordecai:
7: 9 who *g* the report that benefited the king."
8: 1 day King Ahasuerus *g* the house of Haman,
9:14 The king then *g* an order to this effect,
1Mc 3:28 chests, *g* his soldiers a year's pay,
3:34 and *g* him instructions concerning
5:42 beside the stream and *g* them this order:
5:58 They *g* orders to the men of their army who
6:12 and for no cause *g* orders that the
6:15 He *g* him his crown, his robe, and his
6:17 and he *g* him the title Eupator.
6:44 So he *g* up his life to save his people and
6:62 broke the oath he had sworn and *g* orders
8: 8 these from him and *g* them to King Eumenes.
10: 9 and he *g* them back to their parents.
10:58 *g* him his daughter Cleopatra in marriage.
10:60 *g* them and their friends silver and gold
10:89 he also *g* him Ekron and all its territory
11:10 I regret that I *g* him my daughter,
11:58 *g* him the right to drink from gold cups,
12: 4 The Romans *g* them letters addressed to the
12:43 him to all his friends, and *g* him presents.
13:17 he *g* orders to get the money and the boys,
13:50 to Simon for peace, and he *g* them peace.
15:32 When he *g* him the king's message,
15:38 and *g* him infantry and cavalry forces.
16:15 The son of Abubus *g* them a deceitful
2Mc 3:36 Before all men he *g* witness to the deeds
7: 3 *g* orders to have pans and caldrons heated.
7:22 it was not I who *g* you the breath of life,
8:28 they *g* a share of the booty to the
9: 7 the Jews, he *g* orders to drive even faster.
15:10 he *g* his orders and pointed out at the
15:15 As he *g* it to him he said,
Jb 1:21 The LORD *g* and the LORD has taken away;
28:27 wisdom and appraised it, *g* it its setting,
34:13 Who *g* him government over the earth,
42:10 *g* to Job twice as much as he had before.
42:11 one *g* him a piece of money and a gold ring.
42:15 *g* them an inheritance among their brethren.
Ps(s) 18:14 heaven, the Most High *g* forth his voice;
18:51 You who *g* great victories to your king and
21: 5 you *g* him length of days forever and ever.
40: 7 not, but ears open to obedience you *g* me.
69:22 in my thirst they *g* me vinegar to drink.
77:18 the skies *g* forth their voice;
78:15 desert and *g* them water in copious floods.
78:24 them for food and *g* them heavenly bread.
78:46 He *g* their harvest to the caterpillar,
78:48 He *g* over to the hail their beasts and
81:13 *g* them up to the hardness of their hearts;
99: 7 heard his decrees and the law he *g* them.
105:32 For rain he *g* them hail,
105:44 And he *g* them the lands of the nations,
106:14 They *g* way to craving in the desert and
106:15 He *g* them what they asked but sent a
106:41 *g* them over into the hands of the nations,
148: 6 he *g* them a duty which shall not pass away.
Prv 31: 1 The advice which his mother *g* him:
Eccl 12: 7 the life breath returns to God who *g* it.
Sg 8:11 he *g* over the vineyard to caretakers.
Wis 7:17 he *g* me sound knowledge of existing things,
8:21 not otherwise possess her except God *g* it
10: 2 fall, and *g* him power to rule all things.
10:10 of God and *g* him knowledge of holy things;
10:12 And she *g* him the prize for his stern
10:14 him false, and *g* him eternal glory.
10:17 she *g* the holy ones the recompense of
10:21 of the dumb, and *g* ready speech to infants.
11: 7 You *g* them abundant water
12:10 by bit, you *g* them space for repentance.
12:19 And you *g* your sons good ground for hope
12:21 *g* the sworn covenants of goodly promises!
Sir 7:28 what can you give them for all they *g* you?
24: 8 "Then the Creator of all *g* me his command,
44:23 the first-born, and *g* him his inheritance.
45: 3 He *g* him the commandments for his people,
45: 5 face to face, he *g* him the commandments,
45:17 He *g* to him his laws,
46: 5 And God Most High *g* answer to him in
46: 9 And the strength he *g* to Caleb remained
47: 5 who *g* strength to his right arm To defeat
47:19 women and *g* them dominion over your body.
47:22 So he *g* to Jacob a remnant,
49: 5 So he *g* over their power to others,
49:10 *G* new strength to Jacob and saved him by
Is 14:17 its cities, and *g* his captives no release?
20: 2 it, the LORD *g* a warning through Isaiah,
42:24 Who was it that *g* Jacob to be plundered,
45:12 I *g* the order to all their host.
47: 6 inheritance, And I *g* them into your hand;
49: 1 from my mother's womb he *g* me my name.
50: 6 I *g* my back to those who beat me,
51: 2 your father, and to Sarah, who *g* you birth;
57:19 for them, I, the Creator, who *g* them life.
66: 4 my sight, and chose what *g* me displeasure,
Jer 2:20 green tree, you *g* yourself to harlotry.
2:27 father," and to a stone, "You *g* me birth."
3: 8 I put her away and *g* her a bill of divorce,
3:18 which I *g* to your fathers as a heritage.
7: 7 I *g* your fathers long ago and forever.
7:14 place which I *g* to you and your fathers,
7:22 I *g* them no command concerning holocaust
12:14 which I *g* my people Israel as their own:
14:14 *g* them no command nor did I speak to them.
15:10 Woe to me, mother, that you *g* me birth!
16:15 back to the land which I *g* their fathers.
20:14 day my mother *g* me birth never be blessed!
23:39 the city which I *g* to you and your fathers.
24:10 the land which I *g* them and their fathers.
25: 5 land which the LORD *g* you and your fathers,
25:17 *g* drink to all the nations to which the LORD
26:12 Jeremiah *g* this answer to the princes and
30: 3 the land which I have *g* to their fathers;

32:12 This deed of purchase I *g* to Baruch,
32:13 In their presence I *g* Baruch this charge:
32:22 This land you *g* them,
33: 2 made the earth and *g* it form and firmness,
35:15 on the land which I *g* you and your fathers;
36:32 another scroll, and *g* it to his secretary,
38:16 the LORD lives who *g* us the breath of life,
39:11 *g* the following orders through Nebuzaradan,
40: 5 *g* him food and gifts and let him go.
44:20 men and women, who *g* him this answer,
45: 1 that the prophet Jeremiah *g* to Baruch,
46:13 The message which the LORD *g* to the
52:32 He spoke kindly to him and *g* him a throne
Lam 1: 9 she *g* no thought how she would end.
1:17 The LORD *g* orders against Jacob for his
Bar 2:21 may continue in the land I *g* your fathers:
2:35 my people Israel from the land I *g* them.
4:30 who *g* you your name is your encouragement.
Ez 3: 2 my mouth and he *g* me the scroll to eat.
16:10 I *g* you a fine linen sash and silk robes
16:34 you *g* payment instead of receiving it,
16:49 and they *g* no help to the poor and needy.
17:18 Though he *g* his hand in pledge,
20:11 Then I *g* them my statutes and made known
20:12 I also *g* them my sabbaths to be a sign
20:25 I *g* them statutes that were not good,
23: 7 Thus she *g* herself as a harlot to them,
27:15 and ebony wood they *g* you for payment.
28:25 their land which I *g* to my servant Jacob;
31: 6 branches all beasts of the field *g* birth,
36:28 shall live in the land I *g* your fathers;
37:25 on the land which I *g* to my servant Jacob,
Dn 1:16 were to receive, and *g* them vegetables.
1:17 To these four young men God *g* knowledge
2:48 a high post, *g* him many generous presents,
5: 1 King Belshazzar *g* a great banquet for a
5:18 The Most High God *g* your father
6:24 This *g* the king great joy.
9:10 *g* us through your servants the prophets.
Hos 2:10 known that it was I who *g* her the grain,
Jl 4: 3 they *g* a boy for a harlot,
Am 2:12 But you *g* the nazirites wine to drink,
Mi 2: 9 you take away forever the honor I *g* them.
Zec 3: 6 of the LORD then *g* Joshua this assurance:
Mt 3:15 So John *g* in.
8:18 Jesus *g* orders to cross to the other shore.
10: 1 *g* them authority to expel unclean spirits
14: 9 he *g* orders that the request be granted.
14:19 them and *g* the loaves to the disciples,
14:19 who in turn *g* them to the people.
15:23 He *g* her no word of response.
15:36 *g* them to the disciples, who in turn gave
16: 2 He *g* them this reply:
22: 2 a king who *g* a wedding banquet for his son.
25:35 *g* me food, I was thirsty and you gave
25:42 gave me no food, I was thirsty and you *g*
25:43 *g* me no welcome, naked and you gave
26:26 it, broke it, and *g* it to his disciples.
26:27 took a cup, *g* thanks, and gave it to them.
27:34 *g* him a drink of wine flavored with gall,
27:50 in a loud voice, and then *g* up his spirit.
Mk 1:43 Jesus *g* him a stern warning and sent him
2:12 all *g* praise to God,
2:26 He even *g* it to his men."
3:17 Simon to whom he *g* the name Peter;
3:17 James (he *g* these two the name Boanerges,
5:13 He *g* the word,
6:28 gave it to the girl, and the girl *g*
6:41 and *g* them to the disciples to distribute.
8: 6 gave thanks, broke them, and *g* them
8:30 Then he *g* them strict orders not to tell
12:44 *g* from their surplus wealth, but she gave
14:22 blessed and broke it, and *g* it to them.
14:23 took a cup, *g* thanks and passed it to them,
Lk 1:57 for delivery arrived, she *g* birth to a son.
2: 7 She *g* birth to her first-born son and
2:38 she *g* thanks to God and talked about the
4:20 he *g* it back to the assistant and sat down.
5:26 Full of awe, they *g* praise to God,
5:29 *g* a great reception for Jesus in his house,
6: 4 and ate the holy bread and *g* it to his men,
6:14 Simon, to whom he *g* the name Peter,
7:15 Then Jesus *g* him back to his mother.
7:22 Jesus *g* this response:
7:29 even the tax collectors, *g* praise to God,
7:45 You *g* me no kiss,
9: 1 *g* them power and authority to overcome all
9:16 and *g* them to his disciples for
10:35 *g* them to the innkeeper with the request:
15:29 yet you never *g* me so much as a kid goat
16: 8 "The owner then *g* his devious employee
18:43 witnessed it and they too *g* praise to God.
19:13 servants and *g* them sums of ten units each,
19:16 sum you *g* me has earned you another ten.'
22:19 thanks, he broke it and *g* it to them,
23:47 had happened, *g* glory to God by saying,
24:42 They *g* him a piece of cooked fish,
Jn 1:19 The testimony John *g* when the Jews sent
1:32 John *g* this testimony also:
3: 3 Jesus *g* him this answer:
3:16 so loved the world that he *g* his only Son,
4:12 who *g* us this well and drank from it with
6:11 then took the loaves of bread, *g* thanks,
6:31 'He *g* them bread from the heavens to eat.'"
6:32 not Moses who *g* you bread from the heavens;
7:22 Moses *g* you circumcision (though it did
9:32 ever *g* sight to a person blind from birth.
12: 2 There they *g* him a banquet,
13:26 the morsel, then took it and *g* it to Judas,
17: 2 may bestow eternal life on those you *g* him.
17: 4 earth by finishing the work you *g* me to do.
17: 6 known to those you *g* me out of the world.
17: 6 These men you *g* me were yours;
17: 7 that all that you *g* me comes from you.
17:12 guarded them with your name which you *g* me.
17:14 I *g* them your word,
17:22 the glory you *g* me that they may be one,
17:24 *g* me I would have in my company where I am,
18: 9 "I have not lost one of those you *g* me.")
18:22 nearby *g* Jesus a sharp blow on the face.
21:13 came over, took the bread and *g* it to them,
Acts 3: 5 The cripple *g* them his whole attention,
4:36 to whom the apostles *g* the name Barnabas
5:28 "We *g* you strict orders not to teach
9:41 *g* her his hand and helped her to her feet.
10:48 So he *g* orders that they be baptized in
11:17 If God was giving them the same gift he *g*
13:21 for a king, God *g* them Saul son of Kish,
14:22 They *g* their disciples reassurances,
15:31 great delight at the encouragement it *g*.
15:32 *g* them reassurance in a long discourse.
18:21 As he said good-bye he *g* them his promise,
21:17 the brothers there *g* us a warm welcome.
23:22 tell anyone that you *g* me this information."
24:23 He *g* orders to the centurion that Paul was
27:35 bread, *g* thanks to God before all of them,
27:36 This *g* them new courage,
28: 7 and *g* us kind hospitality for three days.
Rom 1:27 and the men *g* up natural intercourse with
4:20 strengthened in faith and *g* glory to God,
11: 8 "God *g* them a spirit of stupor;
1Cor 10:30 blamed for the food over which I *g* thanks?
16: 1 instructions I *g* the churches of Galatia.
2Cor 7: 6 *g* me strength with the arrival of Titus.
8: 5 Beyond our hopes they first *g* themselves
9: 9 "He scattered abroad and *g* to the poor,
Gal 1: 4 Jesus Christ, who *g* himself for our sins,
1:24 and they *g* glory to God on my account.
2: 9 *g* Barnabas and me the handclasp of
2:20 of God, who loved me and *g* himself for me.
Eph 2: 2 as you *g* allegiance to the present age
2: 6 us up and *g* us a place in the heavens,
3: 2 God in his goodness *g* me in your regard.
4: 8 took a host of captives and *g* gifts to men."
4:11 It is he who *g* apostles,
5: 2 He *g* himself for us as an offering to God,
5:25 He *g* himself up for her to make her holy,
Phil 4:10 It *g* me great joy in the Lord that your
Col 1:25 commission God *g* me to preach among you
2:13 God *g* you new life in company with Christ.
1Thes 4: 2 instructions we *g* you in the Lord Jesus.
2Thes 2:16 mercy *g* us eternal consolation and hope,
1Tm 1: 3 I *g* you when I was on my way to Macedonia:
2: 6 Jesus, who *g* himself as a ransom for all."
2Tm 4:17 Lord stood by my side and *g* me strength,
Heb 2: 4 God then *g* witness to it by signs,
7: 4 the patriarch *g* one tenth of his booty!
11:22 and *g* instructions about his burial.
1Pt 1: 3 he who in his great mercy *g* us new birth;
1:21 raised him from the dead and *g* him glory.
1Jn 3:24 from the Spirit that he *g* us.
5:11 God *g* us eternal life,
Rv 1: 1 is the revelation God *g* to Jesus Christ,
10: 3 then *g* a loud cry like the roar of a lion.
11: 1 Someone *g* me a measuring rod and said:
12: 5 She *g* birth to a son
13: 2 The dragon *g* it his own power and throne,
15: 7 One of the four living creatures *g* to the
20:13 The sea *g* up its dead;
20:13 death and the nether world *g* up their dead.
21:23 or moon, for the glory of God *g* it light,

GAY (1)

Sir 30:25 *g* while at table benefits from his food.

GAZA (26)

Gn 10:19 from Sidon all the way to Gerar, near *G*,
Dt 2:23 who once dwelt in villages as far as *G*,
Jos 10:41 Joshua conquered from Kadesh-barnea to *G*,
11:22 However, some survived in *G*,
13: 3 by the five lords of the Philistines in *G*,
15:47 *G* and its towns and villages,
Jgs 1:18 did not occupy *G* with its territory,
6: 4 of the land as far as the outskirts of *G*,
16: 1 Once Samson went to *G*,
16: 2 the men of *G* surrounded him with an ambush
16:21 to *G* and bound him with bronze fetters,
1Sm 6:17 one for Ashdod, one for *G*,
1Kgs 5: 4 west of the Euphrates, from Tiphsah to *G*,
2Kgs 18: 8 all the way to *G* and its territory.
1Mc 11:61 But when he set out for *G*,
11:61 people of *G* locked their gates against him.
11:62 the people of *G* appealed to him for mercy,
Jer 25:20 Ashkelon, *G*, Ekron
47: 1 the Philistines, before Pharaoh attacked *G*:
47: 5 *G* is shaved bald,
Am 1: 6 For three crimes of *G*,
1: 7 I will send fire upon the wall of *G*,
Zep 2: 4 For *G* shall be forsaken,
Zec 9: 5 shall see it and be afraid; *G* also:
9: 5 The king shall disappear from *G*,
Acts 8:26 the road which goes from Jerusalem to *G*,

GAZARA (13)

1Mc 4:15 as far as *G* and the plains of Judea,
7:45 a day's journey, from Adasa to near *G*,
9:52 the city of Beth-zur, *G* and the citadel,
13:43 besieged *G* and surrounded it with troops.
13:53 all his soldiers, with his residence in *G*.
14: 7 of war and made himself master of *G*,
14:34 by the sea and *G* on the border of Azotus,
15:28 Joppa and *G* and the citadel of Jerusalem;
15:35 As for Joppa and *G*,
16: 1 John then went up from *G* and told his
16:19 sent other men to *G* to do away with John.
16:21 brought word to John at *G* that his father
2Mc 10:32 to a well-fortified stronghold called *G*,

GAZE (22)

Gn 13:14 where you are, *g* to the north and south,
Nm 24: 1 omens, but turned his *g* toward the desert.
Jb 3: 9 have none, nor *g* on the eyes of the dawn,
Ps(s) 17:11 crouching to the ground, they fix their *g*,
27: 4 That I may *g* on the loveliness of the LORD
39:14 Turn your *g* from me,
Prv 17:24 man of intelligence fixes his *g* on wisdom,
Sir 9: 7 *G* not about the lanes of the city and
9: 8 *g* not upon the beauty of another's wife
39:20 His *g* spans all the ages;
Is 8:22 He shall *g* at the earth,
Ez 4: 3 Fix your *g* on it:
4: 7 Fixing your *g* on the siege of Jerusalem,
36:34 exposed to the *g* of every passer-by.
Am 9: 3 hide from my *g* in the bottom of the sea,
9: 4 I will fix my *g* upon them for evil,
Ob 1:12 *G* not upon the day of your brother,
1:13 *G* not,
Hb 1:13 do you *g* on the faithless in silence while
Mk 10:27 Jesus fixed his *g* on them and said,
Acts 3: 4 Peter fixed his *g* on the man; so did John.
2Cor 4:18 *g* on what is seen but on what is unseen.

GAZED (6)

Jdt 10:14 men heard her words and *g* upon her face,
Ps(s) 63: 3 Thus have I *g* toward you in the sanctuary
Prv 24:32 And as I *g* at it,
Is 57: 8 you carved the symbol and *g* upon it
Lk 22:56 She *g* at him intently,
Acts 23: 1 Paul *g* intently at the Sanhedrin.

GAZELLE (14)

Dt 12:15 may eat it, as they do the *g* or the deer.
12:22 may eat it as you would the *g* or the deer:
14: 5 the sheep, the goat, the red deer, the *g*,
15:22 it alike, as you would a *g* or a deer.
2Sm 2:18 as fleet of foot as a *g* in the open field,
Prv 6: 5 Free yourself as a *g* from the snare,
Sg 2: 9 My lover is like a *g* or a young stag.
2:17 Like a *g* or a young stag upon the
4: 5 young of a *g* that browse among the lilies.
7: 4 are like twin fawns, the young of a *g*.
8:14 like a *g* or a young stag on the mountains
Sir 27:20 away, he has fled like a *g* from the trap.
Is 13:14 Like a hunted *g*,
Acts 9:36 Tabitha (in Greek Dorcas, meaning a *g*).

GAZELLES (5)

1Kgs 5: 3 and a hundred sheep, not counting harts, *g*,
1Chr 12: 9 were as swift as the *g* on the mountains.
Sg 2: 7 by the *g* and hinds of the field,
3: 5 by the *g* and hinds of the field,
8: 4 by the *g* and hinds of the field,

GAZEZ (2)

1Chr 2:46 Caleb's concubine, bore Haran, Moza, and *G*.
2:46 Haran became the father of *G*.

GAZING (7)

Ex 24:11 After *g* on God,
Sg 2: 9 behind our wall, *g* through the windows,
Sir 41:21 Of *g* at a married woman,
Is 38:14 My eyes grow weak, *g* heavenward:
Mk 3:34 And *g* around him at those seated in the
Acts 1:10 They were still *g* up into the heavens when
2Cor 3:18 *g* on the Lord's glory with unveiled faces,

GAZZAM (2)

Ezr 2:48 sons of Rezin, sons of Nekoda, sons of *G*,
Neh 7:51 sons of Rezin, sons of Nekoda, sons of *G*,

GE-HINNOM (1)

Neh 11:30 They were settled from Beer-sheba to *G*.

GEAR (4)

Gn 27: 3 Take your g,
Ez 27:20 Dedan traded with you for riding g.
Zec 11:15 This time take the g of a foolish shepherd.
Acts 27:19 threw even the ship's g overboard.

GEBA (20)

Jos 18:24 Ophra, Chephar-ammoni, Ophni and G;
21:17 pasture lands, G with its pasture lands,
1Sm 13:16 with them were now occupying G of Benjamin,
13:18 the third took the road for G
14: 2 the threshing floor on the outskirts of G;
14: 5 Michmash, the other to the south, toward G.
14:16 The lookouts of Saul in G of Benjamin saw
2Sm 2:24 of the valley toward the desert near G.
1Kgs 15:22 King Asa built G of Benjamin and Mizpeh.
2Kgs 23: 8 and then defiled, from G to Beer-sheba,
1Chr 6:45 pasture lands, G with its pasture lands,
8: 6 dwelt in G and were deported to Manahath.
2Chr 16: 6 and with them he fortified G and Mizpah.
Ezr 2:26 men of Ramah and G,
Neh 7:30 men of Ramah and G,
11:31 Benjaminites were in G,
12:29 and from the plains of G and Azmaveth (for
Jdt 3:10 set up his camp between G and Scythopolis,
Is 10:29 "We will spend the night at G."
Zec 14:10 And from G to Rimmon in the Negeb,

GEBAL (2)

Ps(s) 83: 8 people of Hagar, G and Ammon and Amalek,
Ez 27: 9 of G were in you to caulk your seams.

GEBALITE (1)

Jos 13: 5 and the G territory;

GEBALITES (1)

1Kgs 5:32 and Hiram's builders, along with the G,

GEBER (2)

1Kgs 4:13 the son of G in Ramoth-gilead,
4:19 G, son of Uri,

GEBIM (1)

Is 10:31 flight, the inhabitants of G seek refuge.

GECKO (1)

Lv 11:30 the various kinds of lizards, the g,

GEDALIAH (32)

2Kgs 25:22 of Babylon, appointed as their governor G,
25:23 king of Babylon had appointed G governor,
25:24 G gave the commanders and their men his
25:25 with ten men, attacked G and killed him,
25:30 governor G, son of Ahikam, son of Shaphan.
1Chr 25: 3 G, Zeri,
25: 9 G was the second;
Ezr 10:18 Maaseiah, Eliezer, Jarib, and G.
Jer 38: 1 Shephatiah, son of Mattan, G,
39:14 quarters of the guard, and entrusted to G,
40: 5 "or go to G, son of Ahikam,
40: 6 Jeremiah went to G,
40: 7 that the king of Babylon had given G,
40: 8 they came with their men to G in Mizpah:
40: 9 G, son of Ahikam,
40:11 in Judah, and had appointed over them G,
40:12 They went to G at Mizpah and had a rich
40:13 armies in the field came to G in Mizpah
40:15 G, son of Ahikam, would not believe them.
40:15 of Kareah, said secretly to G in Mizpah:
40:16 Nevertheless, G,
41: 1 the king's nobles, came with ten men to G,
41: 2 him, rose up and attacked with swords G,
41: 3 G and the Chaldean soldiers who were there.
41: 4 The second day after the murder of G,
41: 7 "Come to G,
41:10 of the bodyguard, had confided to G,
41:16 brought away from Mizpah after he killed G,
41:18 Ishmael, son of Nethaniah, had slain G,
43: 6 of the bodyguard, had entrusted to G,
Zep 1: 1 Zephaniah, the son of Cushi, the son of G,

GEDER (1)

Jos 12:13 Jarmuth, Lachish, Eglon, Gezer, Debir, G,

GEDERAH (3)

Jos 15:36 Socoh, Azekah, Shaaraim, Adithaim, G,
1Chr 4:23 potters and inhabitants of Netaim and G,
12: 5 Jozabad from G;

GEDERITE (1)

1Chr 27:28 of the foothills was Baalhanan the G,

GEDEROTH (2)

Jos 15:41 Eglon, Cabbon, Lahmam, Chitlish, G,
2Chr 28:18 they captured Beth-shemesh, Aijalon, G,

GEDEROTHAIM (1)

Jos 15:36 Azekah, Shaaraim, Adithaim, Gederah, and G;

GEDOR (7)

Jos 15:58 Halhul, Beth-zur, G,
1Chr 4: 4 Penuel was the father of G,
4:18 Egyptian wife bore Jered, the father of G,
4:39 that they went to the approaches of G,
8:31 Abdon, and Zur, Kish, Baal, Ner, Nadab, G,
9:37 then came Zur, Kish, Baal, Ner, Nadab, G,
12: 8 and Zebadiah, sons of Jeroham, from G.

GEHARASHIM (1)

1Chr 4:14 became the father of Joab, the father of G,

GEHAZI (17)

2Kgs 4:12 Then he said to his servant G,
4:13 when she stood before Elisha, he told G,
4:14 G answered. "She has no son,
4:25 the man of God said to his servant G:
4:27 G came near to push her away,
4:29 "Gird your loins," Elisha said to G,
4:31 G had gone on ahead and had laid the staff
4:36 Elisha summoned G and said,
5:20 Naaman had gone some distance when G,
5:21 So G hurried after Naaman.
5:22 "Yes," G replied, "but my master sent
5:23 of his servants, who carried them before G.
5:24 reached the hill, G took what they had,
5:25 who asked him, "Where have you been, G?"
5:27 And G left Elisha, a leper white as snow.
8: 4 The king was talking with G,
8: 5 "My lord king," G said,

GEHENNA (10)

Mt 5:22 him in contempt he risks the fires of G.
5:29 your body than to have it all cast into G.
5:30 your body than to have it all cast into G.
10:28 who can destroy both body and soul in G.
18: 9 eye than be thrown with both into fiery G.
23:33 How can you escape condemnation to G?
Mk 9:43 and enter G with its unquenchable fire.
9:45 than to be thrown into G with both feet.
9:47 than to be thrown with both eyes into G,
Lk 12: 5 power to cast into G after he has killed.

GELDING (1)

Mal 1:14 under his vow sacrifices to the LORD a g;

GELILOTH (1)

Jos 18:17 it extended to En-shemesh, and thence to G,

GEM (1)

Wis 7: 9 nor did I liken any priceless g to her;

GEM-CUTTER (1)

Ex 28:11 As a g engraves a seal,

GEMALLI (1)

Nm 13:12 for the Josephites, with Ammiel, son of G,

GEMARIAH (5)

Jer 29: 3 by Elasah, son of Shaphan, and by G,
36:10 It was in the room of G,
36:11 Now Micaiah, son of G,
36:12 of Shemaiah, Elnathan, son of Achbor, G,
36:25 G urged the king not to burn the scroll,

GEMLIKE (1)

Rv 4: 3 had a g sparkle as of jasper and carnelian.

GEMS (3)

Ex 25: 7 onyx stones and other g for mounting on
35: 9 g for mounting on the ephod
35:27 princes brought onyx stones and other g

GENDER (1)

Jb 21:10 Their bulls g without fail;

GENEALOGICAL (2)

Ex 6:16 of the sons of Levi, in their g order,
6:19 are the clans of Levi in their g order.

GENEALOGIES (2)

1Tm 1: 4 themselves with interminable myths and g,
Ti 3: 9 you abstain from stupid arguments and g,

GENERAL (37)

Gn 26:26 councilor, and Phicol, the g of his army.
Jgs 4: 2 The g of his army was Sisera,
4: 7 I will lead Sisera, the g of Jabin's army,
1Sm 14:50 The name of his g was Abner,
17:55 meet the Philistine, he asked his g Abner,
26: 5 where Saul and Abner, son of Ner, the g,
2Sm 2: 8 Abner, son of Ner, Saul's g,
3:38 that a great g has fallen today in Israel.
10:16 Helam, with Shobach, g of Hadadezer's army,
10:18 Shobach, g of the army,
19:14 become my g permanently in place of Joab.'"
1Kgs 1:19 the priest, and Joab, the g of the army,
2:32 Abner, son of Ner, g of Israel's army,
2:32 Amasa, son of Jether, g of Judah's army.
11:15 conquered Edom, Joab, the g of the army,
11:21 ancestors and that Joab, the g of the army,
16:16 all Israel proclaimed Omri, g of the army,
2Kgs 18:17 The king of Assyria sent the g,
1Chr 19:16 with Shophach, the g of Hadadezer's army,
19:18 he also killed Shophach, the g of the army.
Jdt 2: 4 Holofernes, g in chief of his forces,
10:13 Holofernes, the g in chief of your forces,
13:15 g in charge of the Assyrian army,
Est 1:13 in g consultation with lawyers and jurists.
D:10 not die because of this g decree of ours.
1Mc 8:10 the Greeks a single g who made war on them.
14: 3 The g went forth and defeated the army of
14:42 He shall act as governor g over them,
14:47 agreed to act as high priest, governor g,
2Mc 4: 5 g and particular good of all the people.
9:19 citizens, Antiochus, their king and g,
9:21 to form plans for the g welfare of all.
9:26 remember the g and individual benefits
14:20 and when g agreement was expressed,
Is 20: 1 In the year the g sent by Sargon,
1Cor 7:17 The g rule is that each one should lead
1Tm 5:14 and in g give our enemies no occasion to

GENERALLY (2)

Jos 13:21 the other cities of the tableland and, g,
Jer 44:21 your kings and princes, and the people g?

GENERALS (10)

1Kgs 2: 5 when he slew the two g of Israel's armies,
1Chr 21: 2 to Joab and to the other g of the army,
Jdt 2:14 the g and officers of the Assyrian army.
5: 2 of the Moabites, the g of the Ammonites,
7: 8 together with the g of the seacoast,
14: 3 camp to awaken the g of the Assyrian army.
14:12 went to the g and division leaders and all
1Mc 11:63 Jonathan heard that the g of Demetrius had
12:24 Jonathan heard that the g of Demetrius had
14: 2 he sent one of his g to take him alive.

GENERATION (74)

Gn 50:23 He saw Ephraim's children to the third g,
Ex 1: 6 and all his brothers and that whole g died.
20: 5 hate me, down to the third and fourth g;
20: 6 bestowing mercy down to the thousandth g,
34: 7 and fourth g for their fathers' wickedness!"
Lv 21:17 None of your descendants, of whatever g,
22: 3 or of your descendants in any future g,
Nm 14:18 and fourth g for their fathers' wickedness.'
15:14 Likewise, in any future g,
32:13 until the whole g that had done evil in
Dt 1:35 'Not one man of this evil g shall look
2:14 g of soldiers had perished from the camp,
5: 9 the third and fourth g but bestowing mercy,
5:10 bestowing mercy, down to the thousandth g,
7: 9 thousandth g toward those who love him
23: 3 any descendant of his even to the tenth g.
23: 4 descendants of theirs even to the tenth g,
23: 9 Children born to them may in the third g
Jgs 2:10 of that g were gathered to their fathers,
2:10 a later g arose that did not know the LORD,
2Kgs 10:30 g shall sit upon the throne of Israel."
15:12 g shall sit upon the throne of Israel,"
Tb 13:11 Every g shall give joyful praise in you,
Jdt 8:32 do something that will go down from g
8:32 to g among the descendants of our race.
Est 9:28 to be commemorated and kept in every g,
1Mc 2:61 so, consider this from generation to g,
Ps(s) 12: 8 us and preserve us always from this g,
14: 5 in great fear, for God is with the just g.
22:31 Let the coming g be told of the LORD that
48:14 you may tell a future g that such is God,
71:18 your strength to every g that is to come.
78: 4 we will declare to the g to come The
78: 6 So that the g to come might know,
78: 8 a g wayward and rebellious, A generation
95:10 Forty years I loathed that g, and I said:
102:19 Let this be written for the g to come,
109:13 the next g may their name be blotted out.
112: 2 the upright g shall be blessed.
145: 4 Generation after g praises your works and
Eccl 1: 4 One g passes and another comes,
Wis 3:19 for dire is the end of the wicked g.
Sir 16:25 do and their domains from generation to g.
45:13 sons and them alone, generation after g,
Is 34:10 From g to generation she shall lie waste,
34:17 and dwell there from g to generation.
60:15 of the ages, a joy to g after generation.
Jer 2:31 You, of this g,
7:29 cast off the g that draws down his wrath.
Jl 1: 3 children, and their children to the next g.
Mt 12:41 present g and be the ones to condemn it.
12:42 the present g and be the one to condemn it.
12:45 that is how it will be with this evil g."

23:36 you, will be the fate of the present g.
24:34 the present g will not pass away until all
Mk 13:30 this g will not pass away until all these
Lk 11:31 the judgment along with the men of this g,
11:32 Nineveh will rise along with the present g,
11:50 so that this g will have to account for
11:51 you, this g will have to account for it.
21:32 the present g will not pass away until all
Acts 2:40 from this g which has gone astray."
7:45 The next g of our fathers inherited it.
Phil 2:15 in the midst of a twisted and depraved g—
Heb 3:10 this I was angered with that g and I said,
Jude 1:14 was of the seventh g descended from Adam,

GENERATIONS (72)

Ex 3:15 this is my title for all g.
12:14 which all your g shall celebrate with
12:17 your g as a perpetual institution.
12:42 a vigil for the LORD throughout their g.
27:21 for the Israelites throughout their g.
29:42 Throughout your g this established
30: 8 Throughout your g this shall be the
30:10 Throughout your g this atonement is to be
30:21 him and his descendants throughout their g."
30:31 this shall belong to me throughout your g.
31:13 token between you and me throughout the g,
31:16 throughout their g as a perpetual covenant.
34: 7 continuing his kindness for a thousand g,
40:15 priesthood throughout all future g."
Lv 6:11 of the LORD perpetually throughout your g.
7:36 a perpetual ordinance throughout their g.
10: 9 by a perpetual ordinance throughout your g,
Nm 15:21 Throughout your g you shall give a
15:23 issues the commandment down through your g:
18:23 is a perpetual ordinance for all your g.
Dt 29:21 "Future g,
Jgs 3: 2 those g only of the Isralites who would
1Chr 16:15 which he made binding for a thousand g—
Tb 1: 4 built and consecrated for all g to come.
13:10 he cherish within you for all g to come.
14: 5 yes, it will be rebuilt for all g to come,
Jdt 8:18 there has not risen among us in recent g,
Est F:10 all future g of his people Israel."
Jb 8: 8 If you inquire of the former g,
Ps(s) 33:11 the design of his heart, through all g.
45:18 make your name memorable through all g;
49:12 forever, their dwellings through all g,
61: 7 let his years be many g;
72: 5 the sun, and like the moon through all g.
77: 9 utterly cease, his promise fail for all g?
79:13 through all g we will declare your praise.
85: 6 with us, prolonging your anger to all g?
89: 2 through all g my mouth shall proclaim your
89: 5 and establish your throne for all g."
90: 1 you have been our refuge through all g.
100: 5 forever, and his faithfulness, to all g.
102:13 forever, and your name through all g.
102:25 through all g your years endure.
105: 8 which he made binding for a thousand g—
106:31 to him for merit through all g forever.
119:90 Through all g your truth endures;
135:13 LORD is your title through all g,
145:13 and your dominion endures through all g.
146:10 your God, O Zion, through all g.
Eccl 4:16 yet the later g will not applaud him.
Sir 2:10 Study the g long past and understand;
14:18 So with the g of flesh and blood:
24:31 like prophecy and bestow it on g to come.
39: 9 memory, through all g his name will live;
44:16 succeeding g might learn by his example.]
Is 41: 4 has called forth the g since the beginning.
51: 8 remain forever and my salvation, for all g.
61: 4 the ruined cities, desolate now for g.
Jer 32:18 your kindness through a thousand g;
Bar 3:20 Later g have seen the light,
6: 2 be there many years, a period seven g long;
Dn 3:100 and his dominion endures through all g.
4:31 and his kingdom endures through all g.
Jl 2: 2 after them, even to the years of distant g.
4:20 abide forever, and Jerusalem for all g.
Mt 1:17 Thus the total number of g is:
1:17 from Abraham to David, fourteen g;
1:17 to the Babylonian captivity, fourteen g;
1:17 captivity to the Messiah, fourteen g.
Acts 15:21 for g now Moses has been proclaimed in
Eph 3:21 church and in Christ Jesus through all g.
Col 1:26 g past but now revealed to his holy ones.

GENEROSITY (14)

1Sm 24:19 Great is the g you showed me today,
Est E: 2 through the bountiful g of their patrons.
E:10 blood, and very different from us in g,
Ps(s) 112: 3 his g shall endure forever.
112: 9 his g shall endure forever;
Sir 20:15 fool has no friends, nor thanks for his g;
33:22 you than that you should look to their g.
37:11 a buyer about value, to a miser about g,
Acts 10: 4 and your g have risen in God's sight,
10:31 and your g remembered in God's presence.
2Cor 8: 2 deep poverty have produced an abundant g.
9:13 your g in sharing with them and with all.
Gal 5:22 joy, peace, patient endurance, kindness, g,
Heb 13:16 Do not neglect good deeds and g;

GENEROUS (32)

Gn 33:11 God has been g toward me,
Nm 10:29 Come with us, and we will be g toward you,
2Sm 2: 6 too, will be g to you for having done this.
7:28 have made this g promise to your servant.
1Kgs 8:56 has gone unfulfilled of the entire g promise
2Chr 31: 5 they gave a g tithe of everything.
2Mc 2:22 favored them with all his g assistance.
13:23 and honored the temple with a g donation.
Ps(s) 84: 7 the early rain clothes it with g growth.
109:21 in your g kindness rescue me;
Sir 7:33 Be g to all the living,
14: 5 To whom will he be g who is stingy with
14: 7 If ever he is g,
26: 3 A good wife is a g gift bestowed upon him
29: 8 To a poor man, however, be g;
31:23 On a man g with food,
35: 7 In g spirit pay homage to the LORD,
Is 55: 7 to our God, who is g in forgiving.
Ez 36:11 and be more g to you than in the beginning;
Dn 2:48 to a high post, gave him many g presents,
Hb 1:16 For thanks to them his portion is g,
Mt 20:15 Or are you envious because I am g?'
Mk 14: 7 and you can be g to them whenever you wish,
Rom 12:13 be g in offering hospitality.
2Cor 8: 8 testing your g love against the concern
8:20 over my handling of this g collection.
9:10 the seed you sow and increase your g yield.
Gal 4:17 not courting your favor in any g spirit.
Eph 1: 8 so immeasurably g is God's favor to us.
1Tm 6:18 to do good, to be rich in good works and g,
1Pt 4:10 As g distributors of God's manifold grace,
2Pt 3: 9 Rather, he shows you g patience,

GENEROUSLY (11)

1Sm 24:18 you have treated me g,
24:20 you g for what you have done this day.
1Chr 29: 5 to contribute g this day to the LORD?"
29:17 people here present also giving to you g.
2Mc 1: 3 him and to do his will readily and g.
6:28 and g for the revered and holy laws."
Sir 35: 9 to the Most High as he has given to you, g,
Acts 10: 2 He was in the habit of giving g to the
Rom 12: 8 He who gives alms should do so g;
Jas 1: 5 God who gives g and ungrudgingly to all,
1Pt 5: 2 and not for shameful profit either, but g.

GENIUS (1)

Acts 17:29 or stone, a product of man's g and his art.

GENNAEUS (1)

2Mc 12: 2 Timothy and Apollonius, son of G,

GENNESARET (4)

1Mc 11:67 pitched their camp near the waters of G,
Mt 14:34 the crossing they reached the shore at G;
Mk 6:53 making the crossing they came ashore at G,
Lk 5: 1 As he stood by the Lake of G,

GENTILE (14)

Neh 5: 9 an end to the derision of our G enemies?
1Mc 1:14 in Jerusalem according to the G custom.
5:15 and the whole of G Galilee had joined
Mt 18:17 him as you would a G or a tax collector.
Acts 10:28 with a G or to have dealings with him.
15:19 to cause God's G converts any difficulties.
15:23 to the brothers of G origin in Antioch,
18: 7 to the house of a G named Titus Justus,
21:25 As for the G converts,
Rom 11:12 have meant riches for the G world,
Gal 2:14 according to G ways rather than Jewish,
2:15 are Jews by birth, not sinners of G origin.
Eph 2:11 You men of G stock
Rv 16:19 parts, and the other G cities also fell.

GENTILES (145)

Lv 26:38 You will be lost among the G,
26:45 of Egypt under the very eyes of the G,
Neh 5: 8 our fellow Jews who had been sold to G;
Tb 13: 3 Praise him, you Israelites, before the G,
13: 5 the G among whom you have been scattered.
1Mc 1:11 make an alliance with the G all around us;
1:13 to introduce the way of living of the G.
1:15 the G and sold themselves to wrongdoing.
1:42 the G conformed to the command of the king,
2:12 laid waste, And the G have defiled them!
2:18 as all the G and the men of Judah and
2:19 all the G in the king's realm obey him,
2:40 the G for our lives and our traditions,
2:44 and the survivors fled to the G for safety.
2:48 saved the law from the hands of the G
2:68 Pay back the G what they deserve,
3:10 Then Apollonius gathered the G,
3:25 and dread fell upon the G about them.
3:26 the G talked about the battles of Judas.
3:45 it was a habitation of G.
3:48 the G consulted the images of their idols.
3:52 Now the G are gathered together against us
3:58 be ready to fight these G
4: 7 They saw the army of the G,
4:11 All the G shall know that there is One who
4:14 G were defeated and fled toward the plain.
4:45 shame to them that the G had defiled it;
4:54 of the day on which the G had defiled it,
4:58 now that the disgrace of the G was removed.
4:60 to prevent the G from coming and trampling
5: 1 When the G round about heard that the
5: 9 The G in Gilead assembled to attack and
5:10 "The G around us have combined against us
5:13 the G have carried away their wives and
5:19 do not fight against the G until we return."
5:21 Galilee and fought many battles with the G.
5:22 About three thousand men of the G fell,
5:38 "All the G around us have rallied to him,
5:43 him, and the G were crushed before them;
5:57 out and fighting against the G around us."
5:63 in all Israel and among all the G,
6:18 to harm them and to strengthen the G.
6:53 rescued from the G and brought to Judea.
7:23 Israelites, more than even the G had done,
13:41 the yoke of the G was removed from Israel,
14:36 in driving the G out of their country,
2Mc 1:27 free those who are the slaves of the G,
1:27 and let the G know that you are our God.
6: 4 The G filled the temple with debauchery
8: 5 organized, the G could not withstand him,
8:16 number of the G attacking them unjustly,
8:17 perpetrated by the G against the holy Place
10: 2 destroyed the altars erected by the G
10: 4 them over to blasphemous and barbarous G.
10: 5 the temple had been profaned by the G,
12:13 and inhabited by a mixed population of G.
13:11 to be subjected again to blasphemous G.
14:14 The G from Judea,
14:15 and that the G were rallying to him,
15:10 of the G and their violation of oaths.
Is 8:23 west of the Jordan, the District of the G.
11:10 for the nations, The G shall seek out,
45:20 together, you fugitives from among the g!
Mt 10:18 before them and before the G on my account.
12:18 and he will proclaim justice to the G.
12:21 In his name, the G will find hope."
20:19 They will turn him over to the G,
20:25 authority among the G lord it over them;
Mk 10:34 him to death and hand him over to the G,
10:42 "You know how among the G those who seem
13:10 news must first be proclaimed to all the G.
Lk 2:32 A revealing light to the G,
18:32 He will be delivered up to the G.
21:24 will be led captive in the midst of the G.
21:24 by the Gentiles, until the times of the G
Acts 4:25 'Why did the G rage,
4:27 with the G and the peoples of Israel.
9:15 I have chosen to bring my name to the G,
10:45 should have been poured out on the G also,
11: 1 the apostles and the brothers heard that G,
11:18 life-giving repentance even to the G."
13:46 of everlasting life, we now turn to the G.
13:48 The G were delighted when they heard this
14: 2 remained unconvinced stirred up the G
14: 5 A move was made by G and Jews,
14:16 In past ages he let the G go their way.
14:27 he had opened the door of faith to the G.
15: 3 about the conversion of the G as they went.
15: 5 demanded that such G be circumcised
15: 7 one from whose lips the G would hear
15:12 God had worked among the G through them.
15:14 from among the G a people to bear his name.
18: 6 From now on, I will turn to the G."
21:11 of this belt and hand him over to the G.'"
21:19 among the G through his ministry.
21:21 Jews who live among the G to abandon Moses,
22:21 to send you far from here, among the G.'"
26:20 yes, even to the G.
26:23 proclaim light to our people and to the G."
28:28 of God has been transmitted to the G—
Rom 1: 5 and bring to obedient faith all the G,
1:13 among you, as I have among the other G.
2:14 When G who do not have the law keep it as
2:24 of God is held in contempt among the G."
3:29 Is he not also the God of the G?
3:29 Yes, of the G too.
9:24 from among the Jews, but from among the G.
9:30 G, who were not seeking justice,
11:11 has come to the G to stir Israel to envy.
11:13 I say this now to you G:
11:13 Inasmuch as I am the apostle of the G,
11:25 Israel until the full number of G enter in,
15: 9 the G glorify God because of his mercy.
15: 9 among the G and I will sing to your name."
15:10 Again, "Rejoice, O G, with his people."
15:11 the Lord, all you G and sing his glory,
15:12 the Gentiles; in him the G will find hope."
15:16 be a minister of Christ Jesus among the G,
15:16 gospel of God so that the G may be offered
15:18 to win the G to obedience by word and deed,
15:27 For if the G have shared in the spiritual
16: 4 the churches of the G are grateful to them.
16:26 all the G that they may believe and obey
1Cor 1:23 block to Jews, and an absurdity to G;
10:20 the G sacrifice to demons and not to God,

GENTILES (cont.)

2Cor 11:26 by floods, robbers, my own people, the *G;*
Gal 1:16 the *G* the good tidings concerning him.
2: 2 the gospel as I present it to the *G—*
2: 8 the Jews had been at work in me for the *G),*
2: 9 we should go to the *G* as they to the Jews.
2:12 *G* before others came who were from James.
2:14 do you force the *G* to adopt Jewish ways?"
3: 8 of justifying the *G* would be through faith,
3:14 might descend on the *G* in Christ Jesus,
Eph 3: 1 for Christ Jesus on behalf of you *G,*
3: 6 Jesus the *G* are now co-heirs with the Jews,
3: 8 preach to the *G* the unfathomable riches
Col 1:27 price which this mystery brings to the *G—*
1Thes 2:16 keep us from preaching salvation to the *G.*
4: 5 desire as do the *G* who know not God;
1Tm 3:16 preached among the *G,*
Rv 11: 2 it, for it has been handed over to the *G,*

GENTLE (11)

2Sm 18: 5 "Be *g* with young Absalom for my sake."
2Mc 15:12 man, modest in appearance, *g* in manners,
Ps(s) 107:29 He hushed the storm to a *g* breeze,
Is 45: 8 like *g* rain let the skies drop it down.
Mt 11:29 from me, for I am *g* and humble of heart.
Acts 27:13 When a *g* south wind began to blow,
1Cor 4:21 with a rod, or with love and a *g* spirit?
1Thes 2: 7 we were as *g* as any nursing mother
1Tm 3: 3 ought not to be contentious but, rather, *g,*
6:11 faith, love, steadfastness, and a *g* spirit.
1Pt 3: 4 beauty of a calm and *g* disposition.

GENTLEMEN (1)

Gn 19: 2 face to the ground, he said, "Please, *g,*

GENTLENESS (2)

Est D: 8 But God changed the king's anger to *g.*
Wis 2:19 have proof of his *g* and try his patience.

GENTLY (7)

Est D: 3 on the one she leaned *g* for support,
Jb 15:11 for you, and speech that deals *g* with you?
Sir 21:20 but the prudent man at the most smiles *g.*
Is 8: 6 the waters of Shiloah that flow *g,*
Gal 6: 1 live by the spirit should *g* set him right,
2Tm 2:25 and *g* correcting those who contradict him,
1Pt 3:16 to reply, but speak *g* and respectfully.

GENUBATH (1)

1Kgs 11:20 Tahpenes' sister bore Hadad a son, *G.*

GENUFLECTED (1)

Mk 15:19 they *g* before him and pretended to pay

GENUINE (7)

2Mc 14: 8 of my *g* concern for the king's interests,
Jn 12: 3 costly perfume made from *g* aromatic nard,
Phil 1:18 whether from specious motives or *g* ones,
2:20 for *g* interest in whatever concerns you.
Jas 1:17 gift, every *g* benefit comes from above,
1Pt 1:22 yourselves for a *g* love of your brothers;
2Pt 1: 3 everything necessary for a life of *g* piety,

GENUINENESS (1)

1Pt 1: 7 gold, may by its *g* lead to praise,

GERA (9)

Gn 46:21 Bela, Becher, Ashbel, *G,*
Jgs 3:15 a savior, the Benjaminite Ehud, son of *G,*
2Sm 16: 5 son of *G* of the same clan as Saul's family,
19:17 Shimei, son of *G,*
19:19 When Shimei, son of *G,*
1Kgs 2: 8 "You also have with you Shimei, son of *G,*
1Chr 8: 3 The sons of Bela were Addar and *G,*
8: 5 of Ehud were Abishua, Naaman, Ahoah, *G,*
8: 7 Also Naaman, Ahijah, and *G.*

GERAHS (5)

Ex 30:13 sanctuary shekel, twenty *g* to the shekel.
Lv 27:25 There are twenty *g* to the shekel.
Nm 3:47 sanctuary shekel, twenty *g* to the shekel.
18:16 sanctuary standard, twenty *g* to the shekel.
Ez 45:12 The shekel shall be twenty *g.*

GERAR (10)

Gn 10:19 extended from Sidon all the way to *G,*
20: 1 While he stayed in *G,*
20: 2 So Abimelech, king of *G,*
26: 1 to Abimelech, king of the Philistines in *G.*
26: 6 So Isaac settled in *G.*
26:17 and made the Wadi *G* his regular campsite.
26:20 of *G* quarreled with Isaac's servants,
26:26 had meanwhile come to him from *G,*
2Chr 14:12 those with him pursued them as far as *G,*
14:13 conquered all the cities around *G,*

GERASENE (2)

Mk 5: 1 *G* territory on the other side of the lake.
Lk 8:37 the entire population of the *G* territory

GERASENES (1)

Lk 8:26 They sailed to the country of the *G,*

GERGESITES (1)

Jdt 5:16 Jebusites, the Shechemites, and all the *G;*

GERIZIM (6)

Dt 11:29 shall pronounce the blessing on Mount *G,*
27:12 *G* to pronounce blessings over the people,
Jos 8:33 were facing Mount *G* and half Mount Ebal,
Jgs 9: 7 to him, Jotham went to the top of Mount *G,*
2Mc 5:23 at Mount *G,* Andronicus;
6: 2 and that on Mount *G* to Zeus the Hospitable,

GERMINATE (1)

1Cor 15:36 The seed you sow does not *g* unless it dies.

GERRENES (1)

2Mc 13:24 from Ptolemais to the region of the *G.*

GERSHOM (5)

Ex 2:22 She bore him a son, whom he named *G;*
18: 3 One of these was called *G;*
Jgs 18:30 for themselves, and Jonathan, son of *G,*
1Chr 23:15 The sons of Moses were *G* and Eliezer.
23:16 The sons of *G:*

GERSHON (17)

Gn 46:11 *G,* Kohath, and Merari.
Ex 6:16 Levi, in their genealogical order, are *G,*
6:17 The sons of *G,*
Nm 3:17 The sons of Levi were named *G,*
3:18 The descendants of *G,*
3:21 To *G* belonged the clan of the Libnites and
10:17 the clans of *G* and Merari set out,
26:57 through *G* the clan of the Gershonites,
1Chr 5:27 The sons of Levi were *G,*
6: 1 The sons of Levi were *G,*
6: 2 The sons of *G* were named Libni and Shimei.
6: 5 of *G:* his son Libni,
6:28 son of Shimei, son of Jahath, son of *G,*
15: 7 of the sons of *G,*
23: 6 *G,* Kohath, and Merari.
26:24 and Uzzielites, Shubael, son of *G,*
Ezr 8: 2 Of the sons of Phinehas, *G;*

GERSHONITE (5)

Nm 4:41 census of all the men of the *G* clans
Jos 21:27 The *G* clan of the Levites received from
21:33 to the *G* clans were thirteen in all.
1Chr 26:21 Among the descendants of Ladan the *G,*
29: 8 them into the keeping of Jehiel the *G*

GERSHONITES (14)

Nm 3:21 these were the clans of the *G.*
3:23 clans of the *G* camped behind the Dwelling,
4:22 to Moses, "Take a total among the *G* also,
4:24 This is the task of the clans of the *G,*
4:27 The service of the *G* shall be entirely
4:28 is the task of the *G* in the meeting tent;
4:38 registration was then made among the *G,*
7: 7 to the *G* in proportion to their duties,
26:57 through Gershon the clan of the *G,*
Jos 21: 6 The *G* obtained thirteen cities by lot from
1Chr 6:47 The clans of the *G* obtained thirteen
6:56 *G* received from the half-tribe of Manasseh:
23: 7 To the *G* belonged Ladan and Shimei.
2Chr 29:12 of the *G:*

GESHAN (1)

1Chr 2:47 The sons of Jahdai were Regem, Jotham, *G,*

GESHEM (4)

Neh 2:19 and *G* the Arab mocked us and ridiculed us.
6: 1 reported to Sanballat, Tobiah, *G* the Arab,
6: 2 Sanballat and *G* sent me this message:
6: 6 it has been reported *G* is witness to this

GESHUR (10)

Jos 13: 2 This additional land includes all *G* and
13:13 so that *G* and Maacath survive in the midst
2Sm 3: 3 Maacah the daughter of Talmai, king of *G;*
13:37 went to Talmai, son of Ammihud, king of *G,*
13:38 of Geshur, and stayed in *G* for three years.
14:23 off to *G* and brought Absalom to Jerusalem.
14:32 'Why did I come back from *G?*
15: 8 For while living in *G* in Aram,
1Chr 2:23 *G* and Aram took from them the villages of
3: 2 who was the daughter of Talmai, king of *G,*

GESHURITES (5)

Dt 3:14 far as the border of the *G* and Maacathites,
Jos 12: 5 as the boundary of the *G* and Maacathites,
13:11 and the territory of the *G* and Maacathites,
13:13 did not dislodge the *G* and Maacathites,
1Sm 27: 8 his men went up and made raids on the *G,*

GESTURED (1)

Acts 24:10 The governor then *g* to Paul,

GET (169)

Gn 3:19 of your face shall you *g* bread to eat,
19: 2 can *g* up early to continue your journey."
19:14 *G* up and leave this place,"
19:17 *G* off to the hills at once,
24: 4 to my kindred to *g* a wife for my son Isaac."
24:38 my own relatives, to *g* a wife for my son.'
24:40 and so you will *g* a wife for my son from
27: 9 Go to the flock and *g* me two choice kids.
27:13 Go and *g* me the kids."
28: 6 to Paddan-aram to *g* himself a wife there,
34: 4 father Hamor, *G* me this girl for a wife."
35: 2 *G* rid of the foreign gods that you have
37:13 *G* ready; I will send you to them."
40:14 me to Pharaoh, to *g* me out of this place.
42:16 send one of your number to *g* your brother,
45:18 There *g* your father and your families,
Ex 21:19 provided the other can *g* up and walk
28: 9 *G* two onyx stones and engrave on them the
34: 2 *G* ready for tomorrow morning,
Lv 14: 4 man who is to be purified, to *g* two live,
Nm 11:13 can I *g* meat to give to all this people?
13:20 best to *g* some of the fruit of the land."
17:17 "Speak to the Israelites and *g* one staff
Dt 2:13 *G* ready, then, to cross the Wadi Zered.'
24:19 sheaf there, you shall not go back to *g* it;
30:12 the sky to *g* it for us and tell us of it,
30:13 the sea to *g* it for us and tell us of it,
Jgs 9:29 to Abimelech, *G* a larger army and come out!'"
14: 2 whom I wish you to *g* as a wife for me."
14: 3 Samson answered his father, *G* her for me,
1Sm 6:21 come down and *g* it."
9:26 Samuel called to Saul on the roof, *G* up,
14: 4 Jonathan intended to *g* over to the Philistine
19: 2 *g* out of sight and remain in hiding.
19:17 You have helped my enemy to *g* away!"
26:22 Let an attendant come over to *g* it.
2Sm 13:15 *G* up and leave," he said to her.
19: 8 Now then, *g* up!
1Kgs 3:24 The king continued, *G* me a sword."
14: 2 *G* ready and disguise yourself so that none
17:11 She left to *g* it,
19: 5 him and ordered him to *g* up and eat.
19: 7 touched him, and ordered, *G* up and eat,
20:33 He answered, "Go and *g* him."
21: 7 *G* up.
21:10 *g* two scoundrels to face him and accuse
22: 9 an official and said to him, *G* Micaiah,
2Kgs 3:15 Now *g* me a minstrel."
5:20 run after him and *g* something out of him."
6:18 When the Arameans came down to *g* him,
8: 1 *G* ready!
9: 2 When you *g* there,
9:17 *G* a driver."
9:18 *G* behind me."
9:19 *G* behind me."
2Chr 18: 8 an official, to whom he said, *G* Micaiah,
Neh 5: 2 order to *g* grain to eat that we may live."
Tb 5: 3 but *g* back that money from Gabael."
6: 4 hold of the fish and don't let it *g* away!"
8: 4 bed and said to his wife, "My love, *g* up.
9: 2 *G* the money and then bring him along with
12:13 When you did not hesitate to *g* up and
12:20 *g* up from the ground and praise God.
Jdt 7:13 the inhabitants of Bethulia *g* their water.
12: 3 we *g* more of the same to provide for you?
1Mc 8:18 He did this to *g* rid of the yoke,
9:44 "Let us *g* up now and fight for our lives,
10:23 "Why have we allowed Alexander to *g* ahead
13:17 he gave orders to *g* the money and the boys,
16:13 and sought to *g* control of the country.
2Mc 1:14 to *g* its great treasures by way of dowry.
2:15 them, send messengers to *g* them for you.
4:46 a colonnade, as if to *g* some fresh air,
Prv 4: 5 *G* wisdom, get understanding!
4: 7 *g* wisdom; at the cost of all you have, get
6:33 A degrading beating will he *g,*
22:25 his ways, and *g* yourself into a snare.
23:23 *G* the truth,
Eccl 4: 9 they *g* a good wage for their labor.
Is 2:10 *G* behind the rocks,
Ez 3:22 *G* up and go out into the plain,
22:27 and destroying lives to *g* unjust gain.
Mi 2: 4 measured out, and no one can *g* them back!"
Mt 2: 8 and *g* detailed information about the child.
2:13 *G* up, take the child and his mother,
2:20 *G* up,
8: 8 give an order and my boy will *g* better.
9:16 hole will pull, and the rip only *g* worse.
9:21 his cloak," she thought, "I shall *g* well."
13:54 man *g* such wisdom and miraculous powers?
13:56 Where did he *g* all this?"
14:22 insisted that his disciples *g* into the boat
14:27 *G* hold of yourselves!

15:23 up and began to entreat him, G rid of her.
15:33 "How could we ever g enough bread in this
16:23 on Peter and said, G out of my sight,
17: 7 and laying his hand on them, said, G up!
20:10 appeared they supposed they would g more;
24:17 come down to g anything out of his house.
25:29 who have will g more until they grow rich,
26:46 G up! Let us be on our way!
Mk 2:21 and the tear would g worse.
3:20 impossible for them to g any food whatever.
5:23 on her so that she may g well and live."
5:28 clothing," she thought, "I shall g well."
5:41 koum," which means, "Little girl, g up."
6: 2 "Where did he g all this?
6:45 he insisted that his disciples g into the boat
6:50 G hold of yourselves!
8:33 G out of my sight, you satan!
9:25 G out of him and never enter him again!"
10:49 G up! He is calling you!
13:15 or enter his house to g anything out of it.
14:15 is the place you are to g ready for us."
Lk 5:23 forgiven you,' or to say, G up and walk'?
5:24 "I say to you, g up!
6: 8 was withered, G up and stand here in front."
7:14 He said, "Young man, I bid you g up."
8:54 G up, child."
11: 7 I cannot g up to look after your needs'
11: 8 even though he does not g up and take care
12:33 G purses for yourselves that do not wear
12:45 girls, to eat and drink and g drunk,
12:47 to fulfill them will g a severe beating,
12:48 be flogged will g off with fewer stripes.
14: 7 to g the places of honor at the table:
17:31 the house, he should not go down to g them;
19:13 to them, 'Invest this until I g back.'
19:23 my return I could g it back with interest?'
20:19 high priests tried to g their hands on him,
22: 9 him, "Where do you want us to g it ready?"
Jn 2:16 G them out of here!
4:11 do you expect to g this flowing water?
5: 7 By the time I g there,
6:10 Jesus said, G the people to recline."
7:15 man g his education when he had no teacher?"
11:31 her saw her g up quickly and go out,
21: 3 replied, and went off to g into their boat.
Acts 3: 5 his whole attention, hoping to g something.
8:31 Philip to g in and sit down beside him.
9: 6 G up and go into the city,
9:34 G up and make your bed."
10:13 G up, Peter!
10:26 said as he helped him to his feet, G up!
11: 7 I listened as a voice said to me, G up,
12: 7 "Hurry, g up!"
16:10 made efforts to g across to Macedonia,
16:36 G started, now.
20:16 for he was eager to g to Jerusalem by the
21:34 not g at the truth because of the uproar,
22:10 Lord replied, G up and go into Damascus.
22:28 cost me quite a sum to g my citizenship."
23:23 G ready to leave for Caesarea by nine
26:16 G up now and stand on your feet.
Rom 3: 8 but they will g what they deserve.
1Cor 5: 7 G rid of the old yeast to make of
14: 8 is uncertain, who will g ready for battle?
2Cor 10:14 g as far as you with the gospel of Christ.
Gal 1:18 I went up to Jerusalem to g to know Cephas,
Eph 4:31 G rid of all bitterness,
2Tm 3: 9 But they will not g very far;
4:11 G Mark and bring him with you,
4:21 G here before winter if you can.
Phlm 1:22 And g a room ready for me;
1Pt 2:20 If you do wrong and g beaten for it,
Rv 19:10 worship him, but he said to me, "No, g up!
22: 9 "No, g up!

GETHER (2)

Gn 10:23 Uz, Hul, G, and Mash.
1Chr 1:17 The descendants of Aram were Uz, Hul, G,

GETHSEMANE (2)

Mt 26:36 Jesus went with them to a place called G.
Mk 14:32 They went then to a place named G.

GETS (9)

Prv 28:23 He who rebukes a man g more thanks in the
28:27 but he who ignores them g many a curse.
Mt 28:14 If any word of this g to the procurator,
Mk 4:27 He goes to bed and g up day after day.
Jn 19:24 Let us throw dice to see who g it."
Acts 23:15 are prepared to kill him before he g there."
1Cor 11:21 person goes hungry while another g drunk.
15:56 is sin, and sin g its power from the law.
3Jn 1:12 is one who g a good testimonial from all,

GETTING (17)

Gn 19:31 "Our father is g old,
19:33 not aware of her lying down or her g up.
19:35 not aware of her lying down or her g up.
1Sm 3: 8 G up and going to Eli,
2Kgs 4:14 no son, and her husband is g on in years."
6: 2 where by g one beam apiece we can build
Tb 6:10 entered Media and were g close to Ecbatana,
10: 7 the whole night through, g no sleep at all.
Mt 4:21 g their nets in order with their father,
Mk 5:18 As Jesus was g into the boat,
6:35 It was now g late and his disciples came
14:68 What are you g at?"
Lk 5:19 way of g him through because of the crowd,
Acts 15:36 see how the brothers are g on
1Cor 5: 2 of grieving, and g rid of the offender!
2Cor 12: 7 Satan to beat me and keep me from g proud.
Eph 5:18 Avoid g drunk on wine;

GEZER (15)

Jos 10:33 At that time Horam, king of G,
12:12 Hebron, Jarmuth, Lachish, Eglon, G,
16: 3 to that of the Lower Beth-horon, and to G,
16:10 not drive out the Canaanites living in G,
21:21 also G with its pasture lands,
Jgs 1:29 Gezer, and so the Canaanites live in G
2Sm 5:25 the Philistines from Gibeon as far as G.
1Kgs 9:15 of Jerusalem, Hazor, Megiddo, G (Pharaoh,
9:16 king of Egypt, had come up and taken G and,
9:17 Solomon then rebuilt G),
1Chr 6:52 pasture lands, G with its pasture lands,
7:28 to the east, G and its towns to the west,
14:16 the Philistine army from Gibeon to G.
20: 4 another battle with the Philistines, at G.

GHOST (6)

1Sm 28: 8 to her, "Tell my fortune through a g;
Mt 14:26 "It is a g!"
Mk 6:49 it was a g and they began to cry out.
Lk 24:37 fright they thought they were seeing a g.
24:39 a g does not have flesh and bones as I do."
24:53 a g does not have flesh and bones as I do."

GHOSTS (5)

Dt 18:11 nor one who consults g and spirits or
2Kgs 21: 6 the consulting of g and spirits.
23:24 with the consultation of g and spirits,
Is 19: 3 consult idols and charmers, g and spirits.
29: 4 voice shall be like a g from the earth,

GIANT (6)

1Chr 20: 6 battle, at Gath, they encountered a g,
1Mc 3: 3 and put on his breastplate like a g.
Ps(s) 19: 6 from his bridal chamber and, like a g,
Sir 47: 4 the g and wiped out the people's disgrace,
Is 10:13 treasures I have pillaged, and, like a g,
Rv 16:21 G hailstones like huge weights came

GIANTS (5)

Nm 13:33 g [the Anakim were a race of g;
Jdt 16: 6 bring him low, nor huge g attack him;
Wis 14: 6 old, when the proud g were being destroyed,
Bar 3:26 In it were born the g,

GIBBEAH (1)

Jos 15:57 Jokdeam, Zanoah, Kain, G and Timnah;

GIBBET (7)

Est 2:23 and both of them were hanged on a g.
5:14 his friends said to him, "Have a g set up,
5:14 pleased Haman, and he had the g erected.
6: 4 be hanged on the g he had raised for him.
7: 9 of Haman stands a g fifty cubits high.
7:10 the g which he had made ready for Mordecai,
8: 7 him on the g because he attacked the Jews,

GIBBETED (1)

Lam 5:12 Princes were g by them,

GIBBETHON (6)

Jos 19:44 Timnah, Ekron, Eltekoh, G
21:23 pasture lands, G with its pasture lands,
1Kgs 15:27 struck him down at G of the Philistines,
16:15 The army was besieging G of the
16:17 Omri marched up from G,
1Chr 6:54 pasture lands, G with its pasture lands,

GIBBETS (2)

Est 9:13 let the ten sons of Haman be hanged on g."
9:25 that he and his sons should be hanged on g.

GIBEA (1)

1Chr 2:49 fatherof Machbenah, and the father of G.

GIBEAH (41)

Jos 18:28 city (that is, Jerusalem), G and Kiriath;
Jgs 19:12 are not Israelites, but will go on to G.
19:13 for some other place, either G or Ramah,
19:14 when they were abreast of G of Benjamin.
19:15 they turned off to enter G for the night.
19:16 among the Benjaminite townspeople of G.
20: 4 I went into G of Benjamin for the night.
20: 5 But the citizens of G rose up against me
20: 9 Now as for G, this is what we will do:
20:10 deal fully and suitably with G of Benjamin
20:13 Now give up these corrupt men of G,
20:14 assembled from their other cities to G,
20:15 in addition to the inhabitants of G.
20:19 Israelites advanced on G with their forces.
20:20 array at G for the combat with Benjamin,
20:25 Benjaminites who came out of G
20:29 So Israel set men in ambush around G.
20:30 line of battle at G as on other occasions.
20:33 ambush rushed from their place west of G,
20:36 trusting in the ambush they had set at G.
20:37 men in ambush made a sudden dash into G,
20:43 and were now pursued to a point east of G,
1Sm 10:10 When they were going from there to G,
10:26 Saul also went home to G,
11: 4 When the messengers arrived at G of Saul,
13: 2 were with Jonathan in G of Benjamin.
13: 3 the Philistine garrison which was in G,
13:15 going from Gilgal to G of Benjamin.
15:34 Saul went up to his home in G of Saul.
22: 6 G under a tamarisk tree on the high place,
23:19 the Ziphites went up to Saul in G and said,
26: 1 Men from Ziph came to Saul in G reporting
2Sm 23:29 son of Ribai, from G of the Benjaminites;
1Chr 11:31 Ithai, son of Ribai, from G of Benjamin;
12: 3 with Joash, both sons of Shemaah of G;
2Chr 13: 2 was named Michaiah, daughter of Uriel of G.
Is 10:29 Ramah is in terror, G of Saul has fled.
Hos 5: 8 Blow the horn in G, the trumpet in Ramah!
9: 9 depths of corruption, as in the days of G;
10: 9 Since the days of G you have sinned,
10: 9 war was not to reach them in G.

GIBEATH-ELOHIM (1)

1Sm 10: 5 After that you will come to G,

GIBEATH-HAMMOREH (1)

Jgs 7: 1 of Midian was in the valley north of G.

GIBEATH-HAARALOTH (1)

Jos 5: 3 circumcised the Israelites at G

GIBEON (40)

Jos 9: 3 of G put into effect a device of their own.
9:17 the Israelites came to their cities of G,
10: 1 of G had made their peace with Israel,
10: 2 G was large enough for a royal city,
10: 4 to come to his aid for an attack on G,
10: 5 all their forces and marched against G,
10: 6 the men of G sent an appeal to Joshua in
10:10 inflicted a great slaughter on them at G
10:12 Stand still, O sun, at G,
10:41 to Gaza, and all the land of Goshen to G.
11:19 exception of the Hivites who lived in G,
18:25 Also G, Ramah, Beeroth,
21:17 four cities of G with its pasture lands,
Jgs 20:32 the one led to Bethel, the other to G,
2Sm 2:12 Ishbaal, Saul's son, left Mahanaim for G.
2:13 also set out and met them at the pool of G.
3:30 he killed their brother Asahel in battle at G
5:25 the Philistines from G as far as Gezer.
20: 8 the great stone in G when Amasa met them.
21: 6 we may dismember them before the LORD in G,
1Kgs 3: 4 The king went to G to sacrifice there,
3: 5 In G the LORD appeared to Solomon in a
9: 2 time, as he had appeared to him in G.
1Chr 6:45 G with its pasture lands,
8:29 In Gibeon dwelt Jeiel, the founder of G
9:35 In Gibeon dwelt Jeiel, the founder of G,
14:16 routed the Philistine army from G to Gezer.
16:39 of the LORD on the high place at G,
21:29 were at that time on the high place at G.
2Chr 1: 3 assembly, he went to the high place at G,
1:13 to Jerusalem from the high place at G,
Ezr 2:20 sons of G,
Neh 3: 7 and the men of G and of Mizpah,
7:25 sons of G,
Is 28:21 bestir himself as in the Valley of G,
Jer 28: 1 prophet Hananiah, son of Azzur, from G,
41:12 They overtook him at the Great Waters in G.
41:16 From G, they retreated

GIBEONITE (2)

1Chr 12: 4 Ishmaiah the G,
Neh 3: 7 At their side were Melatiah the G,

GIBEONITES (7)

Jos 9:22 Joshua summoned the G and said to them,
2Sm 21: 1 his family because he put the G to death."
21: 2 So the king called the G and spoke to them.
21: 2 (Now the G were not Israelites,
21: 3 David said to the G,
21: 4 The G answered him,
21: 9 Meholathite, and surrendered them to the G.

GIDDALTI (2)

1Chr 25: 4 Hananiah, Hanani, Eliathah, G,
25:29 The twenty-second fell to G,

GIDDEL (4)

Ezr 2:47 sons of Shamlai, sons of Hanan, sons of G,
2:56 sons of Jaalah, sons of Darkon, sons of G,
Neh 7:49 sons of Shalmai, sons of Hanan, sons of G,

GIDDEL (cont.)
7:58 sons of Jaala, sons of Darkon, sons of G,

GIDDY (1)

Sir 19: 2 Wine and women make the mind g,

GIDEON (45)

Jgs 6:11 While his son G was beating out wheat in
6:13 "My lord," G said to him,
6:19 So G went off and prepared a kid and an
6:22 G, now aware that it had been the angel of
6:24 So G built there an altar to the LORD and
6:27 So G took ten of his servants and did as
6:29 inquiry led them to the conclusion that G,
6:32 So on that day G was called Jerubbaal,
6:34 The spirit of the LORD enveloped G;
6:36 G said to God,
6:39 G then said to God,
7: 1 G) encamped by En-harod with all his
7: 2 The LORD said to G,
7: 3 G put them to this test on the mountain,
7: 4 The LORD said to G,
7: 5 When G led the soldiers down to the water,
7: 7 The LORD said to G,
7: 8 and G ordered the rest of the Israelites
7: 9 That night the LORD said to G,
7:13 When G arrived,
7:14 can only be the sword of the Israelite G,
7:15 When G heard the description and
7:18 camp and cry out, 'For the LORD and for G!' "
7:19 So G and the hundred men who were with him
7:20 cried out, "A sword for the LORD and G!"
7:24 G also sent messengers throughout the
7:25 of Oreb and Zeeb to G beyond the Jordan.
8: 4 When G reached the Jordan and crossed it
8: 7 G said,
8:11 G went up by the route of the nomads east
8:13 Then G,
8:21 So G stepped forward and killed Zebah and
8:22 The Israelites then said to G,
8:23 But G answered them,
8:24 G went on to say,
8:27 G made an ephod out of the gold and placed
8:27 and caused the ruin of G and his family.
8:28 for forty years, during the lifetime of G.
8:30 Now G had seventy sons,
8:32 At a good old age G,
8:33 But after G was dead,
8:35 G for all the good he had done for Israel.
2Sm 2:16 And so that place, which is in G,
Jdt 8: 1 son of Elkiah, son of Ananias, son of G,
Heb 11:32 I have no time to tell of G,

GIDEONI (5)

Nm 1:12 Abidan, son of G from Dan:
2:22 [Their prince was Abidan, son of G,
7:60 day it was the turn of Abidon, son of G,
7:65 This was the offering of Abidan, son of G.
10:24 tribe of Manasseh, and Abidan, son of G,

GIDGAD (2)

Nm 33:32 from Bene-jaakan, they camped at Mount G.
33:33 Setting out from Mount G,

GIDOM (1)

Jgs 20:45 men among them, and chasing them up to G,

GIFT (97)

Gn 23:11 the presence of my kinsmen I make this g.
30:20 said, "God has brought me a precious g.
32:19 they have been sent as a g to my lord Esau;
33:10 me the favor, please accept this g from me,
Nm 18: 6 they are a g to you,
18: 7 I give you the priesthood as a g.
18:11 g in every wave offering of the Israelites;
Jos 15:19 She answered, "Give me an additional g!
Jgs 1:15 Give me an additional g," she answered.
17: 4 to the LORD as my g in favor of my son,
1Sm 2:20 woman for the g she has made to the LORD!"
30:26 "This is a g to you from the spoil of the
2Kgs 5:15 Please accept a g from your servant."
8: 8 a g with you and go call on the man of God.
2Chr 35: 8 also gave a freewill g to the people,
Ezr 3: 5 might offer as a freewill g to the LORD.
2Mc 4:30 cities had been given as a g to Antiochus,
15:16 "Accept this holy sword as a g from God;
Jb 6:22 to offer a g for me from your possessions,
Ps(s) 22:26 g will I utter praise in the vast assembly;
127: 3 Behold, sons are a g from the LORD;
Prv 18:16 A man's g clears the way for him,
20:25 to pledge a sacred g is a trap for a man,
21:14 A secret g allays anger,
Eccl 3:13 the fruit of all his labor is a g of God.
5:18 the fruits of his toil, has a g from God.
Wis 8:21 too, was prudence, to know whose is the g—
Sir 11:17 The LORD's g remains with the just;
18:14 reproach, nor spoil any g by harsh words.
18:15 a burning wind, so does a word improve a g.
18:16 Sometimes the word means more than the g:
18:17 a grudging g wears out the expectant eyes.
20:13 A g from a rogue will do you no good,
20:13 in his eyes the one g is equal to seven.
26: 3 g bestowed upon him who fears the LORD;
26:14 A g from the LORD is her governed speech,
45:21 his food, a g to him and his descendants.
46:19 or secret g have I taken from any man!"
Ez 46:16 If the prince makes a g of part of his
46:17 But if he makes a g of part of his
Mt 5:23 If you bring your g to the altar and there
5:24 against you, leave your g at the altar,
5:24 brother, and then come and offer your g.
8: 4 priest and offer the g Moses prescribed.
10: 8 The g you have received, give as a gift.
23:18 by the g on the altar he is obligated.'
Jn 3:34 he does not ration his g of the Spirit.
4:10 "If only you recognized God's g,
14:27 farewell to you, my peace is my g to you;
17:24 this glory of mine which is your g to me,
Acts 2:38 you will receive the g of the Holy Spirit.
8:20 thinking that God's g can be bought!
10:45 surprised that the g of the Holy Spirit
11:17 If God was giving them the same g he gave
Rom 1:11 you some spiritual g to strengthen you
3:24 now undeservedly justified by the g of God,
5:15 But the g is not like the offense.
5:15 of God and the gracious g of the one man,
5:16 The g is entirely different from the sin
5:16 the g came after many offenses and brought
5:17 receive the overflowing grace and g of justice
6:23 but the g of God is eternal life in Christ
12: 6 One's g may be prophecy;
12: 7 It may be the g of ministry;
12: 7 is a teacher should use his g for teaching;
1Cor 1: 5 with every g of speech and knowledge.
1: 7 among you that you lack no spiritual g
7: 7 Still, each one has his own g from God,
12: 9 Spirit another is given the g of healing,
12:10 One receives the g of tongues,
12:30 all work miracles or have the g of healing?
12:30 have the g of interpretation of tongues?
13: 2 If I have the g of prophecy and,
14: 1 above all, the g of prophecy.
14:13 should pray for the g of interpretation.
14:22 The g of tongues is a sign,
16: 3 have chosen to take your g to Jerusalem.
2Cor 1:11 God may be thanked for the g granted us
9: 5 the bountiful g you have already promised.
9: 5 It should be ready as a gracious g,
9:15 Thanks be to God for his indescribable g!
Gal 2:21 not treat God's gracious g as pointless.
Eph 2: 8 This is not your own doing, it is God's g;
3: 7 Through the g God in his goodness bestowed
5: 2 offering to God, a g of pleasing fragrance.
Phil 4:17 It is not that I am eager for the g;
2Thes 1:12 g of our God and of the Lord Jesus Christ.
1Tm 4:14 Do not neglect the g you received when,
2Tm 1: 6 I remind you to stir into flame the g of God
Heb 6: 4 g and become sharers in the Holy Spirit,
Jas 1:17 Every worthwhile g,
4: 6 Yet he bestows a greater g,
1Pt 1:13 set all your hope on the g to be conferred
3: 7 as much as you to the gracious g of life.
Jude 1: 4 They pervert the gracious g of our God to
Rv 22:17 it accept the g of life-giving water.

GIFTED (2)

2Sm 14: 2 to Tekoa and brought from there a g woman,
Acts 21: 9 four unmarried daughters g with prophecy.

GIFTS (91)

Gn 15: 2 "O Lord GOD, what good will your g be,
24:10 and bearing all kinds of g from his master,
32:21 I first appease him with g that precede me,
32:22 So the g went on ahead of him,
43:11 baggage and take them down to the man as g:
43:15 So the men got the g,
43:25 their g to await Joseph's arrival at noon,
43:26 him with the g they had brought inside,
Ex 28:38 in consecrating any of their sacred g,
Nm 18:19 g which the Israelites make to the LORD;
18:29 From all the g that you receive,
18:32 Do not profane the sacred g of the
Dt 12:26 g or votive offerings that you may have,
15:14 weight him down with g from your flock
33:15 With the finest g of the age-old mountains
2Kgs 20:12 had been ill, he sent letters and g to him.
1Chr 16:29 Bring g, and enter his presence;
2Chr 17: 5 secure, and all Judah gave Jehoshaphat g,
17:11 Jehoshaphat g and a tribute of silver;
21: 3 father gave them numerous g of silver,
29:33 As consecrated g there were six hundred
31:14 in charge of the freewill g made to God;
32:23 Many brought g for the LORD to Jerusalem
Ezr 1: 6 g besides all their freewill offerings.
Neh 9:25 feast themselves on your immense good g.
Tb 11:18 seven happy days, and he received many g.
13:11 their hands their g for the King of heaven.
Jdt 16:18 holocausts, freewill offerings, and g.
Est 2:18 and bestowing g with royal bounty.
9:19 which they send g of food to one another.
9:22 food to one another and g to the poor.
1Mc 2:18 enriched with silver and gold and many g."
3:30 for the g that he had previously given
10:24 words and offer dignities and g,
10:28 many exemptions and will bestow g on you.
10:54 give to you and to her g worthy of you."
10:60 gold and many g and thus won their favor.
16:19 present them with silver, gold, and g.
2Mc 3: 2 the temple with the most magnificent g.
Ps(s) 36: 9 their fill of the prime g of your house;
45:13 And the city of Tyre is here with g;
68:19 high, taken captives, received men as g—
68:30 in Jerusalem let the kings bring you g.
72:10 of Tarshish and the Isles shall offer g;
76:12 let all round about him bring g to the
96: 8 Bring g, and enter his courts;
Prv 6:35 nor be satisfied with the greatest g.
Wis 7:14 g they have from discipline commend them.
Sir 3:17 you will be loved more than a giver of g.
7: 9 "He will appreciate my many g;
20: 9 Some g do one no good,
20:28 Favors and g blind the eyes;
34:18 g who offers in sacrifice ill-gotten goods!
34:19 High approves not the g of the godless,
35: 7 to the LORD, be not sparing of freewill g.
41:22 and of following up your g with insults;
Is 1:23 one of them loves a bribe and looks for g.
18: 7 Then will g be brought to the LORD of
39: 1 his sickness, he sent letters and g to him.
Jer 40: 5 gave him food and g and let him go.
Bar 6:26 one puts g beside them as beside the dead.
Ez 16:33 All harlots receive g.
16:33 rather bestowed your g on all your lovers,
20:26 I let them become defiled by their g,
20:31 By offering your g,
20:39 my holy name with your g and your idols.
Dn 2: 6 from me g and presents and great honors.
5:17 "You may keep your g,
Mi 1:14 you shall give parting g to Moresheth-gath;
Mt 2:11 coffers and presented him with g of gold,
Rom 11:29 God's g and his call are irrevocable.
12: 6 We have g that differ according to the
1Cor 2:12 us to recognize the g he has given us.
12: 1 leave you in ignorance about spiritual g.
12: 4 There are different g but the same Spirit;
12:11 the same Spirit who produces all these g,
12:31 Set your hearts on the greater g.
14: 1 Set your hearts on spiritual g—
14:12 you have set your hearts on spiritual g,
Eph 3:16 g in keeping with the riches of his glory.
4: 8 took a host of captives and gave g to men."
4:10 that he might fill all men with his g.
Heb 2: 4 of the g of the Holy Spirit as he willed.
5: 1 God, to offer g and sacrifices for sins.
8: 3 is appointed to offer g and sacrifices;
8: 4 offering the g which the law prescribes.
9: 9 in which g and sacrifices are offered that
11: 4 borne witness to him on account of his g;
1Pt 4:10 put your g at the service of one another,
Rv 11:10 them and in their merriment exchange g,
21: 7 wins the victory shall inherit these g;

GIGANTIC (1)

Rv 12:14 But the woman was given the wings of a g

GIHON (7)

Gn 2:13 The name of the second river is the G;
1Kgs 1:33 upon my own mule and escort him down to G.
1:38 on King David's mule, escorted him to G.
1:45 Nathan the prophet anointed him king at G,
2Chr 32:30 stopped the upper outflow of water from G
33:14 of David to the west of G in the valley,
Sir 24:25 with knowledge, like the G at vintage time.

GILALAI (1)

Neh 12:36 his brethren Shemaiah, Azarel, Milalai, G,

GILBOA (8)

1Sm 28: 4 they camped on G.
31: 1 and falling mortally wounded on Mount G,
31: 8 Saul and his three sons lying on Mount G.
2Sm 1: 6 Mount G and saw Saul leaning on his spear,
1:21 Mountains of G,
21:12 them at the time they killed Saul on G.
1Chr 10: 1 a number of them fell, slain on Mount G.
10: 8 his sons where they had fallen on Mount G.

GILDED (6)

Bar 6:38 These g and silvered wooden statues are
6:50 They are wooden, g and silvered;
6:54 of these wooden or g or silvered gods,
6:56 these wooden and silvered and g gods;
6:69 that is no protection, are their wooden, g,
6:70 are their silvered and g wooden gods.

GILEAD (105)

Gn 31:21 he headed for the highlands of G.
31:23 up with him in the hill country of G.
31:25 also pitched his tents there, on Mount G.
37:25 a caravan of Ishmaelites coming from G,
Nm 26:29 the clan of the Machirites, through G,
27: 1 Zelophehad, son of Hepher, son of G,

32: 1 land of Jazer and of *G* was grazing country,
32:26 other livestock remain in the towns of *G*,
32:29 you shall give them *G* as their property
32:39 son of Manasseh, invaded *G* and captured it,
32:40 [Moses gave *G* to Machir,
36: 1 houses in the clan of descendants of *G*,
Dt 2:36 the city in the wadi itself, as far as *G*,
3:10 all the cities of the plateau and all *G*
3:12 Arnon, halfway up into the highlands of *G*,
3:13 The rest of *G* and all of Bashan,
3:15 To Machir I gave *G*,
3:16 Gad the territory from *G* to the Wadi Arnon
4:43 Ramoth in *G* for the Gadites;
34: 1 and the LORD showed him all the land *G*,
Jos 12: 2 through half of *G* to the Wadi Jabbok,
12: 5 half of *G* as far as the territory of Sihon,
13:11 also *G* and the territory of the Geshurites
13:25 included Jazer, all the cities of *G*,
13:31 Half of *G*,
17: 1 his eldest son, Machir, the father of *G*,
17: 1 who had already obtained *G* and Bashan,
17: 3 Zelophehad, son of Hepher, son of *G*,
17: 5 the land of *G* and Bashan beyond the Jordan,
17: 6 of *G* fell to the rest of the Manassehites.
20: 8 of Reuben, Ramoth in *G* in the tribe of Gad,
21:38 at Ramoth in *G* with its pasture lands,
22: 9 of Canaan and returned to the land of *G*,
22:13 of *G* an embassy consisting of Phinehas,
22:15 half-tribe of Manasseh in the land of *G*,
22:32 *G* to the Israelites in the land of Canaan,
Jgs 5:17 *G*, beyond the Jordan,
10: 4 possessed thirty cities in the land of *G*;
10: 8 in the Amorite land beyond the Jordan in *G*.
10:17 had gathered for war and encamped in *G*,
10:18 the princes of *G* said to one another,
10:18 be leader of all the inhabitants of *G*."
11: 1 Gileadite Jephthah, born to *G* of a harlot.
11: 5 When this occurred the elders of *G* went to
11: 7 Jephthah replied to the elders of *G*.
11: 8 The elders of *G* said to Jephthah,
11: 8 be the leader of all of us who dwell in *G*."
11: 9 Jephthah answered the elders of *G*,
11:10 The elders of *G* said to Jephthah,
11:11 So Jephthah went with the elders of *G*,
11:29 He passed through *G* and Manasseh,
12: 4 the men of *G* and fought against Ephraim,
12: 4 "You of *G* are Ephraimite fugitives in
12: 5 me pass," the men of *G* would say to him,
12: 7 died and was buried in his city in *G*.
20: 1 Dan to Beer-sheba, and from the land of *G*,
1Sm 13: 7 over the Jordan into the land of Gad and *G*.
2Sm 2: 9 Mahanaim, where he made him king over *G*,
17:26 and Absalom encamped in the territory of *G*.
24: 6 *G* and to the district below Mount Hermon.
1Kgs 4:13 villages of Jair, son of Manasseh, in *G*;
4:19 son of Uri, in the land of *G*
17: 1 Elijah the Tishbite, from Tishbe in *G*,
2Kgs 10:33 east of the Jordan (all the land of *G*,
10:33 on the river Arnon up through *G* and Bashan.
15:25 who had with him fifty men from *G*,
15:29 Hazor, all the territory of Naphtali, *G*,
1Chr 2:21 the daughter of Machir, the father of *G*,
2:22 twenty-three cities in the land of *G*.
2:23 to the sons of Machir, the father of *G*.
5: 9 they had much livestock in the land of *G*.
5:10 tents throughout the region east of *G*.
5:14 son of Huri, son of Jaroah, son of *G*,
5:16 They dwelt in *G*,
6:65 Ramoth in *G* with its pasture lands,
7:14 she bore Machir, the father of *G*.
7:17 These were the descendants of *G*,
26:31 them outstanding officers at Jazer of *G*.
27:21 for the half-tribe of Manasseh in *G*,
Jdt 1: 8 the seacoast, to the peoples of Carmel, *G*,
1Mc 5: 9 The Gentiles in *G* assembled to attack and
5:17 I and my brother Jonathan will go to *G*."
5:20 and eight thousand men to Judas, for *G*.
5:25 all that had happened to the Jews in *G*:
5:27 have been imprisoned in other cities of *G*.
5:36 Maked, Bosor, and the other cities of *G*.
5:45 great and small, who were in *G*,
5:55 Judas and Jonathan were in the land of *G*,
13:22 So he left for *G*.
Ps(s) 60: 9 Mine is *G*,
108: 9 Mine is *G*,
Sg 4: 1 of goats streaming down the mountains of *G*.
6: 5 a flock of goats streaming down from *G*.
Jer 8:22 Is there no balm in *G*, no physician there?
22: 6 Though you be to me like *G*,
46:11 Go up to *G*,
50:19 and Bashan, And on Mount Ephraim and *G*,
Ez 47:18 and *G* on the one side,
Hos 6: 8 *G* is a city of evildoers,
12:12 In *G* is falsehood,
Am 1: 3 they threshed *G* with sledges of iron,
1:13 they ripped open expectant mothers in *G*,
Ob 1:19 of Samaria, And Benjamin shall occupy *G*.
Mi 7:14 Let them feed in Bashan and *G*,
Zec 10:10 I will bring them into *G* and into Lebanon,

GILEADITE (9)

Jgs 10: 3 Jair the *G* came after him and judged
11: 1 There was a chieftain, the *G* Jephthah,
11:40 Jephthah the *G* for four days of the year.
12: 7 Jephthah the *G* died and was buried in his
2Sm 17:27 Lodebar, and Barzillai, the *G* from Rogelim,
19:32 Barzillai the *G* also came down from
1Kgs 2: 7 be kind to the sons of Barzillai the *G*,
Ezr 2:61 the *G* and became known by his name).
Neh 7:63 the *G* and became known by his name).

GILEADITES (4)

Nm 26:29 a descendant of Machir, the clan of the *G*.
26:30 The *G* were: through Abiezer
Jgs 12: 5 The *G* took the fords of the Jordan toward
Jdt 15: 5 The *G* and the Galileans struck the enemy's

GILEAD'S (1)

Jgs 11: 2 *G* wife had also borne him sons,

GILGAL (40)

Dt 11:30 the *G* beside the terebinth of Moreh?]
Jos 4:19 in *G* on the eastern limits of Jericho.
4:20 At *G* Joshua set up the twelve stones which
5: 9 the place is called *G* to the present day.
5:10 encamped at *G* on the plains of Jericho,
9: 6 they journeyed to Joshua in the camp at *G*,
10: 6 sent an appeal to Joshua in his camp at *G*:
10: 7 So Joshua marched up from *G* with his
10: 9 upon them after an all-night march from *G*,
10:15 all Israel returned to the camp at *G*
10:43 with all Israel returned to the camp at *G*.
12:23 (in Naphath-dor), the foreign king of *G*,
14: 6 When the Judahites came up to Joshua in *G*,
15: 7 of the *G* that faces the pass of Adummim,
Jgs 2: 1 the LORD went up from *G* to Bochim and said,
3:19 however, from where the idols are, near *G*,
1Sm 7:16 *G* and Mizpah and judging Israel at each of
10: 8 Now go down ahead of me to *G*,
11:14 go to *G* to inaugurate the kingdom there."
11:15 So all the people went to *G*,
13: 4 the soldiers were called up to Saul in *G*.
13: 7 Saul, however, held out at *G*,
13: 8 When Samuel did not arrive at *G*,
13:12 will come down against me at *G*,
13:15 Samuel set out from *G* and went his own way;
13:15 going from *G* to Gibeah of Benjamin.
15:12 return he had passed on and gone down to *G*.
15:21 sacrifice to the LORD their God in *G*."
15:33 he cut Agag down before the LORD in *G*.
2Sm 19:16 Judah had come to *G* to meet him and to
19:41 Finally the king crossed over to *G*,
2Kgs 2: 1 he and Elisha were on their way from *G*.
4:38 When Elisha returned to *G*,
Hos 4:15 Come not to *G*,
9:15 All their wickedness is in *G*;
12:12 to nought, in *G* they sacrifice to bullocks;
Am 4: 4 Come to Bethel, and sin, to *G*,
5: 5 Do not come to *G*,
5: 5 For *G* shall be led into exile,
Mi 6: 5 from Shittim to *G*,

GILO (2)

2Sm 23:34 Eliam, son of Ahithophel, from *G*;
1Cr 11:36 Ahijah, from *G*

GILOH (2)

Jos 15:51 Anab, Eshtemoh, Anim, Goshen, Holon and *G*;
2Sm 15:12 an invitation to come from his town, *G*,

GILONITE (1)

2Sm 15:12 Absalom also sent to Ahithophel the *G*,

GIMZO (1)

2Chr 28:18 dependencies, and *G* and its dependencies,

GINATH (2)

1Kgs 16:21 divided, half following Tibni, son of *G*,
16:22 prevailed over those of Tibni, son of *G*.

GINNETHON (3)

Neh 10: 7 Harim, Meremoth, Obadiah, Daniel, *G*,
12: 4 Shecaniah, Rehum, Meremoth, Iddo, *G*,
12:16 for *G*,

GIRD (19)

Ex 29: 9 with the tunics, *g* them with the sashes,
Lv 16: 4 *g* himself with the linen sash and put on
1Sm 2: 4 are broken, while the tottering *g*
25:13 to his men, "Let everyone *g* on his sword."
2Sm 3:31 garments, *g* yourselves with sackcloth,
2Kgs 4:29 *G* your loins," Elisha said to Gehazi,
9: 1 *G* your loins, take this flask of oil
Jb 38: 3 *G* up your loins now,
40: 7 *G* up your loins now, like a man.
Ps(s) 45: 4 *G* your sword upon your thigh,
Is 22:21 with your robe, and *g* him with your sash,
Jer 1:17 But do you *g* your loins;
4: 8 So *g* yourselves with sackcloth,
6:26 O daughter of my people, *g* on sackcloth,
Lam 2:10 heads and *g* themselves with sackcloth;
Ez 44:18 they shall not *g* themselves with anything
Jl 1:13 *G* yourselves and weep, O priests!
Na 2: 2 Keep watch on the road, *g* your loins,
1Pt 1:13 So *g* the loins of your understanding;

GIRDED (16)

Lv 8: 7 the tunic on Aaron, *g* him with the sash,
8: 7 and *g* him with the embroidered belt of the
8:13 them with tunics, *g* them with sashes,
Dt 1:41 And each of you *g* on his weapons,
1Sm 17:39 *g* himself with Saul's sword over the tunic.
25:13 everyone, David included, *g* on his sword.
2Sm 22:33 The God who *g* me with strength and kept my
22:40 "You *g* me with strength for war;
1Kgs 18:46 who *g* up his clothing and ran before Ahab
20:32 they dressed in sackcloth *g* at the waist,
Jdt 4:10 slaves also *g* themselves with sackcloth.
4:14 were also *g* with sackcloth as they offered
2Mc 3:19 *g* with sackcloth below their breasts,
Ps(s) 18:33 The God who *g* me with strength and kept
18:40 And you *g* me with strength for war;
Ez 23:15 with sashes *g* about their waists,

GIRDING (1)

2Mc 10:25 their heads and *g* their loins in sackcloth.

GIRDLE (4)

2Kgs 1: 8 "with a leather *g* about his loins."
Jdt 9: 2 had immodestly loosened the maiden's *g*,
Ps(s) 109:19 him, like a *g* which is always about him.
Is 3:24 there will be stench, instead of the *g*,

GIRGASHITE (1)

1Chr 1:14 and the Jebusite, the Amorite, the *G*,

GIRGASHITES (6)

Gn 10:16 of the Jebusites, the Amorites, the *G*,
15:21 the Amorites, the Canaanites, the *G*,
Dt 7: 1 the Hittites, *G*,
Jos 3:10 Hittites, Hivites, Perizzites, *G*,
24:12 Perizzites, Canaanites, Hittites, *G*,
Neh 9: 8 Amorites, Perizzites, Jebusites, and *G*.

GIRL (61)

Gn 24:14 coming out to draw water, if I say to a *g*,
24:16 The *g* was very beautiful,
24:28 Then the *g* ran off and told her mother's
24:55 "Let the *g* stay with us a short while,
24:57 "Let us call the *g* and see what she
29:24 (Laban assigned his slave *g* Zilpah to his
29:29 (Laban assigned his slave *g* Bilhah to his
34: 3 indeed was really in love with the *g*,
34: 4 father Hamor, "Get me this *g* for a wife."
Ex 1:16 but if it is a *g*,
21:31 if it is a boy or a *g* that the ox gores.
Lv 12: 5 If she gives birth to a *g*,
12: 7 who gives birth to a boy or a *g* child.
27: 6 shekels for a boy, and three for a *g*;
Dt 22:15 mother of the *g* shall take the evidence
22:16 father of the *g* shall say to the elders,
22:21 they shall bring the *g* to the entrance of
22:24 the *g* because she did not cry out for help
Ru 2: 5 of his harvesters, "Whose *g* is this?"
2: 6 "She is the Moabite *g* who returned from
4:12 the LORD will give you from this *g*,
1Kgs 1: 3 *g* throughout the territory of Israel,
2Kgs 5: 2 the land of Israel in a raid a little *g*,
5: 4 slave *g* from the land of Israel had said.
Tb 6:12 Now the *g* is sensible,
6:13 tonight we must speak for the *g*,
7:15 the other bedroom and bring the *g* there."
7:16 as she was told, and brought the *g* there.
Est 2: 4 Then the *g* who pleases the king shall
2: 7 The *g* was beautifully formed and lovely to
2: 9 The *g* pleased him and won his favor.
2:12 Each *g* went in turn to visit King
2:13 Then, when the *g* was to visit the king,
Sir 9: 4 With a singing *g* be not familiar,
36:21 one *g* will be more suitable than another:
41:21 Of trifling with a servant *g* you have,
Ez 16:22 remembered nothing of when you were a *g*,
16:43 remember what happened when you were a *g*,
16:60 I made with you when you were a *g*,
23: 8 when they had lain with her as a young *g*,
Jl 4: 3 and sold a *g* for the wine they drank.
Mt 9:24 The little *g* is not dead.
9:25 her by the hand, and the little *g* got up.
14:11 brought in on a platter and given to the *g*,
26:71 another *g* saw him and said to those nearby,
Mk 5:41 "Talitha, koum," which means, "Little *g*,
5:42 The *g*,
6:22 The king told the *g*,
6:25 At that the *g* hurried back to the king's
6:28 the girl, and the *g* gave it to her mother.
14:69 The servant *g*,
Lk 8:42 his only daughter, a *g* of about twelve,

GIRL (cont.)
22:56 g saw him sitting in the light of the fire.
Jn 18:17 servant g who kept the gate said to Peter,
Acts 16:16 met a slave g who had a clairvoyant spirit.
16:17 The g began to follow Paul and the rest of
Gal 4:22 Abraham had two sons, one by the slave g,
4:23 The son of the slave g had been begotten
4:30 "Cast out slave g and son together;
4:31 of a slave g but of a mother who is free.

GIRLHOOD (2)

Ez 23:19 all the more, recalling the days of her g,
23:21 You yearned for the lewdness of your g,

GIRLS (31)

Ex 1:22 Hebrews, but you may let all the g live."
Nm 31:18 all g who had no intercourse with a man.
31:35 thousand g who were still virgins.
Dt 22:19 which they shall give to the g father,
22:20 evidence of the g virginity is not found,
22:29 shall pay the g father fifty silver shekels
Jgs 19: 3 the g father joyfully made him welcome.
19: 4 He was detained by the g father,
19: 5 But the g father said to his son-in-law,
19: 6 Then the g father said to the husband,
19: 8 early to depart, but the g father said,
19: 9 and servant, the g father said to him,
21:21 g of Shiloh come out to do their dancing,
21:21 seize one of the g of Shiloh for a wife,
1Sm 9:11 they met some g coming out to draw water
9:12 The g answered,
2Sm 6:20 the view of the slave g of his followers,
6:22 the slave g you spoke of I will be honored."
Tb 6:13 g father to let us have her as your bride.
8: 1 drinking, the g parents wanted to retire.
8: 4 When the g parents left the bedroom and
8:14 told the g parents that Tobiah was alive,
Jdt 16:12 Sons of slave g pierced them through;
Ez 23: 3 even as young g played the harlot in Egypt.
Dn 13:36 two g and shut the doors of the garden,
13:36 the doors of the garden, dismissing the g.
Zec 8: 5 with boys and g playing in her streets.
Mt 26:69 of the serving g came over to him and said,
Mk 14:66 servant g of the high priest came along.
Lk 12:45 to abuse the housemen and servant g,
Gal 4:30 for the slave g son shall never be an heir

GIRT (12)

Ex 12:11 with your loins g,
Jgs 18:16 The six hundred men g with weapons of war,
1Sm 2:18 the boy Samuel, g with a linen apron,
2Sm 6:14 Then David, g with a linen apron,
21:16 Dadu was g with a new sword and planned to
Neh 4:12 he worked, had his sword g at his side.
Ps(s) 65: 7 by your power, you who are g with might;
93: 1 is the LORD and g about with strength,
Prv 31:17 She is g about with strength,
Sg 4: 4 is like David's tower g with battlements.
Bar 6:42 And their women, g with cords,
Jl 1: 8 Lament like a virgin g with sackcloth for

GIRZITES (1)

1Sm 27: 8 up and made raids on the Geshurites, G,

GISHPA (1)

Neh 11:21 and G were in charge of the temple slaves.

GITH (3)

Is 28:25 does he not scatter g and sow cumin,
28:27 G is not threshed with a sledge,
28:27 But g is beaten out with a staff,

GITTAIM (2)

2Sm 4: 3 the Beerothites fled to G,
Neh 11:33 Anathoth, Nob, Ananiah, Hazor, Ramah, G,

GITTITE (6)

2Sm 6:10 it to the house of Obed-edom the G.
6:11 house of Obed-edom the G for three months,
15:19 before the king, he said to Ittai the G:
15:22 And Ittai the G,
18: 2 and a third under command of Ittai the G.
1Chr 13:13 it instead to the house of Obed-edom the G.

GIVE (1026)

Gn 1:29 I g you every seed-bearing plant all over
1:30 ground, I g all the green plants for food."
4:12 soil, it shall no longer g you its produce.
9: 3 I g them all to you as I did the green
12: 7 "To your descendants I will g this land."
13:15 will g to you and your descendants forever.
13:17 length and breadth, for to you I will g it."
14:21 of Sodom said to Abram, G me the people;
15: 7 to g you this land as a possession."
15:18 "To your descendants I g this land,
17: 8 I will g to you and to your descendants
17:16 bless her, and I will g you a son by her.
17:16 he shall g rise to nations,
17:17 Or can Sarah g birth at ninety?"
19: 9 an immigrant, and now he dares to g orders!
23:11 I g you both the field and the cave in it;
24: 7 'I will g this land to your descendants'
24:14 a drink, and let me g water to your camels,
24:17 "Please g me a sip of water from your jug."
24:43 Please g me a little water from your jug,
24:44 a drink, but I will g water to your camels,
24:54 he said, G me leave to return to my master."
25:31 g me your birthright in exchange for it."
26: 3 your descendants I will g all these lands,
26: 4 in the sky and g them all these lands,
27: 4 may g you my special blessing before I die."
27: 7 that I may g you my blessing with the
27:19 so that you may g me your special blessing."
27:25 I may eat of it and then g you my blessing."
27:28 "May God g to you of the dew of the
27:31 you may then g me your special blessing."
28:13 lying I will g to you and your descendants.
28:20 g me enough bread to eat and clothing
28:22 Of everything you g me,
29:19 to g her to you rather than to an outsider.
29:21 Then Jacob said to Laban, G me my wife,
29:27 one, and then I will g you the other too,
29:35 I will g grateful praise to the LORD";
30: 1 to Jacob, G me children or I shall die!"
30: 3 with her, and let her g birth on my knees,
30:25 G me leave to go to my homeland.
34: 8 Please g her to him in marriage.
34: 9 g your daughters to us,
34:12 only g me the maiden in marriage."
34:14 to g our sister to an uncircumcised man;
34:16 Then we will g you our daughters and take
34:21 and g our daughters to them in marriage.
34:23 Let us, therefore, g in to them,
35:12 gave to Abraham and Isaac I now g to you;
35:12 descendants after you will I g this land."
38:18 asked, "What pledge am I to g to you?"
38:26 am, since I did not g her to my son Shelah."
41:16 God who will g Pharaoh the right answer."
41:24 but none of them can g me an explanation."
42:27 opened his bag to g his donkey some fodder,
45: 3 But his brothers could g him no answer,
47:15 G us food or we shall perish under your
47:16 replied Joseph, g me your livestock,
47:19 only g us seed,
47:24 is in, you must g a fifth of it to Pharaoh,
48: 4 and I will g this land to your descendants
48:22 As for me, I g to you,
Ex 1:19 and g birth before the midwife arrives."
5: 5 yet you would g them rest from their labor!"
6: 4 with them, to g them the land of Canaan,
6: 8 the land which I swore to g to Abraham,
6: 8 I will g it to you as your own possession
12:25 which the LORD will g you as he promised.
13: 5 he swore to your fathers he would g you,
13:11 to you and your fathers he would g you,
13:21 means of a column of fire to g them light.
17: 2 with Moses and said, G us water to drink."
18:19 listen to me, and I will g you some advice,
21:23 injury ensues, you shall g life for life,
22:16 If her father refuses to g her to him,
22:28 You shall g me the first-born of your sons.
22:29 but on the eighth day you must g it to me.
23:13 G heed to all that I have told you.
23:26 and I will g you a full span of life.
24:12 I will g you the stone tablets on which I
25: 2 that his heart prompts him to g.
25:16 to put the commandments which I will g you.
25:21 to put the commandments which I will g you.
25:22 that I wish you to g the Israelites.
28: 3 you shall g instructions to make such
30:12 shall g the LORD a forfeit for his life,
30:14 group must g this contribution to the LORD.
30:15 not give more, nor shall the poor g less,
32:13 I will g your descendants as their
33: 1 and Jacob I would g to their descendants.
33:14 answered, "will go along, to g you rest."
34:24 before you to g you a large territory,
Lv 5: 1 person refuses to g the information which,
5: 1 seen or learned, he has been adjured to g,
5:24 g the owner one fifth of its value.
6: 2 G Aaron and his sons the following command:
7:32 from your peace offering you shall g
7:36 LORD ordered the Israelites to g them
13:54 he shall g orders to have the infected
15:14 tent, he shall g them to the priest,
22:31 the commandments which I, the LORD, g you,
25:38 out of the land of Egypt to g you the land
26: 4 I will g you rain in due season,
26:16 then I, in turn, will g you your deserts.
Nm 1:50 You are to g the Levites charge of the
3: 9 shall g the Levites to Aaron and his sons;
3:48 G this silver to Aaron and his sons as
5: 7 and in addition g one fifth of their value
6:26 LORD look upon you kindly and g you peace!
8: 2 to Moses, and said, G Aaron this command:
10:29 place which the LORD has promised to g us.
11:13 can I get meat to g to all this people?
11:13 are crying to me, G us meat for our food.'
11:18 the LORD will g you meat for food,
11:21 will g them meat to eat for a whole month.'
14: 8 us, he will bring us in and g us that land,
14:16 people into the land he swore to g them;
15: 2 Moses, G the Israelites these instructions:
15: 2 the land I will g you for your homesteads,
15:21 Throughout your generations you shall g a
18: 7 I g you the priesthood as a gift.
18:12 they g to the LORD as their first fruits;
18:24 Israelites g as a contribution to the LORD.
18:26 to Moses, G the Levites these instructions:
20:12 this community into the land I will g them."
21:16 people together, and I will g them water."
21:33 with all his people to g battle at Edrei.
22: 8 g you whatever answer the LORD gives me."
22:11 able to g them battle and drive them out.'"
23:18 g ear to my testimony,
25:12 I hereby g him my pledge of friendship,
27: 7 you shall g them hereditary property among
27: 9 you shall g his heritage to his brothers;
27:10 g his heritage to his father's brothers;
27:11 you shall g his heritage to his nearest
28: 2 Moses, G the Israelites this commandment:
31:30 asses and sheep, and g them to the Levites,
32:29 you shall g them Gilead as their property
34: 2 said to Moses, G the Israelites this order:
35: 2 they shall g the Levites cities for homes,
35: 6 are the cities you shall g to the Levites:
36: 2 commanded by the LORD to g the heritage
Dt 1: 8 I would g to them and their descendants.'
1:17 g ear to the lowly and to the great alike,
1:35 the good land I swore to g to your fathers,
1:36 to his sons I will g the land he trod upon,
1:38 him, for he is to g Israel its heritage.
1:39 to them I will g it,
1:45 did not listen to your cry or g ear to you.
2: 4 G this order to the people:
2: 5 not g you so much as a foot of their land,
2: 9 not g you possession of any of their land,
2:19 for I will not g you possession of any
2:28 and for the water you g me to drink,
2:29 which the LORD, our God, is about to g us.'
3: 1 with all his people to g battle at Edrei.
3:20 g them on the other side of the Jordan.
4: 6 for thus will you g evidence of your
5:31 me and I will g you all the commandments,
6: 3 g you a land flowing with milk and honey.
6:10 Isaac and Jacob, that he would g you,
6:23 on oath to our fathers, and to g it to us.
7:13 he swore to your fathers he would g you.
10: 8 to him, and to g blessings in his name,
10:11 I swore to their fathers I would g them.'
11: 9 he would g to them and their descendants,
11:14 I will g the seasonal rain to your land,
11:21 LORD swore to your fathers he would g them.
12: 9 which the LORD, your God, will g you.
14:21 But you may g it to an alien who belongs
15: 4 he will g you to occupy as your heritage,
15: 9 to your needy kinsman and g him nothing;
15:10 g to him, give freely and not with ill will;
16:17 but each of you with as much as he can g,
17:10 g you in the place which the LORD chooses,
17:11 You shall carry out the directions they g
18: 4 You shall also g him the first fruits of
19: 3 LORD, your God, will g you as a heritage,
19: 8 land he promised your fathers he would g
20: 4 you against your enemies and g you victory.'
21: 5 to him and to g blessings in his name,
21:14 for her, you shall g her her freedom,
22: 2 then g it back to him.
22:19 which they shall g to the girl's father,
26: 3 he swore to our fathers he would g us.'
28:11 he swore to your fathers he would g you.
28:12 heavens, to g your land rain in due season,
28:14 any of the commandments which I now g you,
28:24 the LORD will g your land powdery dust,
28:65 for there the LORD will g you an anguished
30:20 swore he would g to your fathers Abraham,
31: 7 swore to their fathers he would g them;
31:14 tent that I may g him his commission."
32: 1 G ear, O heavens, while I speak;
34: 4 Jacob that I would g to their descendants.
Jos 1: 2 into the land I will g the Israelites.
1: 6 so that you may g this people possession
1: 6 I swore to their fathers I would g them.
1:18 and does not obey every command you g him,
2:12 and g me an unmistakable token that you
5: 6 had promised their fathers he would g us.
6: 5 When they g a long blast on the ram's
7:19 said to Achan, "My son, g to the LORD,
14:12 G me, therefore, this mountain region
15:16 "I will g my daughter Achsah in marriage
15:19 She answered, G me an additional gift!
15:19 in the Negeb, g me also pools of water."
17: 4 Moses to g us a heritage among our kinsmen."
21:43 had sworn to their fathers he would g them.
Jgs 1:12 "I will g my daughter Achsah in marriage
1:15 G me an additional gift," she answered.
1:15 the Negeb to me, g me also pools of water."
4:19 her, "Please g me a little water to drink.
5: 3 G ear, O princes!
6:17 g me a sign that you are speaking with me.
8: 5 you g my followers some loaves of bread?
8: 6 that we should g food to your army?"
8:15 we should g food to your weary followers?'"
8:24 each of you g me a ring from his booty?"
8:25 "We will gladly g them,"

9: 9 answered them, 'Must I *g* up my rich oil,
9:11 I *g* up my sweetness and my good fruit,
9:13 I *g* up my wine that cheers gods and men,
11:17 But the king of Edom did not *g* consent.
12: 6 being able to *g* the proper pronunciation,
14:12 I will *g* you thirty linen tunics and
14:13 you must *g* me thirty tunics and thirty
16: 5 *g* you eleven hundred shekels of silver."
17:10 and I will *g* you ten silver shekels a year,
20:13 Now *g* up these corrupt men of Gibeah,
21: 1 none of them would *g* his daughter
21: 7 to *g* them any of our daughters in marriage?"
21:18 *g* them any of our daughters in marriage,
Ru 4: 7 take off his sandal and *g* it to the other.
4:12 the LORD will *g* you from this girl,
1Sm 1: 4 he used to *g* a portion each to his wife
1:11 *g* your handmaid a male child, I will give
1:28 Now I, in turn, *g* him to the LORD;
2:10 earth, Now may he *g* strength to his king,
2:15 *G* me some meat to roast for the priest.
2:16 he would reply, "No, *g* it to me now,
6: 5 *g* them as a tribute to the God of Israel.
8:14 olive groves, and *g* them to his officials.
8:15 and *g* the revenue to his eunuchs and his
9: 7 and we have no present to *g* the man of God.
9: 8 If I *g* that to the man of God,
9:27 that I may *g* you a message from God."
11: 3 *G* us seven days to send messengers
17:10 *G* me a man and let us fight together."
17:25 him, the king would *g* him great wealth,
18: 8 "They *g* David ten thousands,
18:17 whom I will *g* you in marriage if you
20: 8 Why should you *g* me up to your father?"
20:29 of me, *g* me leave to visit my brothers.'
21: 4 *G* me five loaves,
21:10 There is none to match it. *G* it to me!"
22: 7 of Jesse *g* all of you fields and vineyards?
25: 8 Please *g* your servants and your son David
25:11 and *g* them to men who come from I know not
27: 1 then Saul will *g* up his continual search
30:22 we will not *g* them anything from the booty,
2Sm 3:14 son of Saul, to say, *G* me my wife Michal,
4:10 news for which I ought to *g* him a reward.
7:11 I will *g* you rest from all your enemies.
10:19 afraid to *g* further aid to the Ammonites.
12:11 see it, and will *g* them to your neighbor.
14: 7 *G* up the one who killed his brother.
18:11 to *g* you fifty pieces of silver and a belt."
19:37 Why should the king *g* me this reward?
21: 6 The king replied, "I will *g* them up."
23:15 that someone would *g* me a drink of water
24:23 All this does Araunah *g* to the king."
1Kgs 2:17 to *g* me Abishag the Shunamite for my wife."
3: 5 something of me and I will *g* it to you."
3: 9 *G* your servant,
3:12 I *g* you a heart so wise and understanding
3:13 I *g* you what you have not asked for,
3:14 father David did, I will *g* you a long life."
3:25 *g* half to one woman and half to the other."
3:26 "Please, my lord, *g* her the living child
3:27 answered, *G* the first one the living child!
5:20 *G* orders, then, to have cedars
5:31 to *g* the temple a foundation of hewn stone.
11:11 of the kingdom and *g* it to your servant.
11:21 *G* me leave to return to my own country."
11:31 grasp and will *g* you ten of the tribes.
11:33 The ten I will *g* you because he has
11:35 kingdom from his sons and will *g* it to you
11:36 I will *g* his son one tribe,
11:38 I will *g* Israel to you.
12: 6 answer do you advise me to *g* this people?"
12: 9 answer do you advise me to *g* this people,
13: 7 man of God, "and I will *g* you a present."
13:33 not *g* up his evil ways after this event,
14: 6 been commissioned to *g* you bitter news.
14:16 He will *g* up Israel because of the sins
17:19 *G* me your son," Elijah said to her.
18:23 *G* us two young bulls.
20: 5 sent you word to *g* me your silver and gold,
20: 8 Do not *g* in."
21: 2 *G* me your vineyard to be my vegetable
21: 2 I will *g* you a better vineyard in exchange,
21: 2 prefer, I will *g* you its value in money."
21: 3 I should *g* you my ancestral heritage."
21: 4 "I will not *g* you my ancestral heritage."
21: 6 I will *g* you a vineyard in exchange.'
2Kgs 3: 3 this he did not *g* up.
3:21 that the kings had come to *g* them battle;
4:42 *G* it to the people to eat," Elisha said.
4:43 *G* it to the people to eat,"
5:22 Please *g* them a talent of silver and two
6:28 *G* up your son that we may eat him today;
6:29 'Now *g* up your son that we may eat him.'
10:15 you are," continued Jehu, *g* me your hand."
12:12 They in turn would *g* it to the carpenters
12:16 with the funds to *g* to the workmen,
14: 9 *G* your daughter to my son in marriage,'
15:20 Menahem secured the money to *g* to the king
17:13 *G* up your evil ways and keep my
18:23 I will *g* you two thousand horses if you
22:18 you to consult the LORD, *g* this response:
1Chr 11:17 that someone would *g* me a drink from the
16: 8 *G* thanks to the LORD,
16:18 "To you will I *g* the land of Canaan as
16:28 *G* to the LORD, you families of nations, *g*
16:29 *G* to the LORD the glory due his name!
16:34 *G* thanks to the LORD,
16:35 That we may *g* thanks to your holy name and
16:41 designated by name to *g* thanks to the LORD,
21:12 What answer am I to *g* him who sent me?"
21:23 I also *g* you the oxen for the holocausts,
21:23 I *g* it all to you."
22: 9 and I will *g* him rest from all his enemies
22:12 May the LORD *g* you prudence and
25: 3 a lyre, to *g* thanks and praise to the LORD.
29: 3 I *g* to the house of my God my personal
29:12 is yours to *g* grandeur and strength to all.
29:13 we *g* you thanks and we praise the majesty
29:14 only *g* you what we have received from you.
29:19 *G* to my son Solomon a wholehearted desire
2Chr 1:10 *G* me, therefore, wisdom and knowledge
1:12 but I will also *g* you riches,
5:13 instruments to *g* thanks to the LORD,
10: 6 answer do you advise me to *g* this people?"
10: 7 kindly with this people and *g* in to them,
10: 9 answer do you advise me to *g* this people,
10:10 *g* to this people who have said to you,
12: 7 I will *g* them some deliverance,
20:21 *G* thanks to the LORD,
21: 7 to *g* him and his sons a lamp for all time.
25: 9 "The LORD can *g* you much more than that."
25:18 *G* your daughter to my son for his wife.'
34:26 you to consult the LORD, *g* this response:
Ezr 4:21 *G* orders, therefore, that will stop the work
9:12 *g* your daughters to their sons in marriage,
10:11 But now, *g* praise to the LORD,
Neh 2: 8 that he may *g* me wood for timbering the
9: 6 To all of them you *g* life,
9: 8 made the covenant with him to *g* to him
9:15 you had sworn with upraised hand to *g* them.
9:20 bestowed on them, to *g* them understanding;
9:27 according to your great mercy *g* them
10:33 to *g* a third of a shekel each year for the
Tb 1: 7 in Jerusalem I would *g* the tithe of grain,
1: 7 years, I used to *g* a second tithe in money,
1:17 I would *g* my bread to the hungry and my
2:13 *G* it back to its owners,
2:14 and told her to *g* it back to its owners.
4: 3 "My son, when I die, *g* me a decent burial.
4: 7 *G* alms from your possessions.
4: 8 Son, *g* alms in proportion to what you own.
4: 8 great wealth, *g* alms out of your abundance;
4: 8 But do not hesitate to *g* alms;
4:11 sight of the Most High for all who *g* them.
4:16 *G* to the hungry some of your bread,
4:16 you have left over, *g* away as alms;
4:16 and do not begrudge the alms you *g*.
5: 2 trust me, so that he will *g* me the money?
5: 3 of course, *g* him a salary when you return;
5:15 you are away I will *g* you the normal wages,
6:16 do not *g* another thought to this demon,
6:18 as the demon smells the odor they *g* off,
7:10 have the right to *g* her to anyone but you,
9: 2 Go to Gabael's house and *g* him this bond.
10: 2 and there is no one to *g* him the money."
10: 8 Tobit, and they will *g* him news of you."
12: 1 that you *g* what is due to the man
12: 1 *g* him a bonus too."
12: 2 It would not hurt me at all to *g* him half
12: 3 How much of a bonus should I *g* him?"
12: 6 *G* him the praise and the glory.
12: 8 is better to *g* alms than to store up gold;
12: 9 regularly *g* alms shall enjoy a full life;
13:11 generation shall *g* joyful praise in you,
14: 9 "Now, children, I *g* you this command:
14: 9 to do what is upright and to *g* alms,
Jdt 8:16 the Lord our God *g* surety for his plans.
9: 9 *G* me, a widow, the strong hand
10:13 your forces, to *g* him a trustworthy report;
10:16 *g* him the report you speak of,
11: 6 handmaid, God will *g* you complete success,
12: 3 "But if your provisions *g* out,
12: 6 sent this message to Holofernes, *G* orders,
14:13 slaves have dared come down to *g* us battle,
Est 1:19 authorizing the king to *g* her royal dignity
C:23 the time of our distress and *g* me courage.
1Mc 2:50 be zealous for the law and *g* your lives
4:31 *G* this army into the hands of your people
4:35 Lysias saw his ranks beginning to *g* way,
8: 7 to *g* hostages and a section of Lycia,
8:26 war they shall not *g* nor provide grain,
9:55 a word to *g* orders concerning his house.
10:39 Ptolemais and its confines I *g* as a
10:54 *G* me your daughter for my wife;
10:54 *g* to you and to her gifts worthy of you."
11: 9 I will *g* you my daughter whom Alexander
11:50 *G* us your terms and let the Jews stop
15:30 *g* up the cities you have seized and the
2Mc 1: 3 May he *g* to all of you a heart to worship
1:11 we *g* him great thanks for having fought on
2:27 who thus seeks to *g* enjoyment to others.
2:29 must *g* attention to the whole structure,
7:23 will *g* you back both breath and life,
9:11 he began to *g* up his excessive arrogance,
10:10 shall *g* a summary of the chief evils caused
11:26 to *g* them our assurances of friendship,
12: 8 men of Jamnia planned to *g* like treatment
14:46 and of spirit to *g* these back to him again.
Jb 2: 4 All that a man has will he *g* for his life.
2:11 together to *g* him sympathy and comfort.
5:18 he smites, but his hands *g* healing.
6:22 Have I asked you to *g* me anything,
6:28 Come now, *g* me your attention;
8: 8 and *g* heed to the experience of the
9:14 How much less shall I *g* him any answer,
10: 1 I will *g* myself up to complaint;
11: 3 and shall you deride and no one *g* rebuke?
13:13 that I may speak and *g* vent to my feelings.
13:17 to my speech, and *g* my statement a hearing.
15:35 they *g* birth to failure.
17: 3 who is there that will *g* surety for me?
26: 2 What help you *g* to the powerless,
31:37 Of all my steps I should *g* him an account;
32:21 to anyone, nor *g* flattering titles to any.
35: 7 If you are righteous, what do you *g* him,
39:19 Do you *g* the horse his strength,
40: 2 Let him who would correct God *g* answer!
Ps(s) 2: 8 Ask of me and I will *g* you the nations
2:10 now, O kings, *g* heed; take warning,
7:18 will *g* thanks to the LORD for his justice,
9: 2 I will *g* thanks to you, O LORD,
13: 4 *G* light to my eyes that I may not sleep
18:29 You indeed, O LORD, *g* light to my lamp;
22:24 you descendants of Jacob, *g* glory to him;
23: 4 your rod and your staff that *g* me courage.
27:12 *G* me not up to the wishes of my foes;
28: 4 *g* them their deserts.
28: 7 exults, and with my song I *g* him thanks.
29: 1 *G* to the LORD, you sons of God, give
29: 2 *G* to the LORD the glory due his name;
29:11 May the LORD *g* strength to his people;
30: 5 ones, and *g* thanks to his holy name.
30:10 *g* you thanks or proclaim your faithfulness?
30:13 LORD, my God, forever will I *g* you thanks.
31: 3 of refuge, a stronghold to *g* me safety.
33: 2 *G* thanks to the LORD on the harp;
35:18 I will *g* you thanks in the vast assembly,
36: 9 your delightful stream you *g* them to drink.
37: 8 *G* up your anger,
39:13 to my cry *g* ear;
41: 3 not *g* him over to the will of his enemies.
43: 4 Then will I *g* you thanks upon the harp,
50:19 To your mouth you *g* free rein for evil,
51:14 *G* me back the joy of your salvation,
55: 3 *g* heed to me,
55:19 He will *g* me freedom and peace from those
57:10 I will *g* thanks to you among the peoples,
60:13 *G* us aid against the foe,
61: 3 you will *g* me rest,
71: 3 of refuge, a stronghold to *g* me safety,
71:22 will I *g* you thanks with music on the lyre,
74:19 *G* not to the vulture the life of your dove;
75: 2 We give you thanks, O God, we *g* thanks.
78:20 *g* bread and provide meat for his people?"
79:13 your pasture, will *g* thanks to you forever;
80:19 *g* us new life,
85: 7 Will you not instead *g* us life;
85:13 The LORD himself will *g* his benefits;
86:12 I will *g* thanks to you,
86:16 *g* your strength to your servant,
88:11 Will the shades arise to *g* you thanks?
92: 2 It is good to *g* thanks to the LORD,
96: 7 *G* to the LORD, you families of nations, *g*
96: 8 *g* to the LORD the glory due his name!
97:12 you just, and *g* thanks to his holy name.
100: 4 *G* thanks to him;
104:11 And *g* drink to every beast of the field,
104:27 all look to you to *g* them food in due time.
104:28 When you *g* it to them,
105: 1 *G* thanks to the LORD,
105:11 "To you will I *g* the land of Canaan as
105:39 them and fire to *g* them light by night.
106:47 That we may *g* thanks to your holy name and
107: 1 *G* thanks to the LORD,
107: 8 Let them *g* thanks to the LORD for his
107:15 Let them *g* thanks to the LORD for his
107:21 Let them *g* thanks to the LORD for his
107:31 Let them *g* thanks to the LORD for his
108: 4 I will *g* thanks to you among the peoples,
108:13 *G* us aid against the foe,
111: 1 I will *g* thanks to the LORD with all my
115: 1 your name *g* glory because of your kindness,
118:19 I will enter them and *g* thanks to the LORD.
118:21 I will *g* thanks to you,
118:28 You are my God, and I *g* thanks to you;
118:29 *G* thanks to the LORD,
119: 7 I will *g* you thanks with an upright heart,
119:25 *g* me life according to your word.
119:32 your commands when you *g* me a docile heart.
119:34 *G* me discernment,
119:37 by your way *g* me life.
119:40 in your justice *g* me life.
119:62 At midnight I rise to *g* you thanks because
119:73 *g* me discernment that I may learn your
119:88 In your kindness *g* me life,
119:93 precepts, for through them you *g* me life.
119:107 O LORD, *g* me life according to your word.
119:125 *g* me discernment that I may know your
119:144 *g* me discernment that I may live.

GIVE (cont.)

119:149 according to your ordinance *g* me life.
119:154 for the sake of your promise *g* me life.
119:156 according to your ordinances *g* me life.
119:159 in your kindness *g* me life.
119:169 keeping with your word, *g* me discernment.
122: 4 to *g* thanks to the name of the LORD.
132: 4 will *g* my eyes no sleep my eyelids no rest,
136: 1 *G* thanks to the LORD,
136: 2 *G* thanks to the God of gods,
136: 3 *G* thanks to the Lord of lords,
136:26 *G* thanks to the God of heaven,
138: 1 I will *g* thanks to you, O LORD,
138: 2 your holy temple and *g* thanks to your name,
138: 4 kings of the earth shall *g* thanks to you,
139:14 I *g* you thanks that I am fearfully,
140:14 the just shall *g* thanks to your name:
142: 8 prison, that I may *g* thanks to your name.
144:10 your praise, You who *g* victory to kings,
145:10 Let all your works *g* you thanks,
145:15 and you *g* them their food in due season;
Prv 3:28 I will give," when you can *g* at once.
4: 2 Yes, excellent advice I *g* you;
5: 9 her house, Lest you *g* your honor to others,
6: 4 *G* no sleep to your eyes,
8: 6 *G* heed! for noble things I speak
19: 6 friends of the man who has something to *g*.
22:21 *g* a dependable report to one who sends you?
22:26 one of those who *g* their hand in pledge,
23:26 My son, *g* me your heart,
25:21 *g* him food to eat, if he be thirsty, *g* him
27:23 flocks, *g* careful attention to your herds;
29:17 you comfort, and *g* delight to your soul.
30: 8 from me, *g* me neither poverty nor riches;
30:15 two daughters of the leech are, "Give, *G*."
31: 3 *G* not your vigor to women,
31: 6 *G* strong drink to one who is perishing,
31:31 *G* her a reward of her labors,
Eccl 7:21 Do not *g* heed to every word that is spoken
Sg 1: 7 flock, where you *g* them rest at midday,
2:13 and the vines, in bloom, *g* forth fragrance.
7:13 There will I *g* you my love.
7:14 The mandrakes *g* forth fragrance,
8: 2 There you would teach me to *g* you spiced
Wis 4: 6 For children born of lawless unions *g*
9: 4 *G* me Wisdom,
16:28 one must *g* you thanks before the sunrise,
17: 5 force, even of fire, was able to *g* light,
Sir 4: 3 delay not to *g* to the needy.
4: 5 your eyes, *g* no man reason to curse you;
4: 8 *G* a hearing to the poor man,
4:31 receive and clenched when it is time to *g*.
6:33 if you *g* heed,
7:25 but *g* her to a worthy man.
7:28 what can you *g* them for all they gave you?
7:31 *g* him his portion as you have been
9: 2 *G* no woman power over you to trample upon
9: 6 *G* not yourself to harlots,
12: 4 *G* to the good man,
12: 4 downtrodden, *g* nothing to the proud man.
12: 5 No arms for combat should you *g* him,
14:13 and *g* him a share in what you possess.
14:16 *G*, take, and treat yourself well,
15: 3 and *g* him the water of learning to drink.
15:20 sin, to none does he *g* strength for lies.
17:20 Return to the LORD and *g* up sin,
17:23 *g* praise than those who have never lived;
23: 7 *G* heed, my children, to the instruction
24:15 balm, or precious myrrh, I *g* forth perfume;
29:26 the table, *g* me to eat the food you have!
30:11 *G* him not his own way in his youth,
30:21 Do not *g* in to sadness,
31:17 gorge not yourself, lest you *g* offense.
32:13 Above all, *g* praise to your Creator,
33: 4 upon your training, and then *g* your answer.
33:19 O rulers of the assembly, *g* ear!
33:21 *G* not to another your wealth,
35: 9 *G* to the Most High as he has given to you,
35:10 and he will *g* back to you sevenfold.
36: 5 *G* new signs and work new wonders;
36:14 *G* evidence of your deeds of old;
37:11 pay no attention to any advice they *g*.
38:12 Then *g* the doctor his place lest he leave;
38:13 There are times that *g* him an advantage,
39: 6 wisdom and in prayer *g* thanks to the LORD,
41:19 Of refusing to *g* when asked,
44:21 *g* them an inheritance from sea to sea,
48:15 not repent, nor did they *g* up their sins,
51: 1 I *g* you thanks,
51:17 I will *g* my teacher grateful praise.
51:29 of God, and be not ashamed to *g* him praise.
51:30 in his own time God will *g* you your reward.
Is 5: 5 Take away its hedge, *g* it to grazing,
5:26 He will *g* a signal to a far-off nation,
7:14 the Lord himself will *g* you this sign:
8: 9 *G* ear, all you distant lands!
12: 1 I *g* you thanks,
12: 4 *G* thanks to the LORD,
19:11 of Pharaoh's advisers *g* stupid counsel.
22:21 sash, and *g* over to him your authority.
22:25 the peg fixed in a sure spot shall *g* way,
24:15 in the coastlands, *g* glory to the LORD!
26:17 *g* birth writhes and cries out in her pains,
28:12 is the resting place, *g* rest to the weary;
28:23 *G* ear and hear my voice,
30:20 The Lord will *g* you the bread you need and
30:23 He will *g* rain for the seed that you sow
32: 9 overconfident women, *g* heed to my words.
36: 8 'I will *g* you two thousand horses,
38:12 Day and night you *g* me over to torment;
38:13 [day and night you *g* me over to torment].
38:19 The living, the living *g* you thanks,
40: 1 Comfort, *g* comfort to my people,
41:28 is not one, no one of them to *g* counsel,
42: 8 my glory I *g* to no other,
42:12 Let them *g* glory to the LORD,
43: 3 I *g* Egypt as your ransom,
43: 4 I *g* men in return for you and peoples in
43: 6 *G* them up!
44: 9 of no avail, as they themselves *g* witness.
45: 3 I will *g* you treasures out of the darkness,
46:13 within Zion, and *g* to Israel my glory.
48:11 My glory I will not *g* to another.
51: 4 my folk, *g* ear to me.
53:12 I will *g* him his portion among the great,
56: 5 me and hold fast to my covenant, I will *g*,
56: 5 eternal, imperishable name will I *g* them.
57:11 did not remember me or *g* me any thought?
57:18 I will *g* full comfort to them and to those
58:11 and *g* you plenty even on the parched land.
61: 3 To *g* them oil of gladness in place of
61: 8 I will *g* them their recompense faithfully,
62: 7 LORD, take no rest And *g* no rest to him,
62: 8 I *g* your grain as food to your enemies;
Jer 3:19 you as sons, And *g* you a pleasant land,
6:10 ears are uncircumcised, they cannot *g* heed;
8:10 I will *g* their wives to strangers,
9:14 *g* them wormwood to eat and poison to drink.
9:18 We must leave the land, *g* up our homes!
11: 5 *g* them a land flowing with milk and honey:
11: 8 But they did not listen or *g* ear.
11:12 But these gods will *g* them no help
13:15 *G* ear, listen humbly,
13:16 *G* glory to the LORD,
14:13 I will *g* you lasting peace in this place."
15: 9 I will *g* to the sword before their enemies,
16: 3 place, the mothers who will *g* them birth,
16: 7 they will not *g* them the cup of
16:21 I will *g* them knowledge;
17: 3 and all your treasures I will *g* as spoil.
17:23 though they did not listen or *g* ear,
18: 2 there I will *g* you my message.
19: 7 Their corpses I will *g* as food to the
20: 5 *g* as plunder into the hand of their foes,
23: 6 This is the name they *g* him:
23:15 Behold, I will *g* them wormwood to eat,
23:35 one another, "What answer did the LORD *g*?"
23:37 the prophet, "What answer did the LORD *g*?"
24: 7 I will *g* them a heart with which to
27: 5 and I can *g* them to whomever I think fit.
27: 8 says the LORD until I *g* them into his hand.
28:14 even the beasts of the field I *g* him.
29: 6 your sons and *g* your daughters husbands.
29:11 plans to *g* you a future full of hope.
31:36 these natural laws *g* way in spite of me,
32:39 One heart and one way I will *g* them,
33: 9 all the peaceful benefits I will *g* her.
33:11 singing, *G* thanks to the LORD of hosts,
34:22 I will *g* the command,
35: 2 one of the rooms, and *g* them wine to drink.
37: 7 *G* this answer to the king of Judah who
38:26 *g* them this answer:
50:34 with success, and *g* rest to the earth,
Lam 1:11 They *g* their treasures for food,
1:21 *G* heed to my groaning;
3:65 *G* them hardness of heart,
4: 4 food, but there is no one to *g* it to them.
5:21 *g* us anew such days as we had of old.
Bar 1:12 and that the Lord may *g* us strength,
1:20 *g* us the land flowing with milk and honey,
2:17 will *g* glory and vindication to the Lord.
2:31 I will *g* them hearts, and heedful ears:
3:27 nor did he *g* them the way of understanding;
4: 3 *G* not your glory to another,
4:23 but God will *g* you back to me with
6:10 *g* part of it to the harlots on the terrace.
6:34 they cannot *g* anyone riches or coppers;
6:52 king over the land, nor do they *g* men rain.
Ez 2: 8 open your mouth and eat what I shall *g* you.
11:19 I will *g* them a new heart and put a new
16:41 and you shall never again *g* payment.
16:61 than you, and *g* them to you as daughters,
18:12 commits robbery, does not *g* back a pledge,
20:28 them to the land I had sworn to *g* them,
20:42 land which I swore to *g* to your fathers.
21:27 bidding him to *g* the order for slaying,
23: 8 She did not *g* up the harlotry which she
29: 5 and the birds of the air I *g* you as food,
32: 7 clouds, and the moon shall not *g* its light.
33:25 *G* them this answer:
34:15 I myself will *g* them rest,
36:26 I will *g* you a new heart and place a new
39:11 On that day I will *g* Gog for his tomb a
43:19 *G* a young bull as a sin offering to the
44:28 you shall *g* them no property in Israel,
44:30 shall *g* to the priests to bring a blessing
47:14 land which I swore to *g* to your fathers,
Dn 1:12 *G* us vegetables to eat and water to drink.
2: 4 the dream and we will *g* its meaning."
2: 7 the dream and we will *g* its meaning."
2: 9 you can also *g* its correct interpretation."
2:16 that he might *g* him the interpretation.
2:23 O God of my fathers, I *g* thanks and praise,
2:25 who can *g* the interpretation to the king."
2:36 we shall also *g* in the king's presence.
3:89 *G* thanks to the Lord,
3:90 praise him and *g* him thanks,
4: 3 me to *g* the interpretation of the dream.
4:14 He can *g* it to whom he will,
5:17 gifts, or *g* your presents to someone else;
6:11 kneel in prayer and *g* thanks to his God
9:18 *G* ear, O my God, and listen;
9:22 I have now come to *g* you understanding.
11:17 *g* him a daughter in marriage
11:38 he shall *g* glory to the god of strongholds;
13:20 *g* in to our desire,
14:26 *G* me permission,
14:26 "I *g* you permission," the king said.
Hos 1: 4 *G* him the name Jezreel,
1: 6 *G* her the name Lo-ruhama;
1: 9 *G* him the name Lo-ammi,
2: 7 she said, "who *g* me my bread and my water,
2:17 there I will *g* her the vineyards she had,
3: 1 *G* your love to a woman beloved of a
4:16 will the LORD now *g* them broad pastures as
4:18 is over, they *g* themselves to harlotry;
5: 1 of Israel, O household of the king, *g* ear!
9:14 *G* them, O LORD! *g* them what?
9:14 *G* them an unfruitful womb,
11: 8 How could I *g* you up,
11: 9 I will not *g* vent to my blazing anger,
13:10 whom you said, *G* me a king and princes"?
13:11 I *g* you a king in my anger,
Jl 2:22 the fig tree and the vine *g* their yield.
Am 6: 8 I *g* over the city with everything in it;
Mi 1: 2 Hear, O peoples, all of you, *g* heed,
1:14 shall *g* parting gifts to Moresheth-gath;
3:11 her priests *g* decisions for a salary,
5: 2 (Therefore the Lord will *g* them up,
5: 2 time when she who is to *g* birth has borne,
6: 7 Shall I *g* my first-born for my crime,
Hb 2: 1 and what answer he will *g* to my complaint.
2:15 Woe to you who *g* your neighbors a flood of
2:19 Can such a thing *g* oracles?
Zep 3:19 *g* them praise and renown in all the earth,
3:20 For I will *g* you renown and praise,
Hg 2: 9 And in this place I will *g* you peace,
Zec 3: 7 *g* you access among these standing here.
8:12 crops, and the heavens shall *g* their dew;
11:12 "If it seems good to you, *g* me my wages;
Mal 2: 2 not lay it to heart, to *g* glory to my name,
Mt 1:23 shall be with child and *g* birth to a son,
3: 8 *G* some evidence that you mean to reform.
3:15 *G* in for now.
5:16 acts and *g* praise to your heavenly Father.
5:31 wife, he must *g* her a decree of divorce.'
5:42 *G* to the man who begs from you.
6: 2 When you *g* alms,
6: 5 I *g* you my word, they are already repaid.
6:11 *G* us today our daily bread,
6:24 You cannot *g* yourself to God and money.
7: 6 "Do not *g* what is holy to dogs or toss
7:11 know how to *g* your children what is good,
7:11 *g* good things to anyone who asks him!
8: 8 *g* an order and my boy will get better.
8: 9 If I *g* one man the order,
10: 8 The gift you have received, *g* as a gift.
10:18 to *g* witness before them and before the
14:16 *G* them something to eat yourselves."
15:10 *G* ear and try to understand.
17:27 Take it and *g* it to them for you and me."
18:29 *g* me time and I will pay you back in full.'
19:21 sell your possessions, and *g* to the poor.
19:28 "I *g* you my solemn word,
20: 8 'Call the workmen and *g* them their pay,
20:14 I intend to *g* this man who was hired last
20:23 my right hand or my left is not mine to *g*.
20:28 to *g* his own life as a ransom for the many."
22:17 *G* us your opinion, then, in this case.
22:21 *g* to Caesar what is Caesar's, but *g* to God
22:46 No one could *g* him an answer;
25: 8 to the sensible, *G* us some of your oil.
25:28 and *g* it to the man with the ten thousand.
25:37 you or see you thirsty and *g* you drink?
26:15 willing to *g* me if I hand him over to you?"
26:34 Jesus said to him, "I *g* you my word,
26:48 betrayer had arranged to *g* them a signal,
Mk 3:28 "I *g* you my word,
4:24 In the measure you *g* you shall receive,
5:43 and told them to *g* her something to eat.
6:22 anything you want and I will *g* it to you."
6:25 "I want you to *g* me,
6:37 "You *g* them something to eat,"
8: 4 "How can anyone *g* these people sufficient
10: 3 he said, "What command did Moses *g* you?"
10:21 and sell what you have and *g* to the poor;
10:29 "I *g* you my word,
10:40 right or my left, that is not mine to *g*;
10:45 to *g* his life in ransom for the many."

11:24 I *g* you my word,
11:29 If you *g* me an answer,
12:17 *G* to Caesar what is Caesar's, but *g* to God
14:11 were jubilant and promised to *g* him money.
14:18 of the meal Jesus said, "I *g* you my word,
14:30 Jesus answered, "I *g* you my assurance,
15:23 tried to *g* him wine drugged with myrrh,
Lk 1:31 and bear a son and *g* him the name Jesus.
1:32 will *g* him the throne of David his father.
3: 8 *G* some evidence that you mean to reform.
3:11 man with two coats *g* to him who has none.
4: 6 "I will *g* you all this power and the
4: 6 given to me and I *g* it to whomever I wish.
6:29 you on one cheek, turn and *g* him the other;
6:30 *G* to all who beg from you.
6:38 *G*, and it shall be given to you.
7: 7 *g* the order and my servant will be cured.
8:55 he told them to *g* her something to eat.
9:13 you not *g* them something to eat yourselves?"
11: 3 *G* us each day our daily bread.
11: 8 persistence, and *g* him as much as he needs.
11:11 *g* his son a snake if he asks for a fish,
11:13 know how to *g* your children good things,
11:13 *g* the Holy Spirit to those who ask him."
11:41 But if you *g* what you have as alms,
12:13 to *g* me my share of our inheritance."
12:32 pleased your Father to *g* you the kingdom.
12:33 Sell what you have and *g* alms.
14:12 "Whenever you *g* a lunch or dinner,
15:12 *g* me the share of the estate that is
15:16 but no one made a move to *g* him anything.
16: 2 *G* me an account of your service,
16:12 money, who will *g* you what is your own?
16:13 You cannot *g* yourself to God and money."
17:18 and *g* thanks to God except this foreigner?"
18: 3 saying, *G* me my rights against my opponent.'
18: 8 I tell you, he will *g* them swift justice.
18:11 'I *g* you thanks,
18:22 Sell all you have and *g* to the poor.
19: 8 "I *g* half my belongings,
19:24 he has, and *g* it to the man with the ten.'
20:16 farmers and *g* the vineyard to others."
20:25 *g* to Caesar what is Caesar's, but *g* to God
21:13 be brought to *g* witness on account of it.
21:15 for I will *g* you words and a wisdom which
22: 5 were delighted, and agreed to *g* him money.
Jn 1:22 we can *g* some answer to those who sent us.
2:25 one to *g* him testimony about human nature.
4: 7 water, Jesus said to her, *G* me a drink."
4:14 *g* him will never be thirsty; no, the water I *g*
4:15 The woman said to him, *G* me this water,
5:14 *G* up your sins so that something worse may
6: 7 loaves enough to *g* each of them a mouthful!"
6:27 food which the Son of Man will *g* you;
6:34 "Sir, *g* us this bread always,"
6:51 the bread I will *g* is my flesh,
6:52 saying, "How can he *g* us his flesh to eat?"
8:34 "I *g* you my assurance,
8:45 I deal in the truth, you *g* me no credence.
9:24 born blind and said to him, *G* glory to God!
10:15 for these sheep I will *g* my life.
10:25 in my Father's name *g* witness in my favor,
10:28 I *g* them eternal life,
11:22 God will *g* you whatever you ask of him."
13:15 What I just did was to *g* you an example:
13:21 He went on to *g* this testimony:
13:26 whom I *g* the bit of food I dip in the dish."
13:29 the feast, or to *g* something to the poor.)
13:34 I *g* you a new commandment:
14:15 you love me and obey the commands I *g* you,
14:16 Father and he will *g* you another Paraclete
14:27 not *g* it to you as the world gives peace.
15:16 ask the Father in my name he will *g* you.
15:17 The command I *g* you is this,
16:14 In doing this he will *g* glory to me,
16:23 I *g* you my assurance,
16:23 ask the Father, he will *g* you in my name.
17: 1 *G* glory to your Son that your Son may give
17: 5 you now, Father, *g* me glory at your side,
19: 9 Jesus would not *g* him any answer.
Acts 3: 6 silver nor gold, but what I have I *g* you!
4:17 we must *g* them a stern warning
7: 5 did not *g* him any of it as his heritage,
7: 5 but he promised to *g* it to him and his
8:19 with the request, *G* me that power too,
13:19 *g* them that country as their heritage
13:34 'I will *g* you the benefits assured to
18:14 I would *g* you Jews a patient and
20:32 and *g* you a share among all who are
21:21 to *g* up the circumcision of their children,
21:26 Then he entered the temple precincts to *g*
23:24 *g* him safe conduct to Felix the governor."
27:34 food, which will *g* you strength to survive.
Rom 1: 8 I *g* thanks to God through Jesus Christ for
1:21 did not glorify him as God or *g* him thanks;
12:20 if he is thirsty, *g* him something to drink;
14:11 me and every tongue shall *g* praise to God."
14:12 have to *g* an account of himself before God.
15:14 you are able to *g* advice to one another.
16: 2 If she needs help in anything, *g* it to her,
16: 3 *G* my greetings to Prisca and Aquila;
1Cor 3: 2 and did not *g* you solid food because you
7:10 I *g* this command (though it is not mine;
7:17 This is the rule I *g* in all the churches.
7:21 *G* it no thought.
7:25 I *g* my opinion as one who is trustworthy,
10:13 Along with the test he will *g* you a way
10:32 *G* no offense to Jew or Greek or to the
11:34 I shall *g* instructions when I come.
12:24 as to *g* greater honor to the lowly members,
13: 3 If I *g* everything I have to feed the poor
14:26 a psalm, another some instruction to *g*,
16: 3 When I come I shall *g* letters of
2Cor 4: 1 mercy, we do not *g* in to discouragement.
4:15 to God because they who *g* thanks are many.
8:10 I am about to *g* you some advice on this
8:12 to *g* should accord with one's means,
9: 7 Everyone must *g* according to what he has
10:11 Well, let such people *g* this some thought,
Gal 3:15 Brothers, let me *g* you an everyday example.
Eph 4:27 do not *g* the devil a chance to work on you.
5: 5 Instead, *g* thanks.
5:14 from the dead, and Christ will *g* you light."
5:20 *G* thanks to God the Father always and for
6: 7 *G* your service willingly,
Phil 1: 3 I *g* thanks to my God every time I think of
2: 1 in the name of the solace that love can *g*,
2:16 you *g* me cause to boast that I did not run
3:13 I *g* no thought to what lies behind but
3:21 He will *g* a new form to this lowly body of
4:21 *G* my greetings in Christ Jesus to every
Col 1: 2 May God our Father *g* you grace and peace.
1: 3 We always *g* thanks to God,
3:17 *G* thanks to God the Father through him.
4: 7 the Lord, will *g* you all the news about me.
4:15 *G* our best wishes to the brothers at
1Thes 3: 9 What thanks can we *g* to God for all the
4:12 so that you will *g* good example to
2Thes 2:11 leads them to *g* credence to falsehood,
3:16 May he who is the Lord of peace *g* you
1Tm 1:18 I have a solemn charge to *g* you,
1:19 and I *g* it to you so that under the
3: 8 not overindulge in drink or *g* in to greed.
5:14 and in general *g* our enemies no occasion
5:16 which ought to be free to *g* help to the
Heb 6:17 wishing to *g* the heirs of his promise even
1Pt 2:12 *g* glory to God on the day of visitation.
4: 5 They shall *g* an accounting to him who
5: 2 *g* it a shepherd's care.
3Jn 1:12 We *g* our testimonial as well,
Rv 2:10 death and I will *g* you the crown of life.
2:17 *g* the hidden manna; I will also *g* him
2:23 *g* each of you what your conduct deserves.
2:26 end, I will *g* authority over the nations
2:28 and I will *g* him the morning star.
3:21 I will *g* the victor the right to sit with
4: 9 Whenever these creatures *g* glory and honor
7:15 who sits on the throne will *g* them shelter.
9:20 They did not *g* up the worship of demons,
10: 9 and said to him, *G* me the little scroll."
12: 2 aloud in pain as she labored to *g* birth.
12: 4 stood before the woman about to *g* birth,
12:17 God's commandments and *g* witness to Jesus.
13:15 permitted to *g* life to the beast's image,
14: 7 "Honor God and *g* him glory,
16: 9 but they did not repent or *g* him due honor.
19: 7 us rejoice and be glad, and *g* him glory!
19:10 and your brothers who *g* witness to Jesus.
21: 6 To anyone who thirsts I will *g* to drink
22: 5 sun, for the Lord God shall *g* them light,
22:16 to *g* you this testimony about the churches.
22:18 I myself *g* witness to all who hear the

GIVEN (461)

Gn 15: 3 "See, you have *g* me no offspring,
20:16 I have *g* your brother a thousand shekels
21: 6 then said, "God has *g* me cause to laugh,
24:35 he has *g* him flocks and herds,
24:36 age, and he has *g* him everything he owns.
26:18 the same names that his father had *g* them.)
26:22 said, "The LORD has now *g* us ample room,
27:41 of the blessing his father had *g* him.
29:33 and therefore he has *g* me this one also";
30: 6 he has heeded my plea and *g* me a son."
30:18 "God has *g* me my reward for having let my
38:14 up, she had not been *g* to him in marriage.
40:16 Joseph had *g* this favorable interpretation,
42:25 and provisions *g* them for their journey.
46:18 whom Laban had *g* to his daughter Leah;
46:25 whom Laban had *g* to his daughter Rachel;
48: 9 his father, "whom God has *g* me here."
Ex 16:15 the bread which the LORD has *g* you to eat.
16:29 The LORD has *g* you the sabbath.
21: 2 he shall be *g* his freedom without cost.
21:11 she shall be *g* her freedom absolutely,
29:35 and his sons just as I have *g* them to you.
35:34 He has also *g* both him and Oholiab,
38:24 having previously been *g* as an offering,
38:29 The bronze, *g* as an offering,
Lv 5:16 This is to be *g* to the priest,
6:10 I have *g* it to them as their portion from
7:34 is raised up, and I have *g* them to Aaron,
10:11 that the LORD has *g* them through Moses."
10:17 It has been *g* to you that you might bear
19:20 has not yet been redeemed or *g* her freedom,
24:23 out the command that the LORD had *g* Moses.
27:23 shall be *g* as sacred to the LORD;
Nm 3:16 with the command the LORD had *g* him.
5: 4 the command the LORD had *g* Moses;
7:84 *g* by the princes of Israel on the occasion
8:19 and I have *g* these dedicated Israelites to
8:20 which the LORD had *g* Moses concerning them.
8:22 The command which the LORD had *g* Moses
14:37 these men who had *g* out the bad report
17: 5 which the LORD had *g* him through Moses.
18: 8 "I myself have *g* you charge of the
19: 3 This is to be *g* to Eleazar the priest,
22: 7 When they had *g* him Balak's message,
23:20 is a blessing I have been *g* to pronounce;
26:62 heritage was *g* them among the Israelites.
32: 5 let this land be *g* to your servants
32: 7 crossing to the land the LORD has *g* them?
32: 9 not enter the land the LORD had *g* them.
33:53 I have *g* you the land as your property.
34:13 to be *g* to the nine and one half tribes.
36:10 the command which the LORD had *g* to Moses.
Dt 1: 3 that the LORD had *g* him in their regard.
1: 8 I have *g* that land over to you.
1:21 your God, has *g* this land over to you.
2: 5 *g* Esau possession of the highlands of Seir.
2: 9 since I have *g* Ar to the descendants of
2:12 their heritage which the LORD has *g* them.]
2:19 since I have *g* it to the descendants of
3:18 your God, has *g* you this land as your own.
3:19 remain behind in the towns I have *g* you,
3:20 all return to the possessions I have *g* you.'
8:10 God, for the good country he has *g* you.
9:11 *g* me the two stone tablets of the covenant,
10: 4 After the LORD had *g* them to me,
12: 1 God of your fathers, has *g* you to occupy,
12:10 when he has *g* you rest from all your
12:21 your herd or flock that the LORD has *g* you,
15:18 since the service he has *g* you for six
20:14 which the LORD, your God, has *g* you.
24: 8 with the instructions I have *g* them.
25: 3 Forty stripes may be *g* him,
26:10 of the soil which you, O LORD, have *g* me.'
26:11 things which the LORD, your God, has *g* you.
26:12 tithes, and you have *g* them to the Levite,
26:13 portion and I have *g* it to the Levite,
26:15 people Israel and the soil you have *g* us
28:31 Your flocks will be *g* to your enemies,
28:32 Your sons and daughters will be *g* to a
28:52 land which the LORD your God, has *g* you,
28:53 whom the LORD, your God, has *g* you.
29: 3 the LORD yet *g* you a mind to understand,
32:46 warning which I have now *g* you
Jos 1:15 of the LORD, has *g* you east of the Jordan."
2: 9 "I know that the LORD has *g* you the land,
6:16 has *g* you the city and everything in it.
9:24 that you be *g* the entire land
13: 8 of the LORD, had *g* them east of the Jordan:
14: 2 instructions the LORD had *g* through Moses
14: 3 had already *g* a heritage beyond the Jordan;
14: 3 were *g* no heritage among the tribes,
17: 4 heritage was *g* to each of them
17:14 "Why have you *g* us only one lot and one
18: 3 LORD, the God of your fathers, has *g* you?
21: 2 Moses, that cities be *g* us to dwell in,
21:12 belonging to the city had been *g* to Caleb,
21:13 were *g* the city of asylum for homicides
22: 7 to the other half Joshua had *g* a portion
23: 1 after the LORD had *g* the Israelites rest
23:13 land which the LORD, your God, has *g* you.
23:15 land which the LORD, your God, has *g* you.
23:16 from the good land which he has *g* you."
24:33 which had been *g* to his son Phinehas
Jgs 1:20 Moses had commanded, Hebron was *g* to Caleb,
15: 6 his wife was taken and *g* to his best man."
18:10 God has indeed *g* it into your power:
21:22 Had you yourselves *g* them these wives,
Ru 1: 6 had visited his people and *g* them food.
1Sm 4:20 You have *g* birth to a son."
9:15 the LORD had *g* Samuel the revelation:
12:13 king you want, a king the LORD has *g* you.
14:39 the LORD lives who has *g* victory to Israel,
15:28 day, and has *g* it to a neighbor of yours,
18:19 Merob to be *g* to David, she was given
25:27 be *g* to the young men who follow my lord.
28:17 grasp and has *g* it to your neighbor David.
30:11 food, which he ate, and *g* water to drink;
30:23 my brothers, after what the LORD has *g* us.
2Sm 7: 1 *g* him rest from his enemies on every side,
10: 6 In view of the offense they had *g* to David,
14:15 because the people have *g* me cause to fear.
16: 8 has *g* over the kingdom to your son Absalom.
16:23 Now the counsel *g* by Ahithophel at that
17: 7 time Ahithophel has not *g* good counsel."
17:21 *g* the following counsel in regard to you."
19:43 have portions from his table been *g* to us?"
21: 2 the Israelites had *g* them their oath,
21: 6 men from among his descendants be *g* to us,
22:36 "You have *g* me your saving shield,
1Kgs 2:21 be *g* to your brother Adonijah for his wife."
3:28 Israel heard the judgment the king had *g*.
5:18 LORD, my God, has *g* me peace on all sides.
5:21 who has *g* David a wise son to rule this
8:36 have *g* to your people as their heritage.

GIVEN (cont.)

8:56 LORD who has *g* rest to his people Israel,
8:66 LORD had *g* to his servant David
9:12 Tyre to see the cities Solomon had *g* him,
9:13 "What are these cities you have *g* me,
9:16 city, had *g* it as dowry to his daughter,
10:13 as were *g* her from Solomon's royal bounty.
12: 8 he ignored the advice the elders had *g* him,
12:13 Ignoring the advice the elders had *g* him,
13: 5 man of God had *g* as the word of the LORD.
21:20 "Because you have *g* yourself up to doing
22:31 In the meantime the king of Aram had *g* his
2Kgs 4:17 following year she had *g* birth to a son,
11:15 He had *g* orders that she should not be
12:15 Instead, they were *g* to the workmen,
17:15 and the warnings which he had *g* them.
18: 6 commandments which the LORD had *g* Moses.
22:10 that the priest Hilkiah had *g* him a book,
23:26 all the provocations that Manasseh had *g*,
1Chr 5: 1 his birthright was *g* to the sons of Joseph,
6:41 belonging to the city had been *g* to Caleb,
21:19 Gad's command, *g* in the name of the LORD.
22:18 Has he not *g* you rest on every side?
23:25 God of Israel, has *g* rest to his people,
24:19 keeping with the precepts *g* them by Aaron,
28: 5 for the LORD has *g* me many sons
29:17 With a sincere heart I have willingly *g*
2Chr 1:12 you king, wisdom and knowledge are *g* you;
2:11 for having *g* King David a wise son of
2:13 artistic work that may be *g* him
8: 2 built up the cities which Huram had *g* him,
10: 8 he ignored the advice the elders had *g* him
10:13 Ignoring the advice the elders had *g* him,
13: 5 *g* the kingdom of Israel to David forever,
14: 5 years, because the LORD had *g* him peace.
14: 6 him, and he has *g* us rest on every side."
18:30 had *g* his chariot commanders the order,
20:11 us out of the possession you have *g* us.
20:27 the LORD had *g* them over their enemies.
30:16 sprinkled the blood *g* them by the Levites;
33: 8 the statutes and the ordinances *g* by Moses."
34:14 of the law of the LORD *g* through Moses.
34:18 king, "Hilkiah the priest has *g* me a book."
35: 6 to the word of the LORD *g* through Moses."
36:23 the LORD, the God of heaven, has *g* to me,
Ezr 1: 2 the LORD, the God of heaven, has *g* to me,
7: 6 the law of Moses which was *g* by the LORD,
9: 8 our eyes and *g* us relief in our servitude.
9: 9 Thus he has *g* us a new life to raise again
Neh 2: 7 let letters be *g* to me for the
9:35 good things that you had *g* them
10:30 the law of God which was *g* through Moses,
13:10 due the Levites were no longer being *g*,
Tb 2:14 *g* to me as a bonus over and above my wages."
5:20 *g* us to live on is certainly enough for us."
7:11 I have *g* her in marriage to seven men,
14: 7 of Abraham, which will be *g* over to them.
14:10 Because Ahiqar had *g* alms to me,
Jdt 3: 5 reached Holofernes and *g* him this message,
4: 8 carried out the orders *g* them by Joakim,
8:16 nor human, that he may be *g* an ultimatum.
16:19 of Holofernes that the people had *g* her,
Est 2: 3 of the women, let cosmetics be *g* them.
8: 7 that I have *g* Esther the house of Haman,
1Mc 2: 7 while it is *g* into the hands of enemies,
3:30 had previously *g* with a more liberal hand
3:42 orders which the king had *g* to destroy
4:40 And when the signal was *g* with trumpets,
4:55 and praised Heaven, who had *g* them success.
8:28 attacking them there shall not be *g* grain,
10: 8 king had *g* him authority to gather an army.
10:36 the king's army and allowances be *g* them,
10:37 let some be *g* positions of trust in the affairs
10:89 such as is usually *g* to King's Kinsmen;
11:37 these instructions made and *g* to Jonathan,
12:23 *g* orders that you should be told of this."
14:44 or to contradict the orders *g* by him,
2Mc 3: 9 him about the information that had been *g*,
3:15 who had *g* the law about deposits
3:26 until they had *g* him innumerable blows.
4: 9 if he were *g* authority to establish a
4:30 cities had been *g* as a gift to Antiochus,
6:23 would be loyal to the holy laws *g* by God.
7:30 the law *g* to our forefathers through Moses.
8:19 times when help had been *g* their ancestors;
15: 8 victory would be *g* them by the Almighty.
Jb 3:20 Why is light *g* to the toilers,
9:24 earth is *g* into the hands of the wicked;
15:19 fathers, To whom alone the land was *g*,
16:11 God has *g* me over to the impious;
22: 7 the thirsty you have *g* no water to drink,
32:11 and have *g* ear to your arguments.
35:10 my Maker, who has *g* visions in the night,
39: 5 Who has *g* the wild ass his freedom,
39:17 and has *g* her no share in understanding.
Ps(s) 8: 7 *g* him rule over the works of your hands,
18:36 You have *g* me your saving shield;
20: 7 the LORD has *g* victory to his anointed,
60: 5 you have *g* us stupefying wine.
66: 9 He has *g* life to our souls,
72:15 May he live to be *g* the gold of Arabia,
78:30 They had not *g* over their craving,
79: 2 They have *g* the corpses of your servants
80: 6 and *g* them tears to drink in ample measure.
91:11 to his angels he has *g* command about you,
111: 5 He has *g* food to those who fear him;
115:16 the earth he has *g* to the children of men.
118:27 The LORD is God, and he has *g* us light.
119:49 to your servant since you have *g* me hope.
Prv 6: 1 neighbor, *g* your hand in pledge to another,
Eccl 2:26 to be *g* to whatever man God sees fit.
6:10 Whatever is, was long ago *g* its name,
12:11 spikes are the topics *g* by one collector.
Wis 3:14 For he shall be *g* fidelity's choice
6: 3 Because authority was *g* you by the Lord
7: 7 Therefore I prayed, and prudence was *g* me;
9:17 except you had *g* Wisdom and sent your holy
11: 4 and water was *g* them from the sheer rock,
18: 4 light of the Law was to be *g* to the world.
Sir 11: 6 the honored are *g* into enemy hands.
12:16 has tears in his eyes, if *g* the chance,
15:17 death, whichever he chooses shall be *g* him.
23:16 A man *g* to sins of the flesh,
24:11 Thus in the chosen city he has *g* me rest,
35: 9 Give to the Most High as he has *g* to you,
42: 7 or of recording all that is *g* or received;
42:17 of the LORD, Though God has *g* these,
Is 4: 1 Only let your name be *g* us,
8:18 me and the children whom the LORD has *g* me:
9: 5 For a child is born to us, a son is *g* us;
17: 2 *g* over to flocks to lie in undisturbed.
23: 4 "I have not been in labor, nor *g* birth,
34: 2 doomed them and *g* them over to slaughter.
35: 2 The glory of Lebanon will be *g* to them,
38:16 You have *g* me health and life;
50: 4 Lord GOD has *g* me a well-trained tongue,
Jer 8:14 destruction, he has *g* us poison to drink,
17: 4 hold on your heritage which I have *g* you.
21:10 It shall be *g* into the power of the king
22: 9 And the answer will be *g*:
22:19 The burial of an ass shall he be *g*,
25:31 The godless shall be *g* to the sword,
27: 6 Now I have *g* all these lands into the hand
27: 6 of the field I have *g* him for his use.
31: 2 As Israel comes forward to be *g* his rest,
33:25 and have *g* no laws to heaven and earth,
34:16 slaves to whom you had *g* their freedom;
37:21 and *g* a loaf of bread each day from the
39:10 *g* at the same time vineyards and farms.
40: 7 that the king of Babylon had *g* Gedaliah,
51:59 *g* by the prophet Jeremiah to Seraiah,
52:34 The allowance *g* him by the king of Babylon
Bar 3:37 of understanding, and has *g* her to Jacob,
Ez 10:13 I heard the wheels *g* the name "wheelwork."
11:15 of Israel has been *g* as our possession."
16:17 *g* you and made for yourself male images,
16:19 the food that I had *g* you,
20:15 not to bring them to the land I had *g* them,
21:16 I have *g* it over to the burnisher that he
29:20 his toil I have *g* him the land of Egypt,
33:24 possession the land that has been *g* to us."
33:27 field I have *g* to the wild beasts for food;
34: 8 my sheep have been *g* over to pillage,
35:12 desolate, they have been *g* us to devour."
36: 4 which have been *g* over to the pillage and
46:17 the inheritance *g* to his sons is permanent.
Dn 1: 9 Though God had *g* Daniel the favor and
2:23 because you have *g* me wisdom and power.
2:37 God of heaven has *g* dominion and strength,
4:13 let him be *g* the sense of a beast,
4:22 you shall be *g* grass to eat like an ox and
4:29 you shall be *g* grass to eat like an ox,
5:28 divided and *g* to the Medes and Persians."
7: 4 on two feet like a man, and *g* a human mind.
7: 5 It was *g* the order,
7: 6 To this beast dominion was *g*.
7:27 be *g* to the holy people of the Most High,
9:23 answer was *g* which I have come to announce,
10: 1 of Persia, a revelation was *g* to Daniel,
11: 6 not be recognized, and she shall be *g* up,
11:11 be *g* into his hand and be carried off.
11:21 to whom the royal insignia shall not be *g*.
13:50 God has *g* you the prestige of old age."
14:32 and two sheep had been *g* to them daily.
14:32 But now they were *g* nothing,
Hos 2:14 "These are the hire my lovers have *g* me";
Jl 2:23 He has *g* you the teacher of justice:
Am 6:11 the LORD has *g* the command to shatter the
9: 9 I have *g* the command to sift the house of
9:15 be plucked From the land I have *g* them,
Zep 1:13 Their wealth shall be *g* to pillage and
Mt 6:33 and all these things will be *g* you besides.
10:19 comes, you will be *g* what you are to say.
11:27 has been *g* over to me by my Father.
12:39 will be *g* it but that of the prophet Jonah.
13:11 "To you has been *g* a knowledge of the
13:11 God, but it has not been *g* to the others.
13:12 has, more will be *g* until he grows rich;
14:11 brought in on a platter and *g* to the girl,
16: 4 no sign will be *g* it except that of Jonah."
19:11 only those to whom it is *g* to do so.
19:29 Moreover, everyone who has *g* up home,
21:23 Who has *g* you this power?"
21:43 taken away from you and *g* to a nation
22:30 they neither marry nor are *g* in marriage
26: 9 a good price and the money *g* to the poor."
28:18 been *g* to me both in heaven and on earth;
Mk 4:25 To those who have, more will be *g*;
8:12 I assure you, no such sign will be *g* it!"
10:29 my word, there is no one who has *g* up home,
11:28 Who has *g* you the power to do them?"
12:25 they neither marry nor are *g* in marriage
14: 5 silver pieces and the money *g* to the poor."
Lk 1:53 The hungry he has *g* every good thing,
2:18 at the report *g* them by the shepherds.
2:21 was *g* the child, the name the angel had *g*
4: 6 *g* to me and I give it to whomever I wish.
6:38 Give, and it shall be *g* to you.
8:18 to the man who has, more will be *g*;
10:19 I have *g* you power to tread on snakes and
10:22 has been *g* over to me by my Father.
11:29 sign will be *g* it except the sign of Jonah.
12:48 When much has been *g* a man,
18:43 he was *g* his sight and began to follow him,
19:15 the servants to whom he had *g* the money,
19:26 whoever has will be *g* more,
20:34 of this age marry and are *g* in marriage,
21: 4 her want has *g* what she could not afford
22:19 "This is my body to be *g* for you.
Jn 1:17 For while the law was *g* through Moses,
3:27 anything unless it is *g* him from on high.
3:35 the Son and has *g* everything over to him.
4: 5 land which Jacob had *g* to his son Joseph.
4:10 and he would have *g* you living water."
5:27 The Father has *g* over to him power to pass
5:36 works the Father has *g* me to accomplish.
5:37 me has himself *g* testimony on my behalf.
6:23 the bread after the Lord had *g* thanks.
6:39 I should lose nothing of what he has *g* me;
7:19 Moses has *g* you the law, has he not?
8:17 that evidence *g* by two persons is valid.
10:29 is greater than all, in what he has *g* me,
11:57 chief priests and the Pharisees had *g* orders
12: 5 and the money have been *g* to the poor."
17: 2 you have *g* him authority over all mankind,
17: 4 I have *g* you glory on earth by finishing
17: 9 for the world but for these you have *g* me,
17:11 which you have *g* me [that they may be one,
17:22 I have *g* them the glory you gave me that
18:11 I not to drink the cup the Father has *g* me?"
19:11 whatever unless it were *g* you from above.
19:35 testimony has been *g* by an eyewitness,
Acts 1:17 been *g* a share in this ministry of ours.
3:16 Such faith has *g* him perfect health,
4:12 world *g* to men by which we are to be saved."
5:32 whom God has *g* to those that obey him."
10:33 whatever directives the Lord has *g* you."
16:23 was *g* instructions to guard them well.
20:28 flock the Holy Spirit has *g* you to guard.
23:11 have *g* testimony to me here in Jerusalem,
25:16 confronted with his accusers and *g* a chance
Rom 5: 5 the Holy Spirit who has been *g* to us.
11:35 has *g* him anything so as to deserve return?"
12: 3 Thus, in virtue of the favor *g* to me,
14:17 and the joy that is *g* by the Holy Spirit.
15:15 I take this liberty because God has *g* me
16:27 *g* through Jesus Christ unto endless ages.
1Cor 1:30 it is who has *g* you life in Christ Jesus.
2:12 us to recognize the gifts he has *g* us.
7: 7 *G* my preference,
11:15 Her hair has been *g* her for a covering.
11:24 took bread, and after he had *g* thanks,
12: 7 of the Spirit is *g* for the common good.
12: 9 Spirit another is *g* the gift of healing,
12:10 Prophecy is *g* to one;
12:13 us have been *g* to drink of the one Spirit.
15:57 But thanks be to God who has *g* us the
2Cor 2: 5 has *g* offense he has hurt not only me,
3:11 was destined to pass away was *g* in glory,
5: 5 and has *g* us the Spirit as a pledge of it.
5:18 has *g* us the ministry of reconciliation.
7:12 had *g* the offense or for the one offended,
9:14 of the surpassing grace God has *g* you.
10: 8 Lord has *g* us for your upbuilding
11: 2 I have *g* you in marriage to one husband,
12: 7 conceited I was *g* a thorn in the flesh,
13:10 severity the authority the Lord has *g* me
Gal 3:19 It was *g* in view of transgressions and
3:19 came to whom the promise had been *g*.
3:21 was *g* was such that it could impart life,
4:15 plucked out your eyes and *g* them to me.
Eph 1: 9 God has *g* us the wisdom to understand
1:21 can be *g* in this age or in the age to come.
3: 8 was *g* the grace to preach to the Gentiles
4: 4 is but one hope *g* all of you by your call.
1Tm 5:10 Has she *g* help to those in distress?
2Tm 1: 7 Spirit God has *g* us is no cowardly spirit,
1:16 because he has often *g* me new heart and
Heb 2:13 "Here am I, and the children God has *g* me!"
Jas 1: 5 ungrudgingly to all, and it will be *g* him.
1Pt 3:18 but was *g* life in the realm of the spirit.
2Pt 1: 1 to those who have been *g* a faith like ours
1:14 indications our Lord Jesus Christ has *g* me,
1Jn 4:13 he in us is that he has *g* us of his Spirit.
5: 9 God has *g* on his own Son's behalf.
5:10 testimony he has *g* on his own Son's behalf.
5:16 God, and thus life will be *g* to the sinner.
5:20 has *g* us discernment to recognize the One
2Jn 1: 4 It has *g* me great joy to find some of your

3Jn 1: 3 For it has *g* me great joy to have the
Rv 2:21 I have *g* her a chance to repent but she
6: 2 its rider had a bow, and he was *g* a crown.
6: 4 Its rider was *g* power to rob the earth of
6: 4 For this he was *g* a huge sword.
6: 8 *g* authority over one quarter of the earth,
6:11 of the martyrs was *g* a long white robe,
7: 2 *g* power to ravage the land and the sea,
8: 2 in God's presence were *g* seven trumpets.
8: 3 was *g* large amounts of incense to deposit
9: 1 was *g* the key to the shaft of the abyss;
12:13 the woman who had *g* birth to the boy.
12:14 But the woman was *g* the wings of a
13: 5 The beast was *g* a mouth for uttering proud
16: 6 and prophets, you have *g* blood to drink;
19: 8 *g* a dress to wear made of finest linen,
22:12 be *g* to each man as his conduct deserves.

GIVER (2)

Sir 3:17 you will be loved more than a *g* of gifts.
2Cor 9: 7 not grudgingly, for God loves a cheerful *g*.

GIVES (145)

Ex 4:11 "Who *g* one man speech and makes another
4:11 who *g* sight to one and makes another blind?
16: 8 the LORD *g* you flesh to eat in the evening,"
16:29 the sixth day he *g* you food for two days.
18:23 when God *g* you orders you will be able to
21: 4 But if his master *g* him a wife and she
22: 6 "When a man *g* money or an article to
22: 9 "When a man *g* an ass,
Lv 12: 2 a woman has conceived and *g* birth to a boy,
12: 5 If she *g* birth to a girl,
12: 7 woman who *g* birth to a boy or a girl child.
20: 2 who *g* any of his offspring to Molech shall
24:20 The same injury that a man *g* another
Nm 5:10 property of the priest to whom he *g* them."
15:22 commandments which the LORD *g* to Moses,
22: 8 give you whatever answer the LORD *g* me."
Dt 1:25 land which the LORD, our God, *g* us is good.'
8:18 God, who *g* you the power to acquire wealth,
13:13 the LORD, your God, *g* you to dwell in,
16: 5 which the LORD, your God, *g* you,
17: 2 which the LORD, your God, *g* you,
19: 8 and *g* you all the land he promised your
24:12 not sleep in the mantle he *g* as a pledge,
25:19 *g* you rest from all your enemies round
26: 2 the land which the LORD, your God, *g* you,
28: 8 the land that the LORD, your God, *g* you.
Jos 2:14 to you when the LORD *g* us the land."
Jgs 21:18 'Cursed be he who *g* a woman to Benjamin!' "
1Sm 2: 6 "The LORD puts to death and *g* life;
2: 8 He *g* to the vower his vow,
20:10 me if your father *g* you a harsh answer?"
Tb 4:19 but the Lord himself *g* all good things.
Jb 5:10 He *g* rain upon the earth and sends water
19:16 I call my servant, but he *g* no answer,
20: 2 my understanding a spirit *g* me a reply.
24:23 of his life he *g* safety and support.
32: 8 of the Almighty, that *g* him understanding.
33:13 him that he *g* no account of his doings?
36:31 the nations, and *g* them food in abundance.
38:29 who *g* the hoarfrost its birth in the skies,
38:36 heart, and *g* the cock its understanding?
Ps(s) 6: 6 in the nether world who *g* you thanks?
23: 2 In verdant pastures he *g* me repose;
37:21 the just man is kindly and *g*,
41: 7 when he leaves he *g* voice to it outside.
68: 7 God *g* a home to the forsaken;
68:12 The Lord *g* the word;
68:36 he *g* power and strength to his people.
112: 9 Lavishly he *g* to the poor;
119:50 affliction is that your promise *g* me life.
127: 2 bread, for he *g* to his beloved in sleep.
136:25 Who *g* food to all flesh,
146: 7 for the oppressed, *g* good to the hungry.
146: 8 the LORD *g* sight to the blind.
147: 9 Who *g* food to the cattle,
Prv 2: 6 For the LORD *g* wisdom,
14: 8 man's wisdom *g* him knowledge of his way,
14:30 A tranquil mind *g* life to the body,
17: 4 The evil man *g* heed to wicked lips,
17:18 is the man who *g* his hand in pledge,
21:26 the day, but the just man *g* unsparingly.
22: 9 for he *g* of his sustenance to the poor.
24:26 He *g* a kiss on the lips who makes an
25:14 who boastfully promises what he never *g*.
25:26 is a just man who *g* way before the wicked.
26: 8 in the sling is he who *g* honor to a fool.
28:27 He who *g* to the poor suffers no want,
29: 4 By justice a king *g* stability to the land;
29:11 The fool *g* vent to all his anger;
29:13 the LORD *g* light to the eyes of both.
29:15 The rod of correction *g* wisdom,
Eccl 2:26 sees fit he *g* wisdom and knowledge and joy;
2:26 but to the sinner he *g* the task of
5:17 limited days of the life which God *g* him;
5:18 Any man to whom God *g* riches and property,
6: 2 whom God *g* riches and property and honor,
8:15 of the life which God *g* him under the sun.
Sg 1:12 banquet my nard *g* forth its fragrance.
Sir 3: 9 a father's blessing *g* a family firm roots,
12: 3 comes to him who *g* comfort to the wicked,
17: 2 *g* him and makes him return to earth again.
17: 4 and *g* him rule over beasts and birds.
17:12 of them he *g* precepts about his fellow men.
20:14 He *g* little and criticizes often,
34:17 the eyes, *g* health and life and blessing.
35: 2 *g* alms he presents his sacrifice of praise.
38: 2 and *g* him access to those in authority.
43:15 In his majesty he *g* the storm its power
43:35 and to those who fear him he *g* wisdom.
Is 9:16 sinful, and every mouth *g* vent to folly.
26:19 of light, and the land of shades *g* birth.
33: 8 yet no man *g* it a thought.
38:18 is not the nether world that *g* you thanks,
40:29 He *g* strength to the fainting;
42: 5 Who *g* breath to its people and spirit to
42:23 Who of you *g* ear to this?
53:10 If he *g* his life as an offering for sin,
66: 7 Before she comes to labor, she *g* birth;
66: 8 in labor when she *g* birth to her children.
Jer 5:24 our God, Who *g* us rain early and late,
14:22 nations' idols is there any that *g* rain?
22:13 neighbor without pay, and *g* him no wages.
31:35 LORD, He who *g* the sun to light the day,
Ez 18: 7 one, *g* back the pledge received for a debt,
18: 7 *g* food to the hungry and clothes the naked;
18:16 who *g* his food to the hungry and clothes
Dn 2:21 He *g* wisdom to the wise and knowledge to
4:22 kingdom of men and *g* it to whom he will.
4:29 kingdom of men and *g* it to whom he will."
Hos 1: 2 for the land *g* itself to harlotry,
Hb 3:10 the ocean *g* forth its roar.
Mt 5:15 stand where it *g* light to all in the house.
10:42 And I promise you that whoever *g* a cup of
26:73 Even your accent *g* you away!"
Mk 1:27 *g* orders to unclean spirits and they obey!"
9:41 Any man who *g* you a drink of water because
Jn 1: 9 The real light which *g* light to every man
6:32 Father who *g* you the real heavenly bread.
6:33 down from heaven and *g* life to the world."
6:37 All that the Father *g* me shall come to me;
6:63 It is the spirit that *g* life;
8:54 He who *g* me glory is the Father,
14:27 do not give it to you as the world *g* peace.
Acts 17:25 it is he who *g* to all life and breath and
Rom 7: 3 is still alive, she *g* herself to another.
8:16 The Spirit himself *g* witness with our
12: 8 He who *g* alms should do so generously;
14: 6 to honor the Lord, and he *g* thanks to God.
14: 6 honor the Lord, and he too *g* thanks to God.
1Cor 3: 7 account, only God, who *g* the growth.
9:18 full use of the authority the gospel *g* me.
12: 8 To one the Spirit *g* wisdom in discourse,
15:38 God *g* body to it as he pleases
2Cor 1:12 Conscience *g* testimony to the boast that
3: 6 written law kills, but the Spirit *g* life.
7: 6 who *g* heart to those who are low in spirit,
Gal 5:13 a freedom that *g* free rein to the flesh.
1Tm 5: 6 who *g* herself up to selfish indulgence,
6:13 Before God, who *g* life to all,
Heb 6:16 an oath *g* firmness to a promise and puts
10:23 to our profession which *g* us hope,
Jas 1: 5 who *g* generously and ungrudgingly to all,
1:15 passion has conceived, it *g* birth to sin,
1Jn 4: 6 who has knowledge of God *g* us a hearing,
Rv 22:20 The One who *g* this testimony says,

GIVING (140)

Gn 9:12 the sign that I am *g* for all ages to come,
38:28 While she was *g* birth,
49:33 finished *g* these instructions to his sons,
Ex 1:16 for the Hebrew women and see them *g* birth,
20:12 land which the LORD, your God, is *g* you.
34:11 keep the commandments I am *g* you today.
Lv 14:34 of Canaan, which I am *g* you to possess,
20: 3 for in *g* his offspring to Molech,
20: 4 a man's crime of *g* his offspring to Molech,
20:24 I am *g* it to you as your own,
23:10 you come into the land which I am *g* you,
25: 2 When you enter the land that I am *g* you,
Nm 13: 2 of Canaan, which I am *g* to the Israelites.
16:14 or *g* us fields and vineyards for our
20:24 enter the land I am *g* to the Israelites,
27:12 the land that I am *g* to the Israelites.
31:27 *g* half to those who took active part in
Dt 1:20 Amorites, which the LORD, our God, is *g* us.
4: 1 LORD, the God of your fathers, is *g* you.
4:21 good land which he is *g* you as a heritage,
4:40 which the LORD, your God, is *g* you forever."
5:16 land which the LORD, your God, is *g* you.
5:31 in the land which I am *g* them to possess.'
7: 3 neither *g* your daughters to their sons nor
9: 6 God, is *g* you this good land to possess,
9:23 take possession of the land he was *g* you,
11:17 soon perish from the good land he is *g* you.
11:31 land which the LORD, your God, is *g* you.
12:10 the LORD, your God, is *g* you as a heritage,
15: 7 land which the LORD, your God, is *g* you,
15:15 That is why I am *g* you this command today.
16:18 which the LORD, your God, is *g* you.
16:20 land which the LORD, your God, is *g* you.
17:14 land which the LORD, your God, is *g* you,
18: 9 land which the LORD, your God, is *g* you,
19: 1 removes the nations whose land he is *g* you,
19: 2 the LORD, your God, is *g* you to occupy.
19:10 the LORD, your God, is *g* you as a heritage,
19:14 the LORD, your God, is *g* you to occupy.
20:16 LORD, your God, is *g* you as your heritage,
21: 1 the LORD, your God, is *g* you to occupy,
21:17 *g* him a double share of whatever he
21:23 LORD, your God, is *g* you as an inheritance.
24: 4 the LORD, your God, is *g* you as a heritage.
25:15 the land which the LORD, your God, is *g* you.
25:19 he is *g* you to occupy as your heritage,
26: 1 the LORD, your God, is *g* you as a heritage,
27: 2 land which the LORD, your God, is *g* you,
27: 3 your fathers, is *g* you as he promised you.
31:10 the elders of Israel, *g* them this order:
32:13 *G* them honey to suck from its rocks and
32:49 am *g* to the Israelites as their possession.
32:52 that land which I am *g* to the Israelites."
Jos 1:11 land which the LORD, your God, is *g* you.' "
1:15 land which the LORD, your God, is *g* them.
1Sm 4:19 was with child and at the point of *g* birth.
22:13 son of Jesse by *g* him food and a sword
2Sm 9: 9 "I am *g* your lord's son all that belonged
11:19 *g* the king all the details of the battle,
1Kgs 3:28 in him the wisdom of God for *g* judgment.
12: 7 submit to them, *g* them a favorable answer,
1Chr 29:17 here present also *g* to you generously.
29:25 *g* him a glorious reign such as had not
2Chr 5:13 voice praising and *g* thanks to the LORD,
32:24 the LORD, who answered him by *g* him a sign.
Ezr 5: 2 with the prophets of God *g* them support.
Tb 14: 2 *g* alms and continually blessing God and
Jdt 6:17 He replied by *g* them an account of what
15:11 the camp, *g* Judith the tent of Holofernes,
1Mc 11:12 his daughter away and *g* her to Demetrius,
12:25 them, *g* them no time to enter his province.
14:32 nation's armed forces and *g* them their pay.
2Mc 2: 2 also that the prophet, in *g* them the law,
2:28 our efforts to *g* only a summary outline.
6:27 Therefore, by manfully *g* up my life now,
8:23 the holy book and *g* them the watchword,
9: 7 Far from *g* up his insolence,
13:15 *G* his men the battle cry "God's Victory,"
13:22 *g* them his pledge and receiving theirs,
Jb 1: 4 His sons used to take turns *g* feasts,
Ps(s) 19: 8 is trustworthy, *g* wisdom to the simple.
26: 7 your altar, O LORD, *G* voice to my thanks,
94:13 law you teach, *G* him rest from evil days,
111: 6 *g* them the inheritance of the nations.
119:130 sheds light, *g* understanding to the simple.
Prv 11:15 but he who hates *g* pledges is safe.
Sir 1:10 *g* gladness and joy and length of days.
7:10 in prayers, and neglect not the *g* of alms.
7:25 *G* your daughter in marriage ends a great
18:17 Only a fool upbraids before *g*;
19:10 in labor, like a woman *g* birth to a child.
Is 26:18 and writhed in pain, *g* birth to wind;
28: 7 their visions, tottering when *g* judgment.
45: 4 called you by your name, *g* you a title,
45:10 or a woman, "What are you *g* birth to?"
55:10 *G* seed to him who sows and bread to him
57: 1 are swept away, with no one *g* it a thought.
Jer 13:21 seize you like those of a woman *g* birth?
21: 8 I am *g* you a choice between life and death.
32:16 After *g* the deed of purchase to Baruch,
32:19 of men, *g* to each according to his ways,
Ez 3: 3 your stomach with this scroll I am *g* you.
11: 2 evil and *g* wicked counsel in this city.
29:19 now *g* the land of Egypt to Nebuchadnezzar,
33:15 what is right and just, *g* back pledges,
36:26 your stony hearts and *g* you natural hearts.
39: 4 to the wild beasts I am *g* you to be eaten.
Dn 6: 4 of *g* him authority over the entire kingdom.
Jon 4: 6 *g* shade that relieved him of any
Mt 6: 3 In *g* alms you are not to let your left
9: 8 praised God for *g* such authority to men.
10: 5 after *g* them the following instructions:
15:36 and after *g* thanks he broke them and gave
17:25 house asked, without *g* him time to speak:
28:12 *g* the soldiers a large bribe with the
Mk 6: 7 two, *g* them authority over unclean spirits.
Lk 1:77 *G* his people a knowledge of salvation in
14:16 was *g* a large dinner and he invited many.
17: 2 than *g* scandal to one of these little ones.
18:43 and began to follow him, *g* God the glory.
22:19 Then, taking bread and *g* thanks,
Jn 9:34 from your birth, and you are *g* us lectures?"
Acts 3: 9 people saw him moving and *g* praise to God,
8:25 After *g* their testimony and proclaiming
10: 2 He was in the habit of *g* generously to the
11:17 If God was *g* them the same gift he gave us
15:41 *g* the churches there renewed assurance.
18: 5 preaching and *g* evidence to the Jews
20:35 is more happiness in *g* than receiving.' "
1Cor 9: 8 reasons I am *g* you are merely human ones,
2Cor 5:12 but we are *g* you an opportunity to boast
6: 3 We avoid *g* anyone offense,
8: 8 I am not *g* an order but simply testing
8:11 be matched by *g* according to your means.
Eph 6:22 very purpose of *g* you news about me
Phil 4:15 by *g* me something for what it had received.
Col 1:12 *g* thanks to the Father for having made you

GIVING (cont.)

Rv 11: 7 When they have finished *g* their testimony,
13: 4 dragon for *g* his authority to the beast;
16:19 *g* her the cup filled with the blazing wine

GLAD (72)

Ex 4:15 When he sees you, his heart will be *g*.
1Sm 19: 5 Israel through him, you were *g* to see it.
1Chr 16:31 Let the heavens be *g* and the earth rejoice;
2Chr 7:10 rejoicing and *g* at heart at the good
Tb 8:16 Blessed are you, who have made me *g*;
1Mc 3: 7 He made Jacob *g* by his deeds,
10:26 not gone over to our enemies, and we are *g*.
Jb 3:22 and are *g* when they reach the grave:
Ps(s) 5:12 take refuge in you be *g* and exult forever.
9: 3 I will be *g* and exult in you;
14: 7 then shall Jacob exult and Israel be *g*.
16: 9 my heart is *g* and my soul rejoices,
21: 2 O Lord, in your strength the king is *g*;
31: 8 I will rejoice and be *g* of your kindness,
32: 7 *g* cries of freedom you will ring me round.
32:11 Be *g* in the LORD and rejoice,
34: 3 the lowly will hear me and be *g*.
35:15 stumbled they were *g* and gathered together;
35:26 and confounded who are *g* at my misfortune.
35:27 for joy and be *g* who favor my just cause;
38:17 say, "Let them not be *g* on my account who,
40:17 all who seek you exult and be *g* in you,
48:12 let Mount Zion be *g*,
53: 7 then shall Jacob exult and Israel be *g*.
58:11 just man shall be *g* when he sees vengeance;
64:11 is *g* in the LORD and takes refuge in him;
67: 5 May the nations be *g* and exult because
68: 4 they are *g* and rejoice.
68:12 women bear the *g* tidings,
69:33 "See you lowly ones, and be *g*;
70: 5 may all who seek you exult and be *g* in you,
90:15 Make us *g*,
92: 5 For you make me *g*,
96:11 Let the heavens be *g* and the earth rejoice;
97: 1 let the many isles be *g*.
97: 8 Zion hears and is *g*,
97:12 Be *g* in the LORD,
104:31 may the LORD be *g* in his works!
104:34 I will be *g* in the LORD.
118:24 let us be *g* and rejoice in it.
119:74 Those who fear you shall see me and be *g*,
126: 3 we are *g* indeed.
149: 2 Let Israel be *g* in their maker,
Prv 10: 1 A wise son makes his father *g*,
12:25 depresses it, but a kindly word makes it *g*.
15:13 A *g* heart lights up the face,
15:20 A wise son makes his father *g*,
17: 5 is *g* at calamity will not go unpunished.
29: 3 He who loves wisdom makes his father *g*,
Eccl 3:12 than to be *g* and to do well during life.
10:19 merriment and wine makes the living *g*,
11: 9 your heart be *g* in the days of your youth.
Is 25: 9 us rejoice and be *g* that he has saved us!"
40: 9 a high mountain, Zion, herald of *g* tidings;
41:27 I will pick out a bearer of the *g* tidings."
44:23 Raise a *g* cry, you heavens:
52: 7 are the feet of him who brings *g* tidings,
54: 1 Raise a *g* cry,
61: 1 sent me to bring *g* tidings to the lowly,
66:10 with Jerusalem and be *g* because of her,
Lam 4:21 Though you rejoice and are *g*,
Zep 3:14 Be *g* and exult with all your heart,
Zec 10: 7 Their children shall see it and be *g*
Mt 5:12 Be *g* and rejoice, for your reward is great
10:25 should be *g* to become like his teacher,
Lk 4:18 has sent me to bring *g* tidings to the poor,
Jn 8:56 He saw it and was *g*."
11:15 For your sakes I am *g* I was not there,
Acts 2:26 has been *g* and my tongue has rejoiced,
Eph 1:13 when you heard the *g* tidings of salvation,
Phil 2:17 I am *g* of it and rejoice with all of you.
2:18 May you be *g* on the same score,
Rv 19: 7 Let us rejoice and be *g*,

GLADDEN (7)

Tb 13:10 May he *g* within you all who were captives;
Ps(s) 46: 5 a stream whose runlets *g* the city of God,
86: 4 *G* the soul of your servant,
104:15 the earth, and wine to *g* men's hearts,
Prv 27: 9 Perfume and incense *g* the heart,
27:11 you are wise, my son, you will *g* my heart,
Jer 31:13 console and *g* them after their sorrows.

GLADDENED (4)

Jb 22:19 The just look on and are *g*,
Ps(s) 21: 7 you *g* him with the joy of your presence.
89:43 of his foes, you have *g* all his enemies.
Sir 3: 5 He who honors his father is *g* by children,

GLADDENS (2)

Ps(s) 94:19 abound within me, your comfort *g* my soul.
Sir 35:23 of his people, and *g* them by his mercy.

GLADLY (6)

Jgs 8:25 "We will *g* give them,"
Jdt 12:18 Judith replied, "I will *g* drink,
Est C: 6 *G* would I have kissed the soles of his
2Mc 2:27 many we will *g* endure these inconveniences,
2Cor 11:19 wise yourselves, you *g* put up with fools.
12:15 *g* spend myself and be spent for your sakes.

GLADNESS (38)

Tb 13:18 gates of Jerusalem shall sing hymns of *g*,
Est 9:22 to observe these days with feasting and *g*,
1Mc 4:59 altar should be observed with joy and *g*
5:54 Zion in joy and *g* and offered holocausts,
2Mc 3:30 and commotion, was filled with joy and *g*,
Ps(s) 4: 8 You put *g* into my heart,
27: 6 in his tent sacrifices with shouts of *g*;
30:12 off my sackcloth and clothed me with *g*,
33: 3 the strings skillfully, with shouts of *g*.
43: 4 the altar of God, the God of my *g* and joy;
45: 8 with the oil of *g* above your fellow kings.
45:16 They are borne in with *g* and joy;
47: 2 your hands, shout to God with cries of *g*,
51:10 Let me hear the sounds of joy and *g*;
90:14 we may shout for joy and *g* all our days.
97:11 and *g*, for the upright of heart.
100: 2 serve the LORD with *g*;
Wis 8:16 with her no grief, but rather joy and *g*.
Sir 1: 9 glory and splendor, *g* and a festive crown.
1:10 heart, giving *g* and joy and length of days.
15: 6 Joy and *g* he will find,
30:22 *G* of heart is the very life of man,
Is 16:10 the orchards are taken away joy and *g*,
35:10 They will meet with joy and *g*,
51: 3 Joy and *g* shall be found in thanksgiving
51:11 They will meet with joy and *g*,
61: 3 To give them oil of *g* in place of mourning,
Jer 7:34 will silence the cry of joy, the cry of *g*,
16: 9 place the cry of joy and the cry of *g*,
25:10 an end the song of joy and the song of *g*,
33:11 yet be heard the cry of joy, the cry of *g*,
Bar 2:23 The sounds of joy and the sounds of *g*,
4:23 you back to me with enduring *g* and joy.
Jl 1:16 And from the house of our God, joy and *g*?
Zep 3:17 He will rejoice over you with *g*,
Zec 8:19 shall become occasions of joy and *g*,
Lk 1:14 Joy and *g* will be yours,
Heb 1: 9 with the oil of *g* above your fellow kings."

GLANCE (16)

Ex 14:24 force a *g* that threw it into a panic;
Jdt 16:15 the rocks, like wax, melt before your *g*.
Est D:14 my lord, though your *g* is full of kindness."
Jb 29:25 mourners took comfort from my cheerful *g*.
40:12 Bring down the haughty with a *g*;
Ps(s) 11: 4 behold, his searching *g* is on mankind.
27: 8 you my *g* seeks;
Prv 4:25 ahead and your *g* be directly forward.
6:25 let her not captivate you with her *g*!
15:30 A cheerful *g* brings joy to the heart;
20: 8 of judgment dispels all evil with his *g*.
23: 5 While your *g* flits to it,
30:13 how overbearing their *g*!
Sg 4: 9 ravished my heart with one *g* of your eyes,
Sir 16:17 the earth's foundations, at his mere *g*,
21:23 but a cultured man keeps his *g* cast down.

GLANCED (1)

Lk 21: 1 He *g* up and saw the rich putting their

GLARING (1)

Jer 4:11 "From the *g* heights through the desert a

GLASS (5)

Prv 23:31 when it is red, when it sparkles in the *g*.
Rv 4: 6 was like a sea of *g* that was crystal-clear.
15: 2 like a sea of *g* mingled with fire.
15: 2 On the sea of *g* were standing those who
21:21 city were of pure gold, transparent as *g*.

GLAZED (1)

Prv 26:23 Like a *g* finish on earthenware are smooth

GLEAM (4)

Ps(s) 104:15 hearts, So that their faces *g* with oil,
Ez 1: 7 sparkled with a *g* like burnished bronze.
Hb 3:11 arrows, at the *g* of your flashing spear.
Rv 2:18 fire and whose feet *g* like polished brass,

GLEAMED (6)

1Mc 6:39 the mountains *g* with their brightness and
Ez 1: 4 of the fire] something *g* like electrum.
1:13 The fire *g*,
1:27 his waist I saw what *g* like electrum;
Rv 1:15 *g* like polished brass refined in a furnace,
21:11 It *g* with the splendor of God.

GLEAN (12)

Lv 19: 9 nor shall you *g* the stray ears of grain.
23:22 shall you *g* the stray ears of your grain.
Ru 2: 2 "Let me go and *g* ears of grain in the
2: 3 The field she entered to *g* after the
2: 8 Do not go to *g* in anyone else's field;
2:15 She rose to *g*,
2:15 Boaz instructed his servants to let her *g*
2:16 them for her to *g* without being rebuked.
2:19 said to her, "Where did you *g* today?
Jb 24:11 they *g* in the the vineyard of the wicked.
Jer 6: 9 Glean, *g* like a vine the remnant of Israel;

GLEANED (4)

Ru 2:17 She *g* in the field until evening,
2:17 had *g* it came to about an ephah of barley,
Is 27:12 of Egypt, and you shall be *g* one by one,
Mi 7: 1 gathered, as when the vines have been *g*;

GLEANER (1)

Sir 33:16 to keep vigil, like a *g* after the vintage;

GLEANING (3)

Jgs 8: 2 "Is not the *g* of Ephraim better than the
Ru 2:23 So she stayed *g* with the servants of Boaz
Is 24:13 as with a *g* when the vintage is done.

GLEANINGS (3)

Ru 2: 7 the *g* into sheaves after the harvesters;
Jer 49: 9 came upon you, they would leave no *g*;
Ob 1: 5 came to you, would they not leave some *g*?

GLEANS (1)

Is 17: 5 one *g* the ears in the Valley of Rephaim.

GLEE (2)

Prv 23:24 father of a just man will exult with *g*;
Ez 35:15 In keeping with your *g* over the

GLIDING (1)

Dt 32:24 with the venom of reptiles *g* in the dust.

GLITTERING (1)

Ez 1:22 could be seen, seeming like *g* crystal,

GLOAT (6)

Jdt 4:12 and mocked for the nations to *g* over.
Est C:22 Let them not *g* over our ruin,
Ps(s) 22:18 They look on and *g* over me;
Lam 2:17 Letting the enemy *g* over you and exalting
Bar 4:12 Let no one *g* over me,
Rv 11:10 The earth's inhabitants *g* over them and in

GLOATED (1)

Lam 1: 7 When her foes *g* over her,

GLOATS (1)

Sir 19: 5 He who *g* over evil will meet with evil,

GLOOM (20)

Jb 3: 5 May darkness and *g* claim it,
10:21 return, to the land of darkness and of *g*,
11:17 its *g* shall become as the morning,
12:22 and brings the *g* forth to the light.
23:17 that thick *g* were before me to conceal me.
30:28 I go about in *g*, without the sun;
Ps(s) 107:10 They dwelt in darkness and *g*,
107:14 and *g* and broke their bonds asunder.
Eccl 5:16 of his life are passed in *g* and sorrow,
Is 8:23 is no *g* where but now there was distress.
9: 1 dwell in the land of *g* a light has shone.
29:18 And out of *g* and darkness,
58:10 and the *g* shall become for you like midday;
59: 9 for brightness, but we walk in *g*!
Ez 31:15 I cast *g* over Lebanon because of him,
Jl 2: 2 it is near, a day of darkness and of *g*,
Am 5:20 and not light, *g* without any brightness?
Zep 1:15 and desolation, a day of darkness and *g*,
2Pt 2:17 The darkest *g* has been reserved for them.
Jude 1:13 *g* of darkness has been reserved forever.

GLOOMY (4)

Est A: 7 It was a dark and *g* day.
Wis 17: 5 stars succeed in lighting up that *g* night.
Mt 16: 3 but in the morning, 'Sky red and *g*,
Heb 12:18 nor *g* darkness and storm and trumpet blast,

GLORIED (1)

Ps(s) 44: 9 In God we *g* day by day;

GLORIES (4)

Ps(s) 10: 3 For the wicked man *g* in his greed,
Wis 18:24 and the *g* of the fathers were carved in
Jer 9:23 But rather, let him who *g*,
1Pt 1:11 for Christ and the *g* that would follow.

GLORIFIED (32)

1Mc 2:64 keeping the law, for by it you shall be *g*.

2Mc 3: 2 *g* the temple with the most magnificent
3:30 Lord who had marvelously *g* his holy Place;
Ps(s) 35:27 And may they ever say, "The LORD be *g;*
40:17 your salvation say ever, "The LORD be *g.*"
70: 5 love your salvation say ever, "God be *g!*"
Wis 18: 8 in this you *g* us whom you had summoned.
19:22 you magnified and *g* your people;
Sir 3:19 by the humble he is *g.*
Is 8:23 but in the end he has *g* the seaward road,
55: 5 God, the Holy One of Israel, who has *g* you.
60: 9 God, the Holy One of Israel, who has *g* you.
Ez 28:22 I will be *g* in your midst.
Dn 4:31 I praised and *g* him who lives forever:
Mt 15:31 They *g* the God of Israel.
Jn 7:39 as yet, since Jesus had not yet been *g.)*
11: 4 that through it the Son of God may be *g.*"
12:16 but after Jesus was *g* they recalled that
12:23 hour has come for the Son of Man to be *g.*
12:28 "I have *g* it,
13:31 Son of Man *g* and God is glorified in him.
13:32 [If God has been *g* in him.]
15: 8 My Father has been *g* in your bearing much
17:10 It is in them that I have been *g.*
Acts 3:13 of our fathers, has *g* his Servant Jesus,
Rom 8:17 we suffer with him so as to be *g* with him.
8:30 and those he justified he in turn *g.*
Phil 3:21 it according to the pattern of his *g* body,
2Thes 1:10 to be *g* in his holy ones and adored by all
1:12 Lord Jesus may be *g* in you and you in him,
1Pt 4:11 you God is to be *g* through Jesus Christ:

GLORIFIES (2)

Ps(s) 50:23 He that offers praise as a sacrifice *g* me;
Prv 14:31 but he who is kind to the needy *g* him.

GLORIFY (33)

Dt 32:43 Exult with him, you heavens, *g* him,
Ezr 7:27 to *g* the house of the LORD in Jerusalem.
Ps(s) 34: 4 *G* the LORD with me,
50:15 I will rescue you, and you shall *g* me."
63: 4 my lips shall *g* you.
69:31 song, and I will *g* him with thanksgiving;
76:11 For wrathful Edom shall *g* you,
86: 9 and worship you, O Lord, and *g* your name.
86:12 my heart, and I will *g* your name forever.
91:15 I will deliver him and *g* him;
117: 1 *g* him, all you peoples!
147:12 *G* the LORD, O Jerusalem;
Sir 17:22 Who in the nether world can *g* the Most
17:23 they *g* the LORD who are alive and well.
43:31 Lift up your voices to *g* the LORD,
Jer 30:19 they will not be tiny, for I will *g* them.
Dn 4:34 praise and exalt and *g* the King of heaven,
5:23 whole course of your life, you did not *g.*
11:38 to his fathers he shall *g* with gold,
Jn 8:54 "If I *g* myself,
12:28 Father, *g* your name!"
12:28 "I have glorifed it, and will *g* it again."
13:32 *g* him in himself, and will glorify him soon.
14:13 will do, so as to *g* the Father in the Son.
21:19 sort of death by which Peter was to *g* God.)
Acts 11:18 and instead began to *g* God in these words:
Rom 1:21 did not *g* him as God or give him thanks;
15: 6 with one heart and voice you may *g* God,
15: 9 the Gentiles *g* God because of his mercy.
1Cor 6:20 So *g* God in your body.
Heb 5: 5 *g* himself with the office of high priest;
1Pt 4:16 should rather *g* God in virtue of that name.

GLORIFYING (5)

1Mc 4:24 they were singing hymns and *g* Heaven,
Dn 3:51 with one voice sang, *g* and blessing God:
Lk 2:20 *g* and praising God for all they had heard
Acts 10:46 could hear speaking in tongues and *g* God.
2Cor 9:13 they are *g* God for your obedient faith

GLORIOUS (79)

Ex 28: 2 For the *g* adornment of your brother Aaron
28:40 for the *g* adornment of Aaron's sons you
Dt 28:58 revere the *g* and awesome name of the LORD,
1Sm 2: 8 nobles and make a *g* throne their heritage.
1Chr 22: 5 it will be renowned and *g* in all countries.
29:25 giving him a *g* reign such as had not been
Neh 9: 5 the blessing, "Blessed is your *g* name,
Tb 3:16 heard in the *g* presence of Almighty God.
Jdt 9: 8 defile the tent where your *g* name resides,
16:13 O Lord, great are you and *g,*
Est 1: 4 he displayed the *g* riches of his kingdom
1Mc 2: 9 her *g* ornaments have been carried off as
14: 9 the young men wore the *g* apparel of war.
14:10 his *g* name reached the ends of the earth.
2Mc 6:19 a *g* death to a life of defilement,
8:15 they themselves bore his holy, *g* name.
Ps(s) 8: 2 how *g* is your name over all the earth!
8:10 how *g* is your name over all the earth!
45:14 All *g* is the king's daughter as she enters;
66: 2 proclaim his *g* praise.
72:19 And blessed forever be his *g* name;
78: 4 The *g* deeds of the LORD and his strength
87: 3 *G* things are said of you, O city of God!
145: 5 *g* majesty and tell of your wondrous works.
145:12 might and the *g* splendor of your kingdom.
Prv 4: 9 a *g* crown will she bestow on you."
Wis 3:15 the fruit of noble struggles is a *g* one;
9:10 from your *g* throne dispatch her
19: 5 your people might experience a *g* journey
Sir 17: 7 their hearts, and shows them his *g* works,
17:11 eyes beheld, his *g* voice their ears heard.
24:12 I have struck root among the *g* people,
40:27 its canopy, all that is *g.*
44: 7 All these were *g* in their time,
45: 8 and adorned him with the *g* vestments:
45:12 the insignia of holiness, Majestic, *g,*
47:18 *g* name which was conferred upon Israel.
49:16 *G,* too, were SHEM and SETH and ENOS
50:11 As he ascended the *g* altar and lent
Is 11:10 seek out, for his dwelling shall be *g.*
12: 5 praise to the LORD for his *g* achievement;
24:23 in Jerusalem, *g* in the sight of his elders.
28: 1 To the fading blooms of his *g* beauty,
28: 4 The fading blooms of his *g* beauty on the
28: 5 will be a *g* crown And a brilliant diadem
30:30 The LORD will make his *g* voice heard,
42:21 his justice to make his law great and *g,*
43: 4 you are precious in my eyes and *g,*
49: 5 And I am made *g* in the sight of the LORD,
52: 1 Put on your *g* garments,
61: 3 a *g* mantle instead of a listless spirit.
62: 3 shall be a *g* crown in the hand of the LORD,
63: 7 I will recall, the *g* deeds of the LORD,
63:12 Whose *g* arm was the guide at Moses' right;
63:15 from your holy and *g* palace!
64:10 Our holy and *g* temple in which our fathers
Jer 48:17 How the strong staff is broken, the *g* rod!
Ez 16:12 your ears, and a *g* diadem upon your head.
24:25 away from them their bulwark, their *g* joy,
Dn 3:26 our fathers, and *g* forever is your name.
3:45 are the Lord God, *g* over the whole world."
3:52 And blessed is your holy and *g* name,
3:53 praiseworthy and *g* above all forever.
3:56 of heaven, praiseworthy and *g* forever.
5:18 a great kingdom and *g* majesty.
8: 9 the south, the east, and the *g* country.
11:16 He shall stop in the *g* land,
11:20 send a tax collector through the *g* kingdom,
11:41 shall enter the *g* land and many shall fall,
11:45 between the sea and the *g* holy mountain,
Acts 2:20 coming of that great and *g* day of the Lord.
Rom 8:21 in the *g* freedom of the children of God.
1Cor 15:43 What is sown is ignoble, what rises is *g.*
Eph 1: 6 that all might praise the *g* favor he has
1:18 the wealth of his *g* heritage to be
5:27 the word, to present to himself a *g* church,
1Tm 1:11 that pertains to the *g* gospel of God
Jas 2: 1 your faith in our *g* Lord Jesus Christ must
1Pt 2: 9 for his own to proclaim the *g* works"

GLORIOUSLY (3)

Ex 15: 1 sing to the LORD, for he is *g* triumphant;
15:21 Sing to the LORD, for he is *g* triumphant;
2Mc 2: 8 that the Place might be *g* sanctified."

GLORY (455)

Ex 14: 4 receive *g* through Pharaoh and all his army,
14:17 receive *g* through Pharaoh and all his army,
14:18 when I receive *g* through Pharaoh and his
16: 7 the morning you will see the *g* of the LORD,
16:10 the *g* of the LORD appeared in the cloud!
24:16 The *g* of the LORD settled upon Mount Sinai.
24:17 To the Israelites the *g* of the LORD was
29:43 hence, it will be made sacred by my *g.*
33:18 Then Moses said, "Do let me see your *g!*"
33:22 When my *g* passes I will set you in the
40:34 and the *g* of the LORD filled the Dwelling.
40:35 and the *g* of the LORD filled the Dwelling.
Lv 9: 6 the *g* of the LORD may be revealed to you.
9:23 Then the *g* of the LORD was revealed to all
10: 3 sight of all the people I will reveal my *g.*"
Nm 14:10 But then the *g* of the LORD appeared at the
14:21 the LORD's *g* that fills the whole earth,
14:22 of all the men who have seen my *g* and the
16:19 the *g* of the LORD appeared to the entire
17: 7 covered it and the *g* of the LORD appeared.
20: 6 Then the *g* of the LORD appeared to them,
Dt 5:24 indeed let us see his *g* and his majesty!
10:21 He is your *g,*
26:19 and *g* above all other nations he has made,
33:29 saving shield, and his sword is your *g.*
Jos 7:19 *g* and honor by telling me what you have
Jgs 4: 9 "but you shall not gain the *g* in the
1Sm 4:21 saying, "Gone is the *g* from Israel,"
4:22 She said, "Gone is the *g* from Israel,"
15:29 *G* of Israel neither retracts nor repents,
2Sm 1:19 the *g* of Israel,
1Kgs 3:13 *g* that among kings there is not your like.
8:11 LORD's *g* had filled the temple of the LORD.
2Kgs 14:10 Enjoy your *g,* but stay at home!
1Chr 16:10 *G* in his holy name;
16:24 day after day Tell his *g* among the nations;
16:28 of nations, give to the LORD *g* and praise;
16:29 Give to the LORD the *g* due his name!
16:35 to your holy name and *g* in praising you."
29:11 and power, majesty, splendor, and *g.*
29:28 old age, rich in years and wealth and *g,*
2Chr 1:11 not asked for riches, treasures and *g,*
1:12 also give you riches, treasures and *g,*
5:14 since the LORD's *g* filled the house of God.
7: 1 and the *g* of the LORD filled the house.
7: 2 for the *g* of the LORD had filled the house
7: 3 and the *g* of the LORD was upon the house,
17: 5 so that he enjoyed great wealth and *g.*
18: 1 therefore had wealth and *g* in abundance;
26:18 part in the *g* that comes from the LORD God."
32:27 Hezekiah possessed very great wealth and *g*—
Tb 12: 6 Give him the praise and the *g.*
12:12 of your prayer before the *G* of the Lord;
12:15 enter and serve before the *G* of the Lord."
13:16 your *g* and to praise the King of heaven!
Jdt 1:14 market places, and turned its *g* into shame.
10: 8 for the *g* of the Israelites and the
15: 9 "You are the *g* of Jerusalem,
Est C:20 the *g* of your temple and your altar;
C:26 You know that I hate the *g* of the pagans,
1Mc 1:40 dishonor was as great as her *g* had been,
2:12 and our beauty and our *g* laid waste,
2:51 shall win great *g* and an everlasting name.
2:62 for his *g* ends in corruption and worms.
3: 3 He spread abroad the *g* of his people,
3:14 win *g* in the kingdom by defeating Judas
9:10 kinsmen and not leave a stain upon our *g!*"
11:51 The Jews thus gained *g* in the eyes of the
14: 5 As his crowning *g* he captured the port of
14:21 people have informed us of your *g* and fame,
14:29 have thus brought great *g* to their nation.
14:35 the *g* he planned to bring to his nation,
15: 9 your *g* will be manifest in all the earth."
2Mc 2: 8 *g* of the Lord will be seen in the cloud,
4:15 prized what the Greeks esteemed as *g.*
5:16 by other kings for the advancement, the *g,*
5:20 in his anger was restored in all its *g,*
Jb 19: 9 He has stripped me of my *g,*
29:20 My *g* is fresh within me,
40:10 and array yourself with *g* and splendor.
Ps(s) 3: 4 my *g,* you lift up my head!
7: 6 to the ground, and lay my *g* in the dust.
8: 6 angels, and crowned him with *g* and honor.
19: 2 The heavens declare the *g* of God,
21: 6 Great is his *g* in your victory;
22: 4 enthroned in the holy place, O *g* of Israel!
22:24 you descendants of Jacob, give *g* to him;
24: 7 portals, that the king of *g* may come in!
24: 8 Who is this king of *g?*
24: 9 portals, that the king of *g* may come in!
24:10 Who is this king of *g?*
24:10 The LORD of hosts; he is the king of *g.*
26: 8 you dwell, the tenting-place of your *g.*
29: 1 sons of God, give to the LORD *g* and praise,
29: 2 Give to the LORD the *g* due his name;
29: 3 is over the waters, the God of *g* thunders,
29: 9 the forests, and in his temple all say, *G!*"
34: 3 Let my soul *g* in the LORD;
35:26 with shame and disgrace who *g* over me.
38:17 account who, when my foot slips, *g* over me."
47: 5 for us our inheritance, the *g* of Jacob,
52: 3 Why do you *g* in evil, you champion
56: 5 In God, in whose promise I *g,*
56:11 In God, in whose promise I *g,*
57: 6 above all the earth be your *g!*
57:12 above all the earth be your *g!*
62: 8 With God is my safety and my *g,*
63: 3 sanctuary to see your power and your *g,*
63:12 everyone who swears by him shall *g,*
64:11 in him *g* all the upright of heart.
66: 2 earth, sing praise to the *g* of his name;
71: 8 with your praise, with your *g* day by day.
72:19 may the whole earth be filled with his *g.*
73:24 and in the end you will receive me in *g.*
78:61 captivity, his *g* into the hands of the foe.
79: 9 our savior, because of the *g* of your name;
84:12 grace and *g* he bestows;
85:10 those who fear him, *g* dwelling in our land.
90:16 your servants and your *g* by their children;
94: 3 the wicked, how long shall the wicked *g,*
96: 3 Tell his *g* among the nations;
96: 7 of nations, give to the LORD *g* and praise;
96: 8 give to the LORD the *g* due his name!
97: 6 his justice, and all peoples see his *g.*
97: 7 to shame, who *g* in the things of nought;
102:16 and all the kings of the earth your *g,*
102:17 has rebuilt Zion and appeared in his *g;*
104: 1 You are clothed with majesty and *g,*
104:31 May the *g* of the LORD endure forever;
105: 3 *G* in his holy name;
106: 5 your people, and *g* with your inheritance.
106:20 *g* for the image of a grass-eating bullock.
106:47 to your holy name and *g* in praising you.
108: 6 over all the earth be your *g!*
111: 3 Majesty and *g* are his work,
112: 9 his horn shall be exalted in *g.*
113: 4 above the heavens is his *g.*
115: 1 your name give *g* because of your kindness,
138: 5 "Great is the *g* of the LORD."
145:11 *g* of your kingdom and speak of your might,
149: 5 Let the faithful exult in *g;*
149: 9 This is the *g* of all his faithful.
Prv 14:28 In many subjects lies the *g* of the king;

GLORY (cont.)

16:31 Gray hair is a crown of g;
17: 6 and the g of children is their parentage.
19:11 and it is his g to overlook an offense.
20:29 The g of young men is their strength,
25: 2 God has g in what he conceals, kings have g
Wis 7:25 a pure effusion of the g of the Almighty:
8:10 her sake I should have g among the masses,
9:11 in my affairs and safeguard me by her g;
10:14 defamed him false, and gave him eternal g.
Sir 1: 9 Fear of the LORD is g and splendor,
1:17 heightens the g of those who possess her.
3:10 G not in your father's shame,
3:10 shame, for his shame is no g to you!
3:11 His father's honor is a man's g;
4:13 He who holds her fast inherits g;
6:31 You will wear her as your robe of g,
9:16 in the fear of God be your g.
10:21 or pauper, his g is the fear of the LORD.
17:11 His majestic g their eyes beheld,
24: 1 before her own people she proclaims her g;
25: 6 their g, the fear of the LORD.
31:10 come off safe, and this remains his g;
33:23 let no one tarnish your g.
36: 3 so now use them to show us your g.
36:13 with your majesty, your temple with your g.
37:25 wise for his people wins a heritage of g,
38: 6 the knowledge to g in his mighty works,
39: 8 and g in the law of the LORD's covenant.
42:16 so the g of the LORD fills all his works;
42:17 the strength to stand firm before his g.
43: 1 forth like heaven itself, a vision of g.
43: 9 The beauty, the g, of the heavens
43:12 It spans the heavens with its g,
44: 2 The abounding g of the Most High's portion,
44:13 endure, their g will never be blotted out;
44:19 of many peoples, kept his g without stain:
45: 3 for his people, and revealed to him his g.
45:20 Then he increased the g of Aaron and
45:26 bless the LORD who has crowned you with g!
46: 2 What g was his when he raised his arm,
48: 4 are you, ELIJAH, Whose g is equal to yours?
49: 5 their g to a foolish foreign nation
49:12 holy temple, destined for everlasting g.
50: 1 among his brethren, the g of his people,
50:20 lips, the name of the LORD would be his g.
Is 4: 2 branch of the LORD will be luster and g,
4: 6 all, his g will be shelter and protection:
6: 3 "All the earth is filled with his g!"
10:16 And instead of his g there will be
13:19 kingdoms, the g and pride of the Chaldeans,
14:18 All the kings of the nations lie in g,
16:14 the g of Moab shall be degraded despite
17: 3 shall have the same g as the Israelites,
17: 4 On that day The g of Jacob shall fade,
21:16 all the g of Kedar shall come to an end.
22:18 there, you and the chariots you g in,
22:24 On him shall hang all the g of his family:
24:15 in the coastlands, give g to the LORD!
26:15 LORD, increased the nation to your own g,
35: 2 The g of Lebanon will be given to them,
35: 2 They will see the g of the LORD,
40: 5 Then the g of the LORD shall be revealed,
40: 6 all their g like the flower of the field.
41:16 the LORD, and g in the Holy One of Israel.
42: 8 my g I give to no other,
42:12 Let them give g to the LORD,
43: 7 is named as mine, whom I created for my g,
44:23 Jacob, and shows his g through Israel.
45:25 and the g of all the descendants of Israel."
46:13 within Zion, and give to Israel my g.
48:11 My g I will not give to another.
49: 3 to me, Israel, through whom I show my g.
58: 8 the g of the LORD shall be your rear guard.
59:19 of the LORD, and those in the east, his g;
60: 1 come, the g of the LORD shines upon you.
60: 2 LORD shines, and over you appears his g.
60:13 The g of Lebanon shall come to you:
60:13 and g to the place where I set my feet.
60:19 light forever, your God shall be your g.
60:21 of my planting, my handiwork to show my g.
61: 3 justice, planted by the LORD to show his g.
62: 2 your vindication, and all kings your g;
63:14 led your people, bringing g to your name.
66: 5 LORD show his g that we may see your joy";
66:18 they shall come and see my g.
66:19 or seen my g; and they shall proclaim my g
66:24 they shall come and see my g.
Jer 2:11 have changed their g for useless things.
4: 2 use his name in blessing, and g in him.
9:22 man g in his wisdom, nor the strong man g
9:22 strength, nor the rich man g in his riches;
9:23 But rather, let him who glories, g in this,
13:16 Give g to the LORD,
13:20 to you, the sheep that were your g?
14:21 us not, disgrace not the throne of your g;
17:12 A throne of g, exalted from the beginning
33: 9 shall be my joy, my praise, my g,
48: 2 Moab's g is no more.
48:18 Come down from g, sit on the ground,
49: 4 Why do you g in your strength,
49:25 How can the city of g be forsaken,
51:41 made captive, the g of the whole world!

Lam 1: 6 Gone from daughter Zion is all her g;
2: 1 down from heaven to earth the g of Israel,
Bar 2:17 will give g and vindication to the Lord.
2:18 soul, will declare your g and justice,
4: 3 Give not your g to another,
4:24 g and the splendor of the Eternal God.
4:37 of the Holy One, rejoicing in the g of God.
5: 1 put on the splendor of g from God forever:
5: 2 that displays the g of the eternal name.
5: 4 peace of justice, the g of God's worship.
5: 6 you borne aloft in g as on royal thrones.
5: 7 Israel may advance secure in the g of God.
5: 9 g with his mercy and justice for company.
Ez 1:28 of the likeness of the g of the LORD.
3:12 as the g of the LORD rose from its place:
3:23 g of the LORD was in that place, like the g
8: 4 I saw there the g of the God of Israel,
10: 2 The g of the God of Israel had gone up
10: 4 and the g of the LORD rose from over the
10: 4 court was bright with the g of the LORD.
10:18 Then the g of the LORD left the threshold
10:19 g of the God of Israel was up above them.
11:22 above them was the g of the God of Israel.
11:23 And the g of the LORD rose from the city
31:18 equal in g or size among the trees of Eden?
32:12 They shall lay waste the g of Egypt,
39:13 and gain renown for it, when I reveal my g,
39:21 Thus I will display my g among the nations,
43: 2 and there I saw the g of the God of Israel
43: 2 waters, and the earth shone with his g.
43: 4 I fell prone as the g of the LORD entered
43: 5 temple was filled with the g of the LORD.
44: 4 g of the LORD filling the LORD's temple,
Dn 2:37 given dominion and strength, power and g;
3:43 by your wonders, and bring g to your name,
3:53 are you in the temple of your holy g,
4:33 to me, and for the g of my kingdom,
5:20 his royal throne and deprived of his g;
7:14 before him, He received dominion, g,
11:38 he shall give g to the god of strongholds;
Hos 4: 7 against me, exchanging their g for shame.
9:11 The g of Ephraim flies away like a bird:
10: 5 it, because the g has departed from it.
Mi 1:15 Even to Adullam shall go the g of Israel.
Hb 2:14 of the LORD's g as water covers the sea.
2:16 You are filled with shame instead of g;
2:16 right hand, and utter shame on your g.
3: 3 Covered are the heavens with his g,
Hg 1: 8 I may take pleasure in it and receive my g,
2: 3 you that saw this house in its former g?
2: 7 come in, And I will fill this house with g,
2: 9 the future g of this house than the former,
Zec 2: 9 the LORD, and I will be the g in her midst."
11: 3 of the shepherds, their g has been ruined.
12: 7 g of the house of David and the g
Mal 2: 2 not lay it to heart, to give g to my name,
Mt 16:27 his Father's g accompanied by his angels.
19:28 his seat upon a throne befitting his g,
24:30 clouds of heaven' with power and great g.
25:31 "When the Son of Man comes in his g,
Mk 8:38 with the holy angels in his Father's g."
10:37 at your left, when you come into your g."
13:26 in the clouds with great power and g.
16:20 and immortal g of justification in heaven."
Lk 2: 9 as the g of the Lord shone around them,
2:14 God and saying, G to God in high heaven,
2:32 the Gentiles, the g of your people Israel."
4: 6 all this power and the g of these kingdoms;
9:26 be ashamed of him when he comes in his g
9:31 appeared in g and spoke of his passage,
9:32 they saw his g and likewise saw the two
18:43 and began to follow him, giving God the g.
19:38 Peace in heaven and g in the highest!"
21:27 coming on a cloud with great power and g.
23:47 what had happened, gave g to God by saying,
24:26 undergo all this so as to enter into his g?"
Jn 1:14 dwelling among us, and we have seen his g:
1:14 g of an only Son coming from the Father,
2:11 Thus did he reveal his g,
5:44 seek the g that comes from the One [God]?
7:18 seeks g for him who sent him is truthful;
8:50 I seek no g for myself:
8:54 I glorify myself, that g comes to nothing.
8:54 He who gives me g is the Father,
9:24 blind and said to him, "Give g to God!
11: 4 rather it is for God's g,
11:40 you would see the g of God displayed?"
12:41 these words because he had seen Jesus' g,
12:43 the praise of men to the g of God.
16:14 In doing this he will give g to me,
17: 1 Give g to your Son that your Son may give g
17: 4 I have given you g on earth by finishing
17: 5 give me g at your side, a g I had with you
17:22 the g you gave me that they may be one,
17:24 this g of mine which is your gift to me,
Acts 7: 2 The God of g appeared to our father
7:55 to the sky above and saw the g of God,
Rom 1:23 they exchanged the g of the immortal God
2: 7 eternal life to those who strive for g,
2:10 But there will be g, honor, and peace
3: 7 light God's truth and thus promotes his g,
3:23 sinned and are deprived of the g of God.
4:20 strengthened in faith and gave g to God,

5: 2 and we boast of our hope for the g of God.
6: 4 from the dead by the g of the Father,
8:18 compared with the g to be revealed in us.
9: 4 Theirs were the adoption, the g,
9:23 make known the riches of his g
9:23 mercy, and which he prepared for g—
11:13 of the Gentiles, I g in my ministry,
11:36 To him be g forever.
15: 7 as Christ accepted you, for the g of God.
15:11 the Lord, all you Gentiles and sing his g,
15:17 This means I can take g in Christ Jesus
16:27 may g be given through Jesus Christ unto
1Cor 2: 7 God planned it before all ages for our g.
2: 8 would never have crucified the Lord of g.
10:31 you should do all for the g of God.
11: 7 image of God and the reflection of his g.
11: 7 in turn, is the reflection of man's g.
11:14 while the long hair of a woman is her g?
2Cor 3: 7 was inaugurated with such g that the
3: 7 Moses' face because of the g that shone
3: 7 on it (even though it was a fading g),
3: 8 be the g of the ministry of the Spirit?
3: 9 condemned had g, greater by far is the g
3:10 that limited glory with this surpassing g,
3:10 the former should be declared no g at all.
3:11 was given in g, greater by far is the glory
3:13 could not see the final fading of that g.
3:18 gazing on the Lord's g with unveiled faces,
3:18 from glory to g into his very image
4: 4 the gospel showing forth the g of Christ,
4: 6 the g of God shining on the face of Christ.
4:15 abundance may bring greater g to God
4:17 eternal weight of g beyond all comparison.
8:19 this work of charity for the g of the Lord.
8:23 apostles of the churches, the g of Christ.
Gal 1: 5 to him be g for endless ages.
1:24 and they gave g to God on my account.
Eph 1:12 his g by being the first to hope in Christ.
1:14 God has made his own, to praise his g.
1:17 of our Lord Jesus Christ, the Father of g,
3:13 they are your g.
3:16 gifts in keeping with the riches of his g.
3:21 to him be g in the church and in Christ
Phil 1:11 ripened in you, to the g and praise of God.
2:11 tongue proclaim to the g of God the Father:
3: 3 spirit of God and g in Christ Jesus
3:19 their belly and their g is in their shame.
4:20 g to our God and Father for unending ages!
Col 1:11 By the might of his g you will be endowed
1:27 make known to them the g beyond price
1:27 mystery of Christ in you, your hope of g.
3: 4 then you shall appear with him in g.
1Thes 2: 6 Neither did we seek g from men,
2:12 God who calls you to his kingship and g.
2Thes 1: 9 g of his might on the Day when he comes,
2:14 achieve the g of our Lord Jesus Christ.
1Tm 1:17 only God, be honor and g forever and ever!
3:16 in throughout the world, taken up into g."
2Tm 2:10 in Christ Jesus and with it eternal g.
4:18 To him be g forever and ever.
Ti 2:13 the appearing of the g of the great God
Heb 1: 3 Son is the reflection of the Father's g,
2: 7 you crowned him with g and honor,
2: 9 with g and honor because he suffered death:
2:10 that when bringing many sons to g God,
9: 5 of g overshadowing the place of expiation.
13:21 To Christ be g forever!
1Pt 1: 7 may by its genuineness lead to praise, g,
1: 8 g because you are achieving faith's goal,
1:21 raised him from the dead and gave him g.
1:24 g of men is like the flower of the field.
2:12 may give g to God on the day of visitation.
4:11 him be g and dominion throughout the ages.
4:13 When his g is revealed,
4:14 Spirit in its g has come to rest on you.
5: 1 and sharer in the g that is to be revealed,
5: 4 win for yourselves the unfading crown of g.
5:10 called you to his everlasting g in Christ,
2Pt 1: 3 him who called us by his own g and power.
1:17 He received g and praise from God the
3:18 G be to him now and to the day of eternity!
Jude 1:24 and exultant in the presence of his g.
1:25 G be to this only God our savior,
Rv 1: 6 to him be g and power forever and ever!
4: 9 Whenever these creatures give g and honor
4:11 worthy to receive g and honor and power!
5:12 and strength, honor and g and praise!"
5:13 the Lamb, be praise and honor, g and might,
7:12 Praise and g, wisdom and thanksgiving
14: 7 "Honor God and give him g,
15: 4 refuse you honor, or the g due your name,
15: 8 smoke which arose from God's g
18: 1 that all the earth was lighted up by his g.
19: 1 Salvation, g and might belong to our God,
19: 7 Let us rejoice and be glad, and give him g!
21:23 or moon, for the g of God gave it light,

GLOSSING (1)

Jb 13: 4 You are g over falsehoods and offering

GLOW (2)

2Mc 12: 9 so that the g of the flames was visible as

Ps(s) 78:14 by day, and all night with a *g* of fire.

GLOWED (1)

Est D: 4 She *g* with the perfection of her beauty

GLOWING (2)

Lv 16:12 of *g* embers from the altar before the LORD,
Is 18: 4 I dwell, Like the *g* heat of sunshine,

GLOWS (1)

Ez 24:11 on the coals till its metal *g* red hot,

GLUING (1)

Sir 22: 7 Teaching a fool is like *g* a broken pot,

GLUM (1)

Mt 6:16 you are not to look *g* as the hypocrites do.

GLUTTED (3)

Prv 1:31 own way, and with their own devices be *g.*
25:16 lest you become *g* with it and vomit it up.
30:22 king, and a fool when he is *g* with food;

GLUTTON (7)

Dt 21:20 he is a *g* and a drunkard.'
Prv 23:21 For the drunkard and the *g* come to poverty,
Sir 18:33 Become not a *g* and a winebibber with
31:20 of sleep, and restless tossing for the *g!*
37:28 neither become a *g* for choice foods,
Mt 11:19 they say, 'This one is a *g* and drunkard,
Lk 7:34 and you say, 'Here is a *g* and a drunkard,

GLUTTONS (2)

Prv 28: 7 but the *g'* companion disgraces his father.
Ti 1:12 have ever been liars, beasts, and lazy *g,"*

GLUTTONY (2)

Sir 31:13 Remember that *g* is evil.
37:29 overeating, and *g* brings on biliousness.

GNASH (2)

Ps(s) 112:10 he shall *g* his teeth and pine away;
Lam 2:16 They hiss and *g* their teeth.

GNASHES (2)

Jb 16: 9 wrath assails, he *g* his teeth against me.
Ps(s) 37:12 against the just and *g* his teeth at them;

GNASHING (1)

Ps(s) 35:16 they mocked me, *g* their teeth at me.

GNAT (1)

Mt 23:24 You strain out the *g* and swallow the camel!

GNATS (8)

Ex 8:12 turned into *g* throughout the land of Egypt."
8:13 of the earth and *g* came upon man and beast.
8:13 turned into *g* throughout the land of Egypt.
8:14 tried to bring forth *g* by their magic arts,
8:14 As the *g* infested man and beast,
Ps(s) 105:31 there came swarms of flies; *g,*
Wis 19:10 young of animals the land brought forth *g,*
Sir 10:11 worms and *g* and maggots.

GNAW (2)

Ez 23:34 dry, and *g* at the very sherds of the cup,
Zep 3: 3 that have had no bones to *g* by morning.

GNAWS (2)

Prv 25:20 in wood, sorrow *g* at the human heart.
Jer 50:17 now Nebuchadnezzar of Babylon *g* her bones.

GOAD (2)

Sir 38:25 who thrills in wielding the *g* like a lance,
Acts 26:14 It is hard for you to kick against the *g.'*

GOADS (1)

Eccl 12:11 The sayings of the wise are like *g;*

GOAH (1)

Jer 31:39 to the hill Gareb and then turn to *G.*

GOAL (6)

Jos 1: 8 then you will successfully attain your *g.*
Sir 35:17 it does not rest till it reaches its *g,*
43:13 the arrows of his judgment to their *g.*
Jer 50: 5 to their *g* in Zion they shall ask the way.
1Tm 6:21 some men have missed the *g* of faith.
1Pt 1: 9 glory because you are achieving faith's *g,*

GOAT (60)

Gn 30:33 that is not a speckled or spotted *g,*
37:31 Joseph's tunic, and after slaughtering a *g,*
Ex 25: 4 fine linen and *g* hair;
26: 7 "Also make sheets woven of *g* hair,
35: 6 fine linen and *g* hair;
35:23 or scarlet yarn, fine linen or *g* hair,
35:26 women who possessed the skill, spun *g* hair.
36:14 Sheets of *g* hair were also woven as a tent
Lv 1:10 is from the flock, that is, a sheep or a *g,*
3:12 "If he presents a *g,*
4:23 as his offering an unblemished male *g.*
4:24 the *g* as a sin offering before the LORD,
7:23 not eat the fat of any ox or sheep or *g.*
9:15 *g* that was for the people's sin offering,
10:16 inquired about the *g* of the sin offering,
11:32 article of wood, cloth, leather or *g* hair,
16: 9 *g* that is determined by lot for the LORD,
16:10 But the *g* determined by lot for Azazel he
16:15 slaughter the people's sin-offering *g,*
16:20 Aaron shall bring forward the live *g.*
16:22 Since the *g* is to carry off their
16:26 "The man who has led away the *g* for
16:27 The sin-offering bullock and *g* whose blood
17: 3 who slaughters an ox or a sheep or *g,*
22:19 the ox or sheep or *g* that he offers must
22:27 "When an ox or a lamb or a *g* is born,
23:19 *g* shall be sacrificed as a sin offering,
Nm 7:16 one *g* for a sin offering;
7:22 one *g* for a sin offering;
7:28 one *g* for a sin offering;
7:34 one *g* for a sin offering;
7:40 one *g* for a sin offering;
7:46 one *g* for a sin offering;
7:52 one *g* for a sin offering;
7:58 one *g* for a sin offering;
7:64 one *g* for a sin offering;
7:70 one *g* for a sin offering;
7:76 one *g* for a sin offering;
7:82 one *g* for a sin offering;
15:11 is to be done for each ox, ram, lamb or *g.*
28:15 one *g* shall be sacrificed as a sin
28:22 and offer one *g* as a sin offering in
28:30 one *g* shall be offered as a sin offering
29: 5 one *g* shall be offered as a sin offering
29:11 *g* shall be sacrificed as a sin offering.
29:16 *g* shall be sacrificed as a sin offering.
29:19 as well as one *g* for a sin offering,
29:22 as well as one *g* for a sin offering,
29:25 as well as one *g* for a sin offering,
29:28 as well as one *g* for a sin offering,
29:31 as well as one *g* for a sin offering,
29:34 as well as one *g* for a sin offering,
29:38 as well as one *g* for a sin offering,
Dt 14: 4 the ox, the sheep, the *g,*
1Sm 24: 3 men in the direction of the wild *g* crags.
Tb 2:12 and also gave her a young *g* for the table.
2:13 On entering my house the *g* began to bleat.
2:13 "Where did this *g* come from?
Ez 45:23 he shall offer one male *g* each day.
Lk 15:29 as a kid *g* to celebrate with my friends.

GOATS (52)

Gn 30:32 every spotted or speckled one among the *g.*
30:39 came to drink, the *g* mated by the rods,
Ex 12: 5 may take it from either the sheep or the *g.*
Lv 16: 5 he shall receive two male *g* for a sin offering
16: 7 Taking the two male *g* and setting them
16:18 some of the bullock's and the *g* blood,
16:21 Israelites, and so put them on the *g* head.
Nm 7:17 and two oxen, five rams, five *g,*
7:23 and two oxen, five rams, five *g,*
7:29 and two oxen, five rams, five *g,*
7:35 and two oxen, five rams, five *g,*
7:41 and two oxen, five rams, five *g,*
7:47 and two oxen, five rams, five *g,*
7:53 and two oxen, five rams, five *g,*
7:59 and two oxen, five rams, five *g,*
7:65 and two oxen, five rams, five *g,*
7:71 and two oxen, five rams, five *g,*
7:77 and two oxen, five rams, five *g,*
7:83 and two oxen, five rams, five *g,*
7:87 those for the sin offerings were twelve *g.*
7:88 all, twenty-four oxen, sixty rams, sixty *g,*
18:17 cattle, sheep or *g* shall not be redeemed;
31:20 every article of cloth, leather, *g'* hair,
Dt 32:14 Its Bashan bulls and its *g,*
1Sm 19:13 putting a net of *g* hair at its head and
19:16 bed, with the net of *g* hair at its head.
25: 2 three thousand sheep and a thousand *g.*
1Kgs 20:27 seemed like a couple of small flocks of *g,*
Ezr 8:35 lambs, and twelve *g* as sin-offerings:
Jdt 2:17 sheep, cattle, and *g* for their food supply;
Jb 39: 1 know about the birth of the mountain *g,*
Ps(s) 50: 9 house no bullock, no *g* out of your fold.
50:13 bulls, or is the blood of *g* my drink?
66:15 I will sacrifice oxen and *g.*
104:18 The high mountains are for wild *g;*
Prv 27:26 and the *g* will bring the price of a field,
27:27 there will be ample *g* milk to supply you,
Sg 4: 1 *g* streaming down the mountains of Gilead.
6: 5 a flock of *g* streaming down from Gilead.
Is 1:11 of calves, lambs and *g* I find no pleasure.
34: 6 with fat, With the blood of lambs and *g,*
Jer 51:40 lambs to the slaughter, like rams and *g.*
Ez 27:21 they dealt in lambs, rams, and *g.*
34:17 one sheep and another, between rams and *g.*
39:18 princes of the land [rams, lambs, and *g,*
Mt 25:32 as a shepherd separates sheep from *g.*
25:33 place on his right hand, the *g* on his left.
Heb 9:12 not with the blood of *g* and calves,
9:13 For if the blood of *g* and bulls and the
9:19 people, he took the blood of *g* and calves,
10: 4 the blood of bulls and *g* to take sins away
11:37 about garbed in the skins of sheep or *g,*

GOATS-HAIR (1)

Rv 6:12 *g* tentcloth and the moon grew red as blood.

GOB (2)

2Sm 21:18 another battle with the Philistines in *G.*
21:19 another battle with the Philistines in *G,*

GOBLET (6)

Gn 44: 2 youngest one's bag put also my silver *g,*
44: 4 Why did you steal the silver *g* from me?
44: 9 of your servants is found to have the *g,*
44:12 the *g* turned up in Benjamin's bag.
44:16 one in whose possession the *g* was found."
44:17 the *g* was found shall become my slave;

GOD (4588)

Gn 1: 1 when *G* created the heavens and the earth,
1: 3 *G* said, "Let there be light,"
1: 4 *G* saw how good the light was.
1: 4 *G* then separated the light from the
1: 5 *G* called the light "day,"
1: 6 *G* said, "Let there be a dome
1: 7 *G* made the dome,
1: 8 *G* called the dome "the sky."
1: 9 *G* said, "Let the water under the sky
1:10 *G* called the dry land "the earth,"
1:10 *G* saw how good it was.
1:11 *G* said, "Let the earth bring forth
1:12 *G* saw how good it was.
1:14 *G* said: "Let there be lights in the dome
1:16 *G* made the two great lights,
1:17 *G* set them in the dome of the sky,
1:18 *G* saw how good it was.
1:20 *G* said, "Let the water teem with
1:21 *G* created the great sea monsters and all
1:21 *G* saw how good it was,
1:22 saw how good it was, and *G* blessed them,
1:24 *G* said, "Let the earth bring forth
1:25 *G* made all kinds of wild animals,
1:25 *G* saw how good it was.
1:26 Then *G* said: "Let us make man
1:27 *G* created man in his image;
1:28 *G* blessed them, saying: "Be fertile
1:29 *G* also said: "See, I give you
1:31 *G* looked at everything he had made,
2: 2 Since on the seventh day *G* was finished
2: 3 *G* blessed the seventh day and made it holy,
2: 4 the LORD *G* made the earth and the heavens
2: 5 for the LORD *G* had sent no rain upon the
2: 7 the LORD *G* formed man out of the clay of
2: 8 Then the LORD *G* planted a garden in Eden,
2: 9 Out of the ground the LORD *G* made various
2:15 The LORD *G* then took the man and settled
2:16 The LORD *G* gave man this order:
2:18 The LORD *G* said: "It is not good
2:19 So the LORD *G* formed out of the ground
2:21 So the LORD *G* cast a deep sleep on the man,
2:22 The LORD *G* then built up into a woman the
3: 1 all the animals that the LORD *G* had made.
3: 1 "Did *G* really tell you not to eat from
3: 3 in the middle of the garden that *G* said,
3: 5 *G* knows well that the moment you eat of it
3: 8 When they heard the sound of the LORD *G*
3: 8 the LORD *G* among the trees of the garden.
3: 9 *G* then called to the man and asked him,
3:13 The LORD *G* then asked the woman,
3:14 Then the LORD *G* said to the serpent:
3:21 his wife the LORD *G* made leather garments,
3:22 *G* said: "See! The man has become like
3:23 The LORD *G* therefore banished him from the
4: 3 to the LORD *G* from the fruit of the soil,
4:25 *G* has granted me more offspring in place
5: 1 When *G* created man,
5: 1 man, he made him in the likeness of *G;*
5:24 with *G,* and he was no longer here, for *G*
6:10 in that age, for he walked with *G,*
6:11 In the eyes of *G* the earth was corrupt and
6:12 *G* saw how corrupt the earth had become,
6:22 out all the commands that *G* gave him.
7:16 species they came, as *G* had commanded Noah.
8: 1 then *G* remembered Noah and all the animals,
8: 1 So *G* made a wind sweep over the earth,
8:15 Then *G* said to Noah:
9: 1 *G* blessed Noah and his sons and said to
9: 6 For in the image of *G* has man been made.
9: 8 *G* said to Noah and to his sons with him:
9:12 *G* added: "This is the sign
9:16 between *G* and all living beings
9:17 *G* told Noah: "This is the sign
9:26 "Blessed be the LORD, the *G* of Shem!
9:27 May *G* expand Japheth,

GOD (cont.)

14:18 wine, and being a priest of G Most High,
14:19 "Blessed be Abram by G Most High,
14:20 And blessed be G Most High,
14:22 "I have sworn to the LORD, G Most High,
15: 2 But Abram said, "O Lord G,
15: 8 "O Lord G,"
16:11 the LORD has heard you, G has answered you.
16:13 name, saying, "You are the G of Vision";
16:13 seen G and remained alive after my vision?"
17: 1 "I am G the Almighty.
17: 3 himself, G continued to speak to him:
17: 7 to be your G and the God of your
17: 8 and I will be their G."
17: 9 G also said to Abraham:
17:15 G further said to Abraham:
17:18 Then Abraham said to G,
17:19 G replied: "Nevertheless, your wife
17:19 G and the God of his descendants after him.
17:22 speaking with him, G departed from Abraham.
17:23 on that same day, as G had told him to do.
19:29 when G destroyed the Cities of the Plain,
19:29 upheaval by which G overthrew the cities
20: 3 But G came to Abimelech in a dream one
20: 6 G answered him in the dream:
20:11 would surely be no fear of G in this place,
20:13 G sent me wandering from my father's house,
20:17 God, and G restored health to Abimelech,
20:18 for G had tightly closed every womb in
21: 2 old age, at the set time that G had stated.
21: 4 circumcised him, as G had commanded.
21: 6 then said, G has given me cause to laugh,
21:12 But G said to Abraham:
21:17 G heard the boy's cry,
21:17 G has heard the boy's cry in this plight
21:19 Then G opened her eyes,
21:20 G was with the boy as he grew up.
21:22 G is with you in everything you do.
21:23 swear to me by G at this place that you
21:33 he invoked by name the LORD, G the Eternal.
22: 1 these events, G put Abraham to the test.
22: 2 Then G said: "Take your son Isaac,
22: 3 out for the place of which G had told him.
22: 8 G himself will provide the sheep for the
22: 9 came to the place of which G had told him,
22:12 I know now how devoted you are to G,
23: 6 You are an elect of G among us.
24: 3 LORD, the God of heaven and the G of earth,
24: 7 "The LORD, the G of heaven,
24:12 "LORD, G of my master Abraham,
24:27 be the LORD, the G of my master Abraham,
24:42 'LORD, G of my master Abraham,
24:48 the LORD, the G of my master Abraham,
25:11 death of Abraham, G blessed his son Isaac,
26:24 "I am the G of your father Abraham.
27:20 He answered, "The LORD, your G,
27:28 "May G give to you of the dew of the
28: 3 G Almighty bless you and make you fertile,
28:13 G of your forefather Abraham and the G
28:17 This is nothing else but an abode of G,
28:20 "If G remains with me,
28:21 my father's house, the LORD shall be my G.
30: 2 retorted, "Can I take the place of G,
30: 6 a son, Rachel said, G has vindicated me;
30:17 he slept with her, and G heard her prayer;
30:18 G has given me my reward for having let my
30:20 she said, G has brought me a precious gift.
30:22 Then G remembered Rachel;
30:23 and she said, G has removed my disgrace."
30:27 it is because of you that G has blessed me.
31: 5 but the G of my father has been with me.
31: 7 G, however,
31: 9 Thus G reclaimed your father's livestock
31:13 I am the G who appeared to you in Bethel,
31:16 All the wealth that G reclaimed from our
31:16 Therefore, do just as G has told you."
31:24 But that night G appeared to Laban the
31:29 last night the G of your father said to me,
31:42 If my ancestral G, the God of Abraham
31:42 G saw my plight and the fruits of my toil,
31:50 G will be witness between you and me."
31:53 May the G of Abraham and the god of Nahor
32:10 "O G of my father Abraham and God of my
32:31 "Because I have seen G face to face,"
33: 5 "They are the children whom G has
33:10 me like coming into the presence of G,
33:11 G has been generous toward me,
33:20 there and invoked "El, the G of Israel."
35: 1 G said to Jacob: "Go up now to Bethel.
35: 1 build an altar there to the G
35: 3 G who answered me in my hour of distress
35: 5 from G fell upon the towns round about,
35: 7 for it was there that G had revealed
35: 9 G appeared to him again and blessed him.
35:10 G said to him: "You whose name is Jacob
35:11 G also said to him: "I am G Almighty
35:13 Then G departed from him.
35:14 On the site where G had spoken with him,
35:15 because G had spoken with him there.
39: 9 a wrong and thus stand condemned before G?"
40: 8 "Surely, interpretations come from G.
41:16 G who will give Pharaoh the right answer."
41:25 G has thus foretold to Pharaoh what he is
41:28 G has revealed to Pharaoh what he is about
41:32 by God and that G will soon bring it about.
41:38 "a man so endowed with the spirit of G?"
41:39 "Since G has made all this known to you,
41:51 G has made me forget entirely the
41:52 G has made me fruitful in the land of my
42:28 "What is this that G has done to us?"
43:14 May G Almighty dispose the man to be
43:23 Your God and the G of your father must
43:29 he said to him, "May G be gracious to you,
44:16 G has uncovered your servants' guilt.
45: 5 lives that G sent me here ahead of you.
45: 7 G, therefore,
45: 8 not really you but G who had me come here;
45: 9 G has made me lord of all Egypt;
46: 1 sacrifices to the G of his father Isaac.
46: 2 There G,
46: 3 "I am G, the God of your father.
48: 3 G Almighty appeared to me at Luz in the
48: 9 his father, "whom G has given me here."
48:11 and now G has allowed me to see your
48:15 "May the G in whose ways my fathers
48:15 The G who has been my shepherd from my
48:20 say, G make you like Ephraim and Manasseh,'"
48:21 But G will be with you and will restore
49:25 God of your father, who helps you, G
50:17 that we, the servants of your father's G,
50:19 Can I take the place of G?
50:20 you meant harm to me, G meant it for good,
50:24 G will surely take care of you and lead
50:25 continued, "When G thus takes care of you,
Ex 1:17 The midwives, however, feared G;
1:20 Therefore G dealt well with the midwives.
1:21 And because the midwives feared G,
2:23 As their cry for release went up to G,
3: 1 he came to Horeb, the mountain of G.
3: 4 closely, G called out to him from the bush,
3: 5 G said, "Come no nearer!
3: 6 I am the G of your father,"
3: 6 "the G of Abraham, the G of Isaac, the G
3: 6 his face, for he was afraid to look at G.
3:11 But Moses said to G,
3:12 you will worship G on this very mountain."
3:13 "But," said Moses to G,
3:13 'The G of your fathers has sent me to you,'
3:14 G replied, "I am who am."
3:15 G spoke further to Moses,
3:15 The LORD, the G of your fathers,
3:15 G of Abraham, the G of Isaac, the G
3:16 the God of your fathers, the G of Abraham,
3:18 The LORD, the G of the Hebrews,
3:18 we may offer sacrifice to the LORD, our G.
4: 5 "that the LORD, the G of their fathers,
4: 5 G of Abraham, the G of Isaac, the G
4:16 spokesman, and you shall be as G to him.
4:20 The staff of G he carried with him.
4:26 Then G let Moses go.
4:27 and when they met at the mountain of G,
5: 1 "Thus says the LORD, the G of Israel:
5: 3 "The G of the Hebrews has sent us word.
5: 3 we may offer sacrifice to the LORD, our G;
5: 8 'Let us go to offer sacrifice to our G.'
6: 2 G also said to Moses, "I am the LORD.
6: 3 As G the Almighty I appeared to Abraham,
6: 7 people, and you shall have me as your G.
6: 7 am your G when I free you from the labor
7: 1 I have made you as G to Pharaoh,
7:16 The LORD, the G of the Hebrews,
8: 6 that there is none like the LORD, our G.
8:15 said to Pharaoh, "This is the finger of G."
8:21 and offer sacrifice to your G in this land."
8:22 the sacrifices we offer to the LORD, our G,
8:23 to offer sacrifice to the LORD, our G,
8:24 go to offer sacrifice to the LORD your G,
9: 1 Thus says the LORD, the G of the Hebrews:
9:13 Thus says the LORD, the G of the Hebrews:
9:30 I know, do not yet fear the LORD G."
10: 3 "Thus says the LORD, the G of the Hebrews:
10: 7 the men go to worship the LORD, their G.
10: 8 "You may go and worship the LORD, your G.
10:16 "I have sinned against the LORD, your G,
10:17 sin once more, and pray the LORD, your G,
10:25 holocausts to offer up to the LORD, our G.
10:26 them we must sacrifice to the LORD our G,
13: 5 this rite, after the LORD, your G,
13:11 "When the LORD, your G,
13:17 G did not lead them by way of the
13:19 solomnly that, when G should come to them,
14:19 The angel of G,
15: 2 my G, I praise him; the God of my father
15:26 listen to the voice of the LORD, your G,"
16:12 you may know that I, the LORD, am your G."
17: 9 of the hill with the staff of G in my hand."
18: 1 heard of all that G had done for Moses and
18: 4 for he said, "My father's G is my helper;
18: 5 he was encamped near the mountain of G,
18:12 a holocaust and other sacrifices to G,
18:12 Moses' father-in-law in the meal before G.
18:15 "The people come to me to consult G.
18:19 you some advice, that G may be with you.
18:19 as the people's representative before G,
18:23 when G gives you orders you will be able
19: 3 mountain, Moses went up the mountain to G.
19:17 led the people out of the camp to meet G,
19:19 speaking and G answering him with thunder.
20: 1 Then G delivered all these commandments:
20: 2 "I, the LORD, am your G,
20: 5 For I, the LORD, your God, am a jealous G,
20: 7 not take the name of the LORD, your G,
20:10 day is the sabbath of the LORD, your G.
20:12 life in the land which the LORD, your G,
20:19 but let not G speak to us,
20:20 for G has come to you only to test you and
20:21 Moses approached the cloud where G was.
21: 6 his master shall bring him to G and there,
21:13 down, but caused his death by an act of G,
22: 7 owner of the house shall be brought to G,
22: 8 before God; the one whom G convicts
22:19 "Whoever sacrifices to any g,
22:27 "You shall not revile G,
23:13 "Never mention the name of any other g;
23:17 all your men appear before the Lord G.
23:19 bring to the house of the LORD, your G.
23:25 The LORD, your G,
24:10 of Israel, and they beheld the G of Israel.
24:11 After gazing on G, they could still eat
24:13 his aide, and went up to the mountain of G.
29:45 of the Israelites and will be their G.
29:46 am their G who brought them out of the
29:46 the land of Egypt, so I, the LORD, their G,
32: 1 "Come, make us a g who will be our leader;
32: 4 Then they cried out, "This is your G,
32: 8 to it and crying out, 'This is your G,
32:11 But Moses implored the LORD, his G,
32:16 tablets that were made by G,
32:16 on them that were engraved by G himself.
32:23 said to me, 'Make us a g to be our leader;
32:27 "Thus says the LORD, the G of Israel:
32:31 sin in making a g of gold for themselves!
34: 6 LORD, the LORD, a merciful and gracious G,
34:14 You shall not worship any other g,
34:14 a jealous G is he.
34:23 before the Lord, the LORD G of Israel.
34:24 a year to appear before the LORD, your G.
34:26 bring to the house of the LORD, your G.
Lv 2:13 G be lacking from your cereal offering.
4:22 by some commandment of the LORD, his G,
11:44 For I, the LORD, am your G;
11:45 the land of Egypt that I might be your G,
18: 2 I, the LORD, am your G.
18: 4 I, the LORD, am your G.
18:21 Molech, thus profaning the name of your G.
18:30 I, the LORD, am your G."
19: 2 Be holy, for I, the LORD your G, am holy.
19: 3 I, the LORD, am your G.
19: 4 I, the LORD, am your G.
19:10 I, the LORD, am your G.
19:12 my name, thus profaning the name of your G.
19:14 of the blind, but you shall fear your G.
19:25 I, the LORD, am your G.
19:31 I, the LORD, am your G.
19:32 thus shall you fear your G.
19:34 I, the LORD, am your G.
19:36 I, the LORD, am your G,
20: 7 for I, the LORD, your G,
20:24 to you as your own, I, the LORD, your G,
21: 6 To their G they shall be sacred,
21: 6 oblations of the LORD, the food of their G,
21: 7 for the priest is sacred to his G.
21: 8 sacred who offers up the food of your G;
21:12 he will profane the sanctuary of his G,
21:12 oil upon him, he is dedicated to his G,
21:17 come forward to offer up the food of his G.
21:21 draw near to offer up the food of his G.
21:22 may, however, partake of the food of his G:
22:25 animals to offer up as the food of your G;
22:33 Egypt, that I, the LORD, might be your G."
23:14 day, when you bring your G this offering,
23:22 I, the LORD, am your G."
23:28 is made for you before the LORD, your G.
23:40 shall make merry before the LORD, your G.
23:43 I, the LORD, am your G."
24:15 his G shall bear the penalty of his sin;
24:22 I, the LORD, am your G."
25:17 but stand in fear of your G.
25:17 I, the LORD, am your G.
25:36 but out of fear of G let him live with you.
25:38 I, the LORD, am your G,
25:38 you the land of Canaan and to be your G.
25:43 them harshly, but stand in fear of your G.
25:55 of the land of Egypt, I, the LORD, your G.
26: 1 for I, the LORD, am your G.
26:12 present in your midst, I will be your G,
26:13 for it is I, the LORD, your G,
26:44 for I, the LORD, am their G.
26:45 that I, the LORD, might be their G."
Nm 6: 7 since his head bears his dedication to G.
10: 9 on the trumpets, and the LORD, your G,
10:10 serve as a reminder of you before your G.
10:10 I, the LORD, am your G."
15:40 all my commandments and be holy to your G.
15:41 I, the LORD, am your God who, as G,
15:41 of Egypt that I, the LORD, may be your G."
16: 9 Is it too little for you that the G of
16:22 "O God, G of the spirits of all mankind,
21: 5 the people complained against G and Moses,

22: 9 Then *G* came to Balaam and said,
22:10 Balaam answered *G*,
22:12 But *G* said to Balaam,
22:18 contrary to the command of the LORD, my *G*.
22:20 night *G* came to Balaam and said to him,
22:22 the anger of *G* flared up at him for going,
22:38 I can speak only what *G* puts in my mouth."
23: 4 out on the barren height, and *G* met him.
23: 8 How can I curse whom *G* has not cursed?
23:19 *G* is not man that he should speak falsely,
23:21 The LORD, his *G*,
23:22 It is *G* who brought him out of Egypt,
23:23 and of Israel, "Behold what *G* has wrought!"
23:27 perhaps *G* will approve of your cursing
24: 2 by tribe, the spirit of *G* came upon him,
24: 4 The utterance of one who hears what *G* says,
24: 8 It is *G* who brought him out of Egypt,
24:16 The utterance of one who hears what *G* says,
25: 2 the people to the sacrifices of their *g*,
25: 2 of the sacrifices and worshiped their *g*.
25:13 because he was zealous on behalf of his *G*
27:16 LORD, the *G* of the spirits of all mankind,

Dt 1: 6 *G*, said to us at Horeb,
1:10 *G*, has so multiplied you
1:11 May the LORD, the *G* of your fathers,
1:19 to the command of the LORD, our *G*,
1:20 of the Amorites, which the LORD, our *G*,
1:21 *G*, has given this land over to you.
1:21 it, as the LORD, the *G* of your fathers,
1:25 reported, 'The land which the LORD, our *G*,
1:26 defying the command of the LORD, your *G*,
1:30 *G*, who goes before you,
1:31 where you saw how the LORD, your *G*,
1:32 you would not trust the LORD, your *G*,
1:41 and fight, just as the LORD, our *G*,
2: 7 *G*, has blessed you
2:29 Jordan into the land which the LORD, our *G*,
2:30 *G*, made him stubborn in mind
2:33 but since the LORD, our *G*,
2:37 to the command of the LORD, our *G*,
3: 3 *G*, delivered into our hands Og,
3:18 *G*, has given you this land
3:20 possess the land which the LORD, your *G*,
3:21 eyes have seen all that the LORD, your *G*,
3:22 Fear them not, for the LORD, your *G*,
3:24 then that I besought the LORD, 'O Lord *G*,
3:24 For what *g* in heaven or on earth can
4: 1 land which the LORD, the *G* of your fathers,
4: 2 of the commandments of the LORD, your *G*,
4: 3 *G*, destroyed from your midst everyone
4: 4 but you, who clung to the LORD, your *G*,
4: 5 statutes and decrees as the LORD, my *G*,
4: 7 has gods so close to it as the LORD, our *G*,
4:10 which you stood before the LORD, your *G*,
4:19 *G*, has let fall to the lot of all other nations
4:23 the covenant which the LORD, your *G*,
4:24 *G*, is a consuming fire, a jealous God.
4:25 in his sight provoke the LORD, your *G*,
4:29 there too you shall seek the LORD, your *G*;
4:30 shall finally return to the LORD, your *G*,
4:31 Since the LORD, your God, is a merciful *G*,
4:32 ever since *G* created man upon the earth;
4:33 voice of *G* speaking from the midst of fire,
4:34 Or did any *g* venture to go and take a
4:34 terrors, all of which the LORD, your *G*,
4:35 know the LORD is *G* and there is no other.
4:39 *G* in the heavens above and on earth below,
4:40 life on the land which the LORD, your *G*,
5: 2 *G*, made a covenant with us
5: 6 'I, the LORD, am your *G*,
5: 9 For I, the LORD, your God, am a jealous *G*,
5:11 not take the name of the LORD, your *G*,
5:12 holy the sabbath day as the LORD, your *G*,
5:14 day is the sabbath of the LORD, your *G*.
5:15 slaves in Egypt, and the LORD, your *G*,
5:15 That is why the LORD, your *G*,
5:16 father and mother, as the LORD, your *G*,
5:16 in the land which the LORD, your *G*,
5:24 and elders, and said, 'The LORD, our *G*,
5:24 can still live after *G* has spoken with him.
5:25 If we hear the voice of the LORD, our *G*,
5:26 living *G* speaking from the midst of fire,
5:27 you, and hear all that the LORD, our *G*,
5:27 say, and then tell us what the LORD, our *G*,
5:32 therefore, to do as the LORD, your *G*,
5:33 prescribed for you by the LORD, your *G*,
6: 1 and decrees which the LORD, your *G*,
6: 2 your grandson may fear the LORD, your *G*,
6: 3 promise of the LORD, the *G* of your fathers,
6: 4 The LORD is our *G*, the LORD alone!
6: 5 Therefore, you shall love the LORD, our *G*,
6:10 "When the LORD, your *G*,
6:13 *G*, shall you fear;
6:15 lest the wrath of the LORD, your *G*,
6:15 God, who is in your midst, is a jealous *G*.
6:16 "You shall not put the LORD, your *G*,
6:17 keep the commandments of the LORD, your *G*,
6:20 and decrees mean which the LORD, our *G*,
6:24 these statutes in fear of the LORD, our *G*,
6:25 and our justice before the LORD, our *G*,
7: 1 "When the LORD, your *G*,
7: 2 and when the LORD, your *G*,
7: 6 are a people sacred to the LORD, your *G*;
7: 9 your God, is *G* indeed, the faithful God
7:12 them carefully, the LORD, your *G*,
7:16 all the nations which the LORD, your *G*,
7:18 Rather, call to mind what the LORD, your *G*,
7:19 arm with which the LORD, your *G*,
7:20 Moreover, the LORD, your *G*,
7:21 terrified by them, for the LORD, your *G*,
7:21 is in your midst, is a great and awesome *G*.
7:23 *G*, will deliver them up to you
7:25 it is an abomination to the LORD, your *G*.
8: 2 how for forty years now the LORD, your *G*,
8: 5 So you must realize that the LORD, your *G*,
8: 6 keep the commandments of the LORD, your *G*,
8: 7 For the LORD, your *G*,
8:10 your fill, you must bless the LORD, your *G*,
8:11 Be careful not to forget the LORD, your *G*,
8:14 heart and unmindful of the LORD, your *G*,
8:18 Remember then, it is the LORD, your *G*,
8:19 But if you forget the LORD, your *G*,
8:20 not heeding the voice of the LORD, your *G*.
9: 3 then, today that it is the LORD, your *G*,
9: 4 *G*, has thrust them out of your way
9: 5 *G*, is driving these nations out before you
9: 6 of your merits that the LORD, your *G*,
9: 7 forget how you angered the LORD, your *G*,
9:16 you had sinned against the LORD, your *G*:
9:23 against this command of the LORD, your *G*,
9:26 *G*, destroy not your people
10: 9 in his heritage, as the LORD, your *G*,
10:12 now, Israel, what does the LORD, your *G*,
10:12 ask of you but to fear the LORD, your *G*,
10:12 to love and serve the LORD, your *G*,
10:14 heavens, belong to the LORD your *G*,
10:17 For the LORD, your God, is the *G* of gods,
10:17 the LORD of lords, the great *G*,
10:20 *G*, shall you fear, and him shall you serve
10:21 He is your glory, he, your *G*,
10:22 seventy strong, and now the LORD, your *G*,
11: 1 "Love the LORD, your *G*,
11: 2 the discipline of the LORD, your *G*;
11:12 heavens, a land which the LORD, your *G*,
11:13 loving and serving the LORD, your *G*,
11:22 I enjoin on you, loving the LORD, your *G*,
11:25 the LORD, your *G*,
11:27 the commandments of the LORD, your *G*,
11:28 obey the commandments of the LORD, your *G*,
11:29 When the LORD, your *G*,
11:31 and occupy the land which the LORD, your *G*,
12: 1 land which the LORD, the *G* of your fathers,
12: 4 not how you are to worship the LORD your *G*.
12: 5 to the place which the LORD, your *G*,
12: 7 There, too, before the LORD, your *G*,
12: 7 undertakings, because the LORD, your *G*,
12: 9 place, the heritage which the LORD, your *G*,
12:10 dwell in the land which the LORD, your *G*,
12:11 then to the place which the LORD, your *G*,
12:12 shall make merry before the LORD, your *G*,
12:15 desire as much meat as the LORD, your *G*,
12:18 you must eat before the LORD, your *G*,
12:20 "After the LORD, your *G*,
12:21 and if the place which the LORD, your *G*,
12:27 on the altar of the LORD, your *G*;
12:27 out against the altar of the LORD, your *G*,
12:28 and right in the sight of the LORD, your *G*.
12:29 "When the LORD, your *G*,
12:31 shall not thus worship the LORD, your *G*,
13: 4 *G*, is testing you to learn
13: 5 *G*, shall you follow, and him shall you fear;
13: 6 from the way which the LORD, your *G*,
13: 6 preached apostasy from the LORD, your *G*,
13:11 to lead you astray from the LORD, your *G*,
13:13 any of the cities which the LORD, your *G*,
13:17 a whole burnt offering to the LORD, your *G*.
13:19 have heeded the voice of the LORD, your *G*,
14: 1 "You are children of the LORD, your *G*.
14: 2 are a people sacred to the LORD, your *G*,
14:21 are a people sacred to the LORD, your *G*.
14:23 then in the place which the LORD, your *G*,
14:23 may learn always to fear the LORD, your *G*.
14:24 because the place which the LORD, your *G*,
14:25 go to the place which the LORD, your *G*,
14:26 enjoy, and there before the LORD, your *G*,
14:29 *G*, may bless you in all that you undertake
15: 4 *G*, will bless you abundantly in the land
15: 5 but heed the voice of the LORD, your *G*,
15: 6 will rule over you, since the LORD, your *G*,
15: 7 need in the land which the LORD, your *G*,
15:10 *G*, will bless you for this in all your works
15:14 to the blessing the LORD, your *G*,
15:15 in the land of Egypt, and the LORD, your *G*,
15:18 *G*, will bless you in everything you do.
15:19 shall consecrate to the LORD, your *G*,
15:20 shall eat them before the LORD, your *G*,
15:21 not sacrifice it to the LORD, your *G*,
16: 1 keeping the Passover of the LORD, your *G*,
16: 2 flock or your herd to the LORD, your *G*,
16: 5 of the communities which the LORD, your *G*,
16: 7 and eat it at the place the LORD, your *G*,
16: 8 meeting in honor of the LORD, your *G*;
16:10 of Weeks in honor of the LORD, your *G*,
16:10 to the blessing the LORD, your *G*,
16:11 In the place which the LORD, your *G*,
16:15 feast in honor of the LORD, your *G*,
16:15 since the LORD, your *G*,
16:16 you shall appear before the LORD, your *G*,
16:17 to the blessings which the LORD, your *G*,
16:18 all the communities which the LORD, your *G*,
16:20 possess the land which the LORD, your *G*,
16:21 wood beside the altar of the LORD, your *G*,
16:22 a sacred pillar, such as the LORD, your *G*,
17: 1 shall not sacrifice to the LORD, your *G*,
17: 1 be an abomination to the LORD, your *G*.
17: 2 of the communities which the LORD, your *G*,
17: 2 evil in the sight of the LORD, your *G*,
17: 8 go up to the place which the LORD, your *G*,
17:12 there in the ministry of the LORD, your *G*,
17:14 come into the land which the LORD, your *G*,
17:15 you as your king whom the LORD, your *G*,
17:19 that he may learn to fear the LORD, his *G*,
18: 5 *G*, has chosen him and his sons
18: 7 there in the name of the LORD, his *G*,
18: 9 come into the land which the LORD, your *G*,
18:12 of such abominations the LORD, your *G*,
18:13 altogether sincere toward the LORD, your *G*.
18:14 and fortunetellers, the LORD, your *G*,
18:15 "A prophet like me will the LORD, your *G*,
18:16 what you requested of the LORD, your *G*,
18:16 again hear the voice of the LORD, our *G*,
19: 1 *G*, removes the nations whose land
19: 2 cities in the land which the LORD, your *G*,
19: 3 regions the land which the LORD, your *G*,
19: 8 *G*, enlarges your territory,
19: 9 on you today, loving the LORD, your *G*,
19:10 Thus, in the land which the LORD, your *G*,
19:14 receive in the land which the LORD, your *G*,
20: 1 be afraid of them, for the LORD, your *G*,
20: 4 *G*, who goes with you to fight for you
20:13 siege to it, and when the LORD, your *G*,
20:14 of your enemies which the LORD, your *G*,
20:16 of those nations which the LORD, your *G*,
20:17 *G*, has commanded you,
20:18 and you thus sin against the LORD, your *G*.
21: 1 open on the land which the LORD, your *G*,
21: 5 also be present, for the LORD, your *G*,
21:10 against your enemies and the LORD, your *G*,
21:23 defile the land which the LORD, your *G*,
22: 5 is an abomination to the LORD, your *G*.
23: 6 *G*, would not listen to Balaam
23:15 *G*, journeys along within your camp
23:19 offering in the house of the LORD, your *G*;
23:19 are an abomination to the LORD, your *G*.
23:21 your countryman so that the LORD, your *G*,
23:22 "When you make a vow to the LORD, your *G*,
23:22 will be held guilty, for the LORD, your *G*,
24: 4 guilt upon the land which the LORD, your *G*,
24: 9 Remember what the LORD, your *G*,
24:13 good deed of yours before the LORD, your *G*.
24:18 slaves in Egypt, and the LORD, your *G*,
24:19 or the widow, that the LORD, your *G*,
25:15 life on the land which the LORD, your *G*,
25:16 is an abomination to the LORD, your *G*.
25:18 of any *g* he harassed you along the way,
25:19 Therefore, when the LORD, your *G*,
26: 1 come into the land which the LORD, your *G*,
26: 2 from the land which the LORD, your *G*,
26: 2 go to the place which the LORD, your *G*,
26: 3 'Today I acknowledge to the LORD, my *G*,
26: 4 in front of the altar of the LORD, your *G*.
26: 5 you shall declare before the LORD, your *G*,
26: 7 we cried to the LORD, the *G* of our fathers,
26:10 having set them before the LORD, your *G*,
26:11 these good things which the LORD, your *G*,
26:13 you shall declare before the LORD, your *G*,
26:14 hearkened to the voice of the LORD, my *G*,
26:16 "This day the LORD, your *G*,
26:17 he is to be your *G* and you are to walk in
26:19 be a people sacred to the LORD, your *G*,
27: 2 into the land which the LORD, your *G*,
27: 3 LORD, your *G*, and the *G* of your fathers,
27: 5 you shall also build to the LORD, your *G*,
27: 6 shall make this altar of the LORD, your *G*,
27: 6 offer on it holocausts to the LORD, your *G*.
27: 7 making merry before the LORD, your *G*.
27: 9 have become the people of the LORD, your *G*.
27:10 hearken to the voice of the LORD, your *G*,
28: 1 to heed the voice of the LORD, your *G*,
28: 1 I enjoin on you today, the LORD, your *G*,
28: 2 hearken to the voice of the LORD, your *G*,
28: 8 you in the land that the LORD, your *G*,
28: 9 keep the commandments of the LORD, your *G*,
28:13 obey the commandments of the LORD, your *G*,
28:15 hearken to the voice of the LORD, your *G*,
28:45 hearken to the voice of the LORD, your *G*,
28:47 you would not serve the LORD, your *G*,
28:52 throughout the land which the LORD your *G*,
28:53 sons and daughters whom the LORD, your *G*,
28:58 and awesome name of the LORD, your *G*,
28:62 hearken to the voice of the LORD, your *G*.
29: 5 should know that I, the LORD, am your *G*.'
29: 9 all now standing before the LORD, your *G*—
29:11 into the covenant of the LORD, your *G*,
29:12 you as his people and he may be your *G*,
29:14 now here present before the LORD, our *G*.
29:17 away their hearts from the LORD, our *G*,
29:24 which the LORD, the *G* of their fathers,
30: 1 among whatever nations the LORD, your *G*,

GOD (cont.)
30: 2 your children return to the LORD, your *G*,
30: 3 as I now command you, the LORD, your *G*,
30: 4 even from there will the LORD, your *G*,
30: 5 *G*, will then bring you into the land
30: 6 *G*, will circumcise your hearts
30: 6 that you may love the LORD, your *G*,
30: 7 But all those curses the LORD, your *G*,
30: 9 *G*, will increase in more than goodly
30: 9 *G*, will again take delight
30:10 you heed the voice of the LORD, your *G*,
30:10 law, when you return to the LORD, your *G*,
30:16 obey the commandments of the LORD, your *G*,
30:16 and grow numerous, and the LORD, your *G*,
30:20 may live, by loving the LORD, your *G*,
31: 3 *G*, who will cross before you;
31: 6 dread of them, for it is the LORD, your *G*,
31:11 goes to appear before the LORD, your *G*,
31:12 learn it, and so fear the LORD, your *G*,
31:13 that they too may fear the LORD, your *G*,
31:17 'Is it not because our *G* is not among us
31:26 ark of the covenant of the LORD, your *G*,
32: 3 Oh, proclaim the greatness of our *G*.
32: 4 A faithful *G*,
32: 8 peoples after the number of the sons of *G*;
32:12 their leader, no strange *g* was with him.
32:15 They spurned the *G* who made them and
32:18 you, You forgot the *G* who gave you birth.
32:39 am God, and there is no *g* besides me.
32:43 heavens, glorify him, all you angels of *G*;
33: 1 is the blessing which Moses, the man of *G*,
33:26 is no *g* like the God of the darling,
33:26 is no god like the *G* of the darling,
Jos 1: 9 fear nor be dismayed, for the LORD, your *G*,
1:11 of the land which the LORD, your *G*,
1:13 *G*, will permit you to settle in this land.'
1:15 possess the land which the LORD, your *G*,
1:17 *G*, be with you as he was with Moses.
2:11 since the LORD, your God, is *G* in
3: 3 ark of the covenant of the LORD, your *G*,
3: 9 listen to the words of the LORD, your *G*."
3:10 that there is a living *G* in your midst,
4: 5 in front of the ark of the LORD, your *G*;
4:23 *G*, dried up the waters of the Jordan
4:23 crossed over, just as the LORD, your *G*,
4:24 and that you may fear the LORD, your *G*,
7: 7 "Alas, O Lord *G*,"
7:13 tomorrow, for the LORD, the *G* of Israel,
7:19 son, give to the LORD, the *G* of Israel,
7:20 sinned against the LORD, the *G* of Israel.
8: 7 of the city, which the LORD, your *G*,
8:30 an altar to the LORD, the *G* of Israel,
9: 9 because of the fame of the LORD, your *G*.
9:18 sworn to them by the LORD, the *G* of Israel.
9:19 sworn to them by the LORD, the *G* of Israel,
9:23 drawers of water] for the house of my *G*."
9:24 fully informed of how the LORD, your *G*,
10:19 to their cities, for the LORD, your *G*,
10:40 there, just as the LORD, the *G* of Israel,
10:42 campaign, for the LORD, the *G* of Israel,
13:14 promised them, the LORD, the *G* of Israel,
13:33 since the LORD himself, the *G* of Israel,
14: 6 know what the LORD said to the man of *G*,
14: 8 I was completely loyal to the LORD, my *G*.
14: 9 been completely loyal to the LORD, my *G*.'
14:14 loyal to the LORD, the *G* of Israel.
18: 3 land which the LORD, the *G* of your fathers,
18: 6 lots for you here before the LORD, our *G*.
22: 3 out the commands of the LORD, your *G*.
22: 4 Since, therefore, the LORD, your *G*,
22: 5 love the LORD, your *G*;
22:16 you have committed against the *G* of Israel?
22:19 addition to the altar of the LORD, our *G*.
22:21 "The LORD is the *G* of gods.
22:22 The LORD, the *G* of gods,
22:22 or treachery against the LORD, our *G*,
22:24 you to do with the LORD, the *G* of Israel?
22:29 addition to the altar of the LORD, our *G*,
22:33 who blessed *G* and decided against
22:34 as a witness among them that the LORD is *G*.
23: 3 You have seen all that the LORD, your *G*,
23: 3 for it has been the LORD, your *G*,
23: 5 *G*, will drive them out and dislodge them
23: 5 of their land as the LORD, your *G*,
23: 8 you must remain loyal to the LORD, your *G*,
23:10 thousand, because it is the LORD, your *G*,
23:11 care, however, to love the LORD, your *G*.
23:13 know for certain that the LORD, your *G*,
23:13 from this good land which the LORD, your *G*,
23:14 one of all the promises the LORD, your *G*,
23:15 just as every promise the LORD, your *G*,
23:15 from this good land which the LORD, your *G*,
23:16 the covenant of the LORD, your *G*,
24: 1 When they stood in ranks before *G*,
24: 2 "Thus says the LORD, the *G* of Israel:
24:17 For it was the LORD, our *G*,
24:18 also will serve the LORD, for he is our *G*."
24:19 for he is a holy *G*; he is a jealous *G*
24:23 your hearts to the LORD, the *G* of Israel."
24:24 Joshua, "We will serve the LORD, our *G*,
24:26 he recorded in the book of the law of *G*.
24:27 you, should you wish to deny your *G*."
Jgs 1: 7 As I have done, so has *G* repaid me."
2:12 the LORD, the *G* of their fathers,
3: 7 the LORD by forgetting the LORD, their *G*,
3:20 said, "I have a message from *G* for you."
4: 6 "This is what the LORD, the *G* of Israel,
4:23 on that day *G* humbled the Canaanite king,
5: 3 song, my hymn to the LORD, the *G* of Israel.
5: 5 the presence of the LORD, the *G* of Israel.
6: 8 said to them, "The LORD, the *G* of Israel,
6:10 I, the LORD, am your *G*;
6:20 The angel of *G* said to him,
6:22 angel of the LORD, said, "Alas, Lord *G*,
6:26 proper kind of altar to the LORD, your *G*,
6:31 he whose altar has been destroyed is a *g*,
6:36 Gideon said to *G*,
6:39 Gideon then said to *G*, "Do not be angry
6:40 That night *G* did so;
7:14 *G* has delivered Midian and all the camp
8: 3 power *G* delivered the princes of Midian,
8:33 of Berith their *g* and forgetting the LORD,
8:34 god and forgetting the LORD, their *G*,
9: 7 of Shechem, that *G* may then hear you!
9:23 *G* put bad feelings between Abimelech and
9:27 and went to the temple of their *g*,
9:56 Thus did *G* requite the evil Abimelech had
9:57 *G* also brought all their wickedness home
10:10 forsaken our *G* and have served the Baals."
11:21 *G* of Israel, delivered Sihon
11:23 *G* of Israel, has cleared the Amorites out
11:24 which your *g* Chemosh gave you to possess,
11:24 we not possess all that the LORD, our *G*,
13: 5 is to be consecrated to *G* from the womb.
13: 6 told her husband, "A man of *G* came to me;
13: 6 he had the appearance of an angel of *G*,
13: 7 shall be consecrated to *G* from the womb,
13: 8 he said, "may the man of *G* whom you sent,
13: 9 *G* heard the prayer of Manoah,
13: 9 and the angel of *G* came again to the woman
13:22 will certainly die, for we have seen *G*."
15:19 Then *G* split the cavity in Lehi,
16:17 consecrated to *G* from my mother's womb.
16:23 to their *g* Dagon and to make merry.
16:23 "Our *g* has delivered into our power
16:24 the people saw him, they praised their *g*.
16:24 *g* has delivered into our power our enemy,
16:28 cried out to the LORD and said, "O Lord *G*,
16:28 Strengthen me, O *G*,
18: 5 They said to him, "Consult *G*,
18:10 *G* has indeed given it into your power:
18:24 "You have taken my *g*,
18:31 as long as the house of *G* was in Shiloh.
20: 2 in the assembly of the people of *G*.
20:18 battle, moved on to Bethel and consulted *G*.
20:27 the covenant of *G* was there in those days,
21: 2 and remained there before *G* until evening,
21: 3 They said, "LORD, *G* of Israel,
Ru 1:15 has gone back to her people and her *g*.
1:16 shall be my people, and your God my *G*.
2:12 full reward from the LORD, the *G* of Israel,
1Sm 1:17 and may the *G* of Israel grant you what
2: 1 in the LORD, my horn is exalted in my *G*.
2: 2 there in no Rock like our *G*.
2: 3 God is the LORD, a *G* who judges deeds.
2:27 A man of *G* came to Eli and said to him:
2:30 is the oracle of the LORD, the *G* of Israel:
3: 3 The lamp of *G* was not yet extinguished,
3: 3 temple of the LORD where the ark of *G* was.
3:13 though he knew his sons were blaspheming *G*,
3:17 May *G* do thus and so to you if you hide a
4: 4 and Phinehas, were with the ark of *G*.
4:11 The ark of *G* was captured,
4:13 was troubled at heart about the ark of *G*.
4:17 dead, and the ark of *G* has been captured."
4:18 At this mention of the ark of *G*,
4:21 reference to the capture of the ark of *G*
4:22 because the ark of *G* had been captured.
5: 1 Philistines, having captured the ark of *G*,
5: 2 *G* and brought it into the temple of Dagon,
5: 7 of the *G* of Israel must not remain with us,
5: 7 he is handling us and our *g* Dagon severely."
5: 8 we do with the ark of the *G* of Israel?"
5: 8 "Let them move the ark of the *G* of Israel
5: 9 moved the ark of the *G* of Israel to Gath!
5:10 The ark of *G* was next sent to Ekron;
5:10 brought the ark of the *G* of Israel here
5:11 "Send away the ark of the *G* of Israel.
5:11 the hand of *G* had been very heavy upon it.
6: 3 to send away the ark of the *G* of Israel,
6: 5 give them as a tribute to the *G* of Israel.
6:15 down the ark of *G* and the box beside it,
7: 8 the LORD our *G* unceasingly for us,
9: 6 There is a man of *G* in this city,
9: 7 we have no present to give the man of *G*.
9: 8 If I give that to the man of *G*,
9: 9 anyone who went to consult *G* used to say,
9:10 went to the city where the man of *G* lived.
9:27 that I may give you a message from *G*."
10: 3 met by three men going up to *G* at Bethel;
10: 7 you judge feasible, because *G* is with you.
10: 9 to leave Samuel, *G* gave him another heart.
10:10 him, and the spirit of *G* rushed upon him,
10:18 "Thus says the LORD, the *G* of Israel,
10:19 But today you have rejected your *G*,
11: 6 *G* rushed upon him and he became very angry.
12: 9 But they forgot the LORD their *G*;
12:12 even though the LORD your *G* is your king.
12:14 king who rules you follow the LORD your *G*—
12:19 Samuel, "Pray to the LORD your *G* for us,
13:13 kept the command the LORD your *G* gave you,
14:36 But the priest said, "Let us consult *G*."
14:37 So Saul inquired of *G*: "Shall I go down
14:41 And Saul said to the LORD, the *G* of Israel:
14:41 me or my son Jonathan, LORD, *G* of Israel,
14:44 "May *G* do thus and so to me if you do not
14:45 for *G* was with him in what he did today!"
15:15 and oxen to sacrifice to the LORD, your *G*;
15:21 sacrifice to the LORD their *G* in Gilgal."
15:30 with me that I may worship the LORD your *G*."
16: 7 Not as man sees does *G* see,
16:15 An evil spirit from *G* is tormenting you.
16:16 When the evil spirit from *G* comes over you,
16:23 Whenever the spirit from *G* seized Saul,
17:26 should insult the armies of the living *G*?"
17:36 he has insulted the armies of the living *G*."
17:45 the *G* of the armies of Israel that you
17:46 whole land shall learn that Israel has a *G*.
18:10 day an evil spirit from *G* came over Saul,
19:23 sheds, the spirit of *G* came upon him also,
20:12 "As the LORD, the *G* of Israel,
22: 3 you, until I learn what *G* will do for me."
22:13 and a sword and by consulting *G* for him,
22:15 the first time I have consulted *G* for him?
23: 7 *G* has put him in my grip.
23:10 "O LORD *G* of Israel,
23:11 O LORD *G* of Israel, tell your servant."
25:22 May *G* do thus and so to David,
25:29 the living in the care of the LORD your *G*;
25:32 "Blessed be the LORD, the *G* of Israel,
25:34 Otherwise, as the LORD, the *G* of Israel,
26: 8 *G* has delivered your enemy into your grasp
28:15 war against me and *G* has abandoned me.
29:10 are as acceptable to me as an angel of *G*.
30: 6 But with renewed trust in the LORD his *G*,
30:15 "Swear to me by *G* that you will not kill
2Sm 2:27 Joab replied, "As *G* lives,
3: 9 May *G* do thus and so to Abner if I do not
3:35 "May *G* do thus and so to me if I eat
6: 2 Judah to bring up from there the ark of *G*,
6: 3 The ark of *G* was placed on a new cart and
6: 6 his hand to the ark of *G* and steadied it,
6: 7 *G* struck him on that spot,
6: 7 on that spot, and he died there before *G*.
6:12 David went to bring up the ark of *G* from
7: 2 cedar, while the ark of *G* dwells in a tent!"
7:18 the LORD and said, "Who am I, Lord *G*,
7:19 even this you see as too little, Lord *G*;
7:19 this too you have shown to man, Lord *G*!
7:20 You know your servant, Lord *G*!
7:22 And so—"Great are you, Lord *G*!
7:22 is none like you and there is no *G* but you,
7:23 like your people Israel, which *G* has led,
7:24 and you, LORD, have become their *G*.
7:25 And now, LORD *G*,
7:26 men say, 'The LORD of hosts is *G* of Israel,'
7:27 It is you, LORD of hosts, *G* of Israel,
7:28 GOD, you are *G* and your words are truth;
7:29 for you, Lord *G*,
10:12 of our people and the cities of our *G*;
12: 7 Thus says the LORD *G* of Israel:
12:16 David besought *G* for the child.
14:11 majesty, keep in mind the LORD your *G*,
14:13 same kind of thing against the people of *G*?
14:14 Yet, though *G* does not bring back life,
14:17 my lord the king is like an angel of *G*,
14:17 The LORD your *G* be with you."
14:20 But my lord is as wise as an angel of *G*,
15:24 bearers of the ark of the covenant of *G*,
15:24 and Abiathar brought the ark of *G* to a
15:25 "Take the ark of *G* back to the city.
15:29 of *G* back to Jerusalem and remained there.
15:32 the top, where men used to worship *G*,
18:28 and said, "Blessed be the LORD your *G*,
19:14 May *G* do thus and so to me,
19:28 But my lord the king is like an angel of *G*.
21:14 *G* granted relief to the land.
22: 3 my *G*, my rock of refuge!
22: 7 upon the LORD and cried out to my *G*;
22:22 of the LORD and was not disloyal to my *G*.
22:29 O my *G*, you brighten the darkness
22:30 and by the help of my *G* I leap over a wall.
22:32 "For who is *G* except the LORD?
22:32 Who is a rock save our *G*?
22:33 The *G* who girded me with strength and kept
22:47 Extolled be my *G*,
22:48 be my God, rock of my salvation, O *G*,
23: 1 God raised up, Anointed of the *G* of Jacob,
23: 3 The *G* of Israel spoke;
23: 3 in justice, that rules in the fear of *G*,
23: 5 Is not my house firm before *G*?
24: 3 "May the LORD your *G* increase the number
24:14 Let us fall by the hand of *G*,
24:23 "May the LORD your *G* accept your offering."
24:24 the LORD my *G* holocausts that cost nothing."
1Kgs 1:17 to me your handmaid by the LORD, your *G*,
1:30 swore to you by the LORD, the *G* of Israel,
1:36 May the LORD, the *G* of my lord the king,
1:47 'May *G* make Solomon more famous than you

1:47 And the king in his bed worshiped G,
1:48 'Blessed be the LORD, the G of Israel,
2: 3 Keep the mandate of the LORD, your G,
2:23 "May G do thus and so to me,
2:26 because you carried the ark of the Lord G
3: 5 G said, "Ask something of me
3: 7 O LORD, my G,
3:11 So G said to him: "Because you have asked
3:28 in him the wisdom of G for giving judgment.
5: 9 G gave Solomon wisdom and exceptional
5:17 a temple in honor of the LORD, his G,
5:18 But now the LORD, my G,
5:19 build a temple in honor of the LORD, my G,
8:15 "Blessed be the LORD, the G of Israel,
8:17 to the honor of the LORD, the G of Israel,
8:20 temple to honor the LORD, the G of Israel.
8:23 G of Israel, there is no God like you
8:25 Now, therefore, LORD, G of Israel,
8:26 Now, LORD, G of Israel,
8:27 indeed be that G dwells among men on earth?
8:28 petition of your servant, O LORD, my G,
8:53 brought our fathers out of Egypt, O Lord G."
8:57 May the LORD, our G, be with us
8:59 prayer I have offered to the LORD, our G,
8:60 know the LORD is G and there is no other.
8:61 must be wholly devoted to the LORD, our G,
8:65 the festival before the LORD, our G,
9: 9 'They forsook the LORD, their G,
10: 9 Blessed be the LORD, your G,
10:24 the wisdom which G had put in his heart.
11: 4 was not entirely with the LORD, his G,
11: 9 turned away from the LORD, the G of Israel,
11:23 G raised up against Solomon another
11:31 the LORD, the G of Israel says:
11:33 g of Moab, and Milcom, g of the Ammonites;
12:22 the LORD spoke to Shemaiah, a man of G:
12:28 Here is your G,
13: 1 A man of G came from Judah to Bethel by
13: 4 man of G was crying out against the altar,
13: 5 man of G had given as the word of the LORD.
13: 6 Then the king appealed to the man of G.
13: 6 "Entreat the LORD, your G,"
13: 6 So the man of G entreated the LORD,
13: 7 the king invited the man of G,
13: 8 kingdom," the man of G said to the king,
13:11 the man of G had done that day in Bethel.
13:12 by the man of G who had come from Judah.
13:14 it, he mounted and followed the man of G,
13:14 "Are you the man of G who came from Judah
13:21 to the man of G who had come from Judah:
13:21 keep the command which the LORD, your G,
13:26 "It is the man of G who rebelled against
13:29 body of the man of G and put it on the ass,
13:31 in the grave where the man of G is buried.
14: 7 'This is what the LORD, the G of Israel,
14:13 pleasing to the LORD, the G of Israel,
15: 3 was not entirely with the LORD, his G,
15: 4 Yet for David's sake the LORD, his G,
15:30 he provoked the LORD, the G of Israel,
16:13 provoking the LORD, the G of Israel,
16:26 to provoke to the LORD, the G of Israel,
16:33 more to anger the LORD, the G of Israel,
17: 1 "As the LORD, the G of Israel,
17:12 "As the LORD, your G lives,"
17:14 For the LORD, the G of Israel,
17:18 "Why have you done this to me, O man of G?
17:20 G, will you afflict even the widow
17:21 G, let the life breath return to the body
17:24 indeed I know that you you are a man of G,"
18:10 As the LORD, your G,
18:21 If the LORD is G,
18:24 The God who answers with fire is G."
18:27 for he is a g and may be meditating,
18:36 forward and said, "LORD, G of Abraham,
18:36 let it be known this day that you are G
18:37 are G and that you have brought them back
18:39 fell prostrate and said, "The LORD is G!
18:39 The LORD is G!"
19: 8 days and forty nights to the mountain of G,
19:10 been zealous for the LORD, the G of hosts,
19:14 most zealous for the LORD, the G of hosts.
20:28 G came up and said to the king of Israel:
20:28 is a god of mountains, not a g of plains,
21:10 and accuse him of having cursed G and king.
21:13 accusation, "Naboth has cursed G and king."
22:54 thus provoking the LORD, the G of Israel,
2Kgs 1: 2 and inquire of Baalzebub, the g of Ekron,
1: 3 'Is it because there is no G in Israel
1: 3 to inquire of Baalzebub, the g of Ekron?'
1: 6 Is it because there is no G in Israel that
1: 6 to inquire of Baalzebub, the g of Ekron?
1: 9 "Man of G,"
1:10 "If I am a man of G," Elijah answered
1:11 "Man of G," he called out to Elijah,
1:12 "If I am a man of G,"
1:13 "Man of G," he implored him,
1:16 to inquire of Baalzebub, the g of Ekron,
2:14 said, "Where is the LORD, the G of Elijah?"
4: 7 She went and told the man of G,
4: 9 "I know that he is a holy man of G.
4:16 she protested, "you are a man of G;
4:21 and laid him on the bed of the man of G.
4:22 I must go quickly to the man of G,
4:25 she reached the man of G on Mount Carmel.
4:25 the man of G said to his servant Gehazi:
4:27 she reached the man of G on the mountain,
4:27 to push her away, but the man of G said:
4:40 to eat it, they exclaimed, "Man of G,
4:42 bringing the man of G twenty barley loaves
5: 7 "Am I a g with power over life and death,
5: 8 When Elisha, the man of G,
5:11 and stand there to invoke the LORD his G,
5:14 seven times at the word of the man of G.
5:15 with his whole retinue to the man of G.
5:15 I know that there is no G in all the earth,
5:17 to any other g except to the LORD.
5:20 the servant of Elisha, the man of G,
6: 6 "Where did it fall?" asked the man of G.
6: 9 of G would send word to the king of Israel,
6:10 the place which the man of G had indicated,
6:15 of the man of G arose and went out,
6:31 "May G do thus and so to me,"
7: 2 the king leaned, answered the man of G,
7:17 G had predicted when the king visited him.
7:18 the prophecy of the man of G to the king,
7:19 The adjutant had answered the man of G.
8: 2 got ready and did as the man of G said,
8: 4 with Gehazi, the servant of the man of G.
8: 7 was told that the man of G had come there,
8: 8 gift with you and go call on the man of G.
8:11 The man of G wept,
9: 6 "Thus says the LORD, the G of Israel:
10:31 the law of the LORD, the G of Israel,
13:19 Angry with him, the man of G said:
14:25 Arabah, just as the LORD, the G of Israel,
16: 2 He did not please the LORD, his G,
17: 7 sinned against the LORD, their G,
17: 9 practices toward the LORD, their G.
17:14 who had not believed in the LORD, their G.
17:16 all the commandments of the LORD, their G,
17:19 the commandments of the LORD, their G,
17:26 not know how to worship the G of the land,
17:26 not know how to worship the G of the land."
17:27 them how to worship the G of the land."
17:39 But the LORD, your G,
18: 5 put his trust in the LORD, the G of Israel;
18:12 heeded the warning of the LORD, their G,
18:22 you say to me, We rely on the LORD, our G,
19: 4 the LORD, your G, will hear all the words
19: 4 of Assyria, sent to taunt the living G,
19: 4 him for the words which the LORD, your G,
19:10 'Do not let your G on whom you rely
19:15 G of Israel, enthroned upon the cherubim!
19:15 are G over all the kingdoms of the earth.
19:16 which he sent to taunt the living G.
19:19 Therefore, O LORD, our G,
19:19 may know that you alone, O LORD, are G."
19:20 "Thus says the LORD, the G of Israel,
19:37 worshiping in the temple of his g Nisroch,
20: 5 the LORD the G of your forefather David:
21:12 thus says the LORD, the G of Israel:
21:22 abandoned the LORD, the G of his fathers,
22:15 "Thus says the LORD, the G of Israel:
22:18 'Thus says the LORD, the G of Israel:
23:16 which the man of G had proclaimed
23:16 man of G who had proclaimed these words,
23:17 "It is the grave of the man of G
23:21 observe the Passover of the LORD, their G,
1Chr 4:10 Jabez prayed to the G of Israel:
4:10 And G granted his prayer.
5:20 For during the battle they called on G,
5:22 fallen in battle, for victory is from G;
5:25 they offended the G of their fathers by
5:25 land, whom G had cleared out of their way.
5:26 Therefore the G of Israel incited against
6:33 services of the Dwelling of the house of G.
6:34 for Israel, as Moses, the servant of G,
9:11 of Ahitub, the ruler of the house of G;
9:13 the work of the service of the house of G.
9:26 chambers and treasures of the house of G.
9:27 At night they lodged about the house of G,
11: 2 And now the LORD, your G,
11:19 G forbid that I should do such a thing!
12:18 the G of our fathers see and punish you."
12:19 your G it is who helps you."
13: 2 you, and is so decreed by the LORD our G,
13: 3 us bring the ark of our G here among us,
13: 5 to bring the ark of G from Kiriath-jearim.
13: 6 of Judah, to bring back the ark of G,
13: 7 G on a new cart from the house of Abinadab;
13: 8 danced before G with great enthusiasm,
13:12 David was now afraid of G,
13:12 "How can I bring the ark of G with me?"
13:14 The ark of G remained in the house of
14:10 David inquired of G,
14:11 G has used me to break through my enemies
14:14 and again David inquired of G.
14:14 But G answered him: "Do not try to pursue
14:15 for G has already gone before you to
14:16 David did as G commanded him,
15: 1 and prepared a place for the ark of G,
15: 2 may carry the ark of G except the Levites,
15:12 bring the ark of the LORD, the G of Israel,
15:13 the wrath of the LORD our G burst upon us,
15:14 up the ark of the LORD, the G of Israel.
15:15 the ark of G on their shoulders with poles,
15:24 sounded the trumpets before the ark of G.
16: 1 They brought the ark of G and set it
16: 1 up holocausts and peace offerings to G.
16: 4 and praise the LORD, the G of Israel.
16: 6 before the ark of the covenant of G.
16:14 He, the LORD, is our G;
16:35 And say, "Save us, O G,
16:36 Blessed be the LORD, the G of Israel,
17: 2 whatever you desire, for G is with you."
17: 3 same night the word of G came to Nathan:
17:16 "Who am I, O LORD G,
17:17 even this you now consider too little, O G!
17:17 the most notable of men, O LORD G.
17:20 no one like you and there is no G but you,
17:21 whom a g went to redeem as his people?
17:22 forever, and you, O LORD, became their G.
17:24 your renown as LORD of hosts, G of Israel,
17:25 "Because you, O my G,
17:26 are truly G and have promised this good
19:13 sake of our people and the cities of our G;
21: 7 This command displeased G,
21: 8 Then David said to G, "I have sinned
21:15 G also sent an angel to destroy Jerusalem;
21:17 face to the ground, and David prayed to G:
21:17 G, strike me and my father's family,
21:30 But David could not go there to worship G,
22: 1 said, "This is the house of the LORD G,
22: 2 stone blocks for building the house of G.
22: 6 a house for the LORD, the G of Israel.
22: 7 myself for the honor of the LORD, my G.
22:11 in building the house of the LORD your G,
22:12 that you keep the law of the LORD, your G.
22:18 "Is not the LORD your G with you?
22:19 and souls to seeking the LORD your G.
22:19 to build the sanctuary of the LORD G,
23:14 As for Moses, however, the man of G,
23:25 "The LORD, the G of Israel,
23:28 take part in the service of the house of G.
24:19 their father, as the LORD, the G of Israel,
25: 5 G gave Heman fourteen sons and three
25: 6 harps and lyres, serving in the house of G,
26: 5 Peullethai, the eighth, for G blessed him.
26:20 of G and the stores of votive offerings.
26:32 everything pertaining to G and to the king.
28: 2 LORD, the footstool for the feet of our G;
28: 3 G said to me, 'You may not build a house
28: 4 However, the LORD, the G of Israel,
28: 8 of the LORD, and in the hearing of our G,
28: 8 all the commandments of the LORD, your G,
28: 9 know the G of your father and serve him
28:12 G and the stores of the votive offerings,
28:20 or discouragement, for the LORD God, my G,
28:21 for all the service of the house of G;
29: 1 "My son Solomon, whom alone G has chosen,
29: 1 not intended for man, but for the LORD G.
29: 2 I have stored up for the house of my G,
29: 3 the delight I take in the house of my G,
29: 3 G my personal fortune in gold and silver:
29: 7 for the service of the house of G
29:10 may you be, O LORD, G of Israel our father,
29:13 Therefore, our G, we give you thanks
29:16 G, all this wealth that we have brought
29:17 I know, O my G,
29:18 O LORD, G of our fathers Abraham,
29:20 assembly, "Now bless the LORD your G!"
29:20 blessed the LORD, the G of their fathers,
2Chr 1: 1 hold on the kingdom, for the LORD, his G,
1: 3 at Gibeon, because the meeting tent of G,
1: 4 (The ark of G,
1: 7 G appeared to Solomon and said to him,
1: 8 Solomon answered G: "You have shown great
1: 9 Now, LORD G,
1:11 G then replied to Solomon:
2: 3 a house for the honor of the LORD, my G,
2: 3 moons, and festivals of the LORD, our G:
2: 4 for our G is greater than all other gods.
2:11 "Blessed be the LORD, the G of Israel,
3: 3 by Solomon for building the house of G:
4:11 to do for King Solomon in the house of G:
4:19 all these articles made for the house of G:
5: 1 in the treasuries of the house of G.
5:14 the LORD's glory filled the house of G.
6: 4 "Blessed be the LORD, the G of Israel,
6: 7 to the honor of the LORD, the G of Israel,
6:10 to the honor of the LORD, the G of Israel.
6:14 "LORD, G of Israel, there is no god like you
6:16 Now, therefore, LORD, G of Israel,
6:17 Now, LORD, G of Israel,
6:18 be that G dwells with mankind on earth?
6:19 petition of your servant, O LORD, my G,
6:40 My G, may your eyes be open and your ears
6:41 And now, "Advance, LORD G,
6:41 May your priests, LORD G,
6:42 G, reject not the plea of your anointed,
7: 6 all the people dedicated the house of G.
7:22 forsook the LORD, the G of their fathers,
8:14 was the command of David, the man of G.
9: 8 Blessed be the LORD, your G,
9: 8 on his throne as king for the LORD, your G.
9: 8 Because your G has so loved Israel as to
9:23 the wisdom which G had put in his heart.
11: 2 of the LORD came to Shemaiah, a man of G:
11:16 desired to seek the LORD, the G of Israel,

GOD (cont.)

11:16 to the LORD, the *G* of their fathers.
13: 5 not know that the LORD, the *G* of Israel,
13:10 But as for us, the LORD is our *G*,
13:11 we observe our duties to the LORD, our *G*,
13:12 See, *G* is with us,
13:12 against the LORD, the *G* of your fathers,
13:15 *G* defeated Jeroboam and all Israel before
13:16 and *G* delivered them into their hands.
13:18 relied on the LORD, the *G* of their fathers.
14: 1 was good and pleasing to the LORD, his *G*,
14: 3 to seek the LORD, the *G* of their fathers,
14: 6 ours, for we have sought the LORD, our *G*;
14:10 Asa called upon the LORD, his *G*, praying:
14:10 Help us, O LORD, our *G*,
14:10 *G*; let no man prevail against you."
15: 1 Azariah, son of Oded, came the spirit of *G*.
15: 3 For a long time Israel had no true *G*,
15: 4 they turned to the LORD, the *G* of Israel,
15: 6 for *G* destroyed them by every kind of
15: 9 Israel when they saw that the LORD, his *G*,
15:12 to seek the LORD, the *G* of their fathers,
15:13 would not seek the LORD, the *G* of Israel,
15:18 He brought into the house of *G* his
16: 7 Aram and did not rely on the LORD, your *G*,
17: 4 *G* of his father and observed his commands,
18: 5 *G* will deliver it over to the king."
18:13 answered, "I will say what my *G* tells me."
18:31 *G* induced them to leave him.
19: 3 land and have been determined to seek *G*."
19: 4 back to the LORD, the *G* of their fathers.
19: 7 the LORD, our *G* there is no injustice,
20: 6 *G* of our fathers, are you not the *G* in heaven,
20: 7 Was it not you, our *G*,
20:12 *G*, will you not pass judgment on them?
20:19 the praises of the LORD, the *G* of Israel,
20:20 Trust in the LORD, your *G*,
20:29 And the fear of *G* came upon all the
20:30 for his *G* gave him rest on every side.
20:33 their hearts on the *G* of their fathers.
21:10 forsaken the LORD, the *G* of his fathers.
21:12 the LORD, the *G* of your ancestor David:
22: 7 Now it was willed by *G* for Ahaziah's
22:12 hidden with them in the house of *G*,
23: 3 a covenant with the king in the house of *G*.
23: 9 of king David which were in the house of *G*.
24: 5 repair the house of your *G* over the years.
24: 7 her sons had damaged the house of *G*
24: 9 the tax which Moses, the servant of *G*,
24:13 house of *G* according to its original form,
24:16 with respect to *G* and his temple.
24:18 temple of the LORD, the *G* of their fathers,
24:20 Then the spirit of *G* possessed Zechariah,
24:20 *G* says, 'why are you transgressing
24:24 abandoned the LORD, the *G* of their fathers.
24:27 and of his rebuilding of the house of *G*,
25: 7 But a man of *G* came to him and said:
25: 8 It is *G* who has the power to reinforce or
25: 9 Amaziah answered the man of *G*,
25: 9 The man of *G* replied,
25:16 "that *G* has let you take counsel to your
25:20 for *G* had determined to hand them over
25:24 he found in the house of *G* with Obed-edom,
26: 5 to seek *G* as long as Zechariah lived,
26: 5 Zechariah lived, who taught him to fear *G*;
26: 5 as he sought the LORD, *G* made him prosper.
26: 7 *G* helped him against the Philistines,
26:16 and broke faith with the LORD, his *G*.
26:18 in the glory that comes from the LORD *G*."
27: 6 in the presence of the LORD, his *G*.
28: 5 Therefore the LORD, his *G*,
28: 6 abandoned the LORD, the *G* of their fathers.
28: 9 because the LORD, the *G* of your fathers,
28:10 guilty of a crime against the LORD, your *G*?
28:25 he angered the LORD, the *G* of his fathers.
29: 5 house of the LORD, the *G* of your fathers,
29: 6 did evil in the eyes of the LORD, our *G*.
29: 7 sanctuary to the honor of the *G* of Israel.
29:10 a covenant with the LORD, the *G* of Israel,
29:36 what *G* had reestablished for the people,
30: 1 in honor of the LORD, the *G* of Israel.
30: 5 in honor of the LORD, the *G* of Israel;
30: 6 return to the LORD, the *G* of Abraham,
30: 7 to the LORD, the *G* of their fathers,
30: 8 forever, and serve the LORD, your *G*,
30: 9 and compassionate is the LORD, your *G*,
30:12 the power of *G* brought it about that the
30:16 to the law of Moses, the man of *G*.
30:19 seek God, the LORD, the *G* of his fathers,
30:22 to the LORD, the *G* of their fathers,
31: 6 had been consecrated to the LORD, their *G*;
31:13 of Azariah, the prefect of the house of *G*.
31:14 charge of the freewill gifts made to *G*;
31:20 and faithful before the LORD, his *G*.
31:21 of *G* or for the law and the commandments,
31:21 commandments, was to do the will of his *G*.
32: 8 arm of flesh, but we have the LORD, our *G*,
32:11 by his claim that 'the LORD, our *G*,
32:14 Will your *g*,
32:15 Since no other *g* of any other nation or
32:15 less shall your *g* save you from my hand!"
32:16 LORD *G* and against his servant Hezekiah,
32:17 to deride the LORD, the *G* of Israel,
32:17 Hezekiah's *g* save his people from my hand."
32:19 They spoke of the *G* of Israel as though he
32:21 And when he entered the temple of his *g*,
32:29 numbers, for *G* gave him very great riches.
32:31 in the land, *G* forsook him to test him,
33: 7 in the house of *G*, of which God had said
33:12 he began to appease the LORD, his *G*.
33:12 the *G* of his fathers and prayed to him.
33:13 understood that the LORD is indeed *G*.
33:16 Judah to serve the LORD, the *G* of Israel.
33:17 they now did so to the LORD, their *G*.
33:18 the acts of Manasseh, his prayer to his *G*,
33:18 in the name of the LORD, the *G* of Israel,
34: 3 seek after the *G* of his forefather David,
34: 8 to restore the house of the LORD, his *G*.
34: 9 to the house of *G* which the Levites,
34:23 "Thus says the LORD, the *G* of Israel:
34:26 'Thus says the LORD, the *G* of Israel,
34:27 have humbled yourself before *G*
34:32 covenant of God, the *G* of their fathers.
34:33 were in Israel to serve the LORD, their *G*.
34:33 desert the LORD, the *G* of their fathers.
35: 3 Serve now the LORD, your *G*,
35: 8 and Jehiel, prefects of the house of *G*,
35:21 kingdom, and *G* has told me to hasten.
35:21 Do not interfere with *G* who is with me,
35:22 of Neco that came from the mouth of *G*,
36: 5 did evil in the sight of the LORD, his *G*.
36:12 did evil in the sight of the LORD, his *G*,
36:13 who had made him swear by *G*.
36:13 than return to the LORD, the *G* of Israel.
36:15 often did the LORD, the *G* of their fathers,
36:16 But they mocked the messengers of *G*,
36:18 All the utensils of the house of *G*,
36:19 They burnt the house of *G*,
36:23 of the earth the LORD, the *G* of heaven,
36:23 let him go up, and may his *G* be with him!'"

Ezr 1: 2 of the earth the LORD, the *G* of heaven,
1: 3 let him go up, and may his *G* be with him!
1: 4 offerings for the house of *G* in Jerusalem.'"
1: 5 that is, whom *G* had inspired to do so
1: 7 Jerusalem and placed in the house of his *g*.
2:68 free-will offerings for the house of *G*,
3: 2 set about rebuilding the altar of the *G*
3: 2 in the law of Moses, the man of *G*.
3: 8 coming to the house of *G* in Jerusalem,
3: 9 were engaged in the work on the house of *G*.
4: 1 a temple for the LORD, the *G* of Israel,
4: 2 you, for we seek your *G* just as you do,
4: 3 to build with us a house for our *G*,
4: 3 build it for the LORD, the *G* of Israel,
4:24 on the house of *G* in Jerusalem was halted.
5: 1 Jerusalem in the name of the *G* of Israel.
5: 2 of *G* in Jerusalem, with the prophets of *G*
5: 5 But their *G* watched over the elders of the
5: 8 of Judah and the house of the great *G*:
5:11 the servants of the *G* of heaven and earth,
5:12 provoked the wrath of the *G* of heaven,
5:13 for the rebuilding of this house of *G*.
5:14 silver utensils of the house of *G*
5:15 house of *G* be rebuilt on its former site.
5:16 foundations of the house of *G* in Jerusalem.
5:17 rebuilding of this house of *G* in Jerusalem.
6: 3 The house of *G* in Jerusalem.
6: 5 silver utensils of the house of *G*
6: 5 Jerusalem and deposited in the house of *G*.
6: 7 Jews to continue to work on that house of *G*;
6: 8 Jews in the rebuilding of that house of *G*:
6: 9 lambs for holocausts to the *G* of heaven,
6:10 sacrifices of pleasing odor to the *G*
6:12 And may the *G* who causes his name to dwell
6:12 or to destroy this house of *G* in Jerusalem.
6:14 according to the command of the *G*
6:16 the dedication of this house of *G* with joy.
6:17 For the dedication of this house of *G*,
6:18 for the service of *G* in Jerusalem,
6:21 them in seeking the LORD, the *G* of Israel.
6:22 work on the house of God, the *G* of Israel.
7: 6 was given by the LORD, the *G* of Israel.
7: 6 the hand of the LORD, his *G* was upon him,
7: 9 the favoring hand of his *G* was upon him.
7:12 scribe of the law of the *G* of heaven (then,
7:14 law of your *G* which is in your possession,
7:15 have freely contributed to the *G* of Israel,
7:16 for the house of their *G* in Jerusalem.
7:17 altar of the house of your *G* in Jerusalem.
7:18 gold, conformably to the will of your *G*.
7:19 your God you are to deposit before the *G*
7:20 for the needs of the house of your *G*,
7:21 scribe of the law of the *G* of heaven,
7:23 Let everything that is ordered by the *G* of
7:23 exactly for the house of the *G* of heaven,
7:24 or any other servant of that house of *G*.
7:25 of your *G* which is in your possession,
7:25 all, that is, who know the laws of your *G*.
7:26 the law of your *G* and the law of the king,
7:27 Blessed be the LORD, THE *G* of our fathers,
7:28 and, with the hand of the LORD, my *G*,
8:17 ministers for the house of our *G*.
8:18 for the favoring hand of our *G* was upon us
8:21 we might humble ourselves before our *G*
8:22 hand of our *G* is upon all who seek him,
8:23 So we fasted, and prayed to our *G* for this,
8:25 offered for the house of our *G* by the king,
8:28 to the LORD, the *G* of your fathers.
8:30 them to Jerusalem, to the house of our *G*.
8:31 The hand of our *G* remained upon us,
8:33 our *G* and consigned to the priest Meremoth,
8:35 *G* of Israel twelve bulls for all Israel,
8:36 to the people and to the house of *G*.
9: 4 *G* of Israel on this apostasy of the exiles,
9: 5 stretching out my hands to the LORD my *G*.
9: 6 "My *G*, I am too ashamed
9: 6 to raise my face to you, O my *G*,
9: 8 ago, mercy came to us from the LORD our *G*,
9: 8 thus our *G* has brightened our eyes and
9: 9 our servitude our *G* has not abandoned us;
9: 9 the house of our *G* and restore its ruins,
9:10 But now, O our *G*,
9:13 though you, our *G*,
9:15 O LORD, *G* of Israel,
10: 1 and prostrate before the house of *G*,
10: 2 "We have indeed betrayed our *G* by taking
10: 3 enter into a covenant before our *G*
10: 3 those who fear the commandments of our *G*.
10: 6 of *G* and entered the chamber of Johanan,
10: 9 in the open place before the house of *G*,
10:11 praise to the LORD, the *G* of your fathers,

Neh 1: 4 I fasted and prayed before the *G* of heaven.
1: 5 LORD, God of heaven, great and awesome *G*,
2: 4 the *G* of heaven and then answered the king:
2: 8 for the favoring hand of my *G* was upon me.
2:12 what my *G* had inspired me to do
2:18 favoring hand of my *G* had rested upon me,
2:20 the *G* of heaven who will grant us success.
3:36 Take note, O our *G*, how we were mocked!
4: 3 We prayed to our *G* and posted a watch
4: 9 warned and that *G* had upset their plan,
4:14 our *G* will fight with us."
5: 9 Should you not walk in the fear of our *G*,
5:13 "Thus may *G* shake from his home and his
5:15 But I, because I feared *G*,
5:19 Keep in mind, O my *G*,
6:10 "Let us meet in the house of *G*,
6:12 it was plain to me that *G* had not sent him;
6:14 Keep in mind Tobiah and Sanballat, O my *G*,
7: 5 When my *G* had put it into my mind to
8: 6 Ezra blessed the LORD, the great *G*,
8: 8 plainly from the book of the law of *G*,
8: 9 "Today is holy to the LORD your *G*.
8:16 in the courts of the house of *G*,
8:18 the book of the law of *G* day after day,
9: 3 the book of the law of the LORD their *G*,
9: 3 themselves before the LORD their *G*.
9: 4 Chenani, who cried out to the LORD their *G*,
9: 5 said, "Arise, bless the LORD, your *G*,
9: 7 "You, O LORD, are the *G* who chose Abram,
9:17 But you are a *G* of pardons,
9:18 is your *G* who brought you up out of Egypt,'
9:31 them, for you are a kind and merciful *G*.
9:32 O our God, great, mighty, and awesome *G*,
10:29 of the lands in favor of the law of *G*,
10:30 the law of *G* which was given through Moses,
10:30 was given through Moses, the servant of *G*,
10:33 for the service of the house of our *G*,
10:34 for every service of the house of our *G*.
10:35 it is to be brought to the house of our *G*
10:35 be burnt on the altar of the LORD, our *G*,
10:37 the law, to bring to the house of our *G*,
10:37 priests who serve in the house of our *G*,
10:38 to the chambers of the house of our *G*.
10:39 tithe of the tithes to the house of our *G*,
10:40 We will not neglect the house of our *G*.
11:11 of Ahitub, the ruler of the house of *G*,
11:16 the external affairs of the house of *G*;
11:22 to the service of the house of *G*—
12:24 of the command of David, the man of *G*,
12:36 musical instruments of David, the man of *G*.
12:40 took up a position in the house of *G*;
12:45 who carried out the ministry of their *G*
12:46 hymns of praise and thanksgiving to *G*
13: 1 ever be admitted into the assembly of *G*;
13: 2 our *G* turned the curse into a blessing."
13: 4 our *G* and who was an associate of Tobiah,
13: 7 a chamber in the courts of the house of *G*.
13: 9 there the utensils of the house of *G*,
13:11 "Why is the house of *G* abandoned?"
13:14 Remember this to my credit, O my *G*!
13:14 of my *G* and its services be forgotten!
13:18 with the result that our *G* has brought all
13:22 This, too, remember in my favor, O my *G*,
13:25 and I adjured them by *G*:
13:26 and though he was beloved of his *G* and God
13:27 betraying our *G* by marrying foreign women?"
13:29 Remember against them, O my *G*,
13:31 Remember this in my favor, O my *G*!

Tb 1:12 Because of this wholehearted service of *G*,
2: 2 If he is a sincere worshiper of *G*,
3:16 in the glorious presence of Almighty *G*.
4:19 At all times bless the Lord *G*,
4:21 You will be a rich man if you fear *G*,
4:21 do what is right before the Lord your *G*."
5: 4 did not know that this was an angel of *G*.
5:10 *G* has healing in store for you;
5:14 *G* save you, brother!
5:17 Tobit said, *G* bless you, brother."

5:17 May G in heaven protect you on the way and
7: 7 "My child, G bless you!
7:12 And may the G of heaven grant both of you
8: 5 "Blessed are you, O G of our fathers;
8:15 praised the G of heaven in these words:
8:15 "Blessed are you, O G,
9: 6 Blessed be G,
11:14 "Blessed be G,
11:15 rejoicing and praising G with full voice.
11:16 Rejoicing and praising G,
11:17 Before them all Tobit proclaimed how G had
11:17 Blessed be your G for bringing you to us,
12: 6 "Thank G!
12: 7 of G are to be declared and made known.
12:11 of G are to be made known with due honor.'
12:14 G commissioned me to heal you and your
12:17 Thank G now and forever.
12:20 So now get up from the ground and praise G.
12:22 kept thanking G and singing his praises;
12:22 done when the angel of G appeared to them.
13: 1 Blessed be G who lives forever,
13: 4 the Lord our God, our Father and G forever.
13: 7 "As for me, I exalt my G,
13:11 drawn to you by the name of the Lord G,
13:18 "Blessed be G who has raised you up!
14: 2 blessing G and praising the divine Majesty.
14: 4 by Israel's prophets, whom G commissioned,
14: 4 whatever G has spoken will be accomplished.
14: 5 But G will again have mercy on them and
14: 5 her the temple of G shall also be rebuilt;
14: 6 converted and shall offer G true worship;
14: 7 bless the G of the ages in righteousness.
14: 7 in those days will truly be mindful of G,
14: 7 Those who sincerely love G shall rejoice,
14: 9 serve G faithfully and do what is right
14: 9 to be mindful of G and at all times to
14:10 Yet G made Nadab's disgraceful crime
14:15 Tobiah praised G for all that he had done
14:15 and he blessed the Lord G forever and ever.
Jdt 3: 8 every people and tribe invoke him as a g.
4: 2 and the temple of the Lord, their G.
4: 9 to G with great fervor and did penance
4:12 they cried out fervently to the G of Israel
5: 8 with divine worship the G of heaven,
5: 9 Their G bade them leave their abode and
5:12 But they cried to their G,
5:13 them, G dried up the Red Sea before them,
5:17 of their God, they prospered, for their G,
5:18 temple of their G was razed to the ground,
5:19 now that they have returned to their G,
5:20 at fault, and are sinning against their G,
5:21 their Lord and G will shield them,
6: 2 Israelites because their G protects them?
6: 2 What g is there beside Nebuchadnezzar?
6: 2 Their G will not save them;
6:18 the people fell prostrate and worshiped G;
6:19 "Lord, G of heaven,
6:21 they called upon the G of Israel for help.
7:19 The Israelites cried to the Lord, their G,
7:24 G judge between you and us!
7:25 G has sold us into their power by laying
7:28 you by heaven and earth, and by our G,
7:29 wailing and loud cries to the Lord their G.
7:30 us wait five days more for the Lord our G,
8:11 G and yourselves this oath which you took.
8:12 you should have put G to the test this day,
8:12 in the place of G in human affairs?
8:14 how then can you fathom G,
8:14 my brothers, do not anger the Lord our G.
8:16 the Lord our G give surety for his plans.
8:16 G is not man that he should be moved by
8:20 we acknowledge no other g but the Lord,
8:21 and G will make us pay for its profanation
8:23 turned to our benefit, but the Lord our G,
8:25 we should be grateful to the Lord our G,
8:35 and may the Lord G go before you to take
9: 1 the temple of G in Jerusalem that evening,
9: 2 "Lord, G of my forefather Simeon!
9: 5 "O G, my God, hear me also, a widow.
9:11 but you are the G of the lowly,
9:12 G of my forefather, God of the heritage
9:14 that you are the g of all power and might,
10: 1 ceased her invocation to the G of Israel,
10: 8 the G of our fathers bring you to favor,
10: 8 of Jerusalem"Judith bowed down to G.
11: 6 handmaid, G will give you complete success,
11:10 them, except when they sin against their G.
11:11 their G upon them whenever they do wrong;
11:12 which G in his laws forbade them to eat.
11:13 in the presence of our G in Jerusalem:
11:16 G has sent me to perform with you such
11:17 serving the G of heaven night and day.
11:17 will go out to the ravine and pray to G.
11:22 G has done well in sending you ahead of
11:23 as you have said, your God will be my G;
12: 8 she besought the Lord, the G of Israel,
13: 4 "O Lord, G of all might,
13: 7 "Strengthen me this day, O G of Israel!"
13:11 God, our G, is with us.
13:14 "Praise G, praise him!
13:14 Praise G, who has not withdrawn his mercy
13:17 They bowed down and worshiped G,
13:17 with one accord, "Blessed are you, our G,
13:18 are you, daughter, by the Most High G,
13:18 and blessed be the Lord G,
13:19 by those who tell of the might of G.
13:20 May G make this redound to your
13:20 disaster, walking uprightly before our G."
14:10 seeing all that the G of Israel had done,
15:10 G is pleased with what you have wrought.
16: 1 instruments, a song to my G with timbrels,
16: 2 For the Lord is G;
16:13 "A new hymn I will sing to my G.
16:18 then went to Jerusalem to worship G;
16:19 dedicated, as a votive offering to G,
Est A: 9 Then they cried out to G,
A:11 seen this dream and what G intended to do,
C: 2 "O Lord G,
C: 7 to place the honor of man above that of G.
C: 8 And now, Lord God, King, G of Abraham,
C:14 she prayed to the Lord, the G of Israel,
C:14 "My Lord, our King, you alone are G.
C:29 no joy except in you, O Lord, G of Abraham.
C:30 G, more powerful than all,
D: 2 after invoking the all-seeing G and savior,
D: 8 G changed the king's anger to gentleness.
D:13 "I saw you, my lord, as an angel of G,
E: 4 vindictive judgment of the all-seeing G.
E:16 of the Most High, the living G of majesty,
E:18 Thus swiftly has G,
E:21 For G, the ruler of all,
F: 1 "This is the work of G.
F: 6 is Israel, who cried to G and was saved.
F: 6 G worked signs and great wonders,
F: 7 one for the people of G,
F: 8 before G and among all the nations.
F: 9 G remembered his people and rendered
F:10 together with joy and happiness before G,
1Mc 2:21 G forbid that we should forsake the law
2Mc 1: 2 May G bless you and remember his covenant
1:11 we have been saved by G from grave dangers,
1:17 Forever blessed be our G,
1:20 Many years later, when it so pleased G,
1:24 Lord G, creator of all things,
1:27 let the Gentiles know that you are our G.
2: 7 "The place is to remain unknown until G
2:17 It is G who has saved all his people and
2:18 We trust in G,
3:28 experienced the sovereign power of G.
3:36 high G that he had seen with his own eyes.
4:17 is no light matter to flout the laws of G,
6: 1 and live no longer by the laws of G;
6:23 would be loyal to the holy laws given by G.
7: 6 "The Lord G is looking on,
7:16 not think that our nation is forsaken by G.
7:18 because we have sinned against our G;
7:19 for having dared to fight against G."
7:28 G did not make them out of existing things;
7:31 will not escape the hands of G.
7:35 judgment of the almighty and all-seeing G.
7:36 covenant, but you, by the judgment of G,
7:37 G to show mercy soon to our nation,
7:37 to make you confess that he alone is G.
8:18 he said, "but we trust in almighty G,
8:23 them the watchword, "The Help of G,"
9: 5 So the all-seeing Lord, the G of Israel,
9: 8 clearly manifesting to all the power of G.
9:11 understanding, under the scourge of G,
9:12 he said, "It is right to be subject to G,
9:17 place to proclaim there the power of G.
9:20 are going as you wish, I thank G very much,
10:16 public prayers asking G to be their ally,
10:25 and his men made supplication to G,
11: 9 of them together thanked G for his mercy,
11:13 because the mighty G was their ally.
12: 6 and after calling upon G,
12:16 Capturing the city by the will of G,
14:33 will level this shrine of G to the ground;
15:16 "Accept this holy sword as a gift from G;
15:27 hands and praying to G with their hearts,
Jb 1: 1 named Job, who feared G and avoided evil.
1: 5 sinned and blasphemed G in their hearts."
1: 6 when the sons of G came to present
1: 8 and upright, fearing G and avoiding evil?"
1:22 nor did he say anything disrespectful of G.
2: 1 Once again the sons of G came to present
2: 3 and upright, fearing G and avoiding evil?
2: 9 Curse G and die."
2:10 We accept good things from G;
3: 4 let not G above call for it,
3:23 hidden from them, and whom G has hemmed
4: 9 By the breath of G they perish,
4:17 "Can a man be righteous as against G?
5: 5 [or G shall take it away by blight;]
5: 8 to God, and to G I would state my plea.
5:17 Happy is the man whom G reproves!
6: 4 the terrors of G are arrayed against me.
6: 8 and that G would grant what I long for:
6: 9 Even that G would decide to crush me,
8: 3 Does G pervert judgment,
8: 5 to G and make supplication to the Almighty,
8:13 So is the end of everyone who forgets G,
8:20 Behold, G will not cast away the upright;
9: 2 but how can a man be justified before G?
9: 4 G is wise in heart and mighty in strength;
9:13 He is G and he does not relent;
10: 2 I will say to G:
11: 5 But oh, that G would speak,
11: 6 G will make you answer for your guilt.
11: 7 Can you penetrate the designs of G?
12: 4 one whom G answers when he calls upon him,
12: 6 and those who provoke G are secure.
12: 9 not know that the hand of G has done this?
13: 3 I wish to reason with G.
13: 7 Is it for G that you speak falsehood?
13: 8 Do you play advocate on behalf of G?
15: 4 piety, and you lessen devotion toward G,
15: 8 Are you privy to the counsels of G,
15:11 the consolations of G not enough for you,
15:13 G and let such words escape your mouth!
15:15 If in his holy one G places no confidence,
15:25 G and bade defiance to the Almighty,
16:11 G has given me over to the impious;
16:20 before G my eyes drop tears,
18:21 such is the place of him who knows not G!
19: 6 then that G has dealt unfairly with me,
19:21 friends, for the hand of G has struck me!
19:26 him, And from my flesh I shall see G;
20:15 G shall compel his belly to disown them.
20:23 G shall send against him the fury of his
20:29 man, and the heritage appointed him by G.
21: 9 fear, nor is the scourge of G upon them.
21:14 Yet they say to G,
21:16 counsel of the wicked is repulsive to G,
21:19 May G not store up the man's misery for
21:22 Can anyone teach G knowledge,
22: 2 Can a man be profitable to G?
22:12 G, in the heights of the heavens,
22:13 Yet you say, "What does G know?
22:17 These men said to G, "Depart from us!"
22:26 and you shall lift up your face toward G.
22:30 G delivers him who is innocent;
23:16 Indeed G has made my courage fail;
24:12 out [yet G does not treat it as unseemly].
27: 2 As G lives, who withholds my deserts,
27: 3 me and the breath of G is in my nostrils,
27: 8 he is cut off, when G requires his life?
27: 9 Will G then attend to his cry when
27:13 is the portion of a wicked man from G,
28:23 G knows the way to it;
29: 2 as in the days when G watched over me,
29: 4 flourishing days, when G sheltered my tent;
31: 2 But what is man's lot from G above,
31: 6 Let G weigh me in the scales of justice;
31:14 me, What then should I do when G rose up;
31:18 a father G has reared me from my youth.
31:23 For the dread of G will be upon me,
31:28 for I should have denied G above.
32: 2 himself rather than G to be in the right.
32:13 G may vanquish him out not man!"
33: 4 For the spirit of G has made me,
33: 6 have been taken from the same clay by G.
33:12 for G is greater than man.
33:14 For G does speak,
33:26 He shall pray and G will favor him;
33:29 Lo, all these things G does,
34: 5 innocent, but G has taken what is my due.
34: 9 a man nought that he is pleasing to G."
34:10 far be it from G to do wickedness;
34:12 Surely, G cannot act wickedly,
34:23 of his time to come before G in judgment.
34:31 When anyone says to G,
34:33 Would you then say that G must punish,
34:37 arguments and addressing many words to G.
35: 2 it right to say, "I am just rather than G?"
35: 6 If you sin, what injury do you do to G?
35:10 power of the mighty, Saying, "Where is G,
35:13 But it is idle to say G does not hear or
36: 5 Behold, G rejects the obstinate in heart;
36:22 Behold, G is sublime in his power.
36:26 Lo, G is great beyond our knowledge;
37:10 With his breath G brings the frost,
37:14 Stand and consider the wondrous works of G!
37:15 you know how G lays his commands upon them,
38: 7 and all the sons of G shouted for joy?
38:41 ravens when their young ones cry out to G,
39:17 For G has withheld wisdom from her and has
40: 2 Let him who would correct G give answer!
40: 9 Have you an arm like that of G,
Ps(s) 3: 3 me, "There is no salvation for him in G."
3: 8 Save me, my G!
4: 2 When I call, answer me, O my just G,
5: 3 Heed my call for help, my king and my G!
5: 5 G, delight not in wickedness;
5:11 G; let them fall by their own devices;
7: 2 G, in you I take refuge;
7: 4 G, if I am at fault in this,
7:10 O searcher of heart and soul, O just G.
7:11 A shield before me is G,
7:12 judge is God, a G who punishes day by day.
7:13 be converted, G will sharpen his sword;
9:18 turn back, all the nations that forget G.
10: 4 "There is no G,"
10:11 He says in his heart, G has forgotten;
10:12 O G, lift up your hand!
10:13 Why should the wicked man despise G,
13: 4 Look, answer me, O LORD, my G!
14: 1 fool says in his heart, "There is no G."
14: 2 if there be one who is wise and seeks G.

GOD (cont.)

14: 5 fear, for G is with the just generation.
16: 1 Keep me, O G, for in you I take refuge;
17: 6 call upon you, for you will answer me, O G;
18: 3 My G, my rock of refuge,
18: 7 upon the LORD and cried out to my G;
18:22 of the LORD and was not disloyal to my G;
18:29 O my G,
18:30 and by the help of my G I leap over a wall.
18:32 For who is G except the LORD?
18:32 Who is a rock, save our G?
18:33 The G who girded me with strength and
18:47 Extolled be G my savior.
18:48 O G, who granted me vengeance,
19: 2 The heavens declare the glory of G,
20: 2 the name of the G of Jacob defend you!
20: 6 raise the standards in the name of our G.
20: 8 are strong in the name of the LORD, our G.
22: 2 My God, my G, why have you forsaken
22: 3 G, I cry out by day, and you answer not;
22:11 birth, From my mother's womb you are my G.
24: 5 from the LORD, a reward from G his savior.
24: 6 him, that seeks the face of the G of Jacob.
25: 2 To you I lift up my soul, O LORD, my G.
25: 5 and teach me, for you are G my savior,
25:22 Redeem Israel, O G, from all its distress!
27: 9 forsake me not, O G my savior.
29: 1 Give to the LORD, you sons of G,
29: 3 over the waters, the G of glory thunders,
30: 3 G, I cried out to you and you healed me.
30:13 O LORD, my G,
31: 6 you will redeem me, O LORD, O faithful G.
31:15 I say, "You are my G."
33:12 Happy the nation whose G is the LORD,
35:23 in my cause, my G and my LORD.
35:24 G, let them not rejoice over me.
36: 2 there is no dread of G before his eyes,
36: 7 Your justice is like the mountains of G;
36: 8 How precious is your kindness, O G!
37:31 The law of his G is in his heart,
38:16 you, O LORD my G,
38:22 G, be not far from me!
40: 4 a new song into my mouth, a hymn to our G.
40: 6 How numerous have you made, O LORD, my G,
40: 9 for me, To do your will, O my G,
40:18 G, hold not back!
41:14 Blessed be the LORD, the G of Israel,
42: 2 waters, so my soul longs for you, O G.
42: 3 Athirst is my soul for God, the living g.
42: 3 When shall I go and behold the face of G?
42: 4 say to me day after day, "Where is your G?"
42: 5 led them in procession to the house of G,
42: 6 Hope in G!
42: 6 in the presence of my savior and my G.
42: 9 I have his song, a prayer to my living G.
42:10 I sing to G, my rock:
42:11 say to me day after day, "Where is your G?"
42:12 Hope in G!
42:12 in the presence of my savior and my G.
43: 1 Do me justice, O G,
43: 2 For you, O G, are my strength.
43: 4 the altar of G, the God of my gladness
43: 4 give you thanks upon the harp, O God, my G!
43: 5 Hope in G!
43: 5 in the presence of my savior and my G.
44: 2 G, our ears have heard,
44: 5 You are my king and my G,
44: 9 In G we gloried day by day;
44:21 hands to a strange g, Would not God
44:22 god, Would not G have discovered this?
45: 3 thus G has blessed you forever.
45: 7 Your throne, O G,
45: 8 G, your G, has anointed you with the oil
46: 2 G is our refuge and our strength,
46: 4 our stronghold is the G of Jacob.
46: 5 stream whose runlets gladden the city of G,
46: 6 G is in its midst;
46: 6 G will help it at the break of dawn.
46: 8 our stronghold is the G of Jacob.
46:11 and confess that I am G,
46:12 our stronghold is the G of Jacob.
47: 2 hands, shout to G with cries of gladness,
47: 6 G mounts his throne amid shouts of joy;
47: 7 Sing praise to G,
47: 8 For the king of all the earth is G;
47: 9 G reigns over the nations, G sits upon his
47:10 with the people of the G of Abraham.
48: 2 wholly to be praised in the city of our G.
48: 4 G is with her castles;
48: 9 In the city of our God; G makes it firm
48:10 O G, we ponder your kindness
48:11 G, so also your praise reaches to the ends
48:15 that such is God, Our G forever and ever;
49: 8 himself, or pay his own ransom to G;
49:16 But G will redeem me from the power of the
50: 1 G the LORD has spoken and summoned the
50: 2 Zion, perfect in beauty, G shines forth.
50: 3 May our G come and not be deaf to us!
50: 6 for G himself is the judge.
50: 7 God, your G, am I.
50:14 Offer to G praise as your sacrifice and
50:16 But to the wicked man G says:
50:22 "Consider this, you who forget G,
50:23 right way I will show the salvation of G."
51: 3 Have mercy on me, O G,
51:12 A clean heart create for me, O G,
51:16 me from blood guilt, O God, my saving G;
51:19 My sacrifice, O G,
51:19 a heart contrite and humbled, O G,
52: 7 G himself shall demolish you;
52: 9 who made not G the source of his strength,
52:10 house of G, Trust in the kindness of G
53: 2 fool says in his heart, "There is no G."
53: 3 G looks down from heaven upon the children
53: 3 if there be one who is wise and seeks G.
53: 5 as they eat bread, who call not upon G?
53: 6 For G has scattered the bones of your
53: 6 put to shame, because G has rejected them.
53: 7 G restores the well-being of his people,
54: 3 G, by your name save me,
54: 4 G, hear my prayer;
54: 5 they set not G before their eyes.
54: 6 Behold, G is my helper;
55: 2 G, to my prayer; turn not away
55:15 I walked in procession in the house of G!
55:17 But I will call upon G,
55:20 G will hear me and will humble them from
55:20 is not in them, nor do they fear G.
55:24 G, will bring them down into the pit
56: 2 Have pity on me, O G,
56: 5 G, in whose promise I glory, in G I trust
56: 8 in your wrath bring down the peoples, O G.
56:10 now I know that G is with me.
56:11 In G, in whose promise I glory,
56:12 promise I glory, in G I trust without fear;
56:13 I am bound, O G,
56:14 walk before G in the light of the living.
57: 2 Have pity on me, O G;
57: 3 I call to God the Most High, to G,
57: 4 G send his kindness and his faithfulness.
57: 6 Be exalted above the heavens, O G;
57: 8 My heart is steadfast, O G;
57:12 Be exalted above the heavens, O G;
58: 7 G, smash their teeth in their mouths;
58:12 truly there is a G who is judge on earth!"
59: 2 Rescue me from my enemies, O my G;
59: 6 you are the LORD of hosts, the G of Israel.
59:10 for you, O G, are my stronghold,
59:11 O God, are my stronghold, my gracious G!
59:11 May G come to my aid;
59:12 G, slay them, lest they beguile my people;
59:14 men may know that G is the ruler of Jacob,
59:18 O God, are my stronghold, my gracious G!
60: 3 G, you have rejected us
60: 8 G promised in his sanctuary:
60:12 Have not you, O G,
60:12 us, so that you go not forth, O G,
60:14 Under G we shall do valiantly;
61: 2 Hear, O G, my cry; listen to my prayer!
61: 6 G, have accepted my vows;
61: 8 Let him sit enthroned before G forever;
62: 2 Only in G is my soul at rest;
62: 6 Only in G be at rest,
62: 8 With G is my safety and my glory,
62: 8 my refuge is in G.
62: 9 G is our refuge!
62:12 One thing G said;
62:12 that power belongs to G,
63: 2 G, you are my God whom I seek;
63:12 The king, however, shall rejoice in G;
64: 2 G, my voice in my lament;
64: 8 But G shoots his arrows at them;
64:10 all men fear and proclaim the work of G,
65: 2 To you we owe our hymn of praise, O G,
65: 6 of justice you answer us, O G our savior,
66: 1 Shout joyfully to G,
66: 3 Say to G, "How tremendous are your deeds!
66: 5 Come and see the works of G,
66: 8 Bless our G,
66:10 For you have tested us, O G!
66:16 Hear now, all you who fear G,
66:19 But G has heard;
66:20 Blessed be G who refused me not my prayer
67: 2 May G have pity on us and bless us;
67: 4 May the peoples praise you, O G;
67: 6 May the peoples praise you, O G;
67: 7 its fruits; God, our G, has blessed us.
67: 8 May G bless us,
68: 2 G arises;
68: 3 the fire, so the wicked perish before G.
68: 4 But the just rejoice and exult before G;
68: 5 Sing to G,
68: 6 of widows is G in his holy dwelling.
68: 7 G gives a home to the forsaken;
68: 8 G, when you went forth at the head
68: 9 presence of G, at the presence of G, the G
68:10 A bountiful rain you showered down, O G,
68:11 in your goodness, O G,
68:17 the mountain G has chosen for his throne,
68:18 The chariots of G are myriad,
68:19 the LORD G enters his dwelling.
68:20 G, who is our salvation.
68:21 G is a saving God for us;
68:22 Surely G crushes the heads of his enemies,
68:25 progress, O God, the progress of my G,
68:27 In your choirs bless G;
68:29 Show forth, O G, your power.
68:29 the power, O G,
68:32 let Ethiopia extend its hands to G.
68:33 You kingdoms of the earth, sing to G,
68:35 "Confess the power of G!"
68:36 in his sanctuary is God, the G of Israel;
68:36 Blessed be G!
69: 2 Save me, O G,
69: 4 My eyes have failed with looking for my G.
69: 6 G, you know my folly,
69: 7 to shame through me, O Lord, G of hosts.
69: 7 who seek you blush for me, O G of Israel,
69:14 O LORD, for the time of your favor, O G!
69:30 let your saving help, O G,
69:31 I will praise the name of G in song,
69:33 you who seek G,
69:36 For G will save Zion and rebuild the
70: 2 Deign, O G,
70: 5 your salvation say ever, G be glorified!"
70: 6 O G, hasten to me!
71: 4 G, rescue me from the hand
71: 5 my trust, O G,
71:11 They say, G has forsaken him;
71:12 O G, be not far from me; my God,
71:16 G, I will tell of your singular justice.
71:17 G, you have taught me from my youth,
71:18 And now that I am old and gray, O G,
71:19 Your power and your justice, O G,
71:19 You have done great things; O G,
71:22 on the lyre, for your faithfulness, O my G!
72: 1 G, with your judgment endow the king,
72:18 Blessed be the LORD, the G of Israel,
73: 1 How good G is to the upright;
73:11 And they say, "How does G know?"
73:17 of G and considered their final destiny.
73:26 G is the rock of my heart and my portion
73:28 be near G is my good; to make the LORD G
74: 1 Why, O G, have you cast us off forever?
74: 8 burn all the shrines of G in the land."
74:10 How long, O G, shall the foe blaspheme?
74:12 G, my king from of old,
74:22 Arise, O G:
75: 2 We give you thanks, O G, we give thanks.
75: 8 But G is the judge;
75:10 I will sing praise to the G of Jacob.
76: 2 G is renowned in Judah,
76: 7 At your rebuke, O G of Jacob,
76:10 and was silent When G arose for judgment,
76:12 Make vows to the LORD, your G,
77: 2 Aloud to G I cry; aloud to God, to hear me;
77: 4 When I remember G,
77:10 Has G forgotten pity?
77:14 G, your way is holy;
77:14 what great god is there like our G?
77:15 You are the G who works wonders;
77:17 The waters saw you, O G;
78: 7 hope in G, And not forget the deeds of G
78: 8 steadfast nor its spirit faithful toward G.
78:10 They kept not the covenant with G;
78:18 And they tempted G in their hearts by
78:19 spoke against God, saying, "Can G spread
78:22 believed not G nor trusted in his help.
78:31 When the anger of G rose against them and
78:34 they sought him and inquired after G again,
78:35 G was their rock and the Most High God,
78:41 G and provoked the Holy One of Israel.
78:56 and rebelled against G the Most High,
78:59 G heard and was enraged and utterly
79: 1 G, the nations have come
79: 9 Help us, O G our savior,
79:10 should the nations say, "Where is their G?"
80:11 by its branches, the cedars of G.
81: 2 joyfully to G our strength; acclaim the G
81: 5 in Israel, an ordinance of the G of Jacob,
81:10 g among you nor shall you worship any alien g
81:11 G who led you forth from the land of Egypt;
82: 1 G arises in the divine assembly;
82: 8 Rise, O G;
83: 2 G, do not remain unmoved; be not silent, O G
83:13 take for ourselves the dwelling place of G."
83:14 G, make them like leaves in a whirlwind,
84: 3 and my flesh cry out for the living G.
84: 4 altars, O LORD of hosts, my king and my G!
84: 8 they shall see the G of gods in Zion.
84: 9 hearken, O G of Jacob!
84:10 G, behold our shield,
84:11 my G than dwell in the tents of the wicked.
84:12 For a sun and a shield is the LORD G;
85: 5 Restore us, O G our savior,
85: 9 I will hear what G proclaims;
86: 3 You are my G;
86:10 you alone are G.
86:12 I will give thanks to you, O LORD my G,
86:14 G, the haughty have risen up against me,
86:15 you, O Lord, are a G merciful and gracious,
87: 3 things are said of you, O city of G!
88: 2 my G, by day I cry out;
89: 7 Who is like the LORD among the sons of G?
89: 8 G is terrible in the council of the holy
89: 9 O LORD, G of hosts, who is like you?
89:27 shall say of me, 'You are my father, my G,
90: 2 from everlasting to everlasting you are G.
90:17 gracious care of the Lord our G be ours;

91: 2 LORD, "My refuge and my fortress, my G,
92:14 LORD shall flourish in the courts of our G.
94: 1 God of vengeance, LORD, G of vengeance,
94: 7 the G of Jacob perceives not."
94:22 stronghold, and my G the rock of my refuge.
94:23 the LORD, our G,
95: 3 For the LORD is a great G,
95: 7 For he is our G,
98: 3 the earth have seen the salvation by our G.
99: 5 Extol the LORD, our G,
99: 8 G, you answered them; a forgiving G
99: 9 Extol the LORD, our G,
99: 9 for holy is the LORD, our G.
100: 3 Know that the LORD is G;
102:25 G, Take me not hence
104: 1 O LORD, my G, you are great indeed!
104:21 for the prey and seek their food from G.
104:33 I will sing praise to my G while I live.
105: 7 He, the LORD, is our G;
106:14 the desert and tempted G in the wilderness.
106:21 They forgot the G who had saved them,
106:47 Save us, O LORD, our G,
106:48 Blessed be the LORD, the G of Israel,
107:11 G and scorned the counsel of the Most High.
108: 2 I My heart is steadfast, O G;
108: 6 Be exalted above the heavens, O G;
108: 8 G promised in his sanctuary:
108:12 Have not you, O G, rejected us,
108:12 rejected us, So that you go not forth, O G,
108:14 Under G we shall do valiantly;
109: 1 G, whom I praise, be not silent,
109:21 But do you, O G,
109:26 Help me, O LORD, my G;
113: 5 Who is like the LORD, our G,
114: 7 O earth, before the face of the G of Jacob,
115: 2 should the pagans say, "Where is their G?"
115: 3 Our G is in heaven;
116: 5 yes, our G is merciful.
118:27 The LORD is G, and he has given us light.
118:28 my G, and I give thanks to you; O my G
119:115 and I will observe the commands of my G.
122: 9 Because of the house of the LORD, our G,
123: 2 So are our eyes on the LORD, our G,
135: 2 LORD, in the courts of the house of our G.
136: 2 Give thanks to the G of gods,
136:26 Give thanks to the G of heaven,
139:17 How weighty are your designs, O G;
139:19 If only you would destroy the wicked, O G,
139:21 G With a deadly hatred I hate them;
139:23 Probe me, O G,
140: 7 I say to the LORD, you are my G;
140: 8 G, my Lord, my strength and my salvation;
141: 8 For toward you, O G,
143:10 Teach me to do your will, for you are my G.
144: 9 G, I will sing a new song to you;
144:15 happy the people whose G is the LORD.
145: 1 I will extol you, O my G and King,
146: 2 I will sing praise to my G while I live.
146: 5 Happy he whose help is the G of Jacob,
146: 5 Jacob, whose hope is in the LORD, his G,
146:10 your G, O Zion, through all generations.
147: 1 sing praise to our G,
147: 7 sing praise with the harp to our G,
147:12 praise your G,
149: 6 the high praises of G be in their throats.
Prv 2: 5 the knowledge of G you will find;
2:17 her youth and forgets the pact with her G;
3: 4 win favor and good esteem before G and man.
25: 2 G has glory in what he conceals,
30: 1 "I am not G; I am not God
30: 5 Every word of G is tested;
30: 9 I steal, and profane the name of my G.
Eccl 1:13 G has appointed for men to be busied about.
2:24 this, I realized, is from the hand of G.
2:26 to be given to whatever man G sees fit.
3:10 G has appointed for men to be busied about.
3:11 to end, the work which G has done.
3:13 the fruit of all his labor is a gift of G.
3:14 that whatever G does will endure forever;
3:14 Thus has G done that he may be revered.
3:15 and G restores what would otherwise be
3:17 both the just and the wicked G will judge,
4:17 your step when you go to the house of G.
5: 1 G is in heaven and you are on earth;
5: 3 When you make a vow to G,
5: 3 For G has no pleasure in fools;
5: 5 lest G be angered by such words and
5: 6 Rather, fear G!
5:17 limited days of the life which G gives him;
5:18 man to whom G gives riches and property,
5:18 the fruits of his toil, has a gift from G.
5:19 because G lets him busy himself with the
6: 2 whom G gives riches and property and honor,
6: 2 yet G does not grant him power to partake
6:12 vain life (which G has made like a shadow)?
7:13 Consider the work of G.
7:14 Both the one and the other G has made,
7:18 who fears G will win through at all events.
7:26 He who is pleasing to G will escape her,
7:29 G made mankind straight,
8: 2 the king, and in view of your oath to G,
8:12 it shall be well with those who fear G,
8:13 days, for his lack of reverence toward G.
8:15 the life which G gives him under the sun.
9: 1 wise, and their deeds are in the hand of G.
9: 7 because it is now that G favors your works.
11: 5 So you know not the work of G which he is
11: 9 all this G will bring you to judgment.
12: 7 the life breath returns to G who gave it.
12:13 Fear G and keep his commandments,
12:14 G will bring to judgment every work,
Wis 1: 3 perverse counsels separate a man from G,
1: 6 Because G is the witness of his inmost
1:13 Because G did not make death,
2:13 G and styles himself a child of the Lord.
2:16 the just and boasts that G is his Father.
2:18 For if the just one be the son of G,
2:20 to his own words, G will take care of him."
2:22 they knew not the hidden counsels of G;
2:23 For G formed man to be imperishable;
3: 1 the souls of the just are in the hand of G,
3: 5 because G tried them and found them worthy
4: 1 because both by G is it acknowledged,
4:10 He who pleased G was loved;
5: 5 how he is accounted among the sons of G;
6: 4 law, nor walk according to the will of G,
6:19 incorruptibility makes one close to G;
7:14 this treasure win the friendship of G,
7:15 Now G grant I speak suitably and value
7:25 For she is an aura of the might of G and a
7:26 the spotless mirror of the power of G,
7:27 she produces friends of G and prophets.
7:28 For there is nought G loves,
8: 3 the splendor of companionship with G;
8: 4 is instructress in the understanding of G,
8:21 not otherwise possess her except G gave it
9: 1 G of my fathers, Lord of mercy.
10: 5 the just man, kept him blameless before G,
10:10 of G and gave him knowledge of holy things;
10:12 devotion to G is mightier than all else.
12:13 any g besides you who have the care of all,
12:26 to experience a condemnation worthy of G.
12:27 G whom before they had refused to know;
13: 1 nature foolish who were in ignorance of G,
13: 6 though they seek G and wish to find him.
14: 8 though corruptible, it was termed a g.
14: 9 to G are the evildoer and his evil deed;
14:15 And now honored as a g what was formerly a
14:22 for them to err in their knowledge of G;
14:30 ill of G and devoted themselves to idols,
15: 1 But you, our G, are good and true,
15: 8 a meaningless g form the selfsame clay;
15:16 succeeds in fashioning a g like himself;
15:19 both the approval of G and his blessing.
16:18 they were struck by the judgment of G;
Sir 2: 6 Trust G and he will help you;
3:18 you are, and you will find favor with G.
3:19 For great is the power of G;
4:28 and the LORD your G will battle for you.
6:16 remedy, such as he who fears G finds;
6:17 For he who fears G behaves accordingly,
7:29 With all your soul, fear G,
7:31 Honor G and respect the priest;
9:16 in the fear of G be your glory.
10: 4 over the earth is in the hand of G,
10: 5 over every man is in the hand of G,
10:13 Because of it G sends unheard-of
10:14 The thrones of the arrogant G overturns
10:15 The roots of the proud G plucks up,
10:17 The traces of the proud G sweeps away and
10:19 Those who fear G.
10:20 who fears G is in honor among his people.
10:23 but none is greater than he who fears G.
15: 9 lips, for it is not accorded to him by G.
15:14 When G, in the beginning, created man
15:19 The eyes of G see all he has made;
16:13 man's hope G does not leave unfulfilled.
16:15 "I am hidden from G;
16:24 When at the first G created his works and,
17:17 goodness G cherishes like a signet ring,
17:27 G watches over the hosts of highest heaven,
19:20 with little understanding who fear G,
23: 4 LORD, Father and G of my life,
32:14 He who would find G must accept discipline:
35:12 of extortion, For he is a G of justice,
35:16 He who serves G willingly is heard;
35:19 G indeed will not delay,
36: 1 Come to our aid, O G of the universe,
36: 4 as we know, that there is no G but you.
36:17 of the earth that you are the eternal G.
37:15 to G to set your feet in the path of truth.
38: 1 G it was who established his profession.
38: 2 From G the doctor has his wisdom,
38: 4 G makes the earth yield healing herbs
38: 9 when you are ill, delay not, but pray to G,
38:14 and he too beseeches G That his diagnosis
39:16 The works of G are all of them good;
39:33 The works of G are all of them good;
40: 1 A great anxiety has G allotted,
40:26 but better than either, fear of G.
40:27 The fear of G is a paradise of blessings;
41: 4 Thus G has ordained for all flesh;
42:17 of the LORD, Though G has given these,
43: 9 with their sparkling the heights of G,
43:12 this bow bent by the mighty hand of G.
44:21 G promised him with an oath that in his
44:23 G acknowledged him as the first-born,
45: 1 Dear to G and men,
45: 3 G wrought swift miracles at his words and
45: 4 meekness G selected him from all mankind;
45:15 That he should serve G in his priesthood
45:23 of his line When, zealous for the G of all,
45:24 on him again G conferred the right,
46: 5 G when his enemies beset him on all sides,
46: 5 And G Most High gave answer to him in
46: 6 because he was a devoted follower of G
46:11 were not deceived, Who did not abandon G:
46:16 He, too, called upon G,
47: 5 Since he called upon the Most High G,
47: 8 deed he offered thanks to G Most High,
47:13 peace, for G made tranquil all his borders.
47:13 He built a house to the name of G,
47:22 But G does not withdraw his mercy,
48:18 fist at Zion and blasphemed G in his pride.
48:20 High G and lifted up their hands to him;
48:21 G struck the camp of the Assyrians and
49: 3 He turned to G with his whole heart,
49:12 In their time they built the house of G;
50: 1 In whose time the house of G was renovated,
50:15 a sweet-smelling odor to the Most High G,
50:19 altar by presenting to G the sacrifice due;
50:22 And now, bless the G of all,
51: 1 G of my father; I praise you, O G my savior!
51:29 Let your spirits rejoice in the mercy of G,
51:30 his own time G will give you your reward.
Is 1:10 Listen to the instruction of our G,
2: 3 mountain, to the house of the G of Jacob,
3:15 says the Lord, the G of hosts.
5:16 and G the holy shall be shown holy by his
7:11 Ask for a sign from the LORD, your G;
7:13 you to weary men, must you also weary my G?
8:10 not be carried out, for "With us is G!"
10:21 the remnant of Jacob, to the mighty G.
10:23 he has decreed, the Lord, the G of hosts,
10:24 thus says the Lord, the G of hosts:
12: 2 G indeed is my savior;
13:19 by G like Sodom and like Gomorrah.
14:13 the stars of G I will set up my throne;
17: 6 branches, says the LORD, the G of Israel.
17:10 For you have forgotten G,
17:13 But G shall rebuke them,
21:10 from the LORD of hosts, The G of Israel,
21:17 remain, for the LORD, the G of Israel,
22: 5 confusion, from the Lord, the G of hosts,
22:12 On that day the Lord, the G of hosts,
22:14 you die, says the Lord, the G of hosts.
22:15 Thus says the Lord, the G of hosts:
24:15 to the name of the LORD, the G of Israel!"
25: 1 O LORD, you are my G,
25: 8 G will wipe away the tears from all faces;
25: 9 "Behold our G,
26:13 O LORD, our G,
28:16 Therefore, thus says the Lord G:
28:22 I have heard from the Lord, the G of hosts,
28:26 has learned this rule, instructed by his G.
29:22 says the LORD, the G of the house of Jacob,
29:23 of Jacob, and be in awe of the G of Israel.
30:15 For thus said the Lord G,
30:18 For the LORD is a G of justice:
31: 3 The Egyptians are men, not G,
35: 2 glory of the LORD, the splendor of our G.
35: 4 Here is your G, he comes with vindication;
36: 7 "We rely on the LORD, our G,"
37: 4 Perhaps the LORD, your G,
37: 4 of Assyria, sent to taunt the living G,
37: 4 him for the words which the LORD, your G,
37:10 'Do not let your G on whom you rely
37:16 "O LORD of hosts, G of Israel,
37:16 are G over all the kingdoms of the earth.
37:17 Sennacherib sent to taunt the living G.
37:20 Therefore, O LORD, our G,
37:20 may know that you, O LORD, alone are G."
37:21 Thus says the LORD, the G of Israel:
37:38 worshiping in the temple of his g Nisroch,
38: 5 says the LORD, the G of your father David:
38:19 Fathers declare to their sons, O G,
40: 1 give comfort to my people, says your G.
40: 3 in the wasteland a highway for our G!
40: 8 wilts, the word of our G stands forever."
40: 9 Here is your G!
40:10 Here comes with power the Lord G,
40:18 To whom can you liken G?
40:27 and my right is disregarded by my G"?
40:28 The LORD is the eternal G,
41:10 I am your G.
41:13 For I am the LORD, your G,
41:17 I, the G of Israel,
42: 5 G, the LORD, who created the heavens
43: 3 For I am the LORD, your G,
43:10 Before me no g was formed,
43:12 made it known, not any strange g among you;
43:12 I am G, yes, from eternity I am He;
44: 6 there is no G but me.
44: 8 Is there a G or any Rock besides me?
44:10 the associates of anyone who forms a g,
44:15 another part he makes a g which he adores,
44:17 Of what remains he makes a g,
44:17 implores it, "Rescue me, for you are my g."
45: 3 know that I am the LORD, the G of Israel,

GOD (cont.)
45: 5 is no other, there is no *G* besides me.
45:14 "With you only is *G*,
45:15 with you God is hidden, the *G* of Israel,
45:18 The creator of the heavens, who is *G*,
45:21 the LORD, besides whom there is no other *G*?
45:21 There is no just and saving *G* but me.
45:22 all you ends of the earth, for I am *G*;
46: 6 a *g* before which they fall down in worship.
46: 9 I am *G*, there is no other, I am God,
48: 1 *G* of Israel without sincerity or justice,
48: 2 the holy city and rely on the *G* of Israel,
48:16 "Now the Lord *G* has sent me,
48:17 I, the LORD, your *G*,
49: 4 with the LORD, my recompense is with my *G*.
49: 5 of the LORD, and my *G* is now my strength!
49:22 Thus says the Lord *G*:
50: 4 Lord *G* has given me a well-trained tongue,
50: 7 The Lord *G* is my help,
50: 9 See, the Lord *G* is my help;
50:10 the name of the LORD and relying on his *G*?
51:15 For I am the LORD, your *G*.
51:20 wrath of the LORD, the rebuke of your *G*.
51:22 Thus says the LORD, your Master, your *G*,
52: 4 Thus says the Lord *G*:
52: 7 and saying to Zion, "Your *G* is King!"
52:10 earth will behold the salvation of our *G*.
52:12 and your rear guard is the *G* of Israel.
53: 4 as one smitten by *G* and afflicted.
54: 5 One of Israel, called *G* of all the earth.
54: 6 in youth and then cast off, says your *G*.
55: 5 run to you, Because of the LORD, your *G*,
55: 7 to our *G*,
56: 8 Thus says the LORD *G*,
57:21 No peace for the wicked! says my *G*.
58: 2 just and not abandoned the law of their *G*;
58: 2 is due them, pleased to gain access to *G*.
59: 2 your crimes that separate you from your *G*,
59:13 LORD, turning back from following our *G*,
60: 9 and gold, In the name of the LORD, your *G*,
60:19 light forever, your *G* shall be your glory.
61: 1 The spirit of the LORD *G* is upon me,
61: 2 LORD and a day of vindication by our *G*,
61: 6 ministers of our *G* you shall be called.
61:10 in the LORD, in my *G* is the joy of my soul;
61:11 So will the Lord *G* make justice and praise
62: 3 of the LORD, a royal diadem held by your *G*.
62: 5 his bride so shall your *G* rejoice in you.
64: 3 any *G* but you doing such deeds for those
65:13 me, therefore thus says the Lord *G*:
65:15 The Lord *G* shall slay you,
65:16 in the land shall swear by the *G* of truth;
66: 9 yet close her womb? says your *G*.
Jer 1: 6 "Ah, Lord *G*!"
2:17 Has not the forsaking of the LORD, your *G*,
2:19 bitter is your forsaking the LORD, your *G*,
2:19 fear of me, says the Lord, the *G* of hosts.
2:22 guilt is still before me, says the Lord *G*.
3:13 how you rebelled against the LORD, your *G*,
3:21 their ways and forgotten the LORD, their *G*.
3:22 to you because you are the LORD, our *G*.
3:23 *G*, alone is the salvation of Israel.
3:25 we have sinned against the LORD, our *G*,
3:25 not to the voice of the LORD, our *G*."
4:10 *G*," they will say, "You only deceived us
5: 4 the way of the LORD, their duty to their *G*.
5: 5 the way of the LORD, their duty to their *G*.
5:14 have said, says the LORD, the *G* of hosts
5:24 hearts, "Let us fear the LORD, our *G*,
7: 3 says the LORD of hosts, the *G* of Israel:
7:20 See now, says the Lord *G*,
7:21 says the LORD of hosts, the *G* of Israel:
7:23 will be your *G* and you shall be my people.
7:27 not listen to the voice of the LORD, its *G*,
9:14 says the LORD of hosts, the *G* of Israel:
10:10 The LORD is true *G*, he is the living God,
11: 3 Thus says the LORD, the *G* of Israel:
11: 4 shall be my people, and I will be your *G*.
12: 4 because they say, *G* does not see our ways."
13:12 Thus says the LORD, the *G* of Israel:
13:16 Give glory to the LORD, your *G*,
14:13 Lord *G*, I replied, it is the prophets
14:22 Is it not you alone, O LORD, our *G*,
15:16 I bore your name, O LORD, *G* of hosts.
16: 9 says the LORD of hosts, the *G* of Israel:
16:10 have we committed against the LORD, our *G*—
19: 3 says the LORD of hosts, the *G* of Israel:
19:14 the house of *G* and said to all the people:
19:15 says the LORD of hosts, the *G* of Israel:
21: 4 Thus says the LORD, the *G* of Israel:
22: 9 their covenant with the LORD, their *G*,
23: 2 thus says the LORD, the *G* of Israel,
23:23 Am I a *G* near at hand only,
23:23 only, says the LORD, and not a *G* far off?
23:36 the living God, the LORD of hosts, our *G*.
24: 5 Thus says the LORD, the *G* of Israel:
24: 7 shall be my people and I will be their *G*,
25:15 For thus said the LORD, the *G* of Israel,
25:27 says the LORD of hosts, the *G* of Israel:
26:13 listen to the voice of the LORD your *G*,
26:16 it is in the name of the LORD, our *G*,
27: 4 says the LORD of hosts, the *G* of Israel:
27:21 says the LORD of hosts, the *G* of Israel,
28: 2 says the LORD of hosts, the *G* of Israel:
28:14 says the LORD of hosts, the *G* of Israel:
29: 4 says the LORD of hosts, the *G* of Israel,
29: 8 says the LORD of hosts, the *G* of Israel:
29:21 is what the LORD of hosts, the *G* of Israel,
29:25 says the LORD of hosts, the *G* of Israel:
30: 2 Thus says the LORD, the *G* of Israel:
30: 9 they shall serve the LORD, their *G*,
30:22 shall be my people, and I will be your *G*.
31: 1 will be the *G* of all the tribes of Israel,
31: 6 up, let us go to Zion, to the LORD, our *G*."
31:18 I will return, for you are the LORD, my *G*.
31:23 says the LORD of hosts, the *G* of Israel:
31:33 I will be their *G*,
32:14 says the LORD of hosts, the *G* of Israel:
32:15 says the LORD of hosts, the *G* of Israel:
32:17 Ah, LORD *G*,
32:18 *G*, great and mighty, whose name is LORD
32:25 and yet you tell me, O Lord *G*:
32:27 I am the LORD, the *G* of all mankind!
32:36 thus says the LORD, the *G* of Israel,
32:38 shall be my people, and I will be their *G*.
33: 4 Thus says the LORD, the *G* of Israel,
34: 2 Thus says the LORD, the *G* of Israel:
34:13 Thus says the LORD, the *G* of Israel:
35: 4 of Hanan, son of Igdaliah, the man of *G*,
35:13 says the LORD of hosts, the *G* of Israel:
35:17 the LORD God of hosts, the *G* of Israel:
35:18 says the LORD of hosts, the *G* of Israel:
35:19 says the LORD of hosts, the *G* of Israel:
37: 3 "Pray to the LORD, our *G*, for us."
37: 7 Thus says the LORD, the *G* of Israel:
38:17 says the LORD God of hosts, the *G* of Israel:
39:16 says the LORD of hosts, the *G* of Israel:
40: 2 he said to him, "The LORD your *G*,
42: 2 pray for us to the LORD, your *G*,
42: 3 Let the LORD, your *G*,
42: 4 I will pray to the LORD, your *G*,
42: 5 all the instructions the LORD, your *G*,
42: 6 will obey the command of the LORD, our *G*,
42: 6 for obeying the command of the LORD, our *G*.
42: 9 Thus says the LORD, the *G* of Israel,
42:13 you disobey the voice of the LORD, your *G*,
42:15 says the LORD of hosts, the *G* of Israel:
42:18 says the LORD of hosts, the *G* of Israel:
42:20 me, sending me to the LORD, your *G*,
42:20 saying, "Pray for us to the LORD, our *G*;
42:20 make known to us all that the LORD, our *G*,
42:21 you obey the voice of the LORD, your *G*,
43: 1 all these words of the LORD, their *G*,
43: 2 it was not the LORD, our *G*,
43:10 says the LORD of hosts, the *G* of Israel;
44: 2 says the LORD of hosts, the *G* of Israel:
44: 7 the LORD God of hosts, the *G* of Israel:
44:11 says the LORD of hosts, the *G* of Israel:
44:25 says the LORD of hosts, the *G* of Israel:
44:26 my name saying, "As the LORD *G* lives."
45: 2 Thus says the LORD, *G* of Israel,
46:10 But this is the day of the Lord *G* of hosts,
46:10 for the Lord *G* of hosts holds a slaughter
46:25 The LORD of hosts, the *G* of Israel,
48: 1 says the LORD of hosts, the *G* of Israel:
49: 5 terror upon you, says the LORD *G* of hosts,
50: 4 as they come, to seek the LORD, their *G*;
50:18 says the LORD of hosts, the *G* of Israel:
50:25 For the Lord *G* of hosts has work to do in
50:28 in Zion the vengeance of the LORD, our *G*.
50:31 man of insolence, says the Lord *G* of hosts;
50:40 As when *G* overturned Sodom and Gomorrah,
51: 5 and Judah are not widowed of their *G*,
51:10 let us tell in Zion what the LORD, our *G*,
51:33 says the LORD of hosts, the *G* of Israel:
51:56 The LORD is a *G* who requites,
Lam 3:41 us reach out our hearts toward *G* in heaven!
Bar 1:10 these on the altar of the Lord our *G*,
1:13 "Pray for us also to the Lord, our *G*;
1:13 we have sinned against the Lord, our *G*,
1:15 "Justice is with the Lord, our *G*;
1:18 heeded the voice of the Lord, our *G*,
1:19 have been disobedient to the Lord, our *G*,
1:21 did not heed the voice of the Lord, our *G*,
1:22 did evil in the sight of the Lord, our *G*.
2: 5 because we sinned against the Lord, our *G*,
2: 6 "Justice is with the Lord, our *G*;
2:11 "And now, Lord, *G* of Israel,
2:12 been impious, and violated, O Lord, our *G*,
2:15 may know that you are the Lord, our *G*,
2:19 for mercy in your sight, O Lord, our *G*.
2:27 "But with us, O Lord, our *G*,
2:31 shall know that I, the Lord, am their *G*.
2:35 eternal covenant, that I will be their *G*,
3: 1 "Lord Almighty, *G* of Israel,
3: 2 Hear, O LORD, for you are a *G* of mercy;
3: 4 Lord Almighty, *G* of Israel,
3: 4 not heed the voice of the Lord, their *G*,
3: 6 for you are the Lord our *G*;
3: 8 fathers, who withdrew from the Lord, our *G*."
3:13 Had you walked in the way of *G*,
3:24 O Israel, how vast is the house of *G*,
3:27 Not these did *G* choose,
3:36 Such is our *G*;
4: 1 She is the book of the precepts of *G*,
4: 4 for what pleases *G* is known to us!
4: 6 *G* that you were handed over to your foes.
4: 8 forsook the Eternal *G* who nourished you,
4: 9 indeed saw coming upon you the anger of *G*;
4: 9 *G* has brought great mourning upon me,
4:10 *G* has brought upon my sons and daughters.
4:12 because they turned from the law of *G*,
4:14 brought upon them by the Eternal *G*.
4:20 I live I will cry out to the Eternal *G*.
4:21 call upon *G*,
4:22 trusted in the Eternal *G* for your welfare,
4:23 but *G* will give you back to me with
4:24 glory and the splendor of the Eternal *G*.
4:25 the anger that has come from *G* upon you;
4:27 Fear not, my children; call out to *G*!
4:28 hearts have been disposed to stray from *G*,
4:35 shall come upon her from the Eternal *G*,
4:36 behold the joy that comes to you from *G*.
4:37 the Holy One, rejoicing in the glory of *G*.
5: 1 on the splendor of glory from *G* forever:
5: 2 Wrapped in the cloak of justice from *G*,
5: 3 *G* will show all the earth your splendor:
5: 4 be named by *G* forever the peace of justice,
5: 5 rejoicing that they are remembered by *G*.
5: 6 but *G* will bring them back to you borne
5: 7 For *G* has commanded that every lofty
5: 7 may advance secure in the glory of *G*.
5: 9 For *G* is leading Israel in joy by the
6: 1 to convey to them what *G* had commanded
6: 1 For the sins you committed before *G*,
6:40 forward Bel and ask the *g* to make noise,
6:61 by *G* to proceed across the whole world,
Ez 2: 4 you shall say to them: Thus says the Lord *G*
3:11 Thus says the Lord *G*! whether they heed
3:27 Thus says the Lord *G*! Let him heed who will
4:14 "Oh no, Lord *G*!"
5: 5 Thus says the Lord *G*: This is Jerusalem!
5: 7 Therefore thus says the Lord *G*:
5: 8 therefore thus says the Lord *G*:
5:11 Therefore, as I live, says the Lord *G*,
6: 3 of Israel, hear the word of the Lord *G*.
6: 3 the Lord *G* [to the mountains and hills,
6:11 Thus says the Lord *G*: Clap your hands,
7: 2 Thus says the Lord *G* to the land of Israel:
7: 5 Thus says the Lord *G*: Disaster upon
8: 1 the hand of the Lord *G* fell upon me there
8: 4 I saw there the glory of the *G* of Israel
9: 8 I fell prone, crying out, Alas, Lord *G*!
10: 2 *G* of Israel had gone up from the cherubim,
10: 5 the voice of *G* the Almighty when he speaks.
10:19 glory of the *G* of Israel was up above them.
10:20 the *G* of Israel by the river Chebar,
11: 7 Therefore thus says the Lord *G*:
11: 8 I will bring upon you, says the Lord *G*.
11:13 "Alas, Lord *G*!
11:16 Thus says the Lord *G*: Though I have removed
11:20 shall be my people and I will be their *G*.
11:21 conduct upon their heads, says the Lord *G*.
11:22 them was the glory of the *G* of Israel.
12:10 Thus says the Lord *G*: This oracle concerns
12:19 Thus says the Lord *G* of the inhabitants of
12:23 Thus says the Lord *G*: I will put an end
12:25 speak I will bring about, says the Lord *G*.
12:28 Thus says the Lord *G*: None of my words
12:28 and it shall be done, says the Lord *G*.
13: 3 Thus says the Lord *G*: Woe to those prophets
13: 8 thus says the Lord *G*: Because you have
13: 8 I am coming at you, says the Lord *G*.
13:13 thus says the Lord *G*: In my fury I will let
13:16 when there was no peace, says the Lord *G*.
13:17 against these, prophesy: Thus says the Lord *G*:
13:20 Therefore thus says the Lord *G*:
14: 4 Thus says the Lord *G*;
14: 6 Thus says the Lord *G*: See! I am coming
14:11 and I will be their God, says the Lord *G*.
14:14 by their virtue, says the Lord *G*.
14:16 were in it, as I live, says the Lord *G*,
14:18 were in it, as I live, says the Lord *G*,
14:20 were in it, as I live, says the Lord *G*,
14:21 Thus says the Lord *G*:
14:23 I did to it what I did, says the Lord *G*.
15: 6 thus says the Lord *G*: Even though I send
15: 8 they have broken faith, says the Lord *G*.
16: 3 Thus says the Lord *G* to Jerusalem:
16: 8 you became mine, says the Lord *G*.
16:14 I had bestowed on you, says the Lord *G*.
16:19 them as an appeasing odor, says the Lord *G*.
16:23 says the Lord *G*— you raised for yourself
16:30 says the Lord *G*, that you did all these
16:36 Thus says the Lord *G*: Because you poured
16:43 conduct upon your head, says the Lord *G*.
16:48 As I live, says the Lord *G*,
16:59 thus speaks the Lord *G*: I will deal with
16:63 you for all you have done, says the Lord *G*.
17: 3 Thus speaks the Lord *G*: The great eagle
17: 9 Thus says the Lord *G*: Can it prosper?
17:16 says the Lord *G*, in the home of the king
17:19 Thus says the Lord *G*: As I live, my oath
17:22 Thus says the Lord *G*: I, too, will take
18: 3 says the Lord *G*: I swear that
18: 9 he shall surely live, says the Lord *G*.
18:23 says the Lord *G*. Do I not rather rejoice
18:30 one according to his ways, says the Lord *G*.
18:32 death of anyone who dies, says the Lord *G*.

20: 3 Thus says the Lord G: Have you come
20: 3 to be consulted by you, says the Lord G.
20: 5 Thus speaks the Lord G: The day I chose
20: 5 to them and swore: I am the Lord, your G.
20: 7 the idols of Egypt: I am the Lord, your G.
20:19 I am the LORD, your G: observe my statutes
20:20 and you to show that I am the LORD, your G.
20:27 Thus says the Lord G: In this way also your
20:30 Thus says the Lord G: will you defile
20:31 says the Lord G: I swear, I will not let
20:33 As I live, says the Lord G,
20:36 into judgment with you, says the Lord G.
20:39 you, house of Israel, thus says the Lord G:
20:40 height of Israel, says the Lord G,
20:44 O house of Israel, says the Lord G.
21: 3 Thus says the Lord G: I am kindling a fire
21: 5 G, they say to me, 'Is not this the one
21:12 it is coming, it is here! says the Lord G.
21:18 says the Lord G, since you have spurned
21:29 says the Lord G: Because you have drawn
21:31 crime will be ended, thus says the Lord G:
21:33 G against the Ammonites and their insults:
22: 3 Thus says the Lord G: Woe to the city
22:12 and me you have forgotten, says the Lord G.
22:19 thus says the Lord G: Because all of you
22:28 saying, "Thus says the Lord G,"
22:31 conduct upon their heads, says the Lord G.
23:22 Therefore, Oholibah, thus says the Lord G:
23:28 says the Lord G: I am now handing you over
23:32 says the Lord G: The cup of your sister
23:34 for I have spoken, says the Lord G.
23:35 says the Lord G: Because you have forgotten
23:46 Thus says the Lord G: Summon an assembly
24: 3 Thus says the Lord G: set up the pot
24: 6 says the Lord G: Woe to the bloody city
24: 9 thus says the Lord G: I, too, will heap up
24:14 deeds you shall be judged, says the Lord G.
24:21 Thus says the Lord G: I will now desecrate
25: 3 Thus says the Lord G: Because you cried out
25: 6 thus says the Lord G: Because you clapped
25: 8 Thus says the Lord G: Because Moab said,
25:12 Thus says the Lord G: Because Edon has
25:13 on them, therefore thus says the Lord G:
25:14 shall know my vengeance, says the Lord G.
25:15 Thus says the Lord G: Because the Philistines
25:16 enmity, therefore thus says the Lord G:
26: 3 says the Lord G: See, I am coming at you,
26: 5 I have spoken, says the Lord G:
26: 7 For thus says the Lord G: I am now bringing
26:14 for I have spoken, says the Lord G.
26:15 Thus says the Lord G to Tyre:
26:19 thus says the Lord G: When I make you a city
26:21 but never again found, says the Lord G.
27: 3 Thus says the Lord G: Tyre, you said
28: 2 to the prince of Tyre: Thus says the Lord G:
28: 2 are haughty of heart, and say, "A g am I!
28: 2 And yet you are a man, and not a g,
28: 2 however you may think yourself like a g.
28: 6 therefore thus says the Lord G:
28: 6 thought yourself to have the mind of a g,
28: 9 Will you then say, "I am a g!"
28: 9 No, you are a man, not a g,
28:10 for I have spoken, says the Lord G.
28:12 Thus says the Lord G: you were stamped
28:13 perfect beauty, In Eden, the garden of G,
28:14 you were on the holy mountain of G,
28:16 Then I banned you from the mountain of G;
28:22 says the Lord G: See! I am coming at you,
28:25 says the Lord G: When I gather the house
28:26 shall know that I, the LORD, am their G.
29: 3 says the Lord G: See! I am coming at you
29: 8 therefore thus says the Lord G:
29:13 says the Lord G: At the end of forty years
29:19 says the Lord G: I am now giving the land
29:20 him the land of Egypt, says the Lord G.
30: 2 Thus says the Lord G: Cry, Oh, the day!
30: 6 fall there by the sword, says the Lord G.
30:10 Thus says the Lord G: I will put an end
30:13 Thus says the Lord G: I will put an end
30:22 thus says the Lord G: See! I am coming at
31: 8 in the garden of G were not its equal,
31: 8 tree in the garden of G matched its beauty.
31: 9 of all Eden's trees in the garden of G.
31:10 says the Lord G: Because it became lofty
31:15 says the Lord G: on the day he went down
31:18 and all his hordes, says the Lord G.
32: 3 Thus says the Lord G: I will spread my net
32: 8 darkness over your land, says the Lord G.
32:11 thus says the Lord G: The sword of the king
32:14 streams flow like oil, says the Lord G.
32:16 shall they chant it, says the Lord G.
32:31 Pharaoh and all his army, says the Lord G.
32:32 and all his hordes, says the Lord G.
33:11 As I live, says the Lord G,
33:25 says the Lord G: you eat on the mountains
33:27 Thus says the Lord G: As I live,
34: 2 Thus says the Lord G: Woe to the shepherds
34: 8 As I live, says the Lord G,
34:10 Thus says the Lord G: I swear I am coming
34:11 thus says the Lord G: I myself will look
34:15 will give them rest, says the Lord G.
34:17 As for you, my sheep, says the Lord G,
34:20 thus says the Lord G: Now I will judge
34:24 I, the LORD, will be their G,
34:30 shall know that I, the LORD, am their G,
34:30 the house of Israel, says the Lord G.
34:31 I am your God, says the Lord G
35: 3 Thus says the Lord G: See! I am coming at you
35: 6 therefore, as I live, says the Lord G,
35:11 therefore, as I live, says the Lord G,
35:14 Thus says the Lord G: Just as you rejoiced
36: 2 Thus says the Lord G: Because the enemy
36: 3 Thus says the Lord G: because you have been
36: 4 says the Lord G to the mountains and hills,
36: 5 therefore thus says the Lord G:
36: 6 Thus says the Lord G: with jealous fury I speak
36:13 Thus says the Lord G:
36:14 people of their children, says the Lord G.
36:15 people of their children, says the Lord G.
36:22 Thus says the Lord G: Not for your sakes do I
36:23 know that I am the LORD, says the Lord G,
36:28 shall be my people, and I will be your G.
36:32 for your sakes do I act, says the Lord G—
36:33 Thus says the Lord G: When I purify you
36:37 Thus says the Lord G: This also I will
37: 3 G," I answered, "you alone know that."
37: 5 Thus says the Lord G to these bones:
37: 9 Thus says the Lord G: From the winds come,
37:12 Thus says the Lord G: O my people
37:19 Thus says the Lord G: I will take the stick
37:21 speaks the Lord G: I will take the Israelites
37:23 they may be my people and I may be their G.
37:27 I will be their G,
38: 3 Thus says the Lord G: See! I am coming at you
38:10 Thus says the Lord G: At that time thoughts
38:14 Thus says the Lord G: When my people Israel
38:17 Thus says the Lord G: It is of you that I spoke
38:18 the land of Israel, says the Lord G,
38:21 will summon every terror, says the Lord G,
39: 1 Thus says the Lord G: See! I am coming at you
39: 5 for I have decreed it, says the Lord G.
39: 8 and shall be fulfilled, says the Lord G.
39:10 those who pillaged them, says the Lord G.
39:13 when I reveal my glory, says the Lord G.
39:17 As for you, son of man, says the Lord G,
39:20 soldiers of every kind, says the Lord G.
39:22 shall know that I am the LORD, their G.
39:25 thus says the Lord G: Now I will restore
39:28 shall know that I, the LORD, am their G,
39:29 upon the house of Israel, says the Lord G.
43: 2 of the G of Israel coming from the east.
43:18 Son of man, thus says the Lord G:
43:19 near me to minister to me, says the Lord G.
43:27 Then I will accept you, says the Lord G.
44: 2 since the LORD, the G of Israel,
44: 6 Thus says the Lord G: Enough of all these
44: 9 Thus says the Lord G: No foreigners
44:12 an oath against them, says the Lord G:
44:15 to offer me fat and blood, says the Lord G.
44:27 present his sin offering, says the Lord G.
45: 9 Thus says the Lord G: Enough, you princes
45: 9 stop evicting my people! says the Lord G.
45:15 and atonement sacrifices, says the Lord G.
45:18 Thus says the Lord G: On the first day
46: 1 says the Lord G: The gate toward the east
46:16 says the Lord G: If the prince makes a gift
47:13 says the Lord G: These are the boundaries
47:23 him his inheritance, says the Lord G.
48:29 these are their portions, says the Lord G.

Dn 1: 2 some of the vessels of the temple of G,
1: 2 and placed in the temple treasury of his g.
1: 9 Though G had given Daniel the favor and
1:17 To these four young men G gave knowledge
2:18 the G of heaven in regard to this mystery,
2:19 a vision, and he blessed the G of heaven:
2:20 be the name of G forever and ever,
2:23 To you, O G of my fathers,
2:28 is a G in heaven who reveals mysteries,
2:37 to you the G of heaven has given dominion
2:44 In the lifetime of those kings the G of
2:45 The great G has revealed to the king what
2:47 "Truly your G is the God of gods and Lord
3:12 they will not serve your g or worship the
3:14 Abednego, that you will not serve my g,
3:15 the G that can deliver you out of my hands?"
3:17 If our G, whom we serve, can save us
3:18 that we will not serve your g or worship
3:24 flames, singing to G and blessing the Lord.
3:26 praiseworthy, O Lord, the G of our fathers,
3:45 them know that you alone are the Lord G,
3:51 one voice sang, glorifying and blessing G:
3:52 are you, O Lord, the G of our fathers,
3:90 Bless the G of gods,
3:92 fire, and the fourth looks like a son of G."
3:93 "Servants of the most high G, come out."
3:95 exclaimed, "Blessed be the G of Shadrach,
3:95 or worship any god except their own G.
3:96 that whoever blasphemes the G of Shadrach,
3:96 is no other G who can rescue like this."
3:99 most high G has accomplished in my regard.
4: 5 my g, and in whom is the spirit of the holy G.
4: 6 the spirit of the holy G is in you
4:15 because the spirit of the holy G is in you."
5: 3 of G in Jerusalem had been brought in,
5:11 in whom is the spirit of the holy G;
5:14 have heard that the spirit of G is in you,
5:18 The Most High G gave your father
5:21 Most High G rules over the kingdom of men
5:23 But the G in whose hand is your life
5:26 G has numbered your kingdom and put an end
6: 6 Daniel unless by way of the law of his G."
6: 8 any petition to g or man for thirty days,
6:11 G in the upper chamber three times a day,
6:12 Daniel praying and pleading before his G.
6:13 a petition to g or man for thirty days,
6:17 To Daniel he said, "May your G,
6:21 living G, has the God whom you serve
6:23 My G has sent his angel and closed the
6:24 den, unhurt because he trusted in his G.
6:27 G of Daniel is to be reverenced and feared:
6:27 "For he is the living G,
9: 3 I turned to the Lord G,
9: 4 I prayed to the LORD, my G,
9: 4 "Ah, Lord, great and awesome G,
9: 9 But yours, O LORD, our G,
9:10 no heed to your command, O LORD, our G,
9:11 in the law of Moses, the servant of G,
9:13 As we did not appease the LORD, our G,
9:14 You, O LORD, our G, are just in all
9:15 O Lord, our G, who led your people out
9:17 Hear, therefore, O G, the prayer
9:18 Give ear, O my G, and listen;
9:19 without delay, for your own sake, O my G,
9:20 presenting my petition to the LORD, my G,
10:12 understanding and humble yourself before G,
11:32 loyal to their G shall take strong action.
11:36 and making himself greater than any g;
11:36 dreadful blasphemies against the G of gods.
11:37 for no g shall he have regard,
11:38 glory to the g of strongholds; a g unknown
11:39 he shall station a people of a foreign g.
13:42 "O eternal G,
13:45 G stirred up the holy spirit of a young
13:50 G has given you the prestige of old age."
13:55 "for the angel of G shall receive the
13:59 "for the angel of G waits with a sword to
13:60 G who saves those that hope in him.
13:63 wife praised G for their daughter Susanna,
14: 4 but Daniel adored only his G.
14: 5 but only the living G who made heaven and
14: 6 "You do not think Bel is a living g?
14:24 "you cannot deny that this is a living g,
14:25 the Lord, my God, for he is the living G.
14:37 Habakkuk, "take the lunch G has sent you."
14:38 "You have remembered me, O G,"
14:41 "You are great, O Lord, the G of Daniel,

Hos 1: 7 I will save them by the LORD, their G;
1: 9 not my people, and I will not be your G.
2: 1 be called, "Children of the living G."
2:25 are my people," and he shall say, "My G."
3: 5 turn back and seek the LORD, their G,
4: 1 no mercy, no knowledge of G in the land.
4: 6 Since you have ignored the law of your G,
4:12 they commit harlotry, forsaking their G.
5: 4 do not allow them to return to their G;
6: 6 and knowledge of G rather than holocausts.
7:10 they do not return to the LORD, their G,
8: 2 While to me they cry out, "O, G of Israel,
8: 6 The work of an artisan no g at all,
9: 1 For you have been unfaithful to your G,
9: 8 A prophet is Ephraim's watchman with G,
9: 8 his ways, hostility in the house of his G.
9:17 My G will disown them because they have
10: 2 G shall break down their altars and
11: 7 G, though in unison they cry out to him,
11: 9 For I am G and not man,
12: 1 Judah is still rebellious against G,
12: 4 brother, and as a man he contended with G;
12: 5 he met G and there he spoke with him;
12: 6 The LORD, the G of hosts,
12: 7 You shall return by the help of your G,
12: 7 and do right and always hope in your G.
12:10 I am the LORD, your G,
13: 4 I am the LORD, your G,
13: 4 You know no G besides me,
14: 1 guilt, for she has rebelled against her G.
14: 2 Return, O Israel, to the LORD, your G;
14: 4 We shall say no more, 'Our g,'

Jl 1:13 night in sackcloth, O ministers of my G!
1:13 G is deprived of offering and libation.
1:14 land, Into the house of the LORD, your G,
1:16 And from the house of our G,
2:13 garments, and return to the LORD, your G.
2:14 and libations for the LORD, your G.
2:17 say among the peoples, "Where is their G?"
2:23 exult and rejoice in the LORD, your G!
2:26 shall praise the name of the LORD, your G,
2:27 I am the LORD, your G,
4:17 you know that I, the LORD, am your G,

Am 1: 8 Philistines shall perish, says the LORD G.
2: 8 fined they drink in the house of their g.
3: 7 the Lord G does nothing without revealing
3: 8 The Lord G speaks— who will not prophesy!
3:11 Therefore, thus says the Lord G:
3:13 Jacob, says the Lord GOD, the G of hosts:
4: 2 The Lord G has sworn by his holiness:
4: 5 to do, O men of Israel, says the Lord G.
4:11 as when G overthrew Sodom and Gomorrah:
4:12 deal thus with you, prepare to meet your G,

GOD (cont.)
4:13 The LORD, The *G* of hosts by name.
5: 3 For thus says the Lord *G*:
5:14 Then truly will the LORD, the *G* of hosts,
5:15 it may be that the LORD, the *G* of hosts,
5:16 thus says the LORD, the *G* of hosts,
5:26 your king, and Kaiwan, your star *g*,
5:27 say I, the LORD, the *G* of hosts by name.
6: 8 The Lord *G* has sworn by his very self,
6: 8 very self, say I, the LORD, the *G* of hosts:
6:14 of Israel, say I, the LORD, the *G* of hosts,
7: 1 This is what the Lord *G* showed me:
7: 2 Forgive, O Lord *G*!
7: 3 "It shall not be," said the Lord *G*.
7: 4 Then the Lord *G* showed me this:
7: 5 Cease, O Lord *G*!
7: 6 also shall not be," said the Lord *G*.
7: 7 Then the Lord *G* showed me this:
8: 1 This is what the Lord *G* showed me:
8: 3 wailings on that day, says the Lord *G*.
8: 9 On that day, says the Lord *G*,
8:11 Yes, days are coming, says the Lord *G*,
8:14 idol of Samaria, "By the life of your *g*,
9: 5 and not for good, I, the Lord *G* of hosts,
9: 8 of the Lord *G* are on this sinful kingdom;
9:15 I have given them, say I, the LORD, your *G*.
Ob 1: 1 [Thus says the Lord *G*:
Jon 1: 5 frightened and each one cried to his *g*.
1: 6 Rise up, call upon your *G*!
1: 6 Perhaps *G* will be mindful of us so that we
1: 9 "I worship the LORD, the *G* of heaven,
2: 2 Jonah said this prayer to the LORD, his *G*:
2: 7 my life up from the pit, O LORD, my *G*.
3: 5 when the people of Nineveh believed *G*;
3: 8 with sackcloth and call loudly to *G*;
3: 9 Who knows, *G* may relent and forgive,
3:10 When *G* saw by their actions how they
4: 2 that you are a gracious and merciful *G*,
4: 6 And when the LORD *G* provided a gourd plant,
4: 7 *G* sent a worm which attacked the plant,
4: 8 the sun arose, *G* sent a burning east wind;
4: 9 But *G* said to Jonah,
Mi 1: 2 Let the Lord *G* be witness against you,
3: 7 because there is no answer from *G*.
4: 2 the LORD, to the house of the *G* of Jacob,
4: 5 peoples walk each in the name of its *g*,
4: 5 But we walk in the name of the LORD, our *G*,
5: 3 in the majestic name of the LORD, his *G*;
6: 6 the LORD, and bow before *G* most high?
6: 8 goodness, and to walk humbly with your *G*.
7: 7 my trust in *G* my savior; my *G* will hear
7:10 who said to me, "Where is the LORD, your *G*
7:17 trembling in fear of you [the LORD, our *G*.
7:18 the *G* who removes guilt and pardons sin
Na 1: 2 A jealous and avenging *G* is the LORD,
Hb 1:11 culprit who makes his own strength his *g*!
1:12 you not from eternity, O LORD, my holy *G*,
3: 3 *G* comes from Teman,
3:18 in the LORD and exult in my saving *G*.
3:19 *G*, my Lord, is my strength;
Zep 1: 7 Silence in the presence of the Lord *G*!
2: 7 For the LORD their *G* shall visit them,
2: 9 says the LORD of hosts, the *G* of Israel,
3: 2 trusted, to her *G* she has not drawn near.
3:17 The LORD, your *G*, is in your midst,
Hg 1:12 to the voice of the LORD, their *G*,
1:12 prophet Haggai, because the LORD, their *G*,
1:14 the house of the LORD of hosts, their *G*,
Zec 6:15 carefully the voice of the LORD your *G*.
8: 8 shall be my people, and I will be their *G*,
8:23 you, for we have heard that *G* is with you."
9: 7 He also shall become a remnant for our *G*,
9:14 The Lord *G* shall sound the trumpet,
9:16 their *G*, shall save them on that day,
10: 6 cast them off, for I am the LORD, their *G*,
11: 4 Thus said the LORD, my *G*: Shepherd the flock
12: 5 strength in the LORD of hosts, their *G*."
13: 9 and they shall say, "The LORD is my *G*."
14: 5 Then the LORD, my *G*, shall come,
Mal 1: 9 So now if you implore *G* for mercy on us,
2:10 Has not the one *G* created us?
2:16 divorce, says the LORD, the *G* of Israel,
2:17 or else, "Where is the just *G*?"
3: 8 Dare a man rob *G*?
3:14 You have said, "It is vain to serve *G*,
3:15 prosper, and even tempt *G* with impunity."
3:18 Between him who serves *G*,
Mt 1:23 a name which means *G* is with us."
3: 2 The reign of *G* is at hand."
3: 9 *G* can raise up children to Abraham from
3:16 *G* descend like a dove and hover over him.
4: 3 said to him, "If you are the Son of *G*,
4: 4 utterance that comes from the mouth of *G*.' "
4: 6 and said, "If you are the Son of *G*,
4: 7 shall not put the Lord your *G* to the test.' "
4:10 'You shall do homage to the Lord your *G*;
5: 3 the reign of *G* is theirs.
5: 8 the single-hearted for they shall see *G*.
5: 9 they shall be called sons of *G*.
5:10 the reign of *G* is theirs.
5:19 shall be called least in the kingdom of *G*.
5:19 shall be great in the kingdom of *G*.
5:20 you shall not enter the kingdom of *G*.
6:24 You cannot give yourself to *G* and money.
6:30 If *G* can clothe in such splendor the grass
7:21 will enter the kingdom of *G* but only the
8:11 banquet in the kingdom of *G* with Abraham,
8:29 "Why meddle with us, Son of *G*?
9: 8 praised *G* for giving such authority to men.
10: 7 'The reign of *G* is at hand!'
11:11 into the kingdom of *G* is greater than he.
11:12 now the kingdom of *G* has suffered violence,
12:28 *G* that I expel demons, then the reign of *G*
13:11 of the mysteries of the reign of *G*,
13:24 "The reign of *G* may be likened to a man
13:31 "The reign of *G* is like a mustard seed
13:33 "The reign of *G* is like yeast which a
13:44 "The reign of *G* is like a buried treasure
13:47 "The reign of *G* is also like a dragnet
13:52 reign of *G* is like the head of a household
14:33 "Beyond doubt you are the Son of *G*!"
15: 3 of *G* for the sake of your 'tradition'?
15: 4 For instance, *G* has said,
15: 5 might have had from me is dedicated to *G*,
15:31 They glorified the *G* of Israel.
16:16 Peter answered, "the Son of the living *G*!"
16:22 *G* forbid that any such thing ever happen
18: 1 of greatest importance in the kingdom of *G*?"
18: 3 you will not enter the kingdom of *G*.
18:23 That is why the reign of *G* may be said to
19: 6 let no man separate what *G* has joined."
19:14 The kingdom of *G* belongs to such as these."
19:23 a rich man enter into the kingdom of *G*.
19:24 for a rich man to enter the kingdom of *G*."
19:26 but for *G* all things are possible."
20: 1 "The reign of *G* is like the case of the
21:31 are entering the kingdom of *G* before you.
21:43 the kingdom of *G* will be taken away from
22: 2 "The reign of *G* may be likened to a king
22:21 is Caesar's, but give to *G* what is God's."
22:29 the Scriptures and the power of *G*.
22:31 have you not read what *G* said to you,
22:32 *G* of Abraham, the *G* of Isaac, the *G*
22:32 He is the *G* of the living,
22:37 love the Lord your *G* with your whole heart,
23:13 doors of the kingdom of *G* in men's faces,
25: 1 "The reign of *G* can be likened to ten
26:63 the living *G* whether you are the Messiah,
26:63 whether you are the Messiah, the Son of *G*."
27:43 He relied on God; let *G* rescue him now
27:46 "My *G*, My God, why have you forsaken me?
27:54 and said, "Clearly this was the Son of *G*!"
Mk 1: 1 the gospel of Jesus Christ, the Son of *G*.
1:14 in Galilee proclaiming the good news of *G*:
1:15 The reign of *G* is at hand!
1:24 I know who you are—the holy One of *G*!"
2: 7 Who can forgive sins except *G* alone?"
2:12 all gave praise to *G*,
3:11 feet, and shout, "You are the Son of *G*!"
3:35 *G* is brother and sister and mother to me."
4:11 of the reign of *G* has been confided.
4:26 "This is how it is with the reign of *G*.
4:30 comparison shall we use for the reign of *G*?
5: 7 meddle with me, Jesus, Son of *G* Most High?
7:11 me is korban' (that is, dedicated to *G*),
9: 1 see the reign of *G* established in power."
9:47 Better for you to enter the kingdom of *G*
10: 6 of creation *G* made them male and female;
10: 9 let no man separate what *G* has joined."
10:14 as these that the kingdom of *G* belongs.
10:15 accept the reign of *G* like a little child
10:18 No one is good but *G* alone.
10:23 is for the rich to enter the kingdom of *G*!"
10:24 how hard it is to enter the kingdom of *G*!
10:25 for a rich man to enter the kingdom of *G*."
10:27 "For man it is impossible but not for *G*.
10:27 With *G* all things are possible."
11:22 "Put your trust in *G*.
12:17 is Caesar's, but give to *G* what is God's."
12:24 the Scriptures or the power of *G*.
12:26 how God told him,
12:26 *G* of Abraham, the *G* of Isaac, the *G*
12:27 He is the *G* of the living,
12:29 The Lord our *G* is Lord alone!
12:30 love the Lord your *G* with all your heart,
12:34 him, "You are not far from the reign of *G*."
14:25 day when I drink it new in the reign of *G*."
15:34 "My *G*, my God, why have you forsaken me?
15:39 "Clearly this man was the Son of *G*!"
15:43 who looked forward to the true reign of *G*.
16:20 by spirits to grasp the true power of *G*.
Lk 1: 6 Both were just in the eyes of *G*,
1: 8 his functions as a priest before *G*,
1:16 will he bring back to the Lord their *G*.
1:17 *G* himself will go before him,
1:19 Gabriel, who stand in attendance before *G*.
1:26 from *G* to a town of Galilee named Nazareth,
1:30 You have found favor with *G*.
1:32 The Lord *G* will give him the throne of
1:35 to be born will be called Son of *G*.
1:37 month, for nothing is impossible with *G*."
1:47 Lord, my spirit finds joy in *G* my savior,
1:49 *G* who is mighty has done great things for
1:64 and he began to speak in praise of *G*.
1:68 "Blessed be the Lord the *G* of Israel
1:78 this is the work of the kindness of our *G*;
2:13 the heavenly host, praising *G* and saying,
2:14 and saying, "Glory to *G* in high heaven,
2:20 praising *G* for all they had heard and seen,
2:28 in his arms and blessed *G* in these words:
2:38 she gave thanks to *G* and talked about the
2:40 wisdom, and the grace of *G* was upon him.
2:52 wisdom and age and grace before *G* and men.
3: 2 the word of *G* was spoken to John son of
3: 6 all mankind shall see the salvation of *G*.' "
3: 8 *G* can raise up children to Abraham from
3:38 Enos, son of Seth, son of Adam, son of *G*.
4: 3 said to him, "If you are the Son of *G*,
4: 8 'You shall do homage to the Lord your *G*;
4: 9 said to him, "If you are the Son of *G*,
4:12 shall not put the Lord your *G* to the test.' "
4:34 the Holy One of *G*."
4:41 out as they did so, "You are the Son of *G*!"
4:43 announce the good news of the reign of *G*,
5: 1 pressed in on him to hear the word of *G*,
5:21 Who can forgive sins but *G* alone?"
5:25 had been lying on and went home praising *G*.
5:26 Full of awe, they gave praise to *G*,
6:12 spending the night in communion with *G*.
6:20 the reign of *G* is yours.
7:16 seized them all and they began to praise *G*.
7:16 and, *G* has visited his people."
7:28 into the kingdom of *G* is greater than he."
7:29 even the tax collectors, gave praise to *G*,
8: 1 the good news of the kingdom of *G*.
8:10 of the reign of *G* have been confided,
8:11 The seed is the word of *G*.
8:21 who hear the word of *G* and act upon it."
8:28 of his voice, "Jesus, Son of *G* Most High,
8:39 and recount all that *G* has done for you."
9: 2 the reign of *G* and heal the afflicted.
9:11 them and spoke to them of the reign of *G*,
9:20 Peter said in reply, "The Messiah of *G*."
9:27 taste death until they see the reign of *G*."
9:43 who saw it marveled at the greatness of *G*.
9:60 come away and proclaim the kingdom of *G*."
9:62 looking back is unfit for the reign of *G*."
10: 9 Say to them, 'The reign of *G* is at hand.'
10:11 But know that the reign of *G* is near.'
10:27 love the Lord your *g* with all your heart,
11:20 *G* that I cast out devils, then the reign of *G*
11:28 they who hear the word of *G* and keep it."
11:42 while neglecting justice and the love of *G*.
11:49 That is why the wisdom of *G* has said,
12: 6 Yet not one of them is neglected by *G*.
12: 8 acknowledge him before the angels of *G*.
12: 9 in the presence of the angels of *G*.
12:20 But *G* said to him, 'You fool!
12:21 instead of growing rich in the sight of *G*."
12:24 yet *G* feeds them.
12:28 If *G* clothes in such splendor the grass of
13:13 she stood up straight and began thanking *G*.
13:18 "What does the reign of *G* resemble?
13:20 "To what shall I compare the reign of *G*?
13:28 all the prophets safe in the kingdom of *G*,
13:29 place at the feast in the kingdom of *G*.
14:15 is he who eats bread in the kingdom of *G*."
15:10 the angels of *G* over one repentant sinner."
15:18 I have sinned against *G* and against you;
15:21 I have sinned against *G* and against you;
16:13 You cannot give yourself to *G* and money."
16:15 the eyes of men, but *G* reads your hearts.
16:15 man thinks important, *G* holds in contempt.
17:15 came back praising *G* in a loud voice.
17:18 and give thanks to *G* except this foreigner?"
17:20 Pharisees when the reign of *G* would come,
17:20 watching when the reign of *G* will come.
17:21 The reign of *G* is already in your midst."
18: 2 city who respected neither *G* nor man.
18: 4 he thought, 'I care little for *G* or man,
18: 7 Will not *G* then do justice to his chosen
18:11 'I give you thanks, O *G*,
18:13 he did was beat his breast and say, 'O *G*,
18:16 The reign of *G* belongs to such as these.
18:17 of *G* as a child will not enter into it."
18:19 None is good but *G* alone.
18:24 for the rich to go into the kingdom of *G*!
18:27 are impossible for men are possible for *G*."
18:29 for the sake of the kingdom of *G*
18:43 began to follow him, giving *G* the glory.
18:43 witnessed it and they too gave praise to *G*.
19:11 that the reign of *G* was about to appear.
19:37 disciples began to rejoice and praise *G* loudly
20: 4 baptism of John come from *G* or from men?"
20: 5 someone said, "If we answer, 'From *G*,'
20:16 When they heard this they said, *G* forbid!"
20:21 of persons but teach the way of *G* in truth.
20:25 is Caesar's, but give to *G* what is God's."
20:36 of the resurrection, they are sons of *G*.
20:37 *G* of Abraham, and the God of Isaac, and the *G*
20:38 *G* is not the God of the dead but of the
21:31 I speak, know that the reign of *G* is near.
22:16 until it is fulfilled in the kingdom of *G*."
22:18 vine until the coming of the reign of *G*."
22:69 seat at the right hand of the Power of *G*.' "
22:70 "So you are the Son of *G*?"
23:35 him save himself if he is the Messiah of *G*,
23:40 "Have you no fear of *G*,
23:47 had happened, gave glory to *G* by saying,

23:51 he looked expectantly for the reign of G.
24:19 deed in the eyes of G and all the people;
24:53 constantly, speaking the praises of G.
Jn 1: 1 was in God's presence, and the Word was G.
1: 2 He was present to G in the beginning.
1: 6 There was a man named John sent by G,
1:12 him he empowered to become children of G.
1:13 desire, nor by man's willing it, but by G.
1:18 No one has ever seen G.
1:18 It is G the only Son,
1:29 of G who takes away the sin of the world!
1:36 There is the Lamb of G!"
1:49 said Nathanael, "you are the Son of G;
1:51 angels of G ascending and descending
3: 2 "we know you are a teacher come from G,
3: 2 such as you perform unless G is with him."
3: 3 of G unless he is begotten from above."
3:16 G so loved the world that he gave his only
3:17 G did not send the Son into the world to
3:21 to make clear that his deeds are done in G."
3:33 testimony certifies that G is truthful.
3:34 whom G has sent speaks the words of God;
3:36 see life, but must endure the wrath of G."
4:20 is the place where men ought to worship G."
4:24 G is Spirit,
5:18 still, was speaking of G as his own Father,
5:25 shall hear the voice of the Son of G,
5:42 do not have the love of G in your hearts.
5:44 seek the glory that comes from the One G?
6:27 on him that G the Father has set his seal."
6:28 must we do to perform the works of G?"
6:29 "This is the work of G:
6:45 'They shall all be taught by G,'
6:46 the one who is from G has seen the Father.
7:17 comes from G or is simply spoken on my own.
8:40 you the truth which I have heard from G.
8:41 have but one father and that is G himself."
8:42 "Were G your father you would love me,
8:42 you would love me, for I came forth from G,
8:47 is of God hears every word G speaks.
8:47 you do not hear is that you are not of G."
8:54 Father, the very one you claim for your G,
9:16 G because he does not keep the sabbath."
9:24 blind and said to him, "Give glory to G!
9:29 We know that G spoke to Moses,
9:31 We know that G does not hear sinners,
9:33 If this man were not from G,
10:33 who are only a man are making yourself G."
11: 4 through it the Son of G may be glorified."
11:22 G will give you whatever you ask of him."
11:27 that you are the Messiah, the Son of G:
11:40 you would see the glory of G displayed?"
11:52 into one all the dispersed children of G.)
12:43 the praise of men to the glory of G.
13: 3 he had come from G and was going to God,
13:31 of Man glorified and G is glorified in him.
13:32 [If G has been glorified in him.] G will
14: 1 Have faith in G and faith in me.
16: 2 you to death will claim to be serving G!
16:27 me and have believed that I came from G.
16:30 We do indeed believe you came from G."
17: 3 to know you, the only true G,
20:17 and your Father, to my G and your God!'"
20:28 said in response, "My Lord and my G!"
20:31 that Jesus is the Messiah, the Son of G,
21:19 of death by which Peter was to glorify G.)
Acts 1: 3 and speaking to them about the reign of G.
2:11 about the marvels G has accomplished."
2:17 come to pass in the last days, says G,
2:22 was a man whom G sent to you with miracles,
2:22 These G worded through him in your midst,
2:23 up by the set purpose and plan of G;
2:24 G freed him from death's bitter pangs,
2:30 He was a prophet and knew that G had sworn
2:32 This is the Jesus G has raised up,
2:36 G has made both Lord and Messiah this Jesus
2:39 still far off whom the Lord our G calls."
2:47 praising G and winning the approval of all
3: 8 walking, jumping about, and praising G.
3: 9 saw him moving and giving praise to G,
3:13 G of Abraham, of Isaac, and of Jacob, the G
3:15 But G raised him from the dead,
3:18 G has brought to fulfillment by this means
3:19 Turn to G,
3:21 restoration which G spoke of long ago
3:22 "'The Lord G will raise up for you a
3:25 covenant G made with your fathers
3:26 When G raised up his servant,
4:10 crucified and whom G raised from the dead.
4:19 sight for us to obey you rather than G.
4:21 whom were praising G for what had happened.
4:24 voices in prayer to G on hearing the story:
5: 4 You have lied not to men but to G!"
5:29 "Better for us to obey G than men!
5:30 The G of our fathers has raised up Jesus
5:31 He whom G has exalted at his right hand as
5:32 whom G has given to those that obey him."
5:39 on the other hand, it comes from G,
5:39 to destroy them without fighting G himself."
6: 2 the word of G in order to wait on tables.
6: 7 The word of G continued to spread,
6:11 speaking blasphemies against Moses and G,
7: 2 The G of glory appeared to our father
7: 3 G said to him,
7: 4 G made him move from there to this land
7: 5 G did not give him any of it as his
7: 6 These are the words G used:
7: 7 judge that nation which they serve, G said,
7: 8 G then made a covenant of circumcision
7:10 but G was with him and rescued him from
7:17 of the promise made by G to Abraham,
7:25 G was using him to bring them deliverance;
7:32 the God of your fathers, the G of Abraham,
7:35 was the one whom G,
7:37 G will raise up for you from among your
7:42 But G turned away from them and abandoned
7:43 of Moloch and the star of the g Rephan,
7:44 as G prescribed it when he spoke to Moses,
7:45 G drove out to make room for our fathers.
7:46 who found favor with G and begged that he
7:55 to the sky above and saw the glory of G,
8:10 "He is the power of the great G,"
8:12 kingdom of G and the name of Jesus Christ,
8:14 that Samaria had accepted the word of G,
8:21 Your heart is not steadfastly set on G.
9:20 the synagogues that Jesus was the Son of G.
10: 2 the people and he constantly prayed to G.
10: 3 of G coming toward him and calling,
10:15 G has purified you are not to call unclean."
10:28 But G has made it clear to me that no one
10:33 All of us stand before G at this moment to
10:34 how true it is that G shows no partiality.
10:35 G and acts uprightly is acceptable to him.
10:38 of the way G anointed him with the Holy
10:38 the grip of the devil, and G was with him.
10:40 only to have G raise him up on the third
10:41 as had been chosen beforehand by G—
10:42 by G as judge of the living and the dead.
10:46 hear speaking in tongues and glorifying G.
11: 1 Gentiles, too, had accepted the word of G.
11: 9 G has purified you are not to call unclean.'
11:17 If G was giving them the same gift he gave
11:18 instead began to glorify G in these words:
11:18 then G has granted life-giving repentance
12: 5 church prayed fervently to G on his behalf.
12:22 shouted back, "This is the voice of a g,
12:23 because he did not ascribe the honor to G,
13: 5 the word of G in the Jewish synagogues,
13: 7 Saul and was anxious to hear the word of G.
13:16 and you others who reverence our G,
13:17 The G of the people Israel once chose our
13:21 for a king, G gave them Saul son of Kish,
13:22 Then G removed him and raised up David as
13:22 on his behalf G testified,
13:23 G has brought forth from this man's
13:26 and you others who reverence our G,
13:30 Yet G raised him from the dead,
13:32 news that what G promised our fathers
13:34 again see the decay of death, G declared,
13:37 G has raised up did not undergo corruption.
13:43 urged them to hold fast to the grace of G.
13:44 entire city gathered to hear the word of G.
13:46 G has to be declared to you first of all;
14:15 such follies as these to the living G,
14:22 if we are to enter into the reign of G."
14:26 of G for the task they had now completed.
14:27 all that G had helped them accomplish,
15: 4 all that G had helped them accomplish.
15: 7 from the early days G selected me
15: 8 G, who reads the hearts of men,
15:10 do you put G to the test by trying to
15:12 wonders G had worked among the Gentiles
15:14 Symeon has told you how G first concerned
16:10 concluding that G had summoned us to
16:14 She already reverenced G,
16:17 men are servants of the Most High G;
16:25 to G as their fellow prisoners listened,
16:32 of G to him and to everyone in his house.
16:34 his whole family his newfound faith in G.
17:13 word of G had been proclaimed by Paul
17:23 an altar inscribed, 'To a G Unknown.'
17:24 G who made the world and all that is in it,
17:27 They were to seek G,
17:30 G may well have overlooked bygone periods
18: 7 named Titus Justus, who reverenced G;
18:11 and a half, teaching them the word of G.
18:13 worship G in ways that are against the law."
18:21 he gave them his promise, G willing,
19: 8 arguments, about the kingdom of G.
19:11 Meanwhile G worked extraordinary miracles
20:21 before G and on faith in our Lord Jesus.
20:28 Shepherd the church of G,
21:19 G had accomplished among the Gentiles
21:20 When they heard it they praised G,
22: 3 I was a staunch defender of G,
22:14 'The G of our fathers long ago designated
23: 1 my life with a clear conscience before G."
23: 3 "You are the one G will strike,
24:14 that I worship the G of our fathers.
24:15 and I have the same hope in G as these
24:16 keep my conscience clear before G and man.
26: 6 in the promise made by G to our fathers.
26: 7 worship G day and night in the hope
26: 8 to believe that G raises dead men to life.
26:18 light and from the dominion of Satan to G;
26:20 message of reform and of conversion to G,
26:29 I would to G that not only you but all who
27:23 of the G whose man I am and whom I serve,
27:24 G has granted safety to all who are
27:25 I trust in G that it will all work out
27:35 bread, gave thanks to G before all of them,
28: 6 minds and began to say that he was a g.
28:15 them, he thanked G and took fresh courage.
28:23 witness to the reign of G among men.
28:28 of G has been transmitted to the Gentiles
28:31 G and taught about the Lord Jesus Christ.
Rom 1: 1 set apart to proclaim the gospel of G
1: 4 the flesh but was made Son of G in power
1: 7 G and called to holiness,
1: 7 grace and peace from G
1: 8 I give thanks to G through Jesus Christ
1: 9 The G I worship in the spirit by preaching
1:16 It is the power of G leading everyone who
1:17 of G which begins and ends with faith;
1:18 The wrath of G is being revealed from
1:19 can be known about G is clear to them;
1:21 G, yet they did not glorify him as G
1:23 G for images representing mortal man,
1:24 G delivered them up in their lusts to
1:25 these men who exchanged the truth of G
1:26 G therefore delivered them up to
1:28 acknowledge G, so God delivered them up
1:30 are gossips and slanderers, they hate G,
2: 5 the just judgment of G will be revealed,
2:11 With G there is no favoritism.
2:13 the law who are just in the sight of G;
2:16 G will pass judgment on the secrets of men
2:17 firmly on the law and pride yourself on G.
2:23 law, do you dishonor G by breaking the law?
2:24 G is held in contempt among the Gentiles."
2:29 his praise, not from men, but from G.
3: 2 the Jews were entrusted with words of G.
3: 4 G must be proved true even though every
3: 5 not G unjust when he inflicts punishment?"
3: 6 that were so, how could G judge the world?
3:11 one who understands, no one in search of G.
3:18 the fear of G is not before their eyes."
3:19 the whole world stands convicted before G,
3:21 G has been manifested apart from the law,
3:22 that justice of G which works through
3:23 sinned and are deprived of the glory of G.
3:24 undeservedly justified by the gift of G,
3:25 G made him the means of expiation for all
3:29 Does G belong to the Jews alone?
3:29 Is he not also the G of the Gentiles?
3:30 It is the same G who justifies the
4: 3 "Abraham believed G,
4: 6 G credits justice without requiring deeds:
4:17 G in whom he believed, the G who restores
4:20 strengthened in faith and gave glory to G,
4:21 that G could do whatever he had promised.
5: 1 peace with G through our Lord Jesus Christ.
5: 2 we boast of our hope for the glory of G.
5: 5 because the love of G has been poured out
5: 8 in this that G proves his love for us:
5:11 G our boast through our Lord Jesus Christ,
5:15 of G and the gracious gift of the one man,
6:10 his life is life for G.
6:11 to sin but alive for G in Christ Jesus.
6:13 offer yourselves to G as men who have come
6:13 your bodies to G as weapons for justice.
6:17 Thanks be to G,
6:22 from sin and have become slaves of G,
6:23 G is eternal life in Christ Jesus our Lord.
7: 4 dead, so that we might bear fruit for G.
7:22 My inner self agrees with the law of G,
7:25 All praise to G,
7:25 law of G but with my flesh the law of sin.
8: 3 Then G sent his Son in the likeness of
8: 7 flesh in its tendency is at enmity with G;
8: 8 those who are in the flesh cannot please G.
8: 9 since the Spirit of G dwells in you.
8:14 are led by the Spirit of G are sons of God.
8:16 with our spirit that we are children of G.
8:17 heirs of G, heirs with Christ
8:19 awaits the revelation of the sons of G.
8:21 the glorious freedom of the children of G.
8:27 for the saints as G himself wills.
8:28 We know that G makes all things work
8:31 If G is for us, who can be against us?
8:33 G, who justifies?
8:34 right hand of G and who intercedes for us?
8:39 love of G that comes to us in Christ Jesus,
9: 5 Blessed forever be G who is over all!
9: 8 of the flesh who are the children of G;
9:12 the favor of him who calls" G said to her,
9:14 That G is unjust?
9:18 other words, G has mercy on whom he wishes,
9:20 Friend, who are you to answer G back?
9:22 What if G, wishing to show his wrath
9:26 they shall be called sons of the living G."
10: 1 desire, my prayer to G for the Israelites,
10: 2 for G though their zeal is unenlightened.
10: 3 not subject themselves to the justice of G.
10: 9 your heart that G raised him from the dead,
11: 1 I ask, then, has G rejected his people?
11: 2 G has not rejected his people whom he
11: 2 how he pleaded with G against Israel?
11: 4 How does G answer him?

GOD (cont.)

11: 5 is a remnant chosen by the grace of *G*.
11: 8 *G* gave them a spirit of stupor;
11:21 If *G* did not spare the natural branches,
11:22 the kindness and the severity of *G*—
11:23 grafted back on, for *G* is able to do this.
11:28 the Jews are enemies of *G* for your sake;
11:30 Just as you were once disobedient to *G* and
11:31 since *G* wished to show you mercy
11:32 *G* has imprisoned all in disobedience that
11:33 and the wisdom and the knowledge of *G*!
12: 1 I beg you through the mercy of *G*
12: 1 living sacrifice holy and acceptable to *G*,
12: 3 of faith that *G* has apportioned him.
13: 1 for there is no authority except from *G*,
13: 1 authority that exists is established by *G*.
13: 2 rebels against the ordinance of *G*;
14: 3 After all, *G* himself has made him welcome.
14: 6 honor the Lord, and he gives thanks to *G*.
14: 6 the Lord, and he too gives thanks to *G*.
14:10 to appear before the judgment seat of *G*.
14:11 me and every tongue shall give praise to *G*."
14:12 to give an account of himself before *G*.
14:17 of *G* is not a matter of eating or drinking,
14:18 way pleases *G* and wins the esteem of men.
14:22 as your rule of life in the sight of *G*.
15: 5 May *G*, the source of all patience
15: 6 with one heart and voice you may glorify *G*,
15: 7 as Christ accepted you, for the glory of *G*.
15: 9 Gentiles glorify *G* because of his mercy.
15:13 So may *G*, the source of hope
15:15 I take this liberty because *G* has given me
15:16 duty of preaching the gospel of *G*
15:17 Jesus for the work I have done for *G*.
15:30 struggle by your prayers to *G* on my behalf.
15:32 *G* willing, I may come to you with joy
15:33 May the *G* of peace be with you all.
16:20 Then the *G* of peace will quickly crush
16:26 and, at the command of the eternal *G*,
16:27 to him, the *G* who alone is wise,
1Cor 1: 2 to the church of *G* which is in Corinth;
1: 3 *G* our Father and the Lord Jesus Christ.
1: 4 I continually thank my *G* for you because
1: 9 *G* is faithful,
1:14 Thank *G*, I baptized none of you except
1:18 salvation it is the power of *G*.
1:20 Has not *G* turned the wisdom of this world
1:21 it pleased *G* to save those who believe
1:24 the power of *G* and the wisdom of God.
1:27 *G* chose those whom the world considers
1:29 that mankind can do no boasting before *G*.
1:30 *G* it is who has given you life in Christ
2: 5 on the wisdom of men but on the power of *G*.
2: 7 *G* planned it before all ages for our glory.
2: 9 what *G* has prepared for those who love him."
2:10 Yet *G* has revealed this wisdom to us
2:10 all matters, even the deep things of *G*.
2:11 at the depths of God but the Spirit of *G*.
2:14 accept what is taught by the Spirit of *G*.
3: 6 and Apollos watered it, but *G* made it grow.
3: 7 waters is of any special account, only *G*,
3:10 Thanks to the favor *G* showed me I laid a
3:16 temple of *G*, and that the Spirit of *G* dwells
3:17 destroys God's temple, *G* will destroy him.
3:17 For the temple of *G* is holy,
3:19 wisdom of this world is absurdity with *G*.
4: 1 and administrators of the mysteries of *G*.
4: 5 everyone will receive his praise from *G*.
4: 9 *G* has put us apostles at the end of the
4:20 of *G* does not consist in talk but in power.
5:13 *G* will judge the others.
6: 9 will not fall heir to the kingdom of *G*?
6:11 Jesus Christ and in the Spirit of our *G*.
6:13 and *G* will do away with them both in the
6:14 *G*, who raised up the Lord,
6:15 *G* forbid!
6:19 the Spirit you have received from *G*.
6:20 So glorify *G* in your body.
7: 7 Still, each one has his own gift from *G*,
7:15 *G* has called you to live in peace.
7:24 continue before *G* in the condition of life
7:40 that in this I have the Spirit of *G*.
8: 3 But if anyone loves *G*,
8: 4 nothing, and that there is no *G* but one.
8: 6 for us there is one *G*,
8: 8 Now food does not bring us closer to *G*.
9: 9 Is *G* concerned here for oxen,
9:21 it (not that I am free from the law of *G*,
10: 5 that *G* was not pleased with most of them,
10:13 Besides, *G* keeps his promise.
10:20 Gentiles sacrifice to demons and not to *G*,
10:31 you should do all for the glory of *G*.
10:32 to Jew or Greek or to the church of *G*,
11: 7 image of *G* and the reflection of his glory.
11:12 and all is from *G*.
11:13 proper for a woman to pray to *G* unveiled?
11:16 churches of *G* recognize any other usage.
11:22 you show contempt for the church of *G*,
12: 3 who speaks in the Spirit of *G* ever says,
12: 6 *G* who accomplishes all of them in everyone.
12:18 *G* has set each member of the body in the
12:24 *G* has so constructed the body as to give
12:28 *G* has set up in the church first apostles,
14: 2 a tongue is talking not to men but to *G*.
14:16 your praise of *G* is solely with the spirit,
14:18 Thank *G*, I speak in tongues more
14:25 God, crying out, *G* is truly among you."
14:28 each one speaking only to himself and to *G*.
14:33 the prophets' control, since *G* is a God,
15: 9 fact, because I persecuted the church of *G*,
15:10 not on my own but through the favor of *G*.
15:15 then be exposed as false witnesses of *G*,
15:24 will hand over the kingdom to *G* the Father.
15:25 until *G* has put all enemies under his feet,
15:27 *G* "has placed all things under his feet."
15:28 to him, so that *G* may be all in all.
15:34 Some of you are quite ignorant of *G*;
15:38 *G* gives body to it as he pleases
15:50 and blood cannot inherit the kingdom of *G*;
15:57 But thanks be to *G* who has given us the
2Cor 1: 1 to the church of *G* that is at Corinth and
1: 2 *G* our Father and the Lord Jesus Christ.
1: 3 Praised be *G*,
1: 3 of mercies, and the *G* of all consolation!
1: 9 in ourselves, but in *G* who raises the dead.
1:11 so that on our behalf *G* may be thanked for
1:18 As *G* keeps his word,
1:19 and I preached to you as Son of *G*,
1:20 *G* has made have been fulfilled in him;
1:20 our Amen to *G* when we worship together.
1:21 *G* is the one who firmly establishes us
1:23 I call on *G* as my witness that it was out
2:14 Thanks be to *G*,
2:17 like so many who trade on the word of *G*.
2:17 sent by *G* and of standing in his presence.
3: 3 ink but by the Spirit of the living *G*,
3: 4 This great confidence in *G* is ours,
3: 5 Our sole credit is from *G*,
4: 2 to trickery or falsify the word of *G*.
4: 2 to every man's conscience before *G*.
4: 4 been blinded by the *g* of the present age
4: 4 forth the glory of Christ, the image of *G*.
4: 6 *G*, who said, "Let light shine out of
4: 6 glory of *G* shining on the face of Christ.
4: 7 power comes from *G* and not from us.
4:15 to *G* because they who give thanks are many.
5: 1 we have a dwelling provided for us by *G*,
5: 5 *G* has fashioned us for this very thing and
5:11 men, but what we are is known to *G*.
5:13 up out of ourselves, *G* is the reason;
5:18 All this has been done by *G*,
5:19 I mean that *G*,
5:20 Christ, *G* as it were appealing through us.
5:20 be reconciled to *G*!
5:21 *G* made him who did not know sin to be sin,
5:21 him we might become the very holiness of *G*.
6: 1 you not to receive the grace of *G* in vain.
6: 4 to present ourselves as ministers of *G*,
6: 7 the message of truth and the power of *G*;
6:16 there is between the temple of *G* and idols.
6:16 of the living God, just as *G* has said:
6:16 be their *G* and they shall be my people.
7: 1 and in the fear of *G* strive to fulfill our
7: 6 *G*, who gives heart to those who are low
7: 9 filled with a sorrow that came from *G*;
7:11 fruit of this sorrow which stems from *G*.
7:12 sight of *G* the devotion you have for us.
7:15 he recalls the obedience you showed to *G*
8: 1 *G* conferred on the churches of Macedonia.
8: 5 to God and then to us by the will of *G*.
8:16 Thanks be to *G*,
9: 7 grudgingly, for *G* loves a cheerful giver.
9: 8 *G* can multiply his favors among you so
9:11 us it results in thanks offered to *G*.
9:12 but also overflows in much gratitude to *G*.
9:13 they are glorifying *G* for your obedient faith
9:14 of the surpassing grace *G* has given you.
9:15 Thanks be to *G* for his indescribable gift!
10: 5 raises itself against the knowledge of *G*;
10:13 bounds the *G* of moderation has set for us
11: 2 of you with the jealousy of *G* himself,
11: 7 the gospel of *G* to you free of charge,
11:11 *G* knows I do.
11:15 as ministers of the justice of *G*.
11:31 The *G* and Father of the Lord Jesus knows
12: 2 his body I cannot say, only *G* can say
12: 3 or outside his body I do not know, *G* knows
12:19 Before *G* I tell you,
12:21 again my *G* may humiliate me before you,
13: 4 weakness, but he lives by the power of *G*.
13: 7 We pray *G* that you may do no evil
13:11 the *G* of love and peace will be with you.
13:13 the Lord Jesus Christ, and the love of *G*,
Gal 1: 1 *G* his Father who raised him from the dead
1: 3 *G* our Father and of the Lord Jesus Christ,
1: 4 evil age, as our *G* and Father willed
1:10 men or *G*?
1:13 the church of *G* and tried to destroy it;
1:20 *G* that what I have just written is true.
1:24 and they gave glory to *G* on my account.
2: 6 prominent they were *G* plays no favorites),
2:19 law that I died to the law, to live for *G*.
2:20 but it is a life of faith in the Son of *G*,
3: 5 you have faith in what you heard that *G*
3: 6 "believed *G*, and it was credited to him
3:17 a covenant formally ratified by *G* is not
3:18 that *G* granted Abraham his privilege.
3:20 and *G* is one.
3:21 the law is opposed to the promises [of *G*?
3:26 of *G* because of your faith in Christ Jesus.
4: 4 come, *G* sent forth his Son born of a woman,
4: 6 *G* has sent forth into our hearts the spirit
4: 8 the past, when you did not acknowledge *G*,
4: 9 Now that you have come to know *G*—
4:14 you took me to yourselves as an angel of *G*,
5:21 things will not inherit the kingdom of *G*!
6: 7 mistake about it, no one makes a fool of *G*!
6:16 this rule of life, and on the Israel of *G*.
Eph 1: 1 the will of *G* an apostle of Jesus Christ,
1: 2 *G* our Father and the Lord Jesus Christ.
1: 3 the *G* and Father of our Lord Jesus Christ,
1: 4 *G* chose us in him before the world began,
1: 9 *G* has given us the wisdom to understand
1:11 for in the decree of *G*,
1:14 redemption of a people *G* has made his own,
1:16 I have never stopped thanking *G* for you
1:17 May the *G* of our Lord Jesus Christ,
2: 4 But *G* is rich in mercy;
2:10 deeds which *G* prepared for us in advance.
2:12 without hope and without *G* in the world.
2:16 of us to *G* in one body through his cross,
2:19 saints and members of the household of *G*.
2:22 a dwelling place for *G* in the Spirit.
3: 2 *G* in his goodness gave me in your regard.
3: 7 Through the gift *G* in his goodness
3: 9 design which for ages was hidden in *G*,
3:12 faith in him we can speak freely to *G*,
3:19 may attain to the fullness of *G* himself.
4: 6 one *G* and Father of all,
4:18 They are estranged from a life in *G*
4:32 just as *G* has forgiven you in Christ.
5: 1 Be imitators of *G* as his dear children.
5: 2 He gave himself for us as an offering to *G*,
5: 5 in the kingdom of Christ and of *G*.
5:20 Give thanks to *G* the Father always and for
6:11 Put on the armor of *G* so that you may be
6:13 of *G* if you are to resist on the evil day;
6:17 and the sword of the spirit, the word of *G*.
6:19 for me that *G* may put his word on my lips,
6:23 May *G* the Father and the Lord Jesus Christ
Phil 1: 2 Grace and peace be yours from *G* our Father
1: 3 thanks to my *G* every time I think of you
1: 8 *G* himself can testify how much I long for
1:11 in you, to the glory and praise of *G*.
1:14 to speak the word of *G* fearlessly.
1:28 All this is as *G* intends,
2: 6 Though he was in the form of *G*,
2: 6 equality with *G* something to be grasped at.
2: 9 *G* highly exalted him and bestowed on him
2:11 proclaim to the glory of *G* the Father:
2:13 *G* who, in his good will toward you,
2:15 children of *G* beyond reproach in the midst
2:27 the point of death, but *G* took pity on him;
3: 3 spirit of *G* and glory in Christ Jesus
3: 9 has its origin in *G* and is based on faith.
3:14 I run toward the prize to which *G* calls me
3:15 way, *G* will clarify the difficulty for you.
3:19 Their *g* is their belly and their glory is
4: 6 Present your needs to *G* in every form of
4: 9 Then will the *G* of peace be with you.
4:18 a sacrifice acceptable and pleasing to *G*.
4:19 My *G* in turn will supply your needs fully,
4:20 to our *G* and Father for unending ages!
Col 1: 1 apostle of Christ Jesus by the will of *G*,
1: 2 May *G* our Father give you grace and peace.
1: 3 We always give thanks to *G*,
1:10 every sort and grow in the knowledge of *G*.
1:15 He is the image of the invisible *G*,
1:19 It pleased *G* to make absolute fullness
1:22 by dying, so as to present you to *G* holy,
1:25 through the commission *G* gave me to preach
1:27 *G* has willed to make known to them the
2: 2 by their knowledge of the mystery of *G*—
2:12 power of *G* who raised him from the dead.
2:13 *G* gave you new life in company with Christ.
2:15 did *G* disarm the principalities and powers.
2:19 growth from this source which comes from *G*.
3: 3 Your life is hidden now with Christ in *G*.
3:16 gratefully to *G* from your hearts in psalms,
3:17 Give thanks to *G* the Father through him.
4: 3 that *G* may provide us with an opening to
4:11 are working with me for the kingdom of *G*.
1Thes 1: 1 to *G* the Father and the Lord Jesus Christ.
1: 2 We keep thanking *G* for all of you and we
1: 3 we constantly are mindful before our *G*
1: 4 We know, too, brothers beloved of *G*,
1: 8 every region your faith in *G* is celebrated,
1: 9 you, and how you turned to *G* from idols,
1: 9 serve him who is the living and true *G*
2: 2 we drew courage from our *G* to preach his
2: 4 having met the test imposed on us by *G*,
2: 4 speak like those who strive to please *G*,
2: 5 under any pretext, as *G* is our witness!
2:10 You are witnesses, as is *G* himself,
2:12 *G* who calls you to his kingship and glory.
2:13 That is why we thank *G* constantly that in
2:13 word of *G* at work within you who believe.
2:14 of *G* in Judea which are in Christ Jesus.
2:15 to *G* and hostile to all mankind,

3: 9 What thanks can we give to *G* for all the
3:11 May *G* himself,
3:13 them blameless and holy before our *G*
4: 1 conduct yourselves in a way pleasing to *G*—
4: 5 desire as do the Gentiles who know not *G;*
4: 7 *G* has not called us to immorality but to
4: 8 but *G* who sends his Holy Spirit upon you.
4: 9 *G* himself has taught you to love one
4:14 *G* will bring forth with him from the dead
5: 9 *G* has not destined us for wrath but for
5:23 *G* of peace make you perfect in holiness.
2Thes 1: 1 to *G* our Father and the Lord Jesus Christ.
1: 2 *G* the Father and the Lord Jesus Christ.
1: 3 right that we thank *G* unceasingly for you,
1: 6 justice would require that *G* visit hardships
1: 8 those who do not acknowledge *G* nor heed"
1:11 that our *G* may make you worthy of his call,
1:12 gift of our *G* and of the Lord Jesus Christ.
2: 4 every so-called *g* proposed for worship,
2: 4 temple and even declares himself to be *G*—
2:11 Therefore *G* is sending upon them a
2:13 We are bound to thank *G* for you always,
2:13 of those whom *G* has chosen for salvation,
2:16 may *G* our Father who loved us and in his
3: 5 the love of *G* and the constancy of Christ.
1Tm 1: 1 of *G* our savior and Christ Jesus our hope,
1: 2 *G* the Father and Christ Jesus our Lord.
1: 4 that training in faith which *G* requires.
1:11 that pertains to the glorious gospel of *G*—
1:17 the immortal, the invisible, the only *G,*
2: 3 good, and *G* our savior is pleased with it,
2: 5 *G* is one.
2: 5 One also is the mediator between *G* and men,
3: 5 how can he take care of the church of *G?*
3:15 household, the church of the living *G,*
4: 3 abstinence from foods which *G* created
4: 4 Everything *G* created is good;
4:10 the living *G* who is the savior of all men,
5: 4 this is the way *G* wants it to be.
5: 5 hope on *G* and continues night and day
5:21 I charge you before *G,*
6: 1 *G* and the church's teaching suffer abuse.
6:11 Man of *G* that you are, flee from all this.
6:13 Before *G,* who gives life to all,
6:15 *G* will bring to pass at his chosen time.
6:17 Let them trust in the *G* who provides us
2Tm 1: 1 by the will of *G* an apostle of Christ
1: 2 and peace from *G* the Father and from
1: 3 I thank God, the *G* of my forefathers
1: 6 *G* bestowed when my hands were laid on you.
1: 7 *G* has given us is no cowardly spirit,
1: 8 but with the strength which comes from *G*
1: 9 *G* has saved us and has called us to a holy
2: 9 but there is no chaining the word of *G!*
2:10 for the sake of those whom *G* has chosen,
2:14 *G* to stop disputing about mere words.
2:19 But the foundation *G* has laid stands firm.
2:25 in the hope always that *G* will enable them
2:26 Thus, taken captive by *G* to do his will,
3: 4 lovers of pleasure rather than of *G*
3:16 inspired of *G* and is useful for teaching
3:17 man of *G* may be fully competent
4: 1 In the presence of *G* and of Christ Jesus,
Ti 1: 1 Paul, a servant of *G,*
1: 1 of the faith of those whom *G* has chosen,
1: 2 in the hope of that eternal life which *G,*
1: 3 to me by the command of *G* our Savior.
1: 4 May grace and peace from *G* our Father,
1:16 They claim to "know *G,*"
2: 3 in ways that befit those who belong to *G.*
2: 5 the word of *G* will not fall into disrepute.
2:10 way possible the doctrine of *G* our Savior.
2:11 The grace of *G* has appeared,
2:13 the great *G* and of our Savior Christ Jesus.
3: 4 kindness and love of *G* our savior appeared,
3: 8 to *G* may be careful to do what is right.
Phlm 1: 3 Grace to you and peace from *G* our Father
1: 4 I thank *G* always,
Heb 1: 1 *G* spoke in fragmentary and varied ways to
1: 5 To which of the angels did *G* ever say,
1: 6 "Let all the angels of *G* worship him."
1: 8 but of the Son, "Your throne, O *G,*
1: 9 hated wickedness, therefore God, your *G,*
1:13 To which of the angels has *G* ever said,
2: 4 *G* then gave witness to it by signs,
2: 8 things to him, *G* left nothing unsubjected.
2:10 that when bringing many sons to glory *G,*
2:13 am I, and the children *G* has given me!"
2:17 high priest before *G* on their behalf,
3: 4 by someone, but *G* is the founder of all.
3:12 spirit and fall away from the living *G.*
3:17 With whom was *G* angry for forty years?
4: 3 who enter into that rest, just as *G* said:
4: 4 "And *G* rested from all his work on the
4: 5 in the place we have referred to, *G* says,
4: 7 because of unbelief, *G* once more set a day,
4: 8 *G* would not have spoken afterward of
4: 9 rest still remains for the people of *G.*
4:10 rests from his own work as *G* did from his.
4:14 through the heavens, Jesus, the Son of *G,*
5: 1 and made their representative before *G,*
5: 4 but only when called by *G* as Aaron was.
5: 7 with loud cries and tears to *G,*
5:10 designated by *G* as high priest according
5:12 the basic elements of the oracles of *G;*
6: 1 repentance from dead works, faith in *G,*
6: 3 And, *G* permitting, we shall advance!
6: 5 of *G* and the powers of the age to come,
6: 6 since they are crucifying the Son of *G*
6: 7 is cultivated, receives the blessing of *G.*
6:10 *G* is not unjust;
6:13 When *G* made his promise to Abraham,
6:15 Abraham obtained what *G* had promised.
6:17 *G,* wishing to give the heirs of his
7: 1 of Salem and priest of the Most High *G,*
7: 3 the Son of *G* he remains a priest forever.
7:19 and through it we draw near to *G.*
7:21 an oath, unlike Jesus to whom *G* said:
7:25 to save those who approach *G* through him,
8: 8 But *G,* finding fault with them, says:
8:10 be their *G* and they shall be my people.
9:14 offered himself up unblemished to *G,*
9:14 from dead works to worship the living *G!*
9:20 the covenant which *G* has enjoined upon you."
9:24 he might appear before *G* now on our behalf.
10: 7 the book, I have come to do your will, O *G.*'"
10:12 his seat forever at the right hand of *G;*
10:21 great priest who is over the house of *G,*
10:27 fire to consume the adversaries of *G.*
10:29 is due the man who disdains the Son of *G,*
10:31 to fall into the hands of the living *G.*
11: 2 of faith the men of old were approved by *G.*
11: 3 the worlds were created by the word of *G,*
11: 4 offered *G* a sacrifice greater than Cain's.
11: 4 *G* himself having borne witness to him on
11: 5 "he was seen no more because *G* took him."
11: 5 he was taken up, he was pleasing to *G*—
11: 6 who comes to *G* must believe that he exists,
11: 7 revered *G* and built an ark that his
11:10 foundations, whose designer and maker is *G.*
11:16 God is not ashamed to be called their *G,*
11:19 that *G* was able to raise from the dead,
11:21 of the sons of Joseph, and worshiped *G,*
11:27 as if he were looking on the invisible *G.*
11:40 *G* had made a better plan,
12: 2 his seat at the right of the throne of *G.*
12: 7 Endure your trials as the discipline of *G,*
12:10 but *G* does so for our true profit,
12:15 no man falls away from the grace of *G;*
12:22 Mount Zion and the city of the living *G,*
12:23 enrolled in heaven, to *G* the judge of all,
12:25 to listen as *G* spoke to them on earth,
12:29 For our *G* is a consuming fire.
13: 4 *G* will judge fornicators and adulterers.
13: 5 content with what you have, for *G* has said,
13: 7 leaders who spoke the word of *G* to you;
13: 9 our hearts strengthened by the grace of *G*
13:15 continually offer *G* a sacrifice of praise,
13:16 *G* is pleased by sacrifices of that kind.
13:20 May the *G* of peace,
13:24 your leaders and to all the people of *G.*
Jas 1: 1 servant of *G* and of the Lord Jesus Christ,
1: 5 let him ask it from the *G* who gives
1:13 is free to say, "I am being tempted by *G.*"
1:13 Surely *G,* who is beyond the grasp of evil
1:27 without stain before our *G* and Father.
2: 5 Did not *G* choose those who are poor in the
2:19 Do you believe that *G* is one?
2:23 which says, "Abraham believed *G,*
3: 9 though they are made in the likeness of *G.*
4: 4 that love of the world is enmity to *G?*
4: 6 *G* resists the proud but bestows his favor
4: 7 Therefore submit to *G,*
4: 8 Draw close to *G,*
1Pt 1: 2 to the foreknowledge of *G* the Father,
1: 3 the *G* and Father of our Lord Jesus Christ,
1:21 are believers in God, the *G* who raised
1:21 faith and hope, then, are centered in *G.*
1:23 through the living and enduring word of *G.*
2: 5 acceptable to *G* through Jesus Christ.
2:12 give glory to *G* on the day of visitation.
2:15 Such obedience is the will of *G.*
2:16 In a word, live as servants of *G.*
2:17 love for the brothers, reverence for *G,*
3: 5 on *G* and obedient to their husbands
3:18 unjust, was that he might lead you to *G.*
3:20 *G* patiently waited until the ark was built.
3:21 but the pledge to *G* of an irreproachable
4: 2 life on human desires but on the will of *G.*
4: 6 might live in the spirit in the eyes of *G.*
4:11 to do it with the strength provided by *G.*
4:11 *G* is to be glorified through Jesus Christ:
4:16 rather glorify *G* in virtue of that name.
4:17 who refuse obedience to the gospel of *G?*
5: 2 over it willingly as *G* would have you do,
5: 5 because *G* "is stern with the arrogant but
5:10 The *G* of all grace,
5:12 testimony that this is the true grace of *G.*
2Pt 1: 1 power of our *G* and Savior Jesus Christ;
1: 2 through your knowledge of *G* and of Jesus,
1:17 He received glory and praise from *G* the
2: 4 Did *G* spare even the angels who sinned?
3: 5 all brought into being by the word of *G.*
3:12 of the day of *G* and trying to hasten it!
3:13 his promise, the justice of *G* will reside.
1Jn 1: 5 that *G* is light;
2: 5 has the love of *G* been made perfect in him.
2:14 strong, and the word of *G* remains in you,
3: 1 us in letting us be called children of *G!*
3: 8 works that the Son of *G* revealed himself.
3: 9 No one begotten of *G* acts sinfully because
3: 9 he cannot sin because he is begotten of *G.*
3:10 one whose actions are unholy belongs to *G,*
3:20 for *G* is greater than our hearts and all
3:21 we can be sure that *G* is with us and that
4: 1 to a test to see if they belong to *G,*
4: 2 Christ come in the flesh belongs to *G,*
4: 3 to acknowledge him does not belong to *G.*
4: 4 You are of *G,*
4: 6 *G* and anyone who has knowledge of *G*
4: 6 anyone who is not of *G* refuses to hear us.
4: 7 us love one another because love is of *G;*
4: 7 is begotten of God and has knowledge of *G.*
4: 8 has known nothing of God, for *G* is love.
4:10 not that we have loved *G,*
4:11 Beloved, if *G* has loved us so,
4:12 No one has ever seen *G.*
4:12 Yet if we love one another *G* dwells in us,
4:15 Son of God, God dwells in him and he in *G.*
4:16 and to believe in the love *G* has for us.
4:16 *G* is love,
4:16 abides in love abides in God, and *G* in him.
4:20 If anyone says, "My love is fixed on *G,*"
4:20 has seen cannot love the *G* he has not seen.
4:21 whoever loves *G* must also love his brother.
5: 1 Jesus is the Christ has been begotten of *G.*
5: 2 we love *G* and do what he has commanded.
5: 3 The love of *G* consists in this:
5: 4 Everyone begotten of *G* conquers the world,
5: 5 who believes that Jesus is the Son of *G.*
5: 9 The testimony of *G* is much greater:
5: 9 *G* has given on his own Son's behalf.
5:10 Whoever believes in the Son of *G* possesses
5:10 Whoever does not believe God has made *G* a
5:11 *G* gave us eternal life,
5:12 possess the Son of *G* does not possess life.
5:13 who believe in the name of the Son of *G.*
5:14 We have this confidence in *G:*
5:16 the sin is not deadly, should petition *G,*
5:18 know that no one begotten of *G* commits sin;
5:18 rather, *G* protects the one begotten by him,
5:19 We know that we belong to *G,*
5:20 that the Son of *G* has come and has given
5:20 He is the true *G* and eternal life.
2Jn 1: 3 from *G* the Father and from Jesus Christ,
1: 9 the teaching of Christ does not possess *G,*
3Jn 1: 6 a good thing if, in a way that pleases *G,*
1:11 Whoever does what is good belongs to *G;*
1:11 whoever does what is evil has never seen *G.*
Jude 1: 1 called by God; who have found love in *G*
1: 4 *G* to sexual excess and deny Jesus Christ,
1:25 Glory be to this only *G* our savior,
Rv 1: 1 is the revelation *G* gave to Jesus Christ,
1: 2 of *G* and the testimony of Jesus Christ.
1: 6 priests in the service of his *G* and Father
1: 8 The Lord *G* says,"I am the Alpha
2: 7 of life which grows in the garden of *G.*'
2:18 "'The Son of *G,* whose eyes blaze like fire
3: 1 One who holds the seven spirits of *G,*
3: 2 is less than complete in the sight of my *G.*
3:12 temple of my *G* and he shall never leave it.
3:12 of my *G* and the name of the city of my God,
4: 5 flaming torches, the seven spirits of *G.*
4: 8 "Holy, holy, holy, is the Lord *G* Almighty,
4:11 "O Lord our *G,* you are worthy to receive
5: 6 these eyes are the seven spirits of *G,*
5: 9 for *G* men of every race and tongue,
5:10 them a kingdom, and priests to serve our *G,*
6: 9 of the witness they bore to the word of *G.*
7: 2 the east holding the seal of the living *G.*
7: 3 on the foreheads of the servants of our *G.*"
7:10 a loud voice, "Salvation is from our *G,*
7:11 fell down before the throne to worship *G.*
7:12 power and might, to our *G* forever and ever.
7:17 and *G* will wipe every tear from their eyes."
8: 4 smoke of the incense went up before *G,*
9: 4 had not the seal of *G* on their foreheads.
10: 7 his trumpet, the mysterious plan of *G,*
11:11 life which comes from *G* returned to them.
11:13 that they worshiped the *G* of heaven.
11:16 presence fell down to worship *G* and said:
11:17 the Lord *G* Almighty who is and who was.
12: 5 child was caught up to *G* and to his throne.
12: 6 place had been prepared for her by *G;*
12:10 *G* and the authority of his Anointed One.
12:10 night and day accused them before our *G.*
13: 6 It began to hurl blasphemies against *G,*
14: 4 first fruits of mankind for *G* and the Lamb.
14: 7 "Honor *G* and give him glory,
14:12 commandments of *G* and their faith in Jesus.
15: 2 holding the harps used in worshiping *G,*
15: 3 sang the song of Moses, the servant of *G,*
15: 3 wonderful are your works, Lord *G* Almighty!
15: 7 wrath of the *G* who lives forever and ever.
16: 7 "Yes, Lord *G* Almighty,
16: 9 of *G* who had power to send these plagues,
16:11 tongues in pain and blasphemed the *G*
16:14 battle on the great day of *G* the Almighty.
16:19 *G* remembered Babylon the great,

GOD (cont.)
16:21 blasphemed G for the plague of hailstones,
17:17 For G has put it into their minds to carry
18: 5 heaven, and G keeps count of her crimes.
18: 8 for mighty is the Lord G who condemns her."
18:20 For G has exacted punishment from her on
19: 1 Salvation, glory and might belong to our G,
19: 4 worshiped G seated on the throne and sang,
19: 5 "Praise our G, all you his servants,
19: 6 The Lord is king, our G, the Almighty!
19: 9 they come from G."
19:10 Worship G alone.
19:13 in blood, and his name was the Word of G.
19:15 the blazing wrath of G the Almighty.
19:17 for the great feast G has prepared for you!
20: 4 their witness to Jesus and the word of G,
20: 6 they shall serve G and Christ as priests,
21: 2 city, coming down out of heaven from G,
21: 3 shall be their G who is always with them.
21: 7 I will be his G and he shall be my son.
21:10 Jerusalem coming down out of heaven from G.
21:11 It gleamed with the splendor of G.
21:22 The Lord, G the Almighty,
21:23 or moon, for the glory of G gave it light,
22: 1 which issued from the throne of G
22: 3 throne of G and of the Lamb shall be there,
22: 5 sun, for the Lord G shall give them light,
22: 6 the Lord, the G of prophetic spirits,
22: 9 Worship G alone!"
22:18 G will visit him with all the plagues
22:19 G will take away his share in the tree of

GOD-FEARING (11)
Gn 42:18 for I am a G man.
Ex 18:21 among all the people for able and G men,
2Kgs 4: 1 You know that he was a G man,
Neh 7: 2 was a more trustworthy and G man than most.
Jdt 8: 8 say about her, for she was a very G woman.
8:31 But now, G woman that you are,
11:17 Your handmaid is, indeed, a G woman,
Jb 1: 9 said, "Is it for nothing that Job is G?
Dn 13: 2 who married a very beautiful and G woman,
Acts 10: 1 cohort Italica, who was religious and G.
10:22 Who is an upright and G man,

GOD-GIVEN (2)
2Mc 7:14 G hope of being restored to life by him;
2Cor 1:12 always acted from G holiness and candor;

GOD-HERO (1)
Is 9: 5 They name him Wonder-Counselor, G,

GOD-LIKE (1)
Dn 5:11 to have brilliant knowledge and g wisdom.

GODDESS (6)
1Kgs 11: 5 By adoring Astarte, the g of the Sidonians,
11:33 has worshiped Astarte, g of the Sidonians,
2Mc 1:13 cut to pieces in the temple of the g Nanea
1:14 On the pretext of marrying the g,
Acts 19:27 the great g Artemis will count for nothing.
19:37 They have not insulted our g.

GODLESS (27)
2Mc 8: 2 on the temple, which was profaned by g men;
10:10 the son of that g man and shall give a
15:33 He cut out the tongue of the g Nicanor,
Jb 8:13 and so shall the hope of the g man perish.
Sir 16: 3 rather die childless than have g children!
16: 6 upon a g people wrath flames out.
21:27 When a g man curses his adversary he
27:11 discourses of the devout, but the g man,
34:19 Most High approves not the gifts of the g,
40:15 for the root of the g is on sheer rock;
41:10 to nought, so too the g from void to void.
Jer 12: 1 Why does the way of the g prosper,
23:11 Both prophet and priest are g!
25:31 The g shall be given to the sword,
Rom 5: 6 still powerless, Christ died for us g men.
1Tm 1: 9 and the sinful, the wicked and the g,
2Tm 2:16 who indulge in it become more and more g,
Ti 2:12 us to reject g ways and worldly desires,
Heb 12:16 you no fornicator or g person like Esau,
1Pt 4:18 what is to become of the g and the sinner?
2Pt 2: 5 he brought down that flood on the g earth.
2: 6 what would happen in the future to the g.
3: 7 the day when g men will be destroyed.
Jude 1: 4 wormed their way into your midst, g types,
1:15 the g for every evil deed they have done,
1:15 and convicting those g sinners of every
1:18 be impostors living by their g passions."

GODLIKE (1)
Zec 12: 8 on that day, and the house of David g,

GODLINESS (1)
2Mc 12:45 awaits those who had gone to rest in g,

GODLY (6)
Sir 6:35 Be eager to hear every g discourse;
44: 1 Now will I praise those g men,
44:10 yet these also were g men whose virtues
Ez 28: 2 a g throne in the heart of the sea!—"
Mal 2:15 what does that one require but g offspring?
2Tm 3:12 Anyone who wants to live a g life in

GODS—GOD'S (591)
Gn 3: 5 g who know what is good and what is bad."
21:17 G messenger called to Hagar from heaven:
28:12 G messengers were going up and down on it.
28:22 up as a memorial stone shall be G abode.
31:11 In the dream G messenger called to me,
31:30 father's house, why did you steal my g?"
31:32 But as for your g,
32: 2 Then G messengers encountered Jacob.
32: 3 saw them he said, "This is G encampment."
35: 2 of the foreign g that you have among you;
35: 4 handed over to Jacob all the foreign g
Ex 9:28 we have had enough of G thunder and hail.
12:12 executing judgment on all the g of Egypt
15:11 Who is like to you among the g, O LORD?
18:16 known to them G decisions and regulations."
20: 3 You shall not have other g besides me.
20:23 neither g of silver nor gods of gold shall
23:24 not bow down in worship before their g,
23:32 not make a covenant with them or their g.
23:33 by ensnaring you into worshiping their g."
31:18 stone tablets inscribed by G own finger.
34:15 worship to their g and sacrifice to them,
34:16 render their wanton worship to their g,
34:17 shall not make for yourselves molten g.
Lv 10: 6 but G wrath also on the whole community.
19: 4 to idols, nor make molten g for yourselves.
26: 1 "Do not make false g for yourselves.
Nm 1:53 Otherwise G wrath will strike the
33: 4 on their g,
Dt 1:17 alike, fearing no man, for judgment is G.
4: 7 that has g so close to it as the LORD,
4:28 There you shall serve g fashioned by the
4:28 stone, g which can neither see nor hear,
5: 7 You shall not have other g besides me.
6:14 You shall not follow other g,
7: 4 sons from following me to serving other g,
7:16 lest you be ensnared into serving their g.
7:25 of their g you shall destroy by fire.
8:19 the LORD, your God, and follow other g,
9:10 of stone inscribed, by G own finger,
10:17 For the LORD, your God, is the God of g,
11:16 that you serve other g and worship them.
11:28 I ordain for you today, to follow other g,
12: 2 you are to dispossess worship their g.
12: 3 poles, and shatter the idols of their g,
12:30 g, 'How did these nations worship their g?
12:31 g every abomination that the LORD detests,
12:31 their sons and daughters to their g.
13: 3 or wonder, urging you to follow other g,
13: 7 entices you secretly to serve other g,
13: 8 have not known, g of any other nations,
13:14 to serve other g whom you have not known,
17: 3 his covenant, by serving other g,
18:20 to speak, or speaks in the name of other g,
20:18 offerings as they make to their g,
21:23 G curse rests on him who hangs on a tree,
28:14 in order to follow other g and serve them.
28:36 you will serve strange g of wood and stone,
28:64 you will serve strange g of wood and stone,
29:17 our God, to go and serve these pagan g!
29:25 served other g and adored them, g whom
30:17 led astray and adore and serve other g,
31:16 rendering wanton worship to the strange g
31:18 evil they have done in turning to other g.
31:20 if they turn to other g and serve them,
32:16 g and angered him with abominable idols.
32:17 to g whom they had not known before,
32:37 g whom they relied on as their 'rock'?
Jos 22:21 "The LORD is the God of g.
22:22 The LORD, the God of g,
23: 7 You must not invoke their g,
23:16 on you, serve other g and worship them,
24: 2 dwelt beyond the River and served other g.
24:14 Cast out the g your fathers served beyond
24:15 the g your fathers served beyond the River
24:15 beyond the River or the g of the Amorites
24:16 the LORD for the service of other g.
24:20 you forsake the LORD and serve strange g,
24:23 put away the strange g that are among you
Jgs 2: 3 and their g shall become a snare for you."
2:12 other g of the various nations around them,
2:12 their worship of these g provoked the LORD.
2:17 themselves to the worship of other g.
2:19 following other g in service and worship,
3: 6 their sons in marriage, and served their g.
5: 8 mother in Israel, New g were their choice;
6:10 you shall not venerate the g of the
9: 9 my rich oil, whereby men and g are honored,
9:13 I give up my wine that cheers g and men,
10: 6 the g of Aram, the g of Sidon, the g of
10: 6 g of the Ammonites, and the g of the
10:13 you still forsook me and worshiped other g.
10:14 Go and cry out to the g you have chosen;
10:16 g from their midst and served the LORD,
1Sm 4: 7 They said, G have come to their camp."
4: 8 us from the power of these mighty g?
4: 8 These are the g that struck the Egyptians
6: 5 then he will cease to afflict you, your g,
7: 3 put away your foreign g and your Ashtaroth,
8: 8 day, deserting me and worshiping strange g,
17:43 cursed David by his g and said to him,
26:19 'Go serve other g!'
2Sm 5:21 They abandoned their g there,
7:23 and their g out of the way of your people,
9: 3 Saul's house to whom I may show G kindness
14:16 me and my son as well from G inheritance.'"
22:31 G way is unerring;
1Kgs 9: 6 proceed to venerate and worship strange g,
9: 9 strange g which they worshiped and served.
11: 2 "they will turn your hearts to their g."
11: 4 wives had turned his heart to strange g,
11: 8 burned incense and sacrificed to their g.
11:10 him this very act of following strange g,
14: 9 strange g and molten images to provoke me;
18:24 You shall call on your g,
18:25 Call upon your g,
19: 2 "May the g do thus and so to me if by
20:10 "May the g do thus and so to me if there
20:23 "Their gods are g of mountains.
2Kgs 17: 7 Egypt, and because they venerated other g.
17:29 make their own g in the various cities
17:29 Samarians had made, each people set up g.
17:31 their children by fire to their city g,
17:33 the LORD they served their own g,
17:35 "You must not venerate other g,
17:37 for you, and you must not venerate other g.
17:38 you must not venerate other g.
18:33 Has any of the g of the nations ever
18:34 Where are the g of Hamath and Arpad?
18:34 Where are the g of Sepharvaim,
18:34 Where are the g of the land of Samaria?
18:35 Which of the g for all these lands ever
19:12 Did the g of the nations whom my fathers
19:18 lands, and cast their g into the fire;
19:18 destroyed them because they were not g,
22:17 me and have burned incense to other g,
23:24 ghosts and spirits, with the household g,
1Chr 5:25 after the g of the natives of the land,
10:10 armor they put in the house of their g,
13:10 he died there in G presence,
14:12 The Philistines had left their g there,
15:26 While the Levites, with G help,
16:25 and awesome is he, beyond all g.
16:26 the g of the nations are things of nought,
22:19 covenant of the LORD and G sacred vessels
2Chr 2: 4 for our God is greater than all other g.
7:19 proceed to venerate and worship strange g,
7:22 g and worshiped them and served them.
13: 8 calves which Jeroboam made you for g?
20:15 for the battle is not yours but G.
25:14 back with him the g of the people of Seir,
25:14 of Seir, which he set up as his own g;
25:15 have you had recourse to this people's g
25:20 they had had recourse to the g of Edom.
28:23 to the g of Damascus who had defeated him,
28:23 the g of the kings of Aram who helped them,
28:24 of G house and broke them in pieces.
28:25 high places to offer sacrifice to other g.
30:27 prayer reached heaven, G holy dwelling.
32:13 Were the g of the nations in those lands
32:14 Who among all the g of those nations which
32:17 "As the g of the nations in other lands
32:19 of the g of the other peoples of the earth,
33:15 He removed the foreign g and the idol from
34:25 me and have offered incense to other g,
Ezr 10:14 us our G burning anger over this affair."
Neh 6:16 G help that this work had been completed.
Tb 1: 4 in the place where the temple, G dwelling,
3:17 so that he might again see G sunlight;
4: 7 G face will not be turned away from you.
4:14 If you thus behave as G servant,
5:10 am, a blind man who cannot see G sunlight,
12: 6 Before all men, honor and proclaim G deeds,
12:18 on my part, but because it was G will.
14: 4 flee into Media for I believe G word
14: 4 G temple there shall be burnt to the
Jdt 3: 8 to destroy all the g of the earth,
5: 7 for they did not wish to follow the g of their
5: 8 expelled them from the presence of their g.
8:18 city of ours that worships g made by hands,
Est C:18 our enemies, because we worshiped their g.
C:21 of the heathen to acclaim their false g,
C:23 King of g and Ruler of every power.
1Mc 5:68 altars and burned the statues of their g;
2Mc 2: 4 which Moses climbed to see G inheritance.
3:24 at G power and fainted away in terror.
3:29 all hope of aid, due to an act of G power,
3:34 proclaim to all men the majesty of G power."
7: 1 them to eat pork in violation of G law.
7:36 of never-failing life, under G covenant,
8:13 faith in G justice deserted and got away.
9:18 G punishment had justly come upon him,
11: 4 did not take G power into account at all,
11:23 father has taken his place among the g,
12:11 Judas and his companions, with G help,
13:13 out and settle the matter with G help.

13:15 Giving his men the battle cry *G* Victory,"
15:14 said of him, "This is *G* prophet Jeremiah,
15:27 greatly over this manifestation of *G* power.
Jb 20:28 waters that run off in the day of *G* anger.
25: 4 How can a man be just in *G* sight,
27:11 I will teach you the manner of *G* dealings,
33:26 he shall see *G* face with rejoicing.
35:15 you have done otherwise, *G* anger punishes,
36: 2 are still words to be said on *G* behalf.
37:22 comes, surrounding *G* awesome majesty!
40:19 He came at the beginning of *G* ways,
Ps(s) 16: 4 multiply their sorrows who court other *g*.
18:31 *G* way is unerring,
47:10 For *G* are the guardians of the earth;
58: 2 like *g* pronounce justice and judge fairly,
65:10 *G* watercourses are filled;
82: 1 he judges in the midst of the *g*.
82: 6 You are *g*, all of you sons of
84: 8 they shall see the God of *g* in Zion.
86: 8 There is none like you among the *g*,
95: 3 a great God, and a great king above all *g*;
96: 4 awesome is he, beyond all *g*.
96: 5 the *g* of the nations are things of nought,
97: 7 all *g* are prostrate before him.
97: 9 all the earth, exalted far above all *g*.
106:28 of Peor and ate the sacrifices of dead *g*.
135: 5 our Lord is greater than all *g*.
136: 2 Give thanks to the God of *g*,
Eccl 3:18 it is *G* way of testing them and of showing
5: 1 be quick to make a promise in *G* presence.
8:17 out all *G* work that is done under the sun,
Wis 9:13 For what man knows *G* counsel,
12: 7 receive a worthy colony of *G* children.
12:24 taking for *g* the worthless and disgusting
12:27 tortured by the very things they deemed *g*,
13: 2 governors of the world, they considered *g*.
13: 3 joy in their beauty they thought them *g*,
13:10 who termed *g* things made by human hands:
14:11 they have become abominable amid *G* works,
15:15 esteemed all the idols of the nations *g*
18:13 acknowledged that the people was *G* son.
Sir 11:22 *G* blessing is the lot of the just man,
15:11 "It was *G* doing that I fell away";
34:18 presents from the lawless win not *G* favor.
38: 8 Thus *G* creative work continues without
38:34 Yet they maintain *G* ancient handiwork,
42:15 Now will I recall *G* works;
42:15 *G* word were his works brought into being;
42:17 Yet even *G* holy ones must fail in
44:12 *G* covenant with them their family endures,
45: 2 *G* honor devolved upon him,
46: 1 implies, the great savior of *G* chosen ones,
46: 7 Averted *G* anger from the people and
46:13 At *G* word he established the kingdom and
48: 3 By *G* word he shut up the heavens and three
49:11 who was like a signet ring on *G* right hand,
Is 8:19 should not a people inquire of their *g*,
8:21 enraged, and curse his king and his *g*.
21: 9 images of her *g* are smashed to the ground.'"
36:18 Has any of the *g* of the nations ever
36:19 Where are the *g* of Hamath and Arpad?
36:19 Where are the *g* of Sepharvaim?
36:19 Where are the *g* of Samaria?
36:20 Which of all the *g* of these lands ever
37:12 Did the *g* of the nations whom my fathers
37:19 lands, and cast their *g* into the fire;
37:19 were not *g* but the work of human hands,
41:23 afterward, that we may know that you are *g*!
42:17 Who say to molten images, "You are our *g*."
45:14 the *g* are nought.
45:20 idols and pray to *g* that cannot save.
Jer 1:16 strange *g* and adoring their own handiwork.
2:11 Does any other nation change its *g*—
2:11 yet they are not *g* at all!
2:28 Where are the *g* you made for yourselves?
2:28 For as numerous as your cities are your *g*,
5: 7 forsaken me, they swear by *g* that are not.
5:19 me to serve strange *g* in your own land,
7: 6 or follow strange *g* to your own harm,
7: 9 Baal, go after strange *g* that you know not,
7:18 out to strange *g* in order to hurt me.
10:11 Let the *g* that did not make heaven and
11:10 also have followed and served strange *g*;
11:12 *g* to which they have been offering incense.
11:12 But these *g* will give them no help
11:13 For as numerous as your cities are your *g*,
13:10 follow strange *g* to serve and adore them,
16:11 me, says the LORD, and followed strange *g*,
16:13 you can serve strange *g* day and night,
16:20 Can man make for himself *g*?
16:20 These are not *g*.
19: 4 by burning in it incense to strange *g*
19:13 and poured out libations to strange *g*.
22: 9 God, by worshiping and serving strange *g*."
25: 6 follow strange *g* to serve and adore them,
32:29 out to strange *g* as a provocation to me.
35:15 and not follow strange *g* or serve them,
43:12 Egypt's *g*, and burn the *g* or carry them
43:13 with fire the temples of the Egyptian *g*.
44: 3 did to provoke me, going after strange *g*,
44: 3 sacrificing to them, *g* which neither they,
44: 5 from the evil of sacrificing to strange *g*.
44: 8 by sacrificing to strange *g* here in the
44:15 wives were burning incense to strange *g*,
46:25 of Thebes, and Egypt, her *g* and her kings,
48:35 high place, or to burn incense to his *g*.
Bar 1:22 of our own wicked hearts, served other *g*,
4:13 ways of *G* commandments they did not walk,
4:24 they soon see *G* salvation come to you,
5: 4 peace of justice, the glory of *G* worship.
5: 8 have overshadowed Israel at *G* command;
6: 3 shoulders *g* of silver and gold and wood,
6: 9 furnish crowns for the heads of their *g*.
6: 9 from their *g* and spend it on themselves,
6:10 men, these *g* of silver and gold and wood;
6:14 Thus it is known they are not *g*;
6:16 useless as one's broken tools are their *g*,
6:22 Know, therefore, that they are not *g*,
6:28 Knowing from this that they are not *g*,
6:29 How can they be called *g*?
6:29 to these *g* of silver and gold and wood;
6:31 their *g* as others do at a funeral banquet.
6:39 it be thought or claimed that they are *g*?
6:41 unable to reflect and abandon these *g*,
6:44 that takes place around these *g* is a fraud:
6:44 it be thought or claimed that they are *g*?
6:47 how then can what they have produced be *g*?
6:50 *g*, but human handiwork; and that *G* work
6:51 Who does not know that they are not *g*?
6:54 of these wooden or gilded or silvered *g*,
6:56 it be admitted or thought that they are *g*?
6:56 these wooden and silvered and gilded *g*;
6:58 the joy of its owner, than these false *g*;
6:58 who are within, rather than these false *g*;
6:58 in a palace, rather than these false *g*!
6:62 But these false *g* are not their equal,
6:63 and cannot be claimed, that they are *g*.
6:64 Know, therefore, that they are not *g*,
6:68 no way is it clear to us that they are *g*;
6:69 are their wooden, gilded, silvered *g*.
6:70 are their silvered and gilded wooden *g*.
6:71 them, it can be known that they are not *g*;
Ez 6:13 offered appeasing odors to any of their *g*.
11:24 in Chaldea [in a vision, by *G* spirit].
Dn 2:11 except the *g* who do not dwell among men."
2:47 "Truly your God is the God of *g* and Lord
3:90 Bless the God of *g*,
5: 4 they praised their *g* of gold and silver,
5:23 and you praised the *g* of silver and gold,
11: 8 Even their *g*, with their molten images
11:36 dreadful blasphemies against the God of *g*.
11:37 He shall have no regard for the *g* of his
Hos 3: 1 to other *g* and are fond of raisin cakes.
Zep 2:11 he makes all the *g* of earth to waste away;
Mt 3:15 this if we would fulfill all of *G* demands."
5:34 Do not swear by heaven (it is *G* throne),
9:35 he proclaimed the good news of *G* reign,
12: 4 he entered *G* house and ate the holy bread,
13:19 about *G* reign without understanding it.
15: 6 your tradition you have nullified *G* word.
16:23 not judging by *G* standards but by man's."
19:12 renounced sex for the sake of *G* reign.
22:16 a truthful man and teach *G* way sincerely.
22:21 is Caesar's, but give to God what is *G*."
23:22 swears by heaven is swearing by *G* throne
26:61 'I can destroy *G* sanctuary and rebuild it
27:40 Come down off that cross if you are *G* Son!"
27:43 After all, he claimed, 'I am *G* Son.'"
Mk 2: 3 While he was delivering *G* word to them,
2:26 How he entered *G* house in the days of
5: 7 I implore you in *G* name,
7: 8 You disregard *G* commandment and cling to
7: 9 fine art of setting aside *G* commandment
7:13 That is the way you nullify *G* word in
8:33 not judging by *G* standards but by man's."
12:14 respect but teach *G* way of life sincerely.
12:17 is Caesar's, but give to God what is *G*."
13:19 any between *G* work of creation and now,
16:19 heaven and took his seat at *G* right hand.
Lk 6: 4 how he entered *G* house and took and ate
7:30 baptism defeated *G* plan in their regard.
7:35 *G* wisdom is vindicated by all who accept it."
16:16 good news of *G* kingdom has been proclaimed,
20:25 is Caesar's, but give to God what is *G*."
Jn 1: 1 the Word was in *G* presence,
1:34 and have testified, 'This is *G* chosen One.'"
3: 5 no one can enter into *G* kingdom without
3:18 not believing in the name of *G* only Son.
4:10 "If only you recognized *G* gift,
5:18 own Father, thereby making himself *G* equal.
6:33 *G* bread comes down from heaven and gives
6:69 we are convinced that you are *G* holy one."
9: 3 it was to let *G* works show forth in him.
10:34 in your law, 'I have said, You are *g*'?
10:35 men gods to whom *G* word was addressed
10:36 sent into the world, I said, 'I am *G* Son'?
11: 4 rather it is for *G* glory,
19: 7 he must die because he made himself *G* Son."
Acts 2:33 Exalted at *G* right hand,
4:19 *G* sight for us to obey you rather than God.
4:31 continued to speak *G* word with confidence.
7:40 'Make us *g* that will be our leaders,'
7:55 of God, and Jesus standing at *G* right hand.
7:56 the Son of Man standing at *G* right hand."
8:20 thinking that *G* gift can be bought!
9:32 to *G* holy people living in Lydda.
10: 4 and your generosity have risen in *G* sight,
10:31 your generosity remembered in *G* presence.
11:23 he rejoiced to see the evidence of *G* favor.
13:36 spent a lifetime in carrying out *G* will,
14:11 *G* have come to us in the form of men!"
15:19 cause *G* Gentile converts any difficulties.
17:18 "He sounds like a promoter of foreign *g*,"
17:29 If we are in fact *G* offspring,
18:26 to him *G* new way in greater detail.
18:27 who through *G* favor had become believers.
19:26 them that man-made gods are no *g* at all.
20:24 bearing witness to the gospel of *G* grace.
20:27 announcing to you *G* design in its entirety.
23: 4 "How dare you insult *G* high priest?"
26:10 I sent many of *G* holy people to prison.
26:18 of their sins and a portion among *G* people.'
26:22 But I have had *G* help to this very day,
Rom 1:10 always pleading that somehow by *G* will I
1:20 realities, *G* eternal power and divinity,
1:32 They know *G* just decree that all who do
2: 2 "We know that *G* judgment on men who do
2: 4 Do you not know that *G* kindness is an
3: 3 unbelief put an end to *G* faithfulness?
3: 5 our wrongdoing provides proof of *G* justice,
3: 7 light *G* truth and thus promotes his glory,
3:20 in *G* sight through observance of the law;
4: 2 grounds for boasting, but not in *G* view;
4:20 he never questioned or doubted *G* promise;
5: 9 that we shall be saved by him from *G* wrath.
5:10 if, when we were *G* enemies,
8: 7 it is not subject to *G* law.
8:33 shall bring a charge against *G* chosen ones?
9: 6 Not that *G* word has failed.
9:11 in order that *G* decree might stand fast
9:16 of man's willing or doing but of *G* mercy.
10: 3 Unaware of *G* justice and seeking to
11:29 *G* gifts and his call are irrevocable.
12: 2 mind, so that you may judge what is *G* will,
12:19 leave that to *G* wrath,
13: 4 ruler is *G* servant to work for your good.
13: 4 he is *G* servant,
13: 6 magistrates being *G* ministers who devote
14:20 *G* work for the sake of something to eat.
15: 8 servant of the Jews because of *G* faithfulness
15:19 and marvels, by the power of *G* Spirit.
1Cor 1: 1 by *G* will to be an apostle of Christ Jesus,
1:21 Since in *G* wisdom the world did not come
1:25 For *G* folly is wiser than men,
2: 1 I did not come proclaiming *G* testimony
2: 7 No, what we utter is *G* wisdom:
2:12 is not the world's spirit but *G* Spirit,
3: 9 We are *G* co-workers,
3:17 If anyone destroys *G* temple,
3:23 and you are Christ's, and Christ is *G*.
6: 1 to the wicked and not to *G* holy people?
6:10 or robbers will inherit *G* kingdom.
7:19 What matters is keeping *G* commandments.
8: 5 *g* in the heavens and on the earth
8: 5 to be sure, many such *g*" and "lords"
14:36 the preaching of *G* word originate with you?
15:10 But by *G* favor I am what I am.
2Cor 1: 1 Paul, by *G* will an apostle of Jesus Christ,
1:12 by debased human wisdom, but by *G* goodness.
2:15 We are an aroma of Christ for *G* sake,
4: 1 we possess this ministry through *G* mercy,
7:10 sorrow for *G* sake produces a repentance
8:21 We are concerned not only for *G* approval
10: 4 *G* power for the destruction of strongholds.
13: 4 him, but we live with him by *G* power in us.
Gal 2:21 not treat *G* gracious gift as pointless.
3: 8 Because Scripture saw in advance that *G*
3:11 no one is justified in *G* sight by the law,
4: 7 are a son makes you an heir, by *G* design.
4: 8 as slaves to *g* who are not really divine.
5: 4 from Christ and fallen from *G* favor!
Eph 1: 8 so immeasurably generous is *G* favor to us.
2: 3 by nature deserved *G* wrath like the rest.
2: 8 This is not your own doing, it is *G* gift;
3: 3 *G* secret plan as I have briefly described
3:10 *G* manifold wisdom is made known to the
4: 7 Each of us has received *G* favor in the
4:13 one in faith and in the knowledge of *G* Son,
4:24 put on that new man created in *G* image,
5: 6 that bring *G* wrath down on the disobedient;
6: 6 but do *G* will with your whole heart as
Phil 4: 7 Then *G* own peace,
Col 1: 6 comprehended *G* gracious intention
3: 1 where Christ is seated at *G* right hand.
3: 6 These are the sins which provoke *G* wrath.
3:12 Because you are *G* chosen ones,
4:12 about whatever pertains to *G* will.
1Thes 2: 8 you not only *G* tidings but our very lives,
2: 9 time we preached *G* good tidings to you
3: 2 He is our brother and *G* fellow worker in
4: 3 It is *G* will that you grow in holiness:
4:16 of the archangel's voice and *G* trumpet;
5:18 such is *G* will for you in Christ Jesus.
2Thes 1: 4 so much so that in *G* communities we can
1: 5 these as an expression of *G* just judgment,
2: 4 he who seats himself in *G* temple and even
1Tm 3:15 of conduct befits a member of *G* household,
4: 5 it is made holy by *G* word and by prayer.
6:14 I charge you to keep *G* command without

GODS—GOD'S (cont.)

2Tm 2:15 hard to make yourself worthy of G approval,
Ti 1: 7 The bishop as G steward must be blameless.
Phlm 1: 5 toward the Lord Jesus and all G people.
1: 7 the hearts of G people have been refreshed.
Heb 2: 9 that through G gracious will he might
3: 2 too, "was faithful in all G household,"
3: 5 Moses "was faithful in all G household"
3: 6 faithful as the Son placed over G house.
4: 3 Yet G work was finished when he created
4:10 And he who enters into G rest,
4:12 Indeed, G word is living and effective,
7: 6 blessed him who had received G promises.
10:36 do G will and receive what he has promised.
11:25 wished to be ill-treated along with G people
11:26 Moses considered the reproach borne by G
12:28 kingdom should hold fast to G grace,
Jas 1:20 a man's anger does not fulfill G justice.
1:23 A man who listens to G word but does not
2: 7 that noble name which has made you G own.
2:23 for this he received the title G friend."
4: 4 A man is marked out as G enemy if he
1Pt 1: 5 who are guarded with G power through faith;
2: 4 nonetheless, and precious in G eyes.
2: 8 and fall are the disbelievers in G word;
2:10 were no people, but now you are G people;
2:19 through his awareness of G presence,
2:20 is right, this is acceptable in G eyes.
2:24 to sin, could live in accord with G will.
3: 4 This is precious in G eyes.
3:17 If it should be G will that you suffer,
3:22 He went to heaven and is at G right hand,
4:10 generous distributors of G manifold grace,
4:11 The one who speaks is to deliver G message.
4:14 for then G Spirit in its glory has come to
4:17 has begun, and begun with G own household.
4:19 as G will requires continue in good deeds,
5: 2 G flock is in your midst;
5: 6 Bow humbly under G mighty hand,
2Pt 1:21 Holy Spirit have spoken under G influence.
2: 1 there were false prophets among G people,
3: 7 and earth are reserved by G word for fire;
1Jn 2:17 the man who does G will endures forever.
3: 2 Dearly beloved, we are G children now;
3: 9 sinfully because he remains of G stock;
3:10 That is the way to see who are G children,
3:17 how can G love survive in a man who has
4: 2 This is how you can recognize G Spirit:
4: 9 G love was revealed in our midst in this
5: 2 We can be sure that we love G children
Jude 1: 8 G dominion and revile the angelic beings.
1:21 Persevere in G love,
Rv 1: 9 G word and bore witness to Jesus.
3:14 Witness and true, the Source of G creation,
5: 8 which were the prayers of G holy people.
7:15 was this that brought them before G throne:
8: 2 in G presence were given seven trumpets.
8: 3 with the prayers of all G holy ones.
8: 4 God, and with it the prayers of G people.
9:13 horns of the altar of gold in G presence.
9:20 demons, or of g made from gold and silver,
11: 1 the measurements of G temple and altar,
11:16 elders who were enthroned in G presence
11:19 Then G temple in heaven opened and in the
12:17 G commandments and give witness to Jesus.
13: 7 wage war against G people and conquer them.
13:10 endurance that distinguishes G holy people.
14:10 he too will drink the wine of G wrath,
14:19 them into the huge winepress of G wrath.
15: 1 which would bring G wrath to a climax.
15: 8 with the smoke which arose from G glory
16: 1 upon the earth the seven bowls of G wrath!"
17: 6 drunk with the blood of G holy ones
19: 8 dress is the virtuous deeds of G saints.)
20: 9 beloved city where G people were encamped;
21: 3 "This is G dwelling among men.

GODSPEED (1)

2Sm 19:40 him G as he returned to his own district.

GOG (11)

1Chr 5: 4 whose son was Shemaiah, whose son was G,
Ez 38: 2 of man, turn toward G [the land of Magog],
38: 3 I am coming at you, G,
38:14 prophesy, son of man, and say to G:
38:16 sight I prove my holiness through you, O G.
38:18 the day when G invades the land of Israel,
39: 1 of man, prophesy against G in these words:
39: 1 I am coming at you, G,
39:11 On that day I will give G for his tomb a
39:11 G shall be buried there with all his horde,
Rv 20: 8 muster for war the troops of G and Magog,

GOIIM (2)

Gn 14: 1 king of G made war on Bera king of Sodom,
14: 9 king of Elam, Tidal king of G,

GOLAN (4)

Dt 4:43 and G in Bashan for the Manassehites.
Jos 20: 8 and G in Bashan in the tribe of Manasseh.
21:27 the city of asylum for homicides at G,
1Chr 6:56 G in Bashan with its pasture lands and

GOLD (491)

Gn 2:11 whole land of Havilah, where there is g.
2:12 The g of that land is excellent;
13: 2 was very rich in livestock, silver, and g.
24:22 took out a g ring weighing half a shekel,
24:22 and two g bracelets weighing ten shekels,
24:35 given him flocks and herds, silver and g,
24:53 he brought out objects of silver and g
41:42 linen and put a g chain about his neck.
44: 8 steal silver or g from your master's house?
Ex 3:22 her house guest for silver and g articles
11: 2 for silver and g articles and for clothing."
12:35 articles of silver and g and for clothing.
20:23 gods of g shall you make for yourselves.
25: 3 g, silver and bronze;
25:11 with pure g, and put a molding of g around
25:12 Cast four g rings and fasten them on the
25:13 poles of acacia wood and plate them with g.
25:17 shall then make a propitiatory of pure g,
25:18 g for the two ends of the propitiatory,
25:24 g and make a molding of gold around it.
25:25 high, with a molding of g around the frame.
25:26 You shall also make four rings of g for it
25:28 shall make of acacia wood and plate with g.
25:29 pure g you shall make its plates and cups,
25:31 shall make a lampstand of pure beaten g—
25:36 form but a single piece of pure beaten g.
25:38 shears and trays, must be of pure g.
25:39 Use a talent of pure g for the lampstand
26: 6 Then make fifty clasps of g,
26:29 Plate the boards with g, and make g rings
26:29 bars, which are also to be plated with g.
26:32 g and shall rest on four silver pedestals.
26:37 plated with gold, with their hooks of g;
28: 5 serving as my priests, they shall use g,
28: 6 they shall make of g thread and of violet,
28: 8 from it and, like it, be made of g thread,
28:11 Israel and then mounted in g filigree work.
28:13 Make filigree rosettes of g,
28:14 of gold, as well as two chains of pure g,
28:15 like the ephod with g thread and violet,
28:20 are to be mounted in g filigree work,
28:22 "when the chains of pure g,
28:23 you shall then make two rings of g for it
28:24 The g cords are then to be fastened to the
28:26 Make two other rings of g and put them on
28:27 Then make two more rings of g and fasten
28:33 linen twined, with g bells between them;
28:34 first a g bell,
28:36 make a plate of pure g and engrave on it,
30: 3 and its horns you shall plate with pure g.
30: 3 Put a g molding around it.
30: 4 the molding you shall put g rings,
30: 5 too, of acacia wood and plate them with g.
31: 4 of embroidery, in making things of g,
31: 8 g lampstand with all its appurtenances,
32: 4 and fashioning this g with a graving tool,
32:24 'Let anyone who has g jewelry take it off.'
32:31 sin in making a god of g for themselves!
35: 5 bring as a contribution to the LORD, g,
35:22 necklaces and various other g articles.
35:22 presented an offering of g to the LORD.
35:32 of embroidery, in making things of g,
36:13 Then fifty clasps of g were made,
36:34 plated with gold, and g rings were made
36:34 the bars, which were also plated with g.
36:36 columns of acacia wood, with g hooks,
36:38 capitals and bands, were plated with g;
37: 2 gold, and a molding of g was put around it.
37: 3 Four g rings were cast and put on its four
37: 4 acacia wood were made and plated with g;
37: 6 The propitiatory was made of pure g,
37: 7 Two cherubim of beaten g were made for the
37:11 gold, and a molding of g was put around it.
37:12 it, with a molding of g around the frame.
37:13 rings of g were cast for it and fastened,
37:15 were made of acacia wood and plated with g.
37:16 for pouring libations, were of pure g.
37:17 The lampstand was made of pure beaten g—
37:22 formed but a single piece of pure beaten g.
37:23 shears and trays, were made of pure g.
37:24 A talent of pure g was used for the
37:26 plated with pure g; and a molding of g
37:27 Underneath the molding g rings were placed,
37:28 were made of acacia wood and plated with g.
38:24 All the g used in the entire construction
39: 2 ephod was woven of g thread and of violet,
39: 3 G was first hammered into gold leaf and
39: 5 from it, and like it, was made of g thread,
39: 6 prepared and mounted in g filigree work;
39: 8 like the ephod, with g thread and violet,
39:13 They were mounted in g filigree work.
39:15 Chains of pure g,
39:16 two gold filigree rosettes and two g rings.
39:17 The two g chains were then fastened to the
39:19 Two other g rings were made and put on the
39:20 Two more g rings were made and fastened to
39:25 bells of pure g were also made and put
39:30 diadem was made of pure g and inscribed,
39:37 the pure g lampstand with its lamps set up
Lv 8: 9 miter on his head, attaching the g plate,
24: 4 shall be set up on the pure g lampstand,
24: 6 pile, on the pure g table before the LORD.
Nm 7:14 one g cup of ten shekels' weight filled
7:20 one g cup of ten shekels' weight filled
7:26 one g cup of ten shekels' weight filled
7:32 one g cup of ten shekels' weight filled
7:38 one g cup of ten shekels' weight filled
7:44 one g cup of ten shek-els' weight filled
7:50 one g cup of ten shekels' weight filled
7:56 one g cup of ten shekels' weight filled
7:62 one g cup of ten shekels' weight filled
7:68 one g cup of ten shekels' weight filled
7:74 one g cup of ten shekels' weight filled
7:80 one g cup of ten shekels' weight filled
7:84 twelve silver basins, and twelve g cups.
7:86 The twelve g cups that were filled with
7:86 so that all the g of the cups amounted to
8: 4 g in both its shaft and its branches,
22:18 gave me his house full of silver and g,
24:13 gave me his house full of silver and g,
31:22 Whatever can stand fire, such as g,
31:50 the LORD some g article he has picked up,
31:51 priest Eleazar accepted this g from them,
31:52 The g that they gave as a contribution to
31:54 the g from the clan and company commanders,
Dt 7:25 Do not covet the silver or g on them,
8:13 your herds and flocks, your silver and g,
17:17 accumulate a vast amount of silver and g.
29:16 idols of wood and stone, of g and silver,
Jos 6:19 All silver and g,
6:24 all that was in it, except the silver, g,
7:21 and a bar of g fifty shekels in weight;
7:24 the silver, the mantle, and the bar of g,
22: 8 very numerous livestock, with silver, g,
Jgs 8:24 being Ishmaelites, the enemy had g rings.)
8:26 The g rings that he requested weighed
8:26 weighed seventeen hundred g shekels,
8:27 of the g and placed it in his city Ophrah.
2Sm 1:24 who decked your attire with ornaments of g.
8:10 brought with him articles of silver, g,
8:11 together with the silver and g he had
12:30 weighed a talent, of g and precious stones;
21: 4 Saul and his house for silver or g,
1Kgs 6:21 the interior of the temple with pure g.
6:21 a cedar altar, overlaid it with g,
6:22 The entire temple was overlaid with g so
6:22 the sanctuary was also overlaid with g.
6:28 The cherubim, too, were overlaid with g.
6:30 and the outer rooms was overlaid with g.
6:32 The doors were overlaid with g,
6:35 flowers, over which g was evenly applied.
7:49 the lampstands of pure g,
7:49 with their flowers, lamps, and tongs of g;
7:50 fire pans of pure g; and hinges of g
7:51 his father David, putting the silver, g,
9:11 the cedar wood, fir wood, and g he wished
9:14 one hundred and twenty talents of g.
9:28 and twenty talents of g to King Solomon.
10: 2 camels bearing spices, a large amount of g,
10:10 the king one hundred and twenty g talents,
10:11 fleet, which used to bring g from Ophir,
10:14 The g that Solomon received every year
10:14 six hundred and sixty-six g talents,
10:16 beaten g six hundred g shekels went into
10:17 beaten g (three minas of g went into each
10:18 made, and overlaid it with refined g.
10:21 King Solomon's drinking vessels were of g,
10:21 of the Forest of Lebanon were of pure g.
10:22 ships would come with a cargo of g,
10:25 silver or g articles,
12:28 two calves of g and said to the people:
14:26 as all the g shields made under Solomon.
15:15 and his own votive offerings of silver, g,
15:18 Asa then took all the silver and g
15:19 I am sending you a present of silver and g.
20: 3 'Your silver and g are mine,
20: 5 sent you word to give me your silver and g,
20: 7 for my wives and sons, my silver and my g,
22:49 made Tarshish ships to go to Ophir for g;
2Kgs 5: 5 ten silver talents, six thousand g pieces,
7: 8 tent, ate and drank, and took silver, g,
12:14 trumpets, or any g or silver article.
12:19 and all the g there was in the treasuries
14:14 He took all the g and silver and all the
16: 8 Ahaz took the silver and g that were in
18:14 and thirty talents of g from Hezekiah,
18:16 to be overlaid with g, and gave the gold
20:13 his whole treasury, his silver, g,
23:33 talents of silver and a talent of g.
23:35 Jehoiakim gave the silver and g to Pharaoh,
23:35 silver and g from the people of the land,
24:13 broke up all the g utensils that Solomon,
25:15 bowls which were of g or silver
1Chr 18:10 He also sent David g,
18:11 and g that he had taken from the nations:
20: 2 It was found to weigh a talent of g;
21:25 six hundred shekels of g for the place.
22:14 the LORD a hundred thousand talents of g,
22:16 and every kind of craftsman skilled in g,
28:14 He specified the weight of g to be used in
28:15 of g for each lampstand and its lamps,
28:16 of g for each table to hold the showbread,

28:16 *g* to be used for the forks and pitchers,
28:17 the amount of *g* for each golden bowl and
28:18 the refined *g*, and its weight,
28:18 *g* for what would suggest a chariot throne:
29: 2 was able, gold for what will be made of *g*,
29: 3 my God my personal fortune in *g* and silver:
29: 4 three thousand talents of Ophir *g*,
29: 5 utensils to be made of *g* and silver,
29: 7 talents and ten thousand darics of *g*,
2Chr 1:15 and *g* as common in Jerusalem as stones,
2: 6 Now, send me men skilled at work in *g*,
2:13 he knows how to work with *g*,
3: 4 He overlaid its interior with pure *g*.
3: 5 cypress wood which he covered with fine *g*,
3: 7 walls and its doors, he overlaid with *g*,
3: 7 (The *g* was from Parvaim.)
3: 8 *g* to the amount of six hundred talents.
3: 9 weight of the nails was fifty *g* shekels.
3: 9 upper chambers he likewise covered with *g*.
3:10 which were then overlaid with *g*.
4: 7 He made the lampstands of *g*,
4:20 lampstands and their lamps of pure *g*
4:21 and *g* tongs [this was the purest gold],
4:22 bowls, cups and firepans of pure *g*.
4:22 well as the doors to the nave, were of *g*.
5: 1 the *g* and all the other articles in the
8:18 and fifty talents of *g* to King Solomon.
9: 1 and by camels bearing spices, much *g*,
9: 9 gave the king one hundred and twenty *g*
9:10 of Huram and of Solomon who brought *g*
9:13 The *g* that Solomon received each year
9:13 six hundred and sixty-six *g* talents,
9:14 country, brought *g* and silver to Solomon.
9:15 beaten *g*, six hundred shekels of beaten *g*
9:16 beaten *g*, three hundred shekels of *g*
9:17 ivory throne which he overlaid with fine *g*.
9:18 a footstool of *g* was fastened to it,
9:20 King Solomon's drinking vessels were of *g*,
9:20 of the Forest of Lebanon were of pure *g*;
9:21 would return with a cargo of *g* and silver,
9:24 silver and *g* articles,
12: 9 the *g* bucklers that Solomon had made.
15:18 silver, *g*, and various utensils.
16: 2 Asa then brought out silver and *g* from the
16: 3 See, I am sending you silver and *g*.
21: 3 gifts of silver, *g* and precious objects,
24:14 and basins and other *g* and silver utensils.
25:24 He took away all the *g* and silver and all
32:27 He had treasuries made for his silver, *g*,
36: 3 talents of silver and a talent of *g*.
Ezr 1: 4 the people of that place with silver, *g*,
1: 6 them help in every way, with silver, *g*,
2:69 sixty-one thousand drachmas of *g*,
5:14 the *g* and silver utensils of the house of
6: 5 the *g* and silver utensils of the house of
7:15 bring with you the silver and *g*
7:16 all the silver and *g* which you may receive
7:18 you with the remainder of the silver and *g*,
8:25 out before them the silver and the *g*
8:26 *g*, one hundred talents;
8:27 polished bronze, as precious as *g*.
8:28 the *g* are a freewill offering to the LORD,
8:30 Levites then took over the silver, the *g*,
8:33 On the fourth day, the silver, the *g*,
Neh 7:69 the treasury one thousand drachmas of *g*,
7:70 twenty thousand drachmas of *g* and two
7:71 amounted to twenty thousand drachmas of *g*,
Tb 12: 8 is better to give alms than to store up *g*;
13:16 gold, and their battlements with pure *g*.
Jdt 2:18 much *g* and silver from the royal palace.
5: 9 they settled, and grew very rich in *g*,
8: 7 Manasseh, had left her *g* and silver,
10:21 a canopy with a netting of crimson and *g*,
Est 1: 6 *G* and silver couches were on the pavement,
D: 6 and covered with *g* and precious stones,
8:15 crown of *g* and a cloak of crimson byssus.
1Mc 1:23 the *g* and silver and the precious vessels;
2:18 enriched with silver and *g* and many gifts."
3:41 fetters and a large sum of silver and *g*,
4:23 and his men collected much *g* and silver,
4:57 of the temple with *g* crowns and shields;
6: 1 famous for its wealth in silver and *g*,
6: 2 temple was very rich, containing *g* helmets,
6:12 vessels of *g* and silver that were in it,
6:39 the sun shone on the *g* and bronze shields,
8: 3 of the silver and *g* mines in Spain,
10:20 sent him a purple robe and a crown of *g*.
10:60 *g* and many gifts and thus won their favor.
10:89 He sent him a *g* buckle,
11:24 He brought with him silver, *g* apparel,
11:58 sent him *g* dishes and a dinner service,
11:58 gave him the right to drink from *g* cups,
11:58 in royal purple, and to wear a *g* buckle.
13:37 *g* crown and the palm branch that you sent.
14:24 a great *g* shield weighing a thousand minas,
14:43 right to wear royal purple and *g* ornaments.
14:44 royal purple or wear an official *g* brooch.
15:18 them a *g* shield worth a thousand minas.
15:26 with *g* and silver and much equipment.
15:32 the *g* and silver plate on the sideboard,
16:11 of Jericho, and he had much silver and *g*,
16:19 that he might present them with silver, *g*,
2Mc 2: 2 the *g* and silver idols and their ornaments.
3:11 talents of silver and two hundred of *g*.
4:32 stole some *g* vessels from the temple and
4:39 large number of *g* vessels had been stolen,
5: 2 clad in garments interwoven with *g*—
5: 3 of arrows and flashes of *g* ornaments,
11: 8 white garments and brandishing *g* weapons.
14: 4 him with a *g* crown and a palm branch,
15:15 Jeremiah presented a *g* sword to Judas.
Jb 3:15 had *g* and filled their houses with silver.
22:24 treat raw *g* like dust, and the fine *g* of Ophir
22:25 shall be your *g* and your sparkling silver.
23:10 if he proved me, I should come forth as *g*.
28: 1 silver, and a place for *g* which men refine.
28: 6 of sapphires, and there is *g* in its dust.
28:15 Solid *g* cannot purchase it,
28:16 It cannot be bought with *g* of Ophir,
28:17 *G* or crystal cannot equal it,
31:24 trust in gold or called fine *g* my security;
42:11 one gave him a piece of money and a *g* ring.
Ps(s) 19:11 than gold, than a heap of purest *g*;
21: 4 you placed on his head a crown of pure *g*.
45:10 her place at your right hand in *g* of Ophir.
45:14 her raiment is threaded with spun *g*.
72:15 May he live to be given the *g* of Arabia,
105:37 he led them forth laden with silver and *g*,
115: 4 Their idols are silver and *g*,
119:72 than thousands of *g* and silver pieces.
119:127 For I love your command more than *g*,
135:15 The idols of the nations are silver and *g*,
Prv 3:14 silver, and better than *g* is her revenue;
8:10 silver, and knowledge rather than choice *g*.
8:19 is better than gold, yes, than pure *g*,
16:16 How much better to acquire wisdom than *g*!
17: 3 crucible for silver, and the furnace for *g*,
20:15 Like *g* or a wealth of corals,
22: 1 riches, and high esteem, than *g* and silver.
25:12 a golden earring, or a necklace of fine *g*,
27:21 crucible tests silver and the furnace *g*,
Eccl 2: 8 I amassed for myself silver and *g*,
Sg 1:11 of *g* for you and silver ornaments.
3:10 made its columns of silver, its roof of *g*,
5:11 His head is pure *g*;
5:14 are rods of *g* adorned with chrysolites.
Wis 3: 6 As *g* in the furnace,
7: 9 Because all *g*,
13:10 *G* and silver, the product of art,
Sir 2: 5 For in fire *g* is tested,
7:18 nor a dear brother for the *g* of Ophir.
8: 2 For *g* has dazzled many,
14: 3 and to the miser, of what use is *g*?
21:21 a chain of *g* is learning to a wise man,
28:25 As you seal up your silver and *g*,
29:11 for that will profit you more than the *g*.
30:15 precious than *g* is health and well-being,
31: 5 The lover of *g* will not be free from sin,
31: 6 Many have been ensnared by *g*,
31:10 he has been tested by *g* and come off safe,
32: 5 of *g* is a concert when wine is served.
32: 6 Like a *g* mounting with an emerald seal is
40:25 *G* and silver make one's way secure,
45:10 The sacred vestments of *g*,
45:12 On his turban the diadem of *g*,
47:18 *G* you gathered like so much iron,
50: 9 Like a vessel of beaten *g*,
51:28 you will win silver and *g* through her.
Is 2: 7 Their land is full of silver and *g*,
2:20 silver and *g* which they made for worship.
13:12 rare than pure gold, men, than *g* of Ophir.
13:17 nothing of silver and take no delight in *g*.
31: 7 spurn his sinful idols of silver and *g*,
39: 2 messengers his treasury, the silver and *g*,
40:19 plates with *g* and fits with silver chains?
46: 6 There are those who pour out *g* from a
60: 6 shall come bearing *g* and frankincense,
60: 9 from afar with their silver and *g*,
60:17 In place of bronze I will bring *g*,
Jer 4:30 on purple, bedecking yourself with *g*,
10: 4 with the adze, adorned with silver and *g*.
10: 9 brought from Tarshish, and *g* from Ophir,
52:19 bowls which were of *g* or silver,
Lam 4: 1 How tarnished is the *g*,
4: 2 precious sons, fine *g* their counterpart,
Bar 3:17 up the silver and the *g* in which men trust;
3:30 her, bearing her away rather than choice *g*?
6: 3 shoulders gods of silver and *g* and wood,
6: 7 they are covered with *g* and silver
6: 8 People bring *g*,
6: 9 priests take the silver and *g* from their gods
6:10 men, these gods of silver and *g* and wood;
6:23 the *g* that covers them for adornment,
6:29 to these gods of silver and *g* and wood;
6:57 seize them strip off the *g* and the silver,
Ez 7:19 and their *g* shall be considered refuse.
7:19 Their silver and *g* cannot save them on the
16:13 Thus you were adorned with *g* and silver;
16:17 You took the splendid *g* and silver
27:22 all kinds of precious stones, and *g*.
28: 4 have put *g* and silver into your treasuries.
28:13 Of *g* your pendants and jewels were made,
38:13 your horde, to carry off silver and *g*,
Dn 2:32 The head of the statue was pure *g*,
2:35 bronze, silver, and *g* all crumbled at once,
2:38 you are the head of *g*.
2:45 the tile, iron, bronze, silver, and *g*.
5: 2 *g* and silver vessels which Nebuchadnezzar,
5: 3 When the *g* and silver vessels taken from
5: 4 they praised their gods of *g* and silver,
5:16 in purple, wear a *g* collar about your neck,
5:23 and you praised the gods of silver and *g*,
5:29 in purple, with a *g* collar about his neck,
10: 5 with a belt of fine *g* around his waist.
11: 8 their precious vessels of silver and *g*,
11:38 to his fathers he shall glorify with *g*,
11:43 He shall control the riches of *g* and
Hos 2:10 And her abundance of silver, and of *g*,
8: 4 and *g* they made idols for themselves,
Jl 4: 5 You took my silver and my *g*,
Na 2:10 "Plunder the silver, plunder the *g*!"
Hb 2:19 See, it is overlaid with *g* and silver,
Zep 1:18 Neither their silver nor their *g* shall be
Hg 2: 8 and mine the *g* says the LORD of hosts.
Zec 4: 2 "I see a lampstand all of *g*,
6:11 Silver and *g* you shall take,
9: 3 dust, and *g* like the mire of the streets.
13: 9 and I will test them as *g* is tested.
14:14 nations shall be gathered together, *g*,
Mal 3: 3 Refining them like *g* or like silver that
Mt 2:11 coffers and presented him with gifts of *g*,
10: 9 *g* nor silver nor copper in your belts;
23:16 by the *g* of the temple he is obligated.'
23:17 the *g* or the temple which makes it sacred?
Acts 3: 6 "I have neither silver nor *g*,
17:29 like a statue of *g* or silver or stone,
20:33 silver or *g* or envy the way he dressed.
1Cor 3:12 ones build on this foundation with *g*,
1Tm 2: 9 out in fancy hair styles, *g* ornaments,
2Tm 2:20 of *g* and silver but also of wood and clay,
Heb 9: 4 of the covenant entirely covered with *g*.
Jas 2: 2 dressed, with *g* rings on his fingers,
5: 3 your *g* and silver have corroded,
1Pt 1: 7 than the passing splendor of fire-tried *g*,
1:18 by any diminishable sum of silver or *g*,
Rv 1:12 When I did so I saw seven lampstands of *g*,
1:13 robe, with a sash of *g* about his breast.
1:20 hand, and of the seven lampstands of *g*:
2: 1 the seven lampstands of *g* has this to say:
3:18 Buy from me *g* refined by fire if you would
4: 4 and had crowns of *g* on their heads.
5: 8 vessels of *g* filled with aromatic spices,
8: 3 angel came in holding a censer of *g*.
8: 3 on the altar of *g* in front of the throne,
9: 7 heads they wore something like *g* crowns;
9:13 horns of the altar of *g* in God's presence.
9:20 demons, or of gods made from *g* and silver,
14:14 One like a Son of Man wearing a *g* crown
15: 6 each with a sash of *g* about his breast.
17: 4 adorned with *g* and pearls and other jewels.
17: 4 In her hand she held a *g* cup that was
18:12 their cargoes of *g* and silver,
18:16 Adorned all in *g* and jewels and pearls!
21:15 me held a rod of *g* for measuring the city,
21:18 the city was of pure *g*,
21:21 and the streets of the city were of pure *g*,

GOLD- (1)

Ezr 1:11 Total of the *g*- and silver ware:

GOLD-COVERED (1)

Is 30:22 your silver-plated idols and your *g* images;

GOLD-PLATED (2)

Ex 26:32 be hung on four *g* columns of acacia wood,
36:36 Four *g* columns of acacia wood,

GOLDEN (59)

Ex 32: 2 take off the *g* earrings they are wearing,
39:38 the oil for the light, the *g* altar,
40: 5 Put the *g* altar of incense in front of the
40:26 He placed the *g* altar in the meeting tent,
Nm 4:11 *g* altar they shall spread a violet cloth,
1Sm 6: 4 "Five *g* hemorrhoids and five golden mice
6: 8 it the *g* articles that you are offering,
6:11 *g* mice and the images of the hemorrhoids.
6:15 beside it, in which the *g* articles were,
6:17 The *g* hemorrhoids the Philistines sent
6:18 The *g* mice,
2Sm 8: 7 David also took away the *g* shields used by
1Kgs 6:21 it with gold, and looped it with *g* chains.
7:48 the *g* altar; the golden table on which
2Kgs 10:29 regards the *g* calves at Bethel and at Dan.
1Chr 18: 7 David took the *g* shields that were carried
28:14 weight of gold to be used in the *g* vessels
28:15 likewise for the *g* lampstands and their
28:17 *g* bowl and the silver for each silver bowl;
2Chr 4: 8 and he made a hundred *g* bowls.
4:19 the *g* altar,
13: 8 *g* calves which Jeroboam made you for gods?
13:11 the *g* lampstand burn evening after evening;
Ezr 1:10 *g* bowls,
8:27 twenty *g* bowls valued at a thousand darics;
Est 1: 7 Liquor was served in a variety of *g* cups,
4:11 the king extends to him the *g* scepter,
D:12 Raising the *g* scepter,
5: 2 toward her the *g* staff which he held.

GOLDEN (cont.)

8: 4 stretched forth the *g* scepter to Esther.
1Mc 1:21 the sanctuary and took away the *g* altar,
1:22 *g* censers, the curtain, the crowns, and the *g*
2Mc 3:25 The rider was seen to be wearing *g* armor.
Jb 28:17 it, nor can *g* vessels reach its worth.
Ps(s) 68:14 with silver, and her pinions with a *g* hue.
Prv 11:22 Like a *g* ring in a swine's snout is a
25:11 Like *g* apples in silver settings are words
25:12 Like a *g* earring,
Eccl 12: 6 and the *g* bowl is broken,
Sg 5:15 are columns of marble resting on *g* bases.
Sir 26:18 *G* columns on silver bases are her shapely
45:11 stones with seal engravings in *g* settings,
Jer 51: 7 Babylon was a *g* cup in the hand of the
Dn 3: 1 King Nebuchadnezzar had a *g* statue made,
3: 5 fall down and worship the *g* statue
3: 7 all fell down and worshiped the *g* statue
3:10 should fall down and worship the *g* statue;
3:12 or worship the *g* statue which you set up."
3:14 god, or worship the *g* statue that I set up?
3:18 or worship the *g* statue which you set up."
5: 7 in purple, wear a *g* collar about his neck,
Zec 4:12 out fresh oil through the two *g* channels?"
Heb 9: 4 in which were the *g* altar of incense and
9: 4 ark were the *g* jar containing the manna,
1Pt 3: 3 hairdress, the wearing of *g* jewelry,
Rv 15: 7 gave to the seven angels seven *g* bowls

GOLDEN-BRIDLED (1)

2Mc 10:29 five majestic men riding on *g* horses,

GOLDSMITH (2)

Is 41: 7 The craftsman encourages the *g*,
46: 6 Then they hire a *g* to make it into a god

GOLDSMITHS (5)

Neh 3: 8 son of Harhaiah, a member of the *g*' guild,
3:31 him, Malchijah, a member of the *g*' guild,
3:32 the *g* and the merchants carried out the
Wis 15: 9 he vies with *g* and silversmiths and
Bar 6:45 They are produced by woodworkers and *g*.

GOLDWARE (1)

Ezr 1: 9 sacks of *g*, thirty; sacks of silverware,

GOLGOTHA (3)

Mt 27:33 called *G* (a name which means Skull Place),
Mk 15:22 site of *G* (which means "Skull Place"),
Jn 19:17 the Place of the Skull (in Hebrew, *G*).

GOLIATH (7)

1Sm 17: 4 A champion named *G* of Gath came out from
17:23 the Philistine champion, by name *G* of Gath,
21:10 "The sword of *G* the Philistine,
22:10 and the sword of *G* the Philistine as well."
2Sm 21:19 of Jair from Bethlehem, killed *G* of Gath,
1Chr 20: 5 Jair, slew Lahmi, the brother of *G* of Gath,
Sir 47: 4 the slingstone that crushed the pride of *G*.

GOLIATH'S (1)

1Sm 17:54 but he kept *G* armor in his own tent.

GOMER (6)

Gn 10: 2 *G*, Magog, Madai, Javan, Tubal,
10: 3 The descendants of *G*:
1Chr 1: 5 The descendants of Japheth were *G*,
1: 6 The descendants of *G* were Ashkenaz,
Ez 38: 6 and helmets], *G* with all its troops,
Hos 1: 3 So he went and took *G*,

GOMORRAH (23)

Gn 10:19 near Gaza, and all the way to Sodom, *G*,
13:10 before the LORD had destroyed Sodom and *G*.)
14: 2 on Bera king of Sodom, Birsha king of *G*,
14: 8 the king of Sodom, the king of *G*,
14:10 and as the kings of Sodom and *G* fled,
14:11 of Sodom and *G* and then went their way,
18:20 outcry against Sodom and *G* is so great,
19:24 Sodom and *G* [from the LORD out of heaven].
19:28 and *G* and the whole region of the Plain,
Dt 29:22 of grass, destroyed like Sodom and *G*,
32:32 Sodom's vinestock, from the vineyards of *G*.
Is 1: 9 had become as Sodom, we should be like *G*.
1:10 to the instruction of our God, people of *G*!
13:19 be overthrown by God like Sodom and like *G*.
Jer 23:14 are all like Sodom, its citizens like *G*.
49:18 As when Sodom, *G*,
50:40 As when God overturned Sodom and *G*,
Am 4:11 upheaval as when God overthrew Sodom and *G*:
Zep 2: 9 like Sodom, the land of Ammon like *G*:
Mt 10:15 go easier for the region of Sodom and *G*
Rom 9:29 have become as Sodom, we should be like *G*."
2Pt 2: 6 He blanketed the cities of Sodom and *G* in
Jude 1: 7 Sodom, *G*, and the towns thereabout

GONG (1)

1Cor 13: 1 well, but do not have love, I am a noisy *g*,

GOOD (680)

Gn 1: 4 God saw how *g* the light was.
1:10 "the sea." God saw how *g* it was.
1:12 with its seed in it. God saw how *g* it was.
1:18 the darkness. God saw how *g* it was.
1:21 God saw how *g* it was, and God blessed
1:25 things of the earth. God saw how *g* it was.
1:31 he had made, and he found it very *g*.
2: 9 were delightful to look at and *g* for food,
2: 9 and the tree of the knowledge of *g* and bad.
2:17 except the tree of knowledge of *g* and bad.
2:18 "It is not *g* for the man to be alone.
3: 5 gods who know what is *g* and what is bad."
3: 6 The woman saw that the tree was *g* for food,
3:22 of us, knowing what is *g* and what is bad!
6: 9 Noah, a *g* man and blameless in that age,
15: 2 "O Lord GOD, what *g* will your gifts be,
20: 5 I did it in *g* faith and with clean hands."
20: 6 "Yes, I know you did it in *g* faith.
25:22 this is to be so, what *g* will it do me!"
25:32 What *g* will any birthright do me?"
27:46 these women, what *g* would life be to me?"
30:11 Leah then said, "What *g* luck!"
30:13 and Leah said, "What *g* fortune!"—meaning,
31:39 I made *g* the loss myself.
32:10 land of your birth, and I will be *g* to you.'
32:13 yourself said, 'I will be very *g* to you,
41:35 husband all the food of the coming *g* years,
43:27 Is he still in *g* health?"
43:28 father is thriving and still in *g* health,"
44: 4 to them, 'Why did you repay *g* with evil?
45: 3 "Is my father still in *g* health?"
49:15 When he saw how *g* a settled life was,
50:20 you meant harm to me, God meant it for *g*,
Ex 3: 8 of that land into a *g* and spacious land,
21:34 the owner of the cistern must make *g* by
Lv 5: 4 it, rashly utters an oath to do *g* or evil,
26:43 may make *g* the debt of their guilt for
27:12 in keeping with its *g* or bad qualities,
27:14 value in keeping with its *g* or bad points,
27:33 whether *g* ones or bad ones are thus chosen,
Nm 13:19 Is the country in which they live *g* or bad?
24:13 of my own accord to anything, *g* or evil,
Dt 1:25 which the LORD, our God, gives us is *g*.'
1:35 the *g* land I swore to give to your fathers,
1:39 who as yet do not know *g* from bad
3:25 over and see this *g* land beyond the Jordan,
4:21 not cross the Jordan nor enter the *g* land
4:22 over and take possession of that *g* land.
6:18 is right and *g* in the sight of the LORD,
6:18 may enter in and possess the *g* land
8: 7 your God, is bringing you into a *g* country,
8:10 God, for the *g* country he has given you.
9: 6 God, is giving you this *g* land to possess,
10:13 which I enjoin on you today for your own *g*?
11:17 perish from the *g* land he is giving you.
12:28 is *g* and right in the sight of the LORD,
24:13 will be a *g* deed of yours before the LORD,
26:11 over all these *g* things which the LORD,
Jos 23:13 you perish from this *g* land which the LORD,
23:15 you from this *g* land which the LORD,
23:16 from the *g* land which he has given you."
24:20 If, after the *g* he has done for you,
Jgs 3:26 their delay Ehud made *g* his escape and,
8:32 At a *g* old age Gideon,
8:35 for all the *g* he had done for Israel.
9:11 I give up my sweetness and my *g* fruit,
9:15 wish to anoint me king over you in *g* faith,
9:16 if you have acted in *g* faith and honorably
9:19 you have acted in *g* faith and with honor
16:20 *g* his escape as he had done time and again,
18: 9 for we have seen the land and it is very *g*.
Ru 3:13 and tomorrow, if he wishes to claim you, *g*!
1Sm 2:24 It is not a *g* report that I hear the
12:14 well and *g*.
12:23 you and to teach you the *g* and right way.
20:31 cannot make *g* your claim to the kingship!
25:15 Yet these men were very *g* to us.
25:21 He has repaid *g* with evil.
25:33 *g* judgment and blessed be you yourself,
28: 2 David answered Achish, *G*!
31: 9 and then sent the *g* news throughout the
2Sm 4:10 thinking himself the bearer of *g* news for
14:17 like an angel of God, evaluating *g* and bad.
14:22 day I know that I am in *g* favor with you,
15: 3 say to him, "Your suit is *g* and just,
15:11 They had been invited and went in *g* faith,
17: 7 time Ahithophel has not given *g* counsel."
17:14 had decided to undo Ahithophel's *g* counsel,
18:19 "Let me run to take the *g* news to the
18:20 On some other day you may take the *g* news,
18:20 but today you would not be bringing *g* news,
18:25 "If he is alone, he has *g* news to report."
18:26 responded, "He, too, is bringing *g* news."
18:27 "He is a good man; he comes with *g* news."
18:31 "Let my lord the king receive the *g* news
19:36 Can I distinguish between *g* and bad?
1Kgs 1:42 are a man of worth and must bring *g* news."
14:15 this *g* land which he gave their fathers,
20:33 is my brother," Hearing this as a *g* omen,
22: 8 he prophesies not *g* but evil about me."
22:13 are unanimously predicting *g* for the king.
22:13 be the same as any of theirs; predict *g*."
22:18 you he prophesies not *g* but evil about me?"
2Kgs 4:13 Can we say a *g* word for you to the king or
7: 9 This is a day of *g* news,
1Chr 4:40 They found abundant and *g* pastures,
10: 9 the *g* news to their idols and their people.
13: 2 "If it seems *g* to you,
16:34 Give thanks to the LORD, for he is *g*,
17:26 have promised this *g* thing to your servant,
28: 8 you may continue to possess this *g* land
2Chr 5:13 to "give thanks to the LORD, for he is *g*,
6:41 may your faithful ones rejoice in *g* things.
7: 3 adored, praising the LORD, "for he is *g*,
7:10 the *g* things the LORD had done for David,
12:12 and in Judah moreover, *g* deeds were found.
14: 1 did what was *g* and pleasing to the LORD,
18: 7 prophesies not *g* but always evil about me.
18:12 unanimously predict *g* for the king,
18:12 your word, like each of theirs, predict *g*."
18:17 tell you that he prophesies no *g* about me,
19: 3 Yet some *g* things are to be found in you,
19:11 firmly, and the LORD will be with the *g*."
24:16 the kings, because he had done *g* in Israel,
30:18 them, saying, "May the LORD, who is *g*,
31:20 He did what was *g*,
Ezr 3:11 thanksgiving to the LORD, "for he is *g*,
5: 7 "To King Darius all *g* wishes!
5: 8 and is making *g* progress under their hands.
8:29 Keep *g* watch over them till you weigh them
9: 9 *g* will of the kings of Persia toward us.
Neh 2:18 And they undertook the *g* work with vigor.
5: 5 and our children are as *g* as theirs,
5: 9 "What you are doing is not *g*.
6:19 Thus they would praise his *g* deeds in my
9:13 just ordinances, firm laws, *g* statutes,
9:20 "Your *g* spirit you bestowed on them,
9:25 of houses filled with all *g* things,
9:25 feast themselves on your immense *g* gifts.
9:35 in the midst of the many *g* things that you
9:36 they might eat its fruits and *g* things
Tb 4: 5 Perform *g* works all the days of your life,
4: 6 service, your *g* works will bring success,
4:19 *g* counsel, but the Lord himself gives all *g*
5: 6 *g* two days' travel from Ecbatana to Rages,
5:14 are a kinsman, and from a noble and *g* line!
5:14 your kinsmen are *g* men.
5:14 You are certainly of *g* lineage,
5:16 *g* health we shall leave you, and in *g* health
5:21 in *g* health and come back to us in *g* health.
5:22 For a *g* angel will go with him,
7: 1 *G* health to you, and welcome!"
7: 7 You are the son of a noble and *g* father.
8: 6 said, 'It is not *g* for the man to be alone;
8:21 you go back in *g* health to your father;
8:21 Be of *g* cheer, my son!
9: 6 and good child, son of a noble and *g*,
10:12 hear *g* reports about you as long as I live."
12: 6 the many *g* things he has done for you,
12: 7 Do *g*, and evil will not find its way to you.
12: 8 Prayer and fasting are *g*,
14: 4 and led away into exile from the *G* Land.
Jdt 8:17 will hear our cry if it is his *g* pleasure.
8:28 that you have said was spoken with *g* sense,
15: 8 *g* things that the Lord had done for Israel,
15:10 You have done *g* to Israel,
Est 1: 8 to comply with the *g* pleasure of everyone.
5: 9 That day Haman left happy and in *g* spirits.
5:14 go to the banquet with the king in *g* cheer."
E: 6 slander the sincere *g* will of rulers.
E:11 He so far enjoyed the *g* will which we have
1Mc 4:24 hymns and glorifying Heaven, "for he is *g*,
6:40 marched forward steadily and in *g* order.
9: 8 we can put up a *g* fight against them."
11:33 Because of the *g* will they show us,
11:44 thousand *g* fighting men to him at Antioch.
14: 4 of Simon, who sought the *g* of his nation.
14: 9 the squares, all talking about the *g* times,
16:17 act of treason he repaid *g* with evil.
2Mc 1:10 send greetings and *g* wishes to Aristobulus,
4: 5 general and particular *g* of all the people.
4:32 Menelaus, thinking this a *g* opportunity,
5: 4 prayed that this vision might be a *g* omen.
5:20 afterward participated in their *g* fortune;
9:21 the esteem and *g* will you bear me.
9:26 to show *g* will toward me and my son.
11: 6 and tears to send a *g* angel to save Israel.
11:15 Maccabeus, solicitous for the common *g*,
11:28 We too are in *g* health.
12:30 Jews who lived there testified to the *g* will
13:26 calming them and gaining their *g* will,
14:30 that this coldness betokened no *g*.
15:12 former high priest, a *g* and virtuous man,
15:23 send a *g* angel now to spread fear and
Jb 2:10 We accept *g* things from God;
9:27 lay aside my sadness and be of *g* cheer,
22:18 he had filled their houses with *g* things!
22:21 In this shall *g* come to you:
30:26 Yet when I looked for *g*,
32: 3 found a *g* answer and had not condemned Job.
34: 4 let us learn between us what is *g*.
Ps(s) 5:13 him with the shield of your *g* will.
13: 6 me sing of the LORD, "He has been *g* to me."
14: 1 there is not one who does *g*.

14: 3 there is not one who does g,
16: 2 Apart from you I have no g."
25: 8 G and upright is the LORD;
30: 6 a lifetime, his g will.
30: 8 in your g will you had endowed me with
34: 9 Taste and see how g the LORD is;
34:11 who seek the LORD want for no g thing.
34:15 Turn from evil, and do g;
35:12 They have repaid me evil for g,
36: 4 he has ceased to understand how to do g.
36: 5 he sets out on a way that is not g,
37: 3 Trust in the LORD and do g,
37:27 Turn from evil and do g,
38:21 evil for g harass me for pursuing good.
52: 5 You love evil rather than g,
53: 2 there is not one who does g.
53: 4 there is not one who does g,
63: 4 For your kindness is a greater g than life;
65: 5 be filled with the g things of your house,
73: 1 How g God is to the upright;
73:28 But for me, to be near God is my g;
84:12 g thing from those who walk in sincerity.
86: 5 For you, O Lord, are g and forgiving,
92: 2 It is g to give thanks to the LORD,
100: 5 bless his name, for he is g;
103: 5 He fills your lifetime with g;
104:28 your hand, they are filled with g things.
107: 1 "Give thanks to the LORD, for he is g,
107: 9 and filled the hungry soul with g things.
109: 5 me evil for g and hatred for my love.
116: 7 for the LORD has been g to you.
116:12 the LORD for all the g he has done for me?
118:29 Give thanks to the LORD, for he is g;
119:17 Be g to your servant,
119:39 which I dread, for your ordinances are g.
119:65 You have done g to your servant,
119:68 You are g and bountiful;
119:71 It is g for me that I have been afflicted,
122: 9 the LORD, our God, I will pray for your g.
125: 4 Do g, O LORD, to the good
133: 1 Behold, how g it is,
135: 3 Praise the LORD, for the LORD is g;
136: 1 Give thanks to the LORD, for he is g,
142: 8 around me when you have been g to me.
143:10 May your g spirit guide me on level ground.
145: 9 The LORD is g to all and compassionate
146: 7 for the oppressed, gives g to the hungry.
147: 1 Praise the LORD, for he is g;
Prv 2: 9 and justice, honesty, every g path;
2:20 Thus you may walk in the way of g men,
3: 4 win favor and g esteem before God and man.
3:27 Refuse no one the g on which he has a
11:23 The desire of the just ends only in g;
11:27 He who seeks the g commands favor,
12: 2 The g man wins favor from the LORD,
12: 8 According to his g sense a man is praised,
12:14 his words a man has his fill of g things,
13: 2 the fruit of his words a man eats g things,
13:15 G sense brings favor,
13:21 but the just shall be recompensed with g.
13:22 The g man leaves an inheritance to his
14:14 and the g man reaps the fruit of his paths.
14:19 Evil men must bow down before the g,
14:22 intent on g gain kindness and constancy.
14:29 The patient man shows much g sense,
15: 3 place, keeping watch on the evil and the g.
15:23 a word in season, how g it is!
15:30 g news invigorates the bones.
16:22 G sense is a fountain of life to its
16:29 and leads him into a way that is not g.
17:13 If a man returns evil for g,
17:20 He who is perverse in heart finds no g,
18: 5 It is not g to be partial to the guilty,
19: 2 Without knowledge even zeal is not g;
19:11 It is g sense in a man to be slow to anger,
19:17 LORD, and he will repay him for his g deed.
20:23 to the LORD, and false scales are not g.
21:16 The man who strays from the way of g sense
22: 1 g name is more desirable than great riches,
24:13 If you eat honey, my son, because it is g,
24:23 To show partiality in judgment is not g.
25:25 from thirst is g news from a far country.
25:27 To eat too much honey is not g;
26:16 than seven men who answer with g sense.
27:23 Take g care of your flocks,
28:21 To show partiality is never g;
31:12 She brings him g,
Eccl 2: 1 pleasure and the enjoyment of g things."
2: 2 "What g does this do?"
2:24 himself with g things by his labors.
4: 8 do I toil and deprive myself of g things?"
4: 9 they get a g wage for their labor.
5:17 Here is what I recognize as g:
6:12 For who knows what is g for a man in life,
7: 1 A g name is better than good ointment,
7:11 Wisdom and an inheritance are g,
7:14 On a g day enjoy good things,
7:18 It is g to hold to this rule,
7:20 on earth so just as to do g and never sin.
8:15 because there is nothing g for man under
9: 2 just and the wicked, for the g and the bad,
9: 2 As it is for the g man,
9:18 and a single slip can ruin much that is g."

12:14 all its hidden qualities, whether g or bad.
Wis 2: 6 let us enjoy the g things that are real,
7:11 Yet all g things together came to me in
7:22 certain, Not baneful, loving the g,
8:18 Wisdom, and g pleasure in her friendship,
12:19 And you gave your sons g ground for hope
13: 1 and who from the g things seen did not
14:26 turmoil, perjury, Disturbance of g men,
15: 1 But you, our God, are g and true,
15:19 their looks are they g or desirable beasts,
18: 9 For in secret the holy children of the g
18: 9 share alike the same g things and dangers,
Sir 2: 9 You who fear the LORD, hope for g things,
7:13 lie after lie, for it never results in g.
11:14 G and evil, life and death,
11:31 The talebearer turns g into evil;
12: 1 If you do g, know for whom you are doing
12: 2 g to the just man and reward will be yours,
12: 3 No g comes to him who gives comfort to the
12: 4 Give to the g man,
12: 6 will meet for every g deed you do for him.
13:23 Wealth is g when there is no sin;
13:24 his countenance, either for g or for evil.
13:25 of a g heart is a cheerful countenance;
14:13 Before you die, be g to your friend,
14:14 Deprive not yourself of present g things,
16:14 Whoever does g has his reward,
17: 6 g and evil he shows them.
18: 6 the g, the evil in him, what are these?
20: 9 Some gifts do one no g,
20:13 A gift from a rogue will do you no g,
26: 1 Happy the husband of a g wife,
26: 3 A g wife is a generous gift bestowed upon
29:14 A g man goes surety for his neighbor,
30:19 What g is an offering to an idol that can
30:20 who groans at the g things his eyes behold!
31:17 Be the first to stop, as befits g manners:
31:22 later you will find my advice g.
31:28 g cheer and merriment are wine drunk
33:14 As evil contrasts with g,
37: 9 He may tell you how g your way will be,
37:18 G and evil, death and life,
37:27 For not every food is g for everyone,
39: 5 to learn what is g and evil among men.
39:16 The works of God are all of them g;
39:25 G things for the good he provided from the
39:25 but for the wicked g things and bad.
39:27 For the g all these are good,
39:33 The works of God are all of them g;
39:34 "This is not as g as that";
41:13 of life is for limited days, but a g name,
42:25 vain, For each in turn, as it comes, is g;
46:10 might know how g it is to be a devoted
51:18 the g I persistently strove for.
Is 1:17 learn to do g.
1:19 you shall eat the g things of the land;
5:20 Woe to those who call evil g, and g evil
7:15 learns to reject the bad and choose the g.
7:16 learns to reject the bad and choose the g,
30: 6 humps of camels To a people g for nothing,
40: 9 of your voice, Jerusalem, herald of g news!
41: 7 He says the soldering is g,
41:23 Do something, g or evil,
48:17 your God, teach you what is for your g,
52: 7 tidings, Announcing peace, bearing g news,
60:10 yet in my g will I have shown you mercy.
63: 7 for he is g to the house of Israel,
64: 5 all our g deeds are like polluted rags;
65: 8 them, for there is still g in them";
Jer 4:22 are wise in evil, but know not how to do g.
6:16 the pathways of old Which is the way to g,
10: 5 harm, neither is it in their power to do g.
13: 7 But it was rotted, g for nothing!
13:10 like this loincloth which is g for nothing.
13:23 As easily would you be able to do g,
15:11 LORD, have I not served you for their g?
18:10 of the g with which I promised to bless it.
18:20 Must g be repaid with evil that they
21:10 this city, for its woe and not for its g,
23:32 and they do this people no g at all,
24: 3 "Figs," I replied: "the g ones are very good,
24: 5 Like these g figs,
24: 6 I will look after them for their g,
26:14 do with me what you think g and right.
29:32 to see the g I will do to this people,
32:39 g and that of their children after them.
32:40 covenant, never to cease doing g to them;
32:41 I will take delight in doing g to them:
32:42 bring upon them all the g I promise them.
33: 9 hear of all the g I will do among them.
33:11 to the LORD of hosts, for the LORD is g;
37: 9 that the Chaldeans will leave you for g,
38:22 betrayed you, outdid you, your g friends!
39:16 against this city, for evil and not for g;
40: 4 seems g to you to come with me to Babylon,
40: 4 go wherever you think g and proper";
44:27 I am watching over them to do evil, not g.
Lam 3:25 G is the LORD to one who waits for him,
3:26 It is g to hope in silence for the saving
3:27 It is g for a man to bear the yoke from
3:38 Most High, whether the thing be g or bad!
Ez 15: 4 is scorched, is it still g for anything?
15: 5 when it was whole it was g for nothing;

18:18 and did what was not g among his people,
20:25 I gave them statutes that were not g,
24: 4 Put in it pieces of meat, all g pieces:
34:14 In g pastures will I pasture them,
34:14 they shall lie down on g grazing ground,
36:31 conduct, and that your deeds were not g;
Dn 3:30 have we done as you ordered us for our g.
3:89 Give thanks to the Lord, for he is g,
3:99 It has seemed g to me to publish the signs
4:24 atone for your sins by g deeds,
Hos 8: 3 men of Israel have thrown away what is g;
14: 3 all iniquity, and receive what is g,
Am 5:14 Seek g and not evil,
5:15 Hate evil and love g,
9: 4 my gaze upon them for evil, and not for g,
Mi 1:12 can the inhabitants of Maroth hope for g?
2: 7 words promise g to him who walks uprightly?
3: 2 what is right, You who hate what is g,
6: 8 You have been told, O man, what is g,
Na 1: 7 The LORD is g,
2: 1 there advances the bearer of g news,
Zep 1:12 "Neither g nor evil can the LORD do."
Zec 3: 8 who sit before you are men of g omen.
11:12 I said to them, "If it seems g to you,
Mal 2:17 evildoer is g in the sight of the LORD,
Mt 4:23 proclaimed the g news of the kingdom,
5:13 Then it is g for nothing but to be thrown
5:33 make g to the Lord all your pledges.'
5:45 for his sun rises on the bad and the g,
6:22 If your eyes are g,
7:11 know how to give your children what is g,
7:11 give g things to anyone who asks him!
7:17 Any sound tree bears g fruit,
7:18 more than a decayed tree can bear g fruit.
7:19 Every tree that does not bear g fruit is
9:12 who are in g health do not need a doctor;
9:35 he proclaimed the g news of God's reign,
9:37 harvest is g but laborers are scarce.
11: 5 the poor have the g news preached to them.
12:12 g deeds may be performed on the sabbath."
12:33 Declare a tree g and its fruit good or
12:34 How can you utter anything g,
12:35 A g man produces good from his store of
13: 8 landed on g soil and yielded grain a
13:23 But what was sown on g soil is the man who
13:24 to a man who sowed g seed in his field.
13:27 'Sir, did you not sow g seed in your field?
13:37 farmer sowing g seed is the Son of Man;
13:38 the g seed the citizens of the kingdom.
17: 4 to Jesus, "Lord, how g that we are here!
19:16 g must I do to possess everlasting life?"
19:17 "Why do you question me about what is g?
19:17 There is One who is g.
22:10 up everyone they met, bad as well as g.
23:23 of the law, justice and mercy and g faith.
24:14 This g news of the kingdom will be
26: 9 a g price and the money given to the poor."
26:10 It is a g deed she has done for me.
26:13 g news is proclaimed throughout the world,
28: 8 ran to carry the g news to his disciples.
Mk 1:14 in Galilee proclaiming the g news of God:
1:38 that I may proclaim the g news there also.
1:39 preaching the g news and expelling demons
3: 4 it permitted to do a g deed on the sabbath
3:14 whom he would send to preach the g news;
4: 8 landed on g soil and yielded grain that
4:20 g soil are the ones who listen to the word,
9: 5 "Rabbi, how g it is for us to be here!
10:17 knelt down before him and asked, G Teacher,
10:18 Jesus answered, "Why do you call me g?
10:18 No one is g but God alone.
13:10 But the g news must first be proclaimed to
14: 9 g news is proclaimed throughout the world,
16:10 to announce the g news to his followers,
16:13 and announced the g news to the others;
16:15 and proclaim the g news to all creation.
Lk 1:19 to speak to you and bring you this g news.
1:53 The hungry he has given every g thing,
2:10 I come to proclaim g news to you
3:18 sort, he preached the g news to the people.
4:43 announce the g news of the reign of God,
6: 9 you, is it lawful to do g on the sabbath
6:27 your enemies, do g to those who hate you;
6:33 If you do g to those who do good to you,
6:35 "Love your enemy and do g;
6:35 is g to the ungrateful and the wicked.
6:38 G measure pressed down,
6:43 "A g tree does not produce decayed fruit
6:43 more than a decayed tree produces g fruit.
6:45 A g man produces goodness from the good in
7:22 the poor have the g news preached to them.
8: 1 the g news of the kingdom of God.
8: 8 But some fell on g soil,
8:15 The seed on g ground are those who hear
9: 6 the g news everywhere and curing diseases.
9:33 "Master, how g it is for us to be here.
11:13 know how to give your children g things,
12:16 "There was a rich man who had a g harvest.
14:34 Salt is g, but if salt loses its flavor what g
15:27 calf because he has him back in g health.'
16:16 the g news of God's kingdom has been
18:18 the ruling class asked him then, G teacher,
18:19 Jesus said to him, "Why call me g?

GOOD (cont.)
18:19 None is *g* but God alone.
19:17 *G* man!' he replied
20: 1 in the temple and proclaiming the *g* news,
Jn 1:46 was, "Can anything *g* come from Nazareth?"
6: 9 dried fish, but what *g* is that for so many?"
7:12 Some maintained, "He is a *g* man,"
10:11 I am the *g* shepherd; the *g* shepherd lays
10:14 "I am the *g* shepherd.
10:32 *g* deeds have I shown you from the Father.
10:33 for any *g* deed' that we are stoning you,"
Acts 4: 9 If we must answer today for a *g* deed done
5:42 the *g* news of Jesus the Messiah.
8:12 believe in the *g* news that Philip preached
8:25 went back to Jerusalem bringing the *g*
8:35 point, telling him the *g* news of Jesus.
8:40 and he went about announcing the *g* news in
9:36 by constant *g* deeds and acts of charity.
10:36 the *g* news of peace proclaimed through
10:38 He went about doing *g* works and healing
11:20 the *g* news of the Lord Jesus to them.
11:24 since he himself was a *g* man filled with
13:32 "We ourselves announce to you the *g* news
14: 1 to convince a *g* number of Jews and Greeks.
14: 7 they continued to proclaim the *g* news.
14:15 We are bringing you the *g* news that will
14:21 After they had proclaimed the *g* news in
16:10 summoned us to proclaim the *g* news there.
20:20 from telling you what was for your own *g*,
24:15 resurrection of the *g* and the wicked alike.
Rom 2:10 and peace for everyone who has done *g*,
3: 8 may we not do evil that *g* may come of it?
4:19 which was as *g* as dead (for he was nearly
5: 7 *g* man someone may have the courage to die.
7:12 and the commandment is holy and just and *g*.
7:13 Did this *g* thing then become death for me?
7:13 used what was *g* to bring about my death.
7:16 that very fact I agree that the law is *g*.
7:18 I know that no *g* dwells in me,
7:19 is that I do, not the *g* I will to do,
8:28 makes all things work together for the *g*
9:11 yet unborn and had done neither *g* nor evil,
10:15 are the feet of those who announce *g* news!"
11:20 Well and *g*.
12: 2 may judge what is God's will, what is *g*,
12: 9 Detest what is evil, cling to what is *g*.
12:21 conquered by evil but conquer evil with *g*.
13: 4 ruler is God's servant to work for your *g*.
15: 2 as to do him *g* by building up his spirit.
16:19 to what is *g* and innocent of all evil.
1Cor 6:12 does not mean that everything is *g* for me.
7:26 *g* to me for a person to continue as he is.
7:35 am going into this with you for your own *g*.
7:35 you, but I do want to promote what is *g*,
12: 7 of the Spirit is given for the common *g*.
14: 6 What *g* will I do you if my speech does not
14:26 All well and *g*,
15:33 "Bad company corrupts *g* morals."
2Cor 5:10 one may receive his recompense, *g* or bad,
8:10 help you who began this *g* work last year,
8:21 approval but also for the *g* esteem of men.
9: 8 everything and even a surplus for *g* works,
13: 7 but simply that you may do what is *g*,
Gal 1:16 the Gentiles the *g* tidings concerning him.
3: 8 faith, it foretold this *g* news to Abraham:
6: 9 Let us not grow weary of doing *g*;
6:10 the opportunity, let us do *g* to all men
Eph 2:10 in Christ Jesus to lead the life of *g* deeds
2:17 *g* news of peace to you who were far off,
4:29 say only the *g* things men need to hear,
6: 8 repaid by the Lord for whatever *g* he does.
Phil 1: 6 that he who has begun the *g* work in you
1:15 rivalry, but others do so out of *g* will.
2:13 It is God who, in his *g* will toward you,
Col 1:10 You will multiply *g* works of every sort
2: 5 happy to see *g* order among you and the
4: 6 speech be always gracious and in *g* taste,
1Thes 2: 2 preach his *g* tidings to you in the face
2: 4 God, as men entrusted with the *g* tidings,
2: 9 all the time we preached God's *g* tidings
3: 6 the *g* news of your faith and love,
4:12 so that you will give *g* example to
5:15 good and, for that matter, the *g* of all.
5:21 Test everything; retain what is *g*.
2Thes 1: 8 nor heed" the *g* news of our Lord Jesus.
2:14 through our preaching of the *g* news
2:17 strengthen them for every *g* work and word.
1Tm 1: 5 springs from a pure heart, a *g* conscience,
1: 8 We know that the law is *g*,
1: 9 not at *g* men but at the lawless and unruly,
1:19 fight the *g* fight and hold fast to faith and a *g*
2: 3 Prayer of this kind is *g*,
2:10 their adornment should be *g* deeds.
3: 2 He should be a *g* teacher.
3: 4 must be a *g* manager of his own household,
3:12 must be *g* managers of their children
4: 4 Everything God created is *g*;
4: 6 you will be a *g* servant of Christ Jesus,
5:10 Her *g* character will be attested to by her *g*
5:10 she been eager to do every possible *g* work?
5:23 a little wine for the *g* of your stomach,
5:25 some *g* deeds stand out clearly as such;
6:12 Fight the *g* fight of faith.
6:18 them to do *g*, to be rich in *g* works
2Tm 2: 3 with me as a *g* soldier of Christ Jesus.
2:14 *g* and can be the ruin of those who listen.
3: 3 licentious, brutal, hating the *g*.
3:17 competent and equipped for every *g* work.
4: 7 I have fought the *g* fight,
Ti 1: 3 manifested in his own *g* time as his word,
2: 3 By their *g* example they must teach the
2: 7 you yourself fail to set them *g* example.
3: 8 This is what is *g* and advantageous for men.
Phlm 1: 6 to know all the *g* which is ours in Christ.
Heb 4: 2 We have indeed heard the *g* news,
5:14 by practice to distinguish *g* from evil.
6: 5 when they have tasted the *g* word of God
9:11 of the *g* things which have come to be,
10: 1 had only a shadow of the *g* things to come,
10:23 each other to love and *g* deeds.
11:12 from one man, who was himself as *g* as dead,
13: 9 It is *g* to have our hearts strengthened by
13:16 Do not neglect *g* deeds and generosity;
13:18 are confident that we have a *g* conscience,
13:21 our Lord, furnish you with all that is *g*,
Jas 2:14 what *g* is it to profess faith without
2:16 and you say to them, "Good-bye and *g* luck!
2:16 meet their bodily needs, what *g* is that?
3:13 through a humility filled with *g* sense.
5:13 If a person is in *g* spirits,
1Pt 2: 3 that you have tasted that the Lord is *g*.
2:12 By observing your *g* works they may give
2:15 talk of foolish men by your *g* behavior.
2:18 not only the *g* and reasonable ones but
3:11 He must turn from evil and do *g*,
3:17 to do so for *g* deeds than for evil ones.
4:19 as God's will requires continue in *g* deeds,
2Pt 2: 8 (Day after day that just one, *g* as he was,
3Jn 1: 2 Beloved, I hope you are in *g* health
1: 6 And you will do a *g* thing if,
1:11 do not imitate what is evil but what is *g*.
1:11 Whoever does what is *g* belongs to God;
1:12 is one who gets a *g* testimonial from all,
Rv 14: 6 of everlasting *g* news to the whole world,
14:13 labors, for their *g* works accompany them."

GOOD-BYE (14)
Gn 32: 1 Kissed his grandchild and daughters *g*
2Sm 13:25 began to bid him *g*
1Kgs 19:20 let me kiss my father and mother *g*
2Kgs 4:23 But she bade him *g*,
Tb 10:11 *G*, my son.
10:12 he said *g* to them and sent them away.
10:14 he said *g* to Raguel and his wife Edna,
Acts 18:21 As he said *g* he gave them
20: 1 he said *g* and set out
21: 5 After we had said *g* to one another
2Cor 2:13 I said *g* to them and went off to Macedonia.
13:11 And now, brothers, I must say *g*.
Jas 2:16 day, and you say to them, *G* and good luck!

GOOD-FOR-NOTHING (1)
Wis 13:13 Then the *g* refuse from these remnants,

GOODLY (11)
Ex 2: 2 Seeing that he was a *g* child,
Nm 24: 5 How *g* are your tents,
Dt 28:11 more than *g* measure the fruit of your womb,
30: 9 *g* measure the returns from all your labors,
Tb 4: 9 you will be storing up a *g* treasure for
Ps(s) 21: 4 you welcomed him with *g* blessings
45: 2 My heart overflows with a *g* theme;
Wis 12:21 you gave the sworn covenants of *g* promises!
Jer 2: 7 into the garden land to eat its *g* fruits,
11:16 A spreading olive tree, *g* to behold,
Bar 6:60 lightning, when it flashes, is a *g* sight;

GOODNESS (29)
Ex 18: 9 Jethro rejoiced over all the *g* that the
Tb 13:10 Praise the Lord for his *g*,
Est E: 4 of those to whom *g* has no meaning,
Ps(s) 21: 4 you welcomed him with *g* blessings
23: 6 Only *g* and kindness follow me all the days
25: 7 kindness remember me, because of your *g*,
31:20 How great is the *g*, O LORD,
51: 3 Have mercy on me, O God, in your *g*;
52:11 *g* of your name before your faithful ones.
54: 8 will praise your name, O LORD, for its *g*,
68:11 *g*, O God, you provided it for the needy
145: 7 *g* and joyfully sing of your justice.
Wis 1: 1 think of the Lord in *g*,
7:26 of the power of God, the image of his *g*.
12:22 think earnestly of your *g* when we judge.
Sir 17:17 A man's *g* God cherishes like a signet ring,
31:23 and this testimony to his *g* is lasting;
40:17 But *g* will never be cut off,
50:24 May his *g* toward us endure in Israel as
Am 5:24 like water, and *g* like an unfailing stream.
Mi 6: 8 Only to do right and to love *g*,
Mt 5:16 may see *g* in your acts and give praise
12:35 man produces good from his store of *g*;
Lk 6:45 man produces *g* from the good in his heart;
Rom 15:14 my brothers, that you are filled with *g*,
2Cor 1:12 by debased human wisdom, but by God's *g*.
Eph 3: 2 which God in his *g* gave me in your regard.
3: 7 Through the gift God in his *g* bestowed on
5: 9 every kind of *g* and justice and truth.
Ti 1: 8 contrary, be hospitable and a lover of *g*;

GOODS (47)
Gn 14:21 the *g* you may keep."
Lv 5:21 retaining his neighbor's *g* unjustly,
Nm 5: 7 has done, restore his ill-gotten *g* in full,
5: 8 ill-gotten *g* can be made, the *g* to be restored
Dt 6:11 of *g* of all sorts that you did not garner,
Jos 7: 1 of Judah, took *g* that were under the ban,
7:11 have stealthily taken *g* subject to the ban,
Jgs 18:21 and their *g* at the head of the column.
2Kgs 8: 9 camel loads of the best *g* of Damascus.
Ezr 1: 4 people of that place with silver, gold, *g*,
1: 6 help in every way, with silver, gold, *g*,
7:26 or corporal punishment, or a fine on his *g*,
Neh 13: 8 household *g* thrown outside the chamber.
Tb 1:14 death I would go to Media to buy *g* for him.
2:12 When she sent back the *g* to their owners,
10:10 camels, clothing, money, and household *g*.
Jdt 16:24 her *g* to the relatives of her husband,
Est 3:13 and that their *g* should be seized as spoil.
8:11 and to seize their *g* as spoil throughout
1Mc 5:13 away their wives and children and their *g*,
5:45 with their wives and children and their *g*,
10:43 with all the *g* he possesses in my kingdom.
Jb 20:22 straits, and nought shall be left of his *g*.
22: 6 unjustly kept your kinsmen's *g* in pawn,
Eccl 6: 3 if he has not the full benefit of his *g*,
6: 6 twice a thousand years and not enjoy his *g*,
Wis 13:17 prays about his *g* or marriage or children,
Sir 34:18 gifts who offers in sacrifice ill-gotten *g*!
Jer 49:29 away, their tent curtains and all their *g*;
50:26 Pile up her *g* in heaps and doom it,
Ez 27:13 slaves and articles of bronze for your *g*.
27:17 figs, honey, oil, and balm for your *g*.
27:27 Your wealth, your *g*,
27:27 your seams, those who traded for your *g*,
27:33 With your *g* which you drew from the seas
33:15 giving back pledges, restoring stolen *g*,
38:12 a people concerned with cattle and *g*,
38:13 silver and gold, to take away cattle and *g*,
Lk 12:18 All my grain and my *g* will go there.
16: 9 through your use of this world's *g*,
Acts 2:45 they would sell their property and *g*,
16:14 in purple *g* from the town of Thyatira.
1Tm 6:17 rich in this world's *g* not to be proud,
Heb 10:34 assented to the confiscation of your *g*,
1Jn 3:17 world's *g* yet closes his heart to his brother
Rv 18:15 The merchants who deal in these *g*,

GOPHERWOOD (1)
Gn 6:14 "Make yourself an ark of *g*,

GORE (3)
Dt 33:17 of the wild ox With which to *g* the nations,
1Kgs 22:11 shall *g* Aram until you have destroyed them.
2Chr 18:10 shall *g* Aram until you have destroyed them.

GOREN-HA-ATAD (2)
Gn 50:10 When they arrived at *G*,
50:11 inhabited the land saw the mourning at *G*,

GORES (3)
Ex 21:28 "When an ox *g* a man or a woman to death,
21:31 if it is a boy or a girl that the ox *g*,
21:32 it is a male or a female slave that it *g*,

GORGE (7)
Dt 32:42 and my sword shall *g* itself with flesh
1Sm 23:25 down to the *g* in the desert below Maon.
23:26 As Saul moved along one rim of the *g*,
23:28 place came to be called the *G* of Divisions.
2Sm 17:13 that city and we can drag it into the *g*,
Sir 31:17 *g* not yourself, lest you give offense.
Is 15: 7 they carry across the *G* of the Poplars,

GORGED (2)
Dt 32:15 you became fat and gross and *g*.
Rv 19:21 *g* themselves on the flesh of the slain.

GORGES (2)
Nm 21:15 Arnon and the wadi *g* That reach back
Bar 5: 7 depths and *g* be filled to level ground,

GORGIAS (11)
1Mc 3:38 son of Dorymenes, and Nicanor and *G*,
4: 1 Now *G* took five thousand infantry and a
4: 5 the night *G* came into the camp of Judas,
4:18 *G* and his army are near us on the mountain.
5:59 But *G* and his men came out of the city to
2Mc 8: 9 With him he associated *G*,
10:14 When *G* became governor of the region,
12:32 they lost no time in marching against *G*,
12:35 one of Bacenor's men, caught hold of *G*,
12:35 Then *G* fled to Marisa.
12:37 he charged *G*' men when they were not

GORING (2)

Ex 21:29 in the habit of *g* people and its owner,
21:36 of *g* and its owner would not keep it in,

GORTYNA (1)

1Mc 15:23 Rhodes, Phaselis, Cos, Side, Aradus, *G,*

GOSHEN (16)

Gn 45:10 You will settle in the region of *G,*
46:28 to Joseph, so that he might meet him in *G.*
46:28 On his arrival in the region of *G,*
46:29 and rode to meet his father Israel in *G.*
46:34 that you may stay in the region of *G,*
47: 1 and they are now in the region of *G."*
47: 4 your servants settle in the region of *G."*
47: 5 "They may settle in the region of *G;*
47:27 in the land of Egypt, in the region of *G.*
50: 8 and herds were left in the region of *G.*
Ex 8:18 make an exception of the very land of *G:*
9:26 Only in the land of *G,*
Jos 10:41 to Gaza, and all the land of *G* to Gibeon.
11:16 the entire Negeb all the land of *G,*
15:51 (that is, Debir), Anab, Eshtemoh, Anim, *G,*
Jdt 1: 9 to Tahpanhes, Raamses, all the land of *G,*

GOSPEL (77)

Mk 1: 1 Here begins the *g* of Jesus Christ,
1:15 Reform your lives and believe in the *g!"*
10:29 for me and for the *g* who will not receive
Acts 15: 7 hear the message of the *g* and believe.
20:24 bearing witness to the *g* of God's grace.
Rom 1: 1 set apart to proclaim the *g* of God
1: 3 the *g* concerning his Son,
1: 9 preaching the *g* of his Son
1:15 to preach the *g* to you Romans as well.
1:16 I am not ashamed of the *g.*
1:17 For in the *g* is revealed the justice of
2:16 when, in accordance with the *g* I preach,
10:16 But not all have believed the *g.*
11:28 In respect to the *g,*
15:16 priestly duty of preaching the *g* of God
15:19 I have completed preaching the *g* of Christ
16:25 strengthen you in the *g* which I proclaim
16:25 the *g* which reveals the mystery hidden for
1Cor 1:17 send me to baptize, but to preach the *g*—
1:21 the absurdity of the preaching of the *g.*
4:15 Christ Jesus through my preaching of the *g.*
9:12 any obstacle in the way of the *g* of Christ.
9:14 who preach the *g* should live by the gospel.
9:16 the *g* is not the subject of a boast;
9:18 that when preaching I offer the *g* free of
9:18 full use of the authority the *g* gives me.
9:23 I do all that I do for the sake of the *g*
15: 1 to remind you of the *g* I preached to you,
2Cor 2:12 I came to Troas to preach the *g* of Christ,
4: 3 *g* can be called "veiled" in any sense,
4: 4 of the *g* showing forth the glory of Christ,
8:18 churches praise for his preaching of the *g.*
9:13 for your obedient faith in the *g* of Christ,
10:14 as far as you with the *g* of Christ
10:16 we hope to preach the *g* even beyond your
11: 4 or a *g* other than the gospel you accepted,
11: 7 the *g* of God to you free of charge,
Gal 1: 6 in Christ, and are going over to another *g.*
1: 7 the *g* of Christ must have confused you.
1: 8 should preach to you a *g* not in accord
1: 9 a *g* to you other than the one you received,
1:11 the *g* I proclaimed to you is no mere human
2: 2 the *g* as I present it to the Gentiles
2: 5 *g* might survive intact for your benefit.
2: 7 entrusted with the *g* for the uncircumcised,
2:14 straightforward about the truth of the *g,*
4:13 first occasioned my bringing you the *g.*
Eph 3: 6 the promise through the preaching of the *g.*
3: 7 of his power, I became a minister of the *g.*
6:15 propagate the *g* of peace as your footgear.
6:19 make known the mystery of the *g*—
Phil 1: 5 promote the *g* from the very first day.
1: 7 the solid grounds on which the *g* rests.
1:12 has worked out to the furtherance of the *g.*
1:27 then, in a way worthy of the *g* of Christ.
1:27 with one accord for the faith of the *g.*
2:22 father's side serving the *g* along with me.
4: 3 struggled at my side in promoting the *g,*
Col 1: 5 hope through the message of truth, the *g,*
1:23 hope promised you by the *g* you have heard.
1:23 It is the *g* which has been announced to
1Thes 1: 5 Our preaching of the *g* proved not a mere
3: 2 fellow worker in preaching the *g* of Christ,
1Tm 1:11 that pertains to the glorious *g* of God
2Tm 1: 8 share of the hardship which the *g* entails.
1:10 immortality into clear light through the *g.*
1:11 In the service of this *g* I have been
2: 8 This is the *g* I preach;
4:17 and all the nations might hear the *g.*
Phlm 1:13 your place while I am in prison for the *g;*
1Pt 1:12 to you by those who preach the *g* to you,
1:25 is the *g* which was preached to you.
3: 1 the *g* may be won over apart from preaching,
4: 6 *g* was preached even to the dead was that,
4:17 those who refuse obedience to the *g* of God?

GOSPELS (2)

Mk 8:35 for my sake and the *g* will preserve it.
Phil 1:16 an opportunity to defend the *g* cause;

GOSSAMER (1)

Jb 8:14 a *g* thread and his trust is a spider's web.

GOSSIP (5)

Ps(s) 69:13 They who sit at the gate *g* about me,
Sir 19: 6 Never repeat *g,*
19:11 a man's thigh is *g* in the breast of a fool.
38:18 deserves, One or two days, to prevent *g;*
2Cor 12:20 of anger, selfish ambitions, slander and *g,*

GOSSIPS (6)

Prv 17: 9 but he who *g* about it separates friends.
Sir 28:13 Cursed be *g* and the double-tongued,
Rom 1:29 They are *g* and slanderers,
1Tm 3:11 should be serious, not slanderous *g.*
5:13 time-wasters but *g* and busybodies as well,
Ti 2: 3 not be slanderous *g* or slaves to drink.

GOT (97)

Gn 18: 8 Then he *g* some curds and milk,
19: 1 When Lot saw them, he *g* up to greet them;
21:14 Early the next morning Abraham *g* some
21:21 *g* a wife for him from the land of Egypt.
22: 4 day Abraham *g* sight of the place from afar.
25:34 and Esau ate, drank, *g* up,
27:14 and *g* them and brought them to his mother;
27:42 When Rebekah *g* news of what her older son
30:33 goat, or a dark sheep, *g* there by theft!"
30:37 however, *g* some fresh shoots of poplar,
31:15 even used up the money that he *g* for us!
31:46 So they *g* some stones and made a mound;
38: 6 *g* a wife named Tamar for his first-born,
39: 2 Joseph *g* on very well and was assigned to
39:12 hand, he *g* away from her and ran outside.
42:29 When they *g* back to their father Jacob in
43:15 So the men *g* the gifts,
43:24 feet, and *g* fodder for their donkeys.
44:32 *g* the boy from his father by going surety
47:17 Thus he *g* them through that year with
Ex 2:17 Then Moses *g* up and defended them and
Nm 11:32 *g* the least gathered ten homers of them.
Jgs 4:21 *g* a tent peg and took a mallet in her hand.
13:11 so Manoah *g* up and followed his wife.
1Sm 3:15 when he *g* up early and opened the doors of
13: 3 Gibeah, and the Philistine *g* word of it.
19:10 only the wall, and David *g* away safe.
19:18 Thus David *g* safely away;
23:25 David *g* word of it and went down to the
25:18 quickly *g* together two hundred loaves,
25:42 She *g* up immediately,
26:12 and they *g* away without anyone's seeing or
28:23 to their entreaties, *g* up from the ground,
2Sm 13:21 King David, who *g* word of the whole affair,
1Kgs 3:20 she *g* up and took my son from my side,
19: 8 He *g* up, ate and drank;
2Kgs 7:12 Though it was night, the king *g* up;
8: 2 *g* ready and did as the man of God said,
9: 6 Jehu *g* up and went into the house.
Tb 8: 5 She *g* up, and they started to pray
8: 9 But Raguel *g* up and summoned his servants.
9: 6 The following morning they *g* an early
11:10 Tobit *g* up and stumbled out through the
1Mc 13:22 Trypho *g* all his cavalry ready to go,
2Mc 8: 5 Once Maccabeus *g* his men organized,
8:13 faith in God's justice deserted and *g* away.
11:12 Most of those who *g* away were wounded and
12:28 *g* possession of the city and slaughtered
14:23 He *g* rid of the throngs of ordinary people
14:45 anger, he *g* up and ran through the crowd,
Eccl 2: 8 I *g* for myself male and female singers and
Ez 3:23 So I *g* up and went out into the plain,
Dn 13:19 the two old men *g* up and hurried to her.
Mt 2:14 Joseph *g* up and took the child and his
2:21 He *g* up, took the child and his mother,
8:13 That very moment the boy *g* better.
8:15 She *g* up at once and began to wait on him.
8:23 He *g* into the boat and his disciples
9: 9 Matthew *g* up and followed him.
9:22 That very moment the woman *g* well.
9:25 her by the hand, and the little girl *g* up.
9:28 When he *g* to the house,
13:10 When the disciples *g* near him,
14:29 So Peter *g* out of the boat and began to
15:28 That very moment her daughter *g* better.
15:39 he *g* into the boat and went to the
25: 7 virgins woke up and *g* their torches ready.
27:48 one of them ran off and *g* a sponge.
Mk 2: 1 days and word *g* around that he was at home.
2:14 Levi *g* up and became his follower.
5: 2 As he *g* out of the boat,
5:26 in the process, yet she *g* no relief;
6:33 them leaving, and many *g* to know about it.
6:51 He *g* into the boat with them and the wind
6:56 All who touched him *g* well.
7:17 When he *g* home, away from the crowd
7:30 When she *g* home, she found the child
8:10 He dismissed them and *g* into the boat with
8:13 Then he left them, *g* into the boat again,
Lk 4:39 She *g* up immediately and waited on them.
5: 3 He *g* into one of the boats,
8:22 One day he *g* into a boat with his
8:37 so he *g* into the boat and went back across
8:55 returned to her and she *g* up immediately;
9:15 his instructions and *g* them all seated.
24:12 Peter, however, *g* up and ran to the tomb.
24:33 *g* up immediately and returned to Jerusalem,
Jn 11:29 she *g* up and started out in his direction.
12:13 *g* palm branches and came out to meet him.
Acts 5:22 *g* to the jail they could not find them,
9: 8 Saul *g* up from the ground unable to see,
9:18 He *g* up and was baptized,
9:34 The man *g* up at once.
13:50 and in that way *g* a persecution started
14:20 long he *g* up and went back into the town.
15: 5 Some of the converted Pharisees then *g* up
21:15 we *g* ready and started up toward Jerusalem.

GOTHONIEL (1)

Jdt 6:15 of the tribe of Simeon, Chabris, son of *G,*

GOTTEN (4)

1Mc 8: 3 They had *g* possession of the silver and
15:37 *g* aboard a ship and escaped to Orthosia.
Prv 9:17 is sweet, and bread *g* secretly is pleasing!"
13:11 Wealth quickly *g* dwindles away,

GOUGE (4)

Nm 16:14 inheritance, will you also *g* out our eyes?
1Sm 11: 2 I must *g* out every man's right eye,
Mt 5:29 your trouble, *g* it out and throw it away!
18: 9 downfall, *g* it out and cast it from you!

GOUGED (1)

Jgs 16:21 Philistines seized him and *g* out his eyes.

GOURD (1)

Jon 4: 6 And when the LORD God provided a *g* plant,

GOURDS (4)

1Kgs 6:18 carved in the form of *g* and open flowers;
7:24 Under the brim, *g* encircled it,
7:24 the *g* were in two rows and were cast in
2Kgs 4:39 from which he picked a clothful of wild *g.*

GOVERN (19)

Gn 1:16 one to *g* the day, and the lesser one to
1:18 upon the earth, to *g* the day and the night,
1Sm 9:17 he is to *g* my people."
10: 1 You are to *g* the LORD's people Israel,
1Kgs 3: 9 who is able to *g* this vast people of yours?"
Ps(s) 72: 2 He shall *g* your people with justice and
Prv 8:16 By me princes *g,*
12:24 The diligent hand will *g,*
Wis 8:14 I should *g* peoples,
9: 3 To *g* the world in holiness and justice,
12:15 as you are just, you *g* all things justly;
12:18 clemency, and with much lenience you *g* us;
Sir 37:26 *g* your appetite so that you allow it not
45:26 wisdom of heart to *g* his people in justice,
Is 3: 4 the fickle shall *g* them,
Jer 23: 5 As king he shall reign and *g* wisely,
Dn 11: 5 still and *g* a domain greater than his.
13: 5 elders who were to *g* the people as judges."

GOVERNED (4)

Est E:15 but rather are *g* by very just laws and are
Sir 26:14 A gift from the LORD is her *g* speech,
Bar 2: 1 against our judges, who *g* Israel,
Dn 9:12 against us and against those who *g* us,

GOVERNING (2)

Wis 15: 1 true, slow to anger, and *g* all with mercy.
Sir 43: 6 marks the changing times, *g* the seasons,

GOVERNMENT (22)

Est B: 2 and by making my *g* humane and effective as
B: 5 so that stability of *g* cannot be obtained,
1Mc 6:56 and that he was seeking to take over the *g.*
8:16 entrusted their *g* to one man every year,
2Mc 3:38 have an enemy or a plotter against the *g,*
4: 2 dared to brand as a plotter against the *g*
4: 6 would be impossible to have a peaceful *g,*
5: 7 Even so, he did not gain control of the *g,*
8: 8 to come to the aid of the king's *g.*
9:24 know to whom the *g* had been entrusted,
10:11 put a certain Lysias in charge of the *g*
11: 1 and kinsman of the king and head of the *g,*
11:19 If you maintain your loyalty to the *g,*
13: 2 his guardian, who was in charge of the *g.*
13:14 temple, the city, the country, and the *g,*
13:23 in charge of the *g* in Antioch had rebelled.
Jb 34:13 Who gave him *g* over the earth,
Sir 10: 1 and the *g* of a prudent man is well ordered.
Dn 5: 7 neck, and be third in the *g* of the kingdom."

GOVERNMENT (cont.)
5:16 neck, and be third in the *g* of the kingdom."
5:29 him third in the *g* of the kingdom.
Ti 3: 1 loyally subject to the *g* and its officials,

GOVERNMENTS (1)
Sir 47:21 Thus two *g* came into being,

GOVERNOR (53)
Gn 42: 6 It was Joseph, as *g* of the country,
2Kgs 23: 8 of the Gate of Joshua, *g* of the city,
25:22 of Babylon, appointed as their *g* Gedaliah,
25:23 king of Babylon had appointed Gedaliah *g*,
25:30 Gedaliah, son of Ahikam, son of Shaphan.
Ezr 4: 8 Then Rehum, the *g*,
4: 9 "Rehum, the *g*,
4:17 "To Rehum, the *g*,
4:23 letter had been read before Rehum, the *g*,
5: 3 to them Tattenai, *g* of West-of-Euphrates,
5: 6 Darius by Tattenai, *g* of West-of-Euphrates,
5:14 to a certain Sheshbazzar, whom he named *g*.
6: 6 Tattenai, *g* of West-of-Euphrates,
6: 7 Let the *g* and the elders of the Jews
6:13 Then Tattenai, the *g* of West-of-Euphrates,
Neh 3: 7 jurisdiction of the *g* of West-of-Euphrates.
5:14 appointed me *g* in the land of Judah,
12:26 the *g* and of Ezra the priest-scribe].
1Mc 7: 8 the King's Friends, *g* of West-of-Euphrates,
10:63 military commander and *g* of the province.
10:69 appointed Apollonius *g* of Coelesyria.
11:59 he made Jonathan's brother Simon *g*
13:42 the first year of Simon, high priest, *g*,
14:42 He shall act as *g* general over them,
14:47 agreed to act as high priest, *g* general,
16:11 been appointed *g* of the plain of Jericho,
2Mc 3: 5 time was *g* of Coelesyria and Phoenicia,
4: 4 the *g* of Coelesyria and Phoenicia,
8: 8 to Ptolemy, *g* of Coelesyria and Phoenicia,
10:14 When Gorgias became *g* of the region,
12:32 in marching against Gorgias, *g* of Idumea,
13:24 left him as military and civil *g*
14:12 elephants, and appointed him *g* of Judea.
Is 60:17 I will appoint peace your *g*,
Hg 1: 1 the prophet Haggai to the *g* of Judah,
1:14 stirred up the spirit of the *g* of Judah,
2: 2 Tell this to the *g* of Judah,
2:21 Tell this to Zerubbabel, the *g* of Judah:
Mal 1: 8 Present it to your *g*;
Lk 2: 2 took place while Quirinius was *g* of Syria.
Acts 7:10 and made him the *g* of Egypt and of the
13: 7 court of the proconsular *g* Sergius Paulus,
13: 8 sought to turn the *g* away from the faith.
13:12 When the *g* saw what had happened,
23:24 may give him safe conduct to Felix the *g*."
23:25 then wrote the *g* a letter to this effect:
23:26 sends greetings to His Excellency Felix, *G*.
23:33 to the *g* and brought Paul before him.
23:34 The *g*,
24: 1 presented their case against Paul to the *g*.
24:10 The *g* then gestured to Paul,
25:24 The *g* began to speak:
26:30 *g* and Bernice and the rest of the company.

GOVERNORS (34)
1Kgs 10:15 kings of Arabia and the *g* of the country.
20:14 the retainers of the *g* of the provinces.'"
20:15 up the retainers of the *g* of the provinces,
20:17 the *g* of the provinces marched out first,
20:19 the soldiers of the *g* of the provinces
2Chr 9:14 of Arabia also, and the *g* of the country,
Ezr 8:36 satraps and to the *g* in West-of-Euphrates
Neh 2: 7 given to me for the *g* of West-of-Euphrates,
2: 9 Thus I proceeded to the *g* of
5:14 nor my brethren lived from the *g* allowance.
5:15 The earlier *g*, my predecessors
5:18 this I did not claim the *g* allowance,
Est 1: 3 the nobles, and the *g* of the provinces.
3:12 the royal satraps, the *g* of every province,
B: 1 to Ethiopia, and the *g* subordinate to them,
8: 9 wrote to the Jews and to the satraps, *g*,
E: 1 "King Ahasuerus the Great to the *g* of the
9: 3 of the provinces, the satraps, *g*,
2Mc 5:22 But he left *g* to harass the nation:
12: 2 But some of the local *g*,
Wis 13: 2 luminaries of heaven, the *g* of the world,
Sir 44: 4 of the folk, and *g* with their staves;
Jer 51:28 king of Media, Its *g* and all its prefects,
51:57 her princes and her wise men drunk, her *g*,
Ez 23: 6 warriors dressed in purple, *g* and officers,
23:12 lusted after the Assyrians, *g* and officers,
23:23 young men, all of them *g* and officers,
Dn 3: 2 then ordered the satraps, prefects, and *g*,
3: 3 The satraps, prefects, and *g*,
3:94 When the satraps, prefects, *g*,
6: 8 and *g* are agreed that the following
Mk 13: 9 You will be arraigned before *g* and kings
Lk 21:12 bringing you to trial before kings and *g*,
1Pt 2:14 as sovereign or to the *g* he commissions

GOVERNS (4)
Est E:18 Thus swiftly has God, who *g* all,
Ps(s) 9: 9 he *g* the peoples with equity.
96:10 he *g* the peoples with equity.
Wis 8: 1 end to end mightily and *g* all things well.

GOWN (2)
Is 3:24 for the rich *g*, a sackcloth skirt.
Ez 16:10 I clothed you with an embroidered *g*,

GOWNS (2)
Ez 16:16 *g* and made for yourself gaudy high places,
16:18 You took your embroidered *g* to cover them;

GOZAN (4)
2Kgs 17: 6 them in Halah, at the Habor, a river of *G*,
18:11 them in Halah, at the Habor, a river of *G*,
19:12 *G*, Haran,
1Chr 5:26 Halah, Habor, and Hara, and to the river *G*,

GOZEN (1)
Is 37:12 *G*, Haran, Rezeph, and the Edenites

GRACE (78)
Gn 10: 9 was a mighty hunter by the *g* of the LORD;
10: 9 a mighty hunter by the *g* of the LORD."
Jb 10:12 *G* and favor you granted me,
Ps(s) 42: 9 By day the LORD bestows his *g*,
45: 3 *g* is poured out upon your lips;
84:12 *g* and glory he bestows;
Wis 3: 9 Because *g* and mercy are with his holy ones,
Mi 7:20 faithfulness to Jacob, and *g* to Abraham,
Zec 12:10 of Jerusalem a spirit of *g* and petition;
Lk 2:40 with wisdom, and the *g* of God was upon him.
2:52 in wisdom and age and *g* before God and men.
Acts 6: 8 of was a man filled with *g* and power,
13:43 urged them to hold fast to the *g* of God.
14: 3 his part confirmed the message with his *g*
20:24 bearing witness to the gospel of God's *g*.
Rom 1: 7 *g* and peace from God our Father and the
4:16 all depends on faith, everything is *g*.
5: 2 by faith to the *g* in which we now stand,
5:15 much more did the *g* of God and the
5:17 receive the overflowing *g* and gift of justice
5:20 increase of sin, *g* has far surpassed it,
5:21 *g* may reign by way of justice leading to
6: 1 us continue in sin that *g* may abound"?
6:14 you are now under *g*,
6:15 we are not under the law but under *g*,
11: 5 there is a remnant chosen by the *g* of God.
11: 6 But if the choice is by *g*,
11: 6 otherwise *g* would not be grace.
15:15 God has given me the *g* to be a minister
16:20 the *g* of our Lord Jesus Christ be with you.
1Cor 1: 3 *G* and peace from God our Father and the
2Cor 1: 2 *G* and peace from God our Father and the
1:15 first so that a double *g* might be yours.
4:15 so that the *g* bestowed in abundance may
6: 1 you not to receive the *g* of God in vain.
8: 1 I should like you to know of the *g* of God
9:14 of the surpassing *g* God has given you.
12: 9 He said to me, "My *g* is enough for you,
13:13 The *g* of the Lord Jesus Christ,
Eph 1: 2 *G* and peace to you from God our Father and
3: 8 was given the *g* to preach to the Gentiles
6:24 *G* be with all who love our Lord Jesus
Phil 1: 2 *G* and peace be yours from God our Father
Col 1: 2 May God our Father give you *g* and peace.
4:18 *G* be with you.
1Thes 1: 1 *G* and peace be yours.
5:28 the *g* of our Lord Jesus Christ be with you.
2Thes 1: 2 *G* and peace be yours from God the Father
3:18 *g* of our Lord Jesus Christ be with you all.
1Tm 1: 2 May *g*, mercy, and peace be yours
1:14 and the *g* of our Lord has been granted me
6:21 *G* be with you.
2Tm 1: 2 May *g*, mercy, and peace from God
1: 9 the *g* held out to us in Christ Jesus
2: 1 in the *g* which is ours in Christ Jesus.
4:22 *G* be with you.
Ti 1: 4 May *g* and peace from God our Father,
2:11 The *g* of God has appeared,
3: 7 be justified by his *g* and become heirs,
3:15 May *g* be with you all!
Phlm 1: 3 *G* to you and peace from God our Father and
1:25 The *g* of our Lord Jesus Christ be with
Heb 4:16 approach the throne of *g* to receive mercy
10:29 be ordinary, and insults the Spirit of *g*?
12:15 that no man falls away from the *g* of God;
12:28 kingdom should hold fast to God's *g*,
13: 9 hearts strengthened by the *g* of God
13:25 *G* be with you all.
1Pt 2:19 presence, this is the work of *g* in him.
4:10 generous distributors of God's manifold *g*,
5:10 The God of all *g*,
5:12 testimony that this is the true *g* of God.
2Pt 1: 2 may *g* be yours and peace in abundance
3:18 Grow rather in *g*,
2Jn 1: 3 In truth and love, then, we shall have *g*,
Rv 1: 4 John wishes you *g* and peace
22:21 The *g* of the Lord Jesus be with you all.

GRACED (1)
Est C:28 nor have I *g* the banquet of the king or

GRACEFUL (5)
Prv 1: 9 A *g* diadem will they be for your head;
4: 9 She will put on your head a *g* diadem;
5:19 your youth, your lovely hind, your *g* doe.
Sir 24:16 terebinth, my branches so bright and so *g*.
26:17 are her beauty of face and *g* figure.

GRACIOUS (38)
Gn 43:29 Then he said to him, "May God be *g* to you,
Ex 34: 6 "The LORD, the LORD, a merciful and *g* God,
Nm 6:25 his face shine upon you, and be *g* to you!
Neh 9:17 are a God of pardons, *g* and compassionate,
2Mc 1:25 only king and benefactor, who alone are *g*,
10:26 the altar, they begged him to be *g* to them,
14: 9 *g* consideration that you show toward all.
Ps(s) 59:11 you, O God, are my stronghold, my *g* God!
59:18 you, O God, are my stronghold, my *g* God!
86:15 But you, O Lord, are a God merciful and *g*,
90:17 may the *g* care of the Lord our God be ours;
103: 8 Merciful and *g* is the LORD,
111: 4 *g* and merciful is the LORD.
112: 4 he is *g* and merciful and just.
112: 5 Well for the man who is *g* and lends,
116: 5 *G* is the LORD and just;
145: 8 The LORD is *g* and merciful,
147: 1 sing praise to our God, for he is *g*;
Prv 11:16 A *g* woman wins esteem,
Sir 6: 5 and *g* lips prompt friendly greetings.
7:19 a *g* wife is more precious than corals.
26:13 A *g* wife delights her husband,
36:16 for you are ever *g* to your people;
Is 30:19 He will be *g* to you when you cry out,
Jl 2:13 For *g* and merciful is he,
Jon 4: 2 I knew that you are a *g* and merciful God,
Acts 20:32 that *g* word of his which can enlarge you,
Rom 5:15 grace of God and the *g* gift of the one man,
2Cor 9: 5 It should be ready as a *g* gift,
Gal 1: 6 you in accord with his *g* design in Christ,
2:21 I will not treat God's *g* gift as pointless.
Phil 1: 7 are sharers of my *g* lot when I lie in
Col 1: 6 comprehended God's *g* intention
4: 6 your speech be always *g* and in good taste,
2Thes 1:12 in accord with the *g* gift of our God and
Heb 2: 9 that through God's *g* will he might taste
1Pt 3: 7 just as much as you to the *g* gift of life.
Jude 1: 4 They pervert the *g* gift of our God to

GRACIOUSLY (10)
Gn 24:12 and thus deal *g* with my master Abraham.
24:14 know that you have dealt *g* with my master."
33: 5 whom God has *g* bestowed on your servant."
Jdt 13: 4 in this hour look *g* on my undertaking for
2Mc 3: 9 *g* received by the high priest of the city,
Ps(s) 20: 4 your offerings and *g* accept your holocaust.
Prv 26:25 When he speaks *g*,
Wis 6:16 of her, and *g* appears to them in the ways,
Mt 11:26 You have *g* willed it so.
Lk 10:21 "Yes, Father, you have *g* willed it so.

GRADUALLY (1)
Gn 8: 3 *G* the waters receded from the earth.

GRAFTED (5)
Rom 11:17 have been *g* in among the others and have
11:19 were cut off that I might be *g* in."
11:23 in their unbelief they will be *g* back on,
11:24 nature, were *g* into the cultivated olive,
11:24 by nature be *g* into their own olive tree.

GRAIN (129)
Gn 27:28 of the earth abundance of *g* and wine.
27:37 I have enriched him with *g* and wine.
41: 5 He saw seven ears of *g*,
41: 6 Behind them sprouted seven ears of *g*,
41:22 In another dream I saw seven ears of *g*,
41:23 Behind them sprouted seven ears of *g*,
41:35 collecting the *g* under Pharaoh's authority,
41:49 *g* in quantities like the sands of the sea,
41:56 had *g* and rationed it to the Egyptians,
41:57 came to Joseph to obtain rations of *g*,
42: 1 that *g* rations were available in Egypt,
42: 2 "that rations of *g* are available in Egypt.
42: 3 to buy an emergency supply of *g* from Egypt.
42:25 to have their containers filled with *g*,
45:23 ten jennies loaded with *g* and bread
49:26 the blessings of fresh *g* and blossoms,
Ex 22: 5 so that shocked *g* or standing grain or the
22: 5 *g* or the field itself is burned up,
23:16 You shall also keep the feast of the *g*
Lv 2:14 the form of fresh grits of new ears of *g*,
11:37 Any sort of cultivated *g* remains clean
11:38 but if the *g* has become moistened it
19: 9 nor shall you glean the stray ears of *g*.
23:14 any bread or roasted *g* or fresh kernels.
23:22 shall you glean the stray ears of your *g*.
27:30 whether in *g* from the fields or in fruit

Nm 18:12 new wine and *g* that they give to the LORD
18:27 as if it were *g* from the threshing floor
20: 5 *g* nor figs nor vines nor pomegranates?
Dt 7:13 of your soil, your *g* and wine and oil,
11:14 the late rain, that you may have your *g*,
12:17 partake of your tithe of *g* or wine or oil,
14:23 eat in his presence your tithe of the *g*,
16: 9 the sickle is first put to the standing *g*.
18: 4 first fruits of your *g* and wine and oil,
23:26 do not put a sickle to your neighbor's *g*.
25: 4 not muzzle an ox when it is treading out *g*.
28: 5 be your *g* bin and your kneading bowl!
28:17 be your *g* bin and your kneading bowl!
28:51 they will leave you no *g* or wine or oil,
33:28 been undisturbed In a land of *g* and wine,
Jos 5:11 the form of unleavened cakes and parched *g*.
22:23 *g* offerings or peace offerings upon it,
22:29 an altar for holocaust, *g* offering,
Jgs 15: 5 loose in the standing *g* of the Philistines,
15: 5 both the shocks and the standing *g*,
Ru 2: 2 "Let me go and glean ears of *g* in the
2:14 he handed her some roasted *g* and she ate
1Sm 17:17 *g* and these ten loaves for your brothers,
25:18 dressed sheep, five seahs of roasted *g*,
2Sm 17:19 strewing ground *g* on the cover so that
17:28 well as wheat, barley, flour, roasted *g*,
1Kgs 18:32 the altar large enough for two seahs of *g*.
2Kgs 4:42 the first fruits, and fresh *g* in the ear.
18:32 a land like your own, a land of *g* and wine,
2Chr 31: 5 in great quantities, the best of their *g*,
32:28 also storehouses for the harvest of *g*,
Neh 5: 2 in order to get *g* to eat that we may live."
5: 3 that we may have *g* during the famine."
5:10 lent the people money and *g* without charge.
5:11 with the interest on the money, the *g*,
10:32 any kind of *g* for sale on the sabbath day,
10:40 and Levites bring the offerings of *g*,
13: 5 incense and utensils, the tithes in *g*,
13:12 once more brought in the tithes of *g*,
13:15 that they were bringing in sheaves of *g*,
Tb 1: 7 in Jerusalem I would give the tithe of *g*,
Jdt 10: 5 She filled a bag with roasted *g*,
11:13 they would use up the first fruits of *g*
1Mc 8:26 war they shall not give nor provide *g*,
8:28 attacking them there shall not be given *g*,
10:30 Instead of collecting the third of the *g*
Jb 5:26 as a shock of *g* comes in at its season.
24:24 like ears of *g* they shrivel.
39:12 Can you rely on him to thresh out your *g*
Ps(s) 4: 8 heart, more than when *g* and wine abound.
65:10 you have prepared the *g*.
65:14 flocks and the valleys blanketed with *g*.
72:16 there be an abundance of *g* upon the earth;
Prv 3:10 Then will your barns be filled with *g*,
11:26 Him who monopolizes *g*,
Wis 11:22 whole universe is as a *g* from a balance.
Sir 18: 8 Like a drop of sea water, like a *g* of sand,
Is 17: 5 of stalks when he gathers the standing *g*;
23: 3 The *g* of Shihor,
27:12 The LORD shall beat out the *g* between the
36:17 a land like your own, a land of *g* and wine,
55: 1 who have no money, come, receive *g* and eat;
62: 8 will I give your *g* as food to your enemies;
62: 9 But you who harvest the *g* shall eat it,
Jer 31:12 The *g*, the wine, and the oil,
Ez 36:29 I will order the *g* to be abundant,
Hos 2:10 known that it was I who gave her the *g*,
2:11 I will take back my *g* in its time,
2:24 The earth shall respond to the *g*,
8: 7 of *g* that forms no ear can yield no flour;
14: 8 they shall dwell in his shade and raise *g*;
Jl 1:10 the earth mourns, Because the *g* is ravaged,
1:17 are broken down, for the *g* has failed.
2:19 See, I will send you *g*,
2:24 The threshing floors shall be full of *g*
Am 5:11 the weak and exacted of them levies of *g*,
8: 5 over," you ask, "that we may sell our *g*,
Hg 1:11 Upon the *g*, and upon the wine,
2:16 went to a heap of *g* for twenty measures,
Zec 9:17 *g* that makes the youths flourish,
Mt 3:12 floor and gather his *g* into the barn,
12: 1 Jesus walked through the standing *g*.
12: 1 to pull off the heads of *g* and eat them.
13: 8 *g* a hundred- or sixty- or thirtyfold.
13:26 When the crop began to mature and yield *g*,
Mk 2:23 walking through standing *g* on the sabbath,
2:23 to pull off heads of *g* as they went along.
4: 7 choked it off, and there was no yield of *g*.
4: 8 landed on good soil and yielded *g*
Lk 6: 1 Jesus was walking through the standing *g*.
8: 8 soil, grew up, and yielded *g* a hundredfold."
12:18 pull down my *g* bins and build larger ones.
12:18 All my *g* and my goods will go there.
12:42 to dispense their ration of *g* in season?
17:35 Two women will be grinding *g* together;
Jn 12:24 the *g* of wheat falls to the earth and dies,
12:24 and dies, it remains just a *g* of wheat.
Acts 7:12 Hearing that there was *g* in Egypt,
1Cor 9: 8 not muzzle an ox while it treads out *g*."
9:10 and the harvester expect a share in the *g*.
15:37 but a kernel of wheat or some other *g*.
1Tm 5:18 on an ox when he is threshing the *g*,"
Rv 18:13 wine and olive oil, fine flour and *g*;

GRAIN-HEADS (1)

Lk 6: 1 His disciples were pulling off *g*,

GRAINFIELD (1)

Dt 23:26 When you go through your neighbor's *g*,

GRAINS (2)

Sir 44:21 would make him numerous as the *g* of dust,
Is 48:19 and those born of your stock like its *g*,

GRANARIES (3)

Prv 10: 5 son who fills the *g* in summer is a credit;
Sir 1:15 with choice foods, her *g* with her harvest.
Jer 50:26 Come upon her from every side, open her *g*,

GRANDCHILDREN (8)

Gn 31:28 me a parting kiss to my daughters and *g*!
32: 1 kissed his *g* and his daughters good-bye;
45:10 you and your children and *g*,
Ex 34: 7 but punishing children and *g* to the third
Dt 4:25 "When you have children and *g*,
Jb 42:16 and he saw his children, his *g*,
Prv 17: 6 *G* are the crown of old men,
1Tm 5: 4 If a widow has any children or *g*,

GRANDDAUGHTER (2)

Gn 36: 2 *g* through Anah of Zibeon the Hivite;
36:14 wife Oholibamah *g* through Anah of Zibeon

GRANDDAUGHTERS (1)

Gn 46: 7 his grandsons, his daughters and his *g*—

GRANDEUR (7)

1Chr 29:11 "Yours, O LORD, are *g* and power,
29:12 it is yours to give *g* and strength to all.
Est C:27 that I abhor the sign of *g* which rests on
1Mc 8:14 a crown or wore purple as a display of *g*.
Jb 40:10 Adorn yourself with *g* and majesty,
Ps(s) 96: 6 praise and *g* are in his sanctuary.
Wis 18:24 and your *g* was on the crown upon his head.

GRANDFATHER (2)

2Sm 9: 7 restore to you all the lands of your *g* Saul,
1Kgs 15: 3 his God, like the heart of his *g* David.

GRANDFATHERS (2)

Ex 10: 6 sight your fathers and *g* have not seen
Dn 11:24 do that which his fathers or *g* never did;

GRANDMOTHER (2)

1Kgs 15:13 *g* Maacah from her position as queen mother,
2Tm 1: 5 to your *g* Lois and to your mother Eunice,

GRANDMOTHERS (1)

1Kgs 15:10 His *g* name was Maacah,

GRANDPARENTS (1)

1Tm 5: 4 fittingly support their parents and *g*;

GRANDSON (7)

Gn 11:31 Terah took his son Abram, his *g* Lot,
Ex 10: 2 that you may recount to your son and *g*
Dt 6: 2 and your son and your *g* may fear the LORD,
Ru 4:17 the news that a *g* had been born to Naomi.
2Chr 22: 9 they said, "He was the *g* of Jehoshaphat,
Jb 18:19 He has neither son nor *g* among his people,
Jer 27: 7 shall serve him and his son and his *g*,

GRANDSONS (4)

Gn 46: 7 His sons and his *g*,
Jgs 12:14 thirty *g* who rode on seventy saddle-asses.
2Kgs 17:41 And their sons and *g*,
1Chr 8:40 archers, and many were their sons and *g*:

GRANT (73)

Gn 19:21 "I will also *g* you the favor you now ask.
Ex 10:25 "You must also *g* us sacrifices and
21:11 If he does not *g* her these three things,
33:19 whom I will, I who *g* mercy to whom I will.
Ru 1: 9 May the LORD *g* each of you a husband and a
1Sm 1:17 of Israel *g* you what you have asked of him."
8: 7 *G* the people's every request.
8: 9 Now *g* their request;
8:22 *G* their request and appoint a king to rule
14: 6 no more difficult for the LORD to *g* victory
17:25 and would *g* exemption to his father's
24:16 part, and *g* me justice beyond your reach!"
2Sm 12:22 the LORD will *g* me the child's life.'
14:15 he will *g* the petition of his maidservant.
14:21 "I hereby *g* this request.
1Kgs 8:30 from your heavenly dwelling and *g* pardon.
8:50 you, and *g* them mercy before their captors,
2Chr 1: 7 a request of me, and I will *g* it to you."
30:18 *g* pardon to everyone who has resolved to
Neh 1:11 *G* success to your servant this day,
2:20 is the God of heaven who will *g* us success.
Tb 4:19 *g* success to all your endeavors and plans.
6:18 to show you mercy and *g* you deliverance.
7:11 May he *g* you mercy and peace."
7:12 heaven *g* both of you peace and prosperity."
7:17 of heaven *g* you joy in place of your grief.
8: 4 have mercy on us and to *g* us deliverance."
8:17 *G* them, Master, mercy and deliverance
9: 6 may the LORD *g* heavenly blessing to you
10:11 *g* prosperity to you and to your wife Sarah.
Est 5: 8 to *g* my petition and honor my request,
1Mc 6:59 Let us *g* them freedom to live according to
10:28 We will *g* you many exemptions and will
10:40 I make a yearly personal *g* of fifteen
11:35 From this day on we *g* them release from
13:34 that he *g* the land a release from taxation,
13:37 our official to *g* you release from tribute.
13:45 loud voices, begging Simon to *g* them peace.
2Mc 1: 4 law and his commandments and *g* you peace.
Jb 6: 8 and that God would *g* what I long for:
17: 3 *G* me one to offer you a pledge on my behalf:
Ps(s) 12: 6 "I will *g* safety to him who longs for it."
20: 5 May he *g* you what is in your heart and
20: 6 The LORD *g* all your requests!
20:10 O LORD, *g* victory to the king,
37: 4 and he will *g* you your heart's requests.
85: 8 your kindness, and *g* us your salvation.
86:17 *G* me a proof of your favor,
118:25 O LORD, *g* salvation!
118:25 O LORD, *g* prosperity!
140: 9 *G* not, O LORD, the desires of the wicked
Eccl 6: 2 does not *g* him power to partake of them,
Wis 7:15 Now God *g* I speak suitably and value these
12:11 anyone did you *g* amnesty for their sins.
Sir 6:37 mind, and the wisdom you desire he will *g*.
45:26 May he *g* you wisdom of heart to govern his
50:23 May he *g* you joy of heart and may peace
Jer 16:13 night, because I will not *g* you my mercy.
37:20 Hear now, my lord king, and *g* my petition:
42: 2 prophet Jeremiah and said, *G* our petition;
42:12 I will *g* you mercy,
Bar 2:14 *g* us favor in the presence of our captors,
Mt 14: 7 he would *g* her anything she asked for.
Mk 5:19 Jesus did not *g* his request,
6:23 "I will *g* you whatever you ask,
10:35 they said, "we want you to *g* our request."
Lk 1:73 swore to Abraham our father he would *g* us:
Acts 4:29 *G* to your servants,
10:40 up on the third day and *g* that he be seen,
Rom 8:32 of us all will not *g* us all things besides?
Eph 1:17 *g* you a spirit of wisdom and insight to
6:23 *g* the brothers peace and love and faith.
2Tm 1:18 on the great Day, may the Lord *g* him mercy!

GRANTED (61)

Gn 4:25 has *g* me more offspring in place of Abel,"
31:30 *G* that you had to leave because you were
47:22 lived off the allowance Pharaoh had *g* them,
Jgs 15:18 "You have *g* this great victory by the
1Sm 1:27 for this child, and the LORD *g* my request.
12: 1 "I have *g* your request in every respect,"
25:35 I have *g* your request as a personal favor."
2Sm 14:22 the king has *g* the request of his servant."
21:14 God *g* relief to the land.
22:48 my salvation, O God, who *g* me vengeance,
24:25 The LORD *g* relief to the country,
2Kgs 2:10 me taken up from you, your wish will be *g*;
25:30 The allowance *g* him by the king was a
1Chr 4:10 And God *g* his prayer.
Ezr 7: 6 him, the king *g* him all that he requested.
8:23 our God for this, and our petition was *g*.
9: 9 has *g* us a fence in Judah and Jerusalem.
Neh 2: 8 The king *g* my requests,
Tb 1:13 *g* me favor and status with Shalmaneser,
Est 5: 3 is half of my kingdom, it shall be *g* you."
5: 6 Esther, "Whatever you ask for shall be *g*,
7: 2 you ask, Queen Esther, shall be *g* you.
9:12 You shall again be *g* whatever you ask,
1Mc 5:62 it was *g* to achieve Israel's salvation.
7: 9 Alcimus, to whom he *g* the high priesthood,
11:62 to him for mercy, and he *g* them peace.
11:66 When they sued for peace, he *g* it to them.
15: 5 tax exemptions that the kings before me *g*
2Mc 4:11 He set aside the royal concessions *g* to
11:15 *g* in behalf of the Jews all the written
11:18 the things that were acceptable he has *g*.
11:35 Lysias, kinsman of the king, has *g* you,
Jb 10:12 Grace and favor you *g* me,
Ps(s) 18:48 O God, who *g* me vengeance,
21: 3 You have *g* him his heart's desire;
61: 6 you *g* me the heritage of those who fear
147:14 He has *g* peace in your borders;
Prv 10:24 him, but the desire of the just will be *g*.
Eccl 9: 9 fleeting life that is *g* you under the sun.
Sir 21: 5 at once, and justice is quickly *g* him.
51:22 The LORD has *g* me my lips as a reward,
Dn 7:12 were *g* a prolongation of life for a time
Hos 12:11 I *g* many visions and spoke to the prophets,
Mt 14: 9 he gave orders that the request be *g*.
18:19 it shall be *g* you by my Father in heaven.
Lk 8:32 permit them to enter the swine. This he *g*.
Jn 5:26 he *g* it to the Son to have life in himself.
6:65 to me unless it is *g* him by the Father."

GRANTED (cont.)

19:38 Pilate *g* it,
Acts 3:14 instead to be *g* the release of a murderer.
3:20 *g* you by the Lord when he sends you Jesus,
7:10 He *g* him favor and wisdom in the court of
11:18 then God has *g* life-giving repentance even
27:24 *g* safety to all who are sailing with you.'
1Cor 4:15 *G* you have ten thousand guardians in Christ,
2Cor 1:11 gift *g* us through the prayers of so many.
12:16 *G* that I did not burden you
Gal 3:18 promise that God *g* Abraham his privilege.
1Tm 1:14 Lord has been *g* me in overflowing measure,
2:15 her chastity being taken for *g*.
Rv 13: 7 *g* authority over every race and people,

GRANTING (5)

Est 2:18 *g* a holiday to the provinces and bestowing
1Mc 14:46 " 'All the people approved of *g* Simon the
Prv 8:21 of justice, *G* wealth to those who love me,
Wis 12:20 *g* time and opportunity to abandon
Acts 15: 8 showed his approval by *g* the Holy Spirit

GRANTS (6)

Gn 25: 6 he made *g* while he was still living,
2Mc 10:38 kindness to Israel and *g* them victory.
Jb 36: 6 rights, but *g* vindication to the oppressed,
Eccl 5:18 property, and *g* power to partake of them,
Jn 5:21 dead and grants life, so the Son *g* life

GRAPE (5)

Nm 6: 3 other vinegar, of any kind of *g* juice,
Sir 39:26 wheat, milk and honey, the blood of the *g*,
50:15 hand for the cup, to offer blood of the *g*,
Is 49:26 their own blood as with the juice of the *g*.
Jl 1: 5 of the *g* will be withheld from your mouths.

GRAPES (42)

Gn 40:10 came out, and its clusters ripened into *g*.
40:11 so I took the *g*,
49:11 his garments, his robe in the blood of *g*.
Lv 19:10 bare, nor gather up the *g* that have fallen.
25: 5 nor shall you pick the *g* of your untrimmed
25:11 or pick the *g* from the untrimmed vines.
Nm 6: 3 juice, nor eat either fresh or dried *g*.
6: 4 not even unripe *g* or grapeskins.
13:20 It was then the season for early *g*.
13:23 a branch with a single cluster of *g* on it,
Dt 23:25 you may eat as many of his *g* as you wish,
24:21 When you pick your *g*,
32:14 and the foaming blood of its *g* you drank.
32:32 are their *g* and bitter their clusters.
Jgs 9:27 harvested their *g* and trod them out.
Neh 13:15 on their asses, together with wine, *g*,
1Mc 6:34 *g* and mulberries to provoke them to fight.
Jb 15:33 be like a vine that sheds its *g* unripened,
Sir 51:15 As the blossoms yielded to ripening *g*,
Is 5: 2 of grapes, but what it yielded was wild *g*.
5: 4 crop of grapes, did it bring forth wild *g*?
16:10 In the wine presses no one treads *g*,
17: 6 Only a scattering of *g* shall be left!
18: 5 the blooms are succeeded by ripening *g*,
62: 9 You who gather the *g* shall drink the wine
65: 8 When the juice is pressed from *g*,
Jer 8:13 no *g* on the vine,
25:30 a shout like that of vintagers over the *g*.
31:29 no longer say, "The fathers ate unripe *g*,
31:30 who eats the unripe *g* shall be set on edge.
Ez 18: 2 "Fathers have eaten green *g*,
Hos 9:10 Like *g* in the desert,
Am 9:13 juice of *g* shall drip down the mountains,
Mi 6:15 out the olive, yet pour no oil, and the *g*,
Mt 7:16 Do you ever pick *g* from thornbushes,
21:34 the tenants to obtain his share of the *g*.
21:41 see to it that he has *g* at vintage time."
Lk 6:44 thornbushes, nor *g* picked from brambles.
Rv 14:18 gather the *g* from the vines of the earth,
14:19 the earth and gathered the *g* of the earth.

GRAPESKINS (1)

Nm 6: 4 not even unripe grapes or *g*.

GRAPEVINE (1)

Jas 3:12 cannot produce olives, or a *g* figs;

GRASP (48)

Dt 3: 4 his cities, none of them eluding our *g*,
Jgs 10:12 out to me, and I saved you from their *g*,
1Sm 4: 3 us and save us from the *g* of our enemies."
10: 1 from the *g* of their enemies round about.
12: 9 of Hazor, into the *g* of the Philistines,
14:10 the LORD has delivered them into our *g*.
14:12 has delivered them into the *g* of Israel."
23:12 deliver me and my men into the *g* of Saul?"
23:14 the LORD did not deliver David into his *g*.
23:20 our task to deliver him into the king's *g*."
24: 5 'I will deliver your enemy into your *g*;
24:11 now delivered you into my *g* in the cave.
24:19 me into your *g* and you did not kill me.
26: 8 delivered your enemy into your *g* this day.
26:23 though the LORD delivered you into my *g*,
28:17 *g* and has given it to your neighbor David.
2Sm 3:18 *g* of the Philistines and from the *g* of all their
14:16 free his servant from the *g* of one
18:19 has set him free from the *g* of his enemies."
18:31 from the *g* of all who rebelled against you."
22: 1 rescued him from the *g* of all his enemies
1Kgs 3: 1 With the royal power firmly in his *g*,
11:31 *g* and will give you ten of the tribes.
2Kgs 3:10 three kings to put them in the *g* of Moab."
3:13 together to put them in the *g* of Moab."
3:18 he will also deliver Moab into your *g*.
2Chr 32:11 save us from the *g* of the king of Assyria'?
Jdt 8:14 heart or *g* the workings of the human mind;
Ps(s) 71: 4 from the *g* of the criminal and the violent.
Prv 3:18 She is a tree of life to those who *g* her,
Wis 9:16 is within our *g* we find with difficulty;
Is 41:13 the LORD, your God, who *g* your right hand;
45: 1 his anointed, Cyrus, whose right hand I *g*,
51:18 She has no one to *g* her by the hand,
Jer 15:21 and rescue you from the *g* of the violent.
Mk 16:20 by spirits to *g* the true power of God.
Lk 2:50 But they did not *g* what he said to them.
9:45 from them they did not *g* it at all,
18:34 to them, and they did not *g* his meaning.
Jn 8:27 They did not *g* that he was speaking to
10: 6 did not *g* what he was trying to tell them.
10:39 tried to arrest him, but he eluded their *g*.
Acts 8:30 "Do you really *g* what you are reading?"
Eph 3:18 Thus you will be able to *g* fully,
Phil 3:12 but I am racing to *g* the prize if possible,
Jas 1:13 Surely God, who is beyond the *g* of evil,

GRASPED (12)

Jgs 15:15 he reached out, *g* it,
16:29 Samson *g* the two middle columns on which
2Sm 2:16 Then each one *g* his opponent's head and
22:17 "He reached out from on high and *g* me;
2Kgs 6: 7 And the man reached down and *g* it.
Jdt 13: 7 close to the bed, *g* the hair of his head,
2Mc 12:35 *g* his military cloak and dragged him along
Ps(s) 18:17 He reached out from on high and *g* me;
Is 42: 6 of justice, I have *g* you by the hand;
Mk 1:31 to her and *g* her hand and helped her up,
Phil 2: 6 equality with God something to be *g* at.
3:12 since I have been *g* by Christ [Jesus].

GRASPING (1)

Lk 18:11 God, that I am not like the rest of men *g*,

GRASS (55)

Gn 2: 5 earth and no *g* of the field had sprouted,
41: 2 they grazed in the reed *g*.
41:18 they grazed in the reed *g*.
Nm 22: 4 us as an ox devours the *g* of the field."
24: 8 He shall devour the nations like *g*,
Dt 11:15 forth *g* in your fields for your animals.
29:22 and unfruitful, without a blade of *g*,
32: 2 like the dew, Like a downpour upon the *g*,
1Kgs 18: 5 may find *g* and save the horses and mules,
2Kgs 19:26 like the scorched *g* on the housetops.
Jb 5:25 and your offspring as the *g* of the earth.
6: 5 Does the wild ass bray when he has *g*?
8:11 Can the reed *g* flourish without water?
8:12 and uncut, it withers quicker than any *g*.
40:15 made Behemoth, that feeds on *g* like an ox.
Ps(s) 37: 2 For like *g* they quickly wither,
90: 5 next morning they are like the changing *g*,
92: 8 flourish like *g* and all evildoers thrive,
102: 5 Withered and dried up like *g* is my heart;
102:12 a lengthening shadow, and I wither like *g*.
103:15 Man's days are like those of *g*;
104:14 You raise *g* for the cattle,
129: 6 May they be like *g* on the housetops,
147: 8 Who makes *g* sprout on the mountains and
Prv 19:12 a lion, but his favor, like dew on the *g*.
27:25 When the *g* is taken away and the
Is 5:24 up stubble, as dry *g* shrivels in the flame,
15: 6 The *g* is withered,
30:33 is piled with dry *g* and wood in abundance,
33:11 You conceive dry *g*,
37:27 like the scorched *g* on the housetops.
40: 6 "All mankind is *g*,
40: 7 The *g* withers, the flower wilts,
40: 7 [So then, the people is the *g*
40: 8 Though the *g* withers and the flower wilts,
51:12 who is human only, to be looked upon as *g*,
66:14 and your bodies flourish like the *g*;
Jer 14: 5 her offspring because there is no *g*.
Dn 4:12 iron and bronze, in the *g* of the field.
4:12 to eat, among beasts, the *g* of the earth.
4:20 with iron and bronze in the *g* of the field;
4:22 you shall be given *g* to eat like an ox and
4:29 you shall be given *g* to eat like an ox,
4:30 out from among men, he ate *g* like an ox,
5:21 with wild asses, and ate *g* like an ox;
Am 7: 2 they were eating all the *g* in the land,
Mi 5: 6 from the LORD, like raindrops on the *g*,
Mt 6:30 clothe in such splendor the *g* of the field,
14:19 he ordered the crowds to sit down on the *g*.
Mk 6:39 down on the green *g* in groups or parties.
Lk 12:28 in such splendor the *g* of the field,
Jn 6:10 *g* for them to find a place on the ground.
1Pt 1:24 "All mankind is *g* and the glory of men is
1:24 *g* withers, the flower wilts, but the word
Rv 9: 4 commanded to do no harm to the *g*

GRASS-EATING (1)

Ps(s) 106:20 their glory for the image of a *g* bullock.

GRASSHOPPER (3)

Jl 1: 4 the *g* has eaten; And what the *g* left,
2:25 years which the locust has eaten, The *g*,

GRASSHOPPERS (9)

Lv 11:22 kinds of locusts, the various kinds of *g*,
Nm 13:33 we felt like mere *g*,
Ps(s) 105:34 there came locusts and *g* without number;
Is 40:22 the earth, and its inhabitants are like *g*;
Na 3:15 Multiply like the *g*,
3:17 the stars, your garrisons as many as *g*,
3:17 the *g* will spread their wings and fly,
Mt 3: 4 *G* and wild honey were his food.
Mk 1: 6 His food was *g* and wild honey.

GRASSY (2)

Wis 19: 7 and a *g* plain out of the mighty flood.
Zec 10: 1 for everyone, *g* fields.

GRATE (2)

Ex 30: 3 Its *g* on top,
37:26 Its *g* on top,

GRATEFUL (11)

Gn 29:35 time I will give *g* praise to the LORD";
47:25 "We are *g* to my lord that we can be
Jgs 8:35 Nor were they *g* to the family of Jerubbaal
Jdt 8:25 this, we should be *g* to the Lord our God,
2Mc 3:33 "Be very *g* to the high priest Onias,"
10: 7 they sang hymns of *g* praise to him who had
10:38 they blessed, with hymns of *g* praise,
Sir 51:17 profited, I will give my teacher *g* praise.
Lk 7:42 Which of them was more *g* to him?"
17: 9 Would he be *g* to the servant who was only
Rom 16: 4 the churches of the Gentiles are *g* to them.

GRATEFULLY (1)

Col 3:16 Sing *g* to God from your hearts in psalms,

GRATIFY (1)

Ps(s) 91:16 will *g* him and will show him my salvation.

GRATIFYING (1)

Wis 3:14 and a more *g* heritage in the Lord's temple.

GRATING (5)

Ex 27: 4 Make a *g* of bronze network for it;
35:16 altar of holocausts, with its bronze *g*,
38: 4 A *g* of bronze network was made for the
38: 5 cast for the four corners of the bronze *g*,
39:39 the altar of bronze with its bronze *g*,

GRATINGS (1)

Ex 38:30 *g* and all the appurtenances of the altar,

GRATITUDE (10)

Dt 28:47 with joy and *g* for abundance of every kind,
2Kgs 4:37 She came in and fell at his feet in *g*;
2Chr 32:25 did not then discharge his debt of *g*,
Est E: 4 only do they drive out *g* from among men;
2Mc 2:27 to win the *g* of many we will gladly endure
Wis 14:26 Disturbance of good men, neglect of *g*,
Acts 24: 3 everywhere acknowledge our deep *g* to you.
2Cor 9:12 church but also overflows in much *g* to God.
Phil 4: 6 form of prayer and in petitions full of *g*.
Col 2: 7 as you were taught, and overflowing with *g*.

GRAVE (56)

Gn 18:20 Gomorrah is so great, and their sin so *g*,
35:20 Jacob set up a memorial stone on her *g*,
35:20 same monument marks Rachel's *g* to this day.
Ex 32:21 that you should lead them into so *g* a sin?"
32:30 the people, "You have committed a *g* sin.
32:31 this people has indeed committed a *g* sin
Nm 19:16 or who touches a human bone or a *g*,
19:18 a slain person or other dead body, or a *g*.
Jgs 16:31 bore him up for burial in the *g* of his father
2Sm 3:32 the king wept aloud at the *g* of Abner,
4:12 and buried it in Abner's *g* in Hebron.
1Kgs 2: 6 to go down to the *g* in peaceful old age.
2: 9 send down his hoary head in blood to the *g*."
13:22 not be brought to the *g* of your ancestors.' "
13:30 He laid the man's body in his own *g*,
13:31 me in the *g* where the man of God is buried.
14:13 of Jeroboam's line will be laid in the *g*,
2Kgs 13:21 cast the dead man into the *g* of Elisha,
21:26 buried in his own *g* in the garden of Uzza,
22:20 you shall go to your *g* in peace,
23:16 When the king looked up and saw the *g* of

23:17 "It is the *g* of the man of God who came
23:30 where they buried him in his own *g*.
2Chr 34:28 and you shall be taken to your *g* in peace.
Tb 2: 7 Then at sunset I went out, dug a *g*,
4: 4 she dies, bury her in the same *g* with me.
6:15 mother down to their *g* in sorrow over me.
8: 9 With him they went out to dig a *g*,
8:11 When they had finished digging the *g*,
8:18 his servants to fill in the *g* before dawn.
Jdt 7:24 You have done us *g* injustice in not making
1Mc 7:25 to the king and accused them of *g* crimes.
14:36 temple and inflict *g* injury on its purity.
2Mc 1:11 we have been saved by God from *g* dangers,
Jb 3:22 and are glad when they reach the *g*:
5:26 You shall approach the *g* in full vigor,
10:19 have been taken from the womb to the *g*.
21:32 on the day he is carried to the *g*
33:18 the pit and his life from passing to the *g*.
Ps(s) 5:10 Their throat is an open *g*;
30:10 lifeblood, from my going down into the *g*?
88: 6 the dead, like the slain who lie in the *g*,
88:12 Do they declare your kindness in the *g*,
94:17 help, I would soon dwell in the silent *g*.
Prv 28:17 with human blood were to flee to the *g*,
Sir 9: 9 to her and you go down in blood to the *g*.
46:20 the *g* he raised his voice as a prophet,
Is 14:20 you will never be one with them in the *g*."
53: 9 A *g* was assigned him among the wicked and
Jer 20:17 Then my mother would have been my *g*,
26:23 and his corpse cast into the common *g*.
Ez 32:23 her company is around Egypt's *g*,
32:24 Elam with all her throng about Egypt's *g*,
32:26 Tubal and all their throng about her *g*,
Na 1:14 I will make your *g* a mockery.
Acts 2:29 and his *g* is in our midst to this day.

GRAVEL (2)

Prv 20:17 afterward his mouth will be filled with *g*.
Lam 3:16 He has broken my teeth with *g*,

GRAVEN (3)

Ps(s) 97: 7 All who worship *g* things are put to shame,
Wis 14:16 and *g* things were worshiped by princely
Is 10:11 I not do to Jerusalem and her *g* images?"

GRAVES (10)

2Kgs 23:16 and saw the *g* there on the mountainside,
23:16 taken from the *g* and burned on the altar,
Neh 2: 5 to Judah, to the city of my ancestors' *g*,
Sir 14:12 have you been told the *g* appointed time.
Is 65: 4 the *g* and spending the night in caverns,
Jer 5:16 Their quivers are like open *g*;
8: 1 Jerusalem will be emptied out of their *g*
Ez 32:23 whose *g* have been made in the recesses of
37:12 open your *g* and have you rise from them,
37:13 I open your *g* and have you rise from them,

GRAVEYARD (3)

2Kgs 23: 6 which was then scattered over the common *g*.
2Mc 9: 4 *g* of the Jews as soon as I arrive there."
9:14 it to the ground and making it a common *g*;

GRAVING (1)

Ex 32: 4 and fashioning this gold with a *g* tool,

GRAY (7)

1Sm 12: 2 As for me, I am old and *g*,
2Mc 6:23 age, the merited distinction of his *g* hair,
Ps(s) 71:18 And now that I am old and *g*,
Prv 16:31 *G* hair is a crown of glory;
20:29 and the dignity of old men is *g* hair.
Is 46: 4 even when your hair is *g* I will bear you;
Hos 7: 9 Of *g* hairs,

GRAY-HAIRED (2)

Jb 15:10 There are *g* old men among us more advanced
Sir 25: 4 How becoming to the *g* is judgment,

GRAYBEARD (1)

Jer 6:11 be taken, husband and wife, *g* with ancient.

GRAYING (1)

Sir 6:18 thus will you find wisdom with *g* hair.

GRAZE (5)

Is 5:17 Lambs shall *g* there at pasture,
30:23 day your cattle will *g* in spacious meadows;
65:25 The wolf and the lamb shall *g* alike,
Ez 34:18 enough for you to *g* on the best pasture,
34:19 Thus my sheep had to *g* on what your feet

GRAZED (3)

Gn 41: 2 they *g* in the reed grass.
41:18 they *g* in the reed grass.
1Chr 27:29 that *g* in Sharon was Shitrai the Sharonite,

GRAZES (1)

Jer 6: 3 pitch their tents, each one *g* his portion.

GRAZING (9)

Ex 34: 3 herds are not to go *g* toward this mountain."
Nm 32: 1 land of Jazer and of Gilead was *g* country,
32: 4 the community of Israel, is *g* country.
Jb 1:14 were plowing and the asses *g* beside them,
Is 5: 5 Take away its hedge, give it to *g*,
7:25 they shall be *g* land for cattle and shall
Jer 25:36 For the LORD lays waste their *g* place,
Ez 34:14 heights of Israel shall be their *g* ground.
34:14 There they shall lie down on good *g* ground,

GREASY (2)

Is 34: 6 has a sword filled with blood, *g* with fat,
34: 7 with blood, and their earth *g* with fat.

GREAT (807)

Gn 1:16 God made the two *g* lights,
1:21 God created the *g* sea monsters and all
4:13 "My punishment is too *g* to bear.
6: 5 saw how *g* was man's wickedness on earth,
7:11 the fountains of the *g* abyss burst forth,
12: 2 "I will make of you a *g* nation,
12: 2 I will make your name *g*,
13: 6 so *g* that they could not dwell together.
15: 1 I will make your reward very *g*."
15:14 in the end they will depart with *g* wealth.
15:18 of Egypt to the *G* River [the Euphrates],
17:20 and I will make of him a *g* nation.
18:18 he is to become a *g* and populous nation,
18:20 outcry against Sodom and Gomorrah is so *g*,
19:13 is so *g* that he has sent us to destroy it."
19:19 *g* kindness of intervening to save my life.
21: 8 child's weaning, Abraham held a *g* feast.
21:13 woman, I will make a *g* nation of him also,
21:18 for I will make of him a *g* nation."
35:16 to be in labor and to suffer *g* distress.
36: 7 become too *g* for them to dwell together,
39: 9 could I commit so *g* a wrong and thus stand
41:29 Seven years of *g* abundance are now coming
46: 3 for there I will make you a *g* nation.
48:19 become a tribe, and he too shall be *g*.
50:10 there a very *g* and solemn memorial service;
Ex 7: 4 by *g* acts of judgment I will bring the hosts
14:10 In *g* fright they cried out to the LORD.
14:31 *g* power that the LORD had shown
15: 7 *g* majesty you overthrew your adversaries;
18:11 the LORD is a deity *g* beyond any other;
29:20 hands and the *g* toes of their right feet.
32:10 Then I will make of you a *g* nation."
32:11 such *g* power and with so strong a hand?
Nm 11:33 and he struck them with a very *g* plague.
14:19 people in keeping with your *g* kindness,
14:39 the Israelites, the people felt *g* remorse.
22:18 gold, I could not do anything, small or *g*,
34: 6 you shall have the *G* Sea with its coast;
34: 7 *G* Sea you shall draw a line to Mount Hor,
Dt 1: 7 and as far as the *G* River [the Euphrates].
1:17 give ear to the lowly and to the *g* alike,
3: 5 nothing of the *g* number of unwalled towns.
4: 6 'This *g* nation is truly a wise and
4: 7 For what *g* nation is there that has gods
4: 8 Or what *g* nation has statutes and decrees
4:32 Did anything so *g* ever happen before?
4:34 and outstretched arm, and by *g* terrors,
4:36 on earth he let you see his *g* fire,
4:37 led you out of Egypt by his *g* power,
5:25 Surely this *g* fire will consume us.
6:22 our eyes signs and wonders, *g* and dire,
7: 1 occupy, and dislodges *g* nations before you
7:19 *g* testings which your own eyes have seen,
7:21 is in your midst, is a *g* and awesome God.
9: 2 the sky, the Anakim, a people *g* and tall.
9:29 *g* power and with your outstretched arm.
10:17 God of gods, the LORD of lords, the *g* God,
10:21 who has done for you those *g* and terrible
11: 7 all these *g* deeds that the LORD has done.
17:16 But he shall not have a *g* number of horses;
17:17 Neither shall he have a *g* number of wives,
18:16 our God, nor see this *g* fire any more,
19: 6 Should the distance be too *g*,
26: 5 But there he became a nation *g*,
28:52 in each of your communities, until the *g*,
29: 2 the *g* testings your own eyes have seen,
29: 2 have seen, and those *g* signs and wonders.
Jos 1: 4 *g* river Euphrates and west to the *G* Sea.
3:16 a solid mass for a very *g* distance indeed,
7: 9 What will you do for your *g* name?"
7:26 and piled a *g* heap of stones over him,
8: 4 the city from the rear, at no *g* distance;
8:29 a *g* heap of stones was piled up over it,
9: 1 the coast of the *G* Sea as far as Lebanon:
9:22 say that you lived at a *g* distance from us,
9:24 advance, we were in *g* fear for our lives,
10: 2 them and that there was *g* fear abroad,
10:10 The Israelites inflicted a *g* slaughter on
10:11 the LORD hurled *g* stones from the sky
10:20 the last blows in this very *g* slaughter,
15:12 boundary was the *G* Sea and its coast.
15:47 Wadi of Egypt and the coast of the *G* Sea.
22: 8 returning to your own tents with *g* wealth,
23: 4 the Jordan and the *G* Sea in the west.
23:11 Take *g* care, however, to love the LORD
24:17 He performed those *g* miracles before our
Jgs 2: 7 *g* work which the LORD had done for Israel,
2:15 he would do, till they were in *g* distress.
5:15 of Reuben *g* were the searchings of heart.
5:16 of Reuben *g* were the searchings of heart!
10: 9 Ephraim, so that Israel was in *g* distress.
15: 8 blows, he inflicted a *g* slaughter on them.
15:18 this *g* victory by the hand of your servant.
16: 5 and find out the secret of his *g* strength,
16: 6 "Tell me the secret of your *g* strength
16:15 not told me the secret of your *g* strength!"
16:23 offer a *g* sacrifice to their god Dagon
1Sm 5: 6 he brought upon the city a *g* and deadly
6: 9 he has brought this *g* calamity upon us;
6:15 were, and had placed them on the *g* stone.
6:19 The people went into mourning at this *g*
11:15 celebrated the occasion with *g* joy.
12:16 stand ready to witness the *g* marvel the
12:22 For the sake of his own *g* name the LORD
12:24 in mind the *g* things he has done among you.
14:45 was he who brought Israel this *g* victory?
17:25 kill him, the king would give him *g* wealth,
18:30 officers, and as a result acquired *g* fame.]
19: 5 a *g* victory for all Israel through him,
19: 8 and inflicted a *g* defeat upon them,
20: 2 My father does nothing, *g* or small,
20:34 Jonathan sprang up from the table in *g*
22:15 servant knows nothing at all, *g* or small,
24:19 *G* is the generosity you showed me today,
26:13 remote hilltop at a *g* distance from Abner,
28:15 "I am in *g* straits,
30: 6 Now David found himself in *g* difficulty,
30:19 Nothing was missing, small or *g*,
2Sm 1: 9 and finish me off, for I am in *g* suffering,
3:38 a *g* general has fallen today in Israel.
7: 9 you famous like the *g* ones of the earth.
7:22 And so *G* are you, Lord GOD!
7:26 Your name will be forever *g*,
12: 2 rich man had flocks and herds in *g* numbers.
18:29 "I saw a *g* disturbance when the king's
20: 8 the *g* stone in Gibeon when Amasa met them.
22:36 saving shield, and your help has made me *g*.
22:51 You who gave *g* victories to your king and
23:10 LORD brought about a *g* victory on that day;
23:12 and the LORD brought about a *g* victory.
23:20 from Kabzeel, was a man of *g* achievements.
1Kgs 1:19 oxen, fatlings, and sheep in *g* numbers;
1:25 oxen, fatlings, and sheep in *g* numbers;
3: 6 "You have shown *g* favor to your servant,
3: 6 you have continued this *g* favor toward him,
7:12 The *g* court was enclosed by three courses
8:42 men will learn of your *g* name
10: 4 of Sheba witnessed Solomon's *g* wisdom,
11:19 Hadad won *g* favor with Pharaoh,
2Kgs 3:27 The wrath against Israel was so *g* that
6:23 The king spread a *g* feast for them.
8: 4 "all the *g* things that Elisha has done."
10:19 absent, for I have a *g* sacrifice for Baal.
17:18 him till, in his *g* anger against Israel,
17:21 the LORD, causing them to commit a *g* sin.
17:36 of Egypt with *g* power and outstretched arm:
18:17 a *g* army to King Hezekiah at Jerusalem.
18:19 "Tell Hezekiah, 'Thus says the *g* king,
18:28 "Listen to the words of the *g* king,
23: 2 prophets, and all the people, small and *g*.
25:26 Then all the people, *g* and small,
1Chr 10: 4 But the armor-bearer, in *g* fear, refused.
11:14 Thus the LORD brought about a *g* victory.
12:41 provisions in *g* quantity of meal,
13: 8 Israel danced before God with *g* enthusiasm,
16:25 For *g* is the LORD and highly to be praised;
17: 8 *g* like that of the greatest on the earth.
17:19 your purpose, you have done this *g* thing.
17:21 You won for yourself a name for *g* and
17:24 God of Israel, may be *g* and abide forever,
20: 2 out a *g* amount of booty from the city.
21:13 hand of the LORD, whose mercy is very *g*,
22: 4 brought *g* stores of cedar logs to David,
22: 8 shed much blood, and you have waged *g* wars.
22:14 with *g* effort I have laid up for the house
22:14 *g* quantities that they cannot be weighed.
29: 1 the work, however, is *g*,
29: 2 precious stone, and *g* quantities of marble.
29:22 in the LORD's presence with *g* rejoicing.
2Chr 1: 8 have shown *g* favor to my father David,
1:10 who could rule this *g* people of yours?"
2: 8 to prepare for me a *g* quantity of wood,
2:12 am now sending you a craftsman of *g* skill,
4: 9 *g* courtyard and the gates of the courtyard;
6:32 from a distant land to honor your *g* name,
9: 6 did not tell me the half of your *g* wisdom;
14:14 carried off a *g* number of sheep and camels.
15:13 was to be put to death, whether small or *g*,
16: 8 with *g* numbers of chariots and drivers?
16:14 also burned a very *g* funeral pyre for him.
17: 5 so that he enjoyed *g* wealth and glory.
18:30 the order, "Fight with no one, small or *g*,
20: 2 "A *g* multitude is coming against you from
20:25 three days taking the spoil, so *g* was it.

GREAT (cont.)
21:14 and all that is yours with a *g* plague;
21:19 of the disease and he died in *g* pain.
24:27 his sons, and the *g* tribute imposed on him,
26:13 fighting men of *g* valor to help the king
28: 5 Israel, who defeated him with *g* slaughter.
28:13 Our guilt is already *g*,
30:13 it was a very *g* assembly.
30:21 Bread with *g* rejoicing for seven days,
30:24 priests sanctified themselves in *g* numbers,
30:26 There was *g* rejoicing in Jerusalem,
31: 5 the Israelites brought, in *g* quantities,
31:10 This *g* supply is what was left over."
31:15 to their brethren *g* and small alike,
32: 5 a *g* number of spears and shields prepared.
32:27 Hezekiah possessed very *g* wealth and glory.
32:29 *g* numbers, for God gave him very *g* riches.
33: 6 with the *g* evil that he did in his sight.
34:30 Levites, and all the people, *g* and small;
Ezr 3:11 and all the people raised a *g* shout of joy,
4:10 *g* and illustrious Assurbanipal transported
5: 8 of Judah and the house of the *g* God:
5:11 which a *g* King of Israel
9: 7 even to this day *g* has been our guilt,
9:13 upon us for our evil deeds and our *g* guilt
Neh 1: 3 are in *g* distress and under reproach.
1: 5 "O LORD, God of heaven, *g* and awesome God,
1:10 freed by your *g* might and your strong hand.
2: 2 Though I was seized with *g* fear,
3:27 sector opposite the *g* projecting tower,
4: 8 in mind the Lord who is *g* and to be feared,
5: 1 Then there rose a *g* outcry of the common
6: 3 a *g* enterprise and am unable to come down;
8: 6 Ezra blessed the LORD, the *g* God,
8:12 portions, and to celebrate with *g* joy,
8:17 therefore there was very *g* joy.
9:18 Egypt,' and were guilty of *g* effronteries,
9:19 yet in your *g* mercy you did not forsake
9:26 and they were guilty of *g* effronteries.
9:27 and according to your *g* mercy give them
9:31 Yet in your *g* mercy you did not completely
9:32 "Now, therefore, O our God, *g*,
9:37 We are in *g* distress!"
12:31 the wall, and I arranged two *g* choirs.
12:43 *G* sacrifices were offered on that day,
12:43 *g* feast of the LORD in which they shared.
13:22 on me in accordance with your *g* mercy!
13:27 that you have done this same very *g* evil,
Tb 1:14 a *g* sum of money with my kinsman Gabael,
4: 8 If you have *g* wealth,
4:13 arrogance there is ruin and *g* disorder.
4:20 I have deposited a *g* sum of money
8:16 dealt with us according to your *g* mercy.
11:14 be God, and praised be his *g* name,
13: 2 world, and he brings up from the *g* abyss.
13:15 My spirit blesses the Lord, the *g* King;
Jdt 1: 1 of the Assyrians in the *g* city of Nineveh.
2: 5 "Thus says the *g* king,
3: 2 the servants of Nebuchadnezzar the *g* king,
4: 9 cried to God with *g* fervor and did penance
5: 2 In *g* anger he summoned all the rulers of
5: 9 silver, and a *g* abundance of livestock.
5:10 and grew into such a *g* multitude that the
5:24 your *g* army,
7: 2 a very *g* army.
7: 4 were, they said to one another in *g* dismay:
7:23 up a *g* clamor and said before the elders:
7:32 Throughout the city they were in *g* misery.
8:19 fell with *g* destruction before our enemies.
12:20 charmed by her, drank a *g* quantity of wine,
13: 4 all had departed, and no one, small or *g*,
15: 5 struck the enemy's flanks with *g* slaughter,
15: 6 plundered it, and acquired *g* riches.
16:13 O Lord, *g* are you and glorious,
16:16 sight, one who fears the Lord is forever *g*.
Est A: 1 year of the reign of the *g* King Ahasuerus,
A: 5 Two *g* dragons came on,
A: 7 and distress, evil and *g* confusion,
A: 9 there appeared to come forth a *g* river,
1: 5 palace for all the people, *g* and small,
2:18 Then the king gave a *g* feast in honor of
B: 1 "The *g* King Ahasuerus writes to the
D: 6 precious stones, so that he inspired *g* awe.
D: 8 In *g* anxiety he sprang from his throne,
E: 1 "King Ahasuerus the *G* to the governors of
F: 6 God worked signs and *g* wonders,
1Mc 1:24 with *g* arrogance and shed much blood.
1:25 And there was *g* mourning for Israel,
1:30 the city suddenly, in a *g* onslaught,
1:35 And they became a *g* threat.
1:40 dishonor was as *g* as her glory had been,
2:17 an honorable and *g* man in this city,
2:51 shall win *g* glory and an everlasting name.
3:20 With *g* presumption and lawlessness they
4:23 violet and crimson cloth, and *g* treasure.
4:25 Thus Israel had a *g* deliverance that day.
4:39 tore their clothes and made *g* lamentation;
4:58 There was *g* joy among the people now that
5:16 a *g* assembly convened to consider what
5:23 and brought them to Judea with *g* rejoicing.
5:45 assembled all the Israelites, *g* and small,
5:45 and their goods, a *g* crowd of people,
5:52 to the *g* plain in front of Beth-shan,
6: 4 So he retreated and in *g* dismay withdrew
6:41 for the army was very *g* and strong.
7: 8 West-of-Euphrates, a *g* man in the kingdom,
7:10 in the land of Judah with a *g* army,
7:11 seeing that they had come with a *g* army.
7:19 to him, throwing them into the *g* pit.
7:22 of Judah and caused *g* distress in Israel.
7:35 He went away in *g* anger.
7:48 and observed that day as a *g* festival.
8: 6 Antiochus the *G*, king of Asia,
8: 6 cavalry and chariots and a very *g* army,
9: 6 his men saw the *g* number of the troops,
9:20 All Israel bewailed him in *g* grief.
9:24 In those days there was a very *g* famine,
9:27 There had not been such *g* distress in
9:35 with them their *g* quantity of baggage.
9:37 sons of Jambri are celebrating a *g* wedding,
9:37 of one of the *g* princes of Canaan,
9:56 Finally he died in *g* agony.
9:68 This caused him *g* distress.
10:46 *g* evil that Demetrius had done in Israel,
10:58 celebrated at Ptolemais with *g* splendor
10:86 that city came out to meet him with *g* pomp.
11:26 *g* honor in the presence of all his Friends.
12:49 the *G* Plain to destroy all Jonathan's men.
12:52 Jonathan and his men, and were in *g* fear,
13:44 into the city and caused a *g* tumult there.
13:51 a *g* enemy of Israel had been destroyed.
14:24 a *g* gold shield weighing a thousand minas,
14:28 in Asaramel, in a *g* assembly of priests,
14:29 have thus brought *g* glory to their nation.
15:29 their territories, done *g* harm to the land,
15:35 men of these cities were doing *g* harm
2Mc 1:11 we give him *g* thanks for having fought on
1:14 to get its *g* treasures by way of dowry.
1:22 began to shine, a *g* fire blazed up,
2:18 from *g* perils and has purified his Place.
2:19 of the purification of the *g* temple,
3:14 There was *g* distress throughout the city.
3:27 to the ground, enveloped in *g* darkness.
3:28 entered that treasury with a *g* retinue
4:22 *g* pomp by Jason and the people of the city,
5:20 once the *g* Sovereign became reconciled.
6:13 a sign of *g* kindness to punish sinners
7:17 and you will see how his *g* power will
8:20 thousand and took a *g* quantity of booty,
8:32 man, who had done *g* harm to the Jews.
9:22 have *g* hopes of recovering from my illness.
10:38 the Lord who shows *g* kindness to Israel
12:15 the aid of the *g* Sovereign of the world,
12:24 but with *g* cunning,
13: 3 with *g* duplicity kept urging Antiochus on,
14: 8 our entire nation is suffering *g* affliction
14:13 up Alcimus as high priest of the *g* temple.
14:18 and the *g* courage with which they fought
14:31 the man, he went to the *g* and holy temple,
Jb 1: 3 she-asses, and a *g* number of work animals,
1:19 when suddenly a *g* wind came across the
2:13 for they saw how *g* was his suffering.
3:19 Small and *g* are there the same,
9:10 He does *g* things past finding out,
12:23 He makes nations *g* and he destroys them;
23: 6 he contend against me with his *g* power,
30:18 One with *g* power lays hold of my clothing;
31:25 Or had I rejoiced that my wealth was *g*,
35: 9 In *g* oppression men cry out;
36:26 Lo, God is *g* beyond our knowledge;
37: 5 He does *g* things beyond our knowing;
37:23 his *g* justice owes no one an accounting.
38:21 them, and the number of your years is *g*!
39:11 Will you trust him for his *g* strength and
42: 3 with *g* things that I do not understand;
Ps(s) 14: 5 then they shall be in *g* fear,
18:36 me, and you have stooped to make me *g*.
18:51 You who gave *g* victories to your king and
21: 6 *G* is his glory in your victory;
25:11 LORD, you will pardon my guilt, *g* as it is.
31:20 How *g* is the goodness, O LORD,
33:16 nor is a warrior delivered by *g* strength.
33:17 *g* though its strength,
34:11 The *g* grow poor and hungry;
37:16 the just than the *g* wealth of the wicked,
44:13 You sold your people for no *g* price;
47: 3 awesome, is the *g* king over all the earth.
48: 2 *G* is the LORD and wholly to be praised
48: 3 of the North," is the city of the *g* King.
49:17 when the wealth of his house becomes *g*,
52: 9 But put his trust in his *g* wealth,
53: 6 There they were in *g* fear,
66: 3 your *g* strength your enemies fawn upon you.
69:14 In your *g* kindness answer me with your
69:17 in your *g* mercy turn toward me.
71:19 You have done *g* things;
76: 2 renowned in Judah, in Israel *g* is his name.
77:14 what *g* god is there like our God?
79:11 your *g* power free those doomed to death.
86:10 For you are *g*,
86:13 *G* has been your kindness toward me;
89: 8 *g* and awesome beyond all round about him.
92: 6 How *g* are your works, O LORD!
95: 3 a great God, and a *g* king above all gods;
96: 4 For *g* is the LORD and highly to be praised;
99: 2 The LORD in Zion is *g*,
99: 3 Let them praise your *g* and awesome name;
104: 1 O LORD, my God, you are *g* indeed!
104:25 The sea also, *g* and wide,
104:25 number of living things both small and *g*,
106:21 saved them, who had done *g* deeds in Egypt,
111: 2 *G* are the works of the LORD,
115:13 fear the LORD, both the small and the *g*.
119:156 Your compassion is *g*,
119:165 Those who love your law have *g* peace,
126: 2 "The LORD has done *g* things for them."
126: 3 The LORD has done *g* things for us;
131: 1 I busy not myself with *g* things,
135: 5 For I know that the LORD is *g*;
136: 4 Who alone does *g* wonders,
136: 7 Who made the *g* lights,
136:17 Who smote *g* kings,
138: 2 for you have made *g* above all things your
138: 5 *G* is the glory of the LORD."
145: 3 *G* is the LORD and highly to be praised;
145: 8 merciful, slow to anger and of *g* kindness.
147: 5 *G* is our Lord and mighty in power:
Prv 12:27 but the wealth of the diligent man is *g*.
13: 7 pretends to be poor, yet has *g* wealth.
15:16 of the LORD than a *g* fortune with anxiety.
18:16 way for him, and gains him access to *g* men.
22: 1 good name is more desirable than *g* riches,
25: 6 presence, nor occupy the place of *g* men;
28:12 just are triumphant, there is *g* jubilation;
Eccl 1:16 I have become *g* and stored up wisdom
2: 4 I undertook *g* works;
2: 9 I became *g*, and stored up more than all
2:21 This also is vanity and a *g* misfortune.
5:10 Where there are *g* riches,
5:16 in gloom and sorrow, under *g* vexation,
6: 3 live many years, no matter to what *g* age,
8: 6 it is a *g* affliction for man that he is
9:14 it and threw up *g* siegeworks about it.
10: 4 for mildness abates *g* offenses.
Wis 5: 1 Then shall the just one with *g* assurance
6: 7 he himself made the *g* as well as the small,
6:24 A *g* number of wise men is the safety of
11:21 For with you *g* strength abides always;
14:22 though they live in a *g* war of ignorance,
17: 1 For *g* are your judgments,
18: 1 But your holy ones had very *g* light;
Sir 2: 3 thus will your future be *g*.
3:19 For *g* is the power of God;
5: 6 *G* is his mercy;
6: 1 Say nothing harmful, small or *g*;
7:25 your daughter in marriage ends a *g* task;
11:12 failure, with little strength and *g* misery
16:12 *G* as his mercy is his punishment;
17:24 How *g* the mercy of the LORD,
18: 7 days is *g* if it reaches a hundred years:
19:20 of *g* intelligence who violate the law.
20:26 by his words, a prudent man pleases the *g*.
20:27 who pleases the *g* is pardoned his faults.
23:11 his obligation, his sin is doubly *g*.
24:27 her counsels, than the *g* abyss.
25:10 He who finds wisdom is *g* indeed,
26: 8 A drunken wife arouses *g* anger,
31:12 If you are dining with a *g* man,
33:11 his *g* knowledge the LORD makes men unlike;
33:12 Some he blesses and makes *g*,
35: 1 To keep the law is a *g* oblation,
37:11 harvest, to an idle slave about a *g* task:
39: 4 He is in attendance on the *g*,
40: 1 A *g* anxiety has God allotted,
43: 5 *G* indeed is the LORD who made it,
46: 1 implies, the *g* savior of God's chosen ones,
51: 3 in your *g* mercy From the scourge of a
51:16 time I paid heed, I met with *g* instruction.
Is 8: 7 *g* and mighty [the king of Assyria and all
9: 1 who walked in darkness have seen a *g* light;
9: 2 brought them abundant joy and *g* rejoicing,
12: 6 *g* in your midst is the Holy One of Israel!
16:14 be degraded despite all its *g* multitude;
27: 1 punish with his sword that is cruel, *g*,
27:13 On that day, A *g* trumpet shall blow,
28: 2 Like a flood of water, *g* and overflowing,
28:29 wonderful is his counsel and *g* his wisdom.
29: 6 With thunder, earthquake, and *g* noise,
30:25 On the day of the *g* slaughter,
32: 2 the shade of a *g* rock in a parched land.
33:23 Then the blind will divide *g* spoils and
34: 6 Bozrah, a *g* slaughter in the land of Edom.
36: 2 a *g* army to King Hezekiah in Jerusalem.
36: 4 Thus says the *g* king,
36:13 "Listen to the words of the *g* king,
40:26 By his *g* might and the strength of his
42:21 justice to make his law *g* and glorious,
47: 9 sorceries and the *g* number of your spells;
51:10 dried up the sea, the waters of the *g* deep,
53:12 I will give him his portion among the *g*,
54: 7 but with *g* tenderness I will take you back.
54:13 and *g* shall be the peace of your children.
63: 7 according to him mercy and his *g* kindness.
Jer 4: 6 I bring from the north, and *g* destruction.
5: 5 will go to the *g* ones and speak with them;
6:13 Small and *g* alike,
6:22 from the land of the north, a *g* nation,
8:10 Small and *g* alike,
10: 6 great are you, *g* and mighty is your name.

10:22 closer, a *g* uproar from the northern land:
11:16 be jubilant when you hear the *g* invasion?
13: 9 of Judah to rot, the *g* pride of Jerusalem.
13:22 For your *g* guilt your skirts are stripped
14:17 Over the *g* destruction which overwhelms
16: 6 They shall die, the *g* and the lowly,
16:10 pronounced all these *g* evils against us?
20:15 filling him with *g* joy.
21: 5 arm, in anger, and wrath, and *g* rage!
21: 6 they shall die in a *g* pestilence.
22: 8 has the LORD done this to so *g* a city?"
25:14 be enslaved to *g* nations and mighty kings,
25:32 A *g* storm is unleashed from the ends of
26:19 committing this *g* evil to our own undoing."
27: 5 on the face of the earth, by my *g* power,
27: 7 shall serve *g* nations and mighty kings.
30:15 Because of your *g* guilt,
32:17 have made heaven and earth by your *g* might,
32:18 O God, *g* and mighty,
32:19 whose name is LORD of hosts, *g* in counsel,
32:21 Egypt amid signs and wonders and *g* terror.
32:37 in anger, wrath, and *g* rage I banish them;
32:42 I brought upon this people all this *g* evil,
33: 3 things *g* beyond reach of your knowledge.
36: 7 for *g* is the fury of anger with which the
41:12 overtook him at the *G* Waters in Gibeon.
44: 7 you inflict so *g* an evil upon yourselves?
44:26 I swear by my own *g* name,
45: 5 And do you seek *g* things for yourself?
48: 3 from Horonaim of ruin and *g* destruction!
50: 9 Babylon a band of *g* nations from the north;
50:41 a people comes from the north, a *g* nation,
Lam 2:13 For *g* as the sea is your downfall;
3:23 each morning, so *g* is his faithfulness.
Bar 1: 4 and the whole people, small and *g* alike
2: 2 He brought down upon us evils so *g* that
2:11 hand, with signs and wonders and *g* might,
2:27 all your clemency and in all your *g* mercy.
2:29 surely this *g* and numerous throng will
4: 9 God has brought *g* mourning upon me,
4:24 with *g* glory and the splendor of the
Ez 8: 6 Do you see the *g* abominations that the
9: 9 the house of Israel are *g* beyond measure;
17: 3 The great eagle, with *g* wings,
17: 7 there was another great eagle, *g* of wing,
17:15 to Egypt to obtain horses and a *g* army.
17:17 Pharaoh with a *g* army and numerous troops.
21:19 This *g* sword of slaughter which threatens
22: 5 your foul reputation and your *g* perversity.
24: 9 I, too, will heap up a *g* bonfire,
24:12 even with fire will its *g* rust be removed.
25:17 I will execute *g* acts of vengeance on them,
26: 7 with cavalry and a *g* and mighty army.
27:12 traded with you, so *g* was your wealth,
27:18 traded with you, so *g* was your wealth,
27:27 and all the *g* crowd within you] Sank into
27:33 With your *g* wealth and merchandise you
28: 5 By your *g* wisdom applied to your trading
28:17 cast you to the earth, so *g* was your guilt;
28:18 Because of your *g* guilt,
29: 3 *G* crouching monster amidst your Niles:
30:13 I will put an end to the *g* ones of Memphis
36:23 I will prove the holiness of my *g* name,
38: 4 a *g* horde with bucklers and shields,
38:15 on horses, a *g* horde and a mighty army?
38:19 be a *g* shaking upon the land of Israel.
39:17 a *g* slaughter on the mountains of Israel:
47:10 of fish shall be like those of the *G* Sea,
47:15 from the *G* Sea in the direction of Hethlon,
47:19 to the Wadi of Egypt, and on to the *G* Sea.
47:20 the *G* Sea forms the boundary up to a point
48:28 to the Wadi of Egypt, and on to the *G* Sea.
Dn 2: 6 from me gifts and presents and *g* honors.
2:10 never has any king, however *g* and mighty,
2:35 a *g* mountain and filled the whole earth.
2:45 The *g* God has revealed to the king what
3:42 deal with us in your kindness and *g* mercy.
3:100 How *g* are his signs,
4: 7 of *g* height at the center of the world.
4:19 has become so *g* as to touch the heavens,
4:27 in Babylon, the king said, "Babylon the *g!*
4:27 Was it not I, with my *g* strength,
5: 1 a *g* banquet for a thousand of his lords,
5:18 a *g* kingdom and glorious majesty.
5:19 Because he made him so *g*,
6:24 This gave the king *g* joy.
7: 2 four winds of heaven stirred up the *g* sea,
7: 7 it had *g* iron teeth with which it devoured
7:17 "These four *g* beasts stand for four
8: 3 by the river a ram with two *g* horns,
8: 8 of its power the *g* horn was shattered,
8:21 *g* horn on its forehead is the first king.
9: 4 confessed, "Ah, Lord, *g* and awesome God,
9:18 not on our just deeds, but on your *g* mercy.
10: 1 a *g* war; he understood it from the vision.
10: 4 month I was on the bank of the *g* river,
10: 7 but *g* fear seized the men who were with me;
10: 8 So I was left alone, seeing this *g* vision.
11: 3 king shall appear and rule with *g* might,
11:10 shall prepare and assemble a *g* armed host,
11:11 whose *g* host shall make a stand but shall
11:13 with this large army and *g* resources.
11:25 meet the king of the south with a *g* army;

11:28 turn back toward his land with *g* riches,
11:40 with chariots and horsemen and a *g* fleet,
11:44 out with *g* fury to slay and to doom many.
12: 1 there shall arise Michael, the *g* prince,
14:18 at the table and cried aloud, *G* you are,
14:23 a *g* dragon which the Babylonians worshiped.
14:41 The king cried aloud, "You are *g*,
Hos 3: 2 lands, for *g* shall be the day of Jezreel.
5:13 to Assyria, and Judah sent to the *g* king.
9: 7 Because your iniquity is great, *g*,
10: 6 to Assyria, as an offering to the *g* king.
Jl 2:11 For *g* is the day of the LORD,
2:21 for the LORD has done *g* things.
2:25 cutter, my *g* army which I sent among you.
3: 4 Day of the Lord, the *g* and terrible day
4:13 The vats overflow, for *g* is their malice.
Am 3: 9 and see the *g* disorders within her,
6: 2 and see, go from there to Hamath the *g*,
6:11 the command to shatter the *g* house to bits,
7: 4 It had devoured the *g* abyss,
Jon 1: 2 "Set out for the *g* city of Nineveh,
1:10 were seized with *g* fear and said to him.
1:16 Struck with *g* fear of the LORD,
3: 2 "Set out for the *g* city of Nineveh,
3: 5 a fast and all of them, *g* and small,
4:11 not be concerned over Nineveh, the *g* city,
Mi 7: 3 a price, The *g* man speaks as he pleases,
Na 1: 3 The LORD is slow to anger, yet *g* in power,
3:10 and all her *g* men were put into chains.
Zep 1:14 their wine, Near is the *g* day of the LORD,
Zec 2: 6 *g* is its width and how great its length."
4: 7 What are you, O *g* mountain?
7:13 the LORD of hosts in his *g* anger said that,
9: 5 she shall be in *g* anguish;
12:11 as *g* as the mourning of Hadadrimmon
14:13 be among them a *g* tumult from the LORD:
14:14 gold, silver, and garments, in *g* abundance.
Mal 1: 5 see it, and you will say, *G* is the LORD,
1:11 setting, my name is *g* among the nations;
1:11 For *g* is my name among the nations,
1:14 For a *g* King am I,
3:23 of the LORD comes, the *g* and terrible day.
3:24 of the LORD comes, the *g* and terrible day.
Mt 4:16 living in darkness has seen a *g* light.
4:25 The *g* crowds that followed him came from
5:12 rejoice, for your reward is *g* in heaven;
5:19 commands shall be *g* in the kingdom of God.
5:35 Jerusalem (it is the city of the *g* King);
8: 1 from the mountain, *g* crowds followed him.
9:33 to speak, to the *g* surprise of the crowds.
13: 2 Such *g* crowds gathered around him that he
15:28 said in reply, "Woman, you have *g* faith!
15:31 The result was *g* astonishment in the
19: 2 *G* crowds followed him and he cured them
20:25 their *g* ones make their importance felt.
24:11 will rise in *g* numbers to mislead many.
24:24 performing signs and wonders so *g* as to
24:30 clouds of heaven' with power and *g* glory.
26:47 by a *g* crowd with swords and clubs.
Mk 1: 5 of Jerusalem went out to him in *g* numbers.
2: 2 At that they began to gather in *g* numbers.
3: 7 A *g* crowd followed him from Galilee,
3: 8 equally *g* multitude came to him from Judea,
4: 2 He began to instruct them at *g* length,
4:41 A *g* awe overcame them at this.
6:31 People were coming and going in *g* numbers,
6:34 and he began to teach them at *g* length.
8: 3 Some of them have come a *g* distance."
9:42 a *g* millstone fastened around his neck.
10:42 their *g* ones make their importance felt.
13: 2 said to him, "You see these *g* buildings?
13:26 in the clouds with *g* power and glory.
16: 8 and because of their *g* fear,
Lk 1:15 for he will be *g* in the eyes of the Lord.
1:32 *G* will be his dignity and he will be
1:49 God who is mighty has done *g* things for me,
2:10 of *g* joy to be shared by the whole people.
4:25 years and a *g* famine spread over the land.
5: 6 Upon doing this they caught such a *g*
5:15 and *g* crowds gathered to hear him and to
5:29 gave a *g* reception for Jesus in his house,
6:23 for your reward shall be *g* in heaven.
6:35 Then will your recompense be *g*.
7:16 "A *g* prophet has risen among us,"
7:47 because of her *g* love.
8:37 neighborhood, for a *g* fear had seized them;
14:25 one occasion when a *g* crowd was with him,
15:14 a *g* famine broke out in that country and
16:26 you and us there is fixed a *g* abyss,
21:11 There will be *g* earthquakes,
21:11 and in the sky fearful omens and *g* signs.
21:23 the wrath against this people will be *g*.
21:27 coming on a cloud with *g* power and glory.
21:34 The *g* day will suddenly close in on you
23:27 A *g* crowd of people followed him,
Jn 5:13 so *g* that Jesus had been able to slip away.
5:20 Yes, to your *g* wonderment,
12: 9 The *g* crowd of Jews discovered he was
12:12 The next day the *g* crowd that had come for
21:11 In spite of the *g* number,
Acts 2:20 of that *g* and glorious day of the Lord.
4:33 Jesus, and *g* respect was paid to them all;
5: 5 *G* fear came upon all who later heard of it.

5:11 *G* fear came on the whole church and on all
5:13 fact that the people held them in *g* esteem.
5:14 more believers, men and women in *g* numbers,
6: 8 *g* wonders and signs among the people.
7:11 and *g* trial came upon Egypt and Canaan,
8: 1 a *g* persecution of the church in Jerusalem.
8: 9 himself off as someone of *g* importance.
8:10 "He is the power of the *g* God,"
8:13 signs and the *g* miracles as they occurred,
11:21 *g* number of them believed
11:26 with the church and instructed *g* numbers.
13:17 He made this people *g* during their sojourn
15: 3 story caused *g* joy among the brothers.
15:31 was *g* delight at the encouragement it gave.
17: 4 *g* number of Greeks sympathetic to Judaism,
17:11 and welcomed the message with *g* enthusiasm.
19:17 Lord Jesus came to be held in *g* reverence.
19:26 this Paul has persuaded *g* numbers of
19:27 *g* goddess Artemis will count for nothing.
19:35 custodian of the temple of the *g* Artemis,
20:12 To the *g* comfort of the people,
21:40 A *g* hush fell on them as he began to speak
22: 6 a *g* light from the sky suddenly flashed
24: 2 through your efforts we enjoy *g* peace.
25:23 Agrippa and Bernice came with *g* pomp
26:22 stand here to testify to *g* and small alike.
26:24 And your *g* learning is driving you mad!"
28:23 him and came to his lodgings in *g* numbers.
Rom 9: 2 is *g* grief and constant pain in my heart.
1Cor 13: 2 if I have faith *g* enough to move mountains,
2Cor 2: 4 is why I wrote you in *g* sorrow and anguish,
2: 4 to help you realize the *g* love I bear you.
2: 7 not be crushed by too *g* a weight of sorrow.
3: 4 This *g* confidence in God is ours,
8:22 this work because of his *g* trust in you.
10:10 and his word makes no *g* impact.
12:12 I have performed among you with *g* patience
Eph 1:18 know the *g* hope to which he has called you,
2: 4 because of his *g* love for us he brought us
2: 7 he might display the *g* wealth of his favor,
5:32 This is a *g* foreshadowing;
Phil 4:10 It gave me *g* joy in the Lord that your
Col 4:11 They have been a *g* comfort to me.
1Thes 1: 6 Lord, receiving the word despite *g* trials,
2: 2 tidings to you in the face of *g* opposition.
1Tm 6: 6 There is, of course, *g* gain in religion
6:10 faith, and have come to grief amid *g* pain.
2Tm 1:18 he stands before the Lord on the *g* Day,
4:11 with you, for he can be of *g* service to me.
4:14 the coppersmith did me a *g* deal of harm;
Ti 2:13 the *g* God and of our Savior Christ Jesus.
3: 8 *g* weight on the things I have been saying,
Phlm 1: 7 I find *g* joy and comfort in your love,
Heb 2: 3 if we ignore a salvation as *g* as ours?
4:14 we have a *g* high priest who has passed
10:21 a *g* priest who is over the house of God,
10:32 you endured a *g* contest of suffering.
10:35 it will have *g* reward.
13:20 who brought up from the dead the *g*
Jas 3: 5 a small member, yet it makes *g* pretensions.
1Pt 1: 3 he who in his *g* mercy gave us new birth;
2Pt 1: 4 us the *g* and precious things he promised,
2Jn 1: 4 It has given me *g* joy to find some of your
3Jn 1: 3 For it has given me *g* joy to have the
Jude 1: 6 darkness against the judgment of the *g* day.
Rv 6:17 The *g* day of vengeance has come.
7:14 who have survived the *g* period of trial;
9:14 up on the banks of the *g* river Euphrates!"
11: 8 will lie in the streets of the *g* city,
11:17 You have assumed your *g* power,
11:18 who revere you, the *g* and the small alike;
12: 1 A *g* sign appeared in the sky,
13: 2 and throne, together with *g* authority.
13:13 It performed *g* prodigies;
13:16 It forced all men, small and *g*,
14: 8 "Fallen, fallen is Babylon the *g*,
15: 1 heaven another sign, *g* and awe-inspiring;
16:12 out his bowl on the *g* river Euphrates.
16:14 battle on the *g* day of God the Almighty.
16:19 The *g* city was split into three parts,
16:19 God remembered Babylon the *g*,
17: 1 judgment in store for the *g* harlot
17: 5 written a symbolic name, "Babylon the *g*,
17:18 The woman you saw is the *g* city which has
18: 1 His authority was so *g* that all the earth
18: 2 "Fallen, fallen is Babylon the *g!*
18:10 "Alas, alas, *g* city that you are,
18:16 "Alas, alas, the *g* city,
18:17 hour this *g* wealth has been destroyed!"
18:18 city could have compared with this *g* one!"
18:19 "Alas, alas, the *g* city,
18:21 the *g* city shall be cast down like this,
19: 1 the loud song of a *g* assembly in heaven.
19: 2 He has condemned the *g* harlot who
19: 5 all you his servants, the small and the *g*,
19: 6 what sounded like the shouts of a *g* crowd,
19:17 for the *g* feast God has prepared for you!
19:18 free and the slave, the small and the *g*."
20:12 I saw the dead, the *g* and the lowly,

GREAT-GRANDCHILDREN (1)

Jb 42:16 his grandchildren, and even his *g*.

GREATER (107)

Gn 1:16 great lights, the *g* one to govern the day,
Nm 14:12 of you a nation *g* and mightier then they."
Dt 4:38 your way nations *g* and mightier than you,
7:17 yourselves, 'These nations are *g* than we.
9: 1 nations *g* and stronger than yourselves,
9:14 of you a nation mightier and *g* than they.'
11:23 nations *g* and mightier than yourselves.
20: 1 and chariots and an army *g* than your own,
Jos 11: 8 defeated them and pursued them to *G* Sidon,
19:28 Rehob, Hammon and Kanah, near *G* Sidon.
1Sm 14:30 Philistines by now have been the *g* for it?"
2Sm 19: 8 and this will be a far *g* disaster for you
23:19 and commanded *g* respect than the Thirty,
23:23 and commanded *g* respect than the Thirty.
2Kgs 21: 9 Manasseh misled them into doing even *g* evil
21:11 these abominations and has done *g* evil
1Chr 12:15 over hundreds and the *g* over thousands.
2Chr 2: 4 for our God is *g* than all other gods.
17:12 Jehoshaphat grew steadily *g*.
30:18 The *g* part of the people,
33: 9 doing even *g* evil than the nations
1Mc 4:35 so as to return to Judea with *g* numbers.
14:37 raised the wall of Jerusalem to a *g* height.
2Mc 8:24 and disabled the *g* part of Nicanor's army,
Jb 1: 3 he was *g* than any of the men of the East.
33:12 for God is *g* than man.
Ps(s) 63: 4 For your kindness is a *g* good than life;
135: 5 our Lord is *g* than all gods.
Sir 3:18 Humble yourself the more, the *g* you are,
10:23 but none is *g* than he who fears God.
13: 2 with no one *g* or wealthier than yourself.
25:10 but not *g* than he who fears the LORD.
25:14 a serpent, no venom *g* than that of a woman.
28:10 The more wood, the *g* the fire,
28:10 The *g* a man's strength,
28:10 the greater his power, the *g* his wrath.
30:16 No treasure *g* than a healthy body;
43:29 fathom him, for *g* is he than all his works;
Is 30:26 times *g* [like the light of seven days].
56:12 And tomorrow will be like today, or even *g*."
Lam 4: 6 my people is *g* than the penalty of Sodom,
Ez 8: 6 But you shall see still *g* abominations!
8:13 *g* abominations that they are practicing.
8:15 shall see other abominations, *g* than these!
Dn 4:33 my kingdom, and became much *g* than before.
7:20 which appeared *g* than its fellows.
11: 5 still and govern a domain *g* than his.
11:13 shall raise another army, *g* than before;
11:36 himself and making himself *g* than any god;
11:37 because he shall make himself *g* than all.
Hg 2: 9 *G* will be the future glory of this house
Mt 11:11 man born of woman *g* than John the Baptizer.
11:11 born into the kingdom of God is *g* than he.
12: 6 there is something *g* than the temple here.
12:41 but you have a *g* than Jonah here.
12:42 but you have a *g* than Solomon here.
Mk 12:31 There is no other commandment *g* than
Lk 7:28 there is no man born of woman *g* than John.
7:28 born into the kingdom of God is *g* than he."
11:31 but you have a *g* than Solomon here.
11:32 reformed, but you have a *g* than Jonah here.
14: 8 in case some *g* dignitary has been invited.
16:10 things, you can also trust him in *g*;
16:10 in a slight matter is also unjust in *g*.
22:26 Let the *g* among you be as the junior,
22:27 Who, in fact, is the *g*—
22:44 anguish he prayed with all the *g* intensity,
Jn 1:50 You will see much *g* things than that."
4:12 pretend to be *g* than our ancestor Jacob,
5:20 he will show him even *g* works than these.
5:36 Yet I have testimony *g* than John's,
8:53 pretend to be *g* than our father Abraham,
10:29 My Father is *g* than all,
13:16 assure you, no slave is *g* than his master;
14:12 do the works I do, and *g* far than these.
14:28 to the Father, for the Father is *g* than I.
15:13 There is no *g* love than this:
15:20 no slave is *g* than his master.
19:11 me over to you is guilty of the *g* sin."
Acts 18:26 explained to him God's new way in *g* detail.
1Cor 9:12 right over you, is not our right even *g*?
12:23 honorable by clothing them with *g* care,
12:24 as to give *g* honor to the lowly members,
12:31 Set your hearts on the *g* gifts.
14: 5 is *g* than one who speaks in tongues,
2Cor 3: 8 how much *g* will be the glory of the
3: 9 *g* by far is the glory of the ministry that
3:11 glory, *g* by far is the glory that endures.
4:15 abundance may bring *g* glory to God
7: 7 concern for me, so that my joy is *g* still.
1Thes 4: 1 so you must learn to make still *g* progress.
4:10 Yet we exhort you to even *g* progress,
Heb 6:13 by himself, having no one *g* to swear by.
6:16 Men swear by someone *g* than themselves;
7: 7 that a lesser person is blessed by a *g*.
9:11 passing through the *g* and more perfect
11: 4 Abel offered God a sacrifice *g* than Cain's.
11:26 *g* riches than the treasures of Egypt,
12:25 how much *g* punishment will be ours if we
Jas 4: 6 Yet he bestows a *g* gift,
2Pt 2:11 though *g* than men in strength and power,
1Jn 3:20 *g* than our hearts and all is known to him.
4: 4 is One *g* in you than there is in the world.
5: 9 The testimony of God is much *g*:
Jude 1: 2 peace, and love be yours in ever *g* measure.
Rv 2:19 efforts of recent times are *g* than ever.

GREATEST (24)

Jos 14:15 for Arba, the *g* among the Anakim.
1Chr 17: 8 name great like that of the *g* on the earth.
Jdt 13:13 All the people, from the least to the *g*,
Est 1:20 their husbands, from the *g* to the least."
2Mc 5: 6 over one's own kindred was the *g* failure,
Prv 6:35 nor be satisfied with the *g* gifts.
Sir 50: 1 The *g* among his brethren,
Jer 31:34 All, from least to *g*,
Dn 9:12 bringing upon us in Jerusalem the *g* calamity
11: 2 a fourth shall acquire the *g* riches of all.
Mt 18: 1 is of *g* importance in the kingdom of God?"
18: 4 is of *g* importance in that heavenly reign.
22:36 which commandment of the law is the *g*?"
22:38 This is the *g* and first commandment.
23:11 The *g* among you will be the one who serves
Lk 9:46 among them as to which of them was the *g*.
9:48 for the least one among you is the *g*."
13: 2 think that these Galileans were the *g* sinners
22:24 them about who should be regarded as the *g*.
Jn 7:37 On the last and *g* day of the festival,
1Cor 13:13 hope, and love, and the *g* of these is love.
1Thes 2:17 were seized with the *g* longing to see you.
5:13 them with the *g* love because of their work.
Heb 8:11 for all shall know me, from least to *g*.

GREATLY (50)

Gn 4: 5 Cain *g* resented this and was crestfallen.
7:18 The swelling waters increased *g*,
21:11 Abraham was *g* distressed,
35:22 When Israel heard of it, he was *g* offended.
38: 7 Judah's first-born, *g* offended the LORD;
38:10 What he did *g* offended the LORD,
47:27 property, were fertile, and increased *g*.
Nm 22: 3 the Israelites *g* because of their numbers,
1Sm 12:17 Thus you will see and understand how *g* the
2Kgs 6:11 *G* disturbed over this,
1Chr 14: 2 for his kingdom was *g* exalted for the sake
19: 5 them, for the men had been *g* disgraced.
21: 8 God, "I have sinned *g* in doing this thing.
29: 9 King David also rejoiced *g*.
29:25 Solomon *g* in the eyes of all Israel,
2Chr 16:10 so *g* was he enraged at him over this.
Jdt 2:28 in Azotus and Ascalon also feared him *g*.
4: 2 and *g* alarmed for Jerusalem and the temple
13:17 All the people were *g* astonished.
1Mc 2:70 in Modein, and all Israel mourned him *g*.
3:31 *G* perplexed,
5:63 The valiant Judas and his brothers were *g*
7:48 The people rejoiced *g*,
8:13 and they were *g* exalted.
10:68 Alexander heard of it he was *g* troubled,
11:42 but I will *g* honor you and your nation
13:49 they suffered *g* from hunger,
15: 9 *g* honor you and your nation and the temple,
2Mc 11: 1 being *g* displeased at what had happened,
15:27 *g* over this manifestation of God's power.
Ps(s) 21: 2 in your victory how *g* he rejoices!
65:10 *g* have you enriched it.
105:24 He *g* increased his people and made them
112: 1 the LORD, who *g* delights in his commands.
116:10 even when I said, "I am *g* afflicted";
Wis 3: 5 a little, they shall be *g* blessed,
Is 52:13 he shall be raised high and *g* exalted.
Jer 9:18 Ruined we are, and *g* ashamed;
Dn 5: 9 Then King Belshazzar was *g* terrified;
7:28 I, Daniel, was *g* terrified by my thoughts,
13:64 onward Daniel was *g* esteemed by the people.
Jon 4: 1 But this was *g* displeasing to Jonah,
Mt 2: 3 At this news King Herod became *g* disturbed,
16:21 suffer *g* there at the hands of the elders,
27:19 dream about him today which has *g* upset me."
Mk 15: 5 But *g* to Pilate's surprise,
Lk 22:15 "I have *g* desired to eat this Passover
Acts 9:21 Any who heard it were *g* taken aback.
18:27 he *g* strengthened those who through God's
Rv 17: 6 When I saw her I was *g* astonished.

GREATNESS (24)

Nm 14:17 power of my LORD be displayed in its *g*,
Dt 3:24 to show to your servant your *g* and might.
32: 3 Oh, proclaim the *g* of our God.
Tb 13: 4 them, he has shown you his *g* even there.
Est 5:11 He recounted the *g* of his riches,
E: 3 incapable of bearing such *g*,
10: 2 as a detailed account of the *g* of Mordecai,
1Mc 9:22 and his *g* have not been recorded;
Ps(s) 51: 3 *g* of your compassion wipe out my offense.
145: 3 his *g* is unsearchable.
145: 6 of your terrible deeds and declare your *g*.
Prv 5:23 through the *g* of his folly he will be lost.
Wis 6: 7 shows no partiality, nor does he fear *g*,
13: 5 For from the *g* and the beauty of created
Sir 39:15 Proclaim the *g* of his name,
Is 63: 1 majesty, marching in the *g* of his strength?
Ez 31: 2 What are you like in your *g*?
38:23 I will prove my *g* and holiness and make
Mi 5: 3 his *g* shall reach to the ends of the earth;
Mt 20:26 you who aspires to *g* must serve the rest,
Mk 10:43 you who aspires to *g* must serve the rest;
Lk 1:25 "My being proclaims the *g* of the Lord,
9:43 all who saw it marveled at the *g* of God.
Heb 7: 4 See the *g* of this man to whom Abraham the

GREAVES (1)

1Sm 17: 6 five thousand shekels, and bronze *g*,

GREECE (5)

1Mc 1: 1 king in his place, having first ruled in *G*.
8: 9 of *G* had planned to come and destroy them,
Dn 10:20 When I leave, the prince of *G* will come;
11: 2 he shall rouse all the kingdom of *G*.
Acts 20: 2 Finally he arrived in *G*,

GREED (17)

Jos 6:18 But be careful not to take, in your *g*,
7:21 in my *g* I took them.
1Sm 2:33 to wear out their eyes in consuming *g*;
Jb 20:20 Though he has known no quiet in his *g*,
Ps(s) 10: 3 For the wicked man glories in his *g*,
Prv 19:22 From a man's *g* comes his shame;
23: 7 For in his *g* he is like a storm.
Eccl 4: 8 his toil, and riches do not satisfy his *g*.
Wis 10:11 by him against the *g* of his defrauders,
Sir 14: 7 and in the end he displays his *g*.
Mk 7:22 theft, murder, adulterous conduct, *g*,
Lk 12:15 to the crowd, "Avoid *g* in all its forms.
Rom 1:29 maliciousness, *g*,
1Thes 2: 5 of flattering words or *g* under any pretext,
1Tm 3: 8 not overindulge in drink or give in to *g*.
2Pt 2: 3 with fabricated tales, in a spirit of *g*.
2:14 Their hearts are trained in *g*.

GREEDIER (1)

Sir 31:13 No creature is *g* than the eye:

GREEDILY (1)

Jb 39:30 His young ones *g* drink blood;

GREEDY (14)

Nm 11: 4 The foreign elements among them were so *g*
11:34 it was there that the *g* people were buried.
1Sm 2:29 Why do you keep a *g* eye on my sacrifices
1Mc 4:17 "Do not be *g* for the plunder,
Prv 1:19 This is the fate of everyone *g* of loot:
15:27 is *g* of gain brings ruin on his own house,
28:25 The *g* man stirs up disputes,
Sir 25:20 a woman's beauty, nor be *g* for her wealth;
31:12 man, bring not a *g* gullet to his table,
31:16 table like a favored guest, and be not *g*,
Jer 6:13 Small and great alike, all are *g* for gain;
8:10 Small and great alike, all are *g* for gain,
Hos 4: 8 of my people, and are *g* for their guilt.
Ti 1: 7 arrogant, a drunkard, a violent or *g* man.

GREEK (24)

2Mc 4:10 his countrymen into the *G* way of life.
4:12 the noblest young men to wear the *G* hat.
6: 8 was issued ordering the neighboring *G* cities
11: 2 plan was to make Jerusalem a *G* settlement;
11:24 *G* customs but prefer their own way of life.
13: 2 They led a *G* army of one hundred and ten
Mk 7:26 The woman who was *G*—
Jn 19:20 inscription, in Hebrew, Latin, and *G*,
Acts 6: 1 the ones who spoke *G* complained that their
9:36 woman convert named Tabitha (in *G* Dorcas,
16: 1 and a believer, and whose father was a *G*.
16: 3 knew that it was only his father who was *G*.
17:12 did numerous influential *G* women and men.
21:37 "So you know *G*!"
Rom 1:16 it to salvation, the Jew first, then the *G*.
2: 9 has done evil, the Jew first, then the *G*.
2:10 good, likewise the Jew first, then the *G*.
10:12 there is no difference between Jew and *G*;
1Cor 10:32 to Jew or *G* or to the church of God,
12:13 Spirit that all of us, whether Jew or *G*,
Gal 2: 3 circumcision, despite his being a *G*.
3:28 There does not exist among you Jew or *G*,
Col 3:11 There is no *G* or Jew here,
Rv 9:11 in Hebrew is Abaddon and in *G* Apollyon.

GREEK-SPEAKING (1)

Acts 9:29 addressed the *G* Jews and debated with them.

GREEKS (23)

1Mc 1:10 and thirty-seven of the kingdom of the *G*.
6: 2 king of Macedon, the first king of the *G*.
8:10 *G* a single general who made war on them.
8:18 of the *G* was subjecting Israel to slavery.
2Mc 4:15 highly prized what the *G* esteemed as glory.
4:36 together with the *G* who detested the crime,
6: 9 not consent to adopt the customs of the *G*.
Dn 8:21 The he-goat is the king of the *G*,
Jl 4: 6 people of Judah and Jerusalem to the *G*,

Jn 7:35 not going off to the Diaspora among the G,
12:20 up to worship at the feast were some G.
Acts 11:20 to Antioch began to talk even to the G,
14:1 as to convince a good number of Jews and G.
17:4 a great number of G sympathetic to Judaism,
18:4 in which he persuaded certain Jews and G.
19:10 of the province of Asia, Jews and G alike,
19:17 known to the Jews and G living in Ephesus,
20:21 With Jews and G alike I insisted solemnly
21:28 He has even brought G into the temple area
Rom 1:14 I am under obligation to G and non-Greeks,
3:9 brought the charge against Jews and G alike
1Cor 1:22 demand "signs" and G look for "wisdom,"
1:24 to those who are called, Jews and G alike,

GREEN (32)

Gn 1:30 ground, I give all the g plants for food."
9:3 give them all to you as I did the g plants.
Ex 10:15 Nothing g was left on any tree or plant
1Kgs 14:23 every high hill and under every g tree.
2Kgs 19:26 the plants of the field, like the g growth,
2Mc 10:7 entwined with leaves, g branches and palms,
Jb 8:12 While it is yet g and uncut,
15:32 time, and his branches shall be g no more.
39:8 pasture, and seeks out every patch of g.
Ps(s) 37:2 quickly wither, and like g herbs they wilt.
52:10 I, like a g olive tree in the house of God,
Prv 11:28 fall, but like g leaves the just flourish.
Is 15:6 withered, new growth is gone, nothing is g.
37:27 the plants of the field, like the g growth,
57:5 among the terebinths, under every g tree;
Jer 2:20 On every high hill, under every g tree,
3:6 every g tree she has played the harlot.
3:13 g tree] and would not listen to my voice,
12:4 the g of the whole countryside wither?
17:2 and their sacred poles, beside the g trees,
17:8 the heat when it comes, its leaves stay g;
50:11 Frisk like calves on the g,
Ez 6:13 beneath every g tree and leafy oak,
17:9 so that all its g growth will wither when
17:24 high the lowly tree, Wither up the g tree,
18:2 "Fathers have eaten g grapes,
21:3 devour all trees, the g as well as the dry.
Jl 2:22 for the pastures of the plain are g;
Mk 6:39 down on the g grass in groups or parties.
Lk 23:31 If they do these things in the g wood,
Rv 6:8 Now I saw a horse sickly g in color.
8:7 a third of the trees and every g plant.

GREENISH (2)

Lv 13:49 or on any leather article is g or reddish,
14:37 house consists of g or reddish depressions

GREENS (1)

Prv 27:25 and the mountain g are gathered in,

GREENSWARD (1)

2Sm 23:4 morning, making the g sparkle after rain.'

GREET (32)

Gn 14:17 to g him in the Valley of Shaveh (that is,
18:2 from the entrance of the tent to g them;
19:1 When Lot saw them, he got up to g them;
37:4 him so much that they would not even g him.
1Sm 10:4 They will g you and offer you two wave
13:10 Saul went out to g him,
17:18 G your brothers and bring home some token
25:5 Pay Nabal a visit and g him in my name.
25:14 messengers from the desert to g our master,
2Sm 8:10 King David to g him and to congratulate
2Kgs 4:29 if you meet anyone, do not g him,
1Mc 7:33 elders of the people came out to g him
12:17 also ordered them to come to you and g you,
Jb 3:7 let no joyful outcry g it!
Ps(s) 95:2 Let us g him with thanksgiving;
119:148 My eyes g the night watches
Is 14:9 It awakens the shades to g you,
21:14 land of Tema, g the fugitives with bread.
Mt 5:47 And if you g your brothers only,
25:6 Come out and g him!'
Mk 9:15 They ran up to g him.
Lk 10:4 wear no sandals and g no one along the way.
Rom 16:16 G one another with a holy kiss.
1Cor 16:20 All the brothers g you.
16:20 G one another with a holy kiss.
2Cor 13:12 G one another with a holy kiss.
1Thes 5:26 G all the brothers with a holy embrace.
2Tm 4:19 G Prisca and Aquila and the family of
Ti 3:15 G those who love us in the faith.
1Pt 5:14 G one another with the embrace of true love.
2Jn 1:10 do not even g him,
3Jn 1:15 g the beloved there,

GREETED (22)

Gn 28:1 called Jacob, g him with a blessing,
Ex 18:7 Having g each other,
Jgs 18:15 Levite at the home of Micah and g him.
1Sm 6:13 spied the ark, they g it with rejoicing.
6:19 when they g the ark of the LORD,
15:13 When Samuel came to him, Saul g him:
17:22 the battle line, where he g his brothers.
30:21 On nearing them David g them.
2Sm 18:28 Then Ahimaaz called out and g the king.
1Kgs 8:14 The king turned and g the whole community
2Kgs 10:15 He g him and asked,
2Chr 6:3 the king g the whole community of Israel
Tb 5:10 entered the house, Tobit g him first.
7:1 They g him first.
9:6 He sprang up and g Gabael,
11:17 the wife of his son Tobiah, he g her:
1Mc 7:29 to Judas, and they g one another peaceably.
11:6 g each other and spent the night there.
Lk 1:40 entered Zechariah's house and g Elizabeth.
24:33 They were g with,
Acts 21:7 g the brothers and spent the day with them.
21:19 Paul first g them,

GREETING (11)

Sir 4:8 poor man, and return his g with courtesy;
41:20 appointed share, Of failing to return a g,
Jer 31:23 her cities, they shall again repeat this g:
Lk 1:29 his words, and wondered what his g meant.
1:41 When Elizabeth heard Mary's g,
1:44 The moment your g sounded in my ears,
1Cor 16:21 Paul, who send you this g in my own hand.
Col 4:18 This g is from Paul— in my own hand!
2Thes 3:17 This g is in my own hand—Paul's.
Jas 1:1 God and of the Lord Jesus Christ, sends g.
1Pt 5:13 chosen together with you, sends you g.

GREETINGS (57)

2Kgs 4:26 G," she replied.
Ezr 4:17 West-of-Euphrates, g and the following:
7:12 law of the God of heaven (then, after g):
Tb 5:10 Raphael said, "Hearty g to you!"
7:1 He said to them, G to you too, brothers!
Est E:1 to those responsible for our interests: G!
1Mc 10:18 Alexander sends g to his brother Jonathan.
10:25 Demetrius sends g to the Jewish nation.
11:30 "King Demetrius sends g to his brother
11:32 Demetrius sends g to his father Lasthenes.
12:6 send g to their brothers the Spartans.
12:20 Spartans, sends g to Onias the high priest.
13:36 Demetrius sends g to Simon the high priest,
14:20 of Sparta send g to Simon the high priest,
15:2 "King Antiochus sends g to Simon,
15:16 of the Romans, sends g to King Ptolemy.
2Mc 1:1 the land of Judea send g to their brethren,
1:10 send g and good wishes to Aristobulus,
9:19 sends hearty g and best wishes for their
11:16 "Lysias sends g to the Jewish people.
11:22 Antiochus sends g to his brother Lysias.
11:27 "King Antiochus sends g to the Jewish
11:34 of the Romans, send g to the Jewish people.
Prv 27:6 but the g of an enemy one prays against.
Sir 6:5 and gracious lips prompt friendly g.
Acts 15:23 send g to the brothers of Gentile origin
15:33 they were sent back with g from the
23:26 Lysias sends g to His Excellency Felix,
Rom 1:1 G from Paul, a servant of Christ Jesus,
16:3 Give my g to Prisca and Aquila;
16:5 G to my beloved Epaenetus;
16:6 My g to Mary, who has worked hard
16:8 G to Ampliatus, who is dear to me
16:10 G to Apelles, who proved himself
16:11 G to my kinsman Herodion and to the
16:12 G, too, to Tryphaena and Tryphosa,
16:13 G to Rufus, a chosen servant of the Lord,
16:14 G to Asyncritus,
16:16 All the churches of Christ send you g.
16:21 my fellow worker, sends you his g;
16:22 this letter, send you my g in the Lord.
16:23 G also from Gaius, who is host to me
1Cor 1:2 g to the church of God which is in Corinth;
16:19 The churches of Asia send you g.
16:19 house, send you cordial g in the Lord.
2Cor 13:12 All the holy ones send g to you.
Gal 1:2 with me send g to the churches in Galatia.
Phil 4:21 Give my g in Christ Jesus to every member
Col 4:10 is a prisoner along with me, sends you g.
4:11 Jesus known also as Justus sends g.
4:12 Epaphras, who is one of you, sends g.
4:14 Luke, our dear physician, sends you g.
2Tm 4:21 Claudia, and all the brothers send g.
Ti 3:15 All who are with me send their g.
Heb 13:24 G to all your leaders and to all the
2Jn 1:13 of your elect sister send you their g.
3Jn 1:15 The beloved here send you their g;

GREETS (4)

2Kgs 4:29 do not greet him, and if anyone g you,
Prv 27:14 When one g his neighbor with a loud voice
Phlm 1:23 my fellow prisoner in Christ Jesus, g you,
2Jn 1:11 whoever g him shares in the evil he does.

GREW (86)

Gn 21:8 Isaac g,
21:20 God was with the boy as he g up.
25:27 As the boys g up,
30:43 Thus the man g increasingly prosperous,
43:1 Now the famine in the land g more severe.
Ex 1:20 The people too, increased and g strong.
2:10 When the child g,
16:21 but when the sun g hot,
17:12 Moses' hands, however, g tired;
19:19 The trumpet blast g louder and louder,
Dt 32:15 ate his fill, the darling g fat and frisky;
Jos 17:13 When the Israelites g stronger they
Jgs 1:28 When the Israelites g stronger,
3:25 waited until they finally g suspicious.
13:24 The boy g up and the LORD blessed him;
Ru 1:13 of husbands until those sons g up?
1Sm 2:21 Samuel g up in the service of the LORD.
3:19 Samuel g up,
15:11 At this Samuel g angry and cried out to
17:28 the men, he g angry with David and said:
2Sm 3:1 that of David, in which David g stronger,
5:10 David g steadily more powerful,
12:3 and she g up with him and his children.
12:5 David g very angry with that man and said
21:15 fought the Philistines, but David g tired.
23:10 until his hand g tired and became cramped,
1Kgs 17:17 g more severe until he stopped breathing.
18:45 trice, the sky g dark with clouds and wind,
22:35 The battle g fierce during the day,
2Chr 17:12 Jehoshaphat g steadily greater.
18:34 The battle g fierce during the day,
26:8 as Egypt, for he g stronger and stronger.
Jdt 5:9 Here they settled, and g very rich in gold,
5:10 and g into such a great multitude that the
13:1 When it g late,
Est F:3 the tiny spring that g into a river,
2Mc 4:50 where he g in wickedness and became the
5:27 g wild to avoid sharing the defilement.
Ps(s) 39:4 hot g my heart within me;
105:28 it g dark,
106:40 And the LORD g angry with his people,
Sg 5:4 within me, and I g faint when he spoke.
Wis 16:17 quenches anything, the fire g more active;
Sir 47:24 Their sinfulness g more and more,
Is 43:22 upon me, O Jacob, for you g weary of me,
53:2 He g up like a sapling before him,
Ez 16:7 You g and developed,
17:10 by the east wind, in the bed where it g?
31:5 Thus it g taller than every other tree of
Dn 4:30 his hair g like the feathers of an eagle,
10:20 When he spoke to me, I g strong and said,
Jon 1:13 not, for the sea g ever more turbulent.
4:6 a gourd plant, that g up over Jonah's head,
Mt 13:7 among thorns, which g up and choked it.
22:7 At this the king g furious and sent his
26:8 the disciples saw this they g indignant,
26:20 When it g dark he reclined at table with
28:4 The guards g paralyzed with fear of him
Mk 4:7 among thorns, which g up and choked it off,
4:39 The wind fell off and everything g calm.
5:26 on the contrary, she only g worse.
14:17 As it g dark he arrived with the Twelve.
15:42 As it g dark (it was Preparation Day,
Lk 1:80 The child g up and matured in spirit.
2:40 The child g in size and strength,
8:8 But some fell on good soil, g up,
8:24 The waves subsided and it g calm.
9:34 g fearful as the others entered it.
13:19 It g and became a large shrub and the
14:21 master of the house g angry at the account.
15:28 son g angry at this and would not go in;
18:23 On hearing this he g melancholy,
Jn 13:21 After saying this, Jesus g deeply troubled.
Acts 6:1 those days, as the number of disciples g,
7:17 people in Egypt g more and more numerous,
9:22 Saul for his part g steadily more powerful,
16:5 the congregations g stronger in faith and
17:16 he g exasperated at the sight of idols
22:2 them in Hebrew, they g quieter still.
23:10 the dispute g worse and the commander
Heb 8:9 broke my covenant and I g weary of them,
Rv 6:12 tentcloth and the moon g red as blood.
18:3 g rich from her wealth and wantonness."
18:15 who g rich from business with the city,
18:19 in which all shipowners g rich from their
22:2 On either side of the river g the trees of

GRIDDLE (4)

Lv 2:5 a cereal offering that is fried on a g,
6:14 fried in oil on a g when you bring it in.
7:9 g shall belong to the priest who offers it,
Ez 4:3 Then take an iron g and set it up as an

GRIEF (59)

Gn 42:38 white head down to the nether world in g."
44:29 white head down to the nether world in g.'
44:31 our father down to the nether world in g.
Dt 34:8 the period of g and mourning for Moses.
Tb 3:6 calumnies, and I am overwhelmed with g.
7:17 of heaven grant you joy in place of your g.
9:4 a single day, I would cause him intense g.
10:13 Never cause her g at any time in your life.
Est 6:12 Haman hurried home, his head covered in g.
1Mc 6:8 Sick with g because his designs had failed,
6:13 and now I am dying, in bitter g,
9:20 All Israel bewailed him in great g.
Jb 30:28 I rise up in public to voice my g.

GRIEF (cont.)

Ps(s) 13: 3 in my soul, *g* in my heart day after day?
31:11 is spent with *g* and my years with sighing;
38:18 to falling, and my *g* is with me always.
39: 3 But my *g* was stirred up;
55: 3 I rock with *g*,
Prv 10: 1 but a foolish son is a *g* to his mother.
17:21 To be a fool's parent is *g* for a man;
27: 9 heart, but by *g* the soul is torn asunder.
Eccl 1:18 and he who stores up knowledge stores up *g*.
2:23 his days sorrow and *g* are his occupation;
11:10 Ward off *g* from your heart and put away
Wis 4:19 be in *g* and their memory shall perish.
8: 9 all was well, and my comfort in care and *g*.
8:16 no bitterness and living with her no *g*,
11:12 For a twofold *g* took hold of them and a
14:21 that men enslaved to either *g* or tyranny
Sir 14: 1 Happy the man whose mouth brings him no *g*,
19:22 There is the wicked man who is bowed in *g*,
22: 4 husband, a shameless one is her father's *g*.
26:19 These two bring *g* to my heart,
29:19 The sinner through surety comes to *g*,
30: 9 you, indulge him and he will bring you *g*.
36:20 A deceitful character causes *g*,
38:18 then compose yourself after your *g*,
38:19 For *g* can bring on an extremity and
Is 16: 7 Kir-hareseth they sigh, stricken with *g*.
29: 2 distress upon Ariel, with mourning and *g*.
65:14 *g* of heart and howl for anguish of spirit.
Jer 8:18 My *g* is incurable,
45: 3 the LORD adds *g* to my pain;
Lam 1: 4 she is in bitter *g*.
2: 8 *g* on wall and rampart till both succumbed.
Ez 23:33 so much, Filled with destruction and *g*,
Mt 17:23 these words they were overwhelmed with *g*.
18:14 of these little ones shall ever come to *g*.
Lk 6:25 you shall weep in your *g*.
22:45 only to find them asleep, exhausted with *g*.
Jn 16: 6 to say to you, you are overcome with *g*.
16:20 a time, but your *g* will be turned into joy.
Rom 9: 2 is great *g* and constant pain in my heart.
2Cor 7: 7 you, for he reported your longing, your *g*,
7: 8 that the letter caused you *g* for a time),
1Thes 4:13 otherwise you might yield to *g*,
1Tm 6:10 faith, and have come to *g* amid great pain.
Heb 12:11 seems a cause for *g* and not for joy,
Rv 18: 7 sensuality, repay her in torment and *g*!

GRIEF-STRICKEN (2)

2Sm 13:20 But Tamar remained *g* and forlorn
Tb 3: 1 *G* in spirit, I groaned and wept aloud.

GRIEFS (1)

Jb 9:18 breath, but might fill me with bitter *g*.

GRIEVANCE (4)

Hos 4: 1 a *g* against the inhabitants of the land:
4: 4 with you is my *g*,
12: 3 The LORD has a *g* against Israel:
Mk 11:25 forgive anyone against whom you have a *g*

GRIEVANCES (1)

Col 3:13 whatever *g* you have against one another.

GRIEVE (14)

Dt 28:32 on and *g* for them in constant helplessness.
1Sm 1: 8 Why do you *g*?
16: 1 "How long will you *g* for Saul,
2Sm 1:26 "I *g* for you, Jonathan my brother!
Tb 4: 3 her, and do not *g* her spirit in any way.
13:14 Happy are all the men who shall *g* over you,
Ps(s) 38:19 I *g* over my sin.
55:18 at dawn, and at noon, I will *g* and moan,
Sir 3:12 *g* him not as long as he lives.
4: 2 A hungry man *g* not,
Bar 4:33 so shall she *g* over her own desolation.
Ez 32: 9 I will *g* the hearts of many peoples when I
Zec 12:10 and they shall *g* over him as one grieves
Jn 16:20 you will *g* for a time,

GRIEVED (23)

Gn 6: 6 made man on the earth, and his heart was *g*.
Nm 11:10 that the LORD became very angry, he was *g*.
Jgs 10:16 so that he *g* over the misery of Israel.
1Sm 15:35 Yet he *g* over Saul,
20: 3 must not know of this lest he be *g*.'
20:34 the month, for he was *g* on David's account,
Tb 2:10 and all my kinsmen were *g* at my condition.
3:10 That day she was deeply *g* in spirit.
7: 7 lost his eyesight, he was *g* and wept aloud.
1Mc 14:16 that Jonathan had died, they were deeply *g*.
2Mc 4:37 Antiochus was deeply *g* and full of pity;
Jb 30:25 was not my soul *g* for the destitute?
31:39 payment and *g* the hearts of its tenants;
Ps(s) 78:40 in the desert and *g* him in the wilderness!
Sir 49: 2 For he *g* over our betrayals,
Is 54: 6 back, like a wife forsaken and *g* in spirit,
63:10 But they rebelled, and *g* his holy spirit;
Bar 2:18 He whose soul is deeply *g*,
4: 8 you, and you *g* Jerusalem who fostered you.
Ez 13:22 man with lies when I did not wish him *g*,
Dn 6:15 The king was deeply *g* at this news and he
Mk 3: 5 for he was deeply *g* that they had closed
2Cor 2: 2 can make me happy again but the ones I *g*?

GRIEVES (2)

Jb 14:22 flesh pains him, and his soul *g* for him.
Zec 12:10 grieve over him as one *g* over a first-born.

GRIEVING (4)

2Sm 19: 3 they heard that the king was *g* for his son.
Lam 3:33 no joy in afflicting or *g* the sons of men.
Mk 16:10 his followers, who were now *g* and weeping.
1Cor 5: 2 to be self-satisfied, instead of *g*,

GRIEVOUS (8)

2Chr 24:25 from him, leaving him in *g* suffering,
Eccl 5:12 a *g* evil which I have seen under the sun:
5:15 This too is a *g* evil,
Wis 19:13 their guests with the more *g* hatred.
Sir 18:10 sees and understands that their death is *g*,
Is 17:11 shall disappear on the day of the *g* blow,
Jer 30:12 Incurable is your wound, *g* your bruise;
Am 5:12 how many are your crimes, how *g* your sins:

GRIEVOUSLY (6)

1Sm 2:17 men sinned *g* in the presence of the LORD;
2Sm 24:10 "I have sinned *g* in what I have done.
Neh 1: 7 *G* have we offended you,
Ez 20:13 My sabbaths, too, they desecrated *g*.
23:10 byword for women, for they punished her *g*.
25:12 *g* guilty by taking vengeance on them,

GRIND (10)

Ex 30:36 *G* some of it into fine dust and put this
Nm 11: 8 the people would *g* it between millstones
Jgs 8: 7 I will *g* your flesh in with the thorns and
Jb 19: 2 will you vex my soul, *g* me down with words?
31:10 Then may my wife *g* for another,
Is 47: 2 Take the millstone and *g* flour,
Mt 13:42 where they will wail and *g* their teeth.
13:50 where they will wail and *g* their teeth.
22:13 out into the night to wail and *g* his teeth.'
25:30 outside, where he can wail and *g* his teeth.'

GRINDERS (1)

Eccl 12: 3 And the *g* are idle because they are few,

GRINDING (8)

Jgs 16:21 fetters, and he was put to *g* in the prison.
2Kgs 23:15 up the stones and *g* them to powder,
Is 3:15 and *g* down the poor when they look to you?
Mt 8:12 will be heard there, and the *g* of teeth."
24:41 Two women will be *g* meal;
24:51 There will be wailing then and *g* of teeth.
Lk 13:28 and *g* of teeth when you see Abraham,
17:35 Two women will be *g* grain together;

GRINDS (1)

Mk 9:18 mouth and *g* his teeth and becomes rigid.

GRIP (16)

1Sm 12: 9 and into the *g* of the king of Moab,
23: 7 "God has put him in my *g*.
30:23 into our *g* the band that came against us.
2Sm 5:19 will you deliver them into my *g*?"
5:19 surely deliver the Philistines into your *g*."
19:10 rescued us from the *g* of the Philistines.
2Chr 36:17 he delivered all of them over into his *g*.
Jb 8: 4 he has left them in the *g* of their guilt,
Ps(s) 22:21 sword, my loneliness from the *g* of the dog.
31: 9 Not shutting me up in the *g* of the enemy
Sir 6: 2 Fall not into the *g* of desire,
Is 22:17 He shall *g* you firmly And roll you up and
Lam 1:14 The LORD has delivered me into their *g*,
Lk 4:38 was in the *g* of a severe fever,
Acts 8:23 with gall and caught in the *g* of sin."
10:38 healing all who were in the *g* of the devil,

GRIPPED (8)

Gn 41:56 since the famine had *g* the land of Egypt.
41:57 of grain, for famine had *g* the whole world.
Ex 15:14 anguish *g* the dwellers in Philistia.
2Kgs 2:12 *g* his own garment and tore it in two.
25: 3 fourth month, when famine had *g* the city,
Jdt 5:10 when famine had *g* the whole land of Canaan,
Jer 52: 6 when famine had *g* the city and the people
Rv 11:11 feet sheer terror *g* those who saw them.

GRIPPING (1)

Gn 25:26 His brother came out next, *g* Esau's heel;

GRIPS (2)

Is 33:14 are in dread, trembling *g* the impious:
Dn 11:40 king of the south shall come to *g* with him,

GRITS (3)

Lv 2:14 the form of fresh *g* of new ears of grain,
2:16 shall then burn some of the *g* and oil,
Prv 27:22 with the pestle, amid the *g* in a mortar,

GROAN (19)

Jb 24:12 From the dust the dying *g*,
Prv 5:11 And you *g* in the end,
29: 2 but when the wicked rule, the people *g*.
Sir 12:12 my advice, when you *g* with regret,
Is 24: 7 vine languishes, all the merry-hearted *g*.
Jer 22:23 How you shall *g* when pains come upon you,
51:52 and in her whole land the wounded will *g*.
Lam 1: 4 her gateways are deserted, her priests *g*,
1:11 All her people *g*,
Ez 9: 4 who moan and *g* over all the abominations
21:11 As for you, son of man, *g*!
21:11 strength *g* bitterly while they look on.
24:17 *G* in silence, make no lament for the dead,
24:23 because of your sins and *g* one to another.
Jl 1:18 How the beasts *g*!
Mk 7:34 he looked up to heaven and emitted a *g*.
Rom 8:23 *g* inwardly while we await the redemption
2Cor 5: 2 We *g* while we are here,
5: 4 While we live in our present tent we *g*;

GROANED (5)

Ex 2:23 *g* and cried out because of their slavery.
Tb 3: 1 in spirit, I *g* and wept aloud.
1Mc 1:26 dwelt, and the rulers and the elders *g*.
2Mc 6:30 to die under the blows, he *g* and said:
Dn 13:22 am completely trapped," Susanna *g*.

GROANING (18)

Ex 2:24 he heard their *g* and was mindful of his
6: 5 that I have heard the *g* of the Israelites,
Jdt 14:16 He broke into a loud clamor of weeping, *g*,
Ps(s) 32: 3 my bones wasted away with my *g* all the day,
38:10 from you my *g* is not hid.
102:21 the earth, To hear the *g* of the prisoners,
Wis 5: 3 rueful and *g* through anguish of spirit:
11:12 *g* at the remembrance of the ones
Sir 41: 9 you will beget them only for *g*.
47:20 your descendants, and *g* upon your domain;
Is 21: 2 I will put an end to all *g*!"
Jer 45: 3 I am weary from *g*,
Lam 1:21 "Give heed to my *g*;
2: 5 Judah he has multiplied moaning and *g*.
Ez 21:12 And when they ask you, "Why are you *g*?",
26:15 of your fall, at the *g* of the wounded,
Mal 2:13 LORD you cover with tears, weeping and *g*,
Acts 7:34 my people in Egypt and have heard their *g*,

GROANINGS (2)

Jb 23: 2 bitter, his hand is heavy upon me in my *g*.
Rom 8:26 with *g* that cannot be expressed in speech.

GROANS (5)

Jb 3:24 than food, and my *g* well forth like water.
Sir 30:20 who *g* at the good things his eyes behold!
Lam 1: 8 She herself *g* and turns away.
1:22 My *g* are many,
Rom 8:22 creation *g* and is in agony even until now.

GROOM (17)

Ps(s) 19: 6 like the *g* from his bridal chamber and,
Mt 6:17 it that you *g* your hair and wash your face.
9:15 in mourning so long as the *g* is with them?
9:15 the day comes that the *g* is taken away,
25: 1 torches and went out to welcome the *g*.
25: 5 The *g* delayed his coming,
25: 6 midnight someone shouted, 'The *g* is here!
25:10 they went off to buy it the *g* arrived,
Mk 2:19 fast as long as the *g* is still among them?
2:19 So long as the *g* stays with them,
2:20 when the *g* will be taken away from them;
Lk 5:34 *g* fast while the groom is still with them?
5:35 that the *g* is removed from their midst,
Jn 2: 9 called the *g* over and remarked to him:
3:29 "It is the *g* who has the bride.
Rv 18:23 and *g* shall ever again be heard in you!

GROOM'S (1)

Jn 3:29 The *g* best man waits there listening for

GROPE (5)

Dt 28:29 you will *g* like a blind man in the dark,
Jb 5:14 at noonday they *g* as though it were night,
12:25 till they *g* in the darkness without light;
Is 59:10 Like blind men we *g* along the wall,
Acts 17:27 yes to *g* for him and perhaps eventually to

GROPED (1)

Acts 13:11 and he *g* about for someone to lead him by

GROSS (2)

Dt 32:15 you became fat and *g* and gorged.
Ps(s) 119:70 Their heart has become *g* and fat;

GROUND (283)

Gn 1:26 and all the creatures that crawl on the *g*."
1:30 the living creatures that crawl on the *g*,
2: 6 and was watering all the surface of the *g*—
2: 7 God formed man out of the clay of the *g*
2: 9 Out of the *g* the LORD God made various
2:19 So the LORD God formed out of the *g*
3:17 to eat, "Cursed be the *g* because of you!
3:19 bread to eat, Until you return to the *g*,
3:23 to till the *g* from which he had been taken.
5:29 very *g* that the LORD has put under a curse,
7: 8 and of everything that creeps on the *g*,
8:13 that the surface of the *g* was drying up.
9: 2 on the *g* and all the fishes of the sea;
18: 2 and bowing to the *g*,
19: 1 and bowing down with his face to the *g*,
23: 4 a piece of property for a burial *g*,
23: 6 his burial *g* for the burial of your dead."
24:52 answer, he bowed to the *g* before the LORD.
28:12 a stairway rested on the *g*,
33: 3 ahead of them, bowing to the *g* seven times,
33:19 The plot of *g* on which he had pitched his
37:10 are to come and bow to the *g* before you?"
38: 9 widow, he wasted his seed on the *g*,
42: 6 down before him with their faces to the *g*,
43:26 while they bowed down before him to the *g*.
44:11 lowered his bag to the *g* and opened it,
44:14 they flung themselves on the *g* before him.
48:12 down before him with his face to the *g*.
49:30 from Ephron the Hittite for a burial *g*.
50:13 for a burial *g* from Ephron the Hittite.
Ex 3: 5 for the place where you stand is holy *g*.
4: 3 The LORD then said, "Throw it on the *g*."
4: 3 it on the *g* it was changed into a serpent,
8:17 very *g* on which they stand shall be filled.
10: 5 They shall cover the *g*,
10: 5 so that the *g* itself will not be visible.
14:13 Stand your *g*,
16:14 were fine flakes like hoarfrost on the *g*.
16:25 day you will not find any of it on the *g*.
27: 5 Put it down around the altar, on the *g*.
32:20 in the fire and then *g* it down to powder,
34: 8 at once bowed down to the *g* in worship.
38: 4 the altar and placed round it, on the *g*,
Lv 11:21 have jointed legs for leaping on the *g*;
11:29 "Of the creatures that swarm on the *g*,
11:41 the *g* are loathsome and shall not be eaten.
11:44 any swarming creature that crawls on the *g*.
11:46 move about in the water or swarm on the *g*,
16:12 handful of finely *g* fragrant incense,
Nm 11:31 two cubits from the *g* for the distance
16:30 and the *g* opens its mouth and swallows
16:31 this than the *g* beneath them split open,
22:31 he fell on his knees and bowed to the *g*.
Dt 4:18 of anything that crawls on the *g* or of any
8:15 scorpions, its parched and waterless *g*;
9:21 I *g* it down to powder as fine as dust,
11: 6 when the *g* opened its mouth and swallowed
12:16 but must pour it out on the *g* like water.
12:24 but pour it out on the *g* like water.
15:23 must be poured out on the *g* like water.
22: 6 or eggs in it, in any tree or on the *g*,
28:56 to set the sole of her foot on the *g*,
28:65 no repose, not a foot of *g* to stand upon,
29:18 both the watered soil and the parched *g*,
32:13 and olive oil from its hard, stony *g*;
Jos 3:17 While all Israel crossed over on dry *g*,
3:17 remained motionless on dry *g* in the bed
4:18 soles of their feet regained the dry *g*,
4:22 'Israel crossed the Jordan here on dry *g*.'
5:14 Joshua fell prostrate to the *g* in worship,
7:21 are now hidden in the *g* inside my tent,
24:32 *g* Jacob had bought from the sons of Hamor,
Jgs 4:21 the peg through his temple down into the *g*,
6:37 the fleece alone, while all the *g* is dry,
6:39 be dry, but let there be dew on all the *g*."
6:40 was dry, but there was dew on all the *g*.
8:16 and *g* these men of Succoth into them.
13:20 saw this, they fell prostrate to the *g*;
20:36 for the men of Israel gave *g* to Benjamin,
Ru 2:10 Casting herself prostrate upon the *g*,
1Sm 5: 3 prone on the *g* before the ark of the LORD.
5: 4 prone on the *g* before the ark of the LORD,
7: 6 and poured it out on the *g* before the LORD,
14:25 there was a honeycomb lying on the *g*,
14:32 on the *g* and eating the flesh with blood.
14:45 hair of his head shall fall to the *g*,
17:49 his brow, and he fell prostrate on the *g*.
20:41 *g* three times before Jonathan in homage.
24: 9 bowed to the *g* in homage and asked Saul:
25:23 falling prostrate on the *g* before David,
25:41 Rising and bowing to the *g*,
26: 7 with his spear thrust into the *g* at his head
26: 8 him to the *g* with one thrust of the spear;
26:20 to the *g* far from the presence of the LORD.
28:14 and so he bowed face to the *g* in homage.
28:20 Saul fell full length on the *g*,
28:23 to their entreaties, got up from the *g*,
30: 3 to find it burned to the *g* and their wives,
30:16 the Amalekites scattered all over the *g*,
2Sm 1: 2 Going to David, he fell to the *g* in homage.
2:22 Why must I strike you to the *g*?
8: 2 with a line, making them lie down on the *g*.
12:16 night to lie on the *g* clothed in sackcloth.
12:17 beside him urging him to rise from the *g*:
12:20 Rising from the *g*, David washed
13:31 rent his garments, and then lay on the *g*.
14: 4 king and fell prostrate to the *g* in homage,
14:11 not a hair of your son shall fall to the *g*."
14:14 out on the *g* and cannot be gathered up.
14:22 to the *g* in homage and blessing the king,
14:33 fell on his face to the *g* before the king.
17:12 down upon him as dew alights on the *g*.
17:19 strewing *g* grain on the cover so that
18:11 you not strike him to the *g* on the spot?
18:28 the *g* he paid homage to the king and said,
20:10 so that his entrails burst forth to the *g*,
22:43 I *g* them fine as the dust of the earth;
23:10 but he stood his *g* and fought the
24:20 homage to the king, with face to the *g*.
1Kgs 7:46 the clayey *g* between Succoth and Zarethan.
20:23 But if we fight them on level *g*,
20:25 Let us fight them on level *g*,
2Kgs 2: 8 divided, and both crossed over on dry *g*.
2:15 to meet him, bowing to the *g* before him.
9:26 repay you for it in that very plot of *g*,
9:26 So now take him into this plot of *g*,
13:18 Elisha said to him, "Strike the *g*!"
13:18 He struck the *g* three times and stopped.
1Chr 11:14 He made a stand on the sown *g*,
21:16 prostrated themselves face to the *g*,
21:21 bowed down before David, his face to the *g*.
21:22 "Sell me the *g* of this threshing floor,
2Chr 4:17 the clayey *g* between Succoth and Zeredah.
20:18 knelt down with his face to the *g*,
20:24 they saw only corpses fallen on the *g*,
Neh 8: 6 before the LORD, their faces to the *g*.
9:11 on dry *g* they passed through the midst of
Tb 12:16 with fear, the two men fell to the *g*.
12:20 So now get up from the *g* and praise God.
14: 4 to the *g* and shall be desolate for a while.
Jdt 5:18 for them, they were *g* down steadily,
5:18 temple of their God was razed to the *g*,
10: 2 to the God of Israel, she rose from the *g*.
12:15 went ahead and spread out on the *g* for her
14:18 Here is Holofernes headless on the *g*!"
16: 4 to the sword, Dash my babes to the *g*,
1Mc 4:40 ashes and fell with their faces to the *g*,
6:40 the heights, while some were on low *g*,
6:46 The beast fell to the *g* on top of him,
10:81 But his men held their *g*,
2Mc 3:27 Suddenly he fell to the *g*,
8: 3 and about to be leveled to the *g*;
8: 8 When Philip saw that Judas was gaining *g*
9: 8 to the *g* and had to be carried on a litter,
9:14 to the *g* and making it a common graveyard;
14:33 I will level this shrine of God to the *g*;
Jb 1:20 He cast himself prostrate upon the *g*,
2:13 the *g* with him seven days and seven nights,
5: 6 nor does trouble spring out of the *g*;
15:29 with no shadow to lengthen over the *g*.
16:13 mercy, he pours out my gall upon the *g*.
18:10 A noose for him is hid on the *g*,
38:27 *g* till the desert blooms with verdure?
39:14 on the *g* and deposits them in the sand,
39:24 Frenzied and trembling he devours the *g*;
Ps(s) 7: 6 let him trample my life to the *g*,
17:11 crouching to the *g*,
18:43 I *g* them fine as the dust before the wind;
26:12 My foot stands on level *g*;
80:10 You cleared the *g* for it,
83:11 they became dung on the *g*.
89:45 his luster and hurled his throne to the *g*.
107:33 into desert, water springs into thirsty *g*,
143: 3 he has crushed my life to the *g*;
143:10 May your good spirit guide me on level *g*.
147: 6 the wicked he casts to the *g*.
Eccl 10: 7 while princes walked on the *g* like slaves.
Wis 12:19 And you gave your sons good *g* for hope
Sir 10:16 down their stem to the level of the *g*,
20:17 *g* is less sudden than a slip of the tongue;
50:17 to the *g* In adoration before the Most High,
Is 3:26 mourn, as the city sits desolate on the *g*.
14:12 How are you cut down to the *g*,
21: 9 images of her gods are smashed to the *g*.'"
26: 5 He tumbles it to the *g*,
28: 2 overflowing, levels to the *g* with violence;
30:23 rain for the seed that you sow in the *g*,
30:24 oxen and the asses that till the *g* will eat
35: 7 will become pools, and the thirsty *g*,
41:18 and the dry *g* into springs of water,
44: 3 I will pour out water upon the thirsty *g*,
47: 1 Sit on the *g*,
49:23 Bowing to the *g*,
51:23 While you offered your back like the *g*,
63: 6 and I let their blood run out upon the *g*."
Jer 4: 3 Till your untilled *g*,
8: 2 burial, but will lie like dung upon the *g*.
16: 4 unburied they will lie like dung on the *g*.
23:12 their way shall become for them slippery *g*.
46:21 turn and flee together, stand not their *g*,
48:18 Come down from glory, sit on the *g*,
Lam 2: 2 the *g* in dishonor her king and her princes.
2: 9 Sunk into the *g* are her gates;
2:10 On the *g* in silence sit the old men of
2:10 of Jerusalem bow their heads to the *g*.
2:11 My gall is poured out on the *g* because of
Bar 5: 7 depths and gorges be filled to level *g*,
6:19 of the *g* consume them and their garments,
6:26 confusion because, if they fall to the *g*,
Ez 1:15 living creatures, I saw wheels on the *g*,
1:19 living creatures were raised from the *g*,
13:14 you have whitewashed and level it to the *g*,
16: 5 thrown out on the *g* as something loathsome,
19:12 was torn up in fury and flung to the *g*;
26: 4 the *g* from her and leave her a bare rock;
26:11 your mighty pillars he shall pull to the *g*.
26:16 clothed in mourning and, sitting on the *g*,
34:14 heights of Israel shall be their grazing *g*.
34:14 they shall lie down on good grazing *g*,
36:18 the blood which they poured out on the *g*,
38:20 and all the reptiles that crawl upon the *g*,
38:20 tumble, and every wall shall fall to the *g*.
41:16 around, covered from the *g* to the windows.
41:20 From the *g* to the lintel of the door the
42: 6 *g* than the closest and the middle chambers.
Dn 7: 4 from the *g* to stand on two feet like a man,
8: 5 the whole earth without touching the *g*.
8: 7 not the force to withstand it, to the *g*,
8:12 It cast truth to the *g*,
Hos 2:20 and with the things that crawl on the *g*.
Am 2:13 I will crush you into the *g* as a wagon
2:15 his life, nor the bowman stand his *g*;
3: 5 up from the *g* without catching anything?
3:14 shall be broken off and fall to the *g*.
5: 7 to wormwood and cast justice to the *g*!
9: 9 a sieve, letting no pebble fall to the *g*.
9:15 I will plant them upon their own *g*;
Mi 7:17 like the serpent, like reptiles on the *g*;
Hg 1:11 oil, and upon all that the *g* brings forth;
Mt 7:26 foolish man who built his house on sandy *g*.
10:29 to the *g* without your Father's consent.
13: 5 Part of it fell on rocky *g*,
15:35 the crowd to seat themselves on the *g*.
17: 6 this the disciples fell forward on the *g*,
24:15 on holy *g* (let the reader take note!),
25:18 went off instead and dug a hole in the *g*,
25:25 your thousand silver pieces in the *g*.
Mk 4: 5 landed on rocky *g* where it had little soil;
4:16 those sown on rocky *g* are people who on
4:26 A man scatters seed on the *g*.
8: 6 the crowd to take their places on the *g*.
9:20 As he fell to the *g* he began to roll
14:35 He advanced a little and fell to the *g*,
Lk 4:35 the demon threw him to the *g* before
5:12 he bowed down to the *g* and said to him,
6:49 his house on the *g* without any foundation.
8: 6 Some fell on rocky *g*,
8:13 Those on the rocky *g* are the ones who,
8:15 The seed on good *g* are those who hear the
9:42 spirit threw him into convulsions on the *g*.
13: 7 Why should it clutter up the *g*?'
19: 8 Zacchaeus stood his *g* and said to the Lord:
22:44 like drops of blood falling to the *g*.
24: 5 Terrified, the women bowed to the *g*.
Jn 6:10 of grass for them to find a place on the *g*.
8: 6 started tracing on the *g* with his finger.
8: 8 time he bent down and wrote on the *g*.
9: 6 With that Jesus spat on the *g*,
18: 6 they retreated slightly and fell to the *g*.
20: 5 in, and saw the wrappings lying on the *g*.
20: 6 He observed the wrappings on the *g* and saw
Acts 7:33 for the place where you stand is holy *g*.
7:54 they *g* their teeth in anger at him.
9: 4 He fell to the *g* and at the same time
9: 8 Saul got up from the *g* unable to see,
9:25 wall one night and lowered him to the *g*,
10:11 was lowered to the *g* by its four corners.
20: 9 and fell from the third story to the *g*.
22: 7 fell to the *g* and heard a voice say to me,
26:14 All of us fell to the *g* and I heard a
Eph 6:13 that your duty requires, and hold your *g*.
Heb 6: 7 *G* which drinks in the rain falling on it
Rv 18:18 smoke go up as the city burned to the *g*:

GROUNDED (1)

Col 1:23 to faith, be firmly *g* and steadfast in it,

GROUNDS (9)

1Mc 10:63 any *g* or be troublesome to him in any way."
Sir 13:18 so too the poor are feeding *g* for the rich.
Jer 49:19 of Jordan to the permanent feeding *g*,
50:44 thicket to the permanent feeding *g*,
Dn 6: 5 tried to find *g* for accusation against Daniel
6: 6 "We shall find no *g* for accusation
Mi 1:11 of Beth-ezel finds in you its *g*.
Rom 4: 2 by his deeds he has *g* for boasting,
Phil 1: 7 the solid *g* on which the gospel rests.

GROUP (35)

Ex 30:13 the registered *g* must pay a half-shekel,
30:14 *g* must give this contribution to the LORD.
38:26 or more who entered the registered *g*;
Nm 4:18 "Do not let the *g* of Kohathite clans
7: 5 to each *g* in proportion to its duties."
26:53 with the number of individuals in each *g*.

GROUP (cont.)

26:54 large *g* you shall assign a large heritage,
26:54 to a small *g* a small heritage, each group
26:56 As the lot falls shall each *g*,
33:54 large *g* and a small heritage to a small *g*.
35: 8 a larger *g* and fewer from a smaller one,
35: 8 so that each *g* will cede cities to the
2Sm 2:13 one *g* on one side of the pool and the
2:25 rallied around Abner, forming a single *g*,
13:34 looked about and saw a large *g* coming
1Chr 26:12 of the LORD, for each *g* in the same way.
Est 8:11 city to *g* together and defend their lives,
8:11 every armed *g* of any nation or province
1Mc 2:16 and his sons gathered in a *g* apart.
2:42 Then they were joined by a *g* of Hasideans,
7:12 A *g* of scribes,
9:65 Jonathan, accompanied by a small *g* of men,
Prv 30:11 is a *g* of people that curses its father,
30:12 There is a *g* that is pure in its own eyes,
30:13 There is a *g*— how haughty their eyes!
30:14 There is a *g* whose incisors are swords,
Mi 2:12 I will *g* them like a flock in the fold,
Mt 20: 8 with the last *g* and end with the first.'
20:10 and when the first *g* appeared they
20:12 'This last *g* did only an hour's work,
Lk 24:22 some women of our *g* have just brought us
Gal 2: 4 they wormed their way into the *g* to spy on

GROUPED (1)

Jdt 2:16 and *g* them into a complete combat force.

GROUPINGS (1)

Gn 10:32 These are the *g* of Noah's sons,

GROUPS (20)

Gn 25:16 twelve chieftains of as many tribal *g*.
Ex 18:21 set them as officers over *g* of thousands,
18:25 the people as officers over *g* of thousands,
Nm 26:53 "Among these *g* the land shall be divided
1Sm 8:12 *g* of a thousand and of a hundred soldiers.
29: 2 their *g* of a hundred and a thousand,
2Sm 18: 1 of groups of a thousand and *g* of a hundred.
1Chr 24: 4 sixteen *g*, and the latter into eight *g*,
24: 6 listing two successive family *g* from
2Chr 35:12 gave it to various *g* of the ancestral houses
Neh 4: 7 them by family *g* with their swords,
Am 1: 6 took captive whole *g* to hand over to Edom,
1: 9 they delivered whole *g* captive to Edom,
Mt 21: 9 The *g* preceding him as well as those
25:32 Then he will separate them into two *g*,
Mk 6:39 down on the green grass in *g* or parties.
12:14 The two *g* came and said to him:
Lk 9:14 "Have them sit down in *g* of fifty or so."

GROVE (1)

Ex 23:11 regard to your vineyard and your olive *g*.

GROVEL (1)

1Sm 2:36 your family will come to *g* before him

GROVELS (1)

Sir 40: 3 on a lofty throne or *g* in dust and ashes,

GROVES (9)

Dt 6:11 and olive *g* that you did not plant;
Jos 24:13 and olive *g* which you did not plant.
1Sm 8:14 of your fields, vineyards, and olive *g*,
Neh 5:11 fields, their vineyards, their olive *g*,
9:25 cisterns already dug, vineyards, olive *g*,
Jdt 3: 8 territory and cut down their sacred *g*,
Is 1:29 and blush for the *g* which you chose.
65: 3 in the *g* and burning incense on bricks,
66:17 and purify themselves to go to the *g*,

GROW (80)

Gn 2: 9 LORD God made various trees *g*
18:30 "Let not my Lord *g* impatient if I go on.
18:32 Lord *g* angry if I speak up this last time.
24:60 may you *g* into thousands of myriads;
Ex 9:32 spelt were not ruined, for they *g* later.
Nm 6: 5 shall let the hair of his head *g* freely.
Dt 6: 3 them, that you may *g* and prosper the more,
28:63 took delight in making you *g* and prosper,
30:16 and decrees, you will live and *g* numerous,
Jgs 16:22 began to *g* as soon as it was shaved off.
2Sm 10: 5 "Stay in Jericho until your beards *g*."
2Chr 13:21 died, while Abijah continued to *g* stronger.
27: 6 Thus Jotham continued to *g* strong because
Ezr 4:22 the evil *g* to the detriment of the throne."
9:12 thus you will *g* strong,
Jb 8:11 Can the papyrus *g* up without mire?
14: 8 Even though its root *g* old in the earth,
17: 2 as their provocation mounts, my eyes *g* dim.
21: 7 Why do the wicked surive, *g* old,
29:18 "In my own nest I shall *g* old;
31:40 Then let the thistles *g* instead of wheat
39: 4 When their offspring thrive and *g*,
Ps(s) 34:11 The great *g* poor and hungry;
69:24 their eyes *g* dim so that they cannot see,
92:13 tree, like a cedar of Lebanon shall he *g*.
102:27 though all of them *g* old like a garment.
Prv 28:20 in haste to *g* rich will not go unpunished.
Eccl 12: 3 they who look through the windows *g* blind;
Sir 8: 6 he is old, for some of us, too, will *g* old.
11:20 with it, *g* old while doing your task.
14:18 with the leaves that *g* on a vigorous tree:
16:25 They were not to hunger, nor *g* weary,
Is 17: 4 Jacob shall fade, and his full body *g* thin,
17:11 Though you make them *g* the day you plant
24:23 the moon will blush and the sun *g* pale,
29:22 be ashamed of, nor shall his face *g* pale.
38:14 My eyes *g* weak, gazing heavenward:
40:28 He does not faint nor *g* weary,
40:30 Though young men faint and *g* weary,
40:31 and not grow weary, walk and not *g* faint.
44:14 and the rain made *g* to serve man for fuel.
51: 6 Though the heavens *g* thin like smoke,
55:13 of the thornbush, the cypress shall *g*,
Jer 5:27 Therefore they *g* powerful and rich,
14: 6 Their eyes *g* dim,
20: 9 I *g* weary holding it in,
Lam 5:17 hearts are sick, at this our eyes *g* dim:
Ez 16: 7 your blood and *g* like a plant in the field.
17: 6 he placed it, To sprout and *g* up a vine,
17: 8 waters it was planted, to *g* branches,
31: 4 Waters made it *g*,
31:14 Thus no tree may *g* lofty in stature or
36: 8 you shall *g* branches and bear fruit for my
37: 6 put sinews upon you, make flesh *g* over you,
47:12 river, fruit trees of every kind shall *g*;
Dn 11: 5 "The king of the south shall *g* strong,
11: 5 but one of his princes shall *g* stronger
Mi 4:10 Writhe in pain, *g* faint,
Hb 2:13 flames, and nations *g* weary for nought!
Mt 6:28 a lesson from the way the wild flowers *g*.
13:30 Let them *g* together until harvest;
24:12 of evil, the love of most will *g* cold.
25:29 who have will get more until they *g* rich,
Jn 4:15 so that I shall not *g* thirsty and have to
Rom 12:11 Do not *g* slack but be fervent in spirit;
1Cor 3: 6 and Apollos watered it, but God made it *g*.
4: 6 so that none of you will *g* self-important
2Cor 10:15 may also *g* among you and overflow.
Gal 6: 9 Let us not *g* weary of doing good;
Col 1: 6 and has continued to *g* in your midst,
1:10 every sort and *g* in the knowledge of God.
1Thes 4: 3 It is God's will that you *g* in holiness:
2Thes 3:13 must never *g* weary of doing what is right,
Heb 1:11 all of them will *g* old like a garment.
6:12 Do not *g* lazy,
12: 3 not *g* despondent or abandon the struggle.
1Pt 2: 2 of the spirit to make you *g* into salvation,
2Pt 3:18 *G* rather in grace,
Jude 1:20 *g* strong in your holy faith through prayer

GROWING (26)

Gn 18: 1 of his tent, while the day was *g* hot.
41: 5 fat and healthy, *g* on a single stalk.
41:22 fat and healthy, *g* on a single stalk.
Ex 1: 9 and powerful the Israelite people are *g*,
9:22 and every *g* thing in the land of Egypt."
9:25 it beat down every *g* thing and splintered
Jgs 11: 2 and on *g* up the sons of the wife had
19: 9 father said to him, "It is already *g* dusk.
1Sm 2:26 young Samuel was *g* in stature and in worth
1Kgs 5:13 on Lebanon to the hyssop *g* out of the wall,
Est 9: 4 that he was continually *g* in power.
1Mc 4:38 weeds *g* in the courts as in a forest or on
6:57 "We are *g* weaker every day,
Eccl 2: 7 had *g* herds of cattle and flocks of sheep,
Sir 3: 9 but a mother's curse uproots the *g* plant.
24:14 like a plane tree *g* beside the water.
Jer 12: 2 root, they keep on *g* and bearing fruit.
Dn 3:76 Everything *g* from the earth,
8: 9 little horn which kept *g* toward the south,
Jon 1:11 For the sea was *g* more and more turbulent.
Lk 8: 7 and the thorns *g* up with it stifled it.
12:21 instead of *g* rich in the sight of God."
13: 6 "A man had a fig tree *g* in his vineyard,
Acts 28: 2 for it had began to rain and was *g* cold.
Rom 4:19 *g* weak in faith he thought of his own body,
Col 2: 7 built up in him, *g* ever stronger in faith,

GROWL (5)

Ex 11: 7 and their animals not even a dog shall *g*,
Jdt 11:19 shepherd, and not even a dog will *g* at you.
Is 5:29 They *g* and seize the prey,
59:11 We all *g* like bears,
Jer 51:38 They all roar like lions, *g* like lion cubs.

GROWLING (1)

Is 31: 4 As a lion or a lion cub *g* over its prey,

GROWN (38)

Gn 25: 8 at a ripe old age, *g* old after a full life;
30:30 you had before I came has *g* into very much,
32:11 my staff, I have now *g* into two companies.
38:14 aware that, although Shelah was now *g* up,
49: 9 like a lion's whelp, you have *g* up on prey,
Ex 2:11 On one occasion, after Moses had *g* up,
23:30 until you have *g* numerous enough to take
Lv 13:37 its place and that black hair has *g* on it,
Dt 4:25 grandchildren, and have *g* old in the land,
31:20 and they have eaten their fill and *g* fat,
1Sm 3: 2 had lately *g* so weak that he could not see.
1Kgs 12: 8 had *g* up with him and were in his service.
12:10 young men who had *g* up with him replied,
1Chr 19: 5 them, "until your beards have *g* again;
23: 1 had *g* old and was near the end of his days,
2Chr 10: 8 had *g* up with him and were in his service.
10:10 young men who had *g* up with him replied:
1Mc 2:49 "Arrogance and scorn have now *g* strong;
6: 6 they had *g* strong by reason of the arms,
13:53 Seeing that his son John was now a *g* man,
16: 3 I have now *g* old,
2Mc 5:24 with orders to kill all the *g* men and sell
Jb 17: 7 My eye has *g* blind with anguish,
Ps(s) 88:10 My eyes have *g* dim through affliction;
Wis 2:10 the old man for his hair *g* white with time.
4:16 the many years of the wicked man *g* old.
13:13 remnants, crooked wood *g* full of knots,
Bar 3:10 land of your foes, *g* old in a foreign land,
Ez 16: 7 your breasts were formed, your hair had *g*,
28: 5 your heart has *g* haughty from your riches
Dn 13:52 "How you have *g* evil with age!
Acts 28:27 The mind of this people has *g* sluggish.
1Cor 4: 8 You have *g* rich!
4:18 Some have *g* full of self-importance,
Heb 8:13 and has *g* old is close to disappearing.
11:24 By faith Moses, when he had *g* up,
Jas 5: 2 your fine wardrobe has *g* moth-eaten,
Rv 17: 2 have *g* drunk on the wine of her lewdness."

GROWS (41)

Gn 38:11 father's house until my son Shelah *g* up"
Nm 18:13 and likewise, of whatever *g* on their land,
Dt 14:22 produce that *g* in the field you have sown;
1Sm 29:10 early morning start, as soon as it *g* light,
2Kgs 19:29 aftergrowth, next year, what *g* of itself;
Jb 14:11 a lake fail, or a stream *g* dry and parches,
40:23 If the river *g* violent,
Ps(s) 49:17 Fear not when a man *g* rich,
61: 3 end I call to you as my heart *g* faint.
77: 4 when I ponder, my spirit *g* faint.
Prv 4:18 that *g* in brilliance till perfect day.
11:24 One man is lavish yet *g* still richer;
13:11 away, but amassed little by little, it *g*.
23: 5 for assuredly it *g* wings,
Eccl 7: 3 when the face is sad the heart *g* wiser.
12: 5 and the locust *g* sluggish and the caper
Wis 16:24 *g* tense for punishment against the wicked,
Sir 10: 3 a city *g* through the wisdom of its princes.
11:16 their birth, and evil *g* old with evildoers.
14:17 All flesh *g* old,
19: 1 He who does so *g* no richer;
30: 1 often, that he may be his joy when he *g* up.
30: 8 a son left to himself *g* up unruly.
Is 16:12 When Moab *g* weary on the high places,
37:30 aftergrowth, next year, what *g* of itself;
Jer 8:22 Why *g* not new flesh over the wound of the
13:16 to the LORD, your God, before it *g* dark;
Hos 10: 4 *g* wild like wormwood in a plowed field!
Mt 5:22 everyone who *g* angry with his brother
13:12 has, more will be given until he *g* rich;
24:32 its branch *g* tender and sprouts leaves,
Mk 4:27 and *g* without his knowing how it happens.
Lk 12:21 the way it works with the man who *g* rich
12:28 *g* today and is thrown on the fire tomorrow,
Acts 19:27 The danger *g*,
2Cor 10:15 we hope that as your faith *g* our influence
Eph 4:16 Through him the whole body *g*,
Col 3:10 one who *g* in knowledge as he is formed
2Thes 1: 3 *g* apace and your mutual love increases;
Heb 3:13 no one *g* hardened by the deceit of sin.
Rv 2: 7 tree of life which *g* in the garden of God.'

GROWTH (17)

2Kgs 19:26 the plants of the field, like the green *g*,
Jb 15:30 flame shall wither him up in his early *g*,
Ps(s) 84: 7 the early rain clothes it with generous *g*.
Sg 6:11 to look at the fresh *g* of the valley,
Sir 43:22 When the mountain *g* is scorched with heat,
50:22 fosters men's *g* from their mother's womb,
Is 15: 6 The grass is withered, new *g* is gone,
37:27 the plants of the field, like the green *g*,
61:11 plants, and a garden makes its *g* spring up,
Ez 17: 9 so that all its green *g* will wither when
Hos 2:14 rank *g* and wild beasts shall devour them.
10: 1 a luxuriant vine whose fruit matches its *g*.
Am 7: 1 late *g* began to come up (the late *g* after
1Cor 3: 7 special account, only God, who gives the *g*.
Col 2:19 a *g* from this source which comes from God.
1Pt 2:12 *G* in HolinessBecause of the Lord,

GRUBS (2)

Dt 28:39 wine, for the *g* will eat the vines clean.
Is 51: 8 eaten by moths, like wool consumed by *g*;

GRUDGE (6)

Gn 27:41 Esau bore Jacob a *g* because of the
50:15 "Suppose Joseph has been nursing a *g*

Lv 19:18 no *g* against your fellow countrymen.
Dt 15: 9 you *g* help to your needy kinsman and give
Jer 3: 5 forever, will he hold his *g* to the end?"
Mk 6:19 Herodias harbored a *g* against him for this

GRUDGING (2)

Prv 23: 6 Do not take food with a *g* man,
Sir 18:17 a *g* gift wears out the expectant eyes.

GRUDGINGLY (1)

2Cor 9: 7 not sadly, not *g*,

GRUMBLE (6)

Ex 16: 7 what are we that you should *g* against us?
Nm 14:27 will this wicked community *g* against me?
14:29 registered in the census, who *g* against me,
16:11 Aaron done that you should *g* against him?"
1Cor 10:10 Nor are you to *g* as some of them did,
Jas 5: 9 Do not *g* against one another,

GRUMBLED (6)

Ex 15:24 As the people *g* against Moses,
16: 2 community *g* against Moses and Aaron.
17: 3 for water, the people *g* against Moses,
Nm 14: 2 the Israelites *g* against Moses and Aaron,
17: 6 community *g* against Moses and Aaron,
Jos 9:18 the entire community *g* against the princes,

GRUMBLERS (1)

Jude 1:16 These men are *g* and whiners.

GRUMBLING (11)

Ex 16: 7 the LORD, as he heeds your *g* against him.
16: 8 as he heeds the *g* you utter against him,
16: 8 Your *g* is not against us,
16: 9 before the LORD, for he has heard your *g*."
16:12 "I have heard the *g* of the Israelites.
Nm 14:36 returning had set the whole community *g*
17:20 my presence the Israelites' *g* against you."
17:25 so that their *g* may cease before me;
1Mc 11:39 that all the troops were *g* at Demetrius,
Wis 1:11 Therefore guard against profitless *g*,
Phil 2:14 you do, act without *g* or arguing:

GRUMBLINGS (2)

Nm 14:27 heard the *g* of the Israelites against me.
Wis 1:10 everything, and discordant *g* are no secret.

GUARANTEE (3)

1Mc 13:16 hostages to *g* that when he is set free
Lk 12:15 but his possessions do not *g* him life."
Heb 7:22 Jesus become the *g* of a better covenant.

GUARANTEED (2)

1Mc 13:38 Whatever we have *g* to you remains in force,
Heb 6:17 his purpose would not change, *g* it by oath,

GUARD (147)

Gn 3:24 sword, to *g* the way to the tree of life.
Ex 23:20 to *g* you on the way and bring you to the
Nm 10:25 Finally, as rear *g* for all the camps,
Dt 4: 9 take care and be earnestly on your *g*
4:15 Be strictly on your *g*,
12:29 advance to dispossess them, be on your *g*!
15: 9 Be on your *g* lest,
Jos 6: 9 the rear *g* followed the ark,
6:13 the rear *g* followed the ark of the LORD,
10:18 of the cave and post men over it to *g* them.
22:26 So we decided to *g* our interests by
1Sm 2: 9 will *g* the footsteps of his faithful ones,
19: 2 please be on your *g* tomorrow morning;
19:10 sent messengers to David's house to *g* it,
29: 2 were marching in the rear *g* with Achish.
2Sm 16: 6 all the soldiers, including the royal *g*,
20:10 *g* against the sword in Joab's other hand,
22:24 him, and I was on my *g* against guilt.
1Kgs 14:27 he entrusted to the officers of the *g* on duty
20:39 and brought me a man and said, *G* this man.
2Kgs 6:10 then they would be on *g*.
11: 5 on the sabbath shall *g* the king's palace;
11: 7 *g* over the temple of the LORD for the king.
25:10 troops who were with the captain of the *g*
25:11 Then Nebuzaradan, captain of the *g*,
25:12 poor, Nebuzaradan, captain of the *g*,
25:15 the captain of the *g* also carried off.
25:18 of the *g* also took Seraiah the high priest,
25:20 The captain of the *g*,
1Chr 9:18 *g* at the king's gate on the east side;
9:23 *g* over the gates of the house of the LORD,
2Chr 8:14 the various classes stood *g* at each gate,
12:10 he entrusted to the officers of the *g* on duty
23: 4 in on the sabbath must *g* the thresholds,
Neh 3:25 the Upper Palace at the quarters of the *g*.
4:10 stood *g* behind the whole house of Judah as
4:16 as a *g* by night and a working force by day.
Tb 4:12 "Be on your *g*,
Jdt 2:10 *g* them for me till the day of their
7:13 to *g* against anyone's leaving the city.
10:20 The *g* of Holofernes and all his servants
14: 2 against the advance *g* of the Assyrians,
1Mc 5:18 people, with the rest of the army to *g* it.
10:32 in it such men as he shall choose to *g* it.
12:27 his men to be on *g* and to remain armed,
12:34 He left a garrison there to *g* it.
2Mc 1:26 Israel and *g* and sanctify your heritage.
Ps(s) 18:24 him, and I was on my *g* against guilt.
91:11 you, that they *g* you in all your ways.
121: 7 will *g* you from all evil; he will *g* your life.
121: 8 The LORD will *g* your coming and your going,
127: 1 LORD *g* the city, in vain does the *g* keep
141: 3 my mouth, a *g* at the door of my lips.
Prv 2:11 watch over you, understanding will *g* you;
4:23 With closest custody, *g* your heart,
5: 2 over you, and understanding may *g* you.
28:14 Happy the man who is always on his *g*;
Eccl 4:17 *G* your step when you go to the house
Wis 1:11 Therefore *g* against profitless grumbling,
Sir 4:20 *g* yourself from evil,
6:13 be on your *g* with your friends.
12:11 you, take care to be on your *g* against him.
13: 8 *G* against being presumptuous;
13:13 Be on your *g* and take care never to
22:27 Who will set a *g* over my mouth,
32:23 Whatever you do, be on your *g*,
34:16 the noonday sun, a *g* against stumbling,
Is 27: 3 Lest anyone harm it, night and day I *g* it.
52:12 you, and your rear *g* is the God of Israel.
58: 8 the glory of the LORD shall be your rear *g*.
Jer 9: 3 Be on your *g*,
32: 2 was imprisoned in the quarters of the *g*,
32: 8 to me to the quarters of the *g* and said,
32:12 happened to be in the quarters of the *g*.
33: 1 still imprisoned in the quarters of the *g*:
37:13 of Benjamin, he met the captain of the *g*,
37:21 be confined in the quarters of the *g*,
37:21 Jeremiah remained in the quarters of the *g*.
38: 6 which was in the quarters of the *g*,
38:13 Jeremiah remained in the quarters of the *g*.
38:28 of the *g* till the day Jerusalem was taken.
39:14 taken out of the quarters of the *g*,
39:15 still imprisoned in the quarters of the *g*,
52:14 troops who were with the captain of the *g*
52:15 Then Nebuzaradan, captain of the *g*,
52:16 poor, Nebuzaradan, captain of the *g*,
52:19 these too the captain of the *g* carried off,
52:24 The captain of the *g* also took Seraiah,
52:26 The captain of the *g*, Nebuzaradan,
52:30 Nebuzaradan, captain of the *g*,
Dn 2:14 with Arioch, the captain of the king's *g*,
Mi 7: 5 in your bosom *g* the portals of your mouth.
Na 2: 2 *g* the rampart,
2: 8 forth captive, and her handmaids, under *g*,
Hb 2: 1 I will stand at my *g* post,
Zec 9: 8 as a *g* that none may pass to and fro;
Mt 5:25 the judge, who will hand you over to the *g*,
6: 1 "Be on *g* against performing religious
7:15 "Be on your *g* against false prophets,
10:17 Be on your *g* with respect to others.
24: 4 "Be on *g*! Let no one mislead you.
26:41 Be on *g*, and pray
27:65 Pilate told them, "You have a *g*.
27:66 and kept it under surveillance of the *g*,
28:11 some of the *g* went into the city and
Mk 8:15 Be on your *g* against the yeast of the
12:38 "Be on *g* against the scribes,
13: 5 "Be on your *g*. Let no one mislead you
13: 9 Be constantly on your *g*.
13:23 So be constantly on *g*!
13:37 I say to all: Be on *g*!"
14:38 Be on *g* and pray that you may not be put
14:54 *g* and began to warm himself at the fire.
15:39 The centurion who stood *g* over him,
Lk 12: 1 on *g* against the yeast of the Pharisees,
12:40 Be on *g*, therefore. The Son of Man will come.
17: 3 "Be on your *g*.
21:34 "Be on *g* lest your spirits become bloated
22:52 chief priests, the chiefs of the temple *g*,
Jn 17:15 the world, but to *g* them from the evil one.
Acts 4: 1 the priests, the captain of the temple *g*,
5:22 *g* got to the jail they could not find them,
5:24 the captain of the temple *g* and the high
5:26 went off with the *g* and brought them in,
12: 4 with four squads of soldiers to *g* him.
12:10 They passed the first *g*,
16:23 was given instructions to *g* them well.
20:28 flock the Holy Spirit has given you to *g*.
20:31 Be on *g*, therefore. Do not forget
23:35 to be kept under *g* in Herod's praetorium.
28:16 a soldier was assigned to keep *g* over him.
1Cor 16:13 Be on your *g*, stand firm in the faith,
Phil 3: 2 Be on *g* against those who mutilate.
4: 7 will stand *g* over your hearts and minds,
1Thes 5: 4 that the day should catch you off *g*,
2Thes 3: 3 you and *g* you against the evil one.
1Tm 6:20 Timothy, *g* what has been committed to you.
2Tm 1:12 able to *g* what has been entrusted to me
1:14 *G* the rich deposit of faith with the help
4:15 Meanwhile, you too had better be on *g*,
1Pt 4:12 for you, but it should not catch you off *g*.
2Pt 3:17 Be on your *g* lest you be led astray by the
1Jn 5:21 children, be on your *g* against idols.
Jude 1:23 Even with those you pity, be on your *g*;
Rv 16:15 (Be on your *g*! I come like a thief.

GUARDED (14)

1Sm 25:21 it was in vain that I *g* all this man's
26:15 have you not *g* your lord the king when one
26:16 death because you have not *g* your lord,
2Kgs 12:10 The priests who *g* the entry would put into
1Chr 9:19 just as their fathers had *g* the entrance
9:21 *g* the gate of the meeting tent.
Est 2:21 of the royal eunuchs who *g* the entrance,
6: 2 of the royal eunuchs who *g* the entrance,
Jn 7:12 crowds there was much *g* debate about him.
17:12 I *g* them with your name which you gave me.
Acts 22:20 even *g* the cloaks of those who killed him!'
1Pt 1: 5 who are *g* with God's power through faith;
2Pt 2: 4 pits of darkness, to be *g* until judgment.
Jude 1: 1 and have been *g* safely in Jesus Christ.

GUARDHOUSE (1)

Gn 42:17 he locked them up in the *g* for three days.

GUARDIAN (9)

1Sm 7: 1 son Eleazar as *g* of the ark of the LORD.
2Chr 34:22 son of Hasrah, the *g* of the wardrobe;
2Mc 11: 1 *g* and kinsman of the king and head of the
13: 2 force, and that with him was Lysias, his *g*,
14: 2 doing away with Antiochus and his *g* Lysias.
Ps(s) 121: 4 slumbers nor sleeps, the *g* of Israel.
121: 5 The LORD is your *g*;
Dn 12: 1 the great prince, *g* of your people;
1Pt 2:25 to the Shepherd, the *G* of your souls.

GUARDIANS (9)

2Kgs 10: 1 to the *g* of Ahab's descendants in Samaria.
10: 5 the city, along with the elders and the *g*,
2Chr 34: 9 which the Levites, the *g* of the threshold,
Ps(s) 47:10 For God's are the *g* of the earth;
Eccl 12: 3 When the *g* of the house tremble,
Sg 5: 7 my mantle from me, the *g* of the walls.
Jer 41:16 and the women and children with their *g*,
1Cor 4:15 Granted you have ten thousand *g* in Christ,
Gal 4: 2 supervision of *g* and administrators

GUARDING (5)

Dt 32:10 for them, *g* them as the apple of his eye.
1Chr 9:19 task the *g* of the threshold of the tent,
Prv 2: 8 who walk honestly, *G* the paths of justice,
Lk 22:63 *g* Jesus amused themselves at his expense.
1Thes 4: 4 of you *g* his member in sanctity and honor,

GUARDROOM (2)

1Kgs 14:28 shields, and then return them to the *g*.
2Chr 12:11 and then they would return them to the *g*.)

GUARDS (35)

Jgs 7:19 watch, just after the posting of the *g*.
2Kgs 10:25 holocaust, Jehu said to the *g* and officers,
10:25 So the *g* and officers put them to the
11: 4 the captains of the Carians and of the *g*.
11: 6 third shall be at the gate behind the *g*.
11:11 And the *g*, with drawn weapons, lined up
11:19 with the captains, the Carians, the *g*,
11:19 the LORD through the *g*' gate to the palace,
2Chr 23:19 he stationed *g* at the gates of the LORD's
Neh 4: 7 to attack us, I stationed *g* down below,
Jdt 4: 5 *g* on all the summits of the high mountains,
13:11 Judith shouted to the *g* from a distance:
Est A:12 two eunuchs of the king who were court *g*.
Ps(s) 97:10 he *g* the lives of his faithful ones;
121: 3 may he slumber not who *g* you:
Prv 13: 3 He who *g* his mouth protects his life;
13: 6 Virtue *g* one who walks honestly,
21:23 He who *g* his mouth and his tongue keeps
24:12 He who *g* your life knows it,
Jer 31:10 he *g* them as a shepherd his flock.
Mt 26:58 he sat down with the *g* to see the outcome.
28: 4 The *g* grew paralyzed with fear of him and
Lk 11:21 a strong man fully armed *g* his courtyard,
23:11 Herod and his *g* then treated him with
Jn 7:32 together sent temple *g* to arrest him.
7:45 When the temple *g* came back,
7:46 spoke like that before," the *g* replied.
18: 3 Judas took the cohort as well as *g*
18:12 the Jewish *g* arrested Jesus and bound him.
18:18 and the servants and the *g* who were
18:22 one of the *g* who was standing nearby gave
19: 6 and the temple *g* saw him they shouted,
Acts 5:23 and the *g* at their posts outside the gates,
12: 6 chains, while *g* kept watch at the door.
12:19 he had the *g* tried and executed.

GUDGODAH (2)

Dt 10: 7 out for Gudgodah, and from *G* for Jotbathah,

GUESS (1)

Wis 9:16 And scarce do we *g* the things on earth,

GUEST (15)

Ex 3:22 ask her neighbor and her house *g* for silver
Jgs 19:22 man whose house it was, "Bring out your *g*,
19:23 Since this man is my *g*,
19:26 of the house in which her husband was a *g*,
2Sm 19:34 for your old age as my *g* in Jerusalem."
Est 5:12 again tomorrow I am to be her *g*,
Sir 29:24 for as a *g* you dare not open your mouth.
31:16 Behave at table like a favored *g*,
Is 11: 6 Then the wolf shall be a *g* of the lamb,
Mk 14:14 Where is my *g* room where I may eat the
Lk 19: 7 "He has gone to a sinner's house as a *g*."
22:11 Do you have a *g* room where I may eat the
Acts 10: 6 He is a *g* of Simon the leather-tanner
10:18 inquire whether Simon Peter was a *g* there.
10:32 *g* in the house of Simon the leather-tanner,

GUESTS (28)

Gn 19: 9 But his *g* put out their hands,
1Sm 9:13 the sacrifice will the invited *g* eat.
9:22 where he placed them at the head of the *g*.
9:24 I explained that I was inviting some *g*."
2Sm 19:29 your servant among the *g* at your table.
1Kgs 1:41 and all the *g* who were with him heard it,
1:49 All the *g* of Adonijah left in terror,
5: 7 and for all the *g* at the royal table.
1Chr 29:15 we are only your *g*, like all our fathers.
Jb 19:14 neglect me, and my *g* have forgotten me.
Prv 9:18 the depths of the nether world are her *g*!
Wis 19:13 their *g* with the more grievous hatred.
19:14 but these were enslaving beneficent *g*.
Sir 32: 1 up, but with the *g* be as one of themselves;
Zep 1: 7 slaughter feast, he has consecrated his *g*.
Mt 9:15 "How can wedding *g* go in mourning so long
14: 9 *g* who were present he gave orders that
22: 3 to summon the invited *g* to the wedding,
22:11 "When the king came in to meet the *g*,
Mk 2:19 "How can the *g* at a wedding fast as long
6:22 a dance which delighted Herod and his *g*.
6:26 of his oath and the presence of the *g*,
Lk 5:34 "Can you make *g* of the groom fast while
7:49 his fellow *g* began to ask among themselves,
14: 7 He went on to address a parable to the *g*,
14:10 will win you the esteem of your fellow *g*.
Jn 2:10 then when the *g* have been drinking awhile,
Acts 10:23 invited them in and treated them as *g*.

GUIDANCE (12)

Nm 33: 1 of Egypt under the *g* of Moses and Aaron.
1Chr 25: 2 inspired songs under the *g* of the king.
25: 6 the house of God, under the *g* of the king.
1Mc 14:36 " 'In his time and under his *g* they
Prv 1: 5 an intelligent man will gain sound *g*,
11:14 For lack of *g* a people falls;
20:18 so with wise *g* wage your war.
24: 6 For it is by wise *g* that you wage your war,
Wis 14: 6 for his race, under the *g* of your hand.
Sir 18:13 Merciful to those who accept his *g*,
46:20 Even when he lay buried, his *g* was sought;
1Tm 1:19 Some men, by rejecting the *g* of conscience,

GUIDE (32)

Nm 27:17 all things, to *g* them in all their actions;
1Chr 17: 6 of Israel whom I commanded to *g* my people,
1Mc 6:15 so that he might *g* the king's son
2Mc 5:15 the laws and to his country, served as *g*.
Jb 38:32 their season, or *g* the Bear with its train?
Ps(s) 5: 9 of my enemies, *g* me in your justice;
22:10 have been my *g* since I was first formed,
25: 5 paths, *G* me in your truth and teach me,
31: 4 your name's sake you will lead and *g* me.
48:15 he will *g* us.
67: 5 the nations on the earth you *g*.
73:24 With your counsel you *g* me,
80: 2 hearken, O *g* of the flock of Joseph!
139:10 the sea, Even there your hand shall *g* me,
143:10 May your good spirit *g* me on level ground.
Prv 6:22 wherever you turn, she will *g* you.
23:19 be wise, and *g* your heart in the right way.
Wis 7:15 *g* of Wisdom and the director of the wise.
9:11 and will *g* me discreetly in my affairs and
18: 3 pillar which was a *g* on the unknown way,
Is 11: 6 together, with a little child to *g* them.
42:16 by paths unknown I will *g* them.
51:18 no one to *g* her of all the sons she bore;
58:11 Then the LORD will *g* you always and give
63:12 glorious arm was the *g* at Moses' right;
Jer 31: 9 tears, but I will console them and *g* them;
Lk 1:79 death, to *g* our feet into the way of peace."
6:39 "Can a blind man act as *g* to a blind man?
Jn 16:13 Spirit of truth he will *g* you to all truth.
Rom 2:19 You feel certain that you can *g* the blind
Phil 3:17 *g* those who follow the example that we set.
Jas 3: 3 obey us, we *g* the rest of their bodies.

GUIDED (11)

Ex 15:13 strength you *g* them to your holy dwelling.
Dt 8:15 who *g* you through the vast and terrible
Ru 4: 4 tell me so, that I may be *g* accordingly,
2Sm 6: 3 and Ahio, sons of Abinadab, *g* the cart,
2Kgs 12: 3 lived, because the priest Jehoiada *g* him.
Jdt 13:18 who *g* your blow at the head of the chief
Ps(s) 78:52 sheep and *g* them like a herd in the desert.
78:72 heart, and with skillful hands he *g* them.
Wis 10:10 his brother's anger, *g* him in direct ways,
Acts 1:16 the one who *g* those that arrested Jesus.
Gal 5:18 If you are *g* by the spirit,

GUIDEPOSTS (1)

Jer 31:21 Set up road markers, put up *g*;

GUIDES (13)

1Mc 4: 2 Some men from the citadel were their *g*.
Ps(s) 23: 3 He *g* me in right paths for his name's sake.
25: 9 He *g* the humble to justice,
95: 7 the people he shepherds, the flock he *g*.
Prv 11: 3 The honesty of the upright *g* them;
Wis 14: 3 But your providence, O Father! guides it,
Sir 18:12 teaching, as a shepherd *g* his flock;
38:25 How can he become learned who *g* the plow,
38:25 Who *g* the ox and urges on the bullock,
40:23 A friend, a neighbor, are timely *g*,
Is 49:10 them and *g* them beside springs of water.
Mt 23:16 It is an evil day for you, blind *g*!
23:24 "Blind *g*! You strain out the gnat

GUIDING (3)

1Chr 13: 7 Uzzah and Ahio were *g* the cart,
Jb 31:18 *g* me even from my mother's womb
Is 63:14 the plain, the spirit of the LORD *g* them?

GUILD (16)

1Kgs 20:35 One of the *g* prophets was prompted by the
2Kgs 2: 3 where the *g* prophets went out to Elisha
2: 5 *g* prophets approached Elisha and asked him.
2: 7 Fifty of the *g* prophets followed,
2:15 The *g* prophets in Jericho,
4: 1 woman, the widow of one of the *g* prophets,
4:38 when the *g* prophets were seated before him,
4:38 some vegetable stew for the *g* prophets."
5:22 *g* prophets from the hill country of
6: 1 The *g* prophets once said to Elisha:
9: 1 one of the *g* prophets and said to him:
9: 4 man (the *g* prophet) went to Ramoth-gilead.
1Chr 4:21 of the linen weavers' *g* in Beth-ashbea,
Neh 3: 8 Harhaiah, a member of the goldsmiths' *g*,
3: 8 side was Hananiah, one of the perfumers' *g*.
3:31 Malchijah, a member of the goldsmiths' *g*,

GUILE (11)

Gn 34:13 to Shechem and his father Hamor with *g*,
Jdt 9:10 With the *g* of my lips,
Ps(s) 10: 7 His mouth is full of cursing, *g* and deceit;
32: 2 not guilt, in whose spirit there is no *g*.
34:14 from evil and your lips from speaking *g*;
Wis 14:25 blood and murder, theft and *g*,
Sir 1:29 fear of the LORD with your heart full of *g*.
19:22 is bowed in grief, but is full of *g* within;
Jn 1:47 There is no *g* in him."
2Cor 2:11 whose *g* we know too well
12:16 being crafty, you say, I caught you by *g*.

GUILEFUL (1)

Jdt 9:13 Let my *g* speech bring wound and wale on

GUILT (185)

Gn 20: 9 such monstrous *g* on me and my kingdom?
26:10 and you would have thus brought *g* upon us!"
44:16 God has uncovered your servants' *g*.
Ex 28:38 Since Aaron bears whatever *g* the
28:43 the sanctuary, lest they incur *g* and die.
Lv 5: 1 and thus commits a sin and has *g* to bear;
5: 3 this may be, and then recognizes his *g*;
5:15 he shall bring to the LORD as his *g*
5:17 that he incurs *g* for which he must answer,
5:18 he shall bring as a *g* offering to the
5:19 Such is the offering for *g*; the penalty of the *g*
5:23 since he has incurred *g* by his sin,
5:24 on the day of his *g* offering he shall make
5:25 As his *g* offering he shall bring to the
5:25 this as his *g* offering to the priest,
5:26 forgiven whatever *g* he may have incurred."
6:10 like the sin offering and the *g* offering.
7: 1 "This is the ritual for *g* offerings,
7: 2 also shall the *g* offering be slaughtered.
7: 5 This is the *g* offering.
7: 7 sin offering and the *g* offering are alike,
7: 7 the *g* offering likewise belongs to the
7:18 who eats of it shall have his *g* to bear.
7:37 offerings, sin offerings, *g* offerings,
10:17 that you might bear the *g* of the community
14:12 priest shall present it as a *g* offering,
14:13 the *g* offering belongs to the priest and
14:14 take some of the blood of the *g* offering
14:17 foot, over the blood of the *g* offering.
14:21 shall take one male lamb for a *g* offering,
14:28 foot, over the blood of the *g* offering.
17:16 his body, he shall have the *g* to bear."
19:21 tent a ram as his *g* offering to the LORD.
22:16 they bring down *g* that must be punished;
26:39 away for their own and their fathers' *g*.
26:41 humbled and they make amends for their *g*,
26:43 may make good the debt of their *g* for
Nm 5:15 offering for an appeal in a question of *g*.
5:31 free from *g*, but the woman shall bear such *g*
6:12 bringing a yearling lamb as a *g* offering.
18: 9 offerings or sin offerings or *g* offerings;
18:22 else they will incur *g* deserving death.
18:32 You will incur no *g* so long as you make a
30:16 of them, he is responsible for her *g*."
Dt 21: 8 and let not the *g* of shedding innocent
21: 8 shall be absolved from the *g* of bloodshed,
21: 9 from your midst the *g* of innocent blood,
24: 4 bring such *g* upon the land which the LORD,
24:16 for his own *g* shall a man be put to death.
25: 2 the number of stripes his *g* deserves.
Jos 22:20 man, he did not perish alone for his *g*!"
1Sm 6: 3 make amends to him through a *g* offering.
6: 4 *g* offering should be our amends to him?",
6: 8 you are offering, as amends for your *g*.
6:17 a *g* offering to the LORD were as follows:
12: 3 I accepted a bribe and overlooked his *g*?
14:41 but if this *g* is in your people Israel,
2Sm 22:24 him, and I was on my guard against *g*.
24:10 now, LORD, forgive the *g* of your servant,
1Kgs 17:18 call attention to my *g* and to kill my son?"
1Chr 21: 3 Why will he bring *g* upon Israel?"
21: 8 Take away your servant's *g*,
2Chr 25: 4 for his own *g* shall a man be put to death."
28:13 the LORD and increase our sins and our *g*.
28:13 Our *g* is already great,
33:23 on the contrary, Amon only increased his *g*.
Ezr 9: 6 our heads and our *g* reaches up to heaven.
9: 7 even to this day great has been our *g*,
9:13 us for our evil deeds and our great *g*—
10: 1 Ezra prayed and acknowledged their *g*,
10:10 women as wives has added to Israel's *g*.
10:19 for their *g* they gave a ram from the flock.
Jdt 8:22 he will lay the *g* on our heads.
11:11 But now their *g* has caught up with them,
Jb 7:21 not pardon my offense, or take away my *g*?
8: 4 he has left them in the grip of their *g*,
10: 6 seek for *g* in me and search after my sins,
10:14 and from my *g* you would not absolve me.
11: 6 that God will make you answer for your *g*.
14:17 in a pouch, and you would cover over my *g*.
20:27 The heavens shall reveal his *g*,
31:33 hidden my sins and buried my *g* in my bosom
33: 9 there is no *g* in me.
Ps(s) 7: 4 fault in this, if there is *g* on my hands,
18:24 him, and I was on my guard against *g*.
25:11 name's sake, O LORD, you will pardon my *g*,
32: 2 the man to whom the LORD imputes not *g*,
32: 5 my sin to you, my *g* I covered not.
32: 5 LORD," and you took away the *g* of my sin.
34:22 the enemies of the just pay for their *g*.
34:23 no one incurs *g* who takes refuge in him.
36: 3 that his *g* will not be found out or hated.
38:19 Indeed, I acknowledge my *g*;
39:12 With rebukes for *g* you chasten man;
51: 4 wash me from my *g* and of my sin cleanse me.
51: 7 Indeed, in *g* was I born,
51:11 face from my sins, and blot out all my *g*.
51:16 Free me from blood *g*,
59: 5 no *g* of mine they hurry to take up arms.
68:22 crowns of those who stalk about in their *g*.
69:28 Heap *g* upon their guilt,
85: 3 You have forgiven the *g* of your people;
89:33 crime with a rod and their *g* with stripes.
106:43 counsels and were brought low by their *g*.
109:14 *g* of his fathers be remembered by the LORD;
Prv 14: 9 *G* lodges in the tents of the arrogant,
16: 6 By kindness and piety *g* is expiated,
17:19 He who loves strife loves *g*;
Sir 4:21 There is a sense of shame laden with *g*,
4:26 Be not ashamed to acknowledge your *g*,
23:11 If he swears in error, he incurs *g*;
27:13 is offensive, their laughter is wanton *g*.
Is 5:18 who tug at *g* with cords of perversity,
13:11 for its evil and the wicked for their *g*.
14:21 his sons for the *g* of their fathers;
24: 6 and its inhabitants pay for their *g*;
27: 9 then, shall be the expiation of Jacob's *g*,
30:13 This *g* of yours shall be like a descending
33:24 who live there will be forgiven their *g*.
40: 2 service is at an end, her *g* is expiated;
53: 6 But the LORD laid upon him the *g* of us all.
53:11 justify many, and their *g* he shall bear.
59: 3 stained with blood, your fingers with *g*;
64: 5 and our *g* carries us away like the wind.
64: 6 from us and have delivered us up to our *g*.
64: 8 LORD, keep not our *g* forever in mind;
Jer 2:22 The stain of your *g* is still before me,
3:13 Only know your *g*:
13:22 For your great *g* your skirts are stripped
14:10 now he remembers their *g*,
14:20 LORD, our wickedness, the *g* of our fathers;
16:17 from me, nor does their *g* escape my view.
25:12 and the land of the Chaldeans for their *g*,
30:15 Because of your great *g*,
32:18 and you repay the fathers' *g*,
33: 8 the *g* they incurred by sinning against me;
50: 7 and their enemies said, "We incur no *g*,

50:20 They shall seek Israel's *g*,
51: 5 *g* to be punished by the Holy One of Israel.
51: 6 one save his life, perish not for her *g*;
Lam 2:14 They did not lay bare your *g*,
5: 7 but we bear their *g*.
Ez 16:49 And look at the *g* of your sister Sodom:
18:19 the son charged with the *g* of his father?"
18:20 not be charged with the *g* of his father,
18:20 father be charged with the *g* of his son.
18:30 that they may be no cause of *g* for you.
21:28 and the arrow taken in hand marks their *g*.
21:29 you have drawn attention to your *g*,
28:17 you to the earth, so great was your *g*;
28:18 Because of your great *g*,
29:16 *g* for having turned to follow after them.
33: 8 he [the wicked man] shall die for his *g*,
33: 9 turn from his way, he shall die for his *g*,
40:39 the sin offerings and *g* offerings.
42:13 offerings, sin offerings, and *g* offerings;
44:29 the sin offering, and the *g* offering;
46:20 cook the *g* offerings and the sin offerings,
Dn 9:24 stop and sin will end, *g* will be expiated,
13:23 without *g* than to sin before the Lord."
Hos 4: 8 of my people, and are greedy for their *g*.
5: 5 Ephraim stumbles in his *g*,
5:15 they pay for their *g* and seek my presence.
7: 1 heal Israel, The *g* of Ephraim stands out,
8:13 remember their *g* and punish their sins;
10: 2 heart is false, now they pay for their *g*;
12: 9 shall not suffice him for the *g* of his sin.
13:12 The *g* of Israel is wrapped up,
14: 1 Samaria shall expiate her *g*,
14: 2 you have collapsed through your *g*.
Mi 7:18 the God who removes *g* and pardons sin for
7:19 compassion on us, treading underfoot our *g*?
Zec 3: 5 said, "See, I have taken away your *g*."
3: 9 take away the *g* of the land in one day.
5: 6 This is their *g* in all the land."
Mal 1: 4 And they shall be called the land of *g*,
Mt 12: 5 break the sabbath rest without incurring *g*?
Mk 3:29 He carries the *g* of his sin without end."
Lk 3:20 to his *g* by shutting John up in prison.
11:51 Their *g* stretches from the blood of Abel
Rom 4: 8 is the man to whom the Lord imputes no *g*."
1Jn 1: 8 If we say, "We are free of the *g* of sin,"

GUILT-OFFERING (4)

Lv 5:16 then make atonement for him with the *g* ram,
14:24 Taking the *g* lamb,
14:25 When he has slaughtered the *g* lamb,
Ezr 10:19 and as a *g* for their guilt they gave a ram

GUILT-OFFERINGS (1)

2Kgs 12:17 The funds from *g* and from sin-offerings,

GUILTLESS (4)

Ex 34: 7 yet not declaring the guilty *g*,
Nm 14:18 yet not declaring the guilty *g*,
Jos 2:19 for his own death, and we shall be *g*.
2Chr 19:10 Do that and you shall be *g*.

GUILTY (76)

Gn 18:23 you sweep away the innocent with the *g*?
18:25 die with the *g*, so that the innocent and the *g*
Ex 21:22 the *g* one shall be fined as much as the
22:11 But if the custodian is really *g* of theft,
23: 7 put to death, nor shall you acquit the *g*.
34: 7 yet not declaring the *g* guiltless,
Lv 4: 3 thereby makes the people also become *g*,
4:13 has forbidden and thus makes itself *g*,
4:22 of the LORD, his God, and thus become *g*,
4:27 of the LORD, and thus becomes *g*,
5: 2 creature, and thus becomes unclean and *g*;
5: 4 recognizes that he is *g* of such an oath;
5: 5 then whoever is *g* in any of these cases
17: 4 Dwelling, shall be judged *g* of bloodshed;
26:40 their fathers were *g* of having rebelled
Nm 5: 8 the priest makes amends for the *g* man.
14:18 yet not declaring the *g* guiltless,
15:24 becomes *g* of the fault of inadvertence,
25: 4 execution of the *g* ones before the LORD,
Dt 15: 9 LORD against you and you will be held *g*.
19:10 and you will not become *g* of bloodshed.
19:15 crime or any offense of which he may be *g*;
21:22 "If a man *g* of a capital offense is put
22:26 since she is not *g* of a capital offense.
23:22 otherwise you will be held *g*,
23:23 from making a vow, you will not be held *g*.
24:15 LORD against you, and you will be held *g*.
25: 1 innocent party and condemning the *g* party,
Jos 20: 3 to which one *g* of accidental and
Jgs 21:22 given them these wives, you would now be *g*.'"
1Sm 19: 5 should you become *g* of shedding innocent
20: 8 if I am *g*, kill me yourself!
2Sm 14:13 as he has, the king shows himself *g*,
14:32 If I am *g*, let him put me to death."
19:20 "May my lord not hold me *g*,
1Kgs 1:52 But if he is found *g* of crime,
2Kgs 17: 4 But the king of Assyria found Hoshea *g* of
2Chr 19:10 warn them lest they become *g* before the
28:10 therefore, *g* of a crime against the LORD,
28:13 for what you propose will make us *g* before
Neh 9: 2 sins and the *g* deeds of their fathers.
9:18 Egypt,' and were *g* of great effronteries,
9:26 you, and they were *g* of great effronteries.
Tb 12:10 *g* of sin are their own worst enemies.
14: 7 but those who become *g* of sin shall
Jdt 5:21 But if they are not a *g* nation,
2Mc 13: 6 A man *g* of sacrilege or notorious for
Jb 9:29 If I must be accounted *g*,
Prv 18: 5 It is not good to be partial to the *g*,
Eccl 5: 5 Let not your utterances make you *g*,
Wis 1: 6 acquits not the blasphemer of his *g* lips;
Sir 7: 7 Be *g* of no evil before the city's populace,
8: 5 remember, we all are *g*.
Is 5:23 To those who acquit the *g* for bribes,
Jer 9: 3 supplanter, every friend is *g* of slander.
Lam 1: 8 Through the sin of which she is *g*,
Ez 22: 4 blood which you shed you have been made *g*,
25:12 grievously *g* by taking vengeance on them,
35: 6 the Lord GOD, you have been *g* of blood,
Dn 9:15 even to this day, we have sinned, we are *g*.
13:53 the innocent, and freeing the *g*,
Hos 4:15 harlot, O Israel, let not Judah become *g*!
Na 1: 3 and the LORD never leaves the *g* unpunished.
Mk 14:64 They all concurred in the verdict *g*."
Lk 13: 4 *g* than anyone else who lived in Jerusalem?
23:22 third time, "What wrong is this man *g* of?
Jn 15:22 spoken to them, they would not be *g* of sin;
15:24 done before, they would not be *g* of sin;
19:11 me over to you is *g* of the greater sin."
Acts 23: 9 "We do not find this man *g* of any crime.
23:29 in no way *g* of anything deserving death
24:20 me *g* of when I stood before the Sanhedrin,
25:11 If I am *g*, if I have committed a crime
1Thes 2: 5 We were not *g*,
Jas 2:10 remainder, has become *g* on all counts.

GUISE (2)

Ps(s) 94:20 you, which creates burdens in the *g* of law?
Lk 20:20 the *g* of honest men to trap him in speech,

GULL (2)

Lv 11:16 crows, the ostrich, the nightjar, the *g*,
Dt 14:15 crows, the ostrich, the nightjar, the *g*,

GULLET (1)

Sir 31:12 man, bring not a greedy *g* to his table,

GULLIES (1)

Jer 2: 6 desert, through a land of wastes and *g*,

GULP (1)

Gn 25:30 "Let me *g* down some of that red stuff;

GUM (2)

Gn 37:25 from Gilead, their camels laden with *g*,
43:11 some balm and honey, *g* and resin,

GUNI (4)

Gn 46:24 Jahzeel, *G*, Jezer, and Shillem.
Nm 26:48 through *G* the clan of the Gunites,
1Chr 5:15 Ahi, son of Abdiel, son of *G*,
7:13 The sons of Naphtali were Jahziel, *G*,

GUNITE (2)

2Sm 23:32 Jashen the *G*;
1Chr 11:34 Jashen the *G*:

GUNITES (1)

Nm 26:48 through Guni the clan of the *G*,

GUR (1)

2Kgs 9:27 he rode through the pass of *G* near Ibleam.

GURBAAL (1)

2Chr 26: 7 against the Arabs who dwelt in *G*,

GUSH (2)

Prv 12:23 but the hearts of fools *g* forth folly.
Jas 3:11 Does a spring *g* forth fresh water and foul

GUSHED (5)

Nm 20:11 and water *g* out in abundance for the
1Kgs 18:28 was their custom, until blood *g* over them.
Ps(s) 78:20 when he struck the rock, waters *g* forth,
105:41 He cleft the rock, and the water *g* forth;
Sir 50:27 they *g* forth from my heart's understanding.

GUSHES (2)

Jer 6: 7 As the well *g* out its waters, so she *g* out

GUSHING (2)

2Mc 14:45 with blood *g* from his frightful wounds.
Jer 18:14 Do the *g* waters dry up that flow fresh

GUTTED (2)

Neh 1: 3 and its gates have been *g* with fire."
2:17 in ruins and its gates have been *g* by fire.

GUY-ROPES (1)

Acts 27:40 same time they untied the *g* of the rudders,

GYMNASIUM (3)

1Mc 1:14 Thereupon they built a *g* in Jerusalem
2Mc 4: 9 authority to establish a *g* and a youth club
4:12 a *g* at the very foot of the acropolis,

H

HA (3)

Ez 36: 2 Because the enemy has said of you, *H!*
Mk 15:29 tossing their heads and saying, *H, h!*

HABAIAH (1)

Ezr 2:61 sons of *H*, sons of Hakkoz, sons of

HABAKKUK (6)

Dn 14:33 In Judea there was a prophet, *H*;
14:35 But *H* answered,
14:37 "Daniel, Daniel," cried *H*,
14:39 at once brought *H* back to his own place.
Hb 1: 1 which *H* the prophet received in vision.
3: 1 Prayer of *H*, the prophet.

HABAZZINIAH (1)

Jer 35: 3 Jaazaniah, son of Jeremiah, son of *H*,

HABIT (7)

Ex 21:29 in the *h* of goring people and its owner,
21:36 ox was previously in the *h* of goring
Nm 22:30 in the *h* of treating you this way before?"
Sir 23: 9 Let not your mouth form the *h* of swearing,
23:15 A man who has the *h* of abusive language
Lk 4:16 on the sabbath as he was in the *h* of doing,
Acts 10: 2 He was in the *h* of giving generously to

HABITATION (2)

1Mc 3:45 it was a *h* of Gentiles.
2Cor 5: 2 we yearn to have our heavenly *h* envelop us.

HABITUALLY (2)

Tb 12:10 but those *h* guilty of sin are their own
Jb 1: 5 This Job did *h*.

HABOR (3)

2Kgs 17: 6 Assyria, settling them in Halah, at the *H*,
18:11 and settled them in Halah, at the *H*,
1Chr 5:26 of Manasseh and brought them to Halah, *H*,

HACALIAH (2)

Neh 1: 1 The words of Nehemiah, the son of *H*.
10: 2 His Excellency Nehemiah, son of *H*,

HACHAMONI (2)

2Sm 23: 8 Ishbaal, son of *H*,
1Chr 11:11 Ishbaal, the son of *H*, chief of the Three.

HACHILAH (3)

1Sm 23:19 and again at Horesh, or on the hill of *H*,
26: 1 the hill of *H* at the edge of the wasteland.
26: 3 camped beside the road on the hill of *H*,

HACHMONI (1)

1Chr 27:32 he and Jehiel, the son of *H*,

HACK (4)

Ps(s) 74: 6 and hammer they *h* at all its paneling.
Is 9:19 Though they *h* on the right,
Ez 16:40 to stone you and *h* you with their swords.
23:47 and *h* them to pieces with their swords.

HADAD (16)

Gn 25:15 Adbeel, Mibsam, Mishma, Dumah, Massa, *H*,
36:35 When Husham died, *H*,
36:36 When *H* died,
1Kgs 11:14 *H* the Edomite,
11:17 Meanwhile, *H*, who was only a boy
11:18 Pharaoh, king of Egypt, who gave *H* a house,
11:19 *H* won great favor with Pharaoh,
11:20 Tahpenes' sister bore *H* a son, Genubath.
11:21 When *H* in Egypt heard that David rested
11:25 this added to the harm done by *H*,
2Kgs 17:31 city gods, King *H* and his consort Anath.
1Chr 1:30 Adbeel, Mibsam, Mishma, Dumah, Massa, *H*,
1:46 Husham died and *H*,
1:47 *H* died and Samlah of Masrekah succeeded
1:50 Baal-hanan died and *H* succeeded him.
1:51 After *H* died. . . .

HADADEZER (16)

2Sm 8: 3 David defeated *H,*
8: 5 Arameans of Damascus came to the aid of *H,*
8: 8 From Tebah and Berothai, towns of *H,*
8: 9 David had defeated all the forces of *H,*
8:10 for his victory over *H* in battle
8:10 Toi had been in many battles with *H.*
8:12 the Amalekites, and from the plunder of *H,*
10:16 *H* sent for and enlisted Arameans from
1Kgs 11:23 of Eliada, who had fled from his lord, *H,*
1Chr 18: 3 David then defeated *H,*
18: 5 Arameans of Damascus came to the aid of *H,*
18: 8 away from Tibhath and Cun, cities of *H,*
18: 9 David had defeated the entire army of *H,*
18:10 war against *H;* for *H* had been at war
19:19 of *H* saw themselves vanquished by Israel,

HADADEZER'S (5)

2Sm 8: 7 *H* servants and brought them to Jerusalem.
10:16 to Helam, with Shobach, general of *H* army,
10:19 All of *H* vassal kings,
1Chr 18: 7 *H* attendants and brought them to Jerusalem.
19:16 with Shophach, the general of *H* army,

HADADRIMMON (1)

Zec 12:11 the mourning of *H* in the plain of Megiddo.

HADAR (1)

Gn 36:39 Baal-hanan died, *H* succeeded him as king;

HADASHAH (1)

Jos 15:37 Zenan, *H,*

HADASSAH (1)

Est 2: 7 He was foster father to *H,*

HADID (3)

Ezr 2:33 sons of Lod, *H,*
Neh 7:37 sons of Lod, *H,*
11:34 Nob, Ananiah, Hazor, Ramah, Gittaim, *H,*

HADLAI (1)

2Chr 28:12 son of Shallum, and Amasa, son of *H,*

HADORAM (6)

Gn 10:27 Almodad, Sheleph, Hazarmaveth, Jerah, *H,*
2Sm 8:10 he sent his son *H* to King David to greet
8:10 *H* also brought with him articles of silver,
1Chr 1:21 Almodad, Sheleph, Hazarmaveth, Jerah, *H,*
18:10 he sent his son *H* to wish King David well
2Chr 10:18 King Rehoboam then sent out *H,*

HADRACH (1)

Zec 9: 1 word of the LORD is upon the land of *H,*

HAELEPH (1)

Jos 18:28 Mozah, Rekem, Irpeel, Taralah, Zela, *H,*

HAGAB (1)

Ezr 2:46 sons of Hagabah, sons of Akkub, sons of *H,*

HAGABA (1)

Neh 7:48 sons of Lebana, sone of *H,* sons of Shalmai

HAGABAH (1)

Ezr 2:45 sons of Padon, sons of Lebanah, sons of *H,*

HAGAR (16)

Gn 16: 1 however, an Egyptian maidservant named *H.*
16: 3 wife Sarai took her maid, *H* the Egyptian,
16: 6 her so much that *H* ran away from her.
16: 8 to Shur, and he asked, *H* maid of Sarai,
16:15 *H* bore Abram a son,
16:15 named the son whom *H* bore him Ishmael.
16:16 years old when *H* bore him Ishmael.
21: 9 Sarah noticed the son whom *H* the Egyptian
21:14 and a skin of water and gave them to *H.*
21:17 God's messenger called to *H* from heaven:
21:17 "What is the matter, *H?*
25:12 Abraham's son Ishmael, whom *H* the Egyptian,
Ps(s) 83: 7 the Ishmaelites, Moab and the people of *H,*
Bar 3:23 The sons of *H* who seek knowledge on earth,
Gal 4:24 this is *H.*
4:25 The mountain Sinai *H* is in Arabia and

HAGGADOL (1)

Neh 11:14 Their commander was Zabdiel, son of *H.*

HAGGAI (11)

Ezr 5: 1 Then the prophets *H* and Zechariah,
6:14 message of the prophets, *H* and Zechariah,
Hg 1: 1 the prophet *H* to the governor of Judah,
1: 3 (Then this word of the LORD came through *H,*
1:12 God, and to the words of the prophet *H,*
1:13 And the LORD's messenger, *H,*
2: 1 of the LORD came through the prophet *H:*
2:10 the word of the LORD came to the prophet *H:*
2:13 Then *H* said: If a person unclean
2:14 Then *H* continued: So is this people
2:20 to *H* on the twenty-fourth day of the month:

HAGGI (2)

Gn 46:16 Zephon, *H,*
Nm 26:15 through *H* the clan of the Haggites,

HAGGIAH (1)

1Chr 6:15 whose son was Shimea, whose son was *H,*

HAGGITES (1)

Nm 26:15 through Haggi the clan of the *H,*

HAGGITH (5)

2Sm 3: 4 the fourth, Adonijah, son of *H;*
1Kgs 1: 5 have relations with herAdonijah, son of *H,*
1:11 you not heard that Adonijah, son of *H,*
2:13 firmly established, Adonijah, son of *H,*
1Chr 3: 2 of Geshur, the fourth, Adonijah, son of *H;*

HAGRITE (1)

1Chr 27:31 and over the flocks was Jaziz the *H.*

HAGRITES (3)

1Chr 5:10 reign of Saul they waged war with the *H,*
5:19 waged war against the *H* and against Jetur,
5:20 mastered the *H* and all who were with them.

HAIL (34)

Ex 9:18 this hour I will rain down such fierce *h*
9:19 shall die when the *h* comes upon them."
9:22 *h* may fall upon the entire land of Egypt,
9:23 the LORD sent forth *h* and peals of thunder.
9:23 LORD rained down *h* upon the land of Egypt;
9:24 flashed through the *h,* such fierce hail
9:26 where the Israelites dwelt, was there no *h.*
9:28 we have had enough of God's thunder and *h.*
9:29 will cease, and there will be no more *h.*
9:33 Then the thunder and the *h* ceased,
9:34 that the rain and *h* and thunder had ceased,
10: 5 the remnant you saved unhurt from the *h,*
10:12 the vegetation and whatever the *h* has left."
10:15 fruit of whatever trees the *h* had spared.
Jb 37:11 With *h,* also, the clouds are laden,
38:22 and seen the treasury of the *h* Which I
Ps(s) 78:47 with *h* and their sycamores with frost.
78:48 He gave over to the *h* their beasts and
105:32 For rain he gave them *h,*
147:17 He scatters his *h* like crumbs;
148: 8 Fire and *h,*
Wis 16:22 in the *h* and flashed lightning in the rain.
Sir 39:29 kept for the proper time, are fire and *h,*
Is 28: 2 and a mighty, who, like a downpour of *h,*
28:17 *H* shall sweep away the refuge of lies,
30:30 of consuming fire, in driving storm and *h.*
Hg 2:17 hands with blight, searing wind, and *h,*
Zec 4: 7 amid exclamations of 'Hail, *H'* to it."
Mt 27:29 to their knees before him, saying, "All *h,*
Mk 15:18 on him, and began to salute him, "All *h!*
Jn 19: 3 they came up to him and said, "All *h,*
Rv 8: 7 came *h* and then fire mixed with blood,

HAILED (1)

2Thes 3: 1 may make progress and be *h* by many others,

HAILSTONES (9)

Jos 10:11 *h* than the Israelites slew with the sword.
Wis 5:22 from his sling, wrathful *h* shall be hurled.
Sir 43:15 the storm its power and breaks off the *h.*
46: 5 answer to him in *h* of tremendous power,
Ez 13:11 *h* shall fall, and a stormwind shall break
13:13 and *h* shall fall with destructive wrath.
38:22 flooding rain and *h,*
Rv 16:21 Giant *h* like huge weights came crashing
16:21 and men blasphemed God for the plague of *h,*

HAILSTORM (1)

Rv 11:19 of thunder, an earthquake, and a violent *h.*

HAILSTORMS (1)

Wis 16:16 rains and *h* and unremitting downpours,

HAIR (98)

Ex 25: 4 fine linen and goat *h;*
26: 7 "Also make sheets woven of goat *h,*
35: 6 fine linen and goat *h;*
35:23 or scarlet yarn, fine linen or goat *h,*
35:26 women who possessed the skill, spun goat *h.*
36:14 Sheets of goat *h* were also woven as a tent
Lv 11:32 article of wood, cloth, leather or goat *h,*
13: 3 If the *h* on the sore has turned white and
13: 4 below the skin, nor has the *h* turned white,
13:10 *h* white and that there is raw flesh in it,
13:20 the skin and that the *h* has turned white,
13:21 finds that there is no white *h* in it and
13:25 If the *h* has turned white on the blotch
13:26 finds that there is no white *h* on the
13:30 skin and that there is fine yellow *h* on it,
13:31 skin, though the *h* on it may not be black,
13:32 scall has not spread and has no yellow *h*
13:36 on the skin he need not look for yellow *h;*
13:37 its place and that black *h* has grown on it,
13:40 "When a man loses the *h* of his head,
13:41 if he loses the *h* on the front of his head,
14: 8 and shave off all his *h* and bathe in water;
14: 9 again shave off all the *h* of his head,
14: 9 his eyebrows, and any other *h* he may have,
19:27 Do not clip your *h* at the temples,
Nm 6: 5 nazirite vow, no razor shall touch his *h.*
6: 5 shall let the *h* of his head grow freely.
6:18 shave his dedicated head, collect the *h,*
6:19 nazirite has shaved off his dedicated *h,*
31:20 every article of cloth, leather, goats' *h,*
Dt 14: 1 the *h* above your foreheads for the dead.
Jgs 16:13 "If you weave my seven locks of *h* into
16:14 wove his seven locks of *h* into the web,
16:19 a man who shaved off his seven locks of *h.*
16:22 But the *h* of his head began to grow as
20:16 to sling a stone at a *h* without missing.
1Sm 14:45 *h* of his head shall fall to the ground,
19:13 putting a net of goat's *h* at its head and
19:16 bed, with the net of goat's *h* at its head.
2Sm 14:11 a *h* of your son shall fall to the ground."
14:26 *h* became too heavy for him—the *h* weighed
18: 9 terebinth, his *h* caught fast in the tree.
1Kgs 1:52 worthy, not a *h* shall fall from his head.
2Kgs 9:30 she shadowed her eyes, adorned her *h,*
Ezr 9: 3 mantle, plucked *h* from my head and beard,
Neh 13:25 some of them beaten and their *h* pulled out;
Jdt 10: 3 arranged her *h* and bound it with a fillet,
13: 7 to the bed, grasped the *h* of his head,
Est C:13 put aside, and her *h* was wholly disheveled.
2Mc 6:23 the merited distinction of his gray *h,*
7: 7 tearing off the skin and *h* of his head,
15:13 distinguished by his white *h* and dignity,
Jb 1:20 began to tear his cloak and cut off his *h.*
4:15 before me, and the *h* of my flesh stood up.
Prv 16:31 Gray *h* is a crown of glory;
20:29 and the dignity of old men is gray *h.*
Sg 4: 1 Your *h* is like a flock of goats streaming
6: 5 Your *h* is like a flock of goats streaming
7: 6 your *h* is like draperies of purple;
Wis 2:10 old man for his *h* grown white with time.
Sir 6:18 thus will you find wisdom with graying *h.*
27:14 oath-filled talk makes the *h* stand on end,
Is 7:20 the head, and the *h* between the legs.
46: 4 even when your *h* is gray I will bear you;
Jer 7:29 Cut off your dedicated *h* and throw it away!
Bar 6:30 torn tunic and with shaven *h* and beard,
Ez 5: 1 of scales and divide the *h* you have cut.
8: 2 a hand and seized me by the *h* of my head. . .
16: 7 your breasts were formed, your *h* had grown,
44:20 *h* hang loose, but they shall keep their *h*
Dn 3:94 not a *h* of their heads had been singed,
4:30 his *h* grew like the feathers of an eagle,
7: 9 and the *h* on his head as white as wool;
14:27 Then Daniel took some pitch, fat, and *h;*
14:36 of his head and carried him by the *h;*
Mi 1:16 Make yourself bald, pluck out your *h,*
Mt 3: 4 was clothed in a garment of camel's *h,*
5:36 cannot make a single *h* white or black).
6:17 that you groom your *h* and wash your face.
10:30 you, every *h* of your head has been counted;
Mk 1: 6 John was clothed in camel's *h,*
Lk 7:38 Then she wiped them with her *h,*
7:44 with her tears and wiped them with her *h.*
21:18 yet not a *h* of your head will be harmed.
Jn 11: 2 with perfume and dried his feet with her *h.)*
12: 3 Then she dried his feet with her *h,*
Acts 27:34 Not one of you shall lose a *h* on his head."
1Cor 11: 6 wear a veil, she ought to cut off her *h.*
11: 6 to have her *h* cut off or her head shaved,
11:14 his hair long, while the long *h* of a woman
11:15 Her *h* has been given her for a covering.
1Tm 2: 9 and not be decked out in fancy *h* styles,
Rv 1:14 The *h* of his head was as white as
9: 8 faces but they had hair like women's *h.*

HAIRDRESS (1)

1Pt 3: 3 The affectation of an elaborate *h,*

HAIRLESS (1)

Gn 27:16 up his hands and the *h* parts of his neck.

HAIRS (4)

Ps(s) 40:13 are more numerous than the *h* of my head,
69: 5 the *h* of my head who hate me without cause.
Hos 7: 9 Of gray *h,* too, there is a sprinkling
Lk 12: 7 truth, even the *h* of your head are counted!

HAIRY (6)

Gn 25:25 and his whole body was like a *h* mantle;
27:11 "But my brother Esau is a *h* man,"
27:23 to identify him because his hands were *h,*
2Kgs 1: 8 "Wearing a *h* garment,"

Ps(s) 68:22 the *h* crowns of those who stalk about in
Zec 13: 4 shall he assume the *h* mantle to mislead,

HAKKATAN (1)

Ezr 8:12 of the sons of Azgad, Johanan, son of *H*,

HAKKOZ (5)

1Chr 24:10 the sixth to Mijamin, the seventh to *H*,
Ezr 2:61 sons of Habaiah, sons of *H*,
Neh 3: 4 side Meremoth, son of Uriah, son of *H*,
3:21 him, Meremoth, son of Uriah, son of *H*,
7:63 sons of Hobaiah, sons of *H*,

HAKUPHA (2)

Ezr 2:51 the Nephusites, sons of Bakbuk, sons of *H*,
Neh 7:53 the Nephusites, sons of Bakbuk, sons of *H*,

HALAH (3)

2Kgs 17: 6 Israelites to Assyria, settling them in *H*,
18:11 to Assyria and settled them in *H*,
1Chr 5:26 of Manasseh and brought them to *H*,

HALAK (2)

Jos 11:17 from Mount *H* that rises toward Seir as far
12: 7 valley to Mount *H* which rises toward Seir,

HALE (2)

Mt 10:17 They will *h* you into court,
Jas 2: 6 They are the ones who *h* you into the

HALED (1)

Jdt 6:14 They *h* him before the rulers of the city,

HALF (117)

Gn 15:10 two, and placed each *h* opposite the other;
24:22 took out a gold ring weighing *h* a shekel,
Ex 24: 6 *h* of the blood and put it in large bowls;
24: 6 the other *h* he splashed on the altar.
25:10 of acacia wood, two and a *h* cubits long,
25:10 half cubits long, one and a *h* cubits wide,
25:10 cubits wide, and one and a *h* cubits high.
25:17 a half long, and one and a *h* cubits wide.
25:23 a cubit wide, and a cubit and a *h* high.
26:12 will be an extra *h* sheet of tent covering,
26:16 cubits, and its width one and a *h* cubits.
27: 5 network is to be *h* as high as the altar.
30:23 *h* the amount,
36:21 cubits, and the width one and a *h* cubits.
37: 1 of acacia wood, two and a *h* cubits long,
37: 1 one and a half cubits wide, and one and a *h*
37: 6 two and a *h* cubits long and one and a *h*
37:10 cubit wide, and one and a *h* cubits high.
38: 4 the ground, *h* as high as the altar itself.
Lv 6:13 half in the morning and *h* in the evening.
Nm 12:12 mother's womb with its flesh *h* consumed."
15: 9 of fine flour mixed with *h* a hin of oil,
15:10 of oil, and a libation of *h* a hin of wine,
28:14 shall be *h* a hin of wine for each bullock,
31:27 giving *h* to those who took active part in
31:27 combat, and *h* to the rest of the community.
31:29 asses and sheep in their *h* of the spoil
31:30 From the Israelites' *h* you shall take one
31:36 The *h* that fell to those who had gone out
31:42 The *h* for the other Israelites,
32:33 as well as *h* the tribe of Manasseh,
34:13 to be given to the nine and one *h* tribes.
34:14 Gad, as well as *h* of the tribe of Manasseh,
34:15 these two and one *h* tribes have received
Dt 29: 7 Gadites, and *h* the tribe of Manasseh.
Jos 8:33 *H* of them were facing Mount Gerizim and *h*
12: 2 through *h* of Gilead to the Wadi Jabbok,
12: 5 and over *h* of Gilead as far as the
13: 8 Now the other *h* of the tribe of Manasseh
13:25 and *h* the land of the Ammonites as far as
13:31 *H* of Gilead,
13:31 for *h* the clans descended from Machir.
14: 2 the remaining nine and a *h* tribes.
14: 3 For to two and a *h* tribes Moses had
22: 7 to *h* the tribe of Manasseh Moses had
22: 7 and to the other *h* Joshua had given a
1Sm 14:14 slew about twenty men within *h* a furlong.
2Sm 10: 4 after shaving off *h* their beards and
18: 3 even if *h* of us should die,
19:41 All the people of Judah and *h* of the
1Kgs 3:25 give half to one woman and *h* to the other."
7:31 a receptacle a cubit and a *h* in depth.
7:32 Each wheel was a cubit and a *h* high.
7:35 there was a raised collar *h* a cubit high,
10: 7 that they were not telling me the *h*.
13: 8 "If you gave me *h* your kingdom,"
16: 9 servant Zimri, commander of *h* his chariots,
16:21 of Israel were divided, *h* following Tibni,
16:21 Ginath, to make him king, and *h* for Omri.
1Chr 2:52 were Reaiah, *h* the Manahathites,
2:54 Atroth-beth-Joab, *h* the Manahathites,
2Chr 9: 6 did not tell me the *h* of your great wisdom;
Neh 3: 9 Hur, leader of *h* the district of Jerusalem,
3:12 leader of *h* the district of Jerusalem,
3:16 leader of *h* the district of Beth-zur,
3:17 leader of *h* the district of Keilah.
3:18 leader of *h* the district of Keilah;
3:38 filled in and completed up to *h* its height.
4:10 only *h* my able men took a hand in the work,
4:10 a hand in the work, while the other *h*,
4:15 *h* of the men with spears at the ready,
12:32 by Hoshaiah and *h* the princes of Judah,
12:38 the other *h* of the princes of the people,
12:40 I, too, who had with me *h* the magistrates,
13:24 Of their children, *h* spoke Ashdodite,
Tb 8:21 *h* of whatever I own when you go back in
8:21 *h* will be yours when I and my wife die.
10:10 wife, together with *h* of all his property:
12: 2 It would not hurt me at all to give him *h*
12: 4 receive *h* of all that he brought back."
12: 5 wages *h* of all that you have brought back,
Est 5: 3 Even if it is *h* of my kingdom,
5: 6 be honored, even if it is for *h* my kingdom."
7: 2 shall be honored, even for *h* the kingdom."
1Mc 3:34 He entrusted to him *h* of the army,
3:37 *h* of the army and set out from Antioch,
10:30 third of the grain and the *h* of the fruit
2Mc 8:30 allotting *h* to themselves and the rest to
Ps(s) 55:24 and deceit shall not live out *h* their days.
Wis 18:14 the night in its swift course was *h* spent,
Sir 29: 6 If the lender is able to recover barely *h*,
Is 44:16 *H* of it he burns in the fire,
44:19 to say, *H* of the wood I burned in the fire,
Ez 16:51 Samaria did not commit *h* your sins!
40:42 half cubits long, one and a *h* cubits wide,
Dn 9:27 *H* the week he shall abolish sacrifice and
Zec 14: 2 *h* of the city shall go into exile,
14: 4 very deep valley, and *h* of
14: 4 shall move to the north and *h* of it
14: 8 *h* to the eastern sea, and *h* to the western sea,
Mk 6:23 you whatever you ask, even to *h* my kingdom!"
Lk 4:25 remained closed for three and a *h* years
19: 8 "I give *h* my belongings,
Jn 7:14 The feast was *h* over by the time Jesus
Acts 18:11 ended by settling there for a year and a *h*,
Rv 8: 1 was silence in heaven for about *h* an hour.
11: 9 three and a *h* days but refuse to bury them.
11:11 But after the three and a *h* days,
12:14 for a year and for two and a *h* years more.

HALF-CUBIT (1)

Ez 43:17 cubits wide, with a *h* rim surrounding it.

HALF-DEAD (2)

Wis 18:18 And cast *h*,
Lk 10:30 beat him, and then went off leaving him *h*.

HALF-FEARFUL (1)

Mt 28: 8 away from the tomb half-overjoyed, *h*,

HALF-OVERJOYED (1)

Mt 28: 8 They hurried away from the tomb *h*,

HALF-POMEGRANATE (2)

Sg 4: 3 Your cheek is like a *h* behind your veil.
6: 7 Your cheek is like a *h* behind your veil.

HALF-SHEKEL (4)

Ex 30:13 enters the registered group must pay a *h*,
30:13 of a *h* is a contribution to the LORD.
30:15 than a *h* in this contribution to the LORD
38:26 one bekah apiece, that is, a *h* apiece,

HALF-SISTER (2)

Lv 20:17 marriage with her sister of his *h*,
Dt 27:22 who has relations with his sister or his *h*!'

HALF-TRIBE (30)

Dt 3:13 Argob region, I gave to the *h* of Manasseh.
Jos 1:12 the Gadites, and the *h* of Manasseh:
4:12 The Reubenites, Gadites, and *h* of Manasseh,
12: 6 the Gadites, and the *h* of Manasseh,
13: 7 the nine tribes and the *h* of Manasseh
13:29 gave to the clans of the *h* of Manasseh.
18: 7 and the *h* of Manasseh have already
21: 5 tribe of Dan, and from the *h* of Manasseh.
21: 6 of Naphtali, and from the *h* of Manasseh.
21:25 and from the *h* of Manasseh the two cities
21:27 received from the *h* of Manasseh two cities:
22: 1 and the *h* of Manasseh and said to them:
22: 9 and the *h* of Manasseh left the other
22:10 and the *h* of Manasseh came to the region
22:11 and the *h* of Manasseh had built an altar
22:13 and the *h* of Manasseh in the land of
22:15 the *h* of Manasseh in the land of Gilead,
22:21 and the *h* of Manasseh replied to the
1Chr 5:18 Gadites, and *h* of Manasseh were warriors,
5:23 The numerous members of the *h* of Manasseh
5:26 *h* of Manasseh and brought them to Halah,
6:46 tribe of Dan, and from the *h* of Manasseh.
6:47 and from the *h* of Manasseh in Bashan.
6:55 From the *h* of Manasseh:
6:56 received from the *h* of Manasseh:
12:32 Of the *h* of Manasseh:
12:38 Reubenites, Gadites, and the *h* of Manasseh,
26:32 and the *h* of Manasseh in everything
27:20 for the *h* of Manasseh,
27:21 for the *h* of Manasseh in Gilead,

HALF-WAY (1)

1Chr 19: 4 and their garments cut off *h* at the hips.

HALF-YEAR (2)

Dn 7:25 over to him for a year, two years, and a *h*.
12: 7 it should be for a year, two years, a *h*;

HALFWAY (1)

Dt 3:12 Arnon, *h* up into the highlands of Gilead,

HALHUL (1)

Jos 15:58 *H*, Beth-zur,

HALI (1)

Jos 19:25 Their territory included Helkath, *H*,

HALICARNASSUS (1)

1Mc 15:23 Sicyon, Caria, Samos, Pamphylia, Lycia, *H*,

HALL (15)

Jgs 3:23 Then Ehud went out into the *h*,
1Kgs 7: 2 He built the *h* called the Forest of
7: 6 The porch of the columned *h* he made fifty
7: 6 porch extended the width of the columned *h*,
10:17 put them in the *h* of the Forest of Lebanon.
10:21 and all the utensils in the *h* of the
2Chr 9:16 king put in the *h* of the Forest of Lebanon.
9:20 and all the utensils in the *h* of the
Est 7: 8 the garden of the palace to the banquet *h*,
1Mc 16:16 hand, rushed upon Simon in the banquet *h*,
Sg 2: 4 banquet *h* and his emblem over me is love.
Dn 5:10 lords, she entered the banquet *h* and said,
Mt 22:10 This filled the wedding *h* with banqueters.
Mk 15:16 away into the *h* known as the praetorium;
Acts 19: 9 day to day in the lecture *h* of Tyrannus.

HALLOHESH (2)

Neh 3:12 was carried out by Shallum, son of *H*,
10:25 Anaiah, Hoshea, Hananiah, Hasshub, *H*,

HALLOWED (3)

Wis 6:10 the holy precepts *h* shall be found holy,
Mt 6: 9 'Our Father in heaven, *h* be your name,
Lk 11: 2 "Father, *h* be your name.

HALT (8)

Jos 3: 8 come to a *h* in the Jordan
3:13 down from upstream will *h* in a solid bank."
2Sm 2:23 Asahel had fallen and died, came to a *h*.
2:28 horn, and all the soldiers came to a *h*,
15:24 Abiathar brought the ark of God to a *h*
18:16 because Joab called on them to *h*.
Neh 12:39 [and they came to a *h* at the Prison Gate].
Is 10:32 Even today he will *h* at Nob,

HALTED (9)

Jos 3:16 than the waters flowing from upstream *h*,
10:13 The sun *h* in the middle of the sky;
1Sm 30: 9 where those who were to remain behind *h*.
2Sm 15:17 they *h* opposite the ascent of the Mount of
2Chr 20:20 were going out, Jehoshaphat *h* and said:
Ezr 4:24 on the house of God in Jerusalem was *h*.
Lk 7:14 at this, the bearers *h*.
18:40 *h* and ordered that he be brought to him.
24:18 They *h*, in distress,

HALTING (2)

2Mc 10:27 city, *h* when they were close to the enemy.
Heb 12:13 *h* limbs may not be dislocated but healed.

HALVES (2)

Lv 1:17 down the middle without separating the *h*,
2Sm 10: 4 lower *h* of their garments at the buttocks,

HAM (17)

Gn 5:32 years old, he became the father of Shem, *H*,
6:10 Shem, *H*, and Japheth.
7:13 day named, Noah and his sons Shem, *H*,
9:18 out of the ark were Shem, *H* and Japheth.
9:18 *H* was the father of Canaan.)
9:22 *H*, the father of Canaan,
10: 1 the descendants of Noah's sons, Shem, *H*,
10: 6 The descendants of *H*:
10:20 These are the descendants of *H*,
14: 5 in Ashteroth-karnaim, the Zuzim in *H*,
1Chr 1: 4 Enoch, Methuselah, Lamech, Noah, Shem, *H*,
1: 8 The descendants of *H* were Cush,
4:41 and attacked the tents of *H* (for Hamites
Ps(s) 78:51 first fruits of manhood in the tents of *H*;
105:23 and Jacob sojourned in the land of *H*.
105:27 among them, and wonders in the land of *H*.
106:22 in Egypt, Wondrous deeds in the land of *H*,

HAMAN (58)

Est A:17 H, however,
3: 1 these events King Ahasuerus raised H,
3: 2 royal gate would kneel and bow down to H,
3: 4 would not listen to them, they informed H,
3: 5 When H observed that Mordecai would not
3: 6 they had told H of Mordecai's nationality,
3: 8 Then H said to King Ahasuerus:
3:10 ring from his hand and gave it to H,
3:11 silver you may keep," the king said to H,
3:12 month they wrote, at the dictation of H,
B: 3 as to how this might be accomplished, H,
B: 6 are indicated to you in the letters of H,
3:15 The king and H then sat down to feast,
4: 7 amount of silver H had promised to pay
B: 8 for H, who is second to the king,
C: 5 thus in not bowing down to the proud H.
C:28 have never eaten at the table of H,
5: 4 today with H to a banquet I have prepared."
5: 5 H make haste to fulfill the wish of Esther."
5: 5 with H to the banquet Esther had prepared.
5: 8 come with H tomorrow to a banquet which I
5: 9 That day H left happy and in good spirits.
5:10 H restrained himself,
5:12 "Moreover," H added,
5:14 This suggestion pleased H,
6: 4 Now H had entered the outer court of the
6: 5 answered him, H is waiting in the court."
6: 6 When H entered,
6: 6 Now H thought to himself,
6:10 Then the king said to H:
6:11 So H took the robe and horse,
6:12 to the royal gate, while H hurried home,
6:14 H off to the banquet Esther had prepared.
7: 1 H went to the banquet with Queen Esther.
7: 6 "The enemy oppressing us is this wicked H."
7: 6 H was seized with dread of the king and
7: 7 H stayed to beg Queen Esther for his life,
7: 8 H had thrown himself on the couch on which
7: 8 spoken when the face of H was covered over.
7: 9 of H stands a gibbet fifty cubits high.
7: 9 H prepared it for Mordecai,
7:10 So they hanged H on the gibbet which he
8: 1 day King Ahasuerus gave the house of H,
8: 2 The king removed his signet ring from H,
8: 2 put Mordecai in charge of the house of H.
8: 3 to revoke the harm done by H the Agagite,
8: 5 revoke the letters which that schemer H,
8: 7 that I have given Esther the house of H,
E:10 "For instance, H, son of Hammedatha
E:17 then, to ignore the letter sent by H,
9:10 Aridai, and Vaizatha, the ten sons of H,
9:12 hundred men, as well as the ten sons of H.
9:13 let the ten sons of H be hanged on gibbets."
9:14 So the ten sons of H were hanged,
9:24 H, son of Hammedatha the Agagite,
9:25 writing that the wicked plan H had devised
9:25 Jews should instead be turned against H
F: 4 The two dragons are myself and H.

HAMAN'S (1)

Est 3: 7 was cast in H presence to determine the

HAMATH (38)

Nm 13:21 as far as where Rehob adjoins Labo of H.
34: 8 from Mount Hor to Labo in the land of H,
Jos 13: 5 of Mount Hermon to Labo in the land of H.
Jgs 3: 3 between Baal-hermon and the entrance to H.
2Sm 8: 9 When Toi, king of H,
1Kgs 8:65 from Labo of H to the Wadi of Egypt,
2Kgs 14:25 of Israel from Labo of H
14:28 Damascus and turned back H from Israel,
17:24 people from Babylon, Cuthah, Avva, H,
17:30 the men of H made Ashima,
18:34 Where are the gods of H and Arpad?
19:13 Where are the king of H,
23:33 him prisoner at Riblah in the land of H,
25:21 put to death in Riblah, in the land of H.
1Chr 13: 5 Israel, from Shihor of Egypt to Labo of H,
18: 3 Hadadezer, king of Zobah toward H,
18: 9 When Tou, king of H,
2Chr 7: 8 from Labo of H to the Wadi of Egypt,
8: 3 Solomon went to H of Zoba and conquered it.
8: 4 all the supply cities, which he built in H.
1Mc 12:25 went into the country of H to meet them,
Ps(s) 76:11 survivors of H shall keep your festivals.
Is 10: 9 not Calno like Carchemish, Or H like Arpad,
11:11 Pathros, Ethiopia, and Elam, Shinar, H,
36:19 Where are the gods of H and Arpad?
37:13 Where is the king of H,
Jer 39: 5 was brought to Riblah, in the land of H,
49:23 H and Arpad are covered with shame,
52: 9 and brought to Riblah, in the land of H,
52:27 put to death in Riblah, in the land of H.
Ez 47:15 the direction of Hethlon, past Labo of H,
47:16 along the frontiers of H and Damascus,
47:17 frontier of H and Damascus to the north.
47:20 up to a point parallel to Labo of H.
48: 1 at the northern extremity, adjoining H,
48: 1 to Hethlon through Labo of H to Hazar-enon,
Am 6: 2 and see, go from there to H the great,
6:14 you from Labo of H even to the Wadi Arabah.
Zec 9: 2 as are all the tribes of Israel, H also,

HAMATHITE (1)

1Chr 1:16 the Arvadite, the Zemarite, and the H.

HAMATHITES (1)

Gn 10:18 the Arvadites, the Zemarites, and the H.

HAMITES (1)

1Chr 4:41 tents of Ham (for H dwelt there formerly)

HAMMATH (3)

Jos 19:35 The fortified cities were Ziddim, Zer, H,
21:32 also H with its pasture lands and Rakkath
1Chr 2:55 from H of the ancestor of the Rechabites.

HAMMEDATHA (8)

Est A:17 Haman, however, son of H the Agagite,
3: 1 raised Haman, son of H the Agagite,
3:10 and gave it to Haman, son of H the Agagite,
8: 5 that schemer Haman, son of H the Agagite,
E:10 "For instance, Haman, son of H,
E:17 ignore the letter sent by Haman, son of H,
9:10 Vaizatha, the ten sons of Haman, son of H,
9:24 Haman, son of H the Agagite,

HAMMER (8)

1Kgs 6: 7 stone dressed at the quarry, so that no h,
Ps(s) 74: 6 chisel and h they hack at all its paneling.
Sir 38:28 The clang of the h deafens his ears,
Is 41: 7 goldsmith, the one who beats with the h,
Jer 23:29 says the LORD, like a h shattering rocks?
50:23 How has the h of the whole earth been
51:20 You are my h, my weapon for war;
Na 2: 2 The h comes up against you;

HAMMERED (4)

Ex 39: 3 Gold was first h into gold leaf and then
Nm 17: 3 Have them h into plates to cover the altar,
17: 4 offering h into a covering for the altar,
Jgs 5:26 She h Sisera, crushed his head;

HAMMERS (2)

Is 44:12 works it over the coals, shapes it with h,
Jer 10: 4 With nails and h they are fastened,

HAMMON (2)

Jos 19:28 Cabul, Mishal, Abdon, Rehob, H and Kanah,
1Chr 6:61 pasture lands, H with its pasture lands,

HAMMUEL (1)

1Chr 4:26 The descendants of Mishma were his son H,

HAMON-GOG (2)

Ez 39:11 horde, and it shall be named "Valley of H."
39:15 others have buried it in the Valley of H.

HAMONAH (1)

Ez 39:16 [Also the name of the city shall be H

HAMOR (13)

Gn 33:19 of bullion from the descendants of H,
34: 2 When Shechem, son of H the Hivite,
34: 4 Shechem also asked his father H,
34: 6 Now H, the father of Shechem
34: 8 H appealed to them, saying:
34:13 to Shechem and his father H with guile,
34:18 seemed fair to H and his son Shechem.
34:20 So H and his son Shechem went to their
34:24 the town agreed with H and his son Shechem,
34:26 had put H and his son Shechem to the sword,
Jos 24:32 Jacob had bought from the sons of H,
Jgs 9:28 Zebul once subject to the men of H,
Acts 7:16 with silver from the sons of H at Shechem.

HAMPER (1)

Acts 9:25 him to the ground, using ropes and a h.

HAMPERS (2)

Mt 15:37 fragments left over, these filled seven h.
Mk 8:20 many full h of fragments did you collect?"

HAMPERS-FULL (1)

Mt 16:10 four thousand and how many h you retrieved?

HAMSTRING (1)

Jos 11: 6 h their horses and burn their chariots."

HAMSTRUNG (3)

Jos 11: 9 h their horses and burned their chariots.
2Sm 8: 4 And he h all the chariot horses,
1Chr 18: 4 horses, David h all but one hundred.

HAMUL (3)

Gn 46:12 and the sons of Perez were Hezron and H.
Nm 26:21 through H the clan of the Hamulites.
1Chr 2: 5 The sons of Perez were Hezron and H.

HAMULITES (1)

Nm 26:21 through Hamul the clan of the H.

HAMUTAL (3)

2Kgs 23:31 His mother, whose name was H,
24:18 His mother's name was H,
Jer 52: 1 His mother's name was H,

HANAMEL (4)

Jer 32: 7 H, son of your uncle Shallum,
32: 8 Then, as the LORD foretold, H,
32: 9 the field in Anathoth from my cousin H,
32:12 in the presence of my cousin H

HANAN (12)

1Chr 8:23 Ishpan, Eber, Eliel, Abdon, Zichri, H,
8:38 Ishmael, Sheariah, Azariah, Obadiah, and H;
9:44 Ishmael, Sheariah, Azariah, Obadiah, and H;
11:43 H, from Beth-maacah;
Ezr 2:46 sons of Hagab, sons of Shamlai, sons of H,
Neh 7:49 of Hagaba, sons of Shalmai, sons of H,
8: 7 Maaseiah, Kelita, Azariah, Jozabad, H,
10:11 Shebaniah, Hodiah, Kelita, Pelaiah, H,
10:23 Meshezabel, Zadok, Jaddua, Pelatiah, H,
10:27 Rehum, Hashabnah, Maaseiah, Ahiah, H,
13:13 one of the Levites, together with H,
Jer 35: 4 of the LORD, to the room of the sons of H,

HANANEL (4)

Neh 3: 1 continued the rebuilding to the Tower of H.
12:39 City Gate], the Fish Gate, the Tower of H,
Jer 31:38 from the Tower of H to the Corner Gate.
Zec 14:10 the Tower of H to the king's wine presses,

HANANI (11)

1Kgs 16: 1 spoke against Baasha to Jehu, son of H,
16: 7 [Through the prophet Jehu, son of H,
1Chr 25: 4 Hananiah, H,
25:25 The eighteenth fell to H,
2Chr 16: 7 At that time H the seer came to Asa,
19: 2 Jehu the seer, son of H,
20:34 in the chronicle of Jehu, son of H,
Ezr 10:20 H and Zebadiah; of the sons of Harim:
Neh 1: 2 year, I was in the citadel of Susa when H,
7: 2 Over Jerusalem I placed H,
12:36 Gilalai, Maai, Nethanel, Judah, and H,

HANANIAH (32)

1Chr 3:19 sons of Zerubbabel were Meshullam and H;
3:21 The sons of H were Pelatiah,
8:24 Eber, Eliel, Abdon, Zichri, Hanan, H,
25: 4 H, Hanani, Eliathah,
25:23 The sixteenth fell to H,
2Chr 26:11 the recorder, under the command of H,
Ezr 10:28 Jehohanan, H,
Neh 3: 8 goldsmiths' guild, and at his side was H,
3:30 After him, H,
7: 2 I placed Hanani, my brother, and H,
10:24 Pelatiah, Hanan, Anaiah, Hoshea, H,
12:12 for Jeremiah, H;
12:41 Minjamin, Micaiah, Elioenai, Zechariah, H,
Tb 5:13 "I am Azariah, son of H the elder,
5:14 I knew H and Nathaniah,
1Mc 2:59 H, Azariah and Mishael,
Jer 28: 1 month of the fourth year, the prophet H,
28: 5 Jeremiah answered the prophet H
28:10 Thereupon the prophet H took the yoke from
28:12 Some time after the prophet H had broken
28:13 Go tell H this:
28:15 To the prophet H the prophet Jeremiah said:
28:15 Hear this, H!
28:17 in the seventh month, H the prophet died.
36:12 son of Shaphan, Zedekiah, son of H,
37:13 named Irijah, son of Shelemiah, son of H;
Dn 1: 6 Daniel, H, Mishael, and Azariah.
1: 7 Daniel to Belteshazzar, H to Shadrach,
1:11 had put in charge of Daniel, H,
1:19 them, none was found equal to Daniel, H,
2:17 went home and informed his companions H,
3:88 H, Azariah, Mishael, bless the Lord;

HANANIEL (1)

Tb 1: 1 Tobit, son Tobiel, son of H son of Aduel,

HAND (846)

Gn 3:22 h to take fruit from the tree of life also,
4:11 receive your brother's blood from your h.
8: 9 Putting out his h, he caught the dove
14:20 High, who delivered your foes into your h."
16:12 h against everyone, and everyone's h against
19:16 seized his h and the hands of his wife and
21:18 lift up the boy and hold him by the h;
22:12 "Do not lay your h on the boy,"

24: 2 "Put your *h* under my thigh,
24: 9 So the servant put his *h* under the thigh
24:18 and quickly lowering the jug onto her *h*,
30:40 The sheep, on the other *h*,
32:12 me, I pray, from the *h* of my brother Esau!
38:28 giving birth, one infant put out his *h*;
38:28 taking a crimson thread, tied it on his *h*,
38:29 But as he withdrew his *h*,
39:12 But leaving the cloak in her *h*,
39:13 left his cloak in her *h* as he fled outside,
40:11 Pharaoh's cup was in my *h*;
40:11 into his cup, and put it in Pharaoh's *h*."
41:44 move *h* or foot in all the land of Egypt."
47:29 put your *h* under my thigh as a sign of
48:13 took the two, Ephraim with his right *h*,
48:13 left, and Manasseh with his left *h*,
48:14 right *h* and laid it on the head of Ephraim,
48:14 and his left *h* on the head of Manasseh,
48:17 had laid his right *h* on Ephraim's head,
48:17 so he took hold of his father's *h*,
48:18 lay your right *h* on his head!"
49: 8 your *h* on the neck of your enemies;
Ex 3:20 I will stretch out my *h*,
4: 2 asked him, "What is that in your *h*?"
4: 4 "Now put out your *h*."
4: 4 So he put out his *h* and laid hold of it,
4: 4 hold of it, and it became a staff in his *h*.
4: 6 said to him, "Put your *h* in your bosom."
4: 6 it, to his surprise his *h* was leprous,
4: 7 said, "Now, put your *h* back in your bosom."
4: 7 Moses put his *h* back in his bosom,
4:17 Take this staff in your *h*;
6: 1 Forced by my mighty *h*,
7: 4 Therefore I will lay my *h* on Egypt and by
7: 5 as I stretch out my *h* against Egypt and
7:15 *h* the staff that turned into a serpent.
7:19 out your *h* over the waters of Egypt
8: 1 Stretch out your *h* and your staff over the
8: 2 out his *h* over the waters of Egypt,
8:13 Aaron stretched out his *h*,
9:15 now I would have stretched out my *h*
9:22 Moses, "Stretch out your *h* toward the sky,
10:12 out your *h* over the land of Egypt,
10:21 Moses, "Stretch out your *h* toward the sky,
10:22 Moses stretched out his *h* toward the sky,
12:11 sandals on your feet and your staff in *h*,
13: 3 a strong *h* that the LORD brought you away.
13: 9 your *h* and as a reminder on your forehead;
13: 9 strong *h* the LORD brought you out of Egypt.
13:14 strong *h* the LORD brought us out of Egypt,
13:16 your *h* and as a pendant on your forehead:
13:16 strong *h* the LORD brought us out of Egypt."
14:16 and, with *h* outstretched over the sea,
14:21 Moses stretched out his *h* over the sea,
14:26 Moses, "Stretch out your *h* over the sea,
14:27 So Moses stretched out his *h* over the sea,
15: 6 Your right *h*, O LORD, magnificent
15: 6 O LORD, magnificent in power your right *h*,
15: 9 my *h* shall despoil them!"
15:12 when you stretched out your right *h*,
15:20 sister, took a tambourine in her *h*,
16: 3 died at the LORD's *h* in the land of Egypt,
17: 5 the elders of Israel, holding in your *h*,
17: 9 of the hill with the staff of God in my *h*."
17:16 he said, "The LORD takes in *h* his banner;
19:13 No *h* shall touch him;
21:20 so hard that the slave dies under his *h*,
21:24 eye for eye, tooth for tooth, *h* for hand,
23: 1 Do not join the wicked in putting your *h*,
23:31 *h* over to you to be driven out of your way.
32:11 such great power and with so strong a *h*?
33:22 cover you with my *h* until I have passed by.
33:23 Then I will remove my *h*,
36: 7 there was already enough at *h*,
Lv 1: 4 lay his *h* on the head of the holocaust,
3: 2 lay his *h* on the head of his offering,
3: 8 laying his *h* on the head of his offering,
3:13 LORD, and after laying his *h* on its head,
4: 4 he shall lay his *h* on its head and
4:29 laid his *h* on the head of the sin offering,
4:33 Having laid his *h* on its head,
8:23 right ear, on the thumb of his right *h*,
14:14 man's right ear, the thumb of his right *h*,
14:15 of it into the palm of his own left *h*;
14:17 Of the oil left in his *h* the priest shall
14:17 man's right ear, the thumb of his right *h*,
14:18 The rest of the oil in his *h* the priest
14:25 purified, on the thumb of his right *h*,
14:26 oil into the palm of his own left *h*
14:28 Some of the oil in his *h* the priest shall
14:28 man's right ear, the thumb of his right *h*,
14:29 *h* the priest shall put on the man's head.
21:19 or malformation, or a crippled foot or *h*,
Nm 5:25 offering of jealousy from the woman's *h*,
20:11 Then, raising his *h*,
21: 2 "If you deliver this people into my *h*,
21:34 for into your *h* I will deliver him with
22: 7 the divination fee in *h* and went to Balaam.
22:29 the ass, "that if I but had a sword at *h*,
25: 7 the assembly, and taking a lance in *h*,
27:18 a man of spirit, and lay your *h* upon him.
35:17 stone in his *h* and causes his death,
35:18 club in his *h* and causes his death,
Dt 2:15 it was the LORD's *h* that was against them,
2:31 begun to *h* over to you Sihon and his land,
3: 2 your *h* with all his people and his land.
4:34 with his strong *h* and outstretched arm,
5:15 with his strong *h* and outstretched arm.
6:21 brought us out of Egypt with his strong *h*,
7: 8 his strong *h* from the place of slavery,
7: 8 and ransomed you from the *h* of Pharaoh,
7:19 his strong *h* and outstretched arm with
7:24 He will deliver their kings into your *h*,
8:17 own *h* that has obtained for me this wealth.'
9:26 brought out of Egypt with your strong *h*.
11: 2 majesty, his strong *h* and outstretched arm;
11:10 would sow your seed and then water it by *h*,
13: 8 any other nations, near at *h* or far away,
13:10 *h* shall be the first raised to slay him;
14:25 money and, with the purse of money in *h*,
15: 7 heart nor close your *h* to him in his need.
15: 8 you shall open your *h* to him and freely
15:11 command you to open your *h* to your poor
17: 9 case and then *h* down to you their decision.
17:11 left from the decision they *h* down to you.
19:12 and shall *h* him over to be slain by the
19:21 eye for eye, tooth for tooth, *h* for hand,
20:13 LORD, your God, delivers it into your *h*,
21:10 LORD, your God, delivers them into your *h*,
23:16 "You shall not *h* over to his master a
23:26 may pluck some of the ears with your *h*,
24: 6 "No one shall take a *h* mill or even its
25:11 if she stretches out her *h* and seizes the
25:12 you shall chop off her *h* without pity.
26: 8 with his strong *h* and outstretched arm,
32:27 boast, 'Our own *h* won the victory;
32:35 Close at *h* is the day of their disaster
32:39 them, and from my *h* there is no rescue.
32:40 "To the heavens I raise my *h* and swear:
32:41 and my *h* shall lay hold of my quiver.
33: 2 While at his right *h* a fire blazed forth
33: 3 But all his holy ones were in his *h*;
Jos 4:24 may learn that the *h* of the LORD is mighty,
5:13 one who stood facing him, drawn sword in *h*.
8:18 out the javelin in your *h* toward Ai,
8:18 out the javelin in his *h* toward the city,
8:26 Joshua kept the javelin in his *h* stretched
17:16 on the other *h*,
20: 9 death at the *h* of the avenger of blood,
Jgs 1:35 as the house of Joseph gained the upper *h*,
3:21 *h* drew the dagger from his right thigh,
4:21 got a tent peg and took a mallet in her *h*.
5:26 With her left *h* she reached for the peg,
7: 6 their mouths by *h* numbered three hundred,
9:48 all his soldiers, took his axe in his *h*,
12: 3 in my own *h* and went on to the Ammonites,
15: 4 of tails one of the torches he had at *h*.
15:18 great victory by the *h* of your servant.
16:26 to the attendant who was holding his *h*,
16:29 himself against them, one at his right *h*,
18:19 put your *h* over your mouth.
Ru 1:13 the LORD, has extended his *h* against me."
1Sm 5:11 the *h* of God had been very heavy upon it.
11:12 *H* over the men and we will put them to
14:19 he said to the priest, "Withdraw your *h*."
14:26 one would raise a *h* to his mouth from it,
16:13 Then Samuel, with the horn of oil in *h*,
17:40 staff in *h*, David selected five smooth
17:40 With his sling also ready to *h*,
17:46 the LORD shall deliver you into my *h*;
17:49 his *h* into the bag and took out a stone,
18:16 other *h*, all Israel and Judah loved him
19: 9 in *h* and David was playing the harp nearby.
21: 4 Now what have you on *h*?
21: 5 to David, "I have no ordinary bread on *h*,
21: 7 for no other bread was on *h* except the
21: 9 "Do you have a spear or a sword on *h*?
22:17 lift a *h* to strike the priests of the LORD.
23:11 Will they *h* me over?
23:17 my father Saul shall not lay a *h* to you.
24: 7 the LORD's anointed, as to lay a *h* on him,
24:11 'I will not raise a *h* against my lord,
25:39 the insult I received at the *h* of Nabal,
27: 1 "I shall perish some day at the *h* of Saul.
2Sm 1:14 your *h* to desecrate the LORD's anointed?"
6: 6 his *h* to the ark of God and steadied it,
12: 7 I rescued you from the *h* of Saul.
13: 5 for me to see, I will eat it from her *h*.'"
13: 6 that I may take nourishment from her *h*."
13:10 bedroom, that I may have it from your *h*."
15: 5 him to show homage, he would extend his *h*,
18:14 And taking three pikes in *h*,
20: 9 With his right *h* Joab held Amasa's beard
20:10 guard against the sword in Joab's other *h*,
21:20 on each *h* and six toes on each foot
22: 1 of all his enemies and from the *h* of Saul.
23: 6 they cannot be taken up by *h*.
23:10 until his *h* grew tired and became cramped,
23:21 wrested the spear from the Egyptian's *h*,
24:14 Let us fall by the *h* of God,
24:14 but let me not fall by the *h* of man."
24:16 forth his *h* toward Jerusalem to destroy it,
24:16 "Enough, now! Stay your *h*."
1Kgs 8:15 and by his *h* has brought it to fulfillment.
8:42 your mighty *h* and your outstretched arm),
13: 4 forth his *h* from the altar and said,
13: 4 *h* he stretched forth against him withered,
13: 6 for me that I may be able to withdraw my *h*."
13: 6 the king recovered the normal use of his *h*.
18:44 as small as a man's *h* rising from the sea."
18:46 But the *h* of the LORD was on Elijah,
20:23 other *h*, the servants of the king of Aram
2Kgs 5:11 God, and would move his *h* over the spot,
10:15 are," continued Jehu, "give me your *h*."
10:15 Jehonadab gave him his *h*,
13:16 king of Israel, "Put your *h* on the bow."
14: 5 When Amaziah had the kingdom firmly in *h*,
18:21 pierces the *h* of anyone who leans on it.
18:29 since he cannot deliver you out of my *h*.
18:33 his land from the *h* of the king of Assyria?
18:35 lands ever rescued his land from my *h*?
18:35 the LORD then rescue Jerusalem from my *h*?'"
19:14 from the *h* of the messengers and read it;
20: 6 city from the *h* of the king of Assyria;
1Chr 6:24 His brother Asaph stood at his right *h*.
11:23 wrested the spear from the Egyptian's *h*,
12: 2 could use either the right or the left *h*,
13: 9 stretched out his *h* to steady the ark,
13:10 because he had laid his *h* on the ark.
20: 6 to each *h* and six toes to each foot;
21:13 I prefer to fall into the *h* of the LORD,
21:15 "Enough, now! Stay your *h*!"
21:16 in his *h* stretched out against Jerusalem.
28:19 because the *h* of the LORD was upon him.
29:12 In your *h* are power and might;
2Chr 6:15 and by your own *h* you have brought it to
16: 7 of the king of Aram has escaped your *h*.
20: 6 In your *h* is power and might,
23:10 all the people, each with his spear in *h*,
25:15 not save their own people from your *h*?"
25:20 for God had determined to *h* them over
32:13 lands able to save their lands from my *h*?
32:14 ban was able to save his people from my *h*?
32:14 god, then, be able to save you from my *h*?
32:15 from my *h* or the hands of my fathers,
32:15 the less shall your god save you from my *h*!"
32:17 have not saved their people from my *h*,
32:17 Hezekiah's god save his people from my *h*."
32:22 of Jerusalem from the *h* of Sennacherib,
Ezr 7: 6 Because the *h* of the LORD,
7: 9 for the favoring *h* of his God was upon him.
7:28 took courage, and, with the *h* of the LORD,
8:18 for the favoring *h* of our God was upon us
8:22 *h* of our God is upon all who seek him,
8:31 The *h* of our God remained upon us,
10: 9 the matter at *h* and because it was raining.
Neh 1:10 by your great might and your strong *h*.
2: 8 for the favoring *h* of my God was upon me.
2:18 favoring *h* of my God had rested upon me,
4:10 only half my able men took a *h* in the work,
4:11 one *h* and held a weapon with the other.
4:17 everyone kept his weapon at his right *h*.
9:14 for them, by the *h* of Moses your servant.
9:15 you had sworn with upraised *h* to give them.
Tb 7:12 *h* and gave her to Tobiah with the words:
8: 3 pursued him there and bound him *h* and foot.
11: 4 said to Tobiah, "Have the gall in your *h*!"
11:11 up to him with the fish gall in his *h*,
11:16 briskly, with no one leading him by the *h*,
13: 2 No one can escape his *h*.
Jdt 6:10 Bethulia, and *h* him over to the Israelites.
8: 9 swearing that he would *h* over the city to
8:11 When you promised to *h* over the city to
8:33 the Lord will rescue Israel by my *h*.
9: 2 You put a sword into his *h* to take revenge
9: 9 a widow, the strong *h* to execute my plan.
9:10 crush their pride by the *h* of a woman.
12: 4 by my *h* what he has determined."
13:14 our enemies by my *h* this very night."
13:15 Lord struck him down by the *h* of a woman.
14: 6 saw the head of Holofernes in the *h* of one
15:10 With your own *h* you have done all this;
16: 5 them, by a woman's *h* he confounded them.
Est 3:10 ring from his *h* and gave it to Haman,
C:15 but you, for I am taking my life in my *h*.
1Mc 2:10 realm, and laid its *h* on her possessions?
3: 6 By his *h* redemption was happily achieved,
3:30 a more liberal *h* than the preceding kings.
4:30 mighty one by the *h* of your servant David
4:30 of the Philistines into the *h* of Jonathan,
10:41 *h* over as they had done in the first years,
11:40 urging Imalkue to *h* over the boy to him,
12:34 men had intended to *h* over this stronghold
12:45 I will *h* it over to you together with
15:21 you, *h* them over to Simon the high priest,
16:16 and his men sprang up, weapons in *h*,
2Mc 7:34 your *h* against the children of Heaven.
10: 4 not *h* them over to blasphemous
14:33 *h* toward the temple and swore this oath:
14:33 you do not *h* Judas over to me as prisoner,
15:15 Stretching out his right *h*,
Jb 1:11 your *h* and touch anything that he has,
1:12 only do not lay a *h* upon his person."
2: 5 your *h* and touch his bone and his flesh,
5:15 of the sword and from the *h* of the mighty,
6: 9 he would put forth his *h* and cut me off!
8:20 neither will he take the *h* of the wicked.
9:33 who could lay his *h* upon us both and
10: 7 and that none can deliver me out of your *h*?

HAND (cont.)

12: 9 not know that the *h* of God has done this?
12:10 In his *h* is the soul of every living thing,
13:14 between my teeth, and take my life in my *h*.
13:21 Withdraw your *h* far from me,
15:25 Because he has stretched out his *h* against
17: 1 my burial is at *h*.
19:21 my friends, for the *h* of God has struck me!
23: 2 his *h* is heavy upon me in my groanings.
27:22 *h* pierces the fugitive dragon as from his *h*
28: 9 He sets his *h* to the flinty rock,
29:20 within me, and my bow is renewed in my *h*!"
30:21 mercy and with your strong *h* you buffet me.
30:24 Yet should not a *h* be held out to help a
31:21 If I have raised my *h* against the innocent
31:25 great, or that my *h* had acquired abundance
31:27 enticed to waft them a kiss with my *h*;
34:20 removing the powerful without lifting a *h*;
35: 7 him, or what does he receive from your *h*?
40: 4 I put my *h* over my mouth.
40:14 that your own right *h* can save you.
40:32 Once you but lay a *h* upon him,
Ps(s) 10:12 O God, lift up your *h*!
16: 8 him at my right *h* I shall not be disturbed.
16:11 the delights at your right *h* forever.
17: 7 from their foes to refuge at your right *h*.
17:14 by your sword from the wicked, by your *h*,
18:36 your right *h* has upheld me,
20: 7 the strength of his victorious right *h*.
21: 9 *h* reach all your enemies, may your right *h*
32: 4 For day and night your *h* was heavy upon me;
36:12 me nor the *h* of the wicked disquiet me.
37:24 for the *h* of the LORD sustains him.
38: 3 in me, and your *h* has come down upon me.
39:11 at the blow of your *h* I wasted away.
44: 3 How with your own *h* you rooted out the
44: 4 right *h* and the light of your countenance,
45: 5 may your right *h* show you wondrous deeds.
45:10 her place at your right *h* in gold of Ophir.
48:11 Of justice your right *h* is full;
60: 7 help us by your right *h*,
63: 9 your right *h* upholds me.
71: 4 my God, rescue me from the *h* of the wicked,
73:23 you have hold of my right *h*;
74:11 draw back your *h* and keep your right *h*
75: 9 For a cup is in the LORD's *h*,
77:11 the right *h* of the Most High is changed."
78:42 They remembered not his *h* nor the day he
78:54 land, to the mountains his right *h* had won.
80:16 and protect what your right *h* has planted
80:18 your help be with the man of your right *h*,
81:15 against their foes I would turn my *h*.
82: 4 from the *h* of the wicked deliver them.
89:14 strong is your hand, exalted your right *h*.
89:22 him, That my *h* may be always with him,
89:26 I will set his *h* upon the sea, his right *h*
97:10 from the *h* of the wicked he delivers them.
98: 1 His right *h* has won victory for him,
104:28 when you open your *h*,
106:26 Then with raised *h* he swore against them
107: 2 redeemed from the *h* of the foe
108: 7 ones may escape, help us by your right *h*,
109: 6 and let the accuser stand at his right *h*.
109:27 And let them know that this is your *h*;
109:31 he stood at the right *h* of the poor man,
110: 1 *h* till I make your enemies your footstool."
110: 5 The LORD is at your right *h*;
118:15 right *h* of the LORD has struck with power:
118:16 right *h* of the LORD is exalted; the right *h*
119:173 Let your *h* be ready to help me,
121: 5 he is beside you at your right *h*.
127: 4 *h* of a warrior are the sons of one's youth.
129: 7 With which the reaper fills not his *h*,
136:12 With a mighty *h* and an outstretched arm,
137: 5 Jerusalem, may my right *h* be forgotten!
138: 7 you raise your *h*; your right *h* saves me.
139: 5 you hem me in and rest your *h* upon me.
139:10 *h* shall guide me, and your right *h* hold me
144: 7 Reach out your *h* from on high
145:16 You open your *h* and satisfy the desire of
Prv 1:24 I extended my *h* and no one took notice;
3:16 Long life is in her right *h*,
6: 1 given your *h* in pledge to another,
6: 5 or as a bird from the *h* of the fowler.
10: 4 slack *h* impoverishes, but the *h* of the diligent
12:24 The diligent *h* will govern,
17:16 the fool's *h* are the means to buy wisdom,
17:18 is the man who gives his *h* in pledge,
19:24 The sluggard loses his *h* in the dish;
21: 1 is the king's heart in the *h* of the LORD;
22:26 one of those who give their *h* in pledge,
26: 9 Like a thorn stick brandished by the *h* of
26:15 The sluggard loses his *h* in the dish;
27:10 neighbor near at *h* than a brother far away.
30:32 put your *h* on your mouth;
Eccl 2:24 this, I realized, is from the *h* of God.
4: 1 the *h* of their oppressors comes violence,
5:14 from his labor that he can carry in his *h*.
9: 1 wise, and their deeds are in the *h* of God.
9:10 Anything you can turn your *h* to,
9:13 other *h* I saw this wise deed under the sun,
11: 6 and at evening let not your *h* be idle:
Sg 2: 6 His left *h* is under my head and his right
5: 4 My lover put his *h* through the opening;
8: 3 His left *h* is under my head and his right
Wis 2:18 him and deliver him from the *h* of his foes.
3: 1 the souls of the just are in the *h* of God,
3:14 also the eunuch whose *h* wrought no misdeed,
5:16 beauteous diadem, from the *h* of the Lord
5:16 For he shall shelter them with his right *h*,
7:16 For both we and our words are in his *h*,
10:20 and praised in unison your conquering *h*—
11:17 For not without means was your almighty *h*,
13:10 or useless stone, the work of an ancient *h*.
14: 6 for his race, under the guidance of your *h*.
16:15 But your *h* none can escape.
16:20 them bread from heaven, ready to *h*,
19: 8 the whole nation sheltered by your *h*,
Sir 4: 9 the oppressed from the *h* of the oppressor;
4:31 Let not your *h* be open to receive and
5:14 if not, put your *h* over your mouth.
7:32 To the poor man also extend your *h*,
10: 4 over the earth is in the *h* of God,
10: 5 over every man is in the *h* of God,
12:12 Let him not sit at your right *h*,
12:17 comes upon you, you will find him at *h*;
13: 1 He who touches pitch blackens his *h*;
15:16 whichever you choose, stretch forth your *h*.
21:19 to a fool, like a manacle on his right *h*.
27:19 Like a bird released from the *h*,
29: 1 the precepts who holds out a helping *h*.
29: 5 he kisses the lender's *h* and speaks with
31:14 Toward what he eyes, do not put out a *h*;
31:18 be not the first to reach out your *h*.
36: 2 Raise your *h* against the heathen,
36: 5 forth the splendor of your right *h* and arm;
43:12 this bow bent by the mighty *h* of God.
47: 4 When his *h* let fly the slingstone that
49:11 was like a signet ring on God's right *h*,
50:15 And had stretched forth his *h* for the cup,
51:19 My *h* opened her gate and I came to know
Is 1:25 I will turn my *h* against you,
3: 6 Be our ruler, and take in *h* this ruin!"—
5:25 his people, he raises his *h* to strike them;
5:25 back, and his *h* is still outstretched.
9:11 back, and his *h* is still outstretched!
9:16 turned back, his *h* is still outstretched!
9:20 turned back, his *h* is still outstretched!
10: 4 turned back, his *h* is still outstretched!
10:10 Just as my *h* reached out
10:14 My *h* has seized like a nest the riches of
11: 8 the child lay his *h* on the adder's lair.
11:11 The Lord shall again take it in *h* to
11:15 and wave his *h* over the Euphrates in his
13:22 at *h* and her days shall not be prolonged.
14:26 this the *h* outstretched over all nations.
14:27 His *h* is stretched out;
23:11 His *h* he stretches out over the sea,
25:10 *h* of the LORD will rest on this mountain,
26:11 O LORD, your *h* is uplifted,
31: 3 When the LORD stretches forth his *h*,
36: 6 pierces the *h* of anyone who leans on it.
36:18 his land from the *h* of the king of Assyria?
36:19 Have they saved Samaria from my *h*?
36:20 lands ever rescued his land from my *h*?
36:20 the LORD then save Jerusalem from my *h*?' "
37:14 from the *h* of the messengers and read it;
37:20 O LORD, our God, save us from his *h*,
38: 6 city from the *h* of the king of Assyria;
40: 2 the *h* of the LORD double for all her sins.
40:12 has cupped in his *h* the waters of the sea,
41:10 and uphold you with my right *h* of justice.
41:13 LORD, your God, who grasp your right *h*;
41:20 That the *h* of the LORD has done this,
42: 6 of justice, I have grasped you by the *h*;
43:13 There is none who can deliver from my *h*.
44: 5 Jacob, And this one shall write on his *h*,
44:20 "Is not this thing in my right *h* a fraud?"
45: 1 his anointed, Cyrus, whose right *h* I grasp,
47: 6 inheritance, And I gave them into your *h*;
48:13 my *h* laid the foundations of the earth;
48:13 my right *h* spread out the heavens.
49:22 See, I will lift up my *h* to the nations,
50: 2 Is my *h* too short to ransom?
50:11 This is your fate from my *h*:
51:16 and shielded you in the shadow of my *h*,
51:17 drank at the LORD's *h* the cup of his wrath;
51:18 She has no one to grasp her by the *h*,
51:22 taking from your *h* the cup of staggering;
56: 2 profanation, and his *h* from any evildoing.
59: 1 the *h* of the LORD is not too short to save,
62: 3 be a glorious crown in the *h* of the LORD,
62: 8 sworn by his right *h* and by his mighty arm:
63: 4 my heart, my year for redeeming was at *h*.
66: 2 My *h* made all these things when all of
Jer 1: 9 LORD extended his *h* and touched my mouth,
6: 9 Pass your *h*, like a vintager,
6:12 my *h* against those who dwell in this land,
11:21 else you shall die by our *h*."
12: 7 my soul I deliver into the *h* of her foes.
15: 6 And so I stretched out my *h* to destroy you,
15:17 Under the weight of your *h* I sat alone
15:21 I will free you from the *h* of the wicked,
18: 4 he was making turned out badly in his *h*,
18: 6 the hand of the potter, so are you in my *h*,
19: 7 by the *h* of those that seek their lives.
20: 5 give as plunder into the *h* of their foes,
21: 5 you with outstretched *h* and mighty arm,
21: 7 says the LORD, I will *h* over Zedekiah,
21: 7 and famine, into the *h* of Nebuchadnezzar,
21:12 the oppressed from the *h* of the oppressor,
22: 3 the victim from the *h* of his oppressor.
22:24 of Judah, are a signet ring on my right *h*,
23:23 Am I a God near at *h* only,
25:15 Take this cup of foaming wine from my *h*,
25:17 I took the cup from the *h* of the LORD and
25:28 to take the cup from your *h* and drink,
27: 6 these lands into the *h* of Nebuchadnezzar,
27: 8 says the LORD until I give them into his *h*.
30:16 who pillage you I will *h* over to pillage,
31:11 redeem him from the *h* of his conqueror.
31:32 I took them by the *h* to lead them forth from
32:21 With strong *h* and outstretched arm you
32:28 I will *h* over this city to the Chaldeans,
34: 3 Neither shall you escape his *h*;
34:20 the parts of the calf, I will *h* over,
34:21 princes, I will *h* over to their enemies,
36:14 Scroll in *h*, Baruch, son of Neriah,
38:16 nor will I *h* you over to these men who
43: 3 to *h* us over to the Chaldeans to be killed
44:30 I will *h* over Pharaoh Hophra,
46:26 *h* them over to those who seek their lives,
48:16 Near at *h* is Moab's ruin,
48:37 every *h* is gashed,
51: 7 Babylon was a golden cup in the *h* of the
51:25 I will stretch forth my *h* against you,
Lam 1:10 stretched out his *h* to all her treasures;
1:14 by his *h* they have been plaited:
2: 3 of his right *h* when the enemy approached;
2: 4 in his right *h* He took his stand as a foe,
2: 8 his *h* brought ruin,
3: 3 back his *h* again and again all the day.
4: 6 in an instant without the turning of a *h*.
Bar 2:11 of the land of Egypt with your mighty *h*,
3: 5 of our fathers, but your own *h* and name:
6:14 Each has in its right *h* an axe or dagger,
Ez 1: 3 the *h* of the LORD came upon me.
2: 9 It was then I saw a *h* stretched out to me,
3:14 the *h* of the LORD rested heavily upon me.
3:19 other *h*, you have warned the wicked man
3:21 other *h*, you have warned a virtuous man
3:22 The *h* of the LORD came upon me,
6:14 I will stretch out my *h* against them,
7:21 I will *h* them over as booty to foreigners,
8: 1 the *h* of the Lord GOD fell upon me there.
8: 2 He stretched out what appeared to be a *h*
8:11 each of them with his censer in his *h*,
9: 2 each with a destroying weapon in his *h*.
10: 7 Thereupon its cherub stretched out his *h*
11: 9 of the city, and *h* you over to foreigners,
12: 7 dug a hole through the wall with my *h* and,
12:23 The days are at *h*,
13: 9 But I will stretch out my *h* against the
14: 9 I will stretch out my *h* against him and
14:13 *h* against it and break its staff of bread,
16:27 Therefore I stretched out my *h* against you,
16:39 I will *h* you over to them to tear down
17:18 Though he gave his *h* in pledge,
18:14 On the other *h*, if a man begets a son
20:22 but I stayed my *h*,
20:33 GOD, with a mighty *h* and outstretched arm,
20:34 With a mighty *h* and outstretched arm,
21:12 shall fail, every *h* shall fall helpless,
21:16 burnisher that he might hold it in his *h*,
21:16 burnished to be put in the *h* of a slayer.
21:19 prophesy, brushing one *h* against the other:
21:22 one *h* against the other and wreak my fury.
21:27 In his right *h* is the divining arrow
21:28 and the arrow taken in *h* marks their guilt.
21:29 drawn to you), you shall be taken in *h*.
21:32 and to him I will *h* it over.
21:36 I will *h* you over to ravaging men,
22:13 I am brushing one *h* against the other
23:31 path of your sister, I will *h* you her cup.
25: 7 I will stretch out my *h* against you.
25:10 I will *h* her over,
25:13 I will stretch out my *h* against Edom and
25:16 out my *h* against the Philistines;
29: 7 When they held you in *h*,
30:10 of Egypt by the *h* of Nebuchadnezzar,
30:12 I will *h* over to foreigners to devastate.
30:22 so that the sword drops from his *h*.
30:24 of Babylon, and put my sword in his *h*,
30:25 when I put my sword in the *h* of the king
33:22 The *h* of the LORD had come upon me the
35: 3 I will stretch out my *h* against you and
37: 1 The *h* of the LORD came upon me,
37:17 so that they form one stick in your *h*.
37:19 of Joseph, which is in the *h* of Ephraim,
37:19 they shall be one in my *h*.
38:12 turning my *h* against the ruins that were
39: 3 I will strike the bow from your left *h*,
39:21 executed and the *h* I have laid upon them.
40: 1 that very day the *h* of the LORD came upon
46: 7 ram, for the lambs as much as he has at *h*,
47: 3 the east with a measuring cord in his *h*,
Dn 2:34 a mountain without a *h* being put to it,
2:45 the mountain without a *h* being put to it,
4:32 is no one who can stay his *h* or say to him,

5: 5 the fingers of a human h appeared,
5: 5 the king saw the wrist and h that wrote,
5:23 But the God in whose h is your life breath
5:24 By him were the wrist and h sent,
8:25 shall be broken without a h being raised.
9:15 out of the land of Egypt with a strong h,
10:10 But then a h touched me,
10:16 something like a man's h touched my lips;
11:11 be given into his h and be carried off.
14:29 H Daniel over to us,
14:30 king was forced to h Daniel over to them.
Hos 2:12 and no one can deliver her out of my h.
7: 5 He extends his h among dissemblers;
Am 1: 6 captive whole groups to h over to Edom,
1: 8 I will turn my h against Ekron,
5:19 he were to rest his h against the wall,
7: 7 he was standing by a wall, plummet in h.
9: 2 even from there my h shall bring them out;
Jon 3: 8 evil way and from the violence he has in h.
4:11 distinguish their right h from their left,
Mi 4:10 LORD redeem you from the h of your enemies.
5: 8 Your h shall be lifted above your foes,
Hb 2:16 revert the cup from the LORD's right h,
Zep 1: 4 I will stretch out my h against Judah,
2:13 will stretch out his h against the north,
Hg 1:11 beasts, and upon all that is produced by h.
Zec 2: 5 was a man with a measuring line in his h.
2:13 See, I wave my h over them;
3: 1 Satan stood at his right h to accuse him.
6:13 The priest shall be put at his right h,
8: 4 each with staff in h because of old age,
13: 7 I will turn my h against the little ones.
14:13 seize the h of his neighbor, and the h of each
Mal 2:13 nor accepts it favorably from your h;
Mt 3: 2 The reign of God is at h."
3:12 His winnowing-fan is in his h.
4:17 The kingdom of heaven is at h."
5:25 h you over to the judge, who will h you over
5:30 Again, if your right h is your trouble,
5:40 over your shirt, h him your coat as well.
6: 3 left h know what your right hand is doing.
7: 9 h his son a stone when he asks for a loaf,
8: 3 out his h and touched him and said,
8:15 took her by the h and the fever left her.
9:18 h on her and she will come back to life."
9:25 put out he entered and took her by the h,
10: 7 'The reign of God is at h!'
10:19 When they h you over,
10:21 "Brother will h over brother to death,
12:10 with a shriveled h happened to be there,
12:13 To the man he said, "Stretch out your h."
12:49 extending his h toward his disciples,
13:28 He answered, 'I see an enemy's h in this.'
14:31 at once stretched out his h and caught him.
17: 7 came toward them and laying his h on them,
18: 6 other h, it would be better for anyone
18: 8 If your h or foot is your undoing,
20:21 at your right h and the other at your left,
20:23 my right h or my left is not mine to give.
22:13 'Bind him h and foot and throw him out
22:44 Lord said to my lord, Sit at my right h,
24: 9 will h you over to torture and kill you.
25:33 The sheep he will place on his right h,
26:15 willing to give me if I h him over to you?"
26:16 looking for an opportunity to h him over.
26:23 h into the dish with me is the one who will h
26:51 accompanied Jesus put his h to his sword,
26:64 see the Son of Man seated at the right h
27:29 his head, and stuck a reed in his right h.
Mk 1:15 The reign of God is at h!
1:31 to her and grasped her h and helped her up,
1:41 Moved with pity, Jesus stretched out his h,
3: 1 there was a man whose h was shriveled up.
3: 3 He addressed the man with the shriveled h:
3: 5 he said to the man, "Stretch out your h."
3: 5 did so and his h was perfectly restored.
5:27 in the crowd and put her h to his cloak.
5:41 Taking her h, he said to her, "Talitha,
7:32 and begged him to lay his h on him.
8:23 man's h and led him outside the village.
9:27 him by the h and helped him to his feet.
9:43 "If your h is your difficulty,
10:34 to death and h him over to the Gentiles,
12:36 h until I make your enemies your footstool.'
13: 9 They will h you over to the courts.
13:12 Brother will h over brother for execution
14:10 the chief priests to h Jesus over to them.
14:11 looking for an opportune way to h him over.
14:62 see the Son of Man seated at the right h
16:19 heaven and took his seat at God's right h.
Lk 1:66 "Was not the h of the Lord upon him?"
3:17 His winnowing-fan is in his h to clear his
5:13 stretched out his h to touch him and said,
6: 6 there was a man whose right h was withered.
6: 8 and said to the man whose h was withered,
6:10 and said to the man, "Stretch out your h."
6:10 did so and his h was perfectly restored.
6:49 other h, anyone who has heard my words
7:30 Pharisees and the lawyers, on the other h,
8:54 He took her by the h and spoke these words:
9:62 "Whoever puts his h to the plow but keeps
10: 9 Say to them, 'The reign of God is at h.'
11:12 or h him a scorpion if he asks for an egg?

13:13 He laid his h on her,
20:20 so that they might then h him over to the
20:42 Sit at my right h while I make your
21: 8 saying, 'I am he' and 'The time is at h.'
21:28 high, for your deliverance is near at h."
22: 4 officers about a way to h him over to them.
22: 6 h him over without creating a disturbance.
22:21 h of my betrayer is with me at this table.
22:53 the temple you never raised a h against me.
22:69 seat at the right h of the Power of God.'"
23:10 scribes were at h to accuse him vehemently.
Jn 2: 6 there were at h six stone water jars,
6:64 believe, and the one who would h him over.)
6:71 of the Twelve, was going to h Jesus over.)
10:12 The hired h —who is no shepherd
10:28 No one shall snatch them out of my h.
10:29 me, and there is no snatching out of his h.
12: 4 disciples (the one about to h him over),
13: 2 son of Simon Iscariot, to h him over;
14:30 the Prince of this world is at h.
18: 2 (the one who was to h him over)
18: 5 (Now Judas, the one who was to h him over,
19:42 Jesus there, for the tomb was close at h.
20:25 in the nailmarks and my h into his side."
20:27 Put your h into my side.
21:20 said, "Lord, which one will h you over?").
Acts 2:25 him at my right h I shall not be disturbed.
2:33 Exalted at God's right h,
2:34 Sit at my right h until I make your
3: 7 took him by the right h and pulled him up.
4:30 assurance by stretching forth your h
5:31 He whom God has exalted at his right h as
5:39 If, on the other h, it comes from God,
7:50 Did not my h make all these things?
7:55 God, and Jesus standing at God's right h.
7:56 the Son of Man standing at God's right h."
9: 8 him by the h and lead him into Damascus.
9:41 gave her his h and helped her to her feet.
11:21 The h of the Lord was with them and a
13:11 The Lord's h is upon you even now!
13:11 about for someone to lead him by the h.
21:11 this belt and h him over to the Gentiles.'"
22:11 h and led into Damascus by my companions.
23:19 the h and drew him aside to ask privately,
25:11 no one has a right to h me over to them.
25:16 Roman practice to h an accused man over
26: 1 stretched out his h and began his defense.
28: 3 from the heat, fastened itself on his h.
28: 4 the sight of the snake hanging from his h,
Rom 2:20 h a clear pattern of knowledge and truth.
7:21 leads to wrongdoing is always ready at h.
8:34 right h of God and who intercedes for us?
1Cor 2:15 The spiritual man, on the other h,
5: 5 I h him over to Satan for the destruction
7:34 The married woman, on the other h,
11: 7 A man, on the other h,
12:15 I am not a h I do not belong to the body,"
12:21 The eye cannot say to the h,
13: 3 the poor and h over my body to be burned,
14: 3 The prophet, on the other h,
15:24 will h over the kingdom to God the Father.
16:21 who send you this greeting in my own h.
2Cor 6: 7 of righteousness with right h and left,
Gal 3:10 on observance of the law, on the other h,
Eph 1:20 and seating him at his right h in heaven,
Phil 1:22 If, on the other h,
Col 2:11 with the circumcision administered by h
3: 1 where Christ is seated at God's right h.
4:18 This greeting is from Paul— in my own h!
1Thes 4: 6 cheating his brother in the matter at h;
2Thes 3:17 This greeting is in my own h— Paul's.
2Tm 2: 2 witnesses you must h on to trustworthy men
Phlm 1:19 I, Paul, write this in my own h:
Heb 1: 3 at the right h of the Majesty in heaven,
1:13 "Sit at my right h till I make your
8: 1 h of the throne of the Majesty in heaven,
8: 9 I took them by the h to lead them forth
10:12 his seat forever at the right h of God;
Jas 1:25 There is, on the other h,
5: 8 because the coming of the Lord is at h.
1Pt 3:22 He went to heaven and is at God's right h,
4: 7 The consummation of all is close at h.
5: 6 Bow humbly under God's mighty h,
Rv 1:16 In his right h he held seven stars.
1:17 He touched me with his right h and said:
1:20 of the seven stars you saw in my right h,
2: 1 who holds the seven stars in his right h
5: 1 In the right h of the One who sat on the
5: 7 right h of the One who sat on the throne.
6: 5 of which held a pair of scales in his h.
8: 4 From the angel's h the smoke of the
10: 2 In his h he held a little scroll which had
10: 5 on the land raised his right h to heaven
10: 8 take the open scroll from the h of the
10:10 scroll from the angel's h and ate it.
13:16 image on their right h or their forehead.
14: 9 or accepts its mark on his forehead or h,
14:14 head and holding a sharp sickle in his h.
17: 4 In her h she held a gold cup that was
19: 2 of his servants which was shed by her h."
20: 1 key to the abyss and a huge chain in his h.

HAND-EXECUTED (1)

Eph 2:11 who, in virtue of a h rite on their flesh,

HAND-SPUN (1)

Ex 35:25 who were expert spinners brought h violet,

HAND-TO-HAND (2)

1Mc 4:34 thousand of Lysias' men fell in h fighting.
2Mc 15:17 issue by h combat with the utmost courage,

HANDBREADTH (7)

Ex 25:25 Surround it with a frame, a h high,
37:12 A frame a h high was also put around it,
1Kgs 7:26 It was a h thick,
2Chr 4: 5 It was a h thick,
Ez 40: 5 long, each cubit being a cubit and a h;
40:43 The ledges, a h wide,
43:13 the altar in cubits of one cubit plus a h.

HANDCLASP (1)

Gal 2: 9 gave Barnabas and me the h of fellowship,

HANDCUFFS (1)

Mk 5: 4 frequently been secured with h and chains,

HANDED (86)

Gn 27:17 Then she h her son Jacob the appetizing
35: 4 They therefore h over to Jacob all the
40:21 so that he again h the cup to Pharaoh;
Dt 25: 1 and a decision is h down to them
Ru 2:14 he h her some roasted grain and she ate
2Kgs 4: 5 As they h her the vessels,
18:30 will not be h over to the king of Assyria.
19:10 will not be h over to the king of Assyria.
2Chr 34:17 have h it over to the overseers
Tb 3: 4 So you h us over to plundering,
10:10 promptly h over to Tobiah Sarah his wife,
Jdt 8:19 were h over to the sword and to pillage,
9: 4 Their wives you h over to plunder,
11:15 they will be h over to you for destruction.
13: 9 h over the head of Holofernes to her maid,
Est E: 7 stories that have been h down to us,
1Mc 7:20 he h the province over to Alcimus,
10:41 be h over for the services of the temple.
Wis 14:15 h down to his subjects mysteries
Is 29:11 When it is h to one who can read,
29:12 When it is h to one who cannot read,
36:15 will not be h over to the king of Assyria."'
37:10 will not be h over to the king of Assyria.
Jer 26:24 h over to the people to be put to death.
32: 4 shall he be h over to the king of Babylon.
32:24 the city will be h over to the Chaldeans
32:25 has already been h over to the Chaldeans!
32:36 h over to the king of Babylon amid sword,
32:43 man or beast, h over to the Chaldeans.
37:17 you shall be h over to the king of Babylon.
38: 3 h over to the army of the king of Babylon;
38:19 I may be h over to them,
38:20 You will not be h over, Jeremiah answered.
38:23 you shall be h over to the king of Babylon,
39:17 h over to the men of whom you are afraid.
44:30 seek his life, just as I h over Zedekiah,
46:24 Egypt, h over to the people of the north.
Lam 2: 7 of her towers he has h over to the enemy,
Bar 4: 6 God that you were h over to your foes.
Ez 23: 9 Therefore I h her over to her lovers,
28: 9 a god, h over to those who will slay you.
31:11 h it over to the mightiest of the nations,
39:23 from them and h them over to their foes,
Dn 1: 2 The Lord h over to him Jehoiakim,
2:38 they may dwell, he has h over to you,
3:32 You have h us over to our enemies,
7:25 They shall be h over to him for a year,
14:22 them to death, and h Bel over to Daniel,
Mt 18:34 Then in anger the master h him over to the
20:18 be h over to the chief priests and scribes,
22:19 When they h him a small Roman coin,
25:14 He called in his servants and h his funds
26: 2 Son of Man is to be h over to be crucified."
26:45 is to be h over to the power of evil men.
27: 2 away to be h over to the procurator Pilate.
27: 3 DenialThen Judas, who had h him over,
27:18 out of jealousy that they had h him over.
27:26 then he h him over to be crucified.
Mk 7:13 in favor of the traditions you have h on.
8: 6 and they h them out to the crowd.
10:33 where the Son of Man will be h over to the
14:41 to be h over to the clutches of evil men.
15: 1 led him away, and h him over to Pilate.
15:10 that the chief priests had h him over.
15:15 scourged, he h him over to be crucified.
16:20 sake of sinners that I was h over to death,
Lk 4:17 the book of the prophet Isaiah was h him,
Jn 13: 3 Father who had h everything over to him
18:30 would certainly not have h him over to you."
18:35 chief priests who have h you over to me.
18:36 to save me from being h over to the Jews.
19:11 That is why he who h me over to you is
19:16 end, Pilate h Jesus over to be crucified.

HANDED (cont.)
Acts 3:13 whom you *h* over and disowned in Pilate's
6:14 the customs which Moses *h* down to us."
27: 1 other prisoners were *h* over to a centurion
28:17 I was *h* over to the Romans as a prisoner.
Rom 4:25 the Jesus who was *h* over to death for our
8:32 *h* him over for the sake of us all
15:28 safely *h* over this contribution to them,
1Cor 11: 2 the traditions just as I *h* them on to you.
11:23 received from the Lord what I *h* on to you,
15: 3 I *h* on to you first of all what I myself
1Pt 1:18 way of life your fathers *h* on to you,
2Pt 2:21 their backs on the holy law *h* on to them,
Rv 11: 2 it, for it has been *h* over to the Gentiles,

HANDFUL (12)
Ex 9: 8 "Take a double *h* of soot from a furnace,
Lv 2: 2 shall take a *h* of this fine flour and oil,
5:12 take a *h* of this flour as a token offering,
6: 8 take from it a *h* of its fine flour and oil,
9:17 taking a *h* of it,
16:12 double *h* of finely ground fragrant incense,
Nm 5:26 where he shall take a *h* of the cereal
Dt 4:27 and there shall remain but a *h* of you
1Kgs 17:12 there is only a *h* of flour in my jar and a
1Chr 16:19 When they were few in number, a *h*,
Ps(s) 105:12 When they were few in number, a *h*,
Eccl 4: 6 Better is one *h* with tranquility than two

HANDFULS (4)
Ru 2:16 and even to let drop some *h* and leave them
1Kgs 20:10 in Samaria to make *h* for all my followers."
2Mc 4:41 pieces of wood or *h* of the ashes
Ez 13:19 with *h* of barley and crumbs of bread,

HANDING (9)
Gn 40:13 You will be *h* Pharaoh his cup as you
Nm 18:28 *h* over to Aaron the priest the part to be
Dt 24: 3 house by *h* her a written bill of divorce;
1Kgs 18: 9 are *h* me over to Ahab to have me killed?
Jer 29:21 I am *h* them over to Nebuchadnezzar,
32: 3 am *h* over this city to the king of Babylon,
34: 2 am *h* this city over to the king of Babylon;
Ez 23:28 I am now *h* you over to those whom you hate,
Jas 2: 4 up as judges *h* down corrupt decisions?

HANDIWORK (17)
Ps(s) 19: 2 of God, and the firmament proclaims his *h*.
115: 4 idols are silver and gold, the *h* of men.
128: 2 For you shall eat the fruit of your *h*;
135:15 nations are silver and gold, the *h* of men.
Sg 7: 2 thighs are like jewels, the *h* of an artist.
Wis 13:12 refuse from his *h* in preparing his food,
Sir 14:19 in decay, and his *h* will follow after him.
38:34 Yet they maintain God's ancient *h*,
Is 17: 8 He shall not look to the altars, his *h*,
60:21 bud of my planting, my *h* to show my glory.
Jer 1:16 to strange gods and adoring their own *h*.
10: 9 of the craftsman and the *h* of the smelter,
25: 6 them, lest you provoke me with your *h*,
25: 7 provoked me with your *h* to your own harm.
25:14 own deeds and according to their own *h*.
Bar 6:50 clear that they are not gods, but human *h*;
Eph 2:10 We are truly his *h*, created in Christ Jesus

HANDKERCHIEFS (1)
Acts 19:12 When *h* or cloths which had touched his

HANDLE (4)
Dt 19: 5 the *h* and hits his neighbor a mortal blow,
Bar 6:28 and women in childbed *h* their sacrifices.
Mk 16:18 languages, they will be able to *h* serpents,
Col 2:21 you be bound by rules that say, "Do not *h*!

HANDLING (3)
1Sm 5: 7 for he is *h* us and our god Dagon severely."
2Chr 25: 5 fit for war, capable of *h* lance and shield.
2Cor 8:20 over my *h* of this generous collection.

HANDMADE (1)
Wis 14: 8 but the *h* idol is accursed,

HANDMAID (26)
Ex 2: 5 the reeds, she sent her *h* to fetch it.
Jgs 9:18 and have made Abimelech, the son of his *h*,
1Sm 1:11 look with pity on the misery of your *h*,
1:11 forget me, if you give your *h* a male child,
1:16 Do not think your *h* a ne'er-do-well;
25:24 Please let your *h* speak to you,
25:24 to you, and listen to the words of your *h*.
25:25 I, your *h*, did not see the young men
25:28 forgive the transgression of your *h*,
25:31 benefit on your lordship, remember your *h*."
25:41 "Your *h* would become a slave to wash the
1Kgs 1:13 'Did you not, lord king, swear to your *h*:
1:17 lord, you swore to me your *h* by the LORD,
3:20 and took my son from my side, as I, your *h*,
Jdt 11: 5 and let your *h* speak in your presence!
11: 6 and if you follow out the words of your *h*,
11:16 "As soon as I, your *h*,
11:17 Your *h* is, indeed, a God-fearing woman
11:17 but each night your *h* will go out to the
12: 4 your *h* will not use up her supplies till
12: 6 my lord, to let your *h* go out for prayer."
Est C:28 I, your *h*, have never eaten at the table
C:29 now, your *h* has had no joy except in you,
Ps(s) 86:16 your servant, and save the son of your *h*.
116:16 I am your servant, the son of your *h*;
Wis 9: 5 For I am your servant, the son of your *h*,

HANDMAIDS (4)
Jb 19:15 Even my *h* treat me as a stranger;
Jl 3: 1 Even upon the servants and the *h*,
Na 2: 8 mistress is led forth captive, and her *h*,
Acts 2:18 even on my servants and *h* I will pour out

HANDMILL (1)
Ex 11: 5 the first-born of the slave-girl at the *h*,

HANDS (471)
Gn 5:29 relief from our work and the toil of our *h*."
19: 9 But his guests put out their *h*,
19:16 seized his hand and the *h* of his wife and
20: 5 I did it in good faith and with clean *h*."
27:16 his *h* and the hairless parts of his neck.
27:22 the voice is Jacob's, the *h* are Esau's."
27:23 to identify him because his *h* were hairy,
37:21 this, he tried to save him from their *h*,
37:22 from their *h* and restore him to his father.
41:51 I endured at the *h* of my family";
48:14 But Israel, crossing his *h*,
Ex 3: 8 rescue them from the *h* of the Egyptians
5:21 and have put a sword in their *h* to slay us."
9:29 the city I will extend my *h* to the LORD;
9:33 of the city, he extended his *h* to the LORD.
15:17 O LORD, which your *h* established.
17:11 As long as Moses kept his *h* raised up,
17:11 of the fight, but when he let his *h* rest,
17:12 Moses' *h*, however, grew tired
17:12 Meanwhile Aaron and Hur supported his *h*,
17:12 so that his *h* remained steady till sunset.
18: 9 rescuing them from the *h* of the Egyptians.
18:10 from the *h* of Pharaoh and the Egyptians.
22: 7 did not lay *h* on his neighbor's property.
22:10 did not lay *h* on his neighbor's property;
29:10 and his sons shall lay their *h* on its head.
29:15 and his sons have laid their *h* on its head,
29:19 and his sons have laid their *h* on its head,
29:20 *h* and the great toes of their right feet.
29:24 shall put into the *h* of Aaron and his sons,
29:25 you have received them back from their *h*,
30:19 shall use it in washing their *h* and feet.
30:21 the LORD they must wash their *h* and feet,
32:15 two tablets of the commandments in his *h*,
34:29 two tablets of the commandments in his *h*,
40:31 sons used to wash their *h* and feet there,
Lv 4:15 shall lay their *h* on the bullock's head.
4:24 Having laid his *h* on its head,
7:30 with his own *h* the oblations to the LORD.
8:14 and his sons laid their *h* on its head.
8:18 and his sons laid their *h* on its head.
8:22 and his sons laid their *h* on its head.
8:24 ears, on the thumbs of their right *h*,
8:27 things into the *h* of Aaron and his sons,
9:22 his *h* over the people and blessed them.
15:11 with unrinsed *h* shall wash his garments,
16:21 Laying both *h* on its head,
24:14 heard him have laid their *h* on his head,
Nm 5:18 in her *h* the cereal offering of her appeal,
6:19 shall place them in the *h* of the nazirite.
8:10 the Israelites shall lay their *h* upon them.
8:12 lay their *h* on the heads of the bullocks,
24:24 his people from the *h* of the Kittim?
27:23 his *h* on him and gave him his commission,
Dt 1:27 into the *h* of the Amorites and destroy us.
2:24 I now deliver into your *h* Sihon,
3: 3 the LORD, our God, delivered into our *h* Og,
4:28 by the *h* of man out of wood and stone,
9:15 two tablets of the covenant in both my *h*,
9:17 Raising the two tablets with both *h* I
17: 7 be the first to raise their *h* against him;
21: 6 nearest the corpse shall wash their *h*
21: 7 declare, 'Our *h* did not shed this blood,
24: 1 out a bill of divorce and *h* it to her,
27:15 the LORD, the product of a craftsman's *h*—
33: 7 His own *h* defend his cause and you will be
33:11 and accept the ministry of his *h*.
34: 9 since Moses had laid his *h* upon him;
Jgs 7:20 They held the torches in their left *h*,
8: 6 "Are the *h* of Zebah and Zalmunna already
8:15 'Are the *h* of Zebah and Zalmunna already
13:23 a holocaust and cereal offering from our *h*!
15:14 fire and his bonds melted away from his *h*.
15:18 or fall into the *h* of the uncircumcised?"
19:27 of the house with her *h* on the threshold.
1Sm 5: 4 *h* broken off and lying on the threshold,
14:48 the *h* of those who were plundering them.
17:47 LORD'S and he shall deliver you into our *h*."
19: 5 his life in his *h* and slew the Philistine,
21:14 and acted like a madman in their *h*,
26: 9 for who can lay *h* on the LORD's anointed
28:19 of Israel into the *h* of the Philistines."
28:21 *h* and fulfilled the request you made of me.
2Sm 3:34 Your *h* were not bound with chains,
4:12 killed them and cut off their *h* and feet,
13:19 Then, putting her *h* to her head,
18:12 a thousand pieces of silver in my two *h*,
21:22 fell at the *h* of David and his servants.
22:21 to the cleanness of my *h* he requited me.
22:35 Who trained my *h* for war till my arms
1Kgs 8:22 and stretching forth his *h* toward heaven.
8:38 stretching out his *h* toward this temple,
8:54 with his *h* outstretched toward heaven.
2Kgs 3:11 who poured water on the *h* of Elijah,
4:34 upon the eyes, and his *h* upon the hands.
9:35 of her but the skull, the feet, and the *h*.
10:24 of those whom I shall deliver into your *h*,
11:12 him, clapping their *h* and shouting,
13:16 his *h* over the king's hands and said,
19:18 were not gods, but the work of human *h*,
21:14 inheritance and deliver them into enemy *h*,
22:17 by everything to which they turn their *h*,
1Chr 12:18 my enemies though my *h* have done no wrong,
20: 8 died at the *h* of David and his servants.
21:13 is very great, than into the *h* of men."
2Chr 6: 4 and by his own *h* brought it to fulfillment.
6:12 of Israel and stretched forth his *h*.
6:13 and stretched forth his *h* toward heaven.
6:29 stretches out his *h* toward this temple,
13:16 Judah, and God delivered them into their *h*.
23:18 temple into the *h* of the levitical priests,
24:13 of restoration progressed under their *h*.
28: 9 Judah that he delivered them into your *h*.
29:23 the assembly, who laid their *h* upon them.
30: 6 left from the *h* of the Assyrian kings.
30: 8 extend your *h* to the LORD and come to his
32:15 people from my hand or the *h* of my fathers,
32:19 peoples of the earth, a work of human *h*.
Ezr 5: 8 and is making good progress under their *h*.
9: 5 stretching out my *h* to the LORD my God.
Neh 6: 9 "Their *h* will slacken in the work,
8: 6 and all the people, their *h* raised high,
13:21 If you keep this up, I will lay *h* on you!"
Tb 3:11 At that time, then, she spread out her *h*,
11:13 used both *h* to peel off the cataracts.
13: 9 he scourged you for the works of your *h*,
13:11 their *h* their gifts for the King of heaven.
Jdt 8:18 city of ours that worships gods made by *h*,
11:13 no layman should even touch with his *h*.
15:12 She took branches in her *h* and distributed
16: 2 snatched me from the *h* of my persecutors.
Est A:13 were preparing to lay *h* on King Ahasuerus.
2:21 in anger to lay *h* on King Ahasuerus.
3: 6 was not enough to lay *h* on Mordecai alone.
C:17 delivered us into the *h* of our enemies,
6: 2 for seeking to lay *h* on King Ahasuerus.
1Mc 2: 7 while it is given into the *h* of enemies,
2: 7 and the sanctuary into the *h* of strangers?
2:47 and the work prospered in their *h*.
2:48 They saved the law from the *h* of the
4:31 this army into the *h* of your people Israel;
14:31 their country and to lay *h* on their temple,
2Mc 3:20 all of them with *h* raised toward heaven,
3:32 some foul play at the *h* of the Jews,
4:34 privately and asked him to lay *h* on Onias.
4:34 through sworn pledges with right *h* joined,
5:16 He laid his impure *h* on the sacred vessels
5:16 gathered up with profane *h* the votive
6:26 or dead, escape the *h* of the Almighty.
7: 4 to scalp him and cut off his *h* and feet,
7:10 told to do so, and bravely held out his *h*,
7:14 "It is my choice to die at the *h* of men
7:31 will not escape the *h* of God.
12:24 *h* of the men under Dositheus and Sosipater;
14:34 stretched out their *h* toward heaven,
14:42 rather than fall into the *h* of vile men
14:46 and flung them with both *h* into the crowd,
15:21 stretched out his *h* toward heaven and
15:27 *h* and praying to God with their hearts,
Jb 1:10 You have blessed the work of his *h*,
4: 3 many, and have made firm their feeble *h*.
5:12 so that their *h* achieve no success;
5:18 he smites, but his *h* give healing.
9:24 earth is given into the *h* of the wicked;
9:30 with snow and cleanse my *h* with lye,
10: 3 to oppress, to spurn the work of your *h*,
10: 8 Your *h* have formed me and fashioned me;
11:13 aright and stretch out your *h* toward him,
14:15 you would esteem the work of your *h*.
16:17 eyes, Although my *h* are free from violence,
17: 9 he who has clean *h* increase in strength.
20:10 and his *h* shall yield up his riches.
21: 5 be astonished, put your *h* over your mouths.
21:16 If their happiness is not in their own *h*
22:30 shall be delivered through cleanness of *h*.
29: 9 and covered their mouths with their *h*;
31: 7 my eyes, or any stain clings to my *h*,
34:19 For they are all the work of his *h*:
36:32 In his *h* he holds the lightning,
Ps(s) 7: 4 fault in this, if there is guilt on my *h*,
8: 7 given him rule over the works of your *h*,
9:17 are trapped by the work of their own *h*.
10:14 misery and sorrow, taking them in your *h*.

18:21 to the cleanness of my *h* he requited me;
18:25 to the cleanness of my *h* in his sight.
18:35 Who trained my *h* for war and my arms to
22:17 They have pierced my *h* and my feet;
24: 4 He whose *h* are sinless, whose heart is clean.
26: 6 I wash my *h* in innocence,
26:10 On their hands are crimes, and their right *h*
28: 2 lifting up my *h* toward your holy shrine.
28: 4 For the work of their *h* repay them;
28: 5 deeds of the LORD nor the work of his *h*,
31: 6 Into your *h* I commend my spirit;
31:16 In your *h* is my destiny;
44:21 and stretched out our *h* to a strange god,
47: 2 All you peoples, clap your *h*,
55:21 Each one lays *h* on his associates,
63: 5 lifting up my *h*,
68:32 let Ethiopia extend its *h* to God.
73:13 clean and washed my *h* as an innocent man?
76: 6 the *h* of all the mighty ones have failed.
77: 3 my *h* are stretched out without flagging;
78:61 captivity, his glory into the *h* of the foe.
78:72 heart, and with skillful *h* he guided them.
81: 7 his *h* were freed from the basket.
88:10 to you I stretch out my *h*.
89:43 You have exalted the right *h* of his foes,
90:17 [Prosper the work of our *h*
91:12 Upon their *h* they shall bear you up,
92: 5 at the works of your *h* I rejoice.
95: 4 In his *h* are the depths of the earth,
95: 5 and the dry land, which his *h* have formed.
98: 8 Let the rivers clap their *h*,
102:26 and the heavens are the work of your *h*.
106:10 hostile hands and freed them from the *h*
106:41 gave them over into the *h* of the nations,
111: 7 The works of his *h* are faithful and just;
115: 7 They have *h* but feel not;
119:48 And I will lift up my *h* to your commands
119:73 Your *h* have made me and fashioned me;
119:109 Though constantly I take my life in my *h*,
123: 2 of servants are on the *h* of their masters,
123: 2 of a maid are on the *h* of her mistress,
125: 3 the just put forth to wickedness their *h*.
134: 2 Lift up your *h* toward the sanctuary,
138: 8 forsake not the work of your *h*.
140: 5 Save me, O LORD, from the *h* of the wicked;
141: 2 the lifting up of my *h*,
143: 5 your doings, the works of your *h* I ponder.
143: 6 I stretch out my *h* to you;
144: 1 LORD, my rock, who trains my *h* for battle,
144: 7 me from many waters, from the *h* of aliens,
144: 8 while their right *h* are raised in perjury.
144:11 and rescue me from the *h* of aliens,
144:11 while their right *h* are raised in perjury.
149: 6 And let two-edged swords be in their *h*:
Prv 6:17 tongue, and *h* that shed innocent blood;
12:14 the work of his *h* comes back to reward him.
12:20 Deceit is in the *h* of those who plot evil,
14: 1 but Folly tears hers down with her own *h*.
21:25 slays him, for his *h* refuse to work.
30: 4 who has cupped the wind in his *h*?
30:28 you can catch them with your *h*,
31:13 and flax and makes cloth with skillful *h*.
31:19 She puts her *h* to the distaff,
31:20 She reaches out her *h* to the poor,
Eccl 2:11 to all the works that my *h* had wrought,
5: 5 such words and destroy the works of your *h*.
7:26 is a snare and whose *h* are prison bonds.
10:18 *h* are lazy, the rafters sag; when hands
Sg 5: 5 to my lover, with my *h* dripping myrrh:
Wis 1:12 destruction by the works of your *h*.
1:16 wicked who with *h* and words invited death,
7:11 company, and countless riches at her *h*;
8:12 they would place their *h* upon their mouths.
8:18 unfailing riches in the works of her *h*,
12: 6 took with their own *h* defenseless lives,
12: 6 willed to destroy by the *h* of our fathers,
13:10 who termed gods things made by human *h*:
13:19 hands he asks facility of a thing with *h*
15:15 hear, nor fingers on their *h* for feeling;
15:17 he makes a dead thing with his lawless *h*.
Sir 2:12 Woe to craven hearts and drooping *h*,
2:18 *h* of the LORD and not into the hands
4:19 and deliver him into the *h* of despoilers.
11: 6 the honored are given into enemy *h*.
12:18 head and clap his *h* and hiss repeatedly,
22: 2 whoever touches him wipes his *h*.
25:22 Feeble *h* and quaking knees
33:13 Like clay in the *h* of a potter,
33:13 So are men in the *h* of their Creator,
33:26 his *h* be idle and he will seek to be free.
38:10 let your *h* be just,
38:30 With his *h* he molds the clay,
38:31 All these men are skilled with their *h*,
42: 6 of a lock placed where there are many *h*;
48:20 Most High God and lifted up their *h* to him;
50:13 the offerings to the LORD in their *h*,
50:20 his *h* over all the congregation of Israel.
51:20 my *h* in cleanness I attained to her.
Is 1:15 When you spread out your *h*,
1:15 Your *h* are full of blood!
2: 8 they worship the works of their *h*,
3:11 with the work of his *h* he will be repaid.
5:12 regard not, the work of his *h* they see not.
13: 7 Therefore all *h* fall helpless,
13: 7 bows of the young men fall from their *h*.
19:25 people Egypt, and the work of my *h* Assyria,
25:11 *h* in Moab as a swimmer extends his hands
25:11 low their pride as his *h* sweep over them.
29:23 children see the work of my *h* in his midst,
31: 7 silver and gold, which he made with his *h*.
33:15 his *h* free of contact with a bribe,
34:17 his *h* he marks off their shares of her;
35: 3 Strengthen the *h* that are feeble,
37:19 they were not gods but the work of human *h*,
45: 9 or, "What you are making has no *h*"?
45:11 or prescribe the work of my *h* for me!
45:12 It was my *h* that stretched out the heavens;
49:16 the palms of my *h* I have written your name;
51:23 will put it into the *h* of your tormentors,
55:12 of the countryside shall clap their *h*.
59: 3 For your *h* are stained with blood,
59: 6 and deeds of violence come from their *h*.
64: 7 we are all the work of your *h*.
65: 2 my *h* all the day to a rebellious people,
65:22 shall long enjoy the produce of their *h*.
Jer 2:37 shall you go away with *h* upon your head;
4:31 Zion gasping, as she stretches forth her *h*:
6:24 helpless fall our *h*,
21: 4 I will turn back in your *h* the weapons
21: 7 into the *h* of their enemies and those who
22:25 *h* of those who seek your life; the hands
22:25 the *h* of Nebuchadnezzar,
26:14 As for me, I am in your *h*;
30: 6 *h* on their loins like women in childbirth?
32: 4 of Judah, escape the *h* of the Chaldeans;
32:30 but provoke me with the works of their *h*,
33:13 under the *h* of the one who counts them,
34: 3 you will be captured and fall into his *h*.
38:18 shall fall into the *h* of the Chaldeans,
38:18 fire, and you shall not escape their *h*.
38:23 and you shall not escape their *h*;
40: 4 today from the fetters that bind your *h*;
44: 8 go on provoking me by the works of your *h*,
47: 3 their *h* fall helpless Because of the day
50:43 news of them, and helpless fall his *h*;
51:49 as at the *h* of Babylon have fallen the
Lam 1: 7 When her people fell into enemy *h*,
1:17 Zion stretched out her *h*,
2:15 All who pass by clap their *h* at you;
2:19 Lift up your *h* to him for the lives of
4: 2 earthen jars made by the *h* of a potter!
4:10 The *h* of compassionate women boiled their
5: 8 there is no one to rescue us from their *h*.
Bar 4:18 himself deliver you from your enemies' *h*.
4:21 deliver you from oppression at enemy *h*.
Ez 1: 8 Human *h* were under their wings,
6:11 Clap your *h*,
7:17 All their *h* shall be limp,
7:27 the *h* of the common people shall tremble.
10: 2 fill both your *h* with burning coals from
10: 7 it in the *h* of the one dressed in linen,
10: 8 [Something like human *h* could be seen
10:21 like human *h* were under their wings.
13:21 they shall no longer be prey to your *h*.
22:14 heart remain firm, will your *h* be strong,
23:37 adultery, and blood is on their *h*.
23:45 adultery, and blood is on their *h*.
25: 6 you clapped your *h* and stamped your feet,
28:10 the uncircumcised at the *h* of foreigners,
Dn 3:15 the God that can deliver you out of my *h*?"
3:17 from the white-hot furnace and from your *h*,
10:10 touched me, raising me to my *h* and knees.
12: 7 lifted his right and left *h* to heaven;
13:34 rose up and laid their *h* on her head.
14: 5 "Because I worship not idols made with *h*,
Hos 14: 4 no more, 'Our god,' to the work of our *h*;
Ob 1:13 Lay not *h* upon his possessions on the day
Mi 5:12 shall no longer adore the works of your *h*.
7: 3 Their *h* succeed at evil;
7:16 They shall put their *h* over their mouths;
Na 3:19 this news of you clap their *h* over you;
Hg 2:14 And so are all the works of their *h*;
2:17 you in all the works of your *h* with blight,
Zec 4: 9 The *h* of Zerubbabel have laid the
4: 9 of this house, and his *h* shall finish it;
4:10 the select stone in the *h* of Zerubbabel.
8: 9 Let your *h* be strong,
8:13 do not fear, but let your *h* be strong.
Mal 1:10 will I accept any sacrifice from your *h*,
1:13 Shall I accept it from your *h*?
Mt 4: 6 with their *h* they will support you that
15: 2 They do not wash their *h*,
15:20 As for eating with unwashed *h*—
16:21 greatly there at the *h* of the elders,
17:12 Man will suffer at their *h* in the same way."
17:22 is going to be delivered into the *h* of men,
18: 8 with two *h* or two feet into endless fire.
19:13 he could place his *h* on them in prayer.
19:15 *h* on their heads before he left that place.
26:50 they stepped forward to lay *h* on Jesus,
27:24 and washed his *h* in front of the crowd,
Mk 5:23 *h* on her so that she may get well and live."
5:26 She had received treatment at the *h* of
6: 2 miraculous deeds are accomplished by his *h*?
6: 5 a few who were sick by laying *h* on them,
7: 2 their *h*.
7: 3 eat without scrupulously washing their *h*.
7: 5 take food without purifying their *h*?"
8:23 on his eyes he laid his *h* on him and asked,
8:25 a second time Jesus laid *h* on his eyes,
9:31 the *h* of men who will put him to death;
9:43 to enter life maimed than to keep both *h*
10:16 and blessed them, placing his *h* on them.
14:46 this, they laid *h* on him and arrested him.
14:58 will destroy this temple made by human *h*,'
14:58 will construct another not made by human *h*.'
16:18 upon whom they lay their *h* will recover."
16:20 upon whom they lay their *h* will recover."
Lk 1:71 our enemies and from the *h* of all our foes.
4:11 again, 'With their *h* they will support you,
4:40 he laid *h* on each of them and cured them.
6: 1 grain-heads, shelling them with their *h*,
8:43 duration, incurable at any doctor's *h*,
9:44 of Man must be delivered into the *h* of men."
15:17 'How many hired *h* at my father's place
15:19 Treat me like one of your hired *h*.'
20:19 high priests tried to get their *h* on him,
23:46 into your *h* I recommend my spirit."
24: 7 must be delivered into the *h* of sinful men,
24:39 Look at my *h* and my feet; it is really I.
24:40 said this he showed them his *h* and feet.
24:50 them out near Bethany, and with *h* upraised,
Jn 7:44 However, no one laid *h* on him.
13: 9 only my feet, but my *h* and head as well."
20:20 this, he showed them his *h* and his side.
20:25 without probing the nailprints in his *h*,
20:27 "Take your finger and examine my *h*.
21:18 you are older you will stretch out your *h*,
Acts 5:12 Through the *h* of the apostles,
6: 6 over them and then imposed *h* on them.
7:41 over the product of their own *h*.
7:48 not dwell in buildings made by human *h*,
7:57 their *h* over their ears as they did so.
8:17 The pair upon arriving imposed *h* on them
8:18 *h* that the apostles conferred the Spirit,
8:19 so that if I place my *h* on anyone he will
9:12 coming to him and placing his *h* on him
9:17 the house he laid his *h* on Saul and said,
13: 3 they imposed *h* on them and sent them off.
14: 3 signs and wonders to be done at their *h*.
17:24 not dwell in sanctuaries made by human *h*;
19: 6 As Paul laid his *h* on them,
19:11 extraordinary miracles at the *h* of Paul.
20:34 You yourselves know that these *h* of mine
21:11 belt, tied his own *h* and feet with it.
27:21 All *h* had gone without food for a long
28: 8 praying, laid his *h* on him and cured him.
Rom 10:21 "All day long I stretched out my *h* to an
2Cor 5: 1 heavens, not made by *h* but to last forever.
11:24 Five times at the *h* of the Jews I received
11:33 a window in the wall and escaped his *h*.
Gal 3:19 by angels, at the *h* of a mediator;
Eph 4:28 let him work with his *h* at honest labor so
1Thes 4:11 Work with your *h* as we directed you to do,
1Tm 2: 8 offer prayers with blameless *h* held aloft,
4:14 the presbyters laid their *h* on you.
5:22 Never lay *h* hastily on anyone,
2Tm 1: 6 of God bestowed when my *h* were laid on you.
Heb 1:10 and the heavens are the work of your *h*.
6: 2 about baptisms and laying-on of *h*,
9:11 more perfect tabernacle not made by *h*,
9:24 did not enter into a sanctuary made by *h*,
10:31 thing to fall into the *h* of the living God.
12:12 your drooping *h* and your weak knees.
Jas 4: 8 Cleanse your *h*,
1Jn 3:22 we will receive at his *h* whatever we ask.
Rv 7: 9 robes and holding palm branches in their *h*.
20: 4 its mark on their foreheads or their *h*.

HANDSOME (11)

Gn 39: 6 was strikingly *h* in countenance and body.
41: 2 out of the Nile came seven cows, *h* and fat;
41: 4 the ugly, gaunt cows ate up the seven *h*,
1Sm 9: 2 a son named Saul, who was a *h* young man.
16:12 a youth *h* to behold and making a splendid
16:18 besides being an able speaker, and *h*.
17:42 youthful, and ruddy, and *h* in appearance,
1Kgs 1: 6 Adonijah was also very *h*,
Dn 1: 4 nobility, young men without any defect, *h*,
Zec 11:13 the *h* price at which they valued me."
Acts 7:20 He proved to be an exceedingly *h* child.

HANDSOMELY (2)

Nm 22:17 very *h* and will do anything you ask of me.
Ez 38: 4 army, horses and riders all *h* outfitted,

HANDSOMER (1)

1Sm 9: 2 There was no other Israelite *h* than Saul;

HANDWRITING (1)

Gal 6:11 See, I write to you in my own large *h*!

HANDY (1)

Bar 6:58 his valor, or a *h* tool in a house,

HANES (1)
Is 30: 4 are at Zoan and their messengers reach *H,*

HANG (11)
Ex 26:12 to *h* down over the rear of the Dwelling.
26:33 *H* the veil from clasps.
40: 5 and *h* the curtain at the entrance of the
Tb 3:10 It is far better for me not to *h* myself,
Jdt 14: 1 head and *h* it on the parapet of your wall.
Est 7: 9 The king answered, "*H* him on it."
2Mc 15:33 would *h* up the other wages of his folly
Sg 4: 4 A thousand bucklers *h* upon it,
Is 22:24 On him shall *h* all the glory of his family:
Ez 15: 3 peg from it, to *h* on it any kind of vessel?
44:20 their heads nor let their hair *h* loose,

HANGED (16)
Jos 8:29 the king of Ai *h* on a tree until evening;
10:26 and killed them, and *h* them on five trees,
2Sm 17:23 orders concerning his family, he *h* himself.
21:12 where the Philistines had *h* them at the
Tb 3:10 but she *h* herself because of ill fortune!'
Est 2:23 and both of them were *h* on a gibbet.
5:14 ask the king to have Mordecai *h* on it.
6: 4 be *h* on the gibbet he had raised for him.
7:10 So they *h* Haman on the gibbet which he had
8: 7 and they have *h* him on the gibbet because
E:18 for he who composed it has been *h,*
9:13 let the ten sons of Haman be *h* on gibbets."
9:14 So the ten sons of Haman were *h,*
9:25 he and his sons should be *h* on gibbets.
Mt 27: 5 He went off and *h* himself.
Gal 3:13 "Accursed is anyone who is *h* on a tree."

HANGING (12)
Ex 26:13 length to be left *h* down on either side
Jos 10:26 trees, where they remained *h* until evening.
2Sm 4:12 feet, *h* them up near the pool in Hebron.
18:10 he had seen Absalom *h* from a terebinth.
18:14 of Absalom, still *h* from the tree alive.
Tb 3:10 house with the intention of *h* herself.
2Mc 6:10 with their babies *h* at their breasts
Lk 19:48 was listening to him and *h* on his words.
23:39 criminals *h* in crucifixion blasphemed him:
Acts 5:30 whom you put to death, *h* him on a tree.
10:40 They killed him, finally, *h* him on a tree,
28: 4 At the sight of the snake *h* from his hand,

HANGINGS (17)
Ex 27: 9 court shall have *h* a hundred cubits long,
27:11 the north side there shall be similar *h,*
27:12 the width of the court there shall be *h,*
27:14 shall be *h* to the extent of fifteen cubits,
27:15 shall be *h* to the extent of fifteen cubits,
35:17 the *h* of the court,
38: 9 the south side of the court there were *h,*
38:11 On the north side there were similar *h,*
38:12 On the west side there were *h,*
38:14 were *h* to the extent of fifteen cubits,
38:15 likewise *h* to the extent of fifteen cubits,
38:16 The *h* on all sides of the court were woven
38:18 wide, in keeping with the *h* of the court.
39:40 the *h* of the court with their columns and
Nm 3:26 of the meeting tent, the *h* of the court,
4:26 of the meeting tent, the *h* of the court,
Est 1: 6 were white cotton draperies and violet *h,*

HANGS (6)
Ex 27:21 veil which *h* in front of the commandments.
30: 6 front of the veil that *h* before the ark
Lv 24: 3 veil that *h* in front of the commandments,
Dt 21:23 God's curse rests on him who *h* on a tree,
Prv 26: 7 A proverb in the mouth of a fool *h* limp,
Is 33:23 majestic ship passes, The rigging *h* slack;

HANNAH (12)
1Sm 1: 2 He had two wives, one named *H,*
1: 2 Peninnah had children, but *H* was childless.
1: 5 a double portion to *H* because he loved her,
1: 7 her, and *H* would weep and refuse to eat.
1: 8 *H,* why do you weep,
1: 9 *H* rose after one such meal at Shiloh,
1:13 her mouth, for *H* was praying silently;
1:15 "It isn't that my lord," *H* answered.
1:19 When Elkanah had relations with his wife *H,*
1:22 LORD and to fulfill his vows, *H* did not go,
1:25 father had sacrificed the young bull, *H,*
2:21 The LORD favored *H* so that she conceived

HANNATHON (1)
Jos 19:14 Skirting north of *H,*

HANNIEL (2)
Nm 34:23 *H,* son of Ephod;
1Chr 7:39 The sons of Ulla were Arah, *H,* and Rizia.

HANOCH (6)
Gn 25: 4 descendants of Midian were Ephah, Epher, *H,*
46: 9 *H,* Pallu, Hezron, and Carmi.
Ex 6:14 Reuben, the first-born of Israel, were *H,*
Nm 26: 5 through *H* the clan of the Hanochites,
1Chr 1:33 descendants of Midian were Ephah, Epher, *H,*
5: 3 Reuben, the first-born of Israel, were *H,*

HANOCHITES (1)
Nm 26: 5 through Hanoch the clan of the *H,*

HANUN (12)
2Sm 10: 1 died, and his son *H* succeeded him as king.
10: 2 David thought, "I will be kind to *H,*
10: 2 to *H* for the loss of his father.
10: 3 the Ammonite princes said to their lord *H:*
10: 4 *H,* therefore, seized David's servants
1Chr 19: 2 David said, "I will show kindness to *H,*
19: 2 the land of the Ammonites to comfort *H,*
19: 3 Hanun, the Ammonite princes said to *H,*
19: 4 Thereupon *H* seized David's servants and
19: 6 *H* and the Ammonites sent a thousand
Neh 3:13 by *H* and the inhabitants of Zanoah;
3:30 him, Hananiah, son of Shelemiah, and *H,*

HAPHARAIM (1)
Jos 19:19 included Jezreel, Chesulloth, Shunem, *H,*

HAPHAZARD (1)
Wis 2: 2 For *h* were we born,

HAPPEN (50)
Gn 42:36 Why must such things always *h* to me?"
49: 1 you what is to *h* to you in days to come.
Ex 2: 4 a distance to find out what would *h* to him.
Dt 4:32 Did anything so great ever *h* before?
22: 3 which your kinsman loses and you *h* to find;
1Sm 2:34 a sign in what will *h* to your two sons,
1Kgs 14: 3 He will tell you what will *h* to the child."
2Kgs 2:12 When Elisha saw it *h* he cried out,
7: 2 make windows in heaven, how could this *h?*"
7:19 make windows in heaven, how could this *h?*"
Tb 8:16 what I feared did not *h.*
14: 4 It shall all *h,* and shall overtake Assyria
14: 4 It shall *h,* and not a single word of the
2Mc 9:25 and waiting to see what will *h.*
Eccl 9: 3 Among all the things that *h* under the sun,
Wis 2:17 let us find out what will *h* to him.
Is 41:22 and foretell to us what it is that shall *h!*
47:13 at each new moon what would *h* to you.
Ez 20:32 What you are thinking of shall never *h:*
Dn 2:28 what is to *h* in days to come;
2:29 thoughts about what should *h* in the future,
8:19 is to *h* later in the period of wrath;
10:14 shall *h* to your people in the days to come;
Jon 4: 5 the shade, to see what would *h* to the city.
Mt 16:22 forbid that any such thing ever *h* to you!"
21:21 and thrown into the sea,' even that will *h.*
24: 6 Such things are bound to *h,*
26:54 be fulfilled which say it must *h* this way?"
Mk 10:32 to tell them what was going to *h* to him.
11:23 but believes that what he says will *h,*
13: 7 Such things are bound to *h,*
Lk 12:38 Should he *h* to come at midnight or before
21: 7 will be the sign that it is going to *h?*"
21: 9 These things are bound to *h* first,
21:28 When these things begin to *h,*
22:49 of Jesus saw what was going to *h,*
23:31 in the green wood, what will *h* in the dry?"
Jn 3: 9 "How can such a thing *h?*"
18: 4 Jesus, aware of all that would *h* to him,
Acts 8:24 what you have just said may never *h* to me."
20:22 and not knowing what will *h* to me there
28: 6 and seeing nothing unusual *h* to him,
1Cor 12:17 were all eye, what would *h* to our hearing?
12:17 were all ear, what would *h* to our smelling?
14:30 by, should *h* to receive a revelation,
Gal 4:18 and not only when I *h* to be with you.
Phil 2:12 not only when I *h* to be with you but all
2Pt 2: 6 what would *h* in the future to the godless.
Rv 1: 1 show his servants what must *h* very soon.
22: 6 to show his servants what must *h* very soon."

HAPPENED (118)
Gn 1: 6 body of water from the others." And so it *h:*
1: 9 And so it *h:* the water under the sky
1:11 fruit with its seed in it." And so it *h:*
1:15 shed light upon the earth." And so it *h:*
1:20 dome of the sky." And so it *h:*
1:24 animals of all kinds." And so it *h:*
1:30 green plants for food." And so it *h.*
20: 8 and informed them of everything that had *h,*
26: 8 *h* to look out of a window and was
29:13 then recounted to Laban all that had *h,*
42:29 they told him all that had *h* to them.
44:15 as I could discover by divination what *h.*"
Ex 32: 1 of Egypt, we do not know what has *h* to him."
32:23 of Egypt, we do not know what has *h* to him.'
35:23 Everyone who *h* to have violet,
35:24 and everyone who *h* to have acacia wood for
Nm 14:36 And so it *h* to the men whom Moses had sent
Jgs 6:13 LORD is with us, why has all this *h* to us?
Ru 2: 3 *h* to be the section belonging to Boaz
1Sm 4: 7 This has never *h* before.
4:16 He asked, "What *h,* my son?"
6: 9 struck us, but that an accident *h* to us."
10:11 another, "What has *h* to the son of Kish?
25:37 become sober, his wife told him what had *h.*
2Sm 1: 4 "Tell me what *h,*" David bade him.
20: 1 Sheba, the son of Bichri, *h* to be there.
2Kgs 6:10 This *h* several times.
7:20 And that is what *h* to him,
1Chr 19: 5 was informed of what had *h* to his men,
2Chr 12: 2 *h* that in the fifth year of King Rehoboam,
36: 8 that he did, and what therefore *h* to him,
Tb 3: 7 it so *h* that Raguel's daughter Sarah also
5: 9 back to tell his father Tobit what had *h.*
10: 2 not appear, he said, "I wonder what has *h.*
12:20 down all these things that have *h* to you."
Jdt 6:16 and Uzziah questioned him about what had *h.*
8:18 gods made by hands, as *h* in former days.
8:26 and all that *h* to Jacob in Syrian
15: 1 On hearing what had *h,*
15: 4 country of Israel to report what had *h,*
Est 4: 7 and Mordecai told him all that had *h,*
6:13 his friends everything that had *h* to him,
1Mc 3:30 He feared that, as had *h* more than once,
4:20 that could be seen indicated what had *h.*
5:25 them all that had *h* to the Jews in Gilead:
12:29 they did not know what had *h* until morning.
2Mc 5: 2 It then *h* that all over the city,
7: 1 It also *h* that seven brothers with their
7:18 why such astonishing things have *h* to us.
9: 3 had *h* to Nicanor and to Timothy's forces.
9:24 unexpected *h* or any unwelcome news came,
10:10 relate what *h* under Antiochus Eupator,
10:21 When Maccabeus was told what had *h* he
11: 1 being greatly displeased at what had *h,*
12:42 had seen with their own eyes what had *h*
Wis 19:10 mindful of what had *h* in their sojourn:
Jer 5:30 shocking, horrible thing has *h* in the land:
32:12 who *h* to be in the quarters of the guard.
32:24 What you threatened has *h,*
36:20 When they told him everything that had *h,*
38: 7 *h* just then to be at the Gate of Benjamin,
48:19 say to them, "What has *h?*"
Ez 16:43 not remember what *h* when you were a girl,
Dn 4:25 All this *h* to King Nebuchadnezzar.
13:26 by the side gate to see what had *h* to her.
Jl 1: 2 Has the like of this *h* in your days or in
Mt 1:22 All this *h* to fulfill what the Lord had
8:33 in the town related everything that had *h,*
9:10 Now it *h* that,
12:10 A man with a shriveled hand *h* to be there,
15:22 It *h* that a Canaanite woman living in that
18:31 saw what had *h* they were badly shaken,
22:26 The same thing *h* to the second,
24:37 of Man will repeat what *h* in Noah's time.
26:56 all this has *h* in fulfillment of the
28:11 to the chief priests all that had *h.*
Mk 2:23 It *h* that he was walking through standing
4:37 It *h* that a bad squall blew up.
5:11 It *h* that a large herd of swine was
5:14 and the people came to see what had *h.*
5:16 explained what had *h* to the possessed man,
5:33 to tremble now as she realized what had *h,*
12:21 The same thing *h* to the third;
Lk 8:32 It *h* that a large herd of swine was
8:34 When the swineherds saw what had *h,*
8:35 went out to see for themselves what had *h.*
8:56 ordered them not to tell anyone what had *h.*
10:31 A priest *h* to be going down the same road;
23: 7 who also *h* to be in Jerusalem at the time.
23:47 The centurion, upon seeing what had *h,*
23:48 for this spectacle saw what had *h,*
24:14 discussing as they went all that had *h.*
24:21 today, the third day since these things *h,*
24:35 Then they recounted what had *h* on the road
Jn 1:28 This *h* in Bethany, across the Jordan,
4:46 *h* to be a royal official whose son was ill.
18:26 as it *h,*
20:24 It *h* that one of the Twelve,
Acts 2:12 could make nothing at all of what had *h.*
3:10 utterly stupefied at what had *h* to him.
4:21 of whom were praising God for what had *h.*
5: 7 wife came in, unaware of what had *h.*
7:40 Egypt, we have no idea what has *h* to him.'
8:27 It *h* that an Ethiopian eunuch,
9:43 Thus it *h* that Peter stayed on in Joppa
10:16 This *h* three times;
11:10 This *h* three times; then the canvas
12:18 who did not know what had *h* to Peter.
13:12 When the governor saw what had *h,*
20: 8 As it *h* there were many lamps in the
28: 8 It *h* that Publius' father was sick in bed,
28: 9 After this *h,*
1Cor 10: 6 These things *h* as an example to keep us
10:11 things that *h* to them serve as an example.
Gal 3:14 This has *h* so that through Christ Jesus
4:15 What has *h* to your open-hearted spirit?
Col 4: 9 They will tell you all that has *h* here.
1Thes 3: 4 now it has *h,*

HAPPENING (8)

2Kgs 9:27 Seeing what was *h*, Ahaziah, king of Judah
Est 4:1 When Mordecai learned all that was *h*,
Mt 24:33 Likewise, when you see all these things *h*,
27:54 seeing the earthquake and all that was *h*,
Mk 9:21 "How long has this been *h* to him?"
13:29 the same way, when you see these things *h*,
Lk 9:7 heard of all that was *h* and was perplexed,
21:31 you see all the things *h* of which I speak,

HAPPENINGS (5)

Jdt 15:5 of the *h* in the camp of their enemies.
2Mc 5:11 When these *h* were reported to the king,
Mk 6:51 They were taken aback by these *h*,
Lk 1:65 *h* began to be recounted to the last detail.
7:18 brought their teacher word of all these *h*.

HAPPENS (6)

Dt 21:17 him a double share of whatever he *h* to own,
Ru 3:18 here, my daughter, until you learn what *h*,
Ez 24:24 all that he did you shall do when it *h*.
Mk 4:27 and grows without his knowing how it *h*.
13:18 Keep praying that none of this *h* in winter.
Rom 7:19 What *h* is that I do,

HAPPIER (2)

Mt 18:13 believe me he is *h* about this one than
1Cor 7:40 She will be *h*,

HAPPILY (1)

1Mc 3:6 By his hand redemption was *h* achieved,

HAPPINESS (24)

Tb 8:17 lives to fulfillment with *h* and mercy."
10:14 left Raguel, he was full of *h* and joy,
Est F:10 together with joy and *h* before God,
1Mc 10:66 returned in peace and *h* to Jerusalem.
14:11 to the land, and Israel was filled with *h*.
2Mc 9:19 and best wishes for their health and *h*.
Jb 7:7 I shall not see *h* again.
9:25 they flee away; they see no *h*;
21:16 If their *h* is not in their own hands and
21:25 bitterness of soul, having never tasted *h*.
36:11 their days in prosperity, their years in *h*.
Ps(s) 72:17 all the nations shall proclaim his *h*.
Prv 18:22 He who finds a wife finds *h*;
Sir 4:18 bring him *h* and reveal her secrets to him.
8:19 heart to no man, and banish not your *h*.
25:22 from a wife who brings no *h* to her husband.
30:16 no *h*,
Is 65:18 always be rejoicing and *h* in what I create;
Jer 15:16 they became my joy and the *h* of my heart,
Lam 3:17 of peace, I have forgotten what *h* is;
Acts 20:35 'There is more *h* in giving than receiving.'"
2Cor 1:24 I prefer to work with you toward your *h*.
2:3 enough to be convinced that my *h* is yours.
2Tm 1:4 That would make my *h* complete.

HAPPIZZEZ (1)

1Chr 24:15 seventeenth to Hezir, the eighteenth to *H*.

HAPPY (93)

Dt 6:24 prosperous and *h* a life as we have today;
1Kgs 8:66 rejoicing and *h* over all the blessings the
10:8 *H* are your men, *h* these servants of yours,
2Chr 9:7 *H* are your men, *h* these servants of yours,
Tb 8:7 allow us to live together to a *h* old age."
8:21 So be *h*, son!"
11:18 Tobiah's wedding feast for seven *h* days,
13:14 *H* are those who love you, and *h* those
13:14 *H* are all the men who shall grieve over you,
13:16 *H* for me if a remnant of my offspring
Est 5:9 That day Haman left *h* and in good spirits.
1Mc 4:45 The *h* thought came to them to tear it down,
10:55 *H* the day on which you returned to the
14:21 and fame, and we were *h* that they came.
2Mc 7:24 to make him rich and *h* if he would abandon
Jb 5:17 *H* is the man whom God reproves!
Ps(s) 1:1 *H* the man who follows not the counsel of
2:12 *H* are all who take refuge in him!
32:1 *H* is he whose fault is taken away,
32:2 *H* the man to whom the LORD imputes not
33:12 *H* the nation whose God is the LORD,
34:9 *h* the man who takes refuge in him.
40:5 *H* the man who makes the LORD his trust;
41:2 *H* is he who has regard for the lowly and
41:3 he will make him *h* on the earth,
65:5 *H* the man you choose,
84:5 *H* they who dwell in your house!
84:6 *H* the men whose strength you are!
84:13 LORD of hosts, *h* the men who trust in you!
89:16 *H* the people who know the joyful shout;
94:12 *H* the man whom you instruct,
106:3 *H* are they who observe what is right,
112:1 *H* the man who fears the LORD,
119:1 *H* are they whose way is blameless,
119:2 *H* are they who observe his decrees,
127:5 *H* the man whose quiver is filled with them;
128:1 *H* are you who fear the LORD,
128:2 *h* shall you be,
137:8 *h* the man who shall repay you the evil you
137:9 *H* the man who shall seize and smash your
144:15 *H* the people for whom things are thus; *h*
146:5 *H* he whose help is the God of Jacob,
Prv 3:13 *H* the man who finds wisdom,
3:18 grasp her, and he is *h* who holds her fast.
8:33 *H* the man who obeys me, and happy
8:34 ways, *H* the man watching daily at my gates,
14:21 but *h* is he who is kind to the poor!
16:20 *h* is he who trusts in the LORD!
20:7 and justice, *h* are his children after him!
28:14 *H* the man who is always on his guard;
29:18 but *h* is he who keeps the law.
Sir 1:11 He who fears the LORD will have a *h* end;
11:28 Call no man *h* before his death,
14:1 *H* the man whose mouth brings him no grief,
14:2 *H* the man whose conscience does not
14:20 *H* the man who meditates on wisdom,
25:8 *H* is he who dwells with a sensible wife,
25:8 *H* is he who sins not with his tongue,
25:9 *H* is he who finds a friend and he who
26:1 *H* the husband of a good wife,
28:19 *H* he who is sheltered from it,
31:8 *H* the rich man found without fault,
34:15 *H* the soul that fears the LORD!
50:28 *H* the man who meditates upon these things,
Is 3:10 *H* the just, for it will be well with them,
32:20 *H* are you who sow beside every stream,
56:2 to be revealed, *H* is the man who does this,
Jer 30:19 songs of praise, the laughter of *h* men.
Jon 4:6 Jonah was very *h* over the plant.
Mt 24:46 *H* that servant whom his master discovers
Lk 14:15 *H* is he who eats bread in the kingdom of
23:29 when they will say, *H* are the sterile,
Rom 14:22 *H* the man whose conscience does not
1Cor 16:17 I was very *h* at the arrival of Stephanas,
2Cor 2:2 can make me *h* again but the ones I grieved?
7:8 you grief for a time), I am *h* once again;
Col 2:5 *h* to see good order among you and the
Jas 1:12 *H* the man who holds out to the end through
1Pt 3:14 to suffer for justice' sake, *h* will you be.
4:14 *H* are you when you are insulted for the
Rv 1:3 *H* is the man who reads this prophetic
1:3 and *h* are those who hear it and heed what
14:13 *H* now are the dead who die in the Lord!"
16:15 *H* the man who stays wide awake and fully
19:9 *H* are they who have been invited to the
20:6 *h* and holy are they who share in the first
22:7 *H* the man who heeds the prophetic message
22:14 *H* are they who wash their robes so as to

HAR-HERES (1)

Jgs 1:35 The Amorites had a firm hold in *H*,

HARA (1)

1Chr 5:26 and brought them to Halah, Habor, and *H*,

HARADAH (2)

Nm 33:24 out from Mount Shepher, they camped at *H*.
33:25 Setting out from *H*,

HARAN (21)

Gn 11:26 he became the father of Abram, Nahor and *H*.
11:27 and Haran, and *H* became the father of Lot.
11:28 *H* died before his father Terah,
11:29 of Nahor's wife was Milcah, daughter of *H*,
11:31 his son Abram, his grandson Lot, son of *H*,
11:31 But when they reached *H*,
11:32 then Terah died in *H*.
12:4 was seventy-five years old when he left *H*.
12:5 and the persons they had acquired in *H*,
27:43 flee at once to my brother Laban in *H*,
28:10 from Beer-sheba and proceeded toward *H*.
29:4 "We are from *H*," they replied.
2Kgs 19:12 Gozan, *H*, Rezeph,
1Chr 2:46 Ephah, Caleb's concubine, bore *H*,
2:46 *H* became the father of Gazez.
23:9 of Shimei were Shelomoth, Haziel, and *H*;
Is 37:12 Gozen, *H*, Rezeph, and the Edenites
Ez 27:23 *H*, Canneh,
Acts 7:2 in Mesopotamia and before he settled in *H*.
7:4 the land of the Chaldeans and settled in *H*.

HARARITE (3)

2Sm 23:11 Next to him was Shammah, son of Agee the *H*.
23:33 *H*; Ahiam, son of Sharar the Hararite,

HARASS (9)

Nm 33:55 will *h* you in the country where you live,
1Mc 6:38 to *h* the enemy and to be protected from
15:40 he began to *h* the people and to make
2Mc 5:22 But he left governors to *h* the nation:
Jb 13:25 Will you *h* a wind-driven leaf,
Ps(s) 10:2 Proudly the wicked *h* the afflicted,
38:21 repay evil for good *h* me for pursuing good.
Acts 8:3 so, After that, Saul began to *h* the church.
12:1 to *h* some of the members of the church.

HARASSED (3)

Dt 25:18 fear of any god he *h* you along the way,
Lam 4:19 They *h* us on the mountains and waylaid us
Rv 11:10 these two prophets *h* everyone on earth.

HARASSING (2)

Jos 10:10 *h* them as far as Azekah and Makkedah
2Mc 10:15 important strongholds, were *h* the Jews;

HARASSMENT (1)

Jb 10:17 attack upon me and multiply your *h* of me;

HARBONA (2)

Est 1:10 wine, he instructed Mehuman, Biztha, *H*,
7:9 *H*, one of the eunuchs who attended

HARBOR (8)

2Mc 12:6 In a night attack he set the *h* on fire,
12:9 night, setting fire to the *h* and the fleet,
Ps(s) 13:3 How long shall I *h* sorrow in my soul,
Is 23:10 the *h* is no more.
Mt 9:4 "Why do you *h* evil thoughts?
Mk 2:8 "Why do you *h* these thoughts?
Lk 5:22 "Why do you *h* these thoughts?
Acts 27:12 the *h* was not fit to pass the winter in,

HARBORED (2)

Mk 6:19 Herodias *h* a grudge against him for this
Jas 2:25 when she *h* the messengers and sent them out

HARD (53)

Gn 19:9 With that, they pressed *h* against Lot,
47:9 Few and *h* have been these years of my life,
Ex 1:14 making life bitter for them with *h* work
6:9 because of their dejection and *h* slavery.
21:20 so *h* that the slave dies under his hand,
Lv 26:19 *h* as iron, and your soil as hard
Dt 1:17 that is too *h* for you and I will hear it.'
26:6 and oppressed us, imposing *h* labor upon us,
32:13 from its rocks and olive oil from its *h*,
Jos 23:6 Therefore strive *h* to observe and carry
Jgs 16:30 He pushed *h*, and the temple fell
1Chr 10:2 pressed *h* after Saul and his sons.
1Mc 2:30 because misfortunes pressed so *h* on them.
10:50 He pressed the battle *h* until sunset,
2Mc 8:20 yet when the Macedonians were *h* pressed,
12:11 After a *h* fight, Judas and his companions,
12:21 hard to besiege and even *h* to reach
14:40 such a man he would deal the Jews a *h* blow.
Jb 37:18 of the skies, *h* as a brazen mirror?
41:15 His heart is *h* as stone;
Ps(s) 118:13 I was *h* pressed and was falling,
Wis 11:4 for their thirst from the *h* stone.
Is 14:3 *h* service in which you have been enslaved,
Ez 2:4 *H* of face and obstinate of heart are they
3:8 But I will make your face as *h* as theirs,
Jon 1:13 Still the men rowed *h* to regain the land,
Mt 23:4 They bind up heavy loads, *h* to carry,
24:19 It will be *h* on pregnant or nursing
25:24 lord,' he said, 'I knew you were a *h* man.
Mk 5:10 He pleaded *h* with Jesus not to drive them
10:23 "How *h* it is for the rich to enter the
10:24 how *h* it is to enter the kingdom of God!
Lk 5:5 we have been *h* at it all night long and
18:24 "How *h* it will be for the rich to go into
19:21 was afraid of you because you are a *h* man.
19:22 You knew I was a *h* man,
19:43 you in, and press you *h* from every side.
Jn 6:60 "This sort of talk is *h* to endure!
Acts 20:35 by such *h* work that you must help the weak.
26:8 should find it *h* to believe that God
26:14 It is *h* for you to kick against the goad.'
Rom 2:5 your *h* and impenitent heart is storing up
16:6 to Mary, who has worked *h* for you,
16:12 Tryphosa, who have worked *h* for the Lord;
1Cor 4:12 We work *h* at manual labor.
2Cor 6:5 as men familiar with *h* work,
Col 2:1 I want you to know how *h* I am struggling
2Tm 2:15 Try *h* to make yourself worthy of God's
2Pt 3:16 certain passages in them *h* to understand.
Jude 1:3 encourage you to fight *h* for the faith
Rv 8:12 hit *h* enough to be plunged into darkness.

HARD-EARNED (1)

Ps(s) 127:2 or put off your rest, You that eat *h* bread,

HARD-PRESSED (2)

2Mc 14:9 interest of our country and its *h* people
Is 8:21 He shall pass through it *h* and hungry,

HARD-WON (1)

Prv 5:10 your *h* earnings go to an alien's house;

HARDEN (7)

Gn 11:3 let us mold bricks and *h* them with fire."
Dt 15:7 you shall not *h* your heart nor close your
Ps(s) 95:8 *H* not your hearts as at Meribah,
Is 63:17 and *h* our hearts so that we fear you not?

HARDEN (cont.)

Heb 3: 8 *h* not your hearts as at the revolt in the
3:15 voice, *h* not your hearts as at the revolt,"
4: 7 should hear his voice, *h* not your hearts."

HARDENED (3)

2Chr 36:13 *h* his heart rather than return to the LORD,
Dn 5:20 became proud and his spirit *h* by insolence,
Heb 3:13 that no one grows *h* by the deceit of sin.

HARDENS (1)

Prv 28:14 but he who *h* his heart will fall into evil.

HARDER (5)

Lv 26:24 for your sins seven times *h* than before.
Sir 26: 5 lying testimony are *h* to bear than death,
Jer 5: 3 They set their faces *h* than stone,
Ez 3: 9 as theirs, like diamond, *h* than flint.
1Cor 15:10 I have worked *h* than all the others,

HARDHEARTED (1)

Jer 3:17 will walk no longer in their *h* wickedness.

HARDIER (1)

Gn 30:41 whenever the *h* animals were in heat,

HARDLY (8)

Gn 29: 7 it is *h* the time to bring the animals home.
Ex 14:25 chariot wheels that they could *h* drive.
Jb 41: 4 I need *h* mention his limbs,
Eccl 5:19 will *h* dwell on the shortness of his life,
Sg 3: 4 I had *h* left them when I found him whom
Wis 17: 1 are your judgments, and *h* to be described;
Sir 26:20 A merchant can *h* remain upright,
Mk 9: 6 He *h* knew what to say,

HARDNESS (8)

Ps(s) 81:13 So I gave them up to the *h* of their hearts;
Jer 7:24 They walked in the *h* of their evil hearts
9:13 rather the *h* of their hearts and the Baals,
11: 8 Each one followed the *h* of his evil heart,
16:12 walking in the *h* of his evil heart instead
23:17 And to everyone who walks in *h* of heart,
Lam 3:65 Give them *h* of heart,
Dn 2:41 but yet have some of the *h* of iron.

HARDSHIP (9)

Wis 2:14 merely to see him is a *h* for us,
2Cor 11:27 enduring labor, *h*,
2Tm 1: 8 share of the *h* which the gospel entails.
2: 3 Bear *h* along with me as a good soldier of
4: 5 put up with *h*,
Jas 5:10 your models in suffering *h* and in patience,
5:13 If anyone among you is suffering *h*,
1Pt 2:19 *h* through his awareness of God's presence,
Rv 2: 3 You are patient and endure *h* for my cause.

HARDSHIPS (12)

Ex 18: 8 *h* they had had to endure on their journey,
Nm 20:14 know of all the *h* that have befallen us,
1Kgs 2:26 and shared in all the *h* my father endured."
1Mc 12:13 But many *h* and wars have beset us,
Jb 30:25 Or have I not wept for the *h* of others;
Ps(s) 60: 5 You have made your people feel *h*;
Is 65:16 For the *h* of the past shall be forgotten,
Acts 20:23 city to city that chains and *h* await me.
1Cor 9:12 we put up with all sorts of *h* so as not to
Phil 4:14 was kind of you to want to share in my *h*.
2Thes 1: 6 God visit *h* on those who visit them on you.
2Tm 1:12 and for its sake I undergo present *h*.

HARDWORKING (1)

2Tm 2: 6 The *h* farmer is the one who should have

HARE (2)

Lv 11: 6 the *h*, which indeed chews the cud,
Dt 14: 7 the camel, the *h* and the rock badger,

HAREM (5)

Est 2: 3 virgins to the *h* in the stronghold of Susa.
2: 9 and her maids to the best place in the *h*.
2:11 walk about in front of the court of the *h*,
2:13 *h* to the royal palace whatever she chose.
2:14 return in the morning to a second *h*

HAREPH (2)

1Chr 2:51 Salma, the father of Bethlehem, and *H*,
4: 3 These were the descendants of *H*,

HARHAIAH (1)

Neh 3: 8 was carried out by Uzziel, son of *H*,

HARHAS (1)

2Kgs 22:14 wife of Shallum, son of Tikvah, son of *H*,

HARHUR (2)

Ezr 2:51 of Bakbuk, sons of Hakupha, sons of *H*,
Neh 7:53 sons of Hakupha, sons of *H*.

HARIM (11)

1Chr 24: 8 the second to Jedaiah, the third to *H*,
Ezr 2:32 sons of *H*, three hundred and twenty;
2:39 sons of *H*,
10:21 Hanani and Zebadiah; of the sons of *H*:
10:31 of the sons of *H*:
Neh 3:11 Tower, was repaired by Malchijah, son of *H*,
7:35 sons of *H*,
7:42 sons of *H*,
10: 6 Malchijah, Hattush, Shebaniah, Malluch, *H*,
10:28 Maaseiah, Ahiah, Hanan, Anan, Malluch, *H*,
12:15 for *H*, Adna;

HARIPH (2)

Neh 7:24 sons of *H*,
10:20 Hezekiah, Azzur, Hodiah, Hashum, Bezai, *H*,

HARK (7)

Sg 2: 8 *H*! my lover
Is 5: 7 for justice, but *h*, the outcry!
52: 8 *H*! your watchmen raise a cry,
Mi 6: 9 *H*! the Lord cries to the city.
Zep 1:14 the LORD, near and very swiftly coming, *H*,
Zec 11: 3 *H*! the wailing of the shepherds.
11: 3 *H*! the roaring of the young lions,

HARLOT (50)

Gn 34:31 our sister have been treated like a *h*?"
38:15 When Judah saw her, he mistook her for a *h*,
38:24 daughter-in-law Tamar had played the *h*
Dt 23:18 be no temple *h* among the Israelite women,
Jos 2: 1 went into the house of a *h* named Rahab,
6:17 Only the *h* Rahab and all who are in the
6:25 Because Rahab the *h* had hidden the
Jgs 11: 1 Gileadite Jephthah, born to Gilead of a *h*.
16: 1 to Gaza, where he saw a *h* and visited her.
Prv 7:10 woman comes to meet him, robed like a *h*,
23:27 For the *h* is a deep ditch,
Is 23:15 be for Tyre as in the song about the *h*:
23:16 a harp, go about the city, O forgotten *h*;
Jer 3: 6 every green tree she has played the *h*.
3: 8 she too went off and played the *h*.
Ez 16:15 you used your renown to make yourself a *h*,
16:16 gaudy high places, where you played the *h*.
16:17 images, with which also you played the *h*.
16:20 Was it not enough that you had become a *h*?
16:25 passer-by, playing the *h* countless times.
16:26 You played the *h* with the Egyptians,
16:28 You also played the *h* with the Assyrians,
16:28 and after playing the *h* with them,
16:29 Again and again you played the *h*,
16:35 Therefore, *h*, hear the word of the LORD!
23: 3 even as young girls played the *h* in Egypt.
23: 5 Oholah became a *h* faithless to me;
23: 7 Thus she gave herself as a *h* to them,
23:19 But she played the *h* all the more,
23:19 when she had been a *h* in the land of Egypt.
23:30 because you played the *h* with the nations
23:44 they did come to her as men come to a *h*.
Hos 1: 2 Go, take a *h* wife and harlot's children,
2: 7 Yes, their mother has played the *h*;
3: 3 shall not play the *h* Or belong to any man;
4:10 they shall play the *h* but not increase,
4:13 That is why your daughters play the *h*,
4:15 Though you play the *h*,
5: 3 Now Ephraim has played the *h*,
Jl 4: 3 they gave a boy for a *h*,
Am 7:17 Your wife shall be made a *h* in the city,
Mi 1: 7 As the wages of a *h* they were gathered,
1: 7 and to the wages of a *h* shall they return.
Na 3: 4 For the many debaucheries of the *h*,
Heb 11:31 By faith Rahab the *h* escaped from being
Jas 2:25 Rahab the *h* will illustrate the point.
Rv 17: 1 great *h* who sits by the waters of the deep.
17:15 "The waters on which you saw the *h*
17:16 beast will turn against the *h* with hatred;
19: 2 He has condemned the great *h* who corrupted

HARLOTRIES (3)

Ez 16:22 And through all your abominations and *h*
43: 7 kings profane my holy name with their *h*
Na 3: 4 Who enslaved nations with her *h*,

HARLOTRY (27)

Gn 38:24 harlot and was then with child from her *h*.
Jer 2:20 every green tree, you gave yourself to *h*.
3: 2 You defiled the land by your wicked *h*.
Ez 16:15 and you lavished your *h* on every passer-by,
16:33 to come to you from all sides for your *h*.
16:34 *h* you were different from all other women.
16:36 *h* with your lovers and abominable idols,
16:41 Thus I will put an end to your *h*,
23: 8 give up the *h* which she had begun in Egypt,
23:11 than her sister's, and she outdid her in *h*.
23:14 same path, yet she went further in her *h*.
23:18 Her *h* was discovered and her shame was
23:27 lewdness and to the *h* you began in Egypt;
23:29 and *h* have brought these things upon you,
23:35 to bear the penalty of your lewdness and *h*.
43: 9 me their *h* and the corpses of their kings,
Hos 1: 2 children, for the land gives itself to *h*,
2: 4 Let her remove her *h* from before her,
2: 6 children, for they are the children of *h*.
4:11 have abandoned the LORD to practice *h*.
4:12 *h* has led them astray; they commit *h*,
4:14 Am I then to punish your daughters for *h*,
4:18 is over, they give themselves to *h*;
5: 4 For the spirit of *h* is in them,
6:10 there *h* is found in Ephraim,
Rv 19: 2 harlot who corrupted the earth with her *h*.

HARLOTS (15)

Dt 23:19 You shall not offer a *h* fee or a dog's
Jos 6:22 "Go into the *h* house and bring out the
1Kgs 3:16 *h* came to the king and stood before him.
22:38 licked up his blood and *h* bathed there,
Prv 29: 3 who consorts with *h* squanders his wealth.
Sir 9: 6 Give not yourself to *h*,
19: 2 and the companion of *h* becomes reckless.
Jer 3: 3 But because you have a *h* brow,
5: 7 to the *h* house they throng.
Bar 6:10 or give part of it to the *h* on the terrace.
Ez 16:33 All *h* receive gifts.
Hos 1: 2 Go, take a harlot wife and *h* children,
4:14 You yourselves consort with *h*,
9: 1 loving a *h* hire upon every threshing floor.
Rv 17: 5 of *h* and all the world's abominations."

HARM (85)

Gn 31: 7 God, however, did not let him do me any *h*.
31:24 care not to threaten Jacob with any *h*!"
31:29 I have it in my power to *h* all of you;
31:29 care not to threaten Jacob with any *h*!'
48:16 The Angel who has delivered me from all *h*,
50:20 Even though you meant *h* to me,
Nm 20:19 is no *h* in merely letting us march through."
35:23 he was not his enemy nor seeking to *h* him:
Jos 9:19 the God of Israel, and so we cannot *h* them.
Jgs 15: 3 Philistines cannot blame me if I *h* them."
Ru 2: 9 commanded the young men to do you no *h*.
1Sm 20: 7 you can be sure he has planned some *h*.
23: 9 found out that Saul was planning to *h* him,
24:10 those who say, 'David is trying to *h* you'?
24:12 that I plan no *h* and no rebellion.
24:18 me generously, while I have done you *h*.
25:26 who seek to *h* my lord become as Nabal!
26: 9 But David said to Abishai, "Do not *h* him,
26:21 back, my son David, I will not *h* you again,
26:23 grasp, I would not *h* the LORD's anointed.
2Sm 12:18 He may do some *h*!"
18:12 my two hands, I would not *h* the king's son,
20: 6 may now do us more *h* than Absalom did.
1Kgs 11:25 this added to the *h* done by Hadad,
1Chr 16:22 my anointed, and to my prophets do no *h*."
Ezr 4:13 thus it can only result in *h* to the throne.
Neh 6: 2 They were planning to do me *h*.
Tb 6:15 Because he loves her, he does not *h* her;
Jdt 11: 4 No one at all will *h* you.
Est A:17 sought to *h* Mordecai and his people
7: 4 to compensate for the *h* done to the king."
8: 3 to revoke the *h* done by Haman the Agagite,
8:12 only do they seek to do *h* to our subjects;
9: 2 to attack those who sought to do them *h*,
1Mc 5:48 no one will *h* you;
6:18 to *h* them and to strengthen the Gentiles.
15:19 and countries, that they are not to *h* them,
15:29 territories, done great *h* to the land,
15:35 men of these cities were doing great *h*
2Mc 3:39 down and destroys those who come to *h* it."
8:32 man, who had done great *h* to the Jews.
Ps(s) 37: 8 be not vexed, it will only *h* you.
52: 4 All the day you plot *h*;
57: 2 your wings I take refuge, till *h* pass by.
71:13 in ignominy and disgrace who seek to *h* me.
71:24 how disgraced are those who sought to *h* me!
105:15 my anointed, and to my prophets do no *h*."
121: 6 The sun shall not *h* you by day,
Prv 1:33 in security, in peace, without fear of *h*."
3:30 with one who has done you no *h*.
12:21 No *h* befalls the just,
Wis 14:29 expect no *h* when they have sworn falsely.
18: 2 formerly had been wronged did not *h* them,
Sir 11:24 What *h* can come to me now?"
19:24 he finds the opportunity, he will do *h*.
22:26 But from him who brings *h* to his friend
27:27 Whoever does *h* will be involved in it
33: 1 No evil can *h* the man who fears the LORD;
38:21 it will not help him, but will do you *h*.
42:13 garments, so *h* to women comes from women:
Is 11: 9 be no *h* or ruin on all my holy mountain;
27: 3 Lest anyone *h* it,
Jer 7: 6 or follow strange gods to your own *h*,
10: 5 Fear them not, they can do no *h*,
25: 7 me with your handiwork to your own *h*.
31:28 pull down, to destroy, to ruin, and to *h*.
39:12 let no *h* befall him,
Dn 3:50 way touched them or caused them pain or *h*.

6:23 neither to you have I done any *h,*
Zec 1:15 but a little angry, they added to the *h,*
8:14 As I determined to *h* you when your fathers
Mk 16:18 be able to drink deadly poison without *h,*
16:20 be able to drink deadly poison without *h,*
Lk 4:35 came out of him without doing him any *h.*
Acts 9:13 all the *h* he has done to your holy people
16:28 "Do not *h* yourself!
18:10 No one will attack you or *h* you.
2Tm 4:14 the coppersmith did me a great deal of *h;*
4:18 rescue me from all attempts to do me *h*
1Pt 3:13 Who indeed can *h* you if you are committed
Rv 7: 3 "Do no *h* to the land or the sea or the
9: 4 The locusts were commanded to do no *h* to
9:10 was enough venom to *h* men for five months.
11: 5 If anyone tries to *h* them,
11: 5 to *h* them will surely be slain in this way.

HARMED (6)

Jos 2:19 if anyone in the house with you is *h.*
1Kgs 13:28 not eaten the body nor had it *h* the ass.
Jdt 11: 1 *h* anyone who chose to serve Nebuchadnezzar,
Bar 4:31 Fearful are those who *h* you,
Lk 21:18 me, yet not a hair of your head will be *h.*
Rv 2:11 shall never be *h* by the second death.'

HARMFUL (7)

2Kgs 4:41 there was no longer anything *h* in the pot.
2Mc 15:38 it is *h* to drink wine alone or water alone,
Ps(s) 52: 9 great wealth, and his strength in *h* plots."
Sir 6: 1 Say nothing *h,*
1Cor 11:17 your meetings are not profitable but *h.*
1Tm 6: 9 foolish and *h* desires which drag men down
Heb 13:17 with sorrow, for that would be *h* to you.

HARMING (1)

1Sm 25:34 lives, who has restrained me from *h* you,

HARMONY (5)

Jb 25: 2 are his who brings about *h* in his heavens.
Wis 19:18 elements, in variable *h* among themselves,
Sir 25: 1 *H* among brethren,
Rom 15: 5 you to live in perfect *h* with one another
2Cor 13:11 Live in *h* and peace,

HARMS (3)

Ps(s) 15: 3 Who *h* not his fellow man,
Prv 8:36 But he who misses me *h* himself;
11:17 himself, but a merciless man *h* himself.

HARNEPHER (1)

1Chr 7:36 The sons of Zophah were Suah, *H,*

HARNESS (7)

1Kgs 18:44 *H* up and leave the mountain before the
1Mc 6:37 each elephant, and fastened to it by a *h,*
Ps(s) 50:19 rein for evil, you *h* your tongue to deceit.
Sir 33:25 the yoke and *h* and the rod of his master.
Jer 5: 5 they had broken the yoke, torn off the *h.*
46: 4 *H* the horses, mount, charioteers!
Mi 1:13 *H* steeds to the chariots,

HARNESSED (3)

Dt 22:10 not plow with an ox and an ass *h* together.
Jdt 15:11 She *h* her mules,
Hos 10:11 Ephraim was to be *h,*

HAROD (1)

1Sm 29: 1 encamped at the spring of *H* near Jezreel.

HAROSHETH-HA-GOIIM (2)

Jgs 4: 2 Who dwelt in *H*
4:13 So Sisera assembled from *H* at the Wadi

HARP (32)

1Sm 16:16 look for a man skilled in playing the *h.*
16:23 Saul, David would take the *h* and play,
18:10 playing the *h* as at other times,
19: 9 in hand and David was playing the *h* nearby.
1Mc 3:45 Jacob, and the flute and the *h* were silent.
Jb 21:12 They sing to the timbrel and *h,*
30:31 My *h* is turned to mourning,
Ps(s) 33: 2 Give thanks to the LORD on the *h;*
43: 4 Then will I give you thanks upon the *h,*
49: 5 set forth my riddle to the music of the *h.*
57: 9 Awake, O my soul; awake, lyre and *h!*
71:22 I will sing your praises with the *h,*
81: 3 the timbrel, the pleasant *h* and the lyre.
92: 4 and lyre, with melody upon the *h.*
98: 5 the harp, with the *h* and melodious song.
108: 3 awake, lyre and *h;*
147: 7 sing praise with the *h* to our God,
149: 3 them sing praise to him with timbrel and *h.*
150: 3 the trumpet, praise him with lyre and *h,*
Wis 19:18 among themselves, like strings of the *h,*
Sir 39:15 on the *h* and all stringed instruments;
40:21 The flute and the *h* offer sweet melody,
Is 5:12 With *h* and lyre,
23:16 Take a *h,* go about the city,
24: 8 of the jubilant, stilled is the cheerful *h.*
Dn 3: 4 the sound of the trumpet, flute, lyre, *h,*
3: 7 the sound of the trumpet, flute, lyre, *h,*
3:10 the sound of the trumpet, flute, lyre, *h,*
3:15 the sound of the trumpet, flute, lyre, *h,*
Am 6: 5 Improvising to the music of the *h,*
1Cor 14: 7 produce a sound, such as a flute or a *h,*

HARPERS (1)

Jgs 5:11 them to the strains of the *h* at the wells,

HARPIST (2)

1Sm 16:17 "Find me a skillful *h* and bring him to me."
16:18 sons of Jesse of Bethlehem is a skillful *h.*

HARPISTS (2)

Rv 14: 2 the melody of *h* playing on their harps.
18:22 No tunes of *h* and minstrels,

HARPS (24)

Gn 31:27 singing to the sound of tambourines and *h.*
1Sm 10: 5 by lyres, tambourines, flutes and *h.*
2Sm 6: 5 with singing and with citharas, *h,*
1Kgs 10:12 the king, and *h* and lyres for the chanters.
1Chr 13: 8 amid songs and music on lyres, *h,*
15:16 to play on musical instruments, *h,*
15:20 and Benaiah, played on *h* set to "Alamoth."
15:28 and cymbals, and the music of *h* and lyres.
16: 5 These were to play on *h* and lyres,
25: 1 accompaniment of lyres and *h* and cymbals.
25: 6 the accompaniment of cymbals, *h* and lyres,
2Chr 5:12 in fine linen, with cymbals, *h* and lyres,
9:11 also lyres and *h* for the chanters.
20:28 to the house of the LORD, with *h,*
29:25 *h* and lyres according to the prescriptions
Neh 12:27 hymns and the music of cymbals, *h,*
1Mc 4:54 day it was reconsecrated with songs, *h,*
13:51 the music of *h* and cymbals and lyres,
Ps(s) 137: 2 the aspens of that land we hung up our *h,*
Is 14:11 your pomp is brought, the music of your *h.*
Am 5:23 will not listen to the melodies of your *h.*
Rv 5: 8 Along with their *h,*
14: 2 the melody of harpists playing on their *h.*
15: 2 were holding the *h* used in worshiping God,

HARRIED (1)

Jn 15:20 They will harry you as they *h* me.

HARROW (1)

Jb 39:10 and will he *h* the valleys after you?

HARROWING (1)

Is 28:24 loosening and *h* his land for planting?

HARRY (3)

Jos 10:19 your enemies, and *h* them in the rear.
Jb 18:11 they *h* him at each step.
Jn 15:20 They will *h* you as they harried me.

HARRYING (2)

Gn 49:23 *H* and attacking, the archers opposed
1Sm 7:11 Philistines, *h* them down beyond Beth-car.

HARSH (17)

1Sm 20:10 me if your father gives you a *h* answer?"
25: 3 Nabal himself, a Calebite, was *h*
1Kgs 12: 4 If you now lighten the *h* service and the
12:13 him, the king gave the people a *h* answer.
2Chr 10: 4 If you now lighten the *h* service and the
10:13 given him, the king gave them a *h* answer,
Tb 13:12 are all who speak a *h* word against you;
Jdt 8: 9 heard of the *h* words which the people,
Prv 15: 1 calms wrath, but a *h* word stirs up anger.
Sir 18:14 no reproach, nor spoil any gift by *h* words.
31:31 Use no *h* words with him and distress him
41:22 Of using *h* words with friends,
Is 19: 4 master, A *h* king who shall rule over them,
Dn 2:15 the reason for this *h* order from the king?"
Eph 4:31 bitterness, all passion and anger, *h* words,
1Pt 2:18 reasonable ones but even those who are *h.*
Jude 1:15 every *h* word they have uttered against him."

HARSHA (2)

Ezr 2:52 of Bazluth, sons of Mehida, sons of *H,*
Neh 7:54 of Bazlith, sons of Mehida, sons of *H,*

HARSHER (1)

Phil 1:17 that it will make my imprisonment even *h.*

HARSHLY (7)

Lv 25:43 Do not lord it over them *h,*
25:46 not lord it *h* over any of the Israelites,
25:53 lord it over him *h* under your very eyes.
2Mc 7:33 Though our living Lord treats us *h* for a
Prv 18:23 man implores, but the rich man answers *h.*
Is 53: 7 Though he was *h* treated,
Ez 34: 4 but you lorded it over them *h* and brutally.

HARSHNESS (1)

Sir 42:14 Better a man's *h* than a woman's indulgence,

HARTS (1)

1Kgs 5: 3 oxen, and a hundred sheep, not counting *h,*

HARUM (1)

1Chr 4: 8 well as of the clans of Aharhel, son of *H.*

HARUMAPH (1)

Neh 3:10 and at his side was Jedaiah, son of *H,*

HARUPHITE (1)

1Chr 12: 6 Shephatiah the *H;*

HARUZ (1)

2Kgs 21:19 was Meshullemeth, daughter of *H* of Jotbah.

HARVEST (83)

Gn 8:22 earth lasts cold and heat, seedtime and *h,*
30:14 One day, during the wheat *h,*
45: 6 five more years tillage will yield no *h.*
47:24 But when the *h* is in,
Ex 22:28 the offering of your *h* and your press.
23:16 of the grain *h* with the first of the crop
23:16 at the fruit *h* at the end of the year,
34:22 *h;* likewise, the feast at the fruit harvest
Lv 19: 9 "When you reap the *h* of your land,
23:10 which I am giving you, and reap your *h,*
23:10 the first fruits of your *h* to the priest,
23:22 "When you reap the *h* of your land,
25: 5 aftergrowth of your *h* you shall not reap,
Dt 24:19 *h* in your field and overlook a sheaf there,
26: 2 which you *h* from the land which the LORD,
28:38 seed on your field, you will *h* but little,
Jos 3:15 banks during the entire season of the *h,*
Jgs 15: 1 some time, in the season of the wheat *h,*
Ru 1:22 Bethlehem at the beginning of the barley *h.*
2:21 servants until they complete his entire *h.*"
1Sm 12:17 Are we not in the *h* time for wheat?
2Sm 21: 9 to death during the first days of the *h*—
21: 9 that is, at the beginning of the barley *h.*
21:10 on the rock from the beginning of the *h*
23:13 During the *h* three of the Thirty went down
24:15 Now it was the time of the wheat *h* when
2Chr 32:28 also storehouses for the *h* of grain,
Jdt 2:27 of Damascus at the time of the wheat *h,*
8: 2 clan, had died at the time of the barley *h.*
Jb 24: 6 they *h* at night in the untilled land.
Ps(s) 65:12 and your paths overflow with a rich *h;*
78:46 He gave their *h* to the caterpillar,
Prv 6: 8 summer, stores up her provisions in the *h.*
10: 5 a son who slumbers during *h,*
20: 4 when he looks for the *h,*
25:13 the coolness of snow in the heat of the *h*
26: 1 Like snow in summer, or rain in *h,*
Sir 1:15 choice foods, her granaries with her *h.*
7: 3 of injustice, lest you *h* it sevenfold.
24:24 understanding, like the Jordan at *h* time.
37:11 work, to a seasonal laborer about the *h,*
Is 9: 2 As they rejoice before you as at the *h,*
17:11 The *h* shall disappear on the day of the
18: 4 of sunshine, like a cloud of dew at *h* time.
23: 3 The grain of Shihor, the *h* of the Nile,
32:10 The vintage will fail, there will be no *h.*
62: 9 But you who *h* the grain shall eat it,
Jer 2: 3 was Israel, the first fruits of his *h;*
5:17 They will devour your *h* and your bread,
5:24 for us over the appointed weeks of *h.*"
8:20 "The *h* has passed,
12:13 They recoil before their *h,*
40:12 Mizpah and had a rich *h* of wine and fruit.
48:32 Upon your *h,* upon your vintage
50:16 and him who wields the sickle in *h* time!
51:33 while, and the *h* time will come for her.
Hos 6:11 you also, O Judah, a *h* has been appointed.
Jl 1:11 because the *h* of the field has perished.
4:13 Apply the sickle, for the *h* is ripe;
Am 4: 7 you when the *h* was still three months away;
Mt 9:37 "The *h* is good but laborers are scarce.
9:38 Beg the *h* master to send out laborers to
9:38 to send out laborers to gather his *h.*"
13:30 grow together until harvest; then at *h* time
13:39 The *h* is the end of the world,
21:43 given to a nation that will yield a rich *h.*
Mk 4:29 the sickle, for the time is ripe for *h.*'"
Lk 10: 2 "The *h* is rich but the workers are few;
10: 2 harvest-master to send workers to his *h.*
12:16 "There was a rich man who had a good *h.*
12:17 'I have no place to store my *h.*
Jn 4:35 'Four months more and it will be *h!*'?
4:35 The fields are shining for *h!*
1Cor 9:11 too much to expect a material *h* from you?
Gal 6: 8 the flesh, he will reap a *h* of corruption;
6: 9 efforts, in due time we shall reap our *h.*
Phil 1:11 may be found rich in the *h* of justice
Jas 3:18 The *h* of justice is sown in peace for
Rv 14:15 "Use your sickle and cut down the *h,*

HARVEST (cont.)

14:15 the earth's *h* is fully ripe."
14:16 all the earth and reaped the earth's *h*.

HARVEST-MASTER (1)

Lk 10: 2 ask the *h* to send workers to his harvest.

HARVESTED (4)

Jgs 9:27 fields, *h* their grapes and trod them out.
Ru 2: 9 Watch to see which field is to be *h*,
Jdt 4: 5 since their fields had recently been *h*,
Jas 5: 4 from the farmhands who *h* your fields.

HARVESTER (2)

Jer 9:21 dung on a field, Like sheaves behind the *h*,
1Cor 9:10 hope and the *h* expect a share in the grain.

HARVESTERS (8)

Ru 2: 3 field she entered to glean after the *h*
2: 4 came from Bethlehem and said to the *h*,
2: 5 Boaz asked the overseer of his *h*,
2: 6 The overseer of the *h* answered,
2: 7 the gleanings into sheaves after the *h*;
Mt 13:30 then at harvest time I will order the *h*,
13:39 of the world, while the *h* are the angels.
Jas 5: 4 The cries of the *h* have reached the ears

HARVESTING (3)

Ex 34:21 even during the seasons of plowing and *h*.
1Sm 6:13 were *h* the wheat in the valley.
8:12 will set them to do his plowing and his *h*,

HARVESTS (4)

Ru 2:23 until the end of the barley and wheat *h*.
Sir 11: 3 but she reaps the choicest of all *h*.
Is 16: 9 fruits and *h* the battle cry has fallen.
Acts 14:17 the heavens he sends down rain and rich *h*;

HASADIAH (2)

1Chr 3:20 were Hashubah, Ohel, Berechiah, *H*,
Bar 1: 1 of Mahseiah, son of Zedekiah, son of *H*,

HASHABIAH (15)

1Chr 6:30 son of Abdi, son of Malluch, son of *H*,
9:14 son of Hasshub, son of Azrikam, son of *H*,
25: 3 Gedaliah, Zeri, Jeshaiah, Shimei, *H*,
25:19 twelfth fell to *H*, his sons, and his brethren
26:30 Among the Hebronites, *H* and his brethren,
27:17 for Levi, *H*;
2Chr 35: 9 and his brothers Shemaiah, Nethanel, *H*,
Ezr 8:19 They also sent us *H*,
8:24 priestly leaders along with Sherebiah, *H*,
Neh 3:17 Next to him, for his own district, was *H*,
10:12 Kelita, Pelaiah, Hanan, Mica, Rehob, *H*,
11:15 son of Hasshub, son of Azrikam, son of *H*,
11:22 Jerusalem was Uzzi, son of Bani, son of *H*,
12:21 for Hilkiah, *H*;
12:24 The heads of the Levites were *H*,

HASHABNAH (1)

Neh 10:26 Hallohesh, Pilha, Shobek, Rehum, *H*,

HASHABNEIAH (2)

Neh 3:10 Next to him Hattush, son of *H*,
9: 5 The Levites Jeshua, Kadmiel, Bani, *H*,

HASHBADDANAH (1)

Neh 8: 4 Pedaiah, Mishael, Malchijah, Hashum, *H*,

HASHMONAH (2)

Nm 33:29 Setting out from Mithkah, they camped at *H*.
33:30 Setting out from *H*—

HASHUBAH (1)

1Chr 3:20 The sons of Meshullam were *H*,

HASHUM (5)

Ezr 2:19 sons of *H*,
10:33 of the sons of *H*:
Neh 7:22 sons of *H*,
8: 4 on his left Pedaiah, Mishael, Malchijah, *H*,
10:19 Adin, Ater, Hezekiah, Azzur, Hodiah, *H*,

HASIDEANS (3)

1Mc 2:42 Then they were joined by a group of *H*,
7:13 The *H* were the first among the Israelites
2Mc 14: 6 "Those Jews called *H*,

HASRAH (1)

2Chr 34:22 wife of Shallum, son of Tokhath, son of *H*,

HASSENAAH (1)

Neh 3: 3 Fish Gate was rebuilt by the sons of *H*;

HASSENUAH (2)

1Chr 9: 7 of Meshullam, son of Hodaviah, son of *H*,
Neh 11: 9 was their commander, and Judah, son of *H*,

HASSHUB (5)

1Chr 9:14 Among the Levites were Shemaiah, son of *H*,
Neh 3:11 repaired by Malchijah, son of Harim, and *H*,
3:23 Benjamin and *H* carried out the repair in
10:24 Hanan, Anaiah, Hoshea, Hananiah, *H*,
11:15 Among the Levites were Shemaiah, son of *H*,

HASSOPHERETH (1)

Ezr 2:55 sons of Sotai, sons of *H*,

HASTE (28)

Dt 16: 3 in frightened *h* you left the land of Egypt.
Jgs 13:10 the woman ran in *h* and told her husband.
2Kgs 7:15 the Arameans had thrown away in their *h*.
Ezr 4:23 they went in all *h* to the Jews in Jerusalem
Jdt 6:16 gathered in *h* at the place of assembly.
Est 3:15 set out in *h* at the king's command;
5: 5 Haman make *h* to fulfill the wish of Esther."
8:14 steeds sped forth in *h* at the king's order,
1Mc 6:63 he departed in *h* and returned to Antioch,
2Mc 4:31 went off in *h* to settle the affair,
11:37 Make *h*, then, to send us those who can
Ps(s) 31: 3 your ear to me, make *h* to deliver me!
38:23 Make *h* to help me, O Lord my salvation!
40:14 O LORD, make *h* to help me.
69:18 in my distress, make *h* to answer me.
70: 2 O LORD, make *h* to help me.
71:12 my God, make *h* to help me.
Prv 21: 5 but all rash *h* leads certainly to poverty.
28:20 in *h* to grow rich will not go unpunished.
Is 5:19 say, "Let him make *h* and speed his work,
49:17 Your rebuilders make *h*,
52:12 Yet not in fearful *h* will you come out,
Dn 3:91 rose in *h* and asked his nobles,
13:50 Then all the people returned in *h*.
Lk 1:39 proceeding in *h* into the hill country to
2:16 They went in *h* and found Mary and Joseph,
Acts 22:18 'You must make *h*,' he said.
1Cor 11:21 for everyone is in *h* to eat his own supper.

HASTEN (16)

Ex 12:33 on, to *h* their departure from the land;
2Chr 24: 5 You must *h* this affair."
24: 5 But the Levites did not *h*.
35:21 another kingdom, and God has told me to *h*.
Tb 1: 6 I would *h* to Jerusalem and present them to
Ps(s) 22:20 O my help, *h* to aid me.
55: 9 I would *h* to find shelter from the violent
70: 6 O God, *h* to me!
141: 1 *h* to me;
143: 7 *H* to answer me, O LORD, for my spirit
Prv 1:16 feet run to evil, they *h* to shed blood.]
Sir 36: 7 *H* the day, bring on the time;
Ez 30: 9 On that day messengers shall *h* forth at my
Jl 4:11 *H* and come, all your neighboring peoples,
Am 6: 3 evil day, yet you *h* the reign of violence!
2Pt 3:12 of the day of God and trying to *h* it!

HASTENED (15)

Gn 18: 6 Abraham *h* into the tent and told Sarah,
Jos 7:22 *h* to the tent and found them hidden there,
1Sm 17:22 of the baggage and *h* to the battle line,
2Sm 19:18 servants, *h* to the Jordan before the king.
2Chr 20: 3 frightened, and he *h* to consult the LORD.
20:20 they *h* out to the wilderness of Tekoa.
29:20 Then King Hezekiah *h* to convoke the
2Mc 4:14 and neglecting the sacrifices, they *h*,
12:29 set out from there and *h* on to Scythopolis,
Jb 31: 5 in falsehood and my foot has *h* to deceit;
Wis 18:21 the blameless man *h* to be their champion,
Dn 6:20 the next morning and *h* to the lions' den.
Mt 14:27 Jesus *h* to reassure them:
Mk 6:33 from all the towns *h* on foot to the place,
6:50 He *h* to reassure them:

HASTENING (1)

Hb 1: 8 They fly like the eagle *h* to devour;

HASTENS (2)

Wis 6:13 She *h* to make herself known in
Jer 48:16 hand is Moab's ruin, his disaster *h* apace.

HASTILY (7)

Ex 10:16 *H* Pharaoh summoned Moses and Aaron
1Mc 6:33 force *h* along the road to Beth-zechariah;
6:57 So he *h* resolved to withdraw.
Prv 19: 2 and he who acts *h*,
20:21 Possessions gained *h* at the outset will in
25: 8 seen bring not forth *h* against an opponent;
1Tm 5:22 Never lay hands *h* on anyone,

HASTY (4)

2Sm 4: 4 But in their *h* flight,
Prv 29:20 Do you see a man *h* in his words?
Eccl 5: 1 Be not *h* in your utterance and let not
8: 3 to God, be not *h* to withdraw from the king;

HASUPHA (2)

Ezr 2:43 sons of Ziha, sons of *H*,
Neh 7:46 sons of Ziha, sons of *H*,

HAT (1)

2Mc 4:12 the noblest young men to wear the Greek *h*.

HATCH (4)

Gn 8: 6 Noah opened the *h* he had made in the ark,
Is 34:15 *h* them out and gather them in her shadow;
59: 5 They *h* adders' eggs,
59: 5 of them is pressed, it will *h* as a viper;

HATCHED (1)

Acts 20: 3 a plot was *h* against him by certain Jews;

HATCHING (1)

Jer 11:19 realized that they were *h* plots against me:

HATE (73)

Gn 26:27 you *h* me and have driven me away from you
Ex 18:21 men, trustworthy men who *h* dishonest gain,
20: 5 on the children of those who *h* me,
Nm 10:35 and those who *h* you may flee before you."
Dt 5: 9 on the children of those who *h* me,
32:41 repay my foes and requite those who *h* me.
Jgs 14:16 his wife wept and said, "You must *h* me;
2Sm 19: 7 who *h* you and hating those who love you.
1Kgs 22: 8 but I *h* him because he prophesies not good
2Chr 1:11 glory, nor for the life of those who *h* you,
18: 7 whom we may consult the LORD, but I *h* him,
19: 2 the wicked and love those who *h* the LORD?
Est C:26 You know that I *h* the glory of the pagans,
Jb 8:22 that *h* you shall be clothed with shame,
Ps(s) 5: 6 You *h* all evildoers;
25:19 enemies are many, and they *h* me violently.
26: 5 I *h* the assembly of evildoers,
31: 7 You *h* those who worship vain idols,
45: 8 You love justice and *h* wickedness;
50:17 *h* discipline and cast my words behind you?
68: 2 and those who *h* him flee before him.
69: 5 hairs of my head who *h* me without cause.
83: 3 and they who *h* you lift up their heads.
89:24 him and those who *h* him I will smite.
97:10 The LORD loves those that *h* evil;
101: 3 I *h* him who does perversely;
119:104 therefore I *h* every false way.
119:113 I *h* men of divided heart,
119:128 every false way I *h*.
119:163 Falsehood I *h* and abhor; your law I love.
120: 6 long have I dwelt with those who *h* peace.
129: 5 be put to shame and fall back that *h* Zion.
139:21 Do I not *h*, O LORD, those who hate you?
139:22 God With a deadly hatred I *h* them;
Prv 5:12 And you say, "Oh, why did I *h* instruction,
8:13 [The fear of the LORD is to *h* evil;]
8:13 the evil way, and the perverse mouth I *h*.
8:36 all who *h* me love death."
9: 8 Reprove not an arrogant man, lest he *h* you;
13:19 the soul, but fools *h* to turn from evil.
19: 7 All the poor man's brothers *h* him;
25:17 he have more than enough of you, and *h* you.
29:10 Bloodthirsty men *h* the honest man,
Eccl 3: 8 A time to love, and a time to *h*;
Sir 7:15 *H* not laborious tasks,
10: 7 and the sin of oppression they both *h*.
17:21 away from sin, *h* intensely what he loathes;
25: 2 Three kinds of men I *h*;
27:24 There is nothing that I *h* so much,
28: 7 of the commandments, *h* not your neighbor,
Is 61: 8 what is right, I *h* robbery and injustice;
66: 5 who, because of my name, *h* and reject you,
Jer 44: 4 to commit this horrible deed which I *h*.
Ez 23:28 now handing you over to those whom you *h*.
Am 5:10 They *h* him who reproves at the gate and
5:15 *H* evil and love good,
5:21 I *h*, I spurn your feasts,
6: 8 abhor the pride of Jacob, I *h* his castles,
Mi 3: 2 what is right, You who *h* what is good,
Zec 8:17 For all these things I *h*, says the LORD.
Mal 2:16 For I *h* divorce,
Mt 5:43 love your countryman but *h* your enemy.'
6:24 He will either *h* one and love the other or
Lk 6:22 "Blest shall you be when men *h* you,
6:27 your enemies, do good to those who *h* you;
16:13 Either he will *h* the one and love the
21:17 All will *h* you because of me,
Jn 7: 7 but it does *h* me because of the evidence I
15:23 To hate me is to *h* my Father.
Rom 1:30 are gossips and slanderers, they *h* God,
7:15 do not do what I want to do but what I *h*.

HATED (32)

Gn 37: 4 they *h* him so much that they would not
37: 8 So they *h* him all the more because of his
Jgs 11: 7 *h* me and drove me from my father's house?"
2Sm 13:22 *h* him for having shamed his sister Tamar.

22:41 before me and those who *h* me I destroyed.
1Mc 11:38 had served under his predecessors *h* him.
2Mc 5: 8 all men, *h* as a transgressor of the laws,
14:28 for he *h* to break his agreement with a man
Ps(s) 18:41 me, and those who *h* me you destroyed.
36: 3 that his guilt will not be found out or *h.*
44: 8 foes, and those who *h* us you put to shame.
44:11 those who *h* us plundered us at will,
81:16 who *h* the LORD would seek to flatter me,
105:25 he changed, so that they *h* his people,
Prv 1:29 Because they *h* knowledge,
1:30 and like fools they *h* knowledge:
14:20 Even by his neighbor the poor man is *h,*
Wis 11:24 for what you *h,*
12: 4 land, whom you *h* for deeds most odious
Sir 9:18 speech, and he who talks rashly is *h.*
20: 7 he who pretends to authority is *h.*
21:28 himself, and is *h* by his neighbors.
Is 60:15 Once you were forsaken, *h* and unvisited,
Mal 1: 3 yet I loved Jacob, but *h* Esau;
Mt 10:22 You will be *h* by all on account of me.
24:10 you will be *h* by all nations on my account.
Mk 13:13 of my name, you will be *h* by everyone.
Jn 15:18 hates you know it has *h* me before you.
15:25 'They *h* me without cause.'
17:14 your word, and the world has *h* them for it;
Rom 9:13 says, "I have loved Jacob and *h* Esau."
Heb 1: 9 You have loved justice and *h* wickedness,

HATEFUL (4)

Sir 20:14 *h* indeed is such a man.
27:30 Wrath and anger are *h* things,
Dn 3:32 over to our enemies, lawless and *h* rebels;
Ti 3: 3 envy, *h* ourselves and hating one another.

HATES (30)

Ex 23: 5 who *h* you lying prostrate under its burden,
Dt 7:10 with destruction the person who *h* him;
Jdt 5:17 prospered, for their God, who *h* wickedness,
Ps(s) 11: 5 the lover of violence he *h.*
55:13 he who *h* me had vaunted himself against me,
Prv 6:16 There are six things the LORD *h,*
11:15 but he who *h* giving pledges is safe.
11:16 but she who *h* virtue is covered with shame.
12: 1 knowledge, but he who *h* reproof is stupid.
13: 5 Anything deceitful the just man *h,*
13:24 He who spares his rod *h* his son,
15:10 he who *h* reproof will die.
15:27 own house, but he who *h* bribes will live.
28:16 He who *h* ill-gotten gain prolongs his days.
29: 1 The man who remains stiff-necked and *h*
Sir 12: 7 The Most High himself *h* sinners,
15:11 for what he *h* he does not do.
15:13 Abominable wickedness the LORD *h,*
21: 6 who *h* correction walks the sinner's path,
27:24 I hate so much, and the LORD *h* him as well.
33: 2 He who *h* the law is without wisdom,
Jn 3:20 Everyone who practices evil *h* the light;
12:25 while the man who *h* his life in this world
15:18 *h* you know it has hated me before you.
15:19 the reason it *h* you is that you do not
Eph 5:29 Observe that no one ever *h* his own flesh;
1Jn 2:11 the man who *h* his brother is in darkness.
3:13 to be surprised if the world *h* you.
3:15 Anyone who *h* his brother is a murderer,
4:20 love is fixed on God," yet *h* his brother,

HATHACH (4)

Est 4: 5 Esther then summoned *H,*
4: 6 So *H* went out to Mordecai in the public
4: 9 *H* returned to Esther and told her what
4:10 *H* and gave him this message

HATHATH (1)

1Chr 4:13 The sons of Othniel were *H* and Meonothai;

HATING (7)

2Sm 19: 7 who hate you and *h* those who love you.
Mt 24:10 falter then, betraying and *h* one another.
Jn 7: 7 The world is incapable of *h* you,
15:24 seen, and they go on *h* me and my Father.
2Tm 3: 3 slanderous, licentious, brutal, *h* the good.
Ti 3: 3 envy, hateful ourselves and *h* one another.
1Jn 2: 9 be in light, *h* his brother all the while,

HATIPHA (2)

Ezr 2:54 sons of Temah, sons of Neziah, sons of *H.*
Neh 7:56 sons of Temah, sons of Neziah, sons of *H.*

HATITA (2)

Ezr 2:42 sons of Talmon, sons of Akkub, sons of *H,*
Neh 7:45 sons of Talmon, sons of Akkub, sons of *H,*

HATRED (27)

Lv 19:17 not bear *h* for your brother in your heart.
Nm 35:20 "If a man pushes another out of *h,*
Dt 1:27 in your tents, 'Out of *h* for us the LORD,
9:28 or 'Out of *h* for them,
19:11 in wait for his neighbor out of *h* for him,
Jos 20: 5 unintentionally and not out of previous *h.*
2Sm 13:15 Then Amnon conceived an intense *h* for her,
Est C:24 and turn his heart to *h* for our enemy,
1Mc 11:40 and of the *h* that his soldiers had for him.
13: 6 nations out of *h* have united to destroy us."
2Mc 3: 1 of the high priest Onias and his *h* of evil,
5:23 Out of *h* for the Jewish citizens,
8: 4 and to manifest his *h* of evil.
Ps(s) 109: 3 and with words of *h* they have encompassed
109: 5 repaid me evil for good and *h* for my love.
139:22 With a deadly *h* I hate them;
Prv 10:12 *H* stirs up disputes,
15:17 love is than a fatted ox and *h* with it.
26:26 A man may conceal *h* under dissimulation,
Eccl 9: 1 Love from *h* man cannot tell;
9: 6 and *h* and rivalry have long since perished.
Wis 19:13 their guests with the more grievous *h.*
Ez 23:29 They shall deal with you in *h,*
35: 5 never let die your *h* for the Israelites,
35:11 you have exercised [in your *h* against them.
Hos 9:15 yes, there they incurred my *h.*
Rv 17:16 beast will turn against the harlot with *h;*

HATS (1)

Dn 3:21 the white-hot furnace with their coats, *h,*

HATTIL (2)

Ezr 2:57 of Giddel, sons of Shephatiah, sons of *H,*
Neh 7:59 of Giddel, sons of Shephatiah, sons of *H,*

HATTUSH (5)

1Chr 3:22 The sons of Shecaniah were Shemiah, *H,*
Ezr 8: 2 of the sons of David, *H,*
Neh 3:10 Next to him *H,*
10: 5 Jeremiah, Pashhur, Amariah, Malchijah, *H,*
12: 2 Jeremiah, Ezra, Amariah, Malluch, *H,*

HAUGHTILY (2)

Ps(s) 75: 6 speak not *h* against the Rock.
Ob 1:12 Speak not *h* on the day of distress!

HAUGHTY (31)

Lv 26:19 sins sevenfold, to break your *h* confidence.
Dt 8:14 *h* of heart and unmindful of the LORD,
Jb 22:29 For he brings down the pride of the *h.*
40:12 Bring down the *h* with a glance;
Ps(s) 18:28 people you save but *h* eyes you bring low;
54: 5 For *h* men have risen up against me,
86:14 O God, the *h* have risen up against me,
101: 5 The man of *h* eyes and puffed-up heart I
131: 1 my heart is not proud, nor are my eyes *h;*
Prv 6:17 *H* eyes,
16:18 disaster, and a *h* spirit before a fall.
18:12 Before his downfall a man's heart is *h,*
21: 4 *H* eyes and a proud heart
30:13 There is a group—how *h* their eyes!
Sir 15: 7 attain to her, *h* men will not behold her.
26: 9 *h* stare an unchaste wife can be recognized.
27:15 Wrangling among the *h* ends in bloodshed,
35:21 Till he destroys the *h* root and branch,
39:24 paths are level, to the *h* they are steep;
Is 2:11 The *h* eyes of man will be lowered,
3:16 Because the daughters of Zion are *h,*
5:15 brought low, and the eyes of the *h* lowered,
10:13 heart, and the boastfulness of his *h* eyes.
16: 6 Moab, how very proud he is, With his *h,*
Ez 16:50 they became *h* and committed abominable
28: 2 Because you are *h* of heart,
28: 5 your heart has grown *h* from your riches
28:17 became *h* of heart because of your beauty;
30:18 Her *h* pride shall cease from her,
Rom 1:30 they hate God, are insolent, *h,*
11:20 Do not be *h* on that account, but fearful.

HAUL (1)

Jn 21: 6 so many fish they could not *h* the net in.

HAULED (4)

Lv 14:45 beams and mortar shall be *h* away to an
Tb 6: 4 seized the fish and *h* it up on the shore.
Mt 13:48 When it was full they *h* it ashore and sat
Jn 21:11 *h* ashore the net loaded with sizable fish

HAULS (1)

Hb 1:15 with his hook, he *h* them away with his net,

HAUNCHES (2)

1Kgs 7:25 east, with their *h* all toward the center,
2Chr 4: 4 east, with their *h* all toward the center;

HAUNT (6)

Is 14:23 make it a *h* of hoot owls and a marshland;
34:13 an abode for jackals and a *h* for ostriches.
Jer 9:10 into a heap of ruins, a *h* of jackals;
10:22 cities of Judah into a desert *h* of jackals.
49:33 Hazor shall become a *h* of jackals,
51:37 become a heap of ruins, a *h* of jackals;

HAUNTS (1)

Sg 4: 8 of Senir and Hermon, From the *h* of lions,

HAURAN (2)

Ez 47:16 Hazar-enon which is on the border of the *H.*
47:18 between the *H*— toward Damascus

HAVEN (2)

Ps(s) 107:30 and he brought them to their desired *h.*
Is 23:14 ships of Tarshish, for your *h* is destroyed.

HAVENS (1)

Acts 27: 8 along the coast to a place called Fair *H,*

HAVEN'T (1)

Gn 27:36 he pleaded, *H* you saved a blessing for me?"

HAVILAH (6)

Gn 2:11 one that winds through the whole land of *H,*
10: 7 Seba, *H,* Sabtah, Raamah, and Sabteca.
10:29 Diklah, Obal, Abimael, Sheba, Ophir, *H,*
1Sm 15: 7 Amalek from *H* to the approaches of Shur,
1Chr 1: 9 The descendants of Cush were Seba, *H,*
1:23 Diklah, Ebal, Abimael, Sheba, Ophir, *H,*

HAVILAH-BY-SHUR (1)

Gn 25:18 The Ishmaelites ranged from *H,*

HAVOC (3)

1Mc 7: 7 you trust to go and see all the *h* Judas
Is 54:16 who have created the destroyer to work *h.*
Acts 9:21 "Isn't this the man who worked such *h* in

HAVVOTH-JAIR (3)

Nm 32:41 villages, captured them and called them *H.*
Dt 3:14 called it after his own name Bashan *H*
Jgs 10: 4 these are called *H* to the present day.

HAWK (1)

Jb 39:26 Is it by your discernment that the *h* soars,

HAWKS (3)

Lv 11:16 the gull, the various species of *h,*
Dt 14:15 the gull, the various species of *h,*
Jb 28: 7 knows, nor has the *h* eye seen that path.

HAY (3)

Is 11: 7 the lion shall eat *h* like the ox.
65:25 and the lion shall eat *h* like the ox [but
1Cor 3:12 silver, precious stones, wood, *h* or straw,

HAZAEL (28)

1Kgs 19:15 arrive, you shall anoint *H* as king of Aram.
19:17 If anyone escapes the sword of *H,*
2Kgs 8: 8 of God had come there, the king said to *H,*
8: 9 *H* went to visit him, carrying a present,
8:11 stared him down until *H* became ill at ease.
8:12 The man of God wept, and *H* asked,
8:13 *H* exclaimed, "How can a dog like me
8:14 *H* left Elisha and returned to his master.
8:14 that you would surely recover," replied *H.*
8:15 The next day, however, *H* took a cloth,
8:15 And *H* reigned in his stead.
8:28 Joram, son of Ahab, in battle against *H,*
8:29 on him at Ramah in his battle against *H,*
9:14 been besieging Ramoth-gilead against *H,*
9:15 inflicted on him in the battle against *H,*
10:32 *H* defeated the Israelites throughout their
12:18 Then King *H* of Aram
12:18 it, *H* decided to go on to attack Jerusalem.
12:19 palace, and sent them to King *H* of Aram,
13: 3 a long time left them in the power of *H,*
13: 3 king of Aram, and of Ben-hadad, son of *H.*
13:22 King *H* of Aram oppressed Israel during the
13:24 So when King *H* of Aram died and his son
13:25 of Hazael, the cities which *H* had taken
2Chr 22: 5 Ahab, king of Israel, to battle against *H,*
22: 6 received at Rama in his battle against *H,*
Am 1: 4 iron, I will send fire upon the house of *H,*

HAZAIAH (1)

Neh 11: 5 son of Baruch, son of Colhozeh, son of *H,*

HAZAR-ADDAR (1)

Nm 34: 4 and extend south of Kadesh-barnea to *H;*

HAZAR-ENAN (2)

Nm 34: 9 shall reach to Ziphron and terminate at *H.*
34:10 you shall draw a line from *H* to Shepham.

HAZAR-ENON (3)

Ez 47:16 to *H* which is on the border of the Hauran.
47:17 the border shall extend from the sea to *H,*
48: 1 to Hethlon through Labo of Hamath to *H,*

HAZAR-GADDAH (1)

Jos 15:27 H, Heshmon,

HAZAR-SHUAL (4)

Jos 15:28 Hazar-gaddah, Heshmon, Beth-pelet, H,
19: 3 received Beer-sheba, Shema, Moladah, H,
1Chr 4:28 They dwelt in Beer-sheba, Moladah, H,
Neh 11:27 in Jeshua, Moladah, Beth-pelet, in H

HAZAR-SUSAH (1)

Jos 19: 5 Bethul, Hormah, Ziklag, Beth-marcaboth, H,

HAZAR-SUSIM (1)

1Chr 4:31 Bethuel, Hormah, Ziklag, Beth-marcaboth, H,

HAZARDOUS (1)

Acts 27: 9 lateness of the year sailing had become h.

HAZARMAVETH (2)

Gn 10:26 became the father of Almodad, Sheleph, H,
1Chr 1:20 became the father of Almodad, Sheleph, H,

HAZAZON-TAMAR (2)

Gn 14: 7 and of the Amorites who dwelt in H.
2Chr 20: 2 they are already in H" (which is Engedi).

HAZEROTH (6)

Nm 11:35 Kibroth-hattaavah the people set out for H.
12: 1 While they were in H,
12:16 from H and encamped in the desert of Paran.
33:17 from Kibroth-hattaavah, they camped at H.
33:18 Setting out from H,
Dt 1: 1 Paran and Tophel, Laban, H and Dizahab;

HAZIEL (1)

1Chr 23: 9 The sons of Shimei were Shelomoth, H,

HAZO (1)

Gn 22:22 Kemuel (the father of Aram), Chesed, H,

HAZOR (19)

Jos 11: 1 When Jabin, king of H,
11:10 H and slew its king with the sword; for H
11:11 H itself he burned.
11:13 the cities built on raised sites, except H,
12:19 Hepher, Aphek, Lasharon, Madon, H,
15:23 Dimonah, Adadah, Kedesh, H and Ithnan;
15:25 and Kerioth-hezron (that is, H);
19:36 Rakkath, Chinnereth, Adamah, Ramah, H,
Jgs 4: 2 Canaanite king, Jabin, who reigned in H.
4:17 the Kenite Heber, since Jabin, king of H,
1Sm 12: 9 captain of the army of Jabin, king of H,
1Kgs 9:15 palace, Millo, the wall of Jerusalem, H,
2Kgs 15:29 Ijon, Abel-beth-maacah, Janoah, Kedesh, H,
Neh 11:33 dependencies, Anathoth, Nob, Ananiah, H,
1Mc 11:67 at daybreak they went to the plain of H.
Jer 49:28 Of Kedar and the kingdoms of H,
49:30 hide in deep holes, you that live in H,
49:33 H shall become a haunt of jackals,

HAZOR-HADATTAH (1)

Jos 15:25 Ziph, Telem, Bealoth, H,

HAZZELELPONI (1)

1Chr 4: 3 their sister was named H.

HE-ASSES (1)

Gn 32:16 twenty she-asses and ten h.

HE-GOAT (8)

Lv 9: 3 Take a h for a sin offering,
Nm 15:24 as well as one h as a sin offering.
Prv 30:31 The strutting cock, and the h,
Ez 43:22 present an unblemished h as a sin offering,
43:25 days you shall offer a h as a sin offering,
Dn 8: 5 a h with a prominent horn on its forehead
8: 8 The h became very powerful,
8:21 The h is the king of the Greeks,

HE-GOATS (8)

Gn 30:35 Laban removed the streaked and spotted h
31:10 in which I saw mating h that were streaked,
31:12 All the h in the flock,
32:15 two hundred she-goats and twenty h;
2Chr 17:11 rams and seven thousand seven hundred h.
29:21 seven lambs and seven h were brought for a
29:23 Then the h for the sin offering were led
Ezr 6:17 twelve h as a sin-offering for all Israel,

HEAD (367)

Gn 3:15 He will strike at your h,
4: 7 If you do well, you can hold up your h;
28:11 his h and lay down to sleep at that spot.
28:18 the stone that he had put under his h,
40:13 up your h and restore you to your post.
40:16 In it I had three wicker baskets on my h;
40:17 pecking at them out of the basket on my h."
40:19 up your h and have you impaled on a stake,
42:38 white h down to the nether world in grief."
43:16 Benjamin with them, he told his h steward,
43:19 So they went up to Joseph's h steward and
44: 1 gave his h steward these instructions:
44: 4 city when Joseph said to his h steward:
44:29 white h down to the nether world in grief.'
44:31 your servants will thus send the white h
47:31 Then Israel bowed at the h of the bed.
48:14 right hand and laid it on the h of Ephraim,
48:14 and his left hand on the h of Manasseh,
48:17 had laid his right hand on Ephraim's h,
48:17 remove it from Ephraim's h to Manasseh's,
48:18 lay your right hand on his h!"
49:26 May they rest on the h of Joseph.
Ex 12: 2 shall stand at the h of your calendar;
12: 9 with its h and shanks and inner organs.
14:27 Egyptians were fleeing h on toward the sea,
28:32 have an opening for the h in the center,
29: 6 Put the miter on his h,
29: 7 anoint him with it, pouring it on his h.
29:10 his sons shall lay their hands on its h.
29:15 his sons have laid their hands on its h,
29:17 put them with the pieces and with the h.
29:19 his sons have laid their hands on its h,
Lv 1: 4 lay his hand on the h of the holocaust,
1: 8 of meat, together with the h and the suet,
1:12 lay these, together with the h and suet,
1:15 the priest shall snap its h loose and
3: 2 lay his hand on the h of his offering,
3: 8 laying his hand on the h of his offering,
3:13 LORD, and after laying his hand on its h,
4: 4 on its h and slaughter it before the LORD.
4:11 the bullock and all its flesh, with its h,
4:15 shall lay their hands on the bullock's h.
4:24 Having laid his hands on its h,
4:29 laid his hand on the h of the sin offering,
4:33 Having laid his hand on its h,
5: 8 Snapping its h loose at the neck,
8: 9 Thummim in it, and put the miter on his h,
8:12 some of the anointing oil on Aaron's h,
8:14 and his sons laid their hands on its h.
8:18 and his sons laid their hands on its h.
8:20 up the ram into pieces, he burned the h,
8:22 and his sons laid their hands on its h.
9:13 him the pieces and the h of the holocaust,
13:12 skin of the stricken man from h to foot,
13:29 or a woman has a sore on the h or cheek,
13:30 scall, a leprous disease of the h or cheek.
13:40 "When a man loses the hair of his h,
13:41 he loses the hair on the front of his h,
13:44 him unclean by reason of the sore on his h.
13:45 keep his garments rent and his h bare,
14: 9 again shave off all the hair of his h,
14:18 put on the h of the man being purified.
14:29 hand the priest shall put on the man's h.
16:21 Laying both hands on its h,
16:21 and so put them on the goat's h.
21: 5 shall not make bare the crown of the h,
21:10 upon whose h the anointing oil has been
21:10 shall not bare his h or rend his garments,
24:14 heard him have laid their hands on his h,
Nm 1: 4 each tribe, the h of his ancestral house.
5:18 the priest shall uncover her h and place
6: 5 shall let the hair of his h grow freely.
6: 7 since his h bears his dedication to God.
6: 9 h becomes unclean, he shall shave his head
6:11 reconsecrate his h and begin anew the period
6:12 because his dedicated h became unclean.
6:18 the nazirite shall shave his dedicated h,
17:18 for the h of Levi's ancestral house shall
25:15 daughter of Zur, who was h of a clan,
Dt 3:28 for he shall cross at the h of this
10:11 now and set out at the h of your people,
19: 5 its h flies off the handle and hits his
21:12 she must shave her h and pare her nails
28:13 The LORD will make you the h,
28:35 soles of your feet to the crown of your h.
28:44 He will become the h, you the tail.
33:16 These shall come upon the h of Joseph and
33:20 that has seized the arm and h of the prey.
Jos 8:10 the army and went up to Ai at its h,
Jgs 5:26 She hammered Sisera, crushed his h;
9:39 So Gaal went out at the h of the citizens
9:53 part of a millstone down on Abimelech's h,
13: 5 and bear, no razor shall touch his h,
16:17 and told her, "No razor has touched my h,
16:22 But the hair of his h began to grow as
18:21 and their goods at the h of the column.
1Sm 1:11 drink, and no razor shall ever touch his h."
4:12 clothes torn and his h covered with dirt.
5: 4 his h and hands broken off and lying on
9: 2 he stood h and shoulders above the people.
9:22 he placed them at the h of the guests,
10: 1 Samuel poured oil on Saul's h;
10:23 he was h and shoulders above all the crowd.
14:45 hair of his h shall fall to the ground,
17: 5 He had a bronze helmet on his h and wore a
17: 7 and its iron h weighed six hundred shekels.
17:38 his h and arming him with a coat of mail.
17:46 I will strike you down and cut off your h.
17:51 he dispatched him and cut off his h.
17:54 David took the h of the Philistine and
17:57 David was still holding the Philistine's h.
19:13 at its h and covering it with a spread.
19:16 bed, with the net of goat's hair at its h.
26: 7 spear thrust into the ground at his h,
26:11 spear which is at his h and the water jug,
26:12 water jug from their place at Saul's h,
26:16 spear and the water jug that was at his h?"
31: 9 off Saul's h and stripped him of his armor,
2Sm 1: 2 with his clothes torn and dirt on his h.
1:10 I removed the crown from his h and the
2:16 Then each one grasped his opponent's h and
3: 8 Abner said, "Am I a dog's h in Judah?
4: 7 struck and killed him, and cut off his h.
4: 7 Then, taking the h, they traveled on
4: 8 They brought the h of Ishbaal to David in
4: 8 "This is the h of Ishbaal,
4:12 But he took the h of Ishbaal and buried it
10:16 general of Hadadezer's army, at their h.
12:30 it, he took the crown from Milcom's h.
12:30 it was placed on David's h.
13:19 Tamar put ashes on her h and tore the long
13:19 Then, putting her hands to her h,
14:25 the sole of his foot to the crown of his h.
14:26 When he shaved his h—
15:30 His h was covered,
15:32 with rent garments and dirt upon his h.
16: 9 Let me go over, please, and lop off his h."
20:21 h shall be thrown to you across the wall."
20:22 advice, and they cut off the h of Sheba,
22:44 you made me h over nations.
23:18 son of Zeruiah, was at the h of the Thirty.
1Kgs 1:52 worthy, not a hair shall fall from his h.
2: 9 down his hoary h in blood to the grave."
18:42 the earth, and put his h between his knees.
19: 6 his h was a hearth cake and a jug of water.
21: 9 fast and set Naboth at the h of the people.
21:12 and placed Naboth at the h of the people.
2Kgs 4:19 "My h hurts!"
6:25 ass's h sold for eighty pieces of silver,
6:31 the king exclaimed, "if the h of Elisha,
6:32 is sending someone to cut off my h?
9: 3 From the flask you have, pour oil on his h,
9: 6 young man poured the oil on his h and said,
19:21 Behind you she wags her h,
1Chr 5:15 Guni, was the h of their ancestral houses.
10: 9 They stripped him, cut off his h,
19:16 general of Hadadezer's army, at their h.
20: 2 took the crown of Milcom from the idol's h.
20: 2 stones, which David wore on his own h.
24: 4 into eight groups, each under its family h.
29:11 you are exalted as h over all.
2Chr 13:12 See, God is with us, at our h,
20:21 as it went forth at the h of the army.
20:27 Jerusalem, with Jehoshaphat at their h,
31:10 priest Azariah, h of the house of Zadok,
Ezr 9: 3 mantle, plucked hair from my h and beard,
Neh 12:36 [Ezra the scribe was at their h
Jdt 9: 1 prostrate, with ashes strewn upon her h,
13: 6 to the bedpost near the h of Holofernes,
13: 7 to the bed, grasped the hair of his h,
13: 8 him twice in the neck and cut off his h.
13: 9 over the h of Holofernes to her maid,
13:15 Then she took the h out of the pouch,
13:15 "Here is the h of Holofernes,
13:18 blow at the h of the chief of our enemies.
14: 1 h and hang it on the parapet of your wall.
14: 6 When he came and saw the h of Holofernes
14:11 they hung the h of Holofernes on the wall.
15:13 At the h of all the people,
Est 2:17 h and made her queen in place of Vashti.
C:13 she covered her h with dirt and ashes.
C:27 rests on my h when I appear in public;
D: 7 against the h of the maid in front of her.
6: 8 when the royal crown was placed on his h.
6:12 Haman hurried home, his h covered in grief.
1Mc 7:47 they cut off Nicanor's h and his right arm,
11:13 he thus wore two crowns on his h,
11:17 off Alexander's h and sent it to Ptolemy.
11:71 tore his clothes, threw earth on his h,
2Mc 5:24 h of an army of twenty-two thousand men,
7: 7 tearing off the skin and hair of his h,
8: 9 and sent him at the h of at least twenty
11: 1 of the king and h of the government,
11: 8 Jerusalem, a horseman appeared at their h,
15:30 ordered Nicanor's h and whole right arm to
15:32 He showed them the vile Nicanor's h and
15:35 up Nicanor's h on the wall of the citadel,
Jb 2: 7 soles of his feet to the crown of his h.
10:15 if righteous, I dare not hold up my h,
16: 4 could declaim over you, or wag my h at you;
16: 5 with talk, or shake my h with silent lips.
20: 6 the heavens and his h reach to the clouds,
29: 3 While he kept his lamp shining above my h,
40:31 hide with barbs, or his h with fish spears?
41:24 think the deep had the hoary h of age.
Ps(s) 3: 4 my glory, you lift up my h!
7:17 own h; upon the crown of his head
18:44 you made me h over nations;
21: 4 you placed on his h a crown of pure gold.
23: 5 You anoint my h with oil;
27: 6 Even now my h is held high above my

40:13 are more numerous than the hairs of my *h*,
60: 9 Ephraim is the helmet for my *h*;
68: 8 you went forth at the *h* of your people,
69: 5 hairs of my *h* who hate me without cause.
108: 9 Manasseh, Ephraim is the helmet for my *h*;
110: 7 therefore will he lift up his *h*.
133: 2 upon the *h* runs down over the beard,
141: 5 oil for the *h*, Which my head shall not
Prv 1: 9 A graceful diadem will they be for your *h*;
4: 9 She will put on your *h* a graceful diadem;
10: 6 Blessings are for the *h* of the just,
11:26 upon the *h* of him who distributes it!
25:22 For live coals you will heap on his *h*,
30:31 and the king at the *h* of his people.
Eccl 2:14 The wise man has eyes in his *h*,
9: 8 and spare not the perfume for your *h*.
Sg 2: 6 under my *h* and his right arm embraces me.
5: 2 For my *h* is wet with dew,
5:11 His *h* is pure gold;
7: 6 You *h* rises like Carmel;
8: 3 under my *h* and his right arm embraces me.
Wis 18:24 your grandeur was on the crown upon his *h*.
Sir 4: 7 before a ruler bow your *h*.
10: 2 as the *h* of a city,
11: 1 his *h* high and sets him among princes.
11:13 Lifts up his *h* and exalts him to the
12:18 *h* and clap his hands and hiss repeatedly,
13: 7 will pass you by, and shake his *h* over you.
19:23 He bows his *h* and feigns not to hear,
20:10 from obscurity a man can lift up his *h*.
44:22 the blessing rested upon the *h* of JACOB.
Is 1: 5 The whole *h* is sick,
1: 6 the foot to the *h* there is no sound spot:
7: 8 of Aram, and Rezin the *h* of Damascus;
7: 8 and Remaliah's son the *h* of Samaria.
7:20 the River [with the king of Assyria] the *h*,
9:13 So the LORD severs from Israel *h* and tail,
9:14 [The elder and the noble are the *h*,
15: 2 Every *h* is shaved, every beard sheared off.
19:15 shall have no work to do for *h* or tail,
22:12 to shave your *h* and put on sackcloth.
28: 1 on the *h* of him who is stupefied with wine.
28: 4 glorious beauty on the *h* of the fertile valley
37:22 Behind you she wags her *h*,
58: 5 That a man bow his *h* like a reed,
59:17 salvation, as the helmet on his *h*;
Jer 2:16 and Tahpanhes shave the crown of your *h*.
2:37 shall you go away with hands upon your *h*;
8:23 Oh, that my *h* were a spring of water,
16: 6 will gash himself or shave his *h* for them.
31: 7 for Jacob, exult at the *h* of the nations;
48:27 you shake your *h* whenever you speak of her?
48:37 Every *h* has been made bald,
50: 8 be like the rams at the *h* of the flock.
Lam 3:54 The waters flowed over my *h*,
Bar 5: 2 bear on your *h* the mitre that displays the
Ez 5: 1 razor, passing it over your *h* and beard.
8: 2 a hand and seized me by the hair of my *h*.
13:18 size of *h* so as to entrap their owners.
16:12 ears, and a glorious diadem upon your *h*.
16:43 bringing down your conduct upon your *h*.
17:19 he broke, I swear to bring down upon his *h*.
21:24 Then put a signpost at the *h* of each road,
Dn 2:32 The *h* of the statue was pure gold,
2:38 you are the *h* of gold.
7: 9 and the hair on his *h* as white as wool;
7:20 about the ten horns on its *h*,
13:34 rose up and laid their hands on her *h*.
13:55 "Your fine lie has cost you your *h*,"
13:59 "Your fine lie has cost you also your *h*,"
14:36 crown of his *h* and carried him by the hair;
Hos 2: 2 one *h* and come up from other lands,
Jl 2:11 LORD raises his voice at the *h* of his army;
4: 4 I will return your deed upon your own *h*.
4: 7 I will return your deed upon your own *h*.
Am 8:10 all with sackcloth and make every *h* bald.
Ob 1:15 deed shall come back upon your own *h*;
Jon 2: 6 seaweed clung about my *h*.
4: 6 gourd plant, that grew up over Jonah's *h*,
4: 8 beat upon Jonah's *h* until he became faint.
Mi 2: 3 Nor shall you walk with *h* high,
2:13 before them, and the LORD at their *h*.
Zec 2: 4 so that no man raised his *h* any more;
3: 5 He also said, "Put a clean miter on his *h*."
3: 5 on his *h* and clothed him with the garments.
6:11 place it on the *h* of [Joshua,
Mt 5:36 do not swear by your *h* (you cannot make a
8:20 the Son of Man has nowhere to lay his *h*."
10:25 If they call the *h* of the house Beelzebul,
10:30 you, every hair of your *h* has been counted;
13:52 reign of God is like the *h* of a household
14: 8 me the *h* of John the Baptizer on a platter."
14:11 John's *h* was brought in on a platter and
14:24 in the waves raised by strong *h* winds.
22:20 coin, he asked them, "Whose *h* is this,
26: 7 him at table and began to pour it on his *h*.
27: 9 the value of a man with a price on his *h*,
27:29 crown out of thorns they fixed it on his *h*,
27:30 of the reed and kept striking him on the *h*.
27:37 Above his *h* they had put the charge
Mk 6:16 exclaimed, "John, whose *h* I had cut off,
6:24 answered, "The *h* of John the Baptizer."
6:25 the *h* of John the Baptizer on a platter."
6:27 him to bring back the Baptizer's *h*.
6:28 the *h* on a platter and gave it to the girl,
12: 4 beat over the *h* and treated shamefully.
12:16 *h* is this and whose inscription is it?"
14: 3 she began to pour the perfume on his *h*.
15:19 on the *h* with a reed and spitting at him,
Lk 7:46 You did not anoint my *h* with oil,
9:58 the Son of Man has nowhere to lay his *h*."
12: 7 even the hairs of your *h* are counted!
12:39 You know as well as I that if the *h* of the
18:11 with *h* unbowed prayed in this fashion:
20:24 Whose *h* is this?
21:18 yet not a hair of your *h* will be harmed.
23:38 There was an inscription over his *h*:
Jn 11:44 out bound *h* and foot with linen strips,
13: 9 only my feet, but my hands and *h* as well."
19: 2 a crown of thorns and fixed it on his *h*,
19:30 Then he bowed his *h*,
20: 7 covered the *h* not lying with the wrappings,
20:12 One was seated at the *h* and the other at
Acts 8:26 *H* south toward the road which goes from
18:18 shaved his *h* because of a vow he had taken.
27:15 up in it and could not *h* into the wind,
27:34 Not one of you shall lose a hair on his *h*."
Rom 12:20 you will heap burning coals upon his *h*."
1Cor 11: 3 head of every man is Christ; the *h* of a
11: 3 and the *h* of Christ is the Father.
11: 4 his *h* covered brings shame upon his head.
11: 5 her *h* uncovered brings shame upon her head.
11: 5 It is as if she had had her *h* shaved.
11: 6 to have her hair cut off or her *h* shaved,
11: 7 the other hand, ought not to cover his *h*,
11:10 to have a sign of submission on her *h*,
12:21 any more than the *h* can say to the feet,
Eph 1:22 made him, thus exalted, *h* of the church,
4:15 and the full maturity of Christ the *h*.
5:23 because the husband is *h* of his wife
5:23 just as Christ is *h* of his body the church,
Col 1:18 It is he who is *h* of the body,
2:10 is the *h* of every principality and power.
2:19 he should be in close touch with the *h*.
Heb 11:21 God, leaning on the *h* of his staff.
Rv 1:14 The hair of his *h* was as white as
10: 1 in a cloud, with a rainbow about his *h*;
12: 1 feet, and on her *h* a crown of twelve stars.
14:14 *h* and holding a sharp sickle in his hand.
19:12 like fire, and on his *h* were many diadems.

HEADACHE (1)

Sir 31:29 *H*, bitterness and disgrace

HEADDRESSES (1)

Is 3:20 the *h*,

HEADED (5)

Gn 31:21 he *h* for the highlands of Gilead.
Mt 12:25 torn by strife is *h* for its downfall.
1Cor 1:18 absurdity to those who are *h* for ruin,
2: 6 of this age, who are men *h* for destruction.
2Cor 4: 3 for those who are *h* toward destruction.

HEADLAND (2)

Nm 21:20 at the *h* of Pisgah that overlooks Jeshimon.
Dt 34: 1 Nebo, the *h* of Pisgah which faces Jericho,

HEADLESS (3)

Jdt 14:15 found him lying on the floor, a *h* corpse.
14:18 Here is Holofernes *h* on the ground!"
Ps(s) 58: 8 draw the bow, let their arrows be *h* shafts.

HEADLONG (11)

Lv 26:36 rustle behind them, they will flee *h*,
2Mc 12:22 they rushed away in such *h* flight that in
Jb 18: 8 For he rushes *h* into a net,
Is 22:17 The LORD shall hurl you down *h*,
52:12 will you come out, nor leave in *h* flight,
Jer 12: 5 And if in a land of peace you fall *h*,
23:12 they shall lose their footing, and fall *h*;
46: 5 routed, They flee *h* without making a stand.
49: 5 shall be scattered, each man in *h* flight,
Ez 29: 7 broke, bringing each one of them down *h*;
Acts 1:18 with his unjust gains, and fell *h* upon it.

HEADQUARTERS (6)

Acts 21:34 so he ordered Paul to be led away to *h*.
21:37 as Paul was about to be led into the *h*.
22:24 directed Paul to be brought inside the *h*.
23:10 from their midst and take him back to *h*.
23:16 the plot, and when he did so he came to *h*.
23:32 The next day they returned to *h*,

HEADS (164)

Gn 40:20 *h* of the chief cupbearer and chief baker.
Ex 6:14 These are the *h* of the ancestral houses.
6:17 The sons of Gershon, as *h* of clans,
6:25 *h* of the ancestral clans of the Levites.
Lv 10: 6 "Do not bare your *h* or tear your garments,
Nm 7: 2 of Israel, who were *h* of ancestral houses;
8:12 lay their hands on the *h* of the bullocks,
30: 2 said to the *h* of the Israelite tribes,
31:26 and of the *h* of the ancestral houses,
32:28 and to the *h* of the ancestral tribes of
36: 1 The *h* of the ancestral houses in the clan
36: 1 princes who were the *h* of the ancestral
Dt 5:23 the person of all your tribal *h* and elders,
28:23 The sky over your *h* will be like bronze
32:42 Flesh from the *h* of the enemy leaders."
33:21 while the *h* of the people were gathered.
Jos 7: 6 and they threw dust on their *h*.
14: 1 and the *h* of families in the tribes of the
19:51 and the *h* of families in the tribes of the
21: 1 The *h* of the Levite families came up to
21: 1 and to the *h* of families of the other
Jgs 7:25 carried the *h* of Oreb and Zeeb to Gideon
8:28 no longer did they hold their *h* high.
9:49 they set the crypt on fire over their *h*,
1Sm 29: 4 if not with the *h* of these men of ours?
2Sm 15:30 *h* covered and were weeping as they went.
1Kgs 20:31 in sackcloth, with cords around our *h*,
20:32 waist, and wearing cords around their *h*,
2Kgs 10: 6 count the *h* of your master's sons and come
10: 7 seventy of them, put their *h* in baskets,
10: 8 "They have brought the *h* of the princes,"
1Chr 5:24 were the *h* of their ancestral houses:
5:24 men, and *h* over their ancestral houses.
7: 2 warrior *h* of the ancestral houses of Tola.
7: 7 *h* of their ancestral houses and warriors.
7: 9 *h* of their ancestral houses and warriors.
7:11 *h* of ancestral houses and warriors.
7:40 of Asher, *h* of ancestral houses,
8: 6 family *h* over those who dwelt in Geba and
8:10 These were his sons, family *h*.
8:13 family *h* of those who dwelt in Aijalon,
8:28 These were family *h* over their kindred,
9: 9 named were *h* of their ancestral houses.
9:13 brethren, *h* of their ancestral houses,
9:33 the gatekeepers, family *h* over the Levites.
9:34 the levitical family *h* over their kindred,
12:20 of our *h* he will desert to his master Saul."
15:12 "You, the *h* of the levitical families,
23: 9 These were the *h* of the families of Ladan.
23:24 the family *h* as they were enrolled one by
24: 6 and of the *h* of the ancestral houses of
24:31 *h* of the priestly and levitical families;
26:21 the family *h* were descendants of Jehiel:
26:26 by King David, the *h* of the families,
26:32 two thousand seven hundred *h* of families.
27: 1 is the list of the Israelite family *h*,
28: 1 the leaders of Israel, the *h* of the tribes,
29: 6 Then the *h* of the families,
2Chr 1: 2 princes of all Israel, and the family *h*;
19: 8 priests and some of the family *h* of Israel
23: 2 and also the *h* of the Israelite families.
26:12 The entire number of family *h* over these
Ezr 1: 5 Then the family *h* of Judah and Benjamin
2:68 some of the family *h* made free-will
3:12 of the priests, Levites, and family *h*,
4: 2 and the family *h* and said to them,
4: 3 of the family *h* of Israel answered them,
7:28 *h* to make the return journey with me.
8: 1 This is the list of the family *h* who
9: 6 our *h* and our guilt reaches up to heaven.
10:16 as his assistants men who were family *h*,
Neh 3:36 Turn back their derision upon their own *h*
7:69 of the family *h* contributed to the service.
7:70 Some of the family *h* contributed to the
8:13 the family *h* of the whole people and also
9: 1 in sackcloth, their *h* covered with dust.
9:17 *h* to return to their slavery in Egypt.
11: 3 These are the *h* of the province who took
11:13 of Malchijah, and his brethren, family *h*,
12: 7 *h* and their brethren in the days of Jeshua.
12:12 Joiakim these were the priestly family *h*:
12:22 the family *h* of the priests were written
12:23 the family *h* were written down in the Book
12:24 The *h* of the Levites were Hashabiah,
12:46 For the *h* of the families of the singers
Jdt 4:11 building, with ashes strewn on their *h*,
8:22 he will lay the guilt on our *h*.
9: 9 and send forth your wrath upon their *h*.
1Mc 3:47 ashes on their *h* and tore their clothes.
4:39 they sprinkled their *h* with ashes and fell
9:23 law raised their *h* in every part of Israel,
2Mc 1:16 *h* and tossed them to the people outside.
10:25 *h* and girding their loins in sackcloth.
Jb 2:12 their cloaks and threw dust upon their *h*.
Ps(s) 22: 8 mock me with parted lips, they wag their *h*:
64: 9 all who see them nod their *h*.
66:12 You let men ride over our *h*;
68:22 Surely God crushes the *h* of his enemies,
74:13 smashed the *h* of the dragons in the waters.
74:14 You crushed the *h* of Leviathan,
83: 3 and they who hate you lift up their *h*.
109:25 when they see me, they shake their *h*.
110: 6 he will crush *h* over the wide earth.
140:10 Those who surround me lift up their *h*;
Sir 36: 9 crush the *h* of the hostile rulers.
Is 3:17 scabs, and the LORD shall bare their *h*.
29:10 prophets] and covered your *h* [the seers].
Jer 13:18 From your *h* fall your magnificent crowns.
14: 3 Ashamed, despairing, they cover their *h*
14: 4 farmers are ashamed, they cover their *h*.
18:16 will be amazed, will shake their *h*.
23:19 storm that bursts upon the *h* of the wicked.
30:23 storm that bursts upon the *h* of the wicked.
Lam 2:10 their *h* and gird themselves with sackcloth;

HEADS (cont.)

2:10 of Jerusalem bow their *h* to the ground.
2:15 and wag their *h* over daughter Jerusalem:
5:16 Garlands have fallen from our *h:*
Bar 6: 9 and furnish crowns for the *h* of their gods.
6:21 alight on their bodies and on their *h;*
6:30 hair and beard, and with their *h* uncovered.
Ez 1:22 Over the *h* of the living creatures,
1:22 stretched straight out above their *h.*
1:26 *h* something like a throne could be seen,
7:18 their faces and baldness on all their *h.*
9:10 will bring down their conduct upon their *h.*
11:21 will bring down their conduct upon their *h,*
22:31 brought down their conduct upon their *h,*
23:15 their waists, flowing turbans on their *h,*
23:42 arms and splendid diadems on their *h.*
24:23 Your turbans shall remain on your *h,*
27:30 bitter cries, Strewing dust on their *h,*
27:31 they shave their *h* and put on sackcloth,
29:18 Their *h* became bald and their shoulders
32:27 whose swords were placed under their *h*
44:18 their *h* and linen drawers on their loins;
44:20 their *h* nor let their hair hang loose,
Dn 3:94 not a hair of their *h* had been singed,
7: 6 like those of a bird, and it had four *h.*
Am 2: 7 *h* of the weak into the dust of the earth,
9: 1 you break them off on the *h* of them all!
Mi 6:12 with deceitful tongues in their *h!*
Hb 3:13 You crush the *h* of the wicked,
3:14 You pierce with your shafts the *h* of their
Mt 12: 1 to pull off the *h* of grain and eat them.
19:15 hands on their *h* before he left that place.
27:39 insulting him, tossing their *h* and saying:
Mk 2:23 to pull off *h* of grain as they went along.
15:29 insulting him, tossing their *h* and saying,
Lk 21:28 happen, stand erect and hold your *h* high,
Acts 18: 6 "Your blood be on your own *h.*
21:24 pay the fee for the shaving of their *h.*
Rv 4: 4 garments and had crowns of gold on their *h.*
9: 7 *h* they wore something like gold crowns;
9:17 The horses' *h* were like heads of lions,
9:19 were like snakes with *h* poised to strike.
12: 3 flaming red, with seven *h* and ten horns;
12: 3 on his *h* were seven diadems.
13: 1 out of the sea with ten horns and seven *h;*
13: 1 ten diadems and on its *h* blasphemous names.
13: 3 *h* seemed to have been mortally wounded,
17: 3 This beast had seven *h* and ten horns.
17: 9 The seven *h* are seven hills on which the
18:19 They poured dust on their *h* and cried out,

HEADSHIP (1)

Eph 1:10 and on earth into one under Christ's *h.*

HEADWAY (1)

Acts 27: 7 For many days we made little *h,*

HEADWINDS (1)

Acts 27: 4 side of Cyprus because of strong *h.*

HEAL (40)

Nm 12:13 "Please, not this! Pray, *h* her!"
Dt 32:39 and life, I who inflict wounds and *h* them,
2Kgs 5:10 times in the Jordan, and your flesh will *h,*
20: 5 I will *h* you.
20: 8 "What is the sign that the LORD will *h* me
Tb 3:17 So Raphael was sent to *h* them both:
12:14 me to *h* you and your daughter-in-law,
Ps(s) 6: 3 *h* me, O LORD, for my body is in terror
41: 5 *h* me, though I have sinned against you.
107:20 *h* them and to snatch them from destruction.
Eccl 3: 3 time to kill, and a time to *h*
Wis 16:10 your mercy brought the antidote to *h* them.
Sir 38: 9 delay not, but pray to God, who will *h* you:
Is 19:22 smite Egypt severely, he shall *h* them;
19:22 LORD and he shall be won over and *h* them.
30:26 he will *h* the bruises left by his blows.
38: 5 I will *h* you:
57:18 ways, but I will *h* them and lead them;
57:19 and I will *h* them.
61: 1 to the lowly, to *h* the brokenhearted,
Jer 17:14 *H* me, LORD, that I may be healed;
30:17 of your wounds I will *h* you,
33: 6 I will *h* them,
51: 9 "We have tried to *h* Babylon,
Lam 2:13 who can *h* you?
Ez 34: 4 nor *h* the sick nor bind up the injured.
34:16 the sick I will *h* [but the sleek and the
Hos 5:13 he cannot *h* you nor take away your sore.
6: 1 it is he who has rent, but he will *h* us;
7: 1 of my people, when I would *h* Israel,
14: 5 I will *h* their defection,
Zec 11:16 nor seek the strays, nor *h* the injured,
Mt 10: 8 the sick, raise the dead, *h* the leprous,
13:15 and turn back to me, and I should *h* them.'
Mk 3: 2 see whether he would *h* him on the sabbath,
Lk 4:23 me the proverb, 'Physician, *h* yourself,'
5:17 and the power of the Lord made him *h.*
9: 2 the reign of God and *h* the afflicted.
Jn 12:40 and I should *h* them."
Acts 28:27 and I should have to *h* them.'

HEALED (30)

Lv 13:18 who had a boil on his skin which later *h,*
13:37 has grown on it, the disease has been *h;*
14: 3 the sore of leprosy has *h* in the leper,
14:48 clean, since the infection has been *h.*
1Sm 6: 3 Then you will be *h,*
2Kgs 8:29 King Joram returned to Jezreel to be *h* of
9:15 but had returned to Jezreel to be *h* of the
2Chr 22: 6 He returned to Jezreel to be *h* of the
Ps(s) 30: 3 my God, I cried out to you and you *h* me.
Is 6:10 understand, and they will turn and be *h.*
53: 5 makes us whole, by his stripes we were *h.*
58: 8 dawn, and your wound shall quickly be *h;*
Jer 14:19 have you struck us a blow that cannot be *h?*
15:18 my wound incurable, refusing to be *h?*
17:14 Heal me, LORD, that I may be *h;*
51: 8 balm for her wounds, in case she can be *h.*
51: 9 tried to heal Babylon, but she cannot be *h.*
Mk 10:52 Your faith has *h* you."
Lk 6:18 to hear him and be *h* of their diseases.
9:11 and he *h* all who were in need of healing.
13:14 that Jesus should have *h* on the sabbath,
14: 4 He took the man, *h* him,
18:42 Your faith has *h* you."
22:51 Then he touched the ear and *h* the man.
Jn 5: 6 saw him lying there, "Do you want to be *h?*"
Acts 28: 9 began to come to Paul and they too were *h.*
Heb 12:13 halting limbs may not be dislocated but *h.*
1Pt 2:24 By his wounds, you were *h.*
Rv 13: 3 wounded, but this mortal wound was *h.*
13:12 first beast, whose mortal wound had been *h.*

HEALER (2)

Ex 15:26 for I, the LORD, am your *h.*"
Hos 11: 4 they did not know that I was their *h.*

HEALERS (1)

1Cor 12:28 third teachers, then miracle workers, *h,*

HEALING (20)

Tb 5:10 God has *h* in store for you;
Jb 5:18 he smites, but his hands give *h.*
Prv 12:18 thrusts, but the tongue of the wise is *h.*
13:17 but a trustworthy envoy is a *h* remedy.
Sir 21: 3 when it cuts, there can be no *h.*
28: 3 his fellows and expect *h* from the LORD?
38: 4 God makes the earth yield *h* herbs which
Jer 8:15 for a time of *h,* but terror comes instead
14:19 wait for peace, to no avail; for a time of *h,*
30:13 remedy for your running sore, no *h* for you.
Ez 30:21 bound up with bandages and *h* remedies
Na 3:19 There is no *h* for your hurt,
Mal 3:20 arise the sun of justice with its *h* rays;
Mk 5:30 at once that *h* power had gone out from him.
Lk 5:14 Offer for your *h* what Moses prescribed;
9:11 and he healed all who were in need of *h.*
Acts 10:38 *h* all who were in the grip of the devil,
1Cor 12: 9 same Spirit another is given the gift of *h,*
12:30 Do all work miracles or have the gift of *h?*
Jas 5:16 pray for one another, that you may find *h.*

HEALS (2)

Ps(s) 103: 3 all your iniquities, he *h* all your ills.
147: 3 He *h* the brokenhearted and binds up their

HEALTH (37)

Gn 20:17 with God, and God restored *h* to Abimelech,
43:27 Is he still in good *h?*"
43:28 father is thriving and still in good *h,*"
45: 3 "Is my father still in good *h?*"
Tb 5:16 In good *h* we shall leave you,
5:16 you, and in good *h* we shall return to you,
5:21 good *h* and come back to us in good health.
7: 1 Good *h* to you, and welcome!"
8:21 when you go back in good *h* to your father;
2Mc 9:19 and best wishes for their *h* and happiness.
9:22 I do not despair about my *h* since I have
11:28 We too are in good *h.*
Ps(s) 38: 4 *h* in my flesh because of your indignation;
38: 8 there is no *h* in my flesh.
Prv 3: 8 *h* for your flesh and vigor for your bones.
4:22 find them, to man's whole being they are *h.*
17:22 A joyful heart is the *h* of the body,
Wis 7:10 Beyond *h* and comeliness I loved her,
Sir 1:16 LORD, with blossoms of peace and perfect *h.*
30:15 precious than gold is *h* and well-being,
34:17 to the eyes, gives *h* and life and blessing.
38:19 an extremity and heartache destroy one's *h.*
40:19 and orchards bring flourishing *h;*
Is 38:16 You have given me *h* and life;
Jer 30:17 to pillage, For I will restore you to *h;*
Mt 9:12 who are in good *h* do not need a doctor;
9:22 Your faith has restored you to *h.*"
14:36 as touched it were fully restored to *h.*
Lk 7:10 house, they found the servant in perfect *h.*
15:27 calf because he has him back in good *h.*'
Jn 4:47 him to come down and restore *h* to his son,
5:13 been restored to *h* had no idea who it was.
Acts 3:16 Such faith has given him perfect *h,*
4: 9 and explain how he was restored to *h,*
Jas 5:15 is ill, and the Lord will restore him to *h.*
3Jn 1: 2 Beloved, I hope you are in good *h*—

HEALTHFUL (1)

Prv 16:24 sweet to the taste and *h* to the body.

HEALTHIER (1)

Dn 1:15 after ten days they looked *h* and better

HEALTHY (9)

Gn 41: 5 He saw seven ears of grain, fat and *h,*
41: 7 ears swallowed up the seven fat, *h* ears.
41:22 dream I saw seven ears of grain, fat and *h,*
41:24 thin ears swallowed up the seven *h* ears.
41:26 The seven *h* cows are seven years,
41:26 and the seven *h* ears are seven years
Sir 30:16 No treasure greater than a *h* body;
Mk 2:17 "People who are *h* do not need a doctor;
Lk 5:31 said to them, "The *h* do not need a doctor;

HEAP (28)

Lv 1:16 on the ash *h* at the east side of the altar.
4:12 At the place of the ash *h,*
Dt 13:17 Let it be a *h* of ruins forever,
Jos 7:26 and piled a great *h* of stones over him,
8:29 a great *h* of stones was piled up over it,
Jgs 15:16 of an ass I have piled them in a *h;*
1Sm 2: 8 from the ash *h* he lifts up the poor,
1Kgs 9: 8 and this temple shall become a *h* of ruins.
Neh 3:35 "It is a rubble *h* they are building.
Jb 8:17 About a *h* of stones are his roots entwined;
27:16 Though he *h* up silver like dust and store
Ps(s) 19:11 than gold, than a *h* of purest gold;
69:28 *H* guilt upon their guilt,
Prv 25:22 For live coals you will *h* on his head,
Sg 7: 3 body is a *h* of wheat encircled with lilies.
Sir 3:26 a sinner will *h* sin upon sin.
8: 3 of railing speech, *h* no wood upon his fire.
Is 25: 2 For you have made the city a *h,*
Jer 7:21 *H* your holocausts upon your sacrifices;
9:10 I will turn Jerusalem into a *h* of ruins,
26:18 a plowed field, Jerusalem a *h* of ruins,
27:17 else this city will become a *h* of ruins.
51:37 Babylon shall become a *h* of ruins,
Ez 24: 9 I, too, will *h* up a great bonfire,
Mi 1: 6 I will make Samaria a stone *h* in the field,
Hg 2:16 went to a *h* of grain for twenty measures,
Lk 14:35 fit for neither the soil nor the manure *h;*
Rom 12:20 you will *h* burning coals upon his head."

HEAPED (7)

Dt 13:17 Having *h* up all its spoils in the middle
Ezr 9: 6 for our wicked deeds are *h* up above our
Jb 6:16 black with ice, and with snow *h* upon them,
Sir 47:18 you *h* up silver as though it were lead;
Bar 3:17 They who *h* up the silver and the gold in
Ez 28: 5 to your trading you have *h* up your riches;
Zec 9: 3 a stronghold, and *h* up silver like dust,

HEAPING (2)

Ps(s) 110: 6 do judgment on the nations, *h* up corpses;
Na 3: 3 the spear, the many slain, the *h* corpses,

HEAPS (18)

Ex 8:10 Heaps and *h* of them were gathered up and
2Kgs 10: 8 "Pile them in two *h* at the entrance of
19:25 reduce fortified cities into *h* of ruins,
2Chr 31: 6 these they brought in and set out in *h.*
31: 7 that they began to establish these *h,*
31: 8 and the princes had come and seen the *h,*
31: 9 priests and the Levites concerning the *h,*
Neh 3:34 burnt as they are, from the *h* of dust?"
Ps(s) 39: 7 he *h* up stores,
Wis 18:23 had already fallen one on another in *h,*
Sir 23:11 A man who often swears *h* up obligations;
Is 37:26 reduce fortified cities into *h* of ruins,
Jer 50:26 Pile up her goods in *h* and doom it,
Lam 4: 5 up in purple now cling to the ash *h.*
Hos 12:12 *h* of stones in the furrows of the field.
Hb 1: 9 a stormwind that *h* up captives like sand.
1:10 He laughs at any fortress, *h* up a ramp,

HEAR (402)

Gn 4:23 "Adah and Zillah, *h* my voice;
21: 6 and all who *h* of it will laugh with me.
21:26 about it, nor did I ever *h* of it until now."
41:15 But I *h* it said of you that the moment you
42: 2 I *h,*" he went on, "that rations of grain
Ex 19: 9 when the people *h* me speaking with you,
22:22 cry out to me, I will surely *h* their cry.
22:26 If he cries out to me, I will *h* him;
32:18 the sounds that I *h* are cries of revelry."
Nm 14:13 "Are the Egyptians to *h* this?
Dt 1:17 that is too hard for you and I will *h* it.'
3:26 with me on your account and would not *h* me.
4: 1 *h* the statutes and decrees which I am
4: 6 who will *h* of all these statutes and say,
4:10 I will have them *h* my words,

4:28 stone, gods which can neither see nor *h*,
4:33 Did a people ever *h* the voice of God
4:36 he let you *h* his voice to discipline you;
5: 1 summoned all Israel and said to them, *H*,
5:25 If we *h* the voice of the LORD,
5:27 Go closer, you, and *h* all that the LORD,
6: 3 *H* then, Israel, and be careful to observe
6: 4 *H*, O Israel! The LORD is our God.
9: 1 *H*, O Israel! You are now about to cross
13:13 you *h* it said that certain scoundrels have
18:16 'Let us not again *h* the voice of the LORD,
20: 3 *H*, O Israel! Today you are going into battle
29: 3 understand, or eyes to see, or ears to *h*.
31:12 that they may *h* it and learn it,
31:13 do not know it yet, must *h* it and learn it,
31:28 I may speak these words for them to *h*,
31:30 end, for the whole assembly of Israel to *h*:
32:44 the words of this song for the people to *h*.
Jos 6: 5 on the ram's horns and you *h* that signal,
7: 9 the other inhabitants of the land *h* of it,
Jgs 5: 3 deeds by the people who bless the LORD, *H*,
7:11 When you *h* what they are saying,
9: 7 *H* me, citizens of Shechem,
9: 7 of Shechem, that God may then *h* you!
13:23 all this just now, or *h* what we have heard."
18:25 him, "Let us *h* no further sound from you,
1Sm 2:24 It is not a good report that I *h* the
13: 3 with a proclamation, "Let the Hebrews *h*!"
15:14 my ears, and the lowing of oxen that I *h*?"
16: 2 Saul will *h* of it and kill me."
2Sm 5:24 When you *h* a sound of marching in the tops
15: 3 is no one to *h* you in the king's name."
15:10 to say, "When you *h* the sound of the horn,
15:35 If you *h* anything from the royal palace,
15:36 you shall send on to me whatever you *h*."
17: 5 let us *h* what he too has to say."
1Kgs 5:14 to *h* Solomon's wisdom from all nations,
8:52 *H* them whenever they call upon you,
10:24 to *h* from him the wisdom which God had put
22:19 "Therefore *h* the word of the LORD:
2Kgs 7: 1 *H* the word of the LORD!
7: 6 to *h* the sound of chariots and horses,
19: 4 God, will *h* all the words of the commander,
19:16 *H* the words of Sennacherib which he sent
20:16 *H* the word of the LORD:
1Chr 14:15 When you *h* the sound of marching in the
28: 2 *H* me, my brethren and my people.
2Chr 6:39 place, *h* their prayer and petitions,
7:14 I will *h* them from heaven and pardon their
9:23 to *h* from him the wisdom which God had put
15: 2 *H* me, Asa and all Judah and Benjamin!
18:18 "Therefore *h* the word of the LORD:
18:27 And he said, *H*, O peoples, all of you!"
20: 9 in our affliction, and you will *h* and save!'
25:16 thing and have refused to *h* my counsel."
Neh 4:14 wherever you *h* the trumpet sound,
9:27 to you, and you would *h* them from heaven,
Tb 3: 6 misery in life, and to *h* these insults!"
3:10 I need no longer live to *h* such insults."
3:13 the earth, never again to *h* such insults.
3:15 never again let me *h* these insults!"
5:10 I can *h* a man's voice,
10:12 *h* good reports about you as long as I live."
Jdt 5: 5 lord, *h* this account from your servant;
8:17 will *h* our cry if it is his good pleasure.
9: 5 "O God, my God, *h* me also, a widow.
9:12 King of all you have created, *h* my prayer!
14: 7 who *h* of you will be struck with terror.
Est 1:18 Median ladies who *h* of the queen's conduct
C:10 *H* my prayer; have pity on your inheritance
C:16 As a child I was wont to *h* from the people
4:30 than all, *h* the voice of those in despair.
2Mc 1: 5 May he *h* your prayers,
Jb 3:18 and *h* not the voice of the slave driver.
13: 6 *H* now the rebuke I shall utter and listen
20: 3 A rebuke which puts me to shame I *h*,
22:27 You shall entreat him and he will *h* you,
26:14 his ways, and how faint is the word we *h*!
31:35 Oh, that I had one to *h* my case,
33: 1 Therefore, O Job, *h* my discourse,
34: 2 *H*, O wise men,
34: 2 and you that have knowledge, *h* me!
34:16 Now, do you, O Job, *h* this!
35:13 But it is idle to say God does not *h* or
37: 2 To *h* his angry voice as it rumbles forth
Ps(s) 4: 2 Have pity on me, and *h* my prayer!
4: 4 the LORD will *h* me when I call upon him.
5: 4 at dawn you *h* my voice;
10:17 The desire of the afflicted you *h*,
17: 1 *H*, O LORD, a just suit; attend to my outcry
17: 6 *h* my word.
27: 7 *H*, O LORD, the sound of my call;
28: 2 *H* the sound of my pleading,
30:11 *H*, O LORD, and have pity on me
31:14 I *h* the whispers of the crowd,
34: 3 the lowly will *h* me and be glad.
34:12 Come, children, *h* me; I will teach you
39:13 *H* my prayer,
45:11 *H*, O daughter, and see;
49: 2 *H* this, all you peoples;
50: 7 *H*, my people, and I will speak;
51:10 Let me *h* the sounds of joy and gladness;
54: 4 O God, *h* my prayer;
55:18 grieve and moan, and he will *h* my voice.
55:20 God will *h* me and will humble them from
58: 6 That it may not *h* the voice of enchanters
61: 2 *H*, O God, my cry; listen to my prayer!
64: 2 *H*, O God, my voice in my lament;
65: 2 must vows be fulfilled, you who *h* prayers.
66:16 *H* now, all you who fear God
66:18 in my heart, the Lord would not *h*;
77: 2 aloud to God, to *h* me;
81: 9 *H*, my people, and I will admonish you;
81: 9 O Israel, will you not *h* me?
81:14 If only my people would *h* me,
84: 9 O LORD of hosts, *h* my prayer;
85: 9 I will *h* what God proclaims;
94: 9 Shall he who shaped the ear not *h*?
95: 7 Oh that today you would *h* his voice:
102: 2 O LORD, *h* my prayer,
102:21 earth, To *h* the groaning of the prisoners,
115: 6 They have ears but *h* not;
130: 1 I cry to you, O LORD; Lord, *h* my voice!
135:17 They have ears but *h* not,
138: 4 LORD, when they *h* the words of your mouth;
143: 1 O LORD, *h* my prayer;
143: 8 At dawn let me *h* of your kindness,
Prv 1: 8 *H*, my son, your father's instruction
4: 1 *H*, O children, a father's instruction,
4:10 *H*, my son, and receive my words.
19:27 If a son ceases to *h* instruction,
22:17 Incline your ear, and *h* my words,
23:19 *H*, my son, and be wise,
Eccl 7:21 you *h* your servant speaking ill of you,
Sg 2:14 Let me see you, let me *h* your voice,
8:13 are listening for your voice, let me *h* it!
Wis 6: 1 *H*, therefore, kings, and understand
15:15 nostrils to snuff the air, Nor ears to *h*,
Sir 4: 6 curse you, his Creator will *h* his prayer.
5:13 Be swift to *h*, but slow to answer.
6:35 Be eager to *h* every godly discourse;
19: 9 Let anything you *h* die within you;
19:23 He bows his head and feigns not to *h*,
22:26 friend all will stand aloof who *h* of it.
27:15 bloodshed, their cursing is painful to *h*.
29:25 besides, you will *h* these bitter words:
34:24 curses, whose voice will the Lord *h*?
34:26 Who will *h* his prayer,
36:16 *H* the prayer of your servants,
41:23 Of repeating what you *h*,
43:25 and when we *h* them we are thunderstruck;
45: 5 He permitted him to *h* his voice,
47:16 coasts, and their peoples came to *h* you;
Is 1: 2 *H*, O heavens, and listen
1:10 *H* the word of the LORD, princes of Sodom!
1:17 redress the wronged, *h* the orphan's plea,
6:10 Else their eyes will see, their ears *h*,
21: 3 I am too bewildered to *h*,
24:16 From the end of the earth we *h* songs:
28:14 Therefore, *h* the word of the LORD,
28:23 Give ear and *h* my voice,
29:18 day the deaf shall *h* the words of a book;
30:11 Let us *h* no more of the Holy One of Israel."
32: 3 the ears of those who *h* will be attentive.
32: 9 complacent ladies, rise up and *h* my voice,
33:13 *H*, you who are far off,
33:15 stopping his ears lest he *h* of bloodshed,
34: 1 Come near, O nations, and *h*,
37: 4 God, will *h* the words of the commander,
37:17 *H* all the words of the letter that
39: 5 Hezekiah, *H* the word of the LORD of hosts:
43: 9 themselves right, that one may *h* and say,
44: 1 *H* then, O Jacob, my servant, Israel,
46: 3 *H* me, O house of Jacob,
47: 8 Now *h* this voluptuous one,
48: 1 *H* this, O house of Jacob
48: 3 forth from my mouth, I let you *h* of them;
48: 5 before they took place I let you *h* of them,
48: 7 and beforetime you did not *h* of them,
48:16 Come near to me and *h* this!
49: 1 *H* me, O coastlands, listen,
50: 4 morning he opens my ear that I may *h*;
51: 7 *H* me, you who know justice,
51:21 But now, *h* this,
59: 1 short to save, nor his ear too dull to *h*.
59: 2 hide his face so that he will not *h* you.
66: 5 me displeasure, *H* the word of the LORD,
Jer 2: 2 cry out this message for Jerusalem to *h*!
4:21 I see that signal, *h* that trumpet sound!
4:31 Yes, I *h* the moaning,
5:21 eyes and see not, who have ears and *h* not.
6:18 Therefore *h*, O nations, and know,
6:24 We *h* the report of them;
7: 2 *H* the word of the LORD,
9:19 *H*, you women,
10: 1 *H* the word which the LORD speaks to you,
11: 6 *H* the words of this covenant and obey them.
11:16 be jubilant when you *h* the great invasion?
17:20 *H* the word of the LORD,
17:23 necks so as not to *h* or take correction.
19: 3 who *h* of it will feel their ears tingle.
20:10 Yes, I *h* the whisperings of many:
20:16 Let him *h* war cries in the morning,
21:11 *H* the word of the LORD,
22:29 O land, land, land, *h* the word of the LORD
23:18 of the LORD, to see him and to *h* his word?
26:15 to speak all these things for you to *h*."
28:15 *H* this, Hananiah! The LORD has not sent you
30: 5 A cry of dismay we *h*;
31:10 *H* the word of the LORD,
31:18 I *h*, I hear Ephraim pleading:
33: 9 *h* of all the good I will do among them.
37:20 *H* now, my lord king,
38:25 If the princes *h* I spoke to you,
42:14 more of war, *h* the trumpet alarm no longer,
44:24 *H* the word of the LORD,
46:12 The nations *h* of your shame,
47: 3 They *h* the stamping hooves of his steeds,
49:20 Therefore, *h* the counsel of the LORD.
49:20 *H* the plans he has made against those that
50:45 Therefore *h* the counsel of the LORD which
50:45 *H* the plans he has made against the land
51:54 *H*! loud cries from Babylon,
Lam 3:61 You *h* their insults,
Bar 1: 3 son of Jehoiakim, king of Judah, to *h* it,
2:14 *H*, O Lord, our prayer of supplication,
2:16 turn, O Lord, your ear to *h* us.
2:22 for if you do not *h* the Lord's voice so as
3: 2 *H*, O LORD, for you are a God of mercy
3: 4 of Israel, *h* the prayer of Israel's few,
3: 9 *H*, O Israel, the commandments of life:
4: 9 *H* you neighbors of Zion!
Ez 3:10 *h* them well.
3:17 When you *h* a word from my mouth,
6: 3 *h* the word of the Lord GOD.
9: 1 he cried loud for me to *h*:
12: 2 do not see, and ears to hear but do not *h*,
13: 2 *H* the word of the LORD:
13:19 lying to my people who willingly *h* lies.
16:35 Therefore, harlot, *h* the word of the LORD!
18:25 *H* now, house of Israel:
21: 3 *H* the word of the LORD!
24:26 to you, that you may *h* it for yourself;
25: 3 *H* the word of the LORD!
33: 7 when you *h* me say anything,
33:30 *h* the latest word that comes from the LORD."
33:31 they sit down before you and *h* your words,
34: 7 shepherds, *h* the word of the LORD.
34: 9 of this, shepherds, *h* the word of the LORD:
36: 1 of Israel, *h* the word of the LORD!
36: 4 of Israel, *h* the word of the LORD:
36:15 I permit you to *h* the reproach of nations,
37: 4 Dry bones, *h* the word of the LORD!
Dn 3: 4 when you *h* the sound of the trumpet,
3:15 whenever you *h* the sound of the trumpet,
5:23 neither see nor *h* nor have intelligence.
9:17 *H*, therefore,
9:19 O Lord, *h*! O LORD, pardon!
Hos 4: 1 *H* the word of the LORD,
5: 1 *H* this, O priests, Pay attention
Jl 1: 2 *H* this, you elders!
Am 3: 1 *H* the word, O men of Israel,
3:13 *H* and bear witness against the house of
4: 1 *H* this word, women of the mountain
5: 1 *H* this word which I utter over you,
7:16 Now *h* the word of the LORD!"
8: 4 *H* this, you who trample upon the needy
Mi 1: 2 *H*, O peoples, all of you, give heed
3: 1 *H*, you leaders of Jacob,
3: 9 *H* this, you leaders of the house of Jacob,
6: 1 *H*, then, what the LORD says:
6: 1 mountains, and let the hills *h* your voice!
6: 2 *H*, O mountains, the plea of the LORD,
6: 9 *H*, O tribe and city council,
7: 7 my God will *h* me!
Na 3:19 All who *h* this news of you clap their
Hb 3:16 I *h*, and my body trembles;
Zec 7:11 and stopped their ears so as not to *h*.
7:12 their hearts diamond-hard so as not to *h*
8: 9 you who in these days *h* these words spoken
10: 6 am the LORD, their God, and I will *h* them.
13: 9 shall call upon my name, and I will *h* them.
Mt 10:27 What you *h* in private,
11: 4 back and report to John what you *h* and see:
11: 5 walk, lepers are cured, the deaf *h*,
11:15 Heed carefully what you *h*!
13:13 they listen but do not *h* or understand.
13:15 see with their eyes, and *h* with their ears,
13:16 see and blest are your ears because they *h*.
13:17 it, to hear what you hear but did not *h* it.
18:30 But he would *h* none of it.
21:16 "Do you *h* what they are saying?"
24: 6 You will *h* of wars and rumors of wars.
27:13 *h* how many charges they bring against you?"
Mk 4: 9 "Let him who has ears to *h* me, hear!"
4:15 ones to whom, as soon as they *h* the word,
4:23 Let him who has ears to *h* me, hear!"
4:24 "Listen carefully to what you *h*.
6:11 If any place will not receive you or *h* you,
6:14 King Herod came to *h* of Jesus,
7:14 *H* me, all of you, and try to understand.
7:37 He makes the deaf *h* and the mute speak!"
12:29 *H*, O Israel! The Lord our God
13: 7 When you *h* about wars and threats of war,
Lk 5: 1 pressed in on him to *h* the word of God,
5:15 to *h* him and to be cured of their maladies.
6:18 to *h* him and be healed of their diseases.
6:27 "To you who *h* me, I say:
6:47 will *h* my words and put them into practice.

HEAR (cont.)
7:22 walk, lepers are cured, the deaf *h*,
8:12 Those on the footpath are people who *h*,
8:13 are the ones who, when they *h* the word,
8:14 seed fallen among briers are those who *h*,
8:15 who *h* the word in a spirit of openness,
8:18 Take heed, therefore, how you *h*:
8:21 who *h* the word of God and act upon it."
9: 9 this man about whom I *h* all these reports?"
10:24 and to hear what you *h* but did not hear it."
11:28 are they who *h* the word of God and keep it."
15: 1 sinners were all gathering around to *h* him,
16: 2 him and said, 'What is this I *h* about you?
16:29 Let them *h* them.'
17:10 It is quite the same with you who *h* me.
21: 9 when you *h* of wars and insurrections.
21:38 all the people came to *h* him in the temple.
Jn 3: 8 You *h* the sound it makes but you do not
3:29 for him and is overjoyed to *h* his voice.
5:25 dead shall *h* the voice of the Son of God,
5:28 tombs shall *h* his voice and come forth.
5:30 I judge as I *h*,
8:43 It is because you cannot bear to *h* my word.
8:47 you do not *h* is that you are not of God."
9:27 "Why do you want to *h* it all over again?
9:31 We know that God does not *h* sinners,
10: 3 The sheep *h* his voice as he calls his own
10:16 lead them, too, and they shall *h* my voice.
10:27 My sheep *h* my voice.
11:42 I know that you always *h* me but I have
14:24 Yet the word you *h* is not mine;
Acts 2:33 This is what you now see and *h*.
10:22 There he is to *h* what you have to say."
10:33 stand before God at this moment to *h*
10:46 *h* speaking in tongues and glorifying God.
13: 7 Saul and was anxious to *h* the word of God.
13:44 entire city gathered to *h* the word of God.
15: 7 *h* the message of the gospel and believe.
17:32 must *h* you on this topic some other time."
19:26 But as you can see and *h* for yourselves,
20:38 *h* that they would never see his face again.
21:22 your coming, of which they are sure to *h*?
22: 9 but did not *h* the voice speaking to me.
22:14 Just One, and to *h* the sound of his voice;
23:35 "I shall *h* your case,"
24:24 to *h* him speak about faith in Christ Jesus.
25:22 Festus, "I too should like to *h* this man."
25:22 "Tomorrow you shall *h* him,"
28:22 we are anxious to *h* you present your views.
28:27 see with their eyes, *h* with their ears,
Rom 2:13 *h* the law who are just in the sight of God;
10:14 they *h* unless there is someone to preach?
1Cor 11:18 I *h* that when you gather for a meeting
2Cor 12: 4 to *h* words which cannot be uttered,
Eph 4:29 say only the good things men need to *h*,
Phil 1:27 or *h* about your behavior from a distance,
1:30 me engaged and now *h* that I am caught up.
2Thes 3:11 We *h* that some of you are unruly,
1Tm 4:16 to salvation yourself and all who *h* you.
2Tm 4:17 and all the nations might *h* the gospel.
Heb 3: 7 "Today, if you should *h* his voice,
3:15 says, "Today, if you should *h* his voice,
4: 7 "Today, if you should *h* his voice,
12:20 for they could not bear to *h* the command:
12:25 Do not refuse to *h* him who speaks.
Jas 1:19 Let every man be quick to *h*,
1Jn 4: 6 anyone who is not of God refuses to *h* us.
3Jn 1: 4 Nothing delights me more than to *h* that my
Rv 1: 3 who *h* it and heed what is written in it,
9:20 and wood, which cannot see or *h* or walk.
22:18 all who *h* the prophetic words of this book.

HEARD (616)
Gn 3: 8 When they *h* the sound of the LORD God
3:10 He answered, "I *h* you in the garden;
14:14 Abram *h* that his nephew had been captured,
16:11 name him Ishmael, For the LORD has *h* you,
21:17 God *h* the boy's cry,
21:17 has *h* the boy's cry in this plight of his.
24:30 his sister Rebekah and *h* her words
24:52 When Abraham's servant *h* their answer,
25:21 The LORD *h* his entreaty,
29:13 *h* the news about his sister's son Jacob,
29:33 "It means, 'The LORD *h* that I was unloved,'
30:17 he slept with her, and God *h* her prayer;
30:22 he *h* her prayer and made her fruitful.
34: 5 Jacob *h* that Shechem had defiled his
34: 7 When they *h* the news,
35:22 When Israel *h* of it,
37:17 in fact, I *h* them say,
37:21 When Reuben *h* this, he tried to save him
39:15 When he *h* me scream for help,
39:19 As soon as the master *h* his wife's story
43:25 they had *h* that they were to dine there.
45: 2 sobs were so loud that the Egyptians *h* him,
47: 5 and Pharaoh, king of Egypt, *h* about it,
Ex 2:15 *h* of the affair and sought to put him to
2:24 he *h* their groaning and was mindful of his
3: 7 my people in Egypt and have *h* their cry
4:31 and when they *h* that the LORD was
6: 5 I have *h* the groaning of the Israelites,
15:14 The nations *h* and quaked;
16: 9 the LORD, for he has *h* your grumbling."
16:12 "I have *h* the grumbling of the Israelites.
18: 1 *h* of all that God had done for Moses and
23:13 it shall not be *h* from your lips.
28:35 that its tinkling may be *h* as he enters
32:17 Joshua *h* the noise of the people shouting,
33: 4 When the people *h* this bad news,
Lv 24:14 *h* him have laid their hands on his head,
Nm 7:89 he *h* the voice addressing him from above
11: 1 and when he *h* it his wrath flared up so
11:10 When Moses *h* the people,
12: 2 And the LORD *h* this.
14:14 It has been *h* that you,
14:15 who have *h* such reports of you will say,
14:27 I have *h* the grumblings of the Israelites
14:28 will do to you just what I have *h* you say.
16: 4 When Moses *h* this, he fell prostrate.
20:16 he *h* our cry and sent an angel who led us
21: 1 *h* that the Israelites were coming along
22:36 When Balak *h* that Balaam was coming,
33:40 Canaan, *h* that the Israelites were coming.
Dt 1:34 When the LORD *h* your words,
4:12 You *h* the sound of the words,
4:32 Was it ever *h* of?
4:36 and you *h* him speaking out of the fire.
5:23 *h* the voice from the midst of the darkness,
5:24 We have *h* his voice from the midst of the
5:26 For what mortal has *h*,
5:28 "The LORD *h* your words as you were
5:28 'I have *h* the words these people have
9: 2 know of them and have *h* it said of them,
10:10 again *h* me and decided not to destroy you,
26: 7 and he *h* our cry and saw our affliction,
Jos 2:10 For we have *h* how the LORD dried up the
5: 1 kings of the Canaanites by the sea *h*
6:20 When they *h* the signal horn,
9: 9 For we have *h* reports of all that he did
10: 1 Now Adonizedek, king of Jerusalem, *h* that,
10: 1 He *h* also that the inhabitants of Gibeon
14:12 promised me that day, as you yourself *h*.
22:11 *h* the report that the Reubenites,
22:30 of the Israelites, *h* what the Reubenites,
24:27 *h* all the words which the LORD spoke to us.
Jgs 7:15 When Gideon *h* the description and
9:46 When they *h* of this,
13: 9 God *h* the prayer of Manoah,
13:23 all this just now, or hear what we have *h*."
20: 3 the Benjaminites *h* that the Israelites had
1Sm 1:13 lips were moving, her voice could not be *h*.
2:22 he *h* repeatedly how his sons were treating
4:19 When she *h* the news concerning the capture
7: 7 When the Philistines *h* that the
7: 9 the LORD for Israel, and the LORD *h* him.
14:27 who had not *h* that his father had put the
17:11 they *h* this challenge of the Philistine,
17:28 brother, *h* him speaking with the men,
22: 6 *h* that David and his men had been located.
23:10 your servant has *h* a report that Saul
23:11 will Saul come down as your servant has *h*?
23:25 Saul *h* of this and pursued David into the
25: 4 When David *h* in the desert that Nabal was
25: 7 I have just *h* that shearers are with you.
31:11 *h* what the Philistines had done to Saul,
2Sm 3:28 Later David *h* of it and said:
4: 1 of Saul, *h* that Abner had died in Hebron,
5:17 When the Philistines *h* that David had
7:22 no God but you, just as we have *h* it told.
8: 9 *h* that David had defeated all the forces
11:26 wife of Uriah *h* that her husband had died,
18: 5 All the soldiers *h* the king instruct the
19: 3 *h* that the king was grieving for his son.
22: 7 From his temple he *h* my voice,
22:45 as soon as they *h* me,
1Kgs 1:11 "Have you not *h* that Adonijah,
1:41 and all the guests who were with him *h* it,
1:41 When Joab *h* the sound of the horn,
1:45 That is the noise you *h*.
3:28 Israel *h* the judgment the king had given,
5:14 kings of the earth who had *h* of his wisdom.
5:15 *h* that Solomon had been anointed king in
5:21 When he had *h* the words of Solomon,
6: 7 be *h* in the temple during its construction.)
9: 3 "I have *h* the prayer of petition which
10: 1 queen of Sheba, having *h* of Solomon's fame,
10: 6 "The report I *h* in my country about your
10: 7 and prosperity surpass the report I *h*.
11:21 When Hadad in Egypt *h* that David rested
12:20 all Israel *h* that Jeroboam had returned,
13: 4 When King Jeroboam *h* what the man of God
15:21 When Baasha *h* of it, he left off fortifying
16:16 they *h* that Zimri had formed a conspiracy
17:22 The LORD *h* the prayer of Elijah;
19:13 When he *h* this, Elijah hid his face
20:12 with the kings when he *h* this reply.
20:31 "We have *h* that the kings of the land of
21:27 When Ahab *h* these words,
2Kgs 3:21 all Moab *h* that the kings had come to give
5: 8 *h* that the king of Israel had torn his
6:30 When the king *h* the woman's words,
11:13 Athaliah *h* the noise made by the people,
13: 4 Jehoahaz entreated the LORD, who *h* him,
19: 1 When King Hezekiah *h* this,
19: 4 the words which the LORD, your God, has *h*.
19: 6 not be frightened by the words you have *h*,
19: 8 *h* that the king of Assyria had withdrawn
19: 9 king of Assyria *h* a report that Tirhakah,
19:11 You have *h* what the kings of Assyria have
19:25 " 'Have you not *h*?
20: 5 I have *h* your prayer and seen your tears.
20:12 of Babylon, *h* that Hezekiah had been ill,
22:11 had *h* the contents of the book of the law,
22:18 As for the threats you have *h*,
22:19 you *h* my threats that this place
1Chr 5:20 and he *h* them because they had put their
10:11 *h* what the Philistines had done to Saul,
14: 8 When the Philistines had *h* that David was
14: 8 But when David *h* of this,
18: 9 *h* that David had defeated the entire army
19: 8 When David *h* of this,
21:28 Once David saw that the LORD had *h* him on
2Chr 5:13 When the trumpeters and singers were *h* as
6:21 heavenly dwelling, and when you have *h*,
7:12 "I have *h* your prayer,
9: 1 the queen of Sheba *h* of Solomon's fame,
9: 5 "The account I *h* in my country about your
9: 6 you have surpassed the stories I *h*.
10: 2 *h* of this in Egypt where he had fled from
15: 8 When Asa *h* these words and the prophecy
16: 5 When Baasha *h* of it,
20:29 when they *h* how the LORD had fought
23:12 When Athaliah *h* the din of the people
30:20 The LORD *h* Hezekiah and spared the people.
30:27 was *h* and their prayer reached heaven,
33:13 he *h* his prayer and restored him to his
33:19 His prayer and how his supplication was *h*,
34:19 When the king *h* the words of the law,
34:26 Israel, concerning the threats you have *h*:
Ezr 3:13 a mighty clamor which was *h* afar off.
4: 1 When the enemies of Judah and Benjamin *h*
9: 3 When I had *h* this thing, I tore my cloak
Neh 1: 4 When I *h* this report,
2:10 Tobiah the Ammonite slave had *h* of this,
3:33 *h* that we were rebuilding the wall,
4: 1 and the Ashdodites *h* that the restoration
5: 6 I *h* the reasons they had for complaint.
6:16 When all our enemies had *h* of this,
8: 9 weeping as they *h* the words of the law.
9: 9 in Egypt, you *h* their cry by the Red Sea;
9:28 and you *h* them from heaven and delivered
12:42 were *h* under the leadership of Jezrahiah.
12:43 at Jerusalem could be *h* from afar off.
13: 3 When they had *h* the law,
13:27 Must it also be *h* of you that you have
Tb 3: 6 live, because I have *h* insulting calumnies,
3:16 *h* in the glorious presence of Almighty God.
6:14 I have *h* that this woman has already been
6:14 And I have *h* it said that it was a demon
6:18 *h* Raphael say that she was his kinswoman,
7: 7 when he *h* that Tobit had lost his eyesight,
14:15 he *h* of the destruction of Nineveh and saw
Jdt 4: 1 dwelt in Judea *h* of all that Holofernes,
4:13 The Lord *h* their cry and had regard for
8: 1 son of Simeon, son of Israel, *h* of this.
8: 9 *h* of the harsh words which the people,
10:14 men *h* her words and gazed upon her face,
11: 8 we have *h* of your wisdom and sagacity,
11: 9 speech in your council, we have *h* of it.
13:12 When the citizens *h* her voice,
14:19 of the Assyrian army *h* these words,
1Mc 2:38 When Mattathias and his friends *h* of it,
3:13 *h* that Judas had gathered many about him,
3:27 When Antiochus *h* about these events,
3:41 merchants of the country *h* of their fame,
4: 2 Judas *h* of it, and himself set out
4:27 he *h* it he was disturbed and discouraged,
5: 1 When the Gentiles round about *h* that the
5:16 When Judas and the people *h* this,
5:56 *h* about the brave deeds and the fighting
5:63 the Gentiles, wherever their name was *h*;
6: 1 he *h* that in Persia there was a city
6: 8 When the king *h* this news,
6:28 When the king *h* this he was angry,
6:41 All who *h* the noise of their numbers,
6:55 Lysias *h* that Philip,
8: 1 had *h* of the reputation of the Romans.
8:12 who *h* of their fame were afraid of them.
9: 1 When Demetrius *h* that Nicanor and his army
9:43 When Bacchides *h* of it,
10: 2 When King Demetrius *h* of it,
10: 8 they *h* that the king had given him authority
10:15 King Alexander *h* of the promises that
10:19 We have *h* of you, that you are a mighty
10:22 When Demetrius *h* of these things,
10:26 We have *h* how you have kept the treaty
10:46 When Jonathan and the people *h* these words,
10:68 Alexander *h* of it he was greatly troubled,
10:74 When Jonathan *h* the message of Apollonius,
10:77 When Apollonius *h* of it,
10:88 When King Alexander *h* of these events,
11:15 When Alexander *h* the news,
11:22 When Demetrius *h* this,
11:63 Jonathan *h* that the generals of Demetrius
12:24 Jonathan *h* that the generals of Demetrius
12:28 When the enemy *h* that Jonathan and his men
12:34 for he *h* that its men had intended to hand
13: 1 When Simon *h* that Trypho was gathering a

13: 7 As the people *h* these words,
14: 2 *h* that Demetrius had invaded his
14:16 When people *h* in Rome and even in Sparta
14:17 But when the Romans *h* that his brother
14:25 When the people *h* of these things,
14:40 He had indeed *h* that the Romans had
2Mc 1: 8 prayed to the Lord, and our prayer was *h;*
2: 7 When Jeremiah *h* of this, he reproved them:
10:13 on all sides he *h* himself called a traitor
12: 5 As soon as Judas *h* of the barbarous deed
13:23 Next he *h* that Philip,
14:15 When the Jews *h* of Nicanor's coming,
14:18 *h* of the valor of Judas and his men,
Jb 2:11 Now when three of Job's friends *h* of all
4:16 was before my eyes, and I *h* a still voice:
5:27 This we have *h,* and you should know.
13: 1 my ear has *h* and perceived it.
16: 2 I have *h* this sort of thing many times.
19: 7 I am not *h.* I cry for help,
28:22 Death say, "Only by rumor have we *h* of it."
29:11 Whoever *h* of me blessed me;
34:28 so that he *h* the plea of the afflicted.
42: 5 I had *h* of you by word of mouth,
Ps(s) 6: 9 for the LORD has *h* the sound of my weeping;
6:10 The LORD has *h* my plea;
18: 7 From his temple he *h* my voice,
18:45 as soon as they *h* me they obeyed.
19: 4 word nor a discourse whose voice is not *h;*
22:25 but when he cried out to him, he *h* him."
28: 6 for he has *h* the sound of my pleading;
31:23 Yet you *h* the sound of my pleading when I
34: 7 the afflicted man called out, the LORD *h,*
40: 2 and he stooped toward me and *h* my cry.
44: 2 O God, our ears have *h,* our fathers
48: 9 As we had *h,* so have we seen
62:12 these two things which I *h:*
66:19 But God has *h;*
76: 9 From heaven you made your intervention *h;*
78: 3 What we have *h* and know,
78:21 Then the LORD *h* and was enraged;
78:59 God *h* and was enraged and utterly rejected
81:12 "But my people *h* not my voice,
92:12 *h* of the fall of my wicked adversaries.
99: 7 *h* his decrees and the law he gave them.
106:44 for their affliction when he *h* their cry;
116: 1 because he has *h* my voice in supplication,
132: 6 Behold, we *h* of it in Ephrathah;
138: 1 [for you have *h* the words of my mouth;]
141: 6 and they *h* how pleasant were my words.
Prv 21:13 poor will himself also call and not be *h.*
Eccl 12:13 The last word, when all is *h:*
Sg 2:12 and the song of the dove is *h* in our land.
5: 2 I *h* my lover knocking:
Wis 11:13 For when they *h* that the cause of their
18: 1 who *h* their voices but did not see their
Sir 3: 5 by children, and when he prays he is *h.*
16: 5 seen, even more than these has my ear *h.*
17:11 beheld, his glorious voice their ears *h.*
21: 5 Prayer from a poor man's lips is *h* at once,
23:12 may they never be *h* among Jacob's heirs.
35:16 He who serves God willingly is *h;*
45: 9 step He would be *h* within the sanctuary,
46:17 and the tremendous roar of his voice was *h.*
48: 7 You *h* threats at Sinai,
48:20 He *h* the prayer they uttered and saved
51:11 Thereupon the LORD *h* my voice,
Is 6: 8 Then I *h* the voice of the Lord saying,
15: 4 cry out, they are *h* as far as Jahaz.
16: 6 We have *h* of the pride of Moab,
21:10 What I have *h* from the LORD of hosts,
23: 5 When it is *h* in Egypt they shall be in
28:22 be tightened, For I have *h* from the Lord,
30:30 The LORD will make his glorious voice *h,*
37: 1 When King Hezekiah *h* this,
37: 4 the words which the LORD, your God, has *h.*
37: 6 not be frightened by the words you have *h,*
37: 8 *h* that the king of Assyria had left there,
37: 9 king of Assyria *h* a report that Tirhakah,
37:11 You yourself have *h* what the kings of
37:26 Have you not *h?*
38: 5 I have *h* your prayer and seen your tears.
39: 1 *h* that Hezekiah had recovered from his
40:28 Do you not know or have you not *h?*
41:21 Have you not *h?*
41:26 no one *h* you say,
42: 2 not making his voice *h* in the street.
48: 6 Now that you have *h,*
48: 8 You neither *h* nor knew,
52:15 see, those who have not *h* shall ponder it.
53: 1 Who would believe what we have *h?*
58: 4 fast so as to make your voice *h* on high!
60:18 longer shall violence be *h* of in your land,
64: 3 such as they had not *h* of from of old.
64: 3 No ear has ever *h,* no eye ever seen,
65:19 shall the sound of weeping be *h* there,
66: 8 Who ever *h* of such a thing,
66:19 coastlands that have never *h* of my fame,
Jer 3:21 A cry is *h* on the heights!
4: 5 it in Judah, make it *h* in Jerusalem;
4:19 For I have *h* the sound of the trumpet,
6:10 whom shall I warn, and be *h?*
8:16 From Dan is *h* the snorting of his steeds;
9:18 The dirge is *h* from Zion:
18:13 who has ever *h* the like?
18:22 May cries be *h* from their homes,
20: 1 Jeremiah was *h* prophesying these things by
23:25 I have *h* the prophets who prophesy lies in
26: 7 and all the people *h* Jeremiah speak these
26:11 city, as you have *h* with your own ears."
26:12 this house and city all that you have *h.*
26:21 Uriah *h* of it and fled in fear to Egypt.
31:15 In Ramah is *h* the sound of moaning,
33:10 beast, there shall yet be *h* the cry of joy,
36:11 *h* all the words of the LORD read from the
36:13 had *h* Baruch read publicly from his book.
36:16 it to them, and when they *h* all its words,
37: 5 who were besieging Jerusalem *h* this report
38: 1 *h* Jeremiah speaking these words to all the
38: 7 *h* that they had put Jeremiah into the
38:27 had been *h* of the earlier conversation.
40: 7 all their men *h* that the king of Babylon
40:11 and those in all other lands *h* that the
41:11 leaders with him *h* of the crimes Ishmael,
48: 4 Moab is crushed, their outcry is *h* in Zoar.
48: 5 to Horonaim the cry of destruction is *h.*
48:29 We have *h* of the pride of Moab,
48:34 Heshbon and Elealeh is *h* as far as Jahaz;
49:14 I have *h* a report from the LORD.
49:21 quakes, to the Red Sea the outcry is *h!*
49:23 covered with shame, they have *h* bad news;
50:46 the outcry is *h* among the nations.
51:51 We are ashamed because we have *h* taunts,
51:55 mighty waters, and their clamor was *h* afar.
Lam 3:56 You *h* me call, "Let not your ear be deaf
Bar 3:22 She has not been *h* of in Canaan,
Ez 1:24 Then I *h* the sound of their wings,
2: 2 and I *h* the one who was speaking say to me:
3:12 and I *h* behind me the noise of a loud
9: 5 To the others I *h* him say:
10: 5 could be *h* as far as the outer court;
10:13 I *h* the wheels given the name "wheelwork."
19: 9 would not be *h* on the mountains of Israel.
23:42 *h* the shout of a carefree mob in the city,
26:13 the sound of your lyres shall be *h* no more.
27:30 shore, Making their voice *h* on your behalf,
33: 5 He *h* the trumpet blast yet refused to take
35:12 I have *h* all the contemptuous things you
35:13 I have *h* the insolent and wild words you
37: 7 and even as I was prophesying I *h* a noise;
43: 2 *h* a sound like the roaring of many waters,
43: 6 I *h* someone speaking to me from the temple,
Dn 3: 7 as soon as they *h* the sound of the trumpet,
3:10 everyone who *h* the sound of the trumpet,
5:10 When the queen *h* of the discussion between
5:14 I have *h* that the spirit of God is in you,
5:16 But I have *h* that you can interpret dreams
6:11 Daniel *h* that this law had been signed,
8:13 I *h* a holy one speaking,
8:16 the Ulai I *h* a human voice that cried out,
10: 9 When I *h* the sound of his voice,
10:12 yourself before God, your prayer was *h.*
12: 7 and I *h* him swear by him who lives forever
12: 8 I *h,* but I did not understand;
13:26 in the house *h* the cries from the garden,
13:44 The Lord *h* her prayer.
14:28 When the Babylonians *h* this,
Ob 1: 1 Of Edom we have *h* a message from the LORD,
Jon 2: 3 world I cried for help, and you *h* my voice.
Na 2:14 cry of your lionesses shall be *h* no more.
Hb 3: 2 O LORD, I have *h* your renown,
Zep 1:10 LORD, A cry will be *h* from the Fish Gate,
2: 8 I have *h* the revilings uttered by Moab,
Zec 8:23 you, for we have *h* that God is with you."
Mt 2:18 "A cry was *h* at Ramah,
2:22 He *h,* however, that Archelaus
4:12 When Jesus *h* that John had been arrested,
5:21 "You have *h* the commandment imposed on
5:27 "You have *h* the commandment,
5:33 "You have *h* the commandment imposed on
5:38 "You have *h* the commandment,
5:43 "You have *h* the commandment,
8:12 Wailing will be *h* there,
11: 2 *h* about the works Christ was performing,
12:19 nor will his voice be *h* in the streets.
12:24 When the Pharisees *h* this, they charged.
13:15 They have scarcely *h* with their ears,
14: 1 tetrarch, having *h* of Jesus' reputation,
14:13 When Jesus *h* this,
14:13 The crowds *h* of it and followed him on
15:12 scandalized when they *h* your pronouncement?"
17: 6 When they *h* this the disciples fell
19:25 *h* this they were completely overwhelmed,
20:30 roadside, who *h* that Jesus was passing by,
21:45 priests and the Pharisees *h* these parables,
22:34 *h* that he had silenced the Sadducees,
26:66 Remember, you *h* the blasphemy.
27:47 some of the bystanders who *h* it remark,
Mk 3: 8 Sidon, because they had *h* what he had done.
3:21 *h* of this they came to take charge of him,
5:20 They were all amazed at what they *h.*
5:27 She had *h* about Jesus and came up behind
6:20 he *h* him speak he was very much disturbed;
6:29 Later, when his disciples *h* about this,
6:55 bedrolls to the place where they *h* he was.
7:25 had an unclean spirit, *h* about him.
11:14 His disciples *h* all this.
11:18 The chief priests and the scribes *h* of
12:28 and when he *h* them arguing he realized how
12:37 majority of the crowd *h* this with delight.
14:58 falsely by alleging, "We *h* him declare,
14:64 You have *h* the blasphemy.
14:72 Just then a second cock crow was *h* and
15:35 A few of the bystanders who *h* it remarked,
16:11 But when they *h* that he was alive and had
Lk 1:13 your prayer has been *h.*
1:41 When Elizabeth *h* Mary's greeting,
1:66 *h* stored these things up in their hearts,
2:18 All who *h* of it were astonished at the
2:20 praising God for all they had *h* and seen,
2:47 All who *h* him were amazed at his
3:22 A voice from heaven was *h* to say:
4:23 we have *h* you have done in Capernaum.'
6:49 anyone who has *h* my words but not put them
7: 3 When he *h* about Jesus he sent some Jewish
7:22 report to John what you have seen and *h.*
7:29 The entire populace that had *h* Jesus,
8: 8 who has ears attend to what he has *h."*
8:50 Jesus *h* this, and his response was:
9: 7 Herod the tetrarch *h* of all that was
12: 3 said in the dark will be *h* in the daylight;
15:25 home, he *h* the sound of music and dancing.
16:14 men, *h* all this and began to deride him.
18:22 When Jesus *h* this he said to him:
20:16 When they *h* this they said,
22:71 We have *h* it from his own mouth."
Jn 1:37 The two disciples *h* what he said,
3:32 all] testifies to what he has seen and *h,*
4: 1 Pharisees had *h* that he was winning over
4:42 We have *h* for ourselves,
4:47 When he *h* that Jesus had come back from
5:37 His voice you have never *h,*
6:45 Everyone who has *h* the Father and learned
7:40 the crowd who *h* these words began to say,
8:26 only tell the world what I have *h* from him,
8:38 you do what you have *h* from your father."
8:40 told you the truth which I have *h* from God.
9:35 When Jesus *h* of his expulsion,
11:20 When Martha *h* that Jesus was coming she
11:29 As soon as Mary *h* this,
11:41 "Father, I thank you for having *h* me.
12:12 feast *h* that Jesus was to enter Jerusalem.
12:18 because they *h* he had performed this sign.
12:29 When the crowd of bystanders *h* the voice,
12:34 "We have *h* it said in the law that the
14:28 You have *h* me say,
15:15 known to you all that I *h* from my Father.
18:21 Question those who *h* me when I spoke.
19: 8 When Pilate *h* this kind of talk,
19:13 Pilate *h* what they were saying,
Acts 1: 4 promise, of which you have *h* me speak.
2: 2 driving wind which was *h* all through the
2: 6 These *h* the sound,
2: 6 one *h* these men speaking his own language.
2:37 When they *h* this, they were deeply shaken.
4: 4 of those who had *h* the speech believed;
4:20 help speaking of what we have *h* and seen."
5: 5 Great fear came upon all who later *h* of it.
5: 9 buried your husband can be *h* at the door.
5:11 on the whole church and on all who *h* of it.
5:33 When the Sanhedrin *h* this,
6:11 they had *h* him speaking blasphemies
6:14 We have *h* him claim that Jesus the
7:31 it carefully, the voice of the Lord was *h:*
7:34 people in Egypt and have *h* their groaning,
7:59 was being stoned he could be *h* praying,
8: 6 the crowds that *h* Philip and saw the
8:14 When the apostles in Jerusalem *h* that
8:30 and *h* the man reading the prophet Isaiah.
9: 4 and at the same time *h* a voice saying,
9: 7 They had *h* the voice but could see no one.
9:13 I have *h* from many sources about this man
9:21 Any who *h* it were greatly taken aback.
9:38 the disciples who had *h* that Peter was
10:15 The voice was *h* a second time:
10:31 'your prayer has been *h* and your
11: 1 apostles and the brothers *h* that Gentiles,
11:18 When they *h* this they stopped objecting,
13:48 The Gentiles were delighted when they *h*
14:14 the apostles Barnabas and Paul *h* of this,
15:24 We have *h* that some of our number without
17: 8 the town's magistrates *h* the whole story,
17:18 because he was *h* to speak of "Jesus" and
17:32 When they *h* about the raising of the dead,
18: 8 too, who *h* Paul believed and were baptized.
18:26 When Priscilla and Aquila *h* him,
19: 2 so much as *h* that there is a Holy Spirit."
19: 5 When they *h* this,
19:10 and Greeks alike, *h* the word of the Lord.
19:28 When they *h* this speech,
21:20 When they *h* it they praised God,
22: 2 When they *h* him addressing them in Hebrew,
22: 7 fell to the ground and *h* a voice say to me,
22:15 be his witness to what you have seen and *h.*
23:16 The son of Paul's sister *h* about the plot,
24:22 he *h* these words he adjourned the trial,
26:14 and I *h* a voice saying to me in Hebrew,
28:15 Certain brothers from Rome who *h* about us
Rom 10:14 can they believe unless they have *h* of him?
10:16 who has believed what he has *h* from us?"

HEARD (cont.)
10:17 and what is *h* is the word of Christ.
10:18 I ask you, have they not *h?*
15:21 and they who have never *h* will understand."
1Cor 2: 9 "Eye has not seen, ear has not *h,*
2Cor 6: 2 says, "In an acceptable time I have *h* you;
Gal 1:13 You have *h,*
1:23 they had only *h* that "he who was formerly
3: 2 of the law or through faith in what you *h?*
3: 5 you have faith in what you *h* that God
Eph 1:13 when you *h* the glad tidings of salvation,
1:15 from the time I first *h* of your faith in
3: 2 I am sure you have *h* of the ministry which
Phil 2:26 distressed that you *h* about his illness.
4: 9 what you have *h* me say and seen me do.
Col 1: 4 we have *h* of your faith in Christ Jesus
1: 5 You *h* of this hope through the message of
1: 6 been the case from the day you first *h* it
1: 9 Ever since we *h* this we have been praying
1:23 hope promised you by the gospel you have *h.*
2Tm 1:13 of sound teaching what you have *h* me say,
2: 2 The things which you have *h* from me
Heb 2: 1 must attend all the more to what we have *h,*
2: 3 was confirmed to us by those who had *h* him.
3:16 those that revolted when they *h* that voice?
4: 2 We have indeed *h* the good news,
4: 2 the word which they *h* did not profit them,
5: 7 and he was *h* because of his reverence.
12:19 who *h* begged that they be not addressed
Jas 5:11 You have *h* of the steadfastness of Job,
2Pt 1:18 We ourselves *h* this said from heaven while
1Jn 1: 3 What we have seen and *h* we proclaim in
1: 5 we have *h* from him and announce to you:
2: 7 now old, is the word you have already *h.*
2:18 as you *h* that the antichrist was coming,
2:24 *h* from the beginning remain in your hearts.
2:24 If what you *h* from the beginning does
3:11 is the message you *h* from the beginning:
4: 3 of the antichrist which, as you have *h,*
2Jn 1: 6 and as you have *h* from the beginning,
Rv 1:10 and I *h* behind me a piercing voice like
3: 3 Call to mind how you accepted what you *h;*
4: 1 and I *h* the trumpetlike voice which had
5:11 I *h* the voices of many angels who
5:13 Then I *h* the voices of every creature in
6: 1 and I *h* one of the four living creatures
6: 3 I *h* the second living creature cry out,
6: 5 I *h* the third living creature cry out,
6: 6 I *h* what seemed to be a voice coming from
6: 7 I *h* the voice of the fourth living
7: 4 I *h* the number of those who were so marked
8:13 I *h* an eagle flying in midheaven cry out
9:13 and I *h* a voice coming from between the
9:16 Their cavalry troops, whose count I *h,*
9:16 a number I *h* myself.
10: 4 spoke, but I *h* a voice from heaven say,
10: 8 I *h* from heaven spoke to me again and said,
11:12 *h* a loud voice from heaven say to them,
12:10 Then I *h* a loud voice in heaven say:
14: 2 I *h* a sound from heaven which resembled
14: 2 the sound I *h* was like the melody of
14:13 I *h* a voice from heaven say to me:
16: 1 I *h* a mighty voice from the sanctuary say
16: 5 Then I *h* the angel in charge of the waters
16: 7 Then I *h* the altar cry out:
18: 4 Then I *h* another voice from heaven say:
18:22 trumpeters, shall ever again be *h* in you!
18:22 the millstone shall ever again be *h* in you!
19: 1 After this I *h* what sounded like the loud
19: 6 Then I *h* what sounded like the shouts of a
21: 3 I *h* a loud voice from the throne cry out:
22: 8 is I, John, who *h* and saw all these things,
22: 8 and when I *h* and saw them I fell down to

HEARING (96)

Gn 23:10 Hittite replied to Abraham in the *h*
23:12 addressed Ephron in the *h* of these men:
23:16 had stipulated in the *h* of the Hittites,
27:34 On *h* his father's words,
Lv 10:20 On *h* this, Moses was satisfied.
Nm 11: 1 the people complained in the *h* of the LORD;
11:18 For in the *h* of the LORD you have cried,
Dt 5: 1 which I proclaim in your *h* this day,
13:12 And all Israel, *h* of it,
17:13 And all the people, on *h* of it,
19:20 The rest, on *h* of it,
21:21 your midst, and all Israel, on *h* of it,
29:18 person, upon *h* the words of this curse,
Jgs 17: 2 in my *h* when they were taken from you,
1Sm 4: 6 The Philistines, *h* the noise of shouting,
4:14 *H* the outcry of the men standing near him,
7: 7 *H,* this, the Israelites became afraid
14:22 on *h* that the Philistines were fleeing,
25:39 On *h* that Nabal was dead, David said:
2Sm 5:17 On *h* this, David went down to the refuge.
18:12 in our *h* to protect the youth Absalom
1Kgs 13:26 On *h* it, the prophet who had brought him
14: 6 *h* the sound of her footsteps as she
20:33 is my brother," *H* this as a good omen,
21:16 On *h* that Naboth was dead,
2Kgs 25:23 *H* that the king of Babylon had appointed
1Chr 28: 8 of the LORD, and in the *h* of our God,
2Chr 34:27 humbled yourself before God on *h* his words
Neh 2:19 On *h* of this, Sanballat the Horonite,
13: 1 the book of Moses in the *h* of the people,
Jdt 11:16 the world will be astonished on *h* of them.
15: 1 On *h* what had happened,
15: 5 On *h* this, all the Israelites, with one accord,
1Mc 11:23 On *h* this, Jonathan ordered the siege
16:22 On *h* this, John was utterly astounded.
2Mc 12: 8 On *h* that the men of Jamnia planned to
Jb 13:17 to my speech, and give my statement a *h.*
33: 8 But you have said in my *h,*
Ps(s) 38:14 But I am like a deaf man, *h* not,
Prv 1: 5 man by *h* them will advance in learning,
23: 9 Speak not for the fool's *h;*
25:10 Lest, *h* it, he reproach you,
28: 9 When one turns away his ear from *h* the law,
Eccl 1: 8 with seeing nor is the ear filled with *h.*
Wis 8:15 terrible princes, *h* of me,
Sir 4: 8 Give a *h* to the poor man,
11: 8 Before *h,* answer not,
Is 5: 9 In my *h* the LORD of hosts has sworn:
42:20 your ears are open, but without *h.*
Jer 28: 7 your hearing and the *h* of all the people.
36:24 *H* all these words did not frighten the
Ez 27:28 *H* the shouts of your mariners,
33: 4 anyone *h* but not heeding the warning of
Dn 3:90 *H* them sing, and astonished at seeing them
Am 8:11 for water, but for *h* the word of the LORD.
Mt 6: 7 a *h* by the sheer multiplication of words.
8:10 on *h* this and remarked to his followers,
19:22 *H* these words, the young man went away
20:24 The other ten, on *h* this, became indignant
Mk 6:16 On *h* of Jesus, Herod exclaimed,
8:18 Ears but no *h?*
10:41 The other ten, on *h* this,
10:47 On *h* that it was Jesus of Nazareth,
14:11 *H* what he had to say,
Lk 1:58 upon *h* that the Lord had extended his
4:21 Scripture passage is fulfilled in your *h.*"
7: 1 this discourse in the *h* of the people,
7: 9 Jesus showed amazement on *h* this,
8:10 perceive, and *h* they may not understand.'
18:23 On *h* this he grew melancholy,
18:36 *H* a crowd go by the man asked,
20:45 In the *h* of all the people,
23: 6 On *h* this Pilate asked if the man was a
Jn 1:40 *h* John was Simon Peter's brother Andrew.
6:60 After *h* his words,
7:51 without first *h* him and knowing the facts?"
8:37 me because my word finds no *h* among you.
11: 4 Upon *h* this, Jesus said:
11: 6 Yet, after *h* that Lazarus was sick,
21: 7 On *h* it was the Lord,
Acts 4:24 voices in prayer to God on *h* the story:
5:24 On *h* this report, the captain of the temple
7:12 *H* that there was grain in Egypt,
7:29 On *h* this, Moses fled.
16:38 alarmed at *h* they were Roman citizens.
18:14 give you Jews a patient and reasonable *h.*
21:12 Upon *h* this,
22:26 On *h* this, the centurion ran
24: 4 your indulgence for a brief *h* of our case.
Rom 10:17 Faith, then, comes through *h,*
1Cor 12:17 were all eye, what would happen to our *h?*
2Tm 4:16 At the first *h* of my case in court,
Phlm 1: 5 for I keep *h* of your love and faith toward
2Pt 2: 8 tormented by seeing and *h* about the lawless
1Jn 4: 6 who has knowledge of God gives us a *h,*

HEARKEN (37)

Ex 19: 5 if you *h* to my voice and keep my covenant,
Nm 23:18 Be aroused, O Balak, and *h;*
Dt 26:17 and decrees, and to *h* to his voice.
27:10 shall therefore *h* to the voice of the LORD,
28: 2 When you *h* to the voice of the LORD,
28:15 if you do not *h* to the voice of the LORD,
28:45 you would not *h* to the voice of the LORD,
28:62 you would not *h* to the voice of the LORD,
32: 1 let the earth *h* to the words of my mouth!
2Mc 8: 3 to *h* to the blood that cried out to him;
Jb 9:16 not believe that he would *h* to my words;
32:10 Therefore I say, *h* to me;
33: 1 hear my discourse, and *h* to all my words.
34:10 Therefore, men of understanding, *h* to me:
34:16 *H* to the words I speak!
37:14 *H* to this, O Job!
Ps(s) 5: 2 *H* to my words, O LORD,
17: 1 *h* to my prayer from lips without deceit.
49: 2 *h,* all who dwell in the world,
54: 4 *h* to the words of my mouth.
55: 2 *H,* O God, to my prayer;
78: 1 *H,* my people, to my teaching
80: 2 O shepherd of Israel, *h,*
84: 9 *h,* O God of Jacob!
86: 6 *H,* O LORD, to my prayer
140: 7 *h,* O LORD, to my voice
141: 1 *h* to my voice when I call upon you.
143: 1 *h* to my pleading in your faithfulness;
Eccl 7: 5 It is better to *h* to the wise man's rebuke
7: 5 rebuke than to *h* to the song of fools;
Wis 6: 2 *H,* you who are in power over the multitude
Sir 16:22 *H* to me, my son, take my advice
Is 10:30 *H,* Laishah!
48:18 If you would *h* to my commandments,
65:24 they are yet speaking, I will *h* to them.
Jer 6:17 *H* to the sound of the trumpet!"
6:17 they said, "We will not *h.*"

HEARKENED (3)

Dt 26:14 I have thus *h* to the voice of the LORD,
Ps(s) 66:19 he has *h* to the sound of my prayer.
Mi 5:14 and wrath upon the nations that have not *h.*

HEARKENS (2)

Wis 1:10 Because a jealous ear *h* to everything,
Sir 4:15 who *h* to her dwells in her inmost chambers.

HEARS (53)

Nm 24: 4 The utterance of one who *h* what God says,
24:16 The utterance of one who *h* what God says,
Dt 33: 7 "The LORD *h* the cry of Judah;
1Sm 3:11 the ears of everyone who *h* it to ring.
2Sm 16:21 When all Israel *h* how odious you have made
17: 9 the first attack, whoever *h* of it will say,
2Kgs 19: 7 a spirit that, when he *h* a certain report,
21:12 and Judah that, whenever anyone *h* of it,
Jb 34:34 say to me, every wise man who *h* my views:
39: 7 of the city, and *h* no shouts of a driver.
Ps(s) 34:18 When the just cry out, the LORD *h* them,
38:15 neither *h* nor has in his mouth a retort.
69:34 For the LORD *h* the poor,
97: 8 Zion *h* and is glad,
145:19 fear him, he *h* their cry and saves them.
Prv 15:29 wicked, but the prayer of the just he *h.*
18:13 He who answers before he *h*—
20:12 The ear that *h,*
29:24 he *h* himself put under a curse,
Sir 19: 8 For he who *h* it will hold it against you,
19:10 When a fool *h* something,
21:15 When an intelligent man *h* words of wisdom,
21:15 the wanton *h* them with scorn and casts
35:13 weak, yet he *h* the cry of the oppressed.
Is 30:19 out, as soon as he *h* he will answer you.
37: 7 a spirit that, when he *h* a certain report,
Jer 36: 3 when the house of Judah *h* all the evil I
50:43 The king of Babylon *h* news of them,
Zep 3: 2 She *h* no voice, accepts no correction;
Mt 7:24 "Anyone who *h* my words and puts them into
7:26 Anyone who *h* my words but does not put
13: 9 Let everyone heed what he *h!*"
13:19 The seed along the path is the man who *h*
13:20 man who *h* the message and at first receives
13:22 among briers is the man who *h* the message,
13:23 the man who *h* the message and takes it in.
13:43 Let everyone heed what he *h!*
Mk 7:16 Let everyone heed what he *h!*"
Lk 10:16 "He who *h* you, hears me.
14:35 Let him who *h* this, heed it."
Jn 5:24 the man who *h* my word and has faith in him
8:47 Whoever is of God *h* every word God speaks.
12:47 anyone *h* my words and does not keep them,
16:13 on his own, but will speak only what he *h,*
18:37 Anyone committed to the truth *h* my voice."
Acts 2: 8 each of us *h* them in his native tongue?
2:11 Yet each of us *h* them speaking in his own
2Cor 12: 7 than what he sees in me or *h* from my lips.
1Jn 5:14 that he *h* us whenever we ask for anything
5:15 since we know that he *h* us whenever we ask,
Rv 3:20 If anyone *h* me calling and opens the door,
22:17 Let him who *h* answer, "Come!"

HEARSAY (1)

Is 11: 3 shall he judge, nor by *h* shall he decide,

HEART (572)

Gn 6: 5 his *h* conceived was ever anything but evil,
6: 6 man on the earth, and his *h* was grieved.
8:21 desires of man's *h* are evil from the start;
34: 8 son Shechem has his *h* set on your daughter.
42:21 anguish of his *h* when he pleaded with us,
Ex 4:15 When he sees you, his *h* will be glad.
9:21 did not take the warning of the LORD to *h*
25: 2 that his *h* prompts him to give.
28:29 *h* as a constant reminder before the LORD.
28:30 that they may be over Aaron's *h* whenever
28:30 over his *h* in the LORD's presence.
35: 5 Everyone, as his *h* prompts him,
35:21 as his *h* suggested and his spirit prompted,
35:22 the women, all as their *h* prompted them,
Lv 19:17 not bear hatred for your brother in your *h.*
Dt 1:21 Do not fear or lose *h.*'
2:30 in *h* that he might deliver him up to you,
4:29 him with your whole *h* and your whole soul.
4:39 why you must now know, and fix in your *h,*
6: 5 love the LORD, our God, with all your *h,*
6: 6 *h* these words which I enjoin on you today.
7: 7 the LORD set his *h* on you and chose you,
8:14 haughty of *h* and unmindful of the LORD,
9: 5 your merits or the integrity of your *h*
10:12 God, with all your *h* and all your soul,
11:13 God, with all your *h* and all your soul,
11:16 But be careful lest your *h* be so lured

11:18 these words of mine into your *h* and soul.
13: 4 him with all your *h* and with all your soul.
15: 7 *h* nor close your hand to him in his need.
17:17 number of wives, lest his *h* be estranged,
18: 6 resides, to visit, as his *h* may desire,
26:16 with all your *h* and with all your soul.
28:65 *h* and wasted eyes and a dismayed spirit.
28:67 for dread that your *h* must feel and the
29:18 safely persist in his stubbornness of *h*,
30: 1 dispersed you, you ponder them in your *h*:
30: 2 voice with all your *h* and all your soul,
30: 6 God, with all your *h* and all your soul,
30:10 God, with all your *h* and all your soul.
32:46 "Take to *h* all the warning which I have
Jos 22: 5 and serve him with your whole *h* and soul."
23:14 So now acknowledge with your whole *h* and
Jgs 5: 9 My *h* is with the leaders of Israel,
5:15 of Reuben great were the searchings of *h*.
5:16 of Reuben great were the searchings of *h*!
16:18 this time, for he has opened his *h* to me."
1Sm 2: 1 "My *h* exults in the LORD,
2:35 who shall do what I have in *h* and mind.
4:13 he was troubled at *h* about the ark of God.
7: 3 with your whole *h* to return to the LORD,
10: 9 to leave Samuel, God gave him another *h*.
12:20 but must worship him with your whole *h*.
12:24 worship him faithfully with your whole *h*;
13:14 LORD has sought out a man after his own *h*
16: 7 appearance but the LORD looks into the *h*."
28: 5 he was dismayed and lost *h* completely.
2Sm 6:16 the LORD, and she despised him in her *h*.
7:21 servant's sake and as you have had at *h*,
13:20 Do not take this affair to *h*."
17:10 man with the *h* of a lion will lose courage.
18:14 in hand, he thrust for the *h* of Absalom,
19:20 may he not remember and take to *h*
1Kgs 2: 4 their whole *h* and with their whole soul,
2:44 *h* the evil that you did to my father David.
3: 6 toward you, with justice and an upright *h*;
3: 9 an understanding *h* to judge your people
3:12 I give you a *h* so wise and understanding
8:23 who are faithful to you with their whole *h*.
8:48 if with their whole *h* and soul they turn
9: 3 and my eyes and my *h* shall be there always.
10:24 him the wisdom which God had put in his *h*.
11: 3 concubines, and his wives turned his *h*.
11: 4 his wives had turned his *h* to strange gods,
11: 4 and his *h* was not entirely with the LORD,
11: 4 God, as the *h* of his father David had been.
11: 9 his *h* was turned away from the LORD,
14: 8 and followed me with his whole *h*,
15: 3 and his *h* was not entirely with the LORD,
15: 3 God, like the *h* of his grandfather David.
15:14 yet Asa's *h* was entirely with the LORD as
2Kgs 9:24 his *h* and he collapsed in his chariot.
23:25 to the LORD as he did, with his whole *h*,
1Chr 15:29 and dancing, she despised him in her *h*.
22:13 do not fear or lose *h*.
28: 9 him with a perfect *h* and a willing soul,
29:17 With a sincere *h* I have willingly given
2Chr 6:30 Knowing his *h*, render to everyone
6:38 and with their whole *h* and with their
7:10 rejoicing and glad at *h* at the good things
7:16 eyes and my *h* also shall be there always.
9:23 him the wisdom which God had put in his *h*.
15:12 their fathers, with all their *h* and soul;
15:15 *h* and sought him with complete desire,
15:17 Asa's *h* was undivided as long as he lived.
20:15 lose *h* at the sight of this vast multitude,
20:17 Do not fear or lose *h*.
22: 9 who sought the LORD with his whole *h*."
32:31 that he might know all that was in his *h*.
34:31 and statutes with his whole *h* and soul,
36:13 his *h* rather than return to the LORD,
Ezr 7:10 Ezra had set his *h* on the study and
Neh 2: 2 If you are not sick, you must be sad at *h*."
9: 8 had found his *h* faithful in your sight,
Tb 4:19 and never let them be erased from your *h*.
6: 5 the fish open and take out its gall, *h*,
6: 5 Its gall, *h*, and liver make useful medicines."
6: 6 open, he put aside the gall, *h* and liver.
6: 7 medicinal value is there in the fish's *h*,
6: 8 "As regards the fish's *h* and liver,
6:17 chamber, take the fish's liver and *h*,
6:18 love with her, and his *h* became set on her.
8: 2 and *h* from the bag which he had with him,
13: 6 When you turn back to him with all your *h*,
Jdt 8:14 *h* or grasp the workings of the human mind;
8:29 to the worthy dispositions of your *h*.
10:16 stand before him, have no fear in your *h*;
11: 1 have no fear in your *h*!
12:16 *h* of Holofernes was in rapture over her,
Est C:24 and turn his *h* to hatred for our enemy,
D: 5 lovely, though her *h* was shrunk with fear.
D:13 *h* was troubled with fear of your majesty.
1Mc 1: 3 him, and his *h* became proud and arrogant.
2:24 *h* was moved and his just fury was aroused;
6:10 my eyes, for my *h* is sinking with anxiety.
2Mc 1: 3 May he give to all of you a *h* to worship
1: 4 May he open your *h* to his law and his
3:16 of the high priest was pierced to the *h*,
3:17 who saw him the pain that lodged in his *h*.
7:21 stirred her womanly *h* with manly courage,
Jb 9: 4 God is wise in *h* and mighty in strength;
10:13 Yet these things you have hidden in your *h*;
11:13 If you set your *h* aright and stretch out
17:11 at an end, the cherished purposes of my *h*.
22:22 his mouth, and lay up his words in your *h*.
23:12 of his mouth I have treasured in my *h*.
27: 6 *h* does not reproach me for any of my days.
29:13 me, and the *h* of the widow I made joyful.
31: 7 of the way, and my *h* has followed my eyes,
31: 9 If my *h* has been enticed toward a woman,
31:27 And had my *h* been secretly enticed to waft
36: 5 Behold, God rejects the obstinate in *h*;
36:13 impious in *h* lay up anger for themselves;
37: 1 my *h* trembles and leaps out of its place.
38:36 Who puts wisdom in the *h*,
41:15 His *h* is hard as stone;
Ps(s) 4: 3 of rank, how long will you be dull of *h*?
4: 8 You put gladness into my *h*,
5:10 their *h* teems with treacheries.
7:10 sustain the just, O searcher of *h* and soul,
7:11 me is God, who saves the upright of *h*;
9: 2 give thanks to you, O LORD, with all my *h*;
10: 6 He says in his *h*, "I shall not be disturbed;
10:11 He says in his *h*, "God has forgotten;
10:13 wicked man despise God, saying in his *h*,
11: 2 to shoot in the dark at the upright of *h*.
12: 3 with smooth lips they speak, and double *h*.
13: 3 in my soul, grief in my *h* day after day?
13: 6 Let my *h* rejoice in your salvation;
14: 1 The fool says in his *h*, "There is no God."
15: 2 in his *h* and slanders not with his tongue;
16: 7 even in the night my *h* exhorts me.
16: 9 my *h* is glad and my soul rejoices,
17: 3 Though you test my *h*,
19: 9 of the LORD are right, rejoicing the *h*;
19:15 the thought of my *h* find favor before you,
20: 5 is in your *h* and fulfill your every plan.
22:15 My *h* has become like wax melting away
24: 4 whose hands are sinless, whose *h* is clean.
25:17 and afflicted Relieve the troubles of my *h*,
26: 2 test my soul and my *h*.
27: 3 army encamp against me, my *h* will not fear;
27: 8 Of you my *h* speaks; you my glance seeks;
28: 7 In him my *h* trusts, and I find help;
28: 7 then my *h* exults,
32:11 exult, all you upright of *h*.
33:11 design of his *h*, through all generations
33:15 the earth, He who fashioned the *h* of each,
36: 2 Sin speaks to the wicked man in his *h*;
36:11 your just defense of the upright of *h*.
37:31 The law of his God is in his *h*,
38: 9 I roar with anguish of *h*.
38:11 My *h* throbs; my strength forsakes me;
39: 4 hot grew my *h* within me;
40: 9 my delight, and your law is within my *h*!"
40:11 Your justice I kept not hid within my *h*;
40:13 the hairs of my head, and my *h* fails me.
41: 7 his *h* stores up malice;
44:22 For he knows the secrets of the *h*.
45: 2 My *h* overflows with a goodly theme;
45: 6 the king's enemies lose *h*.
49: 4 prudence shall be the utterance of my *h*.
51: 8 you are pleased with sincerity of *h*,
51:12 A clean *h* create for me,
51:19 a *h* contrite and humbled,
53: 2 The fool says in his *h*, "There is no God
55: 5 My *h* quakes within me;
55:22 butter is his speech, but war is in his *h*;
57: 8 My *h* is steadfast; O God; my heart
61: 3 end I call to you as my *h* grows faint.
62:11 wealth abound, set not your *h* upon it.
64: 7 deep are the thoughts of each *h*.
64:11 in him glory all the upright of *h*.
66:18 Were I to cherish wickedness in my *h*,
69:21 Insult has broken my *h*,
73: 1 the LORD, to those who are clean of *h*!
73:13 Is it but in vain I have kept my *h* clean
73:21 *h* was embittered and my soul was pierced,
73:26 Though my flesh and my *h* waste away,
73:26 is the rock of my *h* and my portion forever.
77: 7 In the night I meditate in my *h*;
78: 8 A generation that kept not its *h* steadfast
78:72 And he tended them with a sincere *h*,
84: 3 *h* and my flesh cry out for the living God.
86:11 direct my *h* that it may fear your name.
86:12 to you, O LORD my God, with all my *h*,
90:12 days aright, that we may gain wisdom of *h*.
94:15 and all the upright of *h* shall follow it.
95:10 They are a people of erring *h*,
97:11 and gladness, for the upright of *h*.
101: 2 I will walk in the integrity of my *h*,
101: 4 A crooked *h* shall be far from me;
101: 5 eyes and puffed-up *h* I will not endure.
102: 5 Withered and dried up like grass is my *h*;
108: 2 My *h* is steadfast, O God; my heart
109:22 and poor, and my *h* is pierced within me.
111: 1 *h* in the company and assembly of the just.
112: 7 his *h* is firm,
112: 8 His *h* is steadfast;
119: 2 decrees, who seek him with all their *h*,
119: 7 I will give you thanks with an upright *h*,
119:10 With all my *h* I seek you;
119:11 Within my *h* I treasure your promise,
119:32 your commands when you give me a docile *h*.
119:34 observe your law and keep it with all my *h*.
119:36 my *h* to your decrees and not to gain.
119:58 I entreat you with all my *h*,
119:69 with all my *h* I will observe your precepts.
119:70 Their *h* has become gross and fat;
119:80 Let my *h* be perfect in your statutes,
119:111 the joy of my *h* they are.
119:112 in my *h* to fulfill your statutes always,
119:113 I hate men of divided *h*, but I love your law
119:145 I call out with all my *h*; answer me
119:161 cause but my *h* stands in awe of your word.
125: 4 LORD, to the good and to the upright of *h*.
131: 1 O LORD, my *h* is not proud,
138: 1 give thanks to you, O LORD, with all my *h*,
139:23 Probe me, O God, and know my *h*;
141: 4 Let not my *h* incline to the evil of
143: 4 within me, my *h* within me is appalled.
Prv 2: 2 wisdom, inclining your *h* to understanding;
2:10 For wisdom will enter your *h*,
3: 5 Trust in the LORD with all your *h*,
4: 4 "Let your *h* hold fast my words:
4:21 of your sight, keep them within your *h*;
4:23 With closest custody, guard your *h*,
5:12 I hate instruction, and my *h* spurn reproof!
6:14 He has perversity in his *h*,
6:18 A *h* that plots wicked schemes,
6:21 Keep them fastened over your *h* always,
6:25 Lust not in your *h* after her beauty,
7: 3 write them on the tablet of your *h*.
7:25 Let not your *h* turn to her ways,
10:20 the *h* of the wicked is of little worth.
11:20 in *h* are an abomination to the LORD,
12:10 but the *h* of the wicked is merciless.
12:25 Anxiety in a man's *h* depresses it,
13:12 Hope deferred makes the *h* sick,
14:10 The *h* knows its own bitterness,
14:13 Even in laughter the *h* may be sad,
14:33 In the *h* of the intelligent wisdom abides,
15: 7 knowledge, but the *h* of fools is perverted.
15:13 A glad *h* lights up the face,
15:30 A cheerful glance brings joy to the *h*;
16: 1 Man may make plans in his *h*,
17:20 He who is perverse in *h* finds no good,
17:22 A joyful *h* is the health of the body,
18:12 Before his downfall a man's *h* is haughty,
19: 3 but his *h* is resentful against the LORD.
19:21 Many are the plans in a man's *h*,
20: 5 *h* is like water far below the surface,
20: 9 Who can say, "I have made my *h* clean,
21: 1 is the king's *h* in the hand of the LORD;
21: 4 Haughty eyes and a proud *h*—
22:11 The LORD loves the pure of *h*;
22:15 Folly is close to the *h* of a child,
22:17 my words, and apply your *h* to my doctrine;
23: 7 says to you, though his *h* is not with you;
23:12 Apply your *h* to instruction,
23:15 My son, if your *h* be wise,
23:15 heart be wise, my own *h* also will rejoice;
23:17 Let not your *h* emulate sinners,
23:19 be wise, and guide your *h* in the right way.
23:26 My son, give me your *h*,
23:33 and your *h* utters disordered thoughts;
24:17 and when he stumbles, let not your *h* exult,
25: 3 in depth, the *h* of kings is unfathomable.
25:20 in wood, sorrow gnaws at the human *h*.
26:23 are smooth lips with a wicked *h*.
26:25 not, for seven abominations are in his *h*.
27: 9 Perfume and incense gladden the *h*,
27:11 are wise, my son, you will gladden my *h*,
27:19 another, so does one human *h* from another.
28:14 he who hardens his *h* will fall into evil.
31:11 Her husband, entrusting his *h* to her,
Eccl 2:10 my *h* rejoiced in the fruit of all my toil.
2:15 concluded in my *h* that this too is vanity.
2:22 *h* with which he has labored under the sun?
5: 1 let not your *h* be quick to make a promise
5:19 him busy himself with the joy of his *h*.
7: 2 man, and the living should take it to *h*.
7: 3 when the face is sad the *h* grows wiser.
7: 4 *h* of the wise is in the house of mourning,
7: 4 the *h* of fools is in the house of mirth.
7: 7 of a wise man, and a bribe corrupts the *h*.
7:22 for you know in your *h* that you have many
7:26 whose *h* is a snare and whose hands are
8: 5 the wise man's *h* knows times and judgments;
8:16 When I applied my *h* to know wisdom and to
9: 7 joy and drink your wine with a merry *h*,
11: 9 your *h* be glad in the days of your youth.
11: 9 Follow the ways of your *h*,
11:10 *h* and put away trouble from your presence,
Sg 1: 7 Tell me, you whom my *h* loves,
3: 1 bed at night I sought him whom my *h* loves
3: 2 crossings I will seek Him whom my *h* loves.
3: 3 Have you seen him whom my *h* loves?
3: 4 them when I found him whom my *h* loves.
3:11 marriage, on the day of the joy of his *h*.
4: 9 You have ravished my *h*,
4: 9 ravished my *h* with one glance of your eyes,
5: 2 I was sleeping, but my *h* kept vigil;
5: 4 my *h* trembled within me.
6:12 my *h* had made me the blessed one of my
8: 6 Set me as a seal on your *h*,

HEART (cont.)

Wis 1: 1 goodness, and seek him in integrity of *h*;
1: 6 of his *h* and the listener to his tongue.
8:17 and reflecting in my *h* That there is
8:21 and besought him, and said with all my *h*:
9: 3 and to render judgment in integrity of *h*:
15:10 Ashes his *h* is!
Sir 1:10 Fear of the LORD warms the *h*,
1:25 LORD, nor approach it with duplicity of *h*.
1:29 fear of the LORD with your *h* full of guile.
2: 2 Be sincere of *h* and steadfast,
2:13 Woe to the faint of *h* who trust not,
4:17 the proof, until his *h* is fully with her.
5: 2 in following the desires of your *h*.
7:27 With your whole *h* honor your father;
8:19 Open your *h* to no man,
9: 9 Lest your *h* be drawn to her and you go
10:12 withdrawing his *h* from his Maker;
12:16 *h* he schemes to plunge you into the abyss.
13:24 The *h* of a man changes his countenance,
13:25 sign of a good *h* is a cheerful countenance;
14:21 Who ponders her ways in his *h*,
17: 5 and imparts to them an understanding *h*.
21: 6 but he who fears the LORD repents in his *h*.
22:19 he who pierces the *h* bares its feelings.
23: 2 be spared, nor the sins of my *h* overlooked;
23: 5 ward off passion from my *h*,
25:12 Worst of all wounds is that of the *h*,
25:22 Depressed mind, saddened face, broken *h*—
26: 4 Be he rich or poor, his *h* is content,
26: 5 are three things at which my *h* quakes,
26:19 These two bring grief to my *h*,
30:16 no happiness, than a joyful *h*!
30:22 Gladness of *h* is the very life of man,
31:28 Joy of *h*, good cheer and merriment
34: 6 by the Most High, fix not your *h* on it;
38:10 hands be just, cleanse your *h* of every sin;
39: 2 men, and goes to the *h* of involved sayings;
39:26 fire, iron and salt, The *h* of the wheat,
39:35 So now with full joy of *h* proclaim and
40: 2 living, His thoughts, the fear in his *h*,
42:18 He plumbs the depths and penetrates the *h*;
45:23 And, at the prompting of his noble *h*,
45:26 of *h* to govern his people in justice,
49: 3 He turned to God with his whole *h*,
50:23 you joy of *h* and may peace abide among you;
50:28 things, wise the man who takes them to *h*!
Is 1: 5 The whole head is sick, the whole *h* faint.
6:10 are to make the *h* of this people sluggish,
6:10 see, their ears hear, their *h* understand,
7: 2 the *h* of the king and heart of the people
9: 8 those who say in arrogance and pride of *h*,
10: 7 Rather, it is in his *h* to destroy,
10:12 of the king of Assyria's proud *h*,
13: 7 Every man's *h* melts in terror;
14:13 You said in your *h*:
15: 5 The *h* of Moab cries out,
16:11 like a lyre, and my *h* for Kir-hareseth.
30:29 a feast is observed, And be merry of *h*,
32: 6 speaks foolishly, planning evil in his *h*:
42:25 it burned them, but they took it not to *h*.
47: 7 But you did not lay these things to *h*,
51: 7 you people who have my teaching at *h*:
57: 1 man perishes, but no one takes it to *h*;
59:13 words of falsehood the *h* has conceived.
60: 5 you see, your *h* shall throb and overflow,
63: 4 For the day of vengeance was in my *h*,
65:14 My servants shall shout for joy of *h*,
65:14 grief of *h* and howl for anguish of spirit.
66:14 your *h* shall rejoice and your bodies
Jer 3:15 appoint over you shepherds after my own *h*,
4: 9 day, says the LORD, The king will lose *h*,
4:14 Cleanse your *h* of evil,
4:18 of yours, how it reaches to your very *h*!
4:19 The walls of my *h*!
4:19 My *h* beats wildly, I cannot be still;
5:23 this people's *h* is stubborn and rebellious;
8:18 is incurable, my *h* within me is faint.
9: 7 friends, but in his *h* he lays an ambush!
9:25 house of Israel, are uncircumcised in *h*.
11: 8 one followed the hardness of his evil *h*,
11:20 O just Judge, searcher of mind and *h*,
12: 3 me, you have found that at *h* I am with you.
12:11 all the land, because no one takes it to *h*.
13:22 ask in your *h* why these things befall you:
15: 1 me, my *h* would not turn toward this people.
15:16 became my joy and the happiness of my *h*,
16:12 of his evil *h* instead of listening to me.
17: 5 in flesh, whose *h* turns away from the LORD.
17: 9 More tortuous than all else is the human *h*,
17:10 LORD, alone probe the mind and test the *h*,
18:12 to the stubbornness of his evil *h*!"
20: 9 then it becomes like fire burning in my *h*,
20:12 who test the just, who probe mind and *h*,
22:17 But your eyes and *h* are set on nothing
23: 2 My *h* within me is broken,
23:17 to everyone who walks in hardness of *h*,
23:20 fulfilled what he has determined in his *h*.
24: 7 I will give them a *h* with which to
24: 7 they shall return to me with their whole *h*.
29:13 Yes, when you seek me with all your *h*,
30:24 fulfilled what he has determined in his *h*.
31:20 My *h* stirs for him,
32:39 One *h* and one way I will give them,
32:41 in this land, with all my *h* and soul.
48:29 his pride, his scorn, his insolence of *h*.
48:36 the wail of flutes for Moab is in my *h*;
48:36 of Kir-heres the wail of flutes is in my *h*;
48:41 are like the *h* of a woman in travail.
49:16 beguiled you, and your presumption of *h*;
49:22 shall be like the *h* of a woman in travail.
Lam 1:20 My *h* recoils within me from my monstrous
1:22 My groans are many, and I am sick at *h*."
2:19 *h* like water in the presence of the Lord;
3:65 Give them hardness of *h*,
Bar 2: 8 turn, each from the figments of his evil *h*.
2:30 captivity they shall have a change of *h*;
Ez 2: 4 of *h* are they to whom I am sending you.
3: 7 is stubborn of brow and obstinate in *h*.
3:10 your *h* all my words that I speak to you;
11:19 a new *h* and put a new spirit within them;
11:19 will remove the stony *h* from their bodies,
11:19 bodies, and replace it with a natural *h*,
14: 4 holding the memory of his idols in his *h*
14: 7 holds the memory of his idols in his *h*
18:31 for yourselves a new *h* and a new spirit.
21:12 when it comes every *h* shall fail,
21:20 all around, That every *h* may tremble;
22:14 Can your *h* remain firm,
25: 6 in your *h* over the land of Israel,
27:25 full and heavily laden in the *h* of the sea.
27:26 east wind smashed you in the *h* of the sea.
27:27 *h* of the sea on the day of your shipwreck.
28: 2 Because you are haughty of *h*,
28: 2 a godly throne in the *h* of the sea!—"
28: 5 your *h* has grown haughty from your riches
28: 8 die a bloodied corpse, in the *h* of the sea.
28:17 became haughty of *h* because of your beauty;
31:10 because it became proud in *h* at its height,
36:26 a new *h* and place a new spirit within you,
44: 7 uncircumcised both in *h* and flesh,
44: 9 uncircumcised in *h* and in flesh,
Dn 3:39 *h* and humble spirit let us be received;
3:41 And now we follow you with our whole *h*,
3:87 Holy men of humble *h*,
5:20 But when his *h* became proud and his spirit
5:22 son, Belshazzar, have not humbled your *h*,
8:25 be proud of *h* and destroy many by stealth.
11:12 In the pride of his *h*,
11:30 confront him, he shall lose *h* and retreat.
Hos 2:16 her into the desert and speak to her *h*.
10: 2 Their *h* is false,
11: 8 My *h* is overwhelmed, my pity is stirred.
13: 6 they became proud of *h* and forgot me.
Jl 2:12 the LORD, return to me with your whole *h*,
Ob 1: 3 The pride of your *h* has deceived you;
1: 3 abode is in the heights, Who say in your *h*,
Jon 2: 4 me into the deep, into the *h* of the sea,
Zep 3:14 Be glad and exult with all your *h*,
Zec 8:17 of you plot evil against another in his *h*,
Mal 2: 2 And if you do not lay it to *h*,
2: 2 cursed it, because you do not lay it to *h*.
Mt 6:21 your treasure is, there your *h* is also.
9:36 of the crowds, his *h* was moved with pity.
11:29 from me, for I am gentle and humble of *h*.
13:15 Sluggish indeed is this people's *h*.
14:14 the vast throng, his *h* was moved with pity,
15: 8 me lip service but their *h* is far from me.
15:32 "My *h* is moved with pity for the crowd.
18:35 of you forgives his brother from his *h*."
22:37 love the Lord your God with your whole *h*,
26:38 them, "My *h* is nearly broken with sorrow.
Mk 4:20 ones who listen to the word, take it to *h*,
7: 6 me lip service but their *h* is far from me.
7:21 come from the deep recesses of the *h*;
8: 2 "My *h* is moved with pity for the crowd.
9:22 of your *h* you can do anything to help us,
12:30 love the Lord your God with all your *h*,
12:33 Yes, 'to love him with all our *h*,
14:34 "My *h* is filled with sorrow to the point
Lk 2:19 things and reflected on them in her *h*.
5:32 invite the self-righteous to a change of *h*,
6:45 produces goodness from the good in his *h*;
10:27 love the Lord your god with all your *h*,
12:34 your treasure lies, there your *h* will be.
18: 1 of praying always and not losing *h*:
21:21 those in the *h* of the city must escape it;
Jn 2:25 He was well aware of what was in man's *h*.
7:18 there is no dishonesty in his *h*.
12:40 see or comprehend, or have a change of *h*—
13:27 Immediately after, Satan entered his *h*.
Acts 2:26 *h* has been glad and my tongue has rejoiced,
4:32 of believers were of one *h* and one mind.
5: 3 why have you let Satan fill your *h*
7:51 people, uncircumcised in *h* and ears,
7:54 to his words were stung to the *h*;
8:21 Your *h* is not steadfastly set on God.
13:22 my own *h* who will fulfill my every wish.'
16:14 her *h* to accept what Paul was saying.
20:33 Never did I set my *h* on anyone's silver or
21:13 you crying and breaking my *h* in this way?
26:20 act in conformity with their change of *h*.
Rom 2: 5 your hard and impenitent *h* is storing up
2:29 and true circumcision is of the *h*;
9: 2 is great grief and constant pain in my *h*.
10: 6 from faith he says, "Do not say in your *h*,
10: 8 you, on your lips and in your *h*" (that is,
10: 9 your *h* that God raised him from the dead,
10:10 Faith in the *h* leads to justification,
15: 6 with one *h* and voice you may glorify God,
1Cor 14:25 and the secret of his *h* will be laid bare.
2Cor 2: 3 saddened by those who should rejoice my *h*.
3: 3 of stone but on tablets of flesh in the *h*.
4:16 We do not lose *h*,
5:12 appearances, and not in what lies in the *h*.
7: 6 who gives *h* to those who are low in spirit,
7:15 His *h* embraces you with an expanding love
8:16 an equal zeal for you in the *h* of Titus!
Eph 6: 6 will with your whole *h* as slaves of Christ.
Col 3: 1 set your *h* on what pertains to higher
3:21 do not nag your children lest they lose *h*.
1Tm 1: 5 is the love that springs from a pure *h*,
2Tm 1:16 me new *h* and has not been ashamed of me,
2:22 those who call on the Lord in purity of *h*.
Phlm 1:12 and that means I am sending my *h*!
1:20 Refresh this *h* of mine in Christ.
Heb 3:10 I said, 'They have always been of erring *h*,
4:12 the reflections and thoughts of the *h*.
12: 5 the Lord nor lose *h* when he reproves you;
1Pt 1:22 love one another constantly from the *h*.
3: 4 is rather the hidden character of the *h*,
1Jn 3:15 that eternal life abides in no murder's *h*.
3:17 *h* to his brother when he sees him in need.
5:10 God possesses that testimony within his *h*.

HEARTACHE (2)

Sir 26: 6 A jealous wife is *h* and mourning and a
38:19 on an extremity and *h* destroy one's health.

HEARTFELT (1)

Col 3:12 beloved, clothe yourselves with *h* mercy,

HEARTH (8)

Lv 6: 2 The holocaust is to remain on the *h* of the
1Kgs 19: 6 his head was a *h* cake and a jug of water.
Jb 18: 5 no flame brightens his *h*.
Is 30:14 from the *h* or dip water from the cistern.
Ez 43:15 the *h* of the altar was four cubits high,
43:15 of the *h* were the four horns of the altar.
43:16 The *h* was a square:
Hos 7: 8 the nations, Ephraim is a *h* cake unturned.

HEARTHS (2)

Jgs 5:16 *h* listening to the lowing of the herds?
Ez 46:23 and *h* were built beneath the stones all

HEARTILY (3)

Is 61:10 I rejoice *h* in the LORD,
Zec 9: 9 Rejoice *h*, O daughter Zion, shout for joy,
Lk 12:19 Eat *h*, drink well.

HEARTS (207)

Gn 42:28 At that their *h* sank.
Ex 36: 2 men whose *h* moved them to come and take
Lv 26:41 when their uncircumcised *h* are humbled and
Nm 15:39 after the desires of your *h* and eyes.
Dt 10:16 Circumcise your *h*,
12:15 to your *h* desire as much meat as the LORD,
12:20 you may eat it at will, to your *h* desire;
12:21 it to your *h* desire in your own community.
29:17 would now turn away their *h* from the LORD,
30: 6 your *h* and the hearts of your descendants,
30: 6 your hearts and the *h* of your descendants,
30:14 you, already in your mouths and in your *h*;
30:17 you turn away your *h* and will not listen,
Jos 24:23 are among you and turn your *h* to the LORD,
Ru 3: 7 Boaz ate and drank to his *h* content.
1Sm 10:26 by warriors whose *h* the LORD had touched.
1Kgs 8:39 You who alone know the *h* of all men,
8:39 according to his conduct; knowing their *h*,
8:58 May he draw our *h* to himself,
11: 2 "they will turn your *h* to their gods."
12:27 the *h* of this people will return to their
2Kgs 23: 3 and decrees with their whole *h* and souls,
1Chr 16:10 rejoice, O *h* that seek the LORD!
22:19 *h* and souls to seeking the LORD your God.
28: 9 *h* and understands all the mind's thoughts.
29:17 that you put *h* to the test and that you
29:18 in the *h* and minds of your people forever,
29:18 forever, and direct their *h* toward you.
2Chr 6:30 conduct, for you alone know the *h* of men.
20:33 fixed their *h* on the God of their fathers.
Jdt 8:27 put them in the crucible to try their *h*,
1Mc 1:62 in their *h* not to eat anything unclean;
12:28 battle, their *h* sank with fear and dread.
2Mc 2: 3 not to let the law depart from their *h*.
11: 9 and their *h* were filled with such courage
15:17 instill valor and stir young *h* to courage,
15:27 hands and praying to God with their *h*,
Jb 1: 5 have sinned and blasphemed God in their *h*."
31:39 payment and grieved the *h* of its tenants;
37:24 none can see him, however wise their *h*.
Ps(s) 10:17 strengthening their *h*,
17:10 they shut up their cruel *h*,
21: 3 You have granted him his *h* desire;

22:27 “May your *h* be ever merry!”
28: 3 their neighbors though evil is in their *h*.
33:21 and our shield, For in him our *h* rejoice;
35:25 Let them not say in their *h*, “Aha!
37: 4 and he will grant you your *h* requests.
37:15 But their swords shall pierce their own *h*,
44:19 Our *h* have not shrunk back,
62: 9 Pour out your *h* before him;
69:33 you who seek God, may your *h* be merry!
73: 7 their fancies overflow their *h*.
74: 8 They said in their *h*, “Let us destroy them;
78:18 their *h* by demanding the food they craved.
78:37 their *h* were not steadfast toward him,
81:13 I gave them up to the hardness of their *h*;
84: 6 their *h* are set upon the pilgrimage:
95: 8 “Harden not your *h* as at Meribah,
104:15 the earth, and wine to gladden men’s *h*,
104:15 oil, and bread fortifies the *h* of men.
105: 3 rejoice, O *h* that seek the LORD!
105:25 Whose *h* he changed, so that they hated
107:12 And he humbled their *h* with trouble;
107:26 their *h* melted away in their plight.
140: 3 men, From those who devise evil in their *h*,
Prv 12:23 but the *h* of fools gush forth folly.
15:11 how much more the *h* of men!
17: 3 for gold, but the tester of *h* is the LORD.
21: 2 own eyes, but it is the LORD who proves *h*.
24: 2 For their *h* plot violence,
24:12 does not he who tests *h* perceive it?
Eccl 3:11 and has put the timeless into their *h*,
8:11 therefore the *h* of men are filled with the
9: 3 and madness is in their *h* during life;
Wis 2: 2 reason is a spark at the beating of our *h*,
Sir 2:12 Woe to craven *h* and drooping hands,
2:17 their *h* and humble themselves before him
16:10 who perished for the impiety of their *h*.
17: 7 He looks with favor upon their *h*,
21:26 mouths, wise men’s words are in their *h*.
31:26 smith, so does wine the *h* of the insolent.
37:13 Then, too, heed your own *h* counsel;
46:11 one of them, whose *h* were not deceived,
48:10 back the *h* of fathers toward their sons,
48:19 The people’s *h* melted within them,
50:27 they gushed forth from my *h* understanding.
51:15 yielded to ripening grapes, the *h* joy,
Is 19: 1 the *h* of the Egyptians melt within them.
29:13 lips alone, though their *h* are far from me,
35: 4 weak, Say to those whose *h* are frightened:
44:18 and their *h* so that they cannot understand.
57:15 dejected, to revive the *h* of the crushed.
63:17 and harden our *h* so that we fear you not?
Jer 4: 4 remove the foreskins of your *h*,
5:24 turn and go away, And say not in their *h*,
7:24 of their evil *h* and turned their backs,
9:13 the hardness of their *h* and the Baals,
13:10 who walk in the stubbornness of their *h*,
17: 1 upon the tablets of their *h*.
23:26 Is my name in the *h* of the prophets who
31:33 within them, and write it upon their *h*;
32:40 into their *h* I will put the fear of me,
48:41 On that day the *h* of Moab’s heroes are
49:22 On that day the *h* of Edom’s heroes shall
Lam 3:41 us reach out our *h* toward God in heaven!
5:15 The joy of our *h* has ceased,
5:17 Over this our *h* are sick,
Bar 1:22 off after the devices of our own wicked *h*,
2:31 I will give them *h*, and heedful ears:
3: 7 this, you put into our *h* the fear of you:
3: 7 have removed from our *h* all the wickedness
4:28 *h* have been disposed to stray from God,
6: 5 Rather, say in your *h*, “You, O Lord,
6:19 it is said their *h* are eaten away.
Ez 6: 9 I have broken their adulterous *h* that turned
11:21 But as for those whose *h* are devoted to
14: 3 memory of their idols fresh in their *h*,
20:16 much were their *h* devoted to their idols,
24:25 of their soul, and the pride of their *h*,
25:15 with destructive malice in their *h*,
32: 9 I will grieve the *h* of many peoples when I
36:26 your stony *h* and giving you natural hearts.
Hos 7: 6 the plotters approach with *h* like ovens.
7:14 their *h* when they wailed upon their beds;
13: 8 young, and tear their *h* from their breasts;
Jl 2:13 Rend your *h*, not your garments,
Na 2:11 melting *h* and trembling knees,
Zep 1:12 thicken on their lees, Who say in their *h*,
Zec 7:10 plot evil against one another in your *h*.
7:12 And they made their *h* diamond-hard so as
10: 7 and their *h* shall be cheered as by wine.
10: 7 Their *h* shall rejoice in the LORD.
Mal 3:24 the *h* of the fathers to their children,
3:24 and the *h* of the children to their fathers,
Mt 13:15 their ears, and understand with their *h*,
Mk 9:50 Keep salt in your *h* and you will be at
Lk 1:17 to turn the *h* of fathers to their children
1:66 heard stored these things up in their *h*,
2:35 the thoughts of many *h* may be laid bare.”
3:15 their *h* whether John might be the Messiah.
6:45 Each man speaks from his *h* abundance.
8:12 of their *h* lest they believe and be saved.
16:15 in the eyes of men, but God reads your *h*.
24:32 “Were not our *h* burning inside us as he
Jn 5:38 do you have his word abiding in your *h*
5:42 you do not have the love of God in your *h*.
12:40 blinded their eyes, and numbed their *h*,
14: 1 “Do not let your *h* be troubled.
16:22 then your *h* will rejoice with a joy no one
Acts 1:24 “O Lord, you read the *h* of men.
2:46 sincere *h* they took their meals in common,
15: 8 God, who reads the *h* of men,
15: 9 purified their *h* by means of faith also.
Rom 1:21 and their senseless *h* were darkened.
2:15 demands of the law are written in their *h*.
5: 5 love of God has been poured out in our *h*
8:27 who searches *h* knows what the Spirit means,
10: 1 Brothers, my *h* desire, my prayer to God
1Cor 4: 5 darkness and manifest the intentions of *h*.
12:31 Set your *h* on the greater gifts.
14: 1 Set your *h* on spiritual gifts
14:12 you have set your *h* on spiritual gifts,
14:39 Set your *h* on prophecy,
2Cor 1:22 the first payment, the Spirit, in our *h*.
3: 2 and read by all men, written on your *h*.
4: 6 out of darkness,” has shone in our *h*,
6:11 to you frankly, opening our *h* wide to you.
6:13 father to his children), open wide your *h*!
7: 2 Make room for us in your *h*!
7: 3 I have already said that you are in our *h*,
Gal 4: 6 God has sent forth into our *h* the spirit
Eph 3:17 May Christ dwell in your *h* through faith,
5:19 Sing praise to the Lord with all your *h*.
6:22 you news about me for your *h*’ consolation.
Phil 4: 7 will stand guard over your *h* and minds,
Col 1:21 in your *h* because of your evil deeds.
2: 2 I wish their *h* to be strengthened and
3:15 Christ’s peace must reign in your *h*,
3:16 gratefully to God from your *h* in psalms,
4: 8 for this purpose, and to comfort your *h*.
1Thes 2: 4 to please God, “the tester of our *h*,”
3:13 May he strengthen your *h*,
2Thes 2:10 their *h* to the truth in order to be saved.
2:17 console your *h* and strengthen them for
3: 5 May the Lord rule your *h* in the love of
Phlm 1: 7 the *h* of God’s people have been refreshed.
Heb 3: 8 harden not your *h* as at the revolt in the
3:15 voice, harden not your *h* as at the revolt,”
4: 7 should hear his voice, harden not your *h*.”
8:10 minds and I will write them upon their *h*;
10:16 *h* and I will write them on their minds,
10:22 our *h* sprinkled clean from the evil which
13: 9 It is good to have our *h* strengthened by
Jas 2: 4 a case like this discriminated in your *h*?
3:14 jealousy and selfish ambition in your *h*,
4: 8 purify your *h*, you backsliders.
5: 8 Steady your *h*,
1Pt 3:15 the Lord, that is, Christ, in your *h*.
2Pt 1:19 and the morning star rises in your *h*.
2:14 Their *h* are trained in greed.
1Jn 2:24 heard from the beginning remain in your *h*.
2:24 from the beginning does remain in your *h*,
2:27 you received from him remains in your *h*.
3:20 greater than our *h* and all is known to him.
Rv 2:23 know that I am the searcher of *h* and minds,

HEARTSICK (2)

2Kgs 22:19 because you were *h* and have humbled
2Chr 34:27 Because you were *h* and have humbled

HEARTY (3)

Tb 5:10 Raphael said, *H* greetings to you!”
2Mc 9:19 sends *h* greetings and best wishes for
Sir 19:26 man’s attire, his *h* laughter and his gait,

HEAT (38)

Gn 8:22 As long as the earth lasts cold and *h*,
30:38 animals were in *h* as they came to drink,
30:41 whenever the hardier animals were in *h*,
31:40 often the scorching *h* ravaged me by day,
Dt 19: 6 the avenger of blood may in the *h* of his
1Sm 11:11 Ammonites until the *h* of the day;
2Sm 4: 5 house of Ishbaal during the *h* of the day,
Tb 2: 9 Because of the *h* I left my face uncovered.
Jb 6:17 in the *h*, they disappear from their place.
30:30 the *h* scorches my very frame.
Ps(s) 19: 7 nothing escapes its *h*.
32: 4 was dried up as by the *h* of summer.
Prv 25:13 Like the coolness of snow in the *h* of the
Wis 2: 4 by the sun’s rays and overpowered by its *h*.
Sir 14:27 Who takes shelter with her from the *h*,
34:16 and strong support, A shelter from the *h*,
38:28 The *h* from the fire sears his flesh,
38:28 flesh, yet he toils away in the furnace *h*.
43: 3 of the earth, and who can bear its fiery *h*?
43:22 the mountain growth is scorched with *h*,
Is 4: 6 shade from the parching *h* of day,
18: 4 Like the glowing *h* of sunshine
25: 4 Shelter from the rain, shade from the *h*.
25: 5 with the cold rain, as with the desert *h*,
57: 5 You who are in *h* among the terebinths,
66:15 *h* and his punishment with fiery flames.
Jer 17: 8 It fears not the *h* when it comes,
36:30 shall be cast out, exposed to the *h* of day,
Lam 5: 9 sustenance, in the face of the desert *h*;
Bar 2:25 to the *h* of day and the frost of night.
Ez 23:20 ass, and whose *h* is like that of stallions.
Dn 3:66 Fire and *h*, bless the Lord;
Hos 7: 5 princes are overcome with the *h* of wine.
Mt 20:12 have worked a full day in the scorching *h*.’
Acts 28: 3 a poisonous snake, escaping from the *h*,
Jas 1:11 with its scorching *h* it parches the meadow,
Rv 7:16 shall the sun or its *h* beat down on them,
16: 9 Those who were scorched by the intense *h*

HEATED (4)

2Mc 7: 3 gave orders to have pans and caldrons *h*.
7: 4 While they were being quickly *h*,
Dn 3:19 He ordered the furnace to be *h* seven times
Hos 7: 7 They are all *h* like ovens,

HEATHEN (4)

2Chr 14: 2 removing the *h* altars and the high places,
Est C:21 of the *h* to acclaim their false gods,
Sir 36: 2 Raise your hand against the *h*,
Mt 4:15 along the sea beyond the Jordan, *h* Galilee:

HEATHENS (1)

Tb 1:10 brothers and relatives ate the food of *h*,

HEAVEN (386)

Gn 6: 2 the sons of *h* saw how beautiful the
6: 4 after the sons of *h* had intercourse with
14:19 God Most High, the creator of *h* and earth;
14:22 God Most High, the creator of *h* and earth,
19:24 and Gomorrah [from the LORD out of *h*.
21:17 and God’s messenger called to Hagar from *h*:
22:11 the LORD’s messenger called to him from *h*,
22:15 called to Abraham from *h* and said:
24: 3 LORD, the God of *h* and the God of earth,
24: 7 “The LORD, the God of *h*,
28:17 abode of God, and that is the gateway to *h*!”
Ex 16: 4 will now rain down bread from *h* for you.
20:22 that I have spoken to you from *h*.
Dt 3:24 For what god in *h* or on earth can perform
4:19 the lot of all other nations under the *h*;
4:26 I call *h* and earth this day to witness
26:15 Look down, then, from *h*,
30:19 *h* and earth today to witness against you:
31:28 call *h* and earth to witness against them.
Jos 2:11 God, is God in *h* above and on earth below.
1Sm 2:10 The Most High in *h* thunders;
20: 2 *H* forbid that you should die!
2Sm 18: 9 He hung between *h* and earth while the mule
22:14 “The LORD thundered from *h*;
1Kgs 8:22 and stretching forth his hands toward *h*.
8:23 God like you in *h* above or on earth below;
8:32 your altar in this temple, listen in *h*;
8:34 listen in *h* and forgive the sin of your
8:36 listen in *h* and forgive the sin of your
8:45 listen in *h* to their prayer and petition,
8:54 with his hands outstretched toward *h*.
22:19 *h* standing by to his right and to his left.
2Kgs 1:10 from *h* and consume you and your fifty men.”
1:10 from *h* and consumed him and his fifty men.
1:12 from *h* and consume you and your fifty men.”
1:12 And divine fire came down from *h*,
1:14 Already fire has come down from *h*,
2: 1 to take Elijah up to *h* in a whirlwind,
2:11 and Elijah went up to *h* in a whirlwind.
7: 2 if the LORD were to make windows in *h*,
7:19 if the LORD were to make windows in *h*,
17:16 pole and worshiped all the host of *h*,
21: 3 worshiped and served the whole host of *h*.
21: 5 altars for the whole host of *h*,
23: 4 for Baal, Asherah, and the whole host of *h*.
23: 5 of the Zodiac, and to the whole host of *h*.
1Chr 21:16 of the LORD standing between earth and *h*,
21:26 fire from *h* upon the altar of holocausts.
29:11 For all in *h* and on earth is yours;
2Chr 2:11 the God of Israel, who made *h* and earth,
6:13 and stretched forth his hands toward *h*.
6:14 there is no god like you in *h* or on earth;
6:23 your altar in this temple, listen from *h*:
6:25 listen from *h* and forgive the sin of your
6:27 listen in *h* and forgive the sin of your
6:35 listen from *h* to their prayer and petition,
7: 1 fire came down from *h* and consumed the
7:13 If I close *h* so that there is no rain,
7:14 I will hear them from *h* and pardon their
18:18 *h* standing by to his right and to his left.
20: 6 of our fathers, are you not the God in *h*,
28: 9 them with a fury that has reached up to *h*.
30:27 voice was heard and their prayer reached *h*,
32:20 son of Amos, prayed and called out to *h*.
33: 3 the whole host of *h* and worshiped them.
33: 5 of *h* in the two courts of the LORD’s house.
36:23 of the earth the LORD, the God of *h*,
Ezr 1: 2 of the earth the Lord, the God of *h*
5:11 ‘We are the servants of the God of *h*
5:12 provoked the wrath of the God of *h*,
6: 9 and lambs for holocausts to the God of *h*,
6:10 of pleasing odor to the God of *h*
7:12 scribe of the law of the God of *h* (then,
7:21 priest, scribe of the law of the God of *h*,
7:23 is ordered by the God of *h* be carried out
7:23 out exactly for the house of the God of *h*,

HEAVEN (cont.)
9: 6 our heads and our guilt reaches up to h.
Neh 1: 4 I fasted and prayed before the God of h.
1: 5 "O LORD, God of h, great and awesome
2: 4 to the God of h and then answered the king:
2:20 is the God of h who will grant us success.
9:13 came down, you spoke with them from h;
9:15 Food from h you gave them in their hunger,
9:27 to you, and you would hear them from h,
9:28 and you heard them from h and delivered
Tb 5:17 May God in h protect you on the way and
6:18 Beg the Lord of h to show you mercy and
7:11 Your marriage to her has been decided in h!
7:11 son, may the Lord of h prosper you both.
7:12 h grant both of you peace and prosperity."
7:17 of h grant you joy in place of your grief.
8:15 Raguel praised the God of h in these words:
10:11 May the Lord of h grant prosperity to you
10:14 and he blessed the Lord of h and earth,
13: 7 and my spirit rejoices in the King of h.
13:11 their hands their gifts for the King of h.
13:16 see your glory and to praise the King of h!
Jdt 5: 8 with divine worship the God of h,
6:19 "Lord, God of h, behold their arrogance!
7:28 We adjure you by h and earth,
9:12 heritage of Israel, Lord of h and earth,
11:17 woman, serving the God of h night and day.
13:18 the Lord God, the creator of h and earth,
Est C: 3 You made h and earth and every wonderful
1Mc 2:37 h and earth are our witnesses that you
2:58 zeal for the law, was taken up to h.
3:18 in the sight of H there is no difference
3:19 army, but on strength that comes from H.
3:50 And they cried aloud to H:
3:59 Whatever H wills, he will do."
4:10 cry to H in the hope that he will favor us,
4:24 they were singing hymns and glorifying H,
4:40 given with trumpets, they cried out to H.
4:55 themselves and adored and praised H,
5:31 to h with trumpet blasts and loud shouting,
9:46 now to H for deliverance from our enemies."
12:15 with the help of H for our support,
16: 3 now grown old, but you, by the mercy of H,
16: 3 and may the help of H be with you!"
2Mc 3:15 and loudly begged him in h who had given
3:20 all of them with hands raised toward h,
3:34 Since you have been scourged by H,
3:39 h watches over that Place and protects it,
7:11 "It was from h that I received these;
7:34 raise your hand against the children of H.
8:20 because of the help they received from H,
9: 4 Yet the condemnation of H rode with him,
9:10 that he could reach the stars of h,
9:20 thank God very much, for my hopes are in h.
14:34 stretched out their hands toward h,
15: 3 wretch asked if there was a ruler in h
15: 4 that there was indeed such a ruler in h,
15: 8 help they had received from h in the past,
15:21 stretched out his hands toward h
15:34 everyone looked toward h and praised the
Jb 1:16 "Lightning has fallen from h and struck
16:19 Even now, behold, my witness is in h,
38:37 Or who tilts the water jars of h So that
Ps(s) 2: 4 He who is throned in h laughs;
11: 4 the LORD's throne is in h.
14: 2 looks down from h upon the children of men,
18:14 And the LORD thundered from h,
20: 7 that he has answered him from his holy h
33:13 From h the LORD looks down; he sees all
36: 6 O LORD, your kindness reaches to h;
53: 3 God looks down from h upon the children of
57: 4 May he send from h and save me;
68: 9 it rained from h at the presence of God,
71:19 power and your justice, O God, reach to h.
73: 9 They set their mouthings in place of h,
73:25 Whom else have I in h?
76: 9 From h you made your intervention heard;
78:23 skies above and the doors of h he opened;
78:69 And he built his shrine like h,
79: 2 your servants as food to the birds of h,
80:15 again, O LORD of hosts, look down from h,
85:12 earth, and justice shall look down from h.
89: 3 in h you have confirmed your faithfulness:
89:30 forever and his throne as the days of h.
102:20 holy height, from h he beheld the earth,
103:19 The LORD has established his throne in h,
104:12 Beside them the birds of h dwell;
105:40 and with bread from h he satisfied them.
107:26 They mounted up to h;
115: 3 Our God is in h;
115:15 blessed by the LORD, who made h and earth.
115:16 H is the heaven of the LORD,
121: 2 is from the LORD, who made h and earth.
123: 1 I lift up my eyes who are enthroned in h.
124: 8 the name of the LORD, who made h and earth.
134: 3 you from Zion, the maker of h and earth.
135: 6 that the LORD wills he does in h and on earth,
136:26 Give thanks to the God of h,
146: 6 in the LORD, his God, Who made h and earth,
148:13 His majesty is above earth and h,
Prv 23: 5 wings, like the eagle that flies toward h.
30: 4 Who has gone up to h and come down again
Eccl 5: 1 God is in h and you are on earth;
Wis 9:16 but when things are in h,
13: 2 the mighty water, or the luminaries of h,
16:20 of angels and furnished them bread from h,
18:16 he still reached to h,
Sir 16:15 in h who remembers me?
16:16 Behold, the heavens, the h of heavens,
17:27 God watches over the hosts of highest h,
24: 5 The vault of h I compassed alone,
43: 1 of the sky shines forth like h itself,
46:17 Then the LORD thundered forth from h,
Is 24: 4 both h and earth languish.
63:15 Look down from h and regard us from your
Jer 7:18 dough to make cakes for the queen of h,
8: 2 sun and the moon and the whole army of h,
10:11 not make h and earth perish from the earth,
19:13 h and poured out libations to strange gods.
23:24 Do I not fill both h and earth?
32:17 have made h and earth by your great might,
33:22 the host of h which cannot be numbered,
33:25 and have given no laws to h and earth,
44:17 queen of h and pour out libations to her,
44:18 of h and pouring out libations to her,
44:19 queen of h and poured out libations to her,
44:25 of h and to pour out libations to her."
51: 9 Her judgment reaches h,
51:48 Then h, and earth, and everything in them
Lam 2: 1 down from h to earth the glory of Israel,
3:41 us reach out our hearts toward God in h!
3:50 Till the LORD from h looks down and sees.
Bar 2: 2 under h what has been done in Jerusalem,
6:54 they are like crows between h and earth.
Dn 2:18 of the God of h in regard to this mystery,
2:19 in a vision, and he blessed the God of h:
2:28 there is a God in h who reveals mysteries,
2:37 God of h has given dominion and strength,
2:44 lifetime of those kings the God of h will set
3:36 their offspring like the stars of h,
3:56 Blessed are you in the firmament of h,
3:63 Stars of h, bless the Lord
4:10 in bed, a holy sentinel came down from h,
4:12 Let him be bathed with the dew of h;
4:20 that came down from h and proclaimed:
4:20 let him be bathed with the dew of h,
4:22 an ox and be bathed with the dew of h;
4:23 once you have learned it is h that rules.
4:28 on the king's lips, a voice spoke from h,
4:30 and his body was bathed with the dew of h,
4:31 I, Nebuchadnezzar, raised my eyes to h;
4:32 does as he pleases with the powers of h
4:34 and exalt and glorify the King of h,
5:21 his body was bathed with the dew of h,
5:23 you have rebelled against the Lord of h.
6:28 signs and wonders in h and on earth,
7: 2 four winds of h stirred up the great sea,
7:13 a son of man coming, on the clouds of h;
8: 8 up four others, facing the four winds of h.
8:10 Its power extended to the host of h,
9:12 calamity that has ever occurred under h.
11: 4 and divided in four directions under h;
12: 7 lifted his right and left hands to h;
13: 9 would not allow their eyes to look to h,
13:35 Through her tears she looked up to h,
14: 5 but only the living God who made h and
Am 9: 6 I have built h, my upper chamber
Jon 1: 9 "I worship the LORD, the God of h,
Zep 1: 5 those who adore the host of h on the roofs,
Zec 2:10 for I scatter you to the four winds of h,
Mal 3:10 I not open for you the floodgates of h,
Mt 4:17 The kingdom of h is at hand."
5:12 rejoice, for your reward is great in h;
5:18 until h and earth pass away,
5:34 Do not swear by h (it is God's throne),
6: 9 'Our Father in h, hallowed be your name
6:10 your will be done on earth as it is in h.
7:21 one who does the will of my Father in h.
10:32 I will acknowledge before my Father in h.
10:33 men I will disown before my Father in h.
11:25 "Father, Lord of h and earth,
13:45 the kingdom of h is like a merchant's
14:19 five loaves and two fish, looked up to h,
16:19 to you the keys of the kingdom of h.
16:19 bound on earth shall be bound in h;
16:19 loosed on earth shall be loosed in h."
18:10 their angels in h constantly behold my
18:18 bound on earth shall be held bound in h,
18:18 loosed on earth shall be held loosed in h.
18:19 it shall be granted you by my Father in h.
19:21 You will then have treasure in h.
22:30 in marriage but live like angels in h.
23: 9 Only one is your father, the One in h.
23:22 The man who swears by h is swearing by
24:29 and the hosts of h will be shaken loose.'
24:30 clouds of h' with power and great glory.
24:36 it, neither the angels in h nor the Son,
25:31 glory, escorted by all the angels of h,
26:64 of the Power and coming on the clouds of h."
28: 2 as the angel of the Lord descended from h.
28:18 been given to me both in h and on earth;
Mk 6:41 the two fish, Jesus raised his eyes to h,
7:34 then he looked up to h and emitted a groan.
10:21 you will then have treasure in h.
12:25 in marriage but live like angels in h.
13:32 neither the angels in h nor even the Son,
14:62 the Power and coming with the clouds of h."
16:19 h and took his seat at God's right hand.
16:20 and immortal glory of justification in h."
Lk 2:14 God and saying, "Glory to God in high h,
2:15 When the angels had returned to h,
3:22 A voice from h was heard to say:
6:23 exult, for your reward shall be great in h.
9:16 the two fish, Jesus raised his eyes to h,
9:54 us call down fire from h to destroy them?"
10:20 you as that your names are inscribed in h."
10:21 you praise, O Father, Lord of h and earth,
11:16 him, were demanding of him a sign from h.
15: 7 there will likewise be more joy in h over
17:29 rained down from h and destroyed them all.
18:13 not even daring to raise his eyes to h.
18:22 You will have treasure in h.
18:25 for a rich man to enter the kingdom of h."
19:38 Peace in h and glory in the highest!"
22:43 appeared to him from h to strengthen him.
24:51 he left them, and was taken up to h.
Jn 3:12 believe when I tell you about those of h?
3:13 h except the One who came down from there
3:13 the Son of Man [who is in h.
3:31 The One who comes from h [who is above
6:33 down from h and gives life to the world."
6:38 my own will that I have come down from h,
6:41 "I am the bread that came down from h."
6:42 How can he claim to have come down from h
6:50 down from h for a man to eat and never die.
6:51 am the living bread come down from h.
6:58 This is the bread that came down from h.
17: 1 these words, Jesus looked up to h and said:
Acts 1: 2 taught until the day he was taken up to h,
2: 5 were devout Jews of every nation under h.
2:34 David did not go up to h,
3:21 Jesus must remain in h until the time of
4:24 who made h and earth and sea and all that
14:15 'the one who made h and earth and the sea
17:24 all that is in it, the Lord of h and earth,
Rom 1:18 The wrath of God is being revealed from h
10: 6 say in your heart, 'Who shall go up into h?'
1Cor 15:47 formed from dust, the second is from h.
15:48 earth, heavenly men are like the man of h.
15:49 we bear the likeness of the man from h.
2Cor 12: 2 a man who was snatched up to the third h.
Gal 1: 8 For even if we, or an angel from h,
Eph 1:20 and seating him at his right hand in h,
3:10 to the principalities and powers of h,
3:15 family in h and on earth takes its name;
6: 9 have a Master in h who plays no favorites.
Phil 3:20 well know, we have our citizenship in h;
Col 1: 4 are by the hope held in store for you in h.
1:16 everything in h and on earth was created,
1:23 been announced to every creature under h,
4: 1 realizing that you too have a master in h.
1Thes 1:10 from h the Son he raised from the dead
4:16 come down from h at the word of command,
2Thes 1: 7 is revealed from h with his mighty angels;
Heb 1: 3 at the right hand of the Majesty in h,
8: 1 hand of the throne of the Majesty in h,
9:24 he entered h itself that he might appear
12:23 assembly of the first-born enrolled in h,
12:25 if we turn away from him who speaks from h!
12:26 will once more shake not only earth but h!"
Jas 5:12 oath at all, either "by h" or "by earth."
1Pt 1: 4 which is kept in h for you who are guarded
1:12 the power of the Holy Spirit sent from h.
3:22 He went to h and is at God's right hand,
2Pt 1:18 We ourselves heard this said from h while
Rv 3:12 Jerusalem which he will send down from h,
4: 1 above me there was an open door to h,
4: 2 A throne was standing there in h,
5: 3 But no one in h or on earth or under the
5:13 I heard the voices of every creature in h
8: 1 was silence in h for about half an hour.
10: 1 angel come down from h wrapped in a cloud,
10: 4 spoke, but I heard a voice from h say,
10: 5 on the land raised his right hand to h
10: 6 who created h and earth and sea along with
10: 8 I heard from h spoke to me again and said,
11:12 heard a loud voice from h say to them,
11:12 to h in a cloud as their enemies looked on.
11:13 terrified that they worshiped the God of h.
11:15 Loud voices in h cried out,
11:19 Then God's temple in h opened and in the
12: 7 Then war broke out in h;
12: 8 were overpowered and lost their place in h.
12:10 Then I heard a loud voice in h say:
13:13 come down from h to earth as men looked on.
14: 2 h which resembled the roaring of the deep,
14: 7 Worship the Creator of h and earth,
14:13 I heard a voice from h say to me:
14:17 out of the temple in h came another angel,
15: 1 I saw in h another sign,
16:11 in pain and blasphemed the God of h
18: 1 I saw another angel coming down from h.
18: 4 Then I heard another voice from h say:
18: 5 For her sins have piled up as high as h,
19: 1 the loud song of a great assembly in h.
19:14 The armies of h were behind him riding
20: 1 Then I saw an angel come down from h,
20: 9 fire came down from h and devoured them.
21: 2 holy city, coming down out of h from God,

21:10 Jerusalem coming down out of *h* from God.

HEAVENLY (55)

Dt 4:19 or the moon or any star among the *h* hosts,
1Kgs 8:30 from your *h* dwelling and grant pardon.
8:39 from your *h* dwelling place and forgive.
8:43 this temple, listen from your *h* dwelling.
8:49 in your honor, listen from your *h* dwelling.
2Chr 6:21 Listen from your *h* dwelling,
6:30 temple, listen from your *h* dwelling place,
6:33 temple, listen from your *h* dwelling place,
6:39 honor, listen from your *h* dwelling place,
Neh 9:6 life, and the *h* hosts bow down before you.
Tb 1:18 judgment decreed against him by the *h* King
9:6 grant *h* blessing to you and to your wife,
2Mc 2:21 and of the *h* manifestations accorded to
11:10 battle order with the aid of their *h* ally.
Ps(s) 78:24 upon them for food and gave them *h* bread.
Mt 5:16 your acts and give praise to your *h* Father.
5:45 prove that you are sons of your *h* Father,
5:48 made perfect as your *h* Father is perfect.
6:1 expect no recompense from your *h* Father.
6:14 your *h* Father will forgive you yours.
6:20 practice instead to store up *h* treasure,
6:26 yet your *h* Father feeds them.
6:32 Your *h* Father knows all that you need.
7:11 how much more will your *h* Father give good
12:50 Whoever does the will of my *h* Father is
15:13 put down by my *h* Father will be uprooted,"
16:17 has revealed this to you, but my *h* Father.
18:4 is of greatest importance in that *h* reign.
18:10 constantly behold my *h* Father's face.
18:14 it is no part of your *h* Father's plan that
18:35 My *h* Father will treat you in exactly the
Mk 8:11 looking for some *h* sign from him as a test.
11:25 you have a grievance so that your *h* Father
13:25 the skies, and the *h* hosts will be shaken.
Lk 2:13 with the angel a multitude of the *h* host,
11:13 how much more will the *h* Father give the
Jn 6:32 my Father who gives you the real *h* bread.
Acts 26:19 I could not disobey that *h* vision.
28:11 with the *H* Twins" as its figurehead.
1Cor 15:40 are *h* bodies and there are earthly bodies.
15:40 The splendor of the *h* bodies is one thing,
15:48 of earth, *h* men are like the man of heaven.
2Cor 5:2 yearn to have our *h* habitation envelop us.
5:4 rather to have the *h* dwelling envelop us,
2Tm 4:18 and will bring me safe to his *h* kingdom.
Heb 3:1 holy brothers who share a *h* calling,
6:4 been enlightened and have tasted the *h* gift
8:5 is only a copy and shadow of the *h* one,
9:23 of the *h* models be purified in this way,
9:23 but the *h* realities themselves called for
11:16 were searching for a better, a *h* home.
12:22 city of the living God, the *h* Jerusalem,
Jas 1:17 from the Father of the *h* luminaries,
Rv 13:6 and the members of his *h* household as well.
15:5 The *h* sanctuary which is the tent of

HEAVENS (233)

Gn 1:1 when God created the *h* and the earth,
2:1 Thus the *h* and the earth and all their
2:4 of the *h* and the earth at their creation.
2:4 the LORD God made the earth and the *h*—
27:28 "May God give to you of the dew of the *h*
27:39 far from the dew of the *h* above!
28:12 ground, with its top reaching to the *h*;
49:25 you, With the blessings of the *h* above,
Ex 17:14 out the memory of Amalek from under the *h*."
20:11 six days the LORD made the *h* and the earth,
31:17 six days the LORD made the *h* and the earth,
Dt 2:25 of you into every nation under the *h*,
4:19 And when you look up to the *h* and behold
4:36 Out of the *h* he let you hear his voice to
4:39 is God in the *h* above and on earth below,
7:24 make their names perish from under the *h*.
9:14 and blot out their name from under the *h*.
10:14 The heavens, even the highest *h*,
11:11 valleys that drinks in rain from the *h*,
11:17 up against you and he will close up the *h*,
11:21 that, as long as the *h* are above the earth,
25:19 out the memory of Amalek from under the *h*.
28:12 for you his rich treasure house of the *h*,
29:19 will blot out his name from under the *h*
32:1 Give ear, O *h*, while I speak;
32:40 "To the *h* I raise my hand and swear:
32:43 Exult with him, you *h*, glorify him,
33:26 the darling, who rides the *h* in his power,
33:28 grain and wine, where the *h* drip with dew.
Jgs 5:4 The earth quaked and the *h* were shaken,
5:20 From the *h* the stars, too, fought
1Sm 5:12 the out-cry from the city went up to the *h*.
2Sm 22:8 the foundations of the *h* trembled and
22:10 He inclined the *h* and came down,
1Kgs 8:27 If the *h* and the highest heavens cannot
2Kgs 14:27 out the name of Israel from under the *h*,
19:15 You have made the *h* and the earth.
1Chr 16:26 things of nought, but the LORD made the *h*.
16:31 Let the *h* be glad and the earth rejoice;
27:23 to multiply Israel like the stars of the *h*.
2Chr 2:5 since the *h* and even the highest heavens
2:5 and even the highest *h* cannot contain him?
6:18 If the *h* and the highest heavens cannot
Neh 9:6 you made the *h*, the highest heavens
9:23 as numerous as the stars of the *h*,
Tb 8:5 *h* and all your creation praise you forever.
Est D:3 and every wonderful thing under the *h*.
2Mc 2:18 everywhere under the *h* to his holy Place,
7:28 to look at the *h* and the earth and see all
10:29 there appeared to the enemy from the *h*
15:23 Sovereign of the *h*,
Jb 9:8 *h* and treads upon the crests of the sea.
11:8 It is higher than the *h*; what can you do?
14:12 Till the *h* are no more,
15:15 and if the *h* are not clean in his sight,
20:6 to the *h* and his head reach to the clouds,
20:27 The *h* shall reveal his guilt,
22:12 Does not God, in the heights of the *h*,
22:14 he walks upon the vault of the *h*!"
25:2 are his who brings about harmony in his *h*.
26:11 The pillars of the *h* tremble and are
28:24 the earth and sees all that is under the *h*.
35:5 regard the *h* high above you.
35:11 us wise rather than the birds of the *h*?"
37:3 Everywhere under the *h* he sends it,
38:33 Do you know the ordinances of the *h*;
41:3 Who under all the *h*?
Ps(s) 8:2 You have exalted your majesty above the *h*.
8:4 When I behold your *h*,
18:10 And he inclined the *h* and came down,
19:2 The *h* declare the glory of God,
19:7 At one end of the *h* it comes forth,
33:6 By the word of the LORD the *h* were made;
50:4 He summons the *h* from above,
50:6 And for the *h* proclaim his justice;
57:6 Be exalted above the *h*,
57:11 For your kindness towers to the *h*,
57:12 Be exalted above the *h*,
68:34 who rides on the heights of the ancient *h*.
69:35 Let the *h* and the earth praise him,
78:26 He stirred up the east wind in the *h*,
89:6 The *h* proclaim your wonders, O LORD
89:12 Yours are the *h*, and yours is the earth
96:5 things of nought, but the LORD made the *h*.
96:11 Let the *h* be glad and the earth rejoice;
97:6 The *h* proclaim his justice,
102:26 and the *h* are the work of your hands.
103:11 For as the *h* are high above the earth,
104:2 have spread out the *h* like a tent-cloth;
108:5 nations, For your kindness towers to the *h*,
108:6 Be exalted above the *h*,
113:4 above the *h* is his glory.
113:6 and looks upon the *h* and the earth below?
119:89 it is firm as the *h*.
136:5 Who made the *h* in wisdom,
139:8 If I go up to the *h*, you are there
144:5 Incline your *h*, O LORD, and come down
147:8 to our God, Who covers the *h* with clouds,
148:1 Praise the LORD from the *h*,
148:4 heavens, and you waters above the *h*.
Prv 3:19 earth, established the *h* by understanding;
8:27 "When he established the *h* I was there,
25:3 As the *h* in height, and the earth in depth
Eccl 2:3 *h* during the limited days of their life.
3:1 and a time for every affair under the *h*.
Wis 9:10 Send her forth from your holy *h* and from
18:15 word from *h* royal throne bounded,
Sir 1:3 *H* height, earth's breadth,
16:16 Behold, the heavens, the heaven of *h*,
24:4 In the highest *h* did I dwell,
26:16 Like the sun rising in the LORD's *h*,
35:16 his petition reaches the *h*.
43:9 The beauty, the glory, of the *h* are the stars
43:12 It spans the *h* with its glory,
45:15 with his family, as permanent as the *h*,
48:3 up the *h* and three times brought down fire.
50:24 in Israel as long as the *h* are above.
Is 1:2 Hear, O *h*, and listen, O earth
13:5 country, and from the end of the *h*,
13:10 constellations of the *h* send forth no light;
13:13 For this I will make the *h* tremble and the
14:12 How have you fallen from the *h*,
14:13 "I will scale the *h*;
24:21 punish the host of the *h* in the heavens,
24:21 punish the host of the heavens in the *h*,
34:4 The *h* shall be rolled up like a scroll,
34:5 When my sword has drunk its fill in the *h*,
37:16 You have made the *h* and the earth.
40:12 the sea, and marked off the *h* with a span?
40:22 He stretches out the *h* like a veil,
42:5 who created the *h* and stretched them out,
44:23 Raise a glad cry, you *h*:
44:24 all things, who alone stretched out the *h*;
45:8 Let justice descend, O *h*,
45:12 It was my hands that stretched out the *h*;
45:18 thus says the LORD, The creator of the *h*,
48:13 my right hand spread out the *h*.
49:13 Sing out, O *h*, and rejoice, O earth
50:3 I clothe the *h* in mourning,
51:6 Raise your eyes to the *h*,
51:6 Though the *h* grow thin like smoke,
51:13 *h* and laid the foundations of the earth?
51:16 of my hand, I, who stretched out the *h*,
55:9 As high as the *h* are above the earth,
55:10 For just as from the *h* the rain and snow
63:19 rend the *h*, and come down
65:17 I am about to create new *h* and a new earth;
66:1 The *h* are my throne,
66:22 As the new *h* and the new earth which I
Jer 2:12 Be amazed at this, O *h*,
4:23 at the *h*, and their light had gone out!
4:28 shall mourn, the *h* above shall darken;
10:2 and have no fear of the signs of the *h*,
10:11 from the earth, and from beneath these *h*!
10:12 and stretched out the *h* by his skill.
10:13 When he thunders, the waters in the *h* roar,
14:22 Or can the mere *h* send showers?
31:37 If the *h* on high can be measured,
49:36 the four winds from the four ends of the *h*:
51:15 and stretched out the *h* by his skill.
51:16 When he thunders, the waters in the *h* roar,
51:53 Though Babylon scale the *h*,
Lam 3:66 wrath and destroy them from under your *h*!
Bar 1:11 the duration of the *h* above the earth;
3:17 and made sport of the birds of the *h*:
3:29 Who has gone up to the *h* and taken her,
6:66 They show the nations no signs in the *h*,
Ez 1:1 exiles by the river Chebar, the *h* opened,
32:7 When I snuff you out I will cover the *h*,
32:8 in the *h* I will darken on your account,
Dn 3:59 You *h*, bless the Lord, praise and exalt him
3:60 All you waters above the *h*,
4:8 and strong, with its top touching the *h*,
4:17 that you saw, with its top touching the *h*,
4:19 has become so great as to touch the *h*,
7:27 majesty of all the kingdoms under the *h*
Hos 2:23 I will respond to the *h*,
Jl 2:10 them the earth trembles, the *h* shake;
3:3 work wonders in the *h* and on the earth,
4:16 The *h* and the earth quake,
Am 9:2 Though they climb to the *h*,
Hb 3:3 Covered are the *h* with his glory,
Hg 1:10 the *h* withheld from you their dew,
2:6 and I will shake the *h* and the earth,
2:21 I will shake the *h* and the earth;
Zec 6:5 "These are the four winds of the *h*,
8:12 its crops, and the *h* shall give their dew;
12:1 Thus says the LORD, who spreads out the *h*,
Mt 3:17 With that, a voice from the *h* said,
24:31 winds, from one end of the *h* to the other.'
24:35 The *h* and the earth will pass away but my
Mk 1:11 Then a voice came from the *h*:
13:31 The *h* and the earth will pass away but my
Lk 4:25 days of Elijah when the *h* remained closed
16:17 It is easier for the *h* and the earth to
21:26 The powers in the *h* will be shaken.
21:33 The *h* and the earth will pass away,
Jn 6:31 'He gave them bread from the *h* to eat.'"
6:32 not Moses who gave you bread from the *h*;
Acts 1:10 They were still gazing up into the *h* when
1:11 just as you saw him go up into the *h*."
2:19 the *h* above and signs on the earth below:
7:42 to the worship of the galaxies in the *h*.
7:49 'The *h* are my throne,
11:9 second time the voice from the *h* spoke out:
14:17 the *h* he sends down rain and rich harvests;
1Cor 8:5 so-called gods in the *h* and on the earth
2Cor 5:1 for us by God, a dwelling in the *h*,
Eph 1:3 Christ every spiritual blessing in the *h*!
1:10 to bring all things in the *h* and on earth
2:6 raised us up and gave us a place in the *h*,
4:10 very one who ascended high above the *h*,
Phil 2:10 Jesus' name every knee must bend in the *h*,
Col 1:20 in his person, both on earth and in the *h*,
Heb 1:10 and the *h* are the work of your hands.
4:14 high priest who has passed through the *h*,
7:26 separated from sinners, higher than the *h*.
2Pt 3:5 into account that of old there were *h*
3:7 The present *h* and earth are reserved by
3:10 on that day the *h* will vanish with a roar;
3:12 the *h* will be destroyed in flames and the
3:13 we await are new *h* and a new earth where,
Rv 12:12 So rejoice, you *h*,
18:20 Rejoice over her, you *h*,
19:11 The *h* were opened, and as I looked on,
21:1 Then I saw new *h* and a new earth.
21:1 *h* and the former earth had passed away,

HEAVENWARD (1)

Is 38:14 My eyes grow weak, gazing *h*:

HEAVIER (8)

Jgs 4:24 their power weighed ever *h* upon him,
1Kgs 12:11 put a heavy yoke on you, I will make it *h*.
12:14 on you a heavy yoke, but I will make it *h*.
2Chr 10:11 put a heavy yoke on you, I will make it *h*!
10:14 a heavy yoke on you, but I will make it *h*.
Prv 27:3 but a fool's provocation is *h* than both.
Sir 22:14 What is *h* than lead,
Lk 20:47 The *h* sentence will be theirs."

HEAVILY (7)

Nm 20:20 them with a large and *h* armed force.
1Kgs 20:16 while Ben-hadad was drinking *h* in the
1Mc 5:3 he defeated them *h*,
Jb 33:7 nor should my presence weigh *h* upon you.

HEAVILY (cont.)
Eccl 6: 1 under the sun, and it weighs *h* upon man:
Ez 3:14 the hand of the LORD rested *h* upon me.
27:25 full and *h* laden in the heart of the sea.

HEAVING (1)
Wis 5:10 Like a ship traversing the *h* water,

HEAVY (40)
Gn 7:12 nights *h* rain poured down on the earth.
Ex 18:18 The task is too *h* for you;
19:16 lightning, and a *h* cloud over the mountain,
Nm 11:14 by myself, for they are too *h* for me.
1Sm 4:17 in fact, the troops suffered *h* losses.
4:18 since he was an old man and *h*,
5:11 the hand of God had been very *h* upon it.
2Sm 14:26 because his hair became too *h* for him
18: 7 and the casualties there that day were *h*—
1Kgs 12: 4 "Your father put on us a *h* yoke.
12: 4 and the *h* yoke your father imposed on us,
12:11 Whereas my father put a *h* yoke on you,
12:14 "My father put on you a *h* yoke,
18:41 drink, for there is the sound of a *h* rain."
18:45 with clouds and wind, and a *h* rain fell.
19:11 A strong and *h* wind was rending the
2Chr 10: 4 "Your father laid a *h* yoke upon us.
10: 4 the *h* yoke that your father imposed on us,
10:10 to you, 'Your father laid a *h* yoke upon us,
10:11 Whereas my father put a *h* yoke on you,
10:14 "My father laid a *h* yoke on you,
Neh 5:15 had laid a *h* burden on the people,
5:18 for the labor lay *h* upon this people.
1Mc 8: 7 kings who succeeded him to pay a *h* tribute,
8:31 *h* upon our friends and allies the Jews?
13:22 go, there was a *h* fall of snow that night,
Jb 23: 2 his hand is *h* upon me in my groanings.
37: 6 likewise to his *h*, drenching rain.
Ps(s) 32: 4 For day and night your hand was *h* upon me;
38: 5 they are like a *h* burden,
66:11 you laid a *h* burden on our backs.
88: 8 Upon me your wrath lies *h*.
Prv 27: 3 Stone is *h*, and sand a burden,
29: 4 but he who imposes *h* taxes ruins it.
Sir 13: 2 Bear no burden too *h* for you;
30:13 Discipline your son, make *h* his yoke,
40: 1 anxiety has God allotted, and a *h* yoke,
Is 47: 6 And upon old men you laid a very *h* yoke.
Mt 23: 4 They bind up *h* loads,
Acts 27:10 is bound to meet with disaster and *h* loss,

HEBER (10)
Gn 46:17 *H* and Malchiel.
Nm 26:45 through *H* the clan of the Heberites,
Jgs 4:11 *H* had detached himself from his own people,
4:17 to the tent of Jael, wife of the Kenite *H*,
4:17 Kenite *H* were at peace with one another.
4:21 Instead Jael, wife of *H*,
1Chr 4:18 wife bore Jered, the father of Gedor, *H*,
7:31 Beriah's sons were *H* and Malchiel,
7:32 *H* became the father of Japhlet,
8:17 Zebadiah, Meshullam, Hizki, *H*,

HEBERITES (1)
Nm 26:45 Beriites, through Heber the clan of the *H*,

HEBREW (30)
Gn 14:13 came and brought the news to Abram the *H*,
39:14 brought in a *H* slave to make sport of us!
39:17 "The *H* slave whom you brought here broke
41:12 There with us was a *H* youth,
Ex 1:15 The king of Egypt told the *H* midwives,
1:16 for the *H* women and see them giving birth,
1:19 *H* women are not like the Egyptian women.
2: 7 of the *H* women to nurse the child for you?"
2:11 labor, he saw an Egyptian striking a *H*,
2:13 "Why are you striking your fellow *H*?"
21: 2 When you purchase a *H* slave,
Dt 15:12 "If your kinsman, a *H* man or woman,
Jdt 12:11 "Go and persuade this *H* woman in your
14:18 A single *H* woman has brought disgrace on
Jer 34: 9 Everyone was to free his *H* slaves,
34:14 his *H* brother who has sold himself to you;
Jon 1: 9 "I am a *H*."
Jn 5: 2 there is a place with the *H* name Bethesda.
19:13 Gabbatha in *H*.
19:17 is called the Place of the Skull (in *H*,
19:20 This inscription, in *H*, Latin, and Greek,
20:16 She turned to him and said [in *H*,
Acts 6: 1 with the widows of those who spoke *H*.
21:40 on them as he began to speak to them in *H*.
22: 2 When they heard him addressing them in *H*,
26:14 and I heard a voice saying to me in *H*,
Phil 3: 5 tribe of Benjamin, a *H* of Hebrew origins;
3: 5 tribe of Benjamin, a Hebrew of *H* origins;
Rv 9:11 name in *H* is Abaddon and in Greek Apollyon.
16:16 kings in a place called in *H* "Armageddon."

HEBREWS (24)
Gn 40:15 I was kidnaped from the land of the *H*,
43:32 (Egyptians may not eat with *H*;
Ex 1:22 the river every boy that is born to the *H*,
2: 6 and said, "It is one of the *H*' children."
2:13 out again, and now two *H* were fighting!
3:18 The LORD, the God of the *H*,
5: 3 "The God of the *H* has sent us word.
7:16 The LORD, the God of the *H*,
9: 1 Thus says the LORD, the God of the *H*:
9:13 Thus says the LORD, the God of the *H*:
10: 3 "Thus says the LORD, the God of the *H*:
1Sm 4: 6 loud shouting in the camp of the *H* mean?"
4: 9 otherwise you will become slaves to the *H*,
13: 3 with a proclamation, "Let the *H* hear!"
13: 7 and other *H* passed over the Jordan into
13:19 the *H* will make swords or spears."
14:11 some *H* are coming out of the holes where
14:21 the *H* who had previously sided with the
29: 3 asked, "What are those *H* doing here?"
Jdt 10:12 "I am a daughter of the *H*,
2Mc 7:31 every kind of affliction for the *H*,
11:13 and came to realize that the *H* were
15:37 in possession of the *H* from that time on,
2Cor 11:22 Are they *H*? So am I.

HEBRON (71)
Gn 13:18 near the terebinth of Mamre, which is at *H*.
23: 2 (that is, *H*) in the land of Canaan,
23:19 Mamre (that is, *H*) in the land of Canaan.
35:27 at Mamre, in Kiriath-arba [that is, *H*,
37:14 So he sent him off from the valley of *H*.
Ex 6:18 of Kohath were Amram, Izhar, *H* and Uzziel.
Nm 3:19 by clans, were Amram, Izhar, *H* and Uzziel.
13:22 Going up by way of Negeb, they reached *H*,
13:22 *H* had been built seven years before Zoan
Jos 10: 3 of Jerusalem, sent for Hoham, king of *H*,
10: 5 The five Amorite kings, of Jerusalem, *H*,
10:23 the cave the five kings, of Jerusalem, *H*,
10:36 Eglon, Joshua went up with all Israel to *H*,
10:39 Debir and its king what had been done to *H*,
11:21 regions and exterminated the Anakim in *H*,
12:10 Ai (which is near Bethel), Jerusalem, *H*,
14:13 Jephunneh, and gave him *H* as his heritage.
14:14 Therefore *H* remains the heritage of the
14:15 *H* was formerly called Kiriath-arba,
15:13 (Arba was the father of Anak), that is, *H*.
15:54 Humtah, Kiriath-arba (that is, *H*),
20: 7 is, *H*) in the mountain region of Judah.
21:11 (Arba was the father of Anak), that is, *H*,
21:13 the city of asylum for homicides at *H*,
Jgs 1:10 against the Canaanites who dwelt in *H*,
1:20 Moses had commanded, *H* was given to Caleb,
16: 3 them to the top of the ridge opposite *H*.
1Sm 30:31 to those in Athach, to those in *H*,
2Sm 2: 1 "Where shall I go?" He replied, "To *H*."
2: 3 and they dwelt in the cities near *H*.
2:11 six months in *H* as king of the Judahites.
2:32 all-night march, and dawn found them in *H*.
3: 2 Sons were born to David in *H*:
3: 5 These were born to David in *H*.
3:19 went to make his own report to David in *H*
3:20 by twenty men, came to David in *H*,
3:22 him in *H* but had gone his way in peace.
3:27 When Abner returned to *H*,
3:32 When they had buried Abner in *H*,
4: 1 of Saul, heard that Abner had died in *H*,
4: 8 Ishbaal to David in *H* and said to the king:
4:12 feet, hanging them up near the pool in *H*.
4:12 and buried it in Abner's grave in *H*.
5: 1 of Israel came to David in *H* and said:
5: 3 the elders of Israel came to David in *H*,
5: 5 seven years and six months in *H* over Judah,
5:13 in Jerusalem after he had come from *H*,
15: 7 to *H* and fulfill a vow I made to the LORD.
15: 8 back to Jerusalem, I will worship him in *H*.'"
15: 9 him a safe journey, and he went off to *H*.
15:10 of the horn, declare Absalom king in *H*."
1Kgs 2:11 in *H* and thirty-three years in Jerusalem.
1Chr 2:42 sons of Mareshah, who was the father of *H*.
2:43 The sons of *H* were Korah,
3: 1 sons of David who were born to him in *H*:
3: 4 Six in all were born to him in *H*,
5:28 The sons of Kohath were Amram, Izhar, *H*,
6: 3 The sons of Kohath were Amram, Izhar, *H*,
6:40 was assigned *H* with its adjacent pasture
6:42 *H* a city of asylum,
11: 1 Then all Israel gathered about David in *H*,
11: 3 elders of Israel came to the king at *H*,
12:24 at *H* to transfer to him Saul's kingdom,
12:39 came to *H* with the resolute intention of
15: 9 hundred of his brethren, of the sons of *H*,
23:12 Amram, Izhar, *H*, and Uzziel:
23:19 The sons of *H*: Jeriah, the chief
24:23 The descendants of *H* were Jeriah,
29:27 in *H* he reigned seven years,
2Chr 11:10 Lachish, Azekah, Zorah, Aijalon, and *H*;
1Mc 5:65 he took *H* and its villages,

HEBRONITES (5)
Nm 3:27 of the Amramites, the Izharites, the *H*,
26:58 clan of the Libnites, the clan of the *H*,
1Chr 26:23 From the Amramites, Izharites, *H*,
26:30 Among the *H*, Hashabiah and his brethren
26:31 Among the *H*, Jerijah was their chief

HEDDLE-BAR (4)
1Sm 17: 7 of his javelin was like a weaver's *h*,
2Sm 21:19 had a spear with a shaft like a weaver's *h*.
1Chr 11:23 a spear that was like a weaver's *h*,
20: 5 whose spear shaft was like a weaver's *h*.

HEDGE (7)
Sir 28:24 As you *h* round your vineyard with thorns,
36:25 A vineyard with no *h* will be overrun;
Is 5: 5 Take away its *h*, give it to grazing,
Hos 2: 8 I will *h* in her way with thorns and erect
Mi 7: 4 a brier, the most upright like a thorn *h*.
Mt 21:33 who planted a vineyard, put a *h* around it,
Mk 12: 1 man planted a vineyard, put a *h* around it,

HEDGEROWS (1)
Lk 14:23 and along the *h* and force them to come in.

HEED (109)
Gn 21:12 *H* the demands of Sarah,
42:21 when he pleaded with us, yet we paid no *h*;
Ex 3:18 "Thus they will *h* your message.
4: 8 you, nor *h* the message of the first sign,
4: 9 even these two signs, nor *h* your plea,
5: 2 that I should *h* his plea to let Israel go?
15:26 if you *h* his commandments and keep all his
23:13 Give *h* to all that I have told you.
23:21 Be attentive to him and *h* his voice.
23:22 *h* his voice and carry out all I tell you,
24: 7 that the LORD has said, we will *h* and do."
Lv 18:30 *H* my charge, then, not to defile yourselves
26:14 "But if you do not *h* me and do not keep
Nm 14:22 already and have failed to *h* my voice,
16:15 to the LORD, "Pay no *h* to their offering.
Dt 4:23 Take *h*, therefore, lest, forgetting
4:30 to the LORD, your God, and *h* his voice.
11: 1 God, therefore, and always *h* his charge:
11:13 you truly *h* my commandments which I enjoin
12:28 *h* all these commandments I enjoin on you,
13: 5 you observe, and his voice shall you *h*,
15: 5 If you but *h* the voice of the LORD,
17:19 and to *h* and fulfill all the words of this
28: 1 if you continue to *h* the voice of the LORD,
30: 2 and *h* his voice with all your heart and
30: 8 must again *h* the LORD'S voice and carry
30:10 if only you *h* the voice of the LORD,
Jgs 11:28 paid no *h* to the message Jephthah sent him.
1Kgs 8:29 may you *h* the prayer which I,
11:38 If, then, you *h* all that I command you,
2Chr 6:20 may you *h* the prayer which I your servant
Neh 1: 6 your eyes open, to *h* the prayer which I,
Tb 6:13 So *h* my words, brother;
1Mc 10:61 accuse him, but the king paid no *h* to them.
Jb 4:20 with no *h* paid to it,
7:17 you make much of him, or pay him any *h*?
8: 8 and give *h* to the experience of the
13:17 Pay careful *h* to my speech,
23: 6 yet, would that he himself might *h* me!
36:21 Take *h*, turn not to evil;
Ps(s) 2:10 And now, O kings, give *h*; take warning
5: 3 *H* my call for help, my king and my God!
10:17 you pay *h* To the defense of the
28: 1 be not deaf to me, Lest, if you *h* me not,
55: 3 give *h* to me, and answer me
119:95 to destroy me, but I pay *h* to your decrees.
142: 5 to see, but there is no one who pays me *h*.
Prv 8: 6 "Give *h*! for noble things I speak;
17: 4 The evil man gives *h* to wicked lips,
21:29 but the upright man pays *h* to his ways.
Eccl 7:21 Do not give *h* to every word that is spoken
11: 4 One who pays *h* to the wind will not sow,
Wis 12:26 But they who took no *h* of punishment
Sir 3: 1 Children, pay *h* to a father's right;
6:24 Listen, my son, and *h* my advice;
6:33 if you give *h*,
23: 7 Give *h*, my children, to the instruction
29:23 no *h* to him who would disparage your home;
37:13 Then, too, *h* your own heart's counsel;
41:14 My children, *h* my instruction about shame;
51:16 In the short time I paid *h*,
Is 21: 7 Then let him pay *h*, very close heed.
32: 9 overconfident women, give *h* to my words.
42:23 listens and pays *h* for the time to come?
55: 2 *H* me, and you shall eat well
Jer 6:10 are uncircumcised, they cannot give *h*;
7:24 But they obeyed not, nor did they pay *h*.
7:26 Yet they have not obeyed me nor paid *h*;
18:19 *H* me, O LORD, and listen
25: 4 Though you refused to listen or pay *h*,
34:14 fathers, however, did not *h* me or obey me.
35:15 but you did not *h* me or obey me.
Lam 1:21 "Give *h* to my groaning;
Bar 1:21 For we did not *h* the voice of the Lord,
2:10 us to do, but we did not *h* his voice,
2:24 But we did not *h* your voice,
2:29 If you do not *h* my voice,
2:30 For I know they will not *h* me,
3: 4 they did not *h* the voice of the Lord,
Ez 2: 5 And whether they *h* or resist
2: 7 my words to them, whether they *h* or resist,
3:11 —whether they *h* or resist!

3:27 Let him *h* who will,
Dn 9:10 against you and paid no *h* to your command,
Mi 1: 2 Hear, O peoples, all of you, give *h*,
Zec 3: 7 If you walk in my ways and *h* my charge,
6:15 *h* carefully the voice of the LORD your God.
Mt 11:15 *H* carefully what you hear!
13: 9 Let everyone *h* what he hears!"
13:43 Let everyone *h* what he hears!
Mk 7:16 Let everyone *h* what he hears!"
Lk 8:18 Take *h*, therefore, how you hear:
14:35 Let him who hears this, *h* it."
Jn 10: 8 and marauders whom the sheep did not *h*.
Acts 28:28 who will *h* it!"
1Cor 14:21 people, and even so they will not *h* me,
2Thes 1: 8 nor *h*" the good news of our Lord Jesus.
1Tm 4: 1 turn away from the faith and will *h* deceitful
Rv 1: 3 who hear it and *h* what is written in it,
2: 7 ears *h* the Spirit's word to the churches!
2:11 ears *h* the Spirit's word to the churches!
2:17 ears *h* the Spirit's word to the churches!
2:29 ears *h* the Spirit's word to the churches!'
3: 6 ears *h* the Spirit's word to the churches!'
3:13 ears *h* the Spirit's word to the churches!
3:22 ears *h* the Spirit's word to the churches.'"
13: 9 Let him who has ears *h* these words!
22: 9 and those who *h* the message of this book.

HEEDED (14)

Gn 16: 2 Abram *h* Sarai's request.
30: 6 indeed he has *h* my plea and given me a son."
Nm 21: 3 when the LORD *h* Israel's prayer and
Dt 13:19 because you have *h* the voice of the LORD,
1Sm 19: 6 Saul *h* Jonathan's plea and swore,
2Kgs 18:12 they had not *h* the warning of the LORD,
Jb 34:27 away from him and *h* none of his ways,
Eccl 9:17 *h* than the shout of a ruler of fools"
Jer 6:19 own schemes, Because they *h* not my words,
23:18 Who has *h* his word, so as to announce it?
35: 8 Now we have *h* Jonadab,
Bar 1:18 We have neither *h* the voice of the Lord,
Dn 3:30 commandments we have not *h* or observed,
Jn 5:25 of God, and those who have *h* it shall live.

HEEDFUL (1)

Bar 2:31 I will give them hearts, and *h* ears:

HEEDFULLY (1)

Is 55: 3 Come to me *h*,

HEEDING (10)

Gn 17:20 As for Ishmael, I am *h* you:
Nm 9:23 ever *h* the charge of the LORD,
Dt 7:12 "As your reward for *h* these decrees and
8:20 too perish for not *h* the voice of the LORD,
30:20 by loving the LORD, your God, *h* his voice,
2Sm 13:14 Not *h* her plea, he overpowered her;
2Kgs 18:12 not *h* and not fulfilling the commandments
Bar 2: 5 against the Lord, our God, not *h* his voice.
Ez 33: 4 anyone hearing but not *h* the warning of
Dn 9:11 your law and went astray, not *h* your voice,

HEEDLESS (1)

Heb 12: 2 him he endured the cross, *h* of its shame.

HEEDLESSLY (1)

Ps(s) 25: 3 shall be put to shame who *h* break faith.

HEEDS (12)

Ex 16: 7 LORD, as he *h* your grumbling against him.
16: 8 he *h* the grumbling you utter against him,
Prv 10: 8 A wise man *h* commands,
10:17 A path to life is his who *h* admonition,
13: 1 but the senseless one *h* no rebuke.
13: 8 for his life, but the poor man *h* no rebuke.
13:18 but he who *h* reproof is honored.
15: 5 but prudent is he who *h* reproof.
15:32 but he who *h* reproof gains understanding.
Sir 28:16 Whoever *h* it has no rest,
Is 50:10 you fears the LORD, *h* his servant's voice,
Rv 22: 7 who *h* the prophetic message of this book!"

HEEL (7)

Gn 3:15 at your head, while you strike at his *h*."
25:26 brother came out next, gripping Esau's *h*;
49:17 by the path, That bites the horse's *h*,
2Sm 2:23 in the abdomen with the *h* of his javelin,
Jb 18: 9 A trap seizes him by the *h*,
Ps(s) 41:10 of my bread, has raised his *h* against me.
Jn 13:18 bread with me has raised his *h* against me.'

HEELS (3)

Gn 49:19 by raiders, but he shall raid at their *h*.
Mt 8:33 The swineherds took to their *h*,
Lk 8:34 they took to their *h* and brought the news

HEGAI (4)

Est 2: 3 Under the care of the royal eunuch *H*,
2: 8 stronghold of Susa under the care of *H*,
2: 8 in to the royal palace under the care of *H*,
2:15 for anything but what the royal eunuch *H*,

HEIFER (16)

Gn 15: 9 him, "Bring me a three-year-old *h*,
Nm 19: 2 Israelites to procure for you a red *h*
19: 5 Then the *h* shall be burned in his sight,
19: 6 the fire in which the *h* is being burned.
19: 8 who burned the *h* shall wash his garments,
19: 9 shall gather up the ashes of the *h*
19: 9 The *h* is a sin offering.
19:10 He who has gathered up the ashes of the *h*
Dt 21: 3 elders of that city shall take a *h*
21: 6 the *h* whose throat was cut in the wadi,
Jgs 14:18 to them, "If you had not plowed with my *h*,
1Sm 16: 2 "Take a *h* along and say,
Is 7:21 a man shall keep a *h* or a couple of sheep,
Jer 46:20 Egypt is a pretty *h*,
Hos 4:16 For Israel is as stubborn as a *h*;
10:11 Ephraim was a trained *h*,

HEIFER'S (2)

Dt 21: 4 shall cut the *h* throat there in the wadi.
Heb 9:13 sprinkling of a *h* ashes can sanctify those

HEIGHT (35)

Gn 6:15 fifty cubits, and its *h* thirty cubits.
22: 2 on a *h* that I will point out to you."
Ex 38: 1 its *h* was three cubits.
Nm 11:31 over the camp site at a *h* of two cubits
23: 3 He went out on the barren *h*,
1Kgs 6: 9 When the temple was built to its full *h*,
7:23 and measured ten cubits across, five in *h*,
Ezr 6: 3 Its *h* is to be sixty cubits and its width
Neh 3:38 filled in and completed up to half its *h*.
Jdt 1: 2 each three cubits in *h* and six in length.
1: 4 gateway he built to a *h* of seventy cubits,
7:10 on the *h* of the mountains where they dwell;
Est D: 7 ablaze with the *h* of majestic anger,
5:14 "Have a gibbet set up, fifty cubits in *h*,
1Mc 14:37 the wall of Jerusalem to a greater *h*.
Ps(s) 102:20 "The LORD looked down from his holy *h*,
Prv 14:29 quick-tempered man displays folly at its *h*.
25: 3 As the heavens in *h*,
Sir 1: 3 Heaven's *h*, earth's breadth,
22:18 open *h* will not remain when the wind blows;
Is 22:16 on a *h* and carved his tomb in the rock:
49: 9 on every bare *h* shall their pastures be.
Jer 12:12 Upon every desert *h* brigands have come up.
Ez 19:11 Stately was her *h* amid the dense foliage;
20:40 holy mountain, on the mountain *h* of Israel,
31:10 because it became proud in heart at its *h*,
40: 5 the width and the *h* of the structure,
41:22 like a wooden altar, three cubits in *h*,
43:13 The *h* of the altar itself was as follows:
Dn 4: 7 tree of great *h* at the center of the world.
8: 8 but at the *h* of its power the great horn
Rom 8:39 neither *h* nor depth nor any other creature,
Eph 3:18 length and *h* and depth of Christ's love,
Rv 21:16 furlongs in length, in width, and in *h*.
21:17 a hundred and forty-four cubits in *h*

HEIGHTENS (1)

Sir 1:17 she *h* the glory of those who possess her.

HEIGHTS (44)

Nm 23: 9 crags I see him, from the *h* I behold him.
Dt 33:29 fawn upon you, as you stride upon their *h*."
Jos 16: 1 went up from Jericho to the *h* at Bethel.
Jgs 5:18 Naphtali, too, on the open *h*!
2Sm 1:19 glory of Israel, Saul, slain upon your *h*;
1:25 the thick of the battle, slain upon your *h*!
22:34 as those of hinds and set me on the *h*;
2Kgs 19:23 my many chariots I climbed the mountain *h*,
19:23 I reached the remotest *h*,
1Mc 6:40 of the king's army extended over the *h*,
Jb 22:12 Does not God, in the *h* of the heavens,
Ps(s) 18:34 as those of hinds and set me on the *h*;
48: 3 His holy mountain, fairest of *h*,
68:34 who rides on the *h* of the ancient heavens.
148: 1 from the heavens, praise him in the *h*;
Prv 8: 2 On the top of the *h* along the road,
9: 3 she calls from the *h* out over the city:
9:14 of her house upon a seat on the city *h*,
Eccl 12: 5 And one fears *h*,
Sir 43: 9 adorn with their sparkling the *h* of God,
Is 33:16 He shall dwell on the *h*,
37:24 my many chariots I climbed the mountain *h*,
37:24 I reached the remotest *h*,
41:18 I will open up rivers on the bare *h*,
58:14 I will make you ride on the *h* of the earth;
Jer 3: 2 Lift your eyes to the *h*,
3:21 A cry is heard on the *h*!
4:11 "From the glaring *h* through the desert a
4:12 this wind from the *h* come at my bidding;
7:29 on the *h* intone an elegy;
14: 6 The wild asses stand on the bare *h*,
18:14 the snow of Lebanon desert the rocky *h*?
31:12 Shouting, they shall mount the *h* of Zion,
49:16 rocky crags, that hold the *h* of the hill:
51:53 and make her strong *h* inaccessible,
Bar 5: 5 stand upon the *h*; look to the east
Ez 17:23 the mountain *h* of Israel I will plant it.
34:14 *h* of Israel shall be their grazing ground.
36: 2 the everlasting *h* have become our
Am 4:13 and strides upon the *h* of the earth:
Ob 1: 3 of the rock, whose abode is in the *h*,
Mi 1: 3 and treads upon the *h* of the earth.
Hb 3:19 of hinds and enables me to go upon the
Rv 2: 5 in mind the *h* from which you have falle

HEINOUS (1)

Jb 31:11 For that would be *h*,

HEIR (20)

Gn 15: 2 and have as my *h* the steward of my house,
15: 3 and so one of my servants will be my *h*."
15: 4 "No, that one shall not be your *h*;
15: 4 your own issue shall be your *h*."
Ru 4: 5 Ruth the Moabite, the widow of the late *h*,
4:14 not failed to provide you today with an *h*!
2Sm 7:12 I will raise up your *h* after you,
14: 7 we must extinguish the *h* also.'
2Kgs 3:27 he took his first-born, his *h* apparent
25:30 *h* governor Gedaliah,
Tb 3:15 and he has no other child to make his *h*,
Eccl 4:15 *h* apparent who will succeed to his place.
Sir 23:22 and offers as *h* her son by a stranger.
Jer 49: 1 has he no *h*?
Lk 20:14 'This is the *h*.
1Cor 6: 9 will not fall *h* to the kingdom of God?
Gal 4: 1 as long as a designated *h* is not of age
4: 7 the fact that you are a son makes you an *h*,
4:30 slave girl's son shall never be an *h*
Heb 1: 2 whom he has made *h* of all things and

HEIRLOOMS (1)

Dt 18: 8 along with his monetary offerings and *h*.

HEIRS (14)

Gn 31:14 still an *h* portion in our father's house?
Jgs 21:17 of Benjamin who survive must have *h*,
Sir 23:12 may they never be heard among Jacob's *h*.
Mt 8:12 while the natural *h* of the kingdom will be
Acts 3:25 you are the *h* of the covenant God made
Rom 4:14 If only those who observe the law are *h*,
8:17 But if we are children, we are *h* as well:
8:17 *h* of God, heirs with Christ,
Ti 3: 7 be justified by his grace and become *h*,
Heb 6:17 wishing to give the *h* of his promise even
11: 9 Isaac and Jacob, *h* of the same promise;
Jas 2: 5 to be rich in faith and *h* of the kingdom
1Pt 3: 7 *h* just as much as you to the gracious gift

HELAH (2)

1Chr 4: 5 of Tekoa, had two wives, *H* and Naarah.
4: 7 The sons of *H* were Zereth,

HELAM (2)

2Sm 10:16 They came to *H*, with Shobach,
10:17 Israel, crossed the Jordan, and went to *H*.

HELBAH (1)

Jgs 1:31 or take possession of Mahaleb, Achzib, *H*,

HELBON (1)

Ez 27:18 wealth, exchanging *H* wine and Zahar wool.

HELD (111)

Gn 8: 2 and the downpour from the sky was *h* back.
21: 8 child's weaning, Abraham *h* a great feast.
31:39 You *h* me responsible for anything stolen
34: 5 he *h* his peace until they came home.
50:10 they *h* there a very great and solemn
Lv 22:32 I, the LORD, must be *h* as sacred.
Nm 16: 3 and *h* an assembly against Moses and Aaron,
18:23 and they alone shall be *h* responsible;
20: 2 they *h* a council against Moses and Aaron.
Dt 15: 9 LORD against you and you will be *h* guilty.
23:22 otherwise you will be *h* guilty,
23:23 making a vow, you will not be *h* guilty.
24:15 LORD against you, and you will be *h* guilty.
33:19 to the mountains where feasts are duly *h*,
Jos 13: 3 though *h* by the five lords of the
Jgs 6: 2 years, so that Midian *h* Israel subject.
6:21 stretched out the tip of the staff he *h*,
7:20 They *h* the torches in their left hands,
9:27 Then they *h* a festival and went to the
1Sm 3:18 told him everything, and *h* nothing back.
9: 6 God in this city, a man *h* in high esteem;
13: 7 Saul, however, *h* out at Gilgal,
17:42 in appearance, he *h* him in contempt.
26:21 because you have *h* my life precious today.
2Sm 1:26 have I *h* love for you than love for women.
18:12 "Even if I already *h* a thousand pieces of
20: 9 Joab *h* Amasa's beard as if to kiss him.
2Kgs 12:16 workmen, because they *h* positions of trust.
13:16 As the king *h* the bow,
22: 7 to them, because they *h* positions of trust.

HELD (cont.)

1Chr 4:22 Joash and Saraph, who *h* property in Moab,
12:30 *h* their allegiance to the house of Saul.
2Chr 7: 9 On the eighth day they *h* a special meeting,
20:26 *h* an assembly in the Valley of Beracah
Ezr 10:16 They *h* sessions to examine the matter,
Neh 4:11 one hand and *h* a weapon with the other.
9:16 they *h* their necks stiff and would not
13:13 for these men were *h* to be trustworthy.
Jdt 7:17 and *h* the water supply and the springs of
Est 1: 6 *h* by cords of crimson byssus from silver
1:14 service and *h* first rank in the realm,
D: 8 *h* her in his arms until she recovered,
5: 2 toward her the golden staff which he *h*.
1Mc 6:37 and fastened to it by a harness, *h*,
9:58 of the law *h* a council and said:
10:81 But his men *h* their ground,
11:27 and in all the honors he had previously *h*,
11:49 that the Jews *h* the city at their mercy,
13:15 in connection with the offices that he *h*.
15:33 a time had been unjustly *h* by our enemies.
2Mc 4:18 were *h* at Tyre in the presence of the king,
7:10 told to do so, and bravely *h* out his hands,
10:15 Idumeans, who *h* some important strongholds,
14:22 But the conference was *h* in the proper way.
Jb 30:24 Yet should not a hand be *h* out to help a
32: 6 therefore I *h* back and was afraid to
36: 8 fetters and *h* fast by bonds of affliction,
Ps(s) 27: 6 is *h* high above my enemies on every side.
106:46 compassion from all who *h* them captive.
Prv 5:22 meshes of his own sin he will be *h* fast;
Sg 7: 6 a king is *h* captive in its tresses.
Wis 3:14 *h* in no wicked thoughts against the Lord
3:17 attain long life, they will be *h* no esteem,
5: 3 "This is he whom once we *h* as a
5:13 nought and *h* no sign of virtue to display,
9: 6 not with him, he shall be *h* in no esteem.
Sir 24: 6 over every people and nation I *h* sway.
26:19 illustrious men *h* in contempt;
45: 1 MOSES, whose memory is *h* in benediction.
48:22 was right and *h* fast to the paths of David,
Is 40:12 has *h* in a measure the dust of the earth,
53: 3 faces, spurned, and we *h* him in no esteem.
62: 3 of the LORD, a royal diadem *h* by your God.
Jer 26:10 *h* court at the New Gate of the house
Ez 20: 7 detestable things that have *h* your eyes;
20: 8 detestable things that had *h* their eyes,
29: 7 When they *h* you in hand,
31:15 so that the deep waters were *h* back.
33:16 sins he committed shall be *h* against him;
Dn 14: 2 Daniel was the king's favorite and was *h*
Ob 1: 2 you are *h* in dire contempt.
Mt 12:36 on judgment day people will be *h*
18:18 bound on earth shall be *h* bound in heaven,
18:18 on earth shall be *h* loosed in heaven.
Mk 6:21 *h* a birthday dinner for his court circle,
Lk 7: 2 had a servant he *h* in high regard,
20: 5 They *h* a brief conference during which
Jn 12: 6 He *h* the purse,
13:29 idea that, since Judas *h* the common purse,
20:23 if you hold them bound, they are *h* bound."
Acts 4:15 of the court while they *h* a consultation.
4:32 rather, everything was *h* in common.
5:13 that the people *h* them in great esteem.
19: 9 and after that *h* his discussions from day
19:17 Lord Jesus came to be *h* in great reverence.
Rom 2:24 of God is *h* in contempt among the Gentiles."
Col 1: 4 by the hope *h* in store for you in heaven.
1Tm 2: 8 offer prayers with blameless hands *h* aloft,
2Tm 1: 9 the grace *h* out to us in Christ Jesus
4:16 May it not be *h* against them!
2Pt 2: 4 He *h* them captive in Tartarus
Rv 1:16 In his right hand he *h* seven stars.
3: 8 yet you have *h* fast to my word and have
6: 5 of which *h* a pair of scales in his hand.
7: 1 they *h* in check the earth's four winds so
10: 2 he *h* a little scroll which had been opened.
14:17 angel, who likewise *h* a sharp sickle.
14:18 voice to the one who *h* the sharp sickle,
17: 4 In her hand she *h* a gold cup that was
21: 9 One of the seven angels who *h* the seven
21:15 me *h* a rod of gold for measuring the city,

HELDAI (3)

1Chr 27:15 the twelfth month, was *H* the Netophathite,
Zec 6:10 Take from the returned captives *H*,
6:14 in the temple of the LORD in favor of *H*,

HELED (2)

2Sm 23:29 *H*, son of Baanah
1Chr 11:30 *H*, son of Baanah,

HELEK (2)

Nm 26:30 through *H* the clan of the Helekites,
Jos 17: 2 of Manasseh, the clans of Abiezer, *H*,

HELEKITES (1)

Nm 26:30 through Helek the clan of the *H*,

HELEPH (1)

Jos 19:33 clans of the Naphtalites extended from *H*,

HELEZ (4)

2Sm 23:26 *H* from Beth-pelet;
1Chr 2:39 Azariah became the father of *H*.
2:39 *H* became the father of Eleasah.
11:27 *H*, from Palti

HELI (1)

Lk 3:23 the son of Joseph, son of *H*,

HELIODORUS (14)

2Mc 3: 7 The king chose his minister *H* and sent him
3: 8 So *H* immediately set out on his journey
3:13 *H* said that in any case the money must be
3:23 them in trust, *H* went on with his plan.
3:24 who had been bold enough to follow *H*
3:25 the horse attacked *H* with its front hoofs.
3:31 of *H* begged Onias to invoke the Most High,
3:32 Fearing that the king might think that *H*
3:33 clothing again appeared and stood before *H*.
3:35 After *H* had offered a sacrifice to the
3:37 When the king asked *H* who would be a
3:40 This was how the matter concerning *H* and
4: 1 it was Onias who threatened *H*
5:18 in so many sins, this man, like *H*,

HELIOPOLIS (3)

Gn 41:45 the daughter of Potiphera, priest of *H*.
41:50 daughter of Potiphera, priest of *H*.
46:20 daughter of Potiphera, priest of *H*,

HELKAI (1)

Neh 12:15 for Meremoth, *H*;

HELKATH (2)

Jos 19:25 Their territory included *H*,
21:31 pasture lands, *H* with its pasture lands,

HELL (1)

Jas 3: 6 from birth, and its fire is kindled by *h*.

HELLENISM (1)

2Mc 4:13 *H* and foreign customs reached such a pitch,

HELLEZ (1)

1Chr 27:10 Seventh, for the seventh month, was *H*,

HELMET (10)

1Sm 17: 5 He had a bronze *h* on his head and wore a
17:38 putting a bronze *h* on his head and arming
Ps(s) 60: 9 Ephraim is the *h* for my head;
108: 9 Manasseh, Ephraim is the *h* for my head;
140: 8 you are my *h* in the day of battle!
Wis 5:18 and shall wear sure judgment for a *h*;
Is 59:17 salvation, as the *h* on his head;
Ez 27:10 shield and *h* they hung upon you,
Eph 6:17 *h* of salvation and the sword of the spirit,
1Thes 5: 8 and the hope of salvation as a *h*.

HELMETS (6)

2Chr 26:14 bucklers, lances, *h*,
1Mc 6: 2 temple was very rich, containing gold *h*,
6:35 men in coats of mail, with bronze *h*,
Jer 46: 4 Fall in with your *h*;
Ez 23:24 *h* they shall array against you everywhere.
38: 5 and Put with them [all with shields and *h*,

HELON (5)

Num 1: 9 Eliab, son of *H*
Nm 2: 7 [Their prince was Eliab, son of *H*,
7:24 day it was the turn of Eliab, son of *H*,
7:29 This was the offering of Eliab, son of *H*.
10:16 tribe of Issachar, and Eliab, son of *H*,

HELP (235)

Gn 4: 1 have produced a man with the *h* of the LORD.
39:15 When he heard me scream for *h*,
39:18 But when I screamed for *h*,
Ex 10:10 "The LORD *h* you," Pharaoh replied
21:19 up and walk around with the *h* of his staff.
23: 5 *h* him, rather, to raise it up.
Lv 25: 6 hired *h* and the tenants who live with you,
Nm 31:26 "With the *h* of the priest Eleazar and of
Dt 15: 9 you grudge *h* to your needy kinsman and
22: 4 see to it that you *h* him lift it up.
22:24 cry out for *h* though she was in the city,
22:27 betrothed maiden may have cried out for *h*,
32:38 of your libations Rise up now and *h* you!
33: 7 and you will be his *h* against his foes."
Jos 1:14 you must *h* them until the LORD has settled
10: 6 *H* us, because all the Amorite kings
10:33 Horam, king of Gezer, came up to *h* Lachish,
Jgs 5:23 my help, as warriors to the *h* of the LORD."
1Sm 9:16 their misery and accept their cry for *h*."
14: 6 Perhaps the LORD will *h* us,
2Sm 10:11 are stronger than I, you shall *h* me.
10:11 stronger than you, I will come to *h* you.
14: 4 to the ground in homage, saying, *H*,
18: 3 that we have you to *h* us from the city."
22:30 and by the *h* of my God I leap over a wall.
22:36 shield, and your *h* has made me great.
22:42 They cried for *h*— but no one saved them
2Kgs 4: 2 "How can I *h* you?"
6:26 the city wall, a woman cried out to him, *H*,
6:27 "No," he replied, "the LORD *h* you!
6:27 Where could I find *h* for you:
14:26 nor freeman, no one at all to *h* Israel.
19:20 to your prayer for *h* against Sennacherib,
1Chr 4:10 *H* me and make me free of misfortune,
5:20 they received *h* so that they mastered the
12:18 "If you come peacefully, to *h* me,
12:20 However, he did not *h* the Philistines,
12:23 *h* until there was a vast encampment,
15:26 While the Levites, with God's *h*,
19: 9 their *h* remained apart in the open field.
19:12 too strong for me, you must come to my *h*;
22:17 of Israel's leaders to *h* his son Solomon:
28:21 they will *h* you in all your work with all
2Chr 14:10 you to *h* the powerless against the strong.
14:10 *H* us, O LORD, our God
19: 2 "Should you *h* the wicked and love those
20: 4 Judah gathered to seek *h* from the LORD;
26:13 valor to *h* the king against his enemies.
26:15 to the marvelous *h* he had received.
28:15 men just named proceeded to *h* the captives.
28:16 an appeal for *h* to the kings of Assyria.
28:20 but to oppress him rather than to *h* him.
28:23 sacrifice to them that they may *h* me also."
32: 8 our God, to *h* us and to fight our battles."
Ezr 1: 6 their neighbors gave them *h* in every way,
6:22 them *h* in their work on the house of God,
Neh 6:16 God's *h* that this work had been completed.
Tb 8: 6 him his wife Eve to be his *h* and support;
Jdt 6:21 they called upon the God of Israel for *h*.
7:25 There is no *h* for us now!
7:31 if those days pass without *h* coming to us,
8:17 from him, let us call upon him to *h* us,
9: 4 of their kinswoman, called on you for *h*.
Est C:14 *H* me, who am alone and have no *h*
C:25 Save us by your power, and *h* me,
E:20 may *h* them on the day set for their ruin,
1Mc 3:15 to *h* him take revenge on the Israelites.
3:53 we be able to resist them unless you *h* us?"
5:39 they have also hired Arabs to *h* them,
7:20 over to Alcimus, leaving troops to *h* him,
8:13 desired to *h* to a kingdom became kings,
8:25 Jewish nation will *h* them wholeheartedly,
8:27 nation, the Romans will *h* them willingly,
10:74 and Simon his brother joined him to *h* him.
12:15 with the *h* of Heaven for our support,
12:53 "Now that they have no leader to *h* them,
14: 1 to obtain *h* so that he could fight Trypho.
16: 3 and may the *h* of Heaven be with you!"
16:18 asking that troops be sent to *h* him and
2Mc 8:19 when *h* had been given their ancestors;
8:20 because of the *h* they received from Heaven,
8:23 giving them the watchword, "The *H* of God,"
8:35 after being humbled through the Lord's *h*
11: 7 in risking their lives to *h* their kinsmen.
12:11 Judas and his companions, with God's *h*,
12:11 cattle and to *h* them in every other way.
13:10 upon the LORD night and day, to *h* them now,
13:13 out and settle the matter with God's *h*.
13:17 with the *h* and protection of the LORD.
15: 7 that he would receive *h* from the LORD.
15: 8 but mindful of the *h* they had received
15:35 and evident proof to all of the LORD's *h*.
Jb 19: 7 I cry for *h*, but there is no redress.
26: 2 What *h* you give to the powerless,
26: 4 With whose *h* have you uttered those words,
29:12 I rescued the poor who cried out for *h*,
30:24 out to *h* a wretched man in his calamity?
35: 9 for *h* because of the power of the mighty,
36:13 they cry not for *h* when he enchains them;
Ps(s) 5: 3 Heed my call for *h*, my king and my God!
12: 2 *H*, O LORD! for no one now is dutiful;
18:30 and by the *h* of my God I leap over a wall.
18:42 They cried for *h*— but no one saved them;
20: 3 May he send you *h* from the sanctuary,
22:12 be near, for I have no one to *h* me.
22:20 O my *h*, hasten to aid me.
28: 7 In him my heart trusts, and I find *h*;
33:20 for the LORD, who is our *h* and our shield,
38:23 Make haste to *h* me, O Lord my salvation!
40:14 O LORD, make haste to *h* me.
40:18 You are my *h* and my deliverer;
41: 4 The LORD will *h* him on his sickbed,
44:27 Arise, *h* us! Redeem us.
46: 2 strength, an ever-present *h* in distress.
46: 6 God will *h* it at the break of dawn.
60: 7 *h* us by your right hand,
60:13 the foe, for worthless is the *h* of men.
63: 8 That you are my *h*,
69:14 kindness answer me with your constant *h*.
69:30 let your saving *h*, O God, protect me.
70: 2 O LORD, make haste to *h* me.
70: 6 You are my *h* and my deliverer;

71:12 my God, make haste to *h* me.
72:12 the afflicted when he has no one to *h* him.
78:22 they believed not God nor trusted in his *h*.
79: 9 *H* us, O God our savior,
80:18 your *h* be with the man of your right hand,
88: 3 incline your ear to my call for *h*,
94:17 Were not the LORD my *h*,
106: 4 visit me with your saving *h*,
107:12 they stumbled, there was no one to *h* them.
108: 7 ones may escape, *h* us by your right hand,
108:13 the foe, for worthless is the *h* of men.
109:26 *H* me, O LORD, my God; save me,
115: 9 he is their *h* and their shield.
115:10 he is their *h* and their shield.
115:11 he is their *h* and their shield.
118: 7 The LORD is with me to *h* me,
119:86 *h* me!
119:173 Let your hand be ready to *h* me,
119:175 praise you, and may your ordinances *h* me.
121: 1 whence shall *h* come to me?
121: 2 My *h* is from the LORD,
124: 8 Our *h* is in the name of the LORD,
146: 5 Happy he whose *h* is the God of Jacob,
Prv 20:22 Trust in the LORD and he will *h* you.
Wis 13:16 for it, knowing that it cannot *h* itself;
13:16 for, truly, it is an image and needs *h*.
Sir 2: 6 Trust God and he will *h* you;
4:10 and *h* their mother as a husband would;
5:10 for it will be no *h* on the day of wrath.
8:16 when there is no one to *h* you,
12:17 feigning to *h*, he will trip you up,
29: 4 adds to the burdens of those who *h* him;
29: 9 Because of the precept, *h* the needy,
34:16 against stumbling, a *h* against falling.
38:21 it will not *h* him, but will do you harm
51: 7 every way, but there was no one to *h* me,
Is 10: 3 To whom will you flee for *h*?
20: 6 *h* and deliverance from the king of Assyria;
22: 5 they cry for *h* to the mountains.
30: 5 gain them nothing, Neither *h* nor benefit,
30: 7 to Egypt whose *h* is futile and vain.
31: 1 Woe to those who go down to Egypt for *h*,
31: 2 wicked and against those who *h* evildoers.
37:21 to your prayer for *h* against Sennacherib,
41:10 I will strengthen you, and *h* you,
41:13 I who say to you, "Fear not, I will *h* you."
41:14 I will *h* you,
44: 2 the Lord who made you, your *h*
49: 8 you, on the day of salvation I *h* you,
50: 7 The Lord GOD is my *h*,
50: 9 See, the Lord GOD is my *h*;
57:13 They shall not *h* you when you cry out,
58: 9 the LORD will answer, you shall cry for *h*,
63: 5 I looked about, but there was no one to *h*,
Jer 11:12 them no *h* whatever when misfortune strikes.
37: 7 out to *h* you will return to its own land,
Lam 1: 7 enemy hands, and she had no one to *h* her;
3: 8 Even when I cry out for *h*,
3:26 in silence for the saving *h* of the LORD.
3:56 "Let not your ear be deaf to my cry for *h*!"
Bar 4:17 What can I do to *h* you?
6:57 was on them, and they cannot *h* themselves.
6:67 The beasts which can *h* themselves by
Ez 16:49 and they gave no *h* to the poor and needy.
30: 8 to Egypt and when all who *h* her are broken.
Dn 10:13 one of the chief princes, came to *h* me.
11:34 When they fall, few people shall *h* them,
11:45 shall come to his end with none to *h* him.
Hos 12: 7 You shall return by the *h* of your God,
13: 9 who is there to *h* you?
Jon 2: 3 midst of the nether world I cried for *h*,
Hb 1: 2 I cry for *h* but you do not listen!
Mt 9: 6 To *h* you realize that the Son of Man has
12:24 expel demons only with the *h* of Beelzebul,
12:27 demons with Beelzebul's *h*, by whose help
15:25 and did him homage with the plea, *H* me,
Mk 3:22 demons with the *h* of the prince of demons."
4:30 What image will *h* to present it?
9:22 of your heart you can do anything to *h* us,
9:24 *H* my lack of trust!"
Lk 5: 7 mates in the other boat to come and *h* them.
10:40 Tell her to *h* me."
Jn 12: 6 to *h* himself to what was deposited there.)
20:31 to *h* you believe that Jesus is the Messiah,
Acts 4:20 *h* speaking of what we have heard and seen."
9:17 to *h* you recover your sight and be filled
12: 9 was taking place through the angel's *h*.
16: 9 him, "Come over to Macedonia and *h* us."
20:35 by such hard work that you must *h* the weak.
21:28 "Fellow Israelites, *h* us!
26:22 But I have had God's *h* to this very day,
Rom 16: 2 If she needs *h* in anything,
16: 2 her, for she herself has been of *h* to many,
1Cor 4: 8 launched upon your reign with no *h* from us.
7:35 what will *h* you to devote yourselves
16:11 *h* him come to me by sending him on his way
2Cor 1:11 But you must *h* us with your prayers,
1:16 receive your *h* on my journey to Judea.
2: 4 to *h* you realize the great love I bear you.
8:10 *h* you who began this good work last year,
Gal 6: 2 *H* carry one another's burdens;
Eph 4:29 to hear, things that will really *h* them.
6:16 it will *h* you extinguish the fiery darts
1Tm 5:10 Has she given *h* to those in distress?
5:16 *h* to the widows who are really in need.
2Tm 1:14 *h* of the Holy Spirit who dwells within us.
Heb 2:16 Surely he did not come to *h* angels,
2:18 he is able to *h* those who are tempted.
4:16 and favor and to find *h* in time of need.
3Jn 1: 6 God, you *h* them to continue their journey.

HELPED (23)

Ru 3:15 measures of barley, *h* her lift the bundle,
1Sm 7:12 explaining, "To this point the LORD *h* us."
19: 4 you, but has *h* you very much by his deeds.
19:17 You have *h* my enemy to get away!"
2Sm 22:49 to me and *h* me escape from my enemies,
1Chr 12: 1 the warriors who *h* him in his battles.
12:22 *h* David by taking charge of his troops,
2Chr 18:31 Jehoshaphat cried out and the LORD *h* him;
26: 7 God *h* him against the Philistines,
28:23 the gods of the kings of Aram who *h* them,
Ps(s) 86:17 that you, O LORD, have *h* and comforted me.
118:13 pressed and was falling, but the LORD *h* me.
Is 31: 3 helper shall stumble, the one *h* shall fall,
Mk 1:31 to her and grasped her hand and *h* her up,
9:27 took him by the hand and *h* him to his feet.
Lk 19:35 and laying their cloaks on it, *h* him mount.
Acts 9:41 He gave her his hand and *h* her to her feet.
10:26 Peter said as he *h* him to his feet,
14:27 related all that God had *h* them accomplish,
15: 4 all that God had *h* them accomplish.
1Cor 14:17 indeed, but the other man will not be *h*.
2Cor 6: 2 on a day of salvation I have *h* you."
Phil 1: 5 have all continually *h* promote the gospel

HELPER (11)

Ex 18: 4 for he said, "My father's God is my *h*;
Jdt 9:11 God of the lowly, the *h* of the oppressed,
Jb 6:13 Have I no *h*, and has advice deserted me?
Ps(s) 10:14 of the fatherless you are the *h*.
27: 9 You are my *h*:
30:11 O LORD, be my *h*."
54: 6 Behold, God is my *h*;
Sir 40:24 A brother, a *h*, for times of stress
51: 2 you have been my *h* against my adversaries.
Is 31: 3 forth his hand, the *h* shall stumble,
Heb 13: 6 "The Lord is my *h*, I will not be afraid

HELPERS (1)

Jb 9:13 the *h* of Rahab bow beneath him.

HELPFUL (2)

2Mc 2:25 things to memory, and to be *h* to all.
8: 7 as being especially *h* for such attacks.

HELPING (3)

1Mc 10:72 I am and who the others are who are *h* me.
Sir 29: 1 the precepts who holds out a *h* hand.
1Cor 2:12 *h* us to recognize the gifts he has given

HELPLESS (11)

Lv 26:37 so *h* will you be to take a stand against
Jgs 16: 5 overcome and bind him so as to keep him *h*.
16: 6 how you may be bound so as to be kept *h*."
2Mc 3:28 his whole bodyguard was carried away *h*,
Sir 29: 5 him and says he is *h* to meet the claim.
Is 13: 7 Therefore all hands fall *h*,
51:20 Your sons lie *h* at every street corner
Jer 6:24 *h* fall our hands,
47: 3 their hands fall *h* Because of the day
50:43 hears news of them, and *h* fall his hands;
Ez 21:12 heart shall fail, every hand shall fall *h*,

HELPLESSNESS (1)

Dt 28:32 look on and grieve for them in constant *h*.

HELPMATE (1)

Sir 36:24 is her husband's richest treasure, a *h*,

HELPS (7)

Gn 49:25 Israel, The God of your father, who *h* you,
1Chr 12:19 who helps you; your God it is who *h*
Ps(s) 37:40 And the LORD *h* them and delivers them;
Wis 17:12 surrender of the *h* that come from reason;
Is 41: 6 One man *h* another,
Rom 8:26 The Spirit too *h* us in our weakness,

HEM (11)

Ex 28:33 All around the *h* at the bottom you shall
28:34 alternating all around the *h* of the robe.
39:24 At the *h* of the robe pomegranates were
39:25 pomegranates all around the *h* of the robe:
39:26 alternating all around the *h* of the robe
Ps(s) 139: 5 you *h* me in and rest your hand upon me.
Sir 45: 8 and robe with pomegranates around the *h*,
Jer 10:18 I will *h* them in,
Ez 5: 3 and tie them in the *h* of your garment.
Zep 1:17 *h* men in till they walk like the blind,
Lk 19:43 encircle you with a rampart, *h* you in,

HEMAM (1)

Gn 36:22 Lotan's descendants were Hori and *H*,

HEMAN (15)

1Kgs 5:11 than Ethan the Ezrahite, or *H*,
1Chr 2: 6 The sons of Zerah were Zimri, Ethan, *H*,
6:18 *H*, the chanter,
15:17 Therefore the Levites appointed *H*,
15:19 The chanters, *H*,
16:41 With them were *H* and Jeduthun and the
25: 1 the descendants of Asaph, *H*
25: 4 Of *H*, these sons of Heman:
25: 5 All these were the sons of *H*,
25: 5 gave *H* fourteen sons and three daughters.
25: 6 these, whether of Asaph, Jeduthun, or *H*,
2Chr 5:12 singers, all who belonged to Asaph, *H*,
29:14 Zechariah and Mattaniah; of the sons of *H*:
35:15 Asaph, *H* and Jeduthun, the king's seer.

HEMDAN (2)

Gn 36:26 The descendants of Dishon were *H*,
1Chr 1:41 The sons of Dishon were *H*,

HEMMED (8)

Jos 8:22 Ai were *h* in by Israelites on either side,
Jgs 1:34 *h* in the Danites in the mountain region,
1Mc 7:46 They *h* them in,
Jb 3:23 is hidden from them, and whom God has *h* in!
18: 7 His vigorous steps are *h* in,
Prv 15:19 way of the sluggard is *h* in as with thorns,
Sir 51: 4 from flames that *h* me in on every side;
Lam 3: 7 He has *h* me in with no escape and weighed

HEMMING (1)

1Mc 6:18 were *h* in Israel around the sanctuary,

HEMORRHAGE (2)

Mk 5:25 been afflicted with a *h* for a dozen years.
Lk 8:43 A woman with a *h* of twelve years' duration,

HEMORRHAGES (1)

Mt 9:20 a woman who had suffered from *h* for twelve

HEMORRHOIDS (7)

1Sm 5: 6 the city and its vicinity with *h*;
5: 9 young and old, and *h* broke out on them.
5:12 who escaped death were afflicted with *h*,
6: 4 "Five golden *h* and five golden mice to
6: 5 make images of the *h* and of the mice that
6:11 the golden mice and the images of the *h*.
6:17 The golden *h* the Philistines sent back

HEMS (1)

Mk 5:31 him, "You can see how this crowd *h* you in,

HENA (3)

2Kgs 18:34 Where are the gods of Sepharvaim, *H*,
19:13 kings of the cities Sepharvaim, *H* and Avva?' "
Is 37:13 of the cities of Sepharvaim, *H* or Ivvah?' "

HENADAD (4)

Ezr 3: 9 with Kadmiel and Binnui, son of *H*,
Neh 3:18 Binnui, son of *H*,
3:24 After him, Binnui, son of *H*,
10:10 Binnui, of the sons of *H*;

HENCE (44)

Gn 10: 9 *h* the saying, "Like Nimrod
22:14 *h* people now say, "On the mountain
26:33 *h* the name of the city, Beer-sheba,
Ex 4:23 *H* I tell you: Let my son go,
10:26 *H*, our livestock also must go with us.
15:23 *H* this place was called Marah.
29:43 *h*, it will be made sacred by my glory
Lv 8:35 *H* you must remain at the entrance of the
11:22 *h* of these you may eat the following:
Nm 11: 3 *H* that place was called Taberah,
21: 3 *H* that place was named Hormah.
21:14 *H* it is said in the "Book of the Wars of
36:12 *h* their heritage remained in the tribe of
Jgs 15:19 *H* that spring in Lehi is called En-hakkore
18:12 *h* to this day the place,
2Chr 20:12 to do, *h* our eyes are turned toward you."
25:27 *h* he fled to Lachish.
Ezr 2:62 *h* they were degraded from the priesthood,
Neh 7:64 *h* they were degraded from the priesthood,
2Mc 5:17 while and *h* disregarded the holy Place.
Ps(s) 102:25 Take me not *h* in the midst of my days;
Eccl 9: 3 *H* the minds of men are filled with evil,
Wis 12:23 *H* those unjust also,
Jer 6:15 *H* they shall be among those who fall;
8:12 *H* they shall be among those who fall;
23:12 *H* their way shall become for them slippery
25: 8 *H*, thus says the LORD of hosts:
32:23 *H* you let all these evils befall them.
44:11 *H*, thus says the LORD of hosts,
48:12 *H*, the days shall come,
48:36 *H* the wail of flutes for Moab is in my

HENCE (cont.)

50:39 *H,* wildcats and desert beasts shall dwell
Lk 1:35 *h,* the holy offspring to be born
Rom 4:16 *H,* all depends on faith,
13:10 *h* love is the fulfillment of the law.
1Cor 15:21 *h* the resurrection of the dead comes
Eph 3:13 *H,* I beg you not to be disheartened by the
Phil 1:21 *h* dying is so much gain.
1Thes 4:8 *h,* whoever rejects these instructions
Heb 8:3 *h* the necessity for this one to have
9:18 *H,* not even the first covenant was
12:3 *h* do not grow despondent or abandon the
Jas 5:16 *H,* declare your sins to one another,
1Pt 2:11 *h* I urge you not to indulge your carnal

HENCEFORTH (11)

Gn 26:29 *H,* 'The LORD's blessing be upon you!' "
Lv 17:5 the Israelites shall *h* offer to the LORD,
1Chr 17:9 them in it to dwell there *h* undisturbed;
17:17 looked on me as *h* the most notable of men,
23:26 *H* the Levites need not carry the Dwelling
1Mc 10:41 shall *h* be handed over for the services of
11:35 all other things that would *h* be due to us,
11:36 *H* none of these provisions shall ever be
Jer 44:26 of Judah shall *h* pronounce my name saying,
Ez 48:35 of the City shall *h* be "The LORD is here."
Gal 6:17 *H,* let no man trouble me,

HENCHMAN (1)

1Sm 21:8 the Edomite, and he was Saul's chief *h.*

HENCHMEN (4)

1Sm 22:17 The king then commanded his *h* standing by:
2Sm 15:1 himself with chariots, horses, and fifty *h.*
1Kgs 1:5 He acquired chariots, drivers, and fifty *h.*
2Mc 4:3 were being committed by one of his *h,*

HENNA (1)

Sg 1:14 cluster of *h* from the vineyards of Engedi.

HEPHER (8)

Nm 26:32 through *H* the clan of the Hepherites.
26:33 Zelophehad, son of *H,*
27:1 Zelophehad, son of *H,*
Jos 12:17 Adullam, Makkedah, Bethel, Tappuah, *H,*
17:2 Helek, Asriel, Shechem, *H* and Shemida,
17:3 Furthermore, Zelophehad, son of *H,*
1Kgs 4:10 as in Socoh and the whole region of *H;*
1Chr 4:6 Naarah bore him Ahuzzam, *H,*

HEPHERITES (1)

Nm 26:32 through Hepher the clan of the *H.*

HEPHZIBAH (1)

2Kgs 21:1 His mother's name was *H.*

HERADONIJAH (1)

1Kgs 1:5 the king did not have relations with *h,*

HERALD (17)

2Sm 1:20 Gath, *h* it not in the streets of Ashkelon,
2Kgs 18:18 and the *h* Joah,
18:37 Shebnah the scribe, and the *h* Joah,
1Chr 18:15 Jehoshaphat, son of Ahilud, was *h:*
Est 10:3 and the *h* of peace for his whole race.
Sir 1:21 words, then the lips of many *h* his wisdom.
Is 36:3 and Shebna the scribe, and the *h* Joah,
36:22 Hilkiah, Shebna the scribe, and the *h* Joah,
40:9 a high mountain, Zion, *h* of glad tidings;
40:9 of your voice, Jerusalem, *h* of good news!
Jer 49:14 a *h* has been sent among the nations:
51:31 One runner meets another, *h* meets herald,
Dn 3:4 A *h* cried out:
Ob 1:1 and a *h* has been sent among the nations:
1Tm 2:7 been made its *h* and apostle (believe me,
Rv 14:6 the *h* of everlasting good news to the

HERALDED (2)

Acts 13:24 John *h* the coming of Jesus by proclaiming
Rom 1:8 your faith is *h* throughout the world.

HERALD'S (3)

Mt 3:3 "A *h* voice in the desert;
Mk 1:3 a *h* voice in the desert,
Lk 3:4 "A *h* voice in the desert,

HERB (1)

Wis 16:12 neither *h* nor application cured them,

HERBAGE (1)

Is 42:15 and hills, all their *h* I will dry up;

HERBS (9)

Ex 12:8 flesh with unleavened bread and bitter *h.*
Nm 9:11 it with unleavened bread and bitter *h,*
2Kgs 4:39 field to gather *h* and found a wild vine,
Ps(s) 37:2 quickly wither, and like green *h* they wilt.
147:8 the mountains and *h* for the service of men;
Prv 15:17 Better a dish of *h* where love is than a
Sg 5:13 beds of spice with ripening aromatic *h.*
Sir 38:4 *h* which the prudent man should not neglect;
Mt 23:23 You pay tithes on mint and *h* and seeds

HERCULES (2)

2Mc 4:19 silver drachmas for the sacrifice to *H.*
4:20 sacrifice to *H* was in fact applied by those

HERD (27)

Gn 18:7 He ran to the *h,*
Ex 34:19 whether in the *h* or in the flock.
Lv 1:2 must be from the *h* or from the flock.
1:3 "If his holocaust offering is from the *h,*
3:1 offering makes his offering from the *h,*
22:21 the *h* or the flock in fulfillment of a vow,
27:32 The tithes of the *h* and the flock shall be
Nm 15:3 oblation from the *h* or from the flock,
Dt 12:17 oil, of the first-born of your *h* or flock,
12:21 *h* or flock that the LORD has given you,
14:23 well as the firstlings of your *h* and flock,
15:19 firstlings of your *h* and of your flock.
16:2 from your flock or your *h* to the LORD,
17:1 from the *h* or from the flock an animal
18:3 the victim is from the *h* or from the flock,
Tb 8:19 he himself went out to the *h* and picked
Ps(s) 68:31 the *h* of strong bulls and the bullocks,
78:52 and guided them like a *h* in the desert.
Mi 2:12 fold, like a *h* in the midst of its corral;
Hb 3:17 the fold and there be no *h* in the stalls,
Mt 8:30 away a large *h* of swine was feeding.
8:31 you expel us, send us into the *h* of swine."
8:32 The whole *h* went rushing down the bluff
Mk 5:11 It happened that a large *h* of swine was
5:13 The *h* of about two thousand went rushing
Lk 8:32 It happened that a large *h* of swine was
8:33 the *h* charged down the bluff into the lake,

HERDED (1)

Ps(s) 49:15 sheep they are *h* into the nether world;

HERDING (1)

Lk 17:7 or *h* sheep and he came in from the fields,

HERDS (42)

Gn 12:16 with Abram, and he received flocks and *h,*
13:5 Abram, also had flocks and *h* and tents,
20:14 Then Abimelech took flocks and *h* and male
24:35 he has given him flocks and *h,*
26:14 He acquired such flocks and *h,*
32:8 him, as well as his flocks, *h* and camels,
33:13 I am encumbered with the flocks and *h,*
34:28 They seized their flocks, *h* and asses,
45:10 and grandchildren, your flocks and *h,*
46:32 have brought with them their flocks and *h,*
47:1 flocks and *h* and everything else they own;
47:17 their flocks of sheep and *h* of cattle,
50:8 and *h* were left in the region of Goshen.
Ex 9:3 your horses, asses, camels, *h* and flocks
10:9 well as our flocks and *h* must accompany us.
10:24 But your flocks and *h* must remain."
12:32 Take your flocks, too, and your *h,*
12:38 livestock, very numerous flocks and *h.*
34:3 even the flocks and the *h* are not to go
Nm 31:9 all their *h* and flocks and wealth as spoil,
32:26 our *h* and other livestock remain in the
35:3 serve their *h* and flocks and other animals.
Dt 7:13 of your *h* and the young of your flocks,
8:13 them, and have increased your *h* and flocks,
12:6 and the firstlings of your *h* and flocks.
28:4 of your *h* and the young of your flocks!
28:18 of your *h* and the young of your flocks!
28:51 no issue of your *h* or young of your flocks,
Jgs 5:16 hearths listening to the lowing of the *h?*
2Sm 12:2 rich man had flocks and *h* in great numbers.
12:4 would not take from his own flocks and *h*
17:29 butter and cheese from the flocks and *h,*
Neh 10:37 the first-born of our flocks and *h.*
Jdt 2:27 fields, destroyed their flocks and *h,*
3:3 all our wheat fields, our flocks and *h,*
Jb 24:2 they steal away *h* and pasture them
Prv 27:23 flocks, give careful attention to your *h;*
Eccl 2:7 growing *h* of cattle and flocks of sheep,
Jer 49:29 Their tents and *h* shall be taken away,
49:32 be your booty, their many *h* your spoil;
Hos 5:6 and their *h* they shall go to seek the LORD,
Jl 1:18 The *h* of cattle are bewildered!

HERDSMANS (1)

Lv 27:32 animal as they are counted by the *h* rod.

HERDSMEN (3)

Gn 13:7 *h* of Abram's livestock and those of Lot's.
13:8 you and me, or between your *h* and mine,
Jb 1:15 They put the *h* to the sword,

HERE (443)

Gn 3:12 "The woman whom you put *h* with me
5:24 walked with God, and he was no longer *h.*
12:19 *H,* then, is your wife.
15:16 time-span the others shall come back *h;*
19:9 they sneered, "came *h* as an immigrant,
19:12 "Who else belongs to you *h?*
19:15 wife and your two daughters who are *h,*
20:15 his wife Sarah to him, he said, *H,*
22:5 "Both of you stay *h* with the donkey,
22:7 continued, *H* are the fire and the wood,
24:13 While I stand *h* at the spring and the
24:43 While I stand *h* at the spring,
24:51 *H* is Rebekah,
27:35 *h* by a ruse and carried off your blessing,"
29:6 *h* comes his daughter Rachel with his flock."
29:8 "until all the shepherds are *h* to roll
30:3 She replied, *H* is my maidservant Bilhah.
31:11 *H!'*
31:32 identify anything *h* as belonging to you,
31:37 produce it *h* before your kinsmen and mine,
31:51 "Here is this mound, and *h* is the memorial
32:11 the Jordan *h* with nothing but my staff,
34:10 in it, and acquire landed property *h."*
37:17 man told him, "They have moved on from *h;*
37:19 *H* comes that master dreamer!
37:20 and throw him into one of the cisterns *h;*
38:21 has never been a temple prostitute *h."*
39:8 "As long as I am *h,"*
39:14 He came in *h* to lie with me,
39:17 slave whom you brought *h* broke in on me,
40:14 is well with you, that I was *h* with you,
40:15 and *h* I have not done anything for which I
42:15 unless your youngest brother comes *h,*
42:15 life of Pharaoh that you shall not leave *h.*
42:16 while the rest of you stay *h* under arrest.
42:28 *H* it is in my bag!"
43:7 he would say, 'Bring your brother down *h'?"*
43:20 came down *h* once before to procure food.
44:16 *H* we are,
45:5 reproach yourselves for having sold me *h.*
45:5 lives that God sent me *h* ahead of you.
45:8 not really you but God who had me come *h;*
45:13 But hurry and bring my father down *h."*
45:18 your families, and then come back *h* to me;
45:19 transport your father on your way back *h.*
46:2 *H* I am," he answered.
46:4 I will also bring you back *h,*
47:23 *h* is your seed for sowing the land.
48:5 the land of Egypt before I joined you *h,*
48:9 his father, "whom God has given me *h."*
Ex 3:4 He answered, *H* I am."
14:11 had to bring us out *h* to die in the desert?
15:25 It was *h* that the LORD,
16:2 *H* in the desert the whole Israelite
17:1 *H* there was no water for the people to
17:3 *H,* then, in their thirst for water
17:3 Was it just to have us die *h* of thirst
19:2 was encamped *h* in front of the mountain,
19:4 on eagle wings and brought you *h* to myself.
24:14 "Wait *h* for us until we return to you.
33:1 *h* to the land which I swore to Abraham,
33:15 yourself, do not make us go up from *h.*
33:21 *H,"* continued the LORD,
34:10 *H,* then," said the LORD, "is the covenant
Lv 4:15 bring it before the meeting tent, and *h,*
Nm 13:17 Moses said to them, "Go up *h* in the Negeb,
13:27 with milk and honey, and *h* is its fruit.
14:2 or that *h* in the desert we were dead!
14:29 *H* in the desert shall your dead bodies fall.
14:32 your bodies shall fall *h* in the desert,
14:33 *h* where your children must wander for
14:35 *h* in the desert they shall die to the last
14:40 up into the foothills, saying, *H* we are,
16:13 not satisfied with having led us *h*
20:1 It was *h* that Miriam died, and here
20:5 *H* there is not even water to drink!"
20:16 Now *h* we are at the town of Kadesh at the
20:18 him, "You shall not pass through *h;*
21:25 Israel seized all the towns *h* and settled
22:5 "A people has come *h* from Egypt who now
22:8 said to them in reply, "Stay *h* overnight,
22:11 'This people that came *h* from Egypt now
22:19 But, you too shall stay *h* overnight,
22:29 sword at hand, I would kill you *h* and now."
22:40 *H* Balak slaughtered oxen and sheep,
23:1 seven bullocks and seven rams for me *h."*
23:3 *h* by your holocaust while I go over there.
23:7 From Aram has Balak brought me *h,*
23:9 *H* is a people that lives apart and does
23:11 was to curse my foes that I brought you *h;*
23:15 said to Balak, "Stand *h* by your holocaust,
23:24 *H* is a people that springs up like a
23:29 *H* build me seven altars; and here prepare
24:10 to curse my foes that I summoned you *h;*
27:12 "Go up *h* into the Abarim Mountains and
32:6 then, to engage in war, while you remain *h?*
32:14 And now *h* you are,
32:16 only to build sheepfolds *h* for our flocks,
32:17 can remain *h* in the fortified towns,
32:22 subdued before him, then you may return *h,*
Dt 1:7 Leave *h* and go to the hill country of the
3:6 so also *h* we doomed all the cities,
5:3 us, all of us who are alive *h* this day.
5:31 Then you wait *h* near me and I will give

9:12 he said to me, 'Go down from *h* now,
11:26 "I set before you *h*,
12: 8 *h*, everyone does what seems right
22:17 But *h* is the evidence of my daughter's
29:14 those who are not *h* among us today
29:14 us who are now *h* present before the LORD,
29:21 who will come *h* from far-off lands,
30:15 *H*, then I have today set before you life
32:49 *h* in the Abarim Mountains [it is in the
Jos 1: 2 So prepare to cross the Jordan *h*,
1:11 from now you shall cross the Jordan *h*,
1:14 land Moses gave you *h* beyond the Jordan.
3: 9 *h* and listen to the words of the LORD,
4:22 'Israel crossed the Jordan *h* on dry ground.'
9:13 *h* are our wineskins,
10: 6 Come up *h* quickly and save us.
14: 1 *H* follow the portions which the Israelites
18: 6 You shall bring *h* to me the description of
18: 6 then cast lots for you *h* before the LORD,
Jgs 4:20 anyone comes and asks, 'Is there someone *h*?'
6:18 Do not depart from *h*,
8:15 Succoth and said, *H* are Zebah and Zalmunna,
14:15 you invite us *h* to reduce us to poverty?"
18: 3 brought you *h* and what are you doing here?"
18: 3 "What is your interest *h*?"
19: 6 to spend the night *h* and enjoy yourself?"
19: 9 Spend the night *h* and enjoy yourself.
20: 7 Now that you are all *h*,
Ru 2: 7 this morning she has remained *h* until now,
2: 8 you are not to leave *h*.
2: 8 Stay *h* with my women servants.
2:14 said to her, "Come *h* and have some food;
3:18 Naomi then said, "Wait *h*,
4: 4 you, bidding you before those *h* present,
1Sm 1:26 lord, I am the woman who stood near you *h*,
3: 4 called to Samuel, who answered, *H* I am."
3: 5 He ran to Eli and said, *H* I am.
3: 6 *H* I am," he said.
3: 8 up and going to Eli, he said, *H* I am.
3:16 He replied, *H* I am."
5:10 God of Israel *h* to kill us and our kindred?"
9:27 of us, but stay *h* yourself for the moment,
10:22 they consulted the LORD, "Has he come *h*?"
12: 3 *H* I stand!
14:12 "Come up *h*,"
14:18 then said to Ahijah, "Bring the ephod *h*."
14:33 Roll a large stone *h* for me."
14:34 Slaughter it *h* and then eat,
14:38 Saul then said, "Come *h*,
16: 6 the LORD'S anointed is *h* before him."
16:11 the sacrificial banquet until he arrives *h*."
16:16 we, your servants *h* in attendance on you,
17:44 his gods and said to him, "Come *h* to me,
21:10 is *h* [wrapped in a mantle] behind an ephod.
21:10 there is no sword *h* except that one."
23: 3 "We are afraid *h* in Judah.
24:12 *h* at this end of your mantle which I hold.
26:22 *H* is the king's spear.
29: 3 asked, "What are those Hebrews doing *h*?"
2Sm 1: 7 When I said, *H* I am,'
1:10 from his arm and brought them *h* to my lord."
2:25 *H* the Benjaminites rallied around Abner,
5: 1 *H* we are, your bone and your flesh.
5: 6 David was told, "You cannot enter *h*:
5: 6 way of saying, "David cannot enter *h*."
7: 2 prophet, *H* I am living in a house of cedar,
11:12 David said to Uriah, "Stay *h* today also,
11:25 for the sword devours now *h* and now there.
14:32 "I was summoning you to come *h*,
18:30 "Step aside and remain in attendance *h*."
19:38 *H* is your servant Chimham.
20: 4 Then present yourself *h*."
20:16 Tell Joab to come *h*,
24:22 *H* are oxen for holocausts,
1Kgs 1:28 King David answered, "Call Bathsheba *h*."
2:30 I will die *h*."
12:28 *H* is your God,
13:17 neither to eat bread nor drink water *h*,
17: 3 "Leave *h*,
18: 8 "Go tell your master, 'Elijah is *h*!'"
18:10 When they replied, 'He is not *h*,'
18:11 Elijah is *h*!'
18:14 Elijah is *h*!'
18:30 said to all the people, "Come *h* to me."
19: 9 of the LORD came to him, "Why are you *h*,
19:13 voice said to him, "Elijah, why are you *h*?"
20:40 while your servant was looking *h* and there,
22: 7 prophet of the LORD *h* whom we may consult
2Kgs 2: 2 "Stay *h*, please," Elijah said to Elisha.
2: 4 Then Elijah said to him, "Stay *h*,
2: 6 Elijah said to Elisha, "Please stay *h*;
3:11 *h* through whom we may inquire of the LORD
3:11 poured water on the hands of Elijah, is *h*."
6: 1 room for us to continue to live *h* with you.
7: 3 "Why should we sit *h* until we die?
7: 4 If we remain *h*, we shall die too.
10:23 is no worshiper of the LORD *h* with you,
19: 4 send up a prayer for the remnant that is *h*.'"
1Chr 4:33 *H* is where they dwelt,
11: 5 said to David, "You shall not enter *h*."
11:11 *H* is the list of David's warriors:
13: 3 let us bring the ark of our God *h* among us,
19: 5 and then you may come back *h*."

29:17 *h* present also giving to you generously.
2Chr 4: 6 *H* were cleansed the victims for the
13:12 and his priests are *h* with trumpets to
18: 6 prophet of the LORD *h* whom we may consult
23: 3 *H* is the king's son who must reign,
28:13 "Do not bring the captives *h*,
Ezr 4: 2 king of Assyria, who had us brought *h*."
5:11 the house built *h* long years ago,
9:15 *H* we are before you in our sins.
Neh 2:14 *h* for my mount to pass with me astride,
9:18 *H* is your God who brought you up out of
Tb 2: 2 from among our kinsmen exiled *h* in Nineveh.
2: 8 escaped, *h* he is again burying the dead!"
5: 5 I have come *h* to work."
5:10 *H* I am, a blind man who cannot see
8:20 not stir from *h*, but shall remain here
10: 6 He will be *h* soon."
14: 8 do not remain *h*.
14:10 For I see that people *h* shamelessly commit
Jdt 5: 9 *H* they settled,
9: 6 decide on come forward and say, *H* we are!'
9: 7 *H* are the Assyrians,
13:15 *H* is the head of Holofernes,
13:15 and *h* is the canopy under which he lay in
14: 5 of Israel and sent him *h* to meet his death."
14:18 *H* is Holofernes headless on the ground!"
Est C:29 From the day I was brought *h* till now,
1Mc 2:65 *H* is your brother Simeon who I know is a
7:40 *H* Judas uttered this prayer:
12:45 That is why I came *h*."
2Mc 1: 6 Even now we are praying for you *h*.
2:32 *H*, then,
14: 7 say, the high priesthood, I have come *h*—
14:33 and erect *h* a splendid temple to Dionysus."
15:37 I will bring my own story to an end *h* too.
Jb 38:11 and *h* shall your proud waves be stilled!
38:35 or will they say to you, *H* we are"?
Ps(s) 45:13 And the city of Tyre is *h* with gifts;
Prv 9: 4 "Let whoever is simple turn in *h*;
9:16 "Let whoever is simple turn in *h*,
Eccl 2:21 For *h* is a man who has labored with wisdom
5:17 *H* is what I recognize as good:
Sg 2: 8 *h* he comes springing across the mountains,
2: 9 *H* he stands behind our wall,
Wis 18:18 And cast half-dead, one *h*,
Sir 29:26 "Come *h*, stranger, set the table
31:12 Nor cry out, "How much food there is *h*!"
Is 6: 8 *H* I am," I said; "send me!"
20: 6 We have fled *h* for help and deliverance
21: 9 *H* he comes now:
22:16 doing *h*, and what people have you here,
22:16 that *h* you have hewn for yourself a tomb?"
28:10 rule on rule, rule on rule, *h* a little,
28:12 *H* is repose
28:13 Rule on rule, rule on rule, *h* a little,
35: 4 *H* is your God,
37: 4 Send up a prayer for the remnant that is *h*.'"
40: 9 *H* is your God!
40:10 *H* comes with power the Lord GOD,
40:10 *H* is his reward with him,
42: 1 *H* is my servant whom I uphold,
45:21 Come *h* and declare in counsel together:
52: 5 But now, what am I to do *h*?
52: 6 It is I who have foretold it. *H* I am!
58: 9 he will say *H* I am!
62:11 *H* is his reward with him,
65: 1 *H* I am! Here I am!
Jer 3:22 *H* we are,
7: 8 But *h* you are,
8:14 Why do we remain *h*?
16:12 *H* you are, every one of you
29:15 raised up for us prophets *h* in Babylon"
32:37 to this place and settle them *h* in safety.
43:10 king of Babylon, and bring him *h*.
44: 8 by sacrificing to strange gods *h* in the
Bar 3:35 When he calls them they answer, *H* we are!"
4:37 *H* come your sons whom you once let go,
Ez 8: 6 that the house of Israel is practicing *h*,
8: 9 abominable evils which they are doing *h*.
8:17 do the abominable things they have done *h*—
21:12 See, it is coming, it is *h*!
40: 4 brought *h* so that I might show it to you.
40:26 with palms *h* and there on its pilasters.
40:34 palms were on its pilasters *h* and there,
40:37 palms were on its pilasters *h* and there,
42:13 *h* the priests who draw near to the LORD
42:13 and *h* they shall keep the most sacred
42:14 *h* the clothing in which they ministered,
43: 7 *h* I will dwell among the Israelites
46:20 *H* the priests cook the guilt offerings and
48:35 City shall henceforth be "The LORD is *h*."
Dn 13:21 maids because a young man was *h* with you,
13:43 *H* I am about to die,
Am 7:10 has conspired against you *h* within Israel;
Zec 2: 4 said, *H* are the horns that scattered Judah,
3: 7 give you access among these standing *h*.
5: 3 it shall every perjurer be expelled from *h*.
6:12 *H* is a man whose name is Shoot,
Mt 2: 5 *H* is what the prophet has written:
8: 9 If I say to another, 'Come *h*,' he comes.
12: 2 "See *h*! Your disciples are doing
12: 6 is something greater than the temple *h*.
12:18 *H* is my servant whom I have chosen,

12:41 but you have a greater than Jonah *h*.
12:42 but you have a greater than Solomon *h*.
14:17 "We have nothing *h*,"
14:18 "Bring them *h*," he said.
16:28 among those standing *h* there are some who
17: 4 to Jesus, "Lord, how good that we are *h*!
17: 4 permission I will erect three booths *h*,
17:17 Bring him *h* to me!"
17:20 to this mountain, 'Move from *h* to there,'
19:27 *H* we have put everything aside to follow
20: 6 'Why have you been standing *h* idle all day?'
21:38 *H* is the one who will inherit everything.
22:12 is it you came in *h* not properly dressed?'
24:23 you at that time, 'Look, the Messiah is *h*,'
25: 6 midnight someone shouted, 'The groom is *h*!
25:25 *H* is your money back.'
26:36 "Stay *h* while I go over there and pray."
26:38 Remain *h* and stay awake with me."
26:46 See, my betrayer is *h*."
26:50 answered, "Friend, do what you are *h* for!"
28: 6 for Jesus the crucified, but he is not *h*.
Mk 1: 1 *H* begins the gospel of Jesus Christ,
3: 3 "Stand up *h* in front!"
6: 3 Are not his sisters our neighbors *h*?"
6:36 *h* and buy themselves something to eat?"
9: 1 among those standing *h* there are some who
9: 5 "Rabbi, how good it is for us to be *h*!
11: 3 it but he will send it back *h* at once.'"
12: 7 *H* is the one who will inherit everything.
13:21 you at that time, 'Look, the Messiah is *h*!'
14:32 "Sit down *h* while I pray,"
14:34 Remain *h* and stay awake."
15:32 come down from that cross *h* and now so
16: 6 He has been raised up; he is not *h*.
Lk 4: 9 Son of God, throw yourself down from *h*,
4:23 'Do *h* in your own country the things we
6: 8 withered, "Get up and stand *h* in front."
7: 8 to another, 'Come *h*,'
7:34 and you say, *H* is a glutton and a drunkard,
9:27 there are some standing *h* who will not
9:33 "Master, how good it is for us to be *h*.
9:41 Bring your son *h* to me."
11:31 but you have a greater than Solomon *h*.
11:32 but you have a greater than Jonah *h*.
13: 7 He said to the vinedresser, 'Look *h*!
13:16 Should not this daughter of Abraham *h* who
15:17 than enough to eat, while *h* I am starving!
16: 4 *H* is a way to make sure that people will
16:25 Now he has found consolation *h*,
16:26 wish to cross from *h* to you cannot do so,
17:21 of reporting that it is *h*' or 'there.'
19:20 *H* is your money,
22:38 They said, "Lord, *h* are two swords!"
24: 6 He is not *h*; he has been raised up.
24:41 to them, "Have you anything *h* to eat?"
24:49 Remain *h* in the city until you are clothed
Jn 2:16 "Get them out of *h*!
4:15 and have to keep coming *h* to draw water."
4:16 call your husband, and then come back *h*."
4:23 Yet an hour is coming, and is already *h*,
4:37 *H* we have the saying verified:
6: 9 "There is a lad *h* who has five barley
6:25 said to him, "Rabbi, when did you come *h*?"
7: 3 "You ought to leave *h* and go to Judea so
7:26 *H* he is speaking in public and they don't
7:39 *H* he was referring to the Spirit,
8:42 me, for I came forth from God, and am *h*.
11:21 "Lord, if you had been *h*,
11:28 "The Teacher is *h*,
11:32 been *h* my brother would never have died."
13:18 purpose *h* is the fulfillment of Scripture:
18:36 As it is, my kingdom is not *h*."
20:30 signs not recorded *h*—
Acts 1:11 do you stand *h* looking up at the skies?
9:10 *H* I am, Lord," came the answer.
9:14 He is *h* now with authorization from the
9:17 Jesus who appeared to you on the way *h*,
9:21 Did he not come *h* purposely to apprehend
10:21 What brought you *h*?"
10:32 to invite Simon known as Peter to come *h*.
16:28 We are all still *h*."
17: 6 they come *h* and Jason has taken them in.
19:37 you have brought *h* are not temple-robbers.
22: 3 *H* I sat at the feet of Gamaliel and was
22:21 I mean to send you far from *h*,
23:11 have given testimony to me *h* in Jerusalem,
23:27 *H* is a man whom the Jews seized and were
24:19 These are the men who should be *h* before
24:20 Let those who are *h* declare what crime
25:14 "There is a prisoner *h*,"
25:17 When they came *h* with me,
25:21 Paul appealed to be kept *h* until there
25:24 and all you who are *h* present with us,
25:24 Jewish community, both *h* and in Jerusalem,
26:22 *h* to testify to great and small alike.
26:26 *h* is well acquainted with these matters.
28:14 *H* we found some of the brothers,
Rom 10:12 *H* there is no difference between Jew and
1Cor 9: 9 Is God concerned *h* for oxen,
14:15 What is my point *h*?
2Cor 5: 2 We groan while we are *h*,
6: 9 dead, yet *h* we are,
10:10 but when he is *h* in person he is

HERE (cont.)
Gal 3:25 But now that faith is *h*,
Eph 4:14 be children no longer, tossed *h* and there,
Phil 1:13 well known throughout the praetorium *h*,
4:21 My brothers *h* send you theirs,
Col 3:11 There is no Greek or Jew *h*,
4: 9 They will tell you all that has happened *h*.
2Thes 2: 2 believing that the day of the Lord is *h*.
1Tm 4: 8 with its promise of life *h* and hereafter.
2Tm 4:21 Get *h* before winter if you can.
Heb 2:13 and again, *H* am I,
13:14 For *h* we have no lasting city;
Jas 2: 3 well-dressed man and say, "Sit right *h*,
5: 4 *H*, crying aloud,
1Pt 1: 6 There is cause for rejoicing *h*.
1Jn 1: 5 *H*, then, is the message we have heard
3Jn 1:15 The beloved *h* send you their greetings;
Rv 3:20 *H* I stand, knocking at the door.
4: 1 "Come up *h* and I will show you what must
10: 9 He said to me, *H*, take it and eat it!
11:12 voice from heaven say to them, "Come up *h*!"
13:18 A certain wisdom is needed *h*;
17: 9 *H* is the clue for one who possesses wisdom!
22:19 tree of life and the holy city described *h*!

HEREAFTER (4)
1Mc 8:30 *h* decide to add or take away anything,
Wis 2: 2 *h* we shall be as though we had not been;
Acts 15:16 *H* I will return and rebuild the fallen hut
1Tm 4: 8 so, with its promise of life here and *h*.

HEREBY (5)
Gn 17:20 I *h* bless him.
Nm 18:21 I *h* assign all tithes in Israel as their
25:12 that I *h* give him my pledge of friendship,
2Sm 14:21 "I *h* grant this request.
Est B: 6 we *h* decree that all those who are

HEREDITARY (12)
Lv 25:33 *h* property in the midst of the Israelites.
25:34 it must always remain their *h* property.
25:46 and leave to your sons as their *h* property,
27:16 to the LORD is a piece of his *h* land,
27:22 purchased and not a part of his *h* property,
27:24 the field shall revert to the *h* owner of
27:28 is a human being or an animal or a *h* field,
Nm 27: 7 *h* property among their father's kinsmen,
32:32 our *h* property on this side of the Jordan."
35: 2 "Tell the Israelites that out of their *h*
Dt 32: 9 portion was Jacob, His *h* share was Israel.
Jgs 2: 6 went to take possession of his own *h* land.

HEREIN (1)
Rv 22:18 visit him with all the plagues described *h*!

HERES (1)
Jgs 8:13 returned from battle by the pass of *H*.

HERESH (1)
1Chr 9:15 descendants of Merari; Bakbakkar; *H*;

HERESIES (1)
2Pt 2: 1 teachers who will smuggle in pernicious *h*.

HERETH (1)
1Sm 22: 5 so David left and went to the forest of *H*.

HERETIC (1)
Ti 3:10 Warn a *h* once and then a second time;

HEREWITH (3)
Gn 41:41 *H*," Pharaoh told Joseph,
Phil 4:18 *H* is my receipt,
1Pt 5:12 *H* are expressed my encouragement and my

HERITAGE (174)
Gn 48: 6 but their *h* shall be recorded in the names
Ex 32:13 give your descendants as their perpetual *h*.'"
Nm 18:20 "You shall not have any *h* in the land of
18:20 will be your portion and your *h* among them.
18:21 assign all tithes in Israel as their *h*
18:23 shall not have any *h* among the Israelites,
18:24 I have assigned to them as their *h* the tithes
18:24 are not to have any *h* among the Israelites."
18:26 I have assigned you from them as your *h*,
26:53 land shall be divided as their *h*
26:54 a large group you shall assign a large *h*,
26:54 small *h*, each group receiving its heritage
26:55 as the *h* of the various ancestral tribes.
26:56 group, large or small, be assigned its *h*."
26:62 no *h* was given them among the Israelites.
27: 7 letting their father's *h* pass on to them.
27: 8 shall let his *h* pass on to his daughter;
27: 9 you shall give his *h* to his brothers;
27:10 shall give his *h* to his father's brothers;
27:11 his *h* to his nearest relative in his clan,
32:18 Israelites has taken possession of his *h*,
32:19 any *h* with them once we cross the Jordan,
32:19 so long as we receive a *h* for ourselves on
33:54 *h* to a large group and a small heritage
33:54 be within the *h* of his ancestral tribe.
34: 2 that shall fall to you as your *h*—
34:14 Manasseh, have already received their *h*;
34:15 one half tribes have received their *h*
34:29 Israelites their *h* in the land of Canaan.
35: 8 to the Levites in proportion to its own *h*."
36: 2 commanded by the LORD to give the *h*
36: 3 their *h* will be withdrawn from our
36: 3 will be withdrawn from our ancestral *h*
36: 3 thus the *h* that fell to us by lot will be
36: 4 the *h* of these women will be permanently
36: 7 so that no *h* of the Israelites will pass
36: 7 will retain their own ancestral *h*.
36: 8 in possession of their own ancestral *h*.
36: 9 no *h* can pass from one tribe to another,
36: 9 tribes will retain their own ancestral *h*."
36:12 hence their *h* remained in the tribe of
Dt 1:38 him, for he is to give Israel its *h*.
2:12 of their *h* which the LORD has given them.]
4:21 good land which he is giving you as a *h*.
4:38 bring you in and to make their land your *h*,
9:26 the *h* which your majesty has ransomed and
9:29 are, after all, your people and your *h*,
10: 9 has no share in the *h* with his brothers;
10: 9 the LORD himself is his *h*,
12: 9 your resting place, the *h* which the LORD,
12:10 the LORD, your God, is giving you as a *h*,
12:12 but has no share of his own in your *h*.
14:27 for he has no share in the *h* with you.
14:29 Levite who has no share in the *h* with you,
15: 4 land he will give you to occupy as your *h*,
18: 1 shall have no share in the *h* with Israel;
18: 2 Levi shall have no *h* among his brothers;
18: 2 the LORD himself is his *h*,
19: 3 the LORD, your God, will give you as a *h*,
19:10 the LORD, your God, is giving you as a *h*,
19:14 *h* you receive in the land which the LORD,
20:16 LORD, your God, is giving you as your *h*,
24: 4 the LORD, your God, is giving you as a *h*.
25:19 he is giving you to occupy as your *h*,
26: 1 the LORD, your God, is giving you as a *h*,
29: 7 we then gave as a *h* to the Reubenites,
31: 7 you must put them in possession of their *h*.
32: 8 Most High assigned the nations their *h*,
Jos 11:23 Joshua gave it to Israel as their *h*,
13: 6 areas in the division of the Israelite *h*,
13: 7 Manasseh the land which is to be their *h*."
13: 8 Gadites, had received their *h* which Moses,
13:14 tribe of Levi Moses assigned no *h* since,
13:14 the LORD, the God of Israel, is their *h*.
13:23 were the *h* of the clans of the Reubenites.
13:28 were the *h* of the clans of the Gadites.
13:33 Moses gave no *h* to the tribe of Levi,
13:33 himself, the God of Israel, is their *h*,
14: 2 the Israelites determined their *h* by lot,
14: 3 had already given a *h* beyond the Jordan;
14: 3 Levites were given no *h* among the tribes,
14: 9 *h* and that of your descendants forever,
14:13 of Jephunneh, and gave him Hebron as his *h*.
14:14 remains the *h* of the Kenizzite Caleb,
15:20 *h* of the clans of the tribe of Judahites:
16: 4 Within the *h* of Manasseh and Ephraim,
16: 5 the dividing line for the *h* of the clans
16: 8 was the *h* of the clans of the Ephraimites,
17: 4 Moses to give us a *h* among our kinsmen."
17: 4 a *h* was given to each of them
17:14 us only one lot and one share as our *h*?
18: 2 Israelites had not yet received their *h*.
18: 7 the priesthood of the LORD is their *h*;
18: 7 the *h* east of the Jordan which Moses,
18:20 This was how the *h* of the clans of the
18:28 was the *h* of the clans of Benjaminites.
19: 1 The *h* of the clans of the tribe of
19: 2 For their *h* they received Beersheba,
19: 8 This was the *h* of the clans of the tribe
19: 9 This *h* of the Simeonites was within the
19: 9 the Simeonites obtained their *h* within it.
19:10 The limit of their *h* was at Sarid.
19:16 the *h* of the clans of the Zebulunites.
19:23 the *h* of the clans of the Issacharites.
19:31 their villages to comprise the *h* of the clans
19:39 to comprise the *h* of the clans of the
19:41 Their *h* was the territory of Zorah,
19:48 *h* of the clans of the tribe of the Danites.
19:49 assigned a *h* in their midst to Joshua,
21: 3 Out of their own *h*,
23: 4 apportioned among your tribes as their *h*
24:28 dismissed the people, each to his own *h*.
24:30 He was buried within the limits of his *h*
24:32 This was a *h* of the descendants of Joseph.
Jgs 2: 9 buried him within the borders of his *h*
18: 1 received no *h* among the tribes of Israel.
21:24 for his own *h* in his own clan and tribe.
1Sm 2: 8 nobles and make a glorious throne their *h*.
10: 1 LORD anoints you commander over his *h*.
10: 1 has anointed you commander over his *h*:
1Kgs 8:36 you have given to your people as their *h*.
12:16 We have no *h* in the son of Jesse.
21: 3 "that I should give you my ancestral *h*."
21: 4 "I will not give you my ancestral *h*."
2Chr 6:27 land which you gave your people as their *h*.
10:16 We have no *h* in the son of Jesse.
Jdt 9:12 of my forefather, God of the *h* of Israel,
13: 5 now is the time for aiding your *h*
Est C:16 among all their ancestors, as a lasting *h*,
C:20 have pronounced, and to destroy your *h*;
1Mc 2:57 as a *h* a throne of everlasting royalty.
15:33 but our ancestral *h* which for a time had
15:34 are holding on to the *h* of our ancestors.
2Mc 1:26 Israel and guard and sanctify your *h*.
2:17 and has restored to all of them their *h*,
14:15 and who always comes to the aid of his *h*.
Jb 20:29 wicked man, and the *h* appointed him by God.
Ps(s) 61: 6 me the *h* of those who fear your name.
135:12 their land a *h*, the heritage of Israel
136:21 And made their land a *h*,
136:22 The *h* of Israel his servant,
Prv 11:29 his household has empty air for a *h*;
Wis 3:14 a more gratifying *h* in the Lord's temple.
Sir 24:12 people, in the portion of the LORD, his *h*.
37:25 One wise for his people wins a *h* of glory,
44:11 families, their *h* with their descendants;
45:22 the people nor shares with them their *h*;
45:25 Was an individual *h* through one son alone;
45:25 the *h* of Aaron is for all his descendants.
Is 58:14 I will nourish you with the *h* of Jacob,
63:17 of your servants, the tribes of your *h*.
Jer 2: 7 defiled my land, you made my *h* loathsome.
3:18 land which I gave to your fathers as a *h*.
3:19 land, a *h* most beautiful among the nations!
12:7 I abandon my house, cast off my *h*;
12: 8 My *h* has turned on me like a lion in the
12: 9 My *h* is a prey for hyenas,
12:10 my vineyard, have trodden my *h* underfoot;
12:14 all my evil neighbors who plunder the *h*
12:15 again and bring them back, each to his *h*,
16:18 and filling my *h* with their abominations.
16:19 "Mere frauds are the *h* of our fathers,
17: 4 your hold on your *h* which I have given you.
Ez 36:12 of you, and you shall be their *h*.
Jl 2:17 people, and make not your *h* a reproach,
Mal 1: 3 a waste, his *h* a desert for jackals.
Jn 13: 8 answered, "you will have no share in my *h*."
Acts 7: 5 God did not give him any of it as his *h*,
13:19 to give them that country as their *h*
Eph 1:18 the wealth of his glorious *h* to be
Heb 11: 8 to the place he was to receive as a *h*;

HERITAGES (1)
Is 49: 8 restore the land and allot the desolate *h*,

HERMAS (1)
Rom 16:14 Asyncritus, Phlegon, Hermes, Patrobas, *H*,

HERMES (2)
Acts 14:12 Paul they called *H*,
Rom 16:14 Greetings to Asyncritus, Phlegon, *H*,

HERMOGENES (1)
2Tm 1:15 all in Asia, including even Phygelus and *H*,

HERMON (15)
Dt 3: 8 territory from the Wadi Arnon to Mount *H*
4:48 *H*) and all the Arabah east of the Jordan,
Jos 11: 3 at the foot of *H* in the land of Mizpah.
11:17 the Lebanon valley at the foot of Mount *H*.
12: 1 Jordan, from the River Arnon to Mount *H*,
12: 5 He ruled over Mount *H*,
13: 5 of Mount *H* to Labo in the land of Hamath.
13:11 Geshurites and Maacathites, all Mount *H*,
2Sm 24: 6 Gilead and to the district below Mount *H*.
1Chr 5:23 as far as Baal-hermon, Senir, and Mount *H*.
Ps(s) 42: 7 you From the land of the Jordan and of *H*,
89:13 Tabor and *H* rejoice at your name.
133: 3 It is a dew like that of *H*,
Sg 4: 8 of Amana, from the top of Senir and *H*,
Sir 24:13 raised aloft, like a cypress on Mount *H*,

HERNIA (1)
Lv 21:20 is afflicted with eczema, ringworm or *h*.

HERO (4)
1Sm 17:51 When they saw that their *h* was dead,
Is 3: 2 *H* and warrior, judge and prophet,
42:13 The LORD goes forth like a *h*,
Jer 46: 6 The swift cannot flee, nor the *h* escape:

HEROD (41)
Mt 2: 1 of Judea during the reign of King *H*,
2: 3 this news King *H* became greatly disturbed,
2: 7 *H* called the astrologers aside and found
2:12 a message in a dream not to return to *H*,
2:13 *H* is searching for the child to destroy him."
2:15 He stayed there until the death of *H*,
2:16 Once *H* realized that he had been deceived
2:22 succeeded his father *H* as king of Judea,
14: 1 On one occasion *H* the tetrarch,

14: 3 Recall that H had had John arrested,
14: 5 H wanted to kill John but was afraid of
14: 6 dance before the court which delighted H
Mk 6:14 King H came to hear of Jesus,
6:16 On hearing of Jesus, H exclaimed,
6:17 H was the one who had ordered John arrested,
6:18 That was because John had told H,
6:20 H feared John,
6:21 Herodias had her chance one day when H
6:22 a dance which delighted H and his guests.
8:15 yeast of the Pharisees and the yeast of H,"
Lk 1: 5 In the days of H, king of Judea
3: 1 procurator of Judea, H tetrarch of Galilee,
3:19 H the tetrarch was censured by John on the
9: 7 H the tetrarch heard of all that was
9: 9 But H said, "John I beheaded.
13:31 H is trying to kill you."
23: 7 Herod's jurisdiction, he sent him to H,
23: 8 H was extremely pleased to see Jesus.
23:11 H and his guards then treated him with
23:12 H and Pilate,
23:15 Neither has H,
Acts 4:27 whom you anointed H and Pontius Pilate in
12: 1 King H started to harass some of the
12: 4 H intended to bring him before the people
12: 6 night before H was to bring him to trial,
12:19 H then initiated a search for him.
12:19 H left Judea to spend some time in
12:20 H had long been infuriated by the people
12:21 On an appointed day H, arrayed in royal
12:23 The angel of the Lord struck H down at
13: 1 had been brought up with H the tetrarch),

HERODIAN (1)

Mt 22:16 to him, accompanied by H sympathizers,

HERODIANS (2)

Mk 3: 6 plot with the H how they might destroy him.
12:13 and H after him to catch him in his speech.

HERODIAS (7)

Mt 14: 3 in chains, and imprisoned on account of H,
14: 6 Then on Herod's birthday H' daughter
Mk 6:17 chained, and imprisoned on account of H,
6:19 H harbored a grudge against him for this
6:21 H had her chance one day when Herod held a
6:22 H' own daughter came in at one point and
Lk 3:19 was censured by John on the subject of H,

HERODION (1)

Rom 16:11 Greetings to my kinsman H and to the

HEROD'S (6)

Mt 2:19 But after H death, the angel of the Lord
14: 6 Then on H birthday Herodias' daughter
Lk 8: 3 out, Joanna, the wife of H steward Chuza,
23: 7 learned that he was under H jurisdiction,
Acts 12:11 sent his angel to rescue me from H clutches
23:35 to be kept under guard in H praetorium.

HEROES (8)

Gn 6: 4 They were the h of old, the men of renown.
2Mc 2:21 h who fought bravely for Judaism so that,
Ps(s) 12: 5 Those who say, "We are h with our tongues;
Jer 46: 5 their h are routed,
48:14 How can you say, "We are h,
48:41 h are like the heart of a woman in travail.
49:22 hearts of Edom's h shall be like the heart
51:56 upon her, [Babylon,] her h are captured,

HERONS (2)

Lv 11:19 the stork, the various species of h,
Dt 14:18 the stork, the various species of h,

HERSELF (56)

Gn 18:12 So Sarah laughed to h and said,
20: 5 'She is my sister,' and she h also stated,
21:16 said to h, "Let me not watch the child
24:57 and see what she h has to say about it."
24:65 The she covered h with her veil.
31:34 a camel cushion, and seated h upon them.
38:14 veiled her face by covering h with a shawl,
Ex 2: 4 His sister stationed h at a distance to
Lv 18:23 h in front of an animal to mate with it;
Nm 5:28 If however, the woman has not defiled h,
30: 4 a vow to the LORD, or binds h to a pledge,
30: 5 bound h and says nothing to her about it,
30: 7 under a rash pledge to which she bound h,
30: 9 the rash pledge to which she had bound h,
30:10 any pledge to which such a woman binds h,
30:11 a vow or binds h under oath to a pledge,
30:14 that she makes under oath to mortify h,
Jgs 5:29 her, and she, too, keeps answering h:
Ru 2:10 Casting h prostrate upon the ground,
1Sm 1: 9 at Shiloh, and presented h before the LORD;
2Sm 21:10 took sackcloth and spread it out for h
2Kgs 4: 5 so, closing the door on h and her children.
Tb 3:10 house with the intention of hanging h.
3:10 But she reconsidered, saying to h:
3:10 but she hanged h because of ill fortune!'
Jdt 8: 5 up a tent for h on the roof of her house.
9: 1 Judith threw h down prostrate,
10: 4 Thus she made h very beautiful,
10:23 She threw h down prostrate before him,
12: 7 she washed h at the spring of the camp.
13: 4 by Holofernes' bed and said within h;
16:19 that she h had taken from his bedroom.
16:22 but she gave h to no man all the days of
Est D: 1 garments and arrayed h in her royal attire.
Wis 6:13 h known in anticipation of men's desire;
7:27 and renews everything while h perduring;
Is 34:14 repose, and find for h a place to rest.
Lam 1: 8 She h groans and turns away.
Ez 22: 3 blood within h so that her time has come,
23: 7 Thus she gave h as a harlot to them,
23: 7 and she defiled h with all those for whom
23:10 took away, and h they slew with the sword.
23:13 I saw that she had defiled h.
Hos 2:15 decked h out with her rings and her jewels,
Zep 2:15 That told h, "There is no other than I!"
Zec 9: 3 Tyre built h a stronghold,
Mt 15:22 woman living in that locality presented h,
Lk 10:39 who seated h at the Lord's feet and
20:32 Finally the widow h died.
Rom 7: 3 is still alive, she gives h to another.
16: 2 to her, for she h has been of help to many,
1Cor 7: 4 does not belong to h but to her husband;
1Tm 5: 6 widow who gives h up to selfish indulgence,
Rv 12: 6 The woman h fled into the desert,
18: 7 she said to h, 'I sit enthroned as a queen.
19: 7 his bride has prepared h for the wedding.

HESED (1)

1Kgs 4:10 the son of H in Arubboth as well as in

HESHBON (37)

Nm 21:25 Amorites, in H and all its dependencies.
21:26 Now H was the capital of Sihon,
21:27 "Come to H, let it be rebuilt,
21:28 from H and a blaze from the city of Sihon;
21:30 Their plowland is ruined from H to Dibon;
21:34 king of the Amorites, who lived in H."
32: 3 of Ataroth, Dibon, Jazer, Nimrah, H,
32:37 The Reubenites rebuilt H,
Dt 1: 4 king of the Amorites, who lived in H,
2:24 your hands Sihon, the Amorite king of H,
2:26 the desert of Kedemoth to Sihon, king of H,
2:30 Sihon, king of H, refused to let us pass
3: 2 king of the Amorites, who lived in H.'
3: 6 As we had done to Sihon, king of H,
4:46 who dwelt in H and whom Moses and the
29: 6 we came to this place, Sihon, king of H,
Jos 9:10 beyond the Jordan, Sihon, king of H,
12: 2 king of the Amorites, who lived in H.
12: 5 far as the territory of Sihon, king of H.
13:10 king of the Amorites, who reigned in H,
13:17 to include H and all its towns which are
13:21 This Amorite king, who reigned in H,
13:26 is, from H to Ramath-mizpeh and Betonim,
13:27 part of the kingdom of Sihon, king of H,
21:39 pasture lands, H with its pasture lands,
Jgs 11:19 to Sihon, king of the Amorites, king of H.
11:26 when Israel occupied H and its villages,
1Chr 6:66 pasture lands, H with its pasture lands,
Neh 9:22 possessed the land of Sihon, king of H,
Sg 7: 5 the pools in H by the gate of Bath-rabbim.
Is 15: 4 H and Elealeh cry out,
16: 8 The terraced slopes of H languish,
16: 9 I water you with tears, H and Elealeh;
Jer 48: 2 Evil they plan against H:
48:34 of H and Elealeh is heard as far as Jahaz;
48:45 For fire breaks forth from H,
49: 3 Howl, H, for the ravager approaches

HESHBONITES (1)

Jdt 5:15 destroyed all the H by main force,

HESHBON'S (1)

Jer 48:45 H shadow stop short the exhausted refugees;

HESHMON (1)

Jos 15:27 Hazar-gaddah, H,

HESITATE (5)

Jgs 18: 9 Are you going to h?
Tb 4: 8 But do not h to give alms;
12:13 When you did not h to get up and leave
Jb 30:10 from me, they do not h to spit in my face!
Ps(s) 119:60 and did not h in keeping your commands.

HESITATED (1)

Gn 19:16 When he h, the men, by the LORD's mercy

HESITATION (1)

Acts 11:12 instructed me to accompany them without h.

HETH (2)

Gn 10:15 father of Sidon, his first-born, and of H;
1Chr 1:13 father of Sidon, his first-born, and H,

HETHLON (2)

Ez 47:15 from the Great Sea in the direction of H,
48: 1 to H through Labo of Hamath to Hazar-enon,

HEW (3)

Dt 29:10 down to those who h wood and draw water
1Chr 22: 2 he appointed them stonecutters to h out
Jer 6: 6 H down her trees, throw up a siege mound

HEWED (2)

1Kgs 5:32 along with the Gebalites, h them out,
Is 5: 2 built a watchtower, and h out a wine press.

HEWERS (4)

Jos 9:21 as h of wood and drawers of water for the
9:23 one of you shall always be a slave h of wood
9:27 h of wood and drawers of water for the
2Chr 2: 9 for your servants, the h who cut the wood,

HEWN (17)

1Kgs 5:31 to give the temple a foundation of h stone.
6:36 of h stones and one course of cedar beams.
7: 9 h to size and trimmed front and back with
7:11 Above were fine stones h to size,
7:12 enclosed by three courses of h stones
2Kgs 12:13 and h stone used in repairing the breaches,
22: 6 of wood and h stone for the temple repairs.
2Chr 16:14 he had h for himself in the City of David,
34:11 buy h stone and timber for the tie beams
Is 22:16 Who has h for himself a sepulcher on a
22:16 that here you have h for yourself a tomb?"
51: 1 Look to the rock from which you were h,
Dn 2:34 a stone which was h from a mountain
2:45 stone you saw h from the mountain
Am 5:11 Though you have built houses of h stone,
Mt 27:60 which had been h from a formation of rock.
Lk 23:53 and laid it in a tomb h out of the rock,

HEWS (1)

Is 10:15 the axe boast against him who h with it?

HEZEKIAH (126)

2Kgs 16:20 His son H succeeded him as king.
18: 1 of Hoshea, son of Elah, king of Israel, H,
18: 6 to the LORD, H never turned away from him,
18: 9 In the fourth year of King H,
18:10 In the sixth year of H,
18:13 In the fourteenth year of King H,
18:14 H, king of Judah, sent this message
18:14 silver and thirty talents of gold from H,
18:15 H paid him all the funds there were in the
18:17 with a great army to King H at Jerusalem.
18:19 The commander said to them, "Tell H,
18:22 whose high places and altars H has removed,
18:29 'Do not let H deceive you,
18:30 Let not H induce you to rely on the LORD,
18:31 Do not listen to H,
18:32 to H when he would seduce you by saying,
18:37 Asaph, came to H with their garments torn,
19: 1 When King H heard this,
19: 3 prophet Isaiah, son of Amoz, "Thus says H:
19: 5 the servants of King H had come to Isaiah,
19: 9 he sent envoys to H with this message:
19:10 "Thus shall you say to H, king of Judah:
19:14 H took the letter from the hand of the
19:20 son of Amoz, sent this message to H:
20: 1 In those days, when H was mortally ill,
20: 3 And H wept bitterly.
20: 5 "Go back and tell H,
20: 8 Then H asked Isaiah, "What is the sign
20:10 shadow to advance ten steps," H answered.
20:12 king of Babylon, heard that H had been ill,
20:13 H was pleased at this,
20:13 in all his realm that H did not show them.
20:14 the prophet came to King H and asked him:
20:14 a distant land, from Babylon," replied H.
20:15 saw everything in my house," answered H.
20:16 Then Isaiah said to H:
20:19 H replied to Isaiah, "The word of the LORD
20:20 The rest of the acts of H,
20:21 H rested with his ancestors and his son
21: 3 places which his father H had destroyed.
1Chr 3:13 whose son was Ahaz, whose son was H,
4:41 by name set out during the reign of H,
2Chr 28:27 His son H succeeded him as king.
29: 1 H was twenty-five years old when he became
29:18 Then they went inside to King H and said:
29:20 Then King H hastened to convoke the
29:27 Then H ordered the holocaust to be
29:30 King H and the princes then commanded the
29:31 H now spoke out this command:
29:36 H and all the people rejoiced over what
30: 1 H sent a message to all Israel and Judah,
30:18 for H prayed for them,
30:20 The LORD heard H and spared the people.
30:22 H spoke encouragingly to all the Levites
30:24 King H of Judah had contributed a thousand
31: 2 H reestablished the classes of the priests

HEZEKIAH (cont.)
31: 8 When *H* and the princes had come and seen
31: 9 Then *H* questioned the priests and the
31:11 *H* then gave orders that chambers be
31:13 by appointment of King *H* and of Azariah,
31:20 This *H* did in all Judah.
32: 2 When *H* saw that Sennacherib was coming
32: 8 from the words of King *H* of Judah.
32: 9 with this message for King *H* of Judah,
32:11 Has not *H* deceived you,
32:12 Has not this same *H* removed his high
32:15 Let not *H* mislead you further and deceive
32:16 the LORD God and against his servant *H*,
32:20 of this, King *H* and the prophet Isaiah,
32:22 Thus the LORD saved *H* and the inhabitants
32:23 and costly objects for King *H* of Judah,
32:24 In those days *H* became mortally ill.
32:25 *H*, however, did not then discharge
32:26 But then *H* humbled himself for his pride
32:26 his anger on them during the time of *H*.
32:27 *H* possessed very great wealth and glory.
32:30 This same *H* stopped the upper outflow of
32:30 *H* prospered in all his undertakings.
32:33 *H* rested with his ancestors;
33: 3 places which his father *H* had torn down,
Ezr 2:16 sons of Ater, who were sons of *H*,
Neh 7:21 sons of Ater who were sons of *H*,
10:18 Bebai, Adonijah, Bigvai, Adin, Ater, *H*,
2Mc 15:22 your angel in the days of King *H* of Judea,
Prv 25: 1 The men of *H*,
Sir 48:17 *H* fortified his city and had water
48:22 For *H* did what was right and held fast to
49: 4 Except for David, *H* and Josiah,
Is 1: 1 in the days of Uzziah, Jotham, Ahaz and *H*,
36: 1 In the fourteenth year of King *H*,
36: 2 with a great army to King *H* in Jerusalem.
36: 4 The commander said to them, "Tell King *H*:
36: 7 one whose high places and altars *H* removed,
36:14 'Do not let *H* deceive you,
36:15 Let not *H* induce you to rely on the LORD,
36:16 Do not listen to *H*,
36:18 Do not let *H* seduce you by saying,
36:22 Asaph, came to *H* with their garments torn,
37: 1 When King *H* heard this,
37: 3 "Thus says *H*: This is a day
37: 5 the servants of King *H* had come to Isaiah,
37: 9 he sent envoys to *H* with this message:
37: 9 "Thus shall you say to *H*, king of Judah:
37:14 *H* took the letter from the hand of the
37:21 son of Amoz, sent this message to *H*:
38: 1 In those days, when *H* was mortally ill,
38: 2 Then *H* turned his face to the wall and
38: 3 And *H* wept bitterly.
38: 5 "Go, tell *H*: Thus says the Lord:
38: 9 The song of *H*, king of Judah
38:22 Then *H* asked, "What is the sign
39: 1 that *H* had recovered from his sickness,
39: 2 *H* was pleased at this,
39: 3 the prophet came to King *H* and asked him,
39: 3 *H* answered, "They came to me
39: 4 *H* replied, "They saw everything
39: 5 Then Isaiah said to *H*, "Hear the word
39: 8 *H* replied to Isaiah,
Jer 15: 4 earth because of what Manasseh, son of *H*,
26:18 used to prophesy in the days of *H*,
26:19 Did *H*, king of Judah,
Hos 1: 1 in the days of Uzziah, Jotham, Ahaz, *H*,
Mi 1: 1 in the days of Jotham, Ahaz, and *H*,
Zep 1: 1 the son of Amariah, the son of *H*,
Mt 1: 9 the father of Ahaz, Ahaz the father of *H*.
1:10 *H* was the father of Manasseh,

HEZEKIAH'S (2)

2Chr 32:17 shall *H* god save his people from my hand."
32:32 The rest of *H* acts,

HEZION (1)

1Kgs 15:18 to Ben-hadad, son of Tabrimmon, son of *H*,

HEZIR (2)

1Chr 24:15 sixteenth to Immer, the seventeenth to *H*,
Neh 10:21 Anathoth, Nebai, Magpiash, Meshullam, *H*,

HEZRAI (1)

2Sm 23:35 *H* from Carmel;

HEZRO (1)

1Chr 11:37 *H*, from Carmel;

HEZRON (20)

Gn 46: 9 Hanoch, Pallu, *H*, and Carmi.
46:12 and the sons of Perez were *H* and Hamul.
Ex 6:14 of Israel, were Hanoch, Pallu, *H* and Carmi;
Nm 26: 6 through *H* the clan of the Hezronites,
26:21 through *H* the clan of the Hezronites,
Jos 15: 3 point south of Kadesh-barnea, across to *H*,
Ru 4:18 Perez was the father of *H*,
4:19 father of Hezron, *H* was the father of Ram,
1Chr 2: 5 The sons of Perez were *H* and Hamul.
2: 9 The sons born to *H* were Jerahmeel,
2:18 By his wife Azubah, Caleb, son of *H*,
2:21 Then *H* had relations with the daughter of
2:24 After the death of *H*,
2:24 with Ephrathah, the widow of his father *H*,
2:25 sons of Jerahmeel, the first-born of *H*,
4: 1 Perez, *H*, Carmi, Hur, and Shobal.
5: 3 of Israel, were Hanoch, Pallu, *H*,
Mt 1: 3 Perez was the father of *H*,
Lk 3:33 son of Admin, son of Arni, son of *H*,

HEZRONITES (2)

Nm 26: 6 through Hezron the clan of the *H*,
26:21 through Hezron the clan of the *H*,

HID (41)

Gn 3: 8 the man and his wife *h* themselves from the
3:10 afraid, because I was naked, so I *h* myself."
Ex 2: 2 a goodly child, she *h* him for three months.
2:12 he slew the Egyptian and *h* him in the sand.
3: 6 Moses *h* his face,
Jos 6:17 because she *h* the messengers we sent.
10:16 who had fled, *h* in a cave at Makkedah.
1Sm 13: 6 difficult situation, *h* themselves in caves,
20:19 Go to the spot where you *h* on the other
20:24 So David *h* in the open country.
1Kgs 18: 4 *h* them away fifty each in two caves,
18:13 I *h* a hundred prophets of the Lord
19:13 Elijah *h* his face in his cloak and went
2Kgs 4:27 LORD *h* it from me and did not let me know."
6:29 But she *h* her son."
7: 8 clothing from it, and went out and *h* them.
7: 8 from it, and again went out and *h* them.
2Chr 22:11 priest, *h* the child from Athaliah's sight,
1Mc 9:38 *h* themselves under cover of the mountain.
2Mc 1:19 *h* it secretly in the hollow of a dry cistern,
Jb 18:10 A noose for him is *h* on the ground,
28:21 It is *h* from the eyes of any beast;
Ps(s) 30: 8 but when you *h* your face I was terrified.
38:10 from you my groaning is not *h*.
40:11 Your justice I kept not *h* within my heart;
69: 6 my folly, and my faults are not *h* from you.
142: 4 which I walk they have *h* a trap for me.
Wis 17: 3 who supposed their secret sins were *h*
Sir 43:34 Beyond these, many things lie *h*;
Is 29:14 the understanding of its prudent men be *h*.
49: 2 me a polished arrow, in his quiver he *h* me.
54: 8 wrath, for a moment I *h* my face from you;
Jer 13: 7 loincloth from the place where I had *h* it.
18:22 capture me, they have *h* snares for my feet;
Ez 39:23 and I *h* my face from them and handed them
Dn 10: 7 they fled and *h* themselves,
Mt 13:44 He *h* it again, and rejoicing at his find
Lk 19:20 money, my lord, which I *h* for safekeeping.
Jn 8:59 but he *h* himself and slipped out of the
Heb 11:23 *h* him for three months after his birth,
Rv 6:15 *h* themselves in caves and mountain crags.

HIDDAI (1)

2Sm 23:30 *H* from Nahale-gaash;

HIDDEN (87)

Dt 7:20 who have *h* from you are destroyed.
29:28 [Both what is still *h* and what has already
33:19 the seas and the *h* treasures of the sand."
Jos 2: 4 woman had taken the two men and *h* them,
2: 6 and *h* them among her stalks of flax spread
6:25 Because Rahab the harlot had *h* the
7:21 are now *h* in the ground inside my tent,
7:22 to the tent and found them *h* there,
10:27 and cast into the cave where they had *h*;
Jgs 9: 5 Jerubbaal, Jotham, escaped, for he was *h*.
2Sm 17: 9 Even now he lies *h* in one of the caves or
1Kgs 10: 3 and there remained nothing *h* from him that
2Kgs 11: 3 he remained *h* in the temple of the LORD,
2Chr 9: 2 and there remained nothing *h* from Solomon
22:12 remained *h* with them in the house of God,
1Mc 1:23 took all the *h* treasures he could find.
16:15 sumptuous banquet, he had his men *h* there.
2Mc 1:16 they opened a *h* trapdoor in the ceiling,
1:20 priests who had *h* the fire to look for it.
1:33 where the exiled priests had *h* the fire,
10:37 Timothy had *h* in a cistern,
12:41 who brings to light the things that are *h*.
Jb 3:21 search for it rather than for *h* treasures,
3:23 Men whose path is *h* from them,
5:21 the scourge of the tongue you shall be *h*,
10:13 Yet these things you have *h* in your heart;
28:11 the streams, and brings *h* things to light.
31:33 *h* my sins and buried my guilt in my bosom
40:13 in the *h* world imprison them.
Ps(s) 55:13 against me, I might have *h* from him.
80:11 The mountains were *h* in its shadow;
90: 8 our *h* sins in the light of your scrutiny.
140: 6 the proud who have *h* a trap for me;
Prv 2: 4 and like *h* treasures search her out:
27: 5 an open rebuke than a love that remains *h*.
Eccl 12:14 every work, with all its *h* qualities,
Wis 2:22 And they knew not the *h* counsels of God;
7:21 as are *h* I learned and such as are plain;
10: 8 they could not even be *h* in their fall.
Sir 3:21 for what is *h* is not your concern.
11: 4 works of the LORD, *h* from men his deeds.
16:15 "I am *h* from God;
17:13 to him, they cannot be *h* from his eyes.
17:16 Their wickedness cannot be *h* from him;
20:29 *H* wisdom and unseen treasure
23:19 step a man takes and peer into *h* corners.
37:10 those who envy you, keep your intentions *h*.
39: 3 is busied with the *h* meanings of the sages.
48:25 end of time, *h* things yet to be fulfilled.
Is 40:27 O Israel, "My way is *h* from the LORD,
42:22 them trapped in holes, *h* away in prisons.
45: 3 darkness, and riches that have been *h* away,
45:15 Truly with you God is *h*,
48: 6 to you, *h* events of which you knew not.
64: 6 For you have *h* your face from us and have
65:16 shall be forgotten, and *h* from my eyes.
Jer 16:17 they are not *h* from me,
Dn 2:22 *h* things and knows what is in the darkness,
13:16 who had *h* themselves and were watching her.
13:18 unaware that the elders were *h* inside.
13:37 A young man, who was *h* there,
13:42 you know what is *h* and are aware of all
Hos 5: 3 know Ephraim, and Israel is not *h* from me;
Mt 5:14 A city set on a hill cannot be *h*.
6:18 who is *h*; and your Father who sees what is *h*
10:26 and nothing *h* that will not become known.
11:25 for what you have *h* from the learned and
13:35 has lain *h* since the creation of the world."
Mk 4:21 under a bushel basket or *h* under a bed?
4:22 are *h* only to be revealed at a later time;
Lk 8:17 is nothing *h* that will not be exposed,
10:21 because what you have *h* from the learned
11:44 like *h* tombs over which men walk unawares."
12: 2 nothing *h* that will not be made known.
Jn 7: 4 to be known publicly keeps his actions *h*.
Acts 14:17 benefits, he has not *h* himself completely,
Rom 16:25 gospel which reveals the mystery *h*
1Cor 2: 7 a mysterious, a *h* wisdom.
4: 5 He will bring to light what is *h* in
Eph 3: 9 design which for ages was *h* in God,
Col 1:26 that mystery *h* from ages and generations
2: 3 treasure of wisdom and knowledge is *h*.
3: 3 Your life is *h* now with Christ in God.
1Tm 5:25 inconspicuous ones cannot be *h* forever.
1Pt 3: 4 is rather the *h* character of the heart,
Rv 2:17 To the victor I will give the *h* manna;

HIDE (83)

Gn 18:17 I *h* from Abraham what I am about to do,
47:18 "We cannot *h* from my lord that,
Ex 2: 3 When she could *h* him no longer,
29:14 But the flesh and *h* and offal of the
Lv 4:11 The *h* of the bullock and all its flesh,
7: 8 the *h* of the holocaust that he has offered.
8:17 with its *h* and flesh and offal he burned
9:11 but the flesh and the *h* he burned up in
13:48 or on a *h* or anything made of leather,
13:49 if the infection on the garment or *h*,
Nm 12:14 would she not *h* in shame for seven days?
19: 5 burned in his sight, with its *h* and flesh,
Dt 31:17 will forsake them and *h* my face from them,
32:20 "I will *h* my face from them,"
Jos 2:16 *H* there for three days,
7:19 do not *h* it from me."
1Sm 3:17 *H* nothing from me!
3:17 to you if you *h* a single thing he told you."
20: 5 go and *h* in the open country until evening.
1Kgs 17: 3 here, go east and *h* in the Wadi Cherith,
22:25 when you retreat into an inside room to *h*."
2Kgs 7:12 have left their camp to *h* in the field,
2Chr 18:24 when you enter an innermost chamber to *h*."
Neh 3:37 *H* not their crime and let not their sin be
Tb 13: 6 to you, and no longer *h* his face from you.
Jb 13:20 me, then from your presence I need not *h*:
13:24 you *h* your face and consider me your enemy?
14:13 that you would *h* me in the nether world
22:14 Clouds *h* him so that he cannot see;
34:22 so dense that evildoers can *h* in it.
40:31 Can you fill his *h* with barbs,
Ps(s) 10: 1 Why *h* in times of distress?
13: 2 How long will you *h* your face from me?
17: 8 *h* me in the shadow of your wings 9 from
27: 5 *h* me in his abode in the day of trouble;
27: 9 *H* not your face from me;
31:21 You *h* them in the shelter of your presence
44:25 Why do you *h* your face,
69:18 *H* not your face from your servant;
78: 4 to us, We will not *h* from their sons;
88:15 why *h* from me your face?
89:47 Will you *h* yourself forever?
102: 3 *H* not your face from me in the day of my
104:29 If you *h* your face,
119:19 *h* not your commands from me.
139:11 If I say, "Surely the darkness shall *h* me,
143: 7 *H* not your face from me lest I become like
Prv 28:12 the wicked gain preeminence, people *h*.
28:28 the wicked gain preeminence, other men *h*;
Wis 6:22 and I shall *h* no secrets from you,
7:13 her riches I do not *h* away;
Sir 4:23 proper time, and *h* not away your wisdom;
18:24 time of vengeance when he will *h* his face.
22:25 in need of support no one need *h* in shame;

23:18 Darkness surrounds me, walls *h* me;
26: 8 great anger, for she does not *h* her shame.
29:10 and *h* it not under a stone to perish;
Is 2:10 Get behind the rocks, *h* in the dust,
3: 9 sin like Sodom they vaunt, They *h* it not.
16: 3 be like the night, To *h* the outcasts,
26:20 *H* yourselves for a brief moment,
29:15 would *h* their plans too deep for the LORD!
30:20 No longer will your Teacher *h* himself,
53: 3 One of those from whom men *h* their faces,
59: 2 *h* his face so that he will not hear you.
Jer 13: 4 there *h* it in a cleft of the rock.
13: 6 the loincloth which I told you to *h* there.
23:24 a man *h* in secret without my seeing him?
33: 5 when I *h* my face from this city for all
38:14 *h* nothing from me."
38:25 do not *h* it from us,
49: 8 Flee, retreat, *h* in deep holes,
49:10 uncover his retreats so that he cannot *h*.
49:30 leave your homes, *h* in deep holes,
50: 2 publish it, *h* it not,
Bar 6:48 themselves where they can *h* with them.
Ez 39:29 No longer will I *h* my face from them,
Am 9: 3 Though they *h* on the summit of Carmel,
9: 3 *h* from my gaze in the bottom of the sea,
Mi 3: 4 shall he *h* his face from them at that time,
1Cor 7:18 He should not try to *h* his circumcision.
2Cor 3:13 who used to *h* his face with a veil so that
Rv 6:16 *H* us from the face of the One who sits on

HIDEOUS (1)

2Mc 9: 9 and while he was still alive in *h* torments,

HIDES (8)

Lv 16:27 where their *h* and flesh and offal shall be
Jb 20:12 in his mouth, and he *h* it under his tongue,
34:29 If he *h* his face, who then can behold him?
Ps(s) 10:11 he *h* his face, he never sees
Prv 22: 3 The shrewd man perceives evil and *h*,
27:12 The shrewd man perceives evil and *h*;
Sir 20:30 *h* his folly than the one who *h* his wisdom.

HIDING (31)

Dt 31:18 Yet I will be *h* my face from them at that
Jos 10:17 been discovered *h* in a cave at Makkedah,
1Sm 10:22 LORD answered, "He is *h* among the baggage."
14:11 out of the holes where they have been *h*."
14:22 who were *h* in the hill country of Ephraim,
19: 2 get out of sight and remain in *h*.
23:19 in Gibeah and said, "David is *h* among us,
23:23 the various *h* places he is holding out.
26: 1 reporting that David was *h* on the hill
2Chr 22: 9 was *h* in Samaria and brought him to Jehu,
Tb 1:19 wanted to put me to death, I went into *h*;
1Mc 1:53 Israel was driven into *h*,
2:31 had gone out to the *h* places in the desert.
2:36 stones, nor blocked up their own *h* places.
2:41 die as our kinsmen died in the *h* places."
10:79 left a thousand cavalry in *h* behind them.
2Mc 14:30 of his men, and went into *h* from Nicanor.
Jb 24: 4 all the poor of the land are driven into *h*.
Ps(s) 10: 8 in *h* he murders the innocent;
17:12 for prey, like young lions lurking in *h*.
56: 7 They gather together in *h*,
74:20 for the *h* places in the land and the
Is 8:17 who is *h* his face from the house of Jacob;
28:15 and in falsehood we have found a *h* place,"—
28:17 lies, and waters shall flood the *h* place.
45:19 *h* nor from some dark place of the earth,
57:17 angry, and struck them, *h* myself in wrath,
Jer 36:19 the princes said to Baruch, "Go into *h*,
Ez 39:24 I dealt with them, *h* my face from them.
Ob 1: 6 they search Esau, seek out his *h* places!
Jn 12:36 utterance, Jesus left them and went into *h*.

HIEL (1)

1Kgs 16:34 his reign, *H* from Bethel rebuilt Jericho.

HIERAPOLIS (1)

Col 4:13 is for you and for those at Laodicea and *H*.

HIERONYMUS (1)

2Mc 12: 2 son of Gennaeus, as also *H* and Demophon,

HIGH (513)

Gn 14:18 and wine, and being a priest of God Most *H*,
14:19 "Blessed be Abram by God Most *H*,
14:20 And blessed be God Most *H*,
14:22 "I have sworn to the LORD, God Most *H*,
34:12 No matter how *h* you set the bridal price,
45:13 *h* position in Egypt and what you have seen.
Ex 25:10 cubits wide, and one and a half cubits *h*.
25:23 a cubit wide, and a cubit and a half *h*.
25:25 Surround it with a frame, a handbreadth *h*,
27: 1 it shall be three cubits *h*.
27: 5 network is to be half as *h* as the altar.
27:18 long, fifty cubits wide, and five cubits *h*.
28:16 folded double, a span *h* and a span wide.
30: 2 long, a cubit wide, and two cubits *h*,
37: 1 cubits wide, and one and a half cubits *h*.
37:10 cubit wide, and one and a half cubits *h*.
37:12 a handbreadth *h* was also put around it,
37:25 long, a cubit wide, and two cubits *h*,
38: 4 the ground, half as *h* as the altar itself.
39: 9 span *h* and a span wide in its folded form.
Lv 26:30 I will demolish your *h* places,
Nm 21:28 and swallowed up the *h* places of the Arnon.
24: 4 God says, and knows what the Most *H* knows,
24:16 God says, and knows what the Most *H* knows,
33:52 images, and demolish all their *h* places.
35:25 stay there until the death of the *h* priest
35:28 of asylum until the death of the *h* priest.
35:28 Only after the death of the *h* priest may
35:32 the land before the death of the *h* priest.
Dt 3: 5 fortified with *h* walls and gates and bars.
12: 2 fail every place on the *h* mountains,
26:19 he will then raise you *h* in praise and
28: 1 you *h* above all the nations of the earth.
32: 8 Most *H* assigned the nations their heritage,
Jos 20: 6 the *h* priest who is in office at the time.
Jgs 8:28 no longer did they hold their heads *h*.
16:25 When their spirits were *h*,
1Sm 2:10 The Most *H* in heaven thunders;
9: 6 God in this city, a man held in *h* esteem;
9:12 have a sacrifice today on the *h* place.
9:13 before he goes up to the *h* place to eat.
9:14 toward them on his way to the *h* place.
9:19 of me to the *h* place and eat with me today.
9:25 came down from the *h* place into the city,
10: 5 down from the *h* place preceded by lyres,
22: 6 under a tamarisk tree on the *h* place,
2Sm 22:14 the Most *H* gave forth his voice.
22:17 "He reached out from on *h* and grasped me;
1Kgs 3: 2 people were sacrificing on the *h* places,
3: 3 and burned incense on the *h* places.
3: 4 because that was the most renowned *h* place.
6: 2 long, twenty wide, and twenty-five *h*.
6:10 with its lowest story five cubits *h*,
6:20 cubits long, twenty wide, and twenty *h*.
6:23 were two cherubim, each ten cubits *h*,
6:26 shape, and each was exactly ten cubits *h*.
7: 2 cubits long, fifty wide, and thirty *h*;
7:15 *h* and twelve cubits in circumference;
7:16 of the columns, each of them five cubits *h*.
7:27 four cubits long, four wide, and three *h*.
7:31 was surmounted by a crown one cubit *h*
7:32 Each wheel was a cubit and a half *h*.
7:35 there was a raised collar half a cubit *h*,
11: 7 Solomon then built a *h* place to Chemosh,
12:31 He also built temples on the *h* places and
12:32 priests of the *h* places he had built.
13: 2 the *h* places who offer sacrifice upon you,
13:32 against all the shrines on the *h* places
13:33 the *h* places from among the common people.
13:33 and became a priest of the *h* places.
14:23 They, too, built for themselves *h* places,
14:23 every *h* hill and under every green tree.
15:14 The *h* places did not disappear;
22:44 the *h* places did not disappear,
22:44 and to burn incense on the *h* places.
2Kgs 12: 4 Still, the *h* places did not disappear;
14: 4 Thus the *h* places did not disappear,
15: 4 Yet the *h* places did not disappear;
15:35 Nevertheless the *h* places did not
16: 4 and burned incense on the *h* places,
17: 9 built *h* places in all their settlements,
17:10 on every *h* hill and under every leafy tree.
17:11 There, on all the *h* places,
17:29 the *h* places which the Samarians had made,
17:32 from their number priests for the *h* places,
17:32 for them in the shrines on the *h* places.
18: 4 It was he who removed the *h* places,
18:22 *h* places and altars Hezekiah has removed,
19:22 your voice And lifted up your eyes on *h*?
21: 3 He rebuilt the *h* places which his father
22: 4 with orders to go to the *h* priest Hilkiah
22: 8 The *h* priest Hilkiah informed the scribe
23: 4 the king commanded the *h* priest Hilkiah,
23: 5 appointed to burn incense on the *h* places
23: 8 *h* places where they had offered incense.
23: 8 also tore down the *h* place of the satyrs,
23: 9 The priests of the *h* places could not
23:13 defiled the *h* places east of Jerusalem,
23:15 at Bethel, the *h* place built by Jeroboam,
23:15 this same altar and *h* place he tore down,
23:19 also removed all the shrines on the *h* places
23:20 of the *h* places that were at the shrines,
25:17 Each of the pillars was eighteen cubits *h*;
25:17 *h*; a bronze capital five cubits *h* surmounted
25:18 the guard also took Seraiah the *h* priest,
1Chr 16:39 of the LORD on the *h* place at Gibeon,
21:29 were at that time on the *h* place at Gibeon.
2Chr 1: 3 assembly, he went to the *h* place at Gibeon,
1: 5 of the LORD's Dwelling on the *h* place.
1:13 to Jerusalem from the *h* place at Gibeon,
3: 4 twenty cubits, and it was twenty cubits *h*.
3:15 he set two columns thirty-five cubits *h*;
4: 1 long, twenty cubits wide and ten cubits *h*.
6:13 five cubits wide, and three cubits *h*,
11:15 *h* places and satyrs and calves he had made.
14: 2 the heathen altars and the *h* places,
14: 4 He removed the *h* places and incense stands
15:17 the *h* places did not disappear from Israel,
17: 6 *h* places and the sacred poles from Judah.
19:11 Amariah is *h* priest over you in everything
20:33 But the *h* places were not removed,
21:11 set up *h* places in the mountains of Judah;
24:11 and an overseer for the *h* priest came,
28: 4 sacrifice and incense on the *h* places,
28:25 *h* places to offer sacrifice to other gods.
31: 1 the *h* places and altars throughout Judah,
32:12 Has not this same Hezekiah removed his *h*
33: 3 He rebuilt the *h* places which his father
33:14 he built it very *h*.
33:17 continued to sacrifice on the *h* places,
33:19 the sites where he built *h* places and
34: 3 purge Judah and Jerusalem of the *h* places,
34: 9 They came to Hilkiah the *h* priest and
Ezr 7: 5 son of Eleazar, son of the *h* priest Aaron
Neh 3: 1 Eliashib the *h* priest and his priestly
3:20 of the house of Eliashib, the *h* priest.
8: 6 and all the people, their hands raised *h*,
13:28 of Joiada, son of Eliashib the *h* priest,
Tb 1:13 the Most *H* granted me favor and status
4:11 sight of the Most *H* for all who give them.
Jdt 1: 2 the wall seventy cubits *h* and fifty thick.
4: 5 on all the summits of the *h* mountains,
4: 6 was *h* priest in Jerusalem in those days,
4: 8 orders given them by Joakim, the *h* priest,
4:14 The *h* priest Joakim,
7: 4 Neither the *h* mountains nor the valleys
13:18 are you, daughter, by the Most *H* God,
15: 8 The *h* priest Joakim and the elders of the
Est A:17 Agagite, who was in *h* honor with the king,
3: 1 son of Hammedatha the Agagite, to *h* rank,
7: 9 of Haman stands a gibbet fifty cubits *h*.
E:16 laws and are the children of the Most *H*,
10: 3 Ahasuerus, in *h* standing among the Jews,
1Mc 1:33 they built up the City of David with a *h*,
4:60 At that time they built *h* walls and strong
6: 7 surrounded with *h* walls both the sanctuary,
7: 5 led by Alcimus, who desired to be *h* priest.
7: 9 to whom he granted the *h* priesthood,
7:21 no pains to maintain his *h* priesthood,
9:50 Tephon, with *h* walls and gates and bars.
10:20 you today to be *h* priest of your nation;
10:32 and I transfer it to the *h* priest,
10:38 obey no other authority than the *h* priest.
10:69 sent this message to Jonathan the *h* priest:
11:27 He confirmed him in the *h* priesthood and
11:57 "I confirm you in the *h* priesthood and
12: 3 "The *h* priest Jonathan and the Jewish
12: 6 "Jonathan the *h* priest,
12: 7 was sent to the *h* priest Onias from Arius,
12:20 sends greetings to Onias the *h* priest.
12:36 *h* barrier between the citadel and the city,
13:27 raised *h* enough to be seen at a distance.
13:33 their fortifications with *h* towers,
13:36 sends greetings to Simon the *h* priest,
13:42 "In the first year of Simon, *h* priest,
14:17 his brother Simon had been made *h* priest
14:20 send greetings to Simon the *h* priest,
14:23 has been made for Simon the *h* priest."
14:27 year under Simon the *h* priest in Asaramel,
14:30 his nation and become their *h* priest,
14:35 they made him their leader and *h* priest
14:38 confirmed him in the *h* priesthood,
14:41 and *h* priest until a true prophet arises.
14:47 accepted and agreed to act as *h* priest,
15:17 Simon the *h* priest and the Jewish people,
15:21 you, hand them over to Simon the *h* priest,
15:24 letter was also sent to Simon the *h* priest.
16:12 gold, being the son-in-law of the *h* priest.
16:24 that he succeeded his father as *h* priest.
2Mc 3: 1 the *h* priest Onias and his hatred of evil,
3: 4 had a quarrel with the *h* priest about the
3: 9 received by the *h* priest of the city,
3:10 The *h* priest explained
3:11 a man who occupied a very *h* position.
3:16 of the *h* priest was pierced to the heart,
3:21 and the *h* priest full of dread and anguish.
3:31 begged Onias to invoke the Most *H*,
3:32 the *h* priest offered a sacrifice for the
3:33 While the *h* priest was offering the
3:33 "Be very grateful to the *h* priest Onias,"
3:36 *h* God that he had seen with his own eyes.
4: 7 obtained the *h* priesthood by corrupt means:
4:24 he secured the *h* priesthood for himself,
4:25 that made him worthy of the *h* priesthood;
4:29 as his substitute in the *h* priesthood,
7:24 his Friend and entrust him with *h* office.
8:30 them, and captured some very *h* fortresses.
10:13 command the respect due to his *h* office,
11: 3 the *h* priesthood up for sale every year.
13: 5 at that place a tower seventy-five feet *h*,
14: 3 A certain Alcimus, a former *h* priest,
14: 7 dignity, that is to say, the *h* priesthood,
14:13 up Alcimus as *h* priest of the great temple.
15:12 Onias, the former *h* priest,
Jb 5:11 He sets up on *h* the lowly,
16:19 is in heaven, and my spokesman is on *h*.
21:22 seeing that he judges those on *h*?
22:12 behold the stars, *h* though they are?
31: 2 his inheritance from the Almighty on *h*?
35: 5 regard the heavens *h* above you.
Ps(s) 7: 8 above them on *h* be enthroned.

HIGH (cont.)
7:18 sing praise to the name of the LORD Most *H.*
9: 3 I will sing praise to your name, Most *H,*
12: 9 strut and in *h* place are the basest of men.
18:14 heaven, the Most *H* gave forth his voice;
18:17 He reached out from on *h* and grasped me;
21: 8 kindness of the Most *H* he stands unshaken.
27: 5 of his tent, he will set me *h* upon a rock.
27: 6 is held *h* above my enemies on every side.
46: 5 of God, the holy dwelling of the Most *H.*
47: 3 of gladness, For the LORD, the Most *H,*
49: 3 in the world, Of lowly birth or *h* degree,
49: 9 Too *h* is the price to redeem one's life;
50:14 and fulfill your vows to the Most *H;*
56: 3 O Most *H,* when I begin to fear
57: 3 I call to God the Most *H,*
61: 3 You will set me *h* upon a rock;
62: 5 my place on *h* they plan to dislodge me;
68:16 *H* the mountains of Bashan;
68:19 You have ascended on *h,*
73: 8 outrage from on *h* they threaten.
73:11 "Is there any knowledge in the Most *H?"*
75: 6 Lift not up your horns against the Most *H;*
77:11 the right hand of the Most *H* is changed."
78:17 against the Most *H* in the wasteland,
78:35 that God was their rock and the Most *H* God,
78:56 and rebelled against God the Most *H,*
78:58 They angered him with their *h* places and
82: 6 are gods, all of you sons of the Most *H;*
83:19 the LORD, the Most *H* over all the earth.
87: 5 who has established her is the Most *H* LORD."
91: 1 who dwell in the shelter of the Most *H,*
91: 9 you have made the Most *H* your stronghold.
91:14 him on *h* because he acknowledges my name.
92: 2 LORD, to sing praise to your name, Most *H,*
92: 9 while you, O LORD, are the Most *H* forever.
93: 4 powerful on *h* is the LORD.
97: 9 O LORD, are the Most *H* over all the earth,
99: 2 is great, he is *h* above all the peoples.
103:11 For as the heavens are *h* above the earth,
104:18 The *h* mountains are for wild goats;
106: 7 rebelled against the Most *H* at the Red Sea.
107:11 God and scorned the counsel of the Most *H.*
107:25 a storm wind which tossed its waves on *h.*
113: 4 *H* above all nations is the LORD;
113: 5 who is enthroned on *h* and looks upon the
144: 7 Reach out your hand from on *h*—
149: 6 the *h* praises of God be in their throats.
Prv 17:19 he who builds his gate *h* courts disaster.
18:11 he fancies it a *h* wall.
22: 1 desirable than great riches, and *h* esteem,
30:19 a rock, The way of a ship on the *h* seas,
Eccl 5: 7 for the *h* official has another higher than
Wis 5:15 and the thought of them is with the Most *H.*
6: 3 by the Lord and sovereignty by the Most *H,*
9:17 Wisdom and sent your holy spirit from on *h?*
Sir 4:10 Thus will you be like a son to the Most *H,*
7: 9 the Most *H* will accept my offerings."
7:15 farming, which was ordained by the Most *H.*
11: 1 his head *h* and sets him among princes.
12: 7 The Most *H* himself hates sinners,
17:21 Turn again to the Most *H* and away from sin,
17:22 nether world can glorify the Most *H*
19:16 will you fulfill the law of the Most *H.*
23:18 Of the Most *H* he is not mindful,
23:23 she has disobeyed the law of the Most *H;*
24: 2 assembly of the Most *H* she opens her mouth,
24: 3 the mouth of the Most *H* I came forth,
29:11 of your treasure as the Most *H* commands,
33:15 See now all the works of the Most *H:*
34: 6 be a vision specially sent by the Most *H,*
34:19 *H* approves not the gifts of the godless,
35: 5 rises as a sweet odor before the Most *H.*
35: 9 Give to the Most *H* as he has given to you,
35:18 will it withdraw till the Most *H* responds,
39: 1 to the study of the law of the Most *H!*
39: 6 LORD, his Maker, to petition the Most *H,*
41: 4 should you reject the will of the Most *H?*
41: 8 men, who forsake the law of the Most *H.*
42: 2 Of the law of the Most *H* and his precepts,
42:18 The Most *H* possesses all knowledge,
43: 2 what a wonderful work of the Most *H!*
43:10 against the flood waters stored on *h,*
44:20 He observed the precepts of the Most *H,*
45:24 should possess the *h* priesthood forever.
46: 5 He called upon the Most *H* God when his
46: 5 And God Most *H* gave answer to him in
47: 5 Since he called upon the Most *H* God,
47: 8 every deed he offered thanks to God Most *H,*
48:20 *H* God and lifted up their hands to him;
49: 4 They abandoned the Law of the Most *H,*
50:14 of the sacrifices for the Most *H,*
50:15 a sweet-smelling odor to the Most *H* God,
50:16 mightily as a reminder before the Most *H.*
50:17 the ground In adoration before the Most *H,*
50:19 As the *h* priest completed the services at
50:21 from him the blessing of the Most *H.*
Is 2:12 that is proud and arrogant, all that is *h,*
2:14 the lofty mountains and all the *h* hills,
6: 1 the Lord seated on a *h* and lofty throne,
7:11 deep as the nether world, or *h* as the sky!
14:14 I will be like the Most *H!"*
15: 2 daughter Dibon to the *h* places to weep;
16: 3 *h* noon let your shadow be like the night,
16:12 When Moab grows weary on the *h* places,
24:18 For the windows on *h* will be opened,
26: 5 He humbles those in *h* places,
30:13 out in a *h* wall whose crash comes suddenly,
30:25 Upon every *h* mountain and lofty hill there
32:15 the spirit from on *h* is poured out on us.
33: 5 The LORD is exalted, enthroned on *h;*
36: 7 whose *h* places and altars Hezekiah removed,
37:23 your voice And lifted up your eyes on *h?*
40: 9 Go up onto a *h* mountain,
40:26 eyes on *h* and see who has created these:
52:13 he shall be raised *h* and greatly exalted.
55: 9 *h* as the heavens are above the earth, so *h*
57: 7 a *h* and lofty mountain you made your bed,
57: 8 Deserting me, you spread out your *h,*
57:15 For thus says he who is *h* and exalted,
57:15 On *h* I dwell, and in holiness
58: 4 fast so as to make your voice heard on *h!*
Jer 2:20 On every *h* hill, under every green tree
3: 6 She has gone up every *h* mountain,
7:31 they have built the *h* place of Topheth
17: 2 beside the green trees, on the *h* hills,
19: 5 They have built *h* places for Baal to
23:39 you on *h* and cast you from my presence,
25:30 The LORD roars from on *h,*
31:37 If the heavens on *h* can be measured,
32:35 They built *h* places to Baal in the Valley
39: 3 officer, Nebushazban, the *h* dignitary,
39:13 and Nebushazban, the *h* dignitary,
42: 1 of Hoshaiah, and all the people, *h* and low,
42: 8 leaders, and all the people, *h* and low,
44:12 *H* and low, they shall die by the sword
48:35 LORD, to offer a holocaust on the *h* place,
49:16 Though you build your nest *h* as the eagle,
52:21 cubits *h* and twelve cubits in diameter;
52:22 five cubits *h* surmounted the one pillar,
52:24 the guard also took Seraiah, the *h* priest,
Lam 1:13 on *h* he sent fire down into my very frame;
3:35 rights in the very sight of the Most *H,*
3:38 it proceeds from the mouth of the Most *H,*
Bar 3:25 Vast and endless, *h* and immeasurable!
6:62 *h* to burn up the mountains and the forests,
Ez 6: 3 you, and I will destroy your *h* places.
6: 6 be made desolate and *h* places laid waste,
6:13 altars, on every *h* hill and mountaintop,
16:16 gowns and made for yourself gaudy *h* places,
17:22 And plant it on a *h* and lofty mountain;
17:24 low the high tree, lift *h* the lowly tree,
20:28 they saw all its *h* hills and leafy trees,
20:29 sort of *h* place do you betake yourselves?—and
20:29 call it a *h* place even to the present day.
21:31 Up with the low and down with the *h!*
34: 6 over all the mountains and *h* hills;
40: 2 where he set me down on a very *h* mountain.
40:42 and a half cubits wide, and one cubit *h.*
41:17 As *h* as the lintel of the door,
43: 7 corpses of their kings [their *h* places].
43:13 base was one cubit *h* and one cubit deep,
43:14 up to the lower edge it was two cubits *h,*
43:14 to the upper ledge it was four cubits *h,*
43:15 the hearth of the altar was four cubits *h,*
47: 5 for the water had risen so *h* it had become
Dn 2:48 He advanced Daniel to a *h* post,
3: 1 made, sixty cubits *h* and six cubits wide,
3:93 "Servants of the most *h* God, come out."
3:99 most *h* God has accomplished in my regard.
4:14 the Most *H* rules over the kingdom of men:
4:21 the Most *H* has passed upon my lord king:
4:22 until you know that the Most *H* rules over
4:29 until you learn that the Most *H* rules over
4:31 restored to me, and I blessed the Most *H,*
5:18 The Most *H* God gave your father
5:21 until he learned that the Most *H* God rules
7:18 of the Most *H* shall receive the kingship,
7:22 in favor of the holy ones of the Most *H,*
7:25 *H* and oppress the holy ones of the Most *H,*
7:27 be given to the holy people of the Most *H,*
Hos 10: 8 The *h* places of Aven shall be destroyed,
Am 7: 9 The *h* places of Isaac shall be laid waste,
Ob 1: 4 Though you go as *h* as the eagle,
Mi 2: 3 Nor shall you walk with head *h,*
4: 1 it shall rise *h* above the hills,
6: 6 before the LORD, and bow before God most *h?*
Hb 2: 9 on *h* to escape the reach of misfortune!
Zep 1:16 fortified cities, against battlements on *h.*
Hg 1: 1 of Shealtiel, and to the *h* priest Joshua,
1:12 son of Shealtiel, and the *h* priest Joshua,
1:14 and the spirit of the *h* priest Joshua,
2: 2 of Shealtiel, and to the *h* priest Joshua,
2: 4 LORD, and take courage, Joshua, *h* priest,
Zec 3: 1 Then he showed me Joshua the *h* priest
3: 8 Listen, O Joshua, *h* priest!
6:11 son of Jehozadak, the *h* priest] Zerubbabel.
Mt 4: 8 The devil then took him up a very *h*
17: 1 led them up on a *h* mountain by themselves.
26: 3 assembled in the palace of the *h* priest,
26:51 it, and slashed at the *h* priest's servant,
26:57 Jesus led him off to Caiaphas the *h* priest,
26:58 as far as the *h* priest's residence.
26:62 The *h* priest rose to his feet and
26:63 The *h* priest then said to him:
26:65 At this the *h* priest tore his robes:
Mk 2:26 in the days of Abiathar the *h* priest
5: 7 meddle with me, Jesus, Son of God Most *H?*
9: 2 with him and led them up a *h* mountain.
13:28 runs *h* and it begins to sprout leaves,
14:47 his sword and struck the *h* priest's slave,
14:53 Then they led Jesus off to the *h* priest,
14:54 right into the *h* priest's courtyard,
14:60 The *h* priest rose to his feet before the
14:61 Once again the *h* priest interrogated him:
14:63 that the *h* priest tore his robes and said:
14:66 servant girls of the *h* priest came along.
Lk 1:32 and he will be called Son of the Most *H.*
1:35 power of the Most *H* will overshadow you;
1:52 thrones and raised the lowly to *h* places.
1:76 shall be called prophet of the Most *H;*
2:14 God and saying, "Glory to God in *h* heaven,
6:35 will rightly be called sons of the Most *H,*
7: 2 had a servant he held in *h* regard,
8:28 of his voice, "Jesus, Son of God Most *H,*
9:22 the elders, the *h* priests and the scribes,
20: 1 the good news, the *h* priests and Pharisees,
20:19 *h* priests tried to get their hands on him,
21:28 happen, stand erect and hold your heads *h,*
22: 2 and the *h* priests and scribes began to
22:50 went so far as to strike the *h* priest's servant
22:54 brought him to the house of the *h* priest,
24:49 until you are clothed with power from on *h."*
Jn 3:27 anything unless it is given him from on *h.*
11:49 named Caiaphas, who was *h* priest that year,
11:51 It was rather as *h* priest for that year
18:10 it and struck the slave of the *h* priest,
18:13 of Caiaphas who was *h* priest that year.
18:15 *h* priest, stayed with Jesus as far as the *h*
18:16 The disciple known to the *h* priest came
18:19 The *h* priest questioned Jesus,
18:22 "Is that the way to answer the *h* priest?"
18:24 sent him, bound, to the *h* priest Caiaphas.
18:26 insisted one of the *h* priest's slaves
Acts 4: 6 next day in Jerusalem, Annas the *h* priest,
5:17 *h* priest and all his supporters (that is,
5:21 When the *h* priest and his supporters
5:24 temple guard and the *h* priests did not know
5:27 the *h* priest began the interrogation in
7: 1 The *h* priest asked whether the charges
7:48 Yet the Most *H* does not dwell in buildings
9: 1 went to the *h* priest and asked him for
16:17 "These men are servants of the Most *H* God;
19:14 the seven sons of Sceva, a Jewish *h* priest,
22: 5 "On this point the *h* priest and the whole
23: 2 the *h* priest Ananias ordered his
23: 4 "How dare you insult God's *h* priest?"
23: 5 I did not know that he was the *h* priest.
24: 1 the *h* priest Ananias came down to Caesarea
Gal 4:26 But the Jerusalem on *h* is freeborn,
Eph 1:21 hand in heaven, *h* above every principality,
4: 8 "When he ascended on *h,*
4:10 very one who ascended *h* above the heavens,
Phil 3:14 life on *h* in Christ Jesus.
Heb 2:17 *h* priest before God on their behalf,
3: 1 and *h* priest whom we acknowledge in faith,
4:14 we have a great *h* priest who has passed
4:15 For we do not have a *h* priest who is
5: 1 Every *h* priest is taken from among men and
5: 5 himself with the office of *h* priest;
5:10 designated by God as *h* priest according to
6:20 being made *h* priest forever according to
7: 1 king of Salem and priest of the Most *H* God,
7:26 that we should have such a *h* priest:
7:27 Unlike the other *h* priests,
7:28 law sets up as *h* priests men who are weak,
8: 1 we have such a *h* priest,
8: 3 Now every *h* priest is appointed to offer
9: 7 only the *h* priest went into the inner one,
9:11 But when Christ came as *h* priest of the
9:25 as the *h* priest enters year after year
13:11 brought into the sanctuary by the *h* priest
Jas 4:10 of the Lord and he will raise you on *h.*
1Pt 5: 6 so that in due time he may lift you *h.*
Rv 14:20 it reached as *h* as a horse's bridle.
18: 5 For her sins have piled up as *h* as heaven,
21:10 in spirit to the top of a very *h* mountain
21:12 Its wall, massive and *h,* had twelve gates

HIGH-PRIESTHOOD (1)
Lk 3: 2 during the *h* of Annas and

HIGH-PRIESTLY (1)
Acts 4: 6 and all who were of the *h* class were there.

HIGH-WALLED (1)
Is 25:12 The *h* fortress he will raze,

HIGHER (21)
Gn 7:19 *H* and higher above the earth rose the
7:20 cubits *h* than the submerged mountains.
Nm 24: 7 His king shall rise *h* than .
Dt 28:13 you will always mount *h* and not decline,
28:43 among you will rise higher and *h* above you,
2Kgs 25:28 gave him a throne *h* than that of the other
Neh 8: 5 was standing *h* up than any of the people);
Jdt 5: 1 fortified the summits of all the *h* peaks,
1Mc 12:36 for making the walls of Jerusalem still *h,*
Jb 11: 8 It is *h* than the heavens; what can you do?

Eccl 5: 7 for the high official has another *h* than
5: 7 him and above these are others *h* still
Jer 52:32 gave him a throne *h* than that of the other
Dn 14: 2 king's favorite and was held in *h* esteem
Mi 4: 1 Shall be established *h* than the mountains;
Lk 4: 5 Then the devil took him up *h* and showed
14:10 you he will say, 'My friend, come up *h*.'
Col 3: 1 set your heart on what pertains to *h* realms
Heb 7:26 separated from sinners, *h* than the heavens.

HIGHEST (17)

Gn 7:19 the *h* mountains everywhere were submerged,
Dt 10:14 The heavens, even the *h* heavens,
1Kgs 8:27 and the *h* heavens cannot contain you,
2Chr 2: 5 and even the *h* heavens cannot contain him?
6:18 and the *h* heavens cannot contain you,
Neh 9: 6 heavens, the *h* heavens and all their host,
1Mc 14:39 Friends, and conferred the *h* honors on him.
Ps(s) 89:28 first-born, *h* of the kings of the earth.
148: 4 Praise him, you *h* heavens,
Sir 17:27 God watches over the hosts of *h* heaven,
24: 4 In the *h* heavens did I dwell,
Is 2: 2 the *h* mountain and raised above the hills.
Ez 27: 6 the *h* oaks of Bashan they made your oars;
41: 7 the lowest to the middle and the *h* story.
Mt 21: 9 Hosanna in the *h!*"
Mk 11:10 Hosanna in the *h!*"
Lk 19:38 Peace in heaven and glory in the *h!*"

HIGHLAND (1)

Jer 17: 3 the peaks in the *h*

HIGHLANDS (18)

Gn 31:21 Euphrates, he headed for the *h* of Gilead.
31:25 Jacob's tents were pitched in the *h;*
36: 8 So Esau settled in the *h* of Seir.
36: 9 ancestor of the Edomites, in the *h* of Seir.
Nm 13:17 "Go up here in the Negeb, up into the *h*,
13:29 Jebusites and Amorites dwell in the *h*,
Dt 1: 2 to Kadesh-barnea by way of the *h* of Seir].
2: 1 around the *h* of Seir for a long time.
2: 3 have wandered round these *h* long enough;
2: 5 given Esau possession of the *h* of Seir.
2:37 the Wadi Jabbok, nor the cities of the *h*.
3:12 Arnon, halfway up into the *h* of Gilead,
2Chr 13: 4 Zemariam, which is in the *h* of Ephraim,
15: 8 cities he had taken in the *h* of Ephraim,
19: 4 from Beer-sheba to the *h* of Ephraim
26:10 vinedressers in the *h* and the garden land.
Jer 13:27 the *h* I see these horrible crimes of yours.

HIGHLY (16)

Gn 34:19 *h* respected than anyone else in his clan.
Ex 11: 3 Moses himself was very *h* regarded by
1Sm 26:24 *h* today, so may the LORD value my life *h*
2Kgs 5: 1 was *h* esteemed and respected by his master,
1Chr 16:25 For great is the LORD and *h* to be praised;
Jdt 6:20 they reassured Achior and praised him *h*.
2Mc 4:15 *h* prized what the Greeks esteemed as glory.
14:37 A man *h* regarded,
Ps(s) 96: 4 For great is the LORD and *h* to be praised;
145: 3 Great is the LORD and *h* to be praised;
Lk 1:28 "Rejoice, O *h* favored daughter!
Acts 5:34 of the law *h* regarded by all the people.
16: 2 in Lystra and Iconium spoke *h* of him,
Rom 12: 3 to think more *h* of himself than he ought.
Phil 2: 9 God *h* exalted him and bestowed on him the

HIGHROAD (1)

2Sm 20:12 covered with blood in the middle of the *h*,

HIGH'S (3)

Sir 24:22 is true of the book of the Most *H* covenant,
28: 7 not your neighbor, of the Most *H* covenant,
44: 2 The abounding glory of the Most *H* portion,

HIGHWAY (16)

Nm 20:19 "We want only to go up along the *h*.
Dt 2:27 me pass through your country by the *h;*
Jgs 21:19 the *h* that goes up from Bethel to Shechem,
2Kgs 18:17 upper pool on the *h* of the fuller's field.
1Chr 26:16 the Shallecheth gate at the ascending *h*.
26:18 at the *h* and two at the large building.
Prv 6:11 will poverty come upon you like a *h* man,
15:19 but the path of the diligent is a *h*.
Is 7: 3 upper pool, on the *h* of the fuller's field,
11:16 There shall be a *h* for the remnant of his
19:23 there shall be a *h* from Egypt to Assyria;
35: 8 A *h* will be there,
36: 2 upper pool, on the *h* of the fuller's field,
40: 3 straight in the wasteland a *h* for our God!
62:10 Build up, build up the *h*,
Jer 31:21 Turn your attention to the *h*,

HIGHWAYMAN (1)

Prv 24:34 Then will poverty come upon you like a *h*,

HIGHWAYS (7)

Jgs 20:32 to draw them away from the city onto the *h*.
20:32 were drawn away from the city onto the *h*,
20:45 But on the *h* the Israelites picked off
Is 33: 8 The *h* are desolate,
49:11 all my mountains, and make my *h* level.
59: 7 thoughts, plunder and ruin are on their *h*.
Lk 14:23 'Go out into the *h* and along the hedgerows

HILKATH (1)

1Chr 6:60 pasture lands, *H* with its pasture lands,

HILKIAH (39)

2Kgs 18:18 who sent out to them Eliakim, son of *H*,
18:26 Then Eliakim, son of *H*,
18:37 master of the palace, Eliakim, son of *H*,
22: 4 with orders to go to the high priest *H*
22: 8 high priest *H* informed the scribe Shaphan,
22: 8 *H* gave the book to Shaphan, who read it.
22:10 that the priest *H* had given him a book,
22:12 and issued this command to *H* the priest,
22:14 So *H* the priest, Ahikam, Achbor,
23: 4 Then the king commanded the high priest *H*,
23:24 *H* had found in the temple of the Lord
1Chr 5:39 Shallum became the father of *H*.
5:39 *H* became the father of Azariah.
6:30 of Hashabiah, son of Amaziah, son of *H*,
9:11 Azariah, son of *H*,
26:11 first-born his father made him chief), *H*,
2Chr 34: 9 They came to *H* the high priest and turned
34:14 *H* the priest found the book of the law of
34:15 *H* gave the book to Shaphan,
34:18 the king, *H* the priest has given me a book."
34:20 his garments and issued this command to *H*,
34:22 Then *H* and the other men from the king
35: 8 *H*, Zechariah and Jehiel,
Ezr 7: 1 son of Seraiah, son of Azariah, son of *H*,
Neh 8: 4 stood Mattithiah, Shema, Anaiah, Uriah, *H*,
11:11 Seraiah, son of *H*
12: 7 and Joiarib, Jedaiah, Sallu, Amok, *H*,
12:21 for *H*, Hashabiah
Jdt 8: 1 son of Ahitob, son of Elijah, son of *H*,
Is 22:20 will summon my servant Eliakim, son of *H;*
36: 3 master of the palace, Eliakim, son of *H*,
36:22 master of the palace, Eliakim, son of *H*,
Jer 1: 1 The words of Jeremiah, son of *H*,
29: 3 son of Shaphan, and by Gemariah, son of *H*,
Bar 1: 1 of Zedekiah, son of Hasadiah, son of *H*,
1: 7 sent to Jerusalem, to Jehoiakim, son of *H*,
Dn 13: 2 woman, Susanna, the daughter of *H;*
13:29 "Send for Susanna, the daughter of *H*,
13:63 *H* and his wife praised God

HILL (71)

Gn 10:30 the way to Sephar, the eastern *h* country.
12: 8 moved on to the *h* country east of Bethel,
14: 6 and the Horites in the *h* country of Seir,
19:30 up from Zoar and settled in the *h* country,
31:23 up with him in the *h* country of Gilead.
Ex 17: 9 of the *h* with the staff of God in my hand."
17:10 to the top of the *h* with Aaron and Hur.
Nm 14:45 that *h* country came down and defeated them,
Dt 1: 7 Leave here and go to the *h* country of the
1:19 direction of the *h* country of the Amorites.
1:20 have come to the *h* country of the Amorites,
1:24 the *h* country as far as the Wadi Eshcol,
1:41 light of going up into the *h* country.
1:43 arrogantly marched off into the *h* country.
3:25 beyond the Jordan, this fine *h* country,
Jos 2:16 "Go up into the *h* country,"
24:33 he was buried on the *h* which had been
1Sm 1: 1 a Zuphite from the *h* country of Ephraim.
7: 1 it into the house of Abinadab on the *h*,
9: 4 they went through the *h* country of Ephraim,
13: 2 in Michmash and in the *h* country of Bethel,
14:22 were hiding in the *h* country of Ephraim,
14:24 in every town in the *h* country of Ephraim.
17: 3 *h* and the Israelites on an opposite hill,
23:14 or in the barren *h* country near Ziph.
23:19 again at Horesh, or on the *h* of Hachilah,
26: 1 *h* of Hachilah at the edge of the wasteland.
26: 3 beside the road on the *h* of Hachilah,
2Sm 2:24 they came to the *h* of Ammah
6: 3 away from the house of Abinadab on the *h*.
20:21 from the *h* country of Ephraim has rebelled
1Kgs 4: 8 the son of Hur in the *h* country of Ephraim;
11: 7 the Ammonites, on the *h* opposite Jerusalem.
12:25 the *h* country of Ephraim and lived there.
14:23 every high *h* and under every green tree.
16:24 He then bought the *h* of Samaria from
16:24 two silver talents and built upon the *h*,
2Kgs 5:22 prophets from the *h* country of Ephraim.
5:24 When they reached the *h*,
17:10 on every high *h* and under every leafy tree.
2Chr 27: 4 he built cities in the *h* country of Judah,
Neh 8:15 "Go out into the *h* country and bring in
1Mc 4:46 in a suitable place on the temple *h*,
11:37 in a conspicuous place on the holy *h*.'"
13:52 of the temple *h* alongside the citadel,
Sg 4: 6 the mountain of myrrh, to the *h* of incense.
Sir 25:19 Like a sandy *h* to aged feet is a railing
Is 10:32 mount of daughter Zion, the *h* of Jerusalem!
30:17 on the mountaintop, like a flag on the *h*.
30:25 *h* there will be streams of running water.
31: 4 wage war upon the mountain and *h* of Zion.
32:19 *H* and tower will become wasteland forever
40: 4 in, every mountain and *h* shall be made low;
Jer 2:20 On every high *h*, under every green tree,
16:16 and *h* and from the clefts of the rocks.
17:26 from the *h* country and the Negeb,
30:18 City shall be rebuilt upon *h*,
31:39 to the *h* Gareb and then turn to Goah.
32:44 the cities of Judah and of the *h* country,
33:13 In the cities of the *h* country,
49:16 crags, that hold the heights of the *h:*
50: 6 From mountain to *h* they wandered,
Ez 6:13 altars, on every high *h* and mountaintop,
34:26 I will place them about my *h*,
Hg 1: 8 Go up into the *h* country;
Mt 5:14 A city set on a *h* cannot be hidden.
Lk 1:39 into the *h* country to a town of Judah,
1:65 throughout the *h* country of Judea these
3: 5 And every mountain and *h* shall be leveled.
4:29 leading him to the brow of the *h* on which

HILLEL (2)

Jgs 12:13 After him the Pirathonite Abdon, son of *H*,
12:15 years, the Pirathonite Abdon, son of *H*,

HILLOCK (1)

Mi 4: 8 And you, O Magdal-eder, *h* of daughter Zion!

HILLS (57)

Gn 19:17 Get off to the *h* at once,
19:19 *h* to keep the disaster from overtaking me,
49:26 mountains, the delights of the eternal *h*.
Dt 8: 7 fountains welling up in the *h* and valleys,
8: 9 iron and in whose *h* you can mine copper.
11:11 land of *h* and valleys that drinks in rain
12: 2 place on the high mountains, on the *h*,
33:15 and the best from the timeless *h;*
Jos 2:22 They went up into the *h*,
2:23 Then the two came back down from the *h*,
Jgs 9:36 him, "You see the shadow of the *h* as men."
2Kgs 16: 4 burned incense on the high places, on *h*,
2Chr 28: 4 and incense on the high places, on *h*,
Jdt 7: 4 valleys and *h* can support the mass of them."
16: 3 the torrents, their horses covered the *h*.
2Mc 5:27 lived like wild animals in the *h*,
Jb 15: 7 or were you brought forth before the *h?*
Ps(s) 65:13 with it, and rejoicing clothes the *h*.
72: 3 peace for the people, and the *h* justice.
114: 4 rams, the *h* like the lambs of the flock.
114: 6 You *h*, like the lambs of the flock?
148: 9 You mountains and all you *h*,
Prv 8:25 were settled into place, before the *h*,
Sg 2: 8 across the mountains, leaping across the *h*.
Wis 17:19 echo resounding from the hollow of the *h*,
Is 2: 2 highest mountain and raised above the *h*.
2:14 the lofty mountains and all the high *h*,
34: 4 with their blood, and all the *h* shall rot;
40:12 mountains in scales and the *h* in a balance?
41:15 and crush them, to make the *h* like chaff.
42:15 I will lay waste mountains and *h*,
54:10 leave their place and the *h* be shaken,
55:12 and *h* shall break out in song before you,
65: 7 the mountains, and disgraced me on the *h*,
Jer 3:23 Deceptive indeed are the *h*,
4:24 trembling, and all the *h* were crumbling!
13:27 On the *h* in the highlands I see these
17: 2 beside the green trees, on the high *h*,
Ez 6: 3 says the Lord GOD [to the mountains and *h*,
20:28 they saw all its high *h* and leafy trees,
34: 6 over all the mountains and high *h;*
35: 8 With the slain I will fill your *h*,
36: 4 says the Lord GOD to the mountains and *h*,
36: 6 of Israel, and say to the mountains and *h*,
Dn 3:75 Mountains and *h*, bless the Lord
Hos 4:13 sacrifice and on the *h* they burn incense,
10: 8 and to the *h*, "Fall upon us!"
Jl 4:18 new wine, and the *h* shall flow with milk;
Am 9:13 mountains, and all the *h* shall run with it.
Mi 4: 1 it shall rise high above the *h*,
6: 1 mountains, and let the *h* hear your voice!
Na 1: 5 quake before him, and the *h* dissolve;
Hb 3: 6 age-old *h* bow low along his ancient ways.
Zep 1:10 the New Quarter, loud crashing from the *h*.
Mt 18:12 out on the *h* and go in search of the stray?
Lk 23:30 the mountains, 'Fall on us,' and to the *h*,
Rv 17: 9 seven *h* on which the woman sits enthroned.

HILLSIDE (4)

Gn 49:22 a wild colt by a spring, a wild ass on a *h*.
2Sm 16:13 Shimei kept abreast of them on the *h*,
Is 5: 1 My friend had a vineyard on a fertile *h;*
Lk 8:32 herd of swine was feeding nearby on the *h*,

HILLSIDES (1)

Mk 5: 5 and day, amid the tombs and on the *h*,

HILLTOP (5)

1Sm 19:22 of the threshing floor on the bare *h*,
19:23 As he set out from the *h* toward the sheds,

HILLTOP (cont.)
26:13 a remote *h* at a great distance from Abner,
2Sm 2:25 a single group, and made a stand on the *h*.
2Kgs 1: 9 was seated on a *h* when he found him.

HILLTOPS (1)
Jgs 9:36 "There are men coming down from the *h!*"

HILT (1)
Jgs 3:22 The *h* also went in after the blade,

HIMSELF (545)
Gn 8:21 LORD smelled the sweet odor, he said to *h:*
13:11 chose for *h* the whole Jordan Plain and set
17: 3 When Abram prostrated *h*,
17:17 prostrated *h* and laughed as he said to *h*
20: 5 He *h* told me, 'She is my sister,'
22: 6 while he *h* carried the fire and the knife.
22: 8 *h* will provide the sheep for the holocaust."
27:41 He said to *h*, "When the time of mourning
28: 6 him to Paddan-aram to get *h* a wife there,
30:36 a three days' journey between *h* and Jacob,
32:19 and Jacob *h* is right behind us.'"
33: 3 He *h* went on ahead of them,
33: 4 embraced him, and flinging *h* on his neck,
33:17 for *h* and made booths for his livestock.
35: 7 it was there that God had revealed *h*
39: 8 not concern *h* with anything in the house,
39:23 The chief jailer did not concern *h* with
41: 1 He saw *h* standing by the Nile,
43:31 he reappeared and, now in control of *h*,
45: 1 *h* in the presence of all his attendants,
45: 1 about when he made *h* known to his brothers.
45:12 yourselves, and Benjamin can see for *h*,
45:14 Thereupon he flung *h* on the neck of his
46:29 he flung *h* on his neck and wept a long
50: 1 Joseph threw *h* on his father's face and
50: 5 had prepared for *h* in the land of Canaan,
Ex 11: 3 Moses *h* was very highly regarded by
14:14 The LORD *h* will fight for you;
21: 8 if her master, who had destined her for *h*,
22: 7 to swear that he *h* did not lay hands on
24: 1 Moses *h* was told, "Come up to the LORD,
32:16 on them that were engraved by God *h*.
Lv 7: 8 someone may keep for *h* the hide
9: 4 for today the LORD will reveal *h* to you."
13: 7 shown *h* to the priest to be declared clean,
13: 7 he shall once more show *h* to the priest.
13:19 pink blotch, he shall show *h* to the priest.
13:33 below the skin, the man shall shave *h*,
13:46 sore is on him he shall declare *h* unclean,
14:21 as a wave offering in atonement for *h*,
16: 4 gird *h* with the linen sash and put on the
16: 6 to atone for *h* and for his household.
16:11 to atone for *h* and for his family.
16:17 has made atonement for *h* and his household,
16:24 in atonement for *h* and for the people,
16:29 shall mortify *h* and shall do no work.
21: 1 None of you shall make *h* unclean for any
21: 3 for these he may make *h* unclean.
21: 4 of his family he shall not make *h* unclean;
22: 8 He shall not make *h* unclean by eating of
23:29 Anyone who does not mortify *h* on this day
25:47 reduced to such poverty that he sells *h*
25:49 if he acquires the means, he may redeem *h*.
26:46 in the pact between *h* and the Israelites.
Nm 5:18 while he *h* shall hold the bitter water
6: 2 the nazirite vow to dedicate *h* to the LORD,
12: 3 Moses *h* was by far the meekest man on the
15:31 He has only *h* to blame."
19:12 he shall purify *h* with the water on the
19:12 *h* on the third and on the seventh day,
19:13 Everyone who fails to purify *h* after
19:20 Any unclean man who fails to have *h*
22:22 angel of the LORD stationed *h* on the road
27:21 He shall present *h* to the priest Eleazar,
30: 3 *h* under oath to a pledge of abstinence,
31:53 soldiers had looted each one kept for *h*.
Dt 1:30 who goes before you, will *h* fight for you,
4:34 for *h* from the midst of another nation,
10: 9 the LORD *h* in his heritage,
12: 8 here, everyone does what seems right to *h*,
15:12 a Hebrew man or woman, sells *h* to you,
18: 2 the LORD *h* is his heritage,
20: 8 he make his fellows as fainthearted as *h*.'
24:13 to him at sunset that he *h* may sleep in it.
28: 9 establish you as a people sacred to *h*,
28:55 his children that he *h* is using for food
29:18 should beguile *h* into thinking that he can
Jos 13:33 to the tribe of Levi, since the LORD *h*,
22:23 upon it, the LORD *h* will exact the penalty.
23: 3 the LORD, your God, *h* who fought for you.
23:10 the LORD, your God, *h* who fights for you,
Jgs 3:16 Ehud made *h* a two-edged dagger a foot long,
3:24 "He must be easing *h* in the cool chamber."
4:11 Heber had detached *h* from his own people,
4:15 Sisera *h* dismounted from his chariot and
6:31 been destroyed is a god, let him act for *h!*"
7:15 explanation of the dream, he prostrated *h*.
16:29 temple rested and braced *h* against them,
19: 1 for *h* a concubine from Bethlehem of Judah.

Ru 2: 4 Boaz *h* came from Bethlehem and said to the
1Sm 12:22 the LORD *h* chose to make you his people.
17:39 girded *h* with Saul's sword over the tunic.
18: 1 he loved him as he loved *h*.
18: 3 bond with David, because he loved him as *h*.
18: 4 Jonathan divested *h* of the mantle he was
18:12 but had departed from Saul *h*
19:22 Saul then went to Ramah *h*.
19:24 he, too, stripped *h* of his garments and he,
20:41 prostrated *h* on the ground three times
22:18 one to the next and killed the priests *h*,
23: 7 Now he has shut *h* in,
25: 3 intelligent and attractive, but Nabal *h*,
26: 5 David *h* then went to the place
26:10 must be the LORD *h* who will strike him,
27: 1 But David said to *h:*
28: 8 disguised *h*, putting on other clothes,
30: 6 Now David found *h* in great difficulty,
2Sm 3:31 King David *h* followed the bier.
4:10 thinking *h* the bearer of good news for
6:20 honored *h* today, exposing *h* to the view
12:20 the ground, David washed and anointed *h*,
14:13 as he has, the king shows *h* guilty,
15: 1 this Absalom provided *h* with chariots,
17:23 orders concerning his family, he hanged *h*.
18:18 and erected it for *h* in the King's Valley,
18:18 *h* is called Yadabshalom to the present day.
18:26 out, "There is another man running by *h*."
23: 7 arm *h* with iron and the shaft of a spear,
1Kgs 1:52 Solomon answered, "If he proves *h* worthy,
2:32 down two men better and more just than *h*,
3: 1 Solomon allied *h* by marriage with Pharaoh,
8:58 May he draw our hearts to *h*,
11:34 take any of the kingdom from Solomon *h*,
12:26 Jeroboam thought to *h:*
14:14 the LORD will raise up for *h* a king of
17:21 Then he stretched *h* out upon the child
18: 2 So Elijah went to present *h* to Ahab.
18: 6 way by himself, Obadiah another way by *h*.
20:38 disguised *h* with a bandage over his eyes.
21:25 no one gave *h* up to the doing of evil in
21:29 you seen that Ahab has humbled *h* before me?
21:29 Since he has humbled *h* before me,
22:11 Chenaanah, made *h* horns of iron and said,
22:21 came forth and presented *h* to the LORD,
22:23 the LORD *h* has decreed evil against you."
22:30 of Israel disguised *h* and entered the fray.
2Kgs 4:34 As Elisha stretched *h* over the child,
5: 3 would present *h* to the prophet in Samaria,"
5:20 of Elisha, the man of God, thought to *h:*
6:32 a man ahead before he *h* should come to him.
8:18 He conducted *h* like the kings of Israel of
8:27 He conducted *h* like the house of Ahab,
13: 2 LORD's sight, conducting *h* like Jeroboam,
16: 3 but conducted *h* like the kings of Israel,
18:16 he *h* had ordered to be overlaid with gold,
19: 1 tore his garments, wrapped *h* in sackcloth,
22: 2 He pleased the LORD and conducted *h*
24:11 *h* arrived at the city while his servants
1Chr 15: 1 David built houses for *h* in the City of
20: 1 while David *h* remained in Jerusalem.
28: 9 seek him, he will let *h* be found by you;
2Chr 6:22 to take an oath of execration against *h*,
10:18 Rehoboam *h* managed to mount his chariot
11:15 he *h* appointed priests for the high places
11:18 Rehoboam took to *h* as wife Mahalath,
12:12 Because he had humbled *h*,
13: 9 Everyone who comes to consecrate *h* with a
13:21 He took to *h* fourteen wives and fathered
14: 9 Asa went out to meet him and set *h* in
16:14 he had hewn for *h* in the City of David,
17:16 son of Zichri, who offered *h* to the LORD,
18:10 Chenaanah, made iron horns for *h* and said:
18:20 came forward and presented *h* to the LORD,
18:22 the LORD *h* has decreed evil against you."
18:29 disguised *h* and they entered the fray.
18:34 and the king of Israel braced *h* up on his
20:35 Judah allied *h* with King Ahaziah of Israel,
21: 6 He conducted *h* like the kings of Israel of
22: 9 Then he looked for Ahaziah *h*.
23:16 between *h* and all the people and the king,
26:20 He *h* fled willingly,
28: 2 but conducted *h* like the kings of Israel
28:24 made for *h* in every corner of Jerusalem.
32: 9 *h* remained at Lachish with all his forces,
32:26 But then Hezekiah humbled *h* for his pride
32:29 He built cities for *h*,
33: 3 and prostrated *h* before the whole host of
33:12 He humbled *h* abjectly before the God of
33:13 The LORD let *h* be won over:
33:19 and carved images before he humbled *h*,
33:23 he did not humble *h* before the LORD as his
36:12 not humble *h* before the prophet Jeremiah,
Ezr 6:20 of whom had purified *h* for the occasion,
10: 8 and *h* be excluded from the assembly of the
Neh 3:12 of Jerusalem, by *h* and his daughters.
Tb 4:19 but the Lord *h* gives all good things.
6:18 will flee and never again show *h* near her.
8: 6 let us make him a partner like *h*,'
8:19 he *h* went out to the herd and picked out
14:10 But Nadab *h* fell into the deadly trap,
Jdt 1:12 he would avenge *h* on all the territories
1:15 *h* he overtook in the mountains of Ragae,

2: 4 of his forces, second to *h* in command,
5: 3 Who has set *h* up as their king and the
7: 7 them, while he *h* returned to his troops.
14: 7 he threw *h* at the feet of Judith in homage,
Est 5:10 Haman restrained *h*,
6: 6 Now Haman thought to *h*,
7: 8 Haman had thrown *h* on the couch on which
1Mc 3: 3 He armed *h* with weapons of war;
3:22 He *h* will crush them before us;
4: 3 and *h* set out with his soldiers to attack
6:44 people and win an everlasting name for *h*.
7:20 help him, while he *h* returned to the king.
7:43 he *h* was the first to fall in the battle.
10:23 of the Jews and thus strengthening *h?*
11:18 But three days later King Ptolemy *h* died,
11:23 exposed *h* to danger by going to the king
12:43 and soldiers to obey him as they would *h*.
13:48 its fortifications and built *h* a residence.
14: 7 of war and made *h* master of Gazara,
2Mc 2:29 *h* with what is needed for ornamentation,
3:24 manifested *h* in so striking a way
3:30 that the almighty Lord had manifested *h*.
4:24 that he secured the high priesthood for *h*,
4:26 and now saw *h* cheated by another man,
4:42 thief *h* they slew near the treasury.
4:45 But Menelaus, seeing *h* on the losing side,
5:10 went unmourned *h* with no funeral
8:23 he *h* took charge of the first division and
9:17 he would become a Jew *h* and visit every
9:18 so he lost hope for *h* and wrote the
10:13 on all sides he heard *h* called a traitor
10:19 while he *h* went off to places where he was
11: 7 Maccabeus *h* was the first to take up arms,
11:12 Lysias *h* escaped only by shameful flight.
12:24 Timothy *h* fell into the hands of the men
12:36 show *h* their ally and leader in the battle.
14:41 on all sides, turned his sword against *h*,
14:43 manly courage threw *h* down into the crowd.
15: 4 such a ruler in heaven, the living LORD *h*,
Jb 1:20 He cast *h* prostrate upon the ground,
2: 8 And he took a potsherd to scrape *h*,
5: 7 But man *h* begets mischief,
15: 2 with airy opinions, or puff *h* up with wind?
15:27 he has blinded *h* with his crassness,
21:19 him requite the man *h* so that he feels it,
22: 2 Though to *h* a wise man be profitable!
22:25 Then the Almighty *h* shall be your gold and
23: 6 power, yet, would that he *h* might heed me!
32: 2 *h* rather than God to be in the right.
34:14 to himself, withdraw to *h* his breath,
Ps(s) 36: 3 For he beguiles *h* with the thought that
49: 8 Yet in no way can a man redeem *h*,
49:19 in his lifetime he counted *h* blessed.
50: 6 for God *h* is the judge.
52: 7 God *h* shall demolish you;
55:13 he who hates me had vaunted *h* against me,
68:17 where the LORD *h* will dwell forever?
85:13 The LORD *h* will give his benefits;
89:49 *h* from the power of the nether world?
135: 4 For the LORD has chosen Jacob for *h*,
Prv 6:32 he who would destroy *h* does it.
8:36 But he who misses me harms *h;*
11:17 himself, but a merciless man harms *h*.
11:25 who refreshes others will *h* be refreshed.
12: 9 Better a lowly man who supports *h* than one
14:16 the fool is reckless and sure of *h*.
14:17 The quick-tempered man makes a fool of *h*,
18:20 with the yield of his lips he sates *h*.
21:13 the poor will *h* also call and not be heard.
21:23 mouth and his tongue keeps *h* from trouble.
22:16 He who oppresses the poor to enrich *h* will
26:16 The sluggard imagines *h* wiser than seven
28: 1 the just man, like a lion, feels sure of *h*.
28:10 an evil way will *h* fall into his own pit.
28:26 He who trusts in *h* is a fool,
29:24 he hears *h* put under a curse,
Eccl 2:24 provide *h* with good things by his labors.
5:19 lets him busy *h* with the joy of his heart.
6: 8 man in knowing how to conduct *h* in life?
Sg 3: 9 made *h* a carriage of wood from Lebanon.
Wis 1: 2 *h* to those who do not disbelieve him.
2:12 he sets *h* against our doings,
2:13 of God and styles *h* a child of the Lord.
3: 5 God tried them and found them worthy of *h*.
3: 6 as sacrificial offerings he took them to *h*.
6: 7 he *h* made the great as well as the small,
15: 8 though he *h* shortly before was made from
15:16 man succeeds in fashioning a god like *h;*
Sir 6:17 accordingly, and his friend will be like *h*.
7:20 nor a laborer who devotes *h* to his task.
8:17 with a fool, for he can keep nothing to *h*.
10:28 Who will acquit him who condemns *h?*
10:28 who will honor him who discredits *h?*
12: 7 The Most High *h* hates sinners,
13:14 loves its own kind, every man a man like *h*.
14: 4 What he denies *h* he collects for others,
14: 5 with *h* and does not enjoy what is his own?
14: 6 more stingy than he who is stingy with *h;*
14: 9 refuses his neighbor and brings ruin on *h*.
16:18 with my ways who will concern *h?*
18:27 sin is rife he keeps *h* from wrongdoing.
20:12 wise man makes *h* popular by a few words,
20:26 A wise man advances *h* by his words,

21:27 curses his adversary he really curses *h.*
21:28 A slanderer besmirches *h,*
22:13 trouble and be spattered when he shakes *h;*
23:18 bed and says to *h* "Who can see me?
30: 4 since he leaves after him one like *h,*
30: 8 a son left to *h* grows up unruly.
31: 4 and if ever he rests, he finds *h* in want.
32:24 He who keeps the law preserves *h;*
33:12 great, some he sanctifies and draws to *h.*
37: 8 For he may be thinking of *h* alone;
37:19 and benefit many, yet be of no use to *h.*
37:24 One wise for *h* has full enjoyment,
39: 1 *h* to the study of the law of the Most High!
39: 1 of old and occupies *h* with the prophecies;
45:22 For the LORD *h* is his portion,
46: 7 God and in Moses' lifetime showed *h* loyal,
Is 7:14 the Lord *h* will give you this sign:
19:21 The LORD shall make *h* known in Egypt,
22:16 Who has hewn for *h* a sepulcher on a height
28:21 bestir *h* as in the Valley of Gibeon,
30:20 No longer will your Teacher hide *h,*
37: 1 tore his garments, wrapped *h* in sackcloth,
40:20 which a skilled craftsman picks out for *h,*
44:15 With a part of their wood he warms *h,*
44:16 he is full, and then warms *h* and says,
51:13 But when he sets *h* to destroy,
53:12 Because he surrendered *h* to death and was
56: 3 say, when he would join *h* to the LORD,
59:17 *h* with garments of vengeance, wrapped *h* in
63: 9 or an angel, but he *h* who saved them.
63: 9 of his love and pity he redeemed them *h,*
63:12 before them, winning for *h* eternal renown;
64: 6 your name, who rouses *h* to cling to you;
Jer 16: 6 one will gash *h* or shave his head for them.
16:20 Can man make for *h* gods?
34:14 his Hebrew brother who has sold *h* to you;
39:12 befall him, but treat him as he *h* requests."
40:10 saying that he *h* would remain in Mizpah,
41: 9 by King Asa to defend *h* against Baasha,
51:14 The LORD of hosts has sworn by *h:*
51:45 save *h* from the burning wrath of the LORD.
Lam 4:16 The LORD *h* has dispersed them,
Bar 4:18 *h* deliver you from your enemies' hands.
Ez 34:12 when he finds *h* among his scattered sheep,
Dn 1: 8 to defile *h* with the king's food or wine;
2:49 Daniel *h* remained at the king's court.
11:17 He shall set *h* to penetrate the entire
11:36 *h* and making himself greater than any god;
11:37 because he shall make *h* greater than all.
14:30 When he saw *h* threatened with violence,
Hos 5: 6 he has withdrawn *h* from them.
13:13 not present *h* where children break forth.
Jon 3: 6 aside his robe, covered *h* with sackcloth,
4: 5 *h* a hut and waited under it in the shade,
Hb 1: 7 he, from *h* derive his law and his majesty.
1:13 wicked man devours one more just than *h?*
2: 5 gathers to *h* all the nations, and rallies to *h*
2: 6 he loads *h* down with debts.
Zec 5: 4 house of him who perjures *h* with my name;
Mt 10:39 *h* brings *h* to ruin, whereas he who brings *h*
14:13 boat from there to a deserted place by *h.*
14:23 he went up on the mountain by *h* to pray,
16:26 whole world and destroy *h* in the process?
18: 4 Whoever makes *h* lowly,
18:26 official prostrated *h* in homage and said,
18:28 owed him a mere fraction of what he *h* owed.
23:12 *h* shall be humbled, but whoever humbles *h*
24:48 if the servant is worthless and tells *h,*
27: 5 He went off and hanged *h.*
27:42 "He saved others but he cannot save *h!*
Mk 3:13 and summoned the men he *h* had decided on,
5: 5 he screamed and gashed *h* with stones.
7:33 took him off by *h* away from the crowd.
8:36 whole world and destroys *h* in the process?
12:36 David *h,* inspired by the Holy Spirit
12:37 If David *h* addresses him as 'Lord,'
14:48 Addressing *h* to them, Jesus said:
14:54 guard and began to warm *h* at the fire.
14:67 When she noticed Peter warming *h,*
15:31 "He saved others but he cannot save *h!*
16:20 Later on it was through them that Jesus *h*
Lk 1:17 God *h* will go before him,
4:39 over her and addressed *h* to the fever,
6:35 *h* is good to the ungrateful and the wicked.
7:39 the Pharisee, saw this, he said to *h,*
9:25 whole world and destroys *h* in the process?
10:29 he wished to justify *h* he said to Jesus,
11:18 If Satan is divided against *h,*
12:17 he asked *h.* I have no place to store
12:21 works with the man who grows rich for *h*
12:45 But if the servant says to *h,*
14: 5 Then he addressed *h* to them:
14:11 *h* shall be humbled and he who humbles *h*
15:15 So he attached *h* to one of the propertied
16: 3 The manager thought to *h,*
17:16 He threw *h* on his face at the feet of
18:14 *h* shall be humbled while he who humbles *h*
19:16 The first presented *h* and said,
20:13 The owner of the vineyard asked *h,*
20:42 Does not David *h* say in the psalms,
23: 2 taxes to Caesar, and calling *h* the Messiah,
23:35 let him save *h* if he is the Messiah of God,
24:30 When he had seated *h* with them to eat,
24:36 *h* stood in their midst [and said to them,
Jn 1: 8 to the light, for he *h* was not the light.
2:24 trust *h* to them because he knew them all.
4: 2 however, it was not Jesus *h* who baptized,
4:44 (Jesus *h* had testified that no one esteems
5:18 own Father, thereby making *h* God's equal.
5:19 you, the Son cannot do anything by *h*—
5:22 The Father *h* judges no one,
5:26 just as the Father possesses life in *h,*
5:26 he granted it to the Son to have life in *h.*
5:37 sent me has *h* given testimony on my behalf.
8:22 he mean he will kill *h* when he claims,
8:41 We have but one father and that is God *h.*"
8:44 beginning, and has never based *h* on truth;
8:59 *h* and slipped out of the temple precincts.
9: 9 The man *h* said, "I am the one."
9:21 He is old enough to speak for *h.*"
12: 6 used to help *h* to what was deposited there.)
13: 4 He picked up a towel and tied it around *h.*
13:27 Jesus addressed *h* to him:
13:32 God will, in turn, glorify him in *h,*
18:18 joined them and stood there warming *h.*
18:25 Peter had been standing there warming *h.*
19: 7 he must die because he made *h* God's Son."
19:12 who makes *h* a king becomes Caesar's rival."
19:17 was led away, and carrying the cross by *h,*
21: 1 showed *h* to the disciples [once again].
Acts 1: 7 The Father has reserved that to *h.*
5: 2 he put aside a part of the proceeds for *h;*
5:36 to pass *h* off as someone of importance.
5:39 to destroy them without fighting God *h.*"
7:13 time, Joseph made *h* known to his brothers,
8: 9 *h* off as someone of great importance.
8:26 of the Lord then addressed *h* to Philip:
8:34 the prophet says this *h* or someone else?"
8:40 Philip found *h* at Azotus next,
9:28 *h* quite openly in the name of the Lord.
11:24 since he *h* was a good man filled with the
14:17 benefits, he has not hidden *h* completely,
15:14 told you how God first concerned *h*
16:27 had escaped, he drew his sword to kill *h;*
17: 6 they dragged Jason *h* and some of the
18:26 to express *h* fearlessly in the synagogue.
19:22 while he *h* stayed on for a time in Asia.
20:10 threw *h* on him, clutching the boy to *h.*
20:35 to recall the words of the Lord Jesus *h,*
24:27 Felix wanted to ingratiate *h* with the Jews,
25: 4 that he *h* would be returning there soon.
25:16 a chance to defend *h* against their charges.
26:24 As Paul went on defending *h* in this way,
Rom 1:19 he *h* made it so.
8:16 The Spirit *h* gives witness with our spirit
8:26 but the Spirit *h* makes intercession for us
8:27 intercedes for the saints as God *h* wills.
12: 3 to think more highly of *h* than he ought.
12: 3 Let him estimate *h* soberly,
14: 3 After all, God *h* has made him welcome.
14:12 have to give an account of *h* before God.
15: 3 with Scripture, Christ did not please *h:*
16:10 Apelles, who proved *h* in Christ's service,
1Cor 2:15 though he *h* can be appraised by no one.
3:15 He *h* will be saved,
3:18 Let no one delude *h.*
7: 4 does not belong to *h* but to his wife.
9: 7 not nourish *h* with the milk of his flock?
9:14 Likewise the Lord *h* ordered that those who
11:28 A man should examine *h* first;
11:29 the body eats and drinks a judgment on *h.*
14: 4 He who speaks in a tongue builds up *h,*
14:28 each one speaking only to *h* and to God.
15:13 of the dead, Christ *h* has not been raised.
15:28 he will then subject *h* to the One who made
2Cor 5:18 who has reconciled us to *h* through Christ
5:19 in Christ, was reconciling the world to *h,*
8: 9 sake he made *h* poor though he was rich,
10:18 It is not the man who recommends *h* who is
11: 2 jealous of you with the jealousy of God *h,*
11:14 Satan disguises *h* as an angel of light.
Gal 1: 4 Lord Jesus Christ, who gave *h* for our sins,
2:20 Son of God, who loved me and gave *h* for me.
3:13 law's curse by *h* becoming a curse for us,
6: 1 trying to avoid falling into temptation *h.*
6: 3 fact he is nothing, he is only deceiving *h.*
Eph 2: 9 accomplished, so let no one pride *h* on it.
2:15 to create in *h* one new man from us who had
2:20 with Christ Jesus *h* as the capstone.
3:19 you may attain to the fullness of God *h.*
5: 2 He gave *h* for us as an offering to God,
5:25 He gave *h* up for her to make her holy,
5:27 word, to present to *h* a glorious church,
5:28 He who loves his wife loves *h.*
5:33 one should love his wife as he loves *h,*
Phil 1: 8 God *h* can testify how much I long for each
2: 7 he emptied *h* and took the form of a slave,
2: 8 and it was thus that he humbled *h,*
3:21 by his power to subject everything to *h.*
1Thes 2:10 You are witnesses, as is God *h,*
3:11 May God *h,*
4: 9 God *h* has taught you to love one another,
4:15 say to you, as if the Lord *h* had said it,
4:16 the Lord *h* will come down from heaven at
2Thes 2: 4 who exalts *h* above every so-called god
2: 4 seats *h* in God's temple and even declares *h*
2:16 May our Lord Jesus Christ *h,*
1Tm 2: 6 Jesus, who gave *h* as a ransom for all."
2Tm 2:13 remain faithful, for he cannot deny *h.*
2:21 if a person will but cleanse *h* of evil things
Ti 2:14 It was he who sacrificed *h* for us,
2:14 and to cleanse for *h* a people of his own,
Heb 2:18 he was *h* tested through what he suffered,
5: 2 for he *h* is beset by weakness and so must
5: 3 offerings for *h* as well as for the people.
5: 5 glorify *h* with the office of high priest;
6:13 made his promise to Abraham, he swore by *h,*
7:27 he did that once for all when he offered *h.*
9: 7 for *h* and for the sins of the people.
9:14 spirit offered *h* up unblemished to God,
9:25 he might offer *h* there again and again,
11: 4 God *h* having borne witness to him on
11:12 from one man, who was *h* as good as dead,
Jas 1:24 he looks at *h,*
1Pt 2:23 *h* up to the One who judges justly.
5:10 glory in Christ, will *h* restore,
2Pt 2: 8 felt *h* tormented by seeing and hearing
1Jn 2: 6 abide in him to conduct *h* just as he did.
2:25 He *h* made us a promise and the promise is
2:28 little ones, so that, when he reveals *h,*
3: 3 has this hope based on him keeps *h* pure,
3: 5 reason he revealed *h* was to take away sins;
3: 8 works that the Son of God revealed *h.*
3Jn 1:10 does he refuse to welcome the brothers *h*
Rv 19:12 person was a name known to no one but *h.*

HIN (22)

Ex 29:40 fourth of a *h* of oil of crushed olives and,
29:40 as its libation, a fourth of a *h* of wine.
30:24 together with a *h* of olive oil;
Lv 19:36 weights, an honest ephah and an honest *h.*
23:13 libation shall be a fourth of a *h* of wine.
Nm 15: 4 flour mixed with a fourth of a *h* of oil,
15: 5 as a libation of a fourth of a *h* of wine,
15: 6 flour mixed with a third of a *h* of oil,
15: 7 and a libation of a third of a *h* of wine,
15: 9 of fine flour mixed with half a *h* of oil,
15:10 of oil, and a libation of half a *h* of wine,
28: 5 a fourth of a *h* of oil of crushed olives.
28: 7 in the sanctuary a fourth of a *h* of wine.
28:14 *h* of wine for each bullock, a third of a *h*
28:14 the ram, and a fourth of a *h* for each lamb.
Ez 4:11 drink shall be the sixth of a *h* by measure;
45:24 he shall offer one *h* of oil for each ephah.
46: 5 the lambs, and a *h* of oil for each ephah.
46: 7 has at hand, and for each ephah a *h* of oil.
46:11 pleases, and a *h* of oil with each ephah.
46:14 of a *h* of oil to moisten the fine flour.

HIND (4)

Gn 49:21 "Naphtali is a *h* let loose which brings
Ps(s) 42: 2 As the *h* longs for the running waters,
Prv 5:19 of the wife of your youth, your lovely *h,*
Jer 14: 5 Even the *h* in the field deserts her

HINDER (6)

Nm 22:22 to *h* him as he was riding along on his ass,
22:32 It is I who have come armed to *h* you
Jdt 12: 7 ordered his bodyguard not to *h* her.
Mt 19:14 "Let the children come to me. Do not *h* them.
Mk 10:14 the children come to me and do not *h* them.
Rom 1:18 in this perversity of theirs, *h* the truth.

HINDERED (3)

Ezr 5: 5 of the Jews so that they were not *h,*
Jb 42: 2 and that no purpose of yours can be *h.*
Rom 15:22 I have so often been *h* from visiting you.

HINDERS (1)

3Jn 1:10 he even *h* those who wish to do so

HINDRANCE (2)

Acts 28:31 full assurance, and without any *h* whatever,
Rom 14:13 stumbling block or *h* in your brother's way.

HINDS (7)

2Sm 22:34 as those of *h* and set me on the heights;
Jb 39: 1 goats, watch for the birth pangs of the *h,*
Ps(s) 18:34 as those of *h* and set me on the heights;
Sg 2: 7 by the gazelles and *h* of the field,
3: 5 by the gazelles and *h* of the field,
8: 4 by the gazelles and *h* of the field,
Hb 3:19 of *h* and enables me to go upon the heights.

HINGES (2)

1Kgs 7:50 *h* of gold for the doors of the inner room,
Prv 26:14 The door turns on its *h,*

HINNOM (2)

Jos 15: 8 which bounds the Valley of *H* on the west.
18:16 continuing down the Valley of *H*

HINT (1)
2Mc 12: 3 There was no *h* of enmity toward them;

HINTERLAND (1)
2Mc 9:23 whenever he went on campaigns in the *h*,

HIP (7)
Gn 32:26 Jacob's *h* at its socket, so that the *h* socket
32:32 Jacob limped along because of his *h*.
32:33 *h* socket, inasmuch as Jacob's *h* socket
Ex 32:27 Put your sword on your *h*,
Dn 5: 6 thoughts terrified him, his *h* joints shook,

HIPS (2)
1Chr 19: 4 their garments cut off half-way at the *h*.
Is 11: 5 waist, and faithfulness a belt upon his *h*.

HIRAH (2)
Gn 38: 1 his tent near a certain Adullamite named *H*.
38:12 company with his friend *H* the Adullamite.

HIRAM (18)
2Sm 5:11 *H*, king of Tyre,
1Kgs 5:15 When *H*, king of tyre,
5:15 for *H* had always been David's friend.
5:16 Solomon sent back this message to *H*:
5:21 words of Solomon, *H* was pleased and said,
5:22 *H* then sent word to Solomon,
5:24 So *H* continued to provide Solomon with all
5:25 while Solomon every year gave *H* twenty
5:26 and there was peace between *H* and Solomon,
7:13 King Solomon had *H* brought from Tyre.
7:40 When *H* made the pots,
7:45 All these articles which *H* made for King
9:11 of the LORD and the palace of the king *H*,
9:11 *H* twenty cities in the land of Galilee.
9:12 *H* left Tyre to see the cities Solomon had
9:14 *H*, however, had sent king Solomon
9:27 In this fleet *H* placed his own expert
1Chr 14: 1 *H*, king of Tyre, sent envoys

HIRAM'S (3)
1Kgs 5:32 Solomon's and *H* builders,
10:11 *H* fleet, which used to bring gold
10:22 of Tarshish ships at sea with *H* fleet.

HIRE (11)
Ex 22:14 this was covered by the price of its *h*.
1Sm 2: 5 The well-fed *h* themselves out for bread,
1Chr 19: 6 *h* chariots and horsemen from Aram Naharaim,
Tb 2:11 my wife Anna worked for *h* at weaving cloth,
Is 23:17 She shall return to her *h* and deal with
23:18 and her *h* shall be sacred to the LORD.
46: 6 Then they *h* a goldsmith to make it into a
Hos 2:14 are the *h* my lovers have given me";
9: 1 a harlot's *h* upon every threshing floor.
Zec 8:10 were no wages for men, or *h* for beasts;
Mt 20: 1 out at dawn to *h* workmen for his vineyard.

HIRED (32)
Ex 12:45 alien or *h* servant may partake of it.
22:14 If it was *h*,
Lv 22:10 *h* servant may eat of any sacred offering.
25: 6 *h* help and the tenants who live with you,
25:40 be like a *h* servant or like your tenant,
25:50 as though he had been *h* as a day laborer.
25:53 him as a servant *h* on an annual basis,
Dt 15:18 six years was worth twice a *h* man's salary;
23: 5 you left Egypt, and because Moab *h* Balaam,
24:14 not defraud a poor and needy *h* servant,
Jgs 9: 4 with which Abimelech *h* shiftless men and
2Sm 10: 6 the Ammonites sent for and *h* twenty
2Kgs 7: 6 "The king of Israel has *h* the kings of
1Chr 19: 7 They *h* thirty-two thousand chariots along
2Chr 24:12 who *h* masons and carpenters to restore the
25: 6 He also *h* a hundred thousand valiant
Ezr 3: 7 They then *h* stonecutters and carpenters,
Neh 13: 2 and water, but they *h* Balaam to curse them,
Tb 5:12 looking for a *h* man to travel with your son?"
Jdt 4:10 All their resident aliens, *h* laborers,
1Mc 5:39 they have also *h* Arabs to help them,
11:38 he had *h* from the islands of the nations.
Is 7:20 shave with the razor *h* from across the River
19:10 all the *h* laborers shall be despondent.
Mal 3: 5 those who defraud the *h* man of his wages,
Mt 20: 7 'No one has *h* us,' they told him.
20: 9 When those *h* late in the afternoon came up
20:14 man who was *h* last the same pay as you.
Mk 1:20 who was in the boat with the *h* men,
Lk 15:17 'How many *h* hands at my father's place
15:19 Treat me like one of your *h* hands.'
Jn 10:12 The *h* hand—who is no shepherd

HIRELING (5)
Jb 7: 1 Are not his days those of a *h*?
7: 2 for the shade, a *h* who waits for his wages.
14: 6 from him and let him be, while, like a *h*,
Is 16:14 In three years, like those of a *h*,
21:16 In another year, like those of a *h*,

HIRES (1)
Prv 26:10 all who pass by is he who *h* a drunken fool.

HISS (4)
Sir 12:18 head and clap his hands and *h* repeatedly,
Lam 2:15 They *h* and wag their heads over daughter
2:16 They *h* and gnash their teeth.
Ez 27:36 The traders among the peoples now *h* at you;

HISSES (2)
Sir 22: 1 everyone *h* at his disgrace.
Zep 2:15 Whoever passes by her *h*,

HISSING (1)
Wis 17: 9 passing of insects and the *h* of reptiles,

HISTORIAN (1)
2Mc 2:30 sides is the task of the professional *h*;

HISTORICAL (3)
Ezr 4:15 be made in the *h* records of your fathers.
4:15 In the *h* records you can discover and
2Mc 2:24 those who wish to plunge into *h* narratives

HISTORY (9)
Gn 25:19 This is the family *h* of Isaac,
37: 2 This is his family *h*. When Joseph was
1Chr 29:29 *h* of Samuel the seer, the *h* of Nathan
29:29 the prophet, and the *h* of Gad the seer.
2Chr 12:15 in the *h* of Shemaiah the prophet and of
33:19 found written down in the *h* of his seers.
1Mc 16:23 Now the rest of the *h* of John,
Mt 11:11 *h* has not known a man born of woman

HIT (8)
1Sm 31: 3 raged around Saul, and the archers *h* him;
1Kgs 22:34 and *h* the king of Israel between the
2Chr 18:33 drew his bow at random and *h* the king of
Mt 26:67 they began to spit in his face and *h* him.
Mk 14:65 They blindfolded him and *h* him,
Jn 18:23 but if I spoke the truth why *h* me?"
Acts 27:41 but the ship *h* a sandbar and ran aground.
Rv 8:12 *h* hard enough to be plunged into darkness.

HITCH (1)
1Sm 6: 7 *h* them to the cart, but drive their calves

HITCHED (3)
Gn 46:29 Joseph *h* the horses to his chariot and
1Sm 6:10 they *h* them to the cart but shut up their
Jdt 15:11 harnessed her mules, *h* her wagons to them,

HITHER (1)
Jer 3:13 How you ran *h* and yon to strangers [under

HITS (1)
Dt 19: 5 handle and *h* his neighbor a mortal blow,

HITTITE (22)
Gn 23:10 So Ephron the *H* replied to Abraham in the
25: 9 the field of Ephron, son of Zohar the *H*,
26:34 married Judith, daughter of Beeri the *H*,
27:46 disgusted with life because of the *H* women.
27:46 If Jacob also should marry a *H* woman,
36: 2 Adah, daughter of Elon the *H*;
49:29 that lies in the field of Ephron the *H*,
49:30 from Ephron the *H* for a burial ground.
50:13 for a burial ground from Ephron the *H*.
1Sm 26: 6 David asked Ahimelech the *H*,
2Sm 11: 3 wife of [Joab's armor-bearer] Uriah the *H*."
11: 6 a message to Joab, "Send me Uriah the *H*."
11:17 army fell, and among them Uriah the *H* died.
11:21 'Your servant Uriah the *H* is also dead.'"
12: 9 have cut down Uriah the *H* with the sword;
23:39 Uriah the *H*—
1Kgs 10:29 these rates to all the *H* and Aramean kings.
15: 5 lived, except in the case of Uriah the *H*.
1Chr 11:41 Uriah the *H*;
2Chr 1:17 middlemen for all the *H* and Aramean kings.
Ez 16: 3 father was an Amorite and your mother a *H*.
16:45 mother was a *H* and your father an Amorite.

HITTITES (35)
Gn 15:20 the *H*, the Perizzites, the Rephaim,
23: 3 side of his dead one and addressed the *H*:
23: 5 The *H* answered Abraham:
23: 7 bow low before the local citizens, the *H*,
23:10 Now Ephron was present with the *H*.
23:10 of the *H* who sat on his town council:
23:16 had stipulated in the hearing of the *H*,
23:18 all the *H* who sat on Ephron's town council.
23:20 from the *H* to Abraham as a burial place.
25:10 field that Abraham had bought from the *H*;
49:32 in it that had been purchased from the *H*."
Ex 3: 8 honey, the country of the Canaanites, *H*,
3:17 Egypt into the land of the Canaanites, *H*,
13: 5 you into the land of the Canaanites, *H*,
23:23 you and bring you to the Amorites, *H*,
23:28 Hivites, Canaanites and *H* out of your way.
33: 2 Driving out the Canaanites, Amorites, *H*,
34:11 out before you the Amorites, Canaanites, *H*,
Nm 13:29 *H*, Jebusites and Amorites dwell
Dt 7: 1 great nations before you—the *H*,
20:17 You must doom them all—the *H*,
Jos 1: 4 domain is to be all the land of the *H*,
3:10 will dispossess the Canaanites, *H*,
9: 1 *H*, Amorites, Canaanites, Perizzites,
11: 3 to the east and west, Amorites, *H*,
12: 8 desert, and the Negeb, belonging to the *H*,
24:12 [the Amorites, Perizzites, Canaanites, *H*,
Jgs 1:26 He then went to the land of the *H*,
3: 5 were living among the Canaanites, *H*,
1Kgs 9:20 the land, descendants of the Amorites, *H*,
11: 1 Ammonites, Edomites, Sidonians, and *H*),
2Kgs 7: 6 Israel has hired the kings of the *H*
2Chr 8: 7 All the people that remained of the *H*,
Ezr 9: 1 and their abominations [Canaanites, *H*,
Neh 9: 8 posterity the land of the Canaanites, *H*,

HIVITE (4)
Gn 26:34 and Basemath, daughter of Elon the *H*.
34: 2 When Shechem, son of Hamor the *H*,
36: 2 through Anah of Zibeon the *H*;
1Chr 1:15 the Amorite, the Girgashite, the *H*,

HIVITES (23)
Gn 10:17 the Amorites, the Girgashites, the *H*,
Ex 3: 8 Amorites, Perizzites, *H* and Jebusites.
3:17 Amorites, Perizzites, *H* and Jebusites,
13: 5 Hittites, Amorites, *H* and Jebusites,
23:23 Perizzites, Canaanites, *H* and Jebusites;
23:28 you I will send hornets to drive the *H*,
33: 2 Hittites, Perizzites, *H* and Jebusites,
34:11 Hittites, Perizzites, *H* and Jebusites.
Dt 7: 1 Amorites, Canaanites, Perizzites, *H*,
20:17 Canaanites, Perizzites, *H* and Jebusites
Jos 3:10 dispossess the Canaanites, Hittites, *H*,
9: 1 Canaanites, Perizzites, *H* and Jebusites,
9: 7 But the men of Israel replied to the *H*,
11: 3 and *H* at the foot of Hermon in the land of
11:19 the exception of the *H* who lived in Gibeon,
12: 8 Canaanites, Perizzites, *H* and Jebusites.
24:12 *H* and Jebusites] out of your way;
Jgs 3: 3 and the *H* who dwell in the mountain region
3: 5 Amorites, Perizzites, *H* and Jebusites.
2Sm 24: 7 to all the cities of the *H* and Canaanites,
1Kgs 9:20 of the Amorites, Hittites, Perizzites, *H*,
2Chr 8: 7 of the Hittites, Amorites, Perizzites, *H*,
Is 17: 9 shall be like those abandoned by the *H*

HIZKI (1)
1Chr 8:17 Zebadiah, Meshullam, *H*,

HIZKIAH (1)
1Chr 3:23 The sons of Neariah were Elioenai, *H*,

HOARDING (1)
Mi 6:10 *h* and the meager ephah that is accursed?

HOARFROST (2)
Ex 16:14 were fine flakes like *h* on the ground.
Jb 38:29 and who gives the *h* its birth in the skies,

HOARY (4)
Dt 32:25 the nursing babe as well as the *h* old man.
1Kgs 2: 9 send down his *h* head in blood to the grave."
Jb 41:24 would think the deep had the *h* head of age.
Wis 4: 9 understanding is the *h* crown for men,

HOBAB (2)
Nm 10:29 out, Moses said to his brother-in-law *H*,
Jgs 4:11 from his own people, the descendants of *H*,

HOBAH (1)
Gn 14:15 them, and pursued them as far as *H*,

HOBAIAH (1)
Neh 7:63 sons of *H*,

HOD (1)
1Chr 7:37 Harnepher, Shual, Beri, Imrah, Bezer, *H*,

HODAVIAH (4)
1Chr 3:24 The sons of Elioenai were *H*,
5:24 Epher, Ishi, Eliel, Azriel, Jeremiah, *H*,
9: 7 were Sallu, son of Meshullam, son of *H*,
Ezr 2:40 sons of Jeshua, Kadmiel, Binnui, and *H*,

HODESH (1)
1Chr 8: 9 his wife *H* he became the father of Jobab,

HODEVIAH (1)

Neh 7:43 sons of Jeshua, Kadmiel, Binnui, *H*,

HODIAH (5)

Neh 8: 7 Sherebiah, Jamin, Akkub, Shabbethai, *H*,
9: 5 Kadmiel, Bani, Hashabneiah, Sherebiah, *H*,
10:11 and their brethren Shebaniah, *H*,
10:14 Hashabiah, Zaccur, Sherebiah, Shebaniah, *H*,
10:19 Bigvai, Adin, Ater, Hezekiah, Azzur, *H*,

HOE (1)

Lk 13: 8 year, while I *h* around it and manure it;

HOED (2)

Is 5: 6 it shall not be pruned or *h*,
7:25 which used to be *h* with the mattock:

HOGLAH (4)

Nm 26:33 daughters whose names were Mahlah, Noah, *H*,
27: 1 had daughters named Mahlah, Noah, *H*,
36:11 Mahlah, Tirzah, *H*,
Jos 17: 3 whose names were Mahlah, Noah, *H*,

HOHAM (1)

Jos 10: 3 Adonizedek, king of Jerusalem, sent for *H*,

HOISTED (4)

Jgs 16: 3 He *h* them on his shoulders and carried
Lk 10:34 He then *h* him on his own beast and brought
Acts 27:17 They *h* it aboard and then made use of
27:40 the rudders, *h* the foresail into the wind,

HOLD (175)

Gn 4: 7 If you do well, you can *h* up your head;
21:18 lift up the boy and *h* him by the hand;
39:12 the house, she laid *h* of him by his cloak,
43: 9 You can *h* me responsible for him.
43: 9 presence, you can *h* it against me forever.
44:32 father, you can *h* it against me forever.'
48:17 so he took *h* of his father's hand,
Ex 4: 4 LORD said to him, "and take *h* of its tail."
4: 4 So he put out his hand and laid *h* of it,
7:17 the water of the river with the staff I *h*,
12:16 first day you shall *h* a sacred assembly,
Lv 23: 7 *h* a sacred assembly and do no sort of work.
23: 8 you shall again *h* a sacred assembly
23:27 when you shall *h* a sacred assembly and
23:36 you shall again *h* a sacred assembly
25:35 poverty and is unable to *h* out beside you,
27:17 period, the full valuation shall *h*;
Nm 5:18 *h* the bitter water that brings a curse.
18:20 Israelites nor *h* any portion among them;
25: 4 and *h* a public execution of the guilty
28:18 these days you shall *h* a sacred assembly,
28:25 seventh day you shall *h* a sacred assembly,
28:26 offering, you shall *h* a sacred assembly,
29: 1 *h* a sacred assembly, and do no sort of work;
29: 7 *h* a sacred assembly, and mortify yourselves
29:12 month you shall *h* a sacred assembly,
29:35 eighth day you shall *h* a solemn meeting,
Dt 10:20 *h* fast to him and swear by his name.
32:41 and my hand shall lay *h* of my quiver.
Jgs 1:27 Canaanites kept their *h* in this district.
1:35 The Amorites had a firm *h* in Har-heres,
8:28 no longer did they *h* their heads high.
Ru 3:15 to her, "Take off your cloak and *h* it out."
1Sm 20: 1 father *h* against me that he seeks my life?"
24:12 here at this end of your mantle which I *h*.
2Sm 4:11 must I *h* you responsible for his death and
15: 5 homage, he would extend his hand, *h* him,
19:20 "May my lord not *h* me guilty,
1Kgs 2:32 will *h* him responsible for his own blood,
8:64 LORD was too small to *h* these offerings.
2Kgs 6:32 close the door and *h* it fast against him.
15:19 in strengthening his *h* on the kingdom.
1Chr 19:13 *H* steadfast and let us show ourselves
28:16 of gold for each table to *h* the showbread,
2Chr 1: 1 David, strengthened his *h* on the kingdom,
6:38 in the land of those who *h* them captive,
7: 7 had made could not *h* the holocausts,
17: 1 king and strengthened his *h* against Israel.
25: 3 he had strengthened his *h* on the kingdom,
Neh 6: 2 let us *h* council together at Caphirim in
6: 7 the king, come, let us *h* council together."
Tb 6: 4 *h* of the fish and don't let it get away!"
6:13 Rages, we will *h* the wedding feast for her.
10: 7 Raguel had sworn to *h* for his daughter,
Jdt 4: 7 them to keep firm *h* of the mountain passes,
Est B: 2 and to *h* sway over the whole world,
1Mc 6:50 and stationed a garrison there to *h* it.
2Mc 12:35 one of Bacenor's men, caught *h* of Gorgias,
Jb 8:17 among the rocks he takes *h*.
9:28 I know that you will not *h* me innocent.
10:15 if righteous, I dare not *h* up my head,
17: 9 Yet the righteous shall *h* to his way,
18: 9 him by the heel, and a snare lays *h* of him.
19:19 All my intimate friends *h* me in horror;
21: 6 dismayed, and horror takes *h* on my flesh.
30: 1 But now they *h* me in derision who are
30:18 One with great power lays *h* of my clothing;
38:13 For taking *h* of the ends of the earth,
41: 9 that they *h* fast and cannot be parted.
Ps(s) 16: 5 and my cup, you it is who *h* fast my lot.
40:18 O my God, *h* not back!
70: 6 O LORD, *h* not back!
73:23 you have *h* of my right hand;
119:67 I went astray, but now I *h* to your promise.
139:10 guide me, and your right hand *h* me fast.
Prv 1:15 them, *h* back your foot from their path!
4: 4 "Let your heart *h* fast my words:
4:13 *H* fast to instruction,
Eccl 7:18 It is good to *h* to this rule,
Sg 3: 4 I took *h* of him and would not let him go
7: 9 palm tree, I will take *h* of its branches.
Wis 4: 3 shall not strike deep root nor take firm *h*.
4:18 They see, and *h* him in contempt;
11:12 For a twofold grief took *h* of them and a
Sir 11:20 My son, *h* fast to your duty,
12:15 but if you slip, he cannot *h* back
19: 8 For he who hears it will *h* it against you,
20: 1 and a man may be wise to *h* his peace.
21:14 no knowledge at all can it *h*.
27: 3 earnestly *h* fast to the fear of the LORD,
28:22 It will not take *h* among the just nor
38: 1 *H* the physician in honor,
Is 4: 1 women will take *h* of one man on that day,
8:11 taking *h* of me and warning me not to walk
13: 8 pangs and sorrows take *h* of them,
33:23 it cannot *h* the mast in place,
43: 6 *H* not back! Bring back my sons
44:14 and lays *h* of other trees of the forest,
48: 9 the sake of my renown I *h* it back from you,
56: 4 what pleases me and *h* fast to my covenant,
56: 6 free from profanation and *h* to my covenant,
58:13 If you *h* back your foot on the sabbath
63:15 O Lord, *h* not back,
64:11 Can you *h* back, O LORD, after all this?
65: 5 broth in their dishes, Crying out, *H* back,
Jer 2:13 broken cisterns, that *h* no water.
3: 5 forever, will he *h* his grudge to the end?"
6:24 fall our hands, Anguish takes *h* of us,
9: 2 not with truth, they *h* forth in the land.
17: 4 *h* on your heritage which I have given you.
26: 8 the priests and prophets laid *h* of him,
34: 9 so that no one should *h* a man of Judah,
49:16 crags, that *h* the heights of the hill:
49:24 Distress and pangs take *h* of her,
50:33 *h* them fast and refuse to let them go.
Ez 3:18 but I will *h* you responsible for his death.
3:20 but I will *h* you responsible for his death
21:16 burnisher that he might *h* it in his hand,
30:21 it may be strong enough to *h* the sword.
33: 6 I will *h* the watchman responsible for that
33: 8 but I will *h* you responsible for his death.
37:20 write you shall *h* up before them to see.
38:21 I will *h* judgment with him in pestilence
Dn 13:39 together, but the man we could not *h*,
Jon 1: 5 Jonah had gone down into the *h* of the ship,
Na 3:14 tread the clay, take *h* of the brick mold!
Zec 8:23 shall take *h*, yes, take *h* of every Jew by
Mt 12:11 Will he not take *h* of it and pull it out?
14:27 "Get *h* of yourselves!
22: 6 The rest laid *h* of his servants,
22:23 Sadducees, who *h* there is no resurrection,
26:48 take *h* of him."
27:30 Afterward they took *h* of the reed and kept
Mk 6:50 "Get *h* of yourselves!
12:18 Then some Sadducees who *h* there is no
Lk 8:29 This spirit had taken *h* of him many a time.
21:28 happen, stand erect and *h* your heads high,
23:26 they laid *h* of one Simon the Cyrenean who
Jn 3:10 "You *h* the office of teacher of Israel
3:27 "No one can lay *h* on anything unless it
8:23 a world which cannot *h* me.
14:30 He has no *h* on me but the world must know
20:23 if you *h* them bound,
21:25 entire world to *h* the books to record them.
Acts 2:24 that death should keep its *h* on him,
7:60 "Lord, do not *h* this sin against them."
13:43 urged them to *h* fast to the grace of God.
17:17 In the synagogue he used to *h* discussions
18:19 synagogue to *h* discussions with the Jews.
Rom 3:28 For we *h* that a man is justified by faith
1Cor 15: 2 you *h* fast to it as I preached it to you.
Eph 6:13 that your duty requires, and *h* your ground.
6:16 *h* faith up before you as your shield;
Phil 1: 7 in your regard since I *h* all of you dear
2:29 in the Lord and *h* men like him in esteem,
Col 1:23 But you must *h* fast to faith,
2Thes 2:15 *H* fast to the traditions you received from
1Tm 1:19 and *h* fast to faith and a good conscience.
3: 9 They must *h* fast to the divinely revealed
6:12 Take firm *h* on the everlasting life to
2Tm 2:12 If we *h* out to the end we shall also reign
Ti 1: 9 he must *h* fast to the authentic message,
Heb 3: 6 It is we who are that house if we *h* fast
4:14 let us *h* fast to our profession of faith.
10:23 Let us *h* unswervingly to our profession
12:28 kingdom should *h* fast to God's grace,
Rv 1:18 I *h* the keys of death and the nether world.
2: 4 I *h* this against you, though:
2:13 and I know you *h* fast to my name and have
2:14 I *h* a few matters against you:
2:15 who *h* to the teaching of the Nicolaitans.
2:20 Nevertheless I *h* this against you:
2:25 case, *h* fast to what you have until I come.
3:11 *H* fast to what you have lest someone rob

HOLDERS (8)

Ex 25:27 as *h* for the poles to carry the table.
26:29 make gold rings on them as *h* for the bars,
30: 4 as *h* for the poles used in carrying it.
36:34 rings were made on them as *h* for the bars,
37:14 as *h* for the poles to carry the table.
37:27 side, as *h* for the poles to carry it.
38: 5 of the bronze grating, as *h* for the poles,
Jer 52:19 The basins also, the fire *h*,

HOLDING (48)

Gn 9:23 took a robe, and *h* it on their backs,
Ex 7:15 *h* in your hand the staff that turned into
9: 2 to let them go and persist in *h* them,
17: 5 of the elders of Israel, *h* in your hand,
Dt 11:22 his ways exactly, and *h* fast to him,
13: 5 heed, serving him and *h* fast to him alone.
30:20 God, heeding his voice, and *h* fast to him.
Jgs 7:19 the horns and broke the jars they were *h*.
16:26 said to the attendant who was *h* his hand,
1Sm 14:27 he was *h* and dipped in into the honey.
14:43 honey from the end of the staff I was *h*.
17:57 David was still *h* the Philistine's head.
18:10 at other times, while Saul was *h* his spear.
20: 6 clan is *h* its seasonal sacrifice there.'
22: 6 tree on the high place, *h* his spear,
23:23 all the various hiding places he is *h* out.
2Sm 23:10 and became cramped, *h* fast to the sword.
2Chr 6:23 man and *h* him responsible for his conduct,
26:19 who was *h* a censer for burning the incense,
Tb 11:11 fish gall in his hand, and *h* him firmly,
1Mc 15:34 are *h* on to the heritage of our ancestors.
Jb 2: 9 him, "Are you still *h* to your innocence?
Is 6: 6 *h* an ember which he had taken with tongs
42:14 silence, I have said nothing, *h* myself in;
Jer 6:11 brims up within me, I am weary of *h* it in;
20: 9 I grow weary *h* it in,
Ez 14: 4 *h* the memory of his idols in his heart and
40: 3 gate, *h* a linen cord and a measuring rod.
40: 5 man was *h* a measuring rod six cubits long,
Lk 18: 9 while *h* everyone else in contempt:
Jn 2: 6 each *h* fifteen to twenty-five gallons.
Acts 7:57 *h* their hands over their ears as they did
8: 9 the town and *h* the Samaritans spellbound.
1Cor 11: 2 you always remember me and are *h* fast
Phil 2:16 the sky while *h* fast to the word of life.
1Tm 6: 3 not *h* to the sound doctrines of our Lord
Heb 6: 6 for themselves and *h* him up to contempt.
Rv 5: 8 the elders were *h* vessels of gold filled
7: 2 from the east *h* the seal of the living God.
7: 9 robes and *h* palm branches in their hands.
8: 3 Another angel came in *h* a censer of gold.
9:14 sixth angel, who was still *h* his trumpet,
14:14 his head and *h* a sharp sickle in his hand.
15: 1 seven angels *h* the seven final plagues
15: 2 were *h* the harps used in worshiping God,
15: 6 came the seven angels *h* the seven plagues.
17: 1 were *h* the seven bowls came to me and said:
20: 1 *h* the key to the abyss and a huge chain in

HOLDINGS (5)

Gn 23: 4 *h* a piece of property for a burial ground,
36:43 their settlements in their territorial *h*.
47:11 them *h* in Egypt on the pick of the land,
Ru 4: 9 acquired from Naomi all the *h* of Elimelech,
2Chr 11:14 their *h* and came to Judah and Jerusalem,

HOLDS (34)

2Mc 3:24 the Lord of spirits who *h* all power
Jb 2: 3 He still *h* fast to his innocence although
12:15 He *h* back the waters and there is drought;
26: 9 He *h* back the appearance of the full moon
36:27 He *h* in check the waterdrops that filter
36:32 In his hands he *h* the lightning,
38:30 that *h* captive the surface of the deep?
39:24 he *h* not back at the sound of the trumpet,
Prv 3:18 grasp her, and he is happy who *h* her fast.
Wis 2:16 he *h* aloof from our paths as from things
Sir 1:21 For a while he *h* back his words,
4:13 He who *h* her fast inherits glory;
29: 1 the precepts who *h* out a helping hand.
45:22 But he *h* no land among the people nor
Is 56: 2 who does this, the son of man who *h* to it;
Jer 20: 5 city, all it has toiled for and *h* dear,
46:10 hosts *h* a slaughter feast in the northland,
48:10 cursed he who *h* back his sword from blood.]
Ez 14: 7 and *h* the memory of his idols in his heart
18: 8 if he *h* off from evildoing,
18:17 who *h* off from evildoing,
23:32 drink, so wide and deep, which *h* so much,
Hos 12: 8 A merchant who *h* a false balance,
Mt 5:22 and if he *h* him in contempt he risks the
10:22 *h* out till the end will escape death.
24:13 The man who *h* out to the end,
Mk 13:13 the man who *h* out till the end is the one

HOLDS (cont.)

Lk 16:15 man thinks important, God *h* in contempt.
Rom 4:16 *h* true for all Abraham's descendants,
2Thes 2: 7 but there is one who *h* him back until
Heb 4: 1 promise of entrance into his rest still *h*,
Jas 1:12 the man who *h* out to the end through trial!
Rv 2: 1 "The One who *h* the seven stars in his
3: 1 " 'The One who *h* the seven spirits of God,

HOLE (11)

Dt 23:14 a *h* and afterward cover up your excrement.
2Kgs 12:10 then took a chest, bored a *h* in its lid,
Ps(s) 7:16 He has opened a *h*,
Ez 8: 7 where I saw there was a *h* in the wall.
12: 5 dig a *h* in the wall and pass through it;
12: 7 dug a *h* through the wall with my hand and,
12:12 through a *h* that he has dug in the wall,
Mt 9:16 thing he has used to cover the *h* will pull,
25:18 went off instead and dug a *h* in the ground,
Mk 2: 4 When they had made a *h*,
2:21 he has used to cover the *h* would pull away

HOLES (7)

1Sm 14:11 out of the *h* where they have been hiding."
Is 2:19 caves in the rocks and into *h* in the earth,
42:22 and plundered, all of them trapped in *h*,
Jer 49: 8 Flee, retreat, hide in deep *h*,
49:30 leave your homes, hide in deep *h*,
Hg 1: 6 wages earned them for a bag with *h* in it.
Heb 11:38 they dwelt in caves and in *h* of the earth.

HOLIDAY (3)

Est 2:18 granting a *h* to the provinces and
9:19 a *h* on which they send gifts of food to
Wis 15:12 and our span of life a *h* for gain;

HOLIDAYS (1)

Jdt 8: 6 feastdays and *h* of the house of Israel.

HOLIES (13)

Ex 26:33 divides the holy place from the holy of *h*.
26:34 ark of the commandments in the holy of *h*.
1Kgs 6:16 enclosing the sanctuary, the holy of *h*.
7:50 the doors of the inner room, or holy of *h*,
8: 6 the sanctuary, the holy of *h* of the temple.
1Chr 6:34 of *h* and of making atonement for Israel,
2Chr 3: 8 He also made the room of the holy of *h*.
3:10 For the room of the holy of *h* he made two
4:22 house, its inner doors to the holy of *h*,
5: 7 the sanctuary, the holy of *h* of the temple.
Ez 41: 4 and said to me, "This is the holy of *h*."
45: 3 shall be the sanctuary, the holy of *h*.
Heb 9: 3 was the tabernacle called the holy of *h*,

HOLIEST (1)

2Mc 5:15 dared to enter the *h* temple in the world;

HOLINESS (51)

Ex 15:11 Who is like to you, magnificent in *h*?
2Chr 30:19 though he be not clean as *h* requires."
2Mc 6:11 In their respect for the *h* of that day,
14:36 Therefore, O holy One, LORD of all *h*,
15: 2 has exalted with *h* above all other days."
Ps(s) 89:36 Once, by my *h*, have I sworn;
93: 5 *h* befits your house,
Wis 2:22 *h* nor discern the innocent souls' reward.
9: 3 you, To govern the world in *h* and justice,
Sir 36: 3 As you have used us to show them your *h*,
45: 6 He raised up also, like Moses in *h*,
45:12 its plate wrought with the insignia of *h*,
Is 57:15 On high I dwell, and in *h*,
Ez 20:41 manifest my *h* in the sight of the nations.
28:22 upon it and use it to manifest my *h*.
28:25 *h* through them in the sight of the nations.
36:23 I will prove the *h* of my great name,
36:23 in their sight I prove my *h* through you.
38:16 in their sight I prove my *h* through you,
38:23 I will prove my greatness and *h* and make
39:27 and will prove my *h* through them in the
44:19 *h* to the people with their garments.
46:20 the risk of transmitting *h* to the people."
Am 4: 2 The Lord GOD has sworn by his *h*:
Mt 5: 6 Blest are they who hunger and thirst for *h*;
5:10 Blest are those persecuted for *h*' sake;
5:20 unless your *h* surpasses that of the
6:33 first his kingship over you, his way of *h*,
21:32 When John came preaching a way of *h*,
Acts 3:12 man walk by some power or *h* of our own?
Rom 1: 4 God in power according to the spirit of *h*,
1: 7 in Rome, beloved of God and called to *h*,
1Cor 7:34 Lord, in pursuit of *h* in body and spirit.
2Cor 1:12 always acted from God-given *h* and candor;
5:21 in him we might become the very *h* of God.
Eph 4:24 whose justice and *h* are born of truth.
5: 3 your *h* forbids this.
1Thes 4: 3 It is God's will that you grow in *h*:
4: 7 has not called us to immorality but to *h*;
5:23 May the God of peace make you perfect in *h*.
2Thes 2:13 in *h* of spirit and fidelity to truth.
1Tm 2:15 she continues in faith and love and *h*—
2Tm 3:16 and training in *h* so that the man of God
Heb 12:10 our true profit, that we may share his *h*.
12:14 *h* without which no one can see the Lord.
2Pt 2: 5 he preserved Noah as a preacher of *h*,
2:21 them not to have recognized the road to *h*
1Jn 2:29 If you consider the *h* that is his,
2:29 who acts in *h* has been begotten by him.
3: 7 the man who acts in *h* is holy indeed,
Rv 22:11 their virtue and the holy ones in their *h*!

HOLLOW (8)

Ex 27: 8 the altar itself in the form of a *h* box,
33:22 I will set you in the *h* of the rock
38: 7 The altar was made in the form of a *h* box.
1Sm 25:29 of your enemies as from the *h* of a sling.
1Kgs 7:15 Two *h* bronze columns were cast,
2Mc 1:19 hid it secretly in the *h* of a dry cistern,
Wis 17:19 an echo resounding from the *h* of the hills,
Jer 52:21 each was four fingers thick, and *h* inside.

HOLLOWS (1)

Zep 2:14 in droves all the wild life of the *h*;

HOLM (1)

Is 44:14 He cuts down cedars, takes a *h* or an oak,

HOLOCAUST (151)

Gn 22: 2 *h* on a height that I will point out to you."
22: 3 with the wood that he had cut for the *h*,
22: 6 *h* and laid it on his son Isaac's shoulders,
22: 7 the wood, but where is the sheep for the *h*?"
22: 8 himself will provide the sheep for the *h*."
22:13 offered it up as a *h* in place of his son.
Ex 18:12 brought a *h* and other sacrifices to God,
29:18 be burned on the altar, since it is a *h*,
29:25 you shall burn them on top of the *h*
29:42 this established *h* shall be offered
30: 9 incense, or any *h* or cereal offering;
Lv 1: 3 "If his *h* offering is from the herd,
1: 4 there lay his hand on the head of the *h*,
1: 6 shall skin the *h* and cut it up into pieces.
1: 9 the whole offering on the altar as a *h*,
1:10 "If his *h* offering is from the flock,
1:13 the whole offering on the altar as a *h*,
1:14 "If he offers a bird as a *h* to the LORD,
1:17 altar, over the wood on the fire, as a *h*,
3: 5 shall then burn on the altar with the *h*,
5: 7 for a sin offering and the other for a *h*.
5:10 shall be offered as a *h* in the usual way.
6: 2 The *h* is to remain on the hearth of the
6: 3 the fire has reduced the *h* on the altar,
6: 5 *h* and burn the fat of the peace offerings.
7: 8 the priest who offers a *h* for someone may
7: 8 the hide of the *h* that he has offered.
8:18 He next brought forward the *h* ram,
8:21 parts of the ram on the altar as a *h*,
8:28 *h* on the altar as the ordination offering,
9: 2 calf for a sin offering and a ram for a *h*,
9: 3 lamb, both unblemished yearlings, for a *h*,
9: 7 your sin offering and your *h* in atonement
9:12 Then Aaron slaughtered his *h*.
9:13 him the pieces and the head of the *h*,
9:14 burned these also with the *h* on the altar.
9:16 forward the *h*, other than the morning *h*
9:22 the sin offering and *h* and peace offering,
9:24 *h* and the remnants of the fat on the altar.
10:19 sin offering and *h* before the LORD today,
12: 6 meeting tent a yearling lamb for a *h*
12: 8 for a *h* and the other for a sin offering.
14:13 the sin offering and the *h* are slaughtered;
14:19 the priest slaughter the *h* and offer it,
14:22 one as a sin offering and the other as a *h*.
14:31 one as a sin offering and the other as a *h*,
15:15 one as a sin offering and the other as a *h*.
15:30 as a sin offering and the other as a *h*.
16: 3 for a sin offering and a ram for a *h*.
16: 5 for a sin offering and one ram for a *h*.
16:24 out and offer his own and the people's *h*,
17: 8 who offers a *h* or sacrifice without
22:18 brings a *h* as a votive offering or as a
23:12 LORD for a *h* an unblemished yearling lamb.
23:18 a *h* of seven unblemished yearling lambs,
Nm 6:11 as a sin offering and the other as a *h*,
6:14 one unblemished yearling lamb for a *h*,
6:16 up the sin offering and the *h* for him.
7:15 one ram, and one yearling lamb for a *h*;
7:21 one ram, and one yearling lamb for a *h*;
7:27 one ram, and one yearling lamb for a *h*;
7:33 one ram, and one yearling lamb for a *h*;
7:39 one ram, and one yearling lamb for a *h*;
7:45 one ram, and one yearling lamb for a *h*;
7:51 one ram, and one yearling lamb for a *h*;
7:57 one ram, and one yearling lamb for a *h*;
7:63 one ram, and one yearling lamb for a *h*;
7:69 one ram, and one yearling lamb for a *h*;
7:75 one ram, and one yearling lamb for a *h*;
7:81 one ram, and one yearling lamb for a *h*;
8:12 offering and the other as a *h* to the LORD,
15: 3 from the herd or from the flock, in *h*,
15: 5 each lamb sacrificed in *h* or otherwise.
15: 8 When you sacrifice an ox as a *h*,
15:24 whole community shall offer the *h*
15:25 brought their *h* as an oblation to the LORD.
23: 3 here by your *h* while I go over there.
23: 6 *h* together with all the princes of Moab.
23:15 then said to Balak, "Stand here by your *h*,
23:17 by his *h* together with the princes of Moab.
28: 3 lambs each day as the established *h*,
28: 6 This is the established *h* that was offered
28:10 sabbath *h* in addition to the established *h*
28:11 offer as a *h* to the LORD two bullocks,
28:13 that the *h* may be a sweet-smelling
28:14 new moon *h* for every new moon of the year.
28:15 to the established *h* and its libation.
28:19 oblation you shall offer a *h* to the LORD,
28:23 in addition to the established morning *h*;
28:24 to the established *h* with its libation,
28:27 sweet-smelling *h* to the LORD two bullocks,
28:31 the established *h* with its cereal offering.
29: 2 a sweet-smelling *h* to the LORD one bullock,
29: 6 new moon *h* with its cereal offering,
29: 6 the established *h* with its cereal offering,
29: 8 a sweet-smelling *h* to the LORD one bullock,
29:11 the established *h* with its cereal offering,
29:13 *h* to the LORD thirteen bullocks,
29:16 *h* with its cereal offering and libation.
29:19 *h* with its cereal offering and libation.
29:22 *h* with its cereal offering and libation.
29:25 *h* with its cereal offering and libation.
29:28 *h* with its cereal offering and libation.
29:31 *h* with its cereal offering and libation.
29:34 *h* with its cereal offering and libation.
29:36 You shall offer up in *h* as a
29:38 *h* with its cereal offering and libation.
Jos 22:29 from the LORD by building an altar for *h*,
Jgs 6:26 bullock and offer it as a *h* on the wood
11:31 I shall offer him up as a *h*."
13:16 if you will, you may offer a *h* to the LORD.
13:23 a *h* and cereal offering from our hands!
1Sm 6:14 the cows were offered as a *h* to the LORD.
7: 9 and offered it entire as a *h* to the LORD.
7:10 While Samuel was offering the *h*,
13: 9 *h* and peace offerings,"
13: 9 and he offered up the *h*.
13:12 So in my anxiety I offered up the *h*."
1Kgs 18:34 "and pour it over the *h* and over the wood."
18:38 LORD'S fire came down and consumed the *h*,
2Kgs 3:27 and offered him as a *h* upon the wall.
5:17 for I will no longer offer *h* or sacrifice
10:25 As soon as he finished offering the *h*,
16:13 on it, burning his *h* and cereal-offering,
16:15 morning *h* and the evening cereal-offering,
16:15 the royal *h* and cereal-offering,
2Chr 7: 1 and consumed the *h* and the sacrifices,
29:24 for "The *h* and the sin offering,"
29:27 the *h* to be sacrificed on the altar,
29:27 and in the same instant that the *h* began,
29:28 trumpets until the *h* had been completed.
29:29 As the *h* was completed,
29:32 all of these as a *h* to the LORD.
35:12 separated what was destined for the *h*
Ezr 3: 5 Thereafter they offered the established *h*,
8:35 all these as a *h* to the LORD.
Neh 10:34 daily cereal offering, for the daily *h*,
Jdt 4:14 sackcloth as they offered the daily *h*,
1Mc 7:33 the *h* that was being offered for the king.
Jb 42: 8 Job, and offer up a *h* for yourselves;
Ps(s) 20: 4 offerings and graciously accept your *h*.
51:18 should I offer a *h*,
Jer 7:22 them no command concerning *h* or sacrifice.
48:35 the LORD, to offer a *h* on the high place,
Ez 45:23 he shall offer as a *h* to the LORD seven bulls
46:13 *h* to the LORD an unblemished yearling lamb;
46:14 LORD is mandatory with the established *h*.
46:15 offered every morning as an established *h*.
Dn 3:38 day no prince, prophet, or leader, no *h*,

HOLOCAUSTS (148)

Gn 8:20 clean bird, he offered *h* on the altar.
Ex 10:25 sacrifices and *h* to offer up to the LORD,
20:24 shall sacrifice your *h* and peace offerings,
24: 5 young men of the Israelites to offer *h*
30:28 the altar of *h* with all its appurtenances,
31: 9 the altar of *h* with all its appurtenances,
32: 6 offered *h* and brought peace offerings.
35:16 the altar of *h*,
38: 1 The altar of *h* was made of acacia wood,
40: 6 Put the altar of *h* in front of the
40:10 the altar of *h* and all its appurtenances,
40:29 He put the altar of *h* in front of the
40:29 and offered *h* and cereal offerings on it,
Lv 4: 7 pour out at the base of the altar of *h*
4:10 the priest shall burn it on the altar of *h*.
4:18 the altar of *h* which is at the entrance
4:24 in the place where the *h* are slaughtered.
4:25 and put it on the horns of the altar of *h*.
4:29 shall slaughter it at the place of the *h*.
4:30 and put it on the horns of the altar of *h*.
4:33 in the place where the *h* are slaughtered.
4:34 and put it on the horns of the altar of *h*.
6: 2 This is the ritual for *h*.
6:18 At the place where *h* are slaughtered,
7: 2 At the place where the *h* are slaughtered,

7:37 This is the ritual for *h*,
14:19 shall the priest slaughter the *h*
23:37 to the LORD *h* and cereal offerings,
Nm 7:87 The animals for the *h* were,
10:10 over your *h* and your peace offerings;
29:39 on your festivals, besides whatever *h*,
Dt 12: 6 you shall bring your *h* and sacrifices,
12:11 your *h* and sacrifices,
12:13 to offer up your *h* in any place you fancy,
12:27 blood of your *h* on the altar of the LORD,
27: 6 and shall offer on it *h* to the LORD,
Jos 8:31 offered *h* and peace offerings to the LORD.
22:23 to secede from the LORD, or to offer *h*,
22:26 not for *h* or for sacrifices,
22:27 the LORD in his presence with our *h*,
22:28 fathers made, not for *h* or for sacrifices,
Jgs 20:26 *h* and peace offerings before the LORD.
21: 4 there and offered *h* and peace offerings.
1Sm 6:15 *h* and sacrifices to the LORD that day.
10: 8 offer *h* and to sacrifice peace offerings.
15:22 "Does the LORD so delight in *h* and
2Sm 6:17 *h* and peace offerings before the LORD.
24:22 Here are oxen for *h*,
24:24 to the LORD my God *h* that cost nothing."
24:25 LORD, and offered *h* and peace offerings.
1Kgs 3: 4 its altar Solomon offered a thousand *h*.
3:15 of the Lord, offered *h* and peace offerings,
8:64 he offered there the *h*,
9:25 Solomon used to offer *h* and peace offerings
10: 5 the *h* he offered in the temple of the LORD,
2Kgs 10:24 they proceeded to offer sacrifices and *h*.
16:15 and cereal-offering, as well as the *h*,
16:15 on it all the blood of *h* and sacrifices.
1Chr 6:34 the altar of *h* and on the altar of incense;
16: 1 offered up *h* and peace offerings to God.
16: 2 offering up the *h* and peace offerings,
16:40 offer *h* to the LORD on the altar of *h*
21:23 See, I also give you the oxen for the *h*,
21:24 LORD, nor offer up *h* that cost me nothing."
21:26 LORD, and offered up *h* and peace offerings.
21:26 down fire from heaven upon the altar of *h*.
21:29 and the altar of *h* were at that time on
22: 1 God, and this is the altar of *h* for Israel."
23:31 offering of *h* to the LORD on sabbaths,
29:21 they offered sacrifices and *h* to the LORD,
2Chr 1: 6 he offered a thousand *h* upon it.
2: 3 the showbread, for *h* morning and evening,
4: 6 Here were cleansed the victims for the *h*;
7: 7 the *h* and the fat of the peace offerings,
7: 7 Solomon had made could not hold the *h*,
8:12 In those times Solomon offered *h* to the
9: 4 the *h* he offered in the house of the LORD,
13:11 They burn *h* to the LORD and fragrant
23:18 the temple for offering the *h* of the LORD,
24:14 utensils for the service and the *h*,
24:14 They offered *h* in the LORD's temple
29: 7 refused to burn incense and offer *h*
29:18 LORD, the altar of *h* with all its utensils,
29:31 all the *h* which were freewill offerings.
29:32 The number of *h* that the assembly brought
29:34 be able to skin all the victims for the *h*,
29:35 Also, the *h* were many,
29:35 offerings and the libations for the *h*.
30:15 and brought *h* into the house of the LORD.
31: 2 whether in regard to *h* or peace offerings,
31: 3 wealth the king allotted a portion for *h*,
35:14 *h* and the fatty portions until night;
35:16 and the *h* offered on the altar of the LORD,
Ezr 3: 2 on it the *h* prescribed in the law of Moses,
3: 3 and offered *h* to the LORD on it,
3: 4 and they offered the daily *h* in the proper
3: 6 month they began to offer *h* to the LORD,
6: 9 rams, and lambs for *h* to the God of heaven,
8:35 offered as *h* to the God of Israel twelve
Jdt 16:16 the fat of all *h* but little in your sight,
16:18 they were purified, they offered their *h*,
1Mc 1:45 to prohibit *h*, sacrifices, and libations
1:54 horrible abomination upon the altar of *h*,
1:59 on the altar erected over the altar of *h*.
4:44 the altar of *h* that had been desecrated.
4:53 on the new altar of *h* that they had made.
4:56 *h* and sacrifices of deliverance and praise.
5:54 Zion in joy and gladness and offered *h*,
2Mc 2:10 and fire came down and burned up the *h*.
Jb 1: 5 early and offering *h* for every one of them.
Ps(s) 40: 7 *H* or sin-offerings you sought not;
50: 8 you, for your *h* are before me always.
51:21 due sacrifices, burnt offerings and *h*;
66:13 I will bring *h* to your house;
66:15 *H* of fatlings I will offer you,
Sir 45:16 mankind to offer *h* and choice offerings,
Is 40:16 for fuel, nor its animals be enough for *h*.
43:23 You did not bring me sheep for your *h*,
56: 7 Their *h* and sacrifices will be acceptable
Jer 6:20 Your *h* find no favor with me,
7:21 Heap your *h* upon your sacrifices;
14:12 If they offer *h* or cereal offerings,
17:26 and the Negeb, to bring *h* and sacrifices,
19: 5 immolate their sons in fire as *h* to Baal:
33:18 Levi ever be lacking, to offer *h* before me,
Bar 1:10 funds, with which you are to procure *h*,
Ez 40:38 of the gate, where the *h* were rinsed.
40:42 There were four tables for *h*,
40:43 with which the *h* were slaughtered.
43:18 when it is set up for the offering of *h*
43:24 on them and offer them to the LORD as *h*.
43:27 your *h* and peace offerings on the altar.
44:11 the *h* and the sacrifices for the people,
45:15 for sacrifice *h* and peace offerings and
45:17 the duty of the prince to provide the *h*,
45:17 the sin offerings, cereal offerings, *h*,
45:25 making the same sin offerings, the same *h*,
46: 2 priests offer his *h* and peace offerings,
46: 4 The *h* which the prince presents to the
46:12 to the LORD, whether *h* or peace offerings,
46:12 *h* or his peace offerings as on the sabbath;
Dn 3:40 As though it were *h* of rams and bullocks,
Hos 6: 6 and knowledge of God rather than *h*.
Am 5:23 But if you would offer me *h*,
Mi 6: 6 Shall I come before him with *h*,
Heb 10: 6 *H* and sin offerings you took no delight in.
10: 8 and offerings, *h* and sin offerings,

HOLOFERNES (51)

Jdt 2: 4 king of the Assyrians, summoned *H*,
2:14 So *H* left the presence of his lord,
2:22 From there *H* took his whole force,
3: 5 had reached *H* and given him this message,
3: 9 At length *H* reached Esdraelon in the
4: 1 who dwelt in Judea heard of all that *H*,
5: 1 It was reported to *H*,
5:22 and the officers of *H* and all the
5:24 your great army, Lord *H*,
6: 1 surrounding the council had subsided, *H*,
6:10 Then *H* ordered the servants who were
6:12 of *H'* servants by hurling stones upon them.
6:17 of what was said in the council of *H*,
6:17 threats of *H* against the house of Israel.
7: 1 The following day *H* ordered his whole army,
7: 6 On the second day *H* led out all his
7: 8 of the seacoast, came to *H* and said:
7:16 words pleased *H* and all his ministers,
7:26 to the troops of *H* and to all his forces;
10:13 I have come to see *H*,
10:17 and these conducted them to the tent of *H*.
10:18 her as she waited outside the tent of *H*,
10:20 The guard of *H* and all his servants came
10:21 Now *H* was reclining on his bed under a
10:23 and when *H* and his servants beheld Judith,
11: 1 *H* said to her: Take courage, lady;
11:20 Her words pleased *H* and all his servants;
11:22 Then *H* said to her: "God has done well
12: 3 *H* asked her. "But if your provisions
12: 5 the servants of *H* led her into the tent,
12: 6 dawn, she rose and sent this message to *H*,
12: 7 *H* ordered his bodyguard not to hinder her.
12:10 *H* gave a banquet for his servants alone,
12:13 So Bagoas left the presence of *H*,
12:15 on the ground for her in front of *H*
12:16 The heart of *H* was in rapture over her,
12:17 *H* said to her, "Drink and be merry
12:20 *H*, charmed by her,
13: 2 Judith was left alone in the tent with *H*,
13: 4 stood by *H'* bed and said within herself;
13: 6 went to the bedpost near the head of *H*,
13: 9 and handed over the head of *H* to her maid,
13:15 "Here is the head of *H*,
13:16 it was my face that seduced *H* to his ruin,
14: 3 run to the tent of *H* and do not find him,
14: 6 When he came and saw the head of *H* in the
14:11 they hung the head of *H* on the wall.
14:13 They came to the tent of *H* and said to the
14:18 Here is *H* headless on the ground!"
15:11 the camp, giving Judith the tent of *H*,
16:19 things of *H* that the people had given her,

HOLON (4)

Jos 15:51 Eshtemoh, Anim, Goshen, *H* and Giloh;
21:15 pasture lands, *H* with its pasture lands,
1Chr 6:43 pasture lands, *H* with its pasture lands,
Jer 48:21 on *H*, Jahzah, and Mephaath,

HOLY (562)

Gn 2: 3 God blessed the seventh day and made it *h*,
Ex 3: 5 for the place where you stand is *h* ground.
15:13 you guided them to your *h* dwelling.
19: 6 be to me a kingdom of priests, a *h* nation.
20: 8 "Remember to keep *h* the sabbath day.
20:11 has blessed the sabbath day and made it *h*.
26:33 the *h* place from the holy of holies.
26:34 ark of the commandments in the *h* of holies.
29:31 ordination ram and boil it in the *h* place.
31:13 that it is I, the LORD, who make you *h*.
Lv 11:44 keep yourselves *h*, because I am holy.
11:45 God, you shall be holy, because I am *h*.
16:19 Thus he shall render it clean and *h*,
19: 2 Be *h*, for I, the LORD your God, am holy.
20: 3 my sanctuary and profaned my *h* name.
20: 7 holy; for I, the LORD, your God, am *h*.
20: 8 observe what I, the LORD, who make you *h*,
21: 6 the food of their God, they must be *h*.
22: 2 else they will profane my *h* name.
22:32 give you, and do not profane my *h* name;
Nm 5:17 vessel he shall meanwhile put some *h* water,
15:40 all my commandments and be *h* to your God.
16: 3 The whole community, all of them, are *h*;
16: 5 who belongs to him and who is the *h* one
16: 7 He whom the LORD then chooses is the *h* one.
Dt 5:12 care to keep *h* the sabbath day as the LORD,
23:15 at your mercy, your camp must be *h*;
26:15 Look down, then, from heaven, your *h* abode,
33: 3 But all his *h* ones were in his hand;
Jos 5:15 the place on which you are standing is *h*."
24:19 able to serve the LORD, for he is a *h* God;
1Sm 2: 2 There is no *H* One like the LORD;
6:20 can stand in the presence of this *H* One?
21: 5 no ordinary bread on hand, only *h* bread;
21: 7 So the priest gave him *h* bread,
1Kgs 6:16 enclosing the sanctuary, the *h* of holies.
7:50 doors of the inner room, or *h* of holies,
8: 6 sanctuary, the *h* of holies of the temple.
8: 8 of the *h* place adjoining the sanctuary;
8:10 When the priests left the *h* place,
2Kgs 4: 9 "I know that he is a *h* man of God.
19:22 Against the *H* One of Israel!
1Chr 6:34 they alone had charge of the *h* of holies
16:10 Glory in his *h* name;
16:27 praise and joy are in his *h* place.
16:29 worship the LORD in *h* attire.
16:35 to your *h* name and glory in praising you."
23:13 was set apart to be consecrated as most *h*,
23:28 and the preservation of everything *h*:
24: 5 for there were officers of the *h* place,
29: 3 to all that I stored up for the *h* house,
29:16 build you a house in honor of your *h* name
2Chr 3: 8 He also made the room of the *h* of holies.
3:10 For the room of the *h* of holies he made
4:22 house, its inner doors to the *h* of holies,
5: 7 sanctuary, the *h* of holies of the temple.
5: 9 part of the *h* place nearest the sanctuary;
5:11 When the priests came out of the *h* place
8:11 where the ark of the LORD has come are *h*."
20:21 praise the *h* Appearance as it went forth
23: 6 They may enter because they are *h*;
30:27 prayer reached heaven, God's *h* dwelling.
31:14 and the most *h* of the consecrated things.
35: 3 the *h* ark in the house built by Solomon,
Ezr 2:63 not to partake of the most *h* foods
9: 2 the *h* race with the peoples of the land.
9: 8 remnant and gave us a stake in his *h* place;
Neh 7:65 not to partake of the most *h* foods
8: 9 "Today is *h* to the LORD your God.
8:10 for today is *h* to our Lord.
8:11 the people saying, "Hush, for today is *h*,
9:14 Your *h* sabbath you made known to them,
10:34 moons, and festivals, for the *h* offerings,
11: 1 in ten to reside in Jerusalem, the *h* city,
11:18 the *h* city was two hundred and eighty-four.
13:22 so that the sabbath day might be kept *h*.
Tb 8:15 you, O God, with every *h* and pure blessing!
11:14 name, and blessed be all his *h* angels.
11:14 *h* name be praised throughout all the ages,
13: 9 O Jerusalem, *h* city,
13:18 you they shall praise his *h* name forever.
Jdt 9:13 against your covenant, your *h* temple,
1Mc 1:15 circumcision and abandoned the *h* covenant;
1:63 unclean food or to profane the *h* covenant;
2: 7 of my people and the ruin of the *h* city,
11:37 in a conspicuous place on the *h* hill.' "
2Mc 1: 7 against the *h* land and the kingdom,
1:12 out those who fought against the *h* city.
1:29 Plant your people in your *h* place,
2:18 under the heavens to his *h* Place,
3: 1 While the *h* city lived in perfect peace
3:30 who had marvelously glorified his *h* Place;
5:17 while and hence disregarded the *h* Place.
5:25 and waited until the *h* day of the sabbath;
6:23 would be loyal to the *h* laws given by God.
6:28 and generously for the revered and *h* laws."
6:30 in his *h* knowledge knows full well that,
8:15 and because they themselves bore his *h*,
8:17 by the Gentiles against the *h* Place
8:23 the *h* book and giving them the watchword,
9:14 on him, that he would set free the *h* city,
9:16 *h* temple which he had previously despoiled;
12:45 in godliness, it was a *h* and pious thought.
13:11 law, their country, and their *h* temple;
14: 3 position and regain access to the *h* altar.
14:31 the man, he went to the great and *h* temple,
14:36 Therefore, O *h* One, LORD of all holiness
15:14 prays for his people and their *h* city."
15:16 "Accept this *h* sword as a gift from God;
15:24 blasphemously come against your *h* people!"
15:32 out against the *h* dwelling of the Almighty.
Jb 5: 1 To which of the *h* ones will you appeal?
6:10 not transgressed the commands of the *H* One.
15:15 If in his *h* one God places no confidence,
Ps(s) 2: 6 have set up my king on Zion, my *h* mountain."
3: 5 LORD, he answers me from his *h* mountain.
5: 8 worship at your *h* temple in fear of you,
11: 4 The LORD is in his *h* temple;
15: 1 Who shall dwell on your *h* mountain?
16: 3 me cherish the *h* ones who are in his land!
20: 7 he has answered him from his *h* heaven
22: 4 Yet you are enthroned in the *h* place,
24: 3 or who may stand in his *h* place?
28: 2 lifting up my hands toward your *h* shrine.

HOLY (cont.)

29: 2 adore the LORD in *h* attire.
30: 5 ones, and give thanks to his *h* name.
33:21 in his *h* name we trust.
34:10 Fear the LORD, you his *h* ones,
43: 3 lead me on And bring me to your *h* mountain,
46: 5 of God, the *h* dwelling of the Most High.
47: 9 the nations, God sits upon his *h* throne.
48: 2 His *h* mountain, fairest of heights
51:13 and your *h* spirit take not from me.
65: 5 your house, the *h* things of your temple!
68: 6 of widows is God in his *h* dwelling.
71:22 praises with the harp, O *H* One of Israel!
77:14 O God, your way is *h*;
78:41 God and provoked the *H* One of Israel.
78:54 And he brought them to his *h* land,
79: 1 they have defiled your *h* temple,
87: 1 His foundation upon the *h* mountains
89: 6 in the assembly of the *h* ones.
89: 8 is terrible in the council of the *h* ones;
89:19 our shield, and to the *H* One of Israel,
89:21 with my *h* oil I have anointed him,
96: 9 worship the LORD in *h* attire.
97:12 you just, and give thanks to his *h* name.
98: 1 hand has won victory for him, his *h* arm.
99: 3 your great and awesome name; *h* is he!
99: 5 *h* is he!
99: 9 his holy mountain; for *h* is the LORD,
102:20 "The LORD looked down from his *h* height,
103: 1 and all my being, bless his *h* name.
105: 3 Glory in his *h* name;
105:42 his *h* word to his servant Abraham.
106:16 the camp, and Aaron, the *h* one of the LORD.
106:47 to your *h* name and glory in praising you.
110: 3 in the day of your birth, in *h* splendor;
111: 9 *h* and awesome is his name.
138: 2 your *h* temple and give thanks to your name,
145:13 in all his words and *h* in all his works.
145:17 in all his ways and *h* in all his works.
145:21 flesh bless his *h* name forever and ever.
Prv 9:10 knowledge of the *H* One is understanding.
30: 3 nor have I the knowledge of the *H* One.
Wis 1: 5 For the *h* spirit of discipline flees
3: 9 grace and mercy are with his *h* ones,
6:10 *h* precepts hallowed shall be found holy,
7:22 For in her is a spirit intelligent, *h*,
7:27 And passing into *h* souls from age to age,
9: 8 You have bid me build a temple on your *h*
9: 8 a copy of the *h* tabernacle which you had
9:10 Send her forth from your *h* heavens and
9:17 Wisdom and sent your *h* spirit from on high?
10:10 of God and gave him knowledge of *h* things;
10:15 The *h* people and blameless race
10:17 the *h* ones the recompense of their labors,
10:20 your *h* name and praised in unison your
11: 1 affairs prosper through the *h* prophet.
12: 3 the ancient inhabitants of your *h* land,
17: 2 lawless thought to enslave the *h* nation,
18: 1 But your *h* ones had very great light;
18: 5 to put to death the infants of the *h* ones,
18: 9 For in secret the *h* children of the good
18: 9 That your *h* ones should share alike the
Sir 4:14 Those who serve her serve the *H* One;
7:31 due sacrifices and *h* offerings.
17: 8 wonders of his deeds and praise his *h* name.
23: 9 or becoming too familiar with the *H* Name.
23:10 the *H* Name will not remain free from sin.
24:10 In the *h* tent I ministered before him,
24:15 like the odor of incense in the *h* place.
26:17 light that shines above the *h* lampstand,
36:12 Take pity on your *h* city,
39:35 proclaim and bless the name of the *H* One.
42:17 Yet even God's *h* ones must fail in
45:15 him and anointed him with the *h* oil,
47:10 So that when the *H* Name was praised,
49: 6 the *h* city and left its streets desolate,
49:12 They erected the *h* temple,
50:17 the Most High, before the *H* One of Israel.
Is 1: 4 the LORD, spurned the *H* One of Israel,
4: 3 that is left in Jerusalem Will be called *h*:
5:16 the *h* shall be shown holy by his justice.
5:19 On with the plan of the *H* One of Israel!
5:24 scorned the word of the *H* One of Israel.
6: 3 *H*, holy, holy is the Lord of hosts!"
6:13 *H* offspring is the trunk.]
10:17 will become a fire, Israel's *H* One a flame,
10:20 lean upon the LORD, the *H* One of Israel,
11: 9 be no harm or ruin on all my *h* mountain;
12: 6 great in your midst is the *H* One of Israel!
17: 7 his eyes turned toward the *H* One of Israel.
27:13 and worship the LORD on the *h* mountain,
29:19 the poor rejoice in the *H* One of Israel.
29:23 name holy; they shall reverence the *H* One
30:11 Let us hear no more of the *H* One of Israel."
30:12 Therefore, thus says the *H* One of Israel:
30:15 said the Lord GOD, the *H* One of Israel:
31: 1 to the *H* One of Israel nor seek the LORD!
35: 8 A highway will be there, called the *h* way;
37:23 Against the *H* One of Israel!
40:25 liken me as an equal? says the *H* One.
41:14 your redeemer is the *H* One of Israel.
41:16 the LORD, and glory in the *H* One of Israel.
41:20 this, the *H* One of Israel has created it.
43: 3 the LORD, your God, the *H* One of Israel,
43:14 LORD, your redeemer, the *H* One of Israel:
43:15 I am the LORD, your *H* One,
43:28 against me Till I repudiated the *h* gates,
45:11 Thus says the LORD, the *H* One of Israel,
47: 4 is the LORD of hosts, the *H* One of Israel.
48: 2 the *h* city and rely on the God of Israel,
48:17 LORD, your redeemer, the *H* One of Israel:
49: 7 LORD, the redeemer and the *H* One of Israel,
49: 7 the *H* One of Israel who has chosen you.
52: 1 glorious garments, O Jerusalem, *h* city.
52:10 his *h* arm in the sight of all the nations;
54: 5 Your redeemer is the *H* One of Israel,
55: 5 of the LORD, your God, the *H* One of Israel,
56: 7 Them I will bring to my *h* mountain and
57:13 the land, and possess my *h* mountain.
57:15 living eternally, whose name is the *H* One:
58:13 following your own pursuits on my *h* day;
58:13 a delight, and the LORD's *h* day honorable;
60: 9 of the LORD, your God, the *H* One of Israel,
60:14 the LORD," "Zion of the *H* One of Israel."
62:12 They shall be called the *h* people,
63:10 they rebelled, and grieved his *h* spirit;
63:11 is he who put his *h* spirit in their midst;
63:15 from your *h* and glorious palace!
63:18 Why have the wicked invaded your *h* place,
64: 9 Your *h* cities have become a desert,
64:10 Our *h* and glorious temple in which our
65:11 forsake the LORD, forgetting my *h* mountain,
65:25 shall hurt or destroy on all my *h* mountain,
66:20 dromedaries, to Jerusalem, my *h* mountain,
Jer 17:12 from the beginning, such is our *h* place.
17:22 no work whatever, but keep *h* the sabbath,
17:24 *h* and abstaining from all work on it,
17:27 you do not obey me and keep *h* the sabbath,
23: 2 of the LORD, because of his *h* words.
25:30 from his *h* dwelling he raises his voice;
31:23 "May the LORD bless you, *h* mountain,
31:40 Gate at the east, shall be *h* to the LORD.
50:29 she insulted the LORD, the *H* One of Israel.
51: 5 to be punished by the *H* One of Israel.
51:51 the *h* places of the house of the LORD.
Bar 2:16 your *h* dwelling and take thought of us;
4:22 joy has come to me from the *H* One
4:37 and from the west By the word of the *H* One,
5: 5 east and the west at the word of the *H* One,
Ez 20:12 that it was I, the LORD, who made them *h*.
20:20 keep *h* my sabbaths,
20:39 my *h* name with your gifts and your idols.
20:40 For on my *h* mountain,
22: 8 What is *h* to me you have spurned,
22:26 violate my law and profane what is *h* to me;
28:14 you were on the *h* mountain of God,
36:20 came], they served to profane my *h* name,
36:21 So I have relented because of my *h* name
36:22 of Israel, but for the sake of my *h* name,
37:28 that it is I, the LORD, who make Israel *h*,
39: 7 my *h* name known among my people Israel;
39: 7 no longer allow my *h* name to be profaned.
39: 7 that I am the LORD, the *H* One in Israel.
39:25 and I will be jealous for my *h* name.
41: 4 and said to me, "This is the *h* of holies."
41:21 In front of the *h* place was something that
41:23 and also the *h* place had a double door.
42:13 for it is a *h* place.
42:14 they shall not leave the *h* place for the
42:14 in which they ministered, for it is *h*.
43: 7 their kings profane my *h* name
43: 8 my *h* name by their abominable deeds;
44:24 all my festivals, and keep my sabbaths *h*.
45: 3 shall be the sanctuary, the *h* of holies.
Dn 3:28 upon Jerusalem, the *h* city of our fathers.
3:35 Isaac your servant, and Israel your *h* one,
3:52 And blessed is your *h* and glorious name,
3:53 are you in the temple of your *h* glory,
3:87 *H* men of humble heart,
4: 5 and in whom is the spirit of the *h* God.
4: 6 I know that the spirit of the *h* God
4:10 in bed, a *h* sentinel came down from heaven,
4:14 is this decided, by order of the *h* ones,
4:15 because the spirit of the *h* God is in you."
4:20 As for the king's vision of a *h* sentinel
5:11 kingdom in whom is the spirit of the *h* God;
7:18 But the *h* ones of the Most High shall
7:21 that horn made war against the *h* ones and
7:22 in favor of the *h* ones of the Most High,
7:22 came when the *h* ones possessed the kingdom.
7:25 and oppress the *h* ones of the Most High,
7:27 be given to the *h* people of the Most High,
8:13 I heard a *h* one speaking,
8:25 his cunning shall be against the *h* ones,
9:16 from your city Jerusalem, your *h* mountain.
9:20 LORD, my God, on behalf of his *h* mountain
9:24 for your people and for your *h* city:
9:24 ratified, and a most *h* will be anointed.
11:28 his mind set against the *h* covenant;
11:30 his rage and energy against the *h* covenant;
11:45 the sea and the glorious *h* mountain,
12: 7 of the *h* people was brought to an end,
13:45 the *h* spirit of a young boy named Daniel,
Hos 11: 9 and not man, the *H* One present among you;
12: 1 rebellious against God, against the *H* One,
Jl 2: 1 in Zion, sound the alarm on my *h* mountain!
4:17 my *h* mountain; Jerusalem shall be holy,
Am 2: 7 the same prostitute, profaning my *h* name.
Ob 1:16 As you have drunk upon my *h* mountain,
1:17 the mountain shall be *h*,
Jon 2: 5 yet would I again look upon your *h* temple."
2: 8 My prayer reached you in your *h* temple.
Mi 1: 2 against you, the Lord from his *h* temple.
Hb 1:12 you not from eternity, O LORD, my *h* God,
2:20 But the LORD is in his *h* temple;
3: 3 from Teman, the *H* One from Mount Paran.
Zep 3: 4 Her priests profane what is *h*,
3:11 no longer exalt yourself on my *h* mountain.
Zec 2:16 possess Judah as his portion of the *h* land,
2:17 for he stirs forth from his *h* dwelling.
8: 3 of the LORD of hosts, the *h* mountain.
14: 5 shall come, and all his *h* ones with him.
14:20 the bells of the horses, *H* to the LORD."
14:21 in Judah shall be *h* to the LORD of hosts;
Mt 1:18 child through the power of the *H* Spirit.
1:20 *H* Spirit that she has conceived this child.
3:11 will baptize you in the *H* Spirit and fire.
4: 5 Next the devil took him to the *h* city,
7: 6 *h* to dogs or toss your pearls before swine.
10:41 he who welcomes a *h* man because he is
10:41 to be *h* receives a holy man's reward.
12: 4 he entered God's house and ate the *h* bread,
12:32 against the *H* Spirit will not be forgiven,
23:28 Thus you present to view a *h* exterior
23:35 from the blood of *h* Abel to the blood of
24:15 on *h* ground (let the reader take note!),
27:19 not interfere in the case of that *h* man.
27:53 entered the *h* city and appeared to many.
28:19 and of the Son, and of the *H* Spirit.
Mk 1: 8 he will baptize you in the *H* Spirit."
1:24 I know who you are—the *h* One of God!"
2:26 Abiathar the high priest and ate the *h* bread
3:29 the *H* Spirit will never be forgiven.
6:20 knowing him to be an upright and *h* man,
8:38 with the *h* angels in his Father's glory."
12:36 David himself, inspired by the *H* Spirit,
13:11 be yourselves speaking but the *H* Spirit.
Lk 1:15 with the *H* Spirit from his mother's womb.
1:35 "The *H* Spirit will come upon you and the
1:35 the *h* offspring to be born will be called
1:41 the *H* Spirit and cried out in a loud voice:
1:49 done great things for me, *h* is his name;
1:67 his father, filled with the *H* Spirit,
1:70 promised through the mouths of his *h* ones,
1:72 and remembered the *h* covenant he made,
1:75 and through all our days be *h* in his sight.
2:25 of Israel, and the *H* Spirit was upon him.
2:26 It was revealed to him by the *H* Spirit
3:16 baptize you in the *H* Spirit and in fire.
3:22 the skies opened and the *H* Spirit
4: 1 Jesus, full of the *H* Spirit,
4:34 the *H* One of God."
6: 4 and ate the *h* bread and gave it to his men,
9:26 and that of his Father and his *h* angels.
10:21 Jesus rejoiced in the *H* Spirit and said:
11:13 give the *H* Spirit to those who ask him."
12:10 the *H* Spirit will never be forgiven.
12:12 The *H* Spirit will teach you at that moment
23:50 an upright and *h* member of the Sanhedrin,
Jn 1:33 is he who is to baptize with the *H* Spirit.'
6:69 we are convinced that you are God's *h* one."
14:26 the *H* Spirit whom the Father will send in
17:11 O Father most *h*, protect them
20:22 "Receive the *H* Spirit.
Acts 1: 2 he had chosen through the *H* Spirit.
1: 5 you will be baptized with the *H* Spirit."
1: 8 power when the *H* Spirit comes down on you;
1:16 Scripture uttered long ago by the *H* Spirit
2: 4 All were filled with the *H* Spirit.
2:33 the promised *H* Spirit from the Father,
2:38 you will receive the gift of the *H* Spirit.
3:14 You disowned the *H* and Just One and
3:21 spoke of long ago through his *h* prophets.
4: 8 Then Peter, filled with the *H* Spirit,
4:25 you have said by the *H* Spirit through the
4:27 in this very city against your *h* Servant,
4:30 in the name of Jesus, your *h* Servant."
4:31 They were filled with the *H* Spirit and
5: 3 so as to make you lie to the *H* Spirit
5:32 So too does the *H* Spirit,
6: 5 a man filled with faith and the *H* Spirit;
6:13 statements against the *h* place and the law."
7:33 for the place where you stand is *h* ground.
7:51 you are always opposing the *H* Spirit just
7:55 meanwhile, filled with the *H* Spirit,
8:15 that they might receive the *H* Spirit.
8:17 on them and they received the *H* Spirit.
8:19 on anyone he will receive the *H* Spirit."
9:13 he has done to your *h* people in Jerusalem.
9:17 your sight and be filled with the *H* Spirit."
9:31 the increased consolation of the *H* Spirit.
9:32 to God's *h* people living in Lydda.
10:22 a *h* messenger to summon you to his house.
10:38 anointed him with the *H* Spirit and power.
10:44 when the *H* Spirit descended upon all
10:45 gift of the *H* Spirit should have been poured
10:47 people who have received the *H* Spirit,
11:15 address them the *H* Spirit came upon them,
11:16 but you will be baptized with the *H* Spirit.'

11:24 man filled with the *H* Spirit and faith.
13: 2 were fasting, the *H* Spirit spoke to them:
13: 4 These two, sent forth by the *H* Spirit,
13: 9 as Paul) was filled with the *H* Spirit;
13:52 but be filled with joy and the *H* Spirit.
15: 8 the *H* Spirit to them just as he did to us.
15:28 'It is the decision of the *H* Spirit,
16: 6 they had been prevented by the *H* Spirit
19: 2 the *H* Spirit when you became believers?"
19: 2 so much as heard that there is a *H* Spirit."
19: 6 the *H* Spirit came down on them and they
20:23 except that the *H* Spirit has been warning
20:28 flock the *H* Spirit has given you to guard.
21:11 Then he said, "Thus says the *H* Spirit:
26:10 I sent many of God's *h* people to prison.
28:25 "The *H* Spirit stated it well when he said
Rom 1: 2 his prophets, as the *h* Scriptures record
5: 5 the *H* Spirit who has been given to us.
7:12 *h* and the commandment is holy
9: 1 My conscience bears me witness in the *H*
12: 1 a living sacrifice *h* and acceptable to God,
14:17 and the joy that is given by the *H* Spirit.
15:13 *H* Spirit you may have hope in abundance.
15:16 sacrifice, consecrated by the *H* Spirit.
16:16 Greet one another with a *h* kiss.
1Cor 1: 2 Christ Jesus and called to be a *h* people,
3:17 For the temple of God is *h*,
6: 1 to the wicked and not to God's *h* people?
6:19 that your body is a temple of the *H* Spirit,
7:14 but as it is, they are *h*.
12: 3 "Jesus is Lord," except in the *H* Spirit.
16:20 Greet one another with a *h* kiss.
2Cor 1: 1 *h* ones of the church who live in Achaia.
6: 6 knowledge, and patience, in the *H* Spirit,
7:11 a measure of *h* zeal it has brought you,
13:12 Greet one another with a *h* kiss.
13:12 All the *h* ones send greetings to you.
13:13 fellowship of the *H* Spirit be with you all!
Eph 1: 1 Jesus Christ, to the *h* ones [at Ephesus],
1: 4 began, to be *h* and blameless in his sight,
1:13 with the *H* Spirit who had been promised.
2:21 and takes shape as a *h* temple in the Lord;
3: 5 the Spirit to the *h* apostles and prophets.
3:18 able to grasp fully, with all the *h* ones,
4:30 Do nothing to sadden the *H* Spirit with
5:26 He gave himself up for her to make her *h*,
5:27 a glorious church, *h* and immaculate,
6:18 and attentively for all in the *h* company.
Phil 1: 1 Jesus, to all the *h* ones at Philippi,
Col 1: 2 our brother, to the *h* ones at Colossae,
1:22 by dying, so as to present you to God *h*,
1:26 past but now revealed to his *h* ones.
3:12 you are God's chosen ones, *h* and beloved,
1Thes 1: 5 *H* Spirit and out of complete conviction.
1: 6 with the joy that comes from the *H* Spirit.
3:13 making them blameless and *h* before our God
3:13 of our Lord Jesus with all his *h* ones.
4: 8 but God who sends his *H* Spirit upon you.
5:26 Greet all the brothers with a *h* embrace.
2Thes 1:10 to be glorified in his *h* ones and adored
1Tm 4: 5 it is made *h* by God's word and by prayer.
2Tm 1: 9 has saved us and has called us to a *h* life,
1:14 help of the *H* Spirit who dwells within us.
Ti 1: 8 steady, just, *h*,
3: 5 of new birth and renewal by the *H* Spirit.
Heb 2: 4 of the gifts of the *H* Spirit as he willed.
3: 1 *h* brothers who share a heavenly calling,
3: 7 Wherefore, as the *H* Spirit says:
6: 4 gift and become sharers in the *H* Spirit,
6:10 service, past and present, to his *h* people.
7:26 *h*, innocent,
9: 2 this was called the *h* place.
9: 3 was the tabernacle called the *h* of holies,
9: 8 The *H* Spirit was showing thereby that
10:15 The *H* Spirit attests this to us,
Jas 5:16 petition of a *h* man is powerful indeed.
1Pt 1:12 the power of the *H* Spirit sent from heaven.
1:15 become *h* yourselves in every aspect of
1:15 the likeness of the *h* One who called you;
1:16 Scripture says, "Be holy, for I am *h*."
2: 5 an edifice of spirit, into a *h* priesthood,
2: 9 race, a royal priesthood, a *h* nation,
3: 5 The *h* women of past ages used to adorn
2Pt 1:18 we were in his company on the *h* mountain.
1:21 It is rather that men impelled by the *H*
2:21 their backs on the *h* law handed on to them,
3: 2 delivered long ago by the *h* prophets,
3:11 How *h* in your conduct and devotion,
1Jn 2:20 the anointing that comes from the *H* One,
3: 7 is holy indeed, even as the Son is *h*.
Jude 1:14 Lord has come with his countless *h* ones
1:20 *h* faith through prayer in the Holy Spirit.
Rv 3: 7 " 'The *h* One,
4: 8 "Holy, holy, *h*, is the Lord God Almighty
5: 8 which were the prayers of God's *h* people.
6:10 long will it be, O Master, *h* and true,
8: 3 with the prayers of all God's *h* ones.
11: 2 will crush the *h* city for forty-two months.
11:18 the prophets and the *h* ones who revere you,
13:10 that distinguishes God's *h* people.
14:10 before the *h* angels and before the Lamb,
14:12 This is what sustains the *h* ones,
15: 4 Since you alone are *h*,
16: 5 "You are just, O *h* One who is and who was,
17: 6 was drunk with the blood of God's *h* ones
20: 6 happy and *h* are they who share in the
21: 2 I also saw a new Jerusalem, the *h* city,
21:10 showed me the *h* city Jerusalem
22:11 virtue and the *h* ones in their holiness!
22:19 tree of life and the *h* city described here!

HOLYDAY (2)

Neh 10:32 from them on the sabbath or on any other *h*.
Sir 50: 6 clouds, like the full moon at the *h* season;

HOMAGE (43)

Gn 27:29 peoples serve you, and nations pay you *h*;
49:10 to him, and he receives the peoples' *h*.
Jgs 8:27 all Israel paid idolatrous *h* to it there,
1Sm 20:41 ground three times before Jonathan in *h*.
24: 9 bowed to the ground in *h* and asked Saul:
25:23 on the ground before David, did him *h*.
28:14 and so he bowed face to the ground in *h*.
2Sm 1: 2 Going to David, he fell to the ground in *h*.
9: 6 came to David, he fell prostrate in *h*.
14: 4 king and fell prostrate to the ground in *h*,
14:22 to the ground in *h* and blessing the king,
14:33 who came to him and in *h* fell on his face
15: 5 Whenever a man approached him to show *h*,
16: 4 "I pay you *h*, my lord the king.
18:28 the ground he paid *h* to the king and said,
24:20 So he went out and paid *h* to the king,
1Kgs 1:16 Bathsheba bowed in *h* to the king,
1:23 and, bowing to the floor, did him *h*.
1:31 Bowing to the floor in *h* to the king,
1:53 altar, and he came and paid *h* to the king.
2:19 king stood up to meet her and paid her *h*.
2Chr 24:17 of Judah came and paid *h* to the king,
Jdt 14: 7 threw himself at the feet of Judith in *h*,
Ps(s) 2:12 with trembling pay *h* to him,
72:11 All kings shall pay him *h*,
119:108 Accept, O LORD, the free *h* of my mouth,
Sir 35: 7 In generous spirit pay *h* to the LORD,
Is 66: 3 burning incense, like paying *h* to an idol.
Mt 2: 2 at its rising and have come to pay him *h*."
2: 8 to me so that I may go and offer him *h* too."
2:11 They prostrated themselves and did him *h*.
4: 9 if you prostrate yourself in *h* before me."
4:10 'You shall do *h* to the Lord your God;
8: 2 a leper came forward and did him *h*,
15:25 forward then and did him *h* with the plea,
18:26 official prostrated himself in *h* and said,
20:20 sons, to do him *h* and ask of him a favor.
28: 9 up and embraced his feet and did him *h*.
28:17 who had entertained doubts fell down in *h*.
Mk 5: 6 at a distance, he ran up and did him *h*,
15:19 before him and pretended to pay him *h*.
Lk 4: 7 Prostrate yourself in *h* before me,
4: 8 it, 'You shall do *h* to the Lord your God;

HOMAM (1)

1Chr 1:39 The sons of Lotan were Hori and *H*;

HOME (207)

Gn 18:33 with Abraham, and Abraham returned *h*.
21:21 with his *h* in the wilderness of Paran.
22:19 for Beer-sheba, where Abraham made his *h*.
25:11 Isaac, who made his *h* near Beer-lahai-roi.
28: 2 to the *h* of your mother's father Bethuel,
29: 7 is hardly the time to bring the animals *h*.
30:14 which he brought *h* to his mother Leah.
30:16 evening, when Jacob came *h* from the fields,
32: 1 then he set out on his journey back *h*,
33:17 There he built a *h* for himself and made
34: 5 he held his peace until they came *h*.
35:27 Jacob went *h* to his father Isaac at Mamre,
39:16 the cloak with her until his master came *h*.
42:19 *h* provisions for your starving families.
42:33 *h* with rations for your starving families.
43:26 When Joseph came *h*, they presented him
46:31 whose *h* is in the land of Canaan,
Ex 16:29 is to stay *h* and no one is to go out."
18:23 and all these people will go *h* satisfied."
Nm 22:34 it has displeased you, I will go back *h*."
24:11 Be off at once, then, to your *h*.
24:25 Then Balaam set out on his journey *h*;
Dt 6: 7 Speak of them at *h* and abroad,
11:19 children, speaking of them at *h* and abroad,
20: 5 Let him return *h*, lest he die in battle
20: 6 Let him return *h*,
20: 7 *h*, lest he die in battle and another take
20: 8 return *h*, lest he make his fellows
21:12 as wife, you may take her *h* to your house.
21:19 to the elders at the gate of his *h* city,
32:25 *h* Shall be the youth and the maiden alike,
Jos 9:12 we brought it from *h* as provisions
19:50 He rebuilt the city and made it his *h*.
20: 6 back *h* to his own city from which he fled."
Jgs 7: 7 So let all the other soldiers go *h*."
8:29 son of Joash, went back *h* to stay.
9:57 all their wickedness *h* to the Shechemites,
18:15 Levite at the *h* of Micah and greeted him.
18:26 they were stronger than he, returned *h*.
19: 9 tomorrow you can start your journey *h*."
19:15 them the shelter of his *h* for the night.
19:18 of Judah and am now going back *h*;
19:28 her on an ass and started out again for *h*.
19:29 On reaching *h*, he took a knife
20: 8 to leave for his tent or return to his *h*.
Ru 1: 9 and a *h* in which you will find rest."
3: 1 must seek a *h* for you that will please you.
3:16 Ruth went *h* to her mother-in-law,
1Sm 1:19 and then returned to their *h* in Ramah.
1:23 And so she remained at *h* and nursed her
2:11 When Elkanah returned *h* to Ramah,
2:20 and his wife, as they were leaving for *h*.
7:17 to return to Ramah, for that was his *h*.
10:13 came out of the prophetic state, he went *h*.
10:26 Saul also went *h* to Gibeah,
15:34 Saul went up to his *h* in Gibeah of Saul.
17:18 brothers and bring *h* some token from them.
23:18 remained, while Jonathan returned to his *h*.
24:23 gave Saul his oath and Saul returned *h*,
25: 1 they buried him at his *h* in Ramah.
25:35 "Go up to your *h* in peace!
26:25 went his way, and Saul returned to his *h*.
2Sm 4:11 have slain an innocent man in bed at *h*,
11:10 David was told that Uriah had not gone *h*.
11:11 Can I go *h* to eat and to drink and to
11:13 servants, and did not go down to his *h*.
13: 7 David then sent *h* a message to Tamar,
14: 8 "Go *h*. I will issue a command
17:23 departed, going to his *h* in his own city.
1Kgs 1:53 Solomon then said to him, "Go to your *h*."
5:28 month in the Lebanon and two months at *h*.
12:24 Let every man return *h*,
13: 7 "Come *h* with me for some refreshment,"
13:15 said, "Come *h* with me and have some bread."
14:12 So leave; go *h*!
21: 4 Ahab went *h* disturbed and angry at the
22:17 Let each of them go back *h* in peace.' "
2Kgs 14:10 Enjoy your glory, but stay at *h*!
16:11 completed by the time the king returned *h*.
19:36 broke camp, and went back *h* to Nineveh.
1Chr 12:20 their lords took counsel and sent him *h*,
16:43 all the people departed, each to his own *h*,
2Chr 11: 4 Let every man return *h*,
18:16 Let each of them go back *h* in peace.' "
25:10 come to him from Ephraim, and sent them *h*.
25:10 and returned *h* blazing with resentment.
25:19 Remain at *h*.
Neh 5:13 "Thus may God shake from his *h* and his
Tb 2: 1 under King Esarhaddon I returned to my *h*,
6: 2 When the boy left *h*,
7: 1 When he brought them into his *h*,
10: 7 *h* to wail and cry the whole night through,
11:17 Welcome to your *h* with blessing and joy.
13:16 shall be rebuilt as his *h* forever.
Jdt 1:16 Then he returned *h* with all his numerous,
6:21 brought him from the assembly to his *h*,
8: 4 remained three years and four months at *h*,
Est 1:22 that every man should be lord in his own *h*.
5:10 restrained himself, however, and went *h*,
6:12 to the royal gate, while Haman hurried *h*,
1Mc 3:56 were afraid, could each return to his *h*,
6:54 the rest scattered each to his own *h*,
11:38 his entire army, every man to his *h*,
12:45 men to stay with you, send the rest back *h*,
12:45 the officials, then I will leave and go *h*.
2Mc 9:29 foster brother Philip brought the body *h*;
11:29 to return *h* and attend to your own affairs.
Jb 34:11 and brings *h* to a man his way of life.
39: 6 his *h* and the salt flats his dwelling.
Ps(s) 68: 7 God gives a *h* to the forsaken;
84: 4 Even the sparrow finds a *h*,
87: 7 "My *h* is within you."
104:17 fir trees are the *h* of the stork.
113: 9 He establishes in her *h* the barren wife as
128: 3 a fruitful vine in the recesses of your *h*;
Prv 7:11 and unruly, in her *h* her feet cannot rest;
7:19 For my husband is not at *h*,
7:20 not till the full moon will he return *h*."
19:14 *H* and possessions are an inheritance from
24:15 not in wait against the *h* of the just man,
27: 8 its nest is a man who is far from his *h*.
30:26 mighty, yet they make their *h* in the crags;
Eccl 12: 5 effect, Because man goes to his lasting *h*,
Sg 3: 4 I should bring him to the *h* of my mother,
8: 2 you, bring you in to the *h* of my mother.
Sir 4:30 Be not a lion at *h*,
14:27 her from the heat, and dwells in her *h*.
21: 4 so too a proud man's *h* is destroyed.
26:16 a virtuous wife is the radiance of her *h*.
29:23 no heed to him who would disparage your *h*;
29:28 abuse at *h* and insults from his creditors.
32:11 be off for *h*!
42: 6 Of a seal to keep an erring wife at *h*,
42:10 Lest she conceive in her father's *h*,
Is 37:37 broke camp and went back *h* to Nineveh.
Jer 39:14 of Ahikam, son of Shaphan, to be brought *h*.
Lam 1:20 the sword bereaves, at *h* death stalks.
Bar 2: 9 over the evils, and brought them *h* to us;
Ez 17:16 the *h* of the king who set him up to rule,
27:26 deep waters your oarsmen brought you *h*,
38:15 from your *h* in the recesses of the north,
Dn 2:17 *h* and informed his companions Hananiah,
4: 1 I, Nebuchadnezzar, was at *h* in my palace,

HOME (cont.)

6:11 he continued his custom of going *h* to kneel
13:13 said to each other, "Let us be off for *h*,
Zep 3:20 At that time I will bring you *h*,
Hg 1: 9 and what you brought *h*,
Mt 1:24 and received her into his *h* as his wife.
8: 6 my serving boy is at *h* in bed paralyzed,
8:13 To the centurion Jesus said, "Go *h*.
9: 6 Roll up your mat, and go *h*."
9: 7 The man stood up and went toward his *h*.
9:10 while Jesus was at table in Matthew's *h*,
10:12 As you enter his *h* bless it.
10:13 If the *h* is deserving,
13:36 Then, dismissing the crowds, he went *h*.
19:29 Moreover, everyone who has given up *h*,
20:14 Take your pay and go *h*.
25:19 came *h* and settled accounts with them.
25:38 from *h* or clothe you in your nakedness?
25:43 away from *h* and you gave me no welcome,
25:44 see you hungry or thirsty or away from *h*
Mk 2: 1 days and word got around that he was at *h*.
2:11 Pick up your mat and go *h*."
5:19 "Go *h* to your family and make it clear to
7:17 When he got *h*, away from the crowd,
7:30 When she got *h*, she found the child
8: 3 If I send them *h* hungry,
8:26 Jesus sent him *h* with the admonition,
9:33 "What were you discussing on the way *h*?"
10:29 word, there is no one who has given up *h*,
13:34 leaves *h* and places his servants in charge,
Lk 1:23 of priestly service was over, he went *h*.
1:56 about three months and then returned *h*.
5:25 had been lying on and went *h* praising God.
7:36 to the Pharisee's *h* and reclined to eat.
7:37 that he was dining in the Pharisee's *h*.
7:44 I came to your *h* and you provided me with
8:39 "Go back *h* and recount all that God has
8:41 he come to his *h* because his only daughter,
9:61 first let me take leave of my people at *h*."
10:38 a woman named Martha welcomed him to her *h*.
15: 6 Once arrived *h*, he invites friends
15:25 As he neared the house on his way *h*,
15:27 The servant answered, 'Your brother is *h*,
17:31 should the man in the field return *h*.
18:14 this man went *h* from the temple justified
18:29 no one who has left *h* or wife or brothers,
23:48 they went *h* beating their breasts.
23:56 they went *h* to prepare spices and perfumes.
Jn 4:50 Jesus told him, "Return *h*.
4:50 word Jesus spoke to him, and started for *h*.
11:20 she went to meet him, while Mary sat at *h*.
20:10 With this, the disciples went back *h*.
Acts 5:42 after day, both in the temple and at *h*,
8:27 to Jerusalem and was returning *h*.
10:30 I was praying at *h* when a man in dazzling
18:26 they took him *h* and explained to him God's
21: 6 we boarded the ship and they returned *h*.
21: 8 we entered the *h* of Philip the evangelist,
1Cor 11:34 If anyone is hungry let him eat at *h*,
14:35 they should ask their husbands at *h*.
2Cor 5: 8 away from the body and at *h* with the Lord.
1Tm 5: 4 let these learn that piety begins at *h*
Ti 2: 5 to be sensible, chaste, busy at *h*,
Heb 11:16 were searching for a better, a heavenly *h*.
Rv 2:13 in your city where Satan has his *h*.

HOMELAND (2)

Gn 30:25 "Give me leave to go to my *h*.
Heb 11:14 they showed that they were seeking a *h*.

HOMELESS (4)

Sir 36:25 a man with no wife becomes a *h* wanderer.
Is 58: 7 sheltering the oppressed and the *h*;
Lam 3:19 of my *h* poverty is wormwood and gall;
1Cor 4:11 clad, roughly treated, wandering about *h*.

HOMELESSNESS (1)

Lam 1: 7 is mindful of the days of her wretched *h*,

HOMER (9)

Lv 27:16 the acreage sown with a *h* of barley seed
Is 5:10 And a *h* of seed shall yield but an ephah.
Ez 45:11 to a tenth of a *h*; by the homer they
45:13 one sixth of an ephah from each *h* of wheat,
45:13 sixth of an ephah from each *h* of barley.
45:14 a homer, for ten liquid measures make a *h*.
Hos 3: 2 of silver and a *h* and a lethech of barley.

HOMERS (1)

Nm 11:32 who got the least gathered ten *h* of them.

HOMES (28)

Nm 32:18 We will not return to our *h* until every
35: 2 they shall give the Levites cities for *h*,
Jgs 9:55 was dead, they all left for their *h*.
2Sm 6:19 With this, all the people left for their *h*.
1Kgs 8:66 the king farewell and went to their *h*,
2Kgs 13: 5 of Aram, dwelt in their own *h* as formerly.
Neh 4: 8 sons and daughters, your wives and your *h*."
Tb 13:12 your towers and set fire to your *h*;
Jdt 7:32 the women and children he sent to their *h*.
9:13 and the *h* your children have inherited.
Jb 21: 9 Their *h* are safe and without fear,
Ps(s) 49:12 Tombs are their *h* forever,
109:10 they be cast out of the ruins of their *h*.
Sir 28:15 *h* and rob them of the fruit of their toil;
41: 5 offspring are in the *h* of the wicked.
Jer 9:18 We must leave the land, give up our *h*!
17:22 Bring no burden from your *h* on the sabbath.
18:22 May cries be heard from their *h*,
49:30 leave your *h*,
51:30 Burned are their *h*, and broken their bars.
Lam 5: 2 over to strangers, our *h* to foreigners.
Ez 45: 4 their *h* and pasture land for their cattle.
Hos 11:11 And I will resettle them in their *h*,
Mk 10:30 present age a hundred times as many *h*,
Lk 16: 4 will take me into their *h* when I am let go.'
Acts 2:46 day, while in their *h* they broke bread.
1Cor 11:22 you not have *h* where you can eat and drink?
2Tm 3: 6 such as these who worm their way into *h*

HOMESICK (1)

Gn 31:30 were desperately *h* for your father's house,

HOMESTEADS (2)

Nm 15: 2 the land I will give you for your *h*,
Is 58:12 shall call you, "Restorer of ruined *h*."

HOMEWARD (5)

1Kgs 20:43 of Israel went off *h* and entered Samaria.
2Kgs 8:21 Then his army fled *h*.
14:12 Israel, and all the Judean soldiery fled *h*.
2Chr 25:22 Israel, and all the Judean soldiers fled *h*.
Jb 38:20 boundaries and set them on their *h* paths?

HOMICIDE (13)

Nm 35: 6 as places where a *h* can take refuge,
35:11 where a *h* who has killed someone
35:12 so that a *h* shall not be put to death
35:25 shall free the *h* from the avenger of blood
35:26 If the *h* of his own accord leaves the
35:28 the *h* was bound to stay in his city of
35:28 may the *h* return to his own district.
Dt 4:42 that a *h* might take refuge there if he
19: 3 that every *h* will be able to find a refuge.
19: 4 "It is in the following case that a *h* may
19: 6 the *h* and overtake him and strike him dead,
Jos 20: 3 one guilty of accidental and unintended *h*
20: 5 they are not to deliver up the *h* who slew

HOMICIDES (6)

Jos 21:13 given the city of asylum for *h* at Hebron,
21:21 the city of asylum for *h* at Shechem in the
21:27 the city of asylum for *h* at Golan,
21:32 city of asylum for *h* at Kedesh in Galilee,
21:36 for *h* at Bezer with its pasture lands,
21:38 the city of asylum for *h* at Ramoth in

HONEST (29)

Gn 42:11 We are *h* men;
42:19 If you have been *h*,
42:31 'We are *h* men: we have never been spies
42:33 'This is how I shall know if you are *h* men:
42:34 I know that you are *h* men and not spies,
Lv 19:36 true weights, an honest ephah and an *h* hin.
1Sm 29: 6 "As the LORD lives, you are *h*,
Jb 6:25 How agreeable are *h* words;
Ps(s) 52: 5 than good, falsehood rather than *h* speech.
Prv 1: 3 conduct, in what is right, just and *h*;
1:11 Let us lie in wait for the *h* man,
2:21 dwell in the land, the *h* will remain in it;
11: 5 The *h* man's virtue makes his way straight,
16:13 The king takes delight in *h* lips,
24:26 a kiss on the lips who makes an *h* reply.
29:10 Bloodthirsty men hate the *h* man,
Sir 29: 3 be *h* with him and you will always come by
Ez 45:10 an honest ephah, and an *h* liquid measure.
Lk 20:20 the guise of *h* men to trap him in speech,
Jn 5:30 and my judgment is *h* because I am not
7:24 by appearances and make an *h* judgment.
Eph 4:28 let him work with his hands at *h* labor so
Phil 4: 8 all that deserves respect, all that is *h*,
2Thes 1:11 power every *h* intention and work of faith.
Ti 3: 1 to be ready to take on any *h* employment.
3:14 Let our people devote themselves to *h* work

HONESTLY (5)

Prv 2: 7 he is the shield of those who walk *h*,
10: 9 He who walks *h* walks securely,
10:29 LORD is a stronghold to him who walks *h*,
13: 6 Virtue guards one who walks *h*,
Is 33:15 He who practices virtue and speaks *h*,

HONESTY (9)

Gn 30:33 wages of mine, let my *h* testify against me:
Jb 29:14 I wore my *h* like a garment;
Prv 2: 9 will understand rectitude and justice, *h*,
8: 6 for noble things I speak; *h* opens my lips.
11: 3 The *h* of the upright guides them;
14:32 but the just man finds a refuge in his *h*.
Is 59:15 *H* is lacking,
Jer 5: 3 O LORD, do your eyes not look for *h*?
Zec 8:16 *h* and peace in the judgments at your gates,

HONEY (62)

Gn 43:11 some balm and *h*,
Ex 3: 8 land, a land flowing with milk and *h*,
3:17 Jebusites, a land flowing with milk and *h*.
13: 5 give you, a land flowing with milk and *h*.
16:31 and it tasted like wafers made with *h*.
33: 3 you to the land flowing with milk and *h*.
Lv 2:11 any leaven or *h* as an oblation to the LORD.
20:24 possession, a land flowing with milk and *h*.
Nm 13:27 It does indeed flow with milk and *h*,
14: 8 that land, a land flowing with milk and *h*,
16:13 away from a land flowing with milk and *h*,
16:14 us to a land flowing with milk and *h*,
Dt 6: 3 to give you a land flowing with milk and *h*.
8: 8 and pomegranates, of olive trees and of *h*,
11: 9 a land flowing with milk and *h*.
26: 9 gave us this land flowing with milk and *h*.
26:15 in the land flowing with milk and *h*
27: 3 the land flowing with milk and *h*,
31:20 into the land flowing with milk and *h*
32:13 Giving them *h* to suck from its rocks and
Jos 5: 6 see the land flowing with milk and *h*
Jgs 14: 8 swarm of bees and *h* in the lion's carcass.
14: 9 So he scooped the *h* out into his palms and
14: 9 had scooped the *h* from the lion's carcass.
14:18 city said to him, "What is sweeter than *h*,
1Sm 14:27 he was holding and dipped in into the *h*.
14:29 are from this small taste of *h* I have had.
14:43 *h* from the end of the staff I was holding.
2Sm 17:29 flour, roasted grain, beans, lentils, *h*,
2Chr 31: 5 the best of their grain, wine, oil and *h*,
Jb 20:17 streams of oil, no torrents of *h* or milk.
Ps(s) 19:11 Sweeter also than syrup or *h* from the comb.
81:17 and with *h* from the rock I would fill them."
119:103 your promises, sweeter than *h* to my mouth!
Prv 5: 3 The lips of an adulteress drip with *h*,
24:13 *h*, my son, because it is good, if virgin *h*
25:16 If you find *h*, eat only what you need,
25:27 To eat too much *h* is not good;
27: 7 One who is full, tramples on virgin *h*;
Sg 4:11 Your lips drip *h*,
5: 1 my spices, I eat my *h* and my sweetmeats,
Sir 24:19 You will remember me as sweeter than *h*,
39:26 salt, The heart of the wheat, milk and *h*,
46: 8 the land flowing with milk and *h*.
49: 1 is his memory, like *h* to the taste,
Is 7:15 He shall be living on curds and *h* by the
7:22 curds and *h* shall be the food of all who
Jer 11: 5 give them a land flowing with milk and *h*:
32:22 under oath, a land flowing with milk and *h*.
41: 8 wheat and barley, oil and *h*."
Bar 1:20 give us the land flowing with milk and *h*,
Ez 3: 3 it, and it was as sweet as *h* in my mouth.
16:13 Fine flour, *h*, and oil were your food.
16:19 the oil, and the *h* with which I fed you,
20: 6 for them, a land flowing with milk and *h*,
20:15 given them, a land flowing with milk and *h*,
27:17 you, exchanging Minnith wheat, figs, *h*,
Mt 3: 4 Grasshoppers and wild *h* were his food.
Mk 1: 6 His food was grasshoppers and wild *h*.
Rv 10: 9 in your mouth it will taste as sweet as *h*."
10:10 In my mouth it tasted as sweet as *h*,

HONEYCOMB (3)

1Sm 14:25 Indeed, there was a *h* lying on the ground,
Prv 16:24 Pleasing words are a *h*,
Sir 24:19 than honey, better to have than the *h*.

HONEYED (1)

Sir 27:23 In your presence he uses *h* talk,

HONOR (188)

Gn 20:16 your *h* has been preserved with everyone."
Ex 20:12 *H* your father and your mother,
Lv 21: 7 has been a prostitute or has lost her *h*,
21: 8 *H* him as sacred who offers up the food of
21: 9 "A priest's daughter who loses her *h* by
21:14 a woman who has lost her *h* as a prostitute,
Nm 25:11 Israelites by his zeal for my *h* among them;
25:11 to the Israelites for the offense to my *h*.
Dt 5:16 *H* your father and your mother,
15: 2 in *h* of the LORD has been proclaimed.
16: 8 shall be a solemn meeting in *h* of the LORD,
16:10 keep the feast of Weeks in *h* of the LORD,
16:15 this pilgrim feast in *h* of the LORD,
Jos 7:19 and *h* by telling me what you have done;
Jgs 9:19 *h* toward Jerubbaal and his family this day,
13:17 we may *h* you when your words come true?"
1Sm 2:29 why do you *h* your sons in preference to me,
2:30 for I will *h* those who honor me,
15:12 where he erected a trophy in his own *h*,
15:30 yet *h* me now before the elders of my
1Kgs 5:17 could not build a temple in *h* of the LORD,

5:19 purpose to build a temple in *h* of the LORD,
5:19 place who shall build the temple in my *h*.'
8:16 for the building of a temple to my *h*;
8:17 to build a temple to the *h* of the LORD,
8:18 him, 'In wishing to build a temple to my *h*,
8:19 you, he shall build the temple to my *h*.'
8:20 and I have built this temple to *h* the LORD,
8:41 comes from a distant land to *h* you
8:43 which I have built is dedicated to your *h*.
8:44 and the temple I have built in your *h*,
8:48 and the temple I have built in your *h*,
9: 7 the temple I have consecrated to my *h*.
18:32 an altar in *h* of the LORD with the stones,
2Kgs 10:20 "Proclaim a solemn assembly in *h* of Baal."
23:10 sons or daughters by fire in *h* of Molech.
23:13 king of Israel, had built in *h* of Astarte,
1Chr 19: 3 to *h* your father?
22: 7 build a house myself for the *h* of the LORD,
22: 8 You may not build a house in my *h*,
22:10 It is he who shall build a house in my *h*;
22:19 into the house built in *h* of the LORD."
28: 3 to me, 'You may not build a house in my *h*,
29:12 "Riches and *h* are from you,
29:16 build you a house in *h* of your holy name
2Chr 1:18 building of a house to *h* the LORD
2: 3 to build a house for the *h* of the LORD,
6: 5 for the building of a temple to my *h*,
6: 7 to build a temple to the *h* of the LORD,
6: 8 'In wishing to build a temple to my *h*,
6: 9 you will beget shall build the temple to my *h*.'
6:10 have built the temple to the *h* of the LORD,
6:32 from a distant land to *h* your great name,
6:33 which I have built is dedicated to your *h*.
6:34 and of the house I have built to your *h*,
6:38 of the house which I have built to your *h*,
7:20 house which I have consecrated to my *h*,
20: 8 they built in it a sanctuary to your *h*,
29: 7 sanctuary to the *h* of the God of Israel.
30: 1 to celebrate the Passover in *h* of the LORD,
30: 5 to celebrate the Passover in *h* of the LORD,
32:33 of Jerusalem paid him *h* at his death.
35: 1 in Jerusalem a Passover to *h* the Lord;
Tb 4: 3 *H* your mother,
10:12 *h* your father-in-law and your
10:14 "May I *h* you all the days of my life!"
12: 6 Before all men, *h* and proclaim God's deeds,
12: 7 Praise them with due *h*.
12:11 of God are to be made known with due *h*.'
Jdt 13:20 make this redound to your everlasting *h*,
15:12 blessed her and performed a dance in her *h*.
Est A:17 Agagite, who was in high *h* with the king,
1:20 as it is, all wives will *h* their husbands,
2:18 Then the king gave a great feast in *h* of
C: 7 to place the *h* of man above that of God.
5: 8 to grant my petition and *h* my request,
6: 3 was done to reward and *h* Mordecai for this?"
1Mc 1:39 Her sabbaths to shame, her *h* to contempt.
10: 3 written in peaceful terms, to pay him *h*;
10:64 saw the *h* paid to him in the proclamation,
11:26 great *h* in the presence of all his Friends.
11:42 but I will greatly *h* you and your nation
12: 8 the envoy with *h* and received the letter,
12:43 Instead, he received him with *h*,
14:23 have voted to receive the men with *h*,
14:40 they had received Simon's envoys with *h*.
15: 9 *h* you and your nation and the temple,
2Mc 5:16 the glory, and the *h* of the Place.
Ps(s) 8: 6 angels, and crowned him with glory and *h*.
Prv 3: 9 *H* the LORD with your wealth,
3:16 right hand, in her left are riches and *h*;
3:35 *H* is the possession of wise men,
5: 9 her house, Lest you give your *h* to others,
8:18 With me are riches and *h*,
21:21 justice and kindness will find life and *h*.
22: 4 humility and fear of the LORD is riches, *h*,
25: 6 Claim no *h* in the king's presence,
25:27 nor to seek honor after *h*.
26: 1 in harvest, *h* for a fool is out of place.
26: 8 in the sling is he who gives *h* to a fool.
29:23 but he who is humble of spirit obtains *h*.
Eccl 6: 2 whom God gives riches and property and *h*,
Wis 6:21 you princes of the peoples, *h* Wisdom,
14:17 they could not *h* him in his presence
14:17 a public image of him they wished to *h*,
Sir 3: 2 LORD sets a father in *h* over his children;
3: 8 In word and deed *h* your father that his
3:11 His father's *h* is a man's glory;
4:21 and a shame that merits *h* and respect.
5:15 *H* and dishonor through talking!
7: 4 authority, nor from the king a place of *h*.
7:27 With your whole heart *h* your father;
7:31 *H* God and respect the priest;
10:19 Whose offspring can be in *h*?
10:19 Which offspring are in *h*?
10:20 is in *h*; he who fears God is in honor
10:22 wise but poor, nor proper to *h* any sinner.
10:23 The prince, the ruler, the judge are in *h*;
10:28 who will *h* him who discredits himself?
29: 6 pays him back, with abuse instead of *h*.
38: 1 Hold the physician in *h*,
45: 2 God's *h* devolved upon him,
45: 7 in *h* and crowned him with lofty majesty;
Is 4: 2 *h* and splendor for the survivors of Israel.
22:23 spot, to be a place of *h* for his family;
25: 3 Therefore a strong people will *h* you,
43:20 Wild beasts *h* me,
43:23 holocausts, nor *h* me with your sacrifices.
58:13 If you *h* it by not following your ways,
Jer 3:17 to *h* the name of the LORD at Jerusalem,
14: 7 action, O LORD, for the *h* of your name
Dn 11:39 him he shall provide with abundant *h*;
Mi 2: 9 you take away forever the *h* I gave them.
Mal 1: 6 I am a father, where is the *h* due to me?
Mt 13:57 is without *h* except in his native place,
15: 4 has said, *H* your father and your mother,'
15: 6 God, need not *h* his father or his mother.'
19:19 *H* your father and your mother';
23: 6 They are fond of places of *h* at banquets
Mk 6: 4 is without *h* except in his native place,
7:10 Moses said, *H* your father and your mother';
10:19 *H* your father and your mother.'"
12:39 synagogues, and places of *h* at banquets.
15: 8 to press their demand that he *h* the custom,
Lk 14: 7 trying to get the places of *h* at the table:
14: 8 do not sit in the place of *h* in case some
18:20 *H* your father and your mother."
20:46 in synagogues, and places of *h* at banquets.
Jn 5:23 honor the Son just as they *h* the Father.
5:23 to *h* the Son refuses to honor the Father
12:26 If anyone serves me, him the Father will *h*.
Acts 12:23 because he did not ascribe the *h* to God,
28:10 They paid us much *h*,
Rom 2: 7 life to those who strive for glory, *h*,
2:10 But there will be glory, *h*,
13: 7 and *h* to everyone who deserves them.
14: 6 who observes the day does so to *h* the Lord.
14: 6 The man who eats does so to *h* the Lord,
14: 6 who does not eat abstains to *h* the Lord,
15:20 It has been a point of *h* with me never to
1Cor 4:10 They *h* you, while they sneer at us!
12:23 We *h* the members we consider less
12:24 as to give greater *h* to the lowly members,
Eph 6: 2 *H* your father and mother" is the first
1Thes 4: 4 you guarding his member in sanctity and *h*,
4:11 Make it a point of *h* to remain at peace
1Tm 1:17 only God, be *h* and glory forever and ever!
5: 3 *H* the claims of widows who are real widows
6:16 To him be *h* and everlasting rule!
Heb 2: 7 you crowned him with glory and *h*,
2: 9 with glory and *h* because he suffered death:
3: 3 but Jesus is more worthy of *h* than he,
5: 4 does not take this *h* on his own initiative,
1Pt 1: 7 glory, and *h* when Jesus Christ appears.
Rv 4: 9 these creatures give glory and *h* and praise
4:11 worthy to receive glory and *h* and power!
5:12 and strength, *h* and glory and praise!"
5:13 throne, and to the Lamb, be praise and *h*,
7:12 and glory, wisdom and thanksgiving and *h*,
13:14 telling them to make an idol in *h* of the beast
14: 7 *H* God and give him glory,
15: 4 Who would dare refuse you *h*,
16: 9 but they did not repent or give him due *h*.

HONORABLE (11)

Tb 14: 1 and received an *h* burial in Nineveh.
1Mc 2:17 a leader, an *h* and great man in this city,
Prv 20: 3 It is *h* for a man to shun strife,
Wis 4: 8 is *h* comes not with the passing of time,
18: 3 way, and the mild sun for an *h* migration.
Is 3: 5 the elder, and the base toward the *h*.
32: 5 noble, nor the trickster be considered *h*.
58:13 a delight, and the LORD's holy day *h*;
Rom 12:17 that your conduct is *h* in the eyes of all.
1Cor 12:23 less *h* by clothing them with greater care,
Heb 3: 3 of a house is more *h* than the house itself.

HONORABLY (2)

Jgs 9:16 and *h* in appointing Abimelech your king,
Rom 13:13 Let us live *h* as in daylight;

HONORED (30)

Jgs 9: 9 up my rich oil, whereby men and gods are *h*,
1Sm 22:14 of your bodyguard, and *h* in your own house?
2Sm 6:20 the king of Israel has *h* himself today,
6:22 the slave girls you spoke of I will be *h*."
1Kgs 8:29 where you have decreed you shall be *h*;
11:36 the city in which I choose to be *h*.
14:21 tribes of Israel, the LORD chose to be *h*.
2Chr 6: 6 I choose Jerusalem, where I shall be *h*,
6:20 where you have decreed you shall be *h*;
12:13 tribes of Israel, the LORD chose to be *h*.
Jdt 12:13 to come to my lord to be *h* by him,
Est 5: 6 and whatever request you make shall be *h*,
7: 2 Whatever request you make shall be *h*,
9:12 ask, and whatever you request shall be *h*."
1Mc 10:63 The king also *h* him by numbering him among
2Mc 3: 2 the kings themselves *h* the Place and
13:23 and *h* the temple with a generous donation.
Jb 14:21 If his sons are *h*,
Prv 13:18 correction, but he who heeds reproof is *h*.
Wis 14:15 And now *h* as a god what was formerly a
14:20 who shortly before was *h* as a man.
Sir 10:29 *h* for his wisdom as the rich man is *h*
10:30 *H* in poverty, how much more so in wealth
11: 6 the *h* are given into enemy hands.
Is 23: 8 whose traders are the earth's *h* men?
23: 9 majesty, to degrade all the earth's *h* men.
1Cor 12:26 if one member is *h*,
2Cor 6: 8 hand and left, whether *h* or dishonored,
Heb 13: 4 Let marriage be *h* in every way and the

HONORING (1)

2Sm 10: 3 "Do you think that David is *h* your father

HONORS (15)

Est E: 2 they were showered with *h*
1Mc 10:88 events, he accorded new *h* to Jonathan.
11:27 and in all the *h* he had previously held,
14:39 and conferred the highest *h* on him.
2Mc 4:15 what their ancestors had regarded as *h*,
Ps(s) 15: 4 while he *h* those who fear the LORD;
Prv 4: 8 she will bring you *h* if you embrace her;
15:33 for wisdom, and humility goes before *h*.
18:12 is haughty, but humility goes before *h*.
Sir 3: 3 He who *h* his father atones for sins;
3: 5 who *h* his father is gladdened by children,
3: 7 He who fears the LORD *h* his father,
Is 29:13 words only and *h* me with their lips alone,
Dn 2: 6 from me gifts and presents and great *h*.
Mal 1: 6 A son *h* his father,

HOODWINKED (1)

Gn 31:20 Jacob had *h* Laban the Aramean by not

HOODWINKING (1)

Gn 31:26 "by *h* me and carrying off my daughters

HOOF (1)

Ez 32:13 nor shall the *h* of beast disturb them.

HOOFBEATS (1)

Jgs 5:28 why are the *h* of his chariots delayed?"

HOOFED (1)

Lv 11:26 All *h* animals that are not cloven-footed

HOOFS (16)

Lv 11: 3 any animal that has *h* you may eat,
11: 4 that only chew the cud or only have *h*:
11: 4 have *h* and is therefore unclean for you;
11: 5 have *h* and is therefore unclean for you;
11: 6 have *h* and is therefore unclean for you;
11: 7 does indeed have *h* and is cloven-footed,
Dt 14: 6 Any animal that has *h* you may eat,
14: 7 only chew the cud or only have cloven *h*:
14: 7 have *h* and are therefore unclean for you;
14: 8 which indeed has *h* and is cloven-footed,
Jgs 5:22 Then the *h* of the horses pounded,
2Mc 3:25 horse attacked Heliodorus with its front *h*.
Is 5:28 The *h* of their horses seem like flint,
Ez 26:11 With the *h* of his horses he shall trample
Mi 4:13 horn I will make iron And your *h* bronze,
Zec 11:16 flesh of the fat ones and tear off their *h*!

HOOK (5)

2Kgs 19:28 my *h* in your nose and my bit in your mouth,
Jb 40:25 Can you lead about Leviathan with a *h*,
Is 19: 8 and lament, all who cast *h* in the Nile;
37:29 my *h* in your nose and my bit in your mouth,
Hb 1:15 He brings them all up with his *h*,

HOOKS (22)

Ex 26:32 which shall have *h* of gold and shall rest
26:37 plated with gold, with their *h* of gold;
27:10 the *h* and bands on the columns shall be of
27:11 the *h* and bands on the columns shall be of
27:17 the court shall have bands and *h* of silver,
36:36 columns of acacia wood, with gold *h*,
36:38 *h* as well as their capitals and bands,
38:10 *h* and bands of the columns being of silver.
38:11 *h* and bands of the columns being of silver.
38:12 *h* and bands of the columns being of silver.
38:17 *h* and bands of the columns were of silver;
38:19 for it, while their *h* were of silver.
38:28 were used for making the *h* on the columns,
2Chr 33:11 they took Manasseh with *h*,
Is 2: 4 and their spears into pruning *h*;
18: 5 cutting of branches with pruning *h*
Ez 19: 4 took him away with *h* to the land of Egypt.
29: 4 I will put *h* in your jaws and make the
Jl 4:10 swords, and your pruning *h* into spears;
Am 4: 2 you When they shall drag you away with *h*,
Mi 4: 3 and their spears into pruning *h*;
2Pt 2:18 bombast while baiting their *h* with passion,

HOOPOE (2)

Lv 11:19 the various species of herons, the *h*,
Dt 14:18 the various species of herons, the *h*,

HOOT (3)

Is 14:23 make it a haunt of *h* owls and a marshland;

HOOT (cont.)

34:11 the desert owl and *h* owl shall possess her,
34:15 There the *h* owl shall nest and lay eggs,

HOOVES (2)

Ps(s) 69:32 oxen or bullocks with horns and divided *h:*
Jer 47: 3 They hear the stamping *h* of his steeds,

HOPE (181)

Gn 32: 6 information in the *h* of gaining your favor.' "
2Sm 14: 7 Thus they will quench my remaining *h* and
Ezr 10: 2 Yet even now there remains a *h* for Israel.
Tb 5:19 I *h* more money is not your chief concern!
Jdt 6: 9 cherish the *h* that they will not be taken,
8:20 we *h* that he will not disdain us or any of
9:11 forsaken, the savior of those without *h.*
13:19 Your deed of *h* will never be forgotten by
1Mc 2:61 none who *h* in him shall fail in strength.
4:10 to Heaven in the *h* that he will favor us,
2Mc 3:29 speechless and deprived of all *h* of aid,
7:11 from him I *h* to receive them again."
7:14 *h* of being restored to life by him;
7:20 courageously because of her *h* in the Lord.
9:18 so he lost *h* for himself and wrote the
13: 3 in the *h* of being established in office.
Jb 4: 6 and your integrity of life your *h?*
5:16 Thus the unfortunate have *h,*
7: 6 they come to an end without *h.*
8:13 so shall the *h* of the godless man perish.
11:18 you shall be secure, because there is *h;*
14: 7 For a tree there is *h,*
14:19 of the land, so you destroy the *h* of man.
17:15 and "my sister," Where then is my *h?*
19:10 my *h* he has uprooted like a tree.
41: 1 Whoever might vainly *h* to do so need only
Ps(s) 9:19 the *h* of the afflicted forever perish.
31:25 be stouthearted, all you who *h* in the LORD.
33:18 him, upon those who *h* for his kindness,
33:22 LORD, be upon us who have put our *h* in you.
39: 8 In you is my *h.*
42: 6 Why do you sigh within me? *H* in God!
42:12 *H* in God!
43: 5 *H* in God! For I shall again be thanking
62: 6 rest, my soul, for from him comes my *h.*
65: 6 The *h* of all the ends of the earth and of
71: 5 For you are my *h,*
71: 6 constant has been my *h* in you.
71:14 always *h* and praise you ever more and more.
78: 7 sons that they should put their *h* in God,
85: 9 and to those who put in him their *h.*
119:43 my mouth, for in your ordinances is my *h;*
119:49 to your servant since you have given me *h.*
119:74 me and be glad, because I *h* in your word.
119:81 I *h* in your word.
119:114 in your word I *h.*
119:116 disappoint me not in my *h.*
119:147 I *h* in your words.
131: 3 O Israel, *h* in the LORD,
143: 9 O LORD, for in you I *h.*
146: 5 the God of Jacob, whose *h* is in the LORD,
147:11 him, with those who *h* for his kindness.
Prv 10:28 The *h* of the just brings them joy,
11: 7 When a wicked man dies his *h* perishes,
13:12 *H* deferred makes the heart sick,
19:18 Chastise your son, for in this there is *h;*
23:18 a future, and your *h* will not be cut off.
24:14 a future, and your *h* will not be cut off.
26:12 There is more *h* for a fool than for him.
Eccl 9: 4 for any among the living there is *h;*
Wis 3: 4 yet is their *h* full of immortality;
3:11 Vain is their *h,*
3:18 no *h* nor comfort in the day of scrutiny;
5:14 the *h* of the wicked is like thistledown
12:19 you gave your sons good ground for *h*
14: 6 being destroyed, the *h* of the universe,
15:10 more worthless than earth is his *h,*
16:29 For the *h* of the ingrate melts like a
Sir 2: 6 make straight your ways and *h* in him.
2: 9 You who fear the LORD, *h* for good things,
2:14 Woe to you who have lost *h!*
14: 2 does not reproach him, who has not lost *h.*
16: 3 length of life, have no *h* in their future.
16:13 man's *h* God does not leave unfulfilled.
17:19 back, he encourages those who are losing *h!*
34:13 LORD, for they put their *h* in their savior;
34:14 for the LORD is his *h.*
38:21 him not, for there is no *h* of his return;
41: 2 with no more sight, with vanished *h.*
49:10 Jacob and saved him by their faith and *h.*
Is 20: 5 and ashamed because of Ethiopia, their *h,*
20: 6 shall say on that day, "Look at our *h!*
40:31 *h* in the LORD will renew their strength,
49:23 who *h* in me shall never be disappointed.
51: 5 In me shall the coastlands *h,*
64: 2 wrought awesome deeds we could not *h* for,
Jer 14: 8 O *H* of Israel, O LORD, our savior
17: 7 trusts in the LORD, whose *h* is the LORD.
17:13 O *h* of Israel, O LORD!
29:11 plans to give you a future full of *h.*
31:17 There is *h* for your future,
50: 7 against the LORD, the *h* of their fathers,
Lam 3:21 call this to mind, as my reason to have *h:*
3:24 therefore will I *h* in him.
3:26 It is good to *h* in silence for the saving
3:29 there may yet be *h.*
Ez 19: 5 vain she had waited, her *h* was destroyed.
37:11 "Our bones are dried up, our *h* is lost,
Dn 13:60 blessing God who saves those that *h* in him.
Hos 2:17 and the valley of Achor as a door of *h.*
12: 7 and do right and always *h* in your God.
Mi 1:12 can the inhabitants of Maroth *h* for good?
Zec 9: 5 Ekron, too, for her *h* shall come to nought.
Mt 12:21 In his name, the Gentiles will find *h.*"
Acts 2:26 has rejoiced, my body will live on in *h,*
23: 6 of my *h* in the resurrection of the dead."
24:15 and I have the same *h* in God as these men
26: 6 But today I stand trial because of my *h* in
26: 7 worship God day and night in the *h*
26: 7 It is because of this *h,*
27:12 put out to sea in the *h* of making Phoenix
27:20 the end, we abandoned any *h* of survival.
28:20 solely because I share the *h* of Israel."
Rom 4:18 Hoping against *h,* Abraham believed
5: 2 and we boast of our *h* for the glory of God.
5: 4 for tested virtue, and tested virtue for *h.*
5: 5 And this *h* will not leave us disappointed,
8:20 yet not without *h,*
8:24 In *h* we were saved.
8:24 But *h* is not hope if its object is seen;
8:24 it possible for one to *h* for what he sees?
12:12 Rejoice in *h,* be patient under trial,
15: 4 that we might derive *h* from the lessons of
15:12 in him the Gentiles will find *h.*"
15:13 So may God, the source of *h,*
15:13 Holy Spirit you may have *h* in abundance.
15:24 out for Spain, I *h* to see you in passing;
1Cor 9:10 for the plowman should plow in *h* and the
9:23 the *h* of having a share in its blessings.
13: 7 to love's forbearance, to its trust, its *h,*
13:13 faith, *h,* and love,
16: 7 I *h* to spend some time with you,
2Cor 1: 7 Our *h* for you is firm because we know that
1:10 We have put our *h* in him who will never
1:13 I *h* that, just as you know us
3:12 Our *h* being such, we speak
5:11 I *h* that it is also known to you in your
10:15 we *h* that as your faith grows our
10:16 we *h* to preach the gospel even beyond your
13: 6 I *h* you will understand that we have not
Gal 5: 5 eagerly await the justification we *h* for,
Eph 1:12 glory by being the first to *h* in Christ.
1:18 the great *h* to which he has called you,
2:12 without *h* and without God in the world.
4: 4 is but one *h* given all of you by your call.
Phil 2:19 I *h,* in the Lord Jesus, to send Timothy
2:23 I *h* to send him as soon as I see how
3:11 Thus do I *h* that I may arrive at
Col 1: 4 by the *h* held in store for you in heaven.
1: 5 of this *h* through the message of truth,
1:23 unshaken in the *h* promised you by the
1:27 mystery of Christ in you, your *h* of glory.
1Thes 1: 3 constancy of *h* in our Lord Jesus Christ.
2:19 all, if not you, will be our *h* or joy,
4:13 yield to grief, like those who have no *h.*
5: 8 and the *h* of salvation as a helmet.
2Thes 2:16 mercy gave us eternal consolation and *h,*
1Tm 1: 1 of God our savior and Christ Jesus our *h,*
3:14 Although I *h* to visit you soon,
5: 5 is one who has set her *h* on God and
2Tm 2:25 in the *h* always that God will enable them
Ti 1: 2 in the *h* of that eternal life which God,
2:13 in this age as we await our blessed *h,*
3: 7 by his grace and become heirs, in *h,*
Phlm 1:22 I *h* that through your prayers I shall be
Heb 3: 6 our confidence and the *h* of which we boast.
6:11 end, fully assured of that for which you *h.*
6:18 to seize the *h* which is placed before us.
6:19 that *h* extends beyond the veil through
7:19 But a better *h* has supervened,
10:23 to our profession which gives us *h,*
11: 1 assurance concerning what we *h* for,
1Pt 1: 3 a birth unto *h* which draws its life from
1:13 set all your *h* on the gift to be conferred
1:21 Your faith and *h,* then, are centered
3:15 ask you the reason for this *h* of yours,
1Jn 3: 3 has this *h* based on him keeps himself pure,
2Jn 1:12 I *h* to visit you and talk with you face to
3Jn 1: 2 Beloved, I *h* you are in good health
1:14 Rather, I *h* to see you soon,

HOPED (9)

Est E:14 For by such measures he *h* to catch us
2Mc 5: 9 among whom he *h* to find protection because
Prv 29:20 More can be *h* for from a fool!
Sir 2:10 anyone *h* in the LORD and been disappointed?
36:15 your name, Reward those who have *h* in you,
Lam 2:16 This at last is the day we *h* for;
3:18 is lost, all that I *h* for from the LORD.
Acts 12:11 clutches and from all that the Jews *h* for."
24:26 he *h* he would be offered a bribe by Paul,

HOPEFULLY (1)

Ps(s) 145:15 The eyes of all look *h* to you,

HOPELESS (2)

Sir 27:21 but he who betrays secrets does *h* damage.
Is 57:10 many misdeeds, you never said, "It is *h*";

HOPES (14)

Ru 1:12 And even if I could offer any *h,*
2Mc 7:34 concern yourself with unfounded *h,*
9:20 God very much, for my *h* are in heaven.
9:22 have great *h* of recovering from my illness.
Jb 6:19 search, the companies of Sheba have *h;*
Wis 13:10 are they, and in dead things are their *h,*
15: 6 and worthy of such *h* are they who make
Sir 11:22 just man, and in due time his *h* bear fruit.
34: 1 Empty and false are the *h* of the senseless,
Jn 5:45 you is Moses on whom you have set your *h.*
1Cor 15:19 *h* in Christ are limited to this life only,
2Cor 8: 5 Beyond our *h* they first gave themselves to
Phil 1:20 I shall never be put to shame for my *h;*
1Tm 4:10 our *h* are fixed on the living God who is

HOPHNI (5)

1Sm 1: 3 where the two sons of Eli, *H* and Phinehas,
2:34 happen to your two sons, *H* and Phinehas:
4: 4 The two sons of Eli, *H* and Phinehas,
4:11 and Eli's two sons, *H* and Phinehas,
4:17 Your two sons, *H* and Phinehas,

HOPHRA (1)

Jer 44:30 I will hand over Pharaoh *H,*

HOPING (10)

2Kgs 7:12 *h* to take us alive and enter our city when
Mt 12:10 *h* to bring an accusation against him:
Mk 3: 2 *h* to be able to bring an accusation
Lk 23: 8 and he was *h* to see him work some miracle.
24:21 We were *h* that he was the one who would
Acts 3: 5 his whole attention, *h* to get something.
23:28 *h* to determine what their charge against
Rom 4:18 *H* against hope, Abraham believed
8:25 And *h* for what we cannot see means
Col 1:28 *h* to make every man complete in Christ.

HOPPED (1)

1Kgs 18:26 they *h* around the altar they had prepared.

HOR (12)

Nm 20:22 whole Israelite community came to Mount *H.*
20:23 There at Mount *H,*
20:25 son Eleazar and bring them up on Mount *H.*
20:27 Mount *H* in view of the whole community,
21: 4 Mount *H* they set out on the Red Sea road,
33:37 Mount *H* on the border of the land of Edom.
33:38 ascended Mount *H* at the LORD's command,
33:39 years old when he died on Mount *H.*
33:41] Setting out from Mount *H*—
34: 7 Sea you shall draw a line to Mount *H,*
34: 8 from Mount *H* to Labo in the land of Hamath,
Dt 32:50 Mount *H* and there was taken to his people;

HORAM (1)

Jos 10:33 At that time *H,* king of Gezer

HORDE (12)

Nm 22: 4 "Soon this *h* will devour all the country
Jdt 1:16 all his numerous, motley *h* of warriors;
Is 29: 5 *h* of your arrogant shall be like fine dust,
29: 5 the *h* of the tyrants like flying chaff.
29: 7 Shall be the *h* of all the nations who war
29: 8 dry, So shall the *h* of all the nations be,
Ez 32:12 down your *h* with the blades of warriors,
38: 4 a great *h* with bucklers and shields,
38: 7 you and all your *h* assembled about you,
38:13 for pillage that you have summoned your *h,*
38:15 on horses, a great *h* and a mighty army?
39:11 Gog shall be buried there with all his *h,*

HORDES (8)

2Mc 2:21 whole land, put to flight the barbarian *h,*
Ez 31: 2 Pharaoh, the king of Egypt, and to his *h:*
31:18 Such are Pharaoh and all his *h,*
32:12 of Egypt, and all her *h* shall be destroyed.
32:16 Egypt and all its *h* shall they chant it,
32:20 shall be made with them for all their *h.*
32:31 comforted for all his *h* slain by the sword
32:32 Pharaoh and all his *h,*

HOREB (18)

Ex 3: 1 the flock across the desert, he came to *H,*
17: 6 there in front of you on the rock in *H.*
33: 6 So, from Mount *H* onward,
Dt 1: 2 it is a journey of eleven days from *H*
1: 6 "The LORD, our God, said to us at *H,*
1:19 *H* and journeyed through the whole desert,
4:10 you stood before the LORD, your God, at *H,*
4:15 to you at *H* from the midst of the fire.
5: 2 our God, made a covenant with us at *H;*
9: 8 At *H* you so provoked the LORD that he was
18:16 your God, at *H* on the day of the assembly,

28:69 the covenant which he made with them at *H.*
1Kgs 8: 9 tablets which Moses had put there at *H,*
19: 8 and forty nights to the mountain of God, *H.*
2Chr 5:10 two tablets which Moses put there on *H,*
Ps(s) 106:19 made a calf in *H* and adored a molten image;
Sir 48: 7 threats at Sinai, at *H* avenging judgments.
Mal 3:22 my servant, which I enjoined him on *H,*

HOREM (1)

Jos 19:38 Edrei, En-hazor, Yiron, Migdal-el, *H,*

HORESH (3)

1Sm 23:15 while he was at *H* in the barrens near Ziph,
23:18 a joint agreement before the LORD in *H,*
23:19 us, now in the refuges, and again at *H,*

HORI (3)

Gn 36:22 Lotan's descendants were *H* and Hemam,
Nm 13: 5 son of *H,* of the tribe of Simeon
1Chr 1:39 The sons of Lotan were *H* and Homam;

HORITE (3)

Gn 36:20 are the descendants of Seir the *H,*
36:21 they are the *H* clans descended from Seir,
36:29 These are the *H* clans:

HORITES (4)

Gn 14: 6 and the *H* in the hill country of Seir,
36:30 they were the clans of the *H,*
Dt 2:12 the former inhabitants were the *H;*
2:22 Seir, by clearing the *H* out of their way,

HORMAH (9)

Nm 14:45 them, beating them back as far as *H.*
21: 3 Hence that place was named *H.*
Dt 1:44 you, cutting you down in Seir as far as *H.*
Jos 12:14 Lachish, Eglon, Gezer, Debir, Geder, *H,*
15:30 Baalah, Iim, Ezem, Eltolad, Chesil, *H,*
19: 4 Balah, Ezem, Eltolad, Bethul, *H,*
Jgs 1:17 the city to destruction, they renamed it *H.*
1Sm 30:30 those in the Kenite cities, to those in *H,*
1Chr 4:30 Bilhah, Ezem, Tolad, Bethuel, *H,*

HORN (44)

Ex 19:13 *h* resounds may they go up to the mountain."
Jos 6:20 When they heard the signal *h,*
Jgs 3:27 the *h* in the mountain region of Ephraim,
6:34 the *h* that summoned Abiezer to follow him.
1Sm 2: 1 in the LORD, my *h* is exalted in my God.
2:10 his king, and exalt the *h* of his anointed!"
13: 3 Saul sounded the *h* throughout the land,
16: 1 Fill your *h* with oil, and be on your way.
16:13 Then Samuel, with the *h* of oil in hand,
2Sm 2:28 Joab then sounded the *h,*
6:15 shouts of joy and to the sound of the *h.*
15:10 to say, "When you hear the sound of the *h,*
18:16 Joab then sounded the *h,*
20: 1 He sounded the *h* and cried out,
20:22 He then sounded the *h,*
22: 3 My shield, the *h* of my salvation,
1Kgs 1:34 of Israel, and you shall blow the *h* and cry,
1:39 Then Zadok the priest took the *h* of oil
1:39 They blew the *h* and all the people shouted,
1:41 When Joab heard the sound of the *h,*
Ps(s) 18: 3 refuge, my shield, the *h* of my salvation,
89:18 and by your favor our *h* is exalted.
89:25 and through my name shall his *h* be exalted.
92:11 You have exalted my *h* like the wild bull's;
98: 6 of the *h* sing joyfully before the King,
112: 9 his *h* shall be exalted in glory.
132:17 will I make a *h* to sprout forth for David;
148:14 and he has lifted up the *h* of his people.
Lam 2: 3 the *h* that was Israel's whole strength;
2:17 over you and exalting the *h* of your foes.
Ez 29:21 make a *h* sprout for the house of Israel,
Dn 7: 8 it had, when suddenly another, a little *h,*
7: 8 This *h* had eyes like a man,
7:11 of the arrogant words which the *h* spoke,
7:20 about the *h* with the eyes and the mouth
7:21 that *h* made war against the holy ones and
8: 5 a he-goat with a prominent *h* on its
8: 8 of its power the great *h* was shattered,
8: 9 *h* which kept growing toward the south,
8:21 great *h* on its forehead is the first king.
Hos 5: 8 Blow the *h* in Gibeah,
Mi 4:13 *h* I will make iron And your hoofs bronze,
Mt 6: 2 do not blow a *h* before you in synagogues
Lk 1:69 He has raised a *h* of saving strength for

HORNED (1)

Gn 49:17 by the roadside, a *h* viper by the path,

HORNETS (3)

Ex 23:28 of you I will send *h* to drive the Hivites,
Dt 7:20 the LORD, your God, will send *h* among them,
Jos 24:12 And I sent the *h* ahead of you which drove

HORNS (80)

Gn 22:13 spied a ram caught by its *h* in the thicket.
Ex 27: 2 At the four corners there are to be *h,*
29:12 your finger put it on the *h* of the altar.
30: 2 high, with *h* that spring directly from it.
30: 3 and its *H* you shall plate with pure gold.
30:10 shall perform the atonement rite on its *h.*
37:25 having *h* that sprang directly from it.
37:26 and its *h* were plated with pure gold;
38: 2 At the four corners *h* were made that
Lv 4: 7 put some of the blood on the *h* of the altar
4:18 put some of the blood on the *h* of the altar
4:25 put it on the *h* of the altar of holocausts.
4:30 put it on the *h* of the altar of holocausts.
4:34 put it on the *h* of the altar of holocausts.
8:15 finger he put it on the *h* around the altar,
9: 9 the blood and put it on the *h* of the altar.
16:18 he shall put it on the *h* around the altar,
Dt 33:17 whose *h* are those of the wild ox With
Jos 6: 4 priests carrying ram's *h* ahead of the ark.
6: 4 times, and have the priests blow the *h.*
6: 5 on the ram's *h* and you hear that signal,
6: 6 ram's *h* in front of the ark of the LORD.
6: 8 *h* before the LORD blowing their horns,
6: 9 with the *h* marched the picked troops;
6: 9 *h* was kept up continually as they marched.
6:13 *h* marched in front of the ark of the LORD,
6:13 of the ark of the LORD, blowing their *h.*
6:13 the blowing of *h* was kept up continually.
6:16 blew the *h* and Joshua said to the people,
6:20 As the *h* blew, the people began to shout.
Jgs 7: 8 Their *h,* and such supplies
7:16 and provided them all with *h* and with
7:18 me blow *h,* you too must blow horns
7:19 the *h* and broke the jars they were holding.
7:20 companies blew *h* and broke their jars.
7:20 and in their right the *h* they were blowing,
7:22 the three hundred men kept blowing the *h,*
1Kgs 1:50 he went and seized the *h* of the altar.
1:51 had seized the *h* of the altar and said,
2:28 of the LORD and seized the *h* of the altar.
22:11 Chenaanah, made himself *h* of iron and said,
1Chr 15:28 with joyful shouting, to the sound of *h,*
2Chr 15:14 with shouting and with trumpets and *h.*
18:10 made iron *h* for himself and said:
Jdt 9: 8 to overthrow with iron the *h* of your altar.
Ps(s) 22:22 from the *h* of the wild bulls,
69:32 oxen or bullocks with *h* and divided hooves:
75: 5 Lift not up your *h.*"
75: 6 Lift not up your *h* against the Most High;
75:11 *h* of all the wicked; the horns of the just
118:27 with leafy boughs up to the *h* of the altar.
Jer 17: 1 [And the *h* of their altars,
Ez 34:21 with your *h* until you have driven them out,
43:15 of the hearth were the four *h* of the altar.
43:20 and put it on the four *h* of the altar,
Dn 7: 8 I was considering the ten *h* it had,
7: 8 *h* were torn away to make room for it.
7:20 about the ten *h* on its head,
7:20 that sprang up, before which three *h* fell;
7:24 The ten *h* shall be ten kings rising out of
8: 3 by the river a ram with two great *h,*
8: 7 blows when they met, and break both its *h.*
Am 3:14 The *h* of the altar shall be broken off and
Zec 2: 1 there were four *h.*
2: 2 "These are the *h* that scattered Judah and
2: 4 "Here are the *h* that scattered Judah,
2: 4 horns of the nations that raised their *h*
Rv 5: 6 He had seven *h* and seven eyes;
9:13 *h* of the altar of gold in God's presence.
12: 3 flaming red, with seven heads and ten *h;*
13: 1 with ten *h* and seven heads; on its horns
13:11 *h* like a ram and it spoke like a dragon.
17: 3 This beast had seven heads and ten *h.*
17:12 The ten *h* you saw represent ten kings who
17:16 The ten *h* you saw on the beast will turn

HORONAIM (4)

Is 15: 5 On the way to *H* they utter rending cries.
Jer 48: 3 a cry from *H* of ruin and great destruction!
48: 5 to *H* the cry of destruction is heard.
48:34 they call from Zoar to *H,*

HORONITE (3)

Neh 2:10 When Sanballat the *H* and Tobiah the
2:19 On hearing of this, Sanballat the *H,*
13:28 was the son-in-law of Sanballat the *H!*

HORRIBLE (12)

1Mc 1:54 *h* abomination upon the altar of holocausts,
Wis 18:17 visions in *h* dreams perturbed them and
Jer 5:30 shocking, *h* thing has happened in the land:
13:27 highlands I see these *h* crimes of yours.
18:13 Truly *h* things has virgin Israel done!
44: 4 not to commit this *h* deed which I hate,
44:22 deeds, the *h* things which you were doing;
Dn 7: 7 from all the others, terrifying, *h,*
9:27 shall be the *h* abomination until the ruin
11:31 sacrifice and setting up the *h* abomination.
12:11 abolished and the *h* abomination is set up,
Hos 6:10 the house of Israel I have seen a *h* thing:

HORRID (1)

Jer 32:34 after me by the *h* idols they set up in it.

HORRIFIED (2)

Gn 20: 8 that had happened, and the men were *h.*
Ez 26:16 tremble at every moment and be *h* at you.

HORROR (32)

2Kgs 23:13 *h,* of Chemosh, the Moabite horror
Jb 18:20 they who went before are struck with *h.*
19:19 All my intimate friends hold me in *h;*
21: 6 am dismayed, and *h* takes hold on my flesh.
Ps(s) 55: 6 and *h* overwhelms me,
Prv 16:12 Kings have a *h* of wrongdoing,
Sir 26:19 to my heart, and the third arouses my *h:*
Jer 2:12 this, O heavens, and shudder with sheer *h,*
8:21 I am disconsolate; *h* has seized me.
15: 4 And I will make them an object of *h* to all
24: 9 of *h* to all the kingdoms of the earth,
25: 9 will doom them, making them an object of *h,*
29:18 of *h* to all the kingdoms of the earth,
34:17 of *h* to all the kingdoms of the earth.
42:18 become an example of malediction and *h,*
44:12 and become an example of malediction, a *h,*
48:39 laughingstock and a *h* to all his neighbors!
49:13 shall become an object of *h* and a disgrace,
49:17 Edom shall become an object of *h.*
50:23 of *h* Babylon has become among the nations!
51:37 A place of *h* and ridicule,
51:41 What a *h* has Babylon become among nations:
Bar 2: 4 a reproach and a *h* among all the nations
Ez 7:18 put on sackcloth, and *h* shall cover them;
12:19 in anxiety and drink their water in *h,*
20:26 so as to make them an object of *h.*
27:36 You have become a *h,*
28:19 You have become a *h,*
32:10 in *h* when they see me brandish my sword,
Dn 9:27 that is decreed is poured out upon the *h.*"
12: 2 shall be an everlasting *h* and disgrace.

HORRORS (2)

2Kgs 23:24 all the other *h* to be seen in the land of
Ps(s) 73:19 They are completely wasted away amid *h.*

HORSE (34)

Ex 15: 1 *h* and chariot he has cast into the sea.
15:21 *h* and chariot he has cast into the sea.
1Kgs 10:29 shekels, a *h* one hundred and fifty shekels;
20:25 army that has deserted you, *h* for horse,
20:25 army that has deserted you, horse for *h,*
2Kgs 11:16 forcibly to the *h* gate of the royal palace,
2Chr 23:15 the entrance to the *H* Gate of the palace,
Neh 3:28 Above the *H* Gate the priests carried out
Jdt 9: 7 force, priding themselves on *h* and rider,
Est 6: 8 *h* on which the king rode
6: 9 The robe and the *h* should be consigned to
6: 9 on the *h* in the public square of the city,
6:10 Take the robe and *h* as you have proposed,
6:11 So Haman took the robe and *h,*
2Mc 3:25 appeared to them a richly caparisoned *h,*
3:25 *h* attacked Heliodorus with its front hoofs.
Jb 39:18 she makes sport of the *h* and his rider.
39:19 Do you give the *h* his strength,
Ps(s) 33:17 Useless is the *h* for safety;
Prv 21:31 The *h* is equipped for the day of battle,
26: 3 The whip for the *h,*
Jer 31:40 as the corner of the *H* Gate at the east,
51:21 With you I shatter *h* and rider,
Zec 1: 8 There appeared the driver of a red *h,*
9:10 from Ephraim, and the *h* from Jerusalem;
10: 3 of Judah, and make them his stately war *h.*
12: 4 LORD, I will strike every *h* with fright,
Rv 6: 2 To my surprise, I saw a white *h;*
6: 4 Another *h* came forth, a red one.
6: 5 This time I saw a black *h,*
6: 8 Now I saw a *h* sickly green in color.
19:11 and as I looked on, a white *h* appeared;
19:19 to do battle with the One riding the *h,*
19:21 of the mouth of the One who rode the *h,*

HORSEBACK (1)

Eccl 10: 7 I have seen slaves on *h,*

HORSEFLY (1)

Jer 46:20 heifer, from the north a *h* lights upon her.

HORSEMAN (5)

2Mc 11: 8 near Jerusalem, a *h* appeared at their head,
12:35 a powerful *h* and one of Bacenor's men,
12:35 when a Thracian *h* attacked Dositheus and
Jer 4:29 of *h* and bowman each city takes to flight;
Am 2:15 shall not escape, nor the *h* save his life.

HORSEMEN (40)

Jos 24: 6 fathers to the Red Sea with chariots and *h.*
1Sm 13: 5 three thousand chariots, six thousand *h,*
2Sm 1: 6 with chariots and *h* closing in on him.
8: 4 *h* and twenty thousand foot soldiers.
2Kgs 13: 7 except fifty *h* with ten chariots and ten

HORSEMEN (cont.)

13:14 "Israel's chariots and h!"
18:24 as you do on Egypt for chariots and h?
1Chr 18: 4 thousand chariots, and seven thousand h.
19: 6 to hire chariots and h from Aram Naharaim,
2Chr 8: 6 for the chariots, the cities for the h,
8: 9 and commanders of his chariots and his h.
9:25 horses, chariots, and twelve thousand h,
12: 3 hundred chariots and sixty thousand h,
Ezr 8:22 ashamed to ask the king for troops and h
Jdt 7: 2 thousand infantry and twelve thousand h,
1Mc 10:77 thousand h and an innumerable infantry.
10:77 he had such a large number of h to rely on.
10:82 When the h were exhausted,
10:83 The h too were scattered over the plain.
15:13 thousand infantry and eight thousand h.
15:41 Kedron and stationed h and infantry there,
16: 4 in the land twenty thousand warriors and h.
16: 5 an immense army of foot soldiers and h,
16: 7 them, for the enemy's h were very numerous.
2Mc 5: 2 days, there appeared h charging in midair,
10:31 and six hundred of their h were slain.
11: 4 of foot soldiers, his thousands of h,
11:11 foot soldiers and sixteen hundred h,
12:10 thousand foot soldiers, and five hundred h.
12:20 foot soldiers and twenty-five hundred h.
12:33 thousand foot soldiers and four hundred h.
13: 2 foot soldiers, fifty-three hundred h,
Is 31: 1 and in h because of their combined power,
36: 9 yet you rely on Egypt for chariots and h!
43:17 waters, Who leads out chariots and h,
Ez 23:23 charioteers and warriors, all of them h.
Dn 11:40 him with chariots and h and a great fleet,
Hos 1: 7 by war, by sword or bow, by horses or h.
Hb 1: 8 His horses prance, his h come from afar:
Zec 10: 5 is with them, and shall put the h to rout.

HORSES—HORSE'S (122)

Gn 46:29 Joseph hitched the h to his chariot and
47:17 he sold them food in return for their h,
49:17 viper by the path, That bites the h heel,
Ex 9: 3 your h,
14: 9 Pharaoh's whole army, his h,
14:23 all Pharaoh's h and chariots and
15:19 They sang thus because Pharaoh's h and
Dt 11: 4 Egyptian army and to their h and chariots,
17:16 But he shall not have a great number of h;
20: 1 you see h and chariots and an army
Jos 11: 4 and with a multitude of h and chariots.
11: 6 hamstring their h and burn their chariots."
11: 9 their h and burned their chariots.
Jgs 5:22 Then the hoofs of the h pounded,
1Sm 8:11 sons and assign them to his chariots and h,
2Sm 8: 4 And he hamstrung all the chariot h,
15: 1 Absalom provided himself with chariots, h,
1Kgs 5: 6 stalls for his twelve thousand chariot h.
5: 8 For the chariot h and draft animals also,
9:19 supplies, cities for chariots and for h,
10:25 garments, weapons, spices, h and mules.
10:28 Solomon's h were imported from Cilicia,
18: 5 We may find grass and save the h and mules,
20: 1 by thirty-two kings with h and chariotry,
20:21 Israel went out, took the h and chariots,
22: 4 my people, your h and my horses as well."
2Kgs 2:11 chariot and flaming h came between them,
3: 7 and mine, and your h and mine as well."
5: 9 Naaman came with his h and chariots and
6:14 there a strong force with h and chariots.
6:15 its h and chariots surrounding the city.
6:17 with h and fiery chariots around Elisha.
7: 6 to hear the sound of chariots and h,
7: 7 fled, abandoning their tents, their h,
7:10 human voice, only the h and asses tethered,
7:13 abandoned h and send scouts to investigate."
7:14 They took two chariots, and h,
9:33 spurted against the wall and against the h.
10: 2 wrote, "and you have the chariots, the h,
14:20 He was brought back on h and buried with
18:23 thousand h if you can put riders on them.
23:11 He did away with the h which the kings of
1Chr 18: 4 Of the chariot h, David hamstrung all
2Chr 1:16 also imported h from Egypt and Cilicia.
1:17 h going for a hundred and fifty shekels.
9:24 garments, weapons, spices, h and mules.
9:25 also had four thousand stalls of h,
9:28 H were imported for Solomon from Egypt
25:28 They brought him back on h and buried him
Ezr 2:66 Their h were seven hundred and thirty-six,
Neh 7:67 Their h were seven hundred and thirty-six,
Jdt 16: 3 the torrents, their h covered the hills.
1Mc 10:81 whereas the enemy's h became tired out.
2Mc 10:29 majestic men riding on golden-bridled h,
Ps(s) 20: 8 Some are strong in chariots; some, in h;
32: 9 Be not senseless like h or mules:
Wis 19: 9 For they ranged about like h,
Sir 48: 9 in a whirlwind, in a chariot with fiery h.
Is 2: 7 Their land is full of h,
5:28 The hoofs of their h seem like flint,
21: 7 If he sees a chariot, a pair of h,
21: 9 a single chariot, a pair of h;
22: 6 takes up the quivers, Aram mounts the h,
22: 7 chariots, and h are posted at the gates,
28:28 crush it with his noisy cartwheels and h.
30:16 "No," you said, "Upon h we will flee."
31: 1 down to Egypt for help, who depend upon h;
31: 3 are men, not God, their h are flesh,
36: 8 'I will give you two thousand h,
63:13 the depths like h in the open country,
66:20 offering to the LORD, on h and in chariots,
Jer 12: 5 wearied you, how will you race against h?
17:25 riding in their chariots or upon their h,
22: 4 riding in chariots or mounted on h,
46: 4 Harness the h, mount, charioteers!
46: 9 Forward, h!
51:27 her, send up h like bristling locusts.
Ez 17:15 to Egypt to obtain h and a great army.
23: 6 attractive young men, knights mounted on h.
23:12 impeccably clothed, knights mounted on h,
26: 7 the king of kings, with h and chariots,
26:10 surge of his h shall cover you with dust,
26:11 of his h he shall trample all your streets;
27:14 From Beth-togarmah h, steeds, and mules
38: 4 h and riders all handsomely outfitted,
38:15 many peoples with you, all mounted on h,
39:20 be filled at my table with h and riders,
Hos 1: 7 by war, by sword or bow, by h or horsemen.
14: 4 not save us, nor shall we have h to mount;
Jl 2: 4 Their appearance is that of h;
Am 4:10 Your h I let be captured,
6:12 Can h run across a cliff?
Mi 5: 9 h from your midst and ruin your chariots;
Na 2: 4 The h are frenzied;
3: 2 h a-gallop, chariots bounding
Hb 1: 8 Swifter than leopards are his h,
1: 8 His h prance, his horsemen come from afar:
Hg 2:22 h shall go down by one another's sword.
Zec 1: 8 behind him were red, sorrel, and white h.
6: 2 red horses, the second chariot black h,
6: 3 black horses, the third chariot white h,
6: 3 spotted horses—all of them strong h.
6: 6 h was turning toward the land of the north,
6: 6 the red and the white h went after them,
6: 7 As these strong h emerged,
12: 4 will strike blind all the h of the peoples,
14:15 plague shall be the plague upon the h,
14:20 day there shall be upon the bells of the h,
Acts 23:24 Also provide h for Paul's journey,
Jas 3: 3 into the mouths of h to make them obey us,
Rv 9: 7 locusts were like h equipped for battle.
9: 9 many chariots and h charging into battle.
9:17 this is how I saw the h and their riders.
9:17 The h' heads were like heads of lions,
9:19 The deadly power of the h was not only in
14:20 around, it reached as high as a h bridle.
18:13 cattle and sheep, h and carriages;
19:14 riding white h and dressed in fine linen,
19:18 and warriors, of h and their riders;

HOSAH (5)

Jos 19:29 it cut back to H and ended at the sea.
1Chr 16:38 Obed-edom, son of Jeduthun, and H,
26:10 H, a descendant of Merari,
26:11 the sons and brethren of H were thirteen.
26:16 To H fell the west side with the

HOSANNA (6)

Mt 21: 9 H to the Son of David!
21: 9 H in the highest!"
21:15 temple precincts, H to the Son of David!"
Mk 11: 9 H! Blessed is he who comes
11:10 H in the highest!"
Jn 12:13 H! Blessed is he who comes

HOSEA (4)

Hos 1: 1 The word of the Lord that came to H,
1: 2 speaking to H, the Lord said to Hosea:
Rom 9:25 As it says in the Book of H:

HOSHAIAH (3)

Neh 12:32 by H and half the princes of Judah,
Jer 42: 1 Johanan, son of Kareah, Azariah, son of H,
43: 2 has sent him to them, Azariah, son of H,

HOSHEA (12)

Nm 13:16 But H, son of Nun, Moses called Joshua.
2Kgs 15:30 H, son of Elah, conspired against Pekah,
17: 1 twelfth year of Ahaz, king of Judah, H,
17: 3 H became his vassal and paid him tribute.
17: 4 But the king of Assyria found H guilty of
17: 5 king of Assyria arrested and imprisoned H;
17: 6 In the ninth year of H,
18: 1 third year of H, son of Elah, king of Israel,
18: 9 Hezekiah, which was the seventh year of H,
18:10 year of Hezekiah, the ninth year of H,
1Chr 27:20 for the sons of Ephraim, H,
Neh 10:24 Zadok, Jaddua, Pelatiah, Hanan, Anaiah, H,

HOSPITABLE (5)

2Mc 6: 2 and that on Mount Gerizim to Zeus the H,
1Tm 3: 2 temper, self-controlled, modest, and h.
5:10 Has she been h to strangers?
Ti 1: 8 the contrary, be h and a lover of goodness;
1Pt 4: 9 Be mutually h without complaining.

HOSPITABLY (1)

Est E:10 us in generosity, was h received by us.

HOSPITALITY (5)

Sir 32: 2 in their joy and win praise for your h.
Lk 10:40 who was busy with all the details of h,
Acts 28: 7 us in and gave us kind h for three days.
Rom 12:13 be generous in offering h.
Heb 13: 2 Do not neglect to show h,

HOST (52)

Gn 17: 4 are to become the father of a h of nations.
17: 5 am making you the father of a h of nations.
Nm 10:14 son of Amminadab, was over their h,
10:15 Zuar, over the h of the tribe of Issachar,
10:16 Helon, over the h of the tribe of Zebulun.
10:18 with Elizur, son of Shedeur, over their h,
10:19 over the h of the tribe of Simeon,
10:20 of Reuel, over the h of the tribe of Gad.
10:22 Elishama, son of Ammihud, over their h,
10:23 over the h of the tribe of Manasseh,
10:24 over the h of the tribe of Benjamin.
10:25 Ahiezer, son of Ammishaddai, over their h,
10:26 Ochran, over the h of the tribe of Asher,
10:27 Enan, over the h of the tribe of Naphtali.
Dt 17: 3 sun or the moon or any of the h of the sky,
Jos 5:14 the h of the LORD and I have just arrived."
5:15 of the h of the LORD replied to Joshua,
Jgs 19:25 When the men would not listen to his h,
1Kgs 22:19 with the whole h of heaven standing by to
2Kgs 17:16 pole and worshiped all the h of heaven,
21: 3 worshiped and served the whole h of heaven.
21: 5 altars for the whole h of heaven,
23: 4 Baal, Asherah, and the whole h of heaven.
23: 5 the Zodiac, and to the whole h of heaven.
2Chr 18:18 with the whole h of heaven standing by to
33: 3 the whole h of heaven and worshiped them.
33: 5 he built altars to the whole h of heaven
Neh 9: 6 the highest heavens and all their h,
1Mc 3:17 as we are, fight such a mighty h as this?
Ps(s) 33: 6 by the breath of his mouth all their h.
Is 24:21 punish the h of the heavens in the heavens,
34: 2 and is wrathful against all their h;
34: 4 scroll, and all their h shall wither away,
45:12 I gave the order to all their h.
Jer 19:13 they burnt incense to the whole h of heaven
33:22 the h of heaven which cannot be numbered,
Ez 32: 3 my net over you [with a h of many nations],
Dn 8:10 Its power extended to the h of heaven,
8:10 it cast down to earth some of the h
8:11 boasted even against the prince of the h,
8:12 sanctuary it cast down, as well as the h,
8:13 there, the sanctuary, and the trampled h?"
11:10 prepare and assemble a great armed h,
11:11 whose great h shall make a stand but shall
Ob 1:20 The captives of the h of the children of
Zep 1: 5 who adore the h of heaven on the roofs,
Lk 2:13 the angel a multitude of the heavenly h,
7:39 When his h, the Pharisee, saw this
14: 9 Then the h might come and say to you,
14:10 when your h approaches you he will say,
Rom 16:23 who is h to me and to the whole church.
Eph 4: 8 took a h of captives and gave gifts to men."

HOSTAGE (1)

1Mc 1:10 son of King Antiochus, once a h at Rome.

HOSTAGES (8)

2Kgs 14:14 treasuries of the palace, and h as well.
2Chr 25:24 the treasures of the palace, and h as well.
1Mc 8: 7 tribute, to give h and a section of Lycia,
9:53 He took as h the sons of the leaders of
10: 6 the h in the citadel be released to him.
10: 9 They released the h to Jonathan,
11:62 chief men as h and sent them to Jerusalem.
13:16 and two of his sons as h to guarantee that

HOSTILE (14)

Gn 31:52 shall be witness, that, with h intent,
1Kgs 8:46 that their captors deport them to a h land,
1Mc 9:29 and those who are h to our nation.
11:41 for they were constantly h to Israel.
15:27 made with Simon and became h toward him.
2Mc 6:29 now became h toward him because what he
14:11 the other Friends who were h to Judas
Ps(s) 8: 3 foes, to silence the h and the vengeful.
106:10 He saved them from h hands and freed them
Sir 36: 9 crush the heads of the h rulers.
46: 6 Which he rained down upon the h army till
47: 7 He destroyed the h Philistines and
Is 11:13 Judah, and Judah shall not be h to Ephraim;
1Thes 2:15 Displeasing to God and h to all mankind,

HOSTILITIES (1)

Gal 5:20 licentiousness, idolatry, sorcery, h,

HOSTILITY (12)

Dt 2: 9 *h* to the Moabites or engage them in battle,
2:19 not show *h* or come in conflict with them,
1Mc 13:17 fear of provoking much *h* among the people,
2Mc 4: 3 When Simon's *h* reached such a point that
Prv 10:18 It is the lips of the liar that conceal *h*;
Sir 37:10 advice from one who regards you with *h*;
Hos 9: 7 iniquity is great, great, too, is your *h*.
9: 8 on all his ways, *h* in the house of his God.
Lk 11:53 Pharisees began to manifest fierce *h* to him
Eph 2:14 down the barrier of *h* that kept us apart.
Col 1:21 you nourished *h* in your hearts because of
Ti 2: 8 to say about us, and *h* will yield to shame.

HOSTS (301)

Ex 7: 4 judgment I will bring the *h* of my people,
12:41 all the *h* of the LORD left the land of
Dt 4:19 the moon or any star among the heavenly *h*,
1Sm 1: 3 of *h* and to sacrifice to him at Shiloh,
1:11 "O LORD of *h*, if you look with pity
4: 4 from there the ark of the LORD of *h*,
15: 2 This is what the LORD of *h* has to say:
17:45 against you in the name of the LORD of *h*,
2Sm 5:10 powerful, for the LORD of *h* was with him.
6: 2 the LORD of *h* enthroned above the cherubim.
6:18 the people in the name of the LORD of *h*.
7: 8 David, 'The LORD of *h* has this to say:
7:26 men say, 'The LORD of *h* is God of Israel,'
7:27 It is you, LORD of *h*, God of Israel
1Kgs 18:15 Elijah answered, "As the LORD of *h* lives,
19:10 been zealous for the LORD, the God of *h*,
19:14 most zealous for the LORD, the God of *h*.
2Kgs 3:14 Then Elisha said, "As the LORD of *h* lives,
19:31 The zeal of the LORD of *h* shall do this.'
1Chr 11: 9 powerful, for the LORD of *h* was with him.
17: 7 my servant David, Thus says the LORD of *h*:
17:24 promised, that your renown as LORD of *h*,
Neh 9: 6 and the heavenly *h* bow down before you.
2Mc 15:21 Maccabeus, contemplating the *h* before him,
Ps(s) 24:10 The LORD of *h*; he is the king of glory.
46: 4 The LORD of *h* is with us;
46: 8 melts away, The LORD of *h* is with us;
46:12 The LORD of *h* is with us;
48: 9 have we seen in the city of the LORD of *h*,
59: 6 and aid me, for you are the LORD of *h*,
68:13 "Kings and their *h* are fleeing,
69: 7 put to shame through me, O Lord, GOD of *h*.
80: 4 O LORD of *h*, restore us;
80: 5 O LORD of *h*, how long will you burn
80: 8 O LORD of *h*, restore us;
80:15 Once again, O LORD of *h*,
80:20 O LORD of *h*, restore us;
84: 2 lovely is your dwelling place, O LORD of *h*!
84: 4 Your altars, O LORD of *h*,
84: 9 O LORD of *h*, hear my prayer
84:13 O LORD of *h*, happy the men who trust
89: 9 O LORD, God of *h*, who is like you?
103:21 Bless the LORD, all you his *h*,
148: 2 you his angels, praise him, all you his *h*.
Sir 17:27 God watches over the *h* of highest heaven,
24: 2 presence of his *h* she declares her worth:
42:17 LORD, Though God has given these, his *h*,
Is 1: 9 the LORD of *h* had left us a scanty remnant,
1:24 therefore, says the Lord, the LORD of *h*,
2:12 For the LORD of *h* will have his day
3: 1 The Lord, the LORD of *h*, shall take away
3:15 says the Lord, the GOD of *h*.
5: 7 of the LORD of *h* is the house of Israel,
5: 9 In my hearing the LORD of *h* has sworn:
5:16 LORD of *h* shall be exalted by his judgment,
5:24 have spurned the law of the LORD of *h*,
6: 3 "Holy, holy, holy is the Lord of *h*!"
6: 5 my eyes have seen the King, the LORD of *h*!"
8:13 But with the LORD of *h* make your alliance
8:18 the LORD of *h* who dwells on Mount Zion.
9: 6 The zeal of the LORD of *h* will do this!
9:12 who struck them, nor seek the LORD of *h*.
9:18 the wrath of the LORD of *h* the land quakes,
10:16 Therefore the Lord, the LORD of *h*,
10:23 he has decreed, the Lord, the GOD of *h*,
10:24 thus says the Lord, the GOD of *h*:
10:26 Then the LORD of *h* will raise against them
10:33 Behold, the Lord, the LORD of *h*,
13: 4 LORD of *h* is mustering an army for battle.
13:13 LORD of *h* on the day of his burning anger.
14:22 rise up against them, says the LORD of *h*,
14:23 broom of destruction, says the LORD of *h*.
14:24 The LORD of *h* has sworn:
14:27 The LORD of *h* has planned;
17: 3 as the Israelites, says the LORD of *h*.
18: 7 LORD of *h* from a people tall and bronzed,
18: 7 where dwells the name of the LORD of *h*.
19: 4 over them, says the LORD, the LORD of *h*.
19:12 the LORD of *h* has planned against Egypt.
19:16 of the LORD of *h* shaking his fist at them.
19:17 which the LORD of *h* has in mind for them.
19:18 of Canaan and swearing by the LORD of *h*;
19:20 to the LORD of *h* in the land of Egypt,
19:25 of the land, when the LORD of *h* blesses it:
21:10 What I have heard from the LORD of *h*,
22: 5 and confusion, from the Lord, the GOD of *h*,
22:12 On that day the Lord, the GOD of *h*,
22:14 This reaches the ears of the LORD of *h*—
22:14 till you die, says the Lord, the GOD of *h*.
22:15 Thus says the Lord, the GOD of *h*:
22:25 On that day, says the LORD of *h*,
23: 9 The LORD of *h* has planned it,
24:23 For the LORD of *h* will reign on Mount Zion
25: 6 On this mountain the LORD of *h* will
28: 5 On that day the LORD of *h* will be a
28:22 I have heard from the Lord, the GOD of *h*,
28:29 This too comes from the LORD of *h*;
29: 6 you shall be visited by the LORD of *h*,
31: 4 So shall the LORD of *h* come down to wage
31: 5 so the LORD of *h* shall shield Jerusalem,
37:16 "O LORD of *h*, God of Israel,
37:32 The zeal of the LORD of *h* shall do this.
39: 5 Hezekiah, "Hear the word of the LORD of *h*:
44: 6 Israel's King and redeemer, the LORD of *h*:
45:13 price or ransom, says the LORD of *h*.
47: 4 our redeemer, Whose name is the LORD of *h*,
48: 2 God of Israel, whose name is the LORD of *h*.
51:15 the LORD of *h* by name.
54: 5 his name is the LORD of *h*;
Jer 2:19 no fear of me, says the Lord, the GOD of *h*.
5:14 have said, says the LORD, the God of *h*—
6: 6 For thus says the LORD of *h*:
6: 9 Thus says the LORD of *h*:
7: 3 says the LORD of *h*, the God of Israel:
7:21 says the LORD of *h*, the God of Israel:
8: 3 to which I banish them, says the LORD of *h*.
9: 6 Therefore, thus says the LORD of *h*:
9:14 therefore, thus says the LORD of *h*,
9:16 says the LORD of *h*: Attention! tell the wailing
10:16 his very own tribe, LORD of *h* is his name.
11:17 The LORD of *h* who planted you has decreed
11:20 But, you, O LORD of *h*, O just Judge,
11:22 Therefore, thus says the LORD of *h*:
15:16 Because I bore your name, O LORD, God of *h*.
16: 9 For thus says the LORD of *h*,
19: 3 Thus says the LORD of *h*,
19:11 Thus says the LORD of *h*: Thus will I smash
19:15 Thus says the LORD of *h*,
20:12 O LORD of *h*, you who test the just,
23:15 says the LORD of *h* against the prophets:
23:16 the LORD of *h*: Listen not to the words
23:36 the words of the living God, the LORD of *h*,
25: 8 Hence, thus says the LORD of *h*:
25:27 Thus says the LORD of *h*,
25:28 Thus says the LORD of *h*:
25:29 who inhabit the earth, says the LORD of *h*.
25:32 Thus says the LORD of *h*:
26:18 Thus says the LORD of *h*:
27: 4 Thus says the LORD of *h*, the God of Israel:
27:18 they would intercede with the LORD of *h*,
27:19 says the LORD of *h* concerning the pillars,
27:21 yes, thus says the LORD of *h*,
28: 2 says the LORD of *h*, the God of Israel:
28:14 For thus says the LORD of *h*,
29: 4 Thus says the LORD of *h*,
29: 8 thus says the LORD of *h*,
29:17 thus says the LORD of *h*:
29:21 This is what the LORD of *h*,
29:25 Thus says the LORD of *h*,
30: 8 On that day, says the LORD of *h*,
31:23 Thus says the LORD of *h*,
31:35 its waves roar, whose name is LORD of *h*:
32:14 Thus says the LORD of *h*,
32:15 For thus says the LORD of *h*,
32:18 great and mighty, whose name is LORD of *h*,
33:11 singing, "Give thanks to the LORD of *h*,
33:12 Thus says the LORD of *h*:
35:13 Thus says the LORD of *h*,
35:17 Now, therefore, says the LORD God of *h*,
35:18 Thus says the LORD of *h*,
35:19 you, thus therefore says the LORD of *h*,
38:17 Thus says the LORD God of *h*,
39:16 Thus says the LORD of *h*,
42:15 Thus says the LORD of *h*,
42:18 For thus says the LORD of *h*,
43:10 Thus says the LORD of *h*,
44: 2 Thus says the LORD of *h*,
44: 7 Now thus says the LORD God of *h*,
44:11 Hence, thus says the LORD of *h*,
44:25 Thus says the LORD of *h*,
46:10 But this is the day of the Lord GOD of *h*,
46:10 *h* holds a slaughter feast in the northland,
46:18 says the King whose name is LORD of *h*,
46:25 The LORD of *h*, the God of Israel, has said
48: 1 Concerning Moab, thus says the LORD of *h*,
48:15 says the King, the LORD of *h* by name.
49: 5 terror upon you, says the LORD GOD of *h*,
49: 7 Concerning Edom, thus says the LORD of *h*:
49:26 On that day, says the LORD of *h*,
49:35 Thus says the LORD of *h*:
50:18 Therefore, thus says the LORD of *h*,
50:25 For the Lord GOD of *h* has work to do in
50:31 man of insolence, says the Lord GOD of *h*;
50:33 Thus says the LORD of *h*:
50:34 is their avenger, whose name is LORD of *h*;
51: 5 not widowed of their God, the LORD of *h*,
51:14 The LORD of *h* has sworn by himself:
51:19 his very own tribe, LORD of *h* is his name.
51:33 For thus says the LORD of *h*,
51:57 says the King, whose name is the LORD of *h*.
51:58 Thus says the LORD of *h*:
Dn 3:61 All you *h* of the Lord,
Hos 12: 6 The LORD, the God of *h*,
Am 3:13 of Jacob, says the Lord GOD, the God of *h*:
4:13 The LORD, The God of *h* by name.
5:14 Then truly will the LORD, the God of *h*,
5:15 it may be that the LORD, the God of *h*,
5:16 thus says the LORD, the God of *h*,
5:27 say I, the LORD, the God of *h* by name.
6: 8 very self, say I, the LORD, the God of *h*:
6:14 of Israel, say I, the LORD, the God of *h*,
9: 5 and not for good, I, the Lord GOD of *h*,
Mi 4: 4 for the mouth of the LORD of *h* has spoken.
Na 2:14 I come against you, says the LORD of *h*;
Hb 2:13 Is not this from the LORD of *h*:
Zep 2: 9 Therefore, as I live, says the LORD of *h*,
2:10 against the people of the LORD of *h*.
Hg 1: 2 Thus says the LORD of *h*:
1: 5 Now thus says the LORD of *h*:
1: 7 Thus says the LORD of *h*:
1: 9 says the LORD of *h*.
1:14 set to work on the house of the LORD of *h*,
2: 4 For I am with you, says the LORD of *h*.
2: 6 For thus says the LORD of *h*:
2: 7 this house with glory, says the LORD of *h*.
2: 8 and mine the gold says the LORD of *h*.
2: 9 house than the former, says the LORD of *h*;
2: 9 I will give you peace, says the LORD of *h*.
2:11 Thus says the LORD of *h*:
2:23 On that day, says the LORD of *h*,
Zec 1: 3 Thus says the LORD of *h*:
1: 3 Return to me, says the LORD of *h*,
1: 3 I will return to you, says the LORD of *h*.
1: 4 Thus says the LORD of *h*.
1: 6 The LORD of *h* has treated us according to
1:12 LORD spoke out and said, "O LORD of *h*,
1:14 Thus says the LORD of *h*:
1:16 shall be built in it, says the LORD of *h*,
1:17 Thus says the LORD of *h*:
2:12 For thus said the LORD of *h* (after he had
2:13 shall know that the LORD of *h* has sent me.
2:15 know that the LORD of *h* has sent me to you.
3: 7 "Thus says the LORD of *h*:
3: 9 its inscription, says the LORD of *h*,
3:10 On that day, says the LORD of *h*,
4: 6 but by my spirit, says the LORD of *h*.
4: 9 know that the LORD of *h* has sent me to you.
5: 4 I will send it forth, says the LORD of *h*,
6:12 Thus says the LORD of *h*:
6:15 know that the LORD of *h* has sent me to you.
7: 3 the priests of the house of the LORD of *h*,
7: 4 this word of the LORD of *h* came to me:
7: 9 Thus says the LORD of *h*:
7:12 message that the LORD of *h* had sent
7:13 the LORD of *h* in his great anger said that,
8: 1 This word of the LORD of *h* came:
8: 2 Thus says the LORD of *h*:
8: 3 city, and the mountain of the LORD of *h*,
8: 4 Thus says the LORD of *h*:
8: 6 Thus says the LORD of *h*:
8: 6 in my eyes also, says the LORD of *h*?
8: 7 Thus says the LORD of *h*:
8: 9 Thus says the LORD of *h*:
8: 9 *h* was laid for the building of the temple.
8:11 as in former days, says the LORD of *h*,
8:14 Thus says the LORD of *h*:
8:14 provoked me to wrath, says the LORD of *h*,
8:18 This word of the LORD of *h* came to me:
8:19 Thus says the LORD of *h*: The fast days
8:20 says the LORD of *h*: These shall yet come
8:22 nations shall come to seek the LORD of *h*
8:23 says the LORD of *h*: In those days ten men
9:15 The LORD of *h* shall be a shield over them,
10: 3 For the LORD of *h* will visit his flock,
12: 5 have their strength in the LORD of *h*.
13: 2 On that day, says the LORD of *h*,
13: 7 who is my associate, says the LORD of *h*.
14:16 year to worship the King, the LORD of *h*,
14:17 to worship the King, the LORD of *h*,
14:21 in Judah shall be holy to the LORD of *h*;
14:21 any merchant in the house of the LORD of *h*.
Mal 1: 4 the ruins," Thus says the LORD of *h*:
1: 6 So says the LORD of *h* to you, O priests
1: 8 it, or welcome you, says the LORD of *h*.
1: 9 says the LORD of *h*.
1:10 no pleasure in you, says the LORD of *h*;
1:11 name among the nations, says the LORD of *h*.
1:13 and you scorn it, says the LORD of *h*;
1:14 For a great King am I, says the LORD of *h*,
2: 2 give glory to my name, says the LORD of *h*,
2: 4 a covenant with Levi, says the LORD of *h*.
2: 7 he is the messenger of the LORD of *h*.
2: 8 the covenant of Levi, says the LORD of *h*.
2:12 anyone to offer sacrifice to the LORD of *h*!
2:16 with injustice, says the LORD of *h*;
3: 1 Yes, he is coming, says the LORD of *h*.
3: 5 who do not fear me, says the LORD of *h*,
3: 7 I will return to you, says the LORD of *h*.
3:10 and try me in this, says the LORD of *h*:
3:11 will not be barren, says the LORD of *h*.
3:12 be a delightful land, says the LORD of *h*.
3:14 penitential dress in awe of the LORD of *h*?
3:17 they shall be mine, says the LORD of *h*,

HOSTS (cont.)

3:19 root nor branch, says the LORD of h.
3:21 the day I take action, says the LORD of h.
3:24 root nor branch, says the LORD of h.
Mt 24:29 and the h of heaven will be shaken loose.'
Mk 13:25 skies, and the heavenly h will be shaken.
Rom 9:29 the Lord of h had left us a remnant,
Jas 5: 4 have reached the ears of the Lord of h.

HOT (11)

Gn 18: 1 of his tent, while the day was growing h.
Ex 11: 8 that he left Pharaoh's presence in h anger.
16:21 but when the sun grew h,
1Sm 11: 9 that tomorrow, while the sun is h,
Neh 7: 3 are not to be opened until the sun is h,
Ps(s) 39: 4 h grew my heart within me;
Ez 24:11 on the coals till its metal glows red h,
Lk 12:55 the south, you say it is going to be h—
Rv 3:15 I know you are neither h nor cold.
3:15 I wish you were one or the other h or cold!
3:16 you are lukewarm, neither h nor cold,

HOTHAM (3)

1Chr 7:32 became the father of Japhlet, Shomer, H,
7:35 The sons of his brother H were Zophah,
11:44 Shama and Jeiel, sons of H,

HOTHEADED (2)

Prv 22:24 Be not friendly with a h man,
29:22 and a h man is the cause of many sins.

HOTHIR (2)

1Chr 25: 4 Romamti-ezer, Joshbekashah, Mallothi, H,
25:28 The twenty-first fell to H,

HOUND (2)

Gn 31:36 "that you should h me so fiercely?
Jb 19:22 Why do you h me as though you were divine,

HOUR (53)

Gn 35: 3 God who answered me in my h of distress
Ex 9:18 tomorrow at this h I will rain down such
Jdt 13: 4 in this h look graciously on my
Est F: 8 These two lots were fulfilled in the h,
2Mc 8:26 to return by reason of the late h,
Ps(s) 104:19 the sun knows the h of its setting.
Sir 10: 4 God, who raises up on it the man of the h;
29: 2 Lend to your neighbor in his h of need,
Mt 10:19 When the h comes, you will be given
24:36 "As for the exact day or h, no one knows
25:13 open, for you know not the day or the h.
26:40 could not stay awake with me for even an h?
26:45 The h is on us when the Son of Man is to
Mk 13:11 In that h, say what you are inspired to say
13:32 "As to the exact day or h,
14:35 it were possible this h might pass him by.
14:37 You could not stay awake for even an h?
14:41 The h is on us.
Lk 1:10 was praying outside at the incense h,
22:14 When the h arrived, he took his place
22:53 But this is your h—
22:59 About an h after that another spoke more
Jn 2: 4 My h has not yet come."
4: 6 The h was about noon.
4:21 an h is coming when you will worship the
4:23 Yet an h is coming, and is already here,
4:53 It was at that very h,
5:25 I solemnly assure you, an h is coming,
5:28 for an h is coming in which all those in
7:30 on him because his h had not yet come.
8:20 because his h had not yet come.
12:23 "The h has come for the Son of Man to be
12:27 Father, save me from this h?
12:27 But it was for this that I came to this h.
13: 1 Jesus realized that the h had come for him
16: 4 when their h comes you may remember
16:32 An h is coming—has indeed already come
17: 1 "Father, the h has come!
19:14 Day for Passover, and the h was about noon.)
19:27 From that h onward, the disciple took her
Acts 3: 1 temple for prayer at the three o'clock h,
10:30 "Just three days ago at this very h,
16:33 At that late h of the night he took them
Rom 13:11 It is now the h for you to wake from sleep,
1Cor 4:11 Up to this very h we go hungry and thirsty,
1Jn 2:18 Children, it is the final h;
2:18 makes us certain that it is the final h.
Rv 8: 1 was silence in heaven for about half an h.
9:15 this was precisely the h,
17:12 along with the beast, but only for an h.
18:10 In a single h your doom has come!"
18:17 h this great wealth has been destroyed!"
18:19 a single h her destruction has come about!"

HOURS (5)

Ps(s) 134: 1 house of the LORD during the h of night.
Mt 20:12 'This last group did only an h work,
Jn 11: 9 "Are there not twelve h of daylight?
Acts 5: 7 Three h later Ananias' wife came in,
19:34 and kept shouting for about two h.

HOUSE (1256)

Gn 12: 1 father's h to a land that I will show you.
14:14 eighteen of his retainers, born in his h,
15: 2 and have as my heir the steward of my h,
17:23 born in his h or acquired with his money
17:27 including the slaves born in his h
19: 2 aside into your servant's h for the night,
19: 3 aside to his place and entered his h.
19: 4 closed in on the h.
19: 5 are the men who came to your h tonight?
19:11 struck the men at the entrance of the h,
20:13 God sent me wandering from my father's h,
24: 7 from my father's h and the land of my kin,
24:23 your father's h for us to spend the night?"
24:27 straight to the h of my master's brother."
24:31 when I have made the h ready for you,
24:38 instead, you shall go to my father's h,
24:40 son from my own kindred of my father's h.
27:15 her older son Esau that she had in the h,
28:21 and I come back safe to my father's h,
29:13 and kissing him, he brought him to his h.
31:14 still an heir's portion in our father's h?
31:30 desperately homesick for your father's h,
34:26 they took Dinah from Shechem's h and left.
38:11 father's h until my son Shelah grows up"
38:11 So Tamar went to live in her father's h.
39: 5 blessed the Egyptian's h for Joseph's sake;
39: 5 he owned, both inside the h and out.
39: 8 not concern himself with anything in the h,
39: 9 no more authority in this h than I do,
39:11 when Joseph came into the h to do his work,
39:11 the household servants were then in the h,
40: 3 in custody in the h of the chief steward
40: 7 were with him in custody in his master's h,
41:10 in custody in the h of the chief steward.
43:16 head steward, "Take these men into the h,
43:17 steward conducted the men to Joseph's h.
43:18 But on being led to his h,
43:19 and talked to him at the entrance of the h.
43:24 then brought the men inside Joseph's h.
44: 8 steal silver or gold from your master's h?
44:14 and his brothers reentered Joseph's h,
Ex 2: 1 of the h of Levi married a Levite woman,
3:22 ask her neighbor and her h guest for silver
7:23 He turned away and went into his h,
8:20 Thick swarms of flies entered the h of
12: 7 every h in which they partake of the lamb.
12:30 for there was not a h without its dead.
12:46 It must be eaten in one and the same h;
12:46 not take any of its flesh outside the h.
19: 3 "Thus shall you say to the h of Jacob;
20:17 "You shall not covet your neighbor's h.
22: 6 and it is stolen from the latter's h,
22: 7 the owner of the h shall be brought to God,
23:19 soil you shall bring to the h of the LORD,
34:26 soil you shall bring to the h of the LORD,
40:38 fire was seen in the cloud by the whole h
Lv 10: 6 Your kinsmen, the rest of the h of Israel,
14:34 infection on any h of the land you occupy,
14:35 the h shall come and report to the priest,
14:35 'It looks to me as if my h were infected.'
14:36 The priest shall then order the h to be
14:36 lest everything in the h become unclean.
14:36 after this is he to go in to examine the h.
14:37 infection on the walls of the h
14:38 of the h behind him and quarantine the h
14:39 priest shall return to examine the h again.
14:41 inside of the h shall then be scraped,
14:42 shall be made and plastered on the h.
14:43 and the h has been scraped and replastered,
14:44 in the h, it is corrosive leprosy, and the h
14:46 Whoever enters a h while it is quarantined
14:47 in such a h shall also wash his garments.
14:48 finds, when he comes to examine the h,
14:48 plastering, he shall declare the h clean,
14:49 To purify the h, he shall take two birds,
14:51 water, and sprinkle the h seven times.
14:52 Thus shall he purify the h with the bird's
14:53 made atonement for it, the h will be clean.
17: 8 whether of the h of Israel or of the
17:10 whether of the h of Israel or of the
22:11 who is born in his h may eat of his food.
22:13 no children, returns to her father's h,
22:18 When anyone of the h of Israel,
25:30 But if such a h in a walled town has not
25:33 Any town h of the Levites in their cities
27:14 dedicates his h as sacred to the LORD,
27:15 who dedicated his h wishes to redeem it,
Nm 1: 4 each tribe, the head of his ancestral h.
1:18 lineage according to clan and ancestral h,
1:44 each according to his ancestral h,
2:34 according to his clan and his ancestral h.
3:24 prince of their ancestral h was Eliasaph,
3:30 prince of their ancestral h was Elizaphan,
3:35 h of the clans of Merari was Zuriel,
12: 7 Throughout my h he bears my trust:
17:17 one staff from them for each ancestral h,
17:18 Levi's ancestral h shall also have a staff.
17:23 Aaron's staff, representing the h of Levi,
18: 1 h shall be responsible for the sanctuary;
20:29 days the whole h of Israel mourned him.
22:18 gave me his h full of silver and gold,
24:13 gave me his h full of silver and gold,
25:14 prince of an ancestral h of the Simeonites.
25:15 who was head of a clan, an ancestral h,
30: 4 while still a maiden in her father's h,
30:11 "If it is in her husband's h that she
30:17 she is still a maiden in her father's h.
Dt 5:21 not desire your neighbor's h or field,
6:22 Egypt and against Pharaoh and his whole h.
7:26 bring any abominable thing into your h,
20: 5 a new h and not yet had the house-warming?
21:12 as wife, you may take her home to your h.
22: 8 "When you build a new h,
22: 8 off, you will bring bloodguilt upon your h.
22:21 girl to the entrance of her father's h
22:21 by her unchasteness in her father's h.
23:19 of votive offering in the h of the LORD,
24: 1 it to her, thus dismissing her from his h:
24: 2 if on leaving his h she goes and becomes
24: 3 h by handing her a written bill of divorce;
24:10 enter his h to receive a pledge from him,
25:14 you keep two different measures in your h,
26:13 'I have purged my h of the sacred portion
28:12 for you his rich treasure h of the heavens,
28:30 Though you build a h,
Jos 2: 1 went into the h of a harlot named Rahab,
2: 3 out the visitors who have entered your h,
2:15 she lived in a h built into the city wall.
2:18 brothers and all your family into your h.
2:19 of them pass outside the doors of your h,
2:19 if anyone in the h with you is harmed.
6:17 are in the h with her are to be spared,
6:22 h and bring out the woman with all her kin,
6:24 in the treasury of the h of the LORD.
9:23 and drawers of water] for the h of my God."
17:17 to Ephraim and Manasseh, the h of Joseph,
18: 5 h of Joseph its territory in the north.
21:45 LORD made to the h of Israel was broken;
22:14 and military leader of his ancestral h.
Jgs 1:22 h of Joseph, too, marched up
1:23 The h of Joseph had a reconnaissance made
1:35 as the h of Joseph gained the upper hand,
6:15 am the most insignificant in my father's h."
9: 5 He then went to his ancestral h in Ophrah,
10: 9 Judah, Benjamin, and the h of Ephraim,
11: 7 hated me and drove me from my father's h?"
11:31 comes out of the doors of my h to meet me
11:34 When Jephthah returned to his h in Mizpah,
12: 1 We will burn your h over you."
17: 4 It remained in the h of Micah.
17: 8 On his journey he came to the h of Micah
17:12 who became his priest, remaining in his h.
18: 2 they traveled as far as the h of Micah in
18: 3 Near the h of Micah,
18:13 of Ephraim and came to the h of Micah.
18:15 they went to the h of the young Levite at
18:17 land went up and entered the h of Micah.
18:31 made as long as the h of God was in Shiloh.
19: 2 for her father's h in Bethlehem of Judah,
19: 3 She brought him into her father's h,
19:18 no one has offered us the shelter of his h.
19:21 to his h and provided fodder for the asses.
19:22 surrounded the h and beat on the door.
19:22 They said to the old man whose h it was,
19:23 owner of the h went out to them and said,
19:26 of the h in which her husband was a guest,
19:27 of the h to start out again on his journey,
19:27 of the h with her hands on the threshold.
20: 5 night and surrounded the h in which I was.
Ru 1: 8 "Go back, each of you, to your mother's h!
4:11 wife come into your h like Rachel and Leah,
4:11 who between them built up the h of Israel.
4:12 may your h become like the house of Perez,
1Sm 2:27 in Egypt as slaves to the h of Pharaoh.
2:35 I will establish a lasting h for him which
7: 1 it into the h of Abinadab on the hill,
18: 2 not allow him to return to his father's h.
18:10 God came over Saul, and he raged in his h.
19: 9 came upon Saul as he was sitting in his h
19:10 sent messengers to David's h to guard it,
20:15 never withdraw your kindness from my h.
21:16 Should this fellow come into my h?"
22:14 your bodyguard, and honored in your own h?
25:36 party in his h like that of a king,
28:24 The woman had a stall-fed calf in the h,
2Sm 3: 1 between the h of Saul and that of David,
3: 1 grew stronger, but the h of Saul weaker.
3: 6 between the h of Saul and that of David,
3: 6 Abner was gaining power in the h of Saul.
3: 8 a kindness to the h of your father Saul,
3:10 take away the kingdom from the h of Saul
3:19 to Israel and to the whole h of Benjamin.
4: 5 h of Ishbaal during the heat of the day,
4: 6 of the h had dozed off while sifting wheat,
4: 7 entered the h while Ishbaal was lying asleep
6: 3 away from the h of Abinadab on the hill.
6:10 it to the h of Obed-edom the Gittite.
6:11 The ark of the LORD remained in the h of
6:11 the LORD blessed Obed-edom and his whole h.
6:12 ark of God from the h of Obed-edom
7: 2 "Here I am living in a h of cedar,
7: 5 Should you build me a h to dwell in?
7: 6 I have not dwelt in a h from the day on
7: 7 Why have you not built me a h of cedar?'

7:11 to you that he will establish a *h* for you.
7:13 It is he who shall build a *h* for my name.
7:16 Your *h* and your kingdom shall endure
7:18 GOD, and who are the members of my *h*,
7:19 *h* of your Servant for a long time to come:
7:25 made concerning your servant and his *h*,
7:26 and the *h* of your servant David stands
7:27 to your servant, 'I will build a *h* for you.'
7:29 bless the *h* of your servant that it may be
7:29 and by your blessing the *h* of your servant
9: 1 "Is there any survivor of Saul's *h*
9: 3 Saul's *h* to whom I may show God's kindness?"
9: 4 Ziba answered, "He is in the *h* of Machir,
9: 5 and had him brought from the *h* of Machir,
11: 4 She then returned to her *h*.
11: 8 "Go down to your *h* and bathe your feet."
11: 9 his lord, and did not go down to his own *h*.
11:10 Why, then, did you not go down to your *h*?"
11:27 sent for her and brought her into his *h*.
12: 8 *h* and your lord's wives for your own.
12: 8 I gave you the *h* of Israel and of Judah.
12:10 the sword shall never depart from your *h*,
12:11 will bring evil upon you out of your own *h*.
12:15 Then Nathan returned to his *h*.
12:17 The elders of his *h* stood beside him
12:20 he went to the *h* of the LORD and worshiped.
12:20 He returned to his own *h*,
13: 7 "Please go to the *h* of your brother Amnon
13: 8 Tamar went to the *h* of her brother Amnon,
13:20 forlorn in the *h* of her brother Absalom.
14:24 the king said, "Let him go to his own *h*;
14:24 his *h* and did not appear before the king.
14:31 went to Absalom in his *h* and asked him,
17:18 They sped on their way and reached the *h*
17:20 servants came to the woman at the *h*,
19:18 Ziba, too, the servant of the *h* of Saul,
19:21 have been the first of the whole *h* of Joseph
19:29 For though my father's entire *h* deserved
21: 4 against Saul and his *h* for silver or gold,
23: 5 Is not my *h* firm before God?
1Kgs 2:27 LORD had made in Shiloh about the *h* of Eli.
2:33 for David, and his descendants, and his *h*,
2:34 he was buried in his *h* in the desert.
2:36 yourself a *h* in Jerusalem and live there.
3:17 same *h*, and I gave birth in the house
3:18 We were alone in the *h*;
6:19 to *h* the ark of the LORD's covenant,
8:13 I have truly built you a princely *h*,
11:18 king of Egypt, who gave Hadad a *h*,
11:28 the entire labor force of the *h* of Joseph.
12:16 Now look to your own *h*, David."
12:19 rebellion against David's *h* to this day.
12:20 David's *h* except the tribe of Judah alone.
12:21 the *h* of Judah and the tribe of Benjamin
12:21 to fight against the *h* of Israel,
12:23 and to the *h* of Judah and to Benjamin,
12:26 "The kingdom will return to David's *h*.
13: 2 'A child shall be born to the *h* of David,
13:18 bring you back with me to my *h*
13:19 and ate bread and drank water in his *h*.
13:34 This was a sin on the part of the *h* of
14: 4 entered the *H* of Ahijah who could not see
14: 8 I deprived the *h* of David of the kingdom
14:10 I am bringing evil upon the *h* of Jeroboam:
14:10 will burn up the *h* of Jeroboam completely,
14:13 *h* has something pleasing to the LORD,
14:14 Israel who will destroy the *h* of Jeroboam.
14:17 Tirzah and crossed the threshold of her *h*,
15:27 son of Ahijah, of the *h* of Issachar,
15:29 he killed off the entire *h* of Jeroboam,
16: 3 your house; I will make your *h* like that
16: 7 LORD had threatened Baasha and his *h*
16: 7 so that he became like the *h* of Jeroboam;
16: 9 drinking to excess in the *h* of Arza,
16:11 he killed off the whole *h* of Baasha,
16:12 Zimri destroyed the entire *h* of Baasha,
17:17 the son of the mistress of the *h* fell sick,
17:23 Elijah brought him down into the *h* from
20: 6 your *h* and the houses of your servants.
21: 2 garden, since it is close by, next to my *h*.
21:22 I will make your *h* like that of Jeroboam,
21:29 upon his *h* during the reign of his son."
2Kgs 4: 2 "Tell me what you have in the *h*."
4: 2 has nothing in the *h* but a jug of oil,"
4:32 When Elisha reached the *h*,
5: 9 and stopped at the door of Elisha's *h*.
5:24 took what they had, carried it into the *h*,
6:32 in his *h* in conference with the elders.
8: 3 to the king to claim her *h* and her field.
8: 5 came to the king to claim her *h* and field.
8:27 He conducted himself like the *h* of Ahab,
9: 6 Jehu got up and went into the *h*.
9: 7 shall destroy the *h* of Ahab your master;
9: 9 of Ahab as I dealt with the *h* of Jeroboam,
9: 9 son of Nebat, and with the *h* of Baasha,
10: 3 throne, and fight for your master's *h*."
10:10 against the *h* of Ahab shall go unfulfilled.
10:30 and have treated the *h* of Ahab as I desire,
13: 6 *h* of Jeroboam had caused Israel to commit,
15: 5 He lived in a *h* apart,
17:21 he tore Israel away from the *h* of David,
19:30 remaining survivors of the *h* of Judah
20: 1 'Put your *h* in order,

20:13 there was nothing in his *h* or in all his
20:15 "What did they see in your *h*?"
20:15 "They saw everything in my *h*,"
20:17 time is coming when all that is in your *h*,
21:13 with the plummet I used for the *h* of Ahab.
25: 9 He burned the *h* of the LORD,
25:13 pillars that belonged to the *h* of the LORD,
25:13 and the bronze sea in the *h* of the LORD,
25:16 Solomon had made for the *h* of the LORD,
1Chr 6:16 with the choir services in the LORD's *h*
6:33 services of the Dwelling of the *h* of God.
7:23 Beriah, since evil had befallen his *h*.
9:11 son of Ahitub, the ruler of the *h* of God;
9:13 the work of the service of the *h* of God.
9:19 his brethren of the same ancestral *h*
9:23 gates of the *h* of the LORD, the house
9:26 the chambers and treasures of the *h* of God.
9:27 At night they lodged about the *h* of God,
10: 6 three sons, his whole *h* died at one time.
10:10 His armor they put in the *h* of their gods,
12:29 with twenty-two princes of his father's *h*.
12:30 had held their allegiance to the *h* of Saul.
13: 7 God on a new cart from the *h* of Abinadab;
13:13 instead to the *h* of Obed-edom the Gittite.
13:14 The ark of God remained in the *h* of
14: 1 and cedar wood to build him a *h*.
15:25 the LORD with joy from the *h* of Obed-edom.
17: 1 David had taken up residence in his *h*,
17: 1 "See, I am living in a *h* of cedar,
17: 4 who are to build a *h* for me to dwell in.
17: 5 For I have never dwelt in a *h*,
17: 6 'Why have you not built me a *h* of cedar?'
17:10 you that I, the LORD, will build you a *h*;
17:12 He it is who shall build me a *h*,
17:14 him in my *h* and in my kingdom forever,
17:23 your servant and his *h* remain firm forever.
17:24 and abide forever, while the *h* of David,
17:25 your servant that you will build him a *h*,
17:27 deigned to bless the *h* of your servant,
22: 1 said, "This is the *h* of the LORD God,
22: 2 out stone blocks for building the *h* of God.
22: 5 but the *h* that is to be built for the LORD
22: 6 commanded him to build a *h* for the LORD,
22: 7 build a *h* myself for the honor of the LORD,
22: 8 You may not build a *h* in my honor,
22:10 It is he who shall build a *h* in my honor;
22:11 in building the *h* of the LORD your God,
22:14 I have laid up for the *h* of the LORD
22:19 into the *h* built in honor of the LORD."
23: 4 to direct the service of the *h* of the LORD,
23:24 work of the service of the *h* of the LORD
23:28 Aaron in the service of the *h* of the LORD,
23:28 take part in the service of the *h* of God.
23:32 in the service of the *h* of the LORD.
24:19 when they functioned in the *h* of the LORD
25: 6 direction in the singing in the *h* of the LORD
25: 6 harps and lyres, serving in the *h* of God,
26:12 in the service of the *h* of the LORD,
26:20 superintended the stores for the *h* of God
26:22 the treasures of the *h* of the LORD.
26:27 for the enhancement of the *h* of the LORD.
28: 2 It was my purpose to build a *h* of repose
28: 3 to me, 'You may not build a *h* in my honor,
28: 6 Solomon who shall build my *h* and my courts,
28:10 chosen you to build a *h* as his sanctuary.
28:12 by way of courts for the *h* of the LORD,
28:12 compartments for the stores for the *h* of God
28:13 work of the service of the *h* of the LORD,
28:13 liturgical vessels of the *h* of the LORD.
28:20 work for the service of the *h* of the LORD.
28:21 ready for all the service of the *h* of God;
29: 2 I have stored up for the *h* of my God,
29: 3 of the delight I take in the *h* of my God,
29: 3 the holy *h*, I give to the *h* of my God
29: 7 contributed for the service of the *h* of God
29: 8 for the treasury of the *h* of the LORD.
29:16 we have brought together to build you a *h*
2Chr 1:18 a house to honor the LORD and also of a *h*
2: 2 him cedars to build a *h* for his dwelling,
2: 3 to build a *h* for the honor of the LORD,
2: 4 And the *h* I intend to build must be large,
2: 5 Yet who is really able to build him a *h*,
2: 5 And who am I that I should build him a *h*,
2: 8 since the *h* I intend to build must be
2:11 build a *h* for the LORD and also a house
3: 1 *h* of the LORD in Jerusalem on Mount Moriah,
3: 3 down by Solomon for building the *h* of God:
3: 4 the width of the *h* was also twenty cubits,
3: 7 The *h*, its beams and thresholds,
3: 8 corresponded to the width of the *h*,
4:11 had to do for King Solomon in the *h* of God:
4:16 from polished bronze for the *h* of the LORD.
4:19 all these articles made for the *h* of God:
4:22 As for the entry to the *h*,
5: 1 articles in the treasuries of the *h* of God.
5:14 since the LORD's glory filled the *h* of God.
6: 2 truly built you a princely *h* and dwelling,
6:33 and knowing that this *h* which I have built
6:34 and of the *h* I have built to your honor,
6:38 of the *h* which I have built to your honor,
7: 1 and the glory of the LORD filled the *h*.
7: 2 priests could not enter the *h* of the LORD,
7: 2 of the LORD had filled the *h* of the LORD.

7: 3 and the glory of the LORD was upon the *h*,
7: 6 and all the people dedicated the *h* of God.
7: 7 court which lay before the *h* of the LORD;
7:11 the *h* of the LORD and the royal palace;
7:11 to the *h* of the LORD and his own house.
7:12 chosen this place for my *h* of sacrifice.
7:16 this *h* that my name may be there forever;
7:20 *h* which I have consecrated to my honor,
7:21 LORD done this to this land and to this *h*?'
8: 1 built the *h* of the LORD and his own house,
8:11 wife of mine shall dwell in the *h* of David,
8:16 foundation of the *h* of the LORD was laid
9: 4 holocausts he offered in the *h* of the LORD,
10:16 Now look to your own *h*, David!"
10:19 in rebellion against David's *h* to this day.
11: 1 together the *h* of Judah and Benjamin,
15:18 He brought into the *h* of God his father's
19: 1 returned in safety to his *h* in Jerusalem.
19:11 is leader of the *h* of Judah in all that
20: 5 in the *h* of the LORD before the new court,
20: 9 we will stand before this *h* and before you,
20: 9 before you, for your name is in this *h*,
20:28 came to Jerusalem, to the *h* of the LORD,
21: 7 LORD would not destroy the *h* of David
21:13 into idolatry, as did the *h* of Ahab,
21:13 your father's *h* who were better than you,
22: 3 too, followed the ways of the *h* of Ahab,
22: 4 sight of the LORD, as did the *h* of Ahab,
22: 7 had anointed to cut down the *h* of Ahab.
22: 8 was executing judgment on the *h* of Ahab,
22: 9 There remained in Ahaziah's *h* no one
22:10 all the royal offspring of the *h* of Judah.
22:12 remained hidden with them in the *h* of God,
23: 3 a covenant with the king in the *h* of God.
23: 6 Let no one enter the LORD's *h* except the
23: 7 Whoever tries to enter the *h* must be slain.
23: 9 of king David which were in the *h* of God.
23:20 land, and led the king out of the LORD's *h*.
23:20 within the upper gate of the king's *h*,
24: 5 repair the *h* of your God over the years.
24: 7 her sons had damaged the *h* of God
24:13 *h* of God according to its original form,
24:27 him, and of his rebuilding of the *h* of God,
25:24 he found in the *h* of God with Obed-edom,
26:19 *h* of the LORD beside the altar of incense,
26:21 *h*, for he was excluded from the house
27: 3 He built the upper gate of the LORD's *h*
28:21 Though Ahaz plundered the LORD's *h*
28:24 of God's *h* and broke them in pieces.
28:24 He closed the doors of the LORD's *h* and
29: 3 doors of the LORD's *h* and repaired them.
29: 5 now and sanctify the *h* of the LORD,
29:15 the LORD's *h* in keeping with his words.
29:16 the interior of the LORD's *h* to cleanse it;
29:16 brought out to the court of the LORD's *h*,
29:17 consecrated the LORD's *h* during eight days,
29:18 have cleansed the entire *h* of the LORD,
29:20 of the city and went up to the LORD's *h*.
29:25 the Levites in the LORD's *h* with cymbals,
29:31 and thank offerings for the *h* of the LORD.
29:35 of the *h* of the LORD was reestablished.
30: 1 they should come to the *h* of the LORD
30:15 brought holocausts into the *h* of the LORD.
31:10 the priest Azariah, head of the *h* of Zadok,
31:10 bring the offerings to the *h* of the LORD,
31:11 be constructed in the *h* of the LORD.
31:13 of Azariah, the prefect of the *h* of God.
31:16 who were eligible to enter the *h* of the LORD
31:21 for the service of the *h* of God or for the
33: 5 heaven in the two courts of the LORD's *h*.
33: 7 an idol that he had carved in the *h* of God,
33: 7 "In this *h* and in Jerusalem which I have
33:15 gods and the idol from the LORD's *h*
33:15 the mount of the LORD's *h* and in Jerusalem,
33:24 him and put him to death in his own *h*.
34: 8 chamberlain, to restore the *h* of the LORD,
34: 9 brought to the *h* of God which the Levites,
34:10 to the master workmen in the *h* of the LORD,
34:10 pay the workmen in the LORD's *h*
34:14 had been deposited in the *h* of the LORD,
34:15 the book of the law in the *h* of the LORD."
34:17 metals deposited in the LORD's *h*
34:30 He went up to the *h* of the LORD with all
34:30 that had been found in the *h* of the LORD.
35: 2 them in the service of the Lord's *h*.
35: 3 the holy ark in the *h* built by Solomon,
35: 8 and Jehiel, prefects of the *h* of God,
36: 7 some of the vessels of the *h* of the LORD
36:18 All the utensils of the *h* of God,
36:18 LORD's *h* and of the king and his princes,
36:19 They burnt the *h* of God,
36:23 charged me to build him a *h* in Jerusalem,
Ezr 1: 2 charged me to build him a *h* in Jerusalem,
1: 4 offerings for the *h* of God in Jerusalem.'"
1: 5 up to build the *h* of the LORD in Jerusalem.
1: 7 had the utensils of the *h* of the LORD
1: 7 Jerusalem and placed in the *h* of his god.
2:36 of Jedaiah, who were of the *h* of Jeshua,
2:68 arrived at the *h* of the LORD in Jerusalem,
2:68 made freewill offerings for the *h* of God,
3: 8 their coming to the *h* of God in Jerusalem,
3: 8 to supervise the work on the *h* of the LORD.
3: 9 were engaged in the work on the *h* of God.

HOUSE (cont.)

3:11 foundation of the LORD's *h* had been laid.
3:12 the old men who had seen the former *h*,
3:12 the foundation of the present *h* being laid.
4: 3 to build with us a *h* for our God,
4:24 on the *h* of God in Jerusalem was halted.
5: 2 again to build the *h* of God in Jerusalem,
5: 3 you to build this *h* and raise this edifice?
5: 8 of Judah and the *h* of the great God:
5: 9 you to build this *h* and raise this edifice?'
5:11 rebuilding the *h* built here long years ago,
5:12 *h* and led the people captive to Babylon.
5:13 decree for the rebuilding of this *h* of God.
5:14 gold and silver utensils of the *h* of God
5:15 the *h* of God be rebuilt on its former site.
5:16 foundations of the *h* of God in Jerusalem.
5:17 rebuilding of this *h* of God in Jerusalem.
6: 3 The *h* of God in Jerusalem.
6: 3 The *h* is to be rebuilt as a place for
6: 5 gold and silver utensils of the *h* of God
6: 5 of Jerusalem and deposited in the *h* of God.
6: 7 the Jews continue to work on that *h* of God;
6: 8 Jews in the rebuilding of that *h* of God:
6:11 edict, a beam is to be taken from his *h*,
6:11 and his *h* is to be reduced to rubble for
6:12 or to destroy this *h* of God in Jerusalem.
6:15 this *h* on the third day of the month Adar,
6:16 the dedication of this *h* of God with joy.
6:17 For the dedication of this *h* of God,
6:22 them help in their work on the *h* of God,
7:16 for the *h* of their God in Jerusalem.
7:17 altar of the *h* of your God in Jerusalem.
7:19 for the service of the *h* of your God
7:20 supply for the needs of the *h* of your God,
7:23 out exactly for the *h* of the God of heaven,
7:24 or any other servant of that *h* of God.
7:27 to glorify the *h* of the LORD in Jerusalem.
8:17 for us ministers for the *h* of our God.
8:25 offered for the *h* of our God by the king,
8:29 in the chambers of the *h* of the LORD.
8:30 them to Jerusalem, to the *h* of our God.
8:33 were weighed out in the *h* of our God
8:36 support to the people and to the *h* of God.
9: 9 the *h* of our God and restore its ruins,
10: 1 weeping and prostrate before the *h* of God,
10: 6 retired from his place before the *h* of God
10: 9 in the open place before the *h* of God,
Neh 1: 6 against you, I and my father's *h* included.
2: 8 city wall and the *h* that I shall occupy."
3:10 Harumaph, who repaired opposite his own *h*.
3:20 to the entrance of the *h* of Eliashib,
3:21 of Eliashib's *h* to the end of the house.
3:23 Annaniah, made the repairs alongside his *h*.
3:24 the *h* of Azariah to the Corner [that is,
3:28 the work of repair, each before his own *h*.
3:29 carried out the repair before his *h*,
4:10 whole *h* of Judah as they rebuilt the wall.
6:10 I went to the *h* of Shemaiah,
6:10 "Let us meet in the *h* of God,
7:39 of Jedaiah who were of the *h* of Jeshua,
8:16 courtyards, in the courts of the *h* of God,
10:33 year for the service of the *h* of our God,
10:34 and for every service of the *h* of our God.
10:35 it is to be brought to the *h* of our God by
10:36 bring each year to the *h* of the LORD
10:37 in the law, to bring to the *h* of our God,
10:37 the priests who serve in the *h* of our God,
10:38 to the chambers of the *h* of our God.
10:39 tithe of the tithes to the *h* of our God,
10:40 We will not neglect the *h* of our God.
11:11 son of Ahitub, the ruler of the *h* of God,
11:16 over the external affairs of the *h* of God;
11:22 appointed to the service of the *h* of God
12:37 top of the wall above the *h* of David
12:40 choirs took up a position in the *h* of God;
13: 4 charge of the chambers of the *h* of our God
13: 7 a chamber in the courts of the *h* of God.
13: 9 replace there the utensils of the *h* of God,
13:11 demanding, "Why is the *h* of God abandoned?"
13:14 *h* of my God and its services be forgotten!
Tb 1: 4 from the *h* of David and from Jerusalem.
2:13 On entering my *h* the goat began to bleat.
3:10 *h* with the intention of hanging herself.
3:17 returned from the courtyard to his *h*,
5:10 When Raphael entered the *h*,
6: 2 Tobiah out of the *h* and went with them.
6:13 her and bring her back with us to your *h*."
7: 1. So he brought him to the *h* of Raguel,
8:11 went back into the *h* and called his wife,
9: 2 Go to Gabael's *h* and give him this bond.
9: 5 in Media, where they stayed at Gabael's *h*.
9: 6 When they entered Raguel's *h*,
11: 3 ahead of your wife to prepare the *h*
Jdt 4:15 look with favor on the whole *h* of Israel.
6:17 of Holofernes against the *h* of Israel.
8: 5 up a tent for herself on the roof of her *h*.
8: 6 feastdays and holidays of the *h* of Israel.
10: 2 her maid and they went down into the *h*,
11: 7 live for Nebuchadnezzar and his whole *h*.
13:14 withdrawn his mercy from the *h* of Israel,
14: 5 one who despised the *h* of Israel
14: 6 So they called Achior from the *h* of Uzziah.
14:10 with the *h* of Israel to the present day.
14:18 disgrace on the *h* of King Nebuchadnezzar.
16:23 to be very old in the *h* of her husband,
16:24 the *h* of Israel mourned her for seven days.
Est 4:14 but you and your father's *h* will perish.
7: 8 the queen while she is with me in my own *h*!"
7: 9 "At the *h* of Haman stands a gibbet fifty
8: 1 day King Ahasuerus gave the *h* of Haman,
8: 2 put Mordecai in charge of the *h* of Haman.
8: 7 that I have given Esther the *h* of Haman,
1Mc 1:28 all the *h* of Jacob was covered with shame.
7:37 *h* to bear your name, to be a *h* of prayer
8:15 They had made for themselves a senate *h*,
9:55 a word to give orders concerning his *h*.
13: 3 *h* have done for the laws and the sanctuary;
14:26 He and his brothers and his father's *h*
16: 2 "I and my brothers and my father's *h* have
2Mc 2:29 As the architect of a new *h* must give
8:33 who had taken refuge in a little *h*;
14:36 preserve forever undefiled this *h*,
Jb 1:13 wine in the *h* of their eldest brother,
1:18 wine in the *h* of their eldest brother,
1:19 desert and smote the four corners of the *h*.
7:10 He shall not again return to his *h*;
20:28 The flood shall sweep away his *h* with the
21:28 you say, "Where is the *h* of the magnate,
27:18 He builds his *h* as of cobwebs,
42:11 and they dined with him in his *h*.
Ps(s) 5: 8 abundant kindness, will enter your *h*;
23: 6 in the *h* of the LORD for years to come.
26: 8 O LORD, I love the *h* in which you dwell,
27: 4 the *h* of the LORD all the days of my life,
36: 9 their fill of the prime gifts of your *h*;
42: 5 and led them in procession to the *h* of God,
45:11 forget your people and your father's *h*.
49:17 when the wealth of his *h* becomes great,
50: 9 I take from your *h* no bullock,
52:10 I, like a green olive tree in the *h* of God,
55:15 I walked in procession in the *h* of God!
65: 5 be filled with the good things of your *h*,
66:13 I will bring holocausts to your *h*;
69:10 sons, Because zeal for your *h* consumes me,
84: 5 Happy they who dwell in your *h*!
84:11 lie at the threshold of the *h* of my God
92:14 They that are planted in the *h* of the LORD
93: 5 holiness befits your *h*, O LORD,
98: 3 his faithfulness toward the *h* of Israel.
101: 2 in the integrity of my heart, within my *h*;
101: 7 not dwell within my *h* who practices deceit.
105:21 of his *h* and ruler of all his possessions,
112: 3 Wealth and riches shall be in his *h*;
114: 1 *h* of Jacob from a people of alien tongue,
115: 9 The *h* of Israel trusts in the LORD;
115:10 The *h* of Aaron trusts in the LORD;
115:12 *h* of Israel; he will bless the *h* of Aaron;
116:19 people, In the courts of the *h* of the LORD,
118: 2 Let the *h* of Israel say,
118: 3 Let the *h* of Aaron say,
118:26 we bless you from the *h* of the LORD.
122: 1 me, "We will go up to the *h* of the LORD.
122: 5 judgment seats, seats for the *h* of David.
122: 9 Because of the *h* of the LORD,
127: 1 Unless the LORD build the *h*,
132: 3 "I will not enter the *h* I live in,
134: 1 *h* of the LORD during the hours of night.
135: 2 *h* of the LORD, in the courts of the house
135:19 *H* of Israel, bless the LORD, house of Aaron,
135:19 of Israel, bless the LORD, *h* of Aaron,
135:20 house of Aaron, bless the LORD, *H* of Levi,
Prv 3:33 of the LORD is on the *h* of the wicked,
5: 8 from her, approach not the door of her *h*,
5:10 your hard-won earnings go to an alien's *h*;
6:31 all the wealth of his *h* he may yield up.
7: 6 For at the window of my *h*,
7: 8 then walking in the direction of her *h*—
7:27 *h* is made up of ways to the nether world,
9: 1 Wisdom has built her *h*,
9:14 of her *h* upon a seat on the city heights,
12: 7 no more, but the *h* of the just stands firm.
14: 1 Wisdom builds her *h*,
14: 9 arrogant, but favor in the *h* of the just.
14:11 The *h* of the wicked will be destroyed,
15: 6 *h* of the just there are ample resources,
15:25 The LORD overturns the *h* of the proud,
15:27 is greedy of gain brings ruin on his own *h*,
17: 1 than a *h* full of feasting with strife.
17:13 for good, from his *h* evil will not depart.
21: 9 than in a roomy *h* with a quarrelsome woman.
21:12 The just man appraises the *h* of the wicked:
21:20 treasure remains in the *h* of the wise,
24: 3 By wisdom is a *h* built,
24:27 afterward you can establish your *h*.
25:17 your foot be seldom in your neighbor's *h*,
25:24 than in a roomy *h* with a quarrelsome woman.
27:10 ruin befalls you, enter not a kinsman's *h*.
Eccl 2: 7 slaves, and slaves were born in my *h*.
4:14 from a prison *h* one comes forth to rule,
4:17 your step when you go to the *h* of God.
7: 2 *h* of mourning than to the *h* of feasting,
7: 4 heart of the wise is in the *h* of mourning,
7: 4 the heart of fools is in the *h* of mirth.
10:18 when hands are slack, the *h* leaks.
12: 3 When the guardians of the *h* tremble,
Sg 1:17 the beams of our *h* are cedars,
Sir 1:15 Her entire *h* she fills with choice foods,
11:29 Bring not every man into your *h*,
14:24 Who encamps near her *h*,
21: 8 He who builds his *h* with another's money
21:18 Like a *h* in ruins is wisdom to a fool;
21:22 The fool steps boldly into a *h*,
21:23 A boor peeps through the doorway of a *h*,
23:11 the scourge will never be far from his *h*.
23:11 just, and all his *h* will suffer affliction.
27: 3 LORD, suddenly your *h* will be thrown down.
29:12 Store up almsgiving in your treasure *h*,
29:21 needs are water, bread, and clothing, a *h*,
29:24 miserable life it is to go from *h* to house,
42:11 that overlooks the approaches to the *h*.
47:13 He built a *h* to the name of God,
48:15 with its rulers from the *h* of David.
49:12 In their time they built the *h* of God;
50: 1 In whose time the *h* of God was renovated,
51:23 take up lodging in the *h* of instruction;
Is 2: 2 The mountain of the LORD's *h* shall be
2: 3 mountain, to the *h* of the God of Jacob,
2: 5 O *h* of Jacob, come, let us walk
2: 6 have abandoned your people, the *h* of Jacob,
3: 6 a man seizes his brother in his father's *h*,
3: 7 in my own *h* there is no bread or clothing!
3:14 loot wrested from the poor is in your *h*.
5: 7 of the LORD of hosts is the *h* of Israel,
5: 8 *h* to house who connect field with field,
6: 4 door shook and the *h* was filled with smoke.
7: 2 word came to the *h* of David that Aram
7:13 Listen, O *h* of David!
7:17 you and your people and your father's *h*
8:17 who is hiding his face from the *h* of Jacob;
10:20 of Israel, the survivors of the *h* of Jacob,
14: 1 them and be counted with the *h* of Jacob.
14: 2 The *h* of Israel will take them and bring
22: 8 to the weapons in the *H* of the Forest;
22:18 glory in, you disgrace to your master's *h*!
22:21 of Jerusalem, and to the *h* of Judah.
22:22 the key of the *H* of David on his shoulder;
24:10 city of chaos, shut against entry, every *h*.
29:22 says the LORD, the God of the *h* of Jacob,
31: 2 He will rise up against the *h* of the
37:31 The remaining survivors of the *h* of Judah
38: 1 Put your *h* in order,
38:20 the *h* of the LORD all the days of our life.
39: 2 there was nothing in his *h* or in his whole
39: 4 "What did they see in your *h*?"
39: 4 replied, "They saw everything in my *h*;
39: 6 shall come when all that is in your *h*,
46: 3 *h* of Jacob, all who remain of the house
48: 1 O *h* of Jacob called by the name of Israel,
56: 5 I will give, in my *h* and within my walls,
56: 7 mountain and make joyful in my *h* of prayer;
56: 7 For my *h* shall be called a house of prayer
58: 1 wickedness, and the *h* of Jacob their sins.
60: 7 and I will enhance the splendor of my *h*.
63: 7 for he is good to the *h* of Israel,
66: 1 What kind of *h* can you build for me;
66:20 to the *h* of the LORD in clean vessels.
Jer 2: 4 to the word of the LORD, O *h* of Jacob!
2: 4 All you clans of the *h* of Israel,
2:26 caught, so shall the *h* of Israel be shamed:
3:18 *h* of Judah will join the house of Israel;
3:20 you been faithless to me, O *h* of Israel,
5: 7 to the harlot's *h* they throng.
5:11 the *h* of Israel and the house of Judah,
5:15 you a nation from afar, O *h* of Israel,
5:20 Announce this to the *h* of Jacob,
7: 2 Stand at the gate of the *h* of the LORD,
7:10 before me in this *h* which bears my name,
7:11 Has this *h* which bears my name become in
7:14 you, I will do to this *h* named after me,
7:30 They have defiled the *h* which bears my
9:25 these nations, like the whole *h* of Israel,
10: 1 the LORD speaks to you, O *h* of Israel.
11:10 the *h* of Israel and the house of Judah
11:15 What right has my beloved in my *h*,
11:17 the *h* of Israel and by the house of Judah,
12: 6 brothers, the members of your father's *h*,
12: 7 I abandon my *h*, cast off my heritage;
12:14 *h* of Judah I will pluck up in their midst.
13:11 *h* of Israel and the whole house of Judah
16: 5 Go not into a *h* of mourning,
16: 8 Enter not a *h* where people are celebrating,
17:26 and thank offerings to the *h* of the LORD.
18: 2 Rise up, be off to the potter's *h*;
18: 3 down to the potter's *h* and there he was,
18: 6 Can I not do to you, *h* of Israel,
18: 6 potter, so are you in my hand, *h* of Israel.
19:14 of the *h* of God and said to all the people:
20: 1 Immer, chief officer in the *h* of the LORD.
20: 2 Gate of Benjamin in the *h* of the LORD.
21:11 To the royal *h* of Judah:
21:12 Hear the word of the LORD, O *h* of David!
22:13 Woe to him who builds his *h* on wrong,
22:14 says, "I will build myself a spacious *h*,
23: 8 brought the descendants of the *h* of Israel up
23:11 In my very *h* I find their wickedness,
23:34 LORD," I will punish that man and his *h*.
26: 2 Stand in the court of the *h* of the LORD
26: 2 who come to worship in the *h* of the LORD;
26: 6 obey them, I will treat this *h* like Shiloh,

26: 7 speak these words in the *h* of the LORD.
26: 9 'This *h* shall be like Shiloh,'
26: 9 about Jeremiah in the *h* of the LORD.
26:10 from the king's palace to the *h* of the LORD
26:10 court at the New Gate of the *h* of the LORD.
26:12 this *h* and city all that you have heard.
27:16 "The vessels of the *h* of the LORD will be
27:18 vessels which remain in the *h* of the LORD
27:21 vessels that remain in the *h* of the LORD,
28: 1 said to me in the *h* of the LORD in the
28: 5 the people assembled in the *h* of the LORD,
28: 6 bringing the vessels of the *h* of the LORD
29:26 be police officers in the *h* of the LORD,
31:27 the *h* of Israel and the house of Judah
31:31 the *h* of Israel and the house of Judah.
31:33 make with the *h* of Israel after those days,
32:34 They defiled the *h* named after me by the
33:11 bring thank offerings to the *h* of the LORD,
33:14 I made to the *h* of Israel and Judah.
33:17 successor on the throne of the *h* of Israel,
34:15 before me in the *h* that is named after me.
35: 2 bring them into the *h* of the LORD,
35: 4 of the Rechabites, into the *h* of the LORD,
35: 7 Build no *h* and sow no seed;
36: 3 when the *h* of Judah hears all the evil I
36: 5 I cannot go to the *h* of the LORD;
36: 6 read publicly in the LORD's *h*
36: 8 he read the LORD's words in the LORD's *h*.
36:10 in the upper court of the LORD's *h*,
36:22 Now the king was sitting in his winter *h*,
37:15 prison in the *h* of Jonathan the scribe,
37:20 me back into the *h* of Jonathan the scribe,
38:14 at the third entrance to the *h* of the LORD.
38:22 All the women left in the *h* of Judah's
38:26 send me back to Jonathan's *h* to die there.' "
41: 5 and incense for the *h* of the LORD.
48:45 Heshbon, and a blaze from the *h* of Sihon:
51:51 the holy places of the *h* of the LORD.
52:13 He burned the *h* of the LORD,
52:17 pillars that belonged to the *h* of the LORD,
52:17 and the bronze sea in the *h* of the LORD,
52:20 Solomon had made for the *h* of the LORD.
Lam 2: 7 in the *h* of the LORD as on a feast day.
Bar 1: 8 he received the vessels of the *h* of the Lord
1:14 which we send you, in the *h* of the Lord,
2:26 And you reduced the *h* which bears your
3:24 O Israel, how vast is the *h* of God,
6:12 of the *h* dust which is thick upon them.
6:19 They are like any beam in the *h*;
6:20 faces are blackened by the smoke of the *h*.
6:58 his valor, or a handy tool in a *h*,
6:58 or the door of a *h*,
Ez 2: 5 for they are a rebellious *h*—
2: 6 their looks, for they are a rebellious *h*.
2: 8 be not rebellious like this *h* of rebellion,
3: 1 scroll, then go, speak to the *h* of Israel.
3: 4 Son of man, go now to the *h* of Israel,
3: 7 *h* of Israel will refuse to listen to you,
3: 7 For the whole *h* of Israel is stubborn of
3: 9 their looks, for they are a rebellious *h*.
3:17 you a watchman for the *h* of Israel.
3:24 Go shut yourself up in your *h*.
3:26 to rebuke them for being a rebellious *h*.
3:27 who will, for they are a rebellious *h*.
4: 3 This shall be a sign for the *h* of Israel.
4: 4 place the sins of the *h* of Israel upon you.
4: 5 you will bear the sins of the *h* of Israel.
4: 6 bear the sins of the *h* of Judah forty days;
5: 4 Say to the whole *h* of Israel:
6:11 of all the abominations of the *h* of Israel,
8: 1 the sixth year, as I was sitting in my *h*,
8: 6 that the *h* of Israel is practicing here,
8:10 beasts [all the idols of the *h* of Israel].
8:11 seventy of the elders of the *h* of Israel,
8:12 the *h* of Israel is doing in his idol room?
8:16 me into the inner court of the LORD's *h*,
8:17 Is it such a trivial matter for the *h* of
9: 9 the *h* of Israel are great beyond measure;
10:19 of the eastern gate of the LORD's *h*,
11: 5 This is the way you talk, *h* of Israel,
11:15 and the whole *h* of Israel that the
12: 2 you live in the midst of a rebellious *h*;
12: 2 do not hear, for they are a rebellious *h*.
12: 3 they will see that they are a rebellious *h*.
12: 6 I have made you a sign for the *h* of Israel.
12: 9 not the house of Israel, that rebellious *h*,
12:10 and the whole *h* of Israel within it.
12:24 divinations within the *h* of Israel,
12:25 In your days, rebellious *h*,
12:27 of man, listen to the *h* of Israel saying,
13: 5 did you build a wall about the *h* of Israel
13: 9 in the register of the *h* of Israel,
14: 4 If anyone of the *h* of Israel,
14: 5 bring back to their senses the *h* of Israel,
14: 6 Therefore say to the *h* of Israel:
14: 7 For if anyone of the *h* of Israel or any
14:11 so that the *h* of Israel may no longer
17: 2 and speak this proverb to the *h* of Israel:
17:12 Son of man, say now to the rebellious *h*:
18: 6 his eyes to the idols of the *h* of Israel:
18:15 his eyes to the idols of the *h* of Israel,
18:25 Hear now, *h* of Israel:
18:29 And yet the *h* of Israel says,
18:29 Is it my way that is not fair, *h* of Israel,
18:30 Therefore I will judge you, *h* of Israel,
18:31 Why should you die, O *h* of Israel?
20: 5 swore to the descendants of the *h* of Jacob;
20:13 But the *h* of Israel rebelled against me in
20:27 Therefore speak to the *h* of Israel,
20:30 Therefore say to the *h* of Israel:
20:31 myself be consulted by you, *h* of Israel?
20:39 As for you, *h* of Israel,
20:40 there the whole *h* of Israel without
20:44 conduct and corrupt actions, O *h* of Israel,
22:18 the *h* of Israel has become dross for me.
23:39 Thus they acted within my *h*
24: 3 Propose this parable to the rebellious *h*:
24:21 Say to the *h* of Israel:
25: 3 of Israel, and the exile of the *h* of Judah,
25: 8 the *h* of Judah is like all other nations,"
25:12 Because Edom has taken vengeance on the *h*
28:24 be a tearing thorn for the *h* of Israel,
28:25 When I gather the *h* of Israel from the
29: 6 have been a reed staff for the *h* of Israel:
29:16 they be for the *h* of Israel to trust in,
29:21 make a horn sprout for the *h* of Israel,
33: 7 appointed watchman for the *h* of Israel;
33:10 you, son of man, speak to the *h* of Israel:
33:11 Why should you die, O *h* of Israel?
33:20 you according to his ways, O *h* of Israel.
34:30 and they are my people, the *h* of Israel,
35:15 of the inheritance of the *h* of Israel,
36:10 of men upon you, the whole *h* of Israel;
36:17 when the *h* of Israel lived in their land,
36:21 holy name which the *h* of Israel profaned
36:22 Therefore say to the *h* of Israel:
36:22 Not for your sakes do I act, *h* of Israel,
36:32 because of your conduct, O *h* of Israel.
36:37 be persuaded to do for the *h* of Israel:
37:11 these bones are the whole *h* of Israel.
37:16 all the *h* of Israel associated with him.
39:12 the *h* of Israel shall need seven months to
39:22 *h* of Israel shall know that I am the LORD,
39:23 its sins the *h* of Israel went into exile;
39:25 and have pity on the whole *h* of Israel,
39:29 poured out my spirit upon the *h* of Israel,
40: 4 Tell the *h* of Israel all that you see."
43:10 describe the temple to the *h* of Israel
44: 6 to that rebellious house, the *h* of Israel:
44: 6 these abominations of yours, O *h* of Israel!
44:12 an occasion of sin to the *h* of Israel,
44:30 to bring a blessing down upon your *h*.
45: 6 this shall belong to the whole *h* of Israel.
45: 8 the *h* of Israel according to their tribes.
45:17 on all the festivals of the *h* of Israel.
45:17 atonement on behalf of the *h* of Israel.
Dn 3:96 shall be cut to pieces and his *h* destroyed.
5: 3 *h* of God in Jerusalem had been brought in,
13: 4 he had a garden near his *h*,
13: 6 their cases, frequented the *h* of Joakim.
13:26 in the *h* heard the cries from the garden,
Hos 1: 4 in a little while I will punish the *h* of Jehu
1: 4 to an end the kingdom of the *h* of Israel;
1: 6 I no longer feel pity for the *h* of Israel;
1: 7 Yet for the *h* of Judah I feel pity;
5: 1 O priests, Pay attention, O *h* of Israel,
5:12 Ephraim, like maggots for the *h* of Judah.
5:14 like a young lion to the *h* of Judah;
6:10 *h* of Israel I have seen a horrible thing:
8: 1 lips, You who watch over the *h* of the LORD!
9: 4 it cannot enter the *h* of the LORD.
9: 8 his ways, hostility in the *h* of his God.
9:15 wicked deeds I will drive them out of my *h*.
12: 1 surrounded me with lies, the *h* of Israel,
Jl 1: 9 and libation from the *h* of the LORD;
1:13 The *h* of your God is deprived of offering
1:14 dwell in the land, Into the *h* of the LORD,
1:16 And from the *h* of our God,
4:18 shall issue from the *h* of the LORD,
Am 1: 4 I will send fire upon the *h* of Hazael,
2: 8 fined they drink in the *h* of their god.
3:13 and bear witness against the *h* of Jacob,
3:15 I strike the winter *h* and the summer house;
5: 1 I utter over you, a lament, O *h* of Israel:
5: 3 shall be left with ten, of the *h* of Israel.
5: 4 For thus says the LORD to the *h* of Israel:
5: 6 *h* of Joseph like a fire That shall consume,
5: 6 with none to quench it for the *h* of Israel:
5:19 Or as if on entering his *h* he were to rest
5:25 forty years in the desert, O *h* of Israel?
6: 9 Should there remain ten men in a single *h*,
6:10 If one says to a man inside a *h*,
6:11 *h* to bits, and reduce the small *h*
6:14 I am raising up against you, O *h* of Israel,
7: 9 attack the *h* of Jeroboam with the sword.
7:16 Israel, preach not against the *h* of Isaac.
9: 9 to sift the *h* of Israel among all nations,
Ob 1:17 And the *h* of Jacob shall take possession
1:18 *h* of Jacob shall be a fire, and the house
1:18 The *h* of Esau shall be stubble,
1:18 Then none shall survive of the *h* of Esau,
Mi 1: 5 pass, and for the sins of the *h* of Israel.
1: 5 And what is the sin of the *h* of Judah?
2: 2 They cheat an owner of his *h*,
2: 7 How can it be said, O *h* of Jacob,
3: 1 of Jacob, rulers of the *h* of Israel!
3: 9 Hear this, you leaders of the *h* of Jacob,
3: 9 of Jacob, you rulers of the *h* of Israel!
4: 1 In days to come the mount of the LORD's *h*
4: 2 of the LORD, to the *h* of the God of Jacob,
6:16 Omri, and all the works of the *h* of Ahab,
Zep 1: 9 *h* of their master with violence and deceit.
2: 7 belong to the remnant of the *h* of Judah;
Hg 1: 2 the time come to rebuild the *h* of the LORD.
1: 4 paneled houses, while this *h* lies in ruins?
1: 8 and build the *h* That I may take pleasure
1: 9 Because my *h* lies in ruins,
1: 9 while each of you hurries to his own *h*.
1:14 set to work on the *h* of the LORD of hosts,
2: 3 you that saw this *h* in its former glory?
2: 7 come in, And I will fill this *h* with glory,
2: 9 the future glory of this *h* than the former,
Zec 1:16 my *h* shall be built in it,
3: 7 you shall judge my *h* and keep my courts,
4: 9 have laid the foundations of this *h*,
5: 4 and it shall come into the *h* of the thief,
5: 4 *h* of him who perjures himself with my name;
5: 4 it shall lodge within his *h*,
6:10 and go the same day to the *h* of Josiah,
7: 3 the priests of the *h* of the LORD of hosts,
8: 9 foundation of the *h* of the LORD of hosts
8:13 nations, O *h* of Judah and house of Israel,
:15 to favor Jerusalem and the *h* of Judah;
8:19 cheerful festivals for the *h* of Judah;
9: 8 I will encamp by my *h* as a guard that
10: 3 hosts will visit his flock, the *h* of Judah,
10: 6 the *h* of Judah, the house of Joseph
11:13 into the treasury in the *h* of the LORD.
12: 4 upon the *h* of Judah I will open my eyes,
12: 7 that the glory of the *h* of David and the
12: 8 on that day, and the *h* of David godlike,
12:10 I will pour out on the *h* of David and on
12:12 the family of the *h* of David,
12:12 the family of the *h* of Nathan,
12:13 the family of the *h* of Levi,
13: 1 On that day there shall be open to the *h*
13: 6 I was wounded in the *h* of my dear ones."
14:20 The pots in the *h* of the LORD shall be as
14:21 any merchant in the *h* of the LORD of hosts.
Mal 3:10 That there may be food in my *h*,
Mt 2:11 at seeing the star, and on entering the *h*,
5:15 stand where it gives light to all in the *h*.
7:24 like the wise man who built his *h* on rock.
7:25 came and the winds blew and buffeted his *h*.
7:26 man who built his *h* on sandy ground.
7:27 the winds blew and lashed against his *h*.
8:14 Jesus entered Peter's *h* and found Peter's
9:23 Jesus arrived at the synagogue leader's *h*
9:28 When he got to the *h*,
10: 6 after the lost sheep of the *h* of Israel.
10:14 what you have to say, leave that *h* or town,
10:25 If they call the head of the *h* Beelzebul,
12: 4 he entered God's *h* and ate the holy bread,
12:29 "How can anyone enter a strong man's *h*
12:29 Only then can he rob his *h*.
13: 1 That same day, on leaving the *h*,
13:57 in his native place, indeed in his own *h*."
15:24 only to the lost sheep of the *h* of Israel,"
17:25 Then Jesus on entering the *h* asked,
21:13 'My *h* shall be called a house of prayer,'
24:17 not come down to get anything out of his *h*.
24:43 if the owner of the *h* knew when the thief
24:43 eye and not allow his *h* to be broken into.
26: 6 in Bethany at the *h* of Simon the leper,
26:18 the Passover with my disciples in your *h*.' "
Mk 1:29 *h* of Simon and Andrew with James and John.
2:15 Jesus was reclining to eat in Levi's *h*,
2:26 How he entered God's *h* in the days of
3:20 *h* with them and again the crowd assembled,
3:27 No one can enter a strong man's *h* and
3:27 Only then can he plunder his *h*.
5:35 from the official's *h* arrived saying,
5:38 approached the *h* of the synagogue leader,
6: 4 among his own kindred, and in his own *h*."
6:10 "Whatever *h* you find yourself in,
7:24 *h* and wanted no one to recognize him;
9:28 *h* his disciples began to ask him privately,
9:33 to Capernaum and Jesus, once inside the *h*,
10:10 Back in the *h* again, the disciples began
11:17 'My *h* shall be called a house of prayer
13:15 or enter his *h* to get anything out of it.
13:35 know when the master of the *h* is coming,
14: 3 at table in the *h* of Simon the leper,
14:14 Whatever *h* he enters, say to the owner,
Lk 1:27 to a man named Joseph, of the *h* of David.
1:32 He will rule over the *h* of Jacob forever
1:40 Zechariah's *h* and greeted Elizabeth.
1:69 for us in the *h* of David his servant,
2: 4 he was of the *h* and lineage of David
2:49 you not know I had to be in my Father's *h*?"
4:38 the synagogue, he entered the *h* of Simon.
5:24 your mat with you, and return to your *h*."
5:29 gave a great reception for Jesus in his *h*,
6: 4 how he entered God's *h* and took and ate
6:48 likened to the man who, in building a *h*,
6:48 came the torrent rushed in on that *h*,
6:49 his *h* on the ground without any foundation.
7: 6 he was only a short distance from the *h*,
7: 6 for I am not worthy to have you enter my *h*.

HOUSE (cont.)

7:10 When the deputation returned to the *h*,
8:27 he did not live in a *h*,
8:49 from the ruler's *h* with the announcement,
8:51 Once he had arrived at the *h*,
9: 4 *h* you enter and proceed from there.
10: 5 any house, first say, 'Peace to this *h*.'
10: 7 one *h* eating and drinking what they have,
10: 7 Do not move from *h* to house.
11:17 Any *h* torn by dissension falls.
11:25 returns, to find the *h* swept and tidied.
11:37 a Pharisee invited him to dine at his *h*.
12:39 if the head of the *h* knew when the thief
12:39 he would not let him break into his *h*.
13:25 When once the master of the *h* has risen to
14: 1 in the *h* of one of the leading Pharisees,
14:21 master of the *h* grew angry at the account.
14:23 I want my *h* to be full,
15: 8 does not light a lamp and sweep the *h*
15:20 With that he set off for his father's *h*.
15:25 As he neared the *h* on his way home,
16:27 my father's *h* where I have five brothers.
17:31 rooftop and his belongings are in the *h*,
19: 5 I mean to stay at your *h* today."
19: 7 "He has gone to a sinner's *h* as a guest."
19: 9 "Today salvation has come to this *h*,
19:46 'My *h* is meant for a house of prayer' but
22:10 Follow him into the *h* he enters,
22:54 brought him to the *h* of the high priest,
Jn 2:16 turning my Father's *h* into a marketplace!"
2:17 "Zeal for your *h* consumes me."
8:53 [Then each went off to his own *h*,
11:31 The Jews who were in the *h* with Mary
12: 3 *h* was filled with the ointment's fragrance.
14: 2 Father's *h* there are many dwelling places;
Acts 2: 2 all through the *h* where they were seated.
2:36 Therefore let the whole *h* of Israel know
7:20 months he was reared in his father's *h*,
7:42 forty years in the desert, O *h* of Israel?
7:46 find a dwelling place for the *h* of Jacob.
7:47 who constructed the building for that *h*.
7:49 What kind of *h* can you build me?
8: 3 He entered *h* after house,
9:11 and at the *h* of Judas ask for a certain
9:17 the *h* he laid his hands on Saul and said,
9:43 for a considerable time at the *h* of Simon,
10: 6 leather-tanner whose *h* stands by the sea."
10:17 at the gate asking for the *h* of Simon.
10:22 by a holy messenger to summon you to his *h*.
10:32 guest in the *h* of Simon the leather-tanner,
11: 3 *h* of uncircumcised men and ate with them."
11:11 came to the *h* where we were staying.
11:12 along with me, and we entered the man's *h*.
11:13 in his *h* and that the angel had said:
12:12 he went to the *h* of Mary the mother of
16:15 believe in the Lord, come and stay at my *h*."
16:32 of God to him and to everyone in his *h*.
16:34 He led them up into his *h*,
16:40 the two first made their way to Lydia's *h*,
17: 5 They marched on the *h* of Jason in an
18: 7 to the *h* of a Gentile named Titus Justus,
18: 7 his *h* was next door to the synagogue.
19:16 they fled from his *h* naked and bruised.
21:16 came along to escort us to the *h* of Mnason,
Rom 16: 5 to the congregation that meets in their *h*.
1Cor 16:19 with the assembly that meets in their *h*,
Col 4:15 and the assembly that meets at his *h*.
1Tm 3: 5 man does not know how to manage his own *h*,
5:13 of leisure, who go about from *h* to house
5:14 younger ones marry, have children, keep *h*,
2Tm 2:21 of the *h* and ready for every noble service.
Phlm 1: 2 and to the church that meets in your *h*.
Heb 3: 3 *h* is more honorable than the house itself.
3: 4 Every *h* is founded by someone,
3: 6 faithful as the Son placed over God's *h*.
3: 6 It is we who are that *h* if we hold fast to
8: 8 *h* of Israel and with the house of Judah.
8:10 make with the *h* of Israel after those days,
10:21 a great priest who is over the *h* of God,
2Jn 1:10 teaching, do not receive him into your *h*;
Rv 3:20 will enter his *h* and have supper with him,

HOUSE-WARMING (1)

Dt 20: 5 built a new house and not yet had the *h*?

HOUSEBORN (2)

Gn 17:12 including *h* slaves and those acquired with
17:13 both the *h* slaves and those acquired with

HOUSEBREAKING (1)

Ex 22: 1 caught in the act of *h* and beaten to death,

HOUSED (1)

Neh 10:40 also are *h* the utensils of the sanctuary,

HOUSEHOLD (103)

Gn 7: 1 "Go into the ark, you and all your *h*,
12:17 But the LORD struck Pharaoh and his *h* with
17:23 male among the members of Abraham's *h*—
17:27 and all the male members of his *h*,
20:18 *h* on account of Abraham's wife Sarah.
24: 2 said to the senior servant of his *h*,
24:28 ran off and told her mother's *h* about it.
24:50 Laban and his *h* said in reply:
30:30 now do something for my own *h* as well."
31:19 appropriated her father's *h* idols.
31:41 years that I have now spent in your *h*,
36: 6 daughters, and all the members of his *h*,
39: 2 assigned to the *h* of his Egyptian master.
39: 4 *h* and entrusted to him all his possessions.
39: 5 in charge of his *h* and all his possessions,
39:11 of the *h* servants were then in the house,
39:14 screamed for her *h* servants and told them,
45: 8 me a father to Pharaoh, lord of all his *h*,
46:31 said to his brothers and his father's *h*:
46:31 'My brothers and my father's *h*,
47:12 his father's whole *h* down to the youngest,
50: 8 of Egypt, as well as Joseph's whole *h*,
50: 8 his brothers, and his father's *h*;
Ex 12: 3 for itself a lamb, one apiece for each *h*.
12: 4 it shall join the nearest *h* in procuring
Lv 16: 6 to atone for himself and for his *h*.
16:17 has made atonement for himself and his *h*,
18: 9 was born in your own *h* or born elsewhere.
Dt 15:16 because he is devoted to you and your *h*,
26: 5 with a small *h* and lived there as an alien.
Jos 24:15 me and my *h*, we will serve the LORD
Jgs 17: 5 He also made an ephod and *h* idols,
18:14 these houses there are an ephod, *h* idols,
18:18 gone in and taken the ephod, the *h* idols,
18:20 priest, agreeing, took the ephod, *h* idols,
1Sm 1:21 Elkanah was going up with the rest of his *h*
19:13 took the *h* idol and laid it in the bed,
19:16 entered, they found the *h* idol in the bed,
2Sm 15:16 king set out, accompanied by his entire *h*,
16: 2 asses are for the king's *h* to ride on.
19:19 king's *h* over and to do whatever he wished.
19:42 the king and his *h* across the Jordan,
1Kgs 4: 7 who supplied food for the king and his *h*,
5:23 furnish the provisions I desire for my *h*."
5:25 kors of wheat to provide for his *h*,
2Kgs 23:24 of ghosts and spirits, with the *h* gods,
1Chr 13:14 Obed-edom's *h* and all that he possessed.
16:43 own home, David returned to bless his *h*.
Neh 13: 8 *h* goods thrown outside the chamber.
Tb 10:10 and camels, clothing, money, and *h* goods.
Jdt 12:11 to Bagoas, the eunuch in charge of his *h*:
Est 1: 8 had instructed all the stewards of his *h*
E:18 been hanged, together with his entire *h*,
Jb 5: 3 his roots, but his *h* suddenly decayed.
5:24 taking stock of your *h*,
Ps(s) 68:13 and the *h* shall divide the spoils.
Prv 11:29 upsets his *h* has empty air for a heritage;
27:27 your *h* and maintenance for your maidens.
31:15 still night, and distributes food to her *h*.
31:21 She fears not the snow for her *h*;
31:27 She watches the conduct of her *h*,
Sir 11:34 and make a stranger of you to your own *h*.
Jer 20: 6 the members of your *h* shall go into exile.
Hos 3: 4 or sacred pillar, without ephod or *h* idols.
5: 1 O house of Israel, O *h* of the king,
Mi 7: 6 and a man's enemies are those of his *h*.
Hb 2: 9 to him who pursues evil gain for his *h*,
2:10 You have devised shame for your *h*,
Mt 10:25 how much more the members of his *h*!
10:36 to make a man's enemies those of his own *h*.
12:25 *h* split into factions cannot last for long.
13:52 reign of God is like the head of a *h*
24:45 charge of his *h* to dispense food at need?
Mk 3:25 *h* is divided according to loyalties, that *h*
7:27 of the *h* satisfy themselves at table first.
Lk 10:40 has left me to do the *h* tasks all alone?
12:52 a *h* of five will be divided three against
Jn 4:53 and his whole *h* thereupon became believers.
Acts 7:10 of Egypt and of the Pharaoh's entire *h*.
10: 1 The same was true of his whole *h*.
11:14 you, you shall be saved, and all your *h*.'
16:15 After she and her *h* had been baptized,
16:31 and you will be saved, and all your *h*."
16:33 then he and his whole *h* were baptized.
18: 8 synagogue, Crispus, along with his whole *h*,
Rom 16:10 to all who belong to the *h* of Aristobulus.
16:11 of the *h* of Narcissus who are in the Lord.
1Cor 1:11 *h* that you are quarreling among yourselves.
1:16 Oh, and I baptized the *h* of Stephanas.
16:15 You know that the *h* of Stephanas is the
Gal 6:10 but especially those of the *h* of the faith.
Eph 2:19 of the saints and members of the *h* of God.
1Tm 3: 4 He must be a good manager of his own *h*,
3:15 of conduct befits a member of God's *h*,
2Tm 2:20 In every large *h* there are vessels not
Heb 3: 2 too, "was faithful in all God's *h*,"
3: 5 Moses "was faithful in all God's *h*" as a
11: 7 and built an ark that his *h* might be saved.
1Pt 2:18 You *h* slaves, obey your masters
4:17 has begun, and begun with God's own *h*.
Rv 13: 6 and the members of his heavenly *h* as well.

HOUSEHOLDS (2)

Ex 1: 1 sons of Israel who, accompanied by their *h*,
1Tm 3:12 managers of their children and their *h*.

HOUSEMEN (1)

Lk 12:45 begins to abuse the *h* and servant girls,

HOUSES (158)

Gn 34:29 and took for loot whatever was in the *h*.
Ex 6:14 These are the heads of the ancestral *h*.
7:28 your bed, into the *h* of your servants too,
8: 5 and your *h* and be left only in the river."
8: 7 The frogs shall leave you and your *h*,
8: 9 the *h* and courtyards and fields died off.
8:17 your servants and your subjects and your *h*.
8:17 The *h* of the Egyptians and the very ground
8:20 house of Pharaoh and the *h* of his servants;
10: 6 They shall fill your *h* and the houses of
12:13 the blood will mark the *h* where you are.
12:15 you shall have your *h* clear of all leaven.
12:19 days no leaven may be found in your *h*.
12:23 come into your *h* to strike you down.
12:27 over the *h* of the Israelites in Egypt;
12:27 struck down the Egyptians, he spared our *h*.'
Lv 14:55 and scall, for leprosy of garments and *h*,
25:31 *h* in villages that are not encircled by
25:32 redeem the town *h* that are their property.
25:33 for the town *h* of the Levites are their
Nm 1: 2 the Israelites, by clans and ancestral *h*,
1:20 by lineage in clans and ancestral *h*:
1:22 by lineage in clans and ancestral *h*:
1:24 by lineage in clans and ancestral *h*:
1:26 by lineage in clans and ancestral *h*:
1:28 by lineage in clans and ancestral *h*:
1:30 by lineage in clans and ancestral *h*:
1:32 by lineage in clans and ancestral *h*:
1:34 by lineage in clans and ancestral *h*:
1:36 by lineage in clans and ancestral *h*:
1:38 by lineage in clans and ancestral *h*:
1:40 by lineage in clans and ancestral *h*:
1:42 by lineage in clans and ancestral *h*:
1:45 service, registered by ancestral *h*,
2: 2 under the ensigns of their ancestral *h*.
2:32 of the Israelites taken by ancestral *h*.
3:15 of the Levites by ancestral *h* and clans,
3:20 the clans of the Levites by ancestral *h*.
4: 2 the Kohathites, by clans and ancestral *h*,
4:22 Gershonites also, by ancestral *h* and clans,
4:29 enroll by clans and ancestral *h* all their men
4:34 the Kohathites, by clans and ancestral *h*,
4:38 the Gershonites, by clans and ancestral *h*,
4:40 as registered by clans and ancestral *h*.
4:42 the Merarites, by clans and ancestral *h*,
4:46 the Levites, by clans and ancestral *h*,
7: 2 of Israel, who were heads of ancestral *h*;
26: 2 priest, "Take a census, by ancestral *h*,
31:26 and of the heads of the ancestral *h*,
34:14 all the ancestral *h* of the tribe of Reuben,
34:14 and the ancestral *h* of the tribe of Gad,
36: 1 *h* in the clan of descendants of Gilead,
36: 1 of the ancestral *h* of the other Israelites.
Dt 6: 9 the doorposts of your *h* and on your gates.
6:11 with *h* full of goods of all sorts that you
8:12 and have built fine *h* and lived in them,
11:20 the doorposts of your *h* and on your gates,
19: 1 and are settled in their cities and *h*,
Jgs 18:14 know that in these *h* there are an ephod,
18:22 when those in the *h* near that of Micah
1Kgs 8: 1 in the ancestral *h* of the Israelites,
9:10 during which Solomon built the two *h*,
20: 6 your house and the *h* of your servants.
2Kgs 25: 9 of the king, and all the *h* of Jerusalem;
1Chr 4:38 and their ancestral *h* spread out to such
5:13 corresponding to their ancestral *h*,
5:15 of Guni, was the head of their ancestral *h*.
5:24 were the heads of their ancestral *h*:
5:24 men, and heads over their ancestral *h*.
7: 2 warrior heads of the ancestral *h* of Tola.
7: 4 Their kindred, by ancestral *h*,
7: 7 heads of their ancestral *h* and warriors.
7: 9 heads of their ancestral *h* and warriors.
7:11 Jediael, heads of ancestral *h* and warriors.
7:40 of Asher, heads of ancestral *h*,
9: 9 named were heads of their ancestral *h*.
9:13 brethren, heads of their ancestral *h*,
12:31 men renowned in their ancestral *h*.
15: 1 David built *h* for himself in the City of
23:24 of Levi according to their ancestral *h*,
24: 6 *h* of the priests and of the Levites,
24:30 the Levites according to their ancestral *h*.
2Chr 5: 2 the princes of the Israelite ancestral *h*,
17:14 mustering according to their ancestral *h*.
25: 5 Benjamin according to their ancestral *h*,
28:21 LORD's house and the *h* of the king
31:16 *h* of males thirty years of age and over,
31:17 records according to their ancestral *h*,
35: 4 Prepare yourselves in your ancestral *h* and
35: 5 of the ancestral *h* of your brethren,
35:12 various groups of the ancestral *h*
Ezr 2:59 *h* and their descent were Israelite:
Neh 3:23 out the repair in front of their *h*;
5: 3 pawn our fields, our vineyards, and our *h*,
5:11 their olive groves, and their *h*,
7: 3 watch posts, and others before their own *h*."
7: 4 small, and none of the *h* had been rebuilt.
7:61 *h* and their descent were Israelite:

8:16 for themselves, on the roof of their *h*,
9:25 of *h* filled with all good things,
10:35 of our family *h* at stated times each year,
Tb 13:18 of gladness, and all her *h* shall cry out,
1Mc 1:31 demolished its *h* and its surrounding walls,
1:55 at the doors of *h* and in the streets.
3:56 proclaimed that those who were building *h*,
13:47 purified the *h* in which there were idols.
2Mc 3:18 *h* in crowds to make public supplication,
5:12 to slay those who took refuge in their *h*.
Jb 3:15 had gold and filled their *h* with silver.
4:19 more with those that dwell in *h* of clay,
15:28 in ruinous cities, in *h* that are deserted,
22:18 he had filled their *h* with good things!
24:16 in the dark he breaks into *h*.
Prv 1:13 we gain, we shall fill our *h* with booty;
Eccl 2: 4 I built myself *h* and planted vineyards;
Is 5: 9 Many *h* shall be in ruins,
6:11 are desolate, without inhabitants, *H*,
8:14 a stumbling stone to both the *h* of Israel,
13:16 their *h* shall be plundered and their wives
13:21 rest there and owls shall fill the *h*;
22:10 You numbered the *h* of Jerusalem,
32:13 For all the joyful *h*,
65:21 They shall live in the *h* they build,
65:22 shall not build *h* for others to live in,
Jer 5:27 Their *h* are as full of treachery as a
6:12 Their *h* will fall to strangers,
19:13 And the *h* of Jerusalem and the palaces of
19:13 all the *h* upon whose roofs they burnt
29: 5 Build *h* to dwell in;
29:28 build *h* to live in;
32:15 *H* and fields and vineyards shall again be
32:29 and set fire to it, burning it and its *h*,
33: 4 concerning the *h* of this city and the
33: 5 and these *h* will be filled with the
35: 9 We build no *h* to live in;
39: 8 the king's palace and the *h* of the people,
52:13 of the king, and all the *h* of Jerusalem;
Bar 6:16 tools are their gods, set up in their *h*;
6:17 their *h* with gates and bars and bolts,
Ez 7:24 who shall take possession of their *h*.
11: 3 we not," they say, "be building *h* soon?
23:47 and daughters, and burn their *h* with fire.
26:12 be torn down, your precious *h* demolished;
28:26 building *h* and planting vineyards.
33:30 along the walls and in the doorways of *h*.
Dn 2: 5 be cut to pieces and your *h* destroyed.
Jl 2: 9 run upon the wall, they climb into the *h*;
Am 5:11 Though you have built *h* of hewn stone,
6:10 be left to carry the dead out of the *h*;
Mi 2: 2 seize them; *h*, and they take them;
2: 9 you drive out from their pleasant *h*;
Zep 1:13 to pillage and their *h* to devastation;
1:13 They will build *h*, but shall not dwell
2: 7 In the *h* of Ashkelon at evening they shall
Hg 1: 4 for you to dwell in your own paneled *h*,
Zec 14: 2 the city shall be taken, *h* plundered,
Acts 4:34 or *h* sold them and donated the proceeds.

HOUSETOP (3)

Ps(s) 102: 8 I am like a sparrow alone on the *h*.
Prv 21: 9 better to dwell in a corner of the *h*
25:24 better to dwell in a corner of the *h*

HOUSETOPS (5)

2Kgs 19:26 growth, like the scorched grass on the *h*.
Ps(s) 129: 6 May they be like grass on the *h*,
Is 22: 1 you have gone up, all of you, to the *h*,
37:27 growth, like the scorched grass on the *h*.
Mt 10:27 you hear in private, proclaim from the *h*.

HOUSEWIFE (1)

2Sm 17:19 and the *h* took the cover and spread it

HOVER (1)

Mt 3:16 of God descend like a dove and *h* over him.

HOVERED (1)

Is 6: 2 their feet, and with two they *h* aloft.

HOVERING (2)

Dt 32:11 its nestlings forth by *h* over its brood,
Is 31: 5 Like *h* birds, so the LORD of hosts

HOWL (9)

Ps(s) 59:16 if they are not filled, they *h*.
Is 13: 6 *H*, for the day of the LORD is near;
13:22 Desert beasts shall *h* in her castles,
14:31 *H*, O gate; cry out, O city!
65:14 grief of heart and *h* for anguish of spirit.
Jer 25:34 *H*, you shepherds, and wail!
48:20 disgraced, yes, destroyed, *h* and cry out;
49: 3 *H*, Heshbon, for the ravager approaches,
51: 8 *h* over her! Bring balm for her wounds,

HOWLING (4)

Dt 32:10 in a wilderness, a wasteland of *h* desert.
Jdt 14:16 a loud clamor of weeping, groaning, and *h*,
14:19 Loud screaming and *h* arose in the camp.
Jer 25:36 shepherds, *h* by the leaders of the flock!

HUBS (1)

1Kgs 7:33 fellies, spokes, and *h* were all cast.

HUDDLE (1)

Lv 26:25 you then *h* together in your walled cities,

HUDDLED (2)

Gn 29: 2 with three droves of sheep *h* near it,
Jb 30: 7 under the nettles they *h* together.

HUE (1)

Ps(s) 68:14 silver, and her pinions with a golden *h*.

HUGE (26)

Nm 13:32 And all the people we saw there are *h* men,
1Kgs 20:13 LORD says, 'Do you see all this *h* army?
1Chr 11:23 the Egyptian, a *h* man five cubits tall.
2Chr 13: 8 simply because you are a *h* multitude and
Jdt 2:20 A *h*, irregular force, too many to count,
16: 6 bring him low, nor *h* giants attack him;
Ez 1: 4 a *h* cloud with flashing fire [enveloped in
Dn 3:22 So *h* a fire was kindled in the furnace
Mt 18:24 one was brought in who owed him a *h* amount.
21: 8 *h* crowd spread their cloaks on the road,
23: 5 their phylacteries and wear *h* tassels.
27:60 Then he rolled a *h* stone across the
Mk 4: 1 Such a *h* crowd gathered around him that he
13: 1 look at the *h* blocks of stone and the
16: 4 (It was a *h* one.)
Jas 3: 5 the spark is that sets a *h* forest ablaze!
Rv 6: 4 For this he was given a *h* sword.
7: 9 After this I saw before me a *h* crowd which
8: 8 something like a *h* mountain all in flames
8:10 a *h* star burning like a torch crashed down
12: 3 it was a *h* dragon,
12: 9 The *h* dragon, the ancient serpent
14:19 them into the *h* winepress of God's wrath.
16:21 Giant hailstones like *h* weights came
18:21 angel picked up a stone like a *h* millstone
20: 1 key to the abyss and a *h* chain in his hand.

HUGGING (2)

Is 16: 1 Send them forth, *h* the earth like reptiles,
Acts 27:13 anchor and proceeded, *h* the coast of Crete.

HUGS (1)

Sir 27:30 things, yet the sinner *h* them tight.

HUKKOK (1)

Jos 19:34 Aznoth-tabor and from there extended to *H*;

HUL (2)

Gn 10:23 Uz, *H*, Gether, and Mash.
1Chr 1:17 The descendants of Aram were Uz, *H*,

HULDAH (2)

2Kgs 22:14 Jerusalem, where the prophetess *H* resided.
2Chr 34:22 from the king went to the prophetess *H*,

HUMAN (117)

Gn 9: 5 man I will demand an accounting for *h* life.
32:29 divine and *h* beings and have prevailed."
Lv 5: 3 aware of it, touches some *h* uncleanness,
7:21 whether the uncleanness be of *h* or of
14:54 law for every kind of *h* leprosy and scall,
24:17 life of any *h* being shall be put to death;
27:28 *h* being or an animal or a hereditary field,
27:29 All *h* beings that are doomed lose the
Nm 9: 6 who were unclean because of a *h* corpse and
19:11 *h* being shall be unclean for seven days;
19:16 or who touches a *h* bone or a grave,
23:19 man that he should speak falsely, nor *h*,
31:26 count up all the *h* captives and the beasts
1Sm 14:15 so that the panic was beyond *h* endurance.
2Sm 7:14 the rod of men and with *h* chastisements;
1Kgs 13: 2 you, and he shall burn *h* bones upon you.' "
2Kgs 7:10 not a *h* voice, only the horses and asses
19:18 were not gods, but the work of *h* hands,
23:14 places where they had been with *h* bones.
23:20 the shrines, and burned *h* bones upon them.
2Chr 32:19 peoples of the earth, a work of *h* hands.
Tb 8: 6 and from these two the *h* race descended.
Jdt 8:12 in the place of God in *h* affairs?
8:14 *h* heart or grasp the workings of the *h*
8:16 that he should be moved by threats, nor *h*,
2Mc 7:28 same way the *h* race came into existence.
Jb 31:33 Had I, out of *h* weakness,
35: 8 and your justice only a fellow *h* being.
Ps(s) 39: 6 only a breath is any *h* existence.
Prv 20: 5 The intention in the *h* heart is like water
25:20 in wood, sorrow gnaws at the *h* heart.
27:19 another, so does one *h* heart from another.
28:17 with *h* blood were to flee to the grave,
30: 2 of men, and have not even *h* intelligence;
Eccl 2: 8 male and female singers and all *h* luxuries.
11: 5 fashions the *h* frame in the mother's womb,
Wis 12: 5 a cannibal feast of *h* flesh and of blood,
13:10 who termed gods things made by *h* hands:
Sir 3:22 when shown things beyond *h* understanding.
33:30 But never lord it over any *h* being,
39:26 of all needs for *h* life are water and fire,
42: 1 ashamed, lest you sin through *h* respect:
Is 2:17 *H* pride will be abased,
37:19 they were not gods but the work of *h* hands,
51:12 you then fear mortal man, who is *h* only,
Jer 17: 5 Cursed is the man who trusts in *h* beings,
17: 9 More tortuous than all else is the *h* heart,
49:33 Where no man lives, no *h* being stays.
50:40 dwell there, no *h* being shall tarry there.
Bar 6:13 a scepter, like the *h* ruler of a district;
6:50 that they are not gods, but *h* handiwork;
Ez 1: 5 their form was *h*,
1: 8 *H* hands were under their wings,
4:12 loaves over *h* excrement in their sight,
4:15 cow's dung in place of *h* excrement;
10: 8 [Something like *h* hands could be seen
10:21 like *h* hands were under their wings.
39:15 pass through, should they see a *h* bone,
Dn 4:13 Let his mind be changed from the *h*;
5: 5 the fingers of a *h* hand appeared,
7: 4 on two feet like a man, and given a *h* mind.
8:16 the Ulai I heard a *h* voice that cired out,
Hos 11: 4 I drew them with *h* cords,
Mt 12:12 more precious a *h* being is than a sheep.
15: 9 reverence, making dogmas out of *h* precepts.'
21:25 Was it divine or merely *h*?"
21:26 while if we say, 'merely *h*,'
22:16 favor and do not act out of *h* respect.
24:22 shortened, not a *h* being would be saved.
Mk 7: 7 they teach as dogmas mere *h* precepts.'
7: 8 and cling to what is *h* tradition."
11:32 But can we say, 'merely *h*'?"
12:14 It is evident you do not act out of *h*
14:58 will destroy this temple made by *h* hands,'
14:58 will construct another not made by *h* hands.'
Jn 2:25 one to give him testimony about *h* nature.
5:34 (Not that I myself accept such *h* testimony
5:41 "It is not that I accept *h* praise
Acts 5:38 purpose or activity is *h* in its origins,
7:48 not dwell in buildings made by *h* hands,
14:15 "We are only men, *h* like you.
17:24 not dwell in sanctuaries made by *h* hands;
Rom 3: 5 (I speak in a merely *h* way.)
6:19 *h* affairs because of your weak *h* nature.)
9: 5 the Messiah (I speak of his *h* origins).
1Cor 2:13 *h* wisdom but in words taught by the Spirit,
3: 4 clear that you are still at the *h* level?
4: 3 you or any *h* court pass judgment on me.
9: 8 reasons I am giving you are merely *h* ones,
13: 1 I speak with *h* tongues and angelic as well,
15:32 beasts at Ephesus for purely *h* motives,
2Cor 1:12 has been prompted, not by debased *h* wisdom,
5:16 look on anyone in terms of mere *h* judgment.
10: 2 ones who accuse us of weak *h* behavior.
10: 3 but we do not wage war with *h* resources.
10: 4 weapons of our warfare are not merely *h*.
11:18 are bragging about their *h* distinctions,
Gal 1:11 I proclaimed to you is no mere *h* invention.
1:16 without seeking *h* advisers or even going
2:20 I still live my *h* life,
6:12 are making a play for *h* approval
Eph 4:14 in *h* trickery and skill in proposing error.
6: 5 obey your *h* masters with the reverence,
6:12 Our battle is not against *h* forces but
Phil 2: 7 He was known to be of *h* estate,
Col 2: 8 philosophy that follows mere *h* traditions,
2:18 inflated with empty pride by his *h* reflections
2:22 based on merely *h* precepts and doctrines.
3:22 I say, obey your *h* masters perfectly,
1Tm 6:16 whom no *h* being has ever seen or can see.
1Pt 2:13 Lord, be obedient to every *h* institution,
4: 2 life on *h* desires but on the will of God.
2Pt 2:16 *h* voice to restrain the prophet's madness.
1Jn 5: 9 Do we not accept *h* testimony?
Rv 18:13 slaves and *h* lives.

HUMANE (1)

Est B: 2 *h* and effective as far as the borders,

HUMBLE (36)

2Chr 7:14 has been pronounced, *h* themselves and pray,
33:23 he did not *h* himself before the LORD as
36:12 not *h* himself before the prophet Jeremiah,
Ezr 8:21 that we might *h* ourselves before our God
Jb 22:29 but the man of *h* mien he saves.
Ps(s) 25: 9 *h* to justice, he teaches the humble his
55:20 me and will *h* them from his eternal throne;
74:21 May the *h* not retire in confusion;
81:15 my ways, Quickly would I *h* their enemies;
Prv 3:34 is stern, but to the *h* he shows kindness.
11: 2 but with the *h* is wisdom.
16:19 It is better to be *h* with the meek than to
29:23 but he who is *h* of spirit obtains honor.
Sir 2:17 their hearts and *h* themselves before him.
3:18 *H* yourself the more,
3:19 by the *h* he is glorified.
7:17 More and more, *h* your pride;

HUMBLE (cont.)

10:15 plucks up, to plant the *h* in their place:
18:20 Before you have fallen, *h* yourself;
36: 6 your anger, pour out wrath, *h* the enemy,
Is 13:11 the insolence of tyrants I will *h*.
Dn 3:39 heart and *h* spirit let us be received;
3:87 Holy men of *h* heart,
4:34 those who walk in pride he is able to *h*.
10:12 understanding and *h* yourself before God,
Na 1:12 I have humbled you, I will *h* you no more.
Zep 2: 3 Seek the LORD, all you *h* of the earth,
2: 5 of the LORD is against you, I will *h* you,
3:12 remnant in your midst a people *h* and lowly,
Mt 11:29 from me, for I am gentle and *h* of heart.
22:44 until I *h* your enemies beneath your feet'?
Rom 9:21 a lofty purpose and another for a *h* one?
Jas 1: 9 Let the brother in *h* circumstances take
1Pt 3: 8 toward one another, kindly disposed, and *h*.
5: 5 arrogant but to the *h* he shows kindness."

HUMBLED (32)

Lv 26:41 are *h* and they make amends for their guilt,
Jgs 4:23 Thus on that day God *h* the Canaanite king,
1Kgs 21:29 you seen that Ahab has *h* himself before me?
21:29 Since he has *h* himself before me,
2Kgs 22:19 you were heartsick and have *h* yourself
2Chr 12: 6 of Israel and the king *h* themselves saying,
12: 7 the LORD saw that they had *h* themselves,
12: 7 "Because they have *h* themselves,
12:12 Because he had *h* himself,
30:11 Zebulun *h* themselves and came to Jerusalem.
32:26 But then Hezekiah *h* himself for his pride
33:12 He *h* himself abjectly before the God of
33:19 and carved images before he *h* himself,
34:27 Because you were heartsick and have *h*
34:27 because you have *h* yourself before me,
Neh 9:24 and you *h* before them the Canaanite
1Mc 12:15 they have been *h*.
2Mc 8:35 after being *h* through the Lord's help by
Ps(s) 51:19 a heart contrite and *h*,
69:11 I *h* myself with fasting,
106:42 them, and they were *h* under their power.
107:12 And he *h* their hearts with trouble;
Prv 25: 7 than that you be *h* before the prince.
Dn 5:19 whomever he wished, he exalted or *h*.
5:22 his son, Belshazzar, have not *h* your heart,
Hos 14: 9 I have *h* him, but I will prosper him.
Na 1:12 Though I have *h* you,
Mt 23:12 Whoever exalts himself shall be *h*,
Lk 14:11 everyone who exalts himself shall be *h*
18:14 everyone who exalts himself shall be *h*
Phil 2: 8 estate, and it was thus that he *h* himself,
Jas 4:10 Be *h* in the sight of the Lord and he will

HUMBLES (6)

1Sm 2: 7 The LORD makes poor and makes rich, he *h*,
Sir 7:11 be mindful of him who exalts and *h*.
Is 26: 5 He *h* those in high places,
Mt 23:12 but whoever *h* himself shall be exalted.
Lk 14:11 and he who *h* himself shall be exalted."
18:14 while he who *h* himself shall be exalted."

HUMBLING (1)

2Cor 11: 7 *h* myself with a view to exalting you?

HUMBLY (6)

Sir 12:11 though he acts *h* and peaceably toward you,
Jer 13:15 Give ear, listen *h*, for the LORD speaks.
Mi 6: 8 love goodness, and to walk *h* with your God.
Phil 2: 3 *h* of others as superior to themselves.
Jas 1:21 *H* welcome the word that has taken root in
1Pt 5: 6 Bow *h* under God's mighty hand,

HUMILIATE (2)

Sir 30:13 make heavy his yoke, lest his folly *h* you.
2Cor 12:21 I come again my God may *h* me before you,

HUMILIATED (2)

2Mc 8:17 Place and the affliction of the *h* city,
Ez 31:11 I *h* it.

HUMILIATION (6)

1Mc 3:51 and your priests are in mourning and *h*.
Prv 29:23 Man's pride causes his *h*,
Sir 2: 5 and worthy men in the crucible of *h*.
20:10 *H* can follow fame,
Acts 8:33 In his *h* he was deprived of justice,
1Thes 2: 2 from the *h* we had suffered at Philippi

HUMILITY (13)

Prv 15:33 for wisdom, and *h* goes before honors.
18:12 heart is haughty, but *h* goes before honors.
22: 4 reward of *h* and fear of the LORD is riches,
Sir 1:24 loyal *h* is his delight.
3:17 My son, conduct your affairs with *h*,
10:27 My son, with *h* have self-esteem;
Zep 2: 3 Seek justice, seek *h*;
Acts 20:19 how I served the Lord in *h* through the
Eph 4: 2 calling you have received, with perfect *h*,
Col 2:23 show of wisdom in their affected piety, *h*,
3:12 with heartfelt mercy, with kindness, *h*,
Jas 3:13 through a *h* filled with good sense.
1Pt 5: 5 one another, clothe yourselves with *h*,

HUMPBACKED (1)

Lv 21:20 or hand, or who is *h* or weakly or walleyed,

HUMPS (1)

Is 30: 6 *h* of camels To a people good for nothing,

HUMTAH (1)

Jos 15:54 Eshan, Janim, Bethtappuah, Aphekah, *H*,

HUNDRED (677)

Gn 5: 3 Adam was one *h* and thirty years old when
5: 4 eight *h* years after the birth of Seth,
5: 5 of Adam was nine *h* and thirty years;
5: 6 When Seth was one *h* and five years old,
5: 7 *h* and seven years after the birth of Enosh,
5: 8 of Seth was nine *h* and twelve years;
5:10 Enosh lived eight *h* and fifteen years
5:11 of Enosh was nine *h* and five years;
5:13 Kenan lived eight *h* and forty years after
5:14 lifetime of Kenan was nine *h* and ten years;
5:16 Mahalalel lived eight *h* and thirty years
5:17 was eight *h* and ninety-five years;
5:18 Jared was one *h* and sixty-two years old,
5:19 eight *h* years after the birth of Enoch,
5:20 of Jared was nine *h* and sixty-two years;
5:22 *h* years after the birth of Methuselah,
5:23 of Enoch was three *h* and sixty-five years.
5:25 was one *h* and eighty-seven years old,
5:26 Methuselah lived seven *h* and eighty-two
5:27 Methuselah was nine *h* and sixty-nine years;
5:28 Lamech was one *h* and eighty-two years old,
5:30 Lamech lived five *h* and ninety-five years
5:31 Lamech was seven *h* and seventy-seven years;
5:32 When Noah was five *h* years old,
6: 3 days shall comprise one *h* and twenty years."
6:15 length of the ark shall be three *h* cubits,
7: 6 Noah was six *h* years old when the flood
7:24 over the earth for one *h* and fifty days,
8: 3 At the end of one *h* and fifty days,
8:13 In the six *h* and first year of Noah's life,
9:28 three *h* and fifty years after the flood.
9:29 of Noah was nine *h* and fifty years;
11:10 When Shem was one *h* years old,
11:11 five *h* years after the birth of Arpachshad,
11:13 Arpachshad lived four *h* and three years
11:15 *h* and three years after the birth of Eber,
11:17 Eber lived four *h* and thirty years after
11:19 *h* and nine years after the birth of Reu,
11:21 *h* and seven years after the birth of Serug,
11:23 lived two *h* years after the birth of Nahor,
11:25 Nahor lived one *h* and nineteen years after
11:32 lifetime of Terah was two *h* and five years;
14:14 three *h* and eighteen of his retainers,
15:13 be enslaved and oppressed for four *h* years.
17:17 be born to a man who is a *h* years old?
21: 5 Abraham was a *h* years old when his son
23: 1 life was one *h* and twenty-seven years.
23:15 of land worth four *h* shekels of silver
23:16 four *h* shekels of silver at the current
25: 7 life was one *h* and seventy-five years.
25:17 life was one *h* and thirty-seven years.
32: 7 to meet you, accompanied by four *h* men."
32:15 two *h* she-goats and twenty he-goats;
32:15 two *h* ewes and twenty rams;
33: 1 saw Esau coming, accompanied by four *h* men.
33:19 he bought for a *h* pieces of bullion
35:28 of Isaac was one *h* and eighty years;
45:22 but to Benjamin he gave three *h* shekels
47: 9 as a wayfarer amount to a *h* and thirty.
47:28 his life came to a *h* and forty-seven years.
50:22 He lived a *h* and ten years.
50:26 Joseph died at the age of a *h* and ten.
Ex 6:16 Levi lived one *h* and thirty-seven years.
6:18 Kohath lived one *h* and thirty-three years.
6:20 Amram lived one *h* and thirty-seven years.
12:37 Succoth, about six *h* thousand men on foot,
12:40 in Egypt was four *h* and thirty years.
12:41 At the end of four *h* and thirty years,
14: 7 six *h* first-class chariots and all the
27: 9 court shall have hangings a *h* cubits long,
27:11 be similar hangings, a *h* cubits long,
27:18 of the court is to be one *h* cubits long,
30:23 five *h* shekels of free-flowing myrrh;
30:23 amount, that is, two *h* and fifty shekels,
30:23 two *h* and fifty shekels of fragrant cane;
30:24 five *h* shekels of cassia
38: 9 of fine linen twined, a *h* cubits long,
38:11 were similar hangings, one *h* cubits long,
38:24 talents and seven *h* and thirty shekels,
38:25 *h* talents and one thousand seven hundred
38:26 six hundred and three thousand five *h*
38:27 One *h* talents of silver were used for
38:27 hundred talents for the one *h* pedestals.
38:28 The remaining one thousand seven *h* and
38:29 talents and two thousand four *h* shekels.
Lv 26: 8 *h* of your foes to flight, and a hundred
Nm 1:21 *h* were enrolled in the tribe of Reuben.
1:23 *h* were enrolled in the tribe of Simeon.
1:25 forty-five thousand six *h* and fifty were
1:27 six *h* were enrolled in the tribe of Judah.
1:29 *h* were enrolled in the tribe of Issachar.
1:31 *h* were enrolled in the tribe of Zebulun.
1:33 *h* were enrolled in the tribe of Ephraim.
1:35 *h* were enrolled in the tribe of Manasseh.
1:37 *h* were enrolled in the tribe of Benjamin.
1:39 seven *h* were enrolled in the tribe of Dan.
1:41 five *h* were enrolled in the tribe of Asher.
1:43 *h* were enrolled in the tribe of Naphtali.
1:46 six hundred and three thousand, five *h*
2: 4 in the census to seventy-four thousand six *h*
2: 6 in the census to fifty-four thousand four *h*
2: 8 the census to fifty-seven thousand four *h*.
2: 9 one *h* and eighty-six thousand four hundred.]
2:11 census to forty-six thousand five *h*
2:13 in the census to fifty-nine thousand three *h*
2:15 to forty-five thousand six *h* and fifty.
2:16 one *h* and fifty-one thousand four hundred
2:19 in the census to forty thousand five *h*
2:21 in the census to thirty-two thousand two *h*
2:23 the census to thirty-five thousand four *h*
2:24 was one *h* and eight thousand one hundred.]
2:26 in the census to sixty-two thousand seven *h*
2:28 in the census to forty-one thousand five *h*
2:30 the census to fifty-three thousand four *h*.
2:31 one *h* and fifty-seven thousand six hundred.]
2:32 six *h* and three thousand five hundred
2:32 and three thousand five *h* and fifty.
3:22 they numbered seven thousand five *h*.
3:28 they numbered eight thousand three *h*.
3:34 they numbered six thousand two *h*.
3:43 thousand two *h* and seventy-three.
3:46 As ransom for the two *h* and seventy-three
3:50 received in silver one thousand three *h*
4:36 numbered two thousand seven *h* and fifty.
4:40 numbered two thousand six *h* and thirty.
4:44 clans, they numbered three thousand two *h*.
4:48 was eight thousand five *h* and eighty,
7:13 silver plate weighing a *h* and thirty shekels
7:19 silver plate weighing a *h* and thirty shekels
7:25 silver plate weighing a *h* and thirty shekels
7:31 silver plate weighing a *h* and thirty shekels
7:37 silver plate weighing a *h* and thirty shekels
7:43 silver plate weighing a *h* and thirty shekels
7:49 silver plate weighing a *h* and thirty shekels
7:55 silver plate weighing a *h* and thirty shekels
7:61 silver plate weighing a *h* and thirty shekels
7:67 silver plate weighing a *h* and thirty shekels
7:73 silver plate weighing one *h* and thirty shekels
7:79 silver plate weighing a *h* and thirty shekels
7:85 plate weighed a *h* and thirty shekels,
7:85 amounted to two thousand four *h* shekels,
7:86 cups amounted to one *h* and twenty shekels.
11:21 around me include six *h* thousand soldiers;
16: 2 son of Reuben] took two *h* and fifty
16:17 Then each of your two *h* and fifty
16:35 consumed the two *h* and fifty men
17:14 thousand seven *h* died from the scourge,
26: 7 seven *h* and thirty men were registered.
26:10 when the fire consumed two *h* and fifty men.
26:14 thousand two *h* men were registered.
26:18 forty thousand five *h* men were registered.
26:22 thousand five *h* men were registered.
26:25 thousand three *h* men were registered.
26:27 sixty thousand five *h* men were registered.
26:34 thousand seven *h* men were registered.
26:37 thousand five *h* men were registered.
26:41 thousand six *h* men were registered.
26:43 thousand four *h* men were registered.
26:47 thousand four *h* men were registered.
26:50 thousand four *h* men were registered.
26:51 These six *h* and one thousand seven hundred
31:28 one out of every five *h* persons,
31:32 to six *h* and seventy-five thousand sheep,
31:36 *h* and thirty-seven thousand five hundred
31:37 *h* and seventy-five fell as tax to the LORD;
31:39 thirty thousand five *h* asses,
31:43 *h* and thirty-seven thousand five hundred
31:45 oxen, thirty thousand five *h* asses,
31:52 sixteen thousand seven *h* and fifty shekels.
33:39 Aaron was a *h* and twenty-three years old
Dt 22:19 besides fining him one *h* silver shekels,
31: 2 "I am now one *h* and twenty years old and
34: 7 one *h* and twenty years old when he died,
Jos 7:21 Babylonian mantle, two *h* shekels of silver,
24:29 the LORD, died at the age of a *h* and ten.
24:32 father of Shechem, for a *h* pieces of money.
Jgs 2: 8 was a *h* and ten years old when he died;
3:31 who slew six *h* Philistines with an oxgoad.
4: 3 for with his nine *h* iron chariots he
4:13 *h* of his iron chariots and all his forces.
7: 6 to their mouths by hand numbered three *h*,
7: 7 "By means of the three *h* who lapped up
7: 8 to their tents, but kept the three *h* men.
7:16 the three *h* men into three companies,
7:19 So Gideon and the *h* men who were with him
7:22 But the three *h* men kept blowing the horns,
8: 4 Jordan and crossed it with his three *h* men,
8:10 a *h* and twenty thousand swordsmen having
8:26 requested weighed seventeen *h* gold shekels,

11:26 Three *h* years have passed;
15: 4 So Samson left and caught three *h* foxes.
16: 5 each give you eleven *h* shekels of silver."
17: 2 "The eleven *h* shekels of silver over
17: 3 eleven *h* shekels of silver to his mother,
17: 3 *h* of them and gave them to the silversmith,
18:11 So six *h* men of the clan of the Danites,
18:16 The six *h* men girt with weapons of war,
20: 2 four *h* thousand foot soldiers who were
20:10 for every hundred, a *h* for every thousand,
20:16 seven *h* picked men who were left-handed,
20:17 four *h* thousand swordsmen ready for battle,
20:35 twenty-five thousand one *h* men of Benjamin,
20:47 But six *h* others who turned and fled
21:12 of Jabesh-gilead four *h* young virgins,
1Sm 8:12 groups of a thousand and of a *h* soldiers.
11: 8 there were three *h* thousand Israelites
13:15 he had with him, who were about six *h*.
14: 2 those with him numbered about six *h* men.
15: 4 and at Telaim reviewed two *h* thousand foot
17: 7 and its iron head weighed six *h* shekels.
18:25 than the foreskins of one *h* Philistines,
18:27 with his men and slew two *h* Philistines.
22: 2 About four *h* men were with him.
22: 7 you an officer over a thousand or a *h* men,
23:13 David and his men, about six *h* in number,
25:13 About four *h* men went up after David,
25:13 while two *h* remained with the baggage.
25:18 Abigail quickly got together two *h* loaves,
25:18 *h* cakes of pressed raisins, and two *h*
27: 2 with his six *h* men and went over to Achish,
29: 2 their groups of a *h* and a thousand,
30: 9 *h* men and came as far as the Wadi Besor,
30:10 four *h* men, but two *h* were too exhausted
30:17 that none escaped except four *h* young men,
30:21 When David came to the two *h* men who had
2Sm 2:31 wounded three *h* and sixty men of Benjamin,
3:14 by paying a *h* Philistine foreskins."
8: 4 from him one thousand seven *h* horsemen
8: 4 preserving only enough for a *h* chariots.
10:18 and David's men killed seven *h* charioteers
14:26 *h* shekels according to the royal standard.
15:11 Two *h* men had accompanied Absalom from
15:18 and the six *h* men of Gath who had
16: 1 asses laden with two *h* loaves of bread,
18: 1 of groups of a thousand and groups of a *h*.
18: 4 out in units of a *h* and of a thousand.
21:16 whose bronze spear weighed three *h* shekels,
23: 8 over eight *h* slain in a single encounter.
23:18 brandished his spear over three *h* slain.
24: 9 *h* thousand men fit for military service;
24: 9 in Judah, five *h* thousand.
1Kgs 5: 3 twenty pasture-fed oxen, and a *h* sheep,
5:30 to three thousand three *h* overseers,
6: 1 In the four *h* and eightieth year from the
7: 2 the Forest of Lebanon one *h* cubits long,
7:18 *h* pomegranates were also cast; two *h*
7:42 four *h* pomegranates in double rows on both
8:63 oxen and one *h* twenty thousand sheep.
9:14 Solomon one *h* and twenty talents of gold.
9:23 in the work numbered five *h* and fifty.
9:28 and brought back four *h* and twenty talents
10:10 the king one *h* and twenty gold talents,
10:14 weighed six *h* and sixty-six gold talents,
10:16 two *h* shields of beaten gold (six hundred
10:17 three *h* bucklers of beaten gold
10:26 *h* chariots and twelve thousand drivers;
10:29 six *h* shekels, a horse one hundred and
11: 3 *h* wives of princely rank and three hundred
12:21 *h* and eighty thousand seasoned warriors
18: 4 of the LORD, Obadiah took a *h* prophets,
18:13 that I hid a *h* of the prophets of the LORD,
18:19 as well as the four *h* and fifty prophets
18:19 four *h* prophets of Asherah who eat
18:22 are four *h* and fifty prophets of Baal.
20:15 of the provinces, two *h* thirty-two of them.
20:29 Israelites struck down one *h* thousand
22: 6 the prophets, about four *h* of them,
2Kgs 3: 4 *h* thousand lambs and the wool of a hundred
3:26 the king of Moab took seven *h* swordsmen to
4:43 "How can I set this before a *h* men?"
14:13 tore down four *h* cubits of the city wall,
18:14 The king of Assyria exacted three *h*
19:35 struck down one *h* and eighty-five thousand
23:33 a *h* talents of silver and a talent of gold.
1Chr 4:42 Five *h* of them (the Simeonites) went to
5:18 *h* and sixty men fit for military service.
5:21 Along with one *h* thousand men they also
5:21 camels, two *h* fifty thousand sheep,
7: 2 thousand six *h* in the time of David.
7: 9 records listed twenty thousand two *h*
7:11 two *h* men fit for military service . . .
8:40 one *h* and fifty.
9: 6 and six *h* and ninety of their brethren.
9: 9 various families were nine *h* and fifty-six.
9:13 were one thousand seven *h* and sixty,
9:22 at the threshold were two *h* and twelve.
11:11 He brandished his spear against three *h*,
11:20 he brandished his spear against three *h*,
12:25 six thousand eight *h* armed troops.
12:26 seven thousand one *h*.
12:27 four thousand six *h*,
12:28 with another three thousand seven *h*,
12:31 twenty thousand eight *h* warriors,
12:33 two *h* chiefs,
12:36 twenty-eight thousand six *h*.
12:38 one *h* and twenty thousand.
15: 5 and one *h* and twenty of his brethren;
15: 6 and two *h* and twenty of his brethren;
15: 7 and one *h* and thirty of his brethren;
15: 8 their chief, and two *h* of his brethren,
15:10 and one *h* and twelve of his brethren.
18: 4 horses, David hamstrung all but one *h*.
21: 5 *h* thousand, and in Judah four hundred
21:25 Ornan six *h* shekels of gold for the place.
22:14 of the LORD a *h* thousand talents of gold,
25: 7 skilled men, was two *h* and eighty-eight.
26:30 one thousand seven *h* police officers,
26:32 two thousand seven *h* heads of families.
29: 7 bronze, and one *h* thousand talents of iron.
2Chr 1:14 he had one thousand four *h* chariots
1:17 and export them at six *h* silver shekels,
1:17 horses going for a *h* and fifty shekels.
2: 1 he placed three thousand six *h* overseers.
2:16 one *h* fifty-three thousand six hundred. *h*.
2:17 six *h* overseers to keep the people working.
3: 8 fine gold to the amount of six *h* talents.
3:16 *h* pomegranates which he set on the chains.
4: 8 and he made a *h* golden bowls.
4:13 four *h* pomegranates for the two networks,
5:12 a *h* and twenty priests blowing trumpets.
7: 5 oxen, and one *h* twenty thousand sheep.
8:10 They were also King Solomon's two *h* and
8:18 back from there four *h* and fifty talents
9: 9 Then she gave the king one *h* and twenty
9:13 weighed six *h* and sixty-six gold talents,
9:15 *h* large shields of beaten gold, six hundred
9:16 *h* bucklers of beaten gold, three hundred
11: 1 a *h* and eighty thousand seasoned warriors,
12: 3 *h* chariots and sixty thousand horsemen,
13: 3 a force of four *h* thousand picked warriors,
13: 3 *h* thousand picked and valiant warriors.
13:17 *h* thousand picked men of Israel fell slain.
14: 7 Asa had an army of three *h* thousand
14: 7 and two *h* and eight thousand from Benjamin
14: 8 of one million men and three *h* chariots,
15:11 seven *h* oxen and seven thousand sheep
17:11 hundred rams and seven thousand seven *h*
17:14 with him three *h* thousand valiant warriors.
17:15 and with him two *h* eighty thousand.
17:16 with him two *h* thousand valiant warriors.
17:17 two *h* thousand armed with bow and buckler.
17:18 one *h* and eighty thousand equipped for war.
18: 5 gathered his prophets, four *h* in number,
24:15 was a *h* and thirty years old when he died.
25: 5 be three *h* thousand picked men fit for war,
25: 6 He also hired a *h* thousand valiant
25: 6 from Israel for a *h* talents of silver.
25: 9 "But what is to be done about the *h*
25:23 Corner Gate, a distance of four *h* cubits.
26:12 valiant warriors was two thousand six *h*,
26:13 three hundred seven thousand five *h* fighting
27: 5 Ammonites paid him one *h* talents of silver,
28: 6 slew one *h* and twenty thousand of Judah in
28: 8 two *h* thousand of their brethren's wives,
29:32 one *h* rams, and two hundred lambs:
29:33 were six *h* oxen and three thousand sheep.
35: 8 two thousand six *h* Passover victims
35: 8 victims together with three *h* oxen.
35: 9 victims, together with five *h* oxen.
36: 3 *h* talents of silver and a talent of gold.
Ezr 1:10 silver bowls, four *h* and ten;
1:11 five thousand four *h* pieces.
2: 3 Parosh, two thousand one *h* and seventy-two;
2: 4 of Shephatiah, three *h* and seventy-two;
2: 5 sons of Arah, seven *h* and seventy-five;
2: 6 and Joab, two thousand eight *h* and twelve;
2: 7 of Elam, one thousand two *h* and fifty-four;
2: 8 sons of Zattu, nine *h* and forty-five;
2: 9 sons of Zaccai, seven *h* and sixty;
2:10 sons of Bani, six *h* and forty-two;
2:11 sons of Bebai, six *h* and twenty-three;
2:12 Azgad, one thousand two *h* and twenty-two;
2:13 sons of Adonikam, six *h* and sixty-six;
2:15 sons of Adin, four *h* and fifty-four;
2:17 sons of Bezai, three *h* and twenty-three;
2:18 sons of Jorah, one *h* and twelve;
2:19 sons of Hashum, two *h* and twenty-three;
2:21 sons of Bethlehem, one *h* and twenty-three;
2:23 men of Anathoth, one *h* and twenty-eight;
2:25 and Beeroth, seven *h* and forty-three;
2:26 of Ramah and Geba, six *h* and twenty-one;
2:27 men of Michmas, one *h* and twenty-two;
2:28 of Bethel and Ai, two *h* and twenty-three;
2:30 sons of Magbish, one *h* and fifty-six;
2:31 Elam, one thousand two *h* and fifty-four;
2:32 sons of Harim, three *h* and twenty;
2:33 Hadid, and Ono, seven *h* and twenty-five;
2:34 sons of Jericho, three *h* and forty-five;
2:35 of Senaah, three thousand six *h* and thirty.
2:36 house of Jeshua, nine *h* and seventy-three;
2:38 one thousand two *h* and forty-seven;
2:41 sons of Asaph, one *h* and twenty-eight.
2:42 of Shobai, one *h* and thirty-nine in all.
2:58 of Solomon was three *h* and ninety-two.
2:60 sons of Nekoda, six *h* and fifty-two.
2:64 to forty-two thousand three *h* and sixty,
2:65 seven thousand three *h* and thirty-seven.
2:65 also had two *h* male and female singers.
2:66 *h* and thirty-six, their mules two hundred
2:67 their camels four *h* and thirty-five,
2:67 asses six thousand seven *h* and twenty.
2:69 silver, and one *h* garments for the priests.
6:17 *h* bulls, two hundred rams, and four hundred
7:22 *h* talents; wheat, one hundred kors;
7:22 wine, one *h* baths; oil, one hundred baths;
8: 3 him one *h* and fifty males were enrolled;
8: 4 son of Zerahiah, and with him two *h* males;
8: 5 of Jahaziel, and with him three *h* males;
8: 9 and with him two *h* and eighteen males;
8:10 and with him one *h* and sixty males;
8:12 Hakkatan, and with him one *h* and ten males;
8:20 the Levites) there were two *h* and twenty.
8:26 silver, six *h* and fifty talents;
8:26 silver utensils, one *h*; gold, one *h* talents;
Neh 5:17 I set my table for a *h* and fifty persons,
7: 8 Parosh, two thousand one *h* and seventy-two;
7: 9 of Shephatiah, three *h* and seventy-two;
7:10 sons of Arah, six *h* and fifty-two;
7:11 Joab, two thousand eight *h* and eighteen;
7:12 of Elam, one thousand two *h* and fifty-four;
7:13 sons of Zattu, eight *h* and forty-five;
7:14 sons of Zaccai, seven *h* and sixty;
7:15 sons of Binnui, six *h* and forty-eight;
7:16 sons of Bebai, six *h* and twenty-eight;
7:17 Azgad, two thousand three *h* and twenty-two;
7:18 sons of Adonikam, six *h* and sixty-seven;
7:20 sons of Adin, six *h* and fifty-five;
7:22 sons of Hashum, three *h* and twenty-eight;
7:23 sons of Bezai, three *h* and twenty-four;
7:24 sons of Hariph, one *h* and twelve;
7:26 and Netophah, one *h* and eighty-eight;
7:27 men of Anathoth, one *h* and twenty-eight;
7:29 and Beeroth, seven *h* and forty-three;
7:30 of Ramah and Geba, six *h* and twenty-one;
7:31 men of Michmas, one *h* and twenty-two;
7:32 of Bethel and Ai, one *h* and twenty-three;
7:34 Elam, one thousand two *h* and fifty-four;
7:35 sons of Harim, three *h* and twenty;
7:36 sons of Jericho, three *h* and forty-five;
7:37 Hadid, and Ono, seven *h* and twenty-one;
7:38 Senaah, three thousand nine *h* and thirty.
7:39 house of Jeshua, nine *h* and seventy-three;
7:40 one thousand two *h* and forty-seven;
7:44 sons of Asaph, one *h* and forty-eight.
7:45 sons of Shobai, one *h* and thirty-eight.
7:60 of Solomon was three *h* and ninety-two.
7:62 sons of Nekoda, six *h* and forty-two.
7:66 to forty-two thousand three *h* and sixty,
7:67 seven thousand three *h* and thirty-seven.
7:67 also had two *h* male and female singers.
7:67 *h* and thirty-six, their mules two hundred
7:68 their camels four *h* and thirty-five,
7:68 asses six thousand seven *h* and twenty.
7:69 for priests, and five *h* minas of silver.
7:70 and two thousand two *h* minas of silver.
11: 6 was four *h* and sixty-eight valiant men.
11: 8 nine *h* and twenty-eight in number.
11:12 the temple service, eight *h* and twenty-two;
11:13 family heads, two *h* and forty-two;
11:14 brethren, warriors, one *h* and twenty-eight.
11:18 in the holy city was two *h* and eighty-four.
11:19 one *h* and seventy-two in number.
12:39 the Tower of Hananel, and the *H* Tower,
Tb 14: 1 peacefully at the age of a *h* and twelve,
14:14 at the venerable age of a *h* and seventeen.
Jdt 1: 3 the gates he raised towers of a *h* cubits,
1:16 and feasted for a *h* and twenty days.
2: 5 a *h* and twenty thousand infantry and
2:15 a *h* and twenty thousand picked troops,
7: 2 Their forces numbered a *h* and seventy
10:17 So they detailed a *h* of their men as an
16:23 reaching the advanced age of a *h* and five.
Est 1: 1 ruled over a *h* and twenty-seven provinces
1: 4 For as many as a *h* and eighty days,
B: 1 satraps of the *h* and twenty-seven provinces
8: 9 and officials of the *h* and twenty-seven
E: 1 provinces in the *h* and twenty-seven satrapies
9: 6 the Jews killed and destroyed five *h* men.
9:12 Jews have killed and destroyed five *h* men,
9:15 of Adar and killed three *h* men in Susa.
9:30 Jews in the *h* and twenty-seven provinces
1Mc 1:10 He became king in the year one *h* and
1:20 Egypt in the year one *h* and forty-three,
1:54 Chislev, in the year one *h* and forty-five,
2:70 He died in the year one *h* and forty-six,
3:24 About eight *h* of their men fell,
3:37 capital, in the year one *h* and forty-seven;
4:52 Chislev, in the year one *h* and forty-eight,
6:16 in Persia in the year one *h* and forty-nine.
6:20 So in the year one *h* and fifty they
6:30 army numbered a *h* thousand foot-soldiers,
6:35 bronze helmets, and five *h* picked cavalry.
6:42 and six *h* men of the king's army fell.
7: 1 In the year one *h* and fifty-one,
7:32 About five *h* men of Nicanor's army fell;
7:41 a *h* and eighty-five thousand of them.
8: 6 against them with a *h* and twenty elephants
8:15 day three *h* and twenty men took counsel,

HUNDRED (cont.)

9: 3 month of the year one *h* and fifty-two,
9: 6 the camp, until only eight *h* men remained.
9:54 In the year one *h* and fifty-three,
10: 1 In the year one *h* and sixty,
10:21 one *h* and sixty at the feast of Booths,
10:57 Ptolemais in the year one *h* and sixty-two.
10:67 In the year one *h* and sixty-five,
11:19 king in the year one *h* and sixty-seven.
11:28 promising him in return three *h* talents.
11:45 populace, one *h* and twenty thousand strong,
11:47 killed about a *h* thousand men in the city,
13:16 if you send us a *h* talents of silver,
13:19 So he sent the boys and the *h* talents;
13:41 Thus in the year one *h* and seventy,
13:51 month, in the year one *h* and seventy-one,
14: 1 In the year one *h* and seventy-two,
14:27 of Elul, in the year one *h* and seventy-two,
15:10 In the year one *h* and seventy-four
15:13 Antiochus encamped before Dor with a *h* and
15:31 pay me five *h* talents of silver for the
15:31 five *h* talents more for the tribute money
15:35 to pay you a *h* talents for these cities."
16:14 in the year one *h* and seventy-seven,
2Mc 1: 7 Demetrius, the year one *h* and sixty-nine,
1:10 Dated in the year one *h* and eighty-eight.
3:11 four *h* talents of silver and two *h*
4: 8 king three *h* and sixty talents of silver,
4: 9 this he agreed to pay a *h* and fifty more,
4:19 to bring there three *h* silver drachmas for
4:24 Jason by three *h* talents of silver.
5:21 off eighteen *h* talents from the temple,
8:19 when a *h* and eighty-five thousand of his
8:20 the eight thousand routed one *h* and twenty
8:22 division, assigning to each fifteen *h* men.
10:31 *h* of their foot soldiers and six hundred
11:11 foot soldiers and sixteen *h* horsemen,
11:21 The year one *h* and forty-eight,
11:33 In the year one *h* and forty-eight,
11:38 In the year one *h* and forty-eight,
12: 4 to sea and drowned at least two *h* of them.
12:10 foot soldiers, and five *h* horsemen.
12:20 who had a force of a *h* and twenty thousand
12:20 foot soldiers and twenty-five *h* horsemen.
12:33 thousand foot soldiers and four *h* horsemen.
13: 1 In the year one *h* and forty-nine,
13: 2 of one *h* and ten thousand foot soldiers,
13: 2 foot soldiers, fifty-three *h* horsemen,
13: 2 and three *h* chariots armed with scythes.
14: 4 Demetrius in the year one *h* and fifty-one
14:39 more than five *h* soldiers to arrest him.
15:22 and he slew a *h* and eighty-five thousand
Jb 1: 3 hundred yoke of oxen, five *h* she-asses,
42:16 After this, Job lived a *h* and forty years;
Prv 17:10 of intelligence than a *h* lashes for a fool.
Eccl 6: 3 man have a *h* children and live many years,
8:12 sinner does evil a *h* times and survives.
Sg 8:12 and two *h* for the caretakers of its fruit.
Sir 16:10 Nor the six *h* thousand foot soldiers who
18: 7 days is great if it reaches a *h* years:
41: 4 one has lived a thousand years, a *h*,
46: 8 spared from the six *h* thousand infantry,
Is 37:36 struck down one *h* and eighty-five thousand
65:20 *h* years, and he who fails of a hundred
Jer 52:23 There were a *h* pomegranates,
52:29 *h* and thirty-two persons from Jerusalem;
52:30 seven *h* and forty-five people of Judah:
52:30 four thousand six *h* persons in all.
Ez 4: 5 same number of days, three *h* and ninety,
4: 9 you lie upon your side, three *h* and ninety.
40:19 it was one *h* cubits between them.
40:23 one *h* cubits from one gate to the other.
40:27 from gate to gate he measured one *h* cubits.
40:47 a *h* cubits long and a hundred cubits wide,
41:13 the temple, which was one *h* cubits long.
41:13 and its walls, was a *h* cubits in length.
41:14 on the east side, was one *h* cubits wide.
41:15 walls on both sides it was one *h* cubits.
42: 2 length was a *h* cubits on the north side,
42: 8 length the wall measured one *h* cubits.
42:16 five *h* cubits by his measuring rod.
42:17 five *h* cubits by the measuring rod.
42:18 five *h* cubits by the measuring rod.
42:19 five *h* cubits by the measuring rod.
42:20 *h* cubits long and five hundred cubits wide.
45: 2 square plot, five *h* by five hundred cubits,
45:15 every two *h* from the pasturage of Israel,
48:16 *h* cubits; the south side, forty-five *h*
48:16 *h* cubits; and the west side, forty-five *h*
48:17 *h* and fifty cubits, south two hundred
48:17 *h* and fifty cubits, and west two hundred
48:30 north side, measuring forty-five *h* cubits,
48:32 east side, measuring forty-five *h* cubits,
48:33 south side, measuring forty-five *h* cubits,
48:34 west side, measuring forty-five *h* cubits,
Dn 6: 2 entire kingdom one *h* and twenty satraps,
8:14 two thousand three *h* evenings and mornings;
12:11 be one thousand two *h* and ninety days.
12:12 one thousand three *h* and thirty-five days.
Am 5: 3 with a thousand shall be left without a *h*,
5: 3 out with a *h* shall be left with ten,
Jon 4:11 in which there are more than a *h* and
Mt 14:24 already several *h* yards out from shore,
18:12 a *h* sheep and one of them wanders away;
Mk 6:37 two *h* days' wages for bread to feed them?"
10:30 this present age a *h* times as many homes,
14: 5 It could have been sold for over three *h*
Lk 7:41 one owed a total of five *h* coins,
15: 4 If he has a *h* sheep and loses one of them,
16: 6 The man replied, 'A *h* jars of oil.'
16: 7 The answer came, 'A *h* measures of wheat,'
Jn 6: 7 "Not even with two *h* days' wages could we
12: 5 could have brought three *h* silver pieces,
19:39 and aloes which weighed about a *h* pounds.
21: 8 no more than a *h* yards.
21:11 one *h* fifty-three of them!
Acts 1:15 been a *h* and twenty gathered together.
5:36 About four *h* men joined him.
7: 6 to slavery and oppressed four *h* years.
13:20 at the end of some four *h* and fifty years.
23:23 o'clock tonight, with two *h* infantrymen,
23:23 seventy cavalrymen, and two *h* spearmen.
27:37 were two *h* and seventy-six of us on board.)
Rom 4:19 as dead (for he was nearly a *h* years old),
1Cor 15: 6 he was seen by five *h* brothers at once,
Gal 3:17 into being four *h* and thirty years later,
Rv 7: 4 one *h* and forty-four thousand from every
9:16 I heard, were two *h* million in number
11: 3 prophesy for those twelve *h* and sixty days,
12: 6 taken care of for twelve *h* and sixty days.
13:18 The man's number is six *h* sixty-six.
14: 1 and with him were the *h* and forty-four
14: 3 This hymn no one could learn except the *h*
14:20 the winepress that for two *h* miles around,
21:17 Its wall measured a *h* and forty-four

HUNDRED- (2)

Mt 13: 8 yielded grain a *h*- or sixty- or thirtyfold.
13:23 a yield of a *h*- or sixty- or thirtyfold."

HUNDREDFOLD (6)

Gn 26:12 that region and reaped a *h* the same year.
2Sm 24: 3 God increase the number of people a *h*
1Chr 21: 3 "May the LORD increase his people a *h*!
Mk 4: 8 at a rate of thirty- and sixty- and a *h*."
4:20 and yield at thirty- and sixty- and a *h*."
Lk 8: 8 good soil, grew up, and yielded grain a *h*."

HUNDREDS (14)

Ex 18:21 as officers over groups of thousands, of *h*,
18:25 as officers over groups of thousands, of *h*,
Dt 1:15 and officials over thousands, over *h*,
1Chr 12:15 over *h* and the greater over thousands.
13: 1 with his commanders of thousands and of *h*,
26:26 the commanders of thousands and of *h*,
27: 1 heads, commanders of thousands and of *h*,
28: 1 the commanders of thousands and of *h*,
29: 6 the commanders of thousands and of *h*,
2Chr 1: 2 to the commanders of thousands and of *h*,
25: 5 under leaders of thousands and of *h*.
1Mc 3:55 among the people, over thousands, over *h*,
Mk 5: 9 "There are *h* of us."
6:40 people took their places in *h* and fifties,

HUNDREDTH (1)

Gn 7:11 In the six *h* year of Noah's life,

HUNG (14)

Ex 26:32 It is to be *h* on four gold-plated columns
40:21 into the Dwelling and *h* the curtain veil,
40:28 He *h* the curtain at the entrance of the
40:33 *h* the curtain at the entrance of the court.
Dt 21:22 is put to death and his corpse *h* on a tree,
2Sm 18: 9 He *h* between heaven and earth while the
Jdt 14:11 they *h* the head of Holofernes on the wall.
1Mc 1:61 decree, with the babies *h* from their necks;
4:51 on the table and *h* up curtains.
2Mc 15:35 Judas *h* up Nicanor's head on the wall of
Ps(s) 137: 2 the aspens of that land we *h* up our harps,
Is 22:25 that *h* on it shall be done away with;
Ez 27:10 shield and helmet they *h* upon you,
27:11 *h* their bucklers all around on your walls,

HUNGER (39)

Gn 41:55 When *h* came to be felt throughout the land
42: 2 we may stay alive rather than die of *h*."
47:13 Egypt and Canaan were languishing from *h*,
Lv 26:26 not enough food to still your *h*.
Dt 8: 3 He therefore let you be afflicted with *h*,
28:48 of every kind, therefore in *h* and thirst,
32:24 "Emaciating *h* and consuming fever and
Neh 9:15 Food from heaven you gave them in their *h*,
Jdt 7:14 wives and children will languish with *h*,
1Mc 13:49 they suffered greatly from *h*,
Jb 30: 3 In want and *h* was their lot,
38:39 the lioness or appease the *h* of her cubs,
Prv 10: 3 The LORD permits not the just to *h*,
13:25 When the just man eats, his *h* is appeased;
Sir 16:25 They were not to *h*,
18:25 the time of *h* in the time of plenty,
24:20 He who eats of me will *h* still,
38:32 and wherever they stay, they need not *h*.
Is 5:13 Their nobles die of *h*,
8:21 and in his *h* he shall become enraged,
49:10 They shall not *h* or thirst,
Jer 14:18 those consumed by *h*.
42:14 trumpet alarm no longer, nor *h* for bread;
42:16 the *h* you dread shall cling to you no less
44:12 fall by the sword or be consumed by *h*.
44:12 low, they shall die by the sword, or by *h*,
44:13 just as I punished Jerusalem with sword, *h*,
44:18 are being destroyed by the sword and by *h*.
Lam 2:19 from *h* at the corner of every street].
4: 9 by the sword than for those who die of *h*,
Bar 2:25 anguish, by *h* and the sword and plague.
Ez 5:12 of pestilence and perish of *h* within you;
5:16 you the cruel, destructive arrows of *h*,
7:15 pestilence and *h* are within.
Mt 5: 6 are they who *h* and thirst for holiness;
Lk 6:20 Blest are you who *h*; you shall be filled.
Rom 8:35 Trial, or distress, or persecution, or *h*,
2Cor 11:27 in *h* and thirst and frequent fastings;
Rv 7:16 Never again shall they know *h* or thirst,

HUNGRY (54)

1Sm 2: 5 out for bread, while the *h* batten on spoil.
2Sm 17:29 been *h* and tired and thirsty in the desert."
Tb 1:17 to the *h* and my clothing to the naked.
4:16 "Give to the *h* some of your bread,
Jb 5: 5 What they have reaped the *h* shall eat up;
22: 7 and from the *h* you have withheld bread;
Ps(s) 17:12 fix their gaze, Like lions *h* for prey,
34:11 The great grow poor and *h*;
50:12 If I were *h*, I should not tell you,
107: 5 *H* and thirsty,
107: 9 and filled the *h* soul with good things.
107:36 And there he settled the *h*,
146: 7 for the oppressed, gives good to the *h*.
Prv 6:30 to satisfy his appetite when he is *h*;
14:21 He sins who despises the *h*;
19:15 deep sleep, and the sluggard must go *h*.
25:21 If your enemy be *h*,
27: 7 but to the man who is *h*,
Sir 4: 2 A *h* man grieve not,
Is 8:21 shall pass through it hard-pressed and *h*,
9:19 Though they hack on the right, they are *h*;
29: 8 As when a *h* man dreams he is eating and
32: 6 To let the *h* go empty and the thirsty be
44:12 He is *h* and weak,
58: 7 Sharing your bread with the *h*,
58:10 bread on the *h* and satisfy the afflicted;
65:13 my servants shall eat, but you shall go *h*;
Ez 18: 7 gives food to the *h* and clothes the naked;
18:16 his food to the *h* and clothes the naked;
Na 3:12 That fall, when shaken, into the *h* mouth.
Mt 4: 2 days and forty nights, and afterward was *h*.
12: 1 His disciples felt *h*,
12: 3 what David did when he and his men were *h*,
15:32 I do not wish to send them away *h*,
21:18 Jesus was returning to the city, he felt *h*.
25:35 For I was *h* and you gave me food,
25:37 when did we see you *h* and feed you or see
25:42 I was *h* and you gave me no food,
25:44 when did we see you *h* or thirsty or away
Mk 2:25 he was in need and he and his men were *h*?
8: 3 If I send them home *h*,
11:12 when they were leaving Bethany he felt *h*.
Lk 1:53 The *h* he has given every good thing,
4: 2 ate nothing, and at the end of it he was *h*.
6: 3 what David did when he and his men were *h*—
6:25 Woe to you who are full; you shall go *h*.
Jn 6:35 No one who comes to me shall ever be *h*,
Acts 10:10 He became *h* and asked for some food,
27:33 you have gone *h*—
Rom 12:20 But "if your enemy is *h*,
1Cor 4:11 Up to this very hour we go *h* and thirsty,
11:21 One person goes *h* while another gets drunk.
11:34 If anyone is *h* let him eat at home,
Phil 4:12 how to eat well or go *h*.

HUNT (11)

Gn 27: 3 out into the country to *h* some game for me.
27: 5 the country to *h* some game for his father,
27:30 when his brother Esau came back from his *h*.
Ex 21:13 He, however, who did not *h* a man down,
1Sm 9: 3 with you and go out and *h* for the asses."
1Mc 4: 5 so he began to *h* for them in the mountains,
Jb 10:16 Should it lift up, you *h* me like a lion:
38:39 Do you *h* the prey for the lioness or
Jer 16:16 I will send many hunters to *h* them out
Am 9: 3 there too I will *h* them and take them away;
Mt 23:34 synagogues and *h* down from city to city;

HUNTED (6)

Gn 27:33 asked, "that *h* game and brought it to me?
Tb 2: 8 Once before he was *h* down for execution
1Mc 9:26 These sought out and *h* down the friends of
2Mc 5: 8 he fled from city to city, *h* by all men,
Is 13:14 Like a *h* gazelle,
Lam 3:52 without cause *h* me down like a bird;

HUNTER (3)

Gn 10: 9 He was a mighty *h* by the grace of the LORD;
10: 9 a mighty *h* by the grace of the LORD."

25:27 boys grew up, Esau became a skillful *h*,

HUNTERS (2)

Eccl 7:26 death I find the woman who is a *h* trap,
Jer 16:16 I will send many *h* to hunt them out from

HUNTING (4)

Lv 17:13 "Anyone *h*, whether of the Israelites
1Sm 24:12 though you are *h* me down to take my life.
26:20 as if he were *h* partridge in the mountains."
1Mc 3: 5 He pursued the wicked, *h* them out,

HUPHAM (3)

Gn 46:21 Ashbel, Gera, Naaman, Ahiram, Shupham, *H*,
Nm 26:39 through *H* the clan of the Huphamites.
1Chr 7:11 Shupham and *H*.

HUPHAMITES (1)

Nm 26:39 through Hupham the clan of the *H*.

HUPPAH (1)

1Chr 24:13 the twelfth to Jakim, the thirteenth to *H*,

HUR (16)

Ex 17:10 to the top of the hill with Aaron and *H*.
17:12 Meanwhile Aaron and *H* supported his hands,
24:14 Aaron and *H* are staying with you.
31: 2 have chosen Bezalel, son of Uri, son of *H*,
35:30 has chosen Bezalel, son of Uri, son of *H*,
38:22 it was Bezalel, son of Uri, son of *H*,
Nm 31: 8 Evi, Rekem, Zur, *H* and Reba;
Jos 13:21 Evi, Rekem, Zur, *H* and Reba;
1Kgs 4: 8 son of *H* in the hill country of Ephraim;
1Chr 2:19 Caleb married Ephrath, who bore him *H*.
2:20 *H* became the father of Uri,
2:50 These were descendants of Caleb, sons of *H*,
4: 1 Perez, Hezron, Carmi, *H*, and Shobal.
4: 4 These were the descendants of *H*,
2Chr 1: 5 made by Bezalel, son of Uri, son of *H*,
Neh 3: 9 was carried out by Rephaiah, son of *H*,

HURAI (1)

1Chr 11:32 *H*, from the valley of Gaash;

HURAM (9)

1Chr 8: 5 Naaman, Ahoah, Gera, Shephuphan, and *H*.
2Chr 2: 2 Moreover, Solomon sent this message to *H*,
2:10 *H*, king of Tyre,
4:11 *H* also made the pots,
4:11 *H* thus completed the work he had to do for
8: 2 built up the cities which *H* had given him,
8:18 *H*, through his servants,
9:10 The servants of *H* and of Solomon who
9:21 went to Tarshish with the servants of *H*.

HURAM-ABI (2)

2Chr 2:12 sending you a craftsman of great skill, *H*,
4:16 *H* made all these articles for King Solomon

HURI (1)

1Chr 5:14 These were the sons of Abihail, son of *H*,

HURL (11)

Ex 9:14 or this time I will *h* all my blows upon
Jgs 5:23 the LORD, *h* a curse at its inhabitants!
1Sm 25:29 but may he *h* out the lives of your enemies
Ps(s) 73:18 you *h* them down to ruin.
Sir 28:23 It will *h* itself against them like a lion;
39:28 they *h* all their force and appease the
Is 22:17 The LORD shall *h* you down headlong,
Mt 13:42 The angels will *h* them into the fiery
13:50 and *h* the wicked into the fiery furnace,
Lk 4:30 built and intending to *h* him over the edge.
Rv 13: 6 It began to *h* blasphemies against God,

HURLED (24)

Ex 10:19 up the locusts and *h* them into the Red Sea.
14:27 sea, when the LORD *h* them into its midst.
15: 4 chariots and army he *h* into the sea;
Jos 10:11 the LORD *h* great stones from the sky above
1Sm 17:49 *h* it with the sling and struck the
Neh 9:11 Their pursuers you *h* into the depths,
2Mc 1:16 *h* stones at the leader and his companions
10:30 arrows and *h* thunderbolts at the enemy,
13: 6 up there and then *h* down to destruction.
Ps(s) 89:45 his luster and *h* his throne to the ground.
Wis 5:22 his sling, wrathful hailstones shall be *h*.
Bar 6:70 of bird, or like a corpse *h* into darkness,
Jon 1: 4 however, *h* a violent wind upon the sea,
Lk 10:15 You shall be *h* down to the realm of death!'
Rv 8: 5 from the altar, and *h* it down to the earth.
8: 7 with blood, which was *h* down to the earth.
12: 4 from the sky and *h* them down to the earth.
12: 9 *h* down to earth and his minions with him.
18:21 millstone and *h* it into the sea and said:
19:20 Both were *h* down alive into the fiery pool
20: 3 The angel *h* him into the abyss,
20:10 was *h* into the pool of burning sulphur,
20:14 nether world were *h* into the pool of fire,
20:15 of the living was *h* into this pool of fire.

HURLING (2)

Jdt 6:12 Holofernes' servants by *h* stones upon them.
2Mc 11:11 *H* themselves upon the enemy like lions,

HURLS (1)

Jb 27:22 *h* the lightning against them relentlessly;

HURRICANE (5)

Sir 43:17 the angry north wind, the *h* and the storm.
Is 5:28 flint, and their chariot wheels like the *h*.
Jer 4:13 clouds he advances, like a *h* his chariots;
Na 1: 3 In *h* and tempest is his path,
Acts 27:14 It was not long before a *h* struck,

HURRIED (15)

Gn 29:13 sister's son Jacob, he *h* out to meet him.
Ex 9:20 *h* their servants and livestock off to shelter.
2Sm 19:17 *h* down with the Judahites to meet King
2Kgs 5:21 So Gehazi *h* after Naaman.
Est 6:12 to the royal gate, while Haman *h* home,
6:14 the king's eunuchs arrived and *h* Haman off
1Mc 2:32 Many *h* out after them,
2Mc 5:21 from the temple, and *h* back to Antioch.
9:25 I made *h* visits to the outlying provinces.
Dn 13:19 left, the two old men got up and *h* to her.
Mt 28: 8 They *h* away from the tomb half-overjoyed,
Mk 6:25 At that the girl *h* back to the king's
Acts 5:23 not find them, and *h* back with the report,
17:13 they *h* there to cause a commotion and stir
20:10 Paul *h* down immediately and threw himself

HURRIEDLY (2)

Gn 41:14 and they *h* brought him from the dungeon.
Jdt 13:13 the least to the greatest, *h* assembled,

HURRIES (1)

Hg 1: 9 while each of you *h* to his own house.

HURRY (18)

Gn 19:22 *H*, escape there!
43:30 With that, Joseph had to *h* out,
45: 9 *H* back, then, to my father and tell him:
45:13 But *h* and bring my father down here."
Jgs 9:48 shoulder, then said to the men with him, *H!*
1Sm 9:12 *H* now; just today he came to the city,
20:38 Again he called to his lad, *H*,
2Sm 15:14 Leave quickly, lest he *h* and overtake us,
2Kgs 4:26 *H* to meet her,
Tb 11: 3 Let us *h* on ahead of your wife to prepare
Jdt 14: 3 They will seize their armor and *h* to their
Est 6:10 *H!* Take the robe
Ps(s) 59: 5 no guilt of mine they *h* to take up arms.
Prv 6: 3 Go, *h*, stir up your neighbor!
Sir 43:14 and like vultures the clouds *h* forth.
Lk 19: 5 he looked up and said, "Zacchaeus, *h* down.
Acts 12: 7 *H*, get up!" he said.
Ti 3:12 or perhaps Tychicus, *h* to me at Nicopolis;

HURRYING (1)

2Mc 9:14 toward which he had been *h* with the

HURT (14)

Ex 21:22 men have a fight and *h* a pregnant woman,
Tb 12: 2 It would not *h* me at all to give him half
Jb 35: 6 your offenses are many, how do you *h* him?
Eccl 5:12 riches kept by their owner to his *h*.
8: 9 one man tyrannizes over another to his *h*.
10: 9 He who moves stones may be *h* by them,
Is 65:25 shall *h* or destroy on all my holy mountain,
Jer 7:18 out to strange gods in order to *h* me.
7:19 Is it I whom they *h*,
Dn 6:23 lions' mouths so that they have not *h* me.
Na 3:19 There is no healing for your *h*,
Jn 21:17 was *h* because he had asked a third time,
Acts 7:26 Why are you trying to *h* each other?'
2Cor 2: 5 has given offense he has *h* not only me,

HURTLED (1)

2Mc 9: 7 As a result he *h* from the dashing chariot,

HURTS (2)

Ex 21:35 ox *h* another's ox so badly that it dies,
2Kgs 4:19 "My head *h!*"

HUSBAND (144)

Gn 3: 6 and she also gave some to her *h*,
3:16 Yet your urge shall be for your *h*,
16: 3 her to her *h* Abram to be his concubine.
18:12 that I am so withered and my *h* is so old,
20: 3 the woman you have taken, for she has a *h*."
29:32 now my *h* will love me.'"
29:34 at last my *h* will become attached to me,
30:15 it not enough for you to take away my *h*,
30:18 for having let my *h* have my maidservant";
30:20 This time my *h* will offer me presents,
39:14 my *h* has brought in a Hebrew slave to make
41:35 *h* all the food of the coming good years,
Ex 21:22 as much as the woman's *h* demands of him,
Lv 21: 7 nor a woman who has been divorced by her *h*;
Nm 5:13 *h* has not sufficient evidence of the fact,
5:19 while under the authority of your *h*,
5:20 while under the authority of your *h*
5:20 other than your *h* have intercourse with you'
5:27 has been impure and unfaithful to her *h*,
5:29 the authority of her *h* and acts impurely,
30: 8 she bound herself, and her *h* learns of it,
30: 9 it her *h* expresses to her his disapproval,
30:12 and her *h* learns of it yet says nothing to
30:13 day he learns of them her *h* annuls them,
30:13 since her *h* has annulled them,
30:14 her *h* can either allow to remain valid or
30:15 But if her *h*,
30:17 the relationship between a *h* and his wife,
Dt 21:13 shall be her *h* and she shall be your wife.
24: 3 the wife of another man, and the second *h*,
24: 4 then her former *h*,
25:11 save her *h* from the blows of his opponent,
28:56 will begrudge her beloved *h* and her son
Jgs 13: 6 The woman went and told her *h*,
13: 9 Since her *h* Manoah was not with her,
13:10 her, the woman ran in haste and told her *h*.
14:15 "Coax your *h* to answer the riddle for us,
19: 3 Her *h* then set out with his servant and a
19: 6 Then the girl's father said to the *h*,
19: 9 and the *h* was ready to go with his
19:25 the *h* seized his concubine and thrust her
19:26 of the house in which her *h* was a guest,
19:27 When her *h* rose that day and opened the
20: 4 the Levite, the *h* of the murdered woman,
Ru 1: 3 Moabite plateau, Elimelech, the *h* of Naomi,
1: 5 left with neither her two sons nor her *h*.
1: 9 a *h* and a home in which you will find rest."
1:12 or if tonight I had a *h* or had borne sons,
2: 1 named Boaz, of the clan of her *h* Elimelech.
4:10 up a family for her late *h* on his estate,
1Sm 1: 8 Her *h* Elkanah used to ask her:
1:18 to her quarters, ate and drank with her *h*,
1:21 The next time her *h* Elkanah was going up
1:22 Hannah did not go, explaining to her *h*,
1:23 Her *h* Elkanah answered her:
2:19 her *h* to offer the customary sacrifice.
4:19 the deaths of her father-in-law and her *h*,
4:21 to her father-in-law and her *h*
25:19 But she did not tell her *h* Nabal.
2Sm 3:15 her and took her away from her *h* Paltiel,
11:26 wife of Uriah heard that her *h* had died,
14: 5 "Alas, I am a widow; my *h* is dead.
14: 7 leave my *h* neither name nor posterity
17: 3 people to you, as a bride returns to her *h*.
2Kgs 4: 1 "My *h*, your servant, is dead.
4: 9 So she said to her *h*,
4:14 no son, and her *h* is getting on in years."
4:22 on him, she went out and called to her *h*,
4:26 ask if all is well with her, with her *h*,
Jdt 8: 2 Her *h*, Manasseh, of her own tribe
8: 7 Her *h*, Manasseh, had left her gold
10: 3 festive attire she had worn while her *h*,
16:22 the time of the death and burial of her *h*,
16:23 to be very old in the house of her *h*,
16:23 they buried her in the tomb of her *h*,
16:24 her goods to the relatives of her *h*,
Prv 7:19 For my *h* is not at home,
12: 4 A worthy wife is the crown of her *h*,
31:11 Her *h*, entrusting his heart to her,
31:23 Her *h* is prominent at the city gates as he
31:28 her *h*, too, extols her:
Sir 4:10 father, and help their mother as a *h* would;
22: 4 daughter becomes a treasure to her *h*,
22: 5 A hussy shames her father and her *h*;
23:22 *h* and offers as heir her son by a stranger.
23:23 secondly, she has wronged her *h*;
25: 1 and the mutual love of *h* and wife.
25:17 When her *h* sits among his neighbors,
25:21 and shame, when a wife supports her *h*.
25:22 a wife who brings no happiness to her *h*.
26: 1 Happy the *h* of a good wife,
26: 2 A worthy wife brings joy to her *h*,
26:13 A gracious wife delights her *h*,
36:21 Though any man may be accepted as a *h*,
42:10 home, or be sterile in that of her *h*.
Is 54: 1 wife than the children of her who has a *h*,
54: 5 For he who has become your *h* is your Maker;
Jer 3: 1 man, Does the first *h* come back to her?
6:11 Yes, all will be taken, *h* and wife,
Ez 16:32 adulterous wife receives, instead of her *h*,
16:45 the mother who spurned her *h* and children,
Dn 11: 6 those who brought her, her son and her *h*.
13:28 people came to her *h* Joakim the next day,
13:63 as did Joakim her *h* and all her relatives,
Hos 2: 4 for she is not my wife, and I am not her *h*.
2: 9 shall say, "I will go back to my first *h*,
2:18 She shall call me "My *h*,"
Mt 1:16 was the father of Joseph the *h* of Mary.
1:19 Joseph her *h*,
Mk 10: 2 permissible for a *h* to divorce his wife.
10:12 her *h* and marries another commits adultery."

HUSBAND (cont.)

Lk 2:36 having lived seven years with her *h* after
16:18 from her *h* likewise commits adultery.
Jn 4:16 He said to her, "Go, call your *h*,
4:17 "I have no *h*," replied the woman.
4:17 "You are right in saying you have no *h!*"
4:18 man you are living with now is not your *h*.
Acts 5: 9 buried your *h* can be heard at the door.
5:10 carried her out for burial beside her *h*.
Rom 7: 2 is bound to her *h* by law while he lives,
7: 3 adulteress if, while her *h* is still alive,
7: 3 if her *h* dies she is freed from that law,
1Cor 7: 2 his own wife and every woman her own *h*.
7: 3 The *h* should fulfill his conjugal
7: 3 his wife, the wife hers toward her *h*.
7: 4 does not belong to herself but to her *h*;
7: 4 a *h* does not belong to himself but to his
7:10 a wife must not separate from her *h*.
7:11 Similarly, a *h* must not divorce his wife.
7:13 And if any woman has a *h* who is an
7:14 *h* is consecrated by his believing wife;
7:14 wife is consecrated by her believing *h*.
7:15 *h* or wife is not bound in such cases.
7:16 your *h*; or you, *h*, that you will not save
7:34 her and is concerned with pleasing her *h*.
7:39 wife is bound to her *h* as long as he lives.
7:39 If her *h* dies she is free to marry,
11: 3 the head of a woman is her *h*;
2Cor 11: 2 I have given you in marriage to one *h*,
Gal 4:27 far more than of her who has a *h!*"
Eph 5:23 because the *h* is head of his wife
5:33 for her part showing respect for her *h*.
Rv 21: 2 as a bride prepared to meet her *h*.

HUSBANDED (1)

Gn 41:48 he *h* all the food of these years of plenty

HUSBANDMEN (1)

Jl 1:11 Be appalled, you *h!*

HUSBANDS (34)

Nm 30:11 "If it is in her *h* house that she makes a
Dt 25: 5 but her *h* brother shall go to her and
Ru 1:11 sons in my womb who may become your *h?*
1:13 yourselves of *h* until those sons grew up?
2:11 for your mother-in-law after your *h* death;
Tb 3: 8 For she had been married to seven *h*,
3: 8 "You are the one who strangles your *h!*
3: 8 you have had no joy with any one of your *h*.
3: 9 Because your *h* are dead?
3:15 I have already lost seven *h*;
6:14 that her *h* died in their bridal chambers.
Est 1:17 disdain upon their *h* when it is reported,
1:20 as it is, all wives will honor their *h*,
Prv 6:34 For vindictive is the *h* wrath,
Sir 36:22 A woman's beauty makes her *h* face light up,
36:24 A wife is her *h* richest treasure,
Jer 29: 6 for your sons and give your daughters *h*.
44:19 was it without our *h* consent that we baked
Ez 16:45 to those who spurned their *h* and children
Dn 13: 7 used to enter her *h* garden for a walk.
Lk 17:27 They ate and drank, they took *h* and wives,
Rom 7: 2 she is released from the law regarding *h*.
1Cor 14:35 anything, they should ask their *h* at home.
Eph 5:22 Wives should be submissive to their *h* as
5:24 should submit to their *h* in every thing.
5:25 *H*, love your wives,
5:28 *H* should love their wives as they do their
Col 3:18 You who are wives, be submissive to your *h*.
3:19 *H*, love your wives.
Ti 2: 4 younger women to love their *h* and children,
2: 5 at home, kindly, submissive to their *h*.
1Pt 3: 1 You married women must obey your *h*,
3: 5 reliant on God and obedient to their *h*—
3: 7 You *h*, too, must show consideration

HUSH (3)

Neh 8:11 Levites quieted all the people saying, *H*,
Tb 10: 6 *H*, do not think about it,
Acts 21:40 A great *h* fell on them as he began to

HUSHA (2)

2Sm 21:18 On that occasion Sibbecai, from *H*,
1Chr 11:29 Sibbecai, from *H*;

HUSHAH (2)

2Sm 23:27 Sibbecai from *H*;
1Chr 4: 4 father of Gedor, and Ezer the father of *H*.

HUSHAI (12)

2Sm 15:32 God, *H* the Archite was there to meet him,
15:37 So David's friend *H* went into the city of
16:16 friend *H* the Archite came to Absalom,
16:17 But Absalom asked *H*:
16:18 *H* replied to Absalom:
17: 5 said, "Now call *H* the Archite also;
17: 6 When *H* came to Absalom,
17: 7 *H* replied to Absalom,
17:14 Israelites pronounced the counsel of *H*
17:15 *H* said to the priests Zadok and Abiathar:
1Kgs 4:16 Baana, son of *H*.
1Chr 27:33 and *H* the Archite was the king's confidant.

HUSHAM (4)

Gn 36:34 When Jobab died, *H*,
36:35 When *H* died,
1Chr 1:45 When Jobab died, *H*,
1:46 *H* died and Hadad,

HUSHATHITE (2)

1Chr 20: 4 At that time, Sibbecai the *H* slew Sippai,
27:11 for the eighth month, was Sibbecai the *H*,

HUSHED (1)

Ps(s) 107:29 He *h* the storm to a gentle breeze,

HUSHIM (4)

Gn 46:23 The sons of Dan: *H*.
1Chr 7:12 The sons of Dan: *H*.
8: 8 he had put away his wives *H* and Baara.
8:11 By *H* he became the father of Abitub and

HUSKS (2)

Sir 27: 4 When a sieve is shaken, the *h* appear;
Lk 15:16 with the *h* that were fodder for the pigs,

HUSSY (1)

Sir 22: 5 A *h* shames her father and her husband;

HUT (5)

Is 1: 8 Zion is left like a *h* in a vineyard,
24:20 a drunkard, and it will sway like a *h*;
Am 9:11 day I will raise up the fallen *h* of David;
Jon 4: 5 a *h* and waited under it in the shade,
Acts 15:16 return and rebuild the fallen *h* of David:

HYACINTH (1)

Rv 21:20 the tenth chrysoprase, the eleventh *h*,

HYDASPES (1)

Jdt 1: 6 the Euphrates, the Tigris, and the *H*,

HYENA (1)

Sir 13:17 there be peace between the *h* and the dog?

HYENAS (2)

1Sm 13:18 the Valley of the *H* toward the desert.
Jer 12: 9 My heritage is a prey for *h*,

HYMENAEUS (2)

1Tm 1:20 of their faith, among them *H* and Alexander;
2Tm 2:17 This is the case with *H* and Philetus,

HYMN (14)

Jgs 5: 3 LORD will sing my song, my *h* to the LORD,
2Chr 20:22 At the moment they began their jubilant *h*,
Tb 13:18 The end of Tobit's *h* of praise.
Jdt 15:14 and the people swelled this *h* of praise:
16:13 "A new *h* I will sing to my God.
1Mc 4:33 all who know your name may *h* your praise."
Ps(s) 40: 4 a new song into my mouth, a *h* to our God.
65: 2 To you we owe our *h* of praise, O God,
Sir 39:14 Send up the sweet odor of your *h* of praise;
Mt 21:16 children you have framed a *h* of praise'?"
Jas 5:13 good spirits, he should sing a *h* of praise.
Rv 5: 9 This is the new *h* they sang:
14: 3 were singing a new *h* before the throne,
14: 3 This *h* no one could learn except the

HYMNS (17)

2Chr 7: 6 when David used them to accompany the *h*.
Neh 12: 8 with his brethren, was in charge of the *h*,
12:27 thanksgiving *h* and the music of cymbals,
12:46 *h* of praise and thanksgiving to God
Tb 13:18 of Jerusalem shall sing *h* of gladness,
Jdt 15:13 armor, wearing garlands and singing *h*.
1Mc 4:24 they were singing *h* and glorifying Heaven,
13:47 the city with *h* and songs of praise.
13:51 lyres, and the singing of *h* and canticles,
2Mc 1:30 Then the priests began to sing *h*.
10: 7 they sang *h* of grateful praise to him who
10:38 they blessed, with *h* of grateful praise,
Ps(s) 47: 8 sing *h* of praise.
Sir 50:18 Then *h* would re-echo,
Acts 16:25 Paul and Silas were praying and singing *h*
Eph 5:19 another in psalms and *h* and inspired songs.
Col 3:16 to God from your hearts in psalms, *h*,

HYPOCRISY (3)

Mt 23:28 exterior while *h* and evil fill you within.
Mk 12:15 Knowing their *h* he said to them,
Lk 12: 1 the yeast of the Pharisees, which is *h*.

HYPOCRITE (4)

Sir 1:26 Play not the *h* before men;
32:15 law masters it, but the *h* finds it a trap.
Mt 7: 5 You *h!* Remove the plank
Lk 6:42 *H*, remove the plank from your own eye first;

HYPOCRITES (10)

Ps(s) 26: 4 worthless men, nor do I consort with *h*.
Mt 6: 2 and streets like *h* looking for applause.
6: 5 do not behave like the *h* who love to stand
6:16 fast, you are not to look glum as the *h* do.
15: 7 "You *h!*
22:18 "Why are you trying to trip me up, you *h?*
24:51 and settle with him as is done with *h*.
Mk 7: 6 prophesied about you *h* when he wrote,
Lk 12:56 You *h!* If you can interpret
13:15 "O you *h!*

HYRCANUS (1)

2Mc 3:11 orphans, and a part was the property of *H*,

HYSSOP (12)

Ex 12:22 Then take a bunch of *h*,
Lv 14: 4 as some cedar wood, scarlet yarn, and *h*.
14: 6 cedar wood, the scarlet yarn and the *h*,
14:49 as well as cedar wood, scarlet yarn, and *h*.
14:51 the cedarwood, the *h* and the scarlet yarn,
14:52 the living bird, the cedar wood, the *h*,
Nm 19: 6 *h* and scarlet yarn and throw them into the
19:18 Then a man who is clean shall take some *h*,
1Kgs 5:13 Lebanon to the *h* growing out of the wall,
Ps(s) 51: 9 Cleanse me of sin with *h*,
Jn 19:29 wine on some *h* and raised it to his lips.
Heb 9:19 with water and crimson wool and *h*,

I

IBEX (1)

Dt 14: 5 deer, the gazelle, the roe deer, the *i*,

IBHAR (3)

2Sm 5:15 Shammua, Shobab, Nathan, Solomon, *I*,
1Chr 3: 6 *I*, Elishua, Eliphelet, Nogah, Nepheg,
14: 5 Shammua, Shobab, Nathan, Solomon, *I*,

IBIS (1)

Dt 14:16 of hawks, the owl, the screech owl, the *i*,

IBLEAM (6)

Jos 17:11 Beth-shean and its towns, *I* and its towns,
21:25 pasture lands and *I* with its pasture lands.
Jgs 1:27 and its towns, those of *I* and its towns,
2Kgs 9:27 as he rode through the pass of Gur near *I*.
15:10 Zechariah, attacked and killed him at *I*,
1Chr 6:55 pasture lands and *I* with its pasture lands.

IBNEIAH (1)

1Chr 9: 8 son of Hodaviah, son of Hassenuah, *I*,

IBNIJAH (1)

1Chr 9: 8 son of Shephatiah, son of Reuel, son of *I*.

IBRI (1)

1Chr 24:27 Shoham, Zaccur, and *I*.

IBSAM (1)

1Chr 7: 2 were Uzzi, Rephaiah, Jeriel, Jahmai, *I*,

IBZAN (2)

Jgs 12: 8 After him *I* of Bethlehem judged Israel.
12:10 years, *I* died and was buried in Bethlehem.

ICE (5)

Jb 6:16 Though they may be black with *i*,
38:29 Out of whose womb comes the *i*,
Wis 16:22 and *i* withstood fire and were not melted,
Sir 43:21 he sends that turn the ponds to lumps of *i*.
Dn 3:70 *I* and snow,

ICELIKE (1)

Wis 19:21 that went about in them, nor melted the *i*,

ICHABOD (2)

1Sm 4:21 [She named the child *I*,
14: 3 Ahijah, son of Ahitub, brother of *I*,

ICONIUM (6)

Acts 13:51 their feet in protest and went on to *I*.
14: 1 In *I* likewise,
14:19 and *I* arrived and won the people over.
14:21 retraced their steps to Lystra and *I* first,
16: 2 in Lystra and *I* spoke highly of him,
2Tm 3:11 persecutions and sufferings in Antioch, *I*,

IDALAH (1)

Jos 19:15 Kattah, Nahalal, Shimron, *I* and Bethlehem,

IDBASH (1)

1Chr 4: 3 Jezreel, Ishma, and *I*;

IDDO (14)

1Kgs 4:14 Ahinadab, son of *I*,
1Chr 6: 6 whose son was Joah, whose son was *I*,
27:21 the half-tribe of Manasseh in Gilead, *I*,
2Chr 9:29 of *I* the seer which concern Jeroboam,
12:15 and of *I* the seer [his family record].
13:22 written in the midrash of the prophet *I*.
Ezr 5: 1 prophets Haggai and Zechariah, son of *I*,
6:14 prophets, Haggai and Zechariah, son of *I*.
8:17 wise leaders, with a command for *I*,
8:17 them what to say to *I* and his brethren,
Neh 12: 4 Hattush, Shecaniah, Rehum, Meremoth, *I*,
12:16 for *I*,
Zec 1: 1 Zechariah, son of Berechiah, son of *I*:
1: 7 Zechariah, son of Berechiah, son of *I*,

IDEA (13)

Gn 21:26 "I have no *i* who did that,"
31:32 had no *i* that Rachel had stolen the idols.
1Sm 17:55 as your majesty is alive, I have no *i*."
1Chr 13: 4 for the *i* was pleasing to all the people.
Lk 19:48 but they had no *i* how to achieve it,
Jn 5:13 restored to health had no *i* who it was.
9:12 He replied, "I have no *i*."
9:21 now, or who opened his eyes, we have no *i*.
9:29 but we have no *i* where this man comes from."
13:29 A few had the *i* that,
Acts 7:40 we have no *i* what has happened to him.'
Gal 1:22 in Judea had no *i* what I looked like;
Jas 4:14 *i* what kind of life will be yours tomorrow.

IDEAL (2)

Prv 31:13 The *I* Wife Like merchant ships,
Jas 1:25 into freedom's *i* law and abides by it.

IDEALS (1)

Phil 2: 2 the one love, united in spirit and *i*.

IDEAS (1)

Lk 24:38 Why do such *i* cross your mind?

IDENTICAL (1)

1Kgs 6:25 The cherubim were *i* in size and shape,

IDENTIFIED (1)

Nm 17:24 each prince *i* his own staff and took it,

IDENTIFY (2)

Gn 27:23 to *i* him because his hands were hairy,
31:32 you *i* anything here as belonging to you,

IDENTITY (1)

Gn 42: 7 own *i* from them and spoke sternly to them.

IDLE (18)

1Mc 2: 7 and to sit *i* while it is given into the
Jb 27:12 then do you spend yourselves in *i* words!
35:13 But it is *i* to say God does not hear or
Ps(s) 74:11 keep your right hand *i* beneath your cloak?
Prv 12:11 but he who follows *i* pursuits is a fool.
28:19 *i* pursuits a man has his fill of poverty.
Eccl 11: 6 and at evening let not your hand be *i*:
12: 3 the grinders are *i* because they are few,
Wis 14: 5 that the products of your Wisdom be not *i*;
Sir 33:26 his hands be *i* and he will seek to be free.
33:28 Force him to work that he be not *i*,
37:11 harvest, to an *i* slave about a great task:
Mt 20: 6 'Why have you been standing here *i* all day?'
1Tm 1: 4 which promote *i* speculations rather than
6:20 *i* talk and the contradictions of what is
2Tm 2:16 Avoid worldly, *i* talk,
Jas 2:20 ignoramus, that without works faith is *i*?
2Pt 2: 3 condemnation has not lain *i* all this time,

IDLENESS (3)

Ex 21:19 *i* and provide for his complete cure.
Prv 31:27 household, and eats not her food in *i*.
Sir 33:28 idle, for *i* is an apt teacher of mischief.

IDLY (2)

Lv 19:16 by *i* when your neighbor's life is at stake.
Jb 39:13 The wings of the ostrich beat *i*;

IDOL (48)

Lv 26: 1 an *i* or a sacred pillar for yourselves,
Dt 4:16 by fashioning an *i* to represent any figure,
4:23 his command an *i* in any form whatsoever.
4:25 by fashioning an *i* in any form
9:12 and have made for themselves a molten *i*,
27:15 molten *i*— an abomination to the LORD,
Jgs 17: 3 of them a carved *i* overlaid with silver.
17: 4 by making a carved *i* overlaid with silver."
18:14 idols, and a carved *i* overlaid with silver?
18:18 and the carved *i* overlaid with silver,
18:20 *i* and went off in the midst of the band.
18:30 Danites set up the carved *i* for themselves,
18:31 They maintained the carved *i* Micah had
1Sm 19:13 the household *i* and laid it in the bed,
19:16 they found the household *i* in the bed,
1Kgs 11: 5 and Milcom, the *i* of the Ammonites,
11: 7 *i* of Moab, and to Molech, the idol
2Kgs 21: 7 The Asherah *i* he had made,
23:13 and of Milcom, the *i* of the Ammonites.
2Chr 33: 7 *i* that he had carved in the house of God,
33:15 He removed the foreign gods and the *i* from
1Mc 10:83 entered Beth-dagon, the temple of their *i*,
Wis 14: 8 but the handmade *i* is accursed,
Sir 30:19 to an *i* that can neither taste nor smell?
Is 40:19 An *i*, cast by a craftsman,
40:20 to set up an *i* that will not be unsteady?
44: 9 *I* makers all amount to nothing,
44:10 forms a god, or casts an *i* to no purpose,
44:13 marks with a stylus the outline of an *i*.
44:15 which he adores, an *i* which he worships.
44:17 Of what remains he makes a god, his *i*,
48: 5 That you might not say, "My *i* did them,
66: 3 incense, like paying homage to an *i*.
Jer 10:14 every artisan is put to shame by his *i*:
13:25 forgotten me, and trusted in the lying *i*,
51:17 every artisan is put to shame by his *i*:
Ez 8:12 the house of Israel is doing in his *i* room?
Dn 14: 3 The Babylonians had an *i* called Bel,
Am 8:14 who swear by the shameful *i* of Samaria,
Acts 7:41 the calf and offered sacrifice to the *i*,
1Cor 8: 4 we know that an *i* is really nothing,
8:10 reclining at table in the temple of an *i*,
10:19 to an *i* is really offered to that idol,
10:19 *i*, or that an *i* is a reality?
10:28 to you, "This was offered in *i* worship,"
Rv 13:14 telling them to make an *i* in honor of the

IDOL-OFFERING (1)

1Cor 8:10 influenced to the point that he eats the *i*?

IDOL-WORSHIPERS (2)

Rv 21: 8 the *i* and deceivers of every sort
22:15 the *i* and all who love falsehood.

IDOLATER (1)

1Cor 5:11 if he is immoral, covetous, an *i*,

IDOLATERS (3)

1Cor 5:10 world, or the covetous or thieves or *i*.
6: 9 no fornicators, *i*,
10: 7 Do not become *i*, as some of them did.

IDOLATOR (1)

Eph 5: 5 in effect an *i*—

IDOLATROUS (3)

Jgs 8:27 all Israel paid *i* homage to it there,
Is 10:10 my hand reached out to *i* kingdoms
Mal 2:11 the LORD loves, and has married an *i* woman.

IDOLATRY (8)

1Sm 15:23 and presumption is the crime of *i*.
2Chr 21:11 of Jerusalem into *i* and seduced Judah.
21:13 and the inhabitants of Jerusalem into *i*,
Ps(s) 40: 5 to *i* or to those who stray after falsehood.
Ez 23:49 and you shall pay for your sins of *i*.
Gal 5:20 lewd conduct, impurity, licentiousness, *i*,
Col 3: 5 evil desires, and that lust which is *i*.
1Pt 4: 3 orgies, carousing, and wanton *i*.

IDOLS (151)

Gn 31:19 appropriated her father's household *i*.
31:32 had no idea that Rachel had stolen the *i*.
31:33 but he did not find the *i*.
31:34 Now Rachel had taken the *i*,
31:35 despite his search, he did not find his *i*.
Ex 20: 4 You shall not carve *i* for yourselves in
Lv 19: 4 "Do not turn aside to *i*,
26:30 and cast your corpses on those of your *i*.
Dt 5: 8 You shall not carve *i* for yourselves in
7: 5 sacred poles, and destroy their *i* by fire.
12: 3 poles, and shatter the *i* of their gods,
29:16 you saw the loathsome *i* of wood and stone,
32:16 gods and angered him with abominable *i*.
32:21 'no-god' and angered me with their vain *i*,
Jgs 3:19 He returned, however, from where the *i* are,
3:26 made good his escape and, passing the *i*,
17: 5 He also made an ephod and household *i*,
18:14 houses there are an ephod, household *i*,
18:18 in and taken the ephod, the household *i*,
18:20 agreeing, took the ephod, household *i*,
1Sm 12:21 *i* which can neither profit nor save;
31: 9 Philistines to their *i* and to the people.
1Kgs 15:12 and removing all the *i* his father had made.
16:13 the God of Israel, to anger by their *i*.
16:26 the God of Israel, to anger by their *i*.
21:26 completely abominable by following *i*,
2Kgs 17:12 that provoked the LORD, and served *i*,
17:41 the LORD, but also served their *i*.
21:11 him, and has led Judah into sin by his *i*,
21:21 and worshiping the *i* his father had served.
23:24 and spirits, with the household gods, *i*,
1Chr 10: 9 the good news to their *i* and their people.
20: 2 took the crown of Milcom from the *i* head.
2Chr 15: 8 remove the detestable *i* from the whole land
24:18 began to serve the sacred poles and the *i*;
28: 2 Israel and even made molten *i* of the Baals.
33:22 the *i* which his father Manasseh had made,
Tb 14: 6 all shall abandon their *i* which have
1Mc 1:43 sacrificed to *i* and profaned the sabbath.
3:48 Gentiles consulted the images of their *i*.
13:47 purified the houses in which there were *i*.
2Mc 2: 2 the gold and silver *i* and their ornaments.
12:40 found amulets sacred to the *i* of Jamnia,
Ps(s) 31: 7 You hate those who worship vain *i*,
78:58 and with their *i* roused his jealousy.
106:36 They served their *i*,
106:38 Whom they sacrificed to the *i* of Canaan,
115: 4 Their *i* are silver and gold,
135:15 The *i* of the nations are silver and gold,
Wis 14:11 *i* of the nations shall a visitation come,
14:12 source of wantonness is the devising of *i*;
14:27 For the worship of infamous *i* is the
14:29 For as their trust is in soulless *i*,
14:30 ill of God and devoted themselves to *i*,
15:13 he creates fragile vessels and *i* alike.
15:15 esteemed all the *i* of the nations gods,
Sir 49: 2 betrayals, and destroyed the abominable *i*.
Is 2: 8 Their land is full of *i*;
2:18 The *i* will perish forever.
2:20 throw to the moles and the bats the *i* of
10:11 Just as I treated Samaria and her *i*,
19: 1 The *i* of Egypt tremble before him,
19: 3 They shall consult *i* and charmers,
30:22 *i* and your gold-covered images;
31: 7 spurn his sinful *i* of silver and gold,
41:29 works are nought, their *i* are empty wind!
42: 8 I give to no other, nor my praise to *i*.
42:17 turned back in utter shame who trust in *i*;
44:18 The *i* have neither knowledge nor reason;
45:20 wooden *i* and pray to gods that cannot save.
46: 1 stoops, their *i* are upon beasts and cattle;
Jer 2: 5 they withdrew from me, Went after empty *i*,
2: 8 by Baal, and went after useless *i*.
7:30 by setting up in it their abominable *i*.
8: 5 Why do they cling to deceptive *i*,
8:19 [Why do they provoke me with their *i*,
10: 3 For the cult *i* of the nations are nothing,
10: 8 these *i* they teach about are wooden:
14:22 nations' *i* is there any that gives rain?
16:18 land with their detestable corpses of *i*,
16:19 heritage of our fathers, empty *i* of no use."
32:34 after me by the horrid *i* they set up in it.
50: 2 images are put to shame, her *i* shattered.
50:38 For it is a land of *i*,
51:47 coming when I will punish the *i* of Babylon;
51:52 says the LORD, when I will punish her *i*,
Bar 6:72 The better for the just man who has no *i*:
Ez 6: 4 cast down your slain ones before your *i*;
6: 6 and laid waste, your *i* broken and removed,
6: 9 me [and their eyes which lusted after *i*.
6:13 when their slain shall lie amid their *i*,
7:20 of them their abominable images [their *i*.
8:10 beasts [all the *i* of the house of Israel].
14: 3 memory of their *i* fresh in their hearts,
14: 4 holding the memory of his *i* in his heart
14: 4 his answer in person because of his many *i*.
14: 5 estranged from me through all their *i*.
14: 6 Return and be converted from your *i*;
14: 7 and holds the memory of his *i* in his heart
16:36 with your lovers and abominable *i*,
18: 6 his eyes to the *i* of the house of Israel:
18:12 give back a pledge, raises his eyes to *i*,
18:15 his eyes to the *i* of the house of Israel,
20: 7 not defile yourselves with the *i* of Egypt:
20: 8 eyes, they did not abandon the *i* of Egypt.
20:16 much were their hearts devoted to their *i*,
20:18 do not defile yourselves with their *i*.
20:24 with eyes only for the *i* of their fathers.
20:30 Will you lust after their detestable *i*?
20:31 with all your *i* even to this day.
20:39 Come, each one of you, destroy your *i*!
20:39 my holy name with your gifts and your *i*.
22: 3 which has made *i* for her own defilement.
22: 4 the *i* you made you have become defiled;
23: 7 for whom she lusted [with all their *i*.
23:30 nations by defiling yourself with their *i*.
23:37 They committed adultery with their *i*;
23:39 day they slew their children for their *i*,
33:25 mountains, you raise your eyes to your *i*,
36:18 ground, and because they defiled it with *i*.
36:25 and from all your *i* I will cleanse you.
37:23 shall they defile themselves with their *i*,
44:10 Israel strayed from me to pursue their *i*,
44:12 used to minister for them before their *i*,
Dn 14: 5 "Because I worship not *i* made with hands,
Hos 3: 4 pillar, without ephod or household *i*.
4:17 Ephraim is an associate of *i*,
8: 4 silver and gold they made *i* for themselves,
11: 2 to the Baals and burning incense to *i*.
13: 2 images, Silver *i* according to their fancy,

IDOLS (cont.)

14: 9 What more has he to do with *i?*
Jon 2: 9 vain *i* forsake their source of mercy.
Mi 1: 7 All her *i* shall be broken to pieces,
Hb 2:18 maker should trust in it, and make dumb *i?*
Zec 13: 2 destroy the names of the *i* from the land,
Acts 15:20 abstain from anything contaminated by *i,*
15:29 to abstain from meat sacrificed to *i,*
17:16 at the sight of *i* everywhere in the city.
21:25 were merely to avoid meat sacrificed to *i,*
Rom 2:22 You who abhor *i,* do you rob temples?
1Cor 8: 1 about meats that have been offered to *i.*
8: 4 eating meats that have been offered to *i:*
8: 7 some were so recently devoted to *i,*
10:14 whom I love, to shun the worship of *i,*
12: 2 were pagans you were led astray to mute *i,*
2Cor 6:16 there is between the temple of God and *i.*
1Thes 1: 9 you, and how you turned to God from *i,*
1Jn 5:21 children, be on your guard against *i.*
Rv 2:14 to *i* and to practice fornication.
2:20 lewdness and to eat food sacrificed to *i.*
9:20 did not repent of the *i* they had made.

IDUMEA (7)

1Mc 3:41 from *I* and from Philistia joined with them.
4:29 They came into *I* and camped at Beth-zur,
4:61 people might have a stronghold facing *I.*
5: 3 the sons of Esau at Akrabattene in *I,*
6:31 through *I* and camped before Beth-zur.
2Mc 12:32 marching against Gorgias, governor of *I,*
Mk 3: 8 came to him from Judea, Jerusalem, *I,*

IDUMEANS (2)

2Mc 10:15 At the same time the *I,*
10:16 quickly against the strongholds of the *I.*

IGAL (2)

2Sm 23:36 *I,* son of Nathan, from Zobah;
1Chr 3:22 sons of Shecaniah were Shemiah, Hattush, *I,*

IGDALIAH (1)

Jer 35: 4 the room of the sons of Hanan, son of *I,*

IGNITED (1)

Lk 12:49 How I wish the blaze were *i!*

IGNOBLE (2)

Wis 15:10 is his hope, and more *i* than clay his life;
1Cor 15:43 What is sown is *i,* what rises is glorious.

IGNOMINY (4)

1Sm 11: 2 eye, that I may thus bring *i* on all Israel."
Jb 10:15 filled with *i* and sodden with affliction!
Ps(s) 69:20 You know my reproach, my shame and my *i;*
71:13 in *i* and disgrace who seek to harm me.

IGNORAMUS (1)

Jas 2:20 Do you want proof, you *i,*

IGNORANCE (13)

2Mc 11:31 in any way for faults committed through *i.*
Jb 38: 2 that obscures divine plans with words of *i?*
Wis 13: 1 by nature foolish who were in *i* of God,
14:22 even though they live in a great war of *i,*
Sir 4:26 guilt, but of your *i* rather be ashamed.
Ez 45:20 who have sinned through inadvertence or *i;*
Acts 3:17 know, my brothers, that you acted out of *i,*
17:23 in *i* I intend to make known to you.
1Cor 12: 1 to leave you in *i* about spiritual gifts.
2Cor 10:12 one another, they only demonstrate their *i.*
Eph 4:18 because of their *i* and their resistance;
5:17 Do not continue in *i,*
1Pt 1:14 the desires that once shaped you in your *i.*

IGNORANT (11)

Eccl 8: 7 for man that he is *i* of what is to come;
Jer 10:14 Every man is stupid, *i;*
51:17 Every man is stupid, *i;*
Rom 11:25 be *i* of this mystery lest you be conceited;
1Cor 15:34 Some of you are quite *i* of God;
1Tm 6: 4 be recognized as both conceited and *i,*
2Tm 2:23 to do with senseless, *i* disputations.
Heb 5:13 alone is *i* of the word that sanctifies,
1Pt 2:15 You must silence the *i* talk of foolish men
2Pt 2:12 pour abuse on things of which they are *i.*
3:16 The *i* and the unstable distort them (just

IGNORE (4)

Est E:17 well, then, to *i* the letter sent by Haman,
Jb 11:11 will he then *i* it?
Hos 4: 6 law of your God, I will also *i* your sons.
Heb 2: 3 if we *i* a salvation as great as ours?

IGNORED (7)

1Kgs 12: 8 he *i* the advice the elders had given him,
2Chr 10: 8 But he *i* the advice the elders had given
Prv 1:25 all my counsel, and my reproof you *i*—
1:30 They *i* my counsel,
Hos 4: 6 Since you have *i* the law of your God,
Mt 22: 5 Some *i* the invitation and went their way,
1Cor 14:38 anyone ignores it, he in turn should be *i.*

IGNORES (6)

Prv 28:27 want, but he who *i* them gets many a curse.
Sir 20: 6 but a boasting fool *i* the proper time.
Mt 18:17 If he *i* them, refer it to the church.
18:17 If he *i* even the church,
1Cor 14:38 If anyone *i* it,
3Jn 1: 9 who enjoys being their leader, *i* us.

IGNORING (2)

1Kgs 12:13 *I* the advice the elders had given him,
2Chr 10:13 *I* the advice the elders had given him,

IIM (1)

Jos 15:29 Baalah, *I,*

IISHVAH (1)

1Chr 7:30 The sons of Asher were Imnah, *I,*

IJON (3)

1Kgs 15:20 They attacked *I,*
2Kgs 15:29 king of Assyria, came and took *I,*
2Chr 16: 4 They attacked *I,*

IKKESH (3)

2Sm 23:26 Ira, son of *I,*
1Chr 11:28 Ira, son of *I,*
27: 9 for the sixth month, was Ira, son of *I,*

ILAI (1)

1Chr 11:29 *I,* from Ahoh;

ILL (51)

Dt 15:10 to him, give freely and not with *i* will;
2Sm 12:15 to David, and it became desperately *i.*
2Kgs 8:11 him down until Hazael became *i* at ease.
9:16 to Jezreel, where Joram lay *i* and Ahaziah,
20: 1 those days, when Hezekiah was mortally *i,*
20:12 of Babylon, heard that Hezekiah had been *i,*
2Chr 32:24 In those days Hezekiah became mortally *i.*
Tb 3:10 she hanged herself because of *i* fortune!'
Est B: 7 whose present *i* will is of long standing,
2Mc 9:21 Now that I am *i,*
Ps(s) 35:13 But I, when they were *i,*
41: 4 take away all his ailment when he is *i.*
41: 9 and 'Now that he lies *i,*
106:32 and Moses fared *i* on their account,
Prv 25:10 reproach you, and your *i* repute cease not.
Eccl 7:21 you hear your servant speaking *i* of you,
7:22 you have many times spoken *i* of others.
Wis 14:30 *i* of God and devoted themselves to idols,
18:19 they perish unaware of why they suffered *i.*
Sir 8: 4 man, lest he speak *i* of your forebears.
14: 3 Wealth *i* becomes the mean man;
38: 9 My son, when you are *i,*
Is 3:11 All goes *i,* with the work of his hands
38: 1 those days, when Hezekiah was mortally *i,*
Bar 6:33 they are treated well or *i* by anyone,
Dn 8:27 I, Daniel, was weak and *i* for some days;
Am 6: 6 are not made *i* by the collapse of Joseph!
Mt 11:21 "It will go *i* with you, Chorazin!
11:21 And just as *i* with you, Bethsaida!
25:36 I was *i* and you comforted me,
25:39 we visit you when you were *i* or in prison?'
25:43 I was *i* and in prison and you did not come
25:44 naked or *i* or in prison
Mk 1:30 Simon's mother-in-law lay *i* with a fever,
1:32 drew on, they brought him all who were *i,*
5:23 "My little daughter is critically *i.*
9:39 my name can at the same time speak *i* of me.
Lk 10:13 It will go *i* with you, Chorazin!
10:13 And just as *i* with you Bethsaida!
Jn 4:46 to be a royal official whose son was *i.*
Acts 9:37 At about that time she fell *i* and died.
19: 9 but chose to speak *i* of the new way in the
24:25 *I* send for you again when I find the time."
28: 5 and suffered no *i* effects from the bite.
Rom 1:29 maliciousness, greed, *i* will,
2Cor 6: 8 honored or dishonored, spoken of well or *i.*
1Tm 5:14 our enemies no occasion to speak *i* of us.
2Tm 4:20 Trophimus I had to leave *i* at Miletus.
Jas 4:11 not, my brothers, speak *i* of one another.
4:11 The one who speaks *i* of his brother or
5:15 in faith will reclaim the one who is *i,*

ILL-FEELING (1)

Sir 7:26 but where there is *i,* trust her not.

ILL-FORMED (1)

Gn 41:19 other cows, scrawny, most *i* and gaunt.

ILL-GOTTEN (5)

Nm 5: 7 he has done, restore his *i* goods in full,
5: 8 restoration of the *i* goods can be made,
Prv 10: 2 *I* treasures profit nothing,
28:16 He who hates *i* gain prolongs his days.
Sir 34:18 his gifts who offers in sacrifice *i* goods!

ILL-PROPORTIONED (1)

Lv 22:23 An ox or a sheep that is in any way *i* or

ILL-TEMPERED (2)

Prv 15:18 An *i* man stirs up strife,
29:22 An *i* man stirs up disputes,

ILL-TREATED (2)

Heb 11:25 he wished to be *i* along with God's people
13: 3 and of the *i* as of yourselves,

ILL-TREATMENT (1)

Acts 5:41 worthy of *i* for the sake of the Name.

ILLEGITIMATE (2)

Hos 5: 7 LORD, for they have begotten *i* children;
Jn 8:41 They cried, "We are no *i* breed!

ILLICIT (5)

Nm 25: 1 having *i* relations with the Moabite women.
1Sm 8: 3 but sought *i* gain and accepted bribes,
Acts 15:20 contaminated by idols, from *i* sexual union,
15:29 strangled animals, and from *i* sexual union.
21:25 of strangled animals, and *i* sexual union."

ILLNESS (12)

2Kgs 8:29 to Jezreel to visit him there in his *i.*
2Chr 22: 6 Because of this *i,*
Jdt 8: 3 and he died of this *i* in Bethulia,
2Mc 9:21 Persia, I fell victim to a troublesome *i;*
9:22 I have great hopes of recovering from my *i.*
Sir 10:10 A slight *i*— the doctor jests,
30:17 bitter life, unending sleep to constant *i.*
31: 2 more than a serious *i* it disturbs repose.
Is 38: 9 had been sick and had recovered from his *i:*
Mt 4:23 cured the people of every disease and *i.*
Mk 5:34 Go in peace and be free of this *i.*"
Phil 2:26 was distressed that you heard about his *i.*

ILLNESSES (1)

1Tm 5:23 stomach, and because of your frequent *i.*

ILLS (2)

Dt 29:21 the *i* with which the LORD has smitten it
Ps(s) 103: 3 all your iniquities, he heals all your *i.*

ILLUMINATED (1)

1Mc 4:50 on the lampstand, and these *i* the temple.

ILLUMINE (1)

Ps(s) 97: 4 His lightnings *i* the world;

ILLUMINED (2)

Ps(s) 77:19 your lightning *i* the world;
Lk 11:36 *i* as when a lamp shines brightly for you."

ILLUMINES (1)

Eccl 8: 1 A man's wisdom *i* his face,

ILLUSION (2)

Ps(s) 62:10 an *i* are men of rank;
Eph 4:22 which deteriorates through *i* and desire,

ILLUSIONS (2)

2Mc 7:18 "Have no vain *i.*
Is 30:10 speak flatteries to us, conjure up *i.*

ILLUSTRATE (1)

Jas 2:25 Rahab the harlot will *i* the point.

ILLUSTRIOUS (4)

Ezr 4:10 the great and *i* Assurbanipal transported
Sir 26:19 *i* men held in contempt;
44: 7 glorious in their time, each *i* in his day.
48:22 David, As ordered by the *i* prophet Isaiah,

ILLYRIA (1)

Rom 15:19 from Jerusalem all the way around to *I.*

IMAGE (43)

Gn 1:26 "Let us make man in our *i,*
1:27 in his *i;* in the divine image he created
5: 3 begot a son in his likeness, after his *i;*
9: 6 For in the *i* of God has man been made.
Tb 9: 6 I have seen the very *i* of my cousin Tobit!"
Ps(s) 106:19 a calf in Horeb and adored a molten *i;*
106:20 glory for the *i* of a grass-eating bullock.
Wis 2:23 the *i* of his own nature he made him.
7:26 of the power of God, the *i* of his goodness.
13:13 and patterns it on the *i* of a man or

13:16 for, truly, it is an *i* and needs help.
14:15 *i* of the child so quickly taken from him,
14:17 a public *i* of him they wished to honor,
15: 5 longs for the inanimate form of a dead *i*.
17:21 an *i* of the darkness that next should come
Sir 17: 1 created man, and in his own *i* he made him.
Is 44:12 The smith fashions an iron *i*,
48: 5 my statue, my molten *i* commanded them."
Jer 44:19 in her *i* and poured out libations to her?
Na 1:14 I will abolish the carved and the molten *i*;
Hb 2:18 Of what avail is the carved *i*,
2:18 Or the molten *i* and lying oracle,
Mt 13:33 He offered them still another *i*:
Mk 4:30 What *i* will help to present it?
Acts 19:35 and of her *i* which fell from the sky?
Rom 8:29 he predestined to share the *i* of his Son,
1Cor 11: 7 *i* of God and the reflection of his glory.
2Cor 3:18 his very *i* by the Lord who is the Spirit.
4: 4 forth the glory of Christ, the *i* of God.
Eph 4:24 put on that new man created in God's *i*,
Col 1:15 He is the *i* of the invisible God,
3:10 he is formed anew in the *i* of his Creator.
Heb 10: 1 good things to come, and no real *i* of them,
Rv 13:15 permitted to give life to the beast's *i*,
13:15 so that the *i* had the power of speech and
13:16 *i* on their right hand or their forehead.
14: 9 "If anyone worships the beast or its *i*,
14:11 or its *i* or accept the mark of its name."
15: 2 won the victory over the beast and its *i*,
16: 2 the mark of the beast or worshiped its *i*.
19:20 the mark of the beast and worship its *i*.
20: 4 the beast or its *i* nor accepted its mark

IMAGES (30)

Nm 33:52 all their stone figures and molten *i*,
Dt 7:25 *i* of their gods you shall destroy by fire.
1Sm 6: 5 make *i* of the hemorrhoids and of the mice
6:11 golden mice and the *i* of the hemorrhoids.
1Kgs 14: 9 strange gods and molten *i* to provoke me;
2Kgs 11:18 They shattered its altars and *i* completely,
2Chr 23:17 They smashed its altars and *i*,
33:19 and carved *i* before he humbled himself,
34: 3 sacred poles and the carved and molten *i*.
34: 4 *i* were shattered and beaten into dust,
34: 7 poles and carved *i* and beat them into dust,
1Mc 3:48 Gentiles consulted the *i* of their idols.
Is 10:10 that had more *i* than Jerusalem and Samaria,
10:11 I not do to Jerusalem and her graven *i*?"
21: 9 And all the *i* of her gods are smashed to
30:22 idols and your gold-covered *i*;
42:17 Who say to molten *i*,
45:16 Those go in disgrace who carve *i*.
Jer 50: 2 her *i* are put to shame,
Ez 7:20 of them their abominable *i* [their idols].
16:17 had given you and made for yourself male *i*,
23:14 the *i* of Chaldeans drawn with vermillion,
Dn 4: 2 *i* and the visions of my mind frightened me.
11: 8 with their molten *i* and their precious
Hos 13: 2 to sin, making for themselves molten *i*,
Am 5:26 the *i* that you have made for yourselves;
Mi 5:12 *i* and the sacred pillars from your midst;
Lk 6:39 He also used *i* in speaking to them:
Acts 7:43 Rephan, the *i* you had made for your cult.
Rom 1:23 immortal God for *i* representing mortal man,

IMAGINATION (1)

Jer 14:14 foolish divination, dreams of their own *i*,

IMAGINE (4)

Est 4:13 "Do not *i* that because you are in the
Ps(s) 41: 8 against me they *i* the worst:
Jn 5:45 Do not *i* that I will be your accuser
Eph 3:20 can do immeasurably more than we ask or *i*—

IMAGINED (1)

2Mc 9: 8 and *i* he could weigh the mountaintops in

IMAGINES (2)

Prv 26:16 The sluggard *i* himself wiser than seven
Jas 1:26 not control his tongue *i* that he is devout,

IMAGINING (1)

2Mc 5: 6 but *i* that he was winning a victory over

IMALKUE (2)

1Mc 11:39 at Demetrius, he went to *I* the Arab,
11:40 kept urging *I* to hand over the boy to him,

IMITATE (15)

Dt 18: 9 to *i* the abominations of the peoples there.
1Kgs 16:31 enough for him to *i* the sins of Jeroboam,
2Kgs 17:15 whom the LORD had commanded them not to *i*.
2Mc 4:16 and whom they desired to *i* in every thing,
Wis 4: 2 When it is present men *i* it,
Bar 6: 4 Take care that you yourselves do not *i*
Ez 18:14 commits, yet fears and does not *i* him;
23:48 will be warned not to *i* your lewdness.
Mt 6: 8 Do not *i* them.
1Cor 11: 1 Imitate me as I *i* Christ.
2Thes 3: 7 You know how you ought to *i* us.
3: 9 ourselves as an example for you to *i*.
Heb 6:12 Do not grow lazy, but *i* those who,
13: 7 how their lives ended, and *i* their faith.
3Jn 1:11 do not *i* what is evil but what is good.

IMITATED (5)

1Kgs 14:24 Judah *i* all the abominable practices of
15: 3 He *i* all the sins his father had committed
16: 2 but you have *i* the conduct of Jeroboam and
16:26 closely *i* the sinful conduct of Jeroboam,
2Kgs 17:22 *i* Jeroboam in all the sins he committed,

IMITATING (3)

1Kgs 15:26 *i* his father's conduct and the sin which
15:34 *i* the conduct of Jeroboam and the sin he
16:19 LORD by *i* the sinful conduct of Jeroboam,

IMITATION (1)

Heb 4:11 in *i* of the example of Israel's unbelief.

IMITATORS (4)

1Cor 4:16 I beg you, then, be *i* of me.
Eph 5: 1 Be *i* of God as his dear children.
Phil 3:17 Be *i* of me, my brothers.
1Thes 1: 6 in turn, became *i* of us and of the Lord,

IMLAH (4)

1Kgs 22: 8 might consult the LORD, Micaiah, son of *I*;
22: 9 and said to him, "Get Micaiah, son of *I*,
2Chr 18: 7 That is Micaiah, son of *I*."
18: 8 to whom he said, "Get Micaiah, son of *I*,

IMMACULATE (1)

Eph 5:27 to himself a glorious church, holy and *i*,

IMMANUEL (2)

Is 7:14 and bear a son, and shall name him *I*.
8: 8 its wings the full width of your land, *I*!

IMMATURE (2)

1Chr 22: 5 "My son Solomon is young and *i*:
29: 1 God has chosen, is still young and *i*;

IMMEASURABLE (2)

Bar 3:25 Vast and endless, high and *i*!
Eph 1:19 the *i* scope of his power in us who believe.

IMMEASURABLY (2)

Eph 1: 8 so *i* generous is God's favor to us.
3:20 in us can do *i* more than we ask or imagine

IMMEDIATE (1)

1Tm 5: 8 and especially for members of his *i* family,

IMMEDIATELY (73)

Jos 2: 5 have to pursue them *i* to overtake them."
8:19 captured the city, and *i* set it on fire.
Jgs 2:23 to remain instead of expelling them *i*,
9:54 *i* called his armor-bearer and said to him,
1Sm 9:13 Go up *i*,
25:42 She got up *i*,
28:20 *I* Saul fell full length on the ground,
2Sm 17:16 So send a warning to David *i*,
1Kgs 20:41 He *i* removed the bandage from his eyes,
2Kgs 1:11 "the king commands you to come down *i*."
Tb 4:14 any man who works for you, but pay him *i*.
8: 3 Then Raphael returned *i*.
1Mc 11:22 was furious, and set out *i* for Ptolemais.
2Mc 3: 8 So Heliodorus *i* set out on his journey
4:10 he *i* initiated his countrymen into the
4:34 regard for justice, he *i* put him to death.
4:38 *i* stripped Andronicus of his purple robe,
6:28 and went *i* to the instrument of torture.
8:11 So he *i* sent word to the coastal cities,
14:12 The king *i* chose Nicanor,
Prv 12:16 The fool *i* shows his anger,
Mt 4:20 They *i* abandoned their nets and became his
4:22 and *i* they abandoned boat and father to
8: 3 *I* the man's leprosy disappeared.
14: 9 The king *i* had his misgivings,
14:22 *I* afterward,
20:34 touched their eyes, and *i* they could see;
21: 2 you will *i* find an ass tethered
24:29 *I* after the stress of that period,
25:16 *I* the man who received the five thousand
26:49 He *i* went over to Jesus,
27:48 *I* one of them ran off and got a sponge.
Mk 1:10 *I* on coming up out of the water he saw the
1:18 They *i* abandoned their nets and became his
1:29 *I* upon leaving the synagogue,
1:31 She *i* began to wait on them.
2: 8 Jesus was *i* aware of their reasoning,
3: 6 they *i* began to plot with the Herodians
4: 5 sprouted *i* because the soil had no depth.
5: 2 he was *i* met by a man from the tombs who
5:29 *I* her flow of blood dried up and the
5:42 stood up *i* and began to walk around.
6:45 *I* afterward he insisted that his disciples
6:54 leaving the boat people *i* recognized him.
9:15 *I* on catching sight of Jesus,
9:20 Jesus and *i* threw the boy into convulsions.
9:24 The boy's father *i* exclaimed,
10:52 *I* he received his sight and started to
Lk 4:39 She got up *i* and waited on them.
5:13 *I* the leprosy left him.
6:49 it *i* fell in and was completely destroyed."
8:44 *I* her bleeding stopped.
8:55 of life returned to her and she got up *i*;
12:54 in the west, you say *i* that rain is coming
13:13 and *i* she stood up straight and began
14: 5 he not *i* rescue him on the sabbath day?"
19:14 and they *i* sent a deputation after him
21: 9 first, but the end does not follow *i*."
24:33 They got up *i* and returned to Jerusalem,
Jn 5: 9 The man was *i* cured;
13:27 *I* after, Satan entered his heart.
19:34 his side, and *i* blood and water flowed out.
Acts 3: 7 *I* the beggar's feet and ankles became
9:18 *I* something like scales fell from his eyes
10:33 I sent for you *i*,
11:11 *I* after that, the three men
16:10 *i* made efforts to get across to Macedonia,
16:26 *I* all the doors flew open and everyone's
16:38 who were *i* alarmed at hearing they were
20:10 hurried down *i* and threw himself on him,
21:30 outside the temple, and *i* closed its gates.
21:32 *I* the commander took his soldiers and
Gal 1:16 *I*, without seeking human advisers or even

IMMENSE (9)

2Sm 12:30 He brought out *i* booty from the city,
Neh 9:25 and feast themselves on your *i* good gifts.
1Mc 16: 5 an *i* army of foot soldiers and horsemen,
Sir 15:18 *I* is the wisdom of the LORD;
Is 13: 4 that of an *i* throng!
Jer 31: 8 they shall return as an *i* throng.
44:15 the women who were present in the *i* crowd,
Dn 7: 3 sea, from which emerged four *i* beasts,
Jl 2:11 For *i* indeed is his camp,

IMMER (10)

1Chr 9:12 Meshullam, son of Meshillemith, son of *I*.
24:14 fifteenth to Bilgah, the sixteenth to *I*,
Ezr 2:37 sons of *I*, one thousand and fifty-two;
2:59 and *I* were unable to prove that their
10:20 Of the sons of *I*:
Neh 3:29 After them Zadok, son of *I*,
7:40 sons of *I*, one thousand and fifty-two
7:61 and *I* were unable to prove that their
11:13 of Ahzai, son of Meshillemoth, son of *I*,
Jer 20: 1 things by the priest Pashhur, son of *I*,

IMMERSED (1)

Mk 10:39 the bath I am *i* in you shall share.

IMMIGRANT (3)

Gn 19: 9 they sneered, "came here as an *i*,
Lv 25:47 to one of the descendants of an *i* family,
2Sm 1:13 replied, "I am the son of an Amalekite *i*."

IMMINENT (4)

1Mc 9: 7 melting away just when the battle was *i*,
Jb 15:23 he knows that his destruction is *i*.
Prv 10:14 but the mouth of a fool is *i* ruin.
Mk 16:20 fulfilled, but other terrible things are *i*.

IMMODERATELY (1)

2Cor 10:15 We do not boast *i* of the work of others;

IMMODESTLY (1)

Jdt 9: 2 who had *i* loosened the maiden's girdle,

IMMOLATE (4)

Is 57: 5 You who *i* children in the wadies,
Jer 7:31 *i* in fire their sons and their daughters,
19: 5 *i* their sons in fire as holocausts to Baal:
Hos 8:13 they offer sacrifice, *i* flesh and eat it,

IMMOLATED (11)

Lv 18:21 any of your offspring to be *i* to Molech,
Nm 8:12 of the bullocks, which shall then be *i*,
2Kgs 16: 3 of Israel, and even *i* his son by fire,
17:17 They *i* their sons and daughters by fire,
17:31 and the men of Sepharvaim *i* their children
21: 6 He *i* his son by fire.
2Chr 28: 3 and *i* his sons by fire according to the
33: 6 who *i* his sons by fire in the Valley of
Jer 32:35 and *i* their sons and daughters to Molech,
Ez 16:21 You slaughtered and *i* my children to them,
23:37 them they *i* the children they had borne me.

IMMOLATES (1)

Dt 18:10 who *i* his son or daughter in the fire,

IMMOLATION (2)
2Kgs 23:10 no longer be an *i* of sons or daughters
Ez 20:26 gifts, by their *i* of every first-born,

IMMORAL (3)
1Cor 5: 9 my letter not to associate with *i* persons.
5:10 of association with *i* people in this world,
5:11 bears the title "brother" if he is *i*,

IMMORALITY (7)
Tb 4:12 your guard, son, against every form of *i*,
Sir 41:15 Before father and mother be ashamed of *i*,
1Cor 6:13 but the body is not for *i*;
7: 2 But to avoid *i*,
1Thes 4: 3 that you abstain from *i*,
4: 7 God has not called us to *i* but to holiness;
Rv 14: 4 have never been defiled by *i* with women.

IMMORTAL (7)
Wis 4: 1 for *i* is its memory:
Sir 17:25 found in men, for not *i* is any son of man.
Hb 1:12 not from eternity, O LORD, my holy God, *i*?
Mk 16:20 and *i* proclamation of eternal salvation.
16:20 and *i* glory of justification in heaven."
Rom 1:23 *i* God for images representing mortal man,
1Tm 1:17 To the King of ages, the *i*,

IMMORTALITY (9)
Wis 3: 4 be punished, yet is their hope full of *i*;
8:13 For her sake I should have *i* and leave to
8:17 That there is *i* in kinship with Wisdom,
15: 3 and to know your might is the root of *i*.
Rom 2: 7 honor, and *i* by patiently doing right;
1Cor 15:53 this mortal body with *i*
15:54 on incorruptibility and the mortal *i*,
1Tm 6:16 *i* and who dwells in unapproachable light,
2Tm 1:10 and *i* into clear light through the gospel.

IMMOVABLE (1)
Ps(s) 125: 1 the LORD are like Mount Zion, which is *i*;

IMMUNE (2)
Nm 5:19 be *i* to the curse brought by this bitter
5:28 *i* and will still be able to bear children.

IMMUNITY (1)
1Mc 10:34 be days of *i* and exemption for every Jew

IMMUTABLE (1)
Dn 6: 9 *i* and irrevocable under Mede and Persian

IMNA (1)
1Chr 7:35 sons of his brother Hotham were Zophah, *I*,

IMNAH (4)
Gn 46:17 *I*, Ishvah,
Nm 26:44 through *I* the clan of the Imnites,
1Chr 7:30 The sons of Asher were *I*,
2Chr 31:14 Kore, the son of *I*,

IMNITES (1)
Nm 26:44 through Imnah the clan of the *I*,

IMPACT (1)
2Cor 10:10 unimpressive and his word makes no great *i*.

IMPALED (6)
Gn 40:19 up your head and have you *i* on a stake,
40:22 but the chief baker he *i*—
41:13 to my post, but the other man was *i*."
1Sm 31:10 temple of Astarte, but *i* his blood
1Chr 10:10 his skull they *i* on the temple of Dagon.
Ezr 6:11 and he is to be lifted up and *i* on it;

IMPART (3)
Sir 16:23 measured wisdom, and *i* accurate knowledge.
Is 28: 9 "To whom would he *i* knowledge?
Gal 3:21 was given was such that it could *i* life,

IMPARTED (2)
Prv 1: 4 resourcefulness may be *i* to the simple,
Rom 6:17 that rule of teaching which was *i* to you;

IMPARTIAL (2)
Dt 16:19 you must be *i*.
Jas 3:17 deeds that are its fruits, *i* and sincere.

IMPARTIALITY (1)
1Tm 5:21 without prejudice, act with complete *i*!

IMPARTIALLY (1)
1Chr 24: 5 Their functions were assigned *i* by lot,

IMPARTS (3)
Ps(s) 19: 3 to day, and night to night *i* knowledge;
Sir 10: 5 of God, who *i* his majesty to the ruler.
17: 5 ears, and *i* to them an understanding heart.

IMPASSABLE (1)
Wis 5: 7 we journeyed through *i* deserts,

IMPATIENCE (1)
Jb 5: 2 *i* kills the fool and indignation slays the

IMPATIENT (4)
Gn 18:30 said, "Let not my Lord grow *i* if I go on.
Jb 4: 5 But now that it comes to you, you are *i*;
21: 4 And why should I not be *i*?
Sir 7:10 Be not *i* in prayers,

IMPECCABLY (1)
Ez 23:12 governors and officers, warriors *i* clothed,

IMPEDED (1)
Prv 4:12 When you walk, your step will not be *i*,

IMPEDIMENT (2)
Mk 7:32 *i* and begged him to lay his hand on him.
7:35 he was freed from the *i*,

IMPELLED (2)
Col 1:29 *i* by that energy of his which is so
2Pt 1:21 It is rather that men *i* by the Holy

IMPELS (1)
2Cor 5:14 The love of Christ *i* us who have reached

IMPENDED (1)
2Mc 6: 9 It was obvious, therefore, that disaster *i*.

IMPENDING (1)
Jas 5: 1 rich, weep and wail over your *i* miseries.

IMPENDS (1)
Wis 6: 8 for those in power a rigorous scrutiny *i*.

IMPENETRABLE (2)
Jer 46:23 her forest, says the LORD, *i* though it be;
Zec 11: 2 of Bashan, for the *i* forest is cut down!

IMPENITENT (1)
Rom 2: 5 your hard and *i* heart is storing up

IMPERFECT (4)
1Cor 13: 9 is *i* and our prophesying is imperfect.
13:10 the perfect comes, the *i* will pass away.
13:12 My knowledge is *i* now;

IMPERIAL (2)
Acts 25:10 "I stand before the *i* bench;
25:21 could be an *i* investigation of his case,

IMPERILED (1)
2Cor 11:26 *i* in the city,

IMPERISHABLE (7)
Wis 2:23 For God formed man to be *i*;
12: 1 for your *i* spirit is in all things!
18: 4 through whom the *i* light of the Law
Is 55:13 the LORD'S renown, an everlasting *i* sign.
56: 5 an eternal, *i* name will I give them.
1Cor 9:25 that withers, but we a crown that is *i*.
1Pt 1: 4 a birth to an *i* inheritance,

IMPERSONATE (2)
Mt 24: 5 Many will come attempting to *i* me.
Mk 13: 6 Any number will come attempting to *i* me.

IMPIETY (2)
Sir 16:10 who perished for the *i* of their hearts.
Rom 11:26 who shall remove all *i* from Jacob;

IMPIOUS (31)
1Mc 3: 8 the cities of Judah destroying the *i* there.
6:21 besieged escaped, joined by *i* Israelites;
7: 5 lawless and *i* men of Israel came to him.
7: 9 He sent him and the *i* Alcimus,
9:25 *i* men and made them masters of the country.
9:73 people and he destroyed the *i* in Israel.
11:25 Although some *i* men of his own nation
2Mc 3:11 Contrary to the calumnies of the *i* Simon,
9: 9 The body of this *i* man swarmed with worms,
Jb 13:16 that no *i* man can come into his presence.
15:34 For the breed of the *i* shall be sterile,
16:11 God has given me over to the *i*;
18:21 is it then with the dwelling of the *i* man,
20: 5 and the joy of the *i* but for a moment?
22:18 But far be from me the mind of the *i*
27: 8 can the *i* man expect when he is cut off,
34:36 since his answers are those of the *i*;
36:13 The *i* in heart lay up anger for themselves;
Ps(s) 43: 1 from the deceitful and *i* man rescue me.
Prv 11: 9 mouth the *i* man would ruin his neighbor,
Wis 12: 4 Works of witchcraft and *i* sacrifices;
14:16 the *i* practice gained strength and was
Sir 4:27 Do not abase yourself before an *i* man,
8:11 Let not the *i* man intimidate you;
13: 1 associates with an *i* man learns his ways.
15: 8 Far from the *i* is she,
21:25 of the *i* talk of what is not their concern,
Is 10: 6 Against an *i* nation I send him,
23:13 She whom the *i* founded,
33:14 are in dread, trembling grips the *i*:
Bar 2:12 we have sinned, been *i*,

IMPLACABLE (1)
2Tm 3: 3 parents, ungrateful, profane, inhuman, *i*,

IMPLANTED (1)
Jas 4: 5 he has *i* in us tends toward jealousy"?

IMPLEMENTED (1)
Jas 2:22 assisting his works and *i* by his works.

IMPLEMENTS (1)
1Sm 8:12 *i* of war and the equipment of his chariots.

IMPLIES (1)
Sir 46: 1 office, Formed to be, as his name *i*,

IMPLORE (9)
1Sm 7: 8 *I* the LORD our God unceasingly for us,
1Mc 3:44 and to pray and *i* mercy and compassion.
Dn 2:18 that they might *i* the mercy of the God of
Zec 7: 2 Regemmelech and his men to *i* favor
8:21 let us go to *i* the favor of the LORD";
8:22 Jerusalem and to *i* the favor of the LORD.
Mal 1: 9 So now if you *i* God for mercy on us,
Mk 5: 7 I *i* you in God's name,
2Cor 5:20 We *i* you, in Christ's name:

IMPLORED (7)
Ex 8: 8 Moses *i* the LORD to fulfill the promise he
32:11 But Moses *i* the LORD,
1Sm 7: 9 He *i* the LORD for Israel,
2Kgs 1:13 "Man of God," he *i* him,
Est 8: 3 Esther fell at his feet and tearfully *i* him
2Mc 8: 2 *i* the Lord to look kindly upon his people,
13:12 and had *i* the merciful LORD continuously

IMPLORES (2)
Prv 18:23 The poor man *i*,
Is 44:17 prostrate before it in worship, he *i* it,

IMPLORING (3)
2Mc 3:22 While they were *i* the almighty Lord to
7:37 *i* God to show mercy soon to our nation,
8:29 *i* the merciful Lord to be completely

IMPORTANCE (8)
Prv 12: 9 than one of assumed *i* who lacks bread.
Mt 18: 1 is of greatest *i* in the kingdom of God?"
18: 4 is of greatest *i* in that heavenly reign.
20:25 their great ones make their *i* felt.
Mk 10:42 their great ones make their *i* felt.
Acts 5:36 tried to pass himself off as someone of *i*.
8: 9 passed himself off as someone of great *i*.
1Thes 2: 7 on our own *i* as apostles of Christ.

IMPORTANT (19)
Ex 18:22 More *i* cases they should refer to you,
2Kgs 8:13 like me, your servant, do anything so *i*?"
1Chr 24:31 the more *i* family did so in the same way
24:31 did so in the same way as the less *i* one.
28: 1 courtiers, the warriors and every *i* man.
2Mc 4:23 and to obtain decisions on some *i* matters.
10:15 the Idumeans, who held some *i* strongholds,
Sir 33: 7 Why is one day more *i* than another,
37:15 Most *i* of all,
Mt 6:26 Are not you more *i* than they?
23:17 Which is more *i*, the gold or the temple
23:19 Which is more *i*, the offering or the altar
Mk 9:34 had been arguing about who was the most *i*.
Lk 12:23 Life is more *i* than food and the body more
12:24 How much more *i* you are than the birds!
16:15 What man thinks *i*, God holds in contempt.
1Cor 12:22 seem less *i* are in fact indispensable.
Gal 2: 6 Those who were regarded as *i*,
Phil 3:16 It is *i* that we continue on our course,

IMPORTED (4)
1Kgs 10:28 Solomon's horses were *i* from Cilicia,
10:29 *i* from Egypt cost six hundred shekels,

2Chr 1:16 also *i* horses from Egypt and Cilicia.
9:28 Horses were *i* for Solomon from Egypt and

IMPORTING (1)

Neh 13:16 *i* fish and every other kind of merchandise

IMPORTS (1)

Rv 18:11 there will be no more market for their *i*—

IMPORTUNED (2)

Jgs 14:17 On the seventh day, since she *i* him,
16:16 She *i* him continually and vexed him with

IMPOSE (12)

Gn 37: 8 "Or *i* your rule on us?"
2Kgs 18:14 I will pay whatever tribute you *i* on me."
Ezr 7:24 you that it is not permitted to *i* taxes,
Neh 10:33 We *i* these commandments on ourselves:
Jb 13: 9 Would you *i* on him as one does on men?
Is 2: 4 the nations, and *i* terms on many peoples.
Dn 13:61 they had plotted to *i* on their neighbor:
Mi 4: 3 and *i* terms on strong and distant nations;
Acts 24: 4 But now, lest I *i* on your time unduly,
2Cor 11:20 you, who *i* upon you and put on airs,
1Thes 2: 9 to you in order not to *i* on you in any way.
2Thes 3: 8 of exhaustion so as not to *i* on any of you.

IMPOSED (19)

Ex 21:30 If, however, a fine is *i* on him,
21:30 for his life whatever amount is *i* on him.
Dt 24: 5 nor shall any public duty be *i* on him.
Jos 6:26 On that occasion Joshua *i* the oath:
1Kgs 12: 4 and the heavy yoke your father *i* on us,
12: 9 me to lighten the yoke my father *i* on them?"
2Kgs 23:33 He *i* a fine upon the land of a hundred
2Chr 10: 4 the heavy yoke that your father *i* on us,
10: 9 me to lighten the yoke my father *i* on them?"
24: 9 had *i* on Israel in the desert should be
24:27 his sons, and the great tribute *i* on him,
Jb 12:18 He loosens the bonds *i* by kings and leaves
Mt 5:21 the commandment *i* on your forefathers,
5:33 the commandment *i* on your forefathers,
Acts 6: 6 prayed over them and then *i* hands on them.
8:17 The pair upon arriving *i* hands on them and
13: 3 they *i* hands on them and sent them off.
1Thes 2: 4 rather, having met the test *i* on us by God,
Heb 9:10 flesh, *i* until the time of the new order.

IMPOSES (1)

Prv 29: 4 but he who *i* heavy taxes ruins it.

IMPOSING (2)

Dt 26: 6 and oppressed us, *i* hard labor upon us,
Sg 5:15 the trees on Lebanon, *i* as the cedars.

IMPOSSIBLE (22)

Jos 8:20 Escape in any direction was *i*,
2Sm 13: 2 it *i* to carry out his designs toward her.
1Mc 5:46 they found it *i* to encircle it on either
2Mc 4: 6 would be *i* to have a peaceful government,
14:10 it is *i* for the state to enjoy peace."
Jer 32:17 nothing is *i* to you.
32:27 Is anything *i* to me?
Dn 6:19 Since sleep was *i* for him,
Zec 8: 6 Even if this should seem *i* in the eyes of
8: 6 it in those days be *i* in my eyes also,
Mt 17:20 Nothing would be *i* for you.
19:26 looked at them and said, "For man it is *i*;
Mk 3:20 it *i* for them to get any food whatever.
6:31 making it *i* for them to so much as eat.
10:27 said, "For man it is *i* but not for God.
Lk 1:37 her sixth month, for nothing is *i* with God."
11:46 You lay *i* burdens on men but will not lift
18:27 that are *i* for men are possible for God."
Acts 2:24 *i* that death should keep its hold on him,
Heb 6: 6 away, it is *i* to make them repent again,
10: 4 because it is *i* for the blood of bulls and
11: 6 but without faith, it is *i* to please him.

IMPOSTERS (1)

2Cor 6: 8 We are called *i*,

IMPOSTOR (1)

Mt 27:63 that *i* while he was still alive
Acts 13:10 "You are an *i* and a thoroughgoing fraud,

IMPOSTORS (2)

Jude 1:18 will be *i* living by their godless passions."
Rv 2: 2 the sort, and discovered that they are *i*.

IMPOSTURE (1)

Mt 27:64 This final *i* would be worse than the first."

IMPOVERISH (2)

Sir 13: 6 you, then without regret he will *i* you.
2Cor 8:13 The relief of others ought not to *i* you;

IMPOVERISHED (2)

Lv 25:39 your countryman becomes so *i* beside you
Prv 11:16 [The slothful become *i*,

IMPOVERISHES (1)

Prv 10: 4 The slack hand *i*,

IMPRECATION (3)

Nm 5:21 adjure the woman with this oath of *i*—
5:21 of malediction and *i* among your people
5:27 become an example of *i* among her people.

IMPRECATIONS (2)

Nm 5:23 The priest shall put these *i* in writing
Dt 29:26 on it all the *i* listed in this book;

IMPRESS (1)

Dt 32:46 you and which you must *i* on your children,

IMPRESSED (7)

Jos 16:10 day, though they have been *i* as laborers.
17:13 stronger they *i* the Canaanites as laborers,
Jgs 1:28 they *i* the Canaanites as laborers,
1:35 the upper hand, they were *i* as laborers.
Jdt 3: 6 them he *i* picked troops as auxiliaries.
Is 31: 8 and his young men shall be *i* as laborers.
Acts 13:12 so *i* was he by the teaching about the Lord.

IMPRESSION (3)

Jgs 20:39 under the *i* that they were defeating them
Sir 38:27 His care is to produce a vivid *i*,
Mt 27:24 *i* and that a riot was breaking out instead.

IMPRINT (1)

Rev 7: 3 until we *i* this seal

IMPRISON (2)

Jb 11:10 If he seize and *i* or call to judgment,
40:13 in the hidden world *i* them.

IMPRISONED (17)

2Kgs 17: 5 the king of Assyria arrested and *i* Hoshea;
2Chr 16:10 with the seer and *i* him in the stocks,
1Mc 5:26 "Many of them have been *i* in Bozrah,
5:27 some have been *i* in other cities of Gilead.
2Mc 13:21 He was found out, arrested, and *i*.
Ps(s) 88: 9 I am *i*, and I cannot escape.
Wis 18: 4 to be deprived of light and *i* by darkness,
Jer 20: 9 fire burning in my heart, *i* in my bones;
32: 2 was *i* in the quarters of the guard,
32: 3 Zedekiah, king of Judah, had *i* him there,
33: 1 was still *i* in the quarters of the guard:
39:15 was still *i* in the quarters of the guard,
Mt 14: 3 in chains, and *i* on account of Herodias,
Mk 6:17 chained, and *i* on account of Herodias.
Acts 22: 4 I arrested and *i* both men and women.
22:19 it is because they know that I *i* those who
Rom 11:32 God has *i* all in disobedience that he

IMPRISONMENT (10)

Ezr 7:26 punishment, or a fine on his goods, or *i*."
Lk 22:33 I am prepared to face *i* and death itself."
Acts 21:13 Lord Jesus I am prepared, not only for *i*,
23:29 guilty of anything deserving death or *i*.
26:31 is doing nothing that deserves death or *i*."
Phil 1:13 My *i* in Christ's cause has become well
1:17 that it will make my *i* even harsher.
Phlm 1:10 my child, whom I have begotten during my *i*.
Heb 11:36 mockery, scourging, even chains and *i*.
13: 3 prisoners as if you were sharing their *i*,

IMPRISONMENTS (2)

2Cor 6: 5 difficulties, distresses, beatings, *i*,
11:23 with my many more labors and *i*,

IMPRISONS (1)

Jb 12:14 if he *i* a man,

IMPROVE (1)

Sir 18:15 a burning wind, so does a word *i* a gift.

IMPROVED (1)

1Mc 13:48 He *i* its fortifications and built himself

IMPROVEMENT (2)

Ps(s) 55:20 For *i* is not in them,
Jn 4:52 them at what time the boy had shown *i*,

IMPROVEMENTS (1)

Acts 24: 2 Many *i* have been made in this nation

IMPROVISING (1)

Am 6: 5 *I* to the music of the harp,

IMPUDENT (3)

Prv 7:13 kisses him, and with an *i* look says to him:
Eccl 8: 1 his face, but an *i* look is resented.
Dn 8:23 arise a king, *i* and skilled in intrigue.

IMPULSE (3)

Mi 2:11 If one, acting on *i*,
1Cor 12: 2 led astray to mute idols, as *i* drove you.
Jas 3: 4 course the steerman's *i* may select.

IMPULSES (1)

Sir 21:11 He who keeps the law controls his *i*;

IMPUNITY (2)

Zec 11: 5 For they who buy them slay them with *i*;
Mal 3:15 prosper, and even tempt God with *i*."

IMPURE (19)

Nm 5:14 wife, whether she was actually *i* or not:
5:27 has been *i* and unfaithful to her husband,
Tb 3:14 that I am innocent of any *i* act with a man,
1Mc 13:48 removing from it everything that was *i*,
2Mc 5:16 He laid his *i* hands on the sacred vessels
Wis 2:16 aloof from our paths as from things *i*.
11: 6 perennial river was troubled with *i* blood
Mt 15:11 goes into a man's mouth that makes him *i*;
15:18 It is things like these that make a man *i*.
15:20 These are the things that make a man *i*.
15:20 that makes no man *i*."
Mk 7:15 enters a man from outside can make him *i*;
7:18 enters a man from outside can make him *i*?
7:20 that and nothing else is what makes him *i*.
7:23 evils come from within and render a man *i*."
Acts 10:14 eaten anything unclean or *i* in my life."
10:28 no one should call any man unclean or *i*.
11: 8 unclean or *i* has ever entered my mouth!'
1Thes 2: 3 or *i* motives or any sort of trickery;

IMPURELY (2)

Nm 5:20 have acted *i* by letting a man other than
5:29 the authority of her husband and acts *i*,

IMPURITIES (6)

1Mc 13:50 them from the citadel and cleansed it of *i*.
14: 7 He cleansed the citadel of its *i*;
Ez 23: 8 breasts and pouring out their *i* on her.
24:11 metal glows red hot, till the *i* in it melt,
36:25 upon you to cleanse you from all your *i*,
36:29 I will save you from all your *i*;

IMPURITY (10)

Lv 15:19 shall be in a state of *i* for seven days.
15:20 lies or sits during her *i* shall be unclean.
15:24 her *i* and shall be unclean for seven days;
Nm 5:13 so that her *i* remains unproved for lack of
5:19 and you have not gone astray by *i* while
1Mc 1:48 with every kind of *i* and abomination,
Mk 7:15 out of him, and only that, constitutes *i*.
Jn 18:28 *i* if they were to eat the Passover supper.
Rom 6:19 enslaved your bodies to *i* and licentiousness
Gal 5:19 lewd conduct, *i*, licentiousness, idolatry

IMPUTED (2)

Ps(s) 106:31 And it was *i* to him for merit through all
Rom 5:13 though sin is not *i* when there is no law

IMPUTES (2)

Ps(s) 32: 2 whom the LORD *i* not guilt,
Rom 4: 8 is the man to whom the Lord *i* no guilt."

IMPUTING (1)

Na 1: 9 What are you *i* to the LORD?

IMRAH (1)

1Chr 7:36 were Suah, Harnepher, Shual, Beri, *I*,

IMRI (2)

1Chr 9: 4 son of Ammihud, son of Omri, son of *I*,
Neh 3: 2 and next to them was Zaccur, son of *I*.

INACCESSIBLE (1)

Jer 51:53 heavens, and make her strong heights *i*,

INACTION (1)

Ezr 4:24 This *i* lasted until the second year of the

INADVERTENCE (6)

Lv 22:14 a one eats of a sacred offering through *i*,
Nm 15:22 "When through *i* you fail to carry out any
15:24 becomes guilty of the fault of *i*,
15:25 they will be forgiven the *i* for which they
15:26 the fault of *i* affects all the people.
Ez 45:20 who have sinned through *i* or ignorance;

INADVERTENT (1)

Tb 3: 3 me not for my sins, nor for my *i* offenses,

INADVERTENTLY (8)

Lv 4: 2 When a person *i* commits a sin against some
4:13 whole community of Israel *i* and without
4:22 "Should a prince commit a sin *i* by doing
4:27 a private person commits a sin *i* by doing
5:15 by *i* cheating in the LORD's sacred dues,
Nm 15:27 if it is an individual who sins *i*,
15:28 before the LORD for him who sinned *i*;
15:29 shall have but one law for him who sins *i*,

INANE (1)

Prv 9:13 The woman Folly is fickle, she is *i*,

INANIMATE (1)

Wis 15: 5 he longs for the *i* form of a dead image.

INANITY (1)

Prv 1:22 long, you simple ones, will you love *i*,

INASMUCH (7)

Gn 32:33 *i* as Jacob's hip socket was struck at the
Jgs 2:20 *I* as this nation has violated my covenant
1Kgs 16: 2 *I* as I lifted you up from the dust and
2Mc 12:43 *i* as he had the resurrection of the dead
Jn 17: 2 *i* as you have given him authority over all
Rom 5:12 thus coming to all men *i* as all sinned
11:13 *I* as I am the apostle of the Gentiles,

INAUGURAL (2)

2Kgs 25:27 Babylon, in the *i* year of his own reign,
Jer 52:31 of Babylon, in the *i* year of his reign,
1Sm 11:14 let us go to Gilgal to *i* the kingdom

INAUGURATED (2)

2Cor 3: 7 was *i* with such glory that the Israelites
Heb 9:18 the first covenant was *i* without blood.

INCALCULABLE (1)

2Mc 3: 6 total sum of money was *i* and out of all

INCALCULABLY (1)

1Tm 4: 8 the discipline of religion is *i* more so,

INCAPABLE (10)

Jdt 5:23 a powerless people, *i* of a strong defense.
Est E: 3 *i* of bearing such greatness,
Bar 6:40 for when they see a deaf mute, *i* of speech,
Mt 15:16 "Are you, too, still *i* of understanding?"
19:12 men are *i* of sexual activity from birth;
Mk 7:18 "Are you, too, *i* of understanding?"
Lk 13:11 quite *i* of standing erect.
Jn 7: 7 The world is *i* of hating you,
Ti 1:16 and thoroughly *i* of any decent action.
1Pt 1: 4 inheritance, *i* of fading or defilement,

INCENSE (148)

Ex 25: 6 the anointing oil and for the fragrant *i*;
30: 1 *i* you shall make an altar of acacia wood,
30: 7 "On it Aaron shall burn fragrant *i*.
30: 8 when he lights the lamps, he shall burn *i*.
30: 8 the established *i* offering before the LORD.
30: 9 you shall not offer up any profane *i*,
30:27 the altar of *i* and the altar of holocausts
30:35 and blend them into *i*.
30:36 *i* shall be treated as most sacred by you.
30:37 make *i* of a like mixture for yourselves;
30:38 Whoever makes an *i* like this for his own
31: 8 all its appurtenances, the altar of *i*,
31:11 oil, and the fragrant *i* for the sanctuary.
35: 8 the anointing oil and for the fragrant *i*;
35:15 the altar of *i*,
35:15 the anointing oil, and the fragrant *i*;
35:28 the light, anointing oil, and fragrant *i*.
37:25 The altar of *i* was made of acacia wood,
37:29 sacred anointing oil and the fragrant *i*
39:38 altar, the anointing oil, the fragrant *i*;
40: 5 *i* in front of the ark of the commandments,
40:27 the veil, and on it he burned fragrant *i*,
40:38 and on it he burned fragrant *i*,
Lv 4: 7 altar of fragrant *i* which is before the LORD
4:18 horns of the altar of fragrant *i* which
10: 1 *i* on the fire they had put in them,
16:12 double handful of finely ground fragrant *i*,
16:13 before the LORD he shall put *i* on the fire,
16:13 so that a cloud of *i* may cover the
26:30 your high places, overthrow your *i* stands,
Nm 4:16 of the oil for the light, the fragrant *i*,
7:14 cup of ten shekels' weight filled with *i*;
7:20 cup of ten shekels' weight filled with *i*,
7:26 cup of ten shekels' weight filled with *i*;
7:32 cup of ten shekels' weight filled with *i*;
7:38 cup of ten shekels' weight filled with *i*;
7:44 cup of ten shekels' weight filled with *i*;
7:50 cup of ten shekels' weight filled with *i*;
7:56 cup of ten shekels' weight filled with *i*;
7:62 cup of ten shekels' weight filled with *i*;
7:68 cup of ten shekels' weight filled with *i*;
7:74 cup of ten shekels' weight filled with *i*;
7:80 cup of ten shekels' weight filled with *i*;
7:86 filled with *i* weighed ten shekels apiece,
16: 7 place *i* in them before the LORD tomorrow.
16:17 shall take his own censer, put *i* in it,
16:18 laying *i* on the fire they had put in them,
16:35 and fifty men who were offering the *i*.
17: 5 the altar to offer *i* before the LORD,
17:11 put fire from the altar in it, lay *i* on it,
17:12 the *i* and made atonement for the people,
1Sm 2:28 priests, to go up to my altar, to burn *i*,
1Kgs 3: 3 sacrifice and burned *i* on the high places.
9:25 to the LORD, and to burn *i* before the LORD;
11: 8 who burned *i* and sacrificed to their gods.
22:44 sacrifice and to burn *i* on the high places.
2Kgs 12: 4 continued to sacrifice and to burn *i* there.
14: 4 to sacrifice and to burn *i* on them.
15: 4 to sacrifice and to burn *i* on them.
15:35 to sacrifice and to burn *i* on them.
16: 4 sacrificed and burned *i* on the high places,
17:11 they burned *i* like the nations whom the
18: 4 time the Israelites were burning *i* to it.
22:17 me and have burned *i* to other gods,
23: 5 kings of Judah had appointed to burn *i* on
23: 5 as well as those who burned *i* to Baal,
23: 8 the high places where they had offered *i*.
1Chr 6:34 altar of holocausts and on the altar of *i*;
28:18 its weight, to be used for the altar of *i*;
2Chr 2: 3 the burning of fragrant *i* in his presence,
2: 5 unless it be to offer *i* in his presence?
13:11 fragrant *i* morning after morning
14: 4 and *i* stands from all the cities of Judah,
26:16 LORD to make an offering on the altar of *i*.
26:18 not for you, Uzziah, to burn *i* to the LORD,
26:19 was holding a censer for burning the *i*,
26:19 house of the LORD beside the altar of *i*,
28: 4 offered sacrifice and *i* on the high places,
29: 7 and refused to burn *i* and offer holocausts
29:11 to him, to be his ministers and to offer *i*."
30:14 of *i* and cast them into the Kidron Valley.
32:12 only, and on it alone you shall offer *i*'?
34: 4 the *i* stands erected above them were torn
34: 7 the *i* stands throughout the land of Israel.
34:25 me and have offered *i* to other gods,
Neh 13: 5 the cereal offerings, *i* and utensils,
13: 9 of God, the cereal offerings, and the *i*.
Tb 6:17 and place them on the embers for the *i*.
8: 2 and placed them on the embers for the *i*.
Jdt 9: 1 While the *i* was being offered in the
1Mc 1:55 They also burnt *i* at the doors of houses
4:49 and brought the lampstand, the altar of *i*,
4:50 Then they burned *i* on the altar and
2Mc 2: 5 put the tent, the ark, and the altar of *i*;
10: 3 for the first time in two years, burned *i*,
Ps(s) 141: 2 Let my prayer come like *i* before you;
Prv 27: 9 Perfume and *i* gladden the heart,
Sg 4: 6 to the mountain of myrrh, to the hill of *i*.
4:14 calamus and cinnamon, with all kinds of *i*;
Wis 18:21 office, prayer and the propitiation of *i*;
Sir 24:15 like the odor of *i* in the holy place.
39:14 Send up the sweet odor of *i*.
49: 1 The name JOSIAH is like blended *i*,
50: 9 like the fire of *i* at the sacrifice;
Is 1:13 your *i* is loathsome to me.
17: 8 the sacred poles or the *i* stands.
27: 9 no sacred poles or *i* altars shall stand.
65: 3 in the groves and burning *i* on bricks,
65: 7 Since they burned *i* on the mountains,
66: 3 burning *i*,
Jer 1:16 And in burning *i* to strange gods and
6:20 Of what use to me *i* that comes from Sheba,
7: 9 adultery and perjury, burn *i* to Baal,
11:12 gods to which they have been offering *i*.
17:26 cereal offerings and *i* and thank offerings
18:15 they burn *i* to a thing that does not exist.
19: 4 by burning in it *i* to strange gods which
19:13 they burnt *i* to the whole host of heaven
32:29 on the roofs of which *i* was burned to Baal
41: 5 offerings and *i* for the house of the LORD.
44:15 their wives were burning *i* to strange gods,
44:17 we will burn *i* to the queen of heaven and
44:18 But since we stopped burning *i* to the
44:19 And when we burned *i* to the queen of
44:21 that you burned *i* in the cities of Judah
44:23 you burned *i* and sinned against the LORD,
44:25 made to burn *i* to the queen of heaven
48:35 the high place, or to burn *i* to his gods.
Bar 6:42 sit by the roads, burning chaff for *i*;
Ez 6: 4 laid waste, your *i* stands shall be broken,
6: 6 removed, and your *i* stands smashed to bits.
8:11 fragrance of the *i* was rising upward.
16:18 my oil and my *i* you set before them;
23:41 it, on which you had set my *i* and oil.
Dn 2:46 and ordered sacrifice and *i* offered to him.
3:38 no holocaust, sacrifice, oblation, or *i*,
Hos 2:15 for whom she burnt *i* While she decked
4:13 sacrifice and on the hills they burn *i*,
11: 2 to the Baals and burning *i* to idols.
Hb 1:16 to his net, and burns *i* to his seine;
Lk 1: 9 the sanctuary of the Lord and offer *i*.
1:10 people was praying outside at the *i* hour,
1:11 standing at the right of the altar of *i*.
Heb 9: 4 golden altar of *i* and the ark of the covenant
Rv 8: 3 *i* and was given large amounts of incense
8: 4 hand the smoke of the *i* went up before God,
14:18 in charge of the fire at the altar of *i*,

INCENSED (1)

Neh 3:33 roused his anger and he became very much *i*.

INCEST (3)

Lv 20:19 whoever does so shall pay the penalty of *i*.
20:21 they shall be childless because of this *i*.
Ez 22:11 who defile their daughters-in-law by *i*,

INCESTUOUS (1)

Dt 23: 3 No child of an *i* union may be admitted

INCIDENT (2)

2Sm 13: 1 Some time later the following *i* occurred.
Mt 18:31 went to their master to report the whole *i*.

INCISED (2)

Sir 44:20 In his own flesh he *i* the ordinance,
45:11 in *i* letters each of the tribes of Israel;

INCISORS (1)

Prv 30:14 There is a group whose *i* are swords,

INCITED (6)

1Sm 26:19 If the LORD has *i* you against me,
2Sm 24: 1 and he *i* David against the Israelites by
1Chr 5:26 of Israel *i* against them the anger of Pul,
Jb 2: 3 *i* me against him to ruin him without cause."
Mk 15:11 the chief priests *i* the crowd to have him
Acts 6:12 and God, and in this way they *i* the people,

INCITES (2)

Dt 32:11 As an eagle *i* its nestlings forth by
Jb 36:33 speaks for him and *i* the fury of the storm.

INCITING (1)

Acts 24:12 find me debating with anyone or *i* a mob.

INCLINE (16)

2Kgs 19:16 *I* your ear, O LORD, and listen!
Ps(s) 17: 6 *i* your ear to me;
31: 3 your justice rescue me, *i* your ear to me,
71: 2 *i* your ear to me, and save me.
78: 1 *i* your ears to the words of my mouth.
86: 1 *I* your ear, O LORD; answer me,
88: 3 *i* your ear to my call for help,
102: 3 *I* your ear to me; in the day when I call,
119:36 *I* my heart to your decrees and not to gain.
141: 4 Let not my heart *i* to the evil of engaging
144: 5 *I* your heavens,
Prv 4:20 be attentive, to my sayings *i* your ear;
5: 1 be attentive, to my knowledge *i* your ear,
5:13 teachers, nor to my instructors *i* my ear!
22:17 *I* your ear, and hear my words, and apply
Is 37:17 *I* your ear, O LORD, and listen!

INCLINED (6)

Dt 31:21 they are *i* to do even at the present time,
1Sm 14: 7 replied, "Do whatever you are *i* to do;
2Sm 22:10 He *i* the heavens and came down,
Ps(s) 18:10 And he *i* the heavens and came down,
116: 2 he has *i* his ear to me the day I called.
1Cor 11:18 among you, and I am *i* to believe it.

INCLINING (2)

Jos 18:17 *I* to the north,
Prv 2: 2 to wisdom, *i* your heart to understanding;

INCLUDE (10)

Lv 7:13 His offering shall also *i* loaves of
Nm 1:49 you shall not enroll nor *i* in the census
11:21 around me *i* six hundred thousand soldiers;
Jos 12: 2 of the Wadi Arnon, to *i* the wadi itself,
13: 6 at least *i* these areas in the division of
13:17 to *i* Heshbon and all its towns which are
15:11 to Mount Baalah, thence to *i* Jabneel,
17: 7 southward to *i* the natives of En-Tappuah,
Jgs 21:11 They were told to *i* under the ban all
1Chr 21: 6 however, he did not *i* in the census,

INCLUDED (12)

Nm 6:21 offering to the LORD which is *i* in his vow
Dt 20:19 men, that they should be *i* in your siege?
Jos 12: 8 It *i* the mountain regions and foothills,
13:25 Their territory *i* Jazer,
13:30 Their territory *i* Mahanaim,
19:18 of the clans of the Issacharites *i* Jezreel,
19:25 Their territory *i* Helkath,
Jgs 20:16 *I* in this total were seven hundred picked
1Sm 25:13 And so everyone, David *i*,
Neh 1: 6 against you, I and my father's house *i*.

Acts 21: 5 wives and children *i*—
Heb 11:40 had made a better plan, a plan which *i* us.

INCLUDES (1)

Jos 13: 2 This additional land *i* all Geshur and all

INCLUDING (35)

Gn 17:12 *i* houseborn slaves and those acquired with
17:27 *i* the slaves born in his house or acquired
34:24 *i* every able-bodied man in the community,
Ex 25:35 *i* a knob below each of the three pairs of
37:21 *i* a knob below each of the three pairs of
Dt 3:10 of Og in Bashan *i* Salecah and Edrei.
3:16 Wadi Arnon *i* the wadi bed and its banks
Jos 8:35 entire community, *i* the women and children,
12: 1 *i* all the eastern section of the Arabah,
16: 9 *i* the villages that belonged to each city
19:33 to Lakkum, *i* Adami-nekeb and Jabneel,
23: 2 he summoned all Israel *i* their elders,
24:18 *i* the Amorites who dwelt in the land.
Jgs 21:10 to the sword, *i* the women and children.
Ru 4: 4 here present, *i* the elders of my people,
4:11 All those at the gate, *i* the elders,
1Sm 6:18 *i* fortified cities and open villages.
14:15 *i* the outpost and the raiding parties,
22:19 city of Nob to the sword, *i* men and women,
2Sm 16: 6 though all the soldiers, *i* the royal guard,
1Kgs 14:26 *i* the treasures of the temple of the LORD
22:39 *i* the ivory palace and all the cities he
1Chr 16:38 sixty-eight of his brethren, *i* Obed-edom,
2Chr 12: 9 *i* the gold bucklers that Solomon had made.
32:32 rest of Hezekiah's acts, *i* his pious works,
Neh 10:37 *i* the first-born of our flocks and herds.
11:20 The rest of Israel, *i* priests and Levites,
Jdt 7:23 All the people, therefore, *i* youths,
Est 3:13 Jews, young and old, *i* women and children,
Jer 44:24 further to all the people, *i* the women:
Mt 8:33 *i* the story about the two possessed men.
Lk 23:27 *i* women who beat their breasts and
Acts 13:38 *i* the remission of all those charges you
Rom 16: 2 herself has been of help to many, *i* myself.
2Tm 1:15 in Asia, *i* even Phygelus and Hermogenes,

INCOME (4)

Tb 1: 6 my *i* and the first shearings of the sheep,
1Mc 3:29 moreover the *i* from the province was small,
2Mc 4: 8 as eighty talents from another source of *i*.
Prv 16: 8 with virtue, than a large *i* with injustice.

INCOMMUNICABLE (1)

Wis 14:21 conferred the *i* Name on stocks and stones.

INCOMPETENT (1)

Wis 13:18 And for aid he beseeches the wholly *i*,

INCONSPICUOUS (1)

1Tm 5:25 even *i* ones cannot be hidden forever.

INCONSTANCY (1)

Jas 3:16 also are *i* and all kinds of vile behavior.

INCONSTANT (1)

Sir 27:11 but the godless man, like the moon, is *i*.

INCONVENIENCES (1)

2Mc 2:27 of many we will gladly endure these *i*,

INCONVENIENT (1)

2Tm 4: 2 with this task whether convenient or *i*—

INCORPORATED (1)

1Mc 10:38 province of Samaria be *i* with Judea

INCORRUPTIBILITY (4)

Wis 6:18 To observe her laws is the basis for *i*;
6:19 and *i* makes one close to God;
1Cor 15:53 corruptible body must be clothed with *i*,
15:54 takes on *i* and the mortal immortality,

INCORRUPTIBLE (2)

1Cor 15:42 earth is subject to decay, what rises is *i*.
15:52 will sound and the dead will be raised *i*,

INCORRUPTION (1)

1Cor 15:50 no more can corruption inherit *i*.

INCREASE (33)

Ex 1:10 deal shrewdly with them to stop their *i*;
5: 9 *I* the work for the men,
Lv 26:18 *i* the chastisement for your sins sevenfold,
Dt 1:11 your fathers, *i* you a thousand times over,
8: 1 on you today, that you may live and *i*,
28:11 The LORD will *i* in more than goodly
30: 9 will *i* in more than goodly measure the
2Sm 24: 3 "May the LORD your God *i* the number of
1Chr 21: 3 "May the LORD *i* his people a hundredfold!
2Chr 28:13 the LORD and *i* our sins and our guilt.
Jb 17: 9 and he who has clean hands *i* in strength.
Ps(s) 73:12 always carefree, while they *i* in wealth.
85:13 our land shall yield its *i*.
144:13 thousands, and *i* to myriads in our meadows;
Eccl 10:10 made easy progress, he must *i* his efforts;
Sir 11:10 My son, why *i* your cares,
18: 4 One cannot lessen, nor *i*,
23: 3 Lest my failings *i*,
Jer 23: 3 there they shall *i* and multiply.
29: 6 There you must *i* in number, not decrease.
Bar 2:34 I will make them *i*;
Ez 36:30 I will *i* the fruit on your trees and the
Dn 12: 4 many shall fall away and evil shall *i*."
Hos 4:10 they shall play the harlot but not *i*,
Mt 24:12 Because of the *i* of evil,
Lk 17: 5 The apostles said to the Lord, *I* our faith,"
Jn 3:30 He must *i*, while I must decrease.
15: 2 ones he trims clean to *i* their yield.
Acts 12:24 word of the Lord continued to spread and *i*.
Rom 5:20 The law came in order to *i* offenses;
5:20 but despite the *i* of sin,
2Cor 9:10 the seed you sow and *i* your generous yield.
1Thes 3:12 And may the Lord *i* you and make you

INCREASED (17)

Gn 7:17 As the waters *i*, they lifted the ark,
7:18 The swelling waters *i* greatly,
47:27 property, were fertile, and *i* greatly.
Ex 1:20 The people too, *i* and grew strong.
Dt 8:13 in them, and have *i* your herds and flocks,
2Sm 15:12 and the people with Absalom *i* in numbers.
2Chr 33:23 on the contrary, Amon only *i* his guilt.
1Mc 4:35 to give way, and the *i* boldness of Judas,
Ps(s) 105:24 He greatly *i* his people and made them
Prv 9:11 be multiplied and the years of your life *i*."
Sir 45:20 Then he *i* the glory of Aaron and bestowed
Is 26:15 *i* the nation, O LORD, increased the nation
Lk 23:23 crucified, and their shouts *i* in violence.
Acts 6: 7 of the disciples in Jerusalem enormously *i*.
9:31 the *i* consolation of the Holy Spirit.
16: 5 stronger in faith and daily *i* in numbers.

INCREASES (8)

2Mc 15:38 makes a more pleasant drink that *i* delight,
Jb 20:18 though his wealth *i*,
Prv 16:21 yet pleasing speech *i* his persuasiveness.
23:28 a robber, and *i* the faithless among men.
28: 8 He who *i* his wealth by interest and
29:16 When the wicked prevail, crime *i*;
Sir 38:24 The scribe's profession *i* his wisdom;
2Thes 1: 3 faith grows apace and your mutual love *i*;

INCREASING (2)

1Sm 14:19 the tumult in the Philistine camp kept *i*.
Ez 27:10 helmet they hung upon you, *i* your splendor.

INCREASINGLY (2)

Gn 30:43 Thus the man grew *i* prosperous,
2Pt 1: 8 Qualities like these, made *i* your own,

INCREDIBLE (1)

Lk 5:26 God, saying, "We have seen *i* things today!"

INCREDULOUS (1)

Lk 24:41 They were still *i* for sheer joy and wonder,

INCREMENT (1)

Lv 22:14 with an *i* of one fifth of the amount.

INCUR (11)

Ex 28:38 bears whatever guilt the Israelites may *i* in
28:43 the sanctuary, lest they *i* guilt and die.
Lv 19:17 fellow man, do not *i* sin because of him.
Nm 18:22 else they will *i* guilt deserving death.
18:32 You will *i* no guilt so long as you make a
1Sm 28:10 LORD lives, you shall *i* no blame for this."
Sir 11:33 only evil, lest you *i* a lasting stain.
Jer 50: 7 and their enemies said, "We *i* no guilt,
1Tm 3: 6 conceited and thus *i* the punishment once
5: 7 about widows, so that no one may *i* blame.
Jas 5:12 In this way you will not *i* condemnation.

INCURABLE (9)

2Chr 21:18 him with an *i* disease of the bowels.
2Mc 9: 5 struck him down with an unseen but *i* blow;
Is 17:11 the day of the grievous blow, the *i* blight.
Jer 8:18 My grief is *i*,
10:19 I am undone, my wound is *i*;
14:17 daughter of my people, over her *i* wound.
15:18 Why is my pain continuous, my wound *i*,
30:12 *I* is your wound,
Lk 8:43 years' duration, *i* at any doctor's hands,

INCURRED (12)

Lv 5: 5 confess the sin he has *i* and as his sin
5:23 therefore, since he has *i* guilt by his sin,
5:26 be forgiven whatever guilt he may have *i*."
Jos 7:12 from among you whoever has *i* the ban.
7:13 from among you whoever has *i* the ban.
7:15 *i* the ban shall be destroyed by fire,
1Mc 13:39 any oversights and defaults *i* up to now,
2Mc 14: 3 *i* defilement at the time of the revolt,
Wis 12:15 power to punish one who has *i* no blame.
Jer 33: 8 all the guilt they *i* by sinning against me;
Hos 9:15 yes, there they *i* my hatred.
Acts 27:21 you would not have *i* this disastrous loss.

INCURRING (1)

Mt 12: 5 can break the sabbath rest without *i* guilt?

INCURS (7)

Lv 5:17 that he *i* guilt for which he must answer,
Nm 35:27 and kills him, the avenger *i* no bloodguilt;
Ps(s) 34:23 no one *i* guilt who takes refuge in him.
Prv 9: 7 he who reproves a wicked man *i* opprobrium.
14:35 servant, but the worthless one *i* his wrath.
20: 2 he who *i* his anger forfeits his life.
Sir 23:11 If he swears in error, he *i* guilt;

INCURSIONS (1)

1Mc 15:40 harass the people and to make *i* into Judea,

INDECENT (4)

Dt 23:15 if he sees anything *i* in your midst,
24: 1 her because he finds in her something *i*,
Is 57: 8 and the doorpost you placed your *i* symbol.
Ez 23:29 naked, so that your *i* nakedness is exposed.

INDECENTLY (1)

Ex 20:26 on which you must not be *i* uncovered.

INDEED (235)

Gn 18:19 *I*, I have singled him out that he may
26:13 all the time, until he was very wealthy *i*.
29:14 to him, "You are *i* my flesh and blood."
30: 6 *i* he has heeded my plea and given me a
34: 3 Jacob, *i* was really in love with the girl,
35:11 A nation, *i* an assembly of nations,
49: 5 "Simeon and Levi, brothers *i*,
Ex 3: 9 *i* the cry of the Israelites has reached me,
11: 3 The LORD *i* made the Egyptians
12:36 The LORD *i* had made the Egyptians so
32:31 this people has *i* committed a grave sin in
33:12 Moses said to the LORD, "You, *i*,
34: 9 This is *i* a stiff-necked people;
Lv 2:12 Such you may *i* present to the LORD in the
7:16 it should *i* be eaten on the day the
11: 4 the camel, which *i* chews the cud,
11: 5 the rock badger, which *i* chews the cud,
11: 6 the hare, which *i* chews the cud,
11: 7 does *i* have hoofs and is cloven-footed,
13: 3 the skin, it is *i* the sore of leprosy;
13: 8 that the eczema has *i* spread on the skin,
13:17 him, find that the sore has *i* turned white,
13:36 If the scall has *i* spread on the skin he
13:49 the thing is *i* infected with leprosy and
22:23 you may *i* present as a freewill offering,
25:44 male and female, you may *i* possess,
Nm 8:17 *I*, all the first-born among the Israelites,
13:27 It does *i* flow with milk and honey,
14:40 for we were *i* doing wrong."
22: 3 *I*, Moab feared the Israelites greatly
Dt 2:30 him up to you, as *i* he has now done.
4:29 and you shall *i* find him when you search
5:24 has *i* let us see his glory and his majesty!
7: 9 then, that the LORD, your God, is God *i*,
10:15 to all other peoples, as *i* he has now done.
12:27 of your other sacrifices the blood *i* must
14: 7 and the rock badger, which *i* chew the cud,
14: 8 which *i* has hoofs and is cloven-footed,
26: 3 that I have *i* come into the land which he
31:17 At that time they will *i* say,
32:31 *I*, their 'rock' is not like our Rock,
32:52 You may *i* view the land at a distance,
Jos 2:24 *i*, all the inhabitants of the land
3:16 a solid mass for a very great distance *i*,
7:20 Joshua, "I have *i* sinned against the LORD,
24:22 They replied, "We are, *i*!"
Jgs 5: 7 beyond the walls, gone *i* from Israel.
6:36 *i* you are going to save Israel through me,
13: 6 appearance of an angel of God, terrible *i*.
18:10 God has *i* given it into your power:
Ru 2:13 would *i* that I were a servant of yours!"
3:12 Now, though *i* I am closely related to you,
1Sm 14:25 *I*, there was a honeycomb lying on the
14:44 do thus and so to me if you do not *i* die,
15:20 "I did *i* obey the LORD and fulfill the
21: 6 "We have *i* been segregated from women as
22:15 No *i*! Let not the king accuse
25:21 *I*, it was in vain that I guarded all this
26:21 *I*, I have been a fool and have made a
2Sm 14:14 We must *i* die;
14:17 *i*, my lord the king is like an angel
19: 7 *I* I am now certain that if Absalom were
19:31 answered the king, *I* let him have it all,
1Kgs 8:27 it *i* be that God dwells among men on earth?
17:24 *i* I know that you you are a man of God,"

INDEED (cont.)

21: 7 "A fine ruler over Israel you are *i!*"
21:25 *I,* no one gave himself up to the doing of
2Kgs 2:19 Elisha, "The site of the city is fine *i,*
14:10 You have *i* conquered Edom,
1Chr 5: 1 (He was *i* the first-born,
22:18 *I,* he has delivered the occupants of the
2Chr 6:18 *i* be that God dwells with mankind on earth?
28:20 king of Assyria, did *i* come to him,
33:13 Manasseh understood that the LORD is *i* God.
35:14 *I* the priests, the sons of Aaron, were busy
Ezr 10: 2 "We have *i* betrayed our God by taking
Tb 2: 2 *I,* son, I shall wait for you to come back."
7: 4 They answered, *I* we do!"
14: 4 *i,* whatever was said by Israel's prophets,
Jdt 7:27 We should *i* be made slaves,
11: 8 *I,* we have heard of your wisdom and
11:17 Your handmaid is, *i,*
1Mc 14:40 He had *i* heard that the Romans had
2Mc 3:38 back well-flogged, if *i* he survives at all;
7:32 We, *i,* are suffering because of our sins.
12:12 they could *i* be useful in many respects,
15: 4 that there was *i* such a ruler in heaven,
Jb 8: 7 for in time to come you will flourish *i.*
15: 7 Are you *i* the first-born of mankind,
17: 2 I am *i* mocked,
19: 4 Be it *i* that I am at fault and that my
22:15 Do you *i* keep to the ancient way trodden
23:16 *I* God has made my courage fail;
28: 1 There is *i* a mine for silver,
30:11 *I,* they have loosed their bonds;
30:23 *I* I know you will turn me back in death to
34:17 Can an enemy of justice *i* be in control,
36: 4 For *i,* my theme cannot fail me:
Ps(s) 16: 6 fair to me *i* is my inheritance.
18:29 You *i,* O LORD, give light to my lamp;
22:17 *I,* many dogs surround me,
38:19 *I,* I acknowledge my guilt;
51: 7 *I,* in guilt was I born,
58: 2 Do you *i* like gods pronounce justice
61: 6 You *i,* O God, have accepted my vows;
73:18 You set them, *i,* on a slippery road;
73:27 For *i,* they who withdraw from you perish;
85:10 *i* is his salvation to those who fear him,
93: 5 Your decrees are worthy of trust *i:*
104: 1 O LORD, my God, you are great *i!*
118:18 Though the LORD has *i* chastised me,
119:96 broad *i* is your command.
121: 4 *I* he neither slumbers nor sleeps,
126: 3 done great things for us; we are glad *i.*
142: 7 Attend to my cry, for I am brought low *i.*
Eccl 8:12 Though *i* I know that it shall be well with
9: 4 *I,* for any among the living there is hope;
Wis 3: 4 For if before men, *i,*
7:30 For that, *i,* night supplants, but wickedness
8: 1 *I,* she reaches from end to end mightily
9: 6 *I,* though one be perfect among the sons of
11:14 out in exposure they *i* mockingly rejected;
11:22 *I,* before you the whole universe is as a
13: 6 For they *i* have gone astray perhaps,
16:12 For *i,* neither herb nor application cured
Sir 20:14 hateful *i* is such a man.
25: 2 their manner of life I loathe *i:*
25:10 He who finds wisdom is great *i,*
35:19 God *i* will not delay,
43: 5 Great *i* is the LORD who made it,
43:11 its Maker, for majestic *i* is its splendor;
43:30 Awful *i* is the LORD's majesty,
Is 12: 2 God *i* is my savior;
33:22 *I* the LORD will be there with us,
40: 2 *I,* she has received from the hand
44:10 *I,* all the associates of anyone who forms
63: 8 They are *i* my people,
Jer 3:23 Deceptive *i* are the hills,
14:13 *I,* I will give you lasting peace in this
15:18 have *i* become for me a treacherous brook,
18: 6 *I,* like clay in the hand of the potter,
20: 4 *I,* I will deliver you to terror,
34:15 Today you *i* repented and did what is right
52: 3 *I,* what was done in Jerusalem and in Judah
Lam 5:22 For now you have *i* rejected us,
Bar 2:25 And *i,* they lie exposed to the heat of day
4: 9 She *i* saw coming upon you the anger of God;
Ez 18:23 Do I *i* derive any pleasure from the death
23:44 And *i* they did come to her as men come to
Jl 2:11 For immense *i* is his camp,
4: 8 *I,* the LORD has spoken.
Am 3: 7 *I,* the Lord GOD does nothing without
6:11 *I,* the LORD has given the command to
Hg 2:19 *I,* the seed has not sprouted,
Zec 1: 2 The LORD was *i* angry with your fathers . . .
Mal 1: 4 They *i* may build, but I will tear down,
3: 9 You are *i* accursed,
3:15 for *i* evildoers prosper,
Mt 11: 9 A prophet *i,* and something more!
12: 8 The Son of Man is *i* Lord of the sabbath."
13:15 Sluggish *i* is this people's heart.
13:57 in his native place, *i* in his own house."
17:11 "Elijah is *i* coming,
24:10 *I,* you will be hated by all nations on my
24:22 *I,* if the period had not been shortened,
Mk 9:12 will *i* come first and restore everything.
13:20 *I,* had the Lord not shortened the period,
Lk 4:25 *I,* let me remind you,
5: 9 For *i,* amazement at the catch
6:19 *i,* the whole crowd was trying to touch him
8:40 *i,* they were all waiting for him,
14:26 his brothers and sisters, *i* his very self,
18:25 *I,* it is easier for a camel to go through
19:48 for *i* the entire populace was listening to
21:22 These *i* will be days of retribution,
Jn 4:23 *I,* it is just such worshipers the Father
5:21 *I,* just as the Father raises the dead and
5:25 assure you, an hour is coming, has *i* come,
5:26 *I,* just as the Father possesses life in
6:40 *I,* this is the will of my Father,
8:41 *I* you are doing your father's works!"
14: 3 I am *i* going to prepare a place for you,
16:28 [I did *i* come from the Father;]
16:30 We do *i* believe you came from God."
16:32 An hour is coming—has *i* already come
Acts 2:14 Jews, *i* all of you staying in Jerusalem!
4:27 *I,* they gathered in this very city against
17:21 *I,* all Athenian citizens,
23: 5 *I,* Scripture has it,
26:11 *I,* so wild was my fury against them that I
28:24 Some, *i,* were convinced by what he said;
Rom 4:15 *I,* the law serves only to bring down wrath,
8: 7 *I,* it cannot be; those who are in the flesh
8:19 *I,* the whole created world eagerly awaits
9: 3 *I,* I could even wish to be separated from
10: 2 *I,* I can testify that they are zealous for
1Cor 7:34 The virgin *i,* any unmarried woman
11: 6 *I,* if a woman will not wear a veil,
12:20 There are, *i,* many different members,
14:17 You will be uttering praise very well *i,*
15:10 *I,* I have worked harder than all the others,
15:15 *I,* we should then be exposed as false
2Cor 3:10 *I,* when you compare that limited glory
4:15 *I,* everything is ordered to your benefit,
5: 1 *I,* we know that when the earthly tent in
5:13 *I,* if we are ever caught up out of
7:10 *I,* sorrow for God's sake produces a
8: 3 *i* I can testify even beyond their means
10: 3 We do *i* live in the body but we do not
10:14 But *i* we did get as far as you with the
12:12 *I,* I have performed among you with great
Gal 2:18 I should then *i* be a transgressor.
3: 4 if *i* they were to no purpose?
Phil 1:18 *I,* I shall continue to rejoice,
1Thes 4: 1 pleasing to God—which you are *i* doing
5:11 upbuild one another, as *i* you are doing.
2Thes 3:10 *I,* when we were with you we used to lay
1Tm 3:16 Wonderful, *i,* is the mystery of our faith,
6:19 for receiving that life which is life *i.*
2Tm 1: 3 as *i* I do constantly, night and day,
Phlm 1:11 you is now useful *i* both to you and to me.
Heb 2:10 *I,* it was fitting that when bringing many
4: 2 We have *i* heard the good news,
4:12 *I,* God's word is living and effective,
6:14 "I will *i* bless you, and multiply you."
12:21 *I,* so fearful was the spectacle that Moses
Jas 5:16 petition of a holy man is powerful *i.*
1Pt 3:13 Who *i* can harm you if you are committed
2Pt 2: 9 The Lord, *i,* knows how to rescue devout
1Jn 1: 4 *I,* our purpose in writing you this is
3: 7 the man who acts in holiness is holy *i,*
3Jn 1: 1 elder to the beloved Gaius, whom *i* I love.
1: 6 *i,* they have testified to your love
Rv 2:10 The devil will *i* cast some of you into
14: 5 they are *i* without flaw.

INDEMNITY (2)

Nm 35:31 "You shall not accept *i* in place of the
35:32 Nor shall you accept *i* to allow a refugee

INDEPENDENT (3)

Sir 11:24 "I am *i.*
1Cor 11:11 not *i* of man nor man independent of woman.

INDESCRIBABLE (2)

2Mc 12:16 *i* slaughter on it that the adjacent pool,
2Cor 9:15 Thanks be to God for his *i* gift!

INDESTRUCTIBLE (1)

1Pt 1:23 not from a destructible but from an *i* seed,

INDIA (4)

Est 1: 1 twenty-seven provinces from *I* to Ethiopia
B: 1 twenty-seven provinces from *I* to Ethiopia,
8: 9 twenty-seven provinces from *I* to Ethiopia:
E: 1 twenty-seven satrapies from *I* to Ethiopia,

INDIAN (1)

1Mc 6:37 by a harness, held, besides the *I* mahout,

INDICATE (2)

Mt 16:21 [the Messiah] started to *i* to his disciples
Acts 9:16 I myself shall *i* to him how much he will

INDICATED (7)

2Kgs 6:10 to the place which the man of God had *i,*
Est B: 6 who are *i* to you in the letters of Haman,
1Mc 4:20 that could be seen *i* what had happened.
Jn 12:33 *i* the sort of death he had to die.)
21:19 (What he said *i* the sort of death by which
1Cor 14:34 law states, submissiveness is *i* for them.
1Thes 4: 6 as we once *i* to you by our testimony.

INDICATES (1)

Rom 7:17 This *i* that it is not I who do it but sin

INDICATING (3)

Jn 18:32 had said *i* the sort of death he had to die.)
Acts 19:33 *i* that he wanted to explain something to
25:27 prisoner without *i* the charges against him."

INDICATIONS (1)

2Pt 1:14 the *i* our Lord Jesus Christ has given me,

INDICTING (1)

Jude 1:15 *i* the godless for every evil deed they

INDICTMENT (3)

Jb 31:35 and that my accuser would write out his *i!*
Jer 25:31 For the LORD has an *i* against the nations,
Acts 24: 9 *i* and maintained that these were the facts.

INDICTMENTS (1)

Jb 13:26 For you draw up bitter *i* against me,

INDIFFERENT (1)

Prv 24:10 If you remain *i* in time of adversity,

INDIGNANT (9)

2Mc 4:35 were *i* and angry over the unjust murder of
4:49 even some Tyrians were *i* over the crime
13:25 *i* that they wanted to annul its provisions.
Mt 20:24 hearing this, became *i* at the two brothers.
21:15 *i* when they observed the wonders he worked,
26: 8 When the disciples saw this they grew *i,*
Mk 10:14 *i* when he noticed it and said to them:
10:41 hearing this, became *i* at James and John.
Lk 13:14 *i* that Jesus should have healed on the

INDIGNANTLY (1)

Mk 14: 4 Some were saying to themselves *i:*

INDIGNATION (12)

Gn 34: 7 the men were shocked and seethed with *i.*
2Mc 14:11 Judas quickly added fuel to Demetrius' *i.*
Jb 5: 2 kills the fool and *i* slays the simpleton.
Ps(s) 38: 4 no health in my flesh because of your *i;*
90: 9 All our days have passed away in your *i;*
90:11 or your *i* toward those who should fear you?
119:53 *I* seizes me because of the wicked who
Jer 15:17 I sat alone because you filled me with *i.*
Ez 21:36 I will pour out my *i* upon you;
Lk 4:28 in the synagogue was filled with *i.*
2Cor 7:11 What *i,* fear, and longing!
11:29 is scandalized that I am not aflame with *i?*

INDISPENSABLE (1)

1Cor 12:22 which seem less important are in fact *i.*

INDISPUTABLE (1)

Heb 7: 7 It is *i* that a lesser person is blessed by

INDISTINCTLY (1)

1Cor 13:12 Now we see *i,*

INDIVIDUAL (9)

Nm 3:47 you shall take five shekels for each *i,*
4:49 they gave them their *i* assignments for
15:27 if it is an *i* who sins inadvertently,
2Sm 20: 1 a rebellious *i* from Benjamin named Sheba,
Jdt 1:11 regarded him as a lone *i* opposed to them,
2Mc 9:26 general and *i* benefits you have received,
Sir 45:25 Was an *i* heritage through one son alone;
Ez 33:24 "Abraham, though but a single *i,*
Acts 1:18 "That *i* bought a piece of land with his

INDIVIDUALLY (4)

Gn 36:40 names of the clans of Esau *i* according
Nm 1: 2 ancestral houses, registering each male *i.*
Acts 20:31 warning you *i* even to the point of tears.
Rom 12: 5 in Christ and *i* members one of another.

INDIVIDUALS (2)

Nm 26:53 keeping with the number of *i* in each group.
Jude 1: 4 Certain *i* have recently wormed their way

INDOORS (4)

1Sm 6: 7 but drive their calves *i* away from them.
6:10 to the cart but shut up their calves *i.*
2Mc 3:19 maidens secluded *i* ran together,
Jb 37: 7 He shuts up all mankind *i;*

INDUCE (3)

2Kgs 18:30 Let not Hezekiah *i* you to rely on the LORD,
2Mc 11:14 also, and to *i* him to become their friend.
Is 36:15 Let not Hezekiah *i* you to rely on the LORD,

INDUCED (6)

Jos 15:18 she *i* him to ask her father for some land.
Jgs 1:14 she *i* him to ask her father for some land.
2Chr 18:31 God *i* them to leave him.
Est E: 5 administration of affairs has *i* many placed
2Mc 4:12 where he *i* the noblest young men to wear
Jn 13: 2 The devil had already *i* Judas,

INDULGE (6)

Gn 33:15 Please *i* me in this, my lord."
Sir 30: 9 for you, *i* him and he will bring you grief.
1Cor 10: 8 us not *i* in lewdness as some of them did,
Col 2:23 chief effect is that they *i* men's pride.
2Tm 2:16 who *i* in it become more and more godless,
1Pt 2:11 I urge you not to *i* your carnal desires.

INDULGED (2)

Prv 13:19 Lust *i* starves the soul,
Jude 1: 7 and the towns thereabout *i* in lust,

INDULGENCE (5)

Sir 42:14 Better a man's harshness than a woman's *i*,
Lk 21:34 with *i* and drunkenness and worldly cares.
Acts 24: 4 beg your *i* for a brief hearing of our case.
Eph 4:19 and the *i* of every sort of lewd conduct.
1Tm 5: 6 A widow who gives herself up to selfish *i*,

INDULGENT (2)

Sir 7:24 keep them chaste, and be not *i* to them.
25:24 no outlet, and be not *i* to an erring wife.

INDUSTRIOUS (3)

1Kgs 11:28 saw that he was also an *i* young man,
Mt 25:21 You are an *i* and reliable servant.
25:23 You too are an *i* and reliable servant.

INEBRIATES (1)

Sir 1:14 she *i* men with her fruits.

INEFFECTUAL (1)

2Pt 1: 8 increasingly your own, are by no means *i*;

INERT (1)

Wis 13:19 of a thing with hands completely *i*.

INESCAPABLE (1)

Wis 17:17 unawares, he served out the *i* sentence;

INEVITABLE (1)

Mt 18: 7 It is *i* that scandal should occur.

INEVITABLY (1)

Lk 17: 1 "Scandals will *i* arise,

INEXCUSABLE (2)

Rom 1:20 Therefore these men are *i*.
2: 1 every one of you who judges another is *i*.

INEXORABLE (2)

Wis 16: 4 upon those oppressors, *i* want had to come;
18:16 bearing the sharp sword of your *i* decree.

INEXORABLY (1)

2Kgs 24: 3 he would *i* put them out of his sight

INEXPRESSIBLE (1)

1Pt 1: 8 and rejoice with *i* joy touched with glory

INFAMOUS (1)

Wis 14:27 For the worship of *i* idols is the reason

INFAMY (1)

Ps(s) 52: 3 do you glory in evil, you champion of *i*?

INFANCY (2)

Is 46: 3 birth, whom I have carried from your *i*.
2Tm 3:15 *i* you have known the sacred Scriptures,

INFANT (8)

Gn 38:28 was giving birth, one *i* put out his hand;
Nm 11:12 bosom, like a foster father carrying an *i*,
Dt 28:57 *i* she brings forth when she secretly uses
Is 49:15 Can a mother forget her *i*,
65:20 be in it an *i* who lives but a few days,
Lam 2:11 As a child and *i* faint away in the open
Hos 11: 4 like one who raises an *i* to his cheeks;
Lk 2:12 find an *i* wrapped in swaddling clothes."

INFANTRY (16)

Jdt 1: 4 chariot forces and the marshaling of his *i*.
2: 5 thousand *i* and twelve thousand cavalry,
2:19 their chariots and cavalry and regular *i*.
2:22 Holofernes took his whole force, the *i*,
7: 2 thousand *i* and twelve thousand horsemen,
7:20 The whole Assyrian camp, *i*,
9: 7 rider, boasting of the power of their *i*,
1Mc 4: 1 thousand *i* and a thousand picked cavalry,
10:77 thousand horsemen and an innumerable *i*.
15:13 thousand *i* and eight thousand horsemen.
15:38 and gave him *i* and cavalry forces.
15:41 Kedron and stationed horsemen and *i* there,
16: 7 Then he divided his *i* into two corps and
2Mc 11: 2 about eighty thousand *i* and all his cavalry
Sir 46: 8 spared from the six hundred thousand *i*,
Acts 23:31 the *i* took Paul and escorted him that

INFANTRYMEN (1)

Acts 23:23 nine o'clock tonight, with two hundred *i*,

INFANTS (14)

1Sm 15: 3 but kill men and women, children and *i*,
22:19 including men and women, children and *i*,
1Mc 2: 9 Her *i* have been murdered in her streets,
2Mc 5:13 and children, a slaughter of virgins and *i*.
Jb 21:11 These folk have *i* numerous as lambs,
Wis 10:21 of the dumb, and gave ready speech to *i*.
11: 7 rebuke to the decree for the slaying of *i*,
12:24 among beasts, deceived like senseless *i*.
18: 5 to put to death the *i* of the holy ones,
Is 13:16 *i* shall be dashed to pieces in their sight;
Jl 2:16 the children and the *i* at the breast;
Mt 21:16 'From the speech of *i* and children you
Acts 7:19 He forced our fathers to abandon their *i*
1Cor 3: 1 but only as men of flesh, as *i* in Christ.

INFECTED (10)

Lv 13:49 the thing is indeed *i* with leprosy and
13:50 quarantine the *i* article for seven days.
13:52 article, whatever it may be, which is *i*;
13:54 give orders to have the *i* article washed
13:55 the *i* article after it has been washed.
13:56 shall tear the *i* part out of the garment,
13:57 and the thing *i* shall be destroyed by fire.
14:35 'It looks to me as if my house were *i*.'
14:40 he shall order the *i* stones to be pulled
Prv 25:19 Like an *i* tooth or an unsteady foot is

INFECTION (19)

Lv 13:47 *i* is on a garment of wool or of linen,
13:49 leather, if the *i* on the garment or hide,
13:50 Having examined the *i*,
13:51 day the priest shall again examine the *i*.
13:51 be its use, the *i* is malignant leprosy,
13:53 But if the priest, on examining the *i*,
13:55 If the *i* has not changed its appearance,
13:56 But if the priest, on examining the *i*,
13:57 the *i* again appears on the garment,
13:58 the washing, the *i* has left the garment,
13:59 leprous *i* on a garment of wool or linen,
14:34 *i* on any house of the land you occupy,
14:36 out before he goes in to examine the *i*,
14:37 finds that the *i* on the walls of the house
14:39 finds that the *i* has spread on the walls,
14:43 "If the *i* breaks out once more after the
14:44 finds that the *i* has spread in the house,
14:48 that the *i* has in fact not spread after
14:48 house clean, since the *i* has been healed.

INFERIOR (5)

Sir 25: 8 his tongue, and he who serves not his *i*.
Dn 2:39 kingdom shall take your place, *i* to yours,
2Cor 11: 5 *i* to the "super-apostles" in nothing.
12:11 I am in no way *i* to the "super-apostles."
12:13 you *i* to the other churches except in this,

INFERS (1)

Wis 8: 8 the things of old, and *i* those yet to come.

INFEST (1)

Dt 28:42 Buzzing insects will *i* all your trees and

INFESTED (2)

Ex 8:14 As the gnats *i* man and beast,
8:20 throughout Egypt the land was *i* with flies.

INFESTING (1)

1Sm 6: 5 mice that are *i* your land and give them

INFIDELITIES (1)

Jer 2:19 chastises you, your own *i* punish you.

INFIDELITY (3)

2Chr 33:19 was heard, all his sins and his *i*,
36:14 and the people added infidelity to *i*,

INFIRM (2)

Sir 42: 8 aged and *i* answering for wanton conduct.
1Cor 11:30 That is why many among you are sick and *i*,

INFIRMITIES (2)

Is 53: 4 Yet it was our *i* that he bore,
Mt 8:17 "It was our *i* he bore,

INFIRMITY (6)

1Kgs 15:23 In his old age, Asa had an *i* in his feet.
Prv 18:14 A man's spirit sustains him in *i*—
Is 53: 3 men, a man of suffering, accustomed to *i*,
53:10 [But the LORD was pleased to crush him in *i*
Hos 5:13 When Ephraim saw his *i*,
Lk 13:12 and said, "Woman, you are free of your *i*."

INFLAMED (7)

2Chr 36:16 people was so *i* that there was no remedy.
2Mc 4:38 *I* with anger,
14:45 Still breathing, and *i* with anger,
Jb 16:16 My face is *i* with weeping and there is
32: 5 mouths of the three men, his wrath was *i*.
Ps(s) 124: 3 When their fury was *i* against us,
Sir 45:18 Men of other families were *i* against him,

INFLAMES (1)

Is 5:11 linger into the night while wine *i* them!

INFLATED (1)

Col 2:18 he is *i* with empty pride by his human

INFLATES (1)

1Cor 8: 1 But whereas "knowledge" *i*,

INFLICT (27)

Ex 32:14 he had threatened to *i* on his people.
Dt 32:39 and life, I who *i* wounds and heal them,
1Sm 20: 9 father is determined to *i* injury upon you,
2Sm 24:12 choose one of them, and I will *i* it on you.'"
2Kgs 8:12 evil that you will *i* upon the Israelites.
1Chr 21:10 choose one of them, and I will *i* it on you."
1Mc 14:36 temple and *i* grave injury on its purity.
Ps(s) 120: 3 What will he *i* on you, with more besides,
Sir 48: 8 You anointed kings who should *i* vengeance,
Jer 25:29 is called by my name, I begin to *i* evil,
26: 3 to *i* upon them for their evil deeds.
44: 7 do you *i* so great an evil upon yourselves?
Ez 5: 8 I will *i* punishments in your midst while
5:10 I will *i* punishments upon you and scatter
6:10 threatened to *i* this calamity upon them.
11: 9 to foreigners, and *i* punishments upon you.
16:38 I will *i* on you the sentence of
16:41 *i* punishments on you while many women
23:49 *i* on you the penalty of your lewdness,
28:22 when I *i* punishments upon it and use it to
28:26 They shall dwell secure while I *i*
30:14 fire to Zoan, and *i* punishments on Thebes.
30:19 Thus will I *i* punishments on Egypt,
Dn 3:44 be routed who *i* evils on your servants;
Zec 14:18 LORD will *i* upon all the nations
Rom 13: 4 to *i* his avenging wrath upon the wrongdoer.
2Thes 1: 8 "with flaming power he will *i* punishment

INFLICTED (23)

Lv 24:20 gives another shall be *i* on him in return.
Jos 10:10 The Israelites *i* a great slaughter on
10:20 Israelites had finally *i* the last blows
Jgs 11:33 so that he *i* a severe defeat on them,
15: 8 blows, he *i* a great slaughter on them.
1Sm 19: 8 Philistines and *i* a great defeat upon them,
23: 5 their cattle and *i* a severe defeat on them,
1Kgs 20:21 chariots, and *i* a severe defeat on Aram.
2Kgs 8:29 wounds which the Arameans had *i* on him
9:15 had *i* on him in the battle against Hazael,
1Chr 5:41 exile which the LORD *i* on Judah
2Chr 13:17 and his people *i* a severe defeat upon them;
1Mc 5:34 him, and he *i* on them a crushing defeat.
8: 4 the earth and had *i* on them severe defeat,
2Mc 9:28 sufferings such as he had *i* on others,
12:16 they *i* such indescribable slaughter on it
Ps(s) 79:12 bosoms the disgrace they have *i* on you,
Dn 13:61 they *i* on them the penalty they had
2Cor 2: 6 *i* by the majority on such a one is enough;
Rv 9: 5 they *i* was like that of a scorpion's sting.
18: 4 with her and sharing the plagues *i* on her!
18:10 for fear of the punishment *i* on her,
18:15 for fear of the punishment *i* on her.

INFLICTING (3)

Ex 20: 5 *i* punishment for their fathers' wickedness
Dt 5: 9 *i* punishments for their fathers'
2Mc 13: 9 mind full of savage plans for *i* on the Jews

INFLICTS (3)

Lv 24:19 Anyone who *i* an injury on his neighbor
Sir 28:21 Dire is the death it *i*,
Rom 3: 5 "Is not God unjust when he *i* punishment?"

INFLUENCE (9)

2Kgs 4: 8 to Shunem, where there was a woman of *i*,
Est E: 7 *i* of those undeserving of authority.
Sir 13: 9 When invited by a man of *i*,
Dn 5: 2 Under the *i* of the wine,
Mt 22:43 David under the Spirit's *i* calls him 'lord,'
Acts 19:20 Lord continue to spread with *i* and power.
2Cor 10:15 our *i* may also grow among you and overflow.
2Tm 2:17 and the *i* of their talk will spread like
2Pt 1:21 the Holy Spirit have spoken under God's *i*.

INFLUENCED (1)

1Cor 8:10 his conscience in its weak state be *i*

INFLUENCING (1)

Acts 18:13 "is *i* people to worship God in ways that

INFLUENTIAL (5)

Ezr 7:28 and with all the most *i* royal officials.
Sir 8: 1 Contend not with an *i* man,
Acts 13:50 But some of the Jews stirred up their *i*
17:12 as did numerous *i* Greek women and men.
1Cor 1:26 not many are *i*;

INFORM (23)

Gn 46:31 "I will go and *i* Pharaoh, telling him:
Dt 32: 7 Ask your father and he will *i* you,
Jos 4:22 what these stones mean, you shall *i* them,
Ru 4: 4 Elimelech, So I thought I would *i* you,
1Sm 8: 9 warn them solemnly and *i* them of the
14: 1 But he did not *i* his father.
22:17 he was a fugitive and yet failed to *i* me."
2Sm 17:21 of the cistern and went on to *i* King David.
18:25 The lookout shouted to *i* the king,
24:13 Gad then went to David to *i* him.
1Kgs 18:12 I go to *i* Ahab and he does not find you,
2Kgs 7: 9 Come, let us go and *i* the palace."
Ezr 4:14 we have sent this message to *i* you,
4:16 We *i* you, O king, that if this city
7:24 We also *i* you that it is not permitted to
Tb 4:20 I wish to *i* you that I have deposited a
2Mc 1:18 Chislev, so we thought it right to *i* you,
11:37 us those who can *i* us of your intentions.
Jb 12: 8 you, and the fish of the sea to *i* you.
Sir 33:18 I would *i* you that not for myself only
Dn 13:50 elders said, "Come, sit with us and *i* us,
Jn 11: 3 The sisters sent word to Jesus to *i* him,
12:22 Philip and Andrew in turn came to *i* Jesus.

INFORMANT (3)

2Sm 1: 6 The youthful *i* replied:
15:13 An *i* came to David with the report,
18:11 Joab said to his *i*:

INFORMATION (16)

Gn 32: 6 this *i* in the hope of gaining your favor.' "
Lv 5: 1 any person refuses to give the *i* which,
Jgs 9:31 to Abimelech in Arumah with the *i*:
1Sm 20:12 toward David or not, I will send you the *i*.
23: 1 David received *i* that the Philistines were
23:23 Then come back to me with sure *i*,
2Sm 1:13 to the young man who had brought him the *i*,
11: 5 had conceived, and sent the *i* to David,
15:28 near the desert until I receive *i* from you."
17:17 A maidservant was to come with *i* for them,
1Kgs 21:14 Then they sent the *i* to Jezebel that
1Mc 11:31 for your *i* a copy of the letter that we
2Mc 3: 9 told him about the *i* that had been given,
Mt 2: 8 "Go and get detailed *i* about the child.
Acts 16:36 The jailer conveyed this *i* to Paul:
23:22 tell anyone that you gave me this *i*."

INFORMED (53)

Gn 20: 8 and *i* them of everything that had happened,
48: 1 Some time afterward, Joseph was *i*,
Ex 4:28 Moses *i* him of all the LORD had said in
9: 7 But though Pharaoh's messengers *i* him that
Dt 17: 4 and if, on being *i* of it,
Jos 9:24 servants were fully *i* of how the LORD,
Jgs 16: 2 *I* that Samson had come there,
1Sm 14:33 *I* that the people were sinning against the
15:12 but was *i* that Saul had gone to Carmel,
19:10 David's wife Michal *i* him,
19:21 *I* of this, Saul sent other messengers,
23:13 was *i* that David had escaped
25:14 was *i* of this by one of the servants,
2Sm 3:23 force he had with him arrived, he was *i*,
4:10 to death the man who *i* me of Saul's death,
15:31 When David was *i* that Ahithophel was among
17:18 But an attendant saw them and *i* Absalom.
19: 9 *i* that the king was sitting at the gate,
21:11 When David was *i* of what Rizpah,
1Kgs 2:39 was *i* that his servants were in Gath.
2:41 When Solomon was *i* that Shimei had gone
18:16 So Obadiah went to meet Ahab and *i* him.
2Kgs 4:31 and *i* him that the boy had not awakened.
6:13 *I* that Elisha was in Dothan,
22: 8 high priest Hilkiah *i* the scribe Shaphan,
22:10 The scribe Shaphan also *i* the king that
1Chr 19: 5 was *i* of what had happened to his men,
Tb 1:19 But a certain citizen of Nineveh *i* the
Jdt 10:18 Holofernes, while he was being *i* about her.
Est A:13 So he *i* the king about them,
2:22 who in turn *i* the king for Mordecai.
3: 4 he would not listen to them, they *i* Haman,
1Mc 7: 3 When he was *i* of this,
11:21 went to the king and *i* him that Jonathan
14:21 people have *i* us of your glory and fame,
2Mc 1:21 *i* us that they could not find any fire,
3: 7 he *i* him about the riches that had been
8:12 Nicanor's advance and *i* his companions
14: 9 have *i* yourself in detail on these matters,
Sir 18:18 Be *i* before speaking;
Jer 11:18 I knew it because the LORD *i* me;
26:10 princes of Judah were *i* of these things,
26:21 officers and princes were *i* of his words,
Dn 2:17 went home and *i* his companions Hananiah,
Mt 2: 5 "In Bethlehem of Judea," they *i* him.
14:12 Afterward, they came and *i* Jesus.
Jn 5:15 The man went off and *i* the Jews that Jesus
Acts 11:13 He *i* us that he had seen an angel standing
21:21 Yet they have been *i* that you teach the
23:30 to be *i* of a plot against this man's life,
24:22 Felix was rather well *i* about the new way,
1Cor 1:11 I have been *i*, my brothers, by certain
Eph 6:21 you *i* as to how I am and what I am doing.

INFORMER (1)

2Mc 4: 1 *i* about the funds against his own country,

INFORMING (2)

1Sm 19:18 *i* him of all that Saul had done to him.
1Mc 12:23 are *i* you that your cattle and your

INFREQUENT (1)

1Sm 3: 1 of the LORD was uncommon and vision *i*.

INFURIATED (2)

Mk 14: 5 They were *i* at her.
Acts 12:20 been *i* by the people of Tyre and Sidon,

INFUSED (1)

Wis 15:11 a quickening soul, and *i* a vital spirit.

INGENIOUS (1)

Rom 1:30 *i* in their wrongdoing and rebellious

INGENUITY (1)

Rv 13:18 with a little *i* anyone can calculate the

INGRAINED (1)

Wis 12:10 their race was wicked and their malice *i*,

INGRATE (2)

Wis 16:29 For the hope of the *i* melts like a wintry
Sir 29:16 and the *i* abandons his protector;

INGRATIATE (2)

Acts 24:27 Felix wanted to *i* himself with the Jews,
Gal 1:10 Is this how I seek to *i* myself with men?

INHABIT (8)

Jdt 5: 3 Which cities do they *i*?
Ps(s) 69:37 it, and those who love his name shall *i* it.
Sir 23:27 and all who *i* the world shall understand,
Is 18: 3 All you who *i* the world,
Jer 25:29 down the sword upon all who *i* the earth,
25:31 To all who *i* the earth to its very ends
Am 9:14 shall rebuild and *i* their ruined cities,
Mt 4:16 those who *i* a land overshadowed by death,

INHABITANT (3)

Is 24:17 pit, and trap are upon you, *i* of the earth;
Jer 2:15 his cities are charred ruins, without *i*.
Zep 2: 5 and leave you to perish without an *i*!

INHABITANTS (188)

Gn 13:13 Now the *i* of Sodom were very wicked in the
19:25 together with the *i* of the cities and the
29:22 invited all the local *i* and gave a feast.
34:30 making me loathsome to the *i* of the land,
Ex 34:12 these *i* of the land that you are to enter;
34:15 make a covenant with the *i* of that land;
Lv 18:25 wickedness, by making it vomit out its *i*.
18:27 by which the previous *i* defiled the land;
25:10 liberty in the land for all its *i*.
Nm 13:32 explored is a country that consumes its *i*.
14:14 they to tell of it to the *i* of this land?
24:22 burning— even as I watch— are your *i*.
33:52 drive out all the *i* of the land before you;
33:55 not drive out the *i* of the land before you,
Dt 2:12 however, the former *i* were the Horites;
2:20 country of the Rephaim from its former *i*,
13:14 led astray the *i* of their city to serve
13:16 shall put the *i* of that city to the sword,
Jos 2: 9 and that all the *i* of the land are
2:24 *i* of the land are overcome with fear of us."
7: 9 and the other *i* of the land hear of it,
8:24 All the *i* of Ai who had pursued the
8:26 had fulfilled the doom on all the *i* of Ai.
9: 3 the *i* of Gibeon put into effect a device
9:11 and all the *i* of our country said to us,
9:24 and that all its *i* be destroyed before you.
10: 1 He heard also that the *i* of Gibeon had
13: 6 I will drive out all the Sidonian *i*
15:15 there he marched up against the *i* of Debir,
Jgs 1:11 there they marched against the *i* of Debir,
1:27 did he dislodge the *i* of Dor and its towns,
1:30 the *i* of Kitron or those of Nahalol;
1:31 drive out the *i* of Acco or those of Sidon,
1:33 *i* of Beth-shemesh or those of Beth-anath,
1:33 the *i* of Beth-shemesh and Beth-anath have
2: 2 not to make a pact with the *i* of this land,
5:23 says the LORD, "hurl a curse at its *i*!
9:45 then killed its *i* and demolished the city,
10:18 shall be leader of all the *i* of Gilead."
20:15 thousand, in addition to the *i* of Gibeah.
20:48 putting to the sword the *i* of the cities,
21: 9 none of the *i* of that city were present.
21:12 Finding among the *i* of Jabesh-gilead four
1Sm 5: 9 he afflicted its *i*, young and old,
6:19 celebration with the *i* of Beth-shemesh
6:21 sent messengers to the *i* of Kiriath-Jearim,
7: 1 So the *i* of Kiriath-jearim came for the
11: 5 of the *i* of Jabesh was repeated to him.
11: 9 the *i* of Jabesh-gilead that tomorrow,
11: 9 came and reported this to the *i* of Jabesh,
23: 5 on them, and thus rescued the *i* of Keilah.
31:11 When the *i* of Jabesh-gilead heard what the
2Sm 12:31 from the city, and also led away the *i*,
2Kgs 2:19 the *i* of the city complained to Elisha,
15:16 *i* of the town and of its whole district,
15:29 and Galilee, deporting the *i* to Assyria.
16: 9 its *i* to Kir and put Rezin to death.
19:26 cities into heaps of ruins, While their *i*,
22:16 upon its *i* all the evil that is threatened
22:19 *i* would become a desolation and a curse;
23: 2 men of Judah and all the *i* of Jerusalem:
1Chr 4:23 were potters and *i* of Netaim and Gederah,
7:21 were slain by the *i* of Gath because they
8:13 and they put the *i* of Gath to flight.
10:11 When all the *i* of Jabesh-gilead had heard
11: 5 The *i* of Jebus said to David,
2Chr 15: 5 were many terrors upon the *i* of the lands.
19: 8 settle quarrels among the *i* of Jerusalem.
20: 7 who drove out the *i* of this land before
20:15 "Listen, all of Judah, *i* of Jerusalem,
20:18 and all Judah and the *i* of Jerusalem fell
20:20 "Listen to me, Judah and *i* of Jerusalem!
20:23 Moabites set upon the *i* of Mount Seir
20:23 when they had finished with the *i* of Seir,
21:11 he led the *i* of Jerusalem into idolatry
21:13 Judah and the *i* of Jerusalem into idolatry,
22: 1 Then the *i* of Jerusalem made Ahaziah,
25:13 thousand of the *i* and took away much booty.
32:22 Thus the LORD saved Hezekiah and the *i* of
32:26 both he and the *i* of Jerusalem;
32:33 *i* of Jerusalem paid him honor at his death.
33: 9 Manasseh misled Judah and the *i* of
34: 9 of Judah, Benjamin, and the *i* of Jerusalem.
34:24 bring evil upon this place and upon its *i*,
34:27 words spoken against this place and its *i*;
34:28 will bring upon this place and upon its *i*.' "
34:30 the men of Judah and the *i* of Jerusalem,
34:32 and the *i* of Jerusalem conformed
35:18 that were present, and the *i* of Jerusalem.
Ezr 2: 1 These are the *i* of the province who
4: 6 against the *i* of Judah and Jerusalem.
Neh 3:13 was repaired by Hanun and the *i* of Zanoah;
7: 3 Appoint as watchmen the *i* of Jerusalem,
7: 6 These are the *i* of the province who
9:24 before them the Canaanite *i* of the land
Tb 13:11 And the *i* of all the limits of the earth,
14:15 the exile of the city's *i* when Cyaxares,
Jdt 1: 6 rallied all the *i* of the mountain region,
1: 7 sent messengers to all the *i* of Persia,
1: 7 to the *i* of Cilicia and Damascus,
1:10 and to all the *i* of Egypt as far as the
1:11 But the *i* of all that land disregarded the
1:12 destroy with his sword all the *i* of Moab,
2:28 him fell upon all the *i* of the coastland,
2:28 in Sur and Ocina, and the *i* of Jamnia.
3: 4 and their *i* are also at your service;
3: 7 The people of these cities and all the *i*
4: 6 to the *i* of Bethulia [and Betomesthaim],
5: 4 me along with all the other *i* of the West?"
5:14 they drove out all the *i* of the desert;
5:22 Holofernes and all the *i* of the seacoast
7:13 is where the *i* of Bethulia get their water.
7:20 of water failed the *i* of Bethulia,
11:14 the *i* there have also done these things.
14: 4 Then you and all the other *i* of the whole
15: 6 The remaining *i* of Bethulia swept down on
1Mc 1:28 the land was shaken on account of its *i*,
1:38 of them the *i* of Jerusalem fled away,
3:34 As for the *i* of Judea and Jerusalem,
5:15 *i* of Ptolemais, Tyre, and Sidon,
6:12 orders that the *i* of Judah be destroyed.
11:18 were killed by the *i* of the strongholds.

11:65 it for many days, and blockaded the *i.*
2Mc 5:17 because of the sins of the city's *i*
6: 2 as the *i* of the place requested.
Jb 26: 5 writhe in terror, the waters, and their *i.*
Ps(s) 83: 8 and Amalek, Philistia with the *i* of Tyre;
107:34 marsh, because of the wickedness of its *i.*
Wis 12: 3 For truly, the ancient *i* of your holy land,
Sir 10: 2 as the head of a city, its *i.*
Is 5: 3 Now, *i* of Jerusalem and men of Judah,
6:11 Until the cities are desolate, without *i,*
10:31 is in flight, the *i* of Gebim seek refuge.
20: 6 *i* of this coastland shall say on that day,
22:21 He shall be a father to the *i* of Jerusalem,
24: 2 he turns it upside down, scattering its *i:*
24: 5 The earth is polluted because of its *i,*
24: 6 the earth, and its *i* pay for their guilt;
26: 9 the earth, the world's *i* learn justice.
26:18 the *i* of the world cannot bring it forth.
26:21 to punish the wickedness of the earth's *i;*
37:27 cities into heaps of ruins, While their *i,*
40:22 the earth, and its *i* are like grasshoppers;
42:11 Let the *i* of Sela exult,
49:19 Now you shall be too small for your *i,*
51: 6 like a garment and its *i* die like flies,
Jer 10:18 I will sling away the *i* of the land;
13:13 with drunkenness all the *i* of this land,
19:12 Thus I will do to this place and to its *i,*
21: 6 I will strike the *i* of this city,
25: 9 them against this land, against its *i,*
44:22 a desert, a thing accursed and without *i,*
51:12 out his threat against the *i* of Babylon.
Lam 4:12 did not believe, nor any of the world's *i,*
Bar 2:23 all the land shall be deserted, without *i.'*
Ez 11:15 of Israel that the *i* of Jerusalem say,
12:19 the *i* of Jerusalem [to the land of Israel]:
12:19 violence of all its *i* that now fills it.
15: 6 for the fire, do I make the *i* of Jerusalem.
35: 9 forever, and leave your cities without *i;*
Hos 4: 1 has a grievance against the *i* of the land:
10: 5 The *i* of Samaria fear for the calf of
Mi 1:11 *i* of Zaanan come not forth from their city.
1:12 How can the *i* of Maroth hope for good?
1:13 steeds to the chariots, O *i* of Lachish;
1:15 to you the conqueror, O *i* of Mareshah;
6:12 whose *i* speak falsehood with deceitful
Zep 1: 4 Judah, and against all the *i* of Jerusalem;
1:11 Wail, O *i* of the Mortar!
Zec 8:20 yet come peoples, the *i* of many cities;
8:21 and the *i* of one city shall approach those
11: 6 shall I spare the *i* of the earth any more,
12: 5 "The *i* of Jerusalem have their strength
12: 7 David and the glory of the *i* of Jerusalem
12: 8 the LORD will shield the *i* of Jerusalem,
12:10 on the *i* of Jerusalem a spirit of grace
13: 1 house of David and to the *i* of Jerusalem,
Acts 1:19 came to be known by the *i* of Jerusalem,
9:35 All the *i* of Lydda and Sharon,
13:27 The *i* of Jerusalem and their rulers failed
19:10 that all the *i* of the province of Asia,
Rv 6:10 avenge our blood among the *i* of the earth?"
8:13 and again woe to the *i* of earth from the
11:10 The earth's *i* gloat over them and in their
13: 8 will be worshiped by all those *i* of earth
13:12 and all its *i* worship the first beast,
13:14 first beast, it led astray the earth's *i,*
17: 2 and the earth's *i* have grown drunk on the

INHABITED (17)

Gn 50:11 When the Canaanites who *i* the land saw the
2Sm 5: 6 against the Jebusites who *i* the region.
2Mc 9:17 *i* place to proclaim there the power of God.
12:13 and *i* by a mixed population of Gentiles.
12:27 city *i* by people of many nationalities.
Ps(s) 107: 4 the way to an *i* city they did not find.
107: 7 them by a direct way to reach an *i* city.
Is 13:20 She shall never be *i,*
44:26 Be *i;* to the cities of Judah:
Jer 17:25 This city will remain *i* forever.
46:26 But later on Egypt shall be *i* again,
Ez 12:20 *I* cities shall be in ruins,
26:19 desolate like cities that are no longer *i,*
34:13 the land's ravines and all its *i* places].
Zec 7: 7 the surrounding cities were *i* and at peace,
7: 7 when the Negeb and the foothills were *i?*
9: 5 from Gaza, and Ashkelon shall not be *i,*

INHABITS (1)

Jdt 5: 5 near you [that *i* this mountain region];

INHALED (1)

Wis 7: 3 And I too, when born, *i* the common air,

INHERIT (30)

Jos 19:49 the portions of the land they were to *i,*
Jgs 11: 2 him, "You shall *i* nothing in our family,
Tb 4:12 that their posterity shall *i* the land.
6:12 father's estate is rightfully yours to *i.*
Ps(s) 25:13 prosperity, and his descendants *i* the land.
69:37 the descendants of his servants shall *i* it,
Prv 3:35 possession of wise men, but fools *i* shame.
Sir 4:16 his descendants too will *i* her.
15: 6 he will find, an everlasting name *i.*
36:10 Jacob, that they may *i* the land as of old,
Is 57:13 he who takes refuge in me shall *i* the land,
65: 9 Judah, those who are to *i* my mountains;
65: 9 My chosen ones shall *i* the land,
Jer 49: 2 Israel shall *i* those who disinherited her,
Mt 5: 5 [Blest are the lowly; they shall *i* the land.]
19:29 many times as much and *i* everlasting life.
21:38 'Here is the one who will *i* everything.
25:34 *I* the kingdom prepared for you from the
Mk 12: 7 'Here is the one who will *i* everything.
16:20 and *i* the spiritual and immortal glory of
Lk 10:25 what must I do to *i* everlasting life?"
Rom 4:13 *i* the world did not depend on the law;
1Cor 6:10 slanderers or robbers will *i* God's kingdom.
15:50 and blood cannot *i* the kingdom of God;
15:50 no more can corruption *i* incorruption.
Gal 3:29 which means you *i* all that was promised.
5:21 such things will not *i* the kingdom of God!
Heb 1:14 sent to serve those who are to *i* salvation?
12:17 he wanted to *i* his father's blessing,
Rv 21: 7 who wins the victory shall *i* these gifts;

INHERITANCE (95)

Gn 21:10 is going to share the *i* with my son Isaac!"
Ex 15:17 planted them on the mountain of your *i*—
Nm 16:14 giving us fields and vineyards for our *i,*
Dt 21:23 the LORD, your God, is giving you as an *i.*
Jos 18: 4 they shall describe for purposes of *i.*
1Sm 26:19 this day I have no share in the LORD's *i,*
2Sm 14:16 me and my son as well from God's *i.'"*
20:19 do you wish to destroy the *i* of the LORD?"
21: 3 that you may bless the *i* of the LORD?"
1Kgs 8:51 For they are your people and your *i,*
8:53 all the peoples of the earth for your *i,*
2Kgs 21:14 of my *i* and deliver them into enemy hands,
1Chr 16:18 give the land of Canaan as your allotted *i."*
28: 8 leave it as an *i* to your children forever.
Ezr 9:12 leave it as an *i* to your children forever.
Neh 11:20 other cities of Judah, each man in his *i.*
Jdt 4:12 the cities of their *i* to be ruined,
8:22 the land, and for the devastation of our *i,*
16:21 days were over, each one returned to his *i.*
Est C: 8 the *i* that was yours from the beginning.
C:10 have pity on your *i* and turn our sorrow
11: 9 his people and rendered justice to his *i.*
1Mc 2:56 the assembly, received an *i* in the land.
2Mc 2: 4 which Moses climbed to see God's *i.*
Jb 27:13 *i* an oppressor receives from the Almighty:
31: 2 God above, his *i* from the Almighty on high?
42:15 father gave them an *i* among their brethren.
Ps(s) 2: 8 I will give you the nations for an *i*
16: 6 fair to me indeed is my *i.*
28: 9 Save your people, and bless your *i;*
33:12 the people he has chosen for his own *i.*
37:18 their *i* lasts forever.
47: 5 He chooses for us our *i,*
68:10 you showered down, O God, upon your *i;*
74: 2 of old, the tribe you redeemed as your *i,*
78:55 he distributed their *i* by lot,
78:62 to the sword and was enraged against his *i.*
78:71 Jacob, his people, and Israel, his *i.*
79: 1 O God, the nations have come into your *i;*
94: 5 they trample down, your *i* they afflict.
94:14 cast off his people, nor abandon his *i;*
105:11 give the land of Canaan as your allotted *i."*
106: 5 joy of your people, and glory with your *i.*
106:40 angry with his people, and abhorred his *i;*
111: 6 works, giving them the *i* of the nations.
119:111 Your decrees are my *i* forever;
Prv 13:22 man leaves an *i* to his children's children,
17: 2 and will share the *i* with the brothers.
19:14 Home and possessions are an *i* from parents,
Eccl 7:11 Wisdom and an *i* are good,
Sir 9: 6 to harlots, lest you surrender your *i.*
17: 9 them knowledge, a law of life as their *i;*
22:23 him, so as to share in his *i* when it comes.
24: 7 in whose *i* should I abide?
24: 8 Jacob make your dwelling, in Israel your *i.'*
24:22 us as an *i* for the community of Jacob.
33:24 at the time of death distribute your *i.*
42: 3 a journey, or of dividing an *i* or property;
44:21 he would give them an *i* from sea to sea,
44:23 him as the first-born, and gave him his *i.*
45:20 glory of Aaron and bestowed upon him his *i:*
45:22 his portion, his *i* in the midst of Israel.
46: 1 the enemy and to win the *i* for Israel.
46: 8 infantry, To lead the people into their *i,*
46: 9 his family too received an *i,*
Is 19:25 and the work of my hands Assyria, and my *i,*
47: 6 Angry at my people, I profaned my *i,*
61: 7 They shall have a double *i* in their land,
Jer 37:12 with his family in the division of an *i.*
Ez 35:15 of the *i* of the house of Israel,
44:28 have no *i,* for I am their inheritance;
46:16 a gift of part of his *i* to any of his sons,
46:16 that property is theirs by *i.*
46:17 of part of his *i* to one of his servants,
46:17 Only the *i* given to his sons is permanent.
46:18 seize any part of the *i* of the people
46:18 an *i* for his sons from his own property,
47:14 that it might fall to you as your *i.*
47:23 resident, there you shall assign him his *i,*
Jl 4: 2 there on behalf of my people and my *i,*
Mi 2: 2 an owner of his house, a man of his *i.*
7:14 with your staff, the flock of your *i,*
7:18 and pardons sin for the remnant of his *i;*
Mt 21:38 us kill him and then we shall have his *i!'*
Mk 12: 7 let us kill him, and the *i* will be ours.'
Lk 12:13 my brother to give me my share of our *i."*
20:14 Let us kill him so that the *i* will be ours.'
Gal 3:18 Clearly, if one's *i* comes through the law,
Eph 1:14 He is the pledge of our *i,*
5: 5 any *i* in the kingdom of Christ and of God.
Col 3:24 will receive an *i* from him as your reward.
Heb 9:15 called may receive the promised eternal *i.*
1Pt 1: 4 a birth to an imperishable *i,*
3: 9 that you may receive a blessing as your *i.*

INHERITANCES (4)

Ez 45: 1 When you apportion the land into *i,*
47:22 You shall allot it as *i* for yourselves and
47:22 shall receive *i* among the tribes of Israel.
48:29 apportion as *i* among the tribes of Israel,

INHERITED (6)

Tb 14:13 Then he *i* Raguel's estate as well as that
Jdt 9:13 Zion, and the homes your children have *i.*
Lam 5: 2 *i* lands have been turned over to strangers,
Acts 7:45 The next generation of our fathers *i* it.
Heb 1: 4 as the name he has *i* is superior to theirs.
11: 7 *i* the justice which comes through faith.

INHERITING (1)

Heb 6:12 faith and patience, are *i* the promises.

INHERITS (3)

Nm 36: 8 every daughter who *i* property in any of
Sir 4:13 He who holds her fast *i* glory;
10:11 When a man dies, he *i* corruption;

INHUMAN (1)

2Tm 3: 3 to their parents, ungrateful, profane, *i,*

INIMICAL (1)

Est B: 5 and alien laws, is *i* to our interests,

INIQUITIES (11)

Lv 16:22 to carry off their *i* to an isolated region,
Tb 13: 5 He scourged you for your *i,*
Jb 22: 5 Are not your *i* endless?
Ps(s) 38: 5 of my sin, For my *i* have overwhelmed me;
79: 8 Remember not against us the *i* of the past;
90: 8 You have kept our *i* before you,
103: 3 He pardons all your *i,*
130: 3 If you, O LORD, mark *i,* LORD, who can
130: 8 And he will redeem Israel from all their *i.*
Prv 5:22 By his own *i* the wicked man will be caught,
Rom 4: 7 "Blest are they whose *i* are forgiven,

INIQUITY (18)

Jb 5:16 have hope, and *i* closes her mouth.
11:11 knows the worthlessness of men and sees *i;*
11:14 If you remove all *i* from your conduct,
15:16 man, who drinks in *i* like water!
22:23 if you put *i* far from your tent,
Ps(s) 7:15 conceived *i* and was pregnant with mischief,
10: 7 under his tongue are mischief and *i.*
73: 7 Out of their crassness comes *i;*
119:133 to your promise, and let no *i* rule over me.
Prv 19:28 and the mouth of the wicked pours out *i.*
22: 8 He who sows *i* reaps calamity,
Eccl 3:16 wickedness, and in the seat of justice, *i.*
Ez 18:26 *i,* and dies, it is because of the iniquity
Hos 9: 7 Because your *i* is great,
9: 9 remember their *i* and punish their sins.
14: 3 Say to him, "Forgive all *i,*
Mi 2: 1 Woe to those who plan *i,*

INITIAL (1)

Heb 6: 1 go beyond the *i* teaching about Christ and

INITIATED (2)

2Mc 4:10 he immediately *i* his countrymen into the
Acts 12:19 Herod then *i* a search for him.

INITIATIVE (2)

Lk 16: 8 Because the worldly take more *i* than the
Heb 5: 4 One does not take this honor on his own *i,*

INJUNCTION (1)

2Thes 3:14 If anyone will not obey our *i,*

INJUNCTIONS (1)

Wis 16:11 For as a reminder of your *i,*

INJURE (6)

1Mc 7:15 will not try to *i* you or your friends."
9:71 try to *i* him for the rest of his life;

INJURE (cont.)

Prv 22:22 *I* not the poor because they are poor,
Zec 12: 3 to lift it shall *i* themselves badly,
Lk 10:19 of the enemy, and nothing shall ever *i* you.
1Cor 6: 8 *i* and cheat your very own brothers.

INJURED (5)

2Kgs 1: 2 his roof terrace at Samaria and had been *i.*
Ez 34: 4 weak nor heal the sick nor bind up the *i.*
34:16 I will bring back, the *i* I will bind up,
Zec 11:16 nor seek the strays, nor heal the *i,*
2Cor 7: 2 We have *i* no one,

INJURES (1)

Sir 27:25 a blow struck in treachery *i* more than one.

INJURIES (1)

1Cor 13: 5 neither does it brood over *i.*

INJURY (22)

Ex 21:22 suffers a miscarriage, but no further *i,*
21:23 But if *i* ensues,
Lv 24:19 Anyone who inflicts an *i* on his neighbor
24:20 The same *i* that a man gives another shall
Dt 17: 8 or of civil rights or of personal *i,*
1Sm 20: 9 father is determined to inflict *i* upon you,
20:13 please my father to bring any *i* upon you,
25: 7 shepherds were with us, we did them no *i,*
25:15 We were done no *i,*
2Sm 13:16 worse than the first *i* you have done me."
2Kgs 1: 2 Ekron, whether I shall recover from this *i.*"
Jdt 10:13 one of his men suffering *i* or loss of life."
1Mc 14:36 temple and inflict grave *i* on its purity.
2Mc 9: 4 *i* done by those who had put him to flight.
Jb 35: 6 If you sin, what *i* do you do to God?
Sir 13:12 and will not refrain from *i* or chains.
Jer 6:14 though it were nought, the *i* to my people:
8:11 the *i* to the daughter of my people:
Mt 5:39 offer no resistance to *i.*
Rom 12:17 Never repay *i* with injury.
Phlm 1:18 he has done you an *i* or owes you anything,

INJUSTICE (19)

Jdt 7:24 *i* in not making peace with the Assyrians.
2Mc 10:12 of the previous *i* that had been done them,
2Ch 19: 7 there is no *i,* no partially
Jb 6:29 Think it over; let there be no *i.*
11:14 conduct, and let not *i* dwell in your tent,
19: 7 If I cry out *I!*" I am not heard.
Prv 16: 8 with virtue, than a large income with *i.*
Wis 1: 5 and when *i* occurs it is rebuked.
Sir 7: 3 Sow not in the furrows of *i,*
28: 2 Forgive your neighbor's *i;*
35: 3 the LORD, and to avoid *i* is an atonement.
40:12 comes from bribes or *i* will be wiped out,
Is 61: 8 love what is right, I hate robbery and *i;*
Jer 22:13 his house on wrong, his terraces on *i;*
Mal 2:16 And covering one's garment with *i,*
Mt 20:13 he said to one in reply, 'I do you no *i.*
1Cor 6: 7 Why not put up with *i,*
2Cor 12:13 Forgive me this *i!*
1Pt 2:19 When a man can suffer *i* and endure

INK (3)

Jer 36:18 "and I wrote them down with *i* in the book."
2Cor 3: 3 with *i* but by the Spirit of the living God,
3Jn 1:13 do not wish to write it out with pen and *i.*

INLAID (1)

Sg 3:10 its framework *i* with ivory.

INLAND (2)

1Mc 3:37 crossed the Euphrates River and advanced *i.*
6: 1 Antiochus was traversing the *i* provinces,

INMOST (16)

Lv 10:18 brought into the *i* part of the sanctuary,
1Sm 24: 4 were occupying the *i* recesses of the cave.
1Kgs 6:27 were placed in the *i* part of the temple,
Jb 19:26 my *i* being is consumed with longing.
Ps(s) 51: 8 and in my *i* being you teach me wisdom.
139:13 Truly you have formed my *i* being;
Prv 18: 8 morsels that sink into one's *i* being.
20:27 it searches through all his *i* being.
20:30 lashes, and a scourging to the *i* being.
23:16 And my *i* being will exult,
26:22 morsels that sink into one's *i* being.
26:24 but in his *i* being he maintains deceit;
Wis 1: 6 Because God is the witness of his *i* self
Sir 4:15 hearkens to her dwells in her *i* chambers.
Jer 12: 2 their lips, but far from their *i* thoughts.
Lk 1:51 has confused the proud in their *i* thoughts.

INN (1)

Lk 10:34 on his own beast and brought him to an *i,*

INNER (55)

Ex 12: 9 with its head and shanks and *i* organs.
29:13 All the fat that covers its *i* organs,
29:17 *i* organs and shanks you shall first wash,
29:22 tail, the fat that covers its *i* organs,
36:12 one *i* sheet, and fifty loops on the inner sheet
Lv 1: 9 The *i* organs and the shanks,
1:13 The *i* organs and the shanks,
3: 3 LORD the fatty membrane over the *i* organs,
3: 9 the fatty membrane over the *i* organs,
3:14 LORD the fatty membrane over the *i* organs,
4: 8 the fatty membrane over the *i* organs,
4:11 its flesh, with its head, legs, *i* organs,
7: 3 tail, the fatty membrane over the *i* organs,
8:16 all the fat that was over the *i* organs,
8:21 the *i* organs and the shanks with water,
8:25 tail and all the fat over the *i* organs,
9:14 Having washed the *i* organs and the shanks,
9:19 tail, the fatty membrane over the *i* organs,
1Kgs 6:29 The walls on all sides of both the *i* and
6:30 The floor of both the *i* and the outer
6:36 The *i* court was walled off by means of
7:12 So also were the *i* court of the temple of
7:50 hinges of gold for the doors of the *i* room,
2Kgs 9: 2 away from his companions into an *i* chamber.
10:25 into the *i* shrine of the temple of Baal,
1Chr 28:11 storerooms, its upper rooms and *i* chambers,
2Chr 4:22 house, its *i* doors to the holy of holies,
Est 4:11 king in the *i* court without being summoned,
5: 1 garments and stood in the *i* courtyard,
1Mc 9:54 *i* court of the sanctuary to be torn down,
Wis 17: 4 even their *i* chambers kept them fearless,
Ez 8:16 me into the *i* court of the LORD's house,
10: 3 man entered, the cloud filled the *i* court,
40:19 the lower gate to the front of the *i* gate;
40:23 The *i* court had a gate opposite the north
40:27 The *i* court also had a southern gate;
40:28 me to the *i* court by the south gate,
40:44 the *i* court where there were two chambers,
41:15 The *i* nave and the outer vestibule were
41:17 on every side in both the *i* and outer rooms
42: 3 Across the twenty cubits of the *i* court
42:15 had finished measuring the *i* temple area,
43: 5 lifted me up and brought me to the *i* court.
44:17 they enter the gates of the *i* court,
44:17 gates of the *i* court or within the temple.
44:21 drink wine when he is to enter the *i* court.
44:27 the *i* court to minister in the sanctuary,
45:19 the doorposts of the gates of the *i* court.
46: 1 The gate toward the east of the *i* court
Mk 11:23 and has no *i* doubts but believes that what
Rom 7:22 My *i* self agrees with the law of God,
2Cor 4:16 because our *i* being is renewed each day
Heb 9: 7 only the high priest went into the *i* one,
Jas 4: 1 Is it not your *i* cravings that make war

INNERMOST (6)

1Kgs 6:19 In the *i* part of the temple was located
2Chr 18:24 day when you enter an *i* chamber to hide."
Sir 42:18 their *i* being he understands.
Mt 24:26 or 'He is in the *i* rooms,'
1Cor 2:11 *i* self but the man's own spirit within him?
Eph 1:18 May he enlighten your *i* vision that you

INNKEEPER (1)

Lk 10:35 and gave them to the *i* with the request:

INNOCENCE (15)

Gn 44:16 How can we plead or how try to prove our *i?*
2Sm 22:25 my justice, according to my *i* in his sight.
1Kgs 8:32 but acquit the just and establish his *i.*
1Mc 2:60 Daniel, for his *i,*
Jb 2: 3 He still holds fast to his *i* although you
2: 9 to him, "Are you still holding to your *i?*
11:15 Surely then you may lift up your face in *i;*
27: 5 till I die I will not renounce my *i.*
31: 6 thus will he know my *i!*
Ps(s) 7: 9 just, and because of the *i* that is mine,
26: 6 I wash my hands in *i,*
Is 43:26 Speak up, prove your *i!*
Hos 8: 5 will they be unable to attain *i* in Israel?
2Cor 6: 6 conducting ourselves with *i,*
7:11 you have displayed your *i* in this matter.

INNOCENT (83)

Gn 18:23 you sweep away the *i* with the guilty?
18:24 there were fifty *i* people in the city;
18:24 the sake of the fifty *i* people within it?
18:25 a thing, to make the *i* die with the guilty,
18:25 *i* and the guilty would be treated alike!
18:26 I find fifty *i* people in the city of Sodom,
18:28 if there are five less than fifty *i* people?
20: 4 would you slay a man even though he is *i?*
Ex 23: 7 *i* and the just you shall not put to death,
Dt 19:10 *i* blood will not be shed and you will not
19:13 from Israel the stain of shedding *i* blood,
21: 8 let not the guilt of shedding *i* blood remain
21: 9 purge from your midst the guilt of *i* blood,
25: 1 *i* party and condemning the guilty party,
27:25 who accepts payment for slaying an *i* man!'
1Sm 19: 5 *i* blood by killing David without cause?"
25:31 for having shed *i* blood or for having
2Sm 3:28 I and my kingdom are forever *i.*
4:11 men have slain an *i* man in bed at home,
14: 9 you and your throne are *i.*"
2Kgs 21:16 shedding so much *i* blood as to fill the
24: 4 especially because of the *i* blood he shed,
2Chr 6:23 but absolving the *i* and rewarding him
Tb 3:14 that I am *i* of any impure act with a man,
Est E: 5 accomplices in the shedding of *i* blood,
1Mc 1:37 And they shed *i* blood around the sanctuary;
2Mc 1: 8 fire to the gatehouse and shedding *i* blood.
4:47 been declared *i* even if they had pleaded
8: 4 criminal slaughter of *i* children
Jb 4: 7 Reflect now, what *i* person perishes?
9:20 were I *i,*
9:21 Though I am *i,* I myself cannot know it;
9:22 Both the *i* and the wicked he destroys.
9:23 he laughs at the despair of the *i.*
9:28 I know that you will not hold me *i.*
17: 8 this, and the *i* aroused against the wicked.
22:19 and are gladdened, and the *i* deride them:
22:30 God delivers him who is *i;*
25: 4 sight, or how can any woman's child be *i?*
27:17 wear, and the *i* shall divide the silver.
31:21 If I have raised my hand against the *i*
33: 9 I am *i;*
34: 5 For Job has said, "I am *i,*
Ps(s) 10: 8 in hiding he murders the *i;*
15: 5 usury and accepts no bribe against the *i.*
19:14 shall I be blameless and *i* of serious sin.
64: 5 words, Shooting from ambush at the *i* man,
73:13 clean and washed my hands as an *i* man?
94:21 the life of the just and condemn *i* blood,
106:38 daughters to demons, And they shed *i* blood,
Prv 1:11 let us, unprovoked, set a trap for the *i;*
6:17 lying tongue, and hands that shed *i* blood;
17:26 It is wrong to fine an *i* man,
20:11 betrays whether his conduct is *i* and right.
21: 8 crooked, but the conduct of the *i* is right.
Wis 2:22 holiness nor discern the *i* souls' reward.
4:12 the whirl of desire transforms the *i* mind.
Sir 51:13 When I was young and *i,* I sought wisdom.
Is 59: 7 evil, and they are quick to shed *i* blood;
Jer 2:34 clothing there is the life-blood of the *i,*
2:35 Yet withal you say, "I am *i;*
7: 6 you no longer shed *i* blood in this place,
19: 4 filled this place with the blood of the *i.*
22: 3 and do not shed *i* blood in this place.
22:17 on your own gain, On shedding *i* blood,
26:15 it is *i* blood you bring on yourselves,
Dn 6:23 For I have been found *i* before him;
13:53 unjust sentences, condemning the *i,*
13:53 *i* and the just you shall not put to death.'
13:62 Thus was *i* blood spared that day.
13:63 she was found *i* of any shameful deed.
Jl 4:19 because they shed *i* blood in their land.
Jon 1:14 do not charge us with shedding *i* blood,
Mt 10:16 must be clever as snakes and *i* as doves.
12: 7 you would not have condemned these *i* men.
27: 4 said, "I did wrong to deliver up an *i* man!"
27:24 so, "I am *i* of the blood of this just man.
Lk 23:47 God by saying, "Surely this was an *i* man."
Rom 16:19 regard to what is good and *i* of all evil.
1Cor 4: 4 does not mean that I am declaring myself *i.*
Phil 2:15 prove yourselves *i* and straightforward,
Heb 7:26 holy, *i,* undefiled, separated from sinners
Jas 3:17 from above, by contrast, is first of all *i.*

INNUMERABLE (3)

Jdt 2:17 *i* sheep, cattle, and goats for their food
1Mc 10:77 three thousand horsemen and an *i* infantry.
2Mc 3:26 until they had given him *i* blows.

INOPPORTUNE (2)

Sir 20: 1 An admonition can be *i,*
22: 6 Like a song in time of mourning is *i* talk,

INQUIRE (18)

Dt 12:30 Do not *i* regarding their gods,
13:15 you must *i* carefully into the matter and
2Kgs 1: 2 "Go and *i* of Baal-zebub,
1: 3 that you are going to *i* of Baal-zebub,
1: 6 that you are sending to *i* of Baal-zebub,
1:16 you sent messengers to *i* of Baal-zebub,
3:11 here through whom we may *i* of the LORD?"
Jdt 8:34 You must not *i* into what I am doing,
1Mc 10:72 *I* and learn who I am and who the others
Jb 8: 8 If you *i* of the former generations,
Is 8:19 *I* of mediums and fortune-tellers
8:19 should not a people *i* of their gods,
Jer 2:10 and see, send to Kedar and carefully *i:*
21: 2 *I* for us of the LORD,
30: 6 *I,* and see: since when do men bear
Jn 9:15 began to *i* how he had recovered his sight.
21:12 Not one of the disciples presumed to *i,*
Acts 10:18 to *i* whether Simon Peter was a guest there.

INQUIRED (24)

Gn 29: 6 He *i* further, "Is he well?"
Ex 18:14 that he was doing for the people, he *i,*
Lv 10:16 *i* about the goat of the sin offering,
1Sm 4:14 outcry of the men standing near him, Eli *i,*
5: 8 all the Philistine lords and *i* of them,

9:11 coming out to draw water and *i* of them,
10:14 Saul's uncle *i* of him and his servant,
14:37 So Saul *i* of God:
16: 4 the city came trembling to meet him and *i,*
19:22 threshing floor on the bare hilltop, he *i,*
20:27 Saul *i* of his son Jonathan,
30: 8 brought him the ephod, David *i* of the LORD,
2Sm 2: 1 After this David *i* of the LORD,
5:19 David *i* of the LORD,
5:23 So David *i* of the LORD, who replied:
9: 3 Then the king *i,*
1Chr 10:14 and had not rather *i* of the LORD.
14:10 David *i* of God, "Shall I advance against
14:14 and again David *i* of God.
Ps(s) 78:34 them they sought him and *i* after God again,
Ez 21:26 has shaken the arrows, *i* of the teraphim,
Dn 2:27 "The mystery about which the king has *i,*
Mt 2: 4 *i* of them where the Messiah was to be born.
Mk 15:44 and *i* whether Jesus was already dead.

INQUIRER (1)

Ez 14:10 *i* and the prophet shall be punished alike,

INQUIRIES (1)

2Sm 11: 3 had *i* made about the woman and was told,

INQUIRING (3)

Gn 43:27 After *i* how they were,
1Sm 23: 2 So he consulted the LORD, *i,*
Mt 2: 2 the east arrived one day in Jerusalem *i,*

INQUIRY (3)

Jgs 6:29 *i* led them to the conclusion that Gideon,
Ezr 4:15 so that *i* may be made in the historical
4:19 When at my command *i* was made,

INS (1)

2Sm 3:25 the *i* and outs of all that you are doing?"

INSANITY (1)

1Sm 21:14 *i* and acted like a madman in their hands,

INSATIABLE (1)

Hb 2: 5 like the nether world, and is *i* as death,

INSATIABLY (1)

Jb 19:22 though you were divine, and *i* prey upon me?

INSCRIBE (4)

Dt 27: 8 *i* all the words of this law very clearly."
Is 8: 1 and *i* on it in ordinary letters:
30: 8 a tablet they can keep, *i* it in a record;
Rv 3:12 I will *i* on him the name of my God and the

INSCRIBED (21)

Ex 31:18 the stone tablets *i* by God's own finger.
39:30 sacred diadem was made of pure gold and *i,*
Dt 9:10 LORD gave me the two tablets of stone *i,*
29:20 of the covenant *i* in this book of the law.
Jos 8:32 Joshua *i* upon the stones a copy of the law
1Chr 4:33 it was *i* of them in their family records.
9: 1 Thus all Israel was *i* in its family
9:22 *i* in the family records of their villages.
2Chr 31:17 The priests were *i* in their family records
31:18 to all who were *i* in the family records,
Est 1:19 *i* among the laws of the Persians and Medes,
1Mc 8:22 *i* on bronze tablets and sent to Jerusalem,
14:18 they sent him *i* tablets of bronze to renew
Jb 19:23 Would that they were *i* in a record:
Dn 5:25 "This is the writing that was *i:*
Lk 10:20 to you as that your names are *i* in heaven."
Acts 17:23 your shrines, I even discovered an altar *i,*
Rv 2:17 a white stone upon which is *i* a new name,
19:12 *I* on his person was a name known to no one
20:15 anyone whose name was not found *i* in the
21:27 Only those shall enter whose names are *i*

INSCRIPTION (12)

1Mc 14:26 So they made an *i* on bronze tablets,
14:27 The following is a copy of the *i:*
14:48 *i* should be engraved on bronze tablets,
Zec 3: 9 I will engrave its *i,*
Mt 22:20 them, "Whose head is this, and whose *i?*"
Mk 12:16 "Whose head is this and whose *i* is it?"
15:26 The *i* proclaiming his offense read,
Lk 20:24 Whose *i* do you read?"
23:38 There was an *i* over his head:
Jn 19:19 Pilate had an *i* placed on the cross which read,
19:20 This *i,* in Hebrew, Latin, and Greek
2Tm 2:19 It bears this *i:* "The LORD knows those

INSCRIPTIONS (1)

Ex 32:16 having *i* on them that were engraved by God

INSCRUTABLE (2)

Sir 21:18 the stupid man knows it only as *i* words.
Rom 11:33 How *i* his judgments,

INSECTS (12)

Lv 11:20 "The various winged *i* that walk on all
11:21 But of the various winged *i* that walk on
11:23 All other winged *i* that have four legs are
Dt 14:19 All winged *i,* too, are unclean for you
28:42 Buzzing *i* will infest all your trees and
1Kgs 8:37 mildew, or a locust swarm, or devouring *i;*
Wis 11:15 worshiping dumb serpents and worthless *i,*
16: 1 and were tormented by a swarm of *i.*
17: 9 passing of *i* and the hissing of reptiles,
Is 18: 1 Ah, land of buzzing *i,*
Bar 6:11 they are not safe from corrosion or *i.*
6:19 Though the *i* out of the ground consume

INSENSATE (2)

2Sm 13:12 Do not commit this *i* deed.
Dn 5:21 from among men and was made *i* as a beast;

INSERTED (1)

2Chr 20:34 is *i* in the book of the kings of Israel.

INSIDE (67)

Gn 6:14 in it, and cover it *i* and out with pitch.
8: 9 the dove and drew it back to him *i* the ark.
9:21 he became drunk and lay naked *i* his tent.
19:10 out their hands, pulled Lot *i* with them,
24:32 The man then went *i;*
31:34 the idols, put them *i* a camel cushion,
39: 5 he owned, both *i* the house and out.
43:18 bags the first time, that we are taken *i;*
43:24 then brought the men *i* Joseph's house.
43:26 him with the gifts they had brought *i,*
Ex 25:11 Plate it *i* and outside with pure gold,
26:33 ark of the commandments you shall bring *i,*
37: 2 The *i* and outside were plated with gold,
Lv 14: 8 is thus made clean may he come *i* the camp;
14:41 whole *i* of the house shall then be scraped,
16: 2 he pleases into the sanctuary, *i* the veil,
16:12 incense, and bringing them *i* the veil.
16:15 goat, and bringing its blood *i* the veil,
Jos 7:21 are now hidden in the ground *i* my tent,
8:24 and put to the sword those *i* the city.
Jgs 7:16 and with empty jars and torches *i* the jars.
1Kgs 14:12 As you step *i* the city, the child will die,
20:30 took refuge within the city, in an *i* room.
22:25 when you retreat into an *i* room to hide."
2Kgs 6:20 and they saw that they were *i* Samaria.
21:13 as one wipes a dish, wiping it *i* and out.
2Chr 29:18 Then they went *i* to King Hezekiah and said:
Neh 4:16 the people to spend the nights *i* Jerusalem,
6:10 in the house of God, *i* the temple building;
Est 1: 9 women *i* the royal palace of King Ahasuerus.
1Mc 1:34 men, who fortified themselves *i* it,
2Mc 10:34 Those *i,* relying on the strength
12:27 *i* were large supplies of machines and
13:20 Judas then sent supplies to the men *i,*
Jb 20:14 it shall be venom of asps *i* him.
Jer 41: 7 When they were once *i* the city,
52:21 each was four fingers thick, and hollow *i.*
Ez 40: 7 of the gate toward the *i* measured one rod.
40: 9 The vestibule of the gate was toward the *i.*
40:15 of the vestibule on the *i* was fifty cubits.
40:22 to it, and its vestibule was toward the *i.*
40:26 its vestibule was toward the *i;*
40:43 wide, were set on the *i* all around,
42: 4 In front of the chambers, to the *i,*
Dn 3:50 and made the *i* of the furnace as though a
13:18 unaware that the elders were hidden *i.*
14: 7 "it is only clay *i* and bronze outside;
Am 6:10 If one says to a man *i* a house,
Zec 5: 7 and there was a woman sitting *i* the bushel.
5: 8 and he thrust her *i* the bushel,
Mt 21:14 to him *i* the temple area and he cured them.
23:25 and leave the *i* filled with loot and lust!
23:26 First cleanse the *i* of the cup so that its
23:27 but *i* full of filth and dead men's bones.
26:58 Going *i,* he sat down with the guards
27:27 The procurator's soldiers took Jesus *i* the
Mk 9:33 to Capernaum and Jesus, once *i* the house,
Lk 1:22 they realized that he had seen a vision *i.*
11: 7 and he from *i* should reply,
11:40 not he who made the outside make the *i* too?
24:32 "Were not our hearts burning *i* us as he
Jn 20:11 Even as she wept, she stooped to peer *i,*
Acts 5:23 but when we opened it we found no one *i.*"
10:12 *I* it were all the earth's four-legged
22:24 Paul to be brought *i* the headquarters.
1Cor 5:12 not those *i* the community you must judge?
Rv 4: 8 had six wings and eyes all over, *i* and out.

INSIGHT (3)

Mk 12:34 approved the *i* of this answer and told him,
Eph 1:17 spirit of wisdom and *i* to know him clearly.
Col 1: 9 through perfect wisdom and spiritual *i.*

INSIGNIA (5)

2Kgs 11:12 son and put the crown and the *i* upon him.
2Chr 23:11 son, set the crown and the *i* upon him,
Sir 45:12 its plate wrought with the *i* of holiness,
Dn 11:21 to whom the royal *i* shall not be given.
Zec 6:13 of the LORD, and taking up the royal *i,*

INSIGNIFICANT (2)

Jgs 6:15 and I am the most *i* in my father's house."
1Sm 18:23 I am poor and *i.*"

INSINCERE (1)

Sir 36:19 by its savor, so does a keen mind *i* words.

INSINCERELY (2)

Jer 3:10 not return to me whole-heartedly, but *i,*
2Cor 1:17 that in making those plans I was acting *i?*

INSINCERITY (1)

Jb 6:30 Is there *i* on my tongue,

INSIPID (2)

Jb 6: 6 Can a thing *i* be eaten without salt?
Sir 20:18 *I* food is the untimely tale;

INSIST (1)

1Sm 20:29 our city, and my brothers *i* on my presence.

INSISTED (18)

Gn 25:33 But Jacob *i,* "Swear to me first!"
Ex 4:13 Yet he *i,* "If you please, Lord,
Nm 20:19 The Israelites *i,* "We want only to go up
2Sm 18:23 But he *i,* "Come what may, I want to run."
2Kgs 4:43 "Give it to the people to eat," Elisha *i.*
Tb 10: 9 But Tobiah *i,* "No, I beg you to let me go
Jer 44:12 of Judah who *i* on coming to dwell in Egypt,
Dn 6:16 But these men *i.*
Mt 14:22 Jesus *i* that his disciples get into the
15:27 "Please, Lord," she *i,* "even the dogs eat
Mk 6:45 Immediately afterward he *i* that his
Lk 8:46 Jesus *i,* "Someone touched me; I know that
23: 5 But they *i,* "He stirs up the people by his
Jn 18:26 *i* one of the high priest's slaves
Acts 12:15 they said to her, but she *i* it was true.
15:38 But Paul *i* that, as he had deserted them
20:21 With Jews and Greeks alike I *i* solemnly on
1Thes 2: 7 even though we could have *i* on our own

INSISTENT (4)

Nm 32:16 But they were *i* with him:
Ps(s) 102: 6 my *i* sighing I am reduced to skin and bone.
Sir 28:11 flare up, and *i* quarrels provoke bloodshed.
32: 9 forward, and with officials be not too *i.*

INSISTENTLY (3)

Jer 35:14 although I spoke to you untiringly and *i.*
Lk 22:59 an hour after that another spoke more *i:*
2Cor 8: 4 they begged us *i* for the favor of sharing

INSISTING (1)

Col 2:18 by *i* on servility in the worship of angels.

INSOFAR (1)

1Pt 3:18 put to death *i* as fleshly existence goes,

INSOLENCE (17)

Dt 17:12 Any man who has the *i* to refuse to listen
32:27 Had I not feared the *i* of their enemies,
Neh 9:10 Because you knew of their *i* toward them;
Est C: 5 that it was not out of *i* or pride or
2Mc 7:34 do not, in your *i,* concern yourself with
9: 7 Far from giving up his *i,*
Ps(s) 31:19 *i* against the just in pride and scorn.
Prv 13:10 The stupid man sows discord by his *i,*
Sir 10:18 *I* is not allotted to a man,
Is 13:11 arrogant, the *i* of tyrants I will humble.
16: 6 *i* that his empty words do not match.
Jer 48:29 his pride, his scorn, his *i* of heart.
50:31 I am against you, man of *i,*
50:32 *I* stumbles and falls;
Ez 7:10 Lawlessness is in full bloom, *i* flourishes,
Dn 5:20 became proud and his spirit hardened by *i,*
Hos 7:16 sword because of the *i* of their tongues;

INSOLENT (12)

Dt 17:13 of it, shall fear, and never again be so *i.*
Neh 9:16 "But they, our fathers, proved to be *i;*
9:29 *i* and would not obey your commandments;
Ps(s) 1: 1 sinners, nor sits in the company of the *i,*
94: 4 the wicked glory, Mouthing *i* speeches,
Sir 31:26 smith, so does wine the hearts of the *i.*
32:18 the proud and *i* man is deterred by nothing.
Is 25: 2 The castle of the *i* is a city no more,
Jer 43: 2 and all the *i* men shouted to Jeremiah:
Ez 35:13 I have heard the *i* and wild words you have
Zep 3: 4 Her prophets are *i,* treacherous men;
Rom 1:30 and slanderers, they hate God, are *i,*

INSOLENTLY (2)

Ex 18:11 took occasion of their being dealt with *i*
1Mc 1:21 He *i* invaded the sanctuary and took away

INSPECT (3)
2Mc 5:18 sent by King Seleucus to *i* the treasury,
Mt 28: 1 came with the other Mary to *i* the tomb.
Lk 14:18 bought some land and must go out and *i* it.

INSPECTED (3)
2Kgs 16:12 from Damascus, the king *i* this altar,
Ez 21:26 inquired of the teraphim, *i* the liver.
Mk 11:11 He *i* everything there,

INSPECTING (2)
Neh 2:15 *i* the wall all the while till I once more
1Mc 16:14 As Simon was *i* the cities of the country

INSPECTION (2)
Neh 3:31 before the Gate of *I* and as far as the
4: 8 I made an *i,* then addressed these words

INSPECTORS (1)
1Mc 1:51 He appointed *i* over all the people,

INSPIRATION (1)
1Tm 1:19 under the *i* of these prophecies

INSPIRE (1)
Zep 2:11 The LORD shall *i* them with fear when he

INSPIRED (17)
1Chr 25: 1 as singers of *i* songs to the accompaniment
25: 2 *i* songs under the guidance of the king.
25: 3 *i* songs to the accompaniment of a lyre,
2Chr 36:22 the LORD *i* King Cyrus of Persia to issue
Ezr 1: 1 the LORD *i* King Cyrus of Persia to issue
1: 5 everyone, that is, whom God had *i* to do so
Neh 2:12 not told anyone what my God had *i* me
Est D: 6 precious stones, so that he *i* great awe.
Is 30: 1 mine, who weave webs that are not *i* by me,
Ez 32:30 because of the terror their might *i;*
Mk 12:36 David himself, *i* by the Holy Spirit,
13:11 In that hour, say what you are *i* to say.
Lk 2:27 He came to the temple now, *i* by the Spirit;
Acts 11:28 One of them named Agabus was *i* to stand up
Eph 5:19 another in psalms and hymns and *i* songs.
Col 3:16 your hearts in psalms, hymns, and *i* songs.
2Tm 3:16 is *i* of God and is useful for teaching

INSPIRES (1)
Heb 12: 2 on Jesus, who *i* and perfects our faith.

INSPIRING (1)
Wis 17:19 of the hills, these sounds, *i* terror,

INSTALLED (3)
Gn 41:43 was Joseph *i* over the whole land of Egypt.
1Mc 1:34 There they *i* a sinful race,
Acts 14:23 In each church they *i* presbyters and,

INSTANCE (3)
Est E:10 "For *i,* Haman, son of Hammedatha,
Mt 15: 4 For *i,* God has said, 'Honor your father
Mk 14:57 Some, for *i,* on taking the stand, testified

INSTANT (15)
Nm 4:20 upon the sacred objects, even for an *i;*
2Chr 29:27 and in the same *i* that the holocaust began,
Prv 6:15 in an *i* he is crushed beyond cure.
Wis 18:12 *i* their nobler offspring were destroyed.
Sir 11:21 it is easy with the LORD suddenly, in an *i,*
Is 29: 5 Then suddenly, in an *i,*
30:13 wall whose crash comes suddenly, in an *i.*
Jer 4:20 In an *i* my tents are ravaged;
49:19 So I, in an *i,* will drive men off;
50:44 permanent feeding grounds, So I, in one *i,*
Lam 4: 6 in an *i* without the turning of a hand.
Hos 7:12 *i* I will send them captive from their land.
Lk 4: 5 the kingdoms of the world in a single *i.*
Acts 22:13 *i* I regained my sight and looked at him.
1Cor 15:52 in an *i,* in the twinkling of an eye,

INSTANTLY (4)
Dn 3: 6 shall be *i* cast into a white-hot furnace."
3:15 shall be *i* cast into the white-hot furnace;
Mt 21:19 and it withered up *i.*
Lk 8:47 touched him and how she had been *i* cured.

INSTEAD (116)
Gn 24:38 *i,* you shall go to my father's house, to
27:12 bring on myself a curse *i* of a blessing."
37:22 *I* of shedding blood,"
37:27 *i* of doing away with him ourselves.
Ex 13:18 *I,* he rerouted them toward the Red Sea by
23:30 *I,* I will drive them out little by little
Lv 27:20 If, *i* of redeeming such a field,
Nm 10:30 *i* to my own country and to my own kindred."
23:11 *i,* you have even blessed them."
24:10 times now you have even blessed them *i!*
Dt 12: 5 *I,* you shall resort to the place which the
15: 8 *I,* you shall open your hand to him and
20:12 peace with you and *i* offers you battle,
29:19 *I,* the LORD's wrath and jealousy will
Jos 23:13 *I* they will be a snare and a trap for you,
Jgs 2:23 to remain *i* of expelling them immediately,
4:21 *I* Jael, wife of Heber, got a tent peg
6:26 You shall build, *i,* the proper kind of altar
15: 2 you may have her *i.*"
20:14 *I,* the Benjaminites assembled from their
1Sm 12:25 If *i* you continue to do evil,
18:19 marriage to Adriel the Meholathite *i*
24:11 of killing you, but I took pity on you *i.*
2Sm 12: 4 *I* he took the poor man's ewe lamb and made
19: 1 If only I had died *i* of you,
23:16 drink it, and *i* poured it out to the LORD,
2Kgs 1: 4 upon which you lie; *i,* you shall die.' "
1: 6 upon which you lie; *i,* you shall die.' "
1:16 upon which you lie; *i* you shall die.' "
12:15 *I,* they were given to the workmen,
1Chr 11:18 *I,* he poured it out as a libation to the
13:13 it *i* to the house of Obed-edom the Gittite.
2Chr 20:10 but *i* they passed them by and did not
21:13 but *i* have walked in the way of the kings
25: 8 *I,* go on your own,
Neh 6: 9 But *i,* I now redoubled my efforts.
Jdt 7:25 *I,* God has sold us into their power by
Est 9:25 should *i* be turned against Haman
1Mc 10:30 *I* of collecting the third of the grain and
11:34 Jerusalem *i* of paying the royal taxes
11:53 *I* of rewarding Jonathan for all the favors
12:43 *I,* he received him with honor,
15:31 or *i,* pay me five hundred talents of silver
2Mc 6:13 promptly *i* of letting them go for long.
Jb 31:40 *i* of wheat and noxious weeds instead
Ps(s) 85: 7 Will you not *i* give us life;
Wis 11: 6 *I* of a spring, when the perennial river
15:12 *I,* he esteemed our life a plaything,
16: 2 *I* of this punishment, you benefited your
16:20 *I* of this, you nourished your people
18: 3 *I* of this, you furnished the flaming pillar
19:10 how *i* of the young of animals the land
19:10 and *i* of fishes the river swarmed with
Sir 6: 1 be not a foe *i* of a friend;
29: 6 pays him back, with abuse *i* of honor.
37:12 *I,* associate with a religious man,
Is 3:24 *I* of perfume there will be stench, *i*
3:24 Then, *i* of beauty: your men will fall
10:16 And *i* of his glory there will be kindling
43:24 *I,*
55:13 the cypress shall grow, *i* of nettles,
60:17 of bronze I will bring gold, *i* of iron,
60:17 In place of wood, bronze, *i* of stones,
61: 3 who mourn in Zion a diadem *i* of ashes,
61: 3 a glorious mantle *i* of a listless spirit.
65:18 *I,* there shall always be rejoicing and
Jer 8:15 for a time of healing, but terror comes *i.*
14:19 for a time of healing, but terror comes *i.*
16:12 of his evil heart *i* of listening to me.
20: 3 *I* of Pashhur, the LORD will name you
30: 9 *i,*
43: 5 *I,* Johanan, son of Karah
Ez 16:32 adulterous wife receives, *i* of her husband,
16:34 Since you gave payment *i* of receiving it,
44: 8 *I* of caring for the service of my temple,
Dn 11:38 *I,* he shall give glory to the god of
Hb 2:16 You are filled with shame *i* of glory;
Mt 2:22 *I,* because of a warning received in a dream,
6:20 practice *i* to store up heavenly treasure,
10: 6 Go *i* after the lost sheep of the house of
18:30 *I,* he had him put in jail until he paid
25:18 went off *i* and dug a hole in the ground,
27:24 and that a riot was breaking out *i,*
Mk 5:19 did not grant his request, but told him *i:*
6: 6 the rounds of the neighboring villages *i,*
7: 5 *i* take food without purifying their hands?"
15:11 the crowd to have him release Barabbas *i.*
Lk 12:21 *i* of growing rich in the sight of God."
12:31 Seek out *i* his kingship over you,
Jn 4:10 for a drink, you would have asked him *i,*
11:54 He withdrew *i* to a town called Ephraim in
15:15 *I,* I call you friends,
19:21 Write *i,* 'This man claimed to be King
Acts 3:14 *i* to be granted the release of a murderer.
11:18 and *i* began to glorify God in these words:
16: 8 Crossing through Mysia *i,*
17: 7 and claim *i* that a certain Jesus is king."
25:19 *I* they differed with him over issues in
27:43 *I,* he ordered those who could swim to jump
Rom 1:22 to be wise, but turned into fools *i:*
14:13 *I* you should resolve to put no stumbling
1Cor 5: 2 to be self-satisfied, *i* of grieving,
6: 8 *I,* you yourselves injure and cheat your
2Cor 12: 9 so I willingly boast of my weaknesses *i,*
Eph 5: 5 *I,* give thanks.
1Tm 1: 6 and *i* have turned to meaningless talk,
6:11 *I,* seek after integrity,
Heb 7:11 *i* of choosing a priest according to the
Jas 3:14 Should you *i* nurse bitter jealousy and
4:15 *I* of saying, "If the Lord wills it,
1Pt 2:23 *I,* he delivered himself up to the One who
3: 9 Return a blessing *i.*
4:13 Rejoice *i,* in the measure that you share
2Jn 1:12 *i,* I hope to visit you and talk with you

INSTIGATED (1)
2Mc 4: 1 and *i* the whole miserable affair.

INSTILL (1)
2Mc 15:17 *i* valor and stir young hearts to courage,

INSTINCT (3)
Rom 2:14 who do not have the law keep it as by *i,*
2Pt 2:12 They act like creatures of *i,*
Jude 1:10 through the very things they know by *i,*

INSTITUTED (1)
Est 9:23 *i* at the written direction of Mordecai.

INSTITUTION (4)
Ex 12:14 pilgrimage to the LORD, as a perpetual *i.*
12:17 your generations as a perpetual *i*—
Wis 18: 9 into effect with one accord the divine *i,*
1Pt 2:13 of the Lord, be obedient to every human *i,*

INSTITUTIONS (1)
2Mc 4:11 *i* and introduced customs contrary to law.

INSTRUCT (23)
Gn 45:19 *I* them further: 'Do this. Take wagons
Ex 11: 2 *I* your people that every man is to ask his
Jos 1:11 "Go through the camp and *i* the people,
4: 3 and *i* them to take up twelve stones from
Jgs 3: 1 of the battles with Canaan [just to *i,*
2Sm 18: 5 All the soldiers heard the king *i* the
2Chr 35: 3 to the Levites who were to *i* all Israel,
Ezr 7:25 *I* those who do not know these laws.
Est 4: 8 He was to *i* her to go to the king;
Jb 12: 8 Or the reptiles on earth to *i* you,
36: 2 Wait yet a little and I will *i* you,
Ps(s) 32: 8 *i* you and show you the way you should walk;
94:12 Happy the man whom you *i,*
119:33 *I* me, O LORD, in the way
Prv 9: 9 *I* a wise man, and he becomes still wiser;
Is 2: 3 God of Jacob, That he may *i* us in his ways,
Dn 11:33 The nation's wise men shall *i* the many;
Mi 4: 2 God of Jacob, That he may *i* us in his ways,
Mk 4: 2 He began to *i* them at great length,
Jn 14:26 send in my name, will *i* you in everything,
1Cor 2:16 known the mind of the Lord so as to *i* him?"
14:19 rather say five intelligible words to *i* others
Col 3:16 made perfect, *i* and admonish one another.

INSTRUCTED (46)
Gn 50:12 Jacob's sons did for him as he had *i* them.
Dt 3:21 "It was then that I *i* Joshua,
Jos 18: 8 journey, Joshua *i* them to survey the land,
Jgs 21:20 And they *i* the Benjaminites,
Ru 2:15 and Boaz *i* his servants to let her glean
3: 6 did just as her mother-in-law had *i* her.
2Sm 11:22 to David all the details as Joab had *i* him.
13:28 But he had *i* his servants:
14: 3 And Joab *i* her what to say.
14:19 It was your servant Joab who *i* me and told
14:30 He therefore *i* his servants:
1Kgs 12:12 to King Rehoboam, as he had *i* them to do.
13: 9 For I was *i* by the word of the LORD not to
2Kgs 11:15 *i* the captains in command of the force:
2Chr 10:12 to King Rehoboam as he had *i* them to do.
34:22 They spoke to her as they had been *i,*
Jdt 4: 7 and *i* them to keep firm hold of the
Est 1: 8 for he had *i* all the stewards of his
1:10 the king was merry with wine, he *i* Mehuman,
Jb 4: 3 Behold, you have *i* many,
Ps(s) 119:102 I turn not away, for you have *i* me.
Prv 21:11 when the wise man is *i,*
Wis 6:11 long for them and you shall be *i.*
Is 28:26 He has learned this rule, *i* by his God.
40:13 of the LORD, or has *i* him as his counselor?
Dn 9:22 He *i* me in these words:
Mt 2: 8 them to Bethlehem, after having *i* them:
28:15 the money and did as they had been *i.*
Mk 6: 8 He *i* them to take nothing on their journey
8:15 So when he *i* them, "Keep your eyes open!
Lk 5:14 Jesus then *i* the man:
Jn 2: 5 His mother *i* those waiting on table,
2: 8 They did as he *i* them.
12:50 whatever I say is spoken just as he *i* me."
Acts 1: 2 having first *i* the apostles he had chosen
10:22 has been *i* by a holy messenger to summon
11:12 *i* me to accompany them without hesitation.
11:26 met with the church and *i* great numbers.
13:47 For thus were we *i* by the Lord:
18:25 Scripture and *i* in the new way of the Lord.
23:30 I have also *i* his accusers to take the
Rom 2:18 *I* by the law, you know his will
1Cor 14:31 one, so that all may be *i* and encouraged.
Gal 6: 6 The man *i* in the word should share all he
Ti 1: 5 As I *i* you, a presbyter must be
Rv 2:14 who *i* Balak to throw a stumbling block in

INSTRUCTING (6)

1Sm 25: 5 his flock, he sent ten young men, *i* them:
2Sm 11:19 the details of the battle, *i* the messenger,
Ezr 8:17 *i* them what to say to Iddo and his
Neh 8: 9 were *i* the people] said to all the people:
Mt 11: 1 Jesus had finished *i* his twelve disciples,
Lk 4:31 where he began *i* them on the sabbath day.

INSTRUCTION (49)

Gn 32:18 To the servant in the lead he gave this *i*:
Ex 24:12 the commandments intended for their *i*."
Dt 32: 2 May my *i* soak in like the rain,
Ru 4:22 used for purposes of edification and *i*.
Jb 22:22 Receive *i* from his mouth,
Ps(s) 25:14 fear him, and his covenant, for their *i*.
Prv 1: 7 wisdom and *i* fools despise.
1: 8 Hear, my son, your father's *i*,
4: 1 Hear, O children, a father's *i*,
4:13 Hold fast to *i*,
5:12 And you say, "Oh, why did I hate *i*,
8:10 Receive my *i* in preference to silver,
8:33 *i* and wisdom do not reject!
19:20 Listen to counsel and receive *i*,
19:27 If a son ceases to hear *i*,
23:12 Apply your heart to *i*,
23:23 wisdom, *i* and understanding.
Wis 3:11 For he who despises wisdom and *i* is doomed.
6:25 so take *i* from my words,
Sir 23: 7 my children, to the *i* that I pronounce,
24:31 Thus do I pour out *i* like prophecy and
41:14 My children, heed my *i* about shame;
47:14 when you were young, overflowing with *i*,
50:27 Wise *i*, appropriate proverbs, I have written
51:16 short time I paid heed, I met with great *i*.
51:23 and take up lodging in the house of *i*;
51:28 Acquire but a little *i*;
Is 1:10 Listen to the *i* of our God,
2: 3 For from Zion shall go forth *i*,
8:16 and the sealed *i* kept among my disciples.
8:20 then this document will furnish its *i*.
29:24 and those who find fault shall receive *i*.
Jer 18:18 not mean the loss of *i* from the priests,
Lam 2: 9 priestly *i* is wanting,
Ez 7:26 *i* shall be lacking to the priest,
Mi 4: 2 For from Zion shall go forth *i*,
Mal 2: 7 and *i* is to be sought from his mouth,
2: 8 and have caused many to falter by your *i*;
Mk 11: 2 sent off two of his disciples with the *i*:
Lk 1: 4 how reliable the *i* was that you received.
22: 8 Jesus sent Peter and John off with the *i*,
Jn 6:59 He said this in a synagogue *i* at Capernaum.
Acts 2:42 to the apostles' *i* and the communal life,
14:22 them to persevere in the faith with this *i*:
Rom 15: 4 before our time was written for our *i*,
1Cor 14: 6 or knowledge, or prophecy, or *i* for you?
14:26 one has a psalm, another some *i* to give,
Eph 6: 4 with the training and *i* befitting the Lord.
Heb 6: 2 *i* about baptisms and laying-on of hands,

INSTRUCTIONS (50)

Gn 26: 5 (my commandments, my ordinances, and my *i*)."
32:20 He gave similar *i* to the second servant
44: 1 Then Joseph gave his head steward these *i*:
44: 2 The steward carried out Joseph's *i*.
49:33 had finished giving these *i* to his sons,
50:16 your father died, he gave us these *i*:
Ex 16: 4 to see whether they follow my *i* or not.
28: 3 you shall give *i* to make such vestments
Nm 15: 2 to Moses, "Give the Israelites these *i*:
18:26 said to Moses, "Give the Levites these *i*:
30: 1 Moses then gave the Israelites these *i*,
35: 1 The LORD gave these *i* to Moses on the
36: 5 Israelites according to the *i* of the LORD:
Dt 24: 8 in accordance with the *i* I have given them.
Jos 3: 3 the camp and issued these *i* to the people:
7: 2 with *i* to go up and reconnoiter the land.
8:33 Ebal, thus carrying out the *i* of Moses,
14: 2 in accordance with the *i* the LORD had
14: 5 carry out the *i* of the LORD to Moses.
Jgs 18: 2 With their *i* to go and scout the land,
1Sm 15:24 the command of the LORD and your *i*.
1Kgs 2: 1 he gave these *i* to his son Solomon:
2Kgs 1: 2 So he sent out messengers with the *i*:
Ezr 6:13 out fully the *i* King Darius had sent them.
Tb 8: 2 this point Tobiah, mindful of Raphael's *i*,
Est 2:20 Esther continued to follow Mordecai's *i*,
1Mc 3:34 him *i* concerning everything he wanted done.
11:37 copy of these *i* made and given to Jonathan,
2Mc 3: 7 with *i* to expropriate the aforesaid wealth.
Jer 42: 5 and faithfully follow all the *i* the LORD,
Mt 10: 5 Twelve, after giving them the following *i*:
21: 2 Jesus sent off two disciples with the *i*:
28:13 the soldiers a large bribe with the *i*:
Mk 14:13 He sent two of his disciples with these *i*:
Lk 9:15 followed his *i* and got them all seated.
19:14 sent a deputation after him with *i* to say,
19:30 he sent two of the disciples with these *i*:
Acts 15:24 without any *i* from us have upset you
16:23 the jailer was given *i* to guard them well.
16:24 upon receipt of these *i*
17:15 who then returned with *i* for Silas and
1Cor 11:34 other matters, I shall give *i* when I come.
16: 1 the *i* I gave the churches of Galatia.
Col 1: 7 intention through the *i* of Epaphras,
4:10 You have received *i* about him:
1Thes 4: 2 know the *i* we gave you in the Lord Jesus.
4: 8 hence, whoever rejects these *i* rejects,
1Tm 4: 6 If you put these *i* before the brotherhood
Heb 11:22 Israelites, and gave *i* about his burial.

INSTRUCTOR (1)

Gal 6: 6 word should share all he has with his *i*.

INSTRUCTORS (1)

Prv 5:13 of my teachers, nor to my *i* incline my ear!

INSTRUCTRESS (1)

Wis 8: 4 For she is *i* in the understanding of God,

INSTRUCTS (4)

Jb 15: 5 God, Because your wickedness *i* your mouth,
36:15 affliction, and *i* them through distress.
Ps(s) 94:10 Shall he who *i* nations not chastise,
Sir 4:11 Wisdom *i* her children and admonishes those

INSTRUMENT (7)

Nm 35:16 with an iron *i* and causes his death,
2Mc 6:19 of his own accord to the *i* of torture,
6:28 and went immediately to the *i* of torture.
Ps(s) 92: 4 the night, With ten-stringed *i* and lyre,
Is 10:10 Assyria *I* of GodJust as my hand reached
Jer 22:28 to be broken up, an *i* that no one wants?
Acts 9:15 This man is the *i* I have chosen to bring

INSTRUMENTS (21)

Gn 4:22 of all who forge *i* of bronze and iron.
1Chr 15:16 as chanters, to play on musical *i*,
16:42 accompaniment, and *i* for the sacred chant.
23: 5 the *i* which David had devised for praise.
2Chr 5:13 musical *i* to "give thanks to the LORD,
7: 6 with the musical *i* of the LORD which King
23:13 their musical *i* were leading the acclaim.
29:26 Levites were stationed with the *i* of David,
29:27 of the trumpets and the *i* of David,
34:12 were skillful with musical *i* were in charge
Neh 12:36 and Hanani, with the musical *i* of David,
Jdt 16: 1 "Strike up the *i*,
Sir 39:15 With music on the harp and all stringed *i*;
Is 13: 5 heavens, The LORD and the *i* of his wrath,
38:20 we shall sing to stringed *i* In the house
Ez 40:43 and on them were laid the *i* with which the
Dn 3: 4 bagpipe, and all the other musical *i*,
3: 7 bagpipe, and all the other musical *i*,
3:10 and all the other musical *i* should fall
3:15 bagpipe, and all the other musical *i*;
Hb 3:19 For the leader; with stringed *i*.

INSUBORDINATE (1)

Ti 1: 6 and are known not to be wild and *i*.

INSUFFICIENT (1)

Lv 14:32 who has *i* means for his purification."

INSULT (25)

1Sm 17:25 He comes up to *i* Israel.
17:26 he should *i* the armies of the living God?"
25:39 the *i* I received at the hand of Nabal,
Tb 3:10 would level this *i* against my father:
8:10 we would be subjected to ridicule and *i*."
2Mc 7:24 Antiochus, suspecting *i* in her words,
Ps(s) 69: 8 of Israel, Since for your sake I bear *i*,
69:21 *I* has broken my heart,
Prv 9: 7 He who corrects an arrogant man earns *i*;
12:16 anger, but the shrewd man passes over an *i*.
22:10 strife and *i* cease.
Sir 8: 6 *I* no man when he is old,
22:22 But a contemptuous *i*,
27:21 A wound can be bound up, and an *i* forgiven,
Jer 15:15 know that for you I have borne *i*.
Mt 5:11 Blest are you when they *i* you and
Lk 6:22 when they ostracize you and *i* you and
11:45 in speaking this way you *i* us too."
23:11 then treated him with contempt and *i*,
Acts 23: 4 "How dare you *i* God's high priest?"
Heb 10:33 you were publicly exposed to *i* and trial;
13:13 the camp, bearing the *i* which he bore.
1Pt 2:23 When he was insulted, he returned no *i*.
3: 9 not return evil for evil or *i* for insult.

INSULTED (16)

Ru 2:22 for in someone else's field you might be *i*."
1Sm 17:36 he has *i* the armies of the living God."
17:45 of the armies of Israel that you have *i*.
2Sm 21:21 And when he *i* Israel,
2Kgs 19:22 Whom have you *i* and blasphemed,
19:23 Through your servants you have *i* the Lord.
Neh 3:37 for they *i* the builders to their face!
Is 37:23 Whom have you *i* and blasphemed,
37:24 Through your servants you have *i* the Lord:
Jer 50:29 has done, do to her, For she *i* the LORD,
Mt 22: 6 The rest laid hold of his servants, *i* them,
Acts 18: 6 When they opposed him and *i* him,
19:37 They have not *i* our goddess.
1Cor 4:12 When we are *i* we respond with a blessing.
1Pt 2:23 When he was *i*, he returned no insult.
4:14 you when you are *i* for the sake of Christ,

INSULTING (5)

Tb 3: 6 to live, because I have heard *i* calumnies,
2Mc 12:14 *i* them and even uttering blasphemies and
Mt 27:39 People going by kept *i* him,
Mk 15:29 People going by kept *i* him,
Lk 22:65 they directed many other *i* words at him.

INSULTINGLY (1)

Jb 16:10 They smite me on the cheek *i*;

INSULTS (17)

Nm 15:30 he be a native or an alien, *i* the LORD,
Tb 3: 6 much misery in life, and to hear these *i*!"
3:10 that I need no longer live to hear such *i*."
3:13 from the earth, never again to hear such *i*.
3:15 never again let me hear these *i*!"
Ps(s) 69:10 *i* of those who blaspheme you fall upon me.
89:51 Remember, O Lord, the *i* to your servants:
Sir 22:20 he who *i* a friend breaks up the friendship.
29: 6 curses and *i* the borrower pays him back,
29:28 are abuse at home and *i* from his creditors.
41:22 and of following up your gifts with *i*;
Lam 3:61 You hear their *i*,
Ez 21:33 Lord GOD against the Ammonites and their *i*:
36:15 of nations, or bear *i* from peoples,
Zep 2: 8 by Moab, and the *i* of the Ammonites,
Col 3: 8 anger and quick temper, the malice, the *i*,
Heb 10:29 to be ordinary, and *i* the Spirit of grace?

INSURGENTS (3)

Mt 27:38 Two *i* were crucified along with him,
27:44 The *i* who had been crucified with him kept
Mk 15:27 With him they crucified two *i*,

INSURRECTION (1)

Lk 23:25 had been thrown in prison for *i* and murder,

INSURRECTIONIST (1)

Jn 18:40 (Barabbas was an *i*.)

INSURRECTIONS (1)

Lk 21: 9 be perturbed when you hear of wars and *i*.

INTACT (3)

1Sm 5: 4 lying on the threshold, his trunk alone *i*.
Prv 15:25 but he preserves *i* the widow's landmark.
Gal 2: 5 gospel might survive *i* for your benefit.

INTEGRITY (21)

Dt 9: 5 *i* of your heart that you are going in to
Jb 4: 6 confidence, and your *i* of life your hope?
Ps(s) 25:21 Let *i* and uprightness preserve me, Let *i*
26: 1 for I have walked in *i*,
26:11 But I walk in *i*;
41:13 But because of my *i* you sustain me and
101: 2 I will persevere in the way of *i*;
101: 2 I will walk in the *i* of my heart,
101: 6 in the way of *i* shall be in my service.
Prv 19: 1 Better a poor man who walks in his *i* than
20: 7 When a man walks in *i* and justice,
28: 6 Better a poor man who walks in his *i* than
Wis 1: 1 in goodness, and seek him in *i* of heart;
9: 3 and to render judgment in *i* of heart:
Sir 7: 6 show favor to the ruler and mar your *i*.
Hb 2: 4 The rash man has no *i*;
Mal 2: 6 He walked with me in *i* and in uprightness,
1Tm 6:11 Instead, seek after *i*, piety, faith, love,
2Tm 2:22 turn from youthful passions and pursue *i*,
Ti 2: 7 Your teaching must have the *i* of serious,

INTELLIGENCE (23)

Dt 4: 6 of your wisdom and *i* to the nations,
1Chr 27:32 Jonathan, David's uncle and a man of *i*,
2Chr 2:11 David a wise son of *i* and understanding,
Jb 12: 3 But I have *i* as well as you;
15: 9 What *i* have you which we have not?
34:35 "Job speaks without *i*,
Prv 1: 2 and discipline, may understand words of *i*;
2: 3 Yes, if you call to *i*,
3: 5 all your heart, on your own *i* rely not;
8: 9 All of them are plain to the man of *i*,
14: 6 but knowledge is easy to the man of *i*.
17:10 man of *i* than a hundred lashes for a fool.
17:24 The man of *i* fixes his gaze on wisdom,
17:27 he who is chary of speech is a man of *i*.
19: 8 He who gains *i* is his own best friend;
20: 5 surface, but the man of *i* draws it forth.
30: 2 stupid of men, and have not even human *i*;
Sir 19:20 and those of great *i* who violate the law.
Is 44:19 reflect, nor have the *i* and sense to say,

INTELLIGENCE (cont.)

Ez 28: 4 your *i* you have made riches for yourself;
Dn 5:23 that neither see nor hear nor have *i*.
Lk 2:47 him were amazed at his *i* and his answers.
Acts 13: 7 a man of *i* who had summoned Barnabas and

INTELLIGENT (19)

Dt 1:13 *i* and experienced men from each of your
4: 6 great nation is truly a wise and *i* people.'
1Sm 25: 3 The woman was *i* and attractive,
Jb 12: 2 No doubt you are the *i* folk,
Prv 1: 5 an *i* man will gain sound guidance,
10:13 On the lips of the *i* is found wisdom,
11:12 has no sense, but the *i* man keeps silent.
14:33 In the heart of the *i* wisdom abides,
14:35 The king favors the *i* servant,
15:14 The mind of the *i* man seeks knowledge,
17: 2 *i* servant will rule over a worthless son,
17:28 if he closes his lips, *i*.
18:15 The mind of the *i* gains knowledge,
19:25 if you rebuke an *i* man,
28:11 but a poor man who is *i* sees through him.
Wis 7:22 For in her is a spirit *i*,
7:23 pervading all spirits, though they be *i*,
Sir 21:15 When an *i* man hears words of wisdom,
Dn 1: 4 without any defect, handsome, *i* and wise,

INTELLIGIBLE (2)

1Cor 14: 9 if you do not utter *i* speech because you
14:19 I would rather say five *i* words to instruct

INTEND (22)

Gn 33: 8 *i* with all those droves that I encountered?"
Dt 25: 7 'My brother-in-law does not *i* to perform
Jgs 6:31 him, "Do you *i* to act in Baal's stead,
1Sm 6: 3 "If you *i* to send away the ark of the God
2Sm 18: 2 soldiers, "I *i* to go out with you myself."
2Chr 2: 3 I *i* to build a house for the honor of the
2: 4 And the house I *i* to build must be large,
2: 8 I *i* to build must be lofty and wonderful.
29:10 Now, I *i* to make a covenant with the LORD,
1Mc 15: 3 kingdom of my ancestors, I *i* to reclaim it,
Ps(s) 21:12 Though they *i* evil against you,
119:112 I *i* in my heart to fulfill your statutes
Jer 21: 4 which you *i* to fight the king of Babylon
Mt 20:14 I *i* to give this man who was hired last
Lk 12:41 Peter said, "Do you *i* this parable for us,
19:22 I *i* to judge you on your own evidence.
Jn 7:35 does he *i* to go that we will not find him?
Acts 17:23 in ignorance I *i* to make known to you.
Rom 7:19 good I will to do, but the evil I do not *i*.
1Cor 16: 8 I *i* to stay in Ephesus until Pentecost.
2Pt 1:12 *i* to recall these things to you constantly,
2Jn 1:12 you, I do not *i* to put it down on paper;

INTENDED (22)

Gn 31:20 Aramean by not telling him of his *i* flight.
Ex 24:12 the commandments *i* for their instruction."
Nm 33:56 I will treat you as I had *i* to treat them."
1Sm 14: 4 ravine through which Jonathan *i* to get
18:25 Saul *i* in this way to bring about David's
2Sm 21: 5 who *i* to destroy us that we might have no
1Chr 29: 1 is great, for this castle is not *i* for man,
2Chr 11:22 his brothers, for he *i* to make him king.
Est A:11 seen this dream and what God *i* to do,
1Mc 4:27 out as he *i* and as the king had ordered.
12:34 for he heard that its men had *i* to hand
13:14 Jonathan, and that he *i* to fight him,
Wis 4:17 do not understand what the Lord *i* for him,
Jer 43:11 the sword, all who are *i* for the sword.
Mk 16: 1 with which they *i* to go and anoint Jesus.
Lk 1:59 *i* to name him after his father Zechariah.
10: 1 him to every town and place he *i* to visit.
Jn 6: 6 (He knew well what he *i* to do but he asked
Acts 12: 4 Herod *i* to bring him before the people
20: 7 Because he *i* to leave the next day,
Rom 4:24 they were *i* for us too.
2Cor 7:12 my writing to you was not *i* for the man

INTENDING (9)

1Mc 11:63 in Galilee, *i* to remove him from office.
2Mc 2: 6 followed him came up *i* to mark the path,
12: 7 *i* to come back later and wipe out the
12:35 *i* to capture the vile wretch alive,
Jer 41:17 where they stopped, *i* to flee into Egypt.
Lk 4:30 was built and *i* to hurl him over the edge.
Jn 6:17 *i* to cross the lake toward Capernaum.
Acts 22:30 *i* to look carefully into the charge which
2Pt 3: 1 *i* them both as reminders urging you to

INTENDS (7)

Gn 27:42 Your brother Esau *i* to settle accounts
1Kgs 8:12 "The LORD *i* to dwell in the dark cloud;
2Chr 6: 1 "The LORD *i* to dwell in the dark cloud.
Wis 9:13 or who can conceive what our Lord *i*?
Is 10: 7 But this is not what he *i*,
Gal 5:17 This is why you do not do what your will *i*.
Phil 1:28 All this is as God *i*,

INTENSE (5)

Ex 10:21 be such *i* darkness that one can feel it."
2Sm 13:15 Then Amnon conceived an *i* hatred for her,
Tb 9: 4 by a single day, I would cause him *i* grief.
Rv 2:22 I will plunge into *i* suffering unless they
16: 9 Those who were scorched by the *i* heat

INTENSELY (2)

Sir 17:21 and away from sin, hate *i* what he loathes;
Zec 8: 2 I am *i* jealous for Zion,

INTENSIFIED (1)

2Mc 6: 3 This *i* the evil in an intolerable and

INTENSIFY (1)

Gn 3:16 "I will *i* the pangs of your childbearing;

INTENSITY (1)

Lk 22:44 anguish he prayed with all the greater *i*.

INTENT (9)

Gn 31:52 shall be witness, that, with hostile *i*,
Ex 32:12 say, 'With evil *i* he brought them out,
1Sm 17:28 I know your arrogance and your evil *i*.
2Sm 18:32 you with evil *i* be as that young man!"
Ps(s) 49: 5 My ear is *i* upon a proverb;
Prv 14:22 *i* on good gain kindness and constancy.
Rom 8: 5 the flesh are *i* on the things of the flesh,
Col 3: 2 Be *i* on things above rather than on things
Jude 1: 3 I was already fully *i* on writing you,

INTENTION (12)

Dt 8: 2 not it was your *i* to keep his commandments.
1Sm 19: 1 Saul discussed his *i* of killing David with
1Chr 12:39 *i* of making David king over all Israel.
2Chr 32: 2 coming with the *i* of attacking Jerusalem,
Tb 3:10 house with the *i* of hanging herself.
2Mc 9:14 hurrying with the *i* of leveling
Prv 20: 5 The *i* in the human heart is like water far
21:27 more so when they offer it with a bad *i*.
Mt 1:20 Such was his *i* when suddenly the angel of
Acts 22: 5 I set out with the *i* of bringing the
Col 1: 7 *i* through the instructions of Epaphras,
2Thes 1:11 his power every honest *i* and work of faith.

INTENTIONS (5)

2Mc 11:37 send us those who can inform us of your *i*.
14: 5 about the dispositions and *i* of the Jews.
Sir 37:10 those who envy you, keep your *i* hidden.
Jer 44:25 You and your wives have stated your *i*,
1Cor 4: 5 in darkness and manifest the *i* of hearts.

INTENTLY (9)

Is 6: 9 Look *i*, but you shall know nothing!
Ez 40: 4 "Son of man, look carefully and listen *i*,
44: 5 and listen *i* to all that I will tell you
Mt 13:14 shall not understand, look *i* as you will,
Mk 4:12 so that they will look *i* and not see,
Lk 22:56 She gazed at him *i*,
Acts 6:15 Sanhedrin who sat there stared at him *i*.
23: 1 Paul gazed *i* at the Sanhedrin.
28:26 you may look *i* yet you will never see.

INTERCEDE (10)

Gn 20: 7 as a spokesman he will *i* for you
23: 8 *I* for me with Ephron,
1Sm 2:25 man, one can *i* for him with the LORD;
2:25 sins against the LORD, who can *i* for him?"
1Kgs 13: 6 "and *i* for me that I may be able to
Est 4: 8 and *i* with him in behalf of her people.
Jer 7:16 You, now, do not *i* for this people;
11:14 Do not *i* on behalf of this people,
14:11 Do not *i* for this people.
27:18 them, they would *i* with the LORD of hosts,

INTERCEDED (4)

Gn 20:17 Abraham then *i* with God,
Tb 1:22 Then Ahiqar *i* on my behalf,
Jer 15:11 Have I not *i* with you in the time of
Lk 4:38 severe fever, and they *i* with him for her.

INTERCEDES (2)

Rom 8:27 *i* for the saints as God himself wills.
8:34 at the right hand of God and who *i* for us?

INTERCEPT (3)

Jos 8:22 Since those in the city came out to *i* them,
2Kgs 1: 3 "Go, *i* the messengers of Samaria's king,
2Chr 35:20 Euphrates, and Josiah went out to *i* him.

INTERCESSION (3)

Jb 42: 9 And the LORD accepted the *i* of Job.
Rom 8:26 but the Spirit himself makes *i* for us with
Heb 7:25 since he forever lives to make *i* for them.

INTERCESSIONS (1)

1Tm 2: 1 of all, I urge that petitions, prayers, *i*,

INTERCESSOR (1)

1Jn 2: 1 the Father, Jesus Christ, an *i* who is just.

INTERCOURSE (40)

Gn 6: 4 of heaven had *i* with the daughters of man,
16: 2 Have *i*, then, with my maid;
16: 4 He had *i* with her,
19: 8 daughters who have never had *i* with men.
30: 3 Have *i* with her,
30: 4 as a consort, and Jacob had *i* with her.
30:10 So Jacob had *i* with Zilpah,
38:16 he said, "Come, let me have *i* with you."
38:16 you pay me for letting you have *i* with me?"
38:18 So he gave them to her and had *i* with her,
Ex 19:15 Have no *i* with any woman."
Lv 18: 6 a close relative to have sexual *i* with her.
18: 7 your father by having *i* with your mother.
18: 7 own mother, you shall not have *i* with her.
18: 8 shall not have *i* with your father's wife,
18: 9 You shall not have *i* with your sister,
18:10 You shall not have *i* with your son's
18:11 You shall not have *i* with the daughter
18:12 shall not have *i* with your father's sister,
18:13 not have *i* with your mother's sister,
18:15 shall not have *i* with your daughter-in-law;
18:16 shall not have *i* with your brother's wife,
18:17 *i* with a woman and also with her daughter,
18:17 nor shall you marry and have *i* with her
18:19 to have *i* with her while she is unclean
20:17 of having had *i* with his own sister.
20:18 *i* with a woman during her menstrual period,
20:19 You shall not have *i* with your mother's
20:20 uncle by having *i* with his uncle's wife,
Nm 5:13 to him by having *i* with another man,
5:19 her, 'If no other man has had *i* with you,
5:20 a man other than your husband have *i* with
31:17 and every woman who has had *i* with a man.
31:18 all girls who had no *i* with a man.
Tb 3: 8 them off before they could have *i* with her,
6:18 Then when you are about to have *i* with her,
2Mc 6: 4 had *i* with women even in the sacred court.
Ez 23:17 love couch, and defiled her with their *i*.
Rom 1:26 women exchanged natural *i* for unnatural,
1:27 and the men gave up natural *i* with women

INTEREST (21)

Ex 22:24 toward him by demanding *i* from him.
Lv 25:36 Do not exact *i* from your countryman either
25:37 neither money at *i* nor food at a profit.
Dt 23:20 "You shall not demand *i* from your
23:20 else on which *i* is usually demanded.
23:21 You may demand *i* from a foreigner,
Jgs 18: 3 "What is your *i* here?"
Neh 5: 7 "You are exacting *i* from your own kinsmen!"
5:11 houses, together with the *i* on the money,
2Mc 14: 9 act in the *i* of our country and its
Jb 21:21 For what *i* has he in his family after him,
Prv 28: 8 He who increases his wealth by *i* and
Ez 18: 8 if he does not lend at *i* nor exact usury;
18:13 things, lends at *i* and exacts usury
18:17 off from evildoing, accepts no *i* or usury,
22:12 You exact *i* and usury;
Dn 11: 6 to the king of the north in the *i* of peace.
Mt 25:27 my return I could have had it back with *i*.
Lk 19:23 on my return I could get it back with *i*?'
1Cor 10:24 his own *i* but rather that of his neighbor.
Phil 2:20 him for genuine *i* in whatever concerns you.

INTERESTED (3)

1Kgs 10: 2 him on every subject in which she was *i*.
2Chr 9: 1 him on every subject in which she was *i*.
Jer 38: 4 he is not *i* in the welfare of our people,

INTERESTS (12)

Jos 22:26 our *i* by building this altar of our own:
Est B: 5 and alien laws, is inimical to our *i*,
E: 1 and to those responsible for our *i*:
1Mc 10:20 after our *i* and preserve amity with us."
2Mc 11:19 endeavor to further your *i* in the future.
14: 8 of my genuine concern for the king's *i*,
Is 58:13 following your ways, seeking your own *i*,
Dn 6: 2 and twenty satraps, to safeguard his *i*;
Mk 7: 9 in the *i* of keeping your traditions!
Phil 2: 4 to others' *i* rather than to his own.
2:21 own *i* rather than those of Christ Jesus.
Rv 13:12 beast to promote its *i* by making the world

INTERFERE (4)

2Chr 35:21 Do not *i* with God who is with me,
Ezr 6: 6 West-of-Euphrates, do not *i* in that place.
Mt 27:19 "Do not *i* in the case of that holy man.
Acts 11:17 Lord Jesus Christ, who was I to *i* with him?"

INTERFERENCE (1)

Ex 2:19 saved us from the *i* of the shepherds.

INTERIOR (8)

1Kgs 6:18 The cedar in the *i* of the temple was
6:21 the *i* of the temple with pure gold.
7:48 made for the *i* of the temple of the LORD:
2Chr 3: 4 He overlaid its *i* with pure gold.
29:16 the *i* of the LORD's house to cleanse it;
1Mc 4:48 *i* of the temple and purified the courts.
Ez 41:17 *i* part of the temple as well as outside,
Acts 19: 1 the *i* of the country and came to Ephesus.

INTERMARRIAGE (1)

Dn 2:43 that they shall seal their alliances by *i*,

INTERMARRY (3)

Gn 34: 9 *I* with us;
Dt 7: 3 You shall not *i* with them,
1Kgs 11: 2 LORD had forbidden the Israelites to *i*,

INTERMARRYING (2)

Jos 23:12 you, by *i* and intermingling with them,
Ezr 9:14 by *i* with these abominable peoples?

INTERMEDIARY (1)

Jer 40:10 as their *i* with the Chaldeans who should

INTERMEDIATE (1)

1Kgs 6: 8 and stairs with *i* landings led up to the

INTERMINABLE (1)

1Tm 1: 4 themselves with *i* myths and genealogies,

INTERMINGLING (1)

Jos 23:12 you, by intermarrying and *i* with them,

INTERMITTENT (1)

Wis 17: 6 But only *i*, fearful fires flashed through

INTERNAL (1)

2Mc 9: 5 pains in his bowels and sharp *i* torment,

INTERPOSED (1)

Jdt 8:11 you *i* between God and yourselves this oath

INTERPRET (13)

Gn 40: 8 but there is no one to *i* them for us."
41: 8 but no one could *i* his dreams for him.
41:15 "I had certain dreams that no one can *i*.
41:15 moment you are told a dream you can *i* it."
Dn 2: 2 be summoned to *i* the dream for him.
5:12 He knew and understood how to *i* dreams,
5:16 you can *i* dreams and solve difficulties;
Mt 16: 3 If you know how to *i* the look of the sky,
Lk 12:56 If you can *i* the portents of earth and sky,
12:56 sky, why can you not *i* the present time?
1Cor 14: 5 also *i* for the upbuilding of the church.
14:27 with another to *i* what they are saying.
14:28 But if there is no one to *i*,

INTERPRETATION (12)

Gn 40:16 saw that Joseph had given this favorable *i*,
40:22 just as Joseph had told them in his *i*.
Dn 2: 9 You have framed a false and deceitful *i* to
2: 9 sure that you can also give its correct *i*."
2:16 the king, that he might give him the *i*.
2:24 and I will tell him the *i* of the dream."
2:25 captives who can give the *i* to the king."
2:36 the *i* we shall also give in the king's
4: 3 before me to give the *i* of the dream.
1Cor 12:30 tongues, all have the gift of *i* of tongues?
14:13 in a tongue should pray for the gift of *i*.
2Pt 1:20 in Scripture which is a personal *i*.

INTERPRETATIONS (1)

Gn 40: 8 said to them, "Surely, *i* come from God.

INTERPRETED (2)

Gn 41:12 he *i* them for us and explained for each of
Lk 24:27 he *i* for them every passage of Scripture

INTERPRETER (1)

Gn 42:23 since he spoke with them through an *i*.

INTERPRETING (3)

Neh 8: 8 *i* it so that all could understand what was
1Cor 2:13 thus *i* spiritual things in spiritual terms.
12:10 of tongues, another that of *i* the tongues.

INTERPRETS (1)

1Cor 14:26 one speaks in a tongue, another *i*.

INTERROGATE (2)

Mk 14:60 feet before the court and began to *i* Jesus:
Acts 22:29 those who were about to *i* him backed away.

INTERROGATED (3)

Mk 14:61 the high priest *i* him: "Are you the Messiah
15: 2 Pilate *i* him: "Are you the king of the Jews
15: 4 Pilate *i* him again:

INTERROGATION (2)

Acts 4: 7 them and began the *i* in this fashion:
5:27 the high priest began the *i* in this way:

INTERRUPT (1)

Sir 11: 8 and *i* no one in the middle of his speech.

INTERRUPTED (3)

1Sm 23:28 Saul *i* his pursuit of David and went to
1Mc 9:55 time he had a stroke, and his work was *i*;
Acts 26:24 himself in this way, Festus *i* with a shout,

INTERRUPTING (1)

2Sm 2:30 Joab, after *i* the pursuit of Abner,

INTERRUPTION (1)

Wis 17:20 light and continued its works without *i*;

INTERVAL (2)

Jer 13: 6 After a long *i*, he said to me:
Acts 16:30 After a brief *i* he led them out and said,

INTERVENE (2)

Is 59:16 and was appalled that there was none to *i*;
Hb 1: 2 but you do not *i*.

INTERVENED (3)

2Mc 4: 6 He saw that unless the king *i*,
Lk 1:60 At this his mother *i*,
Acts 23:27 I *i* with my troops and rescued him.

INTERVENES (2)

Dt 25:11 wife of one *i* to save her husband
Jb 41: 8 each so close to the next that no space *i*;

INTERVENING (1)

Gn 19:19 me the great kindness of *i* to save my life.

INTERVENTION (1)

Ps(s) 76: 9 From heaven you made your *i* heard;

INTERVIEW (1)

2Mc 4: 8 in an *i*, he promised the king

INTERWOVEN (1)

2Mc 5: 2 in midair, clad in garments *i* with gold

INTIMACIES (1)

Gn 19: 5 out to us that we may have *i* with them."

INTIMACY (1)

Sir 20: 3 Like a eunuch lusting for *i* with a maiden

INTIMATE (10)

Ex 33:12 Yet you have said, 'You are my *i* friend,'
33:17 favor with me and you are my *i* friend."
Lv 18:14 father's brother by being *i* with his wife,
Dt 13: 7 or your beloved wife, or your *i* friend,
Jgs 11:39 She had not been *i* with man.
2Sm 3: 7 have you been *i* with my father's concubine?"
Jb 19:19 All my *i* friends hold me in horror;
Sir 9: 3 Be not *i* with a strange woman,
9:15 With the learned be *i*;
27:16 be trusted, he will never find an *i* friend.

INTIMATES (2)

2Kgs 10:11 as well as all his powerful supporters, *i*,
Sir 30: 2 from him, and boast of him among his *i*.

INTIMIDATE (6)

Ezr 4: 4 people of the land set out to *i*
Sir 4:22 let no one *i* you to your own downfall.
8:11 Let not the impious man *i* you;
48:12 no one, nor was any man able to *i* his will.
Mt 10:26 Do not let them *i* you.
2Cor 10: 9 I do not wish to *i* you with my letters.

INTIMIDATED (1)

Phil 1:28 be *i* by your opponents in any situation.

INTIMIDATION (1)

Sir 20:21 shame, and perish through a fool's *i*.

INTOLERABLE (4)

Gn 20: 9 You have treated me in an *i* way.
2Sm 13:12 That is an *i* crime in Israel.
2Mc 6: 3 evil in an *i* and utterly disgusting way.
9:10 transport the man because of this *i* stench.

INTONE (3)

Jer 7:29 on the heights *i* an elegy;
9: 9 over the pasture lands, *i* a dirge:
9:17 Let them come quickly and *i* a dirge for us,

INTRACTABLE (1)

Ti 1:16 They are disgusting *i* and thoroughly

INTREPID (1)

Jb 41:25 earth there is not his like, *i* he was made.

INTRICATE (1)

Est E:13 and by weaving *i* webs of deceit,

INTRIGUE (4)

Prv 11: 6 the faithless are caught in their own *i*.
24: 9 Beyond *i* and folly and sin,
Dn 8:23 arise a king, impudent and skilled in *i*.
Phil 1:17 from pure motives but as an *i* against me,

INTRIGUER (2)

Prv 16:28 An *i* sows discord,
24: 8 men call him an *i*.

INTRODUCE (1)

1Mc 1:13 to *i* the way of living of the Gentiles.

INTRODUCED (5)

1Mc 12:43 him with honor, *i* him to all his friends,
2Mc 4:11 institutions and *i* customs contrary to the law.
4:24 When he had been *i* to the king,
Dn 9:24 expiated, Everlasting justice will be *i*,
Acts 9:27 him in charge and *i* him to the apostles.

INTRODUCING (1)

Acts 17:20 You are *i* subjects unfamiliar to us and we

INTRODUCTION (1)

1Cor 16: 3 When I come I shall give letters of *i* to

INVADE (11)

2Chr 20:10 to *i* when they came from the land of Egypt,
1Mc 3:39 seven thousand cavalry to *i* the land
9:69 men who had advised him to *i* the province.
13: 1 army to *i* and ravage the land of Judah,
13:12 with a large army to *i* the land of Judah,
13:20 Next he began to *i* and ravage the country.
14:31 When the enemies of the Jews sought to *i*
2Mc 13:13 *i* Judea and take possession of the city,
Prv 23:10 landmark, nor *i* the fields of orphans;
Dn 11: 9 shall *i* the land of the king of the south,
Hos 9: 6 silver treasures, and thorns *i* their tents.

INVADED (17)

Nm 32:39 son of Manasseh, *i* Gilead and captured it,
1Sm 11:11 and *i* the camp during the dawn watch.
23:27 because the Philistines have *i* the land."
2Kgs 15:19 reign, Pul, king of Assyria, *i* the land,
2Chr 21:17 They came up against Judah, *i* it,
24:23 They *i* Judah and Jerusalem,
32: 1 He *i* Judah, besieged the fortified cities,
1Mc 1:17 He *i* Egypt with a strong force,
1:21 He insolently *i* the sanctuary and took
14: 2 heard that Demetrius had *i* his territory,
15:10 Antiochus *i* the land of his ancestors,
2Mc 11: 5 So he *i* Judea,
Is 63:18 Why have the wicked *i* your holy place,
Jer 35:11 king of Babylon, *i* this land,
Jl 1: 6 For a people has *i* my land,
Na 2: 1 nevermore shall you be *i* by the scoundrel;
Rv 20: 9 They *i* the whole country and surrounded

INVADERS (1)

Heb 11:34 in battle, and turned back foreign *i*.

INVADES (4)

Ez 38:18 day, the day when Gog *i* the land of Israel,
Mi 5: 4 *i* our country and treads upon our land,
5: 5 it *i* our land and treads upon our borders.
Hb 3:16 Decay *i* my bones,

INVADING (1)

2Mc 13: 1 Eupator was *i* Judea with a large force,

INVALID (1)

Gal 3:17 ratified by God is not set aside as *i* by any

INVASION (2)

Sir 48:18 Sennacherib led an *i* and sent his adjutant;
Jer 11:16 be jubilant when you hear the great *i*?

INVENTED (1)

Ti 1:14 *i* by men who have swerved from the truth.

INVENTION (3)

Neh 6: 8 rather, it is the *i* of your own mind."
Wis 14:12 and their *i* was a corruption of life.
Gal 1:11 I proclaimed to you is no mere human *i.*

INVENTORY (2)

Ezr 1: 9 This was the *i:*
2Mc 3:14 set he went in to take an *i* of the funds.

INVENTS (1)

Jb 33:10 Yet he *i* pretexts against me and reckons

INVEST (4)

Nm 27:20 *I* him with some of your own dignity,
1Kgs 20: 1 proceeded to *i* and attack Samaria.
Mt 25:16 went to *i* it and made another five.
Lk 19:13 saying to them, *I* this until I get back.'

INVESTED (3)

Jgs 9:50 to Thebez, which he *i* and captured.
1Mc 15:14 While he *i* the city,
Ez 24: 2 day the king of Babylon has *i* Jerusalem.

INVESTIGATE (6)

Dt 13:15 into the matter and *i* it thoroughly.
1Sm 14:38 We must *i* and find out how this sin was
2Kgs 7:13 the abandoned horses and send scouts to *i.*"
2Chr 32:31 *i* the sign that had occurred in the land,
Eccl 1:13 I applied my mind to search and *i* in wisdom
Acts 19:39 there is any further matter you want to *i,*

INVESTIGATED (4)

1Sm 14:17 When they had *i,*
Est A-13 He overheard them plotting, *i* their plans,
2:23 The matter was *i* and verified,
1Pt 1:11 They *i* the times and the circumstances

INVESTIGATING (1)

Sir 11: 7 Before *i,*

INVESTIGATION (4)

Dt 17: 4 you find by careful *i* that it is true and
19:18 and if after a thorough *i* the judges find
Acts 25:21 there could be an imperial *i* of his case,
25:26 that from this *i* I may have something to

INVESTMENT (1)

Lk 19:18 The second came and said, 'Your *i,*

INVETERATE (1)

Sir 20:24 Better a thief than an *i* liar,

INVIGORATE (1)

Prv 5:19 Her love will *i* you always,

INVIGORATES (1)

Prv 15:30 good news *i* the bones.

INVINCIBLE (2)

2Mc 11:13 *i* because the mighty God was their ally.
Wis 5:19 He shall take *i* rectitude as a shield and

INVIOLABILITY (1)

2Mc 3:12 *i* of a temple venerated all over the world.

INVIOLABLE (3)

Nm 18:19 this is an *i* covenant to last forever
Est 9:27 the *i* obligation of celebrating these two
2Mc 4:33 withdrawing to the *i* sanctuary at Daphne,

INVISIBLE (7)

Jb 33:21 it cannot be seen, and his bones, once *i,*
Rom 1:20 the creation of the world, *i* realities,
Col 1:15 He is the image of the *i* God,
1:16 earth was created, things visible and *i,*
1Tm 1:17 To the King of ages, the immortal, the *i,*
Heb 11: 3 is visible came into being through the *i.*
11:27 as if he were looking on the *i* God.

INVITATION (5)

2Sm 15:12 counselor, an *i* to come from his town,
2Mc 12: 4 to live on friendly terms, accepted the *i,*
Mt 22: 5 Some ignored the *i* and went their way,
Acts 16:15 had been baptized, she extended us an *i:*
Rom 2: 4 God's kindness is an *i* to you to repent?

INVITATIONS (1)

Jb 1: 4 sending *i* to their three sisters to eat

INVITE (15)

Ex 2:20 *I* him to have something to eat."
34:15 *i* you and you may partake of his sacrifice.
Dt 33:19 You who *i* the tribes to the mountains
Jgs 14:15 Did you *i* us here to reduce us to poverty?"
1Sm 16: 3 *I* Jesse to the sacrifice,
1Kgs 1:10 But he did not *i* the prophet Nathan,
1:26 But me, your servant, he did not *i;*
Jdt 12:10 to which he did not *i* any of the officers.
Zec 3:10 you will *i* one another under your vines
Mt 22: 9 and *i* to the wedding anyone you come upon.'
Lk 5:32 *i* the self-righteous to a change of heart,
14:12 do not *i* your friends or brothers or
14:12 might *i* you in return and thus repay you.
14:13 a reception, *i* beggars and the crippled,
Acts 10:32 to *i* Simon known as Peter to come here.

INVITED (36)

Gn 29:22 So Laban *i* all the local inhabitants and
31:54 and *i* his kinsmen to share in the meal.
Nm 25: 2 These then *i* the people to the sacrifices
1Sm 9:13 the sacrifice will the *i* guests eat.
16: 5 themselves and *i* them to the sacrifice.
2Sm 13:23 near Ephraim, and he *i* all the princes.
15:11 They had been *i* and went in good faith,
1Kgs 1: 9 near En-rogel, Adonijah *i* all his brothers,
1:19 he has *i* all the king's sons,
1:25 he *i* all the king's sons,
13: 7 refreshment," the king *i* the man of God,
Est 5:12 "Queen Esther *i* no one but me to the
2Mc 12: 3 they *i* the Jews who lived among them,
14: 5 when he was *i* to the council by Demetrius
Wis 1:16 wicked who with hands and words *i* death,
Sir 13: 9 When *i* by a man of influence,
Mt 22: 3 to summon the *i* guests to the wedding,
22: 4 'Tell those who were *i,*
22: 8 but those who were *i* were unfit to come.
22:14 The *i* are many, the elect are few."
Lk 7:36 Pharisee who *i* Jesus to dine with him.
11:37 a Pharisee *i* him to dine at his house.
14: 8 you are *i* by someone to a wedding party,
14: 8 in case some greater dignitary has been *i.*
14:10 been *i* is go and sit in the lowest place,
14:12 He said to the one who had *i* him:
14:16 was giving a large dinner and he *i* many.
14:17 time he sent his servant to say to those *i,*
14:24 those *i* shall taste a morsel of my dinner.'"
Jn 2: 2 had likewise been *i* to the celebration.
Acts 8:31 *i* Philip to get in and sit down beside him.
10:23 Peter *i* them in and treated them as guests.
13:42 the people *i* them to speak on this subject
16: 9 of Macedonia stood before him and *i* him,
28:17 Three days later Paul *i* the prominent men
Rv 19: 9 been *i* to the wedding feast of the lamb."

INVITES (2)

Lk 15: 6 he *i* friends and neighbors in and says to
1Cor 10:27 *i* you to his table and you want to go,

INVITING (5)

1Sm 9:24 I explained that I was *i* some guests."
Tb 9: 5 and was *i* him to the wedding celebration.
1Mc 16:19 To the army officers he sent letters *i*
2Mc 8:11 *i* them to buy Jewish slaves and promising
Acts 7:14 father Jacob, *i* him and all his kinsfolk

INVOCATION (1)

Jdt 10: 1 and ceased her *i* to the God of Israel,

INVOICE (2)

Lk 16: 6 The manager said, 'Take your *i,*
16: 7 said, 'Take your *i* and make it eighty.'

INVOKE (16)

Gn 4:26 that time men began to *i* the LORD by name.
Nm 6:27 shall they *i* my name upon the Israelites,
Jos 23: 7 You must not *i* their gods,
2Kgs 5:11 out and stand there to *i* the LORD his God,
1Chr 16: 8 Give thanks to the LORD, *i* his name;
Jdt 3: 8 and every people and tribe *i* him as a god.
Est B: 9 *I* the Lord and speak to the king for us:
2Mc 3:31 Heliodorus begged Onias to *i* the Most High,
Ps(s) 75: 2 and we *i* your name;
105: 1 Give thanks to the LORD, *i* his name;
139:20 Wickedly they *i* your name;
Is 48: 1 *i* the God of Israel without sincerity
Bar 2:32 of their captivity, and shall *i* my name.
Acts 9:14 priests to arrest any who *i* your name."
9:21 in Jerusalem among those who *i* this name?
19:13 Jewish exorcists once tried to *i* the name of

INVOKED (11)

Gn 12: 8 there to the LORD and *i* the LORD by name.
13: 4 and there he *i* the LORD by name.
21:33 and there he *i* by name the LORD,
26:25 an altar there and *i* the LORD by name.
33:20 set up a memorial stone there and *i* "El,
2Kgs 20:11 So the prophet Isaiah *i* the LORD,
2Mc 12:15 But Judas and his men *i* the aid of the
Sir 31:23 a man generous with food, blessings are *i,*
Is 65:16 on whom a blessing is *i* in the land.
Hos 2:19 Baals, so that they shall no longer be *i.*
Heb 11:20 By faith Isaac *i* for Jacob and Esau

INVOKES (1)

Wis 13:17 And for vigor he *i* the powerless;

INVOKING (4)

Gn 24:60 *I* a blessing on Rebekah, they said:
Est D- 2 after *i* the all-seeing God and savior,
2Mc 12:28 *i* the Sovereign who forcibly shatters the
Mt 27:47 who heard it remark, "He is *i* Elijah!"

INVOLVE (4)

Jos 22:19 against the LORD nor *i* us in rebellion,
2Kgs 14:10 Why *i* yourself and Judah with you in
2Chr 25:19 Why *i* yourself,
Jn 2: 4 how does this concern of yours *i* me?

INVOLVED (8)

Ex 22: 1 beaten to death, there is no bloodguilt *i.*
2Sm 14:19 asked, "Is Joab *i* with you in all this?"
Est E- 5 and has *i* them in irreparable calamities
Sir 12:14 of the proud man, who is *i* in his sins:
27:27 Whoever does harm will be *i* in it without
39: 2 men, and goes to the heart of *i* sayings;
Gal 3:20 be no mediator when only one person is *i;*
Jas 1: 2 joy when you are *i* in every sort of trial.

INVOLVES (2)

Wis 8:16 For association with her *i* no bitterness
2Jn 1: 6 This love *i* our walking according to the

INVOLVING (2)

2Sm 3: 8 day you charge me with a crime *i* a woman!
Mt 13:21 or persecution *i* the message occurs,

INVULNERABLE (1)

2Mc 8:36 and that they were *i* for the very reason

INWARD (2)

Jb 30:17 my *i* parts seethe and will not be stilled.
Sir 40:29 spirit to one who understands *i* feelings:

INWARDLY (8)

Ps(s) 62: 5 bless with their mouths, but *i* they curse.
Sir 30: 7 bandage, and will quake *i* at every outcry.
Jer 3:11 is *i* more just than traitorous Judah.
Rom 2:29 He is a real Jew who is one *i,*
8:23 groan *i* while we await the redemption of
2Cor 2:13 Yet I was *i* troubled because I did not
9: 7 give according to what he has *i* decided;
Eph 3:16 you *i* through the working of his Spirit.

IONIAN (1)

Acts 27:27 were still being driven across the *I* Sea,

IPHDEIAH (1)

1Chr 8:25 Hanan, Hananiah, Elam, Anthothijah, *I,*

IPHTAH (1)

Jos 15:43 their villages, Libnah, Ether, Ashan, *I,*

IPHTAHEL (2)

Jos 19:14 the boundary ended at the valley of *I.*
19:27 reached Zebulun and the valley of *I;*

IR (1)

1Chr 4:15 sons of Caleb, son of Jephunneh, were *I,*

IR-HAMELAH (1)

Jos 15:62 Middin, Secacah, Nibshan, *I* and Engedi;

IR-MOAB (1)

Nm 22:36 him at the boundary city *I* on the Arnon

IR-SHEMESH (1)

Jos 19:41 was the territory of Zorah, Eshtaol, *I*

IRA (6)

2Sm 20:26 *I* the Jairite was also David's priest.
23:26 *I,* son of Ikkesh, from Tekoa;
23:38 *I* from Jattir; Gareb from Jattir;
1Chr 11:28 *I,* son of Ikkesh, from Tekoa;
11:40 *I,* from Jattir; Gareb, from Jattir;
27: 9 Sixth, for the sixth month, was *I,*

IRAD (2)

Gn 4:18 Irad, and *I* became the father of Mehujael;

IRAM (2)

Gn 36:43 Kenaz, Teman, Mibzar, Magdiel, and *I.*
1Chr 1:54 Magdiel, and *I* were the chiefs of Edom.

IRI (1)

1Chr 7: 7 were Ezbon, Uzzi, Uzziel, Jerimoth, and *I*—

IRIJAH (2)

Jer 37:13 the captain of the guard, a man named *I*,
37:14 *I* kept Jeremiah in custody and brought him

IRKED (1)

Sir 6:26 and be not *i* at her bonds.

IRKSOME (1)

Sir 6:21 How *i* she is to the unruly!

IRON (101)

Gn 4:22 all who forge instruments of bronze and *i*.
Lv 26:19 will make the sky above you as hard as *i*,
Nm 31:22 fire, such as gold, silver, bronze, *i*,
35:16 with an *i* instrument and causes his death,
Dt 3:11 He had a bed of *i*,
4:20 he has taken and led out of that *i* foundry,
8: 9 *i* and in whose hills you can mine copper.
27: 5 made of stones that no *i* tool has touched.
28:23 and the earth under your feet like *i*.
28:48 He will put an *i* yoke on your neck,
33:25 May your bolts be of *i* and bronze;
Jos 6:19 and gold, and the articles of bronze or *i*,
6:24 gold, and articles of bronze and *i*,
8:31 stones on which no *i* tool had been used,
17:16 in the valley region all have *i* chariots,
17:18 if, despite their strength and *i* chariots,
22: 8 with silver, gold, bronze and *i*,
Jgs 1:19 on the plain, because they had *i* chariots.
4: 3 for with his nine hundred *i* chariots he
4:13 of his *i* chariots and all his forces.
1Sm 17: 7 and its *i* head weighed six hundred shekels.
2Sm 12:31 to work with saws, iron picks, and *i* axes,
23: 7 himself with *i* and the shaft of a spear,
1Kgs 6: 7 or *i* tool was to be heard in the temple
8:51 of Egypt, from the midst of an *i* furnace.
22:11 made himself horns of *i* and said,
2Kgs 6: 5 trunk, the *i* axhead slipped into the water.
6: 6 water, and brought the *i* to the surface.
1Chr 20: 3 and set them to work with saws, *i* picks,
22: 3 *i* to make nails for the doors of the gates,
22:14 and bronze and *i* in such great quantities
22:16 skilled in gold, silver, bronze, and *i*.
29: 2 *i* for what will be made of iron,
29: 7 and one hundred thousand talents of *i*.
2Chr 2: 6 at work in gold, silver, bronze and *i*,
2:13 to work with gold, silver, bronze and *i*,
18:10 made *i* horns for himself and said:
Jdt 9: 8 overthrow with *i* the horns of your altar.
2Mc 11: 9 most savage beasts, yes, even walls of *i*.
Jb 19:24 That with an *i* chisel and with lead they
20:24 Should he escape the *i* weapon,
28: 2 *I* is taken from the earth,
40:18 his frame is like *i* rods.
41:19 He regards *i* as straw,
Ps(s) 2: 9 You shall rule them with an *i* rod;
107:16 the gates of brass and burst the bars of *i*.
149: 8 chains, their nobles with fetters of *i*;
Prv 27:17 As iron sharpens *i*,
Eccl 10:10 If the *i* becomes dull,
Sir 22:15 Sand and salt and an *i* mass are easier to
28:20 of *i* and its chains are chains of bronze!
38:28 standing near his anvil, forging crude *i*,
39:26 human life are water and fire, *i* and salt,
47:18 Gold you gathered like so much *i*,
48:17 With *i* tools he cut through the rock and
Is 44:12 The smith fashions an *i* image,
45: 2 I will shatter, and *i* bars I will snap.
48: 4 is an *i* sinew and your forehead bronze,
60:17 of bronze I will bring gold, instead of *i*,
60:17 of wood, bronze, instead of stones, *i*;
Jer 1:18 made you a fortified city, A pillar of *i*,
11: 4 out of the land of Egypt, that *i* foundry,
17: 1 sin of Judah is written with an *i* stylus,
28:13 a wooden yoke, you forge an *i* yoke!
28:14 A yoke of *i* I will place on the necks of
Ez 4: 3 *i* griddle and set it up as an iron wall
22:18 *i* and lead [in the midst of a furnace]:
22:20 Just as silver, bronze, *i*,
27:12 was your wealth, exchanging silver, *i*,
27:19 Javan exchanged wrought *i*,
Dn 2:33 iron, its feet partly *i* and partly tile.
2:34 put to it, struck its *i* and tile feet,
2:35 The *i*, tile, bronze, silver, and gold all
2:40 shall be a fourth kingdom, strong as *i*;
2:40 just as *i* breaks in pieces and crushes
2:41 partly of potter's tile and partly of *i*,
2:41 but yet have some of the hardness of *i*.
2:41 As you saw the *i* mixed with clay tile,
2:42 and the toes partly *i* and partly tile,
2:43 The *i* mixed with clay tile means that they
2:43 united, any more than *i* mixes with clay.
2:45 to it, which broke in pieces the tile, *i*,
4:12 and roots, fettered with *i* and bronze,
4:20 *i* and bronze in the grass of the field;
5: 4 gods of gold and silver, bronze and *i*,
5:23 the gods of silver and gold, bronze and *i*,
7: 7 it had great *i* teeth with which it
7:19 crushing with its *i* teeth and bronze claws,
Am 1: 3 they threshed Gilead with sledges of *i*,
Mi 4:13 horn I will make *i* And your hoofs bronze,
Acts 12:10 came to the *i* gate leading out to the city,
Rv 2:27 a rod of *i* and shatter them like crockery;
9: 9 of lions, their chests like *i* breastplates.
12: 5 to shepherd all the nations with an *i* rod.
18:12 bronze, *i* and marble;
19:15 He will shepherd them with an *i* rod;

IRON- (1)

2Chr 24:12 and also *i*- and bronze-smiths to repair it.

IRONS (1)

Acts 21:33 Paul and had him bound with double *i*.

IRPEEL (1)

Jos 18:27 Mizpeh, Chephirah, Mozah, Rekem, *I*,

IRREGULAR (1)

Jdt 2:20 A huge, *i* force,

IRRELIGIOUS (2)

Rom 1:18 the *i* and perverse spirit of men who,
1Tm 1: 9 lawless and unruly, the *i* and the sinful,

IRREPARABLE (1)

Est E- 5 and has involved them in *i* calamities by

IRREPROACHABLE (5)

1Thes 2:10 and *i* our conduct was toward you who are
5:23 *i* at the coming of our Lord Jesus Christ.
1Tm 3: 2 A bishop must be *i*,
Ti 1: 6 I instructed you, a presbyter must be *i*,
1Pt 3:21 but the pledge to God of an *i* conscience

IRRESISTIBLE (1)

2Mc 1:13 in Persia with his seemingly *i* army,

IRRESOLUTE (1)

Is 29: 9 Be *i*, stupefied; blind yourselves and stay

IRRESPONSIBLE (2)

Jb 30: 8 *I*, nameless men,
Ti 1:10 There are many *i* teachers,

IRREVOCABLE (5)

Est 1:19 let an *i* royal decree be issued by him and
Dn 6: 9 immutable and *i* under Mede and Persian law."
6:13 absolute, *i* under the Mede and Persian law."
6:16 law every royal prohibition or decree is *i*."
Rom 11:29 God's gifts and his call are *i*.

ISAAC (140)

Gn 17:19 bear you a son, and you shall call him *I*.
17:21 But my covenant I will maintain with *I*,
21: 3 *I* to this son of his whom Sarah bore him.
21: 4 When his son *I* was eight days old,
21: 5 years old when his son *I* was born to him.
21: 8 *I* grew,
21: 9 borne to Abraham playing with her son *I*;
21:10 to share the inheritance with my son *I*!"
21:12 *I* that descendants shall bear your name.
22: 2 "Take your son *I*,
22: 3 his donkey, took with him his son *I*,
22: 7 on together, *I* spoke to his father Abraham.
22: 7 *I* continued, "Here are the fire
22: 9 Next he tied up his son *I*,
24: 4 to my kindred to get a wife for my son *I*."
24:14 you have decided upon for your servant *I*.
24:62 Meanwhile *I* had gone from Beer-lahai-roi
24:66 recounted to *I* all the things he had done.
24:67 Then *I* took Rebekah into his tent;
24:67 In his love for her *I* found solace after
25: 5 everything that he owned to his son *I*.
25: 6 to the land of Kedem, away from his son *I*.
25: 9 His sons *I* and Ishmael buried him in the
25:11 death of Abraham, God blessed his son *I*,
25:19 This is the family history of *I*,
25:19 Abraham had begotten *I*.
25:20 *I* was forty years old when he married
25:21 *I* entreated the LORD on behalf of his wife,
25:26 *I* was sixty years old when they were born.
25:28 *I* preferred Esau,
26: 1 of Abraham), and *I* went down to Abimelech,
26: 6 So *I* settled in Gerar.
26: 8 to see *I* fondling his wife Rebekah.
26: 9 He called for *I* and said: "She must
26: 9 *I* replied, "I thought I might lose my life
26:12 *I* sowed a crop in that region and reaped a
26:16 So Abimelech said to *I*, "Go away from
26:17 *I* left there and made the Wadi Gerar his
26:18 *I* reopened the wells which his father's
26:23 From there *I* went up to Beer-sheba.
26:27 *I* asked them, "Why have you come to me,
26:30 *I* then made a feast for them,
26:31 Then *I* bade them farewell,
26:35 a source of embitterment to *I* and Rebekah.
27: 1 When *I* was so old that his eyesight had
27: 2 *I* then said, "As you can see, I am so old
27: 5 while *I* was speaking to his son Esau.
27:18 Jacob said, "Father!" "Yes?" replied *I*.
27:20 But *I* asked, "How did you succeed so
27:21 *I* then said to Jacob, "Come closer, son,
27:22 When *I* felt him, he said, "Although
27:25 Then *I* said, "Serve me your game, son,
27:25 Jacob served it to him, and *I* ate;
27:26 Finally his father *I* said to him,
27:27 *I* smelled the fragrance of his clothes.
27:30 just after *I* had finished blessing him,
27:32 "Who are you?" his father *I* asked him.
27:33 *I* was seized with a fit of uncontrollable
27:35 When *I* explained, "Your brother came
27:37 *I* replied: "I have already appointed
27:38 *I*, however, made no reply; and Esau wept
27:39 Finally *I* spoke again and said to him:
27:46 Rebekah said to *I*: "I am disgusted with
28: 1 *I* therefore called Jacob,
28: 5 Then *I* sent Jacob on his way;
28: 6 Esau noted that *I* had blessed Jacob when
28: 8 the Canaanite women were to his father *I*,
28:13 your forefather Abraham and the God of *I*;
31:18 go to his father *I* in the land of Canaan.
31:42 God of Abraham and the Awesome One of *I*,
31:53 took the oath by the Awesome One of *I*.
32:10 my father Abraham and God of my father *I*!
35:12 gave to Abraham and *I* I now give to you;
35:27 Jacob went home to his father *I* at Mamre,
35:27 Hebron], where Abraham and *I* had stayed.
35:28 of *I* was one hundred and eighty years;
46: 1 sacrifices to the God of his father *I*.
48:15 whose ways my fathers Abraham and *I* walked,
48:16 and the names of my fathers Abraham and *I*,
49:31 buried, and so are *I* and his wife Rebekah,
50:24 promised on oath to Abraham, *I* and Jacob."
Ex 2:24 of his covenant with Abraham, *I* and Jacob.
3: 6 "the God of Abraham, the God of *I*,
3:15 fathers, the God of Abraham, the God of *I*,
3:16 fathers, the God of Abraham, *I* and Jacob,
4: 5 fathers, the God of Abraham, the God of *I*,
6: 3 I appeared to Abraham, *I* and Jacob,
6: 8 I swore to give to Abraham, *I* and Jacob.
32:13 your servants Abraham, *I* and Israel,
33: 1 *I* and Jacob I would give to their
Lv 26:42 covenant with Jacob, my covenant with *I*,
Nm 32:11 under oath to Abraham and *I* and Jacob.
Dt 1: 8 to your fathers, Abraham, *I* and Jacob,
6:10 to your fathers, Abraham, *I* and Jacob,
9: 5 oath to your fathers, Abraham, *I* and Jacob.
9:27 your servants, Abraham, *I* and Jacob.
29:12 swore to your fathers Abraham, *I* and Jacob.
30:20 give to your fathers Abraham, *I* and Jacob."
34: 4 *I* and Jacob that I would give to their
Jos 24: 3 his descendants numerous, and gave him *I*.
24: 4 To *I* I gave Jacob and Esau.
1Kgs 18:36 and said, "LORD, God of Abraham, *I*,
2Kgs 13:23 because of his covenant with Abraham, *I*,
1Chr 1:28 The sons of Abraham were *I* and Ishmael.
1:34 Abraham became the father of *I*.
1:34 The sons of *I* were Esau and Israel.
16:16 into with Abraham and by his oath to *I*;
29:18 O LORD, God of our fathers Abraham, *I*,
2Chr 30: 6 the LORD, the God of Abraham, *I* and Israel,
Tb 4:12 My boy, keep in mind Noah, Abraham, *I*,
Jdt 8:26 he dealt with Abraham, and how he tried *I*,
2Mc 1: 2 faithful servants, Abraham, *I* and Jacob.
Ps(s) 105: 9 into with Abraham and by his oath to *I*;
Sir 44:22 And for *I* he renewed the same promise
Jer 33:26 rulers for the race of Abraham, *I*,
Bar 2:34 to their fathers, to Abraham, *I* and Jacob;
Dn 3:35 of Abraham, your beloved, *I* your servant,
Am 7: 9 The high places of *I* shall be laid waste,
7:16 Israel, preach not against the house of *I*.
Mt 1: 2 Abraham was the father of *I*,
1: 2 the father of Isaac, *I* the father of Jacob,
8:11 in the kingdom of God with Abraham, *I*,
22:32 'I am the God of Abraham, the God of *I*,
Mk 12:26 'I am the God of Abraham, the God of *I*,
Lk 3:34 son of Judah, son of Jacob, son of *I*,
13:28 grinding of teeth when you see Abraham, *I*,
20:37 Lord the God of Abraham, and the God of *I*,
Acts 3:13 The God of Abraham, of *I*,
7: 8 Abraham, who had become the father of *I*,
7: 8 *I* did the same for Jacob,
7:32 of your fathers, the God of Abraham, of *I*,
Rom 9: 7 *I* shall your descendants be called."
9:10 twin children by one man, our father *I*—
Gal 4:28 are children of the promise, as *I* was.
Heb 11: 7 when put to the test, offered up *I*
11: 9 dwelling in tents with *I* and Jacob,
11:18 *I* shall your descendants be called."
11:19 and so he received *I* back as a symbol.
11:20 By faith *I* invoked for Jacob and Esau
Jas 2:21 when he offered his son *I* on the altar?

ISAAC'S (4)

Gn 22: 6 and laid it on his son *I* shoulders,
26:19 But when *I* servants dug in the wadi and
26:20 of Gerar quarreled with *I* servants,
26:32 That same day *I* servants came and brought

ISAIAH (55)

2Kgs 19: 2 in sackcloth, to tell the prophet *I*,
19: 5 servants of King Hezekiah had come to *I*,
19:20 Then *I*, son of Amoz, sent this message
20: 1 Hezekiah was mortally ill, the prophet *I*,
20: 4 Before *I* had left the central courtyard,
20: 7 *I* then ordered a poultice of figs to be
20: 8 Then Hezekiah asked *I*, "What is the sign
20: 9 *I* replied, "This will be the sign for you
20:11 So the prophet *I* invoked the LORD,
20:14 Then *I* the prophet came to King Hezekiah
20:16 Then *I* said to Hezekiah: "Hear the word
20:19 Hezekiah replied to *I*, "The word of the
2Chr 26:22 The prophet *I*, son of Amos, wrote the rest
32:20 of this, King Hezekiah and the prophet *I*,
32:32 written in the Vision of the Prophet *I*,
Sir 48:20 they uttered and saved them through *I*.
48:22 As ordered by the illustrious prophet *I*,
Is 1: 1 The vision which *I*, son of Amoz,
2: 1 This is what *I*, son of Amoz, saw concerning
7: 3 Then the LORD said to *I*: Go out to meet
13: 1 a vision of *I*, son of Amoz.
20: 2 it, the LORD gave a warning through *I*,
20: 3 Just as my servant *I* has gone naked and
37: 2 in sackcloth, to tell the prophet *I*,
37: 5 servants of King Hezekiah had come to *I*,
37:21 Then *I*, son of Amoz, sent this message to
38: 1 Hezekiah was mortally ill, the prophet *I*,
38: 4 Then the word of the LORD came to *I*:
38: 7 *I* answered:] "This will be the sign
38:21 *I* then ordered a poultice of figs to be
39: 3 Then *I* the prophet came to King Hezekiah
39: 5 Then *I* said to Hezekiah, "Hear the word
39: 8 Hezekiah replied to *I*, "The word of the
Mt 3: 3 that the prophet *I* had spoken when he said:
4:14 what had been said through *I* the prophet:
8:17 what had been said through *I* the prophet:
12:17 what had been said through *I* the prophet:
15: 7 did *I* prophesy about you when he said:
Mk 1: 2 In *I* the prophet it is written: "I send my
7: 6 "How accurately *I* prophesied about you
Lk 3: 4 in the book of the words of *I* the prophet:
4:17 the book of the prophet *I* was handed him,
Jn 1:23 quoting the prophet *I*, "I am 'a voice
12:38 was to fulfill the word of the prophet *I*:
12:39 not believe was that, as *I* says elsewhere:
12:41 *I* uttered these words because he had seen
Acts 8:28 in his carriage reading the prophet *I*.
8:30 and heard the man reading the prophet *I*.
28:25 said to your fathers through the prophet *I*:
Rom 9:27 *I* cries out, referring to Israel
9:29 It is just as *I* predicted: "Unless the Lord
10:16 *I* asks, "Lord, who has believed what he has
10:20 Then *I* says boldly, "I was found by those
15:12 Once more, *I* says, "The root of Jesse will

ISAIAH'S (1)

Mt 13:14 *I* prophecy is fulfilled in them which says:

ISCAH (1)

Gn 11:29 of Haran, the father of Milcah and *I*.

ISCARIOT (11)

Mt 10: 4 Simon the Zealot Party member, and Judas *I*,
26:14 *I* went off to the chief priests and said,
Mk 3:19 Simon of the Zealot Party, and Judas *I*,
14:10 Then Judas *I*, one of the Twelve, went off
Lk 6:16 Zealot, Judas son of James, and Judas *I*,
22: 3 took possession of Judas, the one called *I*,
Jn 6:71 talking about Judas, son of Simon the *I*,
12: 4 Judas *I*, one of his disciples
13: 2 had already induced Judas, son of Simon *I*,
13:26 it and gave it to Judas, son of Simon *I*.
14:22 Judas (not Judas *I*) said to him,

ISHBAAL (21)

2Sm 2: 8 Abner, son of Ner, Saul's general, took *I*,
2:10 *I*, son of Saul, was forty years old
2:12 Abner, son of Ner, and the servants of *I*,
2:15 twelve of the Benjaminites of *I*,
3: 7 *I*, son of Saul, said to Abner, "Why
3: 8 Enraged at the words of *I*,
3:11 *I* was no longer able to say a word to him.
3:14 the same time David sent messengers to *I*,
3:15 *I* sent for her and took her away from her
4: 1 When *I*, son of Saul, heard that Abner
4: 2 *I*, son of Saul, had two company leaders
4: 5 the house of *I* during the heat of the day,
4: 7 while *I* was lying asleep in his bedroom.
4: 8 *I* to David in Hebron and said to the king:
4: 8 "This is the head of *I*,
4:12 *I* and buried it in Abner's grave in Hebron.
23: 8 *I*, son of Hachamoni,
1Chr 11:11 *I*, the son of Hachamoni, chief of the Three.
12: 7 Elkanah, Isshiah, Azarel, Joezer, and *I*,
24:13 thirteenth to Huppah, the fourteenth to *I*,
27: 2 first division for the first month was *I*,

ISHBAH (1)

1Chr 4:17 the father of Miriam, Shammai, and *I*,

ISHBAK (2)

Gn 25: 2 bore him Zimran, Jokshan, Medan, Midian, *I*,
1Chr 1:32 she bore Zimran, Jokshan, Medan, Midian, *I*,

ISHHOD (1)

1Chr 7:18 His sister Molecheth bore *I*,

ISHI (6)

1Chr 2:31 The sons of *I*: Sheshan.
4:19 Shimon the Garmite and *I* the Maacathite.
4:20 son of *I* was Zoheth and the son of Zoheth.
4:42 Neariah, Rephaiah, and Uzziel, sons of *I*.
5:24 Epher, *I*, Eliel, Azriel, Jeremiah, Hodaviah,

ISHMA (1)

1Chr 4: 3 Jezreel, *I*,

ISHMAEL (46)

Gn 16:11 you shall name him *I*.
16:15 Abram named the son whom Hagar bore him *I*.
16:16 eighty-six years old when Hagar bore him *I*.
17:18 to God, "Let but *I* live on by your favor!"
17:20 As for *I*, I am heeding you:
17:23 Abraham took his son *I* and all his slaves,
17:25 his son *I* was thirteen years old
17:26 day Abraham and his son *I* were circumcised;
21:11 especially on account of his son *I*.
25: 9 and *I* buried him in the cave of Machpelah,
25:12 are the descendants of Abraham's son *I*,
25:16 These are the sons of *I*,
28: 9 were to his father Isaac, so he went to *I*,
28: 9 of Abraham's son *I* and sister of Nebaioth.
36: 3 daughter of *I* and sister of Nebaioth.
Nm 24:23 Alas, who shall survive of *I*,
2Kgs 25:23 *I*, son of Nethaniah,
25:25 But in the seventh month *I*,
1Chr 1:28 The sons of Abraham were Isaac and *I*.
1:29 Nebaioth, the first-born of *I*,
1:31 These were the descendants of *I*.
8:38 names were Azrikam, his first-born, *I*,
9:44 names were Azrikam, his first-born, *I*,
2Chr 19:11 to the LORD, and Zebadiah, son of *I*,
23: 1 *I*, son of Jehohanan; Azariah, son of Obed;
Ezr 10:22 Elioenai, Maaseiah, *I*,
Jer 40: 8 *I*, son of Nethaniah;
40:14 the king of the Ammonites, had sent *I*,
40:15 "Let me go and kill *I*,
40:16 you have lied about *I*."
41: 1 In the seventh month *I*,
41: 2 they were together at table in Mizpah, *I*,
41: 3 *I* also slew all the men of Judah of
41: 6 *I* son of Nethaniah, went out from Mizpah
41: 7 When they were once inside the city, *I*,
41: 8 were ten among them who pleaded with *I*:
41: 9 The cistern into which *I* threw all the
41: 9 this cistern *I*, son of Nethaniah, filled with
41:10 *I*, son of Nethaniah,
41:10 With these captives, *I*, son of Nethaniah,
41:11 leaders with him heard of the crimes *I*,
41:12 took all their men and set out to attack *I*,
41:14 All of those whom *I* had brought away from
41:15 But *I*, son of Nethaniah, escaped from
41:16 and children with their guardians, whom *I*,
41:18 were afraid of the Chaldeans, because *I*,

ISHMAELITE (3)

2Sm 17:25 son of an *I* named Ithra
1Chr 2:17 bore Amasa, whose father was Jether the *I*.
27:30 over the camels was Obil the *I*;

ISHMAELITES (8)

Gn 25:18 The *I* ranged from Havilah-by-Shur,
37:25 they saw a caravan of *I* coming from Gilead,
37:27 Rather, let us sell him to these *I*,
37:28 to the *I* for twenty pieces of silver.
39: 1 him from the *I* who had brought him there.
Jgs 8:24 (For being *I*, the enemy had gold rings.)
Jdt 2:23 plundered all the Rassisites and the *I*
Ps(s) 83: 7 The tents of Edom and the *I*,

ISHMAEL'S (4)

Gn 25:13 These are the names of *I* sons,
25:13 Nebaioth *I* first-born),
25:17 The span of *I* life was one hundred
Jer 41:13 the people who were *I* captives rejoiced.

ISHMAIAH (2)

1Chr 12: 4 *I* the Gibeonite,
27:19 for Zebulun, *I*,

ISHMERAI (1)

1Chr 8:18 Zebadiah, Meshullam, Hizki, Heber, *I*,

ISHPAH (1)

1Chr 8:16 Zebadiah, Arad, Eder, Michael, *I*,

ISHPAN (1)

1Chr 8:22 and Shimrath were the sons of Shimei, *I*,

ISHVAH (1)

Gn 46:17 Imnah, *I*, Ishvi, and Beriah,

ISHVI (4)

Gn 46:17 Imnah, Ishvah, *I*,
Nm 26:44 through *I* the clan of the Ishvites,
1Sm 14:49 The sons of Saul were Jonathan, *I*,
1Chr 7:30 The sons of Asher were Imnah, Iishvah, *I*,

ISHVITES (1)

Nm 26:44 Imnites, through Ishvi the clan of the *I*,

ISLAND (10)

Acts 13: 6 traveled over the whole *i* as far as Paphos,
27:16 We passed under the lee of a small *i* named
27:26 we still have to face shipwreck on some *i*."
28: 1 we learned that the *i* was called Malta.
28: 7 of Publius, the chief figure on the *i*.
28: 9 the rest of the sick on the *i* began to
28:11 ship which had passed the winter at the *i*.
Rv 1: 9 found myself on the *i* called Patmos
6:14 mountain and *i* was uprooted from its base.
16:20 Every *i* fled and mountains disappeared.

ISLANDS (7)

Est 10: 1 on the land and on the *i* of the sea.
1Mc 6:29 other kingdoms and from the *i* of the seas.
8:11 All the other kingdoms and *i* that had ever
11:38 he had hired from the *i* of the nations.
15: 1 a letter from the *i* of the sea to Simon,
Sir 43:24 the deep, and plants the *i* in the sea.
Ez 26:18 On this, the day of your fall, the *i* quake!

ISLES (6)

1Mc 14: 5 and made it a gateway to the *i* of the sea.
Ps(s) 72:10 of Tarshish and the *I* shall offer gifts;
97: 1 let the many *i* be glad.
Is 11:11 Elam, Shinar, Hamath, and the *i* of the sea.
Ez 26:15 slays in your midst, shall not the *i* quake?
26:18 *i* in the sea are terrified at your passing.

ISMACHIAH (1)

2Chr 31:13 Asahel, Jerimoth, Jozabad, Eliel, *I*,

ISOLATE (1)

1Mc 12:36 that would *i* the citadel and so prevent

ISOLATED (1)

Lv 16:22 carry off their iniquities to an *i* region,

ISRAEL (1961)

Gn 32:29 no longer be spoken of as Jacob, but as *I*,
33:20 stone there and invoked "El, the God of *I*."
34: 7 What Shechem had done was an outrage in *I*;
35:10 be called Jacob, but *I* shall be your name."
35:10 Thus he was named *I*.
35:21 *I* moved on and pitched his tent beyond
35:22 While *I* was encamped in that region,
35:22 When *I* heard of it, he was greatly offended.
37: 3 *I* loved Joseph best of all his sons,
37:13 flocks at Shechem, *I* said to Joseph,
42: 5 the sons of *I* were among those who came to
43: 6 *I* demanded, "Why did you bring this
43: 8 Then Judah urged his father *I*:
43:11 Their father *I* then told them:
45:21 The sons of *I* acted accordingly.
45:28 "It is enough," said *I*.
46: 1 *I* set out with all that was his.
46: 2 God, speaking to *I* in a vision by night,
46: 5 and the sons of *I* put their father and
46:28 *I* had sent Judah ahead to Joseph,
46:29 and rode to meet his father *I* in Goshen.
46:30 And *I* said to Joseph, "At last I can die,
47:27 Thus *I* settled in the land of Egypt,
47:29 When the time approached for *I* to die,
47:31 Then *I* bowed at the head of the bed.
48: 8 When *I* saw Joseph's sons,
48:11 Then *I* said to Joseph,
48:14 But *I*, crossing his hands, put out his right
48:20 shall the people of *I* pronounce blessings;
48:21 Then *I* said to Joseph: "I am about to die.
49: 2 and listen, sons of Jacob, listen to *I*,
49: 7 them in Jacob, disperse them throughout *I*.
49:16 for his kindred like any other tribe of *I*.
49:24 because of the Shepherd, the Rock of *I*,
49:28 All these are the twelve tribes of *I*,
50: 2 When they embalmed *I*,
50:25 Then, putting the sons of *I* under oath,
Ex 1: 1 These are the names of the sons of *I* who,
3:18 Then you and the elders of *I* shall go to
4:22 *I* is my son, my first-born.

5: 1 said, "Thus says the LORD, the God of *I*:
5: 2 that I should heed his plea to let *I* go?
5: 2 even if I did, I would not let *I* go."
6:14 The sons of Reuben, the first-born of *I*,
9: 4 the livestock of *I* and that of Egypt,
12: 3 Tell the whole community of *I*:
12: 6 with the whole assembly of *I* present,
12:15 day to the seventh shall be cut off from *I*.
12:19 shall be cut off from the community of *I*.
12:21 all the elders of *I* and said to them,
12:47 whole community of *I* must keep this feast.
14: 5 "Why, we have released *I* from our service!"
14:20 the camp of the Egyptians and that of *I*.
14:25 Egyptians sounded the retreat before *I*,
14:30 Thus the LORD saved *I* on that day from the
14:30 When *I* saw the Egyptians lying dead on the
15:22 Then Moses led *I* forward from the Red Sea,
17: 5 along with some of the elders of *I*,
17: 6 did, in the presence of the elders of *I*.
17: 8 Amalek came and waged war against *I*.
17:11 raised up, *I* had the better of the fight,
18: 1 had done for Moses and for his people *I*:
18: 1 how the LORD had brought *I* out of Egypt.
18: 8 and the Egyptians for the sake of *I*,
18: 9 goodness that the LORD had shown *I*
18:12 Aaron came with all the elders of *I*
18:25 He picked out able men from all *I* and put
19: 2 While *I* was encamped here in front of the
24: 1 Abihu, and seventy of the elders of *I*,
24: 4 twelve pillars for the twelve tribes of *I*.
24: 9 Nadab, Abihu, and seventy elders of *I*,
24:10 of Israel, and they beheld the God of *I*.
28: 9 on them the names of the sons of *I*;
28:11 *I* and then mounted in gold filigree work.
28:12 ephod as memorial stones of the sons of *I*.
28:21 them to match the names of the sons of *I*,
28:29 names of the sons of *I* on the breastpiece
32: 4 they cried out, "This is your God, O *I*,
32: 8 it and crying out, 'This is your God, O *I*,
32:13 your servants Abraham, Isaac and *I*,
32:27 them, "Thus says the LORD, the God of *I*:
34:23 appear before the Lord, the LORD God of *I*.
34:27 I have made a covenant with you and with *I*."
39: 6 engravings with the names of the sons of *I*.
39: 7 ephod as memorial stones of the sons of *I*,
39:14 to match the names of the sons of *I*,
40:38 of *I* in all the stages of their journey.
Lv 4:13 "If the whole community of *I* inadvertently
9: 1 his sons, together with the elders of *I*,
9: 3 Tell the elders of *I*, too: Take a he-goat
10: 6 Your kinsmen, the rest of the house of *I*,
17: 8 of *I* or of the aliens residing among them,
17:10 of *I* or of the aliens residing among them,
20: 2 an Israelite or an alien residing in *I*,
22:18 of Israel, or any alien residing in *I*,
Nm 1: 3 in companies all the men in *I* of twenty
1:16 tribes, chiefs of the troops of *I*.
1:20 of Reuben, the first-born of *I*,
1:44 and Aaron and the twelve princes of *I*.
3:13 made all the first-born in *I* sacred to me,
7: 2 an offering was made by the princes of *I*,
7:84 of *I* on the occasion of its anointing:
10: 4 the princes, the chiefs of the troops of *I*,
10:29 for the LORD has promised prosperity to *I*."
10:36 ride upon the clouds, to the troops of *I*.
11:16 for me seventy of the elders of *I*,
11:30 to the camp, along with the elders of *I*.
16: 9 God of *I* has singled you out
16: 9 singled you out from the community of *I*,
16:25 Moses, followed by the elders of *I*,
18:14 Whatever is doomed in *I* shall be yours.
18:21 I hereby assign all tithes in *I* as their
19:13 of the LORD and shall be cut off from *I*.
20:14 "Your brother *I* has this to say:
20:21 their territory, *I* detoured around them.
20:29 days the whole house of *I* mourned him.
21: 2 *I* then made this vow to the LORD:
21:17 Then it was that *I* sang this song:
21:21 Now *I* sent men to Sihon,
21:23 would not let *I* pass through his territory,
21:23 and advanced into the desert against *I*.
21:23 he reached Jahaz, he engaged *I* in battle.
21:24 *I* defeated him at the point of the sword,
21:25 *I* seized all the towns here and settled in
21:31 *I* had settled in the land of the Amorites,
21:32 *I* then captured it with its dependencies
22: 2 Zippor, saw all that *I* did to the Amorites.
23: 7 curse for me on Jacob, come and denounce *I*."
23:21 observed in Jacob, nor misery seen in *I*.
23:23 sorcery against Jacob, nor omen against *I*.
23:23 It shall yet be said of Jacob, and of *I*,
24: 1 that the LORD was pleased to bless *I*,
24: 2 When he raised his eyes and saw *I* encamped,
24: 5 your encampments, O *I*!
24:17 from Jacob, and a staff shall rise from *I*,
24:18 *I* shall do valiantly,
25: 1 While *I* was living at Shittim,
25: 3 When *I* thus submitted to the rites of Baal
25: 3 Peor, the LORD's anger flared up against *I*.
25: 4 blazing wrath may be turned away from *I*."
26: 2 more who are fit for military service in *I*."
26: 5 Of Reuben, the first-born of *I*,
31: 4 From each of the tribes of *I* you shall
31: 5 From the clans of *I*, therefore, a thousand
32: 4 has laid low before the community of *I*,
32:22 of every obligation to the LORD and to *I*,
Dt 1: 1 to all *I* beyond the Jordan [in the desert,
1:38 him, for he is to give *I* its heritage.
4: 1 "Now, *I*, hear the statutes and decrees
5: 1 summoned all *I* and said to them, "Hear, O *I*
6: 3 Hear then, *I*, and be careful to observe them,
6: 4 "Hear, O *I*! The LORD is our God,
9: 1 "Hear, O *I*! You are now about to cross
10:12 "And now, *I*, what does the LORD, your
11: 6 swallowed them up out of the midst of *I*,
13:12 And all *I*, hearing of it, shall fear and never
17: 4 this abomination has been committed in *I*,
17:20 descendants will enjoy a long reign in *I*.
18: 1 have no share in the heritage with *I*;
18: 6 in *I* in which he ordinarily resides,
19:13 *I* the stain of shedding innocent blood,
20: 3 'Hear, O *I*! Today you are going
21: 8 Absolve, O LORD, your people *I*,
21: 8 blood remain in the midst of your people *I*.'
21:21 purge the evil from your midst, and all *I*,
22:19 because the man defamed a virgin in *I*.
22:21 she committed a crime against *I* by her
25: 6 his name may not be blotted out from *I*.
25: 7 to perpetuate his brother's name in *I*.'
25:10 And his lineage shall be spoken of in *I* as
26:15 and bless your people *I* and the soil you
27: 1 Then Moses, with the elders of *I*,
27: 9 the levitical priests, then said to all *I*:
27: 9 "Be silent, O *I* and listen!
27:14 shall proclaim aloud to all the men of *I*:
29: 1 Moses summoned all *I* and said to them,
29: 9 and officials, and all of the men of *I*,
29:20 him out from all the tribes of *I* for doom,
31: 1 finished speaking these words to all *I*,
31: 7 and in the presence of all *I* said to him,
31: 9 of the LORD, and to all the elders of *I*,
31:11 when all *I* goes to appear before the LORD,
31:11 this law aloud in the presence of all *I*.
31:30 end, for the whole assembly of *I* to hear:
32: 9 was Jacob, His hereditary share was *I*.
32:45 speaking all these words to all *I*,
33: 5 people assembled and the tribes of *I* came
33:10 your decisions to Jacob and your law to *I*.
33:21 of the LORD and his decrees respecting *I*."
33:28 *I* has dwelt securely,
33:29 How fortunate you are, O *I*!
34:10 then no prophet has arisen in *I* like Moses,
34:12 that Moses exhibited in the sight of all *I*.
Jos 3: 7 begin to exalt you in the sight of all *I*,
3:12 one from each of the tribes of *I*
3:17 While all *I* crossed over on dry ground,
4:14 LORD exalted Joshua in the sight of all *I*,
4:22 *I* crossed the Jordan here on dry ground.'
6:18 camp of *I* this ban and the misery of it.
6:23 and placed them outside the camp of *I*.
6:25 who continue in the midst of *I* to this day.
7: 6 Joshua, together with the elders of *I*,
7: 8 that *I* has turned its back to its enemies?
7:11 *I* has sinned: They have violated
7:13 tomorrow, for the LORD, the God of *I*,
7:13 You are under the ban, O *I*.
7:15 and has committed a shameful crime in *I*."
7:16 Joshua had *I* come forward by tribes,
7:19 "My son, give to the LORD, the God of *I*,
7:20 sinned against the LORD, the God of *I*.
7:24 Then Joshua and all *I* took Achan,
7:25 And all *I* stoned him to death and piled a
8:10 up to Ai at its head, with the elders of *I*.
8:14 early in the morning to engage *I* in battle
8:24 Then all *I* returned and put to the sword
8:30 built an altar to the LORD, the God of *I*,
8:33 all *I*, stranger and native alike,
8:33 of the people of *I* on this first occasion.
8:35 and the strangers who had accompanied *I*.
9: 2 a common attack against Joshua and *I*.
9: 6 they said to him and to the men of *I*,
9: 7 But the men of *I* replied to the Hivites,
9:16 were from nearby, and would be living in *I*.
9:18 sworn to them by the LORD, the God of *I*.
9:19 sworn to them by the LORD, the God of *I*,
10: 1 of Gibeon had made their peace with *I*,
10:11 before *I* along the descent from Beth-horon,
10:12 to the LORD, and said in the presence of *I*:
10:14 for the LORD fought for *I*.
10:15 and all *I* returned to the camp at Gilgal.]
10:24 Joshua summoned all the men of *I* and said
10:29 on with all *I* from Makkedah to Libnah,
10:30 the LORD delivered into the power of *I*.
10:31 on with all *I* from Libnah to Lachish,
10:32 delivered Lachish into the power of *I*,
10:34 Joshua passed on with all *I* to Eglon;
10:36 Eglon, Joshua went up with all *I* to Hebron,
10:38 all *I* turned back to Debir and attacked it,
10:40 there, just as the LORD, the God of *I*,
10:42 the LORD, the God of Israel, fought for *I*.
10:43 with all *I* returned to the camp at Gilgal.
11: 5 they encamped together to fight against *I*.
11: 6 I will stretch them slain before *I*.
11:13 *I* did not destroy by fire any of the
11:16 the mountain regions and foothills of *I*,
11:20 to encourage them to wage war against *I*,
11:21 Judah, and the entire mountain region of *I*.
11:23 Joshua gave it to *I* as their heritage,
12: 7 Joshua apportioned to the tribes of *I*.
13:13 survive in the midst of *I* to this day.
13:14 had promised them, the LORD, the God of *I*,
13:33 Levi, since the LORD himself, the God of *I*,
14:10 while *I* was journeying through the desert,
14:14 completely loyal to the LORD, the God of *I*.
21:43 And so the LORD gave *I* all the land he had
21:45 the LORD made to the house of *I* was broken;
22:14 ten princes, one from every tribe of *I*,
22:16 you have committed against the God of *I*?
22:18 be angry with the whole community of *I*!
22:20 wrath fall upon the entire community of *I*?
22:22 the God of gods, knows and *I* shall know.
22:24 have you to do with the LORD, the God of *I*?
23: 2 he summoned all *I* (including their elders,
24: 1 together all the tribes of *I* at Shechem,
24: 2 "Thus says the LORD, the God of *I*:
24: 9 king of Moab, prepared to war against *I*.
24:23 your hearts to the LORD, the God of *I*."
24:31 *I* served the LORD during the entire
24:31 and knew all that the LORD had done for *I*.
Jgs 2: 7 great work which the LORD had done for *I*,
2:10 know the LORD, or what he had done for *I*,
2:14 the anger of the LORD flared up against *I*,
2:20 In his anger toward *I* the LORD said,
2:23 or delivering them into the power of *I*.
3: 4 These served to put *I* to the test,
3:10 of the LORD came upon him, and he judged *I*.
3:12 Eglon, king of Moab, against *I*.
3:13 Amalekites, he attacked and defeated *I*,
3:30 brought under the power of *I* at that time;
3:31 with an oxgoad. He, too, rescued *I*.
4: 4 Deborah, wife of Lappidoth, was judging *I*.
4: 6 "This is what the LORD, the God of *I*,
5: 2 Of chiefs who took the lead in *I*,
5: 3 my song, my hymn to the LORD, the God of *I*.
5: 5 in the presence of the LORD, the God of *I*.
5: 7 beyond the walls, gone indeed from *I*.
5: 7 Deborah, rose, when I rose, a mother in *I*,
5: 8 nor a lance, among forty thousand in *I*!
5: 9 My heart is with the leaders of *I*,
5:11 his just deeds that brought freedom to *I*.
6: 2 years, so that Midian held *I* subject.
6: 4 of Gaza, leaving no sustenance in *I*,
6: 6 Thus was *I* reduced to misery by Midian,
6: 7 *I* cried out to the LORD because of Midian,
6: 8 who said to them, "The LORD, the God of *I*,
6:14 have and save *I* from the power of Midian.
6:15 him, "Please, my lord, how can I save *I*?
6:36 indeed you are going to save *I* through me,
6:37 shall know that you will save *I* through me,
7: 2 lest *I* vaunt itself against me and say,
7:15 Then returning to the camp of *I*,
8:27 all *I* paid idolatrous homage to it there,
8:35 for all the good he had done for *I*.
9:22 When Abimelech had ruled *I* for three years,
10: 1 there rose to save *I* the Issacharite Tola,
10: 2 When he had judged *I* twenty-three years,
10: 3 after him and judged *I* twenty-two years.
10: 7 the LORD became angry with *I* and allowed
10: 9 Ephraim, so that *I* was in great distress.
10:16 so that he grieved over the misery of *I*.
11: 4 Some time later, the Ammonites warred on *I*.
11:13 *I* took away my land from the Arnon to the
11:15 *I* did not take the land of Moab or the
11:16 *I* went through the desert to the Red Sea
11:17 *I* then sent messengers to the king of Edom
11:17 So *I* remained in Kadesh.
11:19 Then *I* sent messengers to Sihon,
11:19 *I* said to him, 'Let me pass through your
11:20 to let *I* pass through his territory.
11:20 who encamped at Jahaz and fought *I*.
11:21 But the LORD, the God of *I*,
11:21 Sihon and all his men into the power of *I*,
11:23 If now the LORD, the God of *I*,
11:23 way of his people, are you to dislodge *I*?
11:25 Did he ever quarrel with *I*,
11:26 when *I* occupied Heshbon and its villages,
11:39 It then became a custom in *I* for Israelite
12: 7 After having judged *I* for six years,
12: 8 After him Ibzan of Bethlehem judged *I*.
12: 9 After having judged *I* for seven years,
12:11 After him the Zebulunite Elon judged *I*.
12:11 When he had judged *I* for ten years,
12:13 Abdon, son of Hillel, judged *I*.
12:14 After having judged *I* for eight years,
13: 5 of *I* from the power of the Philistines."
14: 4 for at that time they had dominion over *I*.
15:20 Samson judged *I* for twenty years in the
16:31 He had judged *I* for twenty years.
17: 6 In those days there was no king in *I*;
18: 1 At that time there was no king in *I*.
18: 1 received no heritage among the tribes of *I*.
18:19 to be priest for a tribe and a clan in *I*?"
18:29 it Dan after their ancestor Dan, son of *I*.
19: 1 At that time, when there was no king in *I*,
19:29 sent them throughout the territory of *I*.
20: 2 all the people and all the tribesmen of *I*,
20: 6 through every part of the territory of *I*,
20: 6 monstrous crime they had committed in *I*.
20:10 the tribes of *I* ten men for every hundred,

ISRAEL (cont.)

20:10 Benjamin for the crime it committed in I."
20:11 all the men of I without exception were
20:12 the tribes of I sent men throughout the
20:13 to death and thus purge the evil from I."
20:21 and felled twenty-two thousand men of I.
20:29 So I set men in ambush around Gibeah.
20:33 all the men of I rose from their places.
20:34 Gibeah, ten thousand picked men from all I,
20:35 the LORD defeated Benjamin before I;
20:36 for the men of I gave ground to Benjamin,
20:39 killing off some thirty of the men of I,
20:41 the sky that the men of I wheeled about.
20:42 men of I in the direction of the desert,
20:48 The men of I withdrew through the
21: 1 Now the men of I had sworn at Mizpah that
21: 3 God of I, why has it come to pass in I
21: 3 today one tribe of I should be lacking?"
21: 5 "Are there any among all the tribes of I who
21: 6 one of the tribes of I has been cut off.
21: 8 of I had not come up to the LORD in Mizpah,
21:15 had made a breach among the tribes of I.
21:25 In those days there was no king in I;
Ru 2:12 a full reward from the LORD, the God of I,
4: 7 Now it used to be the custom in I that,
4: 7 This was the form of attestation in I.
4:11 who between them built up the house of I.
4:14 May he become famous in I!
1Sm 1:17 of I grant you what you have asked of him."
2:22 how his sons were treating all I
2:28 of all the tribes of I to be my priests,
2:29 part of every offering of my people I?'
2:30 is the oracle of the LORD, the God of I:
2:32 rival all the benefits enjoyed by I,
3:11 "I am about to do something in I that
3:20 Thus all I from Dan to Beer-sheba came to
4: 1 Philistines gathered for an attack on I.
4: 1 I went out to engage them in battle and
4: 1 and Samuel spoke to all I.
4: 2 then drew up in battle formation against I.
4: 2 struggle I was defeated by the Philistines,
4: 3 retired to the camp, the elders of I said,
4: 5 all I shouted so loudly that the earth
4:10 The Philistines fought and I was defeated;
4:10 which I lost thirty thousand foot soldiers.
4:17 I fled from the Philistines;
4:18 He had judged I for forty years.
4:21 saying, "Gone is the glory from I,"
4:22 She said, "Gone is the glory from I,"
5: 7 'The ark of the God of I must not remain
5: 8 shall we do with the ark of the God of I?"
5: 8 "Let them move the ark of the God of I
5: 9 they moved the ark of the God of I to Gath!
5:10 God of I here to kill us and our kindred?"
5:11 "Send away the ark of the God of I.
6: 3 to send away the ark of the God of I,
6: 5 and give them as a tribute to the God of I.
7: 5 then gave orders, "Gather all I to Mizpah,
7: 7 at Mizpah, their lords went up against I.
7: 9 He implored the LORD for I,
7:10 Philistines advanced to join battle with I.
7:10 confusion that they were defeated by I.
7:13 never again to enter the territory of I,
7:14 had taken from I were restored to them.
7:14 I also freed the territory of these cities
7:14 there was peace between I and the Amorites.
7:15 Samuel judged I as long as he lived.
7:16 and judging I at each of these sanctuaries.
7:17 he judged I and built an altar to the LORD.
8: 1 Samuel appointed his sons judges over I.
8: 4 Therefore all the elders of I came in a
8:22 Samuel thereupon said to the men of I,
9: 9 (In former times in I,
9:16 are to anoint as commander of my people I.
9:20 Whom does I desire ardently if not you and
9:21 of one of the smallest tribes of I,
10: 1 You are to govern the LORD's people I,
10:18 the God of I, 'It was I who brought I
10:20 had all the tribes of I come forward,
11: 2 that I may thus bring ignominy on all I."
11: 3 throughout the territory of I.
11: 7 of I by couriers with the message,
11:13 this day, for today the LORD has saved I."
12: 1 Samuel addressed all I: "I have granted
13: 1 He reigned (two) years over I.
13: 2 Saul chose three thousand men of I,
13: 4 Thus all I learned that Saul had overcome
13: 4 I had brought disgrace upon the Philistines;
13: 5 Moving up against I,
13:13 establish your kingship in I as lasting;
13:19 was to be found in the whole land of I,
13:20 All I, therefore, had to go down
14:12 has delivered them into the grasp of I."
14:23 Thus the LORD saved I that day.
14:37 Will you deliver them into the power of I?"
14:39 the LORD lives who has given victory to I,
14:40 So he said to all I, "Stand on one side,
14:41 And Saul said to the LORD, the God of I:
14:41 in me or my son Jonathan, LORD, God of I,
14:41 but if this guilt is in your people I,
14:45 it was he who brought I this great victory?
14:47 After taking over the kingship of I,
14:48 He defeated Amalek and delivered I from
15: 1 sent to anoint you king over his people I.
15: 2 'I will punish what Amalek did to I when
15:17 are you not leader of the tribes of I?
15:17 you king of I and sent you on a mission,
15:26 LORD and the LORD rejects you as king of I."
15:28 torn the kingdom of I from you this day,
15:29 Glory of I neither retracts nor repents,
15:30 the elders of my people and before I.
15:35 LORD regretted having made him king of I.
16: 1 Saul, whom I have rejected as king of I?
17: 8 He stood and shouted to the ranks of I:
17:10 "I defy the ranks of I today.
17:11 Saul and all the men of I,
17:19 and all I are fighting against the
17:25 He comes up to insult I.
17:25 exemption to his father's family in I."
17:26 Philistine and frees I of the disgrace?
17:45 of the armies of I that you have insulted.
17:46 whole land shall learn that I has a God.
17:52 Then the men of I and Judah,
18: 6 each of the cities of I to meet King Saul,
18:16 the other hand, all I and Judah loved him,
18:18 who are my kin or my father's clan in I
19: 5 a great victory for all I through him,
20:12 "As the LORD, the God of I,
23:10 "O LORD God of I, your servant has heard
23:11 O LORD God of I, tell your servant."
23:17 be king of I and I shall be second to you.
24: 3 picked men from all I and went in search
24:15 whom are you on campaign, O king of I?
24:21 over I shall come into your possession,
25: 1 died, and all I gathered to mourn him;
25:30 you, and appoints you as commander over I,
25:32 "Blessed be the LORD, the God of I,
25:34 Otherwise, as the LORD, the God of I,
26: 2 Ziph with three thousand picked men of I,
26:15 not a man whose like does not exist in I?
26:20 For the king of I has come out to seek a
27: 1 search for me throughout the land of I,
27:12 must certainly be detested by his people I.
28: 1 their military forces to fight against I.
28: 3 had died and, after being mourned by all I,
28: 4 Saul, too, mustered all I;
28:19 Moreover, the LORD will deliver I,
28:19 of I into the hands of the Philistines."
29: 3 is David, the officer of Saul, king of I.
30:25 forward he made it a law and a custom in I,
31: 1 As they pressed their attack on I,
31: 7 men of I had fled and that Saul and his
2Sm 1:12 the soldiers of the LORD of the clans of I,
1:19 the glory of I, Saul, slain upon your heights;
1:24 Women of I, weep over Saul, who clothed
2: 9 Ephraim, Benjamin, and the rest of I.
2:10 forty years old when he became king over I,
2:17 men of I were defeated by David's servants.
2:28 pursuing I no farther and fighting no more.
3:10 I and over Judah from Dan to Beer-sheba."
3:12 will aid you by bringing all I over to you."
3:17 said in discussion with the elders of I:
3:18 I will save my people I from the grasp
3:19 to I and to the whole house of Benjamin.
3:21 go to assemble all I for my lord the king,
3:37 So on that day all the people and all I
3:38 that a great general has fallen today in I.
4: 1 he ceased to resist and all I was alarmed.
5: 1 of I came to David in Hebron and said:
5: 2 people Israel and shall be commander of I.'"
5: 3 the elders of I came to David in Hebron,
5: 3 the LORD, and they anointed him king of I.
5: 5 years in Jerusalem over all I and Judah.
5:12 the LORD had established him as king of I
5:12 his rule for the sake of his people I.
5:17 that David had been anointed king of I,
6: 1 again assembled all the picked men of I,
6:19 each woman in the entire multitude of I,
6:20 the king of I has honored himself today,
6:21 me commander of the LORD's people, I,
7: 7 judges whom I charged to tend my people I,
7: 8 the flock to be commander of my people I.
7:10 I will fix a place for my people I;
7:11 I first appointed judges over my people I.
7:23 on earth is there like your people I,
7:24 yourself your people I as yours forever,
7:26 men say, 'The LORD of hosts is God of I,'
7:27 It is you, LORD of hosts, God of I,
8:15 David reigned over all I,
10: 9 of I and arrayed them against the Arameans.
10:15 by I with a full mustering of troops;
10:17 receiving this news, David assembled all I,
10:18 But the Arameans gave way before I,
10:19 kings, in view of their defeat by I,
11: 1 along with his officers and the army of I,
11:11 ark and I and Judah are lodged in tents,
12: 7 Thus says the LORD God of I:
12: 7 'I anointed you king of I.
12: 8 I gave you the house of I and of Judah.
12:12 bring it about in the presence of all I,
13:12 That is an intolerable crime in I.
13:13 And you would be a discredited man in I.
14:25 In all I there was not a man who could so
15: 2 servant is of such and such a tribe of I,"
15: 6 away the loyalties of the men of I.
15:10 spies throughout the tribes of I to say,
16:18 and all this people and all I have chosen,
16:21 When all I hears how odious you have made
16:22 his father's concubines in view of all I.
17: 4 to Absalom and to all the elders of I.
17:10 For all I knows that your father is a
17:11 Let all I from Dan to Beer-sheba,
17:13 all I shall bring ropes to that city and
17:15 gave Absalom and the elders of I,
17:26 I and Absalom encamped in the territory of
18: 6 army then took the field against I,
18: 7 of I were defeated by David's servants,
19:10 but throughout the tribes of I all the
19:11 When the talk of all I reached the king,
19:23 Should anyone die today in I?
19:23 Am I not aware that today I am king of I?"
19:41 people of I had escorted the king across.
19:43 All the Judahites replied to the men of I:
20: 1 Every man to his tent, O I!"
20:14 all the tribes of I to Abel Beth-maacah.
20:19 to beat down a city that is a mother in I.
20:19 whether loyalty is finished or ended in I.'
20:23 Joab was in command of the whole army of I.
21: 2 off in his zeal for the men of I and Judah.)
21: 4 it our place to put any man to death in I."
21: 5 have no place in all the territory of I,
21:15 battle between the Philistines and I.
21:17 us again lest you quench the lamp of I."
21:21 And when he insulted I,
23: 1 of Jacob, favorite of the Mighty One of I.
23: 3 God of I spoke; of me the Rock of Israel
24: 1 The LORD's anger against I flared again,
24: 1 by prompting him to number I and Judah.
24: 2 "Tour all the tribes in I from Dan to
24: 4 in order to register the people of I.
24: 9 in I, eight hundred thousand men fit
24:15 I from morning until the time appointed,
24:25 country, and the plague was checked in I.
1Kgs 1: 3 girl throughout the territory of I,
1:20 all I is waiting for you to make known to
1:30 I swore to you by the LORD, the God of I,
1:34 the prophet are to anoint him king of I,
1:35 I designate him ruler of I and of Judah."
1:48 'Blessed be the LORD, the God of I,
2: 4 someone of your line on the throne of I.'
2:11 of David's reign over I was forty years:
2:15 was mine, and all I expected me to be king.
3:28 I heard the judgment the king had given,
4: 1 Solomon was king over all I,
4: 7 commissaries for all I who supplied food
4:20 I were as numerous as the sands by the sea;
5: 5 Thus Judah and I lived in security,
5:27 thirty thousand workmen from all I.
6: 1 the fourth year of Solomon's reign over I,
6:13 and will not forsake my people I."
8: 1 of I and all the leaders of the tribes,
8: 2 All the men of I assembled before King
8: 3 When all the elders of I had arrived,
8: 5 Solomon and the entire community of I
8:14 the whole community of I as they stood.
8:15 "Blessed be the LORD, the God of I,
8:16 the day I brought my people I out of Egypt,
8:16 I for the building of a temple to my honor;
8:16 but I choose David to rule my people I.'
8:17 to the honor of the LORD, the God of I,
8:20 father David and sit on the throne of I,
8:20 temple to honor the LORD, the God of I.
8:22 the presence of the whole community of I,
8:23 "LORD, God of I, there is no God like you
8:25 LORD, God of I, keep the further promise
8:25 line to sit before me on the throne of I,
8:26 God of I, may this promise which you made
8:30 people I which they offer in this place.
8:33 "If your people I sin against you and are
8:34 and forgive the sin of your people I,
8:36 sin of your servant and of your people I,
8:38 if then any one [of your entire people I
8:41 likewise, who is not of your people I,
8:43 name, may fear you as do your people I,
8:52 and to the petition of your people I.
8:55 stood and blessed the whole community of I,
8:56 LORD who has given rest to his people I,
8:59 and of his people I as each day requires,
8:62 The king and all I with him offered
8:66 to his servant David and to his people I.
9: 5 your throne of sovereignty over I forever,
9: 5 someone from your line on the throne of I.'
9: 7 I will cut off I from the land I gave them
9: 7 I shall become a proverb and a byword
10: 9 pleased to place you on the throne of I.
10: 9 In his enduring love for I,
11: 9 turned away from the LORD, the God of I,
11:16 Joab and all I remained there six months
11:25 was an enemy of I as long as Solomon lived;
11:25 a rift in I by becoming king over Edom.
11:31 the LORD, the God of I says:
11:32 I have chosen out of all the tribes of I.
11:37 that you desire and shall become king of I.
11:38 I will give I to you.
11:42 in Jerusalem over all I was forty years.
12: 1 where all I had come to proclaim him king.
12:12 third day all I came back to King Rehoboam,
12:16 I saw that the king did not listen to them,
12:16 To your tents, O I!

12:16 So *I* went off to their tents,
12:18 labor, but all *I* stoned him to death.
12:19 and *I* went into rebellion against David's
12:20 all *I* heard that Jeroboam had returned,
12:20 an assembly and made him king over all *I.*
12:21 to fight against the house of *I,*
12:28 Here is your God, O *I,*
14: 7 'This is what the LORD, the God of *I,*
14: 7 people and made you ruler of my people *I.*
14:10 line, whether slave or freeman in *I,*
14:13 die, and all *I* will mourn him and bury him,
14:13 pleasing to the LORD, the God of *I,*
14:14 *I* who will destroy the house of Jeroboam.
14:15 The LORD will strike *I* like a reed tossed
14:15 will pluck out *I* from this good land
14:16 He will give up *I* because of the sins
14:16 has committed and caused *I* to commit."
14:18 He was buried with all *I* mourning him,
14:19 book of the chronicles of the kings of *I.*
14:21 city in which, out of all the tribes of *I,*
15: 9 the twentieth year of Jeroboam, king of *I,*
15:16 was war between Asa and Baasha, king of *I,*
15:17 Baasha, king of *I,* attacked Judah
15:19 break your treaty with Baasha, king of *I,*
15:20 of his troops against the cities of *I.*
15:25 king of *I;* he reigned over Israel
15:26 the sin which he had caused *I* to commit.
15:27 which Nadab and all *I* were besieging.
15:30 Jeroboam committed and caused *I* to commit,
15:30 which he provoked the LORD, the God of *I,*
15:31 book of the chronicles of the kings of *I.*
15:32 was war between Asa and Baasha, king of *I,*
15:33 twenty-four-year reign over *I* in Tirzah.
15:34 and the sin he had caused *I* to commit.
16: 2 dust and made you ruler of my people *I,*
16: 2 and have caused my people *I* to sin,
16: 5 book of the chronicles of the kings of *I.*
16: 8 began his two-year reign over *I* in Tirzah.
16:13 son Elah committed and caused *I* to commit,
16:13 commit, provoking the LORD, the God of *I,*
16:14 book of the chronicles of the kings of *I.*
16:16 that day in the camp all *I* proclaimed Omri,
16:16 Omri, general of the army, king of *I.*
16:17 up from Gibbethon, accompanied by all *I,*
16:19 conduct of Jeroboam, thus causing *I* to sin.
16:20 book of the chronicles of the kings of *I.*
16:21 At that time the people of *I* were divided,
16:23 he reigned over *I* twelve years,
16:26 *I* to sin and to provoke to the LORD,
16:26 and to provoke to the LORD, the God of *I,*
16:27 book of the chronicles of the kings of *I.*
16:29 became king of *I;* he reigned over Israel
16:33 of Israel, than any of the kings of *I*
17: 1 "As the LORD, the God of *I,* lives,
17:14 For the LORD, the God of *I,* says,
18:17 to him, "Is it you, you disturber of *I?*"
18:18 "It is not I who disturb *I,*"
18:19 Now summon all *I* to me on Mount Carmel,
18:31 the LORD had said, "Your name shall be *I.*"
18:36 "LORD, God of Abraham, Isaac, and *I,*
18:36 be known this day that you are God in *I*
19:16 Jehu, son of Nimshi, as king of *I,*
19:18 Yet I will leave seven thousand men in *I*—
20: 2 He sent couriers to Ahab, king of *I,*
20: 4 The king of *I* answered, "As you say, my
20: 7 The king of *I* then summoned all the elders
20:11 The king of *I* replied, "Tell him, 'It is not
20:13 came up to Ahab, king of *I* and said:
20:20 The Arameans fled with *I* pursuing them,
20:21 The king of *I* went out,
20:22 went up to the king of *I* and said to him:
20:26 and went up to Aphek to fight against *I.*
20:28 of God came up and said to the king of *I:*
20:31 kings of the land of *I* are merciful kings.
20:31 our heads, and go out to the king of *I.*
20:32 their heads, they went to the king of *I.*
20:40 The king of *I* said to him,
20:41 of *I* recognized him as one of the prophets.
20:43 of *I* went off homeward and entered Samaria.
21: 7 "A fine ruler over *I* you are indeed!"
21:18 "Start down to meet Ahab, king of *I,*
21:21 line, whether slave or freeman, in *I.*
21:22 you have provoked me by leading *I* into sin."
22: 1 passed without war between Aram and *I.*
22: 2 of Judah came down to the king of *I,*
22: 4 Jehoshaphat answered the king of *I,*
22: 5 Jehoshaphat also said to the king of *I,*
22: 6 king of *I* gathered together the prophets,
22: 8 The king of *I* answered, "There is one other
22: 9 of *I* called an official and said to him,
22:10 The king of *I* and King Jehoshaphat of
22:17 "I see all *I* scattered on the mountains,
22:18 The king of *I* said to Jehoshaphat,
22:26 The king of *I* then said, "Seize Micaiah
22:29 The king of *I* and King Jehoshaphat of
22:30 and the king of *I* said to Jehoshaphat,
22:30 *I* disguised himself and entered the fray.
22:31 with anyone at all except the king of *I.*"
22:32 cried out, "That must be the king of *I!*"
22:33 aware that he was not the king of *I,*
22:34 of *I* between the joints of his breastplate.
22:39 book of the chronicles of the kings of *I.*
22:41 in the fourth year of Ahab, king of *I.*
22:45 also made peace with the king of *I.*
22:52 began to reign over *I* in Samaria in the
22:52 he reigned two years over *I.*
22:53 son of Nebat, who caused *I* to sin.
22:54 thus provoking the LORD, the God of *I,*
2Kgs 1: 1 Ahab's death, Moab rebelled against *I.*
1: 3 'Is it because there is no God in *I* that
1: 6 Is it because there is no God in *I* that
1:18 the book of chronicles of the kings of *I.*
3: 1 became king of *I* in Samaria [in the
3: 3 which Jeroboam, son of Nebat, had lured *I;*
3: 4 used to pay the king of *I* as tribute a
3: 5 of Moab had rebelled against the king of *I.*
3: 6 Joram as king mustered all *I,*
3: 9 So the king of *I* set out,
3:10 exclaimed the king of *I.*
3:11 of the officers of the king of *I* replied,
3:12 So the kings of *I,* Judah, and Edom
3:13 Elisha asked the king of *I.*
3:13 "No," the king of *I* replied.
3:24 But when they reached the camp of *I,*
3:27 The wrath against *I* was so great that they
5: 2 from the land of *I* in a raid a little girl,
5: 4 the slave girl from the land of *I* had said.
5: 5 will send along a letter to the king of *I.*"
5: 6 To the king of *I* he brought the letter,
5: 7 king of *I* tore his garments and exclaimed:
5: 8 that the king of *I* had torn his garments,
5: 8 and find out that there is a prophet in *I.*"
5:12 Pharpar, better than all the waters of *I?*
5:15 is no God in all the earth, except in *I.*
6: 8 When the king of Aram was waging war on *I,*
6: 9 of God would send word to the king of *I,*
6:10 So the king of *I* would send word to the
6:11 them, "who among us is for the king of *I?*"
6:12 *I* the very words you speak in your bedroom."
6:21 When the king of *I* saw them,
6:23 Aramean raiders came into the land of *I.*
6:26 the king of *I* was walking on the city wall,
7: 6 "The king of *I* has hired the kings of the
8:16 year of Joram, son of Ahab, king of *I,*
8:18 like the kings of *I* of the line of Ahab,
8:25 year of Joram, son of Ahab, king of *I.*
8:26 she was daughter of Omri, king of *I.*
9: 3 I anoint you king over *I.*'
9: 6 said, "Thus says the LORD, the God of *I:*
9: 6 king over the people of the LORD, over *I.*
9: 8 Ahab's line, whether slave or freeman in *I.*
9:12 'I anoint you king over *I.*'"
9:14 Joram, with all *I,*
9:21 When they had done so, Joram, king of *I,*
10:21 sent word of it throughout the land of *I.*
10:28 Jehu rooted out the worship of Baal from *I.*
10:29 son of Nebat, had caused *I* to commit,
10:30 generation shall sit upon the throne of *I.*"
10:31 the law of the LORD, the God of *I,*
10:31 the sins which Jeroboam caused *I* to commit.
10:32 At that time the LORD began to dismember *I.*
10:34 book of the chronicles of the kings of *I.*
10:36 over *I* in Samaria was twenty-eight years.
13: 1 his seventeen-year reign over *I* in Samaria.
13: 2 the sin he had caused *I* to commit.
13: 3 The LORD was angry with *I* and for a long
13: 4 to which the king of Aram had subjected *I.*
13: 5 So the LORD gave *I* a savior,
13: 6 house of Jeroboam had caused *I* to commit,
13: 8 book of the chronicles of the kings of *I.*
13:10 his sixteen-year reign over *I* in Samaria.
13:11 son of Nebat, had caused *I* to commit,
13:12 book of the chronicles of the kings of *I.*
13:13 was buried with the kings of *I* in Samaria.]
13:14 King Joash of *I* went down to visit him.
13:16 had done so, Elisha said to the king of *I,*
13:18 Then he said to the king of *I,*
13:22 *I* during the entire reign of Jehoahaz.
13:23 But the Lord was merciful with *I* and
13:25 times, and thus recovered the cities of *I.*
14: 1 year of Joash, son of Jehoahaz, king of *I,*
14: 8 son of Jehoahaz, son of Jehu, king of *I,*
14: 9 of *I* sent this reply to the king of Judah:
14:11 King Jehoash of *I* then advanced,
14:12 Judah was defeated by *I,*
14:13 King Jehoash of *I* captured Amaziah,
14:15 book of the chronicles of the kings of *I.*
14:16 was buried in Samaria with the kings of *I.*
14:17 Jehoash, son of Jehoahaz, king of *I,*
14:23 Judah, Jeroboam, son of Joash, king of *I,*
14:24 son of Nebat, had caused *I* to commit.
14:25 He restored the boundaries of *I* from
14:25 Arabah, just as the LORD, the God of *I,*
14:26 LORD saw the very bitter affliction of *I,*
14:26 slave nor freeman, no one at all to help *I.*
14:27 out the name of *I* from under the heavens,
14:28 Damascus and turned back Hamath from *I,*
14:28 book of the chronicles of the kings of *I.*
14:29 rested with his ancestors, the kings of *I,*
15: 1 twenty-seventh year of Jeroboam, king of *I.*
15: 8 was king of *I* in Samaria for six months.
15: 9 son of Nebat, had caused *I* to commit.
15:11 book of the chronicles of the kings of *I.*
15:12 generation shall sit upon the throne of *I,*"
15:15 book of the chronicles of the kings of *I.*
15:18 son of Nebat, had caused *I* to commit.
15:21 book of the chronicles of the kings of *I.*
15:23 began his two-year reign over *I* in Samaria.
15:24 son of Nebat, had caused *I* to commit.
15:26 book of the chronicles of the kings of *I.*
15:27 his twenty-year reign over *I* in Samaria.
15:28 son of Nebat, had caused *I* to commit.
15:29 During the reign of Pekah, king of *I,*
15:31 book of the chronicles of the kings of *I.*
15:32 year of Pekah, son of Remaliah, king of *I,*
16: 3 but conducted himself like the kings of *I,*
16: 5 and Pekah, son of Remaliah, king of *I,*
16: 7 of the king of Aram and the king of *I,*
17: 1 his nine-year reign over *I* in Samaria.
17: 2 to the extent of the kings of *I* before him.
17: 8 [and the kings of *I* whom they set up].
17:13 *I* and Judah by every prophet and seer,
17:18 him till, in his great anger against *I,*
17:19 God, but followed the rites practiced by *I.*
17:20 So the LORD rejected the whole race of *I.*
17:21 he tore *I* away from the house of David,
17:23 the LORD put *I* away out of his sight as he
17:23 and *I* went into exile from their native
17:34 descendants of Jacob, whom he had named *I.*
18: 1 year of Hoshea, son of Elah, king of *I,*
18: 5 put his trust in the LORD, the God of *I;*
18: 9 year of Hoshea, son of Elah, king of *I,*
18:10 the ninth year of Hosea, king of *I,*
19:15 "O LORD, God of *I,*
19:20 God of *I,* in answer to your prayer
19:22 Against the Holy One of *I!*
21: 3 set up a sacred pole, as Ahab, king of *I,*
21: 7 I have chosen out of all the tribes of *I,*
21: 8 I will not in future allow *I* to be driven
21:12 therefore thus says the LORD, the God of *I:*
22:15 them, "Thus says the LORD, the God of *I:*
22:18 'Thus says the LORD, the God of *I:*
23:13 of Misconduct, which Solomon, king of *I,*
23:15 son of Nebat, who caused *I* to sin
23:19 Samaria which the kings of *I* had erected,
23:22 during the period when the Judges ruled *I,*
23:22 of the kings of *I* and the kings of Judah,
23:27 will I put out of my sight as I did *I.*
24:13 the gold utensils that Solomon, king of *I,*
1Chr 1:34 The sons of Isaac were Esau and *I.*
2: 1 These were the sons of *I:*
2: 7 trouble upon *I* by violating the ban.
4:10 Jabez prayed to the God of *I:*
5: 1 The sons of Reuben, the first-born of *I.*
5: 1 was given to the sons of Joseph, son of *I,*
5: 3 The sons of Reuben, the first-born of *I,*
5:17 king of Judah, and of Jeroboam, king of *I.*
5:26 of *I* incited against them the anger of Pul,
6:23 son of Kohath, son of Levi, son of *I.*
6:34 of holies and of making atonement for *I,*
7:29 the descendants of Joseph, the son of *I.*
9: 1 Thus all *I* was inscribed in its family
9: 1 are recorded in the book of the kings of *I.*
10: 1 Now the Philistines were at war with *I;*
11: 1 Then all *I* gathered about David in Hebron,
11: 2 it was you who led *I* in all its battles.
11: 2 my people *I* and be ruler over them.'"
11: 3 the elders of *I* came to the king at Hebron,
11: 3 and they anointed him king over *I,*
11: 4 Then David and all *I* went to Jerusalem,
11:10 chief warriors who, together with all *I,*
11:10 as the LORD had commanded concerning *I.*
12:33 of the times and who knew what *I* had to do:
12:39 intention of making David king over all *I.*
12:39 The rest of *I* was likewise of one mind to
12:41 For there was rejoicing in *I.*
13: 2 he said to the whole assembly of *I:*
13: 2 our brethren from all the districts of *I,*
13: 5 Then David assembled all *I,*
13: 6 David and all *I* went up to Baalah,
13: 8 *I* danced before God with great enthusiasm,
14: 2 had truly confirmed him as king over *I,*
14: 2 exalted for the sake of his people *I.*
14: 8 that David was anointed king over all *I,*
15: 3 Then David assembled all *I* in Jerusalem to
15:12 bring the ark of the LORD, the God of *I,*
15:14 bring up the ark of the LORD, the God of *I.*
15:25 Thus David, the elders of *I,*
15:28 Thus all *I* brought back the ark of the
16: 4 thank, and praise the LORD, the God of *I.*
16:13 he has uttered, You descendants of *I,*
16:17 statute, for *I* as an everlasting covenant,
16:36 Blessed be the LORD, the God of *I,*
16:40 law of the LORD which he has decreed for *I.*
17: 5 a house, from the time when I led *I* onward,
17: 6 as I have wandered about with all of *I,*
17: 6 of *I* whom I commanded to guide my people,
17: 7 you might become ruler over my people *I.*
17: 9 I will assign a place for my people *I* and
17:10 when I appointed judges over my people *I.*
17:21 "Is there, like your people *I,*
17:22 You made your people *I* your own forever,
17:24 your renown as LORD of hosts, God of *I,*
18:14 David reigned over all *I* and dispensed
19:16 Seeing themselves vanquished by *I,*
19:17 to David, he gathered all *I* together,
19:18 But the Arameans fled before *I,*
19:19 Hadadezer saw themselves vanquished by *I,*
20: 7 He defied *I,*

ISRAEL (cont.)
21: 1 A satan rose up against *I*,
21: 1 he enticed David into taking a census of *I*.
21: 3 Why will he bring guilt upon *I*?"
21: 4 Joab, who departed and traversed all of *I*,
21: 5 in all *I* one million one hundred thousand,
21: 7 displeased God, who began to punish *I*.
21:12 LORD's destroying angel in every part of *I*?
21:14 *I*, and seventy thousand men of Israel
22: 1 and this is the altar of holocausts for *I*."
22: 2 lived in the land of *I* be brought together,
22: 6 build a house for the LORD, the God of *I*.
22: 9 I will bestow peace and tranquillity on *I*.
22:10 the throne of his kingship over *I* forever.'
22:12 when he brings you to rule over *I*,
22:13 decrees which the LORD gave Moses for *I*.
23: 1 days, he made his son Solomon king over *I*.
23: 2 gathered together all the leaders of *I*,
23:25 God of *I*, has given rest to his people,
24:19 their father, as the LORD, the God of *I*,
26:30 had the administration of *I* on the western
27:16 Over the tribes of *I*, for the Reubenites
27:22 were the commanders of the tribes of *I*.
27:23 multiply *I* like the stars of the heavens.
27:24 it, for because of it wrath fell upon *I*.
28: 1 at Jerusalem all the leaders of *I*,
28: 4 the God of *I*, chose me from all my father's
28: 4 father's family to be king over *I* forever.
28: 4 it pleased him to make me king over all *I*.
28: 5 to sit on the LORD's royal throne over *I*.
28: 8 Therefore, in the presence of all *I*,
29: 6 families, the leaders of the tribes of *I*,
29:10 may you be, O LORD, God of *I* our father,
29:18 God of our fathers Abraham, Isaac, and *I*,
29:21 and many other sacrifices for all *I*;
29:23 he prospered, and all *I* obeyed him.
29:25 Solomon greatly in the eyes of all *I*,
29:25 enjoyed by any king over *I* before him.
29:26 the son of Jesse, had reigned over all *I*.
29:27 that he reigned over *I* was forty years:
29:30 all *I* and all the kingdoms of the surrounding
2Chr 1: 2 He sent a summons to all *I*,
1: 2 the judges, the princes of all *I*,
1:13 the meeting tent, and became king over *I*.
2:11 "Blessed be the LORD, the God of *I*,
2:16 alien men who were in the land of *I*
5: 2 of *I* and all the leaders of the tribes,
5: 3 All the men of *I* assembled before the king
5: 4 When all the elders of *I* had arrived,
5: 6 *I* gathered about him before the ark were
6: 3 the whole community of *I* as they stood.
6: 4 "Blessed be the LORD, the God of *I*,
6: 5 *I* for the building of a temple to my honor,
6: 5 any man to be commander of my people *I*;
6: 6 and I choose David to rule my people *I*.'
6: 7 to the honor of the LORD, the God of *I*,
6:10 and have taken my seat on the throne of *I*,
6:10 to the honor of the LORD, the God of *I*.
6:12 of *I* and stretched forth his hands.
6:13 knelt in the presence of the whole of *I*
6:14 "LORD, God of *I*, there is no god like you
6:16 Now, therefore, LORD, God of *I*,
6:16 line to sit before me on the throne of *I*,
6:17 God of *I*, may this promise which you made
6:21 *I* which they direct toward this place.
6:24 When your people *I* have sinned against you
6:25 and forgive the sin of your people *I*,
6:27 sin of your servants and of your people *I*.
6:32 too, who is not of your people, *I*,
6:33 name, fearing you as do your people *I*,
7: 6 priests blew the trumpets and all *I* stood.
7: 8 this occasion Solomon and with him all *I*,
7:10 David, for Solomon, and for his people *I*.
7:18 be lacking someone of yours as ruler in *I*.'
8: 7 Hivites, and Jebusites, who were not of *I*—
8:11 dwell in the house of David, king of *I*,
9: 8 loved *I* as to will to make it last forever,
9:30 in Jerusalem over all *I* for forty years.
10: 1 *I* had come to Shechem to proclaim him king.
10: 3 and he and all *I* said to Rehoboam,
10:16 When all *I* saw that the king would not
10:16 Everyone to your tents, O *I*!
10:16 So all *I* went off to their tents.
10:19 Thus *I* has been in rebellion against
11: 1 against *I* and restore the kingdom to him.
11:13 Now the priests and Levites throughout *I*
11:16 desired to seek the LORD, the God of *I*,
12: 1 the law of the LORD, he and all *I* with him.
12: 6 *I* and the king humbled themselves saying,
12:13 city in which, out of all the tribes of *I*,
13: 4 "Listen to me, Jeroboam and all *I*!
13: 5 of *I*, has given the kingdom of Israel
13:15 Jeroboam and all *I* before Abijah and Judah.
13:17 thousand picked men of *I* fell slain.
15: 3 For a long time *I* had no true God,
15: 4 they turned to the LORD, the God of *I*,
15: 9 to him from *I* when they saw that the LORD,
15:13 who would not seek the LORD, the God of *I*,
15:17 the high places did not disappear from *I*,
16: 1 year of Asa's reign, Baasha, king of *I*,
16: 3 break your treaty with Baasha, king of *I*,
16: 4 of his troops against the cities of *I*.
16:11 in the book of the kings of Judah and *I*.
17: 1 king and strengthened his hold against *I*.
17: 4 his commands, and not the practices of *I*.
18: 3 Ahab, king of *I*, asked Jehoshaphat,
18: 4 Jehoshaphat also said to the king of *I*,
18: 5 The king of *I* gathered his prophets,
18: 7 The king of *I* answered Jehoshaphat,
18: 8 So the king of *I* called an official,
18: 9 The king of *I* and King Jehoshaphat of
18:16 "I see all *I* scattered on the mountains,
18:17 The king of *I* said to Jehoshaphat,
18:19 asked, 'Who will deceive Ahab, king of *I*,
18:25 The king of *I* then said: "Seize Micaiah
18:28 The king of *I* and King Jehoshaphat of
18:29 and the king of *I* said to Jehoshaphat,
18:29 So the king of *I* disguised himself and
18:30 one, small or great, except the king of *I*."
18:31 exclaimed, "That must be the king of *I*!"
18:32 king of *I* and gave up their pursuit of him.
18:33 of *I* between the joints of his breastplate.
18:34 and the king of *I* braced himself up on his
19: 8 family heads of *I* to judge in the name
20: 7 before your people *I* and gave it forever
20:10 you did not allow *I* to invade
20:19 sing the praises of the LORD, the God of *I*,
20:29 LORD had fought against the enemies of *I*.
20:34 is inserted in the book of the kings of *I*.
20:35 allied himself with King Ahaziah of *I*,
21: 4 brothers and also some of the princes of *I*.
21: 6 like the kings of *I* of the line of Ahab,
21:13 have walked in the way of the kings of *I*
22: 5 Jehoram, son of Ahab, king of *I*,
24: 5 collect money from all *I* that you may repair
24: 6 of the LORD, and by the assembly of *I*,
24: 9 had imposed on *I* in the desert should be
24:16 the kings, because he had done good in *I*,
25: 6 from *I* for a hundred talents of silver.
25: 7 *I* go with you, for the LORD is not with *I*,
25: 9 talents that I paid for the troops of *I*?"
25:17 of Jehoahaz, son of Jehu, the king of *I*,
25:18 *I* sent this reply to King Amaziah of Judah:
25:21 Therefore King Joash of *I* advanced and he
25:22 There Judah was defeated by *I*,
25:23 King Joash of *I* captured Amaziah,
25:25 survived Joash, son of Jehoahaz, king of *I*,
25:26 in the book of the kings of Judah and *I*.
27: 7 in the book of the kings of *I* and Judah.
28: 2 *I* and even made molten idols of the Baals.
28: 5 delivered into the power of the king of *I*,
28:13 great, and there is a burning anger upon *I*."
28:19 Judah low because of Ahaz, king of *I*,
28:23 further disaster to him and to all *I*.
28:26 in the book of the kings of Judah and *I*.
28:27 bring him to the tombs of the kings of *I*.
29: 7 the sanctuary to the honor of the God of *I*.
29:10 a covenant with the LORD, the God of *I*,
29:24 the altar to atone for the sin of all *I*;
29:24 the king had said, "is for all *I*."
29:27 and the instruments of David, king of *I*.
30: 1 Hezekiah sent a message to all *I* and Judah,
30: 1 in honor of the LORD, the God of *I*.
30: 5 throughout all *I* from Beer-sheba to Dan,
30: 5 in honor of the LORD, the God of *I*;
30: 6 and his princes, traversed all *I* and Judah,
30: 6 the LORD, the God of Abraham, Isaac and *I*,
30:25 rest of the assembly that had come from *I*,
30:25 land of *I* and those that lived in Judah.
30:26 days of Solomon, son of David, king of *I*,
31: 8 they blessed the LORD and his people *I*.
32:17 letters to deride the LORD, the God of *I*,
32:19 They spoke of the God of *I* as though he
32:32 in the book of the kings of Judah and *I*.
33: 7 tribes of *I* I shall place my name forever.
33:16 Judah to serve the LORD, the God of *I*.
33:18 him in the name of the LORD, the God of *I*,
33:18 in the chronicles of the kings of *I*.
34: 7 incense stands throughout the land of *I*.
34: 9 Ephraim, and all the remnant of *I*,
34:21 and those who are left in *I* and Judah,
34:23 "Thus says the LORD, the God of *I*:
34:26 'Thus says the LORD, the God of *I*,
34:33 all who were in *I* to serve the LORD,
35: 3 to the Levites who were to instruct all *I*,
35: 3 built by Solomon, son of David, king of *I*.
35: 3 now the LORD, your God, and his people *I*.
35: 4 of King David of *I* and his son Solomon.
35:18 in *I* since the time of the prophet Samuel,
35:18 of *I* kept a Passover like that of Josiah,
35:18 all of Judah and *I* that were present,
35:25 These have been made obligatory for *I*,
35:26 in the book of the kings of *I* and Judah.
36: 8 in the book of the kings of *I* and Judah.
36:13 than return to the LORD, the God of *I*.
Ezr 2: 2 The census of the men of *I*:
3: 2 rebuilding the altar of the God of *I* in order
3:10 the manner laid down by David, king of *I*.
3:11 for his kindness to *I* endures forever";
4: 1 a temple for the LORD, the God of *I*,
4: 3 of the family heads of *I* answered them,
4: 3 must build it for the LORD, the God of *I*,
5: 1 and Jerusalem in the name of the God of *I*.
5:11 ago, which a great king of *I* built and finished.
6:14 according to the command of the God of *I*
6:17 he-goats as a sin-offering for all *I*,
6:17 keeping with the number of the tribes of *I*.
6:21 them in seeking the LORD, the God of *I*.
6:22 work on the house of God, the God of *I*.
7: 6 which was given by the LORD, the God of *I*.
7:10 on teaching statutes and ordinances in *I*.
7:11 the LORD's commandments and statutes for *I*:
7:13 my kingdom belonging to the people of *I*,
7:15 have freely contributed to the God of *I*,
8:18 the sons of Mahli, son of Levi, son of *I*,
8:29 and Levites and the family leaders of *I*,
8:35 the God of *I* twelve bulls for all Israel,
9: 4 God of *I* on this apostasy of the exiles,
9:15 O LORD, God of *I*, you are just;
10: 2 Yet even now there remains a hope for *I*.
10: 5 *I* that they would do as had been proposed;
Neh 1: 6 which we of *I* have committed against you,
7: 7 The census of the men of *I*:
7:72 all *I* took up residence in their cities.
8: 1 of Moses which the LORD prescribed for *I*.
10:34 for sin offerings to make atonement for *I*,
11:20 The rest of *I*, including the priests and Levites,
12:47 Thus all *I*, in the days of Zerubbabel
13: 3 separated from *I* every foreign element.
13:18 *I* by once more profaning the sabbath?"
13:26 Did not Solomon, the king of *I*,
13:26 God and God had made him king over all *I*,
Tb 1: 4 lived as a young man in my own country, *I*,
1: 5 the young bull which Jeroboam, king of *I*,
1: 6 prescribed for all *I* by perpetual decree.
14: 4 "As for our kinsmen who dwell in *I*,
14: 4 entire country of *I* shall become desolate;
14: 5 them and bring them back to the land of *I*.
14: 5 just as the prophets of *I* said of her.
Jdt 4: 8 and the senate of the whole people of *I*,
4: 9 All the men of *I* cried to God with great
4:12 *I* not to allow their children to be seized,
4:15 to look with favor on the whole house of *I*.
6:17 of Holofernes against the house of *I*.
6:21 they called upon the God of *I* for help.
8: 1 son of Sarasadai, son of Simeon, son of *I*,
8: 6 feastdays and holidays of the house of *I*.
8:33 enemies, the Lord will rescue *I* by my hand.
9:12 my forefather, God of the heritage of *I*,
9:14 who protects the people of *I* but you alone."
10: 1 and ceased her invocation to the God of *I*,
12: 8 she besought the Lord, the God of *I*,
13: 7 said, "Strengthen me this day, O God of *I*!"
13:11 in *I* and his power against our enemies;
13:14 withdrawn his mercy from the house of *I*,
14: 4 inhabitants of the whole territory of *I*
14: 5 of *I* and sent him here to meet his death."
14:10 seeing all that the God of *I* had done,
14:10 with the house of *I* to the present day.
15: 4 country of *I* to report what had happened,
15: 8 good things that the Lord had done for *I*,
15: 9 of Jerusalem, the surpassing joy of *I*;
15:10 You have done good to *I*,
15:12 All the women of *I* gathered to see her;
15:13 while the men of *I* followed in their armor,
15:14 led all *I* in this song of thanksgiving,
16: 7 garb to raise up the afflicted in *I*.
16:24 the house of *I* mourned her for seven days.
Est C: 2 one to oppose you in your will to save *I*.
C: 6 soles of his feet for the salvation of *I*.
C:11 All *I*, too, cried out with all their strength,
C:14 Then she prayed to the Lord, the God of *I*,
C:16 O Lord, chose *I* from among all peoples,
F: 6 the name of the Jews, but my people is *I*,
F:10 all future generations of his people *I*."
1Mc 1:11 in *I* men who were breakers of the law,
1:20 to *I* and to Jerusalem with a strong force.
1:25 And there was great mourning for *I*,
1:30 and destroyed many of the people in *I*.
1:36 and a wicked adversary to *I* at all times.
1:53 *I* was driven into hiding,
1:58 So they used their power against *I*,
1:62 But many in *I* were determined and resolved
1:63 Terrible affliction was upon *I*.
2:16 Many of *I* joined them,
2:46 boys whom they found in the territory of *I*.
2:55 his commission, became a judge in *I*.
2:70 in Modein, and all *I* mourned him greatly.
3: 8 He turned away wrath from *I*
3:10 army from Samaria, to fight against *I*.
3:35 crush and destroy the power of *I*
3:46 formerly at Mizpah a place of prayer for *I*.
4:11 there is One who redeems and delivers *I*."
4:25 Thus *I* had a great deliverance that day.
4:27 because things in *I* had not turned out as
4:30 "Blessed are you, O Savior of *I*,
4:31 this army into the hands of your people *I*;
4:59 *I* decreed that the days of the dedication
5: 3 in Idumea, because they were blockading *I*;
5:63 in all *I* and among all the Gentiles,
6:18 were hemming in *I* around the sanctuary,
7: 5 lawless and impious men of *I* came to him.
7:22 of Judah and caused great distress in *I*.
7:26 officers, who was a bitter enemy of *I*,
8:18 of the Greeks was subjecting *I* to slavery.
9:20 All *I* bewailed him in great grief.
9:21 the mighty one has fallen, the savior of *I*!"
9:23 law raised their heads in every part of *I*,
9:27 had not been such great distress in *I*

9:51 In each he put a garrison to oppose *I.*
9:73 Then the sword ceased in *I.*
9:73 people and he destroyed the impious in *I.*
10:46 great evil that Demetrius had done in *I,*
11:23 He selected some elders and priests of *I*
11:41 for they were constantly hostile to *I.*
12:52 fear, and all *I* fell into deep mourning.
13: 4 for the sake of these, for the sake of *I,*
13:26 All *I* bewailed him with solemn lamentation,
13:41 yoke of the Gentiles was removed from *I,*
13:51 a great enemy of *I* had been destroyed.
14:11 the land, and *I* was filled with happiness.
16: 2 battles of *I* from our youth until today,
16: 2 and many times we succeeded in saving *I.*
2Mc 1:26 *I* and guard and sanctify your heritage.
9: 5 So the all-seeing Lord, the God of *I,*
10:38 kindness to *I* and grants them victory.
11: 6 and tears to send a good angel to save *I.*
Ps(s) 14: 7 out of Zion would come the salvation of *I!*
14: 7 then shall Jacob exult and *I* be glad.
22: 4 enthroned in the holy place, O glory of *I!*
22:24 revere him, all you descendants of *I!*
25:22 Redeem *I,* O God, from all its distress!
41:14 Blessed be the LORD, the God of *I,*
50: 7 *I,* I will testify against you;
53: 7 out of Zion would come the salvation of *I!*
53: 7 then shall Jacob exult and *I* be glad.
59: 6 you are the LORD of hosts, the God of *I.*
68: 9 God, at the presence of God, the God of *I,*
68:35 Over *I* in his majesty;
68:36 in his sanctuary is God, the God of *I;*
69: 7 who seek you blush for me, O God of *I,*
71:22 praises with the harp, O Holy One of *I!*
72:18 Blessed be the LORD, the God of *I,*
76: 2 renowned in Judah, in *I* great is his name.
78: 5 Jacob, and established it as a law in *I,*
78:21 against Jacob, and anger rose against *I,*
78:31 best men, and laid low the young men of *I.*
78:41 tempted God and provoked the Holy One of *I.*
78:55 and settled the tribes of *I* in their tents.
78:59 and was enraged and utterly rejected *I.*
78:71 him to shepherd Jacob, his people, and *I,*
80: 2 O shepherd of *I,* hearken, O guide
81: 5 For it is a statute in *I,*
81: 9 O *I,* will you not hear me?
81:12 heard not my voice, and *I* obeyed me not;
81:14 would hear me, and *I* walk in my ways,
81:17 *I* I would feed with the best of wheat,
83: 5 let the name of *I* be remembered no more!"
89:19 our shield, and to the Holy One of *I,*
98: 3 and his faithfulness toward the house of *I.*
103: 7 Moses, and his deeds to the children of *I.*
105:10 statute, for *I* as an everlasting covenant,
105:23 Then *I* came to Egypt, and Jacob sojourned
106:48 Blessed be the LORD, the God of *I,*
114: 1 When *I* came forth from Egypt,
114: 2 Judah became his sanctuary, *I* his domain.
115: 9 The house of *I* trusts in the LORD;
115:12 he will bless the house of *I;*
118: 2 Let the house of *I* say, "His mercy endures
121: 4 slumbers nor sleeps, the guardian of *I.*
122: 4 the LORD, According to the decree for *I,*
124: 1 Had not the LORD been with us, let *I* say,
125: 5 Peace be upon *I!*
128: 6 Peace be upon *I!*
129: 1 they oppressed me from my youth, let *I* say,
130: 7 for the dawn, let *I* wait for the LORD,
130: 8 he will redeem *I* from all their iniquities.
131: 3 O *I,* hope in the LORD, both now
135: 4 for himself, *I* for his own possession.
135:12 a heritage, the heritage of *I* his people.
135:19 House of *I,* bless the LORD, house of Aaron,
136:11 And brought out *I* from their midst,
136:14 And led *I* through its midst,
136:22 The heritage of *I* his servant,
147: 2 the dispersed of *I* he gathers.
147:19 his statutes and his ordinances to *I.*
148:14 his faithful ones, from the children of *I,*
149: 2 Let *I* be glad in their maker,
Prv 1: 1 of Solomon, the son of David, king of *I:*
Eccl 1:12 Qo-heleth, was king over *I* in Jerusalem,
Sg 3: 7 men surround it, of the valiant men of *I:*
Sir 17:14 a ruler, but the LORD's own portion is *I.*
24: 8 make your dwelling, in *I* your inheritance.'
36:11 *I,* whom you named your first-born.
37:23 but the life of *I* is days without number.
45: 5 to Jacob, his judgments and decrees to *I.*
45:11 incised letters each of the tribes of *I;*
45:16 memorial, and to atone for the people of *I.*
45:17 and the ritual to the descendants of *I.*
45:22 portion, his inheritance in the midst of *I.*
45:23 noble heart, atoned for the children of *I.*
46: 1 the enemy and to win the inheritance for *I.*
47: 2 of the sacred offerings, so was DAVID in *I.*
47:11 of royalty and established his throne in *I.*
47:18 glorious name which was conferred upon *I.*
47:23 remembered, the sinner who led *I* into sin,
50:13 in the presence of the whole assembly of *I.*
50:17 the Most High, before the Holy One of *I.*
50:20 his hands over all the congregation of *I.*
50:24 in *I* as long as the heavens are above.
Is 1: 3 But *I* does not know,
1: 4 the LORD, spurned the Holy One of *I,*
1:24 the LORD of hosts, the Mighty One of *I:*
4: 2 honor and splendor for the survivors of *I.*
5: 7 of the LORD of hosts is the house of *I,*
5:19 On with the plan of the Holy One of *I!*
5:24 and scorned the word of the Holy One of *I.*
7: 1 Rezin, king of Aram, and Pekah, king of *I,*
8:14 a stumbling stone to both the houses of *I,*
8:18 we are signs and portents in *I* from the
9: 7 sent word against Jacob, it falls upon *I,*
9:11 on the west devour *I* with open mouth.
9:13 So the LORD severs from *I* head and tail,
10:17 The light of *I* will become a fire,
10:20 On that day The remnant of *I,*
10:20 they lean upon the LORD, the Holy One of *I,*
10:22 For though your people, O *I,*
11:12 the nations and gather the outcasts of *I;*
11:16 *I* when he came up from the land of Egypt.
12: 6 great in your midst is the Holy One of *I!*
14: 1 *I* and settles them on their own soil,
14: 2 The house of *I* will take them and bring
17: 6 branches, says the LORD, the God of *I.*
17: 7 his eyes turned toward the Holy One of *I.*
17: 9 Amorites When faced with the children of *I:*
19:24 On that day *I* shall be a third party with
19:25 of my hands Assyria, and my inheritance, *I.*"
21:10 heard from the LORD of hosts, The God of *I,*
21:17 shall remain, for the LORD, the God of *I,*
24:15 sea, to the name of the LORD, the God of *I!*"
27: 6 take root, *I* shall sprout and blossom,
27:12 shall be gleaned one by one, O sons of *I.*
29:19 and the poor rejoice in the Holy One of *I.*
29:23 of Jacob, and be in awe of the God of *I.*
30:11 Let us hear no more of the Holy One of *I.*"
30:12 Therefore, thus says the Holy One of *I:*
30:15 thus said the Lord GOD, the Holy One of *I:*
30:29 mountain of the LORD, toward the Rock of *I,*
31: 1 not to the Holy One of *I* nor seek the LORD!
31: 6 Return, O children of *I,*
37:16 "O LORD of hosts, God of *I,*
37:21 Thus says the LORD, the God of *I:*
37:23 Against the Holy One of *I!*
40:27 O Jacob, do you say, and declare, O *I,*
41: 8 But you, *I,* my servant, Jacob,
41:14 Fear not, O worm Jacob, O maggot *I;*
41:14 your redeemer is the Holy One of *I.*
41:16 the LORD, and glory in the Holy One of *I.*
41:17 I, the God of *I,* will not forsake them.
41:20 this, the Holy One of *I* has created it.
42:24 Jacob to be plundered, *I* to the despoilers?
43: 1 created you, O Jacob, and formed you, O *I:*
43: 3 I am the LORD, your God, the Holy One of *I,*
43:14 the LORD, your redeemer, the Holy One of *I:*
43:15 the LORD, your Holy One, the creator of *I,*
43:22 me, O Jacob, for you grew weary of me, O *I.*
43:28 under the ban, and exposed *I* to scorn.
44: 1 Hear then, O Jacob, my servant, *I,*
44: 5 "The LORD's," and *I* shall be his surname.
44:21 Remember this, O Jacob, you O *I,*
44:21 O *I,* by me you shall never be forgotten:
44:23 Jacob, and shows his glory through *I.*
45: 3 may know that I am the LORD, the God of *I,*
45: 4 of Jacob, my servant, of *I* my chosen one,
45:11 Thus says the LORD, the Holy One of *I,*
45:15 Truly with you God is hidden, the God of *I,*
45:17 *I,* you are saved by the LORD.
45:25 and the glory of all the descendants of *I.*"
46: 3 Jacob, all who remain of the house of *I,*
46:13 within Zion, and give to *I* my glory.
47: 4 is the LORD of hosts, the Holy One of *I.*
48: 1 O house of Jacob called by the name of *I,*
48: 1 the God of *I* without sincerity or justice,
48: 2 the holy city and rely on the God of *I,*
48:12 Listen to me, Jacob *I,* whom I named!
48:17 LORD, your redeemer, the Holy One of *I:*
49: 3 You are my servant, he said to me, *I,*
49: 5 back to him and *I* gathered to him
49: 6 of Jacob, and restore the survivors of *I;*
49: 7 LORD, the redeemer and the Holy One of *I,*
49: 7 the Holy One of *I* who has chosen you.
52:12 you, and your rear guard is the God of *I.*
54: 5 Your redeemer is the Holy One of *I,*
55: 5 of the LORD, your God, the Holy One of *I,*
56: 8 LORD GOD, who gathers the dispersed of *I:*
60: 9 of the LORD, your God, the Holy One of *I,*
60:14 of the LORD," "Zion of the Holy One of *I.*"
63: 7 for he is good to the house of *I,*
63:16 not to know us, nor *I* to acknowledge us,
Jer 2: 3 Sacred to the LORD was *I,*
2: 4 All you clans of the house of *I,*
2:14 Is *I* a slave, a bondman by birth?
2:26 caught, so shall the house of *I* be shamed:
2:31 Have I been a desert to *I,*
3: 6 See now what rebellious *I* has done!
3: 8 the adulteries rebellious *I* had committed,
3:11 Rebel *I* is inwardly more just than
3:12 Return, rebel *I,*
3:18 house of Judah will join the house of *I;*
3:20 you been faithless to me, O house of *I,*
3:23 LORD, our God, alone is the salvation of *I.*
4: 1 If you wish to return, O *I,*
5:11 both the house of *I* and the house of Judah,
5:15 you a nation from afar, O house of *I,*
6: 9 Glean, glean like a vine the remnant of *I;*
7: 3 Thus says the LORD of hosts, the God of *I:*
7:12 because of the wickedness of my people *I.*
7:21 Thus says the LORD of hosts, the God of *I:*
9:14 thus says the LORD of hosts, the God of *I:*
9:25 these nations, like the whole house of *I,*
10: 1 which the LORD speaks to you, O house of *I.*
10:16 *I* is his very own tribe,
11: 3 Thus says the LORD, the God of *I:*
11:10 of *I* and the house of Judah have broken.
11:17 the house of *I* and by the house of Judah,
12:14 which I gave my people *I* as their own:
13:11 so had I made the whole house of *I* and the
13:12 Thus says the LORD, the God of *I:*
14: 8 O Hope of *I,* O LORD, our savior in time
16: 9 thus says the LORD of hosts, the God of *I:*
17:13 O hope of *I,* O LORD!
18: 6 Can I not do to you, house of *I,*
18: 6 potter, so are you in my hand, house of *I.*
18:13 Truly horrible things has virgin *I* done!
19: 3 God of *I:* I am going to bring such evil
19:15 God of *I:* I will surely bring upon
21: 4 God of *I:* I will turn back in your
23: 2 God of *I,* against the shepherds who
23: 6 shall be saved, *I* shall dwell in security.
23: 8 house of *I* up from the land of the north"
23:13 by Baal and led my people *I* astray.
24: 5 God of *I:* Like these good figs,
25:15 God of *I,* to me: Take this cup of
25:27 God of *I:* Drink! become drunk and
27: 4 God of *I:* It was I who made the world
27:21 God of *I,* concerning the vessels that
28: 2 God of *I:* I will break the yoke
28:14 God of *I:* A yoke of iron I will
29: 4 God of *I,* to all the exiles whom I exiled
29: 8 the God of *I:* Do not let yourselves
29:21 God of *I,* has to say about those who
29:23 For they are criminals in *I,*
29:25 God of *I:* Because you sent letters
30: 2 God of *I:* Write all the words I
30: 3 the lot of my people (of *I* and Judah,
30: 4 which the LORD spoke to *I* and to Judah:
30:10 not, says the LORD, be not dismayed, O *I!*
31: 1 I will be the God of all the tribes of *I,*
31: 2 As *I* comes forward to be given his rest,
31: 4 you, and you shall be rebuilt, O virgin *I;*
31: 7 has delivered his people, the remnant of *I.*
31: 9 For I am a father to *I,*
31:10 He who scattered *I,*
31:21 Turn back, O virgin *I,*
31:23 God of *I:* When I change their lot
31:27 when I will seed the house of *I* and the
31:31 with the house of *I* and the house of Judah.
31:33 make with the house of *I* after those days,
31:36 of *I* cease as a nation before me forever.
31:37 race of *I* because of all they have done,
32:14 God of *I:* Take these deeds
32:15 God of *I:* Houses and fields
32:20 day, both in *I* and among all other men,
32:21 you brought your people *I* out of the land
32:36 God of *I,* concerning this city,
33: 4 God of *I,* concerning the houses
33: 7 change the lot of Judah and the lot of *I,*
33:14 promise I made to the house of *I* and Judah.
33:17 successor on the throne of the house of *I,*
34: 2 God of *I:* Go to Zedekiah
34:13 God of *I:* The day I brought your
35:13 God of *I:* Go, say to the men of
35:17 God of *I:* I will bring upon Judah
35:18 God of *I:* Since you have obeyed
35:19 God of *I:* Never shall there fail to be
36: 2 the words I have spoken to you against *I,*
37: 7 God of *I:* Give this answer to the king
38:17 God of *I:* If you surrender to
39:16 God of *I:* Behold, I am now fulfilling
41: 9 defend himself against Baasha, king of *I;*
42: 9 God of *I,* to whom you sent me offer
42:15 God of *I:* If you are determined to go
42:18 God of *I:* Just as my furious anger
43:10 God of *I:* I will send for my servant
44: 2 God of *I:* You have seen all the evil
44: 7 God of *I:* Why do you inflict so great
44:11 God of *I:* I have determined evil
44:25 God of *I:* You and your wives have
45: 2 God of *I,* to you, Baruch, because you said,
46:25 God of *I,* has said: See! I will
46:27 Jacob, fear not; be not dismayed, O *I.*
48: 1 God of *I:* Woe to Nebo
48:13 as *I* was disappointed by Bethel in which
48:27 Is *I* a laughingstock to you?
49: 1 Has *I* no sons? has he no heir?
49: 2 *I* shall inherit those who disinherited her,
50: 4 the men of *I* and of Judah shall come,
50:17 A stray sheep was *I* that lions pursued;
50:18 God of *I:* I will punish the king
50:19 But I will bring back *I* to her fold,
50:29 she insulted the LORD, the Holy One of *I.*
50:33 Oppressed are the men of *I,*
51: 5 *I* and Judah are not widowed of their God,
51: 5 guilt to be punished by the Holy One of *I.*
51:19 *I* is his very own tribe,
51:33 God of *I:* Daughter Babylon is like a
51:49 Babylon, too, must fall, O slain of *I,*
Lam 2: 1 down from heaven to earth the glory of *I,*

ISRAEL (cont.)
2: 5 has become an enemy, he has consumed *I*:
Bar 2: 1 against our judges, who governed *I*,
2: 1 and against the men of *I* and Judah.
2:11 God of *I*, you who led your people
2:15 that *I* and his descendants bear your name.
2:26 the kingdom of *I* and the kingdom of Judah.
2:35 my people *I* from the land I gave them.
3: 1 God of *I*, afflicted souls and dismayed spirits
3: 4 God of *I*, hear the prayer of Israel's few,
3: 9 Hear, O *I*, the commandments of life:
3:10 How is it, *I*, that you are in the land of your
3:24 O *I*, how vast is the house of God,
3:37 has given her to Jacob, his servant, to *I*,
4: 4 O *I*; for what pleases God is known to us!
4: 5 Remember, *I*, You were sold to the nations
5: 7 *I* may advance secure in the glory of God.
5: 8 tree have overshadowed *I* at God's command;
5: 9 For God is leading *I* in joy by the light
Ez 3: 1 scroll, then go, speak to the house of *I*.
3: 4 Son of man, go now to the house of *I*,
3: 7 house of *I* will refuse to listen to you,
3: 7 For the whole house of *I* is stubborn of
3:17 you a watchman for the house of *I*.
4: 3 This shall be a sign for the house of *I*.
4: 4 place the sins of the house of *I* upon you.
4: 5 you will bear the sins of the house of *I*.
5: 4 Say to the whole house of *I*:
6: 2 Son of man, turn toward the mountains of *I*,
6: 3 Mountains of *I*, hear the word of the Lord
6:11 of all the abominations of the house of *I*,
7: 2 Thus says the Lord GOD to the land of *I*:
8: 4 I saw there the glory of the God of *I*,
8: 6 that the house of *I* is practicing here,
8:10 beasts [all the idols of the house of *I*.
8:11 seventy of the elders of the house of *I*,
8:12 the house of *I* is doing in his idol room?
9: 8 *I* when you pour out your fury on Jerusalem?"
9: 9 of the house of *I* are great beyond measure;
10: 2 the God of *I* had gone up from the cherubim,
10:19 glory of the God of *I* was up above them.
10:20 beneath the God of *I* by the river Chebar,
11: 5 This is the way you talk, house of *I*,
11:10 at the boundaries of *I* I will judge you;
11:11 At the boundaries of *I* I will judge you,
11:13 you utterly wipe out what remains of *I*?"
11:15 of *I* that the inhabitants of Jerusalem say,
11:15 land of *I* has been given as our possession."
11:17 and I will restore to you the land of *I*.
11:22 above them was the glory of the God of *I*.
12: 6 I have made you a sign for the house of *I*.
12: 9 Son of man, did not the house of *I*,
12:10 and the whole house of *I* within it.
12:19 inhabitants of Jerusalem [to the land of *I*:
12:22 proverb that you have in the land of *I*:
12:23 they shall never quote it again in *I*.
12:24 divinations within the house of *I*,
12:27 of man, listen to the house of *I* saying,
13: 2 of man, prophesy against the prophets of *I*,
13: 4 foxes among ruins are your prophets, O *I*!
13: 5 did you build a wall about the house of *I*
13: 9 house of Israel, nor enter the land of *I*;
13:16 those prophets of *I* who prophesied to
14: 1 elders of *I* came and sat down before me,
14: 4 If anyone of the house of *I*,
14: 5 bring back to their senses the house of *I*,
14: 6 Therefore say to the house of *I*:
14: 7 house of *I* or any alien resident in Israel
14: 9 him and root him out of my people *I*.
14:11 so that the house of *I* may no longer stray
17: 2 and speak this proverb to the house of *I*:
17:23 the mountain heights of *I* I will plant it.
18: 2 proverb that you recite in the land of *I*:
18: 3 you who will repeat this proverb in *I*.
18: 6 his eyes to the idols of the house of *I*:
18:15 his eyes to the idols of the house of *I*,
18:25 Hear now, house of *I*:
18:29 And yet the house of *I* says,
18:29 Is it my way that is not fair, house of *I*,
18:30 Therefore I will judge you, house of *I*,
18:31 Why should you die, O house of *I*?
19: 1 raise a lamentation over the prince of *I*:
19: 9 would not be heard on the mountains of *I*.
20: 1 some of the elders of *I* came to consult
20: 3 speak with the elders of *I* and say to them:
20: 5 The day I chose *I*,
20:13 of *I* rebelled against me in the desert.
20:27 Therefore speak to the house of *I*,
20:30 Therefore say to the house of *I*:
20:31 let myself be consulted by you, house of *I*?
20:38 but they shall not return to the land of *I*.
20:39 As for you, house of *I*,
20:40 mountain, on the mountain height of *I*,
20:40 of *I* without exception shall worship me;
20:42 when I bring you back to the land of *I*,
20:44 conduct and corrupt actions, O house of *I*,
21: 7 and prophesy against the land of *I*,
21: 8 land of Israel, saying to the land of *I*:
21:17 It is for all the princes of *I*,
21:30 for you, depraved and wicked prince of *I*,
22: 6 the princes of *I*, family by family,
22:18 the house of *I* has become dross for me.
24:21 Say to the house of *I*:
25: 3 the devastation of the land of *I*,
25: 6 in your heart over the land of *I*,
25:14 upon Edom I will entrust to my people *I*,
27:17 and the land of *I* trafficked with you,
28:24 be a tearing thorn for the house of *I*
28:25 When I gather the house of *I* from the
29: 6 have been a reed staff for the house of *I*:
29:16 they be for the house of *I* to trust in,
29:21 make a horn sprout for the house of *I*,
33: 7 appointed watchman for the house of *I*;
33:10 you, son of man, speak to the house of *I*:
33:11 Why should you die, O house of *I*?
33:20 of you according to his ways, O house of *I*.
33:24 in the ruins on the land of *I* reason thus:
33:28 and the mountains of *I* shall be so
34: 2 man, prophesy against the shepherds of *I*,
34: 2 of *I* who have been pasturing themselves!
34:13 pasture them upon the mountains of *I*
34:14 heights of *I* shall be their grazing ground.
34:14 they be pastured on the mountains of *I*.
34:30 and they are my people, the house of *I*,
35:12 have uttered against the mountains of *I*:
35:15 of the inheritance of the house of *I*,
36: 1 son of man, prophesy to the mountains of *I*:
36: 1 Mountains of *I*, hear the word of the LORD!
36: 4 therefore, mountains of *I*,
36: 6 prophesy concerning the land of *I*,
36: 8 As for you, mountains of *I*, you shall grow
36: 8 branches and bear fruit for my people *I*,
36:10 of men upon you, the whole house of *I*;
36:12 [My people *I* are the ones whom I will have
36:17 when the house of *I* lived in their land,
36:21 house of *I* profaned among the nations
36:22 Therefore say to the house of *I*:
36:22 Not for your sakes do I act, house of *I*,
36:32 because of your conduct, O house of *I*.
36:37 will be persuaded to do for the house of *I*:
37:11 man, these bones are the whole house of *I*.
37:12 them, and bring you back to the land of *I*.
37:16 and all the house of *I* associated with him.
37:19 and of the tribes of *I* associated with him,
37:22 upon the land, in the mountains of *I*,
37:28 that it is I, the LORD, who make *I* holy,
38: 8 the mountains of *I* which were long a ruin],
38:14 When my people *I* are dwelling in security,
38:16 my people *I* like a cloud covering the land.
38:17 through my servants, the prophets of *I*,
38:18 the day when Gog invades the land of *I*,
38:19 be a great shaking upon the land of *I*.
39: 2 I will lead you against the mountains of *I*.
39: 4 Upon the mountains of *I* you shall fall,
39: 7 make my holy name known among my people *I*;
39: 7 know that I am the LORD, the Holy One in *I*.
39: 9 in the cities of *I* go out and burn weapons:
39:11 Gog for his tomb a well-known place in *I*,
39:12 of *I* shall need seven months to bury them.
39:17 a great slaughter on the mountains of *I*:
39:22 house of *I* shall know that I am the LORD,
39:23 of its sins the house of *I* went into exile;
39:25 and have pity on the whole house of *I*,
39:29 poured out my spirit upon the house of *I*,
40: 2 me in divine visions to the land of *I*,
40: 4 Tell the house of *I* all that you see."
43: 2 glory of the God of *I* coming from the east.
43:10 *I* [that they may be ashamed of their sins],
44: 2 since the LORD, the God of *I*,
44: 6 to that rebellious house, the house of *I*:
44: 6 these abominations of yours, O house of *I*!
44:10 *I* strayed from me to pursue their idols,
44:12 an occasion of sin to the house of *I*,
44:22 women, but only virgins of the race of *I*;
44:28 you shall give them no property in *I*,
44:29 is under the ban in *I* shall be theirs.
45: 6 this shall belong to the whole house of *I*.
45: 8 This shall be his property in *I*,
45: 8 of *I* will no longer oppress my people,
45: 8 the house of *I* according to their tribes.
45: 9 Enough, you princes of *I*!
45:15 every two hundred from the pasturage of *I*,
45:16 to this offering [for the prince in *I*.
45:17 on all the festivals of the house of *I*.
45:17 make atonement on behalf of the house of *I*.
47:13 tribes of *I* [Joseph having two portions].
47:18 side, and the land of *I* on the other side,
47:21 yourselves according to the tribes of *I*.
47:22 receive inheritances among the tribes of *I*.
48:19 shall be taken from all the tribes of *I*.
48:29 as inheritances among the tribes of *I*,
48:30 of which are named after the tribes of *I*.
Dn 3:35 Isaac your servant, and *I* your holy one,
3:83 O *I*, bless the Lord; praise and exalt him
9: 7 the residents of Jerusalem, and all *I*,
9:11 *I* transgressed your law and went astray,
9:20 my sin and the sin of my people *I*,
13:48 To condemn a woman of *I* without
13:57 is how you acted with the daughters of *I*,
Hos 1: 1 days of Jeroboam, son of Joash, king of *I*.
1: 4 to an end the kingdom of the house of *I*;
1: 5 the bow of *I* in the valley of Jezreel.
1: 6 I no longer feel pity for the house of *I*;
2: 2 Judah and of *I* shall be gathered together
3: 1 Even as the LORD loves the people of *I*,
3: 4 For the people of *I* shall remain many days
3: 5 of *I* shall turn back and seek the LORD,
4: 1 Hear the word of the LORD, O people of *I*,
4:15 Though you play the harlot, O *I*,
4:16 For *I* is as stubborn as a heifer;
5: 1 O priests, Pay attention, O house of *I*,
5: 3 know Ephraim, and *I* is not hidden from me;
5: 3 has played the harlot, *I* is defiled.
5: 5 arrogance of *I* bears witness against him;
5: 9 tribes of *I* I announce what is sure to be.
6:10 house of *I* I have seen a horrible thing:
6:10 harlotry is found in Ephraim, *I* is defiled.
7: 1 of my people, when I would heal *I*,
7:10 arrogance of *I* bears witness against him;
8: 2 While to me they cry out, "O, God of *I*,
8: 3 The men of *I* have thrown away what is good;
8: 5 they be unable to attain innocence in *I*?
8: 8 *I* is swallowed up;
8:14 *I* has forgotten his maker and built palaces.
9: 1 Rejoice not, O *I*, exult not like the nations!
9: 7 Let *I* know it! "The prophet is a fool,
9:10 Like grapes in the desert, I found *I*;
10: 1 *I* is a luxuriant vine whose fruit matches
10: 6 into captivity, *I* be shamed by his schemes.
10: 8 of Aven shall be destroyed, the sin of *I*;
10: 9 the days of Gibeah you have sinned, O *I*.
10:15 At dawn the king of *I* shall perish utterly.
11: 1 When *I* was a child I loved him,
11: 8 you up, O Ephraim, or deliver you up, O *I*?
12: 1 surrounded me with lies, the house of *I*,
12: 3 The LORD has a grievance against *I*:
12:13 for a wife *I* tended sheep.
12:14 a prophet the LORD brought *I* out of Egypt,
13: 1 word caused fear, for he was exalted in *I*;
13: 9 Your destruction, O *I*!
13:12 The guilt of *I* is wrapped up,
14: 2 Return, O *I*, to the LORD, your God;
14: 6 I will be like the dew for *I*:
Jl 2:27 shall know that I am in the midst of *I*;
4: 2 behalf of my people and my inheritance, *I*;
4:16 his people, a stronghold to the men of *I*.
Am 1: 1 which he received in vision concerning *I*,
1: 1 days of Jeroboam, son of Joash, king of *I*,
2: 6 For three crimes of *I*,
2:11 Is this not so, O men of *I*?
3: 1 Hear the word, O men of *I*,
3:14 On the day when I punish *I* for his crimes,
4: 5 For so you love to do, O men of *I*,
4:12 I will deal with you in my own way, O *I*!
4:12 with you, prepare to meet your God, O *I*:
5: 1 I utter over you, a lament, O house of *I*:
5: 2 is fallen, to rise no more, the virgin *I*;
5: 3 shall be left with ten, of the house of *I*.
5: 4 For thus says the LORD to the house of *I*:
5: 6 with none to quench it for the house of *I*:
5:25 forty years in the desert, O house of *I*?
6: 1 to whom the people of *I* have recourse!
6:14 I am raising up against you, O house of *I*,
7: 8 the plummet in the midst of my people *I*;
7: 9 and the sanctuaries of *I* made desolate;
7:10 Bethel, sent word to Jeroboam, king of *I*:
7:10 has conspired against you here within *I*;
7:11 and *I* shall surely be exiled from its land."
7:15 said to me, Go, prophesy to my people *I*.
7:16 prophesy not against *I*,
7:17 *I* shall be exiled far from its land.
8: 2 time is ripe to have done with my people *I*;
9: 7 not like the Ethiopians to me, O men of *I*,
9: 9 to sift the house of *I* among all nations,
9:14 about the restoration of my people *I*;
Ob 1:20 captives of the host of the children of *I*
Mi 1: 5 pass, and for the sins of the house of *I*.
1:13 Because there were in you the crimes of *I*.
1:14 is a deception to the kings of *I*.
1:15 Even to Adullam shall go the glory of *I*.
2:12 one, I will assemble all the remnant of *I*;
3: 1 leaders of Jacob, rulers of the house of *I*!
3: 8 to Jacob his crimes and to *I* his sins.
3: 9 of Jacob, you rulers of the house of *I*!
4:14 they strike on the cheek the ruler of *I*.
5: 1 forth for me one who is to be ruler in *I*;
5: 2 brethren shall return to the children of *I*.)
6: 2 people, and he enters into trial with *I*.
Na 2: 3 restore the vine of Jacob, the pride of *I*,
Zep 2: 9 says the LORD of hosts, the God of *I*,
3:13 the remnant of *I*.
3:14 sing joyfully, O *I*!
3:15 The King of *I*, the LORD, is in your midst,
Zec 2: 2 that scattered Judah and *I* and Jerusalem."
8:13 nations, O house of Judah and house of *I*,
9: 1 the LORD's, as are all the tribes of *I*,
11:14 off the brotherhood between Judah and *I*.
12: 1 the word of the LORD concerning *I*.
Mal 1: 1 The word of the LORD to *I* through Malachi.
1: 5 is the LORD, even beyond the land of *I*."
2:11 thing has been done in *I* and in Jerusalem.
2:16 hate divorce, says the LORD, the God of *I*,
3:22 The statutes and ordinances for all *I*.
Mt 2: 6 a ruler who is to shepherd my people *I*.'"
2:20 his mother, and set out for the land of *I*.
2:21 his mother, and returned to the land of *I*.
8:10 I have never found this much faith in *I*.
9:33 like this has ever been seen in *I*!"
10: 6 after the lost sheep of the house of *I*.

10:23 the towns of *I* before the Son of Man comes.
15:24 only to the lost sheep of the house of *I*."
15:31 They glorified the God of *I*.
19:28 thrones to judge the twelve tribes of *I*.
27:42 So he is the king of *I*!
Mk 12:29 'Hear, O *I*! The Lord our God is Lord
15:32 Let the 'Messiah,' the 'king of *I*,'
Lk 1:16 *I* will he bring back to the Lord their God.
1:54 He has upheld *I* his servant,
1:68 "Blessed be the Lord the God of *I* because
1:80 when he made his public appearance in *I*.
2:25 pious, and awaited the consolation of *I*,
2:32 the Gentiles, the glory of your people *I*."
2:34 be the downfall and the rise of many in *I*,
4:25 there were many widows in *I* in the days of
4:27 in *I* in the time of Elisha the prophet;
22:30 on thrones judging the twelve tribes of *I*.
24:21 that he was the one who would set *I* free.
Jn 1:31 water was that he might be revealed to *I*."
1:49 Son of God; you are the king of *I*."
3:10 "You hold the office of teacher of *I* and
12:13 Blessed is the King of *I*!"
Acts 1: 6 are you going to restore the rule to *I* now?"
2:22 "Men of *I*, listen to me!
2:36 Therefore let the whole house of *I* know
4:10 then you and all the people of *I* must
4:27 with the Gentiles and the peoples of *I*.
5:21 the full council of the elders of *I*.
5:31 repentance to *I* and forgiveness of sins.
7:42 forty years in the desert, O house of *I*?
9:15 and their kings and to the people of *I*.
10:36 the message he has sent to the sons of *I*,
13:17 God of the people *I* once chose our fathers.
13:23 man's descendants Jesus, a savior for *I*.
13:24 of repentance to all the people of *I*.
28:20 solely because I share the hope of *I*."
Rom 9:27 Isaiah cries out, referring to *I*,
9:31 while *I*, seeking a law from which justice
10:19 again, did *I* really not understand?
10:21 *I* he says, "All day long I stretched out
11: 2 Elijah, how he pleaded with God against *I*?
11: 7 *I* did not obtain what she was seeking,
11:11 has come to the Gentiles to stir *I* to envy.
11:25 blindness has come upon part of *I*
11:26 enter in, and then all *I* will be saved.
1Cor 10:18 Look at *I* according to the flesh and see
Gal 6:16 this rule of life, and on the *I* of God.
Eph 2:12 and were excluded from the community of *I*.
Phil 3: 5 the stock of *I* and the tribe of Benjamin,
Heb 8: 8 the house of *I* and with the house of Judah.
8:10 make with the house of *I* after those days,
11:28 angel might not touch the first-born of *I*.
Rv 7: 4 forty-four thousand from every tribe of *I*;
21:12 gates, the names of the twelve tribes of *I*.

ISRAELITE (79)

Ex 1: 9 and powerful the *I* people are growing,
5:15 Then the *I* foremen came and made this
5:19 *I* foremen knew they were in a sorry plight,
16: 1 *I* community came into the desert of Sin,
16: 2 Here in the desert the whole *I* community
16: 9 to Aaron, "Tell the whole *I* community:
16:10 announced this to the whole *I* community,
17: 1 the whole *I* community journeyed by stages,
35: 1 the whole *I* community and said to them,
35: 4 Moses told the whole *I* community,
35:20 the whole *I* community left Moses' presence,
35:29 Every *I* man and woman brought to the LORD
Lv 16: 5 From the *I* community he shall receive two
16:17 as well as for the whole *I* community,
17: 3 *I* who slaughters an ox or a sheep or goat,
19: 2 to the whole *I* community and tell them:
20: 2 an *I* or an alien residing in Israel,
23:42 native *I* among you shall dwell in booths,
24:10 was a man born of an *I* mother (Shelomith,
24:11 man quarreled publicly with another *I*
Nm 1:53 God's wrath will strike the *I* community.
5:10 Each *I* man may dispose of his own sacred
15:25 make atonement for the whole *I* community;
15:26 Not only the whole *I* community,
15:29 a native *I* or an alien residing with you.
17: 6 The next day the whole *I* community
19: 9 lustral water for the *I* community.
20: 1 The whole *I* community arrived in the
20:22 the whole *I* community came to Mount Hor.
25: 5 So Moses told the *I* judges,
25: 6 Yet a certain *I* came and brought in a
25: 6 view of Moses and of the whole *I* community,
25: 8 followed the *I* into his retreat where be
25: 8 the pair of them, the *I* and the woman.
25:14 *I* slain with the Midianite woman was Zimri,
27:20 that the whole *I* community may obey him.
30: 2 Moses said to the heads of the *I* tribes,
31:12 *I* community at their camp
36: 3 they marry into one of the other *I* tribes,
36: 8 who inherits property in any of the *I* tribes
36: 9 but all the *I* tribes will retain their own
Dt 23:18 be no temple harlot among the *I* women,
23:18 nor a temple prostitute among the *I* men.
24: 7 *I* in order to enslave him and sell him,
Jos 5: 2 the *I* nation for the second time."
9:14 the *I* princes partook of their provisions,
13: 6 areas in the division of the *I* heritage,
20: 9 which any *I* or stranger living among them
Jgs 2: 6 each *I* went to take possession of his own
7:14 can only be the sword of the *I* Gideon,
11:40 It then bacame a custom in Israel for *I*
20:23 But though the *I* soldiers took courage and
20:26 So the entire *I* army went up to Bethel,
20:31 thirty of the *I* soldiers in the open field,
21:17 else one of the *I* tribes will be wiped out.
1Sm 7: 2 the whole *I* population turned to the LORD.
9: 2 There was no other *I* handsomer than Saul;
2Sm 1: 3 replied, "I have escaped from the *I* camp."
1Kgs 20:15 Behind them he mustered all the *I* soldiery,
2Kgs 6:12 "The *I* prophet Elisha can tell the king
1Chr 1:43 before they had *I* kings were the following:
16: 3 of the LORD, and distributed to every *I*,
27: 1 This is the list of the *I* family heads,
2Chr 5: 2 the princes of the *I* ancestral houses,
6:29 when any *I* of all your people offers a
11:16 all those of the *I* tribes who firmly
23: 2 Judah and also the heads of the *I* families.
Ezr 2:59 ancestral houses and their descent were *I*:
7:28 I gathered together *I* family heads to make
9: 1 "Neither the *I* laymen nor the priests nor
Neh 7:61 ancestral houses and their descent were *I*:
9: 2 Those of *I* descent separated themselves
Tb 5: 5 He replied "I am an *I*,
5: 9 a man who is one of our own *I* kinsmen!"
Jdt 4:11 And all the *I* men,
14:11 Then all the *I* men took up their arms and
15: 3 Then all the *I* warriors overwhelmed them.
Jn 1:47 "This man is a true *I*.
Rom 11: 1 I myself am an *I*,

ISRAELITES—ISRAELITES' (683)

Gn 32:33 the *I* do not eat the sciatic muscle that
36:31 of Edom before any king reigned over the *I*.
46: 8 These are the names of the *I*,
Ex 1: 7 But the *I* were fruitful and prolific.
1:11 the *I* to oppress them with forced labor.
1:12 the *I* and reduced them to cruel slavery,
2:23 Still the *I* groaned and cried out because
2:25 He saw the *I* and knew. . . .
3: 9 So indeed the cry of the *I* has reached me,
3:10 you to Pharaoh to lead my people, the *I*,
3:11 go to Pharaoh and lead the *I* out of Egypt?"
3:13 God, "when I go to the *I* and say to them,
3:14 added, "This is what you shall tell the *I*:
3:15 to Moses, "Thus shall you say to the *I*:
3:16 "Go and assemble the elders of the *I*,
4:29 went and assembled all the elders of the *I*.
5:14 The foremen of the *I*,
6: 5 that I have heard the groaning of the *I*,
6: 6 Therefore, say to the *I*:
6: 9 But when Moses told this to the *I*,
6:11 king of Egypt, to let the *I* leave his land."
6:12 LORD, "If the *I* would not listen to me,
6:13 the LORD, to bring the *I* out of Egypt,
6:13 orders regarding both the *I* and Pharaoh,
6:26 "Lead the *I* from the land of Egypt,
6:27 king of Egypt, to bring the *I* out of Egypt
7: 2 tell Pharaoh to let the *I* leave his land.
7: 4 will bring the hosts of my people, the *I*,
7: 5 Egypt and lead the *I* out of their midst."
9: 4 so that none belonging to the *I* will die."
9: 6 died, but not one beast belonging to the *I*.
9: 7 even one beast belonging to the *I* had died,
9:26 in the land of Goshen, where the *I* dwelt,
9:35 in his obstinacy he would not let the *I* go,
10:20 obstinate, and he would not let the *I* go.
10:23 But all the *I* had light where they dwelt.
11: 7 But among the *I* and their animals not even
11: 7 between the Egyptians and the *I*.
11:10 and he would not let the *I* leave his land.
12:27 passed over the houses of the *I* in Egypt;
12:28 and the *I* went and did as the LORD had
12:31 my people at once, you and the *I* with you!
12:35 The *I* did as Moses had commanded:
12:37 The *I* set out from Rameses for Succoth,
12:40 The time the *I* had stayed in Egypt was
12:42 so on this same night all the *I* must keep
12:50 All the *I* did just as the LORD had
12:51 the *I* out of Egypt company by company.
13: 2 that opens the womb among the *I*,
13:18 In battle array the *I* marched out of Egypt.
13:19 Joseph had made the *I* swear solomnly that,
14: 2 "Tell the *I* to turn about and camp before
14: 3 'The *I* are wandering about aimlessly in
14: 4 This the *I* did. When it was reported
14: 8 he pursued the *I* even while they were
14:10 Pharaoh was already near when the *I* looked
14:15 Tell the *I* to go forward.
14:16 that the *I* may pass through it on dry land.
14:22 the *I* marched into the midst of the sea on
14:28 army which had followed the *I* into the sea.
14:29 But the *I* had marched on dry land through
15: 1 Moses and the *I* sang this song to the LORD:
15:19 though the *I* had marched on dry land
16: 3 *I* said to them, "Would that he had died
16: 6 So Moses and Aaron told all the *I*,
16:12 "I have heard the grumbling of the *I*.
16:15 On seeing it, the *I* asked one another,
16:17 The *I* did so. Some gathered a large
16:31 The *I* called this food manna.
16:35 The *I* ate this manna for forty years,
17: 7 the *I* quarreled there and tested the LORD,
19: 1 day, the *I* came to the desert of Sinai.
19: 4 tell the *I*: you have seen for yourselves
19: 6 That is what you must tell the *I*."
20:22 Moses, "Thus shall you speak to the *I*:
24: 5 having sent certain young men of the *I*
24:11 Yet he did not smite these chosen *I*.
24:17 To the *I* the glory of the LORD was seen as
25: 2 the *I* to take up a collection for me.
25:22 the commands that I wish you to give the *I*.
27:20 *I* to bring you clear oil of crushed olives,
27:21 for the *I* throughout their generations.
28: 1 "From among the *I* have your brother Aaron,
28:30 *I* over his heart in the LORD's presence.
28:38 Since Aaron bears whatever guilt the *I* may
29:28 are due to Aaron and his sons from the *I*
29:28 too, the *I* shall make a contribution,
29:43 "There, at the altar, I will meet the *I*;
29:45 the midst of the *I* and will be their God.
30:12 a census of the *I* who are to be registered,
30:16 you receive this forfeit money from the *I*,
30:16 it may be the *I'* reminder before the LORD,
30:31 To the *I* you shall say:
31:13 said to Moses, "You must also tell the *I*:
31:16 So shall the *I* observe the sabbath,
31:17 and the *I* it is to be an everlasting token;
32:20 on the water and made the *I* drink.
33: 5 The LORD said to Moses, "Tell the *I*:
33: 6 onward, the *I* laid aside their ornaments.
34:30 and the other *I* saw Moses and noticed how
34:32 Later on, all the *I* came up to him,
34:34 tell the *I* all that had been commanded.
34:35 Then the *I* would see that the skin of
35:30 Moses said to the *I*, "See, the LORD
36: 3 contributions which the *I* had brought
39:32 The *I* did the work just as the LORD had
39:42 The *I* had carried out all the work just as
40:36 the *I* would set out on their journey.
Lv 1: 2 "Speak to the *I* and tell them:
4: 2 The LORD said to Moses, "Tell the *I*:
7:23 The LORD said to Moses, "Tell the *I*:
7:29 The LORD said to Moses, "Tell the *I*:
7:34 for from the peace offerings of the *I* I have
7:34 ordinance as a contribution from the *I*."
7:36 LORD ordered the *I* to give them this share
7:38 commanded the *I* in the wilderness of Sinai
10:11 you must teach the *I* all the laws that the
10:14 your due from the peace offerings of the *I*.
11: 2 and Aaron, "Speak to the *I* and tell them:
12: 2 The LORD said to Moses, "Tell the *I*:
15: 2 and Aaron, "Speak to the *I* and tell them:
15:31 shall warn the *I* of their uncleanness,
16:16 the sinful defilements and faults of the *I*.
16:19 holy, purged of the defilements of the *I*.
16:21 sinful faults and transgressions of the *I*,
16:34 shall be made for all the sins of the *I*."
17: 2 and his sons, as well as to all the *I*,
17: 5 the *I* shall henceforth offer to the LORD,
17:12 That is why I have told the *I*:
17:13 the *I* or of the aliens residing among them,
17:14 body is its blood, I have told the *I*:
18: 2 to Moses, "Speak to the *I* and tell them:
20: 2 The LORD said to Moses, "Tell the *I*:
21:24 to Aaron and his sons and to all the *I*.
22: 2 offerings which the *I* consecrate to me;
22: 3 which the *I* consecrate to the LORD,
22:15 The sacred offerings which the *I*
22:18 to Aaron and his sons and to all the *I*,
22:32 in the midst of the *I* I,
23: 2 to Moses, "Speak to the *I* and tell them:
23:10 to Moses, "Speak to the *I* and tell them:
23:24 The LORD said to Moses, "Tell the *I*:
23:34 The LORD said to Moses, "Tell the *I*:
23:43 when I led the *I* out of the land of Egypt,
23:44 to the *I* the festivals of the LORD.
24: 2 "Order the *I* to bring you clear oil of
24: 8 part of the *I* by an everlasting agreement.
24:10 Among the *I* there was a man born of an
24:15 Tell the *I*: Anyone who curses his God
24:23 When Moses told this to the *I*,
25: 2 Sinai, "Speak to the *I* and tell them:
25:33 hereditary property in the midst of the *I*.
25:46 not lord it harshly over any of the *I*,
25:55 For to me the *I* belong as servants;
26:46 in the pact between himself and the *I*.
27: 2 to Moses, "Speak to the *I* and tell them:
27:34 LORD gave Moses on Mount Sinai for the *I*.
Nm 1: 1 of the *I'* departure from the land of Egypt,
1: 2 a census of the whole community of the *I*,
1:45 The total number of the *I* of twenty years
1:49 in the census along with the other *I*.
1:52 While the other *I* shall camp by companies,
1:54 All this the *I* fulfilled as the LORD had
2: 2 "The *I* shall camp,
2:32 census of the *I* taken by ancestral houses.
2:33 were not registered with the other *I*,
2:34 *I* did just as the LORD had commanded Moses;
3: 8 of the *I* in the service of the Dwelling.
3: 9 aside from among the *I* as dedicated to me.
3:12 I who have chosen the Levites from the *I*

ISRAELITES—ISRAELITES' (cont.)
3:12 first-born that opens the womb among the *I.*
3:38 the obligations of the sanctuary for the *I.*
3:40 males of the *I* a month old or more,
3:41 in place of all the first-born of the *I,*
3:41 the first-born among the cattle of the *I.*"
3:42 a census of all the first-born of the *I,*
3:45 in place of all the first-born of the *I,*
3:46 of the *I* who outnumber the Levites,
3:50 From the first-born of the *I* he received
4:46 when Moses and Aaron and the *I* princes had
5: 2 the *I* to expel from camp every leper,
5: 4 The *I* obeyed the command that the LORD had
5: 6 The LORD said to Moses, "Tell the *I:*
5: 9 The *I* are bound to make
5:12 to Moses, "Speak to the *I* and tell them:
6: 2 "Speak to the *I* and tell them:
6:23 This is how you shall bless the *I.*
6:27 So shall they invoke my name upon the *I,*
8: 6 Levites from among the *I* and purify them.
8: 9 assemble also the whole community of the *I.*
8:10 the *I* shall lay their hands upon them.
8:11 the LORD as a wave offering from the *I,*
8:14 aside the Levites from the rest of the *I,*
8:16 because they, among the *I,*
8:16 first-born that opens the womb among the *I.*
8:17 Indeed, all the first-born among the *I,*
8:18 the first-born *I* I have taken the Levites;
8:19 I have given these dedicated *I* to Aaron
8:19 discharge the duties of the *I* in the meeting
8:19 the *I* should they come near the sanctuary."
8:20 community of the *I* deal with the Levites,
9: 2 "Tell the *I* to celebrate the Passover at
9: 4 told the *I* to celebrate the Passover.
9: 7 at its proper time along with the other *I?*"
9:10 "Speak to the *I* and say:
9:17 rose from the tent, the *I* would break camp;
9:18 At the bidding of the LORD the *I* moved on,
9:19 *I* obeyed the LORD and would not move on;
9:22 the *I* remained in camp and did not depart;
10:12 The *I* moved on from the desert of Sinai by
10:28 This was the order of departure for the *I,*
11: 4 for meat that even the *I* lamented again,
13: 2 land of Canaan, which I am giving to the *I.*
13: 3 All of them were leaders among the *I,*
13:24 It was because of the cluster the *I* cut
13:26 of the *I* in the desert of Paran at Kadesh,
13:32 the *I* about the land they had scouted,
14: 2 All the *I* grumbled against Moses and Aaron,
14: 5 the whole assembled community of the *I;*
14: 7 and said to the whole community of the *I,*
14:10 appeared at the meeting tent to all the *I.*
14:27 heard the grumblings of the *I* against me.
14:39 Moses repeated these words to all the *I,*
15: 2 to Moses, "Give the *I* these instructions:
15:18 to Moses, "Speak to the *I* and tell them:
15:32 While the *I* were in the desert,
15:38 "Speak to the *I* and tell them that they
16: 2 fifty *I* who were leaders in the community,
16:34 all the *I* near them fled at their shrieks,
17: 3 way they shall serve as a sign to the *I.*"
17: 5 to be a reminder to the *I* that no layman,
17:17 "Speak to the *I* and get one staff from
17:20 my presence the *I'* grumbling against you."
17:21 So Moses spoke to the *I,*
17:24 staffs from the LORD's presence to the *I.*
17:27 Then the *I* cried out to Moses,
18: 5 that wrath may not fall again upon the *I.*
18: 6 the Levites, from the body of the *I;*
18: 8 in the various sacred offerings of the *I;*
18:11 the gift in every wave offering of the *I;*
18:19 sacred gifts which the *I* make to the LORD;
18:20 of the *I* nor hold any portion among them;
18:22 *I* may no longer approach the meeting tent;
18:23 shall not have any heritage among the *I,*
18:24 the *I* give as a contribution to the LORD.
18:24 are not to have any heritage among the *I.*"
18:26 When you receive from the *I* the tithes I
18:28 all the tithes you receive from the *I,*
18:32 of the *I* and so bring death on yourselves."
19: 2 Tell the *I* to procure for you a red heifer
19:10 *I* and for the aliens residing among them.
20:12 in showing forth my sanctity before the *I,*
20:13 where the *I* contended against the LORD,
20:19 *I* insisted, "We want only to go up along
20:24 not enter the land I am giving to the *I,*
21: 1 the *I* were coming along the way of Atharim,
21:10 The *I* moved on and encamped in Oboth.
22: 1 Then the *I* moved on and encamped in the
22: 3 the *I* greatly because of their numbers,
25: 8 Thus the slaughter of *I* was checked;
25:11 the *I* by his zeal for my honor among them;
25:11 end to the *I* for the offense to my honor.
25:13 of his God and thus made amends for the *I.*"
26: 2 throughout the community of the *I* of all
26: 4 The *I* who came out of the land of Egypt
26:51 and thirty were the *I* who were registered.
26:62 They were not registered with the other *I,*
26:62 for no heritage was given them among the *I.*
26:63 census of the *I* taken on the plains of Moab
26:64 of the *I* taken in the desert of Sinai.
27: 8 Therefore, tell the *I:* If a man dies without
27:11 This is the legal norm for the *I,*
27:12 view the land that I am giving to the *I.*
27:21 as he directs, Joshua, all the *I* with him,
28: 2 to Moses, "Give the *I* this commandment:
30: 1 Moses then gave the *I* these instructions,
31: 2 to Moses, "Avenge the *I* on the Midianites,
31: 9 But the *I* kept the women of the Midianites
31:16 the *I* toward the LORD in the Peor affair,
31:30 From the *I'* half you shall take one out of
31:42 The half for the other *I,*
31:47 From this, the *I'* share,
31:54 as a memorial for the *I* before the LORD.
32: 7 Why do you wish to discourage the *I* from
32: 9 then so discouraged the *I* that they would
32:13 So in his anger with the *I* the LORD made
32:14 to the LORD's blazing wrath against the *I.*
32:17 will march as troops in the van of the *I,*
32:18 the *I* has taken possession of his heritage,
32:28 the heads of the ancestral tribes of the *I:*
33: 1 *I* journeyed up by companies from the land
33: 3 morrow the *I* went forth in triumph,
33: 5 out from Rameses, the *I* camped at Succoth.
33:38 departure of the *I* from the land of Egypt,
33:40 of Canaan, heard that the *I* were coming.
33:51 "Tell the *I:* When you go across the Jordan
34: 2 said to Moses, "Give the *I* this order:
34:13 Moses also gave this order to the *I:*
34:29 the *I* their heritage in the land of Canaan.
35: 2 "Tell the *I* that out of their hereditary
35: 8 the cities from the property of the *I,*
35:10 The LORD said to Moses, "Tell the *I:*
35:15 shall serve not only the *I* but all the resident
35:34 the LORD who dwells in the midst of the *I.*"
36: 1 of the ancestral houses of the other *I.*
36: 2 to apportion the land by lot among the *I;*
36: 4 When the *I* celebrate the jubilee year,
36: 5 So Moses gave this regulation to the *I*
36: 7 the *I* will pass from one tribe to another,
36: 7 *I* will retain their own ancestral heritage.
36: 8 in order that all the *I* may remain in
36:13 LORD prescribed for the *I* through Moses,
Dt 1: 3 Moses spoke to the *I* all the commands that
2:12 just as the *I* have done in the land of
3:18 over in the vanguard of your brother *I.*
4:44 is the law which Moses set before the *I.*
4:46 the *I* defeated after coming out of Egypt.
10: 6 [The *I* set out from Beeroth Bene-jaakan
28:69 to make with the *I* in the land of Moab,
31:19 Teach it to the *I* and have them recite it,
31:19 song may be a witness for me against the *I.*
31:22 that same day, and he taught it to the *I.*
31:23 it is you who must bring the *I* into the land
32:49 I am giving to the *I* as their possession.
32:51 of you broke faith with me among the *I*
32:51 to manifest my sanctity among the *I.*
32:52 enter that land which I am giving to the *I.*"
33: 1 God, pronounced upon the *I* before he died.
34: 8 the *I* wept for Moses in the plains of Moab,
34: 9 and so the *I* gave him their obedience,
Jos 1: 2 the people into the land I will give the *I.*
2: 2 some *I* had come there that night to spy
3: 1 with all the *I* from Shittim to the Jordan,
3: 9 So Joshua said to the *I,*
4: 4 men whom he had selected from among the *I,*
4: 5 will equal in number the tribes of the *I.*
4: 7 to serve as a perpetual memorial to the *I.*"
4: 8 The twelve *I* did as Joshua had commanded:
4: 8 the Jordan as there were tribes of the *I,*
4:12 armed, marched in the vanguard of the *I,*
4:21 taken from the Jordan, saying to the *I,*
5: 1 before the *I* until they crossed over,
5: 3 and circumcised the *I* at Gibeath-haaraloth,
5: 6 *I* had wandered forty years in the desert,
5:10 While the *I* were encamped at Gilgal on the
5:12 No longer was there manna for the *I,*
6: 1 of siege because of the presence of the *I,*
7: 1 But the *I* violated the ban;
7: 1 anger of the LORD flared up against the *I.*
7:12 If the *I* cannot stand up to their enemies,
7:23 tent, brought them to Joshua and all the *I,*
8:15 *I* fled in seeming defeat toward the desert,
8:17 in this pursuit of Joshua and the *I,*
8:20 because the *I* retreating toward the desert
8:21 when Joshua and the main body of *I* saw
8:22 of Ai were hemmed in by *I* on either side,
8:24 inhabitants of Ai who had pursued the *I*
8:27 the *I* took for themselves as booty the
8:31 keeping with the command to the *I* of Moses,
8:32 There, in the presence of the *I,*
9:16 the *I* learned that these people were from
9:17 road, the *I* came to their cities of Gibeon,
9:26 he saved them from being killed by the *I,*
10: 4 had concluded peace with Joshua and the *I.*
10:10 The *I* inflicted a great slaughter on them
10:11 hailstones than the *I* slew with the sword.
10:12 LORD delivered up the Amorites to the *I,*
10:20 Once Joshua and the *I* had finally
10:21 no man uttering a sound against the *I.*
11: 8 delivered them into the power of the *I,*
11:14 The *I* took all the spoil and livestock of
11:19 in Gibeon, no city made peace with the *I;*
11:22 no Anakim were left in the land of the *I.*
12: 1 *I* conquered and whose lands they occupied,
12: 6 of the LORD, and the *I* conquered them,
12: 7 kings whom Joshua and the *I* conquered
13: 6 At the advance of the *I* I will drive out
13:13 the *I* did not dislodge the Geshurites and
13:22 their slain followers the *I* put to the sword
14: 1 which the *I* received in the land of Canaan.
14: 1 of the *I* determined their heritage by lot,
14: 5 did the *I* carry out the instructions of
17:13 When the *I* grew stronger they impressed
18: 1 community of the *I* assembled at Shiloh,
18: 2 the *I* had not yet received their heritage.
18: 3 Joshua therefore said to the *I,*
18:10 land for the *I* into their separate shares,
19:49 the *I* assigned a heritage in their midst
19:51 tribes of the *I* divided the land by lot
20: 2 "Tell the *I* to designate the cities of
21: 1 of the *I* at Shiloh in the land of Canaan,
21: 3 the *I* gave the Levites the following
21: 8 pasture lands the *I* allotted to the Levites
21:41 cities within the territory of the *I* which,
22: 9 Manasseh left the other *I* at Shiloh
22:11 *I* heard the report that the Reubenites,
22:21 replied to the military leaders of the *I:*
22:30 community, the military leaders of the *I,*
22:31 the *I* free from punishment by the LORD."
22:32 of Gilead to the *I* in the land of Canaan,
22:33 The report satisfied the *I,*
23: 1 after the LORD had given the *I* rest from
24:32 which the *I* had brought up from Egypt,
Jgs 1: 1 death of Joshua the *I* consulted the LORD,
1:28 When the *I* grew stronger,
2: 4 LORD had made these threats to all the *I,*
2:11 *I* offended the LORD by serving the Baals.
2:22 Through these nations the *I* were to be
3: 1 those *I* who had no experience of the battles
3: 2 those generations only of the *I*
3: 5 the *I* were living among the Canaanites,
3: 7 Because the *I* had offended the LORD by
3: 9 But when the *I* cried out to the LORD,
3:12 Again the *I* offended the LORD,
3:14 The *I* then served Eglon,
3:15 But when the *I* cried out to the LORD,
3:15 him that the *I* sent their tribute to Eglon,
3:27 and the *I* went down from the mountains
4: 1 however, the *I* again offended the LORD.
4: 3 But the *I* cried out to the LORD;
4: 3 he sorely oppressed the *I* for twenty years.
4: 5 there the *I* came up to her for judgment.
4:23 the Canaanite king, Jabin, before the *I;*
6: 1 The *I* offended the LORD,
6: 2 For fear of Midian the *I* established the
6: 3 that when the *I* had completed their sowing,
6: 6 Midian, and so the *I* cried out to the LORD.
6: 8 sent a prophet to the *I* who said to them,
7: 8 ordered the rest of the *I* to their tents,
7:23 The *I* were called to arms from Naphtali,
8:22 The *I* then said to Gideon,
8:28 Midian brought into subjection by the *I;*
8:33 *I* again abandoned themselves to the Baals,
9:55 When the *I* saw that Abimelech was dead,
10: 6 The *I* again offended the LORD,
10: 8 the *I* in Bashan, and all the Israelites
10:10 Then the *I* cried out to the LORD,
10:11 The LORD answered the *I:*
10:15 But the *I* said to the LORD,
10:17 the *I* assembled and encamped in Mizpah.
11:27 this day between the *I* and the Ammonites!"
11:33 Ammonites brought into subjection by the *I.*
13: 1 The *I* again offended the LORD,
19:12 off to a city of foreigners, who are not *I,*
19:30 day the *I* came up from the land of Egypt
20: 1 So all the *I* came out as one man:
20: 3 heard that the *I* had gone up to Mizpah.
20: 3 The *I* asked to be told how the crime had
20: 7 Now that you are all here, O *I,*
20:13 to the demand of their brothers, the *I.*
20:14 cities to Gibeah, to do battle with the *I.*
20:17 Meanwhile the other *I* who,
20:18 When the *I* asked who should go first in
20:19 the *I* advanced on Gibeah with their forces.
20:20 On the day the *I* drew up in battle array
20:22 Then the *I* went up and wept before the
20:25 against them felled eighteen thousand *I,*
20:27 When the *I* consulted the LORD (for the ark
20:30 The *I* went up against the Benjaminites for
20:32 The *I,* however, had planned the flight
20:33 and the *I* in ambush rushed from their
20:35 and on that day the *I* killed twenty-five
20:38 the other *I* had agreed with the men in
20:39 the *I* wheeled about to resist as the smoke
20:45 *I* picked off five thousand men among them,
21: 5 Then the *I* asked, "Are there any among
21: 6 The *I* were disconsolate over their brother
21:18 in marriage, because the *I* have sworn,
21:24 Also at that time the *I* dispersed;
1Sm 2:14 That is how all the *I* were treated who
2:28 oblations of the *I* to your father's family.
6: 6 them that the *I* were released and departed?
7: 4 the *I* put away their Baals and Ashtaroth,
7: 6 at Mizpah that Samuel began to judge the *I.*
7: 7 heard that the *I* had gathered at Mizpah,
7: 7 the *I* became afraid of the Philistines and
7:11 Thereupon the *I* sallied forth from Mizpah
10:18 to the LORD at Mizpah and addressed the *I:*

11: 8 thousand *I* and seventy thousand Judahites.
11:15 *I* celebrated the occasion with great joy.
13: 6 Some *I*, aware of the danger
14:18 the ephod in front of the *I* at that time.)
14:21 to join the *I* under Saul and Jonathan.
14:22 all the *I* who were hiding in the hill
15: 6 kind to the *I* when they came up from Egypt."
17: 2 Saul and the *I* also gathered and camped in
17: 3 on one hill and the *I* on an opposite hill,
17:21 The *I* and the Philistines drew up opposite
17:24 When the *I* saw the man,
17:25 The *I* had been saying:
17:53 the Philistines, the *I* looted their camp.
29: 1 and the *I* were encamped at the spring of
31: 1 with the *I* fleeing before them and falling
31: 7 When the *I* on the slope of the valley and
2Sm 5: 2 who led the *I* out and brought them back.
6: 5 while David and all the *I* made merry
6:15 as he and all the *I* were bringing up the
7: 6 I led the *I* out of Egypt to the present,
7: 7 all my wanderings everywhere among the *I*,
10:19 peace with the *I* and became their subjects.
15: 6 the *I* who came to the king for judgment,
15:13 "The *I* have transferred their loyalty to
16: 3 *I* will restore to me my father's kingdom.' "
16:15 entered Jerusalem with all the *I*.
17:14 Then Absalom and all the *I* pronounced the
17:24 the Jordan accompanied by all the *I*.
18:16 turned back from the pursuit of the *I*,
18:17 And all the *I* fled to their own tents.
19: 9 Now the *I* had fled to their separate tents,
19:42 *I* began coming to the king and saying,
19:44 The *I* answered the Judahites:
19:44 turn spoke even more fiercely than the *I*.
20: 2 So all the *I* left David for Sheba,
21: 2 (Now the Gibeonites were not *I*,
21: 2 although the *I* had given them their oath,
23: 9 The *I* had retreated,
24: 1 and he incited David against the *I* by
1Kgs 6: 1 departure of the *I* from the land of Egypt,
6:13 *I* and will not forsake my people Israel."
8: 1 princes in the ancestral houses of the *I*,
8: 9 the LORD made a covenant with the *I*
8:63 all the *I* dedicated the temple of the LORD.
8:65 On this occasion Solomon and all the *I*,
9:21 doom the *I* had been unable to accomplish,
9:22 But Solomon enslaved none of the *I*,
11: 2 the LORD had forbidden the *I* to intermarry,
12:17 the *I* who lived in the cities of Judah.
12:24 march out to fight against your brother *I*.
12:33 chose to establish a feast for the *I*;
14:24 the LORD had cleared out of the *I'* way.
18:20 So Ahab sent to all the *I* and had the
19:10 but the *I* have forsaken your covenant,
19:14 But the *I* have forsaken your covenant,
20:27 The *I*, too, were called to arms
20:27 The *I*, encamped opposite them,
20:29 and the *I* struck down one hundred thousand
21:26 done, whom the LORD drove out before the *I*.
2Kgs 3:24 the *I* rose up and attacked the Moabites,
8:12 the evil that you will inflict upon the *I*.
10:32 Hazael defeated the *I* throughout their
13: 5 the LORD gave Israel a savior, and the *I*,
16: 3 LORD had cleared out of the way of the *I*.
17: 6 Samaria, and deported the *I* to Assyria,
17: 7 because the *I* sinned against the LORD,
17: 8 LORD had cleared out of the way of the *I*
17:21 he drove the *I* away from the LORD,
17:22 The *I* imitated Jeroboam in all the sins he
17:24 cities of Samaria in place of the *I*.
18: 4 that time the *I* were burning incense to it.
18:11 the *I* to Assyria and settled them in Halah,
21: 2 LORD had cleared out of the way of the *I*.
21: 9 LORD had destroyed at the coming of the *I*.
1Chr 6:49 The *I* assigned these cities with their
9: 2 there were certain lay *I*
10: 1 the *I* fled before the Philistines,
10: 7 When all the *I* who were in the valley saw
19:10 some of the best fighters among the *I*
21: 2 the number of the *I* from Beer-sheba to Dan,
2Chr 5:10 with the *I* at their departure from Egypt.
6:11 of the LORD which he made with the *I*."
7: 3 All the *I* looked on while the fire came
8: 2 Huram had given him, and settled *I* there.
8: 8 in the land, whom the *I* had not destroyed
8: 9 did not enslave the *I* for his works.
10:17 those *I* who lived in the cities of Judah.
10:18 labor, but the *I* stoned him to death.
11: 3 and to all the *I* in Judah and Benjamin:
13:12 the LORD, the God of your fathers, O *I*,
13:16 The *I* fled before Judah,
13:18 The *I* were subdued on that occasion and
28: 3 the LORD had cleared out before the *I*.
28: 8 The *I* took away as captives two hundred
30: 6 *I*, return to the LORD,
30:21 Thus the *I* who were in Jerusalem
31: 1 those *I* who had been present went forth to
31: 1 the *I* returned to their various cities,
31: 5 the order was promulgated, the *I* brought,
31: 6 *I* and Judahites living in other cities of
33: 2 LORD had cleared out of the way of the *I*.
33: 9 LORD had destroyed at the coming of the *I*.
34:33 from all the territory belonging to the *I*,
35:17 The *I* who were present on that occasion
Ezr 2:70 Thus all the *I* dwelt in their cities.
3: 1 after the *I* had settled in their cities,
6:16 The *I*— priests, Levites, and the other
6:21 The *I* who had returned from the exile
7: 7 Some of the *I* and some priests,
8:25 officials, and all the *I* of that region.
10: 1 large assembly of *I* gathered about him,
10:25 Among the other *I*: Of the sons of Parosh:
Neh 1: 6 day and night for your servants the *I*,
2:10 had come to seek the welfare of the *I*.
8:14 the *I* must dwell in booths during the feast
8:17 Now the *I* had done nothing of this sort
9: 1 the *I* gathered together fasting and in
9: 5 The *I* answered with the blessing,
10:40 *I* and Levites bring the offerings of grain,
11: 3 (In the cities of Judah dwelt lay *I*,
13: 2 would not succor the *I* with food and water,
Tb 1: 8 and to converts who were living with the *I*.
1:18 In his rage he killed many *I*,
13: 3 Praise him, you *I*,
14: 7 Because all the *I* who are to be saved in
Jdt 4: 1 When the *I* who dwelt in Judea heard of all
4: 8 The *I* carried out the orders given them by
5: 1 army, that the *I* were ready for battle,
5:17 *I* did not sin in the sight of their God,
5:23 "We are not afraid of the *I*,"
6: 2 the *I* because their God protects them?
6:10 to Bethulia, and hand him over to the *I*.
6:14 The *I* came down to him from their city,
7: 1 passes, and engage the *I* in battle.
7: 4 When the *I* saw how many there were,
7: 6 in the sight of the *I* who were in Bethulia.
7:10 These *I* do not rely on their spears,
7:17 the water supply and the springs of the *I*.
7:19 The *I* cried to the Lord,
10: 8 for the glory of the *I* and the exaltation
10:19 regarding the *I* with wonder because of her,
11:17 me when the *I* have committed their crimes.
15: 5 On hearing this, all the *I*,
15: 7 The *I* who returned from the slaughter took
15: 8 priest Joakim and the elders of the *I*,
16:25 her death, no one again disturbed the *I*.
1Mc 1:43 and many *I* were in favor of his religion;
2:42 by a group of Hasideans, valiant *I*,
3:15 with him to help him take revenge on the *I*.
3:41 of silver and gold, to buy the *I* as slaves.
5: 9 destroy the *I* who were in their territory;
5:45 Then he assembled all the *I*,
5:60 and about two thousand *I* fell that day.
6: 6 strong army and been driven back by the *I*;
6:21 the besieged escaped, joined by impious *I*;
7: 9 with orders to take revenge on the *I*.
7:13 first among the *I* to seek peace with them,
7:23 and his men were bringing upon the *I*,
10:61 Some pestilent *I*, transgressors of the law,
Is 17: 3 of Aram shall have the same glory as the *I*,
66:20 just as the *I* bring their offering to the
Jer 16:14 lives, who brought the *I* out of Egypt";
16:15 who brought the *I* out of the land of the
23: 7 brought the *I* out of the land of Egypt";
32:30 The *I* and the Judeans from their youth
32:30 the *I* did nothing but provoke me with the
32:32 for all the wickedness the *I* and Judeans,
Bar 2:28 down your law in the presence of the *I*:
Ez 2: 3 Son of man, I am sending you to the *I*,
4:13 Thus the *I* shall eat their food unclean
35: 5 you never let die your hatred for the *I*,
37:16 and those *I* who are associated with him.
37:21 I will take the *I* from among the nations
43: 7 here I will dwell among the *I* forever.
44: 9 of the foreigners who live among the *I*.
44:15 my sanctuary when the *I* strayed from me,
47:22 The latter shall be to you like native *I*;
48:11 stray along with the *I* as the Levites did,
Dn 1: 3 the *I* of royal blood and of the nobility,
13:48 and continued, "Are you such fools, O *I*!
Hos 2: 1 of the *I* shall be like the sand of the sea,
Am 3:12 So the *I* who dwell in Samaria shall escape
9: 7 Did I not bring the *I* from the land of
Mt 27: 9 a price on his head, a price set by the *I*,
Lk 7: 9 have never found so much faith among the *I*."
Acts 3:12 "Fellow *I*, why does this surprise you?
5:35 and then said to the assembly, "Fellow *I*,
7:23 he decided to visit his kinsmen, the *I*.
7:37 This Moses is the one who said to the *I*,
13:16 *I* and you others who reverence our God,
21:28 "Fellow *I*, help us!
Rom 9: 4 the sake of my brothers, my kinsmen the *I*.
9: 6 For not all *I* are true Israelites nor
9:27 of the *I* should be as the sands of the sea,
10: 1 heart's desire, my prayer to God for the *I*,
2Cor 3: 7 that the *I* could not look on Moses' face
3:13 hide his face with a veil so that the *I* could
11:22 Are they *I*?
Heb 7: 5 tithes from the people, their brother *I*,
11:22 of his life, spoke of the Exodus of the *I*,
11:29 By faith the *I* crossed the Red Sea as if
12:25 For if the *I* did not escape punishment
Rv 2:14 in the way of the *I* by tempting them to eat

ISRAEL'S (30)

Gn 48:10 (Now *I* eyes were dim from age,
48:13 Ephraim with his right hand, to *I* left,
48:13 Manasseh with his left hand, to *I* right,
Ex 14:19 angel of God, who had been leading *I* camp,
Nm 21: 3 *I* prayer and delivered up the Canaanites,
23:10 Jacob, or numbered *I* wind-borne particles?
1Kgs 2: 5 when he slew the two generals of *I* armies,
2:32 Abner, son of Ner, general of *I* army,
2Kgs 2:12 my father! *I* chariots and drivers!"
13:14 *I* chariots and horsemen!"
1Chr 22:17 all of *I* leaders to help his son Solomon:
26:29 of *I* civil affairs as officials and judges.
2Chr 2: 3 such is *I* perpetual obligation.
33: 8 I will not again allow *I* feet to leave the
Ezr 10:10 women as wives has added to *I* guilt.
Tb 1: 4 city had been singled out of all *I* tribes,
14: 4 indeed, whatever was said by *I* prophets,
1Mc 3: 2 him, and they carried on *I* war joyfully.
5:62 whom it was granted to achieve *I* salvation.
14:26 have stood firm and repulsed *I* enemies.
2Mc 1:25 and eternal, *I* savior from all evil,
Ps(s) 68:27 bless the Lord, you of *I* wellspring!
Is 10:17 will become a fire, *I* Holy One a flame,
44: 6 Thus says the LORD, *I* King and redeemer,
Jer 3:21 the plaintive weeping of *I* children,
50:20 They shall seek *I* guilt,
Lam 2: 3 wrath, the horn that was *I* whole strength;
Bar 3: 4 God of Israel, hear the prayer of *I* few,
Heb 4:11 in imitation of the example of *I* unbelief.
11:30 Because of *I* faith,

ISSACHAR (36)

Gn 30:18 so she named him *I*.
35:23 Jacob's first-born, Simeon, Levi, Judah, *I*,
46:13 The sons of *I*:
49:14 *I* is a rawboned ass,
Ex 1: 3 *I*, Zebulun and Benjamin;
Nm 1: 8 Nahshon, son of Amminadab; from *I*:
1:28 Of the descendants of *I*,
1:29 hundred were enrolled in the tribe of *I*.
2: 5 the tribe of *I* [Their prince was Nethanel,
7:18 day Nethanel, son of Zuar, prince of *I*,
10:15 of Zuar, over the host of the tribe of *I*,
13: 7 of the tribe of *I*
26:25 These were the clans of *I*,
34:26 the tribe of *I*:
Dt 27:12 cross the Jordan, Simeon, Levi, Judah, *I*,
33:18 O Zebulun, in your pursuits, and you, *I*,
Jos 17:10 Asher on the north and *I* on the east.
17:11 in *I* and in Asher Manasseh was awarded
19:17 The fourth lot fell to *I*.
21: 6 by lot from the clans of the tribe of *I*,
21:28 From the tribe of *I* they obtained the four
Jgs 5:15 With Deborah were the princes of *I*;
1Kgs 4:17 Jehoshaphat, son of Paruah, in *I*;
15:27 Baasha, son of Ahijah, of the house of *I*,
1Chr 2: 1 Reuben, Simeon, Levi, Judah, *I*,
6:47 thirteen cities from the tribes of *I*,
6:57 From the tribe of *I*:
7: 1 The sons of *I* were Tola,
7: 5 In all the clans of *I* there was a total of
12:41 their neighbors from as far as *I*,
26: 5 Nethanel, the fifth, Ammiel, the sixth, *I*,
27:18 for *I*, Omri, son of Michael;
2Chr 30:18 from Ephraim, Manasseh, *I* and Zebulun,
Ez 48:25 *I*: on the frontier of Simeon,
48:26 on the frontier of *I*,
48:33 the gate of Simeon, the gate of *I*,
Rv 7: 7 Levi, twelve thousand from the tribe of *I*,

ISSACHARITE (1)

Jgs 10: 1 there rose to save Israel the *I* Tola,

ISSACHARITES (4)

Nm 26:23 The *I* by clans were:
Jos 19:17 of the clans of the *I* included Jezreel,
19:23 were the heritage of the clans of the *I*.
1Chr 12:33 Of the *I*, their chiefs who were endowed

ISSHIAH (6)

1Chr 7: 3 were Michael, Obadiah, Joel, and *I*.
12: 7 *I*, Azarel, Joezer, and Ishbaal
23:20 Micah, the chief, and *I*, the second.
24:21 *I*, the chief, of the descendants
24:25 *I*, the brother of Micah;
24:25 and Zechariah, a descendant of *I*.

ISSHIJAH (1)

Ezr 10:31 Eliezer, *I*,

ISSUE (30)

Gn 7: 3 will keep their *i* alive over all the earth.
15: 4 your own *i* shall be your heir."
17:16 and rulers of peoples shall *i* from him."
35:11 you, and kings shall *i* from your loins.
Dt 7:13 the *i* of your herds and the young of your
17: 8 your own community there is a case at *i*
28: 4 the *i* of your herds and the young of your

ISSUE (cont.)
28:18 the *i* of your herds and the young of your
28:51 no *i* of your herds or young of your flocks,
1Sm 2: 3 nor let arrogance *i* from your mouths.
2Sm 14: 8 I will *i* a command on your behalf."
14:20 this to come at the *i* in a roundabout way.
1Kgs 18:21 said, "How long will you straddle the *i*?
2Chr 21:15 your bowels *i* forth because of the disease,
36:22 *i* this proclamation throughout his kingdom,
Ezr 1: 1 *i* this proclamation throughout his kingdom,
6: 8 I also *i* this decree concerning your
6:11 I also *i* this decree:
7:21 *i* this decree to all the treasurers of
Est 1:20 will *i* is published throughout his realm,
2Mc 14:18 he shrank from deciding the *i* by bloodshed.
15:17 decide the *i* by hand-to-hand combat
Wis 3:16 of adulterers will remain without *i*,
Jer 34: 8 in Jerusalem to *i* an edict of emancipation.
Dn 6: 9 *i* the prohibition over your signature,
8:22 four kingdoms that will *i* from his nation,
Jl 4:18 shall *i* from the house of the LORD,
Mt 27:64 You should *i* an order having the tomb kept
Acts 11: 2 some among the circumcised took *i* with him,
1Cor 10:28 to it and on account of the conscience *i*—

ISSUED (33)
Jos 3: 3 and *i* these instructions to the people:
8:27 to the command of the LORD *i* to Joshua.
Jgs 15:19 the cavity in Lehi, and water *i* from it,
2Kgs 22:12 and *i* this command to Hilkiah the priest,
23:21 The king *i* a command to all the people to
2Chr 21:19 his bowels *i* forth because of the disease
30: 5 they *i* a decree to be proclaimed
34:20 his garments and *i* this command to Hilkiah,
Ezr 4:21 until a further decree has been *i* by me.
5: 3 "Who *i* the decree for you to build this
5: 9 'Who *i* the decree for you to build this
5:13 King Cyrus *i* a decree for the rebuilding
5:17 whether a decree really was *i* by King Cyrus
6: 1 Thereupon King Darius *i* an order to search
6: 3 year of King Cyrus, King Cyrus *i* a decree:
6:12 I, Darius, have *i* this decree;
7:13 I have *i* this decree,
Jdt 2: 3 refused to comply with the order he had *i*.
2: 6 they did not comply with the order I *i*.
Est 1:12 at the royal order *i* through the eunuchs.
1:15 of King Ahasuerus *i* through the eunuchs?"
1:19 let an irrevocable royal decree be *i* by him
3: 9 king, let a decree be *i* to destroy them;
8: 5 let a document be *i* to revoke the letters
2Mc 6: 8 a decree was *i* ordering the neighboring
Dn 2:13 was *i* that the wise men should be slain,
3:10 you *i* a decree that everyone who heard the
4: 3 So I *i* a decree that all the wise men of
6:14 to you, O king, or to the decree you *i*;
Mt 27:58 Pilate *i* an order for its release.
Acts 22:24 He *i* orders that he be examined under the
25:21 so I *i* orders that he be kept in custody
Rv 22: 1 which *i* from the throne of God and of the

ISSUES (4)
Nm 15:23 from the time the LORD first *i* the
Dt 28:57 afterbirth that *i* from her womb
Jb 41:12 From his nostrils *i* steam,
Acts 25:19 with him over *i* in their own religion,

ISSUING (1)
Mt 16:12 They finally realized he was not *i* a

ITALICA (1)
Acts 10: 1 named Cornelius, of the Roman cohort *I*,

ITALY (3)
Acts 18: 2 arrived from *I* with his wife Priscilla.
27: 1 it was decided that we were to sail for *I*,
27: 6 an Alexandrian vessel bound for *I*,

ITCH (1)
Dt 28:27 boils and with tumors, eczema and the *i*,

ITHAI (1)
1Chr 11:31 *I*, son of Ribai,

ITHAMAR (20)
Ex 6:23 she bore him Nadab, Abihu, Eleazar and *I*.
28: 1 with his sons Nadab, Abihu, Eleazar and *I*,
38:21 by the Levites under the direction of *I*,
Lv 10: 6 said to Aaron and his sons Eleazar and *I*,
10:12 and his surviving sons, Eleazar and *I*,
10:16 surviving sons of Aaron, Eleazar and *I*,
Nm 3: 2 his first-born, Abihu, Eleazar, and *I*.
3: 4 Thereafter only Eleazar and *I* performed
4:28 they shall be under the supervision of *I*,
4:33 meeting tent under the supervision of *I*,
7: 8 their duties, under the supervision of *I*,
26:60 were born Nadab and Abihu, Eleazar and *I*.
1Chr 5:29 of Aaron were Nadab, Abihu, Eleazar, and *I*.
24: 1 of Aaron were Nadab, Abihu, Eleazar, and *I*.
24: 2 only Eleazar and *I* served as priests.
24: 3 Eleazar, and Ahimelech, a descendant of *I*,
24: 4 found to be more numerous than those of *I*,
24: 5 descended both from Eleazar and from *I*.
24: 6 groups from Eleazar before each one from *I*.
Ezr 8: 2 of the sons of *I*,

ITHIEL (1)
Neh 11: 7 son of Kolaiah, son of Maaseiah, son of *I*,

ITHLAH (1)
Jos 19:42 Irshemesh, Shaalabbin, Aijalon, *I*,

ITHMAH (1)
1Chr 11:46 *I*, from Moab;

ITHNAN (1)
Jos 15:23 Dimonah, Adadah, Kedesh, Hazor and *I*;

ITHRA (1)
2Sm 17:25 was the son of an Ishmaelite named *I*,

ITHRAN (3)
Gn 36:26 of Dishon were Hemdan, Eshban, *I*,
1Chr 1:41 The sons of Dishon were Hemdan, Eshban, *I*,
7:37 Imrah, Bezer, Hod, Shamma, Shilshah, *I*,

ITHREAM (2)
2Sm 3: 5 and the sixth, *I*, of David's wife Eglah.
1Chr 3: 3 the sixth, *I*, by his wife Eglah.

ITHRITES (1)
1Chr 2:53 the *I*, the Puthites, the Shumathites,

ITINERANT (1)
Acts 19:13 Some *i* Jewish exorcists once tried to

ITSELF (93)
Ex 7:18 and the river *i* shall become so polluted
7:21 and the river *i* became so polluted that
10: 5 so that the ground *i* will not be visible.
10:26 to him until we arrive at the place *i*."
12: 3 must procure for *i* a lamb.
22: 5 standing grain or the field *i* is burned up,
24:10 sapphire tilework, as clear as the sky *i*.
25:21 In the ark *i* you are to put the
26: 1 "The Dwelling *i* you shall make out of
26:14 Over the tent *i* you shall make a covering
27: 8 the altar *i* in the form of a hollow box,
29: 5 tunic, the robe of the ephod, the ephod *i*,
38: 4 on the ground, half as high as the altar *i*.
Lv 4:13 LORD has forbidden and thus makes *i* guilty,
5:24 make full restitution of the thing *i*,
11:33 unclean, and the vessel *i* you must break.
11:39 that you could otherwise eat, dies of *i*,
13: 3 sore has turned white and the sore *i* shows
17:15 died of *i* or was killed by a wild beast,
22: 8 of *i* or has been killed by wild beasts.
Nm 15:24 if the community *i* unwittingly becomes
19:22 unclean person touches becomes unclean *i*,
23: 9 and does not reckon *i* among the nations.
Dt 2:36 Arnon and from the city in the wadi *i*,
14:21 not eat any animal that has died of *i*,
24:15 day's wages before sundown on the day *i*,
32:42 and my sword shall gorge *i* with flesh
Jos 6:24 city *i* they burned with all that was in it,
11:11 Hazor *i* he burned.
12: 2 of the Wadi Arnon, to include the wadi *i*,
13: 9 the Wadi Arnon and the city in the wadi *i*,
13:16 Wadi Arnon, and the city in the wadi *i*,
17: 8 although Tappuah *i* was an Ephraimite city
Jgs 7: 2 lest Israel vaunt *i* against me and say,
20:34 Israel, and advanced against the city *i*.
1Sm 17:49 The stone embedded *i* in his brow,
2Kgs 19:29 aftergrowth, next year, what grows of *i*;
1Chr 28:11 of the portico and of the building *i*,
2Chr 29:28 The entire assembly prostrated *i*,
Neh 13:16 In Jerusalem *i* the Tyrians who were
Tb 2:14 Your true character is finally showing *i*!"
2Mc 2:32 to a story and then abbreviate the story *i*.
5:20 Therefore, the Place *i*,
Ps(s) 139:12 For you darkness *i* is not dark,
Sg 5:16 His mouth is sweetness *i*;
Wis 2:11 for weakness proves *i* useless.
11:19 their frightful appearance *i* could slay.
13:16 for it, knowing that it cannot help *i*;
17:13 more one's expectation is of *i* uncertain,
Sir 23:16 not to be quenched till it burns *i* out:
28:23 It will hurl *i* against them like a lion;
34: 3 the reflection of a face is to the face *i*.
34:21 bread of charity is life *i* for the needy;
43: 1 of the sky shines forth like heaven *i*,
43: 8 As its name says, each month it renews *i*;
Is 10:15 the saw exalt *i* above him who wields it?
37:30 aftergrowth, next year, what grows of *i*;
44:20 cannot save *i* when the flame consumes it;
Jer 7:27 the word *i* is banished from their speech.
Bar 6:14 but it cannot save *i* from war or pillage.
Ez 5:13 Thus shall my anger spend *i*,
25:12 made *i* grievously guilty by taking vengeance
29:15 never more to set *i* above the nations.
31:14 by water may stand by *i* in its loftiness.
40:11 the gate's passage *i* was thirteen cubits.
43:13 The height of the altar *i* was as follows:
44:31 of *i* or has been killed by wild beasts.
Hos 1: 2 children, for the land gives *i* to harlotry,
Zec 6:14 The crown *i* shall be a memorial offering
Mt 6:34 Let tomorrow take care of *i*.
12:45 this time seven spirits more evil than *i*.
Mk 4:28 The soil produces of *i* first the blade,
Lk 11:17 kingdom divided against *i* is laid waste.
11:26 with seven other spirits far worse than *i*,
22:33 prepared to face imprisonment and death *i*."
Jn 15: 4 can bear fruit of *i* apart from the vine,
20: 7 wrappings, but rolled up in a place by *i*.
Acts 5:38 is human in its origins, it will destroy *i*.
12:10 to the city, which opened for them of *i*.
27:17 made use of cables to brace the ship *i*.
28: 3 from the heat, fastened *i* on his hand.
Rom 8:21 because the world *i* will be freed from its
14:14 Lord Jesus that nothing is unclean in *i*;
1Cor 9: 8 does not the law *i* speak of these things?
11:14 Does not nature *i* teach you that it is
2Cor 10: 5 that raises *i* against the knowledge of God;
Gal 5: 6 only faith, which expresses *i* through love.
Eph 4:16 supporting ligament, builds *i* up in love.
Heb 3: 3 a house is more honorable than the house *i*.
9:24 he entered heaven *i* that he might appear
3Jn 1:12 testimonial from all, even from truth *i*.
Rv 4: 6 At the very center, around the throne *i*,
19:10 spirit proves *i* by witnessing to Jesus."

ITTAI (8)
2Sm 15:19 before the king, he said to *I* the Gittite:
15:21 But *I* answered the king,
15:22 So the king said to *I*,
15:22 And *I* the Gittite,
18: 2 and a third under command of *I* the Gittite.
18: 5 gave this command to Joab, Abishai and *I*:
18:12 the king charged you and Abishai and *I*
23:29 *I*,

ITURAEA (1)
Lk 3: 1 of the region of *I* and Trachonitis,

IVORY (13)
1Kgs 10:18 The king also had a large *i* throne made,
10:22 would come with a cargo of gold, silver, *i*,
22:39 the *i* palace and all the cities he built,
2Chr 9:17 *i* throne which he overlaid with fine gold.
9:21 return with a cargo of gold and silver, *i*,
Ps(s) 45: 9 from *i* palaces string music brings you joy.
Sg 3:10 its framework inlaid with *i*.
5:14 body is a work of *i* covered with sapphires.
7: 5 Your neck is like a tower of *i*.
Ez 27:15 *i* tusks and ebony wood they gave you for
Am 3:15 The *i* apartments shall be ruined,
6: 4 Lying upon beds of *i*,
Rv 18:12 of *i* pieces and expensive wooden furniture;

IVVAH (1)
Is 37:13 of the cities of Sepharvaim, Hena or *I*?' "

IVY (1)
2Mc 6: 7 in his procession, wearing wreaths of *i*.

IYE-ABARIM (3)
Nm 21:11 *I* in the desert fronting Moab on the east.
33:44 they camped at *I* on the border of Moab.
33:45 Setting out from *I*,

IZARAHIAH (2)
1Chr 7: 3 The sons of Uzzi: *I*.
7: 3 The sons of *I* were Michael,

IZHAR (10)
Ex 6:18 The sons of Kohath were Amram, *I*,
6:21 The sons of *I* were Korah,
Nm 3:19 of Kohath, by clans, were Amram, *I*,
16: 1 Korah, son of *I*,
1Chr 4: 7 The sons of Helah were Zereth, *I*,
5:28 The sons of Kohath were Amram, *I*,
6: 3 The sons of Kohath were Amram, *I*,
6:23 son of Ebiasaph, son of Korah, son of *I*,
23:12 Amram, *I*, Hebron, and Uzziel:
23:18 The sons of *I*:

IZHARITES (4)
Nm 3:27 the clans of the Amramites, the *I*,
1Chr 24:22 Shelomith of the *I*,
26:23 From the Amramites, *I*,
26:29 Among the *I*, Chenaniah and his sons

IZLIAH (1)
1Chr 8:18 Meshullam, Hizki, Heber, Ishmerai, *I*,

IZRI (1)

1Chr 25:11 The fourth fell to *I*.

IZZIAH (1)

Ezr 10:25 Ramiah, *I*,

J

JAAKAN (1)

1Chr 1:42 sons of Ezer were Bilhan, Zaavan, and *J*.

JAAKOBATH (1)

1Chr 4:36 son of Seraiah, son of Asiel, Elioenai, *J*,

JAALA (1)

Neh 7:58 of Sophereth, sons of Perida, sons of *J*,

JAALAH (1)

Ezr 2:56 Hassophereth, sons of Peruda, sons of *J*,

JAAR (1)

Ps(s) 132: 6 we found it in the fields of *J*.

JAARESHIAH (1)

1Chr 8:27 *J*, Elijah, and Zichri were the sons

JAASIEL (2)

1Chr 11:47 Eliel, Obed, and *J* the Mezobian.
27:21 for Benjamin, *J*,

JAASU (1)

Ezr 10:37 Eliashib, Mattaniah, Mattenai, and *J*;

JAAZANIAH (4)

2Kgs 25:23 son of Tanhumeth the Netophathite, and *J*,
Jer 35: 3 So I went and brought *J*,
Ez 8:11 the house of Israel, among whom stood *J*,
11: 1 I saw twenty-five men, among whom were *J*,

JABAL (1)

Gn 4:20 Adah, gave birth to *J*,

JABBOK (7)

Gn 32:23 children, and crossed the ford of the *J*.
Nm 21:24 of his land from the Arnon to the *J*
Dt 2:37 neither the region bordering on the Wadi *J*,
3:16 and to the Wadi *J*,
Jos 12: 2 through half of Gilead to the Wadi *J*,
Jgs 11:13 took away my land from the Arnon to the *J*
11:22 whole territory from the Arnon to the *J*,

JABESH (11)

1Sm 11: 1 All the men of *J* begged Nahash,
11: 3 The elders of *J* said to him:
11: 5 the inhabitants of *J* was repeated to him.
11: 9 and reported this to the inhabitants of *J*,
31:12 wall of Beth-shan, and brought them to *J*,
31:13 buried them under the tamarisk tree in *J*,
2Kgs 15:10 Shallum, son of *J*, conspired against
15:13 Shallum, son of *J*, became king
15:14 he attacked and killed Shallum, son of *J*,
1Chr 10:12 Saul and his sons, and brought them to *J*.
10:12 They buried their bones under the oak of *J*,

JABESH-GILEAD (11)

Jgs 21: 8 found that none of the men of *J* had come
21:10 thousand warriors with orders to go to *J*
21:12 of *J* four hundred young virgins,
21:14 wives the women of *J* whom they had spared;
1Sm 11: 1 the Ammonite went up and laid siege to *J*.
11: 9 "Tell the inhabitants of *J* that tomorrow,
31:11 When the inhabitants of *J* heard what the
2Sm 2: 4 David that the men of *J* had buried Saul.
2: 5 to the men of *J* and said to them:
21:12 his son Jonathan from the citizens of *J*,
1Chr 10:11 inhabitants of *J* had heard

JABEZ (4)

1Chr 2:55 Sopherim dwelling in *J* were the Tirathites,
4: 9 *J* was the most distinguished of the
4: 9 His mother had named him *J*,
4:10 *J* prayed to the God of Israel:

JABIN (7)

Jos 11: 1 When *J*, king of Hazor,
Jgs 4: 2 into the power of the Canaanite king, *J*,
4:17 Jael, wife of the Kenite Heber, since *J*,
4:23 day God humbled the Canaanite king, *J*,
4:24 they destroyed the Canaanite king, *J*.
1Sm 12: 9 of Sisera, the captain of the army of *J*,
Ps(s) 83:10 as with Sisera and *J* at the torrent Kishon,

JABIN'S (1)

Jgs 4: 7 I will lead Sisera, the general of *J* army,

JABNEEL (2)

Jos 15:11 to Mount Baalah, thence to include *J*,
19:33 to Lakkum, including Adami-nekeb and *J*,

JABNEH (1)

2Chr 26: 6 *J* and Ashdod [and built cities in the

JABS (1)

Sir 22:19 One who *j* the eye brings tears:

JACAN (1)

1Chr 5:13 Michael, Meshullam, Sheba, Jorai, *J*,

JACHIN (9)

Gn 46:10 Nemuel, Jamin, Ohad, *J*,
Ex 6:15 of Simeon were Jenuel, Jamin, Ohad, *J*,
Nm 26:12 through *J* the clan of the Jachinites,
1Kgs 7:21 of the temple, one to the right, called *J*,
1Chr 4:24 The sons of Simeon were Nemuel, Jamin, *J*,
9:10 *J*;
24:17 to Jehezkel, the twenty-first to *J*,
2Chr 3:17 the right *J* and the one to the left Boaz.
Neh 11:10 *J*; Seraiah, son of Hilkaiah,

JACHINITES (1)

Nm 26:12 through Jachin the clan of the *J*,

JACINTH (2)

Ex 28:19 in the third row, a *j*,
39:12 in the third row a *j*,

JACKALS (15)

Jb 30:29 I have become the brother of *j*,
Ps(s) 63:11 to the sword, and shall be the prey of *j*.
Is 13:22 castles, and *j* in her luxurious palaces.
34:13 an abode for *j* and a haunt for ostriches.
35: 7 The abode where *j* lurk will be a marsh for
43:20 Wild beasts honor me, *j* and ostriches,
Jer 9:10 into a heap of ruins, a haunt of *j*;
10:22 cities of Judah into a desert haunt of *j*.
14: 6 bare heights, gasping for breath like *j*;
49:33 Hazor shall become a haunt of *j*,
51:37 become a heap of ruins, a haunt of *j*;
Lam 4: 3 Even the *j* bare their breasts and suckle
5:18 should be desolate, with *j* roaming there!
Mi 1: 8 I utter lamentation like the *j*,
Mal 1: 3 a waste, his heritage a desert for *j*.

JACKASS (1)

Jb 11:12 and the wild *j* be made docile?

JACKASSES (1)

Gn 45:23 ten *j* loaded with the finest products

JACOB (388)

Gn 25:18 Birth of Esau and *J*.
25:26 so they named him *J*.
25:27 whereas *J* was a simple man,
25:28 but Rebekah preferred *J*.
25:29 Once, when *J* was cooking a stew,
25:30 He said to *J*, "Let me gulp down some of
25:31 *J* replied, "First give me your birthright
25:33 But *J* insisted, "Swear to me first!"
25:33 So he sold *J* his birthright under oath.
25:34 *J* then gave him some bread and the lentil
27: 6 for his father, Rebekah said to her son *J*,
27:11 hairy man," said *J* to his mother Rebekah,
27:14 So *J* went and got them and brought them to
27:15 and gave them to her younger son *J* to wear;
27:17 Then she handed her son *J* the appetizing
27:18 Bringing them to his father, *J* said,
27:19 *J* answered his father:
27:21 Isaac then said to *J*, "Come closer, son,
27:22 So *J* moved up closer to his father.
27:25 *J* served it to him, and Isaac ate;
27:27 As *J* went up and kissed
27:30 *J* had scarcely left his father,
27:36 Esau exclaimed, "He has been well named *J*!
27:41 Esau bore *J* a grudge because of the
27:41 my father comes, I will kill my brother *J*."
27:42 called her younger son *J* and said to him:
27:46 If *J* also should marry a Hittite woman,
28: 1 Isaac therefore called *J*,
28: 5 Then Isaac sent *J* on his way;
28: 5 of Rebekah, the mother of *J* and Esau.
28: 6 Esau noted that Isaac had blessed *J* when
28: 7 and that *J* had obeyed his father and
28:10 *J* departed from Beer-sheba and proceeded
28:16 When *J* awoke from his sleep,
28:18 Early the next morning *J* took the stone
28:20 *J* then made this vow:
29: 1 After *J* resumed his journey he came to the
29: 4 *J* said to them, "Friends, where are you
29:10 As soon as *J* saw Rachel,
29:11 Then *J* kissed Rachel and burst into tears.
29:13 heard the news about his sister's son *J*,
29:13 *J* then recounted to Laban all that had
29:18 Since *J* had fallen in love with Rachel,
29:20 So *J* served seven years for Rachel,
29:21 *J* said to Laban, "Give me my wife,
29:23 her to Jacob, and *J* consummated
29:25 In the morning *J* was amazed:
29:28 *J* agreed.
29:30 *J* then consummated his marriage with
30: 1 saw that she failed to bear children to *J*,
30: 1 She said to *J*,
30: 2 In anger *J* retorted,
30: 4 a consort, and *J* had intercourse with her.
30: 9 her maidservant Zilpah to *J* as a consort.
30:10 So *J* had intercourse with Zilpah,
30:12 maidservant Zilpah bore a second son to *J*;
30:15 mandrakes, *J* may lie with you tonight."
30:16 evening, when *J* came home from the fields,
30:17 she conceived and bore a fifth son to *J*.
30:19 conceived again and bore a sixth son to *J*;
30:25 gave birth to Joseph, *J* said to Laban:
30:29 *J* replied: "You know what work I did
30:31 *J* answered: "You do not have to pay me
30:36 himself and *J*, while Jacob continued
30:37 *J*, however, got some fresh shoots
30:40 The sheep, on the other hand, *J* kept apart,
30:41 *J* would set the rods in the troughs in
30:42 go to Laban, but the sturdy ones to *J*.
31: 1 *J* learned that Laban's sons were saying, "*J*
31: 2 *J* perceived, too, that Laban's attitude
31: 3 LORD said to *J*, "Return to the land
31: 4 So *J* sent for Rachel and Leah to meet him
31:11 the dream God's messenger called to me, *J*!'
31:17 *J* proceeded to put his children and wives
31:20 *J* had hoodwinked Laban the Aramean by not
31:22 day, word came to Laban that *J* had fled.
31:24 care not to threaten *J* with any harm!"
31:25 When Laban overtook *J*,
31:26 "What do you mean," Laban demanded of *J*,
31:29 'Take care not to threaten *J* with any harm!'
31:31 "I was frightened," *J* replied to Laban,
31:32 *J*, of course, had no idea that Rachel
31:36 *J*, now enraged, upbraided Laban.
31:43 Laban replied to *J*: "The women are mine,
31:45 Then *J* took a stone and set it up as a
31:46 *J* said to his kinsmen,
31:47 it Jegar-sahadutha, but *J* named it Galeed.
31:51 Laban said further to *J*:
31:53 *J* took the oath by the Awesome One of Isaac.
32: 2 home, while *J* continued on his own way.
32: 2 Then God's messengers encountered *J*.
32: 4 *J* sent messengers ahead to his brother
32: 5 'Your servant *J* speaks as follows:
32: 7 When the messengers returned to *J*,
32: 8 *J* was very much frightened.
32:14 *J* selected from what he had with him the
32:19 answer, 'They belong to your brother *J*,
32:19 and *J* himself is right behind us.'"
32:21 to add, 'Your servant *J* is right behind us.'"
32:21 *J* reasoned, "If I first appease him with
32:23 the course of that night, however, *J* arose,
32:25 his possessions, *J* was left there alone.
32:27 But *J* said, "I will not let you go until
32:28 the man asked. He answered, *J*."
32:29 "You shall no longer be spoken of as *J*,
32:30 *J* then asked him, "Do tell me your name,
32:31 *J* named the place Peniel,
32:32 Penuel, *J* limped along because of his hip.
33: 1 *J* looked up and saw Esau coming,
33: 5 *J* answered, "They are the children
33: 8 *J* answered, "It was to gain my lord's
33:10 "No, I beg you!" said *J*.
33:13 But *J* replied: "As my lord can see,
33:15 But *J* said, "For what reason?
33:17 back to Seir, *J* journeyed to Succoth.
33:18 *J* arrived safely at the city of Shechem,
34: 1 the daughter whom Leah had borne to *J*,
34: 3 attracted to Dinah, daughter of *J*,
34: 5 *J* heard that Shechem had defiled his
34: 6 went out to discuss the matter with *J*,
34:27 Then the other sons of *J* followed up the
34:30 *J* said to Simeon and Levi:
35: 1 God said to *J*: "Go up now to Bethel.
35: 2 So *J* told his family and all the others
35: 4 They therefore handed over to *J* all the
35: 5 so that no one pursued the sons of *J*.
35: 6 Thus *J* and all the people who were with
35:10 name is *J* shall no longer be called Jacob,
35:14 spoken with him, *J* set up a memorial stone,
35:15 *J* named the site Bethel.
35:20 *J* set up a memorial stone on her grave,
35:22 The sons of *J* were now twelve.
35:26 of *J* who were born to him in Paddan-aram.
35:27 *J* went home to his father Isaac at Mamre,
35:29 His sons Esau and *J* buried him.
36: 6 of Seir, out of the way of his brother *J*.
37: 1 *J* settled in the land where his father
37:34 Then *J* rent his clothes,
42: 1 When *J* learned that grain rations were
42: 4 Benjamin that *J* did not send with the rest,
42:29 to their father *J* in the land of Canaan,
42:36 Their father *J* said to them:
42:38 But *J* replied: "My son shall not go down
45:25 to their father *J* in the land of Canaan.
45:27 the spirit of their father *J* revived.
46: 2 to Israel in a vision by night, called, *J*!

JACOB (cont.)
46: 2 J!" "Here I am," he answered.
46: 5 So J departed from Beer-sheba,
46: 6 Thus J and all his descendants migrated to
46: 8 of the Israelites, J and his descendants,
46:15 sons whom Leah bore to J in Paddan-aram,
46:18 these she bore to J—
46:22 These were the sons whom Rachel bore to J—
46:25 these she bore to J—
47: 5 J and his sons came to Joseph in Egypt,
47: 7 his father J and presented him to Pharaoh.
47: 7 After J had paid his respects to Pharaoh,
47: 9 J replied: "The years I have lived
47:10 Then J bade Pharaoh farewell and withdrew
47:28 J lived in the land of Egypt for seventeen
48: 2 When J was told,
48: 3 J then said to Joseph: "God Almighty
49: 1 J called his sons and said: "Gather around
49: 2 "Assemble and listen, sons of J,
49: 7 I will scatter them in J,
49:24 By the power of the Mighty One of J,
49:33 When J had finished giving these
50:17 J begs you to forgive the criminal
50:24 promised on oath to Abraham, Isaac and J."
Ex 1: 1 households, migrated with J into Egypt:
1: 5 the direct descendants of J was seventy.
2:24 of his covenant with Abraham, Isaac and J.
3: 6 of Abraham, the God of Isaac, the God of J."
3:15 of Abraham, the God of Isaac, the God of J,
3:16 fathers, the God of Abraham, Isaac and J,
4: 5 of Abraham, the God of Isaac, the God of J,
6: 3 I appeared to Abraham, Isaac and J,
6: 8 I swore to give to Abraham, Isaac and J.
19: 3 "Thus shall you say to the house of J;
33: 1 and J I would give to their descendants.
Lv 26:42 guilt, I will remember my covenant with J,
Nm 23: 7 "Come and lay a curse for me on J,
23:10 Who has ever counted the dust of J,
23:21 Misfortune is not observed in J,
23:23 No, there is no sorcery against J,
23:23 It shall yet be said of J,
24: 5 How goodly are your tents, O J;
24:17 A star shall advance from J,
24:19 valiantly, and J shall overcome his foes.
32:11 under oath to Abraham and Isaac and J.
Dt 1: 8 to your fathers, Abraham, Isaac and J,
6:10 to your fathers, Abraham, Isaac and J,
9: 5 oath to your fathers, Abraham, Isaac and J.
9:27 your servants, Abraham, Isaac and J.
29:12 swore to your fathers Abraham, Isaac and J.
30:20 give to your fathers Abraham, Isaac and J."
32: 9 While the LORD's own portion was J,
32:15 So J ate his fill,
33: 4 he made the community of J his domain,
33:10 your decisions to J and your law to Israel.
33:28 and the fountain of J has been undisturbed
34: 4 J that I would give to their descendants.
Jos 24: 4 To Isaac I gave J and Esau.
24: 4 J and his children went down to Egypt.
24:32 ground J had bought from the sons of Hamor,
1Sm 12: 8 When J and his sons went to Egypt and the
2Sm 23: 1 God raised up, Anointed of the God of J,
1Kgs 18:31 for the number of tribes of the sons of J,
2Kgs 13:23 of his covenant with Abraham, Isaac, and J.
17:34 the LORD enjoined on the descendants of J,
1Chr 16:13 of Israel, his servants, sons of J,
16:17 Which he established for J by statute,
Tb 4:12 keep in mind Noah, Abraham, Isaac, and J,
Jdt 8:26 and all that happened to J in Syrian
1Mc 1:28 all the house of J was covered with shame.
3: 7 He made J glad by his deeds,
3:45 Joy had disappeared from J,
5: 2 the descendants of J who were among them,
2Mc 1: 2 faithful servants, Abraham, Isaac and J.
Ps(s) 14: 7 then shall J exult and Israel be glad.
20: 2 the name of the God of J defend you!
22:24 all you descendants of J,
24: 6 him, that seeks the face of the God of J.
44: 5 and my God, who bestowed victories on J.
46: 4 our stronghold is the God of J.
46: 8 our stronghold is the God of J.
46:12 our stronghold is the God of J.
47: 5 for us our inheritance, the glory of J,
53: 7 then shall J exult and Israel be glad.
59:14 men may know that God is the ruler of J,
75:10 I will sing praise to the God of J.
76: 7 At your rebuke, O God of J,
77:16 your people, the sons of J and Joseph.
78: 5 He set it up as a decree in J,
78:21 and fire blazed up against J,
78:71 the ewes he brought him to shepherd J,
79: 7 devoured J and laid waste his dwelling.
81: 2 acclaim the God of J.
81: 5 in Israel, an ordinance of the God of J,
84: 9 hearken, O God of J!
85: 2 you have restored the well-being of J.
87: 2 gates of Zion, more than any dwelling of J.
94: 7 the God of J perceives not."
99: 4 justice and judgment in J you have wrought.
105: 6 of Abraham, his servants, sons of J,
105:10 Which he established for J by statute,
105:23 Egypt, and J sojourned in the land of Ham.
114: 1 house of J from a people of alien tongue,
114: 7 O earth, before the face of the God of J,
132: 2 to the LORD, vowed to the Mighty One of J:
132: 5 LORD, a dwelling for the Mighty One of J."
135: 4 For the LORD has chosen J for himself,
146: 5 Happy he whose help is the God of J,
147:19 He has proclaimed his word to J,
Sir 24: 8 my tent, Saying, 'In J make your dwelling,
24:22 as an inheritance for the community of J.
36:10 Gather all the tribes of J,
44:22 and the blessing rested upon the head of J.
45: 5 That he might teach his precepts to J,
46:10 That all the people of J might know how
46:14 when he visited the encampments of J.
47:22 So he gave to J a remnant,
48:10 sons, and to reestablish the tribes of J.
49:10 to J and saved him by their faith and hope.
Is 2: 3 mountain, to the house of the God of J,
2: 5 O house of J, come, let us walk in the
2: 6 abandoned your people, the house of J,
8:17 who is hiding his face from the house of J;
9: 7 The Lord has sent word against J,
10:20 Israel, the survivors of the house of J,
10:21 A remnant will return, the remnant of J,
14: 1 When the LORD has pity on J and again
14: 1 them and be counted with the house of J.
17: 4 On that day The glory of J shall fade,
27: 6 In days to come J shall take root,
29:22 says the LORD, the God of the house of J,
29:22 Now J shall have nothing to be ashamed of,
29:23 they shall reverence the Holy One of J,
40:27 Why, O J, do you say, and declare, O Israel,
41: 8 But you, Israel, my servant, J,
41:14 Fear not, O worm J, O maggot Israel;
41:21 forward your reasons, says the King of J.
42:24 Who was it that gave J to be plundered,
43: 1 thus says the LORD, who created you, O J,
43:22 Yet you did not call upon me, O J,
43:28 the holy gates, put J under the ban,
44: 1 Hear then, O J, my servant, Israel,
44: 2 Fear not, O J, my servant, the darling
44: 5 LORD's," another shall be named after J,
44:21 Remember this, O J, you O Israel,
44:23 For the LORD has redeemed J,
45: 4 For the sake of J, my servant,
45:19 I have not said to the descendants of J,
46: 3 Hear me, O house of J,
48: 1 O house of J called by the name of Israel,
48:12 Listen to me, J Israel, whom I named!
48:20 say, "The LORD has redeemed his servant J.
49: 5 that J may be brought back
49: 6 my servant, to raise up the tribes of J,
49:26 savior, your redeemer, the Mighty One of J.
58: 1 wickedness, and the house of J their sins.
58:14 I will nourish you with the heritage of J,
59:20 a redeemer to those of J who turn from sin,
60:16 savior, your redeemer, the mighty one of J.
65: 9 From J I will save offspring,
Jer 2: 4 to the word of the LORD, O house of J!
5:20 Announce this to the house of J,
9: 3 Every brother apes J, the supplanter,
10:16 Not like these is the portion of J:
10:25 For they have devoured J utterly,
30: 7 A time of distress for J,
30:10 But you, my servant J, fear not,
30:10 J shall again find rest,
30:18 I will restore the tents of J,
31: 7 Shout with joy for J,
31:11 The LORD shall ransom J,
33:26 descendants of J and of my servant David,
33:26 for the race of Abraham, Isaac, and J.
46:27 But you, my servant J,
46:27 J shall again find rest,
46:28 You, my servant J, never fear,
Is 49: 5 That J may be brought back to him
51:19 Not like these is the portion of J,
Lam 1:17 against J for his neighbors to be his foes;
2: 2 without pity all the dwellings of J;
2: 3 He blazed up in J like a flaming fire
Bar 2:34 to their fathers, to Abraham, Isaac and J;
3:37 of understanding, and has given her to J,
4: 2 Turn, O J, and receive her:
Ez 20: 5 to the descendants of the house of J;
28:25 their land which I gave to my servant J;
37:25 on the land which I gave to my servant J,
39:25 Now I will restore the fortunes of J and
Hos 10:11 was to plow, J was to break his furrows:
12: 3 he shall punish J for his conduct,
12:13 When J fled to the land of Aram,
Am 3:13 and bear witness against the house of J,
6: 8 I abhor the pride of J,
7: 2 How can J stand? He is so small!
7: 5 Cease, O LORD God! How can J stand?
8: 7 The LORD has sworn by the pride of J:
Ob 1:10 Because of violence to your brother J,
1:17 And the house of J shall take possession
1:18 The house of J shall be a fire,
Mi 1: 5 For the crime of J all this comes to pass,
1: 5 What is the crime of J?
2: 7 How can it be said, O house of J,
2:12 I will gather you, O J, each and every one,
3: 1 Hear, you leaders of J,
3: 8 to J his crimes and to Israel his sins.
3: 9 Hear this, you leaders of the house of J,
4: 2 of the LORD, to the house of the God of J,
5: 6 of J shall be in the midst of many peoples,
5: 7 remnant of J shall be among the nations,
7:20 You will show faithfulness to J,
Na 2: 3 The LORD will restore the vine of J,
Mal 1: 3 yet I loved J, but hated Esau;
2:12 and advocate out of the tents of J,
3: 6 change, nor do you cease to be sons of J.
Mt 1: 2 Isaac the father of J, Jacob the father of
1:15 father of Matthan, Matthan the father of J.
1:16 J was the father of Joseph the husband of
8:11 kingdom of God with Abraham, Isaac, and J,
22:32 Abraham, the God of Isaac, the God of J'?
Mk 12:26 Abraham, the God of Isaac, the God of J'?
Lk 1:32 He will rule over the house of J forever
3:34 son of Perez, son of Judah, son of J,
13:28 of teeth when you see Abraham, Isaac, J,
20:37 and the God of Isaac, and the God of J.
Jn 4: 5 land which J had given to his son Joseph.
4:12 pretend to be greater than our ancestor J,
Acts 3:13 The God of Abraham, of Isaac, and of J,
7: 8 Isaac did the same for J, and Jacob
7:12 J sent our fathers there on a first
7:14 Then Joseph sent for his father J,
7:15 J went down to Egypt and died there,
7:32 the God of Abraham, of Isaac, and of J.'
7:46 find a dwelling place for the house of J.
Rom 9:13 says, "I have loved J and hated Esau."
11:26 who shall remove all impiety from J;
Heb 11: 9 dwelling in tents with Isaac and J,
11:20 J and Esau blessings that were still to be.
11:21 By faith J, when dying, blessed each of

JACOB'S (22)
Gn 27:22 him, he said, "Although the voice is J,
28:10 J Dream at Bethel When he came upon a
31:25 J tents were pitched in the highlands;
31:33 in and searched J tent and Leah's tent,
32:26 over him, he struck J hip at its socket,
32:33 inasmuch as J hip socket was struck at the
34: 7 as J sons were coming in from the fields.
34:13 J sons replied to Shechem and his father
34:19 he was deeply in love with J daughter.
34:25 brothers Simeon and Levi, two of J sons,
35: 9 On J arrival from Paddan-aram,
35:23 Reuben, J first-born,
46: 8 Reuben, J first-born,
46:19 The sons of J wife Rachel:
46:26 J people who migrated to Egypt
46:26 not counting the wives of J sons
46:27 all the people comprising J family who had
50:12 Thus J sons did for him as he had
Sir 23:12 may they never be heard among J heirs.
Is 27: 9 then, shall be the expiation of J guilt,
Mal 1: 3 Was not Esau J brother?
Jn 4: 6 This was the site of J well.

JADA (2)
1Chr 2:28 The sons of Onam were Shammai and J.
2:32 The sons of J,

JADDAI (1)
Ezr 10:43 Jeiel, Mattithiah, Zabad, Zebina, J,

JADDUA (3)
Neh 10:22 Meshullam, Hezir, Meshezabel, Zadok, J,
12:11 and Johanan became the father of J.
12:22 time of Eliashib, Joiada, Johanan, and J,

JADED (1)
Ez 23:43 "Oh, this woman j with adulteries!

JADON (1)
Neh 3: 7 Melatiah the Gibeonite, J the Meronothite,

JAEL (5)
Jgs 4:17 had fled on foot to the tent of J,
4:18 J went out to meet Sisera and said to him,
4:21 Instead J, wife of Heber, got a tent peg
4:22 J went out to meet him and said to him,
5:24 Blessed among women be J,

JAGUR (1)
Jos 15:21 Kabzeel, Eder, J,

JAHATH (8)
1Chr 4: 2 the father of J, and Jahath became the
6: 5 his son Libni, whose son was J,
6:28 son of Zimmah, son of Shimei, son of J,
23:10 The sons of Shimei were J,
23:11 J was the chief and Zizah was second to him;
24:22 and J of the descendants of Shelomith.
2Chr 34:12 their overseers were J and Obadiah,

JAHAZ (7)
Nm 21:23 When he reached J,
Dt 2:32 advanced against us to join battle at J;
Jos 13:18 Dibon, Bamoth-baal, Beth-baal-meon, J,
21:36 pasture lands, J with its pasture lands,

Jgs 11:20 who encamped at *J* and fought Israel.
Is 15: 4 cry out, they are heard as far as *J.*
Jer 48:34 Heshbon and Elealeh is heard as far as *J;*

JAHAZIEL (6)

1Chr 12: 5 *J;* Johanan; Jozabad from Gederah;
16: 6 and the priests Benaiah and *J* were to be
23:19 Jeriah, the chief, Amariah, the second, *J,*
24:23 Jeriah, the chief, Amariah, the second, *J,*
2Chr 20:14 And the spirit of the LORD came upon *J,*
Ezr 8: 5 of the sons of Zattu, Shecaniah, son of *J,*

JAHDAI (1)

1Chr 2:47 The sons of *J* were Regem,

JAHDIEL (1)

1Chr 5:24 Eliel, Azriel, Jeremiah, Hodaviah, and *J*—

JAHDO (1)

1Chr 5:14 of Michael, son of Jeshishai, son of *J,*

JAHLEEL (2)

Gn 46:14 Sered, Elon, and *J.*
Nm 26:26 through *J* the clan of the Jahleelites.

JAHLEELITES (1)

Nm 26:26 through Jahleel the clan of the *J.*

JAHMAI (1)

1Chr 7: 2 of Tola were Uzzi, Rephaiah, Jeriel, *J,*

JAHZAH (2)

1Chr 6:63 pasture lands, *J* with its pasture lands,
Jer 48:21 on Holon, *J,* and Mephaath,

JAHZEEL (2)

Gn 46:24 *J,* Guni, Jezer, and Shillem.
Nm 26:48 through *J* the clan of the Jahzeelites,

JAHZEELITES (1)

Nm 26:48 through Jahzeel the clan of the *J,*

JAHZEIAH (1)

Ezr 10:15 Only Jonathan, son of Asahel, and *J,*

JAHZERAH (1)

1Chr 9:12 Maasai, son of Adiel, son of *J,*

JAHZIEL (1)

1Chr 7:13 The sons of Naphtali were *J,*

JAIL (15)

Gn 39:20 *j* where the royal prisoners were confined.
39:22 in charge of all the prisoners in the *j,*
40: 3 (the same *j* where Joseph was confined).
40: 5 in the *j* both had dreams on the same night,
Jer 37:15 the scribe, which they were using as a *j.*
Mt 18:30 put in *j* until he paid back what he owed.
Acts 4: 3 them and put them in *j* for the night.
5:18 apostles and threw them into the public *j.*
5:19 of the Lord opened the gates of the *j,*
5:21 *j* that the prisoners were to be brought in.
5:22 got to the *j* they could not find them,
5:23 "We found the *j* securely locked and the
5:25 in *j* are standing over there in the temple,
8: 3 men and women out, and threw them into *j.*
16:37 even a trial, then they threw us into *j,*

JAILED (1)

Mk 15: 7 There was a prisoner named Barabbas *j*

JAILER (9)

Gn 39:21 the chief *j* well-disposed toward him.
39:22 The chief *j* put Joseph in charge of all
39:23 The chief *j* did not concern himself with
Lk 12:58 up to the *j,* and the jailer throw you
Acts 16:23 and the *j* was given instructions to guard
16:27 The *j* woke up to see the prison gates wide
16:29 The *j* called for a light,
16:36 The *j* conveyed this information to Paul:

JAIR (12)

Nm 32:41 *J,* a Manassehite clan, campaigned against
Dt 3:14 *J,* a Manassehite clan, took all the region
Jos 13:30 king of Bashan, and all the villages of *J,*
Jgs 10: 3 *J* the Gileadite came after him and judged
10: 5 *J* died and was buried in Kamon.
2Sm 21:19 in which Elhanan, son of *J* from Bethlehem,
1Kgs 4:13 having charge of the villages of *J,*
1Chr 2:22 Segub became the father of *J,*
2:23 and Aram took from them the villages of *J,*
20: 5 Philistines, and Elhanan, the son of *J,*
Est A: 1 first day of Nisan, Mordecai, son of *J,*
2: 5 a certain Jew named Mordecai, son of *J,*

JAIRITE (1)

2Sm 20:26 Ira the *J* was also David's priest.

JAIRUS (2)

Mk 5:22 officials of the synagogue, a man named *J,*
Lk 8:41 A man named *J,*

JAKEH (1)

Prv 30: 1 The words of Agur, son of *J* the Massaite:

JAKIM (2)

1Chr 8:19 *J,* Zichri,
24:12 eleventh to Eliashib, the twelfth to *J,*

JALAM (4)

Gn 36: 5 and Oholibamah bore Jeush, *J* and Korah.
36:14 whom she bore to Esau were Jeush, *J,*
36:18 the clans of Jeush, *J,* and Korah.
1Chr 1:35 sons of Esau were Eliphaz, Reuel, Jeush, *J,*

JALON (1)

1Chr 4:17 of Ezrah were Jether, Mered, Epher, and *J.*

JAMBRES (1)

2Tm 3: 8 Just as Jannes and *J* opposed Moses,

JAMBRI (2)

1Mc 9:36 But the sons of *J* from Medaba made a raid
9:37 sons of *J* are celebrating a great wedding,

JAMES (44)

Mt 4:21 and caught sight of two other brothers, *J,*
10: 2 *J,* Zebedee's son, and his brother John;
10: 3 *J,* son of Alphaeus, and Thaddaeus;
13:55 Isn't Mary known to be his mother and *J,*
17: 1 Six days later Jesus took Peter, *J,*
27:56 and Mary the mother of *J* and Joseph,
Mk 1:19 little farther along, he caught sight of *J,*
1:29 house of Simon and Andrew with *J* and John.
3:17 *J,* son of Zebedee;
3:17 and John, the brother of *J* (he gave
3:18 Matthew, Thomas, *J* son of Alphaeus;
5:37 except Peter, James, and *J'* brother John.
6: 3 brother of *J* and Joses and Judas and Simon?
9: 2 Six days later, Jesus took Peter, *J,*
10:35 Zebedee's sons, *J* and John,
10:41 this, became indignant at *J* and John.
13: 3 of Olives facing the temple, Peter, *J,*
14:33 same time he took along with him Peter, *J,*
15:40 Mary the mother of *J* the younger and Joses,
16: 1 Mary Magdalene, Mary the mother of *J,*
Lk 5:10 all his shipmates, as well as *J* and John,
6:14 Peter, and Andrew his brother, *J* and John,
6:15 Matthew and Thomas, *J* son of Alphaeus,
6:16 Simon called the Zealot, Judas son of *J,*
8:51 to enter with him except Peter, John, *J,*
9:28 saying this he took Peter, John and *J,*
9:54 When his disciples *J* and John saw this,
24:10 Magdala, Joanna, and Mary the mother of *J.*
Acts 1:13 Peter and John and *J* and Andrew;
1:13 *J* son of Alphaeus;
1:13 Zealot party member, and Judas son of *J.*
12: 2 He beheaded *J* the brother of John,
12:17 "Report this to *J* and the brothers,"
15:13 concluded their presentation, *J* spoke up:
21:14 Paul and *J* in Jerusalem.
21:18 to *J* in the presence of all the presbyters.
1Cor 15: 7 Next he was seen by *J;*
Gal 1:19 I did not meet any other apostles except *J,*
2: 9 who were the acknowledged pillars, *J,*
2:12 before others came who were from *J.*
Jas 1: 1 To the twelve tribes in the dispersion, *J,*
5:20 mulgated by blessed *J* the apostle."
Jude 1: 1 servant of Jesus Christ and brother of *J,*

JAMIN (6)

Gn 46:10 Nemuel, *J,*
Ex 6:15 The sons of Simeon were Jenuel, *J,*
Nm 26:12 through *J* the clan of the Jaminites,
1Chr 2:27 the first-born of Jerahmeel, were Maaz, *J,*
4:24 The sons of Simeon were Nemuel, *J,*
Neh 8: 7 [The Levites Jeshua, Bani, Sherebiah, *J,*

JAMINITES (1)

Nm 26:12 through Jamin the clan of the *J,*

JAMLECH (1)

1Chr 4:34 Meshobab, *J,*

JAMNIA (7)

Jdt 2:28 in Sur and Ocina, and the inhabitants of *J.*
1Mc 4:15 and the plains of Judea, to Azotus and *J.*
5:58 who were with them, and marched toward *J.*
10:69 army, Apollonius pitched his camp at *J.*
15:40 When Cendebeus came to *J,*
2Mc 12: 8 On hearing that the men of *J* planned to
12:40 found amulets sacred to the idols of *J,*

JAMNIAN (1)

2Mc 12: 9 them, he attacked the *J* populace by night,

JANAI (1)

1Chr 5:12 in command, and *J* was judge in Bashan.

JANIM (1)

Jos 15:53 Arab, Dumah, Eshan, *J,*

JANNAI (1)

Lk 3:24 son of Levi, son of Melchi, son of *J,*

JANNES (1)

2Tm 3: 8 Just as *J* and Jambres opposed Moses,

JANOAH (2)

Jos 16: 6 and continued east of it to *J;*
2Kgs 15:29 came and took Ijon, Abel-beth-maacah, *J,*

JAPHETH (12)

Gn 5:32 he became the father of Shem, Ham, and *J.*
6:10 Shem, Ham, and *J.*
7:13 named, Noah and his sons Shem, Ham, and *J,*
9:18 came out of the ark were Shem, Ham and *J.*
9:23 Shem and *J,*
9:27 May God expand *J,*
10: 1 of Noah's sons, Shem, Ham, and *J,*
10: 2 The descendants of *J:*
10: 5 These are the descendants of *J,*
1Chr 1: 4 Methuselah, Lamech, Noah, Shem, Ham, and *J.*
1: 5 The descendants of *J* were Gomer,
Jdt 2:25 he proceeded to the southern borders of *J,*

JAPHETH'S (1)

Gn 10:21 *J* oldest brother and the ancestor of all

JAPHIA (5)

Jos 10: 3 king of Hebron, Piram, king of Jarmuth, *J,*
19:12 on to Daberath, and up to *J.*
2Sm 5:15 Nathan, Solomon, Ibhar, Elishua, Nepheg, *J,*
1Chr 3: 7 Elishua, Eliphelet, Nogah, Nepheg, *J,*
14: 6 Ibhar, Elishua, Elpelet, Nogah, Nepheg, *J,*

JAPHLET (3)

1Chr 7:32 Heber became the father of *J,*
7:33 The sons of *J* were Pasach,
7:33 these were the sons of *J.*

JAPHLETITES (1)

Jos 16: 3 descended westward to the border of the *J,*

JAR (15)

1Kgs 14: 3 loaves, some cakes, and a *j* of preserves,
17:12 flour in my *j* and a little oil in my jug.
17:14 says, 'The *j* of flour shall not go empty,
17:16 The *j* of flour did not go empty,
Sir 21:14 A fool's mind is like a broken *j*—
Is 30:14 like a potter's *j* smashed beyond rescue,
Jer 32:14 of purchase, and put them in an earthen *j,*
Mt 26: 7 a woman carrying a *j* of costly perfume
Mk 14: 3 a woman entered carrying an alabaster *j*
14: 3 Breaking the *j,* she began to pour the
14:13 will come upon a man carrying a water *j.*
Lk 22:10 will come upon a man carrying a water *j.*
Jn 4:28 her water *j* and went off into the town.
19:29 There was a *j* there, full of common wine.
Heb 9: 4 ark were the golden *j* containing the manna,

JAR-STAND (1)

Lv 11:35 if it is an oven or a *j,*

JARED (7)

Gn 5:15 years old, he became the father of *J.*
5:16 and thirty years after the birth of *J,*
5:18 *J* was one hundred and sixty-two years old,
5:19 *J* lived eight hundred years after the
5:20 of *J* was nine hundred and sixty-two years;
1Chr 1: 2 Adam, Seth, Enosh, Kenan, Mahalalel, *J,*
Lk 3:37 son of Methuselah, son of Enoch, son of *J,*

JARHA (2)

1Chr 2:34 daughters, had an Egyptian slave named *J.*
2:35 his daughter in marriage to his slave *J,*

JARIB (2)

Ezr 8:16 I sent Eliezer, Ariel, Shemaiah, *J,*
10:18 Maaseiah, Eliezer, *J,* and Gedaliah.

JARMUTH (7)

Jos 10: 3 Hoham, king of Hebron, Piram, king of *J,*
10: 5 Amorite kings, of Jerusalem, Hebron, *J,*
10:23 the five kings, of Jerusalem, Hebron, *J,*
12:11 is near Bethel), Jerusalem, Hebron, *J,*
15:35 Zanoah, Engannim, Tappuah, Enam, *J,*
21:29 pasture lands, *J* with its pasture lands,

JARMUTH (cont.)

Neh 11:29 its dependencies, in En-rimmon, Zorah, *J,*

JAROAH (1)

1Chr 5:14 sons of Abihail, son of Huri, son of *J,*

JARS (14)

Ex 7:19 even in the wooden pails and stone *j.*"
Jgs 7:16 with empty *j* and torches inside the jars.
7:19 horns and broke the *j* they were holding.
7:20 companies blew horns and broke their *j.*
1Kgs 18:34 "Fill four *j* with water,"
Jb 38:37 Or who tilts the water *j* of heaven So
Jer 14: 3 They find no water and return with empty *j.*
40:10 the fruit and the oil, to store them in *j,*
48:12 shall empty his flasks and break his *j.*
Lam 4: 2 earthen *j* made by the hands of a potter!
Lk 16: 6 The man replied, 'A hundred *j* of oil.'
Jn 2: 6 there were at hand six stone water *j,*
2: 7 "Fill those *j* with water,"

JASHAR (2)

Jos 10:13 Is this not recorded in the Book of *J?*
2Sm 1:18 Book of *J* to be taught to the Judahites.

JASHEN (2)

2Sm 23:32 *J* the Gunite;
1Chr 11:34 *J* the Gunite:

JASHUB (4)

Gn 46:13 Tola, Puah, *J,* and Shimron.
Nm 26:24 through *J* the clan of the Jashubites,
1Chr 7: 1 The sons of Issachar were Tola, Puah, *J,*
Ezr 10:29 *J,*

JASHUBITES (1)

Nm 26:24 through Jashub the clan of the *J,*

JASON (20)

1Mc 8:17 son of John, son of Accos, and *J,*
12:16 son of Antiochus, and Antipater, son of *J,*
14:22 son of Antiochus, and Antipater, son of *J,*
2Mc 1: 7 years after *J* and his followers had revolted
2:23 which *J* of Cyrene set forth in detail in
4: 7 Onias' brother *J* obtained the high
4:10 When *J* received the king's approval and
4:13 of the ungodly pseudo-high-priest *J,*
4:19 the vile *J* sent envoys as representatives
4:22 great pomp by *J* and the people of the city,
4:23 Three years later *J* sent Menelaus,
4:24 *J* by three hundred talents of silver.
4:26 Then *J,*
5: 5 *J* gathered fully a thousand men and
5: 6 *J* then slaughtered his fellow citizens
Acts 17: 5 They marched on the house of *J* in an
17: 6 they dragged *J* himself and some of the
17: 7 Now they come here and *J* has taken them in.
17: 9 they released *J* and the others on bail.
Rom 16:21 so, too, do my kinsmen Lucius, *J,*

JASPER (7)

Ex 28:20 fourth row, a chrysolite, an onyx and a *j.*
39:13 fourth row a chrysolite, an onyx and a *j.*
Jb 28:18 Neither coral nor *j* should be thought of;
Ez 28:13 topaz, and beryl, chrysolite, onyx, and *j,*
Rv 4: 3 a gemlike sparkle as of *j* and carnelian.
21:18 The wall was constructed of *j;*
21:19 the first course of stones was *j,*

JATHNIEL (1)

1Chr 26: 2 the second son, Zebadiah, the third, *J,*

JATTIR (8)

Jos 15:48 Shamir, *J,*
21:14 pasture lands, *J* with its pasture lands,
1Sm 30:27 to those in Ramoth-negeb, to those in *J,*
2Sm 23:38 of Zeruiah; Ira from Jattir; Gareb from *J;*
1Chr 6:42 its pasture land, *J* with its pasture lands,
11:40 Ira, from *J;* Gareb, from Jattir;

JAVAN (7)

Gn 10: 2 Gomer, Magog, Madai, *J,*
10: 4 The descendants of *J:*
1Chr 1: 5 of Japheth were Gomer, Magog, Madai, *J,*
1: 7 The descendants of *J* were Elishah,
Is 66:19 Put and Lud, Mosoch, Tubal and *J,*
Ez 27:13 *J,* Tubal, and Meshech were also traders
27:19 *J* exchanged wrought iron,

JAVELIN (10)

Jos 8:18 "Stretch out the *j* in your hand toward Ai,
8:18 out the *j* in his hand toward the city,
8:26 Joshua kept the *j* in his hand stretched
1Sm 17: 7 of his *j* was like a weaver's heddle-bar,
2Sm 2:23 him in the abdomen with the heel of his *j,*
Jb 39:23 quiver, flashes the spear and the *j.*
41:18 will the spear, nor the dart, nor the *j.*
Sir 46: 2 arm, to brandish his *j* against the city!
Jer 6:23 Bow and *j* they wield;
50:42 Bow and *j* they wield, cruel and pitiless

JAW (1)

1Sm 17:35 it attacked me, I would seize it by the *j,*

JAW-TEETH (1)

Ps(s) 58: 7 the *j* of the lions, break, O LORD!

JAWBONE (4)

Jgs 15:15 Near him was the fresh *j* of an ass;
15:16 *j* of an ass I have piled them in a heap;
15:16 *j* of an ass I have slain a thousand men."
15:17 finished speaking he threw the *j* from him;

JAWS (8)

1Mc 2:60 was delivered from the *j* of lions.
Jb 29:17 And I broke the *j* of the wicked man;
Ps(s) 22:16 baked clay, my tongue cleaves to my *j;*
Is 30:28 the *j* of the peoples to send them astray].
Ez 29: 4 I will put hooks in your *j* and make the
Mt 16:18 *j* of death shall not prevail against it.
2Tm 4:17 That is how I was saved from the lion's *j.*
Heb 11:33 they broke the *j* of lions,

JAZER (16)

Nm 21:24 of the Ammonites, whose boundary was at *J.*
21:26 seized all his land from *J* to the Arnon.
21:32 of the Amorites, Moses sent spies to *J;*
32: 1 of *J,* and of Gilead was grazing country,
32: 3 said, "The region of Ataroth, Dibon, *J,*
32:35 Dibon, Ataroth, Aroer, Atroth-shophan, *J,*
Jos 13:25 Their territory included *J,*
21:39 lands, and *J* with its pasture lands.
2Sm 24: 5 and went in the direction of Gad toward *J.*
1Chr 6:66 lands, and *J* with its pasture lands.
26:31 them outstanding officers at *J* of Gilead.
1Mc 5: 8 After seizing *J* and its villages,
Is 16: 8 as far as *J* and scattered over the desert,
16: 9 I weep with *J* for the vines of Sibmah;
Jer 48:32 More than for *J* I weep over you,
48:32 to the sea, as far as *J* they stretched.

JAZIZ (1)

1Chr 27:31 and over the flocks was *J* the Hagrite.

JEALOUS (28)

Ex 20: 5 For I, the LORD, your God, am a *j* God,
34:14 LORD is 'the Jealous One'; a *j* God is he.
Nm 11:29 answered him, "Are you *j* for my sake?
Dt 4:24 your God, is a consuming fire, a *j* God.
5: 9 For I, the LORD, your God, am a *j* God,
6:15 your God, who is in your midst, is a *j* God.
Jos 24:19 he is a *j* God who will not forgive your
1Sm 18: 9 [And from that day on, Saul was *j* of David.
Ps(s) 37: 1 evildoers, nor *j* of those who do wrong;
Wis 1:10 Because a *j* ear hearkens to everything,
Sir 9: 1 Be not *j* of the wife of your bosom,
26: 6 A *j* wife is heartache and mourning and a
30: 3 He who educates his son makes his enemy *j,*
45:18 against him, were *j* of him in the desert,
Is 11:13 Ephraim shall not be *j* of Judah,
Ez 16:42 fury upon you I will cease to be *j* of you.
36: 6 With *j* fury I speak,
39:25 Israel, and I will be *j* for my holy name.
Na 1: 2 A *j* and avenging God is the LORD,
Zec 8: 2 intensely jealous for Zion, stirred to *j*
Acts 13:45 they became very *j* and countered with
Rom 10:19 you *j* of those who are not even a nation;
1Cor 10:22 Do we mean to provoke the Lord to *j* anger?
13: 4 Love is not *j,* it does not put on airs,
2Cor 11: 2 *j* of you with the jealousy of God himself,
Gal 5:26 or challenging, or *j* toward one another.

JEALOUSIES (1)

1Pt 2: 1 pretenses, *j,*

JEALOUSLY (1)

Ps(s) 68:17 Why look you *j,*

JEALOUSY (34)

Nm 5:14 of *j* that makes him suspect his wife,
5:15 it, since it is a cereal offering of *j,*
5:18 appeal, that is, the cereal offering of *j,*
5:25 cereal offering of *j* from the woman's hand,
5:29 "This, then, is the law for *j:*
5:30 or when such a feeling of *j* comes over a
Dt 29:19 wrath and *j* will flare up against that man,
1Mc 8:16 one, and there was no envy or *j* among them.
Ps(s) 78:58 places and with their idols roused his *j.*
79: 5 Will your *j* burn like fire?
Prv 14:30 life to the body, but *j* rots the bones.
27: 4 but before *j* who can stand?
Wis 6:23 shall I admit consuming *j* to my company,
Ez 5:13 in my *j* when I spend my fury upon them.
8: 3 the statue of *j* which stirs up jealousy.
8: 5 of the gate the altar of the statue of *j.*
16:38 I will wreak fury and *j* upon you.
23:25 I will let loose my *j* against you,
36: 5 with burning *j* I speak against the rest of
38:19 In my anger and in my *j,*
Zep 1:18 of his *j* all the earth shall be consumed.
3: 8 of my *j* shall all the earth be consumed.
Mt 27:18 was out of *j* that they had handed him over.
Mk 15:10 that it was out of *j* that the chief
Acts 5:17 party of the Sadducees), filled with *j,*
Rom 13:13 excess and lust, not in quarreling and *j.*
1Cor 3: 3 long as there are *j* and quarrels among you,
2Cor 11: 2 jealous of you with the *j* of God himself,
12:20 I fear I may find discord, *j,*
Gal 5:20 sorcery, hostilities, bickering, *j,*
Jas 3:14 *j* and selfish ambition in your hearts,
3:16 Where there are *j* and strife,
4: 5 he has implanted in us tends toward *j*"?

JEARIM (1)

Jos 15:10 north of the ridge of Mount *J* (that is,

JEBERECHIAH (1)

Is 8: 2 Uriah the priest, and Zechariah, son of *J.*

JEBUS (4)

Jgs 19:10 and traveled till they came opposite *J,*
19:11 they were near *J* with the day far gone,
1Chr 11: 4 all Israel went to Jerusalem, that is, *J,*
11: 5 The inhabitants of *J* said to David,

JEBUSITE (8)

Jos 18:28 Zela, Haeleph, the *J* city (that is,
2Sm 24:16 at the threshing floor of Araunah the *J.*
24:18 on the threshing floor of Araunah the *J.*"
1Chr 1:14 his first-born, and Heth, and the *J,*
21:15 by the threshing floor of Ornan the *J.*
21:18 LORD on the threshing floor of Ornan the *J.*
21:28 him on the threshing floor of Ornan the *J,*
2Chr 3: 1 the threshing floor of Ornan the *J.*

JEBUSITES (34)

Gn 10:16 of the *J,* the Amorites, the Girgashites,
15:21 the Canaanites, the Girgashites, and the *J.*"
Ex 3: 8 Amorites, Perizzites, Hivites and *J.*
3:17 Amorites, Perizzites, Hivites and *J,*
13: 5 Hittites, Amorites, Hivites and *J,*
23:23 Perizzites, Canaanites, Hivites and *J;*
33: 2 Hittites, Perizzites, Hivites and *J,*
34:11 Hittites, Perizzites, Hivites and *J.*
Nm 13:29 *J* and Amorites dwell in the highlands,
Dt 7: 1 Canaanites, Perizzites, Hivites, and *J:*
20:17 Canaanites, Perizzites, Hivites and *J*—
Jos 3:10 Perizzites, Girgashites, Amorites and *J.*
9: 1 Canaanites, Perizzites, Hivites and *J,*
11: 3 Perizzites and *J* in the mountain regions,
12: 8 Canaanites, Perizzites, Hivites and *J.*
15: 8 on the southern flank of the *J* [that is,
15:63 [But the *J* who lived in Jerusalem the
15:63 so the *J* dwell in Jerusalem beside the
18:16 Hinnom along the southern flank of the *J,*
24:12 Girgashites, Hivites and *J* out of your way;
Jgs 1:21 not dislodge the *J* who dwelt in Jerusalem,
1:21 with the result that the *J* live in
3: 5 Amorites, Perizzites, Hivites and *J.*
19:11 city of the *J* and spend the night in it."
2Sm 5: 6 against the *J* who inhabited the region.
5: 8 "All who wish to attack the *J* must strike
1Kgs 9:20 and *J* whose doom the Israelites had been
1Chr 11: 4 the natives of the land were called *J.*
11: 6 *J* first shall be made the chief commander."
2Chr 8: 7 Amorites, Perizzites, Hivites, and *J,*
Ezr 9: 1 [Canaanites, Hittites, Perizzites, *J,*
Neh 9: 8 Hittites, Amorites, Perizzites, *J,*
Jdt 5:16 the Canaanites, the Perizzites, the *J,*
Zec 9: 7 in Judah, and Ekron shall be like the *J.*

JECHOLIAH (1)

2Kgs 15: 2 His mother, whose name was *J,*

JECHONIAH (2)

Mt 1:11 Josiah became the father of *J* and his
1:12 exile *J* was the father of Shealtiel,

JECOLIAH (1)

2Chr 26: 3 His mother, named *J,* was from Jerusalem.

JECONIAH (11)

1Sm 6:19 The descendants of *J* did not join in the
1Chr 3:16 *J,* his son; Zedekiah, his son.
3:17 The sons of *J* the captive were:
Est A: 3 Babylon, had taken from Jerusalem with *J,*
2: 6 Jerusalem with the captives taken with *J,*
Jer 24: 1 of Babylon, had exiled from Jerusalem *J,*
27:20 of Babylon, did not take when he exiled *J,*
28: 4 And I will bring back to this place *J,*
29: 2 This was after King *J* and the queen mother,
Bar 1: 3 read the words of this scroll for *J,*
1: 9 king of Babylon, carried off *J,*

JEDAIAH (13)

1Chr 4:37 son of Shiphi, son of Allon, son of *J,*
9:10 Among the priests were *J;*
24: 7 lot fell to Jehoiarib, the second to *J,*
Ezr 2:36 sons of *J,* who were of the house of Jeshua,
Neh 3:10 of Jerusalem, and at his side was *J,*
7:39 sons of *J* who were of the house of Jeshua,
11:10 *J;* Joiarib;
12: 6 Maadiah, Bilgah, Shemaiah, and Joiarib, *J,*
12: 7 Joiarib, Jedaiah, Sallu, Amok, Hilkiah, *J.*
12:19 for *J,* Uzzi; for Sallu, Kallai;
12:21 for *J,*
Zec 6:10 the returned captives Heldai, Tobijah, *J;*
6:14 of the LORD in favor of Heldai, Tobijah, *J,*

JEDIAEL (6)

1Chr 7: 6 sons of Benjamin were Bela, Becher, and *J*—
7:10 The sons of *J:*
7:11 All these were descendants of *J,*
11:45 *J,*
12:21 Adnah, Jozabad, *J,*
26: 2 Zechariah, the first-born, *J,*

JEDIDAH (1)

2Kgs 22: 1 His mother's name was *J,*

JEDIDIAH (1)

2Sm 12:25 and sent the prophet Nathan to name him *J,*

JEDUTHUN (13)

1Chr 9:16 Shemaiah, son of Galal, a descendant of *J;*
16:38 brethren, including Obed-edom, son of *J,*
16:41 With them were Heman and *J* and the others
16:42 The sons of *J* kept the gate.
25: 1 the descendants of Asaph, Heman, and *J,*
25: 3 Of Jeduthun, these sons of *J:*
25: 3 under the direction of their father *J,*
25: 6 All these, whether of Asaph, *J,*
2Chr 5:12 all who belonged to Asaph, Heman, *J,*
29:14 Jehuel and Shimei; of the sons of *J:*
35:15 Asaph, Heman and *J,* the king's seer.
Neh 11:17 son of Shammua, son of Galal, son of *J.*

JEER (2)

Ez 36: 3 and have become a byword and a popular *j;*
Lk 14:29 for all who saw it would *j* at him,

JEERED (2)

2Kgs 2:23 boys came out of the city and *j* at him.
Mk 15:31 and the scribes also joined in and *j:*

JEERING (3)

Wis 17: 7 a *j* reproof of their vaunted shrewdness.
Mt 27:41 and the elders also joined in the *j:*
Lk 23:35 watching, and the leaders kept *j* at him,

JEGAR-SAHADUTHA (1)

Gn 31:47 Laban called it *J,*

JEHALLEL (1)

2Chr 29:12 Kish, son of Abdi, and Azariah, son of *J;*

JEHALLELEL (1)

1Chr 4:16 The sons of *J* were Ziph,

JEHDEIAH (2)

1Chr 24:20 of the descendants of Amram, and *J,*
27:30 over the she-asses was *J* the Meronothite;

JEHEZKEL (1)

1Chr 24:16 to Pethahiah, the twentieth to *J,*

JEHIEL (16)

1Chr 15:18 Zechariah, Uzziel, Shemiramoth, *J,*
15:20 Zechariah, Uzziel, Shemiramoth, *J,*
16: 5 were Zechariah, Uzziel, Shemiramoth, *J,*
23: 8 *J* the chief, then Zetham and Joel;
26:21 the family heads were descendants of *J:*
26:21 the descendants of *J,*
27:32 he and *J,* the son of Hachmoni,
29: 8 into the keeping of *J* the Gershonite
2Chr 21: 2 sons of Jehoshaphat, were Azariah, *J,*
31:13 *J,* Azaziah,
35: 8 Hilkiah, Zechariah and *J,*
35: 9 Nethanel, Hashabiah, *J* and Jozabad,
Ezr 8: 9 of the sons of Joab, Obadiah, son of *J,*
10: 2 Then Shecaniah, the son of *J,*
10:21 Maaseiah, Elijah, Shemaiah, *J,*
10:26 Mattaniah, Zechariah, *J,*

JEHIZKIAH (1)

2Chr 28:12 Berechiah, son of Meshillemoth, *J,*

JEHOADDAH (4)

1Chr 8:36 Ahaz became the father of *J,* and Jehoaddah
9:42 Ahaz became the father of *J,* and Jehoaddah

JEHOADDAN (1)

2Chr 25: 1 His mother, named *J,* was from Jerusalem.

JEHOADDIN (1)

2Kgs 14: 2 His mother, whose name was *J,*

JEHOAHAZ (23)

2Kgs 10:35 His son *J* succeeded him as king.
13: 1 Joash, son of Ahaziah, king of Judah, *J,*
13: 4 Then *J* entreated the LORD,
13: 7 No soldiers were left to *J,*
13: 8 The rest of the acts of *J,*
13: 9 *J* rested with his ancestors and was buried
13:10 Joash, king of Judah, Jehoash, son of *J,*
13:22 Israel during the entire reign of *J.*
13:25 succeeded him as king, Joash, son of *J,*
13:25 had taken in battle from his father *J,*
14: 1 In the second year of Joash, son of *J,*
14: 8 sent messengers to Jehoash, son of *J,*
14:17 king of Judah, survived Jehoash, son of *J,*
23:30 Then the people of the land took *J,*
23:31 *J* was twenty-three years old when he began
23:34 *J* he took away with him to Egypt,
2Chr 21:17 there was left to him only one son, *J,*
25:17 Judah sent messengers to Joash, son of *J,*
25:23 king of Judah, son of Joash, son of *J,*
25:25 king of Judah, survived Joash, son of *J,*
36: 1 The people of the land took *J,*
36: 2 *J* was twenty-three years old when he became
36: 4 brother *J* away and brought him to Egypt.

JEHOASH (10)

2Kgs 12:19 But King *J* of Judah took all the dedicated
13:10 year of Joash, king of Judah, *J,*
14: 8 Then Amaziah sent messengers to *J,*
14: 9 King *J* of Israel sent this reply to the
14:11 King *J* of Israel then advanced,
14:13 *J* of Israel captured Amaziah, son of *J*
14:15 The rest of the acts of *J,*
14:16 *J* rested with his ancestors;
14:17 son of Joash, king of Judah, survived *J,*

JEHOHANAN (7)

1Chr 26: 3 Jathniel, the fourth, Elam, the fifth, *J,*
2Chr 17:15 Next to him, *J* the commander,
23: 1 Ishmael, son of *J;*
Ezr 10:28 *J,* Hananiah,
Neh 6:18 *J* had married the daughter of Meshullam,
12:13 for Amariah, *J;*
12:42 and Maaseiah, Shemaiah, Eleazar, Uzzi, *J,*

JEHOIACHIN (13)

2Kgs 24: 6 and his son *J* succeeded him as king.
24: 8 *J* was eighteen years old when he began to
24:12 Then *J,* king of Judah,
24:15 He deported *J* to Babylon,
24:17 In place of *J,* the king of Babylon
25:27 the thirty-seventh year of the exile of *J,*
25:27 year of his own reign, raised up *J,*
25:29 *J* took off his prison garb and ate at the
2Chr 36: 8 His son *J* succeeded him as king.
36: 9 *J* was eighteen years old when he became
Jer 52:31 the thirty-seventh year of the exile of *J,*
52:31 year of his reign, took up the case of *J,*
52:33 *J* took off his prison garb and ate at the

JEHOIACHIN'S (1)

Ez 1: 2 the fifth year, that is, of King *J* exile,

JEHOIADA (54)

2Sm 8:18 Benaiah, son of *J,*
20:23 Benaiah, son of *J,*
23:20 Benaiah, son of *J,* a stalwart from Kabzeel,
23:22 the deeds performed by Benaiah, son of *J.*
1Kgs 1: 8 Zadok the priest, Benaiah, son of *J,*
1:26 Zadok the priest, nor Benaiah, son of *J,*
1:32 Nathan the prophet, and Benaiah, son of *J.*
1:36 In answer to the king, Benaiah, son of *J,*
1:38 Nathan the prophet, Benaiah, son of *J,*
1:44 Nathan the prophet, Benaiah, son of *J,*
2:25 Then King Solomon sent Benaiah, son of *J,*
2:29 He sent Benaiah, son of *J,*
2:34 Benaiah, son of *J,* went back, struck him
2:35 The king appointed Benaiah, son of *J,*
2:46 then gave the order to Benaiah, son of *J,*
4: 4 [Benaiah, son of *J*
2Kgs 11: 4 *J* summoned the captains of the Carians and
11: 9 did just as *J* the priest commanded.
11: 9 off duty that week, came to *J* the priest.
11:12 Then *J* led out the king's son and put the
11:15 Then *J* the priest instructed the captains
11:17 Then *J* made a covenant between the LORD as
11:18 temple of the LORD, *J* with the captains,
12: 3 he lived, because the priest *J* guided him.
12: 8 the priest *J* and the other priests.
12:10 The priest *J* then took a chest,
1Chr 11:22 Benaiah, son of *J,* a valiant man
11:24 deeds as these of Benaiah, the son of *J,*
12:28 four thousand six hundred, along with *J,*
18:17 Benaiah, son of *J,* was in command
27: 5 month, was Benaiah, son of *J* the priest,
27:34 After Ahithophel came *J,*
2Chr 22:11 of Ahaziah, and wife of *J* the priest,
23: 1 *J* took courage and entered a conspiracy
23: 3 *J* said to them: "Here is the King's son
23: 8 Judah did just as *J* the priest commanded.
23: 8 since *J* the priest had not dismissed any
23: 9 *J* the priest gave the captains the spears,
23:11 *J* and his sons anointed him,
23:14 Then *J* the priest sent out the captains
23:16 Then *J* made a covenant between himself and
23:18 Then *J* gave the charge of the LORD's
24: 2 to the LORD as long as *J* the priest lived.
24: 3 *J* provided him with two wives,
24: 6 Then the king summoned *J,*
24:12 Then the king and *J* gave it to the workmen
24:14 rest of the money to the king and to *J,*
24:14 continually throughout the lifetime of *J.*
24:15 *J* lived to a ripe old age;
24:17 After the death of *J,*
24:20 possessed Zechariah, son of *J* the priest.
24:22 unmindful of the devotion shown him by *J,*
24:25 of the murder of the son of *J* the priest.
Jer 29:26 you priest in place of the priest *J,*

JEHOIAKIM (39)

2Kgs 23:34 he changed his name to *J.*
23:35 *J* gave the silver and gold to Pharaoh,
23:36 *J* was twenty-five years old when he began
24: 1 and *J* became his vassal for three years.
24: 1 Then *J* turned and rebelled against him.
24: 5 The rest of the acts of *J,*
24: 6 *J* rested with his ancestors,
24:19 the sight of the LORD, just as *J* had done.
1Chr 3:15 the second, *J;*
3:16 The sons of *J* were: Jeconiah, his son;
2Chr 36: 4 and Jerusalem, and changed his name to *J.*
36: 5 *J* was twenty-five years old when he became
36: 8 The rest of the acts of *J,*
Jer 1: 3 and continued through the reign of *J,*
22:18 Therefore, thus says the LORD concerning *J,*
22:24 says the LORD, if you, Coniah, son of *J,*
24: 1 exiled from Jerusalem Jeconiah, son of *J,*
25: 1 people of Judah, in the fourth year of *J,*
26: 1 In the beginning of the reign of *J,*
26:21 When King *J* and all his officers and
26:22 Thereupon King *J* sent Elnathan,
27: 1 [In the beginning of the reign of *J,*
27:20 take when he exiled Jeconiah, son of *J,*
28: 4 back to this place Jeconiah, son of *J,*
35: 1 to Jeremiah from the LORD in the days of *J,*
36: 1 In the fourth year of *J,*
36: 9 the ninth month, in the fifth year of *J,*
36:28 that the first scroll contained, which *J,*
36:29 And against *J,* king of Judah, say this:
36:30 The LORD now says of *J,* king of Judah:
36:32 the words contained in the book which *J,*
37: 1 Coniah, son of *J,*
45: 1 Jeremiah dictated in the fourth year of *J,*
46: 2 king of Babylon, in the fourth year of *J,*
52: 2 the eyes of the LORD, just as *J* had done.
Bar 1: 3 of this scroll for Jeconiah, son of *J,*
1: 7 These they sent to Jerusalem, to *J,*
Dn 1: 1 In the third year of the reign of *J,*
1: 2 The Lord handed over to him *J,*

JEHOIARIB (2)

1Chr 9:10 *J;* Jachin; Azariah, son of Hilkiah,
24: 7 The first lot fell to *J,*

JEHONADAB (4)

2Kgs 10:15 When he had left there, Jehu met *J,*
10:15 "Yes," replied *J.*
10:15 *J* gave him his hand,
10:23 all the garments for them, Jehu, with *J,*

JEHONATHAN (2)

2Chr 17: 8 Zebadiah, Asahel, Shemiramoth, *J,*
Neh 12:18 for Shemaiah, *J;*

JEHORAM (26)

1Kgs 22:51 His son *J* succeeded him as king.
2Kgs 1:17 him as king, in the second year of *J,*
8:16 of Joram, son of Ahab, king of Israel, *J,*
8:21 Thereupon *J* with all his chariots crossed
8:23 The rest of the acts of *J,*
8:24 *J* rested with his ancestors and was buried
8:25 Ahaziah, son of *J,*
8:29 Then Ahaziah, son of *J,*
11: 2 daughter of King *J* and sister of Ahaziah,
12:19 by his forebears, Jehoshaphat, *J,*
2Chr 17: 8 together with the priests Elishama and *J.*
21: 1 *J,* his son, succeeded him as king.
21: 3 he gave to *J* because he was the first-born.
21: 4 When *J* had come into his father's kingdom

JEHORAM (cont.)

21: 5 *J* was thirty-two years old when he became
21: 9 Thereupon *J* crossed over with his officers
21:16 Then the LORD stirred up against *J* the
22: 1 Thus Ahaziah, son of *J*,
22: 5 their counsel when he accompanied *J*,
22: 5 There *J* was wounded by the Arameans.
22: 6 *J*, king of Judah, went down to visit *J*
22: 7 Ahaziah's downfall that he should join *J*,
22: 7 his arrival he rode out with *J* to Jehu,
22:11 Jehosheba, who was the daughter of King *J*,
23: 1 Azariah, son of *J*;

JEHORAM'S (2)

2Kgs 8:20 During *J* reign,
2Chr 21:10 revolted at that time against *J* sovereignty

JEHOSHAPHAT (76)

2Sm 8:16 *J*, son of Ahilud, was chancellor.
20:24 *J*, son of Ahilud, was the chancellor.
1Kgs 4: 3 *J*, son of Ahilud, chancellor;
4:17 *J*, son of Paruah, in Issachar;
15:24 David, and his son *J* succeeded him as king.
22: 2 *J* of Judah came down to the king of Israel,
22: 4 He asked *J*, "Will you come with me
22: 4 *J* answered the king of Israel,
22: 5 *J* also said to the king of Israel,
22: 7 But *J* said, "Is there no other prophet
22: 8 *J* said, "Let not your majesty speak of evil
22:10 of Israel and King *J* of Judah were seated,
22:18 The king of Israel said to *J*,
22:29 King *J* of Judah went up to Ramoth-gilead,
22:30 and the king of Israel said to *J*,
22:32 When the chariot commanders saw *J*,
22:32 But *J* shouted his battle cry,
22:41 *J*, son of Asa, began to reign over Judah
22:42 *J* was thirty-five years old when he began
22:45 *J* also made peace with the king of Israel.
22:46 The rest of the acts of *J*,
22:49 *J* made Tarshish ships to go to Ophir for
22:50 Then Ahaziah, son of Ahab, said to *J*,
22:50 But *J* would not agree.
22:51 *J* rested with his ancestors;
22:52 in Samaria in the seventeenth year of *J*,
2Kgs 1:17 in the second year of Jehoram, son of *J*,
3: 1 in Samaria [in the eighteenth year of *J*,
8:16 of Ahab, king of Israel, Jehoram, son of *J*,
9: 2 you get there, look for Jehu, son of *J*,
9:14 Thus Jehu, son of *J*,
12:19 offerings presented by his forebears, *J*,
1Chr 3:10 whose son was Asa, whose son was *J*,
18:15 *J*, son of Ahilud, was herald:
2Chr 17: 1 *J* succeeded him as king and strengthened
17: 3 The LORD was with *J*,
17: 5 kingdom secure, and all Judah gave *J* gifts,
17:10 Judah, so that they did not war against *J*.
17:11 brought *J* gifts and a tribute of silver;
17:12 *J* grew steadily greater.
18: 1 *J* therefore had wealth and glory in
18: 3 Ahab, king of Israel, asked *J*,
18: 4 But *J* also said to the king of Israel,
18: 6 But *J* said, "Is there no other prophet
18: 7 The king of Israel answered *J*,
18: 9 *J* of Judah were seated each on his throne,
18:17 The king of Israel said to *J*,
18:28 The king of Israel and King *J* of Judah
18:29 and the king of Israel said to *J*,
18:31 When the commanders saw *J*,
18:31 But *J* cried out and the LORD helped him;
19: 1 King *J* of Judah returned in safety to his
19: 2 son of Hanani, met King *J* and said to him:
19: 4 *J* dwelt in Jerusalem;
19: 8 *J* appointed some Levites and priests and
20: 1 them some Meunites came to fight against *J*.
20: 2 The message was brought to *J*:
20: 3 *J* was frightened,
20:15 inhabitants of Jerusalem, and King *J*!
20:18 *J* knelt down with his face to the ground,
20:20 As they were going out, *J* halted and said:
20:25 *J* and his people came to take plunder,
20:27 Judah and Jerusalem, with *J* at their head,
20:31 Thus *J* reigned over Judah.
20:34 The rest of the acts of *J*,
20:35 King *J* of Judah allied himself with King
20:37 from Mareshah, prophesied against *J*,
21: 1 *J* rested with his ancestors;
21: 2 His brothers, sons of *J*,
21: 2 all these were sons of King *J* of Judah.
21:12 not followed the path of your father *J*,
22: 9 for they said, "He was the grandson of *J*,
Jl 4: 2 and bring them down to the Valley of *J*,
4:12 themselves and come up to the Valley of *J*;
Mt 1: 8 of Jehoshaphat, *J* the father of Joram,

JEHOSHAPHAT'S (1)

2Chr 20:30 Thereafter *J* kingdom enjoyed peace,

JEHOSHEBA (3)

2Kgs 11: 2 But *J*, daughter of King Jehoram
2Chr 22:11 But *J*, a royal princess, secretly took
22:11 In this way *J*,

JEHOZABAD (3)

2Kgs 12:22 Jozacar, son of Shimeath, and *J*,
1Chr 26: 4 Shemaiah, the first-born, *J*,
2Chr 24:26 Zabad, son of Shimeath from Ammon, and *J*,

JEHOZADAK (8)

1Chr 5:40 Seraiah became the father of *J*.
5:41 *J* was one of those who went into the exile
Hg 1: 1 and to the high priest Joshua, son of *J*:
1:12 and the high priest Joshua, son of *J*,
1:14 of the high priest Joshua, son of *J*,
2: 2 and to the high priest Joshua, son of *J*,
2: 4 courage, Joshua, high priest, son of *J*,
Zec 6:11 place it on the head of [Joshua, son of *J*,

JEHU (71)

1Kgs 16: 1 The LORD spoke against Baasha to *J*,
16: 7 [Through the prophet *J*,
16:12 to Baasha through the prophet *J*,
19:16 Then you shall anoint Jehu, son of *J*,
19:17 the sword of Hazael, *J* will kill him.
19:17 If he escapes the sword of *J*,
2Kgs 9: 2 When you get there, look for *J*,
9: 5 "For which one of us?" asked *J*.
9: 6 *J* got up and went into the house.
9:11 When *J* rejoined his master's servants,
9:13 spread it under *J* on the bare steps,
9:13 blew the trumpet, and cried out, *J* is king!"
9:14 Thus *J*, son of Jehoshaphat,
9:15 "If you are truly with me," *J* said,
9:16 *J* mounted his chariot and drove to Jezreel,
9:17 saw the troop of *J* coming and reported,
9:18 *J* said. "Get behind me."
9:19 *J* replied. "Get behind me."
9:20 The driving is like that of *J*,
9:21 out, each in his own chariot, to meet *J*.
9:22 Jehu, he asked, "Is all well, *J*?"
9:22 "How can all be well," *J* replied,
9:24 But *J* drew his bow and shot Joram between
9:25 Then *J* said to his adjutant Bidkar,
9:27 *J* pursued him, shouting, "Kill him too!"
9:30 learned that *J* had arrived in Jezreel,
9:31 As *J* came through the gate,
9:32 *J* looked up to the window and shouted,
9:33 *J* rode in over her body and,
9:36 They returned to *J*,
10: 1 *J* prepared letters and sent them to the
10: 5 and the guardians, sent this message to *J*:
10: 6 So *J* wrote them a second letter:
10: 7 in baskets, and sent them to *J* in Jezreel.
10:11 Thereupon *J* slew all who were left of the
10:14 "Take them alive," *J* ordered.
10:15 When he had left there, *J* met Jehonadab,
10:15 "if you are," continued *J*,
10:15 hand, and *J* drew him up into his chariot.
10:17 *J* slew all who remained there of Ahab's
10:18 *J* gathered all the people together and
10:18 some extent, but *J* will serve him yet more.
10:19 This *J* did as a ruse,
10:20 *J* said further,
10:21 and *J* sent word of it throughout the land
10:22 *J* said to the custodian of the wardrobe,
10:23 brought out all the garments for them, *J*,
10:24 Now *J* had stationed eighty men outside
10:25 *J* said to the guards and officers,
10:28 Thus *J* rooted out the worship of Baal from
10:30 The LORD said to *J*, "Because you have done
10:31 But *J* was not careful to observe
10:34 The rest of the acts of *J*,
10:35 *J* rested with his ancestors and was buried
12: 2 began to reign in the seventh year of *J*,
13: 1 king of Judah, Jehoahaz, son of *J*,
14: 8 to Jehoash, son of Jehoahaz, son of *J*,
15:12 Thus the LORD's promise to *J*,
1Chr 2:38 Obed became the father of *J*.
2:38 *J* became the father of Azariah.
4:35 Jamlech, Joshah, son of Amaziah, Joel, *J*,
12: 3 *J* from Anathoth;
2Chr 19: 2 *J* the seer, son of Hanani,
20:34 be found written in the chronicle of *J*,
22: 7 his arrival he rode out with Jehoram to *J*,
22: 8 While *J* was executing judgment on the
22: 9 was hiding in Samaria and brought him to *J*,
25:17 to Joash, son of Jehoahaz, son of *J*,
Hos 1: 4 will punish the house of *J* for the bloodshed

JEHUBBAH (1)

1Chr 7:34 The sons of Shomer were Ahi, Rohgah, *J*,

JEHUCAL (1)

Jer 37: 3 Yet King Zedekiah sent *J*,

JEHUD (1)

Jos 19:45 Ekron, Eltekoh, Gibbethon, Baalath, *J*,

JEHUDI (4)

Jer 36:14 Thereupon the princes sent *J*,
36:21 happened, he sent *J* to fetch the scroll.
36:21 *J* brought it from the room of Elishama the
36:23 Each time *J* finished reading three or four

JEHUEL (1)

2Chr 29:14 *J* and Shimei; of the sons of Jeduthun:

JEHUS (1)

2Kgs 10:36 The length of *J* reign over Israel in

JEIEL (12)

1Chr 5: 7 *J*, the chief,
8:29 In Gibeon dwelt *J*,
9:35 In Gibeon dwelt *J*,
11:44 Shama and *J*, sons of Hotham, from Aroer
15:18 Eliphelehu, Mikneiah, Obed-edom, and *J*.
15:21 and *J* led the chant on lyres set to "the
15:24 and *J* were also gatekeepers before the ark.
16: 5 Eliab, Benaiah, Obed-edom, and *J*.
2Chr 20:14 of Zechariah, son of Benaiah, son of *J*,
26:11 by *J* the scribe and Maaseiah the recorder,
Ezr 8:13 sons, whose names were Eliphelet, *J*,
10:43 *J*, Mattithiah,

JEKABZEEL (1)

Neh 11:25 its dependencies, in *J* and its villages,

JEKAMEAM (2)

1Chr 23:19 the second, Jahaziel, the third, and *J*,
24:23 the second, Jahaziel, the third, *J*,

JEKAMIAH (3)

1Chr 2:41 Shallum became the father of *J*.
2:41 *J* became the father of Elishama.
3:18 Malchiram, Pedaiah, Shenazzar, *J*,

JEKUTHIEL (1)

1Chr 4:18 of Gedor, Heber, the father of Soco, and *J*,

JEMIMAH (1)

Jb 42:14 daughters, of whom he called the first *J*,

JENNIES (1)

Gn 45:23 ten *j* loaded with grain and bread and other

JENUEL (1)

Ex 6:15 The sons of Simeon were *J*,

JEPHTHAH (26)

Jgs 11: 1 There was a chieftain, the Gileadite *J*,
11: 2 up the sons of the wife had driven *J* away,
11: 3 So *J* had fled from his brothers and had
11: 5 went to bring *J* from the land of Tob.
11: 6 "Come," they said to *J*,
11: 7 *J* replied to the elders of Gilead.
11: 8 The elders of Gilead said to *J*,
11: 9 *J* answered the elders of Gilead,
11:10 The elders of Gilead said to *J*,
11:11 So *J* went with the elders of Gilead,
11:11 *J* settled all his affairs before the LORD.
11:13 He answered the messengers of *J*,
11:14 Again *J* sent messengers to the king of the
11:15 saying to him, "This is what *J* says:
11:28 paid no heed to the message *J* sent him.
11:29 The spirit of the LORD came upon *J*.
11:30 *J* made a vow to the LORD.
11:32 *J* then went on to the Ammonites to fight
11:34 When *J* returned to his house in Mizpah,
11:40 *J* the Gileadite for four days of the year.
12: 1 said to *J*, "Why do you go on to fight
12: 2 *J* answered them, "My soldiers and I were
12: 4 Then *J* called together all the men of
12: 7 *J* the Gileadite died and was buried in his
1Sm 12:11 Barak, *J*, and Samson; he delivered you
Heb 11:32 time to tell of Gideon, Barak, Samson, *J*,

JEPHUNNEH (17)

Nm 13: 6 son of *J*, the tribe of Judah;
14: 6 Joshua, son of Nun, and Caleb, son of *J*,
14:30 to settle you, except Caleb, son of *J*,
14:38 Joshua, son of Nun, and Caleb, son of *J*,
26:65 of them was left except Caleb, son of *J*,
32:12 except the Kenizzite Caleb, son of *J*,
Nm 34:19 Caleb, son of *J*
Dt 1:36 to your fathers, except Caleb, son of *J*;
Jos 14: 6 in Gilgal, the Kenizzite Caleb, son of *J*,
14:13 Joshua blessed Caleb, son of *J*,
14:14 heritage of the Kenizzite Caleb, son of *J*,
15:13 commanded, Joshua gave Caleb, son of *J*,
21:12 the city had been given to Caleb, son of *J*,
1Chr 4:15 The sons of Caleb, son of *J*,
6:41 city had been given to Caleb, the son of *J*,
7:38 The sons of Jether were *J*, Pispa, and Ara.
Sir 46: 7 himself loyal, He and CALEB, son of *J*,

JERAH (2)

Gn 10:26 of Almodad, Sheleph, Hazarmaveth, *J*,
1Chr 1:20 of Almodad, Sheleph, Hazarmaveth, *J*,

JERAHMEEL (9)

1Sm 27:10 Negeb of Judah," or "The Negeb of *J*,"
1Chr 2: 9 The sons born to Hezron were *J*,
2:25 The sons of *J*,
2:26 *J* also had another wife,
2:27 The sons of Ram, the first-born of *J*,
2:33 These were the descendants of *J*.
2:42 The descendants of Caleb, the brother of *J*:
24:29 Mahli were Eleazar, who had no sons, and *J*,
Jer 36:26 would not listen to them, but commanded *J*,

JERAHMEELITE (1)

1Sm 30:29 those in Racal, to those in the *J* cities,

JERED (1)

1Chr 4:18 His (Mered's) Egyptian wife bore *J*,

JEREMAI (1)

Ezr 10:33 Mattenai, Mattattah, Zabad, Eliphelet, *J*,

JEREMIAH (152)

2Kgs 23:31 whose name was Hamutal, daughter of *J*,
24:18 name was Hamutal, daughter of *J* of Libnah.
1Chr 5:24 Epher, Ishi, Eliel, Azriel, *J*,
12: 5 *J*; Jahaziel; Johanan; Jozabad from
12:11 Eliab third, Mishmannah fourth, *J* fifth,
12:14 Johanan eighth, Elzabad ninth, *J* tenth,
2Chr 35:25 *J* also composed a lamentation over Josiah,
36:12 not humble himself before the prophet *J*,
36:21 fulfill the word of the LORD spoken by *J*:
36:22 fulfill the word of the LORD spoken by *J*,
Ezr 1: 1 fulfill the word of the LORD spoken by *J*,
Neh 10: 3 Seraiah, Azariah, *J*,
12: 1 Seraiah, *J*,
12:12 for *J*, Hananiah; for Ezra, Meshullam;
12:34 Judah, Benjamin, Shemaiah, and *J*,
2Mc 2: 1 not only that *J* the prophet ordered the
2: 5 When *J* arrived there,
2: 7 When *J* heard of this, he reproved them:
15:14 said of him, "This is God's prophet *J*,
15:15 hand, *J* presented a gold sword to Judas.
Sir 49: 7 its streets desolate, As *J* had foretold;
Jer 1: 1 The words of *J*,
1:11 What do you see, *J*?
1:15 of *J* Opposite her walls all around and
7: 1 following message came to *J* from the LORD:
11: 1 following message came to *J* from the LORD:
14: 1 LORD that came to *J* concerning the drought:
18: 1 This word came to *J* from the LORD:
18:18 said, "let us contrive a plot against *J*.
19:14 When *J* returned from Topheth,
20: 1 *J* was heard prophesying these things by
20: 3 Pashhur had released *J* from the stocks,
21: 1 The message which came to *J* from the LORD
21: 3 But *J* answered them:
24: 3 What do you see, *J*?
25: 1 to *J* concerning all the people of Judah,
25: 2 This word the prophet *J* spoke to all the
25:13 *J* prophesied against all the nations].
26: 7 and all the people heard *J* speak these
26: 8 When *J* finished speaking all that the LORD
26: 9 gathered about *J* in the house of the LORD.
26:12 *J* gave this answer to the princes and all
26:20 things against this city and land as *J* did.
26:24 But Ahikam, son of Shaphan, protected *J*,
27: 1 this message came to *J* from the LORD:
28: 5 The prophet *J* answered the prophet
28:10 the yoke from the neck of the prophet *J*,
28:11 At that, the prophet *J* went away.
28:12 Jeremiah, the word of the LORD came to *J*:
28:15 To the prophet Hananiah the prophet *J* said:
29: 1 the letter which the prophet *J* sent from
29:27 do you not rebuke *J* of Anathoth who poses
29:30 prophet, the word of the LORD came to *J*:
30: 1 following message came to *J* from the LORD:
32: 1 This message came to *J* from the LORD in
32: 2 and the prophet *J* was imprisoned in the
32: 6 message came to me from the LORD, said *J*:
32:26 Then this word of the LORD came to *J*:
33: 1 The word of the LORD came to *J* a second
33:18 This word of the LORD also came to *J*:
33:23 This word of the LORD came to *J*:
34: 1 to *J* from the LORD while Nebuchadnezzar,
34: 6 *J* told all these things to Zedekiah,
34: 8 This is the word that came to *J* from the
34:12 Then this word of the LORD came to *J*:
35: 1 *J* from the LORD in the days of Jehoiakim,
35: 3 So I went and brought Jaazaniah, son of *J*,
35:12 Then this word of the LORD came to *J*:
35:18 to the company of the Rechabites *J* said:
36: 1 Judah, this word came to *J* from the LORD.
36: 4 So *J* called Baruch,
36: 4 who wrote down on a scroll, as *J* dictated,
36: 5 Then *J* charged Baruch:
36: 8 did everything the prophet *J* commanded;
36:10 publicly read the words of *J* from his book.
36:18 *J* dictated all these words to me,"
36:19 to Baruch, "Go into hiding, you and *J*;
36:26 Baruch, the secretary, and the prophet *J*.
36:27 This word of the LORD came to *J*,
36:27 with the text *J* had dictated to Baruch:
36:32 *J* took another scroll,
37: 2 words of the LORD spoken by *J* the prophet.
37: 3 priest, to the prophet *J* with this request:
37: 4 time *J* had not yet been put into prison;
37: 6 of the LORD then came to the prophet *J*:
37:12 *J* set out from Jerusalem for the District
37:13 he seized the prophet *J*,
37:14 *J* answered, "I am not deserting
37:14 Irijah kept *J* in custody and brought him
37:15 and had *J* beaten and thrown into prison in
37:16 And so *J* entered the vaulted dungeon,
37:17 *J* answered: you shall be handed over
37:18 *J* then asked King Zedekiah:
37:21 *J* be confined in the quarters of the guard,
37:21 *J* remained in the quarters of the guard.
38: 1 *J* speaking these words to all the people:
38: 6 And so they took *J* and threw him into the
38: 6 cistern, only mud, and *J* sank into the mud.
38: 7 heard that they had put *J* into the cistern.
38: 9 in all they have done to the prophet *J*,
38:10 *J* out of the cistern before he should die.
38:11 these he sent down to *J* in the cistern,
38:12 Then he said to *J*:
38:12 *J* did so, and they drew him up
38:13 *J* remained in the quarters of the guard.
38:14 Once King Zedekiah summoned the prophet *J*
38:14 question to ask you," the king said to *J*;
38:14 "hide nothing from me." *J* answered Zedekiah:
38:16 But King Zedekiah swore to *J* secretly:
38:17 Thereupon *J* said to Zedekiah;
38:19 King Zedekiah however, said to *J*,
38:20 You will not be handed over, *J* answered.
38:24 Zedekiah said to *J*, "Let no one know
38:27 When all the princes came to *J*,
38:28 Thus *J* stayed in the quarters of the guard
39:11 Concerning *J*, Nebuchadnezzar, king of
39:14 *J* taken out of the quarters of the guard,
39:15 While *J* was still imprisoned in the
40: 1 This word came to *J* from the LORD,
40: 2 captain of the bodyguard took charge of *J*,
40: 6 *J* went to Gedaliah,
42: 1 and low, approached the prophet *J* and said,
42: 4 the prophet *J* answered them:
42: 5 they said to *J*, "May the LORD be our
42: 7 before the word of the LORD came to *J*.
43: 1 When *J* finished speaking to the people all
43: 2 and all the insolent men shouted to *J*:
43: 6 also *J*, the prophet, and Baruch,
43: 8 word of the LORD came to *J* in Tahpanhes:
43:10 his throne upon these stones which I, *J*,
44: 1 This word came to *J* for all the people of
44:15 and Upper Egypt, *J* received this answer:
44:20 women, who gave him this answer, *J* said:
44:24 *J* said further to all the people,
45: 1 message that the prophet *J* gave to Baruch,
45: 1 *J* dictated in the fourth year of Jehoiakim,
46: 1 came to the prophet *J* against the nations.
46:13 *J* concerning the advance of Nebuchadnezzar,
47: 1 the prophet *J* concerning the Philistines,
49:34 LORD against Elam came to the prophet *J*
50: 1 of the Chaldeans, through the prophet *J*:
51:59 errand given by the prophet *J* to Seraiah,
51:60 *J* had written the misfortune that was to
51:61 And *J* said to Seraiah:
51:64 To "weary themselves" are the words of *J*
52: 1 name was Hamutal, daughter of *J* of Libnah.
Bar 6: 1 A copy of the letter which *J* sent to those
Dn 9: 2 of which the LORD spoke to the prophet *J*:
Mt 2:17 through *J* the prophet was then fulfilled:
16:14 still others *J* or one of the prophets."
27: 9 said through *J* the prophet was fulfilled:

JEREMIAH'S (1)

Jer 36:32 he wrote on it at *J* dictation all the

JEREMOTH (8)

1Chr 7: 8 Joash, Eliezer, Elioenai, Omri, *J*,
8:14 Their brethren were Elpaal, Shashak, and *J*.
23:23 Mahli, Eder, and *J*; three in all.
25:22 The fifteenth fell to *J*,
27:19 for Naphtali, *J*,
Ezr 10:26 Mattaniah, Zechariah, Jehiel, Abdi, *J*,
10:27 Elioenai, Eliashib, Mattaniah, *J*,
10:29 Jashub, Sheal, and *J*;

JERIAH (2)

1Chr 23:19 *J*, the chief,
24:23 The descendants of Hebron were *J*,

JERIBAI (1)

1Chr 11:46 *J* and Joshaviah,

JERICHO (70)

Nm 22: 1 other side of the *J* stretch of the Jordan.
26: 3 of Moab along the *J* stretch of the Jordan,
26:63 of Moab along the *J* stretch of the Jordan.
31:12 of Moab, along the *J* stretch of the Jordan.
33:48 of Moab along the *J* stretch of the Jordan.
33:50 *J* stretch of the Jordan and said to him:
34:15 side of the *J* stretch of the Jordan,
35: 1 of Moab beside the *J* stretch of the Jordan:
36:13 of Moab beside the *J* stretch of the Jordan.
Dt 32:49 [it is in the land of Moab facing *J*;
34: 1 the headland of Pisgah which faces *J*,
34: 3 of the Jordan with the lowlands at *J*,
34:12 of the Jordan with the lowlands at *J*,
Jos 2: 1 saying, "Go, reconnoiter the land and *J*."
2: 1 When the two reached *J*,
2: 2 But a report was brought to the king of *J*
2: 3 So the king of *J* sent Rahab the order,
3:16 Thus the people crossed over opposite *J*.
4:13 over before the LORD to the plains of *J*.
4:19 in Gilgal on the eastern limits of *J*.
5:10 encamped at Gilgal on the plains of *J*,
5:13 While Joshua was near *J*,
6: 1 Now *J* was in a state of siege because of
6: 2 delivered *J* and its king into your power.
6:25 whom Joshua had sent to reconnoiter *J*,
6:26 man who attempts to rebuild this city, *J*.
7: 2 Joshua next sent men from *J* to Ai,
8: 2 its king what you did to *J* and its king;
9: 3 learning what Joshua had done to *J* and Ai,
10: 1 its king as he had done to *J* and its king.
10:28 Makkedah what he had done to the king of *J*.
10:30 its king what he had done to the king of *J*.
12: 9 They were the kings of *J*,
13:32 of Moab, beyond the Jordan east of *J*.
16: 1 Jordan at *J* to the waters of Jericho
16: 1 went up from *J* to the heights at Bethel.
16: 7 to Ataroth and Naarah, and skirting *J*,
18:12 and went over the northern flank of *J*,
18:21 *J*, Beth-hoglah,
20: 8 And beyond the Jordan east of *J* they
24:11 Jericho, the men of *J* fought against you,
2Sm 10: 5 "Stay in *J* until your beards grow,"
1Kgs 16:34 his reign, Hiel from Bethel rebuilt *J*.
2Kgs 2: 4 Elisha, for the LORD has sent me on to *J*."
2: 5 They went on to *J*,
2:15 The guild prophets in *J*,
2:18 When they returned to Elisha in *J*,
25: 5 king and overtook him in the desert near *J*,
1Chr 6:63 Across the Jordan at *J* [that is,
19: 5 "Remain at *J*,"
2Chr 28:15 They brought them to *J*,
Ezr 2:34 sons of *J*,
Neh 3: 2 At their side the men of *J* were rebuilding,
7:36 sons of *J*,
Jdt 4: 4 to Kona, Beth-horon, Belmain, and *J*,
1Mc 9:50 the *J* fortress, as well as Emmaus,
16:11 been appointed governor of the plain of *J*,
16:14 Mattathias and Judas went down to *J*
2Mc 12:15 *J* without battering-ram or siege machine;
Sir 24:14 palm tree in Engedi, like a rosebush in *J*,
Jer 39: 5 and captured Zedekiah in the desert near *J*.
52: 8 and overtook Zedekiah in the desert near *J*,
Mt 20:29 were leaving *J* a large crowd followed him,
Mk 10:46 They came to *J* next,
Lk 10:30 Jerusalem to *J* who fell prey to robbers.
18:35 As he drew near *J* a blind man sat at the
19: 1 Entering *J*, he passed through the city.
Heb 11:30 the walls of *J* fell after being encircled

JERIEL (1)

1Chr 7: 2 The sons of Tola were Uzzi, Rephaiah, *J*,

JERIJAH (1)

1Chr 26:31 *J* was their chief according to their

JERIMOTH (6)

1Chr 7: 7 sons of Bela were Ezbon, Uzzi, Uzziel, *J*,
12: 6 *J*; Bealiah; Shemariah;
24:30 of Mushi were Mahli, Eder, and *J*.
25: 4 Mattaniah, Uzziel, Shubael, and *J*;
2Chr 11:18 himself as wife Mahalath, daughter of *J*,
31:13 Jehiel, Azaziah, Nahath, Asahel, *J*,

JERIOTH (1)

1Chr 2:18 Hezron, became the father of a daughter, *J*.

JEROBOAM (92)

1Kgs 11:26 Solomon's servant *J*,
11:28 *J* was a man of means,
11:29 At that time *J* left Jerusalem,
11:31 tore it into twelve pieces, and said to *J*:
11:40 When Solomon tried to have *J* killed for
12: 2 *J*, son of Nebat,
12:15 fulfill the prophecy he had uttered to *J*,
12:20 When all Israel heard that *J* had returned,
12:25 *J* built up Shechem in the hill country of
12:26 *J* thought to himself:
12:32 *J* established a feast in the eighth month
12:33 *J* ascended the altar he built in Bethel on
13: 1 while *J* was standing at the altar to offer
13: 4 When King *J* heard what the man of God was
13:33 *J* did not give up his evil ways after this
13:34 a sin on the part of the house of *J*
14: 1 At that time Abijah, son of *J*, took sick.
14: 2 So *J* said to his wife,
14: 4 The wife of *J* obeyed.

JEROBOAM (cont.)

14: 6 the door, said, "Come in, wife of J.
14: 7 Go, tell J,
14:10 I am bringing evil upon the house of J:
14:10 and will burn up the house of J completely,
14:14 of Israel who will destroy the house of J.
14:16 give up Israel because of the sins J
14:19 The rest of the acts of J,
14:30 constant warfare between Rehoboam and J.
15: 1 In the eighteenth year of King J,
15: 6 There was war between Abijam and J.
15: 9 In the twentieth year of J,
15:25 of Asa, king of Judah, Nadab, son of J,
15:29 J, not leaving a single soul to Jeroboam
15:30 J committed and caused Israel to commit,
15:34 imitating the conduct of J and the sin he
16: 2 J and have caused my people Israel to sin,
16: 3 I will make your house like that of J,
16: 7 so that he became like the house of J;
16:19 LORD by imitating the sinful conduct of J,
16:26 closely imitated the sinful conduct of J,
16:31 enough for him to imitate the sins of J,
21:22 I will make your house like that of J,
22:53 like his father, his mother, and J,
2Kgs 3: 3 but he still clung to the sin to which J,
9: 9 of Ahab as I dealt with the house of J,
10:29 he did not desist from the sins which J,
10:31 the sins which J caused Israel to commit.
13: 2 LORD's sight, conducting himself like J,
13: 6 the house of J had caused Israel to commit,
13:11 not desist from any of the sins which J,
13:13 his ancestors, and J occupied the throne.
14:16 His son J succeeded him as king.
14:23 Amaziah, son of Joash, king of Judah, J,
14:24 not desist from any of the sins which J,
14:27 under the heavens, he saved them through J,
14:28 The rest of the acts of J,
14:29 J rested with his ancestors,
15: 1 king in the twenty-seventh year of J,
15: 8 king of Judah, Zechariah, son of J,
15: 9 and did not desist from the sins which J,
15:18 LORD, not desisting from the sins which J,
15:24 LORD, not desisting from the sins which J,
15:28 LORD, not desisting from the sins which J,
17:21 away from the house of David, they made J,
17:22 imitated J in all the sins he committed,
23:15 was at Bethel, the high place built by J,
23:16 proclaimed as J was standing by the altar
1Chr 5:17 time of Jotham, king of Judah, and of J,
2Chr 9:29 visions of Iddo the seer which concern J,
10: 2 When J, son of Nebat, heard of this
10: 3 J was summoned to the assembly,
10:12 J and all the people came back to King
10:15 the prophecy the LORD had uttered to J,
11: 4 LORD and gave up the expedition against J.
11:14 because J and his sons repudiated them as
12:15 was war continually between Rehoboam and J.
13: 1 In the eighteenth year of King J,
13: 2 There was war between Abijah and J.
13: 3 while J lined up against him in battle
13: 4 "Listen to me, J and all Israel!
13: 6 Yet J, son of Nebat,
13: 8 golden calves which J made you for gods?
13:13 But J had an ambush go around them to come
13:15 J and all Israel before Abijah and Judah.
13:19 Abijah pursued J and took cities from him:
13:20 J did not regain power during the time of
Tb 1: 5 as well as to the young bull which J,
Hos 1: 1 kings of Judah, and in the days of J,
Am 1: 1 king of Judah, and in the days of J,
7: 9 will attack the house of J with the sword.
7:10 the priest of Bethel, sent word to J,
7:11 J shall die by the sword,

JEROBOAM'S (8)

1Kgs 14: 2 so that none will recognize you as J wife.
14: 5 J wife is coming to consult you about her
14:10 I will cut off every male in J line,
14:11 When one of J line dies in the city,
14:13 alone of J line will be laid in the grave,
14:13 J house has something pleasing to the LORD,
14:17 So J wife started back;
14:20 The length of J reign was twenty-two years.

JEROHAM (9)

1Sm 1: 1 He was the son of J,
1Chr 6:12 whose son was Eliab, whose son was J,
6:19 son of Samuel, son of Elkanah, son of J,
8:27 Elijah, and Zichri were the sons of J.
9: 8 son of Hassenuah, Ibneiah, son of J;
9:12 Adaiah, son of J,
12: 8 Joelah, finally, and Zebadiah, sons of J,
27:22 for Dan, Azarel, son of J.
Neh 11:12 Adaiah, son of J,

JERUBBAAL (14)

Jgs 6:32 So on that day Gideon was called J,
7: 1 Early the next morning J (that is,
8:29 Then J,
8:35 they grateful to the family of J [Gideon]
9: 1 Abimelech, son of J,
9: 5 slew his brothers, the seventy sons of J,
9: 5 Only the youngest son of J,
9:16 have dealt well with J and with his family,
9:19 honor toward J and his family this day,
9:24 violence done to the seventy sons of J
9:28 Were not the son of J and his lieutenant
9:57 for the curse of Jotham, son of J,
1Sm 12:11 Accordingly, the LORD sent J,
2Sm 11:21 Who killed Abimelech, son of J?

JERUBBAAL'S (1)

Jgs 9: 2 that seventy men, or all J sons,

JERUEL (1)

2Chr 20:16 wadi which opens on the wilderness of J.

JERUSA (1)

2Chr 27: 1 His mother was named J, daughter of Zadok.

JERUSALEM (933)

Jos 10: 1 Now Adonizedek, king of J,
10: 3 So Adonizedek, king of J,
10: 5 The five Amorite kings, of J,
10:23 to him from the cave the five kings, of J,
12:10 of Jericho, Ai (which is near Bethel), J,
15: 8 flank of the Jebusites [that is, J,
15:63 in J the Judahites could not drive out;
15:63 J beside the Judahites to the present day.]
18:28 Haeleph, the Jebusite city (that is, J),
Jgs 1: 7 He was brought to J, and there he died.
1: 8 Judahites fought against J and captured it,
1:21 not dislodge the Jebusites who dwelt in J,
1:21 Jebusites live in J beside the Benjaminites
19:10 till they came opposite Jebus, which is J.
1Sm 17:54 of the Philistine and brought it to J;
2Sm 5: 5 years in J over all Israel and Judah.
5: 6 Then the king and his men set out for J
5:13 wives in J after he had come from Hebron,
5:13 sons and daughters were born to him in J.
5:14 names of those who were born to him in J:
8: 7 Hadadezer's servants and brought them to J.
8: 7 when he came to J in the days of Rehoboam,
9:13 But Meribbaal lived in J
10:14 attack on the Ammonites and returned to J.
11: 1 David, however, remained in J.
11:12 So Uriah remained in J that day.
12:31 and all the soldiers then returned to J.
14:23 off to Geshur and brought Absalom to J.
14:28 Absalom lived in J for two years without
15: 8 'If the LORD ever brings me back to J,
15:11 men had accompanied Absalom from J.
15:14 to all his servants who were with him in J:
15:29 ark of God back to J and remained there.
15:37 city of J as Absalom was about to enter it.
16: 3 answered the king, "He is staying in J,
16:15 entered J with all the Israelites.
17:20 but found no one, and so returned to J.
19:20 did the day my lord the king left J.
19:26 When he came from J to meet the king,
19:34 provide for your old age as my guest in J."
19:35 that I should go up to J with the king?
20: 2 But from the Jordan to J the Judahites
20: 3 When King David came to his palace in J,
20: 7 from J to campaign in pursuit of Sheba,
20:22 while Joab returned to J to the King.
24: 8 J again after nine months and twenty days.
24:16 forth his hand toward J to destroy it,
1Kgs 2:11 in Hebron and thirty-three years in J.
2:36 yourself a house in J and live there.
2:38 So Shimei stayed in J for a long time.
2:41 that Shimei had gone from J to Gath,
3: 1 temple of the LORD, and the wall around J.
3:15 awoke from his dream, he went to J,
8: 1 the Israelites, came to King Solomon in J,
9:15 LORD, his palace, Millo, the wall of J,
9:19 else Solomon decided should be built in J,
10: 2 arrived in J with a very numerous retinue,
10:26 cities and to the king's service in J.
10:27 king made silver as common in J as stones,
11: 7 of the Ammonites, on the hill opposite J.
11:13 for the sake of my servant David and of J,
11:29 At that time Jeroboam left J,
11:32 the sake of David my servant, and of J,
11:36 may always have a lamp before me in J,
11:42 in J over all Israel was forty years.
12:18 managed to mount his chariot to flee to J,
12:21 On his arrival in J
12:27 sacrifices in the temple of the LORD in J,
12:28 "You have been going up to J long enough.
14:21 king, and he reigned seventeen years in J,
14:25 Shishak, king of Egypt, attacked J.
15: 2 He reigned three years in J.
15: 4 the LORD, his God, gave him a lamp in J,
15: 4 son after him and permitting J to endure
15:10 he reigned forty-one years in J.
22:42 and he reigned twenty-five years in J.
2Kgs 8:17 to reign, and he reigned eight years in J.
8:26 his reign, and he reigned one year in J.
9:28 brought him in a chariot to J and buried
12: 2 of Jehu, and he reigned forty years in J.
12:18 it, Hazael decided to go on to attack J.
12:19 Aram, who then led his forces away from J.
14: 2 and he reigned twenty-nine years in J.
14: 2 whose name was Jehoaddin, was from J.
14:13 He went on to J where he tore down four
14:19 a conspiracy was formed against him in J,
14:20 his ancestors in the City of David in J.
15: 2 reign, and he reigned fifty-two years in J.
15: 2 whose name was Jecholiah, was from J.
15:33 king, and he reigned sixteen years in J.
16: 2 king, and he reigned sixteen years in J.
16: 5 king of Israel, came up to J to attack it.
18: 2 and he reigned twenty-nine years in J.
18:17 with a great army to King Hezekiah at J.
18:17 They went up, and on their arrival in J,
18:22 J to worship before this altar in J
18:35 Will the LORD then rescue J from my hand?'
19:10 saying that J will not be handed over
19:21 Behind you she wags her head, daughter J.
19:31 For out of J shall come a remnant,
21: 1 and he reigned fifty-five years in J.
21: 4 had said, "I will establish my name in J—
21: 7 "In this temple and in J,
21:12 will bring such evil on J and Judah that,
21:13 J with the same cord as I did Samaria,
21:13 I will wipe J clean as one wipes a dish,
21:16 as to fill the length and breadth of J.
21:19 to reign, and he reigned two years in J.
22: 1 and he reigned thirty-one years in J.
22:14 themselves to the Second Quarter in J,
23: 1 and of J summoned together before him.
23: 2 men of Judah and all the inhabitants of J:
23: 4 He had these burned outside J on the
23: 5 cities of Judah and in the vicinity of J,
23: 6 pole, to the Kidron Valley, outside J;
23: 9 function at the altar of the LORD in J;
23:13 king defiled the high places east of J,
23:20 Then he returned to J.
23:23 this Passover of the LORD was kept in J.
23:24 to be seen in the land of Judah and in J,
23:27 I will reject this city, J,
23:30 his body on a chariot from Megiddo to J,
23:31 to reign, and he reigned three months in J.
23:33 land of Hamath, thus ending his reign in J.
23:36 to reign, and he reigned eleven years in J.
24: 4 blood he shed, with which he filled J,
24: 8 to reign, and he reigned three months in J.
24: 8 was Nehushta, daughter of Elnathan of J.
24:10 king of Babylon, attacked J,
24:14 He deported all J:
24:15 J to Babylon the king's mother and wives,
24:18 king, and he reigned eleven years in J.
24:20 The LORD's anger befell J and Judah till
25: 1 and his whole army advanced against J,
25: 8 came to J as the representative of the
25: 9 of the king, and all the houses of J;
25:10 tore down the walls that surrounded J.
1Chr 3: 4 Then he reigned thirty-three years in J,
5:36 as priest in the temple Solomon built in J.
5:41 on Judah and J through Nebuchadnezzar.
6:17 Solomon built the temple of the LORD in J,
8:28 over their kindred, chiefs who dwelt in J.
8:32 too, dwelt with their relatives in J,
9: 3 In J lived Judahites and Benjaminites;
9:34 over their kindred, chiefs who dwelt in J.
9:38 dwelt opposite their brethren in J.
11: 4 Then David and all Israel went to J,
14: 3 David took other wives in J and became the
14: 4 names of those who were born to him in J:
15: 3 Then David assembled all Israel in J to
18: 7 attendants and brought them to J.
19:15 Joab then returned to J.
20: 1 Rabbah, while David himself remained in J.
20: 3 Then he and his whole army returned to J.
21: 4 all of Israel, and then returned to J.
21:15 God also sent an angel to destroy J;
21:16 sword in his hand stretched out against J.
23:25 people, and has taken up his dwelling in J.
28: 1 assembled at J all the leaders of Israel,
29:27 reigned seven years, and in J thirty-three.
2Chr 1: 4 had brought up from Kiriath-jearim to J,
1:13 to J from the high place at Gibeon,
1:14 the chariot cities and with the king in J.
1:15 silver and gold as common in J as stones,
2: 6 craftsmen who are with me in Judah and J,
2:15 of Joppa, whence you may take them up to J."
3: 1 the house of the LORD in J on Mount Moriah,
5: 2 came to J to bring up the ark of the
6: 6 I choose J, where I shall be honored,
8: 6 else Solomon decided should be built in J,
9: 1 to J to test him with subtle questions,
9:25 to the chariot cities and to the king in J.
9:27 king made silver as common in J as stones,
9:30 in J over all Israel for forty years.
10:18 managed to mount his chariot and flee to J.
11: 1 On his arrival in J Rehoboam gathered
11: 5 in J and built fortified cities in Judah.
11:14 their holdings and came to Judah and J,
11:16 Israel, came to J to sacrifice to the LORD,
12: 2 Shishak, king of Egypt, attacked J,
12: 4 cities of Judah and came as far as J.
12: 5 who had gathered at J because of Shishak,
12: 7 not be poured out upon J through Shishak.
12: 9 attacked J and carried off the treasures

12:13 his power in *J* and continued to rule;
12:13 king, and he reigned seventeen years in *J*,
13: 2 he reigned three years in *J*.
14:14 Then they returned to *J*.
15:10 They gathered at *J* in the third month of
17:13 he had soldiers, valiant warriors, in *J*.
19: 1 Judah returned in safety to his house in *J*.
19: 4 Jehoshaphat dwelt in *J*;
19: 8 In *J* also,
19: 8 settle quarrels among the inhabitants of *J*.
20: 5 stood up in the assembly of Judah and *J*
20:15 "Listen, all of Judah, inhabitants of *J*,
20:17 be with you to deliver you, Judah and *J*.
20:18 of *J* fell down before the LORD in worship.
20:20 "Listen to me, Judah and inhabitants of *J*!
20:27 Then all the men of Judah and *J*,
20:27 turned back toward *J* celebrating the
20:28 They came to *J*,
20:31 and he reigned twenty-five years in *J*.
21: 5 king, and he reigned eight years in *J*.
21:11 of *J* into idolatry and seduced Judah.
21:13 and the inhabitants of *J* into idolatry,
21:20 king, and he reigned eight years in *J*.
22: 1 Then the inhabitants of *J* made Ahaziah,
22: 2 became king, and he reigned one year in *J*.
23: 2 When they had come to *J*,
24: 1 king, and he reigned forty years in *J*.
24: 6 from Judah and *J* the tax levied by Moses,
24: 9 Judah and *J* that the tax which Moses,
24:18 of theirs, wrath came upon Judah and *J*.
24:23 They invaded Judah and *J*,
25: 1 and he reigned twenty-nine years in *J*.
25: 1 His mother, named Jehoaddan, was from *J*.
25:23 at Beth-shemesh and brought him to *J*.
25:23 *J* from the Ephraim Gate to the Corner Gate,
25:27 a conspiracy was formed against him in *J*;
26: 3 king, and he reigned fifty-two years in *J*.
26: 3 His mother, named Jecoliah, was from *J*.
26: 9 built towers in *J* at the Corner Gate,
26:15 He also built machines in *J*,
27: 1 king, and he reigned sixteen years in *J*.
27: 8 king, and he reigned sixteen years in *J*.
28: 1 king, and he reigned sixteen years in *J*.
28:10 of Judah and *J* your slaves and bondwomen.
28:24 made for himself in every corner of *J*.
28:27 with his ancestors and was buried in *J*—
29: 1 and he reigned twenty-nine years in *J*.
29: 8 of the LORD has come upon Judah and *J*;
30: 1 come to the house of the LORD in *J*
30: 2 and the entire assembly in *J* had agreed to
30: 3 and the people were not gathered at *J*.
30: 5 that everyone should come to *J* to
30:11 Zebulun humbled themselves and came to *J*.
30:13 Thus many people gathered in *J* to
30:14 to take down the altars that were in *J*;
30:21 Thus the Israelites who were in *J*
30:26 There was great rejoicing in *J*,
31: 4 He also commanded the people living in *J*
32: 2 coming with the intention of attacking *J*,
32: 9 he sent his officials to *J* with this
32: 9 Judah, and all the Judahites who were in *J*:
32:10 relying, while you remain under siege in *J*?
32:12 and altars and commanded Judah and *J*,
32:18 to the people of *J* who were on the wall,
32:22 of *J* from the hand of Sennacherib,
32:23 Many brought gifts for the LORD to *J* and
32:25 descended upon him and upon Judah and *J*.
32:26 both he and the inhabitants of *J*;
32:33 of *J* paid him honor at his death.
33: 1 king, and he reigned fifty-five years in *J*.
33: 4 said, "In *J* shall my name be forever":
33: 7 "In this house and in *J* which I have
33: 9 misled Judah and the inhabitants of *J*
33:13 and restored him to his kingdom in *J*.
33:15 on the mount of the LORD's house and in *J*,
33:21 became king, and he reigned two years in *J*.
34: 1 king, and he reigned thirty-one years in *J*.
34: 3 to purge Judah and *J* of the high places,
34: 5 Thus he purged Judah and *J*.
34: 7 Then he returned to *J*.
34: 9 Judah, Benjamin, and the inhabitants of *J*.
34:22 she dwelt in *J*,
34:29 now convened all the elders of Judah and *J*.
34:30 the men of Judah and the inhabitants of *J*,
34:32 committed all who were of *J* and Benjamin,
34:32 and the inhabitants of *J* conformed
35: 1 in *J* a Passover to honor the Lord;
35:18 were present, and the inhabitants of *J*.
35:24 he had in reserve, and brought him to *J*,
35:24 ancestors, and all Judah and *J* mourned him.
36: 1 made him king in *J* in his father's stead.
36: 2 king, and he reigned three months in *J*.
36: 3 The king of Egypt deposed him in *J* and
36: 4 his brother Eliakim king over Judah and *J*,
36: 5 king, and he reigned eleven years in *J*.
36: 9 reigned three months [and ten days] in *J*.
36:10 his brother Zedekiah king over Judah and *J*,
36:11 king, and he reigned eleven years in *J*.
36:14 temple which he had consecrated in *J*.
36:19 house of God, tore down the walls of *J*,
36:23 also charged me to build him a house in *J*,
Ezr 1: 2 also charged me to build him a house in *J*,
1: 4 offerings for the house of God in *J*.'"
1: 5 go up to build the house of the LORD in *J*.
1: 7 from *J* and placed in the house of his god.
1:11 exiles were brought back from Babylon to *J*.
2: 1 Babylon, and who came back to *J* and Judah,
2:68 arrived at the house of the LORD in *J*,
2:70 the common people took up residence in *J*;
3: 1 the people gathered at *J* as one man.
3: 8 their coming to the house of God in *J*,
3: 8 all who had come from the captivity to *J*,
4: 6 against the inhabitants of Judah and *J*.
4: 8 letter against *J* to King Artaxerxes:
4:12 have arrived at *J* and are now rebuilding
4:20 in *J* who ruled over all West-of-Euphrates,
4:23 *J* and stopped their work by force of arms.
4:24 work on the house of God in *J* was halted.
5: 1 and *J* in the name of the God of Israel.
5: 2 again to build the house of God in *J*,
5:14 *J* and carried off to the temple in Babylon,
5:15 and deposit them in the temple of *J*,
5:16 the foundations of the house of God in *J*.
5:17 the rebuilding of this house of God in *J*.
6: 3 The house of God in *J*.
6: 5 Nebuchadnezzar took from the temple of *J*
6: 5 of *J* and deposited in the house of God.
6: 9 requirements of the priests who are in *J*—
6:12 this or to destroy this house of God in *J*.
6:18 divisions for the service of God in *J*,
7: 7 *J* in the seventh year of King Artaxerxes.
7: 8 Ezra came to *J* in the fifth month of that
7: 9 day of the fifth month he arrived at *J*,
7:13 who is minded to go up to *J* with you,
7:14 seven counselors to supervise Judah and *J*
7:15 the God of Israel, whose dwelling is in *J*,
7:16 contribute for the house of their God in *J*.
7:17 on the altar of the house of your God in *J*.
7:19 God you are to deposit before the God of *J*.
7:27 king to glorify the house of the LORD in *J*.
8:29 weigh them out in *J*
8:30 had been weighed out, to bring them to *J*,
8:31 We set out for *J* from the river of Ahava
8:32 Thus we arrived in *J*,
9: 9 and has granted us a fence in Judah and *J*.
10: 7 Judah and *J* that all the exiles should gather
10: 7 the exiles should gather together in *J*,
10: 9 together in *J* within the three-day period:
Neh 1: 2 preserved after the captivity, and about *J*,
1: 3 Also, the wall of *J* lies breached,
2:11 When I had arrived in *J*,
2:12 my God had inspired me to do for *J*)
2:13 observing how the walls of *J* lay in ruins
2:17 how *J* lies in ruins and its gates have
2:17 Come, let us rebuild the wall of *J*,
2:20 neither share nor claim nor memorial in *J*."
3: 8 *J* as far as the wall of the public square.
3: 9 of Hur, leader of half the district of *J*,
3:12 leader of half the district of *J*,
4: 1 of the walls of *J* was progressing
4: 2 *J* and thus to throw us into confusion.
4:16 the people to spend the nights inside *J*,
6: 7 in *J* to proclaim you king of Judah.
7: 2 Over *J* I placed Hanani,
7: 3 "The gates of *J* are not to be opened
7: 3 Appoint as watchmen the inhabitants of *J*,
7: 6 away, and who came back to *J* and Judah,
8:15 made throughout their cities and in *J*:
11: 1 of the people took up residence in *J*,
11: 1 to bring one man in ten to reside in *J*,
11: 2 willingly agreed to take up residence in *J*.
11: 3 of the province who took up residence in *J*.
11: 4 In *J* dwelt both Judahites and Benjaminites.
11: 6 total of the sons of Perez who dwelt in *J*
11:22 The prefect of the Levites in *J* was Uzzi,
12:27 At the dedication of the wall of *J*,
12:27 were brought to *J* to celebrate
12:28 gathered together from the region about *J*,
12:29 had built themselves settlements about *J*).
12:43 at *J* could be heard from afar off.
13: 6 During all this time I had not been in *J*,
13: 7 asked leave of the king and returned to *J*,
13:15 and bringing them to *J* on the sabbath day.
13:16 In *J* itself the Tyrians who were resident
13:19 on the gates of *J* before the sabbath,
13:20 spent the night once or twice outside *J*,
Tb 1: 4 away from the house of David and from *J*.
1: 6 often make the pilgrimage alone to *J*
1: 6 to *J* and present them to the priests,
1: 7 in *J* I would give the tithe
1: 7 each year I would go and disburse in *J*.
5:14 me they used to make the pilgrimage to *J*,
13: 8 of his majesty, and sing his praises in *J*."
13: 9 O *J*, holy city, he scourged you
13:16 *J* shall be rebuilt as his home forever.
13:16 *J* shall be built with sapphire and emerald,
13:16 The towers of *J* shall be built with gold,
13:17 The streets of *J* shall be paved with
13:18 gates of *J* shall sing hymns of gladness,
14: 4 even Samaria and *J* shall become desolate!
14: 5 and they shall rebuild *J* with splendor.
14: 7 shall be gathered together and go to *J*;
Jdt 1: 9 and west of the Jordan as far as *J*,
4: 2 alarmed for *J* and the temple of the Lord,
4: 6 who was high priest in *J* in those days,
4: 8 the whole people of Israel, which met in *J*.
4:11 women and children who lived in *J*
4:13 the sanctuary of the Lord Almighty in *J*.
5:19 were scattered, and have repossessed *J*,
9: 1 in the temple of God in *J* that evening,
10: 8 of the Israelites and the exaltation of *J*
11:13 minister in the presence of our God in *J*:
11:14 They have sent messengers to *J* to bring
11:19 you through Judea, till you come to *J*,
13: 4 on my undertaking for the exaltation of *J*;
15: 5 Even those from *J* and the rest of the
15: 8 elders of the Israelites, who dwelt in *J*,
15: 9 "You are the glory of *J*,
16:18 The people then went to *J* to worship God;
16:20 celebration in *J* before the sanctuary,
Est A: 3 of Babylon, had taken from *J* with Jeconiah,
2: 6 had been exiled from *J* with the captives
1Mc 1:14 in *J* according to the Gentile custom.
1:20 up to Israel and to *J* with a strong force.
1:29 and he came to *J* with a strong force.
1:35 the plunder they had collected from *J*.
1:38 of them the inhabitants of *J* fled away,
1:44 letters to *J* and to the cities of Judah,
2: 1 of Joarib, left *J* and settled in Modein.
2: 6 were being committed in Judah and in *J*,
2:18 and those who are left in *J* have done.
2:31 king who were in the City of David, in *J*,
3:34 As for the inhabitants of Judea and *J*,
3:35 of *J* and efface their memory from the land.
3:45 *J* was uninhabited,
3:46 they assembled and went to Mizpah near *J*,
6: 7 which he had built upon the altar in *J*;
6:12 But I now recall the evils I did in *J*,
6:26 the citadel in *J* in order to capture it,
6:48 king's army went up to *J* to attack them,
7:17 their blood they have shed round about *J*,
7:19 from *J* and pitched his camp in Beth-zaith.
7:27 Nicanor came to *J* with a large force and
7:39 left *J* and pitched his camp at Beth-horon,
7:47 they brought to *J* and displayed there.
8:22 inscribed on bronze tablets and sent to *J*,
9: 3 and fifty-two, they encamped against *J*.
9:50 On returning to *J*,
9:53 put them in custody in the citadel at *J*.
10: 7 to *J* and read the letter to all the people.
10:10 Thereafter Jonathan dwelt in *J*,
10:31 Let *J* and her territory,
10:32 yield my authority over the citadel in *J*,
10:39 I give as a present to the sanctuary in *J*
10:43 the temple of *J* or in any of its precincts,
10:45 walls of *J* and fortifying it all around,
10:66 returned in peace and happiness to *J*.
10:74 ten thousand men, he set out from *J*,
10:87 He and his men then returned to *J*,
11: 7 called Eleutherus and then returned to *J*.
11:20 men of Judea to attack the citadel in *J*,
11:34 offer sacrifices for us in *J* instead of paying
11:41 of *J* and from the other strongholds,
11:51 Finally they returned to *J* with much spoil.
11:62 chief men as hostages and sent them to *J*.
11:74 Then Jonathan returned to *J*.
12:25 He set out from *J* and went into the
12:36 for making the walls of *J* still higher,
13: 2 were in dread and terror, he went up to *J*.
13:10 and quickly completing the walls of *J*,
13:39 in *J* shall no longer be collected there.
13:49 The men in the citadel in *J* were prevented
14:19 These were read before the assembly in *J*.
14:36 those in the City of David in *J*,
14:37 raised the wall of *J* to a greater height.
15: 7 *J* and its temple shall be free.
15:28 Joppa and Gazara and the citadel of *J*;
15:32 came to *J* and on seeing the splendor of
16:20 to seize *J* and the mount of the temple.
2Mc 1: 1 The Jews in *J* and in the land of Judea
1:10 The people of *J* and Judea,
3: 6 treasury in *J* was so full of untold riches
3: 9 When he arrived in *J* and had been
3:37 be a suitable man to be sent to *J* next,
4: 9 it and to enroll men in *J* as Antiochians.
4:19 representatives of the Antiochians of *J*,
4:22 After going to Joppa, he proceeded to *J*.
5:11 he set out from Egypt and took *J* by storm.
5:22 *J*, Philip, a Phrygian by birth,
5:25 When this man arrived in *J*,
6: 2 in *J* and dedicate it to Olympian Zeus,
8:31 the rest of the spoils they carried to *J*.
8:36 *J* testified that the Jews had a champion,
9: 4 "I will make *J* the common graveyard of
10:15 from *J* and endeavored to continue the war.
11: 2 His plan was to make *J* a Greek settlement;
11: 5 fortified place about twenty miles from *J*,
11: 8 Suddenly, while they were still near *J*,
12: 9 glow of the flames was visible as far as *J*,
12:29 to Scythopolis, seventy-five miles from *J*.
12:31 Finally they arrived in *J*,
12:43 to *J* to provide for an expiatory sacrifice.
14:23 Nicanor stayed on in *J*,
14:37 A certain Razis, one of the elders of *J*,
15:30 right arm to be cut off and taken to *J*.
Ps(s) 51:20 kindness by rebuilding the walls of *J*;
68:30 temple in *J* let the kings bring you gifts.
79: 1 holy temple, they have laid *J* in ruins.
79: 3 out their blood like water round about *J*,

JERUSALEM (cont.)

102:22 and his praise, in *J*,
116:19 the house of the LORD, in your midst, O *J*.
122: 2 we have set foot within your gates, O *J*—
122: 3 *J*,
122: 6 Pray for the peace of *J*!
125: 2 Mountains are round about *J*;
128: 5 prosperity of *J* all the days of your life;
135:21 from Zion be the LORD, who dwells in *J*.
137: 5 If I forget you, *J*,
137: 6 you not, If I place not *J* ahead of my joy.
137: 7 the children of Edom, the day of *J*,
147: 2 The LORD rebuilds *J*;
147:12 Glorify the LORD, O *J*;
Eccl 1: 1 words of David's son, Qoheleth, king in *J*:
1:12 was king over Israel in *J*
1:16 wisdom beyond all who were before me in *J*,
2: 7 more than all who had been before me in *J*.
2: 9 up more than all others before me in *J*;
Sg 1: 5 but lovely, O daughters of *J*—
2: 7 I adjure you, daughters of *J*,
3: 5 I adjure you, daughters of *J*,
3:11 Daughters of *J*, come forth and look upon
5: 8 I adjure you, daughters of *J*,
5:16 and such my friend, O daughters of *J*.
6: 4 as Tirzah, my beloved, as lovely as *J*,
8: 4 I adjure you, daughters of *J*,
Sir 24:11 he has given me rest, in *J* is my domain.
36:12 Take pity on your holy city, *J*,
Is 1: 1 Judah and *J* in the days of Uzziah,
2: 1 son of Amoz, saw concerning Judah and *J*.
2: 3 and the word of the LORD from *J*.
3: 1 shall take away from *J* and from Judah
3: 8 *J* is crumbling, Judah is falling;
4: 3 he that is left in *J* Will be called holy:
4: 3 every one marked down for life in *J*.
5: 3 Now, inhabitants of *J* and men of Judah,
7: 1 son of Remaliah, went up to attack *J*,
8:14 trap and a snare to those who dwell in *J*;
10:10 that had more images than *J* and Samaria,
10:11 shall I not do to *J* and her graven images?"
10:12 end all his work on Mount Zion and in *J*,
10:32 the mount of daughter Zion, the hill of *J*!
22:10 You numbered the houses of *J*,
22:21 shall be a father to the inhabitants of *J*,
24:23 of hosts will reign on Mount Zion and in *J*,
27:13 the LORD on the holy mountain, in *J*.
28:14 you arrogant, who rule this people in *J*:
30:19 O people of Zion, who dwell in *J*,
31: 5 so the LORD of hosts shall shield *J*,
31: 9 who has a fire in Zion and a furnace in *J*.
33:20 let your eyes see *J* as a quiet abode,
36: 2 with a great army to King Hezekiah in *J*.
36: 7 Judah and *J* to worship before this altar?'
36:20 Will the LORD then save *J* from my hand?'"
37:10 *J* will not be handed over to the king
37:22 Behind you she wags her head, daughter *J*.
37:32 For out of *J* shall come a remnant,
40: 2 Speak tenderly to *J*,
40: 9 Cry out at the top of your voice, *J*,
41:27 "For *J* I will pick out a bearer of the
44:26 I say to *J*:
44:28 He shall say of *J*,
51:17 Arise, O *J*, You who drank at the LORD's
52: 1 Put on your glorious garments, O *J*,
52: 2 off the dust, ascend to the throne, *J*;
52: 9 Break out together in song, O ruins of *J*!
52: 9 the Lord comforts his people, he redeems *J*.
62: 6 Upon your walls, O *J*, I have stationed
62: 7 *J* And makes of it the pride of the earth.
64: 9 a desert, Zion is a desert, *J* a waste.
65:18 For I create *J* to be a joy and its people
65:19 I will rejoice in *J* and exult in my people.
66:10 Rejoice with *J* and be glad because of her,
66:13 in *J* you shall find your comfort.
66:20 carts, upon mules and dromedaries, to *J*,
Jer 1: 3 downfall and exile of *J* in the fifth month
1:15 set up his throne at the gateways of *J*
2: 2 Go, cry out this message for *J* to hear!
2:28 *J* are the altars you have set up for Baal.
3:17 time they will call *J* the LORD's throne;
3:17 to honor the name of the LORD at *J*,
4: 3 For the men of Judah and to *J*,
4: 4 hearts, O men of Judah and citizens of *J*;
4: 5 Proclaim it in Judah, make it heard in *J*;
4:11 it will be said of this people and of *J*,
4:14 Cleanse your heart of evil, O *J*,
4:16 known to the nations, announce it to *J*:
5: 1 Roam the streets of *J*,
6: 1 Flee, sons of Benjamin, out of *J*!
6: 6 trees, throw up a siege mound against *J*.
6: 8 Be warned, O *J*, lest I be estranged from
7:17 the cities of Judah, in the streets of *J*?
7:34 streets of *J* I will silence the cry of joy,
8: 1 bones of the citizens of *J* will be emptied
9:10 I will turn *J* into a heap of ruins,
11: 2 the men of Judah and to the citizens of *J*,
11: 6 cities of Judah and in the streets of *J*:
11: 9 the men of Judah and the citizens of *J*,
11:12 citizens of *J* will go and cry out to the gods
11:13 And as many as the streets of *J* are the
13: 9 of Judah to rot, the great pride of *J*.
13:13 and prophets, and all the citizens of *J*.
13:27 Woe to you, *J*,
14: 2 from *J* ascends a cry of anguish.
14:16 the streets of *J* by famine and the sword.
15: 4 son of Hezekiah, king of Judah, did in *J*.
15: 5 Who will pity you, *J*,
17:19 and leave, and at the other gates of *J*.
17:20 you citizens of *J* who enter these gates!
17:21 to bring them in through the gates of *J*.
17:25 the men of Judah, and the citizens of *J*.
17:26 cities of Judah and the neighborhood of *J*,
17:27 come through the gates of *J* on the sabbath,
17:27 gates, which will consume the palaces of *J*.
18:11 to the men of Judah and the citizens of *J*:
19: 3 the LORD, kings of Judah and citizens of *J*:
19: 7 place I will foil the plan of Judah and *J*;
19:13 And the houses of *J* and the palaces of the
22:19 forth and cast out beyond the gates of *J*.
24: 1 of Babylon, had exiled from *J* Jeconiah,
24: 8 the remnant of *J* remaining in this land
25: 2 people of Judah and all the citizens of *J*:
25:18 *J*, the cities of Judah,
26:18 become a plowed field, *J* a heap of ruins,
27: 3 ambassadors who have come to *J* to Zedekiah,
27:18 and in *J* might not be taken to Babylon.
27:20 king of Judah, from *J* to Babylon,
27:20 along with all the nobles of Judah and *J*—
27:21 the palace of the king of Judah, and in *J*:
29: 1 *J* to the remaining elders among the exiles,
29: 1 by Nebuchadnezzar from *J* to Babylon.
29: 2 the courtiers, the princes of Judah and *J*,
29: 2 and the skilled workmen had left *J*.
29: 4 the exiles whom I exiled from *J* to Babylon:
29:20 exiles whom I sent away from *J* to Babylon.
29:25 your own authority to all the people of *J*,
32: 2 of the king of Babylon was besieging *J*,
32:32 the men of Judah and the citizens of *J*,
32:44 the land of Benjamin, in the suburbs of *J*,
33: 9 Then *J* shall be my joy,
33:10 in the streets of *J* that are now deserted,
33:13 the land of Benjamin and the suburbs of *J*,
33:16 shall be safe and *J* shall dwell secure;
34: 1 were all attacking *J* and all her cities:
34: 6 things to Zedekiah, king of Judah, in *J*,
34: 7 *J* and the remaining cities of Judah,
34: 8 in *J* to issue an edict of emancipation.
34:19 The princes of Judah and of *J*,
35:11 we decided to come into *J* to escape the
35:11 that is why we are now living in *J*."
35:13 the men of Judah and to the citizens of *J*:
35:17 citizens of *J* every evil that I threatened;
36: 9 proclaimed for all the people of *J*
36: 9 and all who came from Judah's cities to *J*.
36:31 citizens of *J* and the men of Judah
37: 5 Chaldeans who were besieging *J*
37:11 of *J* at the threat of the army of Pharaoh,
37:12 out from *J* for the District of Benjamin,
38:28 of the guard till the day *J* was taken.
39: 1 his army marched against *J* and besieged it.
39: 8 the people, and demolished the walls of *J*.
40: 1 among the captives of *J* and Judah who were
42:18 was poured out upon the citizens of *J*,
44: 2 brought on *J* and the other cities of Judah.
44: 6 the cities of Judah and the streets of *J*,
44: 9 in the land of Judah and the streets of *J*?
44:13 in Egypt, just as I punished *J* with sword,
44:17 the cities of Judah and the streets of *J*.
44:21 the cities of Judah and the streets of *J*:
51:35 blood upon the people of Chaldea, says *J*.
51:50 LORD from afar, let *J* come to your minds.
52: 1 king, and he reigned eleven years in *J*.
52: 3 what was done in *J* and in Judah so angered
52: 4 and his whole army advanced against *J*,
52:12 came to *J* as the representative of the
52:13 of the king, and all the houses of *J*;
52:14 tore down all the walls that surrounded *J*.
52:29 hundred and thirty-two persons from *J*;
Lam 1: 7 *J* is mindful of the days of her wretched
1: 8 sin of which she is guilty, *J* is defiled;
1:17 *J* has become in their midst a thing
2:10 maidens of *J* bow their heads to the ground.
2:13 can I liken or compare you, O daughter *J*?
2:15 hiss and wag their heads over daughter *J*:
4:12 enemy or foe could enter the gates of *J*.
Bar 1: 2 Chaldeans took *J* and burnt it with fire].
1: 7 These they sent to *J*,
1: 7 the whole people who were with him in *J*.
1: 9 nobles, and the people of the land from *J*,
1:15 shame, we men of Judah and citizens of *J*,
2: 2 under heaven what has been done in *J*,
2:23 Judah and from the streets of *J*
4: 8 you, and you grieved *J* who fostered you.
4:30 Fear not, *J*! He who gave you your name
4:36 Look to the east, *J*!
5: 1 *J*, take off your robe of mourning and
5: 5 Up, *J*! stand upon the heights;
Ez 4: 1 in front of you, and draw on it a city *J*.
4: 7 Fixing your gaze on the siege of *J*,
4:16 man, I am breaking the staff of bread in *J*.
5: 5 Thus says the Lord GOD: This is *J*!
8: 3 air and brought me in divine visions to *J*,
9: 4 Pass through the city [through *J* and mark
9: 8 of Israel when you pour out your fury on *J*?"
11:15 of Israel that the inhabitants of *J* say,
12:10 *J* and the whole house of Israel within it.
12:19 inhabitants of *J* [to the land of Israel]:
13:16 prophets of Israel who prophesied to *J*
14:21 though I send *J* my four cruel punishments,
14:22 on *J* [all that I have brought upon it].
15: 6 the fire, do I make the inhabitants of *J*.
16: 2 of man, make known to *J* her abominations:
16: 3 Thus says the Lord GOD to *J*:
17:12 The king of Babylon came to *J* and took
21: 7 Son of man, look toward *J*,
21:25 of the Ammonites or to Judah's capital, *J*.
21:27 hand is the divining arrow marked *J*,"
22:19 I must gather you together within *J*.
23: 4 Samaria is Oholah, and *J* is Oholibah.]
24: 2 day the king of Babylon has invested *J*.
26: 2 Son of man, because of what Tyre said of *J*:
33:21 the fugitive came to me from *J* and said,
36:38 sheep, the sheep of *J* on its feast days,
Dn 1: 1 of Babylon came and laid siege to *J*.
3:28 that you have brought upon us and upon *J*,
5: 2 father, had taken from the temple in *J*,
5: 3 the house of God in *J* had been brought in,
6:11 a day, with the windows open toward *J*.
9: 2 ruins of *J* seventy years must be fulfilled.
9: 7 the men of Judah, the residents of *J*,
9:12 by bringing upon us in *J* the greatest
9:16 your wrath be turned away from your city *J*,
9:16 *J* and your people have become the reproach
9:25 From the utterance of the word that *J* was
Jl 3: 5 in *J* survivors whom the LORD shall call.
4: 1 would restore the fortunes of Judah and *J*,
4: 6 the people of Judah and *J* to the Greeks,
4:16 from Zion, and from *J* raises his voice;
4:17 *J* shall be holy,
4:20 abide forever, and *J* for all generations.
Am 1: 2 roar from Zion, and from *J* raise his voice:
2: 5 upon Judah, to devour the castles of *J*.
Ob 1:11 entered his gates and cast lots over *J*,
1:20 And the captives of *J* who are in Sepharad
Mi 1: 1 he received concerning Samaria and *J*.
1: 5 Is it not *J*?
1: 9 to the gate of my people, even to *J*.
1:12 come down from the LORD to the gate of *J*.
3:10 Zion with bloodshed, and *J* with wickedness!
3:12 like a field, and *J* reduced to rubble,
4: 2 and the word of the LORD from *J*.
4: 8 be restored, the kingdom of daughter *J*.
Zep 1: 4 and against all the inhabitants of *J*;
1:12 At that time I will explore *J* with lamps;
3:14 exult with all your heart, O daughter *J*!
3:16 On that day, it shall be said to *J*:
Zec 1:12 how long will you be without mercy for *J*
1:14 am deeply moved for the sake of *J* and Zion,
1:16 I will turn to *J* in mercy;
1:16 a measuring line shall be stretched over *J*.
1:17 again comfort Zion, and again choose *J*.
2: 2 that scattered Judah and Israel and *J*."
2: 6 "To measure *J*," he answered
2: 8 will live in *J* as though in open country,
2:16 the holy land, and he will again choose *J*.
3: 2 may the LORD who has chosen *J* rebuke you!
7: 7 when *J* and the surrounding cities were
8: 3 I will dwell within *J*; Jerusalem shall
8: 4 age, shall again sit in the streets of *J*.
8: 8 I will bring them back to dwell within *J*.
8:15 to favor *J* and the house of Judah;
8:22 in *J* and to implore the favor of the LORD.
9: 9 daughter Zion, shout for joy, O daughter *J*!
9:10 from Ephraim, and the horse from *J*;
12: 2 I will make *J* a bowl to stupefy all
12: 2 [Judah will be besieged, even *J*
12: 3 make *J* a weighty stone for all peoples.
12: 5 "The inhabitants of *J* have their strength
12: 6 but *J* shall not abide on its own site.
12: 7 of *J* may not be exalted over Judah.
12: 8 the LORD will shield the inhabitants of *J*,
12: 9 of all nations that come against *J*.
12:10 of *J* a spirit of grace and petition;
12:11 On that day the mourning in *J* shall be as
13: 1 of David and to the inhabitants of *J*,
14: 2 all the nations against *J* for battle:
14: 4 of Olives, which is opposite *J* to the east.
14: 8 that day, living waters shall flow from *J*,
14:10 but *J* shall remain exalted in its place.
14:11 *J* shall abide in security.
14:12 all nations that have fought against *J*:
14:14 Judah also shall fight against *J*.
14:16 *J* shall come up year after year to worship
14:17 does not come up to *J* to worship the King,
14:21 And every pot in *J* and in Judah shall be
Mal 2:11 thing has been done in Israel and in *J*.
Mt 2: 1 the east arrived one day in *J* inquiring,
2: 3 greatly disturbed, and with him all *J*.
3: 5 At that time *J*,
4:25 from Galilee, the Ten Cities, *J* and Judea,
5:35 by *J* (it is the city of the great King);
15: 1 from *J* approached Jesus with the question:
16:21 he must go to *J* and suffer greatly
20:17 As Jesus was starting to go up to *J*,
20:18 "We are going up to *J* now.
21: 1 As they drew near *J*, entering Bethphage
21:10 *J* the whole city was stirred to its depths,
23:37 O Jerusalem, *J*,

Mk 1:5 of J went out to him in great numbers.
3:8 great multitude came to him from Judea, J,
3:22 the scribes who arrived from J asserted,
7:1 who had come from J gathered around him.
10:32 disciples were on the road going up to J,
10:33 "We are on our way up to J,
11:1 on the Mount of Olives, close to J,
11:11 J and went into the temple precincts.
11:15 When they reached J he entered the temple
11:27 They returned once more to J.
15:41 many others who had come up with him to J.
Lk 2:22 the couple brought him up to J so that he
2:25 J at the time a certain man named Simeon.
2:38 who looked forward to the deliverance of J.
2:41 year to J for the feast of the Passover,
2:45 him, they returned to J in search of him.
4:9 Then the devil led him to J,
5:17 village of Galilee and from Judea and J.
6:17 and J and the coast of Tyre and Sidon,
9:31 which he was about to fulfill in J.
9:51 he firmly resolved to proceed toward J,
9:53 welcome him because he was on his way to J.
10:30 from J to Jericho who fell prey to robbers.
13:4 guilty than anyone else who lived in J?
13:22 all the while making his way toward J.
13:33 can be allowed to die anywhere except in J.'
13:34 "O Jerusalem, J, you slay the prophets
17:11 On his journey to J he passed along the
18:31 "We must now go up to J so that all that
19:11 because he was near J where they thought
19:28 thus he went ahead with his ascent to J.
21:20 "When you see J encircled by soldiers,
21:24 J will be trampled by the Gentiles,
23:7 who also happened to be in J at the time.
23:28 "Daughters of J, do not weep for me.
24:13 named Emmaus seven miles distant from J,
24:18 "Are you the only resident of J who does
24:33 They got up immediately and returned to J,
24:47 to all the nations, beginning at J.
24:52 then returned to J filled with joy.
Jn 1:19 sent priests and Levites from J to ask,
2:13 Passover was near, Jesus went up to J.
2:23 he was in J during the Passover festival,
4:20 but you people claim that J is the place
4:21 Father neither on this mountain nor in J.
4:45 all that he had done in J on that occasion.
5:1 of a Jewish feast, Jesus went up to J.
5:2 Now in J by the Sheep Pool there is a
7:25 This led some of the people of J to remark:
10:22 came for the feast of the Dedication in J.
11:18 The village was not far from J—
11:55 went up to J for Passover purification.
12:12 the feast heard that Jesus was to enter J.
Acts 1:4 met with them, he told them not to leave J:
1:8 then you are to be my witnesses in J,
1:12 J from the mount called Olivet near J
1:19 came to be known by the inhabitants of J,
2:5 Staying in J at the time were devout Jews
2:14 are Jews, indeed all of you staying in J!
4:5 the scribes assembled the next day in J,
4:16 Everyone who lives in J knows what a
5:16 from the towns around J would gather,
5:28 yet you have filled J with your teaching
6:7 of the disciples in J enormously increased.
8:1 of a great persecution of the church in J
8:14 When the apostles in J heard that Samaria
8:25 they went back to J bringing the good news
8:26 toward the road which goes from J to Gaza,
8:27 a pilgrimage to J and was returning home.
9:2 arrest and bring to J anyone he might find,
9:13 harm he has done to your holy people in J.
9:21 in J among those who invoke this name?
9:26 in J he tried to join the disciples there;
9:28 moving freely about J and expressing
10:39 he did in the land of the Jews and in J.
11:2 when Peter went up to J some among the
11:22 reached the ears of the church in J,
11:27 prophets came down from J to Antioch.
12:25 to J upon completing the relief mission,
13:13 There John left them and returned to J.
13:27 J and their rulers failed to recognize him,
13:31 who had come up with him from Galilee to J.
15:2 and presbyters in J about this question.
15:4 in J they were welcomed by that church,
15:22 in agreement with the whole J church,
16:4 the apostles and presbyters had made in J.
19:21 and Achaia again, and then go on to J.
20:16 for he was eager to get to J by the feast
20:22 But now, as you see, I am on my way to J,
21:4 to tell Paul that he should not go up to J;
21:11 'This is how the Jews in J will bind the
21:12 of Caesarea urged Paul not to proceed to J.
21:13 only for imprisonment, but for death, in J."
21:15 stay, we got ready and started up toward J.
21:17 On our arrival in J,
21:31 of the cohort that all J was rioting.
22:5 I would arrest back to J for punishment.
22:17 J I was praying in the court of the temple,
22:18 'Leave J at once because they will not
23:11 you have given testimony to me here in J,
24:11 passed since I went to J to worship there.
25:1 province, he went up from Caesarea to J
25:3 Paul, and urging Festus to send him to J.
25:6 After spending eight or ten days in J,
25:7 Jews who had come down from J
25:9 "Are you willing to go up to J and stand
25:15 While I was in J the chief priests and the
25:20 J and stand trial there on these charges.
25:24 Jewish community, both here and in J,
26:4 people from the beginning and later at J,
26:10 That is just what I did in J.
26:20 people of J and all the country of Judea;
28:17 yet in J I was handed over to the Romans
Rom 15:19 from J all the way around to Illyria.
15:25 for J to bring assistance to the saints.
15:26 for those in need among the saints in J.
15:31 J may be well received by the saints there;
1Cor 16:3 you have chosen to take your gift to J.
Gal 1:17 seeking human advisers or even going to J
1:18 that I went up to J to get to know Cephas,
2:1 years, I went up to J again with Barnabas,
4:25 and corresponds to the J of our time,
4:26 But the J on high is freeborn,
Heb 12:22 city of the living God, the heavenly J,
Rv 3:12 new J which he will send down from heaven,
21:2 I also saw a new J,
21:10 city J coming down out of heaven from God.

JERUSALEM'S (4)

Is 4:4 And purges J blood from her midst with the
62:1 be silent, for J sake I will not be quiet,
Jer 23:14 But among J prophets I saw deeds still
23:15 For from J prophets ungodliness has gone

JERUSHA (1)

2Kgs 15:33 His mother's name was J,

JESARELAH (1)

1Chr 25:14 The seventh was J,

JESHAIAH (7)

1Chr 3:21 The sons of Hananiah were Pelatiah, J,
25:3 Gedaliah, Zeri, J, Shimei, Hashabiah
25:15 The eighth was J, his sons
26:25 whose son was Rehabiah, whose son was J,
Ezr 8:7 of the sons of Elam, J,
8:19 also sent us Hashabiah, and with him J,
Neh 11:7 son of Maaseiah, son of Ithiel, son of J,

JESHANAH (2)

1Sm 7:12 stone and placed it between Mizpah and J;
2Chr 13:19 its dependencies, J and its dependencies,

JESHER (1)

1Chr 2:18 Her sons were J, Shobab, and Ardon.

JESHIMON (2)

Nm 21:20 at the headland of Pisgah that overlooks J.
23:28 to the top of Peor, that overlooks J.

JESHISHAI (1)

1Chr 5:14 son of Gilead, son of Michael, son of J,

JESHOHAIAH (1)

1Chr 4:36 son of Asiel, Elioenai, Jaakobath, J,

JESHOSHAPHAT (1)

2Chr 18:7 J said, "Let not your Majesty speak

JESHUA (31)

1Chr 24:11 the eighth to Abijah, the ninth to J,
2Chr 31:15 priestly cities were Eden, Miniamin, J,
Ezr 2:2 (those who returned with Zerubbabel, J,
2:6 Pahath-moab, who were sons of J and Joab,
2:36 of Jedaiah, who were of the house of J,
2:40 sons of J, Kadmiel, Binnui, and Hodaviah,
3:2 Then J, son of Jozadak, together with
3:8 Zerubbabel, son of Shealtiel, and J,
3:9 J and his sons and brethren,
4:3 But Zerubbabel, J,
5:2 Zerubbabel, son of Shealtiel, and J,
8:33 assisted by the Levites Jozabad, son of J,
10:18 Of the sons of J, son of Jozadak,
Neh 3:19 next to him Ezer, son of J,
7:7 (those who returned with Zerubbabel, J,
7:11 of Pahath-moab who were sons of J and Joab,
7:39 of Jedaiah who were of the house of J,
7:43 sons of J,
8:7 [The Levites J, Bani, Sherebiah, Jamin,
8:17 nothing of this sort from the days of J,
9:4 on the platform of the Levites were J,
9:5 The Levites J, Kadmiel, Bani, Hashabneiah,
10:10 J, son of Azaniah;
11:26 in Jekabzeel and its villages, in J,
12:1 with Zerubbabel, son of Shealtiel, and J:
12:7 heads and their brethren in the days of J.
12:8 The Levites were J, Binnui, Kadmiel,
12:10 J became the father of Joiakim,
12:24 the Levites were Hashabiah, Sherebiah, J,
12:26 lived in the time of Joiakim, son of J,
Sir 49:12 a signet ring on God's right hand, And J,

JESHUSH (1)

2Chr 11:19 J, Shemariah and Zaham.

JESIMIEL (1)

1Chr 4:36 Jaakobath, Jeshohaiah, Asaiah, Adiel, J,

JESSE (50)

Ru 4:17 He was the father of J,
4:22 of Jesse, and J became the father of David.
1Sm 16:1 I am sending you to J of Bethlehem,
16:3 Invite J to the sacrifice,
16:5 He also had J and his sons cleanse
16:8 Then J called Abinadab and presented him
16:9 Next J presented Shammah,
16:10 way J presented seven sons before Samuel,
16:10 sons before Samuel, but Samuel said to J,
16:11 Then Samuel asked J,
16:11 J replied, "There is still the youngest,
16:11 Samuel said to J, "Send for him;
16:12 J sent and had the young man brought to
16:18 of J of Bethlehem is a skillful harpist.
16:19 to ask J to send him his son David,
16:20 Then J took five loaves of bread,
16:22 his armor-bearer, and sent J the message,
17:12 was the son of an Ephrathite named J,
17:13 oldest sons of J had followed Saul to war;
17:17 [Now J said to his son David:
17:20 out on his errand, as J had commanded him.
17:58 am the son of your servant J of Bethlehem."
20:27 of J not come to table yesterday or today?"
20:31 long as the son of J lives upon the earth,
22:7 of J give all of you fields and vineyards?
22:8 has made an agreement with the son of J?
22:9 "I saw the son of J come to Ahimelech,
22:13 you conspire against me with the son of J
25:10 Who is the son of J?
2Sm 17:25 of J and sister of Joab's mother Zeruiah.
20:1 in David, nor any share in the son of J.
23:1 "The utterance of David, son of J;
1Kgs 12:16 We have no heritage in the son of J.
1Chr 2:12 Obed became the father of J.
2:13 J became the father of Eliab,
10:14 his kingdom to David, the son of J.
12:19 O David, we are with you, O son of J.
29:26 Thus David, the son of J,
2Chr 10:16 We have no heritage in the son of J.
11:18 of Abihail, daughter of Eliab, son of J.
Ps(s) 72:20 prayers of David the son of J are ended.
Sir 45:25 David, the son of J of the tribe of Judah,
Is 11:1 a shoot shall sprout from the stump of J,
11:10 On that day, The root of J,
Mt 1:5 Obed was the father of J,
1:6 J the father of King David.
Lk 3:32 son of Nathan, son of David, son of J,
Acts 13:22 'I have found David son of J to be a man
Rom 15:12 Isaiah says, "The root of J will appear,

JESSE'S (1)

1Sm 20:30 shame, you are the companion of J son?

JESTS (1)

Sir 10:10 the doctor j,

JESUS (1049)

Sir 50:27 I have written in this book, I, J,
Mt 1:1 A family record of J Christ,
1:16 that J who is called the Messiah was born.
1:18 is how the birth of J Christ came about.
1:21 name him J because he will save his people
1:25 before she bore a son, whom he named J.
2:1 After J' birth in Bethlehem of Judea
3:13 Later J, coming from Galilee,
3:15 J answered: "Give in for now.
3:16 After J was baptized,
4:1 Then J was led into the desert by the
4:4 J replied, "Scripture has it:
4:7 J answered him, "Scripture also has it:
4:10 J said to him, "Away with you, Satan!
4:12 When J heard that John had been arrested,
4:17 time on J began to proclaim this theme:
4:23 J toured all of Galilee.
7:28 J finished this discourse and left the
8:3 J stretched out his hand and touched him
8:4 Then J said to him:
8:5 As J entered Capernaum,
8:10 J showed amazement on hearing this and
8:13 To the centurion J said, "Go home.
8:14 J entered Peter's house and found Peter's
8:18 J gave orders to cross to the other shore.
8:20 J said to him, "The foxes have lairs,
8:22 J told him, "Follow me, and let the dead
8:25 J was sleeping soundly,
8:34 that the entire town came out to meet J.
9:2 J saw their faith he said to the paralytic,
9:4 J was aware of what they were thinking and
9:9 J saw a man named Matthew at his post
9:10 while J was at table in Matthew's home,
9:10 came to join J and his disciples at dinner.
9:15 J said to them: "How can wedding guests
9:18 Before J had finished speaking to them,

JESUS (cont.)
9:19 *J* stood up and followed him,
9:22 *J* turned around and saw her and said,
9:23 When *J* arrived at the synagogue leader's
9:27 As *J* moved on from there,
9:28 *J* said to them, "Are you confident I can
9:30 Then *J* warned them sternly,
9:35 *J* continued his tour of all the towns
10: 5 *J* sent these men on mission as the Twelve,
11: 1 When *J* had finished instructing his twelve
11: 4 In reply, *J* said to them:
11: 7 *J* began to speak to the crowds about John:
11:25 On one occasion *J* spoke thus: "Father,
12: 1 *J* walked through the standing grain.
12:10 be there, and they put this question to *J*,
12:15 *J* was aware of this, and so he withdrew
13: 1 the house, *J* sat down by the lakeshore.
13:34 All these lessons *J* taught the crowds in
13:53 When *J* had finished these parables,
13:54 *J* next went to his native place and spent
13:57 *J* said to them, "No prophet is without honor
14: 1 tetrarch, having heard of *J*' reputation,
14:12 Afterward, they came and informed *J*.
14:13 When *J* heard this, he withdrew by boat
14:16 *J* said to them: "There is no need
14:22 *J* insisted that his disciples get into the
14:27 *J* hastened to reassure them:
14:29 to walk on the water, moving toward *J*.
14:31 *J* at once stretched out his hand and
15: 1 Jerusalem approached *J* with the question:
15:21 Then *J* left that place and withdrew to the
15:24 sheep of the house of Israel," *J* replied.
15:28 *J* then said in reply, "Woman, you have
15:29 *J* left that place and passed along the Sea
15:32 *J* called his disciples to him and said:
15:34 But *J* asked them, "How many loaves
16: 6 When *J* said to them, "Be on the lookout
16: 8 *J* knew their thoughts and said,
16:13 When *J* came to the neighborhood of
16:17 *J* replied, "Blest are you, Simon
16:21 From then on *J* [the Messiah] started to
16:23 *J* turned on Peter and said,
16:24 *J* then said to his disciples:
17: 1 Six days later *J* took Peter,
17: 4 Then Peter said to *J*,
17: 7 *J* came toward them and laying his hand on
17: 8 looked up they did not see anyone but *J*.
17: 9 down the mountainside *J* commanded them,
17:17 In reply *J* said: "What on unbelieving
17:18 Then *J* reprimanded him,
17:19 *J* at that point and asked him privately,
17:22 they met again in Galilee, *J* said to them,
17:25 Then *J* on entering the house asked,
17:26 replied, "From foreigners," *J* observed:
18: 1 disciples came up to *J* with the question,
18:22 "No," *J* replied, "not seven times;
19: 1 When *J* had finished this discourse,
19:14 disciples began to scold them, but *J* said,
19:18 *J* replied, "You shall not kill';
19:21 *J* told him, "If you seek perfection,
19:23 *J* said to his disciples:
19:26 *J* looked at them and said,
19:28 *J* said to them:
20:17 As *J* was starting to go up to Jerusalem,
20:22 In reply *J* said, "You do not know what
20:25 *J* then called them together and said:
20:30 roadside, who heard that *J* was passing by,
20:32 *J* then stopped and called out to them,
20:34 with compassion, *J* touched their eyes,
21: 1 *J* sent off two disciples with the
21: 6 went off and did what *J* had ordered;
21:11 is the prophet *J* from Nazareth in Galilee."
21:12 *J* entered the temple precincts and drove
21:16 *J* said to them, "Of course I do!
21:18 At dawn, as *J* was returning to the city,
21:21 *J* said: "Believe me, if you trust
21:23 After *J* had entered the temple precincts,
21:24 *J* answered: "I too will ask a question
21:27 So their answer to *J* was,
21:31 *J* said to them,
21:42 *J* said to them, "Did you never read in
22: 1 *J* began to address them,
22:15 to plot how they might trap *J* in speech.
22:18 *J* recognized their bad faith and said to
22:29 *J* replied: "You are badly misled
22:37 *J* said to him: "You shall love the Lord
22:41 In turn *J* put a question to the assembled
23: 1 Then *J* told the crowds and his disciples:
24: 1 *J* left the temple precincts then,
24: 4 In reply *J* said to them:
26: 1 when *J* had finished all these discourses,
26: 4 to arrest *J* by some trick and kill him;
26: 6 While *J* was in Bethany at the house of
26:10 *J* became aware of this and said to them:
26:17 Bread, the disciples came up to *J* and said,
26:19 The disciples then did as *J* had ordered,
26:25 *J* answered,
26:26 During the meal *J* took bread,
26:31 *J* then said to them,
26:34 *J* said to him,
26:36 Then *J* went with them to a place called
26:49 He immediately went over to *J*,
26:50 *J* answered,
26:50 they stepped forward to lay hands on *J*,
26:51 accompanied *J* put his hand to his sword,
26:52 *J* said to him: "Put back your sword
26:55 At that very time *J* said to the crowd:
26:57 *J* led him off to Caiaphas the high priest,
26:59 *J* so that they might put him to death.
26:63 But *J* remained silent.
26:64 *J* answered: "It is you who say it.
26:69 said, "You too were with *J* the Galilean."
26:71 nearby, "This man was with *J* the Nazorean."
26:75 Peter remembered the prediction *J* had made:
27: 1 action against *J* to put him to death.
27: 3 him over, seeing that *J* had been condemned,
27:11 *J* was arraigned before the procurator,
27:11 *J* responded, "As you say."
27:17 you, Barabbas or *J* the so-called Messiah?"
27:20 ask for Barabbas and have *J* put to death.
27:22 to them, "Then what am I to do with *J*,
27:26 *J*, however,
27:27 The procurator's soldiers took *J* inside
27:37 "THIS IS JESUS, KING OF THE JEWS."
27:46 midafternoon *J* cried out in a loud tone,
27:50 Once again *J* cried out in a loud voice,
27:53 After *J*' resurrection they came forth from
27:54 keeping watch over *J* were terror-stricken
27:55 *J* from Galilee to attend to his needs.
27:57 He was another of *J*' disciples,
27:58 and had gone to request the body of *J*.
28: 5 I know you are looking for *J* the crucified,
28: 9 warning, *J* stood before them and said,
28:10 *J* said to them, "Do not be afraid!
28:16 the mountain to which *J* had summoned them.
28:18 *J* came forward and addressed them in these
Mk 1: 1 Here begins the gospel of *J* Christ,
1: 9 *J* came from Nazareth in Galilee and was
1:14 *J* appeared in Galilee proclaiming the good
1:17 *J* said to them,
1:24 "What do you want of us, *J* of Nazareth?
1:25 *J* rebuked him sharply:
1:41 Moved with pity, *J* stretched out his hand,
1:43 *J* gave him a stern warning and sent him on
1:45 possible for *J* to enter a town openly.
2: 4 to bring him to *J* because of the crowd,
2: 4 open up the roof over the spot where *J* was.
2: 5 When *J* saw their faith,
2: 8 *J* was immediately aware of their reasoning,
2:15 *J* was reclining to eat in Levi's house,
2:17 Overhearing the remark, *J* said to them,
2:18 People came to *J* with the objection,
2:19 *J* replied: "How can the guests
3: 2 They kept an eye on *J* to see whether he
3: 7 *J* withdrew toward the lake with his
4:38 *J* was in the stern through it all,
5: 6 Catching sight of *J* at a distance,
5: 7 in a loud voice, "Why meddle with me, *J*,
5: 8 *J* had been saying to him,
5: 9 "What is your name," *J* asked him.
5:10 He pleaded hard with *J* not to drive them
5:15 As they approached *J*,
5:18 As *J* was getting into the boat,
5:19 *J* did not grant his request,
5:20 the Ten Cities what *J* had done for him.
5:21 Now when *J* had crossed back to the other
5:22 Seeing *J*, he fell at his feet
5:24 a large crowd followed, pushing against *J*.
5:27 She had heard about *J* and came up behind
5:30 *J* was conscious at once that healing power
5:36 *J* disregarded the report that had been
5:38 *J* was struck by the noise of people
5:40 *J* took the child's father and mother and
6: 4 *J*' response to all this was:
6: 7 *J* summoned the Twelve and began to send
6:14 King Herod came to hear of *J*,
6:16 On hearing of *J*, Herod exclaimed, "John,
6:30 The apostles returned to *J* and reported to
6:32 So *J* and the apostles went off in the boat
6:34 Upon disembarking *J* saw a vast crowd.
6:37 give them something to eat," *J* replied.
6:38 *J* asked. "Go and see."
6:41 the two fish, *J* raised his eyes to heaven,
7:33 *J* took him off by himself away from the
8:23 *J* took the blind man's hand and led him
8:25 a second time *J* laid hands on his eyes,
8:26 *J* sent him home with the admonition,
8:27 Then *J* and his disciples set out for the
9: 2 Six days later, *J* took Peter,
9: 4 the two were in conversation with *J*.
9: 5 Then Peter spoke to *J*:
9: 8 no longer saw anyone with them—only *J*.
9:15 Immediately on catching sight of *J*,
9:20 they did so the spirit caught sight of *J*
9:21 Then *J* questioned the father:
9:23 *J* said, " 'If you can'?
9:25 *J*, on seeing a crowd rapidly gathering,
9:27 But *J* took him by the hand and helped him
9:28 When *J* arrived at the house his disciples
9:33 Teaching They returned to Capernaum and *J*,
9:39 *J* said in reply: "Do not try to stop him
10: 5 *J* told them: "He wrote that commandment
10:14 *J* became indignant when he noticed it and
10:18 *J* answered, "Why do you call me good?
10:21 *J* looked at him with love and told him,
10:23 *J* looked around and said to his disciples,
10:24 So *J* repeated what he had said:
10:27 *J* fixed his gaze on them and said,
10:29 *J* answered: "I give you my word,
10:32 to Jerusalem, with *J* walking in the lead.
10:38 *J* told them, "You do not know what you
10:39 *J* said in response, "From the cup I drink
10:42 *J* called them together and said to them:
10:47 Jesus of Nazareth, he began to call out, *J*,
10:49 Then *J* stopped and said,
10:50 aside his cloak, jumped up and came to *J*.
10:51 *J* asked him, "What do you want me to do
10:52 *J* said in reply, "Be on your way.
11: 6 They answered as *J* had told them to,
11: 7 *J* and threw their cloaks across its back,
11:19 *J* and his disciples went out of the city.
11:22 In reply *J* told them:
11:29 *J* said to them, "I will ask you a question.
11:33 So their answer to *J* was, "We do not know."
11:33 In turn, *J* said to them, "Then neither will
12:17 At that *J* said to them, "Give to Caesar
12:24 *J* said: "You are badly misled,
12:28 he realized how skillfully *J* answered them.
12:29 *J* replied: "This is the first:
12:34 *J* approved the insight of this answer and
12:35 As *J* was teaching in the temple precincts
13: 2 *J* said to him, "You see these great
13: 5 *J* began his discourse:
14: 3 When *J* was in Bethany reclining at table
14: 6 But *J* said: "Let her alone
14:10 the chief priests to hand *J* over to them.
14:18 and in the course of the meal *J* said,
14:27 *J* then said to them: "Your faith in me
14:30 *J* answered, "I give you my assurance,
14:48 Addressing himself to them, *J* said:
14:53 Then they led *J* off to the high priest,
14:55 against *J* that would lead to his death,
14:60 the court and began to interrogate *J*:
14:61 But *J* remained silent; he made no reply.
14:62 Then *J* answered: "I am;
14:67 said, "You too were with *J* of Nazareth."
14:72 recalled the prediction *J* had made to him,
15: 1 They bound *J*, led him away, and handed
15: 2 are the one who is saying it," *J* replied.
15: 5 surprise, *J* made no further response.
15:15 and after he had had *J* scourged,
15:16 The soldiers now led *J* away into the hall
15:19 Continually striking *J* on the head with a
15:22 When they brought *J* to the site of
15:34 At that time *J* cried in a loud voice,
15:37 *J*, uttering a loud cry, breathed his last.
15:41 These women had followed *J* when he was in
15:43 and urgently requested the body of *J*.
15:44 surprised that *J* should have died so soon.
15:44 and inquired whether *J* was already dead.
16: 1 which they intended to go and anoint *J*.
16: 6 You are looking for *J* of Nazareth,
16: 9 *J* rose from the dead early on the first
16:14 at table, *J* was revealed to the Eleven.
16:19 the Lord *J* was taken up into heaven and
16:20 Later on it was through them that *J*
Lk 1:31 and bear a son and give him the name *J*.
2:21 the name *J* was given the child,
2:27 when the parents brought in the child *J*
2:43 *J* remained behind unknown to his parents.
2:52 *J*, for his part, progressed steadily
3:21 and *J* was at prayer after likewise being
3:23 When *J* began his work he was about thirty
4: 1 *J*, full of the Holy Spirit,
4: 4 *J* answered him, "Scripture has it,
4: 8 In reply, *J* said to him, "Scripture has it,
4:12 *J* said to him in reply,
4:14 *J* returned in the power of the Spirit to
4:34 What do you want of us, *J* of Nazareth?
4:35 *J* said to him sharply, "Be quiet!
5: 8 Simon Peter fell at the knees of *J* saying,
5:10 *J* said to Simon, "Do not be afraid.
5:12 Seeing *J*, he bowed down to the ground
5:13 *J* stretched out his hand to touch him and
5:14 *J* then instructed the man:
5:17 One day *J* was teaching,
5:18 to bring him in and lay him before *J*;
5:19 into the middle of the crowd before *J*.
5:20 Seeing their faith, *J* said,
5:22 *J*, however, knew their reasoning
5:29 gave a great reception for *J* in his house,
5:31 *J* said to them, "The healthy do not need
5:34 *J* replied: "Can you make guests
6: 1 *J* was walking through the standing grain.
6: 3 *J* said to them: "Have you not read
6: 9 *J* said to them, "I ask you, is it lawful
6:11 asking one another what could be done to *J*.
7: 3 about *J* he sent some Jewish elders to him,
7: 4 *J* they petitioned him earnestly.
7: 6 *J* set out with them.
7: 9 *J* showed amazement on hearing this,
7:15 Then *J* gave him back to his mother.
7:22 *J* gave this response:
7:24 *J* began to speak about him to the crowds.
7:29 The entire populace that had heard *J*,
7:36 Pharisee who invited *J* to dine with him.
7:36 *J* went to the Pharisee's home and reclined
7:40 In answer to his thoughts, *J* said to him,
7:43 *J* said to him, "You are right."

8:28 On seeing J he began to shriek;
8:28 and exclaimed at the top of his voice, J,
8:29 By now J was ordering the unclean spirit
8:30 "What is your name," J demanded.
8:35 Coming on J, they found the man
8:37 asked J to leave their neighborhood,
8:39 town making public what J had done for him.
8:40 On his return, J was welcomed by the crowd;
8:41 the synagogue, came up and fell at J' feet,
8:42 As J went, the crowds almost crushed him.
8:45 J asked, "Who touched me?"
8:46 J insisted, "Someone touched me;
8:48 J said to her, "Daughter, it is your faith
8:50 J heard this, and his response was:
9: 1 J now called the Twelve together and gave
9: 3 J advised them: "Take nothing for the
9:10 related to J all they had accomplished.
9:14 J said to his disciples,
9:16 the two fish, J raised his eyes to heaven,
9:18 One day when J was praying in seclusion
9:23 J said to all: "Whoever wishes to be
9:33 When these were leaving, Peter said to J:
9:36 the voice fell silent, J was there alone.
9:41 J said in reply: "What an unbelieving
9:42 J then rebuked the unclean spirit,
9:43 that he was doing, J said to his disciples:
9:47 J, who knew their thoughts,
9:50 J told him in reply, "Do not stop him,
9:58 J said to him, "The foxes have lairs,
9:60 J said to him, "Let the dead bury their
9:62 J answered him, "Whoever puts his hand
10:21 J rejoiced in the Holy Spirit and said:
10:26 J answered him: "What is written in the law"
10:28 J said, "You have answered correctly.
10:29 he wished to justify himself he said to J,
10:30 J replied: There was a man going down
10:37 J said to him,
10:38 On their journey J entered a village where
11: 5 J said to them: "If one of you knows
11:14 J was casting out a devil which was mute,
11:46 J answered: "Woe to you lawyers also!
13: 6 J spoke this parable:
13:12 When J saw her,
13:14 that J should have healed on the sabbath,
13:17 at the marvels J was accomplishing.
14: 1 When J came on a sabbath to eat a meal in
14: 3 J asked the lawyers and the Pharisees,
14:16 J responded: "A man was giving
15:11 J said to them: "A man had two sons,
17:13 they raised their voices and said, J,
17:16 at the feet of J and spoke his praises.
17:17 J took the occasion to say,
18:16 but J called for the children,
18:19 J said to him, "Why call me 'good'?
18:22 When J heard this he said to him:
18:24 When J observed this he said:
18:37 came that J of Nazareth was passing by.
18:38 He shouted out, J,
18:40 J halted and ordered that he be brought to
18:40 When he had come close, J asked him,
18:42 J said to him, "Receive your sight.
19: 3 He was trying to see what J was like,
19: 4 a sycamore tree which was along J' route,
19: 5 J came to the spot he looked up and said,
19: 9 J said to him: "Today salvation has come
19:35 Then they led the animal to J, and laying
20: 8 J said to them, "In that case, neither will
20:34 J said to them: "The children of this age
20:41 J then said to them: "How can they say
20:45 of all the people, J said to his disciples:
22: 8 J sent Peter and John off with the
22:34 J replied,
22:47 He approached J to embrace him.
22:48 J said to him, "Judas, would you betray
22:49 of J saw what was going to happen,
22:51 J said in answer to their question, "Enough!"
22:52 J said, "Am I a criminal that you come
22:63 J amused themselves at his expense.
23: 8 Herod was extremely pleased to see J.
23: 9 Jesus at considerable length, but J made
23:20 for he wanted J to be the one he released.
23:25 murder, and delivered J up to their wishes.
23:26 shoulder for him to carry along behind J.
23:28 J turned to them and said:
23:34 J said, "Father, forgive them;
23:42 J, remember me when you enter upon
23:43 And J replied, "I assure you:
23:46 J uttered a loud cry and said,
23:52 Pilate with a request for J' body.
24: 3 they did not find the body of the Lord J.
24:15 J approached and began to walk along with
24:19 those that had to do with J of Nazareth,
Jn 1:17 this enduring love came through J Christ.
1:29 John caught sight of J coming toward him,
1:36 As he watched J walk by he said, "Look!
1:37 heard what he said, and followed J.
1:38 When J turned around and noticed them
1:42 He brought him to J,
1:43 "Follow me," J said to him.
1:45 the prophets too J,
1:47 When J saw Nathanael coming toward him,
1:48 "Before Philip called you," J answered,
1:50 J responded: "Do you believe

2: 1 in Galilee, and the mother of J was there.
2: 2 J and his disciples had likewise been
2: 3 the wine ran out, and J' mother told him,
2: 4 J replied, "Woman, how does this concern
2: 7 "Fill those jars with water," J ordered,
2:11 J performed this first of his signs at
2:13 Passover was near, J went up to Jerusalem.
2:19 "Destroy this temple," was J' answer,
2:22 Only after J had been raised from the dead
2:24 J would not trust himself to them because
3: 3 J gave him this answer: "I solemnly assure
3: 5 J replied:
3:10 J responded: "You hold the office of teacher
3:22 J and his disciples came into Judean
4: 1 Now when J learned that the Pharisees had
4: 2 however, it was not J himself who baptized,
4: 6 J, tired from his journey,
4: 7 woman came to draw water, J said to her,
4:10 J replied: "If only you recognized
4:13 J replied: "Everyone who drinks this water
4:17 you have no husband, J exclaimed.
4:21 J told her: "Believe me woman
4:26 J replied, "I who speak to you am he."
4:27 surprised that J was speaking with a woman.
4:34 J explained to them: "Doing the will of him
4:44 J himself had testified that no one
4:47 that J had come back from Judea to Galilee,
4:48 J replied, "Unless you people see signs
4:50 J told him, "Return home.
4:50 put his trust in the word J spoke to him,
4:53 the father realized, that J had told him,
4:54 This was the second sign that J performed
5: 1 of a Jewish feast, J went up to Jerusalem.
5: 6 J, who knew he had been sick a long time,
5: 8 J said to him, "Stand up!
5:13 so great that J had been able to slip away.
5:14 J found him in the temple precincts and
5:15 Jews that J was the one who had cured him.
5:16 It was because J did things such as this
5:19 This was J' answer:
6: 1 J crossed the Sea of Galilee [to the
6: 3 J then went up the mountain and sat down
6: 5 when J looked up and caught sight of a
6: 8 One of J' disciples,
6:10 J said, "Get the people to recline."
6:11 J then took the loaves of bread,
6:15 J realized that they would come and carry
6:17 was dark, and J had still not joined them;
6:19 miles, they sighted J approaching the boat,
6:22 J had not left in it with his disciples;
6:24 neither J nor his disciples were there,
6:24 boats and went to Capernaum looking for J.
6:26 J answered them: "I assure you you are not
6:29 J replied: "This is the work of God
6:32 J said to them: "I solemnly assure you
6:35 J explained to them: "I myself am the bread
6:42 "Is this not J, the son of Joseph?
6:43 "Stop your murmuring," J told them.
6:53 J said to them: "Let me solemnly assure you
6:61 J was fully aware that his disciples were
6:64 J knew from the start,
6:67 J then said to the Twelve,
6:70 J replied, "Did I not choose the Twelve
6:71 of the Twelve, was going to hand J over.)
7: 1 After this, J moved about within Galilee.
7: 6 J answered them: "It is not yet the right
7:14 The feast was half over by the time J went
7:16 This was J' answer: "My doctrine is not my
7:21 J answered: "I have performed a single
7:28 At this, J, who was teaching in the temple
7:33 J then said to them: "Only a little while
7:37 of the festival, J stood up and cried out:
7:39 as yet, since J had not yet been glorified.)
8: 1 while J went out to the Mount of Olives.
8: 6 J bent down and started tracing on the
8:10 J finally straightened up and said to her,
8:11 J said, "Nor do I condemn you.
8:12 J spoke to them once again.
8:14 J answered: "What if I am my own witness
8:19 J replied: "You know neither me nor my Father
8:25 J answered: "What I have been telling you
8:28 J continued: "When you lift up the Son of Man
8:31 J then went on to say to those Jews who
8:34 J answered them: "I give you my assurance
8:39 J told them: "If you were Abraham's
8:42 J answered: "Were God your father
8:49 J replied: "I am not possessed
8:54 J answered: "If I glorify myself
8:58 J answered them: "I solemnly declare it
8:59 that they picked up rocks to throw at J,
9: 3 "Neither," answered J:
9: 6 With that J spat on the ground,
9:11 call J made mud and smeared it on my eyes,
9:14 (Note that it was on a sabbath that J had
9:22 anyone who acknowledged J as the Messiah
9:35 When J heard of his expulsion,
9:37 "You have seen him," J replied.
9:39 Then J said:] "I came into this world
9:41 To which J replied: "If you were blind
10: 6 Even though J used this figure with them,
10:23 J was walking in the temple area,
10:25 J answered: "I did tell you
10:32 rocks to stone him, J protested to them,

10:34 J answered: "Is it not written in your law
11: 3 The sisters sent word to J to inform him,
11: 4 Upon hearing this, J said:
11: 5 J loved Martha and her sister and Lazarus
11: 9 J answered: "Are there not twelve hours
11:13 J had been speaking about his death,
11:14 Finally J said plainly: "Lazarus is dead.
11:17 When J arrived at Bethany,
11:20 that J was coming she went to meet him,
11:21 Martha said to J: "Lord, if you had been
11:23 brother will rise again," J assured her.
11:25 J told her: "I am the resurrection
11:30 (Actually J had not yet come into the
11:32 When Mary came to the place where J was,
11:33 When J saw her weeping,
11:35 J began to weep,
11:38 troubled in spirit, J approached the tomb.
11:39 "Take away the stone," J directed.
11:40 J replied,
11:41 the stone and J looked upward and said:
11:44 "Untie him," J told them,
11:45 to visit Mary, and had seen what J did,
11:46 the Pharisees and reported what J had done.
11:51 prophesied that J would die for the nation
11:54 J no longer moved about freely in Jewish
11:56 They were on the lookout for J,
12: 1 Six days before Passover J came to Bethany,
12: 1 of Lazarus whom J had raised from the dead.
12: 3 nard, with which she anointed J' feet.
12: 7 To this J replied: "Leave her alone.
12: 9 only because of J but also to see Lazarus,
12:11 because many Jews were going over to J and
12:12 feast heard that J was to enter Jerusalem.
12:14 J found a donkey and mounted it;
12:16 but after J was glorified they recalled
12:21 "Sir, we should like to see J."
12:22 Philip and Andrew in turn came to inform J.
12:23 J answered them: "The hour has come
12:30 J answered,
12:35 J answered: "The light is among you
12:36 J left them and went into hiding.
12:41 these words because he had seen J' glory,
12:44 J proclaimed aloud: "Whoever puts faith
13: 1 J realized that the hour had come for him
13: 3 J— fully aware that he had come from God
13: 7 J answered,
13: 8 "If I do not wash you," J answered,
13:10 J told him, "The man who has bathed
13:21 After saying this, J grew deeply troubled.
13:23 One of them, the disciple whom J loved,
13:24 Peter signaled him to ask J whom he meant.
13:25 back against J' chest and said to him,
13:26 J answered, "The one to whom I give
13:27 J addressed himself to him:
13:28 at table understood why J said this to him.
13:29 J was telling him to buy what was needed
13:31 Once Judas had left, J said:
13:36 J answered: "I am going where you cannot
13:38 J answered. "You will lay down your life
14: 6 J told him: "I am the way and the truth
14: 9 "Philip," J replied, "after I have been
14:23 J answered: "Anyone who loves me
16:19 Since J was aware that they wanted to
16:31 J answered them: "Do you really believe"
17: 1 words, J looked up to heaven and said:
17: 3 God, and him whom you have sent, J Christ.)
18: 1 J went out with his disciples across the
18: 2 J had often met there with his disciples.
18: 4 J, aware of all that would happen to him,
18: 5 J the Nazorean," they replied.
18: 6 As J said to them, "I am he,"
18: 7 J put the question to them again,
18: 7 J the Nazorean," they repeated.
18: 8 "I have told you, I am he," J said.
18:11 At that, J said to Peter,
18:12 the Jewish guards arrested J and bound him.
18:15 another disciple, kept following J closely.
18:15 J as far as the high priests' courtyard,
18:19 The high priest questioned J,
18:20 J answered by saying: "I have spoken
18:22 nearby gave J a sharp blow on the face.
18:23 J replied, "If I said anything wrong
18:28 brought J from Caiaphas to the praetorium.
18:32 (This was to fulfill what J had said
18:33 back into the praetorium and summoned J.
18:34 J answered, "Are you saying this on
18:36 J answered: "My kingdom does not belong
18:37 J replied: "It is you who say
19: 1 move was to take J and have him scourged.
19: 5 When J came out wearing the crown of
19: 9 back into the praetorium, he said to J,
19: 9 J would not give him any answer.
19:11 J answered: "You would have no power
19:13 then brought J outside and took a seat on
19:16 end, Pilate handed J over to be crucified.
19:16 J was led away,
19:18 one on either side, J in the middle.
19:19 J THE NAZOREAN THE KING OF THE JEWS
19:20 where J was crucified was near the city.
19:23 After the soldiers had crucified J they
19:25 Near the cross of J there stood his mother,
19:26 whom he loved, J said to his mother,
19:28 After that, J, realizing that everything

JESUS (cont.)

19:30 When *J* took the wine,
19:32 broke the legs of the men crucified with *J*,
19:33 came to *J* and saw that he was already dead,
19:38 a disciple of *J* (although a secret one for
19:38 Pilate's permission to remove *J'* body.
19:39 first come to *J* at night) likewise came,
19:40 They took *J'* body,
19:42 Jewish Preparation Day they buried *J* there,
20: 2 disciple (the one *J* loved) and told them,
20: 9 Scripture that *J* had to rise from the dead.)
20:12 foot of the place where *J'* body had lain.
20:14 and caught sight of *J* standing there.
20:16 *J* said to her, "Mary!"
20:17 *J* then said: "Do not cling to me,
20:19 of the Jews, *J* came and stood before them.
20:24 means "Twin"), was absent when *J* came.
20:26 locked doors, *J* came and stood before them.
20:29 *J* then said to him: "You become a believer
20:30 *J* performed many other signs
20:31 to help you believe that *J* is the Messiah,
21: 1 *J* showed himself to the disciples [once
21: 4 after daybreak *J* was standing on the shore,
21: 4 though none of the disciples knew it was *J*.
21: 7 the disciple *J* loved cried out to Peter,
21:10 of the fish you just caught," *J* told them.
21:12 "Come and eat your meal," *J* told them.
21:13 *J* came over, took the bread and gave
21:14 This marked the third time that *J* appeared
21:15 eaten their meal, *J* said to Simon Peter,
21:15 At which *J* said, "Feed my lambs."
21:16 *J* replied, "Tend my sheep."
21:17 A third time, *J* asked him,
21:17 *J* said to him, "Feed my sheep."
21:19 *J* had finished speaking he said to him,
21:20 disciple whom *J* loved was following
21:20 *J'* chest during the supper and said,
21:21 Seeing him, Peter was prompted to ask *J*,
21:22 want him to stay until I come," *J* replied,
21:23 *J* never told him,
21:25 are still many other things that *J* did,

Acts 1: 1 I dealt with all that *J* did and taught
1:11 *J* who has been taken from you will return,
1:14 in their company, and Mary the mother of *J*,
1:16 the one who guided those that arrested *J*.
1:21 company while the Lord *J* moved among us,
2:22 *J* the Nazorean was a man whom God sent to
2:32 This is the *J* God has raised up,
2:36 Lord and Messiah this *J* whom you crucified."
2:38 each one of you, in the name of *J* Christ,
3: 6 In the name of *J* Christ,
3:13 our fathers, has glorified his Servant *J*,
3:20 you by the Lord when he sends you *J*,
3:21 *J* must remain in heaven until the time of
4: 2 of the dead in the person of *J*.
4:10 done in the name of *J* Christ the Nazorean
4:11 This *J* is 'the stone rejected by you the
4:13 recognized these men as having been with *J*.
4:18 to speak the name of *J* or teach about him.
4:27 very city against your holy Servant, *J*,
4:30 and wonders to be worked in the name of *J*,
4:33 witness to the resurrection of the Lord *J*,
5:30 has raised up *J* whom you put to death,
5:40 not to speak again about the name of *J*,
5:42 proclaiming the good news of *J* the Messiah.
6:14 We have heard him claim that *J* the
7:55 of God, and *J* standing at God's right hand.
7:59 stoned he could be heard praying, "Lord *J*,
8:12 kingdom of God and the name of *J* Christ,
8:16 been baptized in the name of the Lord *J*.
8:35 point, telling him the good news of *J*.
9: 5 The voice answered, "I am *J*,
9:17 Lord *J* who appeared to you on the way here,
9:20 the synagogues that *J* was the Son of God.
9:22 his proofs that this *J* was the Messiah.
9:27 fearlessly in the name of *J* at Damascus.
9:34 said to him, "Aeneas, *J* Christ cures you!
10:36 through *J* Christ who is Lord of all.
10:37 all over Judea about *J* of Nazareth,
10:48 they be baptized in the name of *J* Christ.
11:17 we first believed in the Lord *J* Christ,
11:20 the good news of the Lord *J* to them.
13:23 forth from this man's descendants *J*,
13:24 John heralded the coming of *J* by
13:31 and for many days thereafter *J* appeared to
13:33 for us, their children, in raising up *J*,
15:11 the favor of the Lord *J* and so are they."
15:26 to the cause of our Lord *J* Christ.
16: 7 again the Spirit of *J* would not allow them.
16:18 "In the name of *J* Christ I command you,
16:31 in the Lord *J* and you will be saved,
17: 3 *J* I am telling you about is the Messiah!"
17: 7 and claim instead that a certain *J* is king."
17:18 to speak of *J*" and "the resurrection,"
18: 5 to the Jews that *J* was the Messiah.
18:25 He spoke and taught accurately about *J*,
18:28 from the Scriptures that *J* is the Messiah.
19: 4 whom they were to believe—that is, *J*."
19: 5 were baptized in the name of the Lord *J*.
19:13 tried to invoke the name of the Lord *J*
19:13 "I adjure you by the *J* whom Paul preaches."
19:15 the evil spirit answered, *J* I recognize,
19:17 Lord *J* came to be held in great reverence.
20:21 before God and on faith in our Lord *J*.
20:24 which I have been assigned by the Lord *J*,
20:35 to recall the words of the Lord *J* himself,
21:13 For the name of the Lord *J* I am prepared,
22: 8 am *J* the Nazorean whom you are persecuting.'
22:18 into a trance and saw *J* speaking to me.
24:24 to hear him speak about faith in Christ *J*.
25:19 and about a certain *J* who had died but who
26: 9 of *J* the Nazorean in every way possible.
26:15 'I am that *J* whom you are persecuting.
28:23 He sought to convince them about *J* by
28:31 of God and taught about the Lord *J* Christ.

Rom 1: 1 from Paul, a servant of Christ *J*,
1: 4 *J* Christ our Lord.
1: 6 who have been called to belong to *J* Christ.
1: 7 from God our Father and the Lord *J* Christ.
1: 8 I give thanks to God through *J* Christ for
2:16 on the secrets of men through Christ *J*.
3:22 faith in *J* Christ for all who believe.
3:24 through the redemption wrought in Christ *J*.
3:26 and might justify those who believe in *J*.
4:24 in him who raised *J* our Lord from the dead,
4:25 the *J* who was handed over to death for our
5: 1 peace with God through our Lord *J* Christ.
5:11 God our boast through our Lord *J* Christ,
5:15 the gracious gift of the one man, *J* Christ,
5:17 and reign through the one man, *J* Christ.
5:21 to eternal life, through *J* Christ our Lord.
6: 3 into Christ *J* were baptized into his death?
6:11 dead to sin but alive for God in Christ *J*.
6:23 God is eternal life in Christ *J* our Lord.
7:25 praise to God, through *J* Christ our Lord!
8: 1 now for those who are in Christ *J*.
8: 2 the spirit of life in Christ *J*, has freed you
8:11 who raised *J* from the dead dwells in you,
8:34 Christ *J*, who died or rather was raised up,
8:39 love of God that comes to us in Christ *J*,
10: 9 you confess with your lips that *J* is Lord,
13:14 put on the Lord *J* Christ and make no
14:14 Lord *J* that nothing is unclean in itself;
15: 5 according to the spirit of Christ *J*,
15: 6 God, the Father of our Lord *J* Christ.
15:16 a minister of Christ *J* among the Gentiles,
15:17 Christ *J* for the work I have done for God.
15:30 Lord *J* Christ and the love of the Spirit,
16: 3 fellow workers in the service of Christ *J*
16:20 the grace of our Lord *J* Christ be with you.
16:25 which I proclaim when I preach *J* Christ,
16:27 given through *J* Christ unto endless ages.

1Cor 1: 1 God's will to be an apostle of Christ *J*,
1: 2 Christ *J* and called to be a holy people,
1: 2 be, call on the name of our Lord *J* Christ,
1: 3 from God our Father and the Lord *J* Christ.
1: 4 favor he has bestowed on you in Christ *J*,
1: 7 for the revelation of our Lord *J* Christ.
1: 8 on the day of our Lord *J* [Christ].
1: 9 fellowship with his Son, *J* Christ our Lord.
1:10 brothers, in the name of our Lord *J* Christ,
1:30 it is who has given you life in Christ *J*.
2: 2 of nothing but *J* Christ and him crucified.
3:11 one that has been laid, namely *J* Christ.
4:15 *J* through my preaching of the gospel.
5: 3 Lord *J* Christ on the man who did this deed.
5: 4 with you and empowered by our Lord *J*,
6:11 Lord *J* Christ and in the Spirit of our God.
8: 6 and one Lord *J* Christ through whom
9: 1 Have I not seen *J* our Lord?
11:23 that the Lord *J* on the night in which he
12: 3 the Spirit of God ever says, "Cursed be *J*."
12: 3 *J* is Lord," except in the Holy Spirit.
15:31 me, which I cherish in Christ *J* our Lord,
15:57 us the victory through our Lord *J* Christ.
16:23 The favor of the Lord *J* be with you.
16:24 My love to all of you in Christ *J*.

2Cor 1: 1 Paul, by God's will an apostle of *J* Christ,
1: 2 from God our Father and the Lord *J* Christ.
1: 3 be God, the Father of our Lord *J* Christ,
1:14 and you ours, on the day of our Lord *J*.
1:19 *J* Christ, whom Silvanus, Timothy,
4: 5 ourselves we preach but Christ *J* as Lord,
4: 5 ourselves as your servants for *J'* sake.
4:10 *J*, so that in our bodies the life of Jesus
4:11 death for *J'* sake, so that the life of Jesus
4:14 Lord *J* will raise us up along with Jesus
8: 9 the favor shown you by our Lord *J* Christ;
11: 4 another *J* than the one we preached,
11:31 The God and Father of the Lord *J* knows
13: 5 do not realize that Christ *J* is in you
13:13 The grace of the Lord *J* Christ,

Gal 1: 1 but by *J* Christ and God his Father who
1: 3 of God our Father and of the Lord *J* Christ,
1:12 It came by revelation from *J* Christ.
2: 4 Christ *J* and thereby to make slaves of us,
2:16 legal observance but by faith in *J* Christ,
3: 1 you before whose eyes *J* Christ was
3:14 Christ *J* the blessing bestowed on Abraham
3:14 might descend on the Gentiles in Christ *J*,
3:22 in consequence of faith in *J* Christ.
3:26 of God because of your faith in Christ *J*.
3:28 All are one in Christ *J*.
4:14 of God, even as if I had been Christ *J*!
5: 6 In Christ *J* neither circumcision nor the
5:24 Those who belong to Christ *J* have
6:14 but the cross of our Lord *J* Christ!
6:17 for I bear the brand marks of *J* in my body.
6:18 of our Lord *J* Christ be with your spirit.

Eph 1: 1 by the will of God an apostle of *J* Christ,
1: 1 ones [at Ephesus], believers in Christ *J*.
1: 2 from God our Father and the Lord *J* Christ.
1: 3 be the God and Father of our Lord *J* Christ,
1: 5 us through Christ *J* to be his adopted sons
1:15 I first heard of your faith in the Lord *J*
1:17 May the God of our Lord *J* Christ,
2: 6 Both with and in Christ *J* he raised us up
2: 7 by his kindness to us in Christ *J*.
2:10 created in Christ *J* to lead the life of
2:13 But now in Christ *J* you who once were far
2:20 with Christ *J* himself as the capstone.
3: 1 for Christ *J* on behalf of you Gentiles,
3: 6 in Christ *J* the Gentiles are now co-heirs
3:11 purpose, carried out in Christ *J* our Lord.
3:21 and in Christ *J* through all generations,
4:21 you in accord with the truth that is in *J*:
5:20 in the name of our Lord *J* Christ.
6:23 May God the Father and the Lord *J* Christ
6:24 love our Lord *J* Christ with unfailing love.

Phil 1: 1 Paul and Timothy, servants of Christ *J*,
1: 1 with their bishops and deacons in Christ *J*.
1: 2 God our Father and from the Lord *J* Christ!
1: 6 right up to the day of Christ *J*.
1: 8 of you with the affection of Christ *J*!
1:11 justice which *J* Christ has ripened in you,
1:19 I receive from the Spirit of *J* Christ.
2:10 So that at *J'* name every knee must bend in
2:11 *J* CHRIST IS LORD!
2:19 I hope, in the Lord *J*,
2:21 interests rather than those of Christ *J*.
3: 3 spirit of God and glory in Christ *J*
3: 8 surpassing knowledge of my Lord *J* Christ.
3:12 since I have been grasped by Christ *J*.
3:14 life on high in Christ *J*.
3:20 coming of our Savior, the Lord *J* Christ.
4: 7 over your hearts and minds, in Christ *J*.
4:19 of his magnificent riches in Christ *J*.
4:21 in Christ *J* to every member of the church.
4:23 of the Lord *J* Christ be with your spirit.

Col 1: 1 an apostle of Christ *J* by the will of God,
1: 3 to God, the Father of our Lord *J* Christ,
1: 4 we have heard of your faith in Christ *J*
2: 6 therefore, to live in Christ *J* the Lord,
3:17 in action, do it in the name of the Lord *J*.
4:11 *J* known also as Justus sends greetings.
4:12 He is a servant of Christ *J* who is always

1Thes 1: 1 to God the Father and the Lord *J* Christ.
1: 3 constancy of hope in our Lord *J* Christ.
1:10 heaven the Son he raised from the dead *J*,
2:14 of God in Judea which are in Christ *J*.
2:15 who killed the Lord *J* and the prophets,
2:19 in, before our Lord *J* Christ at his coming?
3:11 Lord *J* make our path to you a straight one!
3:13 of our Lord *J* with all his holy ones.
4: 1 we beg and exhort you in the Lord *J*
4: 2 the instructions we gave you in the Lord *J*.
4:14 For if we believe that *J* died and rose,
5: 9 salvation through our Lord *J* Christ.
5:18 such is God's will for you in Christ *J*.
5:23 at the coming of our Lord *J* Christ.
5:28 the grace of our Lord *J* Christ be with you.

2Thes 1: 1 to God our Father and the Lord *J* Christ.
1: 2 from God the Father and the Lord *J* Christ.
1: 7 when the Lord *J* is revealed from heaven
1: 8 God nor heed" the good news of our Lord *J*.
1:12 *J* may be glorified in you and you in him,
1:12 gift of our God and of the Lord *J* Christ.
2: 1 *J* Christ and our being gathered to him,
2: 8 and the Lord *J* will destroy him with the
2:14 achieve the glory of our Lord *J* Christ.
2:16 May our Lord *J* Christ himself,
3: 6 brothers, in the name of the Lord *J* Christ,
3:12 we urge them strongly in the Lord *J* Christ,
3:18 grace of our Lord *J* Christ be with you all.

1Tm 1: 1 an apostle of Christ *J* by command of God
1: 1 of God our savior and Christ *J* our hope,
1: 2 from God the Father and Christ *J* our Lord.
1:12 I thank Christ *J* our Lord,
1:14 the faith and love which are in Christ *J*.
1:15 *J* came into the world to save sinners.
1:16 *J* Christ might display all his patience,
2: 5 between God and men, the man Christ *J*,
3:13 much assurance in their faith in Christ *J*.
4: 6 you will be a good servant of Christ *J*,
5:21 I charge you before God, Christ *J*,
6: 3 sound doctrines of our Lord *J* Christ
6:13 gives life to all, and before Christ *J*,
6:14 until our Lord *J* Christ shall appear.

2Tm 1: 1 by the will of God an apostle of Christ *J*
1: 2 and from Christ *J* our Lord be with you.
1: 9 grace held out to us in Christ *J*
1:13 me say, in faith and love in Christ *J*.
2: 1 in the grace which is ours in Christ *J*.
2: 3 with me as a good soldier of Christ *J*.
2: 8 Remember that *J* Christ, a descendant of
2:10 in Christ *J* and with it eternal glory.
3:12 in Christ *J* can expect to be persecuted.
3:15 faith in *J* Christ leads to salvation.
4: 1 In the presence of God and of Christ *J*,

Ti 1: 1 sent as an apostle of *J* Christ for the
1: 4 God our Father, and Christ *J* our Savior,
2:13 the great God and of our Savior Christ *J*.
3: 6 lavished on us through *J* Christ our Savior,
Phlm 1: 1 Paul, a prisoner of Christ *J*,
1: 3 God our Father and from the Lord *J* Christ.
1: 5 toward the Lord *J* and all God's people.
1:23 Epaphras, my fellow prisoner in Christ *J*,
1:25 of our Lord *J* Christ be with your spirit.
Heb 2: 9 but we do see *J* crowned with glory and
2: 9 *J*, who was made for a little while lower
2:14 flesh, *J* likewise had a full share in ours,
3: 1 a heavenly calling, fix your eyes on *J*,
3: 3 but *J* is more worthy of honor than he,
4:14 who has passed through the heavens, *J*,
6:20 extends beyond the veil through which *J*,
7:21 without an oath, unlike *J* to whom God said:
7:22 Thus has *J* become the guarantee of a
7:24 but *J*, because he remains forever,
8: 6 *J* has obtained a more excellent ministry
10: 5 on coming into the world, *J* said:
10:10 of the body of *J* Christ once for all.
10:12 But *J* offered one sacrifice for sins and
10:19 since the blood of *J* assures our entrance
12: 2 let us keep our eyes fixed on *J*,
12:24 spirits of just men made perfect, to *J*,
13: 8 *J* Christ is the same yesterday,
13:12 Therefore *J* died outside the gate,
13:20 blood of the eternal covenant, *J* our Lord,
13:21 Through *J* Christ may he carry out in you
Jas 1: 1 a servant of God and of the Lord *J* Christ,
2: 1 Lord *J* Christ must not allow of favoritism.
1Pt 1: 1 Peter, an apostle of *J* Christ,
1: 2 *J* Christ and purification with his blood.
1: 3 be the God and Father of our Lord *J* Christ,
1: 3 the resurrection of *J* Christ from the dead;
1: 7 glory, and honor when *J* Christ appears.
1:13 be conferred on you when *J* Christ appears.
2: 5 acceptable to God through *J* Christ.
3:21 through the resurrection of *J* Christ.
4:11 God is to be glorified through *J* Christ:
2Pt 1: 1 Peter, servant and apostle of *J* Christ,
1: 1 power of our God and Savior *J* Christ;
1: 2 through your knowledge of God and of *J*,
1: 8 in true knowledge of our Lord *J* Christ.
1:11 *J* Christ will be richly provided for.
1:14 indications our Lord *J* Christ has given me,
1:16 the coming in power of our Lord *J* Christ,
2:20 recognizing the Lord and Savior *J* Christ,
3:18 knowledge of our Lord and Savior *J* Christ.
1Jn 1: 3 with the Father and with his Son, *J* Christ.
1: 7 of his Son *J* cleanses us from all sin.
2: 1 in the presence of the Father, *J* Christ,
2:22 He who denies that *J* is the Christ.
3:23 believe in the name of his Son, *J* Christ,
4: 2 *J* Christ come in the flesh belongs to God,
4:15 acknowledges that *J* is the Son of God,
5: 1 *J* is the Christ has been begotten of God.
5: 5 one who believes that *J* is the Son of God.
5: 6 *J* Christ it is who came through water and
5:20 is true, for we are in his Son *J* Christ.
2Jn 1: 3 from God the Father and from *J* Christ,
1: 7 *J* Christ as coming in the flesh.
Jude 1: 1 a servant of *J* Christ and brother of James,
1: 1 and have been guarded safely in *J* Christ.
1: 4 our God to sexual excess and deny *J* Christ,
1:17 words of the apostles of our Lord *J* Christ;
1:21 Lord *J* Christ which leads to life eternal.
1:25 God our savior, through *J* Christ our Lord.
Rv 1: 1 is the revelation God gave to *J* Christ,
1: 2 word of God and the testimony of *J* Christ.
1: 5 and from *J* Christ the faithful witness,
1: 9 reign and the endurance we have in *J*,
1: 9 God's word and bore witness to *J*.
12:17 God's commandments and give witness to *J*.
14:12 commandments of God and their faith in *J*.
17: 6 of those martyred for their faith in *J*
19:10 and your brothers who give witness to *J*.
19:10 spirit proves itself by witnessing to *J*."
20: 4 for their witness to *J* and the word of God,
22:16 "It is I, *J*,
22:20 Come, Lord *J*!
22:21 The grace of the Lord *J* be with you all.

JETHER (10)

Jgs 8:20 Then he said to his first-born, *J*,
8:20 Since *J* was still a boy,
1Kgs 2: 5 Abner, son of Ner, and Amasa, son of *J*.
2:32 of Israel's army, and Amasa, son of *J*,
1Chr 2:17 Amasa, whose father was *J* the Ishmaelite.
2:32 brother of Shammai, were *J* and Jonathan.
2:32 *J* died without sons.
4:17 The sons of Ezrah were *J*,
4:17 *J* became the father of Miriam,
7:38 The sons of *J* were Jephunneh,

JETHERAI (1)

1Chr 6: 6 Iddo, whose son was Zerah, whose son was *J*.

JETHETH (2)

Gn 36:40 the clans of Timna, Alvah, *J*,
1Chr 1:51 the chiefs of Timna, Aliah, *J*,

JETHRO (9)

Ex 3: 1 tending the flock of his father-in-law *J*,
4:18 to his father-in-law *J* and said to him,
4:18 *J* replied, "Go in peace."
18: 1 Now Moses' father-in-law *J*,
18: 2 So his father-in-law *J* took along Zipporah,
18: 5 his father-in-law *J* came to him in the
18: 6 of God, and he sent word to Moses, "I, *J*,
18: 9 *J* rejoiced over all the goodness that the
18:12 Then *J*,

JETTA (1)

1Chr 6:44 pasture lands, *J* with its pasture lands,

JETUR (3)

Gn 25:15 Mishma, Dumah, Massa, Hadad, Tema, *J*,
1Chr 1:31 Mishma, Dumah, Massa, Hadad, Tema, *J*,
5:19 war against the Hagrites and against *J*,

JEUEL (2)

1Chr 9: 6 Among the Zerahites were *J* and six hundred
2Chr 29:13 Shimri and *J*; of the sons of Asaph:

JEUSH (8)

Gn 36: 5 and Oholibamah bore *J*,
36:14 whom she bore to Esau were *J*,
36:18 the clans of *J*, Jalam, and Korah.
1Chr 1:35 The sons of Esau were Eliphaz, Reuel, *J*,
7:10 The sons of Bilhan were *J*,
8:39 his brother, were Ulam, his first-born, *J*,
23:10 The sons of Shimei were Jahath, Zizah, *J*,
23:11 but *J* and Beriah had not many sons,

JEUZ (1)

1Chr 8:10 father of Jobab, Zibia, Mesha, Malcam, *J*,

JEW (38)

Est A: 2 He was a *J* residing in the city of Susa,
2: 5 of Susa a certain *J* named Mordecai,
3: 4 since he had told them that he was a *J*.
5:13 the *J* Mordecai sitting at the royal gate."
6:10 proposed, and do this for the *J* Mordecai,
8: 7 said to Queen Esther and to the *J* Mordecai:
9:29 daughter of Abihail and of Mordecai the *J*,
9:31 these days of Purim which Mordecai the *J*
10: 3 The *J* Mordecai was next in rank to King
1Mc 2:23 a certain *J* came forward in the sight of
10:34 and exemption for every *J* in my kingdom.
2Mc 6: 6 feasts, nor even admit that he was a *J*.
9:17 he would become a *J* himself and visit
Dn 14:28 "The king has become a *J*,"
Zec 8:23 every *J* by the edge of his garment and say,
Jn 3:25 between John's disciples and a certain *J*.
4: 9 Samaritan woman said to him, "You are a *J*.
18:35 "I am no *J*!"
Acts 10:28 must know that it is not proper for a *J*
18: 2 There he found a *J* named Aquila,
18:24 A *J* named Apollos,
19:34 But when they recognized that he was a *J*,
21:39 Paul replied, "I am a *J*,
22: 3 "I am a *J*, born in Tarsus in Cilicia,
Rom 1:16 believes in it to salvation, the *J* first,
2: 9 every man who has done evil, the *J* first,
2:10 who has done good, likewise the *J* first,
2:17 Let us suppose you bear the name of *J*"
2:28 Appearance does not make a *J*.
2:29 He is a real *J* who is one inwardly,
3: 1 What is the advantage, then, of being a *J*,
10:12 there is no difference between *J* and Greek;
1Cor 9:20 a *J* to the Jews in order to win the Jews.
10:32 to *J* or Greek or to the church of God,
12:13 Spirit that all of us, whether *J* or Greek,
Gal 2:14 "If you who are a *J* are living according
3:28 There does not exist among you *J* or Greek,
Col 3:11 There is no Greek or *J* here,

JEWEL (4)

Is 13:19 And Babylon, the *j* of kingdoms,
Ez 20: 6 with milk and honey, a *j* among all lands.
20:15 with milk and honey, a *j* among all lands.
Rv 21:11 a precious *j* that sparkled like a diamond.

JEWELER (1)

Sir 45:11 in golden settings, the work of the *j*,

JEWELRY (5)

Ex 32:24 'Let anyone who has gold *j* take it off.'
Jdt 10: 4 rings, earrings, and all her other *j*.
Jer 2:32 Does a virgin forget her *j*,
Ez 16:11 I adorned you with *j*:
1Pt 3: 3 hairdress, the wearing of golden *j*,

JEWELS (11)

2Chr 32:27 silver, gold, precious stones, spices, *j*,
Sg 1:10 cheeks lovely in pendants, your neck in *j*.
5:12 seem bathed in milk, and are set like *j*.
7: 2 Your rounded thighs are like *j*,
Is 61:10 a diadem, like a bride bedecked with her *j*.
Ez 25: 9 totally of its cities, the *j* of the land:
28:13 Of gold your pendants and *j* were made,
Hos 2:15 herself out with her rings and her *j*,
Zec 9:16 *j* in a crown raised aloft over his land.
Rv 17: 4 adorned with gold and pearls and other *j*.
18:16 Adorned all in gold and *j* and pearls!

JEWISH (72)

1Chr 4:19 The sons of his *J* wife,
Neh 13:24 and none of them knew how to speak *J*;
Est 6:13 are beginning to decline, is of the *J* race,
1Mc 8:20 and his brothers, with the *J* people,
8:23 the *J* nation at sea and on land forever;
8:25 the *J* nation will help them wholeheartedly,
8:27 way, if war is made first on the *J* nation,
8:29 have made an agreement with the *J* people.
10:25 Demetrius sends greetings to the *J* nation.
11:30 his brother Jonathan and to the *J* nation.
11:33 decided to bestow benefits on the *J* nation,
12: 3 "The high priest Jonathan and the *J* people
12: 6 and the rest of the *J* people send
13:36 kings, and to the elders and the *J* people.
14:20 the priests, and the rest of the *J* people,
14:33 he stationed a garrison of *J* soldiers,
14:35 When the *J* people saw Simon's loyalty and
14:37 In this citadel he stationed *J* soldiers,
14:41 "'The *J* people and their priest have,
14:47 and ethnarch of the *J* people and priests
15: 2 priest and ethnarch, and to the *J* nation.
15:17 by Simon the high priest and the *J* people,
15:39 could launch attacks against the *J* people.
2Mc 5:23 Out of hatred for the *J* citizens,
8: 9 nations to wipe out the entire *J* race.
8:11 inviting them to buy *J* slaves and
9:19 "To my esteemed *J* citizens,
10: 8 prescribed that the whole *J* nation
11:16 "Lysias sends greetings to the *J* people.
11:27 the *J* senate and to the rest of the Jews.
11:34 the Romans, send greetings to the *J* people.
13:21 men inside, but Rhodocus, of the *J* army,
15:12 arms for the whole *J* community.
Dn 5:13 him, "Are you the Daniel, the *J* exile,
6:14 this they replied, "Daniel, the *J* exile,
Lk 7: 3 about Jesus he sent some *J* elders to him,
23:51 He was from Arimathea, a *J* town,
Jn 2: 6 As prescribed for *J* ceremonial washings,
2:13 As the *J* Passover was near,
3: 1 Nicodemus, a member of the *J* Sanhedrin,
5: 1 Later, on the occasion of a *J* feast,
6: 4 The *J* feast of Passover was near;
7: 2 as the *J* feast of Booths drew near,
11:19 and many *J* people had come out to console
11:54 no longer moved about freely in *J* circles.
11:55 The *J* Passover was near,
18:12 the *J* guards arrested Jesus and bound him.
19:40 and in accordance with *J* burial custom
19:42 *J* Preparation Day they buried Jesus there,
Acts 9:22 and reduced the *J* community of Damascus to
10:22 well thought of in the whole *J* community,
13: 5 the word of God in the *J* synagogues,
13: 6 where they came across a *J* magician named
13:43 *J* converts followed Paul and Barnabas,
14: 1 they entered the *J* synagogue and spoke in
16: 1 Timothy, whose mother was *J* and a believer,
17: 1 where there was a *J* synagogue.
17:10 arrival, they went to the *J* synagogue.
18:28 public refutation of the *J* party
19:13 Some itinerant *J* exorcists once tried to
19:14 the seven sons of Sceva, a *J* high priest,
24:24 few days later Felix came with his *J* wife,
25: 2 There the *J* chief priests and the leaders
25: 9 But Festus, wishing to please the *J* people,
25:24 The whole *J* community,
26: 3 in all the various *J* customs and disputes.
28:17 men of the *J* community to visit him.
Gal 1:14 I made progress in *J* observance far beyond
2:14 according to Gentile ways rather than *J*,
2:14 do you force the Gentiles to adopt *J* ways?"
Ti 1:10 especially from among the *J* converts
1:14 and unaffected by *J* myths or rules

JEWS—JEW'S (313)

2Kgs 25:25 along with the *J* and Chaldeans who were in
Ezr 4:12 Let it be known to the king that the *J* who
4:23 they went in all haste to the *J* in Jerusalem
5: 1 began to prophesy to the *J* in Judah and
5: 5 of the *J* so that they were not hindered,
6: 7 *J* continue to work on that house of God;
6: 8 *J* in the rebuilding of that house of God:
6:14 The elders of the *J* continued to make
Neh 1: 2 I asked them about the *J*,
2:16 as yet I had disclosed nothing to the *J*,
3:33 He ridiculed the *J*,
3:34 "What are these miserable *J* trying to do?
4: 6 When the *J* who lived near them had come to
5: 1 wives against certain of their fellow *J*.
5: 8 our fellow *J* who had been sold to Gentiles;
5:17 and fifty persons, *J* and magistrates,
6: 6 you and the *J* are planning a rebellion;
13:23 days I saw *J* who had married Ashdodite,

JEWS—JEW'S (cont.)

Tb 11:17 was joy for all the *J* who lived in Nineveh.
Est 3: 6 he sought to destroy all the *J*,
3:10 Hammedatha the Agagite, the enemy of the *J*.
3:13 all the royal provinces, that all the *J*,
4: 3 reached, the *J* went into deep mourning,
4: 7 royal treasury for the slaughter of the *J*.
4:13 palace, you alone of all the *J* will escape.
4:14 will come to the *J* from another source;
4:16 and assemble all the *J* who are in Susa;
8: 1 gave the house of Haman, enemy of the *J*,
8: 3 and the plan he had devised against the *J*.
8: 5 of the *J* in all the royal provinces.
8: 7 on the gibbet because he attacked the *J*,
8: 8 name what you see fit concerning the *J*
8: 9 they wrote to the *J* and to the satraps,
8: 9 to the *J* in their own script and language.
8:11 these letters the king authorized the *J*
E:15 But we find that the *J*,
E:19 that the *J* may follow their own laws,
8:13 so that the *J* might be prepared on that
8:16 there was splendor and merriment for the *J*,
8:17 banqueting and feasting for the *J*.
8:17 for they were seized with a fear of the *J*.
9: 1 *J* had expected to become masters of them,
9: 1 the *J* became masters of their enemies.
9: 2 The *J* mustered in their cities throughout
9: 3 supported the *J* from fear of Mordecai;
9: 5 The *J* struck down all their enemies with
9: 6 *J* killed and destroyed five hundred men.
9:10 Haman, son of Hammedatha, the foe of the *J*.
9:12 "In the stronghold of Susa the *J* have
9:13 let the *J* in Susa be permitted again
9:15 and the *J* in Susa mustered again on the
9:16 The other *J*, who dwelt in the royal
9:18 (The *J* in Susa, however, mustered
9:19 That is why the rural *J*,
9:20 events and sent letters to all the *J*,
9:22 *J* obtained rest from their enemies
9:23 The *J* took upon themselves for the future
9:24 the Agagite, the foe of all the *J*,
9:25 plan Haman had devised against the *J*
9:27 the *J* established and took upon themselves,
9:28 never to fall into disuse among the *J*,
9:30 peace and security to all the *J*
9:31 and Queen Esther had designated for the *J*,
10: 3 Ahasuerus, in high standing among the *J*,
F: 5 assembled to destroy the name of the *J*,
1Mc 4: 2 camp of the *J* and take them by surprise.
5:23 the *J* who were in Galilee and in Arbatta,
5:25 all that had happened to the *J* in Gilead:
5:44 The *J* captured that city and burnt the
6:47 When the *J* saw the strength of the royal
6:52 The *J* countered by setting up machines of
6:61 he sent peace terms to the *J*,
7:45 The *J* pursued them a day's journey,
7:47 the *J* collected the spoils and the booty;
8:22 the *J* as a record of peace and alliance:
8:31 heavy upon our friends and allies the *J*?
9:40 The *J* rose up against them from their
9:42 *J* returned to the marshes of the Jordan.
10:23 of the *J* and thus strengthening himself?
10:29 now free you, as I also exempt all the *J*.
10:33 Every one of the *J* who has been carried
10:36 "Let thirty thousand *J* be enrolled in the
10:75 When the *J* besieged it,
11:47 So the king called the *J* to his aid.
11:49 that the *J* held the city at their mercy,
11:50 let the *J* stop attacking us and our city."
11:51 The *J* thus gained glory in the eyes of the
12:21 that the Spartans and the *J* are brothers;
12:26 made ready to attack the *J* that very night.
13:42 high priest, governor, and leader of the *J*."
13:51 the *J* entered the citadel with shouts of
14:22 Antipater, son of Jason, envoys of the *J*,
14:31 When the enemies of the *J* sought to invade
14:34 these cities he resettled with *J*,
14:40 the Romans had addressed the *J* as friends,
15: 1 Simon, the priest and ethnarch of the *J*,
15:17 Certain envoys of the *J*,
2Mc 1: 1 The *J* in Jerusalem and in the land of
1: 1 to their brethren, the *J* in Egypt,
1: 7 we *J* wrote to you during the trouble and
1:10 anointed priests, and to the *J* in Egypt.
3:30 the *J* praised the Lord who had marvelously
3:32 some foul play at the hands of the *J*,
4:11 to the *J* through the mediation of John,
4:35 As a result, not only the *J*,
4:36 the region of Cilicia, the *J* of the city,
5:25 then, finding the *J* refraining from work,
6: 1 force the *J* to abandon the customs
6: 7 of the king's birthday the *J* had,
6: 8 to act in the same way against the *J*:
8:10 Romans by selling captured *J* into slavery.
8:20 when only eight thousand *J* fought along
8:32 man, who had done great harm to the *J*.
8:34 the thousand slave dealers to buy the *J*,
8:36 testified that the *J* had a champion,
9: 4 he planned to make the *J* suffer for the
9: 4 of the *J* as soon as I arrive there."
9: 7 Breathing fire in his rage against the *J*,
9:15 equality with the Athenians all the *J*,
9:18 to the *J* in the form of a supplication.
10: 6 The *J* celebrated joyfully for eight days
10:12 taken the lead in treating the *J* fairly
10:14 and used every opportunity to attack the *J*.
10:15 strongholds, were harassing the *J*;
10:24 who had previously been defeated by the *J*,
10:29 on golden-bridled horses, who led the *J* on.
11: 2 all his cavalry and marched against the *J*.
11:15 granted in behalf of the *J* all the written
11:16 of the letter which Lysias wrote to the *J*:
11:24 We understand that the *J* do not agree with
11:27 the Jewish senate and to the rest of the *J*.
11:31 and none of the *J* shall be molested in any
12: 1 king, and the *J* went about their farming.
12: 3 they invited the *J* who lived among them,
12: 4 When the *J*, not suspecting treachery
12: 8 treatment to the *J* who lived among them,
12:10 When the *J* had gone about a mile from
12:11 promised to supply the *J* with cattle
12:17 there were certain *J* known as Toubiani.
12:28 But the *J*, invoking the Sovereign
12:30 But when the *J* who lived there testified
12:34 ensuing battle, a few of the *J* were slain.
12:40 which the law forbids the *J* to wear.
13: 9 inflicting on the *J* worse things
13:13 the *J* should march out and settle the
13:18 king, having had a taste of the *J'* daring,
13:19 Beth-zur, a strong fortress of the *J*;
13:23 Dismayed, he parleyed with the *J*,
14: 5 the dispositions and intentions of the *J*.
14: 6 "Those *J* called Hasideans,
14:14 the *J* would mean prosperity for themselves.
14:15 When the *J* heard of Nicanor's coming,
14:37 of the *J* because of his love for them.
14:39 Nicanor, to show his detestation of the *J*,
14:40 such a man he would deal the *J* a hard blow.
15: 2 *J* who were forced to follow him pleaded,
15:17 to courage, the *J* determined not to delay,
Jer 40:15 All the *J* who have now rallied to you will
Dn 3: 8 and accused the *J* to King Nebuchadnezzar:
3:12 There are certain *J* whom you have made
13: 4 and the *J* had recourse to him often
Mt 2: 2 "Where is the newborn king of the *J*?
27:11 "Are you the king of the *J*?"
27:29 him, saying, "All hail, king of the *J*!"
27:37 "THIS IS JESUS, KING OF THE *J*."
28:15 circulates among the *J* to this very day.
Mk 7: 3 The Pharisees, and in fact all *J*,
15: 2 "Are you the king of the *J*?"
15: 9 me to release the king of the *J* for you?"
15:12 do with the man you call the king of the *J*?"
15:18 King of the *J*!"
15:26 his offense read, "THE KING OF THE *J*.
Lk 23: 3 asked him, "Are you the king of the *J*?"
23:37 and saying, "If you are the king of the *J*,
23:38 "THIS IS THE KING OF THE *J*."
Jn 1:19 The testimony John gave when the *J* sent
2:18 At this the *J* responded,
4: 9 that *J* have nothing to do with Samaritans.)
4:22 after all, salvation is from the *J*.
5:10 *J* began telling the man who had been cured,
5:15 *J* that Jesus was the one who had cured him.
5:18 The reason why the *J* were even more
6:41 At this the *J* started to murmur in protest
6:52 At this the *J* quarreled among themselves,
7: 1 *J* were looking for a chance to kill him.
7:11 naturally, the *J* were looking for him,
7:13 about him, however, for fear of the *J*.
7:15 The *J* were filled with amazement and said,
7:35 caused the *J* to exclaim among themselves:
8:22 At this some of the *J* began to ask,
8:31 on to say to those *J* who believed in him:
8:48 The *J* answered, "Are we not right,
8:52 sure you are possessed," the *J* retorted.
8:57 At this the *J* objected:
9:18 The *J* refused to believe that he had
9:22 fashion because they were afraid of the *J*.
10:19 the *J* were sharply divided once more.
10:24 when the *J* gathered around him and said,
10:31 the *J* again reached for rocks to stone him,
10:33 that we are stoning you," the *J* retorted.
11: 8 the *J* only recently trying to stone you,
11:31 The *J* who were in the house with Mary
11:33 the *J* who had accompanied her also weeping,
11:36 to weep, which caused the *J* to remark,
11:45 many of the *J* who had come to visit Mary,
12: 9 of *J* discovered he was there and came out,
12:11 because many *J* were going over to Jesus
13:33 I say to you now what I once said to the *J*:
18:14 Caiaphas who had proposed to the *J*
18:20 temple area where all the *J* come together.
18:31 not put anyone to death," the *J* answered.
18:33 "Are you the king of the *J*?"
18:36 to save me from being handed over to the *J*.
18:38 went out again to the *J* and said to them:
18:39 me to release to you the king of the *J*?"
19: 3 to him and said, "All hail, king of the *J*!",
19: 7 "We have our law," the *J* responded,
19:12 eager to release him, but the *J* shouted,
19:14 He said to the *J*, "Look at your king!"
19:19 NAZOREAN THE KING OF THE *J*
19:20 and Greek, was read by many of the *J*,
19:21 priests of the *J* tried to tell Pilate,
19:21 not have written, 'The King of the *J*.'
19:21 to be King of the *J*.'" Pilate answered,
19:31 Since it was the Preparation Day the *J* did
19:38 (although a secret one for fear of the *J*),
20:19 place where they were for fear of the *J*,
Acts 2: 5 were devout *J* of every nation under heaven.
2:11 There are even visitors from Rome—all *J*,
2:14 "You who are *J*,
6: 9 Freedmen" (that is, the *J* from Cyrene,
9:23 passed, certain *J* conspired to kill Saul,
9:29 the Greek-speaking *J* and debated with them.
10:39 did in the land of the *J* and in Jerusalem.
11:19 making the message known to none but *J*.
12: 3 he saw that this pleased certain of the *J*,
12:11 clutches and from all that the *J* hoped for."
13:43 many *J* and devout Jewish converts followed
13:45 When the *J* saw the crowds,
13:50 But some of the *J* stirred up their
13:50 The *J* finally expelled them from their
14: 1 to convince a good number of *J* and Greeks.
14: 2 But the *J* who remained unconvinced stirred
14: 4 with the *J* and others with the apostles.
14: 5 A move was made by Gentiles and *J*,
14:19 some *J* from Antioch and Iconium arrived
16: 3 because of the *J* of that region,
16:20 Furthermore, they are *J*,
17: 4 Some of the *J* were convinced and threw in
17: 5 This only aroused the resentment of the *J*,
17:13 But when the *J* of Thessalonica learned
17:17 the *J* and those sympathetic to Judaism,
18: 2 Claudius had ordered all *J* to leave Rome.
18: 4 in which he persuaded certain *J* and Greeks.
18: 5 to the *J* that Jesus was the Messiah.
18:12 the *J* rose in a body against Paul and
18:14 in self-defense when Gallio said to the *J*:
18:14 you *J* a patient and reasonable hearing.
18:19 synagogue to hold discussions with the *J*.
19:10 the province of Asia, *J* and Greeks alike,
19:17 to the *J* and Greeks living in Ephesus,
19:33 Alexander, as the *J* pushed him forward.
20: 3 plot was hatched against him by certain *J*;
20:19 my way from the plottings of certain *J*.
20:21 With *J* and Greeks alike I insisted
21:11 'This is how the *J* in Jerusalem will bind
21:20 many thousands of *J* have come to believe,
21:21 teach the *J* who live among the Gentiles
21:27 *J* from the province of Asia recognized Paul
22: 5 letters to our brother *J* in Damascus.
22:12 spoken of by all the *J* who lived there,
22:30 which the *J* were bringing against him.
23:12 certain *J* formed a conspiracy in which
23:20 "The *J* have agreed among themselves to
23:27 whom the *J* seized and were about to murder.
24: 5 up sedition among the *J* all over the world.
24: 9 The *J* supported this indictment and
24:19 Certain *J* from the province of Asia are
24:27 wanted to ingratiate himself with the *J*,
25: 7 the *J* who had come down from Jerusalem
25: 8 no crime either against the law of the *J*
25:10 I have done the *J* no wrong,
25:15 chief priests and the elders of the *J*
26: 2 have been leveled against me by the *J*,
26: 4 later at Jerusalem, is well known to all *J*.
26: 7 Majesty, that I stand accused by the *J*.
26: 8 Let me ask why you, above all, who are *J*,
26:21 That is why the *J* seized me in the temple
28:19 When the *J* objected, I was forced
Rom 3: 2 the *J* were entrusted with words of God.
3: 9 have already brought the charge against *J*
3:29 Does God belong to the *J* alone?
9:24 whom he called, not only from among the *J*,
11:14 my fellow *J* to envy and save some of them.
11:23 And if the *J* do not remain in their
11:28 the *J* are enemies of God for your sake;
15: 8 Christ became the servant of the *J*
15:27 in the spiritual blessings of the *J*,
1Cor 1:22 *J* demand "signs" and Greeks look for
1:23 a stumbling block to *J*,
1:24 those who are called, *J* and Greeks alike,
9:20 a Jew to the Jews in order to win the *J*.
2Cor 11:24 of the *J* I received forty lashes less one;
Gal 2: 8 *J* had been at work in me for the Gentiles),
2: 9 should go to the Gentiles as they to the *J*.
2:13 rest of the *J* joined in his dissembling,
2:15 We are *J* by birth,
Eph 3: 6 the Gentiles are now co-heirs with the *J*,
1Thes 2:14 fellow countrymen as they did from the *J*
Rv 2: 9 slander you endure from self-styled *J*
3: 9 Jews who are not really *J* but frauds,

JEZANIAH (1)

Jer 40: 8 and *J* of Beth-maacah.

JEZEBEL (21)

1Kgs 16:31 He even married *J*, daughter of Ethbaal,
18: 4 *J* was murdering the prophets of the LORD,
18:13 what I did when *J* was murdering the
19: 1 Ahab told *J* all that Elijah had done
19: 2 *J* then sent a messenger to Elijah and said,
21: 5 His wife *J* came to him and said to him.
21: 7 his wife *J* said to him. "Get up.
21:11 did as *J* had ordered them in writing,
21:14 to *J* that Naboth had been stoned to death.

21:15 When *J* learned that Naboth had been stoned
21:23 (Against *J*, too, the LORD declared.
21:23 shall devour *J* in the district of Jezreel.")
21:25 LORD as did Ahab, urged on by his wife *J*.
2Kgs 9: 7 the other servants of the LORD shed by *J*,
9:10 shall devour *J* at the confines of Jezreel,
9:22 and witchcrafts of your mother *J* continue?"
9:30 *J* learned that Jehu had arrived in Jezreel,
9:36 of Jezreel dogs shall eat the flesh of *J*.
9:37 The corpse of *J* shall be like dung in the
9:37 that no one can say: This was *J*.'"
Rv 2:20 you tolerate a *J*—

JEZEBEL'S (1)

1Kgs 18:19 prophets of Asherah who eat at *J* table."

JEZER (3)

Gn 46:24 Jahzeel, Guni, *J*, and Shillem.
Nm 26:49 through *J* the clan of the Jezerites,
1Chr 7:13 The sons of Naphtali were Jahziel, Guni, *J*,

JEZERITES (1)

Nm 26:49 Gunites, through Jezer the clan of the *J*,

JEZIEL (1)

1Chr 12: 3 also *J* and Pelet,

JEZRAHIAH (1)

Neh 12:42 were heard under the leadership of *J*.

JEZREEL (41)

Jos 15:56 Maon, Carmel, Ziph, Juttah, *J*,
17:16 its towns, and those in the valley of *J*."
19:18 the clans of the Issacharites included *J*,
Jgs 6:33 and crossed over into the valley of *J*,
1Sm 25:43 wife, and David also married Ahinoam of *J*.
27: 3 his two wives, Ahinoam from *J* and Abigail,
28: 1 men must go out on campaign with me to *J*."
29: 1 encamped at the spring of Harod near *J*.
29:11 The Philistines, however, went on up to *J*.
30: 5 two wives, Ahinoam of *J* and Abigail,
2Sm 2: 2 his two wives, Ahinoam of *J* and Abigail,
2: 9 him king over Gilead, the Ashurites, *J*,
3: 2 his first-born, Amnon, of Ahinoam from *J*;
4: 4 news about Saul and Jonathan came from *J*,
1Kgs 4:12 below *J* from Beth-shean to Abel-meholah;
18:45 Ahab mounted his chariot and made for *J*.
18:46 before Ahab as far as the approaches to *J*.
21: 1 a vineyard in *J* next to the palace of Ahab,
21:23 shall devour Jezebel in the district of *J*.")
2Kgs 8:29 King Joram returned to *J* to be healed of
8:29 to *J* to visit him there in his illness.
9:10 shall devour Jezebel at the confines of *J*,
9:15 but had returned to *J* to be healed of the
9:15 one escapes from the city to report in *J*."
9:16 Jehu mounted his chariot and drove to *J*,
9:17 The watchman standing on the tower in *J*
9:30 learned that Jehu had arrived in *J*,
9:36 of *J* dogs shall eat the flesh of Jezebel.
9:37 dung in the field in the confines of *J*,
10: 6 and come to me in *J* at this time tomorrow."
10: 7 in baskets, and sent them to Jehu in *J*.
10:11 who were left of the family of Ahab in *J*,
1Chr 3: 1 the first-born, Amnon, by Ahinoam of *J*;
4: 3 *J*, Ishma, and Idbash; their sister
2Chr 22: 6 He returned to *J* to be healed of the
22: 6 down to visit Jehoram, son of Ahab, in *J*.
Hos 1: 4 Give him the name *J*,
1: 4 house of Jehu for the bloodshed at *J*
1: 5 break the bow of Israel in the valley of *J*.
2: 2 lands, for great shall be the day of *J*.
2:24 and oil, and these shall respond to *J*.

JEZREELITE (8)

1Kgs 21: 1 as Naboth the *J* had a vineyard in Jezreel
21: 4 at the answer Naboth the *J* had made to him:
21: 6 I spoke to Naboth the *J* and said to him,
21: 7 the vineyard of Naboth the *J* for you."
21:15 Naboth the *J* which he refused to sell you,
21:16 way down to the vineyard of Naboth the *J*,
2Kgs 9:21 reached him near the field of Naboth the *J*.
9:25 throw him into the field of Naboth the *J*.

JIBE (1)

Sir 11: 4 worn cloak and *j* at no man's bitter day:

JIDLAPH (1)

Gn 22:22 Chesed, Hazo, Pildash, *J* and Bethuel."

JOAB (134)

1Sm 26: 6 Abishai, son of Zeruiah and brother of *J*,
2Sm 2:13 *J*, son of Zeruiah, and David's servants
2:14 Then Abner said to *J*,
2:14 *J* replied, "All right!"
2:18 The three sons of Zeruiah were there *J*,
2:22 How could I face your brother *J*?"
2:24 *J* and Abishai,
2:26 Then Abner called to *J* and said:
2:27 *J* replied, "As God lives,
2:28 *J* then sounded the horn,
2:30 *J*, after interrupting the pursuit of Abner,
2:32 *J* and his men made an all-night march,
3:22 and *J* were coming in from an expedition,
3:23 When *J* and the whole force he had with him
3:24 So *J* went to the king and said:
3:26 *J* then left David,
3:27 *J* took him aside within the city gate as
3:29 of Ner, be laid to *J* and to all his family.
3:30 *J* and his brother Abishai had lain in wait
3:31 *J* and to all the people who were with him,
8:16 *J*, son of Zeruiah, was in command
10: 7 *J* with the entire levy of trained soldiers.
10: 9 When *J* saw the battle lines drawn up
10:11 *J* said, "If the Arameans are stronger
10:13 When *J* and the soldiers who were with him
10:14 *J* then ceased his attack on the Ammonites
11: 1 David sent out *J* along with his officers
11: 6 therefore sent a message to *J*,
11: 6 So *J* sent Uriah to David.
11: 7 he came, David questioned him about *J*,
11:11 and my lord *J* and your majesty's servants
11:14 wrote a letter to *J* which he sent by Uriah.
11:16 So while *J* was besieging the city,
11:17 men of the city made a sortie against *J*,
11:18 Then *J* sent David a report of all the
11:22 all the details as *J* had instructed him.
11:25 "This is what you shall convey to *J*:
12:26 *J* fought against Rabbah of the Ammonites
14: 1 When *J*,
14: 3 And *J* instructed her what to say.
14:19 "Is *J* involved with you in all this?"
14:19 It was your servant *J* who instructed me
14:20 Your servant *J* did this to come at the
14:21 Then the king said to *J*:
14:22 in homage and blessing the king, *J* said,
14:23 *J* then went off to Geshur and brought
14:29 Joab to send him to the king, but *J*
14:29 him a second time, *J* refused to come.
14:31 *J* went to Absalom in his house and asked
14:32 Absalom answered *J*:
14:33 *J* went to the king and reported this.
18: 2 Abishai, son of Zeruiah and brother of *J*,
18: 5 But the king gave this command to *J*,
18:10 Someone saw this and reported to *J* that he
18:11 *J* said to his informant:
18:12 But the man replied to *J*:
18:14 *J* replied, "I will not waste the time
18:16 *J* then sounded the horn,
18:16 because *J* called on them to halt.
18:20 But *J* said to him:
18:21 Then *J* said to a Cushite,
18:21 The Cushite bowed to *J* and sped away.
18:22 But Ahimaaz, son of Zadok, said to *J* again,
18:22 *J* replied: "Why do you want to run, my son?"
18:23 *J* said to him, "Very well."
18:29 the king's servant *J* sent your servant on,
19: 2 *J* was told that the king was weeping and
19: 6 Then *J* went to his residence and said:
19:14 my general permanently in place of *J*.'"
20: 7 So *J* and the Cherethites and Pelethites
20: 8 Now *J* had a belt over his tunic,
20: 9 And *J* asked Amasa,
20: 9 *J* held Amasa's beard as if to kiss him.
20:10 hand, *J* stabbed him in the abdomen with it,
20:10 *J* and his brother Abishai pursued Sheba,
20:11 who favors Joab and is for David follow *J*."
20:13 went on after *J* in pursuit of Sheba,
20:15 and all the soldiers who were with *J* began
20:16 Tell *J* to come here,
20:17 When *J* had come near her,
20:17 come near her, the woman said, "Are you *J*?"
20:20 *J* answered, "Not at all, not at all!
20:21 Then the woman said to *J*,
20:22 son of Bichri, and threw it out to *J*.
20:22 while *J* returned to Jerusalem to the King.
20:23 *J* was in command of the whole army of
23:18 Abishai, brother of *J*,
23:24 Asahel, brother of *J*. . . .
23:37 Naharai from Beeroth, armor-bearer of *J*,
24: 2 Accordingly the king said to *J* and the
24: 3 But *J* said to the king:
24: 4 overruled *J* and the leaders of the army,
24: 9 *J* then reported to the king the number of
1Kgs 1: 7 He conferred with *J*, son of Zeruiah,
1:19 king's sons, Abiathar the priest, and *J*,
1:41 When *J* heard the sound of the horn,
2: 5 You yourself know what *J*,
2:22 and has with him Abiathar the priest and *J*,
2:28 When the news came to *J*,
2:29 King Solomon was told that *J* had fled to
2:30 king, "This is what *J* said to me in reply."
2:31 the blood which *J* shed without provocation.
2:33 *J* and his descendants shall be responsible
11:15 Earlier, when David had conquered Edom, *J*,
11:16 *J* and all Israel remained there six months
11:21 rested with his ancestors and that *J*,
1Chr 2:16 Abishai, *J*, and Asahel.
4:14 Seraiah became the father of *J*
11: 6 *J*, the son of Zeruiah,
11: 8 while *J* restored the rest of the city.
11:20 Abishai,the brother of *J*.
11:26 Asahel, the brother of *J*;
11:39 from Beeroth, the armor-bearer of *J*,
18:15 *J*, son of Zeruiah,
19: 8 he sent *J* and his whole army of warriors
19:10 When *J* saw that there was a battle line
19:14 *J* therefore advanced with his men to
19:15 *J* then returned to Jerusalem.
20: 1 go to war, *J* led the army out in force,
20: 1 *J* had attacked Rabbah and destroyed it,
21: 2 to *J* and to the other generals of the army,
21: 3 But *J* replied:
21: 4 the king's command prevailed over *J*,
21: 5 *J* reported the result of the census to
21: 6 for the king's command was repugnant to *J*.
26:28 Saul, son of Kish, Abner, son of Ner, *J*,
27: 7 fourth month, was Asahel, brother of *J*,
27:24 *J*, son of Zeruiah,
27:34 The commander of the king's army was *J*.
Ezr 2: 6 who were sons of Jeshua and *J*,
8: 9 of the sons of *J*,
Neh 7:11 Pahath-moab who were sons of Jeshua and *J*,

JOAB'S (11)

2Sm 3:27 for the killing of *J* brother Asahel.
3:29 May the men of *J* family never be without
11: 3 wife of *J* armor-bearer] Uriah the Hittite."
14:30 "You see *J* field that borders mine,
14:30 *J* farmhands came to him with torn garments
17:25 Amasa in command of the army in *J* place.
17:25 of Jesse and sister of *J* mother Zeruiah.
18: 2 third part of the soldiers under *J* command,
18:15 *J* young armor-bearers closed in on Absalom,
20:10 guard against the sword in *J* other hand,
20:11 of *J* attendants stood by Amasa and said,

JOAH (11)

2Kgs 18:18 and the herald *J*,
18:26 and Shebnah and *J* said to the commander:
18:37 Shebnah the scribe, and the herald *J*,
1Chr 6: 6 whose son was Zimmah, whose son was *J*,
26: 4 first-born, Jehozabad, a second son, *J*,
2Chr 29:12 *J*, son of Zimmah, and Eden, son of Joah;
34: 8 Maaseiah, the ruler of the city, and *J*,
Is 36: 3 and Shebna the scribe, and the herald *J*,
36:11 and Shebna and *J* said to the commander,
36:22 Shebna the scribe, and the herald *J*,

JOAHAZ (1)

2Chr 34: 8 the ruler of the city, and Joah, son of *J*,

JOAKIM (10)

Jdt 4: 6 *J*, who was high priest in Jerusalem in
4: 8 carried out the orders given them by *J*,
4:14 The high priest *J*,
15: 8 priest *J* and the elders of the Israelites,
Dn 13: 1 In Babylon there lived a man named *J*,
13: 4 *J* was very rich;
13: 6 their cases, frequented the house of *J*.
13:28 people came to her husband *J* the next day,
13:29 the daughter of Hilkiah, the wife of *J*."
13:63 as did *J* her husband and all her relatives,

JOANAN (1)

Lk 3:27 son of Josech, son of Joda, son of *J*,

JOANNA (2)

Lk 8: 3 from whom seven devils had gone out, *J*,
24:10 The women were Mary of Magdala, *J*,

JOARIB (2)

1Mc 2: 1 son of Simeon, a priest of the family of *J*,
14:29 of the priest Mattathias, descendant of *J*,

JOASH (57)

Jgs 6:11 in Ophrah that belonged to *J* the Abiezrite.
6:29 to the conclusion that Gideon, son of *J*,
6:30 So the townspeople said to *J*,
6:31 But *J* replied to all who were standing
7:14 sword of the Israelite Gideon, son of *J*,"
8:13 Then Gideon, son of *J*,
8:29 Then Jerubbaal, son of *J*,
8:32 At a good old age Gideon, son of *J*,
8:32 his father *J* in Ophrah of the Abiezrites.
1Kgs 22:26 to Amon, prefect of the city, and to *J*,
2Kgs 11: 2 Jehoram and sister of Ahaziah, took *J*,
11:19 where *J* took his seat on the royal throne.
12: 1 *J* was seven years old when he became king.
12: 2 *J* began to reign in the seventh year of
12: 3 *J* did what was pleasing to the LORD as
12: 5 For the priests *J* made this rule:
12: 7 twenty-third year of the reign of King *J*,
12: 8 King *J* summoned the priest Jehoiada and
12:20 The rest of the acts of *J*,
13: 1 In the twenty-third year of *J*,
13: 9 His son *J* succeeded him as king.
13:10 In the thirty-seventh year of *J*,
13:12 [The rest of the acts of *J*,
13:13 *J* rested with his ancestors,
13:13 *J* was buried with the kings of Israel in

JOASH (cont.)
13:14 King J of Israel went down to visit him.
13:25 son Ben-hadad succeeded him as king, J,
13:25 J defeated Ben-hadad three times,
14: 1 In the second year of J,
14: 1 king of Israel, Amaziah, son of J,
14: 3 since he did just as his father J had done.
14:17 Amaziah, son of J,
14:23 the fifteenth year of Amaziah, son of J,
14:23 Joash, king of Judah, Jeroboam, son of J,
14:27 he saved them through Jeroboam, son of J.
1Chr 3:11 whose son was Ahaziah, whose son was J,
4:22 and J and Saraph,
7: 8 The sons of Becher were Zemirah, J,
12: 3 Ahiezer was their chief, along with J,
27:28 and over the stores of oil was J.
2Chr 18:25 of the city, and to J the king's son,
22:11 secretly took Ahaziah's son J from among
24: 1 J was seven years old when he became king,
24: 2 J did what was pleasing to the LORD as
24: 4 J decided to restore the LORD's temple.
24:22 Thus King J was unmindful of the devotion
24:23 year a force of Arameans came up against J.
24:24 So punishment was meted out to J.
25:17 Amaziah of Judah sent messengers to J,
25:18 King J of Israel sent this reply to King
25:21 Therefore King J of Israel advanced and he
25:23 King J of Israel captured Amaziah,
25:23 captured Amaziah, king of Judah, son of J,
25:25 Amaziah, son of J, king of Judah, survived
Hos 1: 1 and in the days of Jeroboam, son of J,
Am 1: 1 and in the days of Jeroboam, son of J,

JOB (59)
Jb 1: 1 was a blameless and upright man named J,
1: 5 J would send for them and sanctify them,
1: 5 For J said, "It may be that my sons
1: 5 This J did habitually.
1: 8 to Satan, "Have you noticed my servant J,
1: 9 "Is it for nothing that J is God-fearing?
1:14 brother, a messenger came to J and said,
1:20 Then J began to tear his cloak and cut off
1:22 In all this J did not sin,
2: 3 to Satan, "Have you noticed my servant J,
2: 7 smote J with severe boils from the soles
2:10 Through all this, J said nothing sinful.
3: 1 J opened his mouth and cursed his day.
3: 2 J spoke out and said:
6: 1 Then J answered and said:
9: 1 Then J answered and said:
12: 1 Then J replied and said:
16: 1 Then J answered and said:
19: 1 Then J answered and said:
21: 1 Then J said in reply:
23: 1 Again J answered and said:
26: 1 Then J spoke again and said:
29: 1 J took up his theme anew and said;
31:37 The words of J are ended.
32: 1 Then the three men ceased to answer J,
32: 2 He was angry with J for considering
32: 3 a good answer and had not condemned J.
32: 4 Elihu bided his time before addressing J.
32:12 behold, there is none who has convicted J,
33: 1 Therefore, O J, hear my discourse
33:31 Be attentive, O J; listen to me!
34: 5 For J has said, "I am innocent,
34: 7 What man is like J?
34:16 Now, do you, O J, hear this!
34:35 J speaks without intelligence,
34:36 Let J be tried to the limit,
35:16 Yet J to no purpose opens his mouth,
37:14 Hearken to this, O J!
38: 1 LORD addressed J out of the storm and said:
40: 1 The LORD then said to J:
40: 3 Then J answered the LORD and said:
40: 6 LORD addressed J out of the storm and said:
42: 1 Then J answered the LORD and said:
42: 7 the LORD had spoken these words to J,
42: 7 rightly concerning me, as has my servant J.
42: 8 and seven rams, and go to my servant J,
42: 8 and let my servant J pray for you;
42: 8 rightly concerning me, as has my servant J."
42: 9 the LORD accepted the intercession of J.
42:10 the LORD restored the prosperity of J,
42:10 gave to J twice as much as he had before.
42:12 days of J more than his earlier ones.
42:15 were as beautiful as the daughters of J;
42:16 this, J lived a hundred and forty years;
42:17 Then J died, old and full of years.
Sir 49: 9 He also referred to J,
Ez 14:14 three men were in it, Noah, Daniel, and J,
14:20 even if Noah, Daniel, and J were in it,
Jas 5:11 You have heard of the steadfastness of J,

JOBAB (9)
Gn 10:29 Obal, Abimael, Sheba, Ophir, Havilah, and J.
36:33 When Bela died, J, son of Zerah,
36:34 When J died,
Jos 11: 1 learned of this, he sent a message to J,
1Chr 1:23 Abimael, Sheba, Ophir, Havilah, and J;
1:44 When Bela died, J, son of Zerah,
1:45 When J died, Husham, from the land
8: 9 his wife Hodesh he became the father of J,
8:18 Izliah, and J were the sons of Elpaal.

JOB'S (1)
Jb 2:11 Now when three of J friends heard of all

JOCHANAN (2)
Sir 50: 1 people, was SIMON the priest, son of J,
50:11 Son of J When he received the sundered

JOCHEBED (2)
Ex 6:20 Amram married his aunt J,
Nm 26:59 Kohath was Amram, whose wife was named J.

JODA (1)
Lk 3:26 son of Semein, son of Josech, son of J,

JOED (1)
Neh 11: 7 Sallu, son of Meshullam, son of J,

JOEL (21)
1Sm 8: 2 His first-born was named J,
1Chr 4:35 Jamlech, Joshah, son of Amaziah, J,
5: 4 His son was J, whose son was Shemaiah,
5: 8 Bela, son of Azaz, son of Shema, son of J.
5:12 J was chief, Shapham was second
6:13 The sons of Samuel were J,
6:18 Heman, the chanter, son of J,
6:21 son of Amasi, son of Elkanah, son of J,
7: 3 sons of Izarahiah were Michael, Obadiah, J,
11:38 J, brother of Nathan,
15: 7 of the sons of Gershon, J,
15:11 and the Levites Uriel, Asaiah, J,
15:17 the Levites appointed Heman, son of J,
23: 8 Jehiel the chief, then Zetham and J;
26:22 of Jehiel, Zetham and his brother J,
27:20 for the half-tribe of Manasseh, J,
2Chr 29:12 Mahath, son of Amasai, and J,
Ezr 10:43 Mattithiah, Zabad, Zebina, Jaddai, J,
Neh 11: 9 J son of Zichri, was their commander,
Jl 1: 1 The word of the LORD which came to J,
Acts 2:16 No, it is what J the prophet spoke of:

JOELAH (1)
1Chr 12: 8 J, finally, and Zebadiah,

JOEZER (1)
1Chr 12: 7 Elkanah, Isshiah, Azarel, J,

JOGBEHAH (2)
Nm 32:35 Ataroth, Aroer, Atroth-shophan, Jazer, J,
Jgs 8:11 route of the nomads east of Nobah and J,

JOGLI (1)
Nm 34:22 Bukki, son of J

JOHA (2)
1Chr 8:16 Ishpah, and J were the sons of Beriah.
11:45 Jediael, son of Shimri, and J,

JOHANAN (28)
2Kgs 25:23 Ishmael, son of Nethaniah, J,
1Chr 3:15 the first-born J;
3:24 were Hodaviah, Eliashib, Pelaiah, Akkub, J,
5:35 Azariah became the father of J.
5:36 J became the father of Azariah,
12: 5 J; Jozabad from Gederah;
12:13 Attai sixth, Eliel seventh, J eighth,
2Chr 28:12 the Ephraimite leaders, Azariah, son of J,
Ezr 8:12 of the sons of Azgad, J,
10: 6 house of God and entered the chamber of J,
Neh 12:11 father of J, and Johanan became
12:22 In the time of Eliashib, Joiada, J,
12:23 Book of Chronicles, up until the time of J,
Jer 40: 8 J, son of Kareah;
40:13 Now J, son of Kareah, and all of the leaders
40:15 Then J, son of Kareah, said secretly
40:16 Gedaliah, son of Ahikam, answered J,
41:11 But when J, son of Kareah, and the other
41:13 At the sight of J,
41:14 brought away from Mizpah went over to J,
41:15 J and fled to the Ammonites with eight men.
41:16 Then J, son of Kareah, and all of his army
42: 1 Then all the army leaders, J,
42: 8 Then he called J, son of Kareah,
43: 2 him to them, Azariah, son of Hoshaiah, J,
43: 4 J, son of Kareah, and the rest of the
43: 5 Instead, J,

JOHN (148)
1Mc 2: 1 In those days Mattathias, son of J,
2: 2 J, who was called Gaddi;
8:17 So Judas chose Eupolemus, son of J,
9:36 and carried off J and everything he had.
9:38 Remembering the blood of J their brother,
13:53 Seeing that his son J was now a grown man,
16: 1 J then went up from Gazara and told his
16: 2 called his two oldest sons, Judas and J,
16: 4 J then mustered in the land twenty
16: 6 J and his men took their position against
16: 6 to cross the stream, J crossed first.
16: 9 but J pursued them until Cendebeus reached
16:10 plain of Azotus, but J set fire to these,
16:19 sent other men to Gazara to do away with J.
16:21 brought word to J at Gazara
16:22 On hearing this, J was utterly astounded.
16:23 Now the rest of the history of J,
2Mc 4:11 to the Jews through the mediation of J,
11:17 J and Absalom, your envoys,
Mt 3: 1 When J the Baptizer made his appearance as
3: 4 J was clothed in a garment of camel's hair,
3:13 J at the Jordan to be baptized by him.
3:14 J tried to refuse him with the protest,
3:15 So J gave in.
4:12 When Jesus heard that J had been arrested,
4:21 James, Zebedee's son, and his brother J.
10: 2 James, Zebedee's son, and his brother J;
11: 2 Now J in prison heard about the works
11: 4 back and report to J what you hear and see:
11: 7 Jesus began to speak to the crowds about J:
11:11 born of woman greater than J the Baptizer.
11:12 From J the Baptizer's time until now the
11:13 as the law spoke prophetically until J.
11:18 J appeared neither eating nor drinking,
14: 2 courtiers, "This man is J the Baptizer
14: 3 Recall that Herod had had J arrested,
14: 4 That was because J had told him,
14: 5 to kill J but was afraid of the people,
14: 8 me the head of J the Baptizer on a platter."
14:10 the order to have J beheaded in prison.
16:14 They replied, "Some say J the Baptizer,
17: 1 and his brother J and led them up on a
17:13 been speaking to them about J the Baptizer.
21:26 the people, who all regard J as a prophet."
21:32 When J came preaching a way of holiness,
Mk 1: 4 that J the Baptizer appeared in the desert,
1: 6 J was clothed in camel's hair,
1: 9 and was baptized in the Jordan by J.
1:19 of James, Zebedee's son, and his brother J.
1:29 house of Simon and Andrew with James and J.
3:17 and J, the brother of James
5:37 except Peter, James, and James' brother J.
6:14 J the Baptizer has been raised from the
6:16 On hearing of Jesus, Herod exclaimed, J,
6:17 was the one who had ordered J arrested,
6:18 That was because J had told Herod,
6:20 Herod feared J,
6:24 answered, "The head of J the Baptizer."
6:25 the head of J the Baptizer on a platter."
6:28 The man went and beheaded J in the prison.
8:28 They replied, "Some, J the Baptizer,
9: 2 and J off by themselves with him and led
9:38 J said to him, "Teacher, we saw a man
10:35 Zebedee's sons, James and J,
10:41 this, became indignant at James and J.
11:32 who all regarded J as a true prophet.)
13: 3 Olives facing the temple, Peter, James, J,
14:33 he took along with him Peter, James, and J.
Lk 1:13 shall bear a son whom you shall name J.
1:60 saying, "No, he is to be called J."
1:63 and wrote the words, "His name is J."
3: 2 spoken to J son of Zechariah in the desert.
3:15 hearts whether J might be the Messiah.
3:16 J answered them all by saying:
3:19 censured by J on the subject of Herodias,
3:20 to his guilt by shutting J up in prison.
5:10 all his shipmates, as well as James and J,
6:14 and Andrew his brother, James and J,
7:18 The disciples of J brought their teacher
7:19 two of them, J sent them to ask the Lord,
7:20 J the Baptizer sends us to you with this
7:22 report to J what you have seen and heard.
7:24 When the messengers of J had set off,
7:28 is no man born of woman greater than J.
7:29 from J the baptismal bath he administered.
7:33 I mean that J the Baptizer came neither
8:51 no one to enter with him except Peter, J,
9: 7 saying, J has been raised from the dead";
9: 9 But Herod said, J I beheaded.
9:19 J the Baptizer," they replied,
9:28 saying this he took Peter, J and James,
9:49 It was J who said,
9:54 When his disciples James and J saw this,
11: 1 us to pray, as J taught his disciples."
16:16 law and the prophets were in force until J.
20: 4 the baptism of J come from God or from men
20: 6 so convinced are they that J was a prophet."
22: 8 sent Peter and J off with the instruction,
Jn 1: 6 There was a man named J sent by God,
1:15 J testified to him by proclaiming:
1:19 The testimony J gave when the Jews sent
1:26 J answered them: I baptize with water
1:28 across the Jordan, where J was baptizing.
1:29 J caught sight of Jesus coming toward him,
1:32 J gave this testimony also:
1:35 The next day J was there again
1:40 hearing J was Simon Peter's brother Andrew.
1:42 him and said, "You are Simon, son of J;
3:23 J too was baptizing at Aenon near Salim
3:24 J, of course, had not yet been thrown

3:26 So they came to *J*, saying, "Rabbi, the man
3:27 *J* answered: "No one can lay hold on
4: 1 baptizing more disciples than *J* (in fact,
5:33 You have sent to *J*,
10:40 place where *J* had been baptizing earlier,
10:41 *J* may never have performed a sign,"
10:41 whatever *J* said about this man was true."
21:15 said to Simon Peter, "Simon, son of *J*,
21:16 he put his question, "Simon, son of *J*,
21:17 time, Jesus asked him, "Simon, son of *J*,
Acts 1: 5 *J* baptized with water,
1:13 Peter and *J* and James and Andrew;
1:22 of *J* until the day he was taken up from us,
3: 1 when Peter and *J* were going up to the
3: 3 When he saw Peter and *J* on their way in,
3: 4 Peter fixed his gaze on the man; so did *J*.
3:11 man stood there clinging to Peter and *J*,
4: 1 and *J* were still addressing the crowd,
4: 6 Annas the high priest, Caiaphas, *J*,
4: 7 They brought Peter and *J* before them and
4:13 the self-assurance of Peter and *J*,
4:19 Peter and *J* answered,
8:14 word of God, they sent Peter and *J* to them.
10:37 in Galilee with the baptism *J* preached;
11:16 *J* baptized with water but you will be
12: 2 He beheaded James the brother of *J*,
12:12 Mary the mother of *J* (also known as Mark),
12:25 relief mission, taking with them *J* Mark.
13: 5 *J* accompanying them as an assistant.
13:13 *J* left them and returned to Jerusalem.
13:24 *J* heralded the coming of Jesus by
15:37 Barnabas wanted to take along *J*,
19: 3 They replied, "With the baptism of *J*."
Gal 2: 9 pillars, James, Cephas, and *J*,
Rv 1: 1 by sending his angel to his servant *J*,
1: 4 *J* wishes you grace and peace
1: 9 I, *J*, your brother, who share with you
22: 8 It is I, *J*, who heard and saw all these

JOHN'S (14)

1Mc 16: 9 was then that *J* brother Judas fell wounded;
Mt 9:14 *J* disciples came to him with the objection,
14:11 *J* head was brought in on a platter and
21:25 What was the origin of *J* baptism?
Mk 1:14 After *J* arrest,
2:18 Now *J* disciples and the Pharisees were
2:18 "Why do *J* disciples and those of the
11:30 was *J* baptism of divine origin or merely
Lk 5:33 *J* disciples fast frequently and offer
Jn 3:25 between *J* disciples and a certain Jew.
5:36 Yet I have testimony greater than *J*,
Acts 13:25 As *J* career was coming to an end,
18:25 Jesus, although he knew only of *J* baptism.
19: 4 *J* baptism was a baptism of repentance.

JOIADA (5)

Neh 3: 6 New City Gate was repaired by *J*,
12:10 and Eliashib became the father of *J*.
12:11 *J* became the father of Johanan,
12:22 In the time of Eliashib, *J*,
13:28 One of the sons of *J*, son of Eliashib

JOIAKIM (4)

Neh 12:10 Joiakim, *J* became the father of Eliashib,
12:12 of *J* these were the priestly family heads:
12:26 All these lived in the time of *J*,

JOIARIB (4)

Neh 11: 5 son of Hazaiah, son of Adaiah, son of *J*,
11:10 *J*; Jachin; Seraiah, son of Hilkaiah,
12: 6 Mijamin, Maadiah, Bilgah, Shemaiah, and *J*,
12:19 and for *J*,

JOIN (58)

Gn 15:15 however, shall *j* your forefathers in peace;
33:14 of my children, until I *j* my lord in Seir."
Ex 1:10 too may *j* our enemies to fight against us,
12: 4 it shall *j* the nearest household in
12:48 *j* in its observance just like the natives.
23: 1 Do not *j* the wicked in putting your hand,
26: 6 with which to *j* the two sets of sheets,
26:11 the loops, to *j* the tent into one whole.
28:27 next to where they *j* the ephod in front,
Lv 20: 5 who *j* him in his wanton worship of Molech.
Nm 27: 3 Although he did not *j* those who banded
Dt 2:32 advanced against us to *j* battle at Jahaz;
13:10 the rest of the people shall *j* in with you.
17: 7 afterward all the people are to *j* in.
1Sm 6:19 The descendants of Jeconiah did not *j* in
7:10 advanced to *j* battle with Israel.
10: 6 and you will *j* them in their prophetic
14:21 *j* the Israelites under Saul and Jonathan.
16: 5 yourselves and *j* me today for the banquet."
2Sm 12:28 *j* the siege against the city and capture
2Kgs 3: 7 Will you *j* me in battle against Moab?"
1Chr 12:18 help me, I am of a mind to have you *j* me.
13: 2 with pasture lands, that they may *j* us;
17:11 been completed and you must *j* your fathers,
2Chr 2: 6 to *j* the craftsmen who are with me in
22: 7 downfall that he should *j* Jehoram,
Ezr 6:21 of the land to *j* them in seeking the LORD,
Neh 4:14 you hear the trumpet sound, *j* us there;
10:30 *j* with their brethren who are their
Tb 3: 9 Then why not *j* them!
Est 9:27 descendants, and all who should *j* them,
2Mc 11: 7 and he exhorted the others to *j* him in
Ps(s) 49:20 He shall *j* the circle of his forebears who
118:27 *J* in procession with leafy boughs up to
Eccl 8: 3 do not *j* in with a base plot,
Is 5: 8 Woe to you who *j* house to house who
14: 1 the aliens will *j* them and be counted with
56: 3 say, when he would *j* himself to the LORD,
56: 6 foreigners who *j* themselves to the LORD,
Jer 3:18 house of Judah will *j* the house of Israel;
50: 5 let us *j* ourselves to the LORD with
Ez 37:17 Then *j* the two sticks together,
37:19 him, and I will *j* to it the stick of Judah,
Dn 11:34 but many shall *j* them out of treachery.
Zec 2:15 shall *j* themselves to the LORD on that day,
Mt 9:10 to *j* Jesus and his disciples at dinner.
18:19 if two of you *j* your voices on earth to
Jn 21: 3 "We will *j* you," they replied,
Acts 5:13 No one else dared to *j* them,
9:26 he tried to *j* the disciples there;
15:38 refusing to *j* them on that mission,
17:15 and Timothy to *j* him as soon as possible.
17:34 A few did *j* him,
21:24 *j* with them in their rite of purification;
Rom 15:30 *j* me in the struggle by your prayers to
2Tm 4: 9 Do your best to *j* me soon,
Heb 13:23 If he is able to *j* me soon,
Jude 1:12 They *j* your solemn feasts without shame

JOINED (68)

Gn 14: 3 *j* forces in the Valley of Siddim (that is,
14:24 the share that is due to the men who *j* me
48: 5 in the land of Egypt before I *j* you here,
49: 6 or my spirit be *j* with their company;
Ex 28: 7 of shoulder straps *j* to its two upper ends.
36:13 *j* so that the Dwelling formed one whole.
36:18 the tent was *j* so that it formed one whole.
39: 4 made for it and *j* to its two upper ends.
39:20 next to where they *j* the ephod in front,
Jos 10: 6 mountain country have *j* forces against us."
11: 5 All these kings *j* forces and marched to
15: 4 it crossed to Azmon and then *j* the Wadi of
Jgs 4: 9 *j* Barak and journeyed with him to Kedesh.
11: 3 A rabble had *j* company with him,
1Sm 10:10 so that he *j* them in their prophetic state.
17:14 While the three oldest had *j* Saul.
22: 2 He was *j* by all those who were in
28:23 his servants *j* the woman in urging him,
1Kgs 6:10 temple, to which it was *j* by cedar beams.
20:29 On the seventh day battle was *j*,
2Kgs 8:28 He *j* Joram,
2Chr 13: 3 Abijah *j* battle with a force of four
13: 7 scoundrels, *j* him and overcame Rehoboam,
20:36 He *j* with him in building ships to sail to
20:37 saying, "Because you have *j* with Ahaziah,
Neh 12:43 The women and the children *j* in,
1Mc 1:52 law, *j* them and committed evil in the land.
2:16 Many of Israel *j* them,
2:42 Then they were *j* by a group of Hasideans,
2:43 the disaster *j* them and supported them.
3: 2 and all who had *j* his father supported him,
3:41 from Idumea and from Philistia *j* with them.
4:14 The battle was *j* and the Gentiles were
5:15 Galilee had *j* forces to destroy them.
6:21 besieged escaped, *j* by impious Israelites;
7:39 at Beth-horon, where the Syrian army *j* him.
9:47 When they *j* battle, Jonathan raised his
10:49 The two kings *j* battle,
10:74 and Simon his brother *j* him to help him.
11:69 out of their places and *j* in the battle.
13:45 of the city, *j* by their wives and children,
2Mc 1:23 a prayer, and all present *j* in with them,
4:34 through sworn pledges with right hands *j*,
8:23 division and *j* in battle with Nicanor.
10:28 As soon as dawn broke, the armies *j* battle,
13: 3 Menelaus also *j* them,
13:12 When they had all *j* in doing this,
Jb 41: 9 So *j* one to another that they hold fast
Mt 19: 6 let no man separate what God has *j*."
23:30 *j* them in shedding the prophets' blood.'
27:41 and the elders also *j* in the jeering:
Mk 2:15 sinners *j* him and his disciples at dinner.
3:13 himself had decided on, who came and *j* him.
10: 9 let no man separate what God has *j*."
15:31 and the scribes also *j* in and jeered:
Lk 5:29 in which he was *j* by a large crowd of tax
Jn 6:17 was dark, and Jesus had still not *j* them;
18:18 *j* them and stood there warming himself.
Acts 5:36 About four hundred men *j* him.
13:36 God's will, fell asleep and *j* his fathers,
16:22 The crowd *j* in the attack on them,
17: 2 Paul *j* the people there and conducted
20: 6 Five days later we *j* them in Troas,
1Cor 6:16 Can you not see that the man who is *j* to a
6:17 *j* to the Lord becomes one spirit with him.
Gal 2:13 The rest of the Jews *j* in his dissembling,
Eph 4:16 proper functioning of the members *j*
Heb 10:34 You even *j* in the sufferings of those who

JOINING (1)

Ez 37: 7 as the bones came together, bone *j* bone.

JOINT (2)

1Sm 23:18 a *j* agreement before the LORD in Horesh,
Ez 29: 7 throwing every shoulder out of *j*;

JOINTED (1)

Lv 11:21 that have *j* legs for leaping on the ground;

JOINTS (7)

1Kgs 22:34 of Israel between the *j* of his breastplate.
2Chr 18:33 of Israel between the *j* of his breastplate.
Ez 24: 4 *j* taken from the pick of the flock.
24: 5 boil these pieces and the *j* that are in it.
Dn 5: 6 thoughts terrified him, his hip *j* shook,
Col 2:19 supported and upheld by *j* and sinews,
Heb 4:12 and divides soul and spirit, *j* and marrow;

JOKDEAM (1)

Jos 15:56 Maon, Carmel, Ziph, Juttah, Jezreel, *J*,

JOKIM (1)

1Chr 4:22 the linen weavers' guild in Bethashbea, *J*;

JOKING (2)

Gn 19:14 But his sons-in-law thought he was *j*.
Prv 26:19 neighbor, and then says, "I was only *j*."

JOKMEAM (1)

1Kgs 4:12 in Taanach and Megiddo, and beyond *J*,

JOKNEAM (4)

Jos 12:22 Taanach, Megiddo, Kedesh, *J* (at Carmel),
19:11 Dabbesheth and the wadi that is near *J*.
21:34 four cities of *J* with its pasture lands,
1Chr 6:62 *J* with its pasture lands,

JOKSHAN (4)

Gn 25: 2 She bore him Zimran, *J*,
25: 3 *J* became the father of Sheba and Dedan.
1Chr 1:32 she bore Zimran, *J*,
1:32 The sons of *J* were Sheba and Dedan.

JOKTAN (6)

Gn 10:25 and the name of his brother was *J*.
10:26 *J* became the father of Almodad,
10:29 All these were descendants of *J*.
1Chr 1:19 world was divided), and his brother was *J*.
1:20 *J* became the father of Almodad,
1:23 all these were the sons of *J*.

JOKTHEEL (2)

Jos 15:38 Hadashah, Migdal-gad, Dilean, Mizpeh, *J*,
2Kgs 14: 7 He renamed it *J*,

JONADAB (11)

2Sm 13: 3 Now Amnon had a friend named *J*,
13: 5 *J* replied, "Lie down on your bed
13:32 But *J*,
13:35 So *J* said to the king:
Jer 35: 6 *J*, Rechab's son, our father, forbade us
35: 8 Now we have heeded *J*,
35:10 do everything our father *J* commanded us.
35:14 The advice of *J*, Rechab's son, by which
35:16 Yes, the children of *J*, Rechab's son,
35:18 Since you have obeyed the command of *J*,
35:19 shall there fail to be a descendant of *J*,

JONAH (29)

2Kgs 14:25 through his servant, the prophet *J*,
Jon 1: 1 is the word of the LORD that came to *J*,
1: 3 But *J* made ready to flee to Tarshish away
1: 5 *J* had gone down into the hold of the ship,
1: 7 So they cast lots, and thus singled out *J*.
1: 9 *J* answered them; "I worship the LORD
1:12 *J* said to them, "Pick me up and throw me
1:15 they took *J* and threw him into the sea,
2: 1 LORD sent a large fish, that swallowed *J*;
2: 2 of the fish *J* said this prayer to the LORD,
2:11 the fish to spew *J* upon the shore.
3: 1 word of the LORD came to *J* a second time:
3: 3 So *J* made ready and went to Nineveh,
3: 4 *J* began his journey through the city,
4: 1 But this was greatly displeasing to *J*,
4: 5 *J* then left the city for a place to the
4: 6 *J* was very happy over the plant.
4: 9 But God said to *J*,
4: 9 "I have reason to be angry," *J* answered,
Mt 12:39 will be given it but that of the prophet *J*.
12:40 Just as *J* spent three days and three
12:41 preaching of *J* they reformed their lives;
12:41 but you have a greater than *J* here.
16: 4 no sign will be given it except that of *J*."
16:17 replied, "Blest are you, Simon son of *J*!
Lk 11:29 sign will be given it except the sign of *J*.

JONAH (cont.)

11:30 Just as *J* was a sign for the Ninevites,
11:32 For at the preaching of *J* they reformed,
11:32 but you have a greater than *J* here.

JONAH'S (2)

Jon 4: 6 a gourd plant, that grew up over *J* head,
4: 8 sun beat upon *J* head

JONAM (1)

Lk 3:30 son of Judah, son of Joseph, son of *J*,

JONATHAN (214)

Jgs 18:30 up the carved idol for themselves, and *J*,
1Sm 13: 2 were with *J* in Gibeah of Benjamin.
13: 3 Now *J* overcame the Philistine garrison
13:16 Saul, his son *J*, and the soldiers they had
13:22 of any of the soldiers with Saul or *J*.
13:22 Only Saul and his son *J* had them.
14: 1 One day *J*, son of Saul, said to his
14: 3 Nor did the soldiers know that *J* had gone.
14: 4 Flanking the ravine through which *J*
14: 6 *J* said to his armor-bearer:
14: 8 *J* continued: "We shall go over to those men
14:12 outpost called to *J* and his armor-bearer.
14:12 So *J* said to his armor-bearer,
14:13 *J* clambered up with his armor-bearer
14:14 In this first exploit *J* and his
14:17 they found *J* and his armor-bearer missing.
14:21 to join the Israelites under Saul and *J*.
14:27 *J*, who had not heard that his father had
14:29 *J* replied: "My father brings trouble
14:39 Israel, even if my son *J* has committed it,
14:40 and I and my son *J* will stand on the other."
14:41 blame for this resides in me or my son *J*,
14:41 *J* and Saul were designated,
14:42 said, "Cast lots between me and my son *J*."
14:42 And *J* was designated.
14:43 Saul said to *J*, "Tell me what you have done."
14:43 *J* replied, "I only tasted a little honey
14:44 and so to me if you do not indeed die, *J*!"
14:45 "Is *J* to die,
14:45 soldiers were able to rescue *J* from death.
14:49 The sons of Saul were *J*,
18: 1 *J* had become as fond of David as if his
18: 3 And *J* entered into a bond with David,
18: 4 *J* divested himself of the mantle he was
19: 1 with his son *J* and with all his servants.
19: 1 But Saul's son *J*, who was very fond of
19: 4 *J* then spoke well of David to his father
19: 7 So *J* summoned David and repeated the whole
19: 7 *J* then brought David to Saul,
20: 1 from the sheds near Ramah, and went to *J*.
20: 2 *J* answered him:
20: 3 *J* must not know of this lest he be grieved.'
20: 4 *J* then said to David, "I will do whatever
20: 9 But *J* answered: "Not I."
20:10 David then asked *J*,
20:11 *J* replied to David
20:12 the open country together, *J* said to David:
20:13 may the LORD do thus and so to *J* if I do
20:16 The name of *J* must never be allowed by the
20:17 love for David, *J* renewed his oath to him,
20:18 *J* then said to him: "Tomorrow is the new
20:25 place against the wall, *J* sat facing him,
20:27 Saul inquired of his son *J*,
20:28 *J* answered Saul: "David urgently asked me
20:30 was extremely angry with *J* and said to him:
20:32 But *J* asked his father Saul:
20:33 and thus *J* learned that his father was
20:34 *J* sprang up from the table in great anger
20:35 The next morning *J* went out into the field
20:37 where *J* had shot the arrow Jonathan
20:39 only *J* and David knew what was meant.
20:40 Then *J* gave his weapons to this boy of his
20:41 the ground three times before *J* in homage.
20:42 At length *J* said to David,
21: 1 his way, while *J* went back into the city.
23:16 in the barrens near Ziph, Saul's son, *J*,
23:18 remained, while *J* returned to his home.
31: 2 Saul and his sons closely, and slew *J*,
2Sm 1: 4 were dead, among them Saul and his son *J*.
1: 5 you know that Saul and his son *J* are dead?"
1:12 until evening for Saul and his son *J*,
1:17 chanted this elegy for Saul and his son *J*,
1:22 valiant, The bow of *J* did not turn back,
1:23 Saul and *J*, beloved and cherished,
1:26 "I grieve for you, *J* my brother!
4: 4 *J*, son of Saul, had a son named
4: 4 news about Saul and *J* came from Jezreel,
9: 1 whom I may show kindness for the sake of *J*?"
9: 6 When Meribbaal, son of *J*,
9: 7 kind to you for the sake of your father *J*.
15:27 your own son Ahimaaz, and Abiathar's son *J*.
15:36 Zadok's son Ahimaaz and Abiathar's son *J*.
17:17 Now *J* and Ahimaaz were staying at En-rogel,
17:20 they asked, "Where are Ahimaaz and *J*?"
17:21 Ahimaaz and *J* came up out of the cistern
21: 7 king, however, spared Meribbaal, son of *J*,
21: 7 a bond between David and Saul's son *J*.
21:12 son *J* from the citizens of Jabesh-gilead,
21:13 there the bones of Saul and of his son *J*,
21:14 Then the bones of Saul and of his son *J*
21:21 And when he insulted Israel, *J*,
23:32 *J*,
1Kgs 1:42 As he was speaking, *J*, son of Abiathar
1:43 *J* answered him. Our lord King David
1Chr 2:32 the brother of Shammai, were Jether and *J*.
2:33 The sons of *J* were Peleth and Zaza.
8:33 Saul became the father of *J*,
8:34 The son of *J* was Meribbaal,
9:39 Saul became the father of *J*,
9:40 The son of *J* was Meribbaal,
10: 2 When the Philistines had killed *J*,
11:34 *J*, son of Shagee, from En-harod;
20: 7 He defied Israel, and *J*,
27:25 cities, the villages, and the towers was *J*,
27:32 *J*, David's uncle and a man of intelligence,
Ezr 8: 6 of the sons of Adin, Ebed, son of *J*,
10:15 Only *J*,
Neh 12:14 for Malluch, *J*;
12:35 trumpets, and also Zechariah, son of *J*,
1Mc 2: 5 Avaran; and *J*, who was called Apphus.
4:30 camp of the Philistines into the hand of *J*,
5:17 I and my brother *J* will go to Gilead."
5:24 Judas Maccabeus and his brother *J* crossed
5:55 Judas and *J* were in the land of Gilead,
9:19 *J* and Simon took their brother Judas and
9:22 Bacchides and *J*.
9:28 of Judas came together and said to *J*:
9:31 From that moment *J* accepted the leadership,
9:33 But *J* and his brother Simon and all the
9:35 *J* sent his brother as leader of the convoy
9:37 was brought to *J* and his brother Simon:
9:44 Then *J* said to his companions,
9:47 *J* raised his arm to strike Bacchides,
9:48 *J* and his men jumped into the Jordan and
9:58 *J* and his companions are living in peace
9:60 telling them to seize *J* and his companions.
9:62 Then *J* and Simon and their companions
9:65 Leaving his brother Simon in the city, *J*,
9:70 *J* learned of this and sent ambassadors to
9:71 He agreed to do as *J* had asked.
9:73 *J* settled in Michmash;
10: 3 a letter to *J* written in peaceful terms,
10: 7 Accordingly *J* went up to Jerusalem and
10: 9 They released the hostages to *J*,
10:10 Thereafter *J* dwelt in Jerusalem,
10:15 the promises that Demetrius had made to *J*;
10:15 the battles and valiant deeds of *J*
10:17 he sent *J* a letter written in these terms:
10:18 Alexander sends greetings to his brother *J*.
10:21 *J* put on the sacred vestments in the
10:46 When *J* and the people heard these words,
10:59 also wrote to *J* to come and meet him.
10:62 He ordered *J* to be divested of his
10:66 So *J* returned in peace and happiness to
10:69 he sent this message to *J* the high priest:
10:74 When *J* heard this message of Apollonius,
10:76 gates, and so *J* took possession of Joppa.
10:78 *J* followed him to Azotus,
10:80 When *J* discovered that there was an ambush
10:81 men held their ground, as *J* had commanded,
10:84 But *J* burned and plundered Azotus with its
10:86 Then *J* left there and pitched his camp at
10:88 these events, he accorded new honors to *J*.
11: 4 charred bodies of those burned by *J*
11: 5 To prejudice the king against *J*,
11: 6 *J* met the king with pomp at Joppa,
11: 7 *J* accompanied the king as far as the river
11:20 At that time *J* gathered together the men
11:21 him that *J* was besieging the citadel.
11:22 He wrote to *J* to discontinue the siege and
11:23 this, *J* ordered the siege to continue.
11:28 *J* asked the king to exempt Judea and the
11:29 letter to *J* about all these matters:
11:30 to his brother *J* and to the Jewish nation.
11:37 of these instructions made and given to *J*,
11:41 Meanwhile *J* sent the request to King
11:42 Demetrius, in turn, sent this word to *J*:
11:44 So *J* sent three thousand good fighting men
11:53 his promises and became estranged from *J*.
11:53 Instead of rewarding *J* for all the favors
11:57 Then young Antiochus wrote to *J*:
11:60 *J* set out and traveled through
11:63 *J* heard that the generals of Demetrius had
11:67 *J* and his army pitched their camp near the
11:71 *J* tore his clothes,
11:74 Then *J* returned to Jerusalem.
12: 1 When *J* saw that the times favored him,
12: 3 "The high priest *J* and the Jewish people
12: 5 of the letter that *J* wrote to the Spartans:
12: 6 *J* the high priest, the senate of the nation,
12:24 *J* heard that the generals of Demetrius had
12:27 *J* ordered his men to be on guard and to
12:28 that *J* and his men were ready for battle,
12:29 But because *J* and his men were watching
12:30 Then *J* pursued them,
12:31 So *J* turned aside against the Arabs who
12:35 When *J* returned, he assembled the elders
12:40 he was afraid that *J* would not permit him,
12:41 *J* marched out against him with forty
12:42 But when Trypho saw that *J* had arrived
12:44 Then he said to *J*: "Why have you put all
12:46 *J* believed him and did as he said.
12:48 Then as soon as *J* had entered Ptolemais,
12:50 upon learning that *J* had been captured and
12:52 of *J* came safely into the land of Judah.
12:52 They mourned over *J* and his men,
13: 8 in place of your brothers Judas and *J*.
13:11 He sent *J*, son of Absalom, to Joppa
13:11 *J* drove out the occupants and remained
13:12 Judah, bringing *J* with him as a prisoner.
13:14 that Simon had succeeded his brother *J*,
13:15 "We have detained your brother *J* on
13:18 who might say that *J* perished because
13:19 broke his promise and would not let *J* go.
13:23 Baskama, he had *J* killed and buried there.
13:25 sent for the remains of his brother *J*,
14:16 in Rome and even in Sparta that *J* had died,
14:18 established with his brothers Judas and *J*.
14:30 After *J* had rallied his nation and become
2Mc 1:23 *J* leading and the rest responding with
8:22 his brothers, Simon, Joseph, and *J*,
Jer 37:15 into prison in the house of *J* the scribe,
37:20 me back into the house of *J* the scribe,

JONATHAN'S (8)

1Sm 19: 6 Saul heeded *J* plea and swore,
20:38 *J* boy picked up the arrow and brought it
2Sm 9: 3 answered the king, "There is still *J* son,
1Mc 9:61 *J* men seized about fifty of the men of the
11:59 he made *J* brother Simon governor of the
11:70 All of *J* men fled;
12:49 and the Great Plain to destroy all *J* men.
Jer 38:26 to send me back to *J* house to die there.' "

JOPPA (27)

Jos 19:46 Me-jarkon and Rakkon, with the coast at *J*.
2Chr 2:15 float them down to you at the port of *J*,
Ezr 3: 7 trees from the Lebanon to the port of *J*,
1Mc 10:75 He pitched camp near *J*,
10:76 and so Jonathan took possession of *J*.
11: 6 Jonathan met the king with pomp at *J*,
12:33 He then turned to *J* and occupied it,
13:11 son of Absalom, to *J* with a large force;
14: 5 he captured the port of *J*
14:34 He also fortified *J* by the sea and Gazara
15:28 *J* and Gazara and the citadel of Jerusalem;
15:35 As for *J* and Gazara, which you demand,
2Mc 4:22 After going to *J*,
12: 3 people of *J* also committed this outrage:
12: 4 the people of *J* took them out to sea and
12: 7 and wipe out the entire population of *J*.
Jon 1: 3 He went down to *J*,
Acts 9:36 Now in *J* there was a certain woman convert
9:38 Since Lydda was near *J*,
9:42 This became known all over *J*,
9:43 Peter stayed on in *J* for a considerable time
10: 5 some men to *J* and summon a certain Simon,
10: 8 to them and dispatched them to *J*.
10:23 accompanied by some of the brothers from *J*.
10:32 Send someone to *J* to invite Simon known as
11: 5 "I was at prayer in the city of *J* when,
11:13 'Send someone to *J* and fetch Simon,

JORAH (1)

Ezr 2:18 sons of *J*,

JORAI (1)

1Chr 5:13 Michael, Meshullam, Sheba, *J*,

JORAM (23)

2Kgs 1:17 son, his brother *J* succeeded him as king,
3: 1 *J*, son of Ahab, became king of Israel
3: 6 *J* as king mustered all Israel,
8:16 In the fifth year of *J*,
8:25 became king in the twelfth year of *J*,
8:28 He joined *J*, son of Ahab, in battle
8:28 where the Arameans wounded *J*.
8:29 King *J* returned to Jezreel to be healed of
9:14 of Nimshi, formed a conspiracy against *J*.
9:14 *J*, with all Israel, had been besieging
9:16 to Jezreel, where *J* lay ill and Ahaziah,
9:17 *J* said, "and send him to meet them
9:19 *J* sent a second driver,
9:21 "Prepare my chariot," said *J*.
9:21 When they had done so, *J*,
9:22 When *J* recognized Jehu,
9:23 *J* reigned about and fled,
9:24 his bow and shot *J* between the shoulders,
9:29 king of Judah in the eleventh year of *J*,
1Chr 3:11 son was Jehoshaphat, whose son was *J*,
26:25 whose son was Jeshaiah, whose son was *J*,
Mt 1: 8 father of Joram, *J* the father of Uzziah.

JORDAN (202)

Gn 13:10 the whole *J* Plain was as far as Zoar,
13:11 the whole *J* Plain and set out eastward.
32:11 the *J* here with nothing but my staff,
50:10 at Goren-ha-atad, which is beyond the *J*,
50:11 It is beyond the *J*.
Nm 13:29 along the seacoast and the banks of the *J*."
22: 1 other side of the Jericho stretch of the *J*.

26: 3 Moab along the Jericho stretch of the *J*,
26:63 of Moab along the Jericho stretch of the *J*.
31:12 Moab, along the Jericho stretch of the *J*.
32: 5 Do not make us cross the *J*."
32:19 heritage with them once we cross the *J*,
32:19 ourselves on this eastern side of the *J*."
32:21 cross the *J* in full force before the LORD
32:29 Gadites and Reubenites cross the *J*
32:32 hereditary property on this side of the *J*."
33:48 of Moab along the Jericho stretch of the *J*.
33:49 Their camp along the *J* on the plains of
33:50 Jericho stretch of the *J* and said to him:
33:51 go across the *J* into the land of Canaan,
34:12 the *J* and terminate with the Salt Sea.
34:15 side of the Jericho stretch of the *J*,
35: 1 Moab beside the Jericho stretch of the *J*:
35:10 go across the *J* into the land of Canaan,
35:14 three beyond the *J*,
36:13 Moab beside the Jericho stretch of the *J*.
Dt 1: 1 to all Israel beyond the *J* [in the desert,
1: 5 the law in the land of Moab beyond the *J*,
2:29 I cross the *J* into the land which the LORD,
3: 8 two kings of the Amorites beyond the *J*
3:17 as well as the Arabah with the *J*
3:20 will give them on the other side of the *J*.
3:25 over and see this good land beyond the *J*,
3:27 Look well, for you shall not cross this *J*.
4:21 swore that I should not cross the *J*
4:22 in this country without crossing the *J*;
4:26 which you will occupy when you cross the *J*.
4:41 three cities in the region east of the *J*,
4:46 the *J* in the ravine opposite Beth-peor,
4:47 the Amorites in the region east of the *J*:
4:49 Hermon) and all the Arabah east of the *J*,
9: 1 You are now about to cross the *J* to enter
11:30 [Are they not beyond the *J*,
11:31 For you are about to cross the *J* to enter
12:10 the *J* and dwell in the land which the LORD,
27: 2 cross the *J* into the land which the LORD,
27: 4 When, moreover, you have crossed the *J*,
27:12 "When you cross the *J*,
30:18 you are crossing the *J* to enter and occupy.
31: 2 has told me that I shall not cross this *J*.
31:13 land which you will cross the *J* to occupy."
32:47 land which you will cross the *J* to occupy."
34: 3 of the *J* with the lowlands at Jericho,
34:12 of the *J* with the lowlands at Jericho,
Jos 1: 2 So prepare to cross the *J* here,
1:11 days from now you shall cross the *J* here,
1:14 the land Moses gave you here beyond the *J*.
1:15 of the LORD, has given you east of the *J*."
2: 7 out along the way to the fords of the *J*,
2:10 the two kings of the Amorites beyond the *J*,
2:23 from the hills, crossed the *J* to Joshua,
3: 1 all the Israelites from Shittim to the *J*,
3: 8 *J* when they reach the edge of the waters."
3:11 whole earth will precede you into the *J*.
3:13 the whole earth, touch the water of the *J*,
3:14 people struck their tents to cross the *J*,
3:15 into the waters at the edge of the *J*,
3:17 dry ground in the bed of the *J*
4: 1 After the entire nation had crossed the *J*,
4: 3 stones from this spot in the bed of the *J*
4: 5 of the *J* in front of the ark of the LORD,
4: 7 'The waters of the *J* ceased to flow before
4: 7 covenant of the LORD when it crossed the *J*.'
4: 8 *J* as there were tribes of the Israelites,
4: 9 twelve stones set up in the bed of the *J*
4:10 ark remained in the bed of the *J*
4:16 of the commandments to come up from the *J*.
4:18 LORD had come up from the bed of the *J*,
4:18 the waters of the *J* resumed their course
4:19 the *J* on the tenth day of the first month,
4:20 stones which had been taken from the *J*,
4:22 'Israel crossed the *J* here on dry ground.'
4:23 *J* in front of you until you crossed over,
5: 1 Amorites to the west of the *J*
5: 1 LORD had dried up the waters of the *J*
7: 7 ever allow this people to pass over the *J*,
7: 7 to dwell on the other side of the *J*.
9: 1 the news reached the kings west of the *J*,
9:10 two kings of the Amorites beyond the *J*,
12: 1 The kings of the land east of the *J*,
12: 7 conquered west of the *J* and whose land,
13: 8 of the LORD, had given them east of the *J*:
13:23 of the Reubenites was the bank of the *J*.
13:27 and in the *J* valley:
13:27 with the bank of the *J* to the southeastern
13:32 of Moab, beyond the *J* east of Jericho.
14: 3 had already given a heritage beyond the *J*;
15: 5 the Salt Sea as far as the mouth of the *J*.
15: 6 from the bay where the *J* meets the sea,
16: 1 Josephites extended from the *J* at Jericho
16: 7 and skirting Jericho, it ended at the *J*.
17: 5 land of Gilead and Bashan beyond the *J*,
18: 7 the heritage east of the *J* which Moses,
18:12 Their northern boundary began at the *J* and
18:19 the Salt Sea, at the southern end of the *J*.
18:20 The *J* bounded it on the east.
19:22 and Beth-shemesh, ending at the *J*.
19:33 and Jabneel, and ended at the *J*.
19:34 Asher on the west, and the *J* on the east.
20: 8 And beyond the *J* east of Jericho they
21:36 also, across the *J*, from the tribe of Reuben,
22: 4 may now return to your tents beyond the *J*;
22: 7 along with their kinsmen west of the *J*.)
22:10 the region of the *J* in the land of Canaan,
22:10 built there at the *J*
22:11 region of the *J* facing the land of Canaan,
22:25 the *J* as a boundary between you and us.
23: 4 the *J* and the Great Sea in the west.
24: 8 of the Amorites who lived east of the *J*.
24:11 Once you crossed the *J* and came to Jericho,
Jgs 3:28 seized the fords of the *J* leading to Moab,
5:17 Gilead, beyond the *J*,
7:24 as far as Beth-barah, as well as the *J*."
7:24 as far as Beth-barah, and the *J* as well.
7:25 of Oreb and Zeeb to Gideon beyond the *J*.
8: 4 When Gideon reached the *J* and crossed it
10: 8 in the Amorite land beyond the *J* in Gilead.
10: 9 also crossed the *J* to fight against Judah,
11:13 and the *J* when they came up from Egypt.
11:22 to the Jabbok, from the desert to the *J*.
12: 5 took the fords of the *J* toward Ephraim.
12: 6 him and kill him at the fords of the *J*.
1Sm 13: 7 over the *J* into the land of Gad and Gilead.
31: 7 those along the *J* saw that the men of Israel
2Sm 2:29 through the Arabah, crosssed the *J*
10:17 David assembled all Israel, crossed the *J*,
16:14 with him arrived at the *J* tired out,
17:22 all his people moved on and crossed the *J*.
17:24 the *J* accompanied by all the Israelites.
18:23 way of the *J* plain and outran the Cushite.
19:16 the king, on his return, reached the *J*,
19:16 to meet him and to escort him across the *J*.
19:18 hastened to the *J* before the king.
19:19 When Shimei, son of Gera, crossed the *J*,
19:32 the king to the *J* for his crossing,
19:37 In escorting the king across the *J*,
19:40 crossed over the *J* but the king remained;
19:42 the king and his household across the *J*,
20: 2 But from the *J* to Jerusalem the Judahites
24: 5 Crossing the *J*, they began near Aroer,
1Kgs 2: 8 Because he came down to meet me at the *J*,
7:46 them cast in the neighborhood of the *J*,
17: 3 hide in the Wadi Cherith, east of the *J*.
17: 5 by the Wadi Cherith, east of the *J*.
2Kgs 2: 6 the LORD has sent me on to the *J*."
2: 7 and when the two stopped at the *J*,
2:13 went back and stood at the bank of the *J*.
5:10 "Go and wash seven times in the *J*,
5:14 Naaman went down and plunged into the *J*
6: 2 Let us go to the *J*,
6: 4 arrived at the *J* they began to fell trees.
7:15 followed the Arameans as far as the *J*,
10:33 east of the *J* (all the land of Gilead,
1Chr 6:63 *J* at Jericho [that is, east of the Jordan]
12:16 It was they who crossed over the *J* when it
12:38 From the other side of the *J*,
19:17 all Israel together, crossed the *J*,
26:30 Israel on the western side of the *J*
2Chr 4:17 The king had them cast in the *J* region,
Jdt 1: 9 and west of the *J* as far as Jerusalem,
5:15 Heshbonites by main force, crossed the *J*,
1Mc 5:24 Jonathan crossed the *J*
5:52 *J* to the great plain in front of Beth-shan,
9:42 the Jews returned to the marshes of the *J*.
9:43 to the banks of the *J* with a large force.
9:45 us are the waters of the *J* on one side,
9:48 the *J* and swam across to the other side,
9:48 enemy did not pursue them across the *J*.
Ps(s) 42: 7 you From the land of the *J* and of Hermon,
114: 3 The sea beheld and fled; *J* turned back.
114: 5 O *J*, that you turn back?
Sir 24:24 understanding, like the *J* at harvest time.
Is 8:23 the seaward road, the land west of the *J*,
Jer 12: 5 what will you do in the thickets of the *J*?
49:19 of *J* to the permanent feeding grounds,
Ez 47:18 the *J* shall form the boundary down to the
Zec 11: 3 lions, the jungle of the *J* is laid waste.
Mt 3: 5 region around the *J* were going out to him.
3: 6 the *J* River as they confessed their sins.
3:13 before John at the *J* to be baptized by him.
4:15 of Naphtali along the sea beyond the *J*,
4:25 Jerusalem and Judea, and from across the *J*.
19: 1 came to the district of Judea across the *J*.
Mk 1: 5 the *J* River as they confessed their sins.
1: 9 Galilee and was baptized in the *J* by John.
10: 1 to the districts of Judea and across the *J*.
Lk 3: 3 He went about the entire region of the *J*
4: 1 then returned from the *J* and was conducted
Jn 1:28 This happened in Bethany, across the *J*,
3:26 the man who was with you across the *J*—
10:40 Then he went back across the *J* to the

JORDAN'S (1)

Jer 50:44 *J* thicket to the permanent feeding grounds,

JORIM (1)

Lk 3:29 son of Joshua, son of Eliezer, son of *J*,

JORKEAM (1)

1Chr 2:44 father of Raham, who was the father of *J*.

JOSECH (1)

Lk 3:26 of Mattathias, son of Semein, son of *J*,

JOSEPH (227)

Gn 30:24 So she named him *J* meaning,
30:25 After Rachel gave birth to *J*,
33: 2 her children next, and Rachel and *J* last.
35:24 *J* and Benjamin;
37: 2 When *J* was seventeen years old,
37: 3 Israel loved *J* best of all his sons,
37: 5 Once *J* had a dream,
37:13 flocks at Shechem, Israel said to *J*,
37:13 "I am ready," *J* answered.
37:14 When *J* reached Shechem,
37:17 So *J* went after his brothers and caught up
37:23 So when *J* came up to them,
37:28 They sold *J* to the Ishmaelites for twenty
37:28 and they pulled *J* up out of the cistern
37:29 the cistern and saw that *J* was not in it,
37:33 *J* has been torn to pieces!"
37:36 meanwhile, sold *J* in Egypt to Potiphar,
39: 1 When *J* was taken down to Egypt,
39: 2 *J* got on very well and was assigned to the
39: 4 to *J* and made him his personal attendant;
39: 6 charge, he gave no thought, with *J* there,
39: 6 Now *J* was strikingly handsome in
39:11 when *J* came into the house to do his work,
39:20 He seized *J* and threw him into the jail
39:21 was in prison, the LORD remained with *J*;
39:22 The chief jailer put *J* in charge of all
40: 3 (the same jail where *J* was confined).
40: 4 The chief steward assigned *J* to them,
40: 6 When *J* came to them in the morning,
40: 8 *J* said to them,
40: 9 Then the chief cupbearer told *J* his dream.
40:12 *J* said to him:
40:16 *J* had given this favorable interpretation,
40:18 *J* said to him in reply:
40:22 as *J* had told them in his interpretation.
40:23 the chief cupbearer gave no thought to *J*;
41:14 Pharaoh therefore had *J* summoned,
41:16 "It is not I," *J* replied to Pharaoh,
41:17 Then Pharaoh said to *J*: "In my dream
41:25 *J* said to Pharaoh: "Both of Pharaoh's dreams
41:39 So Pharaoh said to *J*: "Since God has made
41:41 Herewith," Pharaoh told *J*,
41:43 *J* installed over the whole land of Egypt.
41:44 "I, Pharaoh, proclaim," he told *J*,
41:45 the name of Zaphenath-paneah on *J*,
41:46 *J* was thirty years old when he entered the
41:46 After *J* left Pharaoh's presence,
41:49 *J* garnered grain in quantities like the
41:50 set in, *J* became the father of two sons,
41:54 of famine set in, just as *J* had predicted.
41:55 to go to *J* and do whatever he told them.
41:56 *J* opened all the cities that had grain and
41:57 world came to *J* to obtain rations of grain,
42: 6 *J*, as governor of the country,
42: 8 When *J* recognized his brothers,
42:14 "It is just as I said," *J* persisted;
42:18 On the third day *J* said to them:
42:23 course, that *J* understood what they said,
42:25 Then *J* gave orders to have their
42:36 *J* is gone, and Simeon is gone,
43:15 down to Egypt to present themselves to *J*.
43:16 When *J* saw Benjamin with them,
43:17 Doing as *J* had ordered,
43:26 When *J* came home,
43:30 With that, *J* had to hurry out,
44: 1 *J* gave his head steward these instructions:
44: 4 the city when *J* said to his head steward:
44:15 *J* asked them.
44:17 "Far be it from me to act thus!" said *J*.
45: 1 *J* could no longer control himself in the
45: 3 "I am *J*."
45: 4 "I am your brother *J*,
45: 9 'Thus says your son *J*:
45:12 can see for himself, that it is I, *J*,
45:15 *J* then kissed all his brothers,
45:17 So Pharaoh told *J*:
45:21 *J* gave them the wagons,
45:26 When they told him, *J* is still alive
45:27 recounted to him all that *J* had told them,
45:27 wagons that *J* had sent for his transport,
45:28 "My son *J* is still alive!
46: 4 back here, after *J* has closed your eyes."
46:19 *J* and Benjamin.
46:20 In the land of Egypt *J* became the father
46:28 Israel had sent Judah ahead to *J*,
46:29 *J* hitched the horses to his chariot and
46:30 And Israel said to *J*,
46:30 have seen for myself that *J* is still alive."
46:31 *J* then said to his brothers and his
47: 1 *J* went and told Pharaoh,
47: 5 Pharaoh said to *J*,
47: 5 when Jacob and his sons came to *J* in Egypt,
47: 5 Egypt, heard about it, Pharaoh said to *J*,
47: 7 Then *J* brought his father Jacob and
47:11 *J* settled his father and brothers and gave
47:12 And *J* sustained his father and brothers
47:14 languishing from hunger, *J* gathered in,
47:15 was spent, all the Egyptians came to *J*,

JOSEPH (cont.)

47:16 "Since your money is gone," replied *J*,
47:17 So they brought their livestock to *J*,
47:20 Thus *J* acquired all the farm land of Egypt
47:22 the priests' lands *J* did not take over.
47:23 *J* told the people: "Now that I have acquired
47:26 Thus *J* made it a law for the land in Egypt,
47:29 die, he called his son *J* and said to him:
47:31 So *J* swore to him.
48: 1 Some time afterward, *J* was informed,
48: 2 was told, "Your son *J* has come to you,"
48: 3 Jacob then said to *J*:
48: 9 are my sons," *J* answered his father,
48:10 When *J* brought his sons close to him,
48:11 Then Israel said to *J*,
48:12 *J* removed them from his father's knees and
48:13 Then *J* took the two,
48:17 When *J* saw that his father had laid his
48:21 Then Israel said to *J*: "I am about to die
49:22 *J* is a wild colt, a wild colt by a spring,
49:26 May they rest on the head of *J*.
50: 1 *J* threw himself on his father's face and
50: 4 was over, *J* spoke to Pharaoh's courtiers.
50: 7 So *J* left to bury his father;
50:10 and *J* observed seven days of mourning for
50:14 After *J* had buried his father he returned
50:15 "Suppose *J* has been nursing a grudge
50:16 So they approached *J* and said:
50:17 'You shall say to *J*,
50:17 these words to him, *J* broke into tears.
50:19 But *J* replied to them:
50:22 *J* remained in Egypt,
50:24 *J* said to his brothers:
50:26 *J* died at the age of a hundred and ten.
Ex 1: 5 *J* was already in Egypt.
1: 6 Now *J* and all his brothers and that whole
1: 8 Then a new king, who knew nothing of *J*,
13:19 for *J* had made the Israelites swear
Nm 1:11 for the descendants of *J*
1:32 Of the descendants of *J*—
13: 7 [son of *J*,
26:28 The sons of *J* were Manasseh and Ephraim.
26:37 These were the descendants of *J* by clans.
27: 1 son of Machir, son of Manasseh, son of *J*,
32:33 as half the tribe of Manasseh, son of *J*,
34:25 for the descendants of *J*
36:12 of the descendants of Manasseh, son of *J*;
Dt 27:12 *J* and Benjamin shall stand on Mount
33:13 Of *J* he said:
33:16 These shall come upon the head of *J* and
Jos 14: 4 the descendants of *J* formed two tribes,
16: 4 of Manasseh and Ephraim, sons of *J*,
17: 1 tribe of Manasseh as the first-born of *J*:
17: 2 other male children of Manasseh, son of *J*.
17:14 The descendants of *J* said to Joshua,
17:17 to Ephraim and Manasseh, the house of *J*,
18: 5 the house of *J* its territory in the north.
18:11 the descendants of Judah and those of *J*.
24:32 The bones of *J*, which the Israelites had
24:32 was a heritage of the descendants of *J*.
Jgs 1:22 The house of *J*, too, marched up against
1:23 of *J* had a reconnaissance made of Bethel,
1:35 as the house of *J* gained the upper hand,
2Sm 19:21 first of the whole house of *J* to come down
1Kgs 11:28 the entire labor force of the house of *J*.
1Chr 2: 2 Levi, Judah, Issachar, Zebulun, Dan, *J*,
5: 1 his birthright was given to the sons of *J*,
7:29 In these dwelt the descendants of *J*,
25: 2 Zaccur, *J*, Nethaniah, and Asharelah
25: 9 first lot fell to Asaph, the family of *J*:
Ezr 10:42 Shelemiah, Shemariah, Shallum, Amariah, *J*,
Neh 12:14 for Shebaniah, *J*;
Jdt 8: 1 days Judith, daughter of Merari, son of *J*,
1Mc 2:53 *J*, when in distress, kept the commandment,
5:18 In Judea he left *J*,
5:56 was in Galilee opposite Ptolemais, *J*,
5:60 *J* and Azariah were beaten,
2Mc 8:22 into four, placing his brothers, Simon, *J*,
10:19 a siege, Maccabeus left Simon and *J*,
Ps(s) 77:16 your people, the sons of Jacob and *J*.
78:67 And he rejected the tent of *J*,
80: 2 Israel, hearken, O guide of the flock of *J*!
81: 6 Who made it a decree for *J* when he came
105:17 them, He sent a man before them, *J*,
Sir 49:15 Was ever a man born like *J*?
Ez 37:16 *J* [the stick of Ephraim] and all the house
37:19 [I will take the stick of *J*,
47:13 tribes of Israel *J* having two portions].
48:32 the gate of *J*, the gate of Benjamin,
Am 5: 6 house of *J* like a fire That shall consume,
5:15 hosts, will have pity on the remnant of *J*.
6: 6 they are not made ill by the collapse of *J*!
Ob 1:18 be a fire, and the house of *J* a flame;
Zec 10: 6 house of Judah, the house of *J* I will save;
Mt 1:16 was the father of *J* the husband of Mary.
1:18 When his mother Mary was engaged to *J*,
1:19 *J* her husband, an upright man unwilling
1:20 *J*, son of David, have no fear
1:24 When *J* awoke he did as the angel of the
2:13 appeared in a dream to *J* with the command:
2:14 *J* got up and took the child and his
2:19 in a dream to *J* in Egypt with the command:
2:22 a dream, *J* went to the region of Galilee.
13:55 Mary known to be his mother and James, *J*,
27:56 and Mary the mother of James and *J*
27:57 man from Arimathea arrived, *J* by name.
27:59 *J* wrapped it in fresh linen and laid it in
Mk 15:43 of the sabbath), *J* from Arimathea arrived
15:45 was dead, Pilate released the corpse to *J*.
15:46 bought a linen shroud, *J* took him down,
Lk 1:27 to a virgin betrothed to a man named *J*,
2: 4 And so *J* went from the town of Nazareth in
2:16 They went in haste and found Mary and *J*,
3:23 the son of *J*,
3:24 son of Melchi, son of Jannai, son of *J*,
3:30 son of Simeon, son of Judah, son of *J*,
23:50 There was a man named *J*,
Jn 1:45 Jesus, son of *J*,
4: 5 of land which Jacob had given to his son *J*.
6:42 "Is this not Jesus, the son of *J*?
19:38 Afterward, *J* of Arimathea,
Acts 1:23 they nominated two, *J* (called Barsabbas,
4:36 was a certain Levite from Cyprus named *J*,
7: 9 patriarchs sold *J* into slavery in Egypt,
7:13 time, *J* made himself known to his brothers,
7:14 Then *J* sent for his father Jacob,
7:18 came to power in Egypt, who knew not *J*.
Heb 11:21 when dying, blessed each of the sons of *J*,
11:22 By faith *J*, near the end of his life,
Rv 7: 8 twelve thousand from the tribe of *J*,

JOSEPHITE (1)

Nm 36: 1 one of the *J* clans

JOSEPHITE'S (4)

Nm 13:11 Susi, of the tribe of Manasseh, for the *J*,
36: 5 tribe of the *J* are right in what they say.
Jos 16: 1 The lot that fell to the *J* extended from
17:16 For the *J* said,

JOSEPH'S (25)

Gn 37:31 They took *J* tunic,
39: 5 blessed the Egyptian's house for *J* sake;
39: 6 left everything he owned in *J* charge,
39:23 with anything at all that was in *J* charge,
41:42 off his signet ring and put it on *J* finger.
42: 3 So ten of *J* brothers went down to buy an
42: 4 It was only *J* full brother Benjamin that
42: 6 When *J* brothers came and knelt down before
43:17 the steward conducted the men to *J* house.
43:19 So they went up to *J* head steward and
43:24 then brought the men inside *J* house.
43:25 out their gifts to await *J* arrival at noon,
43:29 *J* eye fell on his full brother Benjamin,
43:34 portions were brought to them from *J* table,
44: 2 The steward carried out *J* instructions.
44:14 Judah and his brothers reentered *J* house,
45:16 Pharaoh's palace that *J* brothers had come,
46:27 with *J* sons who were born to him in Egypt
48: 8 When Israel saw *J* sons,
50: 8 of Egypt, as well as *J* whole household,
50:15 *J* brothers became fearful and thought,
50:23 son Machir were also born on *J* knees.
Ex 13:19 Moses also took *J* bones along,
1Chr 5: 2 from him, though the birthright had been *J*.)
Lk 4:22 They also asked, "Is not this *J* son?"

JOSES (3)

Mk 6: 3 brother of James and *J* and Judas and Simon?
15:40 Mary the mother of James the younger and *J*,
15:47 of *J* observed where he had been laid.

JOSHAH (1)

1Chr 4:34 Meshobab, Jamlech, *J*,

JOSHAPHAT (2)

1Chr 11:43 *J* the Mithnite;
15:24 The priests, Shebaniah, *J*,

JOSHAVIAH (1)

1Chr 11:46 Jeribai and *J*,

JOSHBEKASHAH (2)

1Chr 25: 4 Eliathah, Giddalti, Romamti-ezer, *J*,
25:24 The seventeenth fell to *J*,

JOSHIBIAH (1)

1Chr 4:35 son of Amaziah, Joel, Jehu, son of *J*,

JOSHUA (216)

Ex 17: 9 Moses, therefore, said to *J*,
17:10 So *J* did as Moses told him:
17:13 And *J* mowed down Amalek and his people
17:14 remembered, and recite it in the ears of *J*:
24:13 So Moses set out with *J*,
32:17 *J* heard the noise of the people shouting,
33:11 to the camp, but his young assistant, *J*,
Nm 11:28 Medad are prophesying in the camp," *J*,
13:16 But Hoshea, son of Nun, Moses called *J*.
14: 6 while *J*,
14:30 you, except Caleb, son of Jephunneh, and *J*,
14:38 had gone to reconnoiter the land, only *J*,
26:65 left except Caleb, son of Jephunneh, and *J*,
27:18 And the LORD replied to Moses, "Take *J*,
27:21 and as he directs, *J*,
27:22 Taking *J* and having him stand in the
32:12 Kenizzite Caleb, son of Jephunneh, and *J*,
32:28 their regard to the priest Eleazar, to *J*,
34:17 Eleazar the priest, and *J*,
Dt 1:38 you shall enter there, but your aide *J*,
3:21 "It was then that I instructed *J*,
3:28 Commission *J*,
31: 3 It is *J* who will cross before you,
31: 7 Then Moses summoned *J* and in the presence
31:14 Summon *J*, and present yourselves
31:14 So Moses and *J* went and presented
31:23 Then the LORD commissioned *J*,
32:44 So Moses, together with *J*,
34: 9 Now *J*, son of Nun, was filled with the
Jos 1: 1 had died, the LORD said to Moses' aide *J*,
1:10 So *J* commanded the officers of the people:
1:12 *J* reminded the Reubenites,
1:16 you have commanded us," they answered *J*,
2: 1 Then *J*, son of Nun, secretly sent out
2:23 from the hills, crossed the Jordan to *J*,
2:24 They assured *J*, "The LORD has delivered
3: 1 *J* moved with all the Israelites from
3: 5 *J* also said to the people,
3: 7 Then the LORD said to *J*,
3: 9 So *J* said to the Israelites,
4: 2 crossed the Jordan, the LORD said to *J*,
4: 5 one from each tribe, *J* said to them:
4: 8 twelve Israelites did as *J* had commanded:
4: 9 *J* also had twelve stones set up in the bed
4:10 LORD had commanded *J* to tell the people.
4:14 LORD exalted *J* in the sight of all Israel,
4:15 Then the LORD said to *J*,
4:17 *J* did so, and when the priests carrying
4:20 At Gilgal *J* set up the twelve stones which
5: 2 On this occasion the LORD said to *J*,
5: 3 So *J* made flint knives and circumcised the
5: 7 up in their stead whom *J* circumcised,
5: 9 Then the LORD said to *J*,
5:13 While *J* was near Jericho,
5:13 *J* went up to him and asked,
5:14 *J* fell prostrate to the ground in worship,
5:15 of the host of the LORD replied to *J*,
5:15 And *J* obeyed.
6: 2 And to *J* the LORD said,
6: 6 Summoning the priests, *J*,
6:10 But the people had been commanded by *J* not
6:12 *J* had the priests take up the ark of the
6:16 blew the horns and *J* said to the people,
6:22 *J* directed the two men who had spied out
6:25 *J* had sent to reconnoiter Jericho, Joshua
6:26 On that occasion *J* imposed the oath:
6:27 Thus the LORD was with *J* so that his fame
7: 2 *J* next sent men from Jericho to Ai,
7: 3 Ai, they returned to *J* and advised,
7: 6 *J*, together with the elders of Israel,
7: 7 "Alas, O Lord GOD," *J* prayed,
7:10 The LORD replied to *J*:
7:16 *J* had Israel come forward by tribes,
7:19 *J* said to Achan,
7:20 Achan answered *J*, "I have indeed sinned
7:22 The messengers whom *J* sent hastened to the
7:23 brought them to *J* and all the Israelites,
7:24 Then *J* and all Israel took Achan,
7:25 *J* said, "The LORD bring upon you today
8: 1 The LORD then said to *J*,
8: 3 So *J* and all the soldiers prepared to
8: 3 *J* sent them off by night with these orders:
8: 9 Then *J* sent them away.
8: 9 to the west of Ai, toward Bethel, *J*,
8:10 Early the next morning *J* mustered the army
8:13 and *J* waited overnight among his troops.
8:15 *J* and the main body of the Israelites fled
8:17 in this pursuit of *J* and the Israelites,
8:18 Then the LORD directed *J*,
8:18 *J* stretched out the javelin in his hand
8:21 for when *J* and the main body of Israelites
8:23 whom they took alive and brought to *J*.
8:26 *J* kept the javelin in his hand stretched
8:27 to the command of the LORD issued to *J*.
8:28 Then *J* destroyed the place by fire,
8:29 then at sunset *J* ordered the body removed
8:30 Later *J* built an altar to the LORD,
8:32 *J* inscribed upon the stones a copy of the
8:35 *J* read aloud to the entire community,
9: 2 a common attack against *J* and Israel.
9: 3 learning what *J* had done to Jericho and Ai,
9: 6 they journeyed to *J* in the camp at Gilgal,
9: 8 But they answered *J*,
9: 8 Then *J* asked them, "Who are you?
9:15 So *J* made an alliance with them and
9:22 *J* summoned the Gibeonites and said to them,
9:24 They answered *J*, "Your servants were
9:26 *J* did what he had decided:
10: 1 *J* had done to that city and its king as he
10: 4 concluded peace with *J* and the Israelites.
10: 6 sent an appeal to *J* in his camp at Gilgal:
10: 7 So *J* marched up from Gilgal with his
10: 8 Meanwhile the LORD said to *J*,
10: 9 And when *J* made his surprise attack upon

10:12 to the Israelites, J prayed to the LORD,
10:15 [Then J and all Israel returned to the
10:17 When J was told that the five kings had
10:20 Once J and the Israelites had finally
10:21 safely to J and the camp at Makkedah,
10:22 Then J said, "Open the mouth of the
10:24 J summoned all the men of Israel and said
10:25 Then J said to them,
10:26 Thereupon J struck and killed them,
10:27 from the trees at the command of J
10:28 J captured and put to the sword at that
10:29 J then passed on with all Israel from
10:32 so that on the second day J captured it
10:33 Lachish, but J defeated him and his people,
10:34 J passed on with all Israel to Eglon;
10:36 Eglon, J went up with all Israel to Hebron,
10:37 no survivors, just as J had done to Eglon.
10:38 Then J and all Israel turned back to Debir
10:40 J conquered the entire country;
10:41 J conquered from Kadesh-barnea to Gaza,
10:42 lands J captured in a single campaign,
10:43 Thereupon J with all Israel returned to
11: 6 The LORD said to J, "Do not fear them,
11: 7 J with his whole army came upon them at
11: 9 J did to them as the LORD had commanded:
11:10 At that time J, turning back, captured Hazor
11:12 J thus captured all those kings with their
11:13 raised sites, except Hazor, which J burned.
11:15 commanded Joshua, and J acted accordingly.
11:16 So J captured all this land:
11:18 J waged war against all these kings for a
11:21 At that time J penetrated the mountain
11:21 J fulfilled the doom on them and on their
11:23 Thus J captured the whole country,
11:23 J gave it to Israel as their heritage,
12: 7 This is a list of the kings whom J and the
12: 7 J apportioned to the tribes of Israel.
13: 1 When J was old and advanced in years,
14: 1 Eleazar the priest, J,
14: 6 When the Judahites came up to J in Gilgal,
14:13 J blessed Caleb,
15:13 As the LORD had commanded, J gave Caleb,
17: 4 themselves to Eleazar the priest, to J,
17:14 The descendants of Joseph said to J,
17:15 the LORD has blessed us" J answered them,
17:17 J therefore said to Ephraim and Manasseh,
18: 3 J therefore said to the Israelites,
18: 8 J instructed them to survey the land,
18: 9 and returned to J in the camp at Shiloh.
18:10 J then divided up the land for the
19:49 assigned a heritage in their midst to J,
19:51 portions into which Eleazar the priest, J,
20: 1 The LORD said to J.
21: 1 came up to Eleazar the priest, to J,
22: 1 At that time J summoned the Reubenites,
22: 6 J then blessed them and sent them away to
22: 7 and to the other half J had given a
22: 7 What J said to them when he sent them off
23: 1 and when J was old and advanced in years,
24: 1 J gathered together all the tribes of
24: 2 before God, J addressed all the people:
24:19 J in turn said to the people,
24:21 But the people answered J,
24:22 J therefore said to the people,
24:24 Then the people promised J,
24:25 So J made a covenant with the people that
24:27 And J said to all the people,
24:28 Then J dismissed the people,
24:29 After these events, J,
24:31 LORD during the entire lifetime of J
24:31 elders who outlived J
Jgs 1: 1 of J the Israelites consulted the LORD,
2: 6 When J dismissed the people,
2: 7 the LORD during the entire lifetime of J,
2: 7 elders who outlived J
2: 8 which the LORD had done for Israel, J,
2:21 of the nations which J left when he died."
1Sm 6:14 of J the Beth-shemite and stopped there.
6:18 of J the Beth-shemite at the present time.
1Kgs 16:34 gates, as the LORD had foretold through J,
2Kgs 23: 8 was at the entrance of the Gate of J,
1Chr 7:27 whose son was Nun, whose son was J.
1Mc 2:55 J, for executing his commission,
2Mc 12:15 of the world, who, in the day of J,
Sir 46: 1 Valiant leader was J, son of Nun,
Hg 1: 1 son of Shealtiel, and to the high priest J,
1:12 son of Shealtiel, and the high priest J,
1:14 and the spirit of the high priest J,
2: 2 of Shealtiel, and to the high priest J,
2: 4 says the LORD, and take courage, J,
Zec 3: 1 Then he showed me J the high priest
3: 3 Now J was standing before the angel,
3: 6 of the LORD then gave J this assurance:
3: 8 Listen, O J, high priest!
3: 9 at the stone that I have placed before J,
6:11 place it on the head of J,
Lk 3:29 son of Elmadam, son of Er, son of J,
Acts 7:45 Under J,
Heb 4: 8 if J had led them into the place of rest,

JOSIAH (55)

1Kgs 13: 2 be born to the house of David, J by name,
2Kgs 21:24 and proclaimed his son J king in his stead.
21:26 Uzza, and his son J succeeded him as king.
22: 1 J was eight years old when he began to
22: 3 year, King J sent the scribe Shaphan,
23:16 When J turned and saw the graves there on
23:19 J also removed all the shrines on the high
23:23 until the eighteenth year of king J,
23:24 J did away with the consultation of ghosts
23:28 The rest of the acts of J,
23:29 King J set out to confront him,
23:30 of the land took Jehoahaz, son of J,
23:34 of Josiah, king in place of his father J;
1Chr 3:14 whose son was Amon, whose son was J.
3:15 The sons of J were:
2Chr 33:25 the land, made his son J king in his stead.
34: 1 J was eight years old when he became king,
34:33 J removed every abominable thing from all
35: 1 J celebrated in Jerusalem a Passover to
35: 7 J contributed to the common people a flock
35:16 altar of the LORD, as King J had commanded.
35:18 of Israel kept a Passover like that of J,
35:20 J had done all this to restore the temple,
35:20 Euphrates, and J went out to intercept him.
35:22 But J would not withdraw from him,
35:23 Then the archers shot King J,
35:25 also composed a lamentation over J,
35:25 singers in their lamentations over J.
35:26 The rest of the chronicle of J,
36: 1 son of J and made him king in Jerusalem in
Sir 49: 1 The name J is like blended incense,
49: 4 Except for David, Hezekiah and J,
Jer 1: 2 LORD first came to him in the days of J,
1: 3 through the reign of Jehoiakim, son of J,
1: 3 of the eleventh year of Zedekiah, son of J,
3: 6 The LORD said to me in the days of King J:
22:11 the LORD concerning Shallum, son of J,
22:18 the LORD concerning Jehoiakim, son of J,
25: 1 in the fourth year of Jehoiakim, son of J,
25: 3 Since the thirteenth year of J,
26: 1 of the reign of Jehoiakim, son of J,
27: 1 of the reign of Jehoiakim, son of J,
35: 1 LORD in the days of Jehoiakim, son of J,
36: 1 In the fourth year of Jehoiakim, son of J,
36: 2 day I first spoke to you, in the days of J,
36: 9 in the fifth year of Jehoiakim, son of J,
37: 1 was succeeded by King Zedekiah, son of J;
45: 1 in the fourth year of Jehoiakim, son of J,
46: 2 in the fourth year of Jehoiakim, son of J,
Bar 1: 8 These silver vessels Zedekiah, son of J,
Zep 1: 1 the son of Hezekiah, in the days of J,
Zec 6:10 and go the same day to the house of J,
Mt 1:10 the father of Amos, Amos the father of J,
1:11 J became the father of Jechoniah and his

JOSIAH'S (1)

2Chr 35:19 of J reign that this Passover was observed.

JOSIPHIAH (1)

Ezr 8:10 of the sons of Bani, Shelomith, son of J,

JOSTLED (1)

Gn 25:22 j each other so much that she exclaimed,

JOTBAH (1)

2Kgs 21:19 was Meshullemeth, daughter of Haruz of J.

JOTBATHAH (3)

Nm 33:33 out from Mount Gidgad, they camped at J.
33:34 Setting out from J,
Dt 10: 7 out for Gudgodah, and from Gudgodah for J,

JOTHAM (26)

Jgs 9: 5 Only the youngest son of Jerubbaal, J,
9: 7 to him, J went to the top of Mount Gerizim,
9:21 Then J went in flight to Beer,
9:57 to the Shechemites, for the curse of J,
2Kgs 15: 5 He lived in a house apart, while J,
15: 7 His son J succeeded him as king.
15:30 in his place [in the twentieth year of J,
15:32 Pekah, son of Remaliah, king of Israel, J,
15:36 The rest of the acts of J,
15:38 J rested with his ancestors and was buried
16: 1 of Pekah, son of Remaliah, Ahaz, son of J,
1Chr 2:47 The sons of Jahdai were Regem, J,
3:12 whose son was Azariah, whose son was J,
5:17 in the family records in the time of J,
2Chr 26:21 Therefore his son J was regent of the
26:23 His son J succeeded him as king.
27: 1 J was twenty-five years old when he became
27: 6 Thus J continued to grow strong because he
27: 7 The rest of the acts of J,
27: 9 J rested with his ancestors and was buried
Is 1: 1 and Jerusalem in the days of Uzziah, J,
7: 1 the days of Ahaz, king of Judah, son of J,
Hos 1: 1 son of Beeri, in the days of Uzziah, J,
Mi 1: 1 to Micah of Moresheth in the days of J,
Mt 1: 9 the father of Jotham, J the father of Ahaz,

JOURNEY (121)

Gn 19: 2 you can get up early to continue your j."
28:20 to protect me on this j I am making and to
29: 1 j he came to the land of the Easterners.
30:36 a three days' j between himself and Jacob,
32: 1 then he set out on his j back home,
33:16 day that Esau began his j back to Seir,
42:25 and provisions given them for their j.
42:38 should befall him on the j you must make,
45:21 he supplied them with provisions for the j.
45:23 and bread and other provisions for his j.
48: 7 died, to my sorrow, during the j in Canaan,
Ex 3:18 then, to go a three days' j in the desert,
4:24 On the j, at the place where they spent
5: 3 Let us go a three days' j in the desert,
8:23 We must go a three days' j in the desert
12:39 opportunity even to prepare food for the j.
18: 8 they had had to endure on their j,
19: 2 the j from Rephidim to the desert of Sinai,
40:36 the Israelites would set out on their j.
40:38 of Israel in all the stages of their j.
Nm 9:10 of a corpse, or if he is absent on a j,
9:13 anyone who is clean and not away on a j,
10:33 the mountain of the LORD, a three days' j,
10:33 place went the three days' j with them.
11:31 distance of a day's j all around the camp.
21: 4 But with their patience worn out by the j,
22:32 rash j of yours is directly opposed to me.
22:34 that you stood against me to oppose my j.
24:25 Then Balaam set out on his j home;
33: 8 a three days' j in the desert of Etham,
Dt 1: 2 it is a j of eleven days from Horeb to
1:31 your j until you arrived at this place.'
2: 7 about your j through this vast desert.
14:24 the j is too much for you and you are not
23: 5 and water on your j after you left Egypt,
24: 9 to Miriam on the j after you left Egypt.
25:17 did to you on the j after you left Egypt,
Jos 5: 4 desert during the j after they left Egypt.
5: 5 born in the desert during the j
5: 7 not having been circumcised on the j.
9: 4 They chose provisions for a j,
9:11 provisions for the j and go to meet them.
9:13 which are worn out from the very long j."
18: 8 to map out the land were ready for the j,
24:17 protected us along our entire j
Jgs 14: 7 However, on the j to speak for the woman,
17: 8 On his j he came to the house of Micah in
19: 9 Early tomorrow you can start your j home."
19:27 of the house to start out again on his j,
1Sm 7:16 He made a yearly j,
9:26 "Get up, and I will start you on your j."
21: 6 Whenever I go on a j,
21: 6 even for a secular j.
2Sm 11:10 to Uriah, "Have you not come from a j?
15: 9 The king wished him a safe j,
1Kgs 13:26 who had brought him back from his j said:
14: 4 She made the j to Shiloh and entered the
18:27 or may have retired, or may be on a j.
19: 4 there and went a day's j into the desert,
19: 7 eat, else the j will be too long for you!"
2Kgs 3: 9 After their roundabout j of seven days the
Ezr 7: 9 month he resolved on the j up from Babylon,
7:28 family heads to make the return j with me.
8:21 petition from him a safe j for ourselves,
Neh 2: 6 my j would take and when I would return.
9:12 of fire, To light the way of their j.
9:19 not cease to lead them by day on their j,
Tb 5: 2 which roads to take for the j into Media!"
5: 3 man who will make the j with you.
5: 7 for I need you to make the j with me.
5:17 son, prepare whatever you need for the j,
5:17 Before setting out on his j,
5:17 Tobit said to him, "Have a safe j."
5:22 will go with him, his j will be successful,
6: 6 the rest he salted and kept for the j.
10: 5 of my eyes, that I let you make this j!"
10:11 Have a safe j.
10:14 of all, for making his j so successful.
11: 1 Then they left and began their return j.
11:15 his father that his j had been a success;
12: 1 due to the man who made the j with you;
1Mc 7:45 The Jews pursued them a day's j,
8:19 After making a very long j to Rome,
2Mc 3: 8 Heliodorus immediately set out on his j
9: 4 without stopping until he finished the j.
Jb 16:22 I am on a j from which I shall not return.
Prv 7:19 is not at home, he has gone on a long j;
Wis 19: 5 your people might experience a glorious j
Sir 21:16 A fool's chatter is like a load on a j,
42: 3 sharing the expenses of a business or a j,
Is 35: 9 It is for those with a j to make,
42:16 I will lead the blind on their j;
Jon 1: 3 went aboard to j with them to Tarshish,
3: 4 Jonah began his j through the city,
Mt 21:33 it out to tenant farmers and went on a j.
25:14 of a man who was going on a j is similar.
Mk 6: 8 nothing on their j but a walking stick
9:30 district and began a j through Galilee,
10:17 setting out on a j a man came running up,
12: 1 it to tenant farmers and went on a j.
Lk 2:44 party, they continued their j for a day,
9: 3 "Take nothing for the j,
10:38 On their j Jesus entered a village where a
11: 6 from a j and I have nothing to offer him';

JOURNEY (cont.)

17:11 On his *j* to Jerusalem he passed along the
Jn 4: 5 and his *j* brought him to a Samaritan town
4: 6 Jesus, tired from his *j*,
Acts 1:12 a mere sabbath's *j* away.
8:26 Philip began the *j*.
9:27 them how on his *j* Saul had seen the Lord,
15:40 chose Silas to accompany him on his *j*,
16: 3 anxious to have him come along on the *j*.
20: 1 good-bye and set out on his *j* to Macedonia.
21: 5 when our time was up, we continued our *j*.
23:24 Also provide horses for Paul's *j*,
26:13 On this *j*, Your Majesty, I saw a light
Rom 15:24 I trust that you will send me on my *j*
1Cor 16: 6 me with what I need for the rest of my *j*.
2Cor 1:16 I might receive your help on my *j* to Judea.
Ti 3:13 Zenas the lawyer and Apollos on their *j*,
3Jn 1: 6 God, you help them to continue their *j*.

JOURNEYED (14)

Gn 12: 9 Then Abram *j* on by stages to the Negeb.
20: 1 Abraham *j* on to the region of the Negeb,
33:17 journey back to Seir, Jacob *j* to Succoth.
Ex 17: 1 the whole Israelite community *j* by stages,
Nm 33: 1 stages by which the Israelites *j*
Dt 1:19 from Horeb and *j* through the whole desert,
Jos 9: 6 they *j* to Joshua in the camp at Gilgal,
Jgs 4: 9 joined Barak and *j* with him to Kedesh.
2Chr 23: 2 They *j* about Judah,
Jb 2:11 They met and *j* together to give him
Wis 5: 7 we *j* through impassable deserts,
11: 2 They *j* through the uninhabited desert,
Ez 27:25 Tarshish *j* for you in your merchandising.
Lk 8: 1 After this he *j* through towns and villages

JOURNEYING (3)

Dt 8: 2 God, has directed all your *j* in the desert,
Jos 14:10 me while Israel was *j* through the desert,
Lk 10:33 But a Samaritan who was *j*

JOURNEYS (4)

Dt 1:33 who *j* before you to find you a resting
23:15 *j* along within your camp to defend you and
Ps(s) 139: 3 My *j* and my rest you scrutinize,
Acts 9:32 Once when Peter was making numerous *j*,

JOWLS (1)

Dt 18: 3 the shoulder, the *j* and the stomach.

JOY (219)

Ex 32:25 that, to the scornful *j* of their foes,
Dt 24: 5 to bring *j* to the wife he has married.
28:47 with *j* and gratitude for abundance of
1Sm 11:15 celebrated the occasion with great *j*.
2Sm 6:15 shouts of *j* and to the sound of the horn.
1Chr 15:25 LORD with *j* from the house of Obed-edom.
16:27 praise and *j* are in his holy place.
29:17 given all these things and now with *j*
2Chr 29:30 They sang praises till their *j* was full,
30:23 With *j*, therefore, they continued
Ezr 3:11 all the people raised a great shout of *j*,
3:12 lifted up their voices in shouts of *j*,
6:16 the dedication of this house of God with *j*.
6:22 for the LORD had filled them with *j* by
Neh 8:12 portions, and to celebrate with great *j*,
8:17 therefore there was very great *j*.
Tb 3: 8 had no *j* with any one of your husbands.
3:10 "What *j* is left for me any more?
7: 6 up and kissed him, shedding tears of *j*.
7:17 heaven grant you *j* in place of your grief.
8:20 bring *j* to my daughter's sorrowing spirit.
10:14 Raguel, he was full of happiness and *j*,
11:17 Welcome to your home with blessing and *j*.
11:17 *j* for all the Jews who lived in Nineveh.
13:10 that his tent may be rebuilt in you with *j*.
13:14 in you as they behold all your *j* forever.
Jdt 12:14 be a *j* for me till the day of my death."
14: 9 and their city resounded with shouts of *j*.
15: 9 of Jerusalem, the surpassing *j* of Israel;
Est C:10 inheritance and turn our sorrow into *j*:
4:29 your handmaid has had no *j* except in you,
E:21 of the chosen race into one of *j*.
8:15 The city of Susa shouted with *j*,
9:22 was turned for them from sorrow into *j*,
F:10 together with *j* and happiness before God,
1Mc 3:45 *J* had disappeared from Jacob,
4:58 There was great *j* among the people now
4:59 altar should be observed with *j*
5:54 in *j* and gladness and offered holocausts,
2Mc 3:30 commotion, was filled with *j* and gladness,
6:30 but also suffering it with *j* in my soul
Jb 20: 5 and the *j* of the impious but for a moment?
38: 7 and all the sons of God shouted for *j*?
Ps(s) 5:12 may be the *j* of those who love your name.
20: 6 May we shout for *j* at your victory and
21: 7 gladdened him with the *j* of your presence.
34: 6 to him that you may be radiant with *j*,
35:27 for *j* and be glad who favor my just cause;
42: 5 Amid loud cries of *j* and thanksgiving,
43: 4 of God, the God of my gladness and *j*;
45: 9 ivory palaces string music brings you *j*.
45:16 They are borne in with gladness and *j*;
47: 6 God mounts his throne amid shouts of *j*;
48: 3 of heights, is the *j* of all the earth;
51:10 Let me hear the sounds of *j* and gladness;
51:14 Give me back the *j* of your salvation,
63: 8 in the shadow of your wings I shout for *j*.
65: 9 east and west you make resound with *j*.
65:14 They shout and sing for *j*.
71:23 shall shout for *j* as I sing your praises;
90:14 may shout for *j* and gladness all our days.
98: 8 shout with them for *j*
105:43 people with *j*; with shouts of joy,
106: 5 ones, rejoice in the *j* of your people,
107:22 and declare his works with shouts of *j*.
119:111 the *j* of my heart they are.
132: 9 let your faithful ones shout merrily for *j*.
132:16 faithful ones shall shout merrily for *j*.
137: 6 If I place not Jerusalem ahead of my *j*.
149: 5 let them sing for *j* upon their couches;
Prv 5:18 And have *j* of the wife of your youth,
10:28 The hope of the just brings them *j*,
12:20 evil, but those who counsel peace have *j*.
14:10 and in its *j* no one else shares.
14:13 may be sad, and the end of *j* may be sorrow.
15:21 Folly is *j* to the senseless man,
15:23 There is *j* for a man in his utterance;
15:30 A cheerful glance brings *j* to the heart;
17:21 the father of a numskull has no *j*.
21:15 To practice justice is a *j* for the just,
23:24 who begets a wise son will have *j* in him.
23:25 Let your father and mother have *j*;
Eccl 2:10 them, nor did I deprive myself of any *j*,
2:26 fit he gives wisdom and knowledge and *j*;
5:18 lot and finds *j* in the fruits of his toil,
5:19 him busy himself with the *j* of his heart.
9: 7 *j* and drink your wine with a merry heart,
Sg 3:11 marriage, on the day of the *j* of his heart.
Wis 8:16 her no grief, but rather *j* and gladness.
13: 3 *j* in their beauty they thought them gods,
Sir 1:10 giving gladness and *j* and length of days.
2: 9 for good things, for lasting *j* and mercy.
3:28 and an attentive ear is the wise man's *j*.
6:29 rest in her, and she will become your *j*.
15: 6 *J* and gladness he will find,
18:32 Have no *j* in the pleasures of a moment
25: 7 The man who finds *j* in his children,
26: 2 A worthy wife brings *j* to her husband,
30: 1 that he may be his *j* when he grows up.
30: 5 Whom he looks upon through life with *j*,
31:27 lacks the wine which was created for his *j*?
31:28 *J* of heart, good cheer and merriment
32: 2 *j* and win praise for your hospitality.
35: 8 and pay your tithes in a spirit of *j*.
39:15 sing out with *j* as you proclaim:
39:35 So now with full *j* of heart proclaim and
41: 9 When you stumble, there is lasting *j*;
50:19 the people of the land would shout for *j*,
50:23 *j* of heart and may peace abide among you;
51:15 yielded to ripening grapes, the heart's *j*,
Is 9: 2 them abundant *j* and great rejoicing,
12: 3 With *j* you will draw water at the fountain
16:10 orchards are taken away *j* and gladness,
16:10 there is no singing, no shout of *j*;
24:11 all *j* has disappeared and cheer has left
29:19 The lowly will ever find *j* in the LORD,
35:10 everlasting joy; They will meet with *j*
48:20 With shouts of *j* proclaim this,
51: 3 *J* and gladness shall be found in
51:11 everlasting *j*; They will meet with joy
52: 8 raise a cry, together they shout for *j*,
55:12 Yes, in *j* you shall depart,
60:15 ages, a *j* to generation after generation.
61: 7 their land, everlasting *j* shall be theirs.
61:10 in the LORD, in my God is the *j* of my soul;
65:14 My servants shall shout for *j* of heart,
65:18 to be a *j* and its people to be a delight;
66: 5 show his glory that we may see your *j*";
Jer 7:34 of Jerusalem I will silence the cry of *j*,
15:16 became my *j* and the happiness of my heart,
16: 9 place the cry of *j* and the cry of gladness,
20:15 filling him with great *j*,
25:10 end the song of *j* and the song of gladness,
31: 7 Shout with *j* for Jacob,
31:13 I will turn their mourning into *j*,
33: 9 Then Jerusalem shall be my *j*,
33:11 there shall yet be heard the cry of *j*,
48:33 *J* and jubilation are at an end in the
51:48 in them shall shout over Babylon with *j*,
Lam 2:15 city, the *j* of the whole earth?"
3:33 He has no *j* in afflicting or grieving the
5:15 The *j* of our hearts has ceased,
Bar 2:23 The sounds of *j* and the sounds of gladness,
3:35 shining with *j* for their Maker.
4:11 With *j* I fostered them;
4:22 and *j* has come to me from the Holy One
4:23 back to me with enduring gladness and *j*.
4:29 in saving you, bring you back enduring *j*."
4:36 behold the *j* that comes to you from God.
5: 9 For God is leading Israel in *j* by the
6:58 handy tool in a house, the *j* of its owner,
Ez 24:25 from them their bulwark, their glorious *j*,
25: 3 *j* over the desecration of my sanctuary,
36: 5 wholehearted *j* and utter contempt
Dn 6:24 This gave the king great *j*.
Hos 2:13 I will bring an end to all her *j*,
Jl 1:12 *j* has withered away from among mankind.
1:16 from the house of our God, *j* and gladness?
Zep 3:14 Shout for *j*, O daughter Zion!
Zec 8:19 shall become occasions of *j* and gladness,
9: 9 heartily, O daughter Zion, shout for *j*,
Mt 13:20 message and at first receives it with *j*.
25:21 Come, share your master's *j*!'
25:23 Come, share your master's *j*!'
Lk 1:14 *J* and gladness will be yours,
1:44 my ears, the baby leapt in my womb for *j*.
1:47 Lord, my spirit finds *j* in God my savior,
2:10 great *j* to be shared by the whole people.
8:13 when they hear the word, receive it with *j*.
15: 7 there will likewise be more *j* in heaven
15:10 there will be the same kind of *j* before
24:41 still incredulous for sheer *j* and wonder,
24:52 then returned to Jerusalem filled with *j*.
Jn 3:29 That is my *j*, and it is complete.
15:11 my *j* may be yours and your joy
16:20 time, but your grief will be turned into *j*.
16:21 *j* that a man has been born into the world.
16:22 rejoice with a *j* no one can take from you.
16:24 you shall receive, that your *j* may be full.
17:13 world that they may share my *j* completely.
Acts 2:28 you will fill me with *j* in your presence.'
5:41 left the Sanhedrin full of *j*
13:52 but be filled with *j* and the Holy Spirit.
15: 3 story caused great *j* among the brothers.
Rom 14:17 and the *j* that is given by the Holy Spirit.
15:13 fill you with all *j* and peace in believing
15:24 the *j* of being with you for a little while.
15:32 I may come to you with *j* and be refreshed
1Cor 12:26 is honored, all the members share its *j*.
2Cor 7: 4 my many afflictions my *j* knows no bounds.
7: 7 for me, so that my *j* is greater still.
7:13 rejoiced even more at the *j* of Titus
8: 2 midst of severe trial their overflowing *j*
Gal 5:22 the fruit of the spirit is love, *j*,
Phil 1:18 That is what brings me *j*.
1:25 for your *j* and your progress in the faith.
2: 2 make my *j* complete by your unanimity,
2:28 so that you may renew your *j* on seeing him,
4: 1 long for, you who are my *j* and my crown,
4:10 It gave me great *j* in the Lord that your
Col 1:24 my *j* in the suffering I endure for you.
1Thes 1: 6 with the *j* that comes from the Holy Spirit.
2:19 all, if not you, will be our hope or *j*,
3: 9 *j* we feel in his presence because of you,
Phlm 1: 7 I find great *j* and comfort in your love,
Heb 12: 2 For the sake of the *j* which lay before him
12:11 seems a cause for grief and not for *j*,
13:17 that they may fulfill their task with *j*,
Jas 1: 2 count it pure *j* when you are involved in
4: 9 into mourning and your *j* into sorrow.
1Pt 1: 8 and rejoice with inexpressible *j* touched
1Jn 1: 4 you this is that our *j* may be complete.
2Jn 1: 4 It has given me great *j* to find some of
1:12 face to face, so that our *j* may be full.
3Jn 1: 3 For it has given me great *j* to have the

JOYFUL (20)

1Sm 18: 6 and dancing, with tambourines, *j* songs,
1Chr 15:28 the covenant of the LORD with *j* shouting,
2Chr 20:27 celebrating the *j* victory the LORD
Ezr 3:13 distinguish the sound of the *j* shouting
Neh 12:27 Jerusalem to celebrate a *j* dedication
Tb 13: 1 Then Tobit composed this *j* prayer:
13:11 generation shall give *j* praise in you,
Jb 3: 7 let no *j* outcry greet it!
29:13 me, and the heart of the widow I made *j*.
Ps(s) 35: 9 LORD, I will be *j* because of his salvation.
89:16 Happy the people who know the *j* shout;
96:12 the plains be *j* and all that is in them!
100: 2 come before him with *j* song.
113: 9 barren wife as the *j* mother of children.
118:15 The *j* shout of victory in the tents of
Prv 17:22 A *j* heart is the health of the body,
Sir 30:16 no happiness, than a *j* heart!
Is 32:13 For all the *j* houses,
35: 2 abundant flowers, and rejoice with *j* song.
56: 7 mountain and make *j* in my house of prayer;

JOYFULLY (22)

Jgs 19: 3 him, the girl's father *j* made him welcome.
Ezr 6:22 They *j* kept the feast of Unleavened Bread
1Mc 3: 2 him, and they carried on Israel's war *j*.
4:56 *j* offered holocausts and sacrifices
2Mc 10: 6 *j* for eight days as on the feast of Booths,
15:28 battle was over and they were *j* departing,
Ps(s) 19: 6 and, like a giant, *j* runs its course.
66: 1 Shout *j* to God, all you on earth,
81: 2 Sing *j* to God our strength;
95: 1 Come, let us sing *j* to the LORD;
95: 2 let us *j* sing psalms to him.
98: 4 Sing *j* to the LORD,
98: 6 sound of the horn sing *j* before the King,
100: 1 Sing *j* to the LORD, all you lands;
145: 7 goodness and *j* sing of your justice.
Prv 29: 6 into a snare, but the just man runs on *j*.

Zep 3:14 sing *j,* O Israel!
3:17 in his love, He will sing *j* because of you,
Mk 4:16 to the word accept it *j* at the outset.
Acts 16:34 and *j* celebrated with his whole family his
Col 1:11 fast, even to endure *j* whatever may come,
Heb 10:34 *j* assented to the confiscation of your goods,

JOYOUS (3)

Est 4:30 her countenance was as *j* as it was lovely,
Ps(s) 137: 3 songs, And our despoilers urged us to be *j:*
Bar 4:34 I will take from her the *j* throngs,

JOYOUSLY (1)

Phil 2:29 Welcome him *j* in the Lord and hold men

JOYS (3)

Ps(s) 16:11 of life, fullness of *j* in your presence,
Sir 14:16 in the nether world there are no *j* to seek.
37: 4 A false friend will share your *j,*

JOZABAD (11)

1Chr 12: 5 *J* from Gederah;
12:21 Adnah, *J,* Jediael, Michael, Jozabad,
2Chr 17:18 Next to him, *J,*
31:13 Azaziah, Nahath, Asahel, Jerimoth, *J,*
35: 9 Nethanel, Hashabiah, Jehiel and *J,*
Ezr 8:33 they were assisted by the Levites *J,*
10:22 Elioenai, Maaseiah, Ishmael, Nethanel, *J,*
10:23 *J,* Shimei,
Neh 8: 7 Hodiah, Maaseiah, Kelita, Azariah, *J,*
11:16 Shabbethai and *J,* levitical chiefs

JOZACAR (1)

2Kgs 12:22 *J,* son of Shimeath,

JOZADAK (5)

Ezr 3: 2 Then Jeshua, son of *J,*
3: 8 son of Shealtiel, and Jeshua, son of *J,*
5: 2 son of Shealtiel, and Jeshua, son of *J,*
10:18 Of the sons of Jeshua, son of *J,*
Neh 12:26 son of *J* [and in the time of Nehemiah the

JOZADAK'S (1)

Sir 49:12 on God's right hand, And Jeshua, *J* son?

JUBAL (1)

Gn 4:21 His brother's name was *J;*

JUBILANT (6)

1Sm 11: 9 to the inhabitants of Jabesh, who were *j,*
2Chr 20:22 At the moment they began their *j* hymn,
Is 24: 8 timbrels, ended the shouts of the *j,*
54: 1 who did not bear, break forth in *j* song,
Jer 11:15 be *j* when you hear the great invasion?
Mk 14:11 they were *j* and promised to give him money.

JUBILANTLY (1)

Jb 39:21 He *j* paws the plain and rushes in his

JUBILATION (6)

1Mc 13:51 Jews entered the citadel with shouts of *j,*
Prv 11:10 and when the wicked perish, there is *j.*
28:12 the just are triumphant, there is great *j;*
Jer 48:33 Joy and *j* are at an end in the fruit
Lk 10:17 The seventy-two returned in *j* saying,
15: 5 finds it, he puts it on his shoulders in *j.*

JUBILEE (19)

Lv 25:10 It shall be a *j* for you,
25:11 In this fiftieth year, your year of *j,*
25:12 Since this is the *j,* which shall be sacred
25:13 "In this year of *j,* then, every one of you
25:15 *j* shall you purchase the land from him;
25:28 possession of the purchaser until the *j,*
25:30 nor shall it be released in the *j.*
25:31 time, and in the *j* they must be released.
25:33 not redeemed, shall be released in the *j;*
25:40 tenant, working with you until the *j* year,
25:50 compute the years from the sale to the *j,*
25:52 years there are left before the *j* year,
25:54 together with his children, in the *j* year.
27:17 is made at the beginning of a *j* period,
27:18 number of years left until the next *j* year,
27:21 but at the *j* it shall be released as
27:23 to the number of years until the next *j,*
27:24 at the *j,* however, the field shall revert
Nm 36: 4 When the Israelites celebrate the *j* year,

JUCAL (1)

Jer 38: 1 of Mattan, Gedaliah, son of Pashhur, *J,*

JUDAH (816)

Gn 29:35 therefore she named him *J.*
35:23 Jacob's first-born, Simeon, Levi, *J,*
37:26 *J* said to his brothers:
38: 1 About that time *J* parted from his brothers
38: 6 *J* got a wife named Tamar for his first-born,
38: 8 Then *J* said to Onan,
38:11 *J* said to his daughter-in-law Tamar,
38:12 After *J* completed the period of mourning,
38:15 When *J* saw her,
38:18 *J* asked, "What pledge am I to give
38:20 *J* sent the kid by his friend the
38:22 He went back to *J* and told him,
38:23 "Let her keep the things," *J* replied;
38:24 *J* was told that his daughter-in-law Tamar
38:24 "Bring her out," cried *J;*
38:26 *J* recognized them and said,
43: 3 But *J* replied: "The man strictly warned us
43: 8 Then *J* urged his father Israel:
44:14 As *J* and his brothers reentered Joseph's
44:16 *J* replied: "What can we say to my lord?
44:18 *J* then stepped up to him and said:
46:12 The sons of *J:* Er, Onan, Shelah
46:28 Israel had sent *J* ahead to Joseph,
49: 8 "You, *J,* shall your brothers praise
49: 9 *J,* like a lion's whelp,
49:10 The scepter shall never depart from *J,*
Ex 1: 2 Reuben, Simeon, Levi and *J;*
31: 2 son of Uri, son of Hur, of the tribe of *J,*
35:30 son of Uri, son of Hur, of the tribe of *J,*
38:22 son of Uri, son of Hur, of the tribe of *J,*
Nm 1: 7 Shelumiel, son of Zurishaddai; from *J:*
1:26 Of the descendants of *J,*
1:27 hundred were enrolled in the tribe of *J.*
2: 3 sunrise, shall be the divisional camp of *J,*
2: 5 With *J* shall camp the tribe of Issachar
2: 9 registered by companies in the camp of *J*
7:12 son of Amminadab, prince of the tribe of *J.*
13: 6 Jephunneh of the tribe of *J*
26:19 The sons of *J* who died in the land of
26:22 These were the clans of *J,*
34:19 from the tribe of *J:* Caleb, son of Jephunneh;
Dt 27:12 you cross the Jordan, Simeon, Levi, *J,*
33: 7 The following is for *J.* He said:
33: 7 "The LORD hears the cry of *J;*
34: 2 the land of *J* as far as the Western Sea,
Jos 7: 1 of Zerah, son of Zara of the tribe of *J,*
7:16 tribes, and the tribe of *J* was designated.
7:17 Then he had the clans of *J* come forward,
7:18 of Zabdi, son of Zerah of the tribe of *J,*
11:21 Anab, the entire mountain region of *J,*
18: 5 *J* is to retain its territory in the south,
18:11 the descendants of *J* and those of Joseph.
20: 7 is, Hebron) in the mountain region of *J.*
21: 4 cities by lot from the tribes of *J,*
21:11 is, Hebron, in the mountain region of *J,*
Jgs 1: 2 The LORD answered, *J* shall attack:
1: 3 *J* then said to his brother Simeon,
1: 4 When the forces of *J* attacked,
1:10 *J* also marched against the Canaanites who
1:17 *J* then went with his brother Simeon,
1:18 *J,* however, did not occupy Gaza
1:19 Since the LORD was with *J,*
10: 9 crossed the Jordan to fight against *J,*
15: 9 Philistines went up and, from a camp in *J,*
15:10 When the men of *J* asked,
15:11 Three thousand men of *J* went down to the
17: 7 the tribe of Judah at Bethlehem of *J.*
17: 9 him, "I am a Levite from Bethlehem in *J,*
18:12 in Zorrah and Eshtaol, and camped in *J,*
19: 1 himself a concubine from Bethlehem of *J.*
19: 2 for her father's house in Bethlehem of *J,*
19:18 "We are traveling from Bethlehem of *J*
19:18 Bethlehem of *J* and am now going back home;
20:18 the LORD said, *J* shall go first."
Ru 1: 1 so a man from Bethlehem of *J* departed
1: 2 they were Ephrathites from Bethlehem of *J.*
1: 7 were on the road back to the land of *J,*
4:12 the house of Perez, whom Tamar bore to *J.*"
1Sm 15: 4 foot soldiers and ten thousand men of *J.*
17: 1 forces for battle at Socoh in *J*
17:12 named Jesse, who was from Bethlehem in *J.*
17:52 Then the men of Israel and *J,*
18:16 the other hand, all Israel and *J* loved him,
22: 5 Leave, and go to the land of *J.*"
23: 3 "We are afraid here in *J.*
23:23 search him out among all the families of *J.*"
27: 6 to the kings of *J* up to the present time.
27:10 And David answered, "The Negeb of *J,*"
30:14 of the Cherethites, the territory of *J,*
30:16 of the Philistines and from the land of *J.*
30:26 sent part of the spoil to the elders of *J,*
2Sm 2: 1 I go up into one of the cities of *J?*"
2: 4 Then the men of *J* came there and anointed
3: 8 Abner said, "Am I a dog's head in *J?*
3:10 Israel and over *J* from Dan to Beer-sheba."
5: 5 years and six months in Hebron over *J,*
5: 5 years in Jerusalem over all Israel and *J.*
6: 2 of *J* to bring up from there the ark of God,
11:11 ark and Israel and *J* are lodged in tents,
12: 8 I gave you the house of Israel and of *J.*
19:12 "Say to the elders of *J:*
19:16 *J* had come to Gilgal to meet him and to
19:41 All the people of *J* and half of the people
20: 5 Accordingly Amasa set out to summon *J,*
21: 2 in his zeal for the men of Israel and *J.*)
24: 1 by prompting him to number Israel and *J.*
24: 7 ending up at Beer-sheba in the Negeb of *J.*
24: 9 in *J,*
1Kgs 1: 9 sons, and all the royal officials of *J.*
1:35 I designate him ruler of Israel and of *J.*"
4:20 *J* and Israel were as numerous as the sands
5: 5 Thus *J* and Israel lived in security,
9:18 Baalath, Tamar in the desert of *J,*
12:17 Israelites who lived in the cities of *J.*
12:20 David's house except the tribe of *J* alone.
12:21 the house of *J* and the tribe of Benjamin
12:23 of Judah, and to the house of *J*
12:27 to their master, Rehoboam, king of *J,*
12:32 in Bethel the pilgrimage feast of *J,*
13: 1 from *J* to Bethel by the word of the LORD,
13:12 by the man of God who had come from *J.*
13:14 "Are you the man of God who came from *J?*"
13:21 out to the man of God who had come from *J:*
14:21 Rehoboam, son of Solomon, reigned in *J.*
14:22 *J* did evil in the sight of the LORD,
14:24 *J* imitated all the abominable practices of
14:29 book of the chronicles of the kings of *J.*
15: 1 son of Nebat, Abijam became king of *J;*
15: 7 book of the chronicles of the kings of *J.*
15: 9 Jeroboam, king of Israel, Asa, king of *J,*
15:17 attacked *J* and fortified Ramah to prevent
15:17 prevent communication with Asa, king of *J.*
15:22 King Asa summoned all *J* without exception,
15:23 book of the chronicles of the kings of *J.*
15:25 In the second year of Asa, king of *J,*
15:28 him in the third year of Asa, king of *J,*
15:33 In the third year of Asa, king of *J,*
16: 8 the twenty-sixth year of Asa, king of *J,*
16:10 the twenty-seventh year of Asa, king of *J,*
16:15 the twenty-seventh year of Asa, king of *J,*
16:23 the thirty-first year of Asa, king of *J,*
16:29 the thirty-eighth year of Asa, king of *J,*
19: 3 for his life, going to Beer-sheba of *J.*
22: 2 of *J* came down to the king of Israel,
22:10 and King Jehoshaphat of *J* were seated,
22:29 Jehoshaphat of *J* went up to Ramoth-gilead,
22:41 to reign over *J* in the fourth year of Ahab,
22:46 book of the chronicles of the kings of *J.*
22:52 seventeenth year of Jehoshaphat, king of *J;*
2Kgs 1:17 of Jehoram, son of Jehoshaphat, king of *J.*
3: 1 eighteenth year of Jehoshaphat, king of *J.*
3: 7 Samaria, he sent the king of *J* the message:
3: 9 by the king of *J* and the king of Edom.
3:11 But the king of *J* asked,
3:12 word of the LORD," the king of *J* agreed.
3:12 So the kings of Israel, *J,*
3:14 were it not that I respect the king of *J.*
8:16 Jehoram, son of Jehoshaphat, king of *J,*
8:19 so, the LORD was unwilling to destroy *J,*
8:20 of *J* and chose a king of its own.
8:22 has been in revolt against the rule of *J.*
8:23 book of the chronicles of the kings of *J.*
8:25 Ahaziah, son of Jehoram, king of *J,*
8:29 Then Ahaziah, son of Jehoram, king of *J,*
9:16 where Joram lay ill and Ahaziah, king of *J,*
9:21 king of Israel, and Ahaziah, king of *J,*
9:27 what was happening, Ahaziah, king of *J,*
9:29 king of *J* in the eleventh year of Joram,
10:13 came across kinsmen of Ahaziah, king of *J.*
12:19 But King Jehoash of *J* took all the
12:19 Jehoram, and Ahaziah, kings of *J,*
12:20 book of the chronicles of the kings of *J.*
13: 1 year of Joash, son of Ahaziah, king of *J,*
13:10 thirty-seventh year of Joash, king of *J,*
13:12 he fought against Amaziah, king of *J,*
14: 1 Israel, Amaziah, son of Joash, king of *J,*
14: 9 of Israel sent this reply to the king of *J:*
14:10 and *J* with you in misfortune and failure?"
14:11 *J* met in battle at Beth-shemesh of Judah.
14:12 *J* was defeated by Israel,
14:13 son of Jehoash, son of Ahaziah, king of *J,*
14:15 and how he fought Amaziah, king of *J,*
14:17 Amaziah, son of Joash, king of *J,*
14:18 book of the chronicles of the kings of *J.*
14:21 Thereupon all the people of *J* took the
14:22 who rebuilt Elath and restored it to *J,*
14:23 year of Amaziah, son of Joash, king of *J,*
15: 1 Azariah, son of Amaziah, king of *J,*
15: 6 book of the chronicles of the kings of *J.*
15: 8 thirty-eighth year of Azariah, king of *J,*
15:13 the thirty-ninth year of Uzziah, king of *J;*
15:17 thirty-ninth year of Azariah, king of *J,*
15:23 the fiftieth year of Azariah, king of *J,*
15:27 fifty-second year of Azariah, king of *J,*
15:32 Israel, Jotham, son of Uzziah, king of *J,*
15:36 book of the chronicles of the kings of *J.*
15:37 and Pekah, son of Remaliah, against *J.*
16: 1 Remaliah, Ahaz, son of Jotham, king of *J,*
16:19 book of the chronicles of the kings of *J.*
17: 1 In the twelfth year of Ahaz, king of *J,*
17:13 Israel and *J* by every prophet and seer,
17:18 Only the tribe of *J* was left.
17:19 Even the people of *J,*
18: 1 Israel, Hezekiah, son of Ahaz, king of *J,*
18: 5 anyone like him among all the kings of *J.*
18:13 fortified cities of *J* and captured them.
18:14 Hezekiah, king of *J,*
18:14 talents of gold from Hezekiah, king of *J.*
18:22 commanding *J* and Jerusalem to worship
19:10 shall you say to Hezekiah, king of *J:*
19:30 house of *J* shall again strike root

JUDAH (cont.)

20:20 book of the chronicles of the kings of *J*.
21:11 "Because Manasseh, king of *J*,
21:11 him, and has led *J* into sin by his idols,
21:12 bring such evil on Jerusalem and *J* that,
21:16 to the sin which he caused *J* to commit,
21:17 book of the chronicles of the kings of *J*.
21:25 book of the chronicles of the kings of *J*.
22:13 LORD for me, for the people, for all *J*,
22:16 in the book which the king of *J* has read.
22:18 king of *J* who sent you to consult the LORD,
23: 1 The king then had all the elders of *J* and
23: 2 of *J* and all the inhabitants of Jerusalem:
23: 5 kings of *J* had appointed to burn incense
23: 5 of *J* and in the vicinity of Jerusalem,
23: 8 in all the priests from the cities of *J*,
23:11 the kings of *J* had dedicated to the sun;
23:12 *J* on the roof (the roof terrace of Ahaz),
23:17 grave of the man of God who came from *J*
23:22 of the kings of Israel and the kings of *J*,
23:24 be seen in the land of *J* and in Jerusalem,
23:26 from his fiercely burning anger against *J*.
23:27 "Even *J* will I put out of my sight as I
23:28 book of the chronicles of the kings of *J*.
24: 2 he loosed them against *J* to destroy it,
24: 3 This befell *J* because the LORD had stated
24: 5 book of the chronicles of the kings of *J*.
24:12 Then Jehoiachin, king of *J*,
24:20 *J* till he cast them out from his presence.
25:21 Thus was *J* exiled from her land.
25:22 he had allowed to remain in the land of *J*,
25:27 of the exile of Jehoiachin, king of *J*,
25:27 own reign, raised up Jehoiachin, king of *J*,
1Chr 2: 1 Reuben, Simeon, Levi, *J*,
2: 3 The sons of *J* were: Er, Onan and Shelah;
4: 1 The descendants of *J* were:
4:21 The descendants of Shelah, son of *J*, were:
4:41 during the reign of Hezekiah, king of *J*,
5: 2 *J*, in fact, became powerful among his brothers,
5:17 records in the time of Jotham, king of *J*,
5:41 on *J* and Jerusalem through Nebuchadnezzar.
6:40 adjacent pasture lands in the land of *J*,
9: 1 Now *J* had been carried in captivity to
9: 4 one of the descendants of Perez, son of *J*.
13: 6 Baalah, that is, to Kiriath-jearim, of *J*,
21: 5 and in *J* four hundred and seventy thousand.
27:18 for *J*, Eliab, one of David's brothers;
28: 4 For he chose *J* as leader,
28: 4 Judah as leader, then one family of *J*,
2Chr 2: 6 who are with me in *J* and Jerusalem,
9:11 had not been seen before in the land of *J*.
10:17 Israelites who lived in the cities of *J*,
11: 1 together the house of *J* and Benjamin,
11: 3 *J*, and to all the Israelites in Judah
11: 5 Jerusalem and built fortified cities in *J*.
11:10 were fortified cities in *J* and Benjamin.
11:12 Thus *J* and Benjamin remained his.
11:14 their holdings and came to *J* and Jerusalem,
11:17 the kingdom of *J* and made Rehoboam,
11:23 all the districts of *J* and Benjamin,
12: 4 cities of *J* and came as far as Jerusalem.
12: 5 commanders of *J* who had gathered
12:12 and in *J* moreover,
13: 1 of King Jeroboam, Abijah became king of *J*;
13:13 so that while his army faced *J*,
13:14 When *J* turned and saw that they had to
13:15 Then the men of *J* shouted;
13:15 and all Israel before Abijah and *J*.
13:16 The Israelites fled before *J*,
14: 3 He commanded *J* to seek the LORD,
14: 4 incense stands from all the cities of *J*,
14: 5 He built fortified cities in *J*,
14: 6 He said to *J*: "Let us build these cities
14: 7 thousand shield- and lance-bearers from *J*,
14:11 defeated the Ethiopians before Asa and *J*,
15: 2 "Hear me, Asa and all *J* and Benjamin!
15: 8 detestable idols from the whole land of *J*
15: 9 Then he convened all *J* and Benjamin,
15:15 All *J* rejoiced over the oath,
16: 1 attacked *J* and fortified Ramah to prevent
16: 1 any communication with Asa, king of *J*.
16: 6 Then King Asa commandeered all of *J* to
16: 7 Hanani the seer came to Asa, king of *J*,
16:11 in the book of the kings of *J* and Israel.
17: 2 forces in all the fortified cities of *J*,
17: 2 and put garrisons in the land of *J* and in
17: 5 secure, and all *J* gave Jehoshaphat gifts,
17: 6 high places and the sacred poles from *J*.
17: 7 and Micaiah, to teach in the cities of *J*.
17: 9 They taught in *J*,
17: 9 cities of *J* and taught among the people.
17:10 kingdoms of the countries surrounding *J*,
17:12 built strongholds and store cities in *J*.
17:13 carried out many works in the cities of *J*,
17:14 Of *J*, the commanders of thousands:
17:19 in the fortified cities throughout all *J*.
18: 3 of Israel, asked Jehoshaphat, king of *J*,
18: 9 of *J* were seated each on his throne,
18:28 king of Israel and King Jehoshaphat of *J*
19: 1 King Jehoshaphat of *J* returned in safety
19: 5 the land, in all the fortified cities of *J*,
19:11 of *J* in all that pertains to the king;
20: 3 He proclaimed a fast for all *J*.
20: 4 Then *J* gathered to seek help from the LORD;
20: 4 the cities of *J* they came to seek the LORD.
20: 5 stood up in the assembly of *J*
20:13 All *J* was standing before the LORD,
20:15 "Listen, all of *J*, inhabitants of Jerusalem,
20:17 with you to deliver you, *J* and Jerusalem.
20:18 and all *J* and the inhabitants of Jerusalem
20:20 to me, *J* and inhabitants of Jerusalem!
20:22 of Mount Seir who were coming against *J*,
20:24 When *J* came to the watchtower of the
20:27 Then all the men of *J* and Jerusalem,
20:31 Thus Jehoshaphat reigned over *J*.
20:35 King Jehoshaphat of *J* allied himself with
21: 2 these were sons of King Jehoshaphat of *J*.
21: 3 together with fortified cities in *J*,
21: 8 Edom revolted against the sovereignty of *J*;
21:10 sovereignty of *J* down to the present time.
21:11 set up high places in the mountains of *J*;
21:11 of Jerusalem into idolatry and seduced *J*.
21:12 father Jehoshaphat, nor of Asa, king of *J*,
21:13 led *J* and the inhabitants of Jerusalem
21:17 They came up against *J*,
22: 1 son of Jehoram, reigned as the king of *J*.
22: 6 Ahaziah, son of Jehoram, king of *J*,
22: 8 encountered the princes of *J*
22:10 all the royal offspring of the house of *J*.
23: 2 They journeyed about *J*,
23: 2 Levites from all the cities of *J*
23: 8 The Levites and all *J* did just as Jehoiada
24: 5 "Go out to all the cities of *J* and
24: 6 *J* and Jerusalem the tax levied by Moses,
24: 9 *J* and Jerusalem that the tax which Moses,
24:17 of *J* came and paid homage to the king,
24:18 of theirs, wrath came upon *J* and Jerusalem.
24:23 They invaded *J* and Jerusalem,
24:24 power, because *J* had abandoned the LORD,
25: 5 Judah and placed them, out of all *J*
25:10 however, became furiously angry with *J*,
25:13 the cities of *J* from Samaria to Beth-horon.
25:17 King Amaziah of *J* sent messengers to Joash,
25:18 sent this reply to King Amaziah of *J*:
25:19 Why involve yourself, and *J* with you,
25:21 Amaziah met in battle at Beth-shemesh of *J*.
25:22 There *J* was defeated by Israel,
25:23 of Israel captured Amaziah, king of *J*,
25:25 Amaziah, son of Joash, king of *J*,
25:26 in the book of the kings of *J* and Israel.
25:28 him with his ancestors in the City of *J*.
26: 1 All the people of *J* chose Uzziah,
26: 2 He rebuilt Elath and restored it to *J*;
27: 4 he built cities in the hill country of *J*,
27: 7 in the book of the kings of Israel and *J*.
28: 6 and twenty thousand of *J* in a single day,
28: 9 *J* that he delivered them into your hands.
28:10 *J* and Jerusalem your slaves and bondwomen.
28:17 The Edomites had returned, attacked *J*,
28:18 of the foothills and the Negeb of *J*;
28:19 the LORD had brought *J* low because of Ahaz,
28:19 who let *J* go its own way and proved
28:25 In every city throughout *J* he set up high
28:26 in the book of the kings of *J* and Israel.
29: 8 of the LORD has come upon *J* and Jerusalem;
29:21 the kingdom, for the sanctuary, and for *J*,
30: 1 sent a message to all Israel and *J*,
30: 6 his princes, traversed all Israel and *J*,
30:12 In *J*, however, the power of God
30:24 King Hezekiah of *J* had contributed a
30:25 and the whole assembly of *J* rejoiced,
30:25 land of Israel and those that lived in *J*.
31: 1 cities of *J* and smashed the sacred pillars,
31: 1 the high places and altars throughout *J*,
31: 6 cities of *J* also brought in tithes of oxen,
31:20 This Hezekiah did in all *J*.
32: 1 He invaded *J*, besieged the fortified cities,
32: 8 from the words of King Hezekiah of *J*.
32: 9 with this message for King Hezekiah of *J*,
32:12 and altars and commanded *J* and Jerusalem,
32:23 and costly objects for King Hezekiah of *J*,
32:25 upon him and upon *J* and Jerusalem.
32:32 in the book of the kings of *J* and Israel.
32:33 All *J* and the inhabitants of Jerusalem
33: 9 Manasseh misled *J* and the inhabitants of
33:14 officers in all the fortified cities of *J*.
33:16 and commanded *J* to serve the LORD,
34: 3 purge *J* and Jerusalem of the high places,
34: 5 Thus he purged *J* and Jerusalem.
34: 9 of Israel, as well as from all of *J*,
34:11 kings of *J* had allowed to fall into ruin.
34:21 and those who are left in Israel and *J*,
34:24 that has been read before the king of *J*.
34:26 king of *J* who sent you to consult the LORD,
34:29 convened all the elders of *J* and Jerusalem.
34:30 men of *J* and the inhabitants of Jerusalem,
35:18 all of *J* and Israel that were present,
35:21 "What quarrel is between us, king of *J*?
35:24 and all *J* and Jerusalem mourned him.
35:26 in the book of the kings of Israel and *J*.
36: 4 brother Eliakim king over *J* and Jerusalem,
36: 8 in the book of the kings of Israel and *J*.
36:10 brother Zedekiah king over *J* and Jerusalem.
36:14 Likewise all the princes of *J*,
36:23 him a house in Jerusalem, which is in *J*.
Ezr 1: 2 him a house in Jerusalem, which is in *J*.
1: 5 *J* and Benjamin and the priests and Levites
1: 8 out to Sheshbazzar, the prince of *J*.
2: 1 and who came back to Jerusalem and *J*,
4: 1 When the enemies of *J* and Benjamin heard
4: 4 of *J* so as to keep them from building.
4: 6 against the inhabitants of *J* and Jerusalem.
5: 1 began to prophesy to the Jews in *J* and
5: 8 of *J* and the house of the great God:
7:14 seven counselors to supervise *J*
9: 9 has granted us a fence in *J* and Jerusalem.
10: 7 A proclamation was made throughout *J* and
10: 9 All the men of *J* and Benjamin gathered
10:23 called Kelita), Pethahiah, *J* and Eliezer.
Neh 1: 2 of my brothers, came with other men from *J*.
2: 5 is deserving of your favor, send me to *J*,
2: 7 afford me safe-conduct till I arrive in *J*;
4:10 whole house of *J* as they rebuilt the wall.
5:14 appointed me governor in the land of *J*,
6: 7 in Jerusalem to proclaim you king of *J*.
6:17 were going to Tobiah from the nobles of *J*,
6:18 for many in *J* were in league with him,
7: 6 and who came back to Jerusalem and *J*,
11: 3 (In the cities of *J* dwelt lay Israelites,
11: 9 son of Zichri, was their commander, and *J*,
11:20 Levites, were in all the other cities of *J*,
11:24 a descendant of Zerah, son of *J*,
11:36 of the Levites from *J* settled in Benjamin.
12: 8 Jeshua, Binnui, Kadmiel, Sherebiah, *J*,
12:31 I had the princes of *J* mount the wall,
12:32 by Hoshaiah and half the princes of *J*,
12:34 along with Azariah, Ezra, Meshullam, *J*,
12:36 Milalai, Gilalai, Maai, Nethanel, *J*,
12:44 For *J* rejoiced in its appointed priests
13:12 *J* once more brought in the tithes of grain,
13:15 In those days I perceived that men in *J*
13:17 I took the nobles of *J* to task,
Jdt 14: 7 "Blessed are you in every tent of *J*;
Est A: 3 taken from Jerusalem with Jeconiah, king of *J*.
2: 6 captives taken with Jeconiah, king of *J*,
1Mc 1:29 the Mysian commander to the cities of *J*,
1:44 to Jerusalem and to the cities of *J*,
1:51 the cities of *J* to offer sacrifices,
1:54 cities of *J* they built pagan altars.
2: 6 were being committed in *J* and in Jerusalem,
2:18 all the Gentiles and the men of *J*
3: 8 cities of *J* destroying the impious there.
3:39 thousand cavalry to invade the land of *J*
5:45 crowd of people, to go into the land of *J*.
5:53 whole way, until he reached the land of *J*.
5:68 their cities he returned to the land of *J*.
6: 5 into the land of *J* had been put to flight;
6:12 that the inhabitants of *J* be destroyed.
7:10 in the land of *J* with a great army,
7:22 of *J* and caused great distress in Israel.
7:50 for a short time the land of *J* was quiet.
9: 1 Bacchides and Alcimus into the land of *J*,
9:57 and the land of *J* was quiet for two years.
9:72 he had previously taken from the land of *J*.
10:30 I collect them from the land of *J*
10:33 carried into captivity from the land of *J*
10:37 as the king has commanded in the land of *J*.
12: 4 envoys with safe conduct to the land of *J*.
12:46 troops, and they returned to the land of *J*.
12:52 of Jonathan came safely into the land of *J*.
13: 1 army to invade and ravage the land of *J*
13:12 with a large army to invade the land of *J*,
Ps(s) 48:12 Zion be glad, Let the cities of *J* rejoice,
60: 9 *J*, my scepter;
68:28 the princes of *J* in a body,
69:36 will save Zion and rebuild the cities of *J*.
76: 2 God is renowned in *J*,
78:68 But he chose the tribe of *J*,
97: 8 of *J* rejoice because of your judgments,
108: 9 *J*, my scepter;
114: 2 of alien tongue, *J* became his sanctuary,
Prv 25: 1 The men of Hezekiah, king of *J*,
Sir 45:25 David, the son of Jesse of the tribe of *J*,
48:15 But *J* remained, a tiny people
49: 4 the Law of the Most High, these kings of *J*,
Is 1: 1 *J* and Jerusalem in the days of Uzziah,
1: 1 Jotham, Ahaz and Hezekiah, kings of *J*.
2: 1 of Amoz, saw concerning *J* and Jerusalem.
3: 1 shall take away from Jerusalem and from *J*
3: 8 Jerusalem is crumbling, *J* is falling;
5: 3 Now, inhabitants of Jerusalem and men of *J*,
5: 7 and the men of *J* are his cherished plant;
7: 1 In the days of Ahaz, king of *J*,
7: 6 saying, "Let us go up and tear *J* asunder,
7:17 than any since Ephraim seceded from *J*.
8: 8 It shall pass into *J*, and flood it all
9:20 together they turn on *J*.
11:12 The dispersed of *J* he shall assemble from
11:13 pass away, and the rivalry of *J* be removed;
11:13 of *J*, and Judah shall not be hostile
19:17 of *J* shall be a terror to the Egyptians.
19:17 Every time they remember *J*,
22: 8 gates, and shelter over *J* is removed.
22:21 of Jerusalem, and to the house of *J*.
26: 1 they will sing this song in the land of *J*:
36: 1 fortified cities of *J* and captured them.
36: 7 commanding *J* and Jerusalem to worship
37: 9 shall you say to Hezekiah, king of *J*:
37:31 remaining survivors of the house of *J*

38: 9 The song of Hezekiah, king of *J*,
40: 9 not to cry out and say to the cities of *J*:
44:26 Be inhabited; to the cities of *J*:
48: 1 of Israel, sprung from the stock of *J*,
65: 9 From Jacob I will save offspring, from *J*,
Jer 1: 2 days of Josiah, son of Amon, king of *J*,
1: 3 of Jehoiakim, son of Josiah, king of *J*,
1: 3 year of Zedekiah, son of Josiah, king of *J*.
1:15 around and opposite all the cities of *J*.
2:28 numerous as your cities are your gods, O *J*!
3: 7 even though her traitor sister *J* saw that
3: 8 her traitor sister *J* was not frightened;
3:10 traitor sister *J* did not return
3:11 is inwardly more just than traitorous *J*.
3:18 house of *J* will join the house of Israel;
4: 3 For the men of *J* and to Jerusalem,
4: 4 O men of *J* and citizens of Jerusalem;
4: 5 Proclaim it in *J*,
4:16 their war cry against the cities of *J*."
5:11 the house of Israel and the house of *J*,
5:20 to the house of Jacob, proclaim it in *J*:
7: 2 all you of *J* who enter these gates to
7:17 see what they are doing in the cities of *J*,
7:30 of *J* have done what is evil in my eyes,
7:34 In the cities of *J* and in the streets of
8: 1 the bones of the kings and princes of *J*,
9:10 The cities of *J* I will make into a waste,
9:25 Egypt and *J*,
10:22 cities of *J* into a desert haunt of jackals.
11: 2 men of *J* and to the citizens of Jerusalem,
11: 6 of *J* and in the streets of Jerusalem:
11: 9 the men of *J* and the citizens of Jerusalem.
11:10 of Israel and the house of *J* have broken.
11:12 Then the cities of *J* and the citizens of
11:13 numerous as your cities are your gods, O *J*!
11:17 the house of Israel and by the house of *J*,
12:14 house of *J* I will pluck up in their midst.
13: 9 So also I will allow the pride of *J* to rot,
13:11 and the whole house of *J* cling to me,
13:19 All *J* is banished in universal exile.
14: 2 *J* mourns, her gates are lifeless;
14:19 Have you cast *J* off completely?
15: 4 what Manasseh, son of Hezekiah, king of *J*,
17: 1 sin of *J* is written with an iron stylus,
17:19 where the kings of *J* enter and leave,
17:20 Hear the word of the LORD, you kings of *J*,
17:25 along with their princes, and the men of *J*,
17:26 of *J* and the neighborhood of Jerusalem,
18:11 the men of *J* and the citizens of Jerusalem:
19: 3 LORD, kings of *J* and citizens of Jerusalem:
19: 4 and the kings of *J* have filled this place
19: 7 I will foil the plan of *J* and Jerusalem;
19:13 *J* shall be defiled like the place of Topheth,
20: 4 *J* I will deliver to the king of Babylon,
20: 5 dear, all the treasures of the kings of *J*,
21: 7 I will hand over Zedekiah, king of *J*,
21:11 To the royal house of *J*:
22: 1 king of *J* and there deliver this message:
22: 2 Listen to the word of the LORD, king of *J*,
22: 6 concerning the palace of the king of *J*:
22:11 Shallum, son of Josiah, king of *J*,
22:18 Jehoiakim, son of Josiah, king of *J*:
22:24 you, Coniah, son of Jehoiakim, king of *J*,
22:30 the throne of David as ruler again over *J*.
23: 6 In his days *J* shall be saved,
24: 1 king of *J*, and the princes of Judah
24: 8 so will I treat Zedekiah, king of *J*,
25: 1 Jeremiah concerning all the people of *J*,
25: 1 of *J* (the first year of Nebuchadnezzar,
25: 2 of *J* and all the citizens of Jerusalem:
25: 3 year of Josiah, son of Amon, king of *J*,
25:18 [Jerusalem, the cities of *J*,
26: 1 of Jehoiakim, son of Josiah, king of *J*,
26: 2 cities of *J* who come to worship
26:10 princes of *J* were informed of these things,
26:18 of *J*, and he told all the people of Judah:
26:19 of Judah, and all *J* condemn him to death?
27: 1 of Jehoiakim, son of Josiah, king of *J* . . .
27: 3 come to Jerusalem to Zedekiah, king of *J*,
27:12 To Zedekiah, king of *J*,
27:18 palace of the king of *J*
27:20 Jeconiah, son of Jehoiakim, king of *J*,
27:20 with all the nobles of *J* and Jerusalem
27:21 the LORD, in the palace of the king of *J*,
28: 1 of] the reign of Zedekiah, king of *J*,
28: 4 king of *J*, and all the exiles of Judah
29: 2 courtiers, the princes of *J* and Jerusalem,
29: 3 son of Hilkiah, whom Zedekiah, king of *J*,
29:22 All the exiles of *J* in Babylon will
30: 3 the lot of my people (of Israel and *J*,
30: 4 which the LORD spoke to Israel and to *J*:
31:23 their lot in the land of *J* and her cities,
31:24 *J* and all her cities,
31:27 house of *J* with the seed of man
31:31 the house of Israel and the house of *J*.
32: 1 in the tenth year of Zedekiah, king of *J*,
32: 3 Zedekiah, king of *J*,
32: 4 Neither shall Zedekiah, king of *J*,
32:12 and before all the men of *J* who happened
32:32 the men of *J* and the citizens of Jerusalem,
32:35 daughters to Molech, bringing sin upon *J*;
32:44 in the cities of *J* and of the hill country,
33: 7 change the lot of *J* and the lot of Israel,
33:10 and in the cities of *J*,
33:13 of Jerusalem, and in the cities of *J*,
33:14 I made to the house of Israel and *J*.
33:16 In those days *J* shall be safe and
34: 2 Go to Zedekiah, king of *J*, and tell him:
34: 4 the word of the LORD, Zedekiah, king of *J*,
34: 6 all these things to Zedekiah, king of *J*,
34: 7 Jerusalem and the remaining cities of *J*,
34: 7 were left of the fortified cities of *J*.
34: 9 so that no one should hold a man of *J*,
34:19 The princes of *J* and of Jerusalem,
34:21 Zedekiah, too, king of *J*,
34:22 the cities of *J* I will turn into a desert
35: 1 of Jehoiakim, son of Josiah, king of *J*:
35:13 men of *J* and to the citizens of Jerusalem:
35:17 I will bring upon *J* and all the citizens
36: 1 of Jehoiakim, son of Josiah, king of *J*,
36: 2 I have spoken to you against Israel, *J*,
36: 3 when the house of *J* hears all the evil I
36: 6 the men of *J* who come up from their cities.
36: 9 king of *J* a fast to placate the LORD was
36:28 contained, which Jehoiakim, king of *J*,
36:29 And against Jehoiakim, king of *J*,
36:30 The LORD now says of Jehoiakim, king of *J*:
36:31 men of *J* I will fulfill all the threats of evil
36:32 in the book which Jehoiakim, king of *J*,
37: 1 king over the land of *J* by Nebuchadnezzar,
37: 7 king of *J* who sent you to me to consult me:
38:19 of *J* who have deserted to the Chaldeans;
39: 1 of the ninth year of Zedekiah, king of *J*,
39: 4 When Zedekiah, king of *J* saw them,
39: 6 Babylon, who slew also all the nobles of *J*.
39:10 were left in the land of *J* by Nebuzaradan,
40: 1 and *J* who were being exiled to Babylon.
40: 5 has appointed ruler over the cities of *J*;
40:11 When the people of *J* in Moab,
40:11 king of Babylon had left a remnant in *J*,
40:12 returned to the land of *J*
40:15 dispersed and the remnant of *J* will perish."
41: 3 Ishmael also slew all the men of *J* of
41:18 of Babylon had made ruler in the land of *J*.
42:15 to the word of the LORD, the remnant of *J*:
42:19 LORD who has spoken to you, remnant of *J*;
43: 4 LORD's command to stay in the land of *J*.
43: 5 leaders took along the whole remnant of *J*
43: 5 thence to dwell again in the land of *J*:
43: 9 in Tahpanhes, while the men of *J* look on,
44: 1 the people of *J* who were living in Egypt,
44: 2 on Jerusalem and the other cities of *J*.
44: 6 cities of *J* and the streets of Jerusalem,
44: 7 Will you root out from *J* man and wife,
44: 9 and the kings of *J* and their wives,
44: 9 the land of *J* and the streets of Jerusalem?
44:11 and I will uproot all *J*.
44:12 *J* who insisted on coming to dwell in Egypt,
44:13 None of the remnant of *J* that have come to
44:14 None shall return to the land of *J* though
44:17 cities of *J* and the streets of Jerusalem.
44:21 cities of *J* and the streets of Jerusalem:
44:26 all you people of *J* who live in Egypt;
44:26 whole land of Egypt no man of *J*
44:27 All the men of *J* in Egypt shall perish by
44:28 to the land of *J* shall be few in number.
44:28 The whole remnant of *J* who came to settle
44:30 just as I handed over Zedekiah, king of *J*,
45: 1 of Jehoiakim, son of Josiah, king of *J*:
46: 2 of Jehoiakim, son of Josiah, king of *J*:
49:34 of the reign of Zedekiah, king of *J*:
50: 4 the men of Israel and of *J* shall come,
50:33 men of Israel, and with them the men of *J*;
51: 5 Israel and *J* are not widowed of their God,
52: 3 what was done in Jerusalem and in *J*
52:10 as well as all the princes of *J* at Riblah.
52:27 Thus was *J* exiled from her land.
52:28 thousand and twenty-three people of *J*;
52:30 seven hundred and forty-five people of *J*:
52:31 of the exile of Jehoiachin, king of *J*,
52:31 took up the case of Jehoiachin, king of *J*,
Lam 1: 3 *J* has fled into exile from oppression and
1:15 in the wine press virgin daughter *J*.
2: 2 in his anger the fortresses of daughter *J*;
2: 5 *J* he has multiplied moaning and groaning.
5:11 the enemy, the maidens in the cities of *J*;
Bar 1: 3 for Jeconiah, son of Jehoiakim, king of *J*,
1: 8 temple, to restore them to the land of *J*,
1: 8 Zedekiah, son of Josiah, king of *J*,
1:15 we men of *J* and citizens of Jerusalem,
2: 1 and against the men of Israel and *J*.
2:23 I will make to cease from the cities of *J*
2:26 the kingdom of Israel and the kingdom of *J*.
Ez 4: 6 bear the sins of the house of *J* forty days;
8: 1 house, and the elders of *J* sat before me,
8:17 such a trivial matter for the house of *J*
8: 1 house, and the elders of *J* sat before me,
25: 3 Israel, and the exile of the house of *J*,
25: 8 the house of *J* is like all other nations,"
25:12 vengeance on the house of *J*
27:17 *J* and the land of Israel trafficked with
37:16 *J* and those Israelites who are associated
37:19 him, and I will join to it the stick of *J*,
48: 7 *J*: on the frontier of Reuben
48: 8 On the frontier of *J*,
48:22 between the portions of *J* and of Benjamin
48:31 the gate of Reuben, the gate of *J*,
Dn 1: 1 year of the reign of Jehoiakim, king of *J*,
1: 2 handed over to him Jehoiakim, king of *J*,
1: 6 Among these were men of *J*:
5:13 whom my father, the king, brought from *J*?
9: 7 the men of *J*, the residents of Jerusalem,
13:56 "Offspring of Canaan, not of *J*,"
13:57 of *J* did not tolerate your wickedness.
Hos 1: 1 Jotham, Ahaz, Hezekiah, kings of *J*,
1: 7 Yet for the house of *J* I feel pity;
2: 2 *J* and of Israel shall be gathered together;
4:15 harlot, O Israel, let not *J* become guilty!
5: 5 in his guilt, and *J* stumbles with them.
5:10 The princes of *J* have become like those
5:12 Ephraim, like maggots for the house of *J*.
5:13 Ephraim saw his infirmity, and *J* his sore,
5:13 to Assyria, and *J* sent to the great king.
5:14 like a young lion to the house of *J*;
6: 4 What can I do with you, *J*?
6:11 For you also, O *J*,
8:14 *J*, too, has fortified many cities,
10:11 Ephraim was to be harnessed, *J* was to plow,
12: 1 *J* is still rebellious against God,
Jl 4: 1 restore the fortunes of *J* and Jerusalem,
4: 6 people of *J* and Jerusalem to the Greeks,
4: 8 and your daughters to the people of *J*,
4:18 the channels of *J* shall flow with water:
4:19 of violence done to the people of *J*,
4:20 But *J* shall abide forever,
Am 1: 1 Israel, in the days of Uzziah, king of *J*,
2: 4 For three crimes of *J*,
2: 5 led them astray, I will send fire upon *J*,
7:12 with you, visionary, flee to the land of *J*!
Ob 1:12 the children of *J* on the day of their ruin;
Mi 1: 1 of Jotham, Ahaz, and Hezekiah, kings of *J*:
1: 5 And what is the sin of the house of *J*?
1: 9 rather, it has come even to *J*,
5: 1 too small to be among the clans of *J*,
Na 2: 1 Celebrate your feasts, O *J*,
Zep 1: 1 days of Josiah, the son of Amon, king of *J*.
1: 4 I will stretch out my hand against *J*,
2: 7 belong to the remnant of the house of *J*;
Hg 1: 1 the prophet Haggai to the governor of *J*,
1:14 up the spirit of the governor of *J*,
2: 2 Tell this to the governor of *J*,
2:21 Tell this to Zerubbabel, the governor of *J*:
Zec 1:12 cities of *J* that have felt your anger
2: 2 that scattered *J* and Israel and Jerusalem."
2: 4 "Here are the horns that scattered *J*,
2: 4 their horns to scatter the land of *J*."
2:16 possess *J* as his portion of the holy land,
8:13 nations, O house of *J* and house of Israel,
8:15 to favor Jerusalem and the house of *J*;
8:19 cheerful festivals for the house of *J*;
9: 7 our God, and shall be like a family in *J*,
9:13 For I will bend *J* as my bow,
10: 3 hosts will visit his flock, the house of *J*,
10: 6 I will strengthen the house of *J*,
11:14 off the brotherhood between *J* and Israel.
12: 2 *J* will be besieged, even Jerusalem.]
12: 4 upon the house of *J* I will open my eyes,
12: 5 the princes of *J* shall say to themselves,
12: 6 *J* like a brazier of fire in the woodland,
12: 7 The LORD shall save the tents of *J* first,
12: 7 of Jerusalem may not be exalted over *J*.
14: 5 earthquake in the days of King Uzziah of *J*.
14:14 *J* also shall fight against Jerusalem.
14:21 in *J* shall be holy to the LORD of hosts;
Mal 2:11 *J* has broken faith;
2:11 *J* has profaned the temple which the LORD
Mt 1: 2 Jacob the father of *J* and his brothers.
1: 3 Jesus *J* was the father of Perez and Zerah,
2: 6 'And you, Bethlehem, land of *J*,
2: 6 by no means least among the princes of *J*,
Lk 1:39 hill country to a town of *J*
3:30 son of Levi, son of Simeon, son of *J*,
3:33 son of Hezron, son of Perez, son of *J*,
Heb 7:14 that our Lord rose from the tribe of *J*,
8: 8 house of Israel and with the house of *J*.
Rv 5: 5 The Lion of the tribe of *J*,
7: 5 twelve thousand from the tribe of *J*,

JUDAHITE (1)

Jos 15: 1 The lot for the clans of the *J* tribe fell

JUDAHITES (48)

Nm 2: 3 [The prince of the *J* was Nahshon,
10:14 the LORD through Moses, the camp of the *J*,
26:20 The *J* by clans were:
Jos 14: 6 When the *J* came up to Joshua in Gilgal,
15:12 complete boundary of the clans of the *J*.
15:13 son of Jephunneh, a portion among the *J*,
15:20 heritage of the clans of the tribe of *J*:
15:21 The cities of the tribe of the *J* in the
15:63 in Jerusalem the *J* could not drive out;
15:63 Jerusalem beside the *J* to the present day.]
18:14 which city belonged to the *J*.
19: 1 of Simeonites lay within that of the *J*.
19: 9 was within the confines of the *J*;
21: 9 From the tribes of the *J* and Simeonites
Jgs 1: 8 *J* fought against Jerusalem and captured it,
1: 9 Afterward the *J* went down to fight against

JUDAHITES (cont.)

1:16 came up with the J from the city of palms
1Sm 11: 8 Israelites and seventy thousand J.
2Sm 1:18 the Book of Jashar to be taught to the J.
2: 4 there and anointed David king of the J.
2: 7 is dead, the J have anointed me their king."
2:10 The J alone followed David.
2:11 and six months in Hebron as king of the J.
19:15 He won over all the J as one man,
19:17 down with the J to meet King David,
19:42 "Why did our brothers the J steal you
19:43 All the J replied to the men of Israel:
19:44 The Israelites answered the J:
19:44 Then the J in turn spoke even more
20: 2 the J remained loyal to their king.
20: 4 "Summon the J for me within three days.
1Chr 2:10 the father of Nahshon, a prince of the J.
4:27 clans did not equal the number of the J.
6:50 them by lot from the tribes of the J,
9: 3 In Jerusalem lived J and Benjaminites;
9: 4 Among the J was Uthai,
12:17 and J also came to David at the stronghold.
12:25 J bearing shields and spears:
2Chr 13:18 J were victorious
14:13 J conquered all the cities around Gerar,
25:12 The J also brought back another ten
31: 6 Israelites and J living in other cities of
32: 9 Judah, and all the J who were in Jerusalem:
Neh 4: 4 Meanwhile the J were saying:
11: 4 In Jerusalem dwelt both J and Benjaminites.
11: 4 Of the J: Athaiah, son of Uzziah
11:25 J lived in Kiriath-arba and its
13:16 and selling it to the J on the sabbath.

JUDAH'S (12)

Gn 38: 7 But Er, J first-born, greatly offended
38:12 Years passed, and J wife,
1Kgs 2:32 Amasa, son of Jether, general of J army.
1Chr 2: 3 But J first-born, Er, was wicked
2: 4 J daughter-in-law Tamar bore him Perez and
Jer 1:18 Against J kings and princes,
24: 5 even so will I regard with favor J exiles
33: 4 of this city and the palaces of J kings,
36: 9 all who came from J cities to Jerusalem.
38:22 All the women left in the house of J king
50:20 guilt, but it shall be no more, and J sins,
Ez 21:25 to Rabbah of the Ammonites or to J capital,

JUDAISM (9)

Est 8:17 of the peoples of the land embraced J,
2Mc 2:21 heroes who fought bravely for J so that,
8: 1 others who remained faithful to J,
14:38 of the revolt, he had been convicted of J,
Acts 2:11 all Jews, or those who have come over to J;
6: 5 of Antioch, who had been a convert to J,
17: 4 a great number of Greeks sympathetic to J,
17:17 with the Jews and those sympathetic to J,
Gal 1:13 the story of my former way of life in J.

JUDAS (175)

1Mc 2: 4 J, who was called Maccabeus;
2:66 will be a father to you, And J Maccabeus,
3: 1 Then his son J, who was called Maccabeus
3:11 When J learned of it,
3:12 the sword of Apollonius was taken by J,
3:13 heard that J had gathered many about him,
3:14 kingdom by defeating J and his followers,
3:16 J went out to meet him with a few men.
3:17 army coming against them, they said to J:
3:18 But J said: "It is easy for many to be
3:25 Then J and his brothers began to be feared,
3:26 the Gentiles talked about the battles of J.
3:42 J and his brothers saw that the situation
3:55 this J appointed officers among the people,
3:58 J said: "Arm yourselves and be brave;
4: 2 J heard of it, and himself set out
4: 5 the night Gorgias came into the camp of J,
4: 6 But at daybreak J appeared in the plain
4: 8 J said to the men with him:
4:13 and the men with J blew the trumpet.
4:16 J and the army returned from the pursuit,
4:19 As J was finishing this speech,
4:21 the army of J in the plain ready to attack,
4:23 Then J went back to plunder the camp,
4:29 and J met them with ten thousand men.
4:35 give way, and the increased boldness of J,
4:36 Then J and his brothers said,
4:41 J appointed men to attack those in the
4:59 Then J and his brothers and the entire
4:61 J also placed a garrison there to protect
5: 3 Then J attacked the sons of Esau at
5:10 sent a letter to J and his brothers saying:
5:16 When J and the people heard this,
5:17 J said to his brother Simon:
5:20 into Galilee, and eight thousand men to J,
5:24 J Maccabeus and his brother Jonathan
5:28 J suddenly changed direction with his army,
5:31 When J perceived that the struggle had
5:38 J sent men to spy on the camp,
5:39 So J went forward to attack them.
5:40 As J and his army were approaching the
5:42 But when J reached the running stream,
5:44 subdued, and J met with no more resistance.
5:48 Then J sent them this peaceful message:
5:49 So J ordered a proclamation to be made in
5:53 and J kept rounding up the stragglers and
5:55 J and Jonathan were in the land of Gilead,
5:61 they had not obeyed J and his brothers,
5:63 The valiant J and his brothers were
5:65 Then J and his brothers went out and
5:68 J then turned toward Azotus in the land of
6:19 But J planned to destroy them,
6:32 Then J marched away from the citadel and
6:42 J with his army advanced to fight,
7: 6 J and his brothers have destroyed all your
7: 7 J has done to us and to the king's land,
7:10 to J and his brothers in peaceful terms.
7:23 When J saw all the evils that Alcimus and
7:25 But when Alcimus saw that J and his
7:27 J and his brothers this peaceable message:
7:29 So he came to J,
7:29 But J' enemies were prepared to seize him.
7:30 J was afraid and would not meet him again.
7:31 he went out to fight J near Caphar-salama.
7:35 "If J and his army are not delivered to
7:40 J camped in Adasa with three thousand men.
7:40 Here J uttered this prayer:
8: 1 J had heard of the reputation of the Romans.
8:17 So J chose Eupolemus,
8:20 J, called Maccabeus,
9: 5 J, with three thousand picked men,
9: 7 As J saw that his army was melting away
9:10 But J said: "For be it from me to do such a
9:12 were on J' side also blew their trumpets.
9:14 right, with the main force of his army, J,
9:16 they turned and followed J and his men,
9:18 Then J fell, and the rest fled.
9:19 Jonathan and Simon took their brother J
9:22 The other acts of J,
9:23 After the death of J,
9:26 friends of J and brought them to Bacchides,
9:28 of J came together and said to Jonathan:
9:29 Since your brother J died
9:31 and took the place of J his brother.
11:70 Mattathias, son of Absalom, and J,
13: 8 in place of your brothers J and Jonathan.
14:18 with his brothers J and Jonathan.
16: 2 called his two oldest sons, J and John,
16: 9 then that John's brother J fell wounded;
16:14 he and his sons Mattathias and J went down
2Mc 1:10 and J send greetings and good wishes to
2:14 J also collected for us the books
2:19 the story of J Maccabeus and his brothers,
5:27 But J Maccabeus and about nine others
8: 1 J Maccabeus and his companions entered the
8: 8 When Philip saw that J was gaining ground
8:12 When J learned of Nicanor's advance and
8:21 Then J divided his army into four,
12: 5 As soon as J heard of the barbarous deed
12:11 After a hard fight, J and his companions,
12:11 The defeated nomads begged J to make
12:12 respects, J agreed to make peace with them.
12:14 treated J and his men with contempt,
12:15 But J and his men invoked the aid of the
12:21 When Timothy learned of the approach of J,
12:22 But when J' first cohort appeared,
12:23 J pressed the pursuit vigorously,
12:26 J then marched to Karnion and the shrine
12:31 J and his men thanked them and exhorted
12:36 J called upon the Lord to show himself
12:38 J rallied his army and went to the city of
12:39 J and his men went to gather up the bodies
12:42 The noble J warned the soldiers to keep
13: 1 J and his men learned that Antiochus
13:10 When J learned of this,
13:12 J encouraged them and told them to stand
13:20 J then sent supplies to the men inside,
13:23 he withdrew and attacked J and his men.
14: 1 J and his men learned that Demetrius,
14: 6 Jews called Hasideans, led by J Maccabeus,
14:10 As long as J is around,
14:11 Friends who were hostile to J
14:13 sent him off with orders to put J to death,
14:14 from Judea, who would have banished J,
14:17 J' brother Simon had engaged Nicanor,
14:18 heard of the valor of J and his men,
14:22 J had posted armed men in readiness at
14:24 but he always kept J in his company,
14:25 so J married,
14:26 the state, and that he had appointed J,
14:31 and ordered them to surrender J.
14:33 you do not hand J over to me as prisoner,
15: 1 When Nicanor learned that J and his
15: 6 monument of victory over J and his men.
15:15 hand, Jeremiah presented a gold sword to J.
15:17 Encouraged by J' noble words,
15:26 But J and his men met the army with
15:30 Then J, who was ever in body
15:35 J hung up Nicanor's head on the wall of
Mt 10: 4 the Zealot Party member, and J Iscariot,
13:55 James, Joseph, Simon, and J his brothers?
26:14 Then one of the Twelve whose name was J
26:25 Then J, his betrayer, spoke:
26:47 While he was still speaking, J,
27: 3 J, who had handed him over,
27: 5 J flung the money into the temple and left.
Mk 3:19 Simon of the Zealot Party, and J Iscariot,
6: 3 brother of James and Joses and J and Simon?
14:10 Then J Iscariot, one of the Twelve,
14:43 Even while he was still speaking, J,
Lk 6:16 Zealot, Judas son of James, and J Iscariot,
22: 3 Then Satan took possession of J,
22:47 a crowd came, led by the man named J,
22:48 Jesus said to him, J, would you betray
Jn 6:71 (He was talking about J,
12: 4 J Iscariot,
13: 2 The devil had already induced J,
13:26 the morsel, then took it and gave it to J,
13:29 idea that, since J held the common purse,
13:30 had J eaten the morsel than he went out.
13:31 Once J had left, Jesus said:
14:22 J (not Judas Iscariot) said to him,
18: 2 The place was familiar to J as well (the
18: 3 J took the cohort as well as guards
18: 5 J, the one who was to hand him over
Acts 1:13 Zealot party member, and J son of James.
1:16 David was destined to be fulfilled in J,
1:25 for this apostolic ministry, replacing J,
5:37 J the Galilean at the time of the census.
9:11 of J ask for a certain Saul of Tarsus.
15:22 were leading men of the community, J,
15:27 whom we are sending you are J and Silas,
15:32 J and Silas,

JUDE (1)

Jude 1: 1 J, a servant of Jesus Christ and brother

JUDEA (91)

Tb 1:18 fugitive from J during the days of judgment
Jdt 1:12 of Moab, Ammon, the whole of J,
4: 1 dwelt in J heard of all that Holofernes,
4: 3 all the people of J been gathered together,
4: 7 passes, since these offered access to J.
4:13 fast of many days' duration throughout J,
8:21 If we are taken, all J will fall,
11:19 I will lead you through J,
1Mc 3:34 As for the inhabitants of J and Jerusalem,
4:15 as far as Gazara and the plains of J,
4:35 so as to return to J with greater numbers.
5: 8 Jazer and its villages, he returned to J.
5:18 In J he left Joseph,
5:23 and brought them to J with great rejoicing.
5:60 and were pursued to the frontiers of J,
6:48 established camps in J and at Mount Zion.
6:53 rescued from the Gentiles and brought to J.
7:24 he went about all the borders of J and
7:46 of J people came out and closed in on them.
9:50 Bacchides built strongholds in J:
9:60 letters secretly to all his allies in J,
9:63 force and sent word to those who were in J.
10:38 three districts that have been added to J
10:38 Samaria be incorporated with J
10:45 it all around, and of building walls in J,
11:20 of J to attack the citadel in Jerusalem,
11:28 Jonathan asked the king to exempt J and
11:34 not only of the territory of J,
11:34 were transferred from Samaria to J
12:35 made plans for building strongholds in J,
13:33 his part, built up the strongholds of J,
14:33 He fortified the cities of J,
15:30 of J of which you have taken possession;
15:39 ordered him to move his troops against J
15:40 the people and to make incursions into J,
15:41 could go out and patrol the roads of J.
16:10 He then returned to J in peace.
2Mc 1: 1 land of J send greetings to their brethren,
1:10 The people of Jerusalem and J,
5:11 the king, he thought that J was in revolt.
10:24 then he appeared in J,
11: 5 So he invaded J,
13: 1 Eupator was invading J with a large force,
13:13 invade J and take possession of the city,
14:12 elephants, and appointed him governor of J.
14:14 The Gentiles from J,
15:22 angel in the days of King Hezekiah of J,
Dn 14:33 In J there was a prophet, Habakkuk;
Mt 2: 1 of J during the reign of King Herod,
2: 5 "In Bethlehem of J," they informed him.
2:22 succeeded his father Herod as king of J,
3: 1 as a preacher in the desert of J,
3: 5 At that time Jerusalem, all J,
4:25 Galilee, the Ten Cities, Jerusalem and J,
19: 1 to the district of J across the Jordan.
24:16 those in J must flee to the mountains.
Mk 3: 8 great multitude came to him from J,
10: 1 the districts of J and across the Jordan.
13:14 in J must flee to the mountains.
Lk 1: 5 of JohnIn the days of Herod, king of J,
1:65 throughout the hill country of J
2: 4 from the town of Nazareth in Galilee to J,
3: 1 when Pontius Pilate was procurator of J,
4:44 continued to preach in the synagogues of J.
5:17 of Galilee and from J and Jerusalem.
6:17 crowd of people was with them from all J
7:17 throughout J and the surrounding country.
21:21 J at the time must flee to the mountains;

23: 5 by his teaching throughout the whole of J,
Jn 4: 3 left J and started back for Galilee again.
4:47 that Jesus had come back from J to Galilee,
4:54 performed on returning from J to Galilee.
7: 1 He had decided not to travel in J because
7: 3 "You ought to leave here and go to J so
11: 7 to his disciples, "Let us go back to J."
Acts 1: 8 in Jerusalem, throughout J and Samaria,
2: 9 We live in Mesopotamia, J and Cappadocia,
8: 1 the countryside of J and Samaria.
9:31 Meanwhile throughout all J,
10:37 all over J about Jesus of Nazareth,
11: 1 All through J the apostles and the
11:29 the relief of the brothers who lived in J.
12:19 left J to spend some time in Caesarea.
15: 1 from J and began to teach the brothers:
21:10 a prophet named Agabus arrived from J.
26:20 of Jerusalem and all the country of J;
28:21 "We have had no letters from J about you,
Rom 15:31 be kept safe from the unbelievers in J,
2Cor 1:16 might receive your help on my journey to J.
Gal 1:22 Christ in J had no idea what I looked like;
1Thes 2:14 of God in J which are in Christ Jesus.

JUDEAN (11)

2Kgs 14:12 and all the J soldiery fled homeward.
18:26 Do not speak to us in J within earshot of
18:28 and cried out in a loud voice in J,
2Chr 25:22 and all the J soldiers fled homeward.
32:18 In a loud voice they shouted in the J
Jdt 3: 9 to the main ridge of the J mountain,
Is 36:11 Do not speak to us in J within earshot of
36:13 and cried out in a loud voice in J,
Dn 2:25 "I have found a man among the J captives
Mk 1: 5 All the J countryside and the people of
Jn 3:22 and his disciples came into J territory,

JUDEANS (4)

2Kgs 16: 6 Elath for Edom, driving the J out of it.
Jer 32:30 The Israelites and the J from their youth
32:32 all the wickedness the Israelites and J,
44:24 the LORD, all you J in the land of Egypt:

JUDGE (138)

Gn 18:25 the j of all the world act with justice?"
Ex 2:14 has appointed you ruler and j over us?
5:21 to them, "The LORD look upon you and j!
Lv 19:15 the mighty, but j your fellow men justly.
Dt 17: 9 or to the j who is in office at that time.
17:12 of the LORD, your God, or to the j.
25: 2 the j shall have him lie down and in his
Jgs 2:18 he would be with the j and save them from
2:18 of their enemies as long as the j lived;
2:19 But when the j died,
11:27 against me, Let the LORD, who is j,
1Sm 7: 6 that Samuel began to j the Israelites.
8: 5 over us, as other nations have, to j us."
8: 6 when they asked for a king to j them.
10: 7 fulfilled, do whatever you j feasible,
16: 7 "Do not j from his appearance or from his
24:13 The LORD will j between me and you,
24:16 The LORD will be the j;
2Sm 12: 1 J this case for me!
15: 4 only I could be appointed j in the land!
19:28 Do what you j best.
1Kgs 3: 9 an understanding heart to j your people
1Chr 5:12 in command, and Janai was j in Bashan.
2Chr 19: 8 family heads of Israel to j
Tb 3: 2 you are the j of the world.
Jdt 7:24 "God j between you and us!
1Mc 2:55 his commission, became a j in Israel.
7:42 j him according to his wickedness."
9:73 he began to j the people and he destroyed
2Mc 12: 6 and after calling upon God, the just j,
12:41 the just j who brings to light the things
Jb 12:11 the ear j words as the mouth tastes food?
22:13 Can he j through the thick darkness?
Ps(s) 7:12 A just j is God,
50: 6 for God himself is the j.
58: 2 like gods pronounce justice and j fairly,
58:12 truly there is a God who is j on earth!"
75: 3 the appointed time, I will j with equity.
75: 8 But God is the j;
82: 2 I "How long will you j unjustly and favor
82: 8 j the earth,
94: 2 Rise up, j of the earth;
Eccl 3:17 both the just and the wicked God will j,
Wis 1: 1 Love justice, you who j the earth;
3: 8 They shall j nations and rule over peoples,
9:12 and I shall j your people justly and be
12:18 are master of might, you j with clemency,
12:22 think earnestly of your goodness when we j.
15: 7 either class the worker in clay is the j.
Sir 7: 6 Seek not to become a j if you have not
8:14 Contend not at law with a j,
10: 2 As the people's j, so are his ministers;
10:23 The prince, the ruler, the j are in honor;
18: 1 is the j of all things without exception;
41:14 j of disgrace only according to my rules,
45:17 laws, and authority to prescribe and to j:
46:13 as a prophet, was SAMUEL, the j and priest.

Is 2: 4 He shall j between the nations,
3: 2 Hero and warrior, j and prophet,
5: 3 men of Judah, j between me and my vineyard:
11: 3 Not by appearance shall he j,
11: 4 But he shall j the poor with justice,
16: 5 j upholding right and prompt to do justice.
33:22 yes, the LORD our j,
51: 5 go forth [and my arm shall j the nations];
66:16 LORD shall j all mankind by fire and sword.
Jer 2:35 Behold, I will j you on that word of yours,
11:20 But, you, O LORD of hosts, O just J,
Ez 7: 3 I will unleash my anger against you and j
7: 8 I will j you according to your conduct and
7:27 according to their judgments I will j them;
11:10 at the boundaries of Israel I will j you;
11:11 At the boundaries of Israel I will j you,
18:30 Therefore I will j you,
20: 4 Will you j, them? Will you j, son of man?
21:35 in the land of your origin, I will j you.
22: 2 you judge, would you j the bloody city?
23:25 I will leave it to them to j, and they will j
23:36 of man, would you j Oholah and Oholibah?
33:20 j every one of you according to his ways,
34:17 I will j between one sheep and another,
34:20 I j between the fat and the lean sheep.
34:22 and I will j between one sheep and another.
35:11 make myself known among you when I j you,
Am 2: 3 I will root out the j from her midst,
Mi 4: 3 He shall j between many peoples and impose
7: 3 makes demands, The j is had for a price,
Zec 3: 7 you shall j my house and keep my courts,
Mt 5:25 your opponent may hand you over to the j,
12:27 Let them be the ones to j you.
19:28 thrones to j the twelve tribes of Israel.
Lk 6:37 Do not j, and you will not be judged.
12:14 who has set me up as your j or arbiter?"
12:57 do you not j for yourselves what is just?
12:58 turn you over to the j, and the j deliver
18: 2 "Once there was a j in a certain city who
18: 6 "Listen to what the corrupt j has to say.
19:22 I intend to j you on your own evidence.
Jn 5:30 I j as I hear,
8:16 Even if I do j,
12:48 not accept my words already has his j,
Acts 4:19 J for yourselves whether it is right in
7: 7 But I will j that nation which they serve,
7:27 who has appointed you ruler and j over us?'
7:35 words, 'Who has appointed you ruler and j?',
10:42 by God as j of the living and the dead.
17:31 he is going to j the world with justice'
18:15 I refuse to j such matters."
24:10 been a j over this nation for many years.
Rom 3: 6 If that were so, how could God j the world?
12: 2 mind, so that you may j what is God's will,
14: 4 alone can j whether he stands or falls.
1Cor 4: 4 The Lord is the one to j me,
5:12 What business is it of mine to j outsiders?
5:12 not those inside the community you must j?
5:13 God will j the others.
6: 2 know that the believers will j the world?
6: 3 Do you not know that we are to j angels?
10:15 You may j for yourselves what I am saying.
11:13 I will let you j for yourselves.
14:29 let the rest j the worth of what they say.
2Tm 4: 1 who is coming to j the living and the dead,
4: 8 on that Day the Lord, just j that he is,
Heb 10:30 repay," and "The Lord will j his people."
12:23 enrolled in heaven, to God the j of all,
13: 4 for God will j fornicators and adulterers.
Jas 4:11 j the law you are no observer of the law,
4:11 are no observer of the law, you are its j.
4:12 There is but one Lawgiver and J,
4:12 Who then are you to j your neighbor?
5: 9 The j stands at the gate.
1Pt 4: 5 stands ready to j the living and the dead.
Rv 6:10 before you j our cause and avenge our
11:18 day of wrath and the moment to j the dead:

JUDGED (38)

Lv 17: 4 Dwelling, shall be j guilty of bloodshed;
Jgs 3:10 of the LORD came upon him, and he j Israel.
10: 2 When he had j Israel twenty-three years,
10: 3 after him and j Israel twenty-two years.
12: 7 After having j Israel for six years,
12: 8 After him Ibzan of Bethlehem j Israel.
12: 9 After having j Israel for seven years,
12:11 After him the Zebulunite Elon j Israel.
12:11 When he had j Israel for ten years,
12:13 Abdon, son of Hillel, j Israel.
12:14 After having j Israel for eight years,
15:20 Samson j Israel for twenty years in the
16:31 He had j Israel twenty years.
1Sm 4:18 He had j Israel for forty years.
7:15 Samuel j Israel as long as he lived.
7:17 he j Israel and built an altar to the LORD.
8: 2 they j at Beer-sheba.
2Mc 9:15 whom he had j not even worthy of burial,
Ps(s) 9:20 let the nations be j in your presence.
109: 7 When he is j,
Wis 6: 4 of his kingdom, you j not rightly,
12:21 With what exactitude you j your sons,
12:22 and, when being j, may look for mercy.

Sir 18:19 Before you are j,
46:14 By the law of the LORD he j the nation,
Ez 24:14 your conduct and your deeds you shall be j,
36:19 to their conduct and deeds I j them.
Lk 6:37 Do not judge, and you will not be j.
20:35 but those j worthy of a place in the age
Acts 5:41 full of joy that they had been j worthy
Rom 2:12 by the law will be j in accordance with it.
3: 4 what you say, and win out when you are j."
1Tm 1:12 has made me his servant and j me faithful.
Heb 4: 1 be j to have lost his chance of entering.
9:27 that men die once, and after death be j,
Jude 1: 9 when his case with the devil was being j—
Rv 20:12 The dead were j according to their conduct
20:13 Each person was j according to his conduct.

JUDGES (72)

Ex 21:22 and he shall pay in the presence of the j.
Lv 13: 5 If he j that the sore has remained
13:37 he j that the scall has remained in its
Nm 25: 5 So Moses told the Israelite j,
Dt 1:16 I charged your j at that time,
16:18 "You shall appoint j and officials
17:19 of the priests or j in office at that time;
19:18 after a thorough investigation the j
21: 2 your elders and j shall go out and measure
29: 9 your chiefs and j,
Jos 8:33 alike, with their elders, officers and j,
23: 2 leaders, j and officers) and said to them:
24: 1 their leaders, their j and their officers.
Jgs 2:16 Even when the LORD raised up j to deliver
2:17 they did not listen to their j,
2:18 Whenever the LORD raised up j for them,
Ru 1: 1 of the j there was a famine in the land;
1Sm 2: 3 God is the LORD, a God who j deeds.
2:10 the LORD j the ends of the earth,
3:18 He will do what he j best."
8: 1 Samuel appointed his sons j over Israel.
2Sm 7: 7 j whom I charged to tend my people Israel,
7:11 I first appointed j over my people Israel.
10:12 the LORD will do what he j best."
2Kgs 23:22 during the period when the J ruled Israel,
1Chr 17: 6 Did I ever say a word to any of the j of
17:10 when I appointed j over my people Israel.
23: 4 six thousand were to be officials and j,
26:29 Israel's civil affairs as officials and j.
2Chr 1: 2 of thousands and of hundreds, the j,
19: 5 He appointed j in the land,
19: 6 he j with you.
Ezr 4: 9 Shimshai, the scribe, and their fellow j,
7:25 appoint magistrates and j to administer
Jb 9:24 he covers the faces of its j.
12:17 away barefoot, and of j he makes fools.
21:22 knowledge, seeing that he j those on high?
Ps(s) 7: 9 [The LORD j the nations.]
9: 9 He j the world with justice;
82: 1 he j in the midst of the gods.
141: 6 Their j were cast down over the crag,
148:11 the princes and all the j of the earth,
Wis 2:16 He j us debased;
Sir 4:15 He who obeys her j nations;
16:12 he j men,
35:18 responds, j justly and affirms the right.
38:33 They do not occupy the j bench,
46:11 The J, too, each one of them, whose hearts
Is 1:26 I will restore your j as at first,
Bar 2: 1 against our j, who governed Israel,
Ez 18: 8 j fairly between a man and his opponent;
44:24 In capital cases they shall stand as j,
Dn 3: 2 governors, the counselors, treasurers, j,
3: 3 governors, the counselors, treasurers, j,
13: 5 two elders of the people were appointed j,
13: 5 elders who were to govern the people as j."
13:41 since they were elders and j of the people,
Zep 3: 3 Her j are wolves of the night that have
Lk 11:19 In such case, let them act as your j.
Jn 5:22 The Father himself j no one,
8:50 is one who seeks it, and it is he who j.
19:13 Jesus outside and took a seat on a j bench
Acts 13:20 Later on he set up j to rule them until
Rom 2: 1 one of you who j another is inexcusable.
1Cor 6: 4 j those who have no standing in the church?
11:32 but since it is the Lord who j us,
Heb 4:12 it j the reflections and thoughts of the
Jas 2: 4 set yourselves up as j
4:11 j his brother is speaking against the law.
4:11 It is the law he j.
1Pt 1:17 In prayer you call upon a Father who j
2:23 himself up to the One who j justly.

JUDGING (13)

Jgs 4: 4 Deborah, wife of Lappidoth, was j Israel.
1Sm 7:16 and j Israel at each of these sanctuaries.
2Sm 8:15 j and administering justice to all his
2Chr 19: 6 "Take care what you do, for you are j,
Ps(s) 9: 5 my cause, seated on your throne, j justly.
Jer 5:28 the fatherless or j the cause of the poor.
Ez 44:24 as judges, j them according to my decrees.
Mt 16:23 are not j by God's standards but by man's."
Mk 8:33 are not j by God's standards but by man's."
Lk 22:30 on thrones j the twelve tribes of Israel.
Jn 7:24 Stop j by appearances and make an honest

JUDGING (cont.)

Acts 23: 3 You sit there *j* men according to the law,
1Cor 6: 2 be thought unworthy of *j* in minor matters?

JUDGMENT (200)

Gn 15:14 will bring *j* on the nation they must serve,
31:42 of my toil, and last night he gave *j.*"
Ex 6: 6 outstretched arm and with mighty acts of *j.*
7: 4 of *j* I will bring the hosts of my people,
12:12 and executing *j* on all the gods of Egypt
18:13 The next day Moses sat in *j* for the people,
Lv 19:15 shall not act dishonestly in rendering *j.*
Nm 35:29 wherever you live, for rendering *j.*
Dt 1:17 In rendering *j,* do not consider who a person
1:17 alike, fearing no man, for *j* is God's.
Jos 20: 6 Once he has stood *j* before the community,
Jgs 4: 5 there the Israelites came up to her for *j.*
1Sm 25:33 be your good *j* and blessed be you yourself,
2Sm 15: 6 the Israelites who came to the king for *j,*
1Kgs 3:28 all Israel heard the *j* the king had given,
3:28 had in him the wisdom of God for giving *j.*
7: 7 vestibule of the throne where he gave *j*—
8:32 take action and pass *j* on your servants.
10: 9 made you king to carry out *j* and justice."
2Chr 6:23 take action and pass *j* on your servants,
20: 9 'When evil comes upon us, the sword of *j,*
20:12 O our God, will you not pass *j* on them?
22: 8 Jehu was executing *j* on the house of Ahab,
Ezr 7:26 king, let strict *j* be executed upon him,
10: 8 to the *j* of the leaders and elders,
10:17 passed *j* on all the men
Tb 1:18 fugitive from Judea during the days of *j*
Jdt 9: 6 and your *j* is made with foreknowledge.
11:19 and there I will set up your *j* seat.
16:17 in the day of *j* he will punish them:
Est E: 4 the vindictive *j* of the all-seeing God.
F: 8 of *j* before God and among all the nations.
2Mc 7:35 the *j* of the almighty and all-seeing God.
7:36 God's covenant, but you, by the *j* of God,
11:36 passed *j* should be submitted to the king.
Jb 8: 3 Does God pervert *j,*
9:19 if of *j,* who will call him to account?
9:32 him, that we should come together in *j.*
11:10 If he seize and imprison or call to *j,*
14: 3 eyes so as to bring him into *j* before you,
19:29 that you may know that there is a *j.*
22: 4 that he enters with you into *j?*
23: 3 find him, that I might come to his *j* seat!
34:23 no man of his time to come before God in *j.*
37:23 discover him, preeminent in power and *j;*
Ps(s) 1: 5 Therefore in *j* the wicked shall not stand,
7: 7 wake to the *j* you have decreed.
9: 8 he has set up his throne for *j.*
17: 2 From you let my *j* come;
72: 1 I O God, with your *j* endow the king,
72: 2 justice and your afflicted ones with *j.*
76:10 and was silent When God arose for *j,*
89:15 and *j* are the foundation of your throne;
94:15 But *j* shall again be with justice,
97: 2 and *j* are the foundation of his throne.
99: 4 justice and *j* in Jacob you have wrought.
101: 1 Of kindness and *j* I will sing;
106:30 forth in *j* and the plague was checked;
110: 6 He will do *j* on the nations,
119:84 When will you do *j* on my persecutors?
122: 5 In it are set up *j* seats,
140:13 justice to the afflicted, *j* to the poor.
143: 2 And enter not into *j* with your servant,
Prv 16:10 no *j* he pronounces is false.
20: 8 of *j* dispels all evil with his glance.
24:23 To show partiality in *j* is not good.
Eccl 3:16 the sun in the *j* place I saw wickedness,
3:17 for every affair and on every work a *j.*
6:10 in *j* with one who is stronger than he.
8: 6 for there is a time and a *j* for everything."
11: 9 regards all this God will bring you to *j.*
12:14 because God will bring to *j* every work,
Wis 5:18 and shall wear sure *j* for a helmet;
6: 5 you, because *j* is stern for the exalted
8:11 I should become keen in *j,*
9: 3 and to render *j* in integrity of heart:
9: 5 lacking in comprehension of *j* and of laws.
12:25 you sent your *j* on them as a mockery;
16:18 and know they were struck by the *j* of God;
Sir 3:23 and false reasoning unbalanced their *j.*
19:21 but dishonest, which by duplicity wins a *j.*
25: 4 How becoming to the gray-haired is *j,*
32:16 His *j* is sound who fears the LORD;
40:25 secure, but better than either, sound *j.*
43:13 speeds the arrows of his *j* to their goal.
Is 1:27 Zion shall be redeemed by *j,*
3:14 *j* with his people's elders and princes:
4: 4 her midst with the blast of searing *j,*
5: 7 He looked for *j,*
5:16 LORD of hosts shall be exalted by his *j,*
9: 6 he confirms and sustains By *j* and justice,
10: 2 Depriving the needy of *j* and robbing my
26: 9 When your *j* dawns upon the earth,
28: 6 A spirit of justice to him who sits in *j,*
28: 7 in their visions, tottering when giving *j.*
34: 5 lo, it shall come down in *j* upon Edom,
40:14 Who taught him the path of *j,*
41: 1 let us come together for *j.*
51: 4 shall go forth from my presence, and my *j,*
Jer 4: 2 "As the LORD lives," in truth, in *j,*
25:31 nations, he is to pass *j* upon all mankind:
48:21 For *j* has come on the land of the plateau:
48:47 Thus far the *j* on Moab.
51: 9 Her *j* reaches heaven,
Bar 6:63 They can neither execute *j,*
Ez 5:15 When I execute *j* upon you in anger and
17:20 bring him to Babylon and enter into *j*
20:35 I will enter into *j* with you face to face.
20:36 Just as I entered into *j* with your fathers
20:36 of Egypt, so will I enter into *j* with you,
21:15 You have spurned the rod and every *j!*
25:11 Thus I will execute *j* upon Moab,
38:21 *j* with him in pestilence and bloodshed;
39:21 nations shall see the *j* I have executed
Dn 1: 4 wise, quick to learn, and prudent in *j,*
3:28 By a proper *j* you have done all this
3:31 done to us, you have done by a proper *j.*
7:22 *j* was pronounced in favor of the holy ones
Hos 5: 1 It is you who are called to *j.*
6: 3 his *j* shines forth like the light of day!
Jl 4: 2 And I will enter into *j* with them there on
4:12 sit in *j* upon all the neighboring nations.
Am 5: 7 Woe to those who turn *j* to wormwood and
6:12 Yet you have turned *j* into gall,
7: 4 he called for a *j* by fire.
Mi 3:11 Her leaders render *j* for a bribe,
Hb 1: 4 law is benumbed, and *j* is never rendered:
1: 4 this is why *j* comes forth perverted.
1:12 O LORD you have marked him for *j,*
Zep 3: 5 after morning he renders *j* unfailingly,
3:15 The LORD has removed the *j* against you,
Zec 7: 9 Render true *j,*
Mal 3: 5 I will draw near to you for *j,*
Mt 5:21 every murderer shall be liable to *j.*'
5:22 with his brother shall be liable to *j;*
7: 1 If you want to avoid *j,* stop passing *j.*
10:15 on the day of *j* than it will for that town.
11:22 and Sidon than for you on the day of *j.*
11:24 for Sodom than for you on the day of *j.*"
12:20 will not quench until *j* is made victorious.
12:36 on *j* day people will be held accountable
12:41 At the *j,* the citizens of Nineveh
12:42 At the *j,* the queen of the South
Lk 10:14 day of *j* for Tyre and Sidon than for you.
11:31 *j* along with the men of this generation,
11:32 At the *j,* the citizens of Nineveh
Jn 3:19 The *j* of condemnation is this:
5:22 no one, but has assigned all *j* to the Son,
5:27 power to pass *j* because he is Son of Man;
5:30 and my *j* is honest because I am not
7:24 by appearances and make an honest *j.*
8:15 pass *j* according to appearances but I pass *j*
8:16 *j* of mine is valid because I am not alone:
12:31 "Now has *j* come upon this world,
18:31 and pass *j* on him according to your law?"
Acts 15:19 It is my *j,*
24:25 uprightness, continence, and the coming *j,*
Rom 2: 1 By your *j* you convict yourself,
2: 2 God's *j* on men who do such things is just."
2: 3 suppose, then, that you will escape his *j,*
2: 5 when the just *j* of God will be revealed,
2:16 God will pass *j* on the secrets of men
2:27 keeps the law, he will pass *j* on you who,
14: 3 abstains must not sit in *j* on him who eats.
14: 4 Who are you to pass *j* on another's servant?
14:10 you, how can you sit in *j* on your brother?
14:10 have to appear before the *j* seat of God.
14:13 we must no longer pass *j* on one another.
1Cor 1:10 rather, be united in mind and *j*
4: 3 you or any human court pass *j* on me.
4: 3 I do not even pass *j* on myself.
4: 5 passing *j* before the time of his return.
6: 1 case against another dare bring it for *j*
6: 2 If the *j* of the world is to be yours,
11:29 the body eats and drinks a *j* on himself.
11:31 would not be falling under *j* in this way;
2Cor 5:16 look on anyone in terms of mere human *j.*
Eph 5:10 correct in your *j* of what pleases the Lord.
Col 2:16 to pass *j* on you in terms of what you eat
2Thes 1: 5 these as an expression of God's just *j,*
1Tm 5:24 sins are flagrant and cry out for *j* now,
Heb 6: 2 resurrection of the dead, and eternal *j.*
10:27 only a fearful expectation of *j* and a
Jas 2:12 destined for *j* under the law of freedom.
2:13 the *j* on the man who has not shown mercy;
2:13 but mercy triumphs over *j.*
1Pt 4:17 The season of *j* has begun,
2Pt 2: 4 to pits of darkness, to be guarded until *j.*
2: 9 of the wicked up to the day of *j.*
3: 7 they are kept for the day of *j,*
1Jn 4:17 we should have confidence on the day of *j;*
Jude 1: 6 darkness against the *j* of the great day.
1:15 holy ones about him to pass *j* on all men,
Rv 14: 7 glory, for his time has come to sit in *j.*
17: 1 I will show you the *j* in store for the
19:11 standard in passing *j* and in waging war.
20: 4 sitting on them were empowered to pass *j.*

JUDGMENTS (26)

Nm 33: 4 on their gods, too, the LORD executed *j.*
1Chr 16:12 his portents, and the *j* he has uttered,
16:14 throughout the earth his *j* prevail He
2Chr 19:10 questions of law, command, statutes, or *j,*
Tb 3: 5 your *j* are many and true in dealing with
Ps(s) 10: 5 your *j* are far from his mind;
36: 7 your *j,*
48:12 cities of Judah rejoice, because of your *j.*
97: 8 cities of Judah rejoice because of your *j,*
105: 5 his portents, and the *j* he has uttered,
105: 7 throughout the earth his *j* prevail.
Eccl 8: 5 the wise man's heart knows times and *j;*
Wis 17: 1 For great are your *j,*
Sir 38:33 They set forth no decisions or *j,*
45: 5 to Jacob, his *j* and decrees to Israel.
48: 7 threats at Sinai, at Horeb avenging *j.*
Is 26: 8 Yes, for your way and your *j,*
Ez 7:27 and according to their *j* I will judge them;
Dn 3:27 all your ways right, and all your *j* proper.
3:28 You have executed proper *j* in all that you
13: 9 to heaven, and did not keep in mind just *j.*
Zec 8:16 honesty and peace in the *j* at your gates,
Rom 2:18 able to make sound *j* on disputed points.
11:33 How inscrutable his *j,*
Rv 16: 7 God Almighty, your *j* are true and just!"
19: 2 to our God, for his *j* are true and just!

JUDICIAL (2)

Dt 19:15 a *j* fact shall be established only on the
2Cor 13: 1 "A *j* fact shall be established only on

JUDICIOUS (1)

Prv 8:12 with experience, and *j* knowledge I attain.

JUDITH (35)

Gn 26:34 Esau was forty years old, he married *J,*
Jdt 8: 1 Now in those days *J,*
8: 4 The widowed *J* remained three years and
8: 9 When *J,*
8:32 Then *J* said to them: "Listen to me,
9: 1 *J* threw herself down prostrate,
9: 1 *J* prayed to the Lord with a loud voice:
10: 1 As soon as *J* had thus concluded,
10: 7 When these men saw *J* transformed in looks
10:10 When they did so, *J* and her maid went out.
10:11 As *J* and her maid walked directly across
10:23 when Holofernes and his servants beheld *J,*
11: 5 *J* answered him: "Listen to the words
12: 2 But *J* said,
12: 4 *J* answered him, "As surely as you,
12:13 of Holofernes, and came to *J* and said,
12:16 Then *J* came in and reclined on it.
12:18 *J* replied, "I will gladly drink, my lord,
13: 2 *J* was left alone in the tent with
13: 4 *J* stood by Holofernes' bed and said within
13:11 *J* shouted to the guards from a distance:
13:14 the two, *J* urged them with a loud voice:
14: 1 Then *J* said to them: "Listen to me,
14: 7 threw himself at the feet of *J* in homage,
14: 8 So *J* told him,
14:14 presuming that he was sleeping with *J.*
14:17 entered the tent where *J* had her quarters;
15: 8 for Israel, and to meet and congratulate *J.*
15:11 the camp, giving *J* the tent of Holofernes,
15:14 *J* led all Israel in this song of
16: 6 But *J,* the daughter of Merari,
16:19 *J* dedicated,
16:20 the sanctuary, and *J* remained with them.
16:21 *J* went back to Bethulia and remained on
16:25 of *J* and for a long time after her death,

JUG (18)

Gn 24:14 if I say to a girl, 'Please lower your *j,*
24:15 Nahor) came out with a *j* on her shoulder.
24:16 went down to the spring and filled her *j.*
24:17 give me a sip of water from your *j.*"
24:18 and quickly lowering the *j* onto her hand,
24:20 she quickly emptied her *j* into the
24:43 Please give me a little water from your *j,*
24:45 Rebekah came out with a *j* on her shoulder.
24:46 lowered the *j* she was carrying and said,
Jgs 4:19 she opened a *j* of milk for him to drink,
1Sm 26:11 spear which is at his head and the water *j,*
26:12 water *j* from their place at Saul's head,
26:16 spear and the water *j* that was at his head?"
1Kgs 17:12 flour in my jar and a little oil in my *j.*
17:14 not go empty, nor the *j* of oil run dry,
17:16 did not go empty, nor the *j* of oil run dry,
19: 6 head was a hearth cake and a *j* of water.
2Kgs 4: 2 has nothing in the house but a *j* of oil,"

JUGS (2)

Is 22:24 all the little dishes, from bowls to *j.*
Mk 7: 4 the washing of cups and *j* and kettles.

JUICE (7)

Nm 6: 3 other vinegar, of any kind of grape *j,*
1Mc 6:34 They showed the elephants the *j* of grapes

Sg 8: 2 you spiced wine to drink and pomegranate *j.*
Is 49:26 their own blood as with the *j* of the grape.
65: 8 When the *j* is pressed from grapes,
Jl 1: 5 Because the *j* of the grape will be
Am 9:13 *j* of grapes shall drip down the mountains,

JUICY (1)

Is 25: 6 A feast of rich food and choice wines, *j,*

JULIA (1)

Rom 16:15 to Philologus and *J,*

JULIUS (2)

Acts 27: 1 named *J* from the cohort known as Augusta.
27: 3 where *J* kindly allowed Paul to visit some

JUMP (1)

Acts 27:43 to *j* overboard first and make for land.

JUMPED (6)

1Mc 9:48 Jonathan and his men *j* into the Jordan and
13:44 men who had been on the siege machine *j*
Mk 10:50 aside his cloak, *j* up and came to Jesus.
Jn 21: 7 and *j* into the water.
Acts 3: 8 he *j* up, stood for a moment,
14:10 The man *j* up and began to walk around.

JUMPING (1)

Acts 3: 8 walking, *j* about,

JUNGLE (2)

Jer 12: 8 has turned on me like a lion in the *j;*
Zec 11: 3 lions, the *j* of the Jordan is laid waste.

JUNIAS (1)

Rom 16: 7 hard for you, and to Andronicus and *J,*

JUNIOR (1)

Lk 22:26 Let the greater among you be as the *j,*

JURISDICTION (2)

Neh 3: 7 the *j* of the governor of West-of-Euphrates.
Lk 23: 7 he learned that he was under Herod's *j,*

JURISTS (1)

Est 1:13 in general consultation with lawyers and *j.*

JUSHAB-HESED (1)

1Chr 3:20 Hashubah, Ohel, Berechiah, Hasadiah, *J*—

JUST (668)

Gn 7: 1 in this age have I found to be truly *j.*
7: 5 Noah did *j* as the LORD had commanded him.
7: 9 with Noah, *j* as the LORD had commanded
15: 5 *J* so," he added, "shall your descendants
18:10 at the entrance of the tent, *j* behind him.
18:19 of the LORD by doing what is right and *j,*
19:23 The sun was *j* rising over the earth as Lot
26:29 toward us, *j* as we have not molested you,
27:13 *J* do as I say. Go and get me the kids."
27:30 *j* after Isaac had finished blessing him,
27:33 I finished eating it *j* before you came,
29:15 *j* because you are a relative of mine?
31:16 Therefore, do *j* as God has told you."
34: 7 *j* as Jacob's sons were coming in from the
37:22 *j* throw him into that cistern there in the
40:22 but the chief baker he impaled *j* as Joseph
41:13 And it turned out *j* as he had told us:
41:28 It is *j* as I told Pharaoh:
41:54 famine set in, *j* as Joseph had predicted.
42:14 "It is *j* as I said," Joseph persisted;
Ex 5:17 "It is *j* because you are lazy that you
7:13 listen to them, *j* as the LORD had foretold.
7:22 and Aaron, *j* as the LORD had foretold.
8:11 listen to them *j* as the LORD had foretold.
8:15 listen to them, *j* as the LORD had foretold.
9:12 them, *j* as the LORD had foretold to Moses.
9:27 The LORD is *j;*
10:11 *J* you men can go and worship the LORD.
12:48 join in its observance *j* like the natives.
12:50 All the Israelites did *j* as the LORD had
14: 2 camp in front of Baal-zephon, *j* opposite,
14:24 In the night watch *j* before dawn the LORD
17: 3 Was it *j* to have us die here of thirst
23: 7 and the *j* you shall not put to death,
23: 8 and twists the words even of the *j.*
27: 8 box, *j* as it was shown you on the mountain.
28:27 in front, *j* above its embroidered belt.
29:35 and his sons *j* as I have given them to you.
29:44 *j* as I also consecrate Aaron and his sons
31:11 they shall make *j* as I have commanded you."
33:17 "This request, too, which you have *j* made,
36: 1 the sanctuary, *j* as the LORD has commanded."
39: 7 Israel, *j* as the LORD had commanded Moses.
39:20 in front, *j* above its embroidered belt.
39:21 this was *j* as the LORD had commanded Moses.
39:26 this, *j* as the LORD had commanded Moses.
39:32 work *j* as the LORD had commanded Moses.
39:42 work *j* as the LORD had commanded Moses.
39:43 work was done *j* as the Lord had commanded,
Lv 4:20 doing with this bullock *j* as he did with
4:21 *j* as has been prescribed for the other one.
4:31 *j* as the fat is removed from the peace
4:35 *j* as the fat is removed from the
15:25 unclean, *j* as during her menstrual period.
15:26 unclean *j* as during her menstruation.
18:28 *j* as it vomited out the nations before you.
Nm 2:34 did *j* as the LORD had commanded Moses;
8: 3 *j* as the LORD had commanded Moses.
9: 5 month, *j* as the LORD had commanded Moses.
14:24 him into the land where he has *j* been,
14:28 will do to you *j* what I have heard you say.
15:20 You shall offer it *j* as you offer a
18:18 *j* as the breast and the right leg of the
23:10 May I die the death of the *j,*
27: 7 "The plea of Zelophehad's daughters is *j;*
30: 1 *j* as the LORD had ordered him.
32: 8 That is *j* what your fathers did when I
32:27 before the LORD, *j* as your lordship says."
Dt 1:30 *j* as he took your part before your very
1:41 go up ourselves and fight, *j* as the LORD,
2:12 *j* as the Israelites have done in the land
4: 8 statutes and decrees that are as *j*
16:19 wise and twists the words even of the *j.*
25:15 and just weight, and a true and *j* measure,
26:13 and the widow, *j* as you have commanded me.
26:14 my God, doing *j* as you have commanded me.
28:63 *J* as the LORD once took delight in making
29:14 it is *j* as much with those who are not
30: 2 and all your soul, *j* as I now command you,
31: 4 with them *j* as he dealt with Sihon and Og,
32: 4 without deceit, how *j* and upright he is!
32:17 not known before, To newcomers *j* arrived,
32:50 *j* as your brother Aaron died on Mount Hor
Jos 4:23 you until you crossed over, *j* as the LORD,
5:14 the host of the LORD and I have *j* arrived."
10:32 person in it, *j* as he had done to Libnah.
10:35 person in it, *j* as he had done at Lachish.
10:37 survivors, *j* as Joshua had done to Eglon.
10:40 doom on all who lived there, *j* as the LORD,
11:23 *j* as the LORD had foretold to Moses.
13: 6 heritage, *j* as I have commanded you.
21:44 side, *j* as he had promised their fathers.
23:15 But *j* as every promise the LORD,
Jgs 3: 1 of the battles with Canaan *j* to instruct,
5:11 recount the *j* deeds of the LORD, his *j* deeds
6:39 me make *j* one more test with the fleece.
7:19 watch, *j* after the posting of the guards.
9:48 Do *j* as you have seen me do."
13:23 would he have let us see all this *j* now,
20:31 open field, *j* as on the other occasions.
Ru 3: 6 *j* as her mother-in-law had instructed her.
1Sm 2: 8 his vow, and blesses the sleep of the *j.*
9:12 *j* today he came to the city,
11: 5 *J* then Saul came in from the field,
13:10 He had *j* finished this offering when
17:20 the barricade of the camp *j* as the army,
24:11 LORD *j* now delivered you into my grasp
25: 7 I have *j* heard that shearers are with you.
25:21 When she met them, David had *j* been saying:
25:25 man Nabal, for he is *j* like his name.
2Sm 3:22 *J* then David's servants and Joab were
3:36 *j* as they were pleased with everything
7:22 no God but you, *j* as we have heard it told.
9:11 do *j* as my lord the king has commanded him
11: 4 was *j* purified after her monthly period.
14:19 the king, it is *j* as your majesty has said,
15: 3 say to him, "Your suit is good and *j,*
1Kgs 1:41 heard it, *j* as they ended their banquet.
2:32 two men better and more *j* than himself,
2:38 will do *j* as the king's majesty has said."
8:32 acquit the *j* and establish his innocence.
8:56 to his people Israel, *j* as he promised.
9: 4 uprightly, doing *j* as I have commanded you,
17:12 *J* now I was collecting a couple of sticks,
21:26 idols, *j* as the Amorites had done,
22:54 God of Israel, *j* as his father had done.
2Kgs 2:22 even to this day, *j* as Elisha prophesied.
5: 4 Naaman went and told his lord *j* what the
5:22 to say, 'Two young men have *j* come to me,
7: 7 their asses, the whole camp *j* as it was,
7:10 and the tents *j* as they were left."
7:17 *j* as the man of God had predicted when the
8: 5 *J* as he was relating to the king how his
11: 9 did *j* as Jehoiada the priest commanded.
14: 3 he did *j* as his father Joash had done.
14:25 to the sea of the Arabah, *j* as the LORD,
15: 3 the LORD *j* as his father Amaziah had done.
15:34 the LORD, *j* as his father Uzziah had done.
16:16 priest did *j* as King Ahaz had commanded.
18: 3 LORD, *j* as his forefather David had done.
22: 2 *j* as his ancestor David had done.
23:32 of the LORD, *j* as his forebears had done.
23:37 of the LORD, *j* as his forebears had done.
24: 9 of the LORD, *j* as his forebears had done.
24:19 sight of the LORD, *j* as Jehoiakim had done.
1Chr 4:38 these *j* named were princes in their clans,
4:41 They who have *j* been listed by name set
9:19 *j* as their fathers had guarded the
14:11 my enemies *j* as water breaks through a dam."
17:20 but you, *j* as we have always understood.
2Chr 12: 6 humbled themselves saying, "The LORD is *j.*"
23: 8 did *j* as Jehoiada the priest commanded.
26: 4 the LORD, *j* as his father Amaziah had done.
27: 2 the LORD *j* as his father Uzziah had done,
28:15 men *j* named proceeded to help the captives.
29: 2 LORD *j* as his forefather David had done.
33:22 LORD, *j* as his father Manasseh had done.
Ezr 4: 2 with you, for we seek your God *j* as you do,
9:15 O LORD, God of Israel, you are *j;*
Neh 5:12 We will do *j* what you ask."
9: 8 of yours you fulfilled, for you are *j.*
9:13 You gave them *j* ordinances,
9:33 all that has come upon us you have been *j,*
Tb 2: 3 the market place where he was *j* strangled!"
3: 2 O Lord, and all your deeds are *j;*
5: 9 "I have *j* found a man who is one of our
7: 2 young man looks *j* like my kinsman Tobit!"
11: 1 they were near Kaserin, *j* before Nineveh,
14: 3 *J* before he died, he called his son Tobiah
14: 5 *j* as the prophets of Israel said to her.
Jdt 12: 5 In the night watch *j* before dawn,
Est A: 6 war, to fight against the race of the *j.*
A: 8 The whole race of the *j* were dismayed with
2:20 *j* as she had when she was being brought up
C:18 You are *j,* O Lord.
5:11 and *j* how the king had promoted him and
E:15 rather are governed by very *j* laws
E:18 governs all, brought *j* punishment upon him.
9:31 *j* as they had previously enjoined upon
1Mc 2:24 heart was moved and his *j* fury was aroused;
2:26 for the law, *j* as Phinehas did with Zimri,
3:56 were building houses, or were *j* married,
7:12 and Bacchides to ask for a *j* agreement.
9: 7 away *j* when the battle was imminent,
9:55 *J* at that time he had a stroke,
11:26 the king treated him *j* as his predecessors
2Mc 1:24 things, awesome and strong, *j* and merciful,
1:25 and benefactor, who alone are gracious, *j,*
2: 8 *j* as it appeared in the time of Moses and
2:10 *J* as Moses prayed to the Lord and fire
2:27 *j* as the preparation of a festive banquet
3:24 But *j* as he was approaching the treasury
7:36 receive *j* punishments for your arrogance.
11:14 them to settle everything on *j* terms,
11:31 dietary laws and other laws, *j* as before,
12: 6 and after calling upon God, the *j* judge,
12:41 the *j* judge who brings to light the things
13: 8 It was altogether *j* that he who had
13:11 this nation, which had *j* begun to revive,
13:17 Day was *j* breaking when this was
14: 8 conduct of the people *j* mentioned.
15:38 *J* as it is harmful to drink wine alone or
Jb 12: 4 God answers when he calls upon him, the *j,*
22: 3 of advantage to the Almighty if you are *j?*
22:19 The *j* look on and are gladdened,
25: 4 How can a man be *j* in God's sight,
27:17 What he has stored the *j* man shall wear,
33:12 In this you are not *j,*
34:17 or will you condemn the supreme *J* One,
35: 2 it right to say, "I am *j* rather than God?"
36: 6 He withholds not the *j* man's rights,
Ps(s) 1: 5 shall sinners, in the assembly of the *j.*
1: 6 For the LORD watches over the way of the *j,*
4: 2 When I call, answer me, O my *j* God,
4: 6 Offer *j* sacrifices, and trust in the LORD.
5:13 For you, O LORD, bless the *j* man;
7: 9 Do me justice, O LORD, because I am *j,*
7:10 the *j,* O searcher of heart and soul, O *j*
7:12 A *j* judge is God,
11: 3 are overthrown, what can the *j* man do?"
11: 5 The LORD searches the *j* and the wicked;
11: 7 For the LORD is just, he loves *j* deeds;
14: 4 who eat up my people *j* as they eat bread?
14: 5 fear, for God is with the *j* generation.
17: 1 Hear, O LORD, a *j* suit;
19:10 of the LORD are true, all of them *j;*
31:19 insolence against the *j* in pride and scorn.
32:11 Be glad in the LORD and rejoice, you *j;*
33: 1 Exult, you *j,* in the LORD,
34:16 The LORD has eyes for the *j,*
34:18 When the *j* cry out,
34:20 Many are the troubles of the *j* man,
34:22 the enemies of the *j* pay for their guilt.
35:24 Do me justice, because you are *j,*
35:27 for joy and be glad who favor my *j* cause;
36:11 your *j* defense of the upright of heart.
37:12 the *j* and gnashes his teeth at them;
37:16 the *j* than the great wealth of the wicked,
37:17 be broken, but the LORD supports the *j.*
37:21 the *j* man is kindly and gives,
37:25 have I seen a *j* man forsaken nor his
37:29 The *j* shall possess the land and dwell in
37:30 The mouth of the *j* man tells of wisdom and
37:32 The wicked man spies on the *j,*
37:39 The salvation of the *j* is from the LORD;
52: 8 The *j* shall look on with awe;
53: 5 who eat up my people *j* as they eat bread,
55:23 will he permit the *j* man to be disturbed.
58:11 *j* man shall be glad when he sees vengeance;
58:12 say, "Truly there is a reward for the *j;*
64:11 The *j* man is glad in the LORD and takes
68: 4 But the *j* rejoice and exult before God;

JUST (cont.)

69:29 the living, and not be recorded with the *j!*
75:11 the horns of the *j* shall be lifted up.
92:13 *j* man shall flourish like the palm tree,
92:16 shall they be, Declaring how *j* is the LORD,
94:21 life of the *j* and condemn innocent blood,
97:11 Light dawns for the *j;*
97:12 Be glad in the LORD, you *j,*
106: 3 what is right, who do always what is *j.*
111: 1 heart in the company and assembly of the *j.*
111: 7 The works of his hands are faithful and *j;*
112: 4 he is gracious and merciful and *j.*
112: 6 *j* man shall be in everlasting remembrance.
116: 5 Gracious is the LORD and *j;*
118:15 shout of victory in the tents of the *j:*
118:20 the *j* shall enter it.
119: 7 when I have learned your *j* ordinances.
119:62 you thanks because of your *j* ordinances.
119:75 know, O LORD, that your ordinances are *j,*
119:106 and swear to keep your *j* ordinances.
119:121 I have fulfilled *j* ordinances;
119:123 after your salvation and your *j* promise.
119:137 You are *j,* O LORD,
119:144 Your decrees are forever *j;*
119:160 each of your *j* ordinances is everlasting.
119:164 a day I praise you for your *j* ordinances.
119:172 your promise, for all your commands are *j.*
125: 3 territory of the *j,* Lest the *j* put forth
129: 4 *j* LORD has severed the cords of the wicked.
140:14 the *j* shall give thanks to your name:
141: 5 Let the *j* man strike me;
142: 8 The *j* shall gather around me when you have
143: 2 servant, for before you no living man is *j.*
145:17 The LORD is *j* in all his ways and holy in
146: 8 the LORD loves the *j.*
Prv 1: 3 conduct, in what is right, *j* and honest;
2:20 good men, and keep to the paths of the *j.*
3:33 but the dwelling of the *j* he blesses;
4:18 the path of the *j* is like shining light,
9: 9 teach a *j* man,
10: 3 The LORD permits not the *j* to hunger,
10: 6 Blessings are for the head of the *j,*
10: 7 The memory of the *j* will be blessed,
10:11 A fountain of life is the mouth of the *j,*
10:16 The *j* man's recompense leads to life,
10:20 Like choice silver is the *j* man's tongue;
10:21 The *j* man's lips nourish many,
10:24 but the desire of the *j* will be granted.
10:25 but the *j* man is established forever.
10:28 The hope of the *j* brings them joy,
10:30 The *j* man will never be disturbed,
10:31 The mouth of the *j* yields wisdom,
10:32 The lips of the *j* know how to please,
11: 8 The *j* man escapes trouble,
11: 9 their knowledge the *j* make their escape.
11:10 When the *j* prosper,
11:21 but those who are *j* shall escape.
11:23 The desire of the *j* ends only in good;
11:28 fall, but like green leaves the *j* flourish.
11:31 If the *j* man is punished on earth,
12: 3 the root of the *j* will never be disturbed.
12: 5 The plans of the *j* are legitimate;
12: 7 more, but the house of the *j* stands firm.
12:10 The *j* man takes care of his beast,
12:12 but the root of the *j* is enduring.
12:13 ensnared, but the *j* comes free of trouble.
12:21 No harm befalls the *j,*
12:26 The *j* man surpasses his neighbor,
13: 5 Anything deceitful the *j* man hates,
13: 9 The light of the *j* shines gaily,
13:21 but the *j* shall be recompensed with good.
13:22 of the sinner is stored up for the *j.*
13:25 When the *j* man eats,
14: 9 arrogant, but favor in the house of the *j.*
14:19 and the wicked, at the gates of the *j.*
14:32 the *j* man finds a refuge in his honesty.
15: 6 house of the *j* there are ample resources,
15:28 The *j* man weighs well his utterance,
15:29 wicked, but the prayer of the *j* he hears.
17:15 condones the wicked, he who condemns the *j,*
18:10 the *j* man runs to it and is safe.
21: 3 To do what is right and *j* is more
21:12 *j* man appraises the house of the wicked:
21:15 To practice justice is a joy for the *j,*
21:18 wicked man serves as ransom for the *j,*
21:26 the day, but the *j* man gives unsparingly.
23:24 The father of a *j* man will exult with glee;
24:15 not in wait against the home of the *j* man,
24:16 *j* man falls seven times and rises again,
24:24 who says to the wicked man, "You are *j*—
24:28 against your neighbor without *j* cause,
25:26 is a *j* man who gives way before the wicked.
28: 1 but the *j* man,
28:12 When the *j* are triumphant,
28:28 but at their fall the *j* flourish.
29: 2 When the *j* prevail, the people rejoice;
29: 6 a snare, but the *j* man runs on joyfully.
29: 7 The *j* man has a care for the rights of the
29:16 but their downfall the *j* will behold.
29:27 The evildoer is an abomination to the *j,*
31: 9 Open your mouth, decree what is *j,*
Eccl 3:17 both the *j* and the wicked God will judge,
5:15 a grievous evil, that he goes *j* as he came.
7:15 a *j* man perishing in his justice,
7:16 "Be not *j* to excess,
7:20 on earth so *j* as to do good and never sin.
8:14 there are *j* men treated as though they had
9: 1 the *j,* the wise, and their deeds
9: 2 same lot for all, for the *j* and the wicked,
11: 5 *J* as you know not how the breath of life
Wis 2:10 Let us oppress the needy *j* man;
2:12 Let us beset the *j* one,
2:16 of the *j* and boasts that God is his Father.
2:18 For if the *j* one be the son of God,
3: 1 the souls of the *j* are in the hand of God,
4: 7 But the *j* man,
4:16 *j* man dead condemns the sinful who live,
5: 1 Then shall the *j* one with great assurance
5:15 But the *j* live forever,
10: 4 it, piloting the *j* man on frailest wood.
10: 5 in universal wickedness, knew the *j* man,
10: 6 She delivered the *j* man from among the
10:10 the *j* man fled from his brother's anger,
10:13 did not abandon the *j* man when he was sold,
10:20 Therefore the *j* despoiled the wicked;
11:14 their thirst proved unlike that of the *j.*
12: 9 the wicked vanquished in battle by the *j,*
12:15 But as you are *j,* you govern all things
12:19 deeds, that those who are *j* must be kind;
16:17 For the universe fights on behalf of the *j.*
16:23 fire, again, that the *j* might be nourished,
18: 7 of the *j* and the destruction of their foes.
18:20 of death touched at one time even the *j,*
19:17 others had been at the portals of the *j*—
Sir 9:16 Have *j* men for your table companions;
10:22 *j* to despise a man who is wise but poor,
11:17 The LORD's gift remains with the *j;*
11:22 God's blessing is the lot of the *j* man,
12: 2 good to the *j* man and reward will be yours,
13:16 So it is with the sinner and the *j.*
16:13 a *j* man's hope God does not leave
16:20 Who tells him of *j* deeds and what could I
18: 1 the LORD alone is *j.*
23:10 *J* as a slave that is constantly under
23:11 without reason he cannot be found *j,*
28:22 among the *j* nor scorch them in its flame,
33:14 so are sinners in contrast with the *j;*
35: 5 The *j* man's offering enriches the altar
35: 6 The *j* man's sacrifice is most pleasing,
38:10 let your hands be *j,*
42:13 For *j* as moths come from garments,
44:17 NOAH, found *j* and perfect,
Is 3:10 Happy the *j,* for it will be well with them
5:23 and deprive the *j* man of his rights!
10:10 *j* as my hand reached out
10:11 *J* as I treated Samaria and her idols,
20: 3 *J* as my servant Isaiah has gone naked and
24:16 "Splendor to the *J* One!"
26: 2 up the gates to let in a nation that is *j,*
26: 7 way of the *j* is smooth; the path of the *j*
28: 9 To those *j* weaned from milk,
29:21 and leave the *j* man with an empty claim.
45:21 There is no *j* and saving God but me.
45:23 my *j* decree and my unalterable word:
45:24 "Only in the LORD are *j* deeds and power.
55:10 For *j* as from the heavens the rain and
56: 1 Observe what is right, do what is *j;*
57: 1 The *j* man perishes,
57: 1 of evil, the *j* man enters into peace;
58: 2 *j* and not abandoned the law of their God;
60:21 Your people shall all be *j,*
66:20 *j* as the Israelites bring their offering
Jer 3:11 is inwardly more *j* than traitorous Judah.
7:14 you and your fathers, *j* as I did to Shiloh.
11:20 But, you, O LORD of hosts, O *j* Judge,
20:12 O LORD of hosts, you who test the *j,*
22: 3 Do what is right and *j.*
22:15 He did what was right and *j,*
23: 5 shall do what is *j* and right in the land.
23:27 *j* as their fathers forgot my name
32:42 *J* as I brought upon this people all this
33:15 a *j* shoot; he shall do what is right and *j*
36:12 where the princes were *j* then in session:
38: 7 *j* then to be at the Gate of Benjamin,
42:18 *J* as my furious anger was poured out upon
44:13 *j* as I punished Jerusalem with sword,
44:30 seek his life, *j* as I handed over Zedekiah,
51:10 The LORD has brought to light our *j* cause;
52: 2 eyes of the LORD, *j* as Jehoiakim had done.
Lam 1:18 "The LORD is *j;* I had defied his command.
4:13 Who shed in her midst the blood of the *j*—
Bar 2: 9 *j* in all the works he commanded us to do,
2:19 "Not on the *j* deeds of our fathers and
6:70 *J* like a thornbush in a garden on which
6:72 The better for the *j* man who has no idols:
Ez 10:22 Their faces looked *j* like those I had seen
16:51 and have even made your sisters appear *j,*
16:52 they appear *j* in comparison with you.
16:52 shame of having made your sisters appear *j.*
18: 5 if he does what is right and *j,*
18:19 the son has done what is right and *j,*
18:21 my statutes and does what is right and *j,*
18:27 has committed, does what is right and *j,*
20:36 *J* as I entered into judgment with your
22:20 *J* as silver, bronze, iron, lead, and tin
22:22 by it *j* as silver is smelted in a furnace.
23:45 But *j* men shall punish them with the
33:14 from his sin and does what is right and *j,*
33:16 he has done what is right and *j,*
33:19 wickedness and does what is right and *j,*
35:14 *J* as you rejoiced over my land because it
40:23 the north gate, *j* as at the east gate;
42:11 to the north, just as long and *j* as wide,
45: 9 and oppression, and do what is right and *j!*
Dn 2:40 *j* as iron breaks in pieces and crushes
3:27 For you are *j* in all you have done;
3:86 Spirits and souls of the *j,*
4:34 all his works are right and his ways *j;*
9:14 our God, are *j* in all that you have done,
9:16 O Lord, in keeping with all your *j* deeds,
9:18 before you, we rely not on our *j* deeds,
13: 9 and did not keep in mind *j* judgments.
13:53 and the *j* you shall not put to death.'
Hos 14:10 the paths of the LORD, in them the *j* walk,
Am 2: 6 Because they sell the *j* man for silver,
5:12 Oppressing the *j,* accepting bribes,
Mi 3: 9 You who abhor what is *j,*
6: 5 that you may know the *j* deeds of the LORD.
Hb 1: 4 Because the wicked circumvent the *j;*
1:13 wicked man devours one more *j* than himself?
2: 4 but the *j* man,
Zep 3: 5 The LORD within her is *j,*
Zec 1: 6 and deeds, *j* as he had determined he would."
8:13 *J* as you were a curse among the nations,
9: 9 a *j* savior is he,
Mal 2:17 or else, "Where is the *j* God?"
3:18 distinction between the *j* and the wicked;
Mt 5:45 the good, he rains on the *j* and the unjust.
8: 8 *J* give an order and my boy will get better.
9:18 "My daughter has *j* died.
11:21 And *j* as ill with you, Bethsaida!
12:40 *J* as Jonah spent three days and three
13:40 *J* as weeds are collected and burned,
13:49 separate the wicked from the *j*
18: 1 *J* then the disciples came up to Jesus with
18:14 *J* so, it is no part of your heavenly Father's
18:29 *J* give me time and I will pay you back in
23:35 all the blood of the *j* ones shed on earth,
25:37 Then the *j* will ask him:
25:46 punishment and the *j* to eternal life."
26:74 *J* then a cock began to crow and Peter
27:10 field *j* as the Lord had commanded me."
27:24 "I am innocent of the blood of this *j* man.
Mk 5:28 "If I *j* touch his clothing,"
6:56 let them touch *j* the tassel of his cloak.
9:18 *J* now I asked your disciples to expel him,
10:14 It is to *j* such as these that the kingdom
14:16 city they found it *j* as he had told them,
14:72 *J* then a second cock crow was heard and
16: 2 Very early, *j* after sunrise,
16: 7 where you will see him *j* as he told you.' "
16:20 to Christ, "reveal your *j* authority now."
Lk 1: 6 Both were *j* in the eyes of God,
1:17 and the rebellious to the wisdom of the *j,*
2:25 He was *j* and pious,
6:26 treated the false prophets in *j* this way.
7: 7 *J* give the order and my servant will be
10:13 And *j* as ill with you Bethsaida!
11:30 *J* as Jonah was a sign for the Ninevites,
12:57 do you not judge for yourselves what is *j?*
13: 2 in Galilee *j* because they suffered this?
14:14 be repaid in the resurrection of the *j."*
19:32 errand and found things *j* as he had said.
22:10 *J* as you enter the city,
22:13 off and found everything *j* as he had said;
24:22 have *j* brought us some astonishing news.
24:24 and found it to be *j* as the women said;
Jn 1:50 "Do you believe *j* because I told you I
3:14 *J* as Moses lifted up the serpent in the
4:23 it is *j* such worshipers the Father seeks.
5:21 *j* as the Father raises the dead and grants
5:23 honor the Son *j* as they honor the Father.
5:26 *j* as the Father possesses life in himself,
6:57 *J* as the Father who has life sent me and I
9:26 *J* what did he do to you?
11:18 not far from Jerusalem *j* under two miles
12:24 and dies, it remains *j* a grain of wheat.
12:34 *J* who is this 'Son of Man'?"
12:50 I say is spoken *j* as he instructed me."
13:10 he is entirely cleansed, *j* as you are;
13:12 "Do you understand what I *j* did for you?
13:15 What I *j* did was to give you an example:
17:10 *J* as all that belongs to me is yours,
17:25 *J* Father,
21: 4 *J* after daybreak Jesus was standing on the
21:10 "Bring some of the fish you *j* caught,"
Acts 1:11 *j* as you saw him go up into the heavens."
3:14 You disowned the Holy and *J* One and
3:17 out of ignorance, *j* as your leaders did.
5: 9 The footsteps of the men who have *j* buried
7:51 Spirit *j* as your fathers did before you.
7:52 those who foretold the coming of the *J* One;
8:24 you have *j* said may never happen to me."
10:30 *J* three days ago at this very hour,
11:15 them, *j* as it had upon us at the beginning.
14:15 *j* such follies as these to the living God,
14:19 *J* at that point,
15: 8 the Holy Spirit to them *j* as he did to us.
21:37 *J* as Paul was about to be led into the

22: 3 defender of God, *j* as all of you are today.
22:14 to know his will, to look upon the *J* One,
23:11 *J* as you have given testimony to me here
26:10 That is *j* what I did in Jerusalem.
27:25 it will all work out *j* as I have been told,
28: 3 Paul had *j* fed the fire with a bundle of
Rom 1:17 says, "The *j* man shall live by faith."
1:32 They know God's *j* decree that all who do
2: 2 judgment on men who do such things is *j*."
2: 5 the *j* judgment of God will be revealed,
2:13 hear the law who are *j* in the sight of God;
2:13 those who keep it who will be declared *j*.
3:10 "There is no *j* man,
3:26 so that he might be *j* and might justify
4:18 many nations, *j* as it was once told him,
5: 7 should lay down his life for a *j* man,
5:12 *j* as through one man sin entered the world
5:18 *j* as a single offense brought condemnation
5:19 *J* as through one man's disobedience all
5:19 one man's obedience all shall become *j*.
6: 4 *j* as Christ was raised from the dead by
6:15 *J* because we are not under the law but
6:19 *J* as formerly you enslaved your bodies to
7:12 and the commandment is holy and *j* and good.
8: 4 so that the *j* demands of the law might be
9:13 It is *j* as Scripture says,
9:29 It is *j* as Isaiah predicted:
11: 5 *J* so, in the present time there is a remnant
11: 7 *J* this: Israel did not obtain
11:30 *J* as you were once disobedient to God and
12: 4 *J* as each of us has one body with many
15:25 *J* now I am leaving for Jerusalem to bring
1Cor 1:31 This is *j* as you find it written,
4:17 *j* as I teach them in all the churches.
7:22 *j* as the freeman who has been called is a
10:33 *j* as I try to please all in any way I can
11: 2 traditions *j* as I handed them on to you.
14: 6 *J* suppose, brothers, that I should come
15:22 *J* as in Adam all die,
15:49 *J* as we resemble the man from earth,
16: 7 I do not want to see you *j* in passing.
16:10 He does the Lord's work *j* as I do,
2Cor 1: 7 know that *j* as you share in the sufferings,
1:13 *j* as you know us to a certain degree
6:16 of the living God, *j* as God has said:
7:11 *J* look at the fruit of this sorrow which
7:14 *j* as everything I ever said to you was
8: 7 that *j* as you are rich in every respect,
10: 7 may belong to Christ but *j* as much do we.
11: 3 *j* as the serpent seduced Eve by his
Gal 1: 9 I repeat what I have *j* said:
1:20 God that what I have *j* written is true.
2: 7 *j* as Peter was for the circumcised (for he
3:11 law, for "the *j* man shall live by faith."
4:16 your enemy *j* because I tell you the truth?
4:29 But *j* as in those days the son born in
Eph 4: 4 *j* as there is but one hope given all of
4:32 *j* as God has forgiven you in Christ.
5:23 husband is head of his wife *j* as Christ
Phil 2:27 not *j* on him,
4: 2 plead with Evodia *j* as I do with Syntyche:
1Thes 2:10 as is God himself, of how upright, *j*,
5: 3 *J* when people are saying,
2Thes 1: 5 as an expression of God's *j* judgment,
2Tm 3: 8 *J* as Jannes and Jambres opposed Moses,
4: 8 on that Day the Lord, *j* judge that he is,
Ti 1: 8 steady, *j*,
Heb 4: 3 who enter into that rest, *j* as God said:
5: 6 *j* as he says in another place,
8: 6 *j* as he is mediator of a better covenant,
9:27 *J* as it is appointed that men die once,
10:37 For, *j* a brief moment,
10:38 My *j* man will live by faith,
11: 4 Because of this he was attested to be *j*,
11:33 faith conquered kingdoms, did what was *j*,
12:23 all, to the spirits of *j* men made perfect,
Jas 1:11 *J* so will the rich man wither away amid
5: 6 You condemned, even killed, the *j* man;
1Pt 2:21 you in *j* this way and left you an example,
3: 7 heirs *j* as much as you to the gracious
3:12 has eyes for the *j* and ears for their cry;
3:18 all, the *j* man for the sake of the unjust,
4:18 if the *j* man is saved only with difficulty,
2Pt 2: 7 a *j* man oppressed by the conduct of men
2: 8 (Day after day that *j* one,
2:18 who have *j* come free of a life of errors.
3: 4 *j* as it was when the world was created."
3:16 distort them *j* as they do the rest
1Jn 1: 9 he who is *j* can be trusted to forgive our
2: 1 Jesus Christ, an intercessor who is *j*.
2: 6 in him to conduct himself *j* as he did.
2:18 *j* as you heard that the antichrist was
3:12 were wicked while his brother's were *j*.
4:17 our relation to this world is *j* like his.
2Jn 1: 4 *j* as we were commanded by the Father.
Jude 1: 7 indulged in lust, *j* as those angels did;
Rv 2: 6 practices of the Nicolaitans, *j* as I do.
16: 5 "You are *j*, O holy One who is and who
16: 7 "Yes, Lord God Almighty, your judgments
19: 2 God, for his judgments are true and *j*!

JUSTICE (299)

Gn 18:25 not the judge of all the world act with *j*?"
31:53 ancestral deities] maintain *j* between us!"
49:16 "Dan shall achieve *j* for his kindred like
Ex 23: 2 side with the many in perverting *j*.
Dt 1:16 and administer true *j* to both parties even
6:25 and our *j* before the LORD,
10:18 executes *j* for the orphan and the widow,
16:18 tribes to administer true *j* for the people
16:19 You shall not distort *j*;
16:20 *J* and justice alone shall be your aim,
32:36 Surely, the LORD shall do *j* for his people:
33:21 He carried out the *j* of the LORD and his
1Sm 8: 3 gain and accepted bribes, perverting *j*.
24:13 the LORD will exact *j* from you in my case.
24:16 my part, and grant me *j* beyond your reach!"
26:23 reward each man for his *j* and faithfulness.
2Sm 8:15 and administering *j* to all his people.
15: 4 might come to me and I would render him *j*."
22:21 "The LORD rewarded me according to my *j*;
22:25 the LORD requited me according to my *j*,
23: 3 Israel said, 'He that rules over men in *j*,
1Kgs 3: 6 toward you, with *j* and an upright heart;
10: 9 made you king to carry out judgment and *j*."
1Chr 18:14 dispensed *j* and right to all his people.
2Chr 9: 8 them as king to administer right and *j*."
Ezr 7:25 *j* to all the people in West-of-Euphrates,
Est F: 9 people and rendered *j* to his inheritance.
1Mc 6:22 you fail to do *j* and avenge our kinsmen?
7:18 "There is no truth or *j* among them;
8:32 them *j* and make war on you by land and sea.'"
14:35 the loyalty and *j* he had shown his nation.
2Mc 4:34 Then, without any regard for *j*,
4:44 presented to him the *j* of their cause.
8:13 faith in God's *j* deserted and got away.
Jb 8: 3 judgment, and does the Almighty distort *j*?
16:21 That he may do *j* for a mortal in his
27: 6 *j* I maintain and I will not relinquish it;
29:14 *j* was my robe and my turban.
31: 6 Let God weigh me in the scales of *j*;
31:13 I refused *j* to my manservant or to my maid,
33:23 for him and bring the man back to *j*,
34:12 wickedly, the Almighty cannot violate *j*.
34:17 Can an enemy of *j* indeed be in control,
35: 8 and your *j* only a fellow human being.
37:23 his great *j* owes no one an accounting.
Ps(s) 5: 9 Because of my enemies, guide me in your *j*;
7: 9 Do me *j*, O LORD, because I am just,
7:18 I will give thanks to the LORD for his *j*,
9: 9 He judges the world with *j*;
15: 2 He who walks blamelessly and does *j*;
17:15 But I in *j* shall behold your face;
18:21 The LORD rewarded me according to my *j*;
18:25 the LORD requited me according to my *j*,
22:32 a people yet to be born the *j* he has shown.
25: 9 He guides the humble to *j*,
26: 1 Do me *j*, O LORD!
31: 2 In your *j* rescue me,
33: 5 He loves *j* and right;
35:24 Do me *j*,
35:28 Then my tongue shall recount your *j*,
36: 7 Your *j* is like the mountains of God;
37: 6 He will make *j* dawn for you like the light;
40:10 I announced your *j* in the vast assembly;
40:11 Your *j* I kept not hid within my heart;
43: 1 Do me *j*, O God, and fight my fight
45: 5 the cause of truth and for the sake of *j*;
45: 8 You love *j* and hate wickedness;
48:11 Of *j* your right hand is full;
50: 6 And for the heavens proclaim his *j*;
51:16 then my tongue shall revel in your *j*.
58: 2 like gods pronounce *j* and judge fairly,
65: 6 awe-inspiring deeds of *j* you answer us,
71: 2 In your *j* rescue me,
71:15 My mouth shall declare your *j*,
71:16 O GOD, I will tell of your singular *j*.
71:19 Your power and your *j*,
71:24 day by day shall discourse on your *j*.
72: 1 judgment endow the king, and with your *j*,
72: 2 *j* and your afflicted ones with judgment.
72: 3 peace for the people, and the hills *j*.
72: 7 *J* shall flower in his days,
82: 3 *j* to the afflicted and the destitute.
85:11 *j* and peace shall kiss.
85:12 earth, and *j* shall look down from heaven.
85:14 *J* shall walk before him,
88:13 or your *j* in the land of oblivion?
89:15 *J* and judgment are the foundation of your
89:17 day, and through your *j* they are exalted.
94:15 But judgment shall again be with *j*,
96:13 with *j* and the peoples with his constancy.
97: 2 *j* and judgment are the foundation of his
97: 6 The heavens proclaim his *j*,
98: 2 sight of the nations he has revealed his *j*.
98: 9 world with *j* and the peoples with equity.
99: 4 justice; you have established equity; *j*
103: 6 *j* and the rights of all the oppressed.
103:17 And his *j* toward children's children among
111: 3 are his work, and his *j* endures forever.
112: 5 lends, who conducts his affairs with *j*;
118:19 Open to me the gates of *j*;
119:40 in your *j* give me life.
119:138 decrees in *j* and in perfect faithfulness.
119:142 Your justice is everlasting *j*,
132: 9 May your priests be clothed with *j*;
140:13 that the LORD renders *j* to the afflicted,
143: 1 in your *j* answer me.
143:11 in your *j* free me from distress,
145: 7 goodness and joyfully sing of your *j*.
146: 7 forever, secures *j* for the oppressed,
Prv 2: 8 who walk honestly, Guarding the paths of *j*,
2: 9 Then you will understand rectitude and *j*,
8:15 me kings reign, and lawgivers establish *j*;
8:20 way of duty I walk, along the paths of *j*,
12:28 In the path of *j* there is life,
17:23 concealed bribe to pervert the course of *j*.
19:28 An unprincipled witness perverts *j*,
20: 7 When a man walks in integrity and *j*,
20:28 the king, and he upholds his throne by *j*.
21:15 To practice *j* is a joy for the just,
21:21 *j* and kindness will find life and honor.
28: 5 Evil men understand nothing of *j*,
29: 4 By *j* a king gives stability to the land;
Eccl 3:16 I saw wickedness, and in the seat of *j*,
5: 7 and violation of rights and *j* in the realm,
7:15 a just man perishing in his *j*,
Wis 1: 1 Love *j*, you who judge the earth;
1:15 nether world on earth, For *j* is undying.
2:11 But let our strength be our norm of *j*;
3:10 they neglected *j* and forsook the Lord.
5: 6 and the light of *j* did not shine for us,
5:18 He shall don *j* for a breastplate and shall
8: 7 Or if one loves *j*,
8: 7 moderation and prudence, *j* and fortitude,
9: 3 To govern the world in holiness and *j*,
12:16 For your might is the source of *j*;
14: 7 is the wood through which *j* comes about;
14:30 But on both counts shall *j* overtake them:
15: 3 For to know you well is complete *j*,
Sir 4: 9 let not *j* be repugnant to you.
7: 5 Parade not your *j* before the Lord,
21: 5 at once, and *j* is quickly granted him.
26:19 And the man who passes from *j* to sin,
27: 8 If you strive after *j* you will attain it,
35:12 fruits of extortion, For he is a God of *j*,
40:17 never be cut off, and *j* endures forever.
45:26 wisdom of heart to govern his people in *j*,
Is 1:17 Make *j* your aim:
1:21 *J* used to lodge within her,
1:26 After that you shall be called city of *j*,
1:27 by judgment, and her repentant ones by *j*.
5: 7 for *j*, but hark, the outcry!
5:16 God the holy shall be shown holy by his *j*.
9: 6 he confirms and sustains By judgment and *j*,
10:22 is decreed as overwhelming *j* demands.
11: 4 But he shall judge the poor with *j*,
11: 5 *J* shall be the band around his waist,
16: 5 A judge upholding right and prompt to do *j*.
26: 9 the earth, the world's inhabitants learn *j*.
26:10 The wicked man, spared, does not learn *j*;
28: 6 A spirit of *j* to him who sits in judgment,
28:17 of right a measuring line, of *j* a level,—
30:18 For the LORD is a God of *j*:
32:16 in the desert and *j* abide in the orchard.
32:17 *J* will bring about peace;
33: 5 he fills Zion with right and *j*.
41: 2 stirred up from the East the champion of *j*,
41:10 and uphold you with my right hand of *j*.
42: 1 he shall bring forth *j* to the nations,
42: 4 Until he establishes *j* on the earth;
42: 6 have called you for the victory of *j*,
42:21 his *j* to make his law great and glorious,
45: 8 Let *j* descend, O heavens, like dew
45: 8 let *j* also spring up!
45:13 I who stirred up one for the triumph of *j*;
45:19 I, the LORD, promise *j*,
46:12 you who seem far from the victory of *j*:
46:13 I am bringing on my *j*,
48: 1 the God of Israel without sincerity or *j*,
51: 1 Listen to me, you who pursue *j*,
51: 5 I will make my *j* come speedily;
51: 6 forever and my *j* shall never be dismayed.
51: 7 Hear me, you who know *j*,
51: 8 my *j* shall remain forever and my salvation,
54:14 In *j* shall you be established,
56: 1 for my salvation is about to come, my *j*,
57:12 I will expose your *j* and your works;
59: 9 is far from us and *j* does not reach us.
59:14 Right is repelled, and *j* stands far off;
59:16 victory, and his *j* lent him its support.
59:17 He put on *j* as his breastplate,
60:17 peace your governor, and *j* your ruler.
61: 3 They will be called oaks of *j*,
61:10 and wrapped me in a mantle of *j*,
61:11 So will the Lord GOD make *j* and praise
Jer 4: 2 lives," in truth, in judgment, and in *j*;
5:28 *j* they do not defend By advancing the
9:23 kindness *j* and uprightness on the earth;
21:12 Each morning dispense *j*,
22:16 he dispensed *j* to the weak and the poor,
23: 6 "The LORD our *j*."
31:23 LORD bless you, holy mountain, abode of *j*!"
33:16 "The LORD our *j*."
50: 7 hope of their fathers, their abode of *j*."
Lam 3:59 do me *j*!

JUSTICE (cont.)
Bar 1:15 J is with the Lord,
2: 6 J is with the Lord,
2:18 soul, will declare your glory and j.
4:13 they tread the disciplined paths of his j.
5: 2 Wrapped in the cloak of j from God,
5: 4 be named by God forever the peace of j,
5: 9 his glory with his mercy and j for company.
Ez 22:29 and oppress the resident alien without j.
Dn 9: 7 J, O Lord, is on your side
9:24 expiated, Everlasting j will be introduced,
12: 3 many to j shall be like the stars forever.
Hos 2:21 I will espouse you in right and in j,
10: 4 While j grows wild like wormwood in a
10:12 "Sow for yourself j,
10:12 till he come and rain down j upon you."
Jl 2:23 He has given you the teacher of j:
Am 5: 7 to wormwood and cast j to the ground!
5:15 love good, and let j prevail at the gate;
5:24 holocausts, then let j surge like water,
6:12 gall, and the fruit of j into wormwood.
Mi 7: 9 I will see his j.
Zep 2: 3 Seek j,
Zec 8: 8 will be their God, with faithfulness and j.
Mal 3:20 arise the sun of j with its healing rays;
Mt 12:18 and he will proclaim j to the Gentiles.
23:23 of the law, j and mercy and good faith.
Lk 11:42 while neglecting j and the love of God.
18: 7 Will not God then do j to his chosen who
18: 8 I tell you, he will give them swift j.
Jn 16: 8 prove the world wrong about sin, about j,
16:10 about j—
Acts 8:33 In his humiliation he was deprived of j,
17:31 with j' through a man he has appointed
28: 4 from the sea, J will not let him live."
Rom 1:17 j of God which begins and ends with faith;
3: 5 our wrongdoing provides proof of God's j,
3:21 But now the j of God has been manifested
3:22 that j of God which works through faith in
3:25 He did so to manifest his own j,
3:26 to manifest his j in the present,
4: 3 God, and it was credited to him as j."
4: 5 the sinful, his faith is credited as j.
4: 6 whom God credits j without requiring deeds:
4: 9 that Abraham's faith was "credited as j."
4:11 circumcision as a seal attesting to the j
4:11 for them too faith might be credited as j,
4:13 in view of the j that comes from faith.
4:22 Thus his faith was credited to him as j.
5:17 of j live and reign through the one man,
5:21 reign by way of j leading to eternal life,
6:13 and your bodies to God as weapons for j.
6:16 death, or of obedience, which leads to j.
6:18 from your sin, you became slaves of j.
6:19 the servants of j for their sanctification.
6:20 were slaves of sin, you had freedom from j.
8:10 sin, while the spirit lives because of j.
9:30 That the Gentiles, who were not seeking j,
9:30 the j which comes from faith
9:31 seeking a law from which j would come,
9:32 Because j comes from faith,
10: 3 j and seeking to establish their own,
10: 3 did not subject themselves to the j of God.
10: 4 him, j comes to everyone who believes.
10: 5 writes of the j that comes from the law,
10: 6 But of the j that comes from faith he says,
14:17 a matter of eating or drinking, but of j,
1Cor 1:30 He has made him our wisdom and also our j,
2Cor 7:11 ardent desire to restore the balance of j!
9: 9 gave to the poor, his j endures forever."
11:15 themselves as ministers of the j of God.
Gal 2:21 If j is available through the law,
3: 6 God, and it was credited to him as j."
3:21 then j would be a consequence of the law.
Eph 4:24 whose j and holiness are born of truth.
5: 9 every kind of goodness and j and truth.
6:14 around your waist, j as your breastplate,
Phil 1:11 of j which Jesus Christ has ripened in you,
3: 6 when it came to j based on the law.
3: 9 j of my own based on observance of the law.
3: 9 The j I possess is that which comes
2Thes 1: 6 even if strict j would require that God
Heb 1: 9 You have loved j and hated wickedness,
7: 2 His name means "king of j";
11: 7 inherited the j which comes through faith.
12:11 j to those who are trained in its school.
Jas 1:20 for a man's anger does not fulfill God's j.
2:23 God, and it was credited to him as j";
3:18 The harvest of j is sown in peace for
1Pt 3:14 if you should have to suffer for j' sake,
2Pt 3:13 to his promise, the j of God will reside.
Rv 19:11 J is his standard in passing judgment and

JUSTIFICATION (6)
Mk 16:20 and immortal glory of j in heaven."
Rom 4:25 death for our sins and raised up for our j.
10:10 Faith in the heart leads to j,
Gal 3:24 came to bring about our j through faith.
5: 4 Any of you who seek your j in the law have
5: 5 that we eagerly await the j we hope for,

JUSTIFIED (23)
Jb 9: 2 but how can a man be j before God?
33:32 I should like to see you j.
40: 8 Would you condemn me that you may be j?
Ps(s) 51: 6 That you may be j in your sentence,
Lk 18:14 from the temple j but the other did not.
Rom 3:20 since no one will be j in God's sight
3:24 are now undeservedly j by the gift of God,
3:28 For we hold that a man is j by faith apart
4: 2 j by his deeds he has grounds for boasting,
5: 1 Now that we have been j by faith,
5: 9 Now that we have been j by his blood,
8:30 those he called he also j; and those he j
1Cor 6:11 j in the name of our Lord Jesus Christ and
Gal 2:16 knowing that a man is not j by legal
2:16 in him in order to be j by faith in Christ,
2:16 for by works of the law no one will be j.
2:17 But if, in seeking to be j in Christ,
3:11 that no one is j in God's sight by the law,
Ti 3: 7 might be j by his grace and become heirs,
Jas 2:21 Was not our father Abraham j by his works
2:24 is j by his works and not by faith alone.
2:25 Was she not j by her works when she

JUSTIFIES (4)
Rom 3:30 It is the same God who j the circumcised
4: 5 yet believes in him who j the sinful,
8:33 God, who j?
2Cor 3: 9 by far is the glory of the ministry that j.

JUSTIFY (5)
Sir 1:19 One cannot j unjust anger;
Is 53:11 his suffering, my servant shall j many,
Lk 10:29 he wished to j himself he said to Jesus,
16:15 "You j yourselves in the eyes of men,
Rom 3:26 and might j those who believe in Jesus.

JUSTIFYING (2)
Gal 3: 8 of j the Gentiles would be through faith,
2Pt 1: 1 j power of our God and Savior Jesus Christ;

JUSTLY (16)
Lv 19:15 to the mighty, but judge your fellow men j.
2Mc 7:38 that has j fallen on our whole nation."
9:18 since God's punishment had j come upon him,
Ps(s) 9: 5 cause, seated on your throne, judging j.
Eccl 8:14 men treated as though they had done j.
Wis 9:12 j and be worthy of my father's throne.
12:15 as you are just, you govern all things j;
19:13 For they j suffered for their own misdeeds,
Sir 35:18 responds, judges j and affirms the right.
Is 32: 1 will reign j and princes will rule rightly.
59: 4 No one brings suit j,
Jer 7: 5 if each of you deals j with his neighbor;
Col 4: 1 owners, deal j and fairly with your slaves,
Ti 2:12 worldly desires, and live temperately, j,
1Pt 1:17 each one j on the basis of his actions.
2:23 himself up to the One who judges j.

JUSTUS (3)
Acts 1:23 Barsabbas, also known as J) and Matthias.
18: 7 to the house of a Gentile named Titus J,
Col 4:11 Jesus known also as J sends greetings.

JUTTAH (2)
Jos 15:55 Maon, Carmel, Ziph, J,
21:16 pasture lands, J with its pasture lands,

K

KAB (1)
2Kgs 6:25 k of wild onion for five pieces of silver.

KABZEEL (3)
Jos 15:21 K, Eder,
2Sm 23:20 son of Jehoiada, a stalwart from K,
1Chr 11:22 a valiant man of mighty deeds, from K.

KADESH (17)
Gn 14: 7 back and came to Enmishpat (that is, K),
16:14 It is between K and Bered.
20: 1 Negeb, where he settled between K and Shur.
Nm 13:26 Israelites in the desert of Paran at K,
20: 1 first month, and the people settled at K.
20:14 From K Moses sent men to the king of Edom
20:16 the town of K at the edge
20:22 Setting out from K,
27:14 water of Meribah of K in the desert of Zin.]
33:37 Setting out from K,
Dt 1:46 you had to stay as long as you did at K.
Jgs 11:16 the desert to the Red Sea and came to K.
11:17 So Israel remained in K.
Jdt 1: 9 as far as Jerusalem, Bethany, Chelous, K,
1Mc 11:63 come with a strong force to K in Galilee,
11:73 the enemy as far as their camp in K,
Ps(s) 29: 8 the LORD shakes the wilderness of K.

KADESH-BARNEA (11)
Nm 32: 8 I sent them from K to reconnoiter
34: 4 Zin, and extend south of K to Hazar-addar;
Dt 1: 2 to K by way of the highlands of Seir].
1:19 We had reached K when I said to you,
2:14 our departure from K and that crossing;
9:23 And when he sent you up from K to take
Jos 10:41 Joshua conquered from K to Gaza,
14: 6 man of God, Moses, about you and me in K.
14: 7 sent me from K to reconnoiter the land;
15: 3 through Zin, up to a point south of K,
Jdt 5:14 led them along the route to Sinai and K.

KADMIEL (8)
Ezr 2:40 sons of Jeshua, K, Binnui, and Hodaviah,
3: 9 his sons and brethren, with K and Binnui,
Neh 7:43 sons of Jeshua, K, Binnui, Hodeviah,
9: 4 of the Levites were Jeshua, Binnui, K,
9: 5 *The Levites Jeshua, K,
10:10 K; and their brethren Shebaniah,
12: 8 The Levites were Jeshua, Binnui, K,
12:24 Hashabiah, Sherebiah, Jeshua, Binnui, K.

KADMONITES (1)
Gn 15:19 of the Kenites, the Kenizzites, the K,

KAIN (1)
Jos 15:57 Ziph, Juttah, Jezreel, Jokdeam, Zanoah, K,

KAIWAN (1)
Am 5:26 will carry away Sakkuth, your king, and K,

KALLAI (1)
Neh 12:20 for Sallu, K;

KAMON (1)
Jgs 10: 5 Jair died and was buried in K.

KANAH (3)
Jos 16: 8 to the Wadi K and ended at the sea.
17: 9 same boundary continued down to the Wadi K.
19:28 Cabul, Mishal, Abdon, Rehob, Hammon and K,

KAREAH (14)
2Kgs 25:23 son of Nethaniah, Johanan, son of K,
Jer 40: 8 Johanan, son of K;
40:13 Now Johanan, son of K,
40:15 Then Johanan, son of K,
40:16 son of Ahikam, answered Johanan, son of K,
41:11 But when Johanan, son of K,
41:13 At the sight of Johanan, son of K,
41:14 from Mizpah went over to Johanan, son of K.
41:16 Then Johanan, son of K,
42: 1 all the army leaders, Johanan, son of K,
42: 8 Then he called Johanan, son of K,
43: 2 son of Hoshaiah, Johanan, son of K,
43: 4 Johanan, son of K, and the rest of the leaders
43: 5 Instead, Johanan, son of K,

KARIM (1)
Jos 15:59 Peor, Etam, Kulom, Tatam, Zores, K,

KARKA (1)
Jos 15: 3 from there, looping around K,

KARKOR (1)
Jgs 8:10 Now Zebah and Zalmunna were in K with

KARNAIM (1)
Am 6:13 our own strength, seized for ourselves K?"

KARNION (2)
2Mc 12:21 well as the baggage, to a place called K,
12:26 marched to K and the shrine of Atargatis,

KARTAH (2)
Jos 21:34 pasture lands, K with its pasture lands,
1Chr 6:62 pasture lands, K with its pasture lands,

KASERIN (1)
Tb 11: 1 When they were near K,

KATTAH (1)
Jos 19:15 Thus, with K,

KATYDIDS (1)
Lv 11:22 of grasshoppers, the various kinds of k,

KEDAR (11)
Gn 25:13 Nebaioth (Ishmael's first-born), K,
1Chr 1:29 the first-born of Ishmael, then K,
Ps(s) 120: 5 Meshech, that I dwell amid the tents of K!
Sg 1: 5 As the tents of K,
Is 21:16 all the glory of K shall come to an end.

42:11 cry out, the villages where *K* dwells;
60: 7 the flocks of *K* shall be gathered for you,
Jer 2:10 and see, send to *K* and carefully inquire:
49:28 Of *K* and the kingdoms of Hazor,
49:28 Rise up, attack *K*, ravage the Easterners.
Ez 27:21 of all the sheikhs of *K* belonged to you;

KEDARS (1)

Is 21:17 Few of *K* stalwart archers shall remain,

KEDEM (1)

Gn 25: 6 sent them away eastward, to the land of *K*,

KEDEMAH (2)

Gn 25:15 Massa, Hadad, Tema, Jetur, Naphish, and *K*.
1Chr 1:31 Massa, Hadad, Tema, Jetur, Naphish, and *K*.

KEDEMITE (1)

Jgs 8:10 were all who were left of the whole *K* army,

KEDEMITES (4)

Jgs 6: 3 Midian, Amalek and the *K* would come up,
6:33 Then all Midian and Amalek and the *K*
7:12 and all the *K* lay in the valley,
Is 11:14 west, together they shall plunder the *K*;

KEDEMOTH (4)

Dt 2:26 messengers from the desert of *K* to Sihon,
Jos 13:18 Bamoth-baal, Beth-baal-meon, Jahaz, *K*,
21:37 pasture lands, *K* with its pasture lands,
1Chr 6:64 pasture lands, *K* with its pasture lands,

KEDESH (13)

Jos 12:22 Shimron, Achshaph, Taanach, Megiddo, *K*,
15:23 Eder, Jagur, Kinah, Dimonah, Adadah, *K*,
19:37 Chinnereth, Adamah, Ramah, Hazor, *K*,
20: 7 So they set apart *K* in Galilee in the
21:32 of asylum for homicides at *K* in Galilee,
Jgs 4: 6 Barak, son of Abinoam, from *K* of Naphtali.
4: 9 joined Barak and journeyed with him to *K*.
4:10 Barak summoned Zebulun and Naphtali to *K*,
4:11 terebinth of Zaanannim, which was near *K*.
2Kgs 15:29 took Ijon, Abel-beth-maacah, Janoah, *K*,
1Chr 6:57 *K* with its pasture lands,
6:61 *K* in Galilee with its pasture lands,
Tb 1: 2 is south of *K* Naphtali in upper Galilee,

KEDRON (3)

1Mc 15:39 and to fortify *K* and strengthen its gates,
15:41 he fortified *K* and stationed horsemen and
16: 9 pursued them until Cendebeus reached *K*,

KEEL (1)

Wis 5:10 be found, no path of its *k* in the waves.

KEEN (4)

Wis 7:22 certain, Not baneful, loving the good, *k*,
8:11 I should become *k* in judgment,
Sir 19:21 There is a shrewdness *k* but dishonest,
36:19 savor, so does a *k* mind insincere words.

KEENER (1)

Hb 1: 8 his horses, and *k* than wolves at evening.

KEEP (405)

Gn 4:20 of all who dwell in tents and *k* cattle.
6:19 female, that you may *k* them alive with you.
7: 3 *k* their issue alive over all the earth.
14:21 the goods you may *k*."
15: 2 if I *k* on being childless and have as my
17: 9 you must *k* my covenant throughout the ages.
17:10 your descendants after you that you must *k*:
18:19 posterity to *k* the way of the LORD
19:19 hills to *k* the disaster from overtaking me,
31:49 "May the LORD *k* watch between you and me
32:17 *k* a space between one drove and the next."
33: 9 "you should *k* what is yours,
38:23 "Let her *k* the things,"
42: 1 "Why do you *k* gaping at one another?
43: 8 children are to *k* from starving to death.
47:24 while you *k* four-fifths as seed for your
Ex 5: 9 so that they *k* their mind on it and pay no
5:17 because you are lazy that you *k* saying,
12: 6 You shall *k* it until the fourteenth day of
12:17 *K*, then,
12:42 Israelites must *k* a vigil for the LORD
12:47 community of Israel must *k* this feast.
13:10 you shall *k* this prescribed rite at its
14:14 you have only to *k* still."
15:26 his commandments and *k* all his precepts,
16:19 *k* any of it over until tomorrow morning."
16:23 is left put away and *k* for the morrow."
16:28 you refuse to *k* my commandments and laws?
16:32 *K* an omerful of manna for your descendants,
19: 5 you hearken to my voice and *k* my covenant,
20: 6 those who love me and *k* my commandments.
20: 8 "Remember to *k* holy the sabbath day.
21:29 owner, though warned, would not *k* it in;
21:34 the dead animal, however, he may *k*.
21:36 of goring and its owner would not *k* it in,
21:36 but the dead animal he may *k*.
23: 7 You shall *k* away from anything dishonest.
23:15 You shall *k* the feast of Unleavened Bread.
23:16 You shall also *k* the feast of the grain
25:30 you shall always *k* showbread set before me.
27:20 so that you may *k* lamps burning regularly.
28:32 of a shirt, to *k* it from being torn.
31:13 Take care to *k* my sabbaths,
31:14 you must *k* the sabbath as something sacred.
34:11 *k* the commandments I am giving you today.
34:18 shall *k* the feast of Unleavened Bread.
34:22 "You shall *k* the feast of Weeks with the
39:23 around the opening to *k* it from being torn.
Lv 7: 8 someone may *k* for himself the hide
11:44 and you shall make and *k* yourselves holy,
13:45 *k* his garments rent and his head bare,
18: 5 *K*, then, my statutes and decrees,
18:26 must *k* my statutes and decrees forbidding
19: 3 your mother and father, and *k* my sabbaths.
19:19 *K* my statutes:
19:30 *K* my sabbaths,
22: 9 "They shall *k* my charge and not do wrong
23:24 seventh month you shall *k* a sabbath rest,
23:32 but shall *k* a sabbath of complete rest and
23:32 you shall *k* this sabbath of yours from
23:41 you shall *k* this pilgrim feast of the LORD
24: 2 so that you may *k* lamps burning regularly.
25: 2 the land, too, *k* a sabbath for the LORD.
25:18 and be careful to *k* my regulations,
26: 2 *K* my sabbaths,
26: 6 and *k* the sword of war from sweeping
26:14 me and do not *k* all these commandments,
Nm 6:24 The LORD bless you and *k* you!
9: 6 and so could not *k* the Passover that day.
9:10 he may still *k* the LORD's Passover.
9:11 But he shall *k* it in the second month,
9:13 a journey, who yet fails to *k* the Passover,
9:14 among you wishes to *k* the LORD's Passover,
15:39 you to *k* all the commandments of the LORD,
15:40 Thus you will remember to *k* all my
16:26 *K* away from the tents of these wicked men
31:18 But you may spare and *k* for yourselves all
32:20 "If you *k* your word to march as troops in
Dt 4:13 his covenant, which he commanded you to *k*:
4:40 You must *k* his statutes and commandments
5:10 those who love me and *k* my commandments.
5:12 care to *k* holy the sabbath day as the LORD,
5:29 to fear me and to *k* all my commandments!
6: 2 may fear the LORD, your God, and *k*,
6:17 But *k* the commandments of the LORD,
7: 9 those who love him and *k* his commandments,
7:12 will *k* with you the merciful covenant
8: 2 was your intention to *k* his commandments.
8: 6 *k* the commandments of the LORD,
9: 5 *k* the promise which he made on oath
10:13 to *k* the commandments and statutes of the
11: 8 *K* all the commandments,
16:10 *k* the feast of Weeks in honor of the LORD,
17:19 He shall *k* it with him and read it all the
22: 2 place and *k* it with you until he claims it;
23:10 *k* yourselves from everything offensive.
23:14 *k* a trowel in your equipment and with it,
23:24 But you must *k* your solemn word and
25:13 not *k* two differing weights in your bag,
25:14 you *k* two different measures in your house,
26:18 and provided you *k* all his commandments,
27: 1 *K* all these commandments which I enjoin on
27:10 and *k* his commandments and statutes which
28: 9 that you *k* the commandments of the LORD,
28:45 nor *k* the commandments and statutes he
29: 8 *K* the terms of this covenant,
30:10 and *k* his commandments and statutes that
33: 9 Thus the Levites *k* your words,
Jos 1: 8 *K* this book of the law on your lips.
8: 6 They will *k* coming out after us until we
22: 5 *k* his commandments;
Jgs 2:22 they would *k* to the way of the LORD
16: 5 and bind him so as to *k* him helpless.
1Sm 2:14 the fork brought up, the priest would *k*.
2:29 Why do you *k* a greedy eye on my sacrifices
12:24 *k* in mind the great things he has done
17:37 will also *k* me safe from the clutches of
2Sm 13:13 he will not *k* me from you."
14:11 your majesty, *k* in mind the LORD your God,
22: 3 my savior, from violence you *k* me safe.
1Kgs 1: 1 spread covers over him he could not *k* warm.
2: 3 *K* the mandate of the LORD,
6:12 my ordinances, *k* and obey all my commands,
8:23 you *k* your covenant of kindness with your
8:25 *k* the further promise you made to my
8:58 him in everything and *k* the commands,
9: 6 fail to *k* the commandments and statutes
11:34 but will *k* him a prince as long as he
13:21 and did not *k* the command which the LORD,
2Kgs 2: 3 "Yes, I know it," he replied. *K* still."
2: 5 *K* still."
11: 7 shall *k* guard over the temple of the LORD
17:13 ways and *k* my commandments and statutes,
17:19 did not *k* the commandments of the LORD,
1Chr 22:12 Israel, so that you *k* the law of the LORD,
28: 8 I exhort you to *k* and to carry out all the
29:18 *k* such thoughts in the hearts and minds of
29:19 wholehearted desire to *k* your commandments,
2Chr 2:17 hundred overseers to *k* the people working.
6:14 you *k* your covenant and show kindness to
6:16 *k* the further promise you made to my
34:31 follow the LORD and to *k* his commandments,
Ezr 4: 4 of Judah so as to *k* them from building.
8:29 *K* good watch over them till you weigh them
Neh 1: 5 who love you and *k* your commandments,
1: 9 to me and carefully *k* my commandments,
4: 8 *K* in mind the Lord who is great and to be
5:13 every man who fails to *k* this promise,
5:19 *K* in mind, O my God, in my favor all
6:14 *K* in mind Tobiah and Sanballat,
6:14 *k* in mind as well Noadiah the prophetess
13:21 If you *k* this up,
Tb 4: 5 all your days, my son, *k* the Lord in mind,
4:12 My boy, *k* in mind Noah,
4:14 "Do not *k* with you overnight the wages of
4:14 *K* a close watch on yourself,
4:19 now, my son, *k* in mind my commandments,
6: 5 heart, and liver, and *k* them with you;
6:13 I know that Raguel cannot *k* her from you
10: 7 She would go out and *k* watch all day at
12: 7 A king's secret it is prudent to *k*,
12:11 you, 'A king's secret it is prudent to *k*,
Jdt 4: 7 them to *k* firm hold of the mountain passes,
5:21 then your lordship should *k* his distance;
7:12 Have some of your servants *k* control of
Est 3:11 "The silver you may *k*,"
1Mc 2:20 will *k* to the covenant of our fathers.
10:27 Continue, therefore, to *k* faith with us,
2Mc 3:15 law about deposits to *k* the deposits safe
3:22 almighty Lord to *k* the deposits safe
6: 6 A man could not *k* the sabbath or celebrate
12:42 the soldiers to *k* themselves free from sin,
14: 6 who stir up sedition and *k* the kingdom
Jb 10:14 should sin, you would *k* a watch against me,
11: 3 Shall your babblings *k* men silent,
14:13 and *k* me sheltered till your wrath is past;
14:16 my steps, and not *k* watch for sin in me.
22:15 Do you indeed *k* to the ancient way trodden
Ps(s) 12: 8 will *k* us and preserve us always from this
16: 1 *K* me, O God, for in you I take refuge;
17: 8 *K* me as the apple of your eye;
25:10 those who *k* his covenant and his decrees.
34:14 *K* your tongue from evil and your lips from
36:11 *K* up your kindness toward your friends,
37:34 Wait for the LORD, and *k* his way;
41: 3 The LORD will *k* and preserve him;
43: 2 Why do you *k* me so far away?
50:18 When you see a thief, you *k* pace with him,
56: 8 of their wickedness *k* them in view:
69:24 cannot see, and *k* their back always feeble.
71:10 and they who *k* watch against my life take
74:11 *k* your right hand idle beneath your cloak?
76:11 survivors of Hamath shall *k* your festivals.
77: 5 You *k* my eyes watchful;
78: 7 forget the deeds of God but *k* his commands,
86: 2 *K* my life, for I am devoted to you;
89:32 violate my statutes and *k* not my commands,
103: 9 chide, nor does he *k* his wrath forever.
103:18 among those who *k* his covenant
105:45 might *k* his statutes and observe his laws.
119: 8 I will *k* your statutes;
119:17 servant, that I may live and *k* your words.
119:34 your law and *k* it with all my heart.
119:44 And I will *k* your law continually,
119:55 your name, O LORD, and I will *k* your law.
119:57 O LORD, that my part is to *k* your words.
119:63 of all who fear you and *k* your precepts.
119:88 that I may *k* the decrees of your mouth.
119:101 withhold my feet, that I may *k* your words.
119:106 and swear to *k* your just ordinances.
119:134 of men, that I may *k* your precepts.
119:146 save me, and I will *k* your decrees.
119:167 I *k* your decrees and love them deeply.
119:168 I *k* your precepts and your decrees,
127: 1 the city, in vain does the guard *k* vigil.
132:12 If your sons *k* my covenant and the decrees
141: 9 *K* me from the trap they have set for me,
Prv 2:20 good men, and *k* to the paths of the just.
3: 1 not my teaching, *k* in mind my commands;
3:21 *k* advice and counsel in view;
3:26 and will *k* your foot from the snare.
4: 4 *k* my commands, that you may live!
4:13 *k* her,
4:21 of your sight, *k* them within your heart;
4:27 nor to left, *k* your foot far from evil.
5: 8 *K* your way far from her,
6:21 *K* them fastened over your heart always,
6:24 To *k* you from your neighbor's wife,
7: 1 My son, *k* my words,
7: 2 *K* my commands and live,
7: 5 That they may *k* you from another's wife,
8:33 obeys me, and happy those who *k* my ways,
22:18 will be well if you *k* them in your bosom,
23: 1 with a ruler, *k* in mind who is before you;
23:26 your heart, and let your eyes *k* to my ways.
28: 4 but those who *k* the law war against him.
Eccl 1: 7 place where they go, the rivers *k* on going.
3: 6 a time to *k*,

KEEP (cont.)

4:11 two sleep together, they *k* each other warm.
4:11 How can one alone *k* warm?
4:17 for they know not how to *k* from doing evil.
12:13 Fear God and *k* his commandments,
Wis 6: 4 judged not rightly, and did not *k* the law,
6:10 For those who *k* the holy precepts hallowed
Sir 1:23 If you desire wisdom, *k* the commandments,
1:26 over your lips *k* watch.
2:15 those who love him *k* his ways.
6:13 *K* away from your enemies;
6:27 with all your strength *k* her ways.
7:22 if they are dependable, *k* them.
7:24 If you have daughters, *k* them chaste,
8:17 a fool, for he can *k* nothing to himself.
9:13 *K* far from the man who has power to kill,
13: 9 by a man of influence, *k* your distance;
13:10 *k* not too far away lest you be forgotten.
15:15 If you choose you can *k* the commandments;
18:30 your lusts, but *k* your desires in check.
23:14 *K* your father and mother in mind when you
26:10 *K* a strict watch over an unruly wife,
27:17 Cherish your friend, *k* faith with him;
29: 3 *K* your promise,
29: 8 *k* him not waiting for your alms;
31:15 as you do, and *k* in mind your own dislikes:
32:23 in this way you will *k* the commandments.
33:16 Now I am the last to *k* vigil,
33:23 *K* control over all your affairs;
35: 1 To *k* the law is a great oblation,
37:10 who envy you, *k* your intentions hidden.
42: 6 Of a seal to *k* an erring wife at home,
42:11 *K* a close watch on your daughter,
43:10 At whose command they *k* their place and
Is 7:21 man shall *k* a heifer or a couple of sheep,
26: 3 A nation of firm purpose you *k* in peace;
29:23 in his midst, They shall *k* my name holy;
30: 8 Now come, write it on a tablet they can *k*,
33:23 mast in place, nor *k* the sail spread out.
41: 1 *K* silence before me, O coastlands;
41: 6 helps another, one says to the other, *K* on!"
47:12 *K* up, now, your spells
56: 6 All who *k* the sabbath free from
64: 8 LORD, *k* not our guilt forever in mind;
Jer 3: 5 "Will he *k* his wrath forever,
5: 6 them, Leopards *k* watch round their cities:
12: 2 root, they *k* on growing and bearing fruit.
17:22 no work whatever, but *k* holy the sabbath,
17:27 you do not obey me and *k* holy the sabbath,
44:25 *k* your vows, carry out your resolutions!
49:11 your orphans behind, I will *k* them alive;
Ez 13:18 lives of my people, yet *k* yourselves alive?
14: 3 *k* the occasion of their sin before them.
17:14 and would *k* his covenant and obey him.
20:11 them my ordinances, which everyone must *k*,
20:13 that bring life to those who *k* them.
20:18 of your parents or *k* their ordinances;
20:19 statutes and be careful to *k* my ordinances;
20:20 *k* holy my sabbaths,
20:21 they did not observe my statutes or *k* my
20:24 for they did not *k* my ordinances,
22:30 before me to *k* me from destroying the land;
33:25 yet you would *k* possession of the land?
33:26 yet you would *k* possession of the land?
39:14 For seven months they shall *k* searching.
42:13 they shall *k* the most sacred offerings:
44:20 they shall *k* their hair carefully trimmed.
44:24 all my festivals, and *k* my sabbaths holy.
Dn 5:17 "You may *k* your gifts,
6:16 *K* in mind, O king,"
8:26 Do you, however, *k* this vision undisclosed,
9: 4 you who *k* your merciful covenant toward
12: 4 *k* secret the message and seal the book
13: 9 and did not *k* in mind just judgments.
Hos 13: 7 like a panther by the road I will *k* watch.
Am 2: 4 of the LORD, and did not *k* his statutes;
Na 2: 2 guard the rampart, *K* watch on the road,
Hb 1:17 *k* on brandishing his sword to slay peoples
2: 1 And *k* watch to see what he will say to me,
Zec 3: 7 you shall judge my house and *k* my courts,
Mal 1:10 *k* you from kindling fire on my altar
2: 7 the lips of the priest are to *k* knowledge,
2: 9 all the people, Since you do not *k* my ways,
Mt 6: 4 *K* your deeds of mercy secret,
10:10 The workman, after all, is worth his *k*.
18:15 his fault, but *k* it between the two of you.
19:17 to enter into life, *k* the commandments."
24:20 *K* praying that you will not have to flee
24:43 he would *k* a watchful eye
25:13 *k* your eyes open, for you know not the day
26:43 they could not *k* their eyes open.
28:14 it out with him and *k* you out of trouble."
Mk 8:15 when he instructed them, *K* your eyes open!
9:43 enter life maimed than to *k* both hands
9:50 *K* salt in your hearts and you will be at
10:48 were scolding him to make him *k* quiet,
13:18 *K* praying that none of this happens in
14:40 They could not *k* their eyes open,
Lk 4:42 him they tried to *k* him from leaving them.
11:28 are they who hear the word of God and *k* it."
17:33 whoever loses it will *k* it.
19:40 He replied, "If they were to *k* silence,
20:47 recite long prayers to *k* up appearances.
Jn 2:10 have done is *k* the choice wine until now."
4:15 and have to *k* coming here to draw water."
8:55 Yes, I know him well, and I *k* his word.
9:16 from God because he does not *k* the sabbath."
10:24 long are you going to *k* us in suspense?
12: 7 Let her *k* it against the day they prepare
12:36 you have the light, *k* faith in the light;
12:46 to *k* anyone who believes in me from
12:47 anyone hears my words and does not *k* them,
14:24 who does not love me does not *k* my words.
15:10 live in my love if you *k* my commandments,
16: 1 all this to *k* your faith from being shaken.
Acts 2:24 that death should *k* its hold on him,
5: 3 *k* for yourself some of the proceeds
8:37 What is to *k* me from being baptized?"
9:24 They went so far as to *k* close watch on
15: 5 circumcised and told to *k* the Mosaic law.
20:28 *K* watch over yourselves,
23:11 *K* up your courage!
24:16 *k* my conscience clear before God and man.
27:22 I urge you now to *k* up your courage.
27:25 So *k* up your courage, men.
28:16 a soldier was assigned to *k* guard over him.
Rom 2:13 those who *k* it who will be declared just.
2:14 do not have the law *k* it as by instinct,
1Cor 7:37 his will makes up his mind to *k* his virgin,
10: 6 to *k* us from wicked desires such as theirs.
11:32 he chastens us to *k* us from being
14:30 the first ones should then *k* quiet.
14:34 women should *k* silent in such gatherings.
2Cor 12: 7 to beat me and *k* me from getting proud.
Gal 4:10 You even go so far as to *k* the ceremonial
Eph 5:15 *K* careful watch over your conduct.
6:21 will *k* you informed as to how I am and
1Thes 1: 2 We *k* thanking God for all of you and we
2:16 they try to *k* us from preaching salvation
1Tm 5:14 younger ones marry, have children, *k* house,
5:22 *K* yourself pure.
6:14 I charge you to *k* God's command without
2Tm 2:14 *K* reminding people of these things and
Ti 1:13 an attempt to *k* them close to sound faith,
2: 6 to *k* themselves completely under control
Phlm 1: 5 for I *k* hearing of your love and faith
1:13 I had wanted to *k* him with me,
Heb 12: 2 let us *k* our eyes fixed on Jesus,
13:17 for they *k* watch over you as men who must
Jas 1:19 *K* this in mind, dear brothers.
2:16 *K* warm and well fed,"
1Pt 3: 7 will *k* your prayers from being answered.
3:10 must *k* his tongue from evil and his lips
3:16 *K* your conscience clear,
2Pt 1:19 *K* your attention closely fixed on it,
1Jn 2: 1 ones, I am writing this to *k* you from sin.
2: 3 knowledge of him is to *k* his commandments.
3:24 who *k* his commandments remain in him
5: 3 that we *k* his commandments
Jude 1: 6 too, who did not *k* to their own domain,
Rv 2: 5 *K* firmly in mind the heights from which
3: 3 *k* to it,
3:10 I will *k* you safe in the time of trial
3:17 You *k* saying, "I am so rich and secure
12:17 those who *k* God's commandments and give
14:12 who *k* the commandments of God and their
18:10 They will *k* their distance for fear of the
18:15 will *k* their distance for fear of the

KEEPER (11)

Gn 4: 2 Abel became a *k* of flocks,
4: 9 Am I my brother's *k*?"
1Sm 17:22 entrusted what he had brought to the *k*
2Kgs 22:14 Tikvah, son of Harhas, *k* of the wardrobe.
2Chr 31:14 a Levite and the *k* of the eastern gate,
Neh 2: 8 letter for Asaph, the *k* of the royal park,
3:29 son of Shecaniah, *k* of the East Gate.
Tb 1:22 had been chief cupbearer, *k* of the seal,
Is 27: 3 I, the LORD, am its *k*,
Jer 35: 4 Maaseiah, son of Shallum, *k* of the doorway.
Jn 10: 3 the *k* opens the gate for him.

KEEPERS (4)

Gn 46:32 shepherds, having long been *k* of livestock;
46:34 have been *k* of livestock from the
2Kgs 25:18 priest, and the three *k* of the entry.
Jer 52:24 priest, and the three *k* of the entry.

KEEPING (84)

Gn 26: 5 *k* my mandate (my commandments,
Ex 21: 6 an awl, thus *k* him as his slave forever.
31:16 *k* it throughout their generations as a
38:18 wide, in *k* with the hangings of the court.
Lv 8:29 was in *k* with the LORD's command to Moses.
8:31 in *k* with the command I have received:
9:21 in *k* with the LORD's command to Moses.
10:18 in *k* with the command I had received."
27: 8 ransom in *k* with the means of the one
27:12 value in *k* with its good or bad qualities,
27:14 its value in *k* with its good or bad points,
Nm 3:39 by clans in *k* with the LORD's command,
6:21 dedication in *k* with the vow he has taken."
14:19 this people in *k* with your great kindness,
17: 5 in *k* with the orders which the LORD had
26:53 heritage in *k* with the number of individuals
Dt 6: 3 more, in *k* with the promise of the LORD,
10: 5 in *k* with the command the LORD gave me.
13:19 *k* all his commandments which I enjoin on
16: 1 of Abib by *k* the Passover of the LORD,
29:20 in *k* with all the curses of the covenant
30:16 in his ways, and *k* his commandments,
Jos 8:31 in *k* with the command to the Israelites of
1Sm 20:42 in *k* with what we two have sworn by the
2Sm 3: 8 friends, by *k* you out of David's clutches;
1Kgs 3:14 me by *k* my statutes and commandments,
8:61 his statutes and *k* his commandments,
9: 4 commanded you, *k* my statutes and decrees,
11:38 and please me by *k* my statutes and my
2Kgs 7: 9 is a day of good news, and we are *k* silent.
9:26 of ground, in *k* with the word of the LORD."
1Chr 17:19 servant's sake and in *k* with your purpose,
24:19 in *k* with the precepts given them by Aaron,
28: 7 if he perseveres in *k* my commandments and
29: 8 gave them into the *k* of Jehiel
2Chr 7:17 you and *k* my statutes and ordinances,
29:15 the LORD's house in *k* with his words.
33: 8 *k* the whole law and the statutes and the
Ezr 6:17 *k* with the number of the tribes of Israel.
10: 3 children born of them, in *k* with what you,
Neh 1: 7 we offended you, not *k* the commandments,
Tb 1: 8 and we ate it in *k* with the decree of the
10: 1 Tobit was *k* track of the time Tobiah would
Est 8: 2 and transferred it into the *k* of Mordecai;
1Mc 1:60 were put to death, in *k* with the decree,
2:64 be courageous and strong in *k* the law,
2Mc 8:17 *k* before their eyes the lawless outrage
11:25 in *k* with the customs of their ancestors.
15: 3 who prescribed the *k* of the sabbath day.
Jb 33:17 man from evil and *k* pride away from him,
Ps(s) 19:12 careful of them, very diligent in *k* them,
32: 8 I will counsel you, *k* my eye on you.
42: 5 with the multitude *k* festival.
119: 5 be firm in the ways of *k* your statutes!
119: 9 By *k* to your words.
119:60 and did not hesitate in *k* your commands.
119:169 in *k* with your word,
Prv 15: 3 place, *k* watch on the evil and the good.
Wis 6:18 love means the *k* of her laws;
Sir 31: 1 *K* watch over riches wastes the flesh,
Is 58: 5 of fasting I wish, of *k* a day of penance:
Jer 17:24 *k* the sabbath holy and abstaining from all
Ez 13:19 die and *k* alive those who should not live,
14: 4 and *k* the occasion of his sin before him,
31:11 has dealt with it in *k* with its wickedness.
35:15 In *k* with your glee over the devastation
Dn 9:16 O Lord, in *k* with all your just deeds,
11: 4 descendants or in *k* with his mighty rule,
Mal 3:14 and what do we profit by *k* his command,
Mt 27:54 The centurion and his men who were *k* watch
Mk 7: 9 in the interests of *k* your traditions!
14:69 The servant girl, *k* an eye on him,
Lk 2: 8 *k* night watch by turns over their flocks.
17:12 *K* their distance,
Rom 12: 3 in *k* with the measure of faith that God
1Cor 7:19 What matters is *k* God's commandments.
2Cor 11:32 King Aretas was *k* a close watch on the city
Eph 3:16 gifts in *k* with the riches of his glory.
2Thes 3:11 not *k* busy but acting like busybodies.
1Tm 3: 4 *k* his children under control without
Jas 1:27 *k* oneself unspotted by the world
2Pt 3: 9 The Lord does not delay in *k* his promise
1Jn 2: 4 known him," without *k* his commandments,
3:22 Because we are *k* his commandments and

KEEPS (59)

Dt 7: 9 the faithful God who *k* his merciful
Jgs 5:29 her, and she, too, *k* answering herself:
1Chr 28: 7 commandments and decrees as he *k* them
Tb 4:10 and *k* one from going into the dark abode.
Jb 20:13 let it go but *k* it still within his mouth.
21:33 and over him the funeral mound *k* watch,
33: 4 me, the breath of the Almighty *k* me alive.
34: 8 *K* company with evildoers and goes along
Ps(s) 31:24 The LORD *k* those who are constant,
116: 6 The LORD *k* the little ones;
145:20 The LORD *k* all who love him,
146: 6 Who *k* faith forever,
Prv 11:12 no sense, but the intelligent man *k* silent.
11:13 but a trustworthy man *k* a confidence.
17:28 Even a fool, if he *k* silent,
19: 8 he who *k* understanding will be successful.
19:16 He who *k* the precept keeps his life,
21:23 and his tongue *k* himself from trouble.
27:16 He who *k* her stores up a stormwind;
28: 7 He who *k* the law is a wise son,
29:18 but happy is he who *k* the law.
Eccl 8: 5 who *k* the commandment experiences no evil,
Wis 6:15 *k* vigil shall quickly be free from care;
Sir 18:27 sin is rife he *k* himself from wrongdoing.
19:24 his lack of strength *k* him from sinning,
21:11 He who *k* the law controls his impulses;
21:23 but a cultured man *k* his glance cast down.
23: 7 for he who *k* it will not be enslaved.
32:24 He who *k* the law preserves himself;
37:12 man, who you are sure *k* the commandments;
38:26 he *k* a watch on the beasts in the stalls.

38:27 and he *k* watch till he finishes his design.
38:28 he *k* watch till he perfects it in detail.
38:30 and he *k* watch on the fire of his kiln.
42: 9 is a treasure that *k* her father wakeful,
Is 26: 2 in a nation that is just, one that *k* faith.
26: 9 yes, my spirit within me *k* vigil for you;
56: 2 Who *k* the sabbath free from profanation,
Jer 8: 6 Everyone *k* on running his course,
Bar 6:58 a house, that *k* safe those who are within,
Ez 14: 7 and *k* the occasion of his sin before him,
18:17 *k* my ordinances and lives by my statutes
18:21 if he *k* all my statutes and does what is
Mt 15:23 She *k* shouting after us."
Lk 9:62 hand to the plow but *k* looking back is unfit
Jn 7: 4 to be known publicly *k* his actions hidden.
7:19 Yet not one of you *k* it.
8:52 man shall never know death if he *k* my word.'
Rom 2:26 person *k* the precepts of the law,
2:27 If a man who is uncircumcised *k* the law,
1Cor 10:13 Besides, God *k* his promise.
2Cor 1:18 As God *k* his word,
2Thes 3: 3 every man has faith, but the Lord *k* faith;
Jas 2:10 law, even though he *k* the entire remainder,
1Jn 2: 5 But whoever *k* his word,
3: 3 has this hope based on him *k* himself pure,
Rv 2:26 the victory, who *k* to my ways till the end,
18: 5 as heaven, and God *k* count of her crimes.

KEHELATHAH (2)

Nm 33:22 Setting out from Rissah, they camped at *K.*
33:23 Setting out from *K,*

KEILAH (16)

Jos 15:44 Ether, Ashan, Iphtah, Ashnah, Nezib, *K,*
1Sm 23: 1 *K* and plundering the threshing floors.
23: 2 will defeat the Philistines and rescue *K.*"
23: 3 to *K* against the forces of the Philistines!"
23: 4 the LORD, who answered, "Go down to *K,*
23: 5 men to *K* and fought with the Philistines.
23: 5 and thus rescued the inhabitants of *K.*
23: 6 fled to David, went down with David to *K,*
23: 7 Saul was told that David had entered *K,*
23: 8 go down to *K* and besiege David and his men.
23:10 a report that Saul plans to come to *K,*
23:12 "Will the citizens of *K* deliver me and my
23:13 left *K* and wandered from place to place.
1Chr 4:19 the sister of Naham, the father of *K,*
Neh 3:17 leader of half the district of *K.*
3:18 Henadad, leader of half the district of *K;*

KELAIAH (1)

Ezr 10:23 Jozabad, Shimei, *K* (also called Kelita),

KELITA (3)

Ezr 10:23 Jozabad, Shimei, Kelaiah (also called *K),*
Neh 8: 7 Akkub, Shabbethai, Hodiah, Maaseiah, *K,*
10:11 and their brethren Shebaniah, Hodiah, *K,*

KEMUEL (3)

Gn 22:21 his brother Buz, *K* (the father of Aram),
Nm 34:24 *K,* son of Shiphtan,
1Chr 27:17 for Levi, Hashabiah, son of *K;*

KENAN (6)

Gn 5: 9 years old, he became the father of *K.*
5:10 and fifteen years after the birth of *K,*
5:12 When *K* was seventy years old,
5:13 *K* lived eight hundred and forty years
5:14 of *K* was nine hundred and ten years;
1Chr 1: 2 Adam, Seth, Enosh, *K,*

KENATH (2)

Nm 32:42 Nobah also campaigned against *K,*
1Chr 2:23 villages of Jair, that is, *K* and its towns,

KENAZ (11)

Gn 36:11 were Teman, Omar, Zepho, Gatam, and *K.*
36:15 the clans of Teman, Omar, Zepho, *K,*
36:42 Alvah, Jetheth, Oholibamah, Elah, Pinon, *K,*
Jos 15:17 Othniel, son of Caleb's brother *K,*
Jgs 1:13 Othniel, son of Caleb's younger brother *K,*
3: 9 Othniel, son of Caleb's younger brother *K,*
3:11 for forty years, until Othniel, son of *K,*
1Chr 1:36 Eliphaz were Teman, Omar, Zephi, Gatam, *K,*
1:53 Jetheth, Oholibamah, Elah, Pinon, *K,*
4:13 The sons of *K* were Othniel and Seraiah.
4:15 The sons of Elah were . . . and *K.*

KENITE (5)

Jgs 1:16 The descendants of the *K,*
4:11 Now the *K* Heber had detached himself from
4:17 to the tent of Jael, wife of the *K* Heber,
4:17 the *K* Heber were at peace with one another.
1Sm 30:29 cities, to those in the *K* cities,

KENITES (6)

Gn 15:19 River [the Euphrates], the land of the *K,*
Nm 24:21 Upon seeing the *K,*
1Sm 15: 6 an ambush in the wadi, warned the *K:*
15: 6 After the *K* left, Saul routed Amalek
27:10 of Jerahmeel," or "The Negeb of the *K.*"
1Chr 2:55 They were the *K,* who came from Hammath

KENIZZITE (4)

Nm 32:12 except the *K* Caleb,
Jos 14: 6 came up to Joshua in Gilgal, the *K* Caleb,
14:14 Hebron remains the heritage of the *K* Caleb,

KENIZZITES (1)

Gn 15:19 the land of the Kenites, the *K*

KEPT (242)

Gn 16: 2 "The LORD has *k* me from bearing children.
20: 6 it was I who *k* you from sinning against me;
25:27 was a simple man, who *k* to his tents.
30:40 sheep, on the other hand, Jacob *k* apart,
39:16 She *k* the cloak with her until his master
43: 7 *k* asking about ourselves and our family:
Ex 5:13 while the taskmasters *k* driving them on,
12:10 of it must be *k* beyond the next morning;
16:20 When some *k* a part of it over until the
17:11 As long as Moses *k* his hands raised up,
23:18 my feast be *k* overnight till the next day.
30:35 is to be salted and so *k* pure and sacred.
34:25 feast be *k* overnight for the next day.
Lv 6: 2 the fire is to be *k* burning on the altar.
6: 5 The fire on the altar is to be *k* burning;
6: 6 to be *k* burning continuously on the altar;
7:15 none of it may be *k* till the next day.
24:12 who *k* him in custody till a decision from
Nm 15:34 But they *k* him in custody,
17:25 be *k* there as a warning to the rebellious,
19: 9 There they are to be *k* for preparing
31: 9 But the Israelites *k* the women of the
31:53 soldiers had looted each one *k* for himself.
Dt 16: 4 day shall be *k* overnight for the next day.
Jos 6: 9 horns was *k* up continually as they marched.
6:13 the blowing of horns was *k* up continually.
8:26 Joshua *k* the javelin in his hand stretched
22:31 you have *k* the Israelites free from
Jgs 1:27 Canaanites *k* their hold in this district.
7: 8 their tents, but *k* the three hundred men.
7:22 the three hundred men *k* blowing the horns,
16: 6 you may be bound so as to be *k* helpless."
1Sm 9:24 for it was *k* for you until your arrival;
13:13 *k* the command the LORD your God gave you,
14:19 tumult in the Philistine camp *k* increasing.
15:11 turned from me and has not *k* my command."
15:13 I have *k* the command of the LORD."
17:54 but he *k* Goliath's armor in his own tent.
25:26 it is the LORD who has *k* you from shedding
2Sm 12:16 He *k* a fast,
12:21 living, you fasted and wept and *k* vigil;
16:13 Shimei *k* abreast of them on the hillside,
18:25 As he *k* coming nearer,
22:22 For I *k* the ways of the LORD and was not
22:33 me with strength and *k* my way unerring;
1Kgs 1: 2 your royal majesty, you will be *k* warm."
2:43 have you not *k* the oath of the LORD and
3:22 But the first *k* saying,
8:24 *k* the promise you made to my father David,
9:25 and he *k* the temple in repair.
11:11 and you have not *k* my covenant and my
11:20 the queen *k* him in Pharaoh's palace,
11:34 chose, who *k* my commandments and statutes.
14: 8 who *k* my commandments and followed me
2Kgs 2:17 However, they *k* urging him,
4:25 She *k* going till she reached the man of
23:23 Passover of the LORD was *k* in Jerusalem.
1Chr 9:23 Thus they and their sons *k* guard over the
11:14 made a stand on the sown ground, *k* it safe,
12:23 And from day to day men *k* coming to
16:42 The sons of Jeduthun *k* the gate.
2Chr 6:15 *k* the promise you made to my father David,
30: 5 not many had *k* it in the manner prescribed.
34:21 since our fathers have not *k* the word of
35:17 *k* the Passover and the feast
35:18 of Israel *k* a Passover like that of Josiah,
Ezr 3: 4 They also *k* the feast of Booths in the
6:19 The exiles *k* the Passover on the
6:22 They joyfully *k* the feast of Unleavened
9: 1 nor the Levites have *k* themselves aloof
Neh 4:17 everyone *k* his weapon at his right hand.
8:18 They *k* the feast for seven days,
9:33 for you *k* faith while we have done evil.
9:34 and our fathers have not *k* your law;
11:19 their brethren, who *k* watch over the gates;
12:25 *k* watch over the storerooms at the gates.
13:22 so that the sabbath day might be *k* holy.
Tb 3: 5 For we have not *k* your commandments,
5: 3 it into two parts, and each of us *k* one;
6: 6 the rest he salted and *k* for the journey.
10: 6 But Tobit *k* telling her:
12:22 *k* thanking God and singing his praises;
Jdt 7: 5 bastions, and *k* watch throughout the night.
7:20 *k* them thus surrounded for thirty-four
10:10 The men of the city *k* her in view as she
12: 1 into the room where his silverware was *k,*
15: 2 No one *k* ranks any longer;
Est A:11 He *k* it in mind,
9:28 be commemorated and *k* in every generation,
1Mc 2:53 when in distress, *k* the commandment,
5:53 and Judas *k* rounding up the stragglers and
6:52 their own, and *k* up the fight a long time.
10:26 We have heard how you have *k* the treaty
11:40 Trypho *k* urging Imalkue to hand over the
12:47 But he *k* with him three thousand men,
2Mc 8:27 thanks to the Lord who *k* them safe
10:30 their own armor, *k* him from being wounded.
10:34 *k* repeating outrageous blasphemies and
12:38 to custom and *k* the sabbath there.
13: 3 with great duplicity *k* urging Antiochus on,
14: 4 On that occasion he *k* quiet.
14:24 but he always *k* Judas in his company,
15:34 be he who has *k* his own Place undefiled!"
Jb 3:10 Because it *k* not shut the doors of the
22: 6 unjustly *k* your kinsmen's goods in pawn,
23:11 his way I have *k* and have not turned aside.
29: 3 While he *k* his lamp shining above my head,
Ps(s) 17: 4 of your lips I have *k* the ways of the law.
18:22 For I *k* the ways of the LORD and was not
18:33 me with strength and *k* my way unerring;
39: 3 man was before me I *k* dumb and silent;
40:11 Your justice I *k* not hid within my heart;
69:27 for they *k* after him whom you smote,
73:13 Is it but in vain I have *k* my heart
78: 8 A generation that *k* not its heart
78:10 They *k* not the covenant with God;
78:56 God the Most High, and *k* not his decrees.
90: 8 You have *k* our iniquities before you,
119: 4 that your precepts be deligently *k.*
119:136 of tears because your law has not been *k.*
119:158 because they *k* not to your promise.
Eccl 5:12 riches *k* by their owner to his hurt.
9: 1 All this I have *k* in mind and recognized:
Sg 5: 2 I was sleeping, but my heart *k* vigil;
7:14 my lover, I have *k* in store for you.
Wis 10: 5 the just man, *k* him blameless before God,
17: 4 even their inner chambers *k* them fearless,
17:16 that unbarred prison and was *k* confined.
18: 4 who had *k* your sons confined through whom
Sir 8:18 do nothing that should be *k* secret,
20: 2 admits his fault will be *k* from disgrace.
39:29 his treasury also, *k* for the proper time,
44:19 of many peoples, *k* his glory without stain:
51: 2 death, and *k* back my body from the pit,
51:15 My feet *k* to the level path because from
Is 8:16 sealed instruction *k* among my disciples.
42:14 I have looked away, and *k* silence,
Jer 29:19 I *k* sending them my servants the prophets,
31: 3 so I have *k* my mercy toward you.
32:14 so that they can be *k* there a long time.
32:33 though I *k* teaching them,
35:15 *k* sending you all my servants the prophets,
35:18 *k* all his commands and done everything he
36:26 But the LORD *k* them concealed.
37:14 Irijah *k* Jeremiah in custody and brought
44: 4 Though I *k* sending to you all my servants
44:25 stated your intentions, and *k* them in fact:
48:11 Thus he *k* his taste,
52:11 and *k* in prison until the day of his death.
Lam 1:14 "He has *k* watch over my sins;
Bar 2: 9 And the Lord *k* watch over the evils,
Ez 11:12 and whose ordinances you have not *k;*
16:56 Was not your sister Sodom *k* in bad repute
Dn 7:28 blanched, but I *k* the matter to myself.
8: 9 horn which *k* growing toward the south,
9:14 so the LORD *k* watch over the calamity and
10:15 thus to me, I fell forward and *k* silent.
12: 9 be *k* secret and sealed until the end time.
14:19 laughed and *k* the king from entering.
Am 1:11 in his anger and *k* his wrath to the end,
Mi 6:16 You have *k* the decrees of Omri,
Mal 3: 7 from my statutes, and have not *k* them.
Mt 8:31 The demons *k* appealing to him,
19:20 man said to him, "I have *k* all these;
21: 9 as well as those following *k* crying out:
21:11 And the crowd *k* answering,
26:16 and from that time on he *k* looking for an
26:58 Peter *k* following him at a distance as far
27:30 of the reed and *k* striking him on the head.
27:36 they sat down there and *k* watch over him.
27:39 People going by *k* insulting him,
27:44 with him *k* taunting him in the same way.
27:64 *k* under surveillance until the third day.
27:66 and *k* it under surveillance of the guard,
Mk 1:45 yet people *k* coming to him from all sides.
2: 8 reasoning, though they *k* it to themselves,
2:13 people *k* coming to him in crowds and he
3: 2 They *k* an eye on Jesus to see whether he
3:10 *k* pushing toward him to touch him.
3:12 while he *k* ordering them sternly not to
4:34 while he *k* explaining things privately to
4:41 They *k* saying to one another,
5:32 he *k* looking around to see the woman who
6: 2 in a way that *k* his large audience amazed.
6:20 upright and holy man, and *k* him in custody.
9:10 They *k* this word of his to themselves,
10:20 I have *k* all these since my childhood."
14:11 He for his part *k* looking for an opportune
14:31 But Peter *k* reasserting vehemently,
14:36 He *k* saying, "Abba (O Father),

KEPT (cont.)
15:29 People going by *k* insulting him,
15:32 crucified with him likewise *k* taunting him.
Lk 1:22 He *k* making signs to them,
2:51 meanwhile *k* all these things in memory.
4:37 His renown *k* spreading through the
9:36 The disciples *k* quiet,
14: 4 At this they *k* silent.
18: 3 widow in that city *k* coming to him saying,
18:13 The other man, however, *k* his distance,
18:21 "I have *k* all these since I was a boy."
22: 6 then *k* looking for an opportunity to hand
23:35 watching, and the leaders *k* jeering at him,
Jn 3:23 and people *k* coming to be baptized.
6: 2 a vast crowd *k* following him because they
6:42 They *k* saying: "Is this not Jesus,
7:12 is a good man," while others *k* saying,
7:31 They *k* saying, "When the Messiah comes,
12:13 They *k* shouting: "Hosanna!
12:17 him from the dead *k* testifying to it.
15:10 even as I have *k* my Father's commandments,
16:18 They *k* asking: "What does he mean
17: 6 they have *k* your word.
17:12 I *k* careful watch,
18:15 disciple, *k* following Jesus closely.
18:17 servant girl who *k* the gate said to Peter,
20:25 The other disciples *k* telling him:
Acts 2:40 he used many other arguments, and *k* urging,
9:21 They *k* saying: "Isn't this the man
12: 6 chains, while guards *k* watch at the door.
12:16 Through all this, Peter *k* on knocking.
19:34 and *k* shouting for about two hours.
20: 7 next day, he *k* on speaking until midnight.
23:35 to be *k* under guard in Herod's praetorium.
24:23 be *k* in custody but allowed some freedom,
25: 4 Paul was being *k* in custody at Caesarea,
25:21 Paul appealed to be *k* here until there
25:21 so I issued orders that he be *k* in custody
Rom 1:13 (though up to now I have been *k* from it)
15:31 be *k* safe from the unbelievers in Judea,
2Cor 11: 9 I *k* myself from being burdensome to you,
Eph 2:14 the barrier of hostility that *k* us apart.
2Tm 2: 5 winner's crown unless he has *k* the rules.
4: 7 have finished the race, I have *k* the faith.
Heb 3:19 their unbelief that *k* them from entering.
11:28 By faith he *k* the Passover and sprinkled
13: 4 way and the marriage bed be *k* undefiled,
1Pt 1: 4 which is *k* in heaven for you who are
2Pt 3: 7 they are *k* for the day of judgment,
Jude 1: 6 These the Lord has *k* in perpetual bondage,
1:18 how they *k* telling you,
Rv 3:10 Because you have *k* my plea to stand fast,
21:27 in the book of the living *k* by the Lamb.

KEREN-HAPPUCH (1)
Jb 42:14 the second Keziah, and the third *K.*

KERIOTH (2)
Jer 48:24 and Beth-meon, on *K* and on Bozrah:
Am 2: 2 upon Moab, to devour the castles of *K;*

KERIOTH-HEZRON (1)
Jos 15:25 Bealoth, Hazor-hadattah, and *K* (that is,

KERNEL (1)
1Cor 15:37 but a *k* of wheat or some other grain.

KERNELS (1)
Lv 23:14 eat any bread or roasted grain or fresh *k.*

KEROS (2)
Ezr 2:44 of Hasupha, sons of Tabbaoth, sons of *K,*
Neh 7:47 of Hasupha, sons of Tabbaoth, sons of *K,*

KETTLE (6)
1Sm 2:14 and would thrust it into the basin, *k,*
Jb 41:23 the sea he churns like perfume in a *k.*
Ez 11: 3 The city is the *k,* and we are the meat."
11: 7 they are the meat, and the city is the *k;*
11:11 The city shall not be a *k* for you,
Mi 3: 3 They chop them in pieces like flesh in a *k,*

KETTLES (1)
Mk 7: 4 the washing of cups and jugs and *k.*

KETURAH (4)
Gn 25: 1 married another wife, whose name was *K.*
25: 4 All of these were descendants of *K.*
1Chr 1:32 The descendants of *K,* Abraham's concubine:
1:33 All these were the descendants of *K.*

KEY (6)
Jgs 3:25 room, they took the *k* and opened them.
Is 22:22 *k* of the House of David on his shoulder;
Lk 11:52 You have taken away the *k* of knowledge.
Rv 3: 7 holy One, the true, who wields David's *k,*
9: 1 was given the *k* to the shaft of the abyss;
20: 1 holding the *k* to the abyss and a huge

KEYS (2)
Mt 16:19 to you the *k* of the kingdom of heaven.
Rv 1:18 I hold the *k* of death and the nether world.

KEYSTONE (3)
Mt 21:42 rejected has become the *k* of the structure.
Mk 12:10 builders has become the *k* of the structure.
Lk 20:17 has become the *k* of the structure'?

KEZIAH (1)
Jb 42:14 he called the first Jemimah, the second *K,*

KIBROTH-HATTAAVAH (5)
Nm 11:34 So that place was named *K,*
11:35 From *K* the people set out for Hazeroth.
33:16 from the desert of Sinai, they camped at *K.*
33:17 from *K,* they camped at Hazeroth.
Dt 9:22 "At Taberah, at Massah, and at *K* likewise,

KIBZAIM (2)
Jos 21:22 pasture lands, *K* with its pasture lands.
1Chr 6:53 pasture lands, *K* with its pasture lands,

KICK (1)
Acts 26:14 It is hard for you to *k* against the goad.'

KID (14)
Gn 38:17 "I will send you a *k* from the flock."
38:20 Judah sent the *k* by his friend the
38:23 After all, I did send her the *k,*
Ex 23:19 shall not boil a *k* in its mother's milk.
34:26 shall not boil a *k* in its mother's milk."
Dt 14:21 shall not boil a *k* in its mother's milk.
Jgs 6:19 So Gideon went off and prepared a *k* and an
13:15 you to stay, while we prepare a *k* for you?"
13:19 Then Manoah took the *k* with a cereal
14: 6 tore the lion in pieces as one tears a *k.*
15: 1 Samson visited his wife, bringing a *k.*
1Sm 16:20 loaves of bread, a skin of wine, and a *k,*
Is 11: 6 and the leopard shall lie down with the *k;*
Lk 15:29 as a *k* goat to celebrate with my friends.

KIDNAPED (1)
Gn 40:15 that I was *k* from the land of the Hebrews,

KIDNAPER (2)
Ex 21:16 "A *k,* whether he sells his victim
Dt 24: 7 and sell him, the *k* shall be put to death.

KIDNAPERS (1)
1Tm 1:10 fornicators, sexual perverts, *k,*

KIDNAPING (1)
Dt 24: 7 "If any man is caught *k* a fellow

KIDNEYS (17)
Ex 29:13 as the lobe of its liver and its two *k,*
29:22 its two *k* with the fat that is on them,
Lv 3: 4 adheres to them, as well as the two *k,*
3: 4 liver, which he shall sever above the *k.*
3:10 adheres to them, as well as the two *k,*
3:10 the liver, which he must sever above the *k.*
3:15 adheres to them, as well as the two *k,*
3:15 the liver, which he must sever above the *k.*
4: 9 adheres to them, as well as the two *k,*
4: 9 the liver, which he must sever above the *k.*
7: 4 two *k* with the fat on them near the loins,
7: 4 liver, which must be severed above the *k.*
8:16 of the liver and the two *k* with their fat,
8:25 of the liver and the two *k* with their fat,
9:10 the *k* and the lobe of the liver that were
9:19 membrane over the inner organs, the two *k,*
Is 34: 6 lambs and goats, with the fat of rams' *k;*

KIDRON (11)
2Sm 15:23 and the king crossed the *K* Valley with all
1Kgs 2:37 For if you leave, and cross the *K* Valley,
15:13 this object and burned it in the *K* Valley.
2Kgs 23: 4 of the *K* and their ashes carried to Bethel.
23: 6 removed the sacred pole, to the *K* Valley,
23:12 them and threw the dust into the *K* Valley.
2Chr 15:16 smashed it, and burnt it in the *K* Valley.
29:16 them and carried it out to the *K* Valley.
30:14 of incense and cast them into the *K* Valley.
Jer 31:40 ashes, all the slopes toward the *K* Valley,
Jn 18: 1 out with his disciples across the *K* Valley.

KIDS (8)
Gn 27: 9 Go to the flock and get me two choice *k.*
27:13 Go and get me the *k.*"
27:16 and with the skins of the *k* she covered up
30:39 forth streaked, speckled and spotted *k.*
1Sm 10: 3 one will be bringing three *k,*
2Chr 35: 7 the common people a flock of lambs and *k,*
Sir 47: 3 made sport of lions as though they were *k,*
Is 5:17 and *k* shall eat in the ruins of the rich.

KILL (148)
Gn 4:14 on the earth, anyone may *k* me at sight."
4:15 on Cain, lest anyone should *k* him at sight.
12:12 then they will *k* me, but let you live
20:11 so they would *k* me on account of my wife.
26: 7 place would *k* him on account of Rebekah,
27:41 my father comes, I will *k* my brother Jacob."
37:18 he came up to them, they plotted to *k* him.
37:20 let us *k* him and throw him into one of the
37:22 but don't *k* him outright."
42:37 You may *k* my own two sons if I do not
Ex 1:16 them giving birth, if it is a boy, *k* him;
4:23 let him go, I warn you, I will *k* your son,
20:13 "You shall not *k.*
21:29 should it then *k* a man or a woman,
22:23 flare up, and I will *k* you with the sword;
32:12 that he might *k* them in the mountains and
Nm 22:29 sword at hand, I would *k* you here and now."
25: 5 "Each of you shall *k* those of his men who
Dt 5:17 'You shall not *k.*
13:10 him, to spare or shield him, but *k* him.
Jgs 8:19 had spared their lives, I should not *k* you."
8:20 to his first-born, Jether, "Go *k* them."
8:21 and Zalmunna said, "Come, *k* us yourself,
9:24 who encouraged him to *k* his brothers.
12: 6 him and *k* him at the fords of the Jordan.
13:23 to him, "If the LORD had meant to *k* us,
15:12 to me that you will not *k* me yourselves."
15:13 we will certainly not *k* you but will
16: 2 saying, "Tomorrow morning we will *k* him."
20: 5 Me they attempted to *k,*
1Sm 5:10 God of Israel here to *k* us and our kindred?"
5:11 that it may not *k* us and our kindred."
14:36 them until daybreak and to *k* them all off."
15: 3 Do not spare him, but *k* men and women,
16: 2 Saul will hear of it and *k* me."
17: 9 but if I beat him and *k* him,
17:25 If anyone should *k* him,
17:35 seize it by the jaw, strike it, and *k* it.
19: 2 "My father Saul is trying to *k* you.
19:10 it, that he might *k* him in the morning.
19:15 him up to me in the bed, that I may *k* him."
19:17 threatened me, 'Let me go or I will *k* you.'"
20: 8 if I am guilty, *k* me yourself!
20:33 that his father was resolved to *k* David.
22:17 the rounds and *k* the priests of the LORD,
22:18 "You make the rounds and *k* the priests!"
24:12 an end of your mantle and did not *k* you,
24:19 me into your grasp and you did not *k* me.
26:15 one of his subjects went to *k* the king,
30:15 will not *k* me or deliver me to my master,
2Sm 13:28 merry with wine and I say to you, *K* Amnon,'
21: 2 Saul had attempted to *k* them off in his
21:16 with a new sword and planned to *k* David,
1Kgs 1:51 Solomon first swear that he will not *k* me,
3:26 please do not *k* it!"
3:27 By no means *k* it, for she is the mother."
12:27 king of Judah, and they will *k* me."
17:18 call attention to my guilt and to *k* my son?"
18:12 and he does not find you, he will *k* me.
18:14 He will *k* me!"
19:17 the sword of Hazael, Jehu will *k* him.
19:17 the sword of Jehu, Elisha will *k* him.
20:36 LORD, a lion will *k* you when you leave me."
2Kgs 6:21 saw them, he asked, "Shall I *k* them,
6:22 "You must not *k* them," replied Elisha.
7: 4 spare us, we live; if they *k* us, we die."
9:27 Jehu pursued him, shouting, *K* him too!"
11: 1 she began to *k* off the whole royal family.
11: 8 anyone tries to approach the cordon, *k* him;
2Chr 22:10 she proceeded to *k* off all the royal
25:16 Why should it be necessary to *k* you?"
Neh 4: 5 us, we shall come into their midst, *k* them,
6:10 *k* you; by night they are coming to *k* you."
Tb 14:10 darkness, for he had tried to *k* Ahiqar.
Jdt 11:12 ran low, they decided to *k* their animals,
Est 8:11 together and defend their lives, and to *k,*
1Mc 9:32 learned of it, he sought to *k* him.
11:10 him my daughter, for he has sought to *k* me."
11:45 center of the city in an attempt to *k* him.
12:40 Looking for a way to seize and *k* him,
16:21 that Ptolemy had sent men to *k* him also.
16:22 When the men came to *k* him,
2Mc 5:24 with orders to *k* all the grown men and
Jb 24:14 murderer rises, to *k* the poor and needy.
Eccl 3: 3 A time to *k,* and a time to heal
Sir 9:13 Keep far from the man who has power to *k,*
27:18 For as an enemy might *k* a man,
Is 14:30 But I will *k* your root with famine that
Jer 26:21 of his words, the king sought to *k* him.
38:16 us the breath of life, I will not *k* you;
38:25 do not hide it from us, or we will *k* you,'
40:15 "Let me go and *k* Ishmael,
40:15 Why should he be allowed to *k* you?
41: 8 "Do not *k* us;
41: 8 And so he spared them and did not *k* them,
Dn 2:14 had set out to *k* the wise men of Babylon:
14:26 will *k* this dragon without sword or club."
14:29 to us, or we will *k* you and your family."

Mt 14: 5 to *k* John but was afraid of the people,
19:18 Jesus replied, " 'You shall not *k*;
21:38 Let us *k* him and then we shall have his
23:34 Some you will *k* and crucify,
24: 9 will hand you over to torture and *k* you.
26: 4 to arrest Jesus by some trick and *k* him;
Mk 6:19 wanted to *k* him but was unable to do so.
9:22 You would think it would *k* him.
10:19 'You shall not *k*;
10:34 spit at him, flog him, and finally *k* him.
12: 7 Come, let us *k* him,
14: 1 way to arrest him by some trick and *k* him.
Lk 11:49 some of these they will persecute and *k*';
12: 4 of those who *k* the body and can do no more.
13:31 Herod is trying to *k* you."
15:23 Take the fatted calf and *k* it.
15:30 loose women, you *k* the fatted calf for him.'
18:20 You shall not *k*.
20:14 *k* him so that the inheritance will be ours.'
Jn 5:18 Jews were even more determined to *k* him
7: 1 Jews were looking for a chance to *k* him.
7:19 Why do you look for a chance to *k* me?"
7:20 "Who wants to *k* you?"
7:25 "Is this not the one they want to *k*?
8:22 he mean he will *k* himself when he claims,
8:37 you are trying to *k* me because my word
8:40 The fact is, you are trying to *k* me,
11:53 day onward there was a plan afoot to *k* him.
12:10 the chief priests planned to *k* Lazarus too,
Acts 2:23 made use of pagans to crucify and *k* him.
5:33 were stung to fury and wanted to *k* them.
9:23 passed, certain Jews conspired to *k* Saul,
9:29 their part responded by trying to *k* him.
16:27 escaped, he drew his sword to *k* himself;
21:36 following along shouting, *K* him! *K* him!"
22:22 Paul, but now they began to shout, *K* him!
23:14 by oath to touch no food until we *k* Paul.
23:15 are prepared to *k* him before he gets there."
23:21 oath not to eat or drink until they *k* him.
25: 3 Their plot was to *k* him on the way.
Rom 7:11 first to deceive me, then to *k* me.
1Tm 1: 9 men who *k* their fathers or mothers,
Jas 2:11 adultery," also said, "You shall not *k*."
1Jn 3:12 Why did he *k* him?
Rv 6: 8 to *k* with sword and famine and plague and
9: 5 The locusts were not allowed to *k* them but
9:15 had been prepared, to *k* a third of mankind.
11: 7 war against them and conquer and *k* them.

KILLED (169)

Gn 4: 8 Cain attacked his brother Abel and *k* him.
4:23 I have *k* a man for wounding me,
Ex 2:14 of killing me as you *k* the Egyptian?"
4:24 came upon Moses and would have *k*
13:15 *k* every first-born in the land of Egypt,
19:13 must be stoned to death or *k* with arrows.
22:12 If it has been *k* by a wild beast,
Lv 7:24 natural death or has been *k* by wild beasts
17:15 died of itself or was *k* by a wild beast,
22: 8 of itself or has been *k* by wild beasts.
Nm 22:33 turned away from me, I would have *k* you;
25:18 who was *k* at the time of the slaughter
31: 7 Moses, and *k* every male among them.
31: 8 in battle, they *k* the five Midianite kings:
35:11 *k* someone unintentionally may take refuge.
35:15 so that anyone who has *k* another
Dt 4:42 if he unwittingly *k* his neighbor
9:20 and would have *k* him had I not prayed for
21: 1 to occupy, and it is not known who *k* him,
Jos 7: 5 those at Ai, who *k* some thirty-six of them.
9:26 saved them from being *k* by the Israelites,
10:26 Thereupon Joshua struck and *k* them,
13:21 king, who reigned in Heshbon, Moses had *k*,
20: 9 had *k* a person accidentally might flee
Jgs 8:18 "Where now are the men you *k* at Tabor?"
8:21 stepped forward and *k* Zebah and Zalmunna.
9:18 and have *k* his seventy sons upon one stone,
9:24 upon their brother Abimelech, who *k* them,
9:45 *k* its inhabitants and demolished the city,
9:54 me, lest they say of me that a woman *k* me."
14:19 *k* thirty of their men and despoiled them;
15:15 grasped it, and with it *k* a thousand men.
16:30 *k* at his death were more than those he had *k*
20:31 and in the beginning they *k* off about
20:35 and on that day the Israelites *k*
20:45 *k* another two thousand of them there.
1Sm 17:36 Your servant has *k* both a lion and a bear,
19: 6 "As the LORD lives, he shall not be *k*."
19:10 yourself tonight, tomorrow you will be *k*."
21:10 whom you *k* in the Vale of the Terebinth,
22:18 one to the next and *k* the priests himself,
28: 9 laying snares for my life, to have me *k*?"
2Sm 3:30 *k* their brother Asahel in battle at Gibeon.]
4: 7 They struck and *k* him,
4:12 *k* them and cut off their hands and feet,
10:18 and David's men *k* seven hundred
11:21 Who *k* Abimelech, son of Jerubbaal?
12: 9 him you *k* with the sword of the Ammonites.
13:30 Absalom had *k* all the princes
13:32 that all the young princes have been *k*!
14: 6 one of them struck his brother and *k* him.
14: 7 'Give up the one who *k* his brother.
18:13 Had I been disloyal and *k* him,
18:15 on Absalom, and *k* him with further blows.
21:12 them at the time they *k* Saul on Gilboa.
21:17 assistance and struck and *k* the Philistine.
21:18 that occasion Sibbecai, from Husha, *k* Saph,
21:19 of Jair from Bethlehem, *k* Goliath of Gath,
21:21 son of David's brother Shimei, *k* him.
23:20 He also went down and *k* the lion in the
23:21 hand, then *k* him with his own spear.
1Kgs 2:34 went back, struck him down and *k* him;
11:16 until they had *k* off every male in Edom.
11:40 When Solomon tried to have Jeroboam *k* for
13:24 But a lion met him on the road, and *k* him.
13:26 him to a lion, which mangled and *k* him,
15:28 Baasha *k* him in the third year of Asa,
15:29 he *k* off the entire house of Jeroboam,
16: 7 and because he *k* Nadab.]
16:10 *k* him in the twenty-seventh year of Asa,
16:11 throne, he *k* off the whole house of Baasha,
16:16 had formed a conspiracy and had *k* the king.
18: 9 are handing me over to Ahab to have me *k*?
20:36 company, a lion came upon him and *k* him.
2Kgs 3:23 fought among themselves and *k* one another.
10: 9 my lord and slew him, yet who *k* all these?
12:21 a plot against him and *k* him at Beth-millo.
12:22 of Shomer, were the officials who *k* him.
14:19 But he was pursued to Lachish and *k* there.
15:10 Zechariah, attacked and *k* him at Ibleam,
15:14 Samaria, where he attacked and *k* Shallum,
15:25 *k* him within the palace stronghold in
15:30 he attacked and *k* him,
17:25 among them that *k* some of their number.
25:25 with ten men, attacked Gedaliah and *k* him,
1Chr 2: 3 in the sight of the LORD, so he *k* him.
10: 2 When the Philistines had *k* Jonathan,
11:22 He *k* the two sons of Ariel of Moab,
11:22 he went down and *k* the lion in the cistern.
11:23 hand, and *k* him with his own spear.
19:18 he also *k* Shophach,
2Chr 24:25 They *k* him on his sickbed.
25: 3 those of his servants who had *k* the king,
25:11 and there they *k* ten thousand men of Seir.
25:13 They *k* three thousand of the inhabitants
28: 7 Zichri, an Ephraimite warrior, *k* Maaseiah,
Tb 1:18 In his rage he *k* many Israelites,
3: 8 but the wicked demon Asmodeus *k* them off
6:14 it said that it was a demon who *k* them.
Est 3:13 including women and children, should be *k*,
9: 6 the Jews *k* and destroyed five hundred men.
9: 7 They also *k* Parshandatha,
9:11 when the number of those *k* in the
9:12 Jews have *k* and destroyed five hundred men,
9:15 of Adar and *k* three hundred men in Susa.
9:16 They *k* seventy-five thousand of their foes,
1Mc 1:61 and those who had circumcised them were *k*.
2:24 he sprang forward and *k* him upon the altar.
2:25 he also *k* the messenger of the king who
3:11 out to meet him and defeated and *k* him.
5:13 who were among the Tobiads have been *k*;
5:35 he *k* all the male population,
7: 4 So the soldiers *k* them,
7:16 arrested sixty of them and *k* them
7:41 your angel went out and *k* a hundred and
9: 2 Arbela, they captured it and *k* many people.
9:40 against them from their ambush and *k* them.
9:69 He *k* many of them and resolved to return
11:18 *k* by the inhabitants of the strongholds.
11:47 *k* about a hundred thousand men in the city,
12:48 entered with him, they *k* with the sword.
12:50 had been captured and his companions *k*,
13:23 he had Jonathan *k* and buried there.
13:31 He *k* him and assumed the kingship in his
16:16 upon Simon in the banquet hall, and *k* him,
2Mc 4:42 they wounded many of them and even *k* a few,
8:24 *k* more than nine thousand of the enemy,
8:30 *k* more than twenty thousand of them,
8:32 also *k* the commander of Timothy's forces,
10:37 had hidden in a cistern, but they *k* him,
12:26 where he *k* twenty-five thousand people.
13:15 men and *k* about two thousand in the camp.
Ps(s) 78:47 He *k* their vines with hail and their
105:29 their waters into blood and *k* their fish.
Wis 11:20 they could have been *k* at a single blast,
Sir 27:18 man, you have *k* your neighbor's friendship.
Is 22: 2 not slain with the sword, nor *k* in battle.
Jer 38:15 If I tell you anything, you will have me *k*,
41: 2 and they *k* him.
41: 8 kill them, as he had *k* their companions.
41: 9 threw all the corpses of the men he had *k*
41:16 away from Mizpah after he *k* Gedaliah,
43: 3 the Chaldeans to be *k* or exiled to Babylon."
Ez 44:31 of itself or has been *k* by wild beasts.
Dn 5:19 Whomever he wished, he *k* or let live;
14:28 "he has destroyed Bel, *k* the dragon,
Mt 21:35 They beat one, *k* another,
21:39 him outside the vineyard, and *k* him.
22: 4 My bullocks and corn-fed cattle are *k*;
22: 6 of his servants, insulted them, and *k* them.
Mk 12: 5 He sent yet another and they *k* him.
12: 5 some they *k*.
12: 8 *k* him and dragged him outside the vineyard.
Lk 12: 5 power to cast into Gehenna after he has *k*.
13: 4 who were *k* by a falling tower in Siloam.
15:27 and your father has *k* the fatted calf
20:15 dragged him outside the vineyard and *k* him.
Acts 5:36 However he was *k*,
7:28 killing me as you *k* the Egyptian yesterday?'
10:40 *k* him, finally, hanging him on a tree,
22:20 guarded the cloaks of those who *k* him!'
23:12 not to eat or drink until they had *k* Paul.
Rom 11: 3 "Lord, they have *k* your prophets,
1Cor 10:10 them did, to be *k* by the destroying angel.
1Thes 2:15 Jews who *k* the Lord Jesus and the prophets,
Jas 5: 6 You condemned, even *k*,
1Jn 3:12 belonged to the evil one and *k* his brother.
Rv 11:13 persons were *k* during the earthquake;

KILLER (2)

Jos 20: 4 To one of these cities the *k* shall flee,
20: 6 Then the *k* may go back home to his own

KILLING (25)

Gn 27:42 to settle accounts with you by *k* you.
37:26 by *k* our brother and concealing his blood?
Ex 2:14 of *k* me as you killed the Egyptian?"
Nm 11:15 please do me the favor of *k* me at once,
Jos 10:11 above them all the way to Azekah, *k* many.
Jgs 7:25 *k* Oreb at the rock of Oreb and Zeeb at the
9:56 to his father in *k* his seventy brothers.
20:39 by *k* off some thirty of the men of Israel,
1Sm 19: 1 Saul discussed his intention of *k* David
19: 5 innocent blood by *k* David without cause?"
24:11 I had some thought of *k* you,
30: 2 were in the city, young and old, *k* no one;
2Sm 3:27 revenge for the *k* of Joab's brother Asahel.
3:37 the king had no part in the *k* of Abner,
1Kgs 17:20 widow with whom I am staying by *k* her son
2Kgs 17:26 has sent lions among them that are *k* them,
Est 9: 5 with the sword, *k* and destroying them;
1Mc 6:45 of the phalanx, *k* men right and left,
6:46 elephant and stabbed it in the belly, *k* it.
2Mc 5:13 young and old, a *k* of women and children,
10:17 them, *k* as many as twenty thousand men.
Ez 13:19 *k* those who should not die and keeping
Acts 7:28 *k* me as you killed the Egyptian yesterday?'
8: 1 for his part, concurred in the act of *k*.
27:42 The soldiers thought at first of *k* the

KILLS (13)

Gn 4:15 "If anyone *k* Cain,
Ex 21:14 But when a man *k* another after maliciously
Nm 35:27 finds him beyond these bounds and *k* him,
35:30 "Whenever someone *k* another,
Dt 19: 4 when someone unwittingly *k* his neighbor to
1Sm 17: 9 If he beats me in combat and *k* me,
17:26 "What will be done for the man who *k* this
17:27 is how the man who *k* him will be rewarded."
Tb 14:11 also what wickedness does—it *k*!
Jb 5: 2 impatience *k* the fool and indignation
Prv 1:32 For the self-will of the simple *k* them,
Wis 14:24 but each either waylays and *k* his neighbor,
2Cor 3: 6 The written law *k*, but the Spirit gives life

KILN (1)

Sir 38:30 and he keeps watch on the fire of his *k*.

KIN (15)

Gn 16:12 In opposition to all his *k*
19:38 named him Ammon, saying, "The son of my *k*.
24: 7 my father's house and the land of my *k*,
Nm 5: 8 if the latter has no next of *k* to whom
Dt 17:15 a foreigner, who is no *k* of yours,
Jos 2:13 brothers and sisters, and all their *k*,
6:22 and bring out the woman with all her *k*,
6:23 father, mother, brothers, and all her *k*.
6:25 spared her with her family and all her *k*,
Jgs 9: 3 When his mother's *k* repeated these words
Ru 2:20 a relative of ours, one of our next of *k*."
3: 9 cloak over me, for you are my next of *k*."
4: 4 it if you wish to acquire it as next of *k*.
1Sm 18:18 And who are my *k* or my father's clan in
Jer 30:21 own, and his rulers shall come from his *k*.

KINAH (1)

Jos 15:22 Kabzeel, Eder, Jagur, *K*,

KIND (123)

Gn 1:11 every *k* of plant that bears seed and every *k*
1:12 *k* of plant that bears seed and every *k* of fruit
7:14 *k* of wild beast, every *k* of domestic animal,
7:14 *k* of creeping thing of the earth, and every *k*
8:19 earth left the ark, one *k* after another.
14: 8 Thereupon the *k* of Sodom,
Lv 5: 3 whatever *k* of uncleanness this may be,
14:54 law for every *k* of human leprosy and scall,
22: 5 whose uncleanness, of whatever *k* it may be,
25:36 your countryman either in money or in *k*,
Nm 6: 3 other vinegar, of any *k* of grape juice,
13:18 highlands, and see what *k* of land it is.
Dt 16:21 any *k* of wood beside the altar of the LORD,
23:19 dog's price as any *k* of votive offering
24:10 you make a loan of any *k* to your neighbor,
28:47 and gratitude for abundance of every *k*,

KIND (cont.)

28:61 Should there be any *k* of sickness or
Jgs 6:26 instead, the proper *k* of altar to the LORD,
Ru 1: 8 May the LORD be *k* to you as you were to
1Sm 15: 6 for you were *k* to the Israelites when they
2Sm 2: 6 now may the LORD be *k* and faithful to you.
9: 7 "I will surely be *k* to you for the sake
10: 2 *k* to Hanun, son of Nahash, as his father was *k*
14:13 same *k* of thing against the people of God?
15:20 and may the LORD be *k* and faithful to you."
24: 3 lord the king to order a thing of this *k?*"
1Kgs 2: 7 *k* to the sons of Barzillai the Gileadite,
2Kgs 9:11 You know that *k* of man and his talk,
1Chr 12:34 array with every *k* of weapon for war:
12:38 men equipped with every *k* of weapon of war:
22:15 and every *k* of craftsman skilled in gold,
28:21 their skill in every *k* of craftsmanship.
29: 2 stones, every other *k* of precious stone,
2Chr 6:28 there is a plague or sickness of any *k;*
6:29 offers a prayer or petition of any *k,*
15: 6 God destroyed them by every *k* of adversity.
34:13 all the workers in every *k* of labor.
Neh 9:31 them, for you are a *k* and merciful God.
10:32 any *k* of grain for sale on the sabbath day,
10:32 seventh year, as well as every *k* of debt.
10:36 and of our fruit trees, of whatever *k;*
13:15 grapes, figs, and every other *k* of burden,
13:16 every other *k* of merchandise and selling it
Tb 1:11 but I refrained from eating that *k* of food.
2:11 at weaving cloth, the *k* of work women do.
1Mc 1:48 with every *k* of impurity and abomination,
2Mc 5:10 no funeral of any *k* or any place
7:31 every *k* of affliction for the Hebrews,
12:30 *k* treatment even in times of adversity,
15:11 all by relating a dream, a *k* of vision,
Ps(s) 144:13 be full, affording every *k* of store;
Prv 14:21 but happy is he who is *k* to the poor!
14:31 but he who is *k* to the needy glorifies him.
28: 8 gathers it for him who is *k* to the poor.
Wis 12:19 deeds, that those who are just must be *k;*
19:11 later they saw also a new *k* of bird when,
19:21 icelike, quick-melting *k* of ambrosial food.
Sir 6: 5 A *k* mouth multiplies friends,
13:14 Every living thing loves its own *k,*
13:15 being is drawn to its own *k;* with his own *k*
22:18 on foolish plans withstand fear of any *k.*
27: 9 Birds nest with their own *k,*
51:12 *k* and preserved me in time of trouble.
Is 8:20 That *k* of thing they will surely say.
66: 1 What *k* of house can you build for me;
Jer 24: 2 excellent figs, the early-ripening *k.*
36:32 and many others of the same *k* in addition.
40:16 of Kareah, "You shall do nothing of the *k;*
Bar 5: 8 The forests and every fragrant *k* of tree
6:70 a garden on which perches every *k* of bird,
Ez 15: 3 peg from it, to hang on it any *k* of vessel?
17:23 Birds of every *k* shall dwell beneath it,
18:24 the same *k* of abominable things
39: 4 To birds of prey of every *k* and to the
39:17 of every *k* and to all the wild beasts:
39:20 with warriors and soldiers of every *k,*
44:30 All the choicest first fruits of every *k,*
44:30 all the best of your offerings of every *k,*
47:12 river, fruit trees of every *k* shall grow;
Dn 3:29 from you, and we have done every *k* of evil.
Na 2:10 their wealth in precious things of every *k!*
Mt 5:11 *k* of slander against you because of me.
10: 1 to cure sickness and disease of every *k.*
17:21 *k* does not leave but by prayer and fasting.]"
Mk 6: 2 What *k* of wisdom is he endowed with?
9:29 "This *k* you can drive out only by prayer."
Lk 15:10 there will be the same *k* of joy before the
16: 8 when it comes to dealing with their own *k.*
Jn 2:15 He made a *k* of] whip of cords and drove
13:18 of all, for I know the *k* of men I chose,
19: 8 When Pilate heard this *k* of talk,
Acts 7:49 What *k* of house can you build me?
10:33 and you have been *k* enough to come.
27:14 struck, the *k* called a "northeaster."
28: 7 and gave us *k* hospitality for three days.
Rom 1:29 They are filled with every *k* of wickedness:
7: 8 to rouse in me every *k* of evil desire.
14: 1 a *k* welcome to those who are weak in faith.
1Cor 5: 1 you of a *k* not even found among the pagans
13: 4 Love is patient; love is *k.*
15:35 What *k* of body will they have?"
15:39 Men have one *k* of body, animals another.
15:39 Birds are of their *k,* fish are of theirs.
Eph 4:31 words, slander, and malice of every *k.*
4:32 In place of these, be *k* to one another,
5: 9 every *k* of goodness and justice and truth.
Phil 4:14 *k* of you to want to share in my hardships.
1Thes 1: 9 what *k* of reception we had from you,
1Tm 2: 3 Prayer of this *k* is good,
3:15 you will know what *k* of conduct befits
Heb 13:16 God is pleased by sacrifices of that *k.*
Jas 1:18 be a *k* of first fruits of his creatures.
3:15 It is earthbound, a *k* of animal,
4:14 idea what *k* of life will be yours tomorrow.
1Pt 2: 1 and disparaging remarks of any *k.*
Rv 11: 6 the earth at will with any *k* of plague.
18:12 fragrant wood of every *k,*

KINDLE (5)

Sir 8:10 time of need, *K* not the coals of a sinner,
Is 50:11 *k* flames and carry about you fiery darts;
Jer 21:14 I will *k* a fire in its forest that shall
50:32 I will *k* in his cities a fire that shall
Am 1:14 I will *k* a fire upon the wall of Rabbah,

KINDLED (15)

Jgs 15: 5 He then *k* the torches and set the foxes
2Sm 22: 9 he *k* coals into flame.
22:13 of his presence coals were *k* to flame.
Jb 19:11 His wrath he has *k* against me;
32: 2 the Buzite, of the family of Ram, was *k.*
Ps(s) 18: 9 from his mouth that *k* coals into flame.
18:13 of his presence coals were *k* to flame.
Jer 17: 4 been *k* by my wrath that will burn forever.
Lam 4:11 He has *k* a fire in Zion that has consumed
Ez 21: 4 shall see that I, the LORD have *k* it,
Dn 3:22 So huge a fire was *k* in the furnace that
Hos 7: 4 are all *k* to wrath like a blazing oven,
8: 5 my wrath is *k* against them;
Zec 10: 3 My wrath is *k* against the shepherds,
Jas 3: 6 from birth, and its fire is *k* by hell.

KINDLES (2)

Sir 28: 8 be fewer, for a quarrelsome man *k* disputes,
Is 9:17 It *k* the forest thickets,

KINDLING (5)

Is 10:16 there will be *k* like the kindling of fire.
Ez 21: 3 I am *k* a fire in you that shall devour all
24:10 bonfire, piling on wood and *k* the fire,
Mal 1:10 keep you from *k* fire on my altar in vain!

KINDLY (38)

Gn 26:29 but have always acted *k* toward you and
33:10 of God, now that you have received me so *k.*
50:21 By thus speaking *k* to them,
Nm 6:26 LORD look upon you *k* and give you peace!
20:17 *K* let us pass through your country.
1Sm 1:18 She replied, "Think *k* of your maidservant,"
25: 8 Look *k* on these young men,
2Sm 19: 8 Go out and speak *k* to your servants.
1Kgs 2: 7 *k* when I was fleeing your brother Absalom.
8:28 Look *k* on the prayer and petition of your
2Kgs 25:28 He spoke *k* to him and gave him a throne
2Chr 6:19 Look *k* on the prayer and petition of your
10: 7 *k* with this people and give in to them,
1Mc 6:12 Yet I was *k* and beloved in my rule.'
12:18 *k* send us an answer on this matter."
12:22 this, *k* write to us about your welfare.
2Mc 1:27 *k* on those who are despised and detested,
6:22 *k* because of their old friendship with him.
6:29 who shortly before had been *k* disposed,
8: 2 the Lord to look *k* upon his people,
Ps(s) 37:21 the just man is *k* and gives,
37:26 All the day he is *k* and lends,
109:21 Lord, deal *k* with me for your name's sake;
Prv 11:17 A *k* man benefits himself,
12:25 depresses it, but a *k* word makes it glad.
22: 9 The *k* man will be blessed,
31:26 in wisdom, and on her tongue is *k* counsel.
Wis 1: 6 For wisdom is a *k* spirit,
7:23 good, keen, unhampered, beneficent, *k,*
Sir 18:16 both are offered by a *k* man.
36:23 And if, besides, her speech is *k,*
Jer 52:32 He spoke *k* to him and gave him a throne
Acts 27: 3 where Julius *k* allowed Paul to visit some
Rom 15:26 Macedonia and Achaia have *k* decided to
2Tm 2:24 be quarrelsome but must be *k* toward all.
Ti 2: 5 to be sensible, chaste, busy at home, *k,*
Jas 3:17 and the *k* deeds that are its fruits,
1Pt 3: 8 loving toward one another, *k* disposed,

KINDNESS (161)

Gn 19:19 the great *k* of intervening to save my life.
24:27 let his constant *k* toward my master fail.
32:11 I am unworthy of all the acts of *k* that
39:21 he showed him *k* by making the chief jailer
Ex 34: 6 slow to anger and rich in *k* and fidelity,
34: 7 his *k* for a thousand generations,
Nm 14:18 'The LORD is slow to anger and rich in *k,*
14:19 this people in keeping with your great *k,*
Jos 2:12 showing *k* to you, you in turn will show *k*
2:14 *k* to you when the LORD gives us the land."
Jgs 21:22 to them, 'Release them to us as a *k,*
Ru 2:13 She said, "May I prove worthy of your *k,*
1Sm 20: 8 Do this *k* for your servant because of the
20:14 alive, may you show me the *k* of the LORD.
20:15 I die, never withdraw your *k* from my house.
2Sm 2: 5 this *k* to your lord Saul in burying him.
3: 8 doing a *k* to the house of your father Saul,
9: 1 whom I may show *k* for the sake of Jonathan
9: 3 of Saul's house to whom I may show God's *k*
22:51 to your king and showed *k* to your anointed.
1Kgs 8:23 you keep your covenant of *k* with your
1Chr 16:34 for he is good, for his *k* endures forever;
16:41 the LORD, "because his *k* endures forever,"
19: 2 David said, "I will show *k* to Hanun,
19: 2 Nahash, for his father treated me with *k.*"
2Chr 6:14 you keep your covenant and show *k* to your
Ezr 3:11 for his *k* to Israel endures forever";
Est D:30 my lord, though your glance is full of *k.*"
2Mc 6:13 a sign of great *k* to punish sinners
9:27 mildness and *k* in his relations with you."
10:38 great *k* to Israel and grants them victory.
Jb 6:14 A friend owes *k* to one in despair,
Ps(s) 5: 8 But I, because of your abundant *k,*
6: 5 rescue me because of your *k,*
13: 6 my downfall though I trusted in your *k.*
17: 7 Show your wondrous *k,*
18:51 to your king and showed *k* to your anointed,
21: 8 the *k* of the Most High he stands unshaken.
23: 6 and *k* follow me all the days of my life;
25: 6 O LORD, and your *k* are from of old.
25: 7 in your *k* remember me,
25:10 All the paths of the LORD are *k* and
26: 3 For your *k* is before my eyes,
31: 8 I will rejoice and be glad of your *k,*
31:17 save me in your *k.*
31:22 *k* he has shown me in a fortified city.
32:10 but *k* surrounds him who trust in the LORD.
33: 5 of the *k* of the LORD the earth is full.
33:18 fear him, upon those who hope for his *k,*
33:22 May your *k,*
36: 6 O LORD, your *k* reaches to heaven;
36: 8 How precious is your *k,* O God!
36:11 Keep up your *k* toward your friends,
40:11 *k* and your truth in the vast assembly.
40:12 may your *k* and your truth ever preserve me.
44:27 Redeem us for your *k'* sake.
48:10 God, we ponder your *k* within your temple.
51:20 *k* by rebuilding the walls of Jerusalem;
52:10 Trust in the *k* of God forever and ever.
57: 4 may God send his *k* and his faithfulness.
57:11 nations, For your *k* towers to the heavens,
59:17 strength and revel at dawn in your *k;*
61: 8 bid *k* and faithfulness preserve him.
62:13 belongs to God, and yours, O Lord, is *k;*
63: 4 For your *k* is a greater good than life;
66:20 God who refused me not my prayer or his *k!*
69:14 great *k* answer me with your constant help.
69:17 O LORD, for bounteous is your *k;*
77: 9 Will his *k* utterly cease,
85: 8 Show us, O LORD, your *k,*
85:11 *K* and truth shall meet;
86: 5 abounding in *k* to all who call upon you.
86:13 Great has been your *k* toward me;
86:15 slow to anger, abounding in *k* and fidelity.
88:12 Do they declare your *k* in the grave,
89: 3 have said, "My *k* is established forever";
89:15 *k* and truth go before you.
89:25 My faithfulness and my *k* shall be with him,
89:29 Forever I will maintain my *k* toward him,
89:34 Yet my *k* I will not take from him,
90:14 Fill us at daybreak with your *k,*
92: 3 To proclaim your *k* at dawn and your
94:18 I say, "My foot is slipping," your *k,*
98: 3 He has remembered his *k* and his
100: 5 the LORD, whose *k* endures forever,
101: 1 Of *k* and judgment I will sing;
103: 4 he crowns you with *k* and compassion,
103: 8 LORD, slow to anger and abounding in *k.*
103:11 is his *k* toward those who fear him.
103:17 But the *k* of the LORD is from eternity to
106: 7 They remembered not your abundant *k,*
106:45 covenant and relented, in his abundant *k,*
107: 1 for he is good, for his *k* endures forever!"
107: 8 give thanks to the LORD for his *k*
107:15 give thanks to the LORD for his *k*
107:21 give thanks to the LORD for his *k*
107:31 give thanks to the LORD for his *k*
108: 5 nations, For your *k* towers to the heavens,
109:12 May there be no one to do him a *k,*
109:16 Because he remembered not to show *k,*
109:21 in your generous *k* rescue me;
109:26 save me, in your *k,*
115: 1 to your name give glory because of your *k,*
117: 2 For steadfast is his *k* toward us,
118:29 for his *k* endures forever.
119:41 Let your *k* come to me,
119:64 Of your *k,* O LORD, the earth is full;
119:76 Let your *k* comfort me according to your
119:88 In your *k* give me life,
119:124 Deal with your servant according to your *k,*
119:149 Hear my voice according to your *k,*
119:159 in your *k* give me life.
130: 7 is *k* and with him is plenteous redemption;
138: 2 name, Because of your *k* and your truth;
138: 8 your *k,*
141: 5 that is *k;*
143: 8 At dawn let me hear of your *k,*
143:12 distress, And in your *k* destroy my enemies;
145: 8 and merciful, slow to anger and of great *k.*
147:11 fear him, with those who hope for his *k.*
Prv 3: 3 Let not *k* and fidelity leave you;
3:34 he is stern, but to the humble he shows *k.*
14:22 those intent on good gain *k* and constancy.
16: 6 By *k* and piety guilt is expiated,
20:28 *K* and piety safeguard the king,
21:21 justice and *k* will find life and honor.
Sir 3:14 For *k* to a father will not be forgotten,
3:30 He who does a *k* is remembered afterward;

7:33 and withhold not your *k* from the dead.
12: 1 doing it, and your *k* will have its effect.
29: 1 He does a *k* who lends to his neighbor,
29:15 Forget not the *k* of your backer,
30: 6 and the one to repay his friends with *k*.
51: 8 of the LORD, his *k* through ages past;
Is 38:18 who go down into the pit await your *k*.
63: 7 us according to him mercy and his great *k*.
Jer 9:23 *k* justice and uprightness on the earth;
16: 5 people, says the LORD, my *k* and my pity.
32:18 your *k* through a thousand generations;
Lam 4:16 with favor, nor show *k* to the elders.
Dn 3:42 but deal with us in your *k* and great mercy.
4:24 and for your misdeeds by *k* to the poor;
Jl 2:13 merciful is he, slow to anger, rich in *k*,
Zec 7: 9 show *k* and compassion toward each other.
Mk 9:22 If out of the *k* of your heart you can do
14: 6 She has done me a *k*.
Lk 1:78 All this is the work of the *k* of our God;
Acts 28: 2 The natives showed us extraordinary *k* by
Rom 2: 4 Or do you presume on his *k* and forbearance?
2: 4 God's *k* is an invitation to you to repent?
11:22 Consider the *k* and the severity of God
11:22 *k* toward you, provided you remain in his *k*
2Cor 10: 1 exhort you by the meekness and *k* of Christ,
Gal 5:22 is love, joy, peace, patient endurance, *k*,
Eph 2: 7 manifested by his *k* to us in Christ Jesus.
Col 3:12 yourselves with heartfelt mercy, with *k*,
Ti 3: 4 the *k* and love of God our savior appeared,
Phlm 1:14 that *k* might not be forced on you but
1Pt 5: 5 the arrogant but to the humble he shows *k*."

KINDRED (24)

Gn 24: 4 and to my *k* to get a wife for my son Isaac."
24:40 my son from my own *k* of my father's house.
24:41 If you visit my *k* and they refuse you,
34:16 among you and become one *k* people with
34:22 *k* people with us only on this condition,
49:16 for his *k* like any other tribe of Israel.
49:29 "Since I am about to be taken to my *k*,
49:33 breathed his last, and was taken to his *k*.
Lv 25:41 his *k* and to the property of his ancestors.
Nm 10:30 instead to my own country and to my own *k*.
1Sm 5:10 God of Israel here to kill us and our *k*?"
5:11 place, that it may not kill us and our *k*."
2Sm 24:17 Punish me and my *k*."
1Chr 7: 2 Their *k* numbered twenty-two thousand six
7: 4 Their *k*, by ancestral houses,
7: 9 twenty thousand two hundred of their *k*
8:28 These were family heads over their *k*,
9: 9 Their *k* of various families were nine
9:34 the levitical family heads over their *k*,
2Mc 5: 6 over one's own *k* was the greatest failure,
Wis 7: 3 the common air, and fell upon the *k* earth;
Sir 31: 9 he, of all his *k*, has done wonders,
Is 13:14 turn to his *k* and flee to his own land.
Mk 6: 4 in his native place, among his own *k*,

KINDS (47)

Gn 1:21 monsters and all *k* of swimming creatures
1:21 the water teems, and all *k* of winged birds.
1:24 bring forth all *k* of living creatures:
1:24 creeping things, and wild animals of all *k*."
1:25 *k* of wild animals, all *k* of cattle, and all *k*
6:20 *k* of birds, of all *k* of beasts, and of all *k*
24:10 and bearing all *k* of gifts from his master,
40:17 were all *k* of bakery products for Pharaoh,
Ex 1:14 mortar and brick and all *k* of field work
3:20 by doing all *k* of wondrous deeds there.
35:29 for the various *k* of work which the LORD
36: 4 the various *k* of work for the sanctuary,
Lv 11:22 *k* of locusts, the various *k* of grasshoppers,
11:22 *k* of katydids, and the various *k* of crickets.
11:29 rat, the mouse, the various *k* of lizards,
19:19 of yours with two different *k* of seed;
19:19 woven with two different *k* of thread.
Dt 22: 9 your vineyard with two different *k* of seed;
22:11 wear cloth of two different *k* of thread,
2Chr 2:13 and also how to do all *k* of engraved work
16:14 *k* of aromatics compounded into an ointment.
32:27 and other precious things of all *k*;
32:28 various *k* of cattle and for the flocks.
Neh 5:18 all *k* of wine in abundance every ten days,
13:20 The merchants and sellers of various *k* of
1Mc 9:23 of Israel, and all *k* of evildoers appeared.
Prv 1:13 All *k* of precious wealth shall we gain,
Sg 4:14 and cinnamon, with all *k* of incense;
Wis 16:26 the various *k* of fruits that nourish man,
19: 6 For all creation, in its several *k*,
Sir 25: 2 Three *k* of men I hate;
43:26 stupendous, amazing, all *k* of life,
Jer 15: 3 *k* of scourge I have decreed against them,
Ez 8:10 figures of all *k* of creeping things
27:22 choicest spices, all *k* of precious stones,
47:10 Its *k* of fish shall be like those of the
2Cor 7: 5 I was under all *k* of stress
2Tm 3: 6 with sins and driven by desires of many *k*,
Ti 3: 3 our passions and of pleasures of various *k*.
Heb 13: 9 carried away by all *k* of strange teaching.
Jas 3:16 are inconstancy and all *k* of vile behavior.

KING (2533)

Gn 14: 1 Amraphel *k* of Shinar, Arioch *k* of Ellasar
14: 1 Chedorlaomer *k* of Elam, and Tidal *k* of
14: 2 Bera *k* of Sodom, Birsha *k* of Gomorrah,
14: 2 Shinab *k* of Admah, Shemeber *k* of Zeboiim,
14: 2 of Zeboiim, and the *k* of Bela (that is,
14: 8 *k* of Sodom, the *k* of Gomorrah, the *k* of
14: 8 *k* of Zeboiim, and the *k* of Bela
14: 9 *k* of Elam, Tidal *k* of Goiim,
14: 9 king of Shinar, and Arioch *k* of Ellasar
14:17 the *k* of Sodom went out to greet him in
14:18 Melchizedek, *k* of Salem,
14:21 The *k* of Sodom said to Abram,
14:22 But Abram replied to the *k* of Sodom:
20: 2 So Abimelech, *k* of Gerar,
26: 1 Abimelech, *k* of the Philistines in Gerar.
26: 8 long time, Abimelech, *k* of the Philistines,
36:31 before any *k* reigned over the Israelites.
36:32 Bela, son of Beor, became *k* in Edom;
36:33 of Zerah, from Bozrah, succeeded him as *k*.
36:34 land of the Temanites, succeeded him as *k*.
36:35 Hadad, son of Bedad, succeeded him as *k*.
36:36 Samlah, from Masrekah, succeeded him as *k*.
36:37 Rehoboth-on-the-River, succeeded him as *k*.
36:38 son of Achbor, succeeded him as *k*.
36:39 Baal-hanan died, Hadar succeeded him as *k*;
37: 8 really going to make yourself *k* over us?"
40: 1 gave offense to their lord, the *k* of Egypt.
40: 5 cupbearer and the baker of the *k* of Egypt
41:46 entered the service of Pharaoh, *k* of Egypt.
47: 5 Joseph in Egypt, and Pharaoh, *k* of Egypt,
49: 9 like a lion recumbent, the *k* of beasts
Ex 1: 8 new *k*, who knew nothing of Joseph,
1:15 The *k* of Egypt told the Hebrew midwives,
1:17 not do as the *k* of Egypt had ordered them,
1:18 the *k* summoned the midwives and asked
2:23 passed, during which the *k* of Egypt died.
3:18 shall go to the *k* of Egypt and say to him:
3:19 "Yet I know that the *k* of Egypt will not
5: 4 The *k* of Egypt answered them,
6:11 Moses, "Go and tell Pharaoh, *k* of Egypt,
6:13 the Israelites and Pharaoh, *k* of Egypt.
6:27 the ones who spoke to Pharaoh, *k* of Egypt,
6:29 Repeat to Pharaoh, *k* of Egypt,
14: 5 to the *k* of Egypt that the people had fled,
Nm 20:14 sent men to the *k* of Edom with the message:
21: 1 When the Canaanite *k* of Arad,
21:21 sent men to Sihon, *k* of the Amorites,
21:26 the capital of Sihon, *k* of the Amorites,
21:26 had fought against the former *k* of Moab
21:29 be taken captive by the Amorite *k* Sihon.
21:33 But Og, *k* of Bashan,
21:34 him as you did to Sihon, *k* of the Amorites,
22: 4 son who was *k* of Moab at that time,
22:10 God, "Balak, son of Zippor, *k* of Moab,
23: 7 Aram has Balak brought me here, Moab's *k*,
23:21 with him is the triumph of his *K*.
24: 7 His *k* shall rise higher than .
32:33 the kingdom of Sihon, *k* of the Amorites,
32:33 and the kingdom of Og, *k* of Bashan,]
33:40 Now, when the Canaanite *k* of Arad,
Dt 1: 4 he had defeated Sihon, *k* of the Amorites,
1: 4 who lived in Heshbon, and Og, *k* of Bashan,
2:24 your hands Sihon, the Amorite *k* of Heshbon,
2:26 desert of Kedemoth to Sihon, *k* of Heshbon,
2:30 But Sihon, *k* of Heshbon,
3: 1 But Og, *k* of Bashan,
3: 2 as you did to Sihon, *k* of the Amorites,
3: 3 delivered into our hands Og, *k* of Bashan,
3: 6 As we had done to Sihon, *k* of Heshbon,
3:11 [Og, *k* of Bashan,
4:46 in the land of Sihon, *k* of the Amorites,
4:47 his land and the land of Og, *k* of Bashan,
7: 8 you from the hand of Pharaoh, *k* of Egypt.
11: 3 the Egyptians, on Pharaoh, *k* of Egypt,
17:14 should you then decide to have a *k* over
17:15 that man over you as your *k* whom the LORD,
17:15 you set over you as *k* must be your kinsman;
28:36 you, and your *k* whom you have set over you,
29: 6 king of Heshbon, and Og, *k* of Bashan,
33: 5 his domain, and he became *k* of his darling.
Jos 2: 2 But a report was brought to the *k* of
2: 3 So the *k* of Jericho sent Rahab the order,
6: 2 Jericho and its *k* into your power.
8: 1 have delivered the *k* of Ai into your power,
8: 2 its *k* what you did to Jericho and its king;
8:14 The *k* of Ai saw this,
8:23 any fugitives or survivors except the *k*,
8:29 the *k* of Ai hanged on a tree until evening;
9:10 king of Heshbon, and Og, *k* of Bashan,
10: 1 Now Adonizedek, *k* of Jerusalem,
10: 1 king as he had done to Jericho and its *k*.
10: 3 So Adonizedek, *k* of Jerusalem,
10: 3 Hoham, *k* of Hebron, Piram, *k* of Jarmuth,
10: 3 Japhia, *k* of Lachish, and Debir, *k* of Eglon,
10:28 fulfilled the doom on the city, on its *k*,
10:28 *k* of Makkedah what he had done to the *k*
10:30 Libnah also, with its *k*,
10:30 *k* what he had done to the king of Jericho.
10:33 At that time Horam, *k* of Gezer,
10:37 They put it to the sword with its *k*,
10:39 capturing it with its *k* and all its towns.
10:39 and its *k* what had been done to Hebron,
10:39 to Hebron, as well as to Libnah and its *k*.
11: 1 When Jabin, *k* of Hazor,
11: 1 Jobab, *k* of Madon, to the *k* of Shimron,
11: 1 the king of Shimron, to the *k* of Achshaph,
11:10 Hazor and slew its *k* with the sword;
12: 2 First, Sihon, *k* of the Amorites,
12: 4 Secondly, Og, *k* of Bashan,
12: 5 as the territory of Sihon, *k* of Heshbon.
12:23 (in Naphath-dor), the foreign *k* of Gilgal,
12:24 king of Gilgal, and the *k* of Tirzah:
13:10 of the cities of Sihon, *k* of the Amorites,
13:21 This Amorite *k*, who reigned in Heshbon,
13:27 part of the kingdom of Sihon, *k* of Heshbon,
13:30 the entire kingdom of Og, *k* of Bashan,
24: 9 Then Balak, son of Zippor, *k* of Moab,
Jgs 3: 8 of Cushan-rishathaim, *k* of Aram Naharaim,
3:10 delivered Cushan-rishathaim, *k* of Aram,
3:12 this offense strengthened Eglon, *k* of Moab,
3:14 Israelites then served Eglon, *k* of Moab,
3:15 sent their tribute to Eglon, *k* of Moab.
3:17 presented the tribute to Eglon, *k* of Moab,
3:19 "I have a private message for you, O *k*."
3:19 And the *k* said, "Silence!"
3:20 So the *k* rose from his chair,
4: 2 to fall into the power of the Canaanite *k*,
4:17 the Kenite Heber, since Jabin, *k* of Hazor,
4:23 on that day God humbled the Canaanite *k*,
4:24 at length they destroyed the Canaanite *k*,
9: 6 proceeded to make Abimelech *k*
9: 8 trees went to anoint a *k* over themselves.
9:15 wish to anoint me *k* over you in good faith,
9:16 honorably in appointing Abimelech your *k*,
9:18 handmaid, *k* over the citizens of Shechem,
11:12 to the *k* of the Ammonites to say,
11:14 sent messengers to the *k* of the Ammonites,
11:17 sent messengers to the *k* of Edom saying,
11:17 But the *k* of Edom did not give consent.
11:17 They also sent to the *k* of Moab,
11:19 Sihon, king of the Amorites, *k* of Heshbon.
11:25 than Balak, son of Zippor, *k* of Moab?
11:28 But the *k* of the Ammonites paid no heed to
17: 6 In those days there was no *k* in Israel;
18: 1 At that time there was no *k* in Israel.
19: 1 that time, when there was no *k* in Israel,
21:25 In those days there was no *k* in Israel;
1Sm 2:10 earth, Now may he give strength to his *k*,
8: 5 follow your example, appoint a *k* over us,
8: 6 when they asked for a *k* to judge them.
8: 7 reject, they are rejecting me as their *k*.
8: 9 of the rights of the *k* who will rule them."
8:10 full to those who were asking him for a *k*.
8:11 the *k* who will rule you will be as follows:
8:18 against the *k* whom you have chosen,
8:19 There must be a *k* over us.
8:20 with a *k* to rule us and to lead us in
8:22 their request and appoint a *k* to rule them."
10:19 'Not so, but you must appoint a *k* over us.'
10:24 all the people shouted, "Long live the *k*!"
11:15 the presence of the LORD, they made Saul *k*.
12: 2 *k* over you and now the king is your leader.
12: 9 captain of the army of Jabin, *k* of Hazor,
12: 9 and into the grip of the *k* of Moab,
12:12 when you saw Nahash, *k* of the Ammonites,
12:12 said to me, 'Not so, but a *k* must rule us,'
12:12 even though the LORD your God is your *k*.
12:13 have the *k* you want, a king the LORD
12:14 if both you and the *k* who rules you follow
12:15 will deal severely with you and your *k*,
12:17 is displeased that you have asked for a *k*."
12:19 our other sins the evil of asking for a *k*."
12:25 do evil, both you and your *k* shall perish."
13: 1 when he became *k* and he reigned . . .
14:47 Aram, Beth-rehob, the *k* of Zobah,
15: 1 to anoint you *k* over his people Israel.
15: 8 He took Agag, *k* of Amalek,
15:11 "I regret having made Saul *k*,
15:17 you *k* of Israel and sent you on a mission,
15:26 and the LORD rejects you as *k* of Israel."
15:32 commanded, "Bring Agag, *k* of Amalek,
15:35 LORD regretted having made him *k* of Israel.
16: 1 Saul, whom I have rejected as *k* of Israel?
16: 1 for I have chosen my *k* from among his sons."
17:25 him, the *k* would give him great wealth,
17:56 *k* said, "Find out whose son the lad is."
18: 6 of the cities of Israel to meet *K* Saul,
18:22 "The *k* is fond of you,
18:25 "The *k* desires no other price for the
18:27 and counted them out before the *k*,
20: 5 when I should in fact dine with the *k*.
20:24 new moon, when the *k* sat at table to dine,
21: 3 "The *k* gave me a commission and told me
21:11 from Saul, going to Achish, *k* of Gath.
21:12 "Is this not David, the *k* of the land?
21:13 very much afraid of Achish, *k* of Gath.
22: 3 Mizpeh of Moab and said to the *k* of Moab,
22: 4 He left them with the *k* of Moab,
22:11 *k* sent a summons to Ahimelech the priest,
22:11 and they all came to the *k*.
22:14 Ahimelech answered the *k*:
22:15 Let not the *k* accuse his servant or anyone
22:16 *k* said, "You shall die, Ahimelech,
22:17 *k* then commanded his henchmen standing by:

KING (cont.)
22:18 The *k* therefore commanded Doeg,
23:17 *k* of Israel and I shall be second to you.
23:20 whenever the *k* wishes to come down,
24: 9 the cave, calling to Saul, "My lord the *k!*"
24:15 whom are you on campaign, O *k* of Israel?
24:21 I know that you shall surely be *k*
25:36 party in his house like that of a *k*,
26:15 *k* when one of his subjects went to kill the *k*,
26:17 David answered, "Yes, my lord the *k*."
26:19 the *k* listen to the words of his servant.
26:20 For the *k* of Israel has come out to seek a
27: 2 over to Achish, son of Maoch, *k* of Gath.
28:13 But the *k* said to her, "Have no fear.
29: 3 is David, the officer of Saul, *k* of Israel.
29: 8 fight against the enemies of my lord the *k?*"
2Sm 2: 4 and anointed David *k* of the Judahites.
2: 7 the Judahites have anointed me their *k*."
2: 9 Mahanaim, where he made him *k* over Gilead,
2:10 years old when he became *k* over Israel,
2:11 six months in Hebron as *k* of the Judahites.
3: 3 Maacah the daughter of Talmai, *k* of Geshur;
3:17 time you have been seeking David as your *k*.
3:21 to assemble all Israel for my lord the *k*,
3:21 then be *k* over all whom you wish to rule."
3:24 So Joab went to the *k* and said:
3:31 *K* David himself followed the bier.
3:32 the *k* wept aloud at the grave of Abner,
3:33 And the *k* sang this elegy over Abner:
3:36 pleased with everything that the *k* did.
3:37 the *k* had no part in the killing of Abner,
3:38 The *k* then said to his servants:
3:39 Although I am the anointed *k*,
4: 8 to David in Hebron and said to the *k*:
4: 8 my lord the *k* on Saul and his posterity."
5: 2 In days past, when Saul was our *k*,
5: 3 *K* David made an agreement with them there
5: 3 LORD, and they anointed him *k* of Israel.
5: 4 was thirty years old when he became *k*,
5: 6 Then the *k* and his men set out for
5:11 Hiram, *k* of Tyre, sent ambassadors
5:12 LORD had established him as *k* of Israel
5:17 that David had been anointed *k* of Israel,
6:12 When it was reported to *K* David that the
6:16 saw *K* David leaping and dancing
6:20 the *k* of Israel has honored himself today,
7: 1 *K* David was settled in his palace,
7: 3 Nathan answered the *k*,
7:18 Then *K* David went in and sat before the
8: 3 Hadadezer, son of Rehob, *k* of Zobah,
8: 5 came to the aid of Hadadezer, *k* of Zobah,
8: 7 [These Shishak, *k* of Egypt,
8: 8 *K* David removed a very large quantity of
8: 9 When Toi, *k* of Hamath,
8:10 he sent his son Hadoram to *K* David to
8:11 too, *K* David consecrated to the LORD,
8:12 of Hadadezer, son of Rehob, *k* of Zobah.
9: 2 summoned to David, and the *k* asked him,
9: 3 *k* inquired, "Is there any survivor of Saul's
9: 3 Ziba answered the *k*,
9: 4 The *k* said to him, "Where is he?"
9: 5 So *K* David sent for him and had him
9: 9 The *k* then called Ziba,
9:11 sons and twenty servants, said to the *k*,
9:11 just as my lord the *k* has commanded him."
10: 1 time later the *k* of the Ammonites died,
10: 1 died, and his son Hanun succeeded him as *k*.
10: 5 told of it, *K* David sent out word to them,
10: 6 as the *k* of Maacah with one thousand men,
11:19 giving the *k* all the details of the battle,
11:20 the *k* may become angry and say to you:
12: 7 'I anointed you *k* of Israel.
13: 6 *k* came to visit him, Amnon said to the *k*,
13:13 So please, speak to the *k*;
13:21 *K* David, who got word of the whole affair
13:24 Absalom went to the *k* and said:
13:25 But the *K* said to Absalom,
13:26 *k* asked him, "Why should he go to you?"
13:31 The *k* stood up, rent his garments
13:33 So let not my lord the *k* put faith in the
13:34 telling the *k* that he had seen some men
13:35 So Jonadab said to the *k*:
13:36 The *k*, too, and all his servants wept
13:37 to Talmai, son of Ammihud, *k* of Geshur,
13:39 The *k* continued during all that time to
14: 1 observed how the *k* felt toward Absalom,
14: 3 to the *k* and speak to him in this manner."
14: 4 So the woman of Tekoa went to the *k* and
14: 5 The *k* said to her, "What do you want?"
14: 8 The *k* then said to the woman:
14: 9 me and my family be to blame, my lord *k*;
14:10 *k* said, "If anyone says a word to you,
14:12 say still another word to my lord the *k*."
14:13 as he has, the *k* shows himself guilty,
14:15 'Let me speak to the *k*.
14:16 For the *k* must surely consent to free his
14:17 *k* provide a resting place; indeed, my lord the *k*
14:18 The *k* answered the woman,
14:18 The woman said, "Let my lord the *k* speak."
14:19 *k* asked, "Is Joab involved with you
14:19 "As you live, my lord the *k*,
14:21 Then the *k* said to Joab:
14:22 the ground in homage and blessing the *k*,
14:22 my lord the *k*, since the *k* has granted
14:24 *k* said, "Let him go to his own house;
14:24 his house and did not appear before the *k*.
14:28 two years without appearing before the *k*.
14:29 Then he summoned Joab to send him to the *k*,
14:32 here, that I may send you to the *k* to say:
14:32 Now, let me appear before the *k*.
14:33 Joab went to the *k* and reported this.
14:33 The *k* then called Absalom,
14:33 on his face to the ground before the *k*.
14:33 Then the *k* kissed him.
15: 2 had a lawsuit to be decided by the *k*,
15: 6 Israelites who came to the *k* for judgment,
15: 7 of four years, Absalom said to the *k*:
15: 9 The *k* wished him a safe journey,
15:10 of the horn, declare Absalom *k* in Hebron."
15:15 whatever our lord the *k* chooses to do."
15:16 Then the *k* set out,
15:17 As the *k* left the city,
15:18 city, were passing in review before the *k*,
15:19 Go back and stay with the *k*,
15:21 But Ittai answered the *k*,
15:21 the LORD lives, and as my lord the *k* lives,
15:21 shall be wherever my lord the *k* may be,
15:22 So the *k* said to Ittai,
15:23 and the *k* crossed the Kidron Valley with
15:25 Then the *k* said to Zadok:
15:27 The *k* also said to the priest Zadok:
15:34 to Absalom, 'Let me be your servant, O *k*;
16: 2 The *k* said to Ziba,
16: 3 *k* said, "And where is your lord's son?"
16: 3 Ziba answered the *k*,
16: 4 The *k* therefore said to Ziba, "So!
16: 4 "I pay you homage, my lord the *k*.
16: 8 of Saul, in whose stead you became *k*,
16: 9 Abishai, son of Zeruiah, said to the *k*:
16: 9 should this dead dog curse my lord the *k?*
16:10 But the *k* replied: "What business is it
16:11 *k* said to Abishai and to all his servants:
16:14 The *k* and all the soldiers with him
16:16 "Long live the *k!* Long live the *k!*"
17: 2 him flee, I shall strike down the *k* alone.
17:16 Otherwise the *k* and all the people with
17:17 in turn were to go and report to *K* David.
17:21 the cistern and went on to inform *K* David.
18: 2 The *k* then said to the soldiers,
18: 4 So the *k* said to them,
18: 5 But the *k* gave this command to Joab,
18: 5 All the soldiers heard the *k* instruct the
18:12 for the *k* charged you and Abishai and
18:13 would have come to the attention of the *k*,
18:19 run to take the good news to the *k*
18:21 tell the *k* what you have seen" The
18:25 The lookout shouted to inform the *k*,
18:26 And the *k* responded,
18:27 *k* replied, "He is a good man;
18:28 Then Ahimaaz called out and greeted the *k*.
18:28 ground he paid homage to the *k* and said,
18:28 the men who rebelled against my lord the *k*."
18:29 *k* asked, "Is the youth Absalom safe?"
18:30 The *k* said, "Step aside
18:31 "Let my lord the *k* receive the good news
18:32 But the *k* asked the Cushite,
18:32 "May the enemies of my lord the *k*
19: 1 The *k* was shaken,
19: 2 the *k* was weeping and mourning for Absalom;
19: 3 heard that the *k* was grieving for his son.
19: 5 Meanwhile the *k* covered his face and cried
19: 9 So the *k* stepped out and sat at the gate.
19: 9 that the *k* was sitting at the gate,
19:10 "The *k* delivered us from the clutches of
19:11 silent about restoring the *k* to his palace?"
19:11 When the talk of all Israel reached the *k*,
19:12 you be last to restore the *k* to his palace?
19:13 Why should you be last to restore the *k?*'
19:15 man, and so they summoned the *k* to return,
19:16 *k*, on his return, reached the Jordan,
19:17 down with the Judahites to meet *K* David,
19:18 hastened to the Jordan before the *k*.
19:19 he fell down before the *k* and said to him:
19:20 did the day my lord the *k* left Jerusalem.
19:21 to come down today to meet my lord the *k*."
19:23 Am I not aware that today I am *k* of Israel?"
19:24 Then the *k* said to Shimei,
19:24 And the *k* gave him his oath.
19:25 son of Saul, also went down to meet the *k*.
19:25 day the *k* left until he returned safely.
19:26 to meet the king, the *k* asked him,
19:27 "My lord the *k*, my servant betrayed me.
19:27 that I may ride on it and go with the *k*.'
19:28 your servant before my lord the *k*.
19:28 But my lord the *k* is like an angel of God.
19:29 deserved only death from my lord the *k*,
19:29 still have to make further appeal to the *k?*"
19:30 the *k* said to him: "Why do yo go talking
19:31 Meribbaal answered the *k*,
19:31 the *k* has returned safely to his palace."
19:32 the *k* to the Jordan for his crossing,
19:33 the *k* during his stay in Mahanaim.
19:34 The *k* said to Barzillai,
19:35 But Barzillai answered the *k*:
19:35 I should go up to Jerusalem with the *k?*
19:36 be any further burden to my lord the *k?*
19:37 In escorting the *k* across the Jordan,
19:37 Why should the *k* give me this reward?
19:38 Let him cross over with my lord the *k*.
19:39 *k* said to him, "Chimham shall come over
19:40 crossed over the Jordan but the *k* remained;
19:41 Finally the *k* crossed over to Gilgal,
19:41 people of Israel had escorted the *k* across.
19:42 began coming to the *k* and saying,
19:42 the *k* and his household across the Jordan,
19:43 "Because the *k* is our relative.
19:44 "We have ten shares in the *k*.
19:44 we not first to speak of restoring the *k?*"
20: 2 the Judahites remained loyal to their *k*.
20: 3 *K* David came to his palace in Jerusalem,
20: 4 Then the *k* said to Amasa:
20:21 of Ephraim has rebelled against *K* David.
20:22 while Joab returned to Jerusalem to the *K*.
21: 2 *k* called the Gibeonites and spoke to them.
21: 5 They said to the *k*, "As for the man who
21: 6 The *k* replied, "I will give them up."
21: 7 The *k*, however, spared Meribbaal,
21: 8 But the *k* took Armoni and Meribbaal,
21:14 that the *k* commanded had been carried out.
22:51 *k* and showed kindness to your anointed.
24: 2 Accordingly the *k* said to Joab and the
24: 3 But Joab said to the *k*:
24: 3 lord the *k* to order a thing of this kind?"
24: 4 The *k*, however, overruled Joab
24: 9 to the *k* the number of people registered:
24:20 Now Araunah looked down and noticed the *k*
24:20 So he went out and paid homage to the *k*,
24:21 does my lord the *k* come to his servant?"
24:22 *k* take and offer up whatever he may wish.
24:23 All this does Araunah give to the *k*."
24:23 Araunah then said to the *k*,
24:24 The *k*, however, replied to Araunah,
1Kgs 1: 1 When *K* David was old and advanced in years,
1: 2 virgin be sought to attend you, lord *k*,
1: 3 the Shunamite, whom they brought to the *k*.
1: 4 nursed the *k* and cared for him, but the *k*
1: 5 began to display his ambition to be *k*.
1:11 *k* without the knowledge of our lord David?
1:13 *K* David, and say to him, 'Did you not, lord *k*
1:13 be *k* after me and shall sit upon my throne?
1:13 Why, then, has Adonijah become *k?*'
1:14 you are still there speaking to the *k*,
1:15 So Bathsheba visited the *k* in his room,
1:16 Bathsheba bowed in homage to the *k*,
1:18 has become king, and you, my lord *k*,
1:20 my lord *k*, all Israel is waiting for you
1:21 when my lord the *k* sleeps with his fathers,
1:22 While she was still speaking to the *k*,
1:24 "Have you decided, my lord *k*,
1:25 company and saying, 'Long live *K* Adonijah!'
1:28 *K* David answered,
1:29 presence and stood before him, the *k* swore,
1:31 to the *k*, Bathsheba said, "May the lord, *K*
1:32 Then *K* David summoned Zadok the priest,
1:34 the prophet are to anoint him *k* of Israel,
1:34 blow the horn and cry, 'Long live *K* Solomon!'
1:36 answer to the *k*, Benaiah, son of Jehoiada,
1:36 May the LORD, the God of my lord the *k*,
1:37 even more than that of my lord, *K* David!"
1:38 and mounting Solomon on *K* David's mule,
1:39 the people shouted, "Long live *K* Solomon!"
1:43 "Our lord, King David, has made Solomon *k*.
1:44 The *k* sent with him Zadok the priest,
1:45 Nathan the prophet anointed him *k* at Gihon,
1:47 paid their respects to our lord, *K* David,
1:47 And the *k* in his bed worshiped God,
1:51 that Adonijah, in his fear of *K* Solomon,
1:51 "Let *K* Solomon first swear that he will
1:53 *K* Solomon sent to have him brought down
1:53 and he came and paid homage to the *k*.
2:15 mine, and all Israel expected me to be *k*.
2:17 he said, "Please ask *K* Solomon,
2:18 Bathsheba, "I will speak to the *k* for you."
2:19 to *K* Solomon to speak to him for Adonijah,
2:19 *k* stood up to meet her and paid her homage.
2:20 "Ask it, my mother," the *k* said to her,
2:22 *K* Solomon answered his mother.
2:23 And *K* Solomon swore by the LORD:
2:25 Then *K* Solomon sent Benaiah,
2:26 The *k* said to Abiathar the priest:
2:29 *K* Solomon was told that Joab had fled to
2:30 of the LORD and said to him, "The *k* says,
2:30 Benaiah reported to the *k*,
2:31 The *k* answered him: 'Do as he has said,
2:35 The *k* appointed Benaiah,
2:36 Then the *k* summoned Shimei and said to him:
2:38 Shimei answered the *k*: "I accept.
2:39 away to Achish, son of Maacah, *k* of Gath,
2:42 the *k* summoned Shimei and said to him:
2:44 *k* said to Shimei: "You know in your heart
2:45 But *K* Solomon shall be blessed,
2:46 The *k* then gave the order to Benaiah,
3: 1 by marriage with Pharaoh, *k* of Egypt.
3: 4 The *k* went to Gibeon to sacrifice there,
3: 7 your servant, *k* to succeed my father David;
3:16 harlots came to the *k* and stood before him.
3:22 Thus they argued before the *k*.
3:23 Then the *k* said: "One woman claims,
3:24 The *k* continued, "Get me a sword."

3:26 the anguish she felt for it, said to the *k.*
3:27 *k* then answered, "Give the first one
3:28 Israel heard the judgment the *k* had given,
3:28 because they saw that the *k* had in him the
4: 1 Solomon was *k* over all Israel,
4: 5 son of Nathan, companion to the *k;*
4: 7 supplied food for the *k* and his household,
4:19 *k* of the Amorites, and of Og, *k* of Bashan.
5: 7 provided food for *K* Solomon and for all
5:15 When Hiram, *k* of Tyre,
5:15 had been anointed *k* in place of his father,
5:27 *K* Solomon conscripted thirty thousand
5:31 By order of the *k,*
6: 2 The temple which *K* Solomon built for the
7:13 *K* Solomon had Hiram brought from Tyre.
7:14 to *K* Solomon and did all his metal work.
7:40 for *K* Solomon in the temple of the LORD:
7:45 All these articles which Hiram made for *K*
7:46 The *k* had them cast in the neighborhood of
7:51 When all the work undertaken by *K* Solomon
8: 1 Israelites, came to *K* Solomon in Jerusalem,
8: 2 All the men of Israel assembled before *K*
8: 5 *K* Solomon and the entire community of
8:14 The *k* turned and greeted the whole
8:62 The *k* and all Israel with him offered
8:63 Thus the *k* and all the Israelites
8:64 On that day the *k* consecrated the middle
8:66 the *k* farewell and went to their homes,
9:10 of the LORD and the palace of the *k*—
9:11 Hiram, *k* of Tyre,
9:11 and gold he wished *K* Solomon gave Hiram
9:14 had sent *k* Solomon one hundred and twenty
9:15 forced labor which *K* Solomon levied
9:16 Hazor, Megiddo, Gezer (Pharaoh, *k* of Egypt,
9:26 *K* Solomon also built a fleet at Ezion-geber,
9:28 and twenty talents of gold to *K* Solomon.
10: 3 *K* Solomon explained everything she asked
10: 6 and your wisdom is true," she told the *k.*
10: 9 you *k* to carry out judgment and justice."
10:10 the *k* one hundred and twenty gold talents,
10:10 as the queen of Sheba gave to *K* Solomon.
10:12 With the wood the *k* made supports for the
10:12 of the LORD and for the palace of the *k,*
10:13 *K* Solomon gave the queen of Sheba
10:16 *K* Solomon made two hundred shields of
10:18 The *k* also had a large ivory throne made,
10:21 *K* Solomon's drinking vessels were of gold,
10:22 The *k* had a fleet of Tarshish ships at sea
10:23 Thus *K* Solomon surpassed in riches and
10:27 The *k* made silver as common in Jerusalem
11: 1 *K* Solomon loved many foreign women besides
11:18 went into Egypt to Pharaoh, *k* of Egypt,
11:23 fled from his lord, Hadadezer, *k* of Zobah,
11:24 settled there, and became *k* in Damascus.
11:25 a rift in Israel by becoming *k* over Edom.
11:26 Zeruah, also rebelled against the *k.*
11:27 *K* Solomon was building Millo,
11:37 you desire and shall become *k* of Israel.
11:40 for his rebellion he escaped to *K* Shishak,
11:43 and his son Rehoboam succeeded him as *k.*
12: 1 all Israel had come to proclaim him *k.*
12: 2 in Egypt, where he had fled from *K* Solomon,
12: 6 *K* Rehoboam consulted the elders who had
12:12 day all Israel came back to *K* Rehoboam,
12:13 him, the *k* gave the people a harsh answer.
12:15 The *k* did not listen to the people,
12:16 saw that the *k* did not listen to them,
12:16 listen to them, the people answered the *k:*
12:18 *K* Rehoboam then sent out Adoram,
12:20 an assembly and made him *k* over all Israel.
12:23 Rehoboam, son of Solomon, the *k* of Judah,
12:27 to their master, Rehoboam, *k* of Judah,
12:28 the *k* made two calves of gold and said to
13: 4 When *K* Jeroboam heard what the man of
13: 6 Then the *k* appealed to the man of God.
13: 6 the *k* recovered the normal use of his hand.
13: 7 the *k* invited the man of God,
13: 8 kingdom," the man of God said to the *k,*
13:11 father the words he had spoken to the *k,*
14:14 LORD will raise up for himself a *k* of Israel
14:20 and his son Nadab succeeded him as *k.*
14:21 was forty-one years old when he became *k,*
14:25 year of King Rehoboam, Shishak, *k* of Egypt,
14:27 them, *K* Rehoboam had bronze shields made,
14:28 the *k* visited the temple of the LORD,
14:31 His son Abijam succeeded him as *k.*
15: 1 In the eighteenth year of *K* Jeroboam,
15: 1 son of Nebat, Abijam became *k* of Judah;
15: 8 David, and his son Asa succeeded him as *k.*
15: 9 Jeroboam, king of Israel, Asa, *k* of Judah,
15:16 war between Asa and Baasha, *k* of Israel,
15:17 Baasha, *k* of Israel,
15:17 prevent communication with Asa, *k* of Judah.
15:18 ministers, *K* Asa sent them to Ben-hadad,
15:18 son of Tabrimmon, son of Hezion, *k* of Aram,
15:19 break your treaty with Baasha, *k* of Israel,
15:20 Ben-hadad agreed with *K* Asa and sent the
15:22 *K* Asa summoned all Judah without exception,
15:22 *K* Asa built Geba of Benjamin and Mizpeh.
15:24 and his son Jehoshaphat succeeded him as *k.*
15:25 In the second year of Asa, *k* of Judah,
15:25 Nadab, son of Jeroboam, became *k* of Israel;
15:28 him in the third year of Asa, *k* of Judah,
15:29 Once he was *k,* he killed off the entire
15:32 war between Asa and Baasha, *k* of Israel,
15:33 In the third year of Asa, *k* of Judah,
16: 6 and his son Elah succeeded him as *k.*
16: 8 the twenty-sixth year of Asa, *k* of Judah,
16:10 the twenty-seventh year of Asa, *k* of Judah,
16:15 the twenty-seventh year of Asa, *k* of Judah,
16:16 formed a conspiracy and had killed the *k.*
16:16 Omri, general of the army, *k* of Israel.
16:21 Tibni, son of Ginath, to make him *k,*
16:22 Tibni died and Omri became *k.*
16:23 year of Asa, king of Judah, Omri became *k;*
16:28 and his son Ahab succeeded him as *k.*
16:29 *k* of Judah, Ahab son of Omri, became *k*
16:31 daughter of Ethbaal, *k* of the Sidonians,
19:15 you shall anoint Hazael as *k* of Aram.
19:16 Jehu, son of Nimshi, as *k* of Israel,
20: 1 Ben-hadad, *k* of Aram,
20: 2 He sent couriers to Ahab, *k* of Israel,
20: 4 The *k* of Israel answered,
20: 4 Israel answered, "As you say, my lord *k,*
20: 7 The *k* of Israel then summoned all the
20: 9 of Ben-hadad, "Say to my lord the *k,*
20:11 The *k* of Israel replied,
20:13 came up to Ahab, *k* of Israel and said:
20:20 pursuing them, while Ben-hadad, *k* of Aram,
20:21 The *k* of Israel went out,
20:22 went up to the *k* of Israel and said to him:
20:22 of the year the *k* of Aram will attack you."
20:23 the servants of the *k* of Aram said to him:
20:28 of God came up and said to the *k* of Israel:
20:31 our heads, and go out to the *k* of Israel.
20:32 their heads, they went to the *k* of Israel.
20:32 "Is he still alive?" the *k* asked.
20:33 to him, the *k* had him mount his chariot.
20:38 went on and waited for the *k* on the road,
20:39 *k* was passing, he called out to the *k*
20:40 The *k* of Israel said to him,
20:41 and the *k* of Israel recognized him as one
20:43 the *k* of Israel went off homeward and
21: 1 next to the palace of Ahab, *k* of Samaria,
21:10 and accuse him of having cursed God and *k.*
21:13 accusation, "Naboth has cursed God and *k.*"
21:18 "Start down to meet Ahab, *k* of Israel,
22: 2 *K* Jehoshaphat of Judah came down to the *k*
22: 3 nothing to take it from the *k* of Aram?"
22: 4 Jehoshaphat answered the *k* of Israel,
22: 5 Jehoshaphat also said to the *k* of Israel,
22: 6 *k* of Israel gathered together the prophets,
22: 7 "The LORD will deliver it over to the *k.*"
22: 8 The *k* of Israel answered,
22: 9 So the *k* of Israel called an official and
22:10 The *k* of Israel and King Jehoshaphat of
22:12 The LORD will deliver it over to the *k.*"
22:13 are unanimously predicting good for the *k.*
22:15 he came to the king, the *k* said to him,
22:15 The LORD will deliver it over to the *k.*"
22:16 But the *k* answered him,
22:18 The *k* of Israel said to Jehoshaphat,
22:26 The *k* of Israel then said,
22:29 The *k* of Israel and King Jehoshaphat of
22:30 and the *k* of Israel said to Jehoshaphat,
22:30 So the *k* of Israel disguised himself and
22:31 In the meantime the *k* of Aram had given
22:31 with anyone at all except the *k* of Israel."
22:32 cried out, "That must be the *k* of Israel!"
22:33 aware that he was not the *k* of Israel,
22:34 and hit the *k* of Israel between the joints
22:35 grew fierce during the day, and the *k,*
22:37 every man to his land, for the *k* is dead!"
22:37 went to Samaria, where they buried the *k.*
22:40 and his son Ahaziah succeeded him as *k.*
22:41 in the fourth year of Ahab, *k* of Israel.
22:45 also made peace with the *k* of Israel.
22:48 There was no *k* in Edom,
22:51 His son Jehoram succeeded him as *k.*
22:52 year of Jehoshaphat, *k* of Judah;
2Kgs 1: 3 intercept the messengers of Samaria's *k,*
1: 6 back to the *k* who sent you and tell him:
1: 7 *k* asked them, "What was the man like
1: 9 Then the *k* sent a captain with his company
1: 9 ordered, "the *k* commands you to come down.
1:11 *k* commands you to come down immediately."
1:16 and went down with him and stated to the *k:*
1:17 son, his brother Joram succeeded him as *k,*
1:17 of Jehoram, son of Jehoshaphat, *k* of Judah.
3: 1 became *k* of Israel in Samaria [in the
3: 1 eighteenth year of Jehoshaphat, *k* of Judah,
3: 4 Now Mesha, *k* of Moab,
3: 4 used to pay the *k* of Israel as tribute a
3: 5 *k* of Moab had rebelled against the *k*
3: 6 Joram as *k* mustered all Israel,
3: 7 he sent the *k* of Judah the message:
3: 7 "The *k* of Moab is in rebellion against me.
3: 9 So the *k* of Israel set out,
3: 9 by the king of Judah and the *k* of Edom.
3:10 exclaimed the *k* of Israel.
3:11 But the *k* of Judah asked,
3:11 of the officers of the *k* of Israel replied,
3:12 word of the LORD," the *k* of Judah agreed.
3:13 Elisha asked the *k* of Israel.
3:13 "No," the *k* of Israel replied.
3:14 were it not that I respect the *k* of Judah.
3:26 the *k* of Moab took seven hundred swordsmen
3:26 to break through to the *k* of Aram,
4:13 to the *k* or to the commander of the army?' "
5: 1 the army commander of the *k* of Aram,
5: 5 "Go," said the *k* of Aram.
5: 5 send along a letter to the *k* of Israel."
5: 6 To the *k* of Israel he brought the letter,
5: 7 the *k* of Israel tore his garments and
5: 8 that the *k* of Israel had torn his garments,
5: 8 torn his garments, he sent word to the *k:*
6: 8 the *k* of Aram was waging war on Israel,
6: 9 of God would send word to the *k* of Israel,
6:10 So the *k* of Israel would send word to the
6:11 the *k* of Aram called together his officers.
6:11 "who among us is for the *k* of Israel?"
6:12 "No one, my lord *k,*"
6:12 Elisha can tell the *k* of Israel
6:21 When the *k* of Israel saw them,
6:23 The *k* spread a great feast for them.
6:24 After this, Ben-hadad, *k* of Aram,
6:26 *k* of Israel was walking on the city wall,
6:26 woman cried out to him, "Help, my lord *k!*"
6:28 *k* asked her, "What is your trouble?"
6:30 When the *k* heard the woman's words,
6:31 do thus and so to me," the *k* exclaimed,
6:32 The *k* had sent a man ahead before he
6:33 speaking, the *k* came down to him and said,
7: 2 But the adjutant on whose arm the *k* leaned,
7: 6 "The *k* of Israel has hired the kings of
7:12 Though it was night, the *k* got up;
7:14 and the *k* sent them to reconnoiter the
7:15 The messengers returned and told the *k.*
7:17 The *k* put in charge of the gate the
7:17 God had predicted when the *k* visited him.
7:18 the prophecy of the man of God to the *k,*
8: 3 to the *k* to claim her house and her field.
8: 4 The *k* was talking with Gehazi,
8: 5 Just as he was relating to the *k* how his
8: 5 came to the *k* to claim her house and field.
8: 5 "My lord *k,*" Gehazi said,
8: 6 The *k* questioned the woman,
8: 6 the *k* placed an official at her disposal,
8: 7 at a time when Ben-hadad, *k* of Aram,
8: 8 God had come there, the *k* said to Hazael,
8: 9 and said, "Your son Ben-hadad, *k* of Aram,
8:13 LORD has showed you to me as *k* over Aram,
8:16 year of Joram, son of Ahab, *k* of Israel,
8:16 of Jehoshaphat, king of Judah, became *k.*
8:20 of Judah and chose a *k* of its own.
8:24 His son Ahaziah succeeded him as *k.*
8:25 son of Jehoram, *k* of Judah, became *k*
8:25 year of Joram, son of Ahab, *k* of Israel.
8:26 she was daughter of Omri, *k* of Israel.
8:28 Ahab, in battle against Hazael, *k* of Aram,
8:29 *K* Joram returned to Jezreel to be healed
8:29 in his battle against Hazael, *k* of Aram.
8:29 Then Ahaziah, son of Jehoram, *k* of Judah,
9: 3 I anoint you *k* over Israel.'
9: 6 anoint you *k* over the people of the LORD,
9:12 'I anoint you *k* over Israel.' "
9:13 the trumpet, and cried out, "Jehu is *k!*"
9:14 Ramoth-gilead against Hazael, *k* of Aram,
9:15 in the battle against Hazael, *k* of Aram.
9:16 Joram lay ill and Ahaziah, *k* of Judah,
9:18 "The *k* asks whether all is well."
9:18 The watchman reported to the *k,*
9:19 and said, "The *k* asks whether all is well."
9:21 king of Israel, and Ahaziah, *k* of Judah,
9:27 what was happening, Ahaziah, *k* of Judah,
9:29 *k* of Judah in the eleventh year of Joram,
10: 5 We will proclaim no one *k;*
10:13 came across kinsmen of Ahaziah, *k* of Judah.
10:35 His son Jehoahaz succeeded him as *k.*
11: 2 of *K* Jehoram and sister of Ahaziah,
11: 7 over the temple of the LORD for the *k.*
11: 8 You shall surround the *k,*
11: 8 stay with the *k,*
11:10 the captains *K* David's spears and shields,
11:12 They proclaimed him *k* and anointed him,
11:12 hands and shouting, "Long live the *k!*"
11:14 When she saw the *k* standing by the pillar,
11:17 and the *k* and the people as the other,
11:17 covenant, between the *k* and the people.
11:19 led the *k* down from the temple of the LORD
12: 1 Joash was seven years old when he became *k.*
12: 7 twenty-third year of the reign of *K* Joash,
12: 8 *K* Joash summoned the priest Jehoiada and
12:18 Then *K* Hazael of Aram
12:19 But *K* Jehoash of Judah took all the
12:19 palace, and sent them to *K* Hazael of Aram,
12:22 and his son Amaziah succeeded him as *k.*
13: 1 year of Joash, son of Ahaziah, *k* of Judah,
13: 3 them in the power of Hazael, *k* of Aram,
13: 4 which the *k* of Aram had subjected Israel.
13: 7 since the *k* of Aram had destroyed them and
13: 9 His son Joash succeeded him as *k.*
13:10 thirty-seventh year of Joash, *k* of Judah,
13:12 he fought against Amaziah, *k* of Judah,
13:14 *K* Joash of Israel went down to visit him.
13:16 done so, Elisha said to the *k* of Israel,
13:16 As the *k* held the bow,
13:18 Then he said to the *k* of Israel,
13:22 *K* Hazael of Aram oppressed Israel during

KING (cont.)

13:24 So when *K* Hazael of Aram died and his son
13:24 and his son Ben-hadad succeeded him as *k*,
14: 1 of Joash, son of Jehoahaz, *k* of Israel,
14: 1 Israel, Amaziah, son of Joash, *k* of Judah,
14: 2 twenty-five years old when he became *k*,
14: 5 slew the officials who had murdered the *k*,
14: 8 son of Jehoahaz, son of Jehu, *k* of Israel,
14: 9 *K* Jehoash of Israel sent this reply to the
14: 9 Israel sent this reply to the *k* of Judah:
14:11 *K* Jehoash of Israel then advanced,
14:11 and he and *K* Amaziah of Judah met in
14:13 *K* Jehoash of Israel captured Amaziah,
14:13 son of Jehoash, son of Ahaziah, *k* of Judah,
14:15 and how he fought Amaziah, *k* of Judah,
14:16 His son Jeroboam succeeded him as *k*.
14:17 Amaziah, son of Joash, *k* of Judah,
14:17 Jehoash, son of Jehoahaz, *k* of Israel,
14:21 him *k* to succeed his father Amaziah.
14:22 after *K* Amaziah rested with his ancestors.
14:23 year of Amaziah, son of Joash, *k* of Judah,
14:23 Judah, Jeroboam, son of Joash, *k* of Israel,
14:29 and his son Zechariah succeeded him as *k*.
15: 1 son of Amaziah, *k* of Judah, became *k*
15: 1 year of Jeroboam, *k* of Israel.
15: 5 The LORD afflicted the *k*,
15: 7 His son Jotham succeeded him as *k*.
15: 8 thirty-eighth year of Azariah, *k* of Judah,
15: 8 was *k* of Israel in Samaria for six months.
15:13 *k* in the thirty-ninth year of Uzziah, *k*
15:17 thirty-ninth year of Azariah, *k* of Judah,
15:19 During his reign, Pul, *k* of Assyria,
15:20 money to give to the *k* of Assyria
15:20 The *k* of Assyria did not remain in the
15:22 and his son Pekahiah succeeded him as *k*.
15:23 the fiftieth year of Azariah, *k* of Judah,
15:27 fifty-second year of Azariah, *k* of Judah,
15:29 *k* of Israel, Tiglath-pileser, *k* of Assyria,
15:32 *k* of Israel, Jotham, son of Uzziah, *k* of
15:33 twenty-five years old when he became *k*,
15:37 the LORD first loosed Rezin, *k* of Aram,
15:38 His son Ahaz succeeded him as *k*.
16: 1 Remaliah, Ahaz, son of Jotham, *k* of Judah,
16: 2 was twenty years old when he became *k*,
16: 5 Then Rezin, *k* of Aram,
16: 5 and Pekah, son of Remaliah, *k* of Israel,
16: 6 the *k* of Edom recovered Elath for Edom,
16: 7 to Tiglath-pileser, *k* of Assyria,
16: 7 of the *k* of Aram and the king of Israel,
16: 8 sent them as a present to the *k* of Assyria,
16:10 *K* Ahaz went to Damascus to meet
16:10 to meet Tiglath-pileser, *k* of Assyria.
16:10 *K* Ahaz sent to Uriah the priest a model of
16:11 plans which *K* Ahaz sent him from Damascus,
16:11 completed by the time the *k* returned home.
16:12 from Damascus, the *k* inspected this altar,
16:15 *K* Ahaz commanded Uriah the priest,
16:16 priest did just as *K* Ahaz had commanded.
16:17 *K* Ahaz detached the frames from the bases
16:18 In deference to the *k* of Assyria he
16:18 a throne, and the outer entrance for the *k*.
16:20 His son Hezekiah succeeded him as *k*.
17: 1 In the twelfth year of Ahaz, *k* of Judah,
17: 3 Shalmaneser, *k* of Assyria,
17: 4 But the *k* of Assyria found Hoshea guilty
17: 4 sending envoys to the *k* of Egypt at Sais,
17: 5 the *k* of Assyria arrested and imprisoned
17: 6 of Hoshea, the *k* of Assyria took Samaria,
17: 7 the domination of Pharaoh, *k* of Egypt,
17:21 they made Jeroboam, son of Nebat, *k*;
17:24 *k* of Assyria brought people from Babylon,
17:26 A report reached the *k* of Assyria:
17:27 The *k* of Assyria gave the order,
17:31 city gods, *K* Hadad and his consort Anath.
18: 1 of Israel, Hezekiah, son of Ahaz, *k* of
18: 2 twenty-five years old when he became *k*,
18: 7 the *k* of Assyria and did not serve him.
18: 9 In the fourth year of *K* Hezekiah,
18: 9 king of Israel, Shalmaneser, *k* of Assyria,
18:10 the ninth year of Hosea, *k* of Israel,
18:11 The *k* of Assyria then deported the
18:13 King Hezekiah, Sennacherib, *k* of Assyria,
18:14 Hezekiah, *k* of Judah,
18:14 message to the *k* of Assyria at Lachish:
18:14 The *k* of Assyria exacted three hundred
18:14 talents of gold from Hezekiah, *k* of Judah.
18:16 and gave the gold to the *k* of Assyria.
18:17 The *k* of Assyria sent the general,
18:17 a great army to *K* Hezekiah at Jerusalem.
18:18 They called for the *k*,
18:19 says the great king, the *k* of Assyria:
18:21 *k* of Egypt is to all who rely on him.
18:23 a wager with my lord, the *k* of Assyria:
18:28 words of the great king, the *k* of Assyria.
18:29 Thus says the *k*: 'Do not let Hezekiah
18:30 not be handed over to the *k* of Assyria.
18:31 to Hezekiah, for the *k* of Assyria says:
18:33 his land from the hand of the *k* of Assyria?
18:36 the *k* had ordered them not to answer him.
19: 1 When *K* Hezekiah heard this,
19: 4 whom his master, the *k* of Assyria,
19: 5 servants of *K* Hezekiah had come to Isaiah,
19: 6 of the *k* of Assyria have blasphemed me.
19: 8 *k* of Assyria had withdrawn from Lachish,
19: 9 *k* of Assyria heard a report that Tirhakah,
19: 9 a report that Tirhakah, *k* of Ethiopia,
19:10 shall you say to Hezekiah, *k* of Judah:
19:10 not be handed over to the *k* of Assyria.
19:13 are the king of Hamath, the *k* of Arpad,
19:20 for help against Sennacherib, *k* of Assyria:
19:32 says the LORD concerning the *k* of Assyria:
19:36 So Sennacherib, the *k* of Assyria,
20: 6 city from the hand of the *k* of Assyria;
20:12 son of Baladan, *k* of Babylon,
20:14 prophet came to *K* Hezekiah and asked him:
20:18 servants in the palace of the *k* of Babylon."
20:21 and his son Manasseh succeeded him as *k*.
21: 3 set up a sacred pole, as Ahab, *k* of Israel,
21:11 "Because Manasseh, *k* of Judah,
21:18 His son Amon succeeded him as *k*.
21:23 against him and slew the *k* in his palace,
21:24 slew all who had conspired against *K* Amon,
21:24 proclaimed his son Josiah *k* in his stead.
21:26 and his son Josiah succeeded him as *k*.
22: 3 year, *K* Josiah sent the scribe Shaphan,
22: 9 scribe Shaphan went to the *k* and reported,
22:10 The scribe Shaphan also informed the *k*
22:10 a book, and then read it aloud to the *k*.
22:11 When the *k* had heard the contents of the
22:16 in the book which the *k* of Judah has read.
22:18 "But to the *k* of Judah who sent you to
22:20 This they reported to the *k*.
23: 1 The *k* then had all the elders of Judah
23: 2 The *k* went up to the temple of the LORD
23: 3 the *k* made a covenant before the LORD that
23: 4 the *k* commanded the high priest Hilkiah,
23:10 The *k* also defiled Topheth in the Valley
23:13 The *k* defiled the high places east of
23:13 of Misconduct, which Solomon, *k* of Israel,
23:16 When the *k* looked up and saw the grave of
23:21 The *k* issued a command to all the people
23:23 until the eighteenth year of *k* Josiah,
23:25 been no *k* who turned to the LORD as he did,
23:29 In his time Pharaoh Neco, *k* of Egypt,
23:29 the river Euphrates to the *k* of Assyria.
23:29 *K* Josiah set out to confront him,
23:30 and proclaimed him *k* to succeed his father.
23:34 of Josiah, *k* in place of his father Josiah;
24: 1 his reign Nebuchadnezzar, *k* of Babylon,
24: 6 and his son Jehoiachin succeeded him as *k*.
24: 7 The *k* of Egypt did not again leave his own
24: 7 for the *k* of Babylon had taken all that
24: 7 all that belonged to the *k* of Egypt
24:10 officials of Nebuchadnezzar, *k* of Babylon,
24:11 Nebuchadnezzar, *k* of Babylon,
24:12 Then Jehoiachin, *k* of Judah,
24:12 surrendered to the *k* of Babylon,
24:13 gold utensils that Solomon, *k* of Israel,
24:16 The *k* of Babylon also led captive to
24:17 the *k* of Babylon appointed his uncle
24:17 of Babylon appointed his uncle Mattaniah *k*,
24:18 was twenty-one years old when he became *k*,
24:20 Zedekiah rebelled against the *k* of Babylon.
25: 1 of the month, Nebuchadnezzar, *k* of Babylon,
25: 4 Then the *k* and all the soldiers left the
25: 5 But the Chaldean army pursued the *k* and
25: 6 The *k* was therefore arrested and brought
25: 6 and brought to Riblah to the *k* of Babylon,
25: 8 year of Nebuchadnezzar, *k* of Babylon),
25: 8 as the representative of the *k* of Babylon.
25: 9 house of the LORD, the palace of the *k*,
25:11 those who had deserted to the *k* of Babylon,
25:19 of the *k* who were still in the city,
25:20 brought them to the *k* of Babylon at Riblah,
25:21 the *k* had them struck down and put to
25:22 of Judah, Nebuchadnezzar, *k* of Babylon,
25:23 Hearing that the *k* of Babylon had
25:24 in the country and serve the *k* of Babylon,
25:27 of the exile of Jehoiachin, *k* of Judah,
25:27 twelfth month, Evil-merodach, *k* of Babylon,
25:27 reign, raised up Jehoiachin, *k* of Judah,
25:30 him by the *k* was a perpetual allowance,
1Chr 3: 2 was the daughter of Talmai, *k* of Geshur,
4:41 during the reign of Hezekiah, *k* of Judah,
5: 6 whom Tiglath-pileser, the *k* of Assyria,
5:17 *k* of Judah, and of Jeroboam, *k* of Israel.
5:26 them the anger of Pul, *k* of Assyria,
5:26 and of Tiglath-pileser, *k* of Assyria,
11: 2 Even formerly, when Saul was still the *k*,
11: 3 elders of Israel came to the *k* at Hebron,
11: 3 and they anointed him *k* over Israel,
11:10 in his reign in order to make him true *k*,
12:32 by name to come and make David *k*.
12:39 of making David *k* over all Israel.
12:39 was likewise of one mind to make David *k*.
14: 1 Hiram, *k* of Tyre
14: 2 had truly confirmed him as *k* over Israel,
14: 8 that David was anointed *k* over all Israel,
15:29 when she saw *K* David leaping and dancing,
16:31 The LORD is *k*.
18: 3 Hadadezer, *k* of Zobah toward Hamath,
18: 5 came to the aid of Hadadezer, *k* of Zobah,
18: 9 When Tou, *k* of Hamath,
18: 9 the entire army of Hadadezer, *k* of Zobah,
18:10 he sent his son Hadoram to wish *K* David
18:11 These also *K* David consecrated to the LORD
18:17 sons were the chief assistants to the *k*.
19: 1 Afterward Nahash, *k* of the Ammonites,
19: 1 died and his son succeeded him as *k*.
19: 5 "Remain at Jericho," the *k* told them,
19: 7 along with the *k* of Maacah and his army,
21: 3 *k*, are not all of them my lord's subjects?
21:20 wheat, he turned around and saw the *k*,
21:23 my lord the *k* do what seems best to him.
21:24 But *K* David replied to Ornan:
23: 1 he made his son Solomon *k* over Israel.
24: 6 a record of it in the presence of the *k*,
24:31 cast lots in the presence of *K* David,
25: 2 inspired songs under the guidance of the *k*.
25: 6 house of God, under the guidance of the *k*.
26:26 the votive offerings dedicated by *K* David,
26:30 of the LORD and in the service of the *k*.
26:32 *K* David appointed them to the
26:32 everything pertaining to God and to the *k*.
27: 1 *k* in all that pertained to the divisions,
27:24 into the book of chronicles of *K* David.
27:25 Over the treasures of the *k* was Azmaveth,
27:31 the overseers of *K* David's possessions.
28: 1 who were in the service of the *k*,
28: 2 *K* David rose to his feet and said:
28: 4 family to be *k* over Israel forever.
28: 4 pleased him to make me *k* over all Israel.
29: 1 *K* David then said to the whole assembly:
29: 9 *K* David also rejoiced greatly.
29:20 before the LORD and before the *k*.
29:22 they proclaimed David's son Solomon *k*,
29:23 the LORD as *k* in place of his father David;
29:24 King David, swore allegiance to *K* Solomon.
29:25 enjoyed by any *k* over Israel before him.
29:28 and his son Solomon succeeded him as *k*.
29:29 Now the deeds of *K* David,
2Chr 1: 8 you have allowed me to succeed him as *k*.
1: 9 for you have made me *k* over a people as
1:11 my people over whom I have made you *k*,
1:13 the meeting tent, and became *k* over Israel.
1:14 chariot cities and with the *k* in Jerusalem.
1:15 The *k* made silver and gold as common in
2: 2 sent this message to Huram, *k* of Tyre:
2:10 Huram, *k* of Tyre,
2:10 people, he has placed you over them as *k*."
2:11 for having given *K* David a wise son of
4:11 to do for *K* Solomon in the house of God:
4:16 Huram-abi made all these articles for *K*
4:17 The *k* had them cast in the Jordan region,
5: 3 *k* during the festival of the seventh month.
5: 6 *K* Solomon and the entire community of
6: 3 the *k* greeted the whole community of
7: 4 The *k* and all the people were offering
7: 5 *K* Solomon offered as sacrifice twenty-two
7: 6 Thus the *k* and all the people dedicated
7: 6 *K* David had made for "praising the LORD,
8:10 They were also *K* Solomon's two hundred
8:11 dwell in the house of David, *k* of Israel,
8:18 and fifty talents of gold to *K* Solomon.
9: 5 and your wisdom is true," she told the *k*.
9: 8 place you on his throne as *k* for the LORD,
9: 8 them as *k* to administer right and justice."
9: 9 Then she gave the *k* one hundred and twenty
9: 9 which the queen of Sheba gave to *K* Solomon.
9:11 With the cabinet wood the *k* made stairs
9:11 temple of the LORD and the palace of the *k*;
9:12 *K* Solomon gave the queen of Sheba
9:12 for, more than she had brought to the *k*.
9:15 *K* Solomon made two hundred large shields
9:16 *k* put in the hall of the Forest of Lebanon.
9:17 *K* Solomon also made a large ivory throne
9:20 *K* Solomon's drinking vessels were of gold,
9:21 For the *k* had ships that went to Tarshish
9:22 Thus *K* Solomon surpassed all the other
9:25 chariot cities and to the *k* in Jerusalem.
9:27 The *k* made silver as common in Jerusalem
9:31 and his son Rehoboam succeeded him as *k*.
10: 1 had come to Shechem to proclaim him *k*.
10: 2 in Egypt where he had fled from *K* Solomon,
10: 6 *K* Rehoboam consulted the elders who had
10:12 *K* Rehoboam as he had instructed them to do.
10:13 given him, the *k* gave them a harsh answer,
10:15 The *k* would not listen to the people,
10:16 saw that the *k* would not listen to them,
10:16 listen to them, the people answered the *k*.
10:18 *K* Rehoboam then sent out Hadoram,
11: 3 to Rehoboam, son of Solomon, *k* of Judah,
11:22 brothers, for he intended to make him *k*.
12: 2 year of King Rehoboam, Shishak, *k* of Egypt,
12: 6 Israel and the *k* humbled themselves saying,
12: 9 Therefore Shishak, *k* of Egypt,
12:10 them, *K* Rehoboam made bronze bucklers,
12:11 the *k* visited the temple of the LORD,
12:13 *K* Rehoboam consolidated his power in
12:13 was forty-one years old when he became *k*,
12:16 His son Abijah succeeded him as *k*.
13: 1 of King Jeroboam, Abijah became *k* of Judah;
13:23 His son Asa succeeded him as *k*.
15:16 Maacah, the mother of *K* Asa,
16: 1 year of Asa's reign, Baasha, *k* of Israel,
16: 1 any communication with Asa, *k* of Judah.
16: 2 and sent them to Ben-hadad, *k* of Aram,
16: 3 break your treaty with Baasha, *k* of Israel,
16: 4 Ben-hadad agreed to *K* Asa's request and

16: 6 Then *K* Asa commandeered all of Judah to
16: 7 Hanani the seer came to Asa, *k* of Judah,
16: 7 the *k* of Aram and did not rely on the LORD,
16: 7 of the *k* of Aram has escaped your hand.
17: 1 *k* and strengthened his hold against Israel.
17:19 These were at the service of the *k;*
17:19 in addition were those whom the *k* had
18: 3 *k* of Israel, asked Jehoshaphat, *k* of Judah,
18: 4 Jehoshaphat also said to the *k* of Israel,
18: 5 The *k* of Israel gathered his prophets,
18: 5 "God will deliver it over to the *k.*"
18: 7 The *k* of Israel answered Jehoshaphat,
18: 8 So the *k* of Israel called an official,
18: 9 The *k* of Israel and King Jehoshaphat of
18:11 the LORD will deliver it over to the *k.*"
18:12 unanimously predict good for the *k,*
18:14 he came to the king, the *k* said to him,
18:15 But the *k* said to him,
18:17 The *k* of Israel said to Jehoshaphat,
18:19 asked, 'Who will deceive Ahab, *k* of Israel,
18:25 The *k* of Israel then said: "Seize Micaiah
18:28 The *k* of Israel and King Jehoshaphat of
18:29 and the *k* of Israel said to Jehoshaphat,
18:29 So the *k* of Israel disguised himself and
18:30 the *k* of Aram had given his chariot
18:30 small or great, except the *k* of Israel."
18:31 exclaimed, "That must be the *k* of Israel!"
18:32 aware that he was not the *k* of Israel
18:33 drew his bow at random and hit the *k*
18:34 and the *k* of Israel braced himself up on
19: 1 *K* Jehoshaphat of Judah returned in safety
19: 2 Hanani, met *K* Jehoshaphat and said to him:
19:11 of Judah in all that pertains to the *k;*
20:15 of Jerusalem, and *K* Jehoshaphat!
20:31 thirty-five years old when he became *k,*
20:35 *K* Jehoshaphat of Judah allied himself with
20:35 allied himself with *K* Ahaziah of Israel,
21: 1 Jehoram, his son, succeeded him as *k.*
21: 2 these were sons of *K* Jehoshaphat of Judah.
21: 5 thirty-two years old when he became *k,*
21: 8 they chose a *k* of their own.
21:12 father Jehoshaphat, nor of Asa, *k* of Judah,
21:20 thirty-two years old when he became *k,*
22: 1 Ahaziah, his youngest son, *k* in his stead,
22: 1 son of Jehoram, reigned as the *k* of Judah.
22: 2 was twenty-two years old when he became *k,*
22: 5 Jehoram, son of Ahab, *k* of Israel,
22: 5 to battle against Hazael, *k* of Aram,
22: 6 in his battle against Hazael, *k* of Aram.
22: 6 Ahaziah, son of Jehoram, *k* of Judah,
22:11 who was the daughter of *K* Jehoram,
23: 3 a covenant with the *k* in the house of God.
23: 7 Levites shall surround the *k* on all sides,
23: 7 Stay with the *k* wherever he goes."
23: 9 of *k* David which were in the house of God.
23:11 and the insignia upon him, and made him *k.*
23:11 him, and they cried, "Long live the *k!*"
23:12 the people running and acclaiming the *k,*
23:13 and there was the *k* standing beside his
23:16 himself and all the people and the *k,*
23:20 and led the *k* out of the LORD's house.
23:20 they seated the *k* upon the royal throne.
24: 1 was seven years old when he became *k,*
24: 6 Then the *k* summoned Jehoiada,
24:12 Then the *k* and Jehoiada gave it to the
24:14 rest of the money to the *k* and to Jehoiada,
24:17 the king, and the *k* then listened to them.
24:22 Thus *K* Joash was unmindful of the devotion
24:23 sent all their spoil to the *k* of Damascus.
24:27 His son Amaziah succeeded him as *k.*
25: 1 twenty-five years old when he became *k,*
25: 3 of his servants who had killed the *k,*
25: 7 *k,* let not the army of Israel go with you,
25:16 still speaking, however, the *k* said to him:
25:17 *K* Amaziah of Judah sent messengers to
25:17 of Jehoahaz, son of Jehu, the *k* of Israel,
25:18 *K* Joash of Israel sent this reply to *K* Amaziah
25:21 Therefore *K* Joash of Israel advanced and
25:21 he and *K* Amaziah met in battle
25:23 *K* Joash of Israel captured Amaziah,
25:23 of Israel captured Amaziah, *k* of Judah,
25:25 Amaziah, son of Joash, *k* of Judah,
25:25 Joash, son of Jehoahaz, *k* of Israel,
26: 1 him *k* to succeed his father Amaziah.
26: 2 this was after *K* Amaziah had gone to rest
26: 3 was sixteen years old when he became *k,*
26:13 valor to help the *k* against his enemies.
26:18 They opposed *K* Uzziah, saying to him:
26:21 *K* Uzziah remained a leper to the day of
26:23 His son Jotham succeeded him as *k.*
27: 1 twenty-five years old when he became *k,*
27: 5 the *k* of the Ammonites and conquered them.
27: 8 twenty-five years old when he became *k,*
27: 9 David, and his son Ahaz succeeded him as *k.*
28: 1 was twenty years old when he became *k,*
28: 5 him into the power of the *k* of Aram.
28: 5 into the power of the *k* of Israel,
28: 7 and also Elkanah, who was second to the *k.*
28:16 At that time *K* Ahaz sent an appeal for
28:19 Judah low because of Ahaz, *k* of Israel,
28:20 Tilgath-pilneser, *k* of Assyria,
28:21 the LORD's house and the houses of the *k*
28:21 to make payment to the *k* of Assyria,
28:22 the same *K* Ahaz became even more
28:27 His son Hezekiah succeeded him as *k.*
29: 1 twenty-five years old when he became *k,*
29:15 then they came as the *k* had ordered,
29:18 they went inside to *K* Hezekiah and said:
29:19 All the articles which *K* Ahaz during his
29:20 Then *K* Hezekiah hastened to convoke the
29:23 were led before the *k* and the assembly,
29:24 and the sin offering," the *k* had said,
29:27 and the instruments of David, *k* of Israel.
29:29 the *k* and all who were with him knelt and
29:30 *K* Hezekiah and the princes then commanded
30: 2 The *k,* his princes, and the entire assembly
30: 4 approved by the *k* and the entire assembly,
30: 6 letters written by the *k* and his princes,
30:12 mind to carry out the command of the *k*
30:24 *K* Hezekiah of Judah had contributed a
30:26 days of Solomon, son of David, *k* of Israel,
31: 3 the *k* allotted a portion for holocausts,
31:13 appointment of *K* Hezekiah and of Azariah,
32: 1 by such deeds, Sennacherib, *k* of Assyria,
32: 7 dismayed because of the *k* of Assyria
32: 8 from the words of *K* Hezekiah of Judah.
32: 9 this, while Sennacherib, *k* of Assyria,
32: 9 with this message for *K* Hezekiah of Judah,
32:10 *K* Sennacherib of Assyria has this to say:
32:11 us from the grasp of the *k* of Assyria'?
32:20 of this, *K* Hezekiah and the prophet Isaiah,
32:21 commander in the camp of the Assyrian *k,*
32:22 from the hand of Sennacherib, *k* of Assyria,
32:23 and costly objects for *K* Hezekiah of Judah,
32:33 His son Manasseh succeeded him as *k.*
33: 1 was twelve years old when he became *k,*
33:11 the army commanders of the Assyrian *k;*
33:20 His son Amon succeeded him as *k.*
33:21 was twenty-two years old when he became *k,*
33:25 all those who had conspired against *K* Amon,
33:25 land, made his son Josiah *k* in his stead.
34: 1 was eight years old when he became *k,*
34:16 who brought it to the *k* at the same time
34:18 Shaphan the scribe announced to the *k,*
34:18 And Shaphan read from it before the *k.*
34:19 When the *k* heard the words of the law,
34:22 from the *k* went to the prophetess Huldah,
34:24 that has been read before the *k* of Judah.
34:26 "But to the *k* of Judah who sent you to
34:28 They brought back this message to the *k.*
34:29 The *k* now convened all the elders of Judah
34:31 the *k* made a covenant before the LORD to
35: 3 by Solomon, son of David, *k* of Israel.
35: 4 of *K* David of Israel and his son Solomon.
35:16 of the LORD, as *K* Josiah had commanded.
35:18 nor had any *k* of Israel kept a Passover
35:20 to restore the temple, Neco, *k* of Egypt,
35:21 "What quarrel is between us, *k* of Judah?
35:23 Then the archers shot *K* Josiah,
36: 1 him *k* in Jerusalem in his father's stead.
36: 2 twenty-three years old when he became *k,*
36: 3 The *k* of Egypt deposed him in Jerusalem
36: 4 *k* of Egypt made his brother Eliakim *k* over
36: 5 twenty-five years old when he became *k,*
36: 6 Nebuchadnezzar, *k* of Babylon,
36: 8 His son Jehoiachin succeeded him as *k.*
36: 9 was eighteen years old when he became *k,*
36:10 *K* Nebuchadnezzar sent for him and had him
36:10 Zedekiah *k* over Judah and Jerusalem.
36:11 was twenty-one years old when he became *k,*
36:13 He also rebelled against *K* Nebuchadnezzar,
36:17 up against them the *k* of the Chaldeans,
36:18 LORD's house and of the *k* and his princes,
36:22 In the first year of Cyrus, *k* of Persia,
36:22 the LORD inspired *K* Cyrus of Persia to
36:23 "Thus says Cyrus, *k* of Persia:
Ezr 1: 1 In the first year of Cyrus, *k* of Persia,
1: 1 the LORD inspired *K* Cyrus of Persia to
1: 2 "Thus says Cyrus, *k* of Persia:
1: 7 *K* Cyrus, too, had the utensils of the house
1: 8 Cyrus, *k* of Persia,
2: 1 exiles, whom Nebuchadnezzar, *k* of Babylon,
3: 7 the port of Joppa, as Cyrus, *k* of Persia,
3:10 the manner laid down by David, *k* of Israel.
4: 2 since the days of Esarhaddon, *k* of Assyria,
4: 3 as *K* Cyrus of Persia has commanded us."
4: 5 the remaining years of Cyrus, *k* of Persia,
4: 5 and until the reign of Darius, *k* of Persia.
4: 7 officials to Artaxerxes, *k* of Persia.
4: 8 letter against Jerusalem to *K* Artaxerxes:
4:11 "To *K* Artaxerxes,
4:12 Let it be known to the *k* that the Jews who
4:13 Now let it be known to the *k* that if this
4:14 to look on while the *k* is being dishonored.
4:14 have sent this message to inform you, O *k,*
4:16 We inform you, O *k,*
4:17 The *k* sent this answer: "To Rehum,
4:23 As soon as a copy of *K* Artaxerxes' letter
4:24 year of the reign of Darius, *k* of Persia.
5: 6 of the letter sent to *K* Darius by Tattenai,
5: 7 "To *K* Darius all good wishes!
5: 8 Let it be known to the *k* that we have
5:11 which a great *k* of Israel built and finished.
5:12 the Chaldean, Nebuchadnezzar, *k* of Babylon,
5:13 first year of Cyrus, *k* of Babylon, *K* Cyrus
5:14 *K* Cyrus ordered to be removed from the
5:17 Now, if it please the *k,*
5:17 a decree really was issued by *K* Cyrus
6: 1 Thereupon *K* Darius issued an order to
6: 3 of King Cyrus, *K* Cyrus issued a decree:
6:10 pray for the life of the *k* and his sons.
6:12 his name to dwell there overthrow every *k*
6:13 the instructions *K* Darius had sent them.
6:14 Darius [and of Artaxerxes, *k* of Persia].
6:15 in the sixth year of the reign of *K* Darius.
6:22 making the *k* of Assyria favorable to them,
7: 1 the reign of Artaxerxes, *k* of Persia,
7: 6 the *k* granted him all that he requested.
7: 7 in the seventh year of *K* Artaxerxes.
7: 8 fifth month of that seventh year of the *k.*
7:11 This is a copy of the rescript which *K*
7:12 "Artaxerxes, *k* of kings,
7:14 You are the envoy from the *k* and his seven
7:15 gold which the *k* and his counselors
7:21 I, Artaxerxes the *k,*
7:23 come upon the realm of the *k* and his sons.
7:26 the law of your God and the law of the *k,*
7:27 who thus disposed the mind of the *k*
7:28 and who let me find favor with the *k,*
8: 1 Babylon during the reign of *K* Artaxerxes:
8:22 ashamed to ask the *k* for troops
8:22 along the way, since we had said to the *k,*
8:25 offered for the house of our God by the *k,*
8:36 the orders of the *k* were presented to the
Neh 1:11 for I was cupbearer to the *k.*
2: 1 of the twentieth year of *K* Artaxerxes,
2: 1 I took some and offered it to the *k.*
2: 2 been sad in his presence, the *k* asked me,
2: 3 seized with great fear, I answered the *k:*
2: 3 "May the *k* live forever!
2: 4 The *k* asked me, "What is it,
2: 5 the God of heaven and then answered the *k:*
2: 5 "If it please the *k,*
2: 6 Then the *k,* and the queen seated
2: 6 to him, and the *k* agreed that I might go.
2: 7 I asked the *k* further:
2: 7 "If it please the *k,* let the letters be given
2: 8 The *k* granted my requests,
2: 9 The *k* also sent with me army officers and
2:18 upon me, and what the *k* had said to me.
2:19 "Are you rebelling against the *k?*"
5:14 *K* Artaxerxes appointed me governor
6: 6 and that you are to be their *k*"
6: 7 in Jerusalem to proclaim you *k* of Judah.
6: 7 like these must reach the ear of the *k.*
7: 6 exiles whom Nebuchadnezzar, *k* of Babylon,
9:22 possessed the land of Sihon, *k* of Heshbon,
9:22 Heshbon, and the land of Og, *k* of Bashan.
13: 6 year of Artaxerxes, *k* of Babylon,
13: 6 king of Babylon, I had gone back to the *k.*
13: 6 leave of the *k* and returned to Jerusalem,
13:26 Did not Solomon, the *k* of Israel,
13:26 the many nations there was no *k* like him,
13:26 God and God had made him *k* over all Israel,
Tb 1: 2 the reign of Shalmaneser, *k* of Assyria,
1: 5 the young bull which Jeroboam, *k* of Israel,
1:15 his son Sennacherib succeeded him as *k,*
1:18 decreed against him by the heavenly *K*
1:19 the *k* that it was I who buried the dead.
1:19 When I found out that the *k* knew all about
1:21 the *k* was assassinated by two of his sons,
1:21 son Esarhaddon, who succeeded him as *k,*
1:22 For under Sennacherib, *k* of Assyria,
2: 1 under *K* Esarhaddon I returned to my home,
10:14 the Lord of heaven and earth, the *K* of all,
13: 6 righteousness, and exalt the *K* of the ages.
13: 7 and my spirit rejoices in the *K* of heaven.
13:10 his goodness, and bless the *K* of the ages,
13:11 hands their gifts for the *K* of heaven.
13:15 My spirit blesses the Lord, the great *K;*
13:16 your glory and to praise the *K* of heaven!
14:15 inhabitants when Cyaxares, *k* of Media,
Jdt 1: 1 *k* of the Assyrians in the great city of
1: 5 Then *K* Nebuchadnezzar waged war against
1: 5 war against *K* Arphaxad in the vast plain,
1: 6 the Hydaspes, and *K* Arioch of the Elamites,
1: 7 Now Nebuchadnezzar, *k* of the Assyrians,
1:11 of Nebuchadnezzar, *k* of the Assyrians,
1:13 proceeded with his army against *K* Arphaxad,
2: 1 of Nebuchadnezzar, *k* of the Assyrians,
2: 4 plan, Nebuchadnezzar, *k* of the Assyrians,
2: 5 the great *k,* the lord of all the earth:
2:19 expedition in advance of *K* Nebuchadnezzar,
3: 2 servants of Nebuchadnezzar the great *k,*
4: 1 of Nebuchadnezzar, *k* of the Assyrians,
5: 3 up as their *k* and the leader of their army?
5:11 The *k* of Egypt,
6: 4 utterly perish, says *K* Nebuchadnezzar,
9:12 of the waters, *K* of all you have created,
11: 1 serve Nebuchadnezzar, *k* of all the earth.
11: 4 the servants of my lord, *K* Nebuchadnezzar."
11: 7 life of Nebuchadnezzar, *k* of all the earth,
11:23 dwell in the palace of *K* Nebuchadnezzar,
14:18 disgrace on the house of *K* Nebuchadnezzar.
Est A: 1 year of the reign of the great *K* Ahasuerus,
A: 3 captives whom Nebuchadnezzar, *k* of Babylon,
A: 3 from Jerusalem with Jeconiah, *k*
A:12 two eunuchs of the *k* who were court guards.
A:13 were preparing to lay hands on *K* Ahasuerus.

KING (cont.)

A:13 So he informed the *k* about them,
A:14 the *k* had the two eunuchs questioned and,
A:15 Then the *k* had these things recorded;
A:16 The *k* also appointed Mordecai to serve at
A:17 Agagite, who was in high honor with the *k*,
A:17 people because of the two eunuchs of the *k*.
1: 5 At the end of this time the *k* gave a feast
1: 8 of the *k* the drinking was unstinted,
1: 9 inside the royal palace of *K* Ahasuerus.
1:10 day, when the *k* was merry with wine,
1:10 the seven eunuchs who attended *K* Ahasuerus,
1:15 of *K* Ahasuerus issued through the eunuchs?"
1:16 the presence of the *k* and of the officials,
1:16 "Queen Vashti has not wronged the *k* alone,
1:16 throughout the provinces of *K* Ahasuerus.
1:17 *K* Ahasuerus commanded that Queen Vashti be
1:19 If it please the *k*,
1:19 come into the presence of *K* Ahasuerus
1:19 authorizing the *k* to give her royal
1:20 when the decree which the *k* will issue is
1:21 with the *k* and the officials, and the *k* acted
2: 1 this, when *K* Ahasuerus' wrath had cooled,
2: 2 young virgins be sought for the *k*.
2: 3 Let the *k* appoint commissaries in all the
2: 4 the *k* shall reign in place of Vashti."
2: 4 This suggestion pleased the *k*,
2: 6 *k* of Judah, whom Nebuchadnezzar, *k* of
2:12 Each girl went in turn to visit *K*
2:13 Then, when the girl was to visit the *k*,
2:14 She could not return to the *k* unless he
2:15 when her turn came to visit the *k*,
2:16 Esther was led to *K* Ahasuerus in his
2:17 *k* loved Esther more than all other women,
2:18 Then the *k* gave a great feast in honor of
2:21 in anger to lay hands on *K* Ahasuerus.
2:22 who in turn informed the *k* for Mordecai.
3: 1 these events *K* Ahasuerus raised Haman,
3: 2 is what the *k* had ordered in his regard.
3: 6 throughout the realm of *K* Ahasuerus.
3: 7 Nisan, in the twelfth year of *K* Ahasuerus,
3: 8 Then Haman said to *K* Ahasuerus:
3: 8 They do not obey the laws of the *k*,
3: 8 is not proper for the *k* to tolerate them.
3: 9 If it please the *k*,
3:10 The *k* took the signet ring from his hand
3:11 silver you may keep," the *k* said to Haman,
3:12 It was written in the name of *K* Ahasuerus
B: 1 "The great *K* Ahasuerus writes to the
3:15 The *k* and Haman then sat down to feast,
B: 8 for Haman, who is second to the *k*,
B: 9 Invoke the Lord and speak to the *k* for us:
4: 8 He was to instruct her to go to the *k*;
4:11 "All the servants of the *k* and the people
4:11 who goes to the *k* in the inner court
4:11 the *k* extends to him the golden scepter,
4:11 not been summoned to the *k* for thirty days."
4:16 Thus prepared, I will go to the *k*,
C: 2 "O Lord God, almighty *K*,
C: 8 And now, Lord God, *K*,
C:14 "My Lord, our *K*, you alone are God.
C:21 gods, and to extol an earthly *k* forever.
C:23 *K* of gods and Ruler of every power.
C:28 of the *k* or drunk the wine of libations.
D: 6 till she stood face to face with the *k*,
D:16 The *k* became troubled and all his
5: 1 while the *k* was seated on his royal throne
5: 3 *k* said to her, "What is it, Queen Esther?
5: 5 the *k* ordered, "Have Haman make haste
5: 5 So the *k* went with Haman to the banquet
5: 6 drinking of the wine, the *k* said to Esther,
5: 8 if I have found favor with the *k* and if it
5:11 and just how the *k* had promoted him and
5:12 no one but me to the banquet with the *k*;
5:12 tomorrow I am to be her guest, with the *k*.
5:14 ask the *k* to have Mordecai hanged on it.
5:14 go to the banquet with the *k* in good cheer."
6: 1 That night the *k*,
6: 2 for seeking to lay hands on *K* Ahasuerus.
6: 3 The *k* asked, "What was done to reward
6: 4 "Who is in the court?" the *k* asked.
6: 4 suggest to the *k* that Mordecai should be
6: 5 "Let him come in," the *k* said.
6: 6 When Haman entered, the *k* said to him,
6: 6 for the man whom the *k* wishes to reward?"
6: 6 the *k* more probably wish to reward than me?"
6: 7 So he replied to the *k*:
6: 7 "For the man whom the *k* wishes to reward
6: 8 *k* wore and the horse on which the *k* rode
6: 9 must clothe the man the *k* wishes to reward,
6: 9 for the man whom the *k* wishes to reward!' "
6:10 Then the *k* said to Haman:
6:11 for the man whom the *k* wishes to reward!"
7: 1 So the *k* of Haman went to the banquet
7: 2 drinking of the wine, the *k* said to Esther,
7: 3 "If I have found favor with you, O *k*,
7: 4 to compensate for the harm done to the *k*."
7: 5 where," said *K* Ahasuerus to Queen Esther,
7: 6 was seized with dread of the *k* and queen.
7: 7 The *k* left the banquet in anger and went
7: 7 he saw that the *k* had decided on his doom.
7: 8 When the *k* returned from the garden of the
7: 8 and the *k* exclaimed,
7: 8 Scarcely had the *k* spoken when the face of
7: 9 one of the eunuchs who attended the *k*,
7: 9 who gave the report that benefited the *k*."
7: 9 The *k* answered, "Hang him on it."
7:10 Mordecai, and the anger of the *k* abated.
8: 1 day *K* Ahasuerus gave the house of Haman,
8: 2 The *k* removed his signet ring from Haman,
8: 3 In another audience with the *k*,
8: 4 The *k* stretched forth the golden scepter
8: 7 *K* Ahasuerus then said to Queen Esther and
8: 8 written in the name of the *k* and sealed
8:10 which he wrote in the name of *K* Ahasuerus
8:11 In these letters the *k* authorized the Jews
8:12 throughout the provinces of *K* Ahasuerus;
E: 1 *K* Ahasuerus the Great to the governors of
E:11 that he was proclaimed 'father of the *k*,'
9: 1 decreed by the *k* was to be carried out,
9: 2 provinces of *K* Ahasuerus to attack
9:11 stronghold of Susa was reported to the *k*,
9:14 The *k* then gave an order to this effect,
9:20 far, in all the provinces of *K* Ahasuerus.
9:25 the *k* ordered in writing that the wicked
10: 1 *K* Ahasuerus laid tribute on the land and
10: 2 greatness of Mordecai, whom the *k* promoted,
10: 3 Mordecai was next in rank to *K* Ahasuerus,
F: 3 Esther, whom the *k* married and made queen.
1Mc 1: 1 Darius, *k* of the Persians and Medes,
1: 1 and Medes, he became *k* in his place,
1:10 Antiochus Epiphanes, son of *K* Antiochus,
1:10 He became *k* in the year one hundred and
1:13 among the people promptly went to the *k*,
1:16 Antiochus proposed to become *k* of Egypt,
1:18 fleet, to make war on Ptolemy, *k* of Egypt.
1:29 the *k* sent the Mysian commander to the
1:41 Then the *k* wrote to his whole kingdom that
1:42 conformed to the command of the *k*,
1:44 The *k* sent messengers with letters to
1:50 command of the *k* should be put to death.
1:54 the *k* erected the horrible abomination
2:15 The officers of the *k* in charge of
2:17 the officers of the *k* addressed Mattathias:
2:22 We will not obey the words of the *k* nor
2:25 of the *k* who was forcing them to sacrifice,
2:31 of the *k* who were in the City of David,
3:26 His fame reached the *k*,
3:37 The *k* took the remaining half of the army
3:42 knew of the orders which the *k* had given
4:27 as he intended and as the *k* had ordered.
6: 1 As *K* Antiochus was traversing the inland
6: 2 king of Macedon, the first *k* of the Greeks.
6: 8 When the *k* heard this news,
6:15 son Antiochus and bring him up to be *k*.
6:16 *K* Antiochus died in Persia in the year one
6:17 When Lysias learned that the *k* was dead,
6:17 reared as a child, to be *k* in his place;
6:22 they went to the *k* and said:
6:28 When the *k* heard this he was angry,
6:33 The *k*, rising before dawn, moved his force
6:43 armor, and he thought the *k* must be on it.
6:48 and the *k* established camps in Judea and
6:50 The *k* took Beth-zur and stationed a
6:55 Lysias heard that Philip, whom *K* Antiochus,
6:55 to train his son Antiochus to be *k*,
6:56 with the army that accompanied the *k*,
6:57 He said to the *k*, the leaders of the army,
6:60 found favor with the *k* and the leaders;
6:61 *k* and the leaders swore an oath to them,
6:62 But when the *k* entered Mount Zion and saw
7: 6 accusation to the *k* against the people:
7: 8 Then the *k* chose Bacchides,
7: 8 man in the kingdom, and faithful to the *k*.
7:20 him, while he himself returned to the *k*.
7:25 to the *k* and accused them of grave crimes.
7:26 Then the *k* sent Nicanor,
7:33 holocaust that was being offered for the *k*.
7:41 they who were sent by the *k* blasphemed,
8: 5 Philip and Perseus, *k* of the Macedonians,
8: 6 Antiochus the Great, *k* of Asia,
8: 8 these from him and gave them to *K* Eumenes.
8:31 wrongs that *K* Demetrius has done to them,
9:57 was dead, Bacchides returned to the *k*,
10: 2 When *K* Demetrius heard of it,
10: 8 heard that the *k* had given him authority
10:15 *K* Alexander heard of the promises that
10:18 *K* Alexander sends greetings to his brother
10:25 *K* Demetrius sends greetings to the Jewish
10:37 the *k* has commanded in the land of Judah.
10:43 precincts, because of money he owes the *k*,
10:48 *K* Alexander gathered together a large army
10:51 sent ambassadors to Ptolemy, *k* of Egypt,
10:55 *K* Ptolemy answered in these words:
10:58 There *K* Alexander met him,
10:59 *K* Alexander also wrote to Jonathan to come
10:61 accuse him, but the *k* paid no heed to them.
10:63 The *k* also had him seated at his side.
10:63 The *k* also honored him by numbering him
10:68 When *K* Alexander heard of it he was
10:88 When *K* Alexander heard of these events,
11: 1 The *k* of Egypt gathered his forces,
11: 2 him, as *K* Alexander had ordered them to do,
11: 5 To prejudice the *k* against Jonathan,
11: 5 but the *k* said nothing.
11: 6 Jonathan met the *k* with pomp at Joppa,
11: 7 Jonathan accompanied the *k* as far as the
11: 8 *K* Ptolemy took possession of the cities
11: 9 He sent ambassadors to *K* Demetrius,
11:14 *K* Alexander was in Cilicia at that time,
11:16 *K* Ptolemy's triumph was complete when the
11:18 three days later *K* Ptolemy himself died,
11:19 *k* in the year one hundred and sixty-seven.
11:21 went to the *k* and informed him that
11:24 to danger by going to the *k* at Ptolemais.
11:24 other presents, and found favor with the *k*.
11:26 the *k* treated him just as his predecessors
11:28 Jonathan asked the *k* to exempt Judea and
11:29 The *k* agreed and wrote the following
11:30 *K* Demetrius sends greetings to his brother
11:32 *K* Demetrius sends greetings to his father
11:34 royal taxes that formerly the *k* received
11:38 When *K* Demetrius saw that the land was
11:40 he might make him *k* in his father's place.
11:41 Meanwhile Jonathan sent the request to *K*
11:44 When they came to the *k*,
11:47 So the *k* called the Jews to his aid.
11:49 and cried out to the *k* in supplication,
11:51 in the eyes of the *k* and all his subjects,
11:52 *K* Demetrius was sure of his royal throne,
11:54 who became *k* and wore the royal crown.
12:20 "Arius, *k* of the Spartans,
12:39 Trypho was determined to become *k* of Asia,
12:39 the crown, and do away with *K* Antiochus.
13:31 treacherously with the young *K* Antiochus.
13:34 Simon also sent chosen men to *K* Demetrius
13:35 *K* Demetrius sent him the following letter:
13:36 *K* Demetrius sends greetings to Simon the
14: 1 *K* Demetrius assembled his army and marched
14: 2 When Arsaces, *k* of Persia and Media,
14:38 *K* Demetrius confirmed him in the high
15: 1 Antiochus, son of *K* Demetrius,
15: 2 *K* Antiochus sends greetings to Simon,
15:16 the Romans, sends greetings to *K* Ptolemy.
15:25 When *K* Antiochus was encamped before Dor,
15:36 no reply, but returned to the *k* in anger.
15:36 had seen, the *k* fell into a violent rage.
15:38 Then the *k* appointed Cendebeus
15:39 Meanwhile the *k* went in pursuit of Trypho.
15:41 As the *k* ordered, he fortified Kedron
16:18 an account of this and sent it to the *k*,
2Mc 1:10 counselor of *K* Ptolemy and member of the
1:11 having fought on our side against the *k*;
1:20 Nehemiah, commissioned by the *k* of Persia,
1:24 and merciful, the only *k* and benefactor,
1:33 and the *k* of the Persians was told that,
1:34 people had burned the sacrifices, the *k*,
1:35 To those on whom the *k* wished to bestow
3: 3 Thus Seleucus, *k* of Asia,
3: 6 to bring it all under the control of the *k*.
3: 7 Apollonius had an audience with the *k*,
3: 7 The *k* chose his minister Heliodorus and
3:13 because of the orders he had from the *k*,
3:32 Fearing that the *k* might think that
3:35 and returned with his soldiers to the *k*.
3:37 When the *k* asked Heliodorus who would be
4: 5 So he had recourse to the *k*,
4: 6 He saw that unless the *k* intervened,
4: 8 he promised the *k* three hundred and sixty
4:18 held at Tyre in the presence of the *k*,
4:21 Egypt for the coronation of *K* Philometor,
4:21 that the *k* was opposed to his policies;
4:23 Simon, to deliver the money to the *k*,
4:24 When he had been introduced to the *k*,
4:27 of the money he had promised to the *k*,
4:28 reason, both were summoned before the *k*.
4:31 The *k*, therefore, went off in haste
4:36 the *k* returned from the region of Cilicia,
4:44 When the *k* came to Tyre,
4:45 sum of money if he would win the *k* over.
4:46 retired with the *k* under a colonnade,
4:47 trouble, the *k* acquitted of the charges,
5: 8 to account before Aretas, *k* of the Arabs,
5:11 these happenings were reported to the *k*,
5:15 the *k* dared to enter the holiest temple in
5:18 sent by *K* Seleucus to inspect the treasury,
5:24 Jewish citizens, the *k* sent Apollonius,
6: 1 Not long after this the *k* sent an Athenian
6:21 meat of the sacrifice prescribed by the *k*,
7: 1 tortured with whips and scourges by the *k*,
7: 3 At that the *k*, in a fury,
7: 5 the *k* ordered them to carry him to the
7: 9 but the *K* of the world will raise us up to
7:12 Even the *k* and his attendants marveled at
7:15 Looking at the *k*, he said:
7:24 was still alive, the *k* appealed to him,
7:25 him at all, the *k* appealed to the mother,
7:39 the *k* became enraged and treated him even
8:10 thousand talents of tribute owed by the *k*
9:19 citizens, Antiochus, their *k* and general,
9:25 therefore appointed as *k* my son Antiochus,
11: 1 of the *k* and head of the government,
11:14 and promising to persuade the *k* also,
11:15 and the *k*, on his part, granted in behalf
11:18 to the *k* I called to his attention,
11:22 *K* Antiochus sends greetings to his brother
11:27 *K* Antiochus sends greetings to the Jewish
11:35 Whatever Lysias, kinsman of the *k*,
11:36 judgment should be submitted to the *k*.

12: 1 were made, Lysias returned to the *k*,
13: 4 But the *K* of kings aroused the anger of
13: 4 When the *k* was shown by Lysias that
13: 9 The *k* was advancing,
13:18 The *k*, having had a taste of the Jews'
13:22 The *k* made a second attempt by negotiating
14: 4 So he went to *K* Demetrius in the year one
14: 9 yourself in detail on these matters, O *k*,
14:12 The *k* immediately chose Nicanor,
14:27 villain's calumnies, the *k* became enraged.
14:29 there was no way of opposing the *k*,
15:22 angel in the days of *K* Hezekiah of Judea,
Jb 4:10 roars, though the *k* of beasts cries out,
15:26 shield, like a *k* prepared for the charge.
18:14 and marches him off to the *k* of terrors.
34:18 the supreme Just One, Who says to a *k*,
41:26 he is *k* over all proud beasts.
Ps(s) 2: 6 "I myself have set up my *k* on Zion,
5: 3 Heed my call for help, my *k* and my God!
10:16 The LORD is *k* forever and ever;
18:51 *k* and showed kindness to your anointed,
20:10 O LORD, grant victory to the *k*,
21: 2 O Lord, in your strength the *k* is glad;
21: 8 For the *k* trusts in the LORD,
24: 7 portals, that the *k* of glory may come in!
24: 8 Who is this *k* of glory?
24: 9 portals, that the *k* of glory may come in!
24:10 Who is this *k* of glory?
24:10 The LORD of hosts; he is the *k* of glory.
29:10 the LORD is enthroned as *k* forever.
33:16 A *k* is not saved by a mighty army,
44: 5 You are my *k* and my God,
45: 2 as I sing my ode to the *k*,
45:12 So shall the *k* desire your beauty;
45:15 apparel she is borne in to the *k*;
45:16 they enter the palace of the *k*.
47: 3 awesome, is the great *k* over all the earth.
47: 7 sing praise to our *k*,
47: 8 For the *k* of all the earth is God;
48: 3 of the North," is the city of the great *K*.
63:12 The *k*, however, shall rejoice in God;
68:25 O God, the progress of my God, my *K*,
72: 1 O God, with your judgment endow the *k*,
74:12 Yet, O God, my *k* from of old,
84: 4 altars, O LORD of hosts, my *k* and my God!
89:19 and to the Holy One of Israel, our *k*.
93: 1 The LORD is *k*, in splendor robed;
95: 3 a great God, and a great *k* above all gods;
96:10 The LORD is *k*.
97: 1 The LORD is *k*; let the earth rejoice;
98: 6 of the horn sing joyfully before the *K*,
99: 1 The LORD is *k*; the peoples tremble;
99: 4 The *K* in his might loves justice;
105:20 The *k* sent and released him,
135:11 king of the Amorites, and Og, *k* of Bashan,
136:19 Sihon, *k* of the Amorites,
136:20 And Og, *k* of Bashan,
145: 1 I will extol you, O my God and *K*,
149: 2 the children of Zion rejoice in their *k*.
Prv 1: 1 of Solomon, the son of David, *k* of Israel:
14:28 In many subjects lies the glory of the *k*;
14:35 The *k* favors the intelligent servant,
16:13 The *k* takes delight in honest lips,
20: 2 The dread of the *k* is as when a lion roars;
20: 8 A *k* seated on the throne of judgment
20:26 A wise *k* winnows the wicked,
20:28 Kindness and piety safeguard the *k*,
22:11 of winning speech has the *k* for his friend.
24:21 My son, fear the LORD and the *k*;
25: 1 The men of Hezekiah, *k* of Judah,
25: 5 the wicked from the presence of the *k*,
29: 4 By justice a *k* gives stability to the land;
29:14 a *k* is zealous for the rights of the poor,
30:22 Under a slave when he becomes *k*,
30:27 they have no *k*,
30:31 and the *k* at the head of his people.
31: 1 The words of Lemuel, *k* of Massa.
Eccl 1: 1 of David's son, Qoheleth, *k* in Jerusalem:
1:12 Qo-heleth, was *k* over Israel in Jerusalem,
2:12 will the man do who is to come after the *k*?
4:13 but foolish *k* who no longer knows caution;
5: 8 every respect is a *k* for the arable land.
8: 2 Observe the precept of the *k*,
8: 3 God, be not hasty to withdraw from the *k*;
9:14 with few men in it advanced a mighty *k*,
10:16 Woe to you, O land, whose *k* was a servant,
10:17 are you, O land, whose *k* is of noble birth,
10:20 your thoughts do not make light of the *k*,
Sg 3: 9 *K* Solomon made himself a carriage of wood
3:11 come forth and look upon *K* Solomon In the
7: 6 a *k* is held captive in its tresses.
Wis 3: 8 and the Lord shall be their *K* forever.
6:24 the safety of the world, and a prudent *k*,
7: 5 For no *k* has any different origin or birth,
9: 7 You have chosen me *k* over your people and
11:10 as a stern *k* you probed and condemned.
12:14 Nor can any *k* or prince confront you on
14:17 copied the appearance of the distant *k*
18:11 the plebeian suffered the same as the *k*.
Sir 7: 4 authority, nor from the *k* a place of honor.
7: 5 and before the *k* flaunt not your wisdom.
10: 3 A wanton *k* destroys his people,
10:10 the doctor jests, a *k* today
38: 2 and the *k* provides for his sustenance.
46:20 he made known to the *k* his fate,
48:23 the sun and prolonged the life of the *k*.
Is 6: 1 In the year *K* Uzziah died,
6: 5 yet my eyes have seen the *K*,
7: 1 In the days of Ahaz, *k* of Judah,
7: 1 king of Aram, and Pekah, *k* of Israel,
7: 2 of the *k* and heart of the people trembled,
7: 6 and appoint the son of Tabeel *k* there."
7:17 [This means the *k* of Assyria.]
7:20 the River [with the *k* of Assyria] the head,
8: 4 shall be carried off by the *k* of Assyria.
8: 7 [the *k* of Assyria and all his power].
8:21 enraged, and curse his *k* and his gods.
10:12 of the *k* of Assyria's proud heart,
14: 4 this taunt-song against the *k* of Babylon:
14:28 In the year that *K* Ahaz died,
19: 4 master, A harsh *k* who shall rule over them,
20: 1 the general sent by Sargon, *k* of Assyria,
20: 4 *k* of Assyria lead away captives from Egypt,
20: 6 help and deliverance from the *k* of Assyria;
23:15 With the days of another *k*,
30:33 has long been ready, prepared for the *k*;
32: 1 a *k* will reign justly and princes will
33:17 Your eyes will see a *k* in his splendor,
33:22 the LORD our lawgiver, the LORD our *k*,
36: 1 King Hezekiah, Sennacherib, *k* of Assyria,
36: 2 From Lachish the *k* of Assyria sent his
36: 2 a great army to *K* Hezekiah in Jerusalem.
36: 4 commander said to them, "Tell *K* Hezekiah:
36: 4 Thus says the great king, the *k* of Assyria,
36: 6 That is what Pharaoh, *k* of Egypt,
36: 8 make a wager with my lord the *k* of Assyria:
36:13 words of the great king, the *k* of Assyria.
36:14 Thus says the *k*: 'Do not let Hezekiah
36:15 not be handed over to the *k* of Assyria." '
36:16 to Hezekiah, for the *k* of Assyria says:
36:18 his land from the hand of the *k* of Assyria?
36:21 the *k* had ordered them not to answer him.
37: 1 When *K* Hezekiah heard this,
37: 4 whom his master, the *k* of Assyria,
37: 5 servants of *K* Hezekiah had come to Isaiah,
37: 6 of the *k* of Assyria have blasphemed me.
37: 8 heard that the *k* of Assyria had left there,
37: 9 *k* of Assyria heard a report that Tirhakah,
37: 9 a report that Tirhakah, *k* of Ethiopia,
37: 9 shall you say to Hezekiah, *k* of Judah:
37:10 not be handed over to the *k* of Assyria.
37:13 is the king of Hamath, the *k* of Arpad,
37:13 Arpad, or a *k* of the cities of Sepharvaim,
37:21 for help against Sennacherib, *k* of Assyria,
37:33 says the LORD concerning the *k* of Assyria:
37:37 So Sennacherib, the *k* of Assyria,
38: 6 city from the hand of the *k* of Assyria;
38: 9 The song of Hezekiah, *k* of Judah,
39: 1 son of Baladan, *k* of Babylon,
39: 3 prophet came to *K* Hezekiah and asked him,
39: 7 servants in the palace of the *k* of Babylon."
41:21 forward your reasons, says the *K* of Jacob.
43:15 Holy One, the creator of Israel, your *K*.
44: 6 says the LORD, Israel's *K* and redeemer,
52: 7 and saying to Zion, "Your God is *K*!"
57: 9 you approached the *k* with scented oil,
Jer 1: 2 days of Josiah, son of Amon, *k* of Judah,
1: 3 of Jehoiakim, son of Josiah, *k* of Judah,
1: 3 of Zedekiah, son of Josiah, *k* of Judah.
1:15 Each *k* shall come and set up his throne at
3: 6 LORD said to me in the days of *K* Josiah:
4: 9 day, says the LORD, The *k* will lose heart,
8:19 in Zion, is her *K* no longer in her midst?
10: 7 Who would not fear you, *K* of the nations,
10:10 God, he is the living God, the eternal *K*,
13:18 Say to the *k* and to the queen mother:
15: 4 what Manasseh, son of Hezekiah, *k* of Judah,
20: 4 Judah I will deliver to the *k* of Babylon,
21: 1 the LORD when *K* Zedekiah sent him Pashhur,
21: 2 LORD, because Nebuchadnezzar, *k* of Babylon,
21: 4 fight the *k* of Babylon and the Chaldeans
21: 7 I will hand over Zedekiah, *k* of Judah,
21: 7 the hand of Nebuchadnezzar, *k* of Babylon,
21:10 *k* of Babylon who shall burn it with fire.
22: 1 *k* of Judah and there deliver this message:
22: 2 Listen to the word of the LORD, *k* of Judah,
22: 6 concerning the palace of the *k* of Judah:
22:11 *k* of Judah, who succeeded his father as *k*.
22:18 Jehoiakim, son of Josiah, *k* of Judah:
22:24 you, Coniah, son of Jehoiakim, *k* of Judah,
22:25 the hands of Nebuchadnezzar, *k* of Babylon,
23: 5 As *k* he shall reign and govern wisely,
24: 1 was after Nebuchadnezzar, *k* of Babylon,
24: 1 Jeconiah, son of Jehoiakim, *k* of Judah,
24: 8 even so will I treat Zedekiah, *k* of Judah,
25: 1 Jehoiakim, son of Josiah, *k* of Judah
25: 1 year of Nebuchadnezzar, *k* of Babylon).
25: 3 year of Josiah, son of Amon, *k* of Judah,
25: 9 will send to Nebuchadnezzar, *k* of Babylon,
25:11 shall be enslaved to the *k* of Babylon;
25:12 I will punish the *k* of Babylon and the
25:19 Pharaoh, *k* of Egypt,
25:26 after them the *k* of Sheshach shall drink].
26: 1 of Jehoiakim, son of Josiah, *k* of Judah,
26:18 in the days of Hezekiah, *k* of Judah,
26:19 Did Hezekiah, *k* of Judah,
26:21 When *K* Jehoiakim and all his officers and
26:21 of his words, the *k* sought to kill him.
26:22 Thereupon *K* Jehoiakim sent Elnathan,
26:23 into Egypt to bring Uriah back to the *k*,
27: 1 of Jehoiakim, son of Josiah, *k* of Judah,]
27: 3 come to Jerusalem to Zedekiah, *k* of Judah,
27: 6 the hand of Nebuchadnezzar, *k* of Babylon,
27: 8 not serve Nebuchadnezzar, *k* of Babylon,
27: 8 neck under the yoke of the *k* of Babylon,
27: 9 you, "You need not serve the *k* of Babylon."
27:11 neck to the yoke of the *k* of Babylon
27:12 To Zedekiah, *k* of Judah,
27:12 your necks to the yoke of the *k* of Babylon;
27:13 that will not serve the *k* of Babylon?
27:14 say, "You need not serve the *k* of Babylon,"
27:17 Serve the *k* of Babylon that you may live;
27:18 palace of the *k* of Judah and in Jerusalem
27:20 city, which Nebuchadnezzar, *k* of Babylon,
27:20 Jeconiah, son of Jehoiakim, *k* of Judah,
27:21 the LORD, in the palace of the *k* of Judah,
28: 1 of] the reign of Zedekiah, *k* of Judah,
28: 2 'I will break the yoke of the *k* of Babylon.
28: 3 LORD which Nebuchadnezzar, *k* of Babylon,
28: 4 Jeconiah, son of Jehoiakim, *k* of Judah,
28: 4 I will break the yoke of the *k* of Babylon.' "
28:11 the yoke of Nebuchadnezzar, *k* of Babylon,
28:14 serving Nebuchadnezzar, *k* of Babylon,
29: 2 was after *K* Jeconiah and the queen mother,
29: 3 king of Judah, sent to the *k* of Babylon,
29:16 the *k* who sits on David's throne,
29:21 them over to Nebuchadnezzar, *k* of Babylon,
29:22 the *k* of Babylon roasted in the flames."
30: 9 the LORD, their God, and David, their *k*,
32: 1 in the tenth year of Zedekiah, *k* of Judah,
32: 2 the *k* of Babylon was besieging Jerusalem,
32: 3 Zedekiah, *k* of Judah,
32: 3 handing over this city to the *k* of Babylon,
32: 4 Neither shall Zedekiah, *k* of Judah,
32: 4 he be handed over to the *k* of Babylon.
32:28 for Nebuchadnezzar, *k* of Babylon,
32:36 handed over to the *k* of Babylon amid sword,
33:21 not have a son to be *k* upon his throne,
34: 1 LORD while Nebuchadnezzar, *k* of Babylon,
34: 2 Go to Zedekiah, *k* of Judah, and tell him:
34: 2 handing this city over to the *k* of Babylon;
34: 3 *k* of Babylon and speak to him face to face.
34: 4 the word of the LORD, Zedekiah, *k* of Judah,
34: 6 all these things to Zedekiah, *k* of Judah,
34: 7 while the armies of the *k* of Babylon were
34: 8 after *K* Zedekiah had made an agreement
34:21 Zedekiah, too, *k* of Judah,
34:21 to the soldiers of the *k* of Babylon who
35: 1 of Jehoiakim, son of Josiah, *k* of Judah:
35:11 But when Nebuchadnezzar, *k* of Babylon,
36: 1 of Jehoiakim, son of Josiah, *k* of Judah,
36: 9 *k* of Judah a fast to placate the LORD was
36:16 must certainly tell the *k* all these things."
36:20 they entered the room where the *k* was.
36:21 and read it to the *k* and to all the
36:21 princes who were in attendance on the *k*.
36:22 Now the *k* was sitting in his winter house,
36:23 the *k* would cut off the piece
36:24 did not frighten the *k* and his ministers
36:25 urged the *k* not to burn the scroll,
36:27 after the *k* burned the scroll with the
36:28 contained, which Jehoiakim, *k* of Judah,
36:29 And against Jehoiakim, *k* of Judah,
36:29 Babylon's *k* shall surely come and lay
36:30 The LORD now says of Jehoiakim, *k* of Judah:
36:32 in the book which Jehoiakim, *k* of Judah,
37: 1 of Jehoiakim, was succeeded by *K* Zedekiah,
37: 1 *k* over the land of Judah by Nebuchadnezzar,
37: 1 of Judah by Nebuchadnezzar, *k* of Babylon.
37: 3 Yet *K* Zedekiah sent Jehucal,
37: 7 Give this answer to the *k* of Judah who
37:17 Once *K* Zedekiah had him brought to his
37:17 shall be handed over to the *k* of Babylon.
37:18 Jeremiah then asked *K* Zedekiah:
37:20 who prophesied to you that the *k* of
37:20 Hear now, my lord *k*,
37:21 *K* Zedekiah ordered that Jeremiah be
38: 3 over to the army of the *k* of Babylon;
38: 4 put to death," the princes said to the *k*;
38: 5 *K* Zedekiah answered:
38: 5 for the *k* could do nothing with them.
38: 7 The *k* happened just then to be at the Gate
38: 9 the palace and said to him, "My lord *k*,
38:10 Then the *k* ordered Ebed-melech the Cushite
38:14 Once *K* Zedekiah summoned the prophet
38:14 to ask you," the *k* said to Jeremiah;
38:16 But *K* Zedekiah swore to Jeremiah secretly:
38:17 surrender to the princes of Babylon's *k*,
38:18 surrender to the princes of Babylon's *k*,
38:19 *K* Zedekiah however,
38:22 women left in the house of Judah's *k* shall
38:22 brought out to the princes of Babylon's *k*,
38:23 shall be handed over to the *k* of Babylon,
38:25 ask you, 'Tell us what you said to the *k*;
38:25 kill you,' or 'What did the *k* say to you?'
38:26 'I petitioned the *k* not to send me back to
38:27 them in the very words the *k* had commanded.
39: 1 *k* of Judah, Nebuchadnezzar, *k* of Babylon,
39: 3 All the princes of the *k* of Babylon came

KING (cont.)
39: 3 all the other princes of the *k* of Babylon.
39: 4 When Zedekiah, *k* of Judah saw them,
39: 5 *k* of Babylon pronounced sentence upon him.
39: 6 at Riblah by order of the *k* of Babylon,
39:11 Jeremiah, Nebuchadnezzar, *k* of Babylon,
39:13 and all the nobles of the *k* of Babylon,
40: 5 whom the *k* of Babylon has appointed ruler
40: 7 that the *k* of Babylon had given Gedaliah,
40: 9 in the land and submit to the *k* of Babylon,
40:11 *k* of Babylon had left a remnant in Judah,
40:14 know that Baalis, the *k* of the Ammonites,
41: 2 *k* of Babylon had made ruler over the land;
41: 9 by *K* Asa to defend himself against Baasha,
41: 9 defend himself against Baasha, *k* of Israel;
41:18 whom the *k* of Babylon had made ruler in
42:11 Do not fear the *k* of Babylon,
43:10 my servant Nebuchadnezzar, *k* of Babylon,
44:30 will hand over Pharaoh Hophra, *k* of Egypt,
44:30 just as I handed over Zedekiah, *k* of Judah,
44:30 mortal foe, Nebuchadnezzar, *k* of Babylon.
45: 1 of Jehoiakim, son of Josiah, *k* of Judah:
46: 2 the army of Pharaoh Neco, *k* of Egypt,
46: 2 Euphrates by Nebuchadnezzar, *k* of Babylon,
46: 2 of Jehoiakim, son of Josiah, *k* of Judah:
46:13 advance of Nebuchadnezzar, *k* of Babylon,
46:17 Call Pharaoh, *k* of Egypt,
46:18 says the *K* whose name is LORD of hosts,
46:26 lives, to Nebuchadnezzar, *k* of Babylon,
48:15 goes down to be slaughtered, says the *K*,
49:28 defeated by Nebuchadnezzar, *k* of Babylon,
49:30 against you [Nebuchadnezzar, *k* of Babylon].
49:34 of the reign of Zedekiah, *k* of Judah:
49:38 Elam and destroy from there *k* and princes,
50:17 Formerly the *k* of Assyria devoured her,
50:18 will punish the *k* of Babylon and his land,
50:18 land, as once I punished the *k* of Assyria;
50:43 The *k* of Babylon hears news of them,
51:28 the *k* of Media,
51:31 *k* of Babylon that all his city is taken.
51:34 routed me, [Nebuchadnezzar, *k* of Babylon,]
51:57 eternal sleep, never to awaken, says the *K*,
51:59 when he went to Babylon for the *k*
52: 1 was twenty-one years old when he became *k*,
52: 3 Zedekiah rebelled against the *k* of Babylon.
52: 4 of the month, Nebuchadnezzar, *k* of Babylon,
52: 5 until the eleventh year of *K* Zedekiah.
52: 8 But the Chaldean army pursued the *k* and
52: 9 The *k*, therefore, was arrested
52: 9 in the land of Hamath, to the *k* of Babylon,
52:10 the *k* of Babylon slew his sons as well as
52:12 year of Nebuchadnezzar, *k* of Babylon),
52:12 as the representative of the *k* of Babylon.
52:13 house of the LORD, the palace of the *k*,
52:15 those who had deserted to the *k* of Babylon,
52:20 and the wheeled carts which *K* Solomon had
52:25 of the *k* who were present in the city,
52:26 brought them to the *k* of Babylon at Riblah,
52:31 of the exile of Jehoiachin, *k* of Judah,
52:31 twelfth month, Evil-merodach, *k* of Babylon,
52:31 took up the case of Jehoiachin, *k* of Judah,
52:34 the *k* of Babylon was a perpetual allowance,
Lam 2: 2 ground in dishonor her *k* and her princes.
2: 6 scorned in fierce wrath both *k* and priest.
2: 9 Her *k* and her princes are among the pagans;
Bar 1: 3 for Jeconiah, son of Jehoiakim, *k* of Judah,
1: 8 Zedekiah, son of Josiah, *k* of Judah,
1: 9 made after Nebuchadnezzar, *k* of Babylon,
1:11 the life of Nebuchadnezzar, *k* of Babylon,
1:12 shadow of Nebuchadnezzar, *k* of Babylon,
2:21 to the service of the *k* of Babylon,
2:22 voice so as to serve the *k* of Babylon.
2:24 heed your voice, or serve the *k* of Babylon,
6: 1 to Babylon by the *k* of the Babylonians,
6: 1 by Nebuchadnezzar, *k* of the Babylonians.
6:17 to execution for a crime against the *k*;
6:33 they can neither set up a *k* nor remove him.
6:52 They set no *k* over the land,
6:55 They cannot resist a *k*, or enemy forces.
6:58 much better to be a *k* displaying his valor,
Ez 1: 2 year, that is, of *K* Jehoiachin's exile,
17:12 The *k* of Babylon came to Jerusalem and
17:12 away its *k* and princes with him to Babylon.
17:16 the home of the *k* who set him up to rule,
19: 9 cage and took him away to the *k* of Babylon,
20:33 wrath, I swear I will be *k* over you!
21:24 the sword of the *k* of Babylon can come.
21:26 two roads divide stands the *k* of Babylon,
24: 2 the *k* of Babylon has invested Jerusalem.
26: 7 the north Nebuchadnezzar the *k* of Babylon,
26: 7 the king of Babylon, the *k* of kings,
28:12 of man, utter a lament over the *k* of Tyre,
29: 2 set your face against Pharaoh, *k* of Egypt,
29: 3 I am coming at you, Pharaoh, *k* of Egypt,
29:18 of man, Nebuchadnezzar, the *k* of Babylon,
29:19 of Egypt to Nebuchadnezzar, *k* of Babylon.
30:10 the hand of Nebuchadnezzar, *k* of Babylon.
30:21 broken the arm of Pharaoh, the *k* of Egypt,
30:22 I am coming at Pharaoh, the *k* of Egypt.
30:24 strengthen the arms of the *k* of Babylon,
30:25 make the arms of the *k* of Babylon strong,
30:25 my sword in the hand of the *k* of Babylon
31: 2 Son of man, say to Pharaoh, the *k* of Egypt,
32: 2 a lament over Pharaoh, the *k* of Egypt,
32:11 of the *k* of Babylon shall come upon you.
Dn 1: 1 *k* of Judah, *K* Nebuchadnezzar of Babylon
1: 2 handed over to him Jehoiakim, *k* of Judah,
1: 3 The *k* told Ashpenaz,
1: 5 The *k* allotted them a daily portion of
1:10 to Daniel, "I am afraid of my lord the *k*;
1:10 age, you will endanger my life with the *k*."
1:18 the *k* had specified for their preparation,
1:19 When the *k* had spoken with all of them,
1:20 wisdom or prudence which the *k* put to them,
1:21 there until the first year of *K* Cyrus.
2: 1 *K* Nebuchadnezzar had a dream which left
2: 2 came and presented themselves to the *k*,
2: 4 The Chaldeans answered the *k* [Aramaic]:
2: 4 "O *k*, live forever!
2: 5 The *k* answered the Chaldeans,
2: 7 "Let the *k* tell his servants the dream
2: 8 But the *k* replied: "I know for certain
2:10 The Chaldeans answered the *k*:
2:10 O *k*; never has any *k*, however great
2:11 What you demand, O *k*,
2:11 there is no one who can tell it to the *k*
2:12 At this the *k* became violently angry and
2:15 "O officer of the *k*," he asked,
2:15 the reason for this harsh order from the *k*?"
2:16 Daniel went and asked for time from the *k*,
2:24 whom the *k* had appointed to destroy the
2:24 Bring me before the *k*,
2:24 quickly brought Daniel to the *k* and said,
2:25 who can give the interpretation to the *k*."
2:26 The *k* asked Daniel,
2:27 mystery about which the *k* has inquired,
2:27 and astrologers could not explain to the *k*.
2:28 and he has shown *K* Nebuchadnezzar what is
2:30 its meaning may be made known to the *k*,
2:31 "In your vision, O *k*, you saw a statue,
2:37 You, O king, are the *k* of kings;
2:45 to the *k* what shall be in the future;
2:46 Then *K* Nebuchadnezzar fell down and
2:47 To Daniel the *k* said,
2:49 At Daniel's request the *k* made Shadrach,
3: 1 *K* Nebuchadnezzar had a golden statue made,
3: 3 statue which *K* Nebuchadnezzar had set up.
3: 5 statue which *K* Nebuchadnezzar has set up.
3: 7 statue which *K* Nebuchadnezzar had set up.
3: 9 and accused the Jews to *K* Nebuchadnezzar:
3: 9 "O *k*, live forever!
3:10 O *k*, you issued a decree
3:12 these men, O *k*, have paid no attention
3:13 who were promptly brought before the *k*.
3:14 *K* Nebuchadnezzar questioned them:
3:16 and Abednego answered *K* Nebuchadnezzar,
3:17 white-hot furnace and from your hands, O *k*,
3:18 But even if he will not, know, O *k*,
3:32 to an unjust *k*,
3:91 "Assuredly, O *k*," they answered.
3:91 *K* Nebuchadnezzar rose in haste
3:94 and nobles of the *k* came together,
3:97 Then the *k* promoted Shadrach,
3:98 *K* Nebuchadnezzar to the nations and
4:15 is the dream that I, *K* Nebuchadnezzar,
4:16 "Belteshazzar," the *k* said to him,
4:19 you are that tree, O *k*,
4:21 this is its meaning, O *k*:
4:21 the Most High has passed upon my lord *k*:
4:24 Therefore, O *k*, take my advice;
4:25 All this happened to *K* Nebuchadnezzar.
4:27 of the royal palace in Babylon, the *k* said,
4:28 has been decreed for you, *K* Nebuchadnezzar,
4:34 and exalt and glorify the *K* of heaven,
5: 1 *K* Belshazzar gave a great banquet for a
5: 2 Jerusalem, to be brought in so that the *k*,
5: 3 had been brought in, and while the *k*,
5: 5 the *k* saw the wrist and hand that wrote,
5: 7 The *k* shouted for the enchanters,
5: 8 the writing or tell the *k* what it meant.
5: 9 Then *K* Belshazzar was greatly terrified;
5:10 the discussion between the *k* and his lords,
5:10 entered the banquet hall and said, "O *k*,
5:11 In fact, *K* Nebuchadnezzar,
5:12 this Daniel, whom the *k* named Belteshazzar.
5:13 was brought into the presence of the *k*.
5:13 The *k* asked him, "Are you the Daniel,
5:13 the Jewish exile, whom my father, the *k*,
5:17 Daniel answered the *k*:
5:17 but the writing I will read for you, O *k*,
5:30 the Chaldean *K*, was slain
6: 4 and the *k* thought of giving him authority
6: 7 to the king and said to him, *K* Darius,
6: 8 man for thirty days, except to you, O *k*;
6: 9 Now, O *k*, issue the prohibition
6:10 So *K* Darius signed the prohibition and
6:13 went to remind the *k* about the prohibition:
6:13 "Did you not decree, O *k*,
6:13 man for thirty days, except to you, O *k*;
6:13 *k* answered them, "The decree is absolute,
6:14 exile, has paid no attention to you, O *k*,
6:15 The *k* was deeply grieved at this news and
6:16 "Keep in mind, O *k*,"
6:17 So the *k* ordered Daniel to be brought and
6:18 the *k* sealed with his own ring and the
6:19 the *k* returned to his palace for the night;
6:20 the *k* rose very early the next morning and
6:22 Daniel answered the *k*: "O *k*, live forever!
6:23 neither to you have I done any harm, O *k*!"
6:24 This gave the *k* great joy.
6:25 The *k* then ordered the men who had accused
6:26 Then *K* Darius wrote to the nations and
7: 1 the first year of *K* Belshazzar of Babylon,
8: 1 third year of the reign of *K* Belshazzar.
8:21 The he-goat is the *k* of the Greeks,
8:21 great horn on its forehead is the first *k*.
8:23 their measure, There shall arise a *k*,
10: 1 In the third year of Cyrus, *k* of Persia,
11: 3 *k* shall appear and rule with great might,
11: 5 "The *k* of the south shall grow strong,
11: 6 *k* of the south shall come to the *k* of the
11: 7 enter the stronghold of the *k* of the north,
11: 8 have nothing to do with the *k* of the north.
11: 9 invade the land of the *k* of the south,
11:11 around the stronghold, the *k* of the south,
11:11 go out to fight against the *k* of the north,
11:13 *k* of the north shall raise another army,
11:14 times many shall resist the *k* of the south,
11:15 When the *k* of the north comes,
11:25 meet the *k* of the south with a great army;
11:25 the *k* of the south shall prepare for
11:36 "The *k* shall do as he pleases,
11:40 "At the appointed time the *k* of the south
11:40 but the *k* of the north shall overwhelm him
14: 1 After *K* Astyages was laid with his fathers,
14: 2 esteem than any of the friends of the *k*.
14: 4 The *k* worshiped it and went every day to
14: 5 When the *k* asked him,
14: 6 Then the *k* continued,
14: 7 "Do not be deceived, O *k*,"
14: 8 the *k* called his priests and said to them,
14: 9 Daniel said to the *k*,
14:10 *k* went with Daniel into the temple of Bel,
14:11 Do you, O *k*, set out the food
14:14 departed the *k* set the food before Bel,
14:14 the *k* alone was present.
14:16 the next morning, the *k* came with Daniel.
14:17 Daniel answered, "They are unbroken, O *k*."
14:18 the *k* looked at the table and cried aloud,
14:19 laughed and kept the *k* from entering.
14:20 women, and children!" said the *k*.
14:21 The angry *k* arrested the priests,
14:24 said the *k* to Daniel,
14:26 Give me permission, O *k*,
14:26 "I give you permission," the *k* said.
14:28 they were angry and turned against the *k*.
14:28 "The *k* has become a Jew,"
14:29 They went to the *k* and demanded:
14:30 *k* was forced to hand Daniel over to them.
14:40 seventh day the *k* came to mourn for Daniel.
14:41 The *k* cried aloud, "You are great,
Hos 1: 1 of Jeroboam, son of Joash, *k* of Israel.
3: 4 shall remain many days without *k* or prince,
3: 5 the LORD, their God, and David, their *k*;
5: 1 O house of Israel, O household of the *k*,
5:13 to Assyria, and Judah sent to the great *k*.
7: 3 In their wickedness they regale the *k*,
7: 5 On the day of our *k*,
8:10 *K* and princes shall shortly succumb
10: 3 If they would say, "We have no *k*—
10: 3 fear the LORD, what can the *k* do for them?
10: 6 to Assyria, as an offering to the great *k*.
10: 7 The *k* of Samaria shall disappear,
10:15 dawn the *k* of Israel shall perish utterly.
11: 5 land of Egypt, and Assyria shall be his *k*;
13:10 Where now is your *k*,
13:10 whom you said, "Give me a *k* and princes"?
13:11 I give you a *k* in my anger,
Am 1: 1 Israel, in the days of Uzziah, *k* of Judah,
1: 1 of Jeroboam, son of Joash, *k* of Israel,
1:15 Their *k* shall go into captivity,
2: 1 he burned to ashes the bones of Edom's *k*,
5:26 You will carry away Sakkuth, your *k*,
7:10 Bethel, sent word to Jeroboam, *k* of Israel:
Jon 3: 6 When the news reached the *k* of Nineveh,
3: 7 Nineveh, by decree of the *k* and his nobles:
Mi 2:13 Their *k* shall go through before them,
4: 7 LORD shall be *k* over them on Mount Zion,
4: 9 Are you without a *k*?
6: 5 remember what Moab's *K* Balak planned,
Na 3:18 how your shepherds slumber, O *k* of Assyria,
Zep 1: 1 of Josiah, the son of Amon, *k* of Judah.
3:15 The *K* of Israel, the LORD, is in your midst,
Hg 1: 1 sixth month in the second year of *K* Darius,
2:10 month, in the second year of *K* Darius,
Zec 7: 1 *k* [the word of the LORD came to Zechariah],
9: 5 The *k* shall disappear from Gaza,
9: 9 See, your *k* shall come to you;
11: 6 his neighbor, or into the power of his *k*;
14: 5 in the days of *K* Uzziah of Judah.
14: 9 LORD shall become *k* over the whole earth;
14:16 come up year after year to worship the *K*,
14:17 not come up to Jerusalem to worship the *K*,
Mal 1:14 For a great *K* am I, says the LORD of hosts,
Mt 1: 6 of Jesse, Jesse the father of *K* David.
2: 1 of Judea during the reign of *K* Herod,
2: 2 "Where is the newborn *k* of the Jews?
2: 3 this news *K* Herod became greatly disturbed,
2: 9 After their audience with the *k*,

2:22 succeeded his father Herod as *k* of Judea,
5:35 Jerusalem (it is the city of the great *K);*
14: 9 The *k* immediately had his misgivings,
18:23 reign of God may be said to be like a *k*
21: 5 Your *k* comes to you without display
22: 2 a *k* who gave a wedding banquet for his son.
22: 7 At this the *k* grew furious and sent his
22:11 "When the *k* came in to meet the guests,
22:13 The *k* then said to the attendants,
25:34 The *k* will say to those on his right:
25:40 The *k* will answer them:
27:11 "Are you the *k* of the Jews?"
27:29 him, saying, "All hail, *k* of the Jews!"
27:37 "THIS IS JESUS, *K* OF THE JEWS."
27:42 So he is the *k* of Israel!
Mk 6:14 *K* Herod came to hear of Jesus,
6:22 The *k* told the girl, "Ask for anything
6:26 The *k* bitterly regretted the request;
15: 2 "Are you the *k* of the Jews?"
15: 9 me to release the *k* of the Jews for you?"
15:12 do with the man you call the *k* of the Jews?"
15:18 *K* of the Jews!"
15:26 his offense read, "THE *K* OF THE JEWS.
15:32 Let the 'Messiah,' the *k* of Israel,'
Lk 1: 5 In the days of Herod, *k* of Judea,
14:31 "Or if a *k* is about to march on another *k*
19:12 went to a faraway country to become its *k,*
19:15 He returned, however, crowned as *k.*
19:22 To him the *k* said: 'You worthless lout!
19:27 of mine who do not want me to be *k,*
19:38 he who comes as *k* in the name of the Lord!
23: 2 and calling himself the Messiah, a *k."*
23: 3 asked him, "Are you the *k* of the Jews?"
23:37 and saying, "If you are the *k* of the Jews,
23:38 "THIS IS THE *K* OF THE JEWS."
Jn 1:49 you are the *k* of Israel."
6:15 would come and carry him off to make him *k,*
12:13 Blessed is the *K* of Israel!"
12:15 Your *k* approaches you on a donkey's colt."
18:33 "Are you the *k* of the Jews?"
18:37 said to him, "So, then, you are a *k?"*
18:37 "It is you who say I am a *k.*
18:39 me to release to you the *k* of the Jews?"
19: 3 to him and said, "All hail, *k* of the Jews!",
19:12 makes himself a *k* becomes Caesar's rival."
19:14 He said to the Jews, "Look at your *k!"*
19:15 "Shall I crucify your *k?"*
19:15 priests replied, "We have no *k* but Caesar."
19:19 JESUS THE NAZOREAN THE *K* OF THE JEWS
19:21 not have written, 'The *K* of the Jews.'
19:21 to be *K* of the Jews'" Pilate answered,
Acts 7:10 in the court of the Pharaoh, *k* of Egypt,
7:18 until a new *k* came to power in Egypt,
12: 1 *K* Herod started to harass some of the
13:21 When they asked for a *k,*
13:22 him and raised up David as their *k;*
17: 7 claim instead that a certain Jesus is *k."*
25:13 A few days later *K* Agrippa and Bernice
25:14 Festus referred Paul's case to the *k.*
25:24 *K* Agrippa and all you who are here present
25:26 and in particular before you, *K* Agrippa,
26: 2 leveled against me by the Jews, *K* Agrippa.
26:19 *K* Agrippa, I could not disobey
26:26 The *k* here is well acquainted with these
26:27 Do you believe the prophets, *K* Agrippa?
26:30 the *k* rose, and with him the governor
2Cor 11:32 In Damascus the ethnarch of *K* Aretas was
1Tm 1:17 *K* of ages, the immortal, the invisible,
6:15 the *K* of kings and Lord of lords who alone
Heb 7: 1 *k* of Salem and priest of the Most High God,
7: 2 His name means *k* of justice";
7: 2 also king of Salem, that is, *k* of peace."
Rv 9:11 *k* was the angel in charge of the abyss,
15: 3 and true are your ways, O *K* of the nations!
17:11 no longer, even though it is an eighth *k,*
17:14 he is the Lord of lords and the *K* of kings;
19: 6 The Lord is *k,* our God, the Almighty!
19:10 The *K* of Kings.
19:16 *K* of kings and Lord of lords."

KINGDOM (267)

Gn 10:10 The chief cities of his *k* were Babylon,
20: 9 such monstrous guilt on me and my *k?*
Ex 19: 6 You shall be to me a *k* of priests,
Nm 32:33 of Manasseh, son of Joseph, the *k* of Sihon,
32:33 king of the Amorites, and the *k* of Og,
Dt 3: 4 region of Argob, the *k* of Og in Bashan:
3:10 all the cities of the *k* of Og in Bashan
3:13 of Gilead and all of Bashan, the *k* of Og,
17:18 When he is enthroned in his *k,*
Jos 13:12 as Salecah, the entire *k* in Bashan of Og,
13:21 and, generally, of the *k* of Sihon.
13:27 Zaphon, the other part of the *k* of Sihon,
13:30 all of Bashan, the entire *k* of Og,
1Sm 11:14 us go to Gilgal to inaugurate the *k* there."
13:14 but as things are, your *k* shall not endure.
15:28 has torn the *k* of Israel from you this day,
28:17 he has torn the *k* from your grasp and has
2Sm 3:10 take away the *k* from the house of Saul and
3:28 I and my *k* are forever innocent.
7:12 your loins, and I will make his *k* firm.
7:16 and your *k* shall endure forever before me;
16: 3 will restore to me my father's *k.'"*
16: 8 has given over the *k* to your son Absalom.
1Kgs 2:15 "You know that the *k* was mine,
2:15 the *k* escaped me and became my brother's,
2:22 "Ask the *k* for him as well,
10:20 like this was produced in any other *k.*
11:11 you of the *k* and give it to your servant.
11:13 Nor will I take away the whole *k.*
11:31 'I will tear away the *k* from Solomon's
11:34 not take any of the *k* from Solomon himself,
11:35 *k* from his sons and will give it to you
12:21 of Israel, to restore the *k* to Rehoboam,
12:26 "The *k* will return to David's house.
13: 8 "If you gave me half your *k,"*
14: 8 house of David of the *k* and gave it to you.
18:10 there is no nation or *k* where my master
18:10 *k* and nation swear they could not find you.
2Kgs 14: 5 When Amaziah had the *k* firmly in hand,
15:19 in strengthening his hold on the *k.*
1Chr 10:14 slew him, and transferred his *k* to David,
12:24 at Hebron to transfer to him Saul's *k,*
14: 2 for his *k* was greatly exalted for the sake
16:20 to nation, from one *k* to another people.
17:11 your own sons, and I will establish his *k.*
17:14 him in my house and in my *k* forever,
28: 7 I will establish his *k* forever,
2Chr 1: 1 of David, strengthened his hold on the *k,*
9:19 this had ever been produced in any other *k.*
11: 1 against Israel and restore the *k* to him.
11:17 the *k* of Judah and made Rehoboam,
13: 5 has given the *k* of Israel to David forever,
13: 8 *k* of the LORD commanded by the sons
14: 4 of Judah, and under him the *k* had peace.
17: 5 As a result, the LORD made his *k* secure,
20:30 Thereafter Jehoshaphat's *k* enjoyed peace,
21: 4 father's *k* and had consolidated his power,
25: 3 he had strengthened his hold on the *k,*
29:21 were brought for a sin offering for the *k,*
32:15 no other god of any other nation or *k*
33:13 and restored him to his *k* in Jerusalem.
35:21 you this day, for my war is with another *k,*
36:20 until the *k* of the Persians came to power.
36:22 issue this proclamation throughout his *k,*
Ezr 1: 1 issue this proclamation throughout his *k,*
7:13 in my *k* belonging to the people of Israel,
Neh 9:35 While they were yet in their *k,*
Tb 1:21 in charge of all the accounts of his *k,*
13: 1 forever, because his *k* lasts for all ages.
Jdt 1:12 and swore by his throne and his *k* that he
2:12 as I live, and by the strength of my *k,*
11: 8 throughout the *k* you alone are competent,
Est 1: 4 he displayed the glorious riches of his *k*
3: 8 throughout the provinces of your *k,*
B: 3 who has gained the second rank in the *k,*
5: 3 Even if it is half of my *k,*
5: 6 be honored, even if it is for half my *k."*
7: 2 make shall be honored, even for half the *k."*
E: 8 the *k* undisturbed and peaceful for all men,
E:12 he strove to deprive us of *k* and of life;
E:16 who has maintained the *k* in a flourishing
9:30 and twenty-seven provinces of Ahasuerus' *k.*
1Mc 1: 6 his *k* among them while he was still alive.
1: 8 So his officers took over his *k,*
1:10 and thirty-seven of the *k* of the Greeks.
1:16 When his *k* seemed secure,
1:41 his whole *k* that all should be one people,
1:51 the orders he published throughout his *k.*
3:14 the *k* by defeating Judas and his followers,
3:27 a muster of all the forces of his *k,*
6:14 and put him in charge of his whole *k.*
6:57 duty to take care of the affairs of the *k.*
7: 8 of West-of-Euphrates, a great man in the *k,*
8:13 they desired to help to a *k* became kings,
8:18 for it was obvious that the *k* of the
10:33 of my *k* I set at liberty without ransom;
10:34 and exemption for every Jew in my *k.*
10:37 positions of trust in the affairs of the *k.*
10:43 with all the goods he possesses in my *k.*
11: 1 take Alexander's *k* and add it to his own.
11: 9 and you shall reign over your father's *k.*
11:11 however, was that he coveted Alexander's *k.*
11:51 and they became renowned throughout his *k.*
15: 3 gained control of the *k* of my ancestors,
15: 9 When we recover our *k,*
15:28 these are cities of my *k.*
2Mc 1: 7 revolted against the holy land and the *k,*
2:17 to all of them their heritage, the *k,*
9:25 especially those on the borders of our *k,*
10:11 When Eupator succeeded to the *k,*
11:23 we wish the subjects of our *k* to be
14: 6 keep the *k* from enjoying peace and quiet.
14:26 Judas, the conspirator against the *k,*
Ps(s) 103:19 throne in heaven, and his *k* rules over all.
105:13 to nation and from one *k* to another people,
145:11 glory of your *k* and speak of your might,
145:12 might and the glorious splendor of your *k.*
145:13 Your kingdom is a *k* for all ages,
Wis 6: 4 though you were ministers of his *k,*
6:20 thus the desire for Wisdom leads up to a *k.*
10:10 Showed him the *k* of God and gave him
Sir 46:13 *k* and anointed princes to rule the people.
Is 9: 6 From David's throne, and over his *k,*
17: 3 be lost to Ephraim and the *k* to Damascus;
19: 2 city against city, *k* against kingdom.
60:12 or *k* shall perish that does not serve you;
Jer 18: 7 and tear down and destroy a nation or a *k.*
18: 9 to build up and plant a nation or a *k.*
27: 8 nation or *k* will not serve Nebuchadnezzar,
Bar 2:26 the kingdom of Israel and the *k* of Judah.
Ez 17:14 so that the *k* would remain a modest one,
Dn 1:20 all the magicians and enchanters in his *k.*
2:39 Another *k* shall take your place,
2:39 place, inferior to yours, then a third *k,*
2:40 There shall be a fourth *k,*
2:41 iron, mean that it shall be a divided *k,*
2:42 the *k* shall be partly strong and partly
2:44 the God of heaven will set up a *k*
3:54 Blessed are you on the throne of your *k,*
3:100 his kingdom is an everlasting *k,*
4:14 that the Most High rules over the *k* of men:
4:15 wise men in my *k* can tell me the meaning,
4:22 the *k* of men and gives it to whom he will.
4:23 your *k* shall be preserved for you
4:28 that your *k* is taken from you!
4:29 the *k* of men and gives it to whom he will."
4:31 and his *k* endures through all generations.
4:33 returned to me, and for the glory of my *k,*
4:33 I was restored to my *k,*
5: 7 and be third in the government of the *k."*
5:11 *k* in whom is the spirit of the holy God;
5:16 and be third in the government of the *k."*
5:18 a great *k* and glorious majesty.
5:21 *k* of men and appoints over it whom he will.
5:26 has numbered your *k* and put an end to it;
5:28 your *k* has been divided and given to the
5:29 him third in the government of the *k.*
6: 1 succeeded to the *k* at the age of sixty-two.
6: 2 entire *k* one hundred and twenty satraps,
6: 4 of giving him authority over the entire *k.*
6: 8 All the supervisors of the *k,*
6:27 his *k* shall not be destroyed,
7:22 came when the holy ones possessed the *k.*
7:23 fourth beast shall be a fourth *k* on earth,
7:24 shall be ten kings rising out of that *k;*
7:27 Most High, Whose *k* shall be everlasting:
9: 1 Medes, reigned over the *k* of the Chaldeans;
10:13 but the prince of the *k* of Persia stood in
11: 2 riches, he shall rouse all the *k* of Greece.
11: 4 No sooner shall he appear than his *k* shall
11: 4 for his *k* shall be torn to pieces and
11:17 to penetrate the entire strength of his *k.*
11:17 in marriage in order to destroy the *k,*
11:20 a tax collector through the glorious *k,*
11:21 By stealth and fraud he shall seize the *k.*
14: 1 Cyrus the Persian succeeded to his *k.*
Hos 1: 4 to an end the *k* of the house of Israel;
Am 9: 8 eyes of the Lord GOD are on this sinful *k;*
Mi 4: 8 be restored, the *k* of daughter Jerusalem.
Mt 4:17 The *k* of heaven is at hand."
4:23 proclaimed the good news of the *k,*
5:19 so shall be called least in the *k* of God.
5:19 commands shall be great in the *k* of God.
5:20 Pharisees you shall not enter the *k* of God.
6:10 heaven, hallowed be your name, your *k* come,
7:21 will enter the *k* of God but only the one
8:11 the banquet in the *k* of God with Abraham,
8:12 of the *k* will be driven out into the dark.
11:11 born into the *k* of God is greater than he.
11:12 now the *k* of God has suffered violence,
12:25 "A *k* torn by strife is headed for its
13:38 world, the good seed the citizens of the *k.*
13:41 from his *k* all who draw others to apostasy,
13:43 shine like the sun in their Father's *k.*
13:45 the *k* of heaven is like a merchant's
16:19 entrust to you the keys of the *k* of heaven.
18: 1 is of greatest importance in the *k* of God?"
18: 3 children, you will not enter the *k* of God.
19:14 The *k* of God belongs to such as these."
19:23 will a rich man enter into the *k* of God.
19:24 than for a rich man to enter the *k* of God."
20:21 hand and the other at your left, in your *k."*
21:31 are entering the *k* of God before you.
21:43 the *k* of God will be taken away from you
23:13 the doors of the *k* of God in men's faces,
24: 7 rise against nation, one *k* against another.
24:14 This good news of the *k* will be
25:34 Inherit the *k* prepared for you from the
Mk 3:24 If a *k* is torn by civil strife, that *k* cannot
6:23 you whatever you ask, even to half my *k!"*
9:47 Better for you to enter the *k* of God with
10:14 such as these that the *k* of God belongs.
10:23 it is for the rich to enter the *k* of God!"
10:24 sons, how hard it is to enter the *k* of God!
10:25 than for a rich man to enter the *k* of God."
13: 8 rise against nation, one *k* against another.
Lk 7:28 born into the *k* of God is greater than he."
8: 1 proclaiming the good news of the *k* of God.
9:60 come away and proclaim the *k* of God."
11: 2 your *k* come.
11:17 *k* divided against itself is laid waste.
11:18 against himself, how can his *k* last?—since
12:32 has pleased your Father to give you the *k.*
13:28 and all the prophets safe in the *k* of God,
13:29 their place at the feast in the *k* of God.
14:15 is he who eats bread in the *k* of God."
16:16 good news of God's *k* has been proclaimed,

KING (cont.)
18:17 *k* of God as a child will not enter into it.”
18:24 be for the rich to go into the *k* of God!
18:25 for a rich man to enter the *k* of heaven.”
18:29 for the sake of the *k* of God who will not
21:10 rise against nation and *k* against kingdom.
22:16 until it is fulfilled in the *k* of God.”
22:30 In my *k* you will eat and drink at my table,
Jn 3: 5 no one can enter into God's *k* without
18:36 “My *k* does not belong to this world.
18:36 If my *k* were of this world,
18:36 As it is, my *k* is not here.”
Acts 8:12 the *k* of God and the name of Jesus Christ,
19: 8 persuasive arguments, about the *k* of God.
20:25 the *k* will ever see my face again.
Rom 14:17 The *k* of God is not a matter of eating or
1Cor 4:20 The *k* of God does not consist in talk but
6: 9 unholy will not fall heir to the *k* of God?
6:10 slanderers or robbers will inherit God's *k*.
15:24 he will hand over the *k* to God the Father.
15:50 and blood cannot inherit the *k* of God;
Gal 5:21 such things will not inherit the *k* of God!
Eph 5: 5 inheritance in the *k* of Christ and of God.
Col 1:13 brought us into the *k* of his beloved Son.
4:11 who are working with me for the *k* of God.
2Thes 1: 5 worthy of his *k* —it is for his *k* you suffer
2Tm 4:18 and will bring me safe to his heavenly *k*.
Heb 1: 8 righteous scepter is the scepter of your *k*.
12:28 *k* should hold fast to God's grace,
Jas 2: 5 of the *k* he promised to those who love him?
2: 8 however, if you fulfill the law of the *k*.
2Pt 1:11 everlasting *k* of our Lord and Savior Jesus
Rv 5:10 You made of them a *k*,
11:15 “The *k* of the world now belongs to our
16:10 Its *k* was plunged into darkness;

KINGDOMS (59)

Dt 3:21 the *k* which you will encounter over there.
28:25 example to all the *k* of the earth.
Jos 11:10 formerly was the chief of all those *k*.
1Sm 10:18 the power of all the *k* that oppressed you.'
1Kgs 5: 1 Solomon ruled over all the *k* from the
2Kgs 19:15 alone are God over all the *k* of the earth.
19:19 the *k* of the earth may know that you alone,
1Chr 29:30 and all the *k* of the surrounding lands.
2Chr 12: 8 serve me and what it is to serve earthly *k*.”
17:10 the *k* of the countries surrounding Judah,
20: 6 you not rule over all the *k* of the nations?
20:29 And the fear of God came upon all the *k* of
36:23 ‘All the *k* of the earth the LORD,
Ezr 1: 2 ‘All the *k* of the earth the LORD,
Neh 9:22 You gave them *k* and peoples,
1Mc 1:16 king of Egypt, so as to rule over both *k*.
6:29 other *k* and from the islands of the seas.
8:11 All the other *k* and islands that had ever
Ps(s) 46: 7 Though nations are in turmoil, *k* totter,
68:33 You *k* of the earth, sing to God,
79: 6 upon the *k* that call not upon your name;
102:23 the peoples gather together, and the *k*,
Is 10:10 as my hand reached out to idolatrous *k*
13: 4 the noise of *k*, nations assembled!
13:19 And Babylon, the jewel of *k*,
14:16 who made the earth tremble, and *k* quake?
23:11 stretches out over the sea, he shakes *k*;
23:17 all the world's *k* on the face of the earth.
37:16 alone are God over all the *k* of the earth.
37:20 all the *k* of the earth may know that you,
47: 5 you be called sovereign mistress of *k*.
Jer 1:10 day I set you over nations and over *k*.
1:15 Lo, I am summoning all the *k* of the north,
15: 4 *k* of the earth because of what Manasseh,
24: 9 object of horror to all the *k* of the earth,
25:26 all the *k* upon the face of the earth [and
28: 8 pestilence against many lands and mighty *k*.
29:18 object of horror to all the *k* of the earth,
34: 1 armies and the earth's *k* subject to him,
34:17 object of horror to all the *k* of the earth.
49:28 Of Kedar and the *k* of Hazor,
51:20 I shatter nations, with you I destroy *k*.
51:27 war against her, summon against her the *k*,
Bar 2: 4 us subject to all the *k* round about us,
Ez 29:15 where it will be the lowliest of *k*,
37:22 again shall they be divided into two *k*.
Dn 2:44 pieces all these *k* and put an end to them,
7:17 for four *k* which shall arise on the earth.
7:27 dominion and majesty of all the *k*
8:22 are four *k* that will issue from his nation,
Am 6: 2 Are you better than these *k*,
Na 3: 5 to the nations, to the *k* your shame!
Zep 3: 8 together the nations, to assemble the *k*,
Hg 2:22 thrones of *k*, destroy the power of the *k*
Mt 4: 8 the *k* of the world in their magnificence,
Lk 4: 5 all the *k* of the world in a single instant.
4: 6 all this power and the glory of these *k*;
Heb 11:33 the prophets, who by faith conquered *k*,

KINGLY (4)

1Kgs 1:27 was to succeed to your majesty's *k* throne?”
Sir 44: 2 Subduers of the land in *k* fashion,
2Tm 4: 1 dead, and by his appearing and his *k* power,
Rv 1: 9 share with you the distress and the *k* reign

KINGS—KING'S (573)

Gn 14: 3 All the latter *k* joined forces in the
14: 5 fourteenth year Chedorlaomer and the *k*
14: 9 four *k* against five.
14:10 and as the *k* of Sodom and Gomorrah fled,
14:17 and the *k* who were allied with him,
14:17 Valley of Shaveh (that is, the *K* Valley).
17: 6 *k* shall stem from you.
35:11 you, and *k* shall issue from your loins.
36:31 The following are the *k* who reigned in the
49:20 rich, and he shall furnish dainties for *k*.
Nm 31: 8 battle, they killed the five Midianite *k*:
Dt 3: 8 we took from the two *k* of the Amorites
3:21 LORD, your God, has done to both these *k*;
4:47 the land of these two *k* of the Amorites in
7:24 He will deliver their *k* into your hand,
31: 4 the *k* of the Amorites whom he destroyed,
Jos 2:10 two *k* of the Amorites beyond the Jordan,
5: 1 When all the *k* of the Amorites to the west
5: 1 all the *k* of the Canaanites by the sea
9: 1 the news reached the *k* west of the Jordan,
9:10 two *k* of the Amorites beyond the Jordan,
10: 5 The five Amorite *k*,
10: 6 because all the Amorite *k* of the mountain
10:16 Meanwhile the five *k* who had fled,
10:17 When Joshua was told that the five *k* had
10:22 the cave and bring out those five *k* to me.”
10:23 out to him from the cave the five *k*,
10:24 and put your feet on the necks of these *k*.”
10:40 and the mountain slopes, with all their *k*.
10:42 All these *k* and their lands Joshua
11: 2 and to the northern *k* in the mountain
11: 5 All these *k* joined forces and marched to
11:12 Joshua thus captured all those *k* with
11:17 All their *k* he captured and put to death.
11:18 war against all these *k* for a long time.
12: 1 The *k* of the land east of the Jordan,
12: 7 This is a list of the *k* whom Joshua and
12: 9 They were the *k* of Jericho,
12:24 thirty-one *k* in all.
24: 8 them [the two *k* of the Amorites] before you.
Jgs 1: 7 At this Adonibezek said, “Seventy *k*,
5: 3 the people who bless the LORD, Hear, O *k*!
5:19 The *k* came and fought;
5:19 then they fought, those *k* of Canaan,
8: 5 pursuing Zebah and Zalmunna, *k* of Midian.”
8:12 pursued them and took the two *k* of Midian,
8:26 purple garments worn by the *k* of Midian,
1Sm 18:18 that I should become the *k* son-in-law?”
18:22 You should become the *k* son-in-law.”
18:23 think it easy to become the *k* son-in-law?
18:26 the prospect of becoming the *k* son-in-law.
18:27 that he might thus become the *k* son-in-law.
20:25 facing him, while Abner sat at the *k* side,
20:29 That is why he has not come to the *k* table.”
21: 9 weapons, because the *k* business was urgent.”
22:14 is as loyal as David, the *k* son-in-law,
22:17 But the *k* servants refused to lift a hand
23:20 our task to deliver him into the *k* grasp.”
26:16 where are the *k* spear and the water jug
26:22 “Here is the *k* spear.
27: 6 to the *k* of Judah up to the present time.
2Sm 9:11 at David's table like one of the *k* sons.
9:13 because he always ate at the *k* table.
10:19 All of Hadadezer's vassal *k*,
11: 1 of the year, when *k* go out on campaign,
11: 8 was sent out after him from the *k* table.
11:24 above, and some of the *k* servants died,
15: 3 there is no one to hear you in the *k* name.”
15:15 The *k* officers answered him,
16: 2 asses are for the *k* household to ride on.
16: 6 stones at David and at all the *k* officers,
18:12 my two hands, I would not harm the *k* son,
18:18 and erected it for himself in the *K* Valley,
18:20 good news, for in fact the *k* son is dead.”
18:29 the *k* servant Joab sent your servant on,
19:19 They crossed over the ford to bring the *k*
19:43 we had anything to eat at the *k* expense?
24: 4 so they left the *k* presence in order to
1Kgs 1: 9 invited all his brothers, the *k* sons,
1:19 he has invited all the *k* sons,
1:23 the prophet entered the *k* presence and,
1:25 he invited all the *k* sons,
1:28 the *k* presence and stood before him,
1:32 When they had entered the *k* presence,
1:44 and they mounted him upon the *k* own mule.
1:47 and the *k* servants went in and paid their
2:19 and a throne was provided for the *k* mother,
2:38 will do just as the *k* majesty has said.”
3:13 glory that among *k* there is not your like.
4:19 was one prefect besides, in the *k* own land.
5: 4 from Tiphsah to Gaza, and over all its *k*,
5:14 of the *k* of the earth who had heard of his wisdom.
10:15 and from all the *k* of Arabia and the
10:23 riches and wisdom all the *k* of the earth.
10:26 cities and to the *k* service in Jerusalem.
10:28 Cilicia, where the *k* agents purchased them.
10:29 rates to all the Hittite and Aramean *k*.
14:19 book of the chronicles of the *k* of Israel.
14:29 book of the chronicles of the *k* of Judah.
15: 7 book of the chronicles of the *k* of Judah.
15:23 book of the chronicles of the *k* of Judah.
15:31 book of the chronicles of the *k* of Israel.
16: 5 book of the chronicles of the *k* of Israel.
16:14 book of the chronicles of the *k* of Israel.
16:20 book of the chronicles of the *k* of Israel.
16:27 book of the chronicles of the *k* of Israel.
16:33 than any of the *k* of Israel before him.
20: 1 by thirty-two *k* with horses and chariotry,
20:12 with the *k* when he heard this reply.
20:16 with the thirty-two *k* who were his allies.
20:24 Take the *k* from their posts and put
20:31 *k* of the land of Israel are merciful kings.
22:26 of the city, and to Joash, the *k* son,
22:27 king's son, and say, ‘This is the *k* order:
22:39 book of the chronicles of the *k* of Israel.
22:46 book of the chronicles of the *k* of Judah.
2Kgs 1:18 the book of chronicles of the *k* of Israel.
3:10 three *k* to put them in the grasp of Moab.”
3:12 So the *k* of Israel,
3:13 “The LORD has called these three *k*
3:21 that the *k* had come to give them battle;
3:23 “The *k* have fought among themselves and
7: 6 king of Israel has hired the *k* of the Hittites
7: 6 and the *k* of the borderlands to fight us.”
8:15 in water, and spread it over the *k* face,
8:18 like the *k* of Israel of the line of Ahab,
8:23 book of the chronicles of the *k* of Judah.
9:34 after all, she was a *k* daughter.”
10: 4 said, “If two *k* could not withstand him,
10:34 book of the chronicles of the *k* of Israel.
11: 4 commitment, and then showed them the *k* son.
11: 5 on the sabbath shall guard the *k* palace;
11:11 the altar and the temple on the *k* behalf.
11:12 Then Jehoiada led out the *k* son and put
12:19 Jehoram, and Ahaziah, *k* of Judah,
12:20 book of the chronicles of the *k* of Judah.
13: 8 book of the chronicles of the *k* of Israel.
13:12 book of the chronicles of the *k* of Israel.
13:13 was buried with the *k* of Israel in Samaria.]
13:16 placed his hands over the *k* hands and said,
14:15 book of the chronicles of the *k* of Israel.
14:16 was buried in Samaria with the *k* of Israel.
14:18 book of the chronicles of the *k* of Judah.
14:28 book of the chronicles of the *k* of Israel.
14:29 rested with his ancestors, the *k* of Israel,
15: 5 in a house apart, while Jotham, the *k* son,
15: 6 book of the chronicles of the *k* of Judah.
15:11 book of the chronicles of the *k* of Israel.
15:15 book of the chronicles of the *k* of Israel.
15:21 book of the chronicles of the *k* of Israel.
15:26 book of the chronicles of the *k* of Israel.
15:31 book of the chronicles of the *k* of Israel.
15:36 book of the chronicles of the *k* of Judah.
16: 3 but conducted himself like the *k* of Israel,
16:19 book of the chronicles of the *k* of Judah.
17: 2 the extent of the *k* of Israel before him.
17: 8 [and the *k* of Israel whom they set up].
18: 5 anyone like him among all the *k* of Judah.
19:11 You have heard what the *k* of Assyria have
19:13 Arpad, or the *k* of the cities Sepharviam,
19:17 the *k* of Assyria have laid waste the
20:20 book of the chronicles of the *k* of Judah.
21:17 book of the chronicles of the *k* of Judah.
21:25 book of the chronicles of the *k* of Judah.
22:12 scribe Shaphan, and the *k* servant Asaiah:
23: 5 whom the *k* of Judah had appointed to burn
23:11 the *k* of Judah had dedicated to the sun;
23:12 the altars made by the *k* of Judah
23:19 Samaria which the *k* of Israel had erected,
23:22 of the kings of Israel and the *k* of Judah,
23:28 book of the chronicles of the *k* of Judah.
24: 5 book of the chronicles of the *k* of Judah.
24:15 to Babylon the *k* mother and wives,
25: 4 the two walls which was near the *k* garden.
25:28 the other *k* who were with him in Babylon.
25:29 and ate at the *k* table as long as he lived.
1Chr 1:43 The *k* who reigned in the land of Edom
1:43 they had Israelite *k* were the following:
4:23 Gederah, where they lived in the *k* service.
9: 1 recorded in the book of the *k* of Israel.
9:18 stood guard at the *k* gate on the east side;
16:21 them, and for their sake he rebuked *k*:
19: 9 while the *k* who had come to their help
20: 1 following year, the time when *k* go to war,
21: 4 However, the *k* command prevailed over Joab,
21: 6 for the *k* command was repugnant to Joab.
25: 5 of Heman, the *k* seer in divine matters;
27:32 son of Hachmoni, were tutors of the *k* sons.
27:33 Ahithophel was also the *k* counselor,
27:33 and Hushai the Archite was the *k* confidant.
27:34 The commander of the *k* army was Joab.
28: 1 of all the *k* estates and possessions,
29: 6 and the overseers of the *k* affairs came
2Chr 1:12 and glory, such as *k* before you never had,
1:16 The *k* agents would acquire them by
1:17 for all the Hittite and Aramean *k*.
8:15 There was no deviation from the *k* command
9:14 All the *k* of Arabia also,
9:22 King Solomon surpassed all the other *k* of
9:23 All the *k* of the earth sought audience
9:26 He was ruler over all the *k* from the River
12: 9 of the temple of the LORD and of the *k* palace.
16:11 in the book of the *k* of Judah and Israel.
18:25 of the city, and to Joash the *k* son,

18:26 king's son, and say, 'This is the *k* order:
20:34 is inserted in the book of the *k* of Israel.
21: 6 like the *k* of Israel of the line of Ahab,
21:13 walked in the way of the *k* of Israel
21:17 away all the wealth found in the *k* palace,
21:20 of David, but not in the tombs of the *k*.
22:11 the *k* sons who were about to be slain,
23: 3 "Here is the *k* son who must reign,
23: 5 another third must be at the *k* palace
23:10 the altar and the temple on the *k* behalf.
23:11 Then they brought out the *k* son,
23:20 come within the upper gate of the *k* house,
24: 8 *k* command, therefore, they made a chest,
24:16 buried in the City of David with the *k*,
24:21 and at the *k* order they stoned him to
24:25 of David, but not in the tombs of the *k*.
24:27 in the midrash of the book of the *k*.
25:16 "Have you been made the *k* counselor?
25:26 in the book of the *k* of Judah and Israel.
26:11 of Hananiah, one of the *k* officials.
27: 7 in the book of the *k* of Israel and Judah.
28: 2 but conducted himself like the *k* of Israel
28: 7 warrior, killed Maaseiah, the *k* son,
28:16 an appeal for help to the *k* of Assyria.
28:23 the gods of the *k* of Aram who helped them,
28:26 in the book of the *k* of Judah and Israel.
28:27 bring him to the tombs of the *k* of Israel.
29:25 prescriptions of David, of Gad the *k* seer,
30: 6 and Judah, and at the *k* command they said:
30: 6 left from the hands of the Assyrian *k*.
32: 4 "Why should the *k* of Assyria come and
32:32 in the book of the *k* of Judah and Israel.
33:18 in the chronicles of the *k* of Israel.
34:11 *k* of Judah had allowed to fall into ruin.
34:20 the scribe, and to Asaiah, the *k* servant:
35: 7 these were from the *k* property.
35:10 their classes according to the *k* command.
35:15 Asaph, Heman and Jeduthun, the *k* seer.
35:26 in the book of the *k* of Israel and Judah.
36: 8 in the book of the *k* of Israel and Judah.
Ezr 4:15 which has proved fatal to *k* and provinces,
4:19 risen up against *k* and that rebellion
4:20 Powerful *k* were once in Jerusalem who
5:17 And may the *k* pleasure in this matter be
7:12 "Artaxerxes, king of *k*,
8:36 were presented to the *k* satraps
9: 7 over, we and our *k* and our priests,
9: 7 to the will of the *k* of foreign lands,
9: 9 the good will of the *k* of Persia toward us.
Neh 2: 9 and presented the *k* letters to them.
2:14 over to the Spring Gate and to the *K* Pool.
3:15 of the Aqueduct Pool near the *k* garden
5: 4 "To pay the *k* tax we have borrowed money
9:24 their *k* as well as the peoples of the land,
9:32 disasters that have befallen us, our *k*,
9:32 time of the *k* of Assyria until this day!
9:34 Yes, our *k* our princes, our priests,
9:37 *k* whom you set over us because of our sins,
Tb 1:20 All that I had was taken to the *k* palace,
12: 7 A *k* secret it is prudent to keep,
12:11 to you, 'A *k* secret it is prudent to keep,
Est A: 2 a prominent man who served at the *k* court,
1: 7 freely, as befitted the *k* munificence.
1:12 At this the *k* wrath flared up,
1:13 because the *k* business was conducted in
1:14 Median officials who were in the *k* personal
2: 2 Then the *k* personal attendants suggested:
2: 8 When the *k* order and decree had been
2:19 was passing his time at the *k* gate,
2:21 the time that Mordecai spent at the *k* gate,
2:23 was written in the annals for the *k* use.]
3: 2 All the *k* servants who were at the royal
3: 3 The *k* servants who were at the royal gate
3: 3 Mordecai, "Why do you disobey the *k* order
B: 4 continually disregards the decrees of *k*,
3:15 couriers set out in haste at the *k* command;
4: 3 wherever the *k* legal enactment reached,
4: 5 one of the *k* eunuchs whom he had placed at
4:13 that because you are in the *k* palace,
D: 8 But God changed the *k* anger to gentleness.
6: 3 The *k* attendants replied,
6: 4 entered the outer court of the *k* palace
6: 5 The *k* servants answered him,
6: 9 to one of the noblest of the *k* officials,
6:14 the *k* eunuchs arrived and hurried Haman
8: 1 Mordecai was admitted to the *k* presence,
8: 8 you in turn may write in the *k* name what
8:14 steeds sped forth in haste at the *k* order,
8:15 Mordecai left the *k* presence clothed in a
8:17 every city, wherever the *k* order arrived,
10: 2 chronicles of the *k* of Media and Persia.
1Mc 1: 2 captured fortresses, and put *k* to death.
2:18 now, be the first to obey the *k* command,
2:18 sons shall be numbered among the *K* Friends,
2:19 all the Gentiles in the *k* realm obey him,
2:19 his fathers and consents to the *k* orders,
2:23 altar in Modein according to the *k* order.
2:31 certain men who had flouted the *k* order
2:33 "Come out and obey the *k* command,
2:34 obey the *k* command to profane the sabbath
2:48 the *k* and did not let the sinner triumph.
3: 7 achieved, and he afflicted many *k*;
3:14 followers, who have despised the *k* command.
3:30 a more liberal hand than the preceding *k*.
3:32 in charge of the *k* affairs from the
3:38 Gorgias, capable men among the *K* Friends,
3:39 and ravage it according to the *k* orders.
4: 3 soldiers to attack the *k* army at Emmaus,
6:15 so that he might guide the *k* son Antiochus
6:17 was dead, he set up the *k* son Antiochus,
6:32 Beth-zechariah, on the way to the *k* camp.
6:40 of the *k* army extended over the heights,
6:42 and six hundred men of the *k* army fell.
6:48 *k* army went up to Jerusalem to attack them,
7: 7 Judas has done to us and to the *k* land,
7: 8 king chose Bacchides, one of the *K* Friends,
8: 4 They had crushed the *k* who had come
8: 7 taken him alive and obliged him and the *k*
8:12 They had conquered *k* both far and near,
8:13 desired to help to a kingdom became *k*,
10:20 you are to be called the *K* Friend,
10:36 in the *k* army and allowances be given them,
10:36 them, as is due to all the *k* soldiers.
10:37 Let some of them be stationed in the *k*
10:49 The two *k* joined battle,
10:58 splendor according to the custom of *k*.
10:60 where he met the two *k* and gave them and
10:89 such as is usually given to *K* Kinsmen;
11:48 Thus they saved the *k* life.
11:57 and wish you to be one of the *K* Friends."
12:13 us, and the *k* around us have attacked us.
13:36 Simon the high priest, the friend of *k*,
14:13 the *k* in those days were crushed.
15: 5 tax exemptions that the *k* before me granted
15:15 this addressed to various *k* and countries:
15:19 to write to various *k* and countries,
15:22 consul sent similar letters to *K* Demetrius,
15:32 So Athenobius, the *k* Friend,
15:32 When he gave him the *k* message,
2Mc 2:13 how he collected the books about the *k*,
3: 2 the *k* themselves honored the Place and
3: 8 but in reality to carry out the *k* purpose.
4:10 the *k* approval and came into office,
4:30 as a gift to Antiochis, the *k* mistress.
5:16 made by other *k* for the advancement,
6: 7 celebration of the *k* birthday the Jews had,
7:30 I will not obey the *k* command.
8: 8 to come to the aid of the *k* government.
10:13 accused before Eupator by the *K* Friends.
11:22 The *k* letter read thus:
11:27 The *k* letter to the people was as follows:
13: 4 But the King of *k* aroused the anger of
13:13 before the *k* army could invade Judea and
13:15 he made a night attack on the *k* pavilion
13:26 is how the *k* attack and withdrawal went.
14: 8 of my genuine concern for the *k* interests,
15: 5 take up arms and carry out the *k* business."
Jb 3:14 With *k* and counselors of the earth
12:18 He loosens the bonds imposed by *k* and
12:18 but a waistcloth to bind the *k* own loins.
29:25 I took a *k* place in the armed forces.
36: 7 And with *k* upon thrones he sets them,
Ps(s) 2: 2 The *k* of the earth rise up,
2:10 And now, O *k*, give heed; take warning,
45: 6 the *k* enemies lose heart.
45: 8 the oil of gladness above your fellow *k*.
45:10 The daughters of *k* come to meet you;
45:14 glorious is the *k* daughter as she enters;
48: 5 the *k* assemble, they come on together;
61: 7 Add to the days of the *k* life;
68:13 *K* and their hosts are fleeing,
68:15 While the Almighty dispersed the *k* there,
68:30 in Jerusalem let the *k* bring you gifts.
72: 1 the king, and with your justice, the *k* son;
72:10 The *k* of Tarshish and the Isles shall
72:10 *k* of Arabia and Seba shall bring tribute.
72:11 All *k* shall pay him homage,
76:13 who is terrible to the *k* of the earth.
89:28 first-born, highest of the *k* of the earth.
102:16 and all the *k* of the earth your glory,
105:14 them, and for their sake he rebuked *k*:
105:30 frogs, even in the chambers of their *k*.
110: 5 he will crush *k* on the day of his wrath.
119:46 decrees before *k* without being ashamed.
135:10 He smote many nations and slew mighty *k*:
135:11 king of Bashan, and all the *k* of Canaan;
136:17 Who smote great *k*,
136:18 And slew powerful *k*,
138: 4 *k* of the earth shall give thanks to you,
144:10 your praise, You who give victory to *k*,
148:11 Let the *k* of the earth and all peoples,
149: 8 To bind their *k* with chains,
Prv 8:15 By me *k* reign,
16:10 The *k* lips are an oracle;
16:12 *K* have a horror of wrongdoing,
16:14 The *k* wrath is like messengers of death,
16:15 In the light of the *k* countenance is life,
19:12 The *k* wrath is like the roaring of a lion,
21: 1 is the *k* heart in the hand of the LORD;
22:29 He will stand in the presence of *k*;
25: 2 conceals, *k* have glory in what they fathom.
25: 3 in depth, the heart of *k* is unfathomable.
25: 6 Claim no honor in the *k* presence,
30:28 yet they find their way into *k* palaces.
31: 3 nor your strength to those who ruin *k*.
31: 4 kings, O Lemuel, not for *k* to drink wine;
Eccl 2: 8 gold, and the wealth of *k* and provinces.
Sg 1:12 For the *k* banquet my nard gives forth
Wis 6: 1 Hear, therefore, *k*, and understand;
6:21 Wisdom, that you may reign as *k* forever.
10:16 fearsome *k* with signs and portents;
Sir 45: 3 words and sustained him in the *k* presence.
48: 6 You sent *k* down to destruction,
48: 8 anointed *k* who should inflict vengeance,
49: 4 the Law of the Most High, these *k* of Judah,
Is 1: 1 Jotham, Ahaz and Hezekiah, *k* of Judah.
7:16 two *k* whom you dread shall be deserted.
10: 8 "Are not my commanders all *k*?"
14: 9 *k* of all nations rise from their thrones.
14:18 All the *k* of the nations lie in glory,
19:11 am a disciple of wise men, of ancient *k*?"
24:21 and the *k* of the earth on the earth.
34:12 no more, nor shall *k* be proclaimed there;
37:11 *k* of Assyria have done to all the countries:
37:18 the *k* of Assyria have laid waste all the
41: 2 he delivers the nations and subdues the *k*;
45: 1 him, and making *k* run in his service,
49: 7 When *k* see you,
49:23 *K* shall be your foster fathers,
52:15 because of him *k* shall stand speechless;
60: 3 your light, and *k* by your shining radiance.
60:10 and their *k* shall be your attendants;
60:11 to you the wealth of nations, and their *k*,
62: 2 your vindication, and all *k* your glory;
Jer 1:18 Against Judah's *k* and princes,
2:26 They, their *k* and their princes,
8: 1 the bones of the *k* and princes of Judah,
13:13 land, the *k* who succeed to David's throne,
17:19 where the *k* of Judah enter and leave,
17:20 Hear the word of the LORD, you *k* of Judah,
17:25 *k* who sit upon the throne of David will
19: 3 LORD, *k* of Judah and citizens of Jerusalem:
19: 4 and the *k* of Judah have filled this place
19:13 palaces of the *k* of Judah shall be defiled
20: 5 dear, all the treasures of the *k* of Judah,
22: 4 *k* who succeed to the throne of David will
22:15 among *k* by competing with them in cedar?
25:14 be enslaved to great nations and mighty *k*,
25:18 the cities of Judah, her *k* and her princes,
25:20 all the *k* of the land of Uz;
25:20 all the *k* of the land of the Philistines:
25:22 all the *k* of Tyre,
25:24 [all the *k* of Arabia;]
25:25 all the *k* of Zimri,
25:26 all the *k* of the north,
26:10 they came up from the *k* palace to the
27: 3 Send to the *k* of Edom,
27: 7 shall serve great nations and mighty *k*.
32: 2 the quarters of the guard, at the *k* palace.
32:32 Judeans, with their *k* and their princes,
33: 4 of this city and the palaces of Judah's *k*,
34: 5 the *k* who preceded you from the first;
36:12 So he went down to the *k* palace,
38: 7 a Cushite, a courtier in the *k* palace,
39: 8 the *k* palace and the houses of the people,
41: 1 of royal descent, one of the *k* nobles,
44: 9 and the *k* of Judah and their wives,
44:17 our *k* and princes have done in the cities
44:21 you, your fathers, your *k* and princes,
46:25 of Thebes, and Egypt, her gods and her *k*,
50:41 mighty *k* roused from the ends of the earth.
51:11 has stirred up the spirit of Media's *k*;
52: 7 the two walls which was near the *k* garden.
52:32 the other *k* who were with him in Babylon.
52:33 and ate at the *k* table as long as he lived.
Lam 4:12 The *k* of the earth did not believe,
Bar 1: 4 the nobles, the *k*' sons,
1:16 our *k* and rulers and priests and prophets,
2: 1 governed Israel, against our *k* and princes,
2:19 the just deeds of our fathers and our *k*
2:24 to have the bones of our *k* and the bones
6:50 *k* it will be clear that they are not gods,
6:65 *K* they neither curse nor bless.
Ez 26: 7 the king of Babylon, the king of *k*,
27:33 you enriched the *k* of the earth.
27:35 are aghast over you, Their *k* are terrified,
28:17 I made you a spectacle in the sight of *k*.
32:10 and their *k* shall shudder over you in
32:29 There are Edom, her *k*,
43: 7 Never again shall they and their *k* profane
43: 7 the corpses of their *k* [their high places].
43: 9 harlotry and the corpses of their *k*,
Dn 1: 4 as could take their place in the *k* palace;
1: 5 training they were to enter the *k* service.
1: 8 to defile himself with the *k* food or wine;
1:19 and so they entered the *k* service.
2:14 with Arioch, the captain of the *k* guard,
2:21 and seasons, makes *k* and unmakes them.
2:23 you, you have made known to us the *k* dream
2:27 In the *k* presence Daniel made this reply:
2:36 we shall also give in the *k* presence.
2:37 You, O king, are the king of *k*;
2:44 In the lifetime of those *k* the God of
2:47 and Lord of *k* and a revealer of mysteries;
2:49 Daniel himself remained at the *k* court.
3:22 other garments, for the *k* order was urgent.
3:46 Now the *k* men who had thrown them in
4:20 As for the *k* vision of a holy sentinel
4:28 While these words were still on the *k* lips,

KINGS—KING'S (cont.)
5: 5 on the plaster of the wall in the *k* palace.
5: 8 But though all the *k* wise men came in,
7:24 shall be ten *k* rising out of that kingdom;
7:24 before him, who shall lay low three *k*.
8:20 represents the *k* of the Medes and Persians.
8:27 I arose and took care of the *k* affairs.
9: 6 prophets, who spoke in your name to our *k*,
9: 8 O LORD, we are shamefaced, like our *k*,
10:13 there with the prince of the *k* of Persia,
11: 2 "Three *k* of Persia are yet to come;
11:27 The two *k*, resolved on evil, shall sit
14: 2 Daniel was the *k* favorite and was held in
14:14 sealed the closed door with the *k* ring,
Hos 1: 1 Jotham, Ahaz, Hezekiah, *k* of Judah,
7: 7 All their *k* have fallen;
8: 4 They made *k*, but not by my authority;
Am 7: 1 up (the late growth after the *k* mowing).
7:13 it is the *k* sanctuary and a royal temple."
Mi 1: 1 of Jotham, Ahaz, and Hezekiah, *k* of Judah:
1:14 is a deception to the *k* of Israel.
Hb 1:10 He scoffs at *k*,
Zep 1: 8 I will punish the princes, and the *k* sons,
Zec 14:10 the Tower of Hananel to the *k* wine presses,
Mt 10:18 be brought to trial before rulers and *k*,
17:25 Do the *k* of the world take tax or toll
Mk 6:25 to the *k* presence and made her request:
13: 9 will be arraigned before governors and *k*
Lk 10:24 many prophets and *k* wished to see what you
21:12 you to trial before *k* and governors,
22:25 "Earthly *k* lord it over their people.
Acts 4:26 The *k* of the earth were aligned,
9:15 and their *k* and to the people of Israel.
12:20 supplied with food from the *k* territory.
1Tm 2: 2 especially for *k* and those in authority,
6:15 the King of *k* and Lord of lords who alone
Heb 1: 9 the oil of gladness above your fellow *k*."
7: 1 from his defeat of the *k* and blessed him.
11:23 birth, thereby disregarding the *k* edict,
11:27 he left Egypt, not fearing the *k* wrath,
Rv 1: 5 from the dead and ruler of the *k* of earth.
6:15 The *k* of the earth, the nobles and those
10:11 many peoples and nations, languages and *k*."
16:12 to prepare the way for the *k* of the East.
16:14 They went out to assemble all the *k* of the
16:16 *k* in a place called in Hebrew "Armageddon."
17: 2 The *k* of the earth have committed
17: 9 They are also seven *k*:
17:12 ten *k* who have not yet been crowned;
17:14 he is the Lord of lords and the King of *k*;
17:18 has sovereignty over the *k* of the earth."
18: 3 The *k* of the earth committed fornication
18: 9 The *k* of the earth who committed
19:10 The King of *K*.
19:16 "King of *k* and Lord of lords."
19:18 You are to eat the flesh of *k*,
19:19 I saw the beast and the *k* of the earth,
21:24 *k* of the earth shall bring their treasures.

KINGSHIP (19)
1Sm 10:16 to him of what Samuel had said about the *k*.
13:13 now establish your *k* in Israel as lasting;
14:47 After taking over the *k* of Israel,
18: 8 All that remains for him is the *k*."
20:31 you cannot make good your claim to the *k*!
1Chr 22:10 the throne of his *k* over Israel forever.'
2Chr 21: 3 but the *k* he gave to Jehoram because he
22: 9 no one powerful enough to wield the *k*.
1Mc 13:32 killed him and assumed the *k* in his place,
Sir 47:21 into being, when in Ephraim *k* was usurped.
Dn 7:14 him, He received dominion, glory, and *k*;
7:14 taken away, his *k* shall not be destroyed.
7:18 ones of the Most High shall receive the *k*,
7:27 Then the *k* and dominion and majesty of all
Ob 1:21 of Esau, and the *k* shall be the LORD's.
Mt 6:33 Seek first his *k* over you,
16:28 they see the Son of Man come in his *k*."
Lk 12:31 Seek out instead his *k* over you,
1Thes 2:12 the God who calls you to his *k* and glory.

KINSFOLK (6)
Gn 12: 1 "Go forth from the land of your *k* and
Jgs 14: 3 wife among your *k* or among all our people,
Jb 19:14 My *k* and companions neglect me,
21: 8 before them their *k* and their offspring.
Acts 7: 3 said to him, Leave your country and your *k*,
7:14 father Jacob, inviting him and all his *k*—

KINSHIP (1)
Wis 8:17 That there is immortality in *k* with Wisdom,

KINSMAN (36)
Gn 14:13 Mamre the Amorite, a *k* of Eshcol and Aner;
14:16 back his *k* Lot and his possessions,
24:48 the daughter of my master's *k* for his son.
Lv 25:25 may go and buy back what his *k* has sold.
Nm 36: 2 of our *k* Zelophehad to his daughters.
Dt 15: 2 he must not press his neighbor, his *k*,
15: 3 the claim on your *k* for what is yours.
15: 9 help to your needy *k* and give him nothing;
15:11 to your poor and needy *k* in your country.
15:12 "If your *k*, a Hebrew man or woman,
17:15 you set over you as king must be your *k*;
19:18 witness and has accused his *k* falsely,
19:19 do to him as he planned to do to his *k*.
22: 1 see to it that it is returned to your *k*.
22: 2 If this *k* does not live near you,
22: 3 which your *k* loses and you happen to find;
25: 3 your *k* should be looked upon as disgraced
Jgs 9: 3 with Abimelech, thinking, "He is our *k*."
9:18 citizens of Shechem, because he is your *k*—
Ru 2: 1 Naomi had a prominent *k* named Boaz,
4: 3 of land that belonged to our *k* Elimelech,
Tb 1:14 a great sum of money with my *k* Gabael,
2: 3 to look for some poor *k* of ours
3:15 Nor does he have a close *k* or other
5: 6 I used to stay with our *k* Gabael,
5:14 So it turns out that you are a *k*,
5:17 for the journey, and set out with your *k*.
7: 1 Azariah, lead me straight to our *k* Raguel."
7: 2 young man looks just like my *k* Tobit!"
7: 4 She said, "Do you know our *k* Tobit?"
7: 7 to weep in the arms of his *k* Tobiah.
10:13 "My child and beloved *k*,
1Mc 11:31 we wrote to Lasthenes our *k* concerning you.
2Mc 11: 1 *k* of the king and head of the government,
11:35 Whatever Lysias, *k* of the king,
Rom 16:11 Greetings to my *k* Herodion and to the

KINSMAN'S (3)
Dt 22: 1 "You shall not see your *k* ox or sheep
22: 4 You shall not see your *k* ass or ox
Prv 27:10 if ruin befalls you, enter not a *k* house.

KINSMEN (113)
Gn 13: 8 your herdsmen and mine, for we are *k*.
23:11 in the presence of my *k* I make this gift.
25: 8 and he was taken to his *k*.
25:17 his last and died, he was taken to his *k*.
25:18 camp in opposition to his various *k*.
27:37 assigned to him all his *k* as his slaves;
31:23 Taking his *k* with him,
31:32 If, with my *k* looking on,
31:37 so, produce it here before your *k* and mine,
31:46 Jacob said to his *k*, "Gather some stones."
31:54 and invited his *k* to share in the meal.
35:29 died as an old man and was taken to his *k*.
Ex 2:11 his *k* and witnessed their forced labor,
2:11 striking a Hebrew, one of his own *k*.
4:18 "Let me go back, please, to my *k* in Egypt,
30:33 on a layman, shall be cut off from his *k*."
30:38 its fragrance, shall be cut off from his *k*."
32:27 from gate to gate, and slay your own *k*,
32:29 for you were against your own sons and *k*,
Lv 10: 4 remove your *k* from the sanctuary and carry
10: 6 Your *k*, the rest of the house of Israel,
17: 9 to the LORD, shall be cut off from his *k*.
19:16 go about spreading slander among your *k*;
25:46 harshly over any of the Israelites, your *k*.
Nm 16:10 He has allowed you and your *k*,
18: 2 you also your other *k* of the tribe of Levi,
18: 6 "Remember, it is I who have taken your *k*,
20: 3 perished with our *k* in the LORD's presence!
27: 4 have property among our father's *k*."
27: 7 property among their father's *k*,
32: 6 "Are your *k*, then, to engage in war,
Dt 1:16 time, 'Listen to complaints among your *k*,
1:28 Our *k* have made us fainthearted by
2: 4 to pass through the territory of your *k*,
2: 8 Elath, Ezion-geber, and Seir, where our *k*,
3:20 until the LORD has settled your *k* as well,
15: 7 If one of your *k* in any community is in
18:15 raise up for you from among your own *k*;
18:18 a prophet like you from among their *k*,
Jos 1:14 you must cross over armed ahead of your *k*
1:15 them until the LORD has settled your *k*,
17: 4 Moses to give us a heritage among our *k*."
17: 4 to each of them among their father's *k*.
22: 3 now you have not once abandoned your *k*,
22: 4 has settled your *k* as he promised them,
22: 7 along with their *k* west of the Jordan.)
22: 8 spoils of your enemies with your *k* there."
Jgs 9: 1 went to his mother's *k* in Shechem,
9:26 of Ebed, came over to Shechem with his *k*.
9:31 Ebed, and his *k* have come to Shechem
9:41 Zebul drove Gaal and his *k* from Shechem,
16:31 All his family and *k* went down and bore
18: 8 When the five returned to their *k* in Zorah
18:14 the land of Laish said to their *k*,
Ru 4:10 not perish among his *k* and fellow citizens.
2Kgs 10:13 on the way, he came across *k* of Ahaziah,
10:13 "We are *k* of Ahaziah," they replied.
1Chr 7:22 but after his *k* had come and comforted him,
9:25 Their *k* who had lived in their own
12: 2 They were some of Saul's *k*, from Benjamin.
23:22 the sons of Kish, their *k*,
Neh 4:17 Neither I, nor my *k*,
5: 5 *k* and our children are as good as theirs,
5: 7 are exacting interest from your own *k*!"
5:10 I myself, my *k*,
Tb 1: 3 performed many charitable works for my *k*
1: 5 All my *k*,
1:16 charitable works for my *k* and my people.
2: 2 from among our *k* exiled here in Nineveh.
2:10 and all my *k* were grieved at my condition.
4:12 own *k* and were blessed in their children.
4:13 Therefore, my son, love your *k*.
4:13 *k* the sons and daughters of your people,
5: 5 replied "I am an Israelite, one of your *k*.
5: 9 a man who is one of our own Israelite *k*!"
5:13 of Hananiah the elder, one of your own *k*."
5:14 your *k* are good men.
7:11 to seven men, all of whom were *k* of ours,
10: 6 is trustworthy, and is one of our own *k*.
14: 4 "As for our *k* who dwell in Israel,
Jdt 8:22 For the slaughter of our *k*,
8:24 brothers, let us set an example for our *k*.
1Mc 2:17 man in this city, supported by sons and *k*.
2:20 *k* will keep to the covenant of our fathers.
2:40 "If we all do as our *k* have done,"
2:41 all die as our *k* died in the hiding places."
5:13 All our *k* who were among the Tobiads have
5:16 *k* who were being attacked by enemies.
5:17 yourself, and go, rescue your *k* in Galilee;
5:32 men of his army, "Fight for our *k* today."
6:22 you fail to do justice and avenge our *k*?
9: 9 our lives now, and come back with our *k*,
9:10 our *k* and not leave a stain upon our glory!"
9:39 the bridegroom and his friends and *k*
9:66 He struck down Odomera and his *k* and the
10:89 such as is usually given to King's *K*;
14:30 high priest, he was gathered to his *k*.
2Mc 8: 1 the village secretly, summoned their *k*,
10:21 those men of having sold their *k* for money
11: 7 him in risking their lives to help their *k*.
12: 6 he marched against the murderers of his *k*.
12:39 them with their *k* in their ancestral tombs.
15:18 and children or their brothers and *k*;
Jer 31:34 their friends and *k* how to know the LORD.
34:17 by proclaiming your neighbors and *k* free.
Ez 11:15 Son of man, it is about your *k*,
Acts 3:22 a prophet like me from among your own *k*:
7:23 he was forty, he decided to visit his *k*,
7:25 He assumed that his *k* would understand
7:37 you from among your *k* a prophet like me.'
Rom 9: 3 sake of my brothers, my *k* the Israelites.
16: 7 and Junias, my *k* and fellow prisoners;
16:21 so, too, do my *k* Lucius,

KINSMEN'S (1)
Jb 22: 6 have unjustly kept your *k* goods in pawn,

KINSWOMAN (6)
Nm 25:18 regards Peor and as regards their *k* Cozbi,
Tb 6:18 heard Raphael say that she was his *k*,
7: 9 ask Raguel to let me marry my *k* Sarah."
7:11 *k*; from now on you are her love,
Jdt 9: 4 abhorrence of the defilement of their *k*,
Lk 1:36 your *k* has conceived a son in her old age;

KINSWOMEN (1)
Sg 6:12 heart had made me the blessed one of my *k*.

KIR (5)
2Kgs 16: 9 inhabitants to *K* and put Rezin to death.
Is 15: 1 waste in a night, *K* of Moab is destroyed.
22: 6 the horses, and *K* uncovers the shields.
Am 1: 5 the people of Aram shall be exiled to *K*,
9: 7 from Caphtor and the Arameans from *K*?

KIR-HARESETH (3)
2Kgs 3:25 *K* was left behind its stone walls
Is 16: 7 For the raisin cakes of *K* they sigh,
16:11 moans like a lyre, and my heart for *K*.

KIR-HERES (2)
Jer 48:31 all Moab I cry, over the men of *K* I moan.
48:36 men of *K* the wail of flutes is in my heart;

KIRIATH (1)
Jos 18:28 city (that is, Jerusalem), Gibeah and *K*;

KIRIATH-ARBA (9)
Gn 23: 2 She died in *K* (that is,
35:27 his father Isaac at Mamre, in *K* [that is,
Jos 14:15 Hebron was formerly called *K*,
15:13 namely, *K* (Arba was the father of Anak),
15:54 Bethtappuah, Aphekah, Humtah, *K* (that is,
20: 7 mountain region of Ephraim, and *K* (that is,
21:11 first, *K* (Arba was the father of Anak),
Jgs 1:10 in Hebron, which was formerly called *K*,
Neh 11:25 Judahites lived in *K* and its dependencies,

KIRIATH-BAAL (2)
Jos 15:60 *K* (that is,
18:14 Beth-horon till it reached *K*

KIRIATH-HUZOTH (1)
Nm 22:39 Balaam went with Balak, and they came to *K*.

KIRIATH-JEARIM (19)

Jos 9:17 of Gibeon, Chephirah, Beeroth and *K*,
15: 9 Ephron, and continued to Baalah, or *K*.
15:60 Kiriath-baal (that is, *K)* and Rabbah;
18:14 till it reached Kiriath-baal (that is, *K)*,
18:15 *K* and projected to the spring at Nephtoah.
Jgs 18:12 Eshtaol, and camped in Judah, up near *K*;
18:12 this day the place, which lies west of *K*,
1Sm 6:21 sent messengers to the inhabitants of *K*
7: 1 So the inhabitants of *K* came for the ark
7: 2 day the ark came to rest in *K* a long time
1Chr 2:50 Shobal, the father of *K*,
2:52 The sons of Shobal, the father of *K*,
2:53 half the Manahathites, and the clans of *K*:
13: 5 of Hamath, to bring the ark of God from *K*.
13: 6 Israel went up to Baalah, that is, to *K*,
2Chr 1: 4 David had brought up from *K* to Jerusalem,
Ezr 2:25 men of *K*, Chephirah, and Beeroth,
Neh 7:29 men of *K*, Chephirah, and Beeroth,
Jer 26:20 the LORD, Uriah, son of Shemaiah, from *K*;

KIRIATH-SANNAH (1)

Jos 15:49 Shamir, Jattir, Socoh, Dannah, *K* (that is,

KIRIATH-SEPHER (4)

Jos 15:15 of Debir, which was formerly called *K*.
15:16 to the one who attacks *K* and captures it."
Jgs 1:11 of Debir, which was formerly called *K*.
1:12 to the one who attacks *K* and captures it."

KIRIATHAIM (6)

Nm 32:37 Reubenites rebuilt Heshbon, Elealeh, *K*,
Jos 13:19 Jahaz, Kedemoth, Mephaath, *K*,
1Chr 6:61 lands, and *K* with its pasture lands.
Jer 48: 1 *K* is disgraced and captured,
48:23 on Dibon, Nebo, and Beth-diblathaim, on *K*,
Ez 25: 9 Beth-jesimoth, Baal-meon, and *K*.

KISH (22)

1Sm 9: 1 was a stalwart man from Benjamin named *K*,
9: 3 Now the asses of Saul's father, *K*,
9: 3 *K* said to his son Saul,
10:11 "What has happened to the son of *K*?
10:21 was chosen, and finally Saul, son of *K*,
14:51 *K*, Saul's father,
2Sm 21:14 *K* at Zela in the territory of Benjamin.
1Chr 8:30 his first-born son, Abdon, and Zur, *K*,
8:33 of Kish, and *K* became the father of Saul.
9:36 then came Zur, *K*, Baal, Ner, Nadab,
9:39 of Kish, and *K* became the father of Saul.
12: 1 under banishment from Saul, son of *K*;
23:21 Eleazar and *K*.
23:22 the sons of *K*,
24:29 and Jerahmeel, of the descendants of *K*.
26:28 whatever Samuel the seer, Saul, son of *K*,
2Chr 29:12 *K*, son of Abdi,
Est A: 1 son of Jair, son of Shimei, son of *K*,
2: 5 son of Jair, son of Shimei, son of *K*,
Acts 13:21 for a king, God gave them Saul son of *K*,

KISHI (1)

1Chr 6:29 Ethan, son of *K*,

KISHION (2)

Jos 19:20 Hapharaim, Shion, Anaharath, Rabbith, *K*,
21:28 four cities of *K* with its pasture lands,

KISHON (6)

Jgs 4: 7 of Jabin's army, out to you at the Wadi *K*,
4:13 from Harosheth-ha-goiim at the Wadi *K*
5:21 *K* swept them away; a wadi . . . , the *K*.
1Kgs 18:40 brook *K* and there he slit their throats.
Ps(s) 83:10 as with Sisera and Jabin at the torrent *K*,

KISS (16)

Gn 27:26 said to him, "Come closer, son, and *k* me."
31:28 *k* to my daughters and grandchildren!
2Sm 15: 5 would extend his hand, hold him, and *k* him.
20: 9 Joab held Amasa's beard as if to *k* him.
1Kgs 19:20 let me *k* my father and mother good-bye,
Jb 31:27 enticed to waft them a *k* with my hand;
Ps(s) 85:11 justice and peace shall *k*.
Prv 24:26 a *k* on the lips who makes an honest reply.
Sg 1: 2 Let him *k* me with kisses of his mouth!
8: 1 I would *k* you and none would taunt me.
Hos 13: 2 Men *k* calves!
Lk 7:45 You gave me no *k*,
22:48 would you betray the Son of Man with a *k*?"
Rom 16:16 Greet one another with a holy *k*.
1Cor 16:20 Greet one another with a holy *k*.
2Cor 13:12 Greet one another with a holy *k*.

KISSED (22)

Gn 27:27 As Jacob went up and *k* him
29:11 Then Jacob *k* Rachel and burst into tears.
32: 1 Laban *k* his grandchildren and his
33: 4 himself on his neck, *k* him as he wept.
45:15 Joseph then *k* all his brothers,
48:10 sons close to him, he *k* and embraced them.
50: 1 face and wept over him as he *k* him.
Ex 4:27 met at the mountain of God, Aaron *k* him.
18: 7 bowed down before him, and *k* him.
Ru 1: 9 She *k* them good-bye,
1:14 and Orpah *k* her mother-in-law good-bye,
1Sm 10: 1 poured oil on Saul's head; he also *k* him,
20:41 They *k* each other and wept aloud together.
2Sm 14:33 Then the king *k* him.
19:40 he *k* Barzillai and bade him Godspeed as he
1Kgs 19:18 those who have not knelt to Baal or *k* him."
Tb 5:17 journey, Tobiah *k* his father and mother.
7: 6 Raguel sprang up and *k* him,
10:12 he *k* his daughter Sarah and said to her:
10:13 *k* them both and sent them away in peace.
Est 4:16 Gladly would I have *k* the soles of his
Lk 15:20 threw his arms around his neck, and *k* him.

KISSES (3)

Prv 7:13 When she seizes him, she *k* him,
Sg 1: 2 Let him kiss me with *k* of his mouth!
Sir 29: 5 he *k* the lender's hand and speaks with

KISSING (4)

Gn 29:13 After embracing and *k* him,
Lk 7:38 *k* them and perfuming them with the oil.
7:45 has not ceased *k* my feet since I entered.
Acts 20:37 throwing their arms around him and *k* him,

KITCHENS (1)

Ez 46:24 "These are the *k* where the temple

KITE (1)

Lv 11:14 the eagle, the vulture, the osprey, the *k*,

KITES (2)

Dt 14:13 the osprey, the various *k* and falcons,
Is 34:15 There shall the *k* assemble,

KITRON (1)

Jgs 1:30 the inhabitants of *K* or those of Nahalol;

KITTIM (9)

Gn 10: 4 Elishah, Tarshish, the *K*, and the Rodanim.
Nm 24:24 deliver his people from the hands of the *K*?
1Chr 1: 7 of Javan were Elishah, Tarshish, the *K*,
1Mc 1: 1 Philip's son, who came from the land of *K*,
Is 23: 1 the land of the *K* the news reaches them.
23:12 Arise, pass over to the *K*,
Jer 2:10 Pass over to the coasts of the *K* and see,
Ez 27: 6 made of cypress wood from the coasts of *K*.
Dn 11:30 When ships of the *K* confront him,

KNAVE (1)

Sir 16:21 men, which only the foolish *k* will think.

KNEAD (3)

Gn 18: 6 *K* it and make rolls."
Jer 7:18 and the women *k* dough to make cakes for
Lk 13:21 It is like yeast which a woman took to *k*

KNEADED (5)

Lv 6:14 It shall be well *k* and fried in oil on a
7:12 of fine flour mixed with oil and well *k*.
1Sm 28:24 flour, she *k* it and baked unleavened bread.
Hos 7: 4 once the dough is *k* until it has risen.
Mt 13:33 took and *k* into three measures of flour.

KNEADING (5)

Ex 7:28 even into your ovens and your *k* bowls.
12:34 in their *k* bowls wrapped in their cloaks
Dt 28: 5 be your grain bin and your *k* bowl!
28:17 "Cursed be your grain bin and your *k* bowl!
2Sm 13: 8 Taking dough and *k* it,

KNEE (5)

Is 45:23 To me every *k* shall bend;
Ez 21:12 daunted, and every *k* shall run with water.
Rom 11: 4 men who have not bowed the *k* to Baal."
14:11 every *k* shall bend before me and every
Phil 2:10 name every *k* must bend in the heavens,

KNEE-DEEP (1)

Ez 47: 4 me wade through the water, which was now *k*.

KNEEL (7)

Gn 24:11 the camels *k* by the well outside the city.
Est 3: 2 royal gate would *k* and bow down to Haman,
3: 2 however, would not *k* and bow down.
3: 5 Mordecai would not *k* and bow down to him,
Ps(s) 95: 6 let us *k* before the LORD who made us.
Dn 6:11 going home to *k* in prayer and give thanks
Eph 3:14 That is why I *k* before the Father from

KNEELING (2)

1Kgs 8:54 where he had been *k* with his hands
Mk 1:40 with a request, *k* down as he addressed him:

KNEELS (1)

Jgs 7: 5 to the other, everyone who *k* down to drink."

KNEES (25)

Gn 30: 3 with her, and let her give birth on my *k*,
48:12 Joseph removed them from his father's *k*
50:23 son Machir were also born on Joseph's *k*.
Nm 22:31 he fell on his *k* and bowed to the ground.
Dt 28:35 you cannot be cured, on your *k* and legs,
1Kgs 18:42 the earth, and put his head between his *k*.
2Kgs 1:13 arrived, he fell to his *k* before Elijah,
Ezr 9: 5 with cloak and mantle torn I fell on my *k*,
Jb 3:12 Wherefore did the *k* receive me?
4: 4 you have strengthened his faltering *k*.
Ps(s) 109:24 My *k* totter from my fasting,
Sir 25:22 Feeble hands and quaking *k*—
Is 35: 3 are feeble, make firm the *k* that are weak,
Lam 1:14 neck, he has brought my strength to its *k*;
Ez 7:17 limp, and all their *k* shall run with water.
Dn 5: 6 his hip joints shook, and his *k* knocked.
10:10 touched me, raising me to my hands and *k*.
Na 2:11 melting hearts and trembling *k*,
Mt 18:29 to his *k* and began to plead with him,
27:29 mock him by dropping to their *k* before him,
Lk 5: 8 Simon Peter fell at the *k* of Jesus saying,
22:41 down on his *k* and prayed in these words:
Acts 7:60 to his *k* and cried out in a loud voice,
10:25 dropped to his *k* before him and bowed low.
Heb 12:12 your drooping hands and your weak *k*.

KNELT (11)

Gn 42: 6 When Joseph's brothers came and *k* down
Jgs 7: 6 of the soldiers *k* down to drink the water.
1Kgs 19:18 those who have not *k* to Baal or kissed him."
2Chr 6:13 Solomon *k* in the presence of the whole of
20:18 *k* down with his face to the ground,
29:29 were with him *k* and prostrated themselves.
Mt 17:14 a man came up to him and *k* before him.
Mk 10:17 running up, *k* down before him and asked,
Acts 9:40 then he *k* down and prayed.
20:36 Paul *k* down with them all and prayed.
21: 5 off, and we *k* down on the beach and prayed.

KNEW (96)

Gn 8:11 So Noah *k* that the waters had lessened on
38: 9 *k* that the descendants would not be
Ex 1: 8 Then a new king, who *k* nothing of Joseph,
2:25 He saw the Israelites and *k*. . . .
5:19 foremen *k* they were in a sorry plight,
Dt 34:10 like Moses, whom the LORD *k* face to face.
Jos 24:31 *k* all that the LORD had done for Israel.
1Sm 3:13 though he *k* his sons were blaspheming God,
20:39 *k* nothing; only Jonathan and David knew
22:17 They *k* he was a fugitive and yet failed to
22:21 "I *k* that day,
28:14 Saul *k* that it was Samuel,
2Sm 1:10 I *k* that he could not survive his wound.
5:12 And David *k* that the LORD had established
11:16 place where he *k* the defenders were strong.
1Chr 12:33 the times and who *k* what Israel had to do:
Neh 2:16 The magistrates *k* nothing of where I had
6:16 for they *k* that it was with our God's help
9:10 you *k* of their insolence toward them;
13:24 and none of them *k* how to speak Jewish;
Tb 1:19 When I found out that the king *k* all about
5:14 I *k* Hananiah and Nathaniah,
1Mc 3:42 they *k* of the orders which the king had
6: 9 with sorrow, for he *k* he was going to die.
13:17 Although Simon *k* that they were speaking
16:22 to death, for he *k* what they meant to do.
2Mc 15:21 for he *k* that it is not through arms but
Jb 28:27 it its setting, *k* it through and through.
Ps(s) 35:11 things I *k* not of,
139:14 My soul also you *k* full well;
Eccl 2:14 Yet I *k* that one lot befalls both of them.
Sg 6:12 Before I *k* it, my heart had made me
Wis 2:22 And they *k* not the hidden counsels of God;
3:13 *k* not transgression of the marriage bed;
5: 7 deserts, but the way of the Lord we *k* not.
9:17 Or who ever *k* your counsel,
10: 5 in universal wickedness, *k* the just man,
15:11 Because he *k* not the one who fashioned him,
19: 1 he *k* beforehand what they were yet to do:
Is 45: 4 giving you a title, though you *k* me not.
48: 6 to you, hidden events of which you *k* not.
48: 8 You neither heard nor *k*,
55: 5 nation you *k* not, and nations that *k* you
Jer 1: 5 Before I formed you in the womb I *k* you,
2: 8 Those who dealt with the law *k* me not;
11:18 I *k* it because the LORD informed me;
19: 4 which neither they nor their fathers *k*;
32: 8 I *k* this was what the LORD meant,
41: 4 murder of Gedaliah, before anyone *k* of it,
44: 3 neither they, nor you, nor your fathers *k*.
44:15 From all the men who *k* that their wives
48:17 his neighbors, all you who *k* him well!
50:24 were caught, O Babylon, before you *k* it!
Ez 28:19 peoples, all who *k* you stand aghast at you;
Dn 5:12 *k* and understood how to interpret dreams,

KNEW (cont.)
5:22 humbled your heart, though you *k* all this;
Jon 1:10 *k* that he was fleeing from the LORD,
4: 2 *k* that you are a gracious and merciful God,
Mt 7:23 declare to them solemnly, 'I never *k* you.
16: 8 Jesus *k* their thoughts and said,
24:43 if the owner of the house *k* when the thief
25:24 lord,' he said, 'I *k* you were a hard man.
27:18 *k*, of course, that it was out of jealousy
Mk 1:34 the demons to speak, because they *k* him.
5:42 this the family's astonishment *k* no bounds.
9: 6 He hardly *k* what to say,
12:12 (They *k* well enough that he meant the
12:17 Their amazement at him *k* no bounds.
Lk 4:41 because they *k* that he was the Messiah.
5:22 *k* their reasoning and answered them by
6: 8 He *k* their thoughts,
9:47 Jesus, who *k* their thoughts,
11:17 Because he *k* their thoughts,
12:39 if the head of the house *k* when the thief
12:47 The slave who *k* his master's wishes but
19:22 You *k* I was a hard man,
Jn 2: 9 only the waiters *k*,
2:24 himself to them because he *k* them all.
5: 6 Jesus, who *k* he had been sick a long time,
6: 6 (He *k* well what he intended to do but he
6:64 (Jesus *k* from the start,
8:19 If you *k* me, you would know my Father
11:57 anyone who *k* where he was should report it,
13:11 washed clean," was that he *k* his betrayer.)
14: 7 If you really *k* me,
16: 3 because they *k* neither the Father nor me.
21: 4 none of the disciples *k* it was Jesus.
21:12 for they *k* it was the Lord.
Acts 2:30 He was a prophet and *k* that God had sworn
7:18 came to power in Egypt, who *k* not Joseph.
16: 3 for they all *k* that it was only his father
18:25 although he *k* only of John's baptism.
1Cor 2: 8 of the rulers of this age *k* the mystery;
1Pt 1:12 *k* by revelation that they were providing,

KNIFE (5)
Gn 22: 6 he himself carried the fire and the *k*.
22:10 out and took the *k* to slaughter his son.
Jgs 19:29 he took a *k* to the body of his concubine,
Prv 23: 2 And put a *k* to your throat if you have a
Jer 36:23 would cut off the piece with a scribe's *k*

KNIGHTS (2)
Ez 23: 6 attractive young men, *k* mounted on horses.
23:12 impeccably clothed, *k* mounted on horses,

KNIT (2)
Jb 10:11 me, with bones and sinews *k* me together.
Ps(s) 139:13 you *k* me in my mother's womb.

KNITTED (9)
Lv 13:48 or on woven or *k* material of linen or wool,
13:49 or hide, or on the woven or *k* material,
13:51 the garment, or on the woven or *k* material,
13:52 the woven or *k* material of wool or linen,
13:53 the garment, or on the woven or *k* material,
13:56 or the leather, or the woven or *k* material.
13:57 the garment, or on the woven or *k* material,
13:58 the garment, or the woven or *k* material,
13:59 wool or linen, or on woven or *k* material,

KNIVES (4)
Gn 49: 5 indeed, weapons of violence are their *k*.
Jos 5: 2 "Make flint *k* and circumcise the
5: 3 So Joshua made flint *k* and circumcised the
Prv 30:14 incisors are swords, whose teeth are *k*,

KNOB (6)
Ex 25:33 blossoms, each with its *k* and petals;
25:33 blossoms, each with its *k* and petals;
25:35 including a *k* below each of the three
37:19 blossoms, each with its *k* and petals;
37:19 blossoms, each with its *k* and petals;
37:21 including a *k* below each of the three

KNOBS (6)
Ex 25:31 *k* and petals springing directly from it.
25:34 almond blossoms, with their *k* and petals,
25:36 Their *k* and branches shall so spring from
37:17 *k* and petals springing directly from it.
37:20 almond blossoms, with their *k* and petals,
37:22 The *k* and branches sprang so directly from

KNOCK (4)
Dt 24:20 you *k* down the fruit of your olive trees,
Sir 13: 2 When they *k* together,
Mt 7: 7 *K*, and it will be opened to you.
Lk 11: 9 *k* and it shall be opened to you.'

KNOCKED (4)
Jdt 14:14 went in, and *k* at the entry of the tent,
Dn 5: 6 him, his hip joints shook, and his knees *k*.
Jn 2:15 and *k* over the money-changers' tables,
Acts 12:13 Peter *k* at the door and a maid named Rhoda

KNOCKING (4)
Sg 5: 2 I heard my lover *k*:
Lk 13:25 door and you stand outside *k* and saying,
Acts 12:16 Through all this, Peter kept on *k*.
Rv 3:20 " 'Here I stand, *k* at the door.

KNOCKS (4)
Ex 21:27 *k* out a tooth of his male or female slave,
Mt 7: 8 The one who *k*, enters.
Lk 11:10 whoever *k*,
12:36 a wedding, so that when he arrives and *k*,

KNOLL (1)
Jos 13:19 Zereth-shahar on the *k* within the valley,

KNOTS (1)
Wis 13:13 remnants, crooked wood grown full of *k*,

KNOW (844)
Gn 3: 5 gods who *k* what is good and what is bad."
4: 9 He answered, "I do not *k*.
12:11 "I *k* well how beautiful a woman you are.
15: 8 "How am I to *k* that I shall possess it?"
15:13 *K* for certain that your descendants shall
19: 8 for you *k* they have come under the shelter
20: 6 "Yes, I *k* you did it in good faith.
22:12 I *k* now how devoted you are to God,
24:14 In this way I shall *k* that you have dealt
24:49 let me *k*; but if not, let me know that, too.
28:15 *K* that I am with you;
28:16 is in this spot, although I did not *k* it!"
29: 5 Then he asked them, "Do you *k* Laban,
30:26 You *k* very well the service that I have
30:29 "You *k* what work I did for you and how
31: 6 You well *k* what effort I put into serving
32:30 "Why should you want to *k* my name?"
37:13 said to Joseph, "Your brothers, you *k*,
42:23 They did not *k*,
42:33 is how I shall *k* if you are honest men:
42:34 I *k* that you are honest men and not spies,
43: 7 How could we *k* that he would say,
43:22 not *k* who put the first money in our bags."
44:27 servant our father said to us, 'As you *k*,
47: 5 and if you *k* any of them to be qualified,
48:19 "I *k* it, son," he said, "I know.
Ex 3: 7 so I *k* well what they are suffering.
3:19 "Yet I *k* that the king of Egypt will not
4:14 I *k* that he is an eloquent speaker.
5: 2 I do not *k* the LORD:
6: 7 You will *k* that I, the LORD, am your God
7:17 This is how you shall *k* that I am the LORD.
8:18 that you may *k* that I am the LORD in the
9:14 that you may *k* that there is none like me
9:30 But you and your servants, I *k*,
10: 2 them, so that you may *k* that I am the LORD.
10:26 but we ourselves shall not *k* which ones we
11: 7 so that you may *k* how the LORD
14: 4 the Egyptians will *k* that I am the LORD."
14:18 The Egyptians shall *k* that I am the LORD,
16: 6 "At evening you will *k* that it was the
16:12 fill of bread, so that you may *k* that I,
16:15 for they did not *k* what it was.
18:11 Now I *k* that the LORD is a deity great
23: 9 you well *k* how it feels to be an alien,
29:46 They shall *k* that I, the LORD, am their God
32: 1 we do not *k* what has happened to him."
32:22 You *k* well enough how prone the people are
32:23 we do not *k* what has happened to him.'
33:12 not let me *k* whom you will send with me.
33:13 with you, do let me *k* your ways so that,
34:29 he did not *k* that the skin of his face had
Nm 10:31 you *k* where we can camp in the desert,
11:16 men you *k* for true elders and authorities
16:28 "This is how you shall *k* that it was the
16:30 will *k* that these men have defied the LORD.
20:14 You *k* of all the hardships that have
22: 6 For I *k* that whoever you bless is blessed
22:34 Yet I did not *k* that you stood against me
Dt 1:39 who as yet do not *k* good from bad
3:19 of which I *k* you have a large number,
4:35 *k* the LORD is God and there is no other.
4:39 This is why you must now *k*,
7:15 malignant diseases that you *k* from Egypt,
9: 2 *k* of them and have heard it said of them,
18:22 *k* that, even though a prophet speaks
20:20 you *k* are not fruit trees you may destroy,
22: 2 near you, or you do not *k* who he may be,
28:33 A people whom you do not *k* will consume
29: 5 Thus you should *k* that I,
29:15 "You *k* in what surroundings we lived in
29:25 gods whom they did not *k* and whom he had
31:13 Their children also, who do not *k* it yet,
31:21 For I *k* what they are inclined to do even
31:27 For I already *k* how rebellious and
31:29 For I *k* that after my death you are sure
Jos 2: 4 me, but I did not *k* where they came from.
2: 5 they left, and I do not *k* where they went.
2: 9 "I *k* that the LORD has given you the land,
3: 4 follow it, that you may *k* the way to take,
3: 7 all Israel, that they may *k* I am with you,
3:10 *k* that there is a living God in your midst,
14: 6 *k* what the LORD said to the man of God,
22:22 the God of gods, knows and Israel shall *k*.
22:31 "Now we *k* that the LORD is with us.
23:13 with them, *k* for certain that the LORD,
Jgs 2:10 generation arose that did not *k* the LORD,
6:37 *k* that you will save Israel through me,
14: 4 Now his father and mother did not *k* that
15:11 not *k* that the Philistines are our rulers?
17:13 "Now I *k* that the LORD will prosper me,
18: 5 that we may *k* whether the undertaking we
18:14 *k* that in these houses there are an ephod,
Ru 2:11 to a people whom you did not *k* previously.
3:11 my townspeople *k* you for a worthy woman.
1Sm 3:20 *k* that Samuel was an accredited prophet
6: 9 not, we will *k* it was not he who struck us,
14: 3 did the soldiers *k* that Jonathan had gone.
17:28 I *k* your arrogance and your evil intent.
19: 3 If I learn anything, I will let you *k*."
20: 3 must not *k* of this lest he be grieved.'
20: 9 upon you, I will certainly let you *k*."
20:30 of a rebellious woman, do I not *k* that,
21: 3 let no one *k* anything about the business
24:21 since I *k* that you shall surely be king
25:11 them to men who come from I *k* not where?"
29: 9 "You *k*," Achish answered David,
2Sm 1: 5 "How do you *k* that Saul and his son
2:26 *k* that afterward there will be bitterness?
3:37 *k* that the king had no part in the killing
7:20 You *k* your servant, Lord GOD!
11:20 Did you not *k* that they would shoot from
14:22 day I *k* that I am in good favor with you,
17: 8 "You *k* that your father and his men are
18:29 servant on, but I do not *k* what it was."
24: 2 the people, that I may *k* their number."
1Kgs 1:18 king, and you, my lord king, do not *k* it.
2: 5 You yourself *k* what Joab,
2: 9 You are a prudent man and will *k* how to
2:15 "You *k* that the kingdom was mine,
2:44 "You *k* in your heart the evil that you
3:11 so that you may *k* what is right
5:17 "You *k* that my father David,
5:20 since you *k* that there is no one among us
8:39 You who alone *k* the hearts of all men,
8:43 the peoples of the earth may *k* your name,
8:60 *k* the LORD is God and there is no other.
17:24 indeed I *k* that you you are a man of God,"
18:12 will carry you to some place I do not *k*,
18:37 Answer me, that this people may *k* that you,
20:13 you today, you will *k* that I am the LORD.
20:28 large army, that you may *k* I am the LORD.' "
22: 3 "Do you not *k* that Ramoth-gilead is ours
2Kgs 2: 3 "Do you *k* that the LORD will take your
2: 3 "Yes, I *k* it," he replied.
2: 5 "Do you *k* that the LORD will take your
2: 5 "Yes, I *k* it," he replied.
4: 1 You *k* that he was a God-fearing man,
4: 9 "I *k* that he is a holy man of God.
4:27 LORD hid it from me and did not let me *k*."
5:15 I *k* that there is no God in all the earth,
6:32 "Do you *k* that this son of a murderer is
8:12 "Because I *k* the evil that you will
9:11 You *k* that kind of man and his talk,
10:10 *K* that not a single word which the LORD
17:26 not *k* how to worship the God of the land,
17:26 not *k* how to worship the God of the land."
19:19 kingdoms of the earth may *k* that you alone,
19:27 I *k* whether you come or go,
1Chr 17:18 You *k* your servant.
21: 2 back to me that I may *k* their number."
28: 9 *k* the God of your father and serve him
29:17 I *k*, O my God, that you put hearts
2Chr 2: 6 fabrics, and who *k* how to do engraved work,
2: 7 *k* how to cut the wood of the Lebanon.
6:30 conduct, for you alone *k* the hearts of men.
6:33 the peoples of the earth may *k* your name,
12: 8 that they may *k* what it is to serve me and
13: 5 Do you not *k* that the LORD,
25:16 *k*, however," he said, "that God has let
29: 9 For our fathers, as you *k*,
32:13 Do you not *k* what my fathers and I have
32:31 that he might *k* all that was in his heart.
Ezr 7:25 all, that is, who *k* the laws of your God.
7:25 Instruct those who do not *k* these laws.
Tb 2:10 I did not *k* there were birds perched on
3:14 "You *k*, O Master, that I am innocent
4: 2 let him *k* about this money before I die?"
5: 2 since he does not know me nor do I *k* him?
5: 2 I do not even *k* which roads to take for
5: 4 he did not *k* that this was an angel of God.
5: 5 Tobiah said, "Do you *k* the way to Media?"
5: 6 know the place well and I *k* all the routes.
5:10 I can go with him, for I *k* all the routes.
5:10 so I *k* every road well."
5:12 "I wish to *k* truthfully whose son you are,
6:13 I *k* that Raguel cannot keep her from you
6:16 I *k* that tonight you shall have her for
7: 4 She said, "Do you *k* our kinsman Tobit?"
8: 7 you *k* that I take this wife of mine not
9: 4 you *k* that my father is counting the days.
10: 7 for I *k* that my father and mother do not

11: 2 "You *k* how we left your father.
14: 4 For I *k* and believe that whatever God has
Jdt 9: 7 They do not *k* that " 'You, the Lord
9:14 all the tribes *k* clearly that you are the god
11:18 Then I will come and let you *k*,
Est 4:11 king and the people of his provinces *k*
C: 5 You *k* all things.
C: 5 *k*, O Lord, that it was not out of insolence
C:25 "You *k* all things.
C:26 You *k* that I hate the glory of the pagans,
C:27 You *k* that I am under constraint,
1Mc 2:65 your brother Simeon who I *k* is a wise man;
3:52 You *k* what they plot against us.
4:11 All the Gentiles shall *k* that there is One
4:33 all who *k* your name may hymn your praise."
6:13 I *k* that this is why these evils have
7:42 and let the rest *k* that Nicanor spoke
12:29 did not *k* what had happened until morning.
13: 3 "You *k* what I,
2Mc 1:27 let the Gentiles *k* that you are our God.
7:22 *k* how you came into existence in my womb;
7:28 then you will *k* that God did not make them
9:23 Nevertheless, I *k* that my father,
9:24 people throughout the realm would *k*
14:32 they did not *k* where the wanted man was,
Jb 5:24 And you shall *k* that your tent is secure;
5:25 You shall *k* that your descendants are many,
5:27 This we have heard, and you should *k*.
7:10 his place shall *k* him no more.
9: 2 I *k* well that it is so;
9: 5 He removes the mountains before they *k* it;
9:21 Though I am innocent, I myself cannot *k* it;
9:28 I *k* that you will not hold me innocent.
10: 2 Let me *k* why you oppose me.
10: 7 Even though you *k* that I am not wicked,
10:13 I *k* that they are your purpose:
11: 8 what can you *k*?
12: 3 for who does not *k* such things as these?
12: 9 not *k* that the hand of God has done this?
13: 2 What you know, I also *k*;
13:18 my case, I *k* that I am in the right.
14: 5 You *k* the number of his months;
14:21 are in disgrace, he does not *k* about them.
15: 9 What do you *k* that we do not know?
19: 6 *K* then that God has dealt unfairly with me,
19:25 as for me, I *k* that my Vindicator lives,
19:29 that you may *k* that there is a judgment.
20: 4 Do you not *k* this from olden time,
21:27 Behold, I *k* your thoughts,
22:13 Yet you say, "What does God *k*?
23: 2 Though I *k* my complaint is bitter,
24:13 they *k* not its ways;
24:16 none of them *k* the light,
30:23 Indeed I *k* you will turn me back in death
31: 6 thus will he *k* my innocence!
32:22 For I *k* nought of flattery;
34:33 speak, therefore, what you *k*.
37:15 you *k* how God lays his commands upon them,
37:16 Do you *k* how the clouds are banked,
38: 5 Who determined its size; do you *k*?
38:18 Tell me, if you *k* all:
38:21 You *k*, because you were born before
38:33 Do you *k* the ordinances of the heavens;
39: 1 *k* about the birth of the mountain goats,
42: 2 I *k* that you can do all things,
42: 3 too wonderful for me, which I cannot *k*.
Ps(s) 4: 4 *K* that the LORD does wonders for his
9:21 let the nations *k* that they are but men.
20: 7 Now I *k* that the LORD has given victory
39: 5 Let me *k*, O LORD, my end
40:10 not restrain my lips, as you, O LORD, *k*.
41:12 That you love me I *k* by this,
50:11 I *k* all the birds of the air,
56:10 now I *k* that God is with me.
59:14 men may *k* that God is the ruler of Jacob,
69: 6 O God, you *k* my folly,
69:20 You *k* my reproach,
71:15 salvation, though I *k* not their extent.
73:11 And they say, "How does God *k*?"
78: 3 What we have heard and *k*,
78: 6 So that the generation to come might *k*,
82: 5 "They *k* not, neither do they understand;
87: 4 and Babylon among those that *k* the LORD;
89:16 Happy the people who *k* the joyful shout;
95:10 of erring heart, and they *k* not my ways.
100: 3 *K* that the LORD is God;
101: 4 evil I will not *k*.
109:27 And let them *k* that this is your hand;
119:75 I *k*, O LORD, that your ordinances
119:125 me discernment that I may *k* your decrees.
119:152 Of old I *k* from your decrees,
135: 5 For I *k* that the LORD is great;
139: 1 I O LORD, you have probed me and you *k* me;
139: 2 you *k* when I sit and when I stand;
139: 4 behold, O LORD, you *k* the whole of it.
139:23 *k* my heart; try me, and *k* my thoughts;
140:13 I *k* that the LORD renders justice to the
142: 4 spirit is faint within me, you *k* my path.
Prv 4:19 they *k* not on what they stumble.
5: 6 her paths will ramble, you *k* not where.
10:32 The lips of the just *k* how to please,
24:12 If you say, "I *k* not this man!"
24:14 Such, you must *k*,
27: 1 for you *k* not what any day may bring forth.
30: 4 name, what is his son's name, if you *k* it?"
Eccl 1:17 applied my mind to *k* wisdom and knowledge,
4:17 for they *k* not how to keep from doing evil.
7:22 for you *k* in your heart that you have many
8:12 Though indeed I *k* that it shall be well
8:16 When I applied my heart to *k* wisdom and to
9: 5 *k* that they are to die, but the dead no longer *k*
11: 2 you *k* not what misfortune may come upon
11: 5 Just as you *k* not how the breath of life
11: 5 So you *k* not the work of God which he is
11: 6 *k* not which of the two will be successful,
Sg 1: 8 If you do not *k*, O most beautiful among
Wis 7:17 that I might *k* the organization of the
8:21 too, was prudence, to *k* whose is the gift
9:10 me, that I may *k* what is your pleasure.
10:12 *k* that devotion to God is mightier than all
12:17 and in those who *k* you,
12:27 God whom before they had refused to *k*;
13: 3 let them *k* how far more excellent is the
15: 2 if we sin we are yours, and *k* your might;
15: 3 to *k* you well is complete justice, and to *k*
16:16 For the wicked who refused to *k* you were
16:18 *k* they were struck by the judgment of God;
16:22 that they might *k* that their enemies'
16:28 So that men might *k* that one must give you
Sir 8:18 for you *k* not what it will engender.
9:11 for you *k* not what disaster awaits him.
9:13 *K* that you are stepping among snares and
11:19 He does not *k* how long it will be till he
12: 1 you do good, *k* for whom you are doing it,
12: 8 In our prosperity we cannot *k* our friends;
16:19 all in secret I am disloyal, who is to *k*?
23:27 Thus all who dwell on the earth shall *k*,
36: 4 Thus they will know, as we *k*,
43: 7 which we *k* the feast days and fixed dates,
46: 6 That all the doomed nations might *k* that
46:10 *k* how good it is to be a devoted follower
51:19 her gate and I came to *k* her secrets.
Is 1: 3 But Israel does not *k*,
5: 5 let you *k* what I mean to do to my vineyard:
5:19 let it come to pass, that we may *k* it!"
6: 9 Look intently, but you shall *k* nothing!
8: 9 *K*, O peoples, and be appalled!
9: 8 falls upon Israel, And all the people *k* it,
19:21 the Egyptians shall *k* the LORD in that day:
37:20 the kingdoms of the earth may *k* that you,
37:28 I *k* whether you come or go,
40:21 Do you not *k*?
40:28 Do you not *k* or have you not heard?
41:20 tree and the pine, That all may see and *k*,
41:22 we may reflect on them And *k* their outcome;
41:23 afterward, that we may *k* that you are gods!
41:26 this from the beginning, that we might *k*;
43:10 my servants whom I have chosen To *k* and
44: 9 shame, they neither see nor *k* anything;
45: 3 away, That you may *k* that I am the LORD,
45: 5 It is I who arm you, though you *k* me not,
45: 6 men may *k* that there is none besides me.
47:11 come evil you will not *k* how to predict:
48: 4 Because I *k* that you are stubborn and that
48: 8 Yes, I *k* you are utterly treacherous,
49:23 Then you shall *k* that I am the LORD,
49:26 All mankind shall *k* that I,
50: 4 That I might *k* how to speak to the weary a
51: 7 Hear me, you who *k* justice,
52: 6 on that day my people shall *k* my renown,
56:11 dogs, they *k* not when they have enough.
56:11 are the shepherds who *k* no discretion;
58: 2 me day after day, and desire to *k* my ways,
59: 8 The way of peace they *k* not,
59:12 are present to us, and our crimes we *k*:
60:16 You shall *k* that I, the LORD, am your
63:16 Were Abraham not to *k* us,
Jer 1: 6 I said, "I *k* not how to speak;
2:19 *K* then, and see, how evil and bitter is
3:13 Only *k* your guilt:
4:22 Fools my people are, they *k* me not;
4:22 are wise in evil, but *k* not how to do good.
5: 4 For they *k* not the way of the LORD,
5: 5 For they *k* the way of the LORD,
5:15 nation, a people whose language you *k* not,
6:15 at all ashamed, they *k* not how to blush.
6:18 Therefore hear, O nations, and *k*,
7: 9 Baal, go after strange gods that you *k* not,
8: 7 people do not *k* the ordinance of the LORD.
8:12 at all ashamed, they *k* not how to blush.
9: 2 go from evil to evil, but me they *k* not,
10:23 You *k*, O LORD, that man is not master
10:25 your wrath on the nations that *k* you not,
12: 3 You, O Lord, *k* me,
13:12 "Do we not *k* that every wineflask is
14:18 and the priest forage in a land they *k* not.
15:15 You *k* I have. Remember me, LORD, visit me,
15:15 *k* that for you I have borne insult.
16:21 they shall *k* that my name is LORD.
17: 4 to your enemies in a land that you *k* not:
17:16 You *k* what passed my lips;
18:23 you, O LORD, *k* all their plans to slay me.
22:28 out, why thrown into a land they *k* not?
29:11 I *k* well the plans I have in mind for you,
29:23 I *k*, I am witness, says the LORD.
31:34 friends and kinsmen how to *k* the LORD.
31:34 All, from least to greatest, shall *k* me,
36:19 let no one *k* where you are."
38:24 "Let no one *k* about this conversation,
40:14 asked him whether he did not *k* that Baalis,
40:15 no one will *k* it.
44:28 settle in Egypt shall *k* whose word stands,
44:29 That you may *k* how surely my threats of
48:30 I *k*, says the LORD, his arrogance
Bar 2:15 whole earth may *k* that you are the Lord,
2:30 For I *k* they will not heed me,
2:31 they shall *k* that I,
3: 9 listen and *k* prudence!
3:14 you may *k* also where are length of days,
6:22 *K*, therefore, that they are not gods
6:49 then can one not *k* that these are no-gods,
6:51 Who does not *k* that they are not gods?
6:64 *K*, therefore, that they are not gods
Ez 2: 5 shall *k* that a prophet has been among them.
5:13 they shall *k* that I,
6: 7 midst, and you shall *k* that I am the LORD.
6:10 shall *k* that it was not in vain that I,
6:13 Then shall they *k* that I am the LORD,
6:14 thus shall they *k* that I am the LORD.
7: 4 then shall you *k* that I am the LORD.
7: 9 then shall you *k* that it is I,
7:27 thus they shall *k* that I am the LORD.
11: 5 Israel, and what you are plotting I well *k*.
11:10 thus you shall *k* that I am the LORD.
11:12 you, and you shall *k* that I am the LORD,
12:15 Then shall they *k* that I am the LORD,
12:16 thus they shall *k* that I am the LORD.
12:20 thus you shall *k* that I am the LORD.
13: 9 thus you shall *k* that I am the LORD.
13:14 thus you shall *k* that I am the LORD.
13:21 Thus you shall *k* that I am the LORD.
13:23 Thus you shall *k* that I am the LORD.
14: 8 Thus you shall *k* that I am the LORD.
14:23 for you shall then *k* that it was not
15: 7 Thus you shall *k* that I am the LORD,
16:62 you, that you may *k* that I am the LORD,
17:21 Thus you shall *k* that I,
17:24 all the trees of the field shall *k* that I,
20:38 Thus you shall *k* that I am the LORD.
20:42 Thus you shall *k* that I am the LORD,
20:44 And you shall *k* that I am the LORD when I
21:10 to north, and everyone shall *k* that I,
22:16 thus you shall *k* that I am the LORD.
22:22 Thus you shall *k* that I,
23:49 Thus you shall *k* that I am the LORD.
24:24 Thus you shall *k* that I am the LORD.
24:27 them, and they shall *k* that I am the LORD.
25: 5 Thus you shall *k* that I am the LORD.
25: 7 and thus you shall *k* that I am the LORD.
25:11 Moab, that they may *k* that I am the LORD.
25:14 thus they shall *k* my vengeance,
25:17 Thus they shall *k* that I am the LORD,
26: 6 thus they shall *k* that I am the LORD.
28:22 Then they shall *k* that I am the LORD,
28:23 Thus they shall *k* that I am the LORD,
28:24 thus they shall *k* that I am the LORD.
28:26 thus they shall *k* that I,
29: 6 dwell in Egypt may *k* that I am the LORD.
29: 9 thus they shall *k* that I am the LORD.
29:16 Thus they shall *k* that I am the LORD.
29:21 thus they shall *k* that I am the LORD.
30: 8 Then they shall *k* that I am the LORD,
30:19 Egypt, that they may *k* that I am the LORD.
30:25 Then they shall *k* that I am the LORD,
30:26 Thus they shall *k* that I am the LORD.
32: 9 the nations, to lands which you do not *k*.
32:15 there, they shall *k* that I am the LORD.
33:29 Thus they shall *k* that I am the LORD,
33:33 *k* that there was a prophet among them.
34:27 Thus they shall *k* that I am the LORD when
34:30 Thus they shall *k* that I,
35: 4 thus you shall *k* that I am the LORD.
35: 9 thus you shall *k* that I am the LORD.
35:12 you, and you shall *k* that I am the LORD.
35:15 Thus they shall *k* that I am the LORD.
36:11 thus you shall *k* that I am the LORD.
36:23 the nations shall *k* that I am the LORD,
36:36 nations that remain shall *k* that I,
36:38 thus they shall *k* that I am the LORD.
37: 3 GOD," I answered, "you alone *k* that."
37: 6 may come to life and *k* that I am the LORD.
37:13 Then you shall *k* that I am the LORD,
37:14 thus you shall *k* that I am the LORD.
37:28 Thus the nations shall *k* that it is I,
38:16 my land, that the nations may *k* of me,
38:23 thus they shall *k* that I am the LORD.
39: 6 thus they shall *k* that I am the LORD.
39: 7 the nations shall *k* that I am the LORD,
39:22 house of Israel shall *k* that I am the LORD,
39:23 The nations shall *k* that because of its
39:28 Thus they shall *k* that I,
Dn 2: 3 my spirit no rest until I *k* what it means."
2: 8 "I *k* for certain that you are bargaining
2: 8 for time, since you *k* what I have decided.
3:18 But even if he will not, *k*,
3:45 Let them *k* that you alone are the Lord God,
4: 6 I *k* that the spirit of the holy God is in
4:14 That all who live may *k* that the Most High
4:22 until you *k* that the Most High rules over

KNOW (cont.)

9:25 *K* and understand this:
10:20 "Do you *k*," he asked, "why I have come
13:42 you *k* what is hidden and are aware of all
13:43 you *k* that they have testified falsely
14:35 I have never seen, and I do not *k* the den!"
Hos 2:22 you in fidelity, and you shall *k* the LORD.
5: 3 I *k* Ephraim,
6: 3 Let us know, let us strive to *k* the LORD;
8: 2 they cry out, "O, God of Israel, we *k* you!"
9: 7 Let Israel *k* it!
11: 4 they did not *k* that I was their healer.
13: 4 You *k* no God besides me,
14:10 let him who is prudent *k* them.
Jl 2:27 shall *k* that I am in the midst of Israel;
4:17 Then shall you *k* that I,
Am 3:10 For they *k* not how to do what is right,
5:12 Yes, I *k* how many are your crimes,
Jon 1:12 since I *k* it is because of me that this
Mi 3: 1 Is it not your duty to *k* what is right,
4:12 But they *k* not the thoughts of the LORD,
6: 5 that you may *k* the just deeds of the LORD.
Zec 2:13 shall *k* that the LORD of hosts has sent me.
2:15 and you shall *k* that the LORD of hosts has
4: 5 "Do you not *k* what these things are?"
4: 9 then you shall *k* that the LORD of hosts
4:13 "Do you not *k* what these are?"
6:15 and you shall *k* that the LORD of hosts has
7:14 among all the nations that they did not *k*.
Mal 2: 4 Then you will *k* that I sent you this
Mt 6: 3 left hand *k* what your right hand is doing.
7:11 *k* how to give your children what is good,
7:16 You will *k* them by their deeds.
16: 3 you *k* how to interpret the look of the sky,
20:22 said, "You do not *k* what you are asking.
20:25 "You *k* how those who exercise authority
21:27 their answer to Jesus was, "We do not *k*."
22:16 we *k* you are a truthful man and teach
24:33 happening, you will *k* that he is near,
24:42 You cannot *k* the day your Lord is coming.
25:12 he answered, 'I tell you, I do not *k* you.'
25:13 open, for you *k* not the day or the hour.
25:26 You *k* I reap where I did not sow and
26: 2 "You *k* that in two days' time it will be
26:70 "I do not *k* what you are talking about!"
26:72 "I do not *k* the man!"
26:74 and swore, "I do not even *k* the man!"
28: 5 *k* you are looking for Jesus the crucified,
28:20 And *k* that I am with you always,
Mk 1:24 I *k* who you are—the holy One of God!"
2:10 That you may *k* that the Son of Man has
5:43 them strictly not to let anyone *k* about it,
6:33 them leaving, and many got to *k* about it.
9:30 but he did not want anyone to *k* about it.
10:19 You *k* the commandments:
10:38 them, "You do not *k* what you are asking.
10:42 "You *k* how among the Gentiles those who
11:33 their answer to Jesus was, "We do not *k*."
12:14 "Teacher, we *k* you are a truthful man,
13:28 sprout leaves, you *k* that summer is near.
13:29 happening, you will *k* that he is near,
13:33 do not *k* when the appointed time will come.
13:35 *k* when the master of the house is coming,
14:40 open, nor did they *k* what to say to him.
14:68 "I do not *k* what you are talking about!
14:71 not even *k* the man you are talking about!"
Lk 1:18 "How am I to *k* this?
1:34 "How can this be since I do not *k* man?"
1:36 *K* that Elizabeth your kinswoman has
2:49 you not *k* I had to be in my Father's house?"
4:34 I *k* who you are:
7:39 he would *k* who and what sort of woman this
8:46 I *k* that power has gone forth from me."
9:33 (He did not really *k* what he was saying.)
10:11 But *k* that the reign of God is near.'
11:13 *k* how to give your children good things,
12:18 I *k*!' he said, 'I will put down my grain bins
12:39 You *k* as well as I that if the head of the
12:46 not expect him, at a time he does not *k*.
12:48 whereas the one who did not *k* them and who
13:25 in reply, 'I do not *k* where you come from.'
13:27 tell you, I do not *k* where you come from.
18:20 You *k* the commandments:
20: 7 replying they did not *k* where it came from.
20:21 we *k* that your words and your doctrine are
21:20 soldiers, *k* that its devastation is near.
21:30 and *k* for yourselves that summer is near.
21:31 I speak, *k* that the reign of God is near.
22:34 you have three times denied that you *k* me."
22:57 denied it, saying, "Woman, I do not *k* him."
22:60 I do not *k* what you are talking about."
23:34 they do not *k* what they are doing."]
24:18 who does not *k* the things that went on
24:35 had come to *k* him in the breaking of bread.
Jn 1:10 made, yet the world did not *k* who he was.
1:48 "How do you *k* me?"
3: 2 "we *k* you are a teacher come from God,
3: 8 makes but you do not *k* where it comes from,
3:11 you, we are talking about what we *k*,
4:25 "I *k* there is a Messiah coming."
4:32 "I have food to eat of which you do not *k*."
4:42 and we *k* that this really is the Savior of
5:32 he renders me I *k* can be verified.
5:42 it is simply that I *k* you,
6:42 Do we not *k* his father and mother?
7:17 to do his will will *k* about this doctrine
7:27 Still, we *k* where this man is from.
7:27 comes, no one is supposed to *k* his origins."
7:28 "So you know me, and you *k* my origins?
7:28 the right to send, and him you do not *k*.
7:29 I *k* him because it is from him I come:
8:14 I *k* where I came from and where I am going;
8:14 you *k* neither the one nor the other.
8:19 "You *k* neither me nor my Father.
8:19 If you knew me, you would *k* my Father too."
8:32 then you will *k* the truth,
8:52 shall never *k* death if he keeps my word.'
8:55 for your God, even though you do not *k* him.
8:55 But I *k* him.
8:55 Were I to say I do not *k* him,
8:55 Yes, I *k* him well, and I keep his word.
9:20 *k* this is our son, and we *k* he was blind
9:24 First of all, we *k* this man is a sinner."
9:25 do not *k* whether his is a sinner or not,"
9:25 "I *k* this much:
9:29 We *k* that God spoke to Moses,
9:30 You do not *k* where he comes from,
9:31 We *k* that God does not hear sinners,
10:14 I know my sheep and my sheep *k* me in the
10:15 the Father knows me and I *k* the Father;
10:27 I *k* them, and they follow me.
11:24 "I *k* he will rise again,"
11:42 I *k* that you always hear me but I have
12:35 in the dark does not *k* where he is going.
12:50 *k* that his commandment means eternal life,
13:17 Once you *k* all these things,
13:18 of all, for I *k* the kind of men I chose,
13:35 is how all will *k* you for my disciples:
14: 4 You *k* the way that leads where I go."
14: 5 Thomas, "we do not *k* where you are going.
14: 5 How can we *k* the way?"
14: 7 really knew me, you would *k* my Father also.
14: 7 From this point on you *k* him;
14: 9 you all this time, you still do not *k* me?
14:20 that day you will *k* that I am in my Father,
14:31 the world must *k* that I love the Father
15:15 slave does not *k* what his master is about.
15:18 hates you *k* it has hated me before you.
15:21 for they *k* nothing of him who sent me.
16:18 We do not *k* what he is talking about."
16:30 We are convinced that you *k* everything.
17: 3 to *k* you,
17:23 So shall the world *k* that you sent me,
18:21 be obvious that they will *k* what I said."
19:10 "Do you not *k* that I have the power to
20: 2 We don't *k* where they have put him!"
20:13 and I do not *k* where they have put him."
20:14 But she did not *k* him.
21:15 Lord," he said, "you *k* that I love you."
21:16 Peter said, "you *k* that I love you."
21:17 "Lord, you *k* everything.
21:17 You *k* well that I love you."
21:24 wrote them down and his testimony, we *k*,
Acts 1: 7 "The exact time it is not yours to *k*.
2:22 through him in your midst, as you well *k*.
2:36 Therefore let the whole house of Israel *k*
3:16 limbs of this man whom you see and *k* well.
3:17 "Yet I *k*, my brothers, that you acted
5:24 did not *k* what to make of the affair.
10:28 "You must *k* that it is not proper for a
10:29 of course, like to *k* why you summoned me."
10:37 I take it you *k* what has been reported all
12:11 "Now I *k* for certain that the Lord has
12:18 who did not *k* what had happened to Peter.
15: 7 you *k* well enough that from the early days
17:19 "We are curious to *k* what this new
17:20 we should like to *k* what it is all about."
17:30 bygone periods when men did not *k* him;
19:15 answered, "Jesus I recognize, Paul I *k*;
19:25 *k* that our prosperity depends on this work.
19:35 "what man is there who does not *k* that
20:18 "You *k* how I lived among you from the
20:25 I *k* as I speak these words that none of
20:29 I *k* that when I am gone,
20:34 You yourselves *k* that these hands of mine
21:24 everyone will *k* that there is nothing in
21:37 "So you *k* Greek!"
22:14 long ago designated you to *k* his will,
22:19 it is because they *k* that I imprisoned
23: 5 I did not *k* that he was the high priest.
24:10 "I *k* that you have been a judge over this
28:22 We *k* very well that this sect is denounced
Rom 1:13 I want you to *k* that I have often planned
1:32 They *k* God's just decree that all who do
2: 2 "We *k* that God's judgment on men who do
2: 4 Do you not *k* that God's kindness is an
2:18 you *k* his will and are able to make sound
3:19 We *k* that everything the law says is
5: 3 We *k* that affliction makes for endurance,
6: 6 This we *k*, our old self was crucified
6: 9 We *k* that Christ,
7: 1 (I am speaking to men who *k* what law is),
7: 7 only through the law that I came to *k* sin.
7:14 We *k* that the law is spiritual,
7:18 I *k* that no good dwells in me,
8:22 we *k* that all creation groans and is in
8:26 for we do not *k* how to pray as we ought;
8:28 We *k* that God makes all things work
11: 2 you not *k* what Scripture says about Elijah,
13:11 for you *k* the time in which we are living.
14:14 I *k* with certainty on the authority of the
1Cor 1:21 did not come to *k* him through "wisdom,"
2:14 He cannot come to *k* such teaching because
5: 6 Do you not *k* that a little yeast has its
6: 2 *k* that the believers will judge the world?
6: 3 Do you not *k* that we are to judge angels?
6:19 You must *k* that your body is a temple of
7:12 although I *k* of nothing the Lord has said,
7:16 you *k* that you will not save your husband;
7:31 for the world as we *k* it is passing away.
8: 1 Of course we all *k*" about that.
8: 4 we *k* that an idol is really nothing,
9:24 You *k* that while all the runners in the
10: 5 yet we *k* that God was not pleased with
11: 3 I want you to *k* that theConcerning Idol
12: 2 You *k* that when you were pagans you were
13:12 then I shall *k* even as I am known.
14: 7 how will anyone *k* what is being played if
14: 9 how will anyone *k* what you are saying?
14:11 but if I do not *k* the meaning,
14:16 He will not *k* what you are saying.
14:37 he should *k* that what I have written you
15:58 You *k* that your toil is not in vain when
16:15 You *k* that the household of Stephanas is
2Cor 1: 7 *k* that just as you share in the sufferings,
1:13 as you *k* us to a certain degree already,
1:13 you will in time come to *k* us well,
2: 3 I *k* you all well enough to be convinced
2:11 whose guile we *k* too well
5: 1 we *k* that when the earthly tent in which
5: 6 We *k* that while we dwell in the body we
5:16 we no longer *k* him by this standard.
5:21 God made him who did not *k* sin to be sin,
8: 1 I should like you to *k* of the grace of God
9: 2 I already *k* your willingness,
11: 6 but I *k* that I am not lacking in knowledge.
12: 2 I *k* a man in Christ who,
12: 3 I *k* that this man
12: 3 in or outside his body I do not *k*,
Gal 1:13 You have heard, I *k*,
1:13 You *k* that I went to extremes in
1:18 I went up to Jerusalem to get to *k* Cephas,
4: 9 Now that you have come to *k* God
4:21 do you *k* what the law has to say?
Eph 1:17 of wisdom and insight to *k* him clearly.
1:18 vision that you may *k* the great hope
3: 4 you will realize that I *k* what I am
6: 8 You *k* that each one, whether slave
Phil 1:12 I want you to *k* that my situation has
1:22 and I do not *k* which to prefer.
2:22 You *k* from experience what Timothy's
3:10 I wish to *k* Christ and the power flowing
3:10 likewise to *k* how to share in his
3:20 As you well *k*, we have our citizenship
4:12 yet I *k* what it is to have an abundance.
4:15 You yourselves *k*, my dear Philippians,
Col 2: 1 I want you to *k* how hard I am struggling
3:24 since you *k* full well you will receive an
1Thes 1: 4 We *k*, too, brothers beloved of God,
1: 5 You *k* as well as we do what we proved to
2: 1 You *k* well enough,
2: 2 about which you *k*—
2: 5 We were not guilty, as you well *k*,
2:11 *k* how we exhorted every one of you,
3: 3 You *k* well enough that such trials are our
3: 4 it has happened, and you *k* what we meant.
4: 2 You *k* the instructions we gave you in the
4: 5 desire as do the Gentiles who *k* not God;
5: 2 you *k* very well that the day of the Lord
2Thes 2: 6 You *k* what restrains him until he shall be
3: 7 You *k* how you ought to imitate us.
1Tm 1: 8 We *k* that the law is good,
1:13 did not *k* what I was doing in my unbelief,
2: 4 men to be saved and come to *k* the truth.
3: 5 man does not *k* how to manage his own house,
3:15 *k* what kind of conduct befits a member
4: 3 thanksgiving by believers who *k* the truth.
2Tm 1:12 for I *k* him in whom I have believed,
1:15 You *k* that all in Asia,
1:18 in Ephesus you *k* even better than I.
2:23 As you well *k*, they only breed quarrels,
2:25 will enable them to repent and *k* the truth.
3:11 You *k* what persecutions I have had to bear,
3:11 you *k* how the Lord saved me from them all.
3:14 because you *k* who your teachers were.
Ti 1:16 They claim to *k* God,"
Phlm 1: 6 to *k* all the good which is ours in Christ.
1:16 will *k* him both as a man and in the Lord.
Heb 8:11 'Know the Lord,' for all shall *k* me,
10:30 We *k* who said,
12: 8 If you do not *k* the discipline of sons,
12:17 You *k* that afterward he wanted to inherit
13:23 I must let you *k* that our brother Timothy
2Pt 1:14 I *k*, by the indications our Lord Jesus
1Jn 2:21 you do not *k* the truth but that you do,
3: 2 We *k* that when it comes to light we shall
3: 5 You *k* well that the reason he revealed
3:14 to life we *k* because we love the brothers.
3:15 and you *k* that eternal life abides in no

3:24 And this is how we *k* that he remains in us:
4:13 The way we *k* we remain in him and he in us
4:16 We have come to *k* and to believe in the
5:15 *k* that he hears us whenever we ask, we *k*
5:18 *k* that no one begotten of God commits sin;
5:19 We *k* that we belong to God,
5:20 We *k*, too, that the Son of God has come
2Jn 1: 1 all those who have come to *k* the truth.
3Jn 1:12 well, and you *k* that our testimony is true.
Jude 1:10 through the very things they *k* by instinct,
Rv 2: 2 I *k* your deeds,
2: 2 I *k* you cannot tolerate wicked men;
2: 9 I *k* of your tribulation and your poverty,
2: 9 I *k* the slander you endure from
2:13 I *k* you live in the very place where
2:13 and I *k* you hold fast to my name and have
2:19 I *k* your deeds
2:19 I *k* also that your efforts of recent times
2:23 Thus shall all the churches come to *k* that
2:24 not uphold this teaching and *k* nothing of
3: 1 I *k* your conduct; I know the reputation
3: 3 you like a thief, at a time you cannot *k*.
3: 8 "'I *k* your deeds; that is why I have left
3: 8 I *k* that your strength is limited;
3:15 I know your deeds; I *k* you are neither
7:14 to him, "Sir, you should *k* better than I."
7:16 Never again shall they *k* hunger or thirst,

KNOWING (45)

Gn 3:22 one of us, *k* what is good and what is bad!
Ex 33:13 do let me know your ways so that, in *k* you,
36: 1 skill and understanding in *k* how
Jos 8:14 *k* that there was an ambush behind the city.
Jgs 13:16 "Not *k* that it was the angel of the LORD,
1Sm 26:12 without anyone's seeing or *k* or awakening.
2Sm 15:11 went in good faith, *k* nothing of the plan.
1Kgs 3: 7 I am a mere youth, not *k* at all how to act.
8:39 *k* their hearts,
2Kgs 4:39 of vegetable stew without anybody's *k* it.
7:12 *K* that we are in famine,
2Chr 6:30 *K* his heart, render to everyone according
6:33 and *k* that this house which I have built
Tb 8:12 may bury him without anyone's *k* about it."
Jb 4:21 they die without *k* wisdom."
37: 5 He does great things beyond our *k*;
Ps(s) 83:19 and perish, *K* that you alone are the LORD,
Prv 14: 7 But *k* lips one meets with by surprise.
Eccl 6: 8 man in *k* how to conduct himself in life?
Wis 8: 9 *k* that she would be my counselor while all
8:21 And *k* that I could not otherwise possess
13: 1 seen did not succeed in *k* him who is,
13:16 for it, *k* that it cannot help itself;
15: 2 we will not sin, *k* that we belong to you.
17:13 of not *k* the cause that brings on torment.
Sir 27:27 in it without *k* how it came upon him.
Is 50: 7 flint, *k* that I shall not be put to shame.
Bar 6:28 *K* from this that they are not gods,
Mt 12:25 *K* their thoughts, he said to them:
Mk 4:27 and grows without his *k* how it happens.
6:20 John, *k* him to be an upright and holy man,
12:15 *K* their hypocrisy he said to them,
Jn 2: 9 wine, without *k* where it had come from;
7:51 without first hearing him and *k* the facts?"
Acts 19:32 not even *k* why they had come together.
20:22 and not *k* what will happen to me there
25:20 Not *k* how to decide the case,
2Cor 4:14 *k* that he who raised up the Lord Jesus
Gal 2:16 *k* that a man is not justified by legal
Phlm 1:21 you, *k* that you will do more than I say.
Heb 10:34 *k* that you had better and more permanent
11: 8 forth, moreover, not *k* where he was going.
13: 2 some have entertained angels without *k* it.
1Jn 2:11 walks in shadows, not *k* where he is going,
3:19 This is our way of *k* we are committed to

KNOWINGLY (1)

Ps(s) 35:19 let not my undeserved foes wink *k*.

KNOWLEDGE (179)

Gn 2: 9 and the tree of the *k* of good and bad.
2:17 except the tree of *k* of good and bad.
Ex 31: 3 and understanding and *k* in every craft:
35:31 and understanding and *k* in every craft:
2Sm 3:26 David's *k* sent messengers after Abner,
1Kgs 1:11 king without the *k* of our lord David?
2:32 without my father David's *k*
5: 9 wisdom and exceptional understanding and *k*,
7:14 and *k* of how to produce any work in bronze.
2Chr 1:10 wisdom and *k* to lead this people,
1:11 but have asked for wisdom and *k* in order
1:12 made you king, wisdom and *k* are given you;
2Mc 6:30 Lord in his holy *k* knows full well that,
Jb 8: 9 (As we are but of yesterday and have no *k*,
17: 4 You darken their minds to *k*;
21:22 Can anyone teach God *k*,
32: 6 back and was afraid to declare to you my *k*.
32:10 let me too set forth my *k*!
32:17 I also will show my *k*!
33: 3 my mind, my lips shall utter *k* sincerely;
34: 2 men, my discourse, and you that have *k*,
35:16 his mouth, and without *k* multiplies words.
36: 3 I will bring my *k* from afar,
36: 4 the one perfect in *k* I set before you.
36:12 they die for lack of *k*.
36:26 Lo, God is great beyond our *k*;
37:16 wondrous work of him who is perfect in *k*?
Ps(s) 19: 3 word to day, and night to night imparts *k*;
73:11 And, "Is there any *k* in the Most High?"
94:10 nations not chastise, he who teaches men *k*?
119:66 Teach me wisdom and *k*,
139: 6 Such *k* is too wonderful for me;
Prv 1: 4 simple, to the young man *k* and discretion.
1: 7 The fear of the LORD is the beginning of *k*;
1:29 Because they hated *k*,
1:30 and like fools they hated *k*:
2: 5 the *k* of God you will find;
2: 6 from his mouth come *k* and understanding;
2:10 enter your heart, *k* will please your soul,
3:20 By his *k* the depths break open,
5: 1 be attentive, to my *k* incline your ear,
8: 9 and right to those who attain *k*.
8:10 to silver, and *k* rather than choice gold.
8:12 with experience, and judicious *k* I attain.
9:10 and *k* of the Holy One is understanding.
10:14 Wise men store up *k*,
11: 9 through their *k* the just make their escape.
12: 1 He who loves correction loves *k*,
12:23 A shrewd man conceals his *k*,
14: 6 but *k* is easy to the man of intelligence.
14: 8 shrewd man's wisdom gives him *k* of his way,
14:18 folly, but shrewd men gain the crown of *k*.
15: 2 The tongue of the wise pours out *k*,
15: 7 The lips of the wise disseminate *k*,
15:14 The mind of the intelligent man seeks *k*,
18:15 knowledge, and the ear of the wise seeks *k*.
19: 2 Without *k* even zeal is not good;
19:25 you rebuke an intelligent man, he gains *k*.
19:27 instruction, he wanders from words of *k*.
21:11 the wise man is instructed, he gains *k*.
22:12 The eyes of the LORD safeguard *k*,
22:20 you the "Thirty," with counsels and *k*,
23:12 instruction, and your ears to words of *k*.
24: 4 And by *k* are its rooms filled with every
24: 5 man, and a man of *k* than a man of might;
30: 3 wisdom, nor have I the *k* of the Holy One.
Eccl 1:16 has broad experience of wisdom and *k*";
1:17 I applied my mind to know wisdom and *k*,
1:18 and he who stores up *k* stores up grief.
2:21 has labored with wisdom and *k* and skill,
2:26 he sees fit he gives wisdom and *k* and joy;
7:12 and the advantage of *k* is that wisdom
7:25 I turned my thoughts toward *k*;
9:10 there will be no work, nor reason, nor *k*,
12: 9 being wise, Qoheleth taught the people *k*,
Wis 2:13 He professes to have *k* of God and styles
6:22 search out and bring to light *k* of her,
7:16 as well as all prudence and *k* of crafts.
7:17 For he gave me sound *k* of existing things,
10: 8 Wisdom first were bereft of *k* of the right,
10:10 of God and gave him *k* of holy things;
13: 9 For if they so far succeeded in *k* that
14:22 enough for them to err in their *k* of God;
18: 6 with sure *k* of the oaths in which they put
Sir 1:17 *K* and full understanding she showers down;
3:24 there is no light, and where there is no *k*,
4:24 and *k* through the tongue's rejoinder.
5:14 If you have the *k*, answer your neighbor;
8: 9 obtain the *k* how to answer in time of need,
11:15 Wisdom and understanding and *k* of affairs,
14:20 meditates on wisdom, and reflects on *k*;
16:23 measured wisdom, and impart accurate *k*.
17: 6 With wisdom and *k* he fills them;
17: 9 He has set before them *k*,
19:18 The *k* of wickedness is not wisdom,
21:13 A wise man's *k* wells up in a flood,
21:14 no *k* at all can it hold.
24:25 It sparkles like the Nile with *k*,
25: 4 and a *k* of counsel to those on in years!
33:11 with his great *k* the LORD makes men unlike;
34: 9 A man with training gains wide *k*;
37:21 fruits of his *k* are seen in his own person;
37:22 the fruits of his *k* are enduring:
38: 2 His *k* makes the doctor distinguished,
38: 6 with the *k* to glory in his mighty works,
39: 7 Who will direct his *k* and his counsel,
42:18 The Most High possesses all *k*,
47:15 earth, and, like a sea, filled it with *k*.
Is 11: 2 *k* and of fear of the LORD,
11: 9 earth shall be filled with *k* of the LORD,
28: 9 "To whom would he impart *k*?
33: 6 the riches that save her, are wisdom and *k*;
40:14 Whom did he consult to gain *k*?
40:28 grow weary, and his *k* is beyond scrutiny.
44:18 The idols have neither *k* nor reason;
44:25 wise men back and make their *k* foolish.
45:20 They are without *k* who bear wooden idols
47:10 Your wisdom and your *k* led you astray,
Jer 16:21 I will give them *k*;
22:16 Is this not true *k* of me?
33: 3 you things great beyond reach of your *k*.
Bar 3:23 The sons of Hagar who seek *k* on earth,
3:23 and Teman, the phrasemakers seeking *k*,
3:32 he has probed her by his *k*—
Dn 1:17 To these four young men God gave *k* and
2:21 to the wise and *k* to those who understand.
5:11 to have brilliant *k* and god-like wisdom.
5:14 brilliant *k* and extraordinary wisdom.
Hos 4: 1 no mercy, no *k* of God in the land.
4: 6 My people perish for want of *k*!
4: 6 Since you have rejected *k*,
6: 6 and *k* of God rather than holocausts.
Hb 2:14 But the earth shall be filled with the *k*
Mal 2: 7 For the lips of the priest are to keep *k*,
Mt 13:11 a *k* of the mysteries of the reign of God,
Lk 1:77 *k* of salvation in freedom from their sins,
11:52 You have taken away the key of *k*.
Rom 1:21 They certainly had *k* of God,
2:20 at hand a clear pattern of *k* and truth.
11:33 the riches and the wisdom and the *k* of God!
15:14 with goodness, that you have complete *k*,
1Cor 1: 5 endowed with every gift of speech and *k*.
8: 1 But whereas *k*" inflates, love upbuilds.
8: 7 Not all, of course, possess this *k*."
8:10 If someone sees you, with your *k*,"
8:11 Because of your *k*" the weak one perishes,
12: 8 to another the power to express *k*.
13: 2 the gift of prophecy and, with full *k*,
13: 8 tongues will be silent, *k* will pass away.
13: 9 Our *k* is imperfect and our prophesying is
13:12 My *k* is imperfect now;
14: 6 speech does not have some revelation, or *k*,
2Cor 2:14 diffuse the fragrance of his *k* everywhere!
6: 6 conducting ourselves with innocence, *k*,
8: 7 respect, in faith and discourse, in *k*,
10: 5 that raises itself against the *k* of God;
11: 6 but I know that I am not lacking in *k*.
Eph 3:19 this love which surpasses all *k*,
4:13 one in faith and in the *k* of God's Son,
Phil 3: 8 the surpassing *k* of my Lord Jesus Christ.
Col 1: 9 asking that you may attain full *k* of his will
1:10 of every sort and grow in the *k* of God.
2: 2 by their *k* of the mystery of God
2: 3 every treasure of wisdom and *k* is hidden.
3:10 one who grows in *k* as he is formed anew in
1Tm 6:20 contradictions of what is falsely called *k*.
6:21 In laying claim to such *k*,
2Tm 3: 7 but never able to reach a *k* of the truth.
Ti 1: 1 *k* of the truth as our religion embodies it.
2Pt 1: 2 through your *k* of God and of Jesus,
1: 3 through *k* of him who called us by his own
1: 8 fruit in true *k* of our Lord Jesus Christ.
3:18 the *k* of our Lord and Savior Jesus Christ.
1Jn 2: 3 our *k* of him is to keep his commandments.
2:20 from the Holy One, so that all *k* is yours.
4: 6 anyone who has *k* of God gives us a hearing,
4: 7 loves is begotten of God and has *k* of God.
Jude 1:10 not only revile what they have no *k* of

KNOWN (207)

Gn 41:39 "Since God has made all this *k* to you,
44:15 "You should have *k* that such a man as I
45: 1 when he made himself *k* to his brothers.
Ex 2:14 thought, "The affair must certainly be *k*."
6: 3 my name, LORD, I did not make *k* to them.
18:16 make *k* to them God's decisions
21:36 But if it was *k* that the ox was previously
33:16 how can it be *k* that we, your people and I,
Lv 4:14 on become *k* that the sin was committed,
Nm 16: 5 "May the LORD make *k* tomorrow morning
Dt 9:24 Ever since I have *k* you,
11: 2 who have not *k* it from experience,
11:28 to follow other gods, whom you have not *k*.
13: 3 whom you have not *k* and to serve them:
13: 7 whom you and your fathers have not *k*,
13:14 to serve other gods whom you have not *k*,
21: 1 to occupy, and it is not *k* who killed him,
28:36 which you and your fathers have not *k*,
28:64 such as you and your fathers have not *k*.
32:17 to gods whom they had not *k* before,
Ru 3: 3 Do not make yourself *k* to the man before
3:14 "Let it not be *k* that this woman came to
1Sm 10:11 When all who had *k* him previously saw him
2Sm 22:44 A people I had not *k* became my slaves;
1Kgs 1:20 Israel is waiting for you to make *k* to them
18:36 let it be *k* this day that you are God in
1Chr 13: 6 which was *k* by the name "LORD enthroned
16: 8 make *k* among the nations his deeds.
2Chr 9:29 first and last, are written, as is well *k*,
12:15 first and last, are written, as is well *k*,
25:26 last, can be found written, as is well *k*,
Ezr 2:61 the Gileadite and became *k* by his name).
4:12 Let it be *k* to the king that the Jews who
4:13 Now let it be *k* to the king that if this
5: 8 Let it be *k* to the king that we have
Neh 7:63 the Gileadite and became *k* by his name).
9:14 Your holy sabbath you made *k* to them,
Tb 12: 7 works of God are to be declared and made *k*.
12:11 of God are to be made *k* with due honor.'
Est 1:17 conduct will become *k* to all the women,
2:22 When the plot became *k* to Mordecai,
1Mc 6: 3 because his plan became *k* to the people of
9:60 this, however, because their plot became *k*.
2Mc 1:33 When the event became *k* and the king of
12:17 there were certain Jews *k* as Toubiani.
Jb 13:23 My misdeeds and my sins make *k* to me!
20:20 Though he has *k* no quiet in his greed,

KNOWN (cont.)
36: 9 Then he makes *k* to them what they have
Ps(s) 18:44 A people I had not *k* became my slaves;
25: 4 Your ways, O LORD, make *k* to me;
67: 3 So may your way be *k* upon earth;
77:15 the peoples you have made *k* your power.
78: 5 fathers they should make *k* to their sons;
79:10 Let it be *k* among the nations in our sight
88:13 Are your wonders made *k* in the darkness,
98: 2 The LORD has made his salvation *k*:
103: 7 He has made *k* his ways to Moses,
105: 1 make *k* among the nations his deeds.
106: 8 for his name's sake, to make *k* his power.
111: 6 *k* to his people the power of his works,
145:12 Making *k* to men your might and the
147:20 his ordinances he has not made *k* to them.
Prv 22:19 I make *k* to you the words of Amen-em-Ope.
Eccl 6: 5 though it has not seen or *k* the sun,
6:10 its name, and the nature of man is *k*,
8: 7 for who will make *k* to him how it will be?
Wis 2: 1 *k* to have come back from the nether world.
6:13 herself *k* in anticipation of men's desire;
7:12 had not *k* that she is the mother of these.
18: 6 That night was *k* beforehand to our fathers,
Sir 4:24 is through speech that wisdom becomes *k*,
11:28 his death, for by how he ends, a man is *k*.
16:15 Among so many people I cannot be *k*;
17:13 Their ways are ever *k* to him,
18:28 Any learned man should make wisdom *k*,
19:25 a wise man is *k* as such when first met.
21: 7 Widely *k* is the boastful speaker but the
24:30 like the dawn, to become *k* afar off.
36:17 Thus it will be *k* to the very ends of the
42:19 He makes *k* the past and the future,
46:20 he made *k* to the king his fate,
51: 1 I will make *k* your name,
Is 12: 4 among the nations make *k* his deeds,
12: 5 let this be *k* throughout all the earth.
19:12 Let them tell you and make *k* What the LORD
19:21 The LORD shall make himself *k* in Egypt,
43:12 I who foretold, I who saved; I made it *k*,
48: 7 so that you cannot claim to have *k* them;
48:20 shouts of joy proclaim this, make it *k*;
64: 1 Thus your name would be made *k* to your
66:14 LORD's power shall be *k* to his servants,
Jer 4:16 "Make this *k* to the nations,
9:11 the mouth of the LORD has spoken make it *k*:
9:15 neither they nor their fathers have *k*;
16:13 that neither you nor your fathers have *k*;
42:20 make *k* to us all that the LORD,
42:21 he has commissioned me to make *k* to you.
Bar 3:20 the way to understanding they have not *k*,
3:23 These have not *k* the way to wisdom,
4: 4 for what pleases God is *k* to us!
6:14 Thus it is *k* they are not gods;
6:50 they will later be *k* for frauds.
6:71 them, it can be *k* that they are not gods;
Ez 16: 2 man, make *k* to Jerusalem her abominations:
20: 4 Make *k* to them the abominations of their
20: 9 whose presence I had made myself *k* to them,
20:11 statutes and made *k* to them my ordinances,
22: 2 Then make *k* all her abominations, and say:
23:36 Then make *k* to them their abominations.
35:11 make myself *k* among you when I judge you,
36:32 let this be *k* to you!
38:23 make myself *k* in the sight of many nations;
39: 7 make my holy name *k* among my people Israel;
43:11 make *k* to them the form and design of the
44:23 and make *k* to them the difference between
Dn 2:23 you have made *k* to us the king's dream."
2:30 that its meaning may be made *k* to the king,
7:16 he made *k* to me the meaning of the things:
Hos 2:10 not *k* that it was I who gave her the grain,
Hb 3: 2 it, in the course of the years make it *k*;
Zec 14: 7 shall be one continuous day, *k* to the LORD,
Mt 4:18 watched two brothers, Simon now *k* as Peter,
9:10 many tax collectors and those *k* as sinners
10: 2 first Simon, now *k* as Peter,
10:26 and nothing hidden that will not become *k*.
10:41 *k* to be holy receives a holy man's reward.
11:11 history has not *k* a man born of woman
13:55 Isn't Mary *k* to be his mother and James,
Mk 2:15 many tax collectors and those *k* as sinners
15:16 away into the hall *k* as the praetorium;
Lk 2:15 this event which the Lord has made *k* to us."
6:44 Each tree is *k* by its yield.
7:37 A woman *k* in the town to be a sinner
8:17 that will not be *k* and brought to light.
12: 2 nothing hidden that will not be made *k*.
19:42 only you had *k* the path to peace this day;
22: 1 Bread *k* as the Passover was drawing near,
Jn 7: 4 to be *k* publicly keeps his actions hidden.
15:15 *k* to you all that I heard from my Father.
17: 6 *k* to those you gave me out of the world.
17: 8 They have *k* that in truth I came from you,
17:25 *k* you, but I have *k* you;
17:25 and these men have *k*
18:15 disciple, who was *k* to the high priest,
18:16 The disciple *k* to the high priest came out
Acts 1:19 to be *k* by the inhabitants of Jerusalem,
1:23 Barsabbas, also *k* as Justus) and Matthias.
1:24 Make *k* to us which of these two you choose
7:13 *k* to his brothers, and his family ties became *k*
9:42 This became *k* all over Joppa,
10: 5 and summon a certain Simon, *k* as Peter.
10:32 to invite Simon *k* as Peter to come here.
11:13 to Joppa and fetch Simon, *k* also as Peter.
11:19 making the message *k* to none but Jews.
12:12 Mary the mother of John (also *k* as Mark),
13: 1 Barnabas, Symeon *k* as Niger,
13: 9 *k* as Paul) was filled with the Holy Spirit;
15:18 these things *k* to him from of old.'
15:22 of the community, Judas, *k* as Barsabbas,
16:17 they will make *k* to you a way of salvation."
17:23 in ignorance I intend to make *k* to you.
19:17 *k* to the Jews and Greeks living in Ephesus,
26: 4 later at Jerusalem, is well *k* to all Jews.
27: 1 named Julius from the cohort *k* as Augusta.
Rom 1:19 can be *k* about God is clear to them;
7: 7 I should never have *k* what evil desire was
9:22 to show his wrath and make *k* his power,
9:23 and in order to make *k* the riches of his
11:34 For "who has *k* the mind of the Lord?
15:20 places where Christ's name was already *k*,
16:19 Your obedience is *k* to all,
16:26 made *k* to all the Gentiles that they may
1Cor 2: 8 if they had *k* it,
2:16 "Who has *k* the mind of the Lord so as to
8: 2 means he has never really *k* it as he ought.
8: 3 if anyone loves God, that man is *k* by him.
13:12 then I shall know even as I am *k*.
2Cor 3: 2 You are my letter, *k* and read by all men,
4: 6 that we in turn might make *k* the glory of
5:11 persuade men, but what we are is *k* to God.
5:11 it is also *k* to you in your consciences.
6: 9 nobodies who in fact are well *k*;
Gal 4: 9 or rather, have been *k* by him
Eph 3:10 God's manifold wisdom is made *k* to the
6:19 make *k* the mystery of the gospel
Phil 1:13 well *k* throughout the praetorium here,
2: 7 He was *k* to be of human estate,
Col 1:27 God has willed to make *k* to them the glory
4:11 Jesus *k* also as Justus sends greetings.
2Tm 3:15 infancy you have *k* the sacred Scriptures,
Ti 1: 6 and are *k* not to be wild and insubordinate.
Heb 3:10 of erring heart, and have never *k* my ways.'
11:24 to be *k* as the son of Pharaoh's daughter;
2Pt 2:21 law handed on to them, once they had *k* it.
1Jn 2: 4 The man who claims, "I have *k* him,"
2:13 you have *k* him who is from the beginning.
2:14 you, children, for you have *k* the Father.
2:14 you have *k* him who is from the beginning,
3: 6 man who sins has not seen him or *k* him.
3:20 than our hearts and all is *k* to him.
4: 8 The man without love has *k* nothing of God,
Rv 1: 1 *k* by sending his angel to his servant John,
2:17 name, to be *k* only by him who receives it.'
12: 9 ancient serpent *k* as the devil or Satan,
19:12 person was a name *k* to no one but himself.

KNOWS (110)

Gn 3: 5 God *k* well that the moment you eat of it
Nm 24: 4 God says, and knows what the Most High *k*,
24:16 God says, and knows what the Most High *k*,
Dt 34: 6 this day no one *k* the place of his burial.
Jos 22:22 the God of gods, *k* and Israel shall know.
1Sm 22:15 Your servant *k* nothing at all,
23:17 Even my father Saul *k* this."
2Sm 14:20 of God, so that he *k* all things on earth."
17:10 For all Israel *k* that your father is a
19:21 For your servant *k* that he has done wrong.
2Chr 2:13 he *k* how to work with gold,
Tb 6:13 of Moses, and he *k* that it is your right,
Est 4:14 Who *k* but that it was for a time like this
2Mc 6:30 in his holy knowledge *k* full well that,
Jb 11:11 For he *k* the worthlessness of men and sees
15:23 he *k* that his destruction is imminent.
18:21 and such is the place of him who *k* not God!
23:10 Yet he *k* my way;
28: 7 The path to it no bird of prey *k*,
28:13 Man *k* nothing to equal it,
28:23 God *k* the way to it;
Ps(s) 33:15 heart of each, he who *k* all their works.
39: 7 up stores, and *k* not who will use them.
44:22 For he *k* the secrets of the heart.
74: 9 and no one of us *k* how long. . . .
90:11 Who *k* the fury of your anger or your
92: 7 A senseless man *k* not,
94:11 The LORD *k* the thoughts of men,
103:14 who fear him, For he *k* how we are formed;
103:16 he is gone, and his place *k* him no more.
104:19 the sun *k* the hour of its setting.
138: 6 he sees, and the proud he *k* from afar.
Prv 9:13 is fickle, she is inane, and *k* nothing.
9:18 Little he *k* that the shades are there,
14:10 The heart *k* its own bitterness,
24:12 He who guards your life *k* it,
28: 2 but with a prudent man it *k* security.
28:22 and he *k* not when want will come upon him.
Eccl 2:19 *k* whether he will be a wise man or a fool?
3:21 Who *k* if the life-breath of the children
4:13 but foolish king who no longer *k* caution;
6:12 For who *k* what is good for a man in life,
8: 1 man, and who *k* the explanation of things?
8: 5 the wise man's heart *k* times and judgments;
8:17 and even if the wise man says that he *k*,
9:12 Man no more *k* his own time than fish taken
10:14 Man *k* not what is to come,
10:15 labor, he who *k* not the way to the city?
Wis 1: 7 is all-embracing, and *k* what man says.
8: 8 copious learning, she *k* the things of old,
8: 8 signs and wonders she *k* in advance and the
9: 9 who *k* your works and was present when you
9:11 For she *k* and understands all things,
9:13 For what man *k* God's counsel,
15:13 man more than any *k* that he is sinning,
Sir 1: 5 Who *k* her subtleties?
21: 7 speaker but the wise man *k* his own faults.
21:18 stupid man *k* it only as inscrutable words.
23:20 *k* all things before they exist still *k* them
34:10 One never put to the proof *k* little,
35:12 he is a God of justice, who *k* no favorites.
Is 1: 3 An ox *k* its owner,
8: 4 *k* how to call his father or mother by name,
29:15 dark, saying, "Who sees us, or who *k* us?"
59: 8 crooked, whoever treads them *k* no peace.
Jer 8: 7 Even the stork in the air *k* it seasons;
9:23 that in his prudence he knows me, *K* that I,
Lam 3: 1 who *k* affliction from the rod of his anger,
Bar 3:31 None *k* the way to her,
3:32 Yet he who knows all things *k* her;
Dn 2:22 things and *k* what is in the darkness,
Jon 3: 9 Who *k*, God may relent and forgive,
Na 3:17 wings and fly, and vanish, no one *k* where.
Mt 6: 8 Father *k* what you need before you ask him.
6:32 Your heavenly Father *k* all that you need.
9:30 sternly, "See to it that no one *k* of this."
11:27 *k* the Son but the Father, and no one *k*
24:36 for the exact day or hour, no one *k* it,
Mk 13:32 "As to the exact day or hour, no one *k* it,
Lk 7: 8 too am a man who *k* the meaning of an order,
10:22 *k* the Son except the Father and no one *k*
11: 5 "If one of you *k* someone who comes to him
12:30 Your Father *k* that you need such things.
Jn 7:49 this lot, that *k* nothing about the law
10:15 that the Father *k* me and I know the Father;
19:35 He tells what he *k* is true,
Acts 4:16 Everyone who lives in Jerusalem *k* what a
Rom 8:27 searches hearts *k* what the Spirit means,
14: 2 A man of sound faith *k* he can eat anything,
1Cor 2:11 *k* a man's innermost self but the man's own
2:11 no one *k* what lies at the depths of God
3:20 *k* how empty are the thoughts of the wise."
8: 2 If a man thinks he *k* something,
2Cor 7: 4 my many afflictions my joy *k* no bounds.
11:11 God *k* I do.
11:31 The God and Father of the Lord Jesus *k*—
12: 3 or outside his body I do not know, God *k*—
2Tm 2:19 "The Lord *k* those who are his";
Jas 4:17 *k* the right thing to do and does not do it,
2Pt 2: 9 *k* how to rescue devout men from trial,
2:10 He *k*, especially, how to treat those
Rv 12:12 His fury knows no limits, for he *k* his time

KOA (1)

Ez 23:23 and all of Chaldea, Pekod, Shoa and *K*,

KOHATH (20)

Gn 46:11 Gershon, *K*, and Merari.
Ex 6:16 order, are Gershon, *K* and Merari.
6:18 The sons of *K* were Amram,
6:18 *K* lived one hundred and thirty-three years.
Nm 3:17 of Levi were named Gershon, *K* and Merari.
3:19 The descendants of *K*,
3:27 To *K* belonged the clans of the Amramites,
10:21 The clan of *K* then set out,
16: 1 Korah, son of Izhar, son of *K*,
26:57 through *K* the clan of the Kohathites,
26:58 Among the descendants of *K* was Amram,
1Chr 5:27 The sons of Levi were Gershon, *K*,
5:28 The sons of *K* were Amram,
6: 1 The sons of Levi were Gershon, *K*,
6: 3 The sons of *K* were Amram,
6: 7 The descendants of *K* were:
6:23 son of Korah, son of Izhar, son of *K*,
15: 5 of the sons of *K*,
23: 6 Gershon, *K*, and Merari.
23:12 The sons of *K*: Amram, Izhar

KOHATHITE (7)

Nm 4:18 "Do not let the group of *K* clans perish
4:37 the census of all the men of the *K* clans
Jos 21:10 of Aaron in the *K* clan of the Levites,
21:20 *K* clans among the Levites obtained by lot,
21:26 to the rest of the *K* clans were ten in all.
1Chr 6:55 These belonged to the rest of the *K* clan.
9:32 Benaiah the *K*,

KOHATHITES (20)

Nm 3:27 these were the clans of the *K*.
3:29 *K* camped at the south side of the Dwelling.
4: 2 "Among the Levites take a total of the *K*,
4: 2 *K* between thirty and fifty years of age;
4: 4 "The service of the *K* in the meeting tent
4:15 camp, shall the *K* enter to carry them.
4:15 in the meeting tent that the *K* shall carry.

4:20 but the *K* shall not go in to look upon the
4:34 community made a registration among the *K*,
7: 9 He gave none to the *K*,
26:57 through Kohath the clan of the *K*,
Jos 21: 4 the Levites fell to the clans of the *K*,
21: 5 The rest of the *K* obtained ten cities by
1Chr 6:18 Among the *K*: Heman, the chanter
6:39 of Aaron who belonged to clan of the *K*,
6:46 The other *K* obtained ten cities by lot for
6:51 The clans of the *K* obtained cities by lot
2Chr 20:19 Levites from among the *K* and Korahites
29:12 Joel, son of Azariah, descendants of the *K*;
34:12 and Zechariah and Meshullam, of the *K*,

KOLAIAH (2)

Neh 11: 7 son of Joed, son of Pedaiah, son of *K*,
Jer 29:21 lies to you in my name, Ahab, son of *K*,

KONA (2)

Jdt 4: 4 word to the whole region of Samaria, to *K*,
15: 4 to Betomasthaim, to Choba and *K*,

KOR (1)

Ez 45:14 the *k* of ten liquid measures [or a homer,

KORAH (25)

Gn 36: 5 and Oholibamah bore Jeush, Jalam and *K*.
36:14 she bore to Esau were Jeush, Jalam, and *K*.
36:16 the clans of Teman, Omar, Zepho, Kenaz, *K*,
36:18 the clans of Jeush, Jalam, and *K*.
Ex 6:21 The sons of Izhar were *K*,
6:24 The sons of *K* were Assir,
Nm 16: 1 *K*, son of Izhar,
16: 5 Then he said to *K* and to all his band,
16: 6 take your censers *K* and all his band] and
16: 8 said to *K*, "Listen to me, you Levites!
16:16 Moses said to *K*, "You and all your band
16:19 when *K* had assembled all his band against
16:24 from the space around the Dwelling" [of *K*,
16:35 from the space around the Dwelling [of *K*,
17: 5 lest he meet the fate of *K* and his band.
17:14 in addition to those who died because of *K*.
26:10 *K* too and the band that died
26:11 The descendants of *K*,
1Chr 1:35 were Eliphaz, Reuel, Jeush, Jalam, and *K*.
2:43 The sons of Hebron were *K*,
6: 7 his son Amminadab, whose son was *K*,
6:22 son of Assir, son of Ebiasaph, son of *K*,
9:19 Kore, son of Ebiasaph, a descendant of *K*,
Sir 45:18 and the band of *K* in their defiance.
Jude 1:11 pay, and like *K* they perish in rebellion.

KORAHITES (6)

Ex 6:24 These are the clans of the *K*.
Nm 26:58 clan of the Mushites, the clan of the *K*.
1Chr 9:19 house of the *K* had as their assigned task
12: 7 Azarel, Joezer, and Ishbaal, who were *K*;
26: 1 Of the *K* was Meshelemiah,
2Chr 20:19 and *K* rose to sing the praises of the LORD,

KORAH'S (3)

Nm 16:32 all of *K* men] and all their possessions.
26: 9 *K* band when it rebelled against the LORD].
27: 3 together against the LORD [in *K* band],

KORBAN (1)

Mk 7:11 you might have had from me is *k*' (that is,

KORDAN (1)

Jos 22:10 there at the *K* a conspicuously large altar.

KORE (4)

1Chr 9:19 Shallum, son of *K*, son of Ebiasaph,
26: 1 Korahites was Meshelemiah, the son of *K*,
26:19 gatekeepers, descendants of *K* and Merari.
2Chr 31:14 *K*, the son of Imnah,

KOREITE (1)

1Chr 9:31 Levites, the first-born of Shallum the *K*,

KORS (7)

1Kgs 5: 2 thirty kors of fine flour, sixty *k* of meal,
5:25 *k* of wheat to provide for his household,
2Chr 2: 9 kors of wheat, twenty thousand *k* of barley,
27: 5 *k* of wheat and ten thousand of barley.
Ezr 7:22 wheat, one hundred *k*;

KOUM (1)

Mk 5:41 her hand, he said to her, "Talitha, *k*,"

KOZ (2)

1Chr 4: 7 of Helah were Zereth, Izhar, Ethnan, and *K*.
4: 8 *K* became the father of Anub and Zobebah,

KULOM (1)

Jos 15:59 (that is, Bethlehem), Peor, Etam, *K*,

KUSHAIAH (1)

1Chr 15:17 Merari, their brethren, Ethan, son of *K*;

L

LAADAH (1)

1Chr 4:21 *L*, the father of Mareshah;

LABAN (53)

Gn 24:29 Now Rebekah had a brother named *L*.
24:30 *L* rushed outside to the man at the spring.
24:50 *L* and his household said in reply:
25:20 and the sister of *L* the Aramean.
27:43 flee at once to my brother *L* in Haran,
28: 2 from among the daughters of your uncle *L*.
28: 5 he went to Paddan-aram, to *L*,
29: 5 Then he asked them, "Do you know *L*,
29:10 his uncle *L*, with the sheep of his uncle *L*
29:13 then recounted to *L* all that had happened,
29:13 When *L* heard the news about his sister's
29:14 all that had happened, and *L* said to him,
29:15 *L* said to him: "Should you serve me
29:16 Now *L* had two daughters;
29:18 fallen in love with Rachel, he answered *L*,
29:19 *L* replied, "I prefer to give her to you
29:21 Then Jacob said to *L*, "Give me my wife,
29:22 So *L* invited all the local inhabitants and
29:24 *L* assigned his slave girl Zilpah to his
29:25 So he cried out to *L*:
29:26 not the custom in our country," *L* replied,
29:28 *L* gave him his daughter Rachel in marriage.
29:29 *L* assigned his slave girl Bilhah to his
30:25 gave birth to Joseph, Jacob said to *L*:
30:27 *L* answered him: "If you will please
30:31 "What should I pay you?" *L* asked.
30:34 "Very well," agreed *L*.
30:35 That same day *L* removed the streaked and
30:40 or fully dark-colored animals of *L*.
30:42 So the feeble animals would go to *L*,
31:12 the things that *L* has been doing to you.
31:19 Now *L* had gone away to shear his sheep,
31:20 Jacob had hoodwinked *L* the Aramean by not
31:22 day, word came to *L* that Jacob had fled.
31:24 to *L* the Aramean in a dream and warned him,
31:25 When *L* overtook Jacob,
31:25 *L* also pitched his tents there,
31:26 "What do you mean," *L* demanded of Jacob,
31:31 "I was frightened," Jacob replied to *L*,
31:33 *L* then went in and searched Jacob's tent
31:34 When *L* had rummaged through the rest of
31:36 Jacob, now enraged, upbraided *L*.
31:43 *L* replied to Jacob: "The women are mine
31:47 *L* called it Jegar-sahadutha,
31:48 "This mound," said *L*, "shall be a witness
31:51 *L* said further to Jacob:
32: 1 *L* kissed his grandchildren and his
32: 5 *L* and have been detained there until now.
46:18 whom *L* had given to his daughter Leah;
46:25 whom *L* had given to his daughter Rachel;
Dt 1: 1 Suph, between Paran and Tophel, *L*,
Jdt 8:26 while he was tending the flocks of *L*,

LABAN'S (5)

Gn 29:30 remained in *L* service another seven years.
30:36 continued to pasture the rest of *L* flock.
30:40 own, which he did not put with *L* flock.
31: 1 Jacob learned that *L* sons were saying,
31: 2 that *L* attitude toward him was not what it

LABO (10)

Nm 13:21 as far as where Rehob adjoins *L* of Hamath.
34: 8 from Mount Hor to *L* in the land of Hamath,
Jos 13: 5 of Mount Hermon to *L* in the land of Hamath.
1Kgs 8:65 from *L* of Hamath to the Wadi of Egypt,
1Chr 13: 5 from Shihor of Egypt to *L* of Hamath,
2Chr 7: 8 from *L* of Hamath to the Wadi of Egypt,
Ez 47:15 the direction of Hethlon, past *L* of Hamath,
47:20 up to a point parallel to *L* of Hamath.
48: 1 Hethlon through *L* of Hamath to Hazar-enon,
Am 6:14 from *L* of Hamath even to the Wadi Arabah.

LABOR (60)

Gn 35:16 to be in *l* and to suffer great distress.
Ex 1:11 Israelites to oppress them with forced *l*.
2:11 his kinsmen and witnessed their forced *l*,
5: 4 Off to your *l*!
5: 5 yet you would give them rest from their *l*!"
6: 6 I will free you from the forced *l* of the
6: 7 when I free you from the *l* of the Egyptians
20: 9 Six days you may *l* and do all your work,
Dt 5:13 Six days you may *l* and do all your work;
20:11 be found in it shall serve you in forced *l*.
26: 6 and oppressed us, imposing hard *l* upon us,
28:33 the fruit of your soil and of all your *l*,
1Sm 4:19 she was seized with the pangs of *l*,
2Sm 20:24 Adoram was in charge of the forced *l*.
1Kgs 4: 6 of Abda, superintendent of the forced *l*.
9:15 This is an account of the forced *l* which
11:28 the entire *l* force of the house of Joseph.
12:18 out Adoram, superintendent of the forced *l*,
2Chr 2: 7 My servants will *l* with yours in order to
8: 8 Solomon subjected to forced *l*,
10:18 who was superintendent of the forced *l*,
24:12 in charge of the *l* on the LORD's temple,
34:13 all the workers in every kind of *l*.
Neh 3: 5 not submit to the *l* asked by their lords.
5:18 for the *l* lay heavy upon this people.
Jdt 5:11 shrewdly forced them to *l* at brickmaking,
2Mc 2:26 upon ourselves the *l* of making this digest,
Ps(s) 48: 7 anguish, like a woman's in *l*,
127: 1 the house, they *l* in vain who build it.
Prv 14:23 In all *l* there is profit,
Eccl 1: 3 all the *l* which he toils at under the sun?
2:18 all the fruits of my *l* under the sun,
2:19 all the fruits of my wise *l* under the sun.
2:20 of all the fruits of my *l* under the sun.
3:13 the fruit of all his *l* is a gift of God.
4: 9 they get a good wage for their *l*.
5:14 from his *l* that he can carry in his hand.
5:17 drink and enjoy all the fruits of his *l*
10:15 When will the fool be weary of his *l*,
Wis 15: 4 us, nor the fruitless *l* of painters,
Sir 6:20 in cultivating her you will *l* but little,
19:10 When a fool hears something, he is in *l*,
38:29 So with the potter sitting at his *l*,
Is 13: 8 of them, like a woman in *l* they writhe;
21: 3 have seized me like those of a woman in *l*;
23: 4 "I have not been in *l*,
42:14 But now, I cry out as a woman in *l*,
54: 1 in jubilant song, you who were not in *l*,
66: 7 Before she comes to *l*, she gives birth;
66: 8 in *l* when she gives birth to her children.
Jon 4:10 cost you no *l* and which you did not raise;
Mk 13: 8 This is but the onset of the pains of *l*.
Jn 4:38 Others have done the *l*,
16:21 is in *l* she is sad that her time has come.
1Cor 4:12 We work hard at manual *l*.
2Cor 11:27 enduring *l*,
Gal 4:19 in *l* pains until Christ is formed in you.
Eph 4:28 let him work with his hands at honest *l*
1Thes 3: 5 and all our *l* might have gone for nothing.
5: 3 of pains overtaking a woman in *l*,

LABORED (10)

2Chr 24:13 The workmen *l*, and the task of restoration
Eccl 1: 8 All speech is *l*;
2:21 has *l* with wisdom and knowledge and skill,
2:21 and to another, who has not *l* over it,
2:22 of heart with which he has *l* under the sun?
Wis 14:19 *l* over the likeness to the best of his
Sir 51:27 I have *l* only a little,
Rom 16:12 who has *l* long in the Lord's service.
Phil 4: 3 Clement and the others who have *l* with me,
Rv 12: 2 aloud in pain as she *l* to give birth.

LABORER (6)

Lv 19:13 withhold overnight the wages of your day *l*.
25:50 as though he had been hired as a day *l*.
Sir 7:20 nor a *l* who devotes himself to his task.
34:22 he sheds blood who denies the *l* his wages.
37:11 work, to a seasonal *l* about the harvest,
Lk 10: 7 they have, for the *l* is worth his wage.

LABORERS (14)

Jos 16:10 day, though they have been impressed as *l*.
17:13 they impressed the Canaanites as *l*,
Jgs 1:28 they impressed the Canaanites as *l*,
1:30 live among them, but have become forced *l*.
1:33 Beth-anath have become forced *l* for them.
1:35 the upper hand, they were impressed as *l*.
1Kgs 9:21 Solomon conscripted as forced *l*,
Jdt 4:10 All their resident aliens, hired *l*,
Prv 16:26 The *l* appetite labors for him,
Is 19:10 all the hired *l* shall be despondent.
31: 8 and his young men shall be impressed as *l*.
58: 3 your own pursuits, and drive all your *l*.
Mt 9:37 "The harvest is good but *l* are scarce.
9:38 master to send out *l* to gather his harvest."

LABORING (4)

Eccl 5:11 Sleep is sweet to the *l* man,
Sir 38:27 engraver and designer who, *l* night and day,
1Thes 1: 3 you are proving your faith, and *l* in love,
2Thes 3: 8 *l* to the point of exhaustion so as not to

LABORIOUS (2)

Sir 7:15 Hate not *l* tasks,
13:25 withdrawn and perplexed is the *l* schemer.

LABORIOUSLY (1)

Wis 15: 7 truly the potter, *l* working the soft earth,

LABORS (15)

Dt 30: 9 measure the returns from all your *l*,
Ps(s) 109:11 and strangers plunder the fruit of his *l*.
Prv 16:26 The laborer's appetite *l* for him,
22: 8 reaps calamity, and the rod destroys his *l*.
31:31 Give her a reward of her *l*,

LABORS (cont.)
Eccl 2:24 provide himself with good things by his *l.*
9: 9 life, for the toil of your *l* under the sun.
Wis 3:11 Vain is their hope, fruitless are their *l,*
5: 1 his oppressors who set at nought his *l.*
10:10 *l* and made abundant the fruit of his works,
10:17 the holy ones the recompense of their *l,*
Sir 31: 3 The rich man *l* to pile up wealth,
2Cor 11:23 with my many more *l* and imprisonments,
Rv 2: 2 I know your deeds, your *l,*
14:13 "Yes, they shall find rest from their *l,*

LACERATE (2)
Lv 19:28 Do not *l* your bodies for the dead,
21: 5 the edges of the beard, nor *l* the body.

LACERATED (1)
Hos 7:14 For wheat and wine they *l* themselves,

LACHISH (25)
Jos 10: 3 Piram, king of Jarmuth, Japhia, king of *L,*
10: 5 of Jerusalem, Hebron, Jarmuth, *L* and Eglon,
10:23 of Jerusalem, Hebron, Jarmuth, *L* and Eglon.
10:31 on with all Israel from Libnah to *L,*
10:32 LORD delivered *L* into the power of Israel,
10:33 Horam, king of Gezer, came up to help *L,*
10:34 From *L,* Joshua passed on with all Israel
10:35 person in it, just as he had done at *L.*
12:11 Bethel), Jerusalem, Hebron, Jarmuth, *L,*
15:39 Migdal-gad, Dilean, Mizpeh, Joktheel, *L,*
2Kgs 14:19 against him in Jerusalem, he fled to *L.*
14:19 But he was pursued to *L* and killed there.
18:14 this message to the king of Assyria at *L:*
18:17 and the commander from *L* with a great army
19: 8 the king of Assyria had withdrawn from *L,*
2Chr 11: 9 Adullam, Gath, Mareshah, Ziph, Adoraim, *L,*
25:27 hence he fled to *L.*
25:27 him to *L* and put him to death there.
32: 9 himself remained at *L* with all his forces,
Neh 11:30 and their villages, *L* and its countryside,
Is 36: 2 From *L* the king of Assyria sent his
37: 8 When the commander returned to *L* and heard
Jer 34: 7 remaining cities of Judah, *L* and Azekah,
Mi 1:13 O inhabitants of *L;* Lachish, the beginning

LACK (43)
Lv 11:10 all those that *l* either fins or scales are
Nm 5:13 remains unproved for *l* of a witness
Dt 8: 9 without stint and where you will *l* nothing,
14:10 *l* either fins or scales you shall not eat;
Jgs 18: 7 with no *l* of any natural resources.
1Kgs 11:22 said to him, "What do you *l* with me,
Neh 5:14 from the time that Nehemiah's *L* of
Jdt 8: 9 people, discouraged by their *l* of water,
Jb 4:11 The old lion perishes for *l* of prey,
36:12 they die for *l* of knowledge.
Prv 5:23 He will die from *l* of discipline,
11:14 For *l* of guidance a people falls;
13:23 but some men perish for *l* of a law court.
26:20 For *l* of wood,
Eccl 8:13 days, for his *l* of reverence toward God.
10: 3 in his *l* of understanding he calls
Sg 7: 3 bowl that should never *l* for mixed wine.
Sir 13: 8 be not as those who *l* sense.
19:24 his *l* of strength keeps him from sinning,
22:13 rest and not be wearied by his *l* of sense.
37:30 Through *l* of self-control many have died,
42:20 No understanding does he *l;*
Is 24:11 In the streets they cry out for *l* of wine;
50: 2 Their fish rot for *l* of water,
Jer 7:32 For *l* of space,
19:11 place, for *l* of place to bury elsewhere.
33:17 Never shall David *l* a successor on the
Lam 1: 4 for *l* of pilgrims going to her feasts;
Bar 3:28 They perished for *l* of prudence,
Ez 34: 5 So they were scattered for *l* of a shepherd,
34: 8 for every wild beast, for *l* of a shepherd;
Mt 13: 6 it, it began to wither for *l* of roots.
13:58 miracles there because of their *l* of faith.
Mk 4: 6 it, it began to wither for *l* of roots.
6: 6 so much did their *l* of faith distress him.
9:24 Help my *l* of trust!"
Lk 8: 6 up, then withered through *l* of moisture.
1Cor 1: 7 confirmed among you that you *l* no spiritual
7: 5 tempt you through your *l* of self-control.
7:19 and its *l* makes no difference either.
2Cor 6:12 There is no *l* of room for you in us;
8:15 excess and he who gathered little had no *l.*"
Gal 5: 6 nor the *l* of it counts for anything;

LACKED (3)
1Mc 4: 6 who *l* such armor and swords as they would
2Mc 8:13 the cowardly and those who *l* faith in
Phil 4:10 course, but *l* the opportunity to show it.

LACKING (17)
Lv 2:13 of your God be *l* from your cereal offering.
Dt 15:11 The needy will never be *l* in the land;
Jgs 18:10 a place where no natural resource is *l.*"
21: 3 that today one tribe of Israel should be *l?*"
2Chr 7:18 be *l* someone of yours as ruler in Israel.'
Jb 39:13 her plumage is *l* in pinions.
Ps(s) 34:10 for nought is *l* to those who fear him.
Wis 9: 5 *l* in comprehension of judgment and of laws.
Is 34:16 No one of these shall be *l,*
59:15 Honesty is *l,*
Jer 33:18 nor shall priests of Levi ever be *l,*
Lam 4: 9 pierced through, *l* the fruits of the field!
Ez 7:26 instruction shall be *l* to the priest,
Mk 4:40 Why are you *l* in faith?"
2Cor 11: 6 but I know that I am not *l* in knowledge.
Col 1:24 In my own flesh I fill up what is *l* in the
Jas 1: 4 you may be fully mature and *l* in nothing.

LACKS (7)
Lv 11:12 that *l* fins or scales is loathsome for you.
Prv 9: 4 to him who *l* understanding,
9:16 turn in here, or who *l* understanding;
12: 9 than one of assumed importance who *l* bread.
Eccl 6: 2 that he *l* none of all the things he craves;
Sir 31:27 *l* the wine which was created for his joy?
2Pt 1: 9 Any man who *l* these qualities is

LAD (5)
1Sm 17:56 king said, "Find out whose son the *l* is."
20:38 Again he called to his *l,* "Hurry
Tb 6: 6 After the *l* had cut the fish open,
Jn 6: 9 "There is a *l* here who has five barley
Acts 20: 9 and a certain young *l* named Eutychus who

LADAN (5)
1Chr 7:26 whose son was Tahan, whose son was *L,*
23: 7 To the Gershonites belonged *L* and Shimei.
23: 8 The sons of *L:* Jehiel, the chief
23: 9 These were the heads of the families of *L.*
26:21 Among the descendants of *L* the Gershonite,

LADDER (1)
1Mc 11:59 the *L* of Tyre to the frontier of Egypt.

LADDERS (1)
1Mc 5:30 *l* and devices for capturing the stronghold,

LADEN (12)
Gn 37:25 from Gilead, their camels *l* with gum,
2Sm 16: 1 asses *l* with two hundred loaves of bread,
Tb 3:10 go down to the nether world *l* with sorrow.
1Mc 10:87 returned to Jerusalem, *l* with much booty.
Jb 37:11 With hail, also, the clouds are *l,*
Ps(s) 105:37 he led them forth *l* with silver and gold,
144:14 may our oxen be well *l.*
Sg 3: 6 like a column of smoke *L* with myrrh,
Sir 4:21 There is a sense of shame *l* with guilt,
Is 1: 4 sinful nation, people *l* with wickedness,
Ez 27:25 full and heavily *l* in the heart of the sea.
Am 2:13 as a wagon crushes when *l* with sheaves.

LADIES (3)
Est 1:18 This very day the Persian and Median *l* who
Is 32: 9 O complacent *l,* rise up and hear my voice,
1Tm 5:13 Besides, they learn to be *l* of leisure,

LADY (3)
Jdt 11: 1 "Take courage, *l;*
2Jn 1: 1 to a *L* who is elect and to her children.
1: 5 But now, my *L,* I would make this request

LAEL (1)
Nm 3:24 ancestral house was Eliasaph, son of *L.*

LAGGED (1)
Dt 25:18 cut off at the rear all those who *l* behind.

LAHAD (1)
1Chr 4: 2 Jahath became the father of Ahumai and *L.*

LAHMAM (1)
Jos 15:40 Lachish, Bozkath, Eglon, Cabbon, *L,*

LAHMI (1)
1Chr 20: 5 and Elhanan, the son of Jair, slew *L,*

LAID (199)
Gn 22: 6 and *l* it on his son Isaac's shoulders,
39:12 the house, she *l* hold of him by his cloak,
48:14 right hand and *l* it on the head of Ephraim,
48:17 had *l* his right hand on Ephraim's head,
50:26 and *l* to rest in a coffin in Egypt.
Ex 4: 4 So he put out his hand and *l* hold of it,
29:15 his sons have *l* their hands on its head,
29:19 his sons have *l* their hands on its head,
33: 6 the Israelites *l* aside their ornaments.
Lv 1: 7 on the altar and *l* some wood on them,
4:24 Having *l* his hands on its head,
4:29 *l* his hand on the head of the sin offering,
4:33 Having *l* his hand on its head,
8:14 and his sons *l* their hands on its head.
8:18 and his sons *l* their hands on its head.
8:22 and his sons *l* their hands on its head.
20:18 *l* bare the flowing fountain of her blood.
24:14 heard him have *l* their hands on his head,
26:13 had *l* upon you and letting you walk erect.
Nm 17:22 Then Moses *l* the staffs down before the
19: 2 and on which no yoke has ever been *l.*
21:30 Ar is *l* waste;
27: 5 When Moses *l* their case before the LORD,
27:23 he *l* his hands on him and gave him his
32: 4 has *l* low before the community of Israel,
36: 1 came up and *l* this plea before Moses and
Dt 34: 9 since Moses had *l* his hands upon him;
1Sm 11: 1 went up and *l* siege to Jabesh-gilead.
18: 2 Saul *l* claim to David that day and did not
19:13 the household idol and *l* it in the bed,
2Sm 3:29 of Ner, be *l* to Joab and to all his family.
22:16 the foundations of the earth were *l* bare,
1Kgs 3:20 *l* him in her bosom, after she had *l* her dead
6:15 and its floor was *l* with fir planking.
6:37 *l* in the month of Ziv in the fourth year,
13:30 He *l* the man's body in his own grave,
14:13 of Jeroboam's line will be *l* in the grave,
16:17 by all Israel, and *l* siege to Tirzah.
16:34 son, Abiram, when he *l* the foundation,
17:19 he was staying, and *l* him on his own bed.
18:33 cut up the young bull and *l* it on the wood.
2Kgs 4:21 and *l* him on the bed of the man of God.
4:31 on ahead and had *l* the staff upon the boy,
6:24 his whole army and *l* siege to Samaria.
18: 9 Assyria, attacked Samaria, *l* siege to it,
19:17 have *l* waste the nations and their lands,
1Chr 13:10 because he had *l* his hand on the ark.
20: 1 force, *l* waste the land of the Ammonites,
22: 3 He also *l* up large stores of iron to make
22: 5 death David *l* up materials in abundance.
22:14 with great effort I have *l* up for the
2Chr 3: 3 These were the specifications *l* down by
8:16 foundation of the house of the LORD was *l*
10: 4 "Your father *l* a heavy yoke upon us.
10:10 you, 'Your father *l* a heavy yoke upon us,
10:14 "My father *l* a heavy yoke on you,
16:14 having *l* him upon a couch which was filled
20:22 the LORD *l* an ambush against the Ammonites,
29:23 the assembly, who *l* their hands upon them.
Ezr 3: 6 the temple of the LORD had not yet been *l.*
3:10 had *l* the foundation of the LORD's temple,
3:10 the LORD in the manner *l* down by David,
3:11 foundation of the LORD's house had been *l.*
3:12 foundation of the present house being *l.*
4:12 and the foundations have already been *l.*
5:16 Then this same Sheshbazzar came and *l* the
Neh 5:15 had *l* a heavy burden on the people,
Jdt 2: 2 and nobles, *l* before them his secret plan,
7:14 will be *l* low in the streets of their city.
10: 3 on, *l* aside the garments of her widowhood,
Est 10: 1 King Ahasuerus *l* tribute on the land and
1Mc 2:10 realm, and *l* its hand on her possessions?
2:12 and our beauty and our glory *l* waste,
15: 4 it and *l* waste many cities in my realm.
15:29 You have *l* waste their territories,
2Mc 3:27 Men picked him up and *l* him on a stretcher.
5:16 He *l* his impure hands on the sacred
8:35 *l* aside his fine clothes and fled alone
8:36 that they followed the laws *l* down by him.
11:11 they *l* low eleven thousand foot soldiers
15:27 they *l* low at least thirty-five thousand,
Jb 6: 2 and my calamity *l* with it in the scales,
16:15 my skin, and have *l* my brow in the dust.
24:24 they are *l* low and,
38: 6 pedestals sunk, and who *l* the cornerstone,
38:25 Who has *l* out a channel for the downpour
Ps(s) 18:16 the foundations of the world were *l* bare,
66:11 you *l* a heavy burden on our backs.
78:31 men, and *l* low the young men of Israel.
79: 1 temple, they have *l* Jerusalem in ruins.
79: 7 devoured Jacob and *l* waste his dwelling.
89:41 you have *l* his strongholds in ruins.
119:110 The wicked have *l* a snare for me,
140: 6 by the wayside they have *l* snares for me.
Prv 27:14 morning a curse can be *l* to his charge.
Wis 4:19 They shall be utterly *l* waste and shall be
Sir 44:14 Their bodies are peacefully *l* away,
Is 6:13 in it, then this in turn shall be *l* waste;
14: 8 "Now that you are *l* to rest,
15: 1 Moab is destroyed; *L* waste in a night,
17: 9 they shall be *l* waste.
23:18 It shall not be stored up or *l* away,
24: 3 The earth is utterly *l* waste,
32:19 The city will be utterly *l* low.
37:18 *l* waste all the nations and their lands,
44:28 of the temple, "Let its foundations be *l.*"
47: 6 And upon old men you *l* a very heavy yoke.
48:13 my hand *l* the foundations of the earth;
49:17 you down and *l* you waste go forth from you;
51:13 heavens and *l* the foundations of the earth?
51:16 who *l* the foundations of the earth,
53: 6 the LORD *l* upon him the guilt of us all.
64:10 all that was dear to us is *l* waste.
Jer 4:20 the whole earth is *l* waste.
5: 3 you *l* them low,
10:25 Jacob utterly, and *l* waste his dwelling.
26: 8 the priests and prophets *l* hold of him,

35:16 the command which their father *l* on them;
48: 1 Woe to Nebo, it is *l* waste;
Lam 3:28 and in silence, when it is *l* upon him.
Ez 6: 4 Your altars shall be *l* waste,
6: 6 be made desolate and high places *l* waste,
6: 6 altars will be made desolate and *l* waste,
19: 8 *l* out against him snares all about him;
21:29 with your crimes *l* bare and your
32:27 and whose shields were *l* over their bones,
32:32 is he *l* to rest among the uncircumcised,
36:35 "The cities that were in ruins, *l* waste,
39:21 executed and the hand I have *l* upon them.
40:17 The pavement was *l* all around the court,
40:43 and on them were *l* the instruments with
40:43 On the tables themselves the flesh was *l*.
Dn 1: 1 of Babylon came and *l* siege to Jerusalem.
13:34 rose up and *l* their hands on her head.
14: 1 After King Astyages was *l* with his fathers,
Hos 10:11 I myself *l* a yoke upon her fair neck;
Jl 1: 7 He has *l* waste my vine,
Am 7: 9 The high places of Isaac shall be *l* waste,
Jon 3: 6 he rose from his throne, *l* aside his robe,
Mi 4:14 "They have *l* siege against us!"
Na 1: 5 The earth is *l* waste before him,
Zep 3: 6 nations, their battlements are *l* waste;
Hg 2:15 *l* upon a stone in the temple of the LORD,
Zec 4: 9 have *l* the foundations of this house,
8: 9 hosts was *l* for the building of the temple.
11: 3 lions, the jungle of the Jordan is *l* waste.
Mt 3:10 now the ax is *l* to the root of the tree.
15:30 They *l* them at his feet and he cured them.
19:15 And he *l* his hands on their heads before
21: 7 and the colt and *l* their cloaks on them,
22: 6 The rest *l* hold of his servants,
27:60 Joseph wrapped it in fresh linen and *l*
28: 6 Come and see the place where he was *l*.
Mk 6:29 carried his body away and *l* it in a tomb.
6:56 they *l* the sick in the market places and
8:23 his eyes he *l* his hands on him and asked,
8:25 a second time Jesus *l* hands on his eyes,
14:46 this, they *l* hands on him and arrested him.
15:46 and *l* him in a tomb which had been cut out
15:47 of Joses observed where he had been *l*.
16: 6 See the place where they *l* him.
Lk 2: 7 in swaddling clothes and *l* him in a manger,
2:35 the thoughts of many hearts may be *l* bare."
3: 9 now the ax is *l* to the root of the tree.
4:40 he *l* hands on each of them and cured them.
6:48 dug deeply and *l* the foundation on a rock.
11:17 kingdom divided against itself is *l* waste.
13:13 He *l* his hand on her,
23:26 they *l* hold of one Simon the Cyrenean who
23:53 and *l* it in a tomb hewn out of the rock,
Jn 7:30 but no one *l* a finger on him because his
7:44 However, no one *l* hands on him.
8:17 It is *l* down in your law that evidence
11:34 "Where have you *l* him?"
11:38 It was a cave with a stone *l* across it.
20:15 you have *l* him and I will take him away."
21: 9 there with a fish *l* on it and some bread.
Acts 5: 2 he took and *l* at the feet of the apostles.
5:15 streets and *l* them on cots and mattresses,
9:17 the house he *l* his hands on Saul and said,
9:37 her body and *l* it out in an upstairs room.
13:29 him down from the tree and *l* him in a tomb.
19: 6 As Paul *l* his hands on them,
28: 8 bed, *l* up with chronic fever and dysentery.
28: 8 praying, *l* his hands on him and cured him.
28:23 to evening he *l* the case before them,
Rom 15:20 I did not want to build on a foundation *l*
1Cor 3:10 Thanks to the favor God showed me I *l* a
3:11 other than the one that has been *l*,
14:25 and the secret of his heart will be *l* bare.
2Cor 10:16 Following the rule *l* down for us,
Gal 2: 2 and I *l* out for their scrutiny the gospel
1Tm 4:14 the presbyters *l* their hands on you.
2Tm 1: 6 God bestowed when my hands were *l* on you.
2:19 But the foundation God has *l* stands firm.
2Pt 3: 4 Our forefathers have been *l* to rest,
1Jn 3:16 love was that he *l* down his life for us;

LAIN (8)

2Sm 3:30 [Joab and his brother Abishai had *l* in wait
Jb 3:13 I should have *l* down and been tranquil;
31: 9 and I have *l* in wait at my neighbor's door;
Jer 3: 2 and see, where have men not *l* with you?
Ez 23: 8 when they had *l* with her as a young girl,
Mt 13:35 *l* hidden since the creation of the world."
Jn 20:12 foot of the place where Jesus' body had *l*.
2Pt 2: 3 condemnation has not *l* idle all this time,

LAIR (6)

Ps(s) 10: 9 He waits in secret like a lion in his *l*;
Is 11: 8 the child lay his hand on the adder's *l*.
Jer 4: 7 Up comes the lion from his *l*,
25:38 The lion leaves his *l*,
Hb 3:14 be of devouring the wretched in their *l*.
Zep 2:15 she become a waste, a *l* for wild beasts?

LAIRS (2)

Mt 8:20 Jesus said to him, "The foxes have *l*,
Lk 9:58 Jesus said to him, "The foxes have *l*,

LAISH (6)

Jgs 18: 7 So the five men went on and came to *L*.
18:14 the land of *L* said to their kinsmen,
18:27 the priest he had had, they attacked *L*,
18:29 the name of the city was formerly *L*.
1Sm 25:43 Saul's own daughter, to Palti, son of *L*,
2Sm 3:15 away from her husband Paltiel, son of *L*,

LAISHAH (1)

Is 10:30 Hearken, *L*! Answer her, Anathoth!

LAKE (23)

Dt 33:23 The *l* and south of it are his possession!"
Jb 14:11 As when the waters of a *l* fail,
Mt 8:24 warning a violent storm came up on the *l*,
13:47 is also like a dragnet thrown into the *l*,
14:25 he came walking toward them on the *l*.
17:27 for fear of disedifying them go to the *l*,
Mk 3: 7 withdrew toward the *l* with his disciples.
4: 1 occasion he began to teach beside the *l*.
5: 1 territory on the other side of the *l*.
5:13 went rushing down the bluff into the *l*,
5:21 around him and he stayed close to the *l*.
6:47 on the *l* while he was alone on the land.
6:49 When they saw him walking on the *l*,
Lk 5: 1 As he stood by the *L* of Gennesaret,
5: 2 saw two boats moored by the side of the *l*;
8:22 us cross over to the far side of the *l*."
8:23 A windstorm descended on the *l*,
8:33 the herd charged down the bluff into the *l*,
8:37 into the boat and went back across the *l*.
Jn 6:16 drew on, his disciples came down to the *l*.
6:17 intending to cross the *l* toward Capernaum.
6:22 crowd remained on the other side of the *l*.
6:25 they found him on the other side of the *l*,

LAKESHORE (2)

Mt 13: 1 leaving the house, Jesus sat down by the *l*.
Mk 2:13 time, while he went walking along the *l*,

LAKKUM (1)

Jos 19:33 Heleph, from the oak at Zaanannim to *L*,

LAMA (1)

Mk 15:34 a loud voice, "Eloi, Eloi, *l* sabachthani?"

LAMB (100)

Ex 12: 3 your families must procure for itself a *l*,
12: 4 If a family is too small for a whole *l*,
12: 4 shall share in the *l* in proportion
12: 5 The *l* must be a year-old male and without
12: 7 every house in which they partake of the *l*.
29:39 one *l* in the morning and the other lamb at
29:39 and the other *l* at the evening twilight.
29:40 With the first *l* there shall be a tenth of
29:41 *l* you shall offer at the evening twilight,
Lv 3: 7 If he presents a *l* as his offering,
4:32 for his sin offering he presents a *l*,
4:35 fat is removed from the peace-offering *l*,
5: 6 from the flock, a ewe *l* or a she-goat.
9: 3 for a sin offering, a calf and a *l*,
12: 6 yearling *l* for a holocaust and a pigeon
12: 8 If, however, she cannot afford a *l*,
14:10 lambs, one unblemished yearling ewe *l*,
14:13 (This *l* he shall slaughter in the sacred
14:21 shall take one male *l* for a guilt offering,
14:24 Taking the guilt-offering *l*,
14:25 he has slaughtered the guilt-offering *l*,
22:27 "When an ox or a *l* or a goat is born,
23:12 for a holocaust an unblemished yearling *l*.
Nm 6:12 bringing a yearling *l* as a guilt offering.
6:14 one unblemished yearling *l* for a holocaust,
6:14 yearling ewe *l* for a sin offering,
7:15 ram, and one yearling *l* for a holocaust:
7:21 ram, and one yearling *l* for a holocaust;
7:27 ram, and one yearling *l* for a holocaust;
7:33 ram, and one yearling *l* for a holocaust;
7:39 ram, and one yearling *l* for a holocaust;
7:45 ram, and one yearling *l* for a holocaust;
7:51 ram, and one yearling *l* for a holocaust;
7:57 ram, and one yearling *l* for a holocaust;
7:63 ram, and one yearling *l* for a holocaust;
7:69 ram, and one yearling *l* for a holocaust;
7:75 ram, and one yearling *l* for a holocaust;
7:81 ram, and one yearling *l* for a holocaust;
15: 5 *l* sacrificed in holocaust or otherwise.
15:11 is to be done for each ox, ram, *l* or goat.
28: 4 offering one *l* in the morning and the
28: 7 And as the libation for the first *l*,
28: 8 The other *l*, to be offered
28:13 oil as the cereal offering for each *l*,
28:14 the ram, and a fourth of a hin for each *l*.
1Sm 7: 9 Samuel therefore took an unweaned *l* and
2Sm 12: 3 except one little ewe *l* that he had bought.
12: 4 *l* and made a meal of it for his visitor."
12: 6 He shall restore the ewe *l* fourfold
Sir 13:16 Is a wolf ever allied with a *l*?
46:16 upon God, and offered him a suckling *l*;
Is 11: 6 Then the wolf shall be a guest of the *l*,
53: 7 Like a *l* led to the slaughter or a sheep
65:25 The wolf and the *l* shall graze alike,
66: 3 sacrificing a *l*, like breaking a dog's neck;
Jer 11:19 Yet I, like a trusting *l* led to slaughter,
Ez 46:13 to the LORD an unblemished yearling *l*;
46:15 The *l*, the cereal offering,
Mk 14:12 was customary to sacrifice the paschal *l*,
Lk 22: 7 was appointed to sacrifice the paschal *l*.
Jn 1:29 There is the *L* of God who takes away the
1:36 There is the *L* of God!"
Acts 8:32 like a *l* before its shearer he was silent
1Pt 1:19 unblemished *l* chosen before the world's
Rv 5: 6 a Lamb standing, a *L* that had been slain.
5: 7 The *L* came and received the scroll from
5: 8 twenty-four elders fell down before the *L*.
5:12 "Worthy is the *L* that was slain to
5:13 One seated on the throne, and to the *L*,
6: 1 *L* broke open the first of the seven seals,
6: 3 When the *L* broke open the second seal,
6: 5 When the *L* broke open the third seal,
6: 7 When the *L* broke open the fourth seal,
6: 9 When the *L* broke open the fifth seal,
6:12 When I saw the *L* break open the sixth seal,
6:16 on the throne and from the wrath of the *L*!
7: 9 They stood before the throne and the *L*,
7:10 is seated on the throne, and from the *L*!"
7:14 and made them white in the blood of the *L*.
7:17 the *L* on the throne will shepherd them.
8: 1 When the *L* broke open the seventh seal,
12:11 the *L* and by the word of their testimony;
13: 8 which belongs to the *L* who was slain.
14: 1 Then the *L* appeared in my vision.
14: 4 are pure and follow the *L* wherever he goes.
14: 4 first fruits of mankind for God and the *L*.
14:10 before the holy angels and before the *L*,
15: 3 the servant of God, and the song of the *L*:
17:14 the *L* but the Lamb will conquer them,
19: 7 For this is the wedding day of the *L*;
19: 9 been invited to the wedding feast of the *L*."
21: 9 you the woman who is the bride of the *L*."
21:14 the names of the twelve apostles of the *L*.
21:22 he and the *L*.
21:23 God gave it light, and its lamp was the *L*.
21:27 in the book of the living kept by the *L*.
22: 1 from the throne of God and of the *L*
22: 3 throne of God and of the *L* shall be there,

LAMBS (87)

Gn 21:28 also set apart seven ewe *l* of the flock,
21:29 these seven ewe *l* that you have set apart?"
21:30 "The seven ewe *l* you shall accept from me
Ex 12:21 them, "Go and procure *l* for your families,
29:38 two yearling *l* as the sacrifice
Lv 14:10 day he shall take two unblemished male *l*,
14:12 Taking one of the male *l*,
23:18 holocaust of seven unblemished yearling *l*,
23:19 and two yearling *l* as a peace offering.
23:20 two *l* as a wave offering before the LORD;
Nm 7:17 and five yearling *l* for a peace offering.
7:23 and five yearling *l* for a peace offering.
7:29 and five yearling *l* for a peace offering.
7:35 and five yearling *l* for a peace offering.
7:41 and five yearling *l* for a peace offering.
7:47 and five yearling *l* for a peace offering.
7:53 and five yearling *l* for a peace offering.
7:59 and five yearling *l* for a peace offering.
7:65 and five yearling *l* for a peace offering.
7:71 and five yearling *l* for a peace offering.
7:77 and five yearling *l* for a peace offering.
7:83 and five yearling *l* for a peace offering.
7:87 bulls, twelve rams, and twelve yearling *l*,
7:88 rams, sixty goats, and sixty yearling *l*.
28: 3 *l* each day as the established holocaust,
28: 9 shall offer two unblemished yearling *l*,
28:11 ram, and seven unblemished yearling *l*,
28:19 *l* that you are sure are unblemished,
28:21 and one tenth for each of the seven *l*;
28:27 *l* that you are sure are unblemished,
28:29 ram, and one tenth for each of the seven *l*.
29: 2 one ram, and seven unblemished yearling *l*,
29: 4 ram, and one tenth for each of the seven *l*.
29: 8 *l* that you are sure are unblemished,
29:10 ram, and one tenth for each of the seven *l*.
29:13 fourteen yearling *l* that are unblemished,
29:15 and one tenth for each of the fourteen *l*.
29:17 rams, and fourteen unblemished yearling *l*,
29:18 rams and *l* in proportion to their number,
29:20 rams, and fourteen unblemished yearling *l*,
29:21 rams and *l* in proportion to their number,
29:23 rams, and fourteen unblemished yearling *l*,
29:24 rams and *l* in proportion to their number,
29:26 rams, and fourteen unblemished yearling *l*,
29:27 rams and *l* in proportion to their number,
29:29 rams, and fourteen unblemished yearling *l*,
29:30 rams and *l* in proportion to their number,
29:32 rams, and fourteen unblemished yearling *l*,
29:33 rams and *l* in proportion to their number,
29:36 one ram, and seven unblemished yearling *l*,
29:37 rams and *l* in proportion to their number,
Dt 32:14 its sheep, with the fat of its *l* and rams;
1Sm 15: 9 best of the fat sheep and oxen, and the *l*.

LAMBS (cont.)
2Kgs 3: 4 *l* and the wool of a hundred thousand rams.
1Chr 29:21 bulls, a thousand rams, and a thousand *l*,
2Chr 29:21 seven *l* and seven he-goats were brought
29:22 then they slaughtered the *l* and cast the
29:32 oxen, one hundred rams, and two hundred *l*:
35: 7 to the common people a flock of *l* and kids,
Ezr 6: 9 and *l* for holocausts to the God of heaven,
6:17 two hundred rams, and four hundred *l*,
7:17 to use this money to buy bulls, rams, *l*,
8:35 Israel, ninety-six rams, seventy-seven *l*,
Jb 21:11 These folk have infants numerous as *l*,
Ps(s) 114: 4 rams, the hills like the *l* of the flock.
114: 6 You hills, like the *l* of the flock?
Prv 27:26 in, The *l* will provide you with clothing,
Wis 19: 9 like horses, and bounded about like *l*,
Sir 47: 3 kids, and of bears, like *l* of the flock.
Is 1:11 of calves, *l* and goats I find no pleasure.
5:17 *L* shall graze there at pasture,
34: 6 with fat, With the blood of *l* and goats,
40:11 in his arms he gathers the *l*,
Jer 51:40 bring them down like *l* to the slaughter,
Ez 27:21 they dealt in *l*,
39:18 blood of the princes of the land [rams, *l*,
46: 4 six unblemished *l* and an unblemished ram,
46: 5 for the ram, whatever he pleases for the *l*,
46: 6 bull, also six *l* and a ram without blemish,
46: 7 ram, for the *l* as much as he has at hand,
46:11 ram, but for the *l* as much as one pleases,
Dn 3:40 rams and bullocks, or thousands of fat *l*.
Hos 4:16 them broad pastures as though they were *l*?
Am 6: 4 couches, They eat *l* taken from the flock,
Lk 10: 3 am sending you as *l* in the midst of wolves.
Jn 21:15 At which Jesus said, "Feed my *l*."
Heb 11:28 the Passover and sprinkled the *l* blood,

LAME (22)
Lv 21:18 he who is blind, or *l*,
Dt 15:21 *l* or blind or has any other serious defect,
2Sm 4: 4 he fell and became *l*
5: 6 the blind and the *l* will drive you away!"
5: 8 The *l* and the blind shall be the personal
5: 8 blind and the *l* shall not enter the palace."
9:13 He was *l* in both feet.
19:27 For your servant, who is *l*,
Jb 29:15 eyes to the blind, and feet to the *l* was I;
Is 33:23 spoils and the *l* will carry off the loot.
35: 6 Then will the *l* leap like a stag,
Jer 31: 8 with the blind and the *l* in their midst,
Mi 4: 6 day, says the LORD, I will gather the *l*,
4: 7 I will make of the *l* a remnant,
Zep 3:19 I will save the *l*,
Mal 1: 8 When you offer the *l* or the sick,
1:13 You bring in what you seize, or the *l*,
Mt 21:14 The blind and the *l* came to him inside the
Lk 14:13 and the crippled, the *l* and the blind.
14:21 poor and the crippled, the blind and the *l*.'
Jn 5: 3 *l* or disabled [4][waiting for the movement
Acts 14: 8 there was a man who was *l* from birth;

LAMECH (12)
Gn 4:18 and Methusael became the father of *L*.
4:19 *L* took two wives;
4:23 *L* said to his wives:
4:23 wives of *L*,
4:24 sevenfold, then *L* seventy-sevenfold."
5:25 years old, he became the father of *L*.
5:26 and eighty-two years after the birth of *L*,
5:28 *L* was one hundred and eighty-two years old,
5:30 *L* lived five hundred and ninety-five years
5:31 The whole lifetime of *L* was seven hundred
1Chr 1: 3 Enoch, Methuselah, *L*
Lk 3:36 son of Shem, son of Noah, son of *L*,

LAMENT (30)
Gn 37:35 Thus did his father *l* him.
Jgs 21: 2 evening, raising their voices in bitter *l*.
Est 4: 3 mourning, with fasting, weeping, and *l*;
Ps(s) 64: 2 Hear, O God, my voice in my *l*;
Sir 38:16 one who is dead with wailing and bitter *l*;
Is 3:26 Her gates will *l* and mourn,
19: 8 The fishermen shall mourn and *l*,
23:14 *L*, O ships of Tarshish,
Jer 9:19 this dirge, and each other this *l*.
16: 5 go not there to *l* or offer sympathy.
22:18 They shall not *l* him, "Alas!
22:18 They shall not *l* him, "Alas, Lord!
34: 5 peace, and they will *l* you as their lord,
Bar 4:11 but with mourning and *l* I let them go.
4:23 With mourning and *l* I sent you forth,
Ez 24:17 Groan in silence, make no *l* for the dead,
26:17 Then they shall utter a *l* over you:
27: 2 for you, son of man, utter a *l* over Tyre,
27:31 you they weep in anguish, with bitter *l*.
27:32 In their mourning they utter a *l* over you;
28:12 of man, utter a *l* over the king of Tyre,
32: 2 Son of man, utter a *l* over Pharaoh,
32:18 Son of man, *l* over the throngs of Egypt,
Jl 1: 8 *L* like a virgin girt with sackcloth for
Am 5: 1 Hear this word which I utter over you, a *l*,
5:16 to wail and professional mourners to *l*,
Mi 1: 8 Judgment For this reason I *l* and wail,
Jas 4: 9 Begin to *l*, to mourn, and to weep;
Rv 1: 7 peoples of the earth shall *l* him bitterly.
18: 9 in her sensuality will weep and *l* over her

LAMENTATION (17)
2Chr 35:25 Jeremiah also composed a *l* over Josiah,
Tb 2: 6 into mourning, And all your songs into *l*."
1Mc 1:27 Every bridegroom took up *l*,
4:39 they tore their clothes and made great *l*;
9:41 mourning, and the sound of music into *l*.
13:26 All Israel bewailed him with solemn *l*,
Is 43:14 bars, and the Chaldeans shall cry out in *l*.
Jer 9: 9 the mountains, break out in cries of *l*,
Ez 2:10 *L* and wailing and woe!
19: 1 man, raise a *l* over the prince of Israel:
19:14 This is a *l* and serves as a lamentation.
Am 5:16 In every square there shall be *l*,
5:17 shall be *l* when I pass through your midst,
Mi 1: 8 I utter *l* like the jackals,
1:11 *l* of Beth-ezel finds in you its grounds.
Mt 2:18 cry was heard at Ramah, sobbing and loud *l*:

LAMENTATIONS (4)
2Chr 35:25 and female singers in their *l* over Josiah.
35:25 Israel, and can be found written in the *L*.
2Mc 11: 6 people begged the Lord with *l* and tears
Am 8:10 into mourning and all your songs into *l*.

LAMENTED (3)
Nm 11: 4 for meat that even the Israelites *l* again,
Lk 8:52 While everyone wept and *l* her,
23:27 who beat their breasts and *l* over him.

LAMENTING (1)
Is 15: 3 streets they wear sackcloth, *l* and weeping;

LAMP (36)
1Sm 3: 3 The *l* of God was not yet extinguished,
2Sm 21:17 us again lest you quench the *l* of Israel."
22:29 You are my *l*, O LORD!
1Kgs 11:36 may always have a *l* before me in Jerusalem,
15: 4 LORD, his God, gave him a *l* in Jerusalem,
2Kgs 4:10 for him with a bed, table, chair, and *l*,
8:19 a *l* in the LORD's presence for all time.
2Chr 21: 7 to give him and his sons a *l* for all time.
Tb 8:13 She sent the maid, who lit a *l*,
Jb 17: 1 is broken, my *l* of life extinguished;
18: 6 in spite of him, his *l* goes out.
21:17 How often is the *l* of the wicked put out?
29: 3 While he kept his *l* shining above my head,
Ps(s) 18:29 You indeed, O LORD, give light to my *l*;
119:105 A *l* to my feet is your word,
132:17 I will place a *l* for my anointed.
Prv 6:23 For the bidding is a *l*,
13: 9 gaily, but the *l* of the wicked goes out.
20:20 *l* will go out at the coming of darkness.
20:27 A *L* from the LORD is the breath of man;
24:20 the *l* of the wicked will be put out.
31:18 at night her *l* is undimmed.
Sir 50:29 for the fear of the LORD is his *l*.
Jer 25:10 of the millstone and the light of the *l*.
Mt 5:15 a *l* and then put it under a bushel basket.
6:22 The eye is the body's *l*.
Mk 4:21 "Is a *l* acquired to be put under a bushel
Lk 8:16 "No one lights a *l* and puts it under a
11:33 "One who lights a *l* does not put it in
11:34 The eye is the *l* of your body.
11:36 as when a *l* shines brightly for you."
15: 8 does not light a *l* and sweep the house in
Jn 5:35 He was the *l*,
2Pt 1:19 as you would on a *l* shining in a dark
Rv 18:23 *l* shall ever again shine out in you!
21:23 God gave it light, and its *l* was the Lamb.

LAMPS (34)
Ex 25:37 seven lamps for it and so set up the *l*
27:20 so that you may keep *l* burning regularly.
30: 7 after morning, when he prepares the *l*,
30: 8 the evening twilight, when he lights the *l*,
35:14 lampstand, with its appurtenances, the *l*,
37:23 Its seven *l*,
39:37 pure gold lampstand with its *l* set up
40: 4 in the lampstand and set up the *l* on it.
40:25 and he set up the *l* before the LORD as the
Lv 24: 2 so that you may keep *l* burning regularly.
24: 3 up the *l* to burn before the LORD regularly,
24: 4 the *l* shall be set up on the pure gold
Nm 4: 9 cloth to cover the lampstand with its *l*,
8: 2 When you set up the seven *l*,
8: 3 setting up the *l* to face toward the front
1Kgs 7:49 the sanctuary, with their flowers, *l*,
1Chr 28:15 for the golden lampstands and their *l*
28:15 of gold for each lampstand and its *l*,
28:15 of silver for each lampstand and its *l*,
2Chr 4:20 the lampstands and their *l* of pure gold
4:21 *l* and gold tongs [this was the purest
13:11 and the *l* of the golden lampstand burn
29: 7 of the vestibule, extinguished the *l*,
Jdt 10:22 to the antechamber, preceded by silver *l*;
1Mc 4:50 altar and lighted the *l* on the lampstand,
2Mc 1: 8 the *l* and set out the loaves of bread.
10: 3 two years, burned incense, and lighted *l*.
Bar 6:18 light more *l* for them than for themselves,
Zep 1:12 that time I will explore Jerusalem with *l*;
Zec 4: 2 "on it are seven *l* with their tubes,
Lk 12:35 your waists and your *l* be burning ready.
Acts 20: 8 As it happened there were many *l* in the
Rv 22: 5 They will need no light from *l* or the sun,

LAMPSTAND (39)
Ex 25:31 "You shall make a *l* of pure beaten gold
25:32 are to extend from the sides of the *l*,
25:33 the six branches that extend from the *l*.
25:35 pairs of branches that extend from the *l*.
25:37 their light on the space in front of the *l*.
25:39 gold for the *l* and all its appurtenances.
26:35 veil you shall place the table and the *l*,
30:27 appurtenances, the *l* and its appurtenances,
31: 8 the pure gold *l* with all its appurtenances,
35:14 the *l*,
37:17 The *l* was made of pure beaten gold
37:19 the six branches that extended from the *l*.
37:21 pairs of branches that extended from the *l*.
37:24 for the *l* and its various appurtenances.
39:37 the pure gold *l* with its lamps set up on
40: 4 bring in the *l* and set up the lamps on it.
40:24 He placed the *l* in the meeting tent,
Lv 24: 4 lamps shall be set up on the pure gold *l*,
Nm 3:31 pertained to the ark, the table, the *l*,
4: 9 violet cloth to cover the *l* with its lamps,
4:10 The *l* with all its utensils they shall
8: 2 their light toward the front of the *l*."
8: 3 lamps to face toward the front of the *l*,
8: 4 The *l* was made of beaten gold in both its
1Chr 28:15 weight of gold for each *l* and its lamps,
28:15 weight of silver for each *l* and its lamps,
28:15 on the use to which each *l* was to be put.
2Chr 13:11 of the golden *l* burn evening after evening;
1Mc 1:21 the *l* for the light with all its fixtures,
4:49 made new sacred vessels and brought the *l*,
4:50 the altar and lighted the lamps on the *l*,
Sir 26:17 the light that shines above the holy *l*,
Dn 5: 5 Suddenly, opposite the *l*,
Zec 4: 2 "I see a *l* all of gold,
4:11 two olive trees at each side of the *l*?"
Lk 8:16 on a *l* so that whoever comes in can see it.
11:33 under a bushel basket, but rather on a *l*,
Heb 9: 2 the outer one, in which were the *l*,
Rv 2: 5 to you and remove your *l* from its place.

LAMPSTANDS (12)
1Kgs 7:49 the *l* of pure gold,
1Chr 28:15 likewise for the golden *l* and their lamps
28:15 and for the silver *l* he specified the
2Chr 4: 7 He made the *l* of gold,
4:20 the *l* and their lamps of pure gold which
Jer 52:19 fire holders, the bowls, the pots, the *l*,
Rv 1:12 When I did so I saw seven *l* of gold,
1:13 and among the *l* One like a Son of Man
1:20 my right hand, and of the seven *l* of gold:
1:20 and the seven *l* are the seven churches.
2: 1 among the seven *l* of gold has this to say:
11: 4 two olive trees and the two *l* which stand

LANCE (7)
Nm 25: 7 left the assembly, and taking a *l* in hand,
Jgs 5: 8 Not a shield could be seen, nor a *l*,
1Chr 12:35 and with them, armed with shield and *l*,
2Chr 25: 5 for war, capable of handling *l* and shield.
Ps(s) 35: 3 Brandish the *l*,
Sir 38:25 who thrills in wielding the goad like a *l*,
Jn 19:34 of the soldiers thrust a *l* into his side,

LANCE-BEARERS (1)
2Chr 14: 7 hundred thousand shield- and *l* from Judah,

LANCES (3)
2Chr 26:14 bucklers, *l*,
2Mc 5: 2 fully armed with *l* and drawn swords;
Ez 39: 9 bucklers,] bows and arrows, clubs and *l*;

LAND (1795)
Gn 1: 9 single basin, so that the dry *l* may appear."
1: 9 into its basin, and the dry *l* appeared.
1:10 God called the dry *l* "the earth,"
1:30 food, and to all the animals of the *l*,
2:11 that winds through the whole *l* of Havilah,
2:12 The gold of that *l* is excellent;
2:13 one that winds all through the *l* of Cush.
4:16 presence and settled in the *l* of Nod,
7:22 Everything on dry *l* with the faintest
10:10 and Accad, all of them in the *l* of Shinar.
10:11 From that *l* he went forth to Asshur,
11: 2 in the *l* of Shinar and settled there.
11:28 before his father Terah, in his native *l*,
11:31 of the Chaldeans, to go to the *l* of Canaan.
12: 1 "Go forth from the *l* of your kinsfolk and
12: 1 father's house to a *l* that I will show you.
12: 5 and they set out for the *l* of Canaan.

12: 5 When they came to the *l* of Canaan,
12: 6 *l* as far as the sacred place at Shechem,
12: 6 (The Canaanites were then in the *l*.)
12: 7 "To your descendants I will give this *l*."
12:10 There was famine in the *l*;
12:10 since the famine in the *l* was severe.
13: 6 so that the *l* could not support them if
13: 7 and the Perizzites were occupying the *l*.)
13: 9 Is not the whole *l* at your disposal?
13:12 Abram stayed in the *l* of Canaan,
13:15 all the *l* that you see I will give to you
13:17 Set forth and walk about in the *l*,
15: 7 to give you this *l* as a possession."
15:13 shall be aliens in a *l* not their own,
15:18 "To your descendants I give this *l*,
15:19 [the Euphrates], the *l* of the Kenites,
16: 3 had lived ten years in the *l* of Canaan,
17: 8 you the *l* in which you are now staying,
17: 8 you are now staying, the whole *l* of Canaan,
19:28 the *l* rising like fumes from a furnace.
20:15 said, "Here, my *l* lies at your disposal;
21:21 got a wife for him from the *l* of Egypt.
21:23 will act as loyally toward me and the *l*
21:32 and returned to the *l* of the Philistines.
21:34 in the *l* of the Philistines for many years.
22: 2 whom you love, and go to the *l* of Moriah.
23: 2 (that is, Hebron) in the *l* of Canaan,
23:15 of *l* worth four hundred shekels of silver
23:19 Mamre (that is, Hebron) in the *l* of Canaan.
24: 4 but that you will go to my own *l* and to my
24: 5 woman is unwilling to follow me to this *l*?
24: 5 son back to the *l* from which you migrated?"
24: 7 from my father's house and the *l* of my kin,
24: 7 'I will give this *l* to your descendants'
24:37 of the Canaanites in whose *l* I live;
25: 6 sent them away eastward, to the *l* of Kedem,
26: 1 There was a famine in the *l* (distinct from
26: 2 to camp wherever in this *l* I tell you.
26: 3 Stay in this *l*, and I will be with you
26:22 ample room, and we shall flourish in the *l*."
27:46 marry a Hittite woman, a native of the *l*,
28: 4 possession of the *l* where you are staying,
28:13 the *l* on which you are lying I will give
28:15 you go, and bring you back to this *l*.
29: 1 journey he came to the *l* of the Easterners.
31: 3 Jacob, "Return to the *l* of your fathers,
31:13 Leave this *l* and return to the *l* of your birth.
31:18 go to his father Isaac in the *l* of Canaan.
32: 4 ahead to his brother Esau in the *l* of Seir,
32:10 O LORD, 'Go back to the *l* of your birth,
33:18 of Shechem, which is in the *l* of Canaan,
34: 1 out to visit some of the women of the *l*.
34:10 The *l* is open before you;
34:21 in the *l* and move about in it freely;
34:30 me loathsome to the inhabitants of the *l*,
35: 6 Luz [that is, Bethel] in the *l* of Canaan.
35:12 The *l* I once gave to Abraham and Isaac I
35:12 descendants after you will I give this *l*."
36: 5 who were born to him in the *l* of Canaan.
36: 6 land of Canaan, and went to the *l* of Seir,
36: 7 and the *l* in which they were staying could
36:16 are the clans of Eliphaz in the *l* of Edom;
36:17 are the clans of Reuel in the *l* of Edom;
36:20 the Horite, the original settlers in the *l*:
36:21 descended from Seir, in the *l* of Edom.
36:30 Horites, clan by clan, in the *l* of Seir.
36:31 kings who reigned in the *l* of Edom
36:34 died, Husham, from the *l* of the Temanites,
37: 1 *l* where his father had stayed, the *l* of Canaan.
40:15 I was kidnaped from the *l* of the Hebrews,
41:19 specimens as these in all the *l* of Egypt!
41:29 are now coming throughout the *l* of Egypt;
41:30 in the *l* of Egypt will be forgotten.
41:30 When the famine has ravaged the *l*,
41:31 *l* because of the famine that follows it
41:33 and put him in charge of the *l* of Egypt.
41:34 the *l* during the seven years of abundance.
41:36 follow in the *l* of Egypt, so that the *l*
41:41 you in charge of the whole *l* of Egypt."
41:43 Joseph installed over the whole *l* of Egypt.
41:44 move hand or foot in all the *l* of Egypt."
41:46 he traveled throughout the *l* of Egypt.
41:47 plenty, when the *l* produced abundant crops,
41:48 *l* of Egypt was enjoying and stored
41:52 made me fruitful in the *l* of my affliction."
41:53 enjoyed by the *l* of Egypt came to an end,
41:54 was available throughout the *l* of Egypt.
41:55 hunger came to be felt throughout the *l*
41:56 the famine had spread throughout the *l*,
41:56 the famine had gripped the *l* of Egypt.
42: 5 there was famine in the *l* of Canaan also,
42: 7 They answered, "From the *l* of Canaan,
42: 9 have come to see the nakedness of the *l*."
42:12 have come to see the nakedness of the *l*."
42:29 to their father Jacob in the *l* of Canaan,
42:30 in custody as if we were spying on the *l*.
42:32 present with our father in the *l* of Canaan.'
42:34 and you may move about freely in the *l*.'"
43: 1 Now the famine in the *l* grew more severe.
44: 8 We even brought back to you from the *l* of
45: 6 years now the famine has been in the *l*,
45: 8 and ruler over the whole *l* of Egypt.
45:17 and go without delay to the *l* of Canaan.
45:18 I will assign you the best *l* in Egypt,
45:18 where you will live off the fat of the *l*.'
45:19 Take wagons from the *l* of Egypt for your
45:20 in the whole *l* of Egypt shall be yours.'"
45:25 to their father Jacob in the *l* of Canaan.
45:26 is he who is ruler of all the *l* of Egypt,"
46: 6 they had acquired in the *l* of Canaan.
46:12 but Er and Onan died in the *l* of Canaan;
46:20 In the *l* of Egypt Joseph became the father
46:31 whose home is in the *l* of Canaan,
47: 1 my brothers have come from the *l* of Canaan,
47: 4 your servants' flocks in the *l* of Canaan,
47: 6 to you, the *l* of Egypt is at your disposal;
47: 6 father and brothers in the pick of the *l*."
47:11 holdings in Egypt on the pick of the *l*,
47:18 disposal except our bodies and our farm *l*.
47:19 we and our *l* perish before your very eyes?
47:19 Take us and our *l* in exchange for food,
47:19 Pharaoh's slaves and our *l* his property;
47:19 and that our *l* may not turn into a waste."
47:20 all the farm *l* of Egypt for Pharaoh,
47:20 so the *l* passed over to Pharaoh,
47:22 them, they did not have to sell their *l*.
47:23 *l* for Pharaoh,
47:23 here is your seed for sowing the *l*.
47:26 Joseph made it a law for the *l* in Egypt,
47:26 Only the *l* of the priests did not pass
47:27 Thus Israel settled in the *l* of Egypt,
47:28 in the *l* of Egypt for seventeen years;
48: 3 appeared to me at Luz in the *l* of Canaan,
48: 4 and I will give this *l* to your descendants
48: 5 in the *l* of Egypt before I joined you here,
48:21 will restore you to the *l* of your fathers.
49:30 facing on Mamre, in the *l* of Canaan,
50: 5 prepared for himself in the *l* of Canaan,
50:11 the *l* saw the mourning at Goren-ha-atad,
50:13 They carried him to the *l* of Canaan and
50:24 out of this *l* to the land that he promised

Ex

1: 7 and strong that the *l* was filled with them.
2:15 from him and stayed in the *l* of Midian.
2:22 he said, "I am a stranger in a foreign *l*."
3: 8 that *l* into a good and spacious *l*, a *l*
3:17 of Egypt into the *l* of the Canaanites,
3:17 Jebusites, a *l* flowing with milk and honey.
4: 9 from the river and pour it on the dry *l*.
4: 9 the river will become blood on the dry *l*."
4:20 sons, and started back to the *l* of Egypt,
5: 5 numerous the people of the *l* are already,"
5:12 the *l* of Egypt to gather stubble for straw,
6: 1 arm, he will drive them from his *l*."
6: 4 give them the land of Canaan, the *l* in
6: 8 the *l* which I swore to give to Abraham,
6:11 Egypt, to let the Israelites leave his *l*."
6:26 the Israelites from the *l* of Egypt,
7: 2 Pharaoh to let the Israelites leave his *l*.
7: 3 wonders that I will work in the *l* of Egypt,
7: 4 the Israelites, out of the *l* of Egypt,
7:19 the *l* of Egypt there shall be blood,
7:21 There was blood throughout the *l* of Egypt.
8: 1 to make frogs overrun the *l* of Egypt."
8: 2 frogs came up and covered the *l* of Egypt.
8: 3 too, made frogs overrun the *l* of Egypt.
8:10 up and there was a stench in the *l*.
8:12 into gnats throughout the *l* of Egypt."
8:13 into gnats throughout the *l* of Egypt.
8:18 make an exception of the very *l* of Goshen:
8:20 Egypt the *l* was infested with flies.
8:21 and offer sacrifice to your God in this *l*."
9: 5 "Tomorrow the LORD shall do this in the *l*."
9: 9 turn into fine dust over the whole *l* of Egypt
9: 9 boils on man and beast throughout the *l*."
9:22 hail may fall upon the entire *l* of Egypt,
9:22 and every growing thing in the *l* of Egypt."
9:23 LORD rained down hail upon the *l* of Egypt;
9:24 seen in the *l* since Egypt became a nation.
9:25 was in the open throughout the *l* of Egypt;
9:26 Only in the *l* of Goshen,
10:12 out your hand over the *l* of Egypt,
10:13 out his staff over the *l* of Egypt,
10:13 the *l* all that day and all that night.
10:14 They swarmed over the whole *l* of Egypt and
10:15 They covered the surface of the whole *l*,
10:15 They ate up all the vegetation in the *l*
10:15 tree or plant throughout the *l* of Egypt.
10:21 that over the *l* of Egypt there may be such
10:22 throughout the *l* of Egypt for three days.
11: 3 servants and the people in the *l* of Egypt.
11: 5 Every first-born in this *l* shall die,
11: 6 be loud wailing throughout the *l* of Egypt,
11: 9 may be multiplied in the *l* of Egypt."
11:10 would not let the Israelites leave his *l*.
12: 1 said to Moses and Aaron in the *l* of Egypt,
12:12 striking down every first-born of the *l*,
12:13 thus, when I strike the *l* of Egypt,
12:17 I brought your ranks out of the *l* of Egypt,
12:25 you have entered the *l* which the LORD
12:29 slew every first-born in the *l* of Egypt,
12:33 on, to hasten their departure from the *l*;
12:41 LORD left the *l* of Egypt on this very date.
12:42 LORD, as he led them out of the *l* of Egypt;
13: 5 brought you into the *l* of the Canaanites,
13: 5 give you, a *l* flowing with milk and honey.
13:11 brought you into the *l* of the Canaanites,
13:15 killed every first-born in the *l* of Egypt,
13:17 lead them by way of the Philistines' *l*,
14: 3 are wandering about aimlessly in the *l*.
14:16 Israelites may pass through it on dry *l*.
14:21 the night and so turned it into dry *l*.
14:22 into the midst of the sea on dry *l*,
14:29 on dry *l* through the midst of the sea,
15:19 on dry *l* through the midst of the sea.
16: 1 after their departure from the *l* of Egypt.
16: 3 died at the LORD's hand in the *l* of Egypt
16: 6 LORD who brought you out of the *l* of Egypt;
16:32 when I brought you out of the *l* of Egypt."
16:35 forty years, until they came to settled *l*;
18: 3 he said, "I am a stranger in a foreign *l*."
19: 1 after their departure from the *l* of Egypt,
20: 2 God, who brought you out of the *l* of Egypt,
20:12 have a long life in the *l* which the LORD,
22:20 once aliens yourselves in the *l* of Egypt,
23: 9 once aliens yourselves in the *l* of Egypt.
23:10 may sow your *l* and gather in its produce.
23:11 let the *l* lie untilled and unharvested,
23:26 woman in your *l* will be barren or miscarry;
23:29 else the *l* will become so desolate that
23:30 enough to take possession of the *l*.
23:31 all who dwell in this *l* I will hand over
23:33 They must not abide in your *l*,
29:46 God who brought them out of the *l* of Egypt,
32: 1 Moses who brought us out of the *l* of Egypt,
32: 4 who brought you out of the *l* of Egypt."
32: 7 whom you brought out of the *l* of Egypt,
32: 8 who brought you out of the *l* of Egypt!'
32:11 whom you brought out of the *l* of Egypt
32:13 and all this *l* that I promised,
32:23 Moses who brought us out of the *l* of Egypt,
33: 1 you have brought up from the *l* of Egypt,
33: 1 here to the *l* which I swore to Abraham,
33: 3 you to the *l* flowing with milk and honey.
34:12 inhabitants of the *l* that you are to enter;
34:15 a covenant with the inhabitants of that *l*;
34:24 there will be no one to covet your *l*

Lv

11: 2 *l* animals these are the ones you may eat:
11:45 the *l* of Egypt that I might be your God,
14:34 "When you come into the *l* of Canaan,
14:34 infection on any house of the *l* you occupy,
18: 3 shall not do as they do in the *l* of Egypt,
18: 3 shall you do as they do in the *l* of Canaan,
18:25 Because their *l* has become defiled,
18:27 the previous inhabitants defiled the *l*;
18:28 otherwise the *l* will vomit you out also
19: 9 "When you reap the harvest of your *l*,
19:23 into the *l* and plant any fruit tree there,
19:29 *l* will become corrupt and full of lewdness.
19:33 "When an alien resides with you in your *l*,
19:34 you too were once aliens in the *l* of Egypt.
19:36 God, who brought you out of the *l* of Egypt.
20:22 otherwise the *l* where I am bringing you to
20:24 Their *l* shall be your possession, a *l* flowing
20:25 in the *l* that I have set apart for you.
22:24 You shall neither do this in your own *l*
22:33 sacred and led you out of the *l* of Egypt,
23:10 you come into the *l* which I am giving you,
23:22 "When you reap the harvest of your *l*,
23:39 you have gathered in the produce of the *l*,
23:43 I led the Israelites out of the *l* of Egypt,
25: 2 the land that I am giving you, let the *l*,
25: 4 year the *l* shall have complete rest,
25: 5 in this year of sabbath rest for the *l*.
25: 6 While the *l* has its sabbath,
25: 7 and for the wild animals on your *l*.
25: 9 blast shall re-echo throughout your *l*.
25:10 liberty in the *l* for all its inhabitants.
25:14 any *l* to your neighbor or buy any from him,
25:15 jubilee shall you purchase the *l* from him;
25:18 for then you will dwell securely in the *l*.
25:19 The *l* will yield its fruit and you will
25:23 *l* shall not be sold in perpetuity; for the *l*
25:24 you must permit the *l* to be redeemed.
25:26 the man has no relative to redeem his *l*,
25:28 sufficient means to buy back his *l*,
25:31 as belonging to the surrounding farm *l*;
25:34 the pasture *l* belonging to their cities
25:38 *l* of Egypt to give you the *l* of Canaan
25:42 out of the *l* of Egypt are servants of mine,
25:45 children who are born and reared in your *l*.
25:55 I brought them out of the *l* of Egypt,
26: 1 up a stone figure for worship in your *l*;
26: 4 season, so that the *l* will bear its crops,
26: 5 so that you may dwell securely in your *l*.
26: 6 I will establish peace in the *l*,
26: 6 sword of war from sweeping across your *l*.
26:13 who brought you out of the *l* of the
26:20 your *l* will bear no crops,
26:32 So devastated will I leave the *l* that your
26:34 Then shall the *l* retrieve its lost
26:34 in the *l* of your enemies; then shall the *l*
26:41 them and bring them into their enemies' *l*.
26:42 and of the *l*,
26:43 But the *l* must first be rid of them,
26:44 even while they are in their enemies' *l*,
26:45 whom I brought out of the *l* of Egypt under
27:16 the LORD is a piece of his hereditary *l*,
27:24 of this *l* from whom it had been purchased.
27:30 "All tithes of the *l*, whether in grain

LAND (cont.)

Nm 1: 1 Israelites' departure from the l of Egypt,
3:13 slew all the first-born in the l of Egypt,
8:17 slew all the first-born in the l of Egypt.
9: 1 their departure from the l of Egypt,
9:14 resident alien as for the native of the l."
10: 9 When in your own l you go to war against
11:12 to the l you have promised under oath to
13: 2 "Send men to reconnoiter the l of Canaan,
13:16 whom Moses sent out to reconnoiter the l.
13:17 them to reconnoiter the l of Canaan,
13:18 highlands, and see what kind of l it is.
13:20 best to get some of the fruit of the l."
13:21 So they went up and reconnoitered the l
13:25 the l for forty days they returned,
13:27 "We went into the l to which you sent us.
13:28 people who are living in the l are fierce,
13:30 said, "We ought to go up and seize the l,
13:32 about the l they had scouted, saying, "The l
14: 2 "Would that we had died in the l of Egypt,
14: 3 this l only to have us fall by the sword?
14: 6 had been in the party that scouted the l,
14: 7 through and explored is a fine, rich l.
14: 8 that land, a l flowing with milk and honey.
14: 9 need not be afraid of the people of that l;
14:14 to tell of it to the inhabitants of this l?
14:16 people into the l he swore to give them;
14:23 not one shall see the l which I promised
14:24 him into the l where he has just been,
14:30 the l where I solemnly swore to settle you,
14:31 they shall appreciate the l you spurned.
14:34 Forty days you spent in scouting the l;
14:36 whom Moses had sent to reconnoiter the l
14:36 discouraging reports about the l;
14:37 l were struck down by the LORD and died.
14:38 the men who had gone to reconnoiter the l,
15: 2 the l I will give you for your homesteads,
15:18 When you enter the l into which I will
15:19 and begin to eat of the food of that l,
16:13 away from a l flowing with milk and honey,
16:14 us to a l flowing with milk and honey,
18:13 likewise, of whatever grows on their l,
18:20 have any heritage in the l of the Israelites
20:12 this community into the l I will give them."
20:23 Mount Hor, on the border of the l of Edom,
20:24 enter the l I am giving to the Israelites,
21: 4 the Red Sea road, to by-pass the l of Edom.
21:24 and took possession of his l from the
21:26 seized all his l from Jazer to the Arnon.
21:31 had settled in the l of the Amorites,
21:34 deliver him with all his people and his l.
21:35 to him, and they took possession of his l.
22: 5 on the Euphrates, in the l of the Amawites,
26: 4 came out of the l of Egypt were as follows:
26:19 died in the l of Canaan were Er and Onan.
26:53 "Among these groups the l shall be
26:55 But the l shall be divided by lot,
27:12 the l that I am giving to the Israelites.
32: 1 Noticing that the l of Jazer and of Gilead
32: 5 let this l be given to your servants as
32: 7 crossing to the l the LORD has given them?
32: 8 from Kadesh-barnea to reconnoiter the l.
32: 9 the Wadi Eshcol and reconnoitered the l,
32: 9 not enter the l the LORD had given them.
32:22 of his way and the l is subdued before him,
32:29 when the l has been subdued before you.
32:30 their property with you in the l of Canaan."
32:32 the l of Canaan as troops before the LORD,
32:33 the l with its towns and the districts
33: 1 journeyed up by companies from the l
33:37 Mount Hor on the border of the l of Edom.
33:38 of the Israelites from the l of Egypt,
33:40 who lived in the Negeb in the l of Canaan,
33:51 go across the Jordan into the l of Canaan,
33:52 all the inhabitants of the l before you;
33:53 take possession of the l and settle in it,
33:53 I have given you the l as your property.
33:54 apportion the l among yourselves by lot,
33:55 out the inhabitants of the l before you,
34: 2 When you enter the l of Canaan,
34: 2 the l of Canaan with its boundaries:
34: 8 from Mount Hor to Labo in the l of Hamath,
34:12 "This is the l that shall be yours,
34:13 "This is the l, to be apportioned among
34:17 men who shall apportion the l among you:
34:29 their heritage in the l of Canaan.
35:10 go across the Jordan into the l of Canaan,
35:14 the Jordan, and three in the l of Canaan.
35:32 the l before the death of the high priest.
35:33 shall not desecrate the l where you live.
35:33 desecrates the l, the l can have no atonement
35:34 Do not defile the l in which you live and
36: 2 the l by lot among the Israelites;

Dt 1: 5 the law in the l of Moab beyond the Jordan,
1: 7 the l of the Canaanites in the Arabah,
1: 8 I have given that l over to you.
1: 8 and occupy the l I swore to your fathers,
1:21 your God, has given this l over to you.
1:22 send men ahead to reconnoiter the l
1:25 taking along some of the fruit of the l,
1:25 to us and reported, 'The l which the LORD,
1:27 has brought us up out of the l of Egypt,
1:35 the good l I swore to give to your fathers,
1:36 to his sons I will give the l he trod upon,
2: 5 not give you so much as a foot of their l,
2: 9 not give you possession of any of their l,
2:12 just as the Israelites have done in the l
2:19 you possession of any l of the Ammonites,
2:24 the Amorite king of Heshbon, and his l.
2:29 cross the Jordan into the l which the LORD,
2:30 refused to let us pass through his l,
2:31 begun to hand over to you Sihon and his l,
2:37 not encroach upon any of the Ammonite l,
3: 2 your hand with all his people and his l.
3:12 "When we occupied the l at that time,
3:13 Bashan was once called a l of the Rephaim.
3:18 your God, has given you this l as your own.
3:20 they too possess the l which the LORD,
3:25 over and see this good l beyond the Jordan,
3:28 them in possession of the l you are to see.'
4: 1 take possession of the l which the LORD,
4: 5 them in the l you are entering to occupy.
4:10 in the l and may so teach their children.'
4:14 are to observe over in the l you will occupy.
4:21 l which he is giving you as a heritage,
4:22 over and take possession of that good l.
4:25 and have grown old in the l,
4:26 you shall all quickly perish from the l
4:38 you in and to make their l your heritage,
4:40 may have long life on the l which the LORD,
4:46 opposite Beth-peor, in the l of Sihon,
4:47 l and the l of Og, king of Bashan, as well—
4:47 the l of these two kings
5: 6 God, who brought you out of the l of Egypt,
5:16 and prosperity in the l which the LORD,
5:31 in the l which I am giving them to possess.'
5:33 long life in the l which you are to occupy.
6: 1 l into which you are crossing for conquest,
6: 3 give you a l flowing with milk and honey.
6:10 into the l which he swore to your fathers,
6:10 that he would give you, a l with fine,
6:12 who brought you out of the l of Egypt,
6:15 and he destroy you from the face of the l;
6:18 may enter in and possess the good l
6:23 the l he promised on oath to our fathers,
7: 1 the l which you are to enter and occupy,
7:13 in the l which he swore to your fathers he
8: 1 may enter in and possess the l
8: 7 a good country, a l with streams of water,
8: 8 hills and valleys, a l of wheat and barley,
8: 9 a l where you can eat bread without stint
8: 9 a l whose stones contain iron and in whose
8:14 God, who brought me out of the l of Egypt,
9: 4 LORD has brought me in to possess this l';
9: 5 going in to take possession of their l;
9: 6 God, is giving you this good l to possess,
9: 7 l of Egypt until you arrived in this place,
9:23 take possession of the l he was giving you,
9:28 from whose l you have brought us say,
9:28 to bring them into the l he promised them';
10:11 that they may enter in and occupy the l
10:19 once aliens yourselves in the l of Egypt.
11: 3 Pharaoh, king of Egypt, and on all his l;
11: 8 of the l into which you are crossing,
11: 9 that you may have long life on the l
11: 9 a l flowing with milk and honey.
11:10 "For the l which you are to enter and
11:10 the l of Egypt from which you have come,
11:11 the l into which you are crossing for
11:11 you are crossing for conquest is a l of hills
11:12 rain from the heavens, a l which the LORD,
11:14 I will give the seasonal rain to your l,
11:17 perish from the good l he is giving you.
11:21 your children may live on in the l
11:25 of you through any l where you set foot,
11:29 the l which you are to enter and occupy,
11:31 to enter and occupy the l which the LORD,
12: 1 careful to observe in the l which the LORD,
12:10 Jordan and dwell in the l which the LORD,
12:19 the Levite as long as you live in the l.
12:29 replaced them and are settled in their l,
13: 6 who brought you out of the l of Egypt and
13:11 God, who brought you out of the l of Egypt,
15: 4 will bless you abundantly in the l he will
15: 7 is in need in the l which the LORD,
15:11 The needy will never be lacking in the l;
15:15 you too were once slaves in the l of Egypt,
16: 3 day of your departure from the l of Egypt;
16: 3 frightened haste you left the l of Egypt.
16:20 life and may possess the l which the LORD,
17:14 you have come into the l which the LORD,
18: 9 "When you come into the l which the LORD,
19: 1 the nations whose l he is giving you,
19: 2 apart three cities in the l which the LORD,
19: 3 into three regions the l which the LORD,
19: 8 and gives you all the l he promised your
19:10 Thus, in the l which the LORD,
19:14 you receive in the l which the LORD,
20: 1 who brought you up from the l of Egypt,
20:15 does not belong to the peoples of this l.
21: 1 lying in the open on the l which the LORD,
21:23 tree, you will defile the l which the LORD,
23:21 on the l you are to enter and occupy.
24: 4 bring such guilt upon the l which the LORD,
25:15 have a long life on the l which the LORD,
25:19 all your enemies round about in the l
26: 1 you have come into the l which the LORD,
26: 2 you harvest from the l which the LORD,
26: 3 that I have indeed come into the l which
26: 9 gave us this l flowing with milk and honey.
26:15 the l flowing with milk and honey
27: 2 cross the Jordan into the l which the LORD,
27: 3 into the l flowing with milk and honey,
28: 8 blessing you in the l that the LORD,
28:11 in the l which he swore to your fathers he
28:12 heavens, to give your l rain in due season,
28:21 you from the l you are entering to occupy.
28:24 the LORD will give your l powdery dust,
28:52 in come tumbling down all over your l.
28:52 throughout the l which the LORD your God,
28:63 of the l you are now entering to occupy.
28:69 make with the Israelites in the l of Moab,
29: 1 seen all that the LORD did in the l of Egypt
29: 1 and all his servants and to all his l;
29: 7 we defeated them and took over their l,
29:15 what surroundings we lived in the l of Egypt
29:21 they see the calamities of this l and the ills
29:23 'Why has the LORD dealt thus with this l?
29:24 when he brought them out of the l of Egypt,
29:26 why the LORD was angry with this l
29:27 soil and cast them out into a strange l,
30: 5 the l which your fathers once occupied,
30:16 you in the l you are entering to occupy.
30:18 you will not have a long life on the l
30:20 a long life for you to live on the l which
31: 7 l which the LORD swore to their fathers
31:13 as long as you live on the l which you
31:16 will live in the l they are about to enter.
31:20 For when I have brought them into the l
31:21 brought them into the l which I promised
31:23 into the l which I promised them on oath.
32:13 l and live off the products of its fields,
32:43 of his servants and purges his people's l.
32:47 l which you will cross the Jordan to occupy."
32:49 l of Moab facing Jericho]; and view the l
32:52 l at a distance, but you shall not enter that l
32:52 that l which I am giving to the Israelites."
33:13 "Blessed by the LORD is his l with the
33:28 been undisturbed In a l of grain and wine,
34: 1 and the LORD showed him all the l—
34: 2 l of Ephraim and Manasseh, all the l of Judah
34: 4 "This is the l which I swore to Abraham,
34: 5 So there, in the l of Moab,
34: 6 ravine opposite Beth-peor in the l of Moab,
34:11 perform in the l of Egypt against Pharaoh
34:11 all his servants and against all his l,

Jos 1: 2 into the l I will give the Israelites.
1: 4 domain is to be all the l of the Hittites,
1: 6 may give this people possession of the l
1:11 take possession of the l which the LORD,
1:13 God, will permit you to settle in this l.'
1:14 l Moses gave you here beyond the Jordan.
1:15 they like you possess the l which the LORD,
1:15 you may return and occupy your own l,
2: 1 "Go, reconnoiter the l and Jericho."
2: 2 had come there that night to spy out the l.
2: 3 for they have come to spy out the entire l."
2: 9 know that the LORD has given you the l,
2: 9 of the l are overcome with fear of you.
2:14 to you when the LORD gives us the l."
2:18 When we come into the l,
2:24 has delivered all this l into our power;
2:24 of the l are overcome with fear of us."
5: 6 them see the l flowing with milk and honey
5:11 Passover they ate of the produce of the l
5:12 on which they ate of the produce of the l,
5:12 year ate of the yield of the l of Canaan.
6:22 the two men who had spied out the l,
6:27 so that his fame spread throughout the l.
7: 2 to go up and reconnoiter the l.
7: 9 the other inhabitants of the l hear of it,
8: 1 your power, with his people, city, and l.
9: 6 "We have come from a distant l to propose
9: 7 "You may be living in l that is ours.
9: 9 "Your servants have come from a faroff l,
9:24 Moses that you be given the entire l
10:41 to Gaza, and all the l of Goshen to Gibeon.
11: 3 at the foot of Hermon in the l of Mizpah.
11:16 So Joshua captured all this l:
11:16 the entire Negeb all the l of Goshen,
11:22 were left in the l of the Israelites.
11:23 And the l enjoyed peace.
12: 1 The kings of the l east of the Jordan,
12: 2 and the l northward through half of Gilead
12: 6 he assigned their l to the Reubenites,
12: 7 conquered west of the Jordan and whose l,
13: 1 of the l still remains to be conquered.
13: 2 This additional l includes all Geshur and
13: 4 all the l of the Canaanites from Mearah of
13: 5 of Mount Hermon to Labo in the l of Hamath.
13: 7 the l which is to be their heritage."
13:21 of Midian, who were settled in the l:
13:25 the l of the Ammonites as far as Aroer,
14: 1 the Israelites received in the l of Canaan.
14: 4 no share of the l except cities to live in,
14: 5 Thus, in apportioning the l,
14: 7 from Kadesh-barnea to reconnoiter the l;
14: 9 'The l where you have set foot shall
14:15 And the l enjoyed peace.

15:18 induced him to ask her father for some l.
15:19 you have assigned to me l in the Negeb,
17: 5 l of Gilead and Bashan beyond the Jordan,
17: 6 The l of Gilead fell to the rest of the
17:10 The l on the south belonged to Ephraim and
17:15 in the l of the Perizzites and Rephaim,
17:18 Its adjacent l shall also be yours if,
18: 1 After they had subdued the l,
18: 3 steps to possess the l which the LORD,
18: 4 them to begin a survey of the l,
18: 6 the description of the l in seven sections.
18: 8 map out the l were ready for the journey,
18: 8 Joshua instructed them to survey the l,
18: 9 So they went through the l,
18:10 Joshua then divided up the l for the
19:49 the portions of the l they were to inherit,
19:51 the l by lot in the presence of the LORD,
21: 2 Israelites at Shiloh in the l of Canaan,
21:43 And so the LORD gave Israel all the l he
22: 4 to your own l,
22: 7 Moses had assigned l in Bashan;
22: 9 Israelites at Shiloh in the l of Canaan
22: 9 of Canaan and returned to the l of Gilead,
22:10 region of the Jordan in the l of Canaan,
22:11 of the Jordan facing the l of Canaan,
22:13 half-tribe of Manasseh in the l of Gilead
22:15 half-tribe of Manasseh in the l of Gilead,
22:19 l you now possess unclean, cross over to the l
22:32 Reubenites and the Gadites in the l of Gilead
22:32 to the Israelites in the l of Canaan,
22:33 Gadites or ravaging the l they occupied.
23: 5 take possession of their l as the LORD,
23:13 you perish from this good l which the LORD,
23:15 you from this good l which the LORD,
23:16 from the good l which he has given you."
24: 3 and led him through the entire l of Canaan.
24: 8 I brought you into the l of the Amorites
24: 8 You took possession of their l,
24:13 "I gave you a l which you had not tilled
24:17 and our fathers up out of the l of Egypt,
24:18 including] the Amorites who dwelt in the l.
Jgs 1: 2 I have delivered the l into his power."
1:14 induced him to ask her father for some l.
1:15 you have assigned l in the Negeb to me,
1:26 He then went to the l of the Hittites,
1:32 live among the Canaanite natives of the l,
1:33 live among the Canaanite natives of the l.
2: 1 l which I promised on oath to your fathers.
2: 2 a pact with the inhabitants of this l,
2: 6 to take possession of his own hereditary l.
2:12 who had led them out of the l of Egypt,
3:11 The l then was at rest for forty years,
3:30 and the l had rest for eighty years.
5: 4 Seir, when you marched from the l of Edom,
5:31 And the l was at rest for forty years.
6: 4 of the l as far as the outskirts of Gaza,
6: 5 when they came into the l to lay it waste.
6: 9 them out before you and gave you their l.
6:10 the Amorites in whose l you are dwelling.
8:28 And the l had rest for forty years,
10: 4 possessed thirty cities in the l of Gilead;
10: 8 the Amorite l beyond the Jordan in Gilead.
11: 3 and had taken up residence in the l of Tob.
11: 5 went to bring Jephthah from the l of Tob.
11:12 me that you come to fight with me in my l?"
11:13 "Israel took away my l from the Arnon to
11:15 the l of Moab or the land of the Ammonites.
11:17 Edom saying, 'Let me pass through your l.'
11:18 l of Edom and the l of Moab, went east
11:18 east of the l of Moab
11:19 me pass through your l to my own place.'
11:21 l of the Amorites dwelling in that region,
12:12 was buried in Elon in the l of Zebulun.
12:15 buried in Pirathon in the l of Ephraim
16:24 our power our enemy, the ravager of our l,
18: 2 Eshtaol, to reconnoiter the l and scout it.
18: 2 their instructions to go and scout the l,
18: 9 for we have seen the l and it is very good.
18: 9 beginning your expedition to possess the l.
18:10 are a trusting people, and the l is ample.
18:14 the l of Laish said to their kinsmen,
18:17 l went up and entered the house of Micah.
18:30 until the time of the captivity of the l.
19:30 came up from the l of Egypt to this day.
20: 1 to Beer-sheba, and from the l of Gilead,
21:12 to the camp at Shiloh in the l of Canaan.
21:21 for a wife, and go to the l of Benjamin.
Ru 1: 1 of the judges there was a famine in the l;
1: 7 were on the road back to the l of Judah,
2:11 and your mother and the l of your birth,
4: 3 l that belonged to our kinsman Elimelech,
1Sm 6: 1 The ark of the LORD had been in the l of
6: 5 of the mice that are infesting your l
6: 5 to afflict you, your gods, and your l.
9: 4 of Ephraim, and through the l of Shalishah.
9: 4 through the l of Shaalim without success.
9: 4 They also went through the l of Benjamin,
9: 5 When they came to the l of Zuph,
9:16 send you a man from the l of Benjamin
12: 6 your fathers up from the l of Egypt.
13: 3 Saul sounded the horn throughout the l,
13: 7 the Jordan into the l of Gad and Gilead.
13:19 was to be found in the whole l of Israel,

14:29 "My father brings trouble to the l.
17:46 whole l shall learn that Israel has a God.
21:12 "Is this not David, the king of the l?
22: 5 Leave, and go to the l of Judah."
23:27 because the Philistines have invaded the l."
27: 1 but to escape to the l of the Philistines;
27: 1 search for me throughout the l of Israel,
27: 8 peoples living in the l between Telam,
27: 8 the approach to Shur, and the l of Egypt.
27: 9 In attacking the l David would not leave a
28: 3 mediums and fortune-tellers out of the l.
28: 9 mediums and fortune-tellers out of the l.
29:11 to return to the l of the Philistines.
30:16 l of the Philistines and from the l of Judah.
31: 9 good news throughout the l of the Philistines
2Sm 9:10 sons and servants must till the l for him.
15: 4 only I could be appointed judge in the l!
21:14 God granted relief to the l.
23:11 there was a plot of l full of lentils.
24:13 a three years' famine to come upon your l,
24:13 to have a three days' pestilence in your l?
1Kgs 2:26 "Go to your l in Anathoth.
4:19 Uri, in the land of Gilead, the l of Sihon,
4:19 one prefect besides, in the king's own l.
5: 1 from the River to the l of the Philistines,
5: 4 ruled over all the l west of the Euphrates,
6: 1 of the Israelites from the l of Egypt,
8: 9 at their departure from the l of Egypt.
8:21 when he brought them out of the l of Egypt."
8:34 them back to the l you gave their fathers.
8:36 sending rain upon this l of yours
8:37 there is famine in the l or pestilence;
8:40 as they live on the l you gave our fathers.
8:41 but comes from a distant l to honor you
8:46 their captors deport them to a hostile l,
8:47 the l of their captivity and be converted.
8:47 you in the l of their captors and say,
8:48 the l of the enemies who took them captive,
8:48 to you toward the l you gave their fathers,
9: 7 I will cut off Israel from the l I gave
9: 8 LORD done this to the l and to this temple?'
9: 9 their fathers out of the l of Egypt;
9:11 Hiram twenty cities in the l of Galilee.
9:13 And he called them the l of Cabul,
9:19 and in the entire l under his dominion.
9:20 people who remained in the l,
9:26 the shore of the Red Sea in the l of Edom.
11:18 appointed him rations, and assigned him l.
12:28 who brought you up from the l of Egypt."
14:15 this good l which he gave their fathers,
14:24 There were also cult prostitutes in the l.
15:12 the temple prostitutes from the l
15:20 Chinnereth, besides all the l of Naphtali.
17: 7 dry, because no rain had fallen in the l.
18: 5 let us go through the l to all sources of
18: 6 Dividing the l to explore between them,
20: 7 summoned all the elders of the l and said:
20:31 of the l of Israel are merciful kings.
22:36 man to his city, every man to his l,
22:47 He removed from the l the rest of the cult
2Kgs 2:19 but the water is bad and the l unfruitful."
3:20 the direction of Edom and filled the l.
3:27 up the siege and returned to their own l.
4:38 to Gilgal, there was a famine in the l.
5: 2 the l of Israel in a raid a little girl,
5: 4 slave girl from the l of Israel had said.
6:23 Aramean raiders came into the l of Israel.
8: 1 famine which is coming upon the l."
8: 2 the l of the Philistines for seven years.
8: 3 the woman returned from the l of the
8: 6 from the day she left the l until now."
10:21 sent word of it throughout the l of Israel.
10:33 east of the Jordan (all the l of Gilead,
11: 3 of the LORD, while Athaliah ruled the l.
11:14 of the l rejoicing and blowing trumpets,
11:18 Thereupon all the people of the l went to
11:19 the guards, and all the people of the l,
11:20 of the l rejoiced and the city was quiet,
13:20 of Moabites used to raid the l each year.
15: 5 vizier and regent for the people of the l.
15:19 Pul, king of Assyria, invaded the l,
17: 5 occupied the whole l and attacked Samaria,
17: 7 had brought them up from the l of Egypt,
17:26 not know how to worship the God of the l,
17:26 not know how to worship the God of the l."
17:27 teach them how to worship the God of the l."
17:36 who brought you up from the l of Egypt
18:25 LORD said to me, 'Go up and destroy that l
18:32 land like your own, a l of grain and wine,
18:33 his l from the hand of the king of Assyria?
18:34 Where are the gods of the l of Samaria?
18:35 lands ever rescued his l from my hand?
19: 7 report, he will return to his own l,
19:37 the sword and fled into the l of Ararat.
20:14 "They came from a distant l,
21: 8 be driven off the l I gave their fathers,
21:24 but the people of the l then slew all who
23:24 be seen in the l of Judah and in Jerusalem,
23:30 Then the people of the l took Jehoahaz,
23:33 him prisoner at Riblah in the l of Hamath,
23:33 He imposed a fine upon the l of a hundred
23:35 the l to raise the amount Pharaoh demanded.
23:35 silver and gold from the people of the l,

24: 7 of Egypt did not again leave his own l,
24:14 among the people of the l except the poor.
24:15 functionaries, and the chief men of the l.
25:19 who mustered the people of the l,
25:21 put to death in Riblah, in the l of Hamath.
25:21 Thus was Judah exiled from her l.
25:22 he had allowed to remain in the l of Judah,
1Chr 1:43 The kings who reigned in the l of Edom
1:45 died, Husham, from the l of the Temanites,
2:22 twenty-three cities in the l of Gilead.
4:40 and good pastures, and the l was spacious,
5: 9 they had much livestock in the l of Gilead.
5:11 them in the l of Bashan as far as Salecah.
5:23 in the l of Bashan as far as Baal-hermon,
5:25 after the gods of the natives of the l,
6:40 adjacent pasture lands in the l of Judah,
7:21 Ezer and Elead, who were born in the l,
10: 9 these they sent throughout the l of the
11: 4 the natives of the l were called Jebusites.
14:17 fame was spread abroad through every l,
16:18 l of Canaan as your allotted inheritance."
19: 2 the l of the Ammonites to comfort Hanun,
19: 3 rather come to you to explore the l,
20: 1 force, laid waste the l of the Ammonites,
21:12 LORD's own sword, a pestilence in the l,
22: 2 in the l of Israel be brought together,
22:18 l into my power, and the l is subdued
28: 8 you may continue to possess this good l
2Chr 2:16 alien men who were in the l of Israel
6: 5 I brought my people out of the l of Egypt,
6:25 l which you gave them and their fathers.
6:27 and send rain upon your l which you gave
6:28 When there is famine in the l,
6:31 as they live on the l you gave our fathers.
6:32 from a distant l to honor your great name,
6:36 their captors deport them to another l,
6:37 l where they are captive and are converted,
6:37 you in the l of their captivity and say,
6:38 in the l of those who hold them captive,
6:38 of their l which you gave their fathers,
7:13 if I command the locust to devour the l,
7:14 and pardon their sins and revive their l.
7:20 uproot the people from the l I gave them;
7:21 LORD done this to this l and to this house?'
7:22 who brought them out of the l of Egypt,
8: 6 and in the entire l under his dominion.
8: 8 is, their descendants remaining in the l,
8:17 to Elath on the seashore of the l of Edom.
9:11 had not been seen before in the l of Judah.
9:26 from the River to the l of the Philistines
11:13 to him from all parts of their l,
13:23 time, ten years of peace began in the l.
14: 5 for the l had peace and no war was waged
14: 6 The l is still ours,
15: 8 detestable idols from the whole l of Judah
17: 2 and put garrisons in the l of Judah and in
19: 3 the l and have been determined to seek God."
19: 5 He appointed judges in the l,
20: 7 who drove out the inhabitants of this l
20:10 invade when they came from the l of Egypt,
22:12 of God, while Athaliah ruled over the l.
23:13 of the l rejoicing and blowing trumpets,
23:20 the people, and all the people of the l,
23:21 of the l rejoiced and the city was quiet,
26:10 in the highlands and the garden l.
26:21 the palace and ruled the people of the l.
27: 4 forest l he set up fortresses and towers.
30: 9 with their captors and return to this l;
30:10 passed from city to city in the l of Ephraim
30:25 l of Israel and those that lived in Judah.
32:31 the sign that had occurred in the l,
33: 8 the l which I assigned to your fathers,
33:25 But the people of the l slew all those who
33:25 Amon, and then they, the people of the l,
34: 7 incense stands throughout the l of Israel.
34: 8 to cleanse the temple as well as the l,
36: 1 The people of the l took Jehoahaz,
36: 3 deposed him in Jerusalem and fined the l
36:21 the l has retrieved its lost sabbaths,
Ezr 3: 3 their fear of the peoples of the l,
4: 4 Thereupon the people of the l set out to
6:21 of the l to join them in seeking the LORD,
9: 1 the l and their abominations [Canaanites,
9: 2 the holy race with the peoples of the l.
9:11 the l which you are entering to take as
9:11 l unclean with the filth of the peoples
9:11 with the filth of the peoples of the l,
9:12 grow strong, enjoy the produce of the l,
10: 2 foreign women of the peoples of the l.
10:11 of the l and from these foreign women."
Neh 3:36 them be carried away to a l of captivity!
5:14 appointed me governor in the l of Judah,
5:16 though I had acquired no l of my own,
9: 8 and his posterity the l of the Canaanites,
9:10 all his servants and the people of his l,
9:15 You bade them enter and occupy the l which
9:22 l of Sihon, king of Heshbon, and the l of Og,
9:23 and you brought them into the l which you
9:24 sons went in to take possession of the l,
9:24 l and delivered them over into their power,
9:24 kings as well as the peoples of the l,
9:25 captured fortified cities and fertile l;
9:35 l that you had spread out before them,

LAND (cont.)

9:36 and as for the *l* which you gave our
10:31 our daughters to the peoples of the *l*,
10:32 When the peoples of the *l* bring in
Tb 3:15 or my father's name in the *l* of my exile.
4:12 that their posterity shall inherit the *l*.
13: 6 In the *l* of my exile I praise him,
14: 4 and led away into exile from the Good *L*.
14: 5 and bring them back to the *l* of Israel.
14: 7 they dwell forever in the *l* of Abraham,
14: 7 sin shall completely disappear from the *l*.
Jdt 1: 9 to Tahpanhes, Raamses, all the *l* of Goshen,
1:11 But the inhabitants of all that *l*
1:12 into a violent rage against all that *l*,
2: 6 and proceed against all the *l* of the West,
2: 7 all the *l* with the feet of my soldiers,
5: 7 who were born in the *l* of the Chaldeans.
5: 9 their abode and proceed to the *l* of Canaan.
5:10 famine had gripped the whole *l* of Canaan,
5:12 and he struck the *l* of Egypt with plagues
5:15 then they settled in the *l* of the Amorites,
8:22 for the taking of exiles from the *l*,
16: 4 He threatened to burn my *l*,
16:21 her life she was renowned throughout the *l*.
Est C:16 people of the *l* of my forefathers that you,
8:17 of the peoples of the *l* embraced Judaism,
10: 1 on the *l* and on the islands of the sea.
1Mc 1: 1 son, who came from the *l* of Kittim,
1:19 cities in the *l* of Egypt were captured,
1:19 and Antiochus plundered the *l* of Egypt.
1:28 *l* was shaken on account of its inhabitants,
1:44 them to follow customs foreign to their *l*;
1:52 joined them and committed evil in the *l*.
2:56 assembly, received an inheritance in the *l*.
3:29 distress he had brought upon the *l*
3:35 and efface their memory from the *l*.
3:36 territory and distribute their *l* by lot.
3:39 cavalry to invade the *l* of Judah
5:45 crowd of people, to go into the *l* of Judah.
5:53 whole way, until he reached the *l* of Judah.
5:55 Judas and Jonathan were in the *l* of Gilead,
5:66 He then set out for the *l* of the
5:68 toward Azotus in the *l* of the Philistines.
5:68 their cities he returned to the *l* of Judah.
6: 5 into the *l* of Judah had been put to flight;
6:13 am dying, in bitter grief, in a foreign *l*."
6:49 for that was a sabbath year in the *l*.
7: 7 Judas has done to us and to the king's *l*,
7:10 in the *l* of Judah with a great army,
7:22 They took possession of the *l* of Judah and
7:50 for a short time the *l* of Judah was quiet.
8:10 them, took possession of their *l*,
8:23 the Jewish nation at sea and on *l* forever;
8:32 justice and make war on you by *l* and sea.'"
9: 1 Bacchides and Alcimus into the *l* of Judah,
9:57 and the *l* of Judah was quiet for two years.
9:72 had previously taken from the *l* of Judah.
10:30 I collect them from the *l* of Judah
10:33 carried into captivity from the *l* of Judah
10:37 the king has commanded in the *l* of Judah.
10:55 you returned to the *l* of your fathers
10:67 came from Crete to the *l* of his fathers.
10:72 were twice put to flight in their own *l*.
11:38 When King Demetrius saw that the *l* was
11:52 and the *l* was peaceful under his rule,
12: 4 envoys with save conduct to the *l* of Judah.
12:46 and they returned to the *l* of Judah.
12:52 Jonathan came safely into the *l* of Judah.
13: 1 army to invade and ravage the *l* of Judah,
13:12 with a large army to invade the *l* of Judah,
13:32 Thus he brought much evil on the *l*.
13:34 he grant the *l* a release from taxation,
13:34 all that Trypho did was to plunder the *l*.
14: 4 The *l* was at rest all the days of Simon,
14: 8 cultivated their *l* in peace; the *l* yielded
14:11 He brought peace to the *l*,
14:13 No one was left to attack them in their *l*;
14:37 for the defense of the *l* and the city,
15:10 Antiochus invaded the *l* of his ancestors,
15:14 by *l* and sea and let no one go in or out.
15:29 territories, done great harm to the *l*,
15:33 "We have not seized any foreign *l*;
16: 4 *l* twenty thousand warriors and horsemen.
2Mc 1: 1 The Jews in Jerusalem and in the *l* of
1: 7 against the holy *l* and the kingdom,
2:21 few as they were, they seized the whole *l*,
5:21 *l* navigable and the sea passable on foot,
9:28 death in the mountains of a foreign *l*.
Jb 1: 1 In the *l* of Uz there was a blameless and
1:10 and his livestock are spread over the *l*.
10:21 return, to the *l* of darkness and of gloom,
10:22 *l* where darkness is the only light.
12:15 sends them forth and they overwhelm the *l*.
12:24 understanding from the leaders of the *l*,
14:19 and floods wash away the soil of the *l*,
15:19 fathers, To whom alone the *l* was given,
18:17 His memory perishes from the *l*,
22: 8 As if the *l* belonged to the man of might,
24: 4 the poor of the *l* are driven into hiding.
24: 6 they harvest at night in the untilled *l*.
24:18 Their portion in the *l* is accursed,
28:13 nor is it to be had in the *l* of the living.
30: 8 men, they were driven out of the *l*.
31:38 If my *l* has cried out against me till its
33:30 pit to the light, in the *l* of the living.
34:13 or who else set all the *l* in its place?
37:17 a calm from the south comes over the *l*,
38:26 a path To bring rain to no man's *l*,
42:15 In all the *l* no other women were as
Ps(s) 10:16 the nations have perished out of his *l*.
16: 3 me cherish the holy ones who are in his *l*!
25:13 and his descendants inherit the *l*.
27:13 bounty of the LORD in the *l* of the living
35:20 in the *l* they fashion treacherous speech.
37: 3 you may dwell in the *l* and enjoy security.
37: 9 who wait for the LORD shall possess the *l*.
37:11 But the meek shall possess the *l*,
37:22 those whom he blesses shall possess the *l*,
37:29 possess the *l* and dwell in it forever.
37:34 He will promote you to ownership of the *l*;
42: 7 you From the *l* of the Jordan and of Hermon,
44: 4 their own sword did they conquer the *l*,
45:17 shall make them princes through all the *l*.
52: 7 and uproot you from the *l* of the living.
65:10 You have visited the *l* and watered it;
65:11 Thus have you prepared the *l*:
66: 6 He has changed the sea into dry *l*;
68: 7 only rebels remain in the parched *l*.
68:10 you restored the *l* when it languished;
69:36 They shall dwell in the *l* and own it,
74: 8 burn all the shrines of God in the *l*."
74:15 brought dry *l* out of the primeval waters.
74:17 You fixed all the limits of the *l*;
74:20 the *l* and the plains are full of violence.
78:12 he did wondrous things, in the *l* of Egypt,
78:54 And he brought them to his holy *l*,
80:10 for it, and it took root and filled the *l*.
81: 6 when he came forth from the *l* of Egypt.
81:11 God who led you forth from the *l* of Egypt;
85: 2 You have favored, O LORD, your *l*;
85:10 who fear him, glory dwelling in our *l*.
85:13 our *l* shall yield its increase.
88:13 or your justice in the *l* of oblivion?
95: 5 the sea, for he has made it, and the dry *l*,
101: 6 My eyes are upon the faithful of the *l*,
101: 8 I will destroy all the wicked of the *l*,
105:11 *l* of Canaan as your allotted inheritance."
105:16 *l* and ruined the crop that sustained them,
105:23 Egypt, and Jacob sojourned in the *l* of Ham.
105:27 among them, and wonders in the *l* of Ham.
105:30 Their *l* swarmed with frogs,
105:32 with flashing fires throughout their *l*.
105:35 they devoured every plant throughout the *l*;
105:36 struck every first-born throughout their *l*,
106:22 in Egypt, Wondrous deeds in the *l* of Ham,
106:24 Yet they despised the desirable *l*;
106:38 Canaan, desecrating the *l* with bloodshed;
107:34 thirsty ground, Fruitful *l* into salt marsh,
107:35 of water, waterless *l* into water springs.
135:12 And he made their *l* a heritage,
136:21 And made their *l* a heritage,
137: 2 the aspens of that *l* we hung up our harps,
137: 4 we sing a song of the LORD in a foreign *l*?
140:12 of wicked tongue shall not abide in the *l*;
142: 6 refuge, my portion in the *l* of the living."
143: 6 my soul thirsts for you like parched *l*.
Prv 2:21 For the upright will dwell in the *l*,
2:22 But the wicked will be cut off from the *l*,
10:30 but the wicked will not abide in the *l*.
12:11 He who tills his own *l* has food in plenty,
28: 2 If a *l* is rebellious, its princes will be many;
28:19 cultivates his *l* will have plenty of food,
29: 4 justice a king gives stability to the *l*;
31:23 gates as he sits with the elders of the *l*.
Eccl 5: 8 every respect is a king for the arable *l*.
10:16 Woe to you, O *l*, whose king was a servant,
10:17 Blessed are you, O *l*,
Sg 2:12 and the song of the dove is heard in our *l*.
Wis 12: 3 the ancient inhabitants of your holy *l*,
12: 7 that the *l* that is dearest of all to you
16:19 as to consume the produce of the wicked *l*.
18:15 a fierce warrior, into the doomed *l*,
19: 7 before been water, dry *l* was seen emerging:
19:10 young of animals the *l* brought forth gnats,
19:19 For *l* creatures were changed into water
19:19 and those that swam went over on to the *l*.
Sir 20:27 He who works his *l* has abundant crops,
24: 6 Over waves of the sea, over all the *l*,
36:10 that they may inherit the *l* as of old,
39:23 and turns fertile *l* into a salt marsh.
43: 4 By its fiery darts the *l* is consumed;
43:23 the scattered dew enriches the parched *l*.
44: 2 Subduers of the *l* in kingly fashion,
45:22 But he holds no *l* among the people nor
46: 8 the *l* flowing with milk and honey.
46: 9 he won his way onto the summits of the *l*;
47:24 and caused them to be exiled from their *l*.
48:15 their *l* and scattered all over the earth.
50:19 the people of the *l* would shout for joy,
Is 1: 7 Your *l* before your eyes strangers devour
1:19 you shall eat the good things of the *l*;
2: 7 Their *l* is full of silver and gold,
2: 7 Their *l* is full of horses,
2: 8 Their *l* is full of idols;
5: 8 left to dwell alone in the midst of the *l*!
6:12 away, and the *l* is abandoned more and more.
7:16 the *l* of those two kings whom you dread
7:18 Egypt, and for the bee in the *l* of Assyria.
7:22 be the food of all who remain in the *l*.
7:25 they shall be grazing *l* for cattle and
8: 8 spread its wings the full width of your *l*,
8:23 the land of Zebulun and the *l* of Naphtali;
8:23 the seaward road, the *l* west of the Jordan,
9: 1 dwelt in the *l* of gloom a light has shone.
9:18 wrath of the LORD of hosts the *l* quakes,
10:23 hosts, will carry out within the whole *l*.
11:16 Israel when he came up from the *l* of Egypt.
13: 5 of his wrath, to destroy all the *l*.
13: 9 the *l* and destroy the sinners within it!
13:14 turn to his kindred and flee to his own *l*.
14:20 For you have ruined your *l*,
14:25 in my *l* and trample him on my mountains;
15: 8 For the cry has gone round the *l* of Moab;
15: 9 Moab and for those who remain in the *l*!
16: 4 and they have done with trampling the *l*,
18: 1 Ah, *l* of buzzing insects,
18: 2 conquering, whose *l* is washed by rivers.
18: 6 birds of prey, and to the beasts in the *l*;
18: 7 conquering, whose *l* is washed by rivers
19: 7 All the sown *l* along the Nile shall dry up
19:17 And the *l* of Judah shall be a terror to
19:18 there shall be five cities in the *l* of Egypt
19:19 be an altar to the LORD in the *l* of Egypt,
19:20 to the LORD of hosts in the *l* of Egypt,
19:24 Assyria, a blessing in the midst of the *l*,
21: 1 comes from the desert, from the fearful *l*,
21:14 you who dwell in the *l* of Tema,
22:18 like a ball into an open *l* To perish there,
23: 1 the *l* of the Kittim the news reaches them.
23:10 Cross to your own *l*, O ship of Tarshish;
23:13 [This people is the *l* of the Chaldeans,
24: 2 the LORD empties the *l* and lays it waste;
24:11 has disappeared and cheer has left the *l*.
24:13 Thus it is within the *l*,
26: 1 they will sing this song in the *l* of Judah:
26:10 in an upright *l* he acts perversely,
26:15 and extended far all the borders of the *l*.
26:19 of light, and the *l* of shades gives birth.
27:13 *l* of Assyria and the outcasts in the *l*
28:24 loosening and harrowing his *l* for planting?
30: 6 troubled *l* of the lioness and roaring lion,
32: 2 the shade of a great rock in a parched *l*.
33:17 his splendor, they will look upon a vast *l*.
34: 6 Bozrah, a great slaughter in the *l* of Edom.
34: 7 Their *l* shall be soaked with blood,
34: 9 and her *l* shall become burning pitch;
35: 1 The desert and the parched *l* will exult;
36:10 will that I have come up to destroy this *l*?
36:10 said to me, "Go up and destroy that *l*!"'"
36:17 land like your own, a *l* of grain and wine,
36:18 his *l* from the hand of the king of Assyria?
36:20 lands ever rescued his *l* from my hand?
37: 7 report, he will return to his own *l*,
37:38 the sword and fled into the *l* of Ararat.
38:11 the LORD no more in the *l* of the living.
39: 3 "They came to me from a distant *l*,
40: 4 The rugged *l* shall be made a plain,
44: 3 ground, and streams upon the dry *l*;
46:11 the east a bird of prey, from a distant *l*,
49: 8 the *l* and allot the desolate heritages,
49:12 and the west, and some from the *l* of Syene.
49:19 you were waste and desolate, a *l* of ruins,
53: 8 he was cut off from the *l* of the living,
57:13 who takes refuge in me shall inherit the *l*,
58:11 and give you plenty even on the parched *l*.
60:18 shall violence be heard of in your *l*,
60:21 be just, they shall always possess the *l*,
61: 7 shall have a double inheritance in their *l*,
62: 4 you "Forsaken," or your *l* "Desolate,"
62: 4 "My Delight," and your *l* "Espoused."
62: 4 in you, and makes your *l* his spouse.
65: 9 My chosen ones shall inherit the *l*,
65:16 on whom a blessing is invoked in the *l*.
65:16 in the *l* shall swear by the God of truth;
Jer 1: 1 family in Anathoth, in the *l* of Benjamin.
1:14 will boil over upon all who dwell in the *l*.
1:18 iron, a wall of brass, against the whole *l*:
2: 2 Following me in the desert, in a *l* unsown.
2: 6 LORD who brought us up from the *l* of Egypt,
2: 6 desert, through a *l* of wastes and gullies,
2: 6 Through a *l* of drought and darkness,
2: 6 darkness, through a *l* which no one crosses,
2: 7 into the garden *l* to eat its goodly fruits,
2: 7 fruits, You entered and defiled my *l*,
2:15 They have made his *l* a waste;
2:31 I been a desert to Israel, a *l* of darkness?
3: 1 Would not the *l* be wholly defiled?
3: 2 You defiled the *l* by your wicked harlotry.
3: 9 Eager to sin, she polluted the *l*,
3:16 you multiply and become fruitful in the *l*,
3:18 will come from the *l* of the north to the *l*
3:19 you as sons, And give you a pleasant *l*,
4: 5 Blow the trumpet through the *l*,
4: 7 his place, To turn your *l* into desolation,
4:16 besiegers are coming from the distant *l*,
4:26 and behold, the garden *l* was a desert,
4:27 Waste shall the whole *l* be;
5:19 your own *l*, so shall you serve strangers in a *l*
5:30 horrible thing has happened in the *l*:

6: 8 you into a desert, a l where no man dwells.
6:12 my hand against those who dwell in this l,
6:22 a people comes from the l of the north,
7: 7 in the l which I gave your fathers long
7:22 day I brought them out of the l of Egypt,
7:25 left the l of Egypt even to this day,
7:34 for the l will be turned to rubble.
8:16 of his stallions shakes the whole l.
8:16 come devouring the l and all it contains,
8:19 of my people, far and wide in the l!
9: 2 not with truth, they hold forth in the l.
9:11 Why is the l ravaged,
9:18 We must leave the l,
10:17 Lift your bundle and leave the l,
10:18 I will sling away the inhabitants of the l;
10:22 closer, a great uproar from the northern l:
11: 4 I brought them up out of the l of Egypt,
11: 5 give them a l flowing with milk and honey:
11: 7 up out of the l of Egypt even to this day.
11:19 it lies before me, Desolate, all the l,
12: 5 And if in a l of peace you fall headlong,
12:11 us cut him off from the l of the living,
12:12 The LORD has a sword which consumes the l,
12:14 See, I will pluck them up from their l;
12:15 back, each to his heritage, each to his l.
13:13 drunkenness all the inhabitants of this l,
14: 4 no rain in the l the farmers are ashamed,
14: 8 Why should you be a stranger in this l,
14:15 and famine shall not befall this l":
14:18 and the priest forage in a l they know not.
15:10 man of strife and contention to all the l!
16: 3 the fathers who will beget them in this l:
16: 6 die, the great and the lowly, in this l,
16:13 I will cast you out of this l into a land
16:15 who brought the Israelites out of the l
16:15 back to the l which I gave their fathers.
16:18 l with their detestable corpses of idols,
17: 4 to your enemies in a l that you know not:
17:13 The rebels in the l shall be put to shame;
17:26 the l of Benjamin and from the foothills,
18:16 Their l shall be turned into a desert,
22:10 never again will he see the l of his birth.
22:12 this l he shall not see again.
22:26 different l from the one you were born in;
22:27 come back to the l for which they yearn.
22:28 out, why thrown into a l they know not?
22:29 O land, land, l,
23: 5 shall do what is just and right in the l.
23: 7 the Israelites out of the l of Egypt";
23: 8 of Israel up from the l of the north"
23: 8 they shall again live on their own l.
23:10 l is filled; on their account the land
23:15 has gone forth into the whole l.
24: 5 this place into the l of the Chaldeans.
24: 6 their good, and bring them back to this l,
24: 8 l and those who have settled in the l of Egypt.
24:10 the l which I gave them and their fathers.
25: 5 l which the LORD gave you and your fathers,
25: 9 I will bring them against this l,
25:11 This whole l shall be a ruin and a desert.
25:12 and the l of the Chaldeans for their guilt,
25:12 l I will turn into everlasting desert.
25:13 Against that l I will fulfill all the
25:20 land of Uz; all the kings of the l
25:38 l is made desolate By the sweeping sword,
26:17 some of the elders of the l came forward
26:20 against this city and l as Jeremiah did.
27: 7 and his grandson, until the time of his l,
27:10 in order to drive you far from your l,
27:11 him I will leave in peace on its own l,
30: 3 the l which I have gave to their fathers;
30:10 l, your descendants, from their land
31: 8 bring them back from the l of the north;
31:16 LORD, they shall return from the enemy's l.
31:23 lot in the l of Judah and her cities,
31:32 to lead them forth from the l of Egypt;
32:15 vineyards shall again be bought in this l.
32:20 wonders in the l of Egypt and to this day,
32:21 your people Israel out of the l of Egypt
32:22 This l you gave them,
32:22 oath, a l flowing with milk and honey.
32:41 I will replant them firmly in this l,
32:43 Fields shall again be bought in this l,
32:44 shall be used in the l of Benjamin,
33:13 in the l of Benjamin and the suburbs of
33:15 shall do what is right and just in the l.
34:13 brought your fathers out of the l of Egypt,
35:11 king of Babylon, invaded this l,
35:15 on the l which I gave you and your fathers;
36:29 waste this l and empty it of man and beast?"
37: 1 king over the l of Judah by Nebuchadnezzar,
37: 2 nor the people of the l would listen to
37: 7 out to help you will return to its own l,
37:20 of Babylon would not attack you or this l?
39: 5 was brought to Riblah, in the l of Hamath,
39:10 were left in the l of Judah by Nebuzaradan,
40: 4 See, the whole l is before you;
40: 6 with him among the people left in the l.
40: 7 Gedaliah, son of Ahikam, charge of the l,
40: 9 in the l and submit to the king of Babylon,
40:12 they all returned to the l of Judah from
41: 2 king of Babylon had made ruler over the l;
41:18 Babylon had made ruler in the l of Judah.
42:10 quietly in this l I will build you up,
42:12 sorry for you and let you return to your l.
42:13 God, and decide not to remain in this l,
42:16 you fear shall reach you in the l of Egypt;
43: 4 LORD's command to stay in the l of Judah.
43: 5 thence to dwell again in the l of Judah:
43:11 He shall come and strike the l of Egypt:
43:12 the l of Egypt and depart victorious.
43:13 of the temple of the sun in the l of Egypt
44: 8 the l of Egypt where you have come to live?
44: 9 l of Judah and the streets of Jerusalem?
44:12 In the l of Egypt they shall fall by the
44:13 in the l of Egypt shall escape or survive.
44:14 None shall return to the l of Judah though
44:22 and so your l became a waste,
44:24 LORD, all you Judeans in the l of Egypt:
44:26 in the whole l of Egypt no man of Judah
44:28 from the land of Egypt to the l of Judah
45: 4 I am uprooting even the whole l.
46:13 king of Babylon, to attack the l of Egypt:
46:16 our own people, To the l of our birth
46:27 far-off l, your descendants, from their land
47: 2 It shall flood the l and all that is in it,
47: 2 the people of the l set up a wailing cry.
48:21 judgment has come on the l of the plateau:
48:33 end in the fruit gardens of the l of Moab.
50: 1 Babylon, against the l of the Chaldeans,
50: 3 against her to turn her l into a desert,
50: 8 from Babylon, leave the l of the Chaldeans,
50:16 own people, everyone flees to his own l.
50:18 will punish the king of Babylon and his l,
50:21 Attack the l of Merathaim,
50:22 Battle alarm in the l, dire destruction!
50:25 has work to do in the l of the Chaldeans.
50:28 the escaped from the l of Babylon:
50:38 For it is a l of idols,
50:45 he has made against the l of the Chaldeans:
51: 2 to winnow her and lay waste her l;
51: 4 The slain shall fall in the l of Chaldea,
51: 5 And the Chaldean l is full of guilt to be
51: 9 Leave her, let us go, each to his own l."
51:28 all its prefects, every l in his domain.
51:29 Turning the l of Babylon into a desert
51:43 parched and arid l Where no man lives,
51:46 for fear of rumors spread in the l;
51:46 the rumor comes, then violence in the l,
51:47 her whole l shall be put to shame,
51:52 and in her whole l the wounded will groan.
51:54 destruction from the l of the Chaldeans;
52: 9 and brought to Riblah, in the l of Hamath,
52:25 who mustered the people of the l,
52:27 put to death in Riblah, in the l of Hamath.
52:27 Thus was Judah exiled from her l.
Lam 3:34 underfoot all the prisoners in the l.
4:21 Edom, you who dwell in the l of Uz,
Bar 1: 8 temple, to restore them to the l of Judah,
1: 9 and the people of the l from Jerusalem,
1:19 of the l of Egypt until the present day,
1:20 l of Egypt to give us the l flowing
2:11 of the l of Egypt with your mighty hand,
2:21 may continue in the l I gave your fathers:
2:23 And all the l shall be deserted,
2:30 But in the l of their captivity they shall
2:32 praise me in the l of their captivity,
2:34 And I will bring them back to the l which
2:35 my people Israel from the l I gave them.
3:10 Israel, that you are in the l of your foes,
3:10 of your foes, grown old in a foreign l,
3:20 have seen the light, have dwelt in the l,
6:52 They set no king over the l,
6:60 and the same wind blows over all the l.
6:71 be comsumed, and be a disgrace in the l.
Ez 1: 3 in the l of the Chaldeans by the river
6:14 live I will make the l a desolate waste,
7: 2 Thus says the Lord GOD to the l of Israel:
7: 2 has come upon the four corners of the l!
7: 7 climax has come for you who dwell in the l!
7:23 for the l is filled with bloodshed and
8:12 the LORD has forsaken the l."
8:17 they have filled the l with violence,
9: 9 the l is filled with bloodshed,
9: 9 think that the LORD has forsaken the l,
11:15 to us the l of Israel has been given as
11:17 and I will restore to you the l of Israel.
12: 6 your face that you may not see the l,
12:13 to Babylon, into the l of the Chaldeans
12:19 Then say to the people of the l:
12:19 of Jerusalem [to the l of Israel]:
12:19 that their l may be emptied of the
12:20 be in ruins, and the l shall be a waste;
12:22 proverb that you have in the l of Israel:
13: 9 house of Israel, nor enter the l of Israel;
14:13 when a l sins against me by breaking faith,
14:15 were to cause wild beasts to prowl the l,
14:16 would be saved, and the l would be a waste.
14:17 the l cutting off from it man and beast,
14:19 if I were to send pestilence into this l,
15: 8 I will make the l a waste,
16: 3 and birth you are of the l of Canaan;
16:29 now going to Chaldea, the l of the traders;
17: 4 branch, And brought it to a l of tradesmen,
17: 5 Then he took some seed of the l,
17:13 oath, while removing the nobles of the l,
18: 2 proverb that you recite in the l of Israel:
19: 4 took him away with hooks to the l of Egypt.
19: 7 The l and all in it were appalled at the
19:13 in the desert, in a l dry and parched,
20: 5 in the l of Egypt I revealed myself to
20: 6 l of Egypt to the l I had scouted for them,
20: 6 for them, a l flowing with milk and honey,
20: 8 my anger on them there in the l of Egypt;
20: 9 I would bring them out of the l of Egypt.
20:10 Therefore I led them out of the l of Egypt
20:15 to the l I had given them, a l flowing
20:28 them to the l I had sworn to give them,
20:36 fathers in the desert of the l of Egypt,
20:38 from the l where they sojourned as aliens
20:38 they shall not return to the l of Israel.
20:42 l of Israel, the l which I swore to give
21: 2 against the forest of the southern l.
21: 7 and prophesy against the l of Israel,
21: 8 land of Israel, saying to the l of Israel:
21:24 Both roads shall lead out from the same l.
21:35 you were created, in the l of your origin,
21:37 your blood shall flow throughout the l.
22:24 You are a l unrained on [that is,
22:29 l practice extortion and commit robbery;
22:30 before me to keep me from destroying the l;
23:19 she had been a harlot in the l of Egypt.
23:48 I will put an end to lewdness in the l,
25: 3 the devastation of the l of Israel,
25: 6 in your heart over the l of Israel,
25: 9 totally of its cities, the jewels of the l:
26:20 to take your place in the l of the living.
27:17 and the l of Israel trafficked with you,
28:25 their l which I gave to my servant Jacob;
29: 9 l of Egypt shall become a desolate waste;
29:10 I will make the l of Egypt a waste and a
29:12 the l of Egypt the most desolate of lands,
29:14 the land of Pathros, the l of their origin,
29:19 giving the l of Egypt to Nebuchadnezzar,
29:20 his toil I have given him the l of Egypt,
30:11 shall be brought in to devastate the l.
30:11 Egypt, and fill the l with the slain.
30:12 I will turn the Niles into dry l and sell
30:12 The l and everything in it I will hand
30:13 Memphis and the princes of the l of Egypt,
30:13 I will cast fear into the l of Egypt,
30:25 for him to wield against the l of Egypt.
31:12 land, and all the peoples of the l withdrew
31:14 are destined for death, for the l below,
31:15 the trees in the l dropped on his account.
31:16 In the l below, all Eden's trees
31:18 down with the trees of Eden to the l below.
32: 4 I will leave you on the l;
32: 6 will water the l with what flows from you,
32: 8 And I will spread darkness over your l,
32:15 l shall be devastated of all that is in it;
32:23 who spread terror in the l of the living.
32:24 spread their terror in the l of the living,
32:26 spread their terror in the l of the living.
32:27 men caused terror in the l of the living.
32:32 spread his terror in the l of the living,
33:24 the ruins on the l of Israel reason thus:
33:24 individual, received possession of the l;
33:24 possession the l that has been given to us."
33:25 yet you would keep possession of the l?
33:26 yet you would keep possession of the l?
33:28 I will make the l a desolate waste,
33:29 when I make the l a desolate waste because
34:27 bear their fruits, and the l its crops,
34:29 longer be carried off by famine in the l,
35:14 rejoiced over my l because it was desolate,
36: 5 have considered my l their possession
36: 6 prophesy concerning the l of Israel,
36:13 of you, "You are a l that devours men,
36:17 when the house of Israel lived in their l,
36:20 of the LORD, yet they had to leave their l."
36:24 lands, and bring you back to your own l.
36:28 shall live in the l I gave your fathers;
36:34 the desolate l shall be tilled,
36:35 l has been made into a garden of Eden,"
37:12 and bring you back to the l of Israel.
37:14 live, and I will settle you upon your l;
37:21 all sides to bring them back to their l.
37:22 I will make them one nation upon the l,
37:25 on the l which I gave to my servant Jacob,
37:25 Jacob, the l where their fathers lived;
38: 2 of man, turn toward Gog [the l of Magog],
38:11 "I will go up against a l of open
38:16 people Israel like a cloud covering the l.
38:16 last days I will bring you against my l,
38:18 the day when Gog invades the l of Israel,
38:19 be a great shaking upon the l of Israel.
38:20 the ground, and all men who are on the l.
39:12 To purify the l,
39:13 l shall bury them and gain renown for it,
39:14 the l burying those who lie unburied,
39:14 who lie unburied, so as to purify the l.
39:16 Thus the l shall be purified.
39:18 the blood of the princes of the l [rams,
39:26 on their l with no one to frighten them.
39:28 nations, will gather them back on their l,
40: 2 me in divine visions to the l of Israel,
45: 1 When you apportion the l into inheritances,
45: 1 set apart a sacred tract of l for the LORD,

LAND (cont.)
45: 2 Of this *l* a square plot,
45: 4 part of the *l* belonging to the priests,
45: 4 their homes and pasture *l* for their cattle.
45: 8 boundary to the eastern boundary of the *l*.
45: 8 but will leave the *l* to the house of
45:16 All the people of the *l* shall be bound to
45:22 and on behalf of all the people of the *l*,
46: 3 The people of the *l* shall worship before
46: 9 When the people of the *l* enter the
47:13 the *l* among the twelve tribes of Israel
47:14 *l* which I swore to give to your fathers,
47:15 is the boundary of the *l* on the north side:
47:18 and the *l* of Israel on the other side,
47:21 You shall distribute this *l* among
48:12 tract of *l* their own most sacred domain,
48:14 or alienate this, the best part of the *l*,
48:15 line are profane *l*, assigned to the City
48:21 the *l* on both sides of the sacred tract
48:29 Such is the *l* which you shall apportion as
Dn 1: 2 which he carried off to the *l* of Shinar,
9: 6 our fathers, and all the people of the *l*.
9:15 out of the *l* of Egypt with a strong hand,
11: 9 invade the *l* of the king of the south,
11:16 He shall stop in the glorious *l*,
11:19 turn to the strongholds of his own *l*,
11:28 turn back toward his *l* with great riches,
11:28 shall arrange matters and return to his *l*.
11:39 the many and distribute the *l* as a reward.
11:41 enter the glorious *l* and many shall fall,
11:42 and not even the *l* of Egypt shall escape.
Hos 1: 2 for the *l* gives itself to harlotry,
2: 5 like the desert, reduce her to an arid *l*,
2:17 when she came up from the *l* of Egypt.
2:20 sword and war I will destroy from the *l*,
2:25 I will sow him for myself in the *l*,
4: 1 grievance against the inhabitants of the *l*:
4: 1 no mercy, no knowledge of God in the *l*.
4: 3 Therefore the *l* mourns,
6: 7 But they, in their *l*,
7:12 I will send them captive from their *l*.
7:16 they shall be mocked in the *l* of Egypt.
9: 3 They shall not dwell in the LORD's *l*;
10: 1 The more productive his *l*,
11: 5 He shall return to the *l* of Egypt,
11:11 like sparrows, from the *l* of Assyria,
12:10 the LORD, your God, since the *l* of Egypt;
12:13 When Jacob fled to the *l* of Aram,
13: 4 the LORD, your God, since the *l* of Egypt;
13: 5 I fed you in the desert, in the torrid *l*.
13:15 shall loot his *l* of every precious thing.
Jl 1: 2 Pay attention, all you who dwell in the *l*!
1: 6 For a people has invaded my *l*,
1:14 Gather the elders, all who dwell in the *l*,
2: 1 Let all who dwell in the *l* tremble,
2: 3 the garden of Eden is the *l* before them,
2:18 for his *l* and took pity on his people.
2:20 and drive him out into a *l* arid and waste,
2:21 Fear not, O *l*! exult and rejoice!
4: 2 them among the nations, and divided my *l*.
4:19 they shed innocent blood in their *l*.
Am 2:10 I who brought you up from the *l* of Egypt,
2:10 years, to occupy the *l* of the Amorites:
3: 1 that I brought up from the *l* of Egypt.
3: 9 Ashdod, in the castles of the *l* of Egypt:
3:11 An enemy shall surround the *l*,
5: 2 She lies abandoned upon her *l*,
7: 2 they were eating all the grass in the *l*,
7: 4 the great abyss, and was consuming the *l*,
7:11 Israel shall surely be exiled from its *l*."
7:12 you, visionary, flee to the *l* of Judah!
7:17 Your *l* shall be divided by measuring line,
7:17 *l*; Israel shall be exiled far from its land.
8: 4 the needy and destroy the poor of the *l*!
8: 8 Shall not the *l* tremble because of this,
8:11 GOD, when I will send famine upon the *l*:
9: 7 Did I not bring the Israelites from the *l*
9:15 be plucked From the *l* I have given them,
Ob 1:20 occupy the Canaanite *l* as far as Zarephath,
Jon 1: 9 of heaven, who made the sea and the dry *l*."
1:13 Still the men rowed hard to regain the *l*,
Mi 5: 4 invades our country and treads upon our *l*,
5: 5 land of Assyria with the sword, and the *l*
5: 5 invades our *l* and treads upon our borders.
5:10 your *l* and tear down all your fortresses.
6: 4 For I brought you up from the *l* of Egypt,
7:13 *l* shall be a waste because of its citizens,
7:15 the days when you came from the *l* of Egypt,
Na 2:14 preying on the *l* I will bring to an end,
3:13 foes the gates of your *l* are open wide,
Hb 1: 6 of the *l* to take dwellings not his own.
2: 8 blood shed, and violence done to the *l*,
2:17 blood shed, and violence done to the *l*,
3: 7 are the pavilions of the *l* of Midian.
Zep 2: 5 I will humble you, *l* of the Philistines,
2: 9 like Sodom, the *l* of Ammon like Gomorrah:
Hg 1:11 drought upon the *l* and upon the mountains;
2: 4 all you people of the *l* says the LORD,
2: 6 and the earth, the sea and the dry *l*.
Zec 2: 4 their horns to scatter the *l* of Judah."
2:10 Flee from the *l* of the north,
2:16 possess Judah as his portion of the holy *l*,
3: 9 take away the guilt of the *l* in one day.
5: 6 This is their guilt in all the *l*."
5:11 build a temple for it in the *l* of Shinar;
6: 6 was turning toward the *l* of the north,
6: 6 ones went toward the *l* of the south.
6: 8 they that go forth to the *l* of the north
6: 8 make my spirit rest in the *l* of the north."
7: 5 all the people of the *l* and to the priests:
7:14 Thus the *l* was left desolate after them
7:14 they made the pleasant *l* into a desert.
8: 7 *l* of the rising sun, and from the land
8:12 its fruit, the *l* shall bear its crops,
9: 1 word of the LORD is upon the *l* of Hadrach,
9:16 jewels in a crown raised aloft over his *l*.
10:10 I will bring them back from the *l* of Egypt,
11:16 For I will raise up a shepherd in the *l*
12:12 And the *l* shall mourn,
13: 2 destroy the names of the idols from the *l*,
13: 2 and the spirit of uncleanness from the *l*.
13: 5 soil, for I have owned *l* since my youth."
13: 8 In all the *l*, says the LORD,
14:10 Negeb, all the *l* shall turn into a plain;
Mal 1: 4 And they shall be called the *l* of guilt,
1: 5 is the LORD, even beyond the *l* of Israel."
3:12 blessed, for you will be a delightful *l*,
3:24 Lest I come and strike the *l* with doom.
Mt 2: 6 'And you, Bethlehem, *l* of Judah,
2:20 mother, and set out for the *l* of Israel.
2:21 mother, and returned to the *l* of Israel.
4:15 *L* of Zebulun, *l* of Naphtali along the sea
4:16 who inhabit a *l* overshadowed by death,
5: 5 they shall inherit the *l*
23:15 over sea and *l* to make a single convert,
27:45 over the whole *l* until midafternoon.
Mk 6:47 on the lake while he was alone on the *l*.
Lk 4:25 years and a great famine spread over the *l*.
5:11 With that they brought their boats to *l*,
8:27 When he came to *l*,
14:18 some *l* and must go out and inspect it.
15:13 belongings and went off to a distant *l*,
15:25 "Meanwhile the elder son was out on the *l*.
21:23 The distress in the *l* and the wrath
23:44 darkness came over the whole *l*
Jn 4: 5 *l* which Jacob had given to his son Joseph.
21: 8 Actually they were not far from *l*—
Acts 1:18 bought a piece of *l* with his unjust gains,
7: 3 kinsfolk, and go to the *l* I will show you.
7: 4 *l* of the Chaldeans and settled in Haran.
7: 4 from there to this *l* where you now dwell.
7: 5 it as his heritage, not even a foot of *l*,
7: 6 will be strangers in a foreign *l*,
7:29 residence as an alien in the *l* of Midian,
7:36 wonders and signs in the *l* of Egypt,
7:40 Moses who brought us out of the *l* of Egypt,
7:45 they brought it into the *l* during the
10:39 did in the *l* of the Jews and in Jerusalem.
13:17 during their sojourn in the *l* of Egypt,
13:19 then he destroyed seven nations in the *l*
27:27 sailors began to suspect that *l* was near.
27:39 they did not recognize the *l* they saw.
27:43 to jump overboard first and make for *l*.
Heb 8: 9 to lead them forth from the *l* of Egypt:
11: 9 in the promised *l* as in a foreign country,
11:29 crossed the Red Sea as if it were dry *l*,
Jas 5:17 on the *l* for three years and six months.
5:18 with rain and the *l* produced its crop.
1Pt 1:17 during your sojourn in a strange *l*.
Jude 1: 5 rescued his people from the *l* of Egypt
Rv 7: 1 wind blew on *l* or sea or through any tree.
7: 2 given power to ravage the *l* and the sea,
7: 3 "Do no harm to the *l* or the sea or the
8: 7 A third of the *l* was scorched,
9: 3 Out of the smoke, onto the *l*,
9: 4 to do no harm to the grass in the *l*
10: 2 on the sea and his left foot on the *l*,
10: 5 on the *l* raised his right hand to heaven
10: 8 the angel standing on the sea and on the *l*."

LANDED (9)
Gn 34:10 freely in it, and acquire *l* property here."
Mt 13: 4 Part of what he sowed *l* on a footpath,
13: 8 *l* on good soil and yielded grain a
Mk 4: 4 Some of what he sowed *l* on the footpath,
4: 5 *l* on rocky ground where it had little soil;
4: 7 Again, some *l* among thorns,
4: 8 *l* on good soil and yielded grain that
Jn 21: 9 When they *l*, they saw a charcoal fire
Acts 18:19 When they *l* at Ephesus,

LANDING (2)
1Mc 15: 4 warships to make a *l* in my country
Acts 18:22 On *l* at Caesarea,

LANDINGS (1)
1Kgs 6: 8 and stairs with intermediate *l* led up to

LANDMARK (3)
Prv 15:25 but he preserves intact the widow's *l*.
22:28 the ancient *l* which your fathers set up.
23:10 Remove not the ancient *l*,

LANDMARKS (3)
Dt 19:14 "You shall not move your neighbor's *l*
27:17 'Cursed be he who moves his neighbor's *l*!'
Jb 24: 2 The wicked remove *l*;

LANDS (201)
Gn 10: 5 maritime nations, in their respective *l*—
10:20 and languages, by their *l* and nations.
10:31 clans and languages by their *l* and nations.
26: 3 your descendants I will give all these *l*,
26: 4 in the sky and give them all these *l*,
43:11 Put some of the *l* best products in your
47:13 and the *l* of Egypt and Canaan were
47:22 the priests' *l* Joseph did not take over.
Lv 26:36 "Those of you who survive in the *l* of
26:39 Those of you who survive in the *l* of their
Nm 35: 2 as well as pasture *l* around the cities.
35: 3 and the pasture *l* shall serve their herds
35: 4 The pasture *l* of the cities to be assigned
35: 5 them as the pasture *l* of their cities.
35: 7 their pasture *l* to be assigned the Levites.
Dt 29:21 who will come here from far-off *l*,
Jos 10:42 *l* Joshua captured in a single campaign,
12: 1 conquered and whose *l* they occupied,
14: 4 their pasture *l* for the cattle and flocks.
21: 2 dwell in, with pasture *l* for our livestock."
21: 3 the following cities with their pasture *l*.
21: 8 These cities with their pasture *l* the
21:11 of Judah, with the adjacent pasture *l*,
21:13 lands; also, Libnah with its pasture *l*,
21:14 pasture *l*, Eshtemoa with its pasture lands,
21:15 its pasture *l*, Debir with its pasture lands,
21:16 its pasture *l*, Juttah with its pasture lands,
21:16 and Beth-shemesh with its pasture *l*:
21:17 its pasture *l*, Geba with its pasture lands,
21:18 pasture lands, Anathoth with its pasture *l*,
21:19 These cities which with their pasture *l*
21:21 They were assigned, with its pasture *l*,
21:21 also Gezer with its pasture *l*,
21:22 pasture lands, Kibzaim with its pasture *l*.
21:23 pasture *l*, Gibbethon with its pasture lands,
21:24 *l*, and Gath-rimmon with its pasture lands
21:25 *l* and Ibleam with its pasture lands.
21:26 These cities which with their pasture *l*
21:27 homicides at Golan, with its pasture *l*;
21:27 and also Beth-ashtaroth with its pasture *l*.
21:28 pasture *l*, Daberath with its pasture lands,
21:29 *l*, and En-gannim with its pasture lands;
21:30 pasture *l*, Abdon with its pasture lands,
21:31 *l*, and Rehob with its pasture lands;
21:32 *l*; also Hammath with its pasture lands
21:32 lands and Rakkath with its pasture *l*.
21:33 These cities which with their pasture *l*
21:34 pasture lands, Kartah with its pasture *l*,
21:35 lands, and Nahalal with its pasture *l*;
21:36 pasture lands, Jahaz with its pasture *l*,
21:37 lands, and Mephaath with its pasture *l*:
21:38 lands, also Mahanaim with its pasture *l*,
21:39 lands, and Jazer with its pasture *l*.
21:41 Israelites which, with their pasture *l*,
21:42 cities went the pasture *l* round about it.
2Sam 9: 7 to you all the *l* of your grandfather Saul
2Kgs 18:35 these *l* ever rescued his land from my hand?
19:17 have laid waste the nations and their *l*,
19:24 I dug wells and drank water in foreign *l*;
1Chr 5:16 all the pasture *l* of Sirion to the borders.
6:40 adjacent pasture *l* in the land of Judah,
6:42 Libnah with its pasture *l*
6:42 Jattir with its pasture *l*,
6:42 lands, Eshtemoa with its pasture *l*,
6:43 pasture lands, Debir with its pasture *l*,
6:44 its pasture *l*, Jetta with its pasture lands,
6:44 lands, and Beth-shemesh with its pasture *l*.
6:45 pasture *l*, Geba with its pasture lands,
6:45 pasture lands, Anathoth with its pasture *l*.
6:45 had thirteen cities with their pasture *l*.
6:49 cities with their pasture *l* to the Levites,
6:52 pasture lands, Gezer with its pasture *l*,
6:53 lands, and Beth-horon with its pasture *l*.
6:54 lands, Gibbethon with its pasture *l*,
6:54 lands, and Gath-rimmon with its pasture *l*.
6:55 lands and Ibleam with its pasture *l*.
6:56 *l* and Ashtaroth with its pasture lands.
6:57 lands, Daberath with its pasture *l*,
6:58 lands, and Engannim with its pasture *l*.
6:59 pasture lands, Abdon with its pasture *l*,
6:60 lands, and Rehob with its pasture *l*.
6:61 pasture lands, Hammon with its pasture *l*,
6:61 lands, and Kiriathaim with its pasture *l*.
6:62 pasture lands, Kartah with its pasture *l*,
6:62 lands, and Tabor with its pasture *l*.
6:63 pasture lands, Jahzah with its pasture *l*,
6:64 lands, and Mephaath with its pasture *l*.
6:65 lands, Mahanaim with its pasture *l*,
6:66 lands, and Jazer with its pasture *l*.
13: 2 Levites from their cities with pasture *l*,
29:30 and all the kingdoms of the surrounding *l*.
2Chr 9:28 for Solomon from Egypt and from all the *l*.
11:14 the Levites left their assigned pasture *l*
13: 9 priests like the peoples of foreign *l*?
15: 5 many terrors upon the inhabitants of the *l*.

20:29 all the kingdoms of the surrounding *l*
31:19 lived on the *l* attached to their cities,
32:13 I have done to all the peoples of other *l*?
32:13 lands able to save their *l* from my hand?
32:17 *l* have not saved their people from my hand,
Ezr 9: 7 to the will of the kings of foreign *l*,
Neh 9:22 you divided up among them as border *l*.
9:30 into the power of the peoples of the *l*.
10:29 of the *l* in favor of the law of God,
Jdt 5:18 finally taken as captives into foreign *l*.
Ps(s) 49:12 though they have called *l* by their names.
96: 1 sing to the LORD, all you *l*.
98: 4 Sing joyfully to the LORD, all you *l*;
100: 1 Sing joyfully to the LORD, all you *l*;
105:41 it flowed through the dry *l* like a stream,
105:44 And he gave them the *l* of the nations,
106:27 nations, and to disperse them over the *l*.
107: 3 hand of the foe And gathered from the *l*,
116: 9 before the LORD in the *l* of the living.
Sir 29:18 and sent them wandering through foreign *l*.
39: 5 *l* to learn what is good and evil among men.
Is 8: 9 Give ear, all you distant *l*!
11: 4 and decide aright for the *l* afflicted.
23: 7 feet have taken her to dwell in distant *l*?
36:20 these *l* ever rescued his land from my hand?
37:18 laid waste all the nations and their *l*,
37:25 I dug wells and drank water in foreign *l*;
48:21 not thirst when he led them through dry *l*;
Jer 6:20 from Sheba, or sweet cane from far-off *l*?
9: 9 cries of lamentation, over the pasture *l*,
23: 3 the remnant of my flock from all the *l*
23: 8 from all the *l* to which I banished them;
27: 6 these *l* into the hand of Nebuchadnezzar,
28: 8 against many *l* and mighty kingdoms.
32:37 together from all the *l* to which in anger,
40:11 and those in all other *l* heard that the
Lam 5: 2 *l* have been turned over to strangers,
Ez 6: 8 have been scattered over the foreign *l*,
12:15 nations and scatter them over foreign *l*.
20: 6 with milk and honey, a jewel among all *l*.
20:15 with milk and honey, a jewel among all *l*.
20:23 nations and scatter them over foreign *l*;
20:32 the nations, like the peoples of foreign *l*,
22: 4 and a laughingstock to all foreign *l*.
22:15 the nations and scatter you over foreign *l*,
25: 7 the peoples, and remove you from the *l*.
26:20 and I will make you dwell in the nether *l*,
29:12 the land of Egypt the most desolate of *l*,
29:12 the nations and strew them over foreign *l*.
30: 7 She shall be the most devastated of *l*,
30:23 the nations and strew them over foreign *l*.
30:26 the nations and strew them over foreign *l*
32: 9 the nations, to *l* which you do not know.
34:13 and gather them from the foreign *l*;
34:13 *l* ravines and all its inhabited places].
35:10 two nations and the two *l* have become mine;
36:19 nations, dispersing them over foreign *l*;
36:24 nations, gather you from all the foreign *l*,
39:27 gather them from the *l* of their enemies,
48:17 The pasture *l* of the City shall extend
Hos 3: 2 one head and come up from other *l*,
Ob 1:19 the lands of Ephraim and the *l* of Samaria,
Zec 10: 9 nations, yet in distant *l* they remember me;

LANE (2)

Nm 22:24 narrow *l* between vineyards with a stone wall
Jl 2: 7 They advance, each in his own *l*,

LANES (1)

Sir 9: 7 Gaze not about the *l* of the city and

LANGUAGE (40)

Gn 10: 5 each with its own *l*—
11: 1 The whole world spoke the same *l*,
11: 6 are one people, all speaking the same *l*,
11: 7 us then go down and there confuse their *l*,
2Chr 32:18 they shouted in the Judean *l* to the people
Est 1:22 script and to each people in its own *l*,
3:12 own script and to each people in its own *l*.
8: 9 script and to each people in its own *l*,
8: 9 and to the Jews in their own script and *l*.
2Mc 7: 8 Answering in the *l* of his forefathers,
7:21 *l* of their forefathers with these words:
7:27 to her son and said in their native *l*:
12:37 raising a battle cry in his ancestral *l*,
Sir 23:15 A man who has the habit of abusive *l* will
Is 19:18 land of Egypt speaking the *l* of Canaan
28:11 with stammering lips and in a strange *l*
33:19 speech, stammering in a *l* not understood.
66:18 I come to gather nations of every *l*;
66:24 every *l*; they shall come and see my glory.
Jer 5:15 nation, a people whose *l* you know not,
Ez 3: 5 speech and barbarous *l* am I sending you,
3: 6 *l* whose words you cannot understand.
Dn 1: 4 the *l* and literature of the Chaldeans;
3: 4 "Nations and peoples of every *l*,
3: 7 peoples of every *l* all fell down
3:96 every *l* that whoever blasphemes the God
3:98 to the nations and peoples of every *l*,
5:19 peoples of every *l* dreaded and feared him.
6:26 to the nations and peoples of every *l*,
7:14 nations and peoples of every *l* serve him.
Mt 5:22 any man who uses abusive *l* toward his
Jn 16:25 spoken these things to you in veiled *l*.
16:29 exclaimed, "without talking in veiled *l*!
Acts 1:19 'Akeldama' in their own *l*.
2: 6 one heard these men speaking his own *l*.
Col 3: 8 the malice, the insults, the foul *l*.
1Jn 4: 5 that is why theirs is the *l* of the world
Rv 11: 9 from every people and race, *l* and nation,
13: 7 over every race and people, *l* and nation.
14: 6 to every nation and race, *l* and people.

LANGUAGES (6)

Gn 10:20 of Ham, according to their clans and *l*,
10:31 clans and *l* by their lands and nations.
Neh 13:24 to the *l* of the various other peoples.
Mk 16:17 demons, they will speak entirely new *l*,
1Cor 14:10 *l* in the world and all are marked by sound;
Rv 10:11 for many peoples and nations, *l* and kings."

LANGUISH (6)

Jdt 7:14 wives and children will *l* with hunger,
Jb 31:16 widow to *l* While I ate my portion alone,
Is 16: 8 The terraced slopes of Heshbon *l*,
24: 4 both heaven and earth *l*.
Jer 31:12 watered gardens, never again shall they *l*.
Am 1: 2 The pastures of the shepherds will *l*,

LANGUISHED (2)

1Mc 1:26 Virgins and young men *l*,
Ps(s) 68:10 you restored the land when it *l*;

LANGUISHES (7)

1Sm 2: 5 seven sons, while the mother of many *l*.
Is 24: 4 mourns and fades, the world *l* and fades;
24: 7 The wine mourns, the vine *l*,
33: 9 The country *l* in mourning,
Jer 31:25 every soul that *l* I will replenish.
Hos 4: 3 mourns, and everything that dwells in it *l*:
Jl 1:10 is ravaged, the must has failed, the oil *l*.

LANGUISHING (2)

Gn 47:13 of Egypt and Canaan were *l* from hunger,
Ps(s) 6: 3 Have pity on me, O LORD, for I am *l*;

LANTERNS (1)

Jn 18: 3 and the Pharisees, and came there with *l*,

LAODICEA (5)

Col 4:13 for you and for those at *L* and Hierapolis.
4:15 Give our best wishes to the brothers at *L*
4:16 read the letter that is coming from *L*.
Rv 1:11 Thyatira, Sardis, Philadelphia, and *L*."
3:14 the presiding spirit of the church in *L*,

LAODICEANS (2)

Col 2: 1 I am struggling for you and for the *L*
4:16 is read in the assembly of the *L* as well,

LAP (8)

Jgs 16:19 She had him sleep on her *l*,
Ru 4:16 Naomi took the child, placed him on her *l*,
1Kgs 17:19 Taking him from her *l*, he carried him
2Kgs 4:20 with her until noon, when he died in her *l*.
Ps(s) 131: 2 Like a weaned child on its mother's *l*,
Prv 16:33 When the lot is cast into the *l*,
Is 66:12 carried in her arms, and fondled in her *l*;
Jer 32:18 into the *l* of their sons who follow them.

LAPIS (1)

Gn 2:12 bdellium and *l* lazuli are also there.

LAPPED (3)

Jgs 7: 6 Those who *l* up the water raised to their
7: 7 three hundred who *l* up the water
1Kgs 18:38 dust, and it *l* up the water in the trench.

LAPPIDOTH (1)

Jgs 4: 4 time the prophetess Deborah, wife of *L*,

LAPS (2)

Jgs 7: 5 set to one side everyone who *l* up the water
Is 65: 7 full measure their recompense into their *l*.

LAPSE (2)

Gn 41: 1 After a *l* of two years, Pharaoh had a
Mk 2: 1 He came back to Capernaum after a *l* of

LARGE (159)

Gn 29: 2 A *l* stone covered the mouth of the well.
30:43 and he came to own, not only *l* flocks,
43:34 was five times as *l* as anyone else's.
50: 9 it was a very *l* retinue.
Ex 16:17 Some gathered a *l* and some a small amount.
16:18 gathered a *l* amount did not have too much,
24: 6 half of the blood and put it in *l* bowls;
34:24 before you to give you a *l* territory.
Nm 20:20 them with a *l* and heavily armed force.
26:54 *l* group you shall assign a large heritage,
26:56 the lot falls shall each group, *l* or small,
32: 1 Gadites had a very *l* number of livestock.
33:54 assigning a *l* heritage to a large group
Dt 1:28 cities are *l* and fortified to the sky;
3:19 of which I know you have a *l* number,
6:10 with fine, *l* cities that you did not build,
9: 1 having *l* cities fortified to the sky,
25:13 in your bag, one *l* and the other small;
25:14 in your house, one *l* and the other small.
27: 2 some *l* stones and coat them with plaster.
Jos 10: 2 Gibeon was *l* enough for a royal city,
10:18 "Roll *l* stones to the mouth of the cave
10:27 the mouth of the cave *l* stones were placed,
13: 1 a very *l* part of the land still remains to
14:12 Anakim are there, with *l* fortified cities,
19: 9 portion of the latter was too *l* for them,
22: 8 iron, and with a very *l* supply of clothing,
22:10 at the Kordan a conspicuously *l* altar.
23: 9 LORD has driven out *l* and strong nations,
24:26 Then he took a *l* stone and set it up there
1Sm 6:14 At a *l* stone in the field,
6:18 The *l* stone on which the ark of the LORD
14:33 Roll a *l* stone here for me."
2Sm 8: 8 David removed a very *l* quantity of bronze.
13:34 looked about and saw a *l* group coming
18: 9 passed under the branches of a *l* terebinth,
18:17 *l* mound of stones was erected over him.
21:20 which there was a man of *l* stature
23:21 he, too, who slew an Egyptian of *l* stature.
1Kgs 4:13 sixty *l* walled cities with gates barred
5:31 *l* blocks were quarried to give the temple
7:10 (The foundation was made of fine, *l* blocks,
8:65 who had assembled in *l* numbers from Labo
10: 2 camels bearing spices, a *l* amount of gold,
10:10 gold talents, a very *l* quantity of spices,
10:11 also brought from there a *l* quantity of
10:18 The king also had a *l* ivory throne made,
18:32 the altar *l* enough for two seahs of grain.
20:25 as *l* as the army that has deserted you,
20:28 I will deliver up to you all this *l* army,
2Kgs 4:38 he said to his servant, "Put the *l* pot on,
7: 6 chariots and horses, the din of a *l* army,
12:11 was a *l* amount of silver in the chest,
16:15 "Upon the *l* altar,"
23:11 the eunuch, which was in the *l* building.
25: 9 every *l* building was destroyed by fire.
1Chr 18: 8 of Hadadezer, *l* quantities of bronze,
22: 3 He also laid up *l* stores of iron to make
26:13 gate, the small and the *l* families alike.
26:18 as for the *l* building on the west,
26:18 at the highway and two at the *l* building.
2Chr 2: 4 And the house I intend to build must be *l*,
7: 8 who had assembled in very *l* numbers from
9: 9 talents and a very *l* quantity of spices,
9:15 made two hundred *l* shields of beaten gold,
9:17 King Solomon also made a *l* ivory throne
24:11 until they had collected a *l* sum of money.
24:24 a very *l* force into their power,
26:15 walls to shoot arrows and cast *l* stones.
28: 5 away captive a *l* number of his people,
32: 4 a *l* crowd was gathered which stopped all
36:18 of the house of God, the *l* and the small,
Ezr 10: 1 a very *l* assembly of Israelites gathered
Neh 13: 5 set aside for the latter's use a *l* chamber
Tb 6: 3 a *l* fish suddenly leaped out of the water
Jdt 2:17 He took along a very *l* number of camels,
5: 3 How *l* is their army?
Est 5:11 of his riches, the *l* number of his sons,
8:15 with a *l* crown of gold and a cloak of
1Mc 1:17 chariots and elephants, and with a *l* fleet,
3:10 together with a *l* army from Samaria,
3:15 And again a *l* company of renegades
3:31 provinces, and so raise a *l* sum of money.
3:41 fetters and a *l* sum of silver and gold,
5: 6 *l* body of people with Timothy
5:26 all of these are *l*,
5:38 have rallied to him, making a very *l* force;
5:46 a *l* and strongly fortified city along the
7:27 Nicanor came to Jerusalem with a *l* force
9:37 a *l* escort they are bringing the bride,
9:43 to the banks of the Jordan with a *l* force.
9:60 Bacchides was setting out with a *l* force,
10: 2 he mustered a very *l* army and marched out
10:48 a *l* army and encamped opposite Demetrius.
10:69 Having gathered a *l* army,
10:77 had such a *l* number of horsemen to rely on.
11:48 set on fire and plundered on a *l* scale.
12:42 *l* army he was afraid to offer him violence.
13: 1 Trypho was gathering a *l* army to invade
13:11 son of Absalom, to Joppa with a *l* force;
13:12 with a *l* army to invade the land of Judah,
14:32 spending *l* sums of his own money to equip
15: 3 I have recruited a *l* number of mercenary
2Mc 1:31 of the liquid to be poured upon *l* stones.
1:35 the *l* revenues he received there.
4:39 a *l* number of gold vessels had been stolen,
5:26 men, he cut down a *l* number of people.
8: 6 and put to flight a *l* number of the enemy.
8:16 nor to fear the *l* number of the Gentiles
10:24 collected a *l* number of cavalry from Asia;

LARGE (cont.)
12:27 were *l* supplies of machines and missiles.
13: 1 Eupator was invading Judea with a *l* force,
14:30 he gathered together a *l* number of his men,
Ps(s) 31: 9 enemy but enabling me to move about at *l*.
Prv 14: 4 but the *l* crops come through the strength
16: 8 virtue, than a *l* income with injustice.
Is 5: 9 houses shall be in ruins, *l* ones and fine,
8: 1 Take a *l* cylinder-seal,
Jer 41: 9 killed was the *l* one made by King Asa
43: 9 Take with you *l* stones and sink them in
52:13 every *l* building he destroyed with fire.
Dn 2:31 a statue, very *l* and exceedingly bright,
4: 8 It was *l* and strong,
4:17 The *l*, strong tree that you saw,
4:19 you are that tree, O king, *l* and strong!
11:13 with this *l* army and great resources.
11:25 for battle with a very *l* and strong army,
Jon 2: 1 But the LORD sent a *l* fish,
3: 3 Now Nineveh was an enormously *l* city;
Mt 8:30 away a *l* herd of swine was feeding.
15:30 *L* crowds of people came to him bringing
20:29 leaving Jericho a *l* crowd followed him,
28:12 soldiers a *l* bribe with the instructions:
Mk 2:15 The number of those who followed him was *l*.
5:11 It happened that a *l* herd of swine was
5:21 a *l* crowd gathered around him and he
5:24 went off together and a *l* crowd followed,
6: 2 in a way that kept his *l* audience amazed.
8: 1 about that time another *l* crowd assembled,
9:14 they saw a *l* crowd standing around,
Lk 5:29 in which he was joined by a *l* crowd of tax
6:17 a *l* crowd of people was with them from all
7:11 disciples and a *l* crowd accompanied him.
8: 4 A *l* crowd was gathering,
8:32 It happened that a *l* herd of swine was
9:37 from the mountain and a *l* crowd met them.
13:19 It grew and became a *l* shrub and the birds
14:16 was giving a *l* dinner and he invited many.
Jn 7: 4 as well display yourself to the world at *l*."
Acts 2: 6 the sound, and assembled in a *l* crowd.
11:24 Thereby *l* numbers were added to the Lord.
Gal 6:11 I write to you in my own *l* handwriting!
2Tm 2:20 In every *l* household there are vessels not
Jas 3: 4 however *l* they are,
Rv 8: 3 *l* amounts of incense to deposit on the altar
17:15 enthroned are *l* numbers of peoples
20:11 a *l* white throne and the One who sat on it.

LARGER (8)
Nm 35: 8 a *l* group and fewer from a smaller one,
Jos 10: 2 a royal city, *l* even than the city of Ai,
Jgs 9:29 to Abimelech, 'Get a *l* army and come out!' "
Dn 8: 3 horns, the one *l* and newer than the other.
Mt 25:21 I will put you in charge of *l* affairs.
25:23 I will put you in charge of *l* affairs.
Lk 7:43 I presume, to whom he remitted the *l* sum."
12:18 pull down my grain bins and build *l* ones.

LARGEST (3)
Dt 7: 7 It was not because you are the *l* of all
Mt 13:32 yet when full-grown it is the *l* of plants.
Mk 4:32 sown, springs up to become the *l* of shrubs,

LASEA (1)
Acts 27: 8 called Fair Havens, near the town of *L*.

LASH (2)
Sir 23: 2 Who will apply the *l* to my thoughts,
Acts 22:24 orders that he be examined under the *l*

LASHA (1)
Gn 10:19 Gomorrah, Admah and Zeboiim, near *L*.

LASHARON (1)
Jos 12:18 Bethel, Tappuah, Hepher, Aphek, *L*,

LASHED (2)
Wis 5:11 the fluid air, *l* by the beat of pinions,
Mt 7:27 the winds blew and *l* against his house.

LASHES (5)
Prv 17:10 intelligence than a hundred *l* for a fool.
20:30 Evil is cleansed away by bloody *l*,
Sir 22: 6 *l* and discipline are at all times wisdom.
Acts 16:23 many *l* they were thrown into prison,
2Cor 11:24 of the Jews I received forty *l* less one;

LAST (149)
Gn 2:23 "This one, at *l*, is bone of my bones
18:32 Lord grow angry if I speak up this *l* time.
19: 4 all the people to the *l* man
19:34 *L* night it was I who lay with my father.
25: 8 Then he breathed his *l*,
25:17 After he had breathed his *l* and died,
29:34 at *l* my husband will become attached to me,
31:29 *l* night the God of your father said to me,
31:42 of my toil, and *l* night he gave judgment."
33: 2 her children next, and Rachel and Joseph *l*.
35:18 With her *l* breath
35:28 then he breathed his *l*.
41:49 so vast that at *l* he stopped measuring it,
46:30 Israel said to Joseph, "At *l* I can die,
49:33 drew his feet into the bed, breathed his *l*,
Lv 8:33 for your ordination is to *l* for seven days.
25:15 *l* jubilee shall you purchase the land
26: 5 your threshing will *l* till vintage time,
Nm 2:31 be the *l* of the divisions on the march."
14:33 till the *l* of you lies dead in the desert.
14:35 in the desert they shall die to the *l* man."
17:28 Are we to perish to the *l* man?"
18:19 covenant to *l* forever before the LORD,
Dt 3:11 the *l* remaining survivor of the Rephaim.
Jos 8: 5 a sortie against us as they did the *l* time,
8: 6 are fleeing from them as we did the *l* time.
8:16 till the *l* of the soldiers in the city
8:24 sword there in the open, down to the *l* man.
10:20 the *l* blows in this very great slaughter,
11:14 until they had exterminated the *l* of them,
19:49 When the *l* of them had received the
21:34 The Merarite clans, the *l* of the Levites,
21:40 to the Merarite clans, the *l* of theLevites,
Jgs 6:16 you will cut down Midian to the *l* man."
16:28 this *l* time that for my two eyes I may
1Sm 15:16 tell you what the LORD said to me *l* night."
2Sm 15:23 aloud as the *l* of the soldiers went by,
19:12 you be *l* to restore the king to his palace?
19:13 Why should you be *l* to restore the king?'
23: 1 These are the *l* words of David:
2Kgs 11: 6 and the *l* third shall be at the gate
25:11 the *l* of the people remaining in the city,
25:11 king of Babylon, and the *l* of the artisans.
1Chr 8: 7 The *l*, who led them into exile,
29:29 Now the deeds of King David, first and *l*,
2Chr 9: 8 Israel as to will to make it *l* forever,
9:29 rest of the acts of Solomon, first and *l*,
12:15 The acts of Rehoboam, first and *l*,
16:11 Now the acts of Asa, first and *l*,
20:34 of the acts of Jehoshaphat, first and *l*,
25:26 rest of the acts of Amaziah, first and *l*,
26:22 rest of the acts of Uzziah, first and *l*,
28:26 his deeds and his activities, first and *l*,
35:26 of the LORD, and his acts, first and *l*,
Neh 8:18 day after day, from the first day to the *l*.
Est 3:13 they may at *l* leave our affairs stable and
2Mc 7:41 The mother was *l* to die after her sons.
9:11 At *l*, broken in spirit,
14:46 steep rock, as he lost the *l* of his blood,
Jb 8:15 rely upon his family, but it shall not *l*;
14:18 at *l* and its rock is moved from its place,
19:25 he will at *l* stand forth upon the dust;
27:19 He lies down a rich man, one *l* time;
Eccl 12:13 The *l* word, when all is heard:
Wis 3:17 and dishonored will their old age be at *l*;
18:20 Yet not for long did the anger *l*.
Sir 7:36 In whatever you do, remember your *l* days,
24:26 nor will the *l* succeed in fathoming her.
28: 6 Remember your *l* days,
33:16 Now I am the *l* to keep vigil,
43:28 let the *l* word be,
Is 38:12 like a weaver who severs the *l* thread.
41: 4 the first, and with the *l* I will also be.
44: 6 I am the first and I am the *l*;
48:12 is I who am the first, and also the *l* am I.
Jer 47: 4 from Tyre and Sidon the *l* of their allies.
50:12 See, the *l* of the nations,
Lam 2:12 And breathe their *l* in their mothers' arms.
2:16 This at *l* is the day we hoped for;
3:31 the Lord's rejection does not *l* forever;
Ez 5: 3 [But of the *l* take a small number and tie
38: 8 the *l* years you will come] against a nation
38:16 *l* days I will bring you against my land,
Dn 8:13 vision *l* concerning the daily sacrifice,
Hos 3: 5 the LORD and to his bounty, in the *l* days.
Am 1: 8 and the *l* of the Philistines shall perish,
4: 2 with hooks, the *l* of you with fishhooks;
Hb 2: 6 how long can it *l*!
Zep 1: 4 from this place the *l* vestige of Baal,
Mt 5:26 released until you have paid the *l* penny.
12:25 split into factions cannot *l* for long.
12:26 How, then, can his dominion *l*?
12:45 Thus the *l* state of that man becomes worse
19:30 first shall come *l*, and the last shall come
20: 8 with the *l* group and end with the first.'
20:12 'This *l* group did only an hour's work,
20:14 man who was hired *l* the same pay as you.
20:16 *l* shall be first and the first shall be last."
22:27 *L* of all the woman died too.
Mk 3:24 by civil strife, that kingdom cannot *l*.
4:17 Being rootless, they *l* only a while.
9:35 the *l* one of all and the servant of all."
10:31 come last, and the *l* shall come first."
12: 6 He sent him to them as a *l* resort,
12:22 *L* of all, the woman also died.
15:37 Jesus, uttering a loud cry, breathed his *l*.
Lk 1:65 began to be recounted to the *l* detail.
11:18 against himself, how can his kingdom *l*—
11:26 *l* state of the man is worse than the first."
12:59 from there until you have paid the *l* penny."
13:30 Some who are *l* will be first and some who
13:30 be first and some who are first will be *l*."
15:17 Coming to his senses at *l*, he said:
Jn 6:39 that I should raise it up on the *l* day.
6:40 Him I will raise up on the *l* day."
6:44 I will raise him up on the *l* day.
6:54 and I will raise him up on the *l* day.
7:37 On the *l* and greatest day of the festival,
11:24 "in the resurrection on the *l* day."
12:48 that which will condemn him on the *l* day.
16:29 "At *l* you are speaking plainly,"
Acts 2:17 'It shall come to pass in the *l* days,
27:23 *L* night a messenger of the God whose man I
Rom 1:10 I may at *l* find my way clear to visit you.
1Cor 13:13 There are in the end three things that *l*:
15: 8 *L* of all he was seen by me,
15:26 and the *l* enemy to be destroyed is death.
15:45 the *l* Adam has become a life-giving spirit.
15:52 of an eye, at the sound of the *l* trumpet.
2Cor 5: 1 not made by hands but to *l* forever.
8:10 help you who began this good work *l* year,
9: 2 that Achaia has been ready since *l* year.
1Thes 2:16 but the wrath has descended upon them at *l*.
2Tm 3: 1 there will be terrible times in the *l* days.
Jas 5: 3 up for yourselves against the *l* days.
1Pt 1: 5 stands ready to be revealed in the *l* days.
1:20 and revealed for your sake in these *l* days.
2Pt 2:20 *l* condition is worse than their first.
3: 3 in the *l* days, mocking, sneering men
Jude 1:18 "In the *l* days there will be impostors
Rv 1:17 the First and the *L* and the One who lives.
2: 8 " 'The First and the *L* who once died but
13: 5 it received was to *l* only forty-two months.
17:10 one lives now, and the *l* has not yet come;
21: 9 the seven *l* plagues came and said to me,
22:13 Alpha and the Omega, the First and the *L*,

LAST-MENTIONED (1)
Neh 12: 8 Mattaniah; the *l*, together with his

LASTED (3)
Jgs 14:17 him during the seven days the feast *l*.
Ezr 4:24 This inaction *l* until the second year of
Mk 15:33 whole countryside and *l* until midafternoon.

LASTHENES (2)
1Mc 11:31 we wrote to *L* our kinsman concerning you.
11:32 Demetrius sends greetings to his father *L*.

LASTING (29)
Dt 28:59 constant blows, malignant and *l* maladies.
1Sm 2:35 I will establish a *l* house for him which
13:13 establish your kingship in Israel as *l*;
25:28 establish a *l* dynasty for my lord,
1Kgs 11:38 for you, as I did for David, a *l* dynasty;
2Kgs 17:23 soil to Assyria, an exile *l* to the present.
Est C:16 among all their ancestors, as a *l* heritage,
1Mc 4:45 lest it be a *l* shame to them that the
Eccl 12: 5 effect, Because man goes to his *l* home,
Sir 2: 9 hope for good things, for *l* joy and mercy.
3:14 it will take *l* root.
11:33 breeds only evil, lest you incur a *l* stain.
31:23 and this testimony to his goodness is *l*;
31:24 and this testimony to his stinginess is *l*.
41: 9 When you stumble, there is *l* joy;
43: 6 times, governing the seasons, their *l* sign,
44:18 A *l* agreement was made with him,
45:15 a *l* covenant with him and with his family,
47:13 name of God, and established a *l* sanctuary.
49: 1 incense, made *l* by a skilled performer.
Is 33: 6 That which makes her seasons *l*,
61: 8 a *l* covenant I will make with them.
Jer 14:13 I will give you *l* peace in this place."
18:16 into a desert, an object of *l* ridicule:
20:11 they will be put to utter shame, to *l*,
33: 6 and reveal to them an abundance of *l* peace.
Lk 16: 9 they fail you, a *l* reception will be yours.
16:11 elusive wealth, who will trust you with *l*?
Heb 13:14 For here we have no *l* city;

LASTLY (2)
Gn 33: 7 *L*, Rachel and her children came forward
Rv 20:12 *L*, among the scrolls,

LASTS (7)
Gn 8:22 As long as the earth *l* cold and heat,
Tb 13: 1 because his kingdom *l* for all ages.
Ps(s) 30: 6 For his anger *l* but a moment;
37:18 their inheritance *l* forever.
Prv 27:24 For wealth *l* not forever,
Mt 13:21 he has no roots, so he *l* only for a time.
2Cor 4:18 what is unseen *l* forever.

LATE (20)
Dt 11:14 your land, the early rain and the *l* rain,
Ru 4: 5 Ruth the Moabite, the widow of the *l* heir,
4:10 a family for her *l* husband on his estate,
2Kgs 12: 7 as *l* as the twenty-third year of the reign
Tb 2:12 *L* in winter she finished the cloth and
Jdt 13: 1 When it grew *l*,
2Mc 8:26 obliged to return by reason of the *l* hour,
Jer 5:24 our God, Who gives us rain early and *l*,
Jl 2:23 you, the early and the *l* rain as before.

Am 7: 1 He was forming a locust swarm when the *l*
7: 1 up (the *l* growth after the king's mowing).
Mi 2: 8 of *l* my people has risen up as an enemy:
Hb 2: 3 it, it will surely come, it will not be *l.*
Mt 14:15 is a deserted place and it is already *l.*
20: 6 going out in *l* afternoon he found still
20: 9 When those hired *l* in the afternoon came
Mk 6:35 It was now getting *l* and his disciples
6:35 is a deserted place and it is already *l.*
11:11 since it was already *l* in the afternoon,
Acts 16:33 At that *l* hour of the night he took them

LATELY (3)

1Sm 3: 2 had *l* grown so weak that he could not see.
Jdt 4: 3 Now, they had *l* returned from exile,
Bar 4:24 Zion's neighbors *l* saw you taken captive,

LATENESS (1)

Acts 27: 9 *l* of the year sailing had become hazardous.

LATER (111)

Gn 6: 4 Nephilim appeared on earth (as well as *l*),
11: 6 nothing will *l* stop them from doing
32:21 him with gifts that precede me, then *l,*
38:24 About three months *l,*
41:11 *L,* we both had dreams on the same night,
44:25 *L,* our father told us to come back and buy
Ex 9:32 the spelt were not ruined, for they grow *l.*
13:14 If your son should ask you *l* on,
34:32 *L* on, all the Israelites came up to him,
Lv 4:14 should it *l* on become known that the sin
4:23 if *l* on he learns of the sin he committed,
4:28 he *l* on learn of the sin he committed,
13:18 who had a boil on his skin which *l* healed,
25:26 but *l* on acquires sufficient means to buy
Nm 21: 3 *L,* when the LORD heeded Israel's prayer
Dt 6:20 *L* on, when your son asks you
21:14 if *l* on you lose your liking for her,
24: 1 is *l* displeased with her because he finds
Jos 3: 2 Three days *l* the officers went through the
8:30 *L* Joshua built an altar to the LORD,
23: 1 Many years *l,*
Jgs 1:16 *l* left and settled among the Amalekites.
2:10 and a *l* generation arose that did not know
11: 4 Some time *l,* the Ammonites warred
14: 8 *L,* when he returned to marry the woman who
19: 5 you can go *l* on."
1Sm 11: 1 About a month *l,* Nahash the Ammonite
25:38 ten days *l* the LORD struck him and he died.
2Sm 3:28 *L* David heard of it and said:
10: 1 Some time *l* the king of the Ammonites died,
13: 1 time *l* the following incident occurred.
1Kgs 2:39 But three years *l,*
3:16 *L,* two harlots came to the king and stood
3:20 *L* that night she got up and took my son
17:17 Some time *l* the son of the mistress of the
2Kgs 4:11 Sometime *l* Elisha arrived and stayed in
4:14 *L* Elisha asked,
1Chr 18: 8 which Solomon *l* used to make the bronze
Tb 1:21 But less than forty days *l* the king was
7:15 *L* Raguel called his wife Edna and said,
Jdt 5:10 *L,* when famine had gripped the whole land
1Mc 1:29 Two years *l,* the king sent the Mysian
11:18 But three days *l* King Ptolemy himself died,
2Mc 1:20 Many years *l,*
4:11 Eupolemus who would *l* go on an embassy
4:23 Three years *l* Jason sent Menelaus,
6:15 may not have to punish us more severely *l,*
9:29 Antiochus' son, he *l* withdrew into Egypt,
12: 7 intending to come back *l* and wipe out the
14: 1 Three years *l,* Judas and his men
Prv 25: 8 *l* on when your neighbor puts you to shame?
Eccl 4:16 yet the *l* generations will not applaud him.
Wis 19:11 *l* they saw also a new kind of bird when,
Sir 13: 7 When *l* he sees you he will pass you by,
17:18 *L* he will rise up and repay them,
27:23 But *l* he changes his tone and twists your
31:22 *l* you will find my advice good.
Jer 46:26 But *l* on Egypt shall be inhabited again,
Bar 3:20 *L* generations have seen the light,
6:50 they will *l* be known for frauds.
Dn 4:26 Twelve months *l,* as he was walking
8:19 is to happen *l* in the period of wrath;
11: 6 But *l* a descendant of her line shall
Mt 3:13 *L* Jesus, coming from Galilee,
9:14 *L* on, John's disciples came to him
14:12 *L* his disciples presented themselves to
17: 1 Six days *l* Jesus took Peter,
25:11 *L* the other bridesmaids came back.
26:52 the sword are sooner or *l* destroyed by it.
26:73 A little while *l* some bystanders came over
Mk 4:22 are hidden only to be revealed at a *l* time;
6:29 *L,* when his disciples heard about this,
8:31 be put to death, and rise three days *l.*
9: 2 Six days *l,* Jesus took Peter, James,
10:34 But three days *l* he will rise."
14:70 *l* the bystanders said to Peter once more,
16:12 *L* on, as two of them were walking along
16:20 *L* on it was through them that Jesus
Lk 15:13 Some days *l* this younger son collected all
22:55 *L* they lighted a fire in the middle of the
22:58 while *l* someone else saw him and said,
Jn 3:22 *L* on, Jesus and his disciples
5: 1 *L,* on the occasion of a Jewish feast,
5:14 *L* on, Jesus found him in the temple
6: 1 *L* on, Jesus crossed the Sea of Galilee
13: 7 what I am doing, but *l* you will understand!"
13:36 *l* on you shall come after me."
20:26 A week *l,* the disciples were once more
21: 1 *L,* at the Sea of Tiberias,
Acts 5: 5 Great fear came upon all who *l* heard of it.
5: 7 Three hours *l* Ananias' wife came in,
7:30 "Forty years *l* an angel appeared to him
13:20 *L* on he set up judges to rule them until
18: 7 *L,* Paul withdrew and went to the house of
20: 6 Five days *l* we joined them in Troas,
23:30 When I *l* came to be informed of a plot
24: 1 Five days *l,* the high priest Ananias came
24:24 few days *l* Felix came with his Jewish wife,
25:13 A few days *l* King Agrippa and Bernice
26: 4 from the beginning and *l* at Jerusalem,
28:11 Three months *l* we set sail in a ship which
28:13 A day *l* a south wind began to blow which
28:17 Three days *l* Paul invited the prominent
Gal 1:17 *l* I returned to Damascus.
3:17 into being four hundred and thirty years *l,*
1Tm 1:16 to those who would *l* have faith in him
4: 1 The Spirit distinctly says that in *l* times
5:24 while other men's sins will appear only *l.*
Heb 12:11 but *l* it brings forth the fruit of peace
1Jn 3: 2 we shall *l* be has not yet come to light.
Jude 1: 5 *l* destroyed those who refused to believe.

LATEST (1)

Ez 33:30 hear the *l* word that comes from the LORD."

LATIN (1)

Jn 19:20 This inscription, in Hebrew, *L,* and Greek,

LATRINE (4)

Dt 23:13 have a place set aside to be used as a *l.*
2Kgs 10:27 down the building, and turned it into a *l,*
Mt 15:17 the stomach and is discharged into the *l,*
Mk 7:19 his stomach only and passes into the *l.*"

LATTER (23)

Gn 10:12 and Calah, the *l* being the principal city.
14: 3 All the *l* kings joined forces in the
Ex 26:35 the *l* on the south side of the Dwelling,
Lv 5:12 the *l* shall take a handful of this flour
5:26 the *l* shall make atonement for him before
13:17 should the *l,* on examining him,
13:20 If the *l,* on examination,
13:34 the *l* shall wash his garments,
15: 8 a clean man, the *l* shall wash his garments,
Nm 5: 8 if the *l* has no next of kin to whom
Dt 25: 2 guilty party, if the *l* deserves stripes,
25:11 hand and seizes the *l* by his private parts,
Jos 19: 9 portion of the *l* was too large for them,
1Chr 18: 3 when the *l* was on his way to set up his
24: 4 groups, and the *l* into eight groups,
1Mc 11: 5 Jonathan, he was told what the *l* had done;
Jb 42:12 *l* days of Job more than his earlier ones.
Wis 11:10 the *l* you tested, admonishing them
14: 2 For the urge for profits devised this *l,*
Ez 46:17 to the *l* only until the year of release,
47:22 *l* shall be to you like native Israelites;
Dn 11: 9 Then the *l* shall invade the land of the
2Cor 2:16 to the *l* an odor dealing death,

LATTERS (4)

Ex 22: 6 and it is stolen from the *l* house,
Nm 3:38 were camped Moses and Aaron and the *l* sons.
Neh 13: 5 had set aside for the *l* use a large
1Mc 4: 4 while the *l* forces were still scattered

LATTICE (5)

Jgs 5:28 wailed the mother of Sisera, from the *l:*
2Kgs 1: 2 Ahaziah had fallen through the *l* of his
Prv 7: 6 of my house, through my *l* I looked out
Sir 42:11 See that there is no *l* in her room,
Ez 41:25 the vestibule outside was a wooden *l.*

LATTICES (1)

Sg 2: 9 through the windows, peering through the *l.*

LAUGH (16)

Gn 18:13 "Why did Sarah *l* and say,
18:15 Sarah dissembled, saying, "I didn't *l.*"
21: 6 then said, "God has given me cause to *l,*
21: 6 and all who hear of it will *l* with me.
Jdt 12:12 do not entice her, she will *l* us to scorn."
Jb 5:22 At destruction and want you shall *l;*
Ps(s) 52: 8 then they shall *l* at him:
59: 9 You, O LORD, *l* at them;
Prv 1:26 I, in my turn, will *l* at your doom;
29: 9 he may rage or *l* but can have no peace.
Eccl 3: 4 A time to weep, and a time to *l;*
Sir 7:11 *L* not at an embittered man;
20:16 How many times they *l* him to scorn!
Dn 14: 7 Daniel began to *l.*
Lk 6:21 you shall *l.*
6:25 Woe to you who *l* now;

LAUGHED (6)

Gn 17:17 himself and *l* as he said to himself,
18:12 So Sarah *l* to herself and said,
1Mc 10:70 I am *l* at and put to shame on your account.
Lam 1: 7 her foes gloated over her, *l* at her ruin.
Dn 14:19 Daniel *l* and kept the king from entering.
Lk 8:53 They *l* at him, being certain she was dead.

LAUGHINGSTOCK (13)

Gn 38:23 "otherwise we shall become a *l.*
Jdt 5:21 become the *l* of the whole world."
Jb 12: 4 him, the just, the perfect man," is a *l;*
Ps(s) 31:12 an object of reproach, a *l* to my neighbors,
44:15 among the nations, a *l* among the peoples.
Wis 5: 3 we held as a *l* and as a type for mockery,
Sir 13:12 Mercilessly he will make of you a *l*
Jer 48:26 retches and vomits, and he too becomes a *l.*
48:27 Is Israel a *l* to you?
48:39 a *l* and a horror to all his neighbors!
Lam 3:14 I have become a *l* for all nations,
Ez 22: 4 the nations and a *l* to all foreign lands.
Hb 1:10 He scoffs at kings, and princes are his *l;*

LAUGHS (10)

2Kgs 19:21 " 'She despises you, *l* you to scorn,
Jb 9:23 he *l* at the despair of the innocent.
39:22 He *l* at fear and cannot be deterred;
41:21 he *l* at the crash of the spear.
Ps(s) 2: 4 He who is throned in heaven *l;*
37:13 But the LORD *l* at him,
Prv 31:25 and dignity, and she *l* at the days to come.
Wis 4:18 but the Lord *l* them to scorn.
Is 37:22 She despises you, *l* you to scorn,
Hb 1:10 He *l* at any fortress,

LAUGHTER (12)

Jb 8:21 Once more will he fill your mouth with *l,*
Ps(s) 126: 2 Then our mouth was filled with *l,*
Prv 14:13 Even in *l* the heart may be sad,
Eccl 2: 2 Of *l* I said; "Mad!"
7: 3 Sorrow is better than *l,*
7: 6 of thorns under a pot, so is the fool's *l.*
Sir 19:26 A man's attire, his hearty *l* and his gait,
21:20 A fool raises his voice in *l,*
27:13 is offensive, their *l* is wanton guilt.
Jer 20: 7 All the day I am an object of *l;*
30:19 songs of praise, the *l* of happy men.
Jas 4: 9 let your *l* be turned into mourning and

LAUNCH (2)

Jos 9: 2 *l* a common attack against Joshua
1Mc 15:39 could *l* attacks against the Jewish people.

LAUNCHED (4)

2Mc 4:40 Lysimachus *l* an unjustified attack against
11: 5 Jerusalem, *l* a strong attack against it.
Acts 8:35 Philip *l* out with this Scripture passage
1Cor 4: 8 *l* upon your reign with no help from us.

LAUNCHES (1)

Is 54:17 false that *l* an accusation against you.

LAVA (1)

Jer 17: 6 change of season, But stands in a *l* waste,

LAVER (10)

Ex 30:18 shall make a bronze *l* with a bronze base.
30:28 its appurtenances, and the *l* with its base.
31: 9 all its appurtenances, the *l* with its base,
35:16 the *l,* with its base; the hangings
38: 8 The bronze *l,* with its bronze base,
39:39 all its appurtenances, the *l* with its base,
40: 7 *l* between the meeting tent and the altar,
40:11 Likewise, anoint the *l* with its base,
40:30 the *l* between the meeting tent and altar,
Lv 8:11 with all its appurtenances, and the *l,*

LAVERS (1)

2Kgs 16:17 from the bases and removed the *l* from them;

LAVISH (3)

Tb 4:17 Be *l* with your bread and wine at the
Prv 11:24 One man is *l* yet grows still richer;
Jer 31:14 I will *l* choice portions upon the priests,

LAVISHED (4)

2Kgs 4:13 to her, 'You have *l* all this care on us;
Sir 1: 8 he has *l* her upon his friends.
Ez 16:15 and you *l* your harlotry on every passer-by,
Ti 3: 6 he *l* on us through Jesus Christ our Savior,

LAVISHES (1)

Gal 3: 5 God *l* the Spirit on you and works wonders

LAVISHLY (1)

Ps(s) 112: 9 *L* he gives to the poor;

LAW (492)

Gn 47:26 Joseph made it a *l* for the land in Egypt,
Ex 12:49 The *l* shall be the same forthe resident
13: 9 *l* of the LORD will ever be on your lips,
21:31 This *l* applies if it is a boy or a girl
29: 9 the priesthood be theirs by perpetual *l*,
Lv 11:46 "This is the *l* for animals and birds and
12: 7 Such is the *l* for the woman who gives
13:59 This is the *l* for leprous infection on a
14: 2 "This is the *l* for the victim of leprosy
14:32 This is the *l* for one afflicted with
14:54 "This is the *l* for every kind of human
14:57 This is the *l* for leprosy.
15:32 "This is the *l* for the man who is
15:33 the *l* for male and female;
Nm 5:29 "This, then, is the *l* for jealousy:
5:30 priest shall apply this *l* in full to her.
6:21 "This, then, is the *l* for the nazirite;
6:21 Thus shall he carry out the *l* of his
9:14 You shall have the same *l* for the resident
15:16 with the same *l* and the same application
15:29 but one *l* for him who sins inadvertently,
19: 2 which the *l* of the LORD prescribes.
19:14 "This is the *l*:
31:21 "This is what the *l*,
Dt 1: 5 *l* in the land of Moab beyond the Jordan,
4: 8 *l* which I am setting before you today?
4:44 *l* which Moses set before the Israelites.
17:18 he shall have a copy of this *l* made from
17:19 all the words of this *l* and these statutes.
19:16 to accuse him of a defection from the *l*,
27: 3 time you cross, all the words of this *l*,
27: 8 all the words of this *l* very clearly."
27:26 to fulfill any of the provisions of this *l*!'
28:58 of the *l* which is written in this book,
28:61 not mentioned in this book of the *l*,
29:20 covenant inscribed in this book of the *l*.
29:28 that we may carry out all the words of this *l*
30:10 that are written in this book of the *l*,
31: 9 When Moses had written down this *l*,
31:11 this *l* aloud in the presence of all Israel.
31:12 carefully observe all the words of this *l*.
31:24 the words of the *l* in their entirety,
31:26 "Take this scroll of the *l* and put it
32:46 carry out carefully every word of this *l*.
33: 4 A *l* he gave to us;
33:10 decisions to Jacob and your *l* to Israel.
Jos 1: 7 *l* which my servant Moses enjoined on you.
1: 8 Keep this book of the *l* on your lips.
8:31 the LORD, as recorded in the book of the *l*.
8:32 stones a copy of the *l* written by Moses.
8:34 were read aloud all the words of the *l*,
8:34 exactly as written in the book of the *l*.
22: 5 to observe the precept and *l* which Moses,
23: 6 is written in the book of the *l* of Moses,
24:26 he recorded in the book of the *l* of God.
1Sm 10:25 the *l* of royalty and wrote it in a book,
30:25 he made it a *l* and a custom in Israel,
1Kgs 2: 3 as they are written in the *l* of Moses,
2Kgs 10:31 observe wholeheartedly the *l* of the LORD,
14: 6 written in the book of the *l* of Moses,
17:13 in accordance with the entire *l* which I
17:34 and regulations, the *l* and commandments,
17:37 and regulations, the *l* and commandment,
21: 8 the entire *l* which my servant Moses
22: 8 book of the *l* in the temple of the LORD."
22:11 heard the contents of the book of the *l*,
23:24 carry out the stipulations of the *l* written
23:25 in accord with the entire *l* of Moses;
1Chr 16:40 do all that is written in the *l* of the LORD
22:12 Israel, so that you keep the *l* of the LORD,
2Chr 6:16 so as always to live according to my *l*,
12: 1 powerful, he abandoned the *l* of the LORD,
14: 3 and to observe the *l* and its commands.
15: 3 no true God, no priest-teacher and no *l*,
17: 9 them the book containing the *l* of the LORD;
19:10 it concerns bloodguilt or questions of *l*,
23:18 the LORD, as is written in the *l* of Moses,
25: 4 according to what is written in the *l*,
30:16 for them according to the *l* of Moses,
31: 3 as prescribed in the *l* of the LORD.
31: 4 themselves entirely to the *l* of the LORD.
31:21 of God or for the *l* and the commandments,
33: 8 keeping the whole *l* and the statutes and
34:14 of the *l* of the LORD given through Moses.
34:15 the book of the *l* in the house of the LORD."
34:19 When the king heard the words of the *l*,
35:26 to what is written in the *l* of the LORD,
Ezr 3: 2 holocausts prescribed in the *l* of Moses,
7: 6 the *l* of Moses which was given by the LORD,
7:10 study and practice of the *l* of the LORD
7:12 scribe of the *l* of the God of heaven (then,
7:14 *l* of your God which is in your possession,
7:21 scribe of the *l* of the God of heaven,
7:26 the *l* of your God and the law of the king,
7:26 the law of your God and the *l* of the king,
10: 3 Let the *l* be observed!
Neh 8: 1 bring forth the book of the *l* of Moses
8: 2 priest brought the *l* before the assembly,
8: 3 listened attentively to the book of the *l*.
8: 7 and Pelaiah explained the *l* to the people,
8: 8 read plainly from the book of the *l* of God,
8: 9 weeping as they heard the words of the *l*.
8:13 examined the words of the *l* more closely.
8:14 They found it written in the *l* prescribed
8:15 trees, to make booths, as the *l* prescribes."
8:18 the book of the *l* of God day after day,
9: 3 the book of the *l* of the LORD their God,
9:14 statutes, and *l* you prescribed for them,
9:26 they cast your *l* behind their backs,
9:29 in order to bring them back to your *l*.
9:34 and our fathers have not kept your *l*;
10:29 of the lands in favor of the *l* of God,
10:30 the *l* of God which was given through Moses,
10:35 of the LORD, our God, as the *l* prescribes.
10:37 also as is prescribed in the *l*,
13: 3 When they had heard the *l*,
Tb 1: 8 the Mosaic *l* and the commands of Deborah,
7:12 "Take her according to the *l*.
7:13 according to the decree of the Mosaic *l*.
Est 1:13 with the wise men versed in the *l*,
1:15 "What is to be done by *l* with Queen
3:14 copy of the decree to be promulgated as *l*
4:16 I will go to the king, contrary to the *l*.
8:13 promulgated as *l* in each and every province
1Mc 1:11 in Israel men who were breakers of the *l*,
1:49 the *l* and change all their observances.
1:52 of the people, those who abandoned the *l*,
1:56 *l* which they found they tore up and burnt.
1:57 the covenant, and whoever observed the *l*,
2:21 should forsake the *l* and the commandments.
2:26 Thus he showed his zeal for the *l*,
2:27 "Let everyone who is zealous for the *l*
2:42 all of them devout followers of the *l*.
2:48 They saved the *l* from the hands of the
2:50 be zealous for the *l* and give your lives
2:58 Elijah, for his burning zeal for the *l*,
2:64 be courageous and strong in keeping the *l*,
2:67 gather about you all who observe the *l*,
2:68 deserve, and observe the precepts of the *l*."
3:48 They unrolled the scroll of the *l*,
3:56 return to his home, according to the *l*.
4:42 chose blameless priests, devoted to the *l*;
4:47 took uncut stones, according to the *l*,
4:53 according to the *l* on the new altar
9:23 the transgressors of the *l* raised their
9:58 of the *l* held a council and said:
10:14 had abandoned the *l* and the commandments,
10:61 Israelites, transgressors of the *l*,
11:21 Some transgressors of the *l*,
13:48 he settled there men who observed the *l*.
14:14 his people and was zealous for the *l*;
14:29 their sanctuary and *l* might be maintained,
15:21 he may punish them according to their *l*."
2Mc 1: 4 *l* and his commandments and grant you peace.
2: 2 that the prophet, in giving them the *l*,
2: 3 not to let the *l* depart from their hearts.
2:18 sacred rites, as he promised through the *l*.
3:15 begged him in heaven who had given the *l*
4:11 introduced customs contrary to the *l*.
7: 1 them to eat pork in violation of God's *l*.
7:23 disregard yourselves for the sake of his *l*."
7:30 *l* given to our forefathers through Moses.
10:26 and a foe to their foes, as the *l* declares.
12:40 which the *l* forbids the Jews to wear.
13: 7 was Menelaus, the transgressor of the *l*,
13:11 they were about to be deprived of their *l*,
15: 9 with words from the *l* and the prophets,
Ps(s) 1: 2 law of the LORD and meditates on his *l*
17: 4 of your lips I have kept the ways of the *l*.
19: 8 The *l* of the LORD is perfect,
37:31 The *l* of his God is in his heart,
40: 9 my delight, and your *l* is within my heart!"
78: 5 Jacob, and established it as a *l* in Israel,
78:10 according to his *l* they would not walk;
89:31 *l* and walk not according to my ordinances,
94:12 instruct, O LORD, whom by your *l* you teach,
94:20 which creates burdens in the guise of *l*?
99: 7 heard his decrees and the *l* he gave them.
119: 1 blameless, who walk in the *l* of the LORD.
119:18 that I may consider the wonders of your *l*.
119:29 way of falsehood, and favor me with your *l*.
119:34 your *l* and keep it with all my heart.
119:44 And I will keep your *l* continually,
119:51 at me, I turn not away from your *l*.
119:53 because of the wicked who forsake your *l*.
119:55 your name, O LORD, and I will keep your *l*.
119:61 about me your *l* I have not forgotten.
119:70 as for me, your *l* is my delight.
119:72 The *l* of your mouth is to me more precious
119:77 that I may live, for your *l* is my delight.
119:85 this is against your *l*.
119:92 Had not your *l* been my delight,
119:97 How I love your *l*, O LORD!
119:109 life in my hands, yet I forget not your *l*.
119:113 men of divided heart, but I love your *l*.
119:126 they have broken your *l*.
119:136 of tears because your *l* has not been kept.
119:142 justice, and your *l* is permanent.
119:150 persecutors who are far from your *l*.
119:153 rescue me, for I have not forgotten your *l*.
119:163 Falsehood I hate and abhor; your *l* I love.
119:165 Those who love your *l* have great peace,
119:174 O LORD, and your *l* is my delight.
Prv 13:23 but some men perish for lack of a *l* court.
28: 4 who abandon the *l* praise the wicked man,
28: 4 but those who keep the *l* war against him.
28: 7 He who keeps the *l* is a wise son,
28: 9 one turns away his ear from hearing the *l*,
29:18 but happy is he who keeps the *l*.
31: 5 in drinking they forget what the *l* decrees,
Wis 2:12 Reproaches us for transgressions of the *l*
6: 4 not rightly, and did not keep the *l*,
14:16 gained strength and was observed as *l*,
16: 6 to remind them of the precept of your *L*.
18: 4 of the *L* was to be given to the world.
Sir 2:16 those who love him are filled with his *l*.
8:14 Contend not at *l* with a judge,
9:15 conversation be about the *l* of the LORD.
14:17 the age-old *l* is:
15: 1 is practiced in the *l* will come to wisdom.
17: 9 a *l* of life as their inheritance;
19:16 will you fulfill the *l* of the Most High.
19:17 perfect wisdom is the fulfillment of the *l*.
19:20 of great intelligence who violate the *l*.
21:11 He who keeps the *l* controls his impulses;
23:23 she has disobeyed the *l* of the Most High;
24:22 the *l* which Moses commanded us as an
32:15 He who studies the *l* masters it,
32:17 and distorts the *l* to suit his purpose.
32:24 He who keeps the *l* preserves himself;
33: 2 He who hates the *l* is without wisdom,
33: 3 *l* is dependable for him as a divine oracle.
34: 8 The *l* is fulfilled without fail,
35: 1 To keep the *l* is a great oblation,
39: 1 to the study of the *l* of the Most High!
39: 8 and glory in the *l* of the LORD's covenant.
41: 8 men, who forsake the *l* of the Most High.
42: 2 Of the *l* of the Most High and his precepts,
45: 5 the *l* of life and understanding,
46:14 By the *l* of the LORD he judged the nation,
49: 4 They abandoned the *L* of the Most High,
Is 5:24 have spurned the *l* of the LORD of hosts,
30: 9 who refuse to obey the *l* of the LORD.
42:21 justice to make his *l* great and glorious,
42:24 they refused to walk, his *l* they disobeyed.
51: 4 For *l* shall go forth from my presence,
58: 2 just and not abandoned the *l* of their God;
Jer 2: 8 Those who dealt with the *l* knew me not;
6:19 not my words, because they despised my *l*.
8: 8 "We are wise, we have the *l* of the LORD"?
9:12 Because they have abandoned my *l*,
16:11 forsaken, and my *l* they have not observed.
26: 4 not living according to the *l* I placed
31:33 I will place my *l* within them,
32:23 by your *l* they did not live,
44:10 they do not fear or follow the *l* and the
44:23 voice of the LORD, not living by his *l*,
Bar 2: 2 as was written in the *l* of Moses:
2:28 your *l* in the presence of the Israelites:
4: 1 of God, the *l* that endures forever;
4:12 because they turned from the *l* of God,
Ez 22:26 my *l* and profane what is holy to me;
43:12 This is the *l* of the temple:
Dn 6: 6 Daniel unless by way of the *l* of his God."
6: 9 and irrevocable under Mede and Persian *l*."
6:10 signed the prohibition and made it *l*.
6:11 Daniel heard that this *l* had been signed,
6:13 irrevocable under the Mede and Persian *l*."
6:16 "that under the Mede and Persian *l* every
7:25 to change the feast days and the *l*.
9:10 to live by the *l* you gave us through your
9:11 Israel transgressed your *l* and went astray,
9:11 malediction, recorded in the *l* of Moses,
9:13 As it is written in the *l* of Moses,
13: 3 their daughter according to the *l* of Moses.
13:61 According to the *l* of Moses,
Hos 4: 6 Since you have ignored the *l* of your God,
8: 1 my covenant, and sinned against my *l*,
Am 2: 4 Because they spurned the *l* of the LORD,
Hb 1: 4 This is why the *l* is benumbed,
1: 7 from himself derive his *l* and his majesty.
Zep 2: 3 of the earth, who have observed his *l*;
3: 4 what is holy, and do violence to the *l*.
Mal 3:22 Remember the *l* of Moses my servant,
Mt 1:19 man unwilling to expose her to the *l*,
5:17 come to abolish the *l* and the prophets.
5:18 away, not the smallest letter of the *l*,
5:40 If anyone wants to go to *l* over your shirt,
7:12 this sums up the *l* and the prophets.
9:11 collectors and those who disregard the *l*?"
11:13 as the *l* spoke prophetically until John.
11:19 of tax collectors and those outside the *l*!'
12: 5 Have you not read in the *l* how the priests
22:36 which commandment of the *l* is the greatest?"
22:40 two commandments the whole *l* is based,
23:23 neglecting the weightier matters of the *l*,
Mk 2:16 collectors and offenders against the *l*,
7: 1 and some of the experts in the *l*
Lk 2:22 to purify them according to the *l* of Moses,
2:23 for it is written in the *l* of the Lord,

2:24 with the dictate in the *l* of the Lord.
2:27 for him the customary ritual of the *l*,
2:39 all the prescriptions of the *l* of the Lord,
5:17 by were Pharisees and teachers of the *l*
5:30 tax collectors and non-observers of the *l*?"
10:26 "What is written in the *l*?
16:16 "The *l* and the prophets were in force
16:17 single stroke of a letter of the *l* to pass.
23:56 as a day of rest, in accordance with the *l*.
24:44 everything written about me in the *l* of
Jn 1:17 For while the *l* was given through Moses,
1:45 found the one Moses spoke of in the *l*—
7:19 Moses has given you the *l*, has he not?
7:23 to prevent a violation of Mosaic *l*,
7:49 this lot, that knows nothing about the *l*—
7:51 "Since when does our *l* condemn any man
8: 5 *l*, Moses ordered such women to be stone.
8:17 It is laid down in your *l* that evidence
10:34 "Is it not written in your *l*,
12:34 *l* that the Messiah is to remain forever.
15:25 this only fulfills the text in their *l*:
18:31 pass judgment on him according to your *l*?"
19: 7 "We have our *l*," the Jews responded,
19: 7 "and according to that *l* he must die
Acts 5:34 of the *l* highly regarded by all the people.
6:13 against the holy place and the *l*."
7:53 You who received the *l* through the
13:15 the reading of the *l* and of the prophets,
13:38 never be acquitted of under the *l* of Moses.
15: 5 circumcised and told to keep the Mosaic *l*.
18:13 worship God in ways that are against the *l*."
18:15 terminology and titles and your own *l*,
21:20 all of them staunch defenders of the *l*.
21:24 follow the *l* yourself with due observance.
21:28 everywhere against our people, our *l*,
22: 3 educated strictly in the *l* of our fathers.
22:12 a devout observer of the *l* and well spoken
23: 3 to the law, yet you violate the *l* yourself
23:29 he was accused in matters of their own *l*
24:14 that is written in the *l* and the prophets,
25: 8 no crime either against the *l* of the Jews
28:23 to the *l* of Moses and the prophets.
Rom 2:12 the *l* will perish without reference to it;
2:12 the *l* will be judged in accordance with it.
2:13 the *l* who are just in the sight of God;
2:14 do not have the *l* keep it as by instinct,
2:14 the *l* serve as a law for themselves.
2:14 the law serve as a *l* for themselves.
2:15 of the *l* are written in their hearts.
2:15 bears witness together with that *l*,
2:17 firmly on the *l* and pride yourself on God.
2:18 Instructed by the *l*, you know his will
2:20 because in the *l* you have at hand a clear
2:23 law, do you dishonor God by breaking the *l*?
2:25 be sure, has value if you observe the *l*,
2:26 person keeps the precepts of the *l*,
2:27 If a man who is uncircumcised keeps the *l*,
2:27 who, with your written *l* and circumcision,
3:19 We know that everything the *l* says is
3:20 observance of the law; the *l* does nothing
3:21 apart from the *l*, even though both law
3:27 By what *l*, the law of works?
3:27 By the *l* of faith.
3:28 by faith apart from observance of the *l*.
3:31 we then abolishing the *l* by means of faith?
3:31 On the contrary, we are confirming the *l*.
4:13 inherit the world did not depend on the *l*;
4:14 If only those who observe the *l* are heirs,
4:15 the *l* serves only to bring down wrath,
4:15 there is no *l* there is no transgression.
4:16 have the *l* but for all who have his faith.
5:13 before the *l* there was sin in the world,
5:13 sin is not imputed when there is no *l*—
5:20 The *l* came in order to increase offenses;
6:14 you are now under grace, not under the *l*.
6:15 we are not under the *l* but under grace,
7: 1 know what *l* is), that the law has power
7: 2 bound to her husband by *l* while he lives,
7: 2 is released from the *l* regarding husbands.
7: 3 her husband dies she is freed from that *l*,
7: 4 died to the *l* through the body of Christ,
7: 5 the sinful passions roused by the *l*
7: 6 Now we have been released from the *l*—
7: 7 That the *l* is the same as sin?
7: 7 only through the *l* that I came to know sin.
7: 7 what evil desire was unless the *l* had said,
7: 8 Without *l* sin is dead,
7: 9 is dead, and at first I lived without *l*.
7:12 Yet the *l* is holy and the commandment is
7:14 We know that the *l* is spiritual,
7:16 that very fact I agree that the *l* is good.
7:21 a *l* that leads to wrongdoing is always
7:22 My inner self agrees with the *l* of God,
7:23 another *l* at war with the law of my mind;
7:23 the prisoner of the *l* of sin in my members.
7:25 law of God but with my flesh the *l* of sin.
8: 2 The *l* of the spirit,
8: 2 has freed you from the *l* of sin and death.
8: 3 The *l* was powerless because of its
8: 4 of the *l* might be fulfilled in us who live,
8: 7 it is not subject to God's *l*.
9:31 seeking a *l* from which justice would come,
9:31 would come, did not arrive at that *l*?
10: 4 Christ is the end of the *l*.
10: 5 from the *l*, "The one who observes the law
13: 8 who loves his neighbor has fulfilled the *l*.
13:10 hence love is the fulfillment of the *l*.
1Cor 9: 8 not the *l* itself speak of these things?
9: 8 It is written in the *l* of Moses,
9:20 To those bound by the *l* I became like one
9:20 it), that I might win those bound by the *l*.
9:21 To those not subject to the *l* I became
9:21 law of God, for I am subject to the *l* of
9:21 I might win those not subject to the *l*.
14:21 It is written in the *l*,
14:34 Rather, as the *l* states,
15:56 is sin, and sin gets its power from the *l*.
2Cor 3: 6 covenant not of a written *l* but of spirit.
3: 6 The written *l* kills,
Gal 2:16 observance of the *l*; for by works of the law
2:19 was through the *l* that I died to the law,
2:21 If justice is available through the *l*,
3: 2 the *l* or through faith in what you heard?
3: 5 Is it because you observe the *l* or because
3:10 All who depend on observance of the *l*,
3:10 in the book of the *l* and carry it out."
3:11 one is justified in God's sight by the *l*,
3:12 But the *l* does not depend on faith.
3:17 God is not set aside as invalid by any *l*
3:18 if one's inheritance comes through the *l*,
3:19 What is the relevance of the *l*,
3:21 the *l* is opposed to the promises [of God]?
3:21 If the *l* that was given was such that it
3:21 justice would be a consequence of the *l*.
3:23 we were under the constraint of the *l*,
3:24 the *l* was our monitor until Christ came to
4: 4 his Son born of a woman, born under the *l*,
4: 5 from the *l* those who were subjected to it,
4:21 You who want to be subject to the *l*,
4:21 do you know what the *l* has to say?
5: 3 they are bound to the *l* in its entirety.
5: 4 justification in the *l* have severed yourselves
5:14 The whole *l* has found its fulfillment in
5:18 By the spirit, you are not under the *l*.
5:23 Against such there is no *l*!
6: 2 that way you will fulfill the *l* of Christ.
6:13 do not follow the *l* themselves.
Eph 2:15 the *l* with its commands and precepts,
Phil 3: 6 when it came to justice based on the *l*.
3: 9 of my own based on observance of the *l*.
1Tm 1: 7 wanting to be teachers of the *l* but
1: 8 *l* is good, provided one uses it in the way *l*
Ti 3: 9 all controversies and quarrels about the *l*.
Heb 7: 5 The *l* provides that the priests of the
7:11 basis of which the people received the *l*),
7:12 there is necessarily a change of *l*.
7:16 not in virtue of a *l* expressed in a
7:19 for the *l* brought nothing to perfection.
7:28 *l* sets up as high priests men who are weak,
7:28 after the *l* appoints as priest the Son,
8: 4 offering the gifts which the *l* prescribes.
9:19 the commandments of the *l* to the people,
9:22 *l* almost everything is purified by blood,
10: 1 Since the *l* had only a shadow of the good
10: 8 according to the prescriptions of the *l*.)
10:28 Anyone who rejects the *l* of Moses is put
Jas 1:25 into freedom's ideal *l* and abides by it.
1:25 but one who carries out the *l* in practice.
2: 8 if you fulfill the *l* of the kingdom.
2: 9 are convicted by the *l* as transgressors.
2:10 falls into sin on one point of the *l*,
2:11 you have become a transgressor of the *l*.
2:12 for judgment under the *l* of freedom.
4:11 his brother is speaking against the *l*.
4:11 judge the *l* you are no observer of the law,
4:11 It is the *l* he judges.
2Pt 2:21 backs on the holy *l* handed on to them,

LAWBREAKERS (2)

1Mc 2:44 in their anger and *l* in their wrath,
3: 6 The *l* were cowed by fear of him,

LAWFUL (13)

1Mc 14:44 It shall not be *l* for any of the people or
2Mc 4:11 he abrogated the *l* institutions and
Mt 12:10 "Is it *l* to work a cure on the sabbath?"
22:17 Is it *l* to pay tax to the emperor or not?"
Mk 12:14 it *l* to pay the tax to the emperor or not?
Lk 6: 9 ask you, is it *l* to do good on the sabbath
14: 3 "Is it *l* to cure on the sabbath or not?"
Acts 16:21 not *l* for us Romans to adopt or practice."
19:39 it ought to be settled in the *l* assembly.
1Cor 6:12 "Everything is *l* for me"
10:23 are *l*" but not all are advantageous.
10:23 "All things are *l*—

LAWGIVER (2)

Is 33:22 yes, the LORD our judge, the LORD our *l*,
Jas 4:12 There is but one *L* and Judge,

LAWGIVERS (1)

Prv 8:15 By me kings reign, and *l* establish justice;

LAW-GIVING (1)

Rom 9: 4 adoption, the glory, the covenants, the *l*,

LAWLESS (17)

1Mc 7: 5 *l* and impious men of Israel came to him.
9:69 he was angry with the *l* men who had
14:14 he suppressed all the *l* and the wicked.
2Mc 8:17 keeping before their eyes the *l* outrage
Prv 3:31 not the *l* man and choose none of his ways:
16:29 A *l* man allures his neighbor,
Wis 4: 6 For children born of *l* unions give
4:20 *l* deeds shall convict them to their face.
15:17 he makes a dead thing with his *l* hands.
17: 2 the *l* thought to enslave the holy nation,
Sir 34:18 presents from the *l* win not God's favor.
Dn 3:32 over to our enemies, *l* and hateful rebels;
Mk 16:20 "This *l* and faithless age is under Satan,
2Thes 2: 8 Thereupon the *l* one will be revealed,
2: 9 This *l* one will appear as part of the
1Tm 1: 9 not at good men but at the *l* and unruly,
2Pt 2: 8 the *l* deeds of those among whom he lived.)

LAWLESSLY (2)

Wis 14:28 or live *l* or lightly forswear themselves.
1Jn 3: 4 Everyone who sins acts *l*,

LAWLESSNESS (11)

Gn 6:11 of God the earth was corrupt and full of *l*.
6:13 the earth is full of *l* because of them.
1Mc 3:20 With great presumption and *l* they come
Wis 5:23 Thus *l* shall lay the whole earth waste and
Ez 7:10 *L* is in full bloom,
9: 9 is filled with bloodshed, the city with *l*.
Hos 4: 2 in their *l*, bloodshed follows bloodshed.
2Cor 6:14 what do righteousness and *l* have in common,
2Thes 2: 3 occurred nor the man of *l* been revealed
2: 7 The secret force of *l* is already at work,
1Jn 3: 4 who sins acts lawlessly, for sin is *l*.

LAWS (57)

Ex 16:28 you refuse to keep my commandments and *l*?
Lv 10:11 all the *l* that the LORD has given them
26:46 decrees and *l* which the LORD had Moses
Ezr 7:25 all, that is, who know the *l* of your God.
7:25 Instruct those who do not know these *l*.
Neh 9:13 You gave them just ordinances, firm *l*,
Jdt 11:12 which God in his *l* forbade them to eat.
Est 1:19 among the *l* of the Persians and Medes,
3: 8 with *l* differing from those of every other
3: 8 They do not obey the *l* of the king,
B: 4 which by its *l* is opposed to every other
B: 5 all men, lives by divergent and alien *l*,
E:15 *l* and are the children of the Most High,
E:19 that the Jews may follow their own *l*,
1Mc 3:21 we are fighting for our lives and our *l*.
3:29 the *l* which had been in effect from of old.
6:59 live according to their own *l* as formerly;
6:59 it was on account of their *l*,
10:37 them, and let them follow their own *l*,
13: 3 have done for the *l* and the sanctuary;
2Mc 2:22 *l* that were in danger of being abolished,
3: 1 peace and the *l* were strictly observed
4: 2 and a zealous defender of the *l*.
4:17 is no light matter to flout the *l* of God,
5: 8 all men, hated as a transgressor of the *l*,
5:15 traitor both to the *l* and to his country,
6: 1 and live no longer by the *l* of God;
6: 5 abominable offerings prohibited by the *l*.
6:23 would be loyal to the holy *l* given by God.
6:28 and generously for the revered and holy *l*."
7: 2 than transgress the *l* of our ancestors."
7: 9 It is for his *l* that we are dying."
7:11 for the sake of his *l* I disdain them;
7:37 my body and my life for our ancestral *l*,
8:21 ready to die for their *l* and their country.
8:36 that they followed the *l* laid down by him.
11:31 to observe their dietary *l* and other laws,
13:14 to fight nobly to death for the *l*,
Ps(s) 105:45 might keep his statutes and observe his *l*.
Wis 6:18 love means the keeping of her *l*;
6:18 her *l* is the basis for incorruptibility;
9: 5 in comprehension of judgment and of *l*.
19: 6 made over anew, serving its natural *l*,
Sir 45:17 He gave to him his *l*,
Is 24: 5 its inhabitants, who have transgressed *l*,
Jer 31:36 these natural *l* give way in spite of me,
33:25 and have given no *l* to heaven and earth,
Ez 43:11 and entrances, all its statutes and *l*;
43:11 carefully observe all its *l* and statutes.
44: 5 the statutes and *l* of the LORD's temple;
44:24 my *l* and statutes on all my festivals,
Dn 9: 5 departed from your commandments and your *l*.
Gal 3:13 *l* curse by himself becoming a curse for us,
Ti 3: 1 and its officials, to obey the *l*,
Heb 8:10 I will place my *l* in their minds and I
10:16 I will put my *l* in their hearts and I will

LAWSUIT (6)

Ex 23: 2 nor shall you, when testifying in a *l*,
23: 3 You shall not favor a poor man in his *l*.

LAWSUIT (cont.)

23: 6 your needy fellow men his rights in his *l.*
2Sm 15: 2 someone had a *l* to be decided by the king,
15: 4 Then everyone who has a *l* to be decided
Prv 13:23 A *l* devours the tillage of the poor,

LAWSUITS (2)

Sir 29:19 he who undertakes too much falls into *l.*
1Cor 6: 7 the very fact that you have *l* against one

LAWYER (3)

Mt 22:35 and one of them, a *l,*
Lk 10:25 a *l* stood up to pose him this problem:
Ti 3:13 Zenas the *l* and Apollos on their journey,

LAWYERS (6)

Est 1:13 in general consultation with *l* and jurists.
Lk 7:30 The Pharisees and the *l,*
11:45 In reply one of the *l* said to him,
11:46 "Woe to you *l* also!
11:52 Woe to you *l!*
14: 3 Jesus asked the *l* and the Pharisees,

LAY (184)

Gn 9:21 became drunk and *l* naked inside his tent.
19:33 older one went in and *l* with her father;
19:34 "Last night it was I who *l* with my father.
19:35 the younger one went in and *l* with him;
22:12 "Do not *l* your hand on the boy,"
28:11 his head and *l* down to sleep at that spot.
34: 2 her, he seized her and *l* with her by force.
35:22 that region, Reuben went and *l* with Bilhah,
48:18 *l* your right hand on his head!"
Ex 7: 4 Therefore I will *l* my hand on Egypt and by
14: 9 up with them as they *l* encamped by the sea,
16:13 In the morning a dew *l* all about the camp,
21: 1 are the rules you shall *l* before them.
22: 7 did not *l* hands on his neighbor's property.
22:10 did not *l* hands on his neighbor's property;
29:10 his sons shall *l* their hands on its head.
Lv 1: 4 *l* his hand on the head of the holocaust,
1: 8 on them, they shall *l* the pieces of meat,
1:12 up into pieces, the priest shall *l* these,
3: 2 *l* his hand on the head of his offering,
4: 4 he shall *l* his hand on its head and
4:15 shall *l* their hands on the bullock's head.
6: 3 altar, and *l* them at the side of the altar.
6: 5 On this he shall *l* out the holocaust and
22:10 "Neither a *l* person nor a priest's tenant
26: 7 enemies and *l* them low with your sword.
26:31 I will *l* waste your cities and devastate
Nm 8:10 Israelites shall *l* their hands upon them.
8:12 *l* their hands on the heads of the bullocks,
17:11 fire from the altar in it, *l* incense on it,
17:19 Then *l* them down in the meeting tent,
22:11 Please come and *l* a curse on them for us;
22:17 come and *l* a curse on this people for me."
23: 7 "Come and *l* a curse for me on Jacob,
27:18 a man of spirit, and *l* your hand upon him.
Dt 9:18 I *l* prostrate before the LORD for forty
9:25 nights, I *l* prostrate before the LORD,
20:12 instead offers you battle, *l* siege to it,
20:19 have to *l* siege to it for a long time
21:13 her nails and *l* aside her captive's garb.
32:41 and my hand shall *l* hold of my quiver.
Jos 7: 6 rent his garments and *l* prostrate before
18:11 The territory allotted them *l* between the
19: 1 Simeonites *l* within that of the Judahites.
Jgs 3:25 There on the floor, dead, *l* their lord!
4:22 went in with her, and there *l* Sisera dead,
5:27 At her feet he sank down, fell, *l* still;
6: 5 when they came into the land to *l* it waste.
6:20 unleavened cakes and *l* them on this rock;
7:12 and all the Kedemites *l* in the valley,
19:26 was a guest, where she *l* until the morning.
19:27 again on his journey, there *l* the woman,
Ru 3: 7 went and *l* down at the edge of the sheaves,
3: 7 uncovered a place at his feet, and *l* down.
3:14 So she *l* at his feet until morning,
1Sm 5: 4 Dagon *l* prone on the ground before the ark
19:24 all that day and night he *l* naked.
23:17 my father Saul shall not *l* a hand to you.
24: 7 the LORD's anointed, as to *l* a hand on him,
26: 9 for who can *l* hands on the LORD's anointed
2Sm 13: 6 So Amnon *l* down and pretended to be sick.
13:31 his garments, and then *l* on the ground.
20:12 Amasa *l* covered with blood in the middle
1Kgs 7:48 the golden table on which the showbread *l;*
13:24 His corpse *l* sprawled on the road,
13:31 *L* my remains beside his.
19: 5 He *l* down and fell asleep under the broom
19: 6 After he ate and drank, he *l* down again,
2Kgs 4:29 *L* my staff upon the boy."
4:34 Then he *l* upon the child on the bed,
4:35 and then once more *l* down upon the boy,
8: 7 time when Ben-hadad, king of Aram, *l* sick.
9:16 to Jezreel, where Joram *l* ill and Ahaziah,
1Chr 9: 2 and dwell there were certain *l* Israelites,
2Chr 3: 4 the porch which *l* before the nave along
4:19 the tables on which the showbread *l,*
7: 7 court which *l* before the house of the LORD;
13:13 army faced Judah, his ambush *l* behind them.
Neh 2:13 how the walls of Jerusalem *l* in ruins
5:18 for the labor *l* heavy upon this people.
11: 3 (In the cities of Judah dwelt *l* Israelites,
13:21 If you keep this up, I will *l* hands on you!"
Jdt 8:22 he will *l* the guilt on our heads.
9: 3 blood the bed in which they *l* deceived,
13: 2 Holofernes, who *l* prostrate on his bed,
13:15 canopy under which he *l* in his drunkenness.
Est A: 7 evil and great confusion, *l* upon the earth.
A:13 preparing to *l* hands on King Ahasuerus.
2:21 in anger to *l* hands on King Ahasuerus.
3: 6 not enough to *l* hands on Mordecai alone.
6: 2 for seeking to *l* hands on King Ahasuerus.
1Mc 14:31 country and to *l* hands on their temple,
2Mc 1:21 with the water the wood and what *l* on it.
3:29 While he *l* speechless and deprived of all
4:34 and asked him to *l* hands on Onias.
Jb 1:12 only do not *l* a hand upon his person."
9:27 *l* aside my sadness and be of good cheer,
9:33 who could *l* his hand upon us both and
22:22 mouth, and *l* up his words in your heart.
36:13 impious in heart *l* up anger for themselves;
40:32 Once you but *l* a hand upon him,
Ps(s) 7: 6 to the ground, and *l* my glory in the dust.
35:11 things I knew not of, they *l* to my charge.
38:13 Men *l* snares for me seeking my life;
76: 7 of Jacob, chariots and steeds *l* stilled.
142: 3 before him I *l* bare my distress.
Wis 5:23 Thus lawlessness shall *l* the whole earth
17: 2 they *l* confined beneath their own roofs as
Sir 31: 6 though destruction *l* before their eyes;
46:20 Even when he *l* buried,
Is 11: 8 the child *l* his hand on the adder's lair.
13: 9 To *l* waste the land and destroy the
34:15 There the hoot owl shall nest and *l* eggs,
42:15 I will *l* waste mountains and hills,
47: 7 But you did not *l* these things to heart,
54:11 I *l* your pavements in carnelians,
Jer 36: 7 Perhaps they will *l* their supplication
36:29 Babylon's king shall surely come and *l*
51: 2 to winnow her and *l* waste her land;
Lam 2:14 They did not *l* bare your guilt,
4:22 he will punish, he will *l* bare your sins.
Ez 4: 1 *l* it in front of you,
4: 2 build a tower, *l* out a ramp,
7: 3 according to your conduct and *l* upon you
7: 8 *l* upon you the consequences of all your
21:34 lying divinations to *l* it on the necks
26:16 from their thrones, *l* aside their robes,
31:12 *l* broken in all the ravines of the land,
32:12 They shall *l* waste the glory of Egypt,
40:18 The pavement *l* alongside the gates,
41:15 He measured the building which *l* the
42: 1 on the north that *l* across the free area
Dn 2:28 this was the dream you saw as you *l* in bed.
4: 2 I had a terrifying dream as I *l* in bed,
7: 1 Babylon, Daniel had a dream as he *l* in bed,
7:24 before him, who shall *l* low three kings.
11:12 heart, he shall *l* low tens of thousands,
13:37 who was hidden there, came and *l* with her.
Hos 2:12 So now I will *l* bare her shame before the
2:14 I will *l* waste her vines and fig trees,
Am 7: 8 I will *l* the plummet in the midst of my
Ob 1: 7 who eat your bread *l* snares beneath you:
1:13 *L* not hands upon his possessions on the
Jon 1: 5 hold of the ship, and *l* there fast asleep.
Mi 1: 6 her stones, and *l* bare her foundations.
Hb 3:13 wicked, you *l* bare their bases at the neck.
Mal 2: 2 listen, And if you do not *l* it to heart,
2: 2 it, because you do not *l* it to heart.
Mt 6:19 *l* up for yourselves an earthly treasure.
8:20 the Son of Man has nowhere to *l* his head."
9:18 Please come and *l* your hand on her and she
21: 8 from the trees and *l* them along his path.
23: 4 to carry, to *l* on other men's shoulders,
26:50 they stepped forward to *l* hands on Jesus,
Mk 1:30 Simon's mother-in-law *l* ill with a fever,
5:23 Please come and *l* your hands on her so
5:40 and entered the room where the child *l.*
7:32 and begged him to *l* his hand on him.
16:18 upon whom they *l* their hands will recover."
16:20 upon whom they *l* their hands will recover."
Lk 5:18 to bring him in and *l* him before Jesus;
9:58 the Son of Man has nowhere to *l* his head."
11:46 You *l* impossible burdens on men but will
16:20 At his gate *l* a beggar named Lazarus who
Jn 3:27 "No one can *l* hold on anything unless it
10:17 that I *l* down my life to take it up again.
10:18 I *l* it down freely.
10:18 I have power to *l* it down,
13:37 I will *l* down my life for you!"
13:38 "You will *l* down your life for me,
15:13 to *l* down one's life for one's friends.
Acts 4:35 They used to *l* them at the feet of the
15:28 not to *l* on you any burden beyond that
Rom 5: 7 should *l* down his life for a just man,
1Cor 3:11 No one can *l* a foundation other than the
Eph 4:22 that you must *l* aside your former way of
2Thes 3:10 *l* down the rule that anyone who would not
1Tm 5:22 Never *l* hands hastily on anyone,
Ti 3: 8 I want you to *l* great weight on the things
Heb 10:22 from the evil which *l* on our conscience
12: 1 *l* aside every encumbrance of sin which
12: 2 which *l* before him he endured the cross,
1Jn 3:16 too must *l* down our lives for our brothers.
Rv 11:18 to destroy those who *l* the earth waste."

LAYERS (1)

Jb 36:29 clouds in *l* as the carpeting of his tent.

LAYING (19)

Lv 3: 8 *l* his hand on the head of his offering,
3:13 the LORD, and after *l* his hand on its head,
16:21 *L* both hands on its head,
Nm 16:18 *l* incense on the fire they had put in them,
1Sm 28: 9 Why, then, are you *l* snares for my life,
Jdt 7:25 by *l* us prostrate before them in thirst
8:13 for whom you are *l* down conditions;
1Mc 15:35 harm to our people and *l* waste our country;
Is 28:16 See, I am *l* a stone in Zion,
Ez 13:14 it to the ground, *l* bare its foundations.
Mt 17: 7 came toward them and *l* his hand on them,
Mk 6: 5 a few who were sick by *l* hands on them,
Lk 14:29 He will do that for fear of *l* the
19:35 animal to Jesus, and *l* their cloaks on it,
Acts 4:37 of the money, *l* it at the apostles' feet.
8:18 Simon observed that it was through the *l*
1Tm 6:21 In *l* claim to such knowledge,
Heb 6: 1 not *l* the foundation all over again:
1Pt 2: 6 "See, I am *l* a cornerstone in Zion,

LAYING-ON (1)

Heb 6: 2 instruction about baptisms and *l* of hands,

LAYMAN (13)

Ex 29:33 but no *l* may eat of them,
30:33 this, or whoever puts any of this on a *l,*
Lv 22:12 *l* may not eat of the sacred contributions.
22:13 No *l,* however, may eat of it.
Nm 1:51 *l* who comes near it shall be put to death.
3:10 Any *l* who comes near shall be put to death."
3:38 Any *l* who came near was to be put to death.
17: 5 be a reminder to the Israelites that no *l,*
18: 4 But no *l* shall come near you.
18: 7 Any *l* who draws near shall be put to death."
Jgs 17: 5 Thus the *l* Micah had a sanctuary.
Jdt 11:13 no *l* should even touch with his hands.
Is 24: 2 *L* and priest alike,

LAYMEN (2)

Ezr 8:15 that both *l* and priests were present,
9: 1 "Neither the Israelite *l* nor the priests

LAYS (15)

Jos 6:26 his first-born when he *l* its foundation,
Jb 18: 9 him by the heel, and a snare *l* hold of him.
30:18 One with great power *l* hold of my clothing;
37:15 you know how God *l* his commands upon them,
Ps(s) 55:21 Each one *l* hands on his associates,
80:14 fruit, The boar from the forest *l* it waste,
Sir 27:26 it, and he who *l* a snare is caught in it,
Is 24: 2 the LORD empties the land and *l* it waste;
44:14 and *l* hold of other trees of the forest,
Jer 9: 7 friends, but in his heart he *l* an ambush!
25:36 For the LORD *l* waste their grazing place,
51:55 For the LORD *l* Babylon waste,
Na 1: 2 and *l* up wrath for his enemies;
Zec 12: 1 heavens, *l* the foundations of the earth,
Jn 10:11 shepherd *l* down his life for the sheep.

LAZARUS (19)

Lk 16:20 beggar named *L* who was covered with sores.
16:21 *L* longed to eat the scraps that fell from
16:23 afar off, and *L* resting in his bosom.
16:24 Send *L* to dip the tip of his finger in
16:25 in your lifetime, while *L* was in misery.
Jn 11: 1 was a certain man named *L* who was sick.
11: 2 (This Mary whose brother *L* was sick was
11: 5 Martha and her sister and *L* very much.
11: 6 Yet, after hearing that *L* was sick,
11:11 added, "Our beloved *L* has fallen asleep,
11:14 *L* is dead.
11:17 *L* had already been in the tomb four days.
11:43 Having said this, he called loudly, *L,*
12: 1 of *L* whom Jesus had raised from the dead.
12: 2 *L* was one of those at table with him.
12: 9 only because of Jesus but also to see *L.*
12:10 the chief priests planned to kill *L* too,
12:11 Jesus and believing in him on account of *L.*
12:17 when he called *L* out of the tomb

LAZINESS (1)

Prv 19:15 *L* plunges a man into deep sleep,

LAZULI (1)

Gn 2:12 bdellium and lapis *l* are also there.

LAZY (8)

Ex 5: 8 They are *l;*
5:17 because you are *l* that you keep saying,

Eccl 10:18 When hands are *l*,
Sir 4:29 your speech, nor *l* and slack in your deeds.
37:11 man about mercy, to a *l* man about work,
Mt 25:26 'You worthless, *l* lout!
Ti 1:12 ever been liars, beasts, and *l* gluttons,"
Heb 6:12 Do not grow *l*,

LEAD (106)

Gn 32:18 servant in the *l* he gave this instruction:
50:24 God will surely take care of you and *l* you
Ex 3: 8 *l* them out of that land into a good
3:10 I will send you to Pharaoh to *l* my people,
3:11 Pharaoh and *l* the Israelites out of Egypt?"
3:17 so I have decided to *l* you up out of the
7: 5 and *l* the Israelites out of their midst."
13:17 not *l* them by way of the Philistines' land,
15:10 like *l* they sank in the mighty waters.
16: 3 But you had to *l* us into this desert to
32:21 that you should *l* them into so grave a sin?"
32:34 and *l* the people whither I have told you.
33:12 indeed, are telling me to *l* this people on;
Nm 20: 5 Why did you *l* us out of Egypt,
20:12 you shall not *l* this community into the
31:22 as gold, silver, bronze, iron, tin and *l*,
Dt 4:27 the nations to which the LORD will *l* you.
6:23 He brought us from there to *l* us into the
13: 6 *l* you astray from the way which the LORD,
13:11 he sought to *l* you astray from the LORD,
28:37 the nations to which the LORD will *l* you.
Jgs 4: 7 I will *l* Sisera,
5: 2 Of chiefs who took the *l* in Israel,
7: 4 *L* them down to the water and I will test
7:17 "Watch me and follow my *l*."
1Sm 8:20 to *l* us in warfare and fight our battles."
30:15 "Will you *l* me down to this raiding party?"
30:15 and I will *l* you to the raiding party."
30:16 He did *l* them,
2Kgs 4:24 *L* on!
2Chr 1:10 wisdom and knowledge to *l* this people,
Neh 3:15 steps that *l* down from the City of David.
9:19 cease to *l* them by day on their journey,
Tb 7: 1 *l* me straight to our kinsman Raguel."
Jdt 11:19 I will *l* you through Judea,
12: 1 Then he ordered them to *l* her into the
2Mc 10:12 had taken the *l* in treating the Jews
13:15 also slew the *l* elephant and its rider.
Jb 19:24 with *l* they were cut in the rock forever!
40:25 Can you *l* about Leviathan with a hook,
Ps(s) 27:11 O LORD, your way, and *l* me on a level path,
31: 4 your name's sake you will *l* and guide me.
43: 3 *l* me on And bring me to your holy mountain,
60:11 Who will *l* me into Edom?
68:26 The singers *l*,
108:11 Who will *l* me into Edom?
119:35 *L* me in the path of your commands,
125: 5 may the LORD *l* away with the evildoers!
139:24 way is crooked, and *l* me in the way of old.
142: 8 *L* me forth from prison,
Prv 2:18 death, and her footsteps *l* to the shades;
4:11 you, I *l* you on straightforward paths.
18: 6 The fool's lips *l* him into strife,
Sg 8: 2 I would *l* you,
Wis 16:13 *l* down to the gates of the nether world,
16:13 the gates of the nether world, and *l* back.
Sir 22:14 What is heavier than *l*
46: 8 To *l* the people into their inheritance,
47:18 you heaped up silver as though it were *l*;
Is 20: 4 king of Assyria *l* away captives from Egypt,
42:16 I will *l* the blind on their journey;
43: 8 *L* out the people who are blind though they
48:17 good, and *l* you on the way you should go.
57:18 ways, but I will heal them and *l* them;
60: 9 with the ships of Tarshish in the *l*,
Jer 6:29 roars, the *l* is consumed by the fire;
23:32 and who *l* my people astray by recounting
31: 9 I will *l* them to brooks of water,
31:24 the farmers and those who *l* the flock,
31:32 to *l* them forth from the land of Egypt;
Lam 5:21 *L* us back to you,
Ez 16:40 They shall *l* an assembly against you to
20:35 I will *l* you to the desert of the peoples,
21:24 Both roads shall *l* out from the same land.
22:18 iron and *l* [in the midst of a furnace]:
22:20 Just as silver, bronze, iron, *l*,
27:12 silver, iron, tin, and *l* for your wares.
32: 9 when I *l* you captive among the nations,
34:13 I will *l* them out from among the peoples
38: 4 I will *l* you forth with all your army,
39: 2 will *l* you against the mountains of Israel.
Dn 12: 3 And those who *l* the many to justice
Hos 2:16 I will *l* her into the desert and speak to
Mi 3: 5 the prophets who *l* my people astray;
Mt 21: 2 Untie them and *l* them back to me.
Mk 10:32 to Jerusalem, with Jesus walking in the *l*.
13: 6 they will claim, and will *l* many astray.
14:44 arrest him and *l* him away,
14:55 against Jesus that would *l* to his death,
Lk 18:39 in the *l* sternly ordered him to be quiet,
19:30 Untie it and *l* it back.
Jn 10:16 I must *l* them,
Acts 9: 8 him by the hand and *l* him into Damascus.
13:11 about for someone to *l* him by the hand.
Rom 6:15 What does all this *l* to?
1Cor 7:17 *l* the life the Lord has assigned him,
Gal 5:25 the spirit, let us follow the spirit's *l*.
Eph 2:10 created in Christ Jesus to *l* the life of
Col 1:10 Then you will *l* a life worthy of the Lord
1Tm 2: 2 that we may be able to *l* undisturbed and
Heb 8: 9 to *l* them forth from the land of Egypt:
1Pt 1: 7 gold, may by its genuineness *l* to praise,
3:18 the unjust, was that he might *l* you to God.
2Pt 1: 6 in turn, should *l* to perseverance,
Rv 7:17 *l* them to springs of life-giving water.
20: 3 so that the dragon might not *l* the nations

LEADEN (2)

Zec 5: 7 Then a *l* cover was lifted,
5: 8 pushing the *l* cover into the opening.

LEADER (68)

Ex 32: 1 "Come, make us a god who will be our *l*;
32:23 said to me, 'Make us a god to be our *l*;
Nm 14: 4 "Let us appoint a *l* and go back to Egypt."
27:17 man who shall act as their *l* in all things,
Dt 32:12 The LORD alone was their *l*,
Jos 22:14 and military *l* of his ancestral house.
Jgs 3:27 from the mountains with him as their *l*.
10:18 be *l* of all the inhabitants of Gilead."
11: 8 be the *l* of all of us who dwell in Gilead."
11: 9 delivers them up to me, I shall be your *l*."
11:11 the people made him their *l* and commander.
1Sm 12: 2 a king over you and now the king is your *l*.
15:17 are you not *l* of the tribes of Israel?
22: 2 who were embittered, and he became their *l*.
2Sm 23:19 respect than the Thirty, becoming their *l*.
1Kgs 11:24 men about him and became *l* of a band,
2Kgs 20: 5 back and tell Hezekiah, the *l* of my people:
1Chr 12:28 with Jehoiada, *l* of the line of Aaron,
15:27 singers, and Chenaniah, the *l* of the chant;
27:16 for the Reubenites the *l* was Eliezer,
28: 4 For he chose Judah as *l*,
2Chr 19:11 is *l* of the house of Judah in all that
32:21 *l* and commander in the camp of the
Ezr 8:17 for Iddo, the *l* in the place Casiphia,
Neh 3: 9 Hur, *l* of half the district of Jerusalem,
3:12 *l* of half the district of Jerusalem,
3:14 *l* of the district of Beth-haccherem;
3:15 of Colhozeh, *l* of the district of Mizpah;
3:16 Azbuk, *l* of half the district of Beth-zur,
3:17 *l* of half the district of Keilah.
3:18 Henadad, *l* of half the district of Keilah;
3:19 to him Ezer, son of Jeshua, *l* of Mizpah,
Jdt 5: 3 up as their king and the *l* of their army?
5: 5 the *l* of all the Ammonites said to him:
1Mc 2:17 "You are a *l*,
2:66 shall be the *l* of your army and direct the
5: 6 body of people with Timothy as their *l*.
5:11 Timothy is the *l* of their army.
5:18 of Zechariah, and Azariah, *l* of the people,
9:30 today to be our ruler and *l* in his place,
9:35 Jonathan sent his brother as *l* of the
12:53 "Now that they have no *l* to help them,
13: 8 "You are our *l* in place of your brothers
13:42 high priest, governor, and *l* of the Jews."
14:35 they made him their *l* and high priest
14:41 Simon shall be their permanent *l* and high
2Mc 1:13 When their *l* arrived in Persia with his
1:16 *l* and his companions and struck them down.
10:28 other taking fury as their *l* in the fight.
12:36 himself their ally and *l* in the battle.
14:20 each *l* communicated them to his troops;
Wis 7:12 in them all, because Wisdom is their *l*,
Sir 10:20 Among brethren their *l* is in honor;
46: 1 Valiant *l* was JOSHUA,
Is 55: 4 the peoples, a *l* and commander of nations,
Jer 30:21 His *l* shall be one of his own,
Dn 3:38 have in our day no prince, prophet, or *l*,
9:25 rebuilt Until one who is anointed and a *l*,
9:26 And the people of a *l* who will come shall
11:18 *l* shall put an end to his shameful conduct,
Mi 2:13 With a *l* to break the path they shall
Hb 3:19 For the *l*; with stringed instruments.
Zec 10: 4 From him shall come *l* and chief,
Mt 9:18 speaking to them, a synagogue *l* came up,
Mk 5:38 approached the house of the synagogue *l*,
Lk 22:26 you be as the junior, the *l* as the servant.
Heb 2:10 should make their *l* in the work of
3Jn 1: 9 but Diotrephes, who enjoys being their *l*,

LEADERS—LEADER'S (92)

Ex 16:22 When all the *l* of the community came and
Nm 13: 3 All of them were *l* among the Israelites,
16: 2 Israelites who were *l* in the community,
25: 4 to Moses, "Gather all the *l* of the people,
Dt 1:13 tribes, that I may appoint them as your *l*.'
1:15 them your *l* as officials over thousands,
32:42 Flesh from the heads of the enemy *l*."
Jos 22:21 to the military *l* of the Israelites:
22:30 the military *l* of the Israelites,
23: 2 all Israel (including their elders, *l*,
24: 1 Shechem, summoning their elders, their *l*,
Jgs 5: 9 My heart is with the *l* of Israel,
20: 2 The *l* of all the people and all the
2Sm 4: 2 two company *l* named Baanah and Rechab,
18: 5 the various *l* with regard to Absalom.
24: 2 and the *l* of the army who were with him,
24: 4 overruled Joab and the *l* of the army,
1Kgs 8: 1 of Israel and all the *l* of the tribes,
15:20 agreed with King Asa and sent the *l*
1Chr 12:19 and placed them among the *l* of his troops.
13: 1 that is to say, with every one of his *l*,
22:17 all of Israel's *l* to help his son Solomon:
23: 2 then gathered together all the *l* of Israel,
24: 6 in the presence of the king, and of the *l*,
25: 1 David and the *l* of the liturgical cult set
28: 1 assembled at Jerusalem all the *l* of Israel,
28:21 Also the *l* and all the people will do
29: 6 families, the *l* of the tribes of Israel,
29:24 All the *l* and warriors,
2Chr 5: 2 of Israel and all the *l* of the tribes,
16: 4 sent the *l* of his troops against the cities
25: 5 under *l* of thousands and of hundreds.
28:12 At this, some of the Ephraimite *l*,
Ezr 5:10 you in a list of the men who are their *l*.
8:16 Nathan, Zechariah, and Meshullam, wise *l*,
8:24 of the priestly *l* along with Sherebiah,
8:29 and Levites and the family *l* of Israel,
9: 1 the *l* approached me with this report:
9: 2 the *l* and rulers have taken a leading part
10: 8 to the judgment of the *l* and elders,
10:14 Let our *l* represent the whole assembly;
Neh 10:15 The *l* of the people:
11: 1 The *l* of the people took up residence in
Jdt 7: 8 Edomites and all the *l* of the Ammonites,
14:12 division *l* and all their other commanders.
1Mc 5:56 Zechariah, and Azariah, the *l* of the army,
6:57 He said to the king, the *l* of the army,
6:60 found favor with the king and the *l*;
6:61 the king and the *l* swore an oath to them,
9:53 He took as hostages the sons of the *l* of
2Mc 14:16 At their *l* command,
14:21 on which the *l* would meet by themselves.
Jb 12:24 takes understanding from the *l* of the land,
Sir 16: 7 He forgave not the *l* of old who rebelled
33:19 Listen, to me, O *l* of the multitude;
Is 3:12 O my people, your *l* mislead,
9:15 The *l* of this people mislead them and
14: 9 to greet you, all the *l* of the earth;
22: 3 All your *l* fled away together,
Jer 25:34 roll in the dust, *l* of the flock!
25:35 no escape for the *l* of the flock.
25:36 shepherds, howling by the *l* of the flock!
40: 7 When the army *l* who were still in the
40:13 and all the *l* of the armies in the field
41:11 *l* with him heard of the crimes Ishmael,
41:13 son of Kareah, and the other army *l*,
41:16 *l* took charge of the remnant of the people,
42: 1 Then all the army *l*,
42: 8 called Johanan, son of Kareah, his army *l*,
43: 4 and the rest of the *l* and the people did
43: 5 and all the army *l* took along the whole
Am 6: 1 *L* of a nation favored from the first,
Mi 3: 1 Hear, you *l* of Jacob,
3: 9 Hear this, you *l* of the house of Jacob,
3:11 Her *l* render judgment for a bribe,
Zec 10: 3 the shepherds, and I will punish the *l*;
Mt 9:23 When Jesus arrived at the synagogue *l*
15:14 they are blind *l* of the blind.
Lk 19:47 destroy him, as were the *l* of the people,
23:35 watching, and the *l* kept jeering at him,
24:20 how our chief priests and *l* delivered him
Acts 3:17 acted out of ignorance, just as your *l* did.
4: 5 When the *l*,
4: 8 *L* of the people!
7:40 'Make us gods that will be our *l*,'
14: 5 Gentiles and Jews, together with their *l*,
25: 2 There the Jewish chief priests and the *l*
Gal 2: 2 this in private conference with the *l*,
1Tm 5:17 who do well as *l* deserve to be paid double,
Heb 13: 7 your *l* who spoke the word of God to you;
13:17 Obey your *l* and submit to them,
13:24 to all your *l* and to all the people of God.

LEADERSHIP (5)

1Chr 4:42 went to Mount Seir under the *l* of Pelatiah,
Neh 12:42 were heard under the *l* of Jezrahiah.
1Mc 9:31 From that moment Jonathan accepted the *l*,
2Mc 4:40 thousand armed men under the *l* of Auranus,
10: 1 and his companions under the Lord's *l*,

LEADING (32)

Ex 3: 1 *L* the flock across the desert,
14:19 angel of God, who had been *l* Israel's camp,
Jgs 3:28 seized the fords of the Jordan *l* to Moab,
2Sm 15: 2 and stand alongside the road *l* to the gate.
1Kgs 21:22 you have provoked me by *l* Israel into sin."
2Chr 17: 7 third year of his reign he sent his *l* men,
23:13 musical instruments were *l* the acclaim.
Ezr 9: 2 have taken a *l* part in this apostasy!"
Tb 11:16 briskly, with no one *l* him by the hand,
2Mc 1:23 *l* and the rest responding with Nehemiah.
Ps(s) 68:28 There is Benjamin, the youngest, *l* them;
Prv 7:27 world, *l* down into the chambers of death.
Is 40:11 in his bosom, and *l* the ewes with care.
Bar 5: 9 For God is *l* Israel in joy by the light of

LEADING (cont.)
Mk 6:21 officers, and the *l* men of Galilee.
Lk 4:29 *l* him to the brow of the hill on which it
14: 1 in the house of one of the *l* Pharisees,
Acts 12:10 came to the iron gate *l* out to the city,
13:15 the *l* men of the synagogue sent this
13:50 sympathizers and the *l* men of the town,
15:22 Those chosen were *l* men of the community,
16:12 a *l* city in the district of Macedonia and
18: 8 A *l* man of the synagogue,
18:17 on Sosthenes, a *l* man of the synagogue,
20:30 the truth and *l* astray any who follow them.
25: 5 "Your *l* men can come down with me,"
Rom 1:16 *l* everyone who believes in it to salvation,
5:21 reign by way of justice *l* to eternal life,
8:15 a spirit of slavery *l* you back into fear,
2Cor 7:10 repentance without regrets, *l* to salvation,
10:13 of moderation has set for us *l* us to you.
Col 2:15 show of them, and *l* them off captive,

LEADS (35)
1Mc 13:20 went around by the road that *l* to Adora,
Ps(s) 23: 2 Beside restful waters he *l* me;
68: 7 he *l* forth prisoners to prosperity;
Prv 7:21 with her smooth lips she *l* him astray;
10:16 The just man's recompense *l* to life,
12:26 but the way of the wicked *l* them astray.
12:28 is life, but the abominable way *l* to death.
14:12 to a man, but the end of it *l* to death!
15:24 The path of life *l* the prudent man upward,
16:25 to a man, but the end of it *l* to death!
16:29 and *l* him into a way that is not good.
21: 5 but all rash haste *l* certainly to poverty.
Wis 6:20 the desire for Wisdom *l* up to a kingdom.
Sir 20:25 A liar's way *l* to dishonor,
Is 40:26 He *l* out their army and numbers them,
43:17 waters, Who *l* out chariots and horsemen,
49:10 For he who pities them *l* them and guides
Mt 7:13 The gate that *l* to damnation is wide,
7:14 But how narrow is the gate that *l* to life,
15:14 If one blind man *l* another,
18: 6 it would be better for anyone who *l* astray
Mk 9:42 But it would be better if anyone who *l*
Jn 10: 3 as he calls his own by name and *l* them out.
14: 4 You know the way that *l* where I go."
Rom 6:16 *l* to death, or of obedience, which leads
7:21 *l* to wrongdoing is always ready at hand.
10:10 Faith in the heart *l* to justification,
2Cor 2:14 *l* us on in Christ's triumphal train,
Eph 5:18 that *l* to debauchery.
2Thes 2:11 which *l* them to give credence to falsehood,
1Tm 5: 6 however, *l* a life of living death.
2Tm 3:15 faith in Jesus Christ *l* to salvation.
Heb 1: 6 when he *l* his first-born into the world,
Jude 1:21 Lord Jesus Christ which *l* to life eternal.

LEAF (4)
Gn 8:11 in its bill was a plucked-off olive *l*!
Ex 39: 3 into gold *l* and then cut up into threads,
Jb 13:25 Will you harass a wind-driven *l*,
Is 34: 4 wither away, As the *l* wilts on the vine,

LEAFAGE (1)
Sir 14:26 Who builds his nest in her *l*,

LEAFY (8)
Dt 12: 2 and under every *l* tree where the nations
2Kgs 16: 4 places, on hills, and under every *l* tree.
17:10 on every high hill and under every *l* tree.
2Chr 28: 4 on hills, and under every *l* tree.
Neh 8:15 oleasters, myrtle, palm and other *l* trees,
Ps(s) 118:27 with *l* boughs up to the horns of the altar.
Ez 6:13 beneath every green tree and *l* oak,
20:28 they saw all its high hills and *l* trees,

LEAGUE (5)
Gn 14:13 these were in *l* with Abram.
Neh 6:18 them, for many in Judah were in *l* with him,
Est C:24 and those who are in *l* with him may perish.
Jb 5:23 shall be in *l* with the stones of the field,
Acts 4:27 Herod and Pontius Pilate in *l* with the

LEAGUED (3)
Jgs 20:11 exception were *l* together against the city,
Ps(s) 83: 9 The Assyrians, too, are *l* with them;
94:20 the tribunal of wickedness be *l* with you,

LEAH (29)
Gn 29:16 the older was called *L*,
29:17 *L* had lovely eyes,
29:23 his daughter *L* and brought her to Jacob,
29:24 to his daughter *L* as her maidservant.)
29:25 it was *L*!
29:28 He finished the bridal week for *L*,
29:30 Rachel also, and he loved her more than *L*.
29:31 When the LORD saw that *L* was unloved,
29:32 *L* conceived and bore a son,
30: 9 *L* saw that she had ceased to bear children,
30:11 *L* then said, "What good luck!"
30:13 and *L* said,
30:14 which he brought home to his mother *L*.
30:14 Rachel asked *L*,
30:15 *L* replied, "Was it not enough for you
30:16 from the fields, *L* went out to meet him.
30:18 *L* then said, "God has given me my
30:19 *L* conceived again and bore a sixth son to
31: 4 So Jacob sent for Rachel and *L* to meet him
31:14 Rachel and *L* answered him:
33: 1 So he divided his children among *L*,
33: 2 children first, *L* and her children next,
33: 7 *L* and her children came forward and bowed
34: 1 the daughter whom *L* had borne to Jacob,
35:23 The sons of *L*: Reuben, Jacob's firstborn
46:15 sons whom *L* bore to Jacob in Paddan-aram,
46:18 whom Laban had given to his daughter *L*;
49:31 wife Rebekah, and there, too, I buried *L*—
Ru 4:11 come into your house like Rachel and *L*,

LEAH'S (4)
Gn 30:12 Then *L* maidservant Zilpah bore a second
31:33 in and searched Jacob's tent and *L* tent,
31:33 Leaving *L* tent, he went into Rachel's.
35:26 the sons of *L* maid Zilpah:

LEAK (2)
Prv 19:13 the nagging of a wife is a persistent *l*.
27:15 For a persistent *l* on a rainy day the

LEAKS (1)
Eccl 10:18 when hands are slack, the house *l*.

LEAN (4)
Sir 15: 4 He will *l* upon her and not fall,
Is 10:20 *l* upon him who struck them; But they lean
Ez 34:20 I judge between the fat and the *l* sheep.

LEANED (7)
2Kgs 7: 2 But the adjutant on whose arm the king *l*,
Est D: 3 on the one she *l* gently for support,
D: 7 and *l* weakly against the head of the maid
2Mc 7:27 she *l* over close to her son and said in
Ez 29: 7 When they *l* on you,
Jn 13:25 He *l* back against Jesus' chest and said to
21:20 (the one who had *l* against Jesus' chest

LEANING (3)
2Sm 1: 6 Mount Gilboa and saw Saul *l* on his spear,
Sg 8: 5 up from the desert, *l* upon her lover?
Heb 11:21 worshiped God, *l* on the head of his staff.

LEANNESS (1)
Is 10:16 of hosts, will send among his fat ones *l*,

LEANS (2)
2Kgs 18:21 pierces the hand of anyone who *l* on it.
Is 36: 6 pierces the hand of anyone who *l* on it.

LEAP (8)
2Sm 22:30 and by the help of my God I *l* over a wall.
Jb 41:11 sparks of fire *l* forth.
Ps(s) 18:30 and by the help of my God I *l* over a wall.
29: 6 *l* like a calf and Sirion like a young bull.
Wis 5:21 from a well-drawn bow shall *l* to the mark;
Is 35: 6 Then will the lame *l* like a stag,
Jl 2: 5 of chariots they *l* on the mountaintops;
Zep 1: 9 on that day, all who *l* over the threshold,

LEAPED (1)
Tb 6: 3 a large fish suddenly *l* out of the water

LEAPING (5)
Lv 11:21 that have jointed legs for *l* on the ground;
2Sm 6:16 King David *l* and dancing before the LORD,
1Chr 15:29 and when she saw King David *l* and dancing,
Sg 2: 8 across the mountains, *l* across the hills.
Jn 4:14 within him, *l* up to provide eternal life."

LEAPS (2)
Jb 37: 1 my heart trembles and *l* out of its place.
41:14 in his neck, and terror *l* before him.

LEAPT (2)
Lk 1:41 Mary's greeting, the baby *l* in her womb.
1:44 in my ears, the baby *l* in my womb for joy.

LEARN (80)
Gn 24:21 silently waiting to *l* whether or not the
27:21 to *l* whether you really are my son Esau or
Ex 7: 5 the Egyptians may *l* that I am the LORD,
8: 6 you may *l* that there is none like the LORD,
9:29 you shall *l* that the earth is the LORD's.
Lv 4:28 he later on *l* of the sin he committed,
Nm 9: 8 "Wait until I *l* what the LORD will
22:19 till I *l* what else the LORD may tell me."
Dt 4:10 that they may *l* to fear me as long as they
5: 1 may *l* them and take care to observe them.
13: 4 is testing you to *l* whether you really
14:23 that you may *l* always to fear the LORD,
17:19 of his life that he may *l* to fear the LORD,
18: 9 you shall not *l* to imitate the
31:12 that they may hear it and *l* it,
31:13 do not know it yet, must hear it and *l* it,
32:39 *L* then that I, I alone, am God,
Jos 4:24 may *l* that the hand of the LORD is mighty,
Ru 3:18 my daughter, until you *l* what happens,
1Sm 6: 3 and will *l* why he continues to afflict you."
17:46 whole land shall *l* that Israel has a God.
17:47 shall *l* that it is not by sword or spear
19: 3 If I *l* anything, I will let you know."
22: 3 you, until I *l* what God will do for me."
23:23 "Look around and *l* in which of all the
28: 2 Now you shall *l* what your servant can do."
2Sm 3:25 to *l* the ins and outs of all that you are
1Kgs 8:42 (since men will *l* of your great name
Tb 2: 8 "Will this man never *l*!
5:14 wanting to *l* the truth about your family.
Est 2:11 to *l* how Esther was faring and what was to
1Mc 3:48 to *l* about the things for which the
10:72 Inquire and *l* who I am and who the others
2Mc 11:26 so that, when they *l* of our decision,
Jb 11: 6 So you might *l* that God will make you
21:14 us, for we have no wish to *l* your ways!
23: 5 *l* the words with which he would answer,
34: 4 let us *l* between us what is good.
Ps(s) 14: 4 Will all these evildoers never *l*,
39: 5 of my days, that I may *l* how frail I am.
53: 5 Will all these evildoers never *l*,
119:71 been afflicted, that I may *l* your statutes.
119:73 me discernment that I may *l* your commands.
Prv 6: 6 O sluggard, study her ways and *l* wisdom;
19:25 an arrogant man, the simple *l* a lesson;
22:25 of a wrathful man, Lest you *l* his ways,
Wis 6: 1 *l*,
6: 9 you may *l* wisdom and that you may not sin.
16:26 That your sons whom you loved might *l*,
Sir 6:33 If you are willing to listen, you will *l*;
38: 5 by a twig that men might *l* his power?
39: 5 lands to *l* what is good and evil among men.
44:16 generations might *l* by his example.]
Is 1:17 *l* to do good.
26: 9 earth, the world's inhabitants *l* justice.
26:10 The wicked man, spared, does not *l* justice;
Jer 10: 2 *L* not the customs of the nations,
12:16 And if they carefully *l* my people's custom
Bar 3:14 *L* where prudence is,
Dn 1: 4 intelligent and wise, quick to *l*,
4:29 until you *l* that the Most High rules over
Mt 6:28 *L* a lesson from the way the wild flowers
9:13 Go and *l* the meaning of the words,
11:29 my yoke upon your shoulders and *l* from me,
24:32 From the fig tree *l* a lesson.
Mk 13:28 *L* a lesson from the fig tree.
Lk 19:15 the money, to *l* what profit each had made.
Acts 23:34 came from, only to *l* he was from Cilicia.
24: 8 and *l* for yourself why we are accusing him."
1Cor 4: 6 May you *l* from us not to go beyond what is
14:35 If they want to *l* anything,
2Cor 2: 9 *l* whether you are obedient in all matters.
Gal 3: 2 I want to *l* only one thing from you:
Phil 1:10 *l* to value the things that really matter,
1Thes 4: 1 you must *l* to make still greater progress.
1Tm 1:20 Satan so that they may *l* not to blaspheme.
5: 4 let these *l* that piety begins at home and
5:13 Besides, they *l* to be ladies of leisure,
Rv 3: 9 they will *l* of my love for you in that way.
14: 3 This hymn no one could *l* except the

LEARNED (78)
Gn 9:24 *l* what his youngest son had done to him,
30:27 "I have *l* through divination that it is
31: 1 Jacob *l* that Laban's sons were saying,
42: 1 When Jacob *l* that grain rations were
Lv 5: 1 a witness of something he has seen or *l*,
Nm 30:15 because on the day he *l* of them he said
30:16 them some time after he first *l* of them,
Jos 9:16 *l* that these people were from nearby,
11: 1 When Jabin, king of Hazor, *l* of this,
1Sm 13: 4 Thus all Israel *l* that Saul had overcome
20:33 and thus Jonathan *l* that his father was
1Kgs 12: 2 returned from Egypt as soon as he *l* this.
21:15 *l* that Naboth had been stoned to death,
2Kgs 9:30 Jezebel *l* that Jehu had arrived in Jezreel,
2Chr 22:10 mother of Ahaziah, *l* that her son was dead,
Neh 13:10 I *l*, too, that the portions due the Levites
Jdt 11:16 "As soon as I, your handmaid, *l* all this,
Est 4: 1 When Mordecai *l* all that was happening,
1Mc 3:11 When Judas *l* of it,
6:17 When Lysias *l* that the king was dead,
9:32 When Bacchides *l* of it,
9:63 When Bacchides *l* of this,
9:70 Jonathan *l* of this and sent ambassadors to
12:22 Now that we have *l* this,
13:14 When Trypho *l* that Simon had succeeded his
2Mc 4:21 Antiochus *l* that the king was opposed to
8:12 When Judas *l* of Nicanor's advance and
9: 3 he *l* what had happened to Nicanor and to
11: 6 When Maccabeus and his men *l* that Lysias
12:21 When Timothy *l* of the approach of Judas,
13: 1 Judas and his men *l* that Antiochus Eupator

13:10 When Judas *l* of this,
14: 1 later, Judas and his men *l* that Demetrius,
15: 1 When Nicanor *l* that Judas and his
Ps(s) 106:35 mingled with the nations and *l* their works.
119: 7 heart, when I have *l* your just ordinances.
Prv 24:32 I saw and *l* the lesson:
30: 3 Neither have I *l* wisdom,
Eccl 1:17 I *l* that this also is a chase after wind.
Wis 6:10 those *l* in them will have ready a response.
7:13 Simply I *l* about her,
7:21 as are hidden I *l* and such as are plain;
9:18 straight, and men *l* what was your pleasure,
Sir 8: 9 men which they have *l* from their fathers;
9:15 With the *l* be intimate;
18:28 Any *l* man should make wisdom known,
34:11 my travels, *l* more than ever I could say.
38:25 How can he become *l* who guides the plow,
39: 8 He will show the wisdom of what he has *l*
51:21 whole being was stirred as I *l* about her;
Is 28:26 He has *l* this rule, instructed by his God.
Ez 19: 3 He *l* to seize prey,
19: 6 He *l* to seize prey,
Dn 4:23 once you have *l* it is heaven that rules.
5:21 until he *l* that the Most High God rules
Mt 2:16 of the date he had *l* from the astrologers.
11:25 you have hidden from the *l* and the clever
13:52 "Every scribe who is *l* in the reign of
Mk 6:38 When they *l* the number they answered,
Lk 7:37 *l* that he was dining in the Pharisee's
10:21 you have hidden from the *l* and the clever
23: 7 *l* that he was under Herod's jurisdiction,
Jn 4: 1 Now when Jesus *l* that the Pharisees had
6:45 the Father and *l* from him comes to me.
Acts 9:30 When the brothers *l* of this,
14: 6 When Paul and Barnabas *l* of this,
17:13 But when the Jews of Thessalonica *l* that
23:27 When I *l* that he was a Roman citizen,
28: 1 we *l* that the island was called Malta.
Rom 1:14 non-Greeks, to *l* and unintelligent alike.
Eph 4:20 is not what you learned when you *l* Christ!
Phil 4: 9 according to what you have *l* and accepted,
4:11 myself in I have *l* to be self-sufficient.
4:12 have *l* how to cope with every circumstance
1Thes 4: 1 you *l* from us how to conduct yourselves
2Tm 3:14 faithful to what you have *l* and believed,
Heb 5: 8 was, he *l* obedience from what he suffered;

LEARNERS (1)

Mt 23: 8 among you is your teacher, the rest are *l*.

LEARNING (14)

Jos 9: 3 *l* what Joshua had done to Jericho and Ai,
1Sm 4: 6 On *l* that the ark of the LORD had come
2Sm 10: 7 On *l* this, David sent out Joab
1Mc 12:50 upon *l* that Jonathan had been captured and
Prv 1: 5 man by hearing them will advance in *l*,
9: 9 teach a just man, and he advances in *l*.
Wis 8: 8 Or again, if one yearns for copious *l*,
Sir 15: 3 and give him the water of *l* to drink.
21:19 Like fetters on the legs is *l* to a fool,
21:21 Like a chain of gold is *l* to a wise man,
Mk 15:45 *L* from him that he was dead,
Acts 26:24 And your great *l* is driving you mad!"
Phil 2:19 courage from *l* how things go with you.
2Tm 3: 7 always *l* but never able to reach a

LEARNS (10)

Lv 4:23 if later on he *l* of the sin he committed,
Nm 30: 5 if her father *l* of her vow or the pledge
30: 6 But if on the day he *l* of it her father
30: 8 she bound herself, and her husband *l* of it,
30: 9 But if on the day he *l* of it her husband
30:12 and her husband *l* of it yet says nothing
30:13 day he *l* of them her husband annuls them,
Sir 13: 1 associates with an impious man *l* his ways.
Is 7:15 he *l* to reject the bad and choose the good.
7:16 *l* to reject the bad and choose the good,

LEASE (1)

Mt 21:41 *l* his vineyard out to others

LEASED (3)

Mt 21:33 Then he *l* it out to tenant farmers and
Mk 12: 1 Then he *l* it to tenant farmers and went on
Lk 20: 9 planted a vineyard, *l* it to tenant farmers,

LEASH (1)

Jb 40:29 Can you put him in *l* for your maidens?

LEAST (47)

Gn 18:32 What if there are at *l* ten there?"
22:12 "Do not do the *l* thing to him.
30: 3 I too may have offspring, at *l* through her."
33:15 "Let me at *l* put at your disposal some of
Ex 10:17 God, to take at *l* this deadly pest from me."
Nm 11:32 who got the *l* gathered ten homers of them.
23:25 Balak to Balaam, "at *l* do not bless them."
Jos 13: 6 at *l* include these areas in the division
1Sm 9:21 and is not my clan the *l* among the clans
2Kgs 18:24 even one of the *l* servants of my lord,
Jdt 7:27 be made slaves, but at *l* we should live,
13:13 All the people, from the *l* to the greatest,
Est 1:20 their husbands, from the greatest to the *l*."
2Mc 8: 9 and sent him at the head of at *l* twenty
8:15 at *l* for the sake of the covenants made
10:18 When at *l* nine thousand took refuge in two
12: 4 sea and drowned at *l* two hundred of them.
12:10 numbering at *l* five thousand foot soldiers,
15:27 they laid low at *l* thirty-five thousand,
Jb 21: 2 At *l* listen to my words,
Wis 15:17 he at *l* lives,
Sir 11: 3 *L* is the bee among winged things,
23:21 when he *l* expects it,
Is 36: 9 even one of the *l* servants of my lord?
Jer 2:35 at *l*,
31:34 All, from *l* to greatest,
Ob 1:13 Gaze not, you at *l*,
Mt 2: 6 by no means *l* among the princes of Judah,
5:19 That is why whoever breaks the *l*
5:19 so shall be called *l* in the kingdom of God.
11:11 Yet the *l* born into the kingdom of God is
24:44 of Man is coming at the time you *l* expect.
24:50 when he is not ready and *l* expects him.
25:40 as you did it for one of my *l* brothers,
25:45 neglected to do it to one of these *l* ones,
Lk 7:28 Yet the *l* born into the kingdom of God is
9:48 for the *l* one among you is the greatest."
12:40 Son of Man will come when you *l* expect him."
19: 8 If I have defrauded anyone in the *l*,
Acts 5:15 at *l* his shadow might fall on one
1Cor 9:22 all men in order to save at *l* some of them.
15: 9 I am the *l* of the apostles;
2Cor 2:17 We at *l* are not like so many who trade on
10: 8 this will not embarrass me in the *l*.
Eph 3: 8 To me, the *l* of all believers,
Heb 8:11 for all shall know me, from *l* to greatest.
Jas 3:14 at *l* refrain from arrogant and false

LEATHER (20)

Gn 3:21 and his wife the LORD God made *l* garments,
Lv 11:32 an article of wood, cloth, *l* or goat hair,
13:48 wool, or on a hide or anything made of *l*,
13:49 or on any *l* article is greenish or reddish,
13:51 woven or knitted material, or on the *l*,
13:52 of wool or linen, or the *l* article,
13:53 or knitted material, or on the *l* article,
13:56 infected part out of the garment, or the *l*,
13:57 or knitted material, or on the *l* article,
13:58 or knitted material, or the *l* article,
13:59 or knitted material, or on any *l* article,
15:17 Any piece of cloth or *l* with seed on it
Nm 31:20 also purify every article of cloth, *l*,
2Kgs 1: 8 replied, "with a *l* girdle about his loins."
Jdt 10: 5 maid a *l* flask of wine and a cruse of oil.
Jb 13:28 Though he wears out like a *l* bottle,
Ez 16:10 gown, put sandals of fine *l* on your feet;
Mt 3: 4 hair, and wore a *l* belt around his waist.
Mk 1: 6 hair, and wore a *l* belt around his waist.
Acts 9:43 time at the house of Simon, a tanner of *l*.

LEATHER-TANNER (2)

Acts 10: 6 Simon the *l* whose house stands by the sea."
10:32 He is a guest in the house of Simon the *l*,

LEATHERN (1)

Ps(s) 119:83 I am shriveled like a *l* flask in the smoke,

LEAVE (251)

Gn 19:14 "Get up and *l* this place,"
24:54 said, "Give me *l* to return to my master."
24:59 sister Rebekah and her nurse to take *l*,
28:15 I will never *l* you until I have done what
30:25 "Give me *l* to go to my homeland.
31:13 *L* this land and return to the land of your
31:30 Granted that you had to *l* because you were
38:17 you *l* a pledge until you send it."
42:15 life of Pharaoh that you shall not *l* here.
42:33 *l* one of your brothers with me,
44:22 to my lord, 'The boy cannot *l* his father;
44:22 his father would die if he were to *l* him.'
Ex 1:10 to fight against us, and so *l* our country."
2:20 "Why did you *l* him there?
3:21 toward this people that, when you *l*,
6:11 of Egypt, to let the Israelites *l* his land."
7: 2 Pharaoh to let the Israelites *l* his land.
8: 7 The frogs shall *l* you and your houses,
8:25 "As soon as I *l* your presence I will pray
9:29 "As soon as I *l* the city I will extend my
10:28 *L* my presence,"
11: 8 before me, they shall beg me, *L* us,
11:10 would not let the Israelites *l* his land.
12:31 and Aaron and said, *L* my people at once,
14:12 *L* us alone.
17: 3 saying, "Why did you ever make us *l* Egypt?
20: 7 For the LORD will not *l* unpunished him who
21: 3 comes into service alone, he shall *l* alone;
21: 3 with a wife, his wife shall *l* with him.
21: 4 property and the man shall *l* alone.
23:11 of the field may eat what the poor *l*.
Lv 16:23 he shall strip off and *l* in the sanctuary
19:10 you shall *l* for the poor and the alien.
21:12 he thus become unclean or *l* the sanctuary;
23:22 you shall *l* for the poor and the alien.
25:46 and *l* to your sons as their hereditary
26:32 So devastated will I *l* the land that your
Nm 10:31 Moses said, "Please, do not *l* us;
11:20 you have wailed, 'Why did we ever *l* Egypt?'
35:32 allow a refugee to *l* his city of asylum
Dt 1: 7 *L* here and go to the hill country of the
2:18 to *l* Ar and the territory of Moab behind.
5:11 For the LORD will not *l* unpunished him who
7:15 but will *l* them with all your enemies.
15:16 tells you that he does not wish to *l* you,
20:16 you shall not *l* a single soul alive.
23:15 in your midst, he will *l* your company.
28:51 they will *l* you no grain or wine or oil,
Jos 1: 5 I will not *l* you nor forsake you.
Jgs 7: 3 'If anyone is afraid or fearful, let him *l*.' "
9:43 watched till he saw the people *l* the city,
16:17 If I am shaved, my strength will *l* me,
20: 8 is to *l* for his tent or return to his home.
21:21 *l* the vineyards and each of you seize one
Ru 2: 7 She asked *l* to gather the gleanings into
2: 8 you are not to *l* here.
2:16 drop some handfuls and *l* them for her
1Sm 10: 2 When you *l* me today,
10: 9 As Saul turned to *l* Samuel,
15: 6 *L* Amalek and withdraw,
16:13 When Samuel took his *l*, he went to Ramah.
16:23 better, for the evil spirit would *l* him.
17:44 and I will *l* your flesh for the birds of
17:46 This very day I will *l* your corpse and the
20:29 well of me, give me *l* to visit my brothers.'
22: 5 *L*, and go to the land of Judah."
25:22 if by morning I *l* a single male alive
27: 9 David would not *l* a man or woman alive,
27:11 But David would not *l* a man or woman alive
2Sm 11:15 pull back and *l* him to be struck down dead."
13: 9 he said, "Have everyone *l* me."
13:15 "Get up and *l*," he said to her.
14: 7 *l* my husband neither name nor posterity
15:14 *L* quickly, lest he hurry and overtake us,
17:21 *L*! Cross the water at once,
19:32 for his crossing, taking *l* of him there.
1Kgs 2:37 if you *l*, and cross the Kidron Valley,
3:17 "By your *l*, my lord,
11:13 I will *l* your son one tribe for the sake
11:21 "Give me *l* to return to my own country."
14:12 So *l*; go home!
17: 3 *L* here, go east and hide
18:12 After I *l* you,
18:44 'Harness up and *l* the mountain before the
19:18 Yet I will *l* seven thousand men in Israel
20:36 LORD, a lion will kill you when you *l* me."
2Kgs 1: 4 shall not *l* the bed upon which you lie;
1: 6 you shall not *l* the bed upon which you lie;
1:16 you shall not *l* the bed upon which you lie;
2: 2 live," Elisha replied, "I will not *l* you."
2: 4 live," Elisha replied, "I will not *l* you."
2: 6 live," Elisha replied, "I will not *l* you."
7:12 us alive and enter our city when we *l* it."
8: 1 *L* with your family and settle wherever you
8:19 For he had promised David that he would *l*
18:14 *L* me,
24: 7 king of Egypt did not again *l* his own land,
1Chr 28: 8 *l* it as an inheritance to your children
2Chr 18:31 God induced them to *l* him.
26:18 *L* the sanctuary, for you have broken faith
33: 8 I will not again allow Israel's feet to *l*
35:15 was no need for them to *l* their stations,
Ezr 9:12 and *l* it as an inheritance to your
Neh 6: 3 stop, while I *l* it to come down to you?"
13: 6 *l* of the king and returned to Jerusalem,
Tb 5:16 In good health we shall *l* you,
5:21 Our son will *l* in good health and come
6: 8 the affliction will *l* him completely,
12:13 When you did not hesitate to get up and *l*
14:11 But now my spirit is about to *l* me."
Jdt 5: 9 Their God bade them *l* their abode and
6: 7 *l* you at one of the towns along the ascent.
10:19 It is not wise to *l* one man of them alive,
Est B: 7 they may at last *l* our affairs stable and
1Mc 1:48 animals, to *l* their sons uncircumcised,
9:10 kinsmen and not *l* a stain upon our glory!"
12:45 the officials, then I will *l* and go home.
13:47 He made them *l* the city,
2Mc 2:28 while we *l* the responsibility for exact
4:34 of his suspicions, to *l* the sanctuary.
6:28 and I will *l* to the young a noble example
12:18 except to *l* behind in one place
Jb 16: 6 if I *l* off,
39: 4 thrive and grow, they *l* and do not return.
39:11 and *l* to him the fruits of your toil?
Ps(s) 37: 7 *L* it to the LORD,
37:33 The LORD will not *l* him in his power nor
119:121 *l* me not to my oppressors.
124: 6 who did not *l* us a prey to their teeth.
Prv 2:13 Who *l* the straight paths to walk in the
3: 3 Let not kindness and fidelity *l* you;
Eccl 2:18 *l* them to a man who is to come after me.
2:21 labored over it, he must *l* his property.
Wis 2: 9 let us *l* tokens of our rejoicing,
7: 6 and in one same way they *l* it.
8:13 *l* to those after me an everlasting memory.

LEAVE (cont.)

Sir 14:15 Will you not *l* your riches to others,
16:13 just man's hope God does not *l* unfulfilled.
23:26 She will *l* an accursed memory;
30:12 disobey you, and *l* you disconsolate.
32:11 When it is time to *l*,
38:12 Then give the doctor his place lest he *l*;
Is 10: 3 Where will you *l* your wealth,
29:21 and *l* the just man with an empty claim.
52:12 you come out, nor *l* in headlong flight,
54:10 *l* their place and the hills be shaken,
54:10 *l* you nor my covenant of peace be shaken,
59:21 into your mouth Shall never *l* your mouth,
65:15 and the name you *l* Shall be used by my
Jer 1:17 though I would *l* you crushed before them;
9: 1 I might *l* my people and depart from them.
9:18 We must *l* the land,
10:17 Lift your bundle and *l* the land,
16:21 this time I will *l* them in no doubt Of my
17:19 where the kings of Judah enter and *l*,
27:11 him I will *l* in peace on its own land,
37: 9 *l* you for good, because they shall not leave!
44: 7 and not *l* yourselves even a remnant?
45: 5 LORD, but your life I will *l* you as booty,
48:28 *L* the cities, dwell in the crags,
48:35 I will *l* no one in Moab,
49: 9 came upon you, they would *l* no gleanings;
49:11 *L* your orphans behind,
49:30 *l* your homes,
50: 8 from Babylon, *l* the land of the Chaldeans,
50:26 in heaps and doom it, *l* not a remnant.
51: 9 *L* her, let us go, each to his own land."
51:45 *L* her, my people, let each one save himself
Ez 10:16 even then the wheels did not *l* their sides.
12:16 I will *l* a few of them to escape the sword,
21: 9 Thus my sword shall *l* its sheath against
21:32 Twisted, twisted, twisted will I *l* it;
23:25 I will *l* it to them to judge,
26: 4 the ground from her and *l* her a bare rock;
32: 4 I will *l* you on the land;
32: 5 I will *l* your flesh on the mountains,
35: 9 and *l* your cities without inhabitants;
36:20 of the LORD, yet they had to *l* their land."
42:14 they shall not *l* the holy place for the
44: 3 of the gate, and *l* by the same way.
44:19 *l* them in the chambers of the sanctuary,
45: 8 but will *l* the land to the house of Israel
46: 2 at the threshold of the gate and then *l*;
46: 9 north gate they shall *l* by the south gate,
46: 9 south gate they shall *l* by the north gate;
46: 9 but he shall *l* by the opposite gate.
46:10 they enter, and he shall also *l* with them.
46:12 then he shall *l*,
Dn 4:12 But *l* in the earth its stump and roots,
4:20 it, but *l* in the earth its stump and roots,
10:20 When I *l*, the prince of Greece will come;
14:11 of Bel said, "See, we are going to *l*.
Hos 13:15 dry up his spring, and *l* his fountain dry.
Jl 2:14 again relent and *l* behind him a blessing.
4:21 their blood, and not *l* it unpunished.
Ob 1: 5 to you, would they not *l* some gleanings?
Mi 6:14 satisfied, food that will *l* you empty;
Zep 2: 5 and *l* you to perish without an inhabitant!
3:12 But I will *l* as a remnant in your midst a
Mt 5:24 against you, *l* your gift at the altar,
8:34 they begged him to *l* their neighborhood.
9:24 crowd who were making a din, he said, *L*,
10:11 you come to and stay with him until you *l*.
10:14 what you have to say, *l* that house or town,
17:21 kind does not *l* but by prayer and fasting.]"
18:12 will he not *l* the ninety-nine out on the
19: 5 'For this reason a man shall *l* his father
23:25 and *l* the inside filled with loot and lust!
27:49 Meanwhile the rest said, *L* him alone.
Mk 6:10 in, stay there until you *l* the locality.
6:11 feet in testimony against them as you *l*."
6:46 When he had taken *l* of them,
10: 7 for this reason a man shall *l* his father
Lk 4:34 *L* us alone!
4:36 with authority and power, and they *l*."
5: 8 fell at the knees of Jesus saying, *L* me,
8:37 asked Jesus to *l* their neighborhood,
9: 5 *l* that town and shake its dust from your
9:61 first let me take *l* of my people at home."
11: 7 he from inside should reply, *L* me alone.
13: 8 the man said, 'Sir, *l* it another year,
13:31 *L* this place!
15: 4 does not *l* the ninety-nine in the
19:44 and *l* not a stone on a stone within you,
21:37 and *l* the city to spend the night on the
Jn 6:67 to the Twelve, "Do you want to *l* me too?"
7: 3 "You ought to *l* here and go to Judea so
12: 7 To this Jesus replied: "*L* her alone.
14:18 I will not *l* you orphaned;
Acts 1: 4 with them, he told them not to *l* Jerusalem:
7: 3 to him, *L* your country and your kinsfolk,
16:39 out with the request that they *l* the city.
18: 2 of Claudius had ordered all Jews to *l* Rome.
18:18 *l* of the brothers and sailed for Syria,
20: 7 Because he intended to *l* the next day,
21: 1 When we had finally taken *l* of them,
22:18 *L* Jerusalem at once because they will not
23:23 to *l* for Caesarea by nine o'clock tonight,
28:25 among themselves, they began to *l*.
Rom 5: 5 And this hope will not *l* us disappointed,
12:19 *l* that to God's wrath,
1Cor 5:10 avoid them, you would have to *l* the world!
12: 1 *l* you in ignorance about spiritual gifts.
2Cor 1: 8 we do not wish to *l* you in the dark about
12: 8 I begged the Lord that this might *l* me.
Eph 5:31 reason a man shall *l* his father and mother,
2Tm 4:20 while Trophimus I had to *l* ill at Miletus.
1Jn 2:19 was from our ranks that they took their *l*—
Rv 3:12 temple of my God and he shall never *l* it.
17:16 will strip off her finery and *l* her naked;

LEAVEN (8)

Gn 19: 3 a meal for them, baking cakes without *l*,
Ex 12:15 you shall have your houses clear of all *l*.
12:19 days no *l* may be found in your houses.
13: 3 Nothing made with *l* must be eaten.
13: 7 no *l* and nothing leavened may be found in
Lv 2:11 any *l* or honey as an oblation to the LORD.
6:10 It shall not be baked with *l*.
23:17 of an ephah of fine flour and baked with *l*.

LEAVENED (12)

Ex 12:15 Whoever eats *l* bread from the first day to
12:19 who eats *l* food shall be cut off from the
12:20 Nothing *l* may you eat;
12:34 took their dough before it was *l*,
12:39 they had brought out of Egypt was not *l*,
13: 7 *l* may be found in all your territory.
23:18 the blood of my sacrifice with *l* bread;
34:25 me the blood of sacrifice with *l* bread,
Lv 7:13 offering shall also include loaves of *l* bread
Dt 16: 3 You shall not eat *l* bread with it.
16: 4 Nothing *l* may be found in all your
Am 4: 5 Burn *l* food as a thanksgiving sacrifice,

LEAVES (46)

Gn 2:24 That is why a man *l* his father and mother
3: 7 so they sewed fig *l* together and made
Ex 28:35 and *l* the LORD's presence in the sanctuary;
Lv 26:36 fainthearted that, if *l* rustle behind them,
Nm 35:26 If the homicide of his own accord *l* the
Jdt 15:13 themselves with garlands of olive *l*.
2Mc 10: 7 Carrying rods entwined with *l*,
Jb 12:18 *l* but a waistcloth to bind the king's
14:10 But when a man dies, all vigor *l* him;
39:14 When she *l* her eggs on the ground and
41:24 Behind him he *l* a shining path;
Ps(s) 1: 3 in due season, and whose *l* never fade.
41: 7 when he *l* he gives voice to it outside.
83:14 O my God, make them like *l* in a whirlwind,
Prv 11:28 fall, but like green *l* the just flourish.
13:22 The good man *l* an inheritance to his
28: 3 is like a devastating rain that *l* no food.
Sir 6: 3 Your *l* it will eat,
11:19 will be till he dies and *l* them to others.
14:18 As with the *l* that grow on a vigorous tree:
30: 4 since he *l* after him one like himself,
30: 6 The avenger he *l* against his foes,
40: 1 From the day one *l* his mother's womb to
40:26 Fear of the LORD *l* nothing wanting;
Is 1:30 shall become like a tree with falling *l*,
6:13 whose trunk remains when its *l* have fallen.
64: 5 We have all withered like *l*,
Jer 17: 8 the heat when it comes, its *l* stay green;
21: 9 But whoever *l* and surrenders to the
25:38 The lion *l* his lair,
Lam 3:20 over and over *l* my soul downcast within me.
Ez 41:24 two movable *l*; two leaves were on one
47:12 their *l* shall not fade,
47:12 serve for food, and their *l* for medicine."
Dn 4: 9 *l* were beautiful and its fruit abundant,
4:11 strip off its *l* and scatter its fruit;
Na 1: 3 and the LORD never *l* the guilty unpunished.
1: 4 He rebukes the sea and *l* it dry,
Mt 21:19 to it, but found nothing there except *l*.
24:32 When its branch grows tender and sprouts *l*,
Mk 11:13 When he reached it he found nothing but *l*;
13:28 runs high and it begins to sprout *l*,
13:34 *l* home and places his servants in charge,
1Cor 9:25 do this to win a crown of *l* that withers,
Rv 22: 2 their *l* serve as medicine for the nations.

LEAVING (72)

Gn 31:33 *L* Leah's tent, he went into Rachel's.
39:12 But *l* the cloak in her hand,
Ex 14:19 The column of cloud also, *l* the front,
Lv 26:33 *l* your countryside desolate and your
Nm 9:12 and not *l* any of it over till morning,
27: 3 he died for his own sin without *l* any sons.
27: 8 If a man dies without *l* a son,
Dt 24: 2 if on *l* his house she goes and becomes the
Jos 10:28 and on every person in it, *l* no survivors.
10:30 with every person there, *l* no survivors.
10:33 him and his people, *l* him no survivors.
10:37 and every person there, *l* no survivors.
10:39 doom on every person there, *l* no survivors.
11: 8 They struck them all down, *l* no survivors.
11:14 the last of them, *l* none alive.
16: 2 *L* Bethel for Luz,
Jgs 6: 4 of Gaza, *l* no sustenance in Israel,
1Sm 2:20 and his wife, as they were *l* for home.
1Kgs 15:29 not *l* a single soul to Jeroboam but
2Kgs 10:11 intimates, and priests, *l* him no survivor.
1Chr 23:22 Eleazar died *l* no sons,
24: 2 Abihu died before their father, *l* no sons;
2Chr 24:25 from him, *l* him in grievous suffering,
Tb 2: 4 sprang to my feet, *l* the dinner untouched;
Jdt 7:13 there to guard against anyone's *l* the city.
1Mc 1:18 his presence and fled, *l* many casualties.
2:28 *l* behind in the city all their possessions.
7:20 over to Alcimus, *l* troops to help him,
9:65 *L* his brother Simon in the city,
11:64 them, *l* his brother Simon in the province.
2Mc 4:31 haste to settle the affair, *l* Andronicus,
6:31 *l* in his death a model of courage and an
13:14 *L* the outcome to the Creator of the world,
Ps(s) 49:11 stupid pass away, *l* to others their wealth.
Is 45: 1 doors before him and *l* the gates unbarred:
Jer 3: 1 man sends away his wife and, after *l* him,
36:20 *L* the scroll in safekeeping in the room of
39: 4 *l* the city on the Royal Garden Road
Ez 16:39 your splendid ornaments, *l* you stark naked.
23:29 you have worked for and *l* you stark naked,
39:28 on their land, not *l* any of them behind.
Dn 2:35 the wind blew them away without *l* a trace.
Hos 2: 5 naked, *l* her as on the day of her birth;
Mal 3:19 on fire, *l* them neither root nor branch,
3:24 on fire, *l* them neither root nor branch,
Mt 9:32 As they were *l*, suddenly some people
13: 1 That same day, on *l* the house,
20:29 were *l* Jericho a large crowd followed him,
Mk 1:29 Immediately upon *l* the synagogue,
4:36 *L* the crowd, they took him away
6:33 People saw them *l*,
6:54 As they were *l* the boat people immediately
10:46 and as he was *l* that place with his
11:12 when they were *l* Bethany he felt hungry.
12:19 brother dies *l* a wife but no child,
12:20 eldest took a wife and died, *l* no children.
Lk 4:38 *L* the synagogue, he entered the house
4:42 him they tried to keep him from *l* them.
5:28 *L* everything behind,
9:33 When these were *l*, Peter said to Jesus:
10:30 him, and then went off *l* him half-dead.
20:28 a man's brother dies *l* a wife and no child,
20:31 All seven died without *l* her any children.
Jn 10:12 *l* the sheep to be snatched and scattered
16:28 Now I am *l* the world to go to the Father."
16:32 and each will go his way, *l* me quite alone.
Acts 13:42 As they were *l*, the people invited them
14:19 him out of the town, *l* him there for dead.
23:32 *l* it to the cavalry to go on with him.
Rom 15:25 Just now I am *l* for Jerusalem to bring
2Cor 11:28 *L* other sufferings unmentioned,
Ti 1: 5 My purpose in *l* you in Crete was that you

LEAVINGS (2)

Mt 15:27 the *l* that fall from their masters' tables."
Mk 7:28 dogs under the table eat the family's *l*."

LEBANA (1)

Neh 7:48 sons of Sia, sons of Padon, sons of *L*,

LEBANAH (1)

Ezr 2:45 sons of Siaha, sons of Padon, sons of *L*,

LEBANON (74)

Dt 1: 7 to *L*,
3:25 Jordan, this fine hill country, and the *L*!'
11:24 from the desert and from *L*,
Jos 1: 4 from the desert and from *L* east to the
9: 1 the coast of the Great Sea as far as *L*:
11:17 the *L* valley at the foot of Mount Hermon.
12: 7 from Baalgad in the *L* valley to Mount
13: 5 and all the *L* on the east,
13: 6 regions between *L* and Misrephoth-maim;
Jgs 3: 3 mountain region of *L* between Baal-hermon
9:15 the buckthorn and devour the cedars of *L*.'
1Kgs 5:13 on *L* to the hyssop growing out of the wall,
5:20 to have cedars from the *L* cut down for me.
5:23 bring them down from the *L* to the sea,
5:28 the *L* each month in relays often thousand,
5:28 one month in the *L* and two months at home.
7: 2 the Forest of *L* one hundred cubits long,
9:19 should be built in Jerusalem, in *L*,
10:17 he put them in the hall of the Forest of *L*.
10:21 hall of the Forest of *L* were of pure gold.
2Kgs 14: 9 of *L* sent word to the cedar of Lebanon,
14: 9 but an animal of *L* passed by and trampled
19:23 the mountain heights, the recesses of *L*;
2Chr 2: 7 cedar, cypress and cabinet wood from *L*,
2: 7 servants know how to cut the wood of the *L*.
2:15 For our part, we will cut trees on *L*,
8: 6 should be built in Jerusalem, in the *L*,
9:16 king put in the hall of the Forest of *L*.
9:20 hall of the Forest of *L* were of pure gold;
25:18 *L* sent a message to the cedar of the *L*
25:18 *L* passed by and trampled the thistle down.
Ezr 3: 7 trees from the *L* to the port of Joppa,
Jdt 1: 7 Cilicia and Damascus, *L* and Anti-Lebanon,

Ps(s) 29: 5 cedars, the LORD breaks the cedars of L.
29: 6 He makes L leap like a calf and Sirion
72:16 mountains the crops shall rustle like L;
92:13 palm tree, like a cedar of L shall he grow.
104:16 the trees of the LORD, the cedars of L,
Sg 3: 9 made himself a carriage of wood from L.
4: 8 Come from Lebanon, my bride, come from L,
4:11 of your garments is the fragrance of L.
4:15 a well of water flowing fresh from L.
5:15 His stature is like the trees on L,
7: 5 the tower on L that looks toward Damascus.
Sir 24:13 "Like a cedar on L I am raised aloft,
50: 8 Like the trees of L in summer,
50:12 a garland, like a stand of cedars on L;
Is 2:13 the cedars of L and all the oaks of Bashan,
10:34 with the axe, and L in its splendor falls.
14: 8 rejoice over you, and the cedars of L:
29:17 and L shall be changed into an orchard,
33: 9 in mourning, L withers with shame;
35: 2 The glory of L will be given to them,
37:24 the mountain heights, the recesses of L;
40:16 L would not suffice for fuel,
60:13 The glory of L shall come to you:
Jer 18:14 the snow of L desert the rocky heights?
22: 6 be to me like Gilead, like the peak of L,
22:20 Scale L and cry out,
22:23 You who dwell on L,
Ez 17: 3 with thick plumage, many-hued, came to L.
27: 5 Cedar from L they took to make you a mast;
31: 3 Behold, a cypress [cedar] in L,
31:15 I cast gloom over L because of him,
Hos 14: 6 He shall strike root like the L cedar,
14: 7 tree and his fragrance like the L cedar.
14: 8 and his fame shall be like the wine of L.
Na 1: 4 and Carmel, and the bloom of L fades;
Hb 2:17 For the violence done to L shall cover you,.
Zec 10:10 I will bring them into Gilead and into L,
11: 1 Open your doors, O L,

LEBANON'S (1)

Ez 31:16 trees were consoled, L choice and best,

LEBAOTH (1)

Jos 15:32 Hormah, Ziklag, Madmannah, Sansannah, L,

LEBONAH (1)

Jgs 21:19 up from Bethel to Shechem, and south of L.

LECAH (1)

1Chr 4:21 Er, the father of L;

LECHEROUS (1)

Sir 25: 2 dissembler, and an old man l in his dotage.

LECHERS (1)

Ez 23:20 She lusted for the l of Egypt,

LECTURE (1)

Acts 19: 9 from day to day in the l hall of Tyrannus.

LECTURES (1)

Jn 9:34 from your birth, and you are giving us l?"

LED (216)

Gn 6:12 all mortals l depraved lives on earth,
19:16 and l them to safety outside the city.
24:27 the LORD has l me straight to the house of
24:48 who had l me on the right road to obtain
43:18 But on being l to his house,
43:23 With that, he l Simeon out to them.
48:13 hand, to Israel's right, and l them to him.
Ex 12:42 as he l them out of the land of Egypt;
15:13 your mercy you l the people you redeemed;
15:21 dancing, and she l them in the refrain:
15:22 Moses l Israel forward from the Red Sea,
19:17 l the people out of the camp to meet God,
Lv 16:21 have it l into the desert by an attendant.
16:26 "The man who has l away the goat for
22:33 sacred and l you out of the land of Egypt,
23:43 l the Israelites out of the land of Egypt,
Nm 15:36 So the whole community l him outside the
16:13 Are you not satisfied with having l us
19: 3 to be l outside the camp and slaughtered
20:16 and sent an angel who l us out of Egypt.
32:17 until we have l them to their destination.
Dt 4:19 do not be l astray into adoring them and
4:20 has taken and l out of that iron foundry,
4:37 l you out of Egypt by his great power,
13:14 have l astray the inhabitants of their city
29: 4 'I l you for forty years in the desert.
30:17 l astray and adore and serve other gods,
Jos 2: 6 Now, she had l them to the roof,
6:23 Her entire family they l forth and placed
7:24 and l them off to the Valley of Achor.
8:11 When all the troops he l were drawn up in
24: 3 l him through the entire land of Canaan.
24: 6 Afterward I l you out of Egypt,
Jgs 2: 1 l you into the land which I promised
2:12 who had l them out of the land of Egypt,
6: 8 I l you up from Egypt;
6:29 l them to the conclusion that Gideon,
7: 5 Gideon l the soldiers down to the water,
19:21 So he l them to his house and provided
20:32 the highways, of which the one l to Bethel,
1Sm 18:13 l the people on their military expeditions,
18:16 him, since he l them on their expeditions.
2Sm 5: 2 l the Israelites out and brought them back.
7: 6 which I l the Israelites out of Egypt
7:23 like your people Israel, which God has l,
12:31 the city, and also l away the inhabitants,
1Kgs 6: 8 landings l up to the middle story
12:30 This l to sin,
21:13 And they l him out of the city and stoned
2Kgs 6:19 And he l them to Samaria.
11:12 Then Jehoiada l out the king's son and put
11:16 She was l out forcibly to the horse gate
11:19 l the king down from the temple of the
12:19 who then l his forces away from Jerusalem.
21:11 him, and has l Judah into sin by his idols,
24:15 and also l captive from Jerusalem to
24:16 The king of Babylon also l captive to
25:11 l into exile the last of the people
1Chr 8: 7 The last, who l them into exile,
11: 2 it was you who l Israel in all its battles.
15:21 l the chant on lyres set to "the eighth."
17: 5 from the time when I l Israel onward,
20: 1 go to war, Joab l the army out in force,
2Chr 21:11 he l the inhabitants of Jerusalem into
21:13 l Judah and the inhabitants of Jerusalem
23:20 and l the king out of the LORD's house.
25:12 whom they l to the summit of the Rock and
29:23 were l before the king and the assembly,
32:30 l it underground westward to the City
Ezr 5:12 house and l the people captive to Babylon.
Neh 9:12 With a column of cloud you l them by day,
11:17 psalms, who l the thanksgiving at prayer;
Tb 8: 1 the dining room and l him into the bedroom.
12: 3 He l me back safe and sound;
14: 4 and l away into exile from the Good Land.
14: 6 which have deceitfully l them into error,
14:15 king of Media, l them captive into Media.
Jdt 5:14 and l them along the route to Sinai and
6:11 From there they l him into the mountain
7: 6 On the second day Holofernes l out all his
12: 5 servants of Holofernes l her into the tent,
15:13 the people, she l the women in the dance,
15:14 l all Israel in this song of thanksgiving,
Est 2:16 Esther was l to King Ahasuerus in his
1Mc 5:29 He l his army from that place by night,
7: 5 They were l by Alcimus,
2Mc 2: 2 the Lord or be l astray in their thoughts,
4:22 this, he l his army into Phoenicia.
4:38 and had him l through the whole city to
6:25 of life, they would be l astray by me,
10:29 golden-bridled horses, who l the Jews on.
13: 2 They l a Greek army of one hundred and ten
14: 6 called Hasideans, l by Judas Maccabeus,
Ps(s) 42: 5 l them in procession to the house of God,
66:12 but you have l us out to refreshment.
77:21 You l your people like a flock under the
78:14 He l them with a cloud by day,
78:52 But his people he l forth like sheep and
78:53 He l them on secure and unafraid,
81:11 God who l you forth from the land of Egypt;
105:37 he l them forth laden with silver and gold,
105:43 And he l forth his people with joy;
106: 9 and he l them through the deep as through
107: 7 And he l them by a direct way to reach an
107:14 And he l them forth from darkness and
136:14 And l Israel through its midst,
136:16 Who l his people through the wilderness,
Prv 7:22 like an ox that is l to slaughter;
Sir 31: 5 he who pursues wealth is l astray by it.
34: 7 For dreams have l many astray,
45: 5 hear his voice, and l him into the cloud,
47:23 the sinner who l Israel into sin,
48:18 l an invasion and sent his adjutant;
Is 9:15 them and those to be l are engulfed.
19:13 chiefs of her tribes have l Egypt astray,
28: 7 L astray by strong drink,
47:10 wisdom and your knowledge l you astray,
48:21 thirst when he l them through dry lands;
53: 7 Like a lamb l to the slaughter or a sheep
63:13 Who l them without stumbling through the
63:14 Thus you l your people,
Jer 2: 6 land of Egypt, Who l us through the desert,
11:19 Yet I, like a trusting lamb l to slaughter,
13:17 for the LORD's flock, l away to exile.
23:13 by Baal and l my people Israel astray.
38:23 and sons shall be l forth to the Chaldeans,
40: 7 poor who had not been l captive to Babylon,
41:10 l away the remnant of the people left in
52:15 l into exile the rest of the people left
52:28 people whom Nebuchadnezzar l away captive:
Lam 3: 2 he has l and forced to walk in darkness,
Bar 1:19 From the time the Lord l our fathers out
1:20 at the time he l our fathers forth from
2:11 you who l your people out of the land of
4:16 have l away this widow's cherished sons,
5: 6 L away on foot by their enemies they left
6: 1 were being l captive to Babylon by the king
6: 1 l captive to Babylon by Nebuchadnezzar,
Ez 13:10 very reason that they l my people astray,
20:10 Therefore I l them out of the land of
29:18 has l his army in an exhausting campaign
29:18 from Tyre for the campaign he l against it.
37: 1 and he l me out in the spirit of the LORD
40:22 Seven steps l up to it,
40:24 Then he l me south,
40:44 He then l me to the inner court where
40:49 ten steps l up to it,
41: 7 that l upward to the side chambers,
42: 1 Then he l me north to the outer court,
42:12 of the way which l to the back wall,
43: 1 he l me to the gate which faces the east,
46:21 Then he l me into the outer court and had
47: 2 He l me outside by the north gate,
Dn 9:15 who l your people out of the land of Egypt
13:45 As she was being l to execution,
Hos 4:12 the spirit of harlotry has l them astray;
Am 2: 4 their fathers followed have l them astray,
2:10 l you through the desert for forty years,
5: 5 For Gilgal shall be l into exile,
9: 4 they are l into captivity by their enemies,
Na 2: 8 shudders, Its mistress is l forth captive,
Mt 4: 1 Then Jesus was l into the desert by the
17: 1 l them up on a high mountain by themselves.
26:57 l him off to Caiaphas the high priest,
27: 2 They bound him and l him away to be handed
27:31 own clothes, and l him off to crucifixion.
Mk 1: 4 which l to the forgiveness of sins.
8:23 man's hand and l him outside the village.
9: 2 with him and l them up a high mountain.
14:53 Then they l Jesus off to the high priest,
15: 1 They bound Jesus, l him away,
15:16 The soldiers now l Jesus away into the
15:20 own clothes, and l him out to crucify him.
Lk 3: 3 which l to the forgiveness of sins,
4: 9 Then the devil l him to Jerusalem,
19:35 Then they l the animal to Jesus,
21:24 be l captive in the midst of the Gentiles.
22:47 a crowd came, l by the man named Judas,
22:54 They l him away under arrest and brought
23: 1 assembly rose up and l him before Pilate.
23:26 As they l him away,
23:32 were l along with him to be crucified.
24:50 Then he l them out near Bethany,
Jn 7:25 This l some of the people of Jerusalem to
8: 3 The scribes and the Pharisees l a woman
18:13 They l him first to Annas,
19:16 Jesus was l away,
Acts 5:19 opened the gates of the jail, l them forth,
5:27 When they had l them in and made them
6:12 seized him, and l him off to the Sanhedrin.
7:36 It was he who l them forth,
8:32 "Like a sheep he was l to the slaughter,
13:17 an outstretched arm he l them out of it.
16:30 a brief interval he l them out and said,
16:34 He l them up into his house,
17:19 Then they l him off
18: 4 Paul l discussions in which he persuaded
21:34 ordered Paul to be l away to headquarters.
21:37 was about to be l into the headquarters,
21:38 l a band of four thousand cutthroats out
22:11 hand and l into Damascus by my companions.
23:18 him in charge and l him to the commander,
26: 4 and the life I have l among my own people
Rom 7:10 should have l to life brought me death.
8:14 are l by the Spirit of God are sons of God.
1Cor 12: 2 pagans you were l astray to mute idols,
15:33 Do not be l astray any longer.
2Cor 7: 9 but because your sadness l to repentance.
1Tm 2:14 was she who was l astray and fell into sin.
Heb 3:16 it not all whom Moses had l out of Egypt?
4: 8 Joshua had l them into the place of rest,
2Pt 3:17 you be l astray by the error of the wicked,
Rv 13:14 beast, it l astray the earth's inhabitants,
18:23 you l all nations astray by your sorcery.
19:20 presence the prodigies that l men astray,
20:10 The devil who l them astray was hurled

LEDGE (7)

Ez 43:14 cubits high, and this l was one cubit deep;
43:14 ledge it was four cubits high, and this l
43:17 The upper l was also a square:
43:17 The lower l, likewise a square,
43:20 altar, and on the four corners of the l,
45:19 on the four corners of the l of the altar,

LEDGES (1)

Ez 40:43 The l, a handbreadth wide, were set

LEE (1)

Acts 27:16 We passed under the l of a small island

LEECH (1)

Prv 30:15 The two daughters of the l are,

LEEKS (1)

Nm 11: 5 and the cucumbers, the melons, the l,

LEES (2)

Jer 48:11 from his youth, has rested upon his *l*;
Zep 1:12 punish the men who thicken on their *l*,

LEFT (524)

Gn 4:16 Cain then *l* the LORD's presence and
7:23 Noah and those with him in the ark were *l*.
8:19 creeping creatures of the earth *l* the ark,
12: 4 was seventy-five years old when he *l* Haran.
13: 9 If you prefer the *l*,
13: 9 you prefer the right, I will go to the *l*."
13:14 After Lot had *l*, the LORD said to Abram:
21:32 *l* and returned to the land of the
23: 3 Then he *l* the side of his dead one and
26:17 Isaac *l* there and made the Wadi Gerar his
27:30 Jacob had scarcely *l* his father,
29: 7 "There is still much daylight *l*;
30:35 these he *l* . . .
32:25 his possessions, Jacob was *l* there alone.
32:32 At sunrise, as he *l* Penuel,
34:26 they took Dinah from Shechem's house and *l*.
39: 6 *l* everything he owned in Joseph's charge,
39:13 *l* his cloak in her hand as he fled outside,
39:15 *l* his cloak beside me and ran away outside."
39:18 he *l* his cloak beside me and fled outside."
41:46 After Joseph *l* Pharaoh's presence,
42:38 full brother is dead, he is the only one *l*.
44:20 he is the only one by that mother who is *l*,
45:25 So they *l* Egypt and made their way to
47:18 there is nothing *l* to put at my lord's
48:13 to Israel's *l*, and Manasseh with his left
48:14 and his *l* hand on the head of Manasseh,
50: 7 So Joseph *l* to bury his father;
50: 8 and herds were *l* in the region of Goshen.
Ex 5:20 *l* Pharaoh and came upon Moses and Aaron,
8: 5 and your houses and be *l* only in the river."
8: 7 only in the river shall they be *l*."
8: 8 After Moses and Aaron *l* Pharaoh's presence,
8:26 " When Moses *l* Pharaoh's presence,
9:21 *l* their servants and livestock in the fields.
9:33 When Moses had *l* Pharaoh's presence and
10: 6 With that he turned and *l* Pharaoh.
10:12 the vegetation and whatever the hail has *l*."
10:15 Nothing green was *l* on any tree or plant
10:18 When Moses *l* the presence of Pharaoh,
10:26 Not an animal must be *l* behind.
11: 8 that he *l* Pharaoh's presence in hot anger.
12:10 *l* over in the morning shall be burned up.
12:41 LORD *l* the land of Egypt on this very date.
13:22 ever *l* its place in front of the people.
14:22 like a wall to their right and to their *l*.
14:29 like a wall to their right and to their *l*.
16:23 is *l* put away and keep for the morrow."
26:13 extra cubit's length to be *l* hanging down
35:20 Israelite community *l* Moses' presence,
36: 4 sanctuary, all *l* the work they were doing,
Lv 5:23 retained by him or the deposit *l* with him
7:16 is *l* over may be eaten on the next day.
7:17 the sacrifice be *l* over on the third day,
8:32 What is *l* over of the flesh and bread you
10:12 *l* over from the oblations of the LORD,
13:58 washing, the infection has *l* the garment,
14:15 some of it into the palm of his own *l* hand;
14:17 Of the oil *l* in his hand the priest shall
14:26 into the palm of his own *l* hand
19: 6 Whatever is *l* over until the third day
22:30 of it shall be *l* over until the next day.
25:52 years there are *l* before the jubilee year,
27:18 of years *l* until the next jubilee year,
Nm 3: 4 in the presence of the LORD, and *l* no sons.
3:49 silver as ransom from those who were *l*
11:26 the gathering but had been *l* in the camp.
14: 9 Their defense has *l* them,
14:44 covenant of the LORD nor Moses *l* the camp.
20:17 without turning to the right or the *l*,
21:35 people, until not a survivor was *l* to him,
22: 7 Then the elders of Moab and of Midian *l*
22:26 to move either to the right or to the *l*.
24:18 dispossessed, and no fugitive is *l* in Seir.
25: 7 the priest, saw this, he *l* the assembly,
26:65 and not one of them was *l* except Caleb,
31:32 *l* of the loot which the soldiers had taken,
Dt 2: 8 "Then we *l* behind us
2:27 turning aside to the right or the *l*.
2:34 we *l* no survivor.
3: 3 so completely that we *l* him no survivor.
5:32 turning aside to the right or to the *l*,
9: 7 From the day you *l* the land of Egypt until
16: 3 frightened haste you *l* the land of Egypt.
17:11 *l* from the decision they hand down to you.
17:20 right or to the *l* from these commandments.
23: 5 water on your journey after you *l* Egypt,
24: 9 to Miriam on the journey after you *l* Egypt.
25:17 to you on the journey after you *l* Egypt,
28:14 turning aside to the right or to the *l* from
28:55 when nothing else is *l* him in the straits
28:62 stars in the sky, only a few will be *l*,
Jos 1: 7 from it either to the right or to the *l*,
2: 5 was time for the gate to be shut, they *l*,
2: 7 fords of the Jordan, and once they had *l*,
5: 4 during the journey after they *l* Egypt.
6: 1 Israelites, so that no one *l* or entered.
9:12 as provisions the day we *l* to come to you,
10:40 He *l* no survivors,
11:11 there to the sword, till none was *l* alive.
11:15 He *l* nothing undone that the LORD had
11:22 were *l* in the land of the Israelites.
22: 9 and the half-tribe of Manasseh *l* the other
Jgs 1:16 later *l* and settled among the Amalekites.
2:21 of the nations which Joshua *l* when he died."
3:19 when all his attendants had *l* his presence,
3:21 and then Ehud with his *l* hand drew the
3:24 When Ehud had *l* and the servants came,
5:26 With her *l* hand she reached for the peg,
7: 3 twenty-two thousand of the soldiers *l*,
7:20 They held the torches in their *l* hands,
8:10 all who were *l* of the whole Kedemite army,
9:55 was dead, they all *l* for their homes.
15: 4 So Samson *l* and caught three hundred foxes.
16:19 mistreat him, for his strength had *l* him.
16:20 he did not realize that the LORD had *l* him.
16:29 one at his right hand, the other at his *l*.
18:24 "What is *l* for me?
19: 2 His concubine was unfaithful to him and *l*
21:24 each of them *l* for his own heritage in his
Ru 1: 3 died, and she was *l* with her two sons,
1: 5 and the woman was *l* with neither her two
1: 7 *l* the place where they had been living.
2:11 you have *l* your father and your mother and
2:14 and she ate her fill and had some *l* over.
2:18 gave her what she had *l* over from lunch.
3:15 her lift the bundle, and *l* for the city.
1Sm 1: 6 to her that the LORD had *l* her barren.
1:18 kindly of your maidservant," and *l*.
1:28 She *l* him there;
2:36 Then whoever is *l* of your family will come
6:12 as they went, without turning right or *l*.
11:11 so scattered that no two were *l* together.
13:17 raiders *l* the camp of the Philistines in
14:26 came to the comb the swarm had *l* it;
15: 6 After the Kenites *l*, Saul routed Amalek
17:20 having *l* the flock with a shepherd,
17:28 you *l* those sheep in the desert meanwhile?
20:41 When the boy had *l*,
22: 4 He *l* them with the king of Moab,
22: 5 David *l* and went to the forest of Hereth.
23:13 *l* Keilah and wandered from place to place.
24: 8 Saul then *l* the cave and went on his way.
25:34 not have had a single man or boy *l* alive."
28:20 Moreover, he had no bodily strength *l*,
28:25 Then they stood up and *l* the same night.
29:11 So David and his men *l* early in the
30: 2 they had carried them off when they *l*.
30:21 and whom he had *l* behind at the Wadi Besor,
2Sm 2:12 Ishbaal, Saul's son, *l* Mahanaim for Gibeon.
2:19 turning neither right nor *l* in his pursuit.
2:21 Abner said to him, "Turn right or *l*;
3:26 Joab then *l* David,
6:19 this, all the people *l* for their homes.
11: 8 Uriah *l* the palace,
13: 9 When they had all *l* him,
15:16 he *l* behind to take care of the palace.
15:17 As the king *l* the city,
16: 6 guard, were on David's right and on his *l*.
16:21 he *l* behind to take care of the palace.
17:21 As soon as they *l*,
17:22 there was no one *l* who had not crossed.
17:23 having *l* orders concerning his family,
19:20 did the day my lord the king *l* Jerusalem.
19:25 day the king *l* until he returned safely.
20: 2 So all the Israelites *l* David for Sheba,
20: 3 he had *l* behind to take care of the palace
24: 4 so they *l* the king's presence in order to
1Kgs 1:49 All the guests of Adonijah *l* in terror,
1:50 Adonijah, in fear of Solomon, also *l*;
2:42 that, if you *l* and went anywhere else,
2:46 of Jehoiada, who struck him dead as he *l*.
5: 7 They *l* nothing unprovided.
7:21 called Jachin, and the other to the *l*,
7:49 and five to the *l* before the sanctuary,
8:10 When the priests *l* the holy place,
9:12 Hiram *l* Tyre to see the cities Solomon had
11:18 They *l* Midian and passing through Paran,
11:29 At that time Jeroboam *l* Jerusalem,
12:25 Then he *l* it and built up Penuel.
15:21 heard of it, he *l* off fortifying Ramah,
17: 5 So he *l* and did as the LORD had commanded.
17:10 He *l* and went to Zarephath.
17:11 She *l* to get it,
17:15 She *l* and did as Elijah had said.
19: 3 He *l* his servant there and went a day's
19:10 I alone am *l*,
19:14 I alone am *l*,
19:20 Elisha *l* the oxen,
19:21 Elisha *l* him and,
19:21 he *l* and followed Elijah as his attendant.
20: 9 The couriers *l* and reported this.
22:19 standing by to his right and to his *l*.
22:24 of the LORD, then *l* me to speak with you?"
2Kgs 1:16 So Elijah *l* and went down with him and
3:25 Kirhareseth was *l* behind its stone walls,
4: 6 "There is none *l*," he answered her.
4:37 then she took her son and *l* the room.
4:43 shall eat and there shall be some *l* over.' "
4:44 when they had eaten, there was some *l* over,
5:12 With this, he turned about in anger and *l*.
5:27 And Gehazi *l* Elisha,
7: 5 At twilight they *l* for the Arameans;
7:10 and the tents just as they were *l*."
7:12 have *l* their camp to hide in the field,
7:13 "Since those who are *l* in the city are no
8: 6 from the day she *l* the land until now."
8:14 Hazael *l* Elisha and returned to his master.
10:11 were *l* of the family of Ahab in Jezreel,
10:15 When he had *l* there,
13: 3 a long time *l* them in the power of Hazael,
13: 7 No soldiers were *l* to Jehoahaz,
17:18 Only the tribe of Judah was *l*.
20: 4 Before Isaiah had *l* the central courtyard,
20:17 nothing shall be *l*,
23: 8 city, to the *l* as one enters the city gate.
23:18 So they *l* his bones undisturbed together
24:14 None were *l* among the people of the land
25: 4 Then the king and all the soldiers *l* the
25:12 *l* behind as vinedressers and farmers.
25:26 *l* with the army commanders and went to
1Chr 6:29 brothers, the Merarites, stood at the *l*:
10: 7 in the rout, they *l* their cities and fled;
12: 2 could use either the right or the *l* hand,
14:12 The Philistines had *l* their gods there,
16:37 Then David *l* Asaph and his brethren there
16:38 he also *l* there Obed-edom and sixty-eight
16:39 priestly brethren he *l* before the Dwelling
21:21 Then he *l* the threshing floor and bowed
2Chr 3:17 the right side and the other for the *l*,
3:17 the right Jachin and the one to the *l* Boaz.
4: 6 of them to the right and five to the *l*.
4: 7 nave, five to the right and five to the *l*.
4: 8 nave, five to the right and five to the *l*;
11:14 for the Levites *l* their assigned pasture
16: 5 heard of it, he *l* off fortifying Ramah;
18:18 standing by to his right and to his *l*.
18:23 the LORD go when he *l* me to speak to you?"
21:17 there was *l* to him only one son,
28:14 Therefore the soldiers *l* their captives
30: 6 *l* from the hands of the Assyrian kings.
31:10 eaten to the full and have had much *l* over,
31:10 This great supply is what was *l* over."
34:21 and those who are *l* in Israel and Judah,
Ezr 9: 8 who *l* us a remnant and gave us a stake in
Neh 6: 1 the wall and that there was no breach *l* in
8: 4 and Maaseiah, and on his *l* Pedaiah,
12:38 The second choir proceeded to the *l*,
Tb 1: 8 for when my father died, he *l* me an orphan.
1:20 I was *l* with nothing.
2: 9 Because of the heat I *l* my face uncovered.
2:10 me for two years, until he *l* for Elymais.
4:16 Whatever you have *l* over,
5:10 "What joy is *l* for me any more?
6: 2 When the boy *l* home,
7:17 Courage, my daughter." Then she *l*.
8: 4 When the girl's parents *l* the bedroom and
10: 7 I have already told you how I *l* him."
10:14 When Tobiah *l* Raguel,
11: 1 Then they *l* and began their return journey.
11: 2 "You know how we *l* your father.
Jdt 2:14 So Holofernes *l* the presence of his lord,
6:13 *l* him lying at the foot of the mountain;
7:22 of the city, with no strength *l* in them.
8: 7 Manasseh, had *l* her gold and silver,
12:13 So Bagoas *l* the presence of Holofernes,
13: 2 was *l* alone in the tent with Holofernes,
13: 4 one, small or great, was *l* in the bedroom,
14: 8 *l* till the time she began speaking to them.
15: 7 slaughter took possession of what was *l*.
Est 5: 9 That day Haman *l* happy and in good spirits.
7: 7 The king *l* the banquet in anger and went
E:24 it will be *l* not merely untrodden by men,
8:15 Mordecai *l* the king's presence clothed in
F: 2 not a single detail has been *l* unfulfilled
1Mc 2: 1 Joarib, *l* Jerusalem and settled in Modein.
2:18 and those who are *l* in Jerusalem have done.
3:32 He *l* Lysias, a nobleman of royal blood,
5:18 In Judea he *l* Joseph,
5:46 encircle it on either the right or the *l*;
6: 2 and weapons *l* there by Alexander,
6:36 it moved, they moved too and never *l* it.
6:45 of the phalanx, killing men right and *l*,
7:39 Nicanor *l* Jerusalem and pitched his camp
9:16 But when the men on the *l* wing saw that
10:13 each one of them *l* his place and returned
10:79 *l* a thousand cavalry in hiding behind them.
10:86 *l* there and pitched his camp at Ashkalon,
12:34 He *l* a garrison there to guard it.
13: 4 brothers have perished, and I alone am *l*.
13:22 So he *l* for Gilead.
14:13 No one was *l* to attack them in their land;
15:10 to him, so that few were *l* with Trypho.
15:15 Numenius and his companions *l* Rome with
2Mc 4:29 Menelaus *l* his brother Lysimachus as his
4:29 high priesthood, while Sostratus *l* Crates,
5:22 But he *l* governors to harass the nation:
8:14 But the others sold everything they had *l*,
10:19 a siege, Maccabeus *l* Simon and Joseph,
12:19 men that Timothy had *l* in the stronghold.
13:23 who was *l* in charge of the government in
13:24 He approved of Maccabeus and *l* him as
14:44 as they quickly drew back and *l* an opening,

Jb 8: 4 he has *l* them in the grip of their guilt,
20:22 and nought shall be *l* of his goods.
22: 6 *l* them stripped naked of their clothing.
22:20 where they stood, and such as were *l*,
Ps(s) 80: 7 *l* us to be fought over by our neighbors,
106:11 not one of them was *l*.
143: 3 he has *l* me dwelling in the dark,
Prv 3:16 right hand, in her *l* are riches and honor;
4:27 Turn neither to right nor to *l*,
29:15 a boy *l* to his whims disgraces his mother.
Eccl 8:10 and as they *l* the sacred place,
10: 2 fool's understanding turns him to his *l*.
Sg 2: 6 His *l* hand is under my head and his right
3: 4 I had hardly *l* them when I found him whom
8: 3 His *l* hand is under my head and his right
Wis 10: 8 they *l* mankind a memorial of their folly
14: 6 raft, *l* to the world a future for his race,
Sir 6: 3 destroy, and you will be *l* a dry tree,
22: 9 weep over the fool, for sense has *l* him.
30: 8 a son *l* to himself grows up unruly.
38:23 rally your courage, once the soul has *l*.
44: 8 Some of them have *l* behind a name and men
47:23 father, and *l* behind him one of his sons,
49: 6 the holy city and *l* its streets desolate,
Is 1: 8 Zion is *l* like a hut in a vineyard,
1: 9 LORD of hosts had *l* us a scanty remnant,
4: 3 that is *l* in Jerusalem Will be called holy:
5: 8 *l* to dwell alone in the midst of the land!
9:19 though they eat on the *l*,
10:14 As one takes eggs *l* alone,
11:11 people that is *l* from Assyria and Egypt,
11:16 of his people that is *l* from Assyria,
17: 6 Only a scattering of grapes shall be *l*!
18: 6 all be *l* to the mountain birds of prey,
24: 6 on earth turn pale, and few men are *l*.
24:11 has disappeared and cheer has *l* the land.
28: 8 with filthy vomit, with no place *l* clean.
30:17 are *l* like a flagstaff on the mountaintop,
30:21 you would turn to the right or to the *l*.
30:26 he will heal the bruises *l* by his blows.
37: 8 heard that the king of Assyria had *l* there,
39: 6 nothing shall be *l*,
49:21 I was *l* all alone;
54: 3 spread abroad to the right and to the *l*;
Jer 4: 7 of nations has set out, has *l* his place,
7:25 *l* the land of Egypt even to this day,
10:20 My sons have *l* me, they are no more:
22:11 He has *l* this place never to return.
29: 2 and the skilled workmen had *l* Jerusalem.
34: 7 were *l* of the fortified cities of Judah.
38: 4 the soldiers who are *l* in this city,
38:22 All the women *l* in the house of Judah's
39: 9 the rest of the people *l* in the city,
39:10 were *l* in the land of Judah by Nebuzaradan,
40: 5 and then, before he *l*—
40: 6 with him among the people *l* in the land.
40:11 king of Babylon had *l* a remnant in Judah,
41:10 the people *l* in Mizpah and the princesses,
51:34 Babylon,] he has *l* me as an empty vessel;
52: 7 soldiers took to flight and *l* the city by night
52:15 exile the rest of the people *l* in the city,
52:16 *l* behind as vinedressers and farmers.
Lam 1:13 He *l* me desolate, in pain all the day.
3: 6 He has *l* me to dwell in the dark like
3:11 my ways, set me astray, *l* me desolate.
4:15 If they *l* and wandered among the nations,
Bar 2:13 for we are *l* few in number among the
4:12 the sins of my children I am *l* desolate,
4:16 cherished sons, have *l* me solitary,
4:19 I am *l* desolate.
5: 6 away on foot by their enemies they *l* you:
6:47 They have *l* frauds and opprobrium to their
Ez 1:10 lion, and on the *l* side the face of an ox,
4: 4 Then you shall lie on your *l* side,
9: 8 As they began to strike, I was *l* alone.
9: 8 Will you destroy all that is *l* of Israel
10:18 Then the glory of the LORD *l* the threshold
11:24 Then the vision I had seen *l* me, :
14:22 still some survivors shall be *l* in it who
21:21 to the *l*! wherever your edge is turned.
23:25 what is *l* of you shall fall by the sword.
23:25 what is *l* of you shall be devoured by fire.
24:21 you *l* behind shall fall by the sword.
31:12 cut it down and *l* it on the mountains.
39: 3 I will strike the bow from your *l* hand,
42:14 *l* here the clothing in which they ministered,
47:11 they shall be *l* for salt.
Dn 2: 1 had a dream which *l* his spirit no rest
4:23 *l* means that your kingdom shall be
7: 7 and what was *l* it trampled with its feet.
7:19 and trampling with its feet what was *l*;
10: 8 So I was *l* alone,
10:13 I *l* him there with the prince of the kings
10:16 now no strength or even breath is *l* in me."
12: 7 lifted his right and *l* hands to heaven;
13: 7 When the people *l* at noon,
13:18 they shut the garden doors and *l* by the
13:19 As soon as the maids had *l*,
Hos 9:12 make them childless, till not one is *l*.
Jl 1: 4 What the cutter *l*, the locust swarm has
1: 4 What the locust swarm *l*,
1: 4 And what the grasshopper *l*,
Am 5: 3 a thousand shall be *l* without a hundred,
5: 3 out with a hundred shall be *l* with ten,
6:10 be *l* to carry the dead out of the houses;
9: 1 Those who are *l* I will slay with the sword;
9:12 That they may conquer what is *l* of Edom
Jon 4: 5 *l* the city for a place to the east of it,
4:11 distinguish their right hand from their *l*,
Hg 2: 3 Who is *l* among you that saw this house in
Zec 4: 3 one on the right and the other on the *l*."
7:14 Thus the land was *l* desolate after them
11: 9 that are *l* devour one another's flesh."
12: 6 right and *l* all the surrounding peoples;
13: 8 off and perish and one third shall be *l*.
14:16 All who are *l* of all the nations that came
Mt 2:13 After they had *l*, the angel of the Lord
2:14 and his mother and *l* that night for Egypt.
4:11 At that the devil *l* him,
4:13 He *l* Nazareth and went down to live in
6: 3 *l* hand know what your right hand is doing.
7:28 *l* the crowds spellbound at his teaching.
8:15 took her by the hand and the fever *l* her.
11: 1 he *l* that locality to teach and preach in
12: 9 *l* that place and went into their synagogue.
15:21 Then Jesus *l* that place and withdrew to
15:29 Jesus *l* that place and passed along the
15:37 they gathered up the fragments *l* over,
16: 4 With that he *l* them abruptly.
19: 1 he *l* Galilee and came to the district of
19:15 on their heads before he *l* that place.
20:21 at your right hand and the other at your *l*,
20:23 my right hand or my *l* is not mine to give.
21:17 *l* them and went out of the city to Bethany,
22:22 by this reply, they went off and *l* him.
22:25 had no children, *l* his wife to his brother.
24: 1 Jesus *l* the temple precincts then,
24: 2 you, not one stone will be *l* on another
24:40 one will be taken and one will be *l*.
24:41 one will be taken and one will be *l*.
25:33 on his right hand, the goats on his *l*.
25:41 "Then he will say to those on his *l*:
26:44 He *l* them again,
27: 5 flung the money into the temple and *l*.
27:38 him, one at his right and one at his *l*.
Mk 1:31 and helped her up, and the fever *l* her.
1:42 The leprosy *l* him then and there,
7:29 The demon has already *l* your daughter."
7:31 He then *l* Tyrian territory and returned by
8:13 Then he *l* them,
9:30 They *l* that district and began a journey
10:37 one at your right and the other at your *l*,
10:40 But as for sitting at my right or my *l*,
12:12 Finally they *l* him and went off.
12:19 we were *l* this in writing by Moses:
12:22 none of the seven *l* any children behind.
13: 2 Not one stone will be *l* upon another
14:52 he *l* the cloth behind and ran off naked.
15:27 one at his right and one at his *l*.
Lk 1:38 With that the angel *l* her.
4:13 had finished all the tempting he *l* him,
4:39 himself to the fever, and it *l* her.
4:42 The next morning he *l* the town and set out
5:11 brought their boats to land, *l* everything,
5:13 Immediately the leprosy *l* him.
9:17 What they had *l*, over and above,
10:40 *l* me to do the household tasks all alone?
11:53 After he had *l* this gathering,
17:29 But on the day Lot *l* Sodom,
17:34 one will be taken and the other *l*.
17:35 one will be taken and the other *l*."
18:28 have *l* all we own to become your followers."
18:29 no one who has *l* home or wife or brothers,
21: 6 when not one stone will be *l* on another,
23:33 one on his right and the other on his *l*.
24:51 As he blessed, he *l* them,
Jn 4: 3 *l* Judea and started back for Galilee again.
4:28 *l* her water jar and went off into the town.
4:43 the two days were over, he *l* for Galilee.
4:52 fever *l* him yesterday afternoon about one."
6:12 *l* over so that nothing will go to waste."
6:13 gathered twelve baskets full of pieces *l* over
6:22 Jesus had not *l* in it with his disciples;
8: 9 This *l* him alone with the woman,
12:36 Jesus *l* them and went into hiding.
13:31 Once Judas had *l*, Jesus said:
18:16 while Peter was *l* standing at the gate.
19:31 bodies *l* on the cross during the sabbath,
Acts 5:41 The apostles for their part *l* the
7: 4 So he *l* the land of the Chaldeans and
9:17 With that Ananias *l*.
12:10 alley, when suddenly the angel *l* him.
12:17 then *l* them to go off to another place.
12:19 *l* Judea to spend some time in Caesarea.
13:13 John *l* them and returned to Jerusalem.
14:20 The next day he *l* with Barnabas for Derbe.
16:18 Then and there the spirit *l* her.
17:33 At this point, Paul *l* them.
18: 1 that, Paul *l* Athens and went to Corinth.
18:19 he *l* Priscilla and Aquila behind and
19: 9 of the assembly, Paul simply *l* them.
21: 3 on our *l* as we continued on toward Syria.
24:27 with the Jews, so he *l* Paul in prison.
25:14 he said, "whom Felix *l* behind in custody.
26:31 After they had *l* the chamber,
Rom 9:29 the Lord of hosts had *l* us a remnant,
11: 3 I alone am *l* and they are seeking my life."
11: 4 "I have *l* for myself seven thousand men
2Cor 1: 9 We were *l* to feel like men condemned to
6: 7 of righteousness with right hand and *l*,
Phil 4:15 of my evangelizing, when I *l* Macedonia,
1Tm 5: 5 The real widow, *l* destitute,
2Tm 4:10 world, has *l* me and gone to Thessalonica.
4:13 bring the cloak I *l* in Troas with Carpus,
Ti 1: 5 might accomplish what had been *l* undone,
Heb 2: 8 things to him, God *l* nothing unsubjected.
11:27 By faith he *l* Egypt,
1Pt 2:21 you in just this way and *l* you an example,
Rv 3: 8 that is why I have *l* an open door before
10: 2 foot on the sea and his *l* foot on the land,

LEFT-HANDED (2)

Jgs 3:15 Benjaminite Ehud, son of Gera, who was *l*.
20:16 were seven hundred picked men who were *l*,

LEFTOVERS (2)

Mk 6:43 up enough *l* to fill twelve baskets,
8: 8 they gathered up seven wicker baskets of *l*.

LEG (12)

Ex 25:26 them at the four corners, one at each *l*.
Lv 7:32 priest the right *l* as a raised offering.
7:33 shall have the right *l* as his portion,
7:34 that is waved and the *l* that is raised up,
8:25 with their fat, and likewise the right *l*;
8:26 top of the portions of fat and the right *l*.
10:14 offering and the *l* of the raised offering,
10:15 The *l* of the raised offering and the
Nm 6:20 offering and the *l* of the raised offering.
18:18 right *l* of the wave offering belong to you.
22:25 since she squeezed Balaam's *l* against it,
1Sm 9:24 cook took up the *l* and what went with it,

LEGAL (6)

Nm 27:11 This is the *l* norm for the Israelites,
Est 4: 3 wherever the king's *l* enactment reached,
1Mc 15: 6 own money, as *l* tender in your country.
Acts 22:25 "Is it *l* to flog a Roman citizen without
Gal 2:16 *l* observance but by faith in Jesus Christ,
Phil 3: 5 in *l* observance I was a Pharisee,

LEGALLY (2)

Neh 12:44 *l* assigned to the priests and Levites.
Gal 3:15 or set it aside once it is *l* validated.

LEGATES (1)

2Mc 11:34 Memmius and Titus Manius, *l* of the Romans,

LEGION (3)

Mk 5: 9 *L* is my name," he answered.
5:15 *L* sitting fully clothed and perfectly sane,
Lk 8:30 *L*," he answered,

LEGIONS (1)

Mt 26:53 notice more than twelve *l* of angels?

LEGITIMATE (1)

Prv 12: 5 The plans of the just are *l*;

LEGITIMATELY (1)

2Mc 6:21 his own providing, such as he could *l* eat,

LEGS (22)

Gn 49:10 Judah, or the mace from between his *l*,
Lv 4:11 and all its flesh, with its head, *l*,
9:21 right *l* as a wave offering before the LORD,
11:21 have jointed *l* for leaping on the ground;
11:23 that have four *l* are loathsome for you.
11:42 belly, goes on all fours, or has many *l*,
Dt 28:35 you cannot be cured, on your knees and *l*,
1Kgs 7:33 The four *l* of each stand had cast braces,
Prv 26: 7 of a fool hangs limp, like crippled *l*.
Sg 5:15 His *l* are columns of marble resting on
Sir 21:19 fetters on the *l* is learning to a fool,
Is 7:20 the head, and the hair between the *l*.
47: 2 Strip off your train, bare your *l*,
Ez 1: 7 four wings, and their *l* went straight down;
16:25 spreading your *l* for every passer-by,
Dn 2:33 its belly and thighs bronze, the *l* iron,
Am 3:12 of *l* or the tip of an ear of his sheep,
Hb 3:16 invades my bones, my *l* tremble beneath me.
Jn 19:31 *l* be broken and the bodies be taken away.
19:32 the *l* of the men crucified with Jesus,
19:33 was already dead, they did not break his *l*.
Rv 10: 1 the sun and his *l* like pillars of fire.

LEHABIM (2)

Gn 10:13 father of the Ludim, the Anamim, the *L*,
1Chr 1:11 became the father of the Ludim, Anamim, *L*,

LEHI (5)

Jgs 15: 9 from a camp in Judah, deployed against *L*.
15:14 When he reached *L*,

LEHI (cont.)
15:19 Then God split the cavity in *L*,
15:19 in *L* is called En-hakkore to this day.
2Sm 23:11 The Philistines had assembled at *L*,

LEISURE (1)

1Tm 5:13 Besides, they learn to be ladies of *l*,

LEMA (1)

Mt 27:46 in a loud tone, "Eli, Eli, *l* sabachthani?",

LEMUEL (2)

Prv 31: 1 The words of *L*, king of Massa.
31: 4 It is not for kings, O *L*,

LEND (17)

Ex 22:24 "If you *l* money to one of your poor
Lv 25:37 You are to *l* him neither money at interest
Dt 15: 6 on you today, you will *l* to many nations,
15: 8 and freely *l* him enough to meet his need.
28:12 *l* to many nations and borrow from none.
28:44 He will *l* to you, not you to him.
Sir 8:12 *L* not to one more powerful than yourself;
8:12 and whatever you *l*,
29: 2 *L* to your neighbor in his hour of need,
29: 7 Many refuse to *l*,
Is 63: 5 that there was no one to *l* support;
Jer 15:10 I neither borrow nor *l*, yet all curse me.
Ez 18: 8 he does not *l* at interest nor exact usury;
Lk 6:34 *l* to those from whom you expect repayment,
6:34 Even sinners *l* to sinners,
6:35 *l* without expecting repayment.
11: 5 says to him, 'Friend, *l* me three loaves,

LENDER (3)

Prv 22: 7 and the borrower is the slave of the *l*.
Sir 29: 6 If the *l* is able to recover barely half,
Is 24: 2 buyer as the seller, The *l* as the borrower,

LENDERS (1)

Sir 29: 5 he kisses the *l* hand and speaks with

LENDS (8)

Ps(s) 15: 5 who *l* not his money at usury and
37:26 All the day he is kindly and *l*,
112: 5 Well for the man who is gracious and *l*,
Prv 19:17 has compassion on the poor *l* to the LORD,
Sir 10: 1 wise magistrate *l* stability to his people,
20:14 He *l* today, he asks it back tomorrow;
29: 1 He does a kindness who *l* to his neighbor,
Ez 18:13 things, *l* at interest and exacts usury

LENGTH (55)

Gn 6:15 *l* of the ark shall be three hundred cubits,
13:17 in the land, through its *l* and breadth,
Ex 26: 2 The *l* of each shall be twenty-eight cubits,
26: 8 the *l* of each shall be thirty cubits,
26:13 an extra cubit's *l* to be left hanging down
26:16 The *l* of each board is to be ten cubits,
36: 9 The *l* of each sheet was twenty-eight
36:15 The *l* of each sheet was thirty cubits and
36:21 The *l* of each board was ten cubits,
Lv 19:35 using measures of *l* or weight or capacity.
Dt 2:16 "When at *l* death had put an end to all
4:26 *l* of time but shall be promptly wiped out.
Jgs 4:24 at *l* they destroyed the Canaanite king,
1Sm 20:42 At *l* Jonathan said to David,
28:20 Immediately Saul fell full *l* on the ground,
2Sm 8: 2 for execution, and a full *l* to be spared.
1Kgs 2:11 The *l* of David's reign over Israel was
14:20 *l* of Jeroboam's reign was twenty-two years.
2Kgs 10:36 The *l* of Jehu's reign over Israel in
21:16 as to fill the *l* and breadth of Jerusalem.
2Chr 3: 3 the *l* was sixty cubits according to the
3: 8 *l* corresponded to the width of the house,
3:12 one wing of each cherub, five cubits in *l*,
3:12 the other wing, also five cubits in *l*,
Jdt 1: 2 each three cubits in height and six in *l*.
3: 9 At *l* Holofernes reached Esdraelon in the
7: 3 Balbaim, and in *l* from Bethulia to Cyamon,
2Mc 5: 8 At *l* he met a miserable end.
Jb 12:12 wisdom, and with *l* of days understanding.
Ps(s) 21: 5 you gave him *l* of days forever and ever.
91:16 with *l* of days I will gratify him and
93: 5 befits your house, O LORD, for *l* of days.
Sir 1:10 giving gladness and joy and *l* of days.
1:18 her branches are *l* of days.
16: 3 Count not on their *l* of life,
Bar 3:14 That you may know also where are *l* of days,
Ez 40:15 The *l* of the gate from the front entrance
40:20 north, whose *l* and width he measured.
41: 2 He measured the *l* of the nave,
41:13 and its walls, was a hundred cubits in *l*.
41:15 lay the *l* of the free area and behind it,
42: 2 *l* was a hundred cubits on the north side,
42: 7 *l* before these chambers was fifty cubits,
42: 8 for the *l* of the chambers belonging to the
42: 8 *l* the wall measured one hundred cubits.
45: 7 corresponding in *l* to one of the tribal
Zec 2: 6 how great is its width and how great its *l*."
Mt 4:24 his reputation traveled the *l* of Syria.
13: 3 He addressed them at *l* in parables,
Mk 4: 2 He began to instruct them at great *l*,
6:34 and he began to teach them at great *l*.
Lk 23: 9 He questioned Jesus at considerable *l*,
Eph 3:18 *l* and height and depth of Christ's love,
Rv 21:16 square, its *l* and its width being the same.
21:16 and found it twelve thousand furlongs in *l*,

LENGTHEN (5)

Jb 15:29 clay with no shadow to *l* over the ground.
Sg 2:17 the day breathes cool and the shadows *l*,
4: 6 the day breathes cool and the shadows *l*,
Is 54: 2 *l* your ropes and make firm your stakes.
Jer 6: 4 the day is waning, evening shadows *l*;

LENGTHENING (2)

Ps(s) 102:12 My days are like a *l* shadow,
109:23 Like a *l* shadow I pass away;

LENGTHS (1)

2Sm 8: 2 He told off two *l* of line for execution,

LENIENCE (1)

Wis 12:18 clemency, and with much *l* you govern us;

LENIENT (2)

Wis 12:16 mastery over all things makes you *l* to all.
Jas 3:17 It is also peaceable, *l*,

LENT (8)

Neh 5:10 and my attendants have *l* the people money
5:11 the wine, and the oil that you have *l* them."
Wis 15: 8 the life that was *l* him is demanded back.
15:16 whose spirit has been *l* him fashioned them.
Sir 47:25 more, and they *l* themselves to every evil.
50:11 *l* majesty to the court of the sanctuary.
Is 59:16 victory, and his justice *l* him its support.
63: 5 victory and my own wrath *l* me its support.

LENTIL (1)

Gn 25:34 then gave him some bread and the *l* stew;

LENTILS (3)

2Sm 17:28 barley, flour, roasted grain, beans, *l*,
23:11 where there was a plot of land full of *l*.
Ez 4: 9 take wheat and barley, and beans and *l*,

LEOPARD (4)

Is 11: 6 and the *l* shall lie down with the kid;
Jer 13:23 the *l* his spots?
Dn 7: 6 I looked and saw another beast, like a *l*;
Rv 13: 2 The beast I saw was like a *l*,

LEOPARDS (3)

Sg 4: 8 haunts of lions, from the *l*' mountains.
Jer 5: 6 them, *L* keep watch round their cities:
Hb 1: 8 Swifter than *l* are his horses,

LEPER (15)

Lv 14: 3 the sore of leprosy has healed in the *l*,
Nm 5: 2 the Israelites to expel from camp every *l*,
12:10 the tent, there was Miriam, a snow-white *l*!
12:10 When Aaron turned and saw her a *l*,
2Sm 3:29 one suffering from a discharge, or a *l*,
2Kgs 5: 1 But valiant as he was, the man was a *l*.
5:27 And Gehazi left Elisha, a *l* white as snow.
15: 5 and he was a *l* to the day of his death.
2Chr 26:21 remained a *l* to the day of his death.
26:21 As a *l* he dwelt in a segregated house,
26:23 cemetery, for they said, "He was a *l*."
Mt 8: 2 a *l* came forward and did him homage,
26: 6 in Bethany at the house of Simon the *l*,
Mk 1:40 A *l* approached him with a request,
14: 3 at table in the house of Simon the *l*,

LEPERS (6)

2Kgs 7: 3 gate were four *l* who were deliberating,
7: 8 After the *l* reached the edge of the camp,
Mt 11: 5 their sight, cripples walk, *l* are cured,
Lk 4:27 the many *l* in Israel in the time of Elisha
7:22 their sight, cripples walk, *l* are cured,
17:12 he was entering a village, ten *l* met him.

LEPROSY (38)

Lv 13: 2 blotch which appears to be the sore of *l*,
13: 3 the skin, it is indeed the sore of *l*;
13: 8 it is *l*.
13: 9 "When someone is stricken with *l*,
13:11 it, it is skin *l* that has long developed.
13:12 If *l* breaks out on the skin and,
13:13 find that the *l* does cover his whole body,
13:15 it is *l*.
13:20 sore of *l* that has broken out in the boil.
13:25 it is *l* that has broken out in the burn;
13:25 declare him unclean and stricken with *l*.
13:27 the man unclean and stricken with *l*.
13:42 it is *l* that is breaking out there.
13:43 of skin *l* of the fleshy part of the body,
13:45 "The one who bears the sore of *l* shall
13:49 with *l* and must be shown to the priest.
13:51 be its use, the infection is malignant *l*,
13:52 since it has malignant *l*,
14: 2 of *l* at the time of his purification.
14: 3 that the sore of *l* has healed in the leper,
14: 7 times the man to be purified from his *l*.
14:32 This is the law for one afflicted with *l*
14:44 has spread in the house, it is corrosive *l*,
14:54 law for every kind of human *l* and scall,
14:55 and scall, for *l* of garments and houses,
14:57 This is the law for *l*.
22: 4 of Aaron who is stricken with *l*,
Dt 24: 8 "In an attack of *l* you shall be careful
2Kgs 5: 3 her mistress, "he would cure him of his *l*."
5: 6 to you, that you may cure him of his *l*."
5: 7 should send someone to me to be cured of *l*?
5:11 hand over the spot, and thus cure the *l*.
5:27 The *l* of Naaman shall cling to you and
2Chr 26:19 of incense, *l* broke out on his forehead.
Mt 8: 3 Immediately the man's *l* disappeared.
Mk 1:42 The *l* left him then and there,
Lk 5:12 certain town, a man full of *l* came to him.
5:13 Immediately the *l* left him.

LEPROUS (8)

Ex 4: 6 it, to his surprise his hand was *l*,
Lv 13:30 is scall, a *l* disease of the head or cheek.
13:44 part of the body, the man is *l* and unclean,
13:47 "When a *l* infection is on a garment of
13:59 *l* infection on a garment of wool or linen,
14:34 if I put a *l* infection on any house of the
2Chr 26:20 and when they saw that his forehead was *l*,
Mt 10: 8 Cure the sick, raise the dead, heal the *l*,

LESHEM (2)

Jos 19:47 so the Danites marched up and attacked *L*,
19:47 Once they had taken possession of *L*,

LESS (35)

Gn 18:28 are five *l* than fifty innocent people?
44:16 the rest of us no *l* than the one in whose
Ex 9:11 no *l* than on the rest of the Egyptians.
30:15 not give more, nor shall the poor give *l*,
Lv 25:16 are few, the price shall be so much the *l*.
Jos 14:11 with no *l* vigor whether for war or for
1Kgs 8:27 how much *l* this temple which I have built!
1Chr 24:31 so in the same way as the *l* important one.
2Chr 6:18 how much *l* this temple which I have built!
32:15 the *l* shall your god save you from my hand!"
Ezr 9:13 have made *l* of our sinfulness than it
Tb 1:21 But *l* than forty days later the king was
Jb 9:14 How much *l* shall I give him any answer,
15:16 his sight, How much *l* so is the abominable,
25: 6 How much *l* man, who is but a maggot,
Ps(s) 8: 6 You have made him little *l* than the angels,
Prv 19:10 much *l* should a slave rule over princes.
28:16 The *l* prudent the prince,
Wis 13: 6 But yet, for these the blame is *l*;
Sir 20:17 is *l* sudden than a slip of the tongue;
Jer 42:16 you dread shall cling to you no *l* in Egypt,
Ez 15: 5 how much *l*,
Mt 9: 5 Which is *l* trouble to say,
Lk 10:12 will be *l* severe than that of such a town.
Rom 11:15 Nothing *l* than life from the dead!
1Cor 12:22 seem *l* important are in fact indispensable.
12:23 We honor the members we consider *l*
12:24 thus bestowing on the *l* presentable a
2Cor 11:24 of the Jews I received forty lashes *l* one;
12:15 too much, will I be loved the *l* for that?
Eph 3: 6 It is no *l* than this:
1Tm 1: 7 much *l* the matters they discuss with such
5: 9 should be not *l* than sixty years of age.
1Jn 2:25 promise and the promise is no *l* than this:
Rv 3: 2 is *l* than complete in the sight of my God.

LESSEN (2)

Jb 15: 4 with piety, and you *l* devotion toward God,
Sir 18: 4 One cannot *l*,

LESSENED (5)

Gn 8: 7 to see if the waters had *l* on the earth.
8: 8 to see if the waters had *l* on the earth.
8:11 knew that the waters had *l* on the earth.
2Mc 9:18 come upon him, his sufferings were not *l*,
Phil 2:28 seeing him, and my own anxieties may be *l*.

LESSENS (1)

Sir 31:30 *l* his strength and multiplies his wounds.

LESSER (6)

Gn 1:16 the day, and the *l* one to govern the night;
Ex 18:22 all the *l* cases they can settle themselves.
18:26 all the *l* cases they settled themselves.
1Chr 12:15 the *l* placed over hundreds and the greater
Jn 2:10 have been drinking awhile, a *l* vintage.
Heb 7:7 that a *l* person is blessed by a greater.

LESSON (10)

1Sm 14:12 they said, "and we will teach you a *l*."
Tb 3:4 and death, till we were an object *l*,
Jb 17:6 their object *l* I have become.
Prv 19:25 an arrogant man, the simple learn a *l*;
24:32 I saw and learned the *l*:
Mt 6:28 a *l* from the way the wild flowers grow.
24:32 From the fig tree learn a *l*.
Mk 13:28 Learn a *l* from the fig tree.
Lk 23:16 to release him, once I have taught him a *l*."
2Tm 2:21 The *l* is that if a person will but cleanse

LESSONS (2)

Mt 13:34 All these *l* Jesus taught the crowds in the
Rom 15:4 we might derive hope from the *l* of patience

LEST (172)

Gn 3:3 not eat it or even touch it, *l* you die.'"
4:15 on Cain, *l* anyone should kill him at sight.
14:23 anything that is yours, *l* you should say,
Ex 20:20 put his fear upon you, *l* you should sin."
23:33 *l* they make you sin against me by
28:43 the sanctuary, *l* they incur guilt and die.
30:20 they must wash with water, *l* they die.
30:21 must wash their hands and feet, *l* they die.
Lv 10:6 *l* you bring not only death on yourselves
14:36 *l* everything in the house become unclean.
15:31 uncleanness, *l* by defiling my Dwelling,
26:44 land, I will not reject or spurn them, *l*,
Nm 17:5 *l* he meet the fate of Korah and his band.
18:3 or the altar, *l* both they and you die.
Dt 1:42 *l* you be beaten down before your enemies,
4:23 Take heed, therefore, *l*,
6:15 nations, *l* the wrath of the LORD,
7:16 *l* you be ensnared into serving their gods.
7:22 *l* the wild beasts become too numerous for
7:25 it for yourselves, *l* you be ensnared by it;
7:26 into your house, *l* you be doomed with it;
8:12 *l*, when you have eaten your fill,
9:28 *l* the people from whose land you have
11:16 But be careful *l* your heart be so lured
15:9 Be on your guard *l*,
17:17 number of wives, *l* his heart be estranged,
18:16 nor see this great fire any more, *l* we die.'
20:5 *l* he die in battle and another dedicate it.
20:6 *l* he die in battle and another enjoy its
20:7 *l* he die in battle and another take her to
20:8 *l* he make his fellows as fainthearted as
20:18 *l* they teach you to make any such
25:3 *l*,
Jos 22:24 concern *l* in the future your children
Jgs 7:2 *l* Israel vaunt itself against me and say,
9:54 *l* they say of me that a woman killed me."
18:25 *l* fierce men fall upon you and you and
Ru 4:6 my claim *l* I depreciate my own estate.
1Sm 9:5 *l* my father forget about the asses and
20:3 must not know of this *l* he be grieved.'
29:4 *l* during the battle he become our enemy.
31:4 *l* these uncircumcised come and make sport
2Sm 1:20 *L* the Philistine maidens rejoice, lest
12:28 *l* it be I that capture the city and it be
13:25 us should not go *l* we be a burden to you."
15:14 Leave quickly, *l* he hurry and overtake us,
20:6 *l* he find fortified cities and take
21:17 us again *l* you quench the lamp of Israel."
2Chr 19:10 warn them *l* they become guilty before the
Ezr 4:22 *l* the evil grow to the detriment of the
Jdt 8:31 cisterns, *l* we be weakened still further."
12:2 of them, *l* it be an occasion of sin;
1Mc 4:45 *l* it be a lasting shame to them that the
Ps(s) 2:12 *L* he be angry and you perish from the way,
7:3 me, *L* I become like the lion's prey,
13:5 I may not sleep in death *l* my enemy say,
13:5 *L* my foes rejoice at my downfall though
28:1 O my Rock be not deaf to me, *L*,
50:22 *l* I rend you and there be no one to rescue
59:12 O God, slay them, *l* they beguile my people;
91:12 up, *l* you dash your foot against a stone.
125:3 *L* the just put forth to wickedness their
143:7 Hide not your face from me *l* I become like
Prv 5:6 *L* you see before you the road to life,
5:9 her house, *L* you give your honor to others,
5:10 *L* strangers have their fill of your wealth,
9:8 Reprove not an arrogant man, *l* he hate you;
20:13 not sleep, *l* you be reduced to poverty;
22:25 of a wrathful man, *L* you learn his ways,
24:18 not your heart exult, *L* the LORD see it,
25:10 *L*,
25:16 *l* you become glutted with it and vomit it
25:17 house, *l* he have more than enough of you,
26:4 to his folly, *l* you too become like him.
26:5 folly, *l* he become wise in his own eyes.
30:6 Add nothing to his words, *l* he reprove you,
30:9 *L*,
30:10 a servant to his master, *l* he curse you,
31:5 *L* in drinking they forget what the law
Eccl 5:5 *l* God be angered by such words and destroy
7:16 and be not overwise, *l* you be ruined.
7:21 *l* you hear your servant speaking ill
Sg 1:7 *L* I be found wandering after the flocks of
Wis 4:11 *l* wickedness pervert his mind or deceit
13:16 Thus *l* it fall down he provides for it,
16:11 *L* they should fall into deep forgetfulness
18:19 *l* they perish unaware of why they suffered
Sir 1:27 *l* you fall and bring upon you dishonor;
2:7 for his mercy, turn not away *l* you fall.
6:2 Fall not into the grip of desire, *l*,
7:3 of injustice, *l* you harvest it sevenfold.
8:1 influential man, *l* you fall into his power.
8:2 *l* he pay out the price of your downfall;
8:4 man, *l* he speak ill of your forebears.
8:10 *l* you be consumed in his flaming fire.
8:15 man, *l* he weigh you down with calamity;
9:1 *l* you teach her to do evil against you.
9:3 strange woman, *l* you fall into her snares.
9:4 not familiar, *l* you be caught in her wiles.
9:5 *l* you be enmeshed in damages for her.
9:6 harlots, *l* you surrender your inheritance.
9:9 *L* your heart be drawn to her and you go
9:13 offend him not, *l* he take away your life;
11:33 only evil, *l* you incur a lasting stain.
12:5 give him, *l* he use them against yourself;
12:12 you, *l* he oust you and take your place.
12:12 right hand, *l* he then demand your seat,
13:10 Be not bold with him *l* you be rebuffed,
13:10 keep not too far away *l* you be forgotten.
22:13 Beware of him *l* you have trouble and be
23:3 *L* my failings increase,
23:3 *L* I succumb to my foes,
23:14 *L* in their presence you commit a blunder
26:10 a strict watch over an unruly wife, *l*,
29:20 means, but take care *l* you fall thereby.
30:10 in his frivolity *l* you share in his sorrow,
30:12 he is still small, *L* he become stubborn,
30:13 heavy his yoke, *l* his folly humiliate you.
31:16 and be not greedy, *l* you be despised.
31:17 gorge not yourself, *l* you give offense.
33:21 wealth, *l* then you have to plead with him;
38:12 Then give the doctor his place *l* he leave;
42:1 ashamed, *l* you sin through human respect:
42:9 *L* she pass her prime unmarried,
42:9 or when she is married, *l* she be disliked;
42:10 While unmarried, *l* she be seduced,
42:10 *l* she prove unfaithful; Lest she conceive
42:11 *l* she make you the sport of your enemies,
45:26 *L* their welfare should ever be forgotten,
Is 10:4 *L* it sink beneath the captive or fall
14:21 *L* they rise and possess the earth,
27:3 *L* anyone harm it,
28:22 arrogant no more *l* your bonds be tightened,
33:15 stopping his ears *l* he hear of bloodshed,
33:15 closing his eyes *l* he look on evil
48:9 it back from you, *l* I should destroy you.
Jer 4:4 *L* my anger break out like fire,
6:8 lest I be estranged from you; *L* I turn
10:24 not in anger, *l* you have us dwindle away.
21:12 *L* my fury break out like fire which burns
25:6 them, *l* you provoke me with your handiwork,
Bar 6:17 bolts, *l* they be carried off by robbers.
Ez 12:12 covering his face *l* he be seen by anyone.
20:22 *l* it be profaned in the sight of the
Am 5:6 *l* he come upon the house of Joseph like a
Mal 3:24 *L* I come and strike the land with doom.
Mk 4:12 *l* perhaps they repent and be forgiven."
Lk 8:12 their hearts *l* they believe and be saved.
12:58 on the way *l* he turn you over to the judge,
21:34 "Be on guard *l* your spirits become
Jn 12:40 their hearts, *l* they see or comprehend,
Acts 13:40 *l* what was said by the prophets be
24:4 But now, *l* I impose on your time unduly,
28:27 closed, *L* they should see with their eyes,
Rom 11:25 of this mystery *l* you be conceited;
1Cor 1:17 *l* the cross of Christ be rendered void of
8:9 *l* in exercising your right you become an
10:12 he is standing upright watch out *l* he fall!
2Cor 9:4 *l* any Macedonians come with me and find
12:7 *l* anyone think more of me than what he
Col 3:21 do not nag your children *l* they lose heart.
1Thes 3:3 *l* any one of you be shaken by these trials.
1Tm 3:6 *l* he become conceited and thus incur the
Heb 2:1 to what we have heard, *l* we drift away.
3:12 *l* any of you have an evil and unfaithful
4:1 *l* any one of you be judged to have lost
Jas 5:9 another, my brothers, *l* you be condemned.
2Pt 3:17 Be on your guard *l* you be led astray by
Rv 3:11 you have *l* someone rob you of your crown.

LET (1343)

Gn 1:3 Then God said, *L* there be light,"
1:6 *L* there be a dome in the middle of the
1:9 *L* the water under the sky be gathered into
1:11 said, *L* the earth bring forth vegetation:
1:14 *L* there be lights in the dome of the sky,
1:14 *L* them mark the fixed times,
1:20 *L* the water teem with an abundance of
1:20 *l* birds fly beneath the dome of the sky."
1:22 and *l* the birds multiply on the earth."
1:24 *L* the earth bring forth all kinds of
1:26 *L* us make man in our image,
1:26 *L* them have dominion over the fish of the
4:8 his brother Abel, *L* us go out in the field."
8:17 and *l* them abound on the earth,
9:26 *L* Canaan be his slave.
9:27 and *l* Canaan be his slave."
11:3 *l* us mold bricks and harden them with fire."
11:4 *l* us build ourselves a city and a tower
11:7 *L* us then go down and there confuse their
12:12 then they will killme, but *l* you live.
13:8 *L* there be no strife between you and me,
14:24 *l* them take their share."
17:18 God, *L* but Ishmael live on by your favor!"
18:4 *L* some water be brought,
18:5 your servant, *l* me bring you a little food,
18:30 *L* not my Lord grow impatient if I go on.
18:32 *l* not my Lord grow angry if I speak up
19:8 *L* me bring them out to you,
19:20 *L* me flee there
19:32 *l* us ply our father with wine and then lie
19:34 *L* us ply him with wine again tonight,
20:6 that is why I did not *l* you touch her.
20:16 *L* that serve you as a vindication before
21:16 to herself, *L* me not watch the child die."
21:19 skin with water, and then *l* the boy drink.
23:9 *L* him sell it to me in your presence,
24:12 *l* it turn out favorably for me today and
24:14 *l* me give water to your camels, too,' let
24:19 When she had *l* him drink his fill,
24:27 who has not *l* his constant kindness toward
24:44 too *l* her be the woman whom the LORD has
24:45 I said to her, 'Please *l* me have a drink.'
24:46 and *l* me bring water for your camels,
24:49 let me know; but if not, *l* me know that,
24:55 *L* the girl stay with us a short while,
24:56 *l* me go back to my master."
24:57 *L* us call the girl and see what she
25:30 *L* me gulp down some of that red stuff;
26:28 *L* us make a pact with you:
26:29 toward you and have *l* you depart in peace.
27:13 *L* any curse against you, son, fall on me!
27:20 your God, *l* things turn out well with me."
27:29 *L* peoples serve you,
30:3 with her, and *l* her give birth on my knees,
30:14 *l* me have some of your son's mandrakes."
30:18 having *l* my husband have my maidservant";
30:26 *L* me have my wives,
30:33 of mine, *l* my honesty testify against me:
30:34 *L* it be as you say."
31:7 however, did not *l* him do me any harm.
31:35 *L* not my lord feel offended that I cannot
31:37 and mine, and *l* them decide between us two.
32:27 The man then said, *L* me go,
32:27 "I will not *l* you go until you bless me."
33:12 said, *L* us break camp and be on our way;
33:14 *L* my lord, then, go on ahead of me,
33:15 *L* me at least put at your disposal some of
34:21 *L* them settle in the land and move about
34:23 *L* us, therefore, give in to them,
37:17 I heard them say, *L* us go on to Dothan.'"
37:20 *l* us kill him and throw him into one of
37:27 Rather, *l* us sell him to these Ishmaelites,
38:16 "Come, *l* me have intercourse with you."
38:23 *L* her keep the things,"
41:33 *l* Pharaoh seek out a wise and discerning
43:4 are willing to *l* our brother go with us,
43:8 *L* the boy go with me,
43:14 so that he may *l* your other brother go,
44:18 *l* your servant speak earnestly to my lord,
44:33 *L* me, your servant,
44:33 and *l* the boy go back with his brothers.
45:24 *L* there be no recriminations on the way."
47:4 *l* your servants settle in the region of
47:29 do not *l* me be buried in Egypt.
49:6 *L* not my soul enter their council,
49:17 *L* Dan be a serpent by the roadside,
49:21 *l* loose which brings forth lovely fawns.
50:18 before him and said, *L* us be your slaves!"
Ex 1:10 *l* us deal shrewdly with them to stop
1:17 had ordered them, but *l* the boys live.
1:22 Hebrews, but you may *l* all the girls live."
4:18 Jethro and said to him, *L* me go back,
4:21 so that he will not *l* the people go.
4:23 *L* my son go, that he may serve me.
4:23 If you refuse to *l* him go,
4:26 Then God *l* Moses go.
5:1 *L* my people go,
5:2 that I should heed his plea to *l* Israel go?
5:2 even if I did, I would not *l* Israel go."
5:3 *L* us go a three days' journey in the desert,
5:7 *L* them go and gather straw themselves!
5:8 *L* us go to offer sacrifice to our God.'
5:17 *L* us go and offer sacrifice to the LORD.
6:11 Egypt, to *l* the Israelites leave his land."
7:2 Pharaoh to *l* the Israelites leave his land.
7:14 is obdurate in refusing to *l* the people go.
7:16 *L* my people go to worship me in the desert.
7:26 *L* my people go to worship me,
7:27 to worship me, If you refuse to *l* them go,
8:4 and I will *l* the people go to offer

LET (cont.)

8:16 *L* my people go to worship me.
8:17 If you will not *l* my people go,
8:24 "I will *l* you go to offer sacrifice to
8:25 refusing to *l* the people go to offer sacrifice
8:28 obdurate and would not *l* the people go.
9: 1 *L* my people go to worship me.
9: 2 to *l* them go and persist in holding them,
9: 7 obdurate and would not *l* the people go.
9: 8 Pharaoh *l* Moses scatter it toward the sky.
9:13 *L* my people go to worship me,
9:17 way for my people by refusing to *l* them go?
9:28 Then I will *l* you go;
9:35 obstinacy he would not *l* the Israelites go,
10: 3 *L* my people go to worship me.
10: 4 If you refuse to *l* my people go,
10: 7 *L* the men go to worship the LORD,
10:10 "if I ever *l* your little ones go with you!
10:20 and he would not *l* the Israelites go.
10:27 obstinate, and he would not *l* them go.
11: 1 After that he will *l* you depart.
11: 1 In fact, he will not merely *l* you go;
11:10 would not *l* the Israelites leave his land.
12:23 not *l* the destroyer come into your houses
12:36 they *l* them have whatever they asked for.
13:15 Pharaoh stubbornly refused to *l* us go,
13:16 *L* this, then, be as a sign on your hand
13:17 Now, when Pharaoh *l* the people go,
14:12 *L* us serve the Egyptians'?
16: 5 *l* it be twice as much as they gather on
16:19 *L* no one keep any of it over until
17:11 of the fight, but when he *l* his hands rest,
18:22 *L* these men render decisions for the
20:19 but *l* not God speak to us,
21: 8 dislikes her, he shall *l* her be redeemed.
21:26 he shall *l* the slave go free in
21:27 he shall *l* the slave go free in
22:12 a wild beast, *l* him bring it as evidence,
22:17 "You shall not *l* a sorceress live.
23:11 *l* the land lie untilled and unharvested,
24:14 complaint, *l* him refer the matter to them."
32:10 *L* me alone, then, that my wrath may blaze
32:12 *L* your blazing wrath die down;
32:22 Aaron replied, *L* not my lord be angry.
32:24 *L* anyone who has gold jewelry take it off.'
32:25 foes, Aaron had *l* the people run wild,
32:26 is for the LORD, *l* him come to me!"
33:12 not *l* me know whom you will send with me.
33:13 with you, do *l* me know your ways so that,
33:18 Then Moses said, "Do *l* me see your glory!"
35:10 *L* every expert among you come and make all
36: 6 *L* neither man nor woman make any more
Lv 2:13 Do not *l* the salt of the covenant of your
14: 7 he shall *l* the living bird fly away over
14:53 He shall then *l* the living bird fly away
20: 2 *L* his fellow citizens stone him.
20:16 *l* them both be put to death;
24:14 his head, *l* the whole community stone him.
25: 2 the land that I am giving you, *l* the land,
25: 9 of the seventh month *l* the trumpet resound;
25:36 but out of fear of God *l* him live with you.
25:40 *l* him be like a hired servant or like your
26:35 you would not *l* it have on the sabbaths
Nm 4:18 "Do not *l* the group of Kohathite clans
6: 5 shall *l* the hair of his head grow freely.
6:25 The LORD *l* his face shine upon you,
7:11 *L* one prince a day present his offering
8:11 *L* Aaron then offer the Levites before the
12:12 *L* her not thus be like the stillborn babe
12:14 *L* her be confined outside the camp for
14: 4 *L* us appoint a leader and go back to Egypt."
14:17 *l* the power of my LORD be displayed in its
15:35 *l* the whole community stone him outside
15:39 *l* the sight of them remind you to keep all
18:15 but you must *l* the first-born of man,
20:17 Kindly *l* us pass through your country.
20:21 to *l* them pass through her territory,
21:22 message, *L* us pass through your country.
21:23 not *l* Israel pass through his territory,
21:27 let it be rebuilt, *l* Sihon's capital
21:29 He *l* his sons become fugitives and his
22:13 the LORD has refused to *l* me go with you."
23:27 "Come, *l* me bring you to another place;
24:14 *l* me first warn you what this people will
27: 4 *L* us, therefore, have property among
27: 8 *l* his heritage pass on to his daughter;
32: 5 *l* this land be giv-en to your servants as
Dt 1:22 *L* us send men ahead to reconnoiter the
2:27 *L* me pass through your country by the
2:28 Only *l* me march through,
2:30 refused to *l* us pass through his land,
3:25 *l* me cross over and see this good land
4: 9 nor *l* them slip from your memory as long
4:19 has *l* fall to the lot of all other nations
4:36 he *l* you hear his voice to discipline you;
4:36 on earth he *l* you see his great fire,
5:24 indeed *l* us see his glory and his majesty!
6: 8 *l* them be as a pendant on your forehead.
8: 3 therefore *l* you be afflicted with hunger,
9:14 *L* me be, that I may destroy them
11:18 and *l* them be a pendant on your forehead.
13:17 *L* it be a heap of ruins forever,
15:18 not be reluctant to *l* your slave go free,
17:20 *L* him not become estranged from his
18:10 *L* there not be found among you anyone who
18:16 *L* us not again hear the voice of the LORD,
20: 5 *L* him return home, lest he die in battle
20: 6 *L* him return home,
20: 7 *L* him return home,
20: 8 *L* him return home,
21: 8 and *l* not the guilt of shedding innocent
22: 7 you shall *l* her go,
23:17 *L* him live with you wherever he chooses,
24:19 *l* it be for the alien,
24:20 *l* what remains be for the alien,
24:21 *l* what remains be for the alien,
28:25 *l* you be beaten down before your enemies;
29:17 *L* there be, then, no man or woman,
29:17 *L* there be no root that would bear such
29:25 and whom he had not *l* fall to their lot:
32: 1 *l* the earth hearken to the words of my
32:38 *L* those who ate the fat of your sacrifices
32:38 *L* them be your protection!
33: 6 live and not die out, but *l* his men be few."
34: 4 I have *l* you feast your eyes upon it,
Jos 2:15 *l* them down through the window with a rope;
2:21 *L* it be as you say,"
3: 4 But *l* there be a space of two thousand
5: 6 For the LORD swore that he would not *l*
9:20 *L* us therefore spare their lives and so
9:21 princes recommended that they be *l* live,
Jgs 1: 3 and *l* us engage the Canaanites in battle.
1:25 they *l* the man and his whole clan go free.
6:31 destroyed is a god, *l* him act for himself!"
6:32 the words, *L* Baal take action against him,
6:39 *L* me make just one more test with the
6:39 *L* the fleece alone be dry,
6:39 dry, but *l* there be dew on all the ground."
7: 3 anyone is afraid or fearful, *l* him leave.'"
7: 7 So *l* all the other soldiers go home."
9:15 *l* fire come from the buckthorn and devour
9:20 and *l* fire come forth
10:14 *l* them save you now that you are in
11:17 Edom saying, *L* me pass through your land.'
11:19 *L* me pass through your land to my own
11:20 to *l* Israel pass through his territory.
11:27 wrong me by warring against me, *L* the LORD,
11:37 said to her father, *L* me have this favor.
12: 5 of the fleeing Ephraimites said, *L* me pass,"
13:14 *L* her observe all that I have commanded
13:23 would he have *l* us see all this just now,
14:12 said to them, *L* me propose a riddle to you.
15: 1 he said, *L* me be with my wife in private,"
15: 1 her father would not *l* him enter,
16:30 Samson said, *L* me die with the Philistines!"
18: 9 they replied, "Come, *l* us attack them,
18:25 him, *L* us hear no further sound from you,
19:11 *l* us turn off to this city of the
19:13 servant, *l* us make for some other place,
19:20 him, "but *l* me provide for all your needs,
19:24 Rather *l* me bring out my maiden daughter
19:25 the following dawn, when they *l* her go.
19:28 He said to her, "Come, *l* us go";
Ru 2: 2 *L* me go and glean ears of grain in the
2:15 Boaz instructed his servants to *l* her glean
2:16 and even to *l* drop some handfuls and leave
3:13 *l* him do so.
3:14 *L* it not be known that this woman came to
1Sm 2: 3 nor *l* arrogance issue from your mouths.
2:16 *L* the fat be burned first as is the custom,
4: 3 *L* us fetch the ark of the LORD from Shiloh
5: 8 *L* them move the ark of God of Israel on to
5:11 *L* it return to its own place,
6: 8 Start it on its way, and *l* it go.
9: 5 who was with him, "Come, *l* us turn back,
9: 6 *L* us go there now!
9: 9 used to say, "Come, *l* us go to the seer."
9:10 Come on, *l* us go!"
11:14 *l* us go to Gilgal to inau-gurate the
13: 3 with a proclamation, *L* the Hebrews hear!"
14: 1 "Come *l* us go over to the Philistine
14: 6 "Come *l* us go over to that outpost of the
14:36 *L* us go down in pursuit of the Philistines
14:36 But the priest said, *L* us consult God."
15:16 *L* me tell you what the LORD said to me
17:10 Give me a man and *l* us fight together."
17:32 *L* your majesty not lose courage.
18:17 *l* the Philistines strike him."
19: 3 If I learn anything, I will *l* you know."
19: 4 *L* not your majesty sin against his
19:12 Then Michal *l* David down through a window,
19:17 threatened me, *L* me go or I will kill you.'"
20: 5 *L* me go and hide in the open country until
20: 6 'David urged me to *l* him go on short
20: 9 upon you, I will certainly *l* you know."
20:11 David, "Come, *l* us go out into the field."
20:28 urgently asked me to *l* him go to his city,
20:29 'Please *l* me go,'
21: 3 told me to *l* no one know anything
22: 3 Moab, *L* my father and mother stay with you,
22:15 *L* not the king accuse his servant or
23:20 the king wishes to come down, *l* him do so.
25:13 to his men, *L* everyone gird on his sword."
25:24 "My lord, *l* the blame be mine.
25:24 Please *l* your handmaid speak to you,
25:25 *L* not my lord pay attention to that
25:27 and *l* it be given to the young men who
26: 8 *L* me nail him to the ground with one
26:11 and the water jug, and *l* us be on our way."
26:19 *l* my lord the king listen to the words of
26:19 you against me, *l* an offering appease him;
26:20 Do not *l* my blood flow to the ground far
26:22 *L* an attendant come over to get it.
27: 5 *l* me have a place to live in one of the
28:22 *L* me set something before you to eat,
29: 4 *L* him return to the place you picked out
30:22 *L* them take those along and be on their way."
2Sm 2:14 *L* the young men rise and perform for us."
3:24 Why did you *l* him go peacefully on his way?
10:12 *l* us prove our valor for the sake of our
13: 5 'Please *l* my sister Tamar come and
13: 6 "Please *l* my sister Tamar come and
13:26 please *l* my brother Amnon come to us."
13:32 *L* not my lord think that all the young
13:33 So *l* not my lord the king put faith in the
14: 9 him, *L* me and my family be to blame,
14:12 "Please *l* your servant say stili another
14:15 *L* me speak to the king.
14:17 *L* the word of my lord the king provide a
14:18 The woman said, *L* my lord the king speak."
14:24 the king said, *L* him go to his own house;
14:32 Now, *l* me appear before the king.
14:32 If I am guilty, *l* him put me to death."
15:14 *L* us take flight,
15:26 *l* him do to me as he sees fit."
15:34 and say to Absalom, *L* me be your servant,
16: 9 *L* me go over,
16:11 *L* him alone and let him curse,
17: 1 "Please *l* me choose twelve thousand men,
17: 5 *l* us hear what he too has to say."
17:11 *L* all Israel from Dan to Beer-sheba,
17:18 They *l* themselves down into this,
18:19 *L* me run to take the good news to the king
18:31 *L* my lord the king receive the good news
19:31 the king, "Indeed *l* him have it all,
19:38 Please *l* your servant go back to die in
19:38 *L* him cross over with my lord the king.
20:11 *L* him who favors Joab and is for David
20:18 *L* them ask if they will in Abel or in Dan
21: 6 *l* seven men from among his descendants be
24:14 *L* us fall by the hand of God,
24:14 but *l* me not fall by the hand of man."
24:22 *L* my lord the king take and offer up
1Kgs 1: 2 *L* a young virgin be sought to attend you,
1:12 *l* me advise you so that you may save your
1:51 *L* King Solomon first swear that he will
2: 9 But you must not *l* him go unpunished.
2:21 *L* Abishag the Shunamite be given to your
11:22 "Nothing," he said, "but please *l* me go!"
12:24 *L* every man return home,
17:21 *l* the life breath return to the body of
18: 5 *l* us go through the land to all sources of
18:23 *L* them choose one,
18:36 *l* it be known this day that you are God in
18:40 *L* none of them escape!"
19:20 *l* me kiss my father and mother goodbye,
20:25 *L* us fight them on level ground,
21: 6 But he refused to *l* me have his vineyard."
22: 8 *L* not your majesty speak of evil against
22:13 *L* your word be the same as any of theirs;
22:17 *L* each of them go back home in peace.'"
22:50 *L* my servants accompany your servants in
2Kgs 1:13 *l* my life and the lives of these fifty men,
1:14 But now, *l* my life mean something to you!"
2:16 *L* them go in search of your master.
4:10 *l* us arrange a little room on the roof and
4:22 husband, *L* me have a servant and a donkey.
4:27 *L* her alone, she is in bitter anguish;
4:27 LORD hid it from me and did not *l* me know."
5: 8 *L* him come to me and find out that there
5:17 "If you will not accept, please *l* me,
6: 2 *L* us go to the Jordan,
6:22 *L* them eat and drink,
7: 4 *l* us desert to the camp of the Arameans.
7: 9 Come, *l* us go and inform the palace."
7:12 *L* me tell you what the Arameans have done
7:13 *l* some of us take five of the abandoned
10:25 *L* no one escape."
11:15 her," he added, *L* him die by the sword,"
14: 8 challenge, "Come *l* us meet face to face."
15:16 his way from Tirzah they did not *l* him in.
18:29 'Do not *l* Hezekiah deceive you,
18:30 *L* not Hezekiah induce you to rely on the
19:10 'Do not *l* your God on whom you rely
20:10 "Rather, *l* it go back ten steps."
23:18 him be," he said, *l* no one move his bones."
1Chr 13: 2 *l* us summon the rest of our brethren from
13: 3 and *l* us bring the ark of our God here
16:21 He *l* no one oppress them,
16:31 *L* the heavens be glad and the earth rejoice;
16:31 *l* them say among the nations:
16:32 *L* the sea and what fills it resound; let
16:36 *L* all the people say, Amen!
19:13 Hold steadfast and *l* us show ourselves
21:23 and *l* my lord the king do what seems best
28: 9 him, he will *l* himself be found by you;
2Chr 2:14 *l* my lord send to his servants the wheat,
11: 4 *L* every man return home,
14: 6 *L* us build these cities and surround them

14:10 *l* no man prevail against you."
18: 7 *L* not your Majesty speak of evil against
18:12 predict good for the king, *l* your word,
18:16 *L* each of them go back home in peace.' "
19: 7 now, *l* the fear of the LORD be upon you.
23: 6 *L* no one enter the LORD's house except the
23:14 to follow her, *l* him die by the sword.
25: 7 king, *l* not the army of Israel go with you,
25:16 *l* you take counsel to your own destruction,
25:17 "Come, *l* us meet each other face to face."
28:19 who *l* Judah go its own way and proved
32:15 *L* not Hezekiah mislead you further and
33:13 The LORD *l* himself be won over:
36:23 to any part of his people, *l* him go up,
Ezr 1: 3 to any part of his people, *l* him go up,
1: 4 *L* everyone who has survived,
4: 2 and said to them, *L* us build with you,
4:12 *L* it be known to the king that the Jews
4:13 Now *l* it be known to the king that if this
5: 8 *L* it be known to the king that we have
5:15 and *l* the house of God be rebuilt on its
5:17 *l* a search be made in the royal archives
6: 7 *L* the governor and the elders of the Jews
6: 8 *l* these men be repaid for their expenses,
6:12 *l* it be carefully executed."
7:23 *L* everything that is ordered by the God of
7:26 *l* strict judgment be executed upon him,
7:28 and who *l* me find favor with the king,
10: 3 *L* us therefore enter into a covenant
10: 3 *L* the law be observed!
10:14 *L* our leaders represent the whole assembly;
10:14 then *l* all those in our cities who have
Neh 1:11 day, and *l* him find favor with this man"
2: 7 *l* letters be given to me for the
2:17 Come, *l* us rebuild the wall of Jerusalem,
2:18 They replied, *L* us be up and building!"
3:36 *l* them be carried away to a land
3:37 Hide not their crime and *l* not their sin
5:10 *L* us put an end to this usury!
6: 2 *l* us hold council together at Caphirim in
6: 7 the king, come, *l* us hold council together."
6:10 *L* us meet in the house of God,
6:10 *l* us lock the doors of the temple.
13:14 *L* not the devotion which I showed for the
Tb 3: 6 *l* me go to the everlasting abode;
3:15 never again *l* me hear these insults!"
4: 2 *l* him know about this money before I die?"
4:15 *l* drunkenness accompany you on your way.
4:19 and never *l* them be erased from your heart.
5:19 Rather *l* it be a ransom for our son!
6: 4 hold of the fish and don't *l* it get away!"
6:13 father to *l* us have her as your bride.
6:13 you or *l* her become engaged to another man;
7: 9 Raguel to *l* me marry my kinswoman Sarah."
8: 4 *L* us pray and beg our LORD to have mercy
8: 5 *L* the heavens and all your creation praise
8: 6 *l* us make him a partner like himself,'
8:15 Let all your chosen ones praise you; *l*
10: 5 of my eyes, that I *l* you make this journey!"
10: 7 "Please *l* me go,
10: 7 beg you, father, *l* me go back to my father.
10: 9 I beg you to *l* me go back to my father."
10:11 Bidding them farewell, he *l* them go.
10:12 *l* me hear good reports about you as long
11: 3 *L* us hurry on ahead of your wife to
13: 8 *L* all men speak of his majesty,
Jdt 5:24 *L* us therefore attack them;
7:30 *L* us wait five days more for the Lord our
8:17 from him, *l* us call upon him to help us,
8:24 *l* us set an example for our kinsmen.
8:33 tonight to *l* me pass through with my maid;
9:13 *L* my guileful speech bring wound and wale
9:14 *L* your whole nation and all the tribes
11: 5 and *l* your handmaid speak in your presence!
11:18 Then I will come and *l* you know,
12: 6 lord, to *l* your handmaid go out for prayer."
14: 2 *l* each of you seize his weapons, and let
16:14 *L* your every creature serve you;
Est 1:19 *l* an irrevocable royal decree be issued by
2: 2 *L* beautiful young virgins be sought for
2: 3 *L* the king appoint commissaries in all the
2: 3 of the women, *l* cosmetics be given them.
3: 9 king, *l* a decree be issued to destroy them;
C:22 *L* them not gloat over our ruin,
6: 5 *L* him come in," the king said.
8: 5 *l* a document be issued to revoke the
9:13 *l* the Jews in Susa be permitted again
9:13 and *l* the ten sons of Haman be hanged on
1Mc 1:11 *L* us go and make an alliance with the
1:48 and to *l* themselves be defiled with every
2:27 *L* everyone who is zealous for the law and
2:37 They said, *L* us all die without reproach;
2:41 *L* us fight against anyone who attacks us
2:48 the kings and did not *l* the sinner triumph.
3:43 *L* us restore our people from their ruined
4:10 So now *l* us cry to Heaven in the hope that
4:32 *l* them tremble at their own destruction.
4:36 *l* us go up to purify the sanctuary and
5:57 *L* us also make a name for ourselves by
6:58 Therefore *l* us now come to terms with
6:59 *L* us grant them freedom to live according
7: 7 and *l* him punish them and all their
7:28 *L* there be no fight between me and you.
7:38 and his army, and *l* them fall by the sword.
7:38 blasphemies, and do not *l* them continue."
7:42 and *l* the rest know that Nicanor spoke
9: 8 *L* us go forward to meet our enemies;
9: 9 *L* us save our lives now,
9:10 *l* us die bravely for our kinsmen and not
9:44 *L* us get up now and fight for our lives,
9:58 Now then, *l* us have Bacchides return,
10: 4 *L* us be the first to make peace with
10:16 *L* us now make him our friend and ally."
10:31 *L* Jerusalem and her territory,
10:33 and *l* all their taxes,
10:34 *L* all feast days, sabbaths, new moon
10:35 *L* no man have authority to exact payment
10:36 *L* thirty thousand Jews be enrolled in the
10:37 *L* some of them be stationed in the king's
10:37 *l* some be given positions of trust
10:37 *L* their superiors and their rulers be
10:37 them, and *l* them follow their own laws,
10:38 *L* the three districts that have been added
10:54 and recovered the royal throne *l* us now
10:71 and *l* us test each other's strength there;
11: 9 "Come, *l* us make a pact with each other;
11:50 "Give us your terms and *l* the Jews stop
12:53 *l* us make war on them and wipe out their
13:19 his promise and would not *l* Jonathan go.
13:40 in our service, *l* them be enrolled.
13:40 *L* there be peace between us."
15:14 by land and sea and *l* no one go in or out.
2Mc 1:27 *l* the Gentiles know that you are our God.
2: 3 not to *l* the law depart from their hearts.
6:17 *L* these words suffice for recalling this
8:27 day on which he *l* descend on them
10:20 money lovers *l* themselves be bribed
10:36 the gates and *l* in the rest of the troops,
11:24 us to *l* them retain their own customs.
12:24 asked them to spare his life and *l* him go,
12:25 they *l* him go for the sake of saving their
15:36 never to *l* this day pass unobserved,
15:38 *L* this, then, be the end.
Jb 3: 4 *l* not God above call for it,
3: 6 *l* it not occur among the days of the year,
3: 7 *l* no joyful outcry greet it!
3: 8 *L* them curse it who curse the sea,
6:29 Think it over; *l* there be no injustice.
7:16 *l* me alone,
7:19 and *l* me alone long enough to swallow my
10: 2 *L* me know why you oppose me.
10:20 *L* me alone,
11:14 and *l* not injustice dwell in your tent,
13:13 Be silent, *l* me alone!
13:21 and *l* not the terror of you frighten me.
13:22 or *l* me speak first,
14: 6 Look away from him and *l* him be,
15:13 God and *l* such words escape your mouth!
16:18 not my blood, nor *l* my outcry come to rest!
20:13 will not *l* it go but keeps it still
21: 2 and *l* that be the consolation you offer.
21:18 *L* them be like straw before the wind,
21:19 *l* him requite the man himself so that he
21:20 feels it, *L* his own eyes see the calamity,
21:20 and the wrath of the Almighty *l* him drink!
27: 7 *L* my enemy be as the wicked and my
31: 6 *L* God weigh me in the scales of justice;
31:37 *l* the Almighty answer me!
31:40 Then *l* the thistles grow instead of wheat
32:10 *l* me too set forth my knowledge!
32:20 Let me speak and obtain relief; *l* me open
33:12 In this you are not just, *l* me tell you;
34: 4 *L* us discern for ourselves what is right; let
34:36 *L* Job be tried to the limit,
40: 2 *L* him who would correct God give answer!
40:11 *L* loose the fury of your wrath;
42: 8 and *l* my servant Job pray for you;
Ps(s) 2: 3 *L* us break their fetters and cast their
4: 7 *l* the light of your countenance shine upon
5:11 *l* them fall by their own devices;
5:12 But *l* all who take refuge in you be glad
7: 6 Let the enemy pursue and overtake me; *l*
7: 8 *L* the assembly of the peoples surround you;
7:10 *L* the malice of the wicked come to an end,
9:20 let not man prevail; *l* the nations be judged
9:21 *l* the nations know that they are but men.
10:15 *l* them not survive.
13: 6 *L* my heart rejoice in your salvation; let
17: 2 From you *l* my judgment come;
19:14 *l* it not rule over me.
19:15 *L* the words of my mouth and the thought of
21:10 *l* fire devour them.
22: 9 let him deliver him, *l* him rescue him,
22:31 *L* the coming generation be told of the
25: 2 *l* me not be put to shame, let not my
25:20 *l* me not be put to shame,
25:21 *L* integrity and uprightness preserve me,
30: 2 and did not *l* my enemies rejoice over me.
31: 2 *l* me never be put to shame.
31:17 *L* your face shine upon your servant;
31:18 O LORD, *l* me not be put to shame,
31:18 let the wicked be put to shame; *l* them
31:19 *L* dumbness strike their lying lips that
33: 8 *L* all the earth fear the LORD; let all
34: 3 *L* my soul glory in the LORD;
34: 4 LORD with me, *l* us together extol his name.
35: 4 *L* those be put to shame and disgraced who
35: 4 *L* those be turned back and confounded who
35: 5 *L* them be like chaff before the wind,
35: 6 *L* their way be dark and slippery,
35: 8 *L* ruin come upon them unawares, and let
35: 8 into the pit they have dug *l* them fall.
35:19 *L* not my unprovoked enemies rejoice over me;
35:19 *l* not my undeserved foes wink knowingly.
35:24 my God, *l* them not rejoice over me.
35:25 *L* them not say in their hearts, "Aha!
35:25 *L* them not say,
35:26 *L* all be put to shame and confounded who
35:26 *L* those be clothed with shame and disgrace
35:27 But *l* those shout for joy and be glad who
36:12 *L* not the foot of the proud overtake me
37:33 nor *l* him be condemned when he is on trial.
38:17 say, *L* them not be glad on my account who,
39: 5 *L* me know, O LORD, my end
39: 9 a fool's taunt *l* me not suffer.
40:15 *L* all be put to shame and confusion who
40:15 *L* them be turned back in disgrace who
40:16 *L* them be dismayed in their shame who say
41:13 me and *l* me stand before you forever.
44:11 You have *l* us be driven back by our foes;
48:12 *l* Mount Zion be glad, Let the cities
51:10 *L* me hear the sounds of joy and gladness;
55:16 *L* death surprise them; let them go down
58: 8 *L* them vanish like water flowing off;
58: 8 the bow, *l* their arrows be headless shafts.
58: 9 *L* them dissolve like a melting snail,
58:10 thistles, *l* the whirlwind carry them away.
59:13 lips *l* them be caught in their arrogance,
61: 7 *l* his years be many generations;
61: 8 *L* him sit enthroned before God forever;
66: 4 *L* all on earth worship and sing praise to
66: 6 therefore *l* us rejoice in him.
66: 9 to our souls, and has not *l* our feet slip.
66:12 You *l* men ride over our heads;
67: 2 may he *l* his face shine upon us.
68:30 in Jerusalem *l* the kings bring you gifts.
68:31 *L* them prostrate themselves with bars of
68:32 *L* nobles come from Egypt; let Ethiopia
69: 7 *L* not those who wait for you be put to
69: 7 *L* not those who seek you blush for me,
69:16 *L* not the flood-waters overwhelm me,
69:23 *L* their own table be a snare before them,
69:24 *L* their eyes grow dim so that they cannot
69:25 *l* the fury of your anger overtake them.
69:26 *L* their encampment become desolate;
69:26 in their tents *l* there be no one to dwell.
69:28 and *l* them not attain to your reward.
69:30 *l* your saving help,
69:35 *L* the heavens and the earth praise him,
70: 3 *L* them be put to shame and confounded who
70: 3 *L* them be turned back in disgrace who
70: 4 *L* them retire in their shame who say to me.
71: 1 *l* me never be put to shame.
71:13 *L* them be put to shame and consumed who
71:13 *l* them be wrapped in ignominy and disgrace
74: 8 said in their hearts, *L* us destroy them;
76:12 *l* all round about him bring gifts to the
78:38 anger and *l* none of his wrath be roused.
79:10 *L* it be known among the nations in our
79:11 *L* the prisoners' sighing come before you;
80:17 *L* those who would burn it with fire or
83: 5 say, "Come, *l* us destroy their nation;
83: 5 *l* the name of Israel be remembered no more!"
83:13 *L* us take for ourselves the dwelling place
83:18 *L* them be shamed and put to rout forever;
83:18 *l* them be confounded and perish,
88: 3 *L* my prayer come before you;
90:16 *L* your work be seen by your servants and
95: 1 let us sing joyfully to the LORD; *l* us
95: 2 Let us greet him with thanksgiving; *l* us
95: 6 Come, *l* us bow down in worship; let us
96:11 *L* the heavens be glad and the earth
96:11 *l* the sea and what fills it resound;
96:12 *l* the plains be joyful and all that is in
97: 1 *l* the earth rejoice; let the many isles
98: 7 *L* the sea and what fills it resound,
98: 8 *L* the rivers clap their hands,
99: 3 *L* them praise your great and awesome name;
102: 2 hear my prayer, and *l* my cry come to you.
102:19 *L* this be written for the generation to
102:19 and *l* his future creatures praise the LORD:
105:14 another people, He *l* no man oppress them,
106:26 them to *l* them perish in the desert,
106:48 *L* all the people say, Amen!
107: 2 Thus *l* the redeemed of the LORD say,
107: 8 *L* them give thanks to the LORD for his
107:15 *L* them give thanks to the LORD for his
107:21 *L* them give thanks to the LORD for his
107:22 *L* them make thank offerings and declare
107:31 *L* them give thanks to the LORD for his
107:32 *L* them extol him in the assembly of the
109: 6 and *l* the accuser stand at his right hand.
109: 7 he is judged, *l* him go forth condemned,
109:14 *l* not his mother's sin be blotted out;
109:27 And *l* them know that this is your hand;
109:28 *L* them curse, but do you bless;
109:28 put to shame, but *l* your servant rejoice.
109:29 *L* my accusers be clothed with disgrace and
109:29 and *l* them wear their shame like a mantle.

LET (cont.)
118: 2 L the house of Israel say,
118: 3 L the house of Aaron say,
118: 4 L those who fear the LORD say,
118:24 l us be glad and rejoice in it.
119:10 l me not stray from your commands.
119:31 O LORD, l me not be put to shame.
119:41 L your kindness come to me
119:76 L your kindness comfort me according to
119:77 L your compassion come to me that I may
119:78 L the proud be put to shame for oppressing
119:79 L those turn to me who fear you and
119:80 L my heart be perfect in your statutes,
119:122 l not the proud oppress me.
119:133 promise, and l no iniquity rule over me.
119:169 L my cry come before you
124: 1 not the LORD been with us, l Israel say,
129: 1 oppressed me from my youth, l Israel say,
130: 2 L your ears be attentive to my voice in
130: 7 for the dawn, l Israel wait for the LORD,
132: 7 L us enter into his dwelling.
132: 9 l your faithful ones shout merrily for joy.
141: 2 L my prayer come like incense before you;
141: 4 L not my heart incline to the evil of
141: 4 and l me not partake of their dainties.
141: 5 L the just man strike me; that is kindness; l
141:10 L all the wicked fall,
143: 8 At dawn l me hear of your kindness,
145:10 L all your works give you thanks,
145:10 O LORD, and l your faithful ones bless you.
145:11 L them discourse of the glory of your
148: 5 L them praise the name of the LORD,
148:11 L the kings of the earth and all peoples,
149: 2 Let Israel be glad in their maker, l the
149: 3 L them praise his name in the festive dance,
149: 3 l them sing praise to him with timbrel and
149: 5 L the faithful exult in glory; let them sing
149: 6 l the high praises of God be in their
149: 6 And l two-edged swords be in their hands:
150: 6 L everything that has breath praise the
Prv 1:11 us lie in wait for the honest man, l us,
1:12 L us swallow them up,
3: 3 L not kindness and fidelity leave you;
3:21 My son, l not these slip out of your sight:
4: 4 L your heart hold fast my words:
4:13 Hold fast to instruction, never l her go;
4:21 L them not slip out of your sight,
4:25 L your eyes look straight ahead and your
4:26 for your feet, and l all your ways be sure.
5:17 L your fountain be yours alone,
6:25 l her not captivate you with her glance!
7:18 l us drink our fill of love, until morning,
7:25 L not your heart turn to her ways,
9: 4 L whoever is simple turn in here;
9:16 L whoever is simple turn in here,
23:17 L not your heart emulate sinners,
23:25 Let your father and mother have joy; l
23:26 heart, and l your eyes keep to my ways.
24:17 when he stumbles, l not your heart exult,
25:17 L your foot be seldom in your neighbor's
27: 2 L another praise you
31:31 l her works praise her at the city gates.
Eccl 2: 1 l me try you with pleasure and the
3:22 will l him see what is to come after him?
4:17 L your approach be obedience,
5: 1 Be not hasty in your utterance and l not
5: 1 therefore l your words be few.
5: 5 L not your utterances make you guilty,
7:18 to this rule, and not to l that one go;
9: 8 At all times l your garments be white,
11: 6 and at evening l not your hand be idle:
11: 8 However many years a man may live, l him,
11: 9 while you are young and l your heart be
Sg 2:14 Let me see you, l me hear your voice,
3: 4 I took hold of him and would not l him go
4:16 L my lover come to his garden and eat its
7: 9 Now l your breasts be like clusters of the
7:12 l us go forth to the fields and spend the
7:13 L us go early to the vineyards,
8:13 are listening for your voice, l me hear it!
Wis 2: 6 l us enjoy the good things that are real,
2: 7 L us have our fill of costly wine and
2: 7 and l no springtime blossom pass us by;
2: 8 l us crown ourselves with rosebuds ere
2: 9 L no meadow be free from our wantonness;
2: 9 l us leave tokens of our rejoicing,
2:10 Let us oppress the needy just man; l us
2:11 But l our strength be our norm of justice;
2:12 L us beset the just one,
2:17 L us see whether his words be true; let us
2:19 With revilement and torture l us put him
2:20 L us condemn him to a shameful death;
13: 3 l them know how far more excellent is the
13: 4 l them from these things realize how much
Sir 2:18 L us fall into the hands of the LORD and
4: 9 l not justice be repugnant to you.
4:22 l no one intimidate you to your own
4:31 L not your hand be open to receive and
6: 6 L your acquaintances be many,
6:28 Then when you have her, do not l her go;
6:35 l no wise saying escape you.
6:36 l your feet wear away his doorstep!
6:37 l his commandments be your constant
7:21 L a wise servant be dear to you as your
7:26 have a wife, l her not seem odious to you;
8:11 L not the impious man intimidate you;
9:15 l all your conversation be about the law
12:12 L him not stand near you,
12:12 L him not sit at your right hand,
14:14 things, l no choice portion escape you.
15:13 he does not l it befall those who fear him.
18:22 L nothing prevent the prompt payment of
19: 9 L anything you hear die within you;
23: 6 L not the lustful cravings of the flesh
23: 9 L not your mouth form the habit of swearing,
23:13 L not your mouth become used to coarse talk,
27:19 l your friend go and cannot recapture him;
31:25 L not wine-drinking be the proof of your
32:20 and l not the same thing trip you twice.
33:20 L neither son nor wife,
33:21 in you, l no man have dominion over you.
33:23 l no one tarnish your glory.
33:26 l his hands be idle and he will seek to be
36: 8 L raging fire consume the fugitive,
36:15 in you, and l your prophets be proved true.
38:10 l your hands be just,
38:23 With the departed dead, l memory fade;
42:12 L her not parade her charms before men,
43:28 l the last word be,
43:29 L us praise him the more,
47: 4 When his hand l fly the slingstone that
51:29 L your spirits rejoice in the mercy of God,
Is 1:18 Come now, l us set things right,
2: 3 "Come, l us climb the LORD's mountain,
2: 5 come, l us walk in the light of the LORD!
2:22 As for you, l man alone,
4: 1 Only l your name be given us,
5: 1 L me now sing of my friend,
5: 5 I will l you know what I mean to do to my
5: 5 break through its wall, l it be trampled!
5:19 say, L him make haste and speed his work,
5:19 l it come to pass, that we may know it!"
7: 4 l not your courage fail before these two
7: 6 saying, L us go up and tear Judah asunder,
7:11 l it be deep as the nether world,
12: 5 l this be known throughout all the earth.
14:20 L him not be named forever,
16: 3 high noon l your shadow be like the night,
16: 4 L the outcasts of Moab live with you,
19:12 L them tell you and make known What the
21: 6 a watchman, l him tell what he sees.
21: 7 riding a camel, Then l him pay heed,
22: 4 Turn away from me, l me weep bitterly;
25: 9 l us rejoice and be glad that he has saved
26: 2 up the gates to l in a nation that is just,
26:11 L them be shamed when they see your zeal
26:11 l the fire prepared for your enemies
29: 1 Add year to year, l the feasts come round.
30:11 L us hear no more of the Holy One of Israel."
30:30 and l it be seen how his arm descends In
32: 6 To l the hungry go empty and the thirsty
32:20 stream, and l the ox and the ass go freely!
33:20 l your eyes see Jerusalem as a quiet abode,
34: 1 L the earth and what fills it listen,
36:14 'Do not l Hezekiah deceive you,
36:15 L not Hezekiah induce you to rely on the
36:18 Do not l Hezekiah seduce you by saying,
37:10 'Do not l your God on whom you rely
41: 1 L them draw near and speak; let us
41:22 L them come near and foretell to us what
42:10 L the sea and what fills it resound,
42:11 L the steppe and its cities cry out,
42:11 L the inhabitants of Sela exult,
42:12 L them give glory to the LORD,
43: 9 Let all the nations gather together, l
43: 9 L them produce witnesses to prove
44: 7 L him stand up and speak,
44: 7 L them foretell to us the things to come.
44:28 shall say of Jerusalem, L her be rebuilt,"
44:28 of the temple, L its foundations be laid."
45: 8 L justice descend,
45: 8 like gentle rain l the skies drop it down.
45: 8 L the earth open and salvation bud forth; l
45:13 He shall rebuild my city and l my exiles
47:13 L the astrologers stand forth to save you,
48: 3 forth from my mouth, I l you hear of them;
48: 5 they took place I l you hear of them,
50: 8 wishes to oppose me, l us appear together.
50: 8 L him confront me.
55: 7 L the scoundrel forsake his way,
55: 7 L him turn to the LORD for mercy;
56: 3 L not the foreigner say,
56: 3 Nor l the eunuch say,
56:12 l us carouse with strong drink,
63: 6 I l their blood run out upon the ground."
63:17 Why do you l us wander,
66: 5 L the LORD show his glory that we may see
66: 9 of birth, and yet not l her child be born?
Jer 2:28 L them rise up!
3:25 L us lie down in our shame, let our
4: 5 in, l us march to the fortified cities."
5:24 not in their hearts, L us fear the LORD,
6: 4 l us rush upon her at midday!
6: 5 l us rush upon her by night,
8:14 L us form ranks and enter the walled cities,
9:11 L him to whom the mouth of the LORD has
9:17 L them come quickly and intone a dirge for
9:19 the LORD, l your ears receive his message.
9:22 L not the wise man glory in his wisdom,
9:23 But rather, l him who glories,
10:11 L the gods that did not make heaven and
11:19 "Let us destroy the tree in its vigor; l us
11:20 L me witness the vengeance you take on
14:17 L my eyes stream with tears day and night,
17:15 L it come to pass!"
17:18 persecutors, not me, be confounded; l them,
18:18 l us contrive a plot against Jeremiah.
18:18 l us destroy him by his own tongue; let
18:21 L their wives be made childless and widows;
18:21 l their men die of pestilence,
18:23 L them go down before you,
20: 7 duped me, O LORD, and I l myself be duped;
20:10 l us denounce him!"
20:12 L me witness the vengeance you take on
20:16 L that man be like the cities which the
20:16 L him hear war cries in the morning,
23:28 L the prophet who has a dream recount his
23:28 l him who has my word speak my word
29: 8 Do not l yourselves be deceived by the
30:11 deserve, I will not l you go unpunished.
31: 6 "Rise up, l us go to Zion,
32:23 Hence you l all these evils befall them.
34:14 you, but then you shall l him go free.
36:19 l no one know where you are."
38:24 L no one know about this conversation,
39:12 l no harm befall him,
40: 5 gave him food and gifts and l him go.
40:15 L me go and kill Ishmael,
42: 3 L the LORD,
42:12 for you and l you return to your land.
46:16 l us return to our own people,
46:17 the name "The noise that l its time go by."
46:28 deserve, I will not l you go unpunished.
48: 2 "Come, l us put an end to her as a people."
49:11 your widows, l them trust in me.
50: 5 l us join ourselves to the LORD with
50:27 her oxen, l them go down to the slaughter;
50:29 Encamp around her, l no one escape.
50:33 hold them fast and refuse to l them go.
51: 3 L the bowman draw his bow,
51: 6 l each one save his life,
51: 9 Leave her, l us go,
51:10 come, l us tell in Zion what the LORD,
51:45 l each one save himself from the burning
51:50 from afar, l Jerusalem come to your minds.
Lam 1:22 L all their evil come before you;
2:18 L your tears flow like a torrent day and
2:18 L there be no respite for you,
3:28 L him sit alone and in silence,
3:29 L him put his mouth to the dust;
3:30 L him offer his cheek to be struck, let him
3:40 L us search and examine our ways that we
3:41 L us reach out our hearts toward God in
3:56 L not your ear be deaf to my cry for help!"
Bar 2:13 L your anger be withdrawn from us,
4:11 but with mourning and lament I l them go.
4:12 L no one gloat over me,
4:14 L Zion's neighbors come,
4:37 Here come your sons whom you once l go,
Ez 3:27 L him heed who will, and let him resist
7:12 L not the buyer rejoice nor the seller
13:13 In my fury I will l loose stormwinds;
14:13 I l famine loose upon it and cut off from
20:26 I l them become defiled by their gifts,
20:31 Shall I l myself be consulted by you,
20:31 I will not l myself be consulted by you.
23:25 I will l loose my jealousy against you,
35: 5 never l die your hatred for the Israelites,
36:32 says the Lord GOD l this be known to you!
39:15 bone, l them put up a marker beside it,
40:16 splayed windows l into the cells
44:20 their heads nor l their hair hang loose,
Dn 2: 7 L the king tell his servants the dream and
3:39 heart and humble spirit l us be received;
3:40 So l our sacrifice be in your presence
3:42 Do not l us be put to shame,
3:44 L all those be routed who inflict evils on
3:44 L them be shamed and powerless,
3:45 L them know that you alone are the Lord
3:74 L the earth bless the Lord,
4:11 l the beasts flee its shade,
4:12 L him be bathed with the dew of heaven;
4:13 L his mind be changed from the human;
4:13 l him be given the sense of a beast,
4:16 l not the dream or its meaning terrify
4:20 l him be bathed with the dew of heaven,
4:20 and l his lot be among wild beasts till
5:19 Whomever he wished, he killed or l live;
9:16 l your anger and your wrath be turned away
9:17 l your face shine upon your desolate
13:13 said to each other, L us be off for home,
14: 9 said to the king, L it be as you say!"
Hos 2: 4 L her remove her harlotry from before her,
2:20 I will l them take their rest in security.
4: 4 But let no one protest, l no one complain;
4:15 O Israel, l not Judah become guilty!
4:17 is an associate of idols, l him alone!
6: 1 "Come, l us return to the LORD,
6: 3 Let us know, l us strive to know the LORD;

9: 7 L Israel know it!
11: 9 I will not l the flames consume you.
14:10 L him who is wise understand these things;
14:10 l him who is prudent know them.
Jl 2: 1 L all who dwell in the land tremble,
2:16 L the bridegroom quit his room,
2:17 the porch and the altar l the priests,
4: 9 L all the soldiers report and march!
4:10 l the weak man say,
4:12 L the nations bestir themselves and come
Am 4:10 Your horses I l be captured,
5:15 good, and l justice prevail at the gate;
5:24 then l justice surge like water,
Ob 1: 1 l us go to war against him!"
Jon 1: 7 l us cast lots to find out on whose
1:14 l us not perish for taking this man's life;
Mi 1: 2 L the Lord GOD be witness against you,
1:16 L your baldness be as the eagle's,
2: 6 preach, l them not preach of these things!"
4: 2 "Come, l us climb the mount of the LORD,
4:11 L her be profaned, let our eyes see Zion's
6: 1 mountains, and l the hills hear your voice!
7:14 L them feed in Bashan and Gilead,
Hb 1: 3 Why do you l me see ruin;
Zec 8: 9 L your hands be strong,
8:13 do not fear, but l your hands be strong.
8:16 l there be honesty and peace in the
8:17 and l none of you plot evil against
8:21 l us go to implore the favor of the LORD";
8:23 of his garment and say, L us go with you,
11: 9 let it die; what is to perish, l it perish,
11: 9 and l those that are left devour one
11:12 but if not, l it go."
11:17 L his arm wither away entirely,
Mt 6: 3 In giving alms you are not to l your left
6:34 L tomorrow take care of itself.
7: 4 L me take that speck out of your eye,'
8:21 "Lord, l me go and bury my father first."
8:22 me, and l the dead bury their dead."
10:26 Do not l them intimidate you.
12:27 L them be the ones to judge you.
13: 9 L everyone heed what he hears!"
13:30 L them grow together until harvest;
13:43 L everyone heed what he hears!
14:36 with the plea that he l them do no more
15:14 L them go their way;
18:27 l the official go and wrote off the debt.
19: 6 l no man separate what God has joined."
19: 8 Moses l you divorce your wives,"
19:12 L him accept this teaching who can."
19:14 but Jesus said, L the children come to me.
21: 3 Then he will l them go at once."
21:38 L us kill him and then we shall have his
24: 4 L no one mislead you.
24:15 on holy ground l the reader take note!),
25:20 he said, 'you l me have five thousand.
26:39 if it is possible, l this cup pass me by.
26:39 Still, l it be as you would have it,
26:46 L us be on our way!
27:25 L his blood be on us and on our children."
27:43 l God rescue him now if he wants to.
Mk 1:38 L us move on to the neighboring villages
2: 4 they l down the mat on which the paralytic
4: 9 L him who has ears to hear me, hear!"
4:23 L him who has ears to hear me, hear!"
4:35 them, L us cross over to the farther shore."
5:12 L us enter them."
5:43 strictly not to l anyone know about it,
6:56 l them touch just the tassel of his cloak.
7:16 L everyone heed what he hears!"
7:27 L the sons of the household satisfy
9: 5 L us erect three booths on this site,
9:13 L me assure you, Elijah has already come.
10: 9 l no man separate what God has joined."
10:14 L the children come to me and do not
11: 6 told them to, and the men l them take it.
12: 7 Come, l us kill him,
12:15 Bring me a coin and l me see it."
13: 5 L no one mislead you.
13:14 it should not be l the reader take note!—those
13:36 l him come suddenly and catch you asleep.
14: 6 L her alone.
14:36 But l it be as you would have it,
15:32 L the 'Messiah,' the 'king of Israel,'
Lk 1:38 L it be done to me as you say."
2:12 L this be a sign to you:
2:15 L us go over to Bethlehem and see this
3:11 L the man with two coats give to him who
4:25 Indeed, l me remind you,
5:19 There they l him down with his mat through
6:29 your coat, l him have your shirt as well.
6:42 l me remove the speck from your eye,'
8: 8 L everyone who has ears attend to what he
8:22 L us cross over to the far side of the
9:33 L us set up three booths,
9:59 The man replied, L me bury my father first."
9:60 said to him, L the dead bury their dead;
9:61 first l me take leave of my people at home."
11:19 In such case, l them act as your judges.
12:35 L your belts be fastened around your
12:39 he would not l him break into his house.
13:15 Which of you does not l his ox or ass out
14:35 L him who hears this, heed it."

15:23 L us eat and celebrate because this son
16: 4 take me into their homes when I am l go.'
16:28 L him be a warning to them so that they
16:29 L them hear them.'
18:16 L the little children come to me.
20: 3 L me put a question for you to answer:
20:14 L us kill him so that the inheritance will
21:32 L me tell you this:
22:26 L the greater among you be as the junior,
23:35 l him save himself if he is the Messiah of
Jn 5:43 But l someone come in his own name,
6:47 L me firmly assure you,
6:53 L me solemnly assure you,
7:37 l him come to me; let him drink
8: 7 L the man among you who has no sin be the
9: 3 it was to l God's works show forth in him.
11: 7 to his disciples, L us go back to Judea."
11:15 In any event, l us go to him."
11:16 to his fellow disciples, L us go along,
11:44 Jesus told them, "and l him go free."
11:48 If we l him go on like this,
12: 7 L her keep it against the day they prepare
12:26 If anyone would serve me, l him follow me;
14: 1 "Do not l your hearts be troubled.
14:31 L us be on our way.
18: 8 "If I am the one you want, l these men go."
19:24 L us throw dice to see who gets it."
Acts 1:20 L his encampment be desolate.
2:36 Therefore l the whole house of Israel know
5: 3 why have you l Satan fill your heart so as
5:38 L them alone.
14:16 past ages he l the Gentiles go their way.
15:36 L us go back now and see how the brothers
16:35 officers with orders to l these men go.
16:37 L them come into the prison and escort us
19:30 but his disciples would not l him.
19:38 L the parties argue their case.
21:39 I beg you, l me address these people."
24:20 L those who are here declare what crime
26: 8 L me ask why you,
27:30 they l the ship's boat down into the sea.
27:32 cut the ropes and l the boat drift.
28: 4 from the sea, Justice will not l him live."
Rom 2:17 L us suppose you bear the name of "Jew"
6: 1 L us continue in sin that grace may
6:12 l sin rule your mortal body and make you
11: 9 L their table become a snare and a trap,
11:10 l their eyes be darkened so that they may
12: 3 L him estimate himself soberly,
13: 1 L everyone obey the authorities that are
13:12 L us cast off deeds of darkness and put on
13:13 L us live honorably as in daylight;
14:15 You must not l the food you eat bring to
14:19 L us,
1Cor 1:10 L there be no factions;
1:31 you find it written, L him who would boast,
3:18 L no one delude himself.
3:21 L there be no boasting about men.
5: 8 L us celebrate the feast not with the old
6: 7 injustice, and l yourselves be cheated?
6:12 will not l myself be enslaved by anything.
7:15 wishes to separate, however, l him do so.
7:36 should be done, l him do as he wishes.
9:15 die than l anyone rob me of my boast!
10: 8 L us not indulge in lewdness as some of
10: 9 L us not test the Lord as some of them did,
10:12 l anyone who thinks he is standing upright
10:13 not l you be tested beyond your strength.
11:13 I will l you judge for yourselves.
11:34 If anyone is hungry l him eat at home,
14:27 in tongues l it be at most two or three,
14:29 L no more than two or three prophets speak,
14:29 and l the rest judge the worth of what
15:32 dead are not raised, L us eat and drink,
16:11 I do, so l no one treat him disdainfully.
16:22 not love the Lord, l a curse be upon him.
2Cor 4: 6 who said, L light shine out of darkness,"
7: 1 l us purify ourselves from every
9: 6 L me say this much:
10: 7 belongs to Christ, l him reflect on this:
10:11 Well, l such people give this some thought,
10:17 L him who would boast,
11:16 l no one think me foolish.
11:16 all the way and l me do a little boasting.
Gal 1: 8 we delivered to you, l a curse be upon him!
1: 9 one you received, l a curse be upon him!
3:15 l me give you an everyday example.
5:25 the spirit, l us follow the spirit's lead.
5:26 L us never be boastful,
6: 9 L us not grow weary of doing good;
6:10 the opportunity, l us do good to all men
6:17 Henceforth, l no man trouble me,
Eph 2: 9 so l no one pride himself on it.
4:14 L us, then, be children no longer,
4:15 l us profess the truth in love and and the
4:25 l everyone speak the truth to his
4:26 If you are angry, l it be without sin.
4:28 l him work with his hands at honest labor
4:29 Never l evil talk pass your lips;
5: 3 l them not even be mentioned among you;
5: 6 L no one deceive you with worthless
Phil 2: 3 l all parties think humbly of others as
Col 2:18 L no one rob you of your prize by

3:16 L the word of Christ,
4: 6 L your speech be always gracious and in
1Thes 5: 6 therefore l us not be asleep like the rest,
2Thes 2: 3 L no one seduce you, no matter how.
1Tm 4:12 L no one look down on you because of your
4:15 l them absorb you,
5: 4 l these learn that piety begins at home
5:16 not l them become a burden to the church,
6:17 L them trust in the God who provides us
2Tm 2:19 L everyone who professes the name of the
Ti 2: 1 l your speech be consistent with your
2:15 L no one look down on you.
3:14 L our people devote themselves to honest
Heb 1: 6 says, L all the angels of God worship him."
4:11 L us strive to enter into that rest,
4:14 l us hold fast to our profession of faith.
4:16 So l us confidently approach the throne of
6: 1 L us,
10:22 l us draw near in utter sincerity and
10:23 L us hold unswervingly to our profession
12: 1 l us lay aside every encumbrance of sin
12: 2 l us keep our eyes fixed on Jesus,
13: 4 L marriage be honored in every way and the
13:13 L us go to him outside the camp,
13:15 Through him l us continually offer God a
13:23 I must l you know that our brother Timothy
Jas 1: 4 L endurance come to its perfection so that
1: 5 l him ask it from the God who gives
1: 9 L the brother in humble circumstances take
1:19 L every man be quick to hear,
3:13 l him show this in practice through a
4: 9 l your laughter be turned into mourning
5:12 l it be "yes" if you mean yes and "no"
1Pt 3: 6 do what is right and l no fears alarm you.
4: 8 l your love for one another be constant,
4:19 l those who suffer as God's will requires
1Jn 2:24 l what you heard from the beginning remain
3: 7 Little ones, l no one deceive you;
3:18 l us love in deed and in truth and not
4: 7 l us love one another because love is of
2Jn 1: 5 l us love one another.
Rv 2: 7 L him who has ears heed the Spirit's word
2:11 L him who has ears heed the Spirit's word
2:17 L him who has ears heed the Spirit's word
2:29 L him who has ears heed the Spirit's word
3: 6 L him who has ears heed the Spirit's word
3:13 L him who has ears heed the Spirit's word
3:22 L him who has ears heed the Spirit's word
13: 9 L him who has ears heed these words!
19: 7 L us rejoice and be glad,
22:11 L the wicked continue in their wicked ways,
22:17 L him who hears answer, "Come!"
22:17 Let him who is thirsty come forward; l all

LETHECH (1)

Hos 3: 2 of silver and a homer and a l of barley.

LETS—LET'S (9)

Ex 22: 4 if he l the fire spread so that it burns
Nm 23: 3 then I will tell you whatever he l me see."
2Kgs 10:24 "If one of you l anyone escape of those
Jb 12:19 l their never-failing waters flow away.
Ps(s) 147:18 he l his breeze blow and the waters run.
Eccl 5:19 because God l him busy himself with the
Mt 27:42 L' see him come down from that cross and
27:49 L' see whether Elijah comes to his rescue."
Mk 15:36 "Now l see whether Elijah comes to take

LETTER (81)

2Sm 11:14 wrote a l to Joab which he sent by Uriah.
2Kgs 5: 5 will send along a l to the king of Israel."
5: 6 To the king of Israel he brought the l,
5: 6 l I am sending my servant Naaman to you,
5: 7 When he read the l,
10: 2 when this l reaches you decide which is
10: 6 So Jehu wrote them a second l:
10: 7 When the l arrived,
19:14 Hezekiah took the l from the hand of the
2Chr 21:12 He received a l from the prophet Elijah
Ezr 4: 8 l against Jerusalem to King Artaxerxes:
4:11 is a copy of the l that they sent to him:
4:23 Artaxerxes' l had been read before Rehum,
5: 6 of the l sent to King Darius by Tattenai,
Neh 2: 8 also a l for Asaph,
6: 5 bore an unsealed l containing this text:
Est B: 1 This is a copy of the l:
8: 8 and seal the l with the royal signet ring."
E: 1 The following is a copy of the l:
E:17 well, then, to ignore the l sent by Haman,
E:19 a copy of this l publicly in every place,
8:13 A copy of the l to be promulgated as law
9:26 of all that was contained in this l,
9:27 year in the manner prescribed by this l,
9:29 full authority this second l about Purim,
1Mc 5:10 sent a l to Judas and his brothers saying:
5:14 While they were reading this l,
10: 3 a l to Jonathan written in peaceful terms,
10: 7 Jerusalem and read the l to all the people.
10:17 sent Jonathan a l written in these terms:
11:29 l to Jonathan about all these matters:
11:31 for your information a copy of the l that

LETTER (cont.)

12: 5 the *l* that Jonathan wrote to the Spartans:
12: 7 Long ago a *l* was sent to the high priest
12: 8 the envoy with honor and received the *l*,
12:17 our *l* about the renewal of our brotherhood.
12:19 is a copy of the *l* that was sent to Onias:
13:35 King Demetrius sent him the following *l*:
14:20 is a copy of the *l* that the Spartans sent:
15: 1 a *l* from the islands of the sea to Simon,
15:24 *l* was also sent to Simon the high priest.
2Mc 9:18 wrote the following *l* to the Jews
9:25 I have written to him the *l* copied below.
11:16 of the *l* which Lysias wrote to the Jews:
11:22 The king's *l* read thus:
11:27 The king's *l* to the people was as follows:
11:34 The Romans also sent them a *l* as follows:
Ps(s) 119:112 to fulfill your statutes always, to the *l*.
Is 37:14 Hezekiah took the *l* from the hand of the
37:17 Hear all the words of the *l* that
Jer 29: 1 This is the contents of the *l* which the
29: 3 sent to the king of Babylon, the *l* read:
29:29 Zephaniah read this *l* to the prophet,
Bar 6: 1 A copy of the *l* which Jeremiah sent to
Mt 5:18 pass away, not the smallest *l* of the law,
5:18 of the law, not the smallest part of a *l*,
Lk 16:17 a single stroke of a *l* of the law to pass.
Acts 15:23 They were to deliver this *l*:
15:30 the assembly together to deliver the *l*.
21:25 we sent them a *l* with our decision that
23:25 then wrote the governor a *l* to this effect:
23:33 they delivered the *l* to the governor and
23:34 The governor, upon reading the *l*,
Rom 2:29 its source is the spirit, not the *l*.
7: 6 in the new spirit, not the antiquated *l*.
15:15 in parts of this *l* by way of reminder.
16:22 I, Tertius, who have written this *l*,
1Cor 5: 9 *l* not to associate with immoral persons.
2Cor 3: 2 You are my *l*,
3: 3 *l* of Christ which I have delivered, a letter
7: 8 I saddened you by my *l* I have no regrets.
7: 8 that the *l* caused you grief for a time),
Col 4:16 Once this *l* has been read to you,
4:16 read the *l* that is coming from Laodicea.
1Thes 5:27 the Lord that this *l* be read to them all.
2Thes 2: 2 or rumor, or a *l* alleged to be ours,
2:15 from us, either by our word or by *l*.
3:14 our injunction, delivered through this *l*,
3:17 I append this signature to every *l* I write.
2Pt 3: 1 I am writing you this second *l*,

LETTERS (41)

1Kgs 21: 8 So she wrote *l* in Ahab's name and,
21: 9 This is what she wrote in the *l*:
21:11 writing, through the *l* she had sent them.
2Kgs 10: 1 *l* and sent them to the city rulers,
20:12 had been ill, he sent *l* and gifts to him.
2Chr 30: 1 and even wrote *l* to Ephraim and Manasseh
30: 6 the *l* written by the king and his princes,
32:17 for he had written *l* to deride the LORD,
Neh 2: 7 let *l* be given to me for the governors
2: 9 and presented the king's *l* to them.
6:17 many *l* were going to Tobiah from the
6:17 Judah, and Tobiah's *l* were reaching them,
6:19 and Tobiah sent *l* trying to frighten me.
Est 1:22 He sent *l* to all the royal provinces,
B: 6 *L* were sent by couriers to all the royal
3:13 who are indicated to you in the *l* of Haman,
8: 5 to revoke the *l* which that schemer Haman,
8:10 These *l*, which he wrote in the name
8:11 In these *l* the king authorized the Jews in
9:20 these events and sent *l* to all the Jews,
1Mc 1:44 *l* to Jerusalem and to the cities of Judah,
9:60 sent *l* secretly to all his allies in Judea,
12: 2 He also sent *l* to Sparta and other places
12: 4 The Romans gave them *l* addressed to the
15:15 his companions left Rome with *l*
15:22 consul sent similar *l* to Kings Demetrius,
16:19 To the army officers he sent *l* inviting
2Mc 2:13 and the royal *l* about sacred offerings In
Sir 45:11 in incised *l* each of the tribes of Israel;
Is 8: 1 and inscribe on it in ordinary *l*:
39: 1 his sickness, he sent *l* and gifts to him.
Jer 29:25 Because you sent *l* on your own authority
Acts 9: 2 asked him for *l* to the synagogues
22: 5 received *l* to our brother Jews in Damascus.
28:21 "We have had no *l* from Judea about you,
1Cor 16: 3 When I come I shall give *l* of introduction
2Cor 3: 1 Or do I need *l* of recommendation to you or
10: 9 I do not wish to intimidate you with my *l*.
10:10 His *l*, they say, are severe and forceful,
10:11 are by word, in the *l* during our absence,
2Pt 3:16 with these matters as he does in all his *l*.

LETTING (12)

Gn 38:16 pay me for *l* you have intercourse with me?"
Lv 26:13 had laid upon you and *l* you walk erect.
Nm 5:20 have acted impurely by *l* a man
20:19 is no harm in merely *l* us march through."
27: 7 *l* their father's heritage pass on to them.
Jos 2:18 the window through which you are *l* us down;
2Mc 6:13 promptly instead of *l* them go for long.
Jer 38: 6 of the guard, *l* him down with ropes.
Lam 2:17 *L* the enemy gloat over you and exalting
Am 9: 9 a sieve, *l* no pebble fall to the ground.
1Tm 6: 9 They are *l* themselves be captured by
1Jn 3: 1 on us in *l* us be called children of God!

LETUSHIM (1)

Gn 25: 3 of Dedan were the Ashurim, the *L*,

LEUMMIM (1)

Gn 25: 3 were the Ashurim, the Letushim, and the *L*.

LEVEL (25)

1Kgs 7:20 lotus pattern above the *l* of the nodes
20:23 But if we fight them on *l* ground,
20:25 Let us fight them on *l* ground,
1Chr 12: 4 a warrior on the *l* of the Thirty,
Tb 3:10 would *l* this insult against my father:
2Mc 14:33 I will *l* this shrine of God to the ground;
Ps(s) 26:12 My foot stands on *l* ground;
27:11 O LORD, your way, and lead me on a *l* path,
143:10 May your good spirit guide me on *l* ground.
Sir 10:16 down their stem to the *l* of the ground,
39:24 For the virtuous his paths are *l*,
51:15 My feet kept to the *l* path because from
Is 25:12 raze, and strike it down *l* with the earth,
26: 7 the path of the just you make *l*.
28:17 of right a measuring line, of justice a *l*—
45: 2 I will go before you and *l* the mountains;
45:13 all his ways I make *l*.
49:11 all my mountains, and make my highways *l*.
Jer 31: 9 lead them to brooks of water, on a *l* road,
Bar 5: 7 depths and gorges be filled to *l* ground,
Ez 13:14 have whitewashed and *l* it to the ground,
42: 5 *l* lower than the closest chambers
Lk 6:17 he stopped at a *l* stretch where were many
1Cor 3: 4 clear that you are still at the human *l*?
Eph 2: 3 we lived at the *l* of the flesh,

LEVELED (8)

2Mc 8: 3 destroyed and about to be *l* to the ground;
Jb 30:19 I am *l* with the dust and ashes.
Is 28:25 When he has *l* the surface,
Jer 51:58 of spacious Babylon shall be *l* utterly;
Mt 26:62 no answer to the testimony *l* against you?"
Lk 3: 5 And every mountain and hill shall be *l*.
Acts 25: 7 him and *l* many serious charges against him,
26: 2 charges have been *l* against me by the Jews,

LEVELING (3)

2Mc 9:14 intention of *l* it to the ground
Mk 15: 4 many accusations they are *l* against you."
Acts 4:29 look at the threats they are *l* against us.

LEVELS (4)

Is 26: 5 it to the ground, *l* it with the dust.
28: 2 overflowing, *l* to the ground with violence;
Ez 42: 3 three parallel rows of them on different *l*.
42: 5 for the system of *l* set them at a level

LEVI (63)

Gn 29:34 that is why she named him *L*.
34:25 pain, Dinah's full brothers Simeon and *L*,
34:30 Jacob said to Simeon and *L*:
35:23 Reuben, Jacob's first-born, Simeon, *L*,
46:11 The sons of *L*: Gershon, Kohath, and Merari.
49: 5 "Simeon and *L*, brothers indeed,
Ex 1: 2 Reuben, Simeon, *L* and Judah;
2: 1 of the house of *L* married a Levite woman,
6:16 The names of the sons of *L*,
6:16 *L* lived one hundred and thirty-seven years.
6:19 the clans of *L* in their genealogical order.
Nm 1:49 "The tribe of *L* alone you shall not
3: 6 of *L* and present them to Aaron the priest,
3:17 The sons of *L* were named Gershon,
16: 1 son of Izhar, son of Kohath, son of *L*,
16:10 and your kinsmen, the descendants of *L*,
17:23 staff, representing the house of *L*,
18: 2 also your other kinsmen of the tribe of *L*,
26:58 These also were clans of *L*:
26:59 She also was of the tribe of *L*,
Dt 10: 8 LORD set apart the tribe of *L*
10: 9 *L* has no share in the heritage with his
18: 1 "The whole priestly tribe of *L* shall have
18: 2 *L* shall have no heritage among his brothers;
21: 5 The priests, the descendants of *L*,
27:12 "When you cross the Jordan, Simeon, *L*,
33: 8 Of *L* he said: "To *L* belong your Thummim,
Jos 13:14 of *L* Moses assigned no heritage since,
13:33 Moses gave no heritage to the tribe of *L*,
1Chr 2: 1 Reuben, Simeon, *L*,
5:27 The sons of *L* were Gershon,
6: 1 The sons of *L* were Gershon,
6: 4 The following were the clans of *L*,
6:23 son of Izhar, son of Kohath, son of *L*,
6:28 son of Jahath, son of Gershon, son of *L*.
6:32 son of Mushi, son of Merari, son of *L*.
21: 6 *L* and Benjamin,
23: 6 into classes according to the sons of *L*:
23:14 were counted as part of the tribe of *L*.
23:24 of *L* according to their ancestral houses,
27:17 for *L*,
Ezr 8:18 man, one of the sons of Mahli, son of *L*,
Neh 12:23 The sons of *L*: the family heads
Ps(s) 135:20 of Aaron, bless the LORD, House of *L*,
Sir 45: 6 his brother AARON, of the tribe of *L*.
Jer 33:18 nor shall priests of *L* ever be lacking,
33:21 with the priests of *L* who minister to me.
Ez 48:31 the gate of Judah, and the gate of *L*.
Zec 12:13 the family of the house of *L*,
Mal 2: 4 because I have a covenant with *L*,
2: 8 You have made void the covenant of *L*,
3: 3 and he will purify the sons of *L*,
Mk 2:14 As he moved on he saw *L* the son of
2:14 *L* got up and became his follower.
Lk 3:24 son of Heli, son of Matthat, son of *L*,
3:29 son of Jorim, son of Matthat, son of *L*,
5:27 named *L* sitting at his customs post.
5:28 behind, *L* stood up and became his follower.
5:29 After that *L* gave a great reception for
Heb 7: 5 of *L* should receive tithes from the people,
7: 9 *L*, who receives tithes,
Rv 7: 7 twelve thousand from the tribe of *L*,

LEVIATHAN (6)

Jb 3: 8 the sea, the appointed disturbers of *L*!
40:25 Can you lead about *L* with a hook,
Ps(s) 74:14 You crushed the heads of *L*,
104:26 great, And where ships move about with *L*,
Is 27: 1 *L* the fleeing serpent, Leviathan the

LEVIED (3)

Nm 31: 5 a thousand men of each tribe were *l*,
1Kgs 9:15 *l* in order to build the temple of the LORD,
2Chr 24: 6 Judah and Jerusalem the tax *l* by Moses,

LEVIES (3)

1Sm 28: 4 *l* advanced to Shunem and encamped.
1Mc 10:29 the tribute, the salt tax, and the crown *l*.
Am 5:11 the weak and exacted of them *l* of grain,

LEVI'S (3)

Nm 17:18 on *L* staff, for the head of Levi's
Mk 2:15 Jesus was reclining to eat in *L* house,

LEVITE (35)

Ex 2: 1 man of the house of Levi married a *L* woman,
4:14 "Have you not your brother, Aaron the *L*?
Dt 12:12 as well as with the *L* who belongs to your
12:18 and the *L* who belongs to your community;
12:19 the *L* as long as you live in the land.
14:27 the *L* who belongs to your community,
14:29 that the *L* who has no share in the
16:11 and the *L* who belongs to your community,
16:14 male and female slave, and also the *L*,
18: 6 "When a *L* goes from one of your
26:11 the *L* and the aliens who live among you,
26:12 tithes, and you have given them to the *L*,
26:13 portion and I have given it to the *L*,
Jos 21: 1 *L* families came up to Eleazar the priest,
Jgs 17: 7 There was a young *L* who had resided within
17: 9 him, "I am a *L* from Bethlehem in Judah,
17:11 the young *L* decided to stay with the man,
17:12 Micah consecrated the young *L*,
17:13 me, since the *L* has become my priest."
18: 3 the young *L* and turned in that direction.
18:15 *L* at the home of Micah and greeted him.
19: 1 there was a *L* residing in remote parts of
20: 4 how the crime had taken place, and the *L*,
2Sm 15:24 too [with all the *L* bearers of the ark of
1Chr 24: 6 The scribe Shemaiah, son of Nethanel, a *L*,
2Chr 20:14 son of Mattaniah, a *L* of the clan of Asaph,
31: 2 to each priest and *L* his proper service,
31:12 of these things was Conaniah the *L*,
31:14 a *L* and the keeper of the eastern gate,
31:19 to every *L* listed in the family records.
Ezr 7:24 tributes, or tolls on any priest, *L*,
8:15 but I could not discover a single *L*.
10:15 and Shabbethai the *L* supporting them.
Lk 10:32 there was a *L* who came the same way;
Acts 4:36 was a certain *L* from Cyprus named Joseph,

LEVITES (246)

Ex 6:25 the heads of the ancestral clans of the *L*.
32:26 All the *L* then rallied to him,
32:28 The *L* carried out the command of Moses,
38:21 by the *L* under the direction of Ithamar,
Lv 25:32 "In levitical cities the *L* shall always
25:33 Any town house of the *L* in their cities
25:33 for the town houses of the *L* are their
Nm 1:47 The *L*, however, were not registered
1:50 You are to give the *L* charge of the
1:51 is to move on, the *L* shall take it down;
1:51 pitched, it is the *L* who shall set it up.
1:53 the *L* shall camp around the Dwelling of
1:53 The *L*, then, shall have charge
2:17 *L* shall set out in the middle of the line.
2:33 The *L*, however, were not registered
3: 9 You shall give the *L* to Aaron and his sons;
3:12 "It is I who have chosen the *L* from the
3:12 The *L*, therefore, are mine,

3:15 of the *L* by ancestral houses and clans,
3:20 the clans of the *L* by ancestral houses.
3:32 The chief prince of the *L*,
3:39 The total number of male *L* a month old or
3:41 Then assign the *L* to me,
3:45 "Take the *L* in place of all the
3:45 and the *L'* cattle in place of their cattle,
3:45 their cattle, that the *L* may belong to me.
3:46 of the Israelites who outnumber the *L*,
3:49 when the rest had been redeemed by the *L*.
4: 2 the *L* take a total of the Kohathites,
4:18 clans perish from the body of the *L*.
4:46 completed the registration among the *L*,
7: 5 Assign them to the *L*,
7: 6 and oxen, and assigned them to the *L*.
8: 6 "Take the *L* from among the Israelites and
8: 9 Then have the *L* come forward in front of
8:10 While the *L* are present before the LORD,
8:11 Let Aaron then offer the *L* before the LORD
8:12 The *L* in turn shall lay their hands on the
8:12 to the LORD, in atonement for the *L*.
8:13 have the *L* stand before Aaron and his sons,
8:14 the *L* from the rest of the Israelites,
8:15 "Only then shall the *L* enter upon their
8:18 first-born Israelites I have taken the *L*;
8:20 of the Israelites deal with the *L*,
8:21 When the *L* had cleansed themselves of sin
8:22 Moses concerning the *L* was carried out.
8:24 "This is the rule for the *L*.
8:26 His service with his fellow *L* shall
8:26 you are to regulate the duties of the *L*."
16: 7 Enough from you *L*!"
16: 8 also said to Korah, "Listen to me, you *L*!
18: 6 is I who have taken your kinsmen, the *L*,
18:21 *L*, however, I hereby assign all tithes
18:23 Only the *L* are to perform the service of
18:23 *L*, therefore, shall not have any heritage
18:26 to Moses, "Give the *L* these instructions:
18:30 tithes will be credited to you *L*
26:57 The *L* registered by clans were:
26:62 number of male *L* one month or more of age,
31:30 asses and sheep, and give them to the *L*,
31:47 and of beasts, and gave them to the *L*,
35: 2 they shall give the *L* cities for homes,
35: 4 lands of the cities to be assigned the *L*
35: 6 are the cities you shall give to the *L*:
35: 7 their pasture lands to be assigned the *L*.
35: 8 to the *L* in proportion to its own heritage."
Dt 18: 7 like all his fellow *L* who are in
27:14 "The *L* shall proclaim aloud to all the
31:25 he gave the *L* who carry the ark of the
33: 9 Thus the *L* keep your words,
Jos 14: 3 *L* were given no heritage among the tribes,
14: 4 The *L* themselves received no share of the
18: 7 For the *L* have no share among you,
21: 3 the Israelites gave the *L* the following
21: 4 the *L* fell to the clans of the Kohathites,
21: 8 lands the Israelites allotted to the *L*
21:10 of Aaron in the Kohathite clan of the *L*,
21:20 clans among the *L* obtained by lot,
21:27 The Gershonite clan of the *L* received from
21:34 The Merarite clans, the last of the *L*,
21:40 to the Merarite clans, the last of the *L*
21:41 their pasture lands, belonged to the *L*,
1Sm 6:15 *L*, meanwhile, had taken down the ark
1Kgs 8: 4 (The priests and *L* carried them.)
12:31 from among the people who were not *L*.
1Chr 6:33 Their brother *L* were appointed to all the
6:49 cities with their pasture lands to the *L*,
9: 2 lay Israelites, the priests, the *L*,
9:14 Among the *L* were Shemaiah,
9:18 gatekeepers for the encampments of the *L*.
9:26 These were the *L* who also had charge of
9:31 Mattithiah, one of the *L*,
9:33 the gatekeepers, family heads over the *L*.
12:27 Of the *L*: four thousand six hundred,
13: 2 the *L* from their cities with pasture lands,
15: 2 one may carry the ark of God except the *L*,
15: 4 together the sons of Aaron and the *L*:
15:11 Zadok and Abiathar, and the *L* Uriel,
15:14 the priests and the *L* sanctified
15:15 The *L* bore the ark of God on their
15:16 *L* to appoint their brethren as chanters,
15:17 Therefore the *L* appointed Heman,
15:22 was the chief of the *L* in the chanting;
15:26 While the *L*, with God's help,
15:27 as were all the *L* who carried the ark,
16: 4 *L* to minister before the ark of the LORD,
23: 2 together with the priests and the *L*.
23: 3 *L* thirty years old and above were counted,
23:26 Henceforth the *L* need not carry the
23:27 *L* from the time they were twenty years old.
24: 6 houses of the priests and of the *L*,
24:20 Of the remaining *L*, there were Shubael,
24:30 the *L* according to their ancestral houses.
26:20 Their brother *L* superintended the stores
28:13 as for the divisions of the priests and *L*,
28:21 The classes of the priests and *L* are ready
2Chr 5: 4 Israel had arrived, the *L* took up the ark,
5:12 various classes), the *L* who were singers,
7: 6 standing at their stations, as were the *L*,
8:14 and the *L* according to their functions of
8:15 to the priests and *L* or the treasuries.
11:13 Now the priests and *L* throughout Israel
11:14 for the *L* left their assigned pasture
13: 9 of the LORD, the sons of Aaron, and the *L*,
13:10 Aaron, and the *L* also have their offices.
17: 8 With them he sent the *L*,
19: 8 Jehoshaphat appointed some *L* and priests
19:11 and the *L* will be your officials.
20:19 *L* from among the Kohathites and Korahites
23: 2 gathering the *L* from all the cities of
23: 4 third of your number, both priests and *L*,
23: 6 priests and those *L* who are ministering.
23: 7 The *L* shall surround the king on all sides,
23: 8 The *L* and all Judah did just as Jehoiada
24: 5 the priests and *L* and said to them:
24: 5 But the *L* did not hasten.
24: 6 "Why have you not required the *L* to bring
24:11 brought to the royal officials by the *L*
29: 4 He summoned the priests and *L*,
29: 5 "Listen to me, you *L*!
29:12 Then the *L* arose:
29:16 where the *L* took it from them and carried
29:25 the *L* in the LORD's house with cymbals,
29:26 The *L* were stationed with the instruments
29:30 princes then commanded the *L* to sing
29:34 their brethren the *L* assisted them until
29:34 the *L*, in fact, were more willing than
30:15 The priests and *L*, touched with shame,
30:16 sprinkled the blood given them by the *L*;
30:17 and the *L* were in charge of slaughtering
30:21 and the *L* and the priests sang the praises
30:22 Hezekiah spoke encouragingly to all the *L*
30:25 together with the priests and *L* and the
31: 2 *L* according to their former classification,
31: 4 provide the support of the priests and *L*,
31: 9 the priests and the *L* concerning the heaps,
31:17 and the *L* of twenty years and over
34: 9 brought to the house of God which the *L*,
34:12 and Obadiah, *L* of the line of Merari,
34:12 All those *L* who were skillful with musical
34:13 Some of the other *L* were scribes,
34:30 of Jerusalem, the priests, the *L*,
35: 3 to the *L* who were to instruct all Israel,
35: 5 of the *L* and the families may be the same.
35: 8 gift to the people, the priests and the *L*.
35: 9 the rulers of the *L*, contributed to the *L*
35:10 as did the *L* in their classes according to
35:11 blood and the *L* proceeded to the skinning.
35:14 therefore the *L* prepared for themselves
35:15 their stations, for their brethren, the *L*,
35:18 like that of Josiah, the priests and *L*,
Ezr 1: 5 Judah and Benjamin and the priests and *L*—
2:40 The *L*: sons of Jeshua, Kadmiel,
2:70 The priests, the *L*,
3: 8 the priests and *L* and all who had come
3: 8 began by appointing the *L* twenty years of
3: 9 and their sons and their brethren, the *L*,
3:10 priests with the trumpets and the *L*,
3:12 Many of the priests, *L*,
6:16 priests, *L*,
6:18 *L* in their divisions for the service
6:20 The *L*, every one of whom had purified
7: 7 of the Israelites and some priests, *L*,
7:13 to the people of Israel, its priests or *L*,
8:20 the *L*) there were two hundred and twenty.
8:29 and *L* and the family leaders of Israel,
8:30 priest and the *L* then took over the silver,
8:33 they were assisted by the *L* Jozabad,
9: 1 priests nor the *L* have kept themselves aloof
10: 5 from the *L* and from all Israel that they
10:23 Of the *L*: Jozabad, Shimei,
Neh 3:17 him, the *L* carried out the work of repair:
7: 1 and the *L* were put in charge of them.
7:43 The *L*: sons of Jeshua, Kadmiel.
7:72 The priests, the *L*,
8: 7 [The *L* Jeshua, Bani, Sherebiah,
8: 9 *L* who were instructing the people]
8:11 [And the *L* quieted all the people saying,
8:13 priests and the *L* gathered around Ezra
9: 4 on the platform of the *L* were Jeshua,
9: 5 The *L* Jeshua, Kadmiel, Bani,
10: 1 appear the names of our princes, our *L*,
10:10 The *L*: Jeshua, son of Azaniah;
10:29 The rest of the people, priests, *L*,
10:35 priests, *L*, and people, have determined
10:38 bring to the *L*; they, the *L*, shall take
10:39 *L* when they take the tithe, and the *L*
10:40 and *L* bring the offerings of grain,
11: 3 of Judah dwelt lay Israelites, priests, *L*,
11:15 Among the *L* were Shemaiah,
11:18 The total of the *L* in the holy city was
11:20 rest of Israel, including priests and *L*,
11:22 The prefect of the *L* in Jerusalem was Uzzi,
11:36 of the *L* from Judah settled in Benjamin.
12: 1 priests and *L* who returned with Zerubbabel,
12: 8 The *L* were Jeshua, Binnui, Kadmiel,
12:24 The heads of the *L* were Hashabiah,
12:27 the *L* were sought out wherever they lived
12:30 priests and *L* first purified themselves,
12:44 legally assigned to the priests and *L*.
12:44 rejoiced in its appointed priests and *L*
12:47 offering to the *L*, and the *L* made theirs
13: 5 in grain, wine, and oil allotted to the *L*,
13:10 due the *L* were no longer being given,
13:10 so that the *L* and the singers who should
13:11 Then I brought the *L* together and had them
13:13 the scribe, and Pedaiah, one of the *L*,
13:22 Then I ordered the *L* to purify themselves
13:29 the covenant of the priesthood and the *L*!
13:30 various functions for the priests and *L*,
Tb 1: 7 To the *L* who were doing service in
Is 66:21 Some of these I will take as priests and *L*,
Jer 33:22 servant David and the *L* who minister to me.
Ez 40:46 the only *L* who may come near to minister
43:19 the *L* who are of the line of Zadok,
44:10 But as for the *L* who departed from me when
45: 5 ten thousand wide as property for the *L*,
48:11 along with the Israelites as the *L* did,
48:12 domain, next to the territory of the *L*.
48:13 The *L* shall have a territory corresponding
48:22 property of the *L* and the City property,
Jn 1:19 sent priests and *L* from Jerusalem to ask,

LEVITICAL (18)

Lv 25:32 "In *l* cities the Levites shall always
Dt 17: 9 to the *l* priests or to the judge who is in
17:18 that is in the custody of the *l* priests.
24: 8 out all the directions of the *l* priests.
27: 9 Moses, with the *l* priests,
31: 9 he entrusted it to the *l* priests who carry
Jos 3: 3 our God, which the *l* priests will carry,
8:33 on either side of the ark facing the *l* priests
1Chr 9:34 were the *l* family heads over their kindred,
15:12 "You, the heads of the *l* families,
24:31 the heads of the priestly and *l* families;
2Chr 5: 5 it was the *l* priests who carried them.
23:18 temple into the hands of the *l* priests,
30:27 the *l* priests rose and blessed the people;
Neh 11:16 *l* chiefs who were placed over the external
12:28 The *l* singers gathered together from the
Ez 44:15 As for the *L* priests,
Heb 7:11 had been achieved through the *l* priesthood

LEVY (5)

Ex 5: 8 Yet you shall *l* upon them the same quota
Nm 31:28 You shall *l* a tax for the LORD on the
2Sm 10: 7 Joab with the entire *l* of trained soldiers.
1Mc 3:31 to Persia and *l* tribute on those provinces,
2Mc 11: 3 to *l* tribute on the temple,

LEWD (10)

Ez 16:27 who revolted at your *l* conduct.
22: 9 in your midst are those who do *l* things.
23:44 came to Oholah and Oholibah, the *l* women.
Mt 5:32 his wife *l* conduct is a separate case
19: 9 whoever divorces his wife *l* conduct is a
1Cor 5: 1 It is actually reported that there is *l*
6:18 Shun *l* conduct.
Gal 5:19 *l* conduct,
Eph 4:19 the indulgence of every sort of *l* conduct.
5: 3 As for *l* conduct or promiscuousness or

LEWDNESS (18)

Lv 19:29 the land will become corrupt and full of *l*.
Ez 16:43 add *l* to the rest of your abominable deeds?
16:58 penalty of your *l* and your abominations
23:21 You yearned for the *l* of your girlhood,
23:27 *l* and to the harlotry you began in Egypt;
23:29 Your *l* and harlotry have brought these
23:35 to bear the penalty of your *l* and harlotry.
23:48 Thus I will put an end to *l* in the land,
23:48 women will be warned not to imitate your *l*.
23:49 inflict on you the penalty of your *l*,
24:13 with *l* when I would have purified you,
1Cor 10: 8 us not indulge in *l* as some of them did,
Rv 2:20 *l* and to eat food sacrificed to idols.
2:21 repent but she refuses to turn from her *l*.
14: 8 nations drink the poisoned wine of her *l*!"
17: 2 have grown drunk on the wine of her *l*."
17: 4 the abominable and sordid deeds of her *l*.
18: 3 nations drink the poisoned wine of her *l*.

LIABLE (4)

1Mc 14:45 prescriptions shall be *l* to punishment.
Mt 5:21 every murderer shall be *l* to judgment.'
5:22 with his brother shall be *l* to judgment;
Lk 20:36 like angels and are no longer *l* to death.

LIAR (15)

Prv 10:18 the lips of the *l* that conceal hostility;
19:22 rather be a poor man than a *l*.
Sir 20:24 Better a thief than an inveterate *l*,
34: 4 can the *l* ever speak the truth?
Jer 48:30 liar in boast, *l* in deed.
Jn 8:44 he is a *l* and the father of lies.
8:55 a *l*!
Rom 3: 4 true even though every man be proved a *l*,
1Jn 1:10 him a *l* and his word finds no place in us.
2: 4 without keeping his commandments, is a *l*;
2:22 Who is the *l*? He who denies that Jesus
4:20 on God," yet hates his brother, he is a *l*.
5:10 has made God a *l* by refusing to believe
Rv 21:27 who is a *l* or has done a detestable act.

LIARS (8)

Ps(s) 58: 4 astray from birth have the *l* gone.
Sir 15: 8 impious is she, not to be spoken of by *l.*
20:25 A *l* way leads to dishonor,
Is 44:25 is I who bring to nought the omens of *l,*
1Tm 1:10 sexual perverts, kidnapers, *l,*
4: 2 taught by demons through plausible *l*—
Ti 1:12 has testified, "Cretans have ever been *l,*
1Jn 1: 6 darkness, we are *l* and do not act in truth.

LIBATION (31)

Gn 35:14 and upon it he made a *l* and poured out oil.
Ex 29:40 hin of oil of crushed olives and, as its *l,*
29:41 cereal offering and *l* as in the morning.
30: 9 nor shall you pour out a *l* upon it.
Lv 23:13 its *l* shall be a fourth of a hin of wine.
Nm 6:17 the LORD, with its cereal offering and *l,*
15: 5 well as a *l* of a fourth of a hin of wine,
15: 7 oil, and a *l* of a third of a hin of wine,
15:10 hin of oil, and a *l* of half a hin of wine,
15:24 with its prescribed cereal offering and *l,*
28: 7 And as the *l* for the first lamb,
28: 8 offering and the same *l* as in the morning,
28:10 to the established holocaust and its *l.*
28:15 to the established holocaust and its *l.*
28:24 to the established holocaust with its *l,*
29:16 holocaust with its cereal offering and *l.*
29:19 holocaust with its cereal offering and *l.*
29:22 holocaust with its cereal offering and *l.*
29:25 holocaust with its cereal offering and *l.*
29:28 holocaust with its cereal offering and *l.*
29:31 holocaust with its cereal offering and *l.*
29:34 holocaust with its cereal offering and *l.*
29:38 holocaust with its cereal offering and *l.*
2Kgs 16:13 and cereal-offering, pouring out his *l,*
1Chr 11:18 he poured it out as a *l* to the LORD,
Jl 1: 9 offering and *l* from the house of the LORD;
1:13 of your God is deprived of offering and *l.*
Zec 9:15 till they are filled with it like *l* bowls,
14:20 shall be as the *l* bowls before the altar.
Phil 2:17 poured out as a *l* over the sacrifical service
2Tm 4: 6 part am already being poured out like a *l.*

LIBATIONS (40)

Ex 25:29 as its pitchers and bowls for pouring *l.*
37:16 as its pitchers and bowls for pouring *l,*
Lv 23:18 along with their cereal offering and *l,*
23:37 and cereal offerings, sacrifices and *l,*
Nm 4: 7 as well as the bowls and pitchers for *l;*
6:14 along with their cereal offerings and *l,*
28: 9 flour mixed with oil, and with their *l.*
28:14 Their *l* shall be half a hin of wine for
28:31 these offerings, together with their *l,*
29: 6 together with the *l* prescribed for them,
29:11 with its cereal offering, and their *l.*
29:18 and *l* as prescribed for the bullocks,
29:21 and *l* as prescribed for the bullocks,
29:24 and *l* as prescribed for the bullocks,
29:27 and *l* as prescribed for the bullocks,
29:30 and *l* as prescribed for the bullocks,
29:33 and *l* as prescribed for the bullocks,
29:37 and *l* as prescribed for the bullocks,
29:39 whatever holocausts, cereal offerings, *l,*
Dt 32:38 wine of your *l* Rise up now and help you!
2Kgs 16:15 cereal-offerings, and *l* of the people.
1Chr 29:21 *l* and many other sacrifices for all Israel;
2Chr 29:35 offerings and the *l* for the holocausts.
Ezr 7:17 the cereal offerings and *l* proper to these,
Est C:28 banquet of the king or drunk the wine of *l.*
1Mc 1:45 sacrifices, and *l* in the sanctuary,
Ps(s) 16: 4 Blood *l* to them I will not pour out,
Is 57: 6 To these you poured out *l,*
Jer 7:18 while *l* are poured out to strange gods in
19:13 of heaven and poured out *l* to strange gods.
32:29 *l* were poured out to strange gods
44:17 the queen of heaven and pour out *l* to her,
44:18 queen of heaven and pouring out *l* to her,
44:19 queen of heaven and poured out *l* to her,
44:19 cakes in her image and poured out *l* to her?
44:25 queen of heaven and to pour out *l* to her."
Ez 20:28 odors, and there they poured out their *l.*
45:17 cereal offerings, and *l* on the feasts,
Hos 9: 4 They shall not pour *l* of wine to the LORD,
Jl 2:14 Offerings and *l* for the LORD, your God.

LIBEL (1)

1Pt 3:16 *l* your way of life in Christ may be shamed.

LIBERAL (1)

1Mc 3:30 a more *l* hand than the preceding kings.

LIBERALITY (1)

2Cor 9:11 In every way your *l* is enriched;

LIBERATED (1)

2Mc 2:22 of the world-famous temple, *l* the city,

LIBERTIES (1)

1Tm 6: 2 must not take *l* with them on that account.

LIBERTY (10)

Lv 25:10 *l* in the land for all its inhabitants.
1Mc 10:33 of my kingdom I set at *l* without ransom;
14:26 They have thus preserved its *l.*"
Ps(s) 119:45 And I will walk at *l,*
Is 61: 1 To proclaim *l* to the captives and release
Lk 4:18 to the poor, to proclaim *l* to captives,
Acts 26:32 to Festus, "He could have been set at *l,*
Rom 15:15 I take this *l* because God has given me the
1Cor 10:29 Why should my *l* be restricted by another
Gal 5: 1 It was for *l* that Christ freed us.

LIBNAH (18)

Nm 33:20 out from Rimmon-perez, they camped at *L.*
33:21 Setting out from *L,* they camped at Rissah.
Jos 10:29 on with all Israel from Makkedah to *L,*
10:30 *L* also, with its king,
10:31 on with all Israel from *L* to Lachish,
10:32 person in it, just as he had done to *L.*
10:39 to Hebron, as well as to *L* and its king.
12:15 Gezer, Debir, Geder, Hormah, Arad, *L,*
15:42 sixteen cities and their villages, *L,*
21:13 also, *L* with its pasture lands,
2Kgs 8:22 *L* also revolted at that time.
19: 8 from Lachish, he found him besieging *L.*
23:31 Hamutal, daughter of Jeremiah, was from *L.*
24:18 was Hamutal, daughter of Jeremiah of *L.*
1Chr 6:42 a city of asylum, *L* with its pasture lands,
2Chr 21:10 *L* also revolted at that time against
Is 37: 8 had left there, he found him besieging *L.*
Jer 52: 1 was Hamutal, daughter of Jeremiah of *L.*

LIBNI (5)

Ex 6:17 as heads of clans, were *L* and Shimei.
Nm 3:18 Gershon, by clans, were named *L* and Shimei.
1Chr 6: 2 sons of Gershon were named *L* and Shimei.
6: 5 his son *L,* whose son was Jahath,
6:14 of Merari were Mahli, whose son was *L,*

LIBNITES (2)

Nm 3:21 of the *L* and the clan of the Shimeites;
26:58 the clan of the *L,*

LIBYA (3)

Ez 30: 5 Ethiopia, Put, Lud, all Arabia, *L,*
Dn 11:43 *L* and Ethiopia shall be in his train.
Acts 2:10 Egypt, and the regions of *L* around Cyrene.

LIBYANS (3)

2Chr 12: 3 the army that came with him from Egypt *L,*
16: 8 Were not the Ethiopians and *L* a vast army,
Na 3: 9 Put and the *L* were her auxiliaries.

LICENTIOUS (1)

2Tm 3: 3 inhuman, implacable, slanderous, *l,*

LICENTIOUSNESS (2)

Rom 6:19 to impurity and *l* for their degradation,
Gal 5:19 lewd conduct, impurity, *l,*

LICK (4)

1Kgs 21:19 of Naboth, the dogs shall *l* up your blood,
Ps(s) 72: 9 him, and his enemies shall *l* the dust.
Is 49:23 worship you and *l* the dust at your feet.
Mi 7:17 They shall *l* the dust like the serpent,

LICKED (3)

1Kgs 21:19 where the dogs *l* up the blood of Naboth,
22:38 *l* up his blood and harlots bathed there,
Lk 16:21 The dogs even came and *l* his sores.

LICKING (1)

Dt 32:22 *l* with flames the roots of the mountains,

LICKS (1)

Is 5:24 as the tongue of fire *l* up stubble,

LID (2)

Nm 19:15 that is open, or with its *l* unfastened,
2Kgs 12:10 then took a chest, bored a hole in its *l,*

LIE (119)

Gn 19:32 our father with wine and then *l* with him,
19:34 tonight, and then you go in and *l* with him,
26:10 for one of the men to *l* with your wife,
30:15 mandrakes, Jacob may *l* with you tonight."
39: 7 to look fondly at him and said, *L* with me."
39:10 day, he would not agree to *l* beside her,
39:12 of him by his cloak, saying, *L* with me!"
39:14 He came in here to *l* with me,
45:11 Since five years of famine still *l* ahead,
47:30 When I *l* down with my ancestors,
Ex 23:11 let the land *l* untilled and unharvested,
Lv 15:24 If a man dares to *l* with her,
18:22 shall not *l* with a male as with a woman;
19:11 not *l* or speak falsely to one another.
26: 6 you may *l* down to rest without anxiety.
Dt 25: 2 the judge shall have him *l* down and in his
Jos 9:22 "Why did you *l* to us and say that you
15:46 sea, all the towns that *l* alongside Ashdod,
Jgs 21:20 "Go and *l* in wait in the vineyards.
Ru 3: 4 uncover a place at his feet, and *l* down.
3:13 *L* there until morning."
2Sm 1:21 Upon you *l* begrimed the warriors' shields,
8: 2 a line, making them *l* down on the ground.
12:11 shall *l* with your wives in broad daylight.
12:16 to *l* on the ground clothed in sackcloth.
13: 5 *L* down on your bed and pretend to be sick.
13:11 *L* with me, my sister!"
2Kgs 1: 4 shall not leave the bed upon which you *l;*
1: 6 shall not leave the bed upon which you *l;*
1:16 shall not leave the bed upon which you *l;*
Tb 10: 7 retorted, "Stop it, and do not *l* to me!
Jdt 3: 2 the great king, *l* prostrate before you,
5: 5 no *l* shall escape your servant's lips.
11: 5 I will tell no *l* to my lord this night,
2Mc 5:10 he who had cast out so many to *l* unburied
Jb 6:28 surely I will not *l* to your face.
7:21 For soon I shall *l* down in the dust;
11:18 shall look round you and *l* down in safety,
14:12 parches, So men *l* down and rise not again.
20:11 vigor, this shall *l* with him in the dust.
21:26 Alike they *l* down in the dust,
38:30 When the waters *l* covered as though with
38:40 in their dens, or *l* in wait in the thicket?
Ps(s) 3: 6 When I *l* down in sleep,
4: 9 as I *l* down, I fall peacefully asleep,
37:24 Though he fall, he does not *l* prostrate,
57: 5 I *l* prostrate in the midst of lions which
59: 4 For behold, they *l* in wait for my life;
84:11 I had rather *l* at the threshold of the
88: 6 dead, like the slain who *l* in the grave,
119:25 *l* prostrate in the dust;
132: 3 live in, nor *l* on the couch where I sleep;
Prv 1:11 Let us *l* in wait for the honest man,
1:18 These men *l* in wait for their own blood,
3:24 When you *l* down, you need not be afraid,
6:22 When you *l* down she will watch over you,
14: 5 A truthful witness does not *l,*
15:11 world and the abyss *l* open before the LORD;
24:15 *L* not in wait against the home of the just
Eccl 11: 3 north, wherever it falls, there shall it *l.*
Sir 7:13 Delight not in telling *l* after lie,
20:23 A *l* is a foul blot in a man,
43:34 Beyond these, many things *l* hid;
50:21 Then again the people would *l* prostrate to
Is 11: 6 and the leopard shall *l* down with the kid;
14:18 All the kings of the nations *l* in glory,
14:30 shall eat, and the needy *l* down in safety;
17: 2 given over to flocks to *l* in undisturbed.
26:19 awake and sing, you who *l* in the dust.
27:10 where calves shall browse and *l.*
34:10 generation to generation she shall *l* waste,
43:17 army, Till they *l* prostrate together,
50:11 you shall *l* down in a place of pain.
51:20 Your sons *l* helpless at every street
56:10 Dreaming as they *l* there,
58: 5 like a reed, and *l* in sackcloth and ashes?
Jer 3:25 Let us *l* down in our shame,
4: 7 till your cities *l* waste and empty.
8: 2 but will *l* like dung upon the ground.
9:21 of the slain *l* like dung on a field,
16: 4 they will *l* like dung on the ground.
25:33 they shall *l* like dung on the field.
25:37 place, desolate *l* the peaceful pastures;
37:14 "That is a *l*!"
43: 2 "You *l;* it was not the LORD, our God,
51:47 all her slain shall *l* fallen within her.
Lam 2:21 in the dust of the streets *l* young and old;
4: 1 stones *l* strewn at every street corner!
Bar 2:25 they *l* exposed to the heat of day and the
Ez 4: 4 Then you shall *l* on your left side,
4: 4 As many days as you *l* thus,
4: 6 you finish this, you are to *l* down again,
4: 9 for as many days as you *l* upon your side,
6:13 when their slain shall *l* amid their idols,
31:18 You shall *l* with the uncircumcised,
32:21 and your allies, *l* with the uncircumcised,
32:27 do not *l* with the mighty men fallen of old,
32:28 the midst of the uncircumcised shall you *l,*
32:29 with the uncircumcised they *l,*
32:30 they *l* uncircumcised with those slain by
34:14 they shall *l* down on good grazing ground,
39:14 the land burying those who *l* unburied,
48:22 *l* in the midst of the prince's property,
Dn 13:20 give in to our desire, and *l* with us.
13:55 "Your fine *l* has cost you your head,"
13:59 "Your fine *l* has cost you also your head,"
Mi 7: 2 They all *l* in wait to shed blood,
Zec 13: 3 have spoken a *l* in the name of the LORD."
Acts 5: 3 Satan fill your heart so as to make you *l*
Rom 1:25 exchanged the truth of God for a *l*
9: 1 I do not *l.* My conscience bears
2Cor 11:31 blessed be he forever—that I do not *l.*
Phil 1: 7 sharers of my gracious lot when I *l* in prison
Ti 1: 2 that eternal life which God, who cannot *l,*
Heb 6:18 are unchangeable, in which he could not *l,*
1Jn 2:21 no *l* has anything in common with the truth.
2:27 free from any *l*—

Rv 11: 8 will *l* in the streets of the great city,

LIED (3)

Ps(s) 78:36 mouths and *l* to him with their tongues,
Jer 40:16 you have *l* about Ishmael."
Acts 5: 4 You have *l* not to men but to God!"

LIES (103)

Gn 20:15 said, "Here, my land *l* at your disposal;
49:29 that *l* in the field of Ephron the Hittite,
Ex 22:15 who is not betrothed, and *l* with her,
22:18 who *l* with an animal shall be put to death.
Lv 15: 4 which the man afflicted with the flow *l*,
15:18 "If a man *l* carnally with a woman,
15:20 Anything on which she *l* or sits during her
15:24 on which he then *l* also becomes unclean.
15:26 she *l* during such a flow becomes unclean,
15:33 for the man who *l* with an unclean woman."
20:12 If a man *l* with his daughter-in-law,
20:13 If a man *l* with a male as with a woman,
20:18 If a man *l* in sexual intercourse with a
26:34 sabbaths during all the time it *l* waste,
26:35 during all the time that it *l* desolate,
Nm 14:33 till the last of you *l* dead in the desert.
24: 9 He *l* crouching like a lion,
Dt 19:11 if someone *l* in wait for his neighbor out
33:20 He *l* there like a lion that has seized the
Jgs 16:10 Samson, "You have mocked me and told me *l*.
16:13 to now you have mocked me and told me *l*.
18:12 the place, which *l* west of Kiriath-jearim,
Ru 3: 4 But when he *l* down,
2Sm 2:24 hill of Ammah which *l* east of the valley
17: 9 Even now he *l* hidden in one of the caves
2Chr 36:21 during all the time it *l* waste it shall
Neh 1: 3 Also, the wall of Jerusalem *l* breached,
2: 3 where my ancestors are buried *l* in ruins,
2:17 how Jerusalem *l* in ruins and its gates
Tb 2: 3 His body *l* in the market place where he
Jb 8:19 There he *l* rotting beside the road,
27:19 He *l* down a rich man,
40:21 Under the lotus trees he *l*,
Ps(s) 10: 9 he *l* in wait to catch the afflicted;
10:10 He stoops and *l* prone till by his violence
41: 9 and 'Now that he *l* ill,
59:13 for the *l* they have told under oath.
62: 5 they delight in *l*;
88: 8 Upon me your wrath *l* heavy,
119:69 Though the proud forge *l* against me,
Prv 6:19 to evil, The false witness who utters *l*,
11:14 security *l* in many counselors.
14: 5 does not lie, but a false witness utters *l*.
14:25 lives, but he who utters *l* is a betrayer.
14:28 In many subjects *l* the glory of the king;
19: 5 and he who utters *l* will not escape.
19: 9 and he who utters *l* will perish.
23:28 Yes, she *l* in wait like a robber,
Wis 14:28 go mad with enjoyment, or prophesy *l*,
Sir 11:32 The evil man *l* in wait for blood,
14:22 a scout, and *l* in wait at her entry way;
15:20 sin, to none does he give strength for *l*.
23:13 to coarse talk, for in it *l* sinful matter.
27:28 vengeance *l* in wait for them like a lion.
31:19 When he *l* down, it is without discomfort.
40: 5 Even when he *l* on his bed to rest,
51: 5 From deceiving lips and painters of *l*,
Is 28:15 For we have made *l* our refuge,
28:17 Hail shall sweep away the refuge of *l*,
30:15 in quiet and in trust your strength *l*.
32: 7 How to ruin the poor with *l*,
59: 4 They trust in emptiness and tell *l*;
Jer 12:11 a mournful waste, desolate it *l* before me,
14:14 *L* these prophets utter in my name,
20: 6 because you have prophesied *l* to them.
23:14 Adultery, living in *l*,
23:25 the prophets who prophesy *l* in my name say,
23:26 prophesy *l* and their own deceitful fancies?
23:32 their *l* and by their empty boasting.
27:10 For they prophesy *l* to you,
27:14 of Babylon," for they prophesy *l* to you.
27:16 soon now," for they prophesy *l* to you.
29: 9 For they prophesy *l* to you in my name;
29:21 those who prophesy *l* to you in my name,
Bar 6:43 aside by some passer-by who *l* with her,
Ez 13: 9 who have false visions and who foretell *l*.
13:19 lying to my people who willingly hear *l*.
13:22 man with *l* when I did not wish him grieved,
33:31 for *l* are on their lips and their desires
Dn 11:27 sit at table together and exchange *l*,
14:12 Daniel shall die for his *l* against us."
Hos 7:13 to redeem them, they spoke *l* against me.
12: 1 Ephraim has surrounded me with *l*,
12: 2 His *l* and falsehoods are many:
Jl 1:17 The seed *l* shriveled under its clods;
Am 2: 4 Because the *l* which their fathers followed
5: 2 She *l* abandoned upon her land,
Mi 2: 1 accomplish it when it *l* within their power.
7: 5 Against her who *l* in your bosom guard the
Na 3: 1 Woe to the bloody city, all *l*,
Zep 3:13 They shall do no wrong and speak no *l*;
Hg 1: 4 houses, while this house *l* in ruins?
1: 9 Because my house *l* in ruins,
Mt 11:19 Yet time will prove where wisdom *l*."
24:28 Where the carcass *l*,
Lk 12:34 Wherever your treasure *l*,
Jn 8:44 he is a liar and the father of *l*.
Rom 3:13 The venom of asps *l* behind their lips,
1Cor 2:11 no one knows what *l* at the depths of God
2Cor 5:12 and not in what *l* in the heart.
Phil 3:13 what *l* behind but push on to what is ahead.
Heb 4:13 all *l* bare and exposed to the eyes of him
12: 1 in running the race which *l* ahead;

LIEUTENANT (1)

Jgs 9:28 *l* Zebul once subject to the men of Hamor,

LIFE (754)

Gn 2: 7 and blew into his nostrils the breath of *l*,
2: 9 with the tree of *l* in the middle of the
3:14 dirt shall you eat all the days of your *l*.
3:17 you eat its yield all the days of your *l*.
3:22 hand to take fruit from the tree of *l* also,
3:24 sword, to guard the way to the tree of *l*.
6:13 So I will destroy them and all *l* on earth.
6:17 in which there is the breath of *l*;
7:11 In the six hundredth year of Noah's *l*,
7:15 the breath of *l* entered the ark with Noah.
7:22 breath of *l* in its nostrils died out.
8:13 six hundred and first year of Noah's *l*,
9: 5 I will demand an accounting for human *l*.
12:13 and my *l* may be spared for your sake."
19:17 "Flee for your *l*!
19:19 great kindness of intervening to save my *l*.
19:20 —that my *l* may be saved."
20: 7 that your *l* may be saved.
23: 1 *l* was one hundred and twenty-seven years.
25: 7 *l* was one hundred and seventy-five years.
25: 8 a ripe old age, grown old after a full *l*;
25:17 *l* was one hundred and thirty-seven years.
26: 9 thought I might lose my *l* on her account."
27:46 with *l* because of the Hittite women.
27:46 these women, what good would *l* be to me?"
32:31 he said, "yet my *l* has been spared."
35:29 After a full *l*, he died as an old man
37:21 "We must not take his *l*.
38: 7 so the LORD took his *l*.
38:10 the LORD, and the LORD took his *l* too.
42:15 *l* of Pharaoh that you shall not leave here.
44:30 father, whose very *l* is bound up with his,
47: 9 and hard have been these years of my *l*,
47:28 *l* came to a hundred and forty-seven years.
49:15 When he saw how good a settled *l* was,
Ex 1:14 making *l* bitter for them with hard work in
4:19 for all the men who sought your *l* are dead."
20:12 have a long *l* in the land which the LORD,
21:23 injury ensues, you shall give *l* for life,
21:30 his *l* whatever amount is imposed on him.
23:26 and I will give you a full span of *l*.
30:12 shall give the LORD a forfeit for his *l*,
Lv 17:11 the *l* of a living body is in its blood,
17:11 because it is the blood, as the seat of *l*,
17:14 the *l* of every living body is its blood,
18: 5 carries them out will find *l* through them.
19:16 by idly when your neighbor's *l* is at stake.
20: 9 father or mother, he has forfeited his *l*.
24:17 *l* of any human being shall be put to death;
24:18 whoever takes the *l* of an animal shall
24:18 A *l* for a life!
26:16 and fever to dim the eyes and sap the *l*.
Nm 14:21 by my *l* and the LORD's glory that fills
14:28 By my *l*, says the LORD,
35:31 not accept indemnity in place of the *l*
Dt 4:40 may have long *l* on the land which the LORD,
4:42 his *l* by fleeing to one of these cities:
5:16 that you may have a long *l* and prosperity
5:33 long *l* in the land which you are to occupy.
6: 2 I enjoin on you, and thus have long *l*.
6:24 prosperous and happy a *l* as we have today;
11: 9 and that you may have long *l* on the land
12:23 for blood is *l*,
12:23 not consume this seat of *l* with the flesh.
13:16 dooming the city and all *l* that is in it,
16:20 *l* and may possess the land which the LORD,
17:19 his *l* that he may learn to fear the LORD,
19: 4 take refuge in such a place to save his *l*:
19: 5 in one of these cities to save his *l*.
19:21 Life for *l*, eye for eye, tooth for tooth,
22: 7 you shall have prosperity and a long *l*.
25:15 have a long *l* on the land which the LORD,
30:15 have today set before you *l* and prosperity,
30:18 you will not have a long *l* on the land
30:19 I have set before you *l* and death,
30:19 Choose *l*, then, that you and your
30:20 will mean *l* for you, a long life for you
32:39 It is I who bring both death and *l*,
32:47 rather, it means your very *l*,
32:47 you are to enjoy a long *l* on the land
Jos 4:14 during his whole *l* they respected him
Jgs 9:17 fought for you at the risk of his *l*
12: 3 I took my *l* in my own hand and went on to
1Sm 2: 6 "The LORD puts to death and gives *l*;
18: 1 fond of David as if his *l* depended on him;
19: 5 his *l* in his hands and slew the Philistine,
20: 1 father hold against me that he seeks my *l*?"
22:23 that seeks your *l* must seek my life also.
23:15 because Saul had come out to seek his *l*;
24:12 you are hunting me down to take my *l*.
25:28 evil to be found in you your whole *l* long.
25:29 seek your life, may the *l* of my lord
26:21 because you have held my *l* precious today.
26:24 As I valued your *l* highly today,
26:24 so may the LORD value my *l* highly and
28: 9 Why, then, are you laying snares for my *l*,
28:21 I took my *l* in my hands and fulfilled the
2Sm 1:23 separated neither in *l* nor in death,
4: 8 son of your enemy Saul, who sought your *l*.
12:22 the LORD will grant me the child's *l*.'
14: 7 for the *l* of his brother whom he has slain;
14:14 Yet, though God does not bring back *l*,
15:21 king may be, whether for death or for *l*."
16:11 came forth from my loins, is seeking my *l*,
19: 6 your *l* and your sons' and daughters' lives,
1Kgs 1:12 save your *l* and that of your son Solomon.
2:23 has not proposed this at the cost of his *l*.
3:11 not for a long *l* for yourself,
3:11 for riches, nor for the *l* of your enemies,
3:14 father David did, I will give you a long *l*."
17:21 *l* breath return to the body of this child."
17:22 the *l* breath returned to the child's body
19: 2 with your *l* what was done to each of them."
19: 3 Elijah was afraid and fled for his *l*,
19: 4 Take my *l*, for I am no better than my
19:10 alone am left, and they seek to take my *l*."
19:14 alone am left, and they seek to take my *l*."
20:31 Perhaps he will spare your *l*."
20:32 "Your servant Ben-hadad pleads for his *l*,"
20:39 pay for his life with your *l* or pay out a
20:42 destruction, your life shall pay for his *l*,
2Kgs 1:13 my *l* and the lives of these fifty men,
1:14 But now, let my *l* mean something to you!"
4:31 boy, but there was no sound or sign of *l*.
5: 7 "Am I a god with power over *l* and death,
8: 1 the woman whose son he had restored to *l*:
8: 5 master had restored a dead person to *l*,
8: 5 Elisha had restored to *l* came to the king
8: 5 that son of hers whom Elisha restored to *l*."
10:24 into your hands, he shall pay *l* for life."
13:21 he came back to *l* and rose to his feet.
18:32 Choose *l*, not death.
20: 6 I will add fifteen years to your *l*.
1Chr 29:15 Our *l* on earth is like a shadow that does
2Chr 1:11 *l* of those who hate you, nor even for a long *l*
Ezr 6:10 pray for the *l* of the king and his sons.
9: 9 Thus he has given us a new *l* to raise
Neh 6:11 man like me enter the temple to save his *l*?
9: 6 To all of them you give *l*,
9:29 which men draw *l* when they practice them.
Tb 1: 3 *l* on the paths of truth and righteousness.
3: 6 command my *l* breath to be taken from me,
3: 6 to die than to endure so much misery in *l*,
4: 5 Perform good works all the days of your *l*,
10:13 cause her grief at any time in your *l*.
10:14 "May I honor you all the days of my *l*!"
12: 9 regularly give alms shall enjoy a full *l*;
Jdt 10:13 of his men suffering injury or loss of *l*."
10:15 to see our master, you have saved your *l*.
11: 3 *l* is spared tonight and for the future.
11: 7 By the *l* of Nebuchadnezzar,
12:18 I ever enjoyed *l* as much as I do today."
12:20 had ever drunk on one single day in his *l*.
13:20 *l* when your people were being oppressed,
16:21 her *l* she was renowned throughout the land.
16:22 herself to no man all the days of her *l*
16:25 During the *l* of Judith and for a long time
Est B: 2 my subjects a *l* of complete tranquillity;
4:11 him the golden scepter, thus sparing his *l*.
C:15 but you, for I am taking my *l* in my hand.
7: 3 your majesty, I ask that my *l* be spared,
7: 7 stayed to beg Queen Esther for his *l*,
E:12 strove to deprive us of kingdom and of *l*;
1Mc 3:12 who fought with it the rest of his *l*.
6:44 So he gave up his *l* to save his people and
9:71 try to injure him for the rest of his *l*;
10:47 remained his allies for the rest of his *l*.
11:48 Thus they saved the king's *l*.
13: 5 to save my own *l* in any time of distress,
2Mc 3:31 praying that the *l* of the man who was
3:33 his sake that the Lord has spared your *l*.
3:35 solemn vows to him who had spared his *l*,
4:10 his countrymen into the Greek way of *l*.
4:16 people whose manner of *l* they emulated,
6:19 a glorious death to a *l* of defilement,
6:20 it is unlawful to taste even for love of *l*.
6:23 admirable *l* he had lived from childhood;
6:25 for the sake of a brief moment of *l*,
6:27 Therefore, by manfully giving up my *l* now,
7: 9 you are depriving us of this present *l*,
7:14 hope of being restored to *l* by him;
7:14 you, there will be no resurrection to *l*."
7:22 it was not I who gave you the breath of *l*,
7:23 will give you back both breath and *l*,
7:25 urging her to advise her boy to save his *l*.
7:36 brief pain, have drunk of never-failing *l*,
7:37 up my body and my *l* for our ancestral laws,
8:17 the subversion of their ancestral way of *l*.
10:13 office, he ended his *l* by taking poison.
11:24 customs but prefer their own way of *l*.
12:24 asked them to spare his *l* and let him go,

LIFE (cont.)
14:25 settled down, and shared the common *l*.
14:38 body and *l* in his ardent zeal for it.
14:46 calling upon the LORD of *l* and of spirit
Jb 2: 4 All that a man has will he give for his *l*.
2: 6 "He is in your power; only spare his *l*."
3:20 the toilers, and *l* to the bitter in spirit?
4: 6 and your integrity of *l* your hope?
7: 1 Is not man's *l* on earth a drudgery?
7: 7 Remember that my *l* is like the wind;
9:21 I despise my *l*.
10: 1 I loathe my *l*.
10:20 Are not the days of my *l* few?
11:17 your *l* shall be brighter than the noonday;
12:10 thing, and the *l* breath of all mankind.
13:14 between my teeth, and take my *l* in my hand.
17: 1 is broken, my lamp of *l* extinguished;
24:22 of his *l* he gives safety and support.
27: 3 So long as I still have *l* in me and the
27: 8 he is cut off, when God requires his *l*?
31:30 to sin by uttering a curse against his *l*—
33:18 pit and his *l* from passing to the grave.
33:22 to the pit, his *l* to the place of the dead.
33:28 to the pit, and I behold the light of *l*."
34:11 and brings home to a man his way of *l*.
36: 5 he preserves not the *l* of the wicked.
Ps(s) 6: 5 Return, O LORD, save my *l*;
7: 6 let him trample my *l* to the ground,
16:11 You will show me the path to *l*,
17:14 men whose portion in *l* is in this world,
21: 5 He asked *l* of you:
22:22 the horns of the wild bulls, my wretched *l*.
23: 6 kindness follow me all the days of my *l*;
25:20 Preserve my *l*, and rescue me;
26: 9 of sinners, nor with men of blood my *l*.
27: 4 house of the LORD all the days of my *l*,
31:11 For my *l* is spent with grief and my years
31:14 together against me, plotting to take my *l*.
34:13 Which of you desires *l*,
35: 4 put to shame and disgraced who seek my *l*;
35: 7 without cause they dug a pit against my *l*.
35:17 from the lions, my only *l*.
36:10 For with you is the fountain of *l*,
38:13 Men lay snares for me seeking my *l*;
39: 6 my days, and my *l* is as nought before you;
40:15 confusion who seek to snatch away my *l*.
49: 9 Too high is the price to redeem one's *l*;
54: 5 up against me, and fierce men seek my *l*;
54: 6 the Lord sustains my *l*.
56: 7 As they have waited for my *l*,
59: 4 For behold, they lie in wait for my *l*;
61: 7 Add to the days of the king's *l*;
63: 4 For your kindness is a greater good than *l*;
63:10 But they shall be destroyed who seek my *l*,
64: 2 from the dread enemy preserve my *l*.
66: 9 He has given *l* to our souls,
69: 2 me, O God, for the waters threaten my *l*;
69:19 Come and ransom my *l*;
70: 3 put to shame and confounded who seek my *l*.
71:10 watch against my *l* take counsel together.
71:13 put to shame and consumed who attack my *l*;
74:19 Give not to the vulture the *l* of your dove;
80:19 give us new *l*,
85: 7 Will you not instead give us *l*;
86: 2 Keep my *l*, for I am devoted to you;
86:14 and the company of fierce men seeks my *l*,
88: 4 and my *l* draws near to the nether world.
89:48 Remember how short my *l* is;
94:21 *l* of the just and condemn innocent blood,
103: 4 He redeems your *l* from destruction,
104:33 I will sing to the LORD all my *l*;
107: 5 their *l* was wasting away within them.
116: 4 the name of the LORD, "O LORD, save my *l*!"
119:25 give me *l* according to your word.
119:37 by your way give me *l*.
119:40 in your justice give me *l*.
119:50 affliction is that your promise gives me *l*.
119:88 In your kindness give me *l*,
119:93 precepts, for through them you give me *l*.
119:107 O LORD, give me *l* according to your word.
119:109 Though constantly I take my *l* in my hands,
119:149 according to your ordinance give me *l*.
119:154 for the sake of your promise give me *l*.
119:156 according to your ordinances give me *l*.
119:159 in your kindness give me *l*.
121: 7 he will guard your *l*.
128: 5 of Jerusalem all the days of your *l*;
133: 3 has pronounced his blessing, *l* forever.
141: 8 strip me not of *l*.
142: 5 there is no one who cares for my *l*.
143: 3 he has crushed my *l* to the ground;
146: 2 I will praise the LORD all my *l*;
Prv 1:12 world does, alive, in the prime of *l*,
1:19 takes away the *l* of him who acquires it.
2:19 come back again, or gain the paths of *l*.
3: 2 For many days, and years of *l*,
3:16 Long *l* is in her right hand,
3:18 She is a tree of *l* to those who grasp her,
3:22 So will they be *l* to your soul,
4:10 and the years of your *l* shall be many.
4:13 keep her, for she is your *l*.
4:22 For they are *l* to those who find them,
4:23 your heart, for in it are the sources of *l*.
5: 6 Lest you see before you the road to *l*,
6:23 a way to *l* are the reproofs of discipline;
6:26 married, she is a trap for your precious *l*.
7:23 a snare, unaware that its *l* is at stake.
8:35 For he who finds me finds *l*,
9:11 and the years of your *l* increased."
10:11 A fountain of *l* is the mouth of the just,
10:16 The just man's recompense leads to *l*,
10:17 A path to *l* is his who heeds admonition,
10:27 The fear of the LORD prolongs *l*,
11:19 Virtue directs toward *l*,
11:30 The fruit of virtue is a tree of *l*,
12:28 In the path of justice there is *l*,
13: 3 He who guards his mouth protects his *l*;
13: 8 A man's riches serve as ransom for his *l*,
13:12 sick, but a wish fulfilled is a tree of *l*.
13:14 teaching of the wise is a fountain of *l*,
14:27 The fear of the LORD is a fountain of *l*,
14:30 A tranquil mind gives *l* to the body,
15: 4 A soothing tongue is a tree of *l*,
15:24 The path of *l* leads the prudent man upward,
16:15 the light of the king's countenance is *l*,
16:17 pays attention to his way safeguards his *l*.
16:22 sense is a fountain of *l* to its possessor,
18: 7 his lips are a snare to his *l*.
18:21 Death and *l* are in the power of the tongue;
19:16 He who keeps the precept keeps his *l*,
19:23 The fear of the LORD is an aid to *l*;
20: 2 he who incurs his anger forfeits his *l*.
21:21 justice and kindness will find *l* and honor.
22: 4 fear of the LORD is riches, honor, and *l*.
22: 5 who would safeguard his *l* will shun them.
24:12 He who guards your *l* knows it,
29:10 but the upright show concern for his *l*.
31:12 good, and not evil, all the days of her *l*.
Eccl 2: 3 heavens during the limited days of their *l*.
2:17 Therefore I loathed *l*,
3:12 than to be glad and to do well during *l*.
5:16 of his *l* are passed in gloom and sorrow,
5:17 limited days of the *l* which God gives him;
5:19 hardly dwell on the shortness of his *l*,
6: 8 man in knowing how to conduct himself in *l*?
6:12 a man in *l*, the limited days of his vain *l*
7:12 that wisdom preserves the *l* of its owner.
8: 8 of the breath of *l* so as to retain it,
8:15 of the *l* which God gives him under the sun.
9: 3 and madness is in their hearts during *l*;
9: 9 Enjoy *l* with the wife whom you love,
9: 9 *l* that is granted you under the sun.
9: 9 This is your lot in *l*,
11: 5 Just as you know not how the breath of *l*
12: 7 the *l* breath returns to God who gave it.
Wis 1:12 Court not death by your erring way of *l*,
2: 4 So our *l* will pass away like the traces of
2:15 us, Because his *l* is not like other men's,
3:17 disappear For should they attain long *l*,
4: 9 hoary crown for men, and an unsullied *l*,
5: 4 His *l* we accounted madness,
7: 6 but one is the entry into *l* for all;
8: 5 if riches be a desirable possession in *l*,
8: 7 in *l* is more useful for men than these.
12:23 those unjust also, who lived a *l* of folly,
13:18 and for *l* he entreats the dead;
14:12 and their invention was a corruption of *l*.
15: 8 the *l* that was lent him is demanded back.
15: 9 is to die nor that his span of *l* is brief;
15:10 hope, and more ignoble than clay his *l*;
15:12 our *l* a plaything, and our span of *l*
16:13 For you have dominion over *l* and death;
Sir 3: 6 who reveres his father will live a long *l*;
4:12 He who loves her loves *l*;
9:13 offend him not, lest he take away your *l*;
10: 9 even during *l* man's body decays;
11:14 Good and evil, *l* and death,
11:18 A man may become rich through a miser's *l*,
11:27 when a man dies, his *l* is revealed.
15:17 Before man are *l* and death,
16: 3 Count not on their length of *l*,
16:28 of *l* which must return into it again.
17: 2 Limited days of *l* he gives him and makes
17: 9 knowledge, a law of *l* as their inheritance;
19: 4 strays after them sins against his own *l*.
20:21 One may lose his *l* through shame,
22:10 but worse than death is the *l* of a fool.
23: 1 LORD, Father and Master of my *l*,
23: 4 LORD, Father and God of my *l*,
25: 2 their manner of *l* I loathe indeed:
26: 2 to her husband, peaceful and full is his *l*.
29:15 backer, for he offers his very *l* for you.
29:24 *l* it is to go from house to house,
30: 5 Whom he looks upon through *l* with joy,
30:17 Preferable is death to a bitter *l*,
30:22 Gladness of heart is the very *l* of man,
30:24 Envy and anger shorten one's *l*,
31:27 is very *l* to man if taken in moderation.
33:14 contrasts with good, and death with *l*,
33:21 While breath of *l* is still in you,
33:32 for you need him as you need your *l*:
34:17 the eyes, gives health and *l* and blessing.
34:21 bread of charity is *l* itself for the needy;
37:18 Good and evil, death and *l*,
37:23 days of one man's *l*, but the *l* of Israel is
37:30 but the abstemious man prolongs his *l*.
39:26 all needs for human *l* are water and fire,
40:17 Wealth or wages can make *l* sweet,
40:28 My son, live not the *l* of a beggar,
40:29 table, his life is not really a *l*.
41: 4 in the nether world he has no claim on *l*.
41:13 The boon of *l* is for limited days,
43:26 stupendous, amazing, all kinds of *l*,
45: 5 the law of *l* and understanding,
46:12 bones return to *l* from their resting place,
46:19 When Samuel approached the end of his *l*,
48: 5 a dead man back to *l* from the nether world,
48:13 beneath him flesh was brought back into *l*.
48:14 In *l* he performed wonders,
48:23 the sun and prolonged the *l* of the king.
49:10 bones return to *l* from their resting place!—
51: 1 will make known your name, refuge of my *l*;
51: 3 from the power of those who sought my *l*;
Is 4: 3 every one marked down for *l* in Jerusalem.
26:14 Dead they are, they have no *l*,
38: 5 I will add fifteen years to your *l*.
38:10 said, "In the noontime of *l* I must depart!
38:12 You have folded up my *l*,
38:16 the *l* of my spirit.
38:16 You have given me health and *l*;
38:17 preserved my *l* from the pit of destruction,
38:20 house of the LORD all the days of our *l*.
43: 4 for you and peoples in exchange for your *l*.
53:10 If he gives his *l* as an offering for sin,
53:10 he shall see his descendants in a long *l*,
55: 3 me heedfully, listen, that you may have *l*.
57:19 for them, I, the Creator, who gave them *l*.
Jer 4:30 Your lovers spurn you, they seek your *l*.
8: 3 Death will be preferred to *l* by all the
10:14 He has molded a fraud, without breath of *l*.
11:21 the men of Anathoth who seek your *l*,
15: 9 of seven swoons away, gasping out her *l*;
18:20 that they should dig a pit to take my *l*?
20:13 *l* of the poor from the power of the wicked!
21: 8 am giving you a choice between *l* and death.
21: 9 shall live and have his *l* as booty.
22:25 into the hands of those who seek your *l*;
35: 7 You shall dwell in tents all your *l*,
38: 2 his *l* shall be spared him as booty,
38:16 LORD lives who gave us the breath of *l*,
38:16 hand you over to these men who seek your *l*."
38:17 of Babylon's king, you shall save your *l*;
38:20 well with you, and your *l* will be spared.
39:18 Your *l* shall be spared as booty,
44:30 to his enemies, to those who seek his *l*,
45: 5 LORD, but your *l* I will leave you as booty,
49:37 their foes, before those who seek their *l*;
51: 6 let each one save his *l*,
51:17 He molded a fraud, without breath of *l*.
52:34 days of his *l* until the day of his death.
Lam 1:11 for food, to retain the breath of *l*.
3:58 me in mortal danger, you redeemed my *l*.
4:20 anointed one of the LORD, our breath of *l*,
Bar 1:11 God, and pray for the *l* of Nebuchadnezzar,
3: 9 Hear, O Israel, the commandments of *l*:
3:14 know also where are length of days, and *l*:
Ez 3:19 die for his sin, but you shall save your *l*.
3:21 the warning, and you shall save your own *l*.
7:13 of his sins, no one shall preserve his *l*.
13:22 turn from his evil conduct and save his *l*;
18: 4 the *l* of the father is like the *l* of the son,
18:27 right and just, he shall preserve his *l*;
20:11 everyone must keep, to have *l* through them.
20:13 that bring *l* to those who keep them.
20:21 that bring *l* to those who observe them,
21:30 coming when your *l* of crime will be ended,
32:10 shall continuously tremble for his own *l*.
33: 5 warning he would have escaped with his *l*.
33:15 living by the statutes that bring *l*,
37: 3 Son of man, can these bones come to *l*?
37: 5 spirit into you, that you may come to *l*.
37: 6 may come to *l* and know that I am the LORD.
37: 9 into these slain that they may come to *l*.
Dn 1:10 age, you will endanger my *l* with the king."
5:23 *l* breath and the whole course of your life,
7:12 prolongation of *l* for a time and a season.
Am 2:14 The warrior shall not save his *l*,
2:15 not escape, nor the horseman save his *l*.
8:14 idol of Samaria, "By the *l* of your god,
8:14 "By the *l* of your love, O Beer-sheba!"
Jon 1:14 let us not perish for taking this man's *l*;
2: 6 waters swirled about me, threatening my *l*;
2: 7 But you brought my *l* up from the pit,
4: 3 And now, LORD, please take my *l* from me;
Hb 2:10 off many peoples, forfeiting your own *l*:
2:19 and silver, but there is no *l* breath in it.
Zep 2:14 in droves all the wild *l* of the hollows;
Mal 2: 5 covenant with him was one of *l* and peace;
2:15 You must then safeguard *l* that is your own,
2:16 You must then safeguard *l* that is your own,
Mt 2:20 had designs on the *l* of the child are dead."
6:25 Is not *l* more than food?
7:14 how narrow is the gate that leads to *l*,
9:18 hand on her and she will come back to *l*."
10:28 the body of *l* but cannot destroy the soul.
11: 5 the deaf hear, dead men are raised to *l*,
11:28 you who are weary and find *l* burdensome,
16:25 save his *l* will lose it, but whoever loses his *l*
18: 8 Better to enter *l* maimed or crippled than

18: 9 Better to enter l with one eye than be
19:16 good must I do to possess everlasting l?"
19:17 If you wish to enter into l,
19:29 times as much and inherit everlasting l.
20:28 to give his own l as a ransom for the many."
25:46 punishment and the just to eternal l."
Mk 3: 4 To preserve l— or destroy it?"
8:35 his l will lose it, but whoever loses his l
8:37 What can a man offer in exchange for his l?
9:43 Better for you to enter l maimed than to
9:45 Better for you to enter l crippled than to
10:17 what must I do to share in everlasting l?"
10:30 and in the age to come, everlasting l.
10:45 to give his l in ransom for the many."
12:14 respect but teach God's way of l sincerely.
12:23 resurrection, when they all come back to l,
Lk 6: 9 To preserve l— or destroy it?"
7: 3 him to come and save the l of his servant.
7:22 the deaf hear, dead men are raised to l,
8:14 and pleasures of l and they do not mature.
8:50 needed is trust and her l will be spared."
8:55 The breath of l returned to her and she
9:24 save his l will lose it, and whoever loses his l
10:25 what must I do to inherit everlasting l?"
12:15 but his possessions do not guarantee him l."
12:20 very night your l shall be required of you.
12:22 warn you, Do not be concerned for your l,
12:23 L is more important than food and the body
15:24 of mine was dead and has come back to l.
15:32 of yours was dead, and has come back to l.
17:33 tries to preserve his l will lose it;
18:18 what must I do to share in everlasting l?"
18:30 age and l everlasting in the age to come."
Jn 1: 4 Whatever came to be in him, found l,
1: 4 in him, found life, l for the light of men.
3:15 all who believe may have eternal l in him.
3:16 in him may not die but may have eternal l.
3:36 Whoever believes in the Son has l eternal.
3:36 Whoever disobeys the Son will not see l,
4:14 him, leaping up to provide eternal l."
4:36 wages and gathers a yield for eternal l,
5:21 grants l, so the Son grants l to those
5:24 in him who sent me possesses eternal l.
5:24 but has passed from death to l.
5:26 just as the Father possesses l in himself,
5:26 granted it to the Son to have l in himself.
5:39 in which you think you have eternal l—
5:40 unwilling to come to me to possess that l.
6:27 but for food that remains unto l eternal,
6:33 down from heaven and gives l to the world."
6:35 "I myself am the bread of l.
6:40 and believes in him shall have eternal l.
6:47 assure you, he who believes has eternal l.
6:48 I am the bread of l.
6:51 give is my flesh, for the l of the world."
6:53 and drink his blood, you have no l in you.
6:54 drinks my blood has l eternal
6:57 Father who has l sent me and I have l
6:57 who feeds on me will have l because of me.
6:63 It is the spirit that gives l;
6:63 The words I spoke to you are spirit and l.
6:68 You have the words of eternal l.
8:12 no, he shall possess the light of l."
10:10 they might have l and have it to the full.
10:11 shepherd lays down his l for the sheep.
10:15 for these sheep I will give my l.
10:17 that I lay down my l to take it up again.
10:28 I give them eternal l,
11:12 if he is asleep his l will be saved."
11:25 "I am the resurrection and the l:
11:26 me, though he should die, will come to l;
12:25 l loses it, while the man who hates his l
12:25 in this world preserves it to l eternal.
12:50 know that his commandment means eternal l,
13:37 I will lay down my l for you!"
13:38 "You will lay down your l for me,
14: 6 "I am the way, and the truth, and the l;
14:19 as one who has life, and you will have l.
15:13 to lay down one's l for one's friends.
17: 2 may bestow eternal l on those you gave him.
17: 3 (Eternal l is this: to know you the only true
20:31 this faith you may have l in his name.
Acts 2:28 You have shown me the paths of l;
2:42 apostles' instruction and the communal l,
3:15 You put to death the Author of l.
5:20 preach to the people all about this new l."
7:38 the oracles of l to pass on to you.
8:33 for he is deprived of his l on earth?"
9:36 Her l was marked by constant good deeds
10:14 eaten anything unclean or impure in my l."
13:46 yourselves as unworthy of everlasting l,
13:48 destined for l everlasting believed in it.
14: 8 sit crippled, never having walked in his l.
17:25 to all l and breath and everything else.
20:10 "There is l in him."
20:24 I put no value on my l if only I can
21:31 Attempts were being made on his l when a
23: 1 my l with a clear conscience before God."
23:30 be informed of a plot against this man's l,
26: 4 and the l I have led among my own people
26: 5 if they wish, to my l lived as a Pharisee,
26: 8 to believe that God raises dead men to l.
Rom 2: 7 eternal l to those who strive for glory,
4:17 God who restores the dead to l
5: 7 should lay down his l for a just man,
5:10 been reconciled will be saved by his l.
5:18 act brought all men acquittal and l.
5:21 by way of justice leading to eternal l,
6: 4 of the Father, we too might live a new l.
6:10 his l is life for God.
6:13 men who have come back from the dead to l,
6:22 as you tend toward eternal l.
6:23 God is eternal l in Christ Jesus our Lord.
7: 9 with it sin came to l,
7:10 that should have led to l brought me death.
8: 2 spirit, the spirit of l in Christ Jesus,
8: 6 but that of the spirit toward l and peace.
8:11 will bring your mortal bodies to l also,
8:38 For I am certain that neither death nor l,
11: 3 I alone am left and they are seeking my l."
11:15 Nothing less than l from the dead!
14: 8 Both in l and in death we are the Lord's.
14: 9 is why Christ died and came to l again,
14:22 have as your rule of l in the sight of God.
1Cor 1:30 it is who has given you l in Christ Jesus.
3:22 or Apollos, or Cephas, or the world, or l,
7:17 lead the l the Lord has assigned him,
7:24 of l that was his when he was called.
7:28 But such people will have trials in this l,
15:19 hopes in Christ are limited to this l only,
15:22 die, so in Christ all will come to l again,
2Cor 1: 8 even to the point of despairing of l.
2:16 death, to the former a breath bringing l.
3: 6 written law kills, but the Spirit gives l.
4:10 bodies the l of Jesus may also be revealed.
4:11 so that the l of Jesus may be revealed in
4:12 Death is at work in us, but l in you.
5: 4 that what is mortal may be absorbed by l.
5:10 or bad, according to his l in the body.
7: 3 to the sharing of death and l together.
Gal 1:13 the story of my former way of l in Judaism.
2:20 Christ, and the l I live now is not my own;
2:20 I still live my human l, but it is a l of faith
3:21 was given was such that it could impart l,
6: 8 is the spirit, he will reap everlasting l.
6:16 and mercy on all who follow this rule of l,
Eph 2: 5 to l with Christ when we were dead in sin.
2:10 Christ Jesus to lead the l of good deeds
3:17 be the root and foundation of your l.
4: 1 l worthy of the calling you have received,
4:18 They are estranged from a l in God because
4:22 you must lay aside your former way of l
6: 3 and that you may have long l on the earth."
Phil 1:21 For, to me, l" means Christ;
1:23 be freed from this l and to be with Christ,
2:16 sky while holding fast to the word of l.
2:17 Even if my l is to be poured out as a
2:30 He risked his l in an effort to render me
3:14 God calls me l on high in Christ Jesus.
4: 3 with me, whose names are in the book of l.
Col 1:10 Then you will lead a l worthy of the Lord
2:12 raised to l with him because you believed
2:13 God gave you new l in company with Christ.
2:21 still living a l bounded by this world?
3: 3 Your l is hidden now with Christ in God.
3: 4 When Christ our l appears,
3: 7 sort, when these sins were your very l.
1Tm 1:16 have faith in him and gain everlasting l.
4: 7 Train yourself for the l of piety,
4: 8 with its promise of l here and hereafter.
5: 6 however, leads a l of living death.
6:12 l to which you were called when,
6:13 Before God, who gives l to all,
6:19 for receiving that l which is life indeed.
2Tm 1: 1 sent to proclaim the promise of l in him,
1: 9 saved us and has called us to a holy l,
1:10 brought l and immortality into clear light
2: 4 entangled in the affairs of civilian l;
3:12 Anyone who wants to live a godly l in
Ti 1: 2 in the hope of that eternal l which God,
3: 7 and become heirs, in hope, of eternal l.
Heb 2:15 had been slaves their whole l long.
7: 3 without beginning of days or end of l,
7:16 the power of a l which cannot be destroyed.
11:22 By faith Joseph, near the end of his l,
12:10 prepare us for the short span of mortal l;
Jas 1:12 he will receive the crown of l the Lord
3: 7 Every form of l,
4:14 idea what kind of l will be yours tomorrow.
1Pt 1: 2 consecrated by the Spirit to a l of
1: 3 hope which draws its l from the resurrection
1:18 way of l your fathers handed on to you,
3: 2 the reverent purity of your way of l.
3: 7 as much as you to the gracious gift of l.
3:10 "He who cares for l and wants to see
3:16 your way of l in Christ may be shamed.
3:18 but was given l in the realm of the spirit.
4: 2 l on human desires but on the will of God.
2Pt 1: 3 necessary for a l of genuine piety,
2:18 who have just come free of a l of errors.
1Jn 1: 1 (This l became visible;
1: 1 and we proclaim to you the eternal l that
1: 3 to you so that you may share l with us,
2:16 for the eye, the l of empty show
2:25 is no less than this: eternal l.
3:14 to l we know because we love the brothers.
3:15 that eternal l abides in no murder's heart.
3:16 love was that he laid down his l for us;
4: 9 the world that we might have l through him.
5:11 gave us eternal l, and this life is in his Son.
5:12 Whoever possesses the Son possesses l;
5:12 possess the Son of God does not possess l.
5:13 you realize that you possess eternal l—
5:16 and thus l will be given to the sinner.
5:20 He is the true God and eternal l.
Jude 1:21 Lord Jesus Christ which leads to l eternal.
Rv 2: 7 tree of l which grows in the garden of God.'
2:10 death and I will give you the crown of l.
11:11 of l which comes from God returned to them.
12:11 love for l did not deter them from death.
13:15 permitted to give l to the beast's image,
20: 4 They came to l again and reigned with
20: 5 to l till the thousand years were over.
22: 2 l which produce fruit twelve times a year,
22:14 of l and enter the city through its gates!
22:19 tree of l and the holy city described here!

LIFE-BREATH (3)

Eccl 3:19 Both have the same l,
3:21 Who knows if the l of the children of men
3:21 upward and the l of beasts goes earthward?

LIFE-GIVING (7)

Sir 18:29 dispensing sound proverbs like l waters.
Acts 11:18 granted l repentance even to the Gentiles."
1Cor 15:45 the last Adam has become a l spirit.
Rv 7:17 He will lead them to springs of l water.
21: 6 without cost from the spring of l water.
22: 1 angel then showed me the river of l water,
22:17 who desire it accept the gift of l water.

LIFE-SAVING (1)

Sir 6:16 A faithful friend is a l remedy,

LIFE-SPAN (2)

Mt 6:27 you by worrying can add a moment to his l?
Lk 12:25 you by worrying can add a moment to his l?

LIFEBLOOD (5)

Gn 9: 4 with its l still in it you shall not eat.
9: 5 For your own l, too, I will demand an
Jer 2:34 clothing there is the l of the innocent,
Ps(s) 30:10 "What gain would there be from my l,
Ez 16:36 sacrificed the l of your children to them,

LIFELESS (4)

Ps(s) 63: 2 the earth, parched, l and without water.
Jer 14: 2 Judah mourns, her gates are l;
1Cor 14: 7 the case of l things which produce a sound,
Jas 2:17 It is thoroughly l.

LIFELONG (1)

2Sm 20: 3 to the day of their death, l widows.

LIFES (5)

Jdt 8:21 pay for its profanation with our l blood.
Sir 29:21 L prime needs are water,
33:31 you have acquired him with your l blood;
41: 1 who still can enjoy l pleasures.
Mk 4:19 to the word, but anxieties over l demands,

LIFETIME (42)

Gn 5: 5 The whole l of Adam was nine hundred and
5: 8 The whole l of Seth was nine hundred and
5:11 l of Enosh was nine hundred and five years;
5:14 l of Kenan was nine hundred and ten years;
5:17 The whole l of Mahalalel was eight hundred
5:20 The whole l of Jared was nine hundred and
5:23 The whole l of Enoch was three hundred and
5:27 The whole l of Methuselah was nine hundred
5:31 The whole l of Lamech was seven hundred
9:29 l of Noah was nine hundred and fifty years;
11:32 l of Terah was two hundred and five years;
35:28 The l of Isaac was one hundred and eighty
Jos 24:31 served the LORD during the entire l
Jgs 2: 7 the LORD during the entire l of Joshua,
8:28 for forty years, during the l of Gideon.
16:30 than those he had killed during his l.
1Sm 14:52 against the Philistines during Saul's l.
2Sm 18:18 During his l Absalom had taken a pillar
1Kgs 11:12 I will not do this during your l,
2Kgs 20:19 "There will be peace and security in my l."
2Chr 10: 6 service of his father during Solomon's l,
24:14 continually throughout the l of Jehoiada.
34:33 During his l they did not desert the LORD,
Jb 10: 5 mortal, and are your years as a man's l,
38:12 Have you ever in your l commanded the
Ps(s) 30: 6 a l, his good will
49:19 Though in his l he counted himself blessed.
103: 5 and compassion, He fills your l with good;
Wis 2: 1 "Brief and troublous is our l;
2: 5 For our l is the passing of a shadow;

LIFETIME (cont.)
Sir 22:11 dead, but for the wicked fool a whole *l*.
46: 7 God and in Moses' *l* showed himself loyal,
48:12 During his *l* he feared no one,
48:23 In his *l* he turned back the sun and
Is 39: 8 "There will be peace and security in my *l*."
65:20 old man who does not round out his full *l*;
Jer 16: 9 Before your very eyes and during your *l* I
22:30 childless, who will never thrive in his *l*!
Dn 2:44 In the *l* of those kings the God of heaven
5:11 during the *l* of your father he was
Lk 16:25 'remember that you were well off in your *l*,
Acts 13:36 had spent a *l* in carrying out God's will,

LIFETIMES (1)
Bar 1:11 that their *l* may equal the duration of the

LIFT (55)
Gn 21:18 *l* up the boy and hold him by the hand;
40:13 within three days Pharaoh will *l* up your
40:19 within three days Pharaoh will *l* up your
Ex 14:16 And you, *l* up your staff and,
40:37 But if the cloud did not *l*,
Lv 2: 9 priest shall then *l* from the cereal offering
Dt 22: 4 see to it that you help him *l* it up.
Jos 4: 5 *l* to your shoulders one stone apiece,
Ru 3:15 of barley, helped her *l* the bundle,
1Sm 22:17 *l* a hand to strike the priests of the LORD.
Jb 10:16 Should it *l* up, you hunt me like a lion:
11:15 then you may *l* up your face in innocence;
22:26 and you shall *l* up your face toward God.
Ps(s) 3: 4 my glory, you *l* up my head!
10:12 O God, *l* up your hand!
24: 7 *L* up, O gates, your lintels; reach up,
24: 9 *L*, up,
25: 1 To you I *l* up my soul, O LORD, my God.
75: 5 *L* not up your horns."
75: 6 *L* not up your horns against the Most High;
83: 3 and they who hate you *l* up their heads.
86: 4 for to you, O Lord, I *l* up my soul;
93: 3 The floods *l* up, O LORD, the floods *l*
93: 3 the floods lift up their voice; the floods *l*
110: 7 therefore will he *l* up his head.
119:48 And I will *l* up my hands to your commands
121: 1 I *l* up my eyes toward the mountains;
123: 1 I *l* up my eyes who are enthroned in heaven.
134: 2 *L* up your hands toward the sanctuary,
140:10 Those who surround me *l* up their heads;
143: 8 I should walk, for to you I *l* up my soul.
Prv 19:24 he will not even *l* it to his mouth.
26:15 he is too weary to *l* it to his mouth.
Eccl 4:10 falls, the other will *l* up his companion.
4:10 he should fall, he has no one to *l* him up.
Sir 20:10 from obscurity a man can *l* up his head.
43:31 *L* up your voices to glorify the LORD,
Is 24:14 These *l* up their voice in acclaim;
40:26 *L* up your eyes on high and see who has
46: 7 They *l* it to their shoulders to carry;
49:22 See, I will *l* up my hand to the nations,
58: 1 *l* up your voice like a trumpet blast;
Jer 3: 2 *L* your eyes to the heights,
10:17 *L* your bundle and leave the land,
13:20 *L* up your eyes and see men coming from the
22:20 and cry out, in Bashan *l* up your voice;
23:39 therefore I will *l* you on high and cast
Lam 2:19 *L* up your hands to him for the lives of
Ez 17:24 low the high tree, *l* high the lowly tree,
Zec 12: 3 to *l* it shall injure themselves badly,
Mt 23: 4 will not *l* a finger to budge them.
Lk 11:46 but will not *l* a finger to lighten them.
Jn 8:28 "When you *l* up the Son of Man,
1Pt 5: 6 so that in due time he may *l* you high.

LIFTED (43)
Gn 7:17 As the waters increased, they *l* the ark,
40:20 he *l* up the heads of the chief cupbearer
Ex 40:37 only when it *l* did they go forward.
Nm 9:21 Or if the cloud *l* during the day,
9:22 but when it *l*,
Jgs 9:48 This he *l* to his shoulder,
1Kgs 13:29 The prophet *l* up the body of the man of
16: 2 "Inasmuch as I *l* you up from the dust and
2Kgs 19:22 your voice And *l* up your eyes on high?
Ezr 3:12 *l* up their voices in shouts of joy,
6:11 and he is to be *l* up and impaled on it;
Jdt 14: 7 Then, after they *l* him up,
1Mc 7:47 right arm, which he had *l* up so arrogantly.
Jb 2:12 *l* up their eyes and did not recognize him,
Ps(s) 75:11 the horns of the just shall be *l* up.
102:11 for you *l* me up only to cast me down.
107:41 *L* up the needy out of misery and made the
148:14 and he has *l* up the horn of his people.
Sir 48:20 Most High God and *l* up their hands to him;
Is 33:10 LORD, now will I be exalted, now be *l* up.
37:23 your voice And *l* up your eyes on high?
Jer 37:11 When the Chaldean army *l* the siege of
Ez 3:12 Then spirit *l* me up,
3:14 The spirit which had *l* me up seized me,
8: 3 Spirit *l* me up in the air and brought me
10:16 *l* their wings to rise from the earth,
10:19 These *l* their wings,
11: 1 Spirit *l* me up and brought me to the east
11:22 Then the cherubim *l* their wings,
11:24 Spirit *l* me up and brought me back to
31: 3 stature, amid the very clouds *l* its crest.
43: 5 *l* me up and brought me to the inner court.
Dn 12: 7 *l* his right and left hands to heaven;
Mi 5: 8 Your hand shall be *l* above your foes,
Zec 5: 7 Then a leaden cover was *l*,
5: 9 As they *l* up the bushel into the air,
Mt 21:21 mountain, 'Be *l* up and thrown into the sea,'
Mk 11:23 mountain, 'Be *l* up and thrown into the sea,'
Jn 3:14 as Moses *l* up the serpent in the desert,
3:14 the desert, so must the Son of Man be *l* up,
12:32 once I am *l* up from earth
12:34 you claim that the Son of Man must be *l* up?
Acts 1: 9 No sooner had he said this than he was *l*

LIFTING (5)
Jb 34:20 removing the powerful without *l* a hand;
Ps(s) 28: 2 you, *l* up my hands toward your holy shrine.
63: 5 *l* up my hands,
141: 2 the *l* up of my hands,
Is 63: 9 *L* them and carrying them all the days of

LIFTS (8)
Lv 15:10 whoever *l* up any such thing shall wash his
1Sm 2: 8 from the ash heap he *l* up the poor,
Ps(s) 75: 8 another he *l* up.
113: 7 he *l* up the poor To seat them with princes,
145:14 The LORD *l* up all who are falling and
Sir 11: 1 *l* his head high and sets him among princes.
11:13 *L* up his head and exalts him to the
Is 10:15 As if a rod could sway him who *l* it,

LIGAMENT (1)
Eph 4:16 firmly together by each supporting *l*,

LIGHT (263)
Gn 1: 3 "Let there be light," and there was *l*.
1: 4 God saw how good the *l* was.
1: 4 God then separated the *l* from the darkness.
1: 5 God called the *l* "day,"
1:15 dome of the sky, to shed *l* upon the earth."
1:17 dome of the sky, to shed *l* upon the earth,
1:18 and to separate the *l* from the darkness.
19:11 with such a blinding *l* that they were
Ex 10:23 all the Israelites had *l* where they dwelt.
13:21 means of a column of fire to give them *l*.
25: 6 oil for the *l*;
25:37 *l* on the space in front of the lampstand.
27:20 of crushed olives, to be used for the *l*,
35: 3 You shall not even *l* a fire in any of your
35: 8 oil for *l*;
35:14 the lamps, and the oil for the *l*;
35:28 as well as spices, and oil for the *l*,
39:37 all its appurtenances, the oil for the *l*,
Lv 24: 2 you clear oil of crushed olives for the *l*,
Nm 4:16 shall be in charge of the oil for the *l*,
8: 2 their *l* toward the front of the lampstand."
Dt 1:41 making *l* of going up into the hill country.
28:46 They will *l* on you and your descendants as
1Sm 29:10 early morning start, as soon as it grows *l*,
2Sm 23: 4 *l* at sunrise on a cloudless morning,
1Kgs 3:21 But when I examined him in the morning *l*,
Neh 9:12 of fire, To *l* the way of their journey.
9:19 column of fire by night cease to *l* for them
Tb 5:10 like the dead who no longer see the *l*!
10: 5 "Alas, my child, *l* of my eyes,
11: 8 will again be able to see the *l* of day."
11:14 "I can see you, son, the *l* of my eyes!"
13:11 *l* will shine to all parts of the earth;
14:10 Ahiqar came out again into the *l*,
Jdt 13:13 They made a fire for *l*;
Est A:10 The *l* of the sun broke forth;
F: 3 that grew into a river, the *l* of the sun,
1Mc 1:21 lampstand for the *l* with all its fixtures,
2Mc 1:32 *l* was lost in the brilliance cast from a *l*
2:27 festive banquet is no *l* matter for one
4:17 It is no *l* matter to flout the laws of God,
12:41 who brings to *l* the things that are hidden.
Jb 3: 4 God above call for it, nor *l* shine upon it!
3:16 like babes that have never seen the *l*?
3:20 Why is *l* given to the toilers,
10:22 land where darkness is the only *l*.
12:22 and brings the gloom forth to the *l*.
12:25 they grope in the darkness without *l*;
17:12 is darkness they talk of approaching *l*.
18: 5 Truly, the *l* of the wicked is extinguished;
18: 6 The *l* is darkened in his tent;
18:18 He is driven from *l* into darkness,
22:28 you, and upon your ways the *l* shall shine.
24:13 are those who are rebels against the *l*;
24:14 When there is no *l* the murderer rises,
24:16 none of them know the *l*,
25: 3 Yet to which of them does not his *l* extend?
26:10 the deep as the boundary of *l* and darkness.
28:11 the streams, and brings hidden things to *l*.
29: 3 and by his *l* I walked through darkness;
30:26 when I expected *l*,
33:28 to the pit, and I behold the *l* of life."
33:30 back his soul from the pit to the *l*,
37:11 laden, as they scatter their flashes of *l*.
37:15 makes the *l* shine forth from his clouds?
37:21 it is as the *l* which men see not while it
38:15 But from the wicked the *l* is withheld,
38:19 is the way to the dwelling place of *l*,
41:10 When he sneezes, *l* flashes forth;
Ps(s) 4: 7 the *l* of your countenance shine upon us!
13: 4 Give *l* to my eyes that I may not sleep
18:29 You indeed, O LORD, give *l* to my lamp;
36:10 of life, and in your *l* we see light.
37: 6 will make justice dawn for you like the *l*;
38:11 the very *l* of my eyes has failed me.
43: 3 Send forth your *l* and your fidelity;
44: 4 right hand and the *l* of your countenance,
49:20 his forebears who shall never more see *l*.
56:14 may walk before God in the *l* of the living.
89:16 in the *l* of your countenance,
90: 8 our hidden sins in the *l* of your scrutiny.
97:11 *L* dawns for the just;
104: 2 and glory, robed in *l* as with a cloak.
105:39 them and fire to give them *l* by night.
112: 4 through the darkness, a *l* for the upright;
118:27 The LORD is God, and he has given us *l*.
119:105 to my feet is your word, a *l* to my path.
119:130 The revelation of your words sheds *l*,
139:11 shall hide me, and night shall be my *l*—
139:12 [Darkness and *l* are the same.]
Prv 4:18 the path of the just is like shining *l*,
6:23 bidding is a lamp, and the teaching a *l*,
13: 9 The *l* of the just shines gaily,
16:15 In the *l* of the king's countenance is life,
29:13 the LORD gives *l* to the eyes of both.
Eccl 2:13 much as *l* has the advantage over darkness.
10:20 in your thoughts do not make *l* of the king,
11: 7 *L* is sweet!
12: 2 and the *l*, and the moon, and the stars,
Wis 5: 6 and the *l* of justice did not shine for us,
6:22 search out and bring to *l* knowledge of her,
7:10 And I chose to have her rather than the *l*,
7:26 For she is the refulgence of eternal *l*,
7:29 Compared to *l*, she takes precedence;
17: 5 force, even of fire, was able to give *l*,
17:20 the whole world shone with brilliant *l*
18: 1 But your holy ones had very great *l*;
18: 4 deprived of *l* and imprisoned by darkness,
18: 4 *l* of the Law was to be given to the world.
Sir 3:24 of the eye is missing, there is no *l*,
11:21 but trust in the LORD and wait for his *l*;
22: 9 over the dead man, for his *l* has gone out;
26:17 the *l* that shines above the holy lampstand,
36:22 beauty makes her husband's face *l* up,
43: 4 the eyes are dazzled by its *l*.
Is 2: 5 come, let us walk in the *l* of the LORD!
4: 5 by day and a *l* of flaming fire by night.
5:20 darkness into light, and *l* into darkness,
8:14 with the *l* blacked out by its clouds.
9: 1 walked in darkness have seen a great *l*;
9: 1 dwelt in the land of gloom a *l* has shone.
10:17 The *l* of Israel will become a fire,
13:10 no *l*; The sun is dark when it rises, and the *l*
26:19 For your dew is a dew of *l*,
30:26 The *l* of the moon will be like that of the
30:26 *l* of the sun will be seven times greater
30:26 times greater [like the *l* of seven days].
42: 6 of the people, a *l* for the nations,
42:16 I will turn darkness into *l* before them,
45: 7 I form the *l*,
49: 6 I will make you a *l* to the nations,
50:10 And walks in darkness without any *l*,
50:11 Walk by the *l* of your own fire and by the
51: 4 and my judgment, as the *l* of the peoples.
53:11 he shall see the *l* in fullness of days;
58: 8 your *l* shall break forth like the dawn,
58:10 Then *l* shall rise for you in the darkness,
59: 9 We look for *l*, and lo, darkness;
60: 1 Your *l* has come, the glory of the LORD
60: 3 Nations shall walk by your *l*,
60:19 No longer shall the sun be your *l* by day,
60:19 The LORD shall be your *l* forever,
60:20 For the LORD will be your *l* forever,
Jer 4:23 at the heavens, and their *l* had gone out!
7:18 gather wood, their fathers *l* the fire,
10:19 if I make *l* of my wound, I can bear it.
13:16 the *l* you look for turns to darkness,
25:10 of the millstone and the *l* of the lamp.
31:35 *l* the day, moon and stars to *l* the night;
51:10 The LORD has brought to *l* our just cause;
Lam 3: 2 forced to walk in darkness, not in the *l*;
Bar 1:12 may give us strength, and *l* to our eyes,
3:14 of days, and life, where *l* of the eyes,
3:20 Later generations have seen the *l*,
3:33 He who dismisses the *l*,
4: 2 walk by her *l* toward splendor.
5: 9 leading Israel in joy by the *l* of his glory
6:18 *l* more lamps for them than for themselves,
Ez 32: 7 clouds, and the moon shall not give its *l*.
Dn 2:22 in the darkness, for the *l* dwells with him.
3:72 *L* and darkness,
Hos 6: 3 judgment shines forth like the *l* of day!
Am 5:18 Darkness and not *l*!
5:20 the day of the LORD be darkness and not *l*,
Mi 2: 1 In the morning *l* they accomplish it when
7: 8 though I sit in darkness, the LORD is my *l*.

7: 9 He will bring me forth to the *l*;
Hb 3: 4 His splendor spreads like the *l*;
3:11 shelter, At the *l* of your flying arrows,
Zec 14: 7 for in the evening time there shall be *l*.
Mt 4:16 living in darkness has seen a great *l*.
4:16 a land overshadowed by death, *l* has arisen."
5:14 "You are the *l* of the world.
5:15 Men do not *l* a lamp and then put it under
5:15 stand where it gives *l* to all in the house.
5:16 your *l* must shine before men so that they
6:22 are good, your body will be filled with *l*;
6:23 And if your *l* is darkness,
10:27 I tell you in darkness, speak in the *l*.
11:30 rest, for my yoke is easy and my burden *l*."
17: 2 as the sun, his clothes as radiant as *l*.
24:29 be darkened, the moon will not shed her *l*,
Mk 13:24 be darkened, the moon will not shed its *l*,
Lk 2:32 A revealing *l* to the Gentiles,
8:17 that will not be known and brought to *l*.
11:33 so that they who come in may see the *l*.
11:35 care, then, that your *l* is not darkness.
12:49 "I have come to *l* a fire on the earth.
15: 8 does not *l* a lamp and sweep the house in a
22:56 girl saw him sitting in the *l* of the fire.
Jn 1: 4 in him, found life, life for the *l* of men.
1: 5 The *l* shines on in darkness,
1: 7 who came as a witness to testify to the *l*,
1: 8 to the light, for he himself was not the *l*.
1: 9 The real *l* which gives light to every man
3:19 the *l* came into the world,
3:19 than *l* because their deeds were wicked.
3:20 Everyone who practices evil hates the *l*;
3:21 But he who acts in truth comes into the *l*,
5:35 for a while you exulted willingly in his *l*.
8:12 "I am the *l* of the world.
8:12 no, he shall possess the *l* of life."
9: 5 I am in the world I am the *l* of the world."
11: 9 because he sees the world bathed in *l*.
11:10 he will stumble since there is no *l* in him."
12:35 "The *l* is among you only a little longer.
12:36 faith in the *l*; thus you will become sons of *l*
12:46 I have come to the world as its *l*,
Acts 9: 3 *l* from the sky suddenly flashed about him.
11:14 In the *l* of what he will tell you,
12: 7 Lord stood nearby and *l* shone in the cell.
13:47 'I have made you a *l* to the nations,
16:29 The jailer called for a *l*,
22: 6 a great *l* from the sky suddenly flashed
22: 9 My companions saw the *l* but did not hear
22:11 see because of the brilliance of the *l*,
26:13 I saw a *l* more brilliant than the sun
26:18 to *l* and from the dominion of Satan to God;
26:23 *l* to our people and to the Gentiles."
Rom 3: 7 *l* God's truth and thus promotes his glory,
13:12 of darkness and put on the armor of *l*.
1Cor 4: 5 He will bring to *l* what is hidden in
2Cor 4: 6 who said, "Let *l* shine out of darkness,"
4:17 present burden of our trial is *l* enough,
6:14 what fellowship can *l* have with darkness?
11:14 Satan disguises himself as an angel of *l*.
Eph 5: 8 darkness, but now you are *l* in the Lord.
5: 8 Well, then, live as children of *l*.
5: 9 *L* produces every kind of goodness and
5:13 *l* of day, and all that then appears is *l*
5:14 from the dead, and Christ will give you *l*."
Phil 3: 7 now reappraised as loss in the *l* of Christ.
3: 8 I have come to rate all as loss in the *l*
Col 1:12 worthy to share the lot of the saints in *l*.
1Thes 5: 5 of you are children of *l* and of the day.
1Tm 6:16 and who dwells in unapproachable *l*,
2Tm 1:10 into clear *l* through the gospel.
1Pt 2: 9 you from darkness into his marvelous *l*.
1Jn 1: 5 God is *l*; in him there is no darkness.
1: 7 if we walk in light, as he is in the *l*,
2: 8 is over and the real *l* begins to shine.
2: 9 The man who claims to be in *l*,
2:10 in the *l* is the one who loves his brother;
3: 2 we shall later be has not yet come to *l*.
3: 2 when it comes to *l* we shall be like him,
Rv 8:12 The day lost a third of its *l*,
18:23 No *l* from a burning lamp shall ever again
21:23 or moon, for the glory of God gave it *l*.
21:24 The nations shall walk by its *l*;
22: 5 They will need no *l* from lamps or the sun,
22: 5 sun, for the Lord God shall give them *l*,

LIGHT-GIVER (1)

Sir 43: 7 dates, this *l* which wanes in its course:

LIGHTED (9)

Jdt 7: 5 their weapons, *l* fires on their bastions,
1Mc 4:50 the altar and *l* the lamps on the lampstand,
12:28 They *l* fires and then withdrew.
2Mc 1: 8 we *l* the lamps and set out the loaves of
10: 3 in two years, burned incense, and *l* lamps.
Lk 11:34 eyesight is sound, your whole body is *l* up,
11:36 body is *l* up and not partly in darkness,
22:55 Later they *l* a fire in the middle of the
Rv 18: 1 that all the earth was *l* up by his glory.

LIGHTEN (8)

1Kgs 12: 4 If you now *l* the harsh service and the
12: 9 me to *l* the yoke my father imposed on them?"
12:10 you to *l* the yoke your father put on them:
2Chr 10: 4 If you now *l* the harsh service and the
10: 9 me to *l* the yoke my father imposed on them?"
10:10 heavy yoke upon us, but do you *l* our yoke';
Jon 1: 5 To *l* the ship for themselves,
Lk 11:46 men but will not lift a finger to *l* them.

LIGHTENED (2)

Ex 18:22 Thus, your burden will be *l*,
Acts 27:38 they *l* the ship further by throwing the

LIGHTER (1)

Ps(s) 62:10 In a balance they prove *l*,

LIGHTHEARTED (1)

Prv 15:15 but a *l* man has a continual feast.

LIGHTING (3)

Wis 17: 5 stars succeed in *l* up that gloomy night.
Sir 43:10 high, *l* up the firmament by its brilliance,
Acts 28: 2 by *l* a fire and gathering us all around it,

LIGHTLY (3)

Tb 4:18 think *l* of any advice that can be useful.
Wis 14:28 or live lawlessly or *l* forswear themselves.
Sir 19: 4 He who *l* trusts in them has no sense,

LIGHTNING (35)

Ex 9:23 *L* flashed toward the earth,
9:24 and *l* constantly flashed through the hail,
19:16 day there were peals of thunder and *l*,
20:18 the people witnessed the thunder and *l*,
2Sm 22:15 he flashed *l* and routed them.
Jb 1:16 *L* has fallen from heaven and struck the
27:22 he hurls the *l* against them relentlessly;
36:32 In his hands he holds the *l*,
37: 3 under the heavens he sends it, with his *l*,
Ps(s) 77:19 your *l* illumined the world;
78:48 their beasts and their flocks to the *l*.
135: 7 with the *l* he makes the rain;
144: 6 Flash forth *l*,
Wis 16:22 in the hail and flashed *l* in the rain.
Sir 32:10 Like the *l* that flashes before a storm is
40:13 like a mighty stream with *l* and thunder,
43:13 His rebuke marks out the path for the *l*,
Jer 10:13 He makes the *l* flash in the rain,
51:16 He makes the *l* flash in the rain,
Bar 6:60 Likewise the *l*, when it flashes,
Ez 1:13 and from it came forth flashes of *l*.
21:15 to flash *l* has it been burnished.
21:20 sword for slaughter, Fashioned to flash *l*,
21:33 burnished to consume and to flash *l*,
Dn 10: 6 like chrysolite, his face shown like *l*,
Na 2: 5 like firebrands, flashing like *l* bolts.
Zec 9:14 and his arrow shall shoot forth as *l*;
Mt 24:27 As the *l* from the east flashes to the west,
28: 3 In appearance he resembled a flash of *l*
Lk 10:18 "I watched Satan fall from the sky like *l*.
17:24 Son of Man in his day will be like the *l*
Rv 4: 5 came flashes of *l* and peals of thunder;
8: 5 Peals of thunder and flashes of *l* followed,
11:19 were flashes of *l* and peals of thunder,
16:18 followed *l* flashes and peals of thunder,

LIGHTNINGS (5)

Jb 38:35 Can you send forth the *l* on their way.
Ps(s) 18:15 to flight, with frequent *l* he routed them.
97: 4 His *l* illumine the world;
Wis 5:21 Well-aimed shafts of *l* shall go forth and
Dn 3:73 *L* and clouds,

LIGHTS (11)

Gn 1:14 "Let there be *l* in the dome of the sky,
1:16 God made the two great *l*,
Ex 30: 8 the evening twilight, when he *l* the lamps,
1Mc 12:29 and his men were watching the *l* burning,
Ps(s) 136: 7 Who made the great *l*,
Prv 15:13 A glad heart *l* up the face,
Sir 33: 7 when it is the sun that *l* up every day?
Jer 46:20 from the north a horsefly *l* upon her.
Ez 32: 8 All the shining *l* in the heavens I will
Lk 8:16 "No one *l* a lamp and puts it under a
11:33 "One who *l* a lamp does not put it in the

LIKE-MINDED (2)

Sir 37:12 Who is *l* with yourself and will feel for
1Pt 3: 8 In summary, then, all of you should be *l*,

LIKED (1)

Gn 27:14 an appetizing dish, such as his father *l*.

LIKELY (1)

Jn 11:56 Is he *l* to come for the feast?"

LIKEN (6)

Sg 1: 9 of Pharaoh's chariots would I *l* you,
Wis 7: 9 her, nor did I *l* any priceless gem to her;
Is 40:18 To whom can you *l* God?
40:25 To whom can you *l* me as an equal?
Lam 2:13 To what can I *l* or compare you,
Lk 13:18 To what shall I *l* it?

LIKENED (4)

Mt 13:24 "The reign of God may be *l* to a man who
22: 2 "The reign of God may be *l* to a king who
25: 1 "The reign of God can be *l* to ten
Lk 6:48 He may be *l* to the man who,

LIKENESS (13)

Gn 1:26 us make man in our image, after our *l*.
5: 1 created man, he made him in the *l* of God;
5: 3 years old when he begot a son in his *l*,
Jb 4:16 It paused, but its *l* I could not discern;
Wis 14:19 over the *l* to the best of his skill;
Ez 1:28 vision of the *l* of the glory of the LORD.
Rom 6: 5 united with him through *l* to his death,
8: 3 in the *l* of sinful flesh as a sin offering,
1Cor 15:49 shall we bear the *l* of the man from heaven.
Phil 2: 7 of a slave, being born in the *l* of men.
Heb 7:15 according to the *l* of Melchizedek:
Jas 3: 9 men, though they are made in the *l* of God.
1Pt 1:15 after the *l* of the holy One who called you;

LIKENESSES (1)

Wis 13:10 the product of art, and *l* of beasts,

LIKES (2)

Gn 27: 9 dish for your father, such as he *l*.
Acts 22:22 Rid the earth of the *l* of him!

LIKEWISE (96)

Gn 7: 3 *L*,
Ex 7:11 of Egypt, did *l* by their magic arts.
12:16 a sacred assembly, and *l* on the seventh.
12:33 The Egyptians *l* urged the people on,
26:13 *L*, the sheets of the tent will have an
26:24 at the bottom, and *l* double at the top,
28:40 *L*, for the glorious adornment of Aaron's
30:20 *L* when they approach the altar in their
34:22 *l*,
36:29 at the bottom, and *l* double at the top,
38: 3 forks and fire pans, were *l* made of bronze.
38:15 *l* hangings to the extent of fifteen cubits,
40:11 *L*, anoint the laver with its base,
Lv 6:15 him as the anointed priest shall do *l*.
7: 7 the guilt offering *l* belongs to the priest
7:21 *L*, if someone touches anything unclean,
8:13 Moses *l* brought forward Aaron's sons,
8:25 with their fat, and *l* the right leg;
16:14 *l* sprinkle some of the blood with his finger
19:10 *L*, you shall not pick your vineyard bare,
25: 7 and *l* for your livestock and for the wild
Nm 5: 9 *L*, every sacred contribution that the
15:14 *L*, in any future generation,
18:13 and *l*,
19: 8 *L*, he who burned the heifer shall wash his
19:15 *l*,
Dt 9:22 at Massah, and at Kibroth-hattaavah *l*,
Jgs 1: 3 I will *l* accompany you into the territory
6:35 through Asher, Zebulun and Naphtali, *l*,
9:49 So all the men *l* cut down brushwood,
1Sm 14:22 *L*, all the Israelites who were hiding in
2Sm 1:11 and all the men who were with him did *l*.
1Kgs 7:29 and on the frames *l*,
8:41 "To the foreigner, *l*,
2Kgs 23:15 *L* the altar which was at Bethel,
1Chr 11:23 He *l* slew the Egyptian,
12:39 was *l* of one mind to make David king.
18: 8 He *l* took away from Tibhath and Cun,
23:30 to praise the LORD, and *l* in the evening;
28:15 *l* for the golden lampstands and their
2Chr 3: 9 The upper chambers he *l* covered with gold.
4:16 *l* the pots,
34: 6 He did *l* in the cities of Manasseh,
36:14 *L* all the princes of Judah,
Tb 4:13 *L*, in worthlessness there is decay and
Est 4: 3 *L* in each of the provinces,
C:12 mortal anguish, *l* had recourse to the Lord.
1Mc 4:61 to protect it, and *l* fortified Beth-zur,
10:45 *L* the cost of building the walls of
11:59 *L*, he made Jonathan's brother Simon
12:12 We *l* rejoice in your renown.
12:38 Simon *l* built up Adida in the Shephelah,
Jb 37: 6 *l* to his heavy,
Ps(s) 49:11 *l* the senseless and the stupid pass away,
Bar 6:60 *L* the lightning, when it flashes,
Ez 40:16 *l*,
43:17 The lower ledge, *l* a square,
44:30 *l* the best of your dough you shall give to
Mt 5:32 a divorced woman *l* commits adultery.
19:28 you who have followed me shall *l* take your
24:33 *L*, when you see all these things happening,
Mk 3:15 were *l* to have authority to expel demons.
13:12 for execution and *l* the father his child;

LIKEWISE (cont.)

14:23 He *l* took a cup, gave thanks and passed
15:32 crucified with him *l* kept taunting him.
Lk 3:14 Soldiers *l* asked him, "What about us?"
3:21 Jesus was at prayer after *l* being baptized,
9:32 they saw his glory and *l* saw the two men
10:32 *L* there was a Levite who came the same way;
15: 7 there will *l* be more joy in heaven over
16:18 from her husband *l* commits adultery.
16:22 The rich man *l* died and was buried.
20:12 they *l* maltreated before driving him away.
21:31 *L* when you see all the things happening of
Jn 2: 2 had *l* been invited to the celebration.
5:19 whatever the Father does, the Son does *l*.
19:39 had first come to Jesus at night) *l* came,
Acts 5: 1 wife Sapphira *l* sold a piece of property.
5:37 too built up quite a following, but *l* died,
14: 1 In Iconium *l*,
Rom 2:10 who has done good, *l* the Jew first,
8:30 Those he predestined he *l* called;
1Cor 1: 6 *L*, the witness I bore to Christ has been
9:14 *L* the Lord himself ordered that those who
10:21 of the Lord and *l* the table of demons.
2Cor 10: 5 we *l* bring every thought into captivity to
Gal 4:25 which is *l* in slavery with her children.
Eph 1: 5 he *l* predestined us through Christ Jesus
Phil 3:10 *l* to know how to share in his sufferings
1Thes 2:11 *l* know how we exhorted every one of you,
2Tm 3:15 *L*, from your infancy you have known the
Ti 2: 2 *l* sound in the faith,
Heb 2:14 flesh, Jesus *l* had a full share in ours,
1Pt 2: 8 is *l* "an obstacle and a stumbling stone."
Rv 13: 7 It was *l* granted authority over every race
14:17 another angel, who *l* held a sharp sickle.

LIKHI (1)

1Chr 7:19 The sons of Shemida were Ahian, Shechem, *L*,

LIKING (3)

Gn 39: 4 he took a *l* to Joseph and made him his
Dt 21:14 if later on you lose your *l* for her,
2Cor 12:20 when I come I may not find you to my *l*,

LILIES (6)

Sg 2:16 he browses among the *l*,
4: 5 young of a gazelle that browse among the *l*.
6: 2 To browse in the garden and to gather *l*.
6: 3 he browses among the *l*.
7: 3 body is a heap of wheat encircled with *l*.
Lk 12:27 "Or take the *l*: They do not spin.

LILITH (1)

Is 34:14 There shall the *l* repose,

LILY (5)

Sg 2: 1 a *l* of the valley.
2: 2 As a *l* among thorns, so is my beloved
Sir 39:14 break forth in blossoms like the *l*.
50: 8 like a *l* on the banks of a stream;
Hos 14: 6 he shall blossom like the *l*;

LILY-SHAPED (2)

1Kgs 7:26 its brim resembled that of a cup, being *l*.
2Chr 4: 5 brim was made like that of a cup, being *l*.

LIMB (4)

Lv 24:20 *L* for limb, eye for eye, tooth for tooth!
2Mc 7: 7 than have your body tortured *l* by limb?"

LIMBS (6)

Jb 18:13 the first-born of death consumes his *l*.
31:20 Whose *l* have not blessed me when warmed
41: 4 I need hardly mention his *l*,
Sir 26:18 bases are her shapely *l* and steady feet.
Acts 3:16 *l* of this man whom you see and know well.
Heb 12:13 halting *l* may not be dislocated but healed.

LIMEKILN (1)

Is 33:12 The peoples shall be as in a *l*,

LIMIT (16)

Jos 19:10 The *l* of their heritage was at Sarid.
2Kgs 11:11 to the northern *l* of the enclosure,
Ezr 7:22 salt, without *l*.
Jb 6:11 and what is my *l* that I should be patient?
14: 5 you have fixed the *l* which he cannot pass.
34:36 Let Job be tried to the *l*,
Ps(s) 104: 9 You set a *l* they may not pass,
147: 5 to his wisdom there is no *l*.
Prv 8:29 When he set for the sea its *l*,
Sir 27:12 *L* the time you spend among fools,
33:24 When your few days reach their *l*,
39:18 nothing can *l* his achievement.
Is 5:14 its throat and opens its maw without *l*;
Jer 5:22 I made the sandy shore the sea's *l*,
Rom 7:13 sin might go to the *l* of sinfulness.
1Cor 13: 7 There is no *l* to love's forbearance,

LIMITED (14)

1Chr 6:39 places to which their encampment was *l*.
Jb 15:20 and *l* years are in store for the tyrant;
Ps(s) 139:16 my days were *l* before one of them existed.
Eccl 2: 3 heavens during the *l* days of their life.
5:17 the *l* days of the life which God gives him;
6:12 the *l* days of his vain life (which God has
8:15 accompaniment of his toil during the *l* days
Sir 17: 2 *L* days of life he gives him and makes him
37:23 *L* are the days of one man's life,
41:13 The boon of life is for *l* days,
47:23 his sons, Expansive in folly, *l* in sense,
1Cor 15:19 hopes in Christ are *l* to this life only,
2Cor 3:10 that *l* glory with this surpassing glory,
Rv 3: 8 I know that your strength is *l*;

LIMITS (16)

Gn 23:17 and all the trees anywhere within its *l*,
Ex 19:12 *l* for the people all around the mountain,
19:23 *l* around the mountain to make it sacred."
Jos 4:19 in Gilgal on the eastern *l* of Jericho.
18:15 The southern boundary began at the *l* of
24:30 He was buried within the *l* of his heritage
Ezr 7:22 dispense to him accurately, within these *l*:
Tb 13:11 the inhabitants of all the *l* of the earth,
Jb 38:10 *l* for it and fastened the bar of its door,
Ps(s) 74:17 You fixed all the *l* of the land;
119:96 I see that all fulfillment has its *l*;
139: 9 if I settle at the farthest *l* of the sea,
Ez 42:15 east and measured all the *l* of the court.
Acts 17:26 It is he who set *l* to their epochs and
Rom 10:18 and their words to the *l* of the world."
Rv 12:12 His fury knows no *l*,

LIMP (2)

Prv 26: 7 A proverb in the mouth of a fool hangs *l*,
Ez 7:17 All their hands shall be *l*,

LIMPED (1)

Gn 32:32 Penuel, Jacob *l* along because of his hip.

LINE (68)

Gn 38: 8 and thus preserve your brother's *l*."
Ex 26:17 that shall serve to fasten the boards in *l*.
36:22 board had two arms, fastening them in *l*.
Lv 6:22 priestly *l* may partake of the sin offering,
7: 6 males of the priestly *l* may partake of it;
Nm 2:17 shall set out in the middle of the *l*.
34: 7 Great Sea you shall draw a *l* to Mount Hor,
34:10 shall draw a *l* from Hazar-enan to Shepham.
Dt 25: 6 continue the *l* of the deceased brother,
Jos 16: 5 the dividing *l* for the heritage of the
18:14 the boundary *l* swung south from the
Jgs 20:30 formed their *l* of battle at Gibeah
1Sm 17: 2 up their battle *l* to meet the Philistines.
17:22 the baggage and hastened to the battle *l*,
17:48 *l* in the direction of the Philistine.
2Sm 8: 2 Moab and then measured them with a *l*,
8: 2 He told off two lengths of *l* for execution,
1Kgs 2: 4 someone of your *l* on the throne of Israel.'
8:25 *l* to sit before me on the throne of Israel,
9: 5 from your *l* on the throne of Israel.'
11:14 Edomite, who was of the royal *l* in Edom.
11:39 I will punish David's *l* for this,
14:10 I will cut off every male in Jeroboam's *l*,
14:11 When one of Jeroboam's *l* dies in the city,
14:13 of Jeroboam's *l* will be laid in the grave,
16: 4 If anyone of Baasha's *l* dies in the city,
21:21 and will cut off every male in Ahab's *l*,
21:24 "When one of Ahab's *l* dies in the city,
2Kgs 8:18 like the kings of Israel of the *l* of Ahab,
9: 8 I will cut off every male in Ahab's *l*,
10:17 slew all who remained there of Ahab's *l*,
1Chr 12:28 with Jehoiada, leader of the *l* of Aaron,
19:10 a battle *l* both in front of and behind him,
2Chr 6:16 *l* to sit before me on the throne of Israel,
21: 6 like the kings of Israel of the *l* of Ahab,
34:12 and Obadiah, Levites of the *l* of Merari,
Tb 5:14 are a kinsman, and from a noble and good *l*!
1Mc 7:14 of the *l* of Aaron has come with the army,
9:11 all the valiant men were in the front *l*.
2Mc 15:20 with their troops drawn up in battle *l*,
Jb 21:33 While all the *l* of mankind follows him,
38: 5 Who stretched out the measuring *l* for it?
Sir 41: 5 A reprobate *l* are the children of sinners,
45:23 was the courageous third of his *l* When,
Is 28:17 I will make of right a measuring *l*,
34:11 The LORD will measure her with *l* and
44:13 The carpenter stretches a *l* and marks with
Jer 31:39 The measuring *l* shall be stretched from
Lam 2: 8 He stretched out the measuring *l*;
Ez 17:13 the royal *l* with whom he made a covenant,
43:19 the Levites who are of the *l* of Zadok,
48:15 *l* are profane land,
48:15 *l* are profane land, assigned to the City
48:21 *l* eastward to the eastern boundary,
48:21 *l* to the western boundary,
48:21 *l* eastward to the eastern boundary,
48:21 *l* to the western boundary,
Dn 11: 6 and her *l* shall not be recognized,
11: 7 of her *l* shall succeed to his rank,
Hos 5:10 become like those that move a boundary *l*;
Am 7:17 Your land shall be divided by measuring *l*,
Zec 1:16 *l* shall be stretched over Jerusalem.
2: 5 was a man with a measuring *l* in his hand.
Mt 17:27 them go to the lake, throw in a *l*,
1Cor 4: 9 has put us apostles at the end of the *l*,
9:26 like a man who loses sight of the finish *l*.
Phil 3:13 of myself as having reached the finish *l*.
3:14 My entire attention is on the finish *l* as

LINEAGE (19)

Nm 1:18 *l* according to clan and ancestral house,
1:20 the first-born of Israel, registered by *l*
1:22 descendants of Simeon, registered by *l*
1:24 descendants of Gad, registered by *l*
1:26 descendants of Judah, registered by *l*
1:28 descendants of Issachar, registered by *l*
1:30 descendants of Zebulun, registered by *l*
1:32 descendants of Ephraim, registered by *l*
1:34 descendants of Manasseh, registered by *l*
1:36 descendants of Benjamin, registered by *l*
1:38 descendants of Dan, registered by *l*
1:40 descendants of Asher, registered by *l*
1:42 descendants of Naphtali, registered by *l*
Dt 25:10 And his *l* shall be spoken of in Israel as
Tb 1: 9 I married Anna, a woman of our own *l*.
4:12 marry a woman of the *l* of your forefathers.
5:14 You are certainly of good *l*,
6:18 was his kinswoman, of his own family's *l*,
Lk 2: 4 he was of the house and *l* of David

LINED (5)

1Kgs 6:15 its walls were *l* from floor to ceiling
2Kgs 11:11 *l* up from the southern to the northern
1Chr 19: 9 *l* up for a battle at the gate of the city,
19:11 then *l* up to oppose the Ammonites.
2Chr 13: 3 while Jeroboam *l* up against him in battle

LINEN (98)

Gn 41:42 fine *l* and put a gold chain about his neck.
Ex 25: 4 fine *l* and goat hair;
26: 1 woven of fine *l* twined and of violet,
26:31 and scarlet yarn, and of fine *l* twined,
26:36 and scarlet yarn and of fine *l* twined.
27: 9 cubits long, woven of fine *l* twined,
27:16 and scarlet yarn and of fine *l* twined.
27:18 Fine *l* twined must be used,
28: 5 violet, purple and scarlet yarn and fine *l*.
28: 6 embroidered on cloth of fine *l* twined.
28: 8 and scarlet yarn, and of fine *l* twined.
28:15 and scarlet yarn on cloth of fine *l* twined.
28:33 purple and scarlet yarn and fine *l* twined,
28:39 "The tunic of fine *l* shall be brocaded.
28:39 The miter shall be made of fine *l*.
28:42 You must also make *l* drawers for them,
35: 6 *l* and goat hair; rams' skins dyed red
35:23 *l* or goat hair, rams' skins dyed red
35:25 *l* thread, All the women who possessed
35:35 *l* thread, weaving, and all other arts
36: 8 *l* twined, having cherubim embroidered
36:35 *l* twined, with cherubim embroidered
36:37 *l* twined, woven in a variegated manner.
38: 9 *l* twined, a hundred cubits long,
38:16 of the court were woven of fine *l* twined.
38:18 *l* twined, twenty cubits long
38:23 purple and scarlet yarn and of fine *l*.
39: 2 and scarlet yarn and of fine *l* twined.
39: 3 into an embroidered pattern on the fine *l*.
39: 5 *l* twined, as the LORD had commanded
39: 8 and scarlet yarn on cloth of fine *l* twined.
39:24 fine *l* twined; bells of pure gold
39:27 fine *l*; the miter of fine linen;
39:28 miter of fine *l*; the ornate turbans of fine *l*
39:28 drawers of *l* [of fine linen twined];
39:29 work made of fine *l* twined and of violet,
Lv 6: 3 clothed in his *l* robe and wearing linen
6: 3 robe and wearing *l* drawers on his body,
13:47 infection is on a garment of wool or of *l*,
13:48 on woven or knitted material of *l* or wool,
13:52 woven or knitted material of wool or *l*,
13:59 infection on a garment of wool or *l*,
16: 4 sacred *l* tunic, with the *l* drawers
16: 4 with the linen sash and put on the *l* miter.
16:23 leave in the sanctuary the *l* vestments
16:32 He shall wear the *l* garments,
Dt 22:11 two different kinds of thread, wool and *l*,
Jgs 14:12 *l* tunics and thirty sets of garments.
1Sm 2:18 the boy Samuel, girt with a *l* apron,
22:18 that day eighty-five who wore the *l* ephod.
2Sm 6:14 Then David, girt with a *l* apron,
1Chr 4:21 of the *l* weavers' guild in Bethashbea,
15:27 David was clothed in a robe of fine *l*,
15:27 David was also wearing a *l* ephod.
2Chr 2:13 with purple, violet, fine *l* and crimson,
3:14 veil of violet, purple, crimson and fine *l*,
5:12 sons and brothers, clothed in fine *l*,
Jdt 16: 8 and put on a *l* robe to beguile him.
Prv 7:16 couch, with brocaded cloths of Egyptian *l*;
31:22 fine *l* and purple are her clothing.
Is 3:23 the mirrors, *l* tunics,

Jer 13: 1 Go buy yourself a *l* loincloth;
38:11 went first to the *l* closet in the palace,
Bar 6:71 rotting of the purple and the *l* upon them,
Ez 9: 2 In their midst was a man dressed in *l*,
9: 3 in *l* with the writer's case at his waist,
9:11 Then I saw the man dressed in *l* with the
10: 2 He said to the man dressed in *l*:
10: 6 *l* to take fire from within the wheelwork,
10: 7 it in the hands of the one dressed in *l*,
16:10 you a fine *l* sash and silk robes to wear.
16:13 your garments were of fine *l*,
27: 7 Fine embroidered *l* from Egypt became your
27:16 garnets, purple, embroidered cloth, fine *l*,
40: 3 gate, holding a *l* cord and a measuring rod.
44:17 inner court, they shall wear *l* garments;
44:18 They shall have *l* turbans on their heads
44:18 their heads and *l* drawers on their loins;
Dn 10: 5 I saw a man dressed in *l* with a belt of
12: 6 One of them said to the man clothed in *l*,
12: 7 The man clothed in *l*,
Mt 27:59 Joseph wrapped it in fresh *l* and laid it
Mk 14:51 who was covered by nothing but a *l* cloth.
15:46 Then, having bought a *l* shroud,
15:46 took him down, wrapped him in the *l*,
Lk 16:19 and *l* and feasted splendidly every day.
23:53 He took it down, wrapped it in fine *l*,
Jn 11:44 came out bound head and foot with *l* strips,
Rv 15: 6 The angels were dressed in pure white *l*,
18:12 fine *l* and purple garments,
18:16 dressed in fine *l* and purple and scarlet,
19: 8 given a dress to wear made of finest *l*,
19: 8 (The *l* dress is the virtuous deeds of
19:14 riding white horses and dressed in fine *l*,

LINEN-WORKERS (1)

Is 19: 9 The *l* shall be disappointed,

LINES (3)

2Sm 10: 9 Joab saw the battle *l* drawn up against him,
Jdt 7:19 was no way of slipping through their *l*.
Ps(s) 16: 6 measuring *l* have fallen on pleasant sites;

LINGER (2)

Prv 23:30 Those who *l* long over wine,
Is 5:11 *l* into the night while wine inflames them!

LINTEL (5)

Ex 12: 7 two doorposts and the *l* of every house
12:22 *l* and the two doorposts with this blood.
12:23 the blood on the *l* and the two doorposts,
Ez 41:17 As high as the *l* of the door,
41:20 From the ground to the *l* of the door the

LINTELS (2)

Ps(s) 24: 7 Lift up, O gates, your *l*;
24: 9 Lift, up, O gates, your *l*;

LINUS (1)

2Tm 4:21 Eubulus, Pudens, *L*,

LION (91)

Gn 49: 9 He crouches like a *l* recumbent,
Nm 23:24 like a lioness, and stalks forth like a *l*;
24: 9 He lies crouching like a *l*,
Dt 33:20 He lies there like a *l* that has seized the
Jgs 14: 5 Timnah, a young *l* came roaring to meet him.
14: 6 he tore the *l* in pieces as one tears a kid.
14: 8 aside to look at the remains of the *l*
14:18 than honey, and what is stronger than a *l*?"
1Sm 17:34 and whenever a *l* or bear came to carry off
17:36 servant has killed both a *l* and a bear,
17:37 me from the claws of the *l* and the bear,
2Sm 17:10 with the heart of a *l* will lose courage.
23:20 *l* in the cistern at the time of the snow.
1Kgs 10:19 Next to each arm stood a *l*;
13:24 But a *l* met him on the road,
13:24 remained standing by it, and so did the *l*.
13:25 in the road, with the *l* standing beside it,
13:26 He has delivered him to a *l*,
13:28 with the ass and the *l* standing beside it.
13:28 The *l* had not eaten the body nor had it
20:36 LORD, a *l* will kill you when you leave me."
20:36 company, a *l* came upon him and killed him.
1Chr 11:22 went down and killed the *l* in the cistern.
Est C:24 persuasive words in the presence of the *l*,
1Mc 3: 4 a lion, like a young *l* roaring for prey.
Jb 4:10 Though the *l* roars,
4:11 The old *l* perishes for lack of prey,
10:16 Should it lift up, you hunt me like a *l*:
28: 8 trodden it, nor has the *l* gone that way.
Ps(s) 10: 9 He waits in secret like a *l* in his lair;
91:13 shall trample down the *l* and the dragon.
Prv 19:12 king's wrath is like the roaring of a *l*,
20: 2 The dread of the king is as when a *l* roars;
22:13 The sluggard says, "A *l* is outside;
26:13 "There is a *l* in the street, a *l* in the middle
28: 1 but the just man, like a *l*,
28:15 Like a roaring *l* or a ravenous bear is a
30:30 The *l*, mightiest of beasts,
Eccl 9: 4 a live dog is better off than a dead *l*.
Sir 4:30 Be not a *l* at home,
25:15 With a dragon or a *l* I would rather dwell
27:10 As a *l* crouches in wait for prey,
27:28 vengeance lies in wait for them like a *l*.
28:23 It will hurl itself against them like a *l*;
Is 5:29 Their roar is that of the *l*,
11: 6 calf and the young *l* shall browse together,
11: 7 the *l* shall eat hay like the ox.
30: 6 land of the lioness and roaring *l*,
31: 4 a lion or a *l* cub growling over its prey,
35: 9 No *l* will be there,
38:13 Like a *l* he breaks all my bones;
65:25 and the *l* shall eat hay like the ox [but
Jer 2:30 devoured your prophets like a ravening *l*.
4: 7 Up comes the *l* from his lair,
12: 8 has turned on me like a *l* in the jungle;
25:38 The *l* leaves his lair,
49:19 As when a *l* comes up from the thicket of
50:44 As when a *l* comes up from the Jordan's
51:38 all roar like lions, growl like *l* cubs.
Lam 3:10 bear he has been to me, a *l* in ambush!
Ez 1:10 but on the right side was the face of a *l*,
10:14 that of a man, the third that of a *l*,
19: 2 a lioness was your mother, a *l* of lions!
19: 3 whelp she raised up, a young *l* he became;
19: 5 of her whelps, him she made a young *l*.
19: 6 among the lions, a young *l* he became;
32: 2 *L* of the nations, you are destroyed.
Dn 7: 4 The first was like a *l*,
Hos 5:14 For I am like a *l* to Ephraim, like a young *l*
11:10 shall follow the LORD, who roars like a *l*;
13: 7 Therefore, I will be like a *l* to them,
13: 8 I will devour them on the spot like a *l*,
Jl 1: 6 His teeth are the teeth of a *l*,
Am 3: 4 a *l* roar in the forest when it has no prey?
3: 4 Does a young *l* cry out from its den unless
3: 8 The *l* roars— who will not be afraid!
3:12 shepherd snatches from the mouth of the *l*
5:19 As if a man went to flee from a *l*,
Mi 5: 7 *l* among beasts of the forest, like a young *l*
Na 2:12 lions' den, Where the *l* went in and out,
2:13 The *l* snatched enough for his cubs,
1Pt 5: 8 a roaring *l* looking for someone to devour.
Rv 4: 7 The first creature resembled a *l*,
5: 5 The *L* of the tribe of Judah,
10: 3 then gave a loud cry like the roar of a *l*.
13: 2 had paws like a bear and the mouth of a *l*.

LIONESS (7)

Nm 23:24 Here is a people that springs up like a *l*,
24: 9 He lies crouching like a lion, or like a *l*;
Jb 4:11 prey, and the cubs of the *l* are scattered.
38:39 the *l* or appease the hunger of her cubs,
Is 30: 6 troubled land of the *l* and roaring lion,
Ez 19: 2 What a *l* was your mother, a lion of lions!
Jl 1: 6 of a lion, and his molars those of a *l*.

LIONESSES (2)

Na 2:13 for his cubs, and strangled for his *l*;
2:14 the cry of your *l* shall be heard no more.

LIONS (65)

Gn 49: 9 Judah, like a *l* whelp,
Dt 33:22 "Dan is a *l* whelp,
Jgs 14: 8 a swarm of bees and honey in the *l* carcass.
14: 9 had scooped the honey from the *l* carcass.
2Sm 1:23 swifter than eagles, stronger than *l*!
23:20 It was he who slew the two *l* in Moab.
1Kgs 7:29 panels between the frames there were *l*,
7:29 likewise, above and below the *l* and oxen,
7:36 there was a clear space, cherubim, *l*,
10:20 and twelve other *l* stood on the steps,
2Kgs 17:25 so he sent *l* among them that killed some
17:26 sent *l* among them that are killing them,
1Chr 12: 9 and spear, who bore themselves like *l*,
2Chr 9:18 seat, with two *l* standing beside the arms.
9:19 Twelve other *l* also stood there,
1Mc 2:60 was delivered from the jaws of *l*.
2Mc 11:11 Hurling themselves upon the enemy like *l*,
Jb 4:10 yet the teeth of the young *l* are broken;
Ps(s) 7: 3 rescue me, Lest I become like the *l* prey,
17:12 Like *l* hungry for prey, like young lions
22:14 against me like ravening and roaring *l*.
22:22 Save me from the *l* mouth;
35:17 from the *l*,
57: 5 in the midst of *l* which devour men;
58: 7 the jaw-teeth of the *l*,
104:21 Young *l* roar for the prey and seek their
Sg 4: 8 of Senir and Hermon, From the haunts of *l*,
Wis 11:17 upon them a drove of bears or fierce *l*,
Sir 13:18 *L* prey are the wild asses of the desert;
21: 2 Its teeth are *l* teeth,
47: 3 made sport of *l* as though they were kids,
Is 5:29 of the lion, like the *l* whelps they roar;
15: 9 *L* for those who are fleeing from Moab and
Jer 2:15 Against him *l* roar full-throated cries.
5: 6 Therefore *l* from the forest slay them,
50:17 A stray sheep was Israel that *l* pursued;
51:38 They all roar like *l*,
Ez 19: 2 a lioness was your mother, a lion of *l*!
19: 2 young *l* she couched to rear her whelps.
19: 6 He prowled among the *l*,
22:25 princes are like roaring *l* that tear prey;
38:13 Tarshish and all her young *l* shall ask you:
41:19 *l* face looking at a palmtree on the other;
Dn 6: 8 otherwise he shall be cast into a den of *l*.
6:13 otherwise he shall be cast into a den of *l*?"
6:17 to be brought and cast into the *l*' den.
6:20 next morning and hastened to the *l*' den.
6:21 been able to save you from the *l*?"
6:23 *l*' mouths so that they have not hurt me.
6:25 their wives, to be cast into the *l*' den.
6:25 the *l* overpowered them and crushed all
6:28 and he delivered Daniel from the *l*' power."
14:31 They threw Daniel into a *l*' den,
14:32 In the den were seven *l*,
14:34 have to Daniel in the *l*' den at Babylon."
Na 2:12 Where is the lions' cave, the young *l*' den,
2:14 and the sword shall devour your young *l*;
Zep 3: 3 Her princes in her midst are roaring *l*;
Zec 11: 3 the roaring of the young *l*,
2Tm 4:17 That is how I was saved from the *l* jaws.
Heb 11:33 they broke the jaws of *l*,
Rv 9: 8 Their teeth were like the teeth of *l*,
9:17 The horses' heads were like heads of *l*,

LIP (3)

Ps(s) 120: 2 O LORD, deliver me from lying *l*,
Mt 15: 8 *l* service but their heart is far from me.
Mk 7: 6 *l* service but their heart is far from me.

LIPS (131)

Ex 13: 9 law of the LORD will ever be on your *l*,
23:13 it shall not be heard from your *l*.
Jos 1: 8 Keep this book of the law on your *l*.
1Sm 1:13 though her *l* were moving,
Jdt 5: 5 no lie shall escape your servant's *l*.
9:10 With the guile of my *l*,
Jb 8:21 with laughter, and your *l* with rejoicing.
11: 5 would speak, and open his *l* against you,
13: 6 utter and listen to the reproof from my *l*.
15: 6 you own *l* refute you.
16: 5 with talk, or shake my head with silent *l*.
23:12 the commands of his *l* I have not departed;
27: 4 nostrils, My *l* shall not speak falsehood,
32:20 let me open my *l*,
33: 3 mind, my *l* shall utter knowledge sincerely;
Ps(s) 12: 3 with smooth *l* they speak,
12: 4 LORD destroy all smooth *l*
12: 5 our *l* are our own;
16: 4 nor will I take their names upon my *l*.
17: 1 hearken to my prayer from *l* without deceit.
17: 4 of your *l* I have kept the ways of the law.
21: 3 you refused not the wish of his *l*.
22: 8 they mock me with parted *l*,
31:19 Let dumbness strike their lying *l* that
34:14 from evil and your *l* from speaking guile;
40:10 I did not restrain my *l*,
45: 3 grace is poured out upon your *l*;
51:17 O Lord, open my *l*,
59: 8 mouths, and blasphemies are on their *l*—
59:13 *l* let them be caught in their arrogance,
63: 4 my *l* shall glorify you.
63: 6 with exultant *l* my mouth shall praise you.
66:14 Which my *l* uttered and my words promised
71:23 My *l* shall shout for joy as I sing your
89:35 the promise of my *l* I will not alter.
106:33 and the rash utterance passed his *l*.
119:13 With my *l* I declare all the ordinances of
119:171 My *l* pour forth your praise,
140: 4 the venom of asps is under their *l*.
141: 3 my mouth, a guard at the door of my *l*.
Prv 5: 3 The *l* of an adulteress drip with honey,
6: 2 been snared by the utterance of your *l*,
7:21 with her smooth *l* she leads him astray;
8: 6 honesty opens my *l*.
8: 7 recounts, but the wickedness my *l* abhor.
10:13 the *l* of the intelligent is found wisdom,
10:18 the *l* of the liar that conceal hostility;
10:19 but he who restrains his *l* does well.
10:21 The just man's *l* nourish many,
10:32 The *l* of the just know how to please,
12:13 the sin of his *l* the evil man is ensnared,
12:19 Truthful *l* endure forever,
12:22 Lying *l* are an abomination to the LORD,
13: 3 to open wide one's *l* brings downfall.
14: 3 back, but the *l* of the wise preserve them.
14: 7 But knowing *l* one meets with by surprise.
15: 7 The *l* of the wise disseminate knowledge,
16:10 The king's *l* are an oracle;
16:13 The king takes delight in honest *l*,
16:23 and augments the persuasiveness of his *l*.
16:27 and on his *l* there is a scorching fire.
16:30 he who compresses his *l* has mischief ready.
17: 4 The evil man gives heed to wicked *l*,
17:28 if he closes his *l*,
18: 6 The fool's *l* lead him into strife,
18: 7 his *l* are a snare to his life.
18:20 with the yield of his *l* he sates himself.
20:15 of corals, wise *l* are a precious ornament.
22:18 bosom, if they all are ready on your *l*.
23:16 exult, when your *l* speak what is right.
24: 2 violence, and their *l* speak of foul play.
24:26 a kiss on the *l* who makes an honest reply.

LIPS (cont.)

24:28 cause, thus committing folly with your *l.*
26:23 are smooth *l* with a wicked heart.
26:24 With his *l* an enemy pretends,
27: 2 not your own *l.*
Eccl 10:12 win favor, but the fool's *l* consume him.
Sg 4: 3 Your *l* are like a scarlet strand;
4:11 Your *l* drip honey,
5:13 His *l* are red blossoms;
7:10 lover, spreading over the *l* and the teeth.
Wis 1: 6 not the blasphemer of his guilty *l;*
Sir 1:21 then the *l* of many herald his wisdom.
1:26 over your *l* keep watch.
6: 5 and gracious *l* prompt friendly greetings.
12:16 With his *l* an enemy speaks sweetly,
15: 9 Unseemly is praise on a sinner's *l,*
20:23 it is constantly on the *l* of the unruly.
21: 5 from a poor man's *l* is heard at once,
21:16 charm to be found upon the *l* of the wise.
21:25 The *l* of the impious talk of what is not
22:27 my mouth, and upon my *l* an effective seal,
23: 8 Through his *l* is the sinner ensnared;
39: 6 the Most High, To open his *l* in prayer,
50:20 blessing of the LORD would be upon his *l,*
51: 3 and from *l* that went over to falsehood;
51: 5 From deceiving *l* and painters of lies,
51:22 The LORD has granted me my *l* as a reward,
Is 6: 5 lips, living among a people of unclean *l;*
6: 7 said, "now that this has touched your *l,*
11: 4 breath of his *l* he shall slay the wicked.
28:11 with stammering *l* and in a strange
29:13 only and honors me with their *l* alone,
30:27 His *l* are filled with fury,
59: 3 Your *l* speak falsehood,
Jer 12: 2 You are upon their *l,*
17:16 You know what passed my *l;*
Ez 33:31 for lies are on their *l* and their desires
Dn 4:28 these words were still on the king's *l,*
10:16 something like a man's hand touched my *l;*
Hos 8: 1 A trumpet to your *l,*
Mi 3: 7 They shall cover their *l,*
Hb 3:16 at the sound, my *l* quiver.
Zep 3: 9 change and purify the *l* of the peoples,
Mal 2: 6 and no dishonesty was found upon his *l;*
2: 7 the *l* of the priest are to keep knowledge,
Lk 4:22 appealing discourse which came from his *l.*
Jn 19:29 wine on some hyssop and raised it to his *l.*
Acts 4:25 the *l* of our father David your servant:
15: 7 whose *l* the Gentiles would hear the message
Rom 3:13 The venom of asps lies behind their *l,*
10: 8 on your *l* and in your heart" (that is,
10: 9 you confess with your *l* that Jesus is Lord,
10:10 confession on the *l* to salvation.
2Cor 12: 7 than what he sees in me or hears from my *l.*
Eph 4:29 Never let evil talk pass your *l;*
6:19 for me that God may put his word on my *l,*
Heb 13:15 of *l* which acknowledge his name.
1Pt 3:10 from evil and his *l* from uttering deceit.
Rv 14: 5 On their *l* no deceit has been found;

LIQUID (10)

Lv 11:34 with water, and any *l* that men drink,
2Mc 1:31 of the *l* to be poured upon large stones.
1:33 a *l* was found with which Nehemiah and his
1:36 and his companions called the *l* nephthar,
Is 5:10 of vineyard shall yield but one *l* measure,
Ez 45:10 an honest ephah, and an honest *l* measure.
45:11 the *l* measure shall be of the same size:
45:11 the *l* measure equal to a tenth of a homer;
45:14 by the kor of ten *l* measures [or a homer,
45:14 a homer, for ten *l* measures make a homer].

LIQUOR (3)

1Sm 1:11 neither wine nor *l* shall he drink,
1:15 I have had neither wine nor *l;*
Est 1: 7 *L* was served in a variety of golden cups,

LIST (10)

Nm 11:26 They too had been on the *l,*
Jos 12: 7 This is a *l* of the kings whom Joshua and
1Chr 11:11 Here is the *l* of David's warriors:
25: 1 the *l* of those who performed this service:
27: 1 is the *l* of the Israelite family heads,
Ezr 5:10 in a *l* of the men who are their leaders.
8: 1 This is the *l* of the family heads who
Neh 7: 5 I came upon the family *l* of those who had
Ez 48: 1 This is the *l* of the tribes.

LISTED (13)

Gn 25:13 sons, *l* in the order of their birth:
Dt 29:26 on it all the imprecations *l* in this book;
Jos 18: 9 *l* its cities in writing in seven sections
Jgs 8:14 who upon being questioned *l* for him the
2Sm 23:18 He was *l* among the Thirty and commanded
23:22 He was *l* among the Thirty warriors and
1Chr 4:41 They who have just been *l* by name set out
5: 1 so that he is not *l* in the family records
5: 7 when they were *l* in the family records
5:17 All were *l* in the family records in the
7: 7 *l* twenty-two thousand and thirty-four.
7: 9 Their family records *l* twenty thousand two
2Chr 31:19 to every Levite *l* in the family records.

LISTEN (272)

Gn 4:10 *L:* your brother's blood cries out
4:23 wives of Lamech, *l* to my utterance:
23: 6 "Please, sir, *l* to us!
23: 8 me room for burial of my dead, *l* to me!
23:11 "Please, sir, *l* to me!
23:13 "Ah, if only you would please *l* to me!
23:15 sir, *l* to me!
27: 6 father, Rebekah said to her son Jacob, *L!*
27: 8 Now, son, *l* carefully to what I tell you.
27:42 *L!* Your brother Esau intends to settle
37: 6 *L* to this dream I had.
42:22 But you wouldn't *l!*
49: 2 and listen, sons of Jacob, *l* to Israel,
Ex 4: 1 they will not believe me, nor *l* to my plea?
6: 9 they would not *l* to him because of their
6:12 "If the Israelites would not *l* to me,
6:12 how can it be that Pharaoh will *l* to me,
6:30 how can it be that Pharaoh will *l* to me?"
7: 4 in the land of Egypt, he will not *l* to you.
7:13 was obstinate and would not *l* to them,
7:22 and would not *l* to Moses and Aaron,
8:11 *l* to them just as the LORD had foretold.
8:15 remained obstinate and would not *l* to them,
9:12 obstinate, and he would not *l* to them,
11: 9 "Pharaoh refuses to *l* to you that my
15:26 "If you really *l* to the voice of the LORD,
16:20 But they would not *l* to him.
18:19 Now, *l* to me,
20:19 Moses, "You speak to us, and we will *l;*
Nm 12: 6 he said, "Now *l* to the words of the LORD:
16: 8 Moses also said to Korah, *L* to me,
20:10 the rock, where he said to them, *L* to me,
Dt 1:16 time, *L* to complaints among your kinsmen,
1:43 gave you this warning but you would not *l.*
1:45 did not *l* to your cry or give ear to you.
5:27 we will *l* and obey.'
13: 9 do not yield to him or *l* to him,
17:12 insolence to refuse to *l* to the priest
18:14 *l* to their soothsayers
18:15 to him you shall *l.*
18:19 *l* to my words which he speaks in my name,
21:18 son who will not *l* to his father or mother,
21:20 and unruly fellow who will not *l* to us;
23: 6 would not *l* to Balaam and turned his curse
27: 9 "Be silent, O Israel and *l!*
30:17 you turn away your hearts and will not *l,*
Jos 3: 9 "Come here and *l* to the words of the LORD,
24:10 but I would not *l* to Balaam.
Jgs 2:17 despoilers, they did not *l* to their judges,
14:13 "we will *l* to it."
19:25 When the men would not *l* to his host,
Ru 2: 8 Boaz said to Ruth, *L,* my daughter!
1Sm 8:19 refused to *l* to Samuel's warning and said,
9: 6 The servant replied, *L!*
15: 1 therefore, *l* to the message of the LORD.
22: 7 *L,* men of Benjamin!
22:12 Then Saul said, *L,* son of Ahitub!"
24:10 "Why do you *l* to those who say,
25:24 you, and *l* to the words of your handmaid.
26:19 the king *l* to the words of his servant.
28:22 you, in turn, please *l* to your maidservant.
2Sm 12:18 to him, but he would not *l* to what we said.
13:16 He would not *l* to her,
20:16 the outworks and called out, "Listen, *l!*
20:17 him, *L* to what your maidservant has to say."
1Kgs 8:28 and *l* to the cry of supplication which I,
8:30 *L* to the petitions of your servant and of
8:30 *L* from your heavenly dwelling and grant
8:32 your altar in this temple, *l* in heaven;
8:34 *l* in heaven and forgive the sin of your
8:36 *l* in heaven and forgive the sin of your
8:39 *l* from your heavenly dwelling place and
8:43 this temple, *l* from your heavenly dwelling.
8:45 *l* in heaven to their prayer and petition,
8:49 your honor, *l* from your heavenly dwelling.
10: 8 before you always and *l* to your wisdom.
12:15 The king did not *l* to the people,
12:16 Israel saw that the king did not *l* to them,
20: 8 and all the people said to him, "Do not *l.*
2Kgs 14:11 But Amaziah would not *l.*
17:14 servants the prophets," they did not *l,*
17:40 They did not *l,*
18:28 Judean, *L* to the words of the great king,
18:31 Do not *l* to Hezekiah,
18:32 Do not *l* to Hezekiah when he would seduce
19:16 Incline your ear, O LORD, and *l!*
21: 9 But they did not *l,*
2Chr 6:19 and *l* to the cry of supplication your
6:21 *L* to the petitions of your servant and of
6:21 *L* from your heavenly dwelling,
6:23 your altar in this temple, *l* from heaven:
6:25 *l* from heaven and forgive the sin of your
6:27 *l* in heaven and forgive the sin of your
6:30 *l* from your heavenly dwelling place,
6:33 *l* from your heavenly dwelling place,
6:35 *l* from heaven to their prayer and petition,
6:39 honor, *l* from your heavenly dwelling place,
9: 7 before you always and *l* to your wisdom.
10:15 The king would not *l* to the people,
10:16 saw that the king would not *l* to them,
13: 4 *L* to me, Jeroboam and all Israel!
20:15 *L,* all of Judah, inhabitants of Jerusalem,
20:20 *L* to me, Judah and inhabitants
24:19 the people would not *l* to their warnings.
25:20 But Amaziah would not *l,*
28:11 Now *l* to me:
29: 5 *L* to me, you Levites!
35:22 Therefore he would not *l* to the words of
Neh 9:30 still they would not *l.*
Tb 3: 7 daughter Sarah also had to *l* to abuse,
6:13 you have the right to marry her *l* to me,
6:16 So now *l* to me, brother;
Jdt 7: 9 "Sir, *l* to what we have to say,
8:11 *L* to me, you rulers of the people
8:32 *L* to me! Judith said to them,
11: 5 *L* to the words of your servant,
14: 1 *L* to me, my brothers.
Est 3: 4 day after day and he would not *l* to them,
1Mc 2:65 *l* to him always,
Jb 13: 6 utter and *l* to the reproof from my lips.
15:17 I will show you, if you *l* to me;
21: 2 At least *l* to my words,
33:31 Be attentive, O Job; *l* to me!
33:33 If not, then do you *l* to me;
Ps(s) 59: 8 "Who is there to *l*—
61: 2 Hear, O God, my cry; *l* to my prayer!
Prv 5: 7 So now, O children, *l* to me,
5:13 did I not *l* to the voice of my teachers,
7:24 So now, O children, *l* to me,
8:32 "So now, O children, *l* to me;
19:20 *L* to counsel and receive instruction,
23:22 *L* to your father who begot you,
Sir 6:24 *L,* my son, and heed my advice;
6:33 If you are willing to *l,* you will learn;
21:24 It is rude for one to *l* at a door;
31:22 *L* to me, my son, and scorn me not;
33:19 *L,* to me, O leaders of the multitude;
39:13 *L,* my faithful children:
Is 1: 2 Hear, O heavens, and *l,*
1:10 *L* to the instruction of our God,
1:15 Though you pray the more, I will not *l.*
6: 9 *L* carefully, but you shall not understand!
7:13 *L,* O house of David!
13: 4 *L!* the rumble on the mountains:
13: 4 *L!* the noise of kingdoms.
18: 3 When the trumpet blows, *l!*
28:12 but they would not *l.*
28:23 voice, pay attention and *l* to what I say:
34: 1 Let the earth and what fills it *l,*
36:13 Judean, *L* to the words of the great king,
36:16 Do not *l* to Hezekiah,
42:18 You who are deaf, *l,*
46:12 *L* to me, you fainthearted,
48:12 *L* to me, Jacob Israel, whom I named!
48:14 All of you assemble and *l:*
49: 1 Hear me, O coastlands, *l,*
51: 1 *L* to me, you who pursue justice,
55: 3 Come to me heedfully, *l,*
65:12 did not answer, I spoke and you did not *l,*
Jer 2: 4 *L* to the word of the LORD,
3:13 green tree] and would not *l* to my voice,
4:15 *L!* They proclaim it from Dan,
7:13 says the LORD, because you did not *l,*
7:16 Do not urge me, for I will not *l* to you.
7:23 *L* to my voice; then I will be your God
7:27 to them, they will not *l* to you either;
7:27 which does not *l* to the voice of the LORD,
8: 6 I *l* closely: they speak what is not true;
8:19 *L!* the cry of the daughter of my people
10:22 *L!* a noise! it comes closer,
11: 4 *L* to my voice and do all that I command
11: 8 But they did not *l* or give ear.
11:12 they cry out to me, I will not *l* to them.
11:14 I will not *l* when they call to me at the
13:11 But they did not *l.*
13:15 Give ear, *l* humbly, for the LORD speaks.
13:17 If you do not *l* to this in your pride,
14:12 fast, I will not *l* to their supplication.
17:23 fathers, though they did not *l* or give ear,
18:19 O LORD, and *l* to what my adversaries say.
19: 3 *L* to the word of the LORD,
22: 2 *L* to the word of the LORD,
22:21 secure, but you answered, "I will not *l.*"
22:21 way from your youth, not to *l* to my voice.
23:16 *L* not to the words of your prophets,
25: 3 to you untiringly, but you would not *l.*
25: 4 Though you refused to *l* or pay heed,
25: 7 But you would not *l* to me,
25: 8 Since you would not *l* to my words, lo!
25:36 *L!* Wailing from the shepherds,
26: 3 Perhaps they will *l* and turn back,
26:13 *l* to the voice of the LORD your God,
27: 9 You, however, must not *l* to your prophets,
27:14 *l* to the words of those prophets who say,
27:16 Do not *l* to the words of your prophets who
27:17 Do not *l* to them!
28: 7 *l* to what I am about to say in your
29: 8 not *l* to those among you who dream dreams.
29:12 when you go to pray to me, I will *l* to you.
29:19 For they did not *l* to my words,
29:20 You, now, *l* to the word of the LORD,
32:23 of it, but they did not *l* to your voice;

32:33 them, they would not *l* to my correction.
36:25 to burn the scroll, he would not *l* to them,
37: 2 people of the land would *l* to the words
38:15 If I counsel you, you will not *l* to me!
42:15 then *l* to the word of the LORD,
44: 5 they would not *l* or accept the warning to
44:16 *l* to what you say in the name of the LORD.
44:26 But *l* then to the word of the LORD,
48: 3 *L!* a cry from Horonaim of ruin
50:28 *L!* the fugitives, the escaped
Lam 1:18 *L,* all you peoples,
Bar 3: 9 *l* and know prudence!
Ez 3: 6 to send you to these, they would *l* to you;
3: 7 to listen to you, since they will not *l* to me.
12:27 of man, *l* to the house of Israel saying,
20: 8 rebelled against me and refused to *l* to me;
20:39 Then *l* to me, and never again profane
33:32 They *l* to your words,
40: 4 of man, look carefully and *l* intently,
44: 5 and *l* intently to all that I will tell you
Dn 9:14 have done, for we did not *l* to your voice.
9:18 Give ear, O my God, and *l;*
Am 5:23 I will not *l* to the melodies of your harps.
Hb 1: 2 I cry for help but you do not *l!*
Zec 1: 4 they would not *l* or pay attention to me,
3: 8 *L,* O Joshua, high priest!
7:11 But they refused to *l;* they stubbornly
7:13 called, so he would not *l* when they called,
Mal 2: 1 If you do not *l,*
Mt 10:14 receive you or *l* to what you have to say,
12:42 of the earth to *l* to the wisdom of Solomon;
13:13 see, they *l* but do not hear or understand.
13:14 *L* as you will, you shall not understand,
17: 5 on whom my favor rests. *L* to him."
18:16 If he does not *l,* summon another,
21:33 *L* to another parable.
Mk 4: 3 *L* carefully to this.
4:12 not see, *l* carefully and not understand,
4:20 good soil are the ones who *l* to the word,
4:24 *L* carefully to what you hear.
9: 7 *L* to him."
15:35 of the bystanders who heard it remarked, *L!*
Lk 9:35 *L* to him."
11:31 of the world to *l* to the wisdom of Solomon,
16:31 they do not *l* to Moses and the prophets,
18: 6 *L* to what the corrupt judge has to say.
Jn 4:35 *L* to what I say:
9:27 told you once, but you would not *l* to me,"
18:20 have spoken publicly to any who would *l.*
Acts 2:14 *L* to what I have to say.
2:22 "Men of Israel, *l* to me!
3:22 *l* to him in everything he says to you.
3:23 Anyone who does not *l* to that prophet
7: 2 *L* to me. The God of glory appeared
13:16 reverence our God, *l* to what I have to say!
15:13 "Brothers, *l* to me.
17:21 than to tell about or *l* to something new.)
22: 1 *l* to what I have to say to you in my
26: 3 I beg you to *l* to me patiently.
26:29 who *l* to me today might become what I am
28:26 *l* carefully yet you will never understand;
28:27 They have scarcely used their ears to *l;*
1Tm 2:11 *l* in silence and be completely submissive.
2Tm 2:14 no good and can be the ruin of those who *l.*
Heb 12:25 refused to *l* as God spoke to them on earth,
Jas 1:22 If all you do is *l* to it,
2: 5 *L,* dear brothers.

LISTENED (32)

Gn 3:17 "Because you *l* to your wife and ate from
Ex 7:16 But as yet you have not *l.*
Dt 9:19 Yet once again the LORD *l* to me.
1Sm 8:21 Samuel had *l* to all the people had to say,
11: 6 As he *l* to this report,
17:23 and spoke as before, and David *l.*
28:23 in urging him, he *l* to their entreaties,
2Kgs 16: 9 who *l* to him and moved against Damascus,
19:20 I have *l!*
22:19 I in turn have *l,*
2Chr 24:17 to the king, and the king then *l* to them.
34:27 and have wept before me, I in turn have *l*—
Neh 8: 3 *l* attentively to the book of the law.
Jb 29:21 For me they *l* and waited;
33: 8 hearing, as I *l* to the sound of your words:
Sir 33: 4 Prepare your words and you will be *l* to;
51:11 the LORD heard my voice, he *l* to my appeal;
Is 66: 4 no one answered, when I spoke, no one *l;*
Jer 3:25 we *l* not to the voice of the LORD,
9:12 and have not followed it or *l* to my voice,
Hos 9:17 disown them because they have not *l* to him;
Hg 1:12 of the people *l* to the voice of the LORD,
Zec 7:13 that, as they had not *l* when he called,
Mal 3:16 one another, and the LORD *l* attentively;
Mt 22:33 who *l* were spellbound by his teaching.
Mk 4:18 They have *l* to the word,
Lk 10:39 at the Lord's feet and *l* to his words.
Acts 7:54 who *l* to his words were stung to the heart;
11: 7 I *l* as a voice said to me, 'Get up, Peter!
15:12 They *l* to Barnabas and Paul as the two
16:14 One who *l* was a woman named Lydia,
16:25 hymns to God as their fellow prisoners *l,*

LISTENER (2)

Wis 1: 6 of his heart and the *l* to his tongue.
Jas 1:25 He is no forgetful *l,*

LISTENERS (1)

Lk 18:26 His *l* asked him, "Who, then, can be saved?"

LISTENING (22)

Gn 18:10 Sarah was *l* at the entrance of the tent,
27: 5 *l* while Isaac was speaking to his son Esau.
Jgs 5:16 your hearths *l* to the lowing of the herds?
1Sm 3: 9 reply, 'Speak, LORD, for your servant is *l.*' "
3:10 answered, "Speak, for your servant is *l.*"
2Sm 20:17 "I am *l.*"
1Kgs 18:29 no one answered, and no one was *l.*
Sg 8:13 my friends are *l* for your voice,
Jer 16:12 of his evil heart instead of *l* to me.
26: 5 *l* to the words of my servants the prophets,
37:14 Without *l,*
Mk 4:16 people who on *l* to the word accept it
Lk 2:46 *l* to them and asking them questions.
19:11 While they were *l* to these things he went
19:48 was *l* to him and hanging on his words.
Jn 3:29 The groom's best man waits there *l* for him
Acts 10:44 upon all who were *l* to Peter's message.
14: 9 On one occasion he was *l* to Paul preaching,
22:22 in his speech the crowd had been *l* to Paul,
27:11 the centurion preferred *l* to the pilot and
27:11 the pilot and the shipowner to *l* to Paul.
2Tm 4: 4 They will stop *l* to the truth and will

LISTENS (11)

Prv 12:15 own eyes, but he who *l* to advice is wise.
15:31 He who *l* to salutary reproof will abide
17: 4 *l* to falsehood from a mischievous tongue.
21:28 but he who *l* will finally have his say.
29:12 If a ruler *l* to lying words,
Sir 14:23 through her windows, and *l* at her doors;
Is 42:23 Who *l* and pays heed for the time to come?
Mt 18:15 If he *l* to you,
Jn 9:31 is devout and obeys his will, he *l* to him.
Jas 1:23 A man who *l* to God's word but does not put
1Jn 4: 5 of the world and why the world *l* to them.

LISTING (1)

1Chr 24: 6 *l* two successive family groups from

LISTLESS (2)

Wis 13:13 This wood he models with *l* skill,
Is 61: 3 a glorious mantle instead of a *l* spirit.

LISTS (1)

Sir 33: 9 and others he *l* as ordinary days.

LIT (2)

1Sm 14:27 raised it to his mouth and his eyes *l* up.
Tb 8:13 She sent the maid, who *l* a lamp,

LITERATURE (2)

Dn 1: 4 taught the language and *l* of the Chaldeans;
1:17 and proficiency in all *l* and science,

LITTER (5)

Nm 4:10 covering of tahash skin, and place on a *l.*
4:12 They shall then place them on a *l.*
2Mc 9: 8 the ground and had to be carried on a *l,*
Sg 3: 7 Ah, it is the *l* of Solomon;
Lk 7:14 Then he stepped forward and touched the *l;*

LITTLE (194)

Gn 18: 5 to your servant, let me bring you a *l* food,
24:43 Please give me a *l* water from your jug,
25:34 Esau cared *l* for his birthright.
26:10 *l* for one of the men to lie with your wife,
30:30 the *l* you had before I came has grown into
43: 2 "Go back and procure us a *l* more food."
Ex 10:10 "if I ever let your *l* ones go with you!
10:24 Your *l* ones, too, may go with you.
16:18 gathered a small amount did not have too *l.*
17: 4 A *l* more and they will stone me!"
23:30 will drive them out *l* by little before you,
Nm 14: 3 wives and *l* ones will be taken as booty.
14:31 Your *l* ones,
16: 9 Is it too *l* for you that the God of Israel
16:27 tents with their wives and sons and *l* ones,
31: 9 Midianites with their *l* ones as captives,
Dt 1:39 Your *l* ones,
7:22 these nations before you *l* by little.
28:38 seed on your field, you will harvest but *l,*
Jgs 4:19 her, "Please give me a *l* water to drink.
18:21 turned to depart, they placed their *l* ones,
19: 5 "Fortify yourself with a *l* food;
1Sm 2:19 mother used to make a *l* garment for him,
14:43 "I only tasted a *l* honey from the end of
15:17 "Though *l* in your own esteem,
20:35 a *l* boy for his appointment with David.
2Sm 7:19 Yet even this you see as too *l,*
12: 3 except one *l* ewe lamb that he had bought.
12: 3 She shared the *l* food he had and drank
16: 1 had gone a *l* beyond the top when Ziba,
19:37 the Jordan, your servant is doing *l* enough!
1Kgs 12:10 *l* finger is thicker than my father's body.
17:12 of flour in my jar and a *l* oil in my jug.
17:13 first make me a *l* cake and bring it to me.
2Kgs 4:10 let us arrange a *l* room on the roof and
5: 2 from the land of Israel in a raid a *l* girl,
5:14 became again like the flesh of a *l* child,
8:12 you will dash their *l* children to pieces,
1Chr 17:17 And yet, even this you now consider too *l,*
2Chr 10:10 *l* finger is thicker than my father's body.
20:13 before the LORD, with their *l* ones,
31:18 in the family records, for their *l* ones,
Tb 4: 8 if you have but *l,*
12: 8 A *l* with righteousness is better than
Jdt 7:27 and not have to behold our *l* ones dying
16:16 fat of all holocausts but *l* in your sight,
Est A: 9 river, a flood of water from a *l* spring.
1Mc 16:15 *l* stronghold called Dok which he had built.
2Mc 5:17 that the Lord was angry for a *l* while
7:33 a *l* while to correct us with chastisements,
8: 8 Judas was gaining ground little by *l*
8:11 *l* did he dream of the punishment
8:33 who had taken refuge in a *l* house;
10: 6 Booths, remembering how, a *l* while before,
Jb 8: 7 Your former state will be of *l* moment,
10:20 a *l* Before I go whence I shall not return,
36: 2 Wait yet a *l* and I will instruct you,
40: 4 Behold, I am of *l* account;
Ps(s) 8: 6 You have made him *l* less than the angels,
17:14 bequeath their abundance to their *l* ones.
37:10 Yet a *l* while,
116: 6 The LORD keeps the *l* ones;
137: 9 and smash your *l* ones against the rock!
Prv 6:10 A *l* sleep, a *l* slumber, a *l* folding of the
9:18 *L* he knows that the shades are there,
10:20 the heart of the wicked is of *l* worth.
13:11 dwindles away, but amassed *l* by little,
15:16 Better a *l* with fear of the LORD than a
16: 8 Better a *l* with virtue,
23: 8 The *l* you have eaten you will vomit up,
24:33 little sleep, a *l* slumber, a little folding
Eccl 5:11 laboring man, whether he eats *l* or much,
10: 1 weighty than wisdom or wealth is a *l* folly!
Sg 2:15 the *l* foxes that damage the vineyards;
8: 8 sister is *l* and she has no breasts as yet.
Wis 3: 5 Chastised a *l,*
7: 9 all gold, in view of her, is a *l* sand,
12: 2 Therefore you rebuke offenders *l* by little,
15: 8 was made from the earth And after a *l,*
Sir 6:20 in cultivating her you will labor but *l,*
11:12 failure, with *l* strength and great misery
19: 1 wastes the *l* he has will be stripped bare.
19:20 those with *l* understanding who fear God,
20:11 A man may buy much for *l,*
20:14 He gives *l* and criticizes often,
22:10 Weep but a *l* over the dead man,
29:23 it *l* or much be content with what you have,
31:19 Does not a *l* suffice for a well-bred man?
34:10 One never put to the proof knows *l,*
42: 5 Of acquiring much or *l,*
51:27 I have labored only a *l,*
51:28 Acquire but a *l* instruction;
Is 11: 6 together, with a *l* child to guide them.
22:24 and offspring, all the *l* dishes,
28:10 rule on rule, here a little, there a *l!*' "
28:13 rule on rule, here a little, there a *l!*"
29:17 But a very *l* while,
32:10 In a *l* more than a year you overconfident
49: 6 It is too *l,*
Jer 51:33 Yet a *l* while,
Lam 1: 5 Her *l* ones have gone away,
2:19 hands to him for the lives of your *l* ones
Dn 7: 8 it had, when suddenly another, a *l* horn,
8: 9 *l* horn which kept growing toward the south,
Hos 1: 4 for in a *l* while I will punish the house
14: 1 their *l* ones shall be dashed to pieces,
Na 3:10 even her *l* ones were dashed to pieces at
Hg 1: 6 You have sown much, but have brought in *l;*
1: 9 You expected much, but it came to *l;*
2: 6 One moment yet, a *l* while,
Zec 1:15 whereas I was but a *l* angry,
13: 7 and I will turn my hand against the *l* ones.
Mt 8:26 How *l* faith you have!"
9:24 The *l* girl is not dead.
9:25 her by the hand, and the *l* girl got up.
13: 5 fell on rocky ground, where it had *l* soil.
13:12 man who has not, will lose what *l* he has.
14:31 "How *l* faith you have!"
17:20 "Because you have so *l* trust,"
18: 2 He called a *l* child over and stood him in
18: 3 you change and become like *l* children,
18: 6 one of these *l* ones who believe in me,
18:10 that you never despise one of these *l* ones.
18:14 of these *l* ones shall ever come to grief.
25:29 have not will lose even the *l* they have.
26:39 advanced a *l* and fell prostrate in prayer.
26:73 A *l* while later some bystanders came over
Mk 1:19 Proceeding a *l* farther along,
4: 5 landed on rocky ground where it had *l* soil;
4:25 not, what *l* they have will be taken away."
5:23 "My *l* daughter is critically ill.

LITTLE (cont.)

5:41 "Talitha, koum," which means, *L* girl,
6:31 to an out-of-the-way place and rest a *l*."
9:36 Then he took a *l* child,
10:13 *l* children to him to have him touch them,
10:15 like a *l* child shall not take part in it."
14:35 He advanced a *l* and fell to the ground,
14:70 A *l* later the bystanders said to Peter
Lk 7:47 *L* is forgiven the one whose love is small."
8:18 not, will lose even the *l* he thinks he has."
9:47 took a *l* child and placed it beside him,
9:48 this *l* child on my account welcomes me,
12:32 "Do not live in fear, *l* flock.
16:10 If you can trust a man in *l* things,
17: 2 than giving scandal to one of these *l* ones.
18: 4 he thought, 'I care *l* for God or man,
18:16 "Let the *l* children come to me.
19:26 the one who has not will lose the *l* he has.
22:58 A *l* while later someone else saw him and
24:25 "What *l* sense you have!
Jn 7:33 a *l* while longer am I to be with you,
12:35 "The light is among you only a *l* longer.
14:19 A *l* while now and the world will see me no
Acts 19:24 and brought in no *l* work for his craftsmen.
26:28 At this, Agrippa said, "A *l* more,
26:29 replied, "Whether *l* more or much more,
27: 7 For many days we made *l* headway,
Rom 15:24 the joy of being with you for a *l* while.
1Cor 4: 3 It matters *l* to me whether you or any
5: 6 Do you not know that a *l* yeast has its
2Cor 8:15 excess and he who gathered *l* had no lack."
11: 1 You must endure *l* of my folly.
11:14 And *l* wonder!
11:16 all the way and let me do a *l* boasting.
Gal 5: 9 "A *l* yeast can affect the entire dough."
1Thes 2: 7 as any nursing mother fondling her *l* ones.
1Tm 5:23 Take a *l* wine for the good of your stomach,
Heb 2: 7 him for a *l* while lower than the angels;
2: 9 made for a *l* while lower than the angels,
1Pt 5:10 those who have suffered a *l* while.
1Jn 2: 1 My *l* ones, I am writing this to keep you
2:12 *L* ones, I address you, for through
2:28 Remain in him now, *l* ones,
3: 7 *L* ones, let no one deceive you;
3:18 *L* children, let us love in deed and
4: 4 You are of God, you *l* ones,
5:21 My *l* children, be on your guard
Rv 3:17 *L* do you realize how wretched you are,
6:11 were told to be patient a *l* while longer
10: 2 he held a *l* scroll which had been opened.
10: 9 and said to him, "Give me the *l* scroll."
10:10 *l* scroll from the angel's hand and ate it.
13:18 with a *l* ingenuity anyone can calculate

LITURGICAL (3)

1Chr 9:28 Some of them had charge of the *l* equipment,
25: 1 David and the leaders of the *l* cult set
28:13 all the *l* vessels of the house of the LORD.

LITURGY (1)

Acts 13: 2 in the *l* of the Lord and were fasting,

LIVE (440)

Gn 3:22 also, and thus eat of it and *l* forever."
12:12 then they will killme, but let you *l*.
17:18 God, "Let but Ishmael *l* on by your favor!"
24: 3 of the Canaanites among whom I *l*,
24:37 of the Canaanites in whose land I *l*;
27:40 "By your sword you shall *l*,
34:10 Thus you can *l* among us.
34:22 But the men will agree to *l* with us and
38:11 So Tamar went to *l* in her father's house.
42:18 "Do this, and you shall *l*;
45:18 where you will *l* off the fat of the land.'
Ex 1:16 but if it is a girl, she may *l*."
1:17 Egypt had ordered them, but let the boys *l*.
1:18 you acted thus, allowing the boys to *l*?"
1:22 Hebrews, but you may let all the girls *l*."
2:21 Moses agreed to *l* with him,
18:20 how they are to *l* and what they are to do.
19:13 man or beast, must not be allowed to *l*.
21:35 they shall sell the *l* ox and divide this
22:17 "You shall not let a sorceress *l*.
34:10 people among whom you *l* may see how
Lv 11: 9 the various creatures that *l* in the water,
14: 4 man who is to be purified, to get two *l*,
16:20 Aaron shall bring forward the *l* goat.
23:17 shall bring with you from wherever you *l*
25: 6 hired help and the tenants who *l* with you,
25:19 so that you may *l* there without worry.
25:35 so that he may continue to *l* with you.
25:36 but out of fear of God let him *l* with you.
26: 3 "If you *l* in accordance with my precepts
26:32 who come to *l* there will stand aghast
Nm 4:19 That they may *l* and not die when they
13:19 Is the country in which they *l* good or bad?
13:29 Amalekites *l* in the region of the Negeb;
33:55 harass you in the country where you *l*.
35:29 and all your descendants, wherever you *l*,
35:33 shall not desecrate the land where you *l*.
35:34 you *l* and in the midst of which I dwell;
Dt 2: 4 the descendants of Esau, who *l* in Seir.
2: 8 our kinsmen, the descendants of Esau, *l*;
4: 1 teaching you to observe, that you may *l*,
4: 9 slip from your memory as long as you *l*,
4:10 to fear me as long as they *l* in the land
4:26 You shall not *l* in it for any length of
4:33 from the midst of fire, as you did, and *l*?
5:24 can still *l* after God has spoken with him.
5:33 LORD, your God, that you may *l* and prosper,
8: 1 on you today, that you may *l* and increase,
8: 3 you that not by bread alone does man *l*,
8: 8 and pomegranates, of *l* trees and of honey,
11:21 you and your children may *l* on in the land
11:30 of the Canaanites who *l* in the Arabah,
12: 1 to occupy, as long as you *l* on its soil.
12:10 round about and you *l* there in security,
12:19 the Levite as long as you *l* in the land.
14: 9 the various creatures that *l* in the water,
16: 3 may remember as long as you *l* the day
18: 1 they shall *l* on the oblations of the LORD
21:12 But before she may *l* there,
22: 2 If this kinsman does not *l* near you,
23: 7 peace and prosperity as long as you *l*.
23:17 Let him *l* with you wherever he chooses,
24:14 of the aliens who *l* in your communities.
25: 5 "When brothers *l* together and one of them
26:11 the Levite and the aliens who *l* among you,
28:30 you build a house, you will not *l* in it.
28:66 You will *l* in constant suspense and stand
29:10 children and the aliens who *l* in your camp,
30: 6 your heart and all your soul, and so may *l*.
30:16 and decrees, you will *l* and grow numerous,
30:19 then, that you and your descendants may *l*,
30:20 a long life for you to *l* on the land which
31:12 as the aliens who *l* in your communities
31:13 as long as you *l* on the land which you
31:16 will *l* in the land they are about to enter.
32:13 land and *l* off the products of its fields,
32:40 As surely as I *l* forever,
33: 6 together "May Reuben *l* and not die out,
Jos 1: 5 No one can withstand you while you *l*.
9:21 princes recommended that they be let *l*,
14: 4 no share of the land except cities to *l* in,
16:10 who *l* on within Ephraim to the present day,
20: 4 him a place in which to *l* among them.
20: 6 he shall *l* on in that city till the death
Jgs 1:21 result that the Jebusites *l* in Jerusalem
1:29 the Canaanites *l* in Gezer in their midst.
1:30 the Canaanites *l* among them,
1:32 *l* among the Canaanite natives of the land,
1:33 *l* among the Canaanite natives of the land.
1Sm 1:26 As you *l* my lord, I am the woman
10:24 all the people shouted, "Long *l* the king!"
12: 8 Egypt, and he gave them this place to *l* in.
12:11 so that you were able to *l* in security.
20: 3 as the LORD lives and as you *l*,
25:26 my lord, as the LORD lives, and as you *l*,
27: 5 a place to *l* in one of the country towns.
27: 5 your servant *l* with you in the royal city?"
2Sm 11:11 As the LORD lives and as you *l*,
12:11 will take your wives while you *l* to see it,
14:19 "As you *l*, my lord the king,
16:16 "Long *l* the king! Long *l* the king!"
19:35 "How much longer have I to *l*,
22:47 "The LORD *l*!
1Kgs 1:25 company and saying, 'Long *l* King Adonijah!'
1:31 "May the lord, King David, *l* forever!"
1:34 blow the horn and cry, 'Long *l* King Solomon!'
1:39 the people shouted, "Long *l* King Solomon!"
2:36 yourself a house in Jerusalem and *l* there.
3:17 lord, this woman and I *l* in the same house,
8:25 conduct so that they *l* in my presence,
8:36 teaching them the right way to *l* and
8:40 as they *l* on the land you gave our fathers.
9: 4 if you *l* in my presence as your father
2Kgs 2: 2 the LORD lives, and as you yourself *l*,"
2: 4 the LORD lives, and as you yourself *l*,"
2: 6 the LORD lives, and as you yourself *l*,"
4: 7 what remains, you and your children can *l*."
4:30 "As the LORD lives and as you yourself *l*,
6: 1 room for us to continue to *l* here with you.
6: 2 apiece we can build ourselves a place to *l*."
7: 4 If they spare us, we *l*;
10:19 Whoever is absent shall not *l*."
11:12 hands and shouting, "Long *l* the king!"
2Chr 6:16 so as always to *l* according to my law,
6:27 But teach them the right way to *l*,
6:31 as they *l* on the land you gave our fathers.
7:17 *l* in my presence as your father David did,
23:11 him, and they cried, "Long *l* the king!"
Neh 2: 3 "May the king *l* forever!
5: 2 in order to get grain to eat that we may *l*."
Tb 3: 6 It is better for me to die than to *l*,
3:10 I need no longer *l* to hear such insults."
3:15 why then should I *l* any longer?
4: 6 you, but also to all those who *l* uprightly.
5:20 us to *l* on is certainly enough for us."
8: 7 allow us to *l* together to a happy old age."
10:12 hear good reports about you as long as I *l*."
10:13 and may I *l* long enough to see children of
Jdt 2:12 For as I *l*, and by the strength of my
7:27 be made slaves, but at least we should *l*,
11: 7 *l* for Nebuchadnezzar and his whole house.
12: 4 him, "As surely as you, my lord, *l*,
12:13 who *l* in the palace of Nebuchadnezzar."
Est C:10 we shall *l* to sing praise to your name,
1Mc 2:29 Many who sought to *l* according to
4:35 were ready either to *l* or to die bravely,
6:59 *l* according to their own laws as formerly;
2Mc 6: 1 and *l* no longer by the laws of God;
7: 9 world will raise us up to *l* again forever.
11:25 that they *l* in keeping with the customs
12: 2 would not allow them to *l* in peace.
12: 4 and wishing to *l* on friendly terms,
Jb 7:16 I cannot *l* forever;
14:14 When a man has died, were he to *l* again,
21:13 They *l* out their days in prosperity,
Ps(s) 18:47 The LORD *l*!
22:30 And to him my soul shall *l*;
55:24 and deceit shall not *l* out half their days.
63: 5 Thus will I bless you while I *l*;
72:15 May he *l* to be given the gold of Arabia,
89:49 What man shall *l*, and not see death,
104:33 I will sing praise to my God while I *l*.
111:10 prudent are all who *l* by it.
118:17 I shall not die, but *l*,
119:17 servant, that I may *l* and keep your words.
119:77 your compassion come to me that I may *l*,
119:116 me as you have promised, that I may *l*;
119:144 give me discernment that I may *l*.
119:175 Let my soul *l* to praise you,
132: 3 "I will not enter the house I *l* in,
146: 2 I will sing praise to my God while I *l*.
Prv 4: 4 keep my commands, that you may *l*!
6:28 Or can a man walk on *l* coals,
7: 2 Keep my commands and *l*,
9: 6 Forsake foolishness that you may *l*;
15:27 own house, but he who hates bribes will *l*.
25:22 For *l* coals you will heap on his head,
26:21 What a bellows is to *l* coals,
Eccl 4:15 Then I saw all those who are to *l* and move
6: 3 have a hundred children and *l* many years,
6: 6 Should he *l* twice a thousand years and not
9: 4 a *l* dog is better off than a dead lion.
11: 8 However many years a man may *l*,
Wis 4:16 just man dead condemns the sinful who *l*,
5:15 But the just *l* forever,
8: 9 So I determined to take her to *l* with me,
14:22 though they *l* in a great war of ignorance,
14:28 *l* lawlessly or lightly forswear themselves.
Sir 3: 1 do so that you may *l*.
3: 6 who reveres his father will *l* a long life;
11:21 Admire not how sinners *l*,
25:15 rather dwell than *l* with an evil woman.
27: 9 and fidelity comes to those who *l* by it.
31:27 Does he really *l* who lacks the wine which
33:20 have power over you as long as you *l*.
39: 9 through all generations his name will *l*;
40:28 My son, *l* not the life of a beggar,
50:26 Those who *l* in Seir and Philistia,
Is 5: 9 ones and fine, with no one to *l* in them.
7:22 abundant yield of milk he shall *l* on curds:
16: 4 Let the outcasts of Moab *l* with you,
26:19 But your dead shall *l*,
32:18 My people will *l* in peaceful country,
33:14 "Who of us can *l* with the consuming fire?
33:14 of us can *l* with the everlasting flames?"
33:24 who *l* there will be forgiven their guilt.
38:16 Those *l* whom the LORD protects;
42: 7 from the dungeon, those who *l* in darkness.
49:18 As I *l*, says the LORD,
49:20 too small for me, make room for me to *l* in."
65:21 They shall *l* in the houses they build,
65:22 shall not build houses for others to *l* in,
Jer 12: 1 why *l* all the treacherous in contentment?
21: 9 shall *l* and have his life as booty.
22:24 As I *l*, says the LORD,
23: 8 they shall again *l* on their own land.
27:12 him and his people, so that you may *l*.
27:17 Serve the king of Babylon that you may *l*;
29:28 build houses to *l* in;
32:23 by your law they did not *l*,
35: 7 so that you may *l* long on the earth where
35: 9 We build no houses to *l* in;
35:10 or fields or crops, and we *l* in tents;
38: 2 he who goes out to the Chaldeans shall *l*;
38: 2 be spared him as booty, and he shall *l*.
38:17 with fire, and you and your family shall *l*.
42:14 there we will *l*";
44: 8 the land of Egypt where you have come to *l*?
44:13 Thus will I punish those who *l* in Egypt,
44:14 though they yearn to return and *l* there.
44:26 all you people of Judah who *l* in Egypt;
46:18 As I *l*, says the King
49: 8 hide in deep holes, you who *l* in Dedan:
49:16 You that *l* in rocky crags,
49:20 he has made against those that *l* in Teman:
49:30 hide in deep holes, you that *l* in Hazor,
50: 3 a desert, So that no one shall *l* there,
50:21 of Merathaim, and those who *l* in Pekod;
50:34 but unrest to those who *l* in Babylon.
51: 1 and against those who *l* in Chaldea,
51:24 and all who *l* in Chaldea All the evil they
Lam 4:20 we thought we could *l* on among the nations.
Bar 1:12 that we may *l* under the protective shadow
4: 1 All who cling to her will *l*,

4:20 I *l* I will cry out to the Eternal God.
Ez 3:18 from his wicked conduct so that he may *l*:
3:21 he shall surely *l* because of the warning,
5:11 Therefore, as I *l*, says the Lord GOD,
6:14 *l* I will make the land a desolate waste,
11:20 that they will *l* according to my statutes,
12: 2 you *l* in the midst of a rebellious house;
12: 3 migrate from where you *l* to another place;
13:19 and keeping alive those who should not *l*,
14:16 and these three men were in it, as I *l*,
14:18 and these three men were in it, as I *l*,
14:20 Noah, Daniel, and Job were in it, as I *l*,
16: 6 *L* in your blood and grow like a plant in
16:48 As I *l*, says the Lord GOD,
17:16 As I *l*, says the Lord GOD,
17:19 As I *l*, my oath which he spurned,
18: 3 As I *l*, says the Lord GOD:
18: 9 he shall surely *l*,
18:13 this son certainly shall not *l*.
18:17 the sins of his father, but shall surely *l*.
18:19 observe all my statutes, he shall surely *l*.
18:21 what is right and just, he shall surely *l*,
18:22 *l* because of the virtue he has practiced.
18:23 he turns from his evil way that he may *l*?
18:24 man does, can he do this and still *l*?
18:28 which he committed, he shall surely *l*,
18:32 Return and *l*!
20: 3 As I *l*! I swear I will not allow
20:25 ordinances through which they could not *l*.
20:31 As I *l*! says the Lord GOD,
20:33 As I *l*, says the Lord GOD,
28:25 Then they shall *l* on their land which I
28:26 they shall *l* on it in security,
32:15 when I strike all who *l* there,
33:11 As I *l*, says the Lord GOD,
33:11 the wicked man's conversion, that he may *l*.
33:13 the virtuous man that he shall surely *l*,
33:15 and doing no wrong, he shall surely *l*,
33:16 what is right and just, he shall surely *l*.
33:19 right and just, because of this he shall *l*.
33:24 they who *l* in the ruins on the land of
33:27 As I *l*, those who are in ruins
34: 8 As I *l*, says the Lord GOD,
35: 6 crimes came to an end, therefore, as I *l*,
35:11 therefore, as I *l*, says the Lord GOD,
36:27 within you and make you *l* by my statutes,
36:28 shall *l* in the land I gave your fathers;
37:14 will put my spirit in you that you may *l*,
37:24 they shall *l* by my statutes and carefully
37:25 They shall *l* on the land which I gave to
37:25 they shall *l* on it forever,
39: 6 those who *l* securely in the coastlands;
39: 9 Then shall those who *l* in the cities of
39:26 when they *l* in security on their land with
44: 9 the foreigners who *l* among the Israelites.
45: 5 temple, that they may have cities to *l* in.
47: 9 living creature that can multiply shall *l*,
Dn 2: 4 "O king, *l* forever!
3: 9 "O king, *l* forever!
4:14 That all who *l* may know that the Most High
4:32 who *l* on the earth are counted as nothing;
4:32 as well as with those who *l* on the earth.
5:10 banquet hall and said, "O king, *l* forever!
5:19 Whomever he wished, he killed or let *l*;
6: 7 and said to him, "King Darius, *l* forever!
6:22 "O king, *l* forever!
9:10 to *l* by the law you gave us through your
12: 2 some shall *l* forever,
Hos 6: 2 he will raise us up, to *l* in his presence.
12:10 I will again have you *l* in tents,
Am 1: 5 root out those who *l* in the Valley of Aven,
1: 8 I will root out those who *l* in Ashdod,
5: 4 Seek me, that you may *l*,
5: 6 Seek the LORD, that you may *l*,
5:11 of hewn stone, you shall not *l* in them!
5:14 Seek good and not evil, that you may *l*;
Jon 4: 3 for it is better for me to die than to *l*."
Hb 2: 4 just man, because of his faith, shall *l*.
Zep 1:18 a sudden end, of all who *l* on the earth.
2: 9 Therefore, as I *l*, says the LORD of hosts,
Zec 1: 5 And the prophets, can they *l* forever?
2: 8 *l* in Jerusalem as though in open country,
13: 3 shall say to him, "You shall not *l*,
Mt 4: 4 'Not on bread alone is man to *l* but on
4:13 He left Nazareth and went down to *l* in
14: 4 "It is not right for you to *l* with her."
22:30 in marriage but *l* like angels in heaven.
Mk 5:23 on her so that she may get well and *l*."
6:18 for you to *l* with your brother's wife."
12:25 in marriage but *l* like angels in heaven.
12:44 from her want, all that she had to *l* on."
Lk 4: 4 has it, 'Not on bread alone shall man *l*.'"
8:27 he did not *l* in a house,
10:28 Do this and you shall *l*."
12:32 "Do not *l* in fear, little flock.
21: 4 every penny she had to *l* on."
Jn 4:50 Your son will *l*."
4:51 with the news that his boy was going to *l*.
4:53 had told him, "Your son is going to *l*."
5:25 God, and those who have heeded it shall *l*.
5:29 Those who have done right shall rise to *l*;
6:51 anyone eats this bread he shall *l* forever;
6:58 who feeds on this bread shall *l* forever."
8:31 "If you *l* according to my teaching,
15: 4 *L* on in me, as I do in you.
15: 6 who does not *l* in me is like a withered,
15: 7 If you *l* in me,
15: 9 me, so I have loved you, *L* on in my love.
15:10 *l* in my love if you keep my commandments,
15:10 Father's commandments, and *l* in his love.
17:26 me may live in them, and I may *l* in them."
Acts 2: 9 We *l* in Mesopotamia,
2:26 has rejoiced, my body will *l* on in hope,
17:21 as well as the foreigners who *l* there,
17:28 'In him we *l* and move and have our being,'
19:28 to shout, "Long *l* Artemis of Ephesus!"
19:34 in unison, "Long *l* Artemis of Ephesus!"
21:21 who *l* among the Gentiles to abandon Moses,
22:22 He isn't worthy to *l*!"
25:24 him, clamoring that he should *l* no more.
28: 4 from the sea, Justice will not let him *l*."
Rom 1:17 says, "The just man shall *l* by faith."
5:17 of justice *l* and reign through the one man,
6: 4 of the Father, we too might *l* a new life.
6: 8 we believe that we are also to *l* with him.
8: 4 of the law might be fulfilled in us who *l*,
8: 5 Those who *l* according to the flesh are
8: 5 flesh, those who *l* according to the spirit,
8:12 so that we should *l* according to the flesh.
8:13 If you *l* according to the flesh,
8:13 the evil deeds of the body, you will *l*.
10: 5 one who observes the law shall *l* by it."
12:18 If possible, *l* peaceably with everyone.
13:13 Let us *l* honorably as in daylight;
14: 8 While we *l* we are responsible to the Lord,
14:11 It is written, "As surely as I *l*,
15: 5 enable you to *l* in perfect harmony with
1Cor 7:12 an unbeliever but is willing to *l* with him,
7:13 an unbeliever but is willing to *l* with her,
7:15 God has called you to *l* in peace.
7:29 wives should *l* as though they had none;
7:30 should *l* as though they were not weeping,
8: 6 whom all things come and for whom we *l*;
8: 6 everything was made and through whom we *l*.
9:14 preach the gospel should *l* by the gospel.
2Cor 1: 1 holy ones of the church who *l* in Achaia.
4:11 While we *l* we are constantly being
5: 4 While we *l* in our present tent we groan;
5:15 who *l* might live no longer for themselves,
10: 3 We do indeed *l* in the body but we do not
13: 4 but we *l* with him by God's power in us.
13:11 *L* in harmony and peace,
Gal 1:14 *l* out all the traditions of my ancestors.
2:19 law that I died to the law, to *l* for God.
2:20 Christ, and the life I *l* now is not my own;
2:20 I still *l* my human life,
3:11 law, for "the just man shall *l* by faith."
3:12 does these things shall *l* by them."
5:13 that you have been called to *l* in freedom
5:16 My point is that you should *l* in accord
5:25 Since we *l* by the spirit,
6: 1 you who *l* by the spirit should gently set
Eph 4: 1 to *l* a life worthy of the calling you have
4:17 you must no longer *l* as the pagans do
5: 8 Well, then, *l* as children of light.
Phil 1:20 be exalted through me, whether I *l* or die.
4: 9 *L* according to what you have learned and
Col 2: 6 therefore, to *l* in Christ Jesus the Lord,
1Thes 4:15 Lord himself had said it, that we who *l*,
5: 8 We who *l* by day must be alert,
5:10 awake or asleep, together might *l* with him.
2Thes 3: 7 *l* lives of disorder when we were among you,
2Tm 2:11 died with him we shall also *l* with him;
3:12 Anyone who wants to *l* a godly life in
Ti 2:12 and worldly desires, and *l* temperately,
3:14 may be in position to *l* fruitful lives.
Heb 10:38 My just man will *l* by faith,
10:39 but among those who have faith and *l*.
12: 9 submit to the Father of spirits, and *l*?
Jas 4:15 wills it, we shall *l* to do this or that,"
1Pt 1: 1 *l* as strangers scattered throughout Pontus,
1:13 *l* soberly;
2:16 *L* as free men,
2:16 In a word, *l* as servants of God.
2:24 to sin, could *l* in accord with God's will.
4: 6 might *l* in the spirit in the eyes of God.
2Pt 1:13 I consider it my duty, as long as I *l*,
2:10 how to treat those who *l* for the flesh in
Jude 1:16 They *l* by their passions,
Rv 1:18 Once I was dead but now I *l*—
2:13 I know you *l* in the very place where
8: 5 filled it with *l* coals from the altar,
22:11 The virtuous must *l* on in their virtue and

LIVED (173)

Gn 5: 4 Adam *l* eight hundred years after the birth
5: 7 Seth *l* eight hundred and seven years after
5:10 Enosh *l* eight hundred and fifteen years
5:13 Kenan *l* eight hundred and forty years
5:16 Mahalalel *l* eight hundred and thirty years
5:19 Jared *l* eight hundred years after the
5:22 Enoch *l* three hundred years after the
5:26 Methuselah *l* seven hundred and eighty-two
5:30 Lamech *l* five hundred and ninety-five
9:28 Noah *l* three hundred and fifty years after
11:11 Shem *l* five hundred years after the birth
11:13 Arpachshad *l* four hundred and three years
11:15 Shelah *l* four hundred and three years
11:17 Eber *l* four hundred and thirty years after
11:19 Peleg *l* two hundred and nine years after
11:21 Reu *l* two hundred and seven years after
11:23 Serug *l* two hundred years after the birth
11:25 Nahor *l* one hundred and nineteen years
16: 3 had *l* ten years in the land of Canaan,
19:30 he *l* with his two daughters in a cave.
21:20 He *l* in the wilderness and became an
25:27 a skillful hunter, a man who *l* in the open;
47: 8 asked him, "How many years have you *l*?"
47: 9 "The years I have *l* as a wayfarer amount
47: 9 the years that my ancestors *l* as wayfarers."
47:22 *l* off the allowance Pharaoh had granted
47:28 *l* in the land of Egypt for seventeen years;
50:22 He *l* a hundred and ten years.
Ex 6:16 Levi *l* one hundred and thirty-seven years.
6:18 *l* one hundred and thirty-three years.
6:20 Amram *l* one hundred and thirty-seven years.
Lv 18: 3 do in the land of Egypt, where you once *l*,
26:35 it have on the sabbaths when you *l* there.
Nm 21: 1 Canaanite king of Arad, who *l* in the Negeb,
21:34 king of the Amorites, who *l* in Heshbon."
33:40 who *l* in the Negeb in the land of Canaan,
Dt 1: 4 king of the Amorites, who *l* in Heshbon,
1: 4 of Bashan, who *l* in Ashtaroth and in Edrei,
2:10 [Formerly the Emim *l* there,
3: 2 king of the Amorites, who *l* in Heshbon.'
8:12 and have built fine houses and *l* in them,
26: 5 a small household and *l* there as an alien.
29:15 "You know in what surroundings we *l* in
Jos 2:15 she *l* in a house built into the city wall.
9:10 and Og, king of Bashan, who *l* in Ashtaroth.
9:22 say that you *l* at a great distance from us,
10:40 but fulfilled the doom on all who *l* there,
11:19 exception of the Hivites who *l* in Gibeon,
12: 2 king of the Amorites, who *l* in Heshbon.
12: 4 the Rephaim, who *l* at Ashtaroth and Edrei.
15:63 [But the Jebusites who *l* in Jerusalem the
24: 8 of the Amorites who *l* east of the Jordan.
Jgs 1: 9 Canaanites who *l* in the mountain region,
1:19 not dislodge those who *l* on the plain,
2:18 of their enemies as long as the judge *l*;
8:31 who *l* in Shechem also bore him a son,
18: 7 They saw that the people dwelling there *l*
18:28 that belongs to Beth-rehob, and *l* there.
19:16 though he *l* among the Benjaminite
21:10 and put those who *l* there to the sword,
Ru 1: 4 When they had *l* there about ten years,
1Sm 7:13 was severe with them as long as Samuel *l*.
7:15 Samuel judged Israel as long as he *l*.
9:10 went to the city where the man of God *l*.
12: 2 I have *l* with you from my youth to the
15:35 Never again, as long as he *l*,
23:14 David now *l* in the refuges in the desert,
27: 3 David and his men *l* in Gath with Achish;
27: 7 David *l* a year and four months in the
27:11 as he *l* in the country of the Philistines.
31: 7 the Philistines came and *l* in those cities.
2Sm 9:13 But Meribbaal *l* in Jerusalen,
14:28 Absalom *l* in Jerusalem for two years
1Kgs 5: 1 and were his vassals as long as he *l*.
5: 5 Thus Judah and Israel *l* in security,
5: 5 Dan to Beer-sheba, as long as Solomon *l*.
8:25 my presence, as you have *l* in my presence.'
9: 4 in my presence as your father David *l*,
11:20 where he then *l* with Pharaoh's own sons.
11:25 an enemy of Israel as long as Solomon *l*;
12:17 Israelites who *l* in the cities of Judah.
12:25 in the hill country of Ephraim and *l* there.
13:25 news to the city where the old prophet *l*.
15: 5 any of his commands as long as he *l*,
15:14 was entirely with the LORD as long as he *l*.
15:32 as long as they *l*
1Kgs 21: 8 nobles who *l* in the same city with Naboth.
2Kgs 12: 3 was pleasing to the LORD as long as he *l*,
15: 5 He *l* in a house apart,
25:29 ate at the king's table as long as he *l*.
25:30 fixed daily amounts, for as long as he *l*.
1Chr 4:23 where they *l* in the king's service.
5: 8 The Reubenites *l* in Aroer and as far as
5:11 The Gadites *l* alongside them in the land
5:23 half-tribe of Manasseh *l* in the land
9: 3 In Jerusalem *l* Judahites and Benjaminites;
9:16 *l* in the villages of the Netophathites.
9:25 Their kinsmen who had *l* in their own
22: 2 all the aliens who *l* in the land of Israel
2Chr 6:16 my law, even as you have *l* in my presence.'
10:17 Israelites who *l* in the cities of Judah.
15:17 Asa's heart was undivided as long as he *l*.
16: 2 Ben-hadad, king of Aram, who *l* in Damascus,
24: 2 the LORD as long as Jehoiada the priest *l*.
24:15 Jehoiada *l* to a ripe old age;
26: 5 to seek God as long as Zechariah *l*,
27: 6 *l* resolutely in the presence of the LORD,
30:25 land of Israel and those that *l* in Judah.
31:19 *l* on the lands attached to their cities,
Neh 4: 6 When the Jews who *l* near them had come to
5:14 brethren *l* from the governor's allowance.
11:21 The temple slaves *l* on Ophel.
11:25 *l* in Kiriath-arba and its dependencies,

LIVED (cont.)
12:26 All these *l* in the time of Joiakim,
12:27 Levites were sought out wherever they *l*
Tb 1: 4 When I *l* as a young man in my own country,
1:14 Gabael, son of Gabri, who *l* at Rages,
11:17 was joy for all the Jews who *l* in Nineveh.
14: 2 after he recovered it he *l* in prosperity,
Jdt 4:11 women and children who *l* in Jerusalem
5:16 and they *l* in these mountains a long time.
16:23 She *l* to be very old in the house of her
2Mc 3: 1 While the holy city *l* in perfect peace and
5:27 *l* like wild animals in the hills,
6:23 the admirable life he had *l* from childhood;
12: 3 they invited the Jews who *l* among them,
12: 8 treatment to the Jews who *l* among them,
12:30 But when the Jews who *l* there testified to
Jb 10:19 I should be as though I had never *l*;
42:16 this, Job *l* a hundred and forty years;
Eccl 9:15 But in the city *l* a man who,
Wis 4:10 he who *l* among sinners was transported
12:23 those unjust also, who *l* a life of folly,
14:17 Men who *l* so far away that they could not
Sir 17:23 give praise than those who have never *l*;
38:32 Without them no city could be *l* in,
41: 4 Whether one has *l* a thousand years,
44: 9 And they are as though they had not *l*,
47:12 successor a wise son, who *l* in security:
Is 45:18 to be a waste, but designing it to be *l* in:
Jer 44:15 the people who *l* in Lower and Upper Egypt,
50:39 Never again shall it be peopled, or *l* in,
52:33 ate at the king's table as long as he *l*.
Lam 2:16 we have *l* to see it!"
Bar 1: 4 all who *l* in Babylon by the river Sud.
Ez 3:15 who *l* at Tel-abib by the river Chebar,
5: 6 my ordinances and has not *l* by my statutes.
11:12 LORD, by whose statutes you have not *l*,
20:16 to their idols, they had not *l* by statutes,
36:17 when the house of Israel *l* in their land,
37:25 Jacob, the land where their fathers *l*;
Dn 4:18 for all, under which the wild beasts *l*,
5:21 he *l* with wild asses,
13: 1 In Babylon there *l* a man named Joakim,
Mt 1:18 to Joseph, but before they *l* together,
23:30 'Had we *l* in our forefathers' time we
Lk 1:80 He *l* in the desert until the day when he
2:25 There *l* in Jerusalem at the time a certain
2:36 having *l* seven years with her husband
13: 4 guilty than anyone else who *l* in Jerusalem?
Jn 7:42 from Bethlehem, the village where David *l*?"
Acts 11:29 the relief of the brothers who *l* in Judea.
20:18 "You know how I *l* among you from the
22:12 well spoken of by all the Jews who *l* there,
23: 1 to this day I have *l* my life with a clear
26: 4 "The way I have *l* since my youth,
26: 5 if they wish, to my life *l* as a Pharisee,
Rom 7: 9 sin is dead, and at first I *l* without law.
Eph 2: 3 we *l* at the level of the flesh,
Jas 5: 5 You *l* in wanton luxury on the earth;
2Pt 2: 8 the lawless deeds of those among whom he *l*.)
Rv 13:14 had been wounded by the sword and yet *l*.
16:18 it in all the time men have *l* on the earth.

LIVELIHOOD (4)
Eccl 9:11 battle by the valiant, nor a *l* by the wise,
Sir 4: 1 My son, rob not the poor man of his *l*;
31: 2 Concern for one's *l* banishes slumber;
Mt 6:25 do not worry about your *l*,

LIVELY (3)
Sir 34:13 *L* is the courage of those who fear the LORD,
Mk 9:14 and scribes in *l* discussion with them.
Lk 24:15 In the course of their *l* exchange,

LIVER (20)
Ex 29:13 as the lobe of its *l* and its two kidneys,
29:22 its inner organs, the lobe of its *l*,
Lv 3: 4 near the loins, and the lobe of the *l*,
3:10 them near the loins, and the lobe of the *l*,
3:15 them near the loins, and the lobe of the *l*,
4: 9 them near the loins, and the lobe of the *l*,
7: 4 near the loins, and the lobe of the *l*,
8:16 the *l* and the two kidneys with their fat,
8:25 the *l* and the two kidneys with their fat,
9:10 *l* that were taken from the sin offering,
9:19 that is on them, and the lobe of the *l*,
Tb 6: 5 open and take out its gall, heart, and *l*,
6: 5 gall, heart, and *l* make useful medicines."
6: 6 open, he put aside the gall, heart and *l*.
6: 7 value is there in the fish's heart, *l*
6: 8 "As regards the fish's heart and *l*,
6:17 chamber, take the fish's *l* and heart,
8: 2 took the fish's *l* and heart from the bag
Prv 7:23 the net, till an arrow pierces its *l*;
Ez 21:26 inquired of the teraphim, inspected the *l*.

LIVES (200)
Gn 6:12 since all mortals led depraved *l* on earth,
42:16 if they are untrue, as Pharaoh *l*,
45: 5 *l* that God sent me here ahead of you.
45: 7 your *l* in an extraordinary deliverance.
47:25 "You have saved our *l*!"

Ex 20:10 your beast, or by the alien who *l* with you.
30:15 to the LORD to pay the forfeit for their *l*.
30:16 the LORD, of the forfeit paid for their *l*."
33:20 cannot see, for no man sees me and still *l*.
Lv 17:11 may thereby be made for your own *l*,
20:11 they have forfeited their *l*.
20:12 deed, they have forfeited their *l*.
20:13 they have forfeited their *l*.
20:16 their *l* are forfeit.
Nm 9:14 "If an alien who *l* among you wishes to
17: 3 the censers at the cost of their *l*.
23: 9 Here is a people that *l* apart and does not
Dt 5:14 your beasts, or the alien who *l* with you.
6: 2 and keep, throughout the days of your *l*,
22:19 and he may not divorce her as long as he *l*.
22:29 he may not divorce her as long as he *l*.
Jos 2:14 "We pledge our *l* for yours,"
9:20 Let us therefore spare their *l* and so deal
9:24 advance, we were in great fear for our *l*,
Jgs 8:19 the LORD lives, if you had spared their *l*,
18:25 you and you and your family lose your *l*."
Ru 3:13 does not wish to claim you, as the LORD *l*,
1Sm 1:11 give him to the LORD for as long as he *l*;
1:28 as long as he *l*,
9:18 said, "Please tell me where the seer *l*."
14:39 the LORD *l* who has given victory to Israel,
14:45 *l*, not a single hair of his head shall fall
19: 6 Jonathan's plea and swore, "As the LORD *l*,
20: 3 as the LORD *l* and as you live,
20:12 "As the LORD, the God of Israel, *l*,
20:21 LORD *l*, there will be nothing to fear.
20:31 long as the son of Jesse *l* upon the earth,
25:26 Now, therefore, my lord, as the LORD *l*,
25:29 but may he hurl out the *l* of your enemies
25:34 as the LORD, the God of Israel, *l*,
26:10 As the LORD *l*," David continued,
26:16 As the LORD *l*, you people deserve death
28:10 swore to her by the LORD, "As the LORD *l*,
29: 6 "As the LORD *l*, you are honest
2Sm 2:27 Joab replied, "As God *l*,
4: 9 *l*, who rescued me from all difficulty,
6:21 As the LORD *l*, who preferred me to your
11:11 As the LORD *l* and as you live,
12: 5 *l*, the man who had done this merits death!
14:11 He replied, "As the LORD *l*,
15:21 "As the LORD *l*, and as my lord the king *l*,
19: 6 and daughters' *l*, also the *l* of your wives
23:17 these men who went at the risk of their *l*?"
1Kgs 1:29 him, the king swore, "As the LORD *l*,
2:24 And now, as the LORD *l*,
11:34 as he *l* for the sake of my servant David,
17: 1 "As the LORD, the God of Israel, *l*,
17:12 "As the LORD, your God *l*,"
18:10 As the LORD, your God, *l*,
18:15 Elijah answered, "As the LORD of hosts *l*,
22:14 "As the LORD *l*," Micaiah answered,
2Kgs 1:13 "let my life and the *l* of these fifty men,
2: 2 "As the LORD *l*, and as you yourself live,
2: 4 "As the LORD *l*, and as you yourself live,
2: 6 "As the LORD *l*, and as you yourself live,
3:14 Elisha said, "As the LORD of hosts *l*,
4:30 "As the LORD *l* and as you yourself live,
5:16 "As the LORD *l* whom I serve,
5:20 As the LORD *l*, I will run after him
7: 7 just as it was, and fleeing for their *l*.
1Chr 11:19 the blood of these men who risked their *l*?"
11:19 For at the risk of their *l* they brought it;
2Chr 18:13 "As the LORD *l*," Micaiah answered,
Tb 4: 3 and do not abandon her as long as she *l*.
5: 6 kinsman Gabael, who *l* at Rages in Media.
8:17 and bring their *l* to fulfillment with
10:13 of us be prosperous all the days of our *l*."
13: 1 Blessed be God who *l* forever,
Jdt 5: 5 truth about this people that *l* near you
8:24 Their *l* depend on us,
13:16 As the Lord *l*, who has protected me
Est B: 5 all men, *l* by divergent and alien laws,
7: 3 I beg that you spare the *l* of my people.
8:11 city to group together and defend their *l*,
1Mc 2:33 king's command, and your *l* will be spared."
2:40 the Gentiles for our *l* and our traditions,
2:50 your *l* for the covenant of our fathers.
3:21 but we are fighting for our *l* and our laws.
9: 9 Let us save our *l* now,
9:44 "Let us get up now and fight for our *l*,
12:51 that they were ready to fight for their *l*,
2Mc 11: 7 in risking their *l* to help their kinsmen.
Jb 19:25 as for me, I know that my Vindicator *l*,
27: 2 As God *l*, who withholds my deserts,
Ps(s) 34:23 But the LORD redeems the *l* of his servants;
37:18 watches over the *l* of the wholehearted;
72:13 the *l* of the poor he shall save.
74:19 unmindful of the *l* of your afflicted ones.
97:10 he guards the *l* of his faithful ones;
Prv 1:18 own blood, they set a trap for their own *l*.
3:29 against him who *l* at peace with you.
11:30 a tree of life, but violence takes *l* away.
14:25 The truthful witness saves *l*,
22:23 plunder the *l* of those who plunder them.
Wis 12: 6 took with their own hands defenseless *l*,
14: 5 men trust their *l* even to frailest wood.
14:24 longer safeguard either *l* or pure wedlock;
15:17 he at least *l*,

16: 9 no remedy was found to save their *l*
Sir 3:12 grieve him not as long as he *l*.
14:25 beside her, and *l* as her welcome neighbor;
23:15 never mature in character as long as he *l*.
25: 7 and he who *l* to see his enemies' downfall.
39:11 While he *l* he is one out of a thousand,
42:24 The universe *l* and abides forever;
44:14 laid away, but their name *l* on and on.
Is 65:20 be in it an infant who *l* but a few days,
Jer 4: 2 Then you can swear, "As the LORD *l*,"
5: 1 Who *l* uprightly and seeks to be faithful,
5: 2 Though they say, "As the LORD *l*,"
12:16 of swearing by my name, "As the LORD *l*,"
16:14 will no longer be said, "As the LORD *l*,
16:15 but rather, "As the LORD *l*,
17:21 As you love your *l*,
19: 7 by the hand of those that seek their *l*.
19: 9 those who seek their *l* will confine them.
21: 7 their enemies and those who seek their *l*.
23: 7 they shall no longer say, "As the LORD *l*,
23: 8 but rather, "As the LORD *l*,
34:20 their enemies, to those who seek their *l*:
34:21 their enemies, to those who seek their *l*,
35: 8 All our *l* we have not drunk wine,
38:16 the LORD *l* who gave us the breath of life,
42:20 At the cost of your *l* you have deceived me,
44:26 my name saying, "As the LORD GOD *l*."
46:26 hand them over to those who seek their *l*,
48: 6 "Flee, save your *l*, to survive
49:31 is at peace, that *l* secure says the LORD,
49:33 jackals, a desert forever, Where no man *l*,
51:29 of Babylon into a desert where no one *l*.
51:37 of horror and ridicule, where no one *l*.
51:43 parched and arid land Where no man *l*,
Lam 1: 3 Yet where she *l* among the nations she
2:19 Lift up your hands to him for the *l* of
5: 9 peril of our *l* we bring in our sustenance,
Bar 6: 6 you, and he is the custodian of your *l*.
Ez 7:13 not regain what he sold as long as he *l*,
13:18 Do you think to entrap the *l* of my people,
13:20 bands of yours in which you entrap men's *l*:
17:17 are built for the destruction of many *l*,
18: 4 For all *l* are mine;
18: 9 if he *l* by my statutes and is careful to
18:17 keeps my ordinances and *l* by my statutes
22:27 blood and destroying *l* to get unjust gain.
Dn 4:31 I praised and glorified him who *l* forever:
12: 7 who *l* forever that it should be for a year,
Hos 4:15 up to Beth-aven, to swear, "As the Lord *l*!"
Mt 3: 2 "Reform your *l*! The reign of God is at hand
4:17 "Reform your *l*! the kingdom of heaven
12:41 preaching of Jonah they reformed their *l*;
Mk 1:15 Reform your *l* and believe in the gospel!"
Lk 21:19 By patient endurance you will save your *l*.
Jn 8:34 everyone who *l* in sin is the slave of sin.
14:10 Father who *l* in me accomplishing his works.
15: 5 He who *l* in me
Acts 3:19 Therefore, reform your *l*!
4:16 Everyone who *l* in Jerusalem knows what a
17:30 on all men everywhere to reform their *l*.
27:10 ship and cargo, but to our own *l* as well."
Rom 7: 1 has power over a man only so long as he *l*?
7: 2 is bound to her husband by law while he *l*,
8:10 sin, while the spirit *l* because of justice.
14: 7 None of us *l* as his own master and none of
16: 4 even risked their *l* for the sake of mine.
1Cor 7:39 is bound to her husband as long as he *l*.
2Cor 5:10 The *l* of all of us are to be revealed
13: 4 of weakness, but he *l* by the power of God.
1Thes 2: 8 you not only God's tidings but our very *l*,
2:12 make your *l* worthy of the God
2Thes 3: 7 live *l* of disorder when we were among you,
1Tm 2: 2 tranquil *l* in perfect piety and dignity.
Ti 3:14 they may be in position to live fruitful *l*.
Heb 7: 8 Scripture testifies that this man *l* on.
7:25 he forever *l* to make intercession for them.
13: 7 consider how their *l* ended,
1Pt 3: 7 consideration for those who share your *l*.
4: 3 the pagans enjoy, living *l* of debauchery,
4:19 and entrust their *l* to a faithful Creator.
1Jn 3:16 too must lay down our *l* for our brothers.
Rv 1:18 the First and the Last and the One who *l*.
2: 8 who once died but now *l* has this to say:
4: 9 on the throne, who *l* forever and ever,
4:10 and worship him who *l* forever and ever.
10: 6 an oath by the One who *l* forever and ever,
15: 7 wrath of the God who *l* forever and ever.
17:10 five have already fallen, one *l* now,
18:13 slaves and human *l*.

LIVESTOCK (67)
Gn 13: 2 Now Abram was very rich in *l*,
13: 7 herdsmen of Abram's *l* and those of Lot's.
30:29 and how well your *l* fared under my care;
31: 9 your father's *l* and gave it to me.
31:18 and he drove off with all his *l* and all
33:14 *l* before me and at the pace of my children,
33:17 home for himself and made booths for his *l*.
34: 5 sons were out in the fields with his *l*,
34:23 Would not the *l* they have acquired
36: 6 as well as his *l* comprising various
36: 7 could not support them because of their *l*.

46: 6 They took with them their l and the
46:32 shepherds, having long been keepers of l;
46:34 keepers of l from the beginning until now,'
47: 5 you may put them in charge of my own l."
47:16 gone," replied Joseph, "give me your l,
47:16 I will sell you bread in return for your l."
47:17 So they brought their l to Joseph,
47:17 with bread in exchange for all their l.
47:18 money spent and our l made over to my lord,
Ex 9: 3 LORD will afflict all your l in the field
9: 4 between the l of Israel and that of Egypt,
9: 6 All the l of the Egyptians died,
9:19 order all your l and whatever else you
9:20 their servants and l off to shelter.
9:21 left their servants and l in the fields.
10:26 Hence, our l also must go with us.
12:38 also went up with them, besides their l,
17: 3 here of thirst with our children and our l?"
34:19 male that opens the womb among all your l,
Lv 25: 7 l and for the wild animals on your land.
26:22 you of your children and wipe out your l,
Nm 20: 4 this desert where we and our l are dying?
20: 8 for the community and their l to drink."
20:11 for the community and their l to drink.
20:19 If we or our l drink any of your water,
32: 1 and Gadites had a very large number of l.
32: 4 Now, since your servants have l,"
32:26 and other l remain in the towns of Gilead,
32:30 and l across before you into Canaan,
Dt 2:35 the l and the loot of the captured cities.
3: 7 but all the l and the loot of each city we
3:19 wives and children, as well as your l,
7:14 be childless nor shall your l be barren.
20:14 but the women and children and l and all
28: 4 of your soil and the offspring of your l,
28:11 of your womb, the offspring of your l,
28:18 of your soil and the offspring of your l,
28:51 of your l and the produce of your soil,
30: 9 of your womb, the offspring of your l,
Jos 1:14 and your l shall remain in the land Moses
8: 2 that you may take its spoil and l as booty.
8:27 as booty the l and the spoil of that city,
11:14 spoil and l of these cities as their booty;
21: 2 to dwell in, with pasture lands for our l."
22: 8 with great wealth, with very numerous l,
Jgs 6: 5 For they would come up with their l.
18:21 they placed their little ones, their l,
20:48 sword the inhabitants of the cities, the l,
2Kgs 3:17 you, your l and your pack animals to drink.'
1Chr 5: 9 for they had much l in the land of Gilead.
5:21 thousand men they also captured their l:
7:21 they had gone down to take away their l.
Jdt 5: 9 gold, silver, and a great abundance of l.
8: 7 silver, servants and maids, l and fields,
Jb 1:10 hands, and his l are spread over the land.
Sir 7:22 If you have l, look after them;

LIVID (1)

Dn 3:19 became l with utter rage against Shadrach,

LIVING (270)

Gn 1:20 teem with an abundance of l creatures,
1:24 earth bring forth all kinds of l creatures:
1:28 all the l things that move on the earth."
1:30 the l creatures that crawl on the ground,
2: 7 of life, and so man became a l being.
3:20 because she became the mother of all the l.
6:19 Of all other l creatures you shall bring
7:23 The LORD wiped out every l thing on earth:
8:17 with you every l thing that is with you
8:21 will I ever again strike down all l beings,
9:10 with every l creature that was with you:
9:12 me and you and every l creature with you:
9:15 made between me and you and all l beings,
9:16 established between God and all l beings
14:12 nephew Lot, who had been l in Sodom,
19:29 overthrew the cities where Lot had been l.
24:62 and was l in the region of the Negeb.
25: 6 he made grants while he was still l,
43: 7 'Is your father still l?
Ex 4:18 in Egypt, to see whether they are still l."
6: 4 the land in which they were l as aliens.
12:48 If any aliens l among you wish to
Lv 14: 6 Taking the l bird with the cedar wood,
14: 7 the l bird fly away over the countryside.
14:51 the scarlet yarn, together with the l bird,
14:52 the spring water, along with the l bird,
14:53 He shall then let the l bird fly away over
17:11 Since the life of a l body is in its blood,
17:14 the life of every l body is its blood,
18:18 While your wife is still l you shall not
19:20 who has already been l with another man
Nm 13:18 Are the people l there strong or weak,
13:22 Talmai, descendants of the Anakim, were l.
13:28 people who are l in the land are fierce,
14:25 and Canaanites are l in the valleys,
17:13 standing there between the l and the dead,
18:15 Every l thing that opens the womb,
25: 1 While Israel was l at Shittim,
Dt 1:44 Amorites l there came out against you and,
5:26 the l God speaking from the midst of fire,
11: 6 and every l thing that belonged to them.

Jos 3:10 know that there is a l God in your midst,
6:21 to the sword all l creatures in the city:
9: 7 "You may be l in land that is ours.
9:16 were from nearby, and would be l in Israel.
9:22 us, when you will be l in our very midst?
16:10 not drive out the Canaanites l in Gezer,
17:16 the Canaanites l in the valley region all
20: 9 any Israelite or stranger l among them
Jgs 1:29 not drive out the Canaanites l in Gezer,
3: 5 the Israelites were l among the Canaanites,
Ru 1: 7 left the place where they had been l.
2:20 is ever merciful to the l and to the dead,"
1Sm 17:26 he should insult the armies of the l God?"
17:36 he has insulted the armies of the l God."
25:15 all the while we were l among them
25:29 of the l in the care of the LORD your God;
26: 3 David, who was l in the desert,
27: 8 peoples l in the land between Telam,
2Sm 7: 2 prophet, "Here I am l in a house of cedar,
12:21 While the child was l,
12:22 "While the child was l,
15: 8 For while l in Geshur in Aram,
1Kgs 3:22 The l one is my son, the dead one is yours."
3:22 dead one is your child, the l one is mine!"
3:23 dead one is your child; the l one is mine.'"
3:25 him, he said, "Cut the l child in two,
3:26 "Please, my lord, give her the l child
3:27 answered, "Give the first one the l child!
7: 8 His l quarters were in another court,
9:16 slaying all the Canaanites l in the city,
13:11 There was an old prophet l in the city,
2Kgs 4:13 She replied, "I am l among my own people."
17:29 the various cities in which they were l;
19: 4 king of Assyria, sent to taunt the l God,
19:16 which he sent to taunt the l God.
1Chr 17: 1 prophet, "See, I am l in a house of cedar,
2Chr 19:10 brethren l in their cities bring to you,
31: 4 He also commanded the people l in
31: 6 Israelites and Judahites l in other cities
Ezr 4:17 and their fellow officials l in Samaria
Tb 1: 8 to converts who were l with the Israelites.
10: 4 has perished and is no longer among the l!"
12: 6 Before all the l,
13: 4 Exalt him before every l being,
Jdt 1:12 and those l anywhere in Egypt as far as
10: 3 worn while her husband, Manasseh, was l.
Est 3: 8 kingdom, there is a certain people l apart,
E:16 of the Most High, the l God of majesty,
1Mc 1:13 to introduce the way of l of the Gentiles.
9:58 his companions are l in peace and security.
2Mc 7:33 Though our l Lord treats us harshly for a
10: 6 spent the feast of Booths l like wild animals
15: 4 such a ruler in heaven, the l LORD himself,
Jb 12:10 In his hand is the soul of every l thing,
28:13 nor is it to be had in the land of the l.
33:30 the pit to the light, in the land of the l.
Ps(s) 27:13 bounty of the LORD in the land of the l
42: 3 Athirst is my soul for God, the l god.
42: 9 I have his song, a prayer to my l God.
52: 7 and uproot you from the land of the l.
56:14 may walk before God in the light of the l.
69:29 May they be erased from the book of the l,
84: 3 heart and my flesh cry out for the l God.
104:25 number of l things both small and great,
116: 9 walk before the LORD in the lands of the l.
142: 6 my refuge, my portion in the land of the l."
143: 2 servant, for before you no l man is just.
145:16 and satisfy the desire of every l thing.
Prv 16:31 it is gained by virtuous l.
Eccl 4: 2 in death than are the l to be still alive.
7: 2 man, and the l should take it to heart.
9: 4 Indeed, for any among the l there is hope;
9: 5 For the l know that they are to die,
10:19 forth merriment and wine makes the l glad,
Wis 1:13 he rejoice in the destruction of the l.
8:16 no bitterness and l with her no grief,
18:12 l were not even sufficient for the burial,
18:23 the anger, and cut off the way to the l.
Sir 1: 8 upon every l thing according to his bounty;
7:33 Be generous to all the l,
13:14 Every l thing loves its own kind,
17:22 in place of the l who offer their praise?
21:13 a flood, and his counsel, like a l spring;
34:22 his neighbor who deprives him of his l:
40: 1 day he returns to the mother of all the l,
49:16 of any l being was the splendor of ADAM.
Is 6: 5 lips, l among a people of unclean lips;
7:15 He shall be l on curds and honey by the
8:19 gods, apply to the dead on behalf of the l?"
37: 4 king of Assyria, sent to taunt the l God,
37:17 that Sennacherib sent to taunt the l God.
38:11 see the LORD no more in the land of the l.
38:19 The living, the l give you thanks,
53: 8 he was cut off from the land of the l,
57:15 he who is high and exalted, l eternally,
65: 4 L among the graves and spending the night
Jer 2:13 have forsaken me, the source of l waters;
10:10 The LORD is true God, he is the l God,
10:17 the land, O city l in a state of siege!
11:19 let us cut him off from the land of the l,
17:13 forsaken the source of l waters [the LORD].
23:14 Adultery, l in lies,
23:36 so that you pervert the words of the l God,

26: 4 not l according to the law I placed before
35:11 that is why we are now l in Jerusalem."
44: 1 the people of Judah who were l in Egypt,
44:23 the voice of the LORD, not l by his law,
Lam 3:39 Why should any l man complain,
Ez 1: 5 four l creatures that looked like this:
1:13 In among the l creatures something like
1:13 moving to and fro among the l creatures.
1:15 As I looked at the l creatures,
1:15 one beside each of the four l creatures.
1:19 When the l creatures moved,
1:19 l creatures were raised from the ground,
1:20 living creatures; for the spirit of the l
1:22 Over the heads of the l creatures,
3:13 of the l creatures striking one another,
5: 7 not l by my statutes nor fulfilling my
10:15 l creatures I had seen by the river Chebar.
10:17 for the l creatures' spirit was in them.
10:20 these were the l creatures I had seen
16:46 with her daughters, l to the north of you;
16:46 your younger sister, l to the south of you,
26:20 to take your place in the land of the l.
29:16 but the l reminder of its guilt for having
32:23 who spread terror in the land of the l.
32:24 spread their terror in the land of the l,
32:26 spread their terror in the land of the l.
32:27 men caused terror in the land of the l.
32:32 he spread his terror in the land of the l,
33:15 goods, l by the statutes that bring life,
38:11 l in security, all of them l without walls,
47: 9 of l creature that can multiply shall live,
Dn 2:30 that I am wiser than any other l person,
6:21 "O Daniel, servant of the l God,
6:27 "For he is the l God,
14: 5 but only the l God who made heaven and
14: 6 "You do not think Bel is a l god?
14:24 "you cannot deny that this is a l god,
14:25 the Lord, my God, for he is the l God.
Hos 2: 1 shall be called, "Children of the l God."
Zec 14: 8 day, l waters shall flow from Jerusalem,
Mt 4:16 l in darkness has seen a great light.
15:22 woman l in that locality presented herself,
16:16 Peter answered, "the Son of the l God!"
22:32 He is the God of the l, not of the dead."
26:63 the l God whether you are the Messiah,
Mk 12:27 He is the God of the l, not of the dead.
Lk 2: 8 l in the fields and keeping night watch by
15:13 he squandered his money on dissolute l.
20:38 is not the God of the dead but of the l.
24: 5 do you search for the L One among the dead?
Jn 4:10 and he would have given you l water."
4:18 man you are l with now is not your husband.
6:51 am the l bread come down from heaven.
7:38 within him rivers of l water shall flow.'"
17:23 I living in them, you l in me
Acts 9: 2 man or woman, l according to the new way.
9:32 to God's holy people l in Lydda.
10:42 by God as judge of the l and the dead.
14:15 just such follies as these to the l God,
19:17 known to the Jews and Greeks l in Ephesus,
Rom 6: 2 How can we who died to sin go on l in it?
9:26 they shall be called sons of the l God."
12: 1 a l sacrifice holy and acceptable to God,
13:11 for you know the time in which we are l.
14: 9 might be Lord of both the dead and the l.
1Cor 5: 1 a man l with his father's wife.
9: 6 Barnabas who are forced to work for a l?
15:45 that Adam, the first man, became a l soul;
2Cor 3: 3 with ink but by the Spirit of the l God,
6:16 You are the temple of the l God,
13: 5 to see whether you are l in faith;
Gal 2:14 "If you who are a Jew are l according to
2:20 Christ is l in me.
Phil 1:22 other hand, I am to go on l in the flesh,
Col 2:21 were still l a life bounded by this world?
1Thes 1: 9 to serve him who is the l and true God and
4:17 Then we, the l,
1Tm 3:15 God's household, the church of the l God,
4:10 on the l God who is the savior of all men,
5: 6 however, leads a life of l death.
2Tm 4: 1 who is coming to judge the l and the dead,
Heb 3:12 spirit and fall away from the l God.
4:12 Indeed, God's word is l and effective,
9:14 from dead works to worship the l God!
10:20 into the sanctuary by the new and l path
10:31 thing to fall into the hands of the l God.
12:22 to Mount Zion and the city of the l God,
13: 9 to those who take them as a standard for l.
1Pt 1:23 through the l and enduring word of God.
2: 4 Come to him, a l stone,
2: 5 You too are l stones,
4: 3 the pagans enjoy, l lives of debauchery,
4: 5 stands ready to judge the l and the dead.
1Jn 3:14 man who does not love is among the l dead.
Jude 1:18 be impostors l by their godless passions."
Rv 3: 5 erase his name from the book of the l,
4: 6 stood four l creatures covered with eyes
4: 8 Each of the four l creatures had six wings
5: 6 with the four l creatures and the elders,
5: 8 the four l creatures and the twenty-four
5:11 throne and the l creatures and the elders.
5:14 The four l creatures answered,
6: 1 and I heard one of the four l creatures

LIVING (cont.)
6: 3 I heard the second *l* creature cry out,
6: 5 seal, I heard the third *l* creature cry out,
6: 6 coming from in among the four *l* creatures.
6: 7 the voice of the fourth *l* creature cry out,
7: 2 the east holding the seal of the *l* God.
7:11 elders and the four *l* creatures fell down
8: 9 third of the creatures *l* in the sea died,
13: 8 world's beginning in the book of the *l*,
14: 3 of the four *l* creatures and the elders.
15: 7 One of the four *l* creatures gave to the
16: 3 and every creature *l* in the sea died.
17: 8 not been written in the book of the *l*
19: 4 four *l* creatures fell down and worshiped
20:12 the scrolls, the book of the *l* was opened.
20:15 of the *l* was hurled into this pool of fire.
21:27 in the book of the *l* kept by the Lamb.

LIZARDS (2)
Lv 11:29 rat, the mouse, the various kinds of *l*,
Prv 30:28 *L*— you can catch them with your hands,

LO (40)
Ex 2: 6 On opening it, she looked, and *l*,
16:10 they turned toward the desert, and *l*,
Jb 4:18 *L*, he puts no trust in his servants,
5:27 *L*, this we have searched out; so it is!
13: 1 *L*, all this my eye has seen;
26:14 *L*, these are but the outlines of his ways,
33:29 *L*, all these things God does,
36:26 *L*, God is great beyond our knowledge;
36:29 *L*! he spreads the clouds
Ps(s) 37:36 Yet as I passed by, *l*!
48: 5 For *l*! the Kings assemble,
Prv 1:23 *L*! I will pour out to you my spirit
7:10 And *l*! the woman comes to meet him
Is 13: 9 *L*, the day of the LORD comes cruel,
17: 1 *L*, Damascus shall cease to be a city and
24: 2 *L*, the LORD empties the land and lays it
34: 5 has drunk its fill in the heavens, *l*,
47:14 *L*, they are like stubble,
50: 2 *L*, with my rebuke I dry up the sea,
50: 9 *L*, they will all wear out like cloth,
54:16 *L*, I have created the craftsman who blows
58: 3 *L*, on your fast day you carry out your own
59: 1 *L*, the hand of the LORD is not too short
59: 9 We look for light, and *l*,
65: 6 *L*, before me it stands written;
65:13 *L*, my servants shall eat,
65:17 *L*, I am about to create new heavens and a
66:12 *L*, I will spread prosperity over her like
66:15 *L*, the LORD shall come in fire,
Jer 1:15 *L*, I am summoning all the kingdoms of the
25: 9 Since you would not listen to my words, *l*!
25:32 *L*! calamity stalls from nation to nation
Zec 8: 7 *L*, I will rescue my people from the land
9: 4 *L*, the LORD will strip her of her
14: 1 *L*, a day shall come for the LORD when the
Mal 2: 3 *L*, I will deprive you of the shoulder and
3: 1 *L*, I am sending my messenger to prepare
3:19 *l*, the day is coming, blazing like an oven,
3:23 *L*, I will send you Elijah,
3:24 *L*, I will send you Elijah,

LO-AMMI (3)
Hos 1: 9 Give him the name *L*,
2: 1 Whereas they were called, *L*,"
2:25 I will say to *L*,

LO-RUHAMA (3)
Hos 1: 6 Give her the name *L*;
1: 8 After she weaned *L*, she conceived
2:25 in the land, and I will have pity on *L*.

LOAD (5)
Gn 45:17 *L* up your animals and go without delay to
Neh 4:11 The *l* carriers, too, were armed;
Sir 21:16 A fool's chatter is like a *l* on a journey,
33:29 if he becomes unruly, *l* him with chains.
Is 1:14 they weigh me down, I tire of the *l*.

LOADED (7)
Gn 42:26 they *l* their donkeys with the rations and
45:23 jackasses *l* with the finest products of Egypt
45:23 ten jennies *l* with grain and bread
1Sm 25:18 cakes of pressed figs, and *l* them on asses.
2Kgs 3:25 fertile field till they had *l* it down;
Jdt 15:11 wagons to them, and *l* these things on them.
Jn 21:11 hauled ashore the net *l* with sizable fish

LOADING (1)
Neh 13:15 in sheaves of grain, *l* them on their asses,

LOADS (5)
2Kgs 8: 9 camel *l* of the best goods of Damascus.
Sir 33:25 Fodder and whip and *l* for an ass;
Lam 5:13 boys stagger under their *l* of wood;
Hb 2: 6 he *l* himself down with debts.
Mt 23: 4 They bind up heavy *l*,

LOAF (11)
Lv 8:26 cake, one *l* of bread made with oil,
Jgs 7:13 "that a round *l* of barley bread was
1Sm 2:36 him for a piece of silver or a *l* of bread,
2Sm 6:19 entire multitude of Israel, a *l* of bread,
1Chr 16: 3 to every man and every woman, a *l* of bread,
Prv 6:26 a loose woman may be scarcely a *l* of bread,
Jer 37:21 and given a *l* of bread each day from the
Mt 7: 9 hand his son a stone when he asks for a *l*,
Mk 8:14 one *l* they had none with them in the boat.
1Cor 10:17 Because the *l* of bread is one,
10:17 one body, for we all partake of the one *l*.

LOAFERS (1)
Acts 17: 5 who engaged *l* from the public square to

LOAN (6)
Dt 23:20 countrymen on a *l* of money or of food
24:10 you make a *l* of any kind to your neighbor,
24:11 the *l* brings his pledge outside to you.
Sir 29: 2 pay back your neighbor when a *l* falls due;
29: 4 Many a man who asks for a *l* adds to the
Lk 19:23 then, did you not put my money out on *l*,

LOANED (1)
Dt 15: 2 his claim on what he has *l* his neighbor;

LOATHE (11)
Lv 11:11 not eat, and their dead bodies you shall *l*.
11:13 "Of the birds, these you shall *l* and,
Dt 7:26 *l* and abhor it utterly as a thing that is
Ps(s) 139:21 Those who rise up against you do I not *l*?
Wis 11:24 that are and *l* nothing that you have made;
Sir 25: 2 their manner of life I *l* indeed:
Ez 6: 9 *l* themselves because of their evil deeds,
20:43 and you shall *l* yourselves because of all
36:31 you shall *l* yourselves for your sins and
Jon 4: 2 to anger, rich in clemency, *l* to punish.

LOATHED (3)
Ps(s) 95:10 Forty years I *l* that generation,
107:18 of their sins, They *l* all manner of food,
Eccl 2:17 Therefore I *l* life,

LOATHES (2)
Sir 17:21 away from sin, hate intensely what he *l*;
50:25 My whole being *l* two nations,

LOATHING (2)
Dt 32:19 *l* and anger toward his sons and daughters.
Ps(s) 119:158 I beheld the apostates with *l*,

LOATHSOME (24)
Gn 34:30 making me *l* to the inhabitants of the land,
Lv 7:21 origin or from some *l* crawling creature,
11:10 lack either fins or scales are *l* for you,
11:11 for you, and you shall treat them as *l*.
11:12 that lacks fins or scales is *l* for you.
11:13 birds, these you shall loathe and, as *l*,
11:20 that walk on all fours are *l* for you.
11:23 insects that have four legs are *l* for you.
11:41 on the ground are *l* and shall not be eaten.
11:42 shall eat no swarming creature: they are *l*.
11:43 Do not make yourselves *l* or unclean with
Nm 11:20 of your very nostrils and becomes *l* to you.
Dt 29:16 and you saw the *l* idols of wood and stone,
Jb 6: 7 they are *l* food to me.
19:17 I am *l* to the men of my family.
Wis 15:18 besides, they worship the most *l* beasts
16: 3 creatures sent to plague them were so *l*,
Is 1:13 your incense is *l* to me.
14:19 cast forth without burial, *l* and corrupt,
66:17 who eat swine's flesh, *l* things and mice,
Jer 2: 7 defiled my land, you made my heritage *l*.
14:19 Is Zion *l* to you?
Ez 8:10 all kinds of creeping things and *l* beasts
16: 5 thrown out on the ground as something *l*,

LOAVES (43)
Ex 12:39 leavened, they baked it into unleavened *l*.
29:23 LORD, you shall take one of the *l* of bread,
Lv 7:13 His offering shall also include *l* of
23:17 from wherever you live two *l* of bread
Nm 11: 8 then cook it in a pot and make it into *l*,
Jgs 8: 5 you give my followers some *l* of bread?
1Sm 10: 3 three kids, another three *l* of bread,
16:20 Then Jesse took five *l* of bread,
17:17 grain and these ten *l* for your brothers,
21: 4 Give me five *l*,
25:18 quickly got together two hundred *l*,
2Sm 16: 1 asses laden with two hundred *l* of bread,
1Kgs 14: 3 Take along ten *l*,
2Kgs 4:42 twenty barely *l* made from the first fruits,
Tb 8:19 He asked his wife to bake many *l* of bread;
1Mc 4:51 They also put *l* on the table
2Mc 1: 8 the lamps and set out the *l* of bread.
Ez 4:12 *l* over human excrement in their sight,
Mt 14:17 replied, "but five *l* and a couple of fish."
14:19 He took the five *l* and two fish,
14:19 broke them and gave the *l* to the disciples,
15:34 them, "How many *l* of bread do you have?"
15:36 He took the seven *l* and the fish,
16: 9 Do you not remember the five *l* among five
16:10 Or the seven *l* among four thousand and how
Mk 6:38 "How many *l* have you?"
6:41 Then, taking the five *l* and the two fish,
6:41 pronounced a blessing, broke the *l*,
6:44 had eaten the *l* numbered five thousand men.
6:52 for they had not understood about the *l*.
8: 5 he asked them, "How many *l* do you have?"
8: 6 Taking the seven *l* he gave thanks,
8:19 I broke the five *l* for the five thousand,
8:20 I broke the seven *l* for the four thousand,
Lk 9:13 "We have nothing but five *l* and two fish.
9:16 Then, taking the five *l* and the two fish,
11: 5 and says to him, 'Friend, lend me three *l*,
Jn 6: 7 *l* enough to give each of them a mouthful!"
6: 9 five barley *l* and a couple of dried fish,
6:11 Jesus then took the *l* of bread,
6:13 who had been fed with the five barley *l*.
6:26 because you have eaten your fill of the *l*.
1Cor 5: 7 of yourselves fresh dough, unleavened *l*,

LOBE (11)
Ex 29:13 as the *l* of its liver and its two kidneys,
29:22 its inner organs, the *l* of its liver,
Lv 3: 4 near the loins, and the *l* of the liver,
3:10 near the loins, and the *l* of the liver,
3:15 near the loins, and the *l* of the liver,
4: 9 near the loins, and the *l* of the liver,
7: 4 near the loins, and the *l* of the liver,
8:16 as well as the *l* of the liver and the two
8:25 the *l* of the liver and the two kidneys
9:10 the kidneys and the *l* of the liver that
9:19 that is on them, and the *l* of the liver,

LOCAL (6)
Gn 23: 7 began to bow low before the *l* citizens,
23:12 after bowing low before the *l* citizens,
29:22 all the *l* inhabitants and gave a feast.
2Mc 12: 2 But some of the *l* governors,
13: 4 executed there in the customary *l* method.
Acts 16:19 the main square before the *l* authorities.

LOCALITIES (1)
Gn 36:40 according to their subdivisions and *l*:

LOCALITY (3)
Mt 11: 1 that *l* to teach and preach in their towns.
15:22 woman living in that *l* presented herself,
Mk 6:10 in, stay there until you leave the *l*.

LOCATED (3)
1Sm 22: 6 heard that David and his men had been *l*.
1Kgs 6:19 In the innermost part of the temple was *l*
Jdt 7: 7 to their city and *l* their sources of water;

LOCK (4)
Neh 6:10 let us *l* the doors of the temple.
Sg 5: 5 choice myrrh upon the fittings of the *l*.
Sir 42: 6 of a *l* placed where there are many hands;
Lk 13:25 master of the house has risen to *l* the door

LOCKED (10)
Gn 42:17 *l* them up in the guardhouse for three days.
Jgs 3:24 that the doors of the upper room were *l*,
1Mc 11:61 people of Gaza *l* their gates against him.
2Mc 1:15 the temple, the priests *l* the doors.
Lk 12: 3 what you have whispered in *l* rooms will be
Jn 20:19 even though the disciples had *l* the doors
20:26 Despite the *l* doors,
Acts 5:23 "We found the jail securely *l* and the
Gal 3:22 Scripture has *l* all things in under the
3:23 *l* in until the faith that was coming

LOCKING (1)
Jgs 3:23 doors of the upper room on him and *l* them.

LOCKS (5)
Jgs 16:13 "If you weave my seven *l* of hair into the
16:14 wove his seven *l* of hair into the web,
16:19 a man who shaved off his seven *l* of hair.
Sg 5: 2 dew, my *l* with the moisture of the night."
5:11 his *l* are palm fronds,

LOCUST (13)
Ex 10:19 *l* remained within the confines of Egypt,
1Kgs 8:37 if blight comes, or mildew, or a *l* swarm,
2Chr 7:13 if I command the *l* to devour the land,
Ps(s) 78:46 the fruits of their toil to the *l*.
109:23 I am swept away like the *l*.
Eccl 12: 5 and the *l* grows sluggish and the caper
Jl 1: 4 the cutter left, the *l* swarm has eaten;
1: 4 What the *l* swarm left,
2:25 you for the years which the *l* has eaten,
Am 4: 9 fig trees and olive trees the *l* devoured;

7: 1 He was forming a *l* swarm when the late
Na 3:17 And your scribes as *l* swarms gathered on
Mal 3:11 I will forbid the *l* to destroy your crops;

LOCUSTS (24)

Ex 10: 4 tomorrow I will bring *l* into your country.
10:12 that *l* may swarm over it and eat up all
10:13 At dawn the east wind brought the *l*.
10:14 had there been such a fierce swarm of *l*,
10:19 up the *l* and hurled them into the Red Sea.
Lv 11:22 the various kinds of *l*,
Dt 28:38 little, for the *l* will devour the crops.
Jgs 6: 5 their tents would become as numerous as *l*;
7:12 lay in the valley, as numerous as *l*.
2Chr 6:28 is pestilence, or blight, or mildew, or *l*,
Jdt 2:20 to count, like *l* or the dust of the earth,
Ps(s) 105:34 came *l* and grasshoppers without number;
Prv 30:27 *L*— they have no king, yet they migrate
Wis 16: 9 For the bites of *l* and of flies slew them,
Sir 43:18 it comes to settle like swarms of *l*.
Is 33: 4 they rush upon it like the onrush of *l*.
Jer 46:23 More numerous than *l*,
51:14 I will fill you with men as numerous as *l*,
51:27 her, send up horses like bristling *l*.
Na 3:15 like the grasshoppers, multiply like the *l*!
Rv 9: 3 *l* as powerful as scorpions in their sting.
9: 4 The *l* were commanded to do no harm to the
9: 5 The *l* were not allowed to kill them but
9: 7 the *l* were like horses equipped for battle.

LOD (4)

1Chr 8:12 who built Ono and *L* with its nearby towns,
Ezr 2:33 sons of *L*, Hadid, and Ono,
Neh 7:37 sons of *L*, Hadid, and Ono,
11:35 Ramah, Gittaim, Hadid, Zeboim, Neballat, *L*,

LODEBAR (5)

Jos 13:26 and from Mahanaim to the boundary of *L*);
2Sm 9: 4 the house of Machir, son of Ammiel, in *L*."
9: 5 the house of Machir, son of Ammiel, in *L*.
17:27 Ammonites, Machir, son of Ammiel from *L*,
Am 6:13 You rejoice in *L*,

LODGE (9)

Ru 1:16 go I will go, wherever you *l* I will lodge,
Ps(s) 55: 8 I would *l* in the wilderness.
61: 5 Oh, that I might *l* in your tent forever,
Sir 11:34 *L* a stranger with you,
Is 1:21 Justice used to *l* within her,
Jer 4:14 must your pernicious thoughts *l* within you?
9: 1 that I had in the desert a travelers' *l*!
Zec 5: 4 it shall *l* within his house,

LODGED (12)

Nm 22: 8 So the princes of Moab *l* with Balaam.
Jos 2: 1 of a harlot named Rahab, where they *l*.
3: 1 Jordan, where they *l* before crossing over.
2Sm 11:11 ark and Israel and Judah are *l* in tents,
1Chr 9:27 At night they *l* about the house of God,
Est A:12 Mordecai *l* at the court with Bagathan
2Mc 3:17 who saw him the pain that *l* in his heart.
Jb 31:32 Because no stranger *l* in the street,
Sir 19:11 Like an arrow *l* in a man's thigh is gossip
Lk 2: 7 for them in the place where travelers *l*.
6:42 yourself to see the plank *l* in your own?
Jn 1:39 So they went to see where he was *l*,

LODGES (5)

Jb 18:14 Fiery destruction *l* in his tent,
Prv 14: 9 Guilt *l* in the tents of the arrogant,
Eccl 7: 9 for discontent *l* in the bosom of a fool.
Sir 14:26 nest in her leafage, and *l* in her branches;
36:27 no nest, but *l* where night overtakes him?

LODGING (7)

2Sm 15:25 me back and permit me to see it and its *l*.
1Chr 17: 5 but I have been *l* in tent or pavilion as
Neh 3:30 repaired the place opposite his own *l*.
Sir 51:23 and take up *l* in the house of instruction;
Jer 41:17 to the *l* place of Chimham near Bethlehem,
Lk 9:12 and find themselves *l* and food,
Acts 28:16 Paul was allowed to take a *l* of his own,

LODGINGS (3)

Acts 18: 3 He took up *l* with them and they worked
28:23 him and came to his *l* in great numbers.
28:30 full years Paul stayed on in his rented *l*,

LOFTINESS (3)

Is 8: 6 before the *l* of Rezin and Remaliah's son,
Jer 48:29 His *l*, his pride, his scorn, his insolence
Ez 31:14 fed by water may stand by itself in its *l*.

LOFTY (26)

1Sm 16: 7 from his appearance or from his *l* stature,
2Sm 22:28 though on the *l* your eyes look down.
2Kgs 19:23 I cut down its *l* cedars,
2Chr 2: 8 I intend to build must be *l* and wonderful.
Jb 41:26 All, however *l*, fear him; he is king
Ps(s) 139: 6 too *l* for me to attain.
Eccl 7: 8 is the patient spirit than the *l* spirit.
10: 6 a fool put in *l* position while the rich
Sir 37:14 better than seven watchmen in a *l* tower.
40: 3 on a *l* throne or grovels in dust and ashes,
45: 7 in honor and crowned him with *l* majesty;
Is 2:14 all the *l* mountains and all the high hills,
2:15 every *l* tower and every fortified wall,
6: 1 saw the Lord seated on a high and *l* throne,
10:33 are felled, and the *l* ones brought low;
26: 5 high places, and the *l* city he brings down;
30:25 Upon every high mountain and *l* hill there
37:24 I cut down its *l* cedars,
57: 7 a high and *l* mountain you made your bed,
Jer 51:58 her *l* gates shall be destroyed by fire.
Bar 5: 7 that every *l* mountain be made low,
Ez 17:22 And plant it on a high and *l* mountain;
31: 3 Lebanon, beautiful of branch, *l* of stature,
31:10 Because it became *l* in stature,
31:14 Thus no tree may grow *l* in stature or
Rom 9:21 a *l* purpose and another for a humble one?

LOG (5)

Lv 14:10 for a cereal offering, and one *l* of oil.
14:12 a guilt offering, along with the *l* of oil,
14:15 The priest shall also take a *l* of oil and
14:21 with oil for a cereal offering, a *l* of oil,
14:24 lamb, along with the *l* of oil,

LOGIC (1)

Gal 2:14 by what *l* do you force the Gentiles to

LOGS (1)

1Chr 22: 4 brought great stores of cedar *l* to David,

LOINCLOTH (9)

Is 32:11 bare, with only a *l* to cover you.
Jer 13: 1 Go buy yourself a linen *l*;
13: 2 I bought the *l*,
13: 4 the *l* which you bought and are wearing,
13: 5 I went to the Parath and buried the *l*.
13: 6 fetch the *l* which I told you to hide there.
13: 7 the *l* from the place where I had hid it.
13:10 be like this *l* which is good for nothing.
13:11 as close as the *l* clings to a man's loins,

LOINCLOTHS (1)

Gn 3: 7 leaves together and made *l* for themselves.

LOINS (34)

Gn 35:11 you, and kings shall issue from your *l*.
37:34 rent his clothes, put sackcloth on his *l*,
Ex 12:11 with your *l* girt,
28:42 naked flesh from their *l* to their thighs.
Lv 3: 4 kidneys, with the fat on them near the *l*,
3:10 kidneys, with the fat on them near the *l*,
3:15 kidneys, with the fat on them near the *l*,
4: 9 kidneys, with the fat on them near the *l*,
7: 4 kidneys with the fat on them near the *l*,
2Sm 7:12 up your heir after you, sprung from your *l*,
16:11 "If my own son, who came forth from my *l*,
2Kgs 1: 8 "with a leather girdle about his *l*."
4:29 "Gird your *l*," Elisha said to Gehazi,
9: 1 "Gird your *l*, take this flask of oil with
Jdt 8: 5 about her *l* and wore widow's weeds.
2Mc 10:25 heads and girding their *l* in sackcloth.
Jb 12:18 but a waistcloth to bind the king's own *l*.
15:27 with his crassness, padding his *l* with fat,
38: 3 Gird up your *l* now,
40: 7 Gird up your *l* now, like a man.
40:16 Behold the strength in his *l*,
Ps(s) 38: 8 For my *l* are filled with burning pains;
Is 15: 4 At this the *l* of Moab tremble
21: 3 Therefore my *l* are filled with anguish,
Jer 1:17 But do you gird your *l*;
13: 1 wear it on your *l*,
13:11 as the loincloth clings to a man's *l*,
30: 6 hands on their *l* like women in childbirth
48:37 and the *l* of all are clothed in sackcloth.
Ez 44:18 their heads and linen drawers on their *l*;
Am 8:10 I will cover the *l* of all with sackcloth
Na 2: 2 Keep watch on the road, gird your *l*,
Heb 7:10 father's *l* when Melchizedek met Abraham.
1Pt 1:13 So gird the *l* of your understanding;

LOIS (1)

2Tm 1: 5 grandmother *L* and to your mother Eunice,

LONE (2)

Jdt 1:11 him as a *l* individual opposed to them,
Eccl 4:12 Where a *l* man may be overcome,

LONELINESS (1)

Ps(s) 22:21 the sword, my *l* from the grip of the dog.

LONELY (2)

Lam 1: 1 How *l* she is now, the once crowded city!
Mk 1:35 he went off to a *l* place in the desert;

LONG (393)

Gn 8:22 As *l* as the earth lasts cold and heat,
23:15 you and me, as *l* as you can bury your dead?"
26: 8 But when he had been there for a *l* time,
37: 3 and he made him a *l* tunic.
37:23 they stripped him of the *l* tunic he had on;
37:32 to bring the *l* tunic to their father,
39: 8 "As *l* as I am here,"
46:29 on his neck and wept a *l* time in his arms.
46:32 having *l* been keepers of livestock;
49:18 "[I *l* for your deliverance, O LORD!]
Ex 2:23 A *l* time passed,
10: 3 How *l* will you refuse to submit to me?
10: 7 to him, "How *l* must he be a menace to us?
14:20 coming any closer together all night *l*.
16:28 "How *l* will you refuse to keep my
17:11 As *l* as Moses kept his hands raised up,
20:12 have a *l* life in the land which the LORD,
25:10 of acacia wood, two and a half cubits *l*,
25:17 of pure gold, two cubits and a half *l*,
25:23 make a table of acacia wood, two cubits *l*,
27: 1 square, five cubits *l* and five cubits wide;
27: 9 shall have hangings a hundred cubits *l*,
27:11 be similar hangings, a hundred cubits *l*,
27:12 there shall be hangings, fifty cubits *l*,
27:16 be a variegated curtain, twenty cubits *l*,
27:18 the court is to be one hundred cubits *l*,
30: 2 wood, with a square surface, a cubit *l*,
37: 1 of acacia wood, two and a half cubits *l*,
37: 6 cubits *l* and one and a half cubits wide.
37:10 was made of acacia wood, two cubits *l*,
37:25 of acacia wood, on a square, a cubit *l*,
38: 1 square, five cubits *l* and five cubits wide;
38: 9 of fine linen twined, a hundred cubits *l*,
38:11 similar hangings, one hundred cubits *l*,
38:12 side there were hangings, fifty cubits *l*,
38:13 the east side the court was fifty cubits *l*.
38:18 twenty cubits *l* and five cubits wide,
Lv 13:11 it is skin leprosy that has *l* developed.
13:46 As *l* as the sore is on him he shall
15:25 as *l* as she suffers this unclean flow she
Nm 6: 4 As *l* as he is a nazirite he shall not eat
6: 6 As *l* as he is dedicated to the LORD,
6: 8 As *l* as he is a nazirite he is sacred to
9:18 As *l* as the cloud stayed over the Dwelling,
14:11 Moses, "How *l* will this people spurn me?
14:11 How *l* will they refuse to believe in me,
14:27 "How *l* will this wicked community grumble
18:32 You will incur no guilt so *l* as you make a
19:20 As *l* as the lustral water has not been
20:15 down to Egypt, where we stayed a *l* time,
32:19 so *l* as we receive a heritage for
Dt 1: 6 'You have stayed *l* enough at this mountain.
1:46 you had to stay as *l* as you did at Kadesh.
2: 1 around the highlands of Seir for a *l* time.
2: 3 wandered round these highlands *l* enough;
3:11 iron, nine regular cubits *l* and four wide,
4: 9 slip from your memory as *l* as you live,
4:10 may learn to fear me as *l* as they live
4:40 may have *l* life on the land which the LORD,
5:16 that you may have a *l* life and prosperity
5:33 *l* life in the land which you are to occupy.
6: 2 I enjoin on you, and thus have *l* life.
11: 9 and that you may have *l* life on the land
11:21 as *l* as the heavens are above the earth,
12: 1 to occupy, as *l* as you live on its soil.
12:19 the Levite as *l* as you live in the land.
16: 3 that you may remember as *l* as you live the
17:20 descendants will enjoy a *l* reign in Israel.
20:19 to it for a *l* time before you capture it,
22: 7 you shall have prosperity and a *l* life.
22:19 he may not divorce her as *l* as he lives.
22:29 he may not divorce her as *l* as he lives.
23: 7 peace and prosperity as *l* as you live.
25:15 have a *l* life on the land which the LORD,
28:13 as *l* as you obey the commandments of the
30:18 you will not have a *l* life on the land
30:20 a *l* life for you to live on the land which
31:13 as *l* as you live on the land which you
32:47 you are to enjoy a *l* life on the land
Jos 6: 5 When they give a *l* blast on the ram's
9:13 which are worn out from the very *l* journey."
11:18 war against all these kings for a *l* time.
24: 7 to Egypt, and dwelt a *l* time in the desert,
Jgs 2:18 of their enemies as *l* as the judge lived;
3:16 made himself a two-edged dagger a foot *l*,
5:28 "Why is his chariot so *l* in coming?
16: 2 an ambush at the city gate all night *l*.
18:31 as *l* as the house of God was in Shiloh.
1Sm 1:11 give him to the LORD for as *l* as he lives;
1:12 she remained *l* at prayer before the LORD,
1:14 *l* will you make a drunken show of yourself?
1:28 as *l* as he lives,
7: 2 came to rest in Kiriath-jearim a *l* time
7:13 was severe with them as *l* as Samuel lived.
7:15 Samuel judged Israel as *l* as he lived.
10:24 all the people shouted, *L* live the king!"
15:35 Never again, as *l* as he lived,
16: 1 "How *l* will you grieve for Saul,
20:31 *l* as the son of Jesse lives upon the earth,

LONG (cont.)
22: 4 him as *l* as David remained in the refuge.
25:28 evil to be found in you your whole life *l*.
27:11 This was his custom as *l* as he lived in
2Sm 2:29 marched all night *l* through the Arabah
3: 1 There followed a *l* war between the house
3:17 "For a *l* time you have been seeking David
4: 7 traveled on the Arabah road all night *l*.
7:19 house of your Servant for a *l* time to come:
13:18 Now she had on a *l* tunic,
13:19 tore the *l* tunic in which she was clothed.
14: 2 has been *l* in mourning for a departed one.
16:16 "*L* live the king! *L* live the king!"
1Kgs 1:25 company and saying, *L* live King Adonijah!'
1:34 blow the horn and cry, *L* live King Solomon!'
1:39 the people shouted, *L* live King Solomon!"
2:38 So Shimei stayed in Jerusalem for a *l* time.
3:11 not for a *l* life for yourself,
3:14 father David did, I will give you a *l* life."
5: 1 and were his vassals as *l* as he lived.
5: 5 Dan to Beer-sheba, as *l* as Solomon lived.
6: 2 built for the LORD was sixty cubits *l*,
6:17 front of the sanctuary, was forty cubits *l*.
6:20 of the LORD's covenant, twenty cubits *l*,
7: 2 Forest of Lebanon one hundred cubits *l*,
7: 6 he made fifty cubits *l* and thirty wide.
7:27 also made of bronze, each four cubits *l*,
8: 8 The poles were so *l* that their ends could
8:40 may fear you as *l* as they live on the land
11:25 an enemy of Israel as *l* as Solomon lived;
11:34 but will keep him a prince as *l* as he
12:28 have been going up to Jerusalem *l* enough.
15: 5 any of his commands as *l* as he lived,
15:14 entirely with the LORD as *l* as he lived.
15:16 king of Israel, a *l* as they both reigned.
15:32 Baasha, king of Israel, as *l* as they lived.]
18: 1 *L* afterward, in the third year,
18:21 said, "How *l* will you straddle the issue?
19: 7 else the journey will be too *l* for you!"
2Kgs 9:22 "as *l* as the many fornications and
11:12 their hands and shouting, *L* live the king!"
12: 3 was pleasing to the LORD as *l* as he lived,
13: 3 a *l* time left them in the power of Hazael,
19:25 *L* ago I prepared it,
25:29 ate at the king's table as *l* as he lived.
25:30 fixed daily amounts, for as *l* as he lived.
1Chr 7:22 Their father Ephraim mourned a *l* time,
17: 6 in tent or pavilion as *l* as I have wandered
2Chr 1:11 you, nor even for a *l* life for yourself,
4: 1 he made a bronze altar twenty cubits *l*,
5: 9 The poles were *l* enough so that their ends
6:13 had made a bronze platform five cubits *l*,
6:31 walk in your ways as *l* as they live
15: 3 For a *l* time Israel had no true God,
15:17 Asa's heart was undivided as *l* as he lived.
23:11 him, and they cried, *L* live the king!"
24: 2 the LORD as *l* as Jehoiada the priest lived.
26: 5 to seek God as *l* as Zechariah lived,
26: 5 and as *l* as he sought the LORD,
Ezr 5:11 the house built here *l* years ago,
Neh 2: 6 asked me how *l* my journey would take and
Tb 4: 3 and do not abandon her as *l* as she lives.
5: 8 but do not be *l*."
10:12 hear good reports about you as *l* as I live."
10:13 and may I live *l* enough to see children of
Jdt 5: 8 to Mesopotamia and dwelt there a *l* time.
5:10 stayed there as *l* as they found sustenance,
5:16 and they lived in these mountains a *l* time.
5:17 "As *l* as the Israelites did not sin in
16:25 of Judith and for a *l* time after her death,
Est B: 7 whose present ill will is of *l* standing,
5:13 Yet none of this satisfies me as *l* as I
1Mc 6:22 "How *l* will you fail to do justice and
6:52 their own, and kept up the fight a *l* time.
8:19 After making a very *l* journey to Rome,
12: 7 *L* ago a letter was sent to the high priest
12:10 *l* time has passed since your mission to us.
2Mc 2:32 it would be nonsense to write a *l* preface
6: 1 Not *l* after this the king sent an Athenian
6:13 promptly instead of letting them go for *l*.
6:21 because of their *l* acquaintance with him,
7:26 After he had urged her for a *l* time,
12:36 been fighting for a *l* time and were weary,
14:10 As *l* as Judas is around,
14:20 After a *l* discussion of the terms,
Jb 6: 8 and that God would grant what I *l* for:
7:19 *l* will it be before you look away from me,
7:19 me alone *l* enough to swallow my spittle?
8: 2 How *l* will you utter such things?
19: 2 How *l* will you vex my soul,
27: 3 So *l* as I still have life in me and the
Ps(s) 4: 3 of rank, how *l* will you be dull of heart?
6: 4 but you, O LORD, how *l* . . .
13: 2 How *l*, O LORD?
13: 2 How *l* will you hide your face from me?
13: 3 How *l* shall I harbor sorrow in my soul,
13: 3 How *l* will my enemy triumph over me?
32: 3 As *l* as I would not speak,
35:17 O LORD, how *l* will you look on?
62: 4 How *l* will you set upon a man and all
72: 5 May he endure as *l* as the sun,
72:17 as *l* as the sun his name shall remain.
74: 9 prophet now, and no one of us knows how *l*.
74:10 How *l*, O God, shall the foe blaspheme?
77: 6 the years *l* past I remember.
79: 5 O LORD, how *l*?
80: 5 how *l* will you burn with anger while your
82: 2 I "How *l* will you judge unjustly and
89:47 How *l*, O LORD?
90:13 Return, O LORD, How *l*?
94: 3 How *l*, O LORD, shall the wicked, how *l*
119:40 Behold, I *l* for your precepts;
119:174 I *l* for your salvation,
120: 6 *l* have I dwelt with those who hate peace.
129: 3 *l* did they make their furrows.
143: 3 me dwelling in the dark, like those *l* dead.
Prv 1:22 "How *l*, you simple ones, will you love
1:23 how *l* will you turn away at my reproof?
3:16 *L* life is in her right hand,
6: 9 How *l*, O sluggard, will you rest?
7:19 is not at home, he has gone on a *l* journey;
8:22 the forerunner of his prodigies of *l* ago;
23:30 Those who linger *l* over wine,
Eccl 6:10 Whatever is, was *l* ago given its name,
9: 6 hatred and rivalry have *l* since perished.
11: 1 after a *l* time you may find it again.
Wis 3:17 disappear For should they attain *l* life,
4: 2 it, and they *l* for it when it is gone;
4:13 he reached the fullness of a *l* career;
6:11 *l* for them and you shall be instructed.
15: 6 make them and *l* for them and worship them.
17: 2 with darkness, fettered by the *l* night,
18:20 Yet not for *l* did the anger last.
Sir 2:10 the generations *l* past and understand;
3: 6 who reveres his father will live a *l* life;
3:12 grieve him not as *l* as he lives.
11:19 He does not know how *l* it will be till he
13: 4 As *l* as the rich man can use you he will
13: 5 As *l* as you have anything he will speak
16: 7 of old who rebelled *l* ago in their might;
23:15 never mature in character as *l* as he lives.
33:20 Have power over you as *l* as you live.
50:24 in Israel as *l* as the heavens are above.
51:24 *l* will you be deprived of wisdom's food,
51:24 how *l* will you endure such bitter thirst?
Is 6:11 "How *l*, O Lord?"
22:11 did you consider him who built it *l* ago.
30:33 For the pyre has *l* been ready,
37:26 *L* ago I prepared it,
41:22 What are the things of *l* ago?
43:18 the past, the things of *l* ago consider not;
44: 8 did I not announce and foretell it *l* ago?
46: 8 remember the former things, those *l* ago:
48: 3 Things of the past I foretold *l* ago,
48: 7 Now, not *l* ago,
51: 9 Awake as in the days of old, in ages *l* ago!
53:10 he shall see his descendants in a *l* life,
63:19 *l* have we been like those you do not rule,
65:22 shall *l* enjoy the produce of their hands.
Jer 2:20 *L* ago you broke your yoke,
4:14 How *l* must your pernicious thoughts lodge
4:21 How *l* must I see that signal,
7: 7 I gave your fathers *l* ago and forever.
12: 4 How *l* must the earth mourn,
13: 6 After a *l* interval, he said to me:
13:27 *l* will it yet be before you become clean!
23:26 How *l* will this continue?
29:28 It will be a *l* time;
31:22 How *l* will you continue to stray,
32:14 so that they can be kept there a *l* time.
35: 7 *l* on the earth where you are wayfarers.'
37:16 dungeon, where he remained a *l* time.
47: 5 strength, how *l* will you gash yourself?
47: 6 how *l* till you find rest?
52:33 ate at the king's table as *l* as he lived.
Lam 3: 6 me to dwell in the dark like those *l* dead.
3:14 all nations, their taunt all the day *l*;
5:20 you forget us, abandon us so *l* a time?
Bar 1:12 of Belshazzar, his son, and serve them *l*,
4:35 her from the Eternal God, for a *l* time,
6: 2 many years, a period seven generations *l*;
Ez 7:11 It shall not be *l* in coming,
7:13 not regain what he sold as *l* as he lives,
12:27 "The vision he sees is a *l* way off;
17: 3 eagle, with great wings, with *l* pinions,
38: 8 mountains of Israel which were *l* a ruin],
40: 5 was holding a measuring rod six cubits *l*,
40: 7 The cells were a rod *l* and a rod wide,
40:18 the gates, as wide as the gates were *l*;
40:21 fifty cubits *l* and twenty-five cubits wide.
40:25 fifty cubits *l* and twenty-five cubits wide.
40:29 fifty cubits *l* and twenty-five cubits wide.
40:33 fifty cubits *l* and twenty-five cubits wide.
40:36 fifty cubits *l* and twenty-five cubits wide.
40:42 of cut stone, one and a half cubits *l*,
40:47 hundred cubits *l* and a hundred cubits wide,
41: 4 twenty cubits *l* and twenty cubits wide,
41:13 the temple, which was one hundred cubits *l*.
41:22 three cubits in height, two cubits *l*,
42:11 to the north, just as *l* and just as wide,
42:20 cubits *l* and five hundred cubits wide.
43:16 twelve cubits *l* and twelve cubits wide.
43:17 fourteen cubits *l* and fourteen cubits wide.
43:17 sixteen cubits *l* and sixteen cubits wide,
45: 1 thousand cubits *l* and twenty thousand wide;
45: 3 thousand cubits *l* and ten thousand wide,
45: 5 be a strip twenty-five thousand cubits *l*
45: 6 cubits wide and twenty-five thousand *l*,
46:22 courts, forty cubits *l* and thirty wide,
Dn 4:24 then your prosperity will be *l*."
8:13 "How *l* shall the events of this vision
12: 6 "How *l* shall it be to the end of these
Hos 8: 5 How *l* will they be unable to attain
Hb 1: 2 How *l*, O LORD?
2: 6 how *l* can it last!
Zec 1:12 how *l* will you be without mercy for
5: 2 it is twenty cubits *l* and ten cubits wide."
Mt 9:15 in mourning so *l* as the groom is with them?
11:21 have reformed in sackcloth and ashes *l* ago.
12:25 split into factions cannot last for *l*.
17:17 How *l* must I remain with you?
17:17 How *l* can I endure you?
24:48 himself, 'My master is a *l* time in coming,'
25:19 After a *l* absence, the master of those servants
Mk 1:33 Before *l* the whole town was gathered
2:19 fast as *l* as the groom is still among them?
2:19 So *l* as the groom stays with them,
5:17 Before *l* they were begging him to go away
9:19 How *l* must I remain with you?
9:19 How *l* can I endure you?
9:21 "How *l* has this been happening to him?"
12:40 and recite *l* prayers for appearance sake;
Lk 5: 5 at it all night *l* and have caught nothing;
8:27 For a *l* time he had not worn any clothes;
9:41 How *l* must I remain with you?
9:41 How *l* can I endure you?
10:13 *l* ago have reformed in sackcloth and ashes.
15:20 While he was still a *l* way off,
17:22 "A time will come when you will *l* to see
18: 7 Will he delay *l* over them, do you suppose?
20: 9 tenant farmers, and went away for a *l* time.
20:47 recite *l* prayers to keep up appearances.
23: 8 him he had wanted for a *l* time to see him,
Jn 5: 6 Jesus, who knew he had been sick a *l* time,
10:24 *l* are you going to keep us in suspense?
17:12 As *l* as I was with them,
Acts 1:16 "the saying in Scripture uttered *l* ago by
3:18 announced *l* ago through all the prophets:
3:21 spoke of *l* ago through his holy prophets.
4:28 your powerful providence you planned *l* ago.
5: 4 it not yours so *l* as it remained unsold?
5:36 Not *l* ago a certain Theudas came on the
8:11 the spell of his magic over a *l* period;
12:20 Herod had *l* been infuriated by the people
14:20 *l* he got up and went back into the town.
15:32 gave them reassurance in a *l* discourse.
19:28 began to shout, *L* live Artemis of Ephesus!"
19:29 Before *l*,
19:34 chant in unison, *L* live Artemis of Ephesus!"
20:11 Then he talked for a *l* while
21:30 Before *l* the whole city was in turmoil.
22:14 *l* ago designated you to know his will,
24:25 Before *l* he exclaimed:
26: 5 with me for a *l* time and can testify,
27:14 It was not *l* before a hurricane struck,
27:21 All hands had gone without food for a *l*
Rom 1: 2 he promised *l* ago through his prophets,
1:11 For I *l* to see you and share with you some
7: 1 has power over a man only so *l* as he lives?
8:36 sake we are being slain all the day *l*;
10:21 "All day *l* I stretched out my hands to an
16:12 who has labored *l* in the Lord's service.
1Cor 3: 3 For as *l* as there are jealousy and
7:39 is bound to her husband as *l* as he lives.
11:14 dishonorable for a man to wear his hair *l*,
11:14 while the *l* hair of a woman is her glory?
14:26 so *l* as as everything is done with a
Gal 4: 1 as *l* as a designated heir is not of age
Eph 6: 3 and that you may have *l* life on the earth."
Phil 1: 8 God himself can testify how much I *l* for
1:23 I *l* to be freed from this life and to be
4: 1 my brothers, you whom I so love and *l* for,
Heb 2:15 had been slaves their whole life *l*.
4: 7 when *l* afterward he spoke through David
1Pt 1:12 Into these matters angels *l* to search.
3:20 They had disobeyed as *l* ago as Noah's day,
2Pt 1:13 I consider it my duty, as *l* as I live,
3: 2 delivered *l* ago by the holy prophets,
Jude 1: 4 *l* ago destined for the condemnation I
Rv 6:10 "How *l* will it be, O Master, holy and true,
6:11 of the martyrs was given a *l* white robe,
7: 9 dressed in *l* white robes and holding palm

LONG-LIVED (2)

Jer 5:15 A *l* nation, an ancient nation, a people
Bar 6:46 Even those who produce them are not *l*

LONG-PAST (1)

2Pt 1: 9 He forgets the cleansing of his *l* sins.

LONG-SUFFERING (1)

Jer 15:15 Because of your *l* banish me not;

LONGED (4)

Mt 13:17 *l* to see what you see but did not see it,
Lk 15:16 He *l* to fill his belly with the husks that
16:21 Lazarus *l* to eat the scraps that fell from

Acts 7:39 thrust him aside and *l* to return to Egypt.

LONGER (193)

Gn 4:12 soil, it shall no *l* give you its produce.
5:24 walked with God, and he was no *l* here,
17: 5 No *l* shall you be called Abram;
32:29 "You shall no *l* be spoken of as Jacob,
35:10 name is Jacob shall no *l* be called Jacob,
45: 1 Joseph could no *l* control himself in the
49: 4 Unruly as water, you shall no *l* excel,
Ex 2: 3 When she could hide him no *l*,
5: 7 "You shall no *l* supply the people with
9:28 you need stay no *l*."
9:33 the rain no *l* poured down upon the earth.
Lv 17: 7 No *l* shall they offer their sacrifices to
27:20 to someone else, it may no *l* be redeemed;
Nm 8:25 from the required service and work no *l*.
9:22 Dwelling for two days or for a month or *l*,
11:15 so that I need no *l* face this distress."
18:22 may no *l* approach the meeting tent;
32:15 will make them stay still *l* in the desert,
Dt 10:16 therefore, and be no *l* stiff-necked.
31: 2 old and am no *l* able to move about freely;
Jos 5:12 No *l* was there manna for the Israelites,
18: 3 "How much *l* will you put off taking steps
23:13 no *l* drive these nations out of your way.
Jgs 2:14 whom they were no *l* able to withstand.
8:28 no *l* did they hold their heads high.
1Sm 1:18 her husband, and no *l* appeared downcast.
2: 3 "Speak boastfully no *l*,
10: 2 father is no *l* worried about the asses,
27: 4 had fled to Gath, he no *l* searched for him.
28:15 *l* answers me through prophets or in dreams,
2Sm 1:21 the shield of Saul, no *l* anointed with oil.
2:26 How much *l* will you refrain from ordering
3:11 Ishbaal was no *l* able to say a word to him.
3:22 was no *l* with him in Hebron but had gone
19:35 "How much *l* have I to live,
1Kgs 8:11 could no *l* minister because of the cloud,
2Kgs 2:12 But when he could no *l* see him,
4:41 there was no *l* anything harmful in the pot.
5:17 for I will no *l* offer holocaust or
6:33 Why should I trust in the LORD any *l*?"
12: 8 must no *l* take funds from your clients,
23:10 so that there would no *l* be an immolation
2Chr 26:18 have broken faith and no *l* have a part
29:11 My sons, be not negligent any *l*,
30:23 they continued the festivity seven days *l*.
35: 3 shall no *l* be a burden on your shoulders.
Ezr 4:13 raised up again, they will no *l* pay taxes,
4:16 no *l* own any part of West-of-Euphrates."
9:15 this, we can no *l* stand in your presence."
Neh 2:17 that we may no *l* be an object of derision!"
9:17 They refused to obey and no *l* remembered
13:10 due the Levites were no *l* being given,
Tb 1:15 became unsafe, so I could no *l* go there.
3:10 that I need no *l* live to hear such insults."
3:15 why then should I live any *l*?
5:10 like the dead who no *l* see the light!
10: 4 has perished and is no *l* among the living!"
12:21 rose to their feet and could no *l* see him.
13: 6 to you, and no *l* hide his face from you.
Jdt 15: 2 No one kept ranks any *l*;
1Mc 9:55 so that he could no *l* utter a word to give
13:39 in Jerusalem shall no *l* be collected there.
2Mc 4:14 no *l* cared about the service of the altar.
6: 1 ancestors and live no *l* by the laws of God;
9:12 When he could no *l* bear his own stench,
9:13 the Lord, who would no *l* have mercy on him,
Jb 11: 9 It is *l* than the earth in measure,
Ps(s) 88: 6 no *l* and who are cut off from your care.
Eccl 4:13 but foolish king who no *l* knows caution;
9: 5 to die, but the dead no *l* know anything.
Wis 14:24 *l* safeguard either lives or pure wedlock;
17: 6 times when that sight was no *l* to be seen.
Is 7: 9 Ephraim shall be crushed, no *l* a nation.
21:11 Seir, "Watchman, how much *l* the night?
21:11 Watchman, how much *l* the night?"
26:21 blood upon her, and no *l* conceal her slain.
30:20 No *l* will your Teacher hide himself,
38:11 No *l* shall I behold my fellow men among
47: 1 *l* shall you be called dainty and delicate.
47: 5 No *l* shall you be called sovereign
51:22 The bowl of my wrath you shall no *l* drink.
52: 1 No *l* shall the uncircumcised or the
54: 4 reproach of your widowhood no *l* remember.
60:18 *l* shall violence be heard of in your land,
60:19 No *l* shall the sun be your light by day,
60:20 No *l* shall your sun go down,
65:19 No *l* shall the sound of weeping be heard
65:20 No *l* shall there be in it an infant who
Jer 3:16 the LORD, They will in those days no *l* say,
3:16 They will no *l* think of it,
3:17 walk no *l* in their hardhearted wickedness.
7: 6 if you no *l* oppress the resident alien,
7: 6 you no *l* shed innocent blood in this place,
7:32 of Ben-hinnom will no *l* be called such,
8:19 Is the LORD no *l* in Zion, is her King no *l*
16:14 says the LORD, when it will no *l* be said,
19: 6 this place will no *l* be called Topheth,
23: 4 so that they need no *l* fear and tremble;
23: 7 says the LORD, when they shall no *l* say,
30: 8 Strangers shall no *l* enslave them;
31:29 In those days they shall no *l* say,
31:34 No *l* will they have need to teach their
33:20 day and night no *l* alternate in sequence,
33:24 as if it were no *l* a nation in their eyes.
34:10 so that they should be slaves no *l*.
42:14 more of war, hear the trumpet alarm no *l*,
44:22 The LORD could no *l* bear your evil deeds,
50:20 sins, but these shall no *l* be found;
Ez 12:24 There shall no *l* be any false visions or
12:28 None of my words shall be delayed any *l*;
13:21 that they shall no *l* be prey to your hands.
13:23 therefore you shall no *l* see false visions
14:11 no *l* stray from me and may no *l* be defiled
16:42 I will be quiet and no *l* vexed.
18: 3 I swear that there shall no *l* be anyone
23:27 you shall no *l* look toward it,
24:27 shall be opened and you shall be dumb no *l*.
26:19 like cities that are no *l* inhabited,
28:24 Sidon shall no *l* be a tearing thorn for
29:16 No *l* shall they be for the house of Israel
31: 5 *l* of branch because of the abundant water.
32:13 The foot of man shall stir them no *l*,
33:22 My mouth was opened, and I was dumb no *l*.
34:10 so that they may no *l* pasture themselves.
34:10 they may no *l* be food for their mouths.
34:22 sheep so that they may no *l* be despoiled,
34:28 They shall no *l* be despoiled by the
34:29 no *l* be carried off by famine in the land,
36:30 thus you shall no *l* bear among the nations
37:23 No *l* shall they defile themselves with
39: 7 no *l* allow my holy name to be profaned.
39:29 No *l* will I hide my face from them,
44:13 no *l* draw near me to serve as my priests,
45: 8 of Israel will no *l* oppress my people,
Hos 1: 6 I no *l* feel pity for the house of Israel;
2:19 Baals, so that they shall no *l* be invoked.
9:15 I will love them no *l*;
Am 7: 8 I will forgive them no *l*.
8: 2 I will forgive them no *l*.
Mi 5:11 there shall no *l* be soothsayers among you.
5:12 shall no *l* adore the works of your hands.
6:10 Am I to bear any *l* criminal hoarding and
Zep 3:11 no *l* exalt yourself on my holy mountain.
Zec 14: 6 that day there shall no *l* be cold or frost.
14:21 On that day there shall no *l* be any
Mal 2:13 Because he no *l* regards your sacrifice
Mt 19: 6 Thus they are no *l* two but one flesh.
Mk 1:45 it was no *l* possible for Jesus to enter a
2: 2 There was no *l* any room for them,
5: 3 could no *l* be restrained even with a chain.
9: 8 around they no *l* saw anyone with them
10: 8 They are no *l* two but one flesh.
Lk 15:18 I no *l* deserve to be called your son.
15:21 I no *l* deserve to be called your son.'
20:36 like angels and are no *l* liable to death.
Jn 4:42 "No *l* does our faith depend on your story.
6:66 and would not remain in his company any *l*.
7:33 a little while *l* am I to be with you,
11:54 no *l* moved about freely in Jewish circles.
12:35 "The light is among you only a little *l*.
13:33 children, I am not to be with you much *l*.
14:30 I shall not go on speaking to you *l*;
15:15 I no *l* speak of you as slaves,
16:21 she no *l* remembers her pain for joy that a
16:25 A time will come when I shall no *l* do so,
Acts 18:20 asked him to stay on *l* but he declined.
Rom 6: 6 and we might be slaves to sin no *l*.
6:14 Sin will no *l* have power over you;
14:13 we must no *l* pass judgment on one another.
1Cor 12:15 would it then no *l* belong to the body?
12:16 would it then no *l* belong to the body?
15:33 Do not be led astray any *l*.
2Cor 5:15 who live might live no *l* for themselves,
5:16 Because of this we no *l* look on anyone in
5:16 Christ, we no *l* know him by this standard.
Gal 3:18 is no *l* conferred in virtue of the promise.
3:25 here, we are no *l* in the monitor's charge.
4: 7 You are no *l* a slave but a son!
Eph 2:19 that you are strangers and aliens no *l*.
4:14 Let us, then, be children no *l*,
4:17 that you must no *l* live as the pagans do
4:28 man who has been stealing must steal no *l*;
1Thes 3: 1 That is why, when we could endure it no *l*,
3: 5 when I could stand the suspense no *l*,
Phlm 1:16 no *l* as a slave but as more than a slave,
Rv 6:11 a little while *l* until the quota was filled
17: 8 you saw existed once but now exists no *l*.
17: 8 for it existed once and now exists no *l*,
17:11 which existed once but now exists no *l*,
20:11 his presence until they could no *l* be seen.
21: 1 had passed away, and the sea was no *l*.

LONGING (9)

2Sm 13:39 but his *l* reached out for Absalom as he
Jb 19:26 my inmost being is consumed with *l*.
Ps(s) 107: 9 Because he satisfied the *l* soul and filled
119:20 with *l* for your ordinances at all times.
2Cor 7: 7 received from you, for he reported your *l*,
7:11 What indignation, fear, and *l*!
Phil 2:26 He has been *l* for all of you,
1Thes 2:17 were seized with the greatest *l* to see you.
2Tm 4: 8 have looked for his appearing with eager *l*.

LONGINGLY (1)

2Cor 9:14 They pray for you *l* because of the

LONGS (5)

Jb 7: 2 He is a slave who *l* for the shade,
Ps(s) 12: 6 "I will grant safety to him who *l* for it."
42: 2 *l* for the running waters, so my soul longs
Wis 15: 5 *l* for the inanimate form of a dead image.

LOOK (308)

Gn 2: 9 were delightful to *l* at and good for food,
13:14 *L* about you,
15: 5 *L* up at the sky and count the stars,
19:17 Don't *l* back or stop anywhere on the Plain.
19:20 *L*, this town ahead is near enough to
25:32 *L*," said Esau, "I'm on the point of dying.
26: 8 happened to *l* out of a window and was
39: 7 wife began to *l* fondly at him and said,
39:14 her household servants and told them, *L*!
40: 7 house, "Why do you *l* so sad today?"
44:21 him down to me that my eyes may *l* on him.'
Ex 1: 9 *L* how numerous and powerful the Israelite
3: 3 must go over to *l* at this remarkable sight,
3: 4 him coming over to *l* at it more closely,
3: 6 his face, for he was afraid to *l* at God.
5: 5 *L* how numerous the people of the land are
5:16 *L* how your servants are beaten!
5:21 to them, "The LORD *l* upon you and judge!
18:21 But you should also *l* among all the people
Lv 13:36 on the skin he need not *l* for yellow hair;
19:23 first *l* upon its fruit as if it were
26: 9 I will *l* with favor upon you,
Nm 4:20 not go in to *l* upon the sacred objects,
6:26 LORD *l* upon you kindly and give you peace!
18: 3 *l* after your persons and the whole tent;
Dt 1:35 evil generation shall *l* upon the good land
3:27 to the top of Pisgah and *l* out to the west,
3:27 *L* well, for you shall not cross this Jordan
4:19 And when you *l* up to the heavens and
7:16 You are not to *l* on them with pity,
9:27 *L* not upon the stubbornness of this people
13: 9 or listen to him, nor *l* with pity upon him,
19:13 Do not *l* on him with pity,
19:21 Do not *l* on such a man with pity.
26:15 *L* down, then, from heaven,
28:32 be given to a foreign nation while you *l* on
28:34 driven mad by what your eyes must *l* upon.
Jos 9:13 *L* at our garments and sandals,
22:28 *L* at the model of the altar of the LORD
Jgs 14: 8 he stepped aside to *l* at the remains of
1Sm 1:11 *l* with pity on the misery of your handmaid,
10: 2 asses you went to *l* for have been found.
10:14 Saul replied, "To *l* for the asses.
14:11 outpost of the Philistines, who said, *L*,
14:29 *L* how bright my eyes are from this small
16:16 *l* for a man skilled in playing the harp.
20:21 If in fact I say to him, *L*,
20:22 But if I say to the boy, *L*,
23:23 *L* around and learn in which of all the
24:12 *L* here at this end of your mantle which I
25: 8 *L* kindly on these young men,
26:16 Go, *l*: where are the king's spear
28:14 "What does he *l* like?"
2Sm 16:12 Perhaps the LORD will *l* upon my affliction
20: 6 cities and take shelter while we *l* on."
22:28 though on the lofty your eyes *l* down.
1Kgs 8:25 your descendants *l* to their conduct
8:28 *L* kindly on the prayer and petition of
12:16 Now *l* to your own house, David."
18:43 "Climb up and *l* out to sea,"
18:43 Seven times he said, "Go *l* again!"
22:13 gone to call Micaiah said to him, *L* now,
2Kgs 3:14 neither *l* at you nor notice you at all.
9: 2 When you get there, *l* for Jehu,
1Chr 16:11 *L* to the LORD in his strength;
2Chr 6:16 that your descendants *l* to their conduct
6:19 *L* kindly on the prayer and petition of
10:16 Now *l* to your own house, David!"
18:12 *L* now, the prophets unanimously predict
Ezr 4:14 to *l* on while the king is being dishonored.
Neh 2: 2 the king asked me, "Why do you *l* sad?
2: 3 How could I not *l* sad when the city where
Tb 2: 3 out to *l* for some poor kinsman of ours.
3: 3 be mindful of me, and *l* with favor upon me.
3: 8 *L* at you! You have already been married
3:15 *l* favorably upon me and have pity on me;
5: 4 Tobiah went to *l* for someone acquainted
7:11 I am sure the Lord will *l* after you both."
13: 6 *l* with favor upon you and show you mercy.
Jdt 4:15 *l* with favor on the whole house of Israel.
6:19 and *l* with favor this day on those who
13: 4 in this hour *l* graciously on my
Est 1:17 and they will *l* with disdain upon their
1Mc 6:26 *L*! They have now besieged the citadel
10:20 and you are to *l* after our interests and
2Mc 1:20 who had hidden the fire to *l* for it.
1:27 *l* kindly on those who are despised and
7:28 to *l* at the heavens and the earth and see
8: 2 the Lord to *l* kindly upon his people,

LOOK (cont.)

Jb 3: 9 may it l for daylight,
7: 8 as you l at me,
7:19 long will it be before you l away from me,
11:18 shall l round you and lie down in safety,
14: 6 L away from him and let him be,
17:13 If I l for the nether world as my dwelling,
21: 5 L at me and be astonished,
22:19 The just l on and are gladdened,
30:20 you stand off and l at me,
35: 5 L up to the skies and behold;
Ps(s) 13: 4 L, answer me, O LORD, my God!
22:18 They l on and gloat over me;
25:16 L toward me, have pity on me,
34: 6 L to him that you may be radiant with joy,
35:17 O LORD, how long will you l on?
37:34 the wicked are destroyed, you shall l on.
38:13 they l to my misfortune,
40: 4 shall l on in awe and trust in the LORD.
52: 8 The just shall l on with awe;
54: 9 me, and my eyes l down upon my enemies.
58: 3 on earth you l to the fruits of extortion.
68:17 Why l you jealously,
74:20 L to your covenant,
80:15 again, O LORD of hosts, l down from heaven,
84:10 and l upon the face of your anointed.
85:12 and justice shall l down from heaven.
104:27 all l to you to give them food in due time.
105: 4 L to the LORD in his strength;
118: 7 help me, and I shall l down upon my foes.
142: 5 I l to the right to see,
145:15 The eyes of all l hopefully to you,
Prv 4:25 Let your eyes l straight ahead and your
7:13 him, and with an impudent l says to him:
7:15 So I came out to meet you, to l for you,
23:31 L not on the wine when it is red,
Eccl 8: 1 his face, but an impudent l is resented.
12: 3 they who l through the windows grow blind;
Sg 3:11 come forth and l upon King Solomon In the
6:11 to l at the fresh growth of the valley,
7: 1 turn, turn, that we may l at you!
7: 1 Why would you l at the Shulammite as at
Wis 12:22 and, when being judged, may l for mercy.
Sir 7:22 If you have livestock, l after them;
11:12 the eyes of the LORD l favorably upon him;
23: 5 A brazen l allow me not;
33:22 than that you should l to their generosity.
33:26 a slave work and he will l for his rest;
33:33 in what direction will you l for him?
40:29 When one has to l to another's table,
Is 3: 9 Their very l bears witness against them;
3:15 grinding down the poor when they l to you?
6: 9 L intently, but you shall know nothing!
8:18 L at me and the children whom the LORD has
13: 8 They l aghast at each other,
14: 8 He shall l upward,
17: 7 On that day man shall l to his maker,
17: 8 He shall not l to the altars,
18: 3 the signal is raised on the mountain, l!
18: 4 I will quietly l on from where I dwell,
20: 6 shall say on that day, L at our hope!
21: 3 too bewildered to hear, too dismayed to l.
22:11 But you did not l to the city's Maker,
22:13 But l! you feast and celebrate,
26: 8 and your judgments, O LORD, we l to you;
31: 1 But l not to the Holy One of Israel nor
33:15 closing his eyes lest he l on evil
33:17 his splendor, they will l upon a vast land.
33:19 people of alien tongue you will l no more,
33:20 L to Zion, the city of our festivals;
34:16 L in the book of the LORD and read:
41:28 When I l, there is not one,
42:18 deaf, listen, you who are blind, l and see!
45:19 of Jacob, L for me in an empty waste."
48: 6 Now that you have heard, l at all this;
49:18 L about and see,
51: 1 L to the rock from which you were hewn,
51: 2 L to Abraham,
51: 6 to the heavens, and l at the earth below;
52:14 so marred was his l beyond that of man,
53: 2 him no stately bearing to make us l at him,
59: 9 We l for light,
59:11 We l for right,
60: 4 Raise your eyes and l about;
63:15 L down from heaven and regard us from your
64: 8 l upon us,
Jer 5: 1 streets of Jerusalem, l about and observe,
5: 3 O LORD, do your eyes not l for honesty?
13:16 the light you l for turns to darkness,
14:18 If I walk out into the field, l!
14:18 If I enter the city, l!
14:22 you alone, O LORD, our God, to whom we l?
16:16 L! I will send many fishermen,
16:21 L, then: I will give them knowledge:
24: 6 I will l after them for their good,
27:22 shall remain, until the day I l for them,
29:13 When you l for me, you will find me.
39:12 "Take him and l after him;
40: 4 I will l after you well.
43: 9 in Tahpanhes, while the men of Judah l on,
Lam 1: 9 L, O LORD, upon her misery,
1:11 L O LORD, and see how worthless
1:12 l and see Whether there is any suffering
1:20 L, O LORD, upon my distress:
2:20 L, O LORD, and consider:
3:36 claim, the Lord does not l on unconcerned.
5: 1 Remember, O LORD, what has befallen us, l,
Bar 2:16 l down from your holy dwelling and take
2:17 L directly at us, and behold:
4:36 L to the east, Jerusalem!
5: 5 l to the east and see your children
Ez 5: 8 in your midst while the nations l on.
5:11 not l upon you with pity nor have mercy.
7: 4 not l upon you with pity nor have mercy;
7: 9 not l upon you with pity nor have mercy;
8: 5 Son of man, l toward the north!
8:18 I will not l upon them with pity nor will
9: 5 not l on them with pity nor show any mercy!
9:10 I, however, will not l upon them with pity,
12: 5 while they l on, dig a hole in the wall
12: 6 while they l on, shoulder the burden
16:41 punishments on you while many women l on.
16:49 And l at the guilt of your sister Sodom:
21: 2 Son of man, l southward,
21: 7 Son of man, l toward Jerusalem,
21:11 strength groan bitterly while they l on.
23:27 you shall no longer l toward it,
28:21 Son of man, l toward Sidon,
34: 6 one to l after them or to search for them.
34: 8 my shepherds did not l after my sheep,
34:11 I myself will l after and tend my sheep.
40: 4 of man, l carefully and listen intently,
44: 5 of man, pay strict attention, l carefully,
Dn 1:10 If he sees that you l wretched by
1:13 Then see how we l in comparison with the
3:55 Blessed are you who l into the depths from
5:10 Be not troubled in mind, nor l so pale!
13: 9 would not allow their eyes to l to heaven,
13:14 and then they agreed to l for an occasion
13:20 L," They said, "The garden doors are shut,
14:19 L at the floor,"
14:24 "L!" said the king to Daniel,
Hos 5: 8 L behind you, O Benjamin!"
Jon 2: 5 yet would I again l upon your holy temple."
Mi 7: 7 But as for me, I will l to the LORD,
Hb 1: 3 why must I l at misery?
1: 5 L over the nations and see,
1:13 Too pure are your eyes to l upon evil,
3: 6 his l makes the nations tremble.
Zec 3: 9 L at the stone that I have placed before
12:10 l on him whom they have thrust through,
Mt 6:16 you are not to l glum as the hypocrites do.
6:26 L at the birds in the sky.
7: 3 Why l at the speck in your brother's eye
10:11 L for a worthy person in every town or
11: 3 'He who is to come' or do we l for another?"
13:13 to them because they l but do not see,
13:14 not understand, l intently as you will,
16: 3 you know how to interpret the l of the sky,
23:27 beautiful to l at on the outside but
24:23 If anyone tells you at that time, L,
24:26 so if they tell you, L,
Mk 2:24 L! Why do they do a thing not permitted
4:12 so that they will l intently and not see,
8:24 see people but they l like walking trees!"
11:18 and began to l for a way to destroy him.
11:21 remembered and said to him, "Rabbi, l!
13: 1 l at the huge blocks of stone and the
13:21 If anyone tells you at that time, L,
13:21 L, he is there!'—do
13:35 L around you!
14: 1 scribes began to l for a way to arrest him
Lk 6:41 "Why l at the speck in your brother's eye
7:20 is to come" or do we l for someone else?' "
9:38 "Teacher, I beg you to l at my son;
10:35 L after him,
11: 7 I cannot get up to l after your needs'
13: 7 He said to the vinedresser, L here!
22: 2 began to l for some way to dispose of him;
24:39 L at my hands and my feet;
Jn 1:29 L! There is the Lamb of God.
1:36 As he watched Jesus walk by he said, L!
7:19 Why do you l for a chance to kill me?"
7:34 You will l for me,
7:36 does he mean by saying, 'You will l for me,
7:52 L it up. You will not find the prophet
8:21 l for me but you will die in your sins.
13:33 You will l for me,
19: 5 cloak, Pilate said to them, L at the man!"
19:14 He said to the Jews, L at your king!"
19:37 shall l on him whom they have pierced."
Acts 3: 4 L at us!" Peter said.
4:29 l at the threats they are leveling against
5:25 then came up to them, pointing out, L,
6: 3 L around among your own number,
7:32 Moses began to tremble and dared l no more.
7:56 "L!" he exclaimed, "I see an opening
8:37 came to some water, and the eunuch said, L,
11:25 Barnabas went off to Tarsus to l for Saul;
13:25 Rather, l for the one who comes after me.
13:41 L on in amazement,
15: 6 accordingly convened to l into the matter.
22:14 to know his will, to l upon the Just One,
22:30 intending to l carefully into the charge
25:24 are here present with us, l at this man!
28:26 you may l intently yet you will never see.
Rom 12:13 L on the needs of the saints as your own;
14:10 Or you, how can you l down on your brother?
1Cor 1:22 demand "signs" and Greeks l for "wisdom,"
10:18 L at Israel according to the flesh and see
2Cor 3: 7 Israelites could not l on Moses' face
5:16 Because of this we no longer l on anyone
7:11 Just l at the fruit of this sorrow which
11:12 depriving at every turn those who l for a
Gal 6: 4 Each man should l to his conduct;
Phil 2:16 As I l to the Day of Christ,
1Tm 4:12 no one l down on you because of your youth,
Ti 2:15 Let no one l down on you.
2Jn 1: 8 L out that you yourselves do not lose what
Jude 1:12 without shame and only l after themselves.

LOOKED (147)

Gn 1:31 God l at everything he had made,
4: 4 LORD l with favor on Abel and his offering,
13:10 Lot l about and saw how well watered the
16: 4 she l on her mistress with disdain.
18:16 set out from there and l down toward Sodom;
19:26 But Lot's wife l back,
19:28 As he l down toward Sodom and Gomorrah
22:13 As Abraham l about,
24:63 in the field, and as he l around,
33: 1 Jacob l up and saw Esau coming,
33: 5 When Esau l about,
40: 6 morning, he noticed that they l disturbed.
41:21 done so, because they l as ugly as before.
43:33 they l at one another in amazement;
Ex 2: 6 On opening it, she l,
3: 2 As he l on, he was surprised to see
14:10 was already near when the Israelites l up
Nm 21: 9 by a serpent l at the bronze serpent,
Dt 25: 3 your kinsman should be l upon as disgraced
Jos 8:20 By the time the men of Ai l back,
Jgs 16:27 women l on as Samson provided amusement.
20:36 it had l as though the enemy were defeated,
20:40 It was when Benjamin l back and saw the
1Sm 6:13 When they l up and spied the ark,
10:21 But they l for him in vain.
16: 6 As they came, he l at Eliab and thought.
24: 9 When Saul l back,
2Sm 6:16 Saul's daughter Michal l down through the
13:34 Then the servant on watch l about and saw
18:24 he l about and saw a man running all alone.
24:20 Now Aaaunah l down and noticed the king
1Kgs 18:43 he directed his servant, who went up and l,
19: 6 He l and there at his head was a hearth
2Kgs 9:30 her hair, and l down from her window.
9:32 Jehu l up to the window and shouted,
9:32 two or three eunuchs l down toward him.
13:23 Lord was merciful with Israel and l on them
23:16 When the king l up and saw the grave of
1Chr 15:29 daughter of Saul, l down from her window,
17:17 and you have l on me as henceforth the
21:21 him, he l up and saw that it was David.
2Chr 7: 3 All the Israelites l on while the fire
20:24 of the desert and l toward the throng,
22: 9 Then he l for Ahaziah himself.
23:13 She l, and there was the king standing
32: 5 He then l to his defenses:
Tb 1:18 so when Sennacherib l for them,
Est D: 7 As he l up, his features ablaze with the
1Mc 4:12 l up and saw them marching toward them,
5:30 they l ahead and saw a countless multitude
2Mc 7: 4 rest of his brothers and his mother l on.
15:34 everyone l toward heaven and praised the
Jb 30:26 Yet when I l for good,
31:26 Had I l upon the sun as it shone,
Ps(s) 44:23 we are l upon as sheep to be slaughtered.
69:21 my heart, and I am weak, I l for sympathy,
92:12 And my eye has l down upon my foes,
102:20 "The LORD l down from his holy height,
Prv 7: 6 of my house, through my lattice I l out
Sir 16:27 Then the LORD l upon the earth,
41:24 you would be l upon by everyone with favor.
48:24 By his powerful spirit he l into the
51: 7 one to help me, I l for one to sustain me,
Is 5: 2 Then he l for the crop of grapes,
5: 4 Why, when I l for the crop of grapes,
5: 7 He l for judgment,
22: 8 On that day you l to the weapons in the
25: 9 "Behold our God, to whom we l to save us!
25: 9 This is the LORD for whom we l;
42:14 I have l away,
51:12 who is human only, to be l upon as grass,
63: 5 I l about, but there was no one to help,
Jer 4:23 I l at the earth,
4:24 I l at the mountains,
4:25 I l and behold, there was no man;
4:26 I l and behold, the garden land
39: 6 As Zedekiah l on,
52:10 As Zedekiah l on,
Ez 1: 4 I l, a stormwind came from the North,
1: 5 four living creatures that l like this:
1: 9 their wings] l out on all their four sides;
1:15 As I l at the living creatures,
1:16 and all four of them l the same:
1:27 resembled his waist I saw what l like fire;
8: 2 looked up and saw a form that l like a man.
8: 5 I l toward the north and saw northward of

10: 1 I / and saw in the firmament above the
10: 2 As I / on, he entered.
10:22 Their faces / just like those I had seen
12: 7 the wall with my hand and, while they / on,
16: 5 No one / on you with pity or compassion to
20:17 But I / on them with pity,
41:21 was something that / like a wooden altar,
42:11 These / like the chambers to the north,
44: 4 and when I / I saw the glory of the LORD
Dn 1:15 after ten days they / healthier and better
2:34 While you / at the statue,
7: 6 After this I / and saw another beast,
8: 3 I / up and saw standing by the river a ram
10: 5 As I / up, I saw a man dressed in linen
10: 6 his arms and feet / like burnished bronze,
10:18 The one who / like a man touched me again
12: 5 I, Daniel, / and saw two others,
13:35 Through her tears she / up to heaven,
14:18 the king / at the table and cried aloud,
14:40 As he came to the den and / in,
Zec 2: 1 I raised my eyes and /;
2: 5 Again I raised my eyes and /:
Mt 14:19 five loaves and two fish, / up to heaven,
17: 8 / up they did not see anyone but Jesus.
19:26 Jesus / at them and said,
Mk 1:27 All who / on were amazed.
3: 5 He / around at them with anger,
7:34 then he / up to heaven and emitted a groan.
10:21 Then Jesus / at him with love and told him,
10:23 Jesus / around and said to his disciples,
14:67 she / at him more closely and said,
15:43 another who / forward to the reign of God.
16: 4 When they /, they found that the stone
Lk 1:48 he has / upon his servant in her lowliness;
2:38 / forward to the deliverance of Jerusalem.
6:10 / around at them all and said to the man,
19: 5 Jesus came to the spot he / up and said,
20:17 He / directly at them and said,
22:61 The Lord turned around and / at Peter,
23:51 and he / expectantly for the reign of God.
Jn 1:42 him to Jesus, who / at him and said,
6: 5 when Jesus / up and caught sight of a vast
9: 9 it was not but someone who / like him.
11:41 away the stone and Jesus / upward and said:
13:22 The disciples / at one another,
17: 1 these words, Jesus / up to heaven and said:
Acts 7:55 / to the sky above and saw the glory of
9:40 her eyes, then / at Peter and sat up.
10:11 object come down that / like a big canvas.
14: 9 and Paul / directly at him and saw that he
21: 4 We / for the disciples there and stayed
22:13 instant I regained my sight and / at him.
Rom 8:36 we are / upon as sheep to be slaughtered."
Gal 1:22 Christ in Judea had no idea what I / like;
2Tm 4: 8 / for his appearing with eager longing.
Jas 1:24 off and promptly forgets what he / like.
Rv 4: 7 while the fourth / like an eagle in flight.
11:12 to heaven in a cloud as their enemies / on.
13:13 come down from heaven to earth as men / on.
19:11 The heavens were opened, and as I / on,

LOOKING (71)

Gn 16: 5 she has been / on me with disdain.
18: 2 L up, he saw three men standing nearby.
24:64 Rebekah, too, was / about,
29: 2 L about, he saw a well in the open
31:32 If, with my kinsmen / on,
37:15 "What are you / for?"
37:16 "I am / for my brothers," he answered.
37:25 L up, they saw a caravan of Ishmaelites
Ex 2:12 L about and seeing no one,
25:20 with their faces / toward the propitiatory.
37: 9 with their faces / toward the propitiatory.
Jgs 13:19 While Manoah and his wife were / on,
1Sm 23:25 When Saul and his men came / for him,
2Sm 12:12 of all Israel, and with the sun / down.'"
1Kgs 20:40 while your servant was / here and there,
2Kgs 5: 7 can see he is only / for a quarrel with me!"
2Chr 26:19 while they were / at him in the house of
Tb 5:12 / for a hired man to travel with you son?"
Est 5: 1 inner courtyard, / toward the royal palace,
1Mc 4.19 appeared, / down from the mountain.
12:40 L for a way to seize and kill him,
2Mc 4: 5 but as a man / to the general and
7: 6 "The Lord God is / on,
7:15 L at the king, he said:
Jb 11:20 entreat your favor, but the wicked, / on,
Ps(s) 69: 4 My eyes have failed with / for my God.
Lam 4:17 eyes ever wasted away, / in vain for aid;
Ez 1:26 a throne could be seen, / like sapphire.
12: 3 of man, during the day while they are / on,
12: 3 for exile, and again while they are / on,
12: 4 exile in the daytime while they are / on;
12: 4 in the evening, again while they are / on,
23:15 their heads, all / like chariot warriors,
41:19 a man's face / at a palmtree on one side,
41:19 a lion's face / at a palmtree on the other;
Na 2: 5 wheel in the squares, / like firebrands,
Mt 6: 2 and streets like hypocrites / for applause.
26:16 kept / for an opportunity to hand him over.
27:55 women were present / on from a distance.
28: 5 I know you are / for Jesus the crucified,
Mk 1:37 they told him, "Everybody is / for you!"
5:32 / around to see the woman who had done it.
8:11 They were / for some heavenly sign from
9: 8 Suddenly / around they no longer saw
14:11 / for an opportune way to hand him over.
15:40 also women present / on from a distance.
16: 6 You are / for Jesus of Nazareth,
Lk 2:44 / for him among their relatives and
9:62 keeps / back is unfit for the reign of God."
13: 6 out / for fruit on it but did not find any.
19:47 meanwhile were / for a way to destroy him,
22: 6 then kept / for an opportunity to hand him
Jn 1:38 him, he asked them, "What are you / for?"
6:24 boats and went to Capernaum / for Jesus.
6:26 you are not / for me because you have seen
7: 1 the Jews were / for a chance to kill him.
7:11 naturally, the Jews were / for him,
20:15 Who is it you are / for?"
Acts 1:11 "why do you stand here / up at the skies?
10:21 men and said, "I am the man you are / for.
17:23 As I walked around / at your shrines,
27:13 they thought they had what they were / for,
Rom 10:20 who were not / for me I revealed myself."
2Cor 13: 3 / for a proof of the Christ who speaks in
Phil 2: 4 each of you / to others' interests rather
Heb 11:10 was / forward to the city with foundations,
11:26 of Egypt, for he was / to the reward.
11:27 as if he were / on the invisible God.
Jas 1:27 L after orphans and widows in their
1Pt 5: 8 a roaring lion / for someone to devour.
2Pt 3:12 / for the coming of the day of God and

LOOKOUT (8)

Nm 23:14 him to the / field on the top of Pisgah,
2Sm 18:24 and a / mounted to the roof of the gate
18:25 The / shouted to inform the king,
18:26 coming nearer, the / spied another runner.
18:27 Then the / said,
Mt 16: 6 "Be on the / against the yeast of the
Jn 11:56 They were on the / for Jesus,
2Pt 2:14 Constantly on the / for a woman,

LOOKOUTS (1)

1Sm 14:16 The / of Saul in Geba of Benjamin saw that

LOOKS (35)

Lv 14:35 'It / to me as if my house were infected.'
Nm 21: 8 and if anyone who has been bitten / at it,
Dt 11:12 a land which the LORD, your God, / after;
24:15 since he is poor and / forward to them.
1Sm 16: 7 appearance but the LORD / into the heart."
Tb 7: 2 young man / just like my kinsman Tobit!"
Jdt 10: 7 transformed in / and differently dressed,
11:21 other / so beautiful and speaks so wisely!"
Jb 15:22 the darkness, and / ever for the sword;
Ps(s) 14: 2 The LORD / down from heaven upon the
33:13 From heaven the LORD / down;
53: 3 God / down from heaven upon the children
104:32 He who / upon the earth,
112: 8 fear till he / down upon his foes.
113: 6 / upon the heavens and the earth below?
Prv 20: 4 when he / for the harvest,
Sg 7: 5 tower on Lebanon that / toward Damascus.
Wis 15:19 their / are they good or desirable beasts,
17: 4 and mute phantoms with somber / appeared.
Sir 11: 2 Praise not a man for his /
17: 7 He / with favor upon their hearts,
25:16 Wickedness changes a woman's /,
30: 5 Whom he / upon through life with joy,
Is 1:23 one of them loves a bribe and / for gifts.
Lam 3:50 Till the LORD from heaven / down and sees.
Ez 2: 6 their words nor be dismayed at their /,
3: 9 Fear them not, nor be dismayed at their /,
Dn 3:92 fire, and the fourth / like a son of God."
Hos 2: 9 if she / for them she shall not find them.
Mt 5:28 anyone who / lustfully at a woman has
Jn 6:40 that everyone who / upon the Son and
12:45 whoever / on me is seeing him who sent me.
Jas 1:23 like a man who / into a mirror at the face
1:24 he / at himself,
5: 7 He / forward to it patiently while the

LOOPED (1)

1Kgs 6:21 it with gold, and / it with golden chains.

LOOPING (1)

Jos 15: 3 from there, / around Karka,

LOOPS (13)

Ex 26: 4 Make / of violet yarn along the edge of
26: 5 There are to be fifty / along the edge of
26: 5 and fifty / along the edge of the
26: 5 the / are directly opposite each other.
26:10 Make fifty / along the edge of the end
26:10 and fifty / along the edge of the end
26:11 bronze clasps and put them into the /,
36:11 L of violet yarn were made along the edge
36:12 Fifty / were thus put on one inner sheet,
36:12 / on the inner sheet in the other set,
36:12 with the / directly opposite each other.
36:17 Fifty / were made along the edge of the
36:17 and fifty / along the edge of the

LOOSE (23)

Gn 49:21 hind let / which brings forth lovely fawns.
Ex 8:17 I will / swarms of flies upon you and your
28:28 belt of the ephod and not swing / from it.
39:21 of the ephod and did not swing / from it.
Lv 1:15 the priest shall snap its head / and
5: 8 Snapping its head / at the neck,
Jgs 15: 5 / in the standing grain of the Philistines,
16: 3 and the two gateposts, and tore them /.
1Sm 15:27 to go, Saul seized a / end of his mantle,
Jb 40:11 Let / the fury of your wrath;
Prv 6:26 a / woman may be scarcely a loaf of bread,
Is 5:27 None will have his waist belt /,
52: 2 L the bonds from your neck,
Ez 5:16 When I / against you the cruel,
13:13 In my fury I will let / stormwinds;
14:13 I let famine / upon it and cut off from it
23:25 I will let / my jealousy against you,
44:20 their heads nor let their hair hang /,
Mt 24:29 and the hosts of heaven will be shaken /.'
Lk 15:30 gone through your property with / women,
Acts 16:26 open and everyone's chains were pulled /.
27:40 They cut / the anchors and abandoned them
Rv 6:13 earth like figs shaken / by a mighty wind.

LOOSED (14)

Ex 15: 7 you / your wrath to consume them like
2Kgs 15:37 at that time that the LORD first / Rezin,
24: 2 The LORD / against him bands of Chaldeans,
24: 2 he / them against Judah to destroy it,
Jdt 6:14 came down to him from their city, / him,
Jb 30:11 Indeed, they have / their bonds;
39: 5 his freedom, and who has / him from bonds?
Ps(s) 78:49 He / against them his fierce anger,
116:16 you have / my bonds.
Mt 16:19 loosed on earth shall be / in heaven."
18:18 loosed on earth shall be held / in heaven.
Lk 1:64 his mouth was opened and his tongue /,

LOOSEN (1)

Lk 3:16 I am not fit to / his sandal strap.

LOOSENED (3)

Jdt 9: 2 who had immodestly / the maiden's girdle,
Jb 38:31 to the Pleiades, or / the bonds of Orion?
Sir 22:16 wooden beams is not / by an earthquake;

LOOSENING (1)

Is 28:24 / and harrowing his land for planting?

LOOSENS (1)

Jb 12:18 He / the bonds imposed by kings and leaves

LOOT (10)

Gn 34:29 and took for / whatever was in the houses.
Nm 31:32 left of the / which the soldiers had taken,
Dt 2:35 livestock and the / of the captured cities.
3: 7 but all the livestock and the / of each
Prv 1:19 This is the fate of everyone greedy of /:
Is 3:14 / wrested from the poor is in your house.
10: 6 I order him To seize plunder, carry off /,
33:23 spoils and the lame will carry off the /.
Hos 13:15 shall / his land of every precious thing.
Mt 23:25 leave the inside filled with / and lust!

LOOTED (2)

Nm 31:53 soldiers had / each one kept for himself.
1Sm 17:53 Philistines, the Israelites / their camp.

LOOTING (1)

Na 3: 1 lies, full of plunder, whose / never stops!

LOP (2)

2Sm 16: 9 Let me go over, please, and / off his head."
Dn 4:11 down the tree and / off its branches,

LOPPED-OFF (1)

Is 18: 5 hooks and the discarding of the / shoots.

LOPS (1)

Is 10:33 / off the boughs with terrible violence;

LORD (7827)

Gn 2: 4 the L God made the earth and the heavens
2: 5 for the L God had sent no rain upon the
2: 7 the L God formed man out of the clay of
2: 8 Then the L God planted a garden in Eden,
2: 9 Out of the ground the L God made various
2:15 The L God then took the man and settled
2:16 The L God gave man this order:
2:18 L God said: It is not good for the man
2:19 So the L God formed out of the ground
2:21 So the L God cast a deep sleep on the man,
2:22 The L God then built up into a woman the

LORD (cont.)
3: 1 of all the animals that the L God had made.
3: 8 When they heard the sound of the L God
3: 8 the L God among the trees of the garden.
3: 9 L God then called to the man and asked him,
3:13 The L God then asked the woman,
3:14 Then the L God said to the serpent:
3:21 his wife the L God made leather garments,
3:22 L God said: "See! The man has become
3:23 The L God therefore banished him from the
4: 1 have produced a man with the help of the L."
4: 3 to the L God from the fruit of the soil,
4: 4 The L looked with favor on Abel and his
4: 6 So the L said to Cain:
4: 9 Then the L asked Cain,
4:10 The L then said: "What have you done!
4:13 Cain said to the L: My punishment is too
4:15 L said to him. "If anyone kills Cain,
4:15 So the L put a mark on Cain,
4:26 time men began to invoke the L by name.
5:29 ground that the L has put under a curse,
6: 3 the L said: "My spirit shall not remain
6: 5 When the L saw how great was man's
6: 7 L said: "I will wipe out from the earth
6: 8 But Noah found favor with the L.
7: 1 Then the L said to Noah:
7: 5 Noah did just as the L had commanded him.
7: 9 with Noah, just as the L had commanded him.
7:16 Then the L shut him in.
7:23 L wiped out every living thing on earth:
8:20 Then Noah built an altar to the L,
8:21 When the L smelled the sweet odor,
9:26 "Blessed be the L, the God of Shem!
10: 9 was a mighty hunter by the grace of the L;
10: 9 a mighty hunter by the grace of the L."
11: 5 The L came down to see the city and the
11: 6 L said: "If now, while they are one
11: 8 Thus the L scattered them from there all
11: 9 the L confused the speech of all the world.
12: 1 L said to Abram: "Go forth
12: 4 in you," Abram went as the L directed him,
12: 7 The L appeared to Abram and said,
12: 7 there to the L who had appeared to him.
12: 8 to the LORD and invoked the L by name.
12:17 But the L struck Pharaoh and his household
13: 4 and there he invoked the L by name.
13:10 the L had destroyed Sodom and Gomorrah.)
13:13 in the sins they committed against the L.
13:14 After Lot had left, the L said to Abram:
13:18 There he built an altar to the L.
14:22 "I have sworn to the L,
15: 1 word of the L came to Abram in a vision:
15: 2 But Abram said, "O L GOD,
15: 4 Then the word of the L came to him:
15: 6 Abram put his faith in the L,
15: 7 "I am the L who brought you from Ur of
15: 8 "O L GOD," he asked, "How am I to know
15:13 Then the L said to Abram:
15:18 that the L made a covenant with Abram,
16: 2 "The L has kept me from bearing children.
16: 5 May the L decide between you and me!"
16:11 name him Ishmael, For the L has heard you,
16:13 To the L who spoke to her she gave a name,
17: 1 years old, the L appeared to him and said:
18: 1 The L appeared to Abraham by the terebinth
18:13 L said to Abraham: "Why did Sarah laugh
18:14 Is anything too marvelous for the L to do?
18:17 The L reflected: "Shall I hide
18:19 of the L by doing what is right and just,
18:19 so that the L may carry into effect for
18:20 Then the L said: "The outcry against Sodom
18:22 the L remained standing before Abraham.
18:26 L replied, "If I find fifty innocent people
18:27 "See how I am presuming to speak to my L,
18:30 "Let not my L grow impatient if I go on.
18:31 I have thus dared to speak to my L,
18:32 L grow angry if I speak up this last time.
18:33 The L departed as soon as he had finished
19:13 for the outcry reaching the L against
19:14 "the L is about to destroy the city."
19:18 "Oh, no, my l!"
19:24 at the same time the L rained down
19:24 and Gomorrah [from the L out of heaven].
20: 4 "O L, would you slay a man
21: 1 The L took note of Sarah as he had said he
21:33 and there he invoked by name the L,
22:11 "Yes, L," he answered.
22:14 now say, "On the mountain the L will see."
22:16 "I swear by myself, declares the L,
24: 1 and the L had blessed him in every way.
24: 3 thigh, and I will make you swear by the L,
24: 7 "The L, the God of heaven, who took me
24:12 L, God of my master Abraham,
24:21 not the L had made his errand successful.
24:26 man then bowed down in worship to the L,
24:27 "Blessed be the L,
24:27 the L has led me straight to the house of
24:31 "Come, blessed of the L!
24:35 "The L has blessed my master so
24:40 'The L, in whose presence
24:42 L, God of my master Abraham,
24:44 the L has decided upon for my master's son.'
24:48 in worship to the LORD, blessing the L,
24:50 "This thing comes from the L;
24:51 of your master's son, as the L has said."
24:52 he bowed to the ground before the L.
24:56 that the L has made my errand successful;
25:21 entreated the L on behalf of his wife,
25:21 The L heard his entreaty,
25:22 She went to consult the L,
26: 2 The L appeared to him and said:
26:12 Since the L blessed him,
26:22 said, "The L has now given us ample room,
26:24 same night the L appeared to him and said:
26:25 an altar there and invoked the L by name.
26:28 "We are convinced that the L is with you,
27:20 He answered, "The L,
27:27 of a field that the L has blessed!
28:13 was the L standing beside him and saying:
28:13 "I, the L, am the God of your forefather
28:16 exclaimed, "Truly, the L is in this spot,
28:21 my father's house, the L shall be my God.
29:31 When the L saw that Leah was unloved,
29:32 she said, "It means, 'The L saw my misery;
29:33 means, 'The L heard that I was unloved,'
29:35 I will give grateful praise to the L";
30:24 the L add another son to this one for me!"
31: 3 Then the L said to Jacob,
31:35 "Let not my l feel offended that I cannot
31:44 the L shall be a witness between us."
31:49 "May the L keep watch between you and me
32: 5 "Thus shall you say to my l Esau:
32: 6 I am sending my l this information in the
32:10 You told me, O L,
32:19 they have been sent as a gift to my l Esau;
33:13 "As my l can see, the children are frail.
33:14 Let my l, then, go on ahead of me,
33:14 of my children, until I join my l in Seir."
33:15 Please indulge me in this, my l."
38: 7 greatly offended the L; so the LORD took
38:10 the LORD, and the L took his life too.
39: 2 But since the L was with him,
39: 3 When his master saw that the L was with
39: 5 the L blessed the Egyptian's house for
39:21 was in prison, the L remained with Joseph;
39:23 since the L was with him and brought
40: 1 and baker gave offense to their l,
42:10 "No, my l," they replied.
42:30 "The man who is l of the country,"
42:33 the man who is l of the country said to us:
44: 7 "How can my l say such things?
44:16 "What can we say to my l?
44:16 Here we are, then, the slaves of my l—
44:18 "I beg you, my l,
44:18 let your servant speak earnestly to my l,
44:19 My l asked your servants,
44:20 So we said to my l,
44:22 We replied to my l,
44:24 we reported to him the words of my l.
44:33 in place of the boy as the slave of my l,
45: 8 father to Pharaoh, l of all his household,
45: 9 God has made me l of all Egypt;
47:18 "We cannot hide from my l that,
47:18 spent and our livestock made over to my l,
47:25 to my l that we can be Pharaoh's slaves."
49:18 "[I long for your deliverance, O L
Ex 3: 2 There an angel of the L appeared to him in
3: 4 When the L saw him coming over to look at
3: 7 L said, "I have witnessed the affliction
3:15 The L, the God of your fathers,
3:16 The L, the God of your fathers,
3:18 The L, the God of the Hebrews,
3:18 that we may offer sacrifice to the L,
4: 1 they may say, 'The L did not appear to you.'"
4: 2 The L therefore asked him,
4: 3 L then said, "Throw it on the ground."
4: 4 put out your hand," the L said to him,
4: 5 may believe," he continued, "that the L,
4: 6 Again the L said to him,
4: 7 L then said, "Now, put your hand back
4:10 said to the L, "If you please, Lord, I have
4:11 The L said to him,
4:11 Is it not I, the L?
4:13 Yet he insisted, "If you please, L,
4:14 the L became angry with Moses and said,
4:19 In Midian the L said to Moses,
4:21 The L said to him,
4:22 Thus says the L: Israel is my son,
4:24 the L came upon Moses and would have
4:27 The L said to Aaron,
4:28 him of all the L had said in sending him,
4:30 them everything the L had said to Moses,
4:31 and when they heard that the L was
5: 1 to Pharaoh and said, "Thus says the L,
5: 2 Pharaoh answered, "Who is the L,
5: 2 I do not know the L:
5: 3 that we may offer sacrifice to the L,
5:17 'Let us go and offer sacrifice to the L.
5:21 to them, "The L look upon you and judge!
5:22 to the L and said, "Lord, why do you
6: 1 Then the L answered Moses,
6: 2 God also said to Moses, "I am the L.
6: 3 Abraham, Isaac and Jacob, but my name, L,
6: 6 I am the L.
6: 7 You will know that I, the L,
6: 8 I, the L!"
6:10 Then the L said to Moses,
6:12 But Moses protested to the L,
6:13 Still, the L, to bring the Israelites out
6:26 and this the Moses to whom the L said,
6:28 day the L spoke to Moses in Egypt he said,
6:29 to Moses in Egypt he said, "I am the L.
6:30 But Moses protested to the L,
7: 1 The L answered him, "See!
7: 5 the Egyptians may learn that I am the L,
7: 6 and Aaron did as the L had commanded
7: 8 The L told Moses and Aaron,
7:10 to Pharaoh and did as the L had commanded.
7:13 listen to them, just as the L had foretold.
7:14 Then the L said to Moses,
7:16 The L, the God of the Hebrews,
7:17 L now says: This is how you shall know
7:17 This is how you shall know that I am the L.
7:19 The L then said to Moses, "Say to Aaron:
7:20 and Aaron did as the L had commanded.
7:22 and Aaron, just as the L had foretold.
7:25 passed after the L had struck the river.
7:26 Then the L said to Moses,
7:26 Thus says the L: Let my people go
8: 1 The L then told Moses, "Say to Aaron:
8: 4 "Pray the L to remove the frogs from me
8: 4 the people go to offer sacrifice to the L.
8: 6 may learn that there is none like the L,
8: 8 Moses implored the L to fulfill the
8: 9 and the L did as Moses had asked.
8:11 listen to them just as the L had foretold.
8:12 Thereupon the L said to Moses,
8:15 listen to them, just as the L had foretold.
8:16 Again the L told Moses,
8:16 Thus says the L: Let my people go
8:18 that I am the L in the midst of the earth.
8:20 This the L did.
8:22 so, for the sacrifices we offer to the L,
8:23 in the desert to offer sacrifice to the L,
8:24 go to offer sacrifice to the L your God,
8:25 pray to the L that the flies may depart
8:25 the people go to offer sacrifice to the L.
8:26 Pharaoh's presence, he prayed to the L;
8:27 and the L did as Moses had asked.
9: 1 Then the L said to Moses,
9: 1 Thus says the L, the God of the Hebrews:
9: 3 the L will afflict all your livestock in
9: 4 But the L will distinguish between the
9: 5 L added, "Tomorrow the LORD shall
9: 6 And on the next day the L did so.
9: 8 Then the L said to Moses and Aaron,
9:12 But the L made Pharaoh obstinate,
9:12 them, just as the L had foretold to Moses.
9:13 Then the L told Moses,
9:13 Thus says the L, the God of the Hebrews:
9:20 servants feared the warning of the L
9:21 did not take the warning of the L to heart
9:22 The L then said to Moses,
9:23 the L sent forth hail and peals of thunder.
9:23 L rained down hail upon the land of Egypt;
9:27 The L is just;
9:28 Pray to the L,
9:29 the city I will extend my hands to the L;
9:30 I know, do not yet fear the L God."
9:33 the city, he extended his hands to the L.
9:35 go, as the L had foretold through Moses.
10: 1 Then the L said to Moses,
10: 2 them, so that you may know that I am the L.
10: 3 to Pharaoh and told him, "Thus says the L,
10: 7 Let the men go to worship the L,
10: 8 to them, "You may go and worship the L,
10: 9 That is what a feast of the L means to us."
10:10 "The L help you,"
10:11 Just you men can go and worship the L.
10:12 The L then said to Moses,
10:13 and the L set an east wind blowing over
10:16 and said, "I have sinned against the L,
10:17 me my sin once more, and pray the L,
10:18 presence of Pharaoh, he prayed to the L,
10:19 and the L changed the wind to a very
10:20 of Egypt, the L made Pharaoh obstinate,
10:21 Then the L said to Moses,
10:24 and Aaron and said, "Go and worship the L.
10:25 and holocausts to offer up to the L,
10:26 of them we must sacrifice to the L our God,
10:27 But the L made Pharaoh obstinate,
11: 1 Then the L told Moses,
11: 3 The L indeed made the Egyptians
11: 4 Moses then said, "Thus says the L:
11: 7 so that you may know how the L
11: 9 The L said to Moses,
11:10 presence, the L made Pharaoh obstinate,
12: 1 The L said to Moses and Aaron in the land
12:11 It is the Passover of the L.
12:12 I, the L!
12:14 shall celebrate with pilgrimage to the L,
12:23 For the L will go by,
12:23 the L will pass over that door and not let
12:25 which the L will give you as he promised.
12:27 'This is the Passover sacrifice of the L,
12:28 as the L had commanded Moses and Aaron.
12:29 At midnight the L slew every first-born in
12:31 Go and worship the L as you said.
12:36 The L indeed had made the Egyptians so

12:41 *L* left the land of Egypt on this very date.
12:42 This was a night of vigil for the *L*,
12:42 for the *L* throughout their generations.
12:43 The *L* said to Moses and Aaron,
12:48 wish to celebrate the Passover of the *L*,
12:50 as the *L* had commanded Moses and Aaron.
12:51 On that same day the *L* brought the
13: 1 The *L* spoke to Moses and said,
13: 3 a strong hand that the *L* brought you away.
13: 5 you must celebrate this rite, after the *L*,
13: 6 day shall also be a festival to the *L*.
13: 8 the *L* did for me when I came out of Egypt.'
13: 9 the law of the *L* will ever be on your lips,
13: 9 strong hand the *L* brought you out of Egypt.
13:11 "When the *L*, your God, has brought you
13:12 to the *L* every son that opens the womb;
13:12 of your animals shall belong to the *L*.
13:14 strong hand the *L* brought us out of Egypt,
13:15 the *L* killed every first-born in the land
13:15 That is why I sacrifice to the *L*
13:16 strong hand the *L* brought us out of Egypt."
13:21 The *L* preceded them,
14: 1 Then the *L* said to Moses,
14: 4 the Egyptians will know that I am the *L*."
14: 8 So obstinate had the *L* made Pharaoh that
14:10 In great fright they cried out to the *L*.
14:13 the victory the *L* will win for you today.
14:14 The *L* himself will fight for you;
14:15 Then the *L* said to Moses,
14:18 The Egyptians shall know that I am the *L*,
14:21 and the *L* swept the sea with a strong east
14:24 In the night watch just before dawn the *L*
14:25 because the *L* was fighting for them
14:26 Then the *L* told Moses,
14:27 sea, when the *L* hurled them into its midst.
14:30 Thus the *L* saved Israel on that day from
14:31 that the *L* had shown against the Egyptians,
14:31 they feared the *L* and believed in him and
15: 1 and the Israelites sang this song to the *L*:
15: 1 I will sing to the *L*,
15: 2 My strength and my courage is the *L*,
15: 3 The LORD is a warrior, *L* is his name!
15: 6 Your right hand, O *L*,
15: 6 magnificent in power your right hand, O *L*,
15:11 Who is like to you among the gods, O *L*?
15:16 frozen like stone, while your people, O *L*,
15:17 your seat, O *L*, the sanctuary, O LORD,
15:18 The *L* shall reign forever and ever.
15:19 the *L* made the waters of the sea flow back
15:21 Sing to the *L*,
15:25 he appealed to the *L*,
15:25 It was here that the *L*,
15:26 you really listen to the voice of the *L*,
15:26 for I, the *L*, am your healer."
16: 4 Then the *L* said to Moses,
16: 6 *L* who brought you out of the land of Egypt;
16: 7 morning you will see the glory of the *L*,
16: 8 *L* gives you flesh to eat in the evening,"
16: 8 is not against us, but against the *L*."
16: 9 Present yourselves before the *L*,
16:10 the glory of the *L* appeared in the cloud!
16:11 The *L* spoke to Moses and said,
16:12 bread, so that you may know that I, the *L*,
16:15 the bread which the *L* has given you to eat.
16:16 "Now, this is what the *L* has commanded.
16:23 told them, "That is what the *L* prescribed.
16:23 rest, the sabbath, sacred to the *L*.
16:25 today, for today is the sabbath of the *L*.
16:28 Then the *L* said to Moses,
16:29 The *L* has given you the sabbath.
16.32 said, "This is what the *L* has commanded.
16:33 the *L* in safekeeping for your descendants."
16:34 safekeeping, as the *L* had commanded Moses.
17: 1 journeyed by stages, as the *L* directed,
17: 2 Why do you put the *L* to a test?"
17: 4 So Moses cried out to the *L*,
17: 5 The *L* answered Moses,
17: 7 tested the LORD, saying, "Is the *L* in our
17:14 Then the *L* said to Moses,
17:16 LORD takes in hand his banner; the *L* will
18: 1 how the *L* had brought Israel out of Egypt.
18: 8 all that the *L* had done to Pharaoh
18: 8 and how the *L* had come to their rescue.
18: 9 goodness that the *L* had shown Israel
18:10 "Blessed be the *L*,"
18:11 the *L* is a deity great beyond any other;
19: 3 Then the *L* called to him and said,
19: 7 that the *L* had ordered him to tell them,
19: 8 together, "Everything the *L* has said,
19: 8 back to the *L* the response of the people.
19: 9 *L* the response of the people, the LORD
19:10 the response of the people, the *L* added,
19:11 for on the third day the *L* will come down
19:18 smoke, for the *L* came down upon it in fire.
19:20 the *L* came down to the top of Mount Sinai,
19:21 Then the *L* told Moses,
19:21 through toward the *L* in order to see him;
19:22 approach the *L* must sanctify themselves;
19:23 Moses said to the *L*,
19:24 The *L* repeated, "Go down now!
19:24 not break through to come up to the *L*;
20: 2 "I, the *L*, am your God,
20: 5 For I, the *L*, your God, am a jealous God,
20: 7 "You shall not take the name of the *L*,
20: 7 For the *L* will not leave unpunished him
20:10 the seventh day is the sabbath of the *L*,
20:11 days the *L* made the heavens and the earth,
20:11 That is why the *L* has blessed the sabbath
20:12 have a long life in the land which the *L*,
20:22 The *L* told Moses,
22:10 the custodian shall swear by the *L* that he
22:19 to any god, except to the *L* alone,
23:17 shall all your men appear before the *L* GOD.
23:19 soil you shall bring to the house of the *L*,
23:25 The *L*, your God, you shall worship;
24: 1 himself was told, "Come up to the *L*,
24: 2 but Moses alone is to come close to the *L*;
24: 3 all the words and ordinances of the *L*,
24: 3 will do everything that the *L* has told us."
24: 4 then wrote down all the words of the *L* and,
24: 5 young bulls as peace offerings to the *L*,
24: 7 who answered, "All that the *L* has said,
24: 8 covenant which the *L* has made with you
24:12 The *L* said to Moses, "Come up to me
24:16 glory of the *L* settled upon Mount Sinai.
24:17 To the Israelites the glory of the *L* was
25: 1 This is what the *L* then said to Moses:
27:21 them before the *L* in the meeting tent,
28:12 his shoulders as a reminder before the *L*.
28:29 heart as a constant reminder before the *L*.
28:30 whenever he enters the presence of the *L*.
28:36 as on a seal engraving, "Sacred to the *L*."
28:38 so that they may find favor with the *L*.
29:11 Then slaughter the bullock before the *L*,
29:18 a sweet smelling oblation to the *L*.
29:23 food that you have set before the *L*,
29:24 wave them as a wave offering before the *L*.
29:25 as a sweet-smelling oblation to the *L*.
29:26 wave it as a wave offering before the *L*;
29:28 contribution, their contribution to the *L*.
29:41 this as a sweet-smelling oblation to the *L*.
29:42 the *L* at the entrance of the meeting tent,
29:46 They shall know that I, the *L*,
29:46 them out of the land of Egypt, so I, the *L*,
30: 8 established incense offering before the *L*.
30:10 This altar is most sacred to the *L*."
30:11 *L* also said to Moses, "When you take
30:12 shall give the *L* a forfeit for his life,
30:13 a half-shekel is a contribution to the *L*.
30:14 group must give this contribution to the *L*.
30:15 the *L* to pay the forfeit for their lives.
30:16 be the Israelites' reminder before the *L*,
30:17 *L* said to Moses, "For ablutions you shall
30:20 the *L* they must wash their hands and feet,
30:22 *L* said to Moses, "Take the finest spices:
30:34 The *L* told Moses, "Take these aromatic
30:37 you must treat it as sacred to the *L*.
31: 1 *L* said to Moses, "See, I have chosen
31:12 *L* said to Moses, "You must also tell
31:13 generations, to show that it is I, the *L*,
31:15 sabbath of complete rest, sacred to the *L*.
31:17 days the *L* made the heavens and the earth,
31:18 When the *L* had finished speaking to Moses
32: 5 proclaimed, "Tomorrow is a feast of the *L*."
32: 7 *L* said to Moses, "Go down at once to
32: 9 this people is," continued the *L* to Moses.
32:11 the LORD, his God, saying, "Why, O *L*,
32:14 So the *L* relented in the punishment he had
32:22 Aaron replied, "Let not my *l* be angry.
32:26 the camp and cried, "Whoever is for the *L*,
32:27 him, and he told them, "Thus says the *L*,
32:29 "Today you have been dedicated to the *L*,
32:30 I will go up to the *L*,
32:31 So Moses went back to the *L* and said,
32:33 *L* answered, "Him only who has sinned
32:35 Thus the *L* smote the people for having had
33: 1 *L* told Moses, "You and the people
33: 5 *L* said to Moses, "Tell the Israelites:
33: 7 Anyone who wished to consult the *L* would
33: 9 its entrance while the *L* spoke with Moses.
33:11 The *L* used to speak to Moses face to face,
33:12 said to the *L*, "You, indeed, are telling
33:14 "I myself," the *L* answered,
33:17 *L* said to Moses, "This request,
33:19 your presence I will pronounce my name, *L*';
33:21 Here," continued the *L*,
34: 1 *L* said to Moses, "Cut two stone tablets
34: 4 up Mount Sinai as the *L* had commanded him,
34: 5 the *L* stood with him there and proclaimed
34: 5 with him there and proclaimed his name, *L*."
34: 6 Thus the *L* passed before him and cried out,
34: 6 "The LORD, the *L*, a merciful and gracious
34: 9 he said, "If I find favor with you, O *L*,
34:10 "Here, then," said the *L*,
34:10 awe-inspiring are the deeds which I, the *L*,
34:14 other god, for the *L* is 'the Jealous One';
34:23 before the *L*, the LORD God of Israel.
34:24 three times a year to appear before the *L*,
34:26 soil you shall bring to the house of the *L*,
34:27 Then the *L* said to Moses,
34:28 with the *L* for forty days and forty nights,
34:29 radiant while he conversed with the *L*.
34:32 all that the *L* had told him on Mount Sinai.
34:34 the presence of the *L* to converse with him,
34:35 until he went in to converse with the *L*.
35: 1 is what the *L* has commanded to be done.
35: 2 as the sabbath of complete rest to the *L*.
35: 4 "This is what the *L* has commanded:
35: 5 Take up among you a collection for the *L*.
35: 5 shall bring as a contribution to the *L*,
35:10 and make all that the *L* has commanded:
35:21 brought a contribution to the *L* for the
35:22 presented an offering of gold to the *L*.
35:24 of silver or bronze offered it to the *L*;
35:29 brought to the *L* such voluntary offerings
35:29 the *L* had commanded Moses to have done.
35:30 "See, the *L* has chosen Bezalel,
36: 1 experts whom the *L* has endowed with skill
36: 1 the sanctuary, just as the *L* has commanded."
36: 2 experts whom the *L* had endowed with skill,
36: 5 work which the *L* has commanded us to do."
38:22 who made all that the *L* commanded Moses,
39: 1 for Aaron, as the *L* had commanded Moses.
39: 5 as the *L* had commanded Moses.
39: 7 just as the *L* had commanded Moses.
39:21 was just as the *L* had commanded Moses.
39:26 just as the *L* had commanded Moses.
39:29 scarlet yarn, as the *L* had commanded Moses.
39:30 "Sacred to the *L*."
39:31 ribbon, as the *L* had commanded Moses.
39:32 work just as the *L* had commanded Moses.
39:42 work just as the *L* had commanded Moses.
39:43 work was done just as the *L* had commanded,
40: 1 Then the *L* said to Moses.
40:16 did exactly as the *L* had commanded him.
40:19 of the tent, as the *L* had commanded him.
40:21 commandments, as the *L* had commanded him.
40:23 before the *L*, as the LORD had commanded
40:25 set up the lamps before the *L* as the LORD
40:25 before the LORD as the *L* had commanded
40:27 incense, as the *L* had commanded him.
40:29 on it, as the *L* had commanded him.
40:32 the altar, as the *L* had commanded Moses.
40:34 and the glory of the *L* filled the Dwelling.
40:35 and the glory of the *L* filled the Dwelling.
40:38 cloud of the *L* was seen over the Dwelling;
40:38 incense, as the *L* had commanded him.
Lv 1: 1 The *L* called Moses,
1: 2 to bring an animal offering to the *L*,
1: 3 To find favor with the *L*,
1: 5 then slaughter the bull before the *L*,
1: 9 a sweet-smelling oblation to the *L*.
1:11 the *L* at the north side of the altar.
1:13 a sweet-smelling oblation to the *L*.
1:14 he offers a bird as a holocaust to the *L*,
1:17 a sweet-smelling oblation to the *L*.
2: 1 to bring a cereal offering to the *L*,
2: 2 a sweet-smelling oblation to the *L*.
2: 3 It is a most sacred oblation to the *L*.
2: 8 of these ways you shall bring to the *L*,
2: 9 as a sweet-smelling oblation to the *L*.
2:10 It is a most sacred oblation to the *L*.
2:11 you present to the *L* shall be unleavened,
2:11 leaven or honey as an oblation to the *L*.
2:12 to the *L* in the offering of first fruits,
2:13 to the *L* shall be seasoned with salt.
2:14 cereal offering of first fruits to the *L*,
2:16 the frankincense, as an oblation to the *L*.
3: 1 the *L* either a male or a female animal,
3: 3 *L* the fatty membrane over the inner organs,
3: 5 as a sweet-smelling oblation to the *L*.
3: 6 he presents to the *L* is from the flock,
3: 7 offering, he shall bring it before the *L*,
3: 9 As an oblation to the *L* he shall present
3:12 a goat, he shall bring it before the *L*,
3:14 he shall offer as an oblation to the *L*
3:16 All the fat belongs to the *L*.
4: 1 The *L* said to Moses,
4: 2 the *L* by doing one of the forbidden things,
4: 3 guilty, he shall present to the *L* a young,
4: 4 of the meeting tent, before the *L*,
4: 4 on its head and slaughter it before the *L*.
4: 6 shall sprinkle it seven times before the *L*,
4: 7 which is before the *L* in the meeting tent.
4:13 does something that the *L* has forbidden
4:15 the meeting tent, and here, before the *L*,
4:15 bullock has been slaughtered before the *L*,
4:17 shall sprinkle it seven times before the *L*,
4:18 which is before the *L* in the meeting tent.
4:22 forbidden by some commandment of the *L*,
4:24 the goat as a sin offering before the *L*,
4:27 forbidden by the commandments of the *L*,
4:31 on the altar for an odor pleasing to the *L*.
4:35 altar with the other oblations of the *L*.
5: 6 to the *L* a female animal from the flock,
5: 7 he shall bring to the *L* as the sin
5:12 altar with the other oblations of the *L*.
5:14 *L* said to Moses, "If someone commits a sin
5:15 he shall bring to the *L* as his guilt
5:17 forbidden by some commandment of the *L*,
5:19 penalty of the guilt must be paid to the *L*."
5:20 The *L* said to Moses,
5:21 commits a sin of dishonesty against the *L*
5:25 he shall bring to the *L* an unblemished ram
5:26 shall make atonement for him before the *L*,
6: 1 *L* said to Moses, "Give Aaron and his sons
6: 7 sons shall first present it before the *L*,
6: 8 a sweet-smelling oblation to the *L*.
6:10 their portion from the oblations of the *L*;

LORD (cont.)

6:11 *L* perpetually throughout your generations.
6:12 The *L* said to Moses,
6:13 to the *L* [on the day he is anointed]:
6:14 it as a sweet-smelling oblation to the *L*.
6:15 the *L* the whole offering shall be burned.
6:17 *L* said to Moses, "Tell Aaron and his sons:
6:18 are slaughtered, there also, before the *L*,
7: 5 burn on the altar as an oblation to the *L*.
7:11 offerings that are presented to the *L*.
7:14 one portion as a contribution to the *L*;
7:20 of a peace offering belonging to the *L*,
7:21 of a peace offering belonging to the *L*,
7:22 *L* said to Moses, "Tell the Israelites:
7:25 from which an oblation is made to the *L*,
7:28 *L* said to Moses, "Tell the Israelites:
7:29 He who presents a peace offering to the *L*
7:30 with his own hands the oblations to the *L*.
7:30 be waved as a wave offering before the *L*.
7:35 share from the oblations of the *L*,
7:35 he called them to be the priests of the *L*;
7:36 on the day he anointed them the *L* ordered
7:38 which the *L* enjoined on Moses at Mount
7:38 of Sinai to bring their offerings to the *L*.
8: 1 *L* said to Moses, "Take Aaron and his sons,
8: 4 And Moses did as the *L* had commanded.
8: 5 them what the *L* had ordered to be done.
8: 9 forehead, as the *L* had commanded him to do.
8:13 on them, as the *L* had commanded him to do.
8:17 the camp, as the *L* had commanded him to do.
8:21 oblation to the *L*, as the LORD
8:26 before the *L* he took one unleavened cake,
8:27 wave them as a wave offering before the *L*.
8:28 a sweet-smelling oblation to the *L*.
8:29 waved it as a wave offering before the *L*;
8:34 The *L* has commanded that what has been
8:35 carrying out the prescriptions of the *L*;
8:36 all that the *L* had commanded through Moses.
9: 2 blemish, and offer them before the *L*.
9: 4 offering, to sacrifice them before the *L*,
9: 4 for today the *L* will reveal himself to you."
9: 5 had come forward and stood before the *L*,
9: 6 "This is what the *L* orders you to do,
9: 6 the glory of the *L* may be revealed to you.
9: 7 atonement for them, as the *L* has commanded.
9:10 sin offering, as the *L* had commanded Moses;
9:21 legs as a wave offering before the *L*,
9:23 of the *L* was revealed to all the people.
10: 1 they offered up before the *L* profane fire,
10: 3 said to Aaron, "This is as the *L* said:
10: 7 the anointing oil of the *L* is upon you."
10: 8 The *L* said to Aaron,
10:11 that the *L* has given them through Moses."
10:12 left over from the oblations of the *L*,
10:13 is your due from the oblations of the *L*,
10:15 be waved as a wave offering before the *L*.
10:15 ordinance, as the *L* has commanded."
10:17 and make atonement for them before the *L*.
10:19 offering and holocaust before the *L* today,
10:19 would it have been pleasing to the *L*?"
11: 1 The *L* said to Moses and Aaron,
11:44 For I, the *L*, am your God;
11:45 Since I, the *L*, brought you up
12: 1 The *L* said to Moses,
12: 7 up before the *L* to make atonement for her,
13: 1 The *L* said to Moses and Aaron,
14: 1 The *L* said to Moses, "This is the law
14:11 the *L* at the entrance of the meeting tent.
14:12 them as a wave offering before the *L*.
14:16 sprinkle it seven times before the *L*.
14:18 make atonement for him before the *L*.
14:20 offering, on the altar before the *L*.
14:23 entrance of the meeting tent before the *L*.
14:24 wave them as a wave offering before the *L*.
14:27 sprinkle it seven times before the *L*.
14:29 he make atonement for him before the *L*.
14:31 the *L* for the man who is to be purified.
14:33 The *L* said to Moses and Aaron,
15: 1 The *L* said to Moses and Aaron,
15:14 or two pigeons, and going before the *L*,
15:15 atonement before the *L* for the man's flow.
15:30 before the *L* for her unclean flow.
16: 1 the *L* spoke to Moses and said to him,
16: 7 the *L* at the entrance of the meeting tent,
16: 8 one is for the *L* and which for Azazel.
16: 9 goat that is determined by lot for the *L*,
16:10 Azazel he shall set alive before the *L*,
16:12 embers from the altar before the *L*,
16:13 the *L* he shall put incense on the fire,
16:18 the *L* and make atonement for it also.
16:30 be cleansed of all your sins before the *L*,
16:34 was it done, as the *L* had commanded Moses.
17: 1 The *L* said to Moses,
17: 2 This is what the *L* has commanded.
17: 4 offering to the *L* in front of his Dwelling,
17: 5 shall henceforth offer to the *L*,
17: 5 them there as peace offerings to the *L*.
17: 6 splash the blood on the altar of the *L*
17: 6 burn the fat for an odor pleasing to the *L*.
17: 9 of the meeting tent to offer it to the *L*,
18: 1 *L* said to Moses, "Speak to the Israelites
18: 2 I, the *L*, am your God.
18: 4 I, the *L*, am your God.
18: 5 I am the *L*.
18: 6 I am the *L*.
18:21 I am the *L*.
18:30 I, the *L*, am your God."
19: 1 *L* said to Moses, "Speak to the whole
19: 2 Be holy, for I, the *L* your God, am holy.
19: 3 I, the *L*, am your God.
19: 4 I, the *L*, am your God.
19: 5 sacrifice your peace offering to the *L*,
19: 8 having profaned what is sacred to the *L*.
19:10 I, the *L*, am your God.
19:12 I am the *L*.
19:14 I am the *L*.
19:16 I am the *L*.
19:18 I am the *L*.
19:21 tent a ram as his guilt offering to the *L*.
19:22 before the *L* for the sin he has committed,
19:24 to the *L* as a thanksgiving feast to him.
19:25 I, the *L*, am your God.
19:28 I am the *L*.
19:30 I am the *L*.
19:31 I, the *L*, am your God.
19:32 I am the *L*.
19:34 I, the *L*, am your God.
19:36 I, the *L*, am your God, who brought
19:37 I am the *L*."
20: 1 The *L* said to Moses,
20: 7 for I, the *L*, your God, am holy
20: 8 therefore, to observe what I, the *L*,
20:24 am giving it to you as your own, I, the *L*,
20:26 for I, the *L*, am sacred, I,
21: 1 *L* said to Moses, "Speak to Aaron's sons,
21: 6 they offer up the oblations of the *L*,
21: 8 treat him as sacred, because I, the *L*,
21:12 he is dedicated to his God, to me, the *L*.
21:15 I, the *L*, have made him sacred."
21:16 *L* said to Moses, "Speak to Aaron
21:21 near to offer up the oblations of the *L*;
21:23 that are sacred to me, for it is I, the *L*,
22: 1 *L* said to Moses, "Tell Aaron and his sons
22: 2 I am the *L*.
22: 3 which the Israelites consecrate to the *L*,
22: 3 I am the *L*.
22: 8 I am the *L*.
22: 9 I am the *L* who have consecrated them.
22:15 which the Israelites contribute to the *L*
22:16 it is I, the *L*,
22:17 *L* said to Moses, "Speak to Aaron
22:18 or as a freewill offering to the *L*,
22:21 anyone presents a peace offering to the *L*
22:22 or ringworm, you shall not offer to the *L*;
22:22 on the altar as an oblation to the *L*.
22:24 or cut off you shall not offer to the *L*.
22:26 *L* said to Moses, "When an ox or a lamb
22:27 to be offered as an oblation to the *L*.
22:29 offer a thanksgiving sacrifice to the *L*,
22:30 I am the *L*.
22:31 observe the commandments which I, the *L*,
22:32 in the midst of the Israelites I, the *L*,
22:33 out of the land of Egypt, that I, the *L*,
23: 1 *L* said to Moses, "Speak to the Israelites
23: 2 The following are the festivals of the *L*,
23: 3 shall belong to the *L* wherever you dwell.
23: 4 are the festivals of the *L* which you shall
23: 5 The Passover of the *L* falls on the
23: 8 days you shall offer an oblation to the *L*.
23: 9 *L* said to Moses, "Speak to the Israelites
23:11 the *L* that it may be acceptable for you.
23:12 you shall offer to the *L* for a holocaust
23:13 as a sweet-smelling oblation to the *L*;
23:16 present the new cereal offering to the *L*.
23:17 offering of your first fruits to the *L*,
23:18 you shall offer to the *L* a holocaust of
23:18 as a sweet-smelling oblation to the *L*.
23:20 two lambs as a wave offering before the *L*;
23:20 sacred to the *L* and belong to the priest.
23:22 I, the *L*, am your God."
23:23 *L* said to Moses, "Tell the Israelites:
23:25 and you shall offer an oblation to the *L*."
23:26 *L* said to Moses, "The tenth of this
23:27 yourselves and offer an oblation to the *L*.
23:28 atonement is made for you before the *L*,
23:33 *L* said to Moses, "Tell the Israelites:
23:36 days you shall offer an oblation to the *L*,
23:36 assembly and offer an oblation to the *L*.
23:37 are the festivals of the *L* on which you
23:37 to the *L* holocausts and cereal offerings,
23:38 offerings that you present to the *L*.
23:39 a pilgrim feast of the *L* for a whole week.
23:40 a week you shall make merry before the *L*,
23:41 shall keep this pilgrim feast of the *L*
23:43 I, the *L*, am your God."
23:44 to the Israelites the festivals of the *L*.
24: 1 *L* said to Moses, "Order the Israelites
24: 3 the lamps to burn before the *L* regularly,
24: 4 lampstand, to burn regularly before the *L*.
24: 6 pile, on the pure gold table before the *L*.
24: 7 which shall serve as an oblation to the *L*,
24: 8 shall be set out afresh before the *L*,
24: 9 among the various oblations to the *L*,
24:12 from the *L* should settle the case for them.
24:13 The *L* then said to Moses,
24:16 the name of the *L* shall be put to death.
24:22 I, the *L*, am your God."
24:23 out the command that the *L* had given Moses.
25: 1 The *L* said to Moses on Mount Sinai,
25: 2 the land, too, keep a sabbath for the *L*.
25: 4 have complete rest, a sabbath for the *L*,
25:17 I, the *L*, am your God.
25:38 I, the *L*, am your God,
25:43 Do not *l* it over them harshly,
25:46 *l* it harshly over any of the Israelites,
25:53 *l* it over him harshly under your very eyes.
25:55 them out of the land of Egypt, I, the *L*,
26: 1 for I, the *L*,
26: 2 I am the *L*.
26:13 for it is I, the *L*,
26:44 for I, the *L*,
26:45 very eyes of the Gentiles, that I, the *L*,
26:46 decrees and laws which the *L* had Moses
27: 1 *L* said to Moses, "Speak to the Israelites
27: 2 of offering one or more persons to the *L*,
27: 9 the *L* is an animal that may be sacrificed,
27: 9 every such animal, when vowed to the *L*,
27:11 If the animal vowed to the *L* is unclean
27:14 dedicates his house as sacred to the *L*,
27:16 to the *L* is a piece of his hereditary land,
27:21 it shall be released as sacred to the *L*;
27:22 field that some man dedicates to the *L*
27:23 shall be given as sacred to the *L*;
27:26 which as such already belongs to the *L*,
27:26 ox or a sheep, it shall be ceded to the *L*;
27:28 which a man vows as doomed to the *L*,
27:28 thus doomed becomes most sacred to the *L*.
27:30 in fruit from the trees, belong to the *L*,
27:32 ceding to the *L* as sacred every tenth animal
27:34 These are the commandments which the *L*

Nm 1: 1 the *L* said to Moses in the meeting tent in
1:19 house, as the *L* had commanded Moses.
1:48 For the *L* had told Moses.
1:54 fulfilled as the *L* had commanded Moses.
2: 1 The *L* said to Moses and Aaron:
2:33 for so the *L* had commanded Moses.
2:34 did just as the *L* had commanded Moses;
3: 1 that the *L* spoke to Moses on Mount Sinai.
3: 4 fire before the *L* in the desert of Sinai,
3: 4 they met death in the presence of the *L*,
3: 5 Now the *L* said to Moses:
3:11 *L* said to Moses, "It is I who have chosen
3:13 They belong to me; I am the *L*."
3:14 The *L* said to Moses in the desert of Sinai,
3:16 with the command the *L* had given him.
3:40 *L* then said to Moses, "Take a census
3:41 Then assign the Levites to me, the *L*,
3:42 the Israelites, as the *L* had commanded him.
3:44 *L* said to Moses: "Take the Levites
3:45 I am the *L*.
3:51 and his sons, as the *L* had commanded him.
4: 1 The *L* said to Moses and Aaron:
4:17 The *L* said to Moses and Aaron:
4:21 The *L* said to Moses,
4:37 together with Aaron, as the *L* bade him.
4:45 together with Aaron, as the *L* bade him.
4:49 so the *L* had commanded Moses.
5: 1 *L* said to Moses: "Order the Israelites
5: 4 the command that the *L* had given Moses;
5: 5 *L* said to Moses, "Tell the Israelites:
5: 6 him, thus breaking faith with the *L*,
5:11 Suspected AdultressThe *L* said to Moses,
5:16 woman come forward and stand before the *L*.
5:18 Then, as the woman stands before the *L*,
5:21 'may the *L* make you an example of
5:25 having waved this offering before the *L*,
5:30 he shall have her stand before the *L*,
6: 1 *L* said to Moses: "Speak to the Israelites
6: 2 nazirite vow to dedicate himself to the *L*,
6: 5 period of his dedication to the *L* is over,
6: 6 As long as he is dedicated to the *L*,
6: 8 as he is a nazirite he is sacred to the *L*.
6:12 of his dedication to the *L* as a nazirite,
6:14 bringing as his offering to the *L* one
6:16 priest shall present them before the *L*,
6:17 up the ram as a peace offering to the *L*,
6:20 wave them as a wave offering before the *L*.
6:21 this is the offering to the *L* which is
6:22 The *L* said to Moses: "Speak to Aaron
6:24 The *L* bless you and keep you!
6:25 The *L* let his face shine upon you,
6:26 *L* look upon you kindly and give you peace!
7: 3 The offering they brought before the *L*
7: 4 The *L* then said to Moses,
7:11 *L* said to Moses, Let one prince a day
8: 1 The *L* spoke to Moses,
8: 3 just as the *L* had commanded Moses.
8: 4 to the pattern which the *L* had shown Moses.
8: 5 *L* said to Moses: "Take the Levites
8:10 the Levites are present before the *L*,
8:11 *L* as a wave offering from the Israelites,
8:11 thus devoting them to the service of the *L*.
8:12 and the other as a holocaust to the *L*,
8:13 to be offered as a wave offering to the *L*;
8:20 the *L* had given Moses concerning them.
8:21 them as a wave offering before the *L*,
8:22 The command which the *L* had given Moses
8:23 The *L* said to Moses: "This is the rule
9: 1 the *L* said to Moses in the desert of Sinai,

9: 5 month, just as the *L* had commanded Moses.
9: 8 what the *L* will command in your regard."
9: 9 The *L* then said to Moses:
9:18 bidding of the *L* the Israelites moved on,
9:19 obeyed the *L* and would not move on;
9:20 bidding of the *L* that they stayed in camp,
9:23 at the bidding of the *L* that they encamped,
9:23 ever heeding the charge of the *L*,
10: 1 The *L* said to Moses: "Make two trumpets
10: 9 the alarm on the trumpets, and the *L*,
10:10 I, the *L*, am your God."
10:13 camp at the bidding of the *L* through Moses,
10:29 place which the *L* has promised to give us.
10:29 the *L* has promised prosperity to Israel."
10:32 you the prosperity the *L* will bestow on us."
10:33 They moved on from the mountain of the *L*,
10:33 covenant of the *L* which was to seek out
10:34 cloud of the *L* was over them by day.
10:35 set out, Moses would say, "Arise, O *L*,
10:36 came to rest, he would say, "Return, O *L*,
11: 1 people complained in the hearing of the *L*;
11: 1 wrath flared up so that the fire of the *L*
11: 2 he prayed to the *L* and the fire died out.
11: 3 there the fire of the *L* burned among them.
11:10 tents, so that the *L* became very angry,
11:11 Moses asked the *L*.
11:16 *L* said to Moses, "Assemble for me seventy
11:18 For in the hearing of the *L* you have cried,
11:18 the *L* will give you meat for food,
11:20 have spurned the *L* who is in your midst,
11:23 *L* answered Moses, "Is this beyond
11:24 and told the people what the *L* had said.
11:25 The *L* then came down in the cloud and
11:28 had been Moses' aide, said, "Moses, my *l*,
11:29 all the people of the *L* were prophets!
11:29 the *L* might bestow his spirit on them all!"
11:31 There arose a wind sent by the *L*,
12: 2 it through Moses alone that the *L* speaks?
12: 2 And the *L* heard this.
12: 4 the *L* said to Moses and Aaron and Miriam,
12: 5 the *L* came down in the column of cloud,
12: 6 said, "Now listen to the words of the *L*:
12: 8 The presence of the *L* he beholds.
12: 9 the *L* against them that when he departed,
12:11 turned and saw her a leper, "Ah, my *l*!"
12:13 Then Moses cried to the *L*,
12:14 *L* answered Moses, "Suppose her father
13: 1 *L* said to Moses, "Send men to
13: 3 the desert of Paran, as the *L* had ordered.
14: 3 Why is the *L* bringing us into this land
14: 8 If the *L* is pleased with us,
14: 9 But do not rebel against the *L*!
14: 9 has left them, but the *L* is with us.
14:10 But then the glory of the *L* appeared at
14:11 *L* said to Moses, "How long will this
14:13 But Moses said to the *L*:
14:14 It has been heard that you, O *L*,
14:14 you, *L*, who plainly reveal yourself!
14:16 'The *L* was not able to bring this people
14:17 of my *L* be displayed in its greatness,
14:18 *L* is slow to anger and rich in kindness,
14:20 The *L* answered: "I pardon them
14:26 The *L* also said to Moses and Aaron:
14:28 By my life, says the *L*,
14:35 I, the *L*, have sworn to do this
14:37 land were struck down by the *L* and died.
14:40 to go up to the place that the *L* spoke of:
14:42 go up, because the *L* is not in your midst;
14:43 from following the *L*; therefore the LORD
14:44 covenant of the *L* nor Moses left the camp.
15: 1 The *L* said to Moses,
15: 3 if you make to the *L* a sweet-smelling
15: 4 shall also present to the *L* a cereal offering
15: 7 making a sweet-smelling offering to the *L*.
15: 8 of a vow, or as a peace offering to the *L*,
15:10 as a sweet-smelling oblation to the *L*.
15:13 present a sweet-smelling oblation to the *L*.
15:14 a sweet-smelling oblation to the *L*,
15:15 Before the *L* you and the alien are alike,
15:17 *L* said to Moses, "Speak to the Israelites
15:19 you shall offer the *L* a contribution
15:21 to the *L* from your first batch of dough.
15:22 commandments which the *L* gives to Moses,
15:23 from the time the *L* first issues the
15:24 oblation pleasing to the *L*,
15:25 their holocaust as an oblation to the *L*.
15:28 the *L* for him who sinned inadvertently;
15:30 he be a native or an alien, insults the *L*,
15:31 of the *L* and has broken his commandment,
15:35 *L* said to Moses, "This man shall be put
15:36 him to death, as the *L* had commanded Moses.
15:37 *L* said to Moses, "Speak to the Israelites
15:39 you to keep all the commandments of the *L*,
15:41 I, the *L*, am your God who, as God,
15:41 brought you out of Egypt that I, the *L*,
16: 3 the *L* is in their midst.
16: 5 "May the *L* make known tomorrow morning
16: 7 incense in them before the *L* tomorrow.
16: 7 He whom the *L* then chooses is the holy one.
16:11 It is therefore against the *L* that you and
16:13 the desert, that you must now *l* it over us?
16:15 Moses became very angry and said to the *L*,
16:16 band shall appear before the *L* tomorrow
16:17 put incense in it, and offer it to the *L*;
16:19 of the *L* appeared to the entire community,
16:20 and the *L* said to Moses and Aaron,
16:23 The *L* answered Moses,
16:28 the *L* who sent me to do all I have done,
16:29 mankind, then it was not the *L* who sent me.
16:30 But if the *L* does something entirely new,
16:30 will know that these men have defied the *L*.
16:35 And fire from the *L* came forth which
17: 1 *L* said to Moses, "Tell Eleazar,
17: 3 before the *L* they have become sacred.
17: 5 which the *L* had given him through Moses.
17: 5 the altar to offer incense before the *L*,
17: 7 covered it and the glory of the *L* appeared.
17: 9 tent, and the *L* said to Moses and Aaron,
17:11 forth from the *L* and the blow is falling."
17:16 The *L* now said to Moses,
17:22 the *L* in the tent of the commandments.
17:25 own staff and took it, the *L* said to Moses,
17:26 Moses did as the *L* had commanded him.
17:28 anyone approaches the Dwelling of the *L*,
18: 1 *L* said to Aaron, "You and your sons
18: 6 the *L* for the service of the meeting tent.
18: 8 *L* said to Aaron, "I myself have given you
18:12 they give to the *L* as their first fruits;
18:13 that they bring in to the *L* shall be yours;
18:15 beast, such as are to be offered to the *L*,
18:17 as a sweet-smelling oblation to the *L*,
18:19 gifts which the Israelites make to the *L*;
18:19 covenant to last forever before the *L*,
18:20 *L* said to Aaron, "You shall not have any
18:24 Israelites give as a contribution to the *L*.
18:25 *L* said to Moses, "Give the Levites these
18:26 to make a contribution from them to the *L*,
18:28 priest the part to be contributed to the *L*.
18:29 to the *L* your own full contribution.
19: 1 The *L* said to Moses and Aaron:
19: 2 which the law of the *L* prescribes.
19:13 of the *L* and shall be cut off from Israel.
19:20 because he defiles the sanctuary of the *L*.
20: 6 Then the glory of the *L* appeared to them,
20: 7 appeared to them, and the *L* said to Moses,
20: 9 took the staff from its place before the *L*,
20:12 But the *L* said to Moses and Aaron,
20:13 the Israelites contended against the *L*,
20:16 fathers, and how, when we cried to the *L*,
20:23 of Edom, the *L* said to Moses and Aaron,
20:27 Moses did as the *L* commanded.
21: 2 Israel then made this vow to the *L*:
21: 3 when the *L* heeded Israel's prayer and
21: 6 *L* sent among the people saraph serpents,
21: 7 in complaining against the *L* and you.
21: 7 Pray the *L* to take the serpents from us."
21: 8 for the people, and the *L* said to Moses,
21:14 said in the "Book of the Wars of the *L*":
21:16 was the well of which the *L* said to Moses,
21:34 The *L*, however, said to Moses,
22: 8 give you whatever answer the *L* gives me."
22:13 the *L* has refused to let me go with you."
22:18 great, contrary to the command of the *L*,
22:19 till I learn what else the *L* may tell me."
22:22 and the angel of the *L* stationed himself
22:23 *L* standing on the road with sword drawn,
22:24 Then the angel of the *L* took his stand in
22:25 When the ass saw the angel of the *L* there,
22:26 The angel of the *L* then went ahead,
22:27 When the ass saw the angel of the *L* there,
22:28 But now the *L* opened the mouth of the ass,
22:31 Then the *L* removed the veil from Balaam's
22:31 *L* standing on the road with sword drawn;
22:32 But the angel of the *L* said to him,
22:34 Then Balaam said to the angel of the *L*,
22:35 But the angel of the *L* said to Balaam,
23: 3 Perhaps the *L* will meet me,
23: 5 in Balaam's mouth, the *L* said to him,
23: 8 denounce whom the *L* has not denounced?
23:12 "Is it not what the *L* puts in my mouth
23:16 Then the *L* met Balaam,
23:17 Balak asked him, "What did the *L* say?"
23:21 The *L*, his God, is with him;
23:26 you that I must do all that the *L* tells me?"
24: 1 that the *L* was pleased to bless Israel,
24: 6 a stream, like the cedars planted by the *L*.
24:11 but the *L* has withheld the reward from you!"
24:13 evil, contrary to the command of the *L*"?
24:13 Whatever the *L* says I must repeat.
25: 4 execution of the guilty ones before the *L*,
25:10 *L* said to Moses, "Phinehas, son of Eleazar,
25:16 *L* then said to Moses, "Treat the Midianites
26: 1 slaughter the *L* said to Moses and Eleazar,
26: 4 or more, as the *L* had commanded Moses.
26: 9 band when it rebelled against the *L*.
26:52 *L* said to Moses, "Among these groups
26:61 they offered profane fire before the *L*.
26:65 For the *L* had told them that they would
27: 3 together against the *L* [in Korah's band],
27: 5 When Moses laid their case before the *L*,
27: 6 case before the LORD, the *L* said to him,
27:11 the Israelites, as the *L* commanded Moses.
27:12 *L* said to Moses, "Go up here into
27:15 Then Moses said to the *L*,
27:16 Then Moses said to the LORD, "May the *L*,
27:18 *L* replied to Moses, "Take Joshua,
27:22 Moses did as the *L* had commanded him.
27:23 as the *L* had directed through Moses.
28: 1 *L* said to Moses, "Give the Israelites
28: 3 oblation which you shall offer to the *L*:
28: 6 as a sweet-smelling oblation to the *L*.
28: 7 you shall pour out to the *L* in the
28: 8 as a sweet-smelling oblation to the *L*.
28:11 as a holocaust to the *L* two bullocks,
28:13 may be a sweet-smelling oblation to the *L*.
28:15 be sacrificed as a sin offering to the *L*.
28:16 first month falls the Passover of the *L*,
28:19 you shall offer a holocaust to the *L*,
28:24 for a sweet-smelling oblation to the *L*.
28:26 present to the *L* the new cereal offering,
28:27 holocaust to the *L* two bullocks,
29: 2 holocaust to the *L* one bullock,
29: 6 as a sweet-smelling oblation to the *L*.
29: 8 holocaust to the *L* one bullock,
29:12 celebrate a pilgrimage feast to the *L*.
29:13 holocaust to the *L* thirteen bullocks,
29:36 oblation to the *L* one bullock,
29:39 you shall make to the *L* on your festivals,
30: 1 just as the *L* had ordered him.
30: 2 tribes, "This is what the *L* has commanded:
30: 3 When a man makes a vow to the *L* or binds
30: 4 her father's house, makes a vow to the *L*,
30: 6 and the *L* releases her from it,
30: 9 herself, and the *L* releases her from it.
30:13 them, the *L* releases her from them.
30:17 These are the statutes which the *L*
31: 1 *L* said to Moses, "Avenge the Israelites
31: 7 Midianites, as the *L* had commanded Moses,
31:16 Israelites toward the *L* in the Peor affair,
31:21 the law, as prescribed by the *L* to Moses,
31:25 The *L* said to Moses:
31:28 *L* on the warriors who went out to combat:
31:29 priest Eleazar as a contribution to the *L*.
31:31 did this, as the *L* had commanded Moses.
31:37 and seventy-five fell as tax to the *L*;
31:38 of which seventy-two fell as tax to the *L*;
31:39 of which sixty-one fell as tax to the *L*;
31:40 of whom thirty-two fell as tax to the *L*,
31:41 the LORD, The taxes contributed to the *L*,
31:41 priest Eleazar, as the *L* had commanded him.
31:47 share, Moses, as the *L* had ordered,
31:50 make atonement for ourselves before the *L*,
31:50 the *L* some gold article he has picked up,
31:52 they gave as a contribution to the *L*
31:54 memorial for the Israelites before the *L*.
32: 4 which the *L* has laid low before the
32: 7 crossing to the land the *L* has given them?
32: 9 not enter the land the *L* had given them.
32:10 At that time the wrath of the *L* flared up,
32:12 Nun, who have followed the *L* unreservedly.'
32:13 So in his anger with the Israelites the *L*
32:13 evil in the sight of the *L* had died out.
32:21 full force before the *L* until he has driven
32:22 of every obligation to the *L* and to Israel,
32:22 shall be your possession before the *L*.
32:23 not do this, you will sin against the *L*,
32:25 servants will do as you command, my *l*.
32:27 as armed troops to battle before the *L*,
32:29 with you as combat troops before the *L*,
32:30 with you as combat troops before the *L*,
32:31 "We will do what the *L* has commanded us,
32:32 the land of Canaan as troops before the *L*,
33: 4 all of whom the *L* had struck down;
33: 4 their gods, too, the *L* executed judgments.
33:50 The *L* spoke to Moses on the plains of Moab
34: 1 The *L* said to Moses, "Give the Israelites
34:13 which the *L* has commanded to be given to
34:16 *L* said to Moses, "These are the names
34:29 These are they whom the *L* commanded to
35: 1 The *L* gave these instructions to Moses on
35: 9 *L* said to Moses, "Tell the Israelites:
35:34 for I am the *L* who dwells in the midst of
36: 2 "The *L* commanded you, my lord,
36: 2 you, my *l*, were also commanded by the LORD
36: 5 according to the instructions of the *L*:
36: 6 This is what the *L* commands with regard to
36:10 the command which the *L* had given to Moses.
36:13 which the *L* prescribed for the Israelites
Dt 1: 3 that the *L* had given him in their regard.
1: 6 "The *L*, our God, said to us at Horeb,
1:10 The *L*, your God, has so multiplied you
1:11 May the *L*, the God of your fathers,
1:19 in obedience to the command of the *L*,
1:20 hill country of the Amorites, which the *L*,
1:21 The *L*, your God, has given this land
1:21 Go up and occupy it, as the *L*,
1:25 to us and reported, 'The land which the *L*,
1:26 and after defying the command of the *L*,
1:27 your tents, 'Out of hatred for us the *L*,
1:30 The *L*, your God, who goes before you,
1:31 as in the desert, where you saw how the *L*,
1:32 Despite this, you would not trust the *L*,
1:34 When the *L* heard your words,
1:36 because he has followed the *L* unreservedly.'
1:37 "The *L* was angered against me also on
1:41 said to me, 'We have sinned against the *L*.
1:41 go up ourselves and fight, just as the *L*,
1:42 But the *L* said to me, 'Warn them:
1:45 On your return you wept before the *L*,

LORD (cont.)
2: 1 Red Sea road, as the *L* had commanded me,
2: 2 Finally the *L* said to me,
2: 7 The *L*, your God, has blessed you in all
2: 9 *L* said to me, 'Do not show hostility
2:12 their heritage which the *L* has given them.]
2:14 the camp, as the *L* had sworn they should.
2:17 among the people, the *L* said to me,
2:21 *L* cleared out of the way for the Ammonites,
2:29 cross the Jordan into the land which the *L*,
2:30 us pass through his land, because the *L*,
2:31 *L* said to me, 'Now that I have already
2:33 but since the *L*, our God, had delivered
2:36 for us to whom the *L* had delivered them up.
2:37 in obedience to the command of the *L*,
3: 2 *L*, however, said to me, 'Do not be afraid
3: 3 *L*, our God, delivered into our hands
3:18 'The *L*, your God, has given you this land
3:20 the *L* has settled your kinsmen as well,
3:20 they too possess the land which the *L*,
3:21 'Your eyes have seen all that the *L*,
3:21 will the *L* do to all the kingdoms which
3:22 the *L*, your God, will fight for you.'
3:23 "And it was then that I besought the *L*,
3:24 then that I besought the LORD, 'O *L* GOD,
3:26 But the *L* was angry with me on your
3:26 "Enough!" the *L* said to me.
4: 1 take possession of the land which the *L*,
4: 2 observance of the commandments of the *L*,
4: 3 your own eyes what the *L* did at Baal-peor:
4: 3 *L*, your God, destroyed from your midst
4: 4 but you, who clung to the *L*,
4: 5 you the statutes and decrees as the *L*,
4: 7 that has gods so close to it as the *L*,
4:10 the day on which you stood before the *L*,
4:12 *L* spoke to you from the midst of the fire.
4:14 The *L* charged me at that time to teach you
4:15 "You saw no form at all on the day the *L*
4:19 *L*, your God, has let fall to the lot of all
4:21 Since the *L* was angered against me on your
4:23 lest, forgetting the covenant which the *L*,
4:24 For the *L*, your God, is a consuming fire,
4:25 this evil done in his sight provoke the *L*,
4:27 The *L* will scatter you among the nations,
4:27 the nations to which the *L* will lead you.
4:29 Yet there too you shall seek the *L*,
4:30 you, you shall finally return to the *L*,
4:31 Since the *L*, your God, is a merciful God,
4:34 and by great terrors, all of which the *L*,
4:35 know the *L* is God and there is no other.
4:39 that the *L* is God in the heavens above and
4:40 may have long life on the land which the *L*,
5: 2 The *L*, our God, made a covenant with us
5: 4 The *L* spoke with you face to face on the
5: 5 I stood between the *L* and you at that time,
5: 5 to announce to you these words of the *L*:
5: 6 'I, the *L*, am your God, who brought you
5: 9 I, the *L*, your God, am a jealous God,
5:11 'You shall not take the name of the *L*,
5:11 For the *L* will not leave unpunished him
5:12 care to keep holy the sabbath day as the *L*,
5:14 the seventh day is the sabbath of the *L*,
5:15 too were once slaves in Egypt, and the *L*,
5:15 why the *L*, your God, has commanded you
5:16 'Honor your father and mother, as the *L*,
5:16 and prosperity in the land which the *L*,
5:22 the *L* spoke with a loud voice to your
5:24 tribal heads and elders, and said, 'The *L*,
5:25 If we hear the voice of the *L*,
5:27 Go closer, you, and hear all that the *L*,
5:27 will say, and then tell us what the *L*,
5:28 "The *L* heard your words as you were
5:32 "Be careful, therefore, to do as the *L*,
5:33 the way prescribed for you by the *L*,
6: 1 the statutes and decrees which the *L*,
6: 2 your son and your grandson may fear the *L*,
6: 3 in keeping with the promise of the *L*,
6: 4 The *L* is our God, the LORD alone!
6: 5 Therefore, you shall love the *L*,
6:10 *L*, your God, brings you into the land
6:12 your fill, take care not to forget the *L*,
6:13 The *L*, your God, shall you fear;
6:15 nations, lest the wrath of the *L*,
6:15 the *L*, your God, who is in your midst,
6:16 not put the *L*, your God, to the test,
6:17 But keep the commandments of the *L*,
6:18 is right and good in the sight of the *L*,
6:18 the *L* promised on oath to your fathers,
6:20 statutes and decrees mean which the *L*,
6:21 but the *L* brought us out of Egypt with his
6:24 the *L* commanded us to observe all these
6:24 all these statutes in fear of the *L*,
6:25 and our justice before the *L*,
7: 1 *L*, your God, brings you into the land
7: 2 when the *L*, your God, delivers them
7: 4 and then the wrath of the *L* would flare up
7: 6 For you are a people sacred to the *L*,
7: 7 the *L* set his heart on you and chose you,
7: 8 It was because the *L* loved you and because
7: 9 Understand, then, that the *L*,
7:12 and observing them carefully, the *L*,
7:15 The *L* will remove all sickness from you;
7:16 shall consume all the nations which the *L*,
7:18 Rather, call to mind what the *L*,
7:19 hand and outstretched arm with which the *L*,
7:20 the *L*, your God, will send hornets
7:21 do not be terrified by them, for the *L*,
7:23 *L*, your God, will deliver them up to you
7:25 for it is an abomination to the *L*,
8: 1 the *L* promised on oath to your fathers.
8: 2 Remember how for forty years now the *L*,
8: 3 that comes forth from the mouth of the *L*.
8: 5 So you must realize that the *L*,
8: 6 keep the commandments of the *L*,
8: 7 *L*, your God, is bringing you into a good
8:10 eaten your fill, you must bless the *L*,
8:11 Be careful not to forget the *L*,
8:14 haughty of heart and unmindful of the *L*,
8:18 Remember then, it is the *L*,
8:19 But if you forget the *L*,
8:20 nations which the *L* destroys before you,
8:20 perish for not heeding the voice of the *L*,
9: 3 Understand, then, today that it is the *L*,
9: 3 them quickly, as the *L* promised you.
9: 4 After the *L*, your God, has thrust them out
9: 4 *L* has brought me in to possess this land';
9: 4 that the *L* is driving them out before you.
9: 5 *L*, your God, is driving these nations out
9: 6 is not because of your merits that the *L*,
9: 7 and do not forget how you angered the *L*,
9: 7 you have been rebellious toward the *L*.
9: 8 *L* that he was angry enough to destroy you,
9: 9 of the covenant which the *L* made with you.
9:10 till the *L* gave me the two tablets of
9:10 copy of all the words that the *L* spoke
9:11 when the *L* had given me the two stone
9:13 this people is,' the *L* said to me.
9:16 I saw how you had sinned against the *L*,
9:16 way which the *L* had pointed out to you
9:18 I lay prostrate before the *L* for forty
9:18 *L* and the evil you had done to provoke him.
9:19 the fierce anger of the *L* against you:
9:19 Yet once again the *L* listened to me.
9:20 With Aaron, too, the *L* was deeply angry,
9:22 likewise, you provoked the *L* to anger.
9:23 rebelled against this command of the *L*,
9:24 you, you have been rebels against the *L*.
9:25 nights, I lay prostrate before the *L*,
9:26 O *L* GOD, destroy not your people,
9:28 'The *L* was not able to bring them into the
10: 1 "At that time the *L* said to me,
10: 4 The *L* then wrote on them,
10: 4 After the *L* had given them to me,
10: 5 in keeping with the command the *L* gave me.
10: 8 "At that time the *L* set apart the tribe
10: 8 to carry the ark of the covenant of the *L*,
10: 8 before the *L* and minister to him,
10: 9 the *L* himself is his heritage, as the LORD,
10:10 and the *L* had once again heard me and
10:12 *L*, your God, ask of you but to fear the *L*,
10:12 his ways exactly, to love and serve the *L*,
10:13 statutes of the *L* which I enjoin on you
10:14 highest heavens, belong to the *L* your God,
10:15 *L* was so attached to them as to choose you,
10:17 God, is the God of gods, the *L* of lords,
10:20 The *L*, your God, shall you fear,
10:22 to Egypt seventy strong, and now the *L*,
11: 1 "Love the *L*,
11: 2 now understand the discipline of the *L*,
11: 7 all these great deeds that the *L* has done.
11: 9 land which the *L* swore to your fathers
11:12 rain from the heavens, a land which the *L*,
11:13 on you today, loving and serving the *L*,
11:17 For then the wrath of the *L* will flare up
11:21 *L* swore to your fathers he would give them.
11:22 I enjoin on you, loving the *L*,
11:23 the *L* will drive all these nations out of
11:25 the *L*,
11:27 for obeying the commandments of the *L*,
11:28 you do not obey the commandments of the *L*,
11:29 *L*, your God, brings you into the land
11:31 to enter and occupy the land which the *L*,
12: 1 to observe in the land which the *L*,
12: 4 not how you are to worship the *L* your God.
12: 5 you shall resort to the place which the *L*,
12: 7 There, too, before the *L*,
12: 7 over all your undertakings, because the *L*,
12: 9 resting place, the heritage which the *L*,
12:10 Jordan and dwell in the land which the *L*,
12:11 place which the *L*, your God, chooses
12:11 special offering you have vowed to the *L*.
12:12 You shall make merry before the *L*,
12:14 which the *L* chooses from among your tribes;
12:15 your heart's desire as much meat as the *L*,
12:18 These you must eat before the *L*,
12:18 and there, before the *L*,
12:20 *L*, your God, had enlarged your territory,
12:21 and if the place which the *L*,
12:21 herd or flock that the *L* has given you,
12:25 doing what is right in the sight of the *L*.
12:26 with you to the place which the *L* chooses,
12:27 of your holocausts on the altar of the *L*,
12:27 be poured out against the altar of the *L*,
12:28 is good and right in the sight of the *L*,
12:29 the *L*, your God, removes the nations
12:31 You shall not thus worship the *L*,
12:31 gods every abomination that the *L* detests,
13: 4 *L*, your God, is testing you to learn
13: 5 The *L*, your God, shall you follow,
13: 6 lead you astray from the way which the *L*,
13: 6 take, he has preached apostasy from the *L*,
13:11 he sought to lead you astray from the *L*,
13:13 "If, in any of the cities which the *L*,
13:17 spoils as a whole burnt offering to the *L*,
13:18 that the blazing wrath of the *L* may die
13:19 you have heeded the voice of the *L*,
14: 1 "You are children of the *L*, your God.
14: 2 For you are a people sacred to the *L*,
14:21 for you are a people sacred to the *L*,
14:23 then in the place which the *L*,
14:23 that you may learn always to fear the *L*,
14:24 your tithe, because the place which the *L*,
14:24 you, considering how the *L* has blessed you,
14:25 money in hand, go to the place which the *L*,
14:26 you would enjoy, and there before the *L*,
14:29 so that the *L*,
15: 2 in honor of the *L* has been proclaimed.
15: 4 *L*, your God, will bless you abundantly
15: 5 If you but heed the voice of the *L*,
15: 6 and none will rule over you, since the *L*,
15: 7 is in need in the land which the *L*,
15: 9 *L* against you and you will be held guilty.
15:10 for the *L*, your God, will bless you
15:14 press, in proportion to the blessing the *L*,
15:15 slaves in the land of Egypt, and the *L*,
15:18 then also the *L*, your God, will bless you
15:19 "You shall consecrate to the *L*,
15:20 your family shall eat them before the *L*,
15:21 you shall not sacrifice it to the *L*,
16: 1 of Abib by keeping the Passover of the *L*,
16: 2 from your flock or your herd to the *L*,
16: 5 in any of the communities which the *L*,
16: 7 shall cook and eat it at the place the *L*,
16: 8 be a solemn meeting in honor of the *L*,
16:10 keep the feast of Weeks in honor of the *L*,
16:10 be in proportion to the blessing the *L*,
16:11 In the place which the *L*,
16:15 this pilgrim feast in honor of the *L*,
16:15 since the *L*, your God, has blessed you
16:16 male among you shall appear before the *L*,
16:16 one shall appear before the *L* empty-handed,
16:17 in proportion to the blessings which the *L*,
16:18 people in all the communities which the *L*,
16:20 life and may possess the land which the *L*,
16:21 kind of wood beside the altar of the *L*,
16:22 you erect a sacred pillar, such as the *L*,
17: 1 "You shall not sacrifice to the *L*,
17: 1 that would be an abomination to the *L*,
17: 2 in any one of the communities which the *L*,
17: 2 woman who does evil in the sight of the *L*,
17: 8 shall then go up to the place which the *L*,
17:10 give you in the place which the *L* chooses,
17:12 officiates there in the ministry of the *L*,
17:14 you have come into the land which the *L*,
17:15 that man over you as your king whom the *L*,
17:19 his life that he may learn to fear the *L*,
18: 1 of the *L* and the portions due to him.
18: 2 the *L* himself is his heritage,
18: 5 *L*, your God, has chosen him and his sons
18: 5 to minister in the name of the *L*.
18: 6 may desire, the place which the *L* chooses,
18: 7 may minister there in the name of the *L*,
18: 7 who are in attendance there before the *L*.
18: 9 "When you come into the land which the *L*,
18:12 such things is an abomination to the *L*,
18:12 and because of such abominations the *L*,
18:13 must be altogether sincere toward the *L*,
18:14 soothsayers and fortunetellers, the *L*,
18:15 "A prophet like me will the *L*,
18:16 is exactly what you requested of the *L*,
18:16 'Let us not again hear the voice of the *L*,
18:17 And the *L* said to me, 'This was well said.
18:21 recognize an oracle which the *L* has spoken?'
18:22 a prophet speaks in the name of the *L*,
18:22 it is an oracle which the *L* did not speak.
19: 1 the *L*, your God, removes the nations
19: 2 apart three cities in the land which the *L*,
19: 3 into three regions the land which the *L*,
19: 8 if the *L*, your God, enlarges your territory,
19: 9 which I enjoin on you today, loving the *L*,
19:10 Thus, in the land which the *L*,
19:14 you receive in the land which the *L*,
19:17 in the dispute shall appear before the *L*
20: 1 own, do not be afraid of them, for the *L*,
20: 4 *L*, your God, who goes with you to fight
20:13 battle, lay siege to it, and when the *L*,
20:14 this plunder of your enemies which the *L*,
20:16 the cities of those nations which the *L*,
20:17 as the *L*, your God, has commanded you,
20:18 their gods, and you thus sin against the *L*,
21: 1 lying in the open on the land which the *L*,
21: 5 of Levi, shall also be present, for the *L*,
21: 8 Absolve, O *L*, your people Israel,
21: 9 doing what is right in the sight of the *L*.
21:10 out to war against your enemies and the *L*,
21:23 you will defile the land which the *L*,
22: 5 such things is an abomination to the *L*,
23: 2 be admitted into the community of the *L*.
23: 3 be admitted into the community of the *L*,

23: 4 be admitted into the community of the *L*,
23: 6 though the *L*,
23: 9 be admitted into the community of the *L*.
23:15 Since the *L*, your God, journeys along
23:19 of votive offering in the house of the *L*,
23:19 these things are an abomination to the *L*,
23:21 not from your countryman so that the *L*,
23:22 "When you make a vow to the *L*,
23:22 you will be held guilty, for the *L*,
23:24 offering you have freely promised to the *L*.
24: 4 That would be an abomination before the *L*,
24: 4 bring such guilt upon the land which the *L*,
24: 9 what the *L*, your God, did to Miriam
24:13 will be a good deed of yours before the *L*,
24:15 Otherwise he will cry to the *L* against you,
24:18 you were once slaves in Egypt, and the *L*,
24:19 the orphan or the widow, that the *L*,
25:15 have a long life on the land which the *L*,
25:16 these matters is an abomination to the *L*,
25:19 Therefore, when the *L*,
26: 1 you have come into the land which the *L*,
26: 2 you harvest from the land which the *L*,
26: 2 you shall go to the place which the *L*,
26: 3 say to him, 'Today I acknowledge to the *L*,
26: 4 set it in front of the altar of the *L*,
26: 5 Then you shall declare before the *L*,
26: 7 hard labor upon us, we cried to the *L*,
26:10 of the products of the soil which you, O *L*,
26:10 And having set them before the *L*,
26:11 over all these good things which the *L*,
26:13 community, you shall declare before the *L*,
26:14 have thus hearkened to the voice of the *L*,
26:16 "This day the *L*, your God, commands you
26:17 you are making this agreement with the *L*:
26:18 the *L* is making this agreement with you:
26:19 and you will be a people sacred to the *L*,
27: 2 the Jordan into the land which the *L*,
27: 3 flowing with milk and honey, which the *L*,
27: 5 plaster, you shall also build to the *L*,
27: 6 You shall make this altar of the *L*,
27: 6 and shall offer on it holocausts to the *L*,
27: 7 eat them there, making merry before the *L*,
27: 9 day you have become the people of the *L*,
27:10 therefore hearken to the voice of the *L*,
27:15 an abomination to the *L*,
28: 1 you continue to heed the voice of the *L*,
28: 1 which I enjoin on you today, the *L*,
28: 2 When you hearken to the voice of the *L*,
28: 7 "The *L*, will beat down before you
28: 8 The *L* will affirm his blessing upon you,
28: 8 blessing you in the land that the *L*,
28: 9 that you keep the commandments of the *L*,
28:10 earth see you bearing the name of the *L*,
28:11 The *L* will increase in more than goodly
28:12 The *L* will open up for you his rich
28:13 The *L* will make you the head,
28:13 as you obey the commandments of the *L*,
28:15 you do not hearken to the voice of the *L*,
28:20 "The *L* will put a curse on you,
28:21 The *L* will bring a pestilence upon you
28:22 *L* will strike you with wasting and fever,
28:24 the *L* will give your land powdery dust,
28:25 The *L* will let you be beaten down before
28:27 The *L* will strike you with Egyptian boils
28:28 And the *L* will strike you with madness,
28:35 The *L* will strike you with malignant boils
28:36 "The *L* will bring you,
28:37 the nations to which the *L* will lead you.
28:45 would not hearken to the voice of the *L*,
28:47 Since you would not serve the *L*,
28:48 enemies whom the *L* will send against you.
28:49 "The *L* will raise up against you a nation
28:52 throughout the land which the *L* your God,
28:53 of your own sons and daughters whom the *L*,
28:58 the glorious and awesome name of the *L*,
28:61 that too the *L* will bring upon you until
28:62 would not hearken to the voice of the *L*,
28:63 "Just as the *L* once took delight in
28:64 The *L* will scatter you among all the
28:65 for there the *L* will give you an anguished
28:68 *L* will send you back in galleys to Egypt,
28:69 covenant which the *L* ordered Moses to make
29: 1 "You have seen all that the *L* did in the
29: 3 the *L* yet given you a mind to understand,
29: 5 Thus you should know that I, the *L*,
29: 9 "You are all now standing before the *L*,
29:11 you may enter into the covenant of the *L*,
29:14 us who are now here present before the *L*,
29:17 now turn away their hearts from the *L*,
29:19 the *L* will never consent to pardon him.
29:19 The *L* will blot out his name from under
29:21 ills with which the *L* has smitten it
29:22 which the *L* overthrew in his furious wrath
29:23 'Why has the *L* dealt thus with this land?
29:24 they forsook the covenant which the *L*,
29:26 that is why the *L* was angry with this land
29:27 *L* uprooted them from their soil
30: 1 and from among whatever nations the *L*,
30: 2 you and your children return to the *L*,
30: 3 soul, just as I now command you, the *L*,
30: 4 of the world, even from there will the *L*,
30: 5 The *L*, your God, will then bring you
30: 6 *L*, your God, will circumcise your hearts
30: 6 your descendants, that you may love the *L*,
30: 7 curses the *L*, your God, will assign
30: 9 Then the *L*, your God, will increase in
30: 9 for the *L*,
30:10 if only you heed the voice of the *L*,
30:10 book of the law, when you return to the *L*,
30:16 If you obey the commandments of the *L*,
30:16 will live and grow numerous, and the *L*,
30:20 by loving the *L*, your God,
30:20 land which the *L* swore he would give
31: 2 besides the *L* has told me that I shall not
31: 3 *L*, your God, who will cross before you;
31: 3 will cross before you, as the *L* promised.]
31: 4 The *L* will deal with them just as he dealt
31: 5 therefore, the *L* delivers them up to you,
31: 6 no fear or dread of them, for it is the *L*,
31: 7 *L* swore to their fathers he would give them;
31: 8 It is the *L* who marches before you;
31: 9 carry the ark of the covenant of the *L*,
31:11 all Israel goes to appear before the *L*,
31:12 hear it and learn it, and so fear the *L*,
31:13 learn it, that they too may fear the *L*,
31:14 The *L* said to Moses, "The time is now
31:15 And the *L* appeared at the tent in a column
31:16 *L* said to Moses, "Soon you will be at rest
31:23 Then the *L* commissioned Joshua,
31:25 ark of the covenant of the *L* this order:
31:26 beside the ark of the covenant of the *L*,
31:27 you, you have been rebels against the *L!*
32: 6 Is the *L* to be thus repaid by you,
32:12 The *L* alone was their leader,
32:19 When the *L* saw this,
32:27 the *L* had nothing to do with it.' "
32:30 Rock sold them and the *L* delivered them up?"
32:36 the *L* shall do justice for his people:
32:48 On that very day the *L* said to Moses,
33: 2 "The *L* came from Sinai and dawned on his
33: 7 "The *L* hears the cry of Judah;
33:11 Bless, O *L*, his possessions and accept
33:12 "Benjamin is the beloved of the *L*,
33:13 "Blessed by the *L* is his land with the
33:21 of the *L* and his decrees respecting Israel."
33:23 and filled with the blessings of the *L*;
33:29 Where else is a nation victorious in the *L?*
33:29 The *L* is your saving shield,
34: 1 Jericho, and the *L* showed him all the land
34: 4 The *L* then said to him,
34: 5 of the LORD, died as the *L* had said;
34:10 like Moses, whom the *L* knew face to face.
34:11 *L* sent him to perform in the land of Egypt
Jos 1: 1 servant of the *L*, had died, the LORD said
1: 9 Do not fear nor be dismayed, for the *L*,
1:11 take possession of the land which the *L*,
1:13 Moses, the servant of the *L*, commanded
1:13 *L*, your God, will permit you
1:15 them until the *L* has settled your kinsmen,
1:15 they like you possess the land which the *L*,
1:15 land, which Moses, the servant of the *L*,
1:17 But may the *L*, your God, be with you
2: 9 "I know that the *L* has given you the land,
2:10 For we have heard how the *L* dried up the
2:11 discouraged because of you, since the *L*,
2:12 Now then, swear to me by the *L* that,
2:14 to you when the *L* gives us the land."
2:24 "The *L* has delivered all this land into
3: 3 you see the ark of the covenant of the *L*,
3: 5 the *L* will perform wonders among you."
3: 7 Then the *L* said to Joshua,
3: 9 here and listen to the words of the *L*,
3:11 The ark of the covenant of the *L* of the
3:13 ark of the LORD, the *L* of the whole earth,
3:17 carrying the ark of the covenant of the *L*
4: 2 crossed the Jordan, the *L* said to Joshua,
4: 5 the Jordan in front of the ark of the *L*,
4: 7 of the *L* when it crossed the Jordan.'
4:10 *L* had commanded Joshua to tell the people.
4:11 reached the other side, the ark of the *L*,
4:13 over before the *L* to the plains of Jericho.
4:14 That day the *L* exalted Joshua in the sight
4:15 Then the *L* said to Joshua,
4:18 *L* had come up from the bed of the Jordan,
4:23 For the *L*, your God, dried up the waters
4:23 you until you crossed over, just as the *L*,
4:24 may learn that the hand of the *L* is mighty,
4:24 is mighty, and that you may fear the *L*,
5: 1 *L* had dried up the waters of the Jordan
5: 2 On this occasion the *L* said to Joshua,
5: 6 they had not obeyed the command of the *L*.
5: 6 For the *L* swore that he would not let them
5: 9 Then the *L* said to Joshua,
5:14 the host of the *L* and I have just arrived."
5:14 him, "What has my *l* to say to his servant?"
5:15 of the host of the *L* replied to Joshua,
6: 2 And to Joshua the *L* said,
6: 6 ram's horns in front of the ark of the *L*.
6: 7 troops marching ahead of the ark of the *L*.
6: 8 horns before the *L* blowing their horns,
6: 8 of the covenant of the *L* following them.
6:11 So he had the ark of the *L* circle the city,
6:12 had the priests take up the ark of the *L*.
6:13 horns marched in front of the ark of the *L*,
6:13 the rear guard followed the ark of the *L*,
6:16 for the *L* has given you the city and
6:19 of bronze or iron, are sacred to the *L*.
6:19 They shall be put in the treasury of the *L*."
6:24 in the treasury of the house of the *L*.
6:26 Cursed before the *L* be the man who
6:27 Thus the *L* was with Joshua so that his
7: 1 of the *L* flared up against the Israelites.
7: 6 before the ark of the *L* until evening;
7: 7 "Alas, O *L* GOD,"
7: 8 Pray, *L*, what can I say,
7:10 The *L* replied to Joshua: "Stand up.
7:13 themselves before tomorrow, for the *L*,
7:14 *L* designates shall come forward by clans;
7:14 the clan which the *L* designates shall come
7:14 *L* designates shall come forward one by one.
7:15 he has violated the covenant of the *L*
7:19 said to Achan, "My son, give to the *L*,
7:20 "I have indeed sinned against the *L*,
7:23 and spread them out before the *L*.
7:25 "The *L* bring upon you today the misery
7:26 Then the anger of the *L* relented.
8: 1 *L* then said to Joshua. "Do not be afraid
8: 7 take possession of the city, which the *L*,
8:18 Then the *L* directed Joshua,
8:27 to the command of the *L* issued to Joshua.
8:30 Later Joshua built an altar to the *L*,
8:31 Israelites of Moses, the servant of the *L*,
8:31 holocausts and peace offerings to the *L*.
8:33 carrying the ark of the covenant of the *L*.
8:33 of Moses, the servant of the *L*,
9: 9 faroff land, because of the fame of the *L*,
9:14 without seeking the advice of the *L*.
9:18 the community had sworn to them by the *L*,
9:19 people, "We have sworn to them by the *L*,
9:24 servants were fully informed of how the *L*,
9:27 the community and for the altar of the *L*,
10: 8 Meanwhile the *L* said to Joshua,
10:10 the *L* threw them into disorder before him.
10:11 the *L* hurled great stones from the sky
10:12 when the *L* delivered up the Amorites to
10:12 to the Israelites, Joshua prayed to the *L*,
10:14 *L* obeyed the voice of a man; for the LORD
10:19 them to escape to their cities, for the *L*,
10:25 This is what the *L* will do to all the
10:30 the *L* delivered into the power of Israel.
10:32 The *L* delivered Lachish into the power of
10:40 doom on all who lived there, just as the *L*,
10:42 captured in a single campaign, for the *L*,
11: 6 *L* said to Joshua, "Do not fear them,
11: 8 The *L* delivered them into the power of the
11: 9 Joshua did to them as the *L* had commanded:
11:12 on them, as Moses, the servant of the *L*,
11:15 As the *L* had commanded his servant Moses,
11:15 the *L* had commanded Moses should be done.
11:20 For it was the design of the *L* to
11:20 exterminated, as the *L* had commanded Moses.
11:23 just as the *L* had foretold to Moses.
12: 6 After Moses, the servant of the *L*,
13: 1 and advanced in years, the *L* said to him:
13: 8 heritage which Moses, the servant of the *L*,
13:14 *L* had promised them, the LORD,
13:33 to the tribe of Levi, since the *L* himself,
14: 2 instructions the *L* had given through Moses
14: 5 out the instructions of the *L* to Moses.
14: 6 know what the *L* said to the man of God,
14: 7 forty years old when the servant of the *L*,
14: 8 but I was completely loyal to the *L*,
14: 9 you have been completely loyal to the *L*,
14:10 the *L* has preserved me while Israel was
14:10 years since the *L* spoke thus to Moses;
14:12 region which the *L* promised me that day,
14:12 but if the *L* is with me I shall be able to
14:12 able to drive them out, as the *L* promised."
14:14 because he was completely loyal to the *L*,
15:13 As the *L* had commanded,
17: 4 "The *L* commanded Moses to give us a
17: 4 So in obedience to the command of the *L* a
17:14 *L* has blessed us" Joshua answered them,
18: 3 steps to possess the land which the *L*,
18: 6 then cast lots for you here before the *L*,
18: 7 the priesthood of the *L* is their heritage;
18: 7 Jordan which Moses, the servant of the *L*,
18: 8 lots for them there before the *L* in Shiloh.
18:10 lots for them before the *L* in Shiloh.
19:50 In obedience to the command of the *L*,
19:51 the land by lot in the presence of the *L*,
20: 1 The *L* said to Joshua.
21: 2 and said to them, "The *L* commanded,
21: 3 in obedience to this command of the *L*,
21:43 And so the *L* gave Israel all the land he
21:44 it, the *L* gave them peace on every side,
21:44 the *L* brought all their enemies under
21:45 *L* made to the house of Israel was broken;
22: 2 done all that Moses, the servant of the *L*,
22: 3 carried out the commands of the *L*,
22: 4 Since, therefore, the *L*,
22: 4 land, which Moses, the servant of the *L*,
22: 5 and law which Moses, the servant of the *L*,
22: 5 love the *L*,
22:16 community of the *L* sends this message:
22:16 You have seceded from the *L* this day,
22:17 a plague came upon the community of the *L*.
22:18 You are rebelling against the *L* today and
22:19 *L* possesses, where the Dwelling of the LORD

LORD (cont.)
22:19 against the *L* nor involve us in rebellion,
22:19 your own in addition to the altar of the *L*,
22:21 "The *L* is the God of gods.
22:22 The *L*, the God of gods, knows and Israel
22:22 of rebellion or treachery against the *L*,
22:23 an altar of our own to secede from the *L*,
22:23 it, the *L* himself will exact the penalty.
22:24 'What have you to do with the *L*,
22:25 For the *L* has placed the Jordan as a
22:25 of Reuben and Gad have no share in the *L*.
22:25 would prevent ours from revering the *L*.
22:27 the *L* in his presence with our holocausts,
22:27 our children, 'You have no share in the *L*.'
22:28 the altar of the *L* which our fathers made,
22:29 against the *L* or to secede now from the *L*
22:29 in addition to the altar of the *L*,
22:31 "Now we know that the *L* is with us.
22:31 this act of treachery against the *L*,
22:31 Israelites free from punishment by the *L*."
22:34 as a witness among them that the *L* is God.
23: 1 after the *L* had given the Israelites rest
23: 3 You have seen all that the *L*,
23: 3 for it has been the *L*,
23: 5 The *L*, your God, will dirve them out
23: 5 take possession of their land as the *L*,
23: 8 them, but you must remain loyal to the *L*,
23: 9 *L* has driven out large and strong nations,
23:10 to flight a thousand, because it is the *L*,
23:11 Take great care, however, to love the *L*,
23:13 with them, know for certain that the *L*,
23:13 you perish from this good land which the *L*,
23:14 that not one of all the promises the *L*,
23:15 But just as every promise the *L*,
23:15 you from this good land which the *L*,
23:16 If you transgress the covenant of the *L*,
23:16 the anger of the *L* will flare up against
24: 2 "Thus says the *L*, the God of Israel:
24: 7 Because they cried out to the *L*,
24:14 *L* and serve him completely and sincerely.
24:14 the River and in Egypt, and serve the *L*.
24:15 If it does not please you to serve the *L*,
24:15 me and my household, we will serve the *L*."
24:16 the *L* for the service of other gods.
24:17 it was the *L*, our God, who brought us
24:18 approach the *L* drove out [all the peoples,
24:18 Therefore we also will serve the *L*,
24:19 "You may not be able to serve the *L*,
24:20 you forsake the *L* and serve strange gods,
24:21 Joshua, "We will still serve the *L*."
24:22 that you have chosen to serve the *L*."
24:23 among you and turn your hearts to the *L*,
24:24 promised Joshua, "We will serve the *L*,
24:26 the oak that was in the sanctuary of the *L*.
24:27 all the words which the *L* spoke to us.
24:29 Joshua, son of Nun, servant of the *L*,
24:31 Israel served the *L* during the entire
24:31 knew all that the *L* had done for Israel.
Jgs 1: 1 of Joshua the Israelites consulted the *L*,
1: 2 The *L* answered, "Judah shall attack:
1: 4 the *L* delivered the Canaanites and
1:19 Since the *L* was with Judah,
1:22 up against Bethel, and the *L* was with them.
2: 1 *L* went up from Gilgal to Bochim and said,
2: 4 When the angel of the *L* had made these
2: 5 They offered sacrifice there to the *L*.
2: 7 the *L* during the entire lifetime of Joshua,
2: 7 great work which the *L* had done for Israel,
2: 8 Joshua, son of Nun, the servant of the *L*,
2:10 generation arose that did not know the *L*,
2:11 offended the *L* by serving the Baals.
2:12 Abandoning the *L*,
2:12 their worship of these gods provoked the *L*.
2:14 anger of the *L* flared up against Israel,
2:15 the *L* turned into disaster for them,
2:16 Even when the *L* raised up judges to
2:17 of obedience to the commandments of the *L*.
2:18 Whenever the *L* raised up judges for them,
2:18 it was thus the *L* took pity on their
2:20 In his anger toward Israel the *L* said,
2:22 they would keep to the way of the *L*
2:23 therefore the *L* allowed them to remain
3: 1 the nations which the *L* allowed to remain,
3: 4 they would obey the commandments the *L*
3: 7 had offended the LORD by forgetting the *L*,
3: 8 the anger of the *L* flared up against them,
3: 9 when the Israelites cried out to the *L*,
3:10 The spirit of the *L* came upon him,
3:10 to war, the *L* delivered Cushan-rishathaim,
3:12 Again the Israelites offended the *L*,
3:15 when the Israelites cried out to the *L*,
3:25 There on the floor, dead, lay their *l!*
3:28 "for the *L* has delivered your enemies the
4: 1 the Israelites again offended the *L*.
4: 2 So the *L* allowed them to fall into the
4: 3 But the Israelites cried out to the *L*;
4: 6 "This is what the *L*,
4: 9 for the *L* will have Sisera fall into the
4:14 the *L* has delivered Sisera into your power.
4:14 The *L* marches before you."
4:15 And the *L* put Sisera and all his chariots
4:18 Sisera and said to him, "Come in, my *l*,
5: 2 noble deeds by the people who bless the *L*,
5: 3 LORD will sing my song, my hymn to the *L*,
5: 4 O *L*, when you went out from Seir,
5: 5 *L*, the One of Sinai, in the presence of the *L*,
5: 9 nobles of the people who bless the *L*;
5:11 where men recount the just deeds of the *L*,
5:13 of the *L* came down for me as warriors.
5:23 "Curse Meroz," says the *L*,
5:23 my help, as warriors to the help of the *L*."
5:31 May all your enemies perish thus, O *L!*
6: 1 The Israelites offended the *L*,
6: 6 and so the Israelites cried out to the *L*.
6: 7 cried out to the *L* because of Midian,
6: 8 the Israelites who said to them, "The *L*,
6:10 I, the *L*, am your God;
6:11 Then the angel of the *L* came and sat under
6:12 *L* appeared to him and said, "The LORD
6:13 "My *l*," Gideon said to him, "if the LORD
6:13 said 'Did not the *L* bring us up from Egypt?'
6:13 For now the *L* has abandoned us and has
6:14 The *L* turned to him and said,
6:15 But he answered him, "Please, my *l*,
6:16 "I shall be with you," the *L* said to him,
6:21 the angel of the *L* stretched out the tip
6:21 the angel of the *L* disappeared from sight.
6:22 the angel of the *L*, said, "Alas, Lord GOD,
6:22 have seen the angel of the *L* face to face!"
6:23 The *L* answered him,
6:24 altar to the *L* and called it Yahweh-shalom.
6:25 That same night the *L* said to him,
6:26 instead, the proper kind of altar to the *L*,
6:27 and did as the *L* had commanded him.
6:34 The spirit of the *L* enveloped Gideon;
7: 2 *L* said to Gideon, "You have too many
7: 4 *L* said to Gideon, "There are still too many
7: 5 down to the water, the *L* said to him,
7: 7 *L* said to Gideon, "By means of the three
7: 9 That night the *L* said to Gideon,
7:15 for the *L* has delivered the camp of Midian
7:18 and cry out, 'For the *L* and for Gideon!'"
7:20 cried out, "A sword for the *L* and Gideon!"
7:22 the *L* set the sword of one against another.
8: 7 when the *L* has delivered Zebah and
8:19 "As the *L* lives,
8:23 The *L* must rule over you."
8:34 of Berith their god and forgetting the *L*,
10: 6 The Israelites again offended the *L*,
10: 6 abandoned the *L* and would not serve him,
10: 7 the *L* became angry with Israel and allowed
10:10 Then the Israelites cried out to the *L*,
10:11 The *L* answered the Israelites:
10:15 But the Israelites said to the *L*,
10:16 gods from their midst and served the *L*,
11: 9 Ammonites and the *L* delivers them up to me,
11:10 "The *L* is witness between us that we will
11:11 settled all his affairs before the *L*.
11:21 But the *L*, the God of Israel,
11:23 If now the *L*,
11:24 and should we not possess all that the *L*,
11:27 wrong me by warring against me, Let the *L*,
11:29 The spirit of the *L* came upon Jephthah.
11:30 Jephthah made a vow to the *L*.
11:31 from the Ammonites shall belong to the *L*.
11:32 and the *L* delivered them into his power,
11:35 made a vow to the *L* and I cannot retract."
11:36 replied, "you have made a vow to the *L*.
11:36 because the *L* has wrought vengeance for
12: 3 and the *L* delivered them into my power.
13: 1 The Israelites again offended the *L*,
13: 3 *L* appeared to the woman and said to her,
13: 8 Manoah then prayed to the *L*.
13: 8 "O *L*, I beseech you," he said,
13:13 The angel of the *L* answered Manoah,
13:15 Then Manoah said to the angel of the *L*,
13:16 But the angel of the *L* answered Manoah,
13:16 will, you may offer a holocaust to the *L*.
13:16 knowing that it was the angel of the *L*,
13:18 The angel of the *L* answered him,
13:19 and offered it on the rock to the *L*,
13:20 the *L* ascended in the flame of the altar.
13:21 *L* was seen no more by Manoah and his wife.
13:21 realizing that it was the angel of the *L*,
13:23 to him, "If the *L* had meant to kill us,
13:24 The boy grew up and the *L* blessed him;
13:25 of the *L* first stirred him in Mahaneh-dan,
14: 4 that this had been brought about by the *L*,
14: 6 But the spirit of the *L* came upon Samson,
14:19 The spirit of the *L* came upon him,
15:14 him, the spirit of the *L* came upon him:
15:18 very thirsty, he cried to the *L* and said,
16:20 he did not realize that the *L* had left him.
16:28 Samson cried out to the *L* and said, "O Lord
17: 4 his mother said, "May the *L* bless my son!
17: 4 to the *L* as my gift in favor of my son,
17:13 "Now I know that the *L* will prosper me,
18: 6 the *L* is favorable to the undertaking you
20: 1 community was gathered to the *L* at Mizpah.
20:18 the attack on the Benjaminites, the *L* said,
20:22 up and wept before the *L* until evening.
20:22 they asked the *L*; and the LORD answered
20:26 before the *L* until evening of that day,
20:26 and peace offerings before the *L*.
20:27 When the Israelites consulted the *L* (for
20:28 the *L* said, "Attack!
20:35 the *L* defeated Benjamin before Israel;
21: 3 They said, *L*,
21: 5 did not come up to the *L* for the assembly?"
21: 5 that anyone who did not go up to the *L*
21: 7 since we have sworn by the *L* not to give
21: 8 Israel had not come up to the *L* in Mizpah,
21:15 because the *L* had made a breach
21:19 of the yearly feast of the *L* at Shiloh,
Ru 1: 6 *L* had visited his people and given them
1: 8 May the *L* be kind to you as you were to
1: 9 May the *L* grant each of you a husband and
1:13 lot is too bitter for you, because the *L*,
1:17 May the *L* do so and so to me,
1:21 but the *L* has brought me back destitute.
1:21 since the *L* has pronounced against me and
2: 4 to the harvesters, "The *L* be with you!"
2: 4 and they replied, "The *L* bless you!"
2:12 May the *L* reward what you have done!
2:12 May you receive a full reward from the *L*,
2:13 I prove worthy of your kindness, my *l*:
2:20 "May he be blessed by the *L*,
3:10 He said, "May the *L* bless you,
3:13 does not wish to claim you, as the *L* lives,
4:11 May the *L* make this wife come into your
4:12 the *L* will give you from this girl,
4:13 the *L* enabled her to conceive and she bore
4:14 "Blessed is the *L* who has not failed to
1Sm 1: 3 pilgrimage from his city to worship the *L*
1: 3 were ministering as priests of the *L*.
1: 5 her, though the *L* had made her barren.
1: 6 to her that the *L* had left her barren.
1: 7 pilgrimage to the sanctuary of the *L*,
1: 9 and presented herself before the *L*;
1:10 In her bitterness she prayed to the *L*,
1:11 "O *L* of hosts, if you look with pity
1:11 give him to the *L* for as long as he lives;
1:12 she remained long at prayer before the *L*,
1:15 "It isn't that my *l*," Hannah answered.
1:15 was only pouring out my troubles to the *L*.
1:19 next morning they worshiped before the *L*,
1:19 with his wife Hannah, the *L* remembered her.
1:20 Samuel, since she had asked the *L* for him.
1:21 sacrifice to the *L* and to fulfill his vows,
1:22 before the *L* and to remain there forever;
1:23 the *L* bring your resolve to fulfillment!"
1:24 him at the temple of the *L* in Shiloh.
1:26 "Pardon, my *l!* As you live my lord
1:26 who stood near you here, praying to the *L*.
1:27 this child, and the *L* granted my request.
1:28 Now I, in turn, give him to the *L*;
1:28 he lives, he shall be dedicated to the *L*."
2: 1 and as she worshiped the *L*, she said:
2: 1 "My heart exults in the *L*,
2: 2 There is no Holy One like the *L*;
2: 3 For an all-knowing God is the *L*,
2: 6 "The *L* puts to death and gives life;
2: 7 The *L* makes poor and makes rich,
2:10 the *L* judges the ends of the earth,
2:11 the service of the *L* under the priest Eli.
2:12 neither for the *L* nor for the priests' duties
2:17 grievously in the presence of the *L*;
2:17 the offerings to the *L* with disdain.
2:18 was serving in the presence of the *L*.
2:20 "May the *L* repay you with children from
2:20 woman for the gift she has made to the *L!*"
2:21 The *L* favored Hannah so that she conceived
2:21 Samuel grew up in the service of the *L*.
2:24 the people of the *L* spreading about you.
2:25 man, one can intercede for him with the *L*;
2:25 but if a man sins against the *L*,
2:25 since the *L* had decided on their death.
2:26 in the estimation of the *L* and of men.
2:27 "This is what the *L* says:
2:30 This, therefore, is the oracle of the *L*,
2:30 But now,' the *L* declares, 'away with this!
3: 1 Samuel was minister to the *L* under Eli,
3: 1 revelation of the *L* was uncommon
3: 3 temple of the *L* where the ark of God was.
3: 4 The *L* called to Samuel,
3: 6 Again the *L* called Samuel,
3: 7 not familiar with the *L*, because the LORD
3: 8 The *L* called Samuel again,
3: 8 that the *L* was calling the youth.
3: 9 and if you are called, reply, 'Speak, *L*,
3:10 the *L* came and revealed his presence,
3:11 *L* said to Samuel: "I am about
3:15 opened the doors of the temple of the *L*.
3:18 Eli answered, "He is the *L*.
3:19 Samuel grew up, and the *L* was with him,
3:20 Samuel was an accredited prophet of the *L*.
4: 3 "Why has the *L* permitted us to be
4: 3 Let us fetch the ark of the *L* from Shiloh
4: 4 from there the ark of the *L* of hosts,
4: 5 When the ark of the *L* arrived in the camp,
4: 6 the ark of the *L* had come into the camp,
5: 3 on the ground before the ark of the *L*.
5: 4 on the ground before the ark of the *L*,
5: 6 *L* dealt severely with the people of Ashdod.
5: 9 the *L* threw the city into utter turmoil:
6: 1 The ark of the *L* had been in the land of
6: 2 "What shall we do with the ark of the *L?*
6: 8 the ark of the *L* and place it on the cart,
6:11 they placed the ark of the *L* on the cart,

6:14 cows were offered as a holocaust to the L.
6:15 and sacrifices to the L that day.
6:17 a guilt offering to the L were as follows:
6:18 The large stone on which the ark of the L
6:19 when they greeted the ark of the L,
6:19 with which the L had afflicted them.
6:21 Philistines have returned the ark of the L;
7: 1 Kiriath-jearim came for the ark of the L
7: 1 Eleazar as guardian of the ark of the L.
7: 2 whole Israelite population turned to the L.
7: 3 with your whole heart to return to the L,
7: 3 your Ashtaroth, devote yourselves to the L,
7: 4 and Ashtaroth, and worshiped the L alone.
7: 5 Mizpah, that I may pray to the L for you."
7: 6 poured it out on the ground before the L,
7: 6 confessing, "We have sinned against the L.
7: 8 "Implore the L our God unceasingly for us,
7: 9 offered it entire as a holocaust to the L.
7: 9 implored the L for Israel, and the LORD
7:10 L thundered loudly against the Philistines,
7:12 "To this point the L helped us."
7:13 for the L was severe with them as long as
7:17 judged Israel and built an altar to the L.
8: 6 He prayed to the L,
8:10 Samuel delivered the message of the L in
8:18 but on that day the L will not answer you."
8:21 had to say, he repeated it to the L,
9:15 the L had given Samuel the revelation:
9:17 caught sight of Saul, the L assured him,
10: 1 L anoints you commander over his heritage.
10: 1 sign for you that the L has anointed you
10: 6 The spirit of the L will rush upon you,
10:17 L at Mizpah and addressed the Israelites:
10:18 "Thus says the L, the God of Israel
10:19 the L according to tribes and families."
10:22 Again they consulted the L,
10:22 The L answered, "He is hiding among
10:24 "Do you see the man whom the L has chosen?
10:25 which he placed in the presence of the L.
10:26 by warriors whose hearts the L had touched.
11: 7 In dread of the L, the people turned out
11:13 this day, for today the L has saved Israel."
11:15 to Gilgal, where in the presence of the L,
11:15 peace offerings there before the L,
12: 3 the presence of the L and of his anointed.
12: 5 "The L is witness against you this day,
12: 6 "The L is witness, who appointed Moses
12: 7 and I shall arraign you before the L,
12: 7 the L has done for you and your fathers.
12: 8 them, your fathers appealed to the L,
12: 9 But they forgot the L their God;
12:10 Each time they appealed to the L and said,
12:10 the L and worshiping Baals and Ashtaroth;
12:11 Accordingly, the L sent Jerubbaal.
12:12 even though the L your God is your king.
12:13 king you want, a king the L has given you.
12:14 If you fear the L and worship him,
12:14 king who rules you follow the L your God
12:15 the L and if you rebel against his command,
12:15 the L will deal severely with you and your
12:16 L is about to accomplish before your eyes.
12:17 Yet I shall call to the L,
12:17 understand how greatly the L is displeased
12:18 called to the L, and the LORD sent thunder
12:18 all the people dreaded the L and Samuel.
12:19 to Samuel, "Pray to the L your God for us,
12:20 still, you must not turn from the L,
12:22 name the L will not abandon his people,
12:22 the L himself chose to make you his people.
12:23 far be it from me to sin against the L
12:24 But you must fear the L and worship him
13:13 kept the command the L your God gave you,
13:13 the L would now establish your kingship in
13:14 The L has sought out a man after his own
14: 3 son of Eli, the priest of the L at Shiloh,
14: 6 Perhaps the L will help us,
14: 6 no more difficult for the L to grant victory
14:10 the L has delivered them into our grasp.
14:12 for the L has delivered them into the
14:23 Thus the L saved Israel that day.
14:33 the L by eating the flesh with blood,
14:34 the L by eating the flesh with blood."
14:34 brought to the L whatever ox he had seized,
14:35 and Saul built an altar to the L—
14:35 the first time he built an altar to the L.
14:39 L lives who has given victory to Israel,
14:41 And Saul said to the L, the God of Israel:
14:41 this resides in me or my son Jonathan, L,
14:45 As the L lives,
15: 1 "It was I the L sent to anoint you king
15: 1 therefore, listen to the message of the L.
15: 2 This is what the L of hosts has to say:
15:10 Then the L spoke to Samuel:
15:11 angry and cried out to the L all night.
15:13 "The L bless you!
15:13 I have kept the command of the L."
15:15 best sheep and oxen to sacrifice to the L,
15:16 tell you what the L said to me last night."
15:17 The L anointed you king of Israel and sent
15:19 Why then have you disobeyed the L?
15:19 on the spoil, thus displeasing the L."
15:20 "I did indeed obey the L and fulfill the
15:20 fulfill the mission on which the L sent me.
15:21 sacrifice to the L their God in Gilgal."
15:22 "Does the L so delight in holocausts
15:22 as in obedience to the command of the L?
15:23 you have rejected the command of the L,
15:24 the command of the L and your instructions.
15:25 return with me, that I may worship the L."
15:26 rejected the command of the L and the LORD
15:28 "The L has torn the kingdom of Israel
15:30 with me that I may worship the L your God."
15:31 with him, and Saul worshiped the L.
15:33 he cut Agag down before the L in Gilgal.
15:35 L regretted having made him king of Israel.
16: 1 L said to Samuel: "How long will you
16: 2 To this the L answered: "Take a heifer
16: 2 say, 'I have come to sacrifice to the L.
16: 4 Samuel did as the L had commanded him.
16: 5 I have come to sacrifice to the L.
16: 7 But the L said to Samuel:
16: 7 appearance but the L looks into the heart."
16: 8 who said, "The L has not chosen him."
16: 9 "The L has not chosen this one either."
16:10 "The L has not chosen any one of these."
16:12 The L said, "There— anoint him,
16:13 on, the spirit of the L rushed upon David.
16:14 The spirit of the L had departed from Saul,
16:14 tormented by an evil spirit sent by the L.
16:18 Moreover, the L is with him."
17:37 "The L, who delivered me from the claws
17:37 the L will be with you."
17:45 against you in the name of the L of hosts,
17:46 Today the L shall deliver you into my hand;
17:47 is not by sword or spear that the L saves.
18:12 to fear David, [because the L was with him,
18:14 his enterprises, for the L was with him.
18:17 my champion and fight the battles of the L.
18:28 to recognize that the L was with David;
19: 5 and the L brought about a great victory
19: 6 plea and swore, "As the L lives,
19: 9 Then an evil spirit from the L came upon
20: 3 as the L lives and as you live,
20:12 "As the L, the God of Israel, lives,
20:13 may the L do thus and so to Jonathan if I
20:13 May the L be with you even as he was with
20:14 may you show me the kindness of the L.
20:15 And when the L exterminates all the
20:16 you, or the L will make you answer for it."
20:21 L lives, there will be nothing to fear,
20:22 beyond you,' go, for the L sends you away.
20:23 the L shall be between you and me forever."
20:42 we two have sworn by the name of the L:
20:42 'The L shall be between you and me,
21: 8 was there that day, detained before the L;
22:10 the L for him and gave him supplies,
22:12 He replied, "Yes, my l."
22:17 the rounds and kill the priests of the L,
22:17 lift a hand to strike the priests of the L.
22:21 that Saul had slain the priests of the L,
23: 2 So he consulted the L,
23: 2 The L answered, "Go, for you will defeat
23: 4 Again David consulted the L,
23:10 L God of Israel, your servant has heard
23:11 O L God of Israel, tell your servant."
23:11 The L answered, "He will come down."
23:12 And the L answered, "Yes."
23:14 the L did not deliver David into his grasp.
23:16 and strengthened his resolve in the L.
23:18 a joint agreement before the L in Horesh,
23:21 L bless you for your sympathy toward me.
24: 5 is the day of which the L said to you,
24: 7 "The L forbid that I should do such a
24: 9 the cave, calling to Saul, "My l the king!"
24:11 You see for yourself today that the L just
24:11 'I will not raise a hand against my l,
24:13 L will judge between me and you, and the L
24:16 The L will be the judge;
24:19 when the L delivered me into your grasp
24:20 May the L reward you generously for what
24:22 swear to me by the L that you will not
25:24 "My l, let the blame be mine.
25:25 Let not my l pay attention to that
25:25 did not see the young men whom my l sent.
25:26 Now, therefore, my lord, as the L lives,
25:26 it is the L who has kept you from shedding
25:26 who seek to harm my l become as Nabal!
25:27 your maidservant has brought for my l,
25:27 be given to the young men who follow my l.
25:28 for the L shall certainly establish a
25:28 establish a lasting dynasty for my l,
25:28 lordship is fighting the battles of the L,
25:29 may the life of my l be bound in the
25:29 the living in the care of the L your God;
25:30 And when the LORD carries out for my l the
25:31 qualm or burden on your conscience, my l,
25:31 L confers this benefit on your lordship,
25:32 "Blessed be the L,
25:34 Otherwise, as the L,
25:38 days later the L struck him and he died.
25:39 "Blessed be the L,
26:10 As the L lives," David continued,
26:10 must be the L himself who will strike him,
26:11 But the L forbid that I touch his anointed!
26:12 the L had put them into a deep slumber.
26:15 have you not guarded your l the king when
26:15 his subjects went to kill the king, your l?
26:16 As the L lives, you people deserve death
26:16 death because you have not guarded your l,
26:17 David answered, "Yes, my l the king."
26:18 "Why does my l pursue his servant?
26:19 let my l the king listen to the words of
26:19 If the L has incited you against me,
26:19 if men, may they be cursed before the L,
26:20 the ground far from the presence of the L.
26:23 The L will reward each man for his justice
26:23 though the L delivered you into my grasp,
26:24 so may the L value my life highly and
28: 6 the L; but the LORD gave no answer,
28:10 to her by the L, "As the LORD lives,
28:16 if the L has abandoned you and is with
28:17 The L has done to you what he foretold
28:18 Amalek, the L has done this to you today.
28:19 Moreover, the L will deliver Israel,
28:19 and the L will have delivered the army of
29: 6 "As the L lives, you are honest,
29: 8 fight against the enemies of my l the king?"
30: 6 But with renewed trust in the L his God,
30: 8 him the ephod, David inquired of the L,
30: 8 The L answered him, "Go in pursuit,
30:23 my brothers, after what the L has given us.
30:26 from the spoil of the enemies of the L":

2Sm 1:10 from his arm and brought them here to my l.
1:12 soldiers of the L of the clans of Israel,
2: 1 After this David inquired of the L,
2: 1 The L replied to him, "Yes."
2: 5 L for having done this kindness to your l
2: 6 now may the L be kind and faithful to you.
2: 7 men, for though your l Saul is dead,
3: 9 out for David what the L swore to him
3:18 take action, for the L has said of David,
3:21 to assemble all Israel for my l the king,
3:28 "Before the L; I and my kingdom
3:39 May the L requite the evildoer in
4: 8 Thus has the L this day avenged my lord
4: 9 "As the L lives, who rescued me
5: 2 L said to you, 'You shall shepherd
5: 3 an agreement with them there before the L,
5:10 powerful, for the L of hosts was with him.
5:12 And David knew that the L had established
5:19 David inquired of the L,
5:19 The L replied to David,
5:20 "The L has scattered my enemies before me
5:23 So David inquired of the L, who replied:
5:24 for the L will have gone forth before you
6: 2 L of hosts enthroned above the cherubim.
6: 5 merry before the L with all their strength,
6: 7 But the L was angry with Uzzah;
6: 8 the L had vented his anger on Uzzah.
6: 9 David feared the L that day and said,
6: 9 "How can the ark of the L come to me?"
6:10 would not have the ark of the L brought
6:11 The ark of the L remained in the house of
6:11 L blessed Oded-edom and his whole house.
6:12 L had blessed the family of Obed-edom
6:13 of the ark of the L had advanced six steps,
6:14 came dancing before the L with abandon,
6:15 bringing up the ark of the L with shouts
6:16 of the L was entering the City of David,
6:16 David leaping and dancing before the L,
6:17 The ark of the L was brought in and set in
6:17 and peace offerings before the L.
6:18 the people in the name of the L of hosts.
6:21 "I was dancing before the L.
6:21 As the L lives, who preferred me
6:21 not only will I make merry before the L,
7: 1 and the L had given him rest from his
7: 3 you have in mind, for the L is with you."
7: 4 that night the L spoke to Nathan and said:
7: 5 tell my servant David, 'Thus says the L:
7: 8 David, 'The L of hosts has this to say:
7:11 The L also reveals to you that he will
7:18 the LORD and said, "Who am I, L GOD,
7:19 Yet even this you see as too little, L GOD;
7:19 this too you have shown to man, L GOD!
7:20 You know your servant, L GOD!
7:22 And so—"Great are you, L GOD!
7:24 people Israel as yours forever, and you, L,
7:25 L God, confirm for all time the prophecy
7:26 men say, 'The L of hosts is God of Israel,'
7:27 It is you, L of hosts, God of Israel
7:28 L GOD, you are God and your words are
7:29 for you, L GOD,
8: 6 The L brought David victory in all his
8:11 too, King David consecrated to the L,
8:14 and the L brought David victory in all his
9:11 do just as my l the king has commanded him.
10: 3 the Ammonite princes said to their l Hanun:
10:12 the L will do what he judges best."
11: 9 palace with the other officers of his l,
11:11 and my l Joab and your majesty's servants
11:11 As the L lives and as you live,
11:26 her husband had died, she mourned her l.
11:27 L was displeased with what David had done.
12: 1 The L sent Nathan to David,
12: 5 L lives, the man who had done this
12: 7 Thus says the L God of Israel:
12: 9 spurned the L and done evil in his sight?
12:11 Thus says the L: "I will bring evil

LORD (cont.)
12:13 to Nathan, "I have sinned against the L."
12:13 "The L on his part has forgiven your sin:
12:14 have utterly spurned the L by this deed,
12:15 The L struck the child that the wife of
12:20 went to the house of the L and worshiped.
12:22 the L will grant me the child's life.'
12:24 The L loved him and sent the prophet
12:25 to name him Jedidiah, on behalf of the L.
13:32 "Let not my l think that all the young
13:33 So let not my l the king put faith in the
14: 9 me and my family be to blame, my l king;
14:11 your majesty, keep in mind the L your God,
14:11 He replied, "As the L lives,
14:12 say still another word to my l the king."
14:17 of my l the king provide a resting place;
14:17 my l the king is like an angel of God,
14:17 The L your God be with you."
14:18 The woman said, "Let my l the king speak."
14:19 "As you live, my l the king,
14:20 But my l is as wise as an angel of God,
14:22 I am in good favor with you, my l the king,
15: 7 Hebron and fulfill a vow I made to the L.
15: 8 'If the L ever brings me back to Jerusalem,
15:15 whatever our l the king chooses to do."
15:20 and may the L be kind and faithful to you."
15:21 the LORD lives, and as my l the king lives,
15:21 shall be wherever my l the king may be,
15:25 If I find favor with the L,
15:31 conspirators with Absalom, he said, "O L,
16: 4 "I pay you homage, my l the king.
16: 8 The L has requited you for all the
16: 8 and the L has given over the kingdom to
16: 9 should this dead dog curse my l the king?
16:10 Suppose the L has told him to curse David;
16:11 let him curse, for the L has told him to.
16:12 Perhaps the L will look upon my affliction
16:18 I am his whom the L and all this people
17:14 For the L had decided to undo Ahithophel's
18:19 take the good news to the king that the L
18:28 king and said, "Blessed be the L your God,
18:28 the men who rebelled against my l the king."
18:31 "Let my l the king receive the good news
18:31 that this day the L has taken your part,
18:32 "May the enemies of my l the king and all
19: 8 I swear by the L that if you do not go out,
19:20 "May my l not hold me guilty,
19:20 did the day my l the king left Jerusalem.
19:21 to come down today to meet my l the king."
19:27 "My l the king, my servant betrayed me.
19:28 your servant before my l the king.
19:28 But my l the king is like an angel of God.
19:29 deserved only death from my l the king,
19:31 now that my l the king has returned safely
19:36 be any further burden to my l the king?
19:38 Let him cross over with my l the king.
20:19 wish to destroy the inheritance of the L?"
21: 1 David had recourse to the L,
21: 3 you may bless the inheritance of the L?"
21: 6 may dismember them before the L in Gibeon,
21: 9 them on the mountain before the L.
22: 1 song to the LORD when the L had rescued
22: 4 'Praised be the L,'
22: 7 called upon the L and cried out to my God;
22:14 "The L thundered from heaven;
22:16 were laid bare, At the rebuke of the L,
22:19 of calamity, but the L came to my support.
22:21 L rewarded me according to my justice;
22:22 of the L and was not disloyal to my God.
22:25 the L requited me according to my justice,
22:29 You are my lamp, O L!
22:31 the promise of the L is fire-tried;
22:32 "For who is God except the L?
22:42 to the L—
22:47 "The L live!
22:50 Therefore will I proclaim you, O L,
23: 2 The spirit of the L spoke through me;
23:10 The L brought about a great victory on
23:12 and the L brought about a great victory.
23:16 it, and instead poured it out to the L,
23:17 "The L forbid that I do this!
24: 3 "May the L your God increase the number
24: 3 l the king to order a thing of this kind?"
24:10 numbered the people, and said to the L:
24:10 L, forgive the guilt of your servant,
24:11 the L had spoken to the prophet Gad,
24:12 and say to David, 'This is what the L says:
24:15 [The L then sent a pestilence over Israel
24:16 the L regretted the calamity and said to
24:16 The angel of the L was then standing at
24:17 was striking the people, he said to the L:
24:18 "Go up and build an altar to the L on the
24:19 David went up as the L had commanded.
24:21 does my l the king come to his servant?"
24:21 floor from you to build an altar to the L,
24:22 "Let my l the king take and offer up
24:23 "May the L your God accept your offering."
24:24 the L my God holocausts that cost nothing."
24:25 Then David built an altar there to the L,
24:25 The L granted relief to the country,
1Kgs 1: 2 virgin be sought to attend you, l king,
1:11 king without the knowledge of our l David?
1:13 and say to him, 'Did you not, l king,
1:17 l, you swore to me your handmaid by the L,
1:18 has become king, and you, my l king,
1:20 my l king, all Israel is waiting for you
1:21 when my l the king sleeps with his fathers,
1:24 "Have you decided, my l king,
1:29 him, the king swore, "As the L lives,
1:30 fulfill the oath I swore to you by the L,
1:31 to the king, Bathsheba said, "May the l,
1:36 May the LORD, the God of my l the king,
1:37 As the L has been with your royal majesty,
1:37 his throne even more than that of my l,
1:43 "Our l, King David, has made Solomon king
1:47 went in and paid their respects to our l,
1:48 'Blessed be the L,
2: 3 Keep the mandate of the L,
2: 4 and the L may fulfill the promise he made
2: 8 L that I would not put him to the sword.
2:15 my brother's, for the L gave it to him.
2:23 And King Solomon swore by the L:
2:24 And now, as the L lives,
2:26 because you carried the ark of the L GOD
2:27 from his office of priest of the L,
2:27 thus fulfilling the prophecy with the L
2:28 of the L and seized the horns of the altar.
2:29 to the tent of the L and was at the altar.
2:30 went to the tent of the L and said to him,
2:32 The L will hold him responsible for his
2:33 be the peace of the L forever for David,
2:42 "Did I not have you swear by the L to
2:43 of the L and the command that I gave you?"
2:44 the L requites you for your own wickedness.
2:45 throne shall endure before the L forever."
3: 1 his palace, and the temple of the L,
3: 2 temple had been built to the name of the L.
3: 3 Solomon loved the L,
3: 5 L appeared to Solomon in a dream at night.
3: 7 O L, my God, you have made me
3:10 The L was pleased that Solomon made this
3:15 before the ark of the covenant of the L,
3:17 "By your leave, my l,
3:26 "Please, my l, give her the living child
5:17 L, his God, until such a time as the L
5:18 the L, my God, has given me peace
5:19 to build a temple in honor of the L,
5:19 as the L predicted to my father David when
5:21 and said, "Blessed be the L this day,
5:26 The L, moreover, gave Solomon wisdom
6: 1 of the temple of the L was begun.
6: 2 built for the L was sixty cubits long,
6:11 This word of the L came to Solomon:
7:12 the temple of the L and the temple porch.
7:40 for King Solomon in the temple of the L:
7:45 temple of the L were of burnished bronze.
7:48 for the interior of the temple of the L:
7:51 in the temple of the L was completed,
7:51 in the treasuries of the temple of the L.
8: 4 they carried the ark of the L and the
8: 6 ark of the covenant of the L to its place
8: 9 when the L made a covenant with the
8:10 the cloud filled the temple of the L
8:11 glory had filled the temple of the L.
8:12 "The L intends to dwell in the dark cloud;
8:15 "Blessed be the L,
8:17 to build a temple to the honor of the L,
8:18 LORD, the God of Israel, the L said to him,
8:20 L has fulfilled the promise that he made:
8:20 on the throne of Israel, as the L foretold,
8:20 I have built this temple to honor the L,
8:21 the ark in which is the covenant of the L,
8:22 Solomon stood before the altar of the L in
8:23 L, God of Israel, there is no God like you
8:25 L, God of Israel, keep the further promise
8:26 Now, L, God of Israel, may this promise
8:28 prayer and petition of your servant, O L,
8:44 their enemies, if they pray to you, O L,
8:53 brought our fathers out of Egypt, O L GOD."
8:54 this entire prayer of petition to the L,
8:54 he rose from before the altar of the L,
8:56 L who has given rest to his people Israel,
8:57 May the L, our God, be with us
8:59 May this prayer I have offered to the L,
8:60 know the L is God and there is no other.
8:61 You must be wholly devoted to the L,
8:62 with him offered sacrifices before the L.
8:63 offered as peace offerings to the L
8:63 Israelites dedicated the temple of the L.
8:64 of the court facing the temple of the L,
8:64 L was too small to hold these offerings.
8:65 celebrated the festival before the L,
8:66 happy over all the blessings the L had given
9: 1 finished building the temple of the L,
9: 2 the L appeared to him a second time,
9: 3 The L said to him: "I have heard
9: 8 L done this to the land and to this temple?'
9: 9 'They forsook the L,
9: 9 L has brought down upon them all this evil.' "
9:10 temple of the L and the palace of the king
9:15 in order to build the temple of the L,
9:25 the LORD, and to burn incense before the L;
10: 5 he offered in the temple of the L,
10: 9 Blessed be the L,
10: 9 the L has made you king to carry out
10:12 of the L and for the palace of the king,
11: 2 from nations with which the L had
11: 4 and his heart was not entirely with the L,
11: 6 Solomon did evil in the sight of the L;
11: 9 The L, therefore, became angry
11: 9 his heart was turned away from the L,
11:10 the L had forbidden him this very act
11:11 So the L said to Solomon:
11:14 L then raised up an adversary to Solomon:
11:23 son of Eliada, who had fled from his l,
11:31 the L, the God of Israel says:
12:15 for the L brought this about to fulfill
12:22 However, the L spoke to Shemaiah,
12:24 'Thus says the L: You must not march
12:24 L and gave up the expedition accordingly.
12:27 in the temple of the L in Jerusalem,
13: 1 from Judah to Bethel by the word of the L,
13: 2 out against the altar the word of the L:
13: 2 "O altar, altar, the L says,
13: 3 "This is the sign that the L has spoken:
13: 5 man of God had given as the word of the L.
13: 6 "Entreat the L, your God," he said,
13: 6 So the man of God entreated the L,
13: 9 For I was instructed by the word of the L
13:17 "for I was told by the word of the L
13:18 an angel told me in the word of the L
13:20 the L spoke to the prophet who had brought
13:21 "The L says, 'Because you rebelled against
13:21 and did not keep the command which the L,
13:26 who rebelled against the command of the L.
13:26 and killed him, as the L predicted to him."
13:32 For the word of the L which he proclaimed
14: 5 The L had said to Ahijah:
14: 7 Go, tell Jeroboam, 'This is what the L,
14:11 For the L has spoken!"
14:13 house has something pleasing to the L,
14:14 the L will raise up for himself a king of
14:15 The L will strike Israel like a reed
14:15 for themselves and thus provoked the L.
14:18 as the L had prophesied through his
14:21 of Israel, the L chose to be honored.
14:22 Judah did evil in the sight of the L,
14:24 L had cleared out of the Israelites' way.
14:26 of the L and those of the royal palace,
14:28 the king visited the temple of the L,
15: 3 and his heart was not entirely with the L,
15: 4 Yet for David's sake the L, his God,
15: 5 because David had pleased the L and did
15:11 pleased the L like his forefather David,
15:14 entirely with the L as long as he lived.
15:15 He brought into the temple of the L his
15:18 temple of the L and of the royal palace.
15:29 the L had pronounced through his servant,
15:30 to commit, by which he provoked the L,
16: 1 The L spoke against Baasha to Jehu,
16: 7 the L had threatened Baasha and his house
16: 7 the evil Baasha did in the sight of the L,
16:12 as the L had prophesied to Baasha through
16:13 caused Israel to commit, provoking the L,
16:19 doing evil in the sight of the L
16:26 Israel to sin and to provoke to the L,
16:30 of the L more than any of his predecessors.
16:33 He did more to anger the L,
16:34 as the L had foretold through Joshua,
17: 1 "As the L, the God of Israel, lives
17: 2 The L then said to Elijah:
17: 5 So he left and did as the L had commanded.
17: 8 So the L said to him:
17:12 "As the L, your God lives,"
17:14 For the L, the God of Israel,
17:14 day when the L sends rain upon the earth.' "
17:16 dry, as the L had foretold through Elijah.
17:20 He called out to the L:
17:20 "O L, my God, will you afflict even
17:21 child three times and called out to the L:
17:21 "O L, my God, let the life breath return
17:22 The L heard the prayer of Elijah;
17:24 word of the L comes truly from your mouth."
18: 1 in the third year, the L spoke to Elijah,
18: 4 who was a zealous follower of the L.
18: 4 was murdering the prophets of the L,
18: 7 and asked, "Is it you, my l Elijah?"
18:10 As the L, your God lives
18:12 the spirit of the L will carry you to some
18:12 servant has revered the L from his youth.
18:13 Have you not been told, my l,
18:13 was murdering the prophets of the L—
18:13 I hid a hundred of the prophets of the L,
18:15 Elijah answered, "As the L of hosts lives,
18:18 commands of the L and following the Baals.
18:21 If the L is God,
18:22 am the only surviving prophet of the L,
18:24 on your gods, and I will call on the L.
18:30 altar of the L which had been destroyed.
18:31 the sons of Jacob, to whom the L had said,
18:32 an altar in honor of the L with the stones,
18:36 prophet Elijah came forward and said, L,
18:37 Answer me, L! Answer me, that this people
18:37 me, that this people may know that you, L,
18:39 fell prostrate and said, "The L is God!
18:46 But the hand of the L was on Elijah,
19: 4 "This is enough, O L!
19: 7 the angel of the L came back a second time,
19: 9 But the word of the L came to him,

19:10 been zealous for the L, the God
19:11 Then the L said, "Go outside and stand
19:11 before the LORD; the L will be passing by."
19:11 the LORD— but the L was not in the wind.
19:11 but the L was not in the earthquake.
19:12 but the L was not in the fire.
19:14 "I have been most zealous for the L,
19:15 desert near Damascus," the L said to him.
20: 4 Israel answered, "As you say, my l king,
20: 9 of Ben-hadad, "Say to my l the king,
20:13 "The L says, 'Do you see all this huge
20:13 you today, you will know that I am the L.
20:14 He answered, "The L says,
20:28 LORD says, 'Because Aram has said the L
20:28 large army, that you may know I am the L.' "
20:35 prompted by the L to say to his companion,
20:36 you did not obey the voice of the L,
20:42 He said to him, "The L says,
21: 3 "The L forbid." Naboth answered him.
21:17 But the L said to Elijah the Tishbite:
21:19 'The L says: After murdering
21:19 the L says: In the place where the dogs
21:23 (Against Jezebel, too, the L declared.
21:25 of evil in the sight of the L as did Ahab,
21:26 whom the L drove out before the Israelites.
21:28 Then the L said to Elijah the Tishbite,
22: 5 Israel, "Seek the word of the L at once."
22: 7 "The L will deliver it over to the king."
22: 7 prophet of the L here whom we may consult?"
22: 8 other through whom we might consult the L,
22:11 horns of iron and said, "The L says,
22:12 The L will deliver it over to the king."
22:14 "As the L lives," Micaiah answered
22:14 "I shall say whatever the L tells me."
22:15 The L will deliver it over to the king."
22:16 nothing but the truth in the name of the L?"
22:17 sheep without a shepherd, and the L saying,
22:19 "Therefore hear the word of the L:
22:19 I saw the L seated on his throne,
22:20 The L asked, 'Who will deceive Ahab,
22:21 came forth and presented himself to the L,
22:21 'I will deceive him. The L asked, 'How?'
22:22 The L replied, 'You shall succeed
22:23 the L has put a lying spirit in the mouths
22:23 the L himself has decreed evil against you."
22:24 cheek saying, "Has the spirit of the L,
22:28 in safety, the L has not spoken through me."
22:38 bathed there, as the L had prophesied.
22:53 He did evil in the sight of the L,
22:54 and worshiped Baal, thus provoking the L,
2Kgs 1: 3 angel of the L said to Elijah the Tishbite:
1: 4 For this, the L says: 'You shall not leave
1: 6 L says, Is it because there is no God
1:15 Then the angel of the L said to Elijah,
1:16 "Thus says the L: 'Because you sent
1:17 of the prophecy of the L spoken by Elijah.
2: 1 When the L was about to take Elijah up to
2: 2 "The L has sent me on to Bethel."
2: 2 "As the L lives, and as you yourself live,"
2: 3 "Do you know that the L will take your
2: 4 for the L has sent me on to Jericho."
2: 4 "As the L lives, and as you yourself live,"
2: 5 "Do you know that the L will take your
2: 6 the L has sent me on to the Jordan."
2: 6 "As the L lives, and as you yourself live,"
2:14 in his turn and said, "Where is the L,
2:16 Perhaps the spirit of the L has carried
2:19 the city is fine indeed, as my l can see,
2:21 salt into it, saying, "Thus says the L,
2:24 and he cursed them in the name of the L.
3:10 "The L has called together these three
3:11 "Is there no prophet of the L here
3:11 here through whom we may inquire of the L?"
3:12 "He has the word of the L."
3:13 "The L has called these three kings
3:14 Elisha said, "As the L of hosts lives,
3:15 of the L came upon Elisha and he announced:
3:16 says the L, 'Provide many catch basins
3:17 L says, 'Though you will see neither wind
3:18 since the L does not consider this enough,
4:16 "Please, my l,"
4:27 L hid it from me and did not let me know."
4:28 "Did I ask my l for a son?"
4:30 "As the L lives and as you yourself live,
4:33 the door on them both, and prayed to the L.
4:43 "For thus says the L, 'They shall eat
4:44 was some left over, as the L had said.
5: 1 him the L had brought victory to Aram.
5: 4 Naaman went and told his l just what the
5:11 and stand there to invoke the L his God,
5:16 "As the L lives whom I serve,
5:17 sacrifice to any other god except to the L.
5:18 trust the L will forgive your servant this:
5:18 May the L forgive your servant this."
5:20 As the L lives, I will run after him
6:12 "No one, my l king,"
6:15 "What shall we do, my l?"
6:17 Then he prayed, "O L,
6:17 And the L opened the eyes of the servant,
6:18 down to get him, Elisha prayed to the L,
6:18 prophet's prayer the L struck them blind.
6:20 they entered Samaria, Elisha prayed, "O L,
6:20 The L, opened their eyes, and they saw
6:26 woman cried out to him, "Help, my l king!"
6:27 "No," he replied, "the L help you!
6:33 to him and said, "This evil is from the L.
6:33 Why should I trust in the L any longer?"
7: 1 "Hear the word of the L!
7: 1 Thus says the L, 'At this time tomorrow
7: 2 if the L were to make windows in heaven,
7: 6 The L had caused the army of the Arameans
7:16 of barley for a shekel, as the L had said.
7:19 if the L were to make windows in heaven,
8: 1 because the L has decreed a seven-year
8: 5 "My l king," Gehazi said,
8: 8 Have him consult the L as to whether I
8:10 L has showed me that he will in fact die."
8:12 Hazael asked, "Why are you weeping, my l?"
8:13 L has showed you to me as king over Aram,"
8:19 so, the L was unwilling to destroy Judah,
9: 3 oil on his head, and say, 'Thus says the L:
9: 6 on his head and said, "Thus says the L,
9: 6 annoint you king over the people of the L,
9: 7 other servants of the L shed by Jezebel,
9:12 to him, and finally, "Thus says the L:
9:25 the L delivered this oracle against him:
9:26 and the blood of his sons,' says the L,
9:26 it in that very plot of ground, says the L.'
9:26 ground, in keeping with the word of the L."
9:36 "This is the sentence which the L
10: 9 I conspired against my l and slew him,
10:10 Know that not a single word which the L
10:10 The L has accomplished all that he
10:16 me," he said, "and see my zeal for the L."
10:17 prophecy which the L had spoken to Elijah.
10:23 is no worshiper of the L here with you,
10:30 The L said to Jehu,
10:31 observe wholeheartedly the law of the L,
10:32 that time the L began to dismember Israel.
11: 3 he remained hidden in the temple of the L,
11: 4 them come to him in the temple of the L,
11: 7 over the temple of the L for the king.
11:10 shields, which were in the temple of the L.
11:13 before them in the temple of the L.
11:15 should not be slain in the temple of the L.
11:17 Jehoiada made a covenant between the L
11:18 a detachment for the temple of the L,
11:19 L through the guards' gate to the palace,
12: 3 was pleasing to the L as long as he lived,
12: 5 that are brought to the temple of the L—
12: 5 are freely brought to the temple of the L—
12:10 right as one entered the temple of the L.
12:10 that were brought to the temple of the L.
12:11 the funds that were in the temple of the L,
12:12 the master workmen in the temple of the L.
12:12 builders working in the temple of the L,
12:14 the L were used there to make silver cups,
12:15 them they repaired the temple of the L.
12:17 were not brought to the temple of the L;
13: 3 The L was angry with Israel and for a long
13: 4 Jehoahaz entreated the L, who heard him
13: 5 So the L gave Israel a savior,
13:11 He did evil in the sight of the L;
13:23 But the L was merciful with Israel and
14: 3 He pleased the L, yet not like his forefather
14:14 of the L and the treasuries of the palace,
14:24 He did evil in the sight of the L;
14:25 to the sea of the Arabah, just as the L,
14:26 L saw the very bitter affliction of Israel,
14:27 Since the L had not determined to blot out
15: 3 the L just as his father Amaziah had done.
15: 5 The L afflicted the king,
15: 9 the sight of the L as his fathers had done,
15:18 He did evil in the sight of the L,
15:24 He did evil in the sight of the L,
15:28 He did evil in the sight of the L,
15:34 He pleased the L,
15:35 the Upper Gate of the temple of the L.
15:37 at that time that the L first loosed Rezin,
16: 2 He did not please the L,
16: 3 whom the L had cleared out of the way
16: 8 in the temple of the L and in the palace
16:14 The bronze altar that stood before the L
16:14 the new altar and the temple of the L—
16:18 he removed from the temple of the L
17: 2 He did evil in the sight of the L,
17: 7 the Israelites sinned against the L,
17: 8 whom the L had cleared out of the way
17: 9 adopted unlawful practices toward the L,
17:11 L, and served idols, although the LORD
17:12 served idols, although the L had told them,
17:13 And though the L warned Israel and Judah
17:14 fathers, who had not believed in the L,
17:15 the L had commanded them not to imitate.
17:16 disregarded all the commandments of the L,
17:18 the L put them away out of his sight.
17:19 did not keep the commandments of the L,
17:20 So the L rejected the whole race of Israel.
17:21 he drove the Israelites away from the L,
17:23 the L put Israel away out of his sight as
17:25 there, they did not venerate the L,
17:28 and taught them how to venerate the L.
17:32 They also venerated the L,
17:33 the L they served their own gods,
17:34 L nor observe the statutes and regulations,
17:34 the L enjoined on the descendants of Jacob,
17:36 The L, who brought you up from the land
17:39 But the L, your God, you must venerate;
17:41 Thus these nations venerated the L,
18: 3 He pleased the L,
18: 5 He put his trust in the L,
18: 6 Loyal to the L, Hezekiah never turned away
18: 6 commandments which the L had given Moses.
18: 7 The L was with him,
18:12 they had not heeded the warning of the L,
18:12 of Moses, the servant of the L.
18:15 of the L and in the palace treasuries.
18:16 the uprights of the temple of the L
18:17 sent the general, the l chamberlain,
18:22 But if you say to me, We rely on the L,
18:23 "Now, make a wager with my l,
18:24 even one of the least servants of my l,
18:25 The L said to me, 'Go up and destroy
18:27 you that my l sent me to speak these words?
18:30 LORD, saying, The L will surely save us;
18:32 seduce you by saying, The L will rescue us.
18:35 the L then rescue Jerusalem from my hand?' "
19: 1 and went into the temple of the L.
19: 4 the L, your God, will hear all the words
19: 4 will rebuke him for the words which the L,
19: 6 'Thus says the L:
19:14 then he went up to the temple of the L,
19:15 "O L, God of Israel, enthroned upon
19:16 Incline your ear, O L, and listen!
19:16 Open your eyes, O L, and see!
19:17 Truly, O L, the kings of Assyria have
19:19 Therefore, O L, our God, save us from
19:19 of the earth may know that you alone, O L,
19:20 "Thus says the L,
19:21 the word the L has spoken concerning him:
19:23 your servants you have insulted the L.
19:31 The zeal of the L of hosts shall do this.'
19:32 says the L concerning the king of Assyria:
19:33 says the L I will shield and save this
19:35 That night the angel of the L went forth
20: 1 "Thus says the L: 'Put your house in order
20: 2 his face to the wall and prayed to the L:
20: 3 "O L, remember how faithfully
20: 4 courtyard, the word of the L came to him.
20: 5 the L the God of your forefather David:
20: 8 "What is the sign that the L will heal me
20: 8 up to the temple of the L on the third day?"
20: 9 the L that he will do what he has promised:
20:11 So the prophet Isaiah invoked the L,
20:16 "Hear the word of the L:
20:17 nothing shall be left, says the L.
20:19 the L which you have spoken is favorable."
21: 2 He did evil in the sight of the L,
21: 2 whom the L had cleared out of the way
21: 4 of the LORD, about which the L had said,
21: 7 L had said to David and to his son Solomon:
21: 9 the nations whom the L had destroyed
21:10 L spoke through his servants the prophets:
21:12 by his idols, therefore thus says the L,
21:16 Manasseh did evil in the sight of the L,
21:20 He did evil in the sight of the L,
21:22 He abandoned the L,
21:22 and did not follow the path of the L.
22: 2 He pleased the L and conducted himself
22: 3 to the temple of the L with orders to go
22: 4 had been donated to the temple of the L,
22: 5 the master workmen in the temple of the L,
22: 8 the book of the law in the temple of the L."
22: 9 the master workmen in the temple of the L."
22:13 "Go, consult the L for me,
22:13 L has been set furiously ablaze against us,
22:15 her, she said to them, "Thus says the L,
22:16 man who sent you to me, Thus says the L:
22:18 of Judah who sent you to consult the L,
22:18 'Thus says the L, the God of Israel:
22:19 and have humbled yourself before the L
22:19 I in turn have listened, says the L.
23: 2 The king went up to the temple of the L
23: 2 that had been found in the temple of the L,
23: 3 the king made a covenant before the L
23: 4 to remove from the temple of the L
23: 6 of the L he also removed the sacred pole,
23: 7 which were in the temple of the L,
23: 9 at the altar of the L in Jerusalem;
23:11 at the entrance of the temple of the L,
23:12 in the two courts of the temple of the L.
23:16 it in fulfillment of the word of the L
23:19 had erected, thereby provoking the L;
23:21 people to observe the Passover of the L,
23:23 Passover of the L was kept in Jerusalem.
23:24 Hilkiah had found in the temple of the L.
23:25 been no king who turned to the L as he did,
23:26 the L did not desist from his fiercely
23:27 The L said: "Even Judah will I put out
23:32 He did evil in the sight of the L,
23:37 He did evil in the sight of the L,
24: 2 L loosed against him bands of Chaldeans,
24: 2 as the L had threatened through his
24: 3 This befell Judah because the L had stated
24: 4 filled Jerusalem, the L would not forgive.
24: 9 He did evil in the sight of the L,
24:13 temple of the L and those of the palace,
24:13 temple of the L, as the LORD had foretold.
24:19 He also did evil in the sight of the L,

LORD (cont.)

25: 9 He burned the house of the *L*,
25:13 that belonged to the house of the *L*,
25:13 and the bronze sea in the house of the *L*,
25:16 Solomon had made for the house of the *L*,
1Chr 2: 3 Er, was wicked in the sight of the *L*,
5:41 the *L* inflicted on Judah and Jerusalem
6:17 built the temple of the *L* in Jerusalem,
9:19 the entrance to the encampment of the *L*.
9:20 the *L* be with him!
9:23 guard over the gates of the house of the *L*,
10:13 because of his rebellion against the *L*
10:14 and had not rather inquired of the *L*.
10:14 Therefore the *L* slew him,
11: 2 now the *L*, your God, has said to you
11: 3 with them in the presence of the *L*;
11: 3 word of the *L* as revealed through Samuel.
11: 9 powerful, for the *L* of hosts was with him.
11:10 as the *L* had commanded concerning Israel.
11:14 Thus the *L* brought about a great victory.
11:18 he poured it out as a libation to the *L*,
12:24 him Saul's kingdom, as the *L* had ordained.
13: 2 to you, and is so decreed by the *L* our God,
13: 6 by the name *L* enthroned upon the cherubim."
13:10 *L* became angry with Uzzah and struck him;
13:14 and the *L* blessed Obed-edom's household
14: 2 David now understood that the *L* had truly
14:10 The *L* answered him, "Advance,
14:17 and the *L* made all the nations fear him.
15: 2 for the *L* chose them to carry the ark of
15: 2 of the *L* and to minister to him forever."
15: 3 in Jerusalem to bring the ark of the *L*
15:12 your brethren and bring the ark of the *L*,
15:13 the wrath of the *L* our God burst upon us,
15:14 themselves to bring up the ark of the *L*,
15:15 ordained according to the word of the *L*.
15:25 the *L* with joy from the house of Obed-edom.
15:26 bearing the ark of the covenant of the *L*,
15:28 the covenant of the *L* with joyful shouting,
15:29 of the *L* was entering the City of David,
16: 2 blessed the people in the name of the *L*,
16: 4 *L*, to celebrate, thank, and praise the *L*,
16: 7 for the first time these praises of the *L*:
16: 8 Give thanks to the *L*,
16:10 rejoice, O hearts that seek the *L*!
16:11 Look to the *L* in his strength;
16:14 He, the *L*, is our God;
16:23 Sing to the *L*,
16:25 great is the *L* and highly to be praised;
16:26 of nought, but the *L* made the heavens.
16:28 Give to the *L*, you families of nations,
16:28 of nations, give to the *L* glory and praise;
16:29 Give to the *L* the glory due his name!
16:29 worship the *L* in holy attire.
16:31 The *L* is king.
16:33 the trees of the forest exult before the *L*,
16:34 Give thanks to the *L*,
16:36 Blessed be the *L*,
16:37 before the ark of the covenant of the *L*
16:39 of the *L* on the high place at Gibeon,
16:40 the *L* on the altar of holocausts regularly,
16:40 of the *L* which he has decreed for Israel.
16:41 by name to give thanks to the *L*,
17: 1 covenant of the *L* dwells under tentcloth."
17: 4 says the *L*: It is not you who is to build
17: 7 my servant David, Thus says the *L* of hosts:
17:10 Moreover, I declare to you that I, the *L*,
17:16 "Who am I, O *L* God,
17:17 the most notable of men, O *L* God.
17:19 O *L*, for your servant's sake
17:20 O *L*, there is no one like you
17:22 Israel your own forever, and you, O *L*,
17:23 Therefore, O *L*, may the promise
17:24 promised, that your renown as *L* of hosts,
17:26 Since you, O *L*, are truly God
17:27 since it is you, O *L*, who blessed it
18: 6 Thus the *L* made David victorious in all
18:11 consecrated to the *L* along with all the silver
18:13 Thus the *L* made David victorious in all
19:13 then may the *L* do what seems best to him."
21: 3 the *L* increase his people a hundredfold!
21: 3 My *L* king,
21: 3 why does my *l* seek to do this thing?
21: 9 Then the *L* spoke to Gad,
21:10 Thus says the *L*:
21:11 "Thus says the *L*:
21:13 I prefer to fall into the hand of the *L*,
21:14 the *L* sent pestilence upon Israel,
21:15 the *L* saw and decided against the calamity,
21:15 The angel of the *L* was then standing by
21:16 of the *L* standing between earth and heaven,
21:17 O *L*, my God, strike me
21:18 Then the angel of the *L* commanded Gad to
21:18 to go up and erect an altar to the *L*
21:19 Gad's command, given in the name of the *L*.
21:22 that I may build on it an altar to the *L*.
21:23 my *l* the king do what seems best to him.
21:24 I will not take what is yours for the *L*,
21:26 David then built an altar there to the *L*,
21:26 When he called upon the *L*,
21:27 Then the *L* gave orders to the angel to
21:28 Once David saw that the *L* had heard him on
21:29 The Dwelling of the *L*,
21:30 fearful of the sword of the angel of the *L*.
22: 1 said, "This is the house of the *L* God,
22: 5 the house that is to be built for the *L*
22: 6 commanded him to build a house for the *L*,
22: 7 a house myself for the honor of the *L*,
22: 8 But this word of the *L* came to me:
22:11 Now, my son, the *L* be with you,
22:11 in building the house of the *L* your God,
22:12 May the *L* give you prudence and
22:12 Israel, so that you keep the law of the *L*,
22:13 decrees which the *L* gave Moses for Israel.
22:14 the *L* a hundred thousand talents of gold,
22:16 to work, therefore, and the *L* be with you!"
22:18 "Is not the *L* your God with you?
22:18 is subdued before the *L* and his people.
22:19 hearts and souls to seeking the *L* your God.
22:19 to build the sanctuary of the *L* God,
22:19 that the ark of the covenant of the *L*
22:19 into the house built in honor of the *L*."
23: 4 direct the service of the house of the *L*,
23: 5 four thousand were to praise the *L*
23:13 forever, to offer sacrifice before the *L*,
23:24 of the *L* from twenty years of age upward,
23:25 "The *L*, the God of Israel, has given rest
23:28 in the service of the house of the *L*,
23:30 to offer thanks and to praise the *L*,
23:31 of holocausts to the *L* on sabbaths,
23:31 they must always be present before the *L*.
23:32 in the service of the house of the *L*.
24:19 they functioned in the house of the *L*
24:19 them by Aaron, their father, as the *L*,
25: 3 a lyre, to give thanks and praise to the *L*.
25: 6 of the *L* to the accompaniment of cymbals,
25: 7 who were trained in singing to the *L*,
26:12 in the service of the house of the *L*,
26:22 the treasures of the house of the *L*.
26:27 for the enhancement of the house of the *L*.
26:30 of the *L* and in the service of the king.
27:23 for the *L* had promised to multiply Israel
28: 2 for the ark of the covenant of the *L*,
28: 4 the *L*, the God of Israel, chose me
28: 5 for the *L* has given me many sons
28: 8 of all Israel, the assembly of the *L*,
28: 8 carry out all the commandments of the *L*,
28: 9 for the *L* searches all hearts and
28:10 The *L* has chosen you to build a house as
28:12 by way of courts for the house of the *L*,
28:13 work of the service of the house of the *L*,
28:13 liturgical vessels of the house of the *L*.
28:18 covered the ark of the covenant of the *L*.
28:19 because the hand of the *L* was upon him.
28:20 fear or discouragement, for the *L* God,
28:20 work for the service of the house of the *L*.
29: 1 is not intended for man, but for the *L* God.
29: 5 to contribute generously this day to the *L*?"
29: 8 for the treasury of the house of the *L*.
29: 9 been contributed to the *L* wholeheartedly.
29:10 *L* in the presence of the whole assembly,
29:10 "Blessed may you be, O *L*,
29:11 "Yours, O *L*, are grandeur and power,
29:11 yours, O *L*, is the sovereignty;
29:16 O *L* our God, all this wealth
29:18 O *L*, God of our fathers Abraham, Issac,
29:20 whole assembly, "Now bless the *L* your God!"
29:20 And the whole assembly blessed the *L*,
29:20 before the *L* and before the king.
29:21 sacrifices and holocausts to the *L*,
29:23 the *L* as king in place of his father David;
29:25 And the *L* exalted Solomon greatly in the
2Chr 1: 1 his hold on the kingdom, for the *L*,
1: 5 Solomon and the assembly consulted the *L*,
1: 9 Now, *L* God, may your promise
1:18 the building of a house to honor the *L*
2: 3 to build a house for the honor of the *L*,
2: 3 new moons, and festivals of the *L*,
2:10 "Because the *L* loves his people,
2:11 "Blessed be the *L*, the God of Israel,
2:11 *L* and also a house for his royal estate.
2:13 the craftsmen of my *l* David your father.
2:14 let my *l* send to his servants the wheat,
3: 1 of the *L* in Jerusalem on Mount Moriah,
4:16 polished bronze for the house of the *L*.
5: 1 for the temple of the *L* had been completed,
5: 7 brought the ark of the covenant of the *L*
5:10 tablets of the covenant which the *L* made
5:13 voice praising and giving thanks to the *L*,
5:13 instruments to "give thanks to the *L*,
6: 1 "The *L* intends to dwell in the dark cloud.
6: 4 "Blessed be the *L*, the God of Israel,
6: 7 to build a temple to the honor of the *L*,
6: 8 the God of Israel, but the *L* said to him:
6:10 *L* has fulfilled the promise that he made.
6:10 on the throne of Israel, as the *L* foretold,
6:10 built the temple to the honor of the *L*,
6:11 of the *L* which he made with the Israelites."
6:12 took his place before the altar of the *L*
6:14 *L*, God of Israel, there is no god like you
6:16 Now, therefore, *L*, God of Israel
6:17 Now, *L*, God of Israel, may this promise
6:19 prayer and petition of your servant, O *L*,
6:41 And now, "Advance, *L* God,
6:41 May your priests, *L* God,
6:42 *L* God, reject not the plea of your
7: 1 and the glory of the *L* filled the house.
7: 2 house of the *L*, for the glory of the LORD
7: 2 of the LORD had filled the house of the *L*.
7: 3 and the glory of the *L* was upon the house,
7: 3 to the earth and adored, praising the *L*,
7: 4 were offering sacrifices before the *L*.
7: 6 with the musical instruments of the *L*
7: 6 King David had made for "praising the *L*,
7: 7 court which lay before the house of the *L*;
7:10 the good things the *L* had done for David,
7:11 the house of the *L* and the royal palace;
7:11 to the house of the *L* and his own house.
7:12 The *L* appeared to Solomon during the night
7:21 *L* done this to this land and to this house?'
7:22 'They forsook the *L*,
8: 1 built the house of the *L* and his own house,
8:11 where the ark of the *L* has come are holy."
8:12 Solomon offered holocausts to the *L*
8:12 *L* which he had built in front of the porch,
8:16 *L* was laid until the house of the LORD
9: 4 he offered in the house of the *L*,
9: 8 Blessed be the *L*,
9: 8 place you on his throne as king for the *L*,
9:11 temple of the *L* and the palace of the king;
10:15 the prophecy the *L* had uttered to Jeroboam,
11: 2 the word of the *L* came to Shemaiah,
11: 4 'Thus says the *L*: You must not march out
11: 4 They obeyed this message of the *L* and gave
11:14 sons repudiated them as priests of the *L*.
11:16 tribes who firmly desired to seek the *L*,
11:16 came to Jerusalem to sacrifice to the *L*,
12: 1 powerful, he abandoned the law of the *L*,
12: 2 for they had been unfaithful to the *L*.
12: 5 "Thus says the *L*: 'You have abandoned me,
12: 6 humbled themselves saying, "The *L* is just."
12: 7 the *L* saw that they had humbled themselves,
12: 7 the word of the *L* came to Shemaiah:
12: 9 the temple of the *L* and of the king's palace.
12:11 the king visited the temple of the *L*,
12:12 the anger of the *L* turned from him so that
12:13 of Israel, the *L* chose to be honored.
12:14 he had not truly resolved to seek the *L*.
13: 5 Do you not know that the *L*,
13: 6 has stood up and rebelled against his *l*!
13: 8 of the *L* commanded by the sons of David,
13: 9 you not expelled the priests of the *L*,
13:10 But as for us, the *L* is our God,
13:10 ministering to the *L* are sons of Aaron,
13:11 They burn holocausts to the *L* and fragrant
13:11 for we observe our duties to the *L*,
13:12 Do not battle against the *L*,
13:14 the *L* and the priests sounded the trumpets.
13:18 victorious because they relied on the *L*,
13:20 the *L* struck him down and he died,
14: 1 did what was good and pleasing to the *L*,
14: 3 He commanded Judah to seek the *L*,
14: 5 years, because the *L* had given him peace.
14: 6 is still ours, for we have sought the *L*,
14:10 Asa called upon the *L*, his God, praying:
14:10 "O *L*, there is none like you to help
14:10 Help us, O *L*, our God, for we rely
14:10 You are the *L*, our God; let no man prevail
14:11 And so the *L* defeated the Ethiopians
14:12 were crushed before the *L* and his army,
14:13 Gerar, for the fear of the *L* was upon them;
15: 2 The *L* is with you when you are with him,
15: 4 in their distress they turned to the *L*,
15: 8 *L* which was before the vestibule of the LORD.
15: 9 him from Israel when they saw that the *L*,
15:11 and sacrificed to the *L* at that time seven
15:12 entered into a covenant to seek the *L*,
15:13 and everyone who would not seek the *L*,
15:14 They swore to the *L* with a loud voice with
15:15 And the *L* gave them rest on every side.
16: 2 treasuries of the temple of the *L*
16: 7 king of Aram and did not rely on the *L*,
16: 8 And yet, because you relied on the *L*,
16: 9 eyes of the *L* roam over the whole earth,
16:12 even in his sickness he did not seek the *L*,
17: 3 The *L* was with Jehoshaphat,
17: 5 As a result, the *L* made his kingdom secure,
17: 9 them the book containing the law of the *L*;
17:10 Now the fear of the *L* was upon all the
17:16 of Zichri, who offered himself to the *L*,
18: 4 Israel, "Seek the word of the *L* at once."
18: 6 prophet of the *L* here whom we may consult?"
18: 7 another through whom we may consult the *L*,
18:10 *L* says, 'With these you shall gore Aram
18:11 the *L* will deliver it over to the king."
18:13 "As the *L* lives," Micaiah answered,
18:15 nothing but the truth in the name of the *L*?"
18:16 sheep without a shepherd, and the *L* saying,
18:18 "Therefore hear the word of the *L*:
18:18 I saw the *L* seated on his throne,
18:19 The *L* asked, 'Who will deceive Ahab,
18:20 forward and presented himself to the *L*,
18:20 'I will deceive him.' The *L* asked, 'How?'
18:21 The *L* agreed: "You shall succeed
18:22 So now the *L* has put a lying spirit in the
18:22 the *L* himself has decreed evil against you."
18:23 the *L* go when he left me to speak to you?"
18:27 in safety, the *L* has not spoken through me."
18:31 Jehoshaphat cried out and the *L* helped him;

19: 2 the wicked and love those who hate the L?
19: 2 this reason, wrath is upon you from the L.
19: 4 of Ephraim and brought them back to the L,
19: 6 on behalf of man, but on behalf of the L;
19: 7 And now, let the fear of the L be upon you.
19: 7 Act carefully, for with the L,
19: 8 to judge in the name of the L
19: 9 and wholeheartedly in the fear of the L.
19:10 lest they become guilty before the L
19:11 you in everything that pertains to the L,
19:11 firmly, and the L will be with the good."
20: 3 and he hastened to consult the L.
20: 4 Judah gathered to seek help from the L;
20: 4 cities of Judah they came to seek the L.
20: 5 in the house of the L before the new court,
20: 6 L, God of our fathers,
20:13 All Judah was standing before the L,
20:14 And the spirit of the L came upon Jahaziel,
20:15 The L says to you: 'Do not fear
20:17 how the L will be with you to deliver you,
20:17 to meet them, and the L will be with you.' "
20:18 fell down before the L in worship.
20:19 rose to sing the praises of the L,
20:20 Trust in the L,
20:21 he appointed some to sing to the L
20:21 "Give thanks to the L,
20:22 the L laid an ambush against the Ammonites,
20:26 for there they blessed the L;
20:27 the L had given them over their enemies.
20:28 came to Jerusalem, to the house of the L,
20:29 L had fought against the enemies of Israel.
20:37 with Ahaziah, the L will shatter your work."
21: 6 He did evil in the sight of the L,
21: 7 but the L would not destroy the house of
21:10 sovereignty because he had forsaken the L,
21:12 L, the God of your ancestor David:
21:14 than you, the L will strike your people,
21:16 Then the L stirred up against Jehoram the
21:18 the L afflicted him with an incurable
22: 4 he did evil in the sight of the L,
22: 7 whom the L had anointed to cut down the
22: 9 who sought the L with his whole heart."
23: 3 L promised concerning the sons of David.
23: 6 must observe the prescriptions of the L.
23:12 went to the people in the temple of the L.
23:18 for offering the holocausts of the L,
24: 2 the L as long as Jehoiada the priest lived.
24: 6 tax levied by Moses, the servant of the L,
24: 9 in the desert should be brought to the L.
24:18 They forsook the temple of the L,
24:19 sent to them to convert them to the L,
24:20 Because you have abandoned the L,
24:22 dying, he said, "May the L see and avenge."
24:24 the L surrendered a very large force into
24:24 power, because Judah had abandoned the L,
25: 2 what was pleasing in the sight of the L,
25: 4 in the Book of Moses, as the L commanded:
25: 7 go with you, for the L is not with Israel,
25: 8 L will defeat you in the face of the enemy.
25: 9 "The L can give you much more than that."
25:15 anger of the L blazed out against Amaziah,
25:27 time that Amaziah ceased to follow the L,
26: 4 He pleased the L,
26: 5 and as long as he sought the L,
26:16 own destruction and broke faith with the L,
26:16 He entered the temple of the L to make an
26:17 and with him eighty other priests of the L,
26:18 for you, Uzziah, to burn incense to the L,
26:18 in the glory that comes from the L God."
26:19 house of the L beside the altar of incense,
26:20 willingly, for the L had afflicted him.
26:21 he was excluded from the house of the L.
27: 2 the L just as his father Uzziah had done,
27: 2 he did not enter the temple of the L;
27: 6 lived resolutely in the presence of the L,
28: 1 the L as his forefather David had done,
28: 3 L had cleared out before the Israelites.
28: 5 Therefore the L, his God, delivered him
28: 6 men, because they had abandoned the L,
28: 9 was a prophet of the L by the name of Oded.
28: 9 "It was because the L,
28:10 therefore, guilty of a crime against the L,
28:11 for the burning anger of the L is upon you."
28:13 the L and increase our sins and our guilt.
28:19 L had brought Judah low because of Ahaz,
28:19 way and proved utterly faithless to the L.
28:22 Ahaz became even more unfaithful to the L.
28:25 Thus he angered the L,
29: 2 L just as his forefather David had done.
29: 5 now and sanctify the house of the L,
29: 6 and did evil in the eyes of the L,
29: 8 of the L has come upon Judah and Jerusalem;
29:10 I intend to make a covenant with the L,
29:11 whom the L has chosen to stand before him,
29:17 they arrived at the vestibule of the L;
29:18 have cleansed the entire house of the L,
29:21 to offer them on the altar of the L.
29:25 were from the L through his prophets.
29:27 began, they also began the song of the L,
29:30 Levites to sing the praises of the L
29:31 "You have undertaken a work for the L.
29:31 and thank offerings for the house of the L.
29:32 all of these as a holocaust to the L.
29:35 of the house of the L was reestablished.
30: 1 come to the house of the L in Jerusalem
30: 1 celebrate the Passover in honor of the L,
30: 5 celebrate the Passover in honor of the L,
30: 6 "Israelites, return to the L,
30: 7 brethren who proved faithless to the L,
30: 8 extend your hands to the L and come to his
30: 8 has consecrated forever, and serve the L,
30: 9 For when you return to the L,
30: 9 for merciful and compassionate is the L,
30:12 in accordance with the word of the L.
30:15 brought holocausts into the house of the L.
30:17 could not consecrate them to the L.
30:18 prayed for them, saying, "May the L,
30:19 who has resolved to seek God, the L,
30:20 The L heard Hezekiah and spared the people.
30:21 L day after day with all their strength.
30:22 well skilled in the service of the L.
30:22 offerings and singing praises to the L,
31: 2 in the gates of the encampment of the L.
31: 3 as prescribed in the law of the L.
31: 4 themselves entirely to the law of the L.
31: 6 things that had been consecrated to the L,
31: 8 they blessed the L and his people Israel.
31:10 bring the offerings to the house of the L,
31:10 over, for the L has blessed his people.
31:11 be constructed in the house of the L.
31:14 distributed the offerings made to the L
31:16 were eligible to enter the house of the L
31:20 good, upright and faithful before the L,
32: 8 only an arm of flesh, but we have the L,
32:11 and thirst, by his claim that 'the L,
32:16 the L God and against his servant Hezekiah,
32:17 he had written letters to deride the L,
32:21 Then the L sent an angel,
32:22 Thus the L saved Hezekiah and the
32:23 Many brought gifts for the L to Jerusalem
32:24 He prayed to the L,
32:26 and therefore the L did not vent his anger
33: 2 He did evil in the sight of the L,
33: 2 nations whom the L had cleared out
33: 4 even built altars in the temple of the L,
33: 4 of the LORD, of which the L had said,
33: 6 so that he provoked the L with the great
33: 9 nations which the L had destroyed
33:10 The L spoke to Manasseh and his people,
33:11 Therefore the L brought against them the
33:12 this distress, he began to appease the L,
33:13 The L let himself be won over:
33:13 understood that the L is indeed God.
33:16 He restored the altar of the L,
33:16 and commanded Judah to serve the L,
33:17 the high places, they now did so to the L,
33:18 who spoke to him in the name of the L,
33:22 He did evil in the sight of the L,
33:23 the L as his father Manasseh had done;
34: 2 He pleased the L,
34: 8 chamberlain, to restore the house of the L,
34:10 the master workmen in the house of the L,
34:14 had been deposited in the house of the L,
34:14 of the law of the L given through Moses.
34:15 the book of the law in the house of the L."
34:21 consult the L concerning the words of the
34:21 L has been set furiously ablaze against us,
34:21 fathers have not kept the word of the L
34:23 "Thus says the L, the God of Israel:
34:24 the one who sent you to me, The L says:
34:26 of Judah who sent you to consult the L,
34:26 'Thus says the L, the God of Israel,
34:27 so declares the L.
34:30 He went up to the house of the L with all
34:30 that had been found in the house of the L.
34:31 covenant before the L to follow the LORD
34:33 all who were in Israel to serve the L,
34:33 his lifetime they did not desert the L,
35: 1 in Jerusalem a Passover to honor the L;
35: 3 Israel, and who were consecrated to the L:
35: 3 Serve now the L,
35: 6 to the word of the L given through Moses."
35:12 of the common people to offer to the L,
35:16 Thus the entire service of the L was
35:16 holocausts offered on the altar of the L,
35:26 to what is written in the law of the L,
36: 5 He did evil in the sight of the L,
36: 7 L and put them in his palace in Babylon.
36: 9 He did evil in the sight of the L.
36:10 precious vessels from the temple of the L.
36:12 He did evil in the sight of the L,
36:12 Jeremiah, who spoke the word of the L.
36:13 his heart rather than return to the L,
36:15 Early and often did the L,
36:16 until the anger of the L against his
36:21 the word of the L spoken by Jeremiah:
36:22 LORD spoken by Jeremiah, the L inspired
36:23 'All the kingdoms of the earth the L,
Ezr 1: 1 LORD spoken by Jeremiah, the L inspired
1: 2 'All the kingdoms of the earth the L,
1: 5 to build the house of the L in Jerusalem.
1: 7 utensils of the house of the L brought forth
2:68 arrived at the house of the L in Jerusalem,
3: 3 and offered holocausts to the L on it,
3: 5 and all the festivals sacred to the L,
3: 5 might offer as a freewill gift to the L.
3: 6 they began to offer holocausts to the L,
3: 6 the temple of the L had not yet been laid.
3: 8 supervise the work on the house of the L.
3:10 the L in the manner laid down by David,
3:11 songs of praise and thanksgiving to the L,
3:11 praising the L because the foundation of
4: 1 exiles were building a temple for the L,
4: 3 God, but we alone must build it for the L,
6:21 of the land to join them in seeking the L,
6:22 for the L had filled them with joy by
7: 6 the law of Moses which was given by the L,
7: 6 Because the hand of the L,
7:10 study and practice of the law of the L
7:27 Blessed be the L,
7:27 to glorify the house of the L in Jerusalem.
7:28 took courage, and, with the hand of the L,
8:28 "You are consecrated to the L,
8:28 the gold are a freewill offering to the L,
8:29 in the chambers of the house of the L.
8:35 all these as a holocaust to the L.
9: 5 stretching out my hands to the L my God.
9: 8 ago, mercy came to us from the L our God,
9:15 O L, God of Israel, you are just;
10: 3 of them, in keeping with what you, my l,
10:11 But now, give praise to the L,
Neh 1: 5 "O L, God of heaven, great
1:11 L, may your ear be attentive to my prayer
4: 8 mind the L who is great and to be feared,
5:13 answered, "Amen," and praised the L.
8: 1 of Moses which the L prescribed for Israel.
8: 6 Ezra blessed the L, the great God,
8: 6 and prostrated themselves before the L,
8: 9 "Today is holy to the L your God.
8:10 for today is holy to our L.
8:10 rejoicing in the L must be your strength!"
8:14 law prescribed by the L through Moses
9: 3 the book of the law of the L their God,
9: 3 themselves before the L their God.
9: 4 Chenani, who cried out to the L their God,
9: 5 and Pethahiah said, "Arise, bless the L,
9: 6 "It is you, O L, you are the only one;
9: 7 "You, O L, are the God who chose Abram
10:30 all the commandments of the L, our LORD,
10:35 year, to be burnt on the altar of the L,
10:36 bring each year to the house of the L
12:43 great feast of the L in which they shared.
Tb 3: 2 "You are righteous, O L,
3: 3 O L, may you be mindful of me,
3: 6 L, command me to be delivered from such
3: 6 L, refuse me not.
3:10 myself, but to beg the L to have me die,
3:12 And now, O L, to you I turn my face
3:15 But if it please you, L, not to slay me
4: 5 all your days, my son, keep the L in mind,
4:19 At all times bless the L God,
4:19 but the L himself gives all good things.
4:19 If the L chooses,
4:21 and do what is right before the L your God."
5:20 What the L has given us to live on is
6:18 Beg the L of heaven to show you mercy and
7:11 I am sure the L will look after you both."
7:11 son, may the L of heaven prosper you both.
7:17 May the L of heaven grant you joy in place
8: 4 Let us pray and beg our L to have mercy on
8: 7 him a partner like himself,' Now, L,
9: 6 may the L grant heavenly blessing to you
10:11 May the L of heaven grant prosperity to
10:13 kinsman, may the L bring you back safely,
10:13 L, I entrust my daughter to your care.
10:14 and he blessed the L of heaven and earth,
12:12 of your prayer before the Glory of the L;
12:15 enter and serve before the Glory of the L."
13: 4 living being, because he is the L our God,
13: 6 Bless the L of righteousness,
13:10 Praise the L for his goodness,
13:11 drawn to you by the name of the L God,
13:13 together and shall bless the L of the ages.
13:15 My spirit blesses the L,
14:15 and he blessed the L God forever and ever.
Jdt 2: 5 the great king, the l of all the earth:
2:13 a single one of the orders of your l;
2:14 So Holofernes left the presence of his l,
2:15 picked troops, as his l had commanded,
4: 2 for Jerusalem and the temple of the L,
4:11 their sackcloth covering before the L.
4:13 The L heard their cry and had regard for
4:13 sanctuary of the L Almighty in Jerusalem.
4:14 attendance on the L who served his altar,
4:15 they cried to the L with all their
5: 5 l, hear this account from your servant;
5:20 "So now, my l and master,
5:21 otherwise their L and God will shield them,
5:24 your great army, L Holofernes,
6: 4 King Nebuchadnezzar, l of all the earth;
6:13 then they returned to their l.
6:19 L, God of heaven, behold their arrogance!
7:19 The Israelites cried to the L,
7:28 and by our God, the L of our forefathers,
7:29 wailing and loud cries to the L their God.
7:30 us wait five days more for the L our God,
8:11 within that time the L comes to our aid,
8:13 It is the L Almighty for whom you are
8:14 my brothers, do not anger the L our God.

LORD (cont.)
8:16 the L our God give surety for his plans.
8:20 we acknowledge no other god but the L,
8:23 turned to our benefit, but the L our God,
8:25 we should be grateful to the L our God,
8:27 Not for vengeance did the L put them in
8:31 L may send rain to fill up our cisterns,
8:33 the L will rescue Israel by my hand.
8:35 and may the L God go before you to take
9: 1 Judith prayed to the L with a loud voice:
9: 2 L, God of my forefather Simeon!
9: 8 "'You, the L, crush warfare; Lord is your
9:12 heritage of Israel, L of heaven and earth,
11: 4 treated, as are all the servants of my l,
11: 5 I will tell no lie to my l this night,
11: 6 l will not fail in any of his undertakings.
11:10 So then, my l and master,
11:11 so that my l will not be repulsed and fail,
11:17 Now I will remain with you, my l;
11:22 to those who have despised my l.
12: 4 answered him, "As surely as you, my l,
12: 4 use up her supplies till the L accomplishes
12: 6 to Holofernes, "Give orders, my l,
12: 8 After bathing, she besought the L,
12:13 to come to my l to be honored by him,
12:14 She replied, "Who am I to refuse my l?
12:18 replied, "I will gladly drink, my l,
13: 4 "O L, God of all might, in this hour
13:15 L struck him down by the hand of a woman.
13:16 As the L lives, who has protected me
13:18 and blessed be the L God,
15: 8 good things that the L had done for Israel,
15:10 blessed by the L Almighty forever and ever!"
16: 1 with timbrels, chant to the L with cymbals;
16: 2 For the L is God;
16: 5 "But the L Almighty thwarted them,
16:12 they perished before the ranks of my L.
16:13 O L, great are you and glorious,
16:16 one who fears the L is forever great.
16:17 the L Almighty will requite them;
Est 1:22 that every man should be l in his own home.
B: 9 Invoke the L and speak to the king for us:
C: 1 Recalling all that the L had done,
C: 2 "O L God, almighty King
C: 4 You are L of all,
C: 4 and there is no one who can resist you, L.
C: 5 O L, that it was not out of insolence
C: 7 will not bow down to anyone but you, my L.
C: 8 And now, L God, King, God of Abraham
C:10 live to sing praise to your name, O L.
C:12 anguish, likewise had recourse to the L.
C:14 Then she prayed to the L,
C:14 "My L, our King, you alone are God.
C:16 the land of my forefathers that you, O L,
C:18 You are just, O L.
C:22 "O L, do not relinquish your scepter to
C:23 Be mindful of us, O L.
C:25 who am alone and have no one but you, O L.
C:29 handmaid has had no joy except in you, O L,
D:13 "I saw you, my l, as an angel of God
D:14 For you are awesome, my l,
F: 6 "The L saved his people and delivered us
2Mc 1: 8 But we prayed to the L,
1:24 "Lord, L God, creator of all things,
2: 2 the L or be led astray in their thoughts,
2: 8 Then the L will disclose these things,
2: 8 glory of the L will be seen in the cloud,
2:10 Just as Moses prayed to the L and fire
2:22 while the L favored them with all his
3:22 While they were imploring the almighty L
3:24 the L of spirits who holds all power
3:30 the Jews praised the L who had marvelously
3:30 that the almighty L had manifested himself.
3:33 his sake that the L has spared your life.
3:35 had offered a sacrifice to the L
4:38 L rendered him the punishment he deserved.
5:17 that the L was angry for a little while
5:19 L, however, had not chosen the people
6:14 the L patiently waits until they reach the
6:30 "The L in his holy knowledge knows full
7: 6 "The L God is looking on,
7:20 courageously because of her hope in the L.
7:33 Though our living L treats us harshly for
7:40 undefiled, putting all his trust in the L.
8: 2 the L to look kindly upon his people,
8:14 and at the same time besought the L to
8:15 They begged the L to do this,
8:27 thanks to the L who kept them safe
8:29 imploring the merciful L to be completely
9: 5 So the all-seeing L,
9:13 Then this vile man vowed to the L,
10: 4 prostrated themselves and begged the L
10:28 valor but also their reliance on the L,
10:38 the L who shows great kindness to Israel
11: 6 people begged the L with lamentations
11:10 the L had shown his mercy toward them,
12:36 Judas called upon the L to show himself
12:41 all therefore praised the ways of the L,
13:10 people to call upon the L night and day,
13:12 and had implored the merciful L
13:17 with the help and protection of the L.
14:35 L of all,
14:36 Therefore, O holy One, L of all holiness,
14:46 calling upon the L of life and of spirit
15: 4 a ruler in heaven, the living L himself,
15: 7 that he would receive help from the L.
15:21 and called upon the L who works miracles;
15:22 "You, O L, sent your angel in the days
15:34 the L who manifests his divine power,
Jb 1: 6 came to present themselves before the L,
1: 7 And the L said to Satan,
1: 7 Then Satan answered the L and said,
1: 8 And the L said to Satan,
1: 9 But Satan answered the L and said,
1:12 And the L said to Satan,
1:12 went forth from the presence of the L.
1:21 The LORD gave and the L has taken away;
1:21 blessed be the name of the L!"
2: 1 came to present themselves before the L,
2: 2 L said to Satan, "Whence do you come?"
2: 2 And Satan answered the L and said,
2: 3 L said to Satan, "Have you noticed
2: 4 And Satan answered the L and said,
2: 6 L said to Satan. "He is in your power;
2: 7 went forth from the presence of the L
16: 9 My enemies l it over me;
28:28 Behold, the fear of the L is wisdom;
30:11 they l it over me,
38: 1 L addressed Job out of the storm and said:
40: 1 The L then said to Job:
40: 3 Then Job answered the L and said:
40: 6 L addressed Job out of the storm and said:
42: 1 Then Job answered the L and said:
42: 7 after the L had spoken these words to Job,
42: 7 that the L said to Eliphaz the Temanite,
42: 9 went and did as the L had commanded them.
42: 9 And the L accepted the intercession of Job.
42:10 Also, the L restored the prosperity of Job,
42:10 the L even gave to Job twice as much as he
42:11 the evil which the L had brought upon him;
42:12 Thus the L blessed the latter days of Job
Ps(s) 1: 2 L and meditates on his law day and night.
1: 6 For the L watches over the way of the just,
2: 2 against the L and against his anointed:
2: 4 the L derides them.
2: 7 I will proclaim the decree of the L:
2: 7 The L said to me, "You are my son
2:11 Serve the L with fear,
3: 2 when he fled from his son Absalom I O L,
3: 4 But you, O L, are my shield;
3: 5 When I call out to the L,
3: 6 sleep, I wake again, for the L sustains me.
3: 8 Rise up, O L!
4: 4 the L does wonders for his faithful one;
4: 4 the L will hear me when I call upon him.
4: 6 Offer just sacrifices, and trust in the L.
4: 7 O L, let the light of your countenance
4: 9 fall peacefully asleep, for you alone, O L,
5: 2 Hearken to my words, O L,
5: 4 To you I pray, O L;
5: 7 and the deceitful the L abhors.
5: 9 at your holy temple in fear of you, O L;
5:13 For you, O L, bless the just man;
6: 2 O L, reprove me not in your anger
6: 3 Have pity on me, O L, for I am languishing;
6: 3 heal me, O L, for my body is in terror;
6: 4 but you, O L,
6: 5 Return, O L, save my life;
6: 9 the L has heard the sound of my weeping;
6:10 The LORD has heard my plea; the L has
7: 2 O L, my God, in you I take refuge;
7: 4 O L, my God, if I am at fault in this
7: 7 Rise up, O L, in your anger;
7: 9 [The L judges the nations.]
7: 9 Do me justice, O L, because I am just,
7:18 will give thanks to the L for his justice,
7:18 sing praise to the name of the L Most High.
8: 2 Majesty of God I O LORD, our L,
8:10 O LORD, our L, how glorious is
9: 2 I will give thanks to you, O L,
9: 8 But the L sits enthroned forever;
9:10 The L is a stronghold for the oppressed,
9:11 you forsake not those who seek you, O L.
9:12 Sing praise to the L enthroned in Zion;
9:14 Have pity on me, O L;
9:17 In passing sentence, the L is manifest;
9:20 Rise, O L, let no man prevail;
9:21 Strike them with terror, O L;
10: 1 Why, O L, do you stand aloof?
10: 3 covetous blasphemes, sets the L at nought.
10:12 Rise, O L!
10:16 The L is king forever and ever;
10:17 The desire of the afflicted you hear, O L;
11: 1 In the L I take refuge;
11: 4 The L is in his holy temple;
11: 5 The L searches the just and the wicked;
11: 7 For the L is just,
12: 2 Help, O L! O God lift up your hand!
12: 4 L destroy all smooth lips
12: 5 who is l over us?"
12: 6 sigh, now will I arise," says the L;
12: 7 The promises of the L are sure,
12: 8 You, O L, will keep us and preserve us
13: 2 How long, O L? Will you utterly forget me?
13: 4 Look, answer me, O L, my God!
13: 6 let me sing of the L,
14: 2 The L looks down from heaven upon the
14: 4 They have not called upon the L;
14: 6 of the afflicted, but the L is his refuge.
14: 7 L restores the well-being of his people,
15: 1 O L, who shall sojourn in your tent?
15: 4 while he honors those who fear the L;
16: 2 I say to the LORD, "My L are you.
16: 5 O L, my alloted portion and my cup
16: 7 I bless the L who counsels me;
16: 8 I set the L ever before me;
17: 1 Hear, O L, just suit; attend to my outcry;
17:13 Rise, O L, confront them
17:14 sword from the wicked, by your hand, O L,
18: 2 I love you, O L, my strength,
18: 3 O L, my rock, my fortress, my deliverer.
18: 4 Praised be the L, I exclaim, and I am safe
18: 7 called upon the L and cried out to my God;
18:14 And the L thundered from heaven,
18:16 were laid bare, At the rebuke of the L,
18:19 my calamity, but the L came to my support.
18:21 The L rewarded me according to my justice;
18:22 of the L and was not disloyal to my God;
18:25 the L requited me according to my justice,
18:29 You indeed, O L, give light to my lamp;
18:31 the promise of the L is fire-tried;
18:32 For who is God except the L?
18:42 to the L— but he answered them not
18:47 The L live! And blessed by my Rock!
18:50 Therefore will I proclaim you, O L,
19: 8 The law of the L is perfect,
19: 8 The decree of the L is trustworthy,
19: 9 The precepts of the L are right,
19: 9 The command of the L is clear,
19:10 The fear of the L is pure,
19:10 The ordinances of the L are true,
19:15 of my heart find favor before you, O L,
20: 2 The L answer you in time of distress;
20: 6 The L grant all your requests!
20: 7 the L has given victory to his anointed,
20: 8 but we are strong in the name of the L,
20:10 O L, grant victory to the king,
21: 2 O L, in your strength the king is glad;
21: 8 For the king trusts in the L,
21:10 May the L consume them in his anger;
21:14 Be extolled, O L, in your strength!
22: 9 "He relied on the L; let him deliver him,
22:20 But you, O L, be not far from me
22:24 "You who fear the L, praise him;
22:27 they who seek the L shall praise him:
22:28 earth shall remember and turn to the L;
22:31 the coming generation be told of the L
23: 1 The L is my shepherd; I shall not want.
23: 6 in the house of the L for years to come.
24: 3 Who can ascend the mountain of the L?
24: 5 He shall receive a blessing from the L,
24: 8 The LORD, strong and mighty, the L,
24:10 The L of hosts; he is the king of glory.
25: 1 To you I lift up my soul, O L, my God.
25: 4 Your ways, O L, make known to me;
25: 6 Remember that your compassion, O L,
25: 7 remember me, because of your goodness, O L.
25: 8 Good and upright is the L;
25:10 All the paths of the L are kindness and
25:11 For your name's sake, O L,
25:12 When a man fears the L,
25:14 of the L is with those who fear him,
25:15 My eyes are ever toward the L,
25:21 preserve me, because I wait for you, O L.
26: 1 Do me justice, O L!
26: 1 and in the L I trust without wavering,
26: 2 I trust without wavering, Search me, O L,
26: 6 and I go around your altar, O L,
26: 8 O L, I love the house in which you dwell
26:12 in the assemblies I will bless the L.
27: 4 One thing I ask of the L; this I seek:
27: 4 the house of the L all the days of my life,
27: 4 of the L and contemplate his temple.
27: 6 I will sing and chant praise to the L.
27: 7 Hear, O L, the sound of my call;
27: 8 your presence, O L,
27:10 forsake me, yet will the L receive me.
27:11 Show me, O L, your way,
27:13 I shall see the bounty of the L in the land
27:14 of the living Wait for the L with courage;
27:14 be stouthearted, and wait for the L.
28: 1 To you, O L, I call;
28: 5 deeds of the L nor the work of his hands,
28: 6 Blessed be the L,
28: 7 the L is my strength and my shield.
28: 8 The L is the strength of his people,
29: 1 Give to the L, you sons of God,
29: 1 of God, give to the L glory and praise,
29: 2 L the glory due his name; adore the LORD
29: 3 The voice of the L is over the waters,
29: 3 waters, the God of glory thunders, the L,
29: 4 The voice of the L is mighty;
29: 4 the voice of the L is majestic.
29: 5 L breaks the cedars, the LORD breaks
29: 7 The voice of the L strikes fiery flames;
29: 8 L shakes the desert, the LORD shakes
29: 9 L twists the oaks and strips the forests,
29:10 The L is enthroned above the flood; the L
29:11 L give strength to his people; may the L

30: 2 I will extol you, O *L*,
30: 3 O *L*, my God, I cried out to you
30: 4 O *L*, you brought me up
30: 5 Sing praise to the *L*,
30: 8 O *L*, in your good will
30: 9 To you, O *L*, I cried out; with the LORD
30:11 Hear, O *L*, and have pity on me; O LORD,
30:13 sing praise to you without ceasing; O *L*,
31: 2 In you, O *L*, I take refuge;
31: 6 you will redeem me, O *L*,
31: 7 vain idols, but my trust is in the *L*.
31:10 Have pity on me, O *L*,
31:15 But my trust is in you, O *L*;
31:18 O *L*, let me not be put to shame
31:20 How great is the goodness, O *L*,
31:22 Blessed be the *L* whose wondrous kindness
31:24 Love the *L*, all you his faithful ones!
31:24 The *L* keeps those who are constant,
31:25 be stouthearted, all you who hope in the *L*.
32: 2 the man to whom the *L* imputes not guilt,
32: 5 I said, "I confess my faults to the *L*,"
32:10 kindness surrounds him who trusts in the *L*.
32:11 Be glad in the *L* and rejoice,
33: 1 Exult, you just, in the *L*,
33: 2 Give thanks to the *L* on the harp;
33: 4 For upright is the word of the *L*,
33: 5 of the kindness of the *L* the earth is full.
33: 6 By the word of the *L* the heavens were made;
33: 8 Let all the earth fear the *L*;
33:10 *L* brings to nought the plans of nations;
33:11 But the plan of the *L* stands forever;
33:12 Happy the nation whose God is the *L*,
33:13 From heaven the *L* looks down;
33:18 eyes of the *L* are upon those who fear him,
33:20 Our soul waits for the *L*,
33:22 May your kindness, O *L*,
34: 2 I will bless the *L* at all times;
34: 3 Let my soul glory in the *L*;
34: 4 Glorify the *L* with me,
34: 5 I sought the *L*,
34: 7 the afflicted man called out, the *L* heard,
34: 8 of the *L* encamps around those who fear him,
34: 9 Taste and see how good the *L* is;
34:10 Fear the *L*, you his holy ones,
34:11 who seek the *L* want for no good thing.
34:12 I will teach you the fear of the *L*.
34:16 The *L* has eyes for the just,
34:17 The *L* confronts the evildoers,
34:18 When the just cry out, the *L* hears them,
34:19 The *L* is close to the brokenhearted;
34:20 but out of them all the *L* delivers him;
34:23 the *L* redeems the lives of his servants;
35: 1 Fight, O *L*, against those who fight me;
35: 5 with the angel of the *L* driving them on.
35: 6 with the angel of the *L* pursuing them.
35: 9 But I will rejoice in the *L*,
35:10 All my being shall say, "O *L*,
35:17 O *L*, how long will you look on?
35:22 You, O *L*, have seen; be not silent; Lord,
35:23 in my cause, my God and my *L*.
35:24 Do me justice, because you are just, O *L*;
35:27 may they ever say, "The *L* be glorified;
36: 6 O *L*, your kindness reaches to heaven;
36: 7 man and beast you save, O *L*.
37: 3 Trust in the *L* and do good,
37: 4 Take delight in the *L*,
37: 5 Commit to the *L* your way;
37: 7 Leave it to the *L*, and wait for him;
37: 9 who wait for the *L* shall possess the land.
37:13 But the *L* laughs at him,
37:17 be broken, but the *L* supports the just.
37:18 The *L* watches over the lives of the
37:20 wicked perish, and the enemies of the *L*,
37:23 By the *L* are the steps of a man made firm,
37:24 for the hand of the *L* sustains him.
37:28 For the *L* loves what is right,
37:33 The *L* will not leave him in his power nor
37:34 Wait for the *L*, and keep his way;
37:39 The salvation of the just is from the *L*;
37:40 And the *L* helps them and delivers them;
38: 2 O *L*, in your anger punish me not,
38:10 O *L*, all my desire is before you;
38:16 O LORD, I wait; you, O *L* my God,
38:22 Forsake me not, O *L*; my God, be not far
38:23 Make haste to help me, O *L* my salvation!
39: 5 Let me know, O *L*,
39: 8 And now, for what do I wait, O *L*?
39:13 Hear my prayer, O *L*; to my cry give ear;
40: 2 I have waited, waited for the *L*,
40: 4 shall look on in awe and trust in the *L*.
40: 5 Happy the man who makes the *L* his trust;
40: 6 How numerous have you made, O *L*,
40:10 I did not restrain my lips, as you, O *L*,
40:12 Withhold not, O *L*,
40:14 Deign, O *L*, to rescue me;
40:17 salvation say ever, "The *L* be glorified."
40:18 afflicted and poor, yet the *L* thinks of me.
41: 2 day of misfortune the *L* will deliver him.
41: 3 The *L* will keep and preserve him;
41: 4 The *L* will help him on his sickbed,
41: 5 Once I said, "O *L*, have pity on me;
41:11 But you, O *L*, have pity on me,
41:14 Blessed be the *L*,
42: 9 By day the *L* bestows his grace,
44:24 Why are you asleep, O *L*?
45:12 for he is your *l*,
46: 4 The *L* of hosts is with us;
46: 8 The *L* of hosts is with us;
46: 9 behold the deeds of the *L*,
46:12 The *L* of hosts is with us;
47: 3 For the *L*, the Most High, the awesome,
47: 6 the *L*, amid trumpet blasts.
48: 2 Great is the *L* and wholly to be praised
48: 9 have we seen in the city of the *L* of hosts,
50: 1 the *L* has spoken and summoned the earth,
51:17 O *L*, open my lips, and my mouth
51:20 Be bountiful, O *L*, to Zion in your kindness
54: 6 the *L* sustains my life.
54: 8 I will praise your name, O *L*,
55:10 Engulf them, O *L*; divide their counsels,
55:17 will call upon God, and the *L* will save me.
55:23 Cast your care upon the *L*,
55:24 But I trust in you, O *L*.
57:10 give thanks to you among the peoples, O *L*.
58: 7 the jaw-teeth of the lions, break, O *L*!
59: 4 Not for any offense or sin of mine, O *L*;
59: 6 and aid me, for you are the *L* of hosts,
59: 9 You, O *L*, laugh at them;
59:12 and bring them down, O *L* our shield!
62:13 that power belongs to God, and yours, O *L*,
64:11 is glad in the *L* and takes refuge in him;
66:18 in my heart, the *L* would not hear;
68: 5 upon the clouds, Whose name is the *L*;
68:12 The *L* gives the word;
68:17 where the *L* himself will dwell forever?
68:18 the *L* advances from Sinai to the sanctuary.
68:19 the *L* God enters his dwelling.
68:20 blessed day by day be the *L*,
68:21 the *L*, my Lord, controls the passageways
68:23 The *L* said: "I will fetch them back
68:27 bless the *L*,
68:33 earth, sing to God, chant praise to the *L*.
69: 7 for you be put to shame through me, O *L*,
69:14 But I pray to you, O *L*,
69:17 O *L*, for bounteous is your kindness;
69:32 This will please the *L* more than oxen or
69:34 For the *L* hears the poor,
70: 2 O *L*, make haste to help me.
70: 6 O *L*, hold not back!
71: 1 In you, O *L*, I take refuge;
71: 5 For you are my hope, O *L*;
71:16 I will treat of the mighty works of the *L*;
72:18 Blessed be the *L*, the God of Israel,
73: 1 the *L*, to those who are clean of heart
73:20 the dream of one who had awakened, O *L*,
73:28 to make the *L* GOD my refuge.
74:18 how the enemy has blasphemed you, O *L*,
76:12 Make vows to the *L*, your God, and fulfill
76:12 terrible *L* Who checks the pride of princes,
77: 3 on the day of my distress I seek the *L*.
77: 8 "Will the *L* reject forever and nevermore
77:12 I remember the deeds of the *L*:
78: 4 glorious deeds of the *L* and his strength
78:21 Then the *L* heard and was enraged;
78:65 Then the *L* awoke,
79: 5 O *L*, how long? Will you be angry forever?
79:12 disgrace they have inflicted on you, O *L*.
80: 4 O *L* of hosts, restore us;
80: 5 O *L* of hosts, how long will you burn
80: 8 O *L* of hosts, restore us;
80:15 Once again, O *L* of hosts,
80:20 O *L* of hosts, restore us;
81:11 I, the *L*, am your God
81:16 who hated the *L* would seek to flatter me,
83:17 disgrace, that men may seek your name, O *L*.
83:19 perish, Knowing that you alone are the *L*,
84: 2 is your dwelling place, O *L* of hosts!
84: 3 yearns and pines for the courts of the *L*.
84: 4 Your altars, O *L* of hosts,
84: 9 O *L* of hosts, hear my prayer;
84:12 For a sun and a shield is the *L* God;
84:12 The *L* withholds no good thing from those
84:13 O *L* of hosts, happy the men who trust
85: 2 You have favored, O *L*,
85: 8 Show us, O *L*, your kindness
85: 9 the *L*— for he proclaims peace
85:13 The *L* himself will give his benefits;
86: 1 Incline your ear, O *L*; answer me
86: 3 You are my God; have pity on me, O *L*,
86: 4 for to you, O *L*, I lift up my soul
86: 5 For you, O *L*, are good and forgiving
86: 6 Hearken, O *L*, to my prayer
86: 8 There is none like you among the gods, O *L*,
86: 9 have made shall come and worship you, O *L*,
86:11 Teach me, O *L*, your way
86:12 I will give thanks to you, O *L* my God,
86:15 But you, O *L*, are a God merciful
86:17 may see, to their confusion, that you, O *L*,
87: 2 upon the holy mountains the *L* loves:
87: 4 and Babylon among those that know the *L*;
87: 5 who has established her is the Most High *L*."
88: 2 O *L*, my God, by day I cry out;
88:10 daily I call upon you, O *L*;
88:14 But I, O *L*, cry out to you;
88:15 Why, O *L*, do you reject me;
89: 2 The favors of the *L* I will sing forever;
89: 6 The heavens proclaim your wonders, O *L*,
89: 7 For who in the skies can rank with the *L*?
89: 7 Who is like the *L* among the sons of God?
89: 9 O *L*, God of hosts, who is like you?
89: 9 Mighty are you, O *L*,
89:16 in the light of your countenance, O *L*,
89:19 For to the *L* belongs our shield,
89:47 How long, O *L*?
89:50 Where are your ancient favors, O *L*,
89:51 Remember, O *L*,
89:52 With which your enemies have reviled, O *L*,
89:53 Blessed be the *L* forever.
90: 1 O *L*, you have been our refuge
90:13 Return, O *L*!
90:17 the gracious care of the *L* our God be ours;
91: 2 the shadow of the Almighty, Say to the *L*,
91: 9 Because you have the *L* for your refuge;
92: 2 It is good to give thanks to the *L*,
92: 5 For you make me glad, O *L*,
92: 6 How great are your works, O *L*!
92: 9 you, O *L*, are the Most High forever
92:10 For behold, your enemies, O *L*,
92:14 *L* shall flourish in the courts of our God.
92:16 shall they be, Declaring how just is the *L*,
93: 1 *L* is king, in splendor robed; robed is the *L*
93: 2 from everlasting you are, O *L*.
93: 3 The floods lift up, O *L*,
93: 4 powerful on high is the *L*.
93: 5 holiness befits your house, O *L*,
94: 1 God of vengeance, *L*,
94: 3 How long, O *L*, shall the wicked,
94: 5 Your people, O *L*, they trample down,
94: 7 murder, And they say, "The *L* sees not;
94:11 The *L* knows the thoughts of men,
94:12 Happy the man whom you instruct, O *L*,
94:14 For the *L* will not cast off his people,
94:17 Were not the *L* my help,
94:18 your kindness, O *L*, sustains me;
94:22 innocent blood, Yet the *L* is my stronghold,
94:23 the *L*, our God, will destroy them.
95: 1 Come, let us sing joyfully to the *L*;
95: 3 For the *L* is a great God,
95: 6 let us kneel before the *L* who made us.
96: 1 Sing to the *L* a new song; sing to the LORD
96: 2 Sing to the *L*; bless his name;
96: 4 great is the *L* and highly to be praised;
96: 5 of nought, but the *L* made the heavens.
96: 7 *L*, you families of nations, give to the *L*
96: 8 give to the *L* the glory due his name!
96: 9 worship the *L* in holy attire.
96:10 The *L* is king. He has made the world firm.
96:13 trees of the forest exult before the *L*,
97: 1 The *L* is king;
97: 5 melt like wax before the *L*, before the Lord
97: 8 rejoice because of your judgments, O *L*.
97: 9 Because you, O *L*,
97:10 The *L* loves those that hate evil;
97:12 Be glad in the *L*,
98: 1 Sing to the *L* a new song,
98: 2 The *L* has made his salvation known:
98: 4 Sing joyfully to the *L*,
98: 5 Sing praise to the *L* with the harp,
98: 6 horn sing joyfully before the King, the *L*.
98: 9 shout with them for joy Before the *L*,
99: 1 The *L* is king;
99: 2 The *L* in Zion is great,
99: 5 Extol the *L*,
99: 6 they called upon the *L*,
99: 8 O *L*, our God, you answered them;
99: 9 Extol the *L*, our God,
99: 9 for holy is the *L*, our God.
100: 1 Sing joyfully to the *L*,
100: 2 serve the *L* with gladness;
100: 3 Know that the *L* is God;
100: 5 the *L*, whose kindness endures forever,
101: 1 to you, O *L*, I will sing praise.
101: 8 from the city of the *L* all evildoers.
102: 2 O *L*, hear my prayer,
102:13 But you, O *L*, abide forever
102:16 the nations shall revere your name, O *L*,
102:17 When the *L* has rebuilt Zion and appeared
102:19 and let his future creatures praise the *L*:
102:20 "The *L* looked down from his holy height,
102:22 the name of the *L* may be declared in Zion;
102:23 and the kingdoms, to serve the *L*.
103: 1 Bless the *L*, O my soul; and all my being,
103: 2 Bless the *L*, O my soul,
103: 6 The *L* secures justice and the rights
103: 8 Merciful and gracious is the *L*,
103:13 the *L* has compassion on those who fear him,
103:17 But the kindness of the *L* is from eternity
103:19 The *L* has established his throne in heaven,
103:20 Bless the *L*, all you his angels,
103:21 Bless the *L*, all you his hosts,
103:22 Bless the *L*, all his works,
103:22 Bless the *L*, O my soul!
104: 1 Bless the *L*, O my soul!
104: 1 O *L*, my God, you are great indeed!
104:16 Well watered are the trees of the *L*,
104:24 How manifold are your works, O *L*!
104:31 May the glory of the *L* endure forever;
104:31 may the *L* be glad in his works!
104:33 I will sing to the *L* all my life;

LORD (cont.)

104:34 I will be glad in the L.
104:35 Bless the L, O my soul!
105: 1 Give thanks to the L, invoke his name;
105: 3 rejoice, O hearts that seek the L!
105: 4 Look to the L in his strength;
105: 7 He, the L, is our God;
105:19 pass and the word of the L proved him true.
105:21 He made him l of his house and ruler of
106: 2 Who can tell the mighty deeds of the L,
106: 4 Remember me, O L,
106:16 the camp, and Aaron, the holy one of the L.
106:25 tents, and obeyed not the voice of the L.
106:34 the peoples, as the L had commanded them,
106:40 And the L grew angry with his people,
106:47 Save us, O L, our God, and gather us
106:48 Blessed be the L,
107: 1 "Give thanks to the L, for he is good,
107: 2 Thus let the redeemed of the L say,
107: 6 They cried to the L in their distress;
107: 8 Let them give thanks to the L for his
107:13 They cried to the L in their distress;
107:15 Let them give thanks to the L for his
107:19 They cried to the L in their distress;
107:21 Let them give thanks to the L for his
107:24 of the L and his wonders in the abyss.
107:28 They cried to the L in their distress;
107:31 Let them give thanks to the L for his
107:43 and to understand the favors of the L?
108: 4 give thanks to you among the peoples, O L;
109:14 of his fathers be remembered by the L;
109:15 May they be continually before the L,
109:20 May this be the recompense from the L
109:21 But do you, O GOD, my L,
109:26 Help me, O L,
109:27 that you, O L,
109:30 I will speak my thanks earnestly to the L,
110: 1 The L said to my Lord:
110: 2 power the L will stretch forth from Zion:
110: 4 The L has sworn, and he will not repent
110: 5 The L is at your right hand;
111: 1 I will give thanks to the L with all my
111: 2 Great are the works of the L,
111: 4 gracious and merciful is the L.
111:10 fear of the L is the beginning of wisdom;
112: 1 Happy the man who fears the L,
112: 7 his heart is firm, trusting in the L.
113: 1 of the LORD, praise the name of the L.
113: 2 be the name of the L both now and forever.
113: 3 the sun is the name of the L to be praised.
113: 4 High above all nations is the L;
113: 5 Who is like the L, our God,
114: 7 Before the face of the L, tremble, O earth,
115: 1 O L, not to us but to your name give glory
115: 9 The house of Israel trusts in the L;
115:10 The house of Aaron trusts in the L;
115:11 Those who fear the L trust in the LORD;
115:12 The L remembers us and will bless us:
115:13 He will bless those who fear the L,
115:14 May the L bless you more and more,
115:15 May you be blessed by the L,
115:16 Heaven is the heaven of the L,
115:17 It is not the dead who praise the L,
115:18 But we bless the L,
116: 1 I love the L because he has heard my
116: 4 I called upon the name of the LORD, "O L,
116: 5 Gracious is the L and just;
116: 6 The L keeps the little ones;
116: 7 for the L has been good to you.
116: 9 before the L in the lands of the living.
116:12 the L for all the good he has done for me?
116:13 and I will call upon the name of the L;
116:14 My vows to the L I will pay in the
116:15 of the L is the death of his faithful ones.
116:16 O L, I am your servant;
116:17 and I will call upon the name of the L.
116:18 My vows to the L I will pay in the
116:19 In the courts of the house of the L,
117: 1 Praise the L, all you nations;
117: 2 and the fidelity of the L endures forever.
118: 4 Let those who fear the L say,
118: 5 I called upon the L; the LORD answered
118: 6 The L is with me; I fear not;
118: 7 The L is with me to help me,
118: 8 take refuge in the L than to trust in man.
118: 9 refuge in the L than to trust in princes.
118:10 in the name of the L I crushed them.
118:11 in the name of the L I crushed them.
118:12 in the name of the L I crushed them.
118:13 and was falling, but the L helped me.
118:14 My strength and my courage is the L,
118:15 right hand of the L has struck with power:
118:16 L is exalted; the right hand of the LORD
118:17 but live, and declare the works of the L.
118:18 Though the L has indeed chastised me,
118:19 I will enter them and give thanks to the L.
118:23 By the L has this been done;
118:24 This is the day the L has made;
118:25 O L, grant salvation!
118:25 O L, grant prosperity!
118:26 L; we bless you from the house of the L.
118:27 The L is God, and he has given us light.
118:29 Give thanks to the L, for he is good;
119: 1 is blameless, who walk in the law of the L.
119:12 Blessed are you, O L;
119:31 O L, let me not be put to shame.
119:33 Instruct me, O L,
119:41 Let your kindness come to me, O L,
119:52 I remember your ordinances of old, O L,
119:55 By night I remember your name, O L,
119:57 I have said, O L, that my part is to keep
119:64 Of your kindness, O L,
119:65 have done good to your servant, O L,
119:75 O L, that your ordinances are just,
119:89 Your word, O L, endures forever;
119:97 How I love your law, O L!
119:107 O L, give me life according to your word
119:108 Accept, O L, the free homage of my mouth
119:126 It is time for the L to act:
119:137 You are just, O L,
119:145 O L; I will observe your statutes
119:149 my voice according to your kindness, O L;
119:151 You, O L, are near,
119:156 Your compassion is great, O L;
119:159 See how I love precepts, O L;
119:166 I wait for your salvation, O L,
119:169 Let my cry come before you, O L;
119:174 I long for your salvation, O L,
120: 1 In my distress I called to the L,
120: 2 O L, deliver me from lying lip
121: 2 My help is from the L,
121: 5 The L is your guardian; the LORD is your
121: 7 The L will guard you from all evil;
121: 8 L will guard your coming and your going,
122: 1 me, "We will go up to the house of the L.
122: 4 it the tribes go up, the tribes of the L,
122: 4 to give thanks to the name of the L.
122: 9 Because of the house of the L,
123: 2 of her mistress, So are our eyes on the L,
123: 3 Have pity on us, O L,
124: 1 Had not the L been with us,
124: 2 Israel say, had not the L been with us
124: 6 Blessed be the L, who did not leave us
124: 8 Our help is in the name of the L,
125: 1 who trust in the L are like Mount Zion,
125: 2 so the L is round about his people,
125: 4 Do good, O L, to the good
125: 5 may the L lead away with the evildoers!
126: 1 the L brought back the captives of Zion,
126: 2 "The L has done great things for them."
126: 3 The L has done great things for us;
126: 4 Restore our fortunes, O L,
127: 1 Unless the L build the house,
127: 1 Unless the L guard the city,
127: 3 Behold, sons are a gift from the L;
128: 1 Happy are you who fear the L,
128: 4 thus is the man blessed who fears the L.
128: 5 The L bless you from Zion:
129: 4 just L has severed the cords of the wicked.
129: 8 not, "The blessing of the L be upon you!
129: 8 We bless you in the name of the L!"
130: 1 I cry to you, O L; Lord, hear my voice!
130: 3 If you, O LORD, mark iniquities, L,
130: 5 I trust in the L;
130: 6 L more than sentinels wait for the dawn.
130: 7 for the dawn, let Israel wait for the L,
130: 7 For with the L is kindness and with him is
131: 1 O L, my heart is not proud
131: 3 O Israel, hope in the L,
132: 2 How he swore to the L,
132: 5 no rest, Till I find a place for the L,
132: 8 Advance, O L, to your resting place
132:11 The L swore to David a firm promise from
132:13 For the L has chosen Zion;
133: 3 there the L has pronounced his blessing,
134: 1 bless the L, all you servants of the LORD
134: 1 Who stand in the house of the LORD
134: 2 toward the sanctuary, and bless the L.
134: 3 May the L bless you from Zion,
135: 2 L, in the courts of the house of our God.
135: 3 Praise the LORD, for the L is good;
135: 4 For the L has chosen Jacob for himself,
135: 5 the LORD is great; our L is greater than
135: 6 the L wills he does in heaven and on earth,
135:13 Your name, O L, endures forever; LORD
135:14 generations, For the L defends his people,
135:19 the LORD, house of Aaron, bless the L,
135:20 bless the LORD, House of Levi, bless the L;
135:20 you who fear the LORD, bless the L.
135:21 Blessed from Zion be the L,
136: 1 Give thanks to the L, for he is good,
136: 3 Give thanks to the L of lords,
137: 4 we sing a song of the L in a foreign land?
137: 7 Remember, O L, against the children
138: 1 I will give thanks to you, O L,
138: 4 the earth shall give thanks to you, O L,
138: 5 And they shall sing of the ways of the L:
138: 5 "Great is the glory of the L."
138: 6 The L is exalted, yet the lowly he sees,
138: 8 L will complete what he has done for me;
138: 8 your kindness, O L, endures forever
139: 1 O L, you have probed me
139: 4 before a word is on my tongue, behold, O L,
139:21 Do I not hate, O L, those who hate you?
140: 2 Deliver me, O L, from evil men;
140: 5 Save me, O L, from the hands
140: 7 L, you are my God; hearken, O LORD
140: 8 O GOD, my L, my strength
140: 9 Grant not, O L, the desires of the wicked;
140:13 the L renders justice to the afflicted,
141: 1 O L, to you I call; hasten to me;
141: 3 O L, set a watch before my mouth
141: 8 For toward you, O GOD, my L,
142: 2 LORD; with a loud voice I beseech the L.
142: 6 I cry out to you, O L;
143: 1 O L, hear my prayer;
143: 7 Hasten to answer me, O L,
143: 9 O L, for in you I hope.
143:11 For your name's sake, O L, preserve me;
144: 1 Blessed be the L, my rock,
144: 3 L, what is man, that you notice him;
144: 5 Incline your heavens, O L,
144:15 happy the people whose God is the L.
145: 3 Great is the L and highly to be praised;
145: 8 The L is gracious and merciful,
145: 9 The L is good to all and compassionate
145:10 Let all your works give you thanks, O L,
145:13 The L is faithful in all his words and
145:14 The L lifts up all who are falling and
145:17 The L is just in all his ways and holy in
145:18 The L is near to all who call upon him,
145:20 The L keeps all who love him,
145:21 May my mouth speak the praise of the L,
146: 1 Praise the L, O my soul;
146: 2 I will praise the L all my life;
146: 5 the God of Jacob, whose hope is in the L,
146: 7 The L sets captives free;
146: 8 the L gives sight to the blind.
146: 8 The L raises up those that were bowed down;
146: 8 the L loves the just.
146: 9 The L protects strangers;
146:10 The L shall reign forever;
147: 1 Praise the L, for he is good;
147: 2 The L rebuilds Jerusalem;
147: 5 Great is our L and mighty in power:
147: 6 The L sustains the lowly;
147: 7 Sing to the L with thanksgiving;
147:11 The L is pleased with those who fear him,
147:12 Glorify the L, O Jerusalem;
148: 1 Praise the L from the heavens,
148: 5 Let them praise the name of the L,
148: 7 Praise the L from the earth,
148:13 men and boys, Praise the name of the L,
149: 1 Sing to the L a new song of praise in
149: 4 For the L loves his people,
150: 1 Praise the L in his sanctuary,
150: 6 everything that has breath praise the L!
Prv 1: 7 of the L is the beginning of knowledge;
1:29 and chose not the fear of the L;
2: 5 will you understand the fear of the L;
2: 6 For the L gives wisdom,
3: 5 Trust in the L with all your heart,
3: 7 fear the L and turn away from evil;
3: 9 Honor the L with your wealth,
3:11 The discipline of the L, my son, disdain not;
3:12 For whom the L loves he reproves,
3:19 The L by wisdom founded the earth,
3:26 For the L will be your confidence,
3:32 the L the perverse man is an abomination,
3:33 of the L is on the house of the wicked,
6:16 There are six things the L hates,
8:13 [The fear of the L is to hate evil;]
8:22 "The L begot me, the first-born of his ways,
8:35 me finds life, and wins favor from the L;
9:10 beginning of wisdom is the fear of the L,
10: 3 The L permits not the just to hunger,
10:27 The fear of the L prolongs life,
10:29 The L is a stronghold to him who walks
11: 1 False scales are an abomination to the L,
11:20 in heart are an abomination to the L,
12: 2 The good man wins favor from the L,
12:22 Lying lips are an abomination to the L,
14: 2 He who walks uprightly fears the L,
14:26 In the fear of the L is a strong defense;
14:27 The fear of the L is a fountain of life,
15: 3 The eyes of the L are in every place,
15: 8 of the wicked is an abomination to the L,
15: 9 of the wicked is an abomination to the L,
15:11 world and the abyss lie open before the L;
15:16 of the L than a great fortune with anxiety.
15:25 The L overturns the house of the proud,
15:26 man's schemes are an abomination to the L,
15:29 The L is far from the wicked,
15:33 The fear of the L is training for wisdom,
16: 1 but what the tongue utters is from the L.
16: 2 but it is the L who proves the spirit.
16: 3 Entrust your works to the L,
16: 4 The L has made everything for his own ends,
16: 5 proud man is an abomination to the L;
16: 6 and by the fear of the L man avoids evil.
16: 7 When the L is pleased with a man's ways,
16: 9 his course, but the L directs his steps.
16:11 Balance and scales belong to the L;
16:20 happy is he who trusts in the L!
16:33 its decision depends entirely on the L.
17: 3 gold, but the tester of hearts is the L.
17:15 the just, are both an abomination to the L.
18:10 The name of the L is a strong tower;
18:22 it is a favor he receives from the L.

19: 3 but his heart is resentful against the *L.*
19:14 parents, but a prudent wife is from the *L.*
19:17 compassion on the poor lends to the *L,*
19:21 it is the decision of the *L* that endures.
19:23 The fear of the *L* is an aid to life;
20:10 measures, are both an abomination to the *L.*
20:12 the *L* has made them both.
20:22 Trust in the *L* and he will help you.
20:23 weights are an abomination to the *L,*
20:24 Man's steps are from the *L;*
20:27 A Lamp from the *L* is the breath of man;
21: 1 is the king's heart in the hand of the *L;*
21: 2 eyes, but it is the *L* who proves hearts.
21: 3 is more acceptable to the *L* than sacrifice.
21:30 understanding, no counsel, against the *L.*
22: 2 the *L* is the maker of them all.
22: 4 of humility and fear of the *L* is riches,
22:11 The *L* loves the pure of heart;
22:12 The eyes of the *L* safeguard knowledge,
22:14 with whom the *L* is angry will fall into it.
22:19 That your trust may be in the *L,*
22:23 For the *L* will defend their cause,
23:17 be zealous for the fear of the *L* always;
24:18 not your heart exult, Lest the *L* see it,
24:21 My son, fear the *L* and the king;
25:22 on his head, and the *L* will vindicate you.
28: 5 but those who seek the *L* understand all.
28:25 but he who trusts in the *L* will prosper.
29:13 the *L* gives light to the eyes of both.
29:25 snare, but he who trusts in the *L* is safe.
29:26 but the rights of each are from the *L.*
30: 9 full, I deny you, saying, "Who is the *L?*
31:30 the woman who fears the *L* is to be praised.
Wis 1: 1 think of the *L* in goodness,
1: 7 For the spirit of the *L* fills the world,
1: 9 the sound of his words shall reach the *L,*
2:13 of God and styles himself a child of the *L.*
3: 8 and the *L* shall be their King forever.
3:10 they neglected justice and forsook the *L.*
3:14 who held no wicked thoughts against the *L*—
4:14 for his soul was pleasing to the *L,*
4:17 not understand what the *L* intended for him,
4:18 but the *L* laughs them to scorn.
5: 7 deserts, but the way of the *L* we knew not.
5:15 forever, and in the *L* is their recompense,
5:16 beauteous diadem, from the hand of the *L*—
6: 2 multitude and *l* it over throngs of peoples!
6: 3 by the *L* and sovereignty by the Most High,
6: 7 For the *L* of all shows no partiality,
8: 3 even the *L* of all loved her.
8:21 I went to the *L* and besought him,
9: 1 God of my fathers, *L* of mercy.
9:13 or who can conceive what our *L* intends?
10:20 and they sang, O *L,*
11:13 to these others, they recognized the *L.*
11:26 they are yours, O *L* and lover of souls.
12: 2 their wickedness and believe in you, O *L!*
13: 3 how far more excellent is the *L* than these;
13: 9 how did they not more quickly find its *L?*
16:12 cured them, but your all-healing word, O *L!*
16:26 your sons whom you loved might learn, O *L,*
19: 9 about like lambs, praising you, O *L!*
19:22 For every way, O *L!*
Sir 1: 1 All wisdom comes from the *L*
1: 7 It is the *L;* he created her, has seen her
1: 9 Fear of the *L* is glory and splendor,
1:10 Fear of the *L* warms the heart,
1:11 He who fears the *L* will have a happy end;
1:12 The beginning of wisdom is fear of the *L,*
1:14 Fullness of wisdom is fear of the *L;*
1:16 Wisdom's garland is fear of the *L,*
1:18 The root of wisdom is fear of the *L;*
1:22 of the *L* is an abomination to the sinner.
1:23 and the *L* will bestow her upon you;
1:24 For fear of the *L* is wisdom and culture;
1:25 Be not faithless to the fear of the *L,*
1:28 For then the *L* will reveal your secrets
1:29 of the *L* with your heart full of guile.
2: 1 My son, when you come to serve the *L,*
2: 7 You who fear the *L,* wait for his mercy,
2: 8 You who fear the *L,* trust him,
2: 9 You who fear the *L,* hope for good things
2:10 hoped in the *L* and been disappointed?
2:11 Compassionate and merciful is the *L;*
2:14 will you do at the visitation of the *L?*
2:15 Those who fear the *L* disobey not his words;
2:16 Those who fear the *L* seek to please him,
2:17 Those who fear the *L* prepare their hearts
2:18 of the *L* and not into the hands of men,
3: 2 *L* sets a father in honor over his children;
3: 6 the *L* who brings comfort to his mother.
3: 7 He who fears the *L* honors his father,
4:13 he dwells, the *L* bestows blessings.
4:14 those who love her the *L* loves.
4:28 and the *L* your God will battle for you.
5: 3 for the *L* will exact the punishment.
5: 4 for the *L* bides his time.
5: 8 Delay not your conversion to the *L,*
6:37 Reflect on the precepts of the *L,*
7: 4 Seek not from the *L* authority,
7: 5 Parade not your justice before the *L,*
9:15 conversation be about the law of the *L.*
10: 7 Odious to the *L* and to men is arrogance.
10:21 or pauper, his glory is the fear of the *L.*
11: 4 For strange are the works of the *L,*
11:12 the eyes of the *L* look favorably upon him;
11:14 death, poverty and riches, are from the *L.*
11:15 love and virtuous paths are from the *L.*
11:21 but trust in the *L* and wait for his light;
11:21 For it is easy with the *L* suddenly,
11:26 For it is easy with the *L* on the day of
12: 2 will be yours, if not from him, from the *L.*
15: 1 He who fears the *L* will do this;
15:13 Abominable wickedness the *L* hates,
15:18 Immense is the wisdom of the *L;*
16: 2 in them if they have not the fear of the *L.*
16:27 Then the *L* looked upon the earth,
17: 1 The *L* from the earth created man,
17:16 all of their sins are before the *L.*
17:20 Return to the *L* and give up sin,
17:23 they glorify the *L* who are alive and well.
17:24 How great the mercy of the *L,*
18: 1 the *L* alone is just.
18: 4 nor penetrate the wonders of the *L.*
18: 9 That is why the *L* is patient with men and
18:23 be not one who tries the *L.*
18:26 before the *L* all things are fleeting.
19:17 All wisdom is fear of the *L;*
21: 6 he who fears the *L* repents in his heart.
21:11 who is perfect in fear of the *L* has wisdom.
23: 1 *L,* Father and Master of my life,
23: 4 *L,* Father and God of my life,
23:19 not understand that the eyes of the *L,*
23:27 nothing is better than the fear of the *L,*
24:12 glorious people, in the portion of the *L,*
25: 1 for they are pleasing to the *L* and to men:
25: 6 their glory, the fear of the *L.*
25:10 but not greater than he who fears the *L.*
25:11 Fear of the *L* surpasses all else.
26: 3 gift bestowed upon him who fears the *L;*
26:14 A gift from the *L* is her governed speech,
26:19 sin, for whom the *L* makes ready the sword.
27: 3 earnestly hold fast to the fear of the *L,*
27:24 hate so much, and the *L* hates him as well.
28: 3 his fellows and expect healing from the *L?*
28:23 who forsake the *L* will fall victims to it,
32:16 His judgment is sound who fears the *L;*
32:24 trusts in the *L* shall not be put to shame.
33: 1 No evil can harm the man who fears the *L;*
33: 3 prudent man trusts in the word of the *L,*
33:11 his great knowledge the *L* makes men unlike;
33:30 But never *l* it over any human being,
34:13 is the courage of those who fear the *L,*
34:14 He who fears the *L* is never alarmed,
34:14 for the *L* is his hope.
34:15 Happy the soul that fears the *L!*
34:16 eyes of the *L* are upon those who love him;
34:24 curses, whose voice will the *L* hear?
35: 3 To refrain from evil pleases the *L,*
35: 4 Appear not before the *L* empty-handed,
35: 7 In generous spirit pay homage to the *L,*
35:10 For the *L* is one who always repays,
39: 6 His care is to seek the *L,* his Maker,
39: 6 Then, if it pleases the *L* Almighty,
39: 6 wisdom and in prayer give thanks to the *L,*
39:14 bless the *L* for all he has done!
40:26 Fear of the *L* leaves nothing wanting;
42:16 so the glory of the *L* fills all his works;
42:17 fail in recounting the wonders of the *L,*
43: 5 Great indeed is the *L* who made it,
43:31 Lift up your voices to glorify the *L,*
43:35 It is the *L* who has made all things,
44:16 [ENOCH walked with the *L* and was taken up,
45: 2 the *L* strengthened him with fearful powers;
45:19 But the *L* saw this and became angry,
45:21 The oblations of the *L* are his food,
45:22 For the *L* himself is his portion,
45:26 bless the *L* who has crowned you with glory!
46: 3 him when he fought the battles of the *L?*
46: 6 *L* was watching over his people's battles.
46:10 it is to be a devoted follower of the *L.*
46:13 womb, Consecrated to the *L* as a prophet,
46:14 By the law of the *L* he judged the nation,
46:17 Then the *L* thundered forth from heaven,
46:19 before the *L* and his anointed prince,
47:11 The *L* forgave him his sins and exalted his
48: 5 the nether world, by the will of the *L.*
48:10 an end to wrath before the day of the *L,*
50:13 the offerings to the *L* in their hands,
50:20 blessing of the *L* would be upon his lips,
50:20 lips, the name of the *L* would be his glory.
50:29 for the fear of the *L* is his lamp.
51: 8 then I remembered the mercies of the *L,*
51:10 O *L,* you are my father,
51:11 Thereupon the *L* heard my voice,
51:12 I bless the name of the *L.*
51:22 The *L* has granted me my lips as a reward,
Is 1: 2 and listen, O earth, for the *L* speaks:
1: 4 They have forsaken the *L,*
1: 9 *L* of hosts had left us a scanty remnant,
1:10 Hear the word of the *L,* princes of Sodom!
1:11 number of your sacrifices says the *L*
1:18 now, let us set things right, says the *L:*
1:20 for the mouth of the *L* has spoken!
1:24 therefore, says the Lord, the *L* of hosts,
1:28 those who desert the *L* shall be consumed.
2: 3 and the word of the *L* from Jerusalem.
2: 5 come, let us walk in the light of the *L!*
2:10 of the *L* and the splendor of his majesty!
2:11 be abased, and the *L* alone will be exalted,
2:12 For the *L* of hosts will have his day
2:17 low, And the *L* alone will be exalted,
2:19 of the *L* and the splendor of his majesty,
2:21 of the *L* and the splendor of his majesty,
3: 1 The Lord, the *L* of hosts,
3: 8 speech and their deeds are before the *L,*
3:13 The *L* rises to accuse,
3:14 The *L* enters into judgment with his
3:15 says the *L,* the GOD of hosts.
3:16 The *L* said: Because the daughters of Zion
3:17 The *L* shall cover the scalps of Zion's
3:17 scabs, and the *L* shall bare their heads.
3:18 On that day the *L* will do away with the
4: 2 branch of the *L* will be luster and glory,
4: 4 When the *L* washes away the filth of the
4: 5 searing judgment, Then will the *L* create,
5: 7 of the *L* of hosts is the house of Israel,
5: 9 In my hearing the *L* of hosts has sworn:
5:12 But what the *L* does they regard not,
5:16 But the *L* of hosts shall be exalted by his
5:24 have spurned the law of the *L* of hosts,
5:25 wrath of the *L* blazes against his people,
6: 1 the *L* seated on a high and lofty throne,
6: 3 "Holy, holy, holy is the *L* of hosts!"
6: 5 my eyes have seen the King, the *L* of hosts!"
6: 8 Then I heard the voice of the *L* saying,
6:11 "How long, O *L?*"
6:12 Until the *L* removes men far away,
7: 3 Then the *L* said to Isaiah:
7: 7 Thus says the *L:* This shall not stand
7:10 Again the *L* spoke to Ahaz:
7:11 Ask for a sign from the *L,*
7:12 I will not tempt the *L!*"
7:14 the *L* himself will give you this sign:
7:17 The *L* shall bring upon you and your people
7:18 On that day The *L* shall whistle for the
7:20 On that day the *L* shall shave with the
8: 1 The *L* said to me:
8: 3 The *L* said to me: Name him
8: 5 Again the *L* spoke to me:
8: 7 Therefore the *L* raises against them the
8:11 For thus said the *L* to me,
8:13 But with the *L* of hosts make your alliance
8:17 For I will trust in the *L,*
8:18 and the children whom the *L* has given me:
8:18 the *L* of hosts who dwells on Mount Zion.
9: 6 The zeal of the *L* of hosts will do this!
9: 7 The *L* has sent word against Jacob,
9:10 But the *L* raises up their foes against
9:12 who struck them, nor seek the *L* of hosts.
9:13 So the *L* severs from Israel head and tail,
9:16 the *L* does not spare their young men,
9:18 wrath of the *L* of hosts the land quakes,
10:12 [But when the *L* has brought to an end all
10:16 Therefore the Lord, the *L* of hosts,
10:20 But they lean upon the *L,*
10:23 the destruction he has decreed, the *L,*
10:24 Therefore thus says the *L,*
10:26 Then the *L* of hosts will raise against
10:33 Behold, the Lord, the *L* of hosts,
11: 2 The spirit of the *L* shall rest upon him:
11: 2 spirit of knowledge and of fear of the *L,*
11: 3 his delight shall be the fear of the *L.*
11: 9 shall be filled with knowledge of the *L,*
11:11 The *L* shall again take it in hand to
11:15 The *L* shall dry up the tongue of the Sea
12: 1 I give you thanks, O *L;*
12: 2 My strength and my courage is the *L,*
12: 4 Give thanks to the *L,*
12: 5 to the *L* for his glorious achievement;
13: 4 *L* of hosts is mustering an army for battle.
13: 5 The *L* and the instruments of his wrath,
13: 6 Howl, for the day of the *L* is near;
13: 9 Lo, the day of the *L* comes cruel,
13:13 *L* of hosts on the day of his burning anger.
14: 1 When the *L* has pity on Jacob and again
14: 3 On the day the *L* relieves you of sorrow
14: 5 The *L* has broken the rod of the wicked,
14:22 rise up against them, says the *L* of hosts,
14:22 remnant, progeny and offspring, says the *L.*
14:23 broom of destruction, says the *L* of hosts.
14:24 The *L* of hosts has sworn:
14:27 The *L* of hosts has planned;
14:32 "The *L* has established Zion,
16:13 of the *L* spoke against Moab in times past.
16:14 But now the *L* has spoken:
17: 3 as the Israelites, says the *L* of hosts.
17: 6 five on its fruitful branches, says the *L,*
18: 4 For thus says the *L* to me:
18: 7 *L* of hosts from a people tall and bronzed,
18: 7 where dwells the name of the *L* of hosts.
19: 1 the *L* is riding on a swift cloud on his
19: 4 over them, says the LORD, the *L* of hosts.
19:12 the *L* of hosts has planned against Egypt.
19:14 The *L* has prepared among them a spirit of
19:16 of the *L* of hosts shaking his fist at them.
19:17 which the *L* of hosts has in mind for them.
19:18 of Canaan and swearing by the *L* of hosts;
19:19 be an altar to the *L* in the land of Egypt,

LORD (cont.)
19:19 a sacred pillar to the *L* near the boundary.
19:20 to the *L* of hosts in the land of Egypt,
19:20 cry out to the *L* against their oppressors,
19:21 The *L* shall make himself known in Egypt,
19:21 the Egyptians shall know the *L* in that day:
19:21 and fulfill the vows they make to the *L*.
19:22 Although the *L* shall smite Egypt severely,
19:22 *L* and he shall be won over and heal them.
19:25 the land, when the *L* of hosts blesses it:
20: 2 it, the *L* gave a warning through Isaiah,
20: 3 Then the *L* said: Just as my servant
21: 6 For thus says my *L* to me:
21: 8 cried, "On the watchtower, O my *L*,
21:10 What I have heard from the *L* of hosts,
21:16 For thus says the *L* to me:
21:17 stalwart archers shall remain, for the *L*,
22: 5 of panic, rout and confusion, from the *L*,
22:12 On that day the *L*,
22:14 This reaches the ears of the *L* of hosts
22:14 this wickedness till you die, says the *L*,
22:15 Thus says the *L*, the GOD of hosts:
22:17 The *L* shall hurl you down headlong,
22:25 On that day, says the *L* of hosts,
22:25 for the *L* has spoken.
23: 9 The *L* of hosts has planned it,
23:11 The *L* has ordered the destruction of
23:17 the seventy years the *L* shall visit Tyre.
23:18 and her hire shall be sacred to the *L*.
23:18 those who dwell before the *L* shall eat
24: 2 the *L* empties the land and lays it waste;
24: 3 stripped, for the *L* has decreed this thing.
24:14 the sea they proclaim the majesty of the *L*:
24:15 in the coastlands, give glory to the *L*!
24:15 of the sea, to the name of the *L*,
24:21 On that day the *L* will punish the host of
24:23 For the *L* of hosts will reign on Mount
25: 1 O *L*, you are my God,
25: 6 On this mountain the *L* of hosts will
25: 8 The *L* GOD will wipe away the tears from
25: 8 for the *L* has spoken.
25: 9 This is the *L* for whom we looked;
25:10 hand of the *L* will rest on this mountain,
26: 4 Trust in the *L* forever!
26: 4 For the *L* is an eternal Rock.
26: 8 Yes, for your way and your judgments, O *L*,
26:10 and sees not the majesty of the *L*.
26:11 O *L*, you hand is uplifted,
26:12 O *L*, you mete out peace to us
26:13 O *L*, our God, other lords than you
26:15 You have increased the nation, O *L*,
26:16 O *L*, oppressed by your punishment,
26:17 pains, so were we in your presence, O *L*.
26:21 See, the *L* goes forth from his place,
27: 1 *L* will punish with his sword that is cruel,
27: 3 I, the *L*, am its keeper,
27:12 The *L* shall beat out the grain between the
27:13 and worship the *L* on the holy mountain,
28: 2 the *L* has a strong one and a mighty,
28: 5 On that day the *L* of hosts will be a
28:13 So for them the word of the *L* shall be:
28:14 Therefore, hear the word of the *L*,
28:16 Therefore, thus says the *L* GOD:
28:21 the *L* shall rise up as on Mount Perazim,
28:22 be tightened, For I have heard from the *L*,
28:29 This too comes from the *L* of hosts;
29: 6 you shall be visited by the *L* of hosts,
29:10 For the *L* has poured out on you a spirit
29:13 The *L* said: Since this people
29:15 would hide their plans too deep for the *L*!
29:19 The lowly will ever find joy in the *L*,
29:22 Therefore thus says the *L*,
30: 1 to the rebellious children, says the *L*,
30: 9 who refuse to obey the law of the *L*.
30:15 For thus said the *L* GOD,
30:18 Yet the *L* is waiting to show you favor,
30:18 For the *L* is a God of justice:
30:20 The *L* will give you the bread you need and
30:26 the *L* binds up the wounds of his people,
30:27 of the *L* coming from afar in burning wrath,
30:29 with a flute Toward the mountain of the *L*,
30:30 The *L* will make his glorious voice heard,
30:31 When the *L* speaks, Assyria will be
30:32 the *L* will bring down on him in punishment,
30:33 in abundance, And the breath of the *L*,
31: 1 to the Holy One of Israel nor seek the *L*!
31: 3 When the *L* stretches forth his hand,
31: 4 Thus says the *L* to me: As a lion
31: 4 So shall the *L* of hosts come down to wage
31: 5 so the *L* of hosts shall shield Jerusalem,
31: 9 Says the *L* who has a fire in Zion and a
32: 6 to speak perversely against the *L*,
33: 2 O *L*, have pity on us, for you we wait.
33: 5 The *L* is exalted, enthroned on high
33: 6 the fear of the *L* is her treasure.
33:10 Now will I rise up, says the *L*,
33:22 Indeed the *L* will be there with us,
33:22 yes, the *L* our judge,
33:22 the LORD our lawgiver, the *L* our king,
34: 2 The *L* is angry with all the nations and is
34: 6 The *L* has a sword filled with blood,
34: 6 For the *L* has a sacrifice in Bozrah,
34: 8 For the *L* has a day of vengeance,
34:11 The *L* will measure her with line and
34:16 Look in the book of the *L* and read:
34:16 For the mouth of the *L* has ordered it,
35: 2 They will see the glory of the *L*,
35:10 Those whom the *L* has ransomed will return
36: 7 "We rely on the *L*, our God,"
36: 8 make a wager with my *l* the king of Assyria:
36: 9 even one of the least servants of my *l*?
36:10 The *L* said to me, "Go up and destroy
36:12 that my *l* sent me to speak these words?
36:15 LORD, saying, "The *L* will surely save us;
36:18 seduce you by saying, "The *L* will save us."
36:20 the *L* then save Jerusalem from my hand?' "
37: 1 and went into the temple of the *L*.
37: 4 Perhaps the *L*, your God, will hear
37: 4 will rebuke him for the words which the *L*,
37: 6 'Thus says the *L*: Do not be frightened
37:14 then he went up to the temple of the *L*,
37:15 it out before him, he prayed to the *L*:
37:16 "O *L* of hosts,
37:17 Incline your ear, O *L*, and listen!
37:17 Open your eyes, O *L* and see!
37:18 Truly, O *L*, the kings of Assyria
37:20 Therefore, O *L*, our God, save us
37:20 of the earth may know that you, O *L*,
37:21 Thus says the *L*, the God of Israel:
37:22 the word the *L* has spoken concerning him:
37:24 your servants you have insulted the *L*:
37:32 The zeal of the *L* of hosts shall do this.
37:33 says the *L* concerning the king of Assyria:
37:34 without entering the city, says the *L*.
37:36 The angel of the *L* went forth and struck
38: 1 Thus says the *L*: Put your house
38: 2 his face to the wall and prayed to the *L*:
38: 3 O *L*, remember how faithfully
38: 4 Then the word of the *L* came to Isaiah:
38: 5 Thus says the *L*, the God of your father
38: 7 the *L* that he will do what he has promised:
38:11 the *L* no more in the land of the living.
38:14 O *L*, I am in straits; be my surety!
38:16 Those live whom the *L* protects;
38:20 The *L* is our savior;
38:20 house of the *L* all the days of our life.
38:22 that I shall go up to the temple of the *L*?"
39: 5 "Hear the word of the *L* of hosts:
39: 6 nothing shall be left, says the *L*.
39: 8 the *L* which you have spoken is favorable."
40: 2 the hand of the *L* double for all her sins.
40: 3 In the desert prepare the way of the *L*!
40: 5 Then the glory of the *L* shall be revealed,
40: 5 for the mouth of the *L* has spoken.
40: 7 when the breath of the *L* blows upon it.
40:10 Here comes with power the *L* GOD,
40:13 Who has directed the spirit of the *L*,
40:27 O Israel, "My way is hidden from the *L*,
40:28 The *L* is the eternal God,
40:31 hope in the *L* will renew their strength,
41: 4 I, the *L*, am the first
41:13 For I am the *L*, your God, who grasp
41:14 I will help you, says the *L*;
41:16 But you shall rejoice in the *L*,
41:17 I, the *L*, will answer them
41:20 That the hand of the *L* has done this,
41:21 Present your case, says the *L*;
42: 5 Thus says God, the *L*, who created
42: 6 I, the *L*, have called you for the victory
42: 8 I am the *L*, this is my name;
42:10 Sing to the *L* a new song,
42:12 Let them give glory to the *L*,
42:13 The *L* goes forth like a hero,
42:21 Though it pleased the *L* in his justice to
42:24 Was it not the *L*, against whom
43: 1 now, thus says the *L*, who created you,
43: 3 I am the *L*, your God, the Holy One
43:10 You are my witnesses, says the *L*,
43:11 It is I, I the *L*;
43:12 You are my witnesses, says the *L*.
43:14 Thus says the *L*, your redeemer
43:15 I am the *L*, your Holy One, the creator
43:16 Thus says the *L*, who opens a way
44: 2 Thus says the *L* who made you
44: 6 Thus says the *L*, Israel's King
44: 6 Israel's King and redeemer, the *L* of hosts:
44:14 which the *L* had planted and the rain made
44:23 the *L* has done this; shout
44:23 For the *L* has redeemed Jacob,
44:24 Thus says the *L*, your redeemer
44:24 I am the *L*, who made all things
45: 1 Thus says the *L* to his anointed,
45: 3 away, That you may know that I am the *L*,
45: 5 I am the *L* and there is no other,
45: 6 I am the *L*, there is no other
45: 7 I, the *L*, do all these things.
45: 8 I, the *L*, have created this.
45:11 Thus says the *L*, the Holy One
45:13 price or ransom, says the *L* of hosts.
45:14 Thus says the *L*: The earning of Egypt
45:17 Israel, you are saved by the *L*.
45:18 For thus says the *L*, The creator
45:18 I am the *L*, and there is no other.
45:19 I, the *L*, promise justice,
45:21 Was it not I, the *L*,
45:24 "Only in the *L* are just deeds and power.
45:25 In the *L* shall be the vindication and the
47: 4 redeemer, Whose name is the *L* of hosts,
48: 1 You who swear by the name of the *L* and
48: 2 of Israel, whose name is the *L* of hosts.
48:16 "Now the *L* GOD has sent me,
48:17 Thus says the *L*, your redeemer
48:17 I, the *L*, your God, teach you
48:20 "The *L* has redeemed his servant Jacob.
48:22 no peace for the wicked, says the *L*
49: 1 The *L* called me from birth,
49: 4 my strength, Yet my reward is with the *L*,
49: 5 For now the *L* has spoken who formed me as
49: 5 I am made glorious in the sight of the *L*,
49: 7 Thus says the *L*, the redeemer
49: 7 Because of the *L* who is faithful,
49: 8 Thus says the *L*: In a time of favor
49:13 For the *L* comforts his people and shows
49:14 "The *L* has forsaken me; my Lord has
49:18 As I live, says the *L*, you shall be arrayed
49:22 Thus says the *L* GOD: see I will lift up
49:23 Then you shall know that I am the *L*,
49:24 Thus says the *L*: Can booty be taken
49:26 All mankind shall know that I, the *L*,
50: 1 Thus says the *L*: Where is the bill
50: 4 *L* GOD has given me a well-trained tongue,
50: 7 The *L* GOD is my help,
50: 9 See, the *L* GOD is my help;
50:10 Who among you fears the *L*,
50:10 the name of the *L* and relying on his God?
51: 1 you who pursue justice, who seek the *L*;
51: 3 the *L* shall comfort Zion and have pity on
51: 3 her wasteland like the garden of the *L*;
51: 9 awake, put on strength, O arm of the *L*!
51:11 Those whom the *L* has ransomed will return
51:13 be looked upon as grass, And forget the *L*,
51:15 For I am the *L*, you God, who stirs up
51:15 the *L* of hosts by name.
51:20 They are filled with the wrath of the *L*,
51:22 drunk, but not with wine, Thus says the *L*,
52: 3 For thus says the *L*: You were sold
52: 4 Thus says the *L* GOD: To Egypt
52: 5 What am I to do here? says the *L*
52: 5 rulers make a boast of it, says the *L*;
52: 8 before their eyes, the *L* restoring Zion.
52: 9 For the *L* comforts his people,
52:10 The *L* has bared his holy arm in the sight
52:11 you who carry the vessels of the *L*.
52:12 flight, For the *L* comes before you,
53: 1 To whom has the arm of the *L* been revealed?
53: 6 the *L* laid upon him the guilt of us all.
53:10 *L* was pleased to crush him in infirmity.]
53:10 of the *L* shall be accomplished through him.
54: 1 of her who has a husband, says the *L*.
54: 5 his name is the *L* of hosts;
54: 6 The *L* calls you back,
54: 8 love I take pity on you, says the *L*,
54:10 my covenant of peace be shaken, says the *L*,
54:13 All your sons shall be taught by the *L*,
54:17 This is the lot of the servants of the *L*,
54:17 their vindication from me, says the *L*.
55: 5 not shall run to you, Because of the *L*,
55: 6 Seek the *L* while he may be found,
55: 7 Let him turn to the *L* for mercy;
55: 8 nor are your ways my ways, says the *L*.
56: 1 Thus says the *L*: observe what is right
56: 3 join himself to the *L*, "The LORD will
56: 4 For thus says the *L*: To the eunuchs
56: 6 foreigners who join themselves to the *L*,
56: 6 Loving the name of the *L*
56: 8 Thus says the *L* GOD, who gathers
57:19 peace to the far and the near, says the *L*;
58: 5 this a fast, a day acceptable to the *L*?
58: 8 glory of the *L* shall be your rear guard.
58: 9 Then you shall call, and the *L* will answer,
58:11 Then the *L* will guide you always and give
58:14 Then you shall delight in the *L*,
58:14 father, for the mouth of the *L* has spoken.
59: 1 the hand of the *L* is not too short to save,
59:13 Transgressing, and denying the *L*,
59:19 in the west shall fear the name of the *L*,
59:19 river which the breath of the *L* drives on.
59:20 of Jacob who turn from sin, says the *L*.
59:21 them which I myself have made, says the *L*:
59:21 from now on and forever, says the *L*.
60: 1 come, the glory of the *L* shines upon you.
60: 2 But upon you the *L* shines,
60: 6 and proclaiming the praises of the *L*,
60: 9 silver and gold, In the name of the *L*,
60:14 They shall call you "City of the *L*,"
60:16 You shall know that I, the *L*,
60:19 The *L* shall be your light forever,
60:20 For the *L* will be your light forever,
60:22 I, the *L*, will swiftly accomplish
61: 1 The spirit of the *L* GOD is upon me,
61: 1 is upon me, because the *L* has anointed me;
61: 2 the *L* and a day of vindication by our God,
61: 3 planted by the *L* to show his glory.
61: 6 shall be named priests of the *L*,
61: 8 For I, the *L*, love what is right
61: 9 them as a race the *L* has blessed.
61:10 I rejoice heartily in the *L*,
61:11 So will the *L* GOD make justice and praise
62: 2 new name pronounced by the mouth of the *L*.

62: 3 be a glorious crown in the hand of the *L*,
62: 4 For the *L* delights in you,
62: 6 O you who are to remind the *L*,
62: 8 The *L* has sworn by his right hand and by
62: 9 shall eat it, and you shall praise the *L*;
62:11 the *L* proclaims to the ends of the earth:
62:12 the holy people, the redeemed of the *L*,
63: 7 The favors of the *L* I will recall,
63: 7 will recall, the glorious deeds of the *L*,
63:14 plain, the spirit of the *L* guiding them?
63:15 O *L*, hold not back,
63:16 us, nor Israel to acknowledge us, You, *L*,
63:17 Why do you let us wander, O *L*,
64: 7 Yet, O *L*, you are our father;
64: 8 Be not so very angry, *L*,
64:11 Can you hold back, O *L*, after all this?
65: 7 crimes of your fathers as well, says the *L*.
65: 8 Thus says the *L*: When the juice
65:11 But you who forsake the *L*,
65:13 me, therefore thus says the *L* GOD:
65:15 The *L* GOD shall slay you,
65:23 by the *L* are they and their offspring.
65:25 on all my holy mountain, says the *L*.
66: 1 Thus says the *L*: The heavens are
66: 2 when all of them came to be, says the *L*.
66: 5 me displeasure, Hear the word of the *L*,
66: 5 "Let the *L* show his glory that we may see
66: 6 the *L* repaying his enemies their deserts!
66: 9 says the *L*; Or shall I who allow her
66:12 For thus says the *L*: Lo I will spread
66:15 Lo, the *L* shall come in fire,
66:16 For the *L* shall judge all mankind by fire
66:16 and many shall be slain by the *L*.
66:17 their deeds and their thoughts, says the *L*.
66:20 all the nations as an offering to the *L*,
66:20 Jerusalem, my holy mountain, says the *L*,
66:20 to the house of the *L* in clean vessels.
66:21 take as priests and Levites, says the *L*.
66:22 make Shall endure before me, says the *L*,
66:23 come to worship before me, says the *L*.
Jer 1: 2 *L* first came to him in the days of Josiah,
1: 4 The word of the *L* came to me thus:
1: 6 "Ah, *L* GOD!" I said, "I know not how
1: 7 But the *L* answered me,
1: 8 I am with you to deliver you, says the *L*.
1: 9 *L* extended his hand and touched my mouth,
1:11 word of the *L* came to me with the question:
1:12 Then the *L* said to me:
1:13 word of the *L* came to me with the question:
1:14 And from the north, said the *L* to me,
1:15 all the kingdoms of the north, says the *L*.
1:19 I am with you to deliver you, says the *L*.
2: 1 This word of the *L* came to me:
2: 3 Sacred to the *L* was Israel,
2: 3 of them, evil would befall him, says the *L*.
2: 4 Listen to the word of the *L*,
2: 5 of the house of Israel, thus says the *L*:
2: 6 *L* who brought us up from the land of Egypt,
2: 8 The priests asked not, "Where is the *L*?"
2: 9 will I yet accuse you, says the *L*,
2:12 and shudder with sheer horror, says the *L*,
2:17 Has not the forsaking of the *L*,
2:19 evil and bitter is your forsaking the *L*,
2:19 God, And showing no fear of me, says the *L*,
2:22 guilt is still before me, says the *L* GOD.
2:29 have all rebelled against me, says the *L*.
2:31 generation, take note of the word of the *L*:
2:37 the *L* has rejected those in whom you trust,
3: 1 you would return to me! says the *L*
3: 6 *L* said to me in the days of King Josiah:
3:10 but insincerely, says the *L*.
3:11 Then the *L* said to me: Rebel Israel
3:12 Return, rebel Israel, says the *L*,
3:12 For I am merciful, says the *L*,
3:13 how you rebelled against the *L*,
3:13 would not listen to my voice, says the *L*.
3:14 Return, rebellious children, says the *L*,
3:16 become fruitful in the land, says the *L*,
3:16 say, "The ark of the covenant of the *L*!"
3:17 to honor the name of the *L* at Jerusalem,
3:20 to me, O house of Israel, says the *L*.
3:21 perverted their ways and forgotten the *L*,
3:22 we now come to you because you are the *L*,
3:23 In the *L*, our God, alone is the salvation
3:25 us, for we have sinned against the *L*,
3:25 we listened not to the voice of the *L*,
4: 1 you wish to return, O Israel, says the *L*,
4: 2 Then you can swear, "As the *L* lives,"
4: 3 of Judah and to Jerusalem, thus says the *L*.
4: 4 For the sake of the *L*, be circumcised,
4: 8 wrath of the *L* is not turned away from us."
4: 9 In that day, says the *L*,
4:10 *L* GOD," they will say, "You only deceived
4:17 she has rebelled against me, says the *L*.
4:26 with all its cities destroyed before the *L*,
4:27 For thus says the *L*: Waste shall
5: 2 Though they say, "As the *L* lives,"
5: 3 O *L*, do your eyes not look for honesty?
5: 4 For they know not the way of the *L*,
5: 5 For they know the way of the *L*,
5: 9 says the *L*; On a nation such as this
5:10 her tendrils, they do not belong to the *L*.
5:11 Israel and the house of Judah, says the *L*.
5:12 They denied the *L*, saying, "Not he—
5:14 for this that you have said, says the *L*,
5:15 from afar, O house of Israel, says the *L*;
5:18 Yet even in those days, says the *L*,
5:19 has the *L* done all these things to us?"
5:22 Should you not fear me, says the *L*,
5:24 not in their hearts, "Let us fear the *L*,
5:29 says the *L*; on a nations such as this
6: 6 For thus says the *L* of hosts: Hew
6: 9 Thus says the *L* of hosts: Glean
6:10 *L* has become for them an object of scorn,
6:12 those who dwell in this land, says the *L*.
6:15 punishment they shall go down, says the *L*.
6:16 Thus says the *L*: Stand beside
6:21 Therefore, thus says the *L*: See, I will
6:22 Thus says the *L*: See, a people comes
6:30 be called, for the *L* has rejected them.
7: 1 message came to Jeremiah from the *L*:
7: 2 Stand at the gate of the house of the *L*,
7: 2 Hear the word of the *L*,
7: 2 who enter these gates to worship the *L*!
7: 3 Thus says the *L* of hosts,
7: 4 "This is the temple of the *L*!
7: 4 The temple of the *L*!"
7:11 I too see what is being done, says the *L*.
7:13 committed all these misdeeds, says the *L*,
7:19 Is it I whom they hurt, says the *L*;
7:20 See now, says the *L* GOD,
7:21 Thus says the *L* of hosts, the God
7:27 does not listen to the voice of the *L*,
7:29 For the *L* has rejected and cast off the
7:30 done what is evil in my eyes, says the *L*.
7:32 days will come, says the *L*,
8: 1 At that time, says the *L*, the bones
8: 3 which I banish them, says the *L* of hosts.
8: 4 Thus says the *L*: Tell them: Thus says the *L*
8: 7 people do not know the ordinance of the *L*.
8: 8 "We are wise, we have the law of the *L*"?
8: 9 Since they have rejected the word of the *L*,
8:12 punishment they shall go down, says the *L*.
8:13 I will gather them all in, says the *L*:
8:14 For the *L* has wrought our destruction,
8:14 because we have sinned against the *L*.
8:17 will work when they bite you, says the *L*.
8:19 Is the *L* no longer in Zion,
9: 2 to evil, but me they know not, says the *L*.
9: 5 They refuse to recognize me, says the *L*.
9: 6 Therefore, thus says the *L* of hosts:
9: 8 For these things, says the *L*,
9:11 mouth of the *L* has spoken make it known:
9:12 The *L* answered: Because they have
9:14 therefore, thus says the *L* of hosts,
9:16 Thus says the *L* of hosts: Attention!
9:19 Hear, you women, the word of the *L*,
9:22 Thus says the *L*: Let not the wise
9:23 prudence he knows me, Knows that I, the *L*,
9:23 For with such am I pleased, says the *L*.
9:24 See, days are coming, says the *L*,
10: 1 Hear the word which the *L* speaks to you,
10: 2 Thus says the *L*: Learn not the customs
10: 6 No one is like you, O *L*,
10:10 The *L* is true God, he is the living God,
10:16 his very own tribe, *L* of hosts is his name.
10:18 For thus says the *L*: Behold this time
10:21 stupid as cattle, the *L* they sought not;
10:23 You know, O *L*, that man is not master
10:24 Punish us, O *L*, but with equity,
11: 1 message came to Jeremiah from the *L*:
11: 3 Thus says the *L*, the God of Israel:
11: 5 "Amen, *L*," I answered.
11: 6 Then the *L* said to me: 'Proclaim all
11: 9 has been found, the *L* said to me,
11:11 Therefore, thus says the *L*:
11:16 goodly to behold, the *L* has named you;
11:17 The *L* of hosts who planted you has decreed
11:18 I knew it because the *L* informed me;
11:18 at that time you, O *L*,
11:20 But, you, O *L* of hosts, O just Judge,
11:21 thus says the *L* concerning the men of
11:21 "Do not prophesy in the name of the *L*;
11:22 Therefore, thus says the *L* of hosts:
12: 1 You would be in the right, O *L*,
12: 3 You, O *L*, know me, you see me,
12:12 The *L* has a sword which consumes the land,
12:13 their harvest, the flaming anger of the *L*.
12:14 Thus says the *L* against all my evil
12:16 of swearing by my name, "As the *L* lives,"
12:17 destroy that nation entirely, says the *L*.
13: 1 The *L* said to me: Go buy yourself
13: 2 I bought the loincloth, as the *L* commanded,
13: 3 time the word of the *L* came to me thus:
13: 8 Then the message came to me from the *L*:
13: 9 Thus says the *L*: So also I will allow
13:11 house of Judah cling to me, says the *L*;
13:12 Thus says the *L*, the God of Israel:
13:13 Thus says the *L*: Beware! I am filling
13:14 fathers and sons together, says the *L*;
13:15 Give ear, listen humbly, for the *L* speaks.
13:16 Give glory to the *L*,
13:25 measured out to you from me, says the *L*.
14: 1 The word of the *L* that came to Jeremiah
14: 7 bear witness against us, take action, O *L*,
14: 8 O Hope of Israel, O *L*,
14: 9 You are in our midst, O *L*,
14:10 Thus says the *L* of this people:
14:10 The *L* has no pleasure in them;
14:11 the *L* said to me: Do not, intercede
14:13 *L* GOD, I replied, it is the prophets
14:14 utter in my name, the *L* said to me.
14:15 Therefore, thus says the *L*:
14:20 We recognize, O *L*, our wickedness,
14:22 Is it not you alone, O *L*,
15: 1 The *L* said to me: Even if Moses
15: 2 they should go, tell them, Thus says the *L*:
15: 3 I have decreed against them, says the *L*:
15: 6 You have disowned me, says the *L*,
15: 9 the sword before their enemies, says the *L*.
15:11 Tell me, *L*, have I not served you
15:15 Remember me, *L*, visit me, and avenge
15:16 of my heart, Because I bore your name, O *L*,
15:19 Thus the *L* answered me: If you repent
15:20 you, to deliver and rescue you, says the *L*.
16: 1 This message came to me from the *L*:
16: 3 for thus says the *L* concerning the sons
16: 5 into a house of mourning, the *L* continued:
16: 5 my friendship from this people, says the *L*,
16: 9 For thus says the *L* of hosts,
16:10 "Why has the *L* pronounced all these great
16:10 What sin have we committed against the *L*,
16:11 your fathers have forsaken me, says the *L*,
16:14 days will surely come, says the *L*,
16:14 will no longer be said, "As the *L* lives,
16:15 but rather, "As the *L* lives,
16:16 I will send many fishermen, says the *L*,
16:19 O *L*, my strength, my fortress,
16:21 they shall know that my name is *L*.
17: 5 Thus says the *L*: Cursed is the man
17: 5 flesh, whose heart turns away from the *L*.
17: 7 trusts in the LORD, whose hope is the *L*.
17:10 I, the *L*, alone probe the mind
17:13 O hope of Israel, O *L*!
17:13 the source of living waters [the *L*.
17:14 Heal me, *L*, that I may be healed
17:15 say to me, "Where is the word of the *L*?
17:19 Thus said the *L* to me: Go stand
17:20 Hear the word of the *L*, you kings
17:21 Thus says the *L*: As you love your lives
17:24 If you obey me wholeheartedly, says the *L*,
17:26 and thank offerings to the house of the *L*.
18: 1 This word came to Jeremiah from the *L*:
18: 5 Then the word of the *L* came to me.
18: 6 as this potter has done? says the *L*.
18:11 Thus says the *L*: Take care! I am
18:13 Therefore thus says the *L*: Ask among
18:19 Heed me, O *L*,
18:23 But you, O *L*, know all their plans
19: 1 Thus said the *L*: Go, buy a potter's
19: 3 Listen to the word of the *L*,
19: 3 Thus says the *L* of hosts,
19: 6 Therefore, days will come, says the *L*,
19:11 Thus says the *L* of hosts:
19:12 place and to its inhabitants, says the *L*;
19:14 where the *L* had sent him to prophesy,
19:15 Thus says the *L* of hosts,
20: 1 Immer, chief officer in the house of the *L*.
20: 2 Gate of Benjamin in the house of the *L*.
20: 3 the *L* will name you "Terror on every side."
20: 4 For thus says the *L*: Indeed I will deliver
20: 7 You duped me, O *L*,
20: 8 The word of the *L* has brought me derision
20:11 But the *L* is with me,
20:12 O *L* of hosts, you who test the just,
20:13 Sing to the LORD, praise the *L*,
20:16 cities which the *L* relentlessly overthrew;
21: 1 the *L* when King Zedekiah sent him Pashhur,
21: 2 Inquire for us of the *L*,
21: 2 Perhaps the *L* will deal with us according
21: 4 Thus says the *L*, the God of Israel:
21: 7 After that, says the *L*, I will hand over
21: 8 Thus says the *L*: "See I am giving you
21:10 its woe and not for its good, says the *L*.
21:11 Hear the word of the *L*, O house of David!
21:12 Thus says the *L*: I am giving you
21:13 Valley-site, Rock of the Plain, says the *L*.
21:14 I will punish you, says the *L*,
22: 1 The *L* told me this: Go down to the house
22: 2 Listen to the word of the *L*,
22: 3 Thus says the *L*: Do what is right
22: 5 commands, I swear by myself, says the *L*:
22: 6 For thus says the *L* concerning the palace
22: 8 has the *L* done this to so great a city?"
22: 9 have deserted their covenant with the *L*,
22:11 Thus says the *L* concerning Shallum,
22:16 true knowledge of me? says the *L*.
22:18 thus says the *L* concerning Jehoiakim,
22:18 They shall not lament him, "Alas, *L*!
22:24 As I live, says the *L*,
22:29 O land, land, land, hear the word of the *L*—
22:30 Thus says the *L*:
23: 1 the flock of my pasture, says the *L*.
23: 2 Therefore, thus says the *L*,
23: 2 drunk, overcome by wine, Because of the *L*,
23: 4 and none shall be missing, says the *L*.
23: 5 Behold, the days are coming, says the *L*,
23: 6 "The *L* our justice."
23: 7 Therefore, the days will come, says the *L*,

LORD (cont.)
23: 7 they shall no longer say, "As the . lives,
23: 8 but rather, "As the *L* lives,
23:11 house I find their wickedness, says the *L*.
23:12 the year of their punishment, says the *L*.
23:15 says the *L* of hosts against the prophets:
23:16 Thus says the *L* of hosts: Listen not
23:16 they speak, not from the mouth of the *L*.
23:17 to those who despise the word of the *L*,
23:18 Now, who has stood in the council of the *L*,
23:19 See, the storm of the *L*!
23:20 The anger of the *L* shall not abate until
23:23 Am I a God near at hand only, says the *L*,
23:24 Without my seeing him? says the *L*.
23:24 both heaven and earth? says the *L*.
23:28 to do with the wheat? says the *L*.
23:29 Is not my word like fire, says the *L*,
23:30 I am against the prophets, says the *L*,
23:31 I am against the prophets, says the *L*,
23:32 who prophesy lying dreams, says the *L*,
23:32 do this people no good at all, says the *L*.
23:33 asks you, "What is the burden of the *L*?"
23:33 the burden, and I cast you off, says the *L*."
23:34 else mentions "the burden of the *L*,"
23:35 one another, "What answer did the *L* give?"
23:35 or, "What did the *L* say?"
23:36 burden of the *L* you shall mention no more.
23:36 words of the living God, the *L* of hosts,
23:37 the prophet, "What answer did the *L* give?"
23:37 or, "What did the *L* say?"
23:38 burden of the LORD," then thus says the *L*:
23:38 use this phrase, "the burden of the *L*,"
24: 1 The *L* showed me two baskets of figs placed
24: 1 of figs placed before the temple of the *L*.
24: 3 Then the *L* said to me: What do you see,
24: 4 Thereupon this word of the *L* came to me:
24: 5 Thus says the *L*, the God of Israel:
24: 7 with which to understand that I am the *L*.
24: 8 says the *L*— even so will I treat Zedekiah,
25: 3 the word of the *L* has come to me and I
25: 4 the *L* has sent you without fail all his
25: 5 land which the *L* gave you and your fathers,
25: 7 you would not listen to me, says the *L*,
25: 8 Hence, thus says the *L* of hosts:
25: 9 the *L* (and I will send to Nebuchadnezzar,
25:12 the Chaldeans for their guilt, says the *L*.
25:15 For thus said the *L*, the God of Isreal,
25:17 I took the cup from the hand of the *L* and
25:17 to all the nations to which the *L* sent me:
25:27 Thus says the *L* of hosts, the God of Israel
25:28 Thus says the *L* of hosts:
25:29 who inhabit the earth, says the *L* of hosts.
25:30 The *L* roars from on high,
25:31 *L* has an indictment against the nations,
25:31 shall be given to the sword, says the *L*.
25:32 Thus says the *L* of hosts: Lo! calamity
25:33 those whom the *L* has slain will be strewn
25:36 For the *L* lays waste their grazing place,
25:38 sword, by the burning wrath of the *L*.
26: 1 of Judah, this message came from the *L*:
26: 2 Thus says the *L*: Stand in the court
26: 2 Stand in the court of the house of the *L*
26: 2 who come to worship in the house of the *L*;
26: 4 Thus says the *L*: If you disobey me,
26: 7 speak these words in the house of the *L*.
26: 8 the *L* bade him speak to all the people,
26: 9 Why do you prophesy in the name of the *L*:
26: 9 about Jeremiah in the house of the *L*.
26:10 king's palace to the house of the *L*
26:10 at the New Gate of the house of the *L*.
26:12 "It was the *L* who sent me to prophesy
26:13 listen to the voice of the *L* your God,
26:13 so that the *L* will repent of the evil with
26:15 in truth it was the *L* who sent me to you,
26:16 it is in the name of the *L*,
26:18 Thus says the *L* of hosts: Zion shall
26:19 the *L* and entreat the favor of the LORD,
26:20 man who prophesied in the name of the *L*,
27: 1 this message came to Jeremiah from the *L*:
27: 2 Thus said the *L* to me: "Make for yourself
27: 4 Thus says the *L* of hosts,
27: 8 says the *L* until I give them into his hand.
27:11 leave in peace on its own land, says the *L*,
27:13 with which the *L* has threatened the nation
27:15 I did not send them, says the *L*,
27:16 Thus says the *L*: Do not listen
27:16 "The vessels of the house of the *L* will
27:18 if the word of the *L* were with them,
27:18 they would intercede with the *L* of hosts,
27:18 which remain in the house of the *L*
27:19 says the *L* of hosts concerning the pillars,
27:21 yes, thus says the *L* of hosts,
27:21 vessels that remain in the house of the *L*,
27:22 until the day I look for them, says the *L*;
28: 1 said to me in the house of the *L* in the
28: 2 "Thus says the *L* of hosts,
28: 3 the temple of the *L* which Nebuchadnezzar,
28: 4 of Judah who went to Babylon,' says the *L*,
28: 5 the people assembled in the house of the *L*,
28: 6 thus may the *L* do! May he fulfill the things
28: 6 vessels of the house of the *L*
28: 9 recognized as truly sent by the *L*
28:11 "Thus says the *L*: Within two years
28:12 the word of the *L* came to Jeremiah:
28:13 Thus says the *L*: By breaking the yoke
28:14 For thus says the *L* of hosts,
28:15 The *L* has not sent you,
28:16 says the *L* I will dispatch you from the
28:16 you have preached rebellion against the *L*.
29: 4 Thus says the *L* of hosts,
29: 7 pray for it to the *L*,
29: 8 thus says the *L* of hosts,
29: 9 I did not send them, says the *L*.
29:10 Thus says the *L*: Only after seventy
29:11 plans I have in mind for you, says the *L*,
29:14 you will find me with you, says the *L*,
29:14 to which I have banished you, says the *L*,
29:15 "The *L* has raised up for us prophets here
29:16 Thus says the *L* concerning the king who
29:17 thus says the *L* of hosts:
29:19 did not listen to my words, says the *L*,
29:19 only to have them go unheeded, says the *L*.
29:20 You, now, listen to the word of the *L*,
29:21 This is what the *L* of hosts,
29:22 the *L* make you like Zedekiah and Ahab,
29:23 I know, I am witness, says the *L*.
29:25 Thus says the *L* of hosts,
29:26 "The *L* has appointed you priest in place
29:26 be police officers in the house of the *L*,
29:30 the word of the *L* came to Jeremiah:
29:31 Thus says the *L* concerning Shemaiah,
29:32 and raises false confidence, says the *L*,
29:32 good I will do to this people, says the *L*,
29:32 he preached rebellion against the *L*.
30: 1 message came to Jeremiah from the *L*:
30: 2 Thus says the *L*, the God of Israel:
30: 3 behold, the days will come, says the *L*,
30: 3 people (of Israel and Judah, says the *L*),
30: 4 which the *L* spoke to Israel and to Judah:
30: 5 thus says the *L*: A cry of dismay
30: 8 On that day, says the *L* of hosts,
30: 9 instead, they shall serve the *L*,
30:10 my servant Jacob, fear not, says the *L*,
30:11 for I am with you, says the *L*,
30:12 For thus says the *L*: Incurable
30:17 of your wounds I will heal you, says the *L*.
30:18 Thus says the *L*: See! I will restore
30:21 of approaching me? says the Lord
30:23 See, the storm of the *L*!
30:24 The anger of the *L* will not abate until he
31: 1 At that time, says the *L*, I will be the God
31: 2 Thus says the *L*: The people that escaped
31: 3 his rest, the *L* appears to him from afar:
31: 6 "Rise up, let us go to Zion, to the *L*,
31: 7 For thus says the *L*: shout with joy
31: 7 The *L* has delivered his people,
31:10 Hear the word of the *L*,
31:11 The *L* shall ransom Jacob,
31:14 be filled with my blessings, says the *L*.
31:15 Thus says the *L*: In Ramsah
31:16 Thus says the *L*: Cease your cries
31:16 shown shall have its reward, says the *L*,
31:17 There is hope for your future, says the *L*;
31:18 allow me, I will return, for you are the *L*,
31:20 for him, I must show him mercy, says the *L*.
31:22 *L* has created a new thing upon the earth:
31:23 Thus says the *L* of hosts,
31:23 "May the *L* bless you,
31:27 The days are coming, says the *L*,
31:28 them to build and to plant, says the *L*.
31:31 The days are coming, says the *L*,
31:32 to show myself their master, says the *L*.
31:33 of Israel after those days, says the *L*.
31:34 friends and kinsmen how to know the *L*.
31:34 to greatest, shall know me, says the *L*,
31:35 Thus says the *L*, He who gives the sun
31:35 its waves roar, whose name is *L* of hosts:
31:36 laws give way in spite of me, says the *L*,
31:37 Thus says the *L*: If the heavens
31:37 because of all they have done, says the *L*.
31:38 The days are coming, says the *L*,
31:40 Gate at the east, shall be holy to the *L*.
32: 1 from the *L* in the tenth year of Zedekiah,
32: 3 Thus says the *L*: I am handing over
32: 5 remain, until I attend to him, says the *L*;
32: 6 This message came to me from the *L*,
32: 8 Then, as the *L* foretold,
32: 8 I knew this was what the *L* meant,
32:14 Thus says the *L* of hosts,
32:15 For thus says the *L* of hosts,
32:16 son of Neriah, I prayed thus to the *L*.
32:17 Ah, *L* GOD, you have made heaven
32:18 great and mighty, whose name is *L* of hosts,
32:25 and yet you tell me, O *L* God:
32:26 Then this word of the *L* came to Jeremiah:
32:27 I am the *L*, the God of all mankind!
32:28 This now is what the *L* says:
32:30 with the works of their hands, says the *L*.
32:36 Now, therefore, thus says the *L*,
32:42 thus says the *L*: Just as I brought
32:44 Negeb, when I change their lot, says the *L*.
33: 1 The word of the *L* came to Jeremiah a
33: 2 Thus says the *L* who made the earth and
33: 2 gave it form and firmness, whose name is *L*:
33: 4 Thus says the *L*, the God of Israel,
33:10 Thus says the *L*: In this place
33:11 thank offerings to the house of the *L*,
33:11 "Give thanks to the *L* of hosts, for the *L*
33:11 to the LORD of hosts, for the *L* is good;
33:11 restore this country as of old, says the *L*.
33:12 Thus says the *L* of hosts: In this place
33:13 of the one who counts them, says the *L*.
33:14 The days are coming, says the *L*,
33:16 "The *L* our justice."
33:17 For thus says the *L*: Never shall David
33:18 This word of the *L* also came to Jeremiah:
33:19 Thus says the *L*: If you can break
33:23 This word of the *L* came to Jeremiah:
33:24 "The *L* has rejected the two tribes which
33:25 Thus says the *L*: When I have no covenant
34: 1 Jeremiah from the *L* while Nebuchadnezzar,
34: 2 Thus says the *L*, the God of Israel:
34: 2 Thus says the *L*: I am handing this city
34: 4 But if you obey the word of the *L*,
34: 4 king of Judah, then, says the *L* to you,
34: 5 and they will lament you as their *l*,
34: 5 it is I who make this promise, says the *L*.
34: 8 word that came to Jeremiah from the *L*
34:12 Then this word of the *L* came to Jeremiah:
34:13 Thus says the *L*, the God of Israel:
34:17 Therefore, thus says the *L*: You did not
34:17 I now proclaim you free, says the *L*,
34:22 I will give the command, says the *L*,
35: 1 from the *L* in the days of Jehoiakim,
35: 2 bring them into the house of the *L*,
35: 4 the Rechabites, into the house of the *L*,
35:12 Then this word of the *L* came to Jeremiah:
35:13 Thus says the *L* of hosts,
35:13 obey my words? says the *L*
35:17 Now, therefore, says the *L* God of hosts,
35:18 Thus says the *L* of hosts,
35:19 you, thus therefore says the *L* of hosts,
36: 1 this word came to Jeremiah from the *L*.
36: 4 the words which the *L* had spoken to him.
36: 5 I cannot go to the house of the *L*;
36: 7 will lay their supplication before the *L*
36: 7 which the *L* has threatened this people.
36: 9 king of Judah a fast to placate the *L*
36:11 all the words of the *L* read from the book.
36:26 But the *L* kept them concealed.
36:27 This word of the *L* came to Jeremiah,
36:29 Thus says the *L*: You burned that scroll
36:30 The *L* now says of Jehoiakim,
37: 2 of the *L* spoken by Jeremiah the prophet.
37: 3 "Pray to the *L*, our God, for us."
37: 6 of the *L* then came to the prophet Jeremiah:
37: 7 Thus says the *L*, the God of Israel:
37: 9 Thus says the *L*: Do not deceive
37:17 whether there was any message from the *L*.
37:20 Hear now, my *l* king,
38: 2 Thus says the *L*: He who remains
38: 3 Thus says the *L*: This city shall
38: 9 the palace and said to him, "My *l* king,
38:14 the third entrance to the house of the *L*.
38:16 the *L* lives who gave us the breath of life,
38:17 Thus says the *L* God of hosts,
38:20 the voice of the *L* and do as I tell you;
38:21 to surrender, this is what the *L* shows me:
39:15 the guard, the word of the *L* came to him:
39:16 Thus says the *L* of hosts,
39:17 on that day I will rescue you, says the *L*;
39:18 because you trusted in me, says the *L*.
40: 1 This word came to Jeremiah from the *L*,
40: 2 Jeremiah, he said to him, "The *L* your God,
40: 3 against the *L* and did not obey his voice,
41: 5 and incense for the house of the *L*.
42: 2 pray for us to the *L*,
42: 3 Let the *L*, you God, show us
42: 4 I will pray to the *L*,
42: 4 whatever the *L* answers you,
42: 5 to Jeremiah, "May the *L* be our witness:
42: 5 follow all the instructions the *L*,
42: 6 we will obey the command of the *L*,
42: 6 with us for obeying the command of the *L*,
42: 7 before the word of the *L* came to Jeremiah.
42: 9 Thus says the *L*, the God of Israel,
42:11 do not fear him, says the *L*,
42:13 But if you disobey the voice of the *L*,
42:15 then listen to the word of the *L*,
42:15 Thus says the *L* of hosts, the God of Israel:
42:18 thus says the *L* of hosts, the God of Israel:
42:19 It is the *L* who has spoken to you,
42:20 you have deceived me, sending me to the *L*,
42:20 your God, saying, "Pray for us to the *L*,
42:20 make known to us all that the *L*,
42:21 message, but you obey the voice of the *L*,
43: 1 to the people all these words of the *L*,
43: 1 God, with which the *L* had sent him to them,
43: 2 it was not the *L*, our God, who sent you
43: 8 of the *L* came to Jeremiah in Tahpanhes:
43:10 Thus says the *L* of hosts, the God of Israel;
44: 2 Thus says the *L* of hosts, the God of Israel:
44: 7 Now thus says the *L* God of hosts,
44:11 thus says the *L* of hosts, the God of Israel:
44:16 to what you say in the name of the *L*.
44:21 that the *L* remembered and brought to mind,
44:22 The *L* could no longer bear your evil deeds,
44:23 burned incense and sinned against the *L*,
44:24 Hear the word of the *L*,

44:25 says the *L* of hosts, the God of Israel:
44:26 But listen then to the word of the *L*,
44:26 I swear by my own great name, says the *L*,
44:26 my name saying, "As the *L* GOD lives."
44:29 this shall be a sign to you, says the *L*,
44:30 Thus says the *L*: See I will hand
45: 2 Thus says the *L*,
45: 3 the *L* adds grief to my pain;
45: 4 say this to him, says the *L*:
45: 5 bringing evil on all mankind, says the *L*,
46: 1 This is the word of the *L* that came to the
46: 5 Terror on every side, says the *L*!
46:10 But this is the day of the *L* GOD of hosts,
46:10 for the *L* GOD of hosts holds a slaughter
46:13 The message which the *L* gave to the
46:15 The *L* thrust him down;
46:18 says the King whose name is *L* of hosts,
46:23 They cut down her forest, says the *L*,
46:25 The *L* of hosts, the God of Israel, has said:
46:26 again, as in times past, says the *L*.
46:28 my servant Jacob, never fear, says the *L*,
47: 1 This is the word that came from the *L* to
47: 2 Thus says the *L*: Behold: Waters
47: 4 Yes, the *L* is destroying the Philistines,
47: 6 Alas, sword of the *L*!
47: 7 it find rest when the *L* has commanded it?
48: 1 Concerning Moab, thus says the *L* of hosts,
48: 8 wasted the plain, as the *L* has said.
48:12 Hence, the days shall come, says the *L*,
48:15 says the King, the *L* of hosts by name.
48:25 broken, his might is shattered says the *L*.
48:26 Because he boasted against the *L*,
48:30 I know, says the *L*, his arrogance;
48:35 I will leave no one in Moab, says the *L*,
48:38 wants, says the *L* How terror seizes Moab,
48:40 For thus says the *L*: Behold the eagle
48:42 a people, because he boasted against the *L*.
48:43 be upon you, people of Moab, says the *L*.
48:44 the year of their punishment, says the *L*.
48:47 of Moab in the days to come, says the *L*.
49: 1 Concerning the Ammonites, thus says the *L*:
49: 2 But the days are coming, says the *L*,
49: 2 those who disinherited her, says the *L*.
49: 5 terror upon you, says the *L* GOD of hosts,
49: 6 the lot of the Ammonites, says the *L*.
49: 7 Concerning Edom, thus says the *L* of hosts:
49:12 For thus says the *L*: Even those
49:13 By my own self I have sworn, says the *L*:
49:14 I have heard a report from the *L*,
49:16 there I will drag you down, says the *L*.
49:18 neighbors were overthrown, says the *L*,
49:20 Therefore, hear the counsel of the *L*,
49:26 On that day, says the *L* of hosts,
49:28 king of Babylon, thus says the *L*:
49:30 holes, you that live in Hazor, says the *L*;
49:31 is at peace, that lives secure says the *L*,
49:32 I will bring ruin upon them, says the *L*.
49:34 The following word of the *L* against Elam
49:35 Thus says the *L* of hosts: Behold I will
49:37 upon them, my burning wrath, says the *L*.
49:38 from there king and princes, says the *L*.
49:39 I will change the lot of Elam, says the *L*.
50: 1 The word which the *L* spoke against Babylon,
50: 4 In those days, at that time, says the *L*,
50: 4 come, Weeping as they come, to seek the *L*,
50: 5 to the *L* with covenant everlasting,
50: 7 guilt, Because they sinned against the *L*,
50:10 plunderers shall be enriched, says the *L*.
50:15 Vengeance of the *L* is this!
50:15 for she sinned against the *L*.
50:18 Therefore, thus says the *L* of hosts,
50:20 In those days, at that time, says the *L*:
50:21 Slaughter and doom them, says the *L*,
50:24 and seized, because you challenged the *L*.
50:25 The *L* opens his armory and brings forth
50:25 For the *L* GOD of hosts has work to do in
50:28 announce in Zion the vengeance of the *L*,
50:29 done, do to her, For she insulted the *L*,
50:30 shall perish on that day, says the *L*.
50:31 man of insolence, says the *L* GOD of hosts;
50:33 Thus says the *L* of hosts: Oppressed
50:34 is their avenger, whose name is *L* of hosts;
50:35 A sword upon the Chaldeans, says the *L*,
50:40 with their neighbors, says the *L*,
50:45 the *L* which he has taken against Babylon;
51: 1 Thus says the *L*: See! I rouse
51: 5 not widowed of their God, the *L* of hosts,
51: 6 This is a time of vengeance for the *L*,
51: 7 of the *L* which made the whole earth drunk;
51:10 The *L* has brought to light our just cause;
51:10 come, let us tell in Zion what the *L*,
51:11 The *L* has stirred up the spirit of Media's
51:11 Yes, it is the vengeance of the *L*,
51:12 For the *L* has planned and he will carry
51:14 The *L* of hosts has sworn by himself:
51:19 his very own tribe, *L* of hosts is his name.
51:24 shall see with your own eyes, says the *L*.
51:25 destroyer of the entire earth, says the *L*;
51:26 Ruins forever shall you be, says the *L*.
51:33 For thus says the *L* of hosts,
51:36 thus says the *L*: Surely I will
51:39 sleep, never to awaken, says the *L*.
51:45 himself from the burning wrath of the *L*.
51:48 against her from the north, says the *L*.
51:50 Remember the *L* from afar,
51:51 the holy places of the house of the *L*.
51:52 behold, the days are coming, says the *L*,
51:53 from me shall reach her, says the *L*.
51:55 For the *L* lays Babylon waste,
51:56 The *L* is a God who requites,
51:57 the King, whose name is the *L* of hosts.
51:58 Thus says the *L* of hosts: The walls
51:62 O *L*, you yourself threatened
52: 2 He did what was evil in the eyes of the *L*,
52: 3 *L* that he cast them out from his presence.
52:13 He burned the house of the *L*,
52:17 that belonged to the house of the *L*,
52:17 and the bronze sea in the house of the *L*,
52:20 Solomon had made for the house of the *L*.
Lam 1: 5 The *L* has punished her for her many sins.
1: 9 Look, O *L*, upon her misery
1:11 "Look O *L*, and see how worthless
1:12 has been dealt me When the *L* afflicted me
1:14 The *L* has delivered me into their grip,
1:15 ones in my midst the *L* has cast away;
1:15 The *L* has trodden in the wine press virgin
1:17 The *L* gave orders against Jacob for his
1:18 "The *L* is just; I had defied his command.
1:20 "Look, O *L*, upon my distress:
2: 1 *L* in his wrath has detested daughter Zion!
2: 2 The *L* has consumed without pity all the
2: 5 The *L* has become an enemy,
2: 6 In Zion the *L* has made feast and sabbath
2: 7 The *L* has disowned his altar,
2: 7 in the house of the *L* as on a feast day.
2: 8 The *L* marked for destruction the wall of
2: 9 have not received any vision from the *L*.
2:17 The *L* has done as he decreed:
2:18 Cry out to the *L*; moan, O daughter Zion!
2:19 heart like water in the presence of the *L*;
2:20 "Look, O *L*, and consider:
2:20 to be slain in the sanctuary of the *L*?
3:18 is lost, all that I hoped for from the *L*.
3:22 The favors of the *L* are not exhausted,
3:24 My portion is the *L*,
3:25 Good is the *L* to one who waits for him,
3:26 in silence for the saving help of the *L*.
3:36 claim, the *L* does not look on unconcerned.
3:37 it comes to pass, except the *L* ordains it;
3:40 our ways that we may return to the *L*!
3:50 Till the *L* from heaven looks down and sees.
3:55 I called upon your name, O *L*,
3:59 You see, O *L*, how I am wronged
3:61 You hear their insults, O *L*,
3:64 Requite them as they deserve, O *L*,
4:11 The *L* has spent his anger,
4:16 The *L* himself has dispersed them,
4:20 The anointed one of the *L*,
5: 1 Remember, O *L*, what has befallen us
5:19 You, O *L*, are enthroned forever
5:21 Lead us back to you, O *L*,
Bar 1: 5 wept and fasted and prayed before the *L*,
1: 8 *L* that had been removed from the temple,
1:10 offer these on the altar of the *L* our God,
1:12 and that the *L* may give us strength,
1:13 "Pray for us also to the *L*,
1:13 for we have sinned against the *L*,
1:13 and the wrath and anger of the *L* have not
1:14 which we send you, in the house of the *L*,
1:15 "Justice is with the *L*,
1:18 We have neither heeded the voice of the *L*,
1:18 the precepts which the *L* set before us.
1:19 From the time the *L* led our fathers out of
1:19 day, we have been disobedient to the *L*,
1:20 the curse which the *L* enjoined upon Moses,
1:21 For we did not heed the voice of the *L*,
1:22 gods, and did evil in the sight of the *L*,
2: 1 "And the *L* fulfilled the warning he had
2: 4 about to which the *L* has scattered us.
2: 5 raised up, because we sinned against the *L*,
2: 6 "Justice is with the *L*,
2: 7 the *L* has warned us have come upon us:
2: 8 and we did not plead before the *L*,
2: 9 And the *L* kept watch over the evils,
2: 9 for the *L* is just in all the works he
2:10 precepts of the *L* which he set before us.
2:11 now, *L*, God of Israel, you who led
2:12 sinned, been impious, and violated, O *L*,
2:14 Hear, O *L*, our prayer of supplication
2:15 whole earth may know that you are the *L*,
2:16 O *L*, look down from your holy dwelling
2:16 turn, O *L*, your ear to hear us.
2:17 will give glory and vindication to the *L*.
2:18 will declare your glory and justice, *L*!
2:19 base our plea for mercy in your sight, O *L*,
2:21 'Thus says the *L*: Bend your shoulders
2:27 with us, O *L*, our God, you have dealt
2:31 they shall know that I, the *L*,
2:33 of their fathers who sinned against the *L*.
3: 1 *L* Almighty, God of Israel, afflicted souls
3: 2 Hear, O *L*, for you are a God of mercy
3: 4 *L* Almighty, God of Israel, hear the prayer
3: 4 they did not heed the voice of the *L*,
3: 6 *L* our God; and you O Lord, we will praise!
3: 8 of our fathers, who withdrew from the *L*,
6: 5 Rather, say in your hearts, "You, O *L*,
Ez 1: 3 word of the *L* came to the priest Ezekiel,
1: 3 the hand of the *L* came upon me.
1:28 of the likeness of the glory of the *L*.
2: 4 say to them: Thus says the *L* God!
3:11 Thus says the *L* GOD! —Whether they
3:12 as the glory of the *L* rose from its place:
3:14 the hand of the *L* rested heavily upon me.
3:17 Thus the word of the *L* came to me:
3:22 The hand of the *L* came upon me,
3:23 that the glory of the *L* was in that place,
3:27 Thus says the *L* GOD! Let him heed
4:12 human excrement in their sight, said the *L*.
4:14 "Oh no, *L* GOD!"
5: 5 Thus says the *L* GOD: This is Jerusalem
5: 7 Therefore thus says the *L* GOD:
5: 8 therefore thus says the *L* GOD:
5:11 Therefore, as I live, says the *L* GOD,
5:13 they shall know that I, the *L*,
5:15 I, the *L*, have spoken!
5:17 I, the *L*, have spoken!
6: 1 Thus the word of the *L* came to me:
6: 3 of Israel, hear the word of the *L* GOD.
6: 3 says the *L* GOD [to the mountains and hills,
6: 7 midst, and you shall know that I am the *L*.
6:10 that it was not in vain that I, the *L*,
6:11 Thus says the *L* GOD: Clap your hands
6:13 Then shall they know that I am the *L*,
6:14 thus shall they know that I am the *L*.
7: 1 Thus the word of the *L* came to me:
7: 2 Thus says the *L* GOD to the land of Israel:
7: 4 then shall you know that I am the *L*.
7: 5 Thus says the *L* GOD: Disaster upon
7: 9 then shall you know that it is I, the *L*,
7:10 See, the day of the *L*!
7:27 thus they shall know that I am the *L*.
8: 1 the hand of the *L* GOD fell upon me there.
8:12 *L* cannot see us; the LORD has forsaken
9: 8 I fell prone, crying out, Alas, *L* GOD!
9: 9 think that the *L* has forsaken the land,
9:11 the exiles everything the *L* had shown me.
10: 4 and the glory of the *L* rose from over the
10: 4 court was bright with the glory of the *L*.
10:18 Then the glory of the *L* left the threshold
11: 2 The *L* said to me: Son of man
11: 5 Then the spirit of the *L* fell upon me,
11: 5 Thus says the *L*: This is the way
11: 7 Therefore thus says the *L* GOD:
11: 8 I will bring upon you, says the *L* GOD.
11:10 thus you shall know that I am the *L*.
11:12 you, and you shall know that I am the *L*,
11:13 "Alas, *L* GOD!
11:14 Thus the word of the *L* came to me:
11:15 say, "They are far away from the *L*;
11:16 Thus says the *L* GOD: Though I have
11:21 conduct upon their heads, says the *L* GOD.
11:23 And the glory of the *L* rose from the city
12: 1 Thus the word of the *L* came to me:
12: 8 the morning, the word of the *L* came to me:
12:10 Thus says the *L* GOD: This oracle
12:15 Then shall they know that I am the *L*,
12:16 thus they shall know that I am the *L*.
12:17 Thus the word of the *L* came to me:
12:19 Thus says the *L* GOD of the inhabitants of
12:20 thus you shall know that I am the *L*.
12:21 Thus the word of the *L* came to me:
12:23 Thus says the *L* GOD: I will put an end
12:24 house of Israel, because it is I, the *L*,
12:25 I speak I will bring about, says the *L* GOD.
12:26 Thus the word of the *L* came to me:
12:28 Thus says the *L* GOD: None of my words
12:28 and it shall be done, says the *L* GOD.
13: 1 Thus the word of the *L* came to me:
13: 2 Hear the word of the *L*:
13: 3 Thus says the *L* GOD: Woe to those
13: 5 firm against attack on the day of the *L*.
13: 6 They say, "Thus says the *L*!"
13: 6 though the *L* did not send them;
13: 8 Therefore thus says the *L* GOD:
13: 8 I am coming at you, says the *L* GOD.
13: 9 thus you shall know that I am the *L*.
13:13 Therefore thus says the *L* GOD:
13:14 thus you shall know that I am the *L*.
13:16 when there was no peace, says the *L* GOD.
13:17 prophesy: Thus says the *L* GOD:
13:20 Therefore thus says the *L* GOD:
13:21 Thus you shall know that I am the *L*.
13:23 Thus you shall know that I am the *L*.
14: 2 before me, the word of the *L* came to me:
14: 4 Thus says the *L* GOD; If anyone
14: 4 I, the *L*, will be his answer
14: 6 Thus says the *L* GOD: Return and be
14: 7 a prophet to consult me for him, I, the *L*,
14: 8 Thus you shall know that I am the *L*.
14: 9 beguiled into speaking a word, I, the *L*,
14:11 and I will be their God, says the *L* GOD.
14:12 Thus the word of the *L* came to me:
14:14 themselves by their virtue, says the *L* GOD.
14:16 men were in it, as I live, says the *L* GOD,
14:18 men were in it, as I live, says the *L* GOD,
14:20 Job were in it, as I live, says the *L* GOD,
14:21 Thus says the *L* GOD: Even though I
14:23 I did to it what I did, says the *L* GOD.
15: 1 Thus the word of the *L* came to me:

LORD (cont.)
15: 6 Therefore, thus says the *L* GOD:
15: 7 Thus you shall know that I am the *L*,
15: 8 they have broken faith, says the *L* GOD.
16: 1 Thus the word of the *L* came to me:
16: 3 Thus says the *L* GOD to Jerusalem:
16: 8 you became mine, says the *L* GOD.
16:14 I had bestowed on you, says the *L* GOD.
16:19 them as an appeasing odor, says the *L* GOD.
16:23 says the *L* GOD —you raised for yourself
16:30 says the *L* GOD, that you did all
16:35 Therefore, harlot, hear the word of the *L!*
16:36 Thus says the *L* GOD: Because you
16:43 conduct upon your head, says the *L* GOD.
16:48 As I live, says the *L* GOD,
16:58 you must bear it all, says the *L*.
16:59 For thus speaks the *L* GOD:
16:62 you, that you may know that I am the *L*,
16:63 you for all you have done, says the *L* GOD.
17: 1 Thus the word of the *L* came to me:
17: 3 speaks the *L* GOD: The great eagle
17: 9 Thus says the *L* GOD:
17:11 Thus the word of the *L* came to me:
17:16 As I live, says the *L* GOD,
17:19 Thus says the *L* GOD: As I live
17:21 Thus you shall know that I, the *L*,
17:22 Thus says the *L* GOD: I, too,
17:24 of the field shall know that I, the *L*,
17:24 As I, the *L*, have spoken, so will I do.
18: 1 Thus the word of the *L* came to me:
18: 3 As I live, says the *L* GOD:
18: 9 he shall surely live, says the *L* GOD.
18:23 death of the wicked? says the *L* GOD.
18:30 one according to his ways, says the *L* GOD.
18:32 death of anyone who dies, says the *L* GOD.
20: 1 to consult the *L* and sat down before me.
20: 2 Then the word of the *L* came to me:
20: 3 Thus says the *L* GOD: Have you come
20: 3 to be consulted by you, says the *L* GOD.
20: 5 Thus speaks the *L* GOD: The day I
20: 5 I am the *L*, your God.
20: 7 I am the *L*, your God.
20:12 me and them, to show that it was I, the *L*,
20:19 I am the *L*, your God:
20:20 between me and you to show that I am the *L*,
20:27 Thus says the *L* GOD: In this way
20:30 Thus says the *L* GOD: will you defile
20:31 says the *L* GOD: I swear I will not
20:33 As I live, says the *L* GOD,
20:36 into judgment with you, says the *L* GOD.
20:38 Thus you shall know that I am the *L*.
20:39 you, house of Israel, thus says the *L* GOD:
20:40 mountain height of Israel, says the *L* GOD,
20:42 Thus you shall know that I am the *L*,
20:44 that I am the *L* when I deal with you thus,
20:44 actions, O house of Israel, says the *L* GOD.
21: 1 Thus the word of the *L* came to me:
21: 3 Thus says the *L* GOD: See! I am
21: 4 shall see that I, the *L* have kindled it,
21: 5 *L* GOD, they say to me,
21: 6 Then the word of the *L* came to me:
21: 8 Thus says the *L*: See! I am coming
21:10 and everyone shall know that I, the *L*,
21:12 coming, it is here! says the *L* GOD.
21:13 Thus the word of the *L* came to me:
21:14 Thus says the *L*: A sword, a sword
21:18 says the *L* GOD, since you have spurned
21:22 I, the *L*, have spoken.
21:23 Thus the word of the *L* came to me:
21:29 Therefore thus says the *L* GOD:
21:31 crime will be ended, thus says the *L* GOD:
21:33 Thus says the *L* GOD against the Ammonites
21:37 You shall not be remembered, for I, the *L*,
22: 1 Thus the word of the *L* came to me:
22: 3 Thus says the *L* GOD: Woe to the city
22:12 and me you have forgotten, says the *L* GOD.
22:14 I, the *L*, have spoken, and I will act.
22:16 thus you shall know that I am the *L*.
22:17 Thus the word of the *L* came to me:
22:19 Therefore thus says the *L* GOD:
22:22 Thus you shall know that I, the *L*,
22:23 Thus the word of the *L* came to me;
22:28 Lord GOD," although the *L* has not spoken.
22:31 conduct upon their heads, says the *L* GOD.
23: 1 Thus the word of the *L* came to me:
23:22 Therefore, Oholibah, thus says the *L* GOD:
23:28 For thus says the *L* GOD: I am now
23:32 Thus says the *L* GOD: The cup of your
23:34 for I have spoken, says the *L* GOD.
23:35 Therefore thus says the *L* GOD:
23:36 Then the *L* said to me: "Son of man
23:46 Thus says the *L* GOD: Summon an assembly
23:49 Thus you shall know that I am the *L*.
24: 1 ninth year, the word of the *L* came to me:
24: 3 Thus says the *L* GOD: Set up the pot
24: 6 Therefore, thus says the *L* GOD:
24: 9 Therefore, thus says the *L* GOD:
24:14 I, the *L*, have spoken; it is coming,
24:14 deeds you shall be judged, says the *L* GOD.
24:15 Thus the word of the *L* came to me:
24:20 Thus the word of the *L* came to me:
24:21 Thus says the *L* GOD: I will now
24:24 Thus you shall know that I am the *L*.
24:27 them, and they shall know that I am the *L*.
25: 1 Thus the word of the *L* came to me:
25: 3 Hear the word of the *L!*
25: 3 says the *L* GOD: Because you cried
25: 5 Thus you shall know that I am the *L*.
25: 6 For thus says the *L* GOD: Because you
25: 7 and thus you shall know that I am the *L*.
25: 8 Thus says the *L* GOD: Because Moab said
25:11 Moab, that they may know that I am the *L*.
25:12 Thus says the *L* GOD: Because Edom
25:13 on them, therefore thus says the *L* GOD:
25:14 shall know my vengeance, says the *L* GOD.
25:15 Thus says the *L* GOD: Because the
25:16 enmity, therefore thus says the *L* GOD:
25:17 Thus they shall know that I am the *L*,
26: 1 year, the word of the *L* came to me:
26: 3 therefore thus says the *L* GOD:
26: 5 I have spoken, says the *L* GOD:
26: 6 thus they shall know that I am the *L*.
26: 7 For thus says the *L* GOD: I am now
26:14 rebuilt, for I have spoken, says the *L* GOD.
26:15 Thus says the *L* GOD to Tyre:
26:19 For thus says the *L* GOD: When I make
26:21 but never again found, says the *L* GOD.
27: 1 Thus the word of the *L* came to me:
27: 3 Thus says the *L* GOD: Tyre, you said
28: 1 Thus the word of the *L* came to me:
28: 2 Thus says the *L* GOD: Because you are
28: 6 therefore thus says the *L* GOD:
28:10 for I have spoken, says the *L* GOD.
28:11 Thus the word of the *L* came to me:
28:12 Thus says the *L* GOD: You were stamped
28:20 Thus the word of the *L* came to me:
28:22 Thus says the *L* GOD: See! I am coming
28:22 Then they shall know that I am the *L*,
28:23 Thus they shall know that I am the *L*,
28:24 thus they shall know that I am the *L*.
28:25 Thus says the *L* GOD: When I gather
28:26 thus they shall know that I, the *L*,
29: 1 tenth year, the word of the *L* came to me:
29: 3 Thus says the *L* GOD: See! I am coming
29: 6 dwell in Egypt may know that I am the *L*.
29: 8 therefore thus says the *L* GOD:
29: 9 thus they shall know that I am the *L*.
29:13 Yet thus says the *L* GOD:
29:16 Thus they shall know that I am the *L*.
29:17 year, the word of the *L* came to me:
29:19 Therefore thus says the *L* GOD:
29:20 him the land of Egypt, says the *L* GOD.
29:21 thus they shall know that I am the *L*.
30: 1 Thus the word of the *L* came to me:
30: 2 Thus says the *L* GOD: Cry, Oh, the day!
30: 3 near is the day, near is the day of the *L*;
30: 6 fall there by the sword, says the *L* GOD.
30: 8 Then they shall know that I am the *L*,
30:10 Thus says the *L* GOD: I will put an end
30:12 I, the *L*, have spoken.
30:13 Thus says the *L* GOD: I will put an end
30:19 Egypt, that they may know that I am the *L*.
30:20 year, the word of the *L* came to me:
30:22 Therefore thus says the *L* GOD:
30:25 Then they shall know that I am the *L*,
30:26 Thus they shall know that I am the *L*.
31: 1 year, the word of the *L* came to me:
31:10 Therefore thus says the *L* GOD:
31:15 Thus says the *L* GOD: On the day he went
31:18 Pharaoh and all his hordes, says the *L* GOD.
32: 1 twelfth year, the word of the *L* came to me:
32: 3 Thus says the *L* GOD: I will spread
32: 8 darkness over your land, says the *L* GOD.
32:11 For thus says the *L* GOD: The sword
32:14 streams flow like oil, says the *L* GOD.
32:15 there, they shall know that I am the *L*.
32:16 hordes shall they chant it, says the *L* GOD.
32:17 twelfth year, the word of the *L* came to me:
32:31 Pharaoh and all his army, says the *L* GOD.
32:32 Pharaoh and all his hordes, says the *L* GOD.
33: 1 Thus the word of the *L* came to me:
33:11 As I live, says the *L* GOD,
33:17 say, "The way of the *L* is not fair!";
33:20 you say, "The way of the *L* is not fair"?
33:22 The hand of the *L* had come upon me the
33:23 Thus the word of the *L* came to me:
33:25 Thus says the *L* GOD: You eat on the
33:27 Thus says the *L* GOD: As I live, those
33:29 Thus they shall know that I am the *L*,
33:30 hear the latest word that comes from the *L*."
34: 1 Thus the word of the *L* came to me:
34: 2 Thus says the *L* GOD: Woe to the
34: 7 shepherds, hear the word of the *L*.
34: 8 As I live, says the *L* GOD,
34: 9 of this, shepherds, hear the word of the *L*:
34:10 Thus says the *L* GOD: I swear I am
34:11 thus says the *L* GOD: I myself will
34:15 myself will give them rest, says the *L* GOD.
34:17 As for you, my sheep, says the *L* GOD,
34:20 Therefore thus says the *L* GOD:
34:24 I, the *L*, will be their God
34:24 I, the *L*, have spoken.
34:27 Thus they shall know that I am the *L* when
34:30 Thus they shall know that I, the *L*,
34:30 the house of Israel, says the *L* GOD.
34:31 pasture, and I am your God, says the *L* GOD.]
35: 1 Thus the word of the *L* came to me:
35: 3 Thus says the *L* GOD: See! I am coming
35: 4 thus you shall know that I am the *L*.
35: 6 end, therefore, as I live, says the *L* GOD,
35: 9 thus you shall know that I am the *L*.
35:10 although the *L* was there
35:11 therefore, as I live, says the *L* GOD,
35:12 you, and you shall know that I am the *L*.
35:14 Thus says the *L* GOD: Just as you
35:15 Thus they shall know that I am the *L*.
36: 1 of Israel, hear the word of the *L!*
36: 2 Thus says the *L* GOD: Because the enemy
36: 3 Thus says the *L* GOD:]; because you have
36: 4 of Israel, hear the word of the *L*:
36: 4 says the *L* GOD to the mountains and hills,
36: 5 therefore thus says the *L* GOD:
36: 6 Thus says the *L* GOD: With jealous fury
36:11 thus you shall know that I am the *L*.
36:13 Thus says the *L* GOD: Because they have
36:14 people of their children, says the *L* GOD.
36:15 people of their children, says the *L* GOD.
36:16 Thus the word of the *L* came to me:
36:20 "These are the people of the *L*,
36:22 Thus says the *L* GOD: Not for your sakes
36:23 the nations shall know that I am the *L*,
36:23 know that I am the LORD, says the *L* GOD,
36:32 for your sakes do I act, says the *L* GOD
36:33 Thus says the *L* GOD: When I purify
36:36 that remain shall know that I, the *L*,
36:36 I, the *L*, have promised, and I will do it.
36:37 Thus says the *L* GOD: This also I will
36:38 thus they shall know that I am the *L*.
37: 1 The hand of the *L* came upon me,
37: 1 *L* and set me in the center of the plain,
37: 3 *L* GOD," I answered, "you alone
37: 4 Dry bones, hear the word of the *L!*
37: 5 Thus says the *L* GOD to these bones:
37: 6 may come to life and know that I am the *L*.
37: 9 Thus says the *L* GOD: From the four
37:12 Thus says the *L* GOD: O, my people
37:13 Then you shall know that I am the *L*,
37:14 thus you shall know that I am the *L*.
37:14 promised, and I will do it, says the *L*.
37:15 Thus the word of the *L* came to me:
37:19 Thus says the *L* GOD: I will take the
37:21 Thus speaks the *L* GOD: I will take
37:28 nations shall know that it is I, the *L*,
38: 1 Thus the word of the *L* came to me:
38: 3 Thus says the *L* GOD: See! I am coming
38:10 Thus says the *L* GOD: At that time
38:14 Thus says the *L* GOD: When my people
38:17 Thus says the *L* GOD: It is of you
38:18 invades the land of Israel, says the *L* GOD,
38:21 I will summon every terror, says the *L* GOD,
38:23 thus they shall know that I am the *L*.
39: 1 Thus says the *L* GOD: See! I am coming
39: 5 for I have decreed it, says the *L* GOD.
39: 6 thus they shall know that I am the *L*.
39: 7 the nations shall know that I am the *L*,
39: 8 and shall be fulfilled, says the *L* GOD.
39:10 those who pillaged them, says the *L* GOD.
39:13 it, when I reveal my glory, says the *L* GOD.
39:17 As for you, son of man, says the *L* GOD,
39:20 and soldiers of every kind, says the *L* GOD.
39:22 house of Israel shall know that I am the *L*,
39:25 Therefore, thus says the *L* GOD:
39:28 Thus they shall know that I, the *L*,
39:29 upon the house of Israel, says the *L* GOD.
40: 1 that very day the hand of the *L* came upon
40:46 who may come near to minister to the *L*.
41:22 "This is the table which is before the *L*.
42:13 to the *L* shall eat the most sacred meals,
43: 4 I fell prone as the glory of the *L* entered
43: 5 temple was filled with the glory of the *L*.
43:18 Son of man, thus says the *L* GOD:
43:19 near me to minister to me, says the *L* GOD.
43:24 the flock, and present them before the *L*;
43:24 them and offer them to the *L* as holocausts.
43:27 Then I will accept you, says the *L* GOD.
44: 2 since the *L*, the God of Israel,
44: 3 to eat his meal in the presence of the *L*.
44: 4 glory of the *L* filling the LORD's temple,
44: 6 Thus says the *L* GOD: Enough of all
44: 9 Thus says the *L* GOD: No foreigners
44:12 sworn an oath against them, says the *L* GOD:
44:15 to offer me fat and blood, says the *L* GOD.
44:27 present his sin offering, says the *L* GOD.
45: 1 apart a sacred tract of land for the *L*,
45: 4 who draw near to minister to the *L*;
45: 9 Thus says the *L* GOD: Enough, you
45: 9 evicting my people! says the *L* GOD
45:15 and atonement sacrifices, says the *L* GOD.
45:18 Thus says the *L* GOD: On the first day
45:23 he shall offer as a holocaust to the *L*
46: 1 Thus says the *L* GOD: The gate toward
46: 3 shall worship before the *L* at the door
46: 4 prince presents to the *L* on the sabbath
46: 9 of the *L* to worship on the festivals,
46:12 prince makes a freewill offering to the *L*,
46:13 to the *L* an unblemished yearling lamb;
46:14 This cereal offering to the *L* is mandatory
46:16 Thus says the *L* GOD: If the prince
47:13 Thus says the *L* GOD:

47:23 assign him his inheritance, says the *L* GOD.
48: 9 The tract that you set aside for the *L*
48:10 sanctuary of the *L* shall be in its center.
48:14 of the land, for it is sacred to the *L*.
48:29 these are their portions, says the *L* GOD.
48:35 City shall henceforth be "The *L* is here."
Dn 1: 2 The *L* handed over to him Jehoiakim,
1:10 to Daniel, "I am afraid of my *l* the king;
2:47 and *L* of kings and a revealer of mysteries;
3:24 flames, singing to God and blessing the *L*.
3:26 "Blessed are you, and praiseworthy, O *L*,
3:37 For we are reduced, O *L*,
3:43 wonders, and bring glory to your name, O *L*:
3:45 Let them know that you alone are the *L* God,
3:49 But the angel of the *L* went down into the
3:52 "Blessed are you, O *L*,
3:57 Bless the *L*, all you works of the Lord,
3:58 Angels of the Lord, bless the *L*,
3:59 You heavens, bless the *L*,
3:60 you waters above the heavens, bless the *L*,
3:61 All you hosts of the Lord, bless the *L*;
3:62 Sun and moon, bless the *L*;
3:63 Stars of heaven, bless the *L*;
3:64 Every shower and dew, bless the *L*;
3:65 All you winds, bless the *L*;
3:66 Fire and heat, bless the *L*;
3:67 [Cold and chill, bless the *L*;
3:68 Dew and rain, bless the *L*;
3:69 Frost and chill, bless the *L*;
3:70 Ice and snow, bless the *L*;
3:71 Nights and days, bless the *L*;
3:72 Light and darkness, bless the *L*;
3:73 Lightnings and clouds, bless the *L*;
3:74 Let the earth bless the *L*,
3:75 Mountains and hills, bless the *L*;
3:76 growing from the earth, bless the *L*;
3:77 You springs, bless the *L*;
3:78 Seas and rivers, bless the *L*;
3:79 and all water creatures, bless the *L*,
3:80 All you birds of the air, bless the *L*;
3:81 you beasts, wild and tame, bless the *L*;
3:82 You sons of men, bless the *L*;
3:83 O Israel, bless the *L*;
3:84 Priests of the *L*, bless the Lord;
3:85 Servants of the *L*, bless the Lord;
3:86 and souls of the just, bless the *L*;
3:87 Holy men of humble heart, bless the *L*;
3:88 Hananiah, Azariah, Mishael, bless the *L*;
3:89 Give thanks to the *L*, for he is good,
3:90 the God of gods, all you who fear the *L*;
4:17 "My *l*," Belteshazzar replied, "this dream
4:21 the Most High has passed upon my *l* king:
5:23 you have rebelled against the *L* of heaven.
9: 2 which the *L* spoke to the prophet Jeremiah:
9: 3 I turned to the *L* God,
9: 4 the LORD, my God, and confessed, "Ah, *L*,
9: 7 Justice, O *L*, is on your side
9: 8 O *L*, we are shamefaced, like our kings
9: 9 yours, O *L*, our God, are compassion
9:10 you and paid no heed to your command, O *L*,
9:13 As we did not appease the *L*,
9:14 so the *L* kept watch over the calamity and
9:14 You, O *L*, our God are just in all
9:15 "Now, O *L*, our God, who led
9:16 O *L*, in keeping with all your just deeds
9:17 and for your own sake, O *L*,
9:19 O *L*, hear!
9:19 O *L*, pardon!
9:19 O *L*, be attentive and act without delay,
9:20 Israel, presenting my petition to the *L*,
10:16 and said to the one facing me, "My *l*,
10:16 can my lord's servant speak with you, my *l*?
10:20 me, I grew strong and said, "Speak, my *l*,
12: 8 so I asked, "My *l*, what follows this?"
13: 5 were appointed judges, of whom the *L* said,
13:23 without guilt than to sin before the *L*."
13:35 for she trusted in the *L* wholeheartedly.
13:44 The *L* heard her prayer.
13:53 freeing the guilty, although the *L* says,
14:25 But Daniel answered, "I adore the *L*,
14:34 the field, when an angel of the *L* told him,
14:36 The angel of the *L* seized him by the crown
14:39 the angel of the *L* at once brought
14:41 king cried aloud, "You are great, O *L*,
Hos 1: 1 The word of the *L* that came to Hosea,
1: 2 speaking to Hosea, the *L* said to Hosea:
1: 2 to harlotry, turning away from the *L*.
1: 4 Then the *L* said to him: "Give him the name
1: 6 and bore a daughter, the *L* said to him:
1: 7 I will save them by the *L*,
1: 9 Then the *L* said to him: "Give him the name
2:15 after her lovers, forgot me, says the *L*.
2:18 On that day, says the *L*.
2:22 you in fidelity, and you shall know the *L*.
2:23 On that day I will respond, says the *L*;
3: 1 Again the *L* said to me: Give your love
3: 1 Even as the *L* loves the people of Israel,
3: 5 of Israel shall turn back and seek the *L*,
3: 5 come trembling to the *L* and to his bounty,
4: 1 Hear the word of the *L*,
4: 1 for the *L* has a grievance against the
4:10 have abandoned the *L* to practice harlotry.
4:15 to Beth-aven, to swear, "As the *L* lives!"
4:16 will the *L* now give them broad pastures as
5: 4 in them, and they do not recognize the *L*.
5: 6 their herds they shall go to seek the *L*,
5: 7 They have been untrue to the *L*,
6: 1 "Come, let us return to the *L*,
6: 3 Let us know, let us strive to know the *L*;
7:10 yet they do not return to the *L*,
8: 1 You who watch over the house of the *L*!
8:13 and eat it, the *L* is not pleased with them.
9: 4 shall not pour libations of wine to the *L*,
9: 4 it cannot enter the house of the *L*.
9:14 Give them, O *L*! give them what!
10: 3 Since they do not fear the *L*,
10:12 a new field, for it is time to seek the *L*,
11:10 They shall follow the *L*,
11:11 resettle them in their homes, says the *L*.
12: 3 The *L* has a grievance against Israel:
12: 6 The *L*, the God of hosts,
12: 6 LORD, the God of hosts, the *L* is his name!
12:10 I am the *L*,
12:14 prophet the *L* brought Israel out of Egypt,
12:15 Ephraim has exasperated his *L*;
13: 4 I am the *L*, your God,
13:15 east wind shall come, a wind from the *L*,
14: 2 Return, O Israel, to the *L*,
14: 3 Take with you words, and return to the *L*;
14:10 Straight are the paths of the *L*,
Jl 1: 1 The word of the *L* which came to Joel,
1: 9 and libation from the house of the *L*;
1: 9 are the priests, the ministers of the *L*.
1:14 of the LORD, your God, and cry to the *L*!
1:15 for near is the day of the *L*,
1:19 To you, O *L*, I cry!
2: 1 tremble, for the day of the *L* is coming;
2:11 *L* raises his voice at the head of his army;
2:11 For great is the day of the *L*,
2:12 Yet even now, says the *L*,
2:13 not your garments, and return to the *L*,
2:14 Offerings and libations for the *L*,
2:17 of the LORD weep, And say, "Spare, O *L*,
2:18 Then the *L* was stirred to concern for his
2:19 The *L* answered and said to his people:
2:21 for the *L* has done great things.
2:23 of Zion, exult and rejoice in the *L*,
2:26 and shall praise the name of the *L*,
2:27 I am in the midst of Israel; I am the *L*,
3: 4 At the coming of the Day of the *L*,
3: 5 be rescued who calls on the name of the *L*;
3: 5 shall be a remnant, as the *L* has said,
3: 5 Jerusalem survivors whom the *L* shall call.
4: 8 Indeed, the *L* has spoken.
4:11 [Bring down, O *L*, your warriors!]
4:14 the day of the *L* in the valley of decision.
4:16 The *L* roars from Zion,
4:16 quake, but the *L* is a refuge to his people,
4:17 Then shall you know that I, the *L*,
4:18 shall issue from the house of the *L*,
4:21 The *L* dwells in Zion.
Am 1: 2 The *L* will roar from Zion,
1: 3 Thus says the *L*: For three crimes
1: 5 of Aram shall be exiled to Kir, says the *L*.
1: 6 Thus says the *L*: For three crimes
1: 8 Philistines shall perish, says the *L* God.
1: 9 Thus says the *L*: For these cities
1:11 Thus says the *L*: For three crimes
1:13 Thus says the *L*: For three crimes
1:15 he and his princes with him, says the *L*.
2: 1 Thus says the *L*: For three crimes
2: 3 princes I will slay with him, says the *L*.
2: 4 Thus says the *L*: For three crimes
2: 4 Because they spurned the law of the *L*,
2: 6 Thus says the *L*: For three crimes
2:11 Omen of Israel? says the *L*.
2:16 shall flee naked on that day, says the *L*.
3: 1 of Israel, that the *L* pronounces over you,
3: 6 befalls a city, has not the *L* caused it?
3: 7 the *L* GOD does nothing without revealing
3: 8 The *L* GOD speaks— who will not prophesy!
3:10 not how to do what is right, says the *L*,
3:11 Therefore, thus says the *L* GOD:
3:12 pillage your castles, Thus says the *L*:
3:13 against the house of Jacob, says the *L* GOD,
3:15 many rooms shall be no more, says the *L*.
4: 2 The *L* GOD has sworn by his holiness:
4: 3 shall be cast into the mire, says the *L*.
4: 5 to do, O men of Israel, says the *L* GOD.
4: 6 Yet you returned not to me, says the *L*.
4: 8 Yet you returned not to me, says the *L*.
4: 9 Yet you returned not to me, says the *L*.
4:10 Yet you returned not to me, says the *L*.
4:11 Yet you returned not to me, says the *L*.
4:13 The *L*, The God of hosts by name.
5: 3 For thus says the *L* GOD:
5: 4 For thus says the *L* to the house of Israel:
5: 6 Seek the *L*, that you may live,
5: 9 whose name is *L*.
5:14 Then truly will the *L*,
5:15 Then it may be that the *L*,
5:16 says the LORD, the God of hosts, the *L*:
5:17 when I pass through your midst, says the *L*.
5:18 to those who yearn for the day of the *L*!
5:18 What will this day of the *L* mean for you?
5:20 the day of the *L* be darkness and not light,
5:27 exile you beyond Damascus, say I, the *L*,
6: 8 The *L* GOD has sworn by his very self,
6: 8 has sworn by his very self, say I, the *L*,
6:10 for no one must mention the name of the *L*.
6:11 the *L* has given the command to shatter the
6:14 you, O house of Israel, say I, the *L*,
7: 1 This is what the *L* GOD showed me:
7: 2 Forgive, O *L* GOD!
7: 3 And the *L* repented of this.
7: 3 "It shall not be," said the *L* GOD.
7: 4 Then the *L* GOD showed me this:
7: 5 Cease, O *L* GOD!
7: 6 The *L* repented of this.
7: 6 "This also shall not be," said the *L* GOD.
7: 7 Then the *L* GOD showed me this:
7: 8 The *L* asked me, "What do you see, Amos?"
7: 8 when I answered, "A plummet," the *L* said:
7:15 The *L* took me from following the flock,
7:16 Now hear the word of the *L*!"
7:17 Now thus says the *L*:
8: 1 This is what the *L* GOD showed me:
8: 2 Then the *L* said to me:
8: 3 wailings on that day, says the *L* GOD.
8: 7 The *L* has sworn by the pride of Jacob:
8: 9 On that day, says the *L* GOD,
8:11 Yes, days are coming, says the *L* GOD,
8:11 water, but for hearing the word of the *L*.
8:12 to the east In search of the word of the *L*,
9: 1 I saw the *L* standing beside the altar,
9: 5 and not for good, I, the *L* GOD of hosts,
9: 6 the surface of the earth, I, the *L* by name.
9: 7 to me, O men of Israel, says the *L*?
9: 8 of the *L* GOD are on this sinful kingdom;
9:12 nations shall bear my name, say I, the *L*,
9:13 Yes, days are coming, says the *L*,
9:15 the land I have given them, say I, the *L*,
Ob 1: 1 Thus says the *L* GOD: of Edom we have
1: 1 Edom we have heard a message from the *L*,
1: 4 there will I bring you down, says the *L*.
1: 8 Shall I not, says the *L*,
1:15 is the day of the *L* for all the nations!
1:18 of the house of Esau, for the *L* has spoken.
Jon 1: 1 is the word of the *L* that came to Jonah,
1: 3 ready to flee to Tarshish away from the *L*.
1: 3 with them to Tarshish, away from the *L*.
1: 4 The *L*, however, hurled a violent wind
1: 9 "I worship the *L*, the God of heaven,
1:10 knew that he was fleeing from the *L*,
1:14 Then they cried to the *L*:
1:14 "We beseech you, O *L*, let us not perish
1:14 with shedding innocent blood, for you, *L*,
1:16 Struck with great fear of the *L*,
2: 1 *L* sent a large fish, that swallowed Jonah;
2: 2 the fish Jonah said this prayer to the *L*,
2: 3 Out of my distress I called to the *L*,
2: 7 you brought my life up from the pit, O *L*,
2: 8 fainted within me, I remembered the *L*;
2:10 deliverance is from the *L*.
2:11 Then the *L* commanded the fish to spew
3: 1 word of the *L* came to Jonah a second time:
4: 2 "I beseech you, *L*," he prayed, "is not this
4: 3 And now, *L*, please take my life from me;
4: 4 *L* asked, "Have you reason to be angry?"
4: 6 And when the *L* God provided a gourd plant,
4:10 *L* said, "You are concerned over the plant
Mi 1: 1 The word of the *L* which came to Micah of
1: 2 *L* GOD be witness against you, the Lord
1: 3 For see, the *L* comes forth from his place,
1:12 down from the *L* to the gate of Jerusalem.
2: 3 thus says the *L*: "Behold, I am planning
2: 5 boundaries by lot in the assembly of the *L*.
2: 7 of Jacob, "Is the *L* short of patience,
2:13 before them, and the *L* at their head.
3: 4 they cry to the *L*, he shall not answer
3: 5 Thus says the *L* regarding the prophets who
3: 8 with power, with the spirit of the *L*,
3:11 rely on the *L*, saying "Is not the LORD in
4: 2 "Come, let us climb the mount of the *L*,
4: 2 and the word of the *L* from Jerusalem.
4: 4 for the mouth of the *L* of hosts has spoken.
4: 5 But we will walk in the name of the *L*,
4: 6 On that day, says the *L*, I will gather
4: 7 *L* shall be king over them on Mount Zion,
4:10 *L* redeem you from the hand of your enemies.
4:12 But they know not the thoughts of the *L*,
4:13 spoils to the *L*, and their riches to the *L*
5: 2 (Therefore the *L* will give them up,
5: 3 the LORD, in the majestic name of the *L*,
5: 6 many peoples, Like dew coming from the *L*,
5: 9 On that day, says the *L*, I will destroy
6: 1 Hear, then, what the *L* says:
6: 2 Hear, O mountains, the plea of the *L*,
6: 2 For the *L* has a plea against his people,
6: 5 that you may know the just deeds of the *L*.
6: 6 With what shall I come before the *L*,
6: 7 the *L* be pleased with thousands of rams,
6: 8 is good, and what the *L* requires of you:
6: 9 the *L* cries to the city.
7: 7 But as for me, I will look to the *L*,
7: 8 I sit in darkness, the *L* is my light.
7: 9 The wrath of the *L* I will endure because I
7:10 She who said to me, "Where is the *L*,
7:17 trembling in fear of you [the *L*,

LORD (cont.)

Na 1: 2 A jealous and avenging God is the *L*,
1: 2 God is the LORD, an avenger is the *L*,
1: 2 The *L* brings vengeance on his adversaries,
1: 3 The *L* is slow to anger,
1: 3 the *L* never leaves the guilty unpunished.
1: 7 The *L* is good, a refuge on the day
1: 9 What are you imputing to the *L?*
1:11 you he came who devised evil against the *L*,
1:12 For, says the *L*, be they ever so many
1:14 The *L* has commanded regarding you:
2: 3 The *L* will restore the vine of Jacob,
2:14 I come against you, says the *L* of hosts;
Hb 1: 2 How long, O *L?*
1:12 Are you not from eternity, O *L*,
1:12 O *L* you have marked him for judgment,
2: 2 Then the *L* answered me and said:
2:13 Is not this from the *L* of hosts:
2:20 But the *L* is in his holy temple;
3: 2 O *L*, I have heard your renown,
3: 2 I have heard your renown, and feared, O *L*,
3: 8 Is your anger against the streams, O *L?*
3:18 in the *L* and exult in my saving God.
3:19 God, my *L*, is my strength;
Zep 1: 1 The word of the *L* which came to Zephaniah,
1: 2 from the face of the earth, says the *L*.
1: 3 from the face of the earth, says the *L*.
1: 5 those who adore the *L* but swear by Milcom;
1: 6 the LORD, and those who do not seek the *L*.
1: 7 Silence in the presence of the *L* GOD!
1: 7 of the *L*, Yes, the LORD has prepared
1:10 On that day, says the *L*,
1:12 "Neither good nor evil can the *L* do."
1:14 wine, Near is the great day of the *L*,
1:14 swiftly coming, Hark, the day of the *L!*
1:17 because they have sinned against the *L*;
2: 2 comes upon you the blazing anger of the *L*:
2: 3 Seek the *L*, all you humble of the earth,
2: 5 The word of the *L* is against you,
2: 7 For the *L* their God shall visit them,
2: 9 Therefore, as I live, says the *L* of hosts,
2:10 against the people of the *L* of hosts.
2:11 The *L* shall inspire them with fear when he
2:12 shall be slain by the sword of the *L*.
3: 2 In the *L* she has not trusted,
3: 5 The *L* within her is just,
3: 8 Therefore, wait for me, says the *L*,
3: 9 they all may call upon the name of the *L*,
3:12 Who shall take refuge in the name of the *L*;
3:15 The *L* has removed the judgment against you,
3:15 The King of Israel, the *L*,
3:17 The *L*, your God, is in your midst,
3:20 before your very eyes, says the *L*.
Hg 1: 1 the word of the *L* came through the prophet
1: 2 Thus says the *L* of hosts:
1: 2 time come to rebuild the house of the *L*.
1: 3 this word of the *L* came through Haggai,
1: 5 Now thus says the *L* of hosts:
1: 7 Thus says the *L* of hosts: Consider
1: 8 in it and receive my glory, says the *L*.
1: 9 For what cause? Says the *L* of hosts.
1:12 the people listened to the voice of the *L*,
1:12 of the prophet Haggai, because the *L*,
1:12 and the people feared because of the *L*.
1:13 to the people as the message of the *L*:
1:13 I am with you, says the *L*.
1:14 Then the *L* stirred up the spirit of the
1:14 set to work on the house of the *L* of hosts,
2: 1 of the *L* came through the prophet Haggai:
2: 4 now take courage, Zerubbabel, says the *L*,
2: 4 all you people of the land says the *L*,
2: 4 For I am with you, says the *L* of hosts.
2: 6 For thus says the *L* of hosts:
2: 7 house with glory, says the *L* of hosts.
2: 8 and mine the gold says the *L* of hosts.
2: 9 house than the former, says the *L* of hosts;
2: 9 will give you peace, says the *L* of hosts.
2:10 word of the *L* came to the prophet Haggai:
2:11 Thus says the *L* of hosts: Ask
2:14 so is this nation in my sight, says the *L*:
2:15 laid upon a stone in the temple of the *L*,
2:17 yet you did not return to me, says the *L*.
2:18 on which the temple of the *L* was founded,
2:20 The message of the *L* came a second time to
2:23 On that day, says the *L* of hosts,
2:23 son of Shealtiel, my servant, says the *L*,
2:23 for I have chosen you, says the *L* of hosts.
Zec 1: 1 of the *L* came to the prophet Zechariah,
1: 2 The *L* was indeed angry with your fathers . . .
1: 3 Thus says the *L* of hosts: Return
1: 3 Return to me, says the *L* of hosts,
1: 3 I will return to you, says the *L* of hosts.
1: 4 Thus says the *L* of hosts.
1: 4 listen or pay attention to me, says the *L*.
1: 6 The *L* of hosts has treated us according to
1: 7 of the *L* came to the prophet Zechariah,
1: 9 Then I asked, "What are these, my *l?*";
1:10 whom the *L* has sent to patrol the earth."
1:11 And they answered the angel of the *L* who
1:12 LORD spoke out and said, "O *L* of hosts,
1:13 me, the *L* replied with comforting words.
1:14 Thus says the *L* of hosts: I am deeply
1:16 added to the harm, Therefore, says the *L*:
1:16 shall be built in it, says the *L* of hosts,
1:17 Thus says the *L* of hosts: My cities
1:17 the *L* will again comfort Zion,
2: 3 Then the *L* showed me four blacksmiths.
2: 9 an encircling wall of fire, says the *L*,
2:10 from the land of the north, says the *L*;
2:10 to the four winds of heaven, says the *L*.
2:12 For thus said the *L* of hosts (after he had
2:13 shall know that the *L* of hosts has sent me.
2:14 I am coming to dwell among you, says the *L*.
2:15 shall join themselves to the *L* on that day,
2:15 that the *L* of hosts has sent me to you.
2:16 The *L* will possess Judah as his portion of
2:17 all mankind, in the presence of the *L!*
3: 1 priest standing before the angel of the *L*,
3: 2 And the angel of the *L* said to Satan,
3: 2 LORD said to Satan, "May the *L* rebuke you,
3: 2 the *L* who has chosen Jerusalem rebuke you!
3: 5 Then the angel of the *L*,
3: 6 of the *L* then gave Joshua this assurance:
3: 7 "Thus says the *L* of hosts: If you walk
3: 9 its inscription, says the *L* of hosts,
3:10 On that day, says the *L* of hosts,
4: 4 with me, "What are these things, my *l?*"
4: 5 "No, my *l*," I answered.
4: 6 but by my spirit, says the *L* of hosts.
4: 8 The word of the *L* then came to me:
4: 9 that the *L* of hosts has sent me to you.
4:10 of the *L* that range over the whole earth.
4:13 "No, my *l*," I answered him.
4:14 who stand by the *L* of the whole earth."
5: 4 I will send it forth, says the *L* of hosts,
6: 4 who spoke with me, "What are these, my *l?*"
6: 5 being reviewed by the *L* of all the earth."
6: 9 This word of the *L* then came to me:
6:12 says the *L* of hosts: Here is a man
6:12 and he shall build the temple of the *L*.
6:13 Yes, he shall build the temple of the *L*,
6:14 in the temple of the *L* in favor of Heldai,
6:15 shall come and build the temple of the *L*,
6:15 that the *L* of hosts has sent me to you.
6:15 heed carefully the voice of the *L* your God.
7: 1 king [the word of the *L* came to Zechariah],
7: 2 his men to implore favor of the *L*
7: 3 the priests of the house of the *L* of hosts,
7: 4 this word of the *L* of hosts came to me:
7: 7 the *L* spoke through the former prophets,
7: 8 [This word of the *L* came to Zechariah:
7: 9 Thus says the *L* of hosts:] Render
7:12 message that the *L* of hosts had sent
7:13 *L* of hosts in his great anger said that,
8: 1 This word of the *L* of hosts came:
8: 2 Thus says the *L* of hosts: I am intensely
8: 3 Thus says the *L*: I will return
8: 3 city, and the mountain of the *L* of hosts,
8: 4 Thus says the *L* of hosts: Old men
8: 6 Thus says the *L* of hosts: Even if
8: 6 in my eyes also, says the *L* of hosts?
8: 7 Thus says the *L* of hosts: Lo, I will
8: 9 says the *L* of hosts: Let your hands
8: 9 when the foundation of the house of the *L*
8:11 as in former days, says the *L* of hosts,
8:14 Thus says the *L* of hosts:
8:14 provoked me to wrath, says the *L* of hosts,
8:17 For all these things I hate, says the *L*.
8:18 This word of the *L* of hosts came to me:
8:19 Thus says the *L* of hosts: The fast days
8:20 Thus says the *L* of hosts: There shall
8:21 let us go to implore the favor of the *L*";
8:21 and, "I too will go to seek the *L*."
8:22 strong nations shall come to seek the *L*
8:22 and to implore the favor of the *L*.
8:23 Thus says the *L* of hosts: In those days
9: 1 word of the *L* is upon the land of Hadrach,
9: 4 the *L* will strip her of her possessions,
9:14 The *L* shall appear over them,
9:14 The *L* GOD shall sound the trumpet,
9:15 The *L* of hosts shall be a shield over them,
9:16 *L*, their God, shall save them on that day,
10: 1 Ask of the *L* rain in the spring season!
10: 1 It is the *L* who makes storm clouds.
10: 3 For the *L* of hosts will visit his flock,
10: 5 shall wage war because the *L* is with them,
10: 6 I had never cast them off, for I am the *L*,
10: 7 Their hearts shall rejoice in the *L*.
10:12 I will strengthen them in the *L*,
10:12 they shall walk in his name, says the *L*.
11: 4 Thus said the *L*, my God:
11: 5 who sell them say, "Blessed be the *L*,
11: 6 of the earth any more, says the *L*.
11:11 understood that this was the word of the *L*.
11:13 But the *L* said to me,
11:13 into the treasury in the house of the *L*.
11:15 The *L* said to me: "This time take
12: 1 the word of the *L* concerning Israel.
12: 1 Thus says the *L*, who spreads out
12: 4 On that day, says the *L*, I will strike
12: 5 have their strength in the *L* of hosts,
12: 7 The *L* shall save the tents of Judah first,
12: 8 *L* will shield the inhabitants of Jerusalem,
12: 8 like an angel of the *L* before them.
13: 2 On that day, says the *L* of hosts,
13: 3 you have spoken a lie in the name of the *L*."
13: 7 who is my associate, says the *L* of hosts.
13: 8 In all the land, says the *L*,
13: 9 and they shall say, "The *L* is my God."
14: 1 a day shall come for the *L* when the spoils
14: 3 Then the *L* shall go forth and fight
14: 5 Then the *L*, my God, shall come
14: 7 be one continuous day, known to the *L*,
14: 9 *L* shall become king over the whole earth;
14: 9 on that day the *L* shall be the only one,
14:12 plague with which the *L* shall strike all
14:13 be among them a great tumult from the *L*:
14:16 year to worship the King, the *L* of hosts,
14:17 to worship the King, the *L* of hosts,
14:18 plague which the *L* will inflict upon all
14:20 the bells of the horses, "Holy to the *L*."
14:20 The pots in the house of the *L* shall be as
14:21 in Judah shall be holy to the *L* of hosts;
14:21 merchant in the house of the *L* of hosts.
Mal 1: 1 word of the *L* to Israel through Malachi.
1: 2 I have loved you, says the *L*;
1: 3 Was not Esau Jacob's brother? says the *L*:
1: 4 the ruins," Thus says the *L* of hosts:
1: 4 people with whom the *L* is angry forever.
1: 5 see it, and you will say, "Great is the *L*,
1: 6 So says the *L* of hosts to you,
1: 7 saying the table of the *L* may be slighted!
1: 8 it, or welcome you, says the *L* of hosts.
1: 9 any of you? says the *L* of hosts.
1:10 no pleasure in you, says the *L* of hosts;
1:11 among the nations, says the *L* of hosts.
1:13 and you scorn it, says the *L* of hosts;
1:13 from your hands? says the *L*.
1:14 his vow sacrifices to the *L* a gelding;
1:14 For a great King am I, says the *L* of hosts,
2: 2 give glory to my name, says the *L* of hosts,
2: 4 a covenant with Levi, says the *L* of hosts.
2: 7 he is the messenger of the *L* of hosts.
2: 8 the covenant of Levi, says the *L* of hosts.
2:11 has profaned the temple which the *L* loves,
2:12 May the *L* cut off from the man who does
2:12 to offer sacrifice to the *L* of hosts!
2:13 the altar of the *L* you cover with tears,
2:14 Because the *L* is witness between you and
2:16 For I hate divorce, says the *L*,
2:16 with injustice, says the *L* of hosts;
2:17 You have wearied the *L* with your words,
2:17 evildoer is good in the sight of the *L*,
3: 1 come to the temple the *L* whom you seek,
3: 1 Yes, he is coming, says the *L* of hosts.
3: 3 that they may offer due sacrifice to the *L*.
3: 5 who do not fear me, says the *L* of hosts,
3: 6 says the LORD of hosts, Surely I, the *L*,
3: 7 I will return to you, says the *L* of hosts.
3:10 and try me in this, says the *L* of hosts:
3:11 will not be barren, says the *L* of hosts.
3:12 be a delightful land, says the *L* of hosts.
3:13 You have defied me in word, says the *L*,
3:14 penitential dress in awe of the *L* of hosts?
3:16 they who fear the *L* spoke with one another,
3:16 another, and the *L* listened attentively;
3:16 those who fear the *L* and trust in his name.
3:17 they shall be mine, says the *L* of hosts,
3:19 root nor branch, says the *L* of hosts.
3:21 the day I take action, says the *L* of hosts.
3:23 the prophet, Before the day of the *L* comes,
Mt 1:20 the *L* appeared in a dream and said to him:
1:22 what the *L* had said through the prophet:
1:24 Joseph awoke he did as the angel of the *L*
2:13 the angel of the *L* suddenly appeared in a
2:15 what the *L* had said through the prophet:
2:19 the angel of the *L* appeared in a dream to
3: 3 'Prepare the way of the *L*,
4: 7 shall not put the *L* your God to the test.'"
4:10 'You shall do homage to the *L* your God;
5:33 make good to the *L* all your pledges.'
7:21 None of those who cry out, 'Lord, *L*,'
7:22 comes, many will plead with me, 'Lord, *L*,
8:21 Another, a disciple, said to him, *L*,
8:25 *L*, save us!
9:28 "Yes, *L*," they told him.
11:25 "Father, *L* of heaven and earth,
12: 8 The Son of Man is indeed *L* of the sabbath."
14:28 Peter spoke up and said, *L*,
14:30 he began to sink and cried out, *L*,
15:22 presented herself, crying out to him, *L*,
15:25 did him homage with the plea, "Help me, *L!*"
15:27 "Please, *L*," she insisted, "even the dogs
17: 4 Then Peter said to Jesus, *L*,
17:15 *L*," he said, "take pity on my son,
18:21 Then Peter came up and asked him, *L*,
18:26 himself in homage and said, 'My *l*,
20:25 among the Gentiles *l* it over them;
20:30 Jesus was passing by, began to shout, *L*,
20:31 but they only shouted the louder, *L*,
20:33 *L*," they told him, "open our eyes!"
21: 9 is he who comes in the name of the *L!*
21:42 It was the *L* who did this and we find it
22:37 love the *L* your God with your whole heart,
22:43 under the Spirit's influence calls him *l*,'
22:44 'The *L* said to my lord,
22:45 If David calls him *l*,'
23:39 is he who comes in the name of the *L!*'"
24:42 You cannot know the day your *L* is coming.

25:20 'My *l*,' he said, 'you let me
25:22 'My *l*,' he said, 'you entrusted me
25:24 'My *l*,' he said, 'I knew you
25:37 *L*, when did we see you hungry and feed you
25:44 *L*, when did we see you hungry or thirsty
26:22 one after another, "Surely it is not I, *L*?"
27:10 field just as the *L* had commanded me."
28: 2 the angel of the *L* descended from heaven.
Mk 1: 3 crying, 'Make ready the way of the *L*,
2:28 the Son of Man is *l* even of the sabbath."
5:19 much the *L* in his mercy has done for you."
7:28 "Please, *L*," she replied, "even the dogs
10:42 seem to exercise authority *l* it over them;
11: 9 is he who comes in the name of the *L*!
12:11 It was the *L* who did it and we find it
12:29 The *L* our God is Lord alone!
12:30 love the *L* your God with all your heart,
12:36 Holy Spirit, said, 'The *L* said to my Lord:
12:37 If David himself addresses him as *L*,'
13:20 had the *L* not shortened the period,
16:19 the *L* Jesus was taken up into heaven and
16:20 The *L* continued to work with them
Lk 1: 6 the commandments and ordinances of the *L*.
1: 9 the sanctuary of the *L* and offer incense.
1:11 hour, an angel of the *L* appeared to him,
1:15 for he will be great in the eyes of the *L*.
1:16 will he bring back to the *L* their God.
1:17 prepare for the *L* a people well-disposed."
1:25 these days the *L* is acting on my behalf;
1:25 being proclaims the greatness of the *L*,
1:28 The *L* is with you.
1:32 The *L* God will give him the throne of
1:38 "I am the servant of the *L*.
1:43 that the mother of my *L* should come to me?
1:58 that the *L* had extended his mercy to her,
1:66 and, "Was not the hand of the *L* upon him?"
1:68 "Blessed be the *L* the God of Israel
1:76 the *L* to prepare straight paths for him,
2: 9 The angel of the *L* appeared to them as the
2: 9 as the glory of the *L* shone around them,
2:11 has been born to you, the Messiah and *L*.
2:15 event which the *L* has made known to us."
2:22 so that he could be presented to the *L*,
2:23 for it is written in the law of the *L*,
2:23 male shall be consecrated to the *L*."
2:24 with the dictate in the law of the *L*.
2:26 until he had seen the Anointed of the *L*.
2:39 all the prescriptions of the law of the *L*,
3: 4 crying, 'Make ready the way of the *L*,
4: 8 it, 'You shall do homage to the *L* your God;
4:12 shall not put the *L* your God to the test.'"
4:18 "The spirit of the *L* is upon me;
4:19 To announce a year of favor from the *L*."
5: 8 the knees of Jesus saying, "Leave me, *L*.
5:12 down to the ground and said to him, *L*,
5:17 and the power of the *L* made him heal.
6: 5 "The Son of Man is *L* even of the sabbath."
6:46 Why do you call me 'Lord, *L*,'
7:13 The *L* was moved with pity upon seeing her
7:19 two of them, John sent them to ask the *L*,
8:45 disclaimed doing it, while Peter said, *L*,
9:54 James and John saw this, they said, *L*,
9:61 said to him, "I will be your follower, *L*,
10: 1 the *L* appointed a further seventy-two and
10:21 praise, O Father, *L* of heaven and earth,
10:27 love the *L* your god with all your heart,
10:40 of hospitality, came to him and said, *L*,
10:41 The *L* in reply said to her:
11: 1 one of his disciples asked him, *L*,
11:39 The *L* said to him: You Pharisees!
12:33 a never-failing treasure with the *L* which
12:41 "Do you intend this parable for us, *L*,
12:42 The *L* said,
13:15 *L* said in reply: "O you hypocrites!
13:23 Someone asked him, *L*,
13:35 is he who comes in the name of the *L*.'"
14:22 'Your orders have been carried out, my *l*,
17: 5 apostles said to the *L*, "Increase our faith,
17:37 Where, *L*?"
18: 6 *L* said, "Listen to what the corrupt judge
18:41 *L*," he answered, "I want to see."
19: 8 stood his ground and said to the *L*:
19: 8 "I give half my belongings, *L*, to the poor.
19:16 The first presented himself and said, *L*,
19:18 came and said, 'Your investment, my *l*,
19:20 'Here is your money, my *l*,
19:38 he who comes as king in the name of the *L*!
20:37 when he called the *L* the God of Abraham,
20:42 say in the psalms, 'The *L* said to my lord:
20:44 Now if David accords him the title *l*,'
22:25 "Earthly kings *l* it over their people.
22:33 *L*," he said to him, "at your side I am
22:38 They said, *L*, here are two swords!"
22:49 saw what was going to happen, they said, *L*,
22:61 The *L* turned around and looked at Peter,
22:61 the word that the *L* had spoken to him,
24: 3 they did not find the body of the *L* Jesus.
24:34 were greeted with, "The *L* has been raised!
Jn 1:23 Make straight the way of the *L*!'"
6:23 the bread after the *L* had given thanks.
6:68 Simon Peter answered him, *L*,
9:38][I do believe, *L*."
11: 2 one who anointed the *L* with perfume
11: 3 sent word to Jesus to inform him, *L*,
11:12 At this the disciples objected, *L*,
11:21 *L*, if you had been here,
11:27 "Yes, *L*," she replied. "I have come to
11:32 she fell at his feet and said to him, *L*,
11:34 *L*, come and see," they said.
11:39 the dead man's sister, said to him, *L*,
12:13 is he who comes in the name of the *L*!
12:38 *L*, who has believed what has reached our
12:38 whom has the might of the *L* been revealed?"
13: 6 he came to Simon Peter, who said to him, *L*,
13: 9 *L*," Simon Peter said to him,
13:13 You address me as 'Teacher' and *L*,'
13:14 I who am Teacher and *L*—
13:25 against Jesus' chest and said to him, *L*,
13:36 *L*," Simon Peter said to him,
13:37 *L*," Peter said to him,
14: 5 *L*," said Thomas, "we do not know
14: 8 *L*," Philip said to him, "show us
14:22 Judas (not Judas Iscariot) said to him, *L*,
20: 2 them, "The *L* has been taken from the tomb!
20:13 them, "Because the *L* has been taken away,
20:18 "I have seen the *L*!"
20:20 the sight of the *L* the disciples rejoiced.
20:25 "We have seen the *L*!"
20:28 Thomas said in response, "My *L* and my God!"
21: 7 loved cried out to Peter, "It is the *L*!"
21: 7 On hearing it was the *L*,
21:12 for they knew it was the *L*.
21:15 *L*," he said, "you know that I love you."
21:16 *L*," Peter said, "you know that I love you."
21:17 *L*, you know everything.
21:20 Jesus' chest during the supper and said, *L*,
21:21 Peter was prompted to ask Jesus, "But *L*,
Acts 1: 6 While they were with him they asked, *L*,
1:21 company while the *L* Jesus moved among us,
1:24 "O *L*, you read the hearts of men.
2:20 of that great and glorious day of the *L*.
2:21 be saved who calls on the name of the *L*.'
2:25 'I have set the *L* ever before me,
2:34 yet David says, 'The Lord said to my *L*,
2:36 God has made both *L* and Messiah this Jesus
2:39 still far off whom the *L* our God calls."
2:47 Day by day the *L* added to their number
3:20 you by the *L* when he sends you Jesus,
3:22 "'The *L* God will raise up for you a
4:24 Sovereign *L*, who made heaven and earth
4:26 against the *L* and against his anointed.'
4:29 But now, O *L*, look at the threats
4:33 witness to the resurrection of the *L* Jesus,
5: 9 scheme to put the Spirit of the *L* to test?
5:14 numbers, were continually added to the *L*.
5:19 of the *L* opened the gates of the jail,
7:31 it carefully, the voice of the *L* was heard:
7:33 The *L* said to him: Remove the sandals
7:49 can you build me? asks the *L*.
7:59 stoned he could be heard praying, *L* Jesus,
7:60 his knees and cried out in a loud voice, *L*,
8:16 been baptized in the name of the *L* Jesus.
8:22 Pray that the *L* may pardon you for
8:24 need the prayers of all of you to the *L*,
8:25 and proclaiming the word of the *L*,
8:26 of the *L* then addressed himself to Philip:
8:39 the Spirit of the *L* snatched Philip away
9:10 Ananias to whom the *L* had appeared
9:10 "Here I am, *L*," came the answer.
9:11 The *L* said to him, "Go at once
9:13 *L*, I have heard from many sources about
9:15 The *L* asked to him: "You must go!
9:17 I have been sent by the *L* Jesus who
9:27 how on his journey Saul had seen the *L*,
9:28 himself quite openly in the name of the *L*.
9:31 steady progress in the fear of the *L*;
9:35 upon seeing him, were converted to the *L*.
9:42 of it, many came to believe in the *L*.
10:33 whatever directives the *L* has given you."
10:36 through Jesus Christ who is *L* of all.
11:16 Then I remembered what the *L* had said:
11:17 we first believed in the *L* Jesus Christ,
11:20 the good news of the *L* Jesus to them.
11:21 The hand of the *L* was with them and a
11:21 them believed and were converted to the *L*.
11:23 remain firm in their commitment to the *L*,
11:24 Thereby large numbers were added to the *L*.
12: 7 *L* stood nearby and light shone in the cell.
12:11 "Now I know for certain that the *L* has
12:17 how the *L* had brought him out of prison.
12:23 The angel of the *L* struck Herod down at
12:24 of the *L* continued to spread and increase.
13: 2 in the liturgy of the *L* and were fasting,
13:10 make crooked the straight paths of the *L*?
13:12 was he by the teaching about the *L*.
13:47 For thus were we instructed by the *L*:
13:48 responded to the word of the *L* with praise.
13:49 of the *L* was carried throughout that area.
14: 3 fearlessly, in complete reliance on the *L*.
14:23 to the *L* in whom they had put their faith.
15:11 the favor of the *L* Jesus and so are they."
15:17 that bear my name may seek out the *L*.
15:18 Thus says the *L* who accomplishes these
15:26 to the cause of our *L* Jesus Christ.
15:35 teaching and preaching the word of the *L*.
15:36 where we proclaimed the word of the *L*."
15:40 by the brothers to the favor of the *L*.
16:14 and the *L* opened her heart to accept what
16:15 you are convinced that I believe in the *L*,
16:31 in the *L* Jesus and you will be saved,
17:24 that is in it, the *L* of heaven and earth,
18: 8 whole household, put his faith in the *L*.
18: 9 One night in a vision the *L* said to Paul:
18:25 and instructed in the new way of the *L*.
19: 5 were baptized in the name of the *L* Jesus.
19:10 and Greeks alike, heard the word of the *L*.
19:13 tried to invoke the name of the *L* Jesus
19:17 *L* Jesus came to be held in great reverence.
19:20 Thus did the word of the *L* continue to
20:19 how I served the *L* in humility through
20:21 before God and on faith in our *L* Jesus.
20:24 which I have been assigned by the *L* Jesus,
20:32 I commend you now to the *L*,
20:35 to recall the words of the *L* Jesus himself,
21:13 For the name of the *L* Jesus I am prepared,
22:10 I asked, and the *L* replied,
22:19 *L*, it is because they know that I
23:11 the *L* appeared at Paul's side and said:
26:15 and the *L* answered: "I am that Jesus
28:31 of God and taught about the *L* Jesus Christ.
Rom 1: 4 Jesus Christ our *L*.
1: 7 from God our Father and the *L* Jesus Christ.
4: 8 is the man to whom the *L* imputes no guilt."
4:24 him who raised Jesus our *L* from the dead,
5: 1 peace with God through our *L* Jesus Christ.
5:11 God our boast through our *L* Jesus Christ,
5:21 eternal life, through Jesus Christ our *L*.
6:23 God is eternal life in Christ Jesus our *L*.
7:25 praise to God, through Jesus Christ our *L*!
8:39 that comes to us in Christ Jesus, our *L*.
9:28 will the *L* execute sentence upon the earth."
9:29 the *L* of hosts had left us a remnant,
10: 9 confess with your lips that Jesus is *L*,
10:12 all have the same *L*, rich in mercy
10:13 calls on the name of the *L* will be saved."
10:16 Isaiah asks, *L*, who has believed
11: 3 *L*, they have killed your prophets,
11:34 For "who has known the mind of the *L*?
12:11 he whom you serve is the *L*.
12:19 I will repay,' says the *L*."
13:14 put on the *L* Jesus Christ and make no
14: 4 will, for the *L* is able to make him stand.
14: 6 observes the day does so to honor the *L*.
14: 6 The man who eats does so to honor the *L*,
14: 6 who does not eat abstains to honor the *L*,
14: 8 While we live we are responsible to the *L*,
14: 9 might be *L* of both the dead and the living.
14:11 "As surely as I live, says the *L*,
14:14 *L* Jesus that nothing is unclean in itself;
15: 6 God, the Father of our *L* Jesus Christ.
15:11 "Praise the *L*, all you Gentiles
15:30 *L* Jesus Christ and the love of the Spirit,
16: 2 Please welcome her in the *L*,
16: 8 to Ampliatus, who is dear to me in the *L*;
16:11 household of Narcissus who are in the *L*.
16:12 Tryphosa, who have worked hard for the *L*;
16:13 to Rufus, a chosen servant of the *L*,
16:18 Such men serve, not Christ our *L*,
16:20 grace of our *L* Jesus Christ be with you.
16:22 letter, send you my greetings in the *L*.
1Cor 1: 2 of our Lord Jesus Christ, their *L* and ours.
1: 3 from God our Father and the *L* Jesus Christ.
1: 7 for the revelation of our *L* Jesus Christ.
1: 8 on the day of our *L* Jesus [Christ].
1: 9 with his Son, Jesus Christ our *L*.
1:10 in the name of our *L* Jesus Christ,
1:31 "Let him who would boast, boast in the *L*."
2: 8 would never have crucified the *L* of glory.
2:16 the mind of the *L* so as to instruct him?"
3: 5 of them doing only what the *L* assigned him.
3:20 "The *L* knows how empty are the thoughts
4: 4 The *L* is the one to judge me,
4:17 my beloved and faithful son in the *L*.
4:19 I shall come to you soon, the *L* willing,
5: 3 passed sentence in the name of our *L* Jesus
5: 4 with you and empowered by our *L* Jesus,
5: 5 spirit may be saved on the day of the *L*.
6:11 justified in the name of our *L* Jesus
6:13 is for the Lord, and the *L* is for the body.
6:14 God, who raised up the *L*,
6:17 to the *L* becomes one spirit with him.
7:12 although I know of nothing the *L* has said,
7:17 lead the life the *L* has assigned him,
7:17 continuing as he was when the *L* called him.
7:22 called in the *L* is a freedman of the Lord,
7:22 called in the Lord is a freedman of the *L*,
7:25 not received any commandment from the *L*,
7:32 affairs, concerned with pleasing the *L*;
7:34 is concerned with things of the *L*,
7:35 you to devote yourselves entirely to the *L*.
7:39 but on one condition, that it be in the *L*.
8: 6 and one *L* Jesus Christ through whom
9: 1 Have I not seen Jesus our *L*?
9: 1 And are you not my work in the *L*?
9: 2 the very seal of my apostolate in the *L*.
9: 5 and the brothers of the *L* and Cephas?
9:14 Likewise the *L* himself ordered that those
10: 9 Let us not test the *L* as some of them did,
10:21 cup of the *L* and also the cup of demons.

LORD (cont.)

10:21 of the L and likewise the table of demons.
10:22 we mean to provoke the L to jealous anger?
11:11 Yet, in the L, woman is not independent
11:23 from the L what I handed on to you,
11:23 that the L Jesus on the night in which he
11:26 proclaim the death of the L until he comes!
11:27 eats the bread or drinks the cup of the L
11:27 sins against the body and blood of the L.
11:32 but since it is the L who judges us,
12: 3 "Jesus is L," except in the Holy Spirit.
12: 5 are different ministries but the same L;
14:21 even so they will not heed me, says the L."
15:31 me, which I cherish in Christ Jesus our L,
15:57 us the victory through our L Jesus Christ.
15:58 fully engaged in the work of the L.
15:58 is not in vain when it is done in the L.
16: 7 spend some time with you, if the L permits.
16:19 house, send you cordial greetings in the L.
16:22 If anyone does not love the L,
16:22 O L, come!
16:23 The favor of the L Jesus be with you.
2Cor 1: 2 from God our Father and the L Jesus Christ.
1: 3 be God, the Father of our L Jesus Christ,
1:14 and you ours, on the day of our L Jesus.
2:12 was opened wide for me by the L.
3:16 "But whenever he turns to the L,
3:17 The L is the Spirit,
3:17 Spirit, and where the Spirit of the L is,
3:18 his very image by the L who is the Spirit.
4: 5 ourselves we preach but Christ Jesus as L,
4:14 he who raised up the L Jesus will raise us
5: 6 dwell in the body we are away from the L.
5: 8 away from the body and at home with the L.
5:11 in awe of the L we try to persuade men,
6:17 separate yourselves from them,' says the L;
6:18 sons and daughters,' says the L Almighty."
8: 9 the favor shown you by our L Jesus Christ;
8:19 work of charity for the glory of the L.
10: 8 further claims about the power the L
10:17 "Let him who would boast, boast in the L."
10:18 but the man whom the L recommends.
11:17 L desires but after the manner of a fool.
11:31 The God and Father of the L Jesus knows
12: 1 speak of visions and revelations of the L.
12: 8 I begged the L that this might leave me.
13:10 severity the authority the L has given me
13:13 The grace of the L Jesus Christ,
Gal 1: 3 God our Father and of the L Jesus Christ,
1:19 except James, the brother of the L.
5:10 I trust that, in the L, you will not adopt
6:14 but the cross of our L Jesus Christ!
6:18 of our L Jesus Christ be with your spirit.
Eph 1: 2 from God our Father and the L Jesus Christ.
1: 3 the God and Father of our L Jesus Christ,
1:15 I first heard of your faith in the L Jesus
1:17 May the God of our L Jesus Christ,
2:21 and takes shape as a holy temple in the L;
3:11 purpose, carried out in Christ Jesus our L.
4: 1 with you, then, as a prisoner for the L,
4: 5 There is one L, one faith, one baptism;
4:17 I declare and solemnly attest in the L
5: 8 darkness, but now you are light in the L.
5:10 in your judgment of what pleases the L.
5:17 but try to discern the will of the L.
5:19 Sing praise to the L with all your hearts.
5:20 in the name of our L Jesus Christ.
5:22 as if to the L because the husband is head
6: 1 Children, obey your parents in the L,
6: 4 training and instruction befitting the L.
6: 7 doing it for the L rather than men.
6: 8 repaid by the L for whatever good he does.
6:10 strength from the L and his mighty power.
6:21 brother and faithful minister in the L,
6:23 May God the Father and the L Jesus Christ
6:24 our L Jesus Christ with unfailing love.
Phil 1: 2 God our Father and from the L Jesus Christ!
2:11 JESUS CHRIST IS L!
2:19 I hope, in the L Jesus, to send Timothy
2:24 in the L that I myself will be coming soon.
2:29 in the L and hold men like him in esteem,
3: 1 the rest, my brothers, rejoice in the L.
3: 8 surpassing knowledge of my L Jesus Christ.
3:20 coming of our Savior, the L Jesus Christ.
4: 1 my dear ones, to stand firm in the L.
4: 2 come to some mutual understanding in the L.
4: 4 Rejoice in the L always!
4: 5 The L is near.
4:10 It gave me great joy in the L that your
4:23 of the L Jesus Christ be with your spirit.
Col 1: 3 to God, the Father of our L Jesus Christ,
1:10 of the L and pleasing to him in every way.
2: 6 therefore, to live in Christ Jesus the L,
3:13 Forgive as the L has forgiven you.
3:17 action, do it in the name of the L Jesus.
3:18 This is your duty in the L.
3:20 everything as the acceptable way in the L.
3:22 sincerity and out of reverence for the L.
3:23 Do it for the L rather than for men,
3:24 Be slaves of Christ the L.
4: 7 minister and fellow slave in the L,
4:17 the ministry you have received in the L."
1Thes 1: 1 to God the Father and the L Jesus Christ.
1: 3 constancy of hope in our L Jesus Christ.
1: 6 turn, became imitators of us and of the L,
1: 8 L has echoed forth from you resoundingly.
2:15 who killed the L Jesus and the prophets,
2:19 before our L Jesus Christ at his coming?
3: 8 flourish only if you stand firm in the L!
3:11 and our L Jesus make our path to you a
3:12 And may the L increase you and make you
3:13 of our L Jesus with all his holy ones.
4: 1 we beg and exhort you in the L Jesus that
4: 2 instructions we gave you in the L Jesus.
4: 6 for the L is an avenger of all such things,
4:15 to you, as if the L himself had said it,
4:16 the L himself will come down from heaven
4:17 in the clouds to meet the L in the air.
4:17 we shall be with the L unceasingly.
5: 2 the L is coming like a thief in the night.
5: 9 salvation through our L Jesus Christ.
5:12 authority in the L and admonish you;
5:23 at the coming of our L Jesus Christ.
5:27 the L that this letter be read to them all.
5:28 grace of our L Jesus Christ be with you.
2Thes 1: 1 to God our Father and the L Jesus Christ.
1: 2 from God the Father and the L Jesus Christ.
1: 7 when the L Jesus is revealed from heaven
1: 8 nor heed" the good news of our L Jesus.
1: 9 apart from the presence of the L
1:12 In this way the name of our L Jesus may be
1:12 gift of our God and of the L Jesus Christ.
2: 1 On the question of the coming of our L
2: 2 believing that the day of the L is here.
2: 8 and the L Jesus will destroy him with the
2:13 for you always, beloved brothers in the L,
2:14 achieve the glory of our L Jesus Christ.
2:16 May our L Jesus Christ himself,
3: 1 that the word of the L may make progress
3: 3 every man has faith, but the L keeps faith;
3: 4 In the L we are confident that you are
3: 5 May the L rule your hearts in the love of
3: 6 in the name of the L Jesus Christ,
3:12 urge them strongly in the L Jesus Christ,
3:16 May he who is the L of peace give you
3:16 The L be with you all.
3:18 of our L Jesus Christ be with you all.
1Tm 1: 2 from God the Father and Christ Jesus our L.
1:12 I thank Christ Jesus our L,
1:14 and the grace of our L has been granted me
6: 3 holding to the sound doctrines of our L Jesus
6:14 until our L Jesus Christ shall appear.
6:15 the King of kings and L of lords who alone
2Tm 1: 2 and from Christ Jesus our L be with you.
1: 8 be ashamed of your testimony to our L,
1:16 L have mercy on the family of Onesiphorus,
1:18 he stands before the L on the great Day,
1:18 the great Day, may the L grant him mercy!
2: 7 for the L will make my meaning fully clear.
2:19 "The L knows those who are his";
2:19 professes the name of the L abandon evil."
2:22 those who call on the L in purity of heart.
2:24 and the servant of the L must not be
3:11 you know how the L saved me from them all.
4: 8 on that Day the L, just judge that he is
4:14 L will repay him according to his deeds.
4:17 L stood by my side and gave me strength,
4:18 The L will continue to rescue me from all
4:22 The L be with your spirit.
Phlm 1: 3 God our Father and from the L Jesus Christ.
1: 5 toward the L Jesus and all God's people.
1:16 will know him both as a man and in the L.
1:20 want to make you "useful" to me in the L.
1:25 of our L Jesus Christ be with your spirit.
Heb 1:10 L, of old you established the earth
2: 3 Announced first by the L,
7:14 that our L rose from the tribe of Judah,
7:21 "The L has sworn, and he will not repent:
8: 2 set up, not by man, but by the L.
8: 8 "Days are coming, says the L,
8: 9 and I grew weary of them, says the L,
8:10 of Israel after those days, says the L:
8:11 or their brothers, saying, 'Know the L,'
10:16 with them after those days, says the L:
10:30 repay," and "The L will judge his people."
12: 5 the L nor lose heart when he reproves you;
12: 6 For whom the L loves, he disciplines;
12:14 without which no one can see the L.
13: 6 "The L is my helper,
13:20 of the eternal covenant, Jesus our L,
Jas 1: 1 a servant of God and of the L Jesus Christ,
1: 7 not expect to receive anything from the L.
1:12 the L has promised to those who love him.
2: 1 your faith in our glorious L Jesus Christ
3: 9 it to say, "Praised be the L and Father";
4:10 of the L and he will raise you on high.
4:15 Instead of saying, "If the L wills it,
5: 4 have reached the ears of the L of hosts.
5: 7 my brothers, until the coming of the L.
5: 8 because the coming of the L is at hand.
5:10 prophets who spoke in the name of the L.
5:11 of Job, and have seen what the L,
5:14 him with oil in the Name [of the L.
5:15 ill, and the L will restore him to health.
1Pt 1: 3 the God and Father of our L Jesus Christ,
1:24 but the word of the L endures forever."
2: 3 that you have tasted that the L is good.
2:13 Because of the L, be obedient
3:12 because the L has eyes for the just and
3:12 but against evildoers the L sets his face."
3:15 Venerate the L,
2Pt 1: 2 your knowledge of God and of Jesus, our L.
1: 8 in true knowledge of our L Jesus Christ.
1:11 everlasting kingdom of our L and Savior
1:14 our L Jesus Christ has given me,
1:16 the coming in power of our L Jesus Christ,
2: 9 The L, indeed, knows how to rescue
2:20 recognizing the L and Savior Jesus Christ,
3: 2 new command of the L and Savior
3: 9 L does not delay in keeping his promise
3:10 The day of the L will come like a thief,
3:18 knowledge of our L and Savior Jesus Christ.
Jude 1: 4 deny Jesus Christ, our only master and L.
1: 5 The L first rescued his people from the
1: 6 These the L has kept in perpetual bondage,
1: 9 He simply said, "May the L punish you."
1:14 the L has come with his countless holy
1:17 prophetic words of the apostles of our L
1:21 L Jesus Christ which leads to life eternal.
1:25 God our savior, through Jesus Christ our L.
Rv 1: 8 The L God says, "I am the Alpha
4: 8 "Holy, holy, holy, is the L God Almighty,
4:11 O L our God, you are worthy
11: 4 in the presence of the L of the earth.
11: 8 where also their L was crucified.
11:15 belongs to our L and to his Anointed One,
11:17 you, the L God Almighty who is and who
14:13 Happy now are the dead who die in the L!"
15: 3 wonderful are your works, L God Almighty!
15: 4 you honor, or the glory due your name, O L?
16: 7 L God Almighty, your judgments are true
17:14 he is the L of lords and the King of kings;
18: 8 for mighty is the L God who condemns her."
19: 6 The L is king, our God, the Almighty!
19:16 "King of kings and L of lords."
21:22 The L, God the Almighty, is its temple
22: 5 sun, for the L God shall give them light,
22: 6 the L, the God of prophetic spirits,
22:20 Come, L Jesus!
22:21 The grace of the L Jesus be with you all.

LORDED (4)

Lv 26:17 your enemies and l over by your foes.
2Mc 5:23 who l it over his fellow citizens worse
Bar 3:16 who l it over the wild beasts of the earth,
Ez 34: 4 you l it over them harshly and brutally.

LORDING (1)

1Pt 5: 3 flock, not l it over those assigned to you,

LORDS-LORD'S (337)

Gn 4:16 L presence and settled in the land of Nod,
13:10 was as far as Zoar, like the L own garden,
16: 7 The L messenger found her by a spring in
16: 9 But the L messenger told her:
16:10 so numerous," added the L messenger,
16:11 Besides," the L messenger said to her:
19:16 When he hesitated, the men, by the L mercy,
19:27 place where he had stood in the L presence.
22:11 the L messenger called to him from heaven,
22:15 Again the L messenger called to Abraham
26:29 Henceforth, 'The L blessing be upon you!'"
27: 7 blessing with the L approval before I die.'
30:30 L blessings came upon you in my company.
33: 8 answered, "It was to gain my l favor."
39: 5 the L blessing was on everything he owned,
44: 9 rest of us, we shall become my l slaves."
47:18 there is nothing left to put at my l disposal
Ex 9:29 you shall learn that the earth is the L.
16: 3 died at the L hand in the land of Egypt,
28:30 over his heart in the L presence.
28:35 and leaves the L presence in the sanctuary;
Lv 3:11 on the altar as the food of the L oblation.
5:15 cheating in the L sacred dues,
8:29 in keeping with the L command to Moses.
9:21 in keeping with the L command to Moses.
9:24 Fire came forth from the L presence and
10: 2 from the L presence and consumed them,
10: 6 for those whom the L fire has smitten;
16: 1 died when they approached the L presence,
23: 6 month is the L feast of Unleavened Bread.
23:34 seventh month is the L feast of Booths,
23:38 in addition to those of the L sabbaths,
24:11 and cursed and blasphemed the L name.
24:16 be put to death for blaspheming the L name.
Nm 3:39 by clans in keeping with the L command,
4:41 together with Aaron, at the L bidding.
4:49 According to the L bidding to Moses,
5: 8 be the L and shall fall to the priest;
9: 7 we be deprived of presenting the L offering
9:10 journey, he may still keep the L Passover.
9:13 the L offering at the prescribed time.
9:14 among you wishes to keep the L Passover,
11:23 Moses, "Is this beyond the L reach?
11:33 the L wrath flared up against the people,
14:21 and the L glory that fills the whole earth,
14:41 are you again disobeying the L orders?

16: 3 you set yourselves over the *L* congregation?"
16: 9 near him for the service of the *L* Dwelling
17: 6 "It is you who have slain the *L* people."
17:24 from the *L* presence to the Israelites.
20: 3 with our kinsmen in the *L* presence!
20: 4 Why have you brought the *L* community into
25: 3 Peor, the *L* anger flared up against Israel.
27:17 that the *L* community may not be like sheep
27:21 decisions of the Urim in the *L* presence;
31: 3 and execute the *L* vengeance on them.
31:16 began the slaughter of the *L* community.
31:30 Levites, who have charge of the *L* Dwelling."
31:47 Levites, who had charge of the *L* Dwelling.
32:14 the *L* blazing wrath against the Israelites.
32:20 word to march as troops in the *L* vanguard
33: 2 By the *L* command Moses recorded the
33:38 priest ascended Mount Hor at the *L* command,
Dt 1:43 In defiance of the *L* command you
2:15 it was the *L* hand that was against them,
10:17 God, is the God of gods, the LORD of *l*,
17:16 against the *L* warning that you must never
29:19 the *L* wrath and jealousy will flare up
30: 8 must again heed the *L* voice and carry out
31:29 because you have done evil in the *L* sight,
32: 3 For I will sing the *L* renown.
32: 9 While the *L* own portion was Jacob,
34: 9 thus carrying out the *L* command to Moses.
Jos 4: 8 placed them, according to the *L* direction.
6:17 It is under the *L* ban.
8: 8 set it afire in obedience to the *L* command.
9:27 of the LORD, in the place of the *L* choice.
13: 3 by the five *l* of the Philistines in Gaza,
21: 8 obedience to the *L* command through Moses.
22: 9 according to the *L* command through Moses.
Jgs 3: 3 the five *l* of the Philistines;
16: 5 *l* of the Philistines came to her and said,
16: 8 So the *l* of the Philistines brought her
16:18 she summoned the *l* of the Philistines,
16:18 So the *l* of the Philistines came and
16:23 The *l* of the Philistines assembled to
16:27 all the *l* of the Philistines were there,
16:30 the *l* and all the people who were in it.
1Sm 1: 9 a chair near the doorpost of the *L* temple.
2: 8 For the pillars of the earth are the *L*,
2:10 the *L* foes shall be shattered.
5: 8 all the Philistine *l* and inquired of them,
5:11 to all the Philistine *l* and pleaded:
6: 4 correspond to the number of Philistine *l*,
6: 4 plague has struck all of you and your *l*.
6:12 The Philistine *l* followed them as far as
6:16 *l* returned to Ekron the same day.
6:18 the Philistines belonging to the five *l*,
7: 7 at Mizpah, their *l* went up against Israel.
10: 1 You are to govern the *L* people Israel,
12:14 him and do not rebel against the *L* command,
13:12 and I have not yet sought the *L* blessing.'
13:14 people, because you broke the *L* command."
16: 6 "Surely the *L* anointed is here before him."
17:47 *L* and he shall deliver you into our hands."
20: 8 servant because of the *L* bond between us,
21: 7 removed from the *L* presence and replaced
24: 7 such a thing to my master, the *L* anointed,
24: 7 a hand on him, for he is the *L* anointed."
24:11 he is the *L* anointed and a father to me.'
25:41 a slave to wash the feet of my *l* servants."
26: 9 on the *L* anointed and remain unpunished?
26:16 have not guarded your lord, the *L* anointed.
26:19 day I have no share in the *L* inheritance,
26:23 my grasp, I would not harm the *L* anointed.
28:18 "Because you disobeyed the *L* directive
29: 2 As the Philistine *l* were marching their
29: 6 But you are not welcome to the *l*.
29: 7 that might displease the Philistine *l*."
29:10 you and your *l* servants who came with you,
2Sm 1:14 your hand to desecrate the *L* anointed?"
1:16 you said, 'I dispatched the *L* anointed.'"
5:25 David obeyed the *L* command and routed the
6:21 he appointed me commander of the *L* people,
9: 9 "I am giving your *l* son all that belonged
9:10 shall be food for your *l* family to eat.
9:10 But Meribbaal, your *l* son,
11:13 to sleep on his bed among his *l* servants,
12: 8 lord's house and your *l* wives for your own.
16: 3 the king said, "And where is your *l* son?"
19:22 He cursed the *L* anointed."
20: 6 Take your *l* servants and pursue him,
21: 6 the LORD in Gibeon, on the *L* mountain."
21: 7 because of the *L* oath that formed a bond
24: 1 The *L* anger against Israel flared again,
1Kgs 6:19 to house the ark of the *L* covenant,
6:37 The foundations of the *L* temple were laid
8: 1 to bring up the ark of the *L* covenant from
8:11 *L* glory had filled the temple of the LORD.
15:26 He did evil in the *L* sight,
15:34 He did evil in the *L* sight,
16:25 the *L* sight beyond any of his predecessors.
18:38 The *L* fire came down and consumed the
21:20 yourself up to doing evil in the *L* sight,
22:43 doing what was right in the *L* sight.
2Kgs 3: 2 He did evil in the *L* sight,
8:18 and he did evil in the *L* sight.
8:19 him a lamp in the *L* presence for all time.
8:27 doing evil in the *L* sight as they did,
11:17 other, by which they would be the *L* people;
13: 2 He did evil in the *L* sight,
13:17 exclaimed, "The *L* arrow of victory!
14: 6 obeying the *L* command written in the book
15:12 Thus the *L* promise to Jehu,
17:17 themselves into evil doing in the *L* sight,
18:25 Was it without the *L* will that I have come
19:15 before him, he prayed in the *L* presence:
20: 5 three days you shall go up to the *L* temple;
21: 6 in the *L* sight and provoked him to anger.
24:20 The *L* anger befell Jerusalem and Judah
1Chr 6:16 David with the choir services in the *L* house
12:20 for their *l* took counsel and sent him home,
13:11 the *L* anger had broken out against Uzzah.
17:16 David came in and sat in the *L* presence,
21: 3 king, are not all of them my *l* subjects?
21:12 or three days of the *L* own sword,
21:12 *L* destroying angel in every part of Israel?
28: 5 to sit on the *L* royal throne over Israel.
29:22 in the *L* presence with great rejoicing.
29:22 and they anointed him as the *L* prince,
2Chr 1: 3 made in the desert by Moses, the *L* servant,
1: 5 front of the *L* Dwelling on the high place.
1: 6 Solomon offered sacrifice in the *L* presence
5: 2 bring up the ark of the *L* covenant
5:13 of the *L* temple was filled with a cloud.
5:14 since the *L* glory filled the house of God.
17: 6 he was encouraged to follow the *L* ways,
20:32 doing what was right in the *L* sight.
23: 5 will be in the courts of the *L* temple.
23: 6 Let no one enter the *L* house except the
23:14 must not put her to death in the *L* temple."
23:16 the king, that they should be the *L* people.
23:18 Then Jehoiada gave the charge of the *L*
23:19 stationed guards at the gates of the *L* temple
23:20 land, and led the king out of the *L* house.
24: 4 Joash decided to restore the *L* temple.
24: 7 the dedicated resources of the *L* temple.
24: 8 they put outside the gate of the *L* temple.
24:12 in charge of the labor on the *L* temple,
24:14 had it made into utensils for the *L* temple,
24:14 They offered holocausts in the *L* temple
24:20 'why are you transgressing the *L* commands,
24:21 him to death in the court of the *L* temple.
27: 3 He built the upper gate of the *L* house and
28:21 Though Ahaz plundered the *L* house and the
28:24 He closed the doors of the *L* house and had
29: 3 the doors of the *L* house and repaired them.
29: 6 away their faces from the *L* dwelling,
29:15 the *L* house in keeping with his words.
29:16 the interior of the *L* house to cleanse it;
29:16 and whatever they found in the *L* temple
29:16 brought out to the court of the *L* house,
29:17 consecrated the *L* house during eight days,
29:19 and they are now before the *L* altar."
29:20 of the city and went up to the *L* house.
29:25 the Levites in the *L* house with cymbals,
33: 5 of heaven in the two courts of the *L* house.
33:15 foreign gods and the idol from the *L* house
33:15 the mount of the *L* house and in Jerusalem,
34:10 used it to pay the workmen in the *L* house
34:17 metals deposited in the *L* house
35: 2 them in the service of the *L* house.
36:14 of the nations and polluting the *L* temple
36:18 *L* house and of the king and his princes,
Ezr 3:10 had laid the foundation of the *L* temple,
3:11 foundation of the *L* house had been laid.
7:11 the *L* commandments and statutes for Israel:
Neh 3: 5 not submit to the labor asked by their *l*.
2Mc 8: 5 for the *L* wrath had now changed to mercy.
8:35 after being humbled through the *L* help by
10: 1 and his companions under the *L* leadership,
15:21 not through arms but through the *L* decision
15:35 and evident proof to all of the *L* help.
Ps(s) 3: 9 Salvation is the *L*!
11: 4 the *L* throne is in heaven.
22:29 For dominion is the *L*,
24: 1 The *L* are the earth and its fullness;
75: 9 For a cup is in the *L* hand,
118:20 This gate is the *L*;
136: 3 Give thanks to the Lord of *l*,
Prv 5:21 each man's ways are plain to the *L* sight;
10:22 It is the *L* blessing that brings wealth,
21:31 the day of battle, but victory is the *L*.
Wis 3:14 a more gratifying heritage in the *L* temple.
10:16 She entered the soul of the *L* servant,
Sir 6:11 other self, and *l* it over your servants;
11:17 The *L* gift remains with the just;
17:14 a ruler, but the *L* own portion is Israel.
18:11 man, but the *L* mercy reaches all flesh,
26:16 Like the sun rising in the *L* heavens,
28: 1 The vengeful will suffer the *L* vengeance,
33: 8 It is due to the *L* Wisdom that they differ;
33:17 Since by the *L* blessing I have made
39: 8 and glory in the law of the *L* covenant.
43:30 Awful indeed is the *L* majesty,
46:18 and destroyed all the *l* of the Philistines.
Is 2: 2 The mountain of the *L* house shall be
2: 3 "Come, let us climb the *L* mountain,
14: 2 as male and female slaves on the *L* soil,
16: 8 clusters overpowered the *l* of nations,
26:13 our God, other *l* than you have ruled us;
36:10 'Was it without the *L* will that I have
38: 5 three days you shall go up to the *L* temple;
44: 5 One shall say, "I am the *L*,"
44: 5 this one shall write on his hand, "The *L*,"
48:14 The *L* friend shall do his will against
51:17 drank at the *L* hand the cup of his wrath;
55:13 the myrtle, This shall be to the *L* renown,
58:13 a delight, and the *L* holy day honorable;
66:14 The *L* power shall be known to his servants,
Jer 3:17 time they will call Jerusalem the *L* throne;
13: 5 Obedient to the *L* command,
13:17 eyes will run with tears for the *L* flock,
31:12 shall come streaming to the *L* blessings:
31:38 when the city shall be rebuilt as the *L*,
36: 6 publicly in the *L* house the LORD's words
36: 8 he read the *L* words in the LORD's house.
36:10 Shaphan, in the upper court of the *L* house,
43: 4 the *L* command to stay in the land of Judah.
43: 7 Against the *L* command they went to Egypt,
48:10 [Cursed be he who does the *L* work remissly,
50:13 Because of the *L* wrath she shall be empty,
51:29 the *L* plan against Babylon is carried out,
Lam 3:31 For the *L* rejection does not last forever;
Bar 1:17 sinned in the *L* sight and disobeyed him.
2:22 *L* voice so as to serve the king of Babylon.
Ez 7:19 cannot save them on the day of the *L* wrath.
8:16 me into the inner court of the *L* house,
8:16 and there at the door of the *L* temple,
8:16 *L* temple and their faces toward the east;
10:19 of the eastern gate of the *L* house,
18:25 You say, "The *L* way is not fair!"
18:29 of Israel says, "The *L* way is not fair!"
44: 4 the glory of the LORD filling the *L* temple,
44: 5 the statutes and laws of the *L* temple;
Dn 4:33 My nobles and *l* sought me out;
5: 1 a great banquet for a thousand of his *l*,
5: 2 to be brought in so that the king, his *l*,
5: 3 brought in, and while the king, his *l*,
5: 9 and his *l* were thrown into confusion.
5:10 the discussion between the king and his *l*,
6:18 with his own ring and the rings of the *l*
10:16 How can my *l* servant speak with you,
Hos 1: 2 the beginning of the *L* speaking to Hosea,
9: 3 They shall not dwell in the *L* land;
9: 5 the festival day, the day of the *L* feast?
Am 4: 1 Who say to your *l*, "Brink drink for us!"
Ob 1:21 of Esau, and the kingship shall be the *L*.
Jon 3: 3 to Nineveh, according to the *L* bidding.
Mi 4: 1 In days to come the mount of the *L* house
Hb 2:14 of the *L* glory as water covers the sea.
2:16 shall revert the cup from the *L* right hand,
Zep 1: 8 On the day of the *L* slaughter feast I
1:18 to save them on the day of the *L* wrath,
2: 2 comes upon you the day of the *L* anger.
2: 3 may be sheltered on the day of the *L* anger.
Hg 1:13 *L* messenger, Haggai, proclaimed
Zec 4: 6 me, "This is the *L* message to Zerubbabel:
9: 1 place, For the cities of Aram are the *L*,
14: 5 And the valley of the *L* mountain shall be
Mal 1:12 *L* table and its offering may be polluted,
Lk 1:45 that the *L* words to her would be fulfilled."
10:39 at the *L* feet and listened to his words.
Acts 9: 1 murderous threats against the *L* disciples,
13:11 The *L* hand is upon you even now!
21:14 further except, "The *L* will be done."
Rom 14: 8 Both in life and in death we are the *L*.
16:12 who has labored long in the *L* service.
1Cor 7:10 it is the *L*):
7:25 who is trustworthy, thanks to the *L* mercy.
7:32 unmarried man is busy with the *L* affairs,
8: 5 to be sure, many such "gods" and *l*—
10:26 "The earth and its fullness are the *L*."
11:20 you assemble it is not to eat the *L* Supper,
14:37 I have written you is the *L* commandment.
16:10 He does the *L* work just as I do,
2Cor 3:18 gazing on the *L* glory with unveiled faces,
1Tm 6:15 the King of kings and Lord of *l* who alone
2Pt 2:11 no opprobrious sentence in the *L* presence.
3: 8 In the *L* eyes, one day is as a thousand
3:15 *L* patience is directed toward salvation.
Rv 1:10 On the *L* day I was caught up in ecstasy,
17:14 he is the Lord of *l* and the King of kings;
19:16 "King of kings and Lord of *l*."

LORDSHIP (5)

Nm 32:27 before the LORD, just as your *l* says."
1Sm 16:16 If your *l* will order it,
25:28 your *l* is fighting the battles of the LORD,
25:31 the LORD confers this benefit on your *l*,
Jdt 5:21 then your *l* should keep his distance;

LORE (1)

Acts 7:22 Moses was educated in all the *l* of Egypt.

LOSE (43)

Gn 26: 9 thought I might *l* my life on her account."
27:45 Must I *l* both of you in a single day?"
Lv 27:29 that are doomed *l* the right to be redeemed;
Dt 1:21 Do not fear or *l* heart.'
21:14 if later on you *l* your liking for her,
32:35 against the time they *l* their footing?"
Jos 6:26 He shall *l* his first-born when he lays its

LOSE (cont.)

6:26 and he shall *l* his youngest son when he
Jgs 18:25 you and you and your family *l* your lives."
1Sm 17:32 "Let your majesty not *l* courage.
2Sm 17:10 with the heart of a lion will *l* courage.
1Chr 22:13 do not fear or *l* heart.
2Chr 20:15 'Do not fear or *l* heart at the sight of
20:17 Do not fear or *l* heart.
Ps(s) 45: 6 the king's enemies *l* heart.
Eccl 3: 6 A time to seek, and a time to *l*;
Sir 20: 2 better to admonish than to *l* one's temper,
20:21 One may *l* his life through shame,
Jer 4: 9 day, says the LORD, The king will *l* heart,
23:12 In the darkness they shall *l* their footing,
Dn 11:30 confront him, he shall *l* heart and retreat.
Mt 5:25 *L* no time; settle with your opponent
5:29 Better to *l* part of your body than to have
5:30 Better to *l* part of your body than to have
13:12 man who has not, will *l* what little he has.
16:25 Whoever would save his life will *l* it,
25:29 have not will *l* even the little they have.
Mk 8:35 Whoever would preserve his life will *l* it,
Lk 8:18 will *l* even the little he thinks he has."
9:24 Whoever would save his life will *l* it,
17:33 tries to preserve his life will *l* it;
19:26 one who has not will *l* the little he has.
Jn 6:39 I should *l* nothing of what he has given me;
10:35 and Scripture cannot *l* its force
16:16 Within a short time you will *l* sight of me,
16:17 a short time you will *l* sight of me,
16:19 a short time you will *l* sight of me,
Acts 20:16 past Ephesus so as not to *l* time in Asia,
27:34 Not one of you shall *l* a hair on his head."
2Cor 4:16 We do not *l* heart, because our inner being
Col 3:21 do not nag your children lest they *l* heart.
Heb 12: 5 the Lord nor *l* heart when he reproves you;
2Jn 1: 8 do not *l* what you have worked for;

LOSES (16)

Lv 13:40 "When a man *l* the hair of his head,
13:41 if he *l* the hair on the front of his head,
21: 9 "A priest's daughter who *l* her honor by
Dt 22: 3 your kinsman *l* and you happen to find;
Prv 19:24 The sluggard *l* his hand in the dish;
26:15 The sluggard *l* his hand in the dish;
Mt 16:25 *l* his life for my sake will find it.
Mk 8:35 but whoever *l* his life for my sake and the
Lk 9:24 *l* his life for my sake will save it.
14:34 *l* its flavor what good is it for seasoning?
15: 4 he has a hundred sheep and *l* one of them,
15: 8 If she has ten silver pieces and *l* one,
17:33 whoever *l* it will keep it.
Jn 12:25 The man who loves his life *l* it,
Rom 4:14 empty word and the promise *l* its meaning.
1Cor 9:26 like a man who *l* sight of the finish line.

LOSING (6)

2Kgs 3:26 When he saw that he was *l* the battle,
2Mc 4:45 But Menelaus, seeing himself on the *l* side,
Sir 17:19 back, he encourages those who are *l* hope!
Jer 50: 6 they wandered, *l* the way to their fold.
Lk 18: 1 of praying always and not *l* heart:
2Tm 4: 2 constantly teaching and never *l* patience.

LOSS (21)

Gn 31:39 I made good the *l* myself.
2Sm 10: 2 to Hanun for the *l* of his father.
2Chr 20:12 We are at a *l* what to do,
Jdt 10:13 of his men suffering injury or *l* of life."
Ps(s) 15: 4 Who, though it be to his *l*,
Prv 22:16 yield up his gains to the rich as sheer *l*.
Sir 20: 8 some things gained are a man's *l*.
31:20 Distress and anguish and *l* of sleep,
Is 41: 3 He pursues them, passing on without *l*,
47: 8 a widow, or suffer the *l* of my children"
Jer 7: 8 trust in deceitful words to your own *l*!
18:18 mean the *l* of instruction from the priests,
Lk 24: 4 still at a *l* over what to think of this,
Acts 27:10 bound to meet with disaster and heavy *l*,
27:21 would not have incurred this disastrous *l*.
1Cor 3:15 a man's building burns, he will suffer *l*.
8: 8 We suffer no *l* through failing to eat,
2Cor 7: 9 thus you did not suffer any *l* from us.
Gal 4:20 You have me at a complete *l*!
Phil 3: 7 reappraised as *l* in the light of Christ.
3: 8 I have come to rate all as *l* in the light

LOSSES (2)

1Sm 4:17 in fact, the troops suffered heavy *l*.
Jdt 7: 9 that there may be no *l* among your troops.

LOST (74)

Gn 34:19 man *l* no time in acting in the matter,
Lv 5:22 unjustly, or if, having found a *l* article,
5:23 deposit left with him or the *l* article
21: 7 has been a prostitute or has *l* her honor,
21:14 woman who has *l* her honor as a prostitute,
26:34 Then shall the land retrieve its *l*
26:38 You will be *l* among the Gentiles,
26:43 desolation it may make up its *l* sabbaths,
Nm 17:27 we are lost, we are all *l*!
Jos 5: 1 and *l* courage at their approach.
1Sm 4:10 Israel *l* thirty thousand foot soldiers.
9:20 As for the asses you *l* three days ago,
28: 5 he was dismayed and *l* heart completely.
1Kgs 16:34 He *l* his first-born son, Abiram,
2Chr 36:21 the land has retrieved its *l* sabbaths,
Neh 6:16 *l* much face in the eyes of the nations,
Tb 3:15 I have already *l* seven husbands;
7: 7 he heard that Tobit had *l* his eyesight,
14: 2 sixty-two years old when he *l* his eyesight,
Jdt 10:10 then they *l* sight of her.
Est 2: 7 for she had *l* both father and mother.
1Mc 11:49 they *l* courage and cried out to the king
2Mc 1:32 but its light was *l* in the brilliance cast
5:14 of three days, eighty thousand were *l*,
9:18 so he *l* hope for himself and wrote the
12:32 they *l* no time in marching against Gorgias,
14:46 steep rock, as he *l* the last of his blood,
Ps(s) 73: 2 But, as for me, I almost *l* my balance;
119:176 I have gone astray [like a *l* sheep];
142: 5 I have *l* all means of escape;
Prv 5:23 the greatness of his folly he will be *l*.
Eccl 5:13 the riches be *l* through some misfortune,
9: 5 for them, because all memory of them is *l*.
Sir 2: 8 trust him, and your reward will not be *l*.
2:14 Woe to you who have *l* hope!
8:12 and whatever you lend, count it as *l*.
14: 2 does not reproach him, who has not *l* hope.
41: 6 Their dominion is *l* to sinners' children,
Is 17: 3 *l* to Ephraim and the kingdom to Damascus;
27:13 and the *l* in the land of Assyria and the
49:20 whom you had *l* shall yet say to you,
Jer 48:11 he kept his taste, and his scent was not *l*.
50: 6 *L* sheep were my people,
Lam 3:18 I tell myself my future is *l*,
3:54 flowed over my head, and I said, "I am *l*!"
Ez 34: 4 not bring back the strayed nor seek the *l*,
34:16 The *l* I will seek out,
37:11 "Our bones are dried up, our hope is *l*,
Dn 7:12 beasts, which also *l* their dominion
Mt 8:25 We are *l*!"
10: 6 after the *l* sheep of the house of Israel.
15:24 only to the *l* sheep of the house of Israel,"
Mk 2:22 skins and both wine and skins will be *l*.
Lk 5:37 will spill out, and the skins will be *l*.
8:24 him, saying, "Master, master, we are *l*!"
15: 4 and follow the *l* one until he finds it?
15: 6 with me because I have found my *l* sheep.'
15: 8 search until she has retrieved what she *l*?
15: 9 I have found the silver piece I *l*.'
15:24 He was *l* and is found.'
15:32 He was *l*, and is found.' "
19:10 has come to search out and save what is *l*."
19:42 but you have completely *l* it from view!
Jn 7:49 and they are *l* anyway!"
17:12 careful watch, and not one of them was *l*,
17:12 none but him who was destined to be *l*—
18: 9 "I have not *l* one of those you gave me.")
Acts 27:22 None among you will be *l*— only the ship.
1Tm 6: 5 minds who have *l* all sense of truth.
Heb 4: 1 be judged to have *l* his chance of entering.
2Pt 1:10 surely those who do so will never be *l*.
Rv 8:12 The day *l* a third of its light,
12: 8 overpowered and *l* their place in heaven.

LOT (140)

Gn 11:27 Haran, and Haran became the father of *L*.
11:31 Terah took his son Abram, his grandson *L*,
12: 4 the LORD directed him, and *L* went with him.
12: 5 took his wife Sarai, his brother's son *L*,
13: 1 belonged to him, and *L* accompanied him.
13: 5 *L*, who went with Abram,
13: 8 So Abram said to *L*:
13:10 *L* looked about and saw how well watered
13:11 *L*, therefore, chose for himself
13:12 *L* settled among the cities of the Plain,
13:14 After *L* had left, the LORD said to Abram:
14:12 way, taking with them Abram's nephew *L*,
14:16 back his kinsman *L* and his possessions,
19: 1 as *L* was sitting at the gate of Sodom.
19: 1 *L* saw them, he got up to greet them;
19: 5 They called to *L* and said to him,
19: 6 *L* went out to meet them at the entrance.
19: 9 With that, they pressed hard against *L*,
19:10 out their hands, pulled *L* inside with them,
19:12 Then the angels said to *L*:
19:14 So *L* went out and spoke to his sons-in-law,
19:15 As dawn was breaking the angels urged *L* on,
19:18 "Oh, no, my lord!" replied *L*.
19:23 rising over the earth as *L* arrived in Zoar,
19:29 he was mindful of Abram by sending *L* away
19:29 the cities where *L* had been living.
19:30 Since *L* was afraid to stay in Zoar,
Lv 16: 9 goat that is determined by *l* for the LORD,
16:10 But the goat determined by *l* for Azazel he
Nm 26:55 But the land shall be divided by *l*,
26:56 As the *l* falls shall each group,
33:54 apportion the land among yourselves by *l*,
33:54 Wherever anyone's *l* falls,
34:13 land, to be apportioned among you by *l*,
36: 2 the land by *l* among the Israelites;
36: 3 that fell to us by *l* will be diminished.
Dt 2: 9 Ar to the descendants of *l* as their own.
2:19 it to the descendants of *L* as their own.
4:19 *l* of all other nations under the heaven;
29:25 and whom he had not let fall to their *l*:
30: 3 the LORD, your God, will change your *l*;
Jos 14: 2 Israelites determined their heritage by *l*,
15: 1 The *l* for the clans of the Judahite tribe
16: 1 The *l* that fell to the Josephites extended
17: 1 Now as for the *l* that fell to the tribe of
17:14 only one *l* and one share as our heritage?
18:11 One *l* fell to the clans of the tribe of
19: 1 The second *l* fell to Simeon.
19:10 *l* fell to the clans of the Zebulunites.
19:17 The fourth *l* fell to Issachar.
19:24 The fifth *l* fell to the clans of the tribe
19:32 The sixth *l* fell to the Naphtalites.
19:40 The seventh *l* fell to the clans of the
19:51 the land by *l* in the presence of the LORD,
21: 4 When the first *l* among the Levites fell to
21: 4 cities by *l* from the tribes of Judah,
21: 5 *l* from the clans of the tribe of Ephraim,
21: 6 *l* from the clans of the tribe of Issachar,
21:10 Levites, since the first *l* fell to them:
21:20 clans among the Levites obtained by *l*,
Jgs 20: 9 We will proceed against it by *l*,
Ru 1:13 my *l* is too bitter for you,
1Chr 6:39 Kohathites, since the first *l* fell to them,
6:46 Kohathites obtained ten cities by *l*
6:48 cities by *l* from the tribes of Reuben,
6:50 them by *l* from the tribes of the Judahites,
6:51 cities by *l* from the tribe of Ephraim.
24: 5 functions were assigned impartially by *l*,
24: 7 The first *l* fell to Jehoiarib,
25: 9 The first *l* fell to Asaph,
26:14 When the *l* was cast for the east side,
26:14 and the north side fell to his *l*.
Neh 10:35 by *l* concerning the procurement of wood:
Est 3: 7 year of King Ahasuerus, the pur, or *l*,
3: 7 and the *l* fell on the thirteenth day of
9:24 destroy them and had cast the pur, or *l*,
1Mc 3:36 territory and distribute their land by *l*.
Jb 17: 5 My *l* is described as evil,
30: 3 In want and hunger was their *l*,
31: 2 But what is man's *l* from God above,
Ps(s) 16: 5 and my cup, you it is who hold fast my *l*.
49:14 the end of those contented with their *l*:
50:18 and with adulterers you throw in your *l*.
78:55 he distributed their inheritance by *l*,
83: 9 they are the forces of the sons of *L*.
Prv 1:14 Cast in your *l* with us,
16:33 When the *l* is cast into the lap,
18:18 The *l* puts an end to disputes,
Eccl 2:14 Yet I knew that one *l* befalls both of them.
2:15 if the fool's *l* is to befall me also,
3:19 For the *l* of man and of beast is one lot;
3:22 for this is his *l*.
5:17 for this is his *l*.
5:18 *l* and finds joy in the fruits of his toil,
9: 2 vain, in that there is the same *l* for all,
9: 9 This is your *l* in life,
Wis 2: 9 for this our portion is, and this our *l*.
5: 5 how his *l* is with the saints!
Sir 11:22 God's blessing is the *l* of the just man,
14:15 and your earnings to be divided by *l*?
16: 8 of *L* whom he detested for their pride;
25:18 may she fall to the *l* of the sinner!
27:28 and abuse will be the *l* of the proud,
36:23 kindly, his *l* is beyond that of mortal men.
Is 17:14 despoil us, the *l* of those who plunder us.
34:17 It is he who casts the *l* for them,
54:17 This is the *l* of the servants of the LORD,
57: 6 wadi is your portion, these are your *l*;
Jer 13:25 This is your *l*, the portion measured out
29:14 says the LORD, and I will change your *l*;
30: 3 the *l* of my people (of Israel and Judah,
31:23 *l* in the land of Judah and her cities,
32:44 and of the Negeb, when I change their *l*,
33: 7 the *l* of Judah and the lot of Israel,
33:26 I will change their *l* and show them mercy.
48:47 change the *l* of Moab in the days to come,
49: 6 I will change the *l* of the Ammonites,
49:39 days to come I will change the *l* of Elam,
Lam 3:47 Terror and the pit have been our *l*.
Dn 4:12 his *l* be to eat, among beasts,
4:20 and let his *l* be among wild beasts till
Mi 2: 5 by *l* in the assembly of the LORD.
Mt 17:17 an unbelieving and perverse *l* you are!
Mk 9:19 the crowd, "What an unbelieving *l* you are!
Lk 1: 9 it fell to him by *l* according to priestly
9:41 an unbelieving and perverse *l* you are!
17:28 It was much the same in the days of *L*:
17:29 But on the day *L* left Sodom,
Jn 7:49 this *l*, that knows nothing about the law
Acts 8:21 can have no portion or *l* in this affair.
17: 4 and threw in their *l* with Paul and Silas.
2Cor 6:15 common *l* between believer and unbeliever?
Phil 1: 7 are sharers of my gracious *l* when I lie in
Col 1:12 to share the *l* of the saints in light.
1Thes 3: 3 enough that such trials are our common *l*.
2Pt 2: 7 He did deliver *L*, however, a just man
2:14 An accursed *l* are they!
Rv 21: 8 *l* is the fiery pool of burning sulphur,

LOTAN (5)

Gn 36:20 *L,* Shobal,
36:29 the clans of *L,*
1Chr 1:38 The descendants of Seir were *L,*
1:39 The sons of *L* were Hori and Homam;
1:39 Timna was the sister of *L.*

LOTAN'S (2)

Gn 36:22 *L* descendants were Hori and Hemam,
36:22 Hori and Hemam, and *L* sister was Timna.

LOTS-LOT'S (27)

Gn 13: 7 of Abram's livestock and those of *L.*
19:26 But *L* wife looked back,
19:36 Thus both of *L* daughters became pregnant
Lv 16: 8 he shall cast *l* to determine which one is
Jos 18: 6 then cast *l* for you here before the LORD,
18: 8 *l* for them there before the LORD in Shiloh.
18:10 *l* for them before the LORD in Shiloh.
1Sm 14:42 "Cast *l* between me and my son Jonathan."
1Chr 24:31 cast *l* in the presence of King David,
25: 8 They cast *l* for their functions equally,
26:13 They cast *l* for each gate,
26:14 Then they cast *l* for his son Zechariah,
Neh 11: 1 rest of the people cast *l* to bring one man
Est F: 7 For this purpose he arranged two *l:*
11: 8 These two *l* were fulfilled in the hour,
Jb 6:27 You would even cast *l* for the orphan,
Ps(s) 22:19 among them, and for my vesture they cast *l.*
Ez 24: 6 one by one, without casting *l* for it.
Jl 4: 3 Over my people they have cast *l;*
Ob 1:11 his gates and cast *l* over Jerusalem,
Jon 1: 7 let us cast *l* to find out on whose account
1: 7 they cast *l,* and thus singled out Jonah
Na 3:10 For her nobles they cast *l,*
Mt 27:35 his clothes among them by casting *l;*
Lk 17:32 Remember *L* wife.
Jn 19:24 for my clothing they cast *l.*")
Acts 1:26 Then they drew *l* between the two men.

LOTUS (3)

1Kgs 7:19 columns were finished wholly in a *l* pattern
Jb 40:21 Under the *l* trees he lies,
40:22 The *l* trees cover him with their shade;

LOUD (73)

Gn 27:34 his father's words, Esau burst into *l,*
39:14 with me, but I cried out as *l* as I could.
45: 2 were so *l* that the Egyptians heard him,
Ex 11: 6 be *l* wailing throughout the land of Egypt,
12:30 and there was a *l* wailing throughout Egypt,
19:16 the mountain, and a very *l* trumpet blast,
Nm 14: 1 whole community broke out with *l* cries,
Dt 5:22 the LORD spoke with a *l* voice to your
Jgs 9: 7 there, cried out to them in a *l* voice:
Ru 1: 9 them good-bye, but they wept with *l* sobs,
1Sm 4: 6 *l* shouting in the camp of the Hebrews mean?"
17:52 the men of Israel and Judah, with *l* shouts,
2Sm 19: 5 his face and cried out in a *l* voice,
1Kgs 8:55 community of Israel, saying in a *l* voice:
2Kgs 18:28 and cried out in a *l* voice in Judean,
1Chr 15:16 cymbals, to make a *l* sound of rejoicing.
2Chr 15:14 They swore to the LORD with a *l* voice with
32:18 In a *l* voice they shouted in the Judean
Ezr 10:12 whole assembly cried out with a *l* voice:
Neh 9: 4 out to the LORD their God, with a *l* voice.
Jdt 7:29 wailing and *l* cries to the Lord their God.
9: 1 Judith prayed to the Lord with a *l* voice:
13:14 the two, Judith urged them with a *l* voice:
14:16 He broke into a *l* clamor of weeping,
14:19 *L* screaming and howling arose in the camp.
1Mc 2:19 But Mattathias answered in a *l* voice:
5:31 heaven with trumpet blasts and *l* shouting,
13:45 garments rent, and cried out in *l* voices,
Ps(s) 42: 5 God, Amid *l* cries of joy and thanksgiving,
142: 2 With a *l* voice I cry out to the LORD;
142: 2 with a *l* voice I beseech the LORD.
Prv 27:14 When one greets his neighbor with a *l*
Is 36:13 and cried out in a *l* voice in Judean,
Jer 51:54 *l* cries from Babylon,
51:55 LORD lays Babylon waste, stills her *l* cry,
Ez 3:12 heard behind me the noise of a *l* rumbling
3:13 by the wheels alongside them, a *l* rumbling.
9: 1 of the Idolaters he cried *l* for me to hear:
11:13 I fell prone and cried out in a *l* voice;
Zep 1:10 the New Quarter, *l* crashing from the hills.
Mt 2:18 heard at Ramah, sobbing and *l* lamentation:
27:46 midafternoon Jesus cried out in a *l* tone,
27:50 Once again Jesus cried out in a *l* voice,
Mk 1:26 and with a *l* shriek came out of him.
5: 7 and did him homage, shrieking in a *l* voice,
15:34 At that time Jesus cried in a *l* voice,
15:37 Then Jesus, uttering a *l* cry,
Lk 1:42 the Holy Spirit and cried out in a *l* voice:
4:15 synagogues, and all were *l* in his praise.
4:33 unclean spirit, who shrieked in a *l* voice:
17:15 cured, came back praising God in a *l* voice.
23:23 demanded with *l* cries that he be crucified,
23:46 Jesus uttered a *l* cry and said,
Acts 7:60 to his knees and cried out in a *l* voice,
14:10 He called out to him in a *l* voice,
23: 9 A *l* uproar ensued.
Heb 5: 7 with *l* cries and tears to God,
Rv 5: 2 a mighty angel who proclaimed in a *l* voice:
7:10 They cried out in a *l* voice,
8:13 flying in midheaven cry out in a *l* voice,
10: 3 then gave a *l* cry like the roar of a lion.
11:12 heard a *l* voice from heaven say to them,
11:15 *L* voices in heaven cried out,
12:10 Then I heard a *l* voice in heaven say:
14: 2 roaring of the deep, or *l* peals of thunder;
14: 7 He said in a *l* voice:
14: 9 followed the others and said in a *l* voice:
14:15 angel came out of the temple and in a *l* voice
14:18 cried out in a *l* voice to the one who
16:17 in the sanctuary came a *l* voice which said,
19: 1 the *l* song of a great assembly in heaven.
19:17 He cried out in a *l* voice to all the birds
21: 3 I heard a *l* voice from the throne cry out:

LOUDER (8)

Ex 19:19 The trumpet blast grew *l* and louder,
1Kgs 18:27 "Call *l,* for he is a god
18:28 They called out *l* and slashed themselves
Mt 20:31 to silence, but they only shouted the *l,*
27:23 But they only shouted the *l,*
Mk 10:48 him keep quiet, but he shouted all the *l,*
15:14 They only shouted the *l,* "Crucify him!"

LOUDLY (15)

1Sm 4: 5 shouted so *l* that the earth resounded.
7:10 LORD thundered *l* against the Philistines,
2Sm 13:19 hands to her head, she went away crying *l.*
Jdt 14: 9 her account, the people cheered *l.*
Est 4: 1 through the city crying out *l* and bitterly.
1Mc 3:54 they blew the trumpets and cried out *l.*
2Mc 3:15 and *l* begged him in heaven who had given
Ps(s) 66: 8 our God, you peoples, *l* sound his praise;
Sir 39:15 greatness of his name, *l* sing his praises,
Jon 3: 8 covered with sackcloth and call *l* to God;
Mk 5:38 people wailing and crying *l* on all sides.
Lk 19:37 *l* for the display of power they had seen,
Jn 11:43 Having said this, he called *l,*
Acts 8: 2 Stephen, bewailing him *l* as they did so,
8: 7 spirits, which came out shrieking *l.*

LOUT (2)

Mt 25:26 'You worthless, lazy *l!*
Lk 19:22 'You worthless *l!*

LOVE (389)

Gn 22: 2 your son Isaac, your only one, whom you *l,*
24:67 In his *l* for her Isaac found solace after
29:18 Since Jacob had fallen in *l* with Rachel,
29:20 but a few days because of his *l* for her.
29:32 now my husband will *l* me.' "
34: 3 indeed was really in *l* with the girl,
34:19 he was deeply in *l* with Jacob's daughter.
Ex 20: 6 those who *l* me and keep my commandments.
Lv 19:18 You shall *l* your neighbor as yourself.
19:34 have the same *l* for him as for yourself;
Dt 4:37 For *l* of your fathers he chose their
5:10 those who *l* me and keep my commandments.
6: 5 Therefore, you shall *l* the LORD,
7: 9 those who *l* him and keep his commandments,
7:13 He will *l* and bless and multiply you;
10:12 his ways exactly, to *l* and serve the LORD,
10:15 Yet in his *l* for your fathers the LORD was
11: 1 *L* the LORD, your God
13: 4 testing you to learn whether you really *l* him
30: 6 your descendants, that you may *l* the LORD,
Jos 22: 5 *l* the LORD, your God; follow him
23:11 Take great care, however, to *l* the LORD,
Jgs 14:16 you do not *l* me,
16: 4 After that he fell in *l* with a woman in
16:15 you *l* me when you do not confide in me?
1Sm 18:22 is fond of you, and all his officers *l* you.
20:17 in his *l* for David, Jonathan renewed
2Sm 1:26 have I held *l* for you than love for women.
13: 4 Amnon said to him, "I am in *l* with Tamar,
13:15 far surpassed the *l* he had had for her.
19: 7 who hate you and hating those who *l* you.
1Kgs 10: 9 In his enduring *l* for Israel,
11: 2 But Solomon fell in *l* with them.
2Chr 19: 2 the wicked and *l* those who hate the LORD?
Neh 1: 5 who *l* you and keep your commandments,
Tb 4:13 Therefore, my son, *l* your kinsmen.
5:22 do not worry about them, my *l.*
6:18 lineage, he fell deeply in *l* with her,
7:11 from now on you are her *l,*
7:15 called his wife Edna and said, "My *l,*
8: 4 from bed and said to his wife, "My *l,*
10: 6 "Hush, do not think about it, my *l;*
10: 6 So do not worry over him, my *l.*
13:14 Happy are those who *l* you,
14: 7 Those who sincerely *l* God shall rejoice,
Est 8: 5 I have found favor with you and you *l* me,
1Mc 4:33 them down by the sword of those who *l* you,
2Mc 6:20 it is unlawful to taste even for *l* of life.
14:37 of the Jews because of his *l* for them.
Ps(s) 4: 3 *l* what is vain and seek after falsehood?
5:12 may be the joy of those who *l* your name.
18: 2 I *l* you, O LORD, my strength
26: 8 O LORD, I *l* the house in which you dwell,
31:24 *L* the LORD, all you his faithful ones!
40:17 may those who *l* your salvation say ever,
41:12 That you *l* me I know by this,
44: 4 of your countenance, in your *l* for them.
45: 8 You *l* justice and hate wickedness;
52: 5 You *l* evil rather than good,
52: 6 You *l* all that means ruin,
69:37 and those who *l* his name shall inhabit it.
70: 5 may those who *l* your salvation say ever,
109: 4 In return for my *l* they slandered me,
109: 5 me evil for good and hatred for my *l.*
116: 1 I *l* the LORD because he has heard
119:47 I will delight in your commands, which I *l.*
119:97 How I *l* your law, O LORD!
119:113 men of divided heart, but I *l* your law.
119:119 therefore I *l* your decrees.
119:127 For I *l* your command more than gold,
119:132 pity as you turn to those who *l* your name.
119:159 See how I *l* precepts,
119:163 Falsehood I hate and abhor; your law I *l.*
119:165 Those who *l* your law have great peace,
119:167 I keep your decrees and *l* them deeply.
122: 6 May those who *l* you prosper!
135: 3 sing praise to his name, which we *l;*
145:20 The LORD keeps all who *l* him,
Prv 1:22 long, you simple ones, will you *l* inanity,
4: 6 *l* her, and she will safeguard you
5:19 Her *l* will invigorate you always,
5:19 her *l* you will flourish continually.
7:18 "Come, let us drink our fill of *l,*
7:18 of love, until morning, let us feast on *l!*
8:17 "Those who *l* me I also love,
8:21 justice, Granting wealth to those who *l* me,
8:36 all who hate me *l* death."
9: 8 reprove a wise man, and he will *l* you.
10:12 up disputes, but *l* covers all offenses.
15:17 *l* is than a fatted ox and hatred with it.
20:13 *L* not sleep, lest you be reduced to poverty
27: 5 open rebuke than a *l* that remains hidden.
Eccl 3: 8 A time to *l,* and a time to hate;
9: 1 *L* from hatred man cannot tell;
9: 6 *l* and hatred and rivalry have long since
9: 9 Enjoy life with the wife whom you *l,*
Sg 1: 2 More delightful is your *l* than wine!
1: 3 that is why the maidens *l* you.
2: 4 banquet hall and his emblem over me is *l.*
2: 5 me with apples, for I am faint with *l.*
2: 7 do not stir up *l* before its own time.
3: 5 do not stir up *l* before its own time.
4:10 How beautiful is your *l,*
4:10 much more delightful is your *l* than wine,
5: 1 Drink freely of *l!*
5: 8 that I am faint with *l.*
7: 7 How beautiful you are, how pleasing, my *l,*
7:13 There will I give you my *l.*
8: 4 the field, Do not arouse, do not stir up *l,*
8: 6 For stern as death is *l,*
8: 7 Deep waters cannot quench *l,*
8: 7 one to offer all he owns to purchase *l,*
Wis 1: 1 *L* justice, you who judge the earth
3: 9 and the faithful shall abide with him in *l:*
6:12 is readily perceived by those who *l* her,
6:17 then, care for discipline is *l* of her;
6:18 *l* means the keeping of her laws;
11:24 For you *l* all things that are and loathe
Sir 2:15 those who *l* him keep his ways.
2:16 those who *l* him are filled with his law.
4:14 those who *l* her the LORD loves.
7:30 With all your strength, *l* your Creator,
11:15 *l* and virtuous paths are from the LORD.
25: 1 and the mutual *l* of husband and wife.
34:16 eyes of the LORD are upon those who *l* him;
40:20 soul, but better than either, conjugal *l.*
Is 43: 4 my eyes and glorious, and because I *l* you,
54: 8 But with enduring *l* I take pity on you,
54:10 My *l* shall never leave you nor my covenant
57: 8 And of those whose embraces you *l* you
61: 8 For I, the LORD, *l* what is right,
63: 9 of his *l* and pity he redeemed them himself,
66:10 be glad because of her, all you who *l* her;
Jer 2:25 I *l* these strangers,
2:33 How well you pick your way when seeking *l!*
14:10 They so *l* to wander that they do not spare
17:21 As you *l* your lives,
31: 3 With age-old *l* I have loved you;
Bar 6: 8 gold, as to a maiden in *l* with ornament,
Ez 16: 8 and saw that you were now old enough for *l.*
23:17 Babylonians came to her, to the *l* couch,
Dn 9: 4 who *l* you and observe your commandments!
14:38 "you have not forsaken those who *l* you."
Hos 2:21 in right and in justice, in *l* and in mercy;
3: 1 your *l* to a woman beloved of a paramour,
4:18 in their arrogance they *l* shame.
6: 6 For it is *l* that I desire,
9:15 I will *l* them no longer;
11: 4 them with human cords, with bands of *l;*
14: 5 heal their defection, I will *l* them freely;
Am 4: 5 freewill offerings, For so you *l* to do,
5:15 Hate evil and *l* good,
8:14 "By the life of your *l,* O Beer-sheba!"

LOVE (cont.)

Mi 3: 2 You who hate what is good, and *l* evil?
6: 8 Only to do right and to *l* goodness,
Zep 3:17 you with gladness, and renew you in his *l*,
Zec 8:17 another in his heart, nor *l* a false oath.
8:19 only *l* faithfulness and peace.
Mt 5:43 *l* your countryman but hate your enemy.'
5:44 *l* your enemies,
5:46 If you *l* those who love you,
6: 5 hypocrites who *l* to stand and pray
6:24 He will either hate one and *l* the other or
19:19 and *L* your neighbor as yourself.' "
22:37 *l* the Lord your God with your whole heart,
22:39 'You shall *l* your neighbor as yourself.'
24:12 of evil, the *l* of most will grow cold.
Mk 10:21 Jesus looked at him with *l* and told him,
12:30 *l* the Lord your God with all your heart,
12:31 'You shall *l* your neighbor as yourself.'
12:33 Yes, 'to *l* him with all our heart,
12:33 and to *l* our neighbor as ourselves' is
Lk 6:27 *L* your enemies,
6:32 If you *l* those who love you,
6:32 Even sinners *l* those who love them.
6:35 *L* your enemy and do good;
7:47 because of her great *l*.
7:47 is forgiven the one whose *l* is small."
10:27 *l* the Lord your god with all your heart,
11:42 while neglecting justice and the *l* of God.
11:43 You *l* the front seats in synagogues and
16:13 Either he will hate the one and *l* the
20:13 Perhaps if I send the son I *l*,
20:46 robes, and *l* marks of respect in public,
Jn 1:14 from the Father, filled with enduring *l*.
1:16 *l* following upon love.
1:17 this enduring *l* came through Jesus Christ.
5:42 do not have the *l* of God in your hearts.
8:42 "Were God your father you would *l* me,
11: 3 inform him, "Lord, the one you *l* is sick."
13: 1 and would show his *l* for them to the end.
13:34 *L* one another
13:34 as my *l* has been for you, so must your love
13:35 by your *l* for one another."
14:15 you *l* me and obey the commands I give you,
14:21 I too will *l* him and reveal myself to him."
14:23 true to my word, and my Father will *l* him;
14:24 who does not *l* me does not keep my words.
14:31 I *l* the Father and do as the Father has
15: 9 me, so I have loved you, Live on in my *l*.
15:10 live in my *l* if you keep my commandments,
15:10 Father's commandments, and live in his *l*.
15:12 *l* one another as I have loved you.
15:13 There is no greater *l* than this:
15:17 I give you is this, that you *l* one another.
15:19 to the world, it would *l* you as its own;
17:24 the *l* you bore me before the world began.
17:26 it so that your *l* for me may live in them,
21:15 son of John, do you *l* me more than these?"
21:15 Lord," he said, "you know that I *l* you."
21:16 "Simon, son of John, do you *l* me?"
21:16 Peter said, "you know that I *l* you."
21:17 him, "Simon, son of John, do you *l* me?"
21:17 he had asked a third time, "Do you *l* me?"
21:17 You know well that I *l* you."
Acts 17:21 *l* nothing more than to tell about or
Rom 5: 5 because the *l* of God has been poured out
5: 8 in this that God proves his *l* for us:
8:35 Who will separate us from the *l* of Christ?
8:39 *l* of God that comes to us in Christ Jesus,
12: 9 Your *l* must be sincere.
12:10 *L* one another with the affection of
13: 8 the debt that binds us to *l* one another.
13: 9 "You shall *l* your neighbor as yourself."
13:10 *L* never wrongs the neighbor, hence love
14:15 you have ceased to follow the rule of *l*.
15:30 Lord Jesus Christ and the *l* of the Spirit,
1Cor 2: 9 what God has prepared for those who *l* him."
4:21 with a rod, or with *l* and a gentle spirit?
8: 1 whereas "knowledge" inflates, *l* upbuilds.
10:14 I am telling you, whom I *l*,
13: 1 and angelic as well, but do not have *l*,
13: 2 enough to move mountains, but have not *l*,
13: 3 over my body to be burned, but have not *l*,
13: 4 *L* is patient; love is kind.
13: 4 *L* is not jealous,
13: 5 *L* is never rude,
13: 6 *L* does not rejoice in what is wrong but
13: 8 *L* never fails.
13:13 faith, hope, and *l*,
13:13 and love, and the greatest of these is *l*.
14: 1 Seek eagerly after *l*.
16:14 Do everything with *l*.
16:22 If anyone does not *l* the Lord,
16:24 My *l* to all of you in Christ Jesus.
2Cor 2: 4 to help you realize the great *l* I bear you.
2: 8 beg you to reaffirm your *l* for him.
5:14 The *l* of Christ impels us who have reached
6: 6 in the Holy Spirit, in sincere *l*;
7:15 heart embraces you with an expanding *l*
8: 7 in total concern, and in the *l* we bear you,
8: 8 *l* against the concern which others show.
8:24 show these men the proof of your *l*,
11:11 Because I do not *l* you?
12:15 If I *l* you too much,
13:11 the God of *l* and peace will be with you.
13:13 of the Lord Jesus Christ, and the *l* of God,
Gal 5: 6 faith, which expresses itself through *l*.
5:13 Out of *l*, place yourselves
5:14 "You shall *l* your neighbor as yourself."
5:22 In contrast, the fruit of the spirit is *l*,
Eph 1: 4 blameless in his sight, to be full of *l*;
1:15 your *l* for all the members of the church,
2: 4 because of his great *l* for us he brought
3:18 length and height and depth of Christ's *l*,
3:19 this *l* which surpasses all knowledge,
4:15 let us profess the truth in *l* and and the
4:16 supporting ligament, builds itself up in *l*.
5: 2 Follow the way of *l*,
5:25 Husbands, *l* your wives,
5:28 *l* their wives as they do their own bodies.
5:33 one should *l* his wife as he loves himself,
6:23 grant the brothers peace and *l* and faith.
6:24 Grace be with all who *l* our Lord Jesus
6:24 our Lord Jesus Christ with unfailing *l*.
Phil 1: 9 is that your *l* may more and more abound,
1:16 Some act from unaffected *l*,
2: 1 in the name of the solace that *l* can give,
2: 2 by your unanimity, possessing the one *l*,
4: 1 my brothers, you whom I so *l* and long for,
Col 1: 4 and the *l* you bear toward all the saints
1: 8 it was who told us of your *l* in the Spirit.
2: 2 and themselves to be closely united in *l*,
3:14 Over all these virtues put on *l*,
3:19 Husbands, *l* your wives.
1Thes 1: 3 are proving your faith, and laboring in *l*,
3: 6 the good news of your faith and *l*,
3:12 with *l* for one another and for all,
3:12 and for all, even as our *l* does for you.
4: 9 As regards brotherly *l*,
4: 9 himself has taught you to *l* one another,
5: 8 putting on faith and *l* as a breastplate
5:13 with the greatest *l* because of their work.
2Thes 1: 3 grows apace and your mutual *l* increases;
3: 5 the *l* of God and the constancy of Christ.
1Tm 1: 5 is the *l* that springs from a pure heart,
1:14 the faith and *l* which are in Christ Jesus.
2:15 she continues in faith and *l* and holiness
4:12 youth, but be a continuing example of *l*,
6:10 The *l* of money is the root of all evil.
6:11 seek after integrity, piety, faith, *l*,
2Tm 1: 2 life in him, to Timothy, my child whom I *l*.
1:13 me say, in faith and *l* in Christ Jesus.
2:22 passions and pursue integrity, faith, *l*,
3:10 my resolution, fidelity, patience, *l*,
Ti 2: 4 women to *l* their husbands and children,
3: 4 kindness and *l* of God our savior appeared,
3:15 Greet those who *l* us in the faith.
Phlm 1: 5 for I keep hearing of your *l* and faith
1: 7 I find great joy and comfort in your *l*,
1: 9 done, I prefer to appeal in the name of *l*.
Heb 6:10 the *l* you have shown him by your service,
10:23 the promise each other to *l* and good deeds.
13: 1 *L* your fellow Christians always.
13: 5 *l* money but be content with what you have,
Jas 1:12 the Lord has promised to those who *l* him.
2: 5 the kingdom he promised to those who *l* him?
2: 8 "You shall *l* your neighbor as yourself."
4: 4 aware that *l* of the world is enmity to God?
1Pt 1: 8 you have never seen him, you *l* him,
1:22 for a genuine *l* of your brothers;
1:22 *l* one another constantly from the heart.
2:17 Foster *l* for the brothers,
4: 8 let your *l* for one another be constant,
4: 8 constant, for *l* covers a multitude of sins.
5:14 one another with the embrace of true *l*.
2Pt 1: 7 brother, and care for your brother, to *l*.
1Jn 2: 5 has the *l* of God been made perfect in him.
2:15 Have no *l* for the world,
2:15 world, the Father's *l* has no place in him,
3: 1 See what *l* the Father has bestowed on us
3:10 God, nor anyone who fails to *l* his brother.
3:11 we should *l* one another.
3:14 to life we know because we *l* the brothers.
3:14 who does not *l* is among the living dead.
3:16 *l* was that he laid down his life for us;
3:17 how can God's *l* survive in a man who has
3:18 let us *l* in deed and in truth and not
3:23 we are to *l* one another as he commanded us.
4: 7 us *l* one another because love is of God;
4: 8 The man without *l* has known nothing of God,
4: 8 has known nothing of God, for God is *l*.
4: 9 *l* was revealed in our midst in this way:
4:10 *L*, then, consists in this:
4:11 we must have the same *l* for one another.
4:12 Yet if we *l* one another God dwells in us,
4:12 and his *l* is brought to perfection in us.
4:16 and to believe in the *l* God has for us.
4:16 God is *l*, and he who abides in love
4:17 Our *l* is brought to perfection in this,
4:18 *L* has no room for fear;
4:18 rather, perfect *l* casts out all fear.
4:18 *l* is not yet perfect in one who is afraid.
4:19 for our part, *l* because he first loved us.
4:20 If anyone says, "My *l* is fixed on God,"
4:20 One who has no *l* for the brother he has
4:20 has seen cannot *l* the God he has not seen.
4:21 whoever loves God must also *l* his brother.
5: 1 the father *l* the child he has begotten.
5: 2 we *l* God's children when we love God
5: 3 The *l* of God consists in this:
2Jn 1: 1 In truth I *l* each of you
1: 2 This *l* is based on the truth that abides
1: 3 In truth and *l*,
1: 5 let us *l* one another.
1: 6 This *l* involves our walking according to
3Jn 1: 1 to the beloved Gaius, whom indeed I *l*.
1: 6 have testified to your *l* before the church.
Jude 1: 1 who have found *l* in God the Father and
1: 2 and *l* be yours in ever greater measure.
1:21 Persevere in God's *l*,
Rv 2: 4 you have turned aside from your early *l*.
2:19 your *l* and faith and service
3: 9 will learn of my *l* for you in that way.
12:11 *l* for life did not deter them from death.
22:15 idol-worshipers and all who *l* falsehood.

LOVED (75)

Gn 29:30 Rachel also, and he *l* her more than Leah.
37: 3 Israel *l* Joseph best of all his sons,
37: 4 their father *l* him best of all his sons,
Dt 7: 8 It was because the LORD *l* you and because
1Sm 1: 5 double portion to Hannah because he *l* her,
18: 1 he *l* him as he loved himself.
18: 3 with David, because he *l* him as himself.
18:16 the other hand, all Israel and Judah *l* him,
18:20 Now Saul's daughter Michal *l* David,
18:28 besides, his own daughter Michal *l* David.
20:17 to him, because he *l* him as his very self.]
2Sm 12:24 The LORD *l* him and sent the prophet Nathan
13: 1 named Tamar, and David's son Amnon *l* her.
1Kgs 3: 3 Solomon *l* the LORD,
11: 1 King Solomon *l* many foreign women besides
2Chr 9: 8 Because your God has so *l* Israel as to
11:21 Rehoboam *l* Maacah,
Est 2:17 king *l* Esther more than all other women,
Jb 19:19 those whom I *l* have turned against me!
Ps(s) 60: 7 of bowshot That your *l* ones may escape;
78:68 the tribe of Judah, Mount Zion which he *l*.
108: 7 That your *l* ones may escape,
109:17 He *l* cursing; may it come upon him
Wis 4:10 He who pleased God was *l*;
7:10 Beyond health and comeliness I *l* her,
8: 2 Her I *l* and sought after from my youth;
8: 3 even the Lord of all *l* her.
16:26 That your sons whom you *l* might learn,
Sir 3:17 you will be *l* more than a giver of gifts.
7:35 for these things you will be *l*.
47: 8 *l* his Maker and daily had his praises sung;
Jer 2: 2 of your youth, how you *l* me as a bride,
8: 2 army of heaven, which they *l* and served,
31: 3 With age-old love I have *l* you;
Ez 16:37 whether you *l* them or loved them not;
Hos 9:10 became as abhorrent as the thing they *l*.
11: 1 When Israel was a child I *l* him,
Mal 1: 2 I have *l* you, says the LORD;
1: 2 but you say, "How have you *l* us?"
1: 3 yet I *l* Jacob, but hated Esau;
Mt 12:18 I have chosen, my *l* one in whom I delight.
Mk 12: 6 the son whom he *l*.
Jn 3:16 so *l* the world that he gave his only Son,
3:19 but men *l* darkness rather than light
11: 5 Jesus *l* Martha and her sister and Lazarus
11:36 Jews to remark, "See how much he *l* him!"
13: 1 He had *l* his own in this world,
13:23 One of them, the disciple whom Jesus *l*,
14:21 and he who loves me will be *l* by my Father.
14:28 If you truly *l* me you would rejoice to
15: 9 "As the Father has *l* me,
15: 9 the Father has loved me, so I have *l* you,
15:12 love one another as I have *l* you.
16:27 because you have *l* me and have believed
17:23 me, and that you *l* them as you loved me.
19:26 mother there with the disciple whom he *l*,
20: 2 disciple (the one Jesus *l*) and told them,
21: 7 the disciple Jesus *l* cried out to Peter,
21:20 the disciple whom Jesus *l* was following
Rom 8:37 conquerors because of him who has *l* us.
9:13 says, "I have *l* Jacob and hated Esau."
9:25 those who were not *l* I will call 'Beloved';
2Cor 12:15 too much, will I be *l* the less for that?
Gal 2:20 of God, who *l* me and gave himself for me.
Eph 5: 2 the way of love, even as Christ *l* you.
5:25 love your wives, as Christ *l* the church.
2Thes 2:16 may God our Father who *l* us and in his
Heb 1: 9 You have *l* justice and hated wickedness,
1Jn 4:10 not that we have *l* God,
4:10 but that he has *l* us and has sent his Son
4:11 Beloved, if God has *l* us so,
4:19 for our part, love because he first *l* us.

LOVELINESS (2)

Ps(s) 27: 4 *l* of the LORD and contemplate his temple.
Jas 1:11 and with that the meadow's *l* is gone.

LOVELY (15)

Gn 29:17 Leah had *l* eyes,
49:21 hind let loose which brings forth *l* fawns.

Jdt 8: 7 She was beautifully formed and l to behold.
Est 1:11 and the officials, for she was l to behold.
2: 7 was beautifully formed and l to behold.
D: 5 her countenance was as joyous as it was l,
Ps(s) 84: 2 I How l is your dwelling place,
Prv 5:19 of the wife of your youth, your l hind,
Sg 1: 5 I am as dark—but l,
1:10 Your cheeks l in pendants,
1:16 yes, you are l.
2:14 For your voice is sweet, and you are l."
4: 3 your mouth is l.
6: 4 as Tirzah, my beloved, as l as Jerusalem,
Jer 6: 2 O l and delicate daughter Zion,

LOVER (39)

2Chr 26:10 He was a l of the soil.
Ps(s) 11: 5 the l of violence he hates.
Eccl 5: 9 and the l of wealth reaps no fruit from it;
Sg 1:13 My l is for me a sachet of myrrh to rest
1:14 My l is for me a cluster of henna from
1:16 Ah, you are beautiful, my l—
2: 3 trees of the woods, so is my l among men.
2: 8 my l— here he comes
2: 9 My l is like a gazelle or a young stag.
2:10 My l speaks;
2:16 My l belongs to me and I to him;
2:17 and the shadows lenghten, roam, my l,
4:16 Let my l come to his garden and eat its
5: 2 I heard my l knocking:
5: 4 My l put his hand through the opening;
5: 5 I rose to open to my l,
5: 6 I opened to my l— but my lover had
5: 8 daughters of Jerusalem, if you find my l—
5: 9 How does your l differ from any other,
5: 9 How does your l differ from any other,
5:10 My l is radiant and ruddy;
5:16 Such is my l,
6: 1 Where has your l gone,
6: 1 your l gone that we may seek him with you?
6: 2 My l has come down to his garden,
6: 3 My l belongs to me and I to him;
7:10 that flows smoothly for my l,
7:11 I belong to my l and for me he yearns.
7:12 Come, my l, let us go forth
7:14 Both fresh and mellowed fruits, my l,
8: 5 up from the desert, leaning upon her l?
8:14 Be swift, my l, like a gazelle
8:14 boasts of having found welcome from her l.
Wis 11:26 they are yours, O Lord and l of souls.
Sir 31: 5 The l of gold will not be free from sin,
Jer 3:20 But like a woman faithless to her l,
Mt 11:19 a l of tax collectors and those outside
Ti 1: 8 be hospitable and a l of goodness;

LOVERS (23)

2Mc 10:20 men in Simon's force who were money l
Wis 15: 6 L of evil things,
Jer 3: 1 But you have sinned with many l,
4:30 Your l spurn you, they seek your life.
13:21 you those whom you taught to be your l?
22:20 from Abarim, for all your l are crushed.
22:22 your shepherds, your l shall go into exile.
30:14 All your l have forgotten you,
Lam 1:19 "I cried out to my l, but they failed me.
Ez 16:33 rather bestowed your gifts on all your l,
16:36 harlotry with your l and abominable idols,
16:37 all your l whom you tried to please,
23: 5 she lusted after her l,
23: 9 Therefore I handed her over to her l,
23:22 I will now stir up your l against you,
Hos 2: 7 "I will go after my l,"
2: 9 If she runs after her l,
2:12 bare her shame before the eyes of her l,
2:14 "These are the hire my l have given me";
2:15 and her jewels, and, in going after her l,
8: 9 Ephraim bargained for l.
2Tm 3: 2 Men will be l of self and of money,
3: 4 l of pleasure rather than of God as they

LOVES (77)

Dt 21:15 two wives l one and dislikes the other;
21:16 his first-born the son of the wife he l,
23: 6 into a blessing for you, because he l you.
Ru 4:15 mother is the daughter-in-law who l you.
2Sm 22:20 and rescued me, because he l me.
2Chr 2:10 "Because the LORD l his people,
Tb 6:12 and her father l her dearly."
6:15 Because he l her, he does not harm her
2Mc 15:14 who l his brethren and fervently prays for
Ps(s) 11: 7 For the LORD is just, he l just deeds;
18:20 the open, and rescued me, because he l me.
22: 9 him, let him rescue him, if he l him."
33: 5 He l justice and right;
37:28 For the LORD l what is right,
47: 5 inheritance, the glory of Jacob, whom he l.
87: 2 upon the holy mountains the LORD l:
97:10 The LORD l those that hate evil;
99: 4 The King in his might l justice;
119:140 is very sure, and your servant l it.
146: 8 the LORD l the just.
149: 4 For the LORD l his people,
Prv 3:12 For whom the LORD l he reproves,
12: 1 He who l correction loves knowledge,
13: 1 A wise son l correction,
13:24 he who l him takes care to chastise him.
15: 9 LORD, but he l the man who pursues virtue.
15:12 The senseless man l not to be reproved;
16:13 and the man who speaks what is right he l.
17:19 He who l strife loves guilt;
21:17 He who l pleasure will suffer want;
21:17 he who l wine and perfume will not be rich.
22:11 The LORD l the pure of heart;
29: 3 He who l wisdom makes his father glad,
Sg 1: 7 Tell me, you whom my heart l,
3: 1 bed at night I sought him whom my heart l—
3: 2 crossings I will seek Him whom my heart l.
3: 3 Have you seen him whom my heart l?
3: 4 them when I found him whom my heart l.
Wis 7:28 For there is nought God l,
8: 7 Or if one l justice,
Sir 3:25 end, and he who l danger will perish in it.
4:12 He who l her loves life;
4:14 those who love her the LORD l.
13:14 Every living thing l its own kind,
30: 1 He who l his son chastises him often,
Is 1:23 one of them l a bribe and looks for gifts.
Hos 3: 1 Even as the LORD l the people of Israel,
12: 8 holds a false balance, who l to defraud!
Mal 2:11 has profaned the temple which the LORD l,
Mt 10:37 Whoever l father or mother,
Lk 7: 5 they said, "because he l our people,
Jn 3:35 The Father l the Son and has given
5:20 For the Father l the Son and everything
10:17 The Father l me for this:
12:25 The man who l his life loses it,
14:21 he has from me is the man who l me;
14:21 and he who l me will be loved by my Father.
14:23 "Anyone who l me will be true to my word,
16:27 The Father already l you,
Rom 13: 8 who l his neighbor has fulfilled the law.
1Cor 8: 3 But if anyone l God,
13: 7 There is no limit to l forbearance,
2Cor 9: 7 not grudgingly, for God l a cheerful giver.
Eph 5:28 He who l his wife loves himself.
5:33 one should love his wife as he l himself,
1Tm 3: 3 Nor can he be someone who l money.
Heb 12: 6 For whom the Lord l, he disciplines
1Jn 2:10 in the light is the one who l his brother;
2:15 If anyone l the world,
4: 7 everyone who l is begotten of God and has
4:21 whoever l God must also love his brother.
5: 1 everyone who l the father loves the child
Rv 1: 5 To him who l us and freed us from our sins

LOVING (13)

Dt 11:13 on you today, l and serving the LORD,
11:22 commandments I enjoin on you, l the LORD,
19: 9 which I enjoin on you today, l the LORD,
30:16 God, which I enjoin on you today, l him,
30:20 your descendants may live, by l the LORD,
2Sm 19: 7 servants to shame today by l those who hate
Wis 7:22 certain, Not baneful, l the good,
Is 56: 6 ministering to him, L the name of the LORD,
56:10 Dreaming as they lie there, l their sleep.
Hos 9: 1 l a harlot's hire upon every threshing
2Tm 1: 7 but rather one that makes us strong, l,
Ti 2: 2 likewise sound in the faith, l,
1Pt 3: 8 sympathetic, l toward one another,

LOVINGLY (1)

Eph 4: 2 and patience, bearing with one another l.

LOW (54)

Gn 23: 7 began to bow l before the local citizens,
23:12 after bowing l before the local citizens,
33: 6 their children came forward and bowed l;
33: 7 and her children came forward and bowed l;
33: 7 and her children came forward and bowed l.
Lv 26: 7 enemies and lay them l with your sword.
Nm 32: 4 has laid l before the community of Israel,
2Sm 9: 8 Bowing l, he answered, "What is
2Chr 28:19 LORD had brought Judah l because of Ahaz,
Jdt 7:14 be laid l in the streets of their city.
11:12 food gave out and all their water ran l,
16: 6 struck down, nor did titans bring him l,
1Mc 6:40 the heights, while some were on l ground,
2Mc 11:11 they laid l eleven thousand foot soldiers
15:27 they laid l at least thirty-five thousand,
Jb 6: 5 Does the ox l over his fodder?
24:24 they are laid l and, like all others,
Ps(s) 18:28 you save but haughty eyes you bring l;
75: 8 one he brings l; another he lifts up.
78:31 men, and laid l the young men of Israel.
79: 8 come to us, for we are brought very l.
106:43 counsels and were brought l by their guilt.
107:39 and were brought l through oppression,
116: 6 I was brought l, and he saved me.
142: 7 to my cry, for I am brought l indeed.
Eccl 12: 4 are shut, and the sound of the mill is l;
Sir 6:12 But if you are brought l,
33:12 Others he curses and brings l,
46:18 He brought l the rulers of the enemy and
Is 2: 9 But man is abased, each one brought l.
2:12 that is high, and it will be brought l;
2:17 be abased, the arrogance of men brought l,
5:15 Men shall be abased, each one brought l,
10:33 are felled, and the lofty ones brought l;
25:11 l their pride as his hands sweep over them.
32:19 The city will be utterly laid l.
40: 4 every mountain and hill shall be made l;
60:14 oppressors shall come, bowing l before you;
Jer 5: 3 you laid them l, but they refused
42: 1 Hoshaiah, and all the people, high and l,
42: 8 leaders, and all the people, high and l,
44:12 High and l, they shall die by the sword
Bar 2: 5 We are brought l, not raised up,
5: 7 that every lofty mountain be made l,
Ez 17:24 that I, the LORD, Bring l the high tree,
21:31 Up with the l and down with the high!
31:12 foliage was brought l in all the valleys,
Dn 3:37 brought l everywhere in the world this day
7:24 before him, who shall lay l three kings.
11:12 heart, he shall lay l tens of thousands,
Hb 3: 6 age-old hills bow l along his ancient ways.
Acts 10:25 to his knees before him and bowed l.
2Cor 7: 6 gives heart to those who are l in spirit,
Phil 4:12 I am experienced in being brought l,

LOW-LYING (1)

Ez 17: 6 To sprout and grow up a vine, dense and l,

LOWBORN (1)

1Cor 1:28 He chose the world's l and despised,

LOWER (29)

Gn 24:14 if I say to a girl, 'Please l your jug,
Ex 28:26 them on the two l ends of the breastpiece,
39:19 put on the two l ends of the breastpiece,
Dt 28:43 above you, while you sink l and lower.
Jos 15:19 So he gave her the upper and the l pools.
16: 3 Japhletites, to that of the L Beth-horon,
18:13 on the mountaintop south of L Beth-horon.
Jgs 1:15 So Caleb gave her the upper and the l pool.
2Sm 10: 4 l halves of their garments at the buttocks,
1Kgs 9:17 Solomon then rebuilt Gezer), L Beth-horon,
1Chr 7:24 l and upper Beth-horon and Uzzen-sheerah.
2Chr 8: 5 He built Upper Beth-horon and L Beth-horon,
Jb 41:15 his flesh, as the l millstone.
Is 22: 9 you collected the water of the l pool.
43:14 I will l all the bars,
Jer 44:15 the people who lived in L and Upper Egypt,
Ez 40:18 this was the l pavement.
40:19 the l gate to the front of the inner gate;
42: 5 them at a level l than the closest chambers
42: 6 therefore they were on a l terrace of the
43:14 up to the l edge it was two cubits high,
43:14 from the l to the upper ledge it was four
43:17 The l ledge, likewise a square
Lk 5: 4 deep water and l your nets for a catch."
5: 5 but if you say so, I will l the nets."
Eph 4: 9 descended into the l regions of the earth?
Heb 2: 7 him for a little while l than the angels;
2: 9 made for a little while l than the angels,

LOWERED (10)

Gn 24:46 l the jug she was carrying and said,
44:11 l his bag to the ground and opened it,
Is 2:11 The haughty eyes of man will be l,
5:15 low, and the eyes of the haughty l,
Ez 1:24 when they stood still, they l their wings.]
Acts 9:25 the wall one night and l him to the ground,
10:11 It was l to the ground by its four corners.
11: 5 it was l down to me from the sky by its
27:17 they l the small anchor used for moving
2Cor 11:33 but I was l in a basket through a window

LOWERING (2)

Gn 24:18 and quickly l the jug onto her hand,
Is 30:27 from afar in burning wrath, with l clouds!

LOWEST (8)

Gn 9:25 l of slaves shall he be to his brothers."
1Kgs 6: 6 Its l story was five cubits wide,
6: 8 The entrance to the l floor of the annex
6:10 annex, with its l story five cubits high,
Ez 41: 7 the l to the middle and the highest story.
42: 5 The outermost chambers were the l,
Lk 14: 9 to proceed shamefacedly to the l place.
14:10 been invited is go and sit in the l place,

LOWING (2)

Jgs 5:16 hearths listening to the l of the herds?
1Sm 15:14 to my ears, and the l of oxen that I hear?"

LOWLANDS (2)

Dt 34: 3 of the Jordan with the l at Jericho,
34:12 of the Jordan with the l at Jericho,

LOWLIEST (2)

Ez 29:14 origin, where it will be the l of kingdoms,
Dn 4:14 whom he will, or set over it the l of men.'

LOWLINESS (4)

Jdt 6:19 Have pity on the *l* of our people,
Sir 13:19 A proud man abhors *l*;
Lk 1:48 he has looked upon his servant in her *l*;
Jas 1:10 and the rich man be proud of his *l*,

LOWLY (47)

Dt 1:17 give ear to the *l* and to the great alike,
2Sm 6:22 I will be *l* in your esteem,
22:28 You save *l* people,
Jdt 9:11 but you are the God of the *l*,
16:11 When my *l* ones shouted,
Est A:10 the *l* were exalted and they devoured the
B: 8 "Remember the days of your *l* estate."
1Mc 14:14 He strengthened all the *l* among his people
Jb 5:11 He sets up on high the *l*,
Ps(s) 18:28 For *l* people you save but haughty eyes
22:27 The *l* shall eat their fill;
34: 3 the *l* will hear me and be glad.
41: 2 he who has regard for the *l* and the poor;
49: 3 in the world, Of *l* birth or high degree,
69:33 "See you *l* ones, and be glad;
72:13 He shall have pity for the *l* and the poor;
82: 3 Defend the *l* and the fatherless;
82: 4 Rescue the *l* and the poor;
113: 7 He raises up the *l* from the dust;
138: 6 The LORD is exalted, yet the *l* he sees,
147: 6 LORD sustains the *l*; the wicked he casts
149: 4 people, and he adorns the *l* with victory.
Prv 10:15 the ruination of the *l* is their poverty.
12: 9 Better a *l* man who supports himself than
Eccl 10: 6 position while the rich sit in *l* places.
Wis 6: 6 For the *l* may be pardoned out of mercy
Sir 10:14 and establishes the *l* in their stead.
35:17 The prayer of the *l* pierces the clouds;
Is 29:19 The *l* will ever find joy in the LORD,
61: 1 sent me to bring glad tidings to the *l*,
66: 2 the *l* and afflicted man who trembles at my
Jer 5: 4 It is only the *l*, I thought, who are foolish
16: 6 They shall die, the great and the *l*,
Ez 17:24 low the high tree, lift high the *l* tree,
Am 2: 7 the earth, and force the *l* out of the way.
8: 6 We will buy the *l* man for silver,
Zep 3:12 in your midst a people humble and *l*,
Mt 5: 5 [Blest are the *l*;
10:42 cup of cold water to one of these *l* ones
18: 4 Whoever makes himself *l*,
Lk 1:52 thrones and raised the *l* to high places.
Rom 12:16 and associate with those who are *l*.
1Cor 12:24 as to give greater honor to the *l* members,
2Cor 10: 1 (you say) when present in your midst am *l*,
Phil 3:21 He will give a new form to this *l* body of
Jas 4: 6 the proud but bestows his favor on the *l*."
Rv 20:12 I saw the dead, the great and the *l*,

LOYAL (18)

Jos 14: 8 people, but I was completely *l* to the LORD,
14: 9 you have been completely *l* to the LORD,
14:14 because he was completely *l* to the LORD,
22: 5 remain *l* to him; and serve him
23: 8 them, but you must remain *l* to the LORD,
Ru 3:10 You have been even more *l* now than before
1Sm 22:14 among all your servants is as *l* as David,
2Sm 20: 2 the Judahites remained *l* to their king.
1Kgs 12:20 None remained *l* to David's house except
2Kgs 18: 6 *L* to the LORD,
Est E:23 it may be, for us and for *l* Persians,
2Mc 6:23 would be *l* to the holy laws given by God.
Prv 18:24 but a true friend is more *l* than a brother.
Sir 1:24 *l* humility is his delight.
44:20 ordinance, and when tested he was found *l*.
46: 7 and in Moses' lifetime showed himself *l*,
Dn 11:32 *l* to their God shall take strong action.
Hos 12: 7 *l* and do right and always hope in your God.

LOYALLY (4)

Gn 21:23 but will act as *l* toward me and the land
32:11 that you have *l* performed for your servant:
Lk 22:28 who have stood *l* by me in my temptations.
Ti 3: 1 Remind people to be *l* subject to the

LOYALTIES (2)

2Sm 15: 6 stealing away the *l* of the men of Israel.
Mk 3:25 If a household is divided according to *l*,

LOYALTY (12)

Gn 24:49 have in mind to show true *l* to my master,
47:29 thigh as a sign of your constant *l* to me;
Dt 32:20 race they are, sons with no *l* in them!
2Sm 15:13 have transferred their *l* to Absalom."
20:19 whether *l* is finished or ended in Israel.'
Est B: 3 for constant devotion and steadfast *l*,
1Mc 14:35 When the Jewish people saw Simon's *l* and
14:35 the *l* and justice he had shown his nation.
2Mc 11:19 If you maintain your *l* to the government,
Sir 15:15 it is *l* to do his will.
40:12 will be wiped out, but *l* remains for ages.
Rom 1:31 in them men without conscience, without *l*,

LUCIUS (3)

1Mc 15:16 *L*, Consul of the Romans,
Acts 13: 1 Symeon known as Niger, *L* of Cyrene,
Rom 16:21 so, too, do my kinsmen *L*,

LUCK (2)

Gn 30:11 Leah then said, "What good *l*!"
Jas 2:16 and you say to them, "Good-bye and good *l*!

LUD (7)

Gn 10:22 Elam, Asshur, Arpachshad, *L*, and Aram.
1Chr 1:17 of Shem were Elam, Asshur, Arpachshad, *L*,
Jdt 2:23 He devastated Put and *L*,
Is 66:19 to Tarshish, Put and *L*,
Jer 46: 9 and Put, bearing your shields, Men of *L*,
Ez 27:10 *L* and Put were in your army as warriors;
30: 5 Ethiopia, Put, *L*,

LUDIM (2)

Gn 10:13 Mizraim became the father of the *L*,
1Chr 1:11 Mesraim became the father of the *L*,

LUHITH (2)

Is 15: 5 The ascent of *L* they climb weeping;
Jer 48: 5 The ascent of *L* they climb weeping;

LUKE (3)

Col 4:14 *L*, our dear physician,
2Tm 4:11 I have no one with me but *L*.
Phlm 1:24 as do Mark, Aristarchus, Demas, and *L*,

LUKEWARM (1)

Rv 3:16 But because you are *l*,

LUMBER (1)

1Kgs 5:23 up the rafts, and you shall take the *l*.

LUMBERMEN (2)

2Kgs 12:13 the LORD, and to the *l* and stone cutters,
22: 5 and *l* making repairs on the temple,

LUMINARIES (3)

Gn 1:15 and serve as *l* in the dome of the sky,
Wis 13: 2 or the mighty water, or the *l* of heaven,
Jas 1:17 from the Father of the heavenly *l*,

LUMP (2)

Sir 22: 2 The sluggard is like a *l* of dung;
Rom 9:21 right to make from the same *l* of clay

LUMPS (1)

Sir 43:21 he sends that turn the ponds to *l* of ice.

LUNATICS (1)

Mt 4:24 the possessed, the *l*, the paralyzed.

LUNCH (5)

Ru 2:18 and gave her what she had left over from *l*.
Dn 13:13 "Let us be off for home, it is time for *l*."
14:34 "Take the *l* you have to Daniel in the
14:37 Habakkuk, "take the *l* God has sent you."
Lk 14:12 "Whenever you give a *l* or dinner,

LURE (5)

Am 3: 5 earth by a snare when there is no *l* for it?
Mt 13:22 anxiety and the *l* of money choke it off.
Jas 1:14 and *l* of his own passion tempt every man.
2Pt 2: 2 Their lustful ways will *l* many away.
2:14 They *l* the weaker types.

LURED (3)

Dt 11:16 But be careful lest your heart be so *l*
12:30 land, you will be *l* into following them.
2Kgs 3: 3 which Jeroboam, son of Nebat, had *l* Israel;

LURK (1)

Is 35: 7 *l* will be a marsh for the reed and papyrus.

LURKING (3)

Gn 4: 7 but if not, sin is a demon *l* at the door:
Ps(s) 17:12 for prey, like young lions *l* in hiding.
Lam 3:10 A *l* bear he has been to me,

LURKS (2)

Ps(s) 10: 8 He *l* in ambush near the villages;
Prv 7:12 and at every corner she *l* in ambush

LUST (21)

Tb 8: 7 I take this wife of mine not because of *l*,
Prv 6:25 *L* not in your heart after her beauty,
13:19 *L* indulged starves the soul,
Wis 14:26 besmirching of souls, unnatural *l*,
Sir 9: 8 many perish, for *l* for it burns like fire.
Jer 2:24 who can restrain her *l*?
Ez 16:30 How wild your *l*!
16:36 Because you poured out your *l* and revealed
20:30 Will you *l* after their detestable idols?
23:11 her *l* was more depraved than her sister's,
Dn 13: 8 day for her walk, they began to *l* for her.
13:14 They admitted their *l*,
13:56 you, *l* has subverted your conscience.
Mt 23:25 leave the inside filled with loot and *l*!
Rom 1:27 women and burned with *l* for one another.
13:13 drunkenness, not in sexual excess and *l*,
Eph 4:19 they have abandoned themselves to *l*
5: 3 or promiscuousness or *l* of any sort,
Col 3: 5 evil desires, and that *l* which is idolatry.
2Pt 1: 4 you who have fled a world corrupted by *l*
Jude 1: 7 and the towns thereabout indulged in *l*,

LUSTED (7)

Ez 6: 9 me [and their eyes which *l* after idols].
23: 5 she *l* after her lovers, the Assyrians
23: 7 for whom she *l* [with all their idols].
23: 9 lovers, the Assyrians for whom she had *l*.
23:12 She too *l* after the Assyrians,
23:16 she *l* for them;
23:20 She *l* for the lechers of Egypt,

LUSTER (4)

Ps(s) 89:45 his *l* and hurled his throne to the ground.
Sir 46:12 names receive fresh *l* in their children!
Is 4: 2 The branch of the LORD will be *l* and glory,
Ez 10: 9 appeared to have the *l* of chrysolite stone.

LUSTFUL (8)

Sir 18:31 If you satisfy your *l* appetites they will
23: 6 not the *l* cravings of the flesh master me,
Jer 5: 8 *L* stallions they are,
Ez 16:26 with the Egyptians, your *l* neighbors,
Dn 13:11 to reveal their *l* desire to have her.
Eph 5: 5 no fornicator, no unclean or *l* person
2Pt 2: 2 Their *l* ways will lure many away.
2:18 with passion, with the *l* ways of the flesh,

LUSTFULLY (1)

Mt 5:28 anyone who looks *l* at a woman has already

LUSTING (2)

1Chr 5:25 God of their fathers by *l* after the gods
Sir 20: 3 Like a eunuch *l* for intimacy with a maiden

LUSTRAL (5)

Nm 19: 9 *l* water for the Israelite community.
19:13 the *l* water has not been splashed over him,
19:20 the *l* water has not been splashed over him,
19:21 the *l* water shall wash his garments,
31:23 it must also be purified with *l* water.

LUSTS (5)

Sir 18:30 Go not after your *l*,
Rom 1:24 them up in their *l* to unclean practices;
6:12 your mortal body and make you obey its *l*;
Gal 5:17 The flesh *l* against the spirit and the
2Pt 2: 7 the conduct of men unprincipled in their *l*.

LUXURIANT (2)

Sir 50:10 Like a *l* olive tree thick with fruit,
Hos 10: 1 is a *l* vine whose fruit matches its growth.

LUXURIES (1)

Eccl 2: 8 male and female singers and all human *l*.

LUXURIOUS (1)

Is 13:22 her castles, and jackals in her *l* palaces.

LUXURIOUSLY (3)

Mt 11: 8 someone *l* dressed?
11: 8 dress *l* are to be found in royal palaces.
Lk 7:25 someone dressed *l*?

LUXURY (4)

Prv 19:10 *L* is not befitting a fool;
Lk 7:25 those who dress in *l* and eat in splendor
Jas 5: 5 You lived in wanton *l* on the earth;
Rv 18:14 All your *l* and splendor are gone;

LUZ (7)

Gn 28:19 the former name of the town had been *L*.
35: 6 who were with him arrived in *L* [that is,
48: 3 appeared to me at *L* in the land of Canaan,
Jos 16: 2 Leaving Bethel for *L*,
18:13 over to the southern flank of *L* (that is,
Jgs 1:23 of Bethel, which formerly was called *L*.
1:26 where he built a city and called it *L*,

LYCAONIAN (2)

Acts 14: 6 they fled to the *L* towns of Lystra and
14:11 what Paul had done, they cried out in *L*,

LYCIA (3)

1Mc 8: 8 to give hostages and a section of *L,*
15:23 Sicyon, Caria, Samos, Pamphylia, *L,*
Acts 27: 5 and Pamphylia, and came to Myra in *L.*

LYDDA (4)

1Mc 11:34 of the three districts of Aphairema, *L,*
Acts 9:32 to God's holy people living in *L.*
9:35 All the inhabitants of *L* and Sharon,
9:38 Since *L* was near Joppa,

LYDIA (2)

1Mc 8: 8 and *L* from among their best provinces.
Acts 16:14 One who listened was a woman named *L,*

LYDIA'S (1)

Acts 16:40 the two first made their way to *L* house,

LYE (3)

Jb 9:30 with snow and cleanse my hands with *l,*
Jer 2:22 you scour it with soap, and use much *l,*
Mal 3: 2 the refiner's fire, or like the fuller's *l.*

LYING (86)

Gn 19:33 not aware of her *l* down or her getting up.
19:35 not aware of her *l* down or her getting up.
28:13 *l* I will give to you and your descendants.
Ex 5: 9 mind on it and pay no attention to *l* words."
14:30 When Israel saw the Egyptians *l* dead on
23: 5 who hates you *l* prostrate under its burden,
Lv 20:11 his father by *l* with his father's wife,
Nm 35: 5 with the city *l* in the center.
35:20 *l* in wait for him throws something at him,
35:22 or if without *l* in wait for him he throws
Dt 21: 1 *l* in the open on the land which the LORD,
Jos 7:10 Why are you *l* prostrate?
Jgs 16: 9 She had men *l* in wait in the chamber and
16:12 there were men *l* in wait in the chamber.
Ru 3: 8 around to find a woman *l* at his feet.
1Sm 5: 3 Dagon was *l* prone on the ground before the
5: 4 hands broken off and *l* on the threshold,
14:25 there was a honeycomb *l* on the ground,
26: 7 found Saul *l* asleep within the barricade,
31: 8 Saul and his three sons *l* on Mount Gilboa.
2Sm 4: 7 while Ishbaal was *l* asleep in his bedroom.
1Kgs 3:19 she smothered him by *l* on him.
13:18 He was *l* to him, however.
13:25 Some passers-by saw the body *l* in the road,
13:28 he went off and found the body *l* in the
21: 4 *L* down on his bed, he turned away
22:22 'I will go forth and become a *l* spirit in
22:23 the LORD has put a *l* spirit in the mouths
2Kgs 4:32 reached the house, he found the boy *l* dead.
2Chr 18:21 'I will go forth and become a *l* spirit in
18:22 So now the LORD has put a *l* spirit in the
Jdt 6:13 and left him *l* at the foot of the mountain;
14:15 the bedroom, and found him *l* on the floor,
1Mc 11: 4 its suburbs demolished, corpses *l* about,
2Mc 4:41 wood or handfuls of the ashes *l* there
10:26 *L* prostrate at the foot of the altar,
15:28 Nicanor *l* there in all his armor,
Ps(s) 31:19 Let dumbness strike their *l* lips that
109: 2 They have spoken to me with *l* tongues,
120: 2 O LORD, deliver me from *l* lip,
Prv 6:17 Haughty eyes, a *l* tongue,
12:17 of, but a *l* witness speaks deceitfully.
12:19 Truthful lips endure forever, the *l* tongue,
12:22 *L* lips are an abomination to the LORD,
17: 7 how much more, *l* words in a noble!
21: 6 He who makes a fortune by a *l* tongue is
23:34 like one now *l* in the depths of the sea,
26:28 The *l* tongue is its owner's enemy,
29:12 If a ruler listens to *l* words,
30: 8 Put falsehood and *l* far from me,
Wis 1:11 unpunished, and a *l* mouth slays the soul.
Sir 22:18 Small stones *l* on an open height will not
26: 5 *l* testimony are harder to bear than death,
Jer 8: 8 into falsehood by the *l* pen of the scribes!
9: 2 with *l,* and not with truth
9: 4 They have accustomed their tongues to *l,*
13:25 forgotten me, and trusted in the *l* idol,
14:14 *L* visions, foolish divination
23:32 against the prophets who prophesy *l* dreams,
Ez 13: 6 visions are false and their divination *l.*
13: 7 you saw false, and your divination *l?*
13: 8 spoken falsehood and have seen *l* visions,
13:19 *l* to my people who willingly hear lies.
17: 6 turned toward him, its roots *l* under him.
21:28 In their eyes this is but a *l* oracle;
21:34 planned with false visions and *l* divinations
22:28 are false and performing *l* divinations,
Dn 13:39 We saw them *l* together,
Hos 4: 2 False swearing, *l,*
Am 6: 4 *L* upon beds of ivory,
Hb 2:18 Or the molten image and *l* oracle,
Mt 9: 2 brought to him a paralyzed man *l* on a mat.
9:36 They were *l* prostrate from exhaustion,
Mk 2: 4 down the mat on which the paralytic was *l.*
7:30 the child *l* in bed and the demon gone.
Lk 2:16 and Joseph, and the baby *l* in the manger;
5:25 had been *l* on and went home praising God.
Jn 5: 3 crowded with sick people *l* there blind,
5: 6 a long time, said when he saw him *l* there,
8:44 *L* speech is his native tongue;
20: 5 in, and saw the wrappings *l* on the ground.
20: 7 covered the head not *l* with the wrappings,
Acts 23:21 More than forty of them are *l* in wait;
Eph 4:25 See to it, then, that you put an end to *l;*
Col 3: 9 Stop *l* to one another.
1Tm 2: 7 me, I am not *l* but speak the truth),

LYRE (16)

Gn 4:21 of all who play the *l* and the pipe.
1Chr 25: 3 inspired songs to the accompaniment of a *l,*
Ps(s) 33: 2 with the ten-stringed *l* chant his praises.
57: 9 Awake, O my soul; awake, *l* and harp!
71:22 will I give you thanks with music on the *l,*
81: 3 the timbrel, the pleasant harp and the *l.*
92: 4 night, With ten-stringed instrument and *l,*
108: 3 awake, *l* and harp; I will wake the dawn
144: 9 a ten-stringed *l* I will chant your praise,
150: 3 of the trumpet, praise him with *l* and harp,
Is 5:12 With harp and *l,* timbrel and flute
16:11 for Moab my breast moans like a *l,*
Dn 3: 4 hear the sound of the trumpet, flute, *l,*
3: 7 heard the sound of the trumpet, flute, *l,*
3:10 heard the sound of the trumpet, flute, *l,*
3:15 hear the sound of the trumpet, flute, *l,*

LYRES (17)

1Sm 10: 5 down from the high place preceded by *l,*
1Kgs 10:12 the king, and harps and *l* for the chanters.
1Chr 13: 8 enthusiasm, amid songs and music on *l,*
15:16 to play on musical instruments, harps, *l,*
15:21 led the chant on *l* set to "the eighth."
15:28 and cymbals, and the music of harps and *l.*
16: 5 These were to play on harps and *l,*
25: 1 accompaniment of *l* and harps and cymbals.
25: 6 the accompaniment of cymbals, harps and *l,*
2Chr 5:12 in fine linen, with cymbals, harps and *l,*
9:11 also *l* and harps for the chanters.
20:28 of the LORD, with harps, *l* and trumpets.
29:25 *l* according to the prescriptions of David,
Neh 12:27 and the music of cymbals, harps, and *l.*
1Mc 13:51 the music of harps and cymbals and *l,*
Is 30:29 Israel, accompanied by the timbrels and *l.*
Ez 26:13 the sound of your *l* shall be heard no more.

LYRIC (1)

Sir 44: 5 psalms, or discoursers on *l* themes;

LYRICS (1)

Ps(s) 137: 3 our captors asked of us the *l* of our songs,

LYSANIAS (1)

Lk 3: 1 and Trachonitis, and *L* tetrarch of Abilene,

LYSIAS (28)

1Mc 3:32 He left *L,* a nobleman of royal blood
3:35 *L* was to send an army against them to
3:38 *L* chose Ptolemy, son of Dorymenes
4:26 went and told *L* all that had occurred.
4:34 of *L'* men fell in hand-to-hand fighting.
4:35 When *L* saw his ranks beginning to give way,
6: 6 that *L* had gone at first with a strong
6:17 When *L* learned that the king was dead,
6:55 *L* heard that Philip,
7: 2 Antiochus and *L* to bring them to him.
2Mc 10:11 he put a certain *L* in charge of the
11: 1 Very soon afterward, *L,*
11: 6 that *L* was besieging the strongholds,
11:12 *L* himself escaped only by shameful flight.
11:13 But *L* was not a stupid man.
11:15 common good, agreed to all that *L* proposed;
11:15 all the written requests of Maccabeus to *L.*
11:16 of the letter which *L* wrote to the Jews:
11:16 *L* sends greetings to the Jewish people.
11:22 Antiochus sends greetings to his brother *L.*
11:35 Whatever *L,* kinsman of the king
12: 1 were made, *L* returned to the king,
13: 2 a large force, and that with him was *L,*
13: 4 When the king was shown by *L* that Menelaus
13:26 But *L* took the platform,
14: 2 away with Antiochus and his guardian *L.*
Acts 23:26 *L* sends greetings to His Excellency Felix,
24:22 the case when *L* the commander arrives."

LYSIMACHUS' (6)

2Mc 4:29 Menelaus left his brother *L* as his
4:39 thefts had been committed by *L*
4:39 the people assembled in protest against *L.*
4:40 *L* launched an unjustified attack against
4:41 Reacting against *L'* attack,
4:41 them in wild confusion at *L* and his men.

LYSTRA (6)

Acts 14: 6 *L* and Derbe and to the surrounding country,
14: 8 *L* there was a man who was lame from birth;
14:21 their steps to *L* and Iconium first,
16: 1 next he came to *L,*
16: 2 in *L* and Iconium spoke highly of him,
2Tm 3:11 and sufferings in Antioch, Iconium, and *L.*

M

MAACAH (20)

Gn 22:24 Tebah, Gaham, Tahash, and *M.*
2Sm 3: 3 Absalom, son of *M* the daughter of Talmai,
10: 6 as the king of *M* with one thousand men,
10: 8 and *M* remained apart in the open country.
1Kgs 2:39 servants ran away to Achish, son of *M,*
15: 2 His mother's name was *M,*
15:10 His grandmother's name was *M,*
15:13 *M* from her position as queen mother,
1Chr 2:48 *M,* Caleb's concubine,
3: 2 the third, Absalom, son of *M,*
7:15 Machir took a wife whose name was *M;*
7:16 *M,* Machir's wife, bore a son
8:29 founder of Gibeon whose wife's name was *M;*
9:35 founder of Gibeon, whose wife's name was *M.*
19: 7 along with the king of *M* and his army,
27:16 for the Simeonites, Shephatiah, son of *M;*
2Chr 11:20 After her, he married *M,*
11:21 Rehoboam loved *M,* daughter of Absalom,
11:22 Rehoboam constituted Abijah, son of *M,*
15:16 *M,* the mother of King Asa,

MAACATH (1)

Jos 13:13 so that Geshur and *M* survive in the midst

MAACATHITE (1)

1Chr 4:19 were Shimon the Garmite and Ishi the *M.*

MAACATHITES (4)

Dt 3:14 far as the border of the Geshurites and *M,*
Jos 12: 5 as the boundary of the Geshurites and *M,*
13:11 and the territory of the Geshurites and *M,*
13:13 did not dislodge the Geshurites and *M,*

MAADAI (1)

Ezr 10:34 *M,* Amram,

MAADIAH (2)

Neh 12: 5 Iddo, Ginnethon, Abijah, Mijamin, *M,*
12:17 for *M,* Piltai; for Bilgah, Shammua;

MAAI (1)

Neh 12:36 Shemaiah, Azarel, Milalai, Gilalai, *M,*

MAARATH (1)

Jos 15:59 Halhul, Beth-zur, Gedor, *M,*

MAASAI (1)

1Chr 9:12 *M,* son of Adiel, son of Jahzerah,

MAASEIAH (22)

1Chr 15:18 Jehiel, Unni, Eliab, Benaiah, *M,*
15:20 Shemiramoth, Jehiel, Unni, Eliab, *M,*
2Chr 26:11 by Jeiel the scribe and *M* the recorder,
28: 7 Zichri, an Ephraimite warrior, killed *M,*
34: 8 land, he sent Shaphan, son of Azaliah, *M,*
Ezr 10:18 *M,* Eliezer, Jarib, and Gedaliah.
10:21 *M,* Elijah, Shemaiah, Jehiel, and Uzziah
10:22 Elioenai, *M,*
10:30 Adna, Chelal, Benaiah, *M,*
Neh 3:23 after them, Azariah, son of *M,*
8: 4 Shema, Anaiah, Uriah, Hilkiah, and *M,*
8: 7 Jamin, Akkub, Shabbethai, Hodiah, *M,*
10:26 Pilha, Shobek, Rehum, Hashabnah, *M,*
11: 5 *M,* son of Baruch, son of Colhozeh,
11: 7 son of Pelaiah, son of Kolaiah, son of *M,*
12:41 the magistrates, the priests Eliakim, *M,*
12:42 Hananiah, with the trumpets, and *M,*
Jer 21: 1 and the priest Zephaniah, son of *M,*
29:21 son of Kolaiah, and Zedekiah, son of *M:*
29:25 and to Zephaniah, the priest, son of *M,*
35: 4 to the princes' room, above the room of *M,*
37: 3 and Zephaniah, son of *M* the priest,

MAATH (1)

Lk 3:26 son of Esli, son of Naggai, son of *M,*

MAAZ (1)

1Chr 2:27 Ram, the first-born of Jerahmeel, were *M,*

MAAZIAH (2)

1Chr 24:18 to Delaiah, the twenty-fourth to *M.*
Neh 10: 9 Baruch, Meshullam, Abijah, Mijamin, *M,*

MACCABEUS (31)

1Mc 2: 4 Judas, who was called *M;*
2:66 he will be a father to you, And Judas *M,*
3: 1 Then his son Judas, who was called *M,*
5:24 Judas *M* and his brother Jonathan crossed

MACCABEUS (cont.)

5:34 army of Timothy realized that it was *M*,
8:20 "Judas, called *M*, and his brothers,
2Mc 2:19 is the story of Judas *M* and his brothers,
5:27 But Judas *M* and about nine others withdrew
8: 1 Judas *M* and his companions entered the
8: 5 Once *M* got his men organized,
8:16 *M* assembled his men,
10: 1 When *M* and his companions under the Lord's
10:16 *M* and his companions,
10:19 sustain a siege, *M* left Simon and Joseph,
10:21 When *M* was told what had happened he
10:25 *M* and his men made supplication to God,
10:30 They surrounded *M*, and shielding him
10:33 For four days *M* and his men eagerly
10:35 dawned, twenty young men in the army of *M*,
11: 6 When *M* and his men learned that Lysias was
11: 7 *M* himself was the first to take up arms,
11:15 *M*, solicitous for the common good,
11:15 all the written requests of *M* to Lysias.
12:19 and Sosipater, two of *M'* captains,
12:20 Meanwhile, *M* divided his army into cohorts,
13:24 He approved of *M* and left him as military
14: 6 Jews called Hasideans, led by Judas *M*,
14:27 *M* as a prisoner to Antioch without delay.
14:30 But *M* noticed that Nicanor was becoming
15: 7 *M* remained confident, fully convinced
15:21 *M*, contemplating the hosts before him,

MACE (1)

Gn 49:10 from Judah, or the *m* from between his legs,

MACEDON (1)

1Mc 6: 2 by Alexander, son of Philip, king of *M*,

MACEDONIA (22)

Acts 16: 9 man of *M* stood before him and invited him,
16: 9 invited him, "Come over to *M* and help us."
16:10 made efforts to get across to *M*,
16:12 in the district of *M* and a Roman colony.
18: 5 When Silas and Timothy came down from *M*,
19:21 mind to travel through *M* and Achaia again,
19:22 Timothy and Erastus, into *M* ahead of him,
19:29 Paul's traveling companions from *M*.
20: 1 goodbye and set out on his journey to *M*.
20: 3 so he decided to return by way of *M*.
Rom 15:26 *M* and Achaia have kindly decided to make a
1Cor 16: 5 come to you after I have passed through *M*.
2Cor 1:16 you, both on my way to *M* and on my return,
2:13 I said good-bye to them and went off to *M*.
7: 5 arrived in *M* I was restless and exhausted.
8: 1 of God conferred on the churches of *M*.
11: 9 brothers who came from *M* supplied
Phil 4:15 start of my evangelizing, when I left *M*,
1Thes 1: 7 for all the believers of *M* and Achaia.
1: 8 This is true not only in *M* and Achaia;
4:10 respect to all the brothers throughout *M*.
1Tm 1: 3 I gave you when I was on my way to *M*:

MACEDONIAN (3)

Est E:10 Haman, son of Hammedatha, a *M*,
1Mc 1: 1 After Alexander the *M*, Philip's son,
Acts 27: 2 With us was a *M*, Aristarchus

MACEDONIANS (6)

Est E:14 transfer the rule of the Persians to the *M*.
1Mc 8: 5 Philip and Perseus, king of the *M*,
2Mc 8:20 Jews fought along with four thousand *M*;
8:20 yet when the *M* were hard pressed,
2Cor 9: 2 about you to the *M* with respect to it,
9: 4 any *M* come with me and find you unready;

MACHBANNAI (1)

1Chr 12:14 ninth, Jeremiah tenth, and *M* eleventh.

MACHBENAH (1)

1Chr 2:49 father of Madmannah, Sheva, the father of *M*,

MACHI (1)

Nm 13:15 son of *M*, of the tribe of Gad.

MACHINE (3)

1Mc 13:43 He made a siege *m*,
13:44 men who had been on the siege *m* jumped
2Mc 12:15 Jericho without battering-ram or siege *m*;

MACHINES (8)

2Chr 26:15 He also built *m* in Jerusalem,
1Mc 6:51 the sanctuary, setting up artillery and *m*,
6:52 countered by setting up *m* of their own,
9:64 Bethbasi, and constructing siege *m*
9:67 forth from the city and set fire to the *m*.
11:20 and they set up many *m* against it.
15:25 troops and with the siege *m* he had made.
2Mc 12:27 were large supplies of *m* and missiles.

MACHIR (21)

Gn 50:23 son *M* were also born on Joseph's knees.
Nm 26:29 through *M* the clan of the Machirites,
26:29 through Gilead, a descendant of *M*,
27: 1 son of Hepher, son of Gilead, son of *M*,
32:39 The descendants of *M*,
32:40 [Moses gave Gilead to *M*,
36: 1 clan of descendants of Gilead, son of *M*,
Dt 3:15 To *M* I gave Gilead,
Jos 13:31 in Bashan, fell to the descendants of *M*,
13:31 for half the clans descended from *M*.
17: 1 since his eldest son, *M*,
17: 3 son of Hepher, son of Gilead, son of *M*,
Jgs 5:14 From *M* came down commanders,
2Sm 9: 4 Ziba answered, "He is in the house of *M*,
9: 5 and had him brought from the house of *M*,
17:27 Nahash from Rabbah of the Ammonites, *M*,
1Chr 2:21 had relations with the daughter of *M*,
2:23 all, which had belonged to the sons of *M*,
7:14 she bore *M*, the father of Gilead.
7:15 *M* took a wife whose name was Maacah;
7:17 the descendants of Gilead, the son of *M*,

MACHIRITES (1)

Nm 26:29 through Machir the clan of the *M*,

MACHIR'S (1)

1Chr 7:16 Maacah, *M* wife, bore a son

MACHPELAH (6)

Gn 23: 9 him to sell me the cave of *M* that he owns;
23:17 Thus Ephron's field in *M*,
23:19 wife Sarah in the cave of the field of *M*,
25: 9 and Ishmael buried him in the cave of *M*,
49:30 the Hittite, the cave in the field of *M*,
50:13 buried him in the cave in the field of *M*,

MACRON (1)

2Mc 10:12 Ptolemy, surnamed *M*, had taken the lead

MAD (14)

Dt 28:34 driven *m* by what your eyes must look upon.
1Sm 21:15 "You see the man is *m*.
2Mc 14: 5 opportunity to further his *m* scheme
Eccl 2: 2 Of laughter I said; *M!*"
Wis 14:28 For they either go *m* with enjoyment,
Jer 25:16 and go *m* because of the sword I will send
51: 7 its wine, with this they have become *m*.
Hos 9: 7 is a fool, the man of the spirit is *m!*"
Mt 11:18 nor drinking, and people say, 'He is *m!*'
Lk 7:33 nor drinking wine, and you say, 'He is *m!*'
Jn 7:20 "You are *m!*"
Acts 26:24 with a shout, "Paul, you are *m!*
26:24 And your great learning is driving you *m!*"
26:25 Excellency," answered Paul, "I am not *m*.

MADAI (2)

Gn 10: 2 Gomer, Magog, *M*,
1Chr 1: 5 of Japheth were Gomer, Magog, *M*,

MADE (1159)

Gn 1: 7 God *m* the dome,
1:16 God *m* the two great lights,
1:16 and he *m* the stars.
1:25 God *m* all kinds of wild animals,
1:31 God looked at everything he had *m*,
2: 3 God blessed the seventh day and *m* it holy,
2: 4 the LORD God *m* the earth and the heavens
2: 9 Out of the ground the LORD God *m* various
3: 1 of all the animals that the LORD God had *m*.
3: 7 together and *m* loincloths for themselves.
3:21 his wife the LORD God *m* leather garments,
5: 1 man, he *m* him in the likeness of God;
6: 6 regretted that he had *m* man on the earth,
6: 7 of the air, for I am sorry that I *m* them."
7: 4 earth every moving creature that I have *m*."
8: 1 So God *m* a wind sweep over the earth,
8: 6 Noah opened the hatch he had *m* in the ark,
9: 6 For in the image of God has man been *m*.
9:15 *m* between me and you and all living beings,
14: 2 king of Goiim *m* war on Bera king of Sodom,
14:23 lest you should say, 'I *m* Abram rich.'
15:18 that the LORD *m* a covenant with Abram,
18:19 for Abraham the promises he *m* about him."
21:27 them to Abimelech and the two *m* a pact.
21:32 they had thus *m* the pact in Beer-sheba,
22:19 for Beer-sheba, where Abraham *m* his home.
24: 7 by oath the promise he then *m* to me,
24:10 he *m* his way to the city of Nahor in Aram
24:11 he *m* the camels kneel by the well outside
24:21 not the LORD had *m* his errand successful.
24:31 when I have *m* the house ready for you,
24:56 that the LORD has *m* my errand successful;
25: 6 he *m* grants while he was still living,
25:11 Isaac, who *m* his home near Beerlahai-roi.
26:17 and *m* the Wadi Gerar his regular campsite.
26:30 Isaac then *m* a feast for them,
27:38 Isaac, however, *m* no reply;
28:20 Jacob then *m* this vow:
29:31 that Leah was unloved, he *m* her fruitful,
30:22 he heard her prayer and *m* her fruitful.
30:37 and he *m* white stripes in them by peeling
31:13 a memorial stone and *m* a vow to me.
31:21 Thus he *m* his escape with all that he had.
31:39 I *m* good the loss myself.
31:46 So they got some stones and *m* a mound;
33:17 for himself and *m* booths for his livestock.
35:14 upon it he *m* a libation and poured out oil.
37: 3 and he *m* him a long tunic.
38:29 "What a breach you have *m* for yourself!"
39: 4 to Joseph and *m* him his personal attendant;
41:39 "Since God has *m* all this known to you,
41:51 "God has *m* me forget entirely the
41:52 *m* me fruitful in the land of my affliction."
43:34 So they drank freely and *m* merry with him.
44:12 and opened it, and when a search was *m*,
45: 1 when he *m* himself known to his brothers.
45: 8 and he has *m* of me a father to Pharaoh,
45: 9 God has *m* me lord of all Egypt;
45:25 So they left Egypt and *m* their way to
47:18 spent and our livestock *m* over to my lord,
47:26 Joseph *m* it a law for the land in Egypt,
50: 5 *m* me promise on oath to bury him in the
50: 6 your father, as he *m* you promise on oath."
Ex 5: 8 quota of bricks as they have previously *m*.
5:15 foremen came and *m* this appeal to Pharaoh:
7: 1 I have *m* you as God to Pharaoh,
8: 3 too, *m* frogs overrun the land of Egypt.
8: 8 he had *m* to Pharaoh about the frogs;
9:12 But the LORD *m* Pharaoh obstinate,
10: 1 for I have *m* him and his servants obdurate
10:20 of Egypt, the LORD *m* Pharaoh obstinate,
10:27 But the LORD *m* Pharaoh obstinate,
11: 3 The LORD indeed *m* the Egyptians
11:10 presence, the LORD *m* Pharaoh obstinate,
12:36 The LORD indeed had *m* the Egyptians so
13: 3 Nothing *m* with leaven must be eaten.
13:19 had *m* the Israelites swear solomnly that,
14: 6 So Pharaoh *m* his chariots ready and
14: 8 So obstinate had the LORD *m* Pharaoh that
15:16 the people you had *m* your own passed over.
15:17 place where you *m* your seat, O LORD,
15:19 the LORD *m* the waters of the sea flow back
16:31 and it tasted like wafers *m* with honey.
20:11 days the LORD *m* the heavens and the earth,
20:11 has blessed the sabbath day and *m* it holy.
22:10 the oath, and no restitution is to be *m*.
24: 8 covenant which the LORD has *m* with you
26: 8 Eleven such sheets are to be *m*;
26:17 all the boards of the Dwelling are to be *m*.
26:24 both boards in the corners are to be *m*.
27: 2 *m* that they spring directly from the altar.
28: 2 Aaron you shall have sacred vestments *m*.
28: 8 from it and, like it, be *m* of gold thread,
28:15 of decision you shall also have *m*,
28:22 cords, have been *m* for the breastpiece,
28:39 The miter shall be *m* of fine linen.
28:40 shall have tunics and sashes and turbans *m*.
29:23 of bread, one of the cakes *m* with oil,
29:33 was *m* at their ordination and consecration;
29:43 hence, it will be *m* sacred by my glory.
30:10 atonement is to be *m* once a year
31:17 days the LORD *m* the heavens and the earth,
32: 4 gold with a graving tool, *m* a molten calf.
32:16 tablets that were *m* by God,
32:20 Taking the calf they had *m*,
32:20 on the water and *m* the Israelites drink.
33:17 request, too, which you have just *m*,
34:27 have *m* a covenant with you and with Israel."
36: 6 a proclamation to be *m* throughout the camp:
36: 8 *m* the Dwelling with its ten sheets woven
36:11 Loops of violet yarn were *m* along the edge
36:13 Then fifty clasps of gold were *m*,
36:14 Eleven such sheets were *m*.
36:17 Fifty loops were *m* along the edge of the
36:18 Fifty bronze clasps were *m* with which the
36:19 for the tent was *m* of rams' skins dyed red,
36:20 wood were *m* as walls for the Dwelling.
36:22 way all the boards of the Dwelling were *m*.
36:29 is how both boards in the corners were *m*.
36:31 Bars of acacia wood were also *m*,
36:33 was *m* to reach across from end to end.
36:34 were *m* on them as holders for the bars,
36:36 wood, with gold hooks, were *m* for it,
36:37 the entrance of the tent was *m* of violet,
37: 1 Bezalel *m* the ark of acacia wood,
37: 4 of acacia wood were *m* and plated with gold;
37: 6 The propitiatory was *m* of pure gold,
37: 7 *m* for the two ends of the propitiatory,
37:10 The table was *m* of acacia wood,
37:15 were *m* of acacia wood and plated with gold.
37:17 The lampstand was *m* of pure beaten gold
37:23 shears and trays, were *m* of pure gold.
37:25 The altar of incense was *m* of acacia wood,
37:28 were *m* of acacia wood and plated with gold.
38: 1 altar of holocausts was *m* of acacia wood,
38: 2 were *m* that sprang directly from the altar.
38: 3 and fire pans, were likewise *m* of bronze.
38: 4 was *m* for the altar and placed round it,
38: 6 *m* of acacia wood and plated with bronze.
38: 7 altar was *m* in the form of a hollow box.
38: 8 was *m* from the mirrors of the women who
38: 9 The court was *m* as follows.
38:22 who *m* all that the LORD commanded Moses,
38:30 With this were *m* the pedestals at the
39: 4 *m* for it and joined to its two upper ends.

39: 5 from it, and like it, was *m* of gold thread,
39:15 like cords, were *m* for the breastpiece,
39:19 Two other gold rings were *m* and put on the
39:20 Two more gold rings were *m* and fastened to
39:24 of the robe pomegranates were *m* of violet,
39:25 bells of pure gold were also *m* and put
39:29 work *m* of fine linen twined and of violet,
39:30 diadem was *m* of pure gold and inscribed,
Lv 2: 4 cakes *m* of fine flour mixed with oil,
2: 8 A cereal offering that is *m* in any of
7:12 and cakes *m* of fine flour mixed with oil
7:25 from which an oblation is *m* to the LORD,
8:15 He also *m* atonement for the altar by
8:26 cake, one loaf of bread *m* with oil,
13:48 or on a hide or anything *m* of leather,
14: 8 thus *m* clean may he come inside the camp;
14:20 the priest has thus *m* atonement for him,
14:42 shall be *m* and plastered on the house.
14:53 When he has thus *m* atonement for it,
16:17 *m* atonement for himself and his household,
16:30 atonement is *m* for you to make you clean,
16:32 "This atonement is to be *m* by the priest
16:34 be *m* for all the sins of the Israelites."
17:11 blood, I have *m* you put it on the altar,
17:11 may thereby be *m* for your own lives,
21:15 I, the LORD, have *m* him sacred."
22:32 It is I who *m* you sacred and led you out
23:17 two loaves of bread *m* of two tenths
23:28 atonement is *m* for you before the LORD,
23:43 land of Egypt, I *m* them dwell in booths.
26:45 of the covenant I *m* with their forefathers,
27: 8 with the means of the one who *m* the vow.
27:16 its valuation shall be *m* according to the
27:17 is *m* at the beginning of a jubilee period,
27:25 "Every valuation shall be *m* according to
27:33 are thus chosen, and no exchange may be *m*.
Nm 3:13 I *m* all the first-born in Israel sacred to
4:34 *m* a registration among the Kohathites,
4:38 was then *m* among the Gershonites,
4:42 the registration was *m* among the Merarites,
5: 8 of the ill-gotten goods can be *m*,
7: 2 an offering was *m* by the princes of Israel,
7:18 Zuar, prince of Issachar, *m* his offering.
8: 4 The lampstand was *m* of beaten gold in both
8:21 and *m* atonement for them to purify them.
11: 8 loaves, which tasted like cakes *m* with oil.
13:26 of Paran at Kadesh, *m* a report to them all,
15:28 when atonement has been *m* for him,
17:12 the incense and *m* atonement for the people,
18: 8 charge of the contributions *m* to me
18:30 *m* your contribution from the best part,
21: 2 Israel then *m* this vow to the LORD:
21: 9 Moses accordingly *m* a bronze serpent and
25:13 God and thus *m* amends for the Israelites."
30: 5 vow or any pledge she has *m* remains valid.
30: 6 any pledge she has *m* becomes null and void;
30: 8 the vow or pledge she had *m* remains valid.
30: 9 he thereby annuls the vow she had *m*
30:12 vow or any pledge she has *m* remains valid.
30:15 as valid any vow or any pledge she has *m*;
32:13 *m* them wander in the desert forty years,
Dt 1:15 and *m* them your leaders and officials over
1:28 Our kinsmen have *m* us fainthearted by
2:30 *m* him stubborn in mind and obstinate in
4:23 which the LORD, your God, has *m* with you,
4:31 which under oath he *m* with your fathers.
5: 2 our God, *m* a covenant with us at Horeb;
9: 5 promise which he *m* on oath to your fathers,
9: 9 of the covenant which the LORD *m* with you.
9:12 and have *m* for themselves a molten idol,
9:21 the calf, the sinful object you had *m*,
10: 3 So I *m* an ark of acacia wood,
10: 5 and placed the tablets in the ark I had *m*.
10:22 *m* you as numerous as the stars of the sky.
17:18 he shall have a copy of this law *m*
26:19 glory above all other nations he has *m*,
27: 5 *m* of stones that no iron tool has touched.
28:69 the covenant which he *m* with them at Horeb.
29:24 had *m* with them when he brought them out
31:16 the covenant which I have *m* with them.
32: 6 Has he not *m* you and established you?
32:15 who *m* them and scorned their saving Rock.
33: 4 he *m* the community of Jacob his domain,
33:20 "Blessed be he who has *m* Gad so vast!
Jos 2:17 how we will fulfill the oath you *m* us take:
2:20 be quit of the oath you have *m* us take."
5: 3 So Joshua *m* flint knives and circumcised
7: 4 three thousand of the people *m* the attack,
9:15 So Joshua *m* an alliance with them and
9:27 the Israelites, at the same time he *m* them,
10: 1 of Gibeon had *m* their peace with Israel,
10: 9 And when Joshua *m* his surprise attack upon
11:19 no city *m* peace with the Israelites;
17: 2 now *m* to the other descendants of Manasseh,
19:50 He rebuilt the city and *m* it his home.
21:45 LORD *m* to the house of Israel was broken;
22:28 the altar of the LORD which our fathers *m*,
23:14 God, *m* to you has remained unfulfilled.
23:15 God, *m* to you has been fulfilled for you,
24: 3 I *m* his descendants numerous,
24:25 So Joshua *m* a covenant with the people
24:25 *m* statutes and ordinances for them
Jgs 1:23 of Joseph had a reconnaissance *m* of Bethel,

2: 4 had *m* these threats to all the Israelites,
2:22 Israelites were to be *m* to prove
3:10 into his power, so that he *m* him subject.
3:16 *m* himself a two-edged dagger a foot long,
3:26 their delay Ehud *m* good his escape and,
8: 8 to Penuel and *m* the same request of them,
8:27 Gideon *m* an ephod out of the gold and
9:18 sons upon one stone, and have *m* Abimelech,
11:11 people *m* him their leader and commander.
11:30 Jephthah *m* a vow to the LORD.
11:35 *m* a vow to the LORD and I cannot retract."
11:36 replied, "you have *m* a vow to the LORD.
17: 3 who *m* of them a carved idol overlaid with
17: 5 He also *m* an ephod and household idols,
18:24 "You have taken my god, which I *m*,
18:27 Having taken what Micah had *m*,
18:31 maintained the carved idol Micah had *m*
19: 3 the girl's father joyfully *m* him welcome.
19: 7 The man still *m* a move to go,
20:37 men in ambush *m* a sudden dash into Gibeah,
21:15 had *m* a breach among the tribes of Israel.
Ru 1: 6 She then *m* ready to go back from the
1:20 the Almighty has *m* it very bitter for me.
1Sm 1: 5 her, though the LORD had *m* her barren.
1: 7 each time they *m* their pilgrimage to the
1:11 LORD, weeping copiously, and she *m* a vow,
2:20 woman for the gift she has *m* to the LORD!"
7:16 He *m* a yearly journey,
11:15 the presence of the LORD, they *m* Saul king.
12: 9 the king of Moab, who *m* war against them.
15:11 "I regret having *m* Saul king,
15:33 "As your sword has *m* women childless,
15:35 LORD regretted having *m* him king of Israel.
16:21 very fond of him, *m* him his armor-bearer,
18:27 David *m* preparations and sallied forth
19:12 a window, and he *m* his escape in safety.
20:37 When the boy *m* for the spot where Jonathan
22: 8 has *m* an agreement with the son of Jesse?
23:18 They *m* a joint agreement before the LORD
25:30 promise of success he has *m* concerning you,
26:21 been a fool and have *m* a serious mistake."
27: 8 men went up and *m* raids on the Geshurites,
28:21 and fulfilled the request you *m* of me.
30:25 he *m* it a law and a custom in Israel,
2Sm 2: 9 Mahanaim, where he *m* him king over Gilead,
2:25 single group, and *m* a stand on the hilltop.
2:32 Joab and his men *m* an all-night march,
5: 3 King David *m* an agreement with them there
6: 5 while David and all the Israelites *m* merry
7:23 so that you have *m* yourself renowned by
7:25 *m* concerning your servant and his house,
7:28 *m* this generous promise to your servant.
10: 9 he *m* a selection from all the picked
10:19 then *m* peace with the Israelites and
11: 3 inquiries *m* about the woman and was told,
11:13 ate and drank with David, who *m* him drunk.
11:17 men of the city *m* a sortie against Joab,
12: 4 lamb and *m* a meal of it for his visitor."
15: 7 Hebron and fulfill a vow I *m* to the LORD.
15: 8 in Geshur in Aram, your servant *m* this vow:
16:21 odious you have *m* yourself to your father,
22:12 He *m* darkness the shelter about him,
22:34 Who *m* my feet swift as those of hinds and
22:36 shield, and your help has *m* me great.
22:37 You *m* room for my steps;
22:38 did I turn again till I *m* an end of them.
22:44 you *m* me head over nations.
22:48 who *m* peoples subject to me and helped me
23: 5 He has *m* an eternal covenant with me,
1Kgs 1:43 "Our lord, King David, has *m* Solomon king.
2: 4 the promise he *m* on my behalf when he said,
2:24 David and *m* of me a dynasty as he promised,
2:27 had *m* in Shiloh about the house of Eli.
3: 7 O LORD, my God, you have *m* me,
3:10 was pleased that Solomon *m* this request.
4:20 they ate and drank and *m* merry.
6: 4 with trellises were *m* for the temple,
6:12 you the promise I *m* to your father David.
6:21 *m* in front of the sanctuary a cedar altar,
6:23 each ten cubits high, *m* of olive wood.
6:31 the sanctuary, doors of olive wood were *m*;
7: 6 he *m* fifty cubits long and thirty wide.
7:10 (The foundation was *m* of fine,
7:17 chainlike mesh were *m* to cover the (nodes
7:23 it was *m* with a circular rim,
7:27 Ten stands were also *m* of bronze,
7:37 This was how the ten stands were *m*,
7:38 Ten bronze basins were then *m*,
7:40 When Hiram *m* the pots,
7:45 All these articles which Hiram *m* for King
7:48 Solomon had all the articles *m* for the
8: 9 when the LORD *m* a covenant with the
8:15 who with his own mouth *m* a promise to my
8:20 LORD has fulfilled the promise that he *m*:
8:21 which he *m* with our fathers when he
8:24 kept the promise you *m* to my father David,
8:25 further promise you *m* to my father David,
8:26 promise which you *m* to my father David,
8:56 promise he *m* through his servant Moses.
10: 9 the LORD has *m* you king to carry out
10:12 With the wood the king *m* supports for the
10:16 King Solomon *m* two hundred shields of
10:18 The king also had a large ivory throne *m*,

10:27 *m* silver as common in Jerusalem as stones,
11:25 who *m* a rift in Israel by becoming king
12:20 an assembly and *m* him king over all Israel.
12:28 the king *m* two calves of gold and said to
12:31 temples on the high places and *m* priests
12:32 with sacrifices to the calves he had *m*;
13:33 but again *m* priests for the high places
14: 4 She *m* the journey to Shiloh and entered
14: 7 people and *m* you ruler of my people Israel.
14: 9 you have gone and *m* for yourself strange
14:15 because they *m* sacred poles for themselves
14:26 as all the gold shields *m* under Solomon.
14:27 them, King Rehoboam had bronze shields *m*,
15:12 removing all the idols his father had *m*.
15:13 she had *m* an outrageous object for Asherah.
16: 2 dust and *m* you ruler of my people Israel,
16:33 built in Samaria, and also *m* a sacred pole.
18:10 he *m* each kingdom and nation swear they
18:32 and *m* a trench around the altar large
18:45 Ahab mounted his chariot and *m* for Jezreel.
20:12 and they *m* ready to storm the city.
20:34 So he *m* an agreement with him and then set
21: 4 answer Naboth the Jezreelite had *m* to him:
22:11 *m* himself horns of iron and said,
22:45 also *m* peace with the king of Israel.
22:49 *m* Tarshish ships to go to Ophir for gold;
2Kgs 3: 2 pillar of Baal, which his father had *m*,
4:42 barley loaves *m* from the first fruits,
11:13 Athaliah heard the noise *m* by the people,
11:17 Then Jehoiada *m* a covenant between the
12: 5 For the priests Joash *m* this rule:
12: 7 had not *m* needed repairs on the temple.
17:15 covenant which he had *m* with their fathers,
17:16 and *m* for themselves two molten calves;
17:16 they also *m* a sacred pole and worshiped
17:21 from the house of David, they *m* Jeroboam,
17:29 the high places which the Samarians had *m*,
17:30 the Babylonians *m* Marduk and his consort;
17:30 the men of Cuth *m* Nergal;
17:30 the men of Hamath *m* Ashima,
17:31 the men of Avva *m* Nibhaz and Tartak;
17:35 When he *m* a covenant with them,
17:38 The covenant which I *m* with you,
18: 4 the sacred Nehushtan which Moses had *m*,
19:15 You have *m* the heavens and the earth.
20:11 who *m* the shadow retreat the ten steps it
20:18 descendants shall be taken and *m* servants
21: 7 The Asherah idol he had *m*,
23: 3 the king *m* a covenant before the LORD that
23: 4 all the objects that had been *m* for Baal,
23:12 He also demolished the altars *m* by the
23:12 and the altars *m* by Manasseh in the two
25:16 Solomon had *m* for the house of the LORD,
1Chr 11: 3 and there David *m* a covenant with them in
11: 6 first shall be *m* the chief commander."
11:14 He *m* a stand on the sown ground,
14:17 and the LORD *m* all the nations fear him.
16:15 he *m* binding for a thousand generations
16:26 of nought, but the LORD *m* the heavens.
16:30 he has *m* the world firm,
17:17 For you have *m* a promise regarding your
17:22 You *m* your people Israel your own forever,
17:25 your servant has *m* bold to pray before you.
18: 6 *m* David victorious in all his campaigns.
18:13 *m* David victorious in all his campaigns.
19:19 *m* peace with David and became his subjects.
22: 5 built for the LORD must be *m* so magnificent
23: 1 he *m* his son Solomon king over Israel.
24: 6 *m* a record of it in the presence of the
26:10 not the first-born his father *m* him chief),
26:31 year of David's reign search was *m*,
29: 2 was able, gold for what will be *m* of gold,
29: 2 gold, silver for what will be *m* of silver,
29: 2 bronze for what will be *m* of bronze,
29: 2 of bronze, iron for what will be *m* of iron,
29: 2 of iron, wood for what will be *m* of wood,
29: 5 utensils to be *m* of gold and silver,
29:19 the castle for which I have *m* preparation."
2Chr 1: 3 tent of God, *m* in the desert by Moses,
1: 5 The bronze altar *m* by Bezalel,
1: 9 for you have *m* me king over a people as
1:11 rule my people over whom I have *m* you king,
1:15 The king *m* silver and gold as common in
2:11 the God of Israel, who *m* heaven and earth,
2:17 Of these he *m* seventy thousand carriers
3: 8 He also *m* the room of the holy of holies.
3:10 he *m* two cherubim of carved workmanship,
3:14 He *m* the veil of violet,
3:16 and he *m* a hundred pomegranates which he
4: 1 he *m* a bronze altar twenty cubits long,
4: 2 He also *m* the molten sea.
4: 5 and its brim was *m* like that of a cup,
4: 6 Then he *m* ten basins for washing,
4: 7 He *m* the lampstands of gold,
4: 8 *m* ten tables and had them set in the nave,
4: 8 and he *m* a hundred golden bowls.
4: 9 He *m* the court of the priests and the
4:11 Huram also *m* the pots,
4:14 He *m* the stands, and the basins
4:16 Huram-abi *m* all these articles for King
4:18 Solomon *m* all these vessels,
4:19 all these articles *m* for the house of God:
5:10 tablets of the covenant which the LORD *m*

MADE (cont.)
6: 4 who with his own mouth *m* a promise to my
6:10 LORD has fulfilled the promise that he *m*.
6:11 of the LORD which he *m* with the Israelites."
6:13 had *m* a bronze platform five cubits long,
6:15 kept the promise you *m* to my father David,
6:16 further promise you *m* to my father David,
6:17 you *m* to your servant David be confirmed.
7: 6 King David had *m* for "praising the LORD,
7: 7 had *m* could not hold the holocausts,
9:11 With the cabinet wood the king *m* stairs
9:15 *m* two hundred large shields of beaten gold,
9:17 King Solomon also *m* a large ivory throne
9:27 *m* silver as common in Jerusalem as stones,
11:12 and spears, and he *m* them very strong.
11:15 high places and satyrs and calves he had *m*.
11:17 the kingdom of Judah and *m* Rehoboam,
12: 9 the gold bucklers that Solomon had *m*.
12:10 them, King Rehoboam *m* bronze bucklers,
13: 5 and to his sons, by a covenant *m* in salt?
13: 8 calves which Jeroboam *m* you for gods?
13: 9 and *m* for yourselves priests like the
15:16 she had *m* an outrageous object for Asherah;
17: 5 As a result, the LORD *m* his kingdom secure,
18:10 Zedekiah, son of Chenaanah, *m* iron horns
21: 7 the covenant he had *m* with David
21:19 *m* a pyre for him like that of his fathers.
22: 1 the inhabitants of Jerusalem *m* Ahaziah,
23: 3 the whole assembly *m* a covenant with the
23:11 and the insignia upon him, and *m* him king.
23:16 Then Jehoiada *m* a covenant between himself
24: 8 king's command, therefore, they *m* a chest,
24:14 it *m* into utensils for the LORD's temple,
25:16 "Have you been *m* the king's counselor?
26: 5 as he sought the LORD, God *m* him prosper.
28: 2 and even *m* molten idols of the Baals.
28:24 *m* for himself in every corner of Jerusalem.
29: 8 he has *m* them an object of terror,
31:14 in charge of the freewill gifts *m* to God;
31:14 he distributed the offerings *m* to the LORD
31:15 who faithfully *m* the distribution to their
31:18 A distribution was also *m* to all who were
32:27 He had treasuries *m* for his silver,
33: 3 altars for the Baals, *m* sacred poles,
33:22 the idols which his father Manasseh had *m*,
33:25 land, *m* his son Josiah king in his stead.
34:31 the king *m* a covenant before the LORD to
35:25 These have been *m* obligatory for Israel,
36: 1 son of Josiah and *m* him king in Jerusalem
36: 4 Then the king of Egypt *m* his brother
36:10 He *m* his brother Zedekiah king over Judah
36:13 Nebuchadnezzar, who had *m* him swear
Ezr 2:68 *m* freewill offerings for the house of God,
4:15 so that inquiry may be *m* in the historical
4:19 When at my command inquiry was *m*,
5:17 let a search be *m* in the royal archives of
8:15 Ahava, where we *m* camp for three days.
9:13 have *m* less of our sinfulness than it
10: 2 of the sons of Elam, *m* this appeal to Ezra:
10: 7 A proclamation was *m* throughout Judah and
Neh 3:23 *m* the repairs alongside his house.
4: 8 I *m* an inspection,
5:18 daily preparations were *m* at my expense
8: 4 platform that had been *m* for the occasion;
8:15 *m* throughout their cities and in Jerusalem:
8:16 with which they *m* booths for themselves,
8:17 returned exiles *m* booths and dwelt in them.
9: 3 they *m* their confession and prostrated
9: 6 you *m* the heavens,
9: 8 you *m* the covenant with him to give to him
9:10 you *m* for yourself a name even to this day.
9:14 Your holy sabbath you *m* known to them,
9:18 they *m* for themselves a molten calf,
9:23 "You *m* their children as numerous as the
12:47 They *m* their consecrated offering to the
12:47 the Levites *m* theirs to the sons of Aaron.
13:26 God and God had *m* him king over all Israel,
13:26 yet even he was *m* to sin by foreign women.
Tb 1: 5 Jeroboam, king of Israel, had *m* in Dan.
6: 2 and *m* camp beside the Tigris River.
7:16 She went and *m* the bed in the room,
8: 6 You *m* Adam and you gave him his wife Eve
8:16 Blessed are you, who have *m* me glad;
8:20 Tobiah and *m* an oath in his presence,
11:13 medicine on his eyes, and it *m* them smart.
12: 1 due to the man who *m* the journey with you;
12: 7 of God are to be declared and *m* known.
12:11 of God are to be *m* known with due honor.'
14:10 Yet God *m* Nadab's disgraceful crime
Jdt 1: 2 He *m* the wall seventy cubits high and
7:27 We should indeed be *m* slaves,
8:14 fathom God, who has *m* all these things,
8:18 city of ours that worships gods *m* by hands,
8:29 Not today only is your wisdom *m* evident,
9: 6 and your judgment is *m* with foreknowledge.
10: 4 Thus she *m* herself very beautiful,
13:11 Once more he has *m* manifest his strength
13:13 They *m* a fire for light;
16:14 for you spoke, and they were *m*,
2:17 head and *m* her queen in place of Vashti.
C: 3 You *m* heaven and earth and every wonderful
5: 2 and *m* her welcome by extending toward her
7:10 gibbet which he had *m* ready for Mordecai,
9:17 and *m* it a day of feasting and rejoicing.
9:18 and *m* it a day of feasting and rejoicing.)
F: 3 Esther, whom the king married and *m* queen.
1Mc 3: 7 He *m* Jacob glad by his deeds,
4: 7 with cavalry, and *m* up of expert soldiers.
4:39 tore their clothes and *m* great lamentation;
4:49 They *m* new sacred vessels and brought the
4:53 new altar of holocausts that they had *m*.
5:49 So Judas ordered a proclamation to be *m* in
6:31 but the besieged *m* a sortie and burned
6:49 He *m* peace with the men of Beth-zur,
7: 6 They *m* this accusation to the king against
8:10 Greeks a single general who *m* war on them.
8:15 They had *m* for themselves a senate house,
8:24 But if war is first *m* on Rome,
8:27 if war is *m* first on the Jewish nation,
8:29 have *m* an agreement with the Jewish people.
8:31 'Why have you *m* your yoke heavy upon our
9:25 men and *m* them masters of the country.
9:36 But the sons of Jambri from Medaba *m* a
10:15 promises that Demetrius had *m* to Jonathan;
10:63 *m* him military commander and governor
11:37 these instructions *m* and given to Jonathan,
11:50 So they threw down their arms and *m* peace.
11:59 he *m* Jonathan's brother Simon governor of
12:26 *m* ready to attack the Jews that very night.
12:35 *m* plans for building strongholds in Judea,
13:43 He *m* a siege machine,
13:47 He *m* them leave the city,
13:53 Simon *m* him commander of all his soldiers,
14: 5 and *m* it a gateway to the isles of the sea.
14: 7 of war and *m* himself master of Gazara,
14:15 He *m* the temple splendid and enriched its
14:17 his brother Simon had been *m* high priest
14:23 has been *m* for Simon the high priest."
14:26 So they *m* an inscription on bronze tablets,
14:28 country, the following proclamation was *m*:
14:35 they *m* him their leader and high priest
14:39 high priesthood, *m* him one of his Friends,
14:41 have, therefore, *m* the following decisions.
14:43 All contracts *m* in the country shall be
15:25 and with the siege machines he had *m*.
15:27 *m* with Simon and became hostile toward him.
15:36 Athenobius *m* no reply,
16:13 So he *m* treacherous plans to do away with
2Mc 3:15 deposits safe for those who had *m* them.
3:35 *m* most solemn vows to him who had spared
4: 1 *m* false accusation that it was Onias who
4:25 that *m* him worthy of the high priesthood;
4:33 evidence of the facts, he *m* a public protest,
5:16 *m* by other kings for the advancement,
6:23 But he *m* up his mind in a noble manner,
7: 7 they brought the second to be *m* sport of.
8:15 of the covenants *m* with their forefathers,
8:21 *m* them ready to die for their laws
8:29 was done, they *m* supplication in common,
9:25 *m* hurried visits to the outlying provinces.
10: 3 purifying the temple, they *m* a new altar.
10:25 and his men *m* supplication to God,
12: 1 After these agreements were *m*,
12:46 Thus he *m* atonement for the dead that
13:15 he *m* a night attack on the king's pavilion
13:22 The king *m* a second attempt by negotiating
14:26 other, he took the treaty that had been *m*,
Jb 4: 3 many, and have *m* firm their feeble hands.
9: 9 He *m* the Bear and Orion,
11:12 and the wild jackass be *m* docile?
17: 6 evil, and I am *m* a byword of the people;
23:16 Indeed God has *m* my courage fail;
27: 2 the Almighty, who has *m* bitter my soul,
28:26 When he *m* rules for the rain and a path
29:13 me, and the heart of the widow I *m* joyful.
31: 1 If I have *m* an agreement with my eyes and
31:15 Did not he who *m* me in the womb make him?
33: 4 For the spirit of God has *m* me,
35:11 and *m* us wise rather than the birds of the
38: 9 When I *m* the clouds its garment and thick
38:38 is fused into a mass and its clods *m* solid?
39: 6 I have *m* the wilderness his home and the
40:15 See, besides you I *m* Behemoth,
40:19 and was *m* the taskmaster of his fellows;
41:25 there is not his like, intrepid he was *m*.
Ps(s) 7:16 but he falls into the pit which he has *m*.
8: 6 You have *m* him little less than the angels,
9:16 nations are sunk in the pit they have *m*;
16: 3 How wonderfully has he *m* me cherish the
18:12 And he *m* darkness the cloak about him;
18:34 Who *m* my feet swift as those of hinds
18:37 You *m* room for my steps;
18:38 did I turn again till I *m* an end of them.
18:44 you *m* me head over nations;
18:48 who *m* peoples subject to me and preserved
21: 7 For you *m* him a blessing forever;
33: 6 the word of the LORD the heavens were *m*;
33: 9 For he spoke, and it was *m*;
37:23 By the LORD are the steps of a man *m* firm,
39: 6 A short span you have *m* my days,
40: 3 he *m* firm my steps.
40: 6 How numerous have you *m*,
40:11 I have *m* no secret of your kindness and
44: 3 the peoples, but for them you *m* room.
44:13 you *m* no profit from the sale of them.
44:14 You *m* us the reproach of our neighbors,
44:15 You *m* us a byword among the nations,
50: 5 who have *m* a covenant with me by sacrifice."
52: 9 who *m* not God the source of his strength,
60: 5 You have *m* your people feel hardships;
69:11 fasting, and this was *m* a reproach to me.
69:12 I *m* sackcloth my garment,
71:20 you have *m* me feel many bitter afflictions,
73:19 How suddenly they are *m* desolate!
74:14 and *m* food of him for the dolphins.
74:17 summer and winter you *m*.
76: 9 From heaven you *m* your intervention heard;
77:15 the peoples you have *m* known your power.
78:13 and he *m* the waters stand as in a mound.
78:16 He *m* streams flow from the crag and
80:16 son of man whom you yourself *m* strong].
80:18 the son of man whom you yourself *m* strong.
81: 6 Who *m* it a decree for Joseph when he came
86: 9 you have *m* shall come and worship you,
88: 9 you have *m* me an abomination to them;
88:13 Are your wonders *m* known in the darkness,
89: 4 "I have *m* a covenant with my chosen one,
89:42 he is *m* the reproach of his neighbors.
91: 9 you have *m* the Most High your stronghold.
93: 1 with strength, And he has *m* the world firm,
95: 5 His is the sea, for he has *m* it,
95: 6 let us kneel before the LORD who *m* us.
96: 5 of nought, but the LORD *m* the heavens.
96:10 He has *m* the world firm,
98: 2 The LORD has *m* his salvation known:
100: 3 he *m* us, his we are; his people,
103: 7 He has *m* known his ways to Moses,
104:19 You *m* the moon to mark the seasons;
105: 8 he *m* binding for a thousand generations
105:21 He *m* him lord of his house and ruler of
105:24 people and *m* them stronger than their foes,
106:19 They *m* a calf in Horeb and adored
107:41 and *m* the families numerous like flocks.
111: 6 He has *m* known to his people the power of
115:15 by the LORD, who *m* heaven and earth.
118:24 This is the day the LORD has *m*;
119:73 Your hands have *m* me and fashioned me;
119:98 command has *m* me wiser than my enemies,
121: 2 is from the LORD, who *m* heaven and earth.
124: 8 name of the LORD, who *m* heaven and earth.
135:12 And he *m* their land a heritage,
136: 5 Who *m* the heavens in wisdom,
136: 7 Who *m* the great lights,
136:21 And *m* their land a heritage,
138: 2 for you have *m* great above all things your
139:14 thanks that I am fearfully, wonderfully *m*;
139:15 unknown to you When I was *m* in secret,
146: 6 the LORD, his God, Who *m* heaven and earth,
147:20 his ordinances he has not *m* known to them.
Prv 4:16 *m* no one stumble steals away their sleep.
7:27 house is *m* up of ways to the nether world,
8:26 as yet the earth and the fields were not *m*,
8:28 When he *m* firm the skies above,
16: 4 The LORD has *m* everything for his own ends,
20: 9 Who can say, "I have *m* my heart clean,
20:12 the LORD has *m* them both.
20:18 Plans *m* after advice succeed;
20:25 trap for a man, or to regret a vow once *m*.
24: 3 house built, by understanding is it *m* firm;
25: 5 his throne is *m* firm through righteousness.
Eccl 1:15 What is crooked cannot be *m* straight,
2: 5 I *m* gardens and parks,
3:11 has *m* everything appropriate to its time,
3:20 both were *m* from the dust,
6:12 vain life (which God has *m* like a shadow)?
7:13 can make straight what he has *m* crooked?
7:14 Both the one and the other God has *m*,
7:29 God *m* mankind straight,
10:10 dull, though at first he *m* easy progress,
Sg 3: 3 me as they *m* their rounds of the city:
3: 9 *m* himself a carriage of wood from Lebanon.
3:10 He *m* its columns of silver,
5: 7 upon me as they *m* their rounds of the city;
6:12 had *m* me the blessed one of my kinswomen.
Wis 1:16 and pined for it, and *m* a covenant with it,
2:23 the image of his own nature he *m* him.
4:17 intended for him, or why he *m* him secure.
6: 7 himself *m* the great as well as the small,
9: 1 you who have *m* all things by your word
9: 9 was present when you *m* the world;
9:18 the paths of those on earth *m* straight,
10:10 and *m* abundant the fruit of his works,
11: 1 She *m* their affairs prosper through the
11:24 are and loathe nothing that you have *m*;
13: 4 how much more powerful is he who *m* them.
13:10 who termed gods things *m* by human hands:
14:10 *m* shall be punished with its contriver.
14:15 *m* an image of the child so quickly taken
14:17 *m* a public image of him
15: 8 was *m* from the earth And after a little,
15:16 For a man *m* them;
18: 5 *m* them perish all at once
19: 4 and *m* them forgetful of what had befallen
19: 6 its several kinds, was being *m* over anew,
Sir 15:14 he *m* him subject to his own free choice.
15:19 The eyes of God see all he has *m*;
16:24 God created his works and, as he *m* them,
17: 1 created man, and in his own image he *m* him.
17:10 An everlasting covenant he has *m* with them,

18: 2 has he *m* equal to describing his works,
23:20 still knows them all after they are *m.*
33:17 by the LORD's blessing I have *m* progress
39:17 had but to speak and the reservoirs were *m.*
42:25 another, yet none of them has he *m* in vain,
43: 5 Great indeed is the LORD who *m* it,
43:35 It is the LORD who has *m* all things,
44:18 A lasting agreement was *m* with him,
45: 7 He *m* him perpetual in his office when he
46:20 he *m* known to the king his fate,
47: 3 *m* sport of lions as though they were kids,
47:13 peace, for God *m* tranquil all his borders.
47:23 who by his policy *m* the people rebel;
49: 1 incense, *m* lasting by a skilled performer.
49: 7 who even in the womb had been *m* a prophet,
49:14 on earth have been *m* the equal of ENOCH,
51:21 therefore I have *m* her my prize possession.
Is 2: 8 hands, that which their fingers have *m.*
2:20 silver and gold which they *m* for worship.
14:16 "Is this the man who *m* the earth tremble,
14:17 Who *m* the world a desert,
17: 8 shall he regard what his fingers have *m:*
19:14 have *m* Egypt stagger in whatever she does,
22:11 you *m* a reservoir between the two walls
25: 2 For you have *m* the city a heap,
28:15 you say, "We have *m* a covenant with death,
28:15 and with the nether world we have *m* a pact;
28:15 For we have *m* lies our refuge,
29:16 *m* should say of its maker, "He *m* me not!"
31: 7 silver and gold, which he *m* with his hands.
37:16 You have *m* the heavens and the earth.
39: 7 descendants shall be taken and *m* servants
40: 4 shall be *m* low; The rugged land shall be *m*
43: 7 created for my glory, whom I formed and *m.*
43:12 I *m* it known, not any strange god
44: 2 Thus says the Lord who *m* you
44:14 and the rain *m* grow to serve man for fuel.
44:24 I am the LORD, who *m* all things,
45:12 *m* the earth and created mankind upon it;
49: 2 He *m* of me a sharp-edged sword and
49: 2 He *m* me a polished arrow,
49: 5 I am *m* glorious in the sight of the LORD,
51: 2 I called him, I blessed him and *m* him many.
51:10 Who *m* the depths of the sea into a way for
55: 4 As I *m* him a witness to the peoples,
57: 7 a high and lofty mountain you *m* your bed,
57:16 faint before me, the souls that I have *m.*
59: 8 Their ways they have *m* crooked,
59:21 covenant with them which I myself have *m,*
64: 1 Thus your name would be *m* known to your
66: 2 My hand *m* all these things when all of
Jer 1:18 I this day who have *m* you a fortified city,
2: 7 my land, you *m* my heritage loathsome.
2:15 They have *m* his land a waste;
2:28 Where are the gods you *m* for yourselves?
5:22 I *m* the sandy shore the sea's limit,
7:12 which I *m* the dwelling place of my name in
10:12 He who *m* the earth by his power,
11:10 covenant which I had *m* with their fathers,
12:11 waste, They have *m* it a mournful waste,
13:11 so had I *m* the whole house of Israel and
18:21 Let their wives be *m* childless and widows;
25:38 land is *m* desolate By the sweeping sword,
27: 5 It was I who *m* the earth,
31:32 It will not be like the covenant I *m* with
32:17 *m* heaven and earth by your great might,
33: 2 *m* the earth and gave it form and firmness,
33:14 I *m* to the house of Israel and Judah.
34: 8 after King Zedekiah had *m* an agreement
34:13 were slaves, I *m* this covenant with them:
34:18 of the agreement which they *m* before me,
37: 1 he was *m* king over the land of Judah by
39: 2 a breach was *m* in the city's defenses.
41: 2 king of Babylon had *m* ruler over the land;
41: 9 large one *m* by King Asa to defend himself
41:18 Babylon had *m* ruler in the land of Judah.
44:25 fulfill the vows we have *m* to burn incense
48:37 Every head has been *m* bald,
49:20 he has *m* against those that live in Teman:
49:37 until I have completely *m* an end of them;
50:38 they shall be *m* frantic by fearful things.
50:45 he has *m* against the land of the Chaldeans:
51: 7 of the LORD which *m* the whole earth drunk;
51:15 He has sworn who *m* the earth by his power,
51:41 How has she been seized, *m* captive,
52:20 Solomon had *m* for the house of the LORD.
Lam 1: 1 the provinces has been *m* a toiling slave.
2: 4 Like an enemy he *m* taut his bow;
2: 6 has *m* feast and sabbath to be forgotten;
3:15 food, *m* me drink my fill of wormwood.
3:45 You have *m* us offscourings and refuse
4: 2 earthen jars *m* by the hands of a potter!
Bar 1: 8 of Judah, had had *m* after Nebuchadnezzar,
2: 4 He has *m* us subject to all the kingdoms
2:11 *m* for yourself a name till the present day:
2:24 had *m* through your servants the prophets,
3:17 and *m* sport of the birds of the heavens:
4:33 collapse, and *m* merry at your downfall,
5: 7 that every lofty mountain be *m* low,
Ez 3:13 the noise *m* by the wings of the living
4:14 "Never have I been *m* unclean,
6: 6 be *m* desolate and high places laid waste,
6: 6 altars will be *m* desolate and laid waste,
7:20 they *m* of them their abominable images
10:10 All four of them seemed to be *m* the same,
12: 6 have *m* you a sign for the house of Israel.
16:16 gowns and *m* for yourself gaudy high places,
16:17 given you and *m* for yourself male images,
16:51 and have even *m* your sisters appear just,
16:52 shame of having *m* your sisters appear just.
16:60 covenant I *m* with you when you were a girl,
17:13 the royal line with whom he *m* a covenant,
19: 5 of her whelps, him she *m* a young lion.
20: 9 presence I had *m* myself known to them,
20:11 statutes and *m* known to them my ordinances,
20:12 that it was I, the LORD, who *m* them holy.
22: 3 which has *m* idols for her own defilement.
22: 4 *m* guilty, and with the idols you *m* you
22:13 *m* because of the bloodshed in your midst.
25:12 Judah and has *m* itself grievously guilty
27: 6 highest oaks of Bashan they *m* your oars;
27: 6 Your bridge they *m* of cypress wood from
27:11 on your walls, and *m* perfect your beauty.
28: 4 you have *m* riches for yourself;
28:13 Of gold your pendants and jewels were *m,*
28:17 I *m* you a spectacle in the sight of kings.
29: 3 it is I who *m* them!"
29: 9 it is I who *m* them," therefore see!
31: 4 Waters *m* it grow, the abyss *m* it flourish,
31: 9 I *m* it beautiful, with much foliage,
31:15 world I *m* the abyss close up over him;
31:16 the crash of his fall I *m* the nations rock,
32:20 shall be *m* with them for all their hordes.
32:23 have been *m* in the recesses of the pit;
36:35 land has been *m* into a garden of Eden,"
37: 2 He *m* me walk among them in every direction
40:42 four tables for holocausts, *m* of cut stone,
43:26 Thus atonement shall be *m* for the altar,
47: 9 this water comes the sea shall be *m* fresh.
47:11 marshes and swamps shall not be *m* fresh;
Dn 2:23 you have *m* known to us the king's dream."
2:27 In the king's presence Daniel *m* this reply:
2:30 its meaning may be *m* known to the king,
2:48 *m* him ruler of the whole province of
2:49 At Daniel's request the king *m* Shadrach,
3: 1 King Nebuchadnezzar had a golden statue *m,*
3:12 There are certain Jews whom you have *m*
3:15 fall down and worship the statue I had *m,*
3:50 and *m* the inside of the furnace as though
5:11 your father, *m* him chief of the magicians,
5:19 Because he *m* him so great,
5:21 among men and was *m* insensate as a beast;
6:10 Darius signed the prohibition and *m* it law.
6:15 news and he *m* up his mind to save Daniel;
7:16 he *m* known to me the meaning of the things:
7:21 that horn *m* war against the holy ones and
8:18 he touched me and *m* me stand up.
9:15 and *m* a name for yourself even to this day,
10:12 "from the first day you *m* up your mind to
13:36 The elders *m* this accusation:
14: 5 "Because I worship not idols *m* with hands,
14: 5 but only the living God who *m* heaven and
14:13 under the table they had *m* a secret entrance
14:27 these he boiled together and *m* into cakes.
Hos 8: 4 They *m* kings, but not by my authority;
8: 4 and gold they *m* idols for themselves,
8:11 When Ephraim *m* many altars to expiate sin,
12: 9 I have *m* a fortune!"
Jl 1: 7 its branches are *m* white.
2:23 he has *m* the rain come down for you,
Am 4: 6 Though I have *m* your teeth clean of food
4: 6 have *m* bread scarce in all your dwellings,
4:13 Who *m* the dawn and the darkness,
5: 8 He who *m* the Pleiades and Orion,
5:26 the images that you have *m* for yourselves;
6: 6 are not *m* ill by the collapse of Joseph!
7: 9 and the sanctuaries of Israel *m* desolate;
7:17 Your wife shall be *m* a harlot in the city,
Jon 1: 3 But Jonah *m* ready to flee to Tarshish away
1: 9 of heaven, who *m* the sea and the dry land."
1:16 men offered sacrifice and *m* vows to him.
3: 3 So Jonah *m* ready and went to Nineveh,
Hb 1:14 You have *m* man like the fish of the sea,
Zep 2: 8 and *m* boasts against their territory.
3: 6 I have *m* their streets deserted,
Hg 2: 5 I *m* with you when you came out of Egypt,
Zec 7:12 And they *m* their hearts diamond-hard so as
7:14 they *m* the pleasant land into a desert.
11:10 covenant which I had *m* with all peoples;
Mal 1: 3 I *m* his mountains a waste,
2: 8 You have *m* void the covenant of Levi,
2: 9 have *m* you contemptible and base before
Mt 3: 1 When John the Baptizer *m* his appearance as
5:48 you must be *m* perfect as your heavenly
8:25 they *m* their way toward him and woke him:
9: 1 Then he reentered the boat, *m* the crossing,
12:20 not quench until judgment is *m* victorious.
13:25 weeds through his wheat, and then *m* off.
13:26 the weeds *m* their appearance as well.
15:31 the mute speaking, the deformed *m* sound,
19: 4 *m* them male and female and declared,
19:12 some have been deliberately *m* so;
20:19 to be *m* sport of and flogged and crucified.
25:16 went to invest it and *m* another five.
25:20 See, I have *m* five thousand more.'
25:22 thousand and I have *m* two thousand more.'
26:75 remembered the prediction Jesus had *m:*
27:12 priests and elders, he had *m* no reply.
27:47 This *m* some of the bystanders who heard it
27:63 while he was still alive *m* the claim,
28:16 eleven disciples *m* their way to Galilee,
Mk 1:16 As he *m* his way along the Sea of Galilee,
2: 4 When they had *m* a hole, they let down
2:27 "The sabbath was *m* for man,
5:23 fell at his feet and *m* this earnest appeal:
6: 6 He *m* the rounds of the neighboring
6:25 to the king's presence and *m* her request:
7: 9 "You have *m* a fine art of setting aside
10: 6 of creation God *m* them male and female;
14: 3 of perfume *m* from expensive aromatic nard.
14:43 *m* his appearance accompanied by a crowd
14:58 will destroy this temple *m* by human hands,'
14:58 construct another not *m* by human hands.' "
14:61 But Jesus remained silent; he *m* no reply.
14:72 recalled the prediction Jesus had *m* to him,
15: 5 surprise, Jesus *m* no further response.
16: 8 They *m* their way out and fled from the
Lk 1:72 and remembered the holy covenant he *m,*
1:80 when he *m* his public appearance in Israel.
2:15 event which the Lord has *m* known to us."
3: 5 be *m* straight And the rough ways smooth,
5: 9 had *m* seized him and all his shipmates,
5:17 and the power of the Lord *m* him heal.
11:40 he who *m* the outside make the inside too?
12: 2 nothing hidden that will not be *m* known.
15:16 but no one *m* a move to give him anything.
17:17 to say, "Were not all ten *m* whole?
19:15 the money, to learn what profit each had *m.*
19:46 but you have *m* it 'a den of thieves.' "
22:39 Then he went out and *m* his way,
23: 9 considerable length, but Jesus *m* no answer.
23:36 The soldiers also *m* fun of him,
Jn 1:10 the world, and through him the world was *m,*
1:14 became flesh and *m* his dwelling among us,
2: 9 waiter in charge tasted the water *m* wine,
2:15 He *m* a [kind of] whip of cords and drove
4:46 once more, where he had *m* the water wine.
8: 3 *m* her stand there in front of everyone.
9: 6 spat on the ground, *m* mud with his saliva,
9:11 call Jesus *m* mud and smeared it on my eyes,
9:14 had *m* the mud paste and opened his eyes.)
12: 3 perfume *m* from genuine aromatic nard,
15:15 since I have *m* known to you all that I
17: 6 I have *m* your name known to those you gave
18:18 *m* a charcoal fire to warm themselves by.
19: 7 he must die because he *m* himself God's Son."
21: 6 So they *m* a cast, and took so many fish
Acts 2:23 *m* use of pagans to crucify and kill him.
2:36 God has *m* both Lord and Messiah this Jesus
2:39 and your children that the promise was *m,*
3:12 Why do you stare at us as if we had *m* this
3:25 you are the heirs of the covenant God *m*
4:18 So they called them back and *m* it clear
4:24 who *m* heaven and earth and sea and all
4:37 he owned and *m* a donation of the money,
5:27 in and *m* them stand before the Sanhedrin,
7: 4 God *m* him move from there to this land
7: 8 then *m* a covenant of circumcision with him,
7:10 and *m* him the governor of Egypt and of the
7:13 Joseph *m* himself known to his brothers,
7:17 of the promise *m* by God to Abraham,
7:43 Rephan, the images you had *m* for your cult.
7:48 not dwell in buildings *m* by human hands,
8:18 *m* them an offer of money with the request,
9:39 Dorcas had *m* when she was still with them.
9:40 Peter first *m* everyone go outside;
10:28 But God has *m* it clear to me that no one
11:29 This *m* the disciples determine to set
12:10 and *m* their way down a narrow alley,
13:17 He *m* this people great during their
13:47 'I have *m* you a light to the nations,
14: 5 A move was *m* by Gentiles and Jews,
14:15 'the one who *m* heaven and earth and the
14:21 news in that town and *m* numerous disciples,
15: 3 *m* their way through Phoenicia and Samaria,
15: 9 He *m* no distinction between them and us,
16: 4 As they *m* their way from town to town,
16: 4 apostles and presbyters had *m* in Jerusalem.
16:10 *m* efforts to get across to Macedonia,
16:40 the two first *m* their way to Lydia's house,
17:24 God who *m* the world and all that is in it,
17:24 not dwell in sanctuaries *m* by human hands;
17:26 From one stock he *m* every nation of
19:21 Paul *m* up his mind to travel through
19:24 Demetrius who *m* miniature shrines
20:13 This was the arrangement he had *m,*
21:23 are four men among us who have *m* a vow.
21:26 the offering was to be *m* for each of them.
21:31 Attempts were being *m* on his life when a
22:24 out why they *m* such an outcry against him.
22:30 Paul down and *m* him stand before them.
24: 2 Many improvements have been *m* in this
26: 6 in the promise *m* by God to our fathers.
27: 7 For many days we *m* little headway,
27:17 *m* use of cables to brace the ship itself.
27:40 into the wind, and *m* for the beach;
Rom 1: 4 was *m* Son of God in power
1:19 he himself *m* it so.
1:20 recognized through the things he has *m.*

MADE (cont.)

3:25 God *m* him the means of expiation for all
4:13 Certainly the promise *m* to Abraham and his
4:13 it was *m* in view of the justice that comes
4:17 "I have *m* you father of many nations."
8:20 Creation was *m* subject to futility,
14: 3 After all, God himself has *m* him welcome.
16: 5 the first offering that Asia *m* to Christ.
16:26 *m* known to all the Gentiles that they may
1Cor 1:30 has *m* him our wisdom and also our justice,
3: 6 and Apollos watered it, but God *m* it grow.
3:13 or straw, the work of each will be *m* clear.
8: 6 everything was *m* and through whom we live.
9:19 I *m* myself the slave of all so as to win
9:22 I have *m* myself all things to all men in
11: 8 was not *m* from woman but woman from man.
11:12 In the same way that woman was *m* from man,
15:27 it says that everything has been *m* subject,
15:27 *m* everything subject to Christ is excluded.
15:28 to the One who *m* all things subject to him,
16:17 because they *m* up for your absence.
2Cor 1:20 God has *m* have been fulfilled in him;
3: 6 *m* us qualified ministers of a new covenant,
5: 1 not *m* by hands but to last forever.
5:21 God *m* him who did not know sin to be sin,
8: 9 sake he *m* himself poor though he was rich,
11: 6 We have *m* this evident to you in every
Gal 1:14 I *m* progress in Jewish observance far
2: 6 God plays no favorites), *m* me add nothing.
Eph 1:14 redemption of a people God has *m* his own,
1:22 things under Christ's feet and has *m* him,
2:14 and who *m* the two of us one by breaking
3:10 God's manifold wisdom is *m* known to the
5:31 his wife, and the two shall be *m* into one."
Col 1:12 having *m* you worthy to share the lot
2:15 He *m* a public show of them,
3:16 In wisdom *m* perfect,
1Thes 2:14 you have been *m* like the churches of God
1Tm 1:12 *m* me his servant and judged me faithful.
1:18 with the prophecies *m* in your regard,
1:19 have *m* shipwreck of their faith,
2: 7 been *m* its herald and apostle (believe me,
4: 5 it is *m* holy by God's word and by prayer.
6:12 you *m* your noble profession of faith.
6:13 who in bearing witness *m* his noble
2Tm 1:10 now *m* manifest through the appearance
Heb 1: 2 whom he has *m* heir of all things and
2: 7 You *m* him for a little while lower than
2: 9 *m* for a little while lower than the angels,
5: 1 men and *m* their representative before God,
6:13 When God *m* his promise to Abraham,
6:20 being *m* high priest forever according to
7:28 as priest the Son, *m* perfect forever.
8: 9 It will not be like the covenant I *m* with
9:11 and more perfect tabernacle not *m* by hands,
9:24 did not enter into a sanctuary *m* by hands,
10:23 for he who *m* the promise each other to
11:11 who had *m* the promise was worthy of trust.
11:34 though weak they were *m* powerful,
11:40 God had *m* a better plan,
11:40 Without us, they were not to be *m* perfect.
12:23 all, to the spirits of just men *m* perfect,
Jas 2: 7 that noble name which has *m* you God's own.
3: 9 though they are *m* in the likeness of God.
1Pt 2:23 When he was *m* to suffer,
2Pt 1: 8 like these, *m* increasingly your own,
2: 2 the true way will be *m* subject to contempt.
3:10 earth and all its deeds will be *m* manifest.
1Jn 2: 5 has the love of God been *m* perfect in him.
2:25 He himself *m* us a promise and the promise
5:10 Whoever does not believe God has *m* God a
Rv 1: 1 He *m* it known by sending his angel to his
1: 6 who has *m* us a royal nation of priests in
4:11 by your will they came to be and were *m*."
5:10 You *m* of them a kingdom,
7:14 and *m* them white in the blood of the Lamb.
8: 6 the seven trumpets *m* ready to blow them.
9: 9 Their wings *m* a sound like the roar of
9:20 did not repent of the idols they had *m*.
9:20 demons, or of gods *m* from gold and silver,
14: 8 which *m* all the nations drink the poisoned
18: 3 For she has *m* all the nations drink the
19: 8 given a dress to wear *m* of finest linen,
21:21 twelve pearls, each *m* of a single pearl;

MADLY (2)

Jer 46: 9 drive *m*, chariots!
Na 2: 5 the chariots dash *m* through the streets

MADMAN (3)

1Sm 21:14 insanity and acted like a *m* in their hands,
2Kgs 9:11 Why did that *m* come to you?"
Jn 10:21 "These are not the words of a *m*.

MADMANNAH (2)

Jos 15:31 Ezem, Eltolad, Chesil, Hormah, Ziklag, *M*,
1Chr 2:49 She also bore Shaaph, the father of *M*,

MADMEN (3)

1Sm 21:16 Do I not have enough *m*,
Jer 29:26 all *m* and those who pose as prophets,
48: 2 You, too, *M*, shall be reduced to silence;

MADMENAH (1)

Is 10:31 *M* is in flight,

MADNESS (10)

Dt 28:28 And the LORD will strike you with *m*,
2Mc 6:29 what he had said seemed to them utter *m*.
Eccl 1:17 to know wisdom and knowledge, *m* and folly,
2:12 the consideration of wisdom, *m* and folly.
7:25 that wickedness is foolish and folly is *m*.
9: 3 evil, and *m* is in their hearts during life;
10:13 and the end of his talk is utter *m*;
Wis 5: 4 His life we accounted *m*,
Zec 12: 4 horse with fright, and its rider with *m*.
2Pt 2:16 a human voice to restrain the prophet's *m*.

MADON (2)

Jos 11: 1 he sent a message to Jobab, king of *M*,
12:19 Tappuah, Hepher, Aphek, Lasharon, *M*,

MAGADAN (1)

Mt 15:39 the boat and went to the district of *M*.

MAGBISH (1)

Ezr 2:30 sons of *M*, one hundred and fifty-six;

MAGDAL-EDER (1)

Mi 4: 8 And you, O *M*, hillock of daughter Zion!

MAGDALA (1)

Lk 24:10 The women were Mary of *M*,

MAGDALENE (12)

Mt 27:56 Among them were Mary *M*, and Mary
27:61 But Mary *M* and the other Mary remained
28: 1 Mary *M* came with the other Mary to inspect
Mk 15:40 Among them were Mary *M*,
15:47 Mary *M* and Mary the mother of Joses
16: 1 When the sabbath was over, Mary *M*,
16: 9 He first appeared to Mary *M*,
16:13 put no more faith in them than in Mary *M*.
Lk 8: 2 Mary called the *M*,
Jn 19:25 Mary the wife of Clopas, and Mary *M*.
20: 1 it was still dark, Mary *M* came to the tomb.
20:18 Mary *M* went to the disciples.

MAGDIEL (2)

Gn 36:43 Elah, Pinon, Kenaz, Teman, Mibzar, *M*,
1Chr 1:54 Elah, Pinon, Kenaz, Teman, Mibzar, *M*,

MAGGOT (5)

Jb 17:14 and the *m* "my mother" and "my sister,"
25: 6 How much less man, who is but a *m*,
Prv 25:20 Like a moth in clothing, or a *m* in wood,
Is 14:11 The couch beneath you is the *m*,
41:14 Fear not, O worm Jacob, O *m* Israel;

MAGGOTS (2)

Sir 10:11 worms and gnats and *m*.
Hos 5:12 for Ephraim, like *m* for the house of Judah.

MAGIC (10)

Ex 7:11 of Egypt, did likewise by their *m* arts.
7:22 magicians did the same by their *m* arts.
8: 3 the magicians did the same by their *m* arts.
8:14 tried to bring forth gnats by their *m* arts,
2Chr 33: 6 He practiced augury, divination and *m*,
Prv 17: 8 has a bribe to offer rates it a *m* stone;
Wis 17: 7 mockeries of the *m* art were in readiness,
Acts 8: 9 man named Simon had been practicing *m*
8:11 the spell of his *m* over a long period;
19:19 A number who had been dealing in *m* even

MAGICIAN (4)

Is 3: 3 and the nobleman, counselor, skilled *m*,
Dn 2:10 and mighty, asked such a thing of any *m*,
Acts 13: 6 *m* named Bar-Jesus who posed as a prophet.
13: 8 Elymas—"the *m*," for that is what his name

MAGICIANS (15)

Gn 41: 8 So he summoned all the *m* and sages of
41:24 I have spoken to the *m*,
Ex 7:11 sorcerers, and they also, the *m* of Egypt,
7:22 *m* did the same by their magic arts.
8: 3 But the *m* did the same by their magic arts.
8:14 Though the *m* tried to bring forth gnats by
8:15 man and beast, the *m* said to Pharaoh,
9:11 The *m* could not stand in Moses' presence,
9:11 for there were boils on the *m* no less than
Dn 1:20 all the *m* and enchanters in his kingdom.
2: 2 So he ordered that the *m*,
2:27 has inquired, the wise men, enchanters, *m*,
4: 4 When the *m*, enchanters, Chaldeans,
4: 6 "Belteshazzar, chief of the *m*,
5:11 your father, made him chief of the *m*,

MAGISTRATE (3)

Wis 9: 7 people and *m* for your sons and daughters.
Sir 10: 1 A wise *m* lends stability to his people,
Lk 12:58 with your opponent to appear before a *m*,

MAGISTRATES (23)

Ezr 7:25 appoint *m* and judges to administer justice
10:14 the elders and *m* of each city in question,
Neh 2:16 The *m* knew nothing of where I had gone or
2:16 priests, nor to the nobles, nor to the *m*,
4: 8 addressed these words to the nobles, the *m*,
4:13 me, for I had said to the nobles, the *m*,
5: 7 I called the nobles and *m* to account,
5:17 a hundred and fifty persons, Jews and *m*,
7: 5 mind to gather together the nobles, the *m*,
12:40 I, too, who had with me half the *m*,
13:11 I took the *m* to task,
1Mc 10:63 He said to his *m*:
Wis 6: 1 learn, you *m* of the earth's expanse!
Dn 3: 2 *m* and all the officials of the provinces
3: 3 *m* and all the officials of the provinces,
Acts 16:20 them over to the *m* with this complaint:
16:22 and the *m* stripped them and ordered them
16:35 the *m* dispatched officers with orders to
16:36 "The *m* have sent orders that you are to
16:38 The officers reported this to the *m*,
17: 6 and some of the brothers to the town *m*,
17: 8 When the town's *m* heard the whole story,
Rom 13: 6 *m* being God's ministers who devote

MAGNATE (1)

Jb 21:28 you say, "Where is the house of the *m*,

MAGNIFICENCE (3)

1Mc 14: 4 his power and his *m* throughout his reign.
Mt 4: 8 all the kingdoms of the world in their *m*,
Acts 19:27 world revere may soon be stripped of her *m*."

MAGNIFICENT (10)

Ex 15: 6 hand, O LORD, *m* in power your right hand,
15:11 Who is like to you, *m* in holiness?
2Sm 7:21 this entire *m* disclosure to your servant.
7:23 yourself renowned by doing this *m* deed,
1Chr 22: 5 built for the LORD must be made so *m*
2Mc 3: 2 glorified the temple with the most *m* gifts.
Sir 50:11 Vested in his *m* robes,
Jer 13:18 From your heads fall your *m* crowns.
Lk 23:11 *m* robe on him and sent him back to Pilate.
Phil 4:19 worthy of his *m* riches in Christ Jesus.

MAGNIFIED (1)

Wis 19:22 you *m* and glorified your people;

MAGNIFIES (1)

Wis 17:11 conscience, always *m* misfortunes.

MAGOG (5)

Gn 10: 2 Gomer, *M*, Madai, Javan, Tubal,
1Chr 1: 5 The descendants of Japheth were Gomer, *M*,
Ez 38: 2 of man, turn toward Gog [the land of *M*,
39: 6 I will send fire upon *M* and upon those who
Rv 20: 8 and muster for war the troops of Gog and *M*,

MAGPIASH (1)

Neh 10:21 Hashum, Bezai, Hariph, Anathoth, Nebai, *M*,

MAGPIE (1)

Acts 17:18 "What is this *m* trying to say to us?"

MAHALAB (1)

Jos 19:29 Thus, with *M*, Achzib, Ummah,

MAHALALEEL (1)

Lk 3:37 son of Enoch, son of Jared, son of *M*,

MAHALALEL (6)

Gn 5:12 years old, he became the father of *M*.
5:13 and forty years after the birth of *M*,
5:15 When *M* was sixty-five years old,
5:16 *M* lived eight hundred and thirty years
5:17 *M* was eight hundred and ninety-five years;
1Chr 1: 2 Adam, Seth, Enosh, Kenan, *M*,

MAHALATH (2)

Gn 28: 9 addition to the wives he had, married *M*,
2Chr 11:18 Rehoboam took to himself as wife *M*,

MAHALEB (1)

Jgs 1:31 or those of Sidon, or take possession of *M*,

MAHANAIM (14)

Gn 32: 3 So he named that place *M*.
Jos 13:26 and from *M* to the boundary of Lodebar);
13:30 Their territory included *M*,
21:38 lands, also *M* with its pasture lands,
2Sm 2: 8 son of Saul, and brought him over to *M*,

2:12 of Ishbaal, Saul's son, left *M* for Gibeon.
2:29 long through the morning, and came to *M.*
17:24 Now David had gone to *M* when Absalom
17:27 When David came to *M,*
18: 6 a battle was fought in the forest near *M.*
19:33 provisioned the king during his stay in *M.*
1Kgs 2: 8 cursed me balefully when I was going to *M.*
4:14 Ahinadab, son of Iddo, in *M;*
1Chr 6:65 pasture lands, *M* with its pasture lands,

MAHANATH (1)

Gn 36:23 Shobal's descendants were Alvan, *M,*

MAHANEH-DAN (2)

Jgs 13:25 spirit of the LORD first stirred him in *M,*
18:12 lies west of Kiriath-jearim, is called *M.*

MAHARAI (3)

2Sm 23:28 *M* from Netophah;
1Chr 11:30 *M,* from Netophah;
27:13 for the tenth month, was *M* from Netophah,

MAHATH (3)

1Chr 6:20 son of Zuth, son of Elkanah, son of *M,*
2Chr 29:12 *M,* son of Amasai,
31:13 *M* and Benaiah were supervisors subject to

MAHAVITE (1)

1Chr 11:46 Eliel the *M;*

MAHAZIOTH (2)

1Chr 25: 4 Joshbekashah, Mallothi, Hothir, and *M.*
25:30 The twenty-third fell to *M,* his sons,

MAHLAH (5)

Nm 26:33 but only daughters whose names were *M,*
27: 1 son of Joseph, had daughters named *M,*
36:11 *M,* Tirzah, Hoglah, Milcah and Noah
Jos 17: 3 but only daughters, whose names were *M,*
1Chr 7:18 Molecheth bore Ishhod, Abiezer, and *M.*

MAHLI (12)

Ex 6:19 The sons of Merari were *M* and Mushi.
Nm 3:20 of Merari, by clans, were *M* and Mushi.
1Chr 6: 4 The sons of Merari were *M* and Mushi.
6:14 The descendants of Merari were *M,*
6:32 son of Bani, son of Shemer, son of *M,*
23:21 The sons of Merari: *M* and Mushi
23:21 The sons of *M:* Eleazar and Kish
23:23 *M,* Eder, and Jeremoth; three in all.
24:26 The descendants of Merari were *M,*
24:28 Descendants of *M* were Eleazar,
24:30 The descendants of Mushi were *M,*
Ezr 8:18 well-instructed man, one of the sons of *M,*

MAHLITES (2)

Nm 3:33 the clans of the *M* and the Mushites;
26:58 clan of the Hebronites, the clan of the *M,*

MAHLON (4)

Ru 1: 2 his wife Naomi, and his sons *M* and Chilion;
1: 5 ten years, both *M* and Chilion died also,
4: 9 the holdings of Elimelech, Chilion and *M.*
4:10 take Ruth the Moabite, the widow of *M,*

MAHOUT (1)

1Mc 6:37 by a harness, held, besides the Indian *m,*

MAHSEIAH (3)

Jer 32:12 I gave to Baruch, son of Neriah, son of *M,*
51:59 to Seraiah, son of Neriah, son of *M,*
Bar 1: 1 which Baruch, son of Neriah, son of *M,*

MAID (28)

Gn 16: 2 Have intercourse, then, with my *m;*
16: 3 of Canaan, his wife Sarai took her *m,*
16: 5 I myself gave my *m* to your embrace;
16: 6 "Your *m* is in your power.
16: 8 to Shur, and he asked, "Hagar *m* of Sarai,
35:25 the sons of Rachel's *m* Bilhah:
35:26 the sons of Leah's *m* Zilpah:
Tb 3: 8 So the *m* said to her:
8:13 She sent the *m,* who lit a lamp,
8:14 The *m* went out and told the girl's parents
Jdt 8:10 she sent the *m* who was in charge of all
8:33 tonight to let me pass through with my *m;*
10: 2 her *m* and they went down into the house,
10: 5 She gave her *m* a leather flask of wine and
10: 5 she wrapped up and gave to the *m* to carry.
10:10 they did so, Judith and her *m* went out.
10:11 her *m* walked directly across the valley,
10:17 their men as an escort for her and her *m,*
12:15 Meanwhile her *m* went ahead and spread out
12:19 then took the things her *m* had prepared,
13: 3 *m* to stand outside the bedroom and wait,
13: 9 over the head of Holofernes to her *m,*
16:24 and to the *m* she gave her freedom.
Est D: 7 against the head of the *m* in front of her.
Jb 31:13 justice to my manservant or to my *m,*
Ps(s) 123: 2 of a *m* are on the hands of her mistress,
Is 24: 2 servant and master, The *m* as her mistress,
Acts 12:13 *m* named Rhoda came to answer it.

MAIDEN (23)

Gn 34:12 only give me the *m* in marriage."
Ex 2: 8 *m* went and called the child's own mother.
Lv 21: 3 or daughter, his brother or his *m* sister,
27: 5 shekels for a youth, and ten for a *m;*
Nm 30: 4 while still a *m* in her father's house,
30:17 she is still a *m* in her father's house.
Dt 22:23 city a man comes upon a *m* who is betrothed,
22:25 that a man comes upon such a betrothed *m,*
22:26 You shall do nothing to the *m,*
22:27 betrothed *m* may have cried out for help,
22:28 a man comes upon a *m* that is not betrothed,
32:25 at home Shall be the youth and the *m* alike,
Jgs 19:24 bring out my *m* daughter or his concubine.
2Sm 13:18 is how *m* princesses dressed in olden days.
1Kgs 1: 4 The *m,* who was very beautiful,
2Chr 36:17 building, sparing neither young man nor *m,*
Jdt 12:13 "So fair a *m* should not be reluctant to
Jb 31: 1 and entertained any thoughts against a *m;*
Prv 30:19 high seas, and the way of a man with a *m.*
Sir 20: 3 a *m* is he who does right under compulsion.
Jer 51:22 young, with you I shatter the youth and *m.*
Bar 6: 8 gold, as to a *m* in love with ornament,
Ez 44:25 son, daughter, brother, or *m* sister;

MAIDENS (18)

2Sm 1:20 of Ashkelon, Lest the Philistine *m* rejoice,
Jdt 9: 2 who had immodestly loosened the *m* girdle,
Est 2: 8 decree had been obeyed and many *m* brought
2Mc 3:19 *m* secluded indoors ran together,
Jb 40:29 Can you put him in leash for your *m?*
Ps(s) 68:26 in their midst the *m* play on timbrels.
78:63 young men, and their *m* were not betrothed.
148:12 judges of the earth, Young men too, and *m,*
Prv 9: 3 She has sent out her *m;*
27:27 household,] and maintenance for your *m.*
Sg 1: 3 that is why the *m* love you.
6: 8 *m* without number
Lam 1:18 *m* and my youths have gone into captivity.
2:10 The *m* of Jerusalem bow their heads to the
2:21 *m* and young men have fallen by the sword;
5:11 by the enemy, the *m* in the cities of Judah;
Ez 9: 6 Old men, youths and *m,*
Zec 9:17 the youths flourish, and new wine, the *m?*

MAIDS (16)

Gn 24:61 Then Rebekah and her *m* started out;
33: 2 putting the *m* and their children first,
Ex 2: 5 while her *m* walked along the river bank.
1Sm 25:42 five *m* following in attendance upon her.
Tb 3: 7 to abuse, from one of her father's *m.*
8:12 "Send one of the *m* in to see whether
Jdt 8: 7 left her gold and silver, servants and *m,*
Est 2: 9 out seven *m* for her from the royal palace,
2: 9 and her *m* to the best place in the harem.
4: 4 Esther's *m* and eunuchs came and told her.
4:16 I and my *m* will also fast in the same way.
D: 2 God and savior, she took with her two *m;*
Dn 13:15 the garden as usual, with two *m* only.
13:17 me oil and soap," she said to the *m,*
13:19 As soon as the *m* had left,
13:21 *m* because a young man was here with you,

MAIDSERVANT (18)

Gn 16: 1 had, however, an Egyptian *m* named Hagar.
29:24 girl Zilpah to his daughter Leah as her *m.)*
29:29 Bilhah to his daughter Rachel as her *m.)*
30: 3 She replied, "Here is my *m* Bilhah.
30: 4 So she gave him her *m* Bilhah as a consort,
30: 7 Rachel's *m* Bilhah conceived again and bore
30: 9 gave her *m* Zilpah to Jacob as a consort.
30:12 Leah's *m* Zilpah bore a second son to Jacob;
30:18 for having let my husband have my *m*";
Ex 23:12 of your *m* and the alien may be refreshed.
1Sm 1:18 She replied, "Think kindly of your *m,*"
25:27 then, which your *m* has brought for my lord,
28:21 "Remember, your *m* obeyed you:
28:22 Now you, in turn, please listen to your *m.*
2Sm 14:15 he will grant the petition of his *m.*
17:17 A *m* was to come with information for them,
20:17 to him, "Listen to what your *m* has to say."
Prv 30:23 and a *m* when she displaces her mistress.

MAIDSERVANTS (5)

Gn 20:17 Abimelech, that is, to his wife and his *m,*
31:33 tent, as well as the tents of the two *m;*
32:23 with the two *m* and his eleven children,
33: 1 children among Leah, Rachel and the two *m,*
33: 6 Then the *m* and their children came forward

MAIL (4)

1Sm 17:38 his head and arming him with a coat of *m.*
1Mc 6:35 to it a thousand men in coats of *m,*
Sir 43:21 and clothes each pool with a coat of *m.*
Jer 51: 3 draw his bow, and flaunt his coat of *m;*

MAIMED (7)

Gn 49: 6 slew men, in their willfulness they *m* oxen.
Ex 22: 9 if it dies, or is *m* or snatched away,
22:13 *m* or dies while the owner is not present,
Lv 22:22 One that is blind or crippled or *m,*
2Mc 7: 5 he was completely *m* but still breathing,
Mt 18: 8 Better to enter life *m* or crippled than be
Mk 9:43 Better for you to enter life *m* than to

MAIN (10)

Jos 8:13 with the *m* body north of the city and the
8:15 Joshua and the *m* body of the Israelites
8:21 for when Joshua and the *m* body of
Jdt 3: 9 to the *m* ridge of the Judean mountain,
5:15 destroyed all the Heshbonites by *m* force,
1Mc 9:14 on the right, with the *m* force of his army,
11:46 of the *m* streets and began to fight.
2Mc 12:35 cloak and dragged him along by *m* strength,
Acts 16:19 the *m* square before the local authorities.
Heb 8: 1 The *m* point in what we are saying is this:

MAINLAND (2)

Ez 26: 6 on the *m* shall be slaughtered by the sword;
26: 8 on the *m* he shall slay with the sword;

MAINSTAY (1)

Jer 49:35 the bow of Elam, the *m* of their might,

MAINTAIN (14)

Gn 17: 7 I will *m* my covenant with you and your
17:19 I will *m* my covenant with him as an
17:21 But my covenant I will *m* with Isaac,
31:53 ancestral deities] *m* justice between us!"
Ex 27:21 *m* them before the LORD in the meeting tent,
1Chr 17:14 but I will *m* him in my house and in my
Jdt 8:23 Lord our God, will *m* it to our disgrace.
1Mc 7:21 spared no pains to *m* his high priesthood,
2Mc 11:19 If you *m* your loyalty to the government,
Jb 27: 6 justice I *m* and I will not relinquish it;
Ps(s) 89:29 Forever I will *m* my kindness toward him,
Sir 38:34 Yet they *m* God's ancient handiwork,
Acts 23: 8 *m* that there is no resurrection and that
Heb 3:14 if only we *m* to the end that confidence

MAINTAINED (12)

Gn 7:24 The waters *m* their crest over the earth
Jgs 18:31 They *m* the carved idol Micah had made as
Est E: 6 who has *m* the kingdom in a flourishing
1Mc 8:12 who relied on them, they *m* friendship.
14:29 that their sanctuary and law might be *m,*
2Mc 15:30 and had *m* from youth his affection for his
Wis 19:20 Fire in water *m* its own strength,
Jn 7:12 Some *m,* "He is a good man,"
9: 9 others *m* it was not but someone who looked
10:21 Others *m:* "These are not words
12:29 Others *m,* "An angel was speaking to him."
Acts 24: 9 indictment and *m* that these were the facts.

MAINTAINING (1)

Jdt 8: 7 livestock and fields, which she was *m.*

MAINTAINS (1)

Prv 26:24 but in his inmost being he *m* deceit;

MAINTENANCE (1)

Prv 27:27 your household,] and *m* for your maidens.

MAJESTIC (19)

Lv 23:40 day you shall gather foliage from *m* trees,
Dt 33:17 the prince among his brothers, The *m* bull,
Est D: 7 features ablaze with the height of *m* anger,
2Mc 10:29 five *m* men riding on golden-bridled horses,
15:13 about him of extraordinary, *m* authority.
Jb 37: 4 the *m* sound of his thunder.
Ps(s) 29: 4 the voice of the LORD is *m.*
Sir 17:11 His *m* glory their eyes beheld,
18: 3 Who can measure his *m* power,
43:11 its Maker, for *m* indeed is its splendor;
45:12 wrought with the insignia of holiness, *M,*
Is 28: 1 to the *m* garland of the drunkard Ephraim,
28: 3 the *m* garland of the drunkard Ephraim.
33:21 no boat is rowed, where no *m* ship passes,
33:22 Indeed the LORD will be there with us, *m;*
Ez 17: 8 branches, bear fruit, and become a *m* vine.
17:23 and bear fruit, and become a *m* cedar.
Mi 5: 3 of the LORD, in the *m* name of the LORD,
2Pt 1:17 came to him out of the *m* splendor:

MAJESTY (82)

Ex 15: 7 great *m* you overthrew your adversaries;
Dt 5:24 has indeed let us see his glory and his *m!*
9:26 heritage which your *m* has ransomed
11: 2 his *m,* his strong hand
33:26 his power, and rides the skies in his *m;*
1Sm 17:32 "Let your *m* not lose courage.
17:55 replied, "As truly as your *m* is alive,
19: 4 not your *m* sin against his servant David,
2Sm 13:24 your *m,* come with all your retainers

MAJESTY (cont.)

14: 4 ground in homage, saying, "Help, your *m*!"
14:11 But she went on to say, "Please, your *m*,
14:15 to speak of this matter to your *m*,
14:19 the king, it is just as your *m* has said,
24: 3 your royal *m* to see it with his own eyes.
1Kgs 1: 2 If she sleeps with your royal *m*,
1:20 is to sit on the throne after your royal *m*.
1:37 As the LORD has been with your royal *m*,
2:38 will do just as the king's *m* has said."
22: 8 "Let not your *m* speak of evil against you."
1Chr 16:27 Splendor and *m* go before him;
29:11 O LORD, are grandeur and power, *m*,
29:13 thanks and we praise the *m* of your name."
2Chr 6:41 resting place, you and the ark of your *m*.
18: 7 "Let not your *M* speak of evil against you."
Tb 13: 6 show his power and *m* to a sinful nation.
13: 8 Let all men speak of his *m*,
14: 2 blessing God and praising the divine *M*.
Est D:13 my heart was troubled with fear of your *m*.
5: 4 "If it please your *m*,"
5: 8 if it pleases your *m* to grant my petition
7: 3 you, O king, and if it pleases your *m*,
8: 5 it pleases your *m* and seems proper to you,
E:16 of the Most High, the living God of *m*,
9:13 So Esther said, "If it pleases your *m*,
2Mc 3:34 proclaim to all men the *m* of God's power."
Jb 13:11 Surely will his *m* affright you and the
31:23 be upon me, and his *m* will overpower me.
37:22 comes, surrounding God's awesome *m*!
40:10 Adorn yourself with grandeur and *m*,
Ps(s) 8: 2 You have exalted your *m* above the heavens.
21: 6 *m* and splendor you conferred upon him.
30: 8 you had endowed me with *m* and strength:
45: 4 In your splendor and your *m* ride on
68:35 Over Israel in his *m*;
96: 6 Splendor and *m* go before him;
104: 1 You are clothed with *m* and glory,
111: 3 *M* and glory are his work,
132: 8 resting place you and the ark of your *m*.
145: 5 glorious *m* and tell of your wondrous works.
148:13 His *m* is above earth and heaven,
150: 2 deeds, praise him for his sovereign *m*.
Sir 2:18 equal to his *m* is the mercy that he shows.
6:30 Her fetters will be your throne of *m*;
10: 5 of God, who imparts his *m* to the ruler.
36:13 Fill Zion with your *m*,
43:15 In his *m* he gives the storm its power and
43:30 Awful indeed is the LORD's *m*,
45: 7 him in honor and crowned him with lofty *m*;
50:11 and lent *m* to the court of the sanctuary.
Is 2:10 of the LORD and the splendor of his *m*!
2:19 of the LORD and the splendor of his *m*,
2:21 of the LORD and the splendor of his *m*,
3: 8 LORD, a provocation in the sight of his *m*.
23: 9 planned it, to disgrace all pride of *m*,
24:14 the sea they proclaim the *m* of the LORD:
26:10 perversely, and sees not the *m* of the LORD.
33: 3 when you rise in your *m*,
63: 1 This one arrayed in *m*,
Jer 22:18 "Alas, Lord! alas, *M*!"
Dn 4:19 Your *m* has become so great as to touch the
4:27 as a royal residence for my splendor and *m*?"
4:33 my *m* and my splendor returned to me.
5:18 a great kingdom and glorious *m*.
7:27 *m* of all the kingdoms under the heavens
Hb 1: 7 he, from himself derive his law and his *m*.
Acts 25:25 so when he appealed to His *M* the Emperor,
26: 7 It is because of this hope, Your *M*,
26:13 On this journey, Your *M*,
Heb 1: 3 seat at the right hand of the *M* in heaven,
8: 1 hand of the throne of the *M* in heaven,
2Pt 1:17 we were eyewitnesses of his sovereign *m*.
Jude 1:25 *M*, too, be his, might and power

MAJESTY'S (2)

2Sm 11:11 *m* servants are encamped in the open field.
1Kgs 1:27 who was to succeed to your *m* kingly throne?"

MAJOR-DOMO (1)

1Kgs 4: 6 Ahishar, *m* of the palace;

MAJORITY (4)

Mk 12:37 The *m* of the crowd heard this with delight.
Acts 19:32 *m* not even knowing why they had come
27:12 the *m* preferred to put out to sea in the
2Cor 2: 6 inflicted by the *m* on such a one is enough;

MAKAZ (1)

1Kgs 4: 9 the son of Deker in *M*,

MAKE (941)

Gn 1:26 "Let us *m* man in our image,
2:18 I will *m* a suitable partner for him."
6:14 *M* yourself an ark of gopherwood,
6:16 *M* an opening for daylight in the ark,
6:16 of the ark, which you shall *m* with bottom,
11: 4 in the sky, and so *m* a name for ourselves;
12: 2 "I will *m* of you a great nation,
12: 2 I will *m* your name great,
13:16 I will *m* your descendants like the dust of
15: 1 I will *m* your reward very great."
16:10 I will *m* your descendants so numerous,"
17: 6 I will *m* nations of you;
17:20 I will *m* him fertile and will multiply him
17:20 and I will *m* of him a great nation.
18: 6 Knead it and *m* rolls."
18:25 to *m* the innocent die with the guilty,
21:13 woman, I will *m* a great nation of him also,
21:18 for I will *m* of him a great nation."
22:17 I will bless you abundantly and *m* your
23:11 the presence of my kinsmen I *m* this gift.
24: 3 thigh, and I will *m* you swear by the LORD,
24:40 with you and *m* your errand successful,
24:42 to *m* successful the errand I am engaged on!
26: 4 I will *m* your descendants as numerous as
26:28 Let us *m* a pact with you:
28: 3 God Almighty bless you and *m* you fertile,
31:44 Come, then, we will *m* a pact,
32:13 and I will *m* your descendants like the
37: 8 really going to *m* yourself king over us?"
39:14 brought in a Hebrew slave to *m* sport of us!
39:17 here broke in on me, to *m* sport of me.
42:36 "Must you *m* me childless?
42:38 befall him on the journey you must *m*,
46: 3 for there I will *m* you a great nation.
48: 4 'I will *m* you fertile and numerous and
48:20 'God *m* you like Ephraim and Manasseh,'
Ex 3:21 I will even *m* the Egyptians so
4:21 I will *m* him obstinate,
5:16 and still we are told to *m* bricks.
6: 3 my name, LORD, I did not *m* known to them.
7: 3 Yet I will *m* Pharaoh so obstinate that,
8: 1 to *m* frogs overrun the land of Egypt."
8:18 *m* an exception of the very land of Goshen:
8:19 I will *m* this distinction between my
9:16 to *m* my name resound throughout the earth!
14: 4 Thus will I *m* Pharaoh so obstinate that he
14:17 But I will *m* the Egyptians so obstinate
16: 3 to *m* the whole community die of famine!"
17: 3 "Why did you ever *m* us leave Egypt?
18:16 *m* known to them God's decisions
19:10 *M* them wash their garments and be ready
19:23 limits around the mountain to *m* it sacred."
20:23 Do not *m* anything to rank with me;
20:23 gods of gold shall you *m* for yourselves.
20:24 "An altar of earth you shall *m* for me,
20:25 If you *m* an altar of stone for me,
21:34 the owner of the cistern must *m* good by
21:36 not keep it in, he must *m* full restitution,
22: 2 He must *m* full restitution.
22: 4 he must *m* restitution with the best
22: 5 started the fire must *m* full restitution.
22: 6 if caught, must *m* twofold restitution.
22: 8 must *m* twofold restitution to the other.
22:11 theft, he must *m* restitution to the owner.
22:12 not *m* restitution for the mangled animal.
22:13 is not present, the man must *m* restitution.
22:14 is present, he need not *m* restitution.
23:24 gods, nor shall you *m* anything like them;
23:27 *m* all your enemies turn from you in flight,
23:32 not *m* a covenant with them or their gods.
23:33 lest they *m* you sin against me by
25: 8 "They shall *m* a sanctuary for me,
25: 9 you shall *m* exactly according to the pattern
25:10 "You shall *m* an ark of acacia wood,
25:13 Then *m* poles of acacia wood and plate them
25:17 shall then *m* a propitiatory of pure gold,
25:18 *M* two cherubim of beaten gold for the two
25:23 "You shall also *m* a table of acacia wood,
25:24 gold and *m* a molding of gold around it.
25:26 You shall also *m* four rings of gold for it
25:28 shall *m* of acacia wood and plate with gold.
25:29 pure gold you shall *m* its plates and cups,
25:31 shall *m* a lampstand of pure beaten gold
25:37 You shall then *m* seven lamps for it and so
25:40 See that you *m* them according to the
26: 1 "The Dwelling itself you shall *m* out of
26: 4 *M* loops of violet yarn along the edge of
26: 6 Then *m* fifty clasps of gold,
26: 7 "Also *m* sheets woven of goat hair,
26:10 *M* fifty loops along the edge of the end
26:11 Also *m* fifty bronze clasps and put them
26:14 shall *m* a covering of rams' skins dyed red,
26:15 "You shall *m* boards of acacia wood as
26:26 Also *m* bars of acacia wood:
26:29 and *m* gold rings on them as holders for
26:36 the tent *m* a variegated curtain of violet,
26:37 *M* five columns of acacia wood for this
27: 1 "You shall *m* an altar of acacia wood,
27: 3 *M* pots for removing the ashes,
27: 4 *M* a grating of bronze network for it;
27: 6 also *m* poles of acacia wood for the altar,
27: 8 *M* the altar itself in the form of a hollow
27: 9 shall also *m* a court for the Dwelling.
28: 3 you shall give instructions to *m* such
28: 4 These are the vestments they shall *m*:
28: 6 they shall *m* of gold thread and of violet,
28:13 *M* filigree rosettes of gold,
28:23 you shall then *m* two rings of gold for it
28:26 *M* two other rings of gold and put them on
28:27 Then *m* two more rings of gold and fasten
28:31 you shall *m* entirely of violet material.
28:33 hem at the bottom you shall *m* pomegranates,
28:36 *m* a plate of pure gold and engrave on it,
28:42 You must also *m* linen drawers for them,
29: 2 flour *m* unleavened cakes mixed with oil,
29:28 too, the Israelites shall *m* a contribution,
29:36 each day as a sin offering, to *m* atonement.
30: 1 you shall *m* an altar of acacia wood,
30: 5 *M* the poles, too, of acacia wood
30:18 shall *m* a bronze laver with a bronze base.
30:32 may you *m* any other oil of a like mixture.
30:37 *m* incense of a like mixture for yourselves;
31: 6 experts with the necessary skill to *m* all
31: 6 all the things I have ordered you to *m*:
31:11 they shall *m* just as I have commanded you."
31:13 that it is I, the LORD, who *m* you holy.
32: 1 "Come, *m* us a god who will be our leader;
32:10 Then I will *m* of you a great nation."
32:13 'I will *m* your descendants as numerous as
32:23 said to me, *M* us a god to be our leader;
32:30 I may be able to *m* atonement for your sin."
32:35 for having had Aaron *m* the calf for them.
33:15 yourself, do not *m* us go up from here.
33:19 "I will *m* all my beauty pass before you,
34:10 said the LORD, "is the covenant I will *m*.
34:12 not to *m* a covenant with these inhabitants
34:15 Do not *m* a covenant with the inhabitants
34:16 gods, they will *m* your sons do the same.
34:17 shall not *m* for yourselves molten gods.
35:10 *m* all that the LORD has commanded:
35:24 Whoever could *m* a contribution of silver
36: 6 *m* any more contributions for the sanctuary."
Lv 1: 4 may be acceptable to *m* atonement for him.
4:20 Thus the priest shall *m* atonement for them,
4:26 shall *m* atonement for the prince's sin,
4:31 Thus the priest shall *m* atonement for him,
4:35 priest shall *m* atonement for the man's sin,
5: 6 priest shall then *m* atonement for his sin.
5:10 *m* atonement for the sin the man committed,
5:13 Thus the priest shall *m* atonement for the
5:16 who shall then *m* atonement for him with
5:18 The priest shall then *m* atonement for the
5:22 the sinful oaths that men *m* in such cases,
5:24 *m* full restitution of the thing itself,
5:26 shall *m* atonement for him before the LORD,
6:23 tent to *m* atonement in the sanctuary;
8:34 done today be done to *m* atonement for you.
10:17 and *m* atonement for them before the LORD.
11:43 Do not *m* yourselves loathsome or unclean
11:44 and you shall *m* and keep yourselves holy,
11:44 You shall not *m* yourselves unclean,
12: 7 up before the LORD to *m* atonement for her,
12: 8 The priest shall *m* atonement for her,
13:39 the priest shall *m* an examination.
14:18 *m* atonement for him before the LORD.
14:29 he *m* atonement for him before the LORD.
14:31 Thus shall the priest *m* atonement before
15:15 Thus shall the priest *m* atonement before
15:30 Thus shall the priest *m* atonement before
16:10 so that with it he may *m* atonement by
16:16 Thus he shall *m* atonement for the
16:17 sanctuary to *m* atonement until he departs.
16:18 the LORD and *m* atonement for it also.
16:27 brought into the sanctuary to *m* atonement,
16:30 atonement is made for you to *m* you clean,
16:33 and *m* atonement for the sacred sanctuary,
19: 4 to idols, nor *m* molten gods for yourselves.
19:22 With this ram the priest shall *m* atonement
20: 8 observe what I, the LORD, who *m* you holy,
21: 1 None of you shall *m* himself unclean for
21: 3 for these he may *m* himself unclean.
21: 4 his family he shall not *m* himself unclean;
21: 5 shall not *m* bare the crown of the head,
21:23 for it is I, the LORD, who *m* them sacred."
22: 8 He shall not *m* himself unclean by eating
22:14 he shall *m* restitution to the priest for
22:16 it is I, the LORD, who *m* them sacred."
23:40 a week you shall *m* merry before the LORD,
24:18 shall *m* restitution of another animal.
24:21 slays an animal shall *m* restitution,
25:10 This fiftieth year you shall *m* sacred by
25:27 he shall *m* a deduction from the price in
25:39 his services, do not *m* him work as a slave.
26: 1 "Do not *m* false gods for yourselves.
26: 9 upon you, and *m* you fruitful and numerous,
26:10 have to discard them to *m* room for the new.
26:19 I will *m* the sky above you as hard as iron,
26:25 I will *m* the sword,
26:34 land have rest and *m* up for its sabbaths
26:36 enemies I will *m* so fainthearted that,
26:41 humbled and they *m* amends for their guilt,
26:43 desolation it may *m* up its lost sabbaths,
26:43 may *m* good the debt of their guilt for
26:44 them out, I *m* void my covenant with them;
Nm 4:27 you shall *m* each man of them responsible
5: 9 are bound to *m* shall fall to the priest.
5:21 'may the LORD *m* you an example of
5:22 enter your body to *m* your belly swell and
8:19 meeting tent and to *m* atonement for them,
10: 2 *M* two trumpets of beaten silver,
11: 8 then cook it in a pot and *m* it into loaves,
14:12 Then I will *m* of you a nation greater and
15: 3 if you *m* to the LORD a sweet-smelling
15:13 shall *m* these offerings in the same way,

15:25 Then the priest shall *m* atonement for the
15:28 and the priest shall *m* atonement before
16: 5 "May the LORD *m* known tomorrow morning
16:13 and honey, to *m* us perish in the desert,
16:22 sin *m* you angry with the whole community?"
17:11 to the community to *m* atonement for them;
18:19 gifts which the Israelites *m* to the LORD;
18:26 to *m* a contribution from them to the LORD,
18:28 Thus you too shall *m* a contribution from
18:32 as you *m* a contribution of the best part.
21: 8 Moses, *M* a saraph and mount it on a pole,
28:23 These offerings you shall *m* in addition to
28:24 you shall *m* exactly the same offerings
28:31 You shall *m* these offerings,
29:39 you shall *m* to the LORD on your festivals,
31:50 *m* atonement for ourselves before the LORD,
32: 5 Do not *m* us cross the Jordan."
32:15 *m* them stay still longer in the desert,
Dt 4:38 you in and to *m* their land your heritage,
5: 3 with our fathers did he *m* this covenant,
7: 2 *M* no covenant with them and show them no
7:24 that you may *m* their names perish from
8:16 you, but also *m* you prosperous in the end.
9:14 I will then *m* of you a nation mightier and
10: 1 Also *m* an ark of wood.
12: 7 eat and *m* merry over all your undertakings,
12:12 You shall *m* merry before the LORD,
12:14 *m* whatever offerings I enjoin upon you.
12:18 shall *m* merry over all your undertakings.
12:23 But *m* sure that you do not partake of the
14:26 partake of it and *m* merry with your family.
16:11 you shall *m* merry in his presence together
16:14 You shall *m* merry at your feast,
16:15 you shall do nought but *m* merry.
17:16 nor shall he *m* his people go back again to
18:19 my name, I myself will *m* him answer for it.
20: 8 *m* his fellows as fainthearted as himself.'
20:12 But if it refuses to *m* peace with you and
20:18 *m* any such abominable offers as they *m*
23:22 "When you *m* a vow to the LORD,
24:10 you *m* a loan of any kind to your neighbor,
26:11 shall *m* merry over all these good things
27: 6 You shall *m* this altar of the LORD,
28:13 The LORD will *m* you the head,
28:69 *m* with the Israelites in the land of Moab,
30: 5 and he will *m* you more prosperous and
32:26 'I will *m* an end of them and blot out
32:42 I will *m* my arrows drunk with blood,
Jos 5: 2 *M* flint knives and circumcise the
6: 5 they will be able to *m* a frontal attack."
6:10 by Joshua not to shout or *m* any noise
8: 5 and when they *m* a sortie against us as
9: 6 to propose that you *m* an alliance with us."
9: 7 How, then, can we *m* an alliance with you?"
9:11 we propose that you *m* an alliance with us.'
Jgs 2: 2 *m* a pact with the inhabitants of this land,
5:12 arise, Barak, *m* despoilers your spoil,
6:39 me *m* just one more test with the fleece.
8:24 say, "I should like to *m* a request of you.
9: 6 proceeded to *m* Abimelech king
9:33 tomorrow morning, *m* a raid on the city.
16:20 he thought he could *m* good his escape as
16:23 to their god Dagon and to *m* merry.
19:13 servant, "let us *m* for some other place,
Ru 3: 3 Do not *m* yourself known to the man before
4: 7 to *m* binding a contract of redemption or
4:11 May the LORD *m* this wife come into your
1Sm 1:14 long will you *m* a drunken show of yourself?
2: 8 and *m* a glorious throne their heritage.
2:19 mother used to *m* a little garment for him,
6: 3 *m* amends to him through a guilt offering.
6: 5 *m* images of the hemorrhoids and of the
6: 7 So now set to work and *m* a new cart.
8:12 and to *m* his implements of war and the
11: 1 Jabesh begged Nahash, *M* a treaty with us,
12: 3 I will *m* restitution to you."
12:22 the LORD himself chose to *m* you his people.
13:19 the Hebrews will *m* swords or spears."
18:30 Philistine chiefs continued to *m* forays,
20:16 you, or the LORD will *m* you answer for it."
20:31 cannot *m* good your claim to the kingship!
22: 7 Will he *m* each of you an officer over a
22:17 *M* the rounds and kill the priests of the
22:18 "You *m* the rounds and kill the priests!"
23:22 Go now and *m* sure once more!
29:10 But *m* an early morning start,
31: 4 these uncircumcised come and *m* sport of me."
2Sm 3:12 the moment, to say, *M* an agreement with me,
3:13 well, I will *m* an agreement with you.
3:19 and then went to *m* his own report to David
3:21 that they may *m* an agreement with you;
6:21 not only will I *m* merry before the LORD,
7: 9 And I will *m* you famous like the great
7:12 your loins, and I will *m* his kingdom firm.
7:13 And I will *m* his royal throne firm forever.
7:27 finds the courage to *m* this prayer to you.
16:12 look upon my affliction and *m* it up to me
19:29 still have to *m* further appeal to the king?"
21: 3 I do for you and how must I *m* atonement,
1Kgs 1:20 all Israel is waiting for you to *m* known
1:47 'May God *m* Solomon more famous than you
12:11 a heavy yoke on you, I will *m* it heavier.
12:14 you a heavy yoke, but I will *m* it heavier.
16: 3 I will *m* your house like that of Jeroboam,
16:21 Tibni, son of Ginath, to *m* him king,
17:13 *m* me a little cake and bring it to me.
20:10 Samaria to *m* handfuls for all my followers."
20:34 you may *m* yourself bazaars in Damascus,
21:22 I will *m* your house like that of Jeroboam,
2Kgs 4:38 and *m* some vegetable stew for the guild
6: 8 he would *m* plans with his servants to
7: 2 if the LORD were to *m* windows in heaven,
7:19 if the LORD were to *m* windows in heaven,
12: 6 they must *m* whatever repairs on the temple
12: 9 the people nor *m* the repairs on the temple.
12:14 the LORD were used there to *m* silver cups,
17:29 But these peoples began to *m* their own
18:23 "Now, *m* a wager with my lord,
18:31 *M* peace with me and surrender!
19:28 mouth, and *m* you return the way you came.
1Chr 4:10 Help me and *m* me free of misfortune,
11:10 in his reign in order to *m* him true king,
12:32 by name to come and *m* David king.
12:39 was likewise of one mind to *m* David king.
15:16 cymbals, to *m* a loud sound of rejoicing.
16: 8 *m* known among the nations his deeds.
17: 8 I will *m* your name great like that of the
18: 8 which Solomon later used to *m* the bronze
22: 3 iron to *m* nails for the doors of the gates,
22: 5 Therefore I will *m* preparations for it."
28: 4 pleased him to *m* me king over all Israel.
2Chr 1: 7 Solomon and said to him, *M* a request of me,
7:20 and I will *m* it a proverb and a byword
9: 8 Israel as to will to *m* it last forever,
10:11 a heavy yoke on you, I will *m* it heavier!
10:14 heavy yoke on you, but I will *m* it heavier.
11:22 brothers, for he intended to *m* him king.
26:16 to *m* an offering on the altar of incense.
28:10 And now you are planning to *m* the children
28:13 for what you propose will *m* us guilty
28:21 to *m* payment to the king of Assyria,
29:10 I intend to *m* a covenant with the LORD,
Ezr 6:14 continued to *m* progress in the building,
7:28 heads to *m* the return journey with me.
Neh 8:15 palm and other leafy trees, to *m* booths,
10:34 sin offerings to *m* atonement for Israel,
13:13 to *m* the distribution to their brethren.
Tb 1: 6 would often *m* the pilgrimage alone to
3:15 and he has no other child to *m* his heir,
4:19 and ask him to *m* all your paths straight
5: 2 him to *m* him recognize me and trust me,
5: 3 man who will *m* the journey with you.
5: 7 for I need you to *m* the journey with me.
5:14 they used to *m* the pilgrimage to Jerusalem,
6: 5 gall, heart, and liver *m* useful medicines."
8: 6 let us *m* him a partner like himself,'
10: 5 of my eyes, that I let you *m* this journey!"
11: 8 This medicine will *m* the cataracts shrink
Jdt 3: 3 *m* use of them as you please.
8:16 It is not for you to *m* the Lord our God
8:21 and God will *m* us pay for its profanation
10: 8 to favor, and *m* your undertaking a success,
13:20 *m* this redound to your everlasting honor,
16: 4 babes to the ground, *m* my children a prey,
Est C:22 them and *m* an example of our chief enemy.
5: 5 *m* haste to fulfill the wish of Esther."
5: 6 whatever request you *m* shall be honored,
7: 2 Whatever request you *m* shall be honored,
1Mc 1:11 "Let us go and *m* an alliance with the
1:18 with a large fleet, to *m* war on Ptolemy,
3:14 "I will *m* a name for myself and win glory
4:31 *m* them ashamed of their troops and their
5:49 *m* an attack from the place where he was.
5:57 "Let us also *m* a name for ourselves by
6:58 and *m* peace with them and all their nation.
8:20 to you to *m* a peaceful alliance with you,
8:32 justice and *m* war on you by land and sea.' "
9:70 sent ambassadors to *m* peace with him
10: 4 first to *m* peace with him
10:16 Let us now *m* him our friend and ally."
10:40 I *m* a yearly personal grant of fifteen
10:63 center of the city and *m* a proclamation
10:72 Men say that you cannot *m* a stand against
11: 9 "Come, let us *m* a pact with each other;
11:40 he might *m* him king in his father's place.
12:53 let us *m* war on them and wipe out their
14:42 to *m* regulations concerning its functions
15: 4 troops and equipped warships to *m* a landing
15:31 not do this, we will come and *m* war on you."
15:40 the people and to *m* incursions into Judea,
2Mc 2:25 as well as to *m* it easy for the studious
3:18 houses in crowds to *m* public supplication,
4:27 he did not *m* any payments of the money he
5:21 In his arrogance he planned to *m* the land
6:24 would be unbecoming to *m* such a pretense;
7:24 to *m* him rich and happy if he would
7:24 he would *m* him his Friend and entrust him
7:28 God did not *m* them out of existing things;
7:37 to *m* you confess that he alone is God.
9: 4 he planned to *m* the Jews suffer for the
9: 4 "I will *m* Jerusalem the common graveyard
11: 2 plan was to *m* Jerusalem a Greek settlement;
11:37 *M* haste, then, to send us those who can
12:11 The defeated nomads begged Judas to *m*
12:12 Judas agreed to *m* peace with them.
12:24 of many of them, and could *m* these suffer.
Jb 7:17 What is man, that you *m* much of him,
8: 5 to God and *m* supplication to the Almighty,
11: 6 that God will *m* you answer for your guilt.
13:19 If anyone can *m* a case against me,
13:23 My misdeeds and my sins *m* known to me!
21:12 and *m* merry to the sound of the flute.
22: 3 a gain to him if you *m* your ways perfect?
22:28 When you *m* a decision,
31:15 he who made me in the womb *m* him?
32:15 They are dismayed, they *m* no more reply;
32:16 speak no more, and have ceased to *m* reply,
32:20 let me open my lips, and *m* reply.
33:13 do you *m* complaint against him that he
37:19 we cannot, for the darkness, *m* our plea.
39:20 Do you *m* the steed to quiver while his
40:28 Will he *m* an agreement with you that you
Ps(s) 5: 9 *m* straight your way before me.
18:36 me, and you have stooped to *m* me great.
21:10 *M* them burn as though in a fiery furnace,
25: 4 Your ways, O LORD, *m* known to me;
31: 3 your ear to me, *m* haste to deliver me!
35: 1 war against those who *m* war upon me.
37: 6 will *m* justice dawn for you like the light;
38:23 *M* haste to help me, O Lord my salvation!
40:14 O LORD, *m* haste to help me.
41: 3 he will *m* him happy on the earth,
44: 4 nor did their own arm *m* them victorious,
45:17 shall *m* them princes through all the land.
45:18 I will *m* your name memorable through all
48:13 Go about Zion, *m* the round;
57: 4 he *m* those a reproach who trample upon me;
65: 9 east and west you *m* resound with joy.
69:13 and drunkards *m* me the butt of their songs.
69:18 in my distress, *m* haste to answer me.
70: 2 O LORD, *m* haste to help me.
71:12 my God, *m* haste to help me.
73:28 to *m* the LORD GOD my refuge.
76:12 *M* vows to the LORD,
78: 5 fathers they should *m* known to their sons;
83:12 *M* their nobles like Oreb and Zeeb;
83:14 my God, *m* them like leaves in a whirlwind,
84: 7 of the mastic trees they *m* a spring of it;
89:22 with him, and that my arm may *m* him strong.
89:28 And I will *m* him the first-born,
89:30 I will *m* his posterity endure forever and
90: 5 You *m* an end of them in their sleep;
90:15 *M* us glad, for the days when you afflicted
92: 5 For you *m* me glad, O LORD
102: 9 their rage against me they *m* a curse of me.
104: 3 You *m* the clouds your chariot;
104: 4 You *m* the winds your messengers,
104:26 which you formed to *m* sport of it.
105: 1 *m* known among the nations his deeds.
106: 8 for his name's sake, to *m* known his power.
107:22 Let them *m* thank offerings and declare his
110: 1 hand till I *m* your enemies your footstool."
116:12 How shall I *m* a return to the LORD for all
119:27 *M* me understand the way of your precepts,
129: 3 long did they *m* their furrows.
132:17 will I *m* a horn to sprout forth for David;
140: 4 *m* their tongues sharp as those of serpents;
Prv 3: 6 of him, and he will *m* straight your paths.
11: 9 their knowledge the just *m* their escape.
16: 1 Man may *m* plans in his heart,
18:21 who *m* it a friend shall eat its fruit.
22:19 *m* known to you the words of Amen-em-Ope.
30:26 mighty, yet they *m* their home in the crags;
Eccl 5: 1 be quick to *m* a promise in God's presence.
5: 3 When you *m* a vow to God,
5: 4 You had better not *m* a vow than *m* it
5: 5 Let not your utterances *m* you guilty,
7: 7 For oppression can *m* a fool of a wise man,
7:13 can *m* straight what he has made crooked?
8: 7 for who will *m* known to him how it will be?
10:20 your thoughts do not *m* light of the king,
11: 2 *M* seven or eight portions;
Sg 1:11 We will *m* pendants of gold for you and
Wis 1:13 Because God did not *m* death,
6:13 She hastens to *m* herself known in
15: 6 *m* them and long for them and worship them.
15:12 one must," says he, *m* profit every way,
Sir 2: 6 *m* straight your ways and hope in him.
11:21 in an instant, to *m* a poor man rich.
11:34 *m* a stranger of you to your own household.
13:12 he will *m* of you a laughingstock,
13:21 When a poor man speaks they *m* sport of him;
15: 5 in the assembly she will *m* him eloquent.
17:20 sin, pray to him and *m* your offenses few.
18:28 Any learned man should *m* wisdom known,
18:31 they will *m* you the sport of your enemies.
19: 2 Wine and women *m* the mind giddy,
19: 9 be assured it will not *m* you burst.
22:23 *M* fast friends with a man while he is poor;
24: 8 my tent, Saying, 'In Jacob *m* your dwelling,
26:10 finding an opportunity, she *m* use of it;
27:14 on end, their brawls *m* one stop one's ears.
28:11 Pitch and resin *m* fire flare up
30:13 Discipline your son, *m* heavy his yoke,
33:26 *M* a slave work and he will look for his
40:17 Wealth or wages can *m* life sweet,
40:25 Gold and silver *m* one's way secure,
42:11 lest she *m* you the sport of your enemies,
44:21 would *m* him numerous as the grains of dust,

MAKE (cont.)
51: 1 I will *m* known your name,
Is 1:17 *M* justice your aim:
3: 4 I will *m* striplings their princes;
3: 7 You shall not *m* me ruler of the people."
5: 6 Yes, I will *m* it a ruin:
5:19 say, "Let him *m* haste and speed his work,
6:10 are to *m* the heart of this people sluggish,
7: 6 tear Judah asunder, *m* it our own by force,
8:10 *m* a resolve, and it shall not be carried
8:13 But with the LORD of hosts *m* your alliance
9: 2 as men *m* merry when dividing spoils.
10: 7 destroy, to *m* an end of nations not a few.
12: 4 among the nations *m* known his deeds,
13:12 I will *m* mortals more rare than pure gold,
13:13 For this I will *m* the heavens tremble and
14:21 *M* ready to slaughter his sons for the
14:23 *m* it a haunt of hoot owls and a marshland;
17:11 *m* them grow the day you plant them and *m*
19:12 Let them tell you and *m* known What the
19:21 The LORD shall *m* himself known in Egypt,
19:21 and fulfill the vows they *m* to the LORD.
26: 7 the path of the just you *m* level.
27: 5 *m* peace with me; peace shall he *m* with
28:17 I will *m* of right a measuring line,
29: 8 all the nations be, who *m* war against Zion.
30:30 The LORD will *m* his glorious voice heard,
35: 3 are feeble, *m* firm the knees that are weak,
35: 9 It is for those with a journey to *m*,
36: 8 *m* a wager with my lord the king of Assyria:
36:16 *M* peace with me and surrender!
37:29 mouth, and *m* you return the way you came.
38: 8 I will *m* the shadow cast by the sun on the
40: 3 *M* straight in the wasteland a highway for
41:15 I will *m* of you a threshing sledge,
41:15 and crush them, to *m* the hills like chaff.
41:28 to *m* an answer when I question them.
42:16 before them, and *m* crooked ways straight.
42:21 justice to *m* his law great and glorious,
43:19 In the desert I *m* a way,
44: 7 Let him stand up and speak, *m* it evident,
44:19 I then *m* an abomination out of the rest,
44:25 omens of liars, who *m* fools of diviners;
44:25 men back and *m* their knowledge foolish.
45: 7 darkness, I *m* well-being and create woe:
45:13 all his ways I *m* level.
46: 6 Then they hire a goldsmith to *m* it into a
47:12 Perhaps you can *m* them avail,
48:20 shouts of joy proclaim this, *m* it known;
49: 6 I will *m* you a light to the nations,
49:11 all my mountains, and *m* my highways level.
49:17 Your rebuilders *m* haste,
49:20 too small for me, *m* room for me to live in."
49:26 will *m* your oppressors eat their own flesh,
50: 3 in mourning, and *m* sackcloth their vesture.
51: 3 Her deserts he shall *m* like Eden,
51: 5 I will *m* my justice come speedily;
52: 5 their rulers *m* a boast of it,
53: 2 him no stately bearing to *m* us look at him,
54: 2 lengthen your ropes and *m* firm your stakes.
54:12 I will *m* your battlements of rubies,
56: 7 and *m* joyful in my house of prayer;
57: 4 Of whom do you *m* sport,
58: 4 fast so as to *m* your voice heard on high!
58:14 *m* you ride on the heights of the earth;
59: 2 It is your sins that *m* him hide his face
60:15 Now I will *m* you the pride of the ages,
61: 8 a lasting covenant I will *m* with them.
61:11 So will the Lord GOD *m* justice and praise
66:22 which I will *m* Shall endure before me,
Jer 3:16 or remember it, or miss it, or *m* another.
4: 5 it in Judah, *m* it heard in Jerusalem;
4:16 *M* this known to the nations,
5:14 Behold, I *m* my words in your mouth,
7:18 dough to *m* cakes for the queen of heaven,
9:10 The cities of Judah I will *m* into a waste,
9:11 mouth of the LORD has spoken *m* it known:
10:11 *m* heaven and earth perish from the earth,
10:19 if I *m* light of my wound, I can bear it.
15: 4 And I will *m* them an object of horror to
15:20 And I will *m* you toward this people a
16: 4 Sword and famine will *m* an end of them,
16:20 Can man *m* for himself gods?
19: 7 I will *m* them fall by the sword before
19: 8 I will *m* this city an object of amazement
19:12 I will *m* this city like Topheth.
23:27 to *m* my people forget my name for Baal.
24: 9 I will *m* them an object of horror to all
25:18 her princes, to *m* them a ruin and a desert,
26: 6 and *m* this the city which all the nations
27: 2 *M* for yourself bands and yoke bars and put
27:10 to *m* me banish you so that you will perish.
29:17 I will *m* them like rotten figs,
29:18 and *m* them an object of horror to all the
29:22 the LORD *m* you like Zedekiah and Ahab,
30:11 I will *m* an end of all the nations among
30:11 but of you I will not *m* an end.
30:19 I will *m* them not few,
31:13 Then the virgins shall *m* merry and dance,
31:31 when I will *m* a new covenant with the
31:33 But this is the covenant which I will *m*
32: 8 *m* it yours."
32:40 I will *m* with them an eternal covenant,
34: 5 it is I who *m* this promise,
34:17 I will *m* you an object of horror to all
34:18 will *m* like the calf which they cut in two,
39:18 I will *m* certain that you escape and do
41:10 set out to *m* his way to the Ammonites.
42:20 *m* known to us all that the LORD,
42:21 he has commissioned me to *m* known to you.
46:28 I will *m* an end of all the nations to
46:28 driven you, But of you I will not *m* an end:
48:26 *m* Moab drunk so that he retches and vomits,
49:15 will I *m* you among the despised
51:12 Babylon raise a signal, *m* strong the watch;
51:25 the cliffs, and *m* you a burnt mountain:
51:39 set a drink before them to *m* them drunk,
51:44 and *m* him disgorge what he swallowed;
51:53 and *m* her strong heights inaccessible,
51:57 will *m* her princes and her wise men drunk,
Bar 2:23 I will *m* to cease from the cities of Judah
2:34 I will *m* them increase;
6:40 forward Bel and ask the god to *m* noise,
Ez 3: 8 But I will *m* your face as hard as theirs,
3:26 I will *m* your tongue stick to your palate
4: 9 in a single vessel and *m* bread out of them.
5:14 I will *m* you a waste and a reproach among
6:14 live I will *m* the land a desolate waste,
7:14 sound the trumpet and *m* everything ready,
7:20 For this reason I *m* them refuse.
9:11 the writing case at his waist *m* his report:
13:18 *m* veils for every size of head
14: 8 man, and *m* of him an example and a byword.
15: 3 you use its wood to *m* anything worthwhile?
15: 3 Can you *m* even a peg from it,
15: 6 fire, do I *m* the inhabitants of Jerusalem.
15: 8 I will *m* the land a waste,
16: 2 man, *m* known to Jerusalem her abominations:
16:15 used your renown to *m* yourself a harlot,
17:24 green tree, and *m* the withered tree bloom.
18:31 and *m* for yourselves a new heart and a new
20: 4 *M* known to them the abominations of their
20:26 so as to *m* them an object of horror.
21:24 *m* for yourself two roads over which the
22: 2 Therefore *m* known all her abominations,
22: 4 Therefore I *m* you an object of scorn to
22:25 things, and *m* widows of many within her.
23:36 Then *m* known to them their abominations.
24:17 Groan in silence, *m* no lament for the dead,
25: 5 I will *m* Rabbah a pasture for camels,
25: 7 I will *m* you plunder for the nations,
25:13 I will *m* it a waste from Teman to Dedan;
26:14 I will *m* you a bare rock;
26:19 When I *m* you a city desolate like cities
26:20 and I will *m* you dwell in the nether lands,
26:21 I will *m* you a devastation,
27: 5 from Lebanon they took to *m* you a mast;
29: 4 I will put hooks in your jaws and *m* the
29:10 I will *m* the land of Egypt a waste and a
29:12 I will *m* the land of Egypt the most
29:15 I will *m* them few,
29:21 *m* a horn sprout for the house of Israel,
30:25 *m* the arms of the king of Babylon strong,
32:14 Then will I *m* their waters clear,
33:28 I will *m* the land a desolate waste,
33:29 when I *m* the land a desolate waste because
34:25 I will *m* a covenant of peace with them,
35: 3 against you and *m* you a desolate waste.
35: 7 I will *m* Mount Seir a desolate waste,
35: 9 desolate will I *m* you forever,
35:11 *m* myself known among you when I judge you,
36:27 within you and *m* you live by my statutes,
37: 6 put sinews upon you, *m* flesh grow over you,
37:22 I will *m* them one nation upon the land,
37:26 I will *m* with them a covenant of peace;
37:28 that it is I, the LORD, who *m* Israel holy,
38:23 *m* myself known in the sight of many nations;
39: 2 and I will *m* you come up from the recesses
39: 3 and *m* the arrows drop from your right.
39: 7 I will *m* my holy name known among my
39: 9 seven years they shall *m* fires with them.
39:10 for they shall *m* fires with the weapons.
43:11 *m* known to them the form and design of the
43:20 you shall purify it and *m* atonement for it.
44:23 and *m* known to them the difference between
44:25 They shall not *m* themselves unclean by
44:25 for these they may *m* themselves unclean.
45:13 These are the offerings you shall *m*:
45:14 homer, for ten liquid measures *m* a homer].
45:17 to *m* atonement on behalf of the house of
45:20 thus you shall *m* atonement for the temple.
Dn 3:34 us up forever, or *m* void your covenant.
7: 8 horns were torn away to *m* room for it.
7:19 wished to *m* certain about the fourth beast,
9:27 he shall *m* a firm compact with the many;
10:14 and came to *m* you understand what shall
11:11 whose great host shall *m* a stand but shall
11:32 By his deceit he shall *m* some who were
11:37 he shall *m* himself greater than all.
11:39 he shall *m* them rule over the many and
13:59 you in two so as to *m* an end of you both."
Hos 2: 5 I will *m* her like a desert
2:20 I will *m* a covenant for them on that day,
9:12 up their children, I will *m* them childless,
10: 4 *m* promises, swear false oaths, and *m* alliances,
11: 8 treat you as Admah, or *m* you like Zeboiim?
Jl 2:17 people, and *m* not your heritage a reproach,
2:19 will I *m* you a reproach among the nations.
Am 8: 9 I will *m* the sun set at midday and cover
8:10 all with sackcloth and *m* every head bald.
8:10 I will *m* them mourn as for an only son,
Ob 1: 2 See, I *m* you small among the nations;
1: 8 day *m* the wise men disappear from Edom,
Mi 1: 6 I will *m* Samaria a stone heap in the field,
1:16 *M* yourself bald, pluck out your hair,
2:11 on impulse, should *m* the futile claim:
4: 7 I will *m* of the lame a remnant,
4:13 horn I will *m* iron And your hoofs bronze,
Na 1: 9 It is he who will *m* an end!
1:14 I will *m* your grave a mockery.
3:16 *M* your couriers more numerous than the
Hb 2: 7 Shall not they who *m* you tremble awake?
2:15 of your wrath to drink, and *m* them drunk,
2:18 maker should trust in it, and *m* dumb idols?
3: 2 it, in the course of the years *m* it known;
Zep 1:18 For he shall *m* an end, yes, a sudden end,
2:13 He will *m* Nineveh a waste,
Zec 6: 8 land of the north will *m* my spirit rest
6:11 and gold you shall take, and *m* a crown;
10: 3 of Judah, and *m* them his stately war horse.
12: 2 I will *m* Jerusalem a bowl to stupefy all
12: 3 On that day I will *m* Jerusalem a weighty
12: 6 On that day I will *m* the princes of Judah
Mal 2: 2 you and of your blessing I will *m* a curse.
2:15 Did he not *m* one being,
Mt 3: 3 the way of the Lord, *m* straight his paths.' "
4:19 after me and I will *m* you fishers of men."
5:33 *m* good to the Lord all your pledges.'
5:36 cannot *m* a single hair white or black).
6:20 *M* it your practice instead to store up
10: 7 As you go, *m* this announcement:
10:36 to *m* a man's enemies those of his own
12:16 them not to *m* public what he had done.
12:29 *m* off with his property unless he first ties
15:18 is things like these that *m* a man impure.
15:20 These are the things that *m* a man impure.
16:23 You are trying to *m* me trip and fall.
20:25 their great ones *m* their importance felt.
23:15 over sea and land to *m* a single convert,
23:15 but once he is converted you *m* a devil of
27:48 it on a reed, tried to *m* him drink.
28:19 and *m* disciples of all the nations.
Mk 1: 3 crying, *M* ready the way of the Lord,
1:17 I will *m* you fishers of men."
5:19 "Go home to your family and *m* it clear to
5:39 "Why do you *m* this din with your wailing?
6:39 He told them to *m* the people sit down on
7:15 enters a man from outside can *m* him impure;
7:18 enters a man from outside can *m* him impure?
9: 3 than the work of any bleacher could *m* them.
10:42 their great ones *m* their importance felt.
10:48 were scolding him to *m* him keep quiet,
12:36 hand until I *m* your enemies your footstool.'
15:36 stuck it on a reed to try to *m* him drink.
Lk 3: 4 crying, *M* ready the way of the Lord,
5:24 to *m* it clear to you that the Son of Man
5:34 "Can you *m* guests of the groom fast while
11:40 he who made the outside *m* the inside too?
11:53 to *m* him speak on a multitude of questions,
14: 9 come and say to you, *M* room for this man,'
16: 4 Here is a way to *m* sure that people will
16: 6 invoice, sit down quickly, and *m* it fifty.'
16: 7 said, 'Take your invoice and *m* it eighty.'
16: 9 *M* friends for yourselves through your use
20:16 He will *m* an end to those tenant farmers
20:18 It will *m* dust of anyone on whom it falls."
20:43 while I *m* your enemies your footstool'?
21: 4 They *m* contributions out of their surplus,
Jn 1:23 *M* straight the way of the Lord!' "
3:21 to *m* clear that his deeds are done in God."
6:15 would come and carry him off to *m* him king,
7:24 by appearances and *m* an honest judgment.
8:53 Whom do you *m* yourself out to be?"
9:39 *m* the sightless see and the seeing blind."
14:23 to him and *m* our dwelling place with him.
19: 4 I am going to bring him out to you to *m*
Acts 1:24 *M* known to us which of these two you
2: 4 *m* bold proclamations as the Spirit prompted
2:12 *m* nothing at all of what had happened.
2:35 until I *m* your enemies your footstool.'
5: 3 let Satan fill your heart so as to *m* you lie
5:24 did not know what to *m* of the affair.
5:28 to *m* us responsible for that man's blood."
6:11 They persuaded some men to *m* the charge
7:40 *M* us gods that will be our leaders,'
7:44 *m* it according to the pattern he had seen.
7:45 God drove out to *m* room for our fathers.
7:50 Did not my hand *m* all these things?
9:34 Get up and *m* your bed."
10:17 *m* out the meaning of the vision he had had,
11: 6 *m* out four-legged creatures of the earth,
13:10 *m* crooked the straight paths of the Lord?
16:17 will *m* known to you a way of salvation."
17:23 in ignorance I intend to *m* known to you.
22:18 'You must *m* haste,' he said.
24:10 thus encouraged to *m* my defense before you,
24:17 alms to my own people and to *m*
24:19 to *m* whatever charge they have against me.
26: 2 to *m* my defense today in your presence,

26:28 Paul, and you will *m* a Christian out of me!"
27:39 They could *m* out a bay with a sandy beach,
27:43 to jump overboard first and *m* for land.
28:19 to *m* accusations against my own people.
Rom 2:18 to *m* sound judgments on disputed points.
2:28 Appearance does not *m* a Jew.
5:11 we go so far as to *m* God our boast through
6:12 your mortal body and *m* you obey its lusts;
6:19 *m* them now the servants of justice for
9:20 its molder, "Why did you *m* me like this?"
9:21 Does not a potter have the right to *m* from
9:22 to show his wrath and *m* known his power,
9:23 and in order to *m* known the riches of his
9:33 *m* men stumble and a rock to make them fall;
10:19 "I will *m* you jealous of those who are
10:19 with a senseless nation I will *m* you angry."
11:27 *m* with them when I take away their sins."
13:14 *m* no provision for the desires of the flesh.
14: 4 will, for the Lord is able to *m* him stand.
14:19 *m* it our aim to work for peace and to
15:26 have kindly decided to *m* a contribution
1Cor 3:13 That day will *m* its appearance with fire,
5: 7 old yeast to *m* of yourselves fresh dough,
6:15 and *m* them the members of a prostitute?
7:31 and those who *m* use of the world as though
9:18 do not *m* full use of the authority
14:40 but *m* sure that everything is done
2Cor 2: 2 *m* me happy again but the ones I grieved?
2: 4 not to *m* you sad but to help you realize
4: 6 that we in turn might *m* known the glory of
4: 7 to *m* it clear that its surpassing power
5: 9 we *m* it our aim to please him whether we
7: 2 *M* room for us in your hearts!
7:12 but to *m* plain in the sight of God the
10: 5 into captivity to *m* it obedient to Christ.
10: 8 If I find I must *m* a few further claims
10:13 When we *m* claims we will not go over the
11:30 boast, I will *m* a point of my weaknesses.
Gal 2: 2 to *m* sure the course I was pursuing,
2: 4 Christ Jesus and thereby to *m* slaves of us,
6: 7 *M* no mistake about it,
Eph 2:15 from us who had been two and to *m* peace,
4: 3 *M* every effort to preserve the unity which
5: 5 *M* no mistake about this:
5:16 *M* the most of the present opportunity,
5:26 He gave himself up for her to *m* her holy,
6:19 *m* known the mystery of the gospel
Phil 1:17 it will *m* my imprisonment even harsher.
1:26 should *m* you even prouder of me in Christ.
2: 2 *m* my joy complete by your unanimity,
Col 1:19 It pleased God to *m* absolute fullness
1:27 God has willed to *m* known to them the
1:28 hoping to *m* every man complete in Christ.
2:23 While these *m* a certain show of wisdom in
4: 5 *m* the most of every opportunity.
4:10 if he comes to you, *m* him welcome.
1Thes 2:12 pleaded with you to *m* your lives worthy
3:11 Jesus *m* our path to you a straight one!
3:12 And may the Lord increase you and *m* you
4: 1 you must learn to *m* still greater progress.
4:11 *M* it a point of honor to remain at peace
5:23 the God of peace *m* you perfect in holiness.
2Thes 1:11 that our God may *m* you worthy of his call,
3: 1 *m* progress and be hailed by many others,
1Tm 5: 7 *M* the following rules about widows,
2Tm 1: 4 That would *m* my happiness complete.
2: 7 for the Lord will *m* my meaning fully clear.
2:15 to *m* yourself worthy of God's approval,
3: 5 they *m* a pretense of religion
3: 6 *m* captives of silly women burdened
Ti 2:15 *M* our appeals and corrections with the
Phlm 1:20 want to *m* you "useful" to me in the Lord.
Heb 1:13 till I *m* your enemies your footstool"?
2: 5 For he did not *m* the world to come
2:10 should *m* their leader in the work of
5: 3 so must *m* sin offerings for himself as well
6: 6 it is impossible to *m* them repent again,
7:25 forever lives to *m* intercession for them.
8: 5 "See that you *m* everything according to
8: 8 when I will *m* a new covenant with the
8:10 But this is the covenant I will *m* with the
9: 9 *m* perfect the conscience of the worshiper,
10:16 I will *m* with them after those days,
12:13 *M* straight the paths you walk on,
Jas 1:16 *M* no mistake about this,
1:27 unspotted by the world *m* for pure worship
3: 3 the mouths of horses to *m* them obey us,
4: 1 cravings that *m* war within your members?
4:16 do is *m* arrogant and pretentious claims.
1Pt 2: 2 of the spirit to *m* you grow into salvation,
5: 1 that is to be revealed, *m* this appeal.
2Pt 1: 5 This is reason enough for you to *m* every
1:10 to *m* your call and election permanent,
3:14 *m* every effort to be found without stain
1Jn 1:10 we *m* him a liar and his word finds no
5:13 I have written this to you to *m* you
2Jn 1: 5 I would *m* this request of you (not as if I
Jude 1:24 *m* you stand unblemished and exultant
Rv 3: 9 I mean to *m* some of Satan's assembly,
3:12 " 'I will *m* the victor a pillar in the
12:17 off to *m* war on the rest of her offspring,
13:13 it could even *m* fire come down from heaven
13:14 telling them to *m* an idol in honor of the
21: 5 said to me, "See, I *m* all things new!"

MAKED (2)

1Mc 5:26 in Bosor near Alema, in Chaspho, *M*,
5:36 there he moved on and took Chaspho, *M*,

MAKER (34)

Jb 4:17 Can a mortal be blameless against his *M*?
32:22 if I did, my *M* would soon take me away.
35:10 the mighty, Saying, "Where is God, my *M*,
36: 3 afar, and to my *M* I will accord the right.
Ps(s) 134: 3 you from Zion, the *m* of heaven and earth.
149: 2 Let Israel be glad in their *m*,
Prv 14:31 who oppresses the poor blasphemes his *M*,
17: 5 He who mocks the poor blasphemes his *M*;
22: 2 the LORD is the *m* of them all.
Wis 12:12 perish, who can challenge you, their *m*;
14: 8 idol is accursed, and its *m* as well:
16:24 For your creation, serving you, its *m*,
Sir 10:12 withdrawing his heart from his *M*;
38:15 his *M* will be defiant toward the doctor.
39: 6 His care is to seek the LORD, his *M*,
39:28 force and appease the anger of their *M*.
43:11 Then bless its *M*,
46:13 Beloved of his people, dear to his *M*,
47: 8 loved his *M* and daily had his praises sung;
Is 17: 7 On that day man shall look to his *m*,
22:11 But you did not look to the city's *M*,
27:11 therefore their *m* shall not spare them,
29:16 As though what is made should say of its *m*,
45: 9 Woe to him who contends with his *M*;
45:11 the LORD, the Holy One of Israel, his *m*:
45:18 and *m* of the earth who established it.
51:13 as grass, And forget the LORD, your *m*,
54: 5 he who has become your husband is your *M*;
Bar 3:35 shining with joy for their *M*.
4: 7 provoked your *M* with sacrifices to demons,
Hos 8:14 has forgotten his *m* and built palaces.
Hb 2:18 carved image, that its *m* should carve it?
2:18 oracle, that its very *m* should trust in it,
Heb 11:10 foundations, whose designer and *m* is God.

MAKERS (3)

Ps(s) 115: 8 Their *m* shall be like them,
135:18 Their *m* shall be like them,
Is 44: 9 Idol *m* all amount to nothing,

MAKES (140)

Ex 4:11 one man speech and *m* another deaf and
4:11 who gives sight to one and *m* another blind?
30:38 Whoever *m* an incense like this for his own
Lv 3: 1 offering *m* his offering from the herd,
4: 3 thereby *m* the people also become guilty,
4:13 has forbidden and thus *m* itself guilty,
7: 7 to the priest who *m* atonement with it.
7:12 anyone *m* a peace offering in thanksgiving,
15: 3 it *m* no difference whether the flow drains
17:11 as the seat of life, that *m* atonement.
Nm 5: 8 the priest *m* amends for the guilty man.
5:14 of jealousy that *m* him suspect his wife,
30: 3 When a man *m* a vow to the LORD or binds
30: 4 in her father's house, *m* a vow to the LORD,
30:11 she *m* a vow or binds herself under oath
30:14 that she *m* under oath to mortify herself,
Dt 7:10 a one, but *m* him personally pay for it.
22:14 and *m* monstrous charges against her and
27:15 be the man who *m* a carved or molten idol
1Sm 2: 7 The LORD *m* poor and makes rich,
2Chr 6:19 of supplication your servant *m* before you.
25:19 and thus ambition *m* you proud.
1Mc 10: 4 before he *m* peace with Alexander
2Mc 15:38 whereas mixing wine with water *m* a more
Jb 12:17 away barefoot, and of judges he *m* fools.
12:23 He *m* nations great and he destroys them;
12:25 he *m* them stagger like drunken men.
36: 9 Then he *m* known to them what they have
37:15 *m* the light shine forth from his clouds?
39:16 young and ruthlessly *m* nought of her brood;
39:18 she *m* sport of the horse and his rider.
40:20 to him, and of all wild animals he *m* sport.
41:23 He *m* the depths boil like a pot;
Ps(s) 29: 6 He *m* Lebanon leap like a calf and Sirion
40: 5 Happy the man who *m* the LORD his trust;
48: 9 God *m* it firm forever.
135: 7 with the lightning he *m* the rain;
147: 8 Who *m* grass sprout on the mountains and
Prv 6:13 his feet, *m* signs with his fingers;
10: 1 A wise son *m* his father glad,
11: 5 The honest man's virtue *m* his way straight,
11:18 The wicked man *m* empty profits,
12:25 depresses it, but a kindly word *m* it glad.
13:12 Hope deferred *m* the heart sick,
14:17 The quick-tempered man *m* a fool of himself,
15:20 A wise son *m* his father glad,
16: 7 he *m* even his enemies be at peace with him.
16:23 The mind of the wise man *m* him eloquent,
21: 6 He who *m* a fortune by a lying tongue is
24:26 a kiss on the lips who *m* an honest reply.
29: 3 He who loves wisdom *m* his father glad,
31:13 and flax and *m* cloth with skillful hands.
31:22 She *m* her own coverlets;
31:24 She *m* garments and sells them,
Eccl 10:19 forth merriment and wine *m* the living glad,
Wis 6:16 Because she *m* her own rounds,
6:19 and incorruptibility *m* one close to God;
12:16 over all things *m* you lenient to all.
13:14 man or *m* it resemble some worthless beast.
13:15 He *m* a fitting shrine for it and puts it
15:17 he *m* a dead thing with his lawless hands.
17:13 the more one *m* of not knowing the cause
Sir 6: 4 owner and *m* him the sport of his enemies.
11:25 day of prosperity *m* one forget adversity;
11:25 day of adversity *m* one forget prosperity.
12:15 While you stand firm, he *m* no bold move;
17: 2 gives him and *m* him return to earth again.
20:12 wise man *m* himself popular by a few words,
20:22 A man *m* a promise to a friend out of shame,
25:16 looks, and *m* her sullen as a female bear.
26:19 sin, for whom the LORD *m* ready the sword.
27:14 oath-filled talk *m* the hair stand on end,
28:14 and *m* them refugees among the peoples;
30: 3 who educates his son *m* his enemy jealous,
33:11 his great knowledge the LORD *m* men unlike;
33:12 Some he blesses and *m* great,
36:22 beauty *m* her husband's face light up,
38: 2 His knowledge *m* the doctor distinguished,
38: 4 God *m* the earth yield healing herbs which
42:19 He *m* known the past and the future,
43:16 thunder of his voice *m* the earth writhe;
Is 33: 6 That which *m* her seasons lasting,
40:23 and *m* the rulers of the earth as nothing.
40:29 for the weak he *m* vigor abound.
44:15 himself, or *m* a fire for baking bread;
44:15 another part he *m* a god which he adores,
44:17 Of what remains he *m* a god,
53: 5 him was the chastisement that *m* us whole,
61:11 and a garden *m* its growth spring up,
62: 4 in you, and *m* your land his spouse.
62: 7 And *m* of it the pride of the earth.
64: 1 is set ablaze, or fire *m* the water boil!
Jer 10:13 He *m* the lightning flash in the rain,
51:16 He *m* the lightning flash in the rain,
Ez 15: 2 what *m* the wood of the vine better than
46:12 prince *m* a freewill offering to the LORD,
46:16 If the prince *m* a gift of part of his
46:17 But if he *m* a gift of part of his
47: 8 the sea, the salt waters, which it *m* fresh.
Dn 2:21 and seasons, *m* kings and unmakes them.
Hos 4:12 and their wand *m* pronouncements for them,
9: 4 bread, that *m* unclean all who eat of it;
Mi 7: 3 the prince *m* demands,
Na 1: 8 He *m* an end of his opponents,
Hb 1:11 culprit who *m* his own strength his god!
3: 6 his look *m* the nations tremble.
3:19 he *m* my feet swift as those of hinds and
Zep 2:11 he *m* all the gods of earth to waste away;
Zec 9:17 grain that *m* the youths flourish,
10: 1 It is the LORD who *m* storm clouds.
Mt 15:11 goes into a man's mouth that *m* him impure;
15:20 that *m* no man impure."
18: 4 Whoever *m* himself lowly,
23:17 the gold or the temple which *m* it sacred?
23:19 or the altar which *m* the offering sacred?
Mk 7:20 that and nothing else is what *m* him impure.
7:37 He *m* the deaf hear and the mute speak!"
Lk 9:39 a convulsion and *m* him foam at the mouth,
Jn 3: 8 *m* but you do not know where it comes from,
19:12 *m* himself a king becomes Caesar's rival."
Rom 5: 3 We know that affliction *m* for endurance,
7:23 this *m* me the prisoner of the law of sin
8:26 but the Spirit himself *m* intercession for
8:28 We know that God *m* all things work
9:18 wishes, and whom he wishes he *m* obdurate.
1Cor 7:19 and its lack *m* no difference either.
7:37 his will *m* up his mind to keep his virgin,
2Cor 5:20 This *m* us ambassadors for Christ,
10:10 and his word *m* no great impact.
Gal 2: 6 however (and it *m* no difference to me how
4: 7 the fact that you are a son *m* you an heir,
6: 7 mistake about it, no one *m* a fool of God!
Col 3:14 binds the rest together and *m* them perfect.
1Thes 1: 8 *m* it needless for us to say anything more.
2Tm 1: 7 spirit, but rather one that *m* us strong,
Heb 1: 7 angels he says, "He *m* his angels winds,
Jas 1: 3 your faith is tested this *m* for endurance.
3: 5 a small member, yet it *m* great pretensions.
1Jn 2:18 *m* us certain that it is the final hour.

MAKHELOTH (2)

Nm 33:25 Setting out from Haradah, they camped at *M*.
33:26 Setting out from *M*, they camped at Tahath.

MAKING (117)

Gn 17: 5 I am *m* you the father of a host of nations.
27:12 He will think I am *m* sport of him,
28:20 to protect me on this journey I am *m* and
34:30 "You have brought trouble upon me by *m* me
39:21 he showed him kindness by *m* the chief
Ex 1:14 *m* life bitter for them with hard work in
15:25 LORD, in *m* rules and regulations for them,
28: 4 In *m* these sacred vestments which your
29:36 you purge the altar in *m* atonement for it;
29:37 Seven days you shall spend in *m* atonement

MAKING (cont.)
31: 4 of embroidery, in *m* things of gold,
32: 8 *m* for themselves a molten calf and
32:31 sin in *m* a god of gold for themselves!
35:32 of embroidery, in *m* things of gold,
35:35 the *m* of variegated cloth of violet,
38:28 were used for *m* the hooks on the columns,
Lv 13:46 dwell apart, *m* his abode outside the camp.
18:25 by *m* it vomit out its inhabitants.
19:29 your daughter by *m* a prostitute of her;
25:46 property, *m* them perpetual slaves.
Nm 6:11 thus *m* atonement for him for the sin he
15: 7 *m* a sweet-smelling offering to the LORD.
Dt 1:41 *m* light of going up into the hill country.
9:16 to you by *m* for yourselves a molten calf!
23:23 Should you refrain from *m* a vow,
24:11 man to whom you are *m* the loan
26:17 you are *m* this agreement with the LORD:
26:18 the LORD is *m* this agreement with you:
27: 7 eat them there, *m* merry before the LORD,
28:63 took delight in *m* you grow and prosper,
29:13 with you alone that I am *m* this covenant,
Jos 9: 4 *m* use of old sacks for their asses,
Jgs 8:33 *m* Baal of Berith their god and forgetting
17: 4 by *m* a carved idol overlaid with silver."
1Sm 16:12 to behold and *m* a splendid appearance.
2Sm 6: 6 steadied it, for the oxen were *m* it tip.
6:18 When he finished *m* these offerings,
8: 2 with a line, *m* them lie down on the ground.
23: 4 *m* the greensward sparkle after rain.'
2Kgs 22: 5 and lumbermen *m* repairs on the temple,
1Chr 6:34 of holies and of *m* atonement for Israel,
12:39 intention of *m* David king over all Israel.
2Chr 1: 1 with him, constantly *m* him more renowned.
34:16 same time that he was *m* his report to him.
Ezr 5: 8 and is *m* good progress under their hands.
6:22 by *m* the king of Assyria favorable to them,
Tb 10:14 of all, for *m* his journey so successful.
Jdt 7:24 in not *m* peace with the Assyrians.
Est B: 2 and by *m* my government humane and
D: 2 In *m* her state appearance,
1Mc 5:38 have rallied to him, *m* a very large force;
8:19 After *m* a very long journey to Rome,
12:36 for *m* the walls of Jerusalem still higher,
2Mc 1:19 *m* sure that the place would be unknown to
2:26 upon ourselves the labor of *m* this digest,
2:31 but the man who is *m* an adaptation should
3:20 hands raised toward heaven, *m* supplication.
9:14 to the ground and *m* it a common graveyard;
Ps(s) 145:12 *M* known to men your might and the glorious
Eccl 12:12 Of the *m* of many books there is no end,
Sir 18:23 *m* a vow have the means to fulfill it;
Is 10: 2 of their rights, *M* widows their plunder,
14: 2 *m* captives of its captors and ruling over
42: 2 not *m* his voice heard in the street.
44:13 *m* it like a man in appearance and dignity,
45: 1 before him, and *m* kings run in his service,
45: 9 or, "What you are *m* has no hands"?
54:15 be any attack, it shall not be of my *m;*
55:10 the earth, *m* it fertile and fruitful,
Jer 18: 4 he was *m* turned out badly in his hand,
18: 4 *m* of the clay another object of whatever
18:11 fashioning evil against you and *m* a plan.
25: 9 will doom them, *m* them an object of horror,
34:15 *m* an agreement before me in the house
46: 5 They flee headlong without *m* a stand.
Ez 16:21 children to them, *m* them pass through fire.
20:31 by *m* your children pass through the fire,
27:30 shore, *M* their voice heard on your behalf,
37:19 the stick of Judah, *m* them a single stick;
45:25 the same rites, *m* the same sin offerings,
Dn 2:38 over to you, *m* you ruler over them all;
11:36 himself and *m* himself greater than any god;
Hos 13: 2 to sin, *m* for themselves molten images,
Mt 2:16 *m* his calculations on the basis of the
9:23 players and the crowd who were *m* a din,
14:34 After *m* the crossing they reached the
15: 9 reverence, *m* dogmas out of human precepts.' "
27:24 Pilate finally realized that he was *m* no
27:31 when they had finished *m* a fool of him,
Mk 1:45 whole matter freely, *m* the story public.
3:20 *m* it impossible for them to get any food
6:31 *m* it impossible for them to so much as eat.
6:53 After *m* the crossing they came ashore at
13: 1 As he was *m* his way out of the temple area,
Lk 1:22 He kept *m* signs to them,
8:39 town *m* public what Jesus had done for him.
9:57 As they were *m* their way along,
13:22 all the while *m* his way toward Jerusalem.
24:13 Two of them that same day were *m* their way
Jn 5:18 own Father, thereby *m* himself God's equal.
10:33 You who are only a man are *m* yourself God."
Acts 6:13 "This man never stops *m* statements
9:31 *m* steady progress in the fear of the Lord;
9:32 Once when Peter was *m* numerous journeys,
11:19 *m* the message known to none but Jews.
24:13 the charges they are *m* against me.
27:12 of *m* Phoenix and spending the winter there.
1Cor 7:21 be better off *m* the most of your slavery.
2Cor 1:17 in *m* those plans I was acting insincerely?
Gal 2:10 one thing that I was *m* every effort to do.
3:14 thereby *m* it possible for us to receive
6:12 are *m* a play for human approval
Col 1:20 *m* peace through the blood of his cross.
1Thes 3:13 *m* them blameless and holy before our God
Rv 13:12 promote its interests by *m* the world
17:17 by *m* them agree to bestow their
19:20 *m* them accept the mark of the beast and

MAKKEDAH (9)
Jos 10:10 harrassing them as far as Azekah and *M.*
10:16 kings who had fled, hid in a cave at *M.*
10:17 had been discovered hiding in a cave at *M,*
10:21 safely to Joshua and the camp at *M,*
10:28 *M,* too, Joshua captured
10:28 *M* what he had done to the king of Jericho.
10:29 passed on with all Israel from *M* to Libnah,
12:16 Geder, Hormah, Arad, Libnah, Adullam, *M,*
15:41 Gederoth, Beth-dagon, Naamah and *M;*

MALACHI (1)
Mal 1: 1 The word of the LORD to Israel through *M.*

MALADIES (3)
Dt 28:59 constant blows, malignant and lasting *m.*
Lk 5:15 to hear him and to be cured of their *m.*
8: 2 who had been cured of evil spirits and *m;*

MALCAM (1)
1Chr 8: 9 the father of Jobab, Zibia, Mesha, *M,*

MALCHIAH (3)
Jer 21: 1 King Zedekiah sent him Pashhur, son of *M,*
38: 1 son of Shelemiah, and Pashhur, son of *M,*
38: 6 threw him into the cistern of Prince *M,*

MALCHIEL (3)
Gn 46:17 Heber and *M.*
Nm 26:45 through *M* the clan of the Malchielites.
1Chr 7:31 Beriah's sons were Heber and *M,*

MALCHIELITES (1)
Nm 26:45 through Malchiel the clan of the *M.*

MALCHIJAH (13)
1Chr 6:25 son of Michael, son of Baaseiah, son of *M,*
9:12 son of Jeroham, son of Pashhur, son of *M;*
24: 9 the fourth to Seorim, the fifth to *M,*
Ezr 10:25 Izziah, Malchijah, Mijamin, Eleazar, *M,*
10:31 Eliezer, Isshijah, *M,*
Neh 3:11 far as the Oven Tower, was repaired by *M.*
3:14 The Dung Gate was repaired by *M,*
3:31 *M,* a member of the goldsmiths' guild,
8: 4 and on his left Pedaiah, Mishael, *M,*
10: 4 Azariah, Jeremiah, Pashhur, Amariah, *M,*
11:12 of Zechariah, son of Pashhur, son of *M,*
12:42 Shemaiah, Eleazar, Uzzi, Jehohanan, *M,*

MALCHIRAM (1)
1Chr 3:18 Shealtiel, *M,* Pedaiah, Shenazzar

MALCHISHUA (5)
1Sm 14:49 sons of Saul were Jonathan, Ishvi, and *M;*
31: 2 and slew Jonathan, Abinadab, and *M,*
1Chr 8:33 Saul became the father of Jonathan, *M,*
9:39 Saul became the father of Jonathan, *M,*
10: 2 had killed Jonathan, Abinadab, and *M,*

MALCHUS (1)
Jn 18:10 (The slave's name was *M.)*

MALE (107)
Gn 1:27 *m* and female he created them.
5: 2 he created them *m* and female.
6:19 two into the ark, one *m* and one female,
7: 2 with you seven pairs, a *m* and its mate;
7: 2 animals, one pair, a *m* and its mate;
7: 3 of the air, seven pairs, a *m* and a female,
7: 3 unclean birds, one pair, a *m* and a female.
7: 9 *m* and female entered the ark with Noah,
7:16 Those that entered were *m* and female,
12:16 male and female slaves, *m* and female asses,
17:10 every *m* among you shall be circumcised.
17:12 Throughout the ages, every *m* among you,
17:14 If a *m* is uncircumcised,
17:23 every *m* among the members of Abraham's
17:27 and all the *m* members of his household,
20:14 flocks and herds and *m* and female slaves
24:35 silver and gold, *m* and female slaves,
30:43 *m* and female servants and camels and asses.
32: 6 sheep, as well as *m* and female servants.
34:15 us by having every *m* among you circumcised.
34:22 that every *m* among us be circumcised as
46:15 thirty-three persons in all, *m* and female.
Ex 12: 5 must be a year-old *m* and without blemish.
13:12 and all the *m* firstlings of your animals
13:15 of the *m* sex that opens the womb,
20:10 son or daughter, or your *m* or female slave,
20:17 neighbor's wife, nor his *m* or female slave,
21: 7 she shall not go free as *m* slaves do.
21:20 "When a man strikes his *m* or female slave
21:26 "When a man strikes his *m* or female slave
21:27 out a tooth of his *m* or female slave,
21:32 it is a *m* or a female slave that it gores,
34:19 "To me belongs every first-born *m* that
Lv 1: 3 the herd, it must be a *m* without blemish.
1:10 a goat, he must bring a *m* without blemish.
3: 1 the LORD either a *m* or a female animal,
3: 6 he may offer either a *m* or a female animal,
4:23 as his offering an unblemished *m* goat.
6:11 All the *m* descendants of Aaron may partake
14:10 day he shall take two unblemished *m* lambs,
14:12 Taking one of the *m* lambs,
14:21 shall take one *m* lamb for a guilt offering,
15:33 the law for *m* and female;
16: 5 shall receive two *m* goats for a sin offering
16: 7 Taking the two *m* goats and setting them
18:22 You shall not lie with a *m* as with a woman;
20:13 If a man lies with a *m* as with a woman,
22:19 that he offers must be an unblemished *m.*
23:19 One *m* goat shall be sacrificed as a sin
25: 6 yourself and for your *m* and female slaves,
25:44 "Slaves, *m* and female,
Nm 1: 2 houses, registering each *m* individually.
3:15 registering every *m* of a month or more."
3:39 The total number of *m* Levites a month old
5: 3 *M* and female alike,
18:10 every *m* among you may partake of them.
26:62 of *m* Levites one month or more of age,
31: 7 Moses, and killed every *m* among them.
31:17 every *m* child and every woman who has had
Dt 5:14 son or daughter, or your *m* or female slave,
5:14 *m* and female slave should rest as you do.
5:21 house or field, nor his *m* or female slave,
12:12 and daughters, your *m* and female slaves,
12:18 son and daughter, your *m* and female slave,
15:19 all the *m* firstlings of your herd and of
16:11 son and daughter, your *m* and female slave,
16:14 son and daughter, your *m* and female slave,
16:16 *m* among you shall appear before the LORD,
20:13 your hand, put every *m* in it to the sword;
28:68 to your enemies as *m* and female slaves,
Jos 17: 2 Shemida, the other *m* children of Manasseh,
1Sm 1:11 me, if you give your handmaid a *m* child,
8:16 He will take your *m* and female servants,
25:22 *m* alive among all those who belong to him."
1Kgs 11:15 the slain, put to death every *m* in Edom.
11:16 until they had killed off every *m* in Edom.
14:10 I will cut off every *m* in Jeroboam's line,
16:11 a single *m* relative or friend of his.
21:21 and will cut off every *m* in Ahab's line,
2Kgs 5:26 sheep or cattle, *m* or female servants?
9: 8 I will cut off every *m* in Ahab's line,
2Chr 31:19 portions to every *m* among the priests
35:25 recited to this day by all the *m* and female
Ezr 2:65 not counting their *m* and female slaves,
2:65 also had two hundred *m* and female singers.
Neh 7:67 not counting their *m* and female slaves,
7:67 also had two hundred *m* and female singers.
Tb 10:10 *m* and female slaves,
1Mc 5:28 He slaughtered all the *m* population,
5:35 he killed all the *m* population,
5:51 He slaughtered every *m,*
Eccl 2: 7 I acquired *m* and female slaves,
2: 8 I got for myself *m* and female singers and
Is 14: 2 as *m* and female slaves on the Lord's soil,
66: 7 upon her, she safely delivers a *m* child.
Jer 34: 9 to free his Hebrew slaves, *m* and female,
34:10 to set free their *m* and female servants,
34:11 afterward they took back their *m* and
34:16 taking back your *m* and female slaves
Ez 16:17 given you and made for yourself *m* images,
45:23 he shall offer one *m* goat each day.
Mal 1:14 is the deceiver, who has in his flock a *m,*
Mt 19: 4 made them *m* and female and declared,
Mk 10: 6 of creation God made them *m* and female;
Lk 2:23 *m* shall be consecrated to the Lord."
Gal 3:28 or Greek, slave or freeman, *m* or female.

MALEDICTION (5)
Nm 5:21 LORD make you an example of *m*
Jer 29:18 to all the kingdoms of the earth, of *m,*
42:18 shall become an example of *m* and horror,
44:12 or by hunger, and become an example of *m,*
Dn 9:11 not heeding your voice, the sworn *m,*

MALEFACTOR (1)
1Pt 4:15 suffers for being a murderer, a thief, a *m,*

MALEFACTORS (1)
Ps(s) 64: 3 Shelter me against the council of *m,*

MALES (36)
Gn 34:24 Hamor and his son Shechem, and all the *m,*
34:25 any trouble, and massacred all the *m.*
Ex 12:48 *m* among them must first be circumcised,
Lv 6:22 All the *m* of the priestly line may partake
7: 6 *m* of the priestly line may partake of it;
Nm 1:20 when all the *m* of twenty years or more who
1:22 when all the *m* of twenty years or more who
1:24 when all the *m* of twenty years or more who

1:26 when all the *m* of twenty years or more who
1:28 when all the *m* of twenty years or more who
1:30 when all the *m* of twenty years or more who
1:32 when all the *m* of twenty years or more who
1:34 when all the *m* of twenty years or more who
1:36 when all the *m* of twenty years or more who
1:38 when all the *m* of twenty years or more who
1:40 when all the *m* of twenty years or more who
1:42 when all the *m* of twenty years or more who
3:22 their *m* of a month or more were registered,
3:28 their *m* of a month or more were registered,
3:34 their *m* of a month or more were registered,
3:40 *m* of the Israelites a month old or more,
3:43 *m* of a month or more were registered,
Jgs 21:11 under the ban all *m* and every woman
2Chr 31:16 houses of *m* thirty years of age and over,
Ezr 8: 3 him one hundred and fifty *m* were enrolled;
8: 4 of Zerahiah, and with him two hundred *m;*
8: 5 of Jahaziel, and with him three hundred *m;*
8: 6 son of Jonathan, and with him fifty *m;*
8: 7 son of Athalaiah, and with him seventy *m;*
8: 8 son of Michael, and with him eighty *m;*
8: 9 and with him two hundred and eighteen *m;*
8:10 and with him one hundred and sixty *m;*
8:11 son of Bebai, and with him twenty-eight *m;*
8:12 and with him one hundred and ten *m;*
8:13 and Shemaiah, and with them sixty *m;*
8:14 son of Zakkur, and with him seventy *m.*

MALFORMATION (1)

Lv 21:18 lame, or who has any disfigurement or *m,*

MALICE (20)

Dt 4:42 to whom he had previously borne no *m,*
19: 4 to whom he had previously borne no *m.*
19: 6 he had previously borne the slain man no *m.*
1Mc 5: 4 also remembered the *m* of the sons of Baean,
Jb 15:35 They conceive *m* and bring forth emptiness;
Ps(s) 7:10 Let the *m* of the wicked come to an end,
17: 3 me with fire, you shall find no *m* in me.
41: 7 his heart stores up *m;*
Prv 26:26 but his *m* will be revealed in the assembly.
Wis 12:10 race was wicked and their *m* ingrained,
16:14 Man, however, slays in his *m,*
Is 58:13 your own interests, or speaking with *m*—
59: 4 they conceive mischief and bring forth *m.*
Ez 25:15 with destructive *m* in their hearts,
Jl 4:13 The vats overflow, for great is their *m.*
Na 3:19 not been overwhelmed, steadily, by your *m?*
Eph 4:31 harsh words, slander, and *m* of every kind.
Col 3: 8 all the anger and quick temper, the *m,*
Ti 3: 3 We went our way in *m* and envy,
Jas 3: 6 among our members as a whole universe of *m.*

MALICIOUS (4)

Est E: 6 *m* slander the sincere good will of rulers.
Ps(s) 37: 7 path of the man who does *m* deeds.
119:150 by *m* persecutors who are far from your law.
Is 58: 9 oppression, false accusation and *m* speech;

MALICIOUSLY (2)

Ex 21:14 kills another after *m* scheming to do so,
Ez 25: 6 *m* in your heart over the land of Israel,

MALICIOUSNESS (2)

Mk 7:22 murder, adulterous conduct, greed, *m,*
Rom 1:29 *m,* greed, ill will, envy, murder

MALIGNANT (6)

Lv 13:51 be its use, the infection is *m* leprosy,
13:52 since it has *m* leprosy,
Dt 7:15 of the *m* diseases that you know from Egypt,
28:35 with *m* boils of which you cannot be cured,
28:59 and constant blows, *m* and lasting maladies.
Ps(s) 41: 9 'A *m* disease fills his frame';

MALLET (2)

Jgs 4:21 got a tent peg and took a *m* in her hand.
5:26 peg, with her right, for the workman's *m.*

MALLOTHI (2)

1Chr 25: 4 Giddalti, Romamti-ezer, Joshbekashah, *M,*
25:26 The nineteenth fell to *M,*

MALLUCH (7)

1Chr 6:29 son of Kishi, son of Abdi, son of *M,*
Ezr 10:29 Meshullam, *M,* Adaiah; Jashub,
10:32 Malchijah, Shemaiah, Shimeon, Benjamin, *M,*
Neh 10: 5 Amariah, Malchijah, Hattush, Shebaniah, *M,*
10:28 Maaseiah, Ahiah, Hanan, Anan, *M,*
12: 2 Seraiah, Jeremiah, Ezra, Amariah, *M,*
12:14 for *M,* Jonathan; for Shebaniah, Joseph;

MALLUS (1)

2Mc 4:30 the people of Tarsus and *M* rose in revolt,

MALTA (1)

Acts 28: 1 we learned that the island was called *M.*

MALTREAT (2)

1Chr 10: 4 these uncircumcised may not come and *m* me."
Lk 6:28 who curse you and pray for those who *m* you.

MALTREATED (8)

Ex 5:23 your name, he has *m* this people of yours,
Nm 20:15 how the Egyptians *m* us and our fathers,
Dt 26: 6 When the Egyptians *m* and oppressed us,
2Mc 7:13 and *m* the fourth brother in the same way.
7:15 forward the fifth brother and *m* him.
Hos 5:11 Is Ephraim *m,* his rights violated?
Lk 20:12 they likewise *m* before driving him away.
Acts 7:24 Upon seeing one of them *m,*

MAMRE (10)

Gn 13:18 went on to settle near the terebinth of *M,*
14:13 camping at the terebinth of *M* the Amorite,
14:24 Aner, Eshcol and *M;*
18: 1 appeared to Abraham by the terebinth of *M,*
23:17 Ephron's field in Machpelah, facing *M,*
23:19 the field of Machpelah, facing *M* (that is,
25: 9 son of Zohar the Hittite, which faces *M,*
35:27 Jacob went home to his father Isaac at *M,*
49:30 in the field of Machpelah, facing on *M,*
50:13 in the field of Machpelah, facing on *M,*

MAN (2497)

Gn 1:26 "Let us make *m* in our image,
1:27 God created *m* in his image;
2: 5 earth and there was no *m* to till the soil,
2: 7 the LORD God formed *m* out of the clay of
2: 7 of life, and so *m* became a living being.
2: 8 he placed there the *m* whom he had formed.
2:15 *m* and settled him in the garden of Eden,
2:16 The LORD God gave *m* this order:
2:18 "It is not good for the *m* to be alone.
2:19 to the *m* to see what he would call them;
2:19 *m* called each of them would be its name.
2:20 The *m* gave names to all the cattle,
2:20 to be the suitable partner for the *m.*
2:21 the LORD God cast a deep sleep on the *m,*
2:22 woman the rib that he had taken from the *m.*
2:23 When he brought her to the man, the *m* said:
2:23 for out of 'her *m*' this one has been taken."
2:24 That is why a *m* leaves his father and
2:25 The *m* and his wife were both naked,
3: 8 the *m* and his wife hid themselves from the
3: 9 God then called to the *m* and asked him,
3:12 *m* replied, "The woman whom you put
3:17 To the *m* he said: Because you listened
3:20 The *m* called his wife Eve,
3:21 For the *m* and his wife the LORD God made
3:22 The *m* has become like one of us,
3:24 When he expelled the *m,*
4: 1 The *m* had relations with his wife Eve,
4: 1 produced a *m* with the help of the LORD."
4:23 I have killed a *m* for wounding me,
5: 1 When God created *m,*
5: 2 created, he blessed them and named them *m.*"
6: 2 saw how beautiful the daughters of *m* were
6: 3 "My spirit shall not remain in *m* forever,
6: 4 had intercourse with the daughters of *m,*
6: 6 regretted that he had made *m* on the earth,
6: 9 Noah, a good *m* and blameless in that age,
7:23 *m* and cattle, the creeping things
8:21 again will I doom the earth because of *m,*
9: 5 and from *m* in regard to his fellow man I
9: 6 blood of man, by *m* shall his blood be shed;
9: 6 For in the image of God has *m* been made.
9:20 Now Noah, a *m* of the soil,
16:12 He shall be a wild ass of a *m,*
17:17 be born to a *m* who is a hundred years old?
19: 4 all the people to the last *m*—
19:31 and there is not a *m* on earth to unite
20: 4 you slay a *m* even though he is innocent?
24:16 very beautiful, a virgin, untouched by *m.*
24:21 The *m* watched her the whole time,
24:22 the *m* took out a gold ring weighing half a
24:26 *m* then bowed down in worship to the LORD,
24:30 her words about what the *m* had said to her,
24:30 rushed outside to the *m* at the spring.
24:32 The *m* then went inside;
24:35 abundantly that he has become a wealthy *m;*
24:58 asked her, "Do you wish to go with this *m?*"
24:61 mounted their camels and followed the *m.*
24:65 the servant, "Who is the *m* out there,
25:27 skillful hunter, a *m* who lived in the open;
25:27 whereas Jacob was a simple *m,*
26:11 "Anyone who molests this *m* or his wife
27:11 "But my brother Esau is a hairy *m,*"
30:43 Thus the *m* grew increasingly prosperous,
32:18 you, he may ask you, 'Whose *m* are you?
32:25 Then some *m* wrestled with him until the
32:26 *m* saw that he could not prevail over him,
32:27 *m* then said, "Let me go,
32:28 "What is your name?" the *m* asked.
32:29 *m* said, "You shall no longer spoken
34:14 to give our sister to an uncircumcised *m;*
34:19 *m* lost no time in acting in the matter,
34:24 every able-bodied *m* in the community,
35:29 as an old *m* and was taken to his kinsmen.
37:15 a *m* met him as he was wandering about in
37:15 are you looking for?" the *m* asked him.
37:17 *m* told him, "They have moved on
38:25 "It is by the *m* to whom these things
41:13 to my post, but the other *m* was impaled."
41:33 Pharaoh seek out a wise and discerning *m*
41:38 "a *m* so endowed with the spirit of God?"
42:11 All of us are sons of the same *m.*
42:13 brothers, sons of a certain *m* in Canaan;
42:18 for I am a God-fearing *m.*
42:30 "The *m* who is lord of the country,"
42:33 *m* who is lord of the country said to us:
43: 3 "The *m* strictly warned us.
43: 5 we will not go down, because the *m* told us,
43: 6 telling the *m* that you had another brother?"
43: 7 "The *m* kept asking about ourselves and
43:11 and take them down to the *m* as gifts:
43:13 too, and be off on your way back to the *m.*
43:14 dispose the *m* to be merciful toward you,
44:13 Then, when each *m* had reloaded his donkey,
44:15 "You should have known that such a *m* as I
44:26 *m* if our youngest brother is not with us.
Ex 2: 1 Now a certain *m* of the house of Levi
2:20 "Where is the *m?*"
2:21 and the *m* gave him his daughter Zipporah
4:11 *m* speech and makes another deaf and dumb?
8:13 the earth and gnats came upon *m* and beast.
8:14 As the gnats infested *m* and beast,
9: 9 boils on *m* and beast throughout the land."
9:10 it caused festering boils on *m* and beast.
9:19 Whatever *m* or beast remains in the fields
9:22 on *m* and beast and every growing thing in
9:25 It struck down every *m* and beast that was
11: 2 people that every *m* is to ask his neighbor,
12:12 first-born of the land, both *m* and beast,
12:48 *m* who is uncircumcised may partake of it.
13: 2 among the Israelites, both of *m* and beast,
13:15 Egypt, every first-born of *m* and of beast.
16:16 each *m* providing for those of his own tent."
19:13 Such a one, *m* or beast,
21: 4 property and the *m* shall leave alone.
21: 7 "When a *m* sells his daughter as a slave,
21:12 a *m* a mortal blow must be put to death.
21:13 He, however, who did not hunt a *m* down,
21:14 But when a *m* kills another after
21:20 "When a *m* strikes his male or female
21:26 "When a *m* strikes his male or female
21:28 "When an ox gores a *m* or a woman to death,
21:29 should it then kill a *m* or a woman,
21:33 "When a *m* uncovers or digs a cistern and
21:37 "When a *m* steals an ox or a sheep and
22: 4 a *m* is burning over a field or a vineyard,
22: 6 "When a *m* gives money or an article to
22: 9 "When a *m* gives an ass,
22:13 a *m* borrows an animal from his neighbor,
22:13 not present, the *m* must make restitution.
22:15 a *m* seduces a virgin who is not betrothed,
23: 3 shall not favor a poor *m* in his lawsuit.
25: 2 From every *m* you shall accept the
32: 1 as for the *m* Moses who brought us out of
32:23 as for the *m* Moses who brought us out of
33:11 face to face, as one *m* speaks to another.
33:20 see, for no *m* sees me and still lives.
35:29 Every Israelite *m* and woman brought to the
36: 6 "Let neither *m* nor woman make any more
38:26 was received from every *m* of twenty years
Lv 5:10 make atonement for the sin the *m* committed,
5:13 the *m* committed in any of the above cases,
13: 3 seeing this, shall declare the *m* unclean.
13: 4 quarantine the stricken *m* for seven days.
13: 6 skin, the priest shall declare the *m* clean;
13: 6 The *m* shall wash his garments and so
13: 8 the skin, he shall declare the *m* unclean;
13:11 *m* unclean without first quarantining him,
13:12 skin of the stricken *m* from head to foot,
13:13 he shall declare the stricken *m* clean;
13:13 it has all turned white, the *m* is clean.
13:17 he shall declare the stricken *m* clean,
13:18 "If a *m* who had a boil on his skin which
13:20 white, he shall declare the *m* unclean;
13:22 the *m* is stricken.
13:24 "If a *m* had a burn on his skin,
13:27 the *m* unclean and stricken with leprosy.
13:28 priest shall therefore declare the *m* clean,
13:29 "When a *m* or a woman has a sore on the
13:33 below the skin, the *m* shall shave himself,
13:34 the skin, he shall declare the *m* clean;
13:36 the *m* is surely unclean.
13:37 the *m* is clean,
13:38 "When the skin of a *m* or a woman is
13:40 "When a *m* loses the hair of his head,
13:44 of the body, the *m* is leprous and unclean,
14: 4 he shall order the *m* who is to be purified,
14: 7 the *m* to be purified from his leprosy.
14: 8 The *m* being purified shall then wash his
14:11 shall place the *m* who is being purified,
14:18 put on the head of the *m* being purified.
14:20 atonement for him, the *m* will be clean.
14:21 "If a *m* is poor and cannot afford so much,
14:25 of the right ear of the *m* being purified,
14:30 or pigeons, such as the *m* can afford,
14:31 the LORD for the *m* who is to be purified.
15: 2 Every *m* who is afflicted with a chronic

MAN (cont.)

15: 4 which the *m* afflicted with the flow lies,
15: 6 on which the afflicted *m* was sitting,
15: 7 of the afflicted *m* shall wash his garments,
15: 8 If the afflicted *m* spits on a clean man,
15: 9 Any saddle on which the afflicted *m* rides,
15:11 Anyone whom the afflicted *m* touches with
15:12 touched by the afflicted *m* shall be broken;
15:13 "When a *m* who has been afflicted
15:16 "When a *m* has an emission of seed,
15:18 "If a *m* lies carnally with a woman,
15:24 If a *m* dares to lie with her,
15:32 the *m* who is afflicted with a chronic flow,
15:33 for the *m* who lies with an unclean woman."
16:26 "The *m* who has led away the goat for
17: 4 a *m* shall be cut off from among his people.
18: 5 for the *m* who carries them out will find
19:17 you may have to reprove your fellow *m*,
19:20 "If a *m* has carnal relations with a
19:20 already been living with another *m*
19:21 *m*, moreover, shall bring to the entrance
20: 3 I myself will turn against such a *m* and
20: 5 I myself will set my face against that *m*
20:10 If a *m* commits adultery with his
20:11 If a *m* disgraces his father by lying with
20:11 *m* and his stepmother shall be put to death;
20:12 If a *m* lies with his daughter-in-law,
20:13 If a *m* lies with a male as with a woman,
20:14 If a *m* marries a woman and her mother also,
20:14 the *m* and the two women as well shall be
20:15 If a *m* has carnal relations with an animal,
20:15 an animal, the *m* shall be put to death,
20:17 If a *m* consummates marriage with her
20:17 the *m* shall pay the penalty of having had
20:18 If a *m* lies in sexual intercourse with a
20:20 If a *m* disgraces his uncle by having
20:20 the *m* and his aunt shall pay the penalty
20:21 If a *m* marries his brother's wife and thus
20:27 "A *m* or a woman who acts as a medium or
22: 5 creature or any *m* whose uncleanness,
24:10 a *m* born of an Israelite mother (Shelomith,
24:11 This *m* quarreled publicly with another
24:20 The same injury that a *m* gives another
24:21 whoever slays a *m* shall be put to death.
25:26 the *m* has no relative to redeem his land,
25:42 they shall not be sold as slaves to any *m*.
27: 3 shall be fifty silver shekels for a *m*,
27: 7 sum shall be fifteen shekels for a *m*,
27:22 "If the field that some *m* dedicates to
27:28 which a *m* vows as doomed to the LORD,
Nm 1: 4 you there shall be a *m* from each tribe,
1:18 Every *m* of twenty years or more then
2:17 every *m* shall be in his proper place,
2:34 every *m* according to his clan and his
3:13 sacred to me, both of *m* and of beast.
4:27 you shall make each *m* of them responsible
4:32 You shall designate for each *m* of them all
5: 6 If a *m* (or a woman) commits a fault
5: 6 fault against his fellow *m* and wrongs him,
5: 8 the priest makes amends for the guilty *m*.
5:10 Each Israelite *m* may dispose of his own
5:13 him by having intercourse with another *m*,
5:14 or if a *m* is overcome by a feeling of
5:19 no other *m* has had intercourse with you,
5:20 have acted impurely by letting a *m*
5:30 a *m* that he becomes suspicious of his wife,
5:31 The *m* shall be free from guilt,
6: 2 When a *m* (or a woman) solemnly takes the
8:17 the Israelites, both of *m* and of beast,
9:13 *m* shall bear the consequences of his sin.
11:27 So, when a young *m* quickly told Moses,
12: 3 far the meekest *m* on the face of the earth.
13: 2 shall send one *m* from each ancestral tribe,
14:35 in the desert they shall die to the last *m*."
15:32 a *m* was discovered gathering wood on the
15:35 to Moses, "This *m* shall be put to death;
17:20 staff of the *m* of my choice shall sprout.
17:28 Are we to perish to the last *m*?"
18:15 opens the womb, whether of *m* or of beast,
18:15 but you must let the first-born of *m*,
19: 9 a *m* who is clean shall gather up the ashes
19:14 When a *m* dies in a tent,
19:18 a *m* who is clean shall take some hyssop,
19:19 The clean *m* shall sprinkle the unclean on
19:20 Any unclean *m* who fails to have himself
23:19 God is not *m* that he should speak falsely,
24: 3 the utterance of the *m* whose eye is true,
24:15 the utterance of the *m* whose eye is true,
26:64 Among them there was not a *m* of those who
27: 8 If a *m* dies without leaving a son,
27:16 set over the community a *m* who shall act
27:18 "Take Joshua, son of Nun, a *m* of spirit,
30: 3 When a *m* makes a vow to the LORD or binds
31:17 woman who has had intercourse with a *m*.
31:18 all girls who had no intercourse with a *m*.
35:16 "If a *m* strikes another with an iron
35:17 If a *m* strikes another with a
35:18 If a *m* strikes another with a
35:20 "If a *m* pushes another out of hatred,
35:22 if a *m* pushes another accidentally and not
Dt 1:17 lowly and to the great alike, fearing no *m*,
1:31 God, carried you, as a *m* carries his child,
1:35 'Not one *m* of this evil generation shall
4:16 it be in the form of a *m* or a woman,
4:28 by the hands of *m* out of wood and stone,
4:32 ever since God created *m* upon the earth;
5:24 have found out today that *m* can still live
7:14 no *m* or woman among you shall be childless
7:24 No *m* will be able to stand up against you,
8: 3 you that not by bread alone does *m* live,
8: 5 you even as a *m* disciplines his son.
15:12 "If your kinsman, a Hebrew *m* or woman,
15:12 dismiss him from your service, a free *m*.
17: 2 a *m* or a woman who does evil in the sight
17: 5 you shall bring the *m* (or woman) who has
17:12 Any *m* who has the insolence to refuse to
17:15 that *m* over you as your king whom the LORD,
18:19 If any *m* will not listen to my words which
19: 6 had previously borne the slain *m* no malice.
19:15 shall not take the stand against a *m*
19:16 takes the stand against a *m* to accuse him
19:21 Do not look on such a *m* with pity.
21: 1 "If the corpse of a slain *m* is found
21:15 "If a *m* with two wives loves one and
21:18 "If a *m* has a stubborn and unruly son who
21:22 "If a *m* guilty of a capital offense is
22: 5 shall not wear an article proper to a *m*,
22: 5 man, nor shall a *m* put on a woman's dress;
22:13 "If a *m*, after marrying a woman
22:16 'I gave my daughter to this *m* in marriage,
22:18 elders shall take the *m* and chastise him,
22:19 because the *m* defamed a virgin in Israel.
22:22 "If a *m* is discovered having relations
22:22 both the *m* and the woman with whom he has
22:23 a *m* comes upon a maiden who is betrothed,
22:24 *m* because he violated his neighbor's wife.
22:25 a *m* comes upon such a betrothed maiden,
22:25 relations with her, the *m* alone shall die.
22:26 This case is like that of a *m* who rises up
22:28 "If a *m* comes upon a maiden that is not
22:29 the *m* who had relations with her shall pay
23: 1 "A *m* shall not marry his father's wife,
24: 1 "When a *m*, after marrying a woman
24: 2 goes and becomes the wife of another *m*,
24: 3 or if this second *m* who has married her,
24: 5 "When a *m* is newly wed, he need not go
24: 7 "If any *m* is caught kidnaping a fellow
24:11 but shall wait outside until the *m* to whom
24:12 If he is a poor *m*, you shall not sleep
24:16 his own guilt shall a *m* be put to death.
25: 7 a *m* does not care to marry his brother's
25:10 family of the *m* stripped of his sandal.'
27:15 be the *m* who makes a carved or molten idol
27:18 be he who misleads a blind *m* on his way!'
27:25 accepts payment for slaying an innocent *m*!'
28:29 you will grope like a blind *m* in the dark,
28:30 betroth a wife, another *m* will have her.
28:54 The most refined and fastidious *m* among
29:17 Let there be, then, no *m* or woman,
29:19 and jealousy will flare up against that *m*,
32:25 nursing babe as well as the hoary old *m*.
32:30 "How could one *m* rout a thousand,
33: 1 is the blessing which Moses, the *m* of God,
33: 8 Thummim, to the *m* of your favor your Urim;
Jos 5: 4 every *m* of military age had died in the
6:26 be the *m* who attempts to rebuild this city,
8:17 with every *m* engaged in this pursuit of
8:24 there in the open, down to the last *m*.
10:14 when the LORD obeyed the voice of a *m*;
10:21 *m* uttering a sound against the Israelites.
14: 6 know what the LORD said to the *m* of God,
20: 5 who slew his fellow *m* unintentionally
22:20 Though he was but a single *m*,
Jgs 1:24 a *m* coming out of the city and said to him,
1:25 they let the *m* and his whole clan go free.
3:29 Not a *m* escaped.
4:16 the sword, not even one *m* surviving.
4:22 "Come, I will show you the *m* you seek."
5:30 there must be a damsel or two for each *m*,
6:16 you will cut down Midian to the last *m*."
7: 4 you that a certain *m* is to go with you,
7:13 one *m* was telling another about a dream.
8:14 He captured a young *m* of Succoth,
8:21 for a man's strength is like the *m*."
9: 2 rule over you, or that one *m* rule over you?'
11:39 She had not been intimate with *m*.
13: 2 There was a certain *m* from Zorah,
13: 6 told her husband, "A *m* of God came to me;
13: 8 he said, "may the *m* of God whom you sent,
13:10 "The *m* who came to me the other day has
13:11 When he reached the *m* he said to him,
14:20 the one who had been best *m* at his wedding.
15: 2 so I gave her to your best *m*.
15: 6 his wife was taken and given to his best *m*."
16: 7 her, "I shall be as weak as any other *m*."
16:11 her, "I shall be as weak as any other *m*."
16:13 the pin, I shall be as weak as any other *m*."
16:17 me, and I shall be as weak as any other *m*."
16:19 a *m* who shaved off his seven locks of hair.
17: 1 There was a *m* in the mountain region of
17:11 young Levite decided to stay with the *m*,
18:19 you to be priest for the family of one *m*
19: 7 The *m* still made a move to go,
19:10 *m*, however, refused to stay another night
19:15 The *m* waited in the public square of the
19:16 an old *m* came from his work in the field;
19:17 city, the old *m* asked where he was going,
19:20 "You are welcome," the old *m* said to him,
19:22 They said to the old *m* whose house it was,
19:23 Since this *m* is my guest,
19:24 *m* you must not commit this wanton crime."
19:28 So the *m* placed her on an ass and started
20: 1 So all the Israelites came out as one *m*:
20: 8 All the people rose as one *m* to say,
20:44 thousand of them fell, warriors to a *m*.
20:46 thousand swordsmen, warriors to a *m*.
Ru 1: 1 so a *m* from Bethelehem of Judah departed
1: 2 The *m* was named Elimelech,
2:19 "The *m* at whose place I worked today is
3: 3 Do not make yourself known to the *m* before
3: 8 the *m* gave a start and turned around to
3:16 So she told her all the *m* had done for her,
3:18 what happens, for the *m* will not rest,
4:13 When they came together as *m* and wife,
1Sm 1: 1 There was a certain *m* from Ramathaim,
1: 3 This *m* regularly went on pilgrimage from
2: 9 For not by strength does *m* prevail;
2:15 and say to the *m* offering the sacrifice,
2:16 And if the *m* protested to him,
2:25 If a *m* sins against another man,
2:25 but if a *m* sins against the LORD,
2:27 A *m* of God came to Eli and said to him:
2:31 no *m* in your family shall reach old age.
2:32 shall never be an old *m* in your family.
4:10 every *m* fled to his own tent.
4:13 *m*, however, went into the city to divulge
4:16 *m* quickly came up to Eli and said,
4:18 since he was an old *m* and heavy,
9: 1 was a stalwart *m* from Benjamin named Kish,
9: 2 named Saul, who was a handsome young *m*.
9: 6 There is a *m* of God in this city, a *m* held
9: 7 "If we go, what can we offer the *m*?
9: 7 we have no present to give the *m* of God.
9: 8 If I give that to the *m* of God,
9:10 went to the city where the *m* of God lived.
9:16 this time tomorrow I will send you a *m*
9:17 him, "This is the *m* of whom I told you;
10: 6 state and will be changed into another *m*.
10:24 you see the *m* whom the LORD has chosen?
11: 7 of the LORD, the people turned out to a *m*.
11:13 say, "No *m* is to be put to death this day,
13:14 The LORD has sought out a *m* after his own
14:24 be the *m* who takes food before evening,
14:28 'Cursed be the *m* who takes food this day!'
14:52 When Saul saw any strong or brave *m*,
15:29 for he is not *m* that he should repent."
16: 7 Not as *m* sees does God see, because *m* sees
16:12 sent and had the young *m* brought to them.
16:16 look for a *m* skilled in playing the harp.
17:10 Give me a *m* and let us fight together."
17:24 When the Israelites saw the *m*,
17:25 "Do you see this *m* coming up?
17:26 "What will be done for the *m* who kills
17:27 how the *m* who kills him will be rewarded."
17:58 asked him, "Whose son are you, young *m*?"
21:15 "You see the *m* is mad.
24:20 For if a *m* meets his enemy,
25: 2 was a *m* of Maon who had property in Carmel;
25: 3 The *m* was named Nabal, his wife Abigail.
25:25 pay attention to that worthless *m* Nabal,
25:34 not have had a single *m* or boy left alive."
26:15 a *m* whose like does not exist in Israel?
26:23 each *m* for his justice and faithfulness.
27: 9 David would not leave a *m* or woman alive,
27:11 a *m* or woman alive to be brought to Gath,
28:14 replied, "It is an old *m* who is rising,
29: 4 "Send that *m* back!
30:22 except to each *m* his wife and children.
2Sm 1: 2 On the third day a *m* came from Saul's camp,
1:13 *m* who had brought him the information,
4:10 the *m* who informed me of Saul's death,
4:11 have slain an innocent *m* in bed at home,
6:19 to each *m* and each woman in the entire
7:19 this too you have shown to *m*, Lord GOD!
12: 2 *m* had flocks and herds in great numbers.
12: 3 But the poor *m* had nothing at all except
12: 4 Now, the rich *m* received a visitor,
12: 5 very angry with that *m* and said to Nathan:
12: 5 the *m* who has done this merits death!
12: 7 "You are the *m*!
13:13 And you would be a discredited *m* in Israel.
14:25 In all Israel there was not a *m* who could
15: 5 Whenever a *m* approached him to show homage,
16: 5 was approaching Bahurim, a *m* named Shimei,
16: 7 "Away, away, you murderous and wicked *m*!
17: 3 is the death of only one *m* you are seeking;
17:10 Then even the brave *m* with the heart of a
17:18 reached the house of a *m* in Bahurim
18:12 But the *m* replied to Joab:
18:20 are not the *m* to bring the news today.
18:24 looked about and saw a *m* running all alone.
18:26 "There is another *m* running by himself."
18:27 The king replied, "He is a good *m*;
18:32 you with evil intent be as that young *m*!"
19: 8 a single *m* will remain with you overnight,
19:15 He won over all the Judahites as one *m*,
19:33 old *m* of eighty and very wealthy besides,
20: 1 Every *m* to his tent, O Israel!"
20:12 and the *m* noticed that all the soldiers

20:21 A *m* named Sheba,
21: 4 our place to put any *m* to death in Israel."
21: 5 "As for the *m* who was exterminating us
21:20 was a *m* of large stature with six fingers
22:49 me and from the violent *m* you rescue me.
23: 1 the utterance of the *m* God raised up,
23:20 Kabzeel, was a *m* of great achievements.
24:14 but let me not fall by the hand of *m*."
1Kgs 1:42 are a *m* of worth and must bring good news."
2: 2 Take courage and be a *m*.
2: 9 You are a prudent *m* and will know how to
5: 5 every *m* under his vine or under his fig
8:31 "If a *m* sins against his neighbor and is
8:46 you (for there is no *m* who does not sin),
11:28 Jeroboam was a *m* of means,
11:28 that he was also an industrious young *m*,
12:22 the LORD spoke to Shemaiah, a *m* of God:
12:24 Let every *m* return home,
13: 1 A *m* of God came from Judah to Bethel by
13: 4 *m* of God was crying out against the altar,
13: 5 *m* of God had given as the word of the LORD.
13: 6 Then the king appealed to the *m* of God.
13: 6 So the *m* of God entreated the LORD,
13: 7 the king invited the *m* of God,
13: 8 kingdom," the *m* of God said to the king,
13:11 the *m* of God had done that day in Bethel.
13:12 by the *m* of God who had come from Judah.
13:14 it, he mounted and followed the *m* of God,
13:14 "Are you the *m* of God who came from
13:21 to the *m* of God who had come from Judah:
13:26 "It is the *m* of God who rebelled against
13:29 body of the *m* of God and put it on the ass,
13:31 in the grave where the *m* of God is buried.
17:18 "Why have you done this to me, O *m* of God?
17:24 indeed I know that you you are a *m* of God,"
20: 7 clearly that this *m* wants to ruin us.
20:11 'It is not for the *m* who is buckling his
20:20 each of them struck down his *m*.
20:28 A *m* of God came up and said to the king of
20:37 The prophet met another *m* and said,
20:37 The *m* struck him a blow and wounded him.
20:39 brought me a man and said, 'Guard this *m*.
20:40 looking here and there, the *m* disappeared."
20:42 set free the *m* I doomed to destruction,
22:27 Put this *m* in prison and feed him scanty
22:36 Every *m* to his city, every *m* to his land,
2Kgs 1: 6 "A *m* came up to us,"
1: 7 "What was the *m* like who came up to you
1: 9 *M* of God," he ordered, "the king
1:10 "If I am a *m* of God," Elijah answered
1:11 *M* of God," he called out to Elijah,
1:12 "If I am a *m* of God,"
1:13 *M* of God," he implored him
3:21 every *m* capable of bearing arms was called
4: 1 You know that he was a God-fearing *m*,
4: 7 She went and told the *m* of God,
4: 9 "I know that he is a holy *m* of God.
4:16 she protested, "you are a *m* of God;
4:21 and laid him on the bed of the *m* of God.
4:22 I must go quickly to the *m* of God,
4:25 she reached the *m* of God on Mount Carmel.
4:25 the *m* of God said to his servant Gehazi:
4:27 she reached the *m* of God on the mountain,
4:27 to push her away, but the *m* of God said:
4:40 began to eat it, they exclaimed, *M* of God,
4:42 *m* came from Baal-shalishah bringing the *m*
5: 1 But valiant as he was, the *m* was a leper.
5: 7 that this *m* should send someone to me to
5: 8 When Elisha, the *m* of God,
5:14 seven times at the word of the *m* of God.
5:15 with his whole retinue to the *m* of God.
5:20 the servant of Elisha, the *m* of God,
5:26 "Was I not present in spirit when the *m*
6: 6 asked the *m* of God.
6: 7 And the *m* reached down and grasped it.
6: 9 But the *m* of God would send word to the
6:10 the place which the *m* of God had indicated,
6:15 of the *m* of God arose and went out,
6:19 I will take you to the *m* you want."
6:32 The king had sent a *m* ahead before he
7: 2 arm the king leaned, answered the *m* of God,
7:17 just as the *m* of God had predicted when
7:18 the prophecy of the *m* of God to the king,
7:19 The adjutant had answered the *m* of God.
8: 2 got ready and did as the *m* of God said,
8: 4 with Gehazi, the servant of the *m* of God.
8: 7 was told that the *m* of God had come there,
8: 8 gift with you and go call on the *m* of God.
8:11 The *m* of God wept,
9: 4 The young *m* (the guild prophet) went to
9: 6 *m* poured the oil on his head and said,
9:11 You know that kind of *m* and his talk,
9:12 told them what the young *m* had said to him,
13:19 Angry with him, the *m* of God said:
13:21 Once some people were burying a *m*,
13:21 cast the dead *m* into the grave of Elisha,
13:21 *m* came in contact with the bones of Elisha,
19:19 our God, save us from the power of this *m*,
22:15 'Say to the *m* who sent you to me,
23:16 word of the LORD which the *m* of God
23:16 *m* of God who had proclaimed these words,
23:17 "It is the grave of the *m* of God who came
1Chr 10:12 done to Saul, its warriors rose to a *m*,
11:22 of Jehoiada, a valiant *m* of mighty deeds,
11:23 the Egyptian, a huge *m* five cubits tall.
16: 3 Israelite, to every *m* and every woman,
22: 9 He will be a peaceful *m*,
23:14 As for Moses, however, the *m* of God,
27:32 David's uncle and a *m* of intelligence,
28: 1 the warriors and every important *m*.
28: 3 you are a *m* who fought wars and shed blood.'
29: 1 for this castle is not intended for *m*,
2Chr 6: 5 any *m* to be commander of my people Israel;
6:22 "When any *m* sins against his neighbor and
6:23 requiting the wicked *m* and holding him
6:36 you (for there is no *m* who does not sin),
8:14 was the command of David, the *m* of God.
11: 2 of the LORD came to Shemaiah, a *m* of God:
11: 4 Let every *m* return home,
14:10 let no *m* prevail against you."
15:13 whether small or great, whether *m* or woman.
18:26 Put this *m* in prison and feed him scanty
19: 6 for you are judging, not on behalf of *m*,
25: 4 his own guilt shall a *m* be put to death."
25: 7 But a *m* of God came to him and said:
25: 9 Amaziah answered the *m* of God,
25: 9 The *m* of God replied,
30:16 to the law of Moses, the *m* of God.
36:17 sparing neither young *m* nor maiden,
Ezr 2: 1 each *m* in his own city (those who returned
3: 1 the people gathered at Jerusalem as one *m*.
3: 2 in the law of Moses, the *m* of God.
3: 9 stood as one *m* to supervise those who were
6:11 If any *m* violates this edict,
8:18 a well-instructed *m*,
Neh 1:11 day, and let him find favor with this *m*—
4:16 Jerusalem, each *m* with his own attendant,
5:13 every *m* who fails to keep this promise,
6:11 "A *m* like me take flight?
6:11 Can a *m* like me enter the temple to save
7: 2 trustworthy and God-fearing *m* than most.
7: 6 each *m* to his own city (those who returned
8: 1 *m* in the open space before the Water Gate,
11: 1 bring one *m* in ten to reside in Jerusalem,
11: 3 *m* on the property he owned in his own city.)
11:20 cities of Judah, each *m* in his inheritance.
12:24 of the command of David, the *m* of God,
12:36 musical instruments of David, the *m* of God.
13:10 had deserted, each *m* to his own field.
Tb 1: 4 I lived as a young *m* in my own country,
2: 2 go out and try to find a poor *m* from among
2: 4 and I carried the dead *m* from the street
2: 8 "Will this *m* never learn!
3:14 I am innocent of any impure act with a *m*,
4:14 the wages of any *m* who works for you,
4:18 "Seek counsel from every wise *m*,
4:19 If the Lord chooses, he raises a *m* up;
4:21 You will be a rich *m* if you fear God,
5: 3 *m* who will make the journey with you.
5: 5 Tobiah said to him, "Who are you, young *m*?"
5: 7 said to him, "Wait for me, young *m*,
5: 9 *m* who is one of our own Israelite kinsmen!"
5: 9 Tobit said, "Call the *m*,
5: 9 summon the *m*, saying, "Young *m*,
5:10 a blind *m* who cannot see God's sunlight,
5:12 for a hired *m* to travel with your son?"
6: 8 smoke surrounds a *m* or a woman
6: 9 it on the eyes of a *m* who has cataracts,
6:13 or let her become engaged to another *m*;
6:15 slay any *m* who wishes to come close to her.
7: 2 young *m* looks just like my kinsman Tobit!"
7: 7 *m* should be afflicted with blindness!"
7:10 for no *m* is more entitled to marry my
8: 1 They brought the young *m* out of the dining
8: 6 'It is not good for the *m* to be alone;
9: 6 noble and good, upright and charitable *m*,
10: 6 *m* who is traveling with him is trustworthy,
11: 6 is coming, and the *m* who traveled with him!"
12: 1 due to the *m* who made the journey with you;
Jdt 2:18 abundant provisions for each *m*,
6: 3 will strike them down as one *m*,
8:16 not *m* that he should be moved by threats,
10:19 is not wise to leave one *m* of them alive,
16:22 but she gave herself to no *m* all the days
Est A: 2 *m* who served at the king's court,
1:22 every *m* should be lord in his own home.
4:11 any *m* or woman who goes to the king
C: 7 to place the honor of *m* above that of God.
6: 6 for the *m* whom the king wishes to reward?"
6: 7 "For the *m* whom the king wishes to reward
6: 9 clothe the *m* the king wishes to reward,
6: 9 for the *m* whom the king wishes to reward!' "
6:11 for the *m* whom the king wishes to reward!"
7: 5 "is the *m* who has dared to do this?"
1Mc 2: 8 "Her temple has become like a *m* disgraced,
2:17 an honorable and great *m* in this city,
2:62 Do not fear the words of a sinful *m*,
2:65 brother Simeon who I know is a wise *m*;
5:42 "Do not allow any *m* to pitch a tent;
7: 7 send a *m* whom you trust to go and see all
7: 8 a great *m* in the kingdom,
7:38 Take revenge on this *m* and his army,
8:16 their government to one *m* every year,
10:16 "Shall we ever find another *m* like him?
10:35 Let no *m* have authority to exact payment
10:38 Judea so that they may be under one *m*
11:38 his entire army, every *m* to his home,
13:53 that his son John was now a grown *m*,
14:12 *m* sat under his vine and his fig tree,
2Mc 2:29 while the *m* who undertakes the decoration
2:31 but the *m* who is making an adaptation
3:11 a *m* who occupied a very high position.
3:17 trembling that had come over the *m*
3:28 The *m* who a moment before had entered that
3:31 *m* who was about to expire might be spared.
3:37 a suitable *m* to be sent to Jerusalem next,
4: 2 the *m* who was a benefactor of the city,
4: 5 but as a *m* looking to the general and
4:26 and now saw himself cheated by another *m*,
4:35 and angry over the unjust murder of the *m*.
4:40 *m* as advanced in folly as he was in years.
5:18 become entangled in so many sins, this *m*,
5:22 more cruel than the *m* who appointed him;
5:25 When this *m* arrived in Jerusalem,
6: 6 A *m* could not keep the sabbath or
6:18 a *m* of advanced age and noble appearance,
6:21 ritual meal took the *m* aside privately,
8:32 of Timothy's forces, a most wicked *m*,
9: 9 body of this impious *m* swarmed with worms,
9:10 the *m* because of this intolerable stench.
9:13 Then this vile *m* vowed to the Lord,
10:10 the son of that godless *m* and shall give a
11:13 But Lysias was not a stupid *m*.
12:35 A *m* called Dositheus,
13: 6 A *m* guilty of sacrilege or notorious for
14:24 for he had a cordial affection for the *m*.
14:28 agreement with a *m* who had done no wrong.
14:31 had been disgracefully outwitted by the *m*,
14:32 they did not know where the wanted *m* was,
14:37 A *m* highly regarded,
14:40 a *m* he would deal the Jews a hard blow.
15:12 former high priest, a good and virtuous *m*,
15:13 Then in the same way another *m* appeared,
Jb 1: 1 was a blameless and upright *m* named Job,
2: 4 All that a *m* has will he give for his life.
4:17 "Can a *m* be righteous as against God?
5: 7 But *m* himself begets mischief,
5:17 Happy is the *m* whom God reproves!
6:26 but the sayings of a desperate *m* as wind?
7:17 What is *m*, that you make much of him
8:13 so shall the hope of the godless *m* perish.
9: 2 but how can a *m* be justified before God?
9:32 For he is not a *m* like myself,
10: 4 Do you see as *m* sees?
11: 2 Should not the *m* of many words be answered,
11: 2 must the garrulous *m* necessarily be right?
11:12 Will empty *m* then gain understanding,
12: 4 calls upon him, the just, the perfect *m*,"
12:14 if he imprisons a *m*,
13:16 no impious *m* can come into his presence.
14: 1 *M* born of woman is short-lived and full of
14: 4 a *m* be found who is clean of defilement?
14:10 *m* dies, all vigor leaves him; when *m* expires,
14:14 When a *m* has died, were he to live again,
14:19 of the land, so you destroy the hope of *m*.
15: 2 Should a wise *m* answer with airy opinions,
15:14 What is a *m* that he should be blameless,
15:16 *m*, who drinks in iniquity like water!
15:20 The wicked *m* is in torment all his days,
16:21 and decide between a *m* and his neighbor.
17:10 for I shall not find a wise *m* among you!
18:21 then with the dwelling of the impious *m*,
19:12 His troops advance as one *m*;
20: 4 time, since *m* was placed upon the earth,
20:29 This is the portion of a wicked *m*,
21: 4 Is my complaint toward *m*?
21:19 requite the *m* himself so that he feels it,
21:30 evil *m* is spared calamity when it comes;
22: 2 Can a *m* be profitable to God?
22: 2 Though to himself a wise *m* be profitable!
22: 8 As if the land belonged to the *m* of might,
22:29 but the *m* of humble mien he saves.
23: 7 There the upright *m* might reason with him,
25: 4 How can a *m* be just in God's sight,
25: 6 the son of *m*, who is only a worm?
27: 8 the impious *m* expect when he is cut off,
27:13 This is the portion of a wicked *m* from God,
27:17 What he has stored the just *m* shall wear,
27:19 He lies down a rich *m*,
28:13 *M* knows nothing to equal it,
28:28 *m* he said: Behold, the fear of the Lord
29:17 And I broke the jaws of the wicked *m*;
30:24 out to help a wretched *m* in his calamity?
31:19 clothing, or a poor *m* without covering,
32: 8 But it is a spirit in *m*,
32:13 God may vanquish him out not *m*!"
33:12 for God is greater than *m*.
33:17 By turning *m* from evil and keeping pride
33:19 Or a *m* is chastened on his bed by pain and
33:23 for him and bring the *m* back to justice,
33:29 God does, twice, or thrice, for a *m*,
34: 7 What *m* is like Job?
34: 9 a *m* nought that he is pleasing to God."
34:11 and brings home to a *m* his way of life.
34:15 together, and *m* would return to the dust.
34:21 For his eyes are upon the ways of *m*,
34:23 For he forewarns no *m* of his time to come
34:34 say to me, every wise *m* who hears my views:
35: 8 can affect only a *m* like yourself;

MAN (cont.)
35:15 nor does he show concern that a *m* will die.
36:25 *m* beholds it from afar.
37:20 or when a *m* says he is being destroyed?
38: 3 Gird up your loins now, like a *m*;
40: 7 Gird up your loins now, like a *m*.
Ps(s) 1: 1 Happy the *m* who follows not the counsel of
5: 5 no evil *m* remains with you;
5:13 For you, O LORD, bless the just *m*;
8: 5 is *m* that you should be mindful of him,
8: 5 the son of *m* that you should care for him?
9:20 Rise, O LORD, let not *m* prevail;
10: 3 For the wicked *m* glories in his greed,
10: 4 wicked *m* boasts, "He will not avenge it"
10:13 Why should the wicked *m* despise God,
10:14 On you the unfortunate *m* depends;
10:18 the fatherless and the oppressed, that *m*,
11: 3 are overthrown, what can the just *m* do?"
15: 3 Who harms not his fellow *m*,
17: 4 not transgressed after the manner of *m*;
18:49 from the violent *m* you have rescued me.
22: 7 But I am a worm, not a *m*;
22:25 nor disdained the wretched *m* in his misery,
25:12 When a *m* fears the LORD,
32: 2 the *m* to whom the LORD inputes not guilt,
32: 6 faithful *m* pray to you in time of stress.
34: 7 When the afflicted *m* called out,
34: 9 happy the *m* who takes refuge in him.
34:20 Many are the troubles of the just *m*,
35:10 afflicted *m* from those too strong for him,
36: 2 Sin speaks to the wicked *m* in his heart;
36: 7 *m* and beast you save,
37: 7 path of the *m* who does malicious deeds.
37:10 while, and the wicked *m* shall be no more;
37:12 The wicked *m* plots against the just and
37:21 The wicked *m* borrows and does not repay;
37:21 the just *m* is kindly and gives,
37:23 By the LORD are the steps of a *m* made firm,
37:25 have I seen a just *m* forsaken nor his
37:30 The mouth of the just *m* tells of wisdom
37:32 The wicked *m* spies on the just,
37:35 I saw a wicked *m*,
37:37 for there is a future for the *m* of peace.
38:14 like a deaf *m*, hearing not, like a dumb *m*
38:15 I am become like a *m* who neither hears nor
39: 2 While the wicked *m* was before me
39: 7 A phantom only, *m* goes his ways;
39:12 With rebukes for guilt you chasten *m*;
39:12 only a breath is any *m*.
40: 5 Happy the *m* who makes the LORD his trust;
43: 1 the deceitful and impious *m* rescue me.
49: 8 Yet in no way can a *m* redeem himself,
49:13 Thus *m*, for all his splendor,
49:17 Fear not when a *m* grows rich,
49:21 *M*, for all his splendor,
50:16 But to the wicked *m* God says:
52: 9 "This is the *m* who made not God the
55:23 will he permit the just *m* to be disturbed.
58:11 *m* shall be glad when he sees vengeance;
62: 4 How long will you set upon a *m* and all
64: 5 Shooting from ambush at the innocent *m*,
64:11 The just *m* is glad in the LORD and takes
65: 5 Happy the *m* you choose,
72:12 shall rescue the poor *m* when he cries out,
73:13 clean and washed my hands as an innocent *m*?
80:16 son of *m* whom you yourself made strong].
80:18 *m* of your right hand, with the son of *m*
87: 4 "This *m* was born there."
87: 6 "This *m* was born there."
88: 5 I am a *m* without strength.
89:49 What *m* shall live, and not see death,
90: 3 You turn *m* back to dust,
92: 7 A senseless *m* knows not,
92:13 just *m* shall flourish like the palm tree,
94:12 Happy the *m* whom you instruct,
101: 5 The *m* of haughty eyes and puffed-up heart
104:23 *M* goes forth to his work and to his
105:14 another people, He let no *m* oppress them,
105:17 sustained them, He sent a *m* before them,
109: 6 Raise up a wicked *m* against him,
109:31 he stood at the right hand of the poor *m*,
112: 1 Happy the *m* who fears the LORD,
112: 5 Well for the *m* who is gracious and lends,
112: 6 just *m* shall be in everlasting remembrance.
112:10 The wicked *m* shall see it and be vexed;
116:11 I said in my alarm, "No *m* is dependable."
118: 6 what can *m* do against me?
118: 8 refuge in the LORD than to trust in *m*.
119: 9 shall a young *m* be faultless in his way?
127: 5 the *m* whose quiver is filled with them;
128: 4 thus is the *m* blessed who fears the LORD.
135: 8 in Egypt, both of *m* and of beast.
137: 8 happy the *m* who shall repay you the evil
137: 9 Happy the *m* who shall seize and smash your
140:12 A *m* of wicked tongue shall not abide in
140:12 evil shall abruptly entrap the violent *m*.
141: 5 Let the just *m* strike me;
143: 2 for before you no living *m* is just.
144: 3 is *m* that you notice him; the son of *m*,
144: 4 *M* is like a breath;
146: 3 Put not your trust in princes, in *m*,
Prv 1: 4 to the young *m* knowledge and discretion.
1: 5 *m* by hearing them will advance in learning,
1: 5 an intelligent *m* will gain sound guidance,
1:11 Let us lie in wait for the honest *m*,
3: 4 win favor and good esteem before God and *m*.
3:13 *m* who finds wisdom, the *m* who gains
3:30 Quarrel not with a *m* without cause.
3:31 the lawless *m* and choose none of his ways:
3:32 the LORD the perverse *m* is an abomination,
5:22 own iniquities the wicked *m* will be caught,
6:11 a highway man, and want like an armed *m*.
6:27 Can a *m* take fire to his bosom,
6:28 Or can a *m* walk on live coals,
8: 9 of them are plain to the *m* of intelligence,
8:33 Happy the *m* who obeys me,
8:34 Happy the *m* watching daily at my gates,
9: 7 He who corrects an arrogant *m* earns insult;
9: 7 who reproves a wicked *m* incurs opprobrium.
9: 8 Reprove not an arrogant *m*,
9: 8 reprove a wise *m*, and he will love you.
9: 9 Instruct a wise *m*,
9: 9 teach a just *m*, and he advances
10: 8 A wise *m* heeds commands,
10:23 so is wisdom for the *m* of sense.
10:24 What the wicked *m* fears will befall him,
10:25 wicked *m* is no more; but the just *m*
10:30 The just *m* will never be disturbed,
11: 5 but by his wickedness the wicked *m* falls.
11: 7 When a wicked *m* dies his hope perishes,
11: 8 just *m* escapes trouble, and the wicked *m*
11: 9 the impious *m* would ruin his neighbor,
11:12 sense, but the intelligent *m* keeps silent.
11:13 but a trustworthy *m* keeps a confidence.
11:17 kindly *m* benefits himself, but a merciless *m*
11:18 The wicked *m* makes empty profits,
11:21 Truly the evil *m* shall not go unpunished,
11:24 One *m* is lavish yet grows still richer;
11:29 the fool will become slave to the wise *m*.
11:31 If the just *m* is punished on earth,
12: 2 The good *m* wins favor from the LORD,
12: 3 No *m* is built up by wickedness,
12: 8 According to his good sense a *m* is praised,
12: 9 Better a lowly *m* who supports himself than
12:10 The just *m* takes care of his beast,
12:13 the sin of his lips the evil *m* is ensnared,
12:14 his words a *m* has his fill of good things,
12:16 but the shrewd *m* passes over an insult.
12:23 A shrewd *m* conceals his knowledge,
12:26 The just *m* surpasses his neighbor,
12:27 The slothful *m* catches not his prey,
12:27 but the wealth of the diligent *m* is great.
13: 2 fruit of his words a *m* eats good things,
13: 5 Anything deceitful the just *m* hates,
13: 7 One *m* pretends to be rich,
13: 8 his life, but the poor *m* heeds no rebuke.
13:10 The stupid *m* sows discord by his insolence,
13:14 that a *m* may avoid the snares of death.
13:16 The shrewd *m* does everything with prudence.
13:18 befall the *m* who disregards correction,
13:22 The good *m* leaves an inheritance to his
13:25 When the just *m* eats,
14: 6 The senseless *m* seeks in vain for wisdom,
14: 6 knowledge is easy to the *m* of intelligence.
14: 7 To avoid the foolish *m*, take steps!
14:12 Sometimes a way seems right to a *m*,
14:14 the good *m* reaps the fruit of his paths.
14:15 but the shrewd *m* measures his steps.
14:16 The wise *m* is cautious and shuns evil;
14:17 quick-tempered *m* makes a fool of himself,
14:17 of himself, but the prudent *m* is at peace.
14:20 Even by his neighbor the poor *m* is hated,
14:27 that a *m* may avoid the snares of death.
14:29 The patient *m* shows much good sense,
14:29 *m* displays folly at its height.
14:32 wicked *m* is overthrown by his wickedness,
14:32 the just *m* finds a refuge in his honesty.
15: 9 but he loves the *m* who pursues virtue.
15:10 is in store for the *m* who goes astray;
15:12 The senseless *m* loves not to be reproved;
15:14 mind of the intelligent *m* seeks knowledge,
15:15 a lighthearted *m* has a continual feast.
15:18 ill-tempered *m* stirs up strife, but a patient *m*
15:20 but a fool of a *m* despises his mother.
15:21 senseless *m*, but the *m* of understanding
15:23 There is joy for a *m* in his utterance;
15:24 path of life leads the prudent *m* upward,
15:28 The just *m* weighs well his utterance,
16: 1 *M* may make plans in his heart,
16: 2 ways of a *m* may be pure in his own eyes,
16: 5 proud *m* is an abomination to the LORD;
16: 6 and by the fear of the LORD *m* avoids evil.
16: 9 In his mind a *m* plans his course,
16:13 the *m* who speaks what is right he loves.
16:14 of death, but a wise *m* can pacify it.
16:21 The wise *m* is esteemed for his discernment,
16:23 The mind of the wise *m* makes him eloquent,
16:25 Sometimes a way seems right to a *m*,
16:29 A lawless *m* allures his neighbor,
16:32 A patient *m* is better than a warrior,
17: 4 The evil *m* gives heed to wicked lips,
17: 8 A *m* who has a bribe to offer rates it a
17:10 A single reprimand does more for a *m* of
17:11 On rebellion alone is the wicked *m* bent,
17:13 If a *m* returns evil for good,
17:18 is the *m* who gives his hand in pledge,
17:20 and a double-tongued *m* falls into trouble.
17:21 To be a fool's parent is grief for a *m*;
17:23 The wicked *m* accepts a concealed bribe to
17:24 *m* of intelligence fixes his gaze on wisdom,
17:26 It is wrong to fine an innocent *m*,
17:27 is chary of speech is a *m* of intelligence.
18: 9 The *m* who is slack in his work is own
18: 9 is own brother to the *m* who is destructive.
18:10 the just *m* runs to it and is safe.
18:17 The *m* who pleads his case first seems to
18:20 the fruit of his mouth a *m* has his fill;
18:23 poor *m* implores, but the rich *m* answers
19: 1 Better a poor *m* who walks in his integrity
19: 4 but the friend of the poor *m* deserts him.
19: 6 friends of the *m* who has something to give.
19:11 is good sense in a *m* to be slow to anger,
19:15 Laziness plunges a *m* into deep sleep,
19:19 The *m* of violent temper pays the penalty;
19:22 rather be a poor *m* than a liar.
19:25 If you beat an arrogant *m*,
19:25 if you rebuke an intelligent *m*,
20: 3 It is honorable for a *m* to shun strife,
20: 5 but the *m* of intelligence draws it forth.
20: 7 When a *m* walks in integrity and justice,
20:17 The bread of deceit is sweet to a *m*,
20:24 how, then, can a *m* understand his way?
20:25 to pledge a sacred gift is a trap for a *m*,
20:27 A Lamp from the LORD is the breath of *m*;
21: 2 ways of a *m* may be right in his own eyes,
21:10 The soul of the wicked *m* desires evil;
21:11 When the arrogant *m* is punished,
21:11 when the wise *m* is instructed,
21:12 just *m* appraises the house of the wicked:
21:16 The *m* who strays from the way of good
21:18 The wicked *m* serves as ransom for the just,
21:18 and the faithless *m* for the righteous.
21:22 The wise *m* storms a city of the mighty,
21:24 Arrogant is the name for the *m* of
21:26 the day, but the just *m* gives unsparingly.
21:29 wicked *m* is brazenfaced, but the upright *m*
22: 3 The shrewd *m* perceives evil and hides,
22: 9 The kindly *m* will be blessed,
22:10 Expel the arrogant *m* and discord goes out;
22:11 the *m* of winning speech has the king for
22:24 Be not friendly with a hotheaded *m*,
22:24 man, nor the companion of a wrathful *m*,
22:29 You see a *m* skilled at his work?
23: 6 Do not take food with a grudging *m*,
23:21 to poverty, and torpor clothes a *m* in rags.
23:24 father of a just *m* will exult with glee;
24: 5 wise *m* is more powerful than a strong man,
24: 5 and a *m* of knowledge than a man of might;
24:12 If you say, "I know not this *m*!"
24:15 in wait against the home of the just *m*,
24:16 just *m* falls seven times and rises again,
24:20 For the evil *m* has no future,
24:24 He who says to the wicked *m*,
24:29 I will repay the *m* according to his deeds."
24:30 by the vineyard of the *m* without sense;
24:34 a highwayman, and want like an armed *m*.
25:14 *m* who boastfully promises what he never
25:18 is the *m* who bears false witness against
25:19 on] a faithless *m* in time of trouble.
25:26 a just *m* who gives way before the wicked.
25:28 is the *m* with no check on his feelings.
26:12 You see a *m* wise in his own eyes?
26:17 Like the *m* who seizes a passing dog by the
26:19 arrows Is the *m* who deceives his neighbor,
26:21 is a contentious *m* in enkindling strife.
26:26 A *m* may conceal hatred under dissimulation,
27: 7 but to the *m* who is hungry,
27: 8 its nest is a *m* who is far from his home.
27:12 The shrewd *m* perceives evil and hides;
27:17 iron, so *m* sharpens his fellow man.
27:21 so a *m* is tested by the praise he receives.
28: 1 wicked *m* flees although no one pursues him;
28: 1 just *m*, like a lion, feels sure of himself.
28: 2 but with a prudent *m* it knows security.
28: 3 A rich *m* who oppresses the poor is like a
28: 4 who abandon the law praise the wicked *m*,
28: 6 Better a poor *m* who walks in his integrity
28:11 rich *m* is wise in his own eyes, but a poor *m*
28:14 Happy the *m* who is always on his guard;
28:17 Though a *m* burdened with human blood were
28:19 idle pursuits a *m* has his fill of poverty.
28:20 The trustworthy *m* will be richly blessed;
28:21 even a morsel of bread a *m* may do wrong.
28:22 avaricious *m* is perturbed about his wealth,
28:23 He who rebukes a *m* gets more thanks in the
28:25 The greedy *m* stirs up disputes,
29: 1 The *m* who remains stiff-necked and hates
29: 5 The *m* who flatters his neighbor is
29: 6 wicked *m* steps into a snare, but the just *m*
29: 7 *m* has a care for the rights of the poor;
29: 7 the wicked *m* has no such concern.
29: 9 If a wise *m* disputes with a fool,
29:10 Bloodthirsty men hate the honest *m*,
29:11 by biding his time, the wise *m* calms it.
29:20 Do you see a *m* hasty in his words?
29:21 If a *m* pampers his servant from childhood,
29:22 An ill-tempered *m* stirs up disputes,
29:22 a hotheaded *m* is the cause of many sins.
29:25 The fear of *m* brings a snare,

30: 1 The pronouncement of mortal *m:*
30:19 seas, and the way of a *m* with a maiden.
Eccl 1: 3 What profit has *m* from all the labor which
1: 8 there is nothing *m* can say.
2:12 the *m* do who is to come after the king?
2:14 The wise *m* has eyes in his head,
2:16 Neither of the wise *m* nor of the fool will
2:16 that the wise *m* dies as well as the fool!
2:18 leave them to a *m* who is to come after me.
2:19 whether he will be a wise *m* or a fool?
2:21 For here is a *m* who has labored with
2:22 For what profit comes to a *m* from all the
2:24 There is nothing better for *m* than to eat
2:26 For to whatever *m* he sees fit he gives
2:26 to be given to whatever *m* God sees fit.
3:13 every *m*, moreover, to eat and drink
3:19 For the lot of *m* and of beast is one lot;
3:19 and *m* has no advantage over the beast;
3:22 better for a *m* than to rejoice in his work;
4: 4 work is the rivalry of one *m* for another.
4: 8 a solitary *m* with no companion;
4:10 Woe to the solitary *m!*
4:12 Where a lone *m* may be overcome,
5: 9 covetous *m* is never satisfied with money,
5:11 Sleep is sweet to the laboring *m*,
5:17 it is well for a *m* to eat and drink and
5:18 *m* to whom God gives riches and property,
6: 1 the sun, and it weighs heavily upon *m:*
6: 2 there is the *m* to whom God gives riches
6: 3 Should a *m* have a hundred children and
6: 3 of this *m* I proclaim that the child born
6: 5 dead child is at rest rather than such a *m*.
6: 8 advantage has the wise *m* over the fool,
6: 8 or what advantage has the poor *m* in
6:10 its name, and the nature of *m* is known,
6:11 vanity, what profit is there for a *m?*
6:12 For who knows what is good for a *m* in life,
6:12 a *m* what will come after him under the sun?
7: 2 feasting, For that is the end of every *m*,
7: 7 For oppression can make a fool of a wise *m*,
7:14 *m* cannot find fault with him in anything.
7:15 a just *m* perishing in his justice,
7:19 *m* than would be ten princes in the city,
7:20 yet there is no *m* on earth so just as to
7:28 One *m* out of a thousand have I come upon,
8: 1 Who is like the wise *m*,
8: 6 *m* that he is ignorant of what is to come;
8: 8 There is no *m* who is master of the breath
8: 9 one *m* tyrannizes over another to his hurt.
8:13 it shall not be well with the wicked *m*,
8:15 there is nothing good for *m* under the sun
8:17 I recognized that *m* is unable to find out
8:17 However much *m* toils in searching,
8:17 and even if the wise *m* says that he knows,
9: 1 Love from hatred *m* cannot tell;
9: 2 As it is for the good *m*,
9:12 *M* no more knows his own time than fish
9:15 But in the city lived a *m* who,
9:15 Yet no one remembered this poor *m*.
9:16 *m* is despised and his words go unheeded.
10:14 *M* knows not what is to come,
11: 8 However many years a *m* may live,
11: 9 Rejoice, O young *m*,
12: 5 effect, Because *m* goes to his lasting home,
Wis 1: 3 perverse counsels separate a *m* from God,
1: 7 is all-embracing, and knows what *m* says.
1: 9 of the wicked *m* shall be scrutinized,
2:10 Let us oppress the needy just *m;*
2:10 old *m* for his hair grown white with time.
2:23 For God formed *m* to be imperishable;
4: 7 just *m*, though he die early,
4:16 just *m* dead condemns the sinful who live,
4:16 the many years of the wicked *m* grown old.
4:17 For they see the death of the wise *m* and
7: 1 I too am a mortal *m*,
7: 1 descendant of the first *m* formed on earth.
7: 2 body and blood, from the seed of *m*,
9: 2 *m* to rule the creatures produced by you,
9: 5 a *m* weak and short-lived and lacking in
9:13 For what *m* knows God's counsel,
10: 3 unjust *m* withdrew from her in his anger,
10: 4 it, piloting the just *m* on frailest wood.
10: 5 in universal wickedness, knew the just *m*,
10: 6 She delivered the just *m* from among the
10:10 the just *m* fled from his brother's anger,
10:13 not abandon the just *m* when he was sold,
11:16 they might recognize that a *m* is punished
13:13 patterns it on the image of a *m*
14:15 as a god what was formerly a dead *m*
14:20 who shortly before was honored as a *m*.
15: 5 which arouses yearning in the senseless *m*,
15:13 *m* more than any knows that he is sinning,
15:16 For a *m* made them;
15:16 For no *m* succeeds in fashioning a god like
16:14 *M*, however, slays in his malice,
16:26 various kinds of fruits that nourish *m*,
18:21 blameless *m* hastened to be their champion,
Sir 1:19 anger plunges a *m* to his downfall.
1:20 patient *m* need stand firm but for a time,
3:25 A stubborn *m* will fare badly in the end,
3:26 A stubborn *m* will be burdened with sorrow;
3:27 affliction of the proud *m* there is no cure;
4: 1 son, rob not the poor *m* of his livelihood;
4: 2 hungry man grieve not, a needy *m* anger not;
4: 5 your eyes, give no *m* reason to curse you;
4: 8 Give a hearing to the poor *m*,
4:27 Do not abase yourself before an impious *m*,
6: 1 "That for the evil *m* with double tongue!"
6:36 If you see a *m* of prudence,
7:11 Laugh not at an embittered *m;*
7:17 what awaits *m* is worms.
7:25 but give her to a worthy *m*.
7:32 To the poor *m* also extend your hand,
8: 1 Contend not with an influential *m*,
8: 2 Quarrel not with a rich *m*,
8: 3 Dispute not with a *m* of railing speech,
8: 4 Be not too familiar with an unruly *m*,
8: 6 Insult no *m* when he is old,
8: 7 Rejoice not when a *m* dies;
8:11 Let not the impious *m* intimidate you;
8:15 Travel not with a ruthless *m*,
8:16 no quarrel with a quick-tempered *m*,
8:19 Open your heart to no *m*,
9:13 Keep far from the *m* who has power to kill,
9:18 in the city is the *m* of railing speech,
10: 1 government of a prudent *m* is well ordered.
10: 4 God, who raises up on it the *m* of the hour;
10: 5 over every *m* is in the hand of God,
10:11 When a *m* dies, he inherits corruption
10:18 Insolence is not allotted to a *m*,
10:22 just to despise a *m* who is wise but poor,
10:24 slave, the wise *m* does not complain.
10:29 The poor *m* is honored for his wisdom as
10:29 as the rich *m* is honored for his wealth;
11: 2 Praise not a *m* for his looks
11: 2 despise not a *m* for his appearance
11:18 A *m* may become rich through a miser's life,
11:21 in an instant, to make a poor *m* rich.
11:22 God's blessing is the lot of the just *m*,
11:26 of death to repay *m* according to his deeds.
11:27 when a *m* dies, his life is revealed
11:28 Call no *m* happy before his death,
11:28 death, for by how he ends, a *m* is known.
11:29 Bring not every *m* into your house,
11:32 The evil *m* lies in wait for blood,
11:33 Avoid a wicked *m*,
12: 2 to the just *m* and reward will be yours,
12: 4 Give to the good *m*, refuse the sinner
12: 4 downtrodden, give nothing to the proud *m*.
12: 9 When a *m* is successful even his enemy is
12:14 So is it with the companion of the proud *m*,
13: 1 with an impious *m* learns his ways.
13: 3 The rich *m* does wrong and boasts of it,
13: 3 the poor *m* is wronged and begs forgiveness.
13: 4 rich *m* can use you he will enslave you,
13: 9 When invited by a *m* of influence,
13:14 its own kind, every *m* a man like himself.
13:15 with his own kind every *m* associates.
13:19 proud *m* abhors lowliness; so does the rich *m*
13:20 *m* stumbles he is supported by a friend;
13:20 poor *m* trips he is pushed down by a friend.
13:21 the supporters for a rich *m* when he speaks;
13:21 a poor *m* speaks they make sport of him;
13:22 A rich *m* speaks and all are silent,
13:22 A poor *m* speaks and they say:
13:24 The heart of a *m* changes his countenance,
14: 1 the *m* whose mouth brings him no grief,
14: 2 *m* whose conscience does not reproach him,
14: 3 Wealth ill becomes the mean *m;*
14:20 Happy the *m* who meditates on wisdom,
15:12 for he has no need of wicked *m*.
15:14 When God, in the beginning, created *m*,
15:17 Before *m* are life and death,
15:20 No *m* does he command to sin,
16: 4 Through one wise *m* can a city be peopled;
16:11 And had there been but one stiffnecked *m*,
17: 1 The LORD from the earth created *m*,
17: 3 He endows *m* with a strength of his own,
17:25 in men, for not immortal is any son of *m*.
18: 5 When a *m* ends he is only beginning,
18: 6 What is *m*, of what worth is he?
18:11 *M* may be merciful to his fellow man,
18:16 both are offered by a kindly *m*.
18:27 A wise *m* is circumspect in all things;
18:28 Any learned *m* should make wisdom known,
19:15 Then, too, a *m* can slip and not mean it;
19:19 while the simple *m* may be free from sin.
19:22 is the wicked *m* who is bowed in grief,
19:25 tell a *m* by his appearance; a wise *m* is known
20: 1 and a *m* may be wise to hold his peace.
20: 4 One *m* is silent and is thought wise,
20: 5 *m* is silent because he has nothing to say;
20: 6 wise *m* is silent till the right time comes,
20:10 from obscurity a *m* can lift up his head.
20:11 A *m* may buy much for little,
20:12 *m* makes himself popular by a few words,
20:14 hateful indeed is such a *m*.
20:20 A *m* through want may be unable to sin,
20:22 *m* makes a promise to a friend out of shame,
20:23 A lie is a foul blot in a *m*,
20:26 A wise *m* advances himself by his words,
20:26 his words, a prudent *m* pleases the great.
20:30 Better the *m* who hides his folly than the
21: 7 but the wise *m* knows his own faults.
21:15 an intelligent *m* hears words of wisdom,
21:17 of a prudent *m* are sought in an assembly,
21:18 *m* knows it only as inscrutable words.
21:20 the prudent *m* at the most smiles gently.
21:21 a chain of gold is learning to a wise *m*,
21:22 while the well-bred *m* remains outside;
21:23 a cultured *m* keeps his glance cast down.
21:24 a cultured *m* would be overwhelmed by the
21:27 When a godless *m* curses his adversary he
22: 7 like disturbing a *m* in the depths of sleep;
22: 9 Weep over the dead *m*,
22:10 Weep but a little over the dead *m*,
22:12 Speak but seldom with the stupid *m*,
22:15 mass are easier to bear than a stupid *m*.
22:23 fast friends with a *m* while he is poor;
23: 8 the railer and the arrogant *m* fall thereby.
23:11 A *m* who often swears heaps up obligations;
23:15 A *m* who has the habit of abusive language
23:16 A *m* given to sins of the flesh,
23:18 And the *m* who dishonors his marriage bed
23:19 a *m* takes and peer into hidden corners.
23:21 Such a *m* will be punished in the streets
23:23 she has borne children by another *m*.
24:26 *m* never finished comprehending wisdom,
25: 2 and an old *m* lecherous in his dotage.
25: 7 The *m* who finds joy in his children,
25:19 aged feet is a railing wife to a quiet *m*.
25:21 *m* is a slave, in disgrace and shame,
26:19 A wealthy *m* reduced to want;
26:19 And the *m* who passes from justice to sin,
27: 5 so in his conversation is the test of a *m*.
27: 7 Praise no *m* before he speaks,
27:11 of the devout, but the godless *m*,
27:18 For as an enemy might kill a *m*,
28: 3 Should a *m* nourish anger against his
28: 4 Should a *m* refuse mercy to his fellows,
28: 8 for a quarrelsome *m* kindles disputes,
29: 4 Many a *m* who asks for a loan adds to the
29: 8 To a poor *m*, however, be generous;
29:14 A good *m* goes surety for his neighbor,
29:28 Painful things to a sensitive *m* are abuse
30:14 Better a poor *m* strong and robust,
30:14 robust, than a rich *m* with wasted frame.
30:20 So it is with the afflicted *m* who groans
30:22 Gladness of heart is the very life of *m*,
31: 3 The rich *m* labors to pile up wealth,
31: 4 The poor *m* toils for a meager subsistence,
31: 8 Happy the rich *m* found without fault,
31:12 If you are dining with a great *m*,
31:19 not a little suffice for a well-bred *m?*
31:23 On a *m* generous with food,
31:27 is very life to *m* if taken in moderation.
32: 7 Young *m*, speak only when necessary,
32: 8 in those few words, be like the wise *m*,
32:18 thoughtful *m* will not neglect direction;
32:18 and insolent *m* is deterred by nothing.
33: 1 No evil can harm the *m* who fears the LORD;
33: 3 prudent *m* trusts in the word of the LORD,
33:10 are of clay, for from earth *m* was formed;
33:21 in you, let no *m* have dominion over you.
34: 2 Like a *m* who catches at shadows or chases
34: 8 is found in the mouth of the faithful *m*.
34: 9 A *m* with training gains wide knowledge;
34: 9 a *m* of experience speaks sense.
34:10 travel a *m* adds to his resourcefulness.
34:20 Like the *m* who slays a son in his father's
34:21 he who withholds it is a *m* of blood.
34:23 If one *m* builds up and another tears down,
34:24 If one *m* prays and another curses,
34:25 If a *m* again touches a corpse after he has
34:26 So with a *m* who fasts for his sins,
36:20 experienced *m* can turn the tables on him.
36:21 Though any *m* may be accepted as a husband,
36:25 *m* with no wife becomes a homeless wanderer.
36:27 Or a *m* who has no nest,
37:11 man about mercy, to a lazy *m* about work,
37:12 Instead, associate with a religious *m*,
37:19 A *m* may be wise and benefit many,
37:20 Though a *m* may be wise,
37:21 When a *m* is wise to his own advantage,
37:22 When a *m* is wise to his people's advantage,
37:30 but the abstemious *m* prolongs his life.
38: 4 which the prudent *m* should not neglect;
38:24 is free from toil can become a wise *m*.
39: 1 How different the *m* who devotes himself to
40: 8 is with all flesh, with *m* and with beast,
40:30 mouth of the shameless *m* begging is sweet,
41: 1 for the *m* at peace amid his possessions,
41: 1 For the *m* unruffled and always successful,
41: 2 sentence to the weak *m* of failing strength,
45: 1 to spring the *m* who won the favor of all:
46:19 or secret gift have I taken from any *m!*"
48: 5 dead *m* back to life from the nether world,
48:12 nor was any *m* able to intimidate his will.
49:15 Was ever a *m* born like JOSEPH?
50:28 the *m* who meditates upon these things,
50:28 things, wise the *m* who takes them to heart!
Is 1:31 The strong *m* shall turn to tow,
2: 9 But *m* is abased, each one brought low.
2:11 The haughty eyes of *m* will be lowered,
2:22 As for you, let *m* alone,
3: 5 one another, yes, every *m* his neighbor.
3: 6 *m* seizes his brother in his father's house,
3:11 Woe to the wicked *m!*
4: 1 women will take hold of one *m* on that day,

MAN (cont.)

5:23 and deprive the just *m* of his rights!
6: 5 For I am a *m* of unclean lips,
6:11 without inhabitants, Houses, without a *m*,
7:21 *m* shall keep a heifer or a couple of sheep,
9:18 No *m* spares his brother,
13:14 Every *m* shall turn to his kindred and flee
13:15 to a *m*, they shall fall by the sword.
14:16 "Is this the *m* who made the earth tremble,
14:29 Rejoice not, O Philistia, not a *m* of you,
17: 7 On that day *m* shall look to his maker,
22:17 shall hurl you down headlong, mortal *m!*
26:10 wicked *m*, spared, does not learn justice;
28: 4 when a *m* sees it, he picks and swallows it
29: 8 As when a hungry *m* dreams he is eating and
29: 8 Or when a thirsty *m* dreams he is drinking
29:21 off, those whose mere word condemns a *m*,
29:21 and leave the just *m* with an empty claim.
31: 8 shall fall by a sword not wielded by *m*,
32: 8 But the noble *m* plans noble things,
33: 8 yet no *m* gives it a thought.
40:41 One *m* helps another,
44:13 it like a *m* in appearance and dignity,
44:15 and the rain made grow to serve *m* for fuel.
51:12 Can you then fear mortal *m*,
52:14 so marred was his look beyond that of *m*,
53: 3 and avoided by men, a *m* of suffering,
55: 7 his way, and the wicked *m* his thoughts;
56: 2 Happy is the *m* who does this, the son of *m*
57: 1 *m* perishes, but no one takes it to heart;
57: 1 of evil, the just *m* enters into peace;
57: 2 couch for the sincere, straightforward *m*.
58: 5 That a *m* bow his head like a reed,
59:15 and the *m* who turns from evil is despoiled.
62: 5 As a young *m* marries a virgin,
65:20 *m* who does not round out his full lifetime;
66: 2 and afflicted *m* who trembles at my word.
66: 3 slaughtering an ox is like slaying a *m;*
Jer 2: 6 which no one crosses, where no *m* dwells?"
3: 1 If *m* sends away his wife and,
3: 1 after leaving him, she marries another *m*,
4:25 I looked and behold, there was no *m;*
6: 8 into a desert, a land where no *m* dwells.
7:20 pour out upon this place, upon *m* and beast,
9: 9 They are scorched, and no *m* crosses them,
9:22 wise *m* glory in his wisdom, nor the strong *m*
9:22 nor the rich *m* glory in his riches;
10:14 Every *m* is stupid,
10:23 O LORD, that *m* is not master of his way;
11: 3 Cursed be the *m* who does not observe the
14: 9 Why are you like a *m* dumbfounded,
15:10 *m* of strife and contention to all the land!
16:20 Can *m* make for himself gods?
17: 5 Cursed is the *m* who trusts in human beings,
17: 7 Blessed is the *m* who trusts in the LORD,
17:11 own is the *m* who acquires wealth unjustly:
20:15 be the *m* who brought the news to my father,
20:16 Let that *m* be like the cities which the
21: 6 inhabitants of this city, both *m* and beast;
22:28 Is this *m* Coniah a vessel despised,
22:30 Write this *m* down as one childless,
23: 2 I am like a *m* who is drunk,
23:24 a *m* hide in secret without my seeing him?
23:34 LORD," I will punish that *m* and his house.
23:36 For each *m* his own word becomes the burden
26:11 to all the people, "This *m* deserves death;
26:16 prophets, "This *m* does not deserve death;
26:20 *m* who prophesied in the name of the LORD,
27: 5 and *m* and beast on the face of the earth,
31:22 woman must encompass the *m* with devotion.
31:27 with the seed of *m* and the seed of beast.
32:43 you call a desert, without *m* or beast,
33:10 you say, "How desolate it is, without *m*,
33:10 that are now deserted, without *m*,
33:12 place, now desolate, without *m* or beast,
34: 9 so that no one should hold a *m* of Judah,
34:22 will turn into a desert where no *m* dwells.
35: 4 of Hanan, son of Igdaliah, the *m* of God,
36:29 this land and empty it of *m* and beast?"
37:13 the captain of the guard, a *m* named Irijah,
38: 4 "This *m* ought to be put to death,"
44: 7 Will you root out from Judah *m* and wife,
44:26 in the whole land of Egypt no *m* of Judah
48:19 Ask the *m* who flees,
49: 5 be scattered, each *m* in headlong flight,
49:18 says the LORD, not a *m* shall dwell there:
49:33 a desert forever, Where no *m* lives,
50: 3 there, because *m* and beast have fled away.
50:31 I am against you, *m* of insolence,
50:40 says the LORD, Not a *m* shall dwell there,
51:17 Every *m* is stupid,
51:22 With you I shatter *m* and wife,
51:43 parched and arid land Where no *m* lives,
51:62 neither *m* nor beast should dwell in it,
Lam 3: 1 I am a *m* who knows affliction from the rod
3:27 for a *m* to bear the yoke from his youth.
3:39 Why should any living *m* complain,
Bar 6:17 in like those of a *m* brought to execution
6:35 They neither save a *m* from death,
6:36 To no blind *m* do they restore his sight,
6:36 nor do they save any *m* in an emergency.
6:40 noise, as though the *m* could understand;
6:63 neither execute judgment, nor benefit *m*.
6:72 The better for the just *m* who has no idols:
Ez 1:10 each of the four had the face of a *m*,
1:26 above, one who had the appearance of a *m*.
2: 1 Son of *m*, stand up!
2: 3 Son of *m*, I am sending you
2: 6 But as for you, son of *m*,
2: 8 As for you, son of *m*,
3: 1 Son of *m*, eat what is before you;
3: 3 Son of *m*, he then said to me,
3: 4 Son of *m*, go now to the house of Israel,
3:10 Son of *m*, he said to me,
3:17 Son of *m*, I have appointed you
3:18 If I say to the wicked *m*,
3:18 that wicked *m* shall die for his sin,
3:19 other hand, you have warned the wicked *m*,
3:20 If a virtuous *m* turns away from virtue and
3:21 you have warned a virtuous *m* not to sin,
3:25 [As for you, son of *m*,
4: 1 As for you, son of *m*,
4:16 Son of *m*, I am breaking the staff
5: 1 As for you, son of *m*,
6: 2 Son of *m*, turn toward the mountains
7: 2 Son of *m*, now say:
8: 2 up and saw a form that looked like a *m*
8: 5 Son of *m*, look toward the north!
8: 6 Son of *m*, he asked me, do you see
8: 8 Son of *m*, he ordered, dig
8:12 Do you see, son of *m*,
8:15 Do you see this, son of *m?*
8:17 Do you see, son of *m?*
9: 2 In their midst was a *m* dressed in linen,
9: 3 Then he called to the *m* dressed in linen
9:11 Then I saw the *m* dressed in linen with the
10: 2 He said to the *m* dressed in linen:
10: 3 As the *m* entered, the cloud filled
10: 6 When he commanded the *m* dressed in linen
10: 6 *m* entered and stood by one of the wheels.
10:14 was that of an ox, the second that of a *m*,
11: 2 Son of *m*, these are the men
11: 4 Therefore prophesy against them, son of *m*,
11:15 Son of *m*, it is about your kinsmen,
12: 2 Son of *m*, you live in the midst
12: 3 Now, son of *m*, during the day
12: 9 Son of *m*, did not the house of Israel,
12:18 Son of *m*, eat your bread trembling,
12:22 Son of *m*, what is this proverb
12:27 Son of *m*, listen to the house of Israel
13: 2 Son of *m*, prophesy against the prophets
13:17 Now, son of *m*, turn toward the daughters
13:22 you have disheartened the upright *m*
13:22 and have encouraged the wicked *m* not to
14: 3 Son of *m*, these men have the memory
14: 8 I will turn against that *m*,
14:13 Son of *m*, when a land sins against me
14:13 it and cut off from it both *m* and beast;
14:17 the land cutting off from it *m* and beast,
14:19 fury, cutting off from it *m* and beast,
14:21 pestilence, to cut off from it *m* and beast,
15: 2 Son of *m*, what makes the wood
16: 2 Son of *m*, make known to Jerusalem
17: 2 Son of *m*, propose a riddle,
17:12 Son of *m*, say now to the rebellious house:
17:13 Then he selected a *m* of the royal line
17:15 But this *m* rebelled against him,
18: 1 Son of *m*, what is the meaning
18: 5 If a *m* is virtuous
18: 8 judges fairly between a *m* and his opponent;
18: 9 observe my ordinances, that *m* is virtuous
18:14 On the other hand, if a *m* begets a son who,
18:21 But if the wicked *m* turns away from all
18:24 And if the virtuous *m* turns from the path
18:24 abominable things that the wicked *m* does,
18:26 When a virtuous *m* turns away from virtue
18:27 But if a wicked *m*,
19: 1 As for you, son of *m*, raise a lamentation
20: 3 Son of *m*,
20: 4 Will you judge, son of *m?*
20:27 speak to the house of Israel, son of *m*,
21: 2 Son of *m*, look southward,
21: 7 Son of *m*, look toward Jerusalem,
21:11 As for you, son of *m*, groan!
21:14 Son of *m*, prophesy!
21:17 Cry out and wail, son of *m*,
21:19 As for you, son of *m*,
21:24 Son of *m*, make for yourself two roads
21:33 As for you, son of *m*, prophesy:
22: 2 You, son of *m*, would you judge,
22:18 Son of *m*, the house of Israel
22:24 Son of *m*, say to her:
23: 2 Son of *m*, there were two women,
23:36 Son of *m*, would you judge Oholah
24: 2 Son of *m*, write down this date today,
24:15 Son of *m*, by a sudden blow
24:25 As for you, son of *m*,
25: 2 Son of *m*, turn toward the Ammonites
25:13 Edom and cut off from it *m* and beast.
26: 2 Son of *m*, because of what Tyre said
27: 2 As for you, son of *m*, utter a lament
28: 2 Son of *m*, say to the prince of Tyre:
28: 2 And yet you are a *m*,
28: 9 No, you are a *m*, not a god,
28:12 Son of *m*, utter a lament
28:21 Son of *m*, look toward Sidon,
29: 2 Son of *m*, set your face against Pharaoh,
29: 8 you, and cut off from you both *m* and beast.
29:11 foot of *m* or beast shall pass through it;
29:18 Son of *m*, Nebuchadnezzar, the king
30: 2 Son of *m*, speak this prophecy:
30:21 Son of *m*, I have broken the arm
31: 2 Son of *m*, say to Pharaoh,
32: 2 Son of *m*, utter a lament over Pharaoh,
32:13 The foot of *m* shall stir them no longer,
32:18 Son of *m*, lament over the throngs
33: 2 Son of *m*, speak thus to your countrymen:
33: 7 You, son of *m*, I have appointed
33: 8 tell the wicked *m* that he shall surely die,
33: 8 out to dissuade the wicked *m* from his way,
33: 8 he [the wicked *m* shall die for his guilt,
33: 9 But if you warn the wicked *m*,
33:10 As for you, son of *m*,
33:11 no pleasure in the death of the wicked *m*,
33:12 As for you, son of *m*, tell your countrymen:
33:12 The virtue which a *m* has practiced will
33:12 wickedness that a *m* has done
33:12 his wickedness [nor can the virtuous *m*,
33:13 the virtuous *m* that he shall surely live,
33:14 to the wicked *m* that he shall surely die,
33:18 When a virtuous *m* turns away from what is
33:19 But when a wicked *m* turns away from
33:24 Son of *m*, they who live in the ruins
33:30 As for you, son of *m*,
34: 2 Son of *m*, prophesy against the shepherds
35: 2 Son of *m*, set your face against Mount Seir
36: 1 As for you, son of *m*,
36:17 Son of *m*, when the house of Israel lived
37: 3 Son of *m*, can these bones come to life?
37: 9 Prophesy to the spirit, prophesy, son of *m*,
37:11 Son of *m*, these bones are the whole house
37:16 Now, son of *m*, take a single stick,
38: 2 Son of *m*, turn toward Gog
38:14 Therefore prophesy, son of *m*,
39: 1 Now, son of *m*, prophesy against Gog
39:17 As for you, son of *m*,
40: 3 a *m* whose appearance was that of bronze;
40: 4 *m* said to me, "Son of man, look carefully
40: 5 The *m* was holding a measuring rod six
43: 6 the temple, while the *m* stood beside me.
43: 7 Son of *m*, this is where my throne shall be,
43:10 As for you, son of *m*, describe the temple
43:18 Son of *m*, thus says the Lord GOD:
44: 5 Son of *m*, pay strict attention,
47: 6 asked me, "Have you seen this, son of *m?*"
Dn 2:10 not a *m* on earth who can do what you ask,
2:25 "I have found a *m* among the Judean
5:11 There is a *m* in your kingdom in whom is
6: 8 any petition to god or *m* for thirty days,
6:13 a petition to god or *m* for thirty days,
7: 4 the ground to stand on two feet like a *m*,
7: 8 This horn had eyes like a *m*,
7:13 I saw One like a son of *m* coming,
8:16 "Gabriel, explain the vision to this *m*."
8:17 But he said to me, "Understand, son of *m*,
10: 5 I saw a *m* dressed in linen with a belt of
10:18 a *m* touched me again and strengthened me,
12: 6 One of them said to the *m* clothed in linen,
12: 7 The *m* clothed in linen,
12:12 Blessed is the *m* who has patience and
13: 1 In Babylon there lived a *m* named Joakim,
13:21 maids because a young *m* was here with you,
13:37 A young *m*, who was hidden there,
13:39 together, but the *m* we could not hold,
13:40 this one and asked who the young *m* was,
Hos 3: 3 not play the harlot Or belong to any *m;*
6: 9 As brigands ambush a *m*,
9: 7 is a fool, the *m* of the spirit is mad!"
11: 9 For I am God and not *m*,
12: 4 brother, and as a *m* he contended with God;
Jl 4:10 let the weak *m* say,
Am 2: 6 Because they sell the just *m* for silver,
2: 6 and the poor *m* for a pair of sandals.
2:14 the strong *m* shall not retain his strength;
4:13 the wind, and declares to *m* his thoughts;
5:13 the prudent *m* is silent at this time,
5:19 As if a *m* went to flee from a lion,
6:10 If one says to a *m* inside a house,
8: 6 We will buy the lowly *m* for silver,
8: 6 and the poor *m* for a pair of sandals;
Jon 3: 7 "Neither *m* nor beast,
3: 8 *M* and beast shall be covered with
3: 8 every *m* shall turn from his evil way and
Mi 2: 2 owner of his house, a *m* of his inheritance.
4: 4 Every *m* shall sit under his own vine or
5: 6 on the grass, Which wait for no *m*,
6: 8 You have been told, O *m*,
7: 3 a price, The great *m* speaks as he pleases,
Hb 1:13 *m* devours one more just than himself?
1:14 You have made *m* like the fish of the sea,
2: 4 The rash *m* has no integrity;
2: 4 but the just *m*, because of his faith,
2: 4 the proud, unstable *m*—
Zep 1: 3 I will sweep away *m* and beast,
3: 6 are devastated, with no *m* dwelling in them.
Hg 2:12 If a *m* carries sanctified flesh in the
Zec 1:10 The *m* who was standing among the myrtle
2: 4 so that no *m* raised his head any more;
2: 5 was a *m* with a measuring line in his hand.

2: 8 to him, "Run, tell this to that young *m:*
3: 2 not this *m* a brand snatched from the fire?"
4: 1 me, like a *m* awakened from his sleep.
6:12 Here is a *m* whose name is Shoot,
8:10 for I set every *m* against his neighbor.
12: 1 and forms the spirit of *m* within him:
13: 3 If a *m* still prophesies,
13: 7 against the *m* who is my associate,
14:13 *m* shall seize the hand of his neighbor,
Mal 2:12 May the LORD cut off from the *m* who does
3: 5 those who defraud the hired *m* of his wages,
3: 8 Dare a *m* rob God?
3:17 as a *m* has compassion
Mt 1:19 *m* unwilling to expose her to the law,
4: 4 'Not on bread alone is *m* to live but on
5:22 any *m* who uses abusive language toward his
5:31 also said, 'Whenever a *m* divorces his wife,
5:32 The *m* who marries a divorced woman
5:42 Give to the *m* who begs from you.
6: 6 Then your Father, who sees what no *m* sees,
6:24 No *m* can serve two masters.
7:24 the wise *m* who built his house on rock.
7:26 *m* who built his house on sandy ground.
8: 9 I am a *m* under authority myself and I have
8: 9 If I give one *m* the order,
8:20 the Son of *M* has nowhere to lay his head."
8:27 "What sort of *m* is this,"
9: 2 to him a paralyzed *m* lying on a mat.
9: 3 said to themselves, "The *m* blasphemes."
9: 6 *M* has authority on earth to forgive sins"
9: 6 he then said to the paralyzed *m*—
9: 7 The *m* stood up and went toward his home.
9: 9 Jesus saw a *m* named Matthew at his post
10:23 towns of Israel before the Son of *M* comes.
10:35 come to set a *m* at odds with his father,
10:41 he who welcomes a holy *m* because he is
11: 6 the *m* who finds no stumbling block in me."
11:10 It is about this *m* that Scripture says,
11:11 history has not known a *m* born of woman
11:19 The Son of *M* appeared eating and drinking,
12: 8 The Son of *M* is indeed Lord of the sabbath."
12:10 A *m* with a shriveled hand happened to be
12:13 To the *m* he said, "Stretch out your hand."
12:22 A possessed *m* who was brought to him was
12:22 cured the *m* so that he could speak and see.
12:24 "This *m* can expel demons only with the
12:32 against the Son of *M* will be forgiven,
12:35 *m* produces good from his store of goodness;
12:35 evil *m* produces evil from his evil store.
12:40 so will the Son of *M* spend three days and
12:43 the unclean spirit departs from a *m,*
12:45 of that *m* becomes worse than the first.
13:12 To the *m* who has, more will be given
13:12 *m* who has not, will lose what little he
13:19 The seed along the path is the *m* who hears
13:20 fell on patches of rock is the *m* who hears
13:22 briers is the *m* who hears the message,
13:23 *m* who hears the message and takes it in.
13:24 to a *m* who sowed good seed in his field.
13:37 farmer sowing good seed is the Son of *M;*
13:41 The Son of *M* will dispatch his angels to
13:44 buried treasure which a *m* found in a field.
13:54 *m* get such wisdom and miraculous powers?
14: 2 courtiers, "This *m* is John the Baptizer
15:14 If one blind *m* leads another,
15:18 is things like these that make a *m* impure.
15:20 These are the things that make a *m* impure.
15:20 that makes no *m* impure."
16:13 "Who do people say that the Son of *M* is?"
16:17 No mere *m* has revealed this to you,
16:24 "If a *m* wishes to come after me,
16:26 What profit would a *m* show if he were to
16:26 a *m* offer in exchange for his very self?
16:27 The Son of *M* will come with his Father's
16:27 will repay each *m* according to his conduct.
16:28 they see the Son of *M* come in his kingship."
17: 9 until the Son of *M* rises from the dead."
17:12 The Son of *M* will suffer at their hands in
17:14 a *m* came up to him and knelt before him.
17:22 "The Son of *M* is going to be delivered
18: 7 woe to that *m* through whom scandal comes!
18:12 A *m* owns a hundred sheep and one of them
19: 3 "May a *m* divorce his wife for any reason
19: 5 'For this reason a *m* shall leave his
19: 6 let no *m* separate what God has joined."
19: 9 and the *m* who marries a divorced woman
19:10 "If that is the case between *m* and wife,
19:16 Another time a *m* came up to him and said,
19:20 The young *m* said to him,
19:22 these words, the young *m* went away sad,
19:23 a rich *m* enter into the kingdom of God.
19:24 for a rich *m* to enter the kingdom of God."
19:26 at them and said, "For *m* it is impossible;
19:28 in the new age when the Son of *M* takes his
20:14 *m* who was hired last the same pay as you.
20:18 There the Son of *M* will be handed over to
20:28 is the case with the Son of *M* who has come,
21:28 There was a *m* who had two sons.
21:30 Then the *m* came to his second son and said
21:44 [The *m* who falls upon that stone will be
22:11 *m* not properly dressed for a wedding feast.
22:12 The *m* had nothing to say.
22:16 a truthful *m* and teach God's way sincerely.
22:24 declared, 'If a *m* dies without children,
23:16 a *m* swears by the temple it means nothing,
23:18 a *m* swears by the altar it means nothing,
23:20 The *m* who swears by the altar is swearing
23:21 The *m* who swears by the temple is swearing
23:22 The *m* who swears by heaven is swearing by
24:13 The *m* who holds out to the end,
24:17 If a *m* is on the roof terrace,
24:18 If a *m* is in the field,
24:27 so will the coming of the Son of *M* be.
24:30 of the Son of *M* will appear in the sky,
24:30 they see 'the Son of *M* coming on the clouds
24:37 *M* will repeat what happened in Noah's time.
24:39 will it be at the coming of the Son of *M.*
24:44 *M* is coming at the time you least expect.
25:14 a *m* who was going on a journey is similar.
25:16 Immediately the *m* who received the five
25:17 the *m* who received the two thousand
25:18 The *m* who received the thousand went off
25:20 The *m* who had received the five thousand
25:22 The *m* who had received the two thousand
25:24 "Finally the *m* who had received the
25:24 lord,' he said, 'I knew you were a hard *m.*
25:28 and give it to the *m* with the ten thousand.
25:31 "When the Son of *M* comes in his glory,
26: 2 of *M* is to be handed over to be crucified."
26:18 "Go to this *m* in the city and tell him,
26:23 "The *m* who has dipped his hand into the
26:24 The Son of *M* is departing,
26:24 that *m* by whom the Son of Man is betrayed.
26:45 The hour is on us when the Son of *M* is to
26:48 saying, "The *m* I shall embrace is the one;
26:61 "This *m* has declared,
26:64 Soon you will see the Son of *M* seated at
26:71 "This *m* was with Jesus the Nazorean."
26:72 "I do not know the *m!"*
26:74 and swore, "I do not even know the *m!"*
27: 4 "I did wrong to deliver up an innocent *m!"*
27: 9 the value of a *m* with a price on his head,
27:19 not interfere in the case of that holy *m.*
27:24 am innocent of the blood of this just *m.*
27:32 This *m* they pressed into service to carry
27:57 fell, a wealthy *m* from Arimathea arrived,
Mk 1:23 a *m* with an unclean spirit that shrieked:
1:25 Come out of the *m!"*
1:26 unclean spirit convulsed the *m* violently
1:45 The *m* went off and began to proclaim the
2: 3 arrived bringing a paralyzed *m* to him.
2: 5 their faith, he said to the paralyzed *m,*
2: 7 "Why does the *m* talk in that way?
2:10 That you may know that the Son of *M* has
2:10 sins" (he said to the paralyzed *m),*
2:12 The *m* stood and picked up his mat and went
2:22 no *m* pours new wine into old wineskins.
2:27 was made for man, not *m* for the sabbath.
2:28 the Son of *M* is lord even of the sabbath."
3: 1 there was a *m* whose hand was shriveled up.
3: 3 He addressed the *m* with the shriveled hand:
3: 5 he said to the *m,* "Stretch out your hand."
3: 5 The *m* did so and his hand was perfectly
4:26 A *m* scatters seed on the ground.
5: 2 *m* from the tombs who had an unclean spirit.
5: 3 The *m* had taken refuge among the tombs;
5: 8 him, "Unclean spirit, come out of the *m!")*
5:15 they caught sight of the *m* who had been
5:16 what had happened to the possessed *m,*
5:18 the *m* who had been possessed was pressing
5:20 At that the *m* went off and began to
5:22 of the synagogue, a *m* named Jairus,
6:20 knowing him to be an upright and holy *m,*
6:28 The *m* went and beheaded John in the prison.
7:15 a *m* from outside can make him impure;
7:18 a *m* from outside can make him impure?
7:20 "What emerges from within a *m,*
7:23 come from within and render a *m* impure."
7:32 Some people brought him a deaf *m* who had a
8:22 him a blind *m* and begged him to touch him.
8:24 The *m* opened his eyes and said,
8:31 them that the Son of *M* had to suffer much,
8:34 "If a *m* wishes to come after me,
8:36 What profit does a *m* show who gains the
8:37 can a *m* offer in exchange for his life?
8:38 the Son of *M* will be ashamed of him when
9: 9 the Son of *M* had risen from the dead.
9:12 *M* that he must suffer much and be despised?
9:17 "Teacher," a *m* in the crowd replied,
9:23 Everything is possible to a *m* who trusts."
9:31 "The Son of *M* is going to be delivered
9:38 we saw a *m* using your name to expel demons
9:39 No *m* who performs a miracle using my name
9:41 Any *m* who gives you a drink of water
10: 7 for this reason a *m* shall leave his father
10: 9 let no *m* separate what God has joined."
10:17 out on a journey a *m* came running up,
10:25 for a rich *m* to enter the kingdom of God."
10:27 "For *m* it is impossible but not for God.
10:33 where the Son of *M* will be handed over to
10:45 *M* has not come to be served but to serve
10:49 So they called the blind *m* over,
10:51 "Rabboni," the blind *m* said,
12: 1 "A *m* planted a vineyard,
12: 2 In due time he dispatched a *m* in his
12:14 "Teacher, we know you are a truthful *m,*
13:13 the *m* who holds out till the end is the
13:15 If a *m* is on the roof terrace,
13:16 If a *m* is in the field,
13:26 Then men will see the Son of *M* coming in
13:34 It is like a *m* traveling abroad.
13:34 *m* at the gate to watch with a sharp eye.
14:13 will come upon a *m* carrying a water jar.
14:20 a *m* who dips into the dish with me.
14:21 The Son of *M* is going the way the
14:21 that *m* by whom the Son of Man is betrayed.
14:41 You will see that the Son of *M* is to be
14:44 saying, "The *m* I shall embrace is the one;
14:51 There was a young *m* following him who was
14:62 and you will see the Son of *M* seated at
14:69 the bystanders, "This *m* is one of them."
14:71 not even know the *m* you are talking about!"
15: 6 any *m* they asked for.
15:12 with the *m* you call the king of the Jews?"
15:21 A *m* named Simon of Cyrene,
15:36 *m* said, "Now let's see whether Elijah
15:39 "Clearly this *m* was the Son of God!"
16: 5 they saw a young *m* sitting at the right,
16:16 The *m* who believes in it and accepts
16:16 the *m* who refuses to believe in it will be
Lk 1:18 I am an old *m;* my wife too is advanced
1:27 to a virgin betrothed to a *m* named Joseph,
1:34 "How can this be since I do not know *m?"*
2:25 at the time a certain *m* named Simeon.
3:11 *m* with two coats give to him who has none.
3:11 The *m* who has food should do the same."
4: 4 has it, 'Not on bread alone shall *m* live.'"
4:33 there was a *m* with an unclean spirit,
5: 8 I am a sinful *m."*
5:12 town, a *m* full of leprosy came to him.
5:14 Jesus then instructed the *m:*
5:21 "Who is this *m* who utters blasphemies?
5:24 make it clear to you that the Son of *M*
5:24 he then addressed the paralyzed *m:*
5:25 At once the *m* stood erect before them.
6: 5 "The Son of *M* is Lord even of the sabbath."
6: 6 was a *m* whose right hand was withered.
6: 8 and said to the *m* whose hand was withered,
6: 8 The *m* rose and remained standing.
6:10 around at them all and said to the *m,*
6:10 The *m* did so and his hand was perfectly
6:22 your name as evil because of the Son of *M.*
6:30 When a *m* takes what is yours,
6:39 a blind *m* act as guide to a blind man?
6:45 A good *m* produces goodness from the good
6:45 *m* produces evil out of his store of evil.
6:45 Each *m* speaks from his heart's abundance.
6:47 Any *m* who desires to come to me will hear
6:48 He may be likened to the *m* who,
6:49 like the *m* who built his house on the ground
7: 8 am a *m* who knows the meaning of an order,
7:12 of the town a dead *m* was being carried out,
7:14 He said, "Young *m,* I bid you get up."
7:15 The dead *m* sat up and began to speak.
7:23 that *m* who finds no stumbling block in me."
7:27 This is the *m* of whom Scripture says,
7:28 is no *m* born of woman greater than John.
7:34 Son of *M* came and he both ate and drank,
7:39 to himself, "If this *m* were a prophet,
8:18 *m* who has, more will be given;
8:25 "What sort of *m* can this be who commands
8:27 he was met by a *m* from the town who was
8:29 the unclean spirit to come out of the *m.*
8:29 *m* used to be tied with chains and fetters,
8:33 came out of the *m* and entered the swine,
8:35 they found the *m* from whom the devils had
8:36 how the possessed *m* had been cured.
8:38 The *m* from whom the devils had departed
8:39 The *m* went all through the town making
8:41 *m* named Jairus, who was chief
8:49 He was still speaking when a *m* came from
9: 9 this *m* about whom I hear all these reports?"
9:22 Son of *M,"* he said, "must first endure
9:26 If a *m* is ashamed of me and my doctrine,
9:26 the Son of *M* will be ashamed of him when
9:38 Suddenly a *m* from the crowd exclaimed:
9:44 *M* must be delivered into the hands of men."
9:49 we saw a *m* using your name to expel demons,
9:50 *m* who is not against you is on your side."
9:58 the Son of *M* has nowhere to lay his head."
9:59 *m* replied, "Let me bury my father first."
10: 6 If there is a peaceable *m* there,
10:30 "There was a *m* going down from Jerusalem
10:36 to the *m* who fell in with the robbers?"
11: 8 take care of the *m* because of friendship,
11:14 the devil was cast out the dumb *m* spoke.
11:21 strong *m* fully armed guards his courtyard,
11:24 an unclean spirit has gone out of a *m,*
11:26 state of the *m* is worse than the first."
11:30 the Son of *M* be a sign for the present age.
12: 8 the Son of *M* will acknowledge him before
12: 9 But the *m* who has disowned me in the
12:10 against the Son of *M* will be forgiven,
12:15 A *m* may be wealthy,
12:16 was a rich *m* who had a good harvest.
12:21 That is the way it works with the *m* who
12:40 of *M* will come when you least expect him."
12:48 When much has been given a *m,*
12:48 of a *m* to whom more has been entrusted.

MAN (cont.)
13: 6 *m* had a fig tree growing in his vineyard,
13: 8 In answer, the *m* said,
13:19 which a *m* took and planted in his garden.
14: 2 of him was a *m* who suffered from dropsy.
14: 4 He took the *m,* healed him,
14: 9 and say to you, 'Make room for this *m,*'
14:16 "A *m* was giving a large dinner and he
14:30 *m* began to build what he could not finish.'
15: 2 *m* welcomes sinners and eats with them."
15:11 "A *m* had two sons.
16: 1 "A rich *m* had a manager who was reported
16: 6 The *m* replied, 'A hundred jars of oil.'
16:10 If you can trust a *m* in little things,
16:15 What *m* thinks important,
16:18 The *m* who marries a woman divorced from
16:19 "Once there was a rich *m* who dressed in
16:22 The rich *m* likewise died and was buried.
16:27 I ask you, then,' the rich *m* said,
16:30 'No, Father Abraham,' replied the rich *m.*
17:16 This *m* was a Samaritan.
17:19 He said to the *m,* "Stand up
17:22 day of the Son of *M* but will not see it.
17:24 The Son of *M* in his day will be like the
17:26 so will it be in the days of the Son of *M.*
17:30 that on the day the Son of *M* is revealed.
17:31 if a *m* is on the rooftop and his
17:31 should the *m* in the field return home.
18: 2 city who respected neither God nor *m.*
18: 4 he thought, 'I care little for God or *m,*
18: 8 But when the Son of *M* comes,
18:13 other *m,* however, kept his distance,
18:14 this *m* went home from the temple justified
18:23 grew melancholy, for he was a very rich *m.*
18:25 a rich *m* to enter the kingdom of heaven."
18:31 the Son of *M* may be accomplished.
18:35 *m* sat at the side of the road begging.
18:36 Hearing a crowd go by the *m* asked,
19: 2 There was a *m* there named Zacchaeus,
19: 2 the chief tax collector and a wealthy *m.*
19:10 The Son of *M* has come to search out and
19:12 "A *m* of noble birth went to a faraway
19:14 say, 'We will not have this *m* rule over us.'
19:17 'Good *m!*' he replied
19:21 was afraid of you because you are a hard *m.*
19:22 You knew I was a hard *m,*
19:24 he has, and give it to the *m* with the ten.'
20: 9 "A *m* planted a vineyard,
20:18 The *m* who falls on that stone will be
21:27 men will see the Son of *M* coming on a
21:36 and to stand secure before the Son of *M.*"
22:10 will come upon a *m* carrying a water jar.
22:12 That *m* will show you an upstairs room,
22:22 of *M* is following out his appointed course,
22:22 but woe to that *m* by whom he is betrayed."
22:36 the *m* who has a purse must carry it;
22:36 And the *m* without a sword must sell his
22:47 a crowd came, led by the *m* named Judas,
22:48 would you betray the Son of *M* with a kiss?"
22:51 Then he touched the ear and healed the *m.*
22:57 intently, then said, "This *m* was with him."
22:59 "This *m* was certainly with him,
22:69 the Son of *M* will have his seat at the
23: 2 "We found this *m* subverting our nation,
23: 4 "I do not find a case against this *m.*"
23: 6 this Pilate asked if the *m* was a Galilean;
23:14 *m* before me as one who subverts the people.
23:15 *m* has done nothing that calls for death.
23:18 whole crowd cried out, "Away with this *m;*
23:22 time, "What wrong is this *m* guilty of?
23:41 done, but this *m* has done nothing wrong."
23:47 by saying, "Surely this was an innocent *m.*"
23:50 There was a *m* named Joseph,
23:52 This *m* approached Pilate with a request
24: 7 that the Son of *M* must be delivered into
Jn 1: 6 There was a *m* named John sent by God,
1: 9 light to every *m* was coming into the world.
1:30 me is to come a *m* who ranks ahead of me,
1:47 "This *m* is a true Israelite.
1:51 ascending and descending on the Son of *M.*"
3: 2 for no *m* can perform signs and wonders
3: 4 "How can a *m* be born again once he is old?"
3:13 the Son of *M* [who is in heaven].
3:14 desert, so must the Son of *M* be lifted up,
3:26 the *m* who was with you across the Jordan
3:29 The groom's best *m* waits there listening
4:18 and the *m* you are living with now is not
4:37 'One *m* sows; another reaps.'
4:50 The *m* put his trust in the word Jesus
5: 5 *m* who had been sick for thirty-eight years.
5: 7 "Sir," the sick *m* answered, "I do not have
5: 9 The *m* was immediately cured;
5:10 began telling the *m* who had been cured,
5:11 "It was the *m* who cured me who told me,
5:13 The *m* who had been restored to health had
5:15 The *m* went off and informed the Jews that
5:24 the *m* who hears my word and has faith in
5:27 to pass judgment because he is Son of *M;*
6:27 food which the Son of *M* will give you;
6:50 from heaven for a *m* to eat and never die.
6:53 flesh of the Son of *M* and drink his blood,
6:56 The *m* who feeds on my flesh and drinks my
6:57 so the *m* who feeds on me will have life
6:58 the *m* who feeds on this bread shall live
6:62 Son of *M* ascend to where he was before . . .
7:12 Some maintained, "He is a good *m,*"
7:15 "How did this *m* get his education when he
7:17 Any *m* who chooses to do his will will know
7:18 The *m* who seeks glory for him who sent him
7:22 so, even on a sabbath you circumcise a *m.*
7:23 If a *m* can be circumcised on the sabbath
7:23 me for curing a whole *m* on the sabbath?
7:27 Still, we know where this *m* is from.
7:31 expected to perform more signs than this *m?*"
7:46 "No *m* ever spoke like that before,"
7:50 Nicodemus (the *m* who had come to him),
7:51 condemn any *m* without first hearing him
8: 7 "Let the *m* among you who has no sin be
8:15 to appearances but I pass judgment on no *m.*
8:28 "When you lift up the Son of *M,*
8:40 a *m* who has told you the truth which I
8:44 He brought death to *m* from the beginning,
8:51 if a *m* is true to my word he shall never
8:52 'A *m* shall never know death if he keeps my
9: 1 he saw a *m* who had been blind from birth.
9: 3 no sin, either of this *m* or of his parents.
9: 7 So the *m* went off and washed,
9: 9 The *m* himself said, "I am the one."
9:11 "That *m* they call Jesus made mud and
9:13 *m* who had been born blind to the Pharisees.
9:16 "This *m* cannot be from God because he
9:16 Others objected, "If a *m* is a sinner,
9:17 Then they addressed the blind *m* again:
9:18 the parents of this *m* who now could see.
9:24 *m* who had been born blind and said to him,
9:24 First of all, we know this *m* is a sinner."
9:29 we have no idea where this *m* comes from."
9:33 If this *m* were not from God,
9:35 him, "Do you believe in the Son of *M?*"
10:33 who are only a *m* are making yourself God."
10:41 whatever John said about this *m* was true."
11: 1 was a certain *m* named Lazarus who was sick.
11: 9 If a *m* goes walking by day he does not
11:37 said, "He opened the eyes of that blind *m.*
11:37 done something to stop this *m* from dying?"
11:44 The dead *m* came out bound head and foot
11:47 this *m* performing all sorts of signs?
11:50 better for you to have one *m* die
12:23 has come for the Son of *M* to be glorified.
12:25 *m* who loves his life loses it, while the *m*
12:34 claim that the Son of *M* must be lifted up?
12:34 Just who is this 'Son of *M'?*"
12:35 The *m* who walks in the dark does not know
13:10 "The *m* who has bathed has no need to wash
13:31 of *M* glorified and God is glorified in him.
14:12 the *m* who has faith in me will do the
14:21 he has from me is the *m* who loves me;
15: 6 A *m* who does not live in me is like a
16:21 joy that a *m* has been born into the world.
18:14 of having one *m* die for the people.)
18:26 of the *m* whose ear Peter had severed.
18:29 accusation do you bring against this *m?*"
18:38 for myself, I find no case against this *m.*
19: 5 Pilate said to them, "Look at the *m!*"
19:12 free this *m* you are no 'Friend of Caesar.'
19:21 'This *m* claimed to be King of the Jews'"
19:39 Nicodemus (the *m* who had first come to
21:18 as a young *m* you fastened your belt and
Acts 2:22 was a *m* whom God sent to you with miracles,
3: 2 *m* crippled from birth was being carried in.
3: 4 Peter fixed his gaze on the *m;*
3:11 *m* stood there clinging to Peter and John,
3:12 we had made this *m* walk by some power
3:16 limbs of this *m* whom you see and know well.
4:10 this *m* stands before you perfectly sound.
4:14 When they saw the *m* who had been cured
4:22 the *m* thus miraculously cured was more
5: 1 Another *m* named Ananias and his wife
6: 5 a *m* filled with faith and the Holy Spirit;
6: 8 of was a *m* filled with grace and power,
6:13 "This *m* never stops making statements
7:22 He was a *m* powerful in word and deed.
7:27 the *m* who was wronging his neighbor pushed
7:56 the Son of *M* standing at God's right hand."
7:57 Then they rushed at him as one *m,*
7:58 cloaks at the feet of a young *m* named Saul.
8: 9 A certain *m* named Simon had been
8:30 and heard the *m* reading the prophet Isaiah.
8:31 "How can I," the *m* replied, "unless someone
8:39 the *m* went on his way rejoicing.
9: 2 Jerusalem anyone he might find, *m* or woman,
9:12 (Saul saw in a vision a *m* named Ananias
9:13 heard from many sources about this *m*
9:15 This *m* is the instrument I have chosen to
9:21 "Isn't this the *m* who worked such havoc
9:33 There he found a *m* named Aeneas,
9:34 The *m* got up at once.
10:21 and said, "I am the *m* you are looking for.
10:22 who is an upright and Godfearing *m,*
10:26 I am only a *m* myself."
10:28 no one should call any *m* unclean or impure.
10:30 when a *m* in dazzling robes stood before me.
10:35 the *m* of any nation who fears God and acts
11:24 *m* filled with the Holy Spirit and faith.
12:22 "This is the voice of a god, not a *m!*"
13: 7 a *m* of intelligence who had summoned
13:22 have found David son of Jesse to be a *m*
14: 8 there was a *m* who was lame from birth;
14:10 The *m* jumped up and began to walk around.
16: 9 A *m* of Macedonia stood before him and
17: 7 To a *m,* they disregard the Emperor's
17:31 with justice' through a *m* he has appointed
18: 8 A leading *m* of the synagogue,
18:17 on Sosthenes, a leading *m* of the synagogue,
18:24 native of Alexandria and a *m* of eloquence,
18:25 Apollos was a *m* full of spiritual fervor.
19:16 Then the *m* with the evil spirit sprang at
19:35 "what *m* is there who does not know that
21: 9 This *m* had four unmarried daughters gifted
21:28 This is the *m* who is spreading his
22:26 This *m* is a Roman citizen!"
23: 9 do not find this *m* guilty of any crime.
23:17 said, "Take this young *m* to the commander;
23:27 Here is a *m* whom the Jews seized and were
24: 5 We have found that this *m* is a
24:16 keep my conscience clear before God and *m.*
25: 5 me," he said, "and if this *m* is at fault,
25:15 this *m* and demanded his condemnation.
25:16 Roman practice to hand an accused *m*
25:17 on the bench and ordered the *m* brought in.
25:22 Festus, "I too should like to hear this *m.*"
25:24 are here present with us, look at this *m!*
26:31 "This *m* is doing nothing that deserves
27:23 of the God whose *m* I am and whom I serve,
28: 4 "This *m* must really be a murderer if,
28: 8 Paul went in to see the *m* and praying,
Rom 1:17 says, "The just *m* shall live by faith."
1:23 God for images representing mortal *m,*
2: 6 he will repay every *m* for what he has done:
2: 9 will come upon every *m* who has done evil,
2:27 If a *m* who is uncircumcised keeps the law,
3: 4 true even though every *m* be proved a liar,
3:10 "There is no just *m,*
3:28 For we hold that a *m* is justified by faith
4: 4 Now, when a *m* works,
4: 5 But when a *m* does nothing,
4: 6 Thus David congratulates the *m* to whom God
4: 8 is the *m* to whom the Lord imputes no guilt."
5: 7 should lay down his life for a just *m,*
5: 7 good *m* someone may have the courage to die.
5:12 *m* sin entered the world and with sin death,
5:14 as did Adam, that type of the *m* to come.
5:15 if by the offense of the one *m* all died,
5:15 of God and the gracious gift of the one *m,*
5:16 from the sin committed by the one *m.*
5:17 reign through one *m* because of his offense,
5:17 justice live and reign through the one *m,*
6: 7 A *m* who is dead has been freed from sin.
7: 1 power over a *m* only so long as he lives?
7: 3 adultery by consorting with another *m.*
7:24 What a wretched *m* I am!
9:10 had conceived twin children by one *m,*
13: 2 the *m* who opposes authority rebels against
13: 3 Rulers cause no fear when a *m* does what is
14: 2 *m* of sound faith knows he can eat anything,
14: 3 The *m* who will eat anything must not
14: 3 the *m* who abstains must not sit in
14: 5 One *m* regards this day as better than that;
14: 6 The *m* who observes the day does so to
14: 6 The *m* who eats does so to honor the Lord,
14: 6 The *m* who does not eat abstains to honor
14:14 it is only when a *m* thinks something
14:20 but it is wrong for a *m* to eat when the
14:22 Happy the *m* whose conscience does not
14:23 But if a *m* eats when his conscience has
1Cor 1:20 Where is the wise *m* to be found?
2: 9 nor has it so much as dawned on *m* what God
2:14 The natural *m* does not accept what is
2:15 spiritual *m,* on the other hand, can appraise
3:14 If the building a *m* has raised on this
5: 1 a *m* living with his father's wife.
5: 3 Jesus Christ on the *m* who did this deed.
5:11 clear that you must not eat with such a *m.*
5:13 "Expel the wicked *m* from your midst."
6:16 Can you not see that the *m* who is joined
6:18 other sin a *m* commits is outside his body,
7: 1 A *m* is better off having no relations with
7: 2 every *m* should have his own wife and every
7:32 *m* is busy with the Lord's affairs,
7:33 but the married *m* is busy with this
7:37 *m,* however, who stands firm in his resolve,
7:38 *m* who marries his virgin, acts fittingly;
8: 2 If a *m* thinks he knows something,
8: 3 anyone loves God, that *m* is known by him.
9:24 part in the race, the award goes to one *m.*
9:26 a *m* who loses sight of the finish line.
10:24 No *m* should seek his own interest but
11: 3 head of every *m* is Christ;
11: 4 Any *m* who prays or prophesies with his
11: 7 *m,* on the other hand, ought not to cover
11: 8 *M* was not made from woman but woman from
11: 8 was not made from woman but woman from *m.*
11: 9 was man created for woman but woman for *m.*
11:11 of *m* nor man independent of woman.
11:12 was made from man, so *m* is born of woman;
11:14 dishonorable for a *m* to wear his hair long,
11:28 A *m* should examine himself first;
13:11 I became a *m* I put childish ways aside.
14: 2 A *m* who speaks in a tongue is talking not

14:13 This means that the *m* who speaks in a
14:17 indeed, but the other *m* will not be helped.
14:37 he is a prophet or a *m* of the Spirit,
15:21 Death came through a *m;*
15:21 of the dead comes through a *m* also.
15:45 Scripture has it that Adam, the first *m,*
15:47 The first *m* was of earth,
15:48 Earthly men are like the *m* of earth,
15:48 heavenly men are like the *m* of heaven.
15:49 Just as we resemble the *m* from earth,
15:49 we bear the likeness of the *m* from heaven.
2Cor 2:10 If you forgive a *m* anything, so do I.
7:12 writing to you was not intended for the *m*
10:18 It is not the *m* who recommends himself who
10:18 but the *m* whom the Lord recommends.
12: 2 I know a *m* in Christ who,
12: 2 *m* who was snatched up to the third heaven.
12: 3 I know that this *m*—
12: 4 be uttered, words which no *m* may speak.
12: 5 About this *m* I will boast;
Gal 1: 1 an apostle sent not by men or by any *m,*
1:12 I did not receive it from any *m,*
2:16 knowing that a *m* is not justified by legal
3: 9 blessed along with Abraham, the *m* of faith.
3:11 law, for "the just *m* shall live by faith."
6: 4 Each *m* should look to his conduct;
6: 6 The *m* instructed in the word should share
6: 7 A *m* will reap only what he sows.
6:17 Henceforth, let no *m* trouble me,
Eph 2:15 to create in himself one new *m* from us who
4:13 *m* who is Christ come to full stature.
4:24 put on that new *m* created in God's image,
4:28 The *m* who has been stealing must steal no
5:31 a *m* shall leave his father and mother,
Phil 1: 7 you who, to a *m,* are sharers
Col 1:28 hoping to make every *m* complete in Christ.
3:10 with its past deeds and put on a new *m,*
1Thes 4: 8 rejects these instructions rejects, not *m,*
2Thes 2: 3 nor the *m* of lawlessness been revealed
3: 2 For not every *m* has faith,
1Tm 1:13 a persecutor, a *m* filled with arrogance;
2: 5 between God and men, the *m* Christ Jesus,
2:12 or in any way to have authority over a *m;*
3: 3 but, rather, gentle, a *m* of peace.
3: 5 for if a *m* does not know how to manage
5: 1 Never censure an older *m,*
6: 4 a sick *m* in his passion for polemics and
6:11 *M* of God that you are,
2Tm 3:17 training in holiness so that the *m* of God
Ti 1: 7 a drunkard, a violent or greedy *m.*
1:12 *m* of Crete, one of their own prophets,
Phlm 1:16 will know him both as a *m* and in the Lord.
Heb 2: 6 is *m* that you should be mindful of him,
2: 6 the son of *m* that you should care for him?
7: 4 See the greatness of this *m* to whom
7: 8 Scripture testifies that this *m* lives on.
8: 2 of that true tabernacle set up, not by *m,*
10:29 is due the *m* who disdains the Son of God,
10:38 My just *m* will live by faith,
11:12 this faith, there came forth from one *m,*
12:15 that no *m* falls away from the grace of God;
13: 6 What can *m* do to me?"
Jas 1: 8 *m* of this sort, devious and erratic in all
1:10 and the rich *m* be proud of his lowliness,
1:11 rich *m* wither away amid his many projects.
1:12 *m* who holds out to the end through trial!
1:14 and lure of his own passion tempt every *m.*
1:19 Let every *m* be quick to hear,
1:23 A *m* who listens to God's word but does not
1:23 like a *m* who looks into a mirror
1:25 the *m* who peers into freedom's ideal law
1:25 Blest will this *m* be in whatever he does.
1:26 If a *m* who does not control his tongue
2: 2 into your assembly a *m* fashionably dressed,
2: 2 the same time a poor *m* in shabby clothes.
2: 3 take notice of the well-dressed *m* and say,
2: 3 whereas you were to say to the poor *m,*
2: 6 Yet you treated this poor *m* shamefully.
2:13 judgment on the *m* who has not shown mercy;
3: 2 in speech he is a *m* in the fullest sense,
3: 8 the tongue no *m* can tame.
4: 4 A *m* is marked out as God's enemy if he
4:17 When a *m* knows the right thing to do and
5: 6 You condemned, even killed, the just *m;*
5:16 petition of a holy *m* is powerful indeed.
5:17 Elijah was only a *m* like us,
1Pt 2:17 You must esteem the person of every *m.*
2:19 When a *m* can suffer injustice and endure
3:18 all, the just *m* for the sake of the unjust,
4:18 the just *m* is saved only with difficulty,
2Pt 1: 9 Any *m* who lacks these qualities is
2: 7 a just *m* oppressed by the conduct of men
2:15 He was a *m* attracted to dishonest gain,
1Jn 2: 4 *m* who claims, "I have known him,"
2: 6 for the *m* who claims to abide in him
2: 9 The *m* who claims to be in light,
2:10 The *m* who continues in the light is the
2:11 the *m* who hates his brother is in darkness.
2:17 the *m* who does God's will endures forever.
3: 6 The *m* who remains in him does not sin.
3: 6 *m* who sins has not seen him or known him.
3: 7 the *m* who acts in holiness is holy indeed,
3: 8 The *m* who sins belongs to the devil,
3:14 The *m* who does not love is among the
3:17 how can God's love survive in a *m* who has
4: 8 *m* without love has known nothing of God,
Rv 1: 3 is the *m* who reads this prophetic message,
1:13 a Son of *M* wearing an ankle-length robe,
4: 7 the third had the face of a *m,*
13:16 it did not allow a *m* to buy or sell
13:18 it is a number that stands for a certain *m.*
14:14 One like a Son of *M* wearing a gold crown
16:15 Happy the *m* who stays wide awake and fully
22: 7 Happy the *m* who heeds the prophetic
22:12 be given to each *m* as his conduct deserves.

MAN-MADE (1)

Acts 19:26 tells them that *m* gods are no gods at all.

MANACLE (1)

Sir 21:19 to a fool, like a *m* on his right hand.

MANAEN (1)

Acts 13: 1 *M* (who had been brought up with Herod the

MANAGE (2)

1Sm 25: 8 and your son David whatever you can *m.*' "
1Tm 3: 5 man does not know how to *m* his own house,

MANAGED (4)

1Kgs 12:18 Rehoboam *m* to mount his chariot to flee to
2Chr 10:18 Rehoboam himself *m* to mount his chariot
Mk 1:36 and his companions *m* to track him down,
Acts 16:15 She *m* to prevail on us.

MANAGEMENT (1)

Gn 39:22 had to be done there was done under his *m.*

MANAGER (5)

Lk 16: 1 "A rich man had a *m* who was reported to
16: 3 The *m* thought to himself,
16: 6 *m* said, 'Take your invoice,
16: 7 hundred measures of wheat,' and the *m* said,
1Tm 3: 4 He must be a good *m* of his own household,

MANAGERS (1)

1Tm 3:12 *m* of their children and their households.

MANAGING (1)

Sir 10:25 Flaunt not your wisdom in *m* your affairs,

MANAHATH (2)

1Chr 1:40 The sons of Shobal were Alian, *M,*
8: 6 who dwelt in Geba and were deported to *M.*

MANAHATHITES (2)

1Chr 2:52 of Kiriath-jearim, were Reaiah, half the *M,*
2:54 Netophathites, Atroth-beth-Joab, half the *M,*

MANASSEH (140)

Gn 41:51 He named his first-born *M,*
46:20 Joseph became the father of *M* and Ephraim,
48: 1 along with him his two sons, *M* and Ephraim.
48: 5 Ephraim and *M* shall be mine as much as
48:13 to Israel's left, and *M* with his left hand,
48:14 and his left hand on the head of *M,*
48:20 Manasseh,' " he placed Ephraim before *M.*
Nm 1:10 Elishama, son of Ammihud, and from *M:*
1:34 Of the descendants of *M,*
1:35 hundred were enrolled in the tribe of *M.*
2:20 the tribe of *M* [Their prince was Gamaliel,
10:23 Pedahzur, over the host of the tribe of *M,*
13:11 son of Susi, of the tribe of *M,*
26:28 The sons of Joseph were *M* and Ephraim.
26:34 These were the clans of *M,*
27: 1 son of Gilead, son of Machir, son of *M,*
32:33 as well as half the tribe of *M,*
32:39 The descendants of Machir, son of *M,*
32:40 [Moses gave Gilead to Machir, son of *M,*
34:14 of Gad, as well as half of the tribe of *M,*
34:23 Bukki, son of Jogli;from the tribe of *M:*
36: 1 of Gilead, son of Machir, son of *M*—
36:12 within the clans of the descendants of *M,*
Dt 3:13 region, I gave to the half-tribe of *M.*
29: 7 Gadites, and half the tribe of *M.*
33:17 and these the thousands of *M*
34: 2 all Naphtali, the land of Ephraim and *M,*
Jos 1:12 the Gadites, and the half-tribe of *M:*
4:12 Reubenites, Gadites, and half-tribe of *M,*
12: 6 the Gadites, and the half-tribe of *M,*
13: 7 *M* the land which is to be their heritage."
13: 8 *M* as well as the Reubenites and Gadites,
13:29 gave to the clans of the half-tribe of *M.*
13:31 to the descendants of Machir, son of *M,*
14: 4 of Joseph formed two tribes, *M* and Ephraim.
16: 4 Within the heritage of *M* and Ephraim,
17: 1 the tribe of *M* as the first-born of Joseph:
17: 2 now made to the other descendants of *M,*
17: 2 and Shemida, the other male children of *M,*
17: 3 son of Gilead, son of Machir, son of *M,*
17: 5 Thus ten shares fell to *M* apart from the
17: 6 *M* received each a portion among his sons.
17: 7 *M* bordered on Asher.
17: 8 the district of Tappuah belonged to *M,*
17: 8 was an Ephraimite city on the border of *M.*
17: 9 in *M* were those to the south of that wadi;
17: 9 thus the territory of *M* ran north of the
17:10 to Ephraim and that on the north to *M;*
17:11 *M* was awarded Beth-shean and its towns,
17:17 Joshua therefore said to Ephraim and *M,*
18: 7 and the half-tribe of *M* have already
20: 8 Gad, and Golan in Bashan in the tribe of *M.*
21: 5 tribe of Dan, and from the half-tribe of *M.*
21: 6 of Naphtali, and from the half-tribe of *M.*
21:25 and from the half-tribe of *M* the two
21:27 from the half-tribe of *M* two cities:
22: 1 and the half-tribe of *M* and said to them:
22: 7 of *M* Moses had assigned land
22: 9 and the half-tribe of *M* left the other
22:10 and the half-tribe of *M* came to the region
22:11 and the half-tribe of *M* had built an altar
22:13 and the half-tribe of *M* in the land of
22:15 the half-tribe of *M* in the land of Gilead,
22:21 and the half-tribe of *M* replied to the
Jgs 1:27 *M* did not take possession of Beth-shean
6:15 My family is the meanest in *M,*
6:35 He sent messengers, too, throughout *M,*
7:23 and from all *M* and they pursued Midian.
11:29 He passed through Gilead and *M,*
12: 4 in territory belonging to Ephraim and *M.*"
1Kgs 4:13 charge of the villages of Jair, son of *M,*
2Kgs 20:21 and his son *M* succeeded him as king.
21: 1 *M* was twelve years old when he began to
21: 9 and *M* misled them into doing even greater
21:11 "Because *M,*
21:16 *M* did evil in the sight of the LORD,
21:17 The rest of the acts of *M,*
21:18 *M* rested with his ancestors and was buried
21:20 of the LORD, as his father *M* had done.
23:12 and the altars made by *M* in the two courts
23:26 of all the provocations that *M* had given,
24: 3 sins *M* had committed in all that he did;
1Chr 3:13 whose son was Hezekiah, whose son was *M,*
5:18 Gadites, and half-tribe of *M* were warriors,
5:23 numerous members of the half-tribe of *M*
5:26 half-tribe of *M* and brought them to Halah,
6:46 and from the tribe of *M.*
6:47 and from the half-tribe of *M* in Bashan.
6:55 From the half-tribe of *M:*
6:56 received from the half-tribe of *M:*
7:14 The sons of *M,*
7:17 of Gilead, the son of Machir, the son of *M.*
7:29 *M,* however, had possession of Bethshean
12:20 Men from *M* also deserted to David when he
12:21 therefore, these deserted to him from *M:*
12:21 and Zillethai, chiefs of thousands of *M.*
12:32 Of the half-tribe of *M:*
12:38 Gadites, and the half-tribe of *M,*
26:32 and the half-tribe of *M* in everything
27:20 for the half-tribe of *M,*
27:21 for the half-tribe of *M* in Gilead,
2Chr 15: 9 *M* and Simeon who sojourned with them;
30: 1 even wrote letters to Ephraim and *M*
30:10 of Ephraim and *M* and as far as Zebulun,
30:11 *M* and Zebulun humbled themselves and came
30:18 people, in fact, chiefly from Ephraim, *M,*
31: 1 throughout Judah, Benjamin, Ephraim and *M,*
32:33 His son *M* succeeded him as king.
33: 1 *M* was twelve years old when he became king,
33: 9 *M* misled Judah and the inhabitants of
33:10 The LORD spoke to *M* and his people,
33:11 they took *M* with hooks,
33:13 *M* understood that the LORD is indeed God.
33:18 The rest of the acts of *M,*
33:20 *M* rested with his ancestors and was buried
33:22 of the LORD, just as his father *M* had done.
33:22 all the idols which his father *M* had made,
33:23 before the LORD as his father *M* had done;
34: 6 He did likewise in the cities of *M,*
34: 9 of the threshold, had collected from *M,*
Ezr 10:30 Mattaniah, Bezalel, Binnui, and *M;*
10:33 Mattattah, Zabad, Eliphelet, Jeremai, *M,*
Jdt 8: 2 Her husband, *M,* of her own tribe and clan,
8: 7 Her husband, *M,* had left her gold and silver,
10: 3 attire she had worn while her husband, *M,*
16:22 of the death and burial of her husband, *M.*
16:23 buried her in the tomb of her husband, *M;*
16:24 goods to the relatives of her husband, *M,*
Ps(s) 60: 9 Mine is Gilead, and mine *M;*
80: 3 forth before Ephraim, Benjamin and *M.*
108: 9 Mine is Gilead, and mine *M,*
Is 9:20 *M* devours Ephraim, and Ephraim *M*
Jer 15: 4 kingdoms of the earth because of what *M,*
Ez 48: 4 *M:* on the frontier of Naphtali
48: 5 on the frontier of *M,*
Mt 1:10 father of Manasseh, *M* the father of Amos,
Rv 7: 6 twelve thousand from the tribe of *M,*

MANASSEHITE (2)

Nm 32:41 Jair, a *M* clan, campaigned against the tent
Dt 3:14 Jair, a *M* clan, took all the region of Argob

MANASSEHITES (10)

Nm 7:54 Gamaliel, son of Pedahzur, prince of the *M.*
26:29 The *M* by clans were:
Dt 4:43 and Golan in Bashan for the *M.*
Jos 16: 9 Ephraimites within the territory of the *M.*
17: 6 land of Gilead fell to the rest of the *M.*
17:12 Since the *M* could not conquer these cities,
22:30 the Gadites and the *M* had to say,
22:31 to the Reubenites, the Gadites and the *M,*
2Kgs 10:33 Gilead, of the Gadites, Reubenites and *M),*
1Chr 9: 3 also Ephraimites and *M.*

MANASSEH'S (3)

Gn 48:17 to remove it from Ephraim's head to *M,*
50:23 and the children of *M* son Machir were also
1Chr 7:15 *M* second son was named Zelophehad,

MANDATE (2)

Gn 26: 5 obeyed me, keeping my *m* (my commandments,
1Kgs 2: 3 Keep the *m* of the LORD,

MANDATORY (1)

Ez 46:14 LORD is *m* with the established holocaust.

MANDRAKES (6)

Gn 30:14 *m* which he brought home to his mother Leah.
30:14 "Please let me have some of your son's *m.*"
30:15 that you must now take my son's *m* too?"
30:15 "In exchange for your son's *m,*
30:16 I have paid for you with my son's *m.*"
Sg 7:14 The *m* give forth fragrance,

MANFULLY (3)

1Sm 4: 9 So fight *m!*"
2Sm 13:28 Be resolute and act *m.*"
2Mc 6:27 Therefore, by *m* giving up my life now,

MANGE (1)

Lv 22:22 that has a running sore or *m* or ringworm,

MANGER (5)

Jb 39: 9 you, and to pass the nights by your *m?*
Is 1: 3 its owner, and an ass, its master's *m;*
Lk 2: 7 in swaddling clothes and laid him in a *m,*
2:12 in a *m* you will find an infant wrapped in
2:16 and Joseph, and the baby lying in the *m;*

MANGLED (2)

Ex 22:12 need not make restitution for the *m* animal.
1Kgs 13:26 him to a lion, which *m* and killed him,

MANHANDLE (1)

Lk 21:12 any of this, they will *m* and persecute you,

MANHANDLED (1)

Mk 14:65 while the officers *m* him.

MANHOOD (5)

Gn 49: 3 my strength and the first fruit of my *m,*
Dt 21:17 since he is the first fruits of his *m,*
Tb 1: 9 When I reached *m* I married Anna,
Ps(s) 78:51 the first fruits of *m* in the tents of Ham;
105:36 land, the first fruits of all their *m.*

MANIFEST (18)

Lv 10: 3 who approach me I will *m* my sacredness;
14:57 so that it may be *m* when there is a state
Nm 27:14 rebelled against my order to *m* my sanctity
Dt 32:51 to *m* my sanctity among the Israelites.
Jdt 13:11 Once more he has made *m* his strength in
Est C:23 *M* yourself in the time of our distress and
1Mc 15: 9 that your glory will be *m* in all the earth."
2Mc 8: 4 and to *m* his hatred of evil.
Ps(s) 9:17 In passing sentence, the LORD is *m;*
Ez 20:41 *m* my holiness in the sight of the nations.
28:22 upon it and use it to *m* my holiness.
28:25 then I will *m* my holiness through them in
Lk 11:53 Pharisees began to *m* fierce hostility to him
Rom 3:25 He did so to *m* his own justice,
3:26 to *m* his justice in the present,
1Cor 4: 5 in darkness and *m* the intentions of hearts.
2Tm 1:10 *m* through the appearance of our Savior.
2Pt 3:10 the earth and all its deeds will be made *m.*

MANIFESTATION (3)

2Mc 12:22 fear and terror at the *m* of the All-seeing.
15:27 greatly over this *m* of God's power.
1Cor 12: 7 To each person the *m* of the Spirit is

MANIFESTATIONS (1)

2Mc 2:21 and of the heavenly *m* accorded to the

MANIFESTED (8)

2Mc 3:16 of his face *m* the anguish of his soul.
3:24 Lord of spirits who holds all power *m* himself
3:30 now that the almighty Lord had *m* himself.
Rom 3:21 of God has been *m* apart from the law,
16:26 now *m* through the writings of the prophets,
Eph 2: 7 *m* by his kindness to us in Christ Jesus.
1Tm 3:16 "He was *m* in the flesh,
Ti 1: 3 has now *m* in his own good time as his word,

MANIFESTING (2)

2Mc 9: 8 litter, clearly *m* to all the power of God.
2Thes 2: 8 and annihilate him by *m* his own presence.

MANIFESTS (2)

2Mc 15:34 praised the LORD who *m* his divine power,
Wis 1: 2 and he *m* himself to those who do not

MANIFOLD (5)

Jb 22: 5 Is not your wickedness *m?*
Ps(s) 104:24 How *m* are your works, O LORD!
Wis 7:22 is a spirit intelligent, holy, unique, *M,*
Eph 3:10 God's *m* wisdom is made known to the
1Pt 4:10 As generous distributors of God's *m* grace,

MANIUS (1)

2Mc 11:34 "Quintus Memmius and Titus *M,*

MANKIND (51)

Gn 7:21 swarmed on the earth, as well as all *m.*
Nm 16:22 out, "O God, God of the spirits of all *m,*
16:29 merely suffering the fate common to all *m,*
27:16 the LORD, the God of the spirits of all *m,*
1Kgs 2: 2 "I am going the way of all *m.*
2Chr 6:18 indeed be that God dwells with *m* on earth?
Jb 12:10 living thing, and the life breath of all *m.*
15: 7 Are you indeed the first-born of *m,*
21:33 While all the line of *m* follows him,
36:28 with them and the showers rain down on *m.*
37: 7 He shuts up all *m* indoors;
Ps(s) 11: 4 eyes behold, his searching glance is on *m.*
33:13 the LORD looks down; he sees all *m.*
Eccl 7:29 God made *m* straight,
Wis 10: 8 then they left *m* a memorial of their folly
14:21 And this became a snare for *m,*
Sir 35:22 Till he requites *m* according to its deeds,
39:19 The works of all *m* are present to him;
45: 4 and meekness God selected him from all *m;*
45:16 *m* to offer holocausts and choice offerings,
Is 40: 5 revealed, and all *m* shall see it together;
40: 6 "All *m* is grass,
45:12 I who made the earth and created *m* upon it;
49:26 All *m* shall know that I,
66:16 LORD shall judge all *m* by fire and sword.
66:23 All *m* shall come to worship before me,
66:24 and they shall be abhorrent to all *m.*
Jer 12:12 no peace for all *m.*
25:31 nations, he is to pass judgment upon all *m:*
32:27 I am the LORD, the God of all *m!*
45: 5 I am bringing evil on all *m,*
Dn 14: 5 and earth and has dominion over all *m.*"
Jl 1:12 Yes, joy has withered away from among *m.*
3: 1 I will pour out my spirit upon all *m.*
Zep 1: 3 will destroy *m* from the face of the earth,
Zec 2:17 Silence, all *m,* in the presence of the LORD!
Mk 3:28 *m* and all the blasphemies men utter,
Lk 3: 6 And all *m* shall see the salvation of God.'"
Jn 17: 2 you have given him authority over all *m,*
Acts 2:17 pour out a portion of my spirit on all *m:*
15:17 so that all the rest of *m* and all the
17:26 of *m* to dwell on the face of the earth.
1Cor 1:29 so that *m* can do no boasting before God.
1Thes 2:15 Displeasing to God and hostile to all *m,*
Jas 3: 7 can be tamed, and has been tamed, by *m;*
1Pt 1:24 "All *m* is grass and the glory of men is
Rv 9:15 had been prepared, to kill a third of *m.*
9:18 a third of *m* was slain.
9:20 That part of *m* which escaped the plagues
14: 4 the first fruits of *m* for God and the Lamb.
16:21 came crashing down on *m* from the sky,

MANLIKE (1)

Dn 8:15 I had seen, a *m* figure stood before me,

MANLY (3)

1Sm 4: 9 Take courage and be *m,* Philistines;
2Mc 7:21 stirred her womanly heart with *m* courage,
14:43 with *m* courage threw himself down

MANNA (20)

Ex 16:21 when the sun grew hot, the *m* melted away.
16:23 You may either bake or boil the *m,*
16:31 The Israelites called this food *m.*
16:32 Keep an omerful of *m* for your descendants,
16:33 "Take an urn and put an omer of *m* in it.
16:35 The Israelites ate this *m* for forty years,
16:35 *m* until they reached the borders of Canaan.
Nm 11: 6 we see nothing before us but this *m.*"
11: 7 *M* was like coriander seed and had the
11: 9 dew fell upon the camp, the *m* also fell.
Dt 8: 3 with hunger, and then fed you with *m,*
8:16 rock and fed you in the desert with *m,*
Jos 5:12 of the produce of the land, the *m* ceased.
5:12 No longer was there *m* for the Israelites,
Neh 9:20 *m* you did not withhold from their mouths,
Ps(s) 78:24 He rained *m* upon them for food and gave
Jn 6:31 Our ancestors had *m* to eat in the desert;
6:49 Your ancestors ate *m* in the desert,
Heb 9: 4 ark were the golden jar containing the *m,*
Rv 2:17 To the victor I will give the hidden *m;*

MANNED (1)

2Mc 10:17 the places, drove back all who *m* the walls,

MANNER (28)

Ex 5:15 do you treat your servants in this *m?*
36:37 fine linen twined, woven in a variegated *m.*
Lv 9:16 holocaust, and offered it in the usual *m.*
Dt 12:21 you may slaughter in the *m* I have told you
Jos 6:15 around the city seven times in the same *m;*
Jgs 18: 7 securely after the *m* of the Sidonians,
2Sm 14: 3 go to the king and speak to him in this *m.*"
2Kgs 17:40 but continued in their earlier *m*
1Chr 24:31 They too, in the same *m* as their relatives,
2Chr 30: 5 not many had kept it in the *m* prescribed.
Ezr 3: 4 the feast of Booths in the *m* prescribed,
3:10 the LORD in the *m* laid down by David,
Est 9:27 year in the *m* prescribed by this letter,
2Mc 2:14 In like *m* Judas also collected for us
4:16 very people whose *m* of life they emulated,
6:23 But he made up his mind in a noble *m,*
7: 7 When the first brother had died in this *m,*
13: 7 In such a *m* was Menelaus,
14:46 Such was the *m* of his death.
Jb 27:11 I will teach you the *m* of God's dealings,
Ps(s) 17: 4 has not transgressed after the *m* of man;
107:18 of their sins, They loathed all *m* of food,
Eccl 7:15 have seen all *m* of things in my vain days:
Sir 16:28 *m* of life which must return into it again.
25: 2 their *m* of life I loathe indeed:
Is 58: 5 Is this the *m* of fasting I wish,
Mk 15:39 over him, on seeing the *m* of his death,
2Cor 11:17 the Lord desires but after the *m* of a fool.

MANNERS (3)

2Mc 15:12 man, modest in appearance, gentle in *m,*
Prv 20:11 Even by his *m* the child betrays whether
Sir 31:17 Be the first to stop, as befits good *m:*

MANOAH (16)

Jgs 13: 2 the clan of the Danites, whose name was *M.*
13: 8 *M* then prayed to the LORD.
13: 9 God heard the prayer of *M,*
13: 9 Since her husband *M* was not with her,
13:11 so *M* got up and followed his wife.
13:12 *M* asked, "Now, when that which you say
13:13 The angel of the LORD answered *M,*
13:15 Then *M* said to the angel of the LORD,
13:16 But the angel of the LORD answered *M,*
13:17 was the angel of the LORD, *M* said to him,
13:19 Then *M* took the kid with a cereal offering
13:19 While *M* and his wife were looking on,
13:20 When *M* and his wife saw this,
13:21 LORD was seen no more by *M* and his wife.
13:21 *M,* realizing that it was the angel
16:31 of his father *M* between Zorah and Eshtaol.

MANOKO (1)

Jos 15:59 Tatam, Zores, Karim, Gallim, Bether and *M;*

MAN'S (156)

Gn 6: 5 saw how great was *m* wickedness on earth,
8:21 desires of *m* heart are evil from the start;
20: 7 Therefore, return the *m* wife
43:21 was each *m* money in the mouth of his bag
44: 1 put each *m* money in the mouth of his bag.
Ex 21:35 "When one *m* ox hurts another's ox so
Lv 4:35 priest shall make atonement for the *m* sin,
14:14 and put it on the tip of the *m* right ear,
14:17 put some on the tip of the *m* right ear,
14:19 offering in atonement for the *m* uncleanness
14:28 also put on the tip of the *m* right ear,
14:29 hand the priest shall put on the *m* head.
15:15 atonement before the LORD for the *m* flow.
20: 4 *m* crime of giving his offspring to Molech,
Nm 5:12 If a *m* wife goes astray and becomes
16:22 will one *m* sin make you angry with the
17:17 Mark each *m* name on his staff;
Dt 15:18 six years was worth twice a hired *m* salary;
Jgs 8:21 yourself, for a *m* strength is like the man."
1Sm 11: 2 I must gouge out every *m* right eye,
25:21 I guarded all this *m* possessions in the desert
2Sm 12: 4 Instead he took the poor *m* ewe lamb and
1Kgs 13:30 He laid the *m* body in his own grave,
18:44 as small as a *m* hand rising from the sea."
Tb 5:10 I can hear a *m* voice,
1Mc 16: 3 the mercy of Heaven, have come to *m* estate.
2Mc 3:32 offered a sacrifice for the *m* recovery.
7:12 attendants marveled at the young *m* courage,
7:23 the universe who shapes each *m* beginning,
Jb 7: 1 Is not *m* life on earth a drudgery?
10: 5 and are your years as a *m* lifetime,
21:19 not store up the *m* misery for his children;

31: 2 But what is *m* lot from God above,
36: 6 He withholds not the just *m* rights,
38:26 a path To bring rain to no *m* land,
Ps(s) 103:15 *M* days are like those of grass;
Prv 4:22 them, to *m* whole being they are health.
5:21 each *m* ways are plain to the LORD's sight;
10:15 The rich *m* wealth is his strong city;
10:16 The just *m* recompense leads to life,
10:20 Like choice silver is the just *m* tongue;
10:21 The just *m* lips nourish many,
11: 5 The honest *m* virtue makes his way straight,
12:25 Anxiety in a *m* heart depresses it,
13: 8 A *m* riches serve as ransom for his life,
14: 8 *m* wisdom gives him knowledge of his way,
15:26 *m* schemes are an abomination to the LORD,
16: 7 When the LORD is pleased with a *m* ways,
18: 4 The words from a *m* mouth are deep waters,
18:11 The rich *m* wealth is his strong city;
18:12 Before his downfall a *m* heart is haughty,
18:14 A *m* spirit sustains him in infirmity
18:16 A *m* gift clears the way for him,
19: 3 A *m* own folly upsets his way,
19: 7 All the poor *m* brothers hate him;
19:21 Many are the plans in a *m* heart,
19:22 From a *m* greed comes his shame;
20:24 *M* steps are from the LORD;
25: 9 but another *m* secret do not disclose;
29:23 *M* pride causes his humiliation,
Eccl 5:11 the rich *m* abundance allows him no sleep.
6: 7 All *m* toil is for his mouth,
7: 5 It is better to hearken to the wise *m*
8: 1 A *m* wisdom illumines his face,
8: 5 the wise *m* heart knows times and judgments;
10: 2 *m* understanding turns him to his right;
10:12 Words from the wise *m* mouth win favor,
12:13 keep his commandments, for this is *m* all;
Wis 2: 1 neither is there any remedy for *m* dying,
Sir 3:11 His father's honor is a *m* glory;
3:28 and an attentive ear is the wise *m* joy.
5:15 A *m* tongue can be his downfall.
9:12 Rejoice not at a proud *m* success;
10: 9 even during life *m* body decays;
10:12 beginning of pride is *m* stubbornness
11: 1 The poor *m* wisdom lifts his head high and
11: 4 the worn cloak and jibe at no *m* bitter day:
14:19 All *m* works will perish in decay,
15:10 But praise is offered by the wise *m* tongue;
15:19 he understands *m* every deed.
16:13 just *m* hope God does not leave unfulfilled.
17:17 A *m* goodness God cherishes like a signet
17:17 cherishes like a signet ring, a *m* virtue,
18: 7 The sum of a *m* days is great if it reaches
19:11 *m* thigh is gossip in the breast of a fool.
19:26 *m* attire, his hearty laughter and his gait,
20: 8 some things gained are a *m* loss.
21: 4 so too a proud *m* home is destroyed.
21: 5 Prayer from a poor *m* lips is heard at once,
21:13 A wise *m* knowledge wells up in a flood,
27: 4 so do a *m* faults when he speaks.
27: 6 a *m* speech disclose the bent of his mind.
28:10 The greater a *m* strength,
29:22 Better a poor *m* fare under the shadow of
35: 5 The just *m* offering enriches the altar and
35: 6 The just *m* sacrifice is most pleasing,
37:14 A *m* conscience can tell him his situation
37:23 Limited are the days of one *m* life,
41:11 *M* body is a fleeting thing,
42:14 a *m* harshness than a woman's indulgence,
Is 13: 7 Every *m* heart melts in terror;
Jer 10:23 *M* course is not within his choice,
13:11 close as the loincloth clings to a *m* loins,
Ez 18:20 The virtuous *m* virtue shall be his own,
18:20 as the wicked *m* wickedness shall be his.
33:11 man, but rather the wicked *m* conversion,
38:21 GOD, every *m* sword against his brother.
41:19 a *m* face looking at a palmtree on one side,
Dn 10:16 something like a *m* hand touched my lips;
Jon 1:14 let us not perish for taking this *m* life;
Mi 7: 6 and a *m* enemies are those of his household.
Mt 8: 3 Immediately the *m* leprosy disappeared.
10:36 a *m* enemies those of his own household.
10:41 known to be holy receives a holy *m* reward.
12:29 "How can anyone enter a strong *m* house
15:11 goes into a *m* mouth that makes him impure;
16:23 not judging by God's standards but by *m*."
24:50 that *m* master will return when he is not
25:14 over to them according to each *m* abilities.
Mk 3:27 No one can enter a strong *m* house and
7:33 He put his fingers into the *m* ears and,
7:35 At once, the *m* ears were opened;
8:23 *m* hand and led him outside the village.
8:33 not judging by God's standards but by *m*."
10:22 At these words the *m* face fell.
Lk 16:21 the scraps that fell from the rich *m* table.
20:28 *m* brother dies leaving a wife and no child,
Jn 1:13 nor by carnal desire, nor by *m* willing it,
2:25 He was well aware of what was in *m* heart.
9: 6 and smeared the *m* eyes with the mud.
9:28 "You are the one who is that *m* disciple.
11:39 Martha, the dead *m* sister,
18:17 "Are you not one of this *m* followers?"
Acts 4:17 to mention that *m* name to anyone again."
5:28 to make us responsible for that *m* blood."
11:12 along with me, and we entered the *m* house.
13:23 forth from this *m* descendants Jesus,
17:25 *m* service as if he were in need of it.
17:29 stone, a product of *m* genius and his art.
20:26 that I take the blame for no *m* conscience,
23:30 be informed of a plot against this *m* life,
Rom 5:19 one *m* disobedience all became sinners,
5:19 one *m* obedience all shall become just.
9:16 of *m* willing or doing but of God's mercy.
1Cor 2:11 knows a *m* innermost self but the man's own
3:13 fire will test the quality of each *m* work.
3:15 if a *m* building burns, he will suffer loss.
10:29 be restricted by another *m* conscience?
11: 7 in turn, is the reflection of *m* glory.
2Cor 4: 2 ourselves to every *m* conscience before God.
Gal 1:10 If I were trying to win *m* approval,
3:15 You cannot add anything to a *m* will or set
Jas 1:20 a *m* anger does not fulfill God's justice.
2Pt 1:21 has never been put forward by *m* willing it.
Rv 13:18 The *m* number is six hundred sixty-six.

MANSERVANT (1)

Jb 31:13 I refused justice to my *m* or to my maid,

MANTELET (1)

Na 2: 6 To the wall they rush, the *m* is set up.

MANTLE (24)

Gn 25:25 and his whole body was like a hairy *m*;
Dt 24:12 not sleep in the *m* he gives as a pledge,
Jos 7:21 spoils, I saw a beautiful Babylonian *m*,
7:24 son of Zerah, with the silver, the *m*,
1Sm 15:27 to go, Saul seized a loose end of his *m*,
18: 4 the *m* he was wearing and gave it to David,
21:10 is here [wrapped in a *m* behind an ephod.
24: 5 and stealthily cut off an end of Saul's *m*.
24: 6 that he had cut off an end of Saul's *m*.
24:12 here at this end of your *m* which I hold.
24:12 off an end of your *m* and did not kill you,
28:14 an old man who is rising, clothed in a *m*."
2Kgs 2: 8 Elijah took his *m*,
2:13 up Elijah's *m* which had fallen from him,
2:14 the *m* which had fallen from Elijah,
Ezr 9: 3 this thing, I tore my cloak and my *m*,
9: 5 with cloak and *m* torn I fell on my knees,
Ps(s) 109:29 and let them wear their shame like a *m*.
Sg 5: 7 me, and wounded me, and took my *m* from me,
Is 59:17 vengeance, wrapped himself in a *m* of zeal.
61: 3 a glorious *m* instead of a listless spirit.
61:10 and wrapped me in a *m* of justice,
Mi 2: 8 you have stripped off the *m* covering the
Zec 13: 4 shall he assume the hairy *m* to mislead,

MANTLES (1)

Ez 27:24 with you rich garments, violet *m*,

MANUAL (1)

1Cor 4:12 We work hard at *m* labor.

MANURE (2)

Lk 13: 8 year, while I hoe around it and *m* it;
14:35 is fit for neither the soil nor the *m* heap;

MANY (603)

Gn 6: 2 for their wives as *m* of them as they chose.
16:10 "that they will be too *m* to count.
21:34 in the land of the Philistines for *m* years.
25:16 twelve chieftains of as *m* tribal groups.
26:14 flocks and herds, and so *m* work animals,
37:34 on his loins, and mourned his son *m* days.
47: 8 asked him, "How *m* years have you lived?"
50:20 his present end, the survival of *m* people.
Ex 7: 3 despite the *m* signs and wonders that I
10: 8 But how *m* of you will go?"
16:16 for each person, as *m* of you as there are,
19:21 otherwise *m* of them will be struck down.
23: 2 of the *m* as an excuse for doing wrong,
23: 2 side with the *m* in perverting justice.
Lv 11:42 belly, goes on all fours, or has *m* legs,
25:16 When the years are *m*,
Nm 9:19 Even when the cloud tarried *m* days over
13:18 living there strong or weak, few or *m*?
21: 6 bit the people so that *m* of them died.
23:10 may my descendants be as *m* as theirs!
Dt 15: 6 on you today, you will lend to *m* nations,
15: 6 you will rule over *m* nations,
23:25 you may eat as *m* of his grapes as you wish,
28:12 lend to *m* nations and borrow from none.
31:17 and *m* evils and troubles will befall them.
31:21 when *m* evils and troubles befall them,
Jos 4: 8 they took up as *m* stones from the bed of
10:11 them all the way to Azekah, killing *m*.
17:14 Our people are too *m*,
17:15 Joshua answered them, "If you are too *m*,
22: 3 For *m* years now you have not once
23: 1 *M* years later,
Jgs 7: 2 "You have too *m* soldiers with you for me
7: 4 Gideon, "There are still too *m* soldiers.
7:12 were as *m* as the sands on the seashore.
8:30 his direct descendants, for he had *m* wives.
9:40 and *m* fell slain right up to the entrance
1Sm 2: 5 sons, while the mother of *m* languishes.
14: 6 grant victory through a few than through *m*."
25:10 *m* servants who run away from their masters.
2Sm 1: 4 that *m* of them had fallen and were dead,
8:10 Toi had been in *m* battles with Hadadezer.
1Kgs 8: 5 sheep and oxen too *m* to number or count.
11: 1 King Solomon loved *m* foreign women besides
22:16 "How *m* times must I adjure you to tell me
2Kgs 3:16 LORD, 'Provide *m* catch basins in this wadi.'
4: 3 as *m* empty vessels as you can.
9:22 "as long as the *m* fornications and
19:23 *m* chariots I climbed the mountain heights,
1Chr 4:27 His brothers, however, did not have *m* sons,
5:22 *M* had fallen in battle,
8:40 and *m* were their sons and grandsons:
23:11 but Jeush and Beriah had not *m* sons,
28: 5 for the LORD has given me *m* sons
29:21 and *m* other sacrifices for all Israel;
2Chr 2:15 cut trees on Lebanon, as *m* as you need,
4:18 so *m* in number that the weight of the
15: 5 but there were *m* terrors upon the
15: 9 for *m* had fled to him from Israel when
17:13 carried out *m* works in the cities of Judah,
18:15 "How *m* times must I adjure you to tell me
26:10 dug numerous cisterns, for he had *m* cattle.
29:35 Also, the holocausts were *m*,
30: 5 not *m* had kept it in the manner prescribed.
30:13 Thus *m* people gathered in Jerusalem to
30:17 for *m* in the assembly had not sanctified
32:23 *M* brought gifts for the LORD to Jerusalem
Ezr 1: 6 and with *m* precious gifts besides all
3:12 *M* of the priests, Levites, and family heads,
3:12 *M* others, however, lifted up their voices
10:13 us who have sinned in this regard are *m*.
Neh 6:17 *m* letters were going to Tobiah from the
6:18 for *m* in Judah were in league with him,
9:28 them according to your mercy, *m* times over.
9:30 You were patient with them for *m* years,
9:35 in the midst of the *m* good things that you
13:26 the *m* nations there was no king like him,
Tb 1: 3 I performed *m* charitable works for my
1:16 During Shalmaneser's reign I performed *m*
1:18 In his rage he killed *m* Israelites,
2: 2 and when *m* different dishes were placed
3: 5 your judgments are *m* and true in dealing
4: 4 that she went through *m* trials for your
5: 6 "Yes, I have been there *m* times.
8:19 asked his wife to bake *m* loaves of bread;
11:18 seven happy days, and he received *m* gifts.
12: 6 the *m* good things he has done for you,
13:11 *m* nations shall come to you from afar,
Jdt 1: 6 Thus *m* nations came together to resist the
2:20 A huge, irregular force, too *m* to count,
4:13 fast of *m* days' duration throughout Judea,
7: 4 When the Israelites saw how *m* there were,
16:22 *M* wished to marry her,
Est 1: 4 For as *m* as a hundred and eighty days,
2: 8 *m* maidens brought together to the stronghold
B: 2 When I came to rule *m* peoples and the hold
E: 2 *M* have become the more ambitious the more
E: 5 has induced *m* placed in authority
E:17 And *m* of the peoples of the land embraced
10: 3 was regarded with favor by his *m* brethren,
11: 3 river, the light of the sun, the *m* waters.
1Mc 1: 2 He fought *m* campaigns,
1: 3 earth, gathering plunder from *m* nations;
1: 9 so did their sons after them for *m* years,
1:11 of the law, and they seduced *m* people,
1:11 from them, *m* evils have come upon us."
1:18 presence and fled, leaving *m* casualties.
1:30 and destroyed *m* of the people in Israel.
1:43 *m* Israelites were in favor of his religion;
1:52 *M* of the people,
1:62 But *m* in Israel were determined and
2:16 *M* of Israel joined them,
2:18 enriched with silver and gold and *m* gifts."
2:29 *M* who sought to live according to
2:32 *M* hurried out after them,
3: 7 achieved, and he afflicted *m* kings;
3:11 *M* fell wounded, and the rest fled.
3:13 heard that Judas had gathered *m* about him,
3:18 "It is easy for *m* to be overcome by a few;
3:18 between deliverance by *m* or by few,
5: 7 He fought *m* battles with them,
5:12 us from them, for *m* of us have fallen.
5:21 and fought *m* battles with the Gentiles.
5:26 *M* of them have been imprisoned in Bozrah,
6: 9 There he remained *m* days,
6:24 they have put to death as *m* of us as they
6:31 For *m* days they attacked it;
6:51 For *m* days he besieged the sanctuary,
7:19 *m* of the men arrested who deserted to him,
8:10 *M* were wounded and fell,
9: 2 they captured it and killed *m* people.
9: 6 afraid, and *m* slipped away from the camp,
9:17 and *m* on both sides fell wounded.
9:20 They mourned for him *m* days,
9:22 but they were very *m*.
9:40 *M* fell wounded,
9:64 he fought against it for *m* days.
9:69 He killed *m* of them and resolved to return
10:21 he gathered an army and procured *m* arms.

MANY (cont.)

10:28 *m* exemptions and will bestow gifts on you.
10:60 gold and *m* gifts and thus won their favor.
11: 1 as the sands of the seashore, and *m* ships;
11:20 and they set up *m* machines against it.
11:24 silver, gold apparel, and *m* other presents,
11:40 During his stay there of *m* days,
11:65 besieged Beth-zur, attacked it for *m* days,
12:13 But *m* hardships and wars have beset us,
13:26 lamentation, mourning over him for *m* days.
13:49 hunger, and *m* of them died of starvation.
14: 7 He took *m* enemies prisoners of war and
15: 4 it and laid waste *m* cities in my realm.
15:29 possession of *m* districts in my realm.
16: 2 and *m* times we succeeded in saving Israel.
16: 8 *m* of them fell wounded,
2Mc 1:20 *M* years later, when it so pleased God,
2:27 to win the gratitude of *m* we will gladly
4:35 but *m* people of other nations as well,
4:39 *M* sacrilegious thefts had been committed
4:42 wounded *m* of them and even killed a few,
5: 9 so *m* from their country perished in exile;
5:10 and he who had cast out so *m* to lie
5:18 they had not become entangled in so *m* sins,
6:24 *m* young men would think the
9: 6 bowels of others with *m* barbarous torments.
9:16 all the sacred vessels *m* times over;
10:17 them, killing as *m* as twenty thousand men.
12:12 they could indeed be useful in *m* respects,
12:22 that in *m* cases they wounded one another,
12:23 and destroying as *m* as thirty thousand men.
12:24 the parents and relatives of *m* of them,
12:27 inhabited by people of *m* nationalities.
13: 8 he who had committed so *m* sins
Jb 4: 3 Behold, you have instructed *m*,
5:25 shall know that your descendants are *m*,
11: 2 Should not the man of *m* words be answered,
11:19 *M* shall entreat your favor,
16: 2 I have heard this sort of thing *m* times.
23:14 and *m* such things may yet be in his mind.
27:14 Though his children be *m*,
32: 7 speak, I thought, and *m* years teach wisdom!
32: 9 It is not those of *m* days who are wise,
34:37 arguments and addressing *m* words to God.
35: 6 Even if your offenses are *m*,
Ps(s) 3: 2 O LORD, how *m* are my adversaries!
3: 2 *M* rise up against me!
3: 3 *M* are saying of me,
4: 7 *M* say, "Oh, that we might see
5:11 For their *m* sins,
22:13 *M* bullocks surround me;
22:17 Indeed, *m* dogs surround me,
25:19 Behold, my enemies are *m*,
32:10 *M* are the sorrows of the wicked,
34:20 *M* are the troubles of the just man,
38:20 *m* are my foes without cause.
40: 4 *M* shall look on in awe and trust in the
40: 6 tell them, they would be too *m* to recount.
55:19 against me, for *m* there are who oppose me.
56: 3 yes, *m* fight against me.
61: 7 let his years be *m* generations;
69: 5 Too *m* for my strength are they who
71: 7 A portent am I to *m*,
71:20 you have made me feel *m* bitter afflictions,
93: 4 More powerful than the roar of *m* waters,
97: 1 let the *m* isles be glad.
106:43 *M* times did he rescue them,
107:38 He blessed them, and they became very *m*;
119:84 How *m* are the days of your servant?
119:157 Though my persecutors and my foes are *m*,
135:10 He smote *m* nations and slew mighty kings:
144: 7 Deliver me and rescue me from *m* waters,
Prv 3: 2 For *m* days, and years of life,
4:10 and the years of your life shall be *m*.
7:26 For *m* are those she has struck down dead,
10:19 Where words are *m*, sin is not wanting;
10:21 The just man's lips nourish *m*,
11:14 security lies in *m* counselors.
14:20 hated, but the friends of the rich are *m*.
14:28 In *m* subjects lies the glory of the king;
15:22 but they succeed when counselors are *m*.
19: 4 Wealth adds *m* friends,
19: 6 *M* curry favor with a noble;
19:21 *M* are the plans in a man's heart,
20: 6 *M* are declared to be men of virtue:
28: 2 land is rebellious, its princes will be *m*;
28:27 but he who ignores them gets *m* a curse.
29:22 and a hotheaded man is the cause of *m* sins.
29:26 *M* curry favor with the ruler,
31:29 *M* are the women of proven worth,
Eccl 5: 2 For nightmares come with *m* cares,
5: 2 cares, and a fool's utterance with *m* words.
5:10 riches, there are also *m* to devour them.
6: 3 have a hundred children and live *m* years,
6:11 there are *m* sayings that multiply vanity,
7:22 that you have *m* times spoken ill of others.
7:29 men have had recourse to *m* calculations.
11: 8 However *m* years a man may live,
11: 8 that the days of darkness will be *m*.
12: 9 scrutinized and arranged *m* proverbs.
12:12 Of the making of *m* books there is no end,
Wis 4:16 the *m* years of the wicked man grown old.
9:15 weighs down the mind that has *m* concerns

Sir 1:21 then the lips of *m* herald his wisdom.
3:23 Their own opinion has misled *m*,
5: 6 my *m* sins he will forgive."
6: 6 Let your acquaintances be *m*,
6:23 like her name, she is not accessible to *m*.
7: 9 "He will appreciate my *m* gifts;
8: 2 For gold has dazzled *m*,
9: 8 Through woman's beauty *m* perish,
11:13 and exalts him to the amazement of the *m*.
11:29 for *m* are the snares of the crafty one;
11:31 with a spark he sets *m* coals afire.
13:11 discussion with him, trust not his *m* words;
13:21 *M* are the supporters for a rich man when
16: 2 *M* though they be, exult not in them
16: 5 *M* such things has my eye seen,
16:15 Among so *m* people I cannot be known;
20:16 How *m* times they laugh him to scorn!
27: 1 For the sake of profit *m* sin,
28:13 for they destroy the peace of *m*.
28:14 A meddlesome tongue subverts *m*,
28:18 *M* have fallen by the edge of the sword,
28:18 the sword, but not as *m* as by the tongue.
29: 4 *M* a man who asks for a loan adds to the
29: 7 *M* refuse to lend, not out of meanness,
29:17 Going surety has ruined *m* prosperous men
30:23 For worry has brought death to *m*,
31: 6 *M* have been ensnared by gold,
31:18 If there are *m* with you at table,
31:25 strength, for wine has been the ruin of *m*.
34: 7 For dreams have led *m* astray,
34:19 *m* sacrifices does he forgive their sins.
37:19 A man may be wise and benefit *m*,
37:30 Through lack of self-control *m* have died,
39: 9 *M* will praise his understanding;
42: 6 of a lock placed where there are *m* hands;
43:34 Beyond these, *m* things lie hid;
44:19 ABRAHAM, father of *m* peoples,
48:12 spirit, wrought *m* marvels by his mere word.
51: 3 From *m* a danger you have saved me,
Is 2: 3 *m* peoples shall come and say:
2: 4 the nations, and impose terms on *m* peoples.
5: 9 *M* houses shall be in ruins,
8:15 And *m* among them shall stumble and fall,
17:12 the roaring of *m* peoples that roar like
22: 9 the breaches in the City of David were *m*;
23:16 Pluck the strings skillfully, sing *m* songs,
24:22 and after *m* days they will be punished.
37:24 *m* chariots I climbed the mountain heights,
42:20 You see *m* things without taking note;
47: 9 shall come upon you For your *m* sorceries
47:12 up, now, your spells and your *m* sorceries.
47:13 You wearied yourself with *m* consultations,
51: 2 I called him, I blessed him and made him *m*.
52:14 Even as *m* were amazed at him
52:15 So shall he startle *m* nations,
53:11 his suffering, my servant shall justify *m*,
53:12 And he shall take away the sins of *m*,
57:10 Though worn out by your *m* misdeeds,
59:12 For our offenses before you are *m*,
66:16 and *m* shall be slain by the LORD.
Jer 2:28 And as *m* as the streets of Jerusalem are
3: 1 But you have sinned with *m* lovers,
5: 6 *m* crimes and their numerous rebellions.
11:13 And as *m* as the streets of Jerusalem are
12:10 *M* shepherds have ravaged my vineyard,
13:17 your pride, I will weep in secret *m* tears;
14: 7 Even though our rebellions are *m*,
16:16 I will send *m* fishermen,
16:16 I will send *m* hunters to hunt them out
20:10 Yes, I hear the whisperings of *m*:
22: 8 *M* people will pass by this city and ask
28: 8 against *m* lands and mighty kingdoms.
30:19 I will make them not few, but *m*;
36:32 and *m* others of the same kind in addition.
42: 2 We are now few who once were *m*,
49:32 be your booty, their *m* herds your spoil;
Lam 1: 5 The LORD has punished her for her *m* sins.
1:22 My groans are *m*,
Bar 4:12 no one gloat over me, a widow, bereft of *m*:
6: 2 reach Babylon you will be there *m* years,
Ez 3: 6 nor to the *m* peoples [with difficult
4: 4 As *m* days as you lie thus,
4: 9 it for as *m* days as you lie upon your side,
11: 6 You have slain *m* in this city and have
14: 4 answer in person because of his *m* idols.
16:26 so *m* times that I was provoked to anger.
16:41 punishments on you while *m* women look on.
17: 9 of a mighty arm or *m* people to do this.]
17:17 are built for the destruction of *m* lives,
19:11 Notably tall was she with her *m* clusters.
21:20 for *m* will be the fallen.
22:25 things, and make widows of *m* within her.
23:24 with chariots and wagons and *m* peoples.
26: 3 I will churn up against you *m* nations,
27: 3 the trade of the peoples to *m* a coastland:
27:15 *m* coastlands traded with you;
27:16 traded with you, so *m* were your products,
27:33 drew from the seas you filled *m* peoples;
32: 3 my net over you [with a host of *m* nations],
32: 9 I will grieve the hearts of *m* peoples when
32:10 *M* peoples shall be appalled at you,
33:24 we, therefore, being *m*,
37: 2 *m* they were on the surface of the plain.

38: 6 with all its troops, *m* peoples with you.
38: 8 After *m* days you will be mustered [in the
38: 8 which has been assembled from *m* peoples
38: 9 all your troops and the *m* peoples with you.
38:15 of the north, you and *m* peoples with you,
38:22 troops, and upon the *m* peoples with him.
38:23 myself known in the sight of *m* nations;
39:27 through them in the sight of *m* nations.
43: 2 heard a sound like the roaring of *m* waters,
47: 7 the river I saw very *m* trees on both sides.
Dn 2:48 a high post, gave him *m* generous presents,
8:25 be proud of heart and destroy *m* by stealth.
8:26 undisclosed, because the days are to be *m*."
9:27 he shall make a firm compact with the *m*;
11:14 times *m* shall resist the king of the south,
11:18 He shall turn to the coastland and take *m*,
11:26 be overwhelmed, and *m* shall fall slain.
11:33 nation's wise men shall instruct the *m*;
11:34 but *m* shall join them out of treachery.
11:39 the *m* and distribute the land as a reward.
11:41 enter the glorious land and *m* shall fall,
11:44 out with great fury to slay and to doom *m*.
12: 2 *M* of those who sleep in the dust of the
12: 3 those who lead the *m* to justice
12: 4 *m* shall fall away and evil shall increase."
12:10 *M* shall be refined,
Hos 3: 3 *M* days you shall wait for me;
3: 4 shall remain *m* days without king or prince,
8:11 When Ephraim made *m* altars to expiate sin,
8:12 Though I write for him my *m* ordinances,
8:14 Judah, too, has fortified *m* cities,
10:13 in your chariots, and in your *m* warriors,
12: 2 His lies and falsehoods are *m*:
12:11 *m* visions and spoke to the prophets,
Am 3:15 ruined, and their *m* rooms shall be no more,
4: 9 your *m* gardens and vineyards,
5:12 Yes, I know how *m* are your crimes,
8: 3 *M* shall be the corpses, strewn everywhere
Jon 4:11 their left, not to mention the *m* cattle?"
Mi 4: 2 *M* nations shall come,
4: 3 He shall judge between *m* peoples and
4:11 How *m* nations are gathered against you!
4:13 hoofs bronze, that you may crush *m* peoples;
5: 6 Jacob shall be in the midst of *m* peoples,
5: 7 the nations, in the midst of *m* peoples,
Na 1:12 LORD, be they ever so *m* and so vigorous,
3: 3 sword, the flash of the spear, the *m* slain,
3: 4 For the *m* debaucheries of the harlot,
3:17 your garrisons as *m* as grasshoppers,
Hb 2: 8 Because you despoiled *m* peoples all the
2:10 for your household, cutting off *m* peoples,
Zec 2:15 *M* nations shall join themselves to the
7: 3 month as I have been doing these *m* years?"
8:20 come peoples, the inhabitants of *m* cities;
8:22 *M* people and strong nations shall come to
Mal 2: 6 uprightness, and turned *m* away from evil.
2: 8 caused *m* to falter by your instruction;
Mt 3: 7 When he saw that *m* of the Pharisees and
7:13 road is clear, and *m* choose to travel it.
7:22 When that day comes, *m* will plead with me,
7:22 we not do *m* miracles in your name as well?'
8:11 *M* will come from the east and the west and
8:16 on, they brought him *m* who were possessed.
9:10 *m* tax collectors and those known as
12:15 *M* people followed him and he cured them all,
13:17 *m* a prophet and many a saint longed to see
13:58 And he did not work *m* miracles there
14:36 As *m* as touched it were fully restored to
15:30 the blind, the mute, and *m* others besides.
15:34 them, "How *m* loaves of bread do you have?"
16: 9 and how *m* baskets-full you picked up?
16:10 and how *m* hampers-full you retrieved?
19:22 went away sad, for his possessions were *m*.
19:29 for my sake will receive *m* times as much
19:30 *M* who are first shall come last,
20:28 to give his own life as a ransom for the *m*."
22:14 The invited are *m*, the elect are few."
24: 5 *M* will come attempting to impersonate me.
24: 5 they will claim, and they will deceive *m*.
24: 7 and pestilence and earthquakes in *m* places.
24:10 *M* will falter then,
24:11 will rise in great numbers to mislead *m*.
26:28 in behalf of *m* for the forgiveness of sins.
26:60 the *m* false witnesses who took the stand.
27:13 hear how *m* charges they bring against you?"
27:53 *M* bodies of saints who had fallen asleep
27:53 entered the holy city and appeared to *m*.
27:55 *M* women were present looking on from a
Mk 1:34 who were variously afflicted, were *m*,
2:15 *m* tax collectors and those known as
3:10 Because he had cured *m*,
4:33 By means of *m* such parables he taught them
6:13 They expelled *m* demons,
6:13 the sick with oil, and worked *m* cures.
6:33 them leaving, and *m* got to know about it.
6:38 "How *m* loaves have you?"
7: 4 There are *m* other traditions they observe
7:13 you have *m* other such practices besides."
8: 5 he asked them, "How *m* loaves do you have
8:19 how *m* baskets of fragments you gathered up
8:20 how *m* full hampers of fragments did you
9:26 like a corpse, which caused *m* to say,
10:22 He went away sad, for he had *m* possessions.

10:30 present age a hundred times as *m* homes,
10:31 *M* who are first shall come last,
10:45 to give his life in ransom for the *m.*"
10:48 *M* people were scolding him to make him
11: 8 *M* people spread their cloaks on the road,
12: 5 So too with *m* others; some they beat;
12:41 *M* of the wealthy put in sizable amounts;
13: 6 they will claim, and will lead *m* astray.
14:24 covenant, to be poured out on behalf of *m.*
14:56 *M* spoke against him falsely under oath but
15: 3 brought *m* accusations against him.
15: 4 See how *m* accusations they are leveling
15:41 There were also *m* others who had come up
Lk 1: 1 *M* have undertaken to compile a narrative
1:14 be yours, and *m* will rejoice at his birth;
1:16 *M* of the sons of Israel will he bring back
2:34 the downfall and the rise of *m* in Israel,
2:35 the thoughts of *m* hearts may be laid bare."
2:36 She had seen *m* days,
4:25 there were *m* widows in Israel in the days
4:27 the *m* lepers in Israel in the time of
4:41 Demons departed from *m,*
6:17 stretch where were *m* of his disciples;
7:21 time he was curing *m* of their diseases,
7:21 he also restored sight to *m* who were blind.)
7:47 you, that is why her *m* sins are forgiven
8: 3 and *m* others who were assisting them out
8:29 This spirit had taken hold of him *m* a time.
8:30 the demons who had entered him were *m.*
9:22 he said, "must first endure *m* sufferings,
10:24 *m* prophets and kings wished to see what
10:41 you are anxious and upset about *m* things;
13:24 *M,* I tell you, will try to enter
14:16 was giving a large dinner and he invited *m.*
15:17 'How *m* hired hands at my father's place
21: 8 *M* will come in my name saying,
22:65 directed *m* other insulting words at him.
Jn 2:23 Passover festival, *m* believed in his name,
4:39 *M* Samaritans from that town believed in
4:41 his own spoken word *m* more came to faith.
6: 9 dried fish, but what good is that for so *m?*"
6:60 his words, *m* of his disciples remarked,
6:66 *m* of his disciples broke away and would
7:31 *M* in the crowd came to believe in him.
8:30 spoke this way, *m* came to believe in him.
10:20 *M* were claiming: "He is possessed.
10:32 *M* good deeds have I shown you from the
10:41 while he stayed there *m* people came to him.
10:42 In that place, *m* came to believe in him.
11:19 and *m* Jewish people had come out to
11:45 *m* of the Jews who had come to visit Mary,
11:55 which meant that *m* people from the country
12:11 because *m* Jews were going over to Jesus
12:37 his *m* signs performed in their presence,
12:42 There were *m,* even among the Sanhedrin,
14: 2 Father's house there are *m* dwelling places;
19:20 and Greek, was read by *m* of the Jews,
20:30 performed *m* other signs as well
21: 6 so *m* fish they could not haul the net in.
21:25 are still *m* other things that Jesus did,
Acts 1: 3 in *m* convincing ways that he was alive,
2:40 of his testimony he used *m* other arguments,
2:43 for *m* wonders and signs were performed by
4: 4 *m* of those who had heard the speech
5:12 *m* signs and wonders occurred among the
6: 7 There were *m* priests among those who
8: 7 There were *m* who had unclean spirits,
8: 7 *M* others were paralytics or cripples,
8:25 news to *m* villages of Samaria on the way.
9:13 I have heard from *m* sources about this man
9:42 of it, *m* came to believe in the Lord.
10:27 He found *m* people assembled there,
12:12 where *m* others were gathered in prayer.
13:31 and for *m* days thereafter Jesus appeared
13:43 *m* Jews and devout Jewish converts followed
14:22 "We must undergo *m* trials if we are to
15:35 continued in Antioch, along with *m* others,
16:23 *m* lashes they were thrown into prison,
17: 3 He explained *m* things,
17:12 *M* of them came to believe,
18: 8 *M* of the Corinthians,
18:10 There are *m* of my people in this city."
19:18 *M* who had become believers came forward
20: 2 providing as he went *m* words of
20: 8 As it happened there were *m* lamps in the
21:20 *m* thousands of Jews have come to believe,
24: 2 *M* improvements have been made in this
24:10 been a judge over this nation for *m* years.
25: 7 and leveled *m* serious charges against him,
26: 2 *M* charges have been leveled against me by
26:10 I sent *m* of God's holy people to prison.
26:11 *M* a time, in synagogue after synagogue,
27: 7 For *m* days we made little headway,
27:20 For *m* days neither the sun nor the stars
Rom 4:17 "I have made you father of *m* nations."
4:18 and so became the father of *m* nations,
5:16 after *m* offenses and brought acquittal.
8:29 Son might be the first-born of *m* brothers.
12: 4 as each of us has one body with *m* members,
12: 5 the same function, so too we, though *m,*
15:23 to visit you which I have had for *m* years.
16: 2 her, for she herself has been of help to *m,*
16:25 which reveals the mystery hidden for *m* ages
1Cor 1:26 Not *m* of you are wise,
1:26 not *m* are influential;
1:26 and surely not *m* are well-born.
8: 5 to be sure, *m* such "gods" and "lords"
9:19 of all so as to win over as *m* as possible.
10:17 loaf of bread is one, we, *m* though we are,
10:33 not my own advantage, but that of the *m,*
11:30 is why *m* among you are sick and infirm,
11:30 sick and infirm, and why so *m* are dying.
12:12 The body is one and has *m* members,
12:12 but all the members, *m* though they are,
12:14 Now the body is not one member, it is *m.*
12:20 There are, indeed, *m* different members,
14:10 There are *m* different languages in the
16: 9 but at the same time there are *m* opposed.
2Cor 1:11 granted us through the prayers of so *m.*
2:17 not like so *m* who trade on the word of God.
4:15 to God because they who give thanks are *m.*
6:10 poor, yet we enrich *m.*
7: 4 my *m* afflictions my joy knows no bounds.
8:22 eagerness has been proved to us in *m* ways.
11:18 Since *m* are bragging about their human
11:23 with my *m* more labors and imprisonments,
11:27 labor, hardship, *m* sleepless nights;
12:21 and I may have to mourn over the *m* who
Gal 3:16 your descendants," as if it applied to *m,*
4:27 *m* are the children of the wife deserted
Phil 3:18 *m* go about in a way which shows them to be
Col 2: 1 *m* others who have never seen me
2Thes 3: 1 make progress and be hailed by *m* others,
1Tm 6:12 when, in the presence of *m* witnesses,
2Tm 1:18 And the *m* services he has performed for
2: 2 you have heard from me through *m* witnesses
3: 6 with sins and driven by desires of *m* kinds,
Ti 1:10 There are *m* irresponsible teachers,
Heb 2:10 that when bringing *m* sons to glory God,
7:23 Under the old covenant there were *m*
9:28 up once to take away the sins of *m;*
12:15 up through which *m* may become defiled;
Jas 1:11 rich man wither away amid his *m* projects.
3: 1 Not *m* of you should become teachers,
3: 2 All of us fall short in *m* respects.
1Pt 1: 6 have to suffer the distress of *m* trials:
2Pt 2: 2 Their lustful ways will lure *m* away.
1Jn 2:18 so now *m* such antichrists have appeared.
4: 1 because *m* false prophets have appeared in
2Jn 1: 7 *M* deceitful men have gone out into the
Rv 5:11 I heard the voices of *m* angels who
8:11 *M* people died from this polluted water.
9: 9 *m* chariots and horses charging into battle.
10:11 prophesy again for *m* peoples and nations,
19:12 like fire, and on his head were *m* diadems.

MANY-HUED (1)

Ez 17: 3 with long pinions, with thick plumage, *m,*

MAOCH (1)

1Sm 27: 2 men and went over to Achish, son of *M,*

MAON (7)

Jos 15:55 *M,* Carmel, Ziph, Juttah, Jezreel,
1Sm 23:24 and his men were in the desert below *M,*
23:25 down to the gorge in the desert below *M.*
23:25 and pursued David into the desert below *M.*
25: 1 Then David went down to the desert of *M.*
25: 2 was a man of *M* who had property in Carmel;
1Chr 2:45 *M,* who was the father of Beth-zur.

MAP (1)

Jos 18: 8 *m* out the land were ready for the journey,

MAR (1)

Sir 7: 6 favor to the ruler and *m* your integrity.

MARA (1)

Ru 1:20 Call me *M,* for the Almighty has made

MARAH (4)

Ex 15:23 without finding water, they arrived at *M,*
15:23 Hence this place was called *M.*
Nm 33: 8 in the desert of Etham, they camped at *M.*
33: 9 Setting out from *M,*

MARAUDER (1)

Jn 10: 1 in some other way is a thief and a *m.*

MARAUDERS (1)

Jn 10: 8 thieves and *m* whom the sheep did not heed.

MARBLE (5)

1Chr 29: 2 precious stone, and great quantities of *m.*
Est 1: 6 byssus from silver rings on *m* pillars.
1: 6 on the pavement, which was of porphyry, *m,*
Sg 5:15 are columns of *m* resting on golden bases.
Rv 18:12 bronze, iron and *m;*

MARCH (31)

Ex 14:10 Egyptians were on the *m* in pursuit of them.
Nm 2: 9 These shall be first on the *m.*
2:16 These shall be second on the *m.*
2:17 As in camp, so also on the *m,*
2:24 These shall be third on the *m.*
2:31 be the last of the divisions on the *m.*"
2:34 on the *m* they were in their own divisions,
20:19 is no harm in merely letting us *m* through."
32:17 *m* as troops in the van of the Israelites,
32:20 "If you keep your word to *m* as troops in
Dt 2:28 Only let me *m* through,
20:10 "When you *m* up to attack a city,
Jos 1:11 to *m* in and take possession of the land
6: 4 seventh day *m* around the city seven times,
6:15 did they *m* around the city seven times.
10: 9 upon them after an all-night *m* from Gilgal,
Jgs 4: 6 "go, *m* on Mount Tabor,
2Sm 2:32 Joab and his men made an all-night *m,*
15:22 the king said to Ittai, "Go, then, *m* on."
1Kgs 12:24 You must not *m* out to fight against your
2Chr 11: 4 not *m* out to fight against your brothers.
Jdt 2:21 After a three-day *m* from Nineveh,
1Mc 5:46 they would have to *m* right through it.
5:48 we will only *m* through."
2Mc 6: 7 they were compelled to *m* in his procession,
13:13 the Jews should *m* out and settle the
Is 27: 4 thorns, In battle I should *m* against them;
Jer 4: 5 in, let us *m* to the fortified cities."
46: 3 Prepare shield and buckler! *m* to battle!
Jl 4: 9 Let all the soldiers report and *m!*
Lk 14:31 to *m* on another king to do battle with him,

MARCHED (62)

Gn 14: 8 and the king of Bela (that is, Zoar) *m* out,
Ex 13:18 array the Israelites *m* out of Egypt.
14:22 *m* into the midst of the sea on dry land,
14:29 *m* on dry land through the midst of the sea,
15:19 *m* on dry land through the midst of the sea.
15:22 Sea, and they *m* out to the desert of Shur.
Dt 1:43 you arrogantly *m* off into the hill country.
Jos 4:12 armed, *m* in the vanguard of the Israelites,
6: 9 priests with the horns *m* the picked troops;
6: 9 of horns was kept up continually as they *m.*
6:13 horns *m* in front of the ark of the LORD,
6:13 Ahead of these *m* the picked troops,
6:14 On this second day they again *m* around the
6:15 they *m* around the city seven times in the
10: 5 all their forces and *m* against Gibeon,
10: 7 So Joshua *m* up from Gilgal with his picked
10:24 of the soldiers who had *m* with him,
11: 5 joined forces and *m* to the waters of Merom,
15:15 he *m* up against the inhabitants of Debir,
19:47 so the Danites *m* up and attacked Leshem,
Jgs 1:10 Judah also *m* against the Canaanites who
1:11 they *m* against the inhabitants of Debir,
1:22 house of Joseph, too, *m* up against Bethel,
5: 4 Seir, when you *m* from the land of Edom,
2Sm 2:29 men *m* all night long through the Arabah
2:29 Jordan, *m* all through the morning
15:18 distance, while the whole army *m* past him.
15:22 the dependents that were with him, *m* on.
15:24 until the soldiers had *m* out of the city.
18: 4 soldiers *m* out in units of a hundred
20: 7 all the warriors *m* out behind Abishai
1Kgs 16:17 Omri *m* up from Gibbethon,
20:16 They *m* out at noon,
20:17 the governors of the provinces *m* out first,
20:17 word that some men had *m* out of Samaria.
1Chr 14: 8 David heard of this, he *m* out against them.
19: 9 The Ammonites *m* out and lined up for a
Jdt 2:22 chariots, and *m* into the mountain region.
1Mc 5:24 and *m* for three days through the desert.
5:28 his army, *m* across the desert to Bozrah,
5:29 they *m* toward the stronghold of Dathema.
5:58 who were with them, and *m* toward Jamnia.
6:32 Then Judas *m* away from the citadel and
6:40 they *m* forward steadily and in good order.
10: 2 army and *m* out to engage him in combat.
10:77 He *m* on Azotus as though he were going on
11:15 Ptolemy *m* out and met him with a strong
12:32 Then he *m* on to Damascus and traversed
12:41 Jonathan *m* out against him with forty
14: 1 King Demetrius assembled his army and *m*
16: 5 Modein, rose early, and *m* into the plain.
2Mc 11: 2 and all his cavalry and *m* against the Jews.
12: 6 he *m* against the murderers of his kinsmen.
12:19 *m* out and destroyed the force of more than
12:26 *m* to Karnion and the shrine of Atargatis,
13:19 So he *m* against Beth-zur,
Ps(s) 68: 8 people, when you *m* through the wilderness,
Jer 37: 5 this report they *m* away from the city.
39: 1 army *m* against Jerusalem and besieged it.
Am 5: 3 The city that *m* out with a thousand shall
5: 3 Another that *m* out with a hundred shall be
Acts 17: 5 They *m* on the house of Jason in an attempt

MARCHES (6)

Dt 31: 6 it is the LORD, your God, who *m* with you;
31: 8 It is the LORD who *m* before you;
Jgs 4:14 The LORD *m* before you."
Jb 18:14 tent, and *m* him off to the king of terrors.
Wis 4: 2 And forever it *m* crowned in triumph,
Hb 1: 6 That *m* the breadth of the land to take

MARCHING (14)

Ex 14: 8 even while they were *m* away in triumph.
Jos 6: 3 soldiers circle the city, *m* once around it.
6: 7 troops *m* ahead of the ark of the LORD.
1Sm 17:41 With his shield-bearer *m* before him,
29: 2 *m* their groups of a hundred and a thousand,
29: 2 men were *m* in the rear guard with Achish.
31:12 set out, and after *m* throughout the night,
2Sm 5:24 sound of *m* in the tops of the mastic trees,
1Chr 14:15 sound of *m* in the tops of the mastic trees,
1Mc 4:12 looked up and saw them *m* toward them,
6:41 of their numbers, the tramp of their *m,*
2Mc 12:32 they lost no time in *m* against Gorgias,
Is 30:29 as one *m* along with a flute Toward the
63: 1 *m* in the greatness of his strength?

MARDUK (1)

2Kgs 17:30 the Babylonians made *M* and his consort;

MAREAL (1)

Jos 19:11 through *M,* reaching Dabbesheth

MARESHAH (8)

Jos 15:44 Ashnah, Nezib, Keilah, Achzib, and *M;*
1Chr 2:42 Then the sons of *M,*
4:21 Laadah, the father of *M;*
2Chr 11: 8 Tekoa, Beth-zur, Soco, Adullam, Gath, *M,*
14: 8 hundred chariots, and he came as far as *M.*
14: 9 array in the valley of Zephathah, near *M.*
20:37 But Eliezer, son of Dodavahu from *M,*
Mi 1:15 to you the conqueror, O inhabitants of *M;*

MARINERS (4)

Ez 27: 8 men of Zemer were in you to be your *m;*
27:28 Hearing the shouts of your *m,*
27:29 The sailors, all the *m* of the sea,
Jon 1: 5 Then the *m* became frightened and each one

MARISA (2)

1Mc 5:66 of the Philistines and passed through *M.*
2Mc 12:35 Then Gorgias fled to *M.*

MARITIME (1)

Gn 10: 5 and from them sprang the *m* nations,

MARK (37)

Gn 1:14 Let them *m* the fixed times,
4:15 So the LORD put a *m* on Cain,
17:11 the *m* of the covenant between you and me.
Ex 12:13 the blood will *m* the houses where you are.
Nm 17:17 *M* each man's name on his staff;
17:18 and *m* Aaron's name on Levi's staff,
1Kgs 20:22 *M* well what you do,
1Mc 1:15 They covered over the *m* of their
2Mc 2: 6 him came up intending to *m* the path,
Jb 36:32 and he commands it to strike the *m.*
Ps(s) 37:10 you *m* his place he will not be there.
37:37 the whole hearted man, and *m* the upright;
104:19 You made the moon to *m* the seasons;
130: 3 If you, O LORD, *m* iniquities,
Wis 5:11 no *m* of passage can be found in it.
5:12 Or as, when an arrow has been shot at a *m,*
5:21 from a well-drawn bow shall leap to the *m;*
Jer 26:15 *m* well: if you put me to death
Ez 9: 4 *m* an X on the foreheads of those who moan
Dn 9:23 *m* the answer and understand the vision.
Mi 2: 5 Thus you shall have no one to *m* out
Mt 8:11 *M* what I say!
13:18 *M* well, then, the parable of the sower.
Acts 12:12 Mary the mother of John (also known as *M),*
12:25 relief mission, taking with them John *M.*
15:37 wanted to take along John, called *M.*
15:39 *M* along with him and sailed for Cyprus.
2Cor 10:13 we make claims we will not go over the *m*
Col 4:10 So does *M,* the cousin of Barnabas.
2Tm 4:11 Get *M* and bring him with you,
Phlm 1:24 in Christ Jesus, greets you, as do *M,*
1Pt 5:13 you, sends you greeting, as does *M* my son.
Rv 14: 9 or accepts its *m* on his forehead or hand,
14:11 or its image or accept the *m* of its name."
16: 2 the *m* of the beast or worshiped its image.
19:20 the *m* of the beast and worship its image.
20: 4 its *m* on their foreheads or their hands.

MARKED (22)

Jb 26:10 He has *m* out a circle on the surface of
Ps(s) 44:12 You *m* us out as sheep to be slaughtered;
Prv 8:27 *m* out the vault over the face of the deep;
30: 4 who has *m* out all the ends of the earth?
Is 4: 3 every one *m* down for life in Jerusalem.
40:12 the sea, and *m* off the heavens with a span?
Jer 6: 6 Woe to the city *m* for punishment;
15: 2 Whoever is *m* for death,
15: 2 whoever is *m* for the sword,
15: 2 whoever is *m* for famine,
15: 2 whoever is *m* for captivity,
43:11 with death, whoever is *m* for death;
Lam 2: 8 The LORD *m* for destruction the wall of
Ez 9: 6 But do not touch any *m* with the X;
21:27 hand is the divining arrow *m* "Jerusalem,"
Hb 1:12 O LORD you have *m* him for judgment,
Jn 21:14 This *m* the third time that Jesus appeared
Acts 9:36 Her life was *m* by constant good deeds and
1Cor 14:10 in the world and all are *m* by sound;
Jas 4: 4 A man is *m* out as God's enemy if he
Rv 7: 4 I heard the number of those who were so *m*—
13:17 he was first *m* with the name of the beast

MARKER (1)

Ez 39:15 human bone, let them put up a *m* beside it,

MARKERS (1)

Jer 31:21 Set up road *m,* put up guideposts;

MARKET (8)

Gn 23:16 shekels of silver at the current *m* value.
2Kgs 7: 1 barley for a shekel, in the *m* of Samaria.' "
Tb 2: 3 in the *m* place where he was just strangled!"
2Mc 3: 4 priest about the supervision of the city *m.*
Mk 6:56 they laid the sick in the *m* places and
7: 4 from the *m* without first sprinkling it.
1Cor 10:25 Eat whatever is sold in the *m* without
Rv 18:11 there will be no more *m* for their imports

MARKETING (1)

Ez 27:24 traded with you, *m* with you rich garments,

MARKETPLACE (3)

2Mc 10: 2 in the *m* and the sacred enclosures.
Mt 20: 3 men standing around the *m* without work,
Jn 2:16 Stop turning my Father's house into a *m!"*

MARKETPLACES (1)

Jdt 1:14 and took its towers, sacked its *m*

MARKS (11)

Gn 35:20 same monument *m* Rachel's grave to this day.
Sir 43: 6 The moon, too, that *m* the changing times,
43:13 rebuke *m* out the path for the lightning,
Is 34:17 his hands he *m* off their shares of her;
44:13 and *m* with a stylus the outline of an idol.
Ez 21:28 and the arrow taken in hand *m* their guilt.
Mt 23: 7 of *m* of respect in public and of being
Mk 12:38 robes and accept *m* of respect in public,
Lk 11:43 in synagogues and *m* of respect in public.
20:46 robes, and love *m* of respect in public,
Gal 6:17 for I bear the brand *m* of Jesus in my body.

MAROTH (1)

Mi 1:12 How can the inhabitants of *M* hope for good?

MARRED (1)

Is 52:14 so *m* was his look beyond that of man,

MARRIAGE (61)

Gn 19:14 who had contracted *m* with his daughters.
29:21 wife, that I may consummate my *m* with her,
29:23 and Jacob consummated the *m* with her.
29:28 Laban gave him his daughter Rachel in *m.*
29:30 then consummated his *m* with Rachel also,
34: 8 Please give her to him in *m.*
34:12 only give me the maiden in *m.*"
34:16 you our daughters and take yours in *m;*
34:21 and give our daughters to them in *m.*
38:14 up, she had not been given to him in *m.*
41:45 on Joseph, and he gave him in *m* Asenath,
Ex 2:21 man gave him his daughter Zipporah in *m.*
22:15 he shall pay her *m* price and marry her.
22:16 pay him the customary *m* price for virgins.
Lv 20:17 *m* with her sister of his half-sister,
Nm 12: 1 *m* he had contracted with a Cushite woman.
Dt 22:16 'I gave my daughter to this man in *m,*
Jos 15:16 "I will give my daughter Achsah in *m*
15:17 so Caleb gave him his daughter Achsah in *m.*
15:18 On the day of her *m* to Othniel,
Jgs 1:12 "I will give my daughter Achsah in *m*
1:13 so Caleb gave him his daughter Achsah in *m.*
1:14 On the day of her *m* to Othniel she
3: 6 In fact, they took their daughters in *m,*
3: 6 their own daughters to their sons in *m,*
21: 1 his daughter in *m* to anyone from Benjamin.
21: 7 not to give them any of our daughters in *m?"*
21:18 give them any of our daughters in *m,*
1Sm 18:17 whom I will give you in *m* if you become my
18:19 in *m* to Adriel the Meholathite instead.]
18:27 So Saul gave him his daughter Michal in *m.*
25:39 David then sent a proposal of *m* to Abigail.
1Kgs 3: 1 Solomon allied himself by *m* with Pharaoh,
11:19 gave him in *m* the sister of Queen Tahpenes,
2Kgs 8:27 did, since he was related to them by *m.*
14: 9 'Give your daughter to my son in *m,*'
1Chr 2:35 gave his daughter in *m* to his slave Jarha,
2Chr 18: 1 but he became related to Ahab by *m.*
Ezr 9:12 give your daughters to their sons in *m,*
Tb 7:11 I have given her in *m* to seven men,
7:11 Your *m* to her has been decided in heaven!
7:13 so that he might draw up a *m* contract
1Mc 10:58 gave him his daughter Cleopatra in *m.*
Sg 3:11 mother has crowned him on the day of his *m,*
Wis 3:13 knew not transgression of the *m* bed;
7: 2 man, and the pleasure that accompanies *m.*
13:17 he prays about his goods or *m* or children,
14:26 of souls, unnatural lust, disorder in *m,*
Sir 7:25 your daughter in *m* ends a great task;
23:18 *m* bed and says to himself "Who can see me?
47:20 upon your reputation, shame upon your *m,*
Dn 11:17 in *m* in order to destroy the kingdom,
Mt 22:30 given in *m* but live like angels in heaven.
Mk 12:25 given in *m* but live like angels in heaven.
Lk 2:36 seven years with her husband after her *m*
20:34 of this age marry and are given in *m,*
1Cor 7:36 He commits no sin if there is a *m.*
2Cor 11: 2 since I have given you in *m* to one husband,
1Tm 4: 3 seared consciences who forbid *m*
Heb 13: 4 Let *m* be honored in every way and the
13: 4 every way and the *m* bed be kept undefiled,

MARRIED (73)

Gn 24:67 he *m* her, and thus she became his wife.
25: 1 Abraham *m* another wife,
25:20 was forty years old when he *m* Rebekah,
26:34 When Esau was forty years old, he *m* Judith,
28: 9 addition to the wives he had, *m* Mahalath,
38: 2 daughter of a Canaanite named Shua, *m* her,
Ex 2: 1 man of the house of Levi *m* a Levite woman,
6:20 Amram *m* his aunt Jochebed,
6:23 Aaron *m* Amminadab's daughter,
6:25 son, Eleazar, *m* one of Putiel's daughters,
Lv 21: 4 But for a sister who has *m* out of his
22:12 A priest's daughter who is *m* to a layman
Nm 36:11 *m* relatives on their father's side within
Dt 21:14 since she was *m* to you under compulsion.
22:14 and defames her by saying, 'I *m* this woman,
22:22 relations with a woman who is *m* to another,
24: 3 or if this second man who has *m* her,
24: 5 family, to bring joy to the wife he has *m.*
Jgs 12: 9 had thirty daughters *m* outside the family,
14:20 and Samson's wife was *m* to the one who had
Ru 1: 4 with her two sons, who *m* Moabite women,
1Sm 25:43 wife, and David also *m* Ahinoam of Jezreel.
2Sm 17:25 Ishamelite named Ithra, who had *m* Abigail,
1Kgs 3: 1 The daughter of Pharaoh, whom he *m,*
4:11 who was *m* to Solomon's daughter Taphath,
4:15 Ahimaaz, who was *m* to Basemath,
7: 8 Pharaoh's daughter, whom Solomon had *m.*
16:31 He even *m* Jezebel,
1Chr 2:19 When Azubah died, Caleb *m* Ephrath,
2:21 having *m* her when he was sixty years old.
4:18 the daughter of Pharaoh, whom Mered *m.*
23:22 the sons of Kish, their kinsmen, *m* them.
2Chr 11:20 After her, he *m* Maacah,
Ezr 2:61 sons of Barzillai (he had *m* one of the
Neh 6:18 Jehohanan had *m* the daughter of Meshullam,
7:63 sons of Barzillai (he had *m* one of the
13:23 those days I saw Jews who had *m* Ashdodite,
Tb 1: 9 When I reached manhood I *m* Anna,
3: 8 For she had been *m* to seven husbands,
3: 8 You have already been *m* seven times,
6:14 this woman has already been *m* seven times,
9: 5 and that he had *m* and was inviting him to
11:15 and that he had *m* Raguel's daughter Sarah,
Est F: 3 is Esther, whom the king *m* and made queen.
1Mc 3:56 who were building houses, or were just *m,*
11: 9 give you my daughter whom Alexander has *m,*
2Mc 14:25 Judas *m,* settled down,
Prv 6:26 scarcely a loaf of bread, But if she is *m,*
Sir 9: 9 With a *m* woman dine not,
41:21 Of gazing at a *m* woman,
42: 9 her prime unmarried, or when she is *m,*
42:12 before men, or spend her time with *m* women;
Is 54: 6 A wife *m* in youth and then cast off,
Dn 13: 2 *m* a very beautiful and God-fearing woman,
Mal 2:11 LORD loves, and has *m* an idolatrous woman.
Mt 22:28 will she be, since all seven of them *m* her?"
24:38 eating and drinking, marrying and being *m,*
Mk 6:17 wife of his brother Philip, whom he had *m.*
12:23 All seven *m* her."
Lk 14:20 said, 'I am newly *m* and so I cannot come.'
20:30 The first one *m* and died childless.
20:31 Next, the second brother *m* the widow,
20:33 Remember, seven *m* her."
Rom 7: 2 a *m* woman is bound to her husband by law
1Cor 7: 8 not *m* and to widows I have this to say:
7:10 To those now *m,*
7:33 but the *m* man is busy with this world's
7:34 *m* woman, on the other hand, has the cares
1Tm 3: 2 bishop must be irreproachable, *m* only once,
3:12 Deacons may be *m* but once and must be good
5: 9 She must have been *m* only once.
Ti 1: 6 must be irreproachable, *m* only once,
1Pt 3: 1 You *m* women must obey your husbands,

MARRIES (15)

Lv 20:14 If a man *m* a woman and her mother also,
20:21 If a man *m* his brother's wife and thus
Nm 30: 7 "If she *m* while under a vow or under a
Sir 26: 7 he who *m* her seizes a scorpion.
Is 62: 5 As a young man *m* a virgin,
Jer 3: 1 and, after leaving him, she *m* another man,

Mt 5:32 The man who *m* a divorced woman likewise
19: 9 case) and *m* another commits adultery,
19: 9 who *m* a divorced woman commits adultery."
Mk 10:11 and *m* another commits adultery against her;
10:12 her husband and *m* another commits adultery."
Lk 16:18 his wife and *m* another commits adultery.
16:18 The man who *m* a woman divorced from her
1Cor 7:28 Neither does a virgin commit sin if she *m*.
7:38 man who *m* his virgin, acts fittingly;

MARROW (2)

Jb 21:24 and nourished, and his bones are rich in *m*.
Heb 4:12 and divides soul and spirit, joints and *m*;

MARRY (55)

Gn 27:46 If Jacob also should *m* a Hittite woman,
28: 1 "You shall not *m* a Canaanite woman!
28: 6 his blessing, not to *m* a Canaanite woman,
29:26 "to *m* off a younger daughter before an
34:21 We can *m* their daughters and give our
Ex 22:15 he shall pay her marriage price and *m* her.
Lv 18:17 nor shall you *m* and have intercourse with
18:18 you shall not *m* her sister as her rival;
21: 7 "A priest shall not *m* a woman who has
21:13 "The priest shall *m* a virgin.
21:14 taken from his own people, shall he *m*;
Nm 36: 3 *m* into one of the other Israelite tribes,
36: 3 to that of the tribe into which they *m*;
36: 4 that of the tribe into which they *m*
36: 6 They may *m* anyone they please,
36: 6 *m* into a clan of their ancestral tribe,
36: 8 Israelite tribes shall *m* someone belonging
36:13 ich they *m* and will be withdrawn from that
Dt 23: 1 "A man shall not *m* his father's wife,
25: 5 shall not *m* anyone outside the family;
25: 7 man does not care to *m* his brother's wife,
25: 8 in saying, 'I am not willing to *m* her,'
Jgs 14: 8 he returned to *m* the woman who pleased him,
Ru 1:12 Go, for I am too old to *m* again.
Neh 10:31 *m* our daughters to the peoples of the land,
13:25 "You shall not *m* your daughters to their
Tb 3:15 relative whom I might bide my time to *m*.
3:17 and to *m* Raguel's daughter Sarah to
3:17 before any other who might wish to *m* her.
4:12 *m* a woman of the lineage of your
4:12 Do not *m* a stranger who is not of your
6:12 all other men have the right to *m* her.
6:13 you have the right to *m* her listen to me,
6:13 before all other men, to *m* his daughter.
6:16 you to *m* a woman from your own family.
6:16 another thought to this demon, but *m* Sarah.
7: 9 ask Raguel to let me *m* my kinswoman Sarah."
7:10 entitled to *m* my daughter Sarah than you,
Jdt 16:22 Many wished to *m* her,
2Mc 14:25 He urged him to *m* and have children;
Is 62: 5 marries a virgin, your Builder shall *m* you;
Jer 16: 2 Do not *m* any woman;
Ez 44:22 may *m* women who are the widows of priests.
Mt 19:10 man and wife, it is better not to *m*."
22:30 they neither *m* nor are given in marriage
Mk 12:25 they neither *m* nor are given in marriage
Lk 20:28 the brother should *m* the widow and raise
20:34 of this age *m* and are given in marriage,
1Cor 7: 9 exercise self-control, they should *m*.
7: 9 It is better to *m* than to be on fire.
7:28 Should you *m*, however, you will not
7:39 If her husband dies she is free to *m*,
9: 5 Do we not have the right to *m* a believing
1Tm 5:11 them from Christ they will want to *m*.
5:14 I should like to see the younger ones *m*,

MARRYING (7)

Dt 22:13 *m* a woman and having relations with her,
24: 1 *m* a woman and having relations with her,
25: 5 the duty of a brother-in-law by *m* her.
Neh 13:27 evil, betraying our God by *m* foreign women?"
2Mc 1:14 On the pretext of *m* the goddess,
Mt 22:25 The eldest died after *m*,
24:38 eating and drinking, *m* and being married,

MARSENA (1)

Est 1:14 Admatha, Tarshish, Meres, *M* and Memucan,

MARSH (4)

1Mc 9:45 on one side, *m* and thickets on the other,
Ps(s) 107:34 thirsty ground, Fruitful land into salt *m*,
Sir 39:23 and turns fertile land into a salt *m*.
Is 35: 7 lurk will be a *m* for the reed and papyrus.

MARSHALING (1)

Jdt 1: 4 chariot forces and the *m* of his infantry.

MARSHALL (1)

Na 2: 2 road, gird your loins, *m* all your strength!

MARSHALS (1)

Jgs 5:14 from Zebulun wielders of the *m* staff.

MARSHES (4)

1Mc 9:42 the Jews returned to the *m* of the Jordan.
Is 42:15 into marshes, and the *m* I will dry up.
Ez 47:11 its *m* and swamps shall not be made fresh;

MARSHLAND (2)

Is 14:23 will make it a haunt of hoot owls and a *m*;
41:18 I will turn the desert into a *m*,

MARTHA (13)

Lk 10:38 a woman named *M* welcomed him to her home.
10:40 *M*, who was busy with all the details of
10:41 *M*, Martha, you are anxious
Jn 11: 1 the village of Mary and her sister *M*.
11: 5 *M* and her sister and Lazarus very much.
11:19 to console *M* and Mary over their brother.
11:20 When *M* heard that Jesus was coming she
11:21 *M* said to Jesus:
11:24 "I know he will rise again," *M* replied,
11:30 was still at the spot where *M* had met him.)
11:39 *M*, the dead man's sister,
12: 2 they gave him a banquet, at which *M* served.

MARTYRED (3)

Rv 2:13 *m* in your city where Satan has his home.
6: 9 spirits of those who had been *m*
17: 6 blood of those *m* for their faith in Jesus.

MARTYRS (1)

Rv 6:11 Each of the *m* was given a long white robe,

MARVEL (3)

1Sm 12:16 stand ready to witness the great *m* the
Wis 8:11 judgment, and should be a *m* before rulers.
Mk 10:24 The disciples could only *m* at his words.

MARVELED (9)

Jdt 10:19 They *m* at her beauty,
10:23 they all *m* at the beauty of her face.
11:20 they *m* at her wisdom and exclaimed,
2Mc 1:22 a great fire blazed up, so that everyone *m*.
7:12 attendants *m* at the young man's courage,
Wis 11:14 but in the end of events, they *m* at him,
Lk 4:22 they *m* at the appealing discourse which
9:43 all who saw it *m* at the greatness of God.
Acts 7:31 When Moses saw it, he *m* at the sight.

MARVELING (1)

Lk 2:33 were *m* at what was being said about him.

MARVELOUS (8)

Gn 18:14 Is anything too *m* for the LORD to do?
2Chr 26:15 was ascribed to the *m* help he had received.
Tb 12:22 they continued to acknowledge these *m* deeds
Jb 9:10 finding out, *m* things beyond reckoning.
Sir 48:14 wonders, and after death, *m* deeds.
Mt 21:42 who did this and we find it *m* to behold'?
Mk 12:11 who did it and we find it *m* to behold'?"
1Pt 2: 9 called you from darkness into his *m* light.

MARVELOUSLY (1)

2Mc 3:30 Lord who had *m* glorified his holy Place;

MARVELS (7)

Ex 34:10 I will work such *m* as have never been
Ps(s) 65: 9 at the earth's ends are in fear at your *m*;
78:43 in Egypt and his *m* in the plain of Zoan,
Sir 48:12 spirit, wrought many *m* by his mere word.
Lk 13:17 rejoiced at the *m* Jesus was accomplishing.
Acts 2:11 tongue about the *m* God has accomplished."
Rom 15:19 by word and deed, with mighty signs and *m*,

MARY (55)

Mt 1:16 was the father of Joseph the husband of *M*.
1:18 When his mother *M* was engaged to Joseph,
1:20 have no fear about taking *M* as your wife.
2:11 house, found the child with *M* his mother.
13:55 Isn't *M* known to be his mother and James,
27:56 Among them were *M* Magdalene,
27:56 and *M* the mother of James and Joseph,
27:61 But *M* Magdalene and the other Mary
28: 1 *M* Magdalene came with the other Mary to
28: 1 came with the other *M* to inspect the tomb.
Mk 6: 3 Is this not the carpenter, the son of *M*,
15:40 Among them were *M* Magdalene,
15:40 *M* the mother of James the younger and
15:47 *M* Magdalene and Mary the mother of Joses
16: 1 Mary Magdalene, *M* the mother of James,
16: 9 He first appeared to *M* Magdalene,
16:13 no more faith in them than in *M* Magdalene.
Lk 1:27 The virgin's name was *M*.
1:30 "Do not fear, *M*. You have found favor
1:34 *M* said to the angel, "How can this be
1:38 *M* said: "I am the servant of the Lord
1:39 Thereupon *M* set out,
1:46 Then *M* said: "My being proclaims
1:56 *M* remained with Elizabeth about three
2: 5 to register with *M*,
2:16 They went in haste and found *M* and Joseph,
2:19 *M* treasured all these things and reflected
2:34 blessed them and said to *M* his mother:
8: 2 *M* called the Magdalene,
10:39 She had a sister named *M*,
10:42 *M* has chosen the better portion and she
24:10 The women were *M* of Magdala,
24:10 Magdala, Joanna, and *M* the mother of James.
Jn 11: 1 the village of *M* and her sister Martha.
11: 2 (This *M* whose brother Lazarus was sick was
11:19 to console Martha and *M* over their brother.
11:20 she went to meet him, while *M* sat at home.
11:28 this she went back and called her sister *M*.
11:29 As soon as *M* heard this,
11:31 The Jews who were in the house with *M*
11:32 When *M* came to the place where Jesus was,
11:45 many of the Jews who had come to visit *M*,
12: 3 *M* brought a pound of costly perfume made
19:25 Mary the wife of Clopas, and *M* Magdalene.
20: 1 still dark, *M* Magdalene came to the tomb.
20:11 Meanwhile, *M* stood weeping beside the tomb.
20:16 Jesus said to her, *M*!"
20:18 *M* Magdalene went to the disciples.
Acts 1:14 their company, and *M* the mother of Jesus,
12:12 *M* the mother of John (also known as Mark),
Rom 16: 6 My greetings to *M*,

MARY'S (1)

Lk 1:41 When Elizabeth heard *M* greeting,

MASH (2)

Gn 10:23 Uz, Hul, Gether, and *M*.
1Chr 1:17 of Aram were Uz, Hul, Gether, and *M*.

MASHAL (1)

1Chr 6:59 *M* with its pasture lands,

MASK (1)

Jb 24:15 roams about, and he puts a *m* over his face;

MASONRY (1)

Sir 22:16 *M* bonded with wooden beams is not loosened

MASONS (5)

2Sm 5:11 cedar wood, as well as carpenters and *m*,
1Chr 14: 1 to David along with *m* and carpenters,
22:15 supply of workmen, stonecutters, *m*,
2Chr 24:12 *m* and carpenters to restore the temple,
34:11 *m* to buy hewn stone and timber for the tie

MASREKAH (2)

Gn 36:36 When Hadad died, Samlah, from *M*,
1Chr 1:47 Hadad died and Samlah of *M* succeeded him.

MASS (9)

Jos 3:16 a solid *m* for a very great distance indeed,
Jdt 7: 4 and hills can support the *m* of them."
1Mc 15:12 realizing what a *m* of troubles had come
Jb 38:38 is fused into a *m* and its clods made solid?
Sir 22:15 *m* are easier to bear than a stupid man.
Mt 13:33 the whole *m* of dough began to rise."
Lk 13:21 until the whole *m* of dough began to rise."
Rom 11:16 so too is the whole *m* of dough,
2Thes 2: 3 Since the *m* apostasy has not yet occurred

MASSA (3)

Gn 25:14 Kedar, Adbeel, Mibsam, Mishma, Dumah, *M*,
1Chr 1:30 Kedar, Adbeel, Mibsam, Mishma, Dumah, *M*,
Prv 31: 1 The words of Lemuel, king of *M*.

MASSACRE (4)

1Mc 5: 2 they began to *m* and persecute the people.
2Mc 5:13 There was a *m* of young and old,
15: 2 him pleaded, "Do not *m* them in that way,
Mt 2:16 He ordered the *m* of all the boys two years

MASSACRED (3)

Gn 34:25 without any trouble, and *m* all the males.
1Mc 15:40 where he took people captive or *m* them.
2Mc 5:26 All those who came out to watch, he *m*,

MASSAH (5)

Ex 17: 7 The place was called *M* and Meribah,
Dt 6:16 your God, to the test, as you did at *M*.
9:22 "At Taberah, at *M*,
33: 8 For you put him to the test at *M* and you
Ps(s) 95: 8 Meribah, as in the day of *M* in the desert,

MASSAITE (1)

Prv 30: 1 The words of Agur, son of Jakeh the *M*:

MASSED (2)

1Chr 11:13 where the Philistines had *m* for battle.
1Mc 11:45 had *m* in the center of the city in an

MASSEIAH (1)

2Chr 23: 1 *M,* son of Adaiah;

MASSES (4)

Wis 8:10 her sake I should have glory among the *m,*
14:20 *m* drawn by the charm of the workmanship,
Is 5:13 and their *m* are parched with thirst.
5:14 Down go their nobility and their *m,*

MASSIVE (2)

1Mc 1:33 with a high, *m* wall and strong towers,
Rv 21:12 Its wall, *m* and high, had twelve gates

MAST (3)

Prv 23:34 the sea, now sprawled at the top of the *m.*
Is 33:23 it cannot hold the *m* in place,
Ez 27: 5 from Lebanon they took to make you a *m;*

MASTER (174)

Gn 3:16 for your husband, and he shall be your *m.*"
4: 7 urge is toward you, yet you can be his *m.*"
24: 9 hand under the thigh of his *m* Abraham
24:10 and bearing all kinds of gifts from his *m,*
24:12 "LORD, God of my *m* Abraham,
24:12 and thus deal graciously with my *m* Abraham.
24:14 that you have dealt graciously with my *m.*"
24:27 be the LORD, the God of my *m* Abraham,
24:27 let his constant kindness toward my *m* fail.
24:35 "The LORD has blessed my *m* so abundantly
24:36 Sarah bore a son to my *m* in her old age,
24:37 My *m* put me under oath, saying:
24:39 When I asked my *m,*
24:42 'LORD, God of my *m* Abraham,
24:48 LORD, the God of my *m* Abraham,
24:49 have in mind to show true loyalty to my *m,*
24:54 he said, "Give me leave to return to my *m.*"
24:56 let me go back to my *m.*"
24:65 "That is my *m,*" replied the servant.
27:29 Be *m* of your brothers,
27:37 "I have already appointed him your *m,*
37:19 "Here comes that *m* dreamer!
39: 2 to the household of his Egyptian *m.*
39: 3 When his *m* saw that the LORD was with him
39: 8 "my *m* does not concern himself with
39:16 the cloak with her until his *m* came home.
39:19 As soon as the *m* heard his wife's story
44: 5 *m* drinks and which he uses for divination.
Ex 21: 4 But if his *m* gives him a wife and she
21: 5 devoted to my *m* and my wife and children;
21: 6 his *m* shall bring him to God and there,
21: 8 if her *m,* who had destined her for himself,
Dt 23:16 "You shall not hand over to his *m* a slave
Jgs 19:11 day far gone, the servant said to his *m,*
19:12 his *m* said to him, "We will not turn off
1Sm 20:38 up the arrow and brought it to his *m.*
24: 7 that I should do such a thing to my *m,*
25:14 messengers from the desert to greet our *m,*
25:17 store for our *m* and for his whole family.
30:13 My *m* abandoned me because I fell sick
30:15 will not kill me or deliver me to my *m,*
1Kgs 12:27 of this people will return to their *m,*
18: 8 "Go tell your *m,* 'Elijah is here!'"
18:10 where my *m* has not sent in search of you.
18:11 And now you say, 'Go tell your *m:*
18:14 And now you say, 'Go tell your *m:*
22:17 and the LORD saying, 'These have no *m!*
2Kgs 2: 3 LORD will take your *m* from over you today?"
2: 5 LORD will take your *m* from over you today?"
2:16 "Let them go in search of your *m.*
5: 1 highly esteemed and respected by his *m,*
5: 3 "If only my *m* would present himself to
5:18 when my *m* enters the temple of Rimmon to
5:20 *m* was too easy with this Aramean Naaman,
5:22 Gehazi replied, "but my *m* sent me to say,
5:25 He went in and stood before Elisha his *m,*
6: 5 "O *m,*" he cried out, "it was borrowed!"
6:22 eat and drink, and then go back to their *m.*"
6:23 them away, and they went back to their *m.*
8: 5 his *m* had restored a dead person to life,
8:14 Hazael left Elisha and returned to his *m.*
9: 7 shall destroy the house of Ahab your *m;*
9:31 "Is all well, Zimri, murderer of your *m?*"
12:12 to the *m* workmen in the temple of the LORD.
18:18 son of Hilkiah, the *m* of the palace;
18:27 "Was it to your *m* and to you that my lord
18:37 Then the *m* of the palace,
19: 2 He sent Eliakim, the *m* of the palace,
19: 4 the words of the commander, whom his *m,*
19: 6 he said to them, "Tell this to your *m:*
22: 5 to the *m* workmen in the temple of the LORD,
22: 9 to the *m* workmen in the temple of the LORD."
1Chr 12:20 of our heads he will desert to his *m* Saul."
25: 8 equally, young and old, *m* and pupil alike.
2Chr 18:16 and the LORD saying, 'These have no *m!*
28: 7 son, and Azrikam, the *m* of the palace,
34:10 to the *m* workmen in the house of the LORD,
Tb 3:14 "You know, O *M,* that I am innocent
8:17 Grant them, *M,* mercy and deliverance,
Jdt 5:20 "So now, my lord and *m,*
10:15 coming down thus promptly to see our *m,*
11:10 So then, my lord and *m,*
14:13 charge of all his things, "Waken our *m,*
1Mc 2:53 the commandment, and he became *m* of Egypt.
14: 7 of war and made himself *m* of Gazara,
14:17 and was *m* of the country and the cities,
Jb 3:19 same, and the servant is free from his *m.*
Prv 25:13 [He refreshes the soul of his *m*
27:18 who is attentive to his *m* will be enriched.
30:10 Slander not a servant to his *m,*
Eccl 8: 8 There is no man who is *m* of the breath of
Wis 12:18 But though you are *m* of might,
18:11 with the same retribution as his *m;*
Sir 23: 1 LORD, Father and *M* of my life,
23: 6 not the lustful cravings of the flesh *m* me,
33:25 the yoke and harness and the rod of his *m.*
41:15 of immorality, before *m* and mistress,
Is 19: 4 deliver Egypt into the power of a cruel *m,*
22:15 to that official, Shebna, *m* of the palace,
24: 2 Layman and priest alike, servant and *m,*
36: 3 there came out to him the *m* of the palace,
36:12 "Was it to you and your *m* that my lord
36:22 Then the *m* of the palace,
37: 2 He sent Eliakim, the *m* of the palace,
37: 4 the words of the commander, whom his *m,*
37: 6 "Tell this to your *m:*
51:22 not with wine, Thus says the LORD, your *M,*
Jer 3:14 children, says the LORD, for I am your *M;*
10:23 know, O LORD, that man is not *m* of his way;
31:32 covenant, and I had to show myself their *m,*
Zep 1: 9 house of their *m* with violence and deceit.
Mal 1: 6 his father, and a servant fears his *m;*
1: 6 if I am a *m,* where is the reverence due
Mt 9:38 Beg the harvest *m* to send out laborers to
10:24 pupil outranks his teacher, no slave his *m.*
10:25 like his teacher, the slave like his *m.*
16:22 "May you be spared, *M!*
17:24 said, "Does your *m* not pay the temple tax?"
18:25 of paying it, his *m* ordered him to be sold,
18:27 the *m* let the official go and wrote off
18:31 to their *m* to report the whole incident.
18:32 His *m* sent for him and said,
18:34 Then in anger the *m* handed him over to the
21: 3 says a word to you, say, 'The *M* needs them.'
24:45 farsighted servant whom the *m* has put in
24:46 whom his *m* discovers at work on his return!
24:48 himself, 'My *m* is a long time in coming,'
24:50 that man's *m* will return when he is not
25:11 *M,* master!' they cried.
25:19 the *m* of those servants came home and
25:21 His *m* said to him, 'Well done!
25:23 His *m* said to him, 'Cleverly done!
25:26 His *m* exclaimed: "You worthless, lazy, lout!
Mk 11: 3 'The *M* needs it but he will send it back
13:35 not know when the *m* of the house is coming,
Lk 2:29 "Now, *M,* you can dismiss your servant
5: 5 Simon answered, *M,* we have been hard
8:24 awaken him, saying, "*M, m,* we are lost!"
9:33 *M,* how good it is for us to be here.
9:49 It was John who said, *M,* we saw a man
10:17 returned in jubilation saying, *M,*
12:37 whom the *m* finds wide awake on his return.
12:42 farsighted steward whom the *m* will set
12:43 whom his *m* finds busy when he returns.
12:44 his *m* will put him in charge of all his
12:45 'My *m* is taking his time about coming,'
12:46 that servant's *m* will come back on a day
13:25 When once the *m* of the house has risen to
14:21 returning reported all this to his *m.*
14:21 *m* of the house grew angry at the account.
14:23 The *m* then said to the servant,
16: 5 to the first, 'How much do you owe my *m?*'
17:13 raised their voices and said, "Jesus, *M,*
19:31 say, 'The *M* has need of it.'"
19:34 They explained that the *M* needed it.
20:28 *M,* Moses prescribed that if a man's
Jn 13:16 you, no slave is greater than his *m;*
15:15 a slave does not know what his *m* is about.
15:20 no slave is greater than his *m.*
Rom 14: 4 His *m* alone can judge whether he stands or
14: 7 master and none of us dies as his own *m.*
1Cor 1:20 Where is the *m* of worldly argument?
9:27 I do is discipline my own body and *m* it,
Gal 4: 1 in name he is *m* of all his possessions;
Eph 6: 9 have a *M* in heaven who plays no favorites.
Col 4: 1 realizing that you too have a *m* in heaven.
2Tm 2:21 dedicated and useful to the *m* of the house
1Pt 3: 6 subject to Abraham and called him her *m.*
2Pt 2: 1 deny the *M* who acquired them for his own,
Jude 1: 4 and deny Jesus Christ, our only *m* and Lord.
Rv 6:10 "How long will it be, O *M,*

MASTER-BUILDER (1)

1Cor 3:10 I laid a foundation as a wise *m* might do,

MASTERED (1)

1Chr 5:20 *m* the Hagrites and all who were with them.

MASTERS—MASTER'S (47)

Gn 24:10 The servant then took ten of his *m* camels,
24:27 me straight to the house of my *m* brother."
24:36 My *m* wife Sarah bore a son to my master in
24:44 the LORD has decided upon for my *m* son.'
24:48 the daughter of my *m* kinsman for his son.
24:51 that she may become the wife of your *m* son,
39: 7 his *m* wife began to look fondly at him and
40: 7 were with him in custody in his *m* house,
44: 8 we steal silver or gold from your *m* house?
Ex 21: 4 *m* property and the man shall leave alone.
1Sm 25:10 many servants who run away from their *m.*
29: 4 For how else can he win back his *m* favor,
1Kgs 1:27 Was this done by my royal *m* order without
2Kgs 6:32 His *m* footsteps are echoing behind him."
9:11 When Jehu rejoined his *m* servants,
10: 2 "Since your *m* sons are with you,"
10: 3 best and the fittest of your *m* offspring,
10: 3 throne, and fight for your *m* house."
10: 6 count the heads of your *m* sons and come to
Jdt 8:22 and a reproach in the eyes of our *m.*
13: 1 the attendants from their *m* presence.
Est 9: 1 the Jews had expected to become *m* of them,
9: 1 the Jews became *m* of their enemies.
1Mc 9:25 impious men and made them *m* of the country.
Ps(s) 123: 2 of servants are on the hands of their *m,*
Sir 32:15 He who studies the law *m* it,
Is 1: 3 knows its owner, and an ass, its *m* manger;
22:18 you glory in, you disgrace to your *m* house!
Jer 27: 4 Tell your *m:* "Thus says the LORD
Mt 6:24 No man can serve two *m.*
15:27 leavings that fall from their *m*' tables."
25:18 in the ground, where he buried his *m* money.
25:21 Come, share your *m* joy!'
25:23 Come, share your *m* joy!'
Lk 12:36 men awaiting their *m* return from a wedding,
12:47 The slave who knew his *m* wishes but did
16: 5 "So he called in each of his *m* debtors,
16:13 "No servant can serve two *m.*
Acts 16:16 profit to her *m* by fortune-telling.
16:19 *m* saw that their source of profit was gone,
Eph 6: 5 obey your human *m* with the reverence,
6: 9 *M,* act in a similar way toward your slaves.
Col 3:22 slaves I say, obey your human *m* perfectly,
1Tm 6: 1 regard their *m* as worthy of full respect;
6: 2 Those slaves whose *m* are brothers in the
Ti 2: 9 Slaves are to be submissive to their *m.*
1Pt 2:18 slaves, obey your *m* with all deference,

MASTERY (2)

Eccl 8: 8 it, and none has *m* of the day of death.
Wis 12:16 *m* over all things makes you lenient to all.

MASTIC (6)

2Sm 5:23 rear and meet them before the *m* trees.
5:24 of marching in the tops of the *m* trees,
1Chr 14:14 them from the direction of the *m* trees.
14:15 of marching in the tops of the *m* trees,
Ps(s) 84: 7 of the *m* trees they make a spring of it;
Dn 13:55 "Under a *m* tree," he answered.

MAT (14)

Mt 9: 2 to him a paralyzed man lying on a *m.*
9: 6 Roll up your *m,* and go home."
Mk 2: 4 the *m* on which the paralytic was lying.
2: 9 or to say, 'Stand up, pick up your *m,*
2:11 Pick up your *m* and go home."
2:12 The man stood and picked up his *m* and went
Lk 5:18 men came along carrying a paralytic on a *m.*
5:19 There they let him down with his *m* through
5:24 Take your *m* with you,
5:25 He picked up the *m* he had been lying on
Jn 5: 8 Pick up your *m* and walk!"
5: 9 he picked up his *m* and began to walk.
5:10 you are not allowed to carry that *m* around."
5:11 me who told me, 'Pick up your *m* and walk.'

MATCH (13)

Ex 28:21 them to *m* the names of the sons of Israel,
39:14 to *m* the names of the sons of Israel,
1Sm 14: 7 I will *m* your resolve."
21:10 "There is none to *m* it.
2Chr 13: 7 young and unthinking, and no *m* for them.
13: 8 do you think you are a *m* for the kingdom
Prv 27:15 a rainy day the *m* is a quarrelsome woman.
Wis 3:10 receive a punishment to *m* their thoughts,
Is 16: 6 insolence that his empty words do not *m.*
46: 5 me with, as an equal, or *m* me against,
Ez 31: 8 nor could the fir trees *m* its boughs,
Lk 5:36 the piece taken from it will not *m* the old.
Acts 6:10 but they proved no *m* for the wisdom and

MATCHED (2)

Ez 31: 8 no tree in the garden of God *m* its beauty.
2Cor 8:11 may be *m* by giving according to your means.

MATCHES (1)

Hos 10: 1 a luxuriant vine whose fruit *m* its growth.

MATE (6)

Gn 7: 2 with you seven pairs, a male and its *m;*
7: 2 animals, one pair, a male and its *m;*
31:12 All the he-goats in the flock, as they *m,*
Lv 18:23 herself in front of an animal to *m* with it;

20:16 a woman goes up to any animal to *m* with it,
Is 34:15 assemble, none shall be missing its *m*.

MATED (2)

Gn 30:39 came to drink, the goats *m* by the rods,
30:41 these animals, so that they *m* by the rods;

MATERIAL (13)

Ex 28:31 ephod you shall make entirely of violet *m*.
Lv 13:48 or on woven or knitted *m* of linen or wool,
13:49 or hide, or on the woven or knitted *m*,
13:51 the garment, or on the woven or knitted *m*,
13:52 or the woven or knitted *m* of wool or linen,
13:53 the garment, or on the woven or knitted *m*,
13:56 or the leather, or the woven or knitted *m*.
13:57 the garment, or on the woven or knitted *m*,
13:58 the garment, or the woven or knitted *m*,
13:59 wool or linen, or on woven or knitted *m*,
2Mc 1:21 the *m* for the sacrifices had been prepared,
2:24 narratives where the *m* is abundant,
1Cor 9:11 it too much to expect a *m* harvest from you?

MATERIALS (1)

1Chr 22: 5 his death David laid up *m* in abundance.

MATES (1)

Lk 5: 7 *m* in the other boat to come and help them.

MATING (1)

Gn 31:10 which I saw *m* he-goats that were streaked,

MATRED (2)

Gn 36:39 she was the daughter of *M*,
1Chr 1:50 She was the daughter of *M*,

MATRI (1)

1Sm 10:21 in clans, and the clan of *M* was chosen,

MATTAN (3)

2Kgs 11:18 altars and images completely, and slew *M*,
2Chr 23:17 its altars and images, and they slew *M*,
Jer 38: 1 Shephatiah, son of *M*,

MATTANAH (2)

Nm 21:18 From Beer they went to *M*,
21:19 they went to Mattanah, from *M* to Nahaliel,

MATTANIAH (16)

2Kgs 24:17 king of Babylon appointed his uncle *M* king,
1Chr 9:15 *M*, son of Mica, son of Zichri,
25: 4 Bukkiah, *M*, Uzziel, Shubael,
25:16 The ninth was *M*,
2Chr 20:14 son of Benaiah, son of Jeiel, son of *M*,
29:13 Zechariah and *M*; of the sons of Heman:
Ezr 10:26 *M*, Zechariah, Jehiel, Abdi, Jeremoth,
10:27 Elioenai, Eliashib, *M*,
10:30 Adna, Chelal, Benaiah, Maaseiah, *M*,
10:37 Cheluhi, Vaniah, Meremoth, Eliashib, *M*,
Neh 11:17 *M*, son of Micah; son of Zabdi,
11:22 son of Bani, son of Hashabiah, son of *M*,
12: 8 Binnui, Kadmiel, Sherebiah, Judah, *M*;
12:25 one section opposite the other, were *M*,
12:35 of Jonathan, son of Shemaiah, son of *M*,
13:13 with Hanan, son of Zaccur, son of *M*,

MATTATHA (1)

Lk 3:31 son of Melea, son of Menna, son of *M*,

MATTATHIAS (16)

1Mc 2: 1 In those days *M*, son of John,
2:14 Then *M* and his sons tore their garments,
2:16 *M* and his sons gathered in a group apart.
2:17 Then the officers of the king addressed *M*:
2:19 But *M* answered in a loud voice:
2:24 When *M* saw him, he was filled with zeal;
2:27 Then *M* went through the city shouting,
2:38 When *M* and his friends heard of it,
2:45 *M* and his friends went about and tore down
2:49 When the time came for *M* to die,
11:70 one stayed except the army commanders *M*,
14:29 our country, Simon, son of the priest *M*,
16:14 he and his sons *M* and Judas went down to
2Mc 14:19 Theodotus and *M* to arrange an agreement.
Lk 3:25 son of Jannai, son of Joseph, son of *M*,
3:26 son of Naggai, son of Maath, son of *M*,

MATTATTAH (1)

Ezr 10:33 Mattenai, *M*, Zabad, Eliphelet, Jeremai,

MATTENAI (3)

Ezr 10:33 *M*, Mattattah, Zabad, Eliphelet, Jeremai,
10:37 Vaniah, Meremoth, Eliashib, Mattaniah, *M*,
Neh 12:19 and for Joiarib, *M*; for Jedaiah, Uzzi;

MATTER (75)

Gn 21:12 of Sarah, no *m* what she is asking of you;
21:17 "What is the *m*, Hagar?
34: 6 went out to discuss the *m* with Jacob,
34:12 No *m* how high you set the bridal price,
34:19 young man lost no time in acting in the *m*,
34:20 presented the *m* to their fellow townsmen:
37:11 against him but his father pondered the *m*.
41:32 means that the *m* has been reaffirmed
Ex 18:16 they come to me to have me settle the *m*
24:14 a complaint, let him refer the *m* to them."
Lv 22: 9 keep my charge and not do wrong in this *m*;
27:33 It shall not *m* whether good ones or bad
Dt 13:15 into the *m* and investigate it thoroughly.
17: 8 in a *m* of bloodshed or of civil rights or
32:47 For this is no trivial *m* for you;
Jos 22:32 land of Canaan, and reported the *m* to them.
Ru 3:18 will not rest, but will settle the *m* today."
1Sm 20:23 in the *m* which you and I have discussed,
22:15 at all, great or small, about the whole *m*."
2Sm 14:15 to speak of this *m* to your majesty,
18:13 the whole *m* would have come to the
2Kgs 9:18 "What does it *m* to you how things are?"
9:19 "What does it *m* to you how things are?"
2Chr 16: 9 You have acted foolishly in this *m*,
Ezr 4:22 Take care that you do not neglect this *m*,
5: 5 order be sent back concerning this *m*.
5:17 pleasure in this *m* be communicated to us."
10: 9 the *m* at hand and because it was raining.
10:16 They held sessions to examine the *m*,
Neh 2:16 others who would be concerned about the *m*.
Est 2:23 The *m* was investigated and verified,
1Mc 10:35 them or to molest any of them in any *m*.
12:18 kindly send us an answer on this *m*."
2Mc 2:27 festive banquet is no light *m* for one
2:31 and to omit detailed treatment of the *m*.
3:40 This was how the *m* concerning Heliodorus
4:17 It is no light *m* to flout the laws of God,
13:13 march out and settle the *m* with God's help.
Jb 19:28 that the root of the *m* is found in him?"
Eccl 6: 3 live many years, no *m* to what great age,
Wis 11:17 fashioned the universe from formless *m*,
Sir 10: 6 No *m* the wrong,
23:13 to coarse talk, for in it lies sinful *m*.
33: 6 stallion that neighs, no *m* who the rider.
Is 22: 1 What is the *m* with you now,
Ez 8:17 Is it such a trivial *m* for the house of
Dn 3:16 to defend ourselves before you in this *m*.
7:28 face blanched, but I kept the *m* to myself.
Mt 25:21 Since you were dependable in a small *m* I
25:23 Since you were dependable in a small *m* I
Mk 1:45 and began to proclaim the whole *m* freely,
4:38 it not *m* to you that we are going to drown?"
Lk 9:45 were afraid to question him about the *m*.
16:10 in a slight *m* is also unjust in greater.
17:21 *m* of reporting that it is 'here' or 'there.'
19:17 'You showed yourself capable in a small *m*.
Jn 7: 5 (As a *m* of fact, not even his brothers
21:23 Jesus never told him, as a *m* of fact,
Acts 15: 6 accordingly convened to look into the *m*.
19:39 is any further *m* you want to investigate,
23:30 his accusers to take the *m* up with you."
25:17 came here with me, I did not delay the *m*.
Rom 14:17 of God is not a *m* of eating or drinking,
1Cor 8: 4 about this *m* of eating meats that have
11:22 Certainly not in this *m*!
2Cor 7:11 have displayed your innocence in this *m*.
8:10 you some advice on this *m* of rich and poor.
Phil 1:10 learn to value the things that really *m*,
3:16 course, no *m* what stage we have reached.
1Thes 1: 5 a mere *m* of words for you but one of power;
4: 6 or cheating his brother in the *m* at hand;
5:15 seek one another's good and, for that *m*,
2Thes 2: 3 Let no one seduce you, no *m* how.
Heb 7:15 The *m* is clearer still if another priest
1Jn 3:20 *m* what our consciences may charge us with;

MATTERS (39)

Dt 25:16 of these *m* is an abomination to the LORD,
1Sm 5: 7 On seeing how *m* stood,
1Chr 25: 5 of Heman, the king's seer in divine *m*;
Ezr 9: 1 When these *m* had been concluded,
Neh 6: 7 since *m* like these must reach the ear of
Est E: 9 treatment *m* coming to our attention.
1Mc 11:29 letter to Jonathan about all these *m*:
2Mc 4:23 to obtain decisions on some important *m*.
11:17 and asked about the *m* contained in it.
11:20 On the details of these *m* I have authorized
11:36 But the *m* on which he passed judgment
14: 9 informed yourself in detail on these *m*,
Jb 32:18 For I am full of *m* to utter;
Dn 11:28 he shall arrange *m* and return to his land.
Mt 23:23 neglecting the weightier *m* of the law,
Jn 3:10 and still you do not understand these *m*?
Acts 18:15 I refuse to judge such *m*."
23:29 he was accused in *m* of their own law
26:26 king here is well acquainted with these *m*.
26:31 *m* over among themselves and admitted,
1Cor 2:10 The Spirit scrutinizes all *m*,
4: 3 It *m* little to me whether you or any human
6: 2 be thought unworthy of judging in minor *m*?
6: 4 If you have such *m* to decide,
7: 1 Now for the *m* you wrote about.
7:12 As for the other *m*, although I know
7:19 What *m* is keeping God's commandments.
11:34 As for other *m*, I shall give instructions
2Cor 2: 9 learn whether you are obedient in all *m*.
Gal 6:15 All that *m* is that one is created anew.
Phil 1:18 All that *m* is that in any and every way,
1Tm 1: 7 the *m* they discuss with such assurance.
3:14 I am writing you about these *m* so that if
Heb 9:10 but can only cleanse in *m* of food and
10: 2 Were *m* otherwise, the priests would
1Pt 1:12 Into these *m* angels long to search.
2Pt 3:16 with these *m* as he does in all his letters.
Rv 2:14 Nevertheless, I hold a few *m* against you:
21: 5 Then he said, "Write these *m* down,

MATTHAN (2)

Mt
1:15 father of Matthan, *M* the father of Jacob.

MATTHAT (2)

Lk 3:24 son of Joseph, son of Heli, son of *M*,
3:29 son of Eliezer, son of Jorim, son of *M*,

MATTHEW (6)

Mt 9: 9 *M* at his post where taxes were collected.
9: 9 *M* got up and followed him.
10: 3 Thomas and *M* the tax collector;
Mk 3:18 Andrew, Philip, Bartholomew, *M*,
Lk 6:15 John, Philip and Bartholomew, *M* and Thomas,
Acts 1:13 Philip and Thomas, Bartholomew and *M*;

MATTHEW'S (1)

Mt 9:10 that, while Jesus was at table in *M* home,

MATTHIAS (2)

Acts 1:23 Barsabbas, also known as Justus) and *M*.
1:26 to *M* who was added to the eleven apostles.

MATTITHIAH (8)

1Chr 9:31 *M*, one of the Levites,
15:18 Jehiel, Unni, Eliab, Benaiah, Maaseiah, *M*,
15:21 But *M*, Eliphelehu, Mikneiah,
16: 5 Zechariah, Uzziel, Shemiramoth, Jehiel, *M*,
25: 3 Zeri, Jeshaiah, Shimei, Hashabiah, and *M*;
25:21 The fourteenth was *M*,
Ezr 10:43 Jeiel, *M*, Zabad, Zebina, Jaddai, Joel,
Neh 8: 4 at his right side stood *M*,

MATTOCK (1)

Is 7:25 which used to be hoed with the *m*:

MATTOCKS (2)

1Sm 13:20 Philistines to sharpen their plowshares, *m*,
13:21 and *m* was two-thirds of a shekel,

MATTRESS (1)

1Sm 9:25 city, a *m* was spread for Saul on the roof,

MATTRESSES (1)

Acts 5:15 the streets and laid them on cots and *m*,

MATURE (8)

Sir 23:15 never *m* in character as long as he lives.
Mt 13:26 When the crop began to *m* and yield grain,
Lk 8:14 and pleasures of life and they do not *m*.
1Cor 2: 6 which we express among the spiritually *m*.
14:20 far as evil is concerned, but in mind be *m*.
Phil 3:15 are spiritually *m* must have this attitude.
Heb 5:14 Solid food is for the *m*,
Jas 1: 4 you may be fully *m* and lacking in nothing.

MATURED (1)

Lk 1:80 The child grew up and *m* in spirit.

MATURITY (3)

Eph 4:15 love and the full *m* of Christ the head.
Heb 6: 1 teaching about Christ and advance to *m*,
Jas 1:15 and when sin reaches *m* it begets death.

MAW (1)

Is 5:14 its throat and opens its *m* without limit;

MAXIMS (1)

Jb 13:12 Your reminders are ashy *m*,

MAXIMUM (1)

Acts 16:24 instructions he put them in *m* security,

MAYHAP (1)

Wis 14:19 *m* in his determination to please the ruler,

MAZZAROTH (1)

Jb 38:32 Can you bring forth the *M* in their season,

ME-JARKON (1)

Jos 19:46 Bene-berak, Gath-rimmon, *M* and Rakkon,

MEADOW (4)

Ps(s) 72: 6 He shall be like rain coming down on the *m*,
Wis 2: 9 Let no *m* be free from our wantonness;
Jer 23: 3 them and bring them back to their *m*;
Jas 1:11 with its scorching heat it parches the *m*,

MEADOWS (5)

Ps(s) 37:20 of the LORD, like the beauty of the *m*,
65:13 The untilled *m* overflow with it,
144:13 and increase to myriads in our *m*;
Is 30:23 day your cattle will graze in spacious *m*;
Jas 1:11 and with that the *m* loveliness is gone.

MEAGER (2)

Sir 31: 4 The poor man toils for a *m* subsistence,
Mi 6:10 hoarding and the *m* ephah that is accursed?

MEAL (30)

Gn 19: 3 He prepared a *m* for them,
31:46 and they had a *m* there at the mound.
31:54 and invited his kinsmen to share in the *m*.
37:25 They then sat down to their *m*.
43:31 of himself, gave the order, "Serve the *m*."
Ex 18:12 Moses' father-in-law in the *m* before God.
Nm 5:15 for her a tenth of an ephah of barley *m*.
1Sm 1: 9 Hannah rose after one such *m* at Shiloh,
28:25 She set the *m* before Saul and his servants,
2Sm 12: 4 a *m* for the wayfarer who had come to him.
12: 4 lamb and made a *m* of it for his visitor."
1Kgs 5: 2 kors of fine flour, sixty kors of *m*,
2Kgs 4:41 "Bring some *m*," Elisha said.
1Chr 12:41 provisions in great quantity of *m*,
Tb 2: 2 you, so that he can share this *m* with me.
2Mc 6:21 ritual *m* took the man aside privately,
Ez 44: 3 to eat his *m* in the presence of the LORD.
Mt 15: 2 hands, for example, before eating a *m*."
24:41 Two women will be grinding *m*;
26:21 In the course of the *m* he said,
26:26 During the *m* Jesus took bread,
Mk 14:18 and in the course of the *m* Jesus said,
14:22 During the *m* he took bread,
Lk 14: 1 When Jesus came on a sabbath to eat a *m* in
22:27 reclines at table or he who serves the *m*?
Jn 13: 4 rose from the *m* and took off his cloak.
21:12 "Come and eat your *m*," Jesus told them.
21:15 When they had eaten their *m*,
1Cor 11:33 my brothers, when you assemble for the *m*,
Heb 12:16 like Esau, who sold his birthright for a *m*.

MEALS (6)

2Chr 35:13 and also cooked the sacred *m* in pots,
2Mc 7:42 sacrificial *m* and the excessive cruelties.
Ez 42:13 to the LORD shall eat the most sacred *m*,
Mk 7: 2 disciples eating *m* without having purified
Acts 2:46 sincere hearts they took their *m* in common,
Gal 2:12 He had been taking his *m* with the Gentiles

MEALTIME (1)

Ru 2:14 At *m* Boaz said to her,

MEAN (73)

Gn 18:21 I *m* to find out."
31:26 "What do you *m*," Laban demanded
Ex 5: 4 of Egypt answered them, "What do you *m*,
12:26 ask you, 'What does this rite of yours *m*?'
13:14 should ask you later on, 'What does this *m*?'
Dt 6:20 statutes and decrees *m* which the LORD,
15: 9 the *m* thought that the seventh year,
30:20 For that will *m* life for you,
Jos 4: 6 ask you what these stones *m* to you,
4:21 you ask their fathers what these stones *m*,
Jgs 2: 2 What did you *m* by this?
1Sm 4: 6 loud shouting in the camp of the Hebrews *m*?"
4:14 Eli inquired, "What does this commotion *m*?"
25:17 He is so *m* that no one can talk to him."
2Sm 19: 7 officers and servants *m* nothing to you.
1Kgs 1:41 "What does this uproar in the city *m*?"
2Kgs 1:14 But now, let my life *m* something to you!"
2Mc 14:14 the Jews would *m* prosperity for themselves.
Ps(s) 119:141 I am *m* and contemptible,
Prv 3: 8 This will *m* health for your flesh and
20:13 eyes wide open *m* abundant food.
Sir 14: 3 Wealth ill becomes the *m* man;
19:15 Thus, too, a man can slip and not *m* it;
Is 3:15 What do you *m* by crushing my people,
5: 5 let you know what I *m* to do to my vineyard:
Jer 4:30 doomed, what do you *m* by putting on purple,
18:18 *m* the loss of instruction from the priests,
Ez 24:19 these things that you are doing *m* for us?"
37:18 you not tell us what you *m* by all this?",
Dn 2:41 iron, *m* that it shall be a divided kingdom,
5:25 Mene, Tekel, Peres. These words *m*:
Am 5:18 What will this day of the LORD *m* for you?
Mt 3: 8 Give some evidence that you *m* to reform.
5:37 Say, 'Yes' when you *m* 'Yes'
5:37 and 'No' when you *m* 'No.'
Mk 1:27 "What does this *m*? A completely new teaching
11: 5 them, "What do you *m* by untying that colt?"
Lk 3: 8 Give some evidence that you *m* to reform.
7:33 I *m* that John the Baptizer came neither
12:41 for us, Lord, or do you *m* it for everyone?"
19: 5 I *m* to stay at your house today."
20:17 "What do the Scriptures *m* when they say,
23:16 Therefore I *m* to release him,
Jn 7:36 What does he *m* by saying,
8:22 he *m* he will kill himself when he claims,
8:33 What do you *m* by saying,
13:22 one another, puzzled as to whom he could *m*.
13:36 Peter said to him, "Where do you *m* to go?"
16:17 "What can he *m*, 'Within a short
16:18 "What does he *m* by this 'short time'?
18:38 "Truth!" said Pilate. "What does that *m*?"
Acts 2:12 "What does this *m*?" they asked one another.
21:39 no *m* city;
22:21 I *m* to send you far from here,
Rom 11:11 stumbling *m* that they are forever fallen?
11:15 the world, what will their acceptance *m*?
1Cor 1:12 This is what I *m*: One of you will say,
4: 4 not *m* that I am declaring myself innocent.
6:12 does not *m* that everything is good for me.
10:20 I *m* that the Gentiles sacrifice to demons
10:22 we *m* to provoke the Lord to jealous anger?
10:23 does not *m* that everything is constructive.
15:50 This is what I *m*, brothers:
2Cor 5:19 I *m* that God, in Christ, was reconciling
10:11 we *m* to be in action when we are present.
Gal 2:17 does that *m* that Christ is encouraging sin?
3:21 Does this *m* that the law is opposed to the
Eph 4: 9 what does this *m* but that he had first
5:32 *m* that it refers to Christ and the church.
Jas 5:12 and "no" if you mean no.
5:12 Rather, let it be "yes" if you mean yes
Rv 2:22 I *m* to cast her down on a bed of pain;
3: 9 I *m* to make some of Satan's assembly,

MEANEST (1)

Jgs 6:15 My family is the *m* in Manasseh,

MEANING (52)

Gn 30:13 and Leah said, "What good fortune!" *m*,
30:24 So she named him Joseph *m*,
37:10 "What is the *m* of this dream of yours?"
40: 5 the same night, each dream with its own *m*.
41:11 and each of our dreams had its own *m*.
41:12 for each of us the *m* of his dream.
41:25 "Both of Pharaoh's dreams have the same *m*.
41:51 He named his first-born Manasseh, *m*,
41:52 and the second he named Ephraim, *m*,
1Sm 15:14 is the *m* of this bleating of sheep that
Est A:11 way, until night, to understand its *m*.
E: 4 of those to whom goodness has no *m*,
2Mc 1:36 called the liquid nephthar, *m* purification,
Ez 18: 2 what is the *m* of this proverb that you
Dn 2: 4 servants the dream and we will give its *m*."
2: 5 unless you tell me the dream and its *m*,
2: 6 But if you tell me the dream and its *m*,
2: 6 Now tell me the dream and its *m*."
2: 7 servants the dream and we will give its *m*."
2:26 tell me the dream that I had, and its *m*?"
2:30 that its *m* may be made known to the king,
2:45 That is the *m* of the stone you saw hewn
2:45 what you dreamed, and its *m* is sure."
4: 4 but none of them could tell me its *m*.
4: 6 *m* of the visions that I saw in my dream.
4:15 Now, Belteshazzar, tell me its *m*.
4:15 wise men in my kingdom can tell me the *m*,
4:16 "let not the dream or its *m* terrify you."
4:17 for your enemies, and its *m* for your foes.
4:21 this is its *m*,
5:15 me to read this writing and tell me its *m*,
7:16 he made known to me the *m* of the things:
8:15 sought the *m* of the vision I had seen,
Mt 9:13 Go and learn the *m* of the words,
12: 7 If you understood the *m* of the text,
Mk 6:52 completely closed to the *m* of the events.
Lk 7: 8 I too am a man who knows the *m* of an order,
8: 9 him what the *m* of this parable might be.
8:11 This is the *m* of the parable.
9:45 its *m* was so concealed from them they did
18:34 to them, and they did not grasp his *m*.
Jn 20:16 "Rabouni!" *m* "Teacher").
Acts 4:36 name Barnabas *m* "son of encouragement").
8:27 Candace (a name *m* queen) of the Ethiopians,
9:36 Tabitha (in Greek Dorcas, *m* a gazelle).
10:17 to make out the *m* of the vision he had had,
Rom 4:14 an empty word and the promise loses its *m*.
1Cor 1:17 cross of Christ be rendered void of its *m*!
14:11 but if I do not know the *m*,
2Tm 2: 7 for the Lord will make my *m* fully clear.
Heb 10:20 the veil (the "veil" *m* his flesh),
Rv 1:20 This is the secret *m* of the seven stars

MEANINGLESS (3)

1Sm 12:21 *m* idols which can neither profit nor save;
Wis 15: 8 he molds a *m* god from the selfsame clay;
1Tm 1: 6 these and instead have turned to *m* talk,

MEANINGS (1)

Sir 39: 3 is busied with the hidden *m* of the sages.

MEANNESS (1)

Sir 29: 7 Many refuse to lend, not out of *m*,

MEANS (116)

Gn 29:32 for she said, "It *m*,
29:33 again and bore a son, and said, "It *m*,
40:12 "This is what it *m*. The three branches
40:18 "This is what it *m*. The three baskets
41:32 That Pharaoh had the same dream twice *m*
49:13 by the seashore [This *m* a shore for ships],
Ex 10: 9 That is what a feast of the LORD *m* to us."
13:21 in the daytime by *m* of a column of cloud
13:21 at night by *m* of a column of fire to give
23: 5 under its burden, by no *m* desert him;
Lv 14:32 has insufficient *m* for his purification."
25:26 *m* to buy it back in his own name,
25:28 acquire sufficient *m* to buy back his land,
25:49 or, if he acquires the *m*,
27: 8 with the *m* of the one who made the vow.
Nm 6:21 from anything else which his *m* may allow.
14:34 you will realize what it *m* to oppose me.
27:14 my sanctity to them by *m* of the water."
Dt 32:47 rather, it *m* your very life,
32:47 since it is by this *m* that you are to
Jgs 7: 7 "By *m* of the three hundred who lapped up
1Sm 6: 3 not send it alone, but must, by all *m*,
1Kgs 3:27 By no *m* kill it, for she is the mother."
6:36 The inner court was walled off by *m* of
11:28 Jeroboam was a man of *m*,
1Chr 29:14 should have the *m* to contribute so freely?
Ezr 2:69 According to their *m* they contributed to
Neh 9:30 through your spirit, by *m* of your prophets;
1Mc 14:10 food and equipped them with *m* of defense,
2Mc 4: 7 obtained the high priesthood by corrupt *m*:
Ps(s) 52: 6 You love all that *m* ruin,
142: 5 I have lost all *m* of escape;
Prv 17:16 in the fool's hand are the *m* to buy wisdom,
22:27 For if you have not the *m* to pay,
Eccl 5:13 he may have a son when he is without *m*.
Wis 6:18 love *m* the keeping of her laws;
11:17 For not without *m* was your almighty hand,
16: 9 they deserved to be punished by such *m*;
Sir 8:13 Go not surety beyond your *m*;
18:16 Sometimes the word *m* more than the gift;
18:23 making a vow have the *m* to fulfill it;
29:20 for your neighbor according to your *m*,
35: 9 to you, generously, according to your *m*.
38:11 a rich offering according to your *m*.
Is 7:17 [This *m* the king of Assyria.]
Ez 5:10 *m* that fathers within you shall eat sons,
17:12 Do you not understand what this *m*?
20:41 and by *m* of you I will manifest my
Dn 2: 3 my spirit no rest until I know what it *m*."
2:43 The iron mixed with clay tile *m* that they
4:23 tree are to be left *m* that your kindgom
5: 7 reads this writing and tells me what it *m*,"
5:12 summon Daniel to tell you what this *m*."
5:16 to read the writing and tell me what it *m*,
5:17 for you, O king, and tell you what it *m*.
Mi 5:11 abolish the *m* of divination from your use,
Mt 1:23 a name which *m* "God is with us."
2: 6 by no *m* least among the princes of Judah,
15: 6 This *m* that for the sake of your tradition
23:16 a man swears by the temple it *m* nothing,
23:18 'If a man swears by the altar it *m* nothing,
27:33 Golgotha (a name which *m* Skull Place),
Mk 4:33 By *m* of many such parables he taught them
5:41 he said to her, "Talitha, koum," which *m*,
15:22 site of Golgotha (which *m* "Skull Place"),
15:34 which *m* "My God,
Lk 8: 3 who were assisting them out of their *m*.
13: 3 By no *m*! But I tell you
19: 9 this is what it *m* to be a son of Abraham.
Jn 1:38 said to him, "Rabbi (which *m* Teacher),
1:41 (This term *m* the Anointed.)
4:25 (This term *m* Anointed.)
9: 7 (This name *m* "One who has been sent.")
10:38 it *m* that the Father is in me and I in him."
11:16 *m* "Twin") said to his fellow disciples,
12:50 I know that his commandment *m* eternal life,
17:17 Consecrate them by *m* of truth
20:24 the Twelve, Thomas (the name *m* "Twin"),
Acts 3:18 God has brought to fulfillment by this *m*
11:29 something aside, each according to his *m*,
13: 8 magician," for that is what his name *m*—
13:47 a *m* of salvation to the ends of the earth."
15: 9 purified their hearts by *m* of faith also.
16:21 which *m* they advocate customs which are
Rom 3:19 This *m* that every mouth is silenced and
3:25 him the *m* of expiation for all who believe.
3:31 we then abolishing the law by *m* of faith?
6:15 are we free to sin? By no *m*!
7:21 This *m* that even though I want to do what
8:25 see *m* awaiting it with patient endurance.
8:27 searches hearts knows what the Spirit *m*,
9: 8 That *m* that it is not the children of the
15:17 This *m* I can take glory in Christ Jesus
1Cor 3: 7 This *m* that neither he who plants nor he

7:33 This *m* he is divided.
8: 2 *m* he has never really known it as he ought.
11:27 This *m* that whoever eats the bread or
14:13 This *m* that the man who speaks in a tongue
2Cor 5:17 This *m* that if anyone is in Christ,
8: 3 According to their *m*—
8: 3 I can testify even beyond their *m*—
8:11 be matched by giving according to your *m*.
8:12 to give should accord with one's *m*,
Gal 3: 7 This *m* that those who believe are sons of
3:29 which *m* you inherit all that was promised.
6:15 It *m* nothing whether one is circumcised or
Eph 2:19 This *m* that you are strangers and aliens
Phil 1:21 For, to me, "life" *m* Christ;
1:22 the flesh, that *m* productive toil for me
Col 1:20 fullness reside in him and by *m* of him,
1Tm 6: 5 religion only as a *m* of personal gain.
Phlm 1:12 and that *m* I am sending my heart!
Heb 7: 2 His name *m* "king of justice";
13: 2 for by that *m* some have entertained angels
2Pt 1: 8 your own, are by no *m* ineffectual;
1Jn 2:27 *m* you have no need for anyone to teach you.

MEANT (28)

Gn 16:13 she *m*, "Have I really seen God
50:20 you meant harm to me, God *m* it for good,
Jgs 13:23 out to him, "If the LORD had *m* to kill us,
1Sm 20:39 only Jonathan and David knew what was *m*.
Est 4: 5 action of Mordecai *m* and the reason for it.
1Mc 16:22 to death, for he knew what they *m* to do.
2Mc 6:12 chastisements were *m* not for the ruin
Jb 30: 2 Such strength as they had, to me *m* nought;
Prv 27: 6 from a friend may be accepted as well *m*,
Jer 13:12 wineflask is *m* to be filled with wine.
13:12 wineflask is *m* to be filled with wine?"
32: 8 I knew this was what the LORD *m*,
Dn 5: 8 the writing or tell the king what it *m*.
5:15 but they could not say what the words *m*.
7:16 and asked him what all this *m* in truth;
Mk 4:21 Is it not *m* to be put on a stand?
6:48 He *m* to pass them by.
9:10 discuss what "to rise from the dead" *m*.
12:12 well enough that he *m* the parable for them.)
Lk 1:29 words, and wondered what his greeting *m*.
19:46 'My house is *m* for a house of prayer' but
Jn 11:13 thought he *m* sleep in the sense of slumber.
11:55 which *m* that many people from the country
13:24 Peter signaled him to ask Jesus whom he *m*.
Rom 11:12 have *m* riches for the Gentile world,
11:15 has *m* reconciliation for the world,
1Thes 3: 4 it has happened, and you know what we *m*.

MEANTIME (4)

Dt 2:14 in the *m* the whole generation of soldiers
Jgs 4:17 Sisera, in the *m*, had fled on foot
2Sm 16:15 In the *m* Absalom, accompanied by
1Kgs 22:31 In the *m* the king of Aram had given his

MEARAH (1)

Jos 13: 4 from *M* of the Sidonians to Aphek,

MEASURE (55)

Gn 15:16 not have reached its full *m* until then."
41:49 stopped measuring it, for it was beyond *m*.
Nm 35: 5 Thus you shall *m* out two thousand cubits
Dt 16:10 and the *m* of your own freewill offering
21: 2 judges shall go out and *m* the distances
25:15 and just weight, and a true and just *m*,
28:11 more than goodly *m* the fruit of your womb,
30: 9 goodly *m* the returns from all your labors,
2Kgs 21:13 I will *m* Jerusalem with the same cord as I
2Chr 3: 3 was sixty cubits according to the old *m*,
2Mc 6:14 *m* of their sins before he punishes them;
Jb 11: 9 It is longer than the earth in *m*,
Ps(s) 60: 8 Shechem, and *m* off the valley of Succoth.
80: 6 and given them tears to drink in ample *m*.
108: 8 Shechem, and *m* off the valley of Succoth;
Prv 24:22 and the ruin from either one, who can *m*?
Wis 11:20 all things by *m* and number and weight.
Sir 9:14 As best you can, take your neighbors' *m*,
18: 3 Who can *m* his majestic power,
Is 5:10 of vineyard shall yield but one liquid *m*,
34:11 The LORD will *m* her with line and plummet
40:12 Who has held in a *m* the dust of the earth,
65: 7 in full *m* their recompense into their laps.
Lam 5:22 and in full *m* turned your wrath against us.
Ez 4:11 you drink shall be the sixth of a hin by *m*;
9: 9 of the house of Israel are great beyond *m*;
45: 3 Also from this sector *m* off a strip,
45:10 an honest ephah, and an honest liquid *m*.
45:11 and the liquid *m* shall be of the same size:
45:11 the liquid *m* equal to a tenth of a homer;
45:14 for every *m* of oil,
45:14 for every measure of oil, a tenth of a *m*,
Dn 8:23 reign, when sinners have reached their *m*,
Zec 2: 6 "To *m* Jerusalem,"
Mal 3:10 to pour down blessing upon you without *m*?
Mt 7: 2 The *m* with which you measure will be used
7: 2 which you *m* will be used to measure you.
Mk 4:24 In the *m* you give you shall receive,
16:20 "The *m* of the years of Satan's power has
Lk 6:38 Good *m* pressed down,
6:38 you *m* with will be measured back to you.
Rom 12: 3 *m* of faith that God has apportioned him.
2Cor 2: 5 he has hurt not only me, but in some *m*,
7:11 What a *m* of holy zeal it has brought you,
Eph 4: 7 favor in the *m* in which Christ bestows it.
Phil 2:13 in you any *m* of desire or achievement.
Col 1:28 men and teach them in the full *m* of wisdom,
1Tm 1:14 Lord has been granted me in overflowing *m*,
1Pt 4:10 one another, each in the *m* he has received.
4:13 the *m* that you share Christ's sufferings.
Jude 1: 2 peace, and love be yours in ever greater *m*.
Rv 11: 2 do not *m* it, for it has been handed over

MEASURED (56)

Ex 16:18 But when they *m* it out by the omer,
2Sm 8: 2 defeated Moab and then *m* them with a line,
1Kgs 6:24 Each wing of a cherub *m* five cubits so
7:23 a circular rim, and *m* ten cubits across,
Jb 6: 2 could my anguish but be *m* and my calamity
Ps(s) 78:50 When he *m* the course of his anger he
Wis 4: 8 of time, nor can it be *m* in terms of years.
Sir 16:23 mind to my words, While I propose *m* wisdom,
Jer 13:25 your lot, the portion *m* out to you from me,
31:37 If the heavens on high can be *m*,
Ez 4:16 water which they have *m* out fearfully,
40: 5 he *m* the width and the height of the
40: 6 its steps, and *m* the gate's threshold,
40: 7 pilasters between the cells *m* five cubits.
40: 7 of the gate toward the inside *m* one rod.
40: 8 He *m* the vestibule of the gate,
40:11 He *m* the gate's entrance,
40:13 He *m* the gate from the back wall of one
40:14 He *m* the vestibule,
40:19 He *m* the width of the court from the front
40:20 facing north, whose length and width he *m*.
40:23 he *m* one hundred cubits from one gate to
40:24 whose cells, pilasters, and vestibule he *m*;
40:27 from gate to gate he *m* one hundred cubits.
40:28 the south gate, where he *m* the south gate.
40:32 gate facing the east, where he *m* the gate,
40:35 where he *m* the dimensions of its cells,
40:47 " Then he *m* the court,
40:48 temple and *m* the pilasters on each side,
40:48 on either side of the door *m* three cubits.
41: 1 brought me to the nave and *m* the pilasters,
41: 2 at either side of it *m* five cubits each.
41: 2 He *m* the length of the nave,
41: 3 and *m* the pilasters flanking that entrance,
41: 4 He *m* the space beyond the nave,
41: 5 Then he *m* the wall of the temple,
41:12 and it *m* ninety cubits from side to side.
41:13 He *m* the temple,
41:15 He *m* the building which lay the length of
42: 8 length the wall *m* one hundred cubits.
42:15 east and *m* all the limits of the court.
42:16 He *m* the east side:
42:17 Then he turned and *m* the north side:
42:18 *m* five hundred cubits by the measuring
42:19 *m* five hundred cubits by the measuring rod.
42:20 Thus he *m* it in the four directions,
47: 3 he *m* off a thousand cubits and had me wade
47: 4 He *m* off another thousand and once more
47: 4 Again he *m* off a thousand and had me wade;
47: 5 Once more he *m* off a thousand,
Hos 2: 1 sea, which can be neither *m* nor counted.
Mi 2: 4 captors, The fields of my people are *m* out,
Mt 23:32 up the vessel *m* out by your forefathers.
Lk 6:38 you measure with will be *m* back to you.
Rv 21:16 He *m* the city with the rod and found it
21:17 Its wall *m* a hundred and forty-four cubits

MEASUREMENT (1)

Rv 21:17 in height by the unit of *m* the angel used.

MEASUREMENTS (4)

Ez 40:21 had the same *m* as those of the first gate;
43:10 of their sins], both its *m* and its design;
43:13 These were the *m* of the altar in cubits of
Rv 11: 1 and take the *m* of God's temple and altar,

MEASURES (25)

Lv 19:35 in using *m* of length or weight or capacity.
Dt 25:14 you keep two different *m* in your house,
Ru 3:15 she did so, he poured out six *m* of barley,
3:17 "He gave me these six *m* of barley because
1Kgs 5:25 and twenty thousand *m* of pure oil.
7:26 Its capacity was two thousand *m*.
7:38 in diameter with a capacity of forty *m*,
1Chr 23:29 mixing, and of all *m* of quantity and size.
2Chr 2: 9 kors of barley, twenty thousand *m* of wine,
2: 9 of wine, and twenty thousand *m* of oil."
4: 5 It had a capacity of three thousand *m*.
Est 8:12 For by such *m* he hoped to catch us
2Mc 4:21 so he took *m* for his own security.
Prv 14:15 everything, but the shrewd man *m* his steps.
20:10 Varying weights, varying *m*,
Sir 42: 4 and balances, or of tested *m* and weights;
Is 44:13 with a plane and *m* it off with a compass,
Ez 45:14 by the kor of ten liquid *m* [or a homer,
45:14 a homer, for ten liquid *m* make a homer].
Dn 14: 3 fine flour, forty sheep, and six *m* of wine.
Hg 2:16 one went to a heap of grain for twenty *m*,
2:16 another went to the vat to draw fifty *m*,
Mt 13:33 took and kneaded into three *m* of flour.
Lk 13:21 woman took to knead into three *m* of flour
16: 7 The answer came, 'A hundred *m* of wheat,'

MEASURING (23)

Gn 41:49 sea, so vast that at last he stopped *m* it,
Jb 38: 5 Who stretched out the *m* line for it?
Ps(s) 16: 6 the *m* lines have fallen on pleasant sites;
Is 28:17 I will make of right a *m* line,
Jer 31:39 The *m* line shall be stretched from there
Lam 2: 8 He stretched out the *m* line;
Ez 40: 3 the gate, holding a linen cord and a *m* rod.
40: 5 man was holding a *m* rod six cubits long,
42:15 he had finished *m* the inner temple area,
42:16 five hundred cubits by his *m* rod.
42:17 five hundred cubits by the *m* rod.
42:18 five hundred cubits by the *m* rod
42:19 measured five hundred cubits by the *m* rod.
47: 3 off to the east with a *m* cord in his hand,
48:30 north side, *m* forty-five hundred cubits,
48:32 the east side, *m* forty-five hundred cubits,
48:33 south side, *m* forty-five hundred cubits,
48:34 the west side, *m* forty-five hundred cubits,
Am 7:17 Your land shall be divided by *m* line,
Zec 1:16 a *m* line shall be stretched over Jerusalem.
2: 5 there was a man with a *m* line in his hand.
Rv 11: 1 Someone gave me a *m* rod and said:
21:15 to me held a rod of gold for *m* the city,

MEAT (60)

Lv 1: 8 on them, they shall lay the pieces of *m*,
17:14 shall not partake of the blood of any *m*.
19:26 "Do not eat *m* with the blood still in it.
Nm 11: 4 *m* that even the Israelites lamented again,
11: 4 again, "Would that we had *m* for food!
11:13 can I get *m* to give to all this people?
11:13 are crying to me, 'Give us *m* for our food.'
11:18 for tomorrow, when you shall have *m* to eat.
11:18 have cried, 'Would that we had *m* for food!
11:18 the LORD will give you *m* for food,
11:21 will give them *m* to eat for a whole month.'
11:33 while the *m* was still between their teeth,
18:18 oblation to the LORD, Their *m*,
Dt 12:15 your heart's desire as much *m* as the LORD,
12:20 he promised you, when you wish *m* for food,
16: 4 and none of the *m* which you sacrificed on
Jgs 6:19 the *m* in a basket and the broth in a pot,
6:20 "Take the *m* and unleavened cakes and lay
6:21 and touched the *m* and unleavened cakes.
6:21 which consumed the *m* and unleavened cakes,
1Sm 2:13 fork, while the *m* was still boiling,
2:15 "Give me some *m* to roast for the priest.
2:15 accept boiled meat from you, only raw *m*."
25:11 my *m* that I have slaughtered for my own
2Sm 6:19 Israel, a loaf of bread, a cut of roast *m*,
1Kgs 17: 6 brought him bread and *m* in the morning,
17: 6 morning, and bread and *m* in the evening,
1Chr 16: 3 every woman, a loaf of bread, a piece of *m*,
2Mc 6:19 a life of defilement, he spat out the *m*,
6:21 urged him to bring *m* of his own providing,
6:21 *m* of the sacrifice prescribed by the king,
Jb 31:31 "Who has not been fed with his *m*!"
Ps(s) 78:20 give bread and provide *m* for his people?"
78:27 And he rained *m* upon them like dust,
Prv 9: 2 She has dressed her *m*,
23:20 nor with those who eat *m* to excess;
Sir 36:19 As the palate tests *m* by its savor,
Is 22:13 butcher sheep, You eat *m* and drink wine:
44:16 fire, and on its embers he roasts his *m*;
44:19 I baked bread and roasted *m* which I ate.
Jer 11:15 *m* turn away your misfortune from you?
Bar 6:27 Even their wives cure parts of the *m*,
Ez 4:14 never has any unclean *m* entered my mouth."
11: 3 The city is the kettle, and we are the *m*."
11: 7 you have placed within it, they are the *m*,
11:11 for you, nor shall you be the *m* within it.
24: 4 Put in it pieces of *m*, all good pieces:
24:10 the fire, Till the *m* has been cooked,
Dn 10: 3 I ate no savory food, I took no *m* or wine,
Mi 3: 3 flesh in a kettle, and like *m* in a caldron.
Zec 9: 7 and take from his mouth his bloody *m*,
Acts 15:20 union, from the *m* of strangled animals,
15:29 to abstain from *m* sacrificed to idols,
15:29 blood, from the *m* of strangled animals,
21:25 were merely to avoid *m* sacrificed to idols,
Rom 14:21 nobly if you abstained from eating *m*,
1Cor 8: 7 so recently devoted to idols, they eat *m*,
8:13 my brother to sin I will never eat *m* again,
10:19 that *m* offered to an idol is really

MEATS (2)

1Cor 8: 1 about *m* that have been offered to idols.
8: 4 eating *m* that have been offered to idols:

MECHANICAL (1)

1Mc 6:51 *m* bows for shooting arrows and slingstones.

MECONAH (1)

Neh 11:28 in Ziklag, in *M* and its dependencies,

MEDABA (1)

1Mc 9:36 But the sons of Jambri from *M* made a raid

MEDAD (2)

Nm 11:26 two men, one named Eldad and the other *M*,
11:27 "Eldad and *M* are prophesying in the camp,"

MEDAN (2)

Gn 25: 2 She bore him Zimran, Jokshan, *M*,
1Chr 1:32 she bore Zimran, Jokshan, *M*,

MEDDLE (4)

Sir 3:22 With what is too much for you *m* not,
Mt 8:29 "Why *m* with us, Son of God?
Mk 5: 7 shrieking in a loud voice, "Why *m* with me,
Lk 8:28 Son of God Most High, why do you *m* with me?

MEDDLES (1)

Prv 26:17 ears is he who *m* in a quarrel not his own.

MEDDLESOME (2)

Sir 28:14 A *m* tongue subverts many,
28:15 A *m* tongue can drive virtuous women from

MEDE (4)

Dn 6: 1 and Darius the *M* succeeded to the kingdom
6: 9 and irrevocable under *M* and Persian law."
6:13 irrevocable under the *M* and Persian law."
6:16 "that under the *M* and Persian law every

MEDEBA (5)

Nm 21:30 fires blaze as far as *M*."
Jos 13: 9 through the tableland of *M* and Dibon,
13:16 itself, through the tableland about *M*,
1Chr 19: 7 his army, who came and encamped before *M*.
Is 15: 2 Over Nebo and over *M* Moab wails.

MEDES (12)

2Kgs 17: 6 river of Gozan, and in the cities of the *M*.
18:11 river of Gozan, and in the cities of the *M*.
Jdt 1: 1 time Arphaxad ruled over the *M* in Ecbatana.
16:10 her daring, the *M* appalled at her boldness.
Est 1:19 among the laws of the Persians and *M*,
1Mc 1: 1 Darius, king of the Persians and *M*,
Is 13:17 I am stirring up against them the *M*,
Jer 25:25 all the kings of Zimri, of Elam, of the *M*;
Dn 5:28 divided and given to the *M* and Persians."
8:20 represents the kings of the *M* and Persians.
9: 1 son of Ahasuerus, of the race of the *M*,
Acts 2: 9 We are Parthians, *M*, and Elamites.

MEDIA (29)

Ezr 6: 2 the stronghold in the province of *M*,
Tb 1:14 death I would go to *M* to buy goods for him.
1:14 son of Gabri, who lived at Rages, in *M*.
1:15 him as king, the roads to *M* became unsafe,
3: 7 On the same day, at Ecbatana in *M*,
4: 1 had deposited with Gabael at Rages in *M*,
4:20 with Gabri's son Gabael at Rages in *M*.
5: 2 which roads to take for the journey into *M*!"
5: 4 the roads who would travel with him to *M*.
5: 5 Tobiah said, "Do you know the way to *M*?"
5: 6 I have often traveled to *M*;
5: 6 kinsman Gabael, who lives at Rages in *M*.
5:10 "My son Tobiah wants to go to *M*.
5:10 *M* and crossed all its plains and mountains;
6: 7 traveled on together till they were near *M*.
6:10 *M* and were getting close to Ecbatana,
9: 5 and two camels, traveled to Rages in *M*,
14: 4 take your children and flee into *M* for I
14: 4 be safer in *M* than in Assyria or Babylon.
14:12 departed with his wife and children for *M*,
14:13 and he buried them at Ecbatana in *M*.
14:15 king of Media, led them captive into *M*.
Est 10: 2 chronicles of the kings of *M* and Persia.
1Mc 6:56 *M* with the army that accompanied the king,
14: 1 assembled his army and marched into *M*
14: 2 When Arsaces, king of Persia and *M*,
Is 21: 2 "Go up, Elam; besiege, O *M*;
Jer 51:28 the king of *M*,

MEDIAN (3)

Est 1: 3 the Persian and *M* aristocracy,
1:14 the seven Persian and *M* officials who were
1:18 This very day the Persian and *M* ladies who

MEDIA'S (1)

Jer 51:11 LORD has stirred up the spirit of *M* kings;

MEDIATION (1)

2Mc 4:11 granted to the Jews through the *m* of John,

MEDIATOR (7)

Jb 33:23 him an angel, one out of a thousand, a *m*,
Gal 3:19 by angels, at the hands of a *m*;
3:20 be no *m* when only one person is involved;
1Tm 2: 5 One also is the *m* between God and men,
Heb 8: 6 now, just as he is *m* of a better covenant,
9:15 This is why he is *m* of a new covenant:
12:24 perfect, to Jesus, the *m* of a new covenant,

MEDICINAL (1)

Tb 6: 7 what *m* value is there in the fish's heart,

MEDICINE (4)

Tb 11: 8 This *m* will make the cataracts shrink and
11:12 Next he smeared the *m* on his eyes,
Ez 47:12 serve for food, and their leaves for *m*."
Rv 22: 2 their leaves serve as *m* for the nations.

MEDICINES (2)

Tb 6: 5 Its gall, heart, and liver make useful *m*."
Sir 38: 7 pain and the druggist prepares his *m*;

MEDIOCRE (1)

2Mc 15:38 if it is poorly done and *m*,

MEDITATE (8)

Ps(s) 63: 7 through the night-watches I will *m* on you:
77: 7 In the night I *m* in my heart;
77:13 And I *m* on your works;
119:15 *m* on your precepts and consider your ways.
119:27 and I will *m* on your wondrous deeds.
119:48 to your commands and *m* on your statutes.
119:78 I will *m* on your precepts.
143: 5 I *m* on all your doings,

MEDITATES (5)

Ps(s) 1: 2 of the LORD and *m* on his law day and night.
119:23 me, your servant *m* on your statutes.
Sir 14:20 Happy the man who *m* on wisdom,
39: 7 his counsel, as he *m* upon his mysteries.
50:28 Happy the man who *m* upon these things,

MEDITATING (1)

1Kgs 18:27 louder, for he is a god and may be *m*,

MEDITATION (4)

Ps(s) 119:97 It is my *m* all the day.
119:99 all my teachers when your decrees are my *m*.
119:148 the night watches in *m* on your promise.
Sir 6:37 let his commandments be your constant *m*;

MEDIUM (3)

Lv 20:27 "A man or a woman who acts as a *m* or
1Sm 28: 7 servants, "Find me a woman who is a *m*,
28: 7 "There is a woman in Endor who is a *m*."

MEDIUMS (5)

Lv 19:31 not go to the *m* or consult fortune-tellers,
20: 6 Should anyone turn to *m* and fortune-tellers
1Sm 28: 3 *m* and fortune-tellers out of the land.
28: 9 the *m* and fortune-tellers out of the land.
Is 8:19 "Inquire of *m* and fortune-tellers

MEEK (3)

Ps(s) 37:11 But the *m* shall possess the land,
Prv 16:19 the *m* than to share plunder with the proud.
Zec 9: 9 a just savior is he, *M*,

MEEKEST (1)

Nm 12: 3 by far the *m* man on the face of the earth.

MEEKNESS (4)

Sir 45: 4 and *m* God selected him from all mankind;
2Cor 10: 1 exhort you by the *m* and kindness of Christ,
Eph 4: 2 have received, with perfect humility, *m*,
Col 3:12 mercy, with kindness, humility, *m*,

MEET (144)

Gn 19: 6 Lot went out to *m* them at the entrance.
29:13 son Jacob, he hurried out to *m* him.
30:16 from the fields, Leah went out to *m* him.
31: 4 So Jacob sent for Rachel and Leah to *m* him
32: 7 He is now coming to *m* you,
33: 4 Esau ran to *m* him,
46:28 Joseph, so that he might *m* him in Goshen.
46:29 and rode to *m* his father Israel in Goshen.
Ex 4:14 Besides, he is now on his way to *m* you.
4:27 to Aaron, "Go into the desert to *m* Moses."
5:20 and Aaron, who were waiting to *m* them,
18: 7 Moses went out to *m* his father-in-law,
19:17 led the people out of the camp to *m* God,
25:22 There I will *m* you and there,
29:42 tent, where I will *m* you and speak to you.
29:43 at the altar, I will *m* the Israelites;
30: 6 the ark of commandments where I will *m* you.
30:36 in the meeting tent where I will *m* you.
Lv 26:28 will *m* you with fiery defiance and will
27: 8 the vow is too poor to *m* the fixed sum,
Nm 17: 5 lest he *m* the fate of Korah and his band.
17:19 front of the commandments, where I *m* you.
22:36 he went out to *m* him at the boundary city
23: 3 Perhaps the LORD will *m* me,
31:13 community, went outside the camp to *m* them,
Dt 1:28 What shall we *m* with up there?
15: 8 and freely lend him enough to *m* his need.
Jos 9:11 for the journey and go to *m* them.
Jgs 4:18 Jael went out to *m* Sisera and said to him,
4:22 Jael went out to *m* him and said to him,
6:35 and these tribes advanced to *m* the others.
11:31 out of the doors of my house to *m* me
14: 5 Timnah, a young lion came roaring to *m* him.
15:14 and the Philistines came shouting to *m* him,
20:31 The Benjaminites went out to *m* them,
1Sm 10: 2 you will *m* two men near Rachel's tomb at
10: 5 that city, you will *m* a band of prophets,
13:15 went up after Saul to *m* the soldiers,
15:12 Early in the morning he went to *m* Saul,
16: 4 city came trembling to *m* him and inquired,
17: 2 up their battle line to *m* the Philistines.
17:48 then moved to *m* David at close quarters,
17:55 Saul saw David go out to *m* the Philistine,
18: 6 of the cities of Israel to *m* King Saul,
21: 2 Nob, who came trembling to *m* him
23:28 of David and went to *m* the Philistines.
25:32 God of Israel, who sent you to *m* me today.
25:34 if you had not come so promptly to *m* me,
27: 5 "If I *m* with your approval,
30:21 came out to *m* David and the men with him.
2Sm 5:23 rear and *m* them before the mastic trees.
6:20 daughter Michal came out to *m* him and said,
15:32 God, Hushai the Archite was there to *m* him,
19:16 *m* him and to escort him across the Jordan.
19:17 down with the Judahites to *m* King David,
19:21 to come down today to *m* my lord the king."
19:25 son of Saul, also went down to *m* the king.
19:26 When he came from Jerusalem to *m* the king,
1Kgs 2: 8 Because he came down to *m* me at the Jordan,
2:19 king stood up to *m* her and paid her homage.
18:16 So Obadiah went to *m* Ahab and informed him.
18:16 Ahab came to *m* Elijah,
21:18 "Start down to *m* Ahab,
2Kgs 2:15 They went to *m* him,
4:26 Hurry to *m* her,
4:29 if you *m* anyone, do not greet him,
4:31 He returned to *m* Elisha and informed him
9:17 to *m* them and to ask whether all is well."
9:18 So a driver went out to *m* him and said.
9:21 out, each in his own chariot, to *m* Jehu.
14: 8 challenge, "Come let us *m* face to face."
16:10 Ahaz went to Damascus to *m* Tiglath-pileser,
1Chr 12:18 *m* them and addressed them in these words:
19: 5 to his men, he sent messengers to *m* them,
2Chr 14: 9 Asa went out to *m* him and set himself in
15: 2 He went forth to *m* Asa and said to him:
20:17 Tomorrow go out to *m* them,
25:17 "Come, let us *m* each other face to face."
28: 9 He went out to *m* the army returning to
Neh 6:10 "Let us *m* in the house of God,
Tb 11:16 gate of Nineveh to *m* his daughter-in-law.
Jdt 5: 4 Why have they refused to come out to *m* me
7:15 and their refusal to *m* you peacefully."
14: 5 of Israel and sent him here to *m* his death."
15: 8 Israel, and to *m* and congratulate Judith.
1Mc 3:11 out to *m* him and defeated and killed him.
3:16 Judas went out to *m* him with a few men.
5:59 came out of the city to *m* them in battle.
7:28 come with a few men to *m* you peaceably."
7:30 Judas was afraid and would not *m* him again.
9: 8 "Let us go forward to *m* our enemies;
9:39 kinsmen had come out to *m* the bride's party
10:56 but *m* me in Ptolemais,
10:59 also wrote to Jonathan to come and *m* him.
10:86 city came out to *m* him with great pomp.
11:22 to *m* him for a conference at Ptolemais
11:64 So he went to *m* them,
12:25 went into the country of Hamath to *m* them,
2Mc 13: 8 fire and ashes should *m* his death in ashes.
14:21 on which the leaders would *m* by themselves.
Jb 5:14 They *m* with darkness in the daytime,
Ps(s) 45:10 The daughters of kings come to *m* you;
85:11 Kindness and truth shall *m*;
109:13 May his posterity *m* with destruction;
119:23 Though princes *m* and talk against me,
Prv 7:10 the woman comes to *m* him,
7:15 So I came out to *m* you,
Sir 12: 6 will *m* for every good deed you do for him.
15: 2 Motherlike she will *m* him,
19: 5 He who gloats over evil will *m* with evil,
29: 5 him and says he is helpless to *m* the claim.
36: 8 and your people's oppressors *m* destruction.
42:24 to *m* each need, each creature is preserved.
Is 7: 3 Go out to *m* Ahaz,
21:14 *M* the thirsty, bring them water;
34:14 Wildcats shall *m* with desert beasts,
35:10 They will *m* with joy and gladness,
51:11 They will *m* with joy and gladness,
64: 4 Would that you might *m* us doing right,
Jer 2:24 in her month they will *m* her.
14:15 famine shall these prophets *m* their end.

32: 4 They shall *m* and speak face to face,
41: 6 Nethaniah, went out from Mizpah to *m* them,
Dn 11:25 *m* the king of the south with a great army;
13:14 an occasion when they could *m* her alone.
Am 2: 2 Moab shall *m* death amid uproar
4:12 deal thus with you, prepare to *m* your God,
5:19 flee from a lion, and a bear should *m* him;
Zec 2: 7 and another angel came out to *m* him,
Mt 8:34 that the entire town came out to *m* Jesus.
22:11 "When the king came in to *m* the guests,
Lk 15:20 He ran out to *m* him,
Jn 4:30 that they set out from the town to *m* him.
11:20 that Jesus was coming she went to *m* him,
12:13 got palm branches and came out to *m* him.
12:18 The crowd came out to *m* him because they
Acts 5:12 they used to *m* in Solomon's Portico.
10:25 As Peter entered, Cornelius went to *m* him,
27:10 is bound to *m* with disaster and heavy loss,
28:15 of Appius and the Three Taverns to *m* us.
Gal 1:19 did not *m* any other apostles except James,
1Thes 4:17 in the clouds to *m* the Lord in the air.
Jas 2:16 fed," but do not *m* their bodily needs,
Rv 21: 2 as a bride prepared to *m* her husband.

MEETING (160)

Ex 27:21 them before the LORD in the *m* tent,
28:43 wear them whenever they go into the *m* tent
29: 4 also bring to the entrance of the *m* tent,
29:10 forward the bullock in front of the *m* tent.
29:11 the LORD, at the entrance of the *m* tent.
29:30 who is to enter the *m* tent to minister
29:32 At the entrance of the *m* tent Aaron and
29:42 the LORD at the entrance of the *m* tent,
29:44 I will consecrate the *m* tent and the altar,
30:16 donate it to the service of the *m* tent,
30:18 Place it between the *m* tent and the altar,
30:20 When they are about to enter the *m* tent,
30:26 the *m* tent and the ark of the commandments,
30:36 in the *m* tent where I will meet you.
31: 7 *m* tent, the ark of the commandments
33: 7 The tent, which was called the *m* tent,
33: 7 would go to this *m* tent outside the camp.
35:21 LORD for the construction of the *m* tent,
38: 8 who served at the entrance of the *m* tent.
38:30 pedestals at the entrance of the *m* tent,
39:32 the Dwelling of the *m* tent was completed.
39:40 the service of the Dwelling of the *m* tent;
40: 2 you shall erect the Dwelling of the *m* tent.
40: 6 the entrance of the Dwelling of the *m* tent.
40: 7 the laver between the *m* tent and the altar,
40:12 and his sons to the entrance of the *m* tent,
40:22 He put the table in the *m* tent,
40:24 He placed the lampstand in the *m* tent,
40:26 He placed the golden altar in the *m* tent,
40:29 the entrance of the Dwelling of the *m* tent,
40:30 the laver between the *m* tent and altar,
40:32 into the *m* tent or approached the altar,
40:34 Then the cloud covered the *m* tent,
40:35 Moses could not enter the *m* tent,
Lv 1: 1 and from the *m* tent gave him this message:
1: 3 shall bring it to the entrance of the *m* tent
1: 5 which is at the entrance of the *m* tent.
3: 2 slaughter it at the entrance of the *m* tent;
3: 8 he shall slaughter it before the *m* tent;
3:13 he shall slaughter it before the *m* tent;
4: 4 the bullock to the entrance of the *m* tent,
4: 5 blood and bring it into the *m* tent,
4: 7 which is before the LORD in the *m* tent.
4: 7 which is at the entrance of the *m* tent.
4:14 They shall bring it before the *m* tent,
4:16 bring some of its blood into the *m* tent,
4:18 which is before the LORD in the *m* tent.
4:18 which is at the entrance of the *m* tent.
6: 9 the court of the *m* tent they shall eat it.
6:19 a sacred place, in the court of the *m* tent.
6:23 *m* tent to make atonement in the sanctuary;
8: 3 community at the entrance of the *m* tent."
8: 4 assembled at the entrance of the *m* tent,
8:31 the flesh at the entrance of the *m* tent,
8:33 the entrance of the *m* tent for seven days,
8:35 of the *m* tent day and night for seven days,
9:23 Moses and Aaron went into the *m* tent.
10: 7 not you go beyond the entry of the *m* tent,
10: 9 Aaron, "When you are to go to the *m* tent,
12: 6 entrance of the *m* tent a yearling lamb
14:11 the LORD at the entrance of the *m* tent.
14:23 the entrance of the *m* tent before the LORD.
15:14 the LORD, to the entrance of the *m* tent,
15:29 the priest at the entrance of the *m* tent.
16: 7 the LORD at the entrance of the *m* tent,
16:16 He shall do the same for the *m* tent,
16:17 No one else may be in the *m* tent from the
16:20 the sanctuary, the *m* tent and the altar,
16:23 Aaron has again gone into the *m* tent,
16:33 sacred sanctuary, the *m* tent and the altar,
17: 4 bringing it to the entrance of the *m* tent
17: 5 to the priest at the entrance of the *m* tent
17: 6 entrance of the *m* tent and there burn the fat
17: 9 of the *m* tent to offer it to the LORD,
19:21 entrance of the *m* tent a ram as his guilt
24: 3 In the *m* tent, outside the veil that hangs
Nm 1: 1 Moses in the *m* tent in the desert of Sinai:
2: 2 They shall camp around the *m* tent,
2:17 "Then the *m* tent and the camp of the
3: 7 the *m* tent by serving at the Dwelling.
3: 8 custody of all the furnishings of the *m* tent
3:25 At the *m* tent they had charge of whatever
3:25 the curtain at the entrance of the *m* tent,
3:38 Dwelling, that is, in front of the *m* tent,
4: 3 undertake obligatory tasks in the *m* tent.
4: 4 *m* tent concerns the most sacred objects.
4:15 the *m* tent that the Kohathites shall carry.
4:23 undertake obligatory tasks in the *m* tent.
4:25 the *m* tent with its covering and the outer
4:25 the curtain at the entrance of the *m* tent,
4:28 the task of the Gershonites in the *m* tent;
4:30 undertake obligatory tasks in the *m* tent.
4:31 the years of their service in the *m* tent:
4:33 *m* tent under the supervision of Ithamar,
4:35 undertake obligatory tasks in the *m* tent,
4:37 clans who were to serve in the *m* tent,
4:39 undertake obligatory tasks in the *m* tent,
4:41 clans who were to serve in the *m* tent,
4:43 undertake obligatory tasks in the *m* tent,
4:47 of service or transport of the *m* tent,
6:10 the priest at the entrance of the *m* tent.
6:13 he shall go to the entrance of the *m* tent,
6:18 Then at the entrance of the *m* tent the
7: 5 be put to use in the service of the *m* tent.
7:89 Moses entered the *m* tent to speak with him,
8: 9 come forward in front of the *m* tent,
8:15 enter upon their service in the *m* tent.
8:19 the *m* tent and to make atonement for them,
8:22 they enter upon their service in the *m* tent
8:24 perform the required service in the *m* tent.
8:26 their responsibilities in the *m* tent,
10: 3 round you at the entrance of the *m* tent;
11:16 the people, and bring them to the *m* tent.
12: 4 "Come out, you three, to the *m* tent."
14:10 at the *m* tent to all the Israelites.
16:18 of the *m* tent along with Moses and Aaron.
16:19 against them at the entrance of the *m* tent,
17: 7 Moses and Aaron turned toward the *m* tent,
17: 8 and Aaron came to the front of the *m* tent,
17:15 to Moses at the entrance of the *m* tent.
17:19 Then lay them down in the *m* tent,
18: 4 of all the work connected with the *m* tent.
18: 6 to the LORD for the service of the *m* tent.
18:21 for the service they perform in the *m* tent.
18:22 may no longer approach the *m* tent;
18:23 are to perform the service of the *m* tent,
18:31 your recompense for service at the *m* tent.
19: 4 seven times toward the front of the *m* tent.
20: 6 the assembly to the entrance of the *m* tent,
23:15 holocaust, while I seek a *m* over there."
25: 6 were weeping at the entrance of the *m* tent.
27: 2 community at the entrance of the *m* tent,
29:35 the eighth day you shall hold a solemn *m*,
31:54 and put it in the *m* tent as a memorial for
Dt 16: 8 shall be a solemn *m* in honor of the LORD,
31:14 *m* tent that I may give him his commission."
31:14 and presented themselves at the *m* tent.
Jos 18: 1 at Shiloh, where they set up the *m* tent.
19:51 LORD, at the door of the *m* tent in Shiloh.
1Sm 2:22 women serving at the entry of the *m* tent].
21: 3 I have arranged a *m* place with my men.
1Kgs 8: 4 carried the ark of the LORD and the *m* tent
1Chr 6:17 singers before the Dwelling of the *m* tent
9:21 guarded the gate of the *m* tent.
23:32 prescribed for them concerning the *m* tent,
2Chr 1: 3 place at Gibeon, because the *m* tent of God,
1: 6 presence on the bronze altar at the *m* tent;
1:13 the high place at Gibeon, from the *m* tent,
5: 5 and they carried the ark and the *m* tent
7: 9 On the eighth day they held a special *m*,
2Mc 5:14 lost, forty thousand *m* a violent death,
8:14 Nicanor had sold before even *m* them.
13:13 After a private *m* with the elders,
Sir 6:12 low, he turns against you and avoids *m* you.
Jn 11:47 the Pharisees called a *m* of the Sanhedrin.
Acts 7:44 "Our fathers in the desert had the *m* tent
19:25 He called a *m* of these men and other
19:40 These words of his broke up the *m*.
22:30 priests and the whole Sanhedrin to a *m*;
1Cor 11:18 for a *m* there are divisions among you,

MEETINGS (1)

1Cor 11:17 your *m* are not profitable but harmful.

MEETS (12)

Gn 32:18 "When my brother Esau *m* you,
Jos 15: 6 from the bay where the Jordan *m* the sea,
1Sm 16:22 in my service, for he *m* with my approval."
24:20 For if a man *m* his enemy,
Prv 14: 7 But knowing lips one *m* with by surprise.
Wis 6:16 the ways, and *m* them with all solicitude.
Jer 51:31 One runner meets another, herald *m* herald,
Rom 16: 5 to the congregation that *m* in their house.
1Cor 16:19 with the assembly that *m* in their house,
Col 4:15 and the assembly that *m* at his house.
Phlm 1: 2 and to the church that *m* in your house.

MEGIDDO (12)

Jos 12:21 Hazor, Shimron, Achshaph, Taanach, *M*,
17:11 and *M* and its towns and natives [the third
Jgs 1:27 and its towns, or those of *M* and its towns.
5:19 of Canaan, At Taanach by the waters of *M*;
1Kgs 4:12 Baana, son of Ahilud, in Taanach and *M*,
9:15 Millo, the wall of Jerusalem, Hazor, *M*,
2Kgs 9:27 his flight as far as *M* and died there.
23:29 but was slain at *M* at the first encounter.
23:30 his body on a chariot from *M* to Jerusalem,
1Chr 7:29 Taanach and its towns, *M* and its towns,
2Chr 35:22 but went out to fight in the plain of *M*.
Zec 12:11 mourning of Hadadrimmon in the plain of *M*.

MEHALLALEL (1)

Neh 11: 4 of Amariah, son of Shephatiah, son of *M*,

MEHETABEL (3)

Gn 36:39 (His wife's name was *M*;
1Chr 1:50 city was Pai, and his wife's name was *M*.
Neh 6:10 of Shemaiah, son of Delaiah, son of *M*,

MEHIDA (2)

Ezr 2:52 of Harhur, sons of Bazluth, sons of *M*,
Neh 7:54 of Harur, sons of Bazlith, sons of *M*,

MEHIR (1)

1Chr 4:11 brother of Shuhah, became the father of *M*,

MEHOLATHITE (2)

1Sm 18:19 given in marriage to Adriel the *M* instead.]
2Sm 21: 8 borne to Adriel, son of Barzillai the *M*,

MEHUJAEL (2)

Gn 4:18 Irad, and Irad became the father of *M*;
4:18 *M* became the father of Methusael,

MEHUMAN (1)

Est 1:10 king was merry with wine, he instructed *M*,

MELANCHOLY (1)

Lk 18:23 On hearing this he grew *m*,

MELATIAH (1)

Neh 3: 7 At their side were *M* the Gibeonite,

MELCHI (2)

Lk 3:24 son of Matthat, son of Levi, son of *M*,
3:28 son of Shealtiel, son of Neri, son of *M*,

MELCHIEL (1)

Jdt 6:15 son of Gothoniel, and Charmis, son of *M*.

MELCHIZEDEK (12)

Gn 14:18 *M*, king of Salem,
Ps(s) 110: 4 forever, according to the order of *M*."
Heb 5: 6 forever, according to the order of *M*."
5:10 as high priest according to the order of *M*.
6:20 priest forever according to the order of *M*.
7: 1 This *M*, king of Salem
7: 6 *M*, who was not of their ancestry
7:10 in his father's loins when *M* met Abraham.
7:11 a priest according to the order of *M*,
7:15 appointed according to the likeness of *M*:
7:17 priest forever according to the order of *M*."
7:21 forever, according to the order of *M*.'"

MELEA (1)

Lk 3:31 son of Jonam, son of Eliakim, son of *M*,

MELECH (2)

1Chr 8:35 The sons of Micah were Pithon, *M*,
9:41 The sons of Micah were Pithon, *M*,

MELLOWED (1)

Sg 7:14 Both fresh and *m* fruits,

MELODIES (1)

Am 5:23 I will not listen to the *m* of your harps.

MELODIOUS (3)

Ps(s) 98: 5 with the harp, with the harp and *m* song.
Wis 17:18 or the *m* song of birds in the spreading
Sir 44: 5 Composers of *m* psalms,

MELODY (6)

Ps(s) 81: 3 Take up a *m*, and sound the timbrel,
92: 4 instrument and lyre, with *m* upon the harp.
Wis 19:18 like strings of the harp, produce new *m*,
Sir 40:21 The flute and the harp offer sweet *m*,
47: 9 providing sweet *m* for the psalms So that
Rv 14: 2 the *m* of harpists playing on their harps.

MELON (1)

Is 1: 8 in a vineyard, Like a shed in a *m* patch,

MELONS (1)

Nm 11: 5 cost in Egypt, and the cucumbers, the *m,*

MELT (9)

2Kgs 12:11 and they would *m* down all the funds that
Jdt 16:15 the rocks, like wax, *m* before your glance.
Ps(s) 97: 5 The mountains *m* like wax before the LORD,
Sir 3:15 warmth upon frost it will *m* away your sins.
Is 19: 1 the hearts of the Egyptians *m* within them.
Ez 24:11 glows red hot, till the impurities in it *m,*
Am 9: 5 GOD of hosts, I *m* the earth with my touch,
Mi 1: 4 *m* under him and the valleys split open,
2Pt 3:12 and the elements will *m* away in a blaze.

MELTED (10)

Ex 15:15 All the dwellers in Canaan *m* away;
16:21 when the sun grew hot, the manna *m* away.
Jos 7: 5 confidence of the people *m* away like water.
Jgs 15:14 fire and his bonds *m* away from his hands.
Jb 28: 2 the earth, and copper is *m* out of stone.
Ps(s) 107:26 their hearts *m* away in their plight.
Wis 16:22 and ice withstood fire and were not *m,*
16:27 merely warmed by a momentary sunbeam, *m;*
19:21 that went about in them, nor *m* the icelike,
Sir 48:19 The people's hearts *m* within them,

MELTING (4)

1Mc 9: 7 *m* away just when the battle was imminent,
Ps(s) 22:15 has become like wax *m* away within my bosom.
58: 9 Let them dissolve like a *m* snail,
Na 2:11 *m* hearts and trembling knees,

MELTS (7)

Ps(s) 46: 7 his voice resounds, the earth *m* away,
68: 3 as wax *m* before the fire,
147:18 He sends his word and *m* them;
Wis 16:29 For the hope of the ingrate *m* like a
Is 8: 6 And *m* with fear before the loftiness of
13: 7 Every man's heart *m* in terror;
14:31 Philistia, all of you *m* away!

MEMBER (22)

Neh 3: 8 of Harhaiah, a *m* of the goldsmiths' guild,
3:31 Malchijah, a *m* of the goldsmiths' guild,
2Mc 1:10 *m* of the family of the anointed priests,
Mt 10: 4 Simon the Zealot Party *m,*
Mk 15:43 a distinguished *m* of the Sanhedrin.
Lk 22: 3 the one called Iscariot, a *m* of the Twelve.
23:50 an upright and holy *m* of the Sanhedrin,
Jn 3: 1 Nicodemus, a *m* of the Jewish Sanhedrin,
Acts 1:13 Simon, the Zealot party *m,*
5:34 Then a *m* of the Sanhedrin stood up,
17:34 a *m* of the court of the Areopagus,
1Cor 6: 5 between one *m* of the church and another?
12:14 Now the body is not one *m,* it is many.
12:18 God has set each *m* of the body in the
12:26 If one *m* suffers, all the members suffer
12:26 if one *m* is honored,
12:27 Every one of you is a *m* of it.
Phil 4:21 in Christ Jesus to every *m* of the church.
1Thes 4: 4 you guarding his *m* in sanctity and honor,
1Tm 3:15 of conduct befits a *m* of God's household,
5:16 church *m* has relatives who are widows,
Jas 3: 5 It is a small *m,* yet it makes great

MEMBERS (56)

Gn 17:23 male among the *m* of Abraham's household
17:27 and all the male *m* of his household,
36: 6 daughters, and all the *m* of his household,
50: 7 officials who were senior *m* of his court
Nm 16: 2 *m* of the council and men of note.
18: 1 *m* of your ancestral house shall be responsible
2Sm 7:18 Lord GOD, and who are the *m* of my house,
1Chr 5:23 The numerous *m* of the half-tribe of
Jer 12: 6 own brothers, the *m* of your father's house,
20: 6 *m* of your household shall go into exile.
Ez 23:20 of Egypt, whose *m* are like that of an ass,
Mt 10:25 how much more the *m* of his household!
Acts 6: 9 Certain *m* of the so-called "Synagogue of
6:15 The *m* of the Sanhedrin who sat there
8: 4 The *m* of the church who had been dispersed
12: 1 to harass some of the *m* of the church.
17:11 Its *m* were better disposed than those in
Rom 6:13 *m* of your body to sin as weapons for evil.
7: 5 in our *m* and we bore fruit for death.
7:23 but I see in my body's *m* another law at
7:23 me the prisoner of the law of sin in my *m.*
12: 4 as each of us has one body with many *m,*
12: 4 and not all the *m* have the same function,
12: 5 Christ and individually *m* one of another.
16:11 to the *m* of the household of Narcissus
1Cor 1:11 by certain *m* of Chloe's household that you
6:15 not see that your bodies are *m* of Christ?
6:15 Would you have me take Christ's *m* and make
6:15 and make them the *m* of a prostitute?
12:12 The body is one and has many *m,*
12:12 but all the *m,* many though they are
12:19 If all the *m* were alike,
12:20 There are, indeed, many different *m,*
12:22 Even those *m* of the body which seem less
12:23 We honor the *m* we consider less honorable
12:24 as to give greater honor to the lowly *m,*
12:25 all the *m* may be concerned for one another.
12:26 member suffers, all the *m* suffer with it;
12:26 member is honored, all the *m* share its joy.
2Cor 8: 4 sharing in this service to *m* of the church.
9: 1 this collection for the *m* of the church.
9:12 supplies the needs of the *m* of the church
Eph 1:15 and your love for all the *m* of the church,
1:18 be distributed among the *m* of the church,
2:19 the saints and *m* of the household of God.
3: 6 *m* of the same body and sharers of the
4:16 proper functioning of the *m* joined firmly
4:25 his neighbor, for we are *m* of one another.
5:30 for we are *m* of his body.
Col 3:15 since as *m* of the one body you have been
1Tm 5: 8 especially for *m* of his immediate family,
Heb 7:13 of whose *m* ever officiated at the altar.
Jas 3: 6 among our *m* as a whole universe of malice.
4: 1 inner cravings that make war within your *m?*
Rv 2: 9 nothing other than *m* of Satan's assembly.
13: 6 the *m* of his heavenly household as well.

MEMBRANE (6)

Lv 3: 3 the LORD the fatty *m* over the inner organs,
3: 9 spine, the fatty *m* over the inner organs,
3:14 the LORD the fatty *m* over the inner organs,
4: 8 the fatty *m* over the inner organs,
7: 3 tail, the fatty *m* over the inner organs,
9:19 tail, the fatty *m* over the inner organs,

MEMMIUS (1)

2Mc 11:34 "Quintus *M* and Titus Manius,

MEMOIRS (1)

2Mc 2:13 Nehemiah's *M* how he collected the books

MEMORABLE (2)

Est E:22 you too must celebrate this *m* day among
Ps(s) 45:18 make your name *m* through all generations;

MEMORANDUM (1)

Ezr 6: 2 the following text: "*M.*

MEMORIAL (23)

Gn 28:18 put under his head, set it up as a *m* stone,
28:22 set up as a *m* stone shall be God's abode.
31:13 anointed a *m* stone and made a vow to me.
31:45 took a stone and set it up as a *m* stone.
31:51 and here is the *m* stone that I have set up
31:52 witness, and this *m* stone shall be witness,
33:20 He set up a *m* stone there and invoked "El,
35:14 spoken with him, Jacob set up a *m* stone,
35:20 Jacob set up a *m* stone on her grave,
50:10 there a very great and solemn *m* service;
Ex 12:14 "This day shall be a *m* feast for you,
28:12 ephod as *m* stones of the sons of Israel.
39: 7 ephod as *m* stones of the sons of Israel,
Nm 31:54 as a *m* for the Israelites before the LORD.
Jos 4: 7 serve as a perpetual *m* to the Israelites."
Jgs 9: 6 the terebinth at the *m* pillar in Shechem.
Neh 2:20 neither share nor claim nor *m* in Jerusalem."
1Mc 13:29 he carved suits of armor as a perpetual *m,*
Wis 10: 8 then they left mankind a *m* of their folly
Sir 45:16 To burn sacrifices of sweet odor for a *m,*
Jer 48: 9 Set up a *m* for Moab,
Zec 6:14 The crown itself shall be a *m* offering in
Mt 26:13 what she did will be spoken of as her *m.*"

MEMORIES (1)

Dt 32:26 them and blot out their name from men's *m,*'

MEMORY (30)

Ex 17:14 out the *m* of Amalek from under the heavens."
Dt 4: 9 them slip from your *m* as long as you live,
25:19 out the *m* of Amalek from under the heavens.
1Mc 3: 7 by his deeds, and his *m* is blessed forever.
3:35 Jerusalem and efface their *m* from the land.
12:53 them and wipe out their *m* from among men."
2Mc 2:25 studious who wish to commit things to *m,*
Jb 18:17 His *m* perishes from the land,
Ps(s) 109:15 the *m* of these parents from the earth,
Prv 10: 7 The *m* of the just will be blessed,
Eccl 9: 5 for them, because all *m* of them is lost.
Wis 4: 1 for immortal is its *m:*
4:19 shall be in grief and their *m* shall perish.
5:14 *m* of the nomad camping for a single day.
8:13 leave to those after me an everlasting *m.*
Sir 10:17 and effaces the *m* of them from the earth.
23:26 She will leave an accursed *m;*
38:23 With the departed dead, let *m* fade;
39: 9 Unfading will be his *m,*
44: 9 But of others there is no *m,*
45: 1 men, MOSES, whose *m* is held in benediction.
46:11 may their *m* be ever blessed,
49: 1 Precious is his *m,*
49:13 Extolled be the *m* of NEHEMIAH!
Is 26:14 them, and wiped out all *m* of them.
Ez 14: 3 the *m* of their idols fresh in their hearts,
14: 4 holding the *m* of his idols in his heart
14: 7 and holds the *m* of his idols in his heart
Mk 14: 9 what she has done will be told in her *m.*"
Lk 2:51 meanwhile kept all these things in *m.*

MEMPHIS (9)

Jdt 1:10 the land of Goshen, Tanis, *M* and beyond,
Is 19:13 fools, the princes of *M* have been deceived.
Jer 2:16 the people of *M* and Tahpanhes shave the
44: 1 in Egypt, at Migdol, Tahpanhes, and *M,*
46:14 in Migdol, proclaim it in *M* and Tahpanhes!
46:19 *M* shall become a desert,
Ez 30:13 of *M* and the princes of the land of Egypt,
30:15 stronghold, and cut down the crowds in *M.*
Hos 9: 6 shall gather them in, *M* shall bury them.

MEMUCAN (3)

Est 1:14 Admatha, Tarshish, Meres, Marsena and *M,*
1:16 the king and of the officials, *M* answered:
1:21 and the king acted on the advice of *M.*

MEN (1700)

Gn 4:26 time *m* began to invoke the LORD by name.
6: 1 When *m* began to multiply on earth and
6: 4 were the heroes of old, the *m* of renown.
6: 7 from the earth the *m* whom I have created,
6: 7 whom I have created, and not only the *m,*
11: 2 While *m* were migrating in the east,
11: 5 city and the tower that the *m* had built.
12:20 Then Pharaoh gave *m* orders concerning him,
14:24 share that is due to the *m* who joined me
18: 2 Looking up, he saw three *m* standing nearby.
18:16 The *m* set out from there and looked down
18:22 the two *m* walked on farther toward Sodom,
19: 5 are the *m* who came to your house tonight?
19: 8 who have never had intercourse with *m.*
19: 8 But don't do anything to these *m,*
19:11 struck the *m* at the entrance of the house,
19:16 When he hesitated, the *m,*
20: 8 had happened, and the *m* were horrified.
21:25 that Abimelech's *m* had seized by force.
23:12 addressed Ephron in the hearing of these *m:*
24:32 and the feet of the *m* who were with him.
24:54 he and the *m* with him had eaten and drunk,
24:59 along with Abraham's servant and his *m.*
26: 7 When the *m* of the place asked questions
26: 7 the *m* of the place would kill him on
26:10 for one of the *m* to lie with your wife,
26:11 therefore gave this warning to all his *m:*
32: 7 to meet you, accompanied by four hundred *m.*
33: 1 Esau coming, accompanied by four hundred *m.*
33:15 disposal some of the *m* who are with me."
34: 7 the *m* were shocked and seethed with
34:21 "These *m* are friendly toward us.
34:22 But the *m* will agree to live with us and
34:24 All the able-bodied *m* of the town agreed
34:30 I have so few *m* that,
38:21 So he asked the *m* of the place,
38:22 the *m* of the place said there was no
42:11 We are honest *m;* your servants have never
42:31 'We are honest *m:* we have never been spies.'
42:33 is how I shall know if you are honest *m:*
42:34 I know that you are honest *m* and not spies,
43:15 So the *m* got the gifts,
43:16 steward, "Take these *m* into the house,
43:17 steward conducted the *m* to Joseph's house.
43:24 then brought the *m* inside Joseph's house.
44: 3 the *m* and their donkeys were sent off.
44: 4 "Go at once after the *m!*
46:32 The *m* are shepherds,
49: 6 For in their fury they slew *m,*
Ex 4:19 all the *m* who sought your life are dead."
5: 9 Increase the work for the *m,*
7:11 in turn, summoned wise *m* and sorcerers,
10: 7 Let the *m* go to worship the LORD,
10:11 Just you *m* can go and worship the LORD.
10:23 *M* could not see one another,
12:37 about six hundred thousand *m* on foot,
17: 9 said to Joshua, "Pick out certain *m,*
18:21 God-fearing men, trustworthy *m* who hate
18:22 Let these *m* render decisions for the
18:25 He picked out able *m* from all Israel and
21:18 "When *m* quarrel and one strikes the other
21:22 *m* have a fight and hurt a pregnant woman,
22:30 "You shall be *m* sacred to me.
23: 6 needy fellow *m* his rights in his lawsuit.
23:17 all your *m* appear before the Lord GOD.
24: 5 having sent certain young *m* of the
34:23 all your *m* shall appear before the Lord,
35:22 Both the *m* and the women,
36: 2 *m* whose hearts moved them to come and take
38:26 three thousand five hundred and fifty *m.*
Lv 5: 4 such as *m* are accustomed to utter rashly,
5:22 the sinful oaths that *m* make in such cases,
11:32 Any such article that *m* use,
11:34 with water, and any liquid that *m* drink,
19:15 the mighty, but judge your fellow *m* justly.

Nm 1: 3 Aaron shall enroll in companies all the *m*
1:17 Aaron took these *m* who had been designated,
4: 2 all the *m* of the Kohathites between thirty
4:23 *m* between thirty and fifty years of age;
4:30 *m* between thirty and fifty years of age;
4:35 *m* between thirty and fifty years of age.
4:37 Such was the census of all the *m* of the
4:39 *m* between thirty and fifty years of age.
4:41 Such was the census of all the *m* of the
4:43 the *m* from thirty up to fifty years of age.
4:45 *m* of the Merarite clans which Moses took,
4:47 of all the *m* between thirty and fifty
9: 6 These *m* came up to Moses and Aaron that
11:16 *m* you know for true elders and authorities
11:26 Now two *m*, one named Eldad
13: 2 "Send *m* to reconnoiter the land of Canaan,
13:16 These are the names of the *m* whom Moses
13:31 But the *m* who had gone up with him said,
13:32 all the people we saw there are huge *m*,
14:22 of all the *m* who have seen my glory and
14:29 Of all your *m* of twenty years or more,
14:36 so it happened to the *m* whom Moses had
14:37 these *m* who had given out the bad report
14:38 the *m* who had gone to reconnoiter the land,
16: 2 members of the council and *m* of note.
16:26 *m* and do not touch anything that is theirs:
16:29 if these *m* die an ordinary death,
16:30 know that these *m* have defied the LORD.
16:32 all of Korah's *m* and all their possessions.
16:35 and fifty *m* who were offering the incense.
20:14 *m* to the king of Edom with the message:
21:21 Now Israel sent *m* to Sihon,
22: 9 and said, "Who are these *m* visiting you?"
22:20 him, "If these *m* have come to summon you,
22:35 the LORD said to Balaam, "Go with the *m*;
25: 5 "Each of you shall kill those of his *m*
26: 7 seven hundred and thirty *m* were registered.
26:10 the fire consumed two hundred and fifty *m*.
26:14 thousand two hundred *m* were registered.
26:18 thousand five hundred *m* were registered.
26:22 thousand five hundred *m* were registered.
26:25 thousand three hundred *m* were registered.
26:27 thousand five hundred *m* were registered.
26:34 thousand seven hundred *m* were registered.
26:37 thousand five hundred *m* were registered.
26:41 thousand six hundred *m* were registered.
26:43 thousand four hundred *m* were registered.
26:47 thousand four hundred *m* were registered.
26:50 thousand four hundred *m* were registered.
26:54 to the number of *m* registered in it.
26:63 were the *m* registered by Moses and the
31: 3 *m* from your midst and arm them for war,
31: 4 shall send a band of one thousand *m* to war."
31: 5 a thousand *m* of each tribe were levied,
31: 5 there were twelve thousand *m* armed for war.
32:11 none of these *m* of twenty years or more
34:17 *m* who shall apportion the land among you:
Dt 1:13 and experienced *m* from each of your tribes,
1:15 So I took outstanding *m* of your tribes,
1:22 'Let us send *m* ahead to reconnoiter the
1:23 I chose twelve *m* from your number,
2:34 cities and doomed them all, with their *m*,
3: 6 we doomed all the cities, with their *m*,
20:19 After all, are the trees of the field *m*,
23:18 a temple prostitute among the Israelite *m*.
25: 1 *m* have a dispute and bring it to court,
25:11 "When two *m* are fighting and the wife of
27:14 proclaim aloud to all the *m* of Israel:
29: 9 and officials, and all of the *m* of Israel,
31:12 Assemble the people *m*,
32:30 or two *m* put ten thousand to flight,
33: 6 live and not die out, but let his *m* be few."
Jos 2: 4 woman had taken the two *m* and hidden them,
2: 4 "True, the *m* you speak of came to me,
2:14 our lives for yours," the *m* answered her.
2:17 The *m* answered her,
3:12 [Now choose twelve *m*,
4: 2 Joshua, "Choose twelve *m* from the people,
4: 4 Summoning the twelve *m* whom he had
5: 5 all the *m* who came out were circumcised,
6:21 *m* and women, young and old,
6:22 the two *m* who had spied out the land,
7: 2 Joshua next sent *m* from Jericho to Ai,
8:12 [He took about five thousand *m* and set
8:19 so, the *m* in ambush rose from their post,
8:20 By the time the *m* of Ai looked back,
8:21 in smoke, they struck back at the *m* of Ai.
8:22 the *m* of Ai were hemmed in by Israelites
8:25 day a total of twelve thousand *m* and women,
9: 6 they said to him and to the *m* of Israel,
9: 7 But the *m* of Israel replied to the Hivites,
10: 2 the city of Ai, and all its *m* were brave.
10: 6 the *m* of Gibeon sent an appeal to Joshua
10:18 the cave and post *m* over it to guard them.
10:24 Joshua summoned all the *m* of Israel and
18: 4 Choose three *m* from each of your tribes;
23:14 as you see, I am going the way of all *m*.
24:11 the *m* of Jericho fought against you,
Jgs 3:29 Moabites, all of them strong and valiant *m*.
4:10 to Kedesh, and ten thousand *m* followed him.
4:14 Tabor, followed by his ten thousand *m*.
5:11 where *m* recount the just deeds of the LORD,
7: 8 their tents, but kept the three hundred *m*.
7:16 the three hundred *m* into three companies,
7:19 So Gideon and the hundred *m* who were with
7:22 the three hundred *m* kept blowing the horns,
8: 4 and crossed it with his three hundred *m*,
8: 5 So he said to the *m* of Succoth,
8: 8 but the *m* of Penuel answered him as had
8: 8 answered him as had the *m* of Succoth.
8: 9 So to the *m* of Penuel,
8:10 their force of about fifteen thousand *m*;
8:15 So he went to the *m* of Succoth and said,
8:16 and ground these *m* of Succoth into them.
8:17 tower of Penuel and slew the *m* of the city.
8:18 "Where now are the *m* you killed at Tabor?"
9: 2 seventy *m*, or all Jerubbaal's sons,
9: 4 shiftless *m* and ruffians as his followers.
9: 9 rich oil, whereby *m* and gods are honored,
9:13 I give up my wine that cheers gods and *m*,
9:25 *m* in ambush for him on the mountaintops,
9:28 Zebul once subject to the *m* of Hamor,
9:32 the fields, you and the *m* who are with you.
9:36 are *m* coming down from the hilltops!"
9:36 "You see the shadow of the hills as *m*."
9:37 *M* are coming down from the region of
9:38 not the *m* for whom you expressed contempt?
9:43 divided the *m* he had into three companies,
9:48 his shoulder, then said to the *m* with him,
9:49 So all the *m* likewise cut down brushwood,
9:49 about a thousand *m* and women,
9:51 of the city, and all the *m* and women,
11:21 and all his *m* into the power of Israel,
12: 1 The *m* of Ephraim gathered together and
12: 4 the *m* of Gilead and fought against Ephraim,
12: 5 pass," the *m* of Gilead would say to him,
14:10 was customary for the young *m* to do this.
14:11 they brought thirty *m* to be his companions.
14:18 the sun set, the *m* of the city said to him,
14:19 thirty of their *m* and despoiled them;
15:10 When the *m* of Judah asked,
15:11 Three thousand *m* of Judah went down to the
15:15 it, and with it killed a thousand *m*.
15:16 of an ass I have slain a thousand *m*."
16: 2 the *m* of Gaza surrounded him with an
16: 9 She had *m* lying in wait in the chamber and
16:12 there were *m* lying in wait in the chamber.
16:27 The temple was full of *m* and women:
16:27 from the roof about three thousand *m*
18: 2 of five valiant *m* of Zorah and Eshtaol,
18: 7 So the five *m* went on and came to Laish.
18:11 six hundred *m* of the clan of the Danites,
18:14 The five *m* who had gone to reconnoiter the
18:16 The six hundred *m* girt with weapons of war,
18:17 Meanwhile the five *m* who had gone to
18:25 lest fierce *m* fall upon you and you and
19: 6 and the two *m* ate and drank together.
19:22 enjoying themselves, the *m* of the city,
19:25 When the *m* would not listen to his host,
20:10 tribes of Israel ten *m* for every hundred,
20:11 all the *m* of Israel without exception were
20:12 *m* throughout the tribe of Benjamin to say,
20:13 Now give up these corrupt *m* of Gibeah,
20:16 hundred picked *m* who were left-handed,
20:21 and felled twenty-two thousand *m* of Israel.
20:29 So Israel set *m* in ambush around Gibeah.
20:33 all the *m* of Israel rose from their places.
20:34 ten thousand picked *m* from all Israel,
20:35 thousand one hundred *m* of Benjamin,
20:36 the *m* of Israel gave ground to Benjamin,
20:37 *m* in ambush made a sudden dash into Gibeah,
20:38 Israelites had agreed with the *m* in ambush
20:39 And though the *m* of Benjamin had begun by
20:39 killing off some thirty of the *m* of Israel,
20:41 the sky that the *m* of Israel wheeled about.
20:41 *m* of Benjamin were thrown into confusion,
20:42 *m* of Israel in the direction of the desert,
20:43 The *m* of Benjamin had been surrounded,
20:45 picked off five thousand *m* among them,
20:48 The *m* of Israel withdrew through the
21: 1 Now the *m* of Israel had sworn at Mizpah
21: 8 they found that none of the *m* of
21:12 virgins, who had had no relations with *m*,
Ru 2: 9 commanded the young *m* to do you no harm.
2: 9 from the vessels the young *m* have filled."
3:10 than before in not going after the young *m*,
3:14 rose before *m* could recognize one another.
1Sm 2:17 Thus the young *m* sinned grievously in the
2:26 in the estimation of the LORD and of *m*.
2:33 *m* of your family shall die by the sword.
4: 2 about four thousand *m* on the battlefield.
4:14 the outcry of the *m* standing near him,
5: 7 how matters stood, the *m* of Ashdod decided,
5: 8 The *m* of Gath replied,
6:15 The *m* of Beth-shemesh also offered other
6:20 The *m* of Beth-shemesh asked,
8:22 Samuel thereupon said to the *m* of Israel,
10: 2 you will meet two *m* near Rachel's tomb at
10: 3 met by three *m* going up to God at Bethel;
10:27 But certain worthless *m* said,
11: 1 All the *m* of Jabesh begged Nahash,
11:12 over the *m* and we will put them to death."
13: 2 Saul chose three thousand *m* of Israel,
13: 8 Gilgal, the *m* began to slip away from Saul.
13:11 saw that the *m* were slipping away from me,
14: 2 with him numbered about six hundred *m*.
14: 8 over to those *m* and show ourselves to them.
14:12 The *m* of the outpost called to Jonathan
14:14 slew about twenty *m* within half a furlong.
14:20 his *m* shouted and rushed into the fight,
15: 3 Do not spare him, but kill *m* and women,
15: 4 foot soldiers and ten thousand *m* of Judah.
15:15 The *m* spared the best sheep and oxen to
15:21 from the spoil the *m* took sheep and oxen,
17: 8 Choose one of your *m*,
17:11 Saul and all the *m* of Israel,
17:26 David now said to the *m* standing by:
17:28 brother, heard him speaking with the *m*,
17:52 Then the *m* of Israel and Judah,
18:27 his *m* and slew two hundred Philistines.
21: 3 I have arranged a meeting place with my *m*.
21: 5 if the *m* have abstained from women,
21: 6 a journey, all the young *m* are consecrated
22: 2 About four hundred *m* were with him.
22: 6 that David and his *m* had been located.
22: 7 "Listen, *m* of Benjamin!
22: 7 an officer over a thousand or a hundred *m*,
22:19 of Nob to the sword, including *m* and women,
23: 3 But David's *m* said to him:
23: 5 David then went with his *m* to Keilah and
23: 8 down to Keilah and besiege David and his *m*.
23:12 deliver me and my *m* into the grasp of Saul?"
23:13 So David and his *m*,
23:24 and his *m* were in the desert below Maon,
23:25 When Saul and his *m* came looking for him,
23:26 gorge, David and his *m* took to the other.
23:26 and Saul and his *m* were attempting to
23:26 David and his *m* in order to capture them,
24: 3 So Saul took three thousand picked *m* from
24: 3 *m* in the direction of the wild goat crags.
24: 4 David and his *m* were occupying the inmost
24: 7 He said to his *m*, "The LORD forbid
24: 8 *m* and would not permit them to attack Saul.
24:23 David and his *m* went up to the refuge.
25: 5 shearing his flock, he sent ten young *m*,
25: 8 Look kindly on these young *m*,
25: 9 When David's young *m* arrived,
25:11 them to *m* who come from I know not where
25:12 So David's young *m* retraced their steps
25:13 Thereupon David said to his *m*,
25:13 About four hundred *m* went up after David,
25:15 Yet these *m* were very good to us.
25:20 David and his *m* were also coming down from
25:25 did not see the young *m* whom my lord sent.
25:27 be given to the young *m* who follow my lord.
26: 1 *M* from Ziph came to Saul in Gibeah
26: 2 with three thousand picked *m* of Israel,
26: 7 Abner and his *m* sleeping around him.
26:19 if *m*, may they be cursed before the LORD,
27: 2 his six hundred *m* and went over to Achish,
27: 3 David and his *m* lived in Gath with Achish;
27: 8 *m* went up and made raids on the Geshurites,
28: 1 that you and your *m* must go out on
29: 2 David and his *m* were marching in the rear
29: 4 if not with the heads of these *m* of ours?
29:11 So David and his *m* left early in the
30: 1 and his *m* reached Ziklag on the third day,
30: 3 David and his *m* arrived at the city to
30: 6 difficulty, for the *m* spoke of stoning him,
30: 9 *m* and came as far as the Wadi Besor,
30:10 continued the pursuit with four hundred *m*,
30:17 none escaped except four hundred young *m*,
30:21 *m* who had been too exhausted to follow him,
30:21 came out to meet David and the *m* with him.
30:22 But all the stingy and worthless *m* among
30:31 the places frequented by David and his *m*.
31: 7 along the Jordan saw that the *m* of Israel
2Sm 1:11 all the *m* who were with him did likewise.
2: 3 also brought up his *m* with their families,
2: 4 Then the *m* of Judah came there and
2: 4 the *m* of Jabesh-gilead had buried Saul.
2: 5 to the *m* of Jabesh-gilead and said to them:
2: 7 therefore, and prove yourselves valiant *m*.
2:14 "Let the young *m* rise and perform for us."
2:17 Abner and the *m* of Israel were defeated by
2:21 *m* and take what you can strip from him."
2:29 Abner and his *m* marched all night long
2:30 the pursuit of Abner, assembled all the *m*.
2:31 three hundred and sixty *m* of Benjamin,
2:32 Joab and his *m* made an all-night march,
3:20 When Abner, accompanied by twenty *m*,
3:20 for Abner and for the *m* who were with him.
3:29 May the *m* of Joab's family never be
3:34 as *m* fall before the wicked,
3:39 king, I am weak this day, and these *m*,
4:11 when wicked *m* have slain an innocent man
4:12 the young *m* killed them and cut off their
5: 6 Then the king and his *m* set out for
5:21 and David and his *m* carried them away.
6: 1 again assembled all the picked *m* of Israel,
7:14 the rod of *m* and with human chastisements;
7:26 name will be forever great, when *m* say,
10: 3 your father by sending *m* with condolences?
10: 5 to them, since the *m* were quite ashamed.
10: 6 men, and twelve thousand *m* from Tob.
10: 8 Rehob and the *m* of Tob and Maacah
10:18 and David's *m* killed seven hundred
11:17 *m* of the city made a sortie against Joab,
11:23 "The *m* had us at a disadvantage and came

MEN (cont.)
12: 1 In a certain town there were two *m*,
13:34 he had seen some *m* coming down
15: 6 away the loyalties of the *m* of Israel.
15:11 *m* had accompanied Absalom from Jerusalem.
15:18 and the six hundred *m* of Gath who had
15:22 with all his *m* and all the dependents that
15:32 the top, where *m* used to worship God,
16:13 David and his *m* continued on the road,
17: 1 "Please let me choose twelve thousand *m*,
17: 8 that your father and his *m* are warriors,
18: 7 twenty thousand *m*.
18:28 *m* who rebelled against my lord the king."
19: 4 that day like *m* shamed by flight in battle.
19:18 accompanied by a thousand *m* from Benjamin.
19:42 the Jordan, along with all David's *m*?"
19:43 the Judahites replied to the *m* of Israel:
21: 2 in his zeal for the *m* of Israel and Judah.)
21: 6 let seven *m* from among his descendants be
21:17 Then David's *m* swore to him,
23: 3 said, 'He that rules over *m* in justice,
23:17 *m* who went at the risk of their lives?"
24: 9 thousand *m* fit for military service;
1Kgs 2:32 two *m* better and more just than himself,
5:11 He was wiser than all other *m*—
5:14 *M* came to hear Solomon's wisdom from all
8: 2 All the *m* of Israel assembled before King
8:27 indeed be that God dwells among *m* on earth?
8:39 You who alone know the hearts of all *m*,
8:42 (since *m* will learn of your great name
9: 9 *M* will answer: 'They forsook the LORD
10: 8 Happy are your *m*,
11:18 Paran, where they picked up additional *m*,
11:24 *m* about him and became leader of a band,
12: 8 and consulted the young *m* who had grown up
12:10 young *m* who had grown up with him replied,
12:14 said to them, as the young *m* had advised:
19:18 I will leave seven thousand *m* in Israel
20:17 that some *m* had marched out of Samaria.
20:33 *m* quickly took him at his word and said,
2Kgs 1: 9 with his company of fifty *m* after Elijah.
1:10 heaven and consume you and your fifty *m*."
1:10 heaven and consumed him and his fifty *m*.
1:11 with his company of fifty *m* after Elijah.
1:12 heaven and consume you and your fifty *m*."
1:12 from heaven, consuming him and his fifty *m*.
1:13 sent a captain with his company of fifty *m*.
1:13 my life and the lives of these fifty *m*,
1:14 captains with their companies of fifty *m*.
2:16 "Among your servants are fifty brave *m*,"
2:17 So they sent the fifty *m*,
4:40 The stew was poured out for the *m* to eat,
4:43 "How can I set this before a hundred *m*?"
5:22 to say, 'Two young *m* have just come to me,
5:24 the house, and sent the *m* on their way.
10: 6 in the care of prominent *m* of the city,
10:24 eighty *m* outside with this warning,
11: 9 Each one with his *m*,
12:16 no reckoning was asked of the *m* who were
15:20 from all the *m* of substance in the country,
15:25 who had with him fifty *m* from Gilead,
17:30 the *m* of Cuth made Nergal;
17:30 the *m* of Hamath made Ashima,
17:31 the *m* of Avva made Nibhaz and Tartak;
17:31 and the *m* of Sepharvaim immolated their
18:27 it not rather to the *m* sitting on the wall,
19:35 eighty-five thousand *m* in Assyrian camp.
20:14 "What did these *m* say to you?
23: 2 temple of the LORD with all the *m* of Judah
23:17 The *m* of the city replied,
24:14 all the officers and *m* of the army,
24:15 functionaries, and the chief *m* of the land.
24:16 Babylon all seven thousand *m* of the army,
25:19 five *m* in the personal service of the king
25:23 with their *m* came to him at Mizpah:
25:24 gave the commanders and their *m* his oath.
25:25 of royal descent, came with ten *m*,
1Chr 4:12 These were the *m* of Recah.
4:22 the *m* of Cozeba;
5:18 *m* who bore shield and sword and who drew
5:18 and sixty *m* fit for military service.
5:21 *m* they also captured their livestock:
5:24 Hodaviah, and Jahdiel *m* who were warriors,
5:24 famous *m*, and heads over their ancestral
7: 4 thousand *m* in organized military troops,
7:11 two hundred *m* fit for military service . . .
7:40 of ancestral houses, distinguished *m*,
7:40 thousand *m* fit for military service.
11:19 blood of these *m* who risked their lives?"
12: 1 The following *m* came to David in Ziklag
12:20 *M* from Manasseh also deserted to David
12:23 And from day to day *m* kept coming to
12:31 *m* renowned in their ancestral houses.
12:34 From Zebulun, *m* fit for military service,
12:34 thousand *m* rallying with a single purpose.
12:35 shield and lance, thirty-seven thousand *m*.
12:38 *m* equipped with every kind of weapon of
17: 9 nor shall wicked *m* ever again oppress them,
17:17 on me as henceforth the most notable of *m*,
18: 5 also slew twenty-two thousand of their *m*.
19: 5 informed of what had happened to his *m*,
19: 5 them, for the *m* had been greatly disgraced.
19:14 his *m* to engage the Arameans in battle;
21: 5 of *m* capable of wielding a sword,
21:13 is very great, than into the hands of *m*."
21:14 and seventy thousand *m* of Israel died.
23: 3 was found to be thirty-eight thousand *m*.
25: 7 singing to the LORD, all of them skilled *m*,
26: 7 also his brethren who were *m* of might,
26: 8 sons and their brethren, were mighty *m*,
26: 9 eighteen sons and brethren, mighty *m*.
26:12 of gatekeepers, under their chief *m*,
27: 1 divisions, of twenty-four thousand *m* each,
27: 2 his division were twenty-four thousand *m*;
27: 4 his division were twenty-four thousand *m*.
27: 5 his division were twenty-four thousand *m*.
27: 7 his division were twenty-four thousand *m*.
27: 8 his division were twenty-four thousand *m*.
27: 9 his division were twenty-four thousand *m*.
27:10 his division were twenty-four thousand *m*.
27:11 his division were twenty-four thousand *m*.
27:12 his division were twenty-four thousand *m*.
27:13 his division were twenty-four thousand *m*.
27:14 his division were twenty-four thousand *m*.
27:15 his division were twenty-four thousand *m*.
2Chr 2: 1 He conscripted seventy thousand *m* to carry
2: 6 Now, send me *m* skilled at work in gold,
2:16 Solomon took a census of all the alien *m*
5: 3 All the *m* of Israel assembled before the
6:30 for you alone know the hearts of *m*.
7:22 *m* will answer: 'They forsook the Lord
9: 7 Happy are your *m*,
10: 8 consulted the young *m* who had grown up
10:10 young *m* who had grown up with him replied:
10:14 according to the advice of the young *m*:
13: 7 Worthless *m*, scoundrels, joined him
13:15 Then the *m* of Judah shouted;
13:17 thousand picked *m* of Israel fell slain.
14: 8 one million *m* and three hundred chariots,
17: 7 year of his reign he sent his leading *m*,
20:27 Then all the *m* of Judah and Jerusalem,
23: 8 Each brought his *m*,
24:24 Though the Aramean force came with few *m*,
25: 5 hundred thousand picked *m* fit for war,
25:11 there they killed ten thousand *m* of Seir.
26:13 seven thousand five hundred fighting *m*
26:17 other priests of the LORD, courageous *m*,
28: 6 in a single day, all of them valiant *m*,
28:15 Then the *m* just named proceeded to help
31:19 had in every city *m* designated by name to
34:12 The *m* worked faithfully at their task;
34:13 in charge of the *m* who carried the burdens,
34:22 Then Hilkiah and the other *m* from the king
34:30 house of the LORD with all the *m* of Judah
36:17 young *m* in their own sanctuary building,
Ezr 2: 2 The census of the *m* of Israel:
2:22 *m* of Netophah,
2:23 *m* of Anathoth,
2:24 *m* of Beth-azmaveth,
2:25 *m* of Kiriath-jearim,
2:26 *m* of Ramah and Geba,
2:27 *m* of Michmas,
2:28 *m* of Bethel and Ai,
2:62 These *m* searched their family records,
3:12 the old *m* who had seen the former house,
4:11 your servants, the *m* of West-of-Euphrates,
4:21 that will stop the work of these *m*.
5: 4 of the *m* who are building this structure?"
5:10 in a list of the *m* who are their leaders.
6: 8 let these *m* be repaid for their expenses,
8:18 with his sons and brethren, eighteen *m*.
8:19 their brethren and their sons, twenty *m*.
8:20 All these *m* were enrolled by name.
10: 1 of Israelites gathered about him, *m*,
10: 9 All the *m* of Judah and Benjamin gathered
10:16 as his assistants *m* who were family heads,
10:17 *m* who had taken foreign women for wives.
Neh 1: 2 my brothers, came with other *m* from Judah.
2:12 set out by night with only a few other *m*
3: 2 side the *m* of Jericho were rebuilding,
3: 5 some of their outstanding *m* would not
3: 7 and the *m* of Gibeon and of Mizpah,
3:22 the priests, *m* of the surrounding country.
4:10 half my able *m* took a hand in the work,
4:15 half of the *m* with spears at the ready,
5:12 *m* that they would do as they had promised.
5:15 then too, their *m* oppressed the people.
5:16 all my *m* were gathered there for the work.
6:10 For *m* are coming to kill you;
7: 7 The census of the *m* of Israel:
7:26 *m* of Bethlehem and Netophah,
7:27 *m* of Anathoth, one hundred and
7:28 *m* of Beth-azmaveth, fortytwo;
7:29 *m* of Kiriath-jearim, Chephirah,
7:30 *m* of Ramah and Geba,
7:31 *m* of Michmas, one hundred and twenty-two;
7:32 *m* of Bethel and Ai, one hundred and
7:33 *m* of Nebo, fifty-two; sons of another Elam,
7:64 These *m* searched their family records,
8: 2 before the assembly, which consisted of *m*,
8: 3 till midday, in the presence of the *m*,
9:29 which *m* draw life when they practice them.
11: 2 The people applauded all those *m* who
11: 6 was four hundred and sixty-eight valiant *m*.
12:44 At that time *m* were appointed over the
13:13 for these *m* were held to be trustworthy.
13:15 In those days I perceived that *m* in Judah
13:19 I posted some of my own *m* at the gates so
Tb 5:14 your kinsmen are good *m*.
6:12 all other *m* have the right to marry her.
6:13 that it is your right, before all other *m*,
7:11 I have given her in marriage to seven *m*,
12: 6 the two *m* aside privately and said to them:
12: 6 all *m*, honor and proclaim God's deeds,
12:16 with fear, the two *m* fell to the ground.
13: 8 Let all *m* speak of his majesty,
13:14 are all the *m* who shall grieve over you,
Jdt 2: 5 presence, take with you *m* of proven valor,
4: 9 All the *m* of Israel cried to God with
4:11 And all the Israelite *m*,
6:12 When the *m* of the city saw them,
6:16 and all their young *m*,
7: 2 day all their fighting *m* went into action.
7: 2 train or the *m* who accompanied it on foot
7:13 we and our *m* will go up to the summits of
7:18 and they sent some of their *m* to the south
7:32 Then he dispersed the *m* to their posts,
9:11 does your power depend upon stalwart *m*;
10: 4 the eyes of all the *m* who should see her.
10: 7 When these *m* saw Judith transformed in
10:10 The *m* of the city kept her in view as she
10:12 The *m* took her in custody and asked her,
10:13 of his *m* suffering injury or loss of life."
10:14 *m* heard her words and gazed upon her face,
10:15 *m* will accompany you to present you to him.
10:17 their *m* as an escort for her and her maid,
11: 7 not only do *m* serve him through you;
11: 9 When the *m* of Bethulia spared him,
14: 2 and let all the able-bodied *m* rush out of
14: 6 one of the *m* in the assembly of the people,
14:11 Then all the Israelite *m* took up their
15:13 the *m* of Israel followed in their armor,
Est 1:13 with the wise *m* versed in the law,
B: 2 to restore the peace desired by all *m*.
B: 5 is continually at variance with all *m*,
E: 4 do they drive out gratitude from among *m*;
E: 8 undisturbed and peaceful for all *m*,
E:24 it will be left not merely untrodden by *m*,
9: 6 Jews killed and destroyed five hundred *m*.
9:12 have killed and destroyed five hundred *m*,
9:15 of Adar and killed three hundred *m* in Susa.
1Mc 1:11 in Israel *m* who were breakers of the law,
1:26 Virgins and young *m* languished,
1:34 they installed a sinful race, perverse *m*,
2: 9 her young *m* by the sword of the enemy.
2:18 as all the Gentiles and the *m* of Judah and
2:31 that certain *m* who had flouted the king's
3:13 an assembly of faithful *m* ready for war.
3:16 Judas went out to meet him with a few *m*.
3:24 About eight hundred of their *m* fell,
3:38 capable *m* among the King's Friends,
3:39 with them he sent forty thousand *m*
3:50 "What shall we do with these *m*,
4: 2 Some *m* from the citadel were their guides.
4: 6 in the plain with three thousand *m*,
4: 8 Judas said to the *m* with him:
4:13 and the *m* with Judas blew the trumpet.
4:15 About three thousand of their *m* fell.
4:23 and his *m* collected much gold and silver,
4:28 picked *m* and five thousand cavalry,
4:29 and Judas met them with ten thousand *m*.
4:34 of Lysias' *m* fell in hand-to-hand fighting.
4:35 whose *m* were ready either to live or to
4:41 appointed *m* to attack those in the citadel,
5:13 they have slain there about a thousand *m*."
5:17 "Choose *m* for yourself,
5:20 Three thousand *m* were allotted to Simon,
5:20 Galilee, and eight thousand *m* to Judas,
5:22 three thousand *m* of the Gentiles fell,
5:32 shouting, he said to the *m* of his army,
5:34 eight thousand of their *m* fell that day.
5:38 Judas sent *m* to spy on the camp,
5:47 But the *m* in the city shut them out and
5:50 the *m* of the army took up their positions,
5:58 to the *m* of their army who were with them,
5:59 But Gorgias and his *m* came out of the city
5:62 did not belong to the family of those *m*
5:64 and *m* gathered about them and praised them.
6: 6 had grown strong by reason of the arms, *m*,
6:18 The *m* in the citadel were hemming in
6:35 to it a thousand *m* in coats of mail,
6:42 and six hundred *m* of the king's army fell.
6:45 of the phalanx, killing *m* right and left,
6:49 He made peace with the *m* of Beth-zur,
6:54 Few *m* remained in the sanctuary;
6:58 let us now come to terms with these *m*
7: 1 with a few *m* in a city on the seacoast,
7: 5 and impious *m* of Israel came to him.
7:19 many of the *m* arrested who deserted to him,
7:23 his *m* were bringing upon the Israelites,
7:24 and took revenge on the *m* who had deserted,
7:28 come with a few *m* to meet you peaceably."
7:32 five hundred *m* of Nicanor's army fell;
7:40 camped in Adasa with three thousand *m*.
8: 9 When the *m* of Greece had planned to come
8:15 three hundred and twenty *m* took counsel,
9: 4 twenty thousand *m* and two thousand cavalry.
9: 5 Judas, with three thousand picked *m*,
9: 6 his *m* saw the great number of the troops,

9: 6 camp, until only eight hundred *m* remained.
9:11 all the valiant *m* were in the front line.
9:16 But when the *m* on the left wing saw that
9:16 they turned and followed Judas and his *m*,
9:25 *m* and made them masters of the country.
9:33 and all the *m* with him discovered this,
9:48 Jonathan and his *m* jumped into the Jordan
9:49 *m* on Bacchides' side fell that day.
9:61 Jonathan's *m* seized about fifty of the men
9:65 accompanied by a small group of *m*,
9:66 these *m* had set out to go up to the siege
9:67 Simon and his *m* then sallied forth from
9:69 he was angry with the lawless *m* who had
10: 7 The *m* in the citadel were struck with fear
10:32 it such *m* as he shall choose to guard it.
10:72 *M* say that you cannot make a stand against
10:74 Choosing ten thousand *m*,
10:75 but the *m* in the city shut him out because
10:76 the *m* of the city became afraid and opened
10:80 evening they showered his *m* with arrows.
10:81 But his *m* held their ground,
10:84 Dagon and the *m* who had taken refuge in it.
10:85 alive, came to about eight thousand *m*.
10:87 He and his *m* then returned to Jerusalem,
11:18 and his *m* in the fortified cities were
11:20 Jonathan gathered together the *m* of Judea
11:25 Although some impious *m* of his own nation
11:43 therefore, of sending *m* to fight for me,
11:44 thousand good fighting *m* to him at Antioch.
11:47 about a hundred thousand *m* in the city,
11:62 *m* as hostages and sent them to Jerusalem.
11:69 Then the *m* in ambush rose out of their
11:70 All of Jonathan's *m* fled;
11:73 Those of his *m* who were running away saw
12: 1 he sent selected *m* to Rome to confirm and
12: 3 the *m* entered the senate chamber and said,
12:27 his *m* to be on guard and to remain armed,
12:28 Jonathan and his *m* were ready for battle,
12:29 and his *m* were watching the lights burning,
12:34 for he heard that its *m* had intended to
12:41 picked fighting *m* and came to Beth-shan.
12:45 Pick out a few *m* to stay with you,
12:47 But he kept with him three thousand *m*,
12:48 the *m* of the city closed the gates and
12:49 Great Plain to destroy all Jonathan's *m*.
12:52 Thus all these *m* of Jonathan came safely
12:52 They mourned over Jonathan and his *m*,
12:53 and wipe out their memory from among *m*."
13:10 So Simon mustered all the *m* able to fight,
13:21 *m* in the citadel sent messengers to Trypho,
13:34 Simon also sent chosen *m* to King Demetrius
13:44 The *m* who had been on the siege machine
13:45 *m* of the city, joined by their wives
13:48 he settled there *m* who observed the law.
13:49 The *m* in the citadel in Jerusalem were
14: 9 Old *m* sat in the squares,
14: 9 young *m* wore the glorious apparel of war.
14:23 have voted to receive the *m* with honor,
14:32 sums of his own money to equip the *m*
15:35 the *m* of these cities were doing great
16: 6 *m* took their position against the enemy.
16: 6 that his *m* were afraid to cross the stream,
16: 6 When his *m* saw this,
16:15 banquet, he had his *m* hidden there.
16:16 drunk freely, Ptolemy and his *m* sprang up,
16:19 other *m* to Gazara to do away with John.
16:21 that Ptolemy had sent *m* to kill him also.
16:22 When the *m* came to kill him,
2Mc 3:26 Then two other young *m*,
3:27 *M* picked him up and laid him on a stretcher.
3:33 the same young *m* in the same clothing
3:34 to all *m* the majesty of God's power."
3:36 Before all *m* he gave witness to the deeds
4: 9 to enroll *m* in Jerusalem as Antiochians.
4:12 the noblest young *m* to wear the Greek hat.
4:40 armed *m* under the leadership of Auranus,
4:41 in wild confusion at Lysimachus and his *m*.
4:44 three *m* sent by the senate presented to
4:47 he condemned to death those poor *m*
4:50 to the covetousness of the *m* in power,
5: 5 thousand *m* and suddenly attacked the city.
5: 8 fled from city to city, hunted by all *m*,
5:24 head of an army of twenty-two thousand *m*,
5:24 with orders to kill all the grown *m* and
5:24 sell the women and young *m* into slavery.
5:25 he ordered his *m* to parade fully armed.
5:26 and running through the city with armed *m*,
6:20 as *m* ought to do who have the courage to
6:24 many young *m* would think the
6:26 time being, I avoid the punishment of *m*,
7:14 is my choice to die at the hands of *m*
7:16 "Since you have power among *m*,
7:34 But you, wretch, vilest of all *m!*
8: 1 to Judaism, assembled about six thousand *m*.
8: 2 temple, which was profaned by godless *m;*
8: 5 Once Maccabeus got his *m* organized,
8: 9 head of at least twenty thousand armed *m*
8:16 Maccabeus assembled his *m*,
8:19 thousand of his *m* were destroyed,
8:22 assigning to each fifteen hundred *m*.
9: 2 to arms, and Antiochus' *m* were routed,
10:17 them, killing as many as twenty thousand *m*.
10:19 Joseph, along with Zacchaeus and his *m*,
10:20 But some of the *m* in Simon's force who
10:20 be bribed by some of the *m* in the towers;
10:21 accused those *m* of having sold their kinsmen
10:23 twenty thousand *m* in the two strongholds.
10:25 and his *m* made supplication to God,
10:29 majestic *m* riding on golden-bridled horses,
10:33 and his *m* eagerly besieged the fortress.
10:35 twenty young *m* in the army of Maccabeus,
11: 6 When Maccabeus and his *m* learned that
11: 9 they were ready to assault not only *m*,
12: 5 against his countrymen, he summoned his *m;*
12: 8 On hearing that the *m* of Jamnia planned to
12:14 treated Judas and his *m* with contempt,
12:15 But Judas and his *m* invoked the aid of the
12:19 *m* that Timothy had left in the stronghold.
12:22 pierced by the swords of their own *m*.
12:23 destroying as many as thirty thousand *m*.
12:24 of the *m* under Dositheus and Sosipater;
12:27 Robust young *m* took up their posts in
12:31 Judas and his *m* thanked them and exhorted
12:35 powerful horseman and one of Bacenor's *m*,
12:36 After Esdris and his *m* had been fighting
12:37 he charged Gorgias' *m* when they were not
12:39 Judas and his *m* went to gather up the
12:40 that this was why these *m* had been slain.
13: 1 Judas and his *m* learned that Antiochus
13:15 his *m* the battle cry "God's Victory,"
13:15 picked force of the bravest young *m*
13:20 Judas then sent supplies to the *m* inside,
13:22 by negotiating with the *m* of Beth-zur.
13:23 he withdrew and attacked Judas and his *m*.
14: 1 Judas and his *m* learned that Demetrius,
14:18 heard of the valor of Judas and his *m*,
14:22 Judas had posted armed *m* in readiness at
14:30 gathered together a large number of his *m*,
14:42 rather than fall into the hands of vile *m*
15: 6 monument of victory over Judas and his *m*.
15: 8 He urged his *m* not to fear the enemy,
15:22 thousand *m* of Sennacherib's army.
15:25 Nicanor and his *m* advanced to the sound of
15:26 But Judas and his *m* met the army with
Jb 1: 3 was greater than any of the *m* of the East.
3:23 *M* whose path is hidden from them,
4:13 of the night, when deep sleep falls on *m*,
7:20 what can I do to you, O watcher of *m?*
11: 3 Shall your babblings keep *m* silent,
11:11 the worthlessness of *m* and sees iniquity;
12:25 he makes them stagger like drunken *m*.
13: 9 Would you impose on him as one does on *m?*
14:12 parches, So *m* lie down and rise not again.
15:10 There are gray-haired old *m* among us more
15:18 What wise *m* relate and have not
17: 8 Upright *m* are astonished at this,
17:12 Such *m* change the night into day;
19:17 I am loathsome to the *m* of my family.
22:15 to the ancient way trodden by worthless *m*,
22:17 These *m* said to God, "Depart from us!"
28: 1 and a place for gold which *m* refine.
29: 8 Then the young *m* saw me and withdrew,
29: 9 The chief *m* refrained from speaking and
30: 5 They were banished from among *m*,
30: 8 Irresponsible, nameless *m*,
31:31 Had not the *m* of my tent exclaimed,
32: 1 Then the three *m* ceased to answer Job,
32: 4 But since these *m* were older than he,
32: 5 was no reply in the mouths of the three *m*,
33:15 falls upon *m* as they slumber in their beds,
33:16 the ears of *m* and as a warning to them,
33:27 He shall sing before *m* and say,
34: 2 Hear, O wise *m*, my discourse,
34: 8 evildoers and goes along with wicked *m*,
34:10 Therefore, *m* of understanding,
34:11 Rather, he requites *m* for their conduct,
34:34 *M* of understanding will say to me,
35: 9 In great oppression *m* cry out;
36:24 his work, which *m* have praised in song.
36:25 All *m* contemplate it;
37:21 it is as the light which *m* see not while
37:24 Therefore *m* revere him,
Ps(s) 4: 3 *M* of rank, how long will you be dull
9:21 let the nations know that they are but *m*.
12: 2 faithfulness has vanished from among *m*.
12: 9 and in high place are the basest of *m*.
14: 2 down from heaven upon the children of *m*,
17:14 by your hand, O LORD, from mortal *m*:
17:14 *m* whose portion in life is in this world,
21:11 the earth and their posterity from among *m*.
22: 7 scorn of *m*, despised by the people.
26: 4 I stay not with worthless *m*,
26: 9 of sinners, nor with *m* of blood my life.
31:20 refuge in you, you show in the sight of *m*.
31:21 of your presence from the plottings of *m;*
36: 8 *m* take refuge in the shadow of your wings.
38:13 *M* lay snares for me seeking my life;
45: 3 in beauty are you than the sons of *m;*
49:11 For he can see that wise *m* die,
53: 3 down from heaven upon the children of *m*
54: 5 For haughty *m* have risen up against me,
54: 5 up against me, and fierce *m* seek my life;
55:24 *M* of blood and deceit shall not live out
56: 2 pity on me, O God, for *m* trample upon me;
57: 5 in the midst of lions which devour *m;*
58: 2 justice and judge fairly, you *m* of rank?
58:12 *m* shall say, "Truly there is a reward
59: 3 from bloodthirsty *m* save me.
59: 4 mighty *m* come together against me.
59:14 *m* may know that God is the ruler of Jacob,
60:13 the foe, for worthless is the help of *m*.
62:10 Only a breath are mortal *m;*
62:10 an illusion are *m* of rank;
64:10 all *m* fear and proclaim the work of God,
66: 5 of God, his tremendous deeds among *m*.
66:12 You let *m* ride over our heads;
68:19 high, taken captives, received *m* as gifts
73: 5 and are not afflicted like the rest of *m*.
74: 5 *m* coming up with axes to a clump of trees;
78:25 The bread of the mighty was eaten by *m;*
78:31 men, and laid low the young *m* of Israel.
78:60 in Shiloh, the tent where he dwelt among *m*.
78:63 Fire consumed their young *m*,
82: 7 Yet like *m* you shall die,
83:17 with disgrace, that *m* may seek your name,
84: 6 Happy the *m* whose strength you are!
84:13 of hosts, happy the *m* who trust in you!
86:14 and the company of fierce *m* seeks my life,
89:48 frail you created all the children of *m!*
90: 3 to dust, saying, "Return, O children of *m*."
94:10 not chastise, he who teaches *m* knowledge?
94:11 The LORD knows the thoughts of *m*,
104:15 oil, and bread fortifies the hearts of *m*.
107: 8 his wondrous deeds to the children of *m*,
107:15 his wondrous deeds to the children of *m*,
107:21 his wondrous deeds to the children of *m*,
107:27 They reeled and staggered like drunken *m*,
107:31 his wondrous deeds to the children of *m*.
108:13 the foe, for worthless is the help of *m*.
115: 4 are silver and gold, the handiwork of *m*.
115:16 earth he has given to the children of *m*.
119:113 I hate *m* of divided heart,
119:134 Redeem me from the oppression of *m*,
124: 2 When *m* rose up against us,
126: 1 captives of Zion, we were like *m* dreaming.
135:15 are silver and gold, the handiwork of *m*.
139:19 and the *m* of blood were to depart from me!
140: 2 Deliver me, O LORD, from evil *m;*
140: 2 preserve me from violent *m*,
140: 5 from violent *m* Who plan to trip up my feet
141: 4 of wickedness With *m* who are evildoers;
145:12 Making known to *m* your might and the
147: 8 mountains and herbs for the service of *m;*
147:10 nor is he pleased with the fleetness of *m*.
148:12 all the judges of the earth, Young *m* too,
148:12 Young men too, and maidens, old *m* and boys,
Prv 1: 2 *m* may appreciate wisdom and discipline,
1:18 These *m* lie in wait for their own blood,
2:12 way of evil men, from *m* of perverse speech,
2:20 Thus you may walk in the way of good *m*,
3:35 Honor is the possession of wise *m*,
4:14 walk not on the way of evil *m;* I call;
6:30 *M* despise not the thief if he steals to
7: 7 simple ones, I observed among the young *m*,
8: 4 "To you, O *m*, I call;
8: 4 my appeal is to the children of *m*.
8:31 and I found delight in the sons of *m*.
10:14 Wise *m* store up knowledge,
12:12 stronghold of evil *m* will be demolished,
12:18 prating of some *m* is like sword thrusts,
13:20 Walk with wise *m* and you will become wise,
13:23 but some *m* perish for lack of a law court.
14:18 but shrewd *m* gain the crown of knowledge.
14:19 Evil *m* must bow down before the good,
15:11 how much more the hearts of *m!*
15:12 to wise *m* he will not go.
17: 6 Grandchildren are the crown of old *m*,
18:16 for him, and gains him access to great *m*.
20: 6 Many are declared to be *m* of virtue:
20:29 The glory of young *m* is their strength,
20:29 and the dignity of old *m* is gray hair.
22:29 not stand in the presence of obscure *m*.
23:28 and increases the faithless among *m*.
24: 1 Be not emulous of evil *m*,
24: 8 *m* call him an intriguer.
24: 9 it is arrogance that *m* find abominable.
24:24 *m* will curse him,
25: 1 The *m* of Hezekiah,
25: 6 presence, nor occupy the place of great *m;*
26:16 than seven *m* who answer with good sense.
27:20 so too the eyes of *m*.
28: 5 Evil *m* understand nothing of justice,
28:10 [And blameless *m* will gain prosperity.]
28:28 the wicked gain pre-eminence, other *m* hide;
29: 8 Arrogant *m* set the city ablaze,
29: 8 the city ablaze, but wise *m* calm the fury.
29:10 Bloodthirsty *m* hate the honest man,
30: 2 Why, I am the most stupid of *m*,
30:14 from the earth, and the poor from among *m*.
Eccl 1:11 There is no remembrance of the *m* of old;
1:13 God has appointed for *m* to be busied about.
2: 3 I should understand what is best for *m*
2:12 What *m* have already done!
3:10 God has appointed for *m* to be busied about.
3:18 As for the children of *m*,
3:21 life-breath of the children of *m* goes upward
7:29 *m* have had recourse to many calculations.
8:10 I saw wicked *m* approach and enter;
8:11 therefore the hearts of *m* are filled with

MEN (cont.)
8:14 there are just *m* treated as though they
8:14 *m* treated as though they had done justly.
9: 3 Hence the minds of *m* are filled with evil,
9:12 like these the children of *m* are caught
9:14 with few *m* in it advanced a mighty king,
12: 3 house tremble, and the strong *m* are bent,
Sg 2: 3 of the woods, so is my lover among *m*.
3: 7 sixty valiant *m* surround it,
3: 7 surround it, of the valiant *m* of Israel:
4: 4 hang upon it, all the shields of valiant *m*.
Wis 3: 4 For if before *m*, indeed, they be punished,
4: 1 both by God is it acknowledged, and by *m*.
4: 2 When it is present *m* imitate it,
4: 9 understanding is the hoary crown for *m*,
6:24 of wise *m* is the safety of the world,
7:14 For to *m* she is an unfailing treasure;
7:20 Powers of the winds and thoughts of *m*,
8: 7 in life is more useful for *m* than these.
9: 6 though one be perfect among the sons of *m*,
9:18 and *m* learned what was your pleasure,
11:23 the sins of *m* that they may repent.
12: 8 But even these, as they were *m*,
12:12 your presence as vindicator of unjust *m*?
13: 1 For all *m* were by nature foolish who were
14: 5 *m* trust their lives even to frailest wood.
14:11 *m* and a trap for the feet of the senseless.
14:14 the vanity of *m* they came into the world,
14:17 *M* who lived so far away that they could
14:21 that *m* enslaved to either grief or tyranny
14:26 turmoil, perjury, Disturbance of good *m*,
16:28 So that *m* might know that one must give
Sir 1:13 With devoted *m* was she created from of old,
1:14 she inebriates *m* with her fruits.
1:26 Play not the hypocrite before *m*;
2: 5 worthy *m* in the crucible of humiliation.
2:18 of the LORD and not into the hands of *m*,
8: 9 Reject not the tradition of old *m* which
9:16 Have just *m* for your table companions;
10: 7 Odious to the LORD and to *m* is arrogance.
10:13 afflictions and brings *m* to utter ruin.
10:19 Can be in honor? Those of *m*.
10:19 Can be in disgrace? Those of *m*.
10:24 When free *m* serve a prudent slave,
11: 4 works of the LORD, hidden from *m* his deeds.
13:13 take care never to accompany *m* of violence.
15: 7 Worthless *m* will not attain to her,
15: 7 to her, haughty *m* will not behold her.
16:12 he judges *m*, each according to his deeds
16:21 Such are the thoughts of senseless *m*,
17:12 them he gives precepts about his fellow *m*.
17:25 The like cannot be found in *m*,
17:27 heaven, while all *m* are dust and ashes.
18: 9 with *m* and showers upon them his mercy.
21: 2 lion's teeth, destroying the souls of *m*.
23:16 Two types of *m* multiply sins,
23:19 not mindful, fearing only the eyes of *m*;
25: 1 for they are pleasing to the LORD and to *m*:
25: 2 Three kinds of *m* I hate;
25: 6 The crown of old *m* is wide experience;
26:19 illustrious *m* held in contempt;
27: 7 speaks, for it is then that *m* are tested.
27:12 but frequent the company of thoughtful *m*.
29:17 Going surety has ruined many prosperous *m*
29:18 Has exiled *m* of prominence and sent them
33:10 So too, all *m* are of clay,
33:11 great knowledge the LORD makes *m* unlike;
33:13 So are *m* in the hands of their Creator,
35:22 and repays *m* according to their thoughts;
36:23 kindly, his lot is beyond that of mortal *m*.
38: 5 by a twig that *m* might learn his power?
38: 6 He endows *m* with the knowledge to glory in
38:31 All these *m* are skilled with their hands,
39: 1 He explores the wisdom of the *m* of old and
39: 2 He treasures the discourses of famous *m*,
39: 5 to learn what is good and evil among *m*.
40: 1 and a heavy yoke, to the sons of *m*;
41: 8 Woe to you, O sinful *m*,
42: 8 and recognized by all *m* as discreet.
42:12 Let her not parade her charms before *m*,
44: 1 Now will I praise those godly *m*,
44: 2 fashion, *m* of renown for their might,
44: 6 Stalwart *m*, solidly established
44: 8 and *m* recount their praiseworthy deeds;
44:10 *m* whose virtues have not been forgotten;
45: 1 Dear to God and *m*, MOSES, whose
45:18 *M* of other families were inflamed against
Is 2:11 lowered, the arrogance of *m* will be abased,
2:17 be abased, the arrogance of *m* brought low,
2:19 *M* will go into caves in the rocks and into
2:20 On that day *m* will throw to the moles and
3:25 Your *m* will fall by the sword,
5: 3 inhabitants of Jerusalem and *m* of Judah,
5: 7 and the *m* of Judah are his cherished plant;
5:15 *M* shall be abased,
6:12 Until the LORD removes *m* far away,
7:13 Is it not enough for you to weary *m*,
7:24 *M* shall go there with bow and arrows;
9: 2 as *m* make merry when dividing spoils.
9:16 the Lord does not spare their young *m*,
13: 7 bows of the young *m* fall from their hands.
13:12 make mortals more rare than pure gold, *m*,
19:11 to Pharaoh, "I am a disciple of wise *m*,
19:12 Where then are your wise *m*?
23: 4 labor, nor given birth, nor raised young *m*,
23: 8 whose traders are the earth's honored *m*?
23: 9 to degrade all the earth's honored *m*.
24: 6 on earth turn pale, and few *m* are left.
29:13 routine observance of the precepts of *m*,
29:14 The wisdom of its wise *m* shall perish and
29:14 the understanding of its prudent *m* be hid.
31: 3 The Egyptians are *m*,
31: 8 his young *m* shall be impressed as laborers.
33: 4 *M* gather spoil as caterpillars are
33: 7 See, the *m* of Ariel cry out in the streets,
36:12 it not rather to the *m* sitting on the wall,
38:11 *m* among those who dwell in the world."
39: 3 asked him, "What did these *m* say to you?
40:30 Though young *m* faint and grow weary,
43: 4 I give *m* in return for you and peoples in
44: 9 and they are more deaf than *m* are.
44:25 *m* back and make their knowledge foolish.
45: 6 *m* may know that there is none besides me.
47: 6 And upon old *m* you laid a very heavy yoke.
51: 7 Fear not the reproach of *m*,
53: 3 spurned and avoided by *m*, a *m* of suffering,
53: 3 One of those from whom *m* hide their faces,
57: 1 Devout *m* are swept away,
59:10 Like blind *m* we grope along the wall,
62: 4 No more shall *m* call you "Forsaken,"
64: 5 all of us have become like unclean *m*,
65: 8 the juice is pressed from grapes, *m* say,
66:24 corpses of the *m* who rebelled against me;
Jer 3: 2 and see, where have *m* not lain with you?
4: 3 For the *m* of Judah and to Jerusalem,
4: 4 O *m* of Judah and citizens of Jerusalem;
5:26 they set traps, but it is *m* they catch.
6:11 street, upon the young *m* gathered together.
11: 2 Speak to the *m* of Judah and to the
11: 9 *m* of Judah and the citizens of Jerusalem.
12: 5 If running against *m* has wearied you,
11:21 the *m* of Anathoth who seek your life,
11:22 The young *m* shall die by the sword;
11:23 bring misfortune upon the *m* of Anathoth,
12: 5 If running against *m* has wearied you,
13:20 your eyes and see *m* coming from the north.
17:25 with their princes, and the *m* of Judah,
18:11 *m* of Judah and the citizens of Jerusalem:
18:21 let their *m* die of pestilence,
18:21 young *m* be slain by the sword in battle.
19:10 in the sight of the *m* who went with you,
30: 6 since when do *m* bear children?
30: 6 Why, then, do I see all these *m*,
30:19 songs of praise, the laughter of happy *m*.
31:13 and dance, and young *m* and old as well.
32:12 and before all the *m* of Judah who happened
32:19 whose eyes are open to all the ways of *m*,
32:20 day, both in Israel and among all other *m*,
32:32 *m* of Judah and the citizens of Jerusalem,
33: 5 *m* come to battle the Chaldeans,
34:18 The *m* who violated my covenant and did not
35: 5 I set before these Rechabite *m* bowls full
35:13 say to the *m* of Judah and to the citizens
36: 6 *m* of Judah who come up from their cities.
36:31 citizens of Jerusalem and the *m* of Judah
38: 9 these *m* have been at fault in all they
38:10 the Cushite to take three *m* along with him,
38:11 Ebed-melech took the *m* along with him,
38:16 you over to these *m* who seek your life."
38:19 "I am afraid of the *m* of Judah who have
39:17 over to the *m* of whom you are afraid.
40: 7 were still in the field with all their *m*
40: 7 son of Ahikam, charge of the land, of *m*,
40: 8 came with their *m* to Gedaliah in Mizpah:
40: 9 *m* not to be afraid to serve the Chaldeans·
41: 1 king's nobles, came with ten *m* to Gedaliah,
41: 3 Ishmael also slew all the *m* of Judah of
41: 5 of it, eighty *m* with beards shaved off,
41: 7 and his *m* slew them and threw them into
41: 9 Ishmael threw all the corpses of the *m*
41:12 all their *m* and set out to attack Ishmael,
41:15 and fled to the Ammonites with eight *m*.
42:17 *m* who determine to go to Egypt to stay,
43: 2 and all the insolent *m* shouted to Jeremiah:
43: 6 *m*, women, and children, the princesses
43: 9 in Tahpanhes, while the *m* of Judah look on,
44:15 From all the *m* who knew that their wives
44:20 To all the people, *m* and women,
44:27 All the *m* of Judah in Egypt shall perish
46: 9 and Put, bearing your shields, *M* of Lud,
48:14 say, "We are heroes, *m* valiant in war"?
48:31 Moab I cry, over the *m* of Kir-heres I moan.
48:36 for the *m* of Kir-heres the wail of flutes
49:15 among the despised nations among *m*!
49:19 So I, in an instant, will drive *m* off;
49:26 now her young *m* shall fall in her streets,
50: 4 the *m* of Israel and of Judah shall come,
50:30 her young *m* shall fall in her streets,
50:33 Oppressed are the *m* of Israel,
50:33 of Israel, and with them the *m* of Judah;
50:35 Babylon's people, her princes and wise *m*!
51: 3 Spare not her young *m*,
51:14 fill you with *m* as numerous as locusts,
51:57 will make her princes and her wise *m* drunk,
52:25 and seven *m* in the personal service of the
Lam 1:15 an army against me to crush my young *m*;
2:10 in silence sit the old *m* of daughter Zion:
2:21 and young *m* have fallen by the sword;
3:33 in afflicting or grieving the sons of *m*.
4:18 *M* dogged our steps so that we could not
5:14 The old *m* have abandoned the gate,
5:14 the gate, the young *m* their music.
Bar 1:15 we *m* of Judah and citizens of Jerusalem,
2: 1 and against the *m* of Israel and Judah.
3:17 the silver and the gold in which *m* trust;
3:38 has appeared on earth, and moved among *m*.
6:10 They trick them out in garments like *m*,
6:52 over the land, nor do they give *m* rain.
Ez 8:16 were about twenty-five *m* with their backs
9: 2 With that I saw six *m* coming from the
9: 6 Old *m*, youths and maidens, women
9: 6 So they began with the *m* [the elders] who
11: 1 entrance of the gate I saw twenty-five *m*,
11: 2 these are the *m* who are planning evil and
14: 3 these *m* have the memory of their idols
14:14 and even if these three *m* were in it,
14:16 wild beasts, and these three *m* were in it,
14:18 and beast, and these three *m* were in it,
19: 3 He learned to seize prey, *m* he devoured,
19: 6 He learned to seize prey, *m* he devoured;
21:34 on the necks of depraved and wicked *m*
21:36 I will hand you over to ravaging *m*,
22:11 *m* who defile their daughters-in-law by
22:11 by incest, *m* who coerce their sisters,
23: 6 officers, all of them attractive young *m*,
23:12 on horses, all of them attractive young *m*.
23:14 When she saw *m* drawn on the wall,
23:23 the *m* of Babylon and all of Chaldea,
23:23 all those of Assyria, attractive young *m*,
23:40 they sent for *m* who had to come from afar,
23:42 these were *m* brought in from the desert,
23:44 they did come to her as *m* come to a harlot.
23:45 But just *m* shall punish them with the
27: 8 *m* of Zemer were in you to be your mariners;
27:11 The *m* of Arvad were all about your walls,
30:17 The young *m* of On and of Pibeseth shall
32:27 do not lie with the mighty *m* fallen of old,
32:27 *m* caused terror in the land of the living.
36:10 and I will settle crowds of *m* upon you,
36:11 settle crowds of *m* and beasts upon you,
36:13 of you, "You are a land that devours *m*,
36:14 *m* or rob your people of their children,
36:38 ruins shall be filled with flocks of *m*;
38:20 the ground, and all *m* who are on the land.
39:14 *M* shall be permanently employed to pass
Dn 1: 4 the nobility, young *m* without any defect,
1: 6 Among these were *m* of Judah:
1:10 with the other young *m* of your age,
1:13 other young *m* who eat from the royal table,
1:15 the young *m* who ate from the royal table.
1:17 To these four young *m* God gave knowledge
2:11 except the gods who do not dwell among *m*."
2:12 the wise *m* of Babylon to be put to death.
2:13 was issued that the wise *m* should be slain,
2:14 had set out to kill the wise *m* of Babylon:
2:18 with the rest of the wise *m* of Babylon.
2:24 appointed to destroy the wise *m* of Babylon,
2:24 not put the wise *m* of Babylon to death.
2:27 which the king has inquired, the wise *m*,
2:38 *m*, wild beasts, and birds of the air,
2:48 prefect over all the wise *m* of Babylon.
3:12 these *m*, O king, have paid no attention
3:20 the strongest *m* in his army bind Shadrach,
3:22 flames devoured the *m* who threw Shadrach,
3:46 Now the king's *m* who had thrown them in
3:82 You sons of *m*, bless the Lord;
3:87 Holy *m* of humble heart,
3:91 we not cast three *m* bound into the fire?"
3:92 "I see four *m* unfettered and unhurt,
3:94 had no power over the bodies of these *m*;
4: 3 So I issued a decree that all the wise *m*
4: 9 all *m* ate of it.
4:14 the Most High rules over the kingdom of *m*:
4:14 he will, or set over it the lowliest of *m*.'
4:15 *m* in my kingdom can tell me the meaning,
4:22 from among *m* and dwell with wild beasts;
4:22 kingdom of *m* and gives it to whom he will.
4:29 You shall be cast out from among *m*,
4:29 kingdom of *m* and gives it to whom he will."
4:30 Nebuchadnezzar was cast out from among *m*,
5: 7 means," he said to the wise *m* of Babylon,
5: 8 But though all the king's wise *m* came in,
5:15 the wise *m* and enchanters were brought in
5:21 among *m* and was made insensate as a beast;
5:21 of *m* and appoints over it whom he will.
6: 6 Then these *m* said to themselves,
6:12 So these *m* rushed in and found Daniel
6:16 But these *m* insisted.
6:25 then ordered the *m* who had accused Daniel,
9: 7 *m* of Judah, the residents of Jerusalem
10: 7 great fear seized the *m* who were with me;
11:33 nation's wise *m* shall instruct the many;
11:35 Of the wise *m*, some shall fall,
13: 6 These *m*, to whom all brought their cases,
13: 8 old *m* saw her enter every day for her walk,
13:19 the two old *m* got up and hurried to her.
13:24 and the old *m* also shouted at her,
13:27 At the accusations by the old *m*,
13:32 but those wicked *m* ordered her to uncover

13:43 with which these wicked *m* have charged me."
14:20 "I see the footprints of *m*,
Hos 8: 3 *m* of Israel have thrown away what is good;
13: 2 offer sacrifice." *M* kiss calves!
Jl 3: 1 prophesy, your old *m* shall dream dreams,
3: 1 dreams, your young *m* shall see visions;
4:16 people, a stronghold to the *m* of Israel.
Am 2:11 sons, and nazirites among your young *m*.
2:11 Is this not so, O *m* of Israel?
3: 1 Hear the word, O *m* of Israel,
4: 5 For so you love to do, O *m* of Israel,
4:10 and with the sword I slew your young *m*;
6: 9 there remain ten *m* in a single house,
8:13 and young *m* shall faint from thirst;
9: 7 like the Ethiopians to me, O *m* of Israel,
Ob 1: 8 day make the wise *m* disappear from Edom,
Jon 1:10 Now the *m* were seized with great fear and
1:13 Still the *m* rowed hard to regain the land,
1:16 *m* offered sacrifice and made vows to him.
Mi 2:12 they shall not be thrown into panic by *m*.
5: 4 it seven shepherds, eight *m* of royal rank;
5: 6 for no man, nor tarry for the sons of *m*.
6:12 You whose rich *m* are full of violence,
7: 2 the earth, among *m* the upright are no more!
Na 3:10 and all her great *m* were put into chains.
Zep 1:12 punish the *m* who thicken on their lees,
1:17 hem *m* in till they walk like the blind,
3: 4 Her prophets are insolent, treacherous *m*;
Hg 1:11 Upon *m* and upon beasts,
Zec 2: 8 the multitude of *m* and beasts in her midst.
3: 8 who sit before you are *m* of good omen.
7: 2 Bethelsarezer sent Regemmelech and his *m*
8: 4 Old *m* and old women,
8:10 those days there were no wages for *m*,
8:23 In those days ten *m* of every nationality,
10: 1 And sends *m* the pouring rain;
10: 7 Then Ephraim shall be valiant *m*,
Mt 4:19 after me and I will make you fishers of *m*."
5:15 *M* do not light a lamp and then put it
5:16 your light must shine before *m* so that
8:27 the *m* were dumbfounded.
8:28 encountered two *m* coming out of the tombs.
8:33 the story about the two possessed *m*.
9: 8 praised God for giving such authority to *m*.
9:27 two blind *m* came after him crying out,
9:28 the house, the blind *m* caught up with him.
10: 5 sent these *m* on mission as the Twelve,
10:32 Whoever acknowledges me before *m* I will
10:33 *m* I will disown before my Father in heaven.
11: 5 the deaf hear, dead *m* are raised to life,
12: 3 David did when he and his *m* were hungry,
12: 4 him and his *m* or anyone other than priests?
12: 7 would not have condemned these innocent *m*.
12:31 sin, every blasphemy, will be forgiven *m*,
14:35 and when the *m* of that place recognized
17:22 going to be delivered into the hands of *m*,
19:12 Some *m* are incapable of sexual activity
20: 3 saw other *m* standing around the marketplace
20:30 two blind *m* sitting by the roadside,
23:34 send you prophets and wise *m* and scribes.
24:40 Two *m* will be out in the field;
26:45 to be handed over to the power of evil *m*.
27:54 The centurion and his *m* who were keeping
28: 4 with fear of him and fell down like dead *m*.
Mk 1:17 I will make you fishers of *m*."
1:20 who was in the boat with the hired *m*,
2:25 was in need and he and his *m* were hungry?
2:26 He even gave it to his *m*."
3:13 summoned the *m* he himself had decided on,
3:28 mankind and all the blasphemies *m* utter,
6:21 officers, and the leading *m* of Galilee.
6:44 eaten the loaves numbered five thousand *m*.
9:31 the hands of *m* who will put him to death;
11: 6 told them to, and the *m* let them take it.
11:15 and the stalls of the *m* selling doves;
11:30 baptism of divine origin or merely from *m*?"
12:40 These *m* devour the savings of widows and
13:11 When *m* take you off into custody,
13:26 Then *m* will see the Son of Man coming in
14:41 be handed over to the clutches of evil *m*.
14:60 answer to what these *m* testify against you?"
15:32 The *m* who had been crucified with him
16:13 These *m* retraced their steps and announced
Lk 1:25 has seen fit to remove my reproach among *m*."
2:52 wisdom and age and grace before God and *m*.
5:10 From now on you will be catching *m*."
5:18 *m* came along carrying a paralytic on a mat.
6: 3 David did when he and his *m* were hungry
6: 4 ate the holy bread and gave it to his *m*,
6:22 "Blest shall you be when *m* hate you,
7:20 When the *m* came to him they said,
7:22 the deaf hear, dead *m* are raised to life,
7:31 comparison can I use for the *m* of today?
7:41 *m* owed money to a certain money-lender;
9:14 (There were about five thousand *m*.)
9:30 Suddenly two *m* were talking with him
9:32 saw the two *m* who were standing with him.
9:44 Man must be delivered into the hands of *m*."
11:31 along with the *m* of this generation,
11:44 hidden tombs over which *m* walk unawares."
11:46 You lay impossible burdens on *m* but will
12: 8 you, whoever acknowledges me before *m*—
12: 9 who has disowned me in the presence of *m*
12:36 Be like *m* awaiting their master's return
14:31 and consider whether, with ten thousand *m*,
16:14 The Pharisees, who were avaricious *m*,
16:15 "You justify yourselves in the eyes of *m*,
17:34 that night there will be two *m* in one bed;
18:10 "Two *m* went up to the temple to pray;
18:11 O God, that I am not like the rest of *m*—
18:27 are impossible for *m* are possible for God."
20: 4 baptism of John come from God or from *m*?"
20: 6 whereas if we say, 'From *m*,'
20:20 guise of honest *m* to trap him in speech,
20:47 These *m* are going through the savings of
21:26 *M* will die of fright in anticipation of
21:27 *m* will see the Son of Man coming on a
22:63 Meanwhile the *m* guarding Jesus amused
24: 4 *m* in dazzling garments stood beside them.
24: 5 *m* said to them: "Why do you search
24: 7 be delivered into the hands of sinful *m*,
Jn 1: 4 him, found life, life for the light of *m*.
1: 7 so that through him all *m* might believe
3:19 but *m* loved darkness rather than light
4:20 is the place where *m* ought to worship God."
5:23 so that all *m* may honor the Son just as
6:10 though the *m* numbered about five thousand,
10:35 *m* gods to whom God's word was addressed
12:32 will draw all *m* to myself."
12:43 the praise of *m* to the glory of God.
13:18 of all, for I know the kind of *m* I chose,
17: 6 These *m* you gave me were yours;
17:25 and these *m* have known that you sent me.
18: 8 "If I am the one you want, let these *m* go."
19:32 the legs of the *m* crucified with Jesus,
Acts 1:10 two *m* dressed in white stood beside them.
1:11 *M* of Galilee," they said, "why do you
1:24 "O Lord, you read the hearts of *m*.
1:26 Then they drew lots between the two *m*.
2: 6 heard these *m* speaking his own language.
2: 7 all of these *m* who are speaking Galileans?
2:15 must realize that these *m* are not drunk,
2:17 your young *m* shall see visions and your
2:17 visions and your old *m* shall dream dreams.
2:22 *M* of Israel, listen to me!
4: 4 of the *m* came to about five thousand.
4: 7 whose name have *m* of your stripe done this?"
4:12 given to *m* by which we are to be saved."
4:13 speakers were uneducated *m* of no standing,
4:13 these *m* as having been with Jesus.
4:15 "What shall we do with these *m*?
5: 4 You have lied not to *m* but to God!"
5: 6 Some of the young *m* came forward,
5: 9 The footsteps of the *m* who have just
5:10 young *m* came in, found her dead,
5:14 believers, *m* and women in great numbers,
5:25 Those *m* you put in jail are standing over
5:29 "Better for us to obey God than *m*!
5:35 what you are going to do with these *m*.
5:36 About four hundred *m* joined him.
5:38 that you have nothing to do with these *m*.
6: 3 for seven *m* acknowledged to be deeply
6: 6 They presented these *m* to the apostles,
6:11 They persuaded some *m* to make the charge
8: 2 Devout *m* buried Stephen,
8: 3 house after house, dragged *m* and women out,
8:12 Christ, *m* and women alike accepted baptism.
9: 7 The *m* who were traveling with him stood
9:38 sent two *m* to him with the urgent request,
10: 5 some *m* to Joppa and summon a certain Simon,
10: 9 as the *m* were traveling along and
10:17 the *m* sent by Cornelius arrived at the
10:19 "There are two *m* in search of you.
10:21 Peter went down to the *m* and said,
11: 3 house of uncircumcised *m* and ate with them."
11:11 the three *m* who had been sent to me from
11:20 some *m* of Cyprus and Cyrene among them
13:15 the leading *m* of the synagogue sent this
13:50 sympathizers and the leading *m* of the town,
14:11 "Gods have come to us in the form of *m*!"
14:15 "We are only *m*, human like you.
15: 1 Some *m* came down to Antioch from Judea
15: 8 God, who reads the hearts of *m*,
15:22 chosen were leading *m* of the community,
16:17 *m* are servants of the Most High God;
16:20 "These *m* are agitators disturbing the
16:30 brief interval he led them out and said, *M*,
16:35 officers with orders to let these *m* go.
17: 6 "These *m* have been creating a disturbance
17:12 did numerous influential Greek women and *m*.
17:22 *M* of Athens, I note that in every respect
17:30 bygone periods when *m* did not know him;
17:30 on all *m* everywhere to reform their lives.
19: 7 were in the company about twelve *m* in all.
19:25 *m* and other workers in the same craft.
19:25 *M*," he said, "you know that our prosperity
19:37 These *m* whom you have brought here are not
20:30 *m* will present themselves distorting the
21:23 are four *m* among us who have made a vow.
21:26 Paul gathered the *m* together and went
22: 4 I arrested and imprisoned both *m* and women.
22:15 before all *m* you are to be his witness to
23: 3 sit there judging *m* according to the law,
24:15 I have the same hope in God as these *m*
24:19 These are the *m* who should be here before
25: 5 "Your leading *m* can come down with me,"
25:11 to the charges these *m* bring against me,
25:23 officers and prominent *m* of the city.
26: 8 to believe that God raises dead *m* to life.
27:10 *M*, I can see that this voyage is bound to
27:21 *M*, you should have taken my advice and not
27:25 So keep up your courage, *m*.
27:31 "If these *m* do not stay with the ship,
28:17 *m* of the Jewish community to visit him.
28:23 witness to the reign of God among *m*.
Rom 1:18 irreligious and perverse spirit of *m* who,
1:20 Therefore these *m* are inexcusable.
1:25 these *m* who exchanged the truth of God for
1:27 and the *m* gave up natural intercourse with
1:27 *M* did shameful things with men,
1:31 One sees in them *m* without conscience,
2: 2 judgment on *m* who do such things is just."
2:14 these *m* although without the law serve as
2:16 on the secrets of *m* through Christ Jesus.
2:29 Such a one receives his praise, not from *m*,
3:23 All *m* have sinned and are deprived of the
3:24 All *m* are now undeservedly justified by
5: 6 powerless, Christ died for us godless *m*.
5:12 coming to all *m* inasmuch as all sinned
5:18 offense brought condemnation to all *m*,
5:18 act brought all *m* acquittal and life.
6:13 *m* who have come back from the dead to life,
7: 1 (I am speaking to *m* who know what law is),
9:33 *m* stumble and a rock to make them fall;
10:15 And how can *m* preach unless they are sent?
11: 4 *m* who have not bowed the knee to Baal."
14:18 way pleases God and wins the esteem of *m*.
16:18 Such *m* serve, not Christ our Lord,
1Cor 1:25 For God's folly is wiser than *m*,
1:25 men, and his weakness more powerful than *m*.
1:26 many of you are wise, as *m* account wisdom;
2: 5 on the wisdom of *m* but on the power of God.
2: 6 this age, who are *m* headed for destruction.
3: 1 as spiritual *m* but only as men of flesh,
3: 3 is not your behavior that of ordinary *m*?
3:21 Let there be no boasting about *m*.
4: 1 *M* should regard us as servants of Christ
4: 9 line, like *m* doomed to die in the arena.
4: 9 to the universe, to angels and *m* alike.
7:23 Do not enslave yourselves to *m*.
9:22 *m* in order to save at least some of them.
10:13 been sent you that does not come to all *m*.
14: 2 a tongue is talking not to *m* but to God.
14: 3 hand, speaks to *m* for their upbuilding,
15:19 life only, we are the most pitiable of *m*.
15:39 *M* have one kind of body, animals another.
15:48 Earthly *m* are like the man of earth,
15:48 heavenly *m* are like the man of heaven.
16:13 stand firm in the faith, and act like *m*.
16:16 I urge you to serve under such *m* and under
16:18 You should recognize the worth of such *m*.
2Cor 1: 9 We were left to feel like *m* condemned to
3: 2 You are my letter, known and read by all *m*,
5:11 in awe of the Lord we try to persuade *m*,
6: 5 as *m* familiar with hard work,
6: 7 as *m* with the message of truth and the
6:11 *M* of Corinth, we have spoken to you
8:21 approval but also for the good esteem of *m*.
8:24 show these *m* the proof of your love,
11:13 Such *m* are false apostles.
12:17 of you through any of the *m* I sent to you?
Gal 1: 1 an apostle sent not by *m* or by any man,
1:10 am trying to please at this point *m* or God?
1:10 how I seek to ingratiate myself with *m*?
6:10 the opportunity, let us do good to all *m*—
Eph 2:11 You *m* of Gentile stock
3: 5 unknown to *m* in former ages but now
3: 9 to enlighten all *m* on the mysterious design
4: 8 a host of captives and gave gifts to *m*."
4:10 that he might fill all *m* with his gifts.
4:29 say only the good things *m* need to hear,
5:15 not act like fools, but like thoughtful *m*.
6: 6 for appearance only and to please *m*,
6: 7 doing it for the Lord rather than *m*.
Phil 2: 7 a slave, being born in the likeness of *m*.
2:29 the Lord and hold *m* like him in esteem,
Col 1:28 we proclaim while we admonish all *m*
3:22 attracting attention and pleasing *m*
3:23 Do it for the Lord rather than for *m*,
1Thes 2: 4 God, as *m* entrusted with the good tidings,
2: 4 tester of our hearts," rather than *m*.
2: 6 Neither did we seek glory from *m*,
2:13 from us you took it, not as the word of *m*,
2Thes 3: 2 may be delivered from confused and evil *m*.
1Tm 1: 9 at good *m* but at the lawless and unruly,
1: 9 *m* who kill their fathers or mothers,
1:19 Some *m*, by rejecting the guidance
2: 1 and thanksgiving be offered for all *m*,
2: 4 *m* to be saved and come to know the truth.
2: 5 also is the mediator between God and *m*,
2: 8 that in every place the *m* shall offer
4: 2 *m* with seared consciences who forbid marriage
4:10 the living God who is the savior of all *m*,
5: 1 You should treat younger *m* as brothers,
6: 5 the bickering of *m* with twisted minds who
6: 5 Such *m* value religion only as a means of
6: 9 which drag *m* down to ruin and destruction.
6:10 Some *m* in their passion for it have
6:21 some *m* have missed the goal of faith.

MEN (cont.)
2Tm 2: 2 *m* who will be able to teach others.
3: 2 *M* will be lovers of self and of money,
3: 8 Moses, so these *m* also oppose the truth;
3: 9 with those two *m*, the stupidity of these
3:13 *m* and charlatans will go from bad to worse,
Ti 1: 9 he will be able both to encourage *m*
1:10 *m* who are empty talkers and deceivers.
1:14 by *m* who have swerved from the truth.
2: 2 the older *m* that they must be temperate,
2: 6 Tell the young *m* to keep themselves
2:11 has appeared, offering salvation to all *m*.
3: 2 display a perfect courtesy toward all *m*.
3: 8 is what is good and advantageous for *m*.
Heb 2: 9 he might taste death for the sake of all *m*.
2:14 the children are *m* of blood and flesh,
5: 1 *m* and made their representative before God,
6: 4 For when *m* have once been enlightened and
6:16 *M* swear by someone greater than themselves;
7: 8 whereas *m* subject to death receive tithes,
7:28 law sets up as high priests *m* who are weak,
9:27 Just as it is appointed that *m* die once,
11: 2 of faith the *m* of old were approved by God.
12:14 Strive for peace with all *m*,
12:23 all, to the spirits of just *m* made perfect,
13:17 over you as *m* who must render an account.
Jas 2:12 Always speak and act as *m* destined for
3: 9 then we use it to curse *m*,
1Pt 1: 1 to *m* chosen according to the foreknowledge
1:24 glory of *m* is like the flower of the field.
2: 4 a living stone, rejected by *m* but approved,
2:15 talk of foolish *m* by your good behavior.
2:16 Live as free *m*,
4: 6 condemned in the flesh in the eyes of *m*,
5: 5 younger *m* must be obedient to your elders.
2Pt 1:21 It is rather that *m* impelled by the Holy
2: 7 conduct of *m* unprincipled in their lusts.
2: 9 knows how to rescue devout *m* from trial,
2:10 These bold and arrogant *m* have no qualms
2:11 greater than *m* in strength and power,
2:12 These *m* pour abuse on things of which they
2:17 These *m* are waterless springs,
2:20 When *m* have fled a polluted world by
3: 3 sneering *m* who are ruled by their passions
3: 7 the day when godless *m* will be destroyed.
3:11 this way, what sort of *m* must you not be!
1Jn 2:13 Young *m*, I address you,
2:14 the beginning, I address you, young *m*,
2Jn 1: 7 deceitful *m* have gone out into the world,
1: 7 *m* who do not acknowledge Jesus Christ as
3Jn 1: 8 we owe it to such *m* to support them and
Jude 1:12 *m* are blotches on your Christian banquets.
1:15 ones about him to pass judgment on all *m*,
1:16 These *m* are grumblers and whiners.
Rv 2: 2 I know you cannot tolerate wicked *m*;
3:10 on the whole world, to test all *m* on earth.
5: 9 for God *m* of every race and tongue,
6: 4 by allowing *m* to slaughter one another.
9: 4 only to those *m* who had not the seal of God
9: 6 *m* will seek death but will not find it;
9:10 was enough venom to harm *m* for five months.
11: 9 *M* from every people and race,
13: 4 *M* worshiped the dragon for giving his
13:13 down from heaven to earth as *m* looked on.
13:16 It forced all *m*,
14: 4 These are *m* who have never been defiled by
16: 2 festering boils broke out on the *m*
16: 8 He was commissioned to burn *m* with fire.
16:10 *m* bit their tongues in pain and blasphemed
16:18 in all the time *m* have lived on the earth.
16:21 and *m* blasphemed God for the plague of
17: 8 All the *m* of the earth whose names have
18:17 navigator, all sailors and seafaring *m*,
19:18 flesh of all *m*, the free and the slave,
19:20 presence the prodigies that led *m* astray,
21: 3 "This is God's dwelling among *m*.

MENACE (1)
Ex 10: 7 to him, "How long must he be a *m* to us?

MENAHEM (8)
2Kgs 15:14 *M*, son of Gadi,
15:16 At that time, *M* punished Tappuah,
15:17 year of Azariah, king of Judah, *M*,
15:19 and *M* gave him a thousand talents of
15:20 *M* secured the money to give to the king of
15:21 The rest of the acts of *M*,
15:22 *M* rested with his ancestors,
15:23 king of Judah, Pekahiah, son of *M*,

MEND (1)
2Cor 13:11 *M* your ways.

MENDED (1)
Jos 9: 4 their asses, and old wineskins, torn and *m*.

MENE (2)
Dn 5:25 *M*, TEKEL, and PERES.
5:26 *M*, God has numbered your kingdom and put

MENELAUS (18)
2Mc 4:23 Three years later Jason sent *M*,
4:27 Although *M* had obtained the office,
4:29 *M* left his brother Lysimachus as his
4:32 *M*, thinking this is a good opportunity,
4:34 Thereupon *M* approached Andronicus
4:39 in the city with the connivance of *M*.
4:43 about this affair were brought against *M*.
4:45 *M*, seeing himself on the losing side,
4:47 *M*, who was the cause of all the trouble,
4:50 *M*, thanks to the covetousness of the men
5: 5 being taken, *M* took refuge in the citadel.
5:15 *M*, that traitor both to the laws
5:23 *M*, who lorded it over his fellow citizens
11:29 *M* has told us of your wish to return home
11:32 I have also sent *M* to reassure you.
13: 3 *M* also joined them,
13: 4 that *M* was to blame for all the trouble,
13: 7 In such a manner was *M*,

MENESTHEUS (2)
2Mc 4: 4 was serious and that Apollonius, son of *M*,
4:21 When Apollonius, son of *M*,

MENNA (1)
Lk 3:31 son of Eliakim, son of Melea, son of *M*,

MEN'S (26)
Gn 44: 1 *m* bags with as much food as they can carry,
Dt 32:26 and blot out their name from *m* memories,'
Ps(s) 104:14 for the cattle, and vegetation for *m* use,
104:15 the earth, and wine to gladden *m* hearts,
Eccl 3:11 their hearts, without *m* ever discovering,
Wis 2:15 us, Because his life is not like other *m*,
6:13 herself known in anticipation of *m* desire;
15: 4 the evil creation of *m* fancy deceive us,
Sir 17: 5 He forms *m* tongues and eyes and ears,
21:26 mouths, wise *m* words are in their hearts.
50:22 fosters *m* growth from their mother's womb,
Lam 3:35 When he distorts *m* rights in the very
Bar 6: 3 you will see borne upon *m* shoulders gods
6:25 no feet, they are carried on *m* shoulders,
Ez 13:20 bands of yours in which you entrap *m* lives:
Hb 2: 8 Because of *m* blood shed,
2:17 Because of *m* blood shed,
Mt 23: 4 hard to carry, to lay on other *m* shoulders,
23:13 the doors of the kingdom of God in *m* faces,
23:27 but inside full of filth and dead *m* bones.
Jn 20:23 If you forgive *m* sins,
2Cor 5:19 not counting *m* transgressions against them,
Col 2:23 chief effect is that they indulge *m* pride.
1Tm 5:24 Some *m* sins are flagrant and cry out for
5:24 while other *m* sins will appear only later.
Rv 9: 7 their faces were like *m* faces but they had

MENSTRUAL (8)
Lv 12: 2 the same uncleanness as at her *m* period.
15:19 "When a woman has her *m* flow,
15:25 for several days outside her *m* period,
15:25 be unclean, just as during her *m* period.
15:33 well as for the woman who has her *m* period,
20:18 with a woman during her *m* period,
Ez 18: 6 relations with a woman in her *m* period;
22:10 those who coerce women in their *m* period.

MENSTRUATION (4)
Lv 12: 5 days she shall be as unclean as at her *m*,
15:26 becomes unclean, as it would during her *m*,
15:26 sits becomes unclean just as during her *m*.
18:19 with her while she is unclean from *m*.

MENSTRUOUS (2)
Bar 6:28 the *m* and women in childbed handle their
Ez 36:17 was like the defilement of a *m* woman.

MENTAL (1)
Prv 15:13 but by *m* anguish the spirit is broken.

MENTALITY (1)
1Pt 4: 1 therefore, arm yourselves with his same *m*.

MENTION (13)
Ex 23:13 "Never *m* the name of any other god;
Dt 2:25 so that at the *m* of your name they will
Jgs 14: 7 *m* to his father or mother what he had done.
1Sm 4:18 At this *m* of the ark of God,
Jb 41: 4 I need hardly *m* his limbs,
Jer 20: 9 I say to myself, I will not *m* him,
23:36 the burden of the LORD you shall *m* no more.
Am 6:10 for no one must *m* the name of the LORD.
Jon 4:11 from their left, not to *m* the many cattle?"
Acts 4:17 never to *m* that man's name to anyone again."
Rom 1: 9 witness that I constantly *m* you in prayer,
Eph 5:12 to *m* the things these people do in secret;
Phlm 1:19 not to *m* that you owe me your very self!

MENTIONED (9)
Dt 28:61 or calamity not *m* in this book of the law,
29:19 curse *m* in this book will alight on him.
Jos 21:16 nine cities from the two tribes *m*.
1Sm 10:16 But he *m* nothing to him of what Samuel had
18:23 But when Saul's servants *m* this to David,
2Mc 4: 1 The Simon *m* above as the informer about
14: 8 unreasonable conduct of the people just *m*.
Zec 13: 2 the land, so that they shall be *m* no more;
Eph 5: 3 any sort, let them not even be *m* among you;

MENTIONING (1)
Gn 40:14 please do me the favor of *m* me to Pharaoh,

MENTIONS (1)
Jer 23:34 or anyone else *m* "the burden of the LORD,"

MEONOTHAI (2)
1Chr 4:13 The sons of Othniel were Hathath and *M*;
4:14 *M* became the father of Ophrah.

MEPHAATH (4)
Jos 13:18 Beth-baal-meon, Jahaz, Kedemoth, *M*,
21:37 lands, and *M* with its pasture lands:
1Chr 6:64 lands, and *M* with its pasture lands.
Jer 48:21 on Holon, Jahzah, and *M*,

MERAIAH (1)
Neh 12:12 for Seraiah, *M*; for Jeremiah, Hananiah;

MERAIOTH (6)
1Chr 5:32 Zerahiah became the father of *M*.
5:33 *M* became the father of Amariah.
6:37 whose son was Zerahiah, whose son was *M*,
9:11 son of Meshullam, son of Zadok, son of *M*,
Ezr 7: 3 son of Amariah, son of Azariah, son of *M*,
Neh 11:11 son of Meshullam, son of Zadok, son of *M*,

MERARI (29)
Gn 46:11 Gershon, Kohath, and *M*.
Ex 6:16 order, are Gershon, Kohath and *M*.
6:19 The sons of *M* were Mahli and Mushi.
Nm 3:17 of Levi were named Gershon, Kohath and *M*.
3:20 The descendants of *M*,
3:33 To *M* belonged the clans of the Mahlites
3:33 these were the clans of *M*.
3:35 house of the clans of *M* was Zuriel,
10:17 the clans of Gershon and *M* set out,
26:57 through *M* the clan of the Merarites.
1Chr 5:27 sons of Levi were Gershon, Kohath, and *M*.
6: 1 sons of Levi were Gershon, Kohath, and *M*.
6: 4 The sons of *M* were Mahli and Mushi.
6:14 The descendants of *M* were Mahli,
6:32 son of Mahli, son of Mushi, son of *M*,
9:14 of Hashabiah, one of the descendants of *M*;
15: 6 of the sons of *M*, Asaiah, their chief
15:17 among the sons of *M*, their brethen, Ethan,
23: 6 Gershon, Kohath, and *M*.
23:21 sons of *M*: Mahli and Mushi.
24:26 The descendants of *M* were Mahli,
24:27 descendants of *M* through his son Uzziah:
26:10 Hosah, a descendant of *M*, had these sons:
26:19 the gatekeepers, descendants of Kore and *M*.
2Chr 29:12 of the sons of *M*:
34:12 and Obadiah, Levites of the line of *M*,
Ezr 8:19 and with him Jeshaiah, sons of *M*,
Jdt 8: 1 Now in those days Judith, daughter of *M*,
16: 6 But Judith, the daughter of *M*,

MERARITE (3)
Nm 4:45 of the men of the *M* clans which Moses took,
Jos 21:34 *M* clans, the last of the Levites,
21:40 cities which were allotted to the *M* clans,

MERARITES (10)
Nm 3:36 The *M* were charged with the care of
4:29 "Among the *M*, too, you shall enroll
4:33 is the task of the clans of the *M* during
4:42 the registration was made among the *M*,
7: 8 to the *M* in proportion to their duties,
26:57 through Merari the clan of the *M*.
Jos 21: 7 The clans of the *M* obtained twelve cities
1Chr 6:29 Their brothers, the *M*, stood at the left:
6:48 The clans of the *M* obtained twelve cities
6:62 the *M* received from the tribe of Zebulun:

MERATHAIM (1)
Jer 50:21 Attack the land of *M*,

MERCENARIES (4)
2Chr 25:13 the *m* whom Amaziah had dismissed from
Jdt 6: 1 of the Moabites, and of the Ammonite *m*:
1Mc 4:35 began to recruit *m* so as to return to Judea
Jer 46:21 The *m* in her ranks are like fatted calves;

MERCENARY (3)
Jdt 6: 5 As for you, Achior, you Ammonite *m*,
1Mc 6:29 *M* forces also came to him from other
15: 3 I have recruited a large number of *m*

MERCHANDISE (7)

Neh 10:32 When the peoples of the land bring in *m* or
13:16 importing fish and every other kind of *m*
13:20 sellers of various kinds of *m* spent the night
Is 23:18 *m* and her hire shall be sacred to the LORD.
23:18 but from her *m* those who dwell before the
Ez 26:12 wealth shall be plundered, your *m* pillaged;
27:33 and *m* you enriched the kings of the earth.

MERCHANDISING (1)

Ez 27:25 of Tarshish journeyed for you in your *m*.

MERCHANT (7)

Prv 31:14 Like *m* ships, she secures her provisions
Sir 26:20 A *m* can hardly remain upright,
37:11 a coward about war, to a *m* about business,
42: 5 or of bargaining in dealing with a *m*;
Is 23: 3 her revenue, and she the *m* among nations.
Hos 12: 8 A *m* who holds a false balance,
Zec 14:21 be any *m* in the house of the LORD of hosts.

MERCHANTS (23)

1Kgs 10:15 the Tarshish fleet, from the traffic of *m*,
2Chr 9:14 from travelers and what the *m* brought.
Neh 3:31 quarters of the temple slaves and the *m*,
3:32 and the *m* carried out the work of repair.
13:20 The *m* and sellers of various kinds of
1Mc 3:41 the *m* of the country heard of their fame,
Jb 40:30 Will the *m* divide him up?
Prv 31:24 sells them, and stocks the *m* with belts.
Is 23: 2 you who dwell on the coast, you *m* of Sidon,
23: 8 bestower of crowns, Whose *m* are princes,
Bar 3:23 on earth, the *m* of Midian and Teman,
Ez 17: 4 a land of tradesmen, set it in a city of *m*.
27:22 *m* of Sheba and Raamah also traded with you,
27:23 Haran, Canneh, and Eden, the *m* of Sheba,
38:13 the *m* of Tarshish and all her young lions
Zep 1:11 for all the *m* will be destroyed,
Zec 11: 7 flock to be slaughtered for the sheep *m*.
11:11 The sheep *m* who were watching me
Mt 13:45 heaven is like a *m* search for fine pearls.
Rv 18: 3 and the world's *m* grew rich from her
18:11 The *m* of the world will weep and mourn
18:15 The *m* who deal in these goods,
18:23 Because your *m* were the world's nobility,

MERCIES (5)

Sir 18: 3 power, or exhaust the tale of his *m*?
51: 8 But then I remembered the *m* of the LORD,
Lam 3:22 are not exhausted, his *m* are not spent;
3:32 he takes pity, in the abundance of his *m*;
2Cor 1: 3 of our Lord Jesus Christ, the Father of *m*,

MERCIFUL (36)

Gn 43:14 dispose the man to be *m* toward you,
Ex 34: 6 "The LORD, the LORD, a *m* and gracious God,
Dt 4:31 Since the LORD, your God, is a *m* God,
7: 9 the faithful God who keeps his *m* covenant
7:12 will keep with you the *m* covenant which he
Ru 2:20 is ever *m* to the living and to the dead,"
2Sm 24:14 fall by the hand of God, for he is most *m*;
1Kgs 8:50 captors, so that these will be *m* to them.
20:31 kings of the land of Israel are *m* kings.
2Kgs 13:23 But the Lord was *m* with Israel and looked
2Chr 30: 9 for *m* and compassionate is the LORD,
Neh 9:31 them, for you are a kind and *m* God.
Tb 8:17 for you were *m* toward two only children.
Jdt 16:15 to those who fear you, you are very *m*.
2Mc 1:24 things, awesome and strong, just and *m*,
8:29 imploring the *m* Lord to be completely
13:12 and had implored the *m* LORD continuously
Ps(s) 78:38 Yet he, being *m*, forgave their sin
86:15 But you, O Lord, are a God *m* and gracious,
103: 8 *M* and gracious is the LORD,
111: 4 gracious and *m* is the LORD.
112: 4 he is gracious and *m* and just.
116: 5 yes, our God is *m*.
135:14 his people, and is *m* to his servants.
145: 8 The LORD is gracious and *m*,
Sir 2:11 Compassionate and *m* is the LORD;
18:11 Man may be *m* to his fellow man,
18:13 *M* to those who accept his guidance,
50:19 would shout for joy, praying to the *M* One,
Jer 3:12 For I am *m*, says the LORD,
Dn 9: 4 you who keep your *m* covenant toward those
Jl 2:13 For gracious and *m* is he,
Jon 4: 2 I knew that you are a gracious and *m* God,
Lk 18:13 his breast and say, 'O God, be *m* to me,
Heb 2:17 that he might be a *m* and faithful high
Jas 5:11 what the Lord, who is compassionate and *m*,

MERCIFULLY (5)

Tb 11:17 how God had *m* restored sight to his eyes.
Mt 18:33 not have dealt *m* with your fellow servant,
Lk 1:72 He has dealt *m* with our fathers and
1Tm 1:13 in my unbelief, I have been treated *m*,
1:16 on that very account I was dealt with *m*,

MERCILESS (8)

Prv 5: 9 honor to others, and your years to a *m* one;
11:17 himself, but a *m* man harms himself.
12:10 beast, but the heart of the wicked is *m*.
17:11 but a *m* messenger will be sent against him.
Wis 12: 5 These *m* murderers of children,
19: 1 the wicked, *m* wrath assailed until the end.
Sir 35:20 the *m* and wreaks vengeance upon the proud;
Jas 2:13 *M* is the judgment on the man who has not

MERCILESSLY (1)

Sir 13:12 *M* he will make of you a laughingstock,

MERCY (212)

Gn 19:16 he hesitated, the men, by the LORD's *m*,
Ex 15:13 In your *m* you led the people you redeemed;
20: 6 *m* down to the thousandth generation,
33:19 whom I will, I who grant *m* to whom I will.
Dt 5:10 and fourth generation but bestowing *m*,
7: 2 no covenant with them and show them no *m*.
13:18 he may show you mercy and in his *m* for you
23:15 you and to put your enemies at your *m*,
Jos 11:20 in destruction and thus receive no *m*,
1Sm 12: 7 recount for you all the acts of *m* the LORD
1Kgs 8:50 you, and grant them *m* before their captors,
1Chr 21:13 hand of the LORD, whose *m* is very great,
2Chr 5:13 for he is good, for his *m* endures forever,"
7: 3 he is good, for his *m* endures forever."
7: 6 the LORD, for his *m* endures forever,"
20:21 to the LORD, for his *m* endures forever."
30: 9 your children will find *m* with their captors
Ezr 9: 8 ago, *m* came to us from the LORD our God,
Neh 1: 5 you who preserve your covenant of *m* toward
9:17 compassionate, slow to anger and rich in *m*;
9:19 *m* you did not forsake them in the desert.
9:27 and according to your great *m* give them
9:28 and delivered them according to your *m*,
9:31 Yet in your great *m* you did not completely
9:32 you who in your *m* preserve the covenant,
13:22 and have *m* on me in accordance with your
13:22 on me in accordance with your great *m*!
Tb 3: 2 All your ways are *m* and truth;
6:18 to show you *m* and grant you deliverance.
7:11 May he grant you *m* and peace."
8: 4 have *m* on us and to grant us deliverance."
8: 7 Call down your *m* on me and on her,
8:16 dealt with us according to your great *m*.
8:17 Grant them, Master, *m* and deliverance,
8:17 lives to fulfillment with happiness and *m*."
11:15 me, and it is he who has had *m* on me.
13: 2 For he scourges and then has *m*;
13: 5 but will again have *m* on you all.
13: 6 look with favor upon you and show you *m*.
14: 5 But God will again have *m* on them and
Jdt 7:30 the Lord our God, to show his *m* toward us;
13:14 withdrawn his *m* from the house of Israel,
Est B: 6 of their enemies, without any pity or *m*,
1Mc 3:44 and to pray and implore *m* and compassion.
4:24 he is good, for his *m* endures forever."
11:49 that the Jews held the city at their *m*,
11:62 the people of Gaza appealed to him for *m*,
13:46 they said, "but according to your *m*."
16: 3 now grown old, but you, by the *m* of Heaven,
2Mc 2: 7 his people together again and shows them *m*.
2:18 that he will soon have *m* on us and gather
5: 6 slaughtered his fellow citizens without *m*,
5:12 his soldiers to cut down without *m*
6:16 He never withdraws his *m* from us.
7:23 the origin of everything, he, in his *m*,
7:29 of *m* I may receive you again with them."
7:37 imploring God to show *m* soon to our nation,
8: 3 to have *m* on the city,
8: 5 for the Lord's wrath had now changed to *m*.
8:27 let descend on them the first dew of his *m*.
9:13 Lord, who would no longer have *m* on him,
11: 9 of them together thanked God for his *m*,
11:10 that the Lord had shown his *m* toward them,
Jb 16:13 directions, He pierces my sides without *m*,
30:21 *m* and with your strong hand you buffet me.
37:13 of the earth, whether for punishment or *m*,
Ps(s) 51: 3 Have *m* on me, O God, in your goodness;
69:17 in your great *m* turn toward me.
102:14 You will arise and have *m* on Zion,
118: 2 of Israel say, "His *m* endures forever."
118: 3 of Aaron say, "His *m* endures forever."
118: 4 fear the LORD say, "His *m* endures forever."
136: 1 for he is good, for his *m* endures forever;
136: 2 the God of gods, for his *m* endures forever;
136: 3 Lord of lords, for his *m* endures forever;
136: 4 great wonders, for his *m* endures forever;
136: 5 in wisdom, for his *m* endures forever;
136: 6 upon the waters, for his *m* endures forever;
136: 7 great lights, for his *m* endures forever;
136: 8 over the day, for his *m* endures forever;
136: 9 over the night, for his *m* endures forever;
136:10 first-born, for his *m* endures forever;
136:11 their midst, for his *m* endures forever;
136:12 arm, for his *m* endures forever;
136:13 Sea in twain, for his *m* endures forever;
136:14 its midst, for his *m* endures forever;
136:15 the Red Sea, for his *m* endures forever;
136:16 the wilderness, for his *m* endures forever;
136:17 great kings, for his *m* endures forever;
136:18 powerful kings, for his *m* endures forever;
136:19 the Amorites, for his *m* endures forever;
136:20 king of Bashan, for his *m* endures forever;
136:21 land a heritage, for his *m* endures forever;
136:22 his servant, for his *m* endures forever;
136:23 our abjection, for his *m* endures forever;
136:24 from our foes, for his *m* endures forever;
136:25 to all flesh, for his *m* endures forever.
136:26 God of heaven, for his *m* endures forever.
Prv 28:13 who confesses and forsakes them obtains *m*.
Wis 3: 9 Because grace and *m* are with his holy ones,
6: 6 For the lowly may be pardoned out of *m*
9: 1 God of my fathers, Lord of *m*,
11:23 But you have *m* on all,
12:22 and, when being judged, may look for *m*.
15: 1 slow to anger, and governing all with *m*.
16:10 your *m* brought the antidote to heal them.
Sir 2: 7 You who fear the LORD, wait for his *m*,
2: 9 for good things, for lasting joy and *m*.
2:18 to his majesty is the *m* that he shows.
5: 6 Great is his *m*; my many sins he will forgive
5: 7 For *m* and anger alike are with him;
12: 3 wicked, nor is it an act of *m* that he does.
16:11 For *m* and anger alike are with him who
16:12 Great as his *m* is his punishment;
17:24 How great the *m* of the LORD,
18: 9 with men and showers upon them his *m*.
18:11 man, but the LORD's *m* reaches all flesh,
28: 4 Should a man refuse *m* to his fellows,
35:23 of his people, and gladdens them by his *m*.
35:24 Welcome is his *m* in time of distress as
36:11 Show *m* to the people called by your name;
37:11 about generosity, to a cruel man about *m*,
47:22 But God does not withdraw his *m*,
51: 3 *m* From the scourge of a slanderous tongue,
51:29 Let your spirits rejoice in the *m* of God,
Is 16: 5 the land, A throne shall be set up in *m*,
27:11 shall he who formed them have *m* on them.
47: 6 but you showed them no *m*,
49:13 his people and shows *m* to his afflicted.
54:10 be shaken, says the LORD, who has *m* on you.
55: 7 Let him turn to the LORD for *m*;
60:10 yet in my good will I have shown you *m*.
63: 7 according to him *m* and his great kindness.
63:15 your might, your surge of pity and your *m*?
Jer 16:13 night, because I will not grant you my *m*.
21: 7 sword, without quarter, without pity or *m*.
31: 3 so I have kept my *m* toward you.
31:20 My heart stirs for him, I must show him *m*,
33:11 his *m* endures forever."
33:26 I will change their lot and show them *m*.
42:12 I will grant you *m*,
Bar 2:19 do we base our plea for *m* in your sight,
2:27 all your clemency and in all your great *m*,
3: 2 you are a God of *m*; and have *m* on us
4:22 Because of the *m* that will swiftly reach you
5: 9 glory with his *m* and justice for company.
Ez 5:11 not look upon you with pity nor have *m*.
7: 4 not look upon you with pity nor have *m*;
7: 9 not look upon you with pity nor have *m*;
8:18 look upon them with pity nor will I show *m*.
9: 5 not look on them with pity nor show any *m*!
9:10 look upon them with pity, nor show any *m*.
Dn 2:18 that they might implore the *m* of the God
3:35 Do not take away your *m* from us,
3:42 deal with us in your kindness and great *m*.
3:89 for he is good, for his *m* endures forever.
3:90 him thanks, because his *m* endures forever."
9:18 not on our just deeds, but on your great *m*.
Hos 2:21 in right and in justice, in love and in *m*;
4: 1 There is no fidelity, no *m*,
Jon 2: 9 vain idols forsake their source of *m*.
Hb 1:17 his sword to slay peoples without *m*?
Zec 1:12 how long will you be without *m* for
1:16 I will turn to Jerusalem in *m*;
10: 6 bring them back, because I have *m* on them,
Mal 1: 9 So now if you implore God for *m* on us,
Mt 5: 7 are they who show *m*; mercy shall be theirs.
6: 4 Keep your deeds of *m* secret,
9:13 words, 'It is *m* I desire and not sacrifice.'
12: 7 text, 'It is *m* I desire and not sacrifice,'
23:23 of the law, justice and *m* and good faith.
Mk 5:19 much the Lord in his *m* has done for you."
Lk 1:50 *m* is from age to age on those who fear him.
1:54 his servant, ever mindful of his *m*;
1:58 that the Lord had extended his *m* to her,
1:78 shall visit us in his *m* To shine on those
Rom 9:15 "I will show *m* to whomever I choose;
9:16 of man's willing or doing but of God's *m*.
9:18 other words, God has *m* on whom he wishes,
9:23 of his glory toward the vessels for *m*,
10:12 rich in *m* toward all who call upon him.
11:30 have received *m* through their disobedience,
11:31 to show you *m*— that they too may receive *m*.
11:32 disobedience that he might have *m* on all.
12: 1 I beg you through the *m* of God to offer
12: 8 works of *m* should do so cheerfully.
15: 9 the Gentiles glorify God because of his *m*.
1Cor 7:25 who is trustworthy, thanks to the Lord's *m*.
2Cor 4: 1 we possess this ministry through God's *m*,
Gal 6:16 and *m* on all who follow this rule of life,

MERCY (cont.)
Eph 2: 4 But God is rich in *m;*
Col 3:12 clothe yourselves with heartfelt *m,*
2Thes 2:16 his *m* gave us eternal consolation and hope,
1Tm 1: 2 May grace, *m,* and peace be yours
2Tm 1: 2 May grace, *m,* and peace from God
1:16 Lord have *m* on the family of Onesiphorus,
1:18 on the great Day, may the Lord grant him *m!*
Ti 3: 5 deeds we had done, but because of his *m.*
Heb 4:16 approach the throne of grace to receive *m*
10:28 law of Moses is put to death without *m*
Jas 2:13 not shown *m;* but *m* triumphs over judgment.
1Pt 1: 3 he who in his great *m* gave us new birth;
2:10 no mercy for you, but now you have found *m.*
2Jn 1: 3 and love, then, we shall have grace, *m,*
Jude 1: 2 May *m,* peace, and love be yours
1:21 and welcome the *m* of our Lord Jesus Christ

MERE (25)
Nm 13:33 we felt like *m* grasshoppers,
1Kgs 3: 7 but I am a *m* youth,
2Kgs 18:20 Do you think *m* words substitute for
2Mc 7:24 the king appealed to him, not with *m* words,
8:18 *m* nod destroy not only those who attack us,
Prv 14:23 is profit, but *m* talk tends only to penury.
Wis 18:25 for the *m* trial of anger was enough.
Sir 16:17 the earth's foundations, at his *m* glance,
48:12 spirit, wrought many marvels by his *m* word.
Is 17: 5 Like the reaper's *m* armful of stalks when
29:21 off, those whose *m* word condemns a man,
36: 5 Do you think *m* words substitute for
65:20 a *m* youth who reaches but a hundred years,
Jer 14:22 Or can the *m* heavens send showers?
16:19 *M* frauds are the heritage of our fathers,
Mt 16:17 No *m* man has revealed this to you,
18:28 him a *m* fraction of what he himself owed.
Mk 7: 7 they teach as dogmas *m* human precepts.'
Acts 1:12 a *m* sabbath's journey away.
2Cor 5:16 on anyone in terms of *m* human judgment.
Gal 1:11 proclaimed to you is no *m* human invention.
Col 2: 8 philosophy that follows *m* human traditions,
1Thes 1: 5 *m* matter of words for you but one of power;
2Tm 2:14 before God to stop disputing about *m* words.
Heb 9:24 made by hands, a *m* copy of the true one;

MERED (2)
1Chr 4:17 The sons of Ezrah were Jether, *M,*
4:18 the daughter of Pharaoh, whom *M* married.

MERED'S (1)
1Chr 4:18 His *(M)* Egyptian wife bore Jered,

MERELY (30)
Ex 11: 1 In fact, he will not *m* let you go;
Lv 13: 6 it was *m* eczema.
13:23 spreading, it is *m* the scar of the boil;
13:28 dying out, it is *m* the scab of the burn;
13:40 is not unclean *m* because of his bald crown.
13:41 not unclean *m* because of his bald forehead.
Nm 16:29 *m* suffering the fate common to all mankind,
20:19 is no harm in *m* letting us march through."
27: 4 from his clan *m* because he had no son?
Jos 17:17 You shall have not *m* one share,
Est E:24 it will be left not *m* untrodden by men,
Wis 2:14 *m* to see him is a hardship for us,
16:27 when *m* warmed by a momentary sunbeam,
Is 66: 3 *M* slaughtering an ox is like slaying a man;
Ob 1: 5 they not steal *m* till they had enough?
Mt 21:25 Was it divine or *m* human?"
21:26 while if we say, *m* human,'
Mk 11:30 baptism of divine origin or *m* from men?"
11:32 But can we say, *m* human'?"
Acts 15:20 We should *m* write to them to abstain from
21:25 were *m* to avoid meat sacrificed to idols,
24:22 words he adjourned the trial, saying *m,*
Rom 3: 5 (I speak in a *m* human way.)
4:12 those circumcised who are not *m* so
1Cor 9: 8 reasons I am giving you are *m* human ones,
2Cor 10: 4 The weapons of our warfare are not *m* human.
Col 2:22 based on *m* human precepts and doctrines.
1Jn 3:18 deed and in truth and not *m* talk about it.
Rv 19:10 I am *m* a fellow servant with you and your
22: 9 I am *m* a fellow servant with you and your

MEREMOTH (7)
Ezr 8:33 of our God and consigned to the priest *M,*
10:36 Uel, Benaiah, Bedeiah, Cheluhi, Vaniah, *M,*
Neh 3: 4 At their side *M,* son of Uriah,
3:21 After him, *M,* son of Uriah,
10: 6 Hattush, Shebaniah, Malluch, Harim, *M,*
12: 3 Malluch, Hattush, Shecaniah, Rehum, *M,*
12:15 for *M,* Helkai;

MERES (1)
Est 1:14 Carshena, Shethar, Admatha, Tarshish, *M,*

MEREST (2)
Mt 11:25 clever you have revealed to the *m* children.
Lk 10:21 clever you have revealed to the *m* children.

MERIBAH (8)
Ex 17: 7 The place was called Massah and *M.*
Nm 20:13 These are the waters of *M,*
20:24 against my commandment at the waters of *M.*
27:14 water of *M* of Kadesh in the desert of Zin.]
Dt 33: 8 you contended with him at the waters of *M.*
Ps(s) 81: 8 I tested you at the waters of *M.*
95: 8 "Harden not your hearts as at *M,*
106:32 They angered him at the waters of *M.*

MERIBATH-KADESH (4)
Dt 32:51 among the Israelites at the waters of *M*
33: 2 forth from Mount Paran and advanced from *M.*
Ez 47:19 from Tamar to the waters of *M,*
48:28 extend from Tamar to the waters of *M,*

MERIBBAAL (19)
2Sm 4: 4 Saul, had a son named *M* with crippled feet.
9: 6 When *M,* son of Jonathan, son of Saul
9: 6 David said, *M,*" and he answered
9:10 *M,* your lord's son, shall always eat
9:11 And so *M* ate at David's table like one of
9:12 *M* had a young son whose name was *M*
9:12 the tenants of Ziba's family worked for *M.*
9:13 But *M* lived in Jerusalen,
16: 1 the top when Ziba, the servant of *M,*
16: 4 Everything *M* had is yours."
19:25 *M,* son of Saul, also went down
19:26 asked him, "Why did you not go with me, *M?*"
19:31 *M* answered the king, "Indeed let him have
21: 7 The king, however, spared *M,*
21: 8 But the king took Armoni and *M,*
1Chr 8:34 Meribbaal, and *M* became the father of Micah.
8:34 The son of Jonathan was *M*
9:40 The son of Jonathan was *M,* and *M* became

MERIT (8)
Dt 19: 6 even though he does not *m* death since he
Ps(s) 106:31 him for *m* through all generations forever.
Sir 18:19 Before you are judged, seek *m* for yourself,
23:12 There are words which *m* death;
Jer 17:10 his ways, according to the *m* of his deeds.
Mt 5:46 who love you, what *m* is there in that?
Lk 6:34 repayment, what *m* is there in it for you?
2Tm 1: 9 not because of any *m* of ours but according

MERITED (2)
2Mc 6:23 age, the *m* distinction of his gray hair,
2Tm 4: 8 From now on a *m* crown awaits me;

MERITS (6)
Dt 9: 4 'It is because of my *m* that the LORD has
9: 5 it is not because of your *m* or the
9: 6 it is not because of your *m* that the LORD,
2Sm 12: 5 lives, the man who has done this *m* death!
Sir 4:21 and a shame that *m* honor and respect.
47:12 his *m* he had as his successor a wise son,

MEROB (4)
1Sm 14:49 his two daughters were named, the elder, *M,*
18:17 to David, "There is my older daughter, *M,*
18:19 for Saul's daughter *M* to be given to David,
2Sm 21: 8 daughter *M* that she had borne to Adriel,

MERODACH (1)
Jer 50: 2 is taken, Bel confounded, *M* shattered;

MERODACH-BALADAN (2)
2Kgs 20:12 At that time, when *M,* son of Baladan
Is 39: 1 At that time when *M,* son of Baladan

MEROM (2)
Jos 11: 5 forces and marched to the waters of *M,*
11: 7 at the waters of *M* in a surprise attack.

MERONOTHITE (2)
1Chr 27:30 over the she-asses was Jehdeiah the *M;*
Neh 3: 7 were Melatiah the Gibeonite, Jadon the *M,*

MEROZ (1)
Jgs 5:23 "Curse *M,*" says the LORD, "hurl a curse

MERRILY (2)
Ps(s) 132: 9 let your faithful ones shout *m* for joy.
132:16 her faithful ones shall shout *m* for joy.

MERRIMENT (5)
Est 8:16 and there was splendor and *m* for the Jews,
8:17 order arrived, there was *m* and exultation,
Eccl 10:19 forth *m* and wine makes the living glad,
Sir 31:28 good cheer and *m* are wine drunk freely at
Rv 11:10 over them and in their *m* exchange gifts,

MERRY (30)
Gn 31:27 and I would have sent you off with *m*
43:34 So they drank freely and made *m* with him.
Lv 23:40 a week you shall make *m* before the LORD,
Dt 12: 7 eat and make *m* over all your undertakings,
12:12 You shall make *m* before the LORD,
12:18 shall make *m* over all your undertakings.
14:26 partake of it and make *m* with your family.
16:11 you shall make *m* in his presence together
16:14 You shall make *m* at your feast,
16:15 you shall do nought but make *m.*
26:11 shall make *m* over all these good things
27: 7 eat them there, making *m* before the LORD,
Jgs 16:23 sacrifice to their god Dagon and to make *m.*
1Sm 25:36 and Nabal was *m* because he was very drunk.
2Sm 6: 5 *m* before the LORD with all their strength,
6:21 not only will I make *m* before the LORD,
13:28 When Amnon is *m* with wine and I say to you,
1Kgs 4:20 they ate and drank and made *m.*
Tb 7:10 "Eat and drink and be *m* tonight,
Jdt 12:17 said to her, "Drink and be *m* with us!"
Est 1:10 seventh day, when the king was *m* with wine,
Jb 21:12 harp, and make *m* to the sound of the flute.
Ps(s) 22:27 "May your hearts be ever *m!*"
69:33 you who seek God, may your hearts be *m!*
Eccl 9: 7 joy and drink your wine with a *m* heart,
Sir 31:31 nor put him to shame while he is *m;*
Is 9: 2 as men make *m* when dividing spoils.
30:29 a feast is observed, And be *m* of heart,
Jer 31:13 Then the virgins shall make *m* and dance,
Bar 4:33 your collapse, and made *m* at your downfall,

MERRY-HEARTED (1)
Is 24: 7 the vine languishes, all the *m* groan.

MERRYMAKERS (2)
Jer 15:17 not sit celebrating in the circle of *m;*
31: 4 you shall go forth dancing with the *m.*

MESH (1)
1Kgs 7:17 Two pieces of network with a chainlike *m*

MESHA (3)
2Kgs 3: 4 Now *M,* king of Moab, who raised sheep,
1Chr 2:42 *M* his first-born,
8: 9 he became the father of Jobab, Zibia, *M,*

MESHACH (14)
Dn 1: 7 Hananiah to Shadrach, Mishael to *M,*
2:49 request the king made Shadrach, *M,*
3:12 Shadrach, *M,* Abednego; these men, O king
3:13 flew into a rage and sent for Shadrach, *M,*
3:14 "Is it true, Shadrach, *M,*
3:16 Shadrach, *M,* and Abednego answered
3:19 livid with utter rage against Shadrach, *M,*
3:20 men in his army bind Shadrach, *M,*
3:22 devoured the men who threw Shadrach, *M,*
3:93 furnace and called to Shadrach, *M,*
3:93 Thereupon Shadrach, *M,*
3:95 "Blessed be the God of Shadrach, *M,*
3:96 whoever blasphemes the God of Shadrach, *M,*
3:97 Then the king promoted Shadrach, *M,*

MESHECH (8)
Gn 10: 2 Gomer, Magog, Madai, Javan, Tubal, *M,*
1Chr 1: 5 were Gomer, Magog, Madai, Javan, Tubal, *M,*
Ps(s) 120: 5 Woe is me that I sojourn in *M,*
Ez 27:13 Tubal, and *M* were also traders with you,
32:26 There are *M* and Tubal and all their throng
38: 2 of Magog], the chief prince of *M* and Tubal,
38: 3 at you, Gog, chief prince of *M* and Tubal.
39: 1 I am coming at you, Gog, chief prince of *M*

MESHELEMIAH (4)
1Chr 9:21 Zechariah, son of *M,*
26: 1 Of the Korahites was *M,*
26: 9 Of *M,* eighteen sons and brethren,
26:14 was cast for the east side, it fell to *M.*

MESHELEMIAH'S (1)
1Chr 26: 2 *M* sons: Zechariah,

MESHES (1)
Prv 5:22 the *m* of his own sin he will be held fast;

MESHEZABEL (3)
Neh 3: 4 Meshullam, son of Berechiah, son of *M;*
10:22 Nebai, Magpiash, Meshullam, Hezir, *M,*
11:24 Pethahiah, son of *M,*

MESHILLEMITH (1)
1Chr 9:12 of Jahzerah, son of Meshullam, son of *M,*

MESHILLEMOTH (2)
2Chr 28:12 son of Johanan, Berechiah, son of *M,*
Neh 11:13 son of Azarel, son of Ahzai, son of *M,*

MESHOBAB (1)
1Chr 4:34 *M,* Jamlech, Joshah, son of Amaziah,

MESHULLAM (27)

2Kgs 22: 3 scribe Shaphan, son of Azaliah, son of *M*,
1Chr 3:19 The sons of Zerubbabel were *M* and Hananiah;
3:20 The sons of *M* were Hashubah,
5:13 Michael, *M*, Sheba, Jorai, Jacan,
8:17 Zebadiah, *M*, Hizki, Heber, Ishmerai,
9: 7 the Benjaminites were Sallu, son of *M*,
9: 8 *M*, son of Shephatiah,
9:11 Azariah, son of Hilkiah, son of *M*,
9:12 son of Adiel, son of Jahzerah, son of *M*,
2Chr 34:12 of the line of Merari, and Zechariah and *M*,
Ezr 8:16 Jarib, Elnathan, Nathan, Zechariah, and *M*,
10:15 with *M* and Shabbethai the Levite
10:29 *M*, Malluch,
Neh 3: 4 next to him was *M*,
3: 6 *M*, son of Besodeiah;
3:30 after them, *M*, son of Berechiah,
6:18 Jehohanan had married the daughter of *M*,
8: 4 Hashum, Hashbaddanah, Zechariah, *M*.
10: 8 Obadiah, Daniel, Ginnethon, Baruch, *M*,
10:21 Hariph, Anathoth, Nebai, Magpiash, *M*,
11: 7 Sallu, son of *M*,
11:11 Seraiah, son of Hilkaiah, son of *M*,
12:13 for Ezra, *M*;
12:16 for Ginnethon, *M*;
12:25 *M*, Talmon, and Akkub were gatekeepers.
12:33 of Judah, along with Azariah, Ezra, *M*,

MESHULLEMETH (1)

2Kgs 21:19 His mother's name was *M*,

MESOPOTAMIA (6)

Jdt 2:24 the Euphrates, he went through *M*,
5: 7 They formerly dwelt in *M*,
5: 8 they fled to *M* and dwelt there a long time.
8:26 *M* while he was tending the flocks of Laban,
Acts 2: 9 We live in *M*,
7: 2 still in *M* and before he settled in Haran.

MESRAIM (2)

1Chr 1: 8 The descendants of Ham were Cush, *M*,
1:11 *M* became the father of the Ludim,

MESSAGE (145)

Gn 32: 5 of Seir, the country of Edom, with this *m*:
37:32 the long tunic to their father, with the *m*:
49:28 and gave to each of them an appropriate *m*,
Ex 3:18 "Thus they will heed your *m*.
4: 8 *m* of the first sign, they should believe the *m*
7:16 of the Hebrews, sent me to you with the *m*:
Lv 1: 1 and from the meeting tent gave him this *m*:
Nm 20:14 sent men to the king of Edom with the *m*:
21:21 to Sihon, king of the Amorites, with the *m*,
22: 7 When they had given him Balak's *m*,
22:10 son of Zippor, king of Moab, sent me the *m*:
Jos 11: 1 learned of this, he sent a *m* to Jobab,
22:16 whole community of the LORD sends this *m*:
Jgs 3:19 and said, "I have a private *m* for you,
3:20 Ehud said, "I have a *m* from God for you."
11:28 paid no heed to the *m* Jephthah sent him.
21:13 a *m* to the Benjaminites at the rock Rimmon,
1Sm 8:10 Samuel delivered the *m* of the LORD in full
9:27 moment, that I may give you a *m* from God."
11: 5 The *m* of the inhabitants of Jabesh was
11: 7 of Israel by couriers with the *m*,
15: 1 therefore, listen to the *m* of the LORD.
16:22 his armor-bearer, and sent Jesse the *m*,
25: 9 this *m* fully to Nabal in David's name,
28:20 for he was badly shaken by Samuel's *m*.
2Sm 11: 6 child,"David therefore sent a *m* to Joab,
13: 7 David then sent home a *m* to Tamar,
1Kgs 5:16 Solomon sent back this *m* to Hiram:
12:24 They accepted this *m* of the LORD and gave
20: 3 "This is Ben-hadad's *m*:
20: 5 again and said, "This is Ben-hadad's *m*:
20:10 Ben-hadad then sent him the *m*,
2Kgs 3: 7 Samaria, he sent the king of Judah the *m*:
5:10 The prophet sent him the *m*:
9: 5 "I have a *m* for you, commander," he said.
10: 5 and the guardians, sent this *m* to Jehu:
18:14 this *m* to the king of Assyria at Lachish:
19: 9 he sent envoys to Hezekiah with this *m*:
19:20 son of Amoz, sent this *m* to Hezekiah:
2Chr 2: 2 Moreover, Solomon sent this *m* to Huram,
11: 4 They obeyed this *m* of the LORD and gave up
16: 2 Aram, who lived in Damascus, with this *m*:
20: 2 The *m* was brought to Jehoshaphat:
21:12 letter from the prophet Elijah with this *m*:
25:18 sent a *m* to the cedar of the Lebanon,
30: 1 Hezekiah sent a *m* to all Israel and Judah,
32: 9 with this *m* for King Hezekiah of Judah,
34:28 They brought back this *m* to the king.
Ezr 4:14 we have sent this *m* to inform you,
6:14 supported by the *m* of the prophets,
Neh 6: 2 Sanballat and Geshem sent me this *m*:
6: 5 sent me the same *m* by one of his servants,
Jdt 3: 5 reached Holofernes and given him this *m*,
12: 6 she rose and sent this *m* to Holofernes,
Est 4:10 to Hathach and gave him this *m* for Mordecai:
1Mc 5:14 from Galilee to deliver a similar *m*:
5:48 Then Judas sent them this peaceful *m*:
7:27 to Judas and his brothers this peaceable *m*:
10:25 So he sent them this *m*:
10:51 to Ptolemy, king of Egypt, with this *m*:
10:69 he sent this *m* to Jonathan the high priest:
10:74 When Jonathan heard the *m* of Apollonius,
13:14 him, he sent envoys to him with this *m*:
15:32 When he gave him the king's *m*,
2Mc 11:13 He therefore sent a *m* persuading them to
14:28 this *m* reached Nicanor he was dismayed,
Ps(s) 19: 5 and to the ends of the world, their *m*.
Is 28: 9 To whom would he convey the *m*?
28:19 terror alone shall convey the *m*.
37: 9 he sent envoys to Hezekiah with this *m*:
37:21 son of Amoz, sent this *m* to Hezekiah:
Jer 2: 2 Go, cry out this *m* for Jerusalem to hear!
7: 1 following *m* came to Jeremiah from the LORD:
7: 2 of the LORD, and there proclaim this *m*:
9:19 of the LORD, let your ears receive his *m*.
11: 1 following *m* came to Jeremiah from the LORD:
13: 8 Then the *m* came to me from the LORD:
16: 1 This *m* came to me from the LORD:
18: 2 there I will give you my *m*.
20: 8 cry out, violence and outrage is my *m*;
21: 1 The *m* which came to Jeremiah from the LORD
22: 1 the king of Judah and there deliver this *m*:
25: 5 all his servants the prophets with this *m*:
26: 1 king of Judah, this *m* came from the LORD:
27: 1 this *m* came to Jeremiah from the LORD:
29:25 the priest, son of Maaseiah, with this *m*:
29:28 For he sent us in Babylon this *m*:
29:31 Send the *m* to all the exiles:
30: 1 following *m* came to Jeremiah from the LORD:
32: 1 This *m* came to Jeremiah from the LORD in
32: 6 This *m* came to me from the LORD,
37:17 whether there was any *m* from the LORD.
42:21 Today I proclaim his *m*,
45: 1 *m* that the prophet Jeremiah gave to Baruch,
46:13 The *m* which the LORD gave to the prophet
Bar 1:10 Their *m* was: We send you funds
Dn 12: 4 the *m* and seal the book until the end time;
Ob 1: 1] Of Edom we have heard a *m* from the LORD,
Jon 3: 2 announce to it the *m* that I will tell you."
Hg 1:13 to the people as the *m* of the LORD:
2:20 The *m* of the LORD came a second time to
Zec 4: 6 me, "This is the LORD's *m* to Zerubbabel:
7:12 *m* that the LORD of hosts had sent
Mt 2:12 a *m* in a dream not to return to Herod,
11: 2 and sent a *m* by his disciples to ask him,
13:19 along the path is the man who hears the *m*
13:20 the *m* and at first receives it with joy.
13:21 or persecution involving the *m* occurs,
13:22 among briers is the man who hears the *m*,
13:23 is the man who hears the *m* and takes it in.
27:19 on the bench, his wife sent him a *m*:
28: 7 That is the *m* I have for you."
Mk 4:33 them the *m* in a way they could understand.
16:20 *m* through the signs which accompanied them.
Jn 17: 8 to them the *m* you entrusted to me,
Acts 2:41 Those who accepted his *m* were baptized;
10:36 is the *m* he has sent to the sons of Israel,
10:44 upon all who were listening to Peter's *m*.
11:19 making the *m* known to none but Jews.
13:15 men of the synagogue sent this *m* to them:
13:26 us that this *m* of salvation was sent forth.
14: 3 He for his part confirmed the *m* with his
14:25 After preaching the *m* in Perga,
15: 7 would hear the *m* of the gospel and believe.
15:27 who will convey this *m* by word of mouth:
16: 6 preaching the *m* in the province of Asia.
17:11 and welcomed the *m* with great enthusiasm.
26:20 a *m* of reform and of conversion to God,
26:25 The *m* I proclaim is the sober truth.
1Cor 1:18 The *m* of the cross is complete absurdity
2: 4 My *m* and my preaching had none of the
2Cor 5:19 entrusted the *m* of reconciliation to us.
6: 7 with the *m* of truth and the power of God;
Col 1: 5 heard of this hope through the *m* of truth,
1Thes 2:13 in receiving his *m* from us you took it,
4:17 Console one another with this *m*.
Ti 1: 9 he must hold fast to the authentic *m*,
1Pt 4:11 The one who speaks is to deliver God's *m*.
2Pt 1:19 *m* as something altogether reliable.
1Jn 1: 5 is the *m* we have heard from him and
3:11 is the *m* you heard from the beginning:
Rv 1: 3 is the man who reads this prophetic *m*,
22: 7 man who heeds the prophetic *m* of this book!"
22: 9 and those who heed the *m* of this book.

MESSAGES (2)

Prv 26: 6 down violence, who sends *m* by a fool.
Jer 18:18 from the wise, nor of *m* from the prophets.

MESSENGER (44)

Gn 16: 7 *m* found her by a spring in the wilderness,
16: 9 But the LORD's *m* told her:
16:10 so numerous," added the LORD's *m*,
16:11 Besides," the LORD's *m* said to her:
21:17 and God's *m* called to Hagar from heaven:
22:11 But the LORD's *m* called to him from heaven,
22:12 not lay your hand on the boy," said the *m*.
22:15 *m* called to Abraham from heaven and said:
24: 7 he will send his *m* before you,
24:40 *m* with you and make your errand successful,
31:11 In the dream God's *m* called to me,
1Sm 4:17 And the *m* answered:
23:27 to capture them, when a *m* came to Saul,
2Sm 11:19 details of the battle, instructing the *m*,
11:22 The *m* set out,
11:25 David said to the *m*: "This is what you
1Kgs 19: 2 Jezebel then sent a *m* to Elijah and said,
22:13 *m* who had gone to call Micaiah said to him,
2Kgs 6:32 When the *m* comes, see that you close
9:18 to the king, "The *m* has reached them,
9:20 reported, "The *m* has reached them,
10: 8 of the princes," a *m* came in and told him.
2Chr 18:12 *m* who had gone to call Micaiah said to him:
1Mc 2:25 he also killed the *m* of the king who was
6: 5 a *m* brought him news that the armies sent
Jb 1:14 eldest brother, a *m* came to Job and said,
Prv 10:26 the sluggard to those who use him as a *m*.
13:17 A wicked *m* brings on disaster,
17:11 but a merciless *m* will be sent against him.
25:13 is a faithful *m* for the one who sends him.
Sir 43:27 For him each *m* succeeds,
Is 42:19 but my servant, or deaf like the *m* I send?
63: 9 It was not a *m* or an angel,
Hg 1:13 LORD's *m*, Haggai, proclaimed to the people
Mal 2: 7 because he is the *m* of the LORD of hosts.
3: 1 sending my *m* to prepare the way before me;
3: 1 And the *m* of the covenant whom you desire.
Mt 11:10 Scripture says, 'I send my *m* ahead of you,
Lk 7:27 'I send my *m* ahead of you to prepare your
Jn 13:16 no *m* outranks the one who sent him.
Acts 10: 3 a *m* of God coming toward him and calling,
10: 7 *m* who spoke these words had disappeared,
10:22 by a holy *m* to summon you to his house.
27:23 Last night a *m* of the God whose man I am

MESSENGERS (87)

Gn 28:12 and God's *m* were going up and down on it.
32: 2 Then God's *m* encountered Jacob.
32: 4 Jacob sent *m* ahead to his brother Esau in
32: 7 When the *m* returned to Jacob,
Ex 9: 7 But though Pharaoh's *m* informed him that
Nm 22: 5 of Moab at that time, sent *m* to Balaam,
24:12 I not warn the very *m* whom you sent to me.
Dt 2:26 *m* from the desert of Kedemoth to Sihon,
Jos 6:17 be spared, because she hid the *m* we sent.
6:25 Rahab the harlot had hidden the *m*
7:22 The *m* whom Joshua sent hastened to the
Jgs 6:35 He sent *m*, too, throughout Manasseh,
6:35 he sent *m* and these tribes advanced to
7:24 Gideon also sent *m* throughout the mountain
9:31 was angry and sent *m* to Abimelech in
11:12 sent *m* to the king of the Ammonites to say,
11:13 He answered the *m* of Jephthah,
11:14 sent *m* to the king of the Ammonites,
11:17 then sent *m* to the king of Edom saying,
11:19 Then Israel sent *m* to Sihon,
1Sm 6:21 sent *m* to the inhabitants of Kiriathjearim,
11: 3 *m* throughout the territory of Israel.
11: 4 When the *m* arrived at Gibeah of Saul,
11: 9 To the *m* who had come he said,
11: 9 The *m* came and reported this to the
16:19 *m* to ask Jesse to send him his son David,
19:10 Saul sent *m* to David's house to guard it,
19:14 When Saul sent *m* to arrest David,
19:15 *m* back to see David and commanded them,
19:16 But when the *m* entered,
19:20 near Ramah, he sent *m* to arrest David.
19:21 Informed of this, Saul sent other *m*,
19:21 For the third time Saul sent *m*,
25:14 sent *m* from the desert to greet our master,
25:42 mounted an ass, and followed David's *m*,
2Sm 2: 5 So David sent *m* to the men of
3:12 Then Abner sent *m* to David in Telam,
3:14 At the same time David sent *m* to Ishbaal,
3:26 David's knowledge sent *m* after Abner,
10: 3 it, that David has sent his *m* to you?"
11: 4 Then David sent *m* and took her.
12:27 He sent *m* to David with the word:
2Kgs 1: 2 So he sent out *m* with the instructions:
1: 3 "Go, intercept the *m* of Samaria's king,
1: 5 The *m* then returned to Ahaziah,
1:16 you sent *m* to inquire of Baal-zebub,
7:15 The *m* returned and told the king.
14: 8 Then Amaziah sent *m* to Jehoash,
16: 7 Meanwhile, Ahaz sent *m* to Tiglath-pileser,
19:14 letter from the hand of the *m* and read it;
20:13 therefore showed the *m* his whole treasury,
1Chr 19: 5 to his men, he sent *m* to meet them,
19:16 the Arameans sent *m* to bring out the
2Chr 25:17 King Amaziah of Judah sent *m* to Joash,
35:21 Neco sent *m* to him, saying:
36:15 God of their fathers, send his *m* to them,
36:16 But they mocked the *m* of God,
Neh 6: 3 However, I sent *m* to them with this reply:
Tb 10: 8 I am sending *m* to your father Tobit,
Jdt 1: 7 sent *m* to all the inhabitants of Persia,
3: 1 *m* to him to sue for peace in these words:
11:14 They have sent *m* to Jerusalem to bring
15: 4 Uzziah sent *m* to Betomasthaim,
1Mc 1:44 The king sent *m* with letters to Jerusalem

MESSENGERS (cont.)

5:14 reading this letter, suddenly other *m,*
7:10 sent *m* who spoke deceitfully to Judas and
13:21 The men in the citadel sent *m* to Trypho,
2Mc 2:15 you need them, send *m* to get them for you.
11:26 please send them *m* to give them our
Ps(s) 78:49 fury and strife, a detachment of *m* of doom.
104: 4 You make the winds your *m,*
Prv 16:14 The king's wrath is like *m* of death,
Is 14:32 What will one answer the *m* of the nation?
18: 2 Go, swift *m,* to a nation tall and bronzed,
23: 2 of Sidon, Whose *m* crossed the sea
30: 4 are at Zoan and their *m* reach Hanes,
33: 7 the streets, the *m* of Shalem weep bitterly.
37:14 letter from the hand of the *m* and read it;
39: 2 and therefore showed the *m* his treasury,
44:26 I carry out the plan announced by my *m;*
Ez 23:16 on them than she sent *m* to them in Chaldea.
23:40 had to come from afar, to whom *m* were sent.
30: 9 On that day *m* shall hasten forth at my
Mt 11: 7 As the *m* set off, Jesus began to speak
Lk 7:24 When the *m* of John had set off,
9:51 Jerusalem, and sent *m* on ahead of him.
Jas 2:25 *m* and sent them out by a different route?

MESSIAH (60)

Mt 1:16 that Jesus who is called the *M* was born.
1:17 from the Babylonian captivity to the *M,*
2: 4 of them where the *M* was to be born.
16:16 "You are the *M,*" Simon Peter answered,
16:20 not to tell anyone that he was the *M.*
16:21 From then on Jesus [the *M* started to
22:42 "What is your opinion about the *M?*
23:10 Only one is your teacher, the *M.*
24: 5 'I am the *M!*'
24:23 you at that time, 'Look, the *M* is here,'
26:63 the living God whether you are the *M,*
26:68 "Play the prophet for us, *M!*
27:17 for you, Barabbas or Jesus the so-called *M?*"
27:22 am I to do with Jesus, the so-called *M?*"
Mk 8:29 Peter answered him, "You are the *M!*"
12:35 the scribes claim, 'The *M* is David's son'?
13:21 you at that time, 'Look, the *M* is here!'
14:61 "Are you the *M,*
15:32 Let the *M,*' the 'king of Israel,' come down
Lk 2:11 has been born to you, the *M* and Lord.
3:15 their hearts whether John might be the *M.*
4:41 speak because they knew that he was the *M.*
9:20 Peter said in reply, "The *M* of God."
20:41 they say that the *M* is the son of David?
22:66 they said, "Tell us, are you the *M?*"
23: 2 taxes to Caesar, and calling himself the *M,*
23:35 let him save himself if he is the *M* of God,
23:39 "Aren't you the *M?*
24:26 Did not the *M* have to undergo all this so
24:46 "Thus it is written that the *M* must
Jn 1:20 was the direct statement, "I am not the *M.*"
1:25 "If you are not the *M,*
1:41 Simon and tell him, "We have found the *M!*"
3:28 'I am not the *M;* I am sent before him.'
4:25 "I know there is a *M* coming."
4:29 Could this not be the *M?*"
7:26 have decided that this is the *M.*
7:27 When the *M* comes,
7:31 They kept saying, "When the *M* comes,
7:41 Others were claiming, "He is the *M.*"
7:41 the *M* is not to come from Galilee?
7:42 Does not Scripture say that the *M,*
9:22 as the *M* would be put out of the synagogue.
10:24 If you really are the *M,*
11:27 have come to believe that you are the *M,*
12:34 in the law that the *M* is to remain forever.
20:31 to help you believe that Jesus is the *M,*
Acts 2:31 beforehand the resurrection of the *M.*
2:36 Lord and *M* this Jesus whom you crucified."
3:18 that his *M* would suffer.
3:20 you Jesus, already designated as your *M.*
5:42 proclaiming the good news of Jesus the *M.*
8: 5 town of Samaria and there proclaimed the *M.*
9:22 with his proofs that this Jesus was the *M.*
17: 3 the *M* had to suffer and rise from the dead:
17: 3 Jesus I am telling you about is the *M!*"
18: 5 evidence to the Jews that Jesus was the *M.*
18:28 from the Scriptures that Jesus is the *M.*
26:23 namely, that the *M* must suffer,
Rom 9: 5 came the *M* (I speak of his human origins).

MESSIAHS (2)

Mt 24:24 False *m* and false prophets will appear,
Mk 13:22 False *m* and false prophets will appear

MET (73)

Gn 37:15 a man *m* him as he was wandering about in
38: 2 *m* the daughter of a Canaanite named Shua,
Ex 4:27 and when they *m* at the mountain of God,
Nm 3: 4 they *m* death in the presence of the LORD,
13:26 *m* Moses and Aaron and the whole community
23: 4 out on the barren height, and God *m* him.
23:16 Then the LORD *m* Balaam,
Jgs 14:11 When they *m* him, they brought thirty men
20:24 *m* the Benjaminites for the second time,
1Sm 9:11 they *m* some girls coming out to draw water
9:18 Saul *m* Samuel in the gateway and said,
10: 3 *m* by three men going up to God at Bethel;
10:10 there to Gibeah, a band of prophets *m* him,
25:20 When she *m* them, David had just been
2Sm 2:13 set out and *m* them at the pool of Gibeon.
16: 1 *m* him with saddled asses laden with two
20: 8 great stone in Gibeon when Amasa *m* them.
1Kgs 7:42 of the capitals where they *m* the columns,
11:29 Ahijah the Shilonite *m* him on the road.
13:24 But a lion *m* him on the road,
18: 7 As Obadiah was on his way, Elijah *m* him.
20:37 The prophet *m* another man and said,
2Kgs 10:15 When he had left there, Jehu *m* Jehonadab,
14:11 Judah *m* in battle at Beth-shemesh of Judah.
1Chr 19:17 together, crossed the Jordan, and *m* them.
2Chr 19: 2 Hanani, *m* King Jehoshaphat and said to him:
25:21 *m* in battle at Beth-shemesh of Judah.
Jdt 4: 8 people of Israel, which *m* in Jerusalem.
1Mc 4:29 and Judas *m* them with ten thousand men.
5:25 There they *m* some Nabateans,
5:44 and Judas *m* with no more resistance.
7:43 The armies *m* in battle on the thirteenth
10:58 There King Alexander *m* him,
10:60 where he *m* the two kings and gave them and
11: 6 Jonathan *m* the king with pomp at Joppa,
11:15 Ptolemy marched out and *m* him with a
2Mc 5: 8 At length he *m* a miserable end.
5:12 cut down without mercy those whom they *m*
14:30 with unaccustomed rudeness when they *m;*
15:26 *m* the army with supplication and prayers.
Jb 2:11 They *m* and journeyed together to give him
32:13 Yet do not say, "We have *m* wisdom.
Sg 8: 1 If I *m* you out of doors,
Wis 19: 5 those others *m* an extraordinary death.
Sir 19:25 a wise man is known as such when first *m.*
45:23 of all, he *m* the crisis of his people And,
51:16 I paid heed, I *m* with great instruction.
Is 35: 9 nor beast of prey go up to be *m* upon it.
Jer 37:13 of Benjamin, he *m* the captain of the guard,
41: 7 son of Ahikam," he said as he *m* them.
Dn 8: 7 the ram with furious blows when they *m,*
13:14 both turned back, and when they *m* again,
Hos 12: 5 he *m* God and there he spoke with him;
Jon 1: 7 account we have *m* with this misfortune."
Mt 17:22 When they *m* again in Galilee,
18:28 But when that same official went out he *m*
22:10 the byroads and rounded up everyone they *m,*
27:32 way out they *m* a Cyrenian named Simon.
Mk 5: 2 he was immediately *m* by a man from the
Lk 8:27 he was *m* by a man from the town who was
9:37 from the mountain and a large crowd *m* them.
11:51 who *m* his death between the altar and the
17:12 was entering a village, ten lepers *m* him.
Jn 4:51 on his way there when his servants *m* him
11:30 still at the spot where Martha had *m* him.)
18: 2 Jesus had often *m* there with his disciples.
Acts 1: 4 On one occasion when he *m* with them,
11:26 For a whole year they *m* with the church
16:16 we *m* a slave girl who had a clairvoyant
20:14 When he *m* us at Assos we took him aboard
1Thes 2: 4 having *m* the test imposed on us by God,
Heb 7: 1 *m* Abraham returning from his defeat of the
7:10 father's loins when Melchizedek *m* Abraham.

METAL (8)

1Kgs 6:34 each door was banded by a *m* strap,
7:14 to King Solomon and did all his *m* work.
7:15 their *m* was of four fingers' thickness.
Sir 13: 2 can the earthen pot go with the *m* cauldron?
43: 4 Like a blazing furnace of solid *m,*
50:16 priests, on their trumpets of beaten *m;*
Lam 4: 1 is the gold, how changed the noble *m;*
Ez 24:11 on the coals till its *m* glows red hot,

METALS (3)

2Kgs 22: 4 have him smelt down the precious *m*
22: 9 "Your servants have smelted down the *m*
2Chr 34:17 have turned into bullion the *m* deposited

METE (1)

Is 26:12 O LORD, you *m* out peace to us,

METED (3)

2Chr 24:24 So punishment was *m* out to Joash.
Ez 23:45 *m* out to adulteresses and murderesses,
1Tm 3: 6 the punishment once *m* out to the devil.

METHOD (1)

2Mc 13: 4 executed there in the customary local *m.*

METHUSAEL (2)

Gn 4:18 Mehujael became the father of *M,* and *M*

METHUSELAH (7)

Gn 5:21 years old, he became the father of *M.*
5:22 three hundred years after the birth of *M,*
5:25 When *M* was one hundred and eighty-seven
5:26 *M* lived seven hundred and eighty-two years
5:27 of *M* was nine hundred and sixty-nine years;
1Chr 1: 3 Enosh, Kenan, Mahalalel, Jared, Enoch, *M,*
Lk 3:37 son of Noah, son of Lamech, son of *M,*

MEUNITES (5)

1Chr 4:41 formerly) and also the *M* who were there.
2Chr 20: 1 some *M* came to fight against Jehoshaphat.
26: 7 who dwelt in Gurbaal, and against the *M.*
Ezr 2:50 of Besai, sons of Asnah, sons of the *M,*
Neh 7:52 of Paseah, sons of Besai, sons of the *M,*

MEZAHAB (2)

Gn 36:39 she was the daughter of Matred, son of *M.)*
1Chr 1:50 of Matred, who was the daughter of *M.*

MEZOBIAN (1)

1Chr 11:47 Eliel, Obed, and Jaasiel the *M.*

MIAMIN (1)

Neh 12:17 for Abijah, Zichri; for *M,*

MIBSAM (3)

Gn 25:13 (Ishmael's first-born), Kedar, Adbeel, *M,*
1Chr 1:29 of Ishmael, then Kedar, Adbeel, *M,*
4:25 whose son was Shallum, whose son was *M,*

MIBZAR (2)

Gn 36:42 Oholibamah, Elah, Pinon, Kenaz, Teman, *M,*
1Chr 1:53 Oholibamah, Elah, Pinon, Kenaz, Teman, *M,*

MICA (3)

2Sm 9:12 had a young son whose name was *M;*
1Chr 9:15 Mattaniah, son of *M,*
Neh 10:12 Hodiah, Kelita, Pelaiah, Hanan, *M,*

MICAH (33)

Jgs 17: 1 region of Ephraim whose name was *M.*
17: 4 It remained in the house of *M.*
17: 5 Thus the layman *M* had a sanctuary.
17: 8 of *M* in the mountain region of Ephraim.
17: 9 *M* said to him, "Where do you come from
17:10 "Stay with me," *M* said to him.
17:12 *M* consecrated the young Levite,
17:13 *M* said, "Now I know that the LORD
18: 2 of *M* in the mountain region of Ephraim,
18: 3 Near the house of *M,*
18: 4 "This is how *M* treats me,"
18:13 of Ephraim and came to the house of *M.*
18:15 Levite at the home of *M* and greeted him.
18:17 land went up and entered the house of *M.*
18:22 that of *M* took up arms and overtook them.
18:23 Danites, who turned about and said to *M,*
18:26 The Danites then went on their way, and *M,*
18:27 Having taken what *M* had made,
18:31 They maintained the carved idol *M* had made
1Chr 5: 5 whose son was Shimei, whose son was *M,*
8:34 and Meribbaal became the father of *M.*
8:35 The sons of *M* were Pithon,
9:40 and Meribbaal became the father of *M.*
9:41 The sons of *M* were Pithon,
23:20 *M,* the chief, and Isshiah, the second.
24:24 The descendants of Uzziel were *M;*
24:24 Shamir, of the descendants of *M;*
24:25 Isshiah, the brother of *M;*
Neh 11:17 Mattaniah, son of *M;*
11:22 of Hashabiah, son of Mattaniah, son of *M;*
Jdt 6:15 Uzziah, son of *M* of the tribe of Simeon,
Jer 26:18 *M* of Moresheth used to prophesy in the
Mi 1: 1 to *M* of Moresheth in the days of Jotham,

MICAIAH (28)

1Kgs 22: 8 through whom we might consult the LORD, *M,*
22: 9 an official and said to him, "Get *M,*
22:13 who had gone to call *M* said to him,
22:14 "As the LORD lives," *M* answered,
22:15 came to the king, the king said to him, *M,*
22:17 So *M* said: I see all Israel scattered
22:19 *M* continued: "Therefore hear the word
22:24 came up and slapped *M* on the cheek saying,
22:25 "You shall find out," *M* replied,
22:26 said, "Seize *M* and take him back to Amon,
22:28 *M* said, "If ever you return in safety
2Kgs 22:12 Ahikam, son of Shaphan, Achbor, son of *M,*
2Chr 17: 7 Obadiah, Zechariah, Nethanel and *M,*
18: 7 That is *M,* son of Imlah."
18: 8 an official, to whom he said, "Get *M,*
18:12 who had gone to call *M* said to him:
18:13 "As the LORD lives," *M* answered,
18:14 came to the king, the king said to him, *M,*
18:16 Then *M* answered: I see all Israel
18:18 *M* continued: "Therefore hear the word
18:23 came up and slapped *M* on the cheek saying,
18:24 "You shall find out," *M* replied,
18:25 "Seize *M* and take him back to Amon,
18:27 *M* said, "If ever you return in safety,
Neh 12:35 of Shemaiah, son of Mattaniah, son of *M,*
12:41 priests Eliakim, Maaseiah, Minjamin, *M,*
Jer 36:11 Now *M,* son of Gemariah,
36:13 To them *M* reported all that he had heard

MICE (6)

1Sm 5: 6 great and deadly plague of *m* that swarmed
6: 4 golden hemorrhoids and five golden *m*
6: 5 images of the hemorrhoids and of the *m*
6:11 golden *m* and the images of the hemorrhoids.
6:18 golden *m*, however, corresponded
Is 66:17 eat swine's flesh, loathsome things and *m*,

MICHAEL (15)

Nm 13:13 son of *M*, of the tribe of Asher;
1Chr 5:13 *M*, Meshullam,
5:14 son of Jaroah, son of Gilead, son of *M*,
6:25 son of Berechiah, son of Shimea, son of *M*,
7: 3 The sons of Izarahiah were *M*,
8:16 Zebadiah, Arad, Eder, *M*,
12:21 Adnah, Jozabad, Jediael, *M*,
27:18 for Issachar, Omri, son of *M*;
2Chr 21: 2 Zechariah, Azariah, *M* and Shephatiah;
Ezr 8: 8 sons of Shephatiah, Zebadiah, son of *M*,
Dn 10:13 way for twenty-one days, until finally *M*,
10:21 against all these except *M*
12: 1 "At that time there shall arise *M*,
Jude 1: 9 Even the archangel *M*,
Rv 12: 7 *M* and his angels battled against the

MICHAH (1)

2Chr 34:20 son of Shaphan, to Abdon, son of *M*,

MICHAIAH (1)

2Chr 13: 2 His mother was named *M*,

MICHAL (17)

1Sm 14:49 the elder, Merob, and the younger, *M*.
18:20 Now Saul's daughter *M* loved David,
18:27 Saul gave him his daughter *M* in marriage.
18:28 besides, his own daughter *M* loved David.
19:10 David's wife *M* informed him,
19:12 Then *M* let David down through a window,
19:13 *M* took the household idol and laid it in
19:17 Saul therefore asked *M*: "Why did you play
19:17 *M* answered Saul: "He threatened
25:43 but Saul gave David's wife *M*,
2Sm 3:13 appear before me unless you bring back *M*,
3:14 son of Saul, to say, "Give me my wife *M*,
6:16 Saul's daughter *M* looked down through the
6:20 daughter *M* came out to meet him and said,
6:21 David replied to *M*: I was dancing
6:23 *M* was childless to the day of her death.
1Chr 15:29 LORD was entering the City of David, *M*,

MICHMAS (2)

Ezr 2:27 men of *M*, one hundred and twenty-two;
Neh 7:31 men of *M*, one hundred and twenty-two;

MICHMASH (10)

1Sm 13: 2 him in *M* and in the hill country of Bethel,
13: 5 up against Israel, they encamped in *M*,
13:11 and with the Philistines assembled at *M*,
13:16 and the Philistines were encamped at *M*.
13:23 had pushed forward to the pass of *M*.
14: 5 One crag was to the north, toward *M*,
14:31 were routed that day from *M* to Aijalon,
Neh 11:31 Benjaminites were in Geba, *M*,
1Mc 9:73 Jonathan settled in *M*;
Is 10:28 Migron, at *M* his supplies are stored.

MICHMETHATH (2)

Jos 16: 6 From *M* on the north,
17: 7 From *M* near Shechem,

MICHRI (1)

1Chr 9: 8 Elah, son of Uzzi, son of *M*;

MIDAFTERNOON (5)

Mt 20: 5 again around noon and *m* and did the same.
27:45 was darkness over the whole land until *m*.
27:46 toward *m* Jesus cried out in a loud tone,
Mk 15:33 the whole countryside and lasted until *m*.
Lk 23:44 land until *m* with an eclipse of the sun.

MIDAIR (1)

2Mc 5: 2 there appeared horsemen charging in *m*,

MIDDAY (11)

Dt 28:29 so that even at *m* you will grope like a
Neh 8: 3 read out of the book from daybreak till *m*,
Sg 1: 7 your flock, where you give them rest at *m*,
Is 58:10 and the gloom shall become for you like *m*;
59:10 We stumble at *m* as at dusk,
Jer 6: 4 let us rush upon her at *m*!
15: 8 the mother of youths the spoiler at *m*;
Am 8: 9 I will make the sun set at *m* and cover the
Zep 2: 4 a waste, Ashdod they shall drive out at *m*,
Lk 23:44 It was now around *m*,
Acts 26:13 than the sun shining in the sky at *m*.

MIDDIN (1)

Jos 15:61 Beth-arabah, *M*,

MIDDLE (36)

Gn 1: 6 there be a dome in the *m* of the waters,
2: 9 with the tree of life in the *m* of the
3: 3 tree in the *m* of the garden that God said,
Ex 26:28 The center bar, at the *m* of the boards,
36:33 The center bar, at the *m* of the boards,
Lv 1:17 down the *m* without separating the halves,
Nm 2:17 Levites shall set out in the *m* of the line.
Dt 13:17 up all its spoils in the *m* of its square,
Jos 10:13 The sun halted in the *m* of the sky;
Jgs 7:19 the camp at the beginning of the *m* watch,
9:51 was a strong tower in the *m* of the city,
16:29 Samson grasped the two *m* columns on which
Ru 3: 8 In the *m* of the night,
2Sm 20:12 with blood in the *m* of the highroad,
23:12 stand in the *m* of the plot and defended it.
1Kgs 6: 6 cubits wide, the *m* one six cubits wide,
6: 8 led up to the *m* story and from the *m* story
6:27 wing, pointing toward the *m* of the room,
8:64 On that day the king consecrated the *m* of
2Chr 6:13 he had placed in the *m* of the courtyard.
7: 7 Then Solomon consecrated the *m* part of the
1Mc 6:45 He dashed up to it in the *m* of the phalanx,
2Mc 14:44 he fell into the *m* of the empty space.
Prv 26:13 the street, a lion in the *m* of the square!"
Sir 11: 8 interrupt no one in the *m* of his speech.
Jer 39: 3 of Babylon came and occupied the *m* gate:
Ez 15: 4 both ends and even the *m* is scorched,
41: 7 the lowest to the *m* and the highest story.
42: 6 ground than the closest and the *m* chambers.
48:21 sanctuary of the temple shall be in the *m*.
Lk 5:19 tiles into the *m* of the crowd before Jesus.
11: 5 him in the *m* of the night and says to him,
22:55 Later they lighted a fire in the *m* of the
Jn 19:18 one on either side, Jesus in the *m*.
Rv 22: 2 Lamb and flowed down the *m* of the streets.

MIDDLEMEN (1)

2Chr 1:17 as *m* for all the Hittite and Aramean kings.

MIDHEAVEN (3)

Rv 8:13 eagle flying in *m* cry out in a loud voice,
14: 6 Then I saw another angel flying in *m*,
19:17 a loud voice to all the birds flying in *m*.

MIDIAN (50)

Gn 25: 2 She bore him Zimran, Jokshan, Medan, *M*,
25: 4 The descendants of *M* were Ephah,
Ex 2:15 fled from him and stayed in the land of *M*.
2:16 seven daughters of a priest of *M* came to
3: 1 his father-in-law Jethro, the priest of *M*.
4:19 In *M* the LORD said to Moses,
18: 1 father-in-law Jethro, the priest of *M*,
Nm 22: 4 So Moab said to the elders of *M*,
22: 7 Then the elders of Moab and of *M* left with
25:15 head of a clan, an ancestral house, in *M*.
Jos 13:21 killed, with his vassals, the princes of *M*,
Jgs 6: 1 them into the power of *M* for seven years,
6: 2 years, so that *M* held Israel subject.
6: 2 For fear of *M* the Israelites established
6: 3 Israelites had completed their sowing, *M*,
6: 6 Thus was Israel reduced to misery by *M*,
6: 7 Israel cried out to the LORD because of *M*,
6:13 and has delivered us into the power of *M*."
6:14 have and save Israel from the power of *M*.
6:16 "and you will cut down *M* to the last man."
6:33 Then all *M* and Amalek and the Kedemites
7: 1 The camp of *M* was in the valley north of
7: 2 you for me to deliver *M* into their power,
7: 7 you and will deliver *M* into your power.
7: 8 camp of *M* was beneath him in the valley.
7:13 bread was rolling into the camp of *M*.
7:14 *M* and all the camp into his power."
7:15 delivered the camp of *M* into your power."
7:23 and from all Manasseh and they pursued *M*.
7:24 Ephraim to say, "Go down to confront *M*,
7:25 They captured the two princes of *M*,
7:25 Then they pursued *M* and carried the heads
8: 1 us when you went to fight against *M*?"
8: 3 your power God delivered the princes of *M*,
8: 5 pursuing Zebah and Zalmunna, kings of *M*."
8:12 pursued them and took the two kings of *M*,
8:22 for you rescued us from the power of *M*."
8:26 purple garments worn by the kings of *M*,
8:28 Thus was *M* brought into subjection by the
9:17 when he saved you from the power of *M*;
1Kgs 11:18 They left *M* and passing through Paran,
1Chr 1:32 she bore Zimran, Jokshan, Medan, *M*,
1:33 The descendants of *M* were Ephah,
Ps(s) 83:10 Deal with them as with *M*;
Is 9: 3 you have smashed, as on the day of *M*.
10:26 such as struck *M* at the rock of Oreb;
60: 6 fill you, dromedaries from *M* and Ephah;
Bar 3:23 on earth, the merchants of *M* and Teman,
Hb 3: 7 are the pavilions of the land of *M*.
Acts 7:29 residence as an alien in the land of *M*,

MIDIANITE (7)

Gn 37:28 Some *M* traders passed by,
Nm 10:29 brother-in-law Hobab, son of Reuel the *M*,
25: 6 brought in a *M* woman to his clansmen
25:14 Israelite slain with the *M* woman was Zimri,
25:15 The slain *M* woman was Cozbi,
25:18 Cozbi, the daughter of a *M* prince,
31: 8 in battle, they killed the five *M* kings:

MIDIANITES (12)

Gn 36:34 He defeated the *M* in the country of Moab;
37:36 *M*, meanwhile, sold Joseph in Egypt
Nm 25:17 "Treat the *M* as enemies and crush them,
31: 2 Moses, "Avenge the Israelites on the *M*,
31: 3 *M* and execute the LORD's vengeance on them.
31: 7 They waged war against the *M*,
31: 9 the *M* with their little ones as captives,
Jgs 6:11 in the wine press to save it from the *M*,
7:12 *M*, Amalekites, and all the Kedemites
10:12 the Amalekites, and the *M* oppress you?
1Chr 1:46 He overthrew the *M* on the Moabite plateau,
Jdt 2:26 He surrounded all the *M*,

MIDLIFE (1)

Jer 17:11 In *m* it will desert him;

MIDMORNING (1)

Mt 20: 3 He came out about *m* and saw other men

MIDNIGHT (12)

Ex 11: 4 At *m* I will go forth through Egypt.
12:29 At *m* the LORD slew every first-born in the
Jgs 16: 3 Samson rested there until *m*.
Jdt 12: 5 her into the tent, where she slept till *m*.
Jb 34:20 in a moment they die, even at *m*.
Ps(s) 119:62 At *m* I rise to give you thanks because of
Mt 25: 6 At *m* someone shouted, 'The groom is here!
Mk 13:35 the house is coming, whether at dusk, at *m*,
Lk 12:38 *m* or before sunrise and find them prepared,
Acts 16:25 About *m*, while Paul and Silas were praying
20: 7 the next day, he kept on speaking until *m*.
27:27 when toward *m* the sailors began to suspect

MIDPOINT (1)

Wis 7:18 beginning and the end and the *m* of times,

MIDRASH (2)

2Chr 13:22 are written in the *m* of the prophet Iddo.
24:27 account in the *m* of the book of the kings.

MIDST (207)

Ex 7: 5 and lead the Israelites out of their *m*."
8:18 that I am the LORD in the *m* of the earth.
14:22 marched into the *m* of the sea on dry land,
14:23 after them right into the *m* of the sea.
14:27 sea, when the LORD hurled them into its *m*.
14:29 on dry land through the *m* of the sea,
15: 8 flood waters congealed in the *m* of the sea.
15:19 on dry land through the *m* of the sea.
17: 7 saying, "Is the LORD in our *m* or not?"
23:25 I will remove all sickness from your *m*;
24:16 he called to Moses from the *m* of the cloud.
24:18 But Moses passed into the *m* of the cloud
25: 8 for me, that I may dwell in their *m*.
29:45 *m* of the Israelites and will be their God.
Lv 15:31 defiling my Dwelling, which is in their *m*,
16:16 among them in the *m* of their uncleanness.
22:32 in the *m* of the Israelites I,
23:30 I will remove him from the *m* of his people.
25:33 property in the *m* of the Israelites.
26:12 Ever present in your *m*,
Nm 11:20 have spurned the LORD who is in your *m*,
14:14 you, O LORD, are in the *m* of this people;
14:42 go up, because the LORD is not in your *m*;
16: 3 the LORD is in their *m*.
31: 3 men from your *m* and arm them for war,
35:34 you live and in the *m* of which I dwell;
35:34 LORD who dwells in the *m* of the Israelites."
Dt 1:42 your enemies, for I will not be in your *m*.'
4: 3 *m* everyone that followed the Baal of Peor;
4:12 LORD spoke to you from the *m* of the fire.
4:15 to you at Horeb from the *m* of the fire.
4:33 voice of God speaking from the *m* of fire,
4:34 for himself from the *m* of another nation,
5: 4 on the mountain from the *m* of the fire.
5:22 from the *m* of the fire and the dense cloud.
5:23 heard the voice from the *m* of the darkness,
5:24 We have heard his voice from the *m* of the
5:26 the living God speaking from the *m* of fire,
6:15 for the LORD, your God, who is in your *m*,
7:21 for the LORD, your God, who is in your *m*,
9:10 *m* of the fire on the day of the assembly.
10: 4 *m* of the fire on the day of the assembly.
11: 6 swallowed them up out of the *m* of Israel,
13: 6 Thus shall you purge the evil from your *m*.
13:12 never again do such evil as this in your *m*.
13:15 abomination has been committed in your *m*,
17: 7 Thus shall you purge the evil from your *m*.
17:12 Thus shall you purge the evil from your *m*.

MIDST (cont.)

19:19 Thus shall you purge the evil from your *m.*
21: 8 remain in the *m* of your people Israel.'
21: 9 from your *m* the guilt of innocent blood,
21:21 Thus shall you purge the evil from your *m,*
22:21 Thus shall you purge the evil from your *m.*
22:22 Thus shall you purge the evil from your *m.*
22:24 Thus shall you purge the evil from your *m.*
23:15 if he sees anything indecent in your *m,*
24: 7 Thus shall you purge the evil from your *m.*
Jos 3:10 know that there is a living God in your *m,*
6:25 continue in the *m* of Israel to this day.
9:22 us, when you will be living in our very *m?*
13:13 survive in the *m* of Israel to this day.
19:49 assigned a heritage in their *m* to Joshua,
24: 5 the prodigies which I wrought in her *m.*
Jgs 1:29 so the Canaanites live in Gezer in their *m.*
10:16 gods from their *m* and served the LORD,
18:20 idol and went off in the *m* of the band.
20:42 In their very *m,*
1Sm 16:13 anointed him in the *m* of his brothers;
1Kgs 3: 8 the *m* of the people whom you have chosen,
6:13 I will dwell in the *m* of the Israelites
8:51 of Egypt, from the *m* of an iron furnace.
2Chr 20:14 clan of Asaph, in the *m* of the assembly,
Neh 4: 5 it or see us, we shall come into their *m,*
9:11 they passed through the *m* of the sea;
9:35 in the *m* of the many good things that you
Est E: 7 the wicked deeds perpetrated in your *m*
2Mc 10:29 In the *m* of the fierce battle,
Ps(s) 22:23 in the *m* of the assembly I will praise you:
46: 6 God is in its *m;* it shall not be disturbed;
55:11 Evil and mischief are in its *m;*
55:12 [treachery is in its *m* oppression and
55:16 is in their dwellings, in their very *m.*
57: 5 in the *m* of lions which devour men;
68:26 in their *m* the maidens play on timbrels.
78:28 *m* of their camp round about their tents.
82: 1 he judges in the *m* of the gods.
102:25 Take me not hence in the *m* of my days;
109:30 in the *m* of the throng I will praise him,
110: 2 "Rule in the *m* of your enemies.
116:19 courts of the house of the LORD, in your *m,*
135: 9 He sent signs and wonders into your *m,*
136:11 And brought out Israel from their *m,*
136:14 And led Israel through its *m,*
Wis 4:14 he sped him out of the *m* of wickedness.
12: 5 human flesh and of blood, from the *m* of . . .
18:23 he stood in the *m* and checked the anger,
Sir 45:22 his inheritance in the *m* of Israel.
51: 4 From the *m* of unremitting fire,
51:10 of trouble, in the *m* of storms and dangers.
Is 4: 4 her *m* with the blast of searing judgment,
5: 8 left to dwell alone in the *m* of the land!
12: 6 great in your *m* is the Holy One of Israel!
19:24 Assyria, a blessing in the *m* of the land,
29:23 see the work of my hands in his *m,*
58: 9 If you remove from your *m* oppression,
63:11 is he who put his holy spirit in their *m;*
Jer 8:19 in Zion, is her King no longer in her *m?*
12:14 house of Judah I will pluck up in their *m.*
12:16 shall be built up in the *m* of my people.
14: 9 You are in our *m,*
21: 4 I will pile up in the *m* of this city,
31: 8 with the blind and the lame in their *m,*
Lam 1:15 mighty ones in my *m* the LORD has cast away;
1:17 has become in their *m* a thing unclean.
4:13 Who shed in her *m* the blood of the just!—
Ez 1: 4 from the *m* of which [the midst of the fire]
5: 4 them in the *m* of the fire and burn them.]
5: 5 In the *m* of the nations I placed her,
5: 8 in your *m* while the nations look on.
6: 7 [The slain shall fall in your *m,*
7: 4 of your abominations shall be in your *m;*
7: 9 of your abominations shall be in your *m;*
9: 2 In their *m* was a man dressed in linen,
12: 2 you live in the *m* of a rebellious house;
14: 8 I will cut him off from the *m* of my people.
22: 7 in your *m,* they extort from the resident
22: 9 in your *m* are those who do lewd things.
22:13 because of the bloodshed in your *m.*
22:18 tin, iron and lead [in the *m* of a furnace]:
22:26 so that I have been profaned in their *m.*
24: 7 For the blood she shed is in her *m:*
26: 5 drying place for nets in the *m* of the sea.
26:15 wounded, when the sword slays in your *m,*
27: 4 the *m* of the sea your builders placed you,
27:32 destroyed like Tyre in the *m* of the sea?
28:18 out fire from your *m* which will devour you.
28:22 I will be glorified in your *m.*
29: 4 then draw you up from the *m* of your Niles
29:21 I will cause you to speak out in their *m:*
32:20 In the *m* of those slain by the sword shall
32:20 Then from the *m* of the nether world,
32:25 in the *m* of the slain they are placed.
32:28 the *m* of the uncircumcised shall you lie,
36:23 nations, in whose *m* you have profaned it.
43: 9 kings, and I will dwell in their *m* forever.
46:10 prince shall be in their *m* when they enter,
47:22 in your *m* who have bred children among you.
48:22 lie in the *m* of the prince's property,
Dn 3:23 bound, into the *m* of the white-hot furnace.
7: 8 a little horn, sprang out of their *m,*
13:34 In the *m* of the people the two elders rose
13:48 He stood in their *m* and continued,
Jl 2:27 shall know that I am in the *m* of Israel;
Am 2: 3 I will root out the judge from her *m,*
3: 9 within her, the oppression in her *m.*"
5:17 be lamentation when I pass through your *m,*
7: 8 the plummet in the *m* of my people Israel;
Jon 2: 3 the *m* of the nether world I cried for help,
Mi 2:12 fold, like a herd in the *m* of its corral;
3:11 saying "Is not the LORD in the *m* of us?
5: 6 of Jacob shall be in the *m* of many peoples,
5: 7 the nations, in the *m* of many peoples,
5: 9 horses from your *m* and ruin your chariots;
5:12 images and the sacred pillars from your *m;*
5:13 will tear out the sacred poles from your *m,*
7:14 apart in a woodland, in the *m* of Carmel.
Na 3:13 See, the troops are women in your *m;*
Zep 2:14 In her *m* shall settle in droves all the
3: 3 Her princes in her *m* are roaring lions;
3:11 I remove from your *m* the proud braggarts,
3:12 in your *m* a people humble and lowly,
3:15 King of Israel, the LORD, is in your *m,*
3:17 The LORD, your God, is in your *m,*
Hg 2: 5 Egypt, And my spirit continues in your *m;*
Zec 2: 8 the multitude of men and beasts in her *m.*
2: 9 the LORD, and I will be the glory in her *m.*"
14: 1 when the spoils shall be divided in your *m.*
Mt 18: 2 over and stood him in their *m* and said:
18:20 gathered in my name, there am I in their *m.*"
Mk 9:36 took a little child, stood him in their *m,*
Lk 1: 1 events which have been fulfilled in our *m,*
2:46 temple sitting in the *m* of the teachers,
4:30 straight through their *m* and walked away.
5:35 that the groom is removed from their *m,*
9:43 In the *m* of their amazement at all
10: 3 am sending you as lambs in the *m* of wolves.
10:13 in your *m* had occurred in Tyre and Sidon,
17:21 The reign of God is already in your *m.*"
21:24 be led captive in the *m* of the Gentiles.
22:27 I am in your *m* as the one who serves you.
24:36 himself stood in their *m* [and said to them,
Acts 2:22 These God worked through him in your *m,*
2:29 and his grave is in our *m* to this day.
23:10 their *m* and take him back to headquarters.
Rom 15:28 Spain, passing through your *m* on the way.
1Cor 5:13 "Expel the wicked man from your *m.*"
2Cor 8: 2 In the *m* of severe trial their overflowing
10: 1 (you say) when present in your *m* am lowly,
Gal 3: 5 Spirit on you and works wonders in your *m?*
Phil 2:15 beyond reproach in the *m* of a twisted
Col 1: 6 fruit, and has continued to grow in your *m,*
Heb 2:12 your praise in the *m* of the assembly";
1Pt 4:12 a trial by fire is occurring in your *m.*
5: 2 God's flock is in your *m;*
1Jn 4: 9 God's love was revealed in our *m*
Jude 1: 4 recently wormed their way into your *m,*

MIDWIFE (3)

Gn 35:17 pangs were most severe, her *m* said to her,
38:28 *m,* taking a crimson thread, tied it on
Ex 1:19 robust and give birth before the *m* arrives."

MIDWIVES (7)

Ex 1:15 The king of Egypt told the Hebrew *m,*
1:16 "When you act as *m* for the Hebrew women
1:17 *m,* however, feared God;
1:18 So the king summoned the *m* and asked them,
1:19 *m* answered Pharaoh, "The Hebrew women
1:20 Therefore God dealt well with the *m.*
1:21 And because the *m* feared God,

MIEN (1)

Jb 22:29 but the man of humble *m* he saves.

MIGDAL-EDER (1)

Gn 35:21 moved on and pitched his tent beyond *M.*

MIGDAL-EL (1)

Jos 19:38 Hazor, Kedesh, Edrei, En-hazor, Yiron, *M,*

MIGDAL-GAD (1)

Jos 15:37 Zenan, Hadashah, *M,*

MIGDAL-SHECHEM (3)

Jgs 9:46 all the citizens of *M* went into the crypt
9:47 the citizens of *M* were gathered together.
9:49 that that every one of the citizens of *M,*

MIGDOL (6)

Ex 14: 2 before Pi-hahiroth, between *M* and the sea.
Nm 33: 7 Baal-zephon, and they camped opposite *M.*
Jer 44: 1 of Judah who were living in Egypt, at *M,*
46:14 Announce it in Egypt, publish it in *M,*
Ez 29:10 a waste and a desolation from *M* to Syene,
30: 6 from *M* to Syene they shall fall there by

MIGHTIER (6)

Nm 14:12 of you a nation greater and *m* then they."
Dt 4:38 of your way nations greater and *m* than you,
9:14 of you a nation *m* and greater than they.'
11:23 nations greater and *m* than yourselves.
Wis 10:12 that devotion to God is *m* than all else.
Lk 3:16 but there is one to come who is *m* than I.

MIGHTIEST (2)

Prv 30:30 The lion, *m* of beasts,
Ez 31:11 handed it over to the *m* of the nations,

MIGHTILY (4)

Wis 6: 6 but the mighty shall be *m* put to the test.
8: 1 end to end *m* and governs all things well.
Sir 50:16 *m* as a reminder before the Most High.
Jer 25:30 *M* he roars over the range,

MIGHTY (150)

Gn 1: 2 while a *m* wind swept over the waters.
10: 9 He was a *m* hunter by the grace of the LORD;
10: 9 a *m* hunter by the grace of the LORD."
49:24 By the power of the *M* One of Jacob,
Ex 6: 1 Forced by my *m* hand,
6: 6 arm and with *m* acts of judgment.
15:10 like lead they sank in the *m* waters.
Lv 19:15 to the weak nor deference to the *m,*
Dt 3:24 on earth can perform deeds as *m* as yours?
10:17 of lords, the great God, *m* and awesome,
Jos 4:24 may learn that the hand of the LORD is *m,*
Jgs 5:13 Then down came the fugitives with the *m,*
1Sm 2: 4 The bows of the *m* are broken,
4: 8 deliver us from the power of these *m* gods?
2Sm 22:18 He rescued me from my *m* enemy,
23: 1 of Jacob, favorite of the *M* One of Israel.
1Kgs 8:42 and your *m* hand and your outstretched arm),
1Chr 11:22 son of Jehoiada, a valiant man of *m* deeds,
26: 8 their sons and their brethren, were *m* men,
26: 9 eighteen sons and brethren, *m* men.
2Chr 6:32 to honor your great name, your *m* power,
26:13 and at their disposal was a *m* army of
Ezr 3:13 raised a *m* clamor which was heard afar off.
8:22 his *m* wrath is against all who forsake him."
Neh 9:11 the depths, like a stone into the *m* waters.
9:32 "Now, therefore, O our God, great, *m,*
Jdt 16: 6 Not by youths was their *m* one struck down,
Est A: 5 They uttered a *m* cry,
1Mc 3:17 few as we are, fight such a *m* host as this?
4:30 who broke the rush of the *m* one by the
9:21 and they said, "How the *m* one has fallen,
10:19 a *m* warrior and worthy to be our friend.
2Mc 11:13 because the *m* God was their ally.
Jb 5:15 of the sword and from the hand of the *m,*
8: 2 words from your mouth are like a *m* wind!
9: 4 God is wise in heart and *m* in strength;
9:19 If it be a question of strength, he is *m;*
21: 7 wicked surive, grow old, become *m* in power?
24:23 He sustains the *m* by his strength,
34:24 Without a trial he breaks the *m,*
35: 9 for help because of the power of the *m,*
41:17 When he rises up, the *m* are afraid;
Ps(s) 18:18 me from my *m* enemy and from my foes,
24: 8 strong and mighty, the LORD, *m* in battle.
29: 4 The voice of the LORD is *m;*
33:16 A king is not saved by a *m* army,
35:18 in the *m* throng I will praise you.
36: 7 your judgments, like the *m* deep;
45: 4 Gird your sword upon your thigh, O *m* one!
59: 4 *m* men come together against me.
71:16 I will treat of the *m* works of the Lord;
76: 6 the hands of all the *m* ones have failed.
78:25 The bread of the *m* was eaten by men;
89: 9 *M* are you, O LORD,
89:14 Yours is a *m* arm;
103:20 all you his angels, you *m* in strength,
106: 2 Who can tell the *m* deeds of the LORD,
112: 2 His posterity shall be *m* upon the earth;
132: 2 to the LORD, vowed to the *M* One of Jacob:
132: 5 LORD, a dwelling for the *M* One of Jacob."
135:10 He smote many nations and slew *m* kings:
136:12 With a *m* hand and an outstretched arm,
147: 5 Great is our Lord and *m* in power:
150: 2 Praise him for his *m* deeds,
Prv 18:18 is decisive in a controversy between the *m.*
21:22 The wise man storms a city of the *m,*
30:26 species not *m,* yet they make their home
Eccl 9:14 city with few men in it advanced a *m* king,
Wis 5:23 A *m* wind shall confront them and a tempest
6: 6 the *m* shall be mightily put to the test.
11:20 and winnowed out by your *m* spirit;
13: 2 the circuit of the stars, or the *m* water,
18: 5 them perish all at once in the *m* water.
19: 7 and a grassy plain out of the *m* flood.
Sir 15:18 he is *m* in power,
18: 2 his works, and who can probe his *m* deeds?
23:14 mother in mind when you sit among the *m,*
34:16 he is their *m* shield and strong support,
38: 6 with the knowledge to glory in his *m* works,
40:13 like a *m* stream with lightning and thunder,
43:12 glory, this bow bent by the *m* hand of God.
Is 1:24 the LORD of hosts, the *M* One of Israel:
8: 7 *m* [the king of Assyria and all his power].
10:21 return, the remnant of Jacob, to the *m* God.
17:12 that surge like the surging of *m* waves!

28: 2 Behold, the LORD has a strong one and a *m*,
43:16 way in the sea and a path in the *m* waters,
49:26 savior, your redeemer, the *M* One of Jacob.
53:12 and he shall divide the spoils with the *m*,
60:16 savior, your redeemer, the *m* one of Jacob.
60:22 a thousand, the youngest, a *m* nation;
62: 8 sworn by his right hand and by his *m* arm:
63: 1 announce vindication, I who am *m* to save."
Jer 6: 1 from the north, and *m* destruction.
10: 6 great are you great and *m* is your name.
20:11 But the LORD is with me, like a *m* champion:
21: 5 you with outstretched hand and *m* arm,
25:14 be enslaved to great nations and *m* kings,
27: 7 turn shall serve great nations and *m* kings.
28: 8 against many lands and *m* kingdoms.
30: 7 How *m* is that day— none like it!
32:18 O God, great and *m*,
32:19 LORD of hosts, great in counsel, *m* in deed,
46:15 has Apis fled, your *m* one failed to stand?
50:41 *m* kings roused from the ends of the earth.
51:13 You who dwell by *m* waters,
51:55 her waves were roaring like *m* waters,
Lam 1:15 *m* ones in my midst the LORD has cast away;
Bar 2:11 out of the land of Egypt with your *m* hand,
Ez 1:24 their wings, like the roaring of *m* waters,
17: 9 need of a *m* arm or many people to do this.]
20:33 GOD, with a *m* hand and outstretched arm,
20:34 With a *m* hand and outstretched arm,
26: 7 with cavalry and a great and *m* army.
26:11 your *m* pillars he shall pull to the ground.
26:17 Once she was *m* on the sea,
26:19 against you, and its *m* waters cover you,
32:18 for the *m* nations have thrust them down to
32:20 world, the *m* warriors shall speak to Egypt:
32:27 do not lie with the *m* men fallen of old,
32:27 though the *m* men caused terror in the land
38:15 on horses, a great horde and a *m* army?.
Dn 2:10 never has any king, however great and *m*,
3:100 How great are his signs, how *m* his wonders;
11: 4 descendants or in keeping with his *m* rule,
Jl 1: 6 has invaded my land, *m* and without number;
2: 2 the mountains, a people numerous and *m!*
2: 5 Like a *m* people arrayed for battle.
2:11 For immense indeed is his camp, yes, *m*,
Zep 3:17 your God, is in your midst, a *m* savior;
Zec 11: 2 are fallen, the *m* have been despoiled.
Mt 24:31 his angels 'with a *m* trumpet blast,
28: 2 Suddenly there was a *m* earthquake as the
Lk 1:49 God who is *m* has done great things for me,
1:52 He has deposed the *m* from their thrones
Rom 15:19 word and deed, with *m* signs and marvels,
Eph 6:10 strength from the Lord and his *m* power.
2Thes 1: 7 is revealed from heaven with his *m* angels;
1Pt 5: 6 Bow humbly under God's *m* hand,
Rv 5: 2 a *m* angel who proclaimed in a loud voice:
6:13 earth like figs shaken loose by a *m* wind.
10: 1 Then I saw another *m* angel come down from
15: 3 *M* and wonderful are your works,
15: 4 Your *m* deeds are clearly seen."
16: 1 I heard a *m* voice from the sanctuary say
18: 8 for *m* is the Lord God who condemns her."
18:10 great city that you are, Babylon the *m!*
19: 6 roaring of the deep, or *m* peals of thunder,

MIGRATE (2)

Prv 30:27 they have no king, yet they *m* all in array;
Ez 12: 3 on, *m* from where you live to another place;

MIGRATED (5)

Gn 24: 5 your son back to the land from which you *m?"*
46: 6 Jacob and all his descendants *m* to Egypt.
46: 8 Jacob and his descendants, who *m* to Egypt.
46:26 Jacob's people who *m* to Egypt
Ex 1: 1 their households, *m* with Jacob into Egypt:

MIGRATING (2)

Gn 11: 2 While men were *m* in the east,
Dt 2:23 So also the Caphtorim, *m* from Caphtor,

MIGRATION (1)

Wis 18: 3 way, and the mild sun for an honorable *m*.

MIGRON (1)

Is 10:28 he has reached Aiath, passed through *M*,

MIJAMIN (4)

1Chr 24: 9 the fifth to Malchijah, the sixth to *M*,
Ezr 10:25 Ramiah, Izziah, Malchijah, *M*,
Neh 10: 8 Ginnethon, Baruch, Meshullam, Abijah, *M*,
12: 5 Meremoth, Iddo, Ginnethon, Abijah, *M*,

MIKLOTH (4)

1Chr 8:31 Ner, Nadab, Gedor, Ahio, Zecher, and *M*.
8:32 *M* became the father of Shimeah.
9:37 Ner, Nadab, Gedor, Ahio, Zechariah, and *M*.
9:38 *M* became the father of Shimeah.

MIKNEIAH (2)

1Chr 15:18 Maaseiah, Mattithiah, Eliphelehu, *M*,
15:21 But Mattithiah, Eliphelehu, *M*,

MILALAI (1)

Neh 12:36 and his brethren Shemaiah, Azarel, *M*,

MILCAH (11)

Gn 11:29 Sarai, and the name of Nahor's wife was *M*,
11:29 of Haran, the father of *M* and Iscah.
22:20 *M* too has borne sons,
22:23 These eight *M* bore to Abraham's brother
24:15 (who was born to Bethuel, son of *M*,
24:24 am the daughter of Bethuel the son of *M*,
24:47 Bethuel, son of Nahor, borne to Nahor by *M*.'
Nm 26:33 were Mahlah, Noah, Hoglah, *M* and Tirzah.
27: 1 daughters named Mahlah, Noah, Hoglah, *M*,
36:11 Mahlah, Tirzah, Hoglah, *M* and Noah,
Jos 17: 3 whose names were Mahlah, Noah, Hoglah, *M*,

MILCH (3)

Gn 32:16 thirty *m* camels and their young;
1Sm 6: 7 two *m* cows that have not borne the yoke;
6:10 Taking two *m* cows,

MILCOM (7)

1Kgs 11: 5 the goddess of the Sidonians, and *M*,
11:33 Sidonians, Chemosh, god of Moab, and *M*,
2Kgs 23:13 of Chemosh, the Moabite horror, and of *M*,
1Chr 20: 2 took the crown of *M* from the idol's head.
Jer 49: 1 Why then has *M* disinherited Gad,
49: 3 For *M* goes into exile along with his
Zep 1: 5 those who adore the LORD but swear by *M;*

MILCOM'S (1)

2Sm 12:30 captured it, he took the crown from *M* head.

MILD (2)

Prv 15: 1 A *m* answer calms wrath,
Wis 18: 3 and the *m* sun for an honorable migration.

MILDEW (2)

1Kgs 8:37 or if blight comes, or *m*,
2Chr 6:28 when there is pestilence, or blight, or *m*,

MILDLY (1)

Wis 11: 9 had been tried, though only *m* chastised,

MILDNESS (3)

2Mc 9:27 *m* and kindness in his relations with you."
Eccl 10: 4 for *m* abates great offenses.
Gal 5:23 endurance, kindness, generosity, faith, *m*,

MILE (3)

2Mc 12:10 When the Jews had gone about a *m* from
12:16 which was about a quarter of a *m* wide,
Mt 5:41 anyone press you into service for one *m*,

MILES (9)

2Mc 11: 5 place about twenty *m* from Jerusalem,
12: 9 visible as far as Jerusalem, thirty *m* away.
12:17 When they had gone on some ninety *m*,
12:29 Scythopolis, seventy-five *m* from Jerusalem.
Mt 5:41 service for one mile, go with him two *m*.
Lk 24:13 Emmaus seven *m* distant from Jerusalem,
Jn 6:19 when they had rowed three or four *m*,
11:18 just under two *m*—
Rv 14:20 winepress that for two hundred *m* around,

MILETUS (3)

Acts 20:15 and on the day after that we put in at *M*.
20:17 Paul sent word from *M* to Ephesus,
2Tm 4:20 while Trophimus I had to leave ill at *M*.

MILITARY (41)

Nm 1: 3 years or more who are fit for *m* service.
1:20 who were fit for *m* service were polled,
1:22 who were fit for *m* service were polled,
1:24 who were fit for *m* service were polled,
1:26 who were fit for *m* service were polled,
1:28 who were fit for *m* service were polled,
1:30 who were fit for *m* service were polled,
1:32 who were fit for *m* service were polled,
1:34 who were fit for *m* service were polled,
1:36 who were fit for *m* service were polled,
1:38 who were fit for *m* service were polled,
1:40 who were fit for *m* service were polled,
1:42 who were fit for *m* service were polled,
1:45 years or more who were fit for *m* service,
26: 2 more who are fit for *m* service in Israel."
Dt 20: 9 *m* officers shall be appointed over the
24: 5 wed, he need not go out on a *m* expedition,
Jos 5: 4 every man of *m* age had died in the desert
22:14 prince and *m* leader of his ancestral house.
22:21 replied to the *m* leaders of the Israelites:
22:30 community, the *m* leaders of the Israelites,
1Sm 18: 4 gave it to David, along with his *m* dress,
18:13 led the people on their *m* expeditions,
28: 1 their *m* forces to fight against Israel.
2Sm 24: 9 hundred thousand men fit for *m* service;
1Chr 5:18 hundred and sixty men fit for *m* service.
7: 4 thousand men in organized *m* troops,
7:11 two hundred men fit for *m* service . . .
7:40 twenty-six thousand men fit for *m* service.
12:34 From Zebulun, men fit for *m* service,
12:37 fit for *m* service and set in battle array:
Jdt 11: 8 and distinguished in *m* strategy.
1Mc 10:63 *m* commander and governor of the province.
2Mc 8: 9 Gorgias, a professional *m* commander,
12:35 grasped his *m* cloak and dragged him along
13:21 army, betrayed *m* secrets to the enemy.
13:24 left him as *m* and civil governor
Jer 41: 3 also slew all the men of Judah of *m* age
Mt 27:28 and wrapped him in a scarlet *m* cloak.
Mk 6:21 dinner for his court circle, *m* officers,
Acts 25:23 *m* officers and prominent men of the city.

MILK (54)

Gn 18: 8 Then he got some curds and *m*,
49:12 than wine, and his teeth are whiter than *m*.
Ex 3: 8 land, a land flowing with *m* and honey,
3:17 Jebusites, a land flowing with *m* and honey.
13: 5 give you, a land flowing with *m* and honey.
23:19 shall not boil a kid in its mother's *m*.
33: 3 you to the land flowing with *m* and honey.
34:26 shall not boil a kid in its mother's *m*."
Lv 20:24 a land flowing with *m* and honey.
Nm 13:27 It does indeed flow with *m* and honey,
14: 8 that land, a land flowing with *m* and honey.
16:13 away from a land flowing with *m* and honey,
16:14 us to a land flowing with *m* and honey,
Dt 6: 3 give you a land flowing with *m* and honey.
11: 9 a land flowing with *m* and honey.
14:21 shall not boil a kid in its mother's *m*.
26: 9 gave us this land flowing with *m* and honey.
26:15 in the land flowing with *m* and honey
27: 3 into the land flowing with *m* and honey,
31:20 into the land flowing with *m* and honey
32:14 Butter from its cows and *m* from its sheep,
Jos 5: 6 see the land flowing with *m* and honey
Jgs 4:19 But she opened a jug of *m* for him to drink,
5:25 He asked for water, she gave him *m;*
Jb 10:10 Did you not pour me out as *m*,
20:17 streams of oil, no torrents of honey or *m*.
29: 6 When my footsteps were bathed in *m*,
Prv 27:27 there will be ample goat's *m* to supply you,
30:33 For the stirring of *m* brings forth curds,
Sg 4:11 sweetmeats and *m* are under your tongue;
5: 1 my sweetmeats, I drink my wine and my *m*.
5:12 waters, His teeth would seem bathed in *m*,
Sir 39:26 salt, The heart of the wheat, *m* and honey,
46: 8 the land flowing with *m* and honey.
Is 7:22 abundant yield of *m* he shall live on curds:
28: 9 To those just weaned from *m*,
55: 1 paying and without cost, drink wine and *m!*
60:16 You shall suck the *m* of nations,
66:11 you may suck fully of the *m* of her comfort,
Jer 11: 5 give them a land flowing with *m* and honey:
32:22 oath, a land flowing with *m* and honey.
Lam 4: 7 than snow were her princes, whiter than *m*,
Bar 1:20 give us the land flowing with *m* and honey,
Ez 20: 6 for them, a land flowing with *m* and honey,
20:15 them, a land flowing with *m* and honey,
25: 4 shall eat your fruits and drink your *m*.
34: 3 You have fed off their *m*,
Jl 4:18 new wine, and the hills shall flow with *m;*
1Cor 3: 2 I fed you with *m*,
9: 7 nourish himself with the *m* of his flock?
Heb 5:12 you need *m*,
5:13 Everyone whose food is *m* alone is ignorant
1Pt 2: 2 eager for *m* as newborn babies—pure *m*

MILL (2)

Dt 24: 6 "No one shall take a hand *m* or even its
Eccl 12: 4 are shut, and the sound of the *m* is low;

MILLET (1)

Ez 4: 9 and beans and lentils, and *m* and spelt;

MILLING (1)

Lk 8:45 the crowds are *m* and pressing around you!"

MILLION (4)

1Chr 21: 5 in all Israel one *m* one hundred thousand,
22:14 talents of gold, a *m* talents of silver,
2Chr 14: 8 of one *m* men and three hundred chariots,
Rv 9:16 I heard, were two hundred *m* in number

MILLO (6)

2Sm 5: 9 he built up the area from *M* to the palace.
1Kgs 9:15 the temple of the LORD, his palace, *M*,
9:24 which he had built for her, Solomon built *M*.
11:27 King Solomon was building *M*,
1Chr 11: 8 all sides, from the *M* all the way around,
2Chr 32: 5 He strengthened the *M* of the City of David

MILLSTONE (10)

Jgs 9:53 upper part of a *m* down on Abimelech's head,
2Sm 11:21 threw a *m* down on him from the wall above,

MILLSTONE (cont.)

Jb 41:15 his flesh, as the lower *m*.
Is 47:2 Take the *m* and grind flour,
Jer 25:10 sound of the *m* and the light of the lamp.
Mt 18:6 me, to be drowned by a *m* around his neck,
Mk 9:42 with a great *m* fastened around his neck.
Lk 17:2 thrown into the sea with a *m* around his neck
Rv 18:21 huge *m* and hurled it into the sea and said:
18:22 of the *m* shall ever again be heard in you!

MILLSTONES (2)

Nm 11:8 grind it between *m* or pound it in a mortar,
Lam 5:13 The youths carry the *m*,

MINA (1)

Ez 45:12 plus fifteen shekels shall be your *m*.

MINAS (7)

1Kgs 10:17 (three *m* of gold went into each buckler);
Ezr 2:69 of gold, five thousand *m* of silver,
Neh 7:69 for priests, and five hundred *m* of silver.
7:70 and two thousand two hundred *m* of silver.
7:71 drachmas of gold, two thousand *m* of silver,
1Mc 14:24 great gold shield weighing a thousand *m*,
15:18 with them a gold shield worth a thousand *m*.

MINCES (1)

Prv 7:22 Like a stag that *m* toward the net,

MINCING (1)

Is 3:16 necks outstretched Ogling and *m* as they go,

MIND (156)

Gn 24:49 in *m* to show true loyalty to my master,
27:42 news of what her older son Esau had in *m*,
Ex 5:9 so that they keep their *m* on it and pay no
10:10 Clearly, you have some evil in *m*.
Nm 23:19 nor human, that he should change his *m*.
Dt 2:30 made him stubborn in *m* and obstinate in
5:29 that they might always be of such a *m*,
7:18 Rather, call to *m* what the LORD,
9:7 "Bear in *m* and do not forget how you
25:17 "Bear in *m* what Amalek did to you on the
29:3 the LORD yet given you a *m* to understand,
Jos 23:4 Bear in *m* that I have apportioned among
1Sm 2:35 who shall do what I have in heart and *m*.
12:24 *m* the great things he has done among you.
18:17 " Saul had in *m*, "I shall not touch him;
2Sm 7:3 the king, "Go do whatever you have in *m*,
14:11 your majesty, keep in *m* the LORD your God,
1Chr 12:18 help me, I am of a *m* to have you join me.
12:39 was likewise of one *m* to make David king.
28:12 pattern for all else that he had in *m*
2Chr 30:12 people were of one *m* to carry out
Ezr 7:27 who thus disposed the *m* of the king to
Neh 4:8 *m* the Lord who is great and to be feared,
5:19 Keep in *m*, O my God,
6:8 rather, it is the invention of your own *m*."
6:14 Keep in *m* Tobiah and Sanballat,
6:14 keep in *m* as well Noadiah the prophetess
7:5 it into my *m* to gather together the nobles,
Tb 4:5 all your days, my son, keep the Lord in *m*,
4:12 My boy, keep in *m* Noah,
4:19 So now, my son, keep in *m* my commandments,
Jdt 8:14 or grasp the workings of the human *m*;
8:14 has made all these things, discern his *m*,
11:10 not disregard his word, but bear it in *m*,
16:9 his eyes, and her beauty captivated his *m*.
Est A:11 He kept it in *m*, and tried in every way,
1Mc 7:30 had come to him with treachery in *m*,
2Mc 4:46 air, and persuaded him to change his *m*.
6:23 But he made up his *m* in a noble manner,
9:25 bearing in *m* that the neighboring rulers,
13:9 his *m* full of savage plans for inflicting
Jb 4:2 attempts a word with you, will you *m*?
22:18 But far be from me the *m* of the impious!]
23:14 and many such things may yet be in his *m*.
33:3 I will state directly what is in my *m*,
Ps(s) 10:5 your judgments are far from his *m*;
83:6 Yes, they consult together with one *m*,
Prv 3:1 not my teaching, keep in *m* my commands;
12:8 but one with a warped *m* is despised.
14:30 A tranquil *m* gives life to the body,
15:14 *m* of the intelligent man seeks knowledge,
16:9 In his *m* a man plans his course,
16:23 The *m* of the wise man makes him eloquent,
17:16 to buy wisdom, since he has no *m* for it?
18:15 The *m* of the intelligent gains knowledge,
23:1 with a ruler, keep in *m* who is before you;
Eccl 1:13 and I applied my *m* to search and
1:16 and my *m* has broad experience of wisdom
1:17 applied my *m* to know wisdom and knowledge,
2:3 though my *m* was concerned with wisdom,
2:23 even at night his *m* is not at rest.
8:9 *m* to every work that is done under the sun,
9:1 All this I have kept in *m* and recognized:
Wis 4:11 pervert his *m* or deceit beguile his soul;
4:12 whirl of desire transforms the innocent *m*.
9:15 earthen shelter weighs down the *m*
15:14 senseless, and worse than childish in *m*,
Sir 3:13 Even if his *m* fail, be considerate with him;
3:28 The *m* of a sage appreciates proverbs,
6:37 Then he will enlighten your *m*,
16:22 take my advice, apply your *m* to my words,
19:2 Wine and women make the *m* giddy,
21:14 A fool's *m* is like a broken jar
23:2 my thoughts, to my *m* the rod of discipline,
23:14 mother in *m* when you sit among the mighty,
25:7 There are nine who come to my *m* as blessed,
25:22 Depressed *m*, saddened face, broken heart
27:6 a man's speech disclose the bent of his *m*.
31:15 as you do, and keep in *m* your own dislikes:
31:20 slumber and a clear *m* next day on rising.
33:5 the wheel of a cart is the *m* of a fool;
34:5 what you already expect, the *m* depicts.
36:19 savor, so does a keen *m* insincere words.
37:17 The root of all conduct is the *m*;
43:19 eyes, the *m* is baffled by its steady fall.
51:26 yoke, that your *m* may accept her teaching.
Is 10:7 he intends, nor does he have this in *m*;
19:17 which the LORD of hosts has in *m* for them.
21:4 My *m* reels, shuddering assails me;
33:18 Your *m* will dwell on the terror:
46:8 this and be firm, bear it well in *m*,
64:8 LORD, keep not our guilt forever in *m*;
65:17 past shall not be remembered or come to *m*.
Jer 7:31 a thing as I never commanded or had in *m*.
11:20 O just Judge, searcher of *m* and heart,
17:10 LORD, alone probe the *m* and test the heart,
19:5 spoke of, nor did it ever enter my *m*
20:12 who test the just, who probe *m* and heart,
29:11 I know well the plans I have in *m* for you,
32:35 nor did it even enter my *m* that they
34:16 But then you changed your *m* and profaned
36:3 all the evil I have in *m* to do to them,
44:21 that the LORD remembered and brought to *m*,
Lam 3:21 But I will call this to *m*,
Bar 3:23 to wisdom, nor have they her paths in *m*.
Ez 28:6 thought yourself to have the *m* of a god,
38:10 that time thoughts shall arise in your *m*,
Dn 2:30 may understand the thoughts in your own *m*.
4:2 and the visions of my *m* frightened me.
4:13 Let his *m* be changed from the human;
5:10 Be not troubled in *m*, nor look so pale!
5:12 extraordinary *m* possessed by this Daniel,
6:15 news and he made up his *m* to save Daniel;
6:16 "Keep in *m*, O king," they said,
7:1 and was terrified by the visions of his *m*.
7:4 two feet like a man, and given a human *m*.
7:15 and I was terrified by the visions of my *m*.
10:12 you made up your *m* to acquire understanding
11:28 his *m* set against the holy covenant;
13:9 and did not keep in *m* just judgments.
Mt 12:34 The mouth speaks whatever fills the *m*.
13:19 him to steal away what was sown in his *m*.
15:18 comes out of the mouth originates in the *m*?
15:19 From the *m* stem evil designs
22:37 with your whole soul, and with all your *m*.'
Mk 3:21 of him, saying, "He is out of his *m*";
12:30 heart, with all your soul, with all your *m*,
Lk 10:27 all your strength, and with all your *m*;
20:19 he had told the parable with them in *m*.
24:38 Why do such ideas cross your *m*?
Jn 10:20 "He is possessed by a devil—out of his *m*!
Acts 4:32 of believers were of one heart and one *m*.
15:24 discussions and disturbed your peace of *m*.
19:21 Paul made up his *m* to travel through
28:27 The *m* of this people has grown sluggish.
Rom 7:23 another law at war with the law of my *m*;
7:25 So with my *m* I serve the law of God but
11:34 For "who has known the *m* of the Lord?
12:2 be transformed by the renewal of your *m*,
1Cor 1:10 rather, be united in *m* and judgment.
2:16 the *m* of the Lord so as to instruct him?"
2:16 But we have the *m* of Christ.
4:4 *M* you, I have nothing on my conscience.
7:37 his will makes up his *m* to keep his virgin,
14:14 is at prayer but my *m* contributes nothing.
14:15 with my spirit, and also to pray with my *m*.
14:15 sing with my spirit and with my *m* as well.
14:20 as evil is concerned, but in *m* be mature.
2Cor 1:17 I change my *m* from one minute to the next?
7:13 his *m* has been set at rest by all of you.
1Thes 2:17 in sight, not in *m*— we were seized
2Thes 2:7 of lawlessness is already at work, *m* you,
Jas 1:19 Keep this in *m*, dear brothers.
3Jn 1:13 is much more that I had in *m* to write you,
Rv 2:5 *m* the heights from which you have fallen.
3:3 Call to *m* how you accepted what you heard;

MINDED (1)

Ezr 7:13 who is *m* to go up to Jerusalem with you,

MINDFUL (25)

Gn 19:29 he was *m* of Abram by sending Lot away
Ex 2:24 and was *m* of his covenant with Abraham,
6:5 treating as slaves, I am *m* of my covenant.
Lv 26:42 and of the land, too, I will be *m*.
Tb 3:3 And now, O Lord, may you be *m* of me,
8:2 point Tobiah, *m* of Raphael's instructions,
14:7 saved in those days will truly be *m* of God,
14:9 to be *m* of God and at all times to bless
Est C:23 Be *m* of us, O Lord.
2Mc 15:8 but *m* of the help they had received from
Ps(s) 8:5 What is man that you should be *m* of him,
106:45 sake he was *m* of his covenant and relented,
111:5 he will forever be *m* of his covenant.
Prv 3:6 In all your ways be *m* of him,
Wis 19:10 *m* of what had happened in their sojourn:
Sir 7:11 be *m* of him who exalts and humbles.
23:18 Of the Most High he is not *m*,
Is 64:4 right, that we were *m* of you in our ways!
Lam 1:7 *m* of the days of her wretched homelessness,
Jon 1:6 will be *m* of us so that we may not perish."
Lk 1:54 Israel his servant, ever *m* of his mercy;
Gal 2:10 was that we should be *m* of the poor
1Thes 1:3 for we constantly are *m* before our God and
Heb 2:6 "What is man that you should be *m* of him,
13:3 Be as *m* of prisoners as if you were

MINDS (28)

Ex 13:17 might change their *m* and return to Egypt.
14:5 his servants changed their *m* about them.
1Chr 28:9 hearts and understands all the *m* thoughts.
29:18 in the hearts and *m* of your people forever,
Jb 17:4 You darken their *m* to knowledge;
Eccl 9:3 Hence the *m* of men are filled with evil,
Sir 40:6 by day, Terrified by what his *m* eye sees,
Jer 51:50 from afar, let Jerusalem come to your *m*.
Mk 3:5 that they had closed their *m* against him.
6:52 their *m* were completely closed to the
8:17 Are your *m* completely blinded?
Lk 24:45 *m* to the understanding of the Scriptures.
Acts 14:2 and poisoned their *m* against the brothers.
28:6 their *m* and began to say that he was a god.
28:27 with their ears, understand with their *m*,
1Cor 14:23 they not say that you are out of your *m*?
2Cor 3:14 Their *m*, of course, were dulled.
4:4 Their unbelieving *m* have been blinded by
Eph 4:17 their *m* empty,
Phil 4:6 Dismiss all anxiety from your *m*.
4:7 will stand guard over your hearts and *m*,
1Tm 6:5 twisted *m* who have lost all sense of truth.
2Tm 3:8 with perverted *m* they falsify the faith.
Ti 1:15 Their very *m* and consciences are tainted.
Heb 8:10 *m* and I will write them upon their hearts;
10:16 hearts and I will write them on their *m*,
Rv 2:23 that I am the searcher of hearts and *m*,
17:17 put it into their *m* to carry out his plan,

MINES (1)

1Mc 8:3 of the silver and gold *m* in Spain,

MINGLE (2)

1Sm 14:34 *M* with the people and tell each of them to
Ps(s) 102:10 like bread and *m* my drink with tears,

MINGLED (2)

Ps(s) 106:35 *m* with the nations and learned their works.
Rv 15:2 something like a sea of glass *m* with fire.

MINGLES (1)

Hos 7:8 Ephraim *m* with the nations,

MINGLING (1)

Jos 23:7 or *m* with these nations while they survive

MINIAMIN (1)

2Chr 31:15 him in the priestly cities were Eden, *M*,

MINIATURE (1)

Acts 19:24 Demetrius who made *m* shrines of Artemis

MINIONS (1)

Rv 12:9 hurled down to earth and his *m* with him.

MINISTER (40)

Ex 28:43 approach the altar to *m* in the sanctuary,
29:30 enter the meeting tent to *m* in the sanctuary
Nm 16:9 stand before the community to *m* for them?
Dt 10:8 in attendance before the LORD and *m* to him,
18:5 in attendance to *m* in the name of the LORD.
18:7 he may *m* there in the name of the LORD,
21:5 *m* to him and to give blessings in his name,
1Sm 2:30 family should *m* in my presence forever.
3:1 young Samuel was *m* to the Lord under Eli,
1Kgs 8:11 could no longer *m* because of the cloud,
1Chr 15:2 ark of the LORD and to *m* to him forever."
16:4 Levites to *m* before the ark of the LORD,
16:37 ark of the covenant of the LORD to *m*
23:13 sacrifice before the LORD, to *m* to him,
2Chr 5:14 not continue to *m* because of the cloud,
29:11 chosen to stand before him, to *m* to him,
Jdt 11:13 *m* in the presence of our God in Jerusalem:
2Mc 3:7 The king chose his *m* Heliodorus and sent
Jer 33:21 with the priests of Levi who *m* to me.
33:22 servant David and the Levites who *m* to me.
Ez 40:46 Levites who may come near to *m* to the LORD.
43:19 line of Zadok, who draw near me to *m* to me,
44:11 stand before the people to *m* for them.

44:12 they used to *m* for them before their idols,
44:15 me, they shall draw near me to *m* to me,
44:16 who shall approach my table to *m* to me,
44:17 not put on anything woolen when they *m*
44:27 the inner court to *m* in the sanctuary,
45: 4 sanctuary, who draw near to *m* to the LORD;
Rom 15:16 be a *m* of Christ Jesus among the Gentiles,
1Cor 9:13 and those who *m* at the altar share the
2Cor 11: 8 support from them in order to *m* to you.
Eph 3: 7 of his power, I became a *m* of the gospel.
6:21 my dear brother and faithful *m* in the Lord,
Col 1: 7 represents us as a faithful *m* of Christ.
1:25 I became a *m* of this church through the
4: 7 faithful *m* and fellow slave in the Lord,
Heb 8: 2 *m* of the sanctuary and of that true
Rv 7:15 day and night they *m* to him in his temple;
8: 2 the seven angels who *m* in God's presence

MINISTERED (4)

Neh 12: 9 their brethren *m* opposite them by turns.
Sir 24:10 In the holy tent I *m* before him,
Ez 42:14 left here the clothing in which they *m*,
44:19 take off the garments in which they *m*

MINISTERING (11)

Ex 28:35 Aaron shall wear it when *m*,
Jgs 20:28 son of Aaron, was *m* to him in those days),
1Sm 1: 3 Phinehas, were *m* as priests of the LORD.
2Chr 13:10 priests *m* to the LORD are sons of Aaron,
23: 6 the priests and those Levites who are *m*.
31: 2 or *m* in the gates of the encampment of the
Neh 10:40 of the sanctuary, and the *m* priests,
Is 56: 6 who join themselves to the LORD, *m* to him,
Dn 7:10 Thousands upon thousands were *m* to him,
Heb 1:14 Are they not all *m* spirits,
10:11 Every other priest stands *m* day by day,

MINISTERS (43)

Nm 1:50 all its equipment and who shall be its *m*.
1Kgs 9:22 for they were his fighting force, his *m*,
10: 5 food at his table, the seating of his *m*,
15:18 Entrusting them to his *m*,
2Kgs 24:12 of Judah, together with his mother, his *m*,
2Chr 9: 4 food at his table, the seating of his *m*,
29:11 to him, to be his *m* and to offer incense."
Ezr 8:17 for us *m* for the house of our God.
Jdt 2: 2 He summoned all his *m* and nobles,
7:16 words pleased Holofernes and all his *m*,
Est 1: 3 over a feast for all his officers and *m*:
2:18 of Esther to all his officials and *m*,
1Mc 1:46 desecrate the sanctuary and the sacred *m*,
Ps(s) 103:21 Bless the LORD, all you his hosts, his *m*,
104: 4 your messengers, and flaming fire your *m*.
Wis 6: 4 Because, though you were *m* of his kingdom,
Sir 7:30 love your Creator, forsake not his *m*.
10: 2 As the people's judge, so are his *m*;
Is 61: 6 the LORD, *m* of our God you shall be called.
Jer 21: 7 and his *m* and the people in this city who
22: 2 sit on the throne of David, you, your *m*,
22: 4 or mounted on horses, with their *m*,
36:24 his *m* or cause them to rend their garments.
36:31 descendants and his *m* for their wickedness;
37: 2 Neither he, nor his *m*,
37:18 In what have I wronged you, or your *m*,
46:26 Nebuchadnezzar, king of Babylon, and his *m*.
Ez 45: 4 to the priests, the *m* of the sanctuary,
45: 5 for the Levites, the *m* of the temple,
46:24 temple *m* cook the sacrifices of the people."
Jl 1: 9 are the priests, the *m* of the LORD.
1:13 wail, O *m* of the altar!
1:13 the night in sackcloth, O *m* of my God!
2:17 let the priests, the *m* of the LORD weep,
Lk 1: 2 original eyewitnesses and *m* of the word.
Rom 13: 6 magistrates being God's *m* who devote
1Cor 3: 5 Simply *m* through whom you became believers,
2Cor 3: 6 has made us qualified *m* of a new covenant,
6: 4 we strive to present ourselves as *m* of God,
11:15 surprise that his *m* disguise themselves as *m*
11:23 Are they *m* of Christ?
Heb 1: 7 his angels winds, and his *m* flaming fire";

MINISTRIES (1)

1Cor 12: 5 there are different *m* but the same Lord;

MINISTRY (30)

Ex 30:20 when they approach the altar in their *m*,
31:10 the vestments for his sons in their *m*,
35:19 the vestments worn by his sons in their *m*."
39:26 which was to be worn in performing the *m*—
39:41 to be worn by his sons in their *m*.
Nm 3:31 which the *m* of the sanctuary was exercised,
Dt 17:12 who officiates there in the *m* of the LORD,
33:11 possessions and accept the *m* of his hands.
2Chr 8:14 of praise and *m* alongside the priests,
Neh 12:45 Levites who carried out the *m* of their God
12:45 *m* of purification (as did the singers
Acts 1:17 had been given a share in this *m* of ours.
1:25 these two you choose for this apostolic *m*,
6: 4 on prayer and the *m* of the word."
7:53 the *m* of angels have not observed it."
21:19 among the Gentiles through his *m*.
Rom 11:13 apostle of the Gentiles, I glory in my *m*,
12: 7 It may be the gift of *m*;
2Cor 3: 7 If the *m* of death,
3: 8 will be the glory of the *m* of the Spirit?
3: 9 *m* of the covenant that condemned had glory,
3: 9 far is the glory of the *m* that justifies.
4: 1 we possess this *m* through God's mercy,
5:18 and has given us the *m* of reconciliation.
6: 3 offense, so that our *m* may not be blamed.
11:12 *m* they work on the same terms as we do.
Eph 3: 2 I am sure you have heard of the *m* which
Col 4:17 the *m* you have received in the Lord."
2Tm 4: 5 your work as an evangelist, fulfill your *m*.
Heb 8: 6 Jesus has obtained a more excellent *m* now,

MINJAMIN (1)

Neh 12:41 the priests Eliakim, Maaseiah, *M*,

MINNI (1)

Jer 51:27 against her the kingdoms, Ararat, *M*,

MINNITH (2)

Jgs 11:33 from Aroer to the approach of *M* (twenty
Ez 27:17 trafficked with you, exchanging *M* wheat,

MINOR (2)

Ez 46:22 in the four corners of the court, *m* courts,
1Cor 6: 2 thought unworthy of judging in *m* matters?

MINSTREL (2)

2Kgs 3:15 Now get me a *m*."
3:15 the *m* played, the power of the LORD came

MINSTRELS (2)

Ps(s) 68:26 The singers lead, the *m* follow,
Rv 18:22 No tunes of harpists and *m*,

MINT (2)

Mt 23:23 You pay tithes on *m* and herbs and seeds
Lk 11:42 on *m* and rue and all the garden plants,

MINUTE (2)

2Cor 1:17 I change my mind from one *m* to the next?
1:18 is not "yes" one *m* and "no" the next.

MINUTES (1)

Acts 5:34 accused ordered out of court for a few *m*,

MIRACLE (5)

Sir 45:19 He brought down upon them a *m*,
Mk 6: 5 He could work no *m* there,
9:39 No man who performs a *m* using my name
Lk 23: 8 and he was hoping to see him work some *m*.
1Cor 12:28 prophets, third teachers, then *m* workers,

MIRACLES (16)

Jos 24:17 He performed those great *m* before our very
Neh 9:17 remembered the *m* you had worked for them.
2Mc 15:21 and called upon the LORD who works *m*;
Sir 45: 3 God wrought swift *m* at his words and
Mt 7:22 Did we not do many *m* in your name as well?'
11:20 towns where most of his *m* had been worked,
11:21 If the *m* worked in you had taken place in
11:23 *m* worked in you had taken place in Sodom,
13:58 *m* there because of their lack of faith.
Lk 10:13 If the *m* worked in your midst had occurred
Acts 2:22 was a man whom God sent to you with *m*,
8: 6 saw the *m* he performed attended closely
8:13 the signs and the great *m* as they occurred,
19:11 extraordinary *m* at the hands of Paul.
1Cor 12:29 Do all work *m* or have the gift of healing?
Heb 2: 4 God then gave witness to it by signs, *m*,

MIRACULOUS (5)

Mt 13:54 did this man get such wisdom and *m* powers?
14: 2 is why such *m* powers are at work in him!"
Mk 6: 2 such *m* deeds are accomplished by his hands?
6:14 is why such *m* powers are at work in him."
1Cor 12:10 of healing, and still another *m* powers.

MIRACULOUSLY (1)

Acts 4:22 *m* cured was more than forty years of age.

MIRAGE (1)

Acts 12: 9 The whole thing seemed to him a *m*.

MIRE (11)

Jb 8:11 Can the papyrus grow up without *m*?
30:19 He has cast me into the *m*;
41:22 spreads like a threshing sledge upon the *m*.
Ps(s) 69:15 Rescue me out of the *m*; may I not sink!
Wis 7: 9 before her, silver is to be accounted *m*.
Is 25:10 down as a straw is trodden down in the *m*.
Am 4: 3 way, And you shall be cast into the *m*,
Mi 7:10 underfoot, like the *m* in the streets.
Zec 9: 3 dust, and gold like the *m* of the streets.
10: 5 trampling the *m* of the streets in battle;
2Pt 2:22 and, "A sow bathes by wallowing in the *m*."

MIRIAM (13)

Ex 6:20 Jochebed, who bore him Aaron, Moses, and *M*.
15:20 The prophetess *M*, Aaron's sister, took
Nm 12: 1 *M* and Aaron spoke against Moses on the
12: 4 the LORD said to Moses and Aaron and *M*,
12: 5 entrance of the tent, called Aaron and *M*.
12:10 cloud withdrew from the tent, there was *M*,
12:15 So *M* was confined outside the camp for
20: 1 It was here that *M* died,
26:59 bore Aaron and Moses and their sister *M*.
Dt 24: 9 to *M* on the journey after you left Egypt.
1Chr 4:17 Jether became the father of *M*,
5:29 children of Amram were Aaron, Moses, and *M*.
Mi 6: 4 And I sent before you Moses, Aaron, and *M*.

MIRMAH (1)

1Chr 8:10 Zibia, Mesha, Malcam, Jeuz, Sachia, and *M*.

MIRROR (5)

Jb 37:18 firmament of the skies, hard as a brazen *m*?
Wis 7:26 light, the spotless *m* of the power of God,
Sir 12:11 Rub him as one polishes a brazen *m*,
1Cor 13:12 Now we see indistinctly, as in a *m*;
Jas 1:23 into a *m* at the face he was born with;

MIRRORS (2)

Ex 38: 8 was made from the *m* of the women who
Is 3:23 *m*, linen tunics, turbans, and shawls.

MIRTH (4)

Eccl 2: 2 and of *m*: "What good does this do?"
7: 4 the heart of fools is in the house of *m*.
8:15 Therefore I commend *m*,
8:15 the sun except eating and drinking and *m*:

MISCARRIAGE (2)

Ex 21:22 a pregnant woman, so that she suffers a *m*,
2Kgs 2:21 again shall death or *m* spring from it.'"

MISCARRIED (1)

Gn 31:38 you, no ewe or she-goat of yours ever *m*,

MISCARRY (2)

Ex 23:26 woman in your land will be barren or *m*;
Jb 21:10 their cows calve and do not *m*.

MISCHIEF (16)

1Mc 9:61 ringleaders in the *m* and put them to death.
Jb 4: 8 it, those who plow for *m* and sow trouble,
5: 6 For *m* comes not out of the earth,
5: 7 But man himself begets *m*,
Ps(s) 7:15 conceived iniquity and was pregnant with *m*,
7:17 His *m* shall recoil upon his own head;
10: 7 under his tongue are *m* and iniquity.
55:11 Evil and *m* are in its midst;
140:10 the *m* which they threaten overwhelm them.
Prv 16:30 he who compresses his lips has *m* ready.
Wis 5: 7 had our fill of the ways of *m* and of ruin;
Sir 7:12 Plot no *m* against your brother,
27:22 eyes plots *m* and no one can ward him off;
33:28 idle, for idleness is an apt teacher of *m*.
Is 7: 5 because of the *m* that Aram [Ephraim and
59: 4 they conceive *m* and bring forth malice.

MISCHIEVOUS (1)

Prv 17: 4 and listens to falsehood from a *m* tongue.

MISCONDUCT (2)

2Kgs 23:13 of Jerusalem, south of the Mount of *M*,
Dn 6: 5 of neglect or *m* was to be found in him.

MISDEED (2)

Prv 17: 9 He who covers up a *m* fosters friendship,
Wis 3:14 also the eunuch whose hand wrought no *m*,

MISDEEDS (12)

Jb 13:23 My *m* and my sins make known to me!
14:17 My *m* would be sealed up in a pouch,
Ps(s) 99: 8 you were to them, though requiting their *m*.
Wis 19:13 For they justly suffered for their own *m*,
Is 1:16 Put away your *m* from before my eyes;
57:10 Though worn out by your many *m*,
Jer 4:18 Your conduct, your *m*, have done this
7:13 because you have committed all these *m*,
Bar 3: 5 at this time not the *m* of our fathers,
3: 8 a requital for all the *m* of our fathers,
Dn 4:24 and for your *m* by kindness to the poor;
1Tm 5:22 or you may be sharing in the *m* of others.

MISER (2)

Sir 14: 3 to the *m*, of what use is gold?
37:11 buyer about value, to a *m* about generosity,

MISERABLE (6)

Neh 3:34 "What are these *m* Jews trying to do?
2Mc 4: 1 and instigated the whole *m* affair.
5: 8 At length he met a *m* end.
9:28 *m* death in the mountains of a foreign land.
Prv 15:15 Every day is *m* for the depressed,
Sir 29:24 A *m* life it is to go from house to house,

MISERIES (1)

Jas 5: 1 rich, weep and wail over your impending *m.*

MISERLINESS (1)

Sir 14: 6 he punishes his own *m.*

MISERLY (1)

Sir 31:24 who is *m* with food is denounced in public,

MISERS (4)

Sir 11:18 A man may become rich through a *m* life,
14: 8 In the *m* opinion his share is too small;
14:10 The *m* eye is rapacious for bread,
1Cor 6:10 perverts, sodomites, thieves, *m,*

MISERY (27)

Gn 29:32 she said, "It means, 'The LORD saw my *m;*
Ex 3:17 *m* of Egypt into the land of the Canaanites,
Nm 23:21 observed in Jacob, nor *m* seen in Israel.
Jos 6:18 camp of Israel this ban and the *m* of it.
7:25 the *m* with which you have afflicted us!"
Jgs 6: 6 Thus was Israel reduced to *m* by Midian,
10:16 so that he grieved over the *m* of Israel.
1Sm 1:11 look with pity on the *m* of your handmaid,
1:16 has been prompted by my deep sorrow and *m.*"
9:16 their *m* and accept their cry for help."
Tb 3: 6 me to die than to endure so much *m* in life,
Jdt 7:32 Throughout the city they were in great *m.*
Jb 7: 3 So I have been assigned months of *m,*
11:16 For then you shall forget your *m,*
21:19 not store up the man's *m* for his children;
Ps(s) 10:14 You do see, for you behold *m* and sorrow,
22:25 nor disdained the wretched man in his *m,*
44:20 of *m* and covered us over with darkness.
107:41 Lifted up the needy out of *m* and made the
Prv 31: 7 When they drink, they will forget their *m,*
Sir 11:12 failure, with little strength and great *m*—
Lam 1: 9 Look, O LORD, upon her *m,*
Bar 5: 1 take off your robe of mourning and *m;*
Hb 1: 3 why must I look at *m?*
1:13 evil, and the sight of *m* you cannot endure.
Lk 16:25 in your lifetime, while Lazarus was in *m.*
Rom 3:16 ruin and *m* strew their course.

MISFORTUNE (37)

Lv 10:19 the LORD today, yet this *m* has befallen me.
Nm 23:21 *M* is not observed in Jacob,
2Kgs 14:10 and Judah with you in *m* and failure?"
1Chr 4:10 Help me and make me free of *m,*
2Chr 25:19 and Judah with you, in *m* and failure?"
Tb 7: 7 But what a terrible *m* that such a
Jb 2:11 heard of all the *m* that had come upon him,
Ps(s) 10: 6 from age to age I shall be without *m.*"
35:26 shame and confounded who are glad at my *m.*
38:13 they look to my *m,* they speak of ruin,
41: 2 in the day of *m* the LORD will deliver him.
Prv 12:21 but the wicked are overwhelmed with *m.*
13:21 *M* pursues sinners,
16:17 The path of the upright avoids *m;*
19:23 eats and sleeps without being visited by *m.*
Eccl 2:21 This also is vanity and a great *m.*
5:13 Should the riches be lost through some *m,*
11: 2 know not what *m* may come upon the earth.
Sir 2: 4 befalls you, in crushing *m* be patient;
29:16 turn a pledge on their behalf into *m,*
37: 9 will be, and then stand by to watch your *m.*
Jer 11:11 bring upon them *m* which they cannot escape.
11:12 give them no help whatever when *m* strikes.
11:14 they call to me at the time of their *m.*
11:15 and sacred meat turn away your *m* from you?
11:17 who planted you has decreed *m* for you
11:23 I will bring *m* upon the men of Anathoth,
15:11 with you in the time of *m* and anguish?
17:17 be my ruin, you, my refuge in the day of *m.*
17:18 Bring upon them the day of *m,*
44:17 we suffered no *m.*
51:60 Jeremiah had written the *m* that was to
Lam 1:21 All my enemies rejoice at my *m:*
Ob 1:13 upon his *m* on the day of his calamity;
Jon 1: 7 on whose account we have met with this *m.*"
Hb 2: 9 his nest on high to escape the reach of *m!*
Zep 3:15 your midst, you have no further *m* to fear.

MISFORTUNES (9)

1Mc 2:30 cattle, because *m* pressed so hard on them.
2Mc 5:20 itself, having shared in the people's *m,*
6:12 book not to be disheartened by these *m,*
6:16 Although he disciplines us with *m,*
10: 4 they might never again fall into such *m,*
14:14 thinking that the *m* and calamities of the
Wis 17:11 distressed conscience, always magnifies *m.*
Sir 20: 8 Some *m* bring success;
Is 51:19 Your *m* are double;

MISGIVINGS (2)

Mt 14: 9 The king immediately had his *m,*
Rom 14:23 when his conscience has *m* about eating,

MISGUIDED (1)

Jb 34:31 When anyone says to God, "I was *m;*

MISHAEL (10)

Ex 6:22 The sons of Uzziel were *M,*
Lv 10: 4 Then Moses summoned *M* and Elzaphan,
Neh 8: 4 and Maaseiah, and on his left Pedaiah, *M,*
1Mc 2:59 Hananiah, Azariah and *M,*
Dn 1: 6 Daniel, Hananiah, *M,* and Azariah.
1: 7 Hananiah to Shadrach, *M* to Meshach,
1:11 had put in charge of Daniel, Hananiah, *M,*
1:19 was found equal to Daniel, Hananiah, *M,*
2:17 and informed his companions Hananiah, *M,*
3:88 Hananiah, Azariah, *M,* bless the Lord;

MISHAL (3)

Jos 19:26 Achshaph, Allammelech, Amad and *M,*
19:28 and Neiel, it extended to Cabul, *M,*
21:30 four cities of *M* with its pasture lands,

MISHAM (1)

1Chr 8:12 The sons of Elpaal were Eber, *M,*

MISHMA (4)

Gn 25:14 first-born), Kedar, Adbeel, Mibsam, *M,*
1Chr 1:30 of Ishmael, then Kedar, Adbeel, Mibsam, *M,*
4:25 whose son was Mibsam, whose son was *M.*
4:26 descendants of *M* were his son Hammuel,

MISHMANNAH (1)

1Chr 12:11 Obadiah was second, Eliab third, *M* fourth,

MISHRAITES (1)

1Chr 2:53 the Puthites, the Shumathites, and the *M.*

MISLEAD (11)

2Chr 32:15 Let not Hezekiah *m* you further and deceive
Is 3:12 O my people, your leaders *m,*
9:15 *m* them and those to be led are engulfed.
Jer 23: 1 who *m* and scatter the flock of my pasture,
50: 6 were my people, their shepherds *m* them,
Zec 13: 4 shall he assume the hairy mantle to *m,*
Mt 24: 4 "Be on guard! Let no one *m* you.
24:11 will rise in great numbers to *m* many.
24:24 to *m* even the chosen if that were possible.
Mk 13: 5 "Be on guard! Let no one *m* you.
13:22 appear performing signs and wonders to *m,*

MISLEADERS (1)

Jb 12:16 the misled and the *m* are his.

MISLEADING (2)

Lam 2:14 for you in vision false and *m* portents.
Jn 7:12 he is only *m* the crowd!"

MISLEADS (1)

Dt 27:18 'Cursed be he who *m* a blind man on his way!'

MISLED (8)

2Kgs 21: 9 and Manasseh *m* them into doing even
2Chr 33: 9 Manasseh *m* Judah and the inhabitants of
Jb 12:16 the *m* and the misleaders are his.
Wis 11:15 which *m* them into worshiping dumb serpents
Sir 3:23 Their own opinion has *m* many,
Mt 22:29 "You are badly *m* because you fail to
Mk 12:24 "You are badly *m,* because you fail
Lk 21: 8 He said, "Take care not to be *m.*

MISMATCH (1)

2Cor 6:14 yoke yourselves in a *m* with unbelievers.

MISPERETH (2)

Ezr 2: 2 Seraiah, Reelaiah, Mordecai, Bilshan, *M,*
Neh 7: 7 Raamiah, Nahamani, Mordecai, Bilshan, *M,*

MISREPHOTH-MAIM (2)

Jos 11: 8 and pursued them to Greater Sidon, to *M,*
13: 6 mountain regions between Lebanon and *M;*

MISS (6)

1Sm 25: 7 neither did they *m* anything all the while
25:15 neither did we *m* anything all the while we
Jb 5:24 of your household, you shall *m* nothing.
Jer 3:16 think of it, or remember it, or *m* it,
Mt 7: 3 eye when you *m* the plank in your own?
Lk 6:41 eye when you *m* the plank in your own?

MISSED (4)

1Sm 20:18 and you will be *m,*
20:19 following day you will be *m* all the more.
25:21 in the desert so that he *m* nothing.
1Tm 6:21 some men have *m* the goal of faith.

MISSES (2)

1Sm 20: 6 If it turns out that your father *m* me,
Prv 8:36 But he who *m* me harms himself;

MISSILES (2)

2Mc 12:27 were large supplies of machines and *m.*
Jb 20:23 wrath and rain down his *m* of war upon him.

MISSING (13)

Gn 44:30 die as soon as he sees that the boy is *m;*
Nm 31:49 under our command, and not one is *m.*
Jgs 20:16 able to sling a stone at a hair without *m.*
1Sm 14:17 the troops and find out if any of us are *m.*"
14:17 they found Jonathan and his armor-bearer *m.*
30:19 Nothing was *m,* small or great,
2Sm 2:30 nineteen other servants of David were *m.*
1Kgs 20:39 If he is *m,* you shall have to pay
Eccl 1:15 straight, and what is *m* cannot be supplied.
Sir 3:24 Where the pupil of the eye is *m,*
Is 34:15 kites assemble, none shall be *m* its mate.
40:26 strength of his power not one of them is *m!*
Jer 23: 4 and none shall be *m,*

MISSION (18)

Ex 5:22 And why did you send me on such a *m?*
1Sm 15:18 you king of Israel and sent you on a *m,*
15:20 fulfill the *m* on which the LORD sent me.
18: 5 every *m* on which Saul sent him.
1Mc 12:10 a long time has passed since your *m* to us.
Jer 23:32 From me they have no *m* or command,
29:31 prophesies to you without a *m* from me,
Dn 10:11 stand up, for my *m* now is to you."
Mt 10: 5 Jesus sent these men on *m* as the Twelve,
10:34 that my *m* on earth is to spread peace.
10:34 My *m* is to spread,
15:24 "My *m* is only to the lost sheep of the
Lk 22:35 "When I sent you on *m* without purse or
Acts 7:12 Jacob sent our fathers there on a first *m.*
12:25 to Jerusalem upon completing the relief *m,*
15:38 Pamphylia, refusing to join them on that *m,*
2Cor 2:16 For such a *m* as this,
Rv 11: 6 rain will fall during the time of their *m.*

MISSPENT (1)

Wis 15: 8 And with *m* toil he molds a meaningless god

MISSTEP (1)

Jer 20:10 friends are on the watch for any *m* of mine.

MIST (3)

Ps(s) 148: 8 Fire and hail, snow and *m,*
Wis 2: 4 and will be dispersed like a *m* Pursued by
Is 44:22 offenses like a cloud, your sins like a *m;*

MISTAKE (8)

Gn 43:12 it may have been a *m.*
1Sm 26:21 have been a fool and have made a serious *m.*"
Eccl 5: 5 before his representative, "It was a *m,*"
10: 5 like a *m* that proceeds from the ruler:
Sir 14: 7 If ever he is generous, it is by *m;*
Gal 6: 7 Make no *m* about it,
Eph 5: 5 Make no *m* about this:
Jas 1:16 Make no *m* about this, my dear brothers.

MISTAKEN (1)

Mk 12:27 You are very much *m.*"

MISTAKENLY (1)

Dt 32:27 feared that these foes would *m* boast,

MISTLIKE (1)

Sir 24: 3 High I came forth, and *m* covered the earth.

MISTOOK (1)

Gn 38:15 When Judah saw her, he *m* her for a harlot,

MISTREAT (6)

Gn 31:50 If you *m* my daughters,
Jgs 16:19 Then she began to *m* him,
2Mc 1:28 who tyrannize over us and arrogantly *m* us.
Sir 7:20 *M* not a servant who faithfully serves,
33:33 If you *m* him and he runs away,
Jer 38:19 be handed over to them, and they will *m* me."

MISTREATMENT (1)

2Cor 12:10 I am content with weakness, with *m,*

MISTREATS (1)

Prv 19:26 He who *m* his father,

MISTRESS (16)

Gn 16: 4 she looked on her *m* with disdain.
16: 8 answered, "I am running away from my *m*,
16: 9 your *m* and submit to her abusive treatment.
1Kgs 17:17 the son of the *m* of the house fell sick,
2Kgs 5: 3 prophet in Samaria," she said to her *m*,
2Mc 4:30 given as a gift to Antiochis, the king's *m*.
Ps(s) 123: 2 eyes of a maid are on the hands of her *m*,
Prv 30:23 and a maidservant when she displaces her *m*.
Sir 37:18 and life, their absolute *m* is the tongue.
41:15 of immorality, before master and *m*,
Is 24: 2 servant and master, The maid as her *m*,
47: 5 you be called sovereign *m* of kingdoms.
47: 7 shall remain always a sovereign *m* forever!"
Lam 1: 1 Widowed is she who was *m* over nations;
Na 2: 8 shudders, Its *m* is led forth captive,
3: 4 fair and charming, a *m* of witchcraft,

MISTS (2)

Jb 36:27 that filter in rain through his *m*,
2Pt 2:17 waterless springs, *m* whipped by the gale.

MISTY (2)

Ps(s) 18:12 dark, *m* rain-clouds his wrap.
Acts 13:11 At once a *m* darkness came over him,

MISUSING (1)

Rom 7:13 It did so that, by *m* the commandment,

MITER (14)

Ex 28: 4 a robe, a brocaded tunic, a *m* and a sash.
28:37 This plate is to be tied over the *m* with a
28:37 a way that it rests on the front of the *m*,
28:39 The *m* shall be made of fine linen.
29: 6 *m* on his head, the sacred diadem on the *m*.
39:28 the *m* of fine linen;
39:31 was tied over the *m* with a violet ribbon,
Lv 8: 9 Thummim in it, and put the *m* on his head,
8: 9 sacred diadem, over the front of the *m*,
16: 4 with the linen sash and put on the linen *m*.
Bar 5: 2 bear on your head the *m* that displays
Zec 3: 5 He also said, "Put a clean *m* on his head."
3: 5 And they put a clean *m* on his head and

MITHKAH (2)

Nm 33:28 Setting out from Terah, they camped at *M*.
33:29 Setting out from *M*,

MITHNITE (1)

1Chr 11:43 Joshaphat the *M*;

MITHREDATH (2)

Ezr 1: 8 had them brought forth by the treasurer *M*,
4: 7 *M* wrote in concert with Tabeel and the

MITYLENE (1)

Acts 20:14 Assos we took him aboard and sailed to *M*.

MIXED (51)

Ex 12:38 crowd of *m* ancestry also went up with them,
29: 2 flour make unleavened cakes *m* with oil,
29:40 ephah of fine flour *m* with a fourth of a hin
Lv 2: 4 cakes made of fine flour *m* with oil,
2: 5 be of fine flour *m* with oil and unleavened.
7:10 offerings that are offered up dry or *m* with oil
7:12 he shall offer unleavened cakes *m* with oil,
7:12 of fine flour *m* with oil and well kneaded.
9: 4 along with a cereal offering *m* with oil;
14:10 flour *m* with oil for a cereal offering,
14:21 flour *m* with oil for a cereal offering,
23:13 of an ephah of fine flour *m* with oil,
Nm 6:15 unleavened cakes of fine flour *m* with oil
7:13 flour *m* with oil for a cereal offering;
7:19 fine flour *m* with oil for cereal offering;
7:25 flour *m* with oil for a cereal offering;
7:31 flour *m* with oil for a cereal offering;
7:37 flour *m* with oil for a cereal offering;
7:43 flour *m* with oil for a cereal offering;
7:49 flour *m* with oil for a cereal offering;
7:55 flour *m* with oil for a cereal offering;
7:61 flour *m* with oil for a cereal offering;
7:67 flour *m* with oil for a cereal offering;
7:73 flour *m* with oil for a cereal offering;
7:79 flour *m* with oil for a cereal offering;
8: 8 cereal offering of fine flour *m* with oil;
15: 4 fine flour *m* with a fourth of a hin of oil,
15: 6 fine flour *m* with a third of a hin of oil,
15: 9 of fine flour *m* with half a hin of oil,
28: 5 ephah of fine flour *m* with a fourth of a hin
28: 9 of an ephah of fine flour *m* with oil,
28:12 three tenths of an ephah of fine flour *m*
28:12 two tenths of an ephah of fine flour *m*
28:13 tenth of an ephah of fine flour *m* with oil
28:20 cereal offerings of fine flour *m* with oil;
28:28 offerings of fine flour *m* ed with oil;
29: 3 cereal offerings of fine flour *m* with oil;
29: 9 cereal offerings of fine flour *m* with oil;
29:14 cereal offerings of fine flour *m* with oil;
1Chr 9:30 however, who *m* the spiced ointments.
Est B: 4 *m* in with all the races throughout the
2Mc 12:13 inhabited by a *m* population of Gentiles.
Prv 9: 2 She has dressed her meat, *m* her wine,
9: 5 of my food, and drink of the wine I have *m!*
Sg 7: 3 bowl that should never lack for *m* wine.
Is 1:22 turned to dross, your wine is *m* with water.
Dn 2:41 As you saw the iron *m* with clay tile,
2:43 The iron *m* with clay tile means that they
14:33 he *m* some bread in a bowl with the stew he
Lk 13: 1 blood Pilate had *m* with their sacrifices.
Rv 8: 7 there came hail and then fire *m* with blood,

MIXES (1)

Dn 2:43 any more than iron *m* with clay

MIXING (3)

1Chr 23:29 unleavened bread, and of the baking and *m*,
2Mc 15:38 whereas *m* wine with water makes a more
Is 5:22 wine, the valiant at *m* strong drink!

MIXTURE (3)

Ex 30:32 nor may you make any other oil of a like *m*.
30:37 make incense of a like *m* for yourselves;
Jn 19:39 bringing a *m* of myrrh and aloes which

MIZAR (1)

Ps(s) 42: 7 of the Jordan and of Hermon, from Mount *M*.

MIZPAH (39)

Gn 31:49 why it was named Galeed—and also *M*,
Jos 11: 3 at the foot of Hermon in the land of *M*.
Jgs 10:17 the Israelites assembled and encamped in *M*.
11:11 In *M*, Jephthah settled all his affairs
11:34 When Jephthah returned to his house in *M*,
20: 1 community was gathered to the LORD at *M*.
20: 3 heard that the Israelites had gone up to *M*.
21: 1 Now the men of Israel had sworn at *M* that
21: 5 at *M* should be put to death without fail.
21: 8 Israel had not come up to the LORD in *M*,
1Sm 7: 5 then gave orders, "Gather all Israel to *M*,
7: 6 When they were gathered at *M*,
7: 6 " It was at *M* that Samuel began to judge
7: 7 that the Israelites had gathered at *M*,
7:11 forth from *M* and pursued the Philistines,
7:12 stone and placed it between *M* and Jeshanah;
7:16 Gilgal and *M* and judging Israel at each of
10:17 the LORD at *M* and addressed the Israelites:
2Kgs 25:23 commanders with their men came to him at *M*:
25:25 Jews and Chaldeans who were in *M* with him.
2Chr 16: 6 and with them he fortified Geba and *M*.
Neh 3: 7 and the men of Gibeon and of *M*,
3:15 of Colhozeh, leader of the district of *M*;
3:19 to him Ezer, son of Jeshua, leader of *M*,
1Mc 3:46 assembled and went to *M* near Jerusalem,
3:46 formerly at *M* a place of prayer for Israel.
Jer 40: 6 went to Gedaliah, son of Ahikam, in *M*,
40: 8 they came with their men to Gedaliah in *M*:
40:10 saying that he himself would remain in *M*,
40:12 *M* and had a rich harvest of wine and fruit.
40:13 armies in the field came to Gedaliah in *M*
40:15 of Kareah, said secretly to Gedaliah in *M*:
41: 1 ten men to Gedaliah, son of Ahikam, at *M*.
41: 1 while they were together at table in *M*,
41: 6 Nethaniah, went out from *M* to meet them,
41:10 of the people left in *M* and the princesses,
41:14 brought away from *M* went over to Johanan,
41:16 away from *M* after he killed Gedaliah,
Hos 5: 1 For you have become a snare at *M*,

MIZPAH-GILEAD (1)

Jgs 11:29 Gilead and Manasseh, and through *M* as well,

MIZPEH (5)

Jos 11: 8 and eastward to the valley of *M*.
15:38 Zenan, Hadashah, Migdal-gad, Dilean, *M*,
18:26 Ramah, Beeroth, *M*,
1Sm 22: 3 to *M* of Moab and said to the king of Moab,
1Kgs 15:22 them King Asa built Geba of Benjamin and *M*.

MIZRAIM (2)

Gn 10: 6 Cush, *M*, Put, and Canaan.
10:13 *M* became the father of the Ludim,

MIZZAH (3)

Gn 36:13 Reuel were Nahath, Zerah, Shammah, and *M*.
36:17 the clans of Nahath, Zerah, Shammah, and *M*.
1Chr 1:37 Reuel were Nahath, Zerah, Shammah, and *M*.

MNASON (1)

Acts 21:16 came along to escort us to the house of *M*,

MOAB (154)

Gn 19:37 one gave birth to a son whom she named *M*,
36:34 the Midianites in the country of *M*;
Ex 15:15 trembling seized the chieftains of *M*;
Nm 21:11 in the desert fronting *M* on the east.
21:15 site of Ar and slant to the border of *M*."
21:20 Bamoth to the cleft in the plateau of *M*
21:26 had fought against the former king of *M*
21:28 It consumed the cities of *M* and swallowed
21:29 Woe to you, O *M!*
22: 1 moved on and encamped in the plains of *M*
22: 3 *M* feared the Israelites greatly because of
22: 4 So *M* said to the elders of Midian,
22: 4 son who was king of *M* at that time,
22: 7 Then the elders of *M* and of Midian left
22: 8 So the princes of *M* lodged with Balaam.
22:10 God, "Balak, son of Zippor, king of *M*,
22:14 of *M* went back to Balak with the report,
22:21 ass, and went off with the princes of *M*.
23: 6 together with all the princes of *M*.
23:17 holocaust together with the princes of *M*.
24:17 Israel, That shall smite the brows of *M*,
26: 3 *M* along the Jericho stretch of the Jordan,
26:63 *M* along the Jericho stretch of the Jordan.
31:12 at their camp on the plains of *M*,
33:44 camped at Iye-abarim on the border of *M*.
33:48 *M* along the Jericho stretch of the Jordan.
33:49 camp along the Jordan on the plains of *M*
33:50 LORD spoke to Moses on the plains of *M*
35: 1 *M* beside the Jericho stretch of the Jordan:
36:13 *M* beside the Jericho stretch of the Jordan.
Dt 1: 5 the law in the land of *M* beyond the Jordan,
2: 8 and we went on toward the desert of *M*.
2:18 to leave Ar and the territory of *M* behind.
23: 5 you left Egypt, and because *M* hired Balaam,
28:69 make with the Israelites in the land of *M*,
32:49 [it is in the land of *M* facing Jericho];
34: 1 went up from the plains of *M* to Mount Nebo,
34: 5 So there, in the land of *M*,
34: 6 opposite Beth-peor in the land of *M*,
34: 8 wept for Moses in the plains of *M*,
Jos 13:32 Moses gave when he was in the plains of *M*,
24: 9 Then Balak, son of Zippor, king of *M*,
Jgs 3:12 this offense strengthened Eglon, king of *M*,
3:14 Israelites then served Eglon, king of *M*,
3:15 sent their tribute to Eglon, king of *M*.
3:17 presented the tribute to Eglon, king of *M*,
3:28 the fords of the Jordan leading to *M*,
3:30 Thus was *M* brought under the power of
10: 6 of Aram, the gods of Sidon, the gods of *M*,
11:15 the land of *M* or the land of the Ammonites.
11:17 They also sent to the king of *M*,
11:18 land of *M*, went east of the land of *M*
11:18 Moab, for the Arnon is the boundary of *M*.
11:25 than Balak, son of Zippor, king of *M*?
Ru 1: 1 and two sons to reside on the plateau of *M*.
1: 6 ready to go back from the plateau of *M*
1:22 accompanied her back from the plateau of *M*.
2: 6 returned from the plateau of *M* with Naomi.
1Sm 12: 9 and into the grip of the king of *M*,
14:47 war on all their surrounding enemies *M*,
22: 3 Mizpeh of *M* and said to the king of Moab,
22: 4 He left them with the king of *M*,
2Sm 8: 2 *M* and then measured them with a line,
8:12 from Edom and *M*,
23:20 It was he who slew the two lions in *M*.
1Kgs 11: 7 a high place to Chemosh, the idol of *M*,
11:33 of the Sidonians, Chemosh, god of *M*,
2Kgs 1: 1 Ahab's death, *M* rebelled against Israel.
3: 4 Now Mesha, king of *M*, who raised sheep
3: 5 *M* had rebelled against the king of Israel.
3: 7 "The king of *M* is in rebellion against me.
3: 7 Will you join me in battle against *M*?"
3:10 three kings to put them in the grasp of *M*."
3:13 together to put them in the grasp of *M*."
3:18 he will also deliver *M* into your grasp.
3:21 all *M* heard that the kings had come to
3:26 the king of *M* took seven hundred swordsmen
1Chr 4:22 Joash and Saraph, who held property in *M*,
11:22 He killed the two sons of Ariel of *M*,
11:46 Ithmah, from *M*;
18: 2 He also defeated *M*,
18:11 from Edom, *M*,
2Chr 24:26 and Jehozabad, son of Shimrith from *M*.
Jdt 1:12 with his sword all the inhabitants of *M*,
5:22 of *M* alike said he should be cut to pieces.
Ps(s) 60:10 *M* shall serve as my washbowl;
83: 7 the Ishmaelites, *M* and the people of Hagar,
108:10 *M* shall serve as my washbowl;
Is 11:14 Edom and *M* shall be their possessions,
15: 1 Oracle on *M*; Laid waste in a night
15: 1 Ar of *M* is destroyed;
15: 1 Laid waste in a night, Kir of *M*
15: 2 Over Nebo and over Medeba *M* wails.
15: 4 At this the loins of *M* tremble,
15: 5 The heart of *M* cries out,
15: 8 For the cry has gone round the land of *M*;
15: 9 *M* and for those who remain in the land!
16: 2 daughters of *M* at the fords of the Arnon.
16: 4 Let the outcasts of *M* live with you,
16: 6 We have heard of the pride of *M*,
16: 7 Therefore *M* wails for Moab,
16:11 for *M* my breast moans like a lyre,
16:12 When *M* grows weary on the high places,
16:13 of the LORD spoke against *M* in times past.
16:14 the glory of *M* shall be degraded despite
25:10 but *M* will be trodden down as a straw is
25:11 *M* as a swimmer extends his hands to swim;
Jer 9:25 *M* and the desert dwellers who shave their

MOAB (cont.)

25:21 Edom *M*, and the Ammonites;
27: 3 Send to the kings of Edom, of *M*,
40:11 When the people of Judah in *M*,
48: 1 Concerning *M*, thus says the LORD
48: 4 *M* is crushed, their outcry is heard in Zoar.
48: 9 Set up a memorial for *M*,
48:11 *M* has been tranquil from his youth,
48:13 Chemosh shall disappoint *M*,
48:15 The ravager of *M* and his cities advances,
48:20 *M* is disgraced, yes, destroyed,
48:20 Publish it at the Arnon, *M* is ruined!
48:24 on all the cities of *M*, far and near.
48:26 make *M* drunk so that he retches and vomits,
48:28 dwell in the crags, you that dwell in *M*,
48:29 We have heard of the pride of *M*,
48:31 And so I wail over Moab, over all *M* I cry,
48:33 end in the fruit gardens of the land of *M*.
48:35 I will leave no one in *M*,
48:36 the wail of flutes for *M* is in my heart;
48:38 *M* and in all his squares there is mourning;
48:38 shattered *M* like a pot that no one wants,
48:39 wants, says the LORD How terror seizes *M*,
48:39 *M* has become a laughingstock and a horror
48:40 eagle he soars, spreads his wings over *M*.
48:42 *M* shall be destroyed,
48:43 pit, and trap be upon you, people of *M*,
48:44 upon *M* in the year of their punishment,
48:45 It consumes the brow of *M*,
48:46 Woe to you, O *M*, you are ruined,
48:47 change the lot of *M* in the days to come,
48:47 Thus far the judgment on *M*.
Ez 25: 8 Because *M* said, "See!
25: 9 the shoulder of *M* totally of its cities,
25:11 Thus I will execute judgment upon *M*,
Dn 11:41 land and many shall fall, except Edom, *M*,
Am 2: 1 For three crimes of *M*,
2: 2 of Edom's king, I will send fire upon *M*,
2: 2 *M* shall meet death amid uproar
Zep 2: 8 I have heard the revilings uttered by *M*,
2: 9 God of Israel, *M* shall become like Sodom,

MOABITE (17)

Nm 22:36 on the Arnon at the end of the *M* territory.
25: 1 having illicit relations with the *M* women.
Dt 23: 4 No Ammonite or *M* may ever be admitted into
Ru 1: 2 time after their arrival on the *M* plateau,
1: 4 with her two sons, who married *M* women,
1:22 Naomi returned with the *M* daughter-in-law,
2: 2 Ruth the *M* said to Naomi,
2: 6 "She is the *M* girl who returned from the
2:21 "He even told me," added Ruth the *M*,
4: 3 who has come back from the *M* plateau,
4: 5 from Naomi, you must take also Ruth the *M*,
4:10 I also take Ruth the *M*,
2Kgs 23:13 Sidonian horror, of Chemosh, the *M* horror,
1Chr 1:46 overthrew the Midianites on the *M* plateau,
8: 8 Shaharaim became a father on the *M* plateau
Neh 13: 1 written there that "no Ammonite or *M* may
13:23 married Ashdodite, Ammonite, or *M* wives.

MOABITES (23)

Gn 19:37 He is the ancestor of the *M* of today.
Dt 2: 9 to the *M* or engage them in battle,
2:11 It was the *M* who called them Emim.
2:29 Seir and the *M* who dwell in Ar have done,
Jgs 3:28 your enemies the *M* into your power."
3:29 occasion they slew about ten thousand *M*,
2Sm 8: 2 Thus the *M* became tributary to David.
1Kgs 11: 1 women besides the daughter of Pharaoh *M*,
2Kgs 3:22 the *M* saw the water at a distance as red
3:23 To the spoils, *M*!"
3:24 the Israelites rose up and attacked the *M*,
3:24 the countryside striking down the *M*,
13:20 bands of *M* used to raid the land each year.
24: 2 him bands of Chaldeans, Arameans, *M*,
1Chr 18: 2 Moab, and the *M* became his subjects,
2Chr 20: 1 After this the *M*,
20:10 And now, see the Ammonites, *M*,
20:22 laid an ambush against the Ammonites, *M*,
20:23 For the Ammonites and *M* set upon the
Ezr 9: 1 Perizzites, Jebusites, Ammonites, *M*,
Jdt 5: 2 anger he summoned all the rulers of the *M*,
6: 1 throng of coastland peoples, of the *M*,
7:17 Thereupon the *M* moved camp,

MOAB'S (8)

Nm 21:13 Arnon forms *M* boundary with the Amorites.
23: 7 Aram has Balak brought me here, *M* king,
Jer 48: 2 *M* glory is no more.
48:16 Near at hand is *M* ruin,
48:18 *M* ravager has come up against you,
48:25 *M* strength is broken,
48:41 On that day the hearts of *M* heroes are
Mi 6: 5 remember what *M* King Balak planned,

MOAN (8)

Ps(s) 55:18 at dawn, and at noon, I will grieve and *m*,
77: 4 When I remember God, I *m*;
102: 8 I am sleepless, and I *m*;
Is 38:14 I *m* like a dove.
59:11 bears, like doves we *m* without ceasing.
Jer 48:31 Moab I cry, over the men of Kir-heres I *m*.
Lam 2:18 Cry out to the LORD; *m*, O daughter Zion!
Ez 9: 4 mark an X on the foreheads of those who *m*

MOANING (4)

Jer 4:31 Yes, I hear the *m*, as of a woman in travail,
31:15 In Ramah is heard the sound of *m*,
Lam 2: 5 Judah he has multiplied *m* and groaning.
Na 2: 8 her handmaids, under guard, *M* like doves,

MOANS (1)

Is 16:11 Therefore for Moab my breast *m* like a lyre,

MOB (5)

Ez 23:42 the shout of a carefree *m* in the city,
Acts 17: 5 to form a *m* and start a riot in the town.
19:35 Finally the town clerk quieted the *m*.
21:35 soldiers because of the violence of the *m*.
24:12 me debating with anyone or inciting a *m*.

MOBILE (1)

Wis 7:24 For Wisdom is *m* beyond all motion,

MOBILIZE (1)

1Kgs 20:25 *M* an army as large as the army that has

MOBILIZED (1)

1Kgs 20:26 Ben-hadad *m* Aram and went up to Aphek to

MOCHMUR (1)

Jdt 7:18 Egrebel, near Chusi, which is on Wadi *M*.

MOCK (9)

Jb 21: 3 and after I have spoken, you can *m*!
Ps(s) 22: 8 they *m* me with parted lips,
42:11 It crushes my bones that my foes *m* me,
80: 7 by our neighbors, and our enemies *m* us.
Prv 1:26 I will *m* when terror overtakes you;
Sir 11: 4 *M* not the worn cloak and jibe at no man's
34:18 *M* presents from the lawless win not God's
Mt 27:29 Then they began to *m* him by dropping to
Mk 10:34 Gentiles, who will *m* him and spit at him,

MOCKED (14)

Jgs 16:10 Samson, "You have *m* me and told me lies.
16:13 "Up to now you have *m* me and told me lies.
16:15 Three times already you have *m* me,
2Chr 36:16 But they *m* the messengers of God,
Neh 2:19 and Geshem the Arab *m* us and ridiculed us.
3:36 Take note, O our God, how we were *m*!
Tb 2: 8 The neighbors *m* me, saying to one another:
Jdt 4:12 and *m* for the nations to gloat over.
1Mc 7:34 But he *m* and ridiculed them,
Jb 17: 2 I am indeed *m*,
Ps(s) 35:16 they *m* me, gnashing their teeth at me.
Sg 8: 7 to purchase love, he would be roundly *m*.
Hos 7:16 thus they shall be *m* in the land of Egypt.
Lk 18:32 He will be *m* and outraged and spat upon.

MOCKERIES (1)

Wis 17: 7 And *m* of the magic art were in readiness,

MOCKERY (13)

2Chr 29: 8 an object of terror, astonishment and *m*,
Jdt 8:22 we shall be a *m* and a reproach in the eyes
Jb 30: 9 Yet now they sing of me in *m*;
Ps(s) 44:14 the *m* and the scorn of those around us.
109:25 And I am become a *m* to them;
123: 4 more than sated with the *m* of the arrogant,
Wis 4:19 corpses and an unceasing *m* among the dead.
5: 3 as a laughingstock and as a type for *m*,
12:25 you sent your judgment on them as a *m*;
Sir 27:28 *M* and abuse will be the lot of the proud,
Ez 36: 4 and *m* of the remaining nations round about;
Na 1:14 I will make your grave a *m*.
Heb 11:36 Still others endured *m*, scourging,

MOCKING (2)

Mk 15:20 When they had finished *m* him,
2Pt 3: 3 in the last days, *m*, sneering men

MOCKINGLY (1)

Wis 11:14 out in exposure they indeed *m* rejected;

MOCKS (5)

Ps(s) 44:17 At the voice of him who *m* and blasphemes,
Prv 17: 5 He who *m* the poor blasphemes his Maker;
30:17 The eye that *m* a father,
Jer 20: 7 I am an object of laughter; everyone *m* me.
Bar 6:43 she *m* her neighbor who has not been

MODEIN (9)

1Mc 2: 1 of Joarib, left Jerusalem and settled in *M*.
2:15 the city of *M* to organize the sacrifices.
2:23 altar in *M* according to the king's order.
2:70 buried in the tombs of his fathers in *M*,
9:19 him in the tomb of their fathers at *M*.
13:25 his brother Jonathan, and buried him in *M*,
13:30 he built at *M* is there to the present day.
16: 4 Cendebeus, they spent the night at *M*,
2Mc 13:14 the government, he pitched his camp near *M*.

MODEL (5)

Jos 22:28 'Look at the *m* of the altar of the LORD
2Kgs 16:10 King Ahaz sent to Uriah the priest a *m*
2Mc 6:31 leaving in his death a *m* of courage and an
1Thes 1: 7 Thus you became a *m* for all the believers
2Tm 1:13 Take as a *m* of sound teaching what you

MODELER (1)

Is 45: 9 Dare the clay say to its *m*,

MODELING (1)

Wis 15: 9 bronze, and takes pride in *m* counterfeits.

MODELS (3)

Wis 13:13 This wood he *m* with listless skill,
Heb 9:23 of the heavenly *m* be purified in this way,
Jas 5:10 *m* in suffering hardship and in patience,

MODERATE (2)

Sir 31:20 *M* eating ensures sound slumber and a
31:22 In whatever you do, be *m*,

MODERATION (4)

2Mc 10: 4 he might chastise them with *m* and not hand
Wis 8: 7 For she teaches *m* and prudence,
Sir 31:27 Wine is very life to man if taken in *m*.
2Cor 10:13 the bounds the God of *m* has set for us

MODEST (4)

2Mc 15:12 a good and virtuous man, *m* in appearance,
Sir 26:15 Choicest of blessings is a *m* wife,
Ez 17:14 so that the kingdom would remain a *m* one,
1Tm 3: 2 once, of even temper, self-controlled, *m*,

MODESTLY (1)

1Tm 2: 9 They should dress *m* and quietly,

MODESTY (1)

Sir 32:10 a storm is the esteem that shines on *m*.

MOISTEN (1)

Ez 46:14 third of a hin of oil to *m* the fine flour.

MOISTENED (1)

Lv 11:38 but if the grain has become *m* it becomes

MOISTURE (2)

Sg 5: 2 with dew, my locks with the *m* of the night."
Lk 8: 6 up, then withered through lack of *m*.

MOLADAH (4)

Jos 15:26 Amam, Shema, *M*,
19: 2 they received Beer-sheba, Shema, *M*,
1Chr 4:28 They dwelt in Beer-sheba, *M*,
Neh 11:26 Jekabzeel and its villages, in Jeshua, *M*,

MOLARS (1)

Jl 1: 6 of a lion, and his *m* those of a lioness.

MOLD (4)

Gn 11: 3 let us *m* bricks and harden them with fire."
1Kgs 7:24 rows and were cast in one *m* with the sea.
2Chr 4: 3 of these cast in the same *m* with the sea.
Na 3:14 tread the clay, take hold of the brick *m*!

MOLDED (7)

1Kgs 6:32 also *m* to the cherubim and the palm trees.
Wis 7: 1 in my mother's womb I was *m* into flesh
Sir 33:13 potter, to be *m* according to his pleasure,
Jer 10:14 He has *m* a fraud, without breath of life.
51:17 He *m* a fraud, without breath of life.
Bar 6:23 did they feel anything when they were *m*.
Rom 9:20 Does something *m* say to its molder,

MOLDER (1)

Rom 9:20 Does something molded say to its *m*,

MOLDERS (1)

Wis 15: 9 and silversmiths and emulates *m* of bronze,

MOLDING (10)

Ex 25:11 and put a *m* of gold around the top of it.
25:24 pure gold and make a *m* of gold around it.
25:25 high, with a *m* of gold around the frame.
30: 3 Put a gold *m* around it.
30: 4 Underneath the *m* you shall put gold rings,
37: 2 gold, and a *m* of gold was put around it.

37:11 gold, and a *m* of gold was put around it.
37:12 it, with a *m* of gold around the frame.
37:26 and a *m* of gold was put around it.
37:27 Underneath the *m* gold rings were placed,

MOLDS (4)

Wis 15: 7 *m* for our service each several article:
15: 8 *m* a meaningless god from the selfsame clay;
Sir 27: 5 of what the potter *m* is in the furnace,
38:30 With his hands he *m* the clay,

MOLE (1)

Lv 11:30 chameleon, the agama, the skink, and the *m*.

MOLECH (8)

Lv 18:21 any of your offspring to be immolated to *M*,
20: 2 his offspring to *M* shall be put to death.
20: 3 for in giving his offspring to *M*,
20: 4 man's crime of giving his offspring to *M*,
20: 5 who join him in his wanton worship of *M*.
1Kgs 11: 7 Chemosh, the idol of Moab, and to *M*,
2Kgs 23:10 of sons or daughters by fire in honor of *M*.
Jer 32:35 immolated their sons and daughters to *M*,

MOLECHETH (2)

1Chr 7:15 his sister's name was *M*.
7:18 His sister *M* bore Ishhod,

MOLES (1)

Is 2:20 On that day men will throw to the *m* and

MOLEST (5)

Ex 22:20 "You shall not *m* or oppress an alien,
Lv 19:33 with you in your land, do not *m* him.
Dt 23:17 Do not *m* him.
1Mc 10:35 them or to *m* any of them in any matter.
Ps(s) 56: 6 All the day they *m* me in my efforts;

MOLESTED (2)

Gn 26:29 toward us, just as we have not *m* you,
2Mc 11:31 and none of the Jews shall be *m* in any way

MOLESTS (1)

Gn 26:11 "Anyone who *m* this man or his wife shall

MOLID (1)

1Chr 2:29 was named Abihail, bore him Ahban and *M*.

MOLOCH (1)

Acts 7:43 tent of *M* and the star of the god Rephan,

MOLTEN (22)

Ex 32: 4 gold with a graving tool, made a *m* calf.
32: 8 for themselves a *m* calf and worshiping it,
34:17 "You shall not make for yourselves *m* gods.
Lv 19: 4 to idols, nor make *m* gods for yourselves.
Nm 33:52 all their stone figures and *m* images,
Dt 9:12 them and have made for themselves a *m* idol,
9:16 to you by making for yourselves a *m* calf!
27:15 be the man who makes a carved or *m* idol
1Kgs 14: 9 strange gods and *m* images to provoke me;
2Kgs 17:16 God, and made for themselves two *m* calves;
2Chr 4: 2 He also made the *m* sea.
28: 2 Israel and even made *m* idols of the Baals.
34: 3 sacred poles and the carved and *m* images.
34: 4 *m* images were shattered and beaten
Neh 9:18 Though they made themselves a *m* calf,
Ps(s) 106:19 made a calf in Horeb and adored a *m* image;
Is 42:17 Who say to *m* images, "You are our gods.
48: 5 my statue, my *m* image commanded them."
Dn 11: 8 with their *m* images and their precious
Hos 13: 2 to sin, making for themselves *m* images,
Na 1:14 I will abolish the carved and the *m* image;
Hb 2:18 Or the *m* image and lying oracle,

MOMENT (62)

Gn 2:17 the *m* you eat from it you are surely
3: 5 God knows well that the *m* you eat of it
39: 5 From the *m* that he put him in charge of
41:15 But I hear it said of you that the *m* you
Ex 33: 5 I to go up in your company even for a *m*,
1Sm 9:27 of us, but stay here yourself for the *m*,
2Sm 3:12 to David in Telam, where he was at the *m*,
1Kgs 14:14 Today, at this very *m*, the LORD will raise
2Chr 20:22 At the *m* they began their jubilant hymn,
26:19 the *m* he showed his anger to the priests,
Tb 3:17 In the very *m* that Tobit returned from the
Jdt 6: 5 for saying these things in a *m* of
1Mc 9:31 that *m* Jonathan accepted the leadership,
2Mc 3:28 The man who a *m* before had entered that
6:25 for the sake of a brief *m* of life,
15:20 Everyone now awaited the decisive *m*.
Jb 7:18 with each new day and try him at every *m*!
8: 7 Your former state will be of little *m*,
20: 5 and the joy of the impious but for a *m*?
34:20 in a *m* they die, even at midnight.
Ps(s) 30: 6 For his anger lasts but a *m*;
Prv 12:19 forever, the lying tongue, for only a *m*.
Sir 18:32 of a *m* which bring on poverty redoubled;
22:16 careful deliberation shaken in a *m* of fear.
Is 10:25 For only a brief *m* more,
26:20 Hide yourselves for a brief *m*,
27: 3 LORD, am its keeper, I water it every *m*;
54: 7 For a brief *m* I abandoned you,
54: 8 of wrath, for a *m* I hid my face from you;
66: 8 one day, or a nation be born in a single *m*?
Ez 26:16 tremble at every *m* and be horrified at you.
Dn 13:15 while they were waiting for the right *m*,
14:42 they were devoured in a *m* before his eyes.
Hg 2: 6 One *m* yet, a little while, and I will shake
Mt 6:27 by worrying can add a *m* to his life-span?
8:13 That very *m* the boy got better.
9:22 That very *m* the woman got well.
15:28 That very *m* her daughter got better.
17:18 That very *m* the boy was cured.
26:50 At that *m* they stepped forward to lay
Mk 14:68 [At that *m* a cock crowed.]
15:38 At that *m* the curtain in the sanctuary was
Lk 1:44 The *m* your greeting sounded in my ears,
1:64 At that *m* his mouth was opened and his
2:38 Coming on the scene at this *m*,
7: 2 was at that *m* sick to the point of death.
10:21 At that *m* Jesus rejoiced in the Holy
12:12 you at that *m* all that should be said."
12:25 by worrying can add a *m* to his life-span?
18:43 At that very *m* he was given his sight and
22:60 At the very *m* he was saying this,
Jn 18:27 At that *m* a cock began to crow.
Acts 3: 8 he jumped up, stood for a *m*,
10:33 All of us stand before God at this *m* to
11: 8 'Not for a *m*, sir!
1Cor 4: 8 At the *m* you are completely satisfied.
7:36 because a critical *m* has come and it seems
15: 2 You are being saved by it at this very *m*
Gal 2: 5 us, but we did not submit to them for a *m*.
Heb 10:37 For, just a brief *m*,
Rv 11:13 At that *m* there was a violent earthquake
11:18 day of wrath and the *m* to judge the dead:

MOMENTARY (1)

Wis 16:27 by fire, when merely warmed by a *m* sunbeam,

MOMENTS (4)

Ru 2: 7 here until now, with scarcely a *m* rest."
Sir 11:27 A *m* affliction brings forgetfulness of
Mt 26:53 call on my Father to provide at a *m* notice
1Thes 5: 1 As regards specific times and *m*,

MONETARY (1)

Dt 18: 8 along with his *m* offerings and heirlooms.

MONEY (141)

Gn 17:12 those acquired with *m* from any foreigner
17:13 those acquired with *m* must be circumcised.
17:23 born in his house or acquired with his *m*—
17:27 or acquired with his *m* from foreigners,
31:15 has even used up the *m* that he got for us!
42:25 grain, their *m* replaced in each one's sack,
42:27 to see his *m* in the mouth of his bag.
42:28 "My *m* has been returned!"
43:12 Also take extra *m* along,
43:15 took double the amount of *m* with them,
43:18 the *m* put back in our bags the first time,
43:21 *m* in the mouth of his bag—our *m* in the full
43:22 have brought other *m* to procure food with.
43:22 not know who put the first *m* in our bags."
43:23 As for your *m*, I received it."
44: 1 put each man's *m* in the mouth of his bag.
44: 2 together with the *m* for his rations."
44: 8 *m* that we found in the mouths of our bags.
47:14 *m* that was to be found in Egypt and Canaan,
47:15 all the *m* in Egypt and Canaan was spent,
47:15 for our *m* is gone."
47:16 "Since your *m* is gone,"
47:18 with our *m* spent and our livestock made
Ex 12:44 has been bought for *m* may partake of it,
21:35 shall sell the live ox and divide this *m*
22: 6 "When a man gives *m* or an article to
22:24 "If you lend *m* to one of your poor
30:16 this forfeit *m* from the Israelites,
Lv 25:36 your countryman either in *m* or in kind,
25:37 neither *m* at interest nor food at a profit.
27: 2 are to be ransomed at a fixed sum of *m*,
27:18 the priest shall estimate its *m* value
Dt 14:25 tithe for *m* and, with the purse of *m* in hand,
14:26 exchange the *m* for whatever you desire,
23:20 on a loan of *m* or of food or of anything else
Jos 24:32 of Shechem, for a hundred pieces of *m*.
Jgs 16:18 came and brought up the *m* with them.
1Kgs 21: 2 you prefer, I will give you its value in *m*."
2Kgs 5:26 this a time to take *m* or to take garments,
12: 5 census tax, personal redemption *m*,
15:20 Menahem secured the *m* to give to the king
2Chr 24: 5 cities of Judah and collect *m* from all Israel
24:11 and they saw that it contained much *m*,
24:11 until they had collected a large sum of *m*.
24:14 rest of the *m* to the king and to Jehoiada,
34: 9 turned over the *m* brought to the house
34:14 When they brought out the *m* that had been
Ezr 7:17 therefore, to use this *m* to buy bulls,
Neh 5: 4 borrowed *m* on our fields and our vineyards.
5:10 lent the people *m* and grain without charge.
5:11 together with the interest on the *m*,
Tb 1: 7 years, I used to give a second tithe in *m*,
1:14 a great sum of *m* with my kinsman Gabael,
4: 1 That same day Tobit remembered the *m* he
4: 2 and let him know about this *m* before I die?"
4:20 I have deposited a great sum of *m*
5: 2 shall I be able to obtain the *m* from him,
5: 2 trust me, so that he will give me the *m*?
5: 3 his copy I put with the *m*.
5: 3 already passed since I deposited that *m*!
5: 3 but get back that *m* from Gabael."
5:19 I hope more *m* is not your chief concern!
9: 2 Get the *m* and then bring him along with
10: 2 and there is no one to give him the *m*."
10:10 and sheep, asses and camels, clothing, *m*,
11:15 that he had brought back the *m*;
12: 3 he brought the *m* back with me:
1Mc 3:29 that this exhausted the *m* in his treasury;
3:31 provinces, and so raise a large sum of *m*.
8:26 shall not give nor provide grain, arms, *m*,
8:28 there shall not be given grain, arms, *m*,
10:43 precincts, because of *m* he owes the king,
13:15 on account of the *m* that he owed the royal
13:17 he gave orders to get the *m* and the boys,
13:18 would not send Trypho the *m* and the boys.
14:32 spending large sums of his own *m* to equip
15: 6 I authorize you to coin your own *m*,
15:30 tribute *m* of the districts outside the territory
15:31 more for the tribute *m* of the cities.
2Mc 3: 6 total sum of *m* was incalculable
3:10 *m* was a care fund for widows and orphans,
3:13 *m* must be confiscated for the royal treasury.
4:19 the *m* should not be spent on a sacrifice,
4:23 Simon, to deliver the *m* to the king,
4:27 of the *m* he had promised to the king,
4:45 sum of *m* if he would win the king over.
8:25 They also seized the *m* of those who had
10:20 men in Simon's force who were *m* lovers
10:21 men of having sold their kinsmen for *m*
Jb 42:11 one gave him a piece of *m* and a gold ring.
Ps(s) 15: 5 who lends not his *m* at usury and
Prv 7:20 A bag of *m* he took with him,
Eccl 5: 9 covetous man is never satisfied with *m*,
7:12 of wisdom is as the protection of *m*;
10:19 living glad, but *m* answers for everything.
Sir 7:18 Barter not a friend for *m*,
21: 8 He who builds his house with another's *m*
29:10 Spend your *m* for your brother and friend,
Is 43:24 You did not buy me sweet cane for *m*,
52: 3 and without *m* you shall be redeemed.
55: 1 You who have no *m*,
55: 2 Why spend your *m* for what is not bread;
Jer 32: 9 from my cousin Hanamel, paying him the *m*,
32:25 Buy the field with *m*, call in witnesses.
32:44 Fields shall be bought with *m*,
Bar 3:18 They schemed anxiously for *m*,
Mi 3:11 for a salary, her prophets divine for *m*,
Mt 6:24 You cannot give yourself to God and *m*.
13:22 anxiety and the lure of *m* choke it off.
20:15 I am free to do as I please with my *m*,
25:18 the ground, where he buried his master's *m*.
25:25 Here is your *m* back.'
25:27 reason to deposit my *m* with the bankers,
26: 9 a good price and the *m* given to the poor."
27: 5 Judas flung the *m* into the temple and left.
27: 6 in the temple treasury since it is blood *m*."
28:15 the *m* and did as they had been instructed.
Mk 12:41 crowd putting *m* into the collection box.
14: 5 silver pieces and the *m* given to the poor."
14:11 were jubilant and promised to give him *m*.
Lk 7:41 "Two men owed *m* to a certain money-lender;
9: 3 no bread, no *m*.
14:28 if he has enough *m* to complete the project?
15:13 he squandered his *m* on dissolute living.
16:12 not been trustworthy with someone else's *m*,
16:13 You cannot give yourself to God and *m*."
19:15 the servants to whom he had given the *m*,
19:20 'Here is your *m*, my lord, which I hid
19:23 then, did you not put my *m* out on loan,
22: 5 were delighted, and agreed to give him *m*.
Jn 12: 5 and the *m* have been given to the poor."
Acts 4:37 that he owned and made a donation of the *m*,
5: 4 you sold it, was not the *m* still yours?
8:18 made them an offer of *m* with the request,
8:20 "May you and your *m* rot
1Tm 3: 3 Nor can he be someone who loves *m*.
6:10 The love of *m* is the root of all evil.
2Tm 3: 2 Men will be lovers of self and of *m*,
Heb 13: 5 love *m* but be content with what you have,

MONEY-CHANGER'S (2)

Mt 21:12 He overturned the *m'* tables and the stalls
Mk 11:15 He overturned the *m'* tables and the stalls
Jn 2:15 area, and knocked over the *m'* tables,

MONEY-LENDER (1)

Lk 7:41 "Two men owed money to a certain *m*;

MONEYBAG (1)

Gn 42:35 sacks, there in each one's sack was his *m!*

MONEYBAGS (2)

Gn 42:35 At the sight of their *m,*
Tb 9: 5 Gabael promptly checked over the sealed *m,*

MONITOR (1)

Gal 3:24 the law was our *m* until Christ came to

MONITOR'S (1)

Gal 3:25 is here, we are no longer in the *m* charge.

MONKEYS (2)

1Kgs 10:22 cargo of gold, silver, ivory, apes, and *m.*
2Chr 9:21 of gold and silver, ivory, apes and *m.*

MONOPOLIZES (1)

Prv 11:26 Him who *m* grain,

MONSTER (3)

Jb 7:12 Am I the sea, or a *m* of the deep,
Ez 29: 3 Egypt, Great crouching *m* amidst your Niles:
32: 2 You were like a *m* in the sea,

MONSTERS (3)

Gn 1:21 God created the great sea *m* and all kinds
Ps(s) 148: 7 from the earth, you sea *m* and all depths;
Sir 43:26 all kinds of life, and the *m* of the deep.

MONSTROUS (7)

Gn 20: 9 brought such *m* guilt on me and my kingdom?
Dt 22:14 and makes *m* charges against her and
22:17 her, and now brings *m* charges against her,
Jgs 20: 6 the *m* crime they had committed in Israel.
Wis 17: 9 For even though no *m* thing frightened them,
Lam 1:20 recoils within me from my *m* rebellion.
Hos 6: 9 on the way to Shechem, committing *m* crime.

MONTH (237)

Gn 7:11 year of Noah's life, in the second *m,*
7:11 month, on the seventeenth day of the *m:*
8: 4 had so diminished that, in the seventh *m,*
8: 4 month, on the seventeenth day of the *m,*
8: 5 continued to diminish until the tenth *m,*
8: 5 tenth *m* the tops of the mountains appeared.
8:13 first year of Noah's life, in the first *m,*
8:13 first month, on the first day of the *m,*
8:14 second *m,* on the twenty-seventh day of the *m,*
Ex 12: 2 *m* shall stand at the head of your calendar;
12: 2 shall reckon it the first *m* of the year.
12: 3 On the tenth of this *m* every one of your
12: 6 it until the fourteenth day of this *m,*
12:18 fourteenth day of the first *m* until the evening
12:18 of this *m* you shall eat unleavened bread.
13: 4 day of your departure is in the *m* of Abib.
13: 5 this *m* that you must celebrate this rite,
16: 1 on the fifteenth day of the second *m*
19: 1 In the third *m* after their departure from
23:15 at the prescribed time in the *m* of Abib,
34:18 *m* of Abib you are to eat unleavened bread,
34:18 for in the *m* of Abib you came out of Egypt.
40: 2 "On the first day of the first *m* you
40:17 On the first day of the first *m* of the
Lv 16:29 tenth day of the seventh *m* everyone of you,
23: 5 falls on the fourteenth day of the first *m,*
23: 6 *m* is the LORD's feast of Unleavened Bread.
23:24 seventh *m* you shall keep a sabbath rest,
23:27 of this seventh *m* is the Day of Atonement,
23:32 on the evening of the ninth of the *m,*
23:34 seventh *m* is the LORD's feast of Booths,
23:39 the fifteenth day, then, of the seventh *m,*
23:41 whole week in the seventh *m* of the year.
25: 9 of the seventh *m* let the trumpet resound;
27: 6 between the ages of one *m* and five years,
Nm 1: 1 Egypt, on the first day of the second *m,*
1:18 community on the first day of the second *m.*
3:15 registering every male of a *m* or more."
3:22 their males of a *m* or more were registered,
3:28 their males of a *m* or more were registered,
3:34 their males of a *m* or more were registered,
3:39 The total number of male Levites a *m* old
3:40 males of the Israelites a *m* old or more,
3:43 males of a *m* or more were registered,
9: 1 In the first *m* of the year following their
9: 3 twilight of the fourteenth day of this *m*
9: 5 of the fourteenth day of the first *m,*
9:11 But he shall keep it in the second *m,*
9:11 twilight of the fourteenth day of that *m,*
9:22 Dwelling for two days or for a *m* or longer,
10:11 on the twentieth day of the second *m,*
11:20 or ten, or twenty days, but for a whole *m*—
11:21 will give them meat to eat for a whole *m.*'
18:16 for a boy is to be paid when he is a *m* old;
20: 1 in the desert of Zin in the first *m,*
26:62 of male Levites one *m* or more of age,
28:11 "On the first of each *m* you shall offer
28:16 the first *m* falls the Passover of the LORD,
28:17 day of this *m* is the pilgrimage feast.
29: 1 seventh *m* you shall hold a sacred assembly,
29: 7 seventh *m* you shall hold a sacred assembly,
29:12 seventh *m* you shall hold a sacred assembly,
33: 3 month, on the fifteenth day of the first *m.*
33:38 of Egypt, on the first day of the fifth *m.*
Dt 1: 3 year, on the first day of the eleventh *m,*
16: 1 "Observe the *m* of Abib by keeping the
16: 1 since it was in the *m* of Abib that he
21:13 her father and mother for a full *m,*
Jos 4:19 Jordan on the tenth day of the first *m,*
5:10 on the evening of the fourteenth of the *m.*
1Sm 11: 1 About a *m* later, Nahash the Ammonite
20:20 the third day of the *m* I will shoot arrows,
20:27 On the next day, the second day of the *m,*
20:34 and took no food that second day of the *m,*
1Kgs 4: 7 having to provide for one *m* in the year.
5: 7 These commissaries, one for each *m,*
5:28 Lebanon each *m* in relays of ten thousand,
5:28 *m* in the Lebanon and two months at home.
6: 1 the month of Ziv, which is the second *m,*
6:37 laid in the *m* of Ziv in the fourth year,
6:38 to plan, in the month of Bul, the eighth *m,*
8: 2 in the *m* of Ethanim (the seventh month).
12:32 in the eighth *m* of the fifteenth day of the *m*
12:33 fifteenth day of the eighth *m,* the *m* in which
2Kgs 15:13 he reigned one *m* in Samaria.
25: 1 *m* of the ninth year of Zedekiah's reign,
25: 1 reign, on the tenth day of the *m,*
25: 3 On the ninth day of the fourth *m,*
25: 8 On the seventh day of the fifth *m* (this
25:25 But in the seventh *m* Ishmael,
25:27 the twenty-seventh day of the twelfth *m,*
1Chr 12:16 overflowing both its banks in the first *m,*
27: 1 and went *m* by month throughout the year.
27: 2 division for the first *m* was Ishabaal,
27: 3 the commanders of the army for the first *m.*
27: 4 the division of the second *m* was Eleazar,
27: 5 army commander, chief for the third *m,*
27: 7 Fourth, for the fourth *m,* was Asahel,
27: 8 Fifth, for the fifth *m,* was the commander
27: 9 Sixth, for the sixth *m,* was Ira,
27:10 Seventh, for the seventh *m,* was Hellez
27:11 Eighth, for the eighth *m,* was Sibbecai
27:12 Ninth, for the ninth *m,* was Abiezer
27:13 Tenth, for the tenth *m,* was Maharai
27:14 Eleventh, for the eleventh *m,* was Benaiah
27:15 Twelfth, for the twelfth *m,* was Heldai
2Chr 3: 2 second *m* of the fourth year of his reign.
5: 3 king during the festival of the seventh *m.*
7:10 *m* he sent the people back to their tents,
15:10 *m* of the fifteenth year of Asa's reign,
29: 3 the first *m* of the first year of his reign,
29:17 on the first day of the first *m,*
29:17 and on the eighth day of the *m* they
29:17 and on the sixteenth day of the first *m,*
30: 2 the Passover during the second *m,*
30:13 feast of Unleavened Bread in the second *m;*
30:15 on the fourteenth day of the second *m.*
31: 7 *m* that they began to establish these heaps,
31: 7 and they completed them in the seventh *m.*
35: 1 on the fourteenth day of the first *m.*
Ezr 3: 1 Now when the seventh *m* came,
3: 6 From the first day of the seventh *m* they
3: 8 of God in Jerusalem, in the second *m,*
6:15 this house on the third day of the *m* Adar,
6:19 on the fourteenth day of the first *m.*
7: 8 fifth *m* of that seventh year of the king.
7: 9 On the first day of the first *m* he
7: 9 day of the fifth *m* he arrived at Jerusalem,
8:31 of Ahava on the twelfth day of the first *m.*
10: 9 ninth month, on the twentieth day of the *m.*
10:16 with the first day of the first *m.*
10:17 By the first day of the tenth *m* they had
Neh 1: 1 In the *m* Chislev of the twentieth year,
2: 1 In the *m* Nisan of the twentieth year of
8: 1 Now when the seventh *m* came,
8: 2 On the first day of the seventh *m,*
8:14 booths during the feast of the seventh *m;*
9: 1 On the twenty-fourth day of this *m,*
Jdt 2: 1 on the twenty-second day of the first *m,*
3:10 and stayed there a whole *m* to refurbish
Est 2:16 Ahasuerus in his palace in the tenth *m,*
3: 7 In the first *m,* Nisan, in the twelfth year
3: 7 day and the *m* for the destruction
3: 7 on the thirteenth day of the twelfth *m,*
3:12 thirteenth day of the first *m* they wrote,
3:13 day, the thirteenth day of the twelfth *m,*
B: 6 on the fourteenth day of the twelfth *m,*
8: 9 on the twenty-third day of the third *m,*
8:12 day, the thirteenth of the twelfth *m,*
E:19 ruin, the thirteenth day of the twelfth *m,*
9: 1 out, the thirteenth day of the twelfth *m,*
9:15 mustered again on the fourteenth of the *m*
9:17 on the thirteenth day of the *m* of Adar.
9:17 On the fourteenth of the *m* they rested,
9:18 on the thirteenth and fourteenth of the *m.*
9:19 celebrate the fourteenth of the *m* of Adar
9:21 fourteenth and the fifteenth of the *m* of Adar
9:22 *m* which was turned for them from sorrow
F:10 fourteenth and fifteenth of the *m* Adar
1Mc 1:54 On the fifteenth day of the *m* Chislev,
1:58 against those who were caught, each *m,*
1:59 On the twenty-fifth day of each *m* they
4:52 the ninth month, that is, the *m* of Chislev,
4:59 from the twenty-fifth day of the *m* Chislev.
7:43 battle on the thirteenth day of the *m* Adar.
9: 3 *m* of the year one hundred and fifty-two,
9:54 hundred and fifty-three, in the second *m,*
10:21 sacred vestments in the seventh *m* of the year
13:51 On the twenty-third day of the second *m,*
16:14 the eleventh month (that is, the *m* Shebat).
2Mc 1: 9 the feast of Booths in the *m* of Chislev.
1:18 on the twenty-fifth day of the *m* Chislev,
10: 5 is, the twenty-fifth of the same *m* Chislev,
15:36 it on the thirteenth day of the twelfth *m,*
Sir 43: 8 As its name says, each *m* it renews itself;
Jer 1: 3 fifth *m* of the eleventh year of Zedekiah,
2:24 in her *m* they will meet her.
28: 1 Judah, in the fifth *m* of the fourth year,
28:17 That same year, in the seventh *m,*
36: 9 In the ninth *m,* in the fifth year
36:22 winter house, since it was the ninth *m,*
39: 1 the tenth *m* of the ninth year of Zedekiah,
39: 2 On the ninth day of the fourth *m,*
41: 1 In the seventh *m* Ishmael,
52: 4 the tenth *m* of the ninth year of his reign,
52: 4 of his reign, on the tenth day of the *m,*
52: 6 On the ninth day of the fourth *m,*
52:12 On the tenth day of the fifth *m* (this was
52:31 on the twenty-fifth day of the twelfth *m,*
Bar 1: 2 fifth year [on the seventh day of the *m,*
Ez 1: 1 year, on the fifth day of the fourth *m,*
1: 2 On the fifth day of the *m,*
8: 1 On the fifth day of the sixth *m,*
20: 1 year, on the tenth day of the fifth *m,*
24: 1 On the tenth day of the tenth *m,*
26: 1 *m* in the eleventh year,
29: 1 day of the tenth *m* in the tenth year,
29:17 of the first *m* in the twenty-seventh year,
30:20 day of the first *m* in the eleventh year,
31: 1 day of the third *m* in the eleventh year,
32: 1 day of the twelfth *m* in the twelfth year,
32:17 day of the first *m* in the twelfth year,
33:21 On the fifth day of the tenth *m,*
40: 1 On the tenth day of the *m* beginning the
45:18 On the first day of the first *m* you shall
45:20 this on the first day of the seventh *m*
45:21 On the fourteenth day of the first *m* you
45:25 On the fifteenth day of the seventh *m,*
47:12 Every *m* they shall bear fresh fruit,
Dn 10: 4 *m* I was on the bank of the great river,
Hg 1: 1 sixth *m* in the second year of King Darius,
1:15 on the twenty-fourth day of the sixth *m.*
2: 1 on the twenty-first day of the seventh *m,*
2:10 On the twenty-fourth day of the ninth *m,*
2:18 from the twenty-fourth day of the ninth *m.*
2:20 Haggai on the twenty-fourth day of the *m:*
Zec 1: 1 the second year of Darius, in the eighth *m,*
1: 7 day of Shebat, the eleventh *m,*
7: 1 on the fourth day of Chislev, the ninth *m,*
7: 3 *m* as I have been doing these many years?"
7: 5 and in the seventh *m* these seventy years,
11: 8 *m* I did away with the three shepherds.
Lk 1:26 In the sixth *m,* the angel Gabriel was sent
1:36 to be sterile is now in her sixth *m,*
Rv 9:15 was precisely the hour, the day, the *m,*
22: 2 fruit twelve times a year, once each *m;*

MONTHLY (3)

2Sm 11: 4 she was just purified after her *m* period.
2Mc 6: 7 at the *m* celebration of the king's
Col 2:16 drink or what you do on yearly or *m* feasts,

MONTHS (56)

Gn 38:24 About three *m* later, Judah
Ex 2: 2 a goodly child, she hid him for three *m.*
Dt 33:14 year, and the choicest sheaves of the *m;*
Jgs 11:37 Spare me for two *m,*
11:38 he replied, and sent her away for two *m.*
11:39 of the two *m* she returned to her father,
19: 2 of Judah, where she stayed for some four *m.*
20:47 Rimmon, where they remained for four *m.*
1Sm 6: 1 in the land of the Philistines seven *m*
27: 7 four *m* in the country of the Philistines.
2Sm 2:11 six *m* in Hebron as king of the Judahites.
5: 5 seven years and six *m* in Hebron over Judah,
6:11 of Obededom the Gittite for three *m,*
24: 8 again after nine *m* and twenty days.
24:13 your enemy three *m* while he pursues you,
1Kgs 5:28 month in the Lebanon and two *m* at home.
11:16 Joab and all Israel remained there six *m*
2Kgs 15: 8 was king of Israel in Samaria for six *m.*
23:31 reign, and he reigned three *m* in Jerusalem.
24: 8 reign, and he reigned three *m* in Jerusalem.
1Chr 3: 4 where he reigned seven years and six *m.*
13:14 of Obed-edom with his family for three *m,*
21:12 or three *m* of fleeing your enemies,
2Chr 36: 2 king, and he reigned three *m* in Jerusalem.
36: 9 three *m* [and ten days] in Jerusalem.
Jdt 8: 4 remained three years and four *m* at home,
16:20 For three *m* the people continued their
Est 2:12 *m*' preparation decreed for the women.
2:12 six *m* were spent with oil of myrrh,
2:12 other six *m* with perfumes and cosmetics.

2Mc 7:27 me, who carried you in my womb for nine *m*,
Jb 3: 6 year, nor enter into the count of the *m!*
7: 3 So I have been assigned *m* of misery,
14: 5 You know the number of his *m;*
21:21 him, when the number of his *m* is finished?
29: 2 Oh, that I were as in the *m* past!
39: 2 hinds, Number the *m* that they must fulfill,
Ez 39:12 of Israel shall need seven *m* to bury them.
39:14 For seven *m* they shall keep searching.
Dn 4:26 Twelve *m* later, as he was walking
Am 4: 7 when the harvest was still three *m* away;
Zec 8:19 and the tenth *m* shall become occasions of
Lk 1:24 She went into seclusion for five *m*,
1:56 about three *m* and then returned home.
Jn 4:35 'Four *m* more and it will be harvest!'?
Acts 7:20 *m* he was reared in his father's house,
19: 8 synagogue, and over a period of three *m*,
20: 3 in Greece, where he stayed for three *m*.
28:11 Three *m* later we set sail in a ship which
Gal 4:10 the ceremonial observance of days and *m*,
Heb 11:23 hid him for three *m* after his birth,
Jas 5:17 on the land for three years and six *m*.
Rv 9: 5 them but only to torture them for five *m;*
9:10 was enough venom to harm men for five *m*.
11: 2 will crush the holy city for forty-two *m*.
13: 5 it received was to last only forty-two *m*.

MONUMENT (4)

Gn 35:20 same *m* marks Rachel's grave to this day.
1Mc 13:27 his father and his brothers a *m* of stones,
2Mc 15: 6 public *m* of victory over Judas and his men.
Is 56: 5 a *m* and a name Better than sons and

MONUMENTS (2)

Jb 21:29 wayfarers and do you not recognize their *m?*
Mt 23:29 prophets and decorate the *m* of the saints.

MOOD (2)

1Sm 30:16 and in a festive *m* because of all the rich
Mk 10:32 Their *m* was one of wonderment,

MOOING (1)

1Sm 6:12 continued along this road, *m* as they went,

MOON (67)

Gn 37: 9 *m* and eleven stars were bowing down to me."
Nm 28:14 *m* holocaust for every new moon of the year.
29: 6 new *m* holocaust with its cereal offering,
Dt 4:19 the *m* or any star among the heavenly hosts,
17: 3 sun or the *m* or any of the host of the sky,
Jos 10:12 Stand still, O sun, at Gibeon, O *m*,
10:13 And the sun stood still, and the *m* stayed,
1Sm 20: 5 "Tomorrow is the new *m*, when I should
20:18 "Tomorrow is the new *m;*
20:24 On the day of the new *m*, when the king sat
2Kgs 4:23 "It is neither the new *m* nor the sabbath."
23: 5 who burned incense to Baal, to the sun, *m*,
Jdt 8: 6 and sabbaths, new *m* eves and new moons,
1Mc 10:34 all feast days, sabbaths, new *m* festivals,
Jb 25: 5 even the *m* is not bright and the stars are
26: 9 full *m* by spreading his clouds before it.
31:26 or the *m* in the splendor of its progress,
Ps(s) 8: 4 the *m* and the stars which you set in place
72: 5 and like the *m* through all generations.
72: 7 and profound peace, till the *m* be no more.
74:16 you fashioned the *m* and the sun.
81: 4 trumpet at the new moon, at the full *m*,
89:38 Like the *m*, which remains forever
104:19 You made the *m* to mark the seasons;
121: 6 not harm you by day, nor the *m* by night.
136: 9 The *m* and the stars to rule over the night,
148: 3 Praise him, sun and *m;*
Prv 7:20 not till the full *m* will he return home."
Eccl 12: 2 and the light, and the *m*,
Sg 6:10 like the dawn, as beautiful as the *m*,
Sir 27:11 devout, but the godless man, like the *m*,
39:12 theme to shine like the *m* in its fullness!
43: 6 *m*, too, that marks the changing times,
50: 6 like the full *m* at the holyday season;
Is 1:13 New *m* and sabbath, calling of assemblies
13:10 and the light of the *m* does not shine.
24:23 the *m* will blush and the sun grow pale,
30:26 The light of the *m* will be like that of
47:13 at each new *m* what would happen to you.
60:19 of the *m* shine upon you at night;
60:20 shall your sun go down, or your *m* withdraw,
66:23 From one new *m* to another,
Jer 8: 2 sun and the *m* and the whole army of heaven,
31:35 the day, *m* and stars to light the night;
Bar 6:59 The sun and *m* and stars are bright,
6:66 like the sun, nor shining like the *m*.
Ez 32: 7 clouds, and the *m* shall not give its light.
46: 1 on the day of the new *m* it shall be open.
46: 6 On the day of the new *m* he shall provide
Dn 3:62 Sun and *m*, bless the Lord;
Hos 5: 7 *m* devour them together with their fields.
Jl 2:10 The sun and the *m* are darkened,
3: 4 be turned to darkness, and the *m* to blood.
4:15 Sun and *m* are darkened,
Am 8: 5 "When will the new *m* be over,"
Hb 3:11 to rise, the *m* remains in its shelter,
Mt 24:29 be darkened, the *m* will not shed her light,
Mk 13:24 be darkened, the *m* will not shed its light,
Lk 21:25 "There will be signs in the sun, the *m*,
Acts 2:20 *m* to blood before the coming
1Cor 15:41 has a splendor of its own, so has the *m*,
Rv 6:12 tentcloth and the *m* grew red as blood.
8:12 a third of the sun, a third of the *m*,
12: 1 with the sun, with the *m* under her feet,
21:23 The city had no need of sun or *m*,

MOONS (11)

1Chr 23:31 holocausts to the LORD on sabbaths, new *m*,
2Chr 2: 3 and evening, and for the sabbaths, new *m*,
8:13 particular on the sabbaths, at the new *m*,
31: 3 and those on sabbaths, new *m* and festivals,
Ezr 3: 5 *m* and all the festivals sacred to the LORD,
Neh 10:34 daily holocaust, for the sabbaths, new *m*,
Jdt 8: 6 and sabbaths, new moon eves and new *m*,
Is 1:14 Your new *m* and festivals I detest;
Ez 45:17 and libations on the feasts, new *m*,
46: 3 of this gate on the sabbaths and new *m*.
Hos 2:13 end to all her joy, her feasts, her new *m*,

MOORED (1)

Lk 5: 2 he saw two boats *m* by the side of the lake;

MORAL (2)

Mt 25:13 The *m* is: keep your eyes open
Lk 19:26 He responded with, 'The *m* is:

MORALS (1)

1Cor 15:33 "Bad company corrupts good *m*."

MORDECAI (62)

Ezr 2: 2 Jeshua, Nehemiah, Seraiah, Reelaiah, *M*,
Neh 7: 7 Nehemiah, Azariah, Raamiah, Nahamani, *M*,
Est A: 1 Ahasuerus, on the first day of Nisan, *M*,
A:11 dream and what God intended to do, *M* awoke.
A:12 *M* lodged at the court with Bagathan and
A:15 *M*,
A:16 also appointed *M* to serve at the court,
A:17 sought to harm *M* and his people because of
2: 5 stronghold of Susa a certain Jew named *M*,
2: 7 *M* had taken her as his own daughter.
2:10 for *M* had commanded her not to do so.
2:11 Day by day *M* would walk about in front of
2:15 adopted daughter of his nephew *M*,
2:19 *M* was passing his time at the king's gate,
2:20 nationality, because *M* had told her not to;
2:21 the time that *M* spent at the king's gate,
2:22 When the plot became known to *M*,
2:22 who in turn informed the king for *M*.
3: 2 *M*, however, would not kneel and bow down.
3: 3 who were at the royal gate said to *M*,
3: 5 that *M* would not kneel and bow down to him,
3: 6 it was not enough to lay hands on *M* alone.
4: 1 When *M* learned all that was happening,
4: 4 anguish, she sent garments for *M* to put on,
4: 5 action of *M* meant and the reason for it.
4: 6 So Hathach went out to *M* in the public
4: 7 gate, and *M* told him all that had happened,
B: 8 *M* had him say, "when you were brought
4: 9 to Esther and told her what *M* had said.
4:10 to Hathach and gave him this message for *M:*
4:12 When Esther's words were reported to *M*,
4:15 Esther sent back to *M* the response:
C: 1 *M* went away and did exactly as Esther had
5: 9 saw that *M* at the royal gate did not rise,
5:13 to see the Jew *M* sitting at the royal gate."
5:14 ask the king to have *M* hanged on it.
6: 2 in which *M* reported Bagathan and Teresh,
6: 3 was done to reward and honor *M* for this?"
6: 4 suggest to the king that *M* should be hanged
6:10 have proposed, and do this for the Jew *M*,
6:11 Haman took the robe and horse, clothed *M*,
6:12 *M* then returned to the royal gate,
6:13 and his wife Zeresh said to him, "If *M*,
7: 9 Haman prepared it for *M*,
7:10 the gibbet which he had made ready for *M*,
8: 1 and *M* was admitted to the king's presence,
8: 2 keeping of *M;* and Esther put *M* in charge
8: 7 then said to Queen Esther and to the Jew *M:*
8: 9 Exactly as *M* dictated,
E:13 deceit, he demanded the destruction of *M*,
8:15 *M* left the king's presence clothed in a
9: 3 supported the Jews from fear of *M;*
9: 4 for *M* was powerful in the royal palace,
9:20 *M* recorded these events and sent letters
9:23 instituted at the written direction of *M*.
9:29 daughter of Abihail and of *M* the Jew,
9:30 when *M* sent documents concerning peace and
9:31 these days of Purim which *M* the Jew and
10: 2 a detailed account of the greatness of *M*,
10: 3 Jew *M* was next in rank to King Ahasuerus,
F: 1 Then *M* said: "This is the work of God.

MORDECAI'S (6)

Est 2:20 Esther continued to follow *M* instructions,
3: 4 see whether *M* explanation was acceptable,
3: 6 Since they had told Haman of *M* nationality,
3: 6 sought to destroy all the Jews, *M* people,
3: 7 destruction of *M* people on a single day,
2Mc 15:36 called Adar in Aramaic, the eve of *M* Day.

MORE (651)

Gn 4:25 granted me *m* offspring in place of Abel,"
8:10 *m* and again sent the dove out from the ark.
8:12 days and then released the dove once *m;*
18:31 Lord, what if there are no *m* than twenty?"
24:20 and ran back to the well to draw *m* water,
29:30 Rachel also, and he loved her *m* than Leah.
29:35 Once *m* she conceived and bore a son,
33:14 while I proceed *m* slowly at the pace of
34:19 Moreover he was *m* highly respected than
37: 8 the *m* because of his talk about his dreams.
38:26 said, "She is *m* in the right than I am,
39: 9 no *m* authority in this house than I do,
43: 1 Now the famine in the land grew *m* severe.
43: 2 "Go back and procure us a little *m* food."
45: 6 five *m* years tillage will yield no harvest.
Ex 1: 9 people are growing, *m* so than we ourselves!
1:12 *m* they were oppressed, the *m* they multiplied
3: 4 him coming over to look at it *m* closely,
8:28 But once *m* Pharaoh became obdurate and
9:29 will cease, and there will be no *m* hail.
10:17 But now, do forgive me my sin once *m*,
11: 1 "One *m* plague will I bring upon Pharaoh
17: 4 A little *m* and they will stone me!"
18:22 *M* important cases they should refer to you,
18:26 *m* difficult cases they referred to Moses,
28:27 Then make two *m* rings of gold and fasten
30:14 Everyone of twenty years or *m* who enters
30:15 The rich need not give *m*,
36: 5 "The people are bringing much *m* than is
36: 6 make any *m* contributions for the sanctuary."
36: 7 enough at hand, in fact, *m* than enough,
38:26 or *m* who entered the registered group;
39:20 Two *m* gold rings were made and fastened to
Lv 12: 4 days *m* in becoming purified of her blood;
13: 6 and once *m* examine him on the seventh day.
13: 7 he shall once *m* show himself to the priest.
14:22 or pigeons, which he can *m* easily afford,
14:43 "If the infection breaks out once *m* after
25:16 many, the price shall be so much the *m;*
25:51 The *m* such years there are, the *m* of the sale
25:52 jubilee year, the *m* he has to his credit;
27: 2 of offering one or *m* persons to the LORD,
27: 7 for persons of sixty or *m*,
27:13 shall pay one fifth *m* than this valuation.
27:15 fifth *m* than the price thus established,
27:19 fifth *m* than the price thus established,
27:27 by paying one fifth *m* than its fixed value.
27:31 he shall pay one fifth *m* than their value.
Nm 1: 3 or *m* who are fit for military service.
1:18 Every man of twenty years or *m* then
1:20 when all the males of twenty years or *m*
1:22 twenty years or *m* who were fit for military
1:24 when all the males of twenty years or *m*
1:26 when all the males of twenty years or *m*
1:28 when all the males of twenty years or *m*
1:30 when all the males of twenty years or *m*
1:32 when all the males of twenty years or *m*
1:34 when all the males of twenty years or *m*
1:36 when all the males of twenty years or *m*
1:38 when all the males of twenty years or *m*
1:40 when all the males of twenty years or *m*
1:42 when all the males of twenty years or *m*
1:45 or *m* who were fit for military service,
3:15 registering every male of a month or *m*."
3:22 males of a month or *m* were registered,
3:28 males of a month or *m* were registered,
3:34 males of a month or *m* were registered,
3:39 month old or *m* whom Moses had registered
3:40 males of the Israelites a month old or *m*,
3:43 males of a month or *m* were registered,
14:29 Of all your men of twenty years or *m*,
22:15 who were *m* numerous and more distinguished
26: 2 twenty years or *m* who are fit for military
26: 4 registered those of twenty years or *m*,
26:62 of male Levites one month or *m* of age,
32:11 none of these men of twenty years or *m*
32:14 to add still *m* to the LORD's blazing wrath
35: 8 take *m* from a larger group and fewer from
Dt 3:26 'Speak to me no *m* of this.
5:22 "These words, and nothing *m*,
5:25 hear the voice of the LORD, our God, any *m*,
6: 3 them, that you may grow and prosper the *m*,
7: 1 nations *m* numerous and powerful than you
15: 4 Nay, *m!* since the LORD, your God,
18:16 our God, nor see this great fire any *m*,
25: 3 Forty stripes may be given him, but no *m;*
25: 3 he were beaten with *m* stripes than these,
28:11 The LORD will increase in *m* than goodly
30: 5 and he will make you *m* prosperous and
30: 9 will increase in *m* than goodly measure the
31:27 How much *m*, then after I am dead!
33:24 *M* blessed than the other sons be Asher!
Jos 10:11 *M* died from these hailstones than the
Jgs 2:21 any *m* of the nations which Joshua left
6:39 not be angry with me if I speak once *m*.
6:39 me make just one *m* test with the fleece.

MORE (cont.)

10:13 Therefore I will save you no *m.*
13:21 LORD was seen no *m* by Manoah and his wife.
15: 2 Her younger sister is *m* beautiful than she;
16:30 Those he killed at his death were *m* than
Ru 1:17 the LORD do so and so to me, and *m* besides,
3:10 You have been even *m* loyal now than before
4:15 She is worth *m* to you than seven sons!"
1Sm 1: 8 Am I not *m* to you than ten sons?"
2:21 birth to three *m* sons and two daughters,
14: 6 because it is no *m* difficult for the LORD
14:30 What is *m,* if the people had eaten freely
18:29 all the *m* [and was his enemy ever after].
18:30 David was *m* successful against them than
20:19 following day you will be missed all the *m.*
21: 6 All the *m* so today,
23: 3 How much *m* so if we go to Keilah against
23:22 Go now and make sure once *m!*
30: 4 him wept aloud until they could weep no *m.*
2Sm 1:26 *M* precious have I held love for you than
2:22 Once *m* Abner said to Asahel:
2:28 Israel no farther and fighting no *m.*
4:11 How much *m* now, when wicked men
5:10 David grew steadily *m* powerful,
5:13 David took *m* concubines and wives in
5:13 and *m* sons and daughters were born to him
6:22 the LORD, but I will demean myself even *m.*
7:20 What *m* can David say to you?
12: 8 enough, I could count up for you still *m.*
16:11 how much *m* might this Benjaminite do so!
18: 8 *m* combatants that day than did the sword.
19: 7 us dead, you would think that *m* suitable.
19:44 spoke even *m* fiercely than the Israelites.
20: 6 may now do us *m* harm than Absalom did.
1Kgs 1:37 his throne even *m* than that of my lord,
1:47 'May God make Solomon *m* famous than you
1:47 you and exalt his throne *m* than your own!'
2:23 and *m* besides if Adonijah has not proposed
2:32 two men better and *m* just than himself,
10:12 No *m* such wood was brought or seen to the
14:22 him even *m* than their fathers had done.
16:30 of the LORD *m* than any of his predecessors.
16:33 He did *m* to anger the LORD,
17:17 grew *m* severe until he stopped breathing.
18:25 prepare it first, for there are *m* of you.
2Kgs 4:35 and then once *m* lay down upon the boy,
5:13 All the *m* now, since he said to you,
6:23 No *m* Aramean raiders came into the land of
10:18 some extent, but Jehu will serve him yet *m.*
25: 3 the city, and the people had no *m* bread,
1Chr 7: 4 since they had *m* wives and sons than their
11: 9 David became *m* and more powerful,
11:25 He was *m* famous than any of the Thirty,
14: 3 became the father of *m* sons and daughters.
17:18 What *m* can David say to you?
24: 4 to be *m* numerous than those of Ithamar,
24:31 the *m* important family did so in the same
2Chr 1: 1 with him, constantly making him *m* renowned.
9:12 for, *m* than she had brought to the king.
11:21 *m* than all his other wives and sixty
25: 9 "The LORD can give you much *m* than that."
28:22 Ahaz became even *m* unfaithful to the LORD.
29:34 were *m* willing than the priests to
32: 7 him, for there is *m* with us than with him.
32:16 His officials said still *m* against the
Neh 2:15 till I once *m* reached the Valley Gate,
7: 2 who was a *m* trustworthy and God-fearing
8:13 examined the words of the law *m* closely.
13:12 once *m* brought in the tithes of grain,
13:18 Israel by once *m* profaning the sabbath?"
Tb 2:10 but the *m* they anointed my eyes with
cataracts became, until I could see no *m.*
5:10 "What joy is left for me any *m?*
5:19 I hope *m* money is not your chief concern!
7:10 for no man is *m* entitled to marry my
Jdt 5:18 they were ground down steadily, *m* and more,
7:30 us wait five days *m* for the Lord our God,
12: 3 we get *m* of the same to provide for you?
12:20 *m* than he had ever drunk on one single day
13:11 Once *m* he has made manifest his strength
Est 1:19 her royal dignity to one *m* worthy than she.
2:17 king loved Esther *m* than all other women,
C:30 O God, *m* powerful than all,
6: 6 the king *m* probably wish to reward than me?"
E: 2 "Many have become the *m* ambitious the *m*
E: 7 but *m* fully when one considers the wicked
1Mc 3:30 feared that, as had happened *m* than once,
3:30 a *m* liberal hand than the preceding kings.
5:44 and Judas met with no *m* resistance.
7:23 *m* than even the Gentiles had done,
15:31 *m* for the tribute money of the cities.
2Mc 4: 9 he agreed to pay a hundred and fifty *m,*
5:22 *m* cruel than the man who appointed him;
6:15 may not have to punish us *m* severly later,
8: 8 advances were becoming *m* frequent,
8:24 killed *m* than nine thousand of the enemy,
8:30 killed *m* than twenty thousand of them,
9: 7 he was all the *m* filled with arrogance.
10:19 to places where he was *m* urgently needed.
10:23 he destroyed *m* than twenty thousand men in
12:19 destroyed the force of *m* than ten thousand
14:39 *m* than five hundred soldiers to arrest him.
15:38 a *m* pleasant drink that increases delight,

Jb 3:24 sighing comes *m* readily to me than food,
4:19 *m* with those that dwell in houses of clay,
4:19 who are crushed *m* easily than the moth!
7: 8 eye that now sees me shall no *m* behold me;
7: 9 to the nether world shall come up no *m.*
7:10 his place shall know him no *m.*
8:21 *m* will he fill your mouth with laughter,
8:22 and the tent of the wicked shall be no *m.*
14:12 Till the heavens are no *m,*
15:10 us *m* advanced in years than your father.
15:32 time, and his branches shall be green no *m.*
20: 9 The eye which saw him does so no *m;*
29:22 Once I spoke, they said no *m,*
32:15 They are dismayed, they make no *m* reply;
32:16 Now that they speak no *m,*
34:19 nor respects the rich *m* than the poor?
34:31 I will offend no *m.*
34:32 if I have done wrong, I will do so no *m,*"
35: 3 advantage have I *m* than if I had sinned?"
40: 5 though twice, I will do so no *m.*
42:12 latter days of Job *m* than his earlier ones.
Ps(s) 4: 8 heart, *m* than when grain and wine abound.
10:18 man, who is of earth, may terrify no *m.*
19:11 They are *m* precious than gold,
31:24 but *m* than requites those who act proudly
37:10 while, and the wicked man shall be no *m;*
37:36 he was no *m;* I sought him,
39:14 may find respite ere I depart and be no *m.*
40:13 are *m* numerous than the hairs of my head,
49:20 his forebears who shall never *m* see light.
59:14 consume, till they are no *m;*
69:32 This will please the LORD *m* than oxen or
71:14 always hope and praise you ever *m* and more.
71:20 of the earth you will once *m* raise me.
72: 7 and profound peace, till the moon be no *m.*
78:17 But they sinned yet *m* against him,
78:32 still *m* and believed not in his wonders.
80:19 Then we will no *m* withdraw from you;
83: 5 let the name of Israel be remembered no *m!*"
87: 2 of Zion, *m* than any dwelling of Jacob.
93: 4 *M* powerful than the roar of many waters,
93: 4 *m* powerful than the breakers of the sea
103:16 he is gone, and his place knows him no *m.*
104:35 from the earth, and may the wicked be no *m.*
115:14 May the LORD bless you *m* and more,
119:72 The law of your mouth is to me *m* precious
119:99 I have *m* understanding than all my
119:100 I have *m* descernment than the elders,
119:127 For I love your command *m* than gold,
120: 3 will he inflict on you, with *m* besides,
123: 3 us, for we are *m* than sated with contempt;
123: 4 Our souls are *m* than sated with the
130: 6 LORD *m* than sentinels wait for the dawn.
130: 6 *M* than sentinels wait for the dawn,
Prv 3:15 She is *m* precious than corals,
10:25 tempest passes, the wicked man is no *m;*
11:31 how much *m* the wicked and the sinner!
12: 7 The wicked are overthrown and are no *m,*
15:11 how much *m* the hearts of men!
16:16 understanding is *m* desirable than silver.
17: 7 how much *m,* lying words in a noble!
17:10 A single reprimand does *m* for a man of
18:24 a true friend is *m* loyal than a brother.
19: 7 how much *m* do his friends shun him!
21: 3 is *m* acceptable to the LORD than sacrifice.
21:27 the *m* so when they offer it with a bad
22: 1 good name is *m* desirable than great riches,
24: 5 A wise man is *m* powerful than a strong man,
25:17 house, lest he have *m* than enough of you,
26:12 There is *m* hope for a fool than for him.
28:16 the prince, the *m* his deeds oppress.
28:23 He who rebukes a man gets *m* thanks in the
29:20 *M* can be hoped for from a fool!
31: 7 misery, and think no *m* of their burdens.
Eccl 2: 7 *m* than all who had been before me in
2: 9 *m* than all others before me in Jerusalem;
4: 2 I declared *m* fortunate in death than are
6: 3 the child born dead is *m* fortunate than he.
7:26 *M* bitter than death I find the woman who
9:12 Man no *m* knows his own time than fish
10: 1 *M* weighty than wisdom or wealth is a
12:12 As to *m* than these, my son, beware.
Sg 1: 2 *M* delightful is your love than wine!
4:10 much *m* delightful is your love than wine,
Wis 3:14 *m* gratifying heritage in the Lord's temple.
8: 5 in life, what is *m* rich than Wisdom,
8: 7 in life is *m* useful for men than these.
13: 3 how far *m* excellent is the Lord than these;
13: 4 how much *m* powerful is he who made them.
13: 9 how did they not *m* quickly find its Lord?
14: 1 *m* unsound than the boat that bears him.
15:10 *m* worthless than earth is his hope, and *m*
15:13 man *m* than any knows that he is sinning,
16:17 quenches anything, the fire grew *m* active;
17:13 *m* one's expectation is of itself uncertain,
17:13 the *m* one makes of not knowing the cause
17:21 themselves *m* burdensome than the darkness.
19:13 their guests with the *m* grievous hatred.
Sir 3:17 you will be loved *m* than a giver of gifts.
3:18 Humble yourself the *m,*
4:10 he will be *m* tender to you than a mother.
7:17 More and *m,* humble your pride;
7:19 a gracious wife is *m* precious than corals.

8:12 Lend not to one *m* powerful than yourself;
10:30 in poverty, how much *m* so in wealth!
10:30 in wealth, in poverty how much the *m!*
11:11 and drive, and fall short all the *m.*
13: 9 then he will urge you all the *m.*
14: 6 None is *m* stingy than he who is stingy
16: 5 seen, even *m* than these has my ear heard.
17:23 No *m* can the dead give praise than those
18:10 and so he forgives them all the *m.*
18:16 Sometimes the word means *m* than the gift;
21: 1 My son, if you have sinned, do so no *m,*
23:27 *m* salutary than to obey his commandments.
24:20 he who drinks of me will thirst for *m;*
27:25 struck in treachery injures *m* than one.
28:10 *m* wood, the greater the fire, the *m* underlying
29:11 for that will profit you *m* than the gold.
29:27 Away, stranger, for one *m* worthy;
30:15 *M* precious than gold is health and
31: 2 *m* than a serious illness it disturbs
31:30 *M* and more wine is a snare for the fool;
32: 7 when they have asked you *m* than once;
33: 7 Why is one day *m* important than another,
34:11 travels, learned *m* than ever I could say.
36:18 yet some foods are *m* agreeable than others;
36:21 one girl will be *m* suitable than another:
37:13 for what have you that you can depend on *m?*
39:12 Once *m* I will set forth my theme to shine
40: 8 with beast, but for sinners seven times *m.*
41: 2 and always rebuffed, with no *m* sight,
43:28 *M* than this we need not add;
43:29 Let us praise him the *m,*
47:24 Their sinfulness grew *m* and more,
Is 1:13 Trample my courts no *m!*
1:13 Bring no *m* worthless offerings;
1:15 Though you pray the *m,*
5: 4 What *m* was there to do for my vineyard
6:12 away, and the land is abandoned *m* and more.
10:10 had *m* images than Jerusalem and Samaria,
10:20 will no *m* lean upon him who struck them;
10:25 For only a brief moment *m,*
13:12 I will make mortals *m* rare than pure gold,
15: 9 blood, but I will bring still *m* upon Dimon:
19: 7 shall dry up and blow away, and be no *m.*
23:10 the harbor is no *m.*
23:12 You shall exult no *m,*
25: 2 The castle of the insolent is a city no *m,*
28:22 arrogant no *m* lest your bonds be tightened,
29:20 be no *m* and the arrogant will have gone;
30:11 Let us hear no *m* of the Holy One of Israel."
30:19 who dwell in Jerusalem, no *m* will you weep;
32: 5 No *m* will the fool be called noble,
32:10 In a little *m* than a year you
33:19 people of alien tongue you will look no *m,*
34:12 Her nobles shall be no *m,*
38:11 the LORD no *m* in the land of the living.
40:15 the coastlands weigh no *m* than powder.
43:25 your sins I remember no *m.*
44: 9 and they are *m* deaf than men are.
53: 8 would have thought any *m* of his destiny?
54: 1 For *m* numerous are the children of the
62: 4 No *m* shall men call you "Forsaken,"
62: 8 No *m* will I give your grain as food to
Jer 2:31 We will come to you no *m*"?
3:11 is inwardly *m* just than traitorous Judah.
10:20 My sons have left me, they are no *m:*
11:19 so that his name will be spoken no *m.*"
15: 8 Their widows were *m* numerous before me
17: 9 *M* tortuous than all else is the human heart,
20: 9 mention him, I will speak in his name no *m.*
23:14 prophets I saw deeds still *m* shocking:
23:36 burden of the LORD you shall mention no *m.*
31:15 be consoled because her children are no *m.*
31:34 evildoing and remember their sin no *m.*
34:16 you forced them once *m* into slavery.
38: 9 spot, for there is no *m* food in the city."
38:27 They said no *m* to him,
42:14 go to Egypt, where we will see no *m* of war,
46:23 *M* numerous than locusts,
48: 2 Moab's glory is no *m.*
48:32 *M* than for Jazer I weep over you,
48:33 the wine vats, the treader treads no *m,*
48:42 Moab shall be destroyed, no *m* a people,
49: 7 Is there no *m* wisdom in Teman,
49:10 and neighbors, so that he is no *m.*
50:20 seek Israel's guilt, but it shall be no *m,*
51:44 peoples shall stream to him no *m.*
52: 6 the city and the people had no *m* bread,
Lam 4: 2 Now worth no *m* than earthen jars made by
4: 7 *M* ruddy than coral, more precious than
4:16 has dispersed them, he regards them no *m;*
5: 7 Our fathers, who sinned, are no *m;*
Bar 4:28 God, turn now ten times the *m* to seek him;
6:18 light *m* lamps for them than for themselves,
Ez 5: 6 my ordinances *m* wickedly than the nations,
5: 6 and against my statutes *m* than the foreign
5: 7 Because you have been *m* rebellious than
16:47 *m* corrupt in all your ways than they.
16:51 have done *m* abominable things than they,
16:52 sinful deeds, *m* abominable than theirs,
17: 7 *m* freely than the bed where it was planted.
23:11 her lust was *m* depraved than her sister's,
23:19 But she played the harlot all the *m,*
26:13 sound of your lyres shall be heard no *m.*

26:21 you a devastation, and you shall be no *m;*
27:36 become a horror, and you shall be no *m.*
28:19 have become a horror, you shall be no *m.*
28:24 a brier that scratches them *m* than all
29:15 never *m* to set itself above the nations.
30:13 the land of Egypt, that they may be no *m.*
36:11 be *m* generous to you than in the beginning;
36:15 No *m* will I permit you to hear the
47: 4 and once *m* had me wade through the water,
47: 5 Once *m* he measured off a thousand,
Dn 2:43 united, any *m* than iron mixes with clay.
3:19 furnace to be heated seven times *m*
11:19 shall stumble and fall, to be found no *m.*
11:30 who forsake it he shall once *m* single out.
Hos 10: 1 *m* abundant his fruit, the *m* altars he built;
10: 1 *m* productive his land, the *m* sacred pillars
11: 2 The *m* I called them,
14: 4 We shall say no *m,*
14: 9 What *m* has he to do with idols?
Jl 2:19 No *m* will I make you a reproach among the
4:17 and strangers shall pass through her no *m.*
Am 3: 2 *m* than all the families of the earth;
3:15 ruined, and their many rooms shall be no *m,*
4: 4 Bethel, and sin, to Gilgal, and sin the *m;*
5: 2 She is fallen, to rise no *m,*
Jon 1:11 the sea was growing *m* and more turbulent.
1:13 not, for the sea grew ever *m* turbulent.
3: 4 days *m* and Nineveh shall be destroyed,"
4:11 in which there are *m* than a hundred and
Mi 7: 2 the earth, among men the upright are no *m!*
Na 1:12 I have humbled you, I will humble you no *m.*
2:14 cry of your lionesses shall be heard no *m.*
3:16 your couriers *m* numerous than the stars,
Hb 1:13 wicked man devours one *m* just than himself?
Zep 3: 7 Yet all the *m* eagerly have they done all
Zec 2: 4 so that no man raised his head any *m;*
11: 6 I spare the inhabitants of the earth any *m,*
13: 2 so that they shall be mentioned no *m;*
Mt 2:18 no comfort for her, since they are no *m.*"
3:11 who will follow me is *m* powerful than I.
6:25 Is not life *m* than food?
6:25 Is not the body *m* valuable than clothes?
6:26 Are not you *m* important than they?
6:30 will he not provide much *m* for you,
7:11 how much *m* will your heavenly Father give
7:18 *m* than a decayed tree can bear good fruit.
10:25 how much *m* the members of his household!
10:31 worth *m* than an entire flock of sparrows.
10:37 or daughter, *m* than me is not worthy of me.
11: 9 A prophet indeed, and something *m!*
12:12 *m* precious a human being is than a sheep.
12:45 this time seven spirits *m* evil than itself.
13:12 has, *m* will be given until he grows rich;
14:36 do no *m* than touch the tassel of his cloak.
20:10 appeared they supposed they would get *m;*
21:36 he dispatched even *m* slaves than before,
22: 1 to address them, once *m* using parables.
23:17 Which is *m* important, the gold or the
23:19 Which is *m* important, the offering
24:21 for those days will be *m* filled with
25:20 See, I have made five thousand *m.*'
25:22 thousand and I have made two thousand *m.*'
25:27 All the *m* reason to deposit my money with
25:29 who have will get *m* until they grow rich,
26:43 Once *m,* on his return, he found them
26:53 notice *m* than twelve legions of angels?
Mk 1: 7 *m* powerful than I is to come after me.
4:24 you give you shall receive, and *m* besides.
4:25 To those who have, *m* will be given;
7:12 to do nothing *m* for his father or mother.
7:36 but the *m* he ordered them not to,
7:36 them not to, the *m* they proclaimed it.
10: 1 Once *m* crowds gathered around him,
10:21 him, "There is one thing *m* you must do.
10:32 Taking the Twelve aside once *m,*
11:27 They returned once *m* to Jerusalem.
12: 1 began to address them once *m* in parables:
12:33 *m* than any burnt offering or sacrifice."
12:34 had the courage to ask him any *m* questions.
12:43 widow contributed *m* than all the others
13:19 Those times will be *m* distressful than any
14:67 she looked at him *m* closely and said,
14:70 later the bystanders said to Peter once *m,*
16:13 no *m* faith in them than in Mary Magdalene.
16:20 might return to the truth and sin no *m,*
Lk 5:15 His reputation spread *m* and more,
6:43 *m* than a decayed tree produces good fruit.
7:26 He is that, I assure you, and something *m.*
7:42 Which of them was *m* grateful to him?"
8:18 to the man who has, *m* will be given;
11:13 how much *m* will the heavenly Father give
12: 4 of those who kill the body and can do no *m.*
12: 7 You are worth *m* than a flock of sparrows.
12:23 *m* important than food and the body
12:24 much *m* important you are than the birds!
12:28 how much *m* will he provide for you,
12:48 *M* will be asked of a man to whom more has
13: 4 Do you think they were *m* guilty than
15: 7 there will likewise be *m* joy in heaven
15:17 father's place have *m* than enough to eat,
16: 8 Because the worldly take *m* initiative than
17:10 We have done no *m* than our duty.'"
18:39 to be quiet, but he cried out all the *m,*
19:26 whoever has will be given *m,*
21: 3 poor widow has put in *m* than all the rest.
22:59 after that another spoke *m* insistently:
Jn 2: 3 mother told him, "They have no *m* wine."
4: 1 baptizing *m* disciples than John (in fact,
4:35 'Four months *m* and it will be harvest!'?
4:41 his own spoken word many *m* came to faith.
4:46 He went to Cana in Galilee once *m,*
5:18 The reason why the Jews were even *m*
7:31 expected to perform *m* signs than this man?"
10:19 the Jews were sharply divided once *m.*
11: 6 he stayed on where he was for two days *m.*
13:12 cloak back on and reclined at table once *m.*
14:19 while now and the world will see me no *m;*
15: 4 No *m* than a branch can bear fruit of
16:10 go to the Father and you can see me no *m;*
16:12 I have much *m* to tell you,
17:11 I am in the world no *m,*
17:14 world [any *m* than I belong to the world].
17:16 world, any *m* than I belong to the world.
19: 8 kind of talk, he was *m* afraid than ever.
20:26 the disciples were once *m* in the room,
21: 8 no *m* than a hundred yards.
21:15 son of John, do you love me *m* than these?"
Acts 4:22 cured was *m* than forty years of age.
5:14 Nevertheless *m* and more believers,
7:17 people in Egypt grew *m* and more numerous,
7:32 Moses began to tremble and dared look no *m.*
8:39 Philip away and the eunuch saw him no *m.*
9:22 Saul for his part grew steadily *m* powerful,
17:21 love nothing *m* than to tell about or
20:35 is *m* happiness in giving than receiving.'"
23:13 (There were *m* than forty of them who took
23:15 would like to examine his case *m* carefully.
23:20 that they want to question him *m* carefully.
23:21 *M* than forty of them are lying in wait;
24:11 Not *m* than twelve days have passed since I
25:24 him, clamoring that he should live no *m.*
26:13 I saw a light *m* brilliant than the sun
26:28 At this, Agrippa said, "A little *m,*
26:29 replied, "Whether little *m* or much more,
Rom 5: 9 it is all the *m* certain that we shall be
5:10 it is all the *m* certain that we who have
5:15 much *m* did the grace of God and the
5:17 much *m* shall those who receive the
6: 9 death has no *m* power over him.
6:13 no *m* shall you offer the members of your
8:37 Yet in all this we are *m* than conquerors
11:12 world, how much *m* their full number!
11:24 so much the *m* will they who belong to it
12: 3 to think *m* highly of himself than he ought.
15:12 Once *m,* Isaiah says, "The root of Jesse
15:23 I have no *m* work to do in these regions,
1Cor 1:25 men, and his weakness *m* powerful than men.
12:21 any *m* than the head can say to the feet,
12:24 which the *m* presentable already have.
14:18 God, I speak in tongues *m* than any of you,
14:29 Let no *m* than two or three prophets speak,
15:50 no *m* can corruption inherit incorruption.
16:12 will go when circumstances are *m* favorable.
2Cor 2: 5 only me, but in some measure, to say no *m,*
7:13 we have rejoiced even *m* at the joy of
8:22 He is now *m* eager than ever for this work
11:23 I am really talking like a fool—I am *m:*
11:23 with my many *m* labors and imprisonments,
12: 7 lest anyone think *m* of me than what he
Gal 4: 9 seem willing to enslave yourselves once *m?*
4:27 far *m* than of her who has a husband!"
5: 3 I point out once *m* to all who receive
5:11 the cross would be a stumbling block no *m.*
Eph 3:20 do immeasurably *m* than we ask or imagine
Phil 1: 9 is that your love may *m* and more abound,
1:24 yet it is *m* urgent that I remain alive for
2:12 you but all the *m* now that I am absent.
3: 4 in external evidence, all the *m* can I!
4:10 that your concern for me bore fruit once *m.*
4:18 says that I have been fully paid and *m.*
1Thes 1: 8 makes it needless for us to say anything *m.*
2:18 I, Paul, tried *m* than once
2Thes 1: 3 It is no *m* than right that we thank God
1Tm 4: 8 of religion is incalculably *m* so,
6: 2 must perform their tasks even *m* faithfully,
2Tm 2:16 indulge in it become *m* and more godless,
Phlm 1:16 no longer as a slave but as *m* than a slave,
1:16 and how much *m* to you,
1:21 you, knowing that you will do *m* than I say.
Heb 2: 1 attend all the *m* to what we have heard,
3: 3 but Jesus is *m* worthy of honor than he,
3: 3 house is *m* honorable than the house itself.
4: 7 because of unbelief, God once *m* set a day,
8: 6 has obtained a *m* excellent ministry now,
8:12 and their sins I will remember no *m.*"
9:11 and *m* perfect tabernacle not made by hands,
9:14 how much *m* will the blood of Christ,
10:17 their transgressions I will remember no *m.*"
10:25 *m* because you see that the Day draws near.
10:34 you had better and *m* permanent possessions.
11: 5 "he was seen no *m* because God took him."
11:32 What *m* shall I recount?
12: 9 all the *m* submit to the Father of spirits,
12:24 speaks *m* eloquently than that of Abel.
12:26 once *m* shake not only earth but heaven!"
12:27 And that "once *m*" shows that shaken,
Jas 3:12 *m* can a brackish source yield fresh water.
1Pt 1: 7 which is *m* precious than the passing
2Pt 2:20 up and overcome in pollution once *m,*
2Jn 1:12 there is much *m* that I could write you,
3Jn 1: 4 Nothing delights me *m* than to hear that my
1:13 is much *m* that I had in mind to write you,
Rv 3:18 on your eyes, if you would see once *m.*
9:12 There are two *m* to come.
10: 6 "There shall be no *m* delay.
12:14 for a year and for two and a half years *m.*
17: 8 abyss once *m* before going to final ruin.
18:11 will be no *m* market for their imports
19: 3 Once *m* they sang "Alleluia!"
21: 4 and there shall be no *m* death or mourning,
22: 5 The night shall be no *m.*

MOREH (2)

Gn 12: 6 place at Shechem, by the terebinth of *M.*
Dt 11:30 opposite the Gilgal beside the terebinth of *M*

MOREOVER (77)

Gn 6:21 *M,* you are to provide yourself with all
30:41 *M,* whenever the hardier animals were in
34:19 *M* he was more highly respected than anyone
45:23 *M,* what he sent to his father was ten
Lv 7:32 *M,* from your peace offering you shall
8:33 *M,* you are not to depart from the entrance
19:21 The man, *m,* shall bring to the entrance
22: 4 *M,* if anyone touches a person who has
25:34 *M,* the pasture land belonging to their
Nm 19:16 *M,* everyone who in the open country
19:22 *M,* whatever the unclean person touches
28:15 *M,* one goat shall be sacrificed as a sin
28:30 *M,* one goat shall be offered as a sin
29: 5 *M,* one goat shall be offered as a sin
29:11 *M,* one goat shall be sacrificed as a sin
29:16 *M,* one goat shall be sacrificed as a sin
31:19 *M,* you shall stay outside the camp for
Dt 7:20 *M,* the LORD, your GOD, will send hornets
12:17 *M,* you shall not, in your own communities,
22:19 *M,* she shall remain his wife,
22:29 *M,* he may not divorce her as long as he
27: 4 When, *m,* you have crossed the Jordan,
Jos 17:11 *M,* in Issachar and in Asher Manasseh was
Jgs 18: 1 *M* the tribe of Danites were in search of a
20:48 *M* they destroyed by fire all the cities
1Sm 7:14 *M* there was peace between Israel and the
16:18 *M,* the LORD is with him."
28:19 *M,* the LORD will deliver Israel,
28:20 *M,* he had no bodily strength left,
30:20 *M,* David took all the sheep and oxen,
2Sm 13:22 Absalom, *m,* said nothing at all to Amnon,
15: 2 *M,* Absalom used to rise early and stand
17: 8 *M,* since your father is skilled in warfare,
1Kgs 5: 9 *M,* God gave Solomon wisdom and exceptional
5:26 The LORD, *m,* gave Solomon wisdom
7: 3 *M,* it had a ceiling of cedar above the
10:16 *M,* King Solomon made two hundred shields
13: 5 *M,* the altar broke up and the ashes from
2Kgs 12:16 *M,* no reckoning was asked of the men who
1Chr 12:41 *M,* their neighbors from as far as Issachar,
17:10 *M,* I declare to you that I, the LORD,
22:15 *M,* you have available an unlimited supply
2Chr 2: 2 *M,* Solomon sent this message to Huram,
9:15 *M,* King Solomon made two hundred large
12:12 in Judah *m,* good deeds were found.
23:19 *M,* he stationed guards at the gates of the
26: 9 *M,* Uzziah built towers in Jerusalem at the
27: 4 *M,* he built cities in the hill country of
28: 3 *M,* he offered sacrifice in the Valley of
33:23 *M,* he did not humble himself before the
Ezr 5:14 *M,* the gold and silver utensils of the
Neh 5:14 *M,* from the time that Nehemiah's Lack of
5:16 *M,* though I had acquired no land of my own,
Est 3: 6 *M,* he thought it was not enough to lay
5:12 *M,*" Haman added, "Queen Esther invited
9: 3 *M,* all the officials of the provinces,
1Mc 3:29 *m* the income from the province was small,
8:31 *M,* concerning the wrongs that King
10:42 *M,* the dues of five thousand silver
2Mc 6: 7 *M,* at the monthly celebration of the
Eccl 3:13 For every man, *m,* to eat and drink
Ez 23:40 *M,* they sent for men who had to come from
Jl 4: 4 *M,* what are you to me,
Mt 19:29 *M,* everyone who has given up home,
Mk 7: 4 *M,* they never eat anything from the market
11:16 *m,* he would not permit anyone to carry
Lk 1: 7 *m,* both were advanced in years.
5:37 *M,* no one pours new wine into old wineskins.
Jn 5:37 *M,* the Father who sent me has himself
6:18 *m,* with a strong wind blowing,
Acts 3:24 *M,* all the prophets who have spoken,
1Tm 2:14 *m,* it was not Adam who was deceived
Heb 3:19 We see, *m,* that it was their unbelief
11: 8 he went forth, *m,* not knowing where
12: 5 *M,* you have forgotten the encouraging
Rv 2: 3 *M,* you do not become discouraged.
13:16 *M,* it did not allow a man to buy or sell

MORESHETH (2)

Jer 26:18 "Micah of *M* used to prophesy in the days

MORESHETH (cont.)
Mi 1: 1 came to Micah of *M* in the days of Jotham,

MORESHETH-GATH (1)
Mi 1:14 you shall give parting gifts to *M;*

MORIAH (2)
Gn 22: 2 whom you love, and go to the land of *M.*
2Chr 3: 1 house of the LORD in Jerusalem on Mount *M,*

MORNING (195)
Gn 1: 5 evening came, and *m* followed—the first day.
1: 8 came, and *m* followed—the second day.
1:13 Evening came, and *m* followed—the third day.
1:19 came, and *m* followed—the fourth day
1:23 Evening came, and *m* followed—the fifth day
1:31 Evening came, and *m* followed—the sixth day
19:27 Early the next *m* Abraham went to the
20: 8 Early the next *m* Abimelech called all his
21:14 Early the next *m* Abraham got some bread
22: 3 the next *m* Abraham saddled his donkey,
24:54 When they were up the next *m,*
26:31 Early the next *m* they exchanged oaths.
28:18 Early the next *m* Jacob took the stone that
29:25 In the *m* Jacob was amazed:
32: 1 Early the next *m,* Laban kissed
40: 6 When Joseph came to them in the *m,*
41: 8 Next *m* his spirit was agitated.
Ex 7:15 Tomorrow *m,* when he sets out
8:16 "Early tomorrow *m* present yourself to
9:13 "Early tomorrow *m* present yourself to
12:10 next *m;* whatever is left over in the *m* shall
12:22 But none of you shall go outdoors until *m.*
16: 7 the *m* you will see the glory of the LORD,
16: 8 Moses, "and in the *m* your fill of bread,
16:12 in the *m* you shall have your fill of bread,
16:13 In the *m* a dew lay all about the camp,
16:19 one keep any of it over until tomorrow *m.*"
16:20 a part of it over until the following *m,*
16:21 Morning after *m* they gathered it,
18:13 who waited about him from *m* until evening.
18:14 to stand about you from *m* till evening?"
19:16 On the *m* of the third day there were peals
27:21 From evening to *m* Aaron and his sons shall
29:39 one lamb in the *m* and the other lamb at
29:41 cereal offering and libation as in the *m.*
30: 7 *M* after *m* when he prepares the lamps,
34: 2 Get ready for tomorrow *m,*
34: 4 and early the next *m* he went up Mount
36: 3 *m* after morning the people continued to
Lv 6: 2 of the altar all night until the next *m,*
6: 5 *m* the priest shall put firewood on it.
6:13 half in the *m* and half in the evening.
9:16 the holocaust, other than the *m* holocaust,
24: 3 the LORD regularly, from evening till *m.*
Nm 9:12 and not leaving any of it over till *m,*
9:15 but from evening until *m* it took on the
9:21 evening until *m;* and when it rose in the *m*
14:40 next *m* they started up into the foothills,
16: 5 "May the LORD make known tomorrow *m*
22:13 The next *m* Balaam arose and told the
22:21 So the next *m* when Balaam arose,
22:41 next *m* Balak took Balaam up on Bamoth-baal,
28: 4 offering one lamb in the *m* and the other
28: 8 and the same libation as in the *m,*
28:23 in addition to the established *m* holocaust;
Dt 16: 7 then in the *m* you may return to your tents.
28:67 In the *m* you will say,
28:67 you will say, 'Would that it were *m!*'
Jos 3: 1 Early the next *m,* Joshua moved with all
6:12 Early the next *m,* Joshua had the priests
7:14 *m* you must present yourselves by tribes.
7:16 *m* Joshua had Israel come forward by tribes,
8:10 Early the next *m* Joshua mustered the army
8:14 army came out very early in the *m* to engage
Jgs 6:28 Early the next *m* the townspeople found
6:31 for him, he shall be put to death by *m.*
6:38 next *m* he wrung the dew from the fleece,
7: 1 Early the next *m* Jerubbaal (that is,
9:33 Promptly at sunrise tomorrow *m,*
16: 2 saying, "Tomorrow *m* we will kill him."
19: 5 rose early in the *m* and he prepared to go.
19: 8 On the fifth *m* he rose early to depart,
19:26 was a guest, where she lay until the *m.*
Ru 2: 7 this *m* she has remained here until now,
3:13 Lie there until *m.*"
3:14 So she lay at his feet until *m,*
1Sm 1:19 the next *m* they worshiped before the LORD,
3:15 Samuel then slept until *m,*
5: 3 people of Ashdod rose early the next *m,*
5: 4 But the next *m* early,
9:19 In the *m,* before dismissing you,
15:12 Early in the *m* he went to meet Saul,
17:16 his stand *m* and evening for forty days.
17:20 Early the next *m,* having left the flock
19: 2 please be on your guard tomorrow *m;*
19:10 guard it, that he might kill him in the *m.*
20:35 The next *m* Jonathan went out into the
25:22 if by *m* I leave a single male alive among
25:36 nothing at all before daybreak the next *m.*
29:10 But make an early *m* start,
29:11 *m* to return to the land of the Philistines.
2Sm 2:27 from the pursuit of their brothers until *m.*"
2:29 Jordan, marched all through the *m,*
11:14 The next *m* David wrote a letter to Joab
13: 4 why are you so dejected *m* after morning?
23: 4 morning light at sunrise on a cloudless *m,*
24:11 When David rose in the *m,*
24:15 Israel from *m* until the time appointed,
1Kgs 3:21 I rose in the *m* to nurse my child,
3:21 But when I examined him in the *m* light,
17: 6 brought him bread and meat in the *m,*
18:26 it and called on Baal from *m* to noon,
2Kgs 3:20 In the *m,*
3:22 Early that *m,*
6:15 Early the next *m,*
7: 9 If we wait until *m* breaks,
10: 8 heaps at the entrance of the city until *m,*"
10: 9 Going out in the *m,*
16:15 "burn the *m* holocaust and the evening
19:35 Early the next *m,*
1Chr 9:27 and they had the duty of opening it each *m.*
16:40 of holocausts regularly, *m* and evening,
23:30 *m* to offer thanks and to praise the LORD,
2Chr 2: 3 showbread, for holocausts *m* and evening,
13:11 fragrant incense *m* after morning and
20:20 In the early *m* they hastened out to the
31: 3 of *m* and evening and those on sabbaths,
Ezr 3: 3 to the LORD on it, both *m* and evening.
Tb 9: 6 The following *m* they got an early start
Est 2:14 return in the *m* to a second harem
5:14 and in the *m* ask the king to have Mordecai
1Mc 3:58 in the *m* be ready to fight these Gentiles
4:52 Early in the *m* on the twenty-fifth day of
5:30 When *m* came, they looked ahead
9:13 and the battle raged from *m* until evening.
10:80 From *m* until evening they showered his men
12:29 did not know what had happened until *m.*
Jb 4:20 *M* or evening they may be shattered;
11:17 its gloom shall become as the *m,*
38: 7 While the *m* stars sang in chorus and all
38:12 you ever in your lifetime commanded the *m*
Ps(s) 88:14 with my *m* prayer I wait upon you.
90: 5 next *m* they are like the changing grass,
101: 8 Each *m* I will destroy all the wicked of
Prv 7:18 let us drink our fill of love, until *m,*
27:14 early *m* a curse can be laid to his charge.
Eccl 10:16 a servant, and whose princes dine in the *m!*
11: 6 In the *m* sow your seed,
Wis 11:22 a drop of *m* dew come down upon the earth.
Sir 18:26 Between *m* and evening the weather changes;
Is 5:11 drink as soon as they rise in the *m,*
14:12 have you fallen from the heavens, O *m* star,
17:11 make your sprouts blossom on the next *m,*
17:14 the evening, they spread terror, before *m,*
21:12 The watchman replies, *M* has come,
28:19 *m* after morning it shall pass,
33: 2 Be our strength every *m,*
37:36 Early the next *m,* there they were,
50: 4 *M* after *m* he opens my ear that I may hear;
Jer 20: 3 next *m,* after Pashhur had released Jeremiah
20:16 Let him hear war cries in the *m,*
21:12 Each *m* dispense justice,
Lam 3:23 They are renewed each *m,*
Ez 12: 8 in the *m,* the word of the LORD came
24:18 the next *m* I did as I had been commanded.
24:19 I therefore spoke to the people that *m,*
33:22 when the fugitive reached me in the *m.*
46:13 this he shall offer every *m.*
46:14 With it every *m* he shall provide as a
46:15 every *m* as an established holocaust.
Dn 6:20 the next *m* and hastened to the lions' den.
14:12 has eaten it all when you return in the *m,*
14:16 Early the next *m,* the king came
Hos 6: 4 Your piety is like a *m* cloud,
7: 6 in the *m* it flares like a blazing fire.
13: 3 they shall be like a *m* cloud or like the
Am 4: 4 Each *m* bring your sacrifices,
Jon 4: 7 But the next *m* at dawn God sent a worm
Mi 2: 1 In the *m* light they accomplish it when it
Zep 3: 3 night that have had no bones to gnaw by *m.*
3: 5 *M* after morning he renders judgment
Mt 14:25 At about three in the *m,* he came walking
16: 3 in the *m,* 'Sky red and gloomy,
Mk 1:35 Rising early the next *m,* he went off
6:48 time was between three and six in the *m.*
11:20 Early next *m,* as they were walking along,
15:25 nine in the *m* when they crucified him.
Lk 4:42 The next *m* he left the town and set out
Jn 20: 1 in the *m* on the first day of the week,
Acts 2:15 It is only nine in the *m!*
28:23 *m* to evening he laid the case before them,
2Pt 1:19 appear and the *m* star rises in your hearts.
Rv 2:28 and I will give him the *m* star.
22:16 of David, the *M* Star shining bright."

MORNINGS (3)
Gn 49:27 *m* he devours the prey,
Dn 8:14 two thousand three hundred evenings and *m;*
8:26 vision of the evenings and the *m* is true,

MORROW (3)
Ex 16:23 is left put away and keep for the *m.*"
16:24 When they put it away for the *m,*
Nm 33: 3 *m* the Israelites went forth in triumph,

MORSEL (5)
1Sm 2:36 that I may have a *m* of bread to eat.'"
Prv 28:21 for even a *m* of bread a man may do wrong.
Lk 14:24 those invited shall taste a *m* of my dinner.'"
Jn 13:26 He dipped the *m,*
13:30 had Judas eaten the *m* than he went out.

MORSELS (2)
Prv 18: 8 dainty *m* that sink into one's inmost being.
26:22 dainty *m* that sink into one's inmost being.

MORTAL (39)
Gn 9:15 become a flood to destroy all *m* beings.
9:16 all *m* creatures that are on earth."
9:17 me and all *m* creatures that are on earth."
Ex 21:12 a man a *m* blow must be put to death.
Dt 5:26 For what *m* has heard,
19: 5 the handle and hits his neighbor a *m* blow,
2Sm 1:15 and the youth struck him a *m* blow.
Est C:12 Queen Esther, seized with *m* anguish,
2Mc 7:16 have power among men, *m* though you are,
9:12 God, and not to think one's *m* self divine."
Jb 4:17 Can a *m* be blameless against his Maker?
10: 5 Are your days as the days of a *m,*
16:21 That he may do justice for a *m* in his
Ps(s) 17:14 wicked, by your hand, O LORD, from *m* men:
17:14 From *m* men whose portion in life is in
62:10 Only a breath are *m* men;
89:11 You have crushed Rahab with a *m* blow;
Prv 30: 1 The pronouncement of *m* man:
Wis 7: 1 I too am a *m* man,
15:17 being *m,* he makes a dead thing
Sir 36:23 is kindly, his lot is beyond that of *m* men.
Is 22:17 LORD shall hurl you down headlong, *m* man!
31: 8 by man, no *m* sword shall devour him;
51:12 Can you then fear *m* man,
Jer 44:30 king of Judah, to his enemy and *m* foe,
Lam 3:39 Why should any living man complain, any *m,*
3:58 You defended me in *m* danger,
Na 3:19 no healing for your hurt, your wound is *m.*
Rom 1:23 immortal God for images representing *m* man,
6:12 your *m* body and make you obey its lusts;
8:11 dead will bring your *m* bodies to life also,
1Cor 15:53 this *m* body with immortality.
15:54 on incorruptibility and the *m* immortality,
2Cor 4:11 of Jesus may be revealed in our *m* flesh.
5: 4 so that what is *m* may be absorbed by life.
Col 1:22 for you in his *m* body by dying,
Heb 12:10 to prepare us for the short span of *m* life;
Rv 13: 3 wounded, but this *m* wound was healed.
13:12 first beast, whose *m* wound had been healed.

MORTALLY (8)
Ex 21:18 with a stone or with his fist, not *m,*
Dt 19:11 and rising up against him, strikes him *m,*
1Sm 17:50 he struck the Philistine *m,*
31: 1 them and falling *m* wounded on Mount Gilboa,
2Kgs 20: 1 In those days, when Hezekiah was *m* ill,
2Chr 32:24 In those days Hezekiah became *m* ill.
Is 38: 1 In those days, when Hezekiah was *m* ill,
Rv 13: 3 heads seemed to have been *m* wounded,

MORTALS (7)
Gn 6:12 since all *m* led depraved lives on earth,
6:13 decided to put an end to all *m* on earth;
Ps(s) 73: 5 They are free from the burdens of *m,*
Wis 9:14 For the deliberations of *m* are timid,
Is 13:12 I will make *m* more rare than pure gold,
52:14 man, and his appearance beyond that of *m*—
Ez 31:14 for the land below, For the company of *m,*

MORTAR (9)
Gn 11: 3 used bricks for stone, and bitumen for *m.*
Ex 1:14 in *m* and brick and all kinds of field work
Lv 14:41 and the *m* that has been scraped off shall
14:42 *m* shall be made and plastered on the house.
14:45 beams and *m* shall be hauled away to an
Nm 11: 8 it between millstones or pound it in a *m,*
Prv 27:22 with the pestle, amid the grits in a *m,*
Jer 43: 9 sink them in *m* in the brickyard
Zep 1:11 Wail, O inhabitants of the *M!*

MORTIFICATION (1)
Sir 34:26 prayer, and what has he gained by his *m?*

MORTIFY (7)
Lv 16:29 shall *m* himself and shall do no work.
16:31 for you, on which you must *m* yourselves.
23:27 hold a sacred assembly and *m* yourselves
23:29 Anyone who does not *m* himself on this day
23:32 sabbath of complete rest and *m* yourselves.
Nm 29: 7 hold a sacred assembly, and *m* yourselves,
30:14 that she makes under oath to *m* herself,

MOSAIC (6)
1Chr 29: 2 settings for them, carnelian and *m* stones,

Tb 1: 8 of the *M* law and the commands of Deborah,
7:13 wife according to the decree of the *M* law.
Jn 7:23 sabbath to prevent a violation of *M* law,
Acts 15: 1 are circumcised according to *M* practice,
15: 5 be circumcised and told to keep the *M* law.

MOSERAH (1)

Dt 10: 6 set out from Beeroth Bene-jaakan for *M*,

MOSEROTH (1)

Nm 33:31 Setting out from *M*,

MOSES (814)

Ex 2:10 adopted him as her son and called him *M*;
2:11 On one occasion, after *M* had grown up,
2:14 Then *M* became afraid and thought,
2:15 But *M* fled from him and stayed in the land
2:17 Then *M* got up and defended them and
2:21 *M* agreed to live with him,
3: 1 Meanwhile *M* was tending the flock of his
3: 3 So *M* decided, "I must go over to look
3: 4 God called out to him from the bush, *M*!
3: 4 *M*!" *M*!" He answered, "Here I am."
3: 6 *M* hid his face, for he was afraid
3:11 *M* said to God, "Who am I that I should
3:13 "But," said *M* to God, "when I go
3:15 God spoke further to *M*, "Thus shall you
4: 1 "But," objected *M*, "suppose they will not
4: 3 into a serpent, and *M* shied away from it.
4: 7 *M* put his hand back in his bosom,
4:10 *M*, however, said to the LORD,
4:14 Then the LORD became angry with *M* and said,
4:18 After this *M* returned to his father-in-law
4:19 In Midian the LORD said to *M*,
4:20 So *M* took his wife and his sons,
4:24 LORD came upon *M* and would have killed
4:26 Then God let *M* go.
4:27 to Aaron, "Go into the desert to meet *M*."
4:28 *M* informed him of all the LORD had said in
4:29 Then *M* and Aaron went and assembled all
4:30 them everything the LORD had said to *M*,
5: 1 that, *M* and Aaron went to Pharaoh and said,
5: 4 them, "What do you mean, *M* and Aaron,
5:20 left Pharaoh and came upon *M* and Aaron,
5:22 *M* again had recourse to the LORD and said,
6: 1 Then the LORD answered *M*,
6: 2 God also said to *M*, "I am the LORD.
6: 9 But when *M* told this to the Israelites,
6:10 Then the LORD said to *M*,
6:12 But *M* protested to the LORD,
6:13 spoke to *M* and Aaron and gave them his
6:20 his aunt Jochebed, who bore him Aaron, *M*,
6:26 this the *M* to whom the LORD said, "Lead
6:27 the same *M* and Aaron.
6:28 day the LORD spoke to *M* in Egypt he said,
6:30 But *M* protested to the LORD,
7: 6 *M* and Aaron did as the LORD had commanded
7: 7 *M* was eighty years old and Aaron
7: 8 The LORD told *M* and Aaron,
7:10 Then *M* and Aaron went to Pharaoh and did
7:14 Then the LORD said to *M*,
7:19 The LORD then said to *M*, "Say to Aaron:
7:20 *M* and Aaron did as the LORD had commanded.
7:22 and would not listen to *M* and Aaron,
7:26 Then the LORD said to *M*, "Go to Pharaoh
8: 1 The LORD then told *M*, "Say to Aaron:
8: 4 Pharaoh summoned *M* and Aaron and said,
8: 5 *M* answered Pharaoh, "Do me the favor
8: 6 *M* replied, "It shall be as you have said,
8: 8 After *M* and Aaron left Pharaoh's presence,
8: 8 *M* implored the LORD to fulfill the promise
8: 9 and the LORD did as *M* had asked.
8:12 Thereupon the LORD said to *M*,
8:16 Again the LORD told *M*,
8:21 summoned *M* and Aaron and said to them,
8:22 *M* replied, "It is not right to do so,
8:25 *M* answered, "As soon as I leave
8:26 " When *M* left Pharaoh's presence,
8:27 and the LORD did as *M* had asked.
9: 1 Then the LORD said to *M*, "Go to Pharaoh
9: 8 Then the LORD said to *M* and Aaron,
9: 8 of Pharaoh let *M* scatter it toward the sky.
9:10 *M* scattered it toward the sky,
9:11 magicians could not stand in *M*' presence,
9:12 them, just as the LORD had foretold to *M*.
9:13 LORD told *M*, "Early tomorrow morning
9:22 The LORD then said to *M*,
9:23 *M* stretched out his staff toward the sky,
9:27 summoned *M* and Aaron and said to them,
9:29 *M* replied, "As soon as I leave the city
9:33 When *M* had left Pharaoh's presence and
9:35 go, as the LORD had foretold through *M*.
10: 1 Then the LORD said to *M*,
10: 3 *M* and Aaron went to Pharaoh and told him,
10: 8 *M* and Aaron were brought back to Pharaoh,
10: 9 and old must go with us," *M* answered,
10:12 The LORD then said to *M*,
10:13 So *M* stretched out his staff over the land
10:16 Pharaoh summoned *M* and Aaron and said,
10:18 When *M* left the presence of Pharaoh,
10:21 LORD said to *M*, "Stretch out your hand
10:22 So *M* stretched out his hand toward the sky,
10:24 Pharaoh then summoned *M* and Aaron and said,
10:25 *M* replied, "You must also grant us
10:29 *M* replied, "Well said!
11: 1 LORD told *M*, "One more plague will I bring
11: 3 *M* himself was very highly regarded by
11: 4 *M* then said, "Thus says the LORD:
11: 9 LORD said to *M*, "Pharaoh refuses to listen
11:10 although *M* and Aaron performed these
12: 1 said to *M* and Aaron in the land of Egypt,
12:21 *M* called all the elders of Israel and said
12:28 did as the LORD had commanded *M*
12:31 Pharaoh summoned *M* and Aaron and said,
12:35 The Israelites did as *M* had commanded:
12:43 The LORD said to *M* and Aaron,
12:50 just as the LORD had commanded *M*
13: 1 The LORD spoke to *M* and said,
13: 3 *M* said to the people, "Remember this day
13:19 *M* also took Joseph's bones along,
14: 1 LORD said to *M*, "Tell the Israelites
14:11 And they complained to *M*,
14:13 But *M* answered the people, "Fear not!
14:15 LORD said to *M*, "Why are you crying
14:21 Then *M* stretched out his hand over the sea,
14:26 LORD told *M*, "Stretch out your hand
14:27 So *M* stretched out his hand over the sea,
14:31 and believed in him and in his servant *M*.
15: 1 Then *M* and the Israelites sang this song
15:22 Then *M* led Israel forward from the Red Sea,
15:24 As the people grumbled against *M*,
16: 2 community grumbled against *M* and Aaron.
16: 4 LORD said to *M*, "I will now rain down
16: 6 So *M* and Aaron told all the Israelites,
16: 8 to eat in the evening," continued *M*,
16: 9 *M* said to Aaron, "Tell the whole Israelite
16:11 The LORD spoke to *M* and said,
16:15 *M* told them, "This is the bread
16:19 *M* also told them, "Let no one keep any
16:20 Therefore *M* was displeased with them.
16:22 the community came and reported this to *M*,
16:24 put it away for the morrow, as *M* commanded,
16:25 *M* then said, "Eat it today,
16:28 LORD said to *M*, "How long will you
16:32 *M* said, "This is what the LORD
16:33 *M* then told Aaron, "Take an urn
16:34 safekeeping, as the LORD had commanded *M*.
17: 2 They quarreled, therefore, with *M* and said,
17: 2 *M* replied, "Why do you quarrel with me?
17: 3 for water, the people grumbled against *M*,
17: 4 *M* cried out to the LORD, "what shall I do
17: 5 LORD answered *M*, "Go over there in front
17: 6 *M* did, in the presence of the elders
17: 9 *M*, therefore, said to Joshua, "Pick out
17:10 So Joshua did as *M* told him:
17:10 he engaged Amalek in battle after *M* had
17:11 As long as *M* kept his hands raised up,
17:12 *M*' hands, however, grew tired;
17:14 LORD said to *M*, "Write this down
17:15 *M* also built an altar there,
18: 1 Now *M*' father-in-law Jethro,
18: 1 had done for *M* and for his people Israel:
18: 2 Moses' wife, whom *M* had sent back to him,
18: 5 Together with *M*' wife and sons,
18: 6 mountain of God, and he sent word to *M*,
18: 7 *M* went out to meet his father-in-law,
18: 8 *M* then told his father-in-law of all that
18:12 Then Jethro, the father-in-law of *M*,
18:12 *M*' father-in-law in the meal before God.
18:13 next day *M* sat in judgment for the people,
18:15 *M* answered his father-in-law,
18:24 *M* followed the advice of his father-in-law
18:26 more difficult cases they referred to *M*,
18:27 Then *M* bade farewell to his father-in-law,
19: 3 mountain, *M* went up the mountain to God.
19: 7 So *M* went and summoned the elders of the
19: 8 Then *M* brought back to the LORD the
19: 9 When *M*, then, had reported to the LORD
19:14 Then *M* came down from the mountain to the
19:17 But *M* led the people out of the camp to
19:19 while *M* was speaking and God answering him
19:20 *M* to the top of the mountain, and *M* went up
19:21 LORD told *M*, "Go down and warn
19:23 *M* said to the LORD, "The people cannot go
19:25 So *M* went down to the people and told them
20:19 position much farther away and said to *M*,
20:20 *M* answered the people, "Do not be afraid,
20:21 while *M* approached the cloud where God was.
20:22 LORD told *M*, "Thus shall you speak
24: 1 *M* himself was told, "Come up to the LORD,
24: 2 but *M* alone is to come close to the LORD;
24: 2 the people shall not come up at all with *M*."
24: 3 When *M* came to the people and related all
24: 4 *M* then wrote down all the words of the
24: 6 *M* took half of the blood and put it in
24: 9 *M* then went up with Aaron,
24:12 LORD said to *M*, "Come up to me
24:13 *M* set out with Joshua, his aide,
24:15 After *M* had gone up, a cloud covered
24:16 he called to *M* from the midst of the cloud.
24:18 But *M* passed into the midst of the cloud
25: 1 This is what the LORD then said to *M*:
30:11 LORD also said to *M*, "When you take
30:17 LORD said to *M*, "For ablutions you shall
30:22 LORD said to *M*, "Take the finest spices:
30:34 LORD told *M*, "Take these aromatic
31: 1 LORD said to *M*, "See, I have chosen Bezalel,
31:12 LORD said to *M*, "You must also tell
31:18 had finished speaking to *M* on Mount Sinai,
32: 1 *M*' delay in coming down from the mountain,
32: 1 *M* who brought us out of the land of Egypt,
32: 7 With that, the LORD said to *M*,
32: 9 this people is," continued the LORD to *M*.
32:11 But *M* implored the LORD,
32:15 *M* then turned and came down the mountain
32:17 noise of the people shouting, he said to *M*,
32:18 *M* answered, "It does not sound like cries
32:19 With that, *M*' wrath flared up,
32:21 *M* asked Aaron, "What did this people
32:23 *M* who brought us out of the land of Egypt,
32:25 When *M* realized that, to the scornful joy
32:28 The Levites carried out the command of *M*,
32:29 *M* said, "Today you have been dedicated
32:30 On the next day *M* said to the people,
32:31 So *M* went back to the LORD and said,
33: 1 LORD told *M*, "You and the people
33: 5 The LORD said to *M*, "Tell the Israelites:
33: 7 *M* used to pitch at some distance away,
33: 8 Whenever *M* went out to the tent,
33: 8 watching *M* until he entered the tent.
33: 9 *M* entered the tent, the column of cloud
33: 9 its entrance while the LORD spoke with *M*.
33:11 The LORD used to speak to *M* face to face,
33:11 *M* would then return to the camp,
33:12 *M* said to the LORD, "You, indeed, are
33:15 *M* replied, "If you are not going yourself,
33:17 The LORD said to *M*,
33:18 *M* said, "Do let me see your glory!"
34: 1 LORD said to *M*, "Cut two stone tablets
34: 4 *M* then cut two stone tablets like the
34: 8 *M* at once bowed down to the ground in
34:13 *M* then spoke to them
34:27 LORD said to *M*, "Write down these words,
34:28 So *M* stayed there with the LORD for forty
34:29 As *M* came down from Mount Sinai with the
34:30 and the other Israelites saw *M* and noticed
34:31 Only after *M* called to them did Aaron and
34:31 *M* then spoke to them
34:34 Whenever *M* entered the presence of the
34:35 see that the skin of *M*' face was radiant;
35: 1 *M* assembled the whole Israelite community
35: 4 *M* told the whole Israelite community,
35:20 whole Israelite community left *M*' presence,
35:29 the LORD had commanded *M* to have done.
35:30 *M* said to the Israelites,
36: 2 *M* then called Bezalel and Oholiab and all
36: 3 They received from *M* all the contributions
36: 3 to bring their voluntary offerings to *M*.
36: 5 left the work they were doing, and told *M*,
36: 6 *M*, therefore, ordered a proclamation
38:21 drawn up at the command of *M*
38:22 who made all that the LORD commanded *M*,
39: 1 for Aaron, as the LORD had commanded *M*.
39: 5 linen twined, as the LORD had commanded *M*.
39: 7 Israel, just as the LORD had commanded *M*.
39:21 this was just as the LORD had commanded *M*.
39:26 all this, just as the LORD had commanded *M*.
39:29 scarlet yarn, as the LORD had commanded *M*.
39:31 violet ribbon, as the LORD had commanded *M*.
39:32 the work just as the LORD had commanded *M*.
39:33 They then brought to *M* the Dwelling,
39:42 the work just as the LORD had commanded *M*.
39:43 So when *M* saw that all the work was done
40: 1 Then the LORD said to *M*.
40:16 *M* did exactly as the LORD had commanded
40:18 It was *M* who erected the Dwelling.
40:31 *M* and Aaron and his sons used to wash
40:32 the altar, as the LORD had commanded *M*.
40:33 Thus *M* finished all the work.
40:35 *M* could not enter the meeting tent,
Lv 1: 1 The LORD called *M*, and from the meeting
4: 1 The LORD said to *M*, "Tell the Israelites:
5:14 The LORD said to *M*, "If someone commits
5:20 The LORD said to *M*, "If someone commits
6: 1 The LORD said to *M*, "Give Aaron
6:12 The LORD said to *M*, "This is the offering
6:17 The LORD said to *M*, "Tell Aaron
7:22 The LORD said to *M*, "Tell the Israelites:
7:28 The LORD said to *M*, "Tell the Israelites:
7:38 which the LORD enjoined on *M* at Mount
8: 1 The LORD said to *M*, "Take Aaron
8: 4 And *M* did as the LORD had commanded.
8: 5 *M* told them what the LORD had ordered to
8:10 *M* anointed and consecrated the Dwelling,
8:13 *M* likewise brought forward Aaron's sons,
8:15 Then *M* slaughtered it,
8:16 with their fat, *M* burned them on the altar.
8:19 *M* splashed its blood on all sides of the
8:23 *M* took some of its blood and put it on the
8:24 *M* had the sons of Aaron also come forward,
8:28 *M* burned them with the holocaust on the
8:29 was *M*' own portion of the ordination ram.
8:29 in keeping with the LORD's command to *M*.
8:30 *M* sprinkled with it Aaron and his
8:31 Finally, *M* said to Aaron and his sons,
8:36 all that the LORD had commanded through *M*.
9: 1 eighth day *M* summoned Aaron and his sons,

MOSES (cont.)
9: 5 So they brought what *M* had ordered.
9: 6 forward and stood before the LORD, *M* said,
9: 7 Come up to the altar," *M* then told Aaron,
9:10 sin offering, as the LORD had commanded *M;*
9:21 in keeping with the LORD's command to *M.*
9:23 *M* and Aaron went into the meeting tent.
10: 3 *M* then said to Aaron, "This is as the LORD
10: 4 Then *M* summoned Mishael and Elzaphan,
10: 5 outside the camp, as *M* had commanded.
10: 6 *M* said to Aaron and his sons Eleazar and
10: 7 So they did as *M* told them.
10:11 that the LORD has given them through *M.*"
10:12 *M* said to Aaron and his surviving sons,
10:16 When *M* inquired about the goat of the sin
10:19 Aaron answered *M,*
10:20 On hearing this, *M* was satisfied.
11: 1 The LORD said to *M* and Aaron,
12: 1 The LORD said to *M,* "Tell the Israelites:
13: 1 The LORD said to *M* and Aaron,
14: 1 The LORD said to *M,* "This is the law
14:33 The LORD said to *M* and Aaron,
15: 1 The LORD said to *M* and Aaron,
16: 1 the LORD spoke to *M* and said to him,
16:34 was it done, as the LORD had commanded *M.*
17: 1 The LORD said to *M,* "Speak to Aaron
18: 1 LORD said to *M,* "Speak to the Israelites
19: 1 The LORD said to *M,*
20: 1 The LORD said to *M,* "Tell the Israelites:
21: 1 LORD said to *M,* "Speak to Aaron's sons,
21:16 The LORD said to *M,* "Speak to Aaron
21:24 *M,* therefore, told this to Aaron
22: 1 The LORD said to *M,*
22:17 The LORD said to *M,*
22:26 LORD said to *M,* "When an ox or a lamb
23: 1 The LORD said to *M,* "Speak to the Israelites
23: 9 LORD said to *M,* "Speak to the Israelites
23:23 The LORD said to *M,* "Tell the Israelites:
23:26 The LORD said to *M,*
23:33 The LORD said to *M,* "Tell the Israelites:
23:44 Thus did *M* announce to the Israelites the
24: 1 LORD said to *M,* "Order the Israelites
24:11 So the people brought him to *M,*
24:13 The LORD then said to *M,*
24:23 When *M* told this to the Israelites,
24:23 out the command that the LORD had given *M.*
25: 1 The LORD said to *M* on Mount Sinai,
26:46 laws which the LORD had *M* promulgate
27: 1 The LORD said to *M,*
27:34 gave *M* on Mount Sinai for the Israelites.
Nm 1: 1 the LORD said to *M* in the meeting tent in
1:17 So *M* and Aaron took these men who had been
1:19 house, as the LORD had commanded *M.*
1:44 in the census taken by *M* and Aaron and the
1:48 For the LORD had told *M.*
1:54 fulfilled as the LORD had commanded *M.*
2: 1 The LORD said to *M* and Aaron:
2:33 for so the LORD had commanded *M.*
2:34 did just as the LORD had commanded *M;*
3: 1 were the descendants of Aaron and *M*
3: 1 that the LORD spoke to *M* on Mount Sinai.
3: 5 Now the LORD said to *M:*
3:11 The LORD said to *M,* "It is I who have
3:14 The LORD said to *M* in the desert of Sinai,
3:16 *M,* therefore, took their census in accordance
3:38 camped *M* and Aaron and the latter's sons.
3:39 male Levites a month old or more whom *M*
3:40 The LORD then said to *M,* "Take a census
3:42 So *M* took a census of all the first-born
3:44 The LORD said to *M:* "Take the Levites
3:49 So *M* took the silver as ransom from those
4: 1 The LORD said to *M* and Aaron:
4:17 The LORD said to *M* and Aaron:
4:21 The LORD said to *M,*
4:34 So *M* and Aaron and the princes of the
4:37 to serve in the meeting tent, which *M* took,
4:41 to serve in the meeting tent, which *M* took,
4:45 the men of the Merarite clans which *M* took,
4:46 when *M* and Aaron and the Israelites
4:49 According to the LORD's bidding to *M,*
4:49 so the LORD had commanded *M.*
5: 1 The LORD said to *M:* "Order the Israelites
5: 4 the command that the LORD had given *M;*
5: 5 The LORD said to *M,* "Tell the Israelites:
5:11 The LORD said to *M,* "Speak to the Israelites
6: 1 The LORD said to *M:*
6:22 The LORD said to *M:*
7: 1 when *M* had completed the erection of the
7: 4 The LORD then said to *M,*
7: 6 So *M* accepted the wagons and oxen,
7:11 LORD said to *M,* "Let one prince a day
7:89 When *M* entered the meeting tent to speak
8: 1 The LORD spoke to *M,*
8: 3 just as the LORD had commanded *M.*
8: 4 to the pattern which the LORD had shown *M.*
8: 5 The LORD said to *M:*
8:20 did *M* and Aaron and the whole community of
8:20 which the LORD had given *M* concerning them.
8:22 *M* concerning the Levites was carried out.
8:23 The LORD said to *M:*
9: 1 the LORD said to *M* in the desert of Sinai,
9: 4 *M,* therefore, told the Israelites
9: 5 month, just as the LORD had commanded *M.*
9: 6 up to *M* and Aaron that same day and said,
9: 8 *M* answered them, "Wait until I learn what
9: 9 The LORD then said to *M:*
9:23 the LORD, as he had bidden them through *M.*
10: 1 The LORD said to *M:*
10:13 camp at the bidding of the LORD through *M,*
10:29 out, *M* said to his brother-in-law Hobab,
10:31 *M* said, "Please, do not leave us;
10:35 Whenever the ark set out, *M* would say,
11: 2 But when the people cried out to *M,*
11:10 When *M* heard the people,
11:11 *M* asked the LORD, "Why are you so displeased
11:16 LORD said to *M,* "Assemble for me seventy
11:21 But *M* said, "The people around me include
11:23 The LORD answered *M,* "Is this beyond
11:24 So *M* went out and told the people what the
11:25 Taking some of the spirit that was on *M,*
11:27 So, when a young man quickly told *M,*
11:28 his youth had been Moses' aide, said, *M,*
11:29 But *M* answered him, "Are you jealous
11:30 Then *M* retired to the camp,
12: 1 Miriam and Aaron spoke against *M*
12: 2 it through *M* alone that the LORD speaks?
12: 3 *M* himself was by far the meekest man on
12: 4 the LORD said to *M* and Aaron and Miriam,
12: 7 Not so with my servant *M!*
12: 8 you not fear to speak against my servant *M?*"
12:11 he said to *M,* "please do not charge us
12:13 *M* cried to the LORD, "Please, not this!
12:14 But the LORD answered *M,*
13: 1 LORD said to *M,* "Send men to reconnoiter
13: 3 *M* dispatched them from the desert of Paran,
13:16 whom *M* sent out to reconnoiter the land.
13:16 But Hoshea, son of Nun, *M* called Joshua.
13:17 the land of Canaan, *M* said to them,
13:26 met *M* and Aaron and the whole community of
13:27 They told *M:* "We went into the land
13:30 however, to quiet the people toward *M,*
14: 2 Israelites grumbled against *M* and Aaron,
14: 5 But *M* and Aaron fell prostrate before the
14:11 And the LORD said to *M,*
14:13 But *M* said to the LORD: "Are the Egyptians
14:26 The LORD also said to *M* and Aaron:
14:36 And so it happened to the men whom *M* had
14:39 When *M* repeated these words to all the
14:41 *M* said, "Why are you again disobeying
14:44 covenant of the LORD nor *M* left the camp.
15: 1 The LORD said to *M,* "Give the Israelites
15:17 The LORD said to *M,* "Speak to the Israelites
15:22 commandments which the LORD gives to *M,*
15:23 LORD gives to Moses, and through *M* to you,
15:33 him to *M* and Aaron and the whole assembly.
15:35 Then the LORD said to *M,* "This man shall
15:36 him to death, as the LORD had commanded *M.*
15:37 The LORD said to *M,*
16: 2 They stood before *M,* and held an assembly
16: 3 and held an assembly against *M* and Aaron,
16: 4 When *M* heard this, he fell prostrate.
16: 8 *M* also said to Korah, "Listen to me,
16:15 *M* became very angry and said to the LORD,
16:16 *M* said to Korah, "You and all your band
16:18 of the meeting tent along with *M* and Aaron.
16:20 and the LORD said to *M* and Aaron,
16:23 The LORD answered *M,*
16:25 *M,* followed by the elders of Israel,
16:28 wives and sons and little ones, *M* said,
17: 1 The LORD said to *M,* "Tell Eleazar,
17: 5 which the LORD had given him through *M.*
17: 6 community grumbled against *M* and Aaron,
17: 7 *M* and Aaron turned toward the meeting tent,
17: 8 Then *M* and Aaron came to the front of the
17: 9 tent, and the LORD said to *M* and Aaron,
17:11 Then *M* said to Aaron, "Take your censer,
17:12 Obeying the orders of *M,*
17:15 to *M* at the entrance of the meeting tent.
17:16 The LORD now said to *M,*
17:21 So *M* spoke to the Israelites,
17:22 Then *M* laid the staffs down before the
17:23 The next day, when *M* entered the tent,
17:24 *M* thereupon brought out all the staffs
17:25 own staff and took it, the LORD said to *M,*
17:26 And *M* did as the LORD had commanded him.
17:27 Then the Israelites cried out to *M,*
18:25 The LORD said to *M,* "Give the Levites
19: 1 The LORD said to *M* and Aaron:
20: 2 they held a council against *M* and Aaron.
20: 3 The people contended with *M,*
20: 6 But *M* and Aaron went away from the
20: 7 appeared to them, and the LORD said to *M,*
20: 9 So *M* took the staff from its place before
20:11 *M* struck the rock twice with his staff,
20:12 But the LORD said to *M* and Aaron,
20:14 From Kadesh *M* sent men to the king of Edom
20:23 land of Edom, the LORD said to *M* and Aaron,
20:27 *M* did as the LORD commanded.
20:28 *M* stripped Aaron of his garments and put
20:28 *M* and Eleazar came down from the mountain,
21: 5 the people complained against God and *M,*
21: 7 Then the people came to *M* and said,
21: 7 So *M* prayed for the people,
21: 8 for the people, and the LORD said to *M,*
21: 9 *M* accordingly made a bronze serpent and
21:16 was the well of which the LORD said to *M,*
21:32 of the Amorites, *M* sent spies to Jazer;
21:34 The LORD, however, said to *M,*
25: 4 he said to *M,* "Gather all the leaders
25: 5 So *M* told the Israelite judges,
25: 6 of *M* and of the whole Israelite community,
25:10 Then the LORD said to *M,*
25:16 The LORD then said to *M,*
26: 1 slaughter the LORD said to *M* and Eleazar,
26: 3 *M* and the priest Eleazar registered those
26: 4 years or more, as the LORD had commanded *M.*
26: 9 who revolted against *M* and Aaron [like
26:52 LORD said to *M,* "Among these groups
26:59 bore Aaron and *M* and their sister Miriam.
26:63 were the men registered by *M* and the
26:64 man of those who had been registered by *M*
27: 2 and standing in the presence of *M,*
27: 5 When *M* laid their case before the LORD,
27:11 the Israelites, as the LORD commanded *M.*
27:12 The LORD said to *M,* "Go up here
27:15 Then *M* said to the LORD,
27:18 And the LORD replied to *M,*
27:22 *M* did as the LORD had commanded him.
27:23 as the LORD had directed through *M.*
28: 1 The LORD said to *M,* "Give the Israelites
30: 1 *M* then gave the Israelites these
30: 2 *M* said to the heads of the Israelite tribes,
30:17 which the LORD prescribed through *M*
31: 1 LORD said to *M,* "Avenge the Israelites
31: 3 *M* told the people, "Select men from your
31: 6 *M* sent them out on the campaign,
31: 7 Midianites, as the LORD had commanded *M,*
31:12 to *M* and the priest Eleazar and to the
31:13 When *M* and the priest Eleazar,
31:14 *M* became angry with the officers of the
31:21 the law, as prescribed by the LORD to *M,*
31:25 The LORD said to *M:*
31:31 So *M* and the priest Eleazar did this,
31:31 did this, as the LORD had commanded *M.*
31:41 to the LORD, *M* gave to the priest Eleazar,
31:42 when *M* had taken it from the soldiers,
31:47 From this, the Israelites' share, *M,*
31:48 of the army came up to *M* and said to him,
31:51 *M* and the priest Eleazar accepted this
31:54 *M,* then, and the priest Eleazar accepted
32: 2 they came to *M* and the priest Eleazar and
32: 6 But *M* answered the Gadites and Reubenites:
32:20 *M* said to them in reply:
32:25 The Gadites and Reubenites answered *M,*
32:28 *M,* therefore, gave this order
32:33 So *M* gave them [the Gadites and Reubenites,
32:40 *M* gave Gilead to Machir,
33: 1 of Egypt under the guidance of *M* and Aaron.
33: 2 By the LORD's command *M* recorded the
33:50 The LORD spoke to *M* on the plains of Moab
34: 1 The LORD said to *M,* "Give the Israelites
34:13 *M* also gave this order to the Israelites:
34:16 The LORD said to *M,* "These are the names
35: 1 The LORD gave these instructions to *M* on
35: 9 The LORD said to *M,* "Tell the Israelites:
36: 1 came up and laid this plea before *M* and
36: 5 So *M* gave this regulation to the
36:10 the command which the LORD had given to *M.*
36:13 prescribed for the Israelites through *M,*
Dt 1: 1 These are the words which *M* spoke to all
1: 3 *M* spoke to the Israelites all the commands
1: 5 *M* began to explain the law in the land of
4:41 Then *M* set apart three cities in the
4:44 the law which *M* set before the Israelites.
4:46 who dwelt in Heshbon and whom *M* and the
5: 1 *M* summoned all Israel and said to them,
27: 1 Then *M,* with the elders of Israel, gave
27: 9 *M,* with the levitical priests,
27:11 That same day *M* gave the people this order:
28:69 of the covenant which the LORD ordered *M*
29: 1 *M* summoned all Israel and said to them,
31: 1 When *M* had finished speaking these words
31: 7 Then *M* summoned Joshua and in the presence
31: 9 When *M* had written down this law,
31:14 The LORD said to *M,* "The time is now
31:14 So *M* and Joshua went and presented
31:16 The LORD said to *M,* "Soon you will be
31:22 So *M* wrote this song that same day,
31:24 When *M* had finished writing out on a
31:30 Then *M* recited the words of this song from
32:44 So *M,* together with Joshua, son of Nun,
32:45 When *M* had finished speaking all these
32:48 On that very day the LORD said to *M,*
33: 1 This is the blessing which *M,*
34: 1 Then *M* went up from the plains of Moab to
34: 5 So there, in the land of Moab, *M,*
34: 7 *M* was one hundred and twenty years old
34: 8 wept for *M* in the plains of Moab,
34: 8 the period of grief and mourning for *M.*
34: 9 since *M* had laid his hands upon him;
34: 9 thus carrying out the LORD's command to *M.*
34:10 no prophet has arisen in Israel like *M,*
34:12 *M* exhibited in the sight of all Israel.
Jos 1: 1 After *M,* the servant of the LORD, had died,
1: 1 had died, the LORD said to *M'* aide Joshua,
1: 2 "My servant *M* is dead.
1: 3 As I promised *M,*
1: 5 I will be with you as I was with *M:*
1: 7 law which my servant *M* enjoined on you.

1:13 "Remember what *M*,
1:14 the land *M* gave you here beyond the Jordan.
1:15 return and occupy your own land, which *M*,
1:16 will obey you as completely as we obeyed *M*.
1:17 your God, be with you as he was with *M*.
3: 7 may know I am with you, as I was with *M*.
4:12 of the Israelites, as *M* had ordered.
4:14 they respected him as they had respected *M*.
8:31 with the command to the Israelites of *M*,
8:32 the stones a copy of the law written by *M*.
8:33 thus carrying out the instructions of *M*,
8:35 Every single word that *M* had commanded,
9:24 commanded his servant *M* that you be given
11:12 sword, fulfilling the doom on them, as *M*,
11:15 his servant Moses, so *M* commanded Joshua,
11:15 the LORD had commanded *M* should be done.
11:20 exterminated, as the LORD had commanded *M*.
11:23 just as the LORD had foretold to *M*.
12: 6 After *M*, the servant of the LORD,
13: 8 had received their heritage which *M*,
13:12 *M* conquered and occupied these territories,
13:14 tribe of Levi *M* assigned no heritage since,
13:15 What *M* gave to the Reubenite clans:
13:21 king, who reigned in Heshbon, *M* had killed,
13:24 What *M* gave to the Gadite clans:
13:29 What *M* gave to the clans of the half-tribe
13:32 *M* gave when he was in the plains of Moab,
13:33 *M* gave no heritage to the tribe of Levi,
14: 2 instructions the LORD had given through *M*
14: 3 For to two and a half tribes *M* had already
14: 5 out the instructions of the LORD to *M*.
14: 6 what the LORD said to the man of God, *M*,
14: 7 years old when the servant of the LORD, *M*,
14: 9 On that occasion *M* swore this oath,
14:10 years since the LORD spoke thus to *M*;
14:11 today as I was the day *M* sent me forth,
17: 4 *M* to give us a heritage among our kinsmen."
18: 7 the heritage east of the Jordan which *M*,
20: 2 cities of which I spoke to them through *M*,
21: 2 to them, "The LORD commanded, through *M*,
21: 8 obedience to the LORD's command through *M*.
22: 2 "You have done all that *M*,
22: 4 to your own land, which *M*,
22: 5 to observe the precept and law which *M*,
22: 7 of Manasseh *M* had assigned land
22: 9 according to the LORD's command through *M*.
23: 6 is written in the book of the law of *M*,
24: 5 "Then I sent *M* and Aaron,
Jgs 1:16 of the Kenite, *M*' father-in-law,
1:20 As *M* had commanded,
3: 4 had enjoined on their fathers through *M*.
4:11 descendants of Hobab, *M*' brother-in-law,
18:30 and Jonathan, son of Gershom, son of *M*,
1Sm 12: 6 LORD is witness, who appointed *M* and Aaron,
12: 8 *M* and Aaron to bring them out of Egypt,
1Kgs 2: 3 as they are written in the law of *M*,
8: 9 tablets which *M* had put there at Horeb,
8:53 as you declared through your servant *M*
8:56 promise he made through his servant *M*.
2Kgs 14: 6 written in the book of the law of *M*,
18: 4 the sacred Nehushtan which *M* had made,
18: 6 commandments which the LORD had given *M*.
18:12 and not fulfilling the commandments of *M*,
21: 8 law which my servant *M* enjoined upon them."
23:25 in accord with the entire law of *M*;
1Chr 5:29 The children of Amram were Aaron, *M*,
6:34 and of making atonement for Israel, as *M*,
15:15 as *M* had ordained according to the word of
21:29 the LORD, which *M* had built in the desert,
22:13 decrees which the LORD gave *M* for Israel.
23:13 The sons of Amram were Aaron and *M*.
23:14 *M*, however, the man of God, his sons
23:15 The sons of *M* were Gershom and Eliezer.
26:24 Shubael, son of Gershon, son of *M*,
2Chr 1: 3 tent of God, made in the desert by *M*,
5:10 the two tablets which *M* put there on Horeb,
8:13 day by day according to the command of *M*,
23:18 the LORD, as is written in the law of *M*,
24: 6 Judah and Jerusalem the tax levied by *M*,
24: 9 Judah and Jerusalem that the tax which *M*,
25: 4 is written in the law, in the Book of *M*,
30:16 for them according to the law of *M*,
33: 8 the statutes and the ordinances given by *M*."
34:14 of the law of the LORD given through *M*.
35: 6 to the word of the LORD given through *M*."
35:12 LORD, as is prescribed in the book of *M*.
Ezr 3: 2 the holocausts prescribed in the law of *M*,
6:18 as is prescribed in the book of *M*.
7: 6 the law of *M* which was given by the LORD,
Neh 1: 7 which you committed to your servant *M*.
1: 8 pray, the promise which you gave through *M*,
8: 1 of *M* which the LORD prescribed for Israel.
8:14 the law prescribed by the LORD through *M*
9:14 for them, by the hand of *M* your servant.
10:30 the law of God which was given through *M*,
13: 1 the book of *M* in the hearing of the people,
Tb 6:13 according to the decree in the Book of *M*,
7:11 according to the decree of the Book of *M*.
7:12 written in the Book of *M* she is your wife.
2Mc 1:29 people in your holy place, as *M* promised."
2: 4 which *M* climbed to see God's inheritance.
2: 8 just as it appeared in the time of *M*
2:10 Just as *M* prayed to the Lord and fire

2:11 *M* had said, "Because it had not been eaten
7: 6 on us, as *M* declared in his canticle,
7:30 the law given to our forefathers through *M*.
Ps(s) 77:21 like a flock under the care of *M* and Aaron.
99: 6 *M* and Aaron were among his priests,
103: 7 He has made known his ways to *M*,
105:26 He sent *M* his servant;
106:16 They envied *M* in the camp,
106:23 he spoke of exterminating them, but *M*,
106:32 Meribah, and *M* fared ill on their account,
Sir 24:22 the law which *M* commanded us as an
45: 1 Dear to God and men, *M*,
45: 6 He raised up also, like *M* in holiness,
45:15 For *M* ordained him and anointed him with
46: 1 assistant to *M* in the prophetic office,
46: 7 and in *M*' lifetime showed himself loyal,
Is 63:11 they remembered the days of old and *M*,
63:12 glorious arm was the guide at *M*' right;
Jer 15: 1 Even if *M* and Samuel stood before me,
Bar 1:20 the curse which the Lord enjoined upon *M*,
2: 2 Jerusalem, as was written in the law of *M*:
2:28 was your warning through your servant *M*,
Dn 9:11 malediction, recorded in the law of *M*,
9:13 As it is written in the law of *M*,
13: 3 their daughter according to the law of *M*.
13:61 According to the law of *M*, they inflicted
Mi 6: 4 And I sent before you *M*,
Mal 3:22 Remember the law of *M* my servant,
Mt 8: 4 the priest and offer the gift *M* prescribed.
17: 3 Suddenly *M* and Elijah appeared to them
17: 4 three booths here, one for you, one for *M*,
19: 7 "Then why did *M* command divorce and the
19: 8 stubbornness *M* let you divorce your wives,"
22:24 "Teacher, *M* declared, 'If a man dies
23: 2 the Pharisees have succeeded *M* as teachers;
Mk 1:44 and offer for your cure what *M* prescribed.
7:10 *M* said, 'Honor your father
9: 4 Elijah appeared to them along with *M*;
9: 5 on this site, one for you, one for *M*,
10: 3 he said, "What command did *M* give you?"
10: 4 *M* permitted divorce and the writing of a
12:19 we were left this in writing by *M*:
12:26 dead, have you not read in the book of *M*,
Lk 2:22 to purify them according to the law of *M*,
5:14 Offer for your healing what *M* prescribed.
9:30 two men were talking with him *M* and Elijah.
9:33 up three booths, one for you, one for *M*,
16:29 answered, 'They have *M* and the prophets.
16:31 they do not listen to *M* and the prophets,
20:28 *M* prescribed that if a man's brother dies
20:37 *M* in the passage about the bush showed
24:27 then, with *M* and all the prophets,
24:44 written about me in the law of *M*
Jn 1:17 For while the law was given through *M*,
1:45 have found the one *M* spoke of in the law
3:14 as *M* lifted up the serpent in the desert,
5:45 you is *M* on whom you have set your hopes.
5:46 you believed *M* you would then believe me,
6:32 not *M* who gave you bread from the heavens;
7:19 *M* has given you the law, has he not?
7:22 *M* gave you circumcision (though it did not
7:22 originate with *M* but with the patriarchs).
8: 5 the law, *M* ordered such women to be stoned.
9:28 We are disciples of *M*.
9:29 We know that God spoke to *M*,
Acts 3:22 For *M* said: The LORD GOD will raise
6:11 him speaking blasphemies against *M* and God,
6:14 the customs which *M* handed down to us."
7:20 "It was at this time that *M* was born.
7:22 *M* was educated in all the lore of Egypt.
7:27 was wronging his neighbor pushed *M* aside.
7:29 On hearing this, *M* fled.
7:31 When *M* saw it, he marveled at the sight.
7:32 *M* began to tremble and dared look no more.
7:35 *M* whom they had rejected with the words,
7:37 *M* is the one who said to the Israelites,
7:40 *M* who brought us out of the land of Egypt,
7:44 as God prescribed it when he spoke to *M*,
13:38 never be acquitted of under the law of *M*.
15:21 for generations now *M* has been proclaimed
21:21 who live among the Gentiles to abandon *M*,
26:22 from what the prophets and *M* foretold:
28:23 to the law of *M* and the prophets.
Rom 5:14 I say, from Adam to *M* death reigned,
9:15 He says to *M*, "I will show mercy
10: 5 *M* writes of the justice that comes from
10:19 *M* says, "I will make you jealous of those
1Cor 9: 8 It is written in the law of *M*,
10: 2 the sea all of them were baptized into *M*.
2Cor 3: 7 the Israelites could not look on *M*' face
3:13 We are not like *M*,
3:15 when *M* is read a veil covers their
2Tm 3: 8 Just as Jannes and Jambres opposed *M*,
Heb 3: 2 *M*, too, "was faithful in all God's
3: 5 *M* "was faithful in all God's household"
3:16 Was it not all whom *M* had led out of Egypt?
7:14 which *M* said nothing about priests.
8: 5 and shadow of the heavenly one, for *M*,
9:19 When *M* had read all the commandments of
10:28 Anyone who rejects the law of *M* is put to
11:23 By faith *M*' parents hid him for three
11:24 By faith *M*, when he had grown up, refused
11:26 *M* considered the reproach borne by God's

12:21 so fearful was the spectacle that *M* said,
Jude 1: 9 a dispute over *M*' body
Rv 15: 3 God, and they sang the song of *M*,

MOSOCH (1)

Is 66:19 to Tarshish, Put and Lud, *M*,

MOST (211)

Gn 3: 1 Now the serpent was the *m* cunning of all
14:18 and wine, and being a priest of God *M* High,
14:19 "Blessed be Abram by God *M* High,
14:20 And blessed be God *M* High,
14:22 "I have sworn to the LORD, God *M* High,
35:17 When her pangs were *m* severe,
41:19 cows, scrawny, *m* ill-formed and gaunt.
Ex 23: 8 for a bribe blinds even the *m*
29:37 Then the altar will be *m* sacred,
30:10 This altar is *m* sacred to the LORD."
30:29 consecrated them, they shall be *m* sacred;
30:36 shall be treated as *m* sacred by you.
40:10 it, so that it will be *m* sacred.
Lv 2: 3 It is a *m* sacred oblation to the LORD.
2:10 It is a *m* sacred oblation to the LORD.
6:10 it is *m* sacred, like the sin offering
6:18 It is *m* sacred.
6:22 of the sin offering, since it is *m* sacred.
7: 1 for guilt offerings, which are *m* sacred.
7: 6 in a sacred place, since it is *m* sacred.
10:12 Since it is *m* sacred,
10:17 in the sacred place, since it is *m* sacred?
14:13 belongs to the priest and is *m* sacred.)
16:31 it shall be a *m* solemn sabbath for you,
21:10 "The *m* exalted of the priests,
21:22 is *m* sacred as well as of what is sacred.
24: 9 as something *m* sacred among the various
27:28 thus doomed becomes *m* sacred to the LORD.
Nm 4: 4 meeting tent concerns the *m* sacred objects.
4:19 when they approach the *m* sacred objects,
18: 9 share in the oblations that are *m* sacred,
18:10 them you shall treat them as *m* sacred;
24: 4 God says, and knows what the *M* High knows,
24:16 God says, and knows what the *M* High knows,
Dt 28:54 The *m* refined and fastidious man among you
28:56 The *m* refined and delicate woman among you,
32: 8 *M* High assigned the nations their heritage,
Jgs 6:15 the *m* insignificant in my father's house."
1Sm 2:10 The *M* High in heaven thunders;
2Sm 1:26 *m* dear have you been to me;
22:14 the *M* High gave forth his voice.
24:14 by the hand of God, for he is *m* merciful;
1Kgs 3: 4 because that was the *m* renowned high place.
19:14 "I have been *m* zealous for the LORD,
1Chr 4: 9 was the *m* distinguished of the brothers.
12:30 *m* of them had held their allegiance to the
17:17 on me as henceforth the *m* notable of men,
23:13 was set apart to be consecrated as *m* holy,
2Chr 31:14 and the *m* holy of the consecrated things.
Ezr 2:63 not to partake of the *m* holy foods
7:28 with all the *m* influential royal officials.
Neh 7: 2 trustworthy and God-fearing man than *m*.
7:65 not to partake of the *m* holy foods
Tb 1:13 the *M* High granted me favor and status
4:11 sight of the *M* High for all who give them.
Jdt 13:18 are you, daughter, by the *M* High God,
Est B: 5 that this *m* singular people is continually
E:15 laws and are the children of the *M* High,
1Mc 9:14 all the *m* stouthearted rallying to him,
13:37 We are willing to be on *m* peaceful terms
2Mc 1:36 but *m* people named it naphtha.
3: 2 the temple with the *m* magnificent gifts.
3:31 begged Onias to invoke the *M* High,
3:35 made *m* solemn vows to him
3:36 witness to the deeds of the *m* high God
7:20 *M* admirable and worthy of everlasting
8:32 of Timothy's forces, a *m* wicked man,
9:25 before entrusted and commended to *m* of you,
11: 9 not only men, but the *m* savage beasts,
11:12 *M* of those who got away were wounded and
Ps(s) 7:18 sing praise to the name of the LORD *M* High.
9: 3 I will sing praise to your name, *M* High,
18:14 heaven, the *M* High gave forth his voice;
21: 8 kindness of the *M* High he stands unshaken.
46: 5 of God, the holy dwelling of the *M* High.
47: 3 of gladness, For the LORD, the *M* High,
50:14 and fulfill your vows to the *M* High;
56: 3 O *M* High, when I begin to fear,
57: 3 I call to God the *M* High,
73:11 "Is there any knowledge in the *M* High?"
75: 6 Lift not up your horns against the *M* High;
77:11 the right hand of the *M* High is changed."
78:17 against the *M* High in the wasteland,
78:35 that God was their rock and the *M* High God,
78:56 and rebelled against God the *M* High,
82: 6 are gods, all of you sons of the *M* High;
83:19 the LORD, the *M* High over all the earth.
87: 5 who has established her is the *M* High LORD."
90:10 strong, And *m* of them are fruitless toil,
91: 1 You who dwell in the shelter of the *M* High,
91: 9 you have made the *M* High your stronghold.
92: 2 LORD, to sing praise to your name, *M* High,
92: 9 while you, O LORD, are the *M* High forever.
97: 9 O LORD, are the *M* High over all the earth,

MOST (cont.)
106: 7 rebelled against the *M* High at the Red Sea.
107:11 God and scorned the counsel of the *M* High.
Prv 30: 2 Why, I am the *m* stupid of men,
Sg 1: 8 you do not know, O *m* beautiful among women,
5: 9 from any other, O *m* beautiful among women?
6: 1 lover gone, O *m* beautiful among women?
Wis 5:15 and the thought of them is with the *M* High.
6: 3 by the Lord and sovereignty by the *M* High,
12: 4 land, whom you hated for deeds *m* odious
15:18 they worship the *m* loathsome beasts
Sir 4:10 Thus will you be like a son to the *M* High,
7: 9 the *M* High will accept my offerings."
7:15 farming, which was ordained by the *M* High.
12: 7 The *M* High himself hates sinners,
17:21 Turn again to the *M* High and away from sin,
17:22 nether world can glorify the *M* High
19:16 will you fulfill the law of the *M* High.
21:20 but the prudent man at the *m* smiles gently.
23:18 Of the *M* High he is not mindful,
23:23 she has disobeyed the law of the *M* High;
24: 2 assembly of the *M* High she opens her mouth,
24: 3 the mouth of the *M* High I came forth,
24:22 true of the book of the *M* High's covenant,
28: 7 your neighbor, of the *M* High's covenant,
29:11 of your treasure as the *M* High commands,
33:15 See now all the works of the *M* High:
34: 6 be a vision specially sent by the *M* High,
34:19 The *M* High approves not the gifts of the
35: 5 rises as a sweet odor before the *M* High.
35: 6 The just man's sacrifice is *m* pleasing,
35: 9 Give to the *M* High as he has given to you,
35:18 will it withdraw till the *M* High responds,
37:15 *M* important of all, pray to God
39: 1 to the study of the law of the *M* High!
39: 6 LORD, his Maker, to petition the *M* High,
41: 4 should you reject the will of the *M* High?
41: 8 men, who forsake the law of the *M* High.
42: 2 Of the law of the *M* High and his precepts,
42:18 The *M* High possesses all knowledge,
43: 2 what a wonderful work of the *M* High!
44: 2 abounding glory of the *M* High's portion,
44:20 He observed the precepts of the *M* High,
46: 5 He called upon the *M* High God when his
46: 5 And God *M* High gave answer to him in
47: 5 Since he called upon the *M* High God,
47: 8 every deed he offered thanks to God *M* High,
48:20 But they called upon the *M* High God and
49: 4 They abandoned the Law of the *M* High,
50:14 of the sacrifices for the *M* High,
50:15 a sweet-smelling odor to the *M* High God,
50:16 mightily as a reminder before the *M* High.
50:17 the ground In adoration before the *M* High,
50:21 from him the blessing of the *M* High.
Is 14:14 I will be like the *M* High!"
Jer 3:19 a heritage *m* beautiful among the nations!
Lam 3:35 rights in the very sight of the *M* High,
3:38 it proceeds from the mouth of the *M* High,
Ez 25: 6 rejoicing *m* maliciously in your heart over
26:17 gone from the seas, city *m* prized!
28: 7 you foreigners, the *m* barbarous of nations.
29:12 the land of Egypt the *m* desolate of lands,
29:12 the *m* deserted of cities for forty years;
30: 7 She shall be the *m* devastated of lands,
30: 7 her cities shall be the *m* desolate of all.
30:11 people with him, the *m* ruthless of nations,
31:12 Foreigners, the *m* ruthless of the nations,
32:12 all of them the *m* ruthless of the nations;
42:13 to the LORD shall eat the *m* sacred meals,
42:13 they shall keep the *m* sacred offerings:
43:12 area on the mountain top shall be *m* sacred.
44:13 my sacred things, or the *m* sacred things.
48:12 tract of land their own *m* sacred domain,
Dn 3:93 "Servants of the *m* high God, come out."
3:99 *m* high God has accomplished in my regard.
4:14 the *M* High rules over the kingdom of men:
4:21 the *M* High has passed upon my lord king:
4:22 until you know that the *M* High rules over
4:29 until you learn that the *M* High rules over
4:31 restored to me, and I blessed the *M* High,
5:18 The *M* High God gave your father
5:21 until he learned that the *M* High God rules
7:18 of the *M* High shall receive the kingship,
7:22 in favor of the holy ones of the *M* High,
7:25 *M* High and oppress the holy ones of the *M*
7:27 be given to the holy people of the *M* High,
9:24 ratified, and a *m* holy will be anointed.
13: 4 because he was the *m* respected of them all.
Am 2:16 And the *m* stouthearted of warriors shall
4: 3 breached walls each by the *m* direct way,
Mi 6: 6 before the LORD, and bow before God *m* high?
7: 4 a brier, the *m* upright like a thorn hedge.
Mt 11:20 where *m* of his miracles had been worked,
24:12 of evil, the love of *m* will grow cold.
Mk 5: 7 meddle with me, Jesus, Son of God *M* High?
9:34 been arguing about who was the *m* important.
Lk 1:32 and he will be called Son of the *M* High.
1:35 power of the *M* High will overshadow you;
1:76 shall be called prophet of the *M* High;
6:35 will rightly be called sons of the *M* High,
8:28 of his voice, "Jesus, Son of God *M* High,
Jn 17:11 O Father *m* holy, protect them with your
Acts 7:48 Yet the *M* High does not dwell in buildings
14: 4 *M* of the townspeople were divided over them,
16:17 "These men are servants of the *M* High God;
19:26 but throughout *m* of the province of Asia,
1Cor 7:21 be better off making the *m* of your slavery.
10: 5 that God was not pleased with *m* of them,
14:27 in tongues let it be at *m* two or three,
15: 6 at once, *m* of whom are still alive,
15:19 life only, we are the *m* pitiable of men.
2Cor 9: 2 Your zeal has stirred up *m* of them.
Gal 1:14 far beyond *m* of my contemporaries,
Eph 5:16 Make the *m* of the present opportunity,
Phil 1:14 *m* of my brothers in Christ,
Col 4: 5 make the *m* of every opportunity.
Heb 7: 1 king of Salem and priest of the *M* High God,

MOTH (6)
Jb 4:19 who are crushed more easily than the *m!*
13:28 like a garment that the *m* has consumed?
Prv 25:20 Like a *m* in clothing,
Is 50: 9 wear out like cloth, the *m* will eat them up.
Hos 5:12 I am like a *m* for Ephraim,
Lk 12:33 no thief comes near nor any *m* destroys.

MOTH-EATEN (1)
Jas 5: 2 rotted, your fine wardrobe has grown *m,*

MOTHER (283)
Gn 2:24 his father and *m* and clings to his wife,
3:20 because she became the *m* of all the living.
21:21 His *m* got a wife for him from the land of
24:53 gave costly presents to her brother and *m.*
24:55 Her brother and *m* replied,
24:67 solace after the death of his *m* Sarah.
27:11 a hairy man," said Jacob to his *m* Rebekah,
27:13 His *m,* however, replied: "Let any curse
27:14 and got them and brought them to his *m;*
28: 5 of Rebekah, the *m* of Jacob and Esau.
28: 7 his father and *m* and gone to Paddan-aram.
30:14 which he brought home to his *m* Leah.
37:10 "Can it be that I and your *m* and your
44:20 he is the only one by that *m* who is left,
48: 7 returning from Paddan, your *m* Rachel died,
Ex 2: 8 maiden went and called the child's own *m.*
20:12 "Honor your father and your *m,*
21:15 his father or *m* shall be put to death.
21:17 his father or *m* shall be put to death.
22:29 days the firstling may stay with its *m,*
Lv 18: 7 father by having intercourse with your *m.*
18: 7 Besides, since she is your own *m,*
19: 3 Revere your *m* and father,
20: 9 his father or *m* shall be put to death;
20: 9 since he has cursed his father or *m,*
20:14 If a man marries a woman and her *m* also,
21: 2 for his nearest relatives, his *m* or father,
21:11 Not even for his father or *m* may he thus
22:27 it shall remain with its *m* for seven days;
24:10 a man born of an Israelite *m* (Shelomith,
Nm 6: 7 Not even for his father or *m,*
Dt 5:16 'Honor your father and your *m,*
21:13 mourned her father and her *m* for a full month,
21:18 who will not listen to his father or *m,*
21:19 his father and *m* shall have him
22: 6 ground, and the *m* bird is sitting on them,
22: 6 take away the *m* bird along with her brood;
22:15 the father and the *m* of the girl shall
27:16 be he who dishonors his father or his *m!*'
Jos 2:13 that you are to spare my father and *m,*
2:18 and gather your father and *m,*
6:23 and brought out Rahab, with her father, *m,*
Jgs 5: 7 Deborah, rose, when I rose, a *m* in Israel,
5:28 peered down and wailed the *m* of Sisera,
14: 2 On his return he told his father and *m,*
14: 3 His father and *m* said to him,
14: 4 Now his father and *m* did not know that
14: 5 went down to Timnah with his father and *m.*
14: 7 to his father or *m* what he had done.
14: 9 When he came to his father and *m,*
14:16 have not told it even to my father or my *m,*
17: 2 He said to his *m,*
17: 3 eleven hundred shekels of silver to his *m,*
17: 4 Then his *m* said, "May the LORD bless
Ru 2:11 and your *m* and the land of your birth,
4:15 his *m* is the daughter-in-law who loves you.
1Sm 1:25 Hannah, his *m,* approached Eli and said:
2: 5 seven sons, while the *m* of many languishes.
2:19 *m* used to make a little garment for him,
15:33 so shall your *m* be childless among women."
22: 3 Moab, "Let my father and *m* stay with you,
2Sm 17:25 of Jesse and sister of Joab's *m* Zeruiah.
19:38 own city by the tomb of his father and *m.*
20:19 to beat down a city that is a *m* in Israel.
1Kgs 1: 6 and next in age to Absalom by the same *m.*
1:11 Then Nathan said to Bathsheba, Solomon's *m:*
2:13 went to Bathsheba, the *m* of Solomon.
2:19 and a throne was provided for the king's *m,*
2:20 "Ask it, my *m,*" the king said to her,
2:22 King Solomon answered his *m.*
3:27 By no means kill it, for she is the *m.*"
11:26 Ephraimite from Zeredah with a widowed *m,*
14:21 His *m* was the Ammonite named Naamah.
14:31 His *m* was the Ammonite named Naamah.
15:13 Maacah from her position as queen *m,*
17:23 from the upper room and gave him to his *m.*
19:20 let me kiss my father and *m* goodbye,
22:53 the LORD, behaving like his father, his *m,*
2Kgs 3: 2 though not as much as his father and *m.*
3:13 your father and to the prophets of your *m.*"
4:19 "Carry him to his *m.*"
4:20 picked him up and carried him to his *m;*
4:21 The *m* took him upstairs and laid him on
4:30 But the boy's *m* cried out:
9:22 and witchcrafts of your *m* Jezebel continue?"
10:13 the princes and the family of the queen *m.*"
11: 1 Athaliah, the *m* of Ahaziah,
12: 2 His *m,* who was named Zibiah,
14: 2 His *m,* whose name was Jehoaddin,
15: 2 His *m,* whose name was Jecholiah,
23:31 His *m,* Whose name was Hamutal,
24:12 king of Judah, together with his *m,*
24:15 to Babylon the king's *m* and wives,
1Chr 2:26 Atarah by name, who was the *m* of Onam.
4: 9 His *m* had named him Jabez,
2Chr 12:13 Rehoboam's *m* was named Naamah,
13: 2 His *m* was named Michaiah,
15:16 *m* of King Asa, he deposed as queen *m*
20:31 His *m* was named Azubah,
22: 2 His *m* was named Athaliah,
22: 3 his *m* counseled him to act sinfully.
22:10 When Athaliah, *m* of Ahaziah,
24: 1 His *m,* named Zibiah, was from Beer-sheba.
25: 1 His *m,* named Jehoaddan,
26: 3 His *m,* named Jecoliah, was from Jerusalem.
27: 1 His *m* was named Jerusa, daughter of Zadok.
29: 1 His *m* was named Abia,
Tb 1: 8 of Deborah, the *m* of my father Tobiel;
4: 3 Honor your *m,* and do not abandon her
4:13 for worthlessness is the *m* of famine.
5:17 journey, Tobiah kissed his father and *m.*
5:18 But his *m* began to weep.
6:15 *m* down to their grave in sorrow over me.
7:13 her *m* and told her to bring a scroll,
7:13 Her *m* brought the scroll,
8:21 I am your father, and Edna is your *m;*
9: 6 your wife, and to your wife's father and *m.*
10: 7 for I know that my father and *m* do not
10:13 From now on I am your *m,*
11:17 Blessed are your father and your *m.*
14:10 The day you bury your *m* next to me,
14:12 When Tobiah's *m* died, he buried her next
Est 2: 7 for she had lost both father and *m.*
2: 7 On the death of her father and *m,*
1Mc 13:28 his father and his *m* and his four brothers.
2Mc 7: 1 seven brothers with their *m* were arrested
7: 4 rest of his brothers and his *m* looked on.
7: 5 *m* encouraged one another to die bravely,
7:20 of everlasting remembrance was the *m,*
7:25 to him at all, the king appealed to the *m,*
7:41 The *m* was last to die after her sons.
Jb 17:14 and the maggot "my *m*" and "my sister,"
Ps(s) 27:10 Though my father and *m* forsake me,
35:14 like one bewailing a *m,*
51: 7 was I born, and in sin my *m* conceived me;
113: 9 barren wife as the joyful *m* of children.
Prv 4: 3 child, frail, yet the darling of my *m,*
10: 1 but a foolish son is a grief to his *m.*
15:20 glad, but a fool of a man despises his *m.*
19:26 mistreats his father, or drives away his *m,*
20:20 If one curses his father or *m,*
23:22 and despise not your *m* when she is old.
23:25 Let your father and *m* have joy;
28:24 defrauds father or *m* and calls it no sin,
29:15 a boy left to his whims disgraces his *m.*
30:11 curses its father, and blesses not its *m.*
30:17 that mocks a father, or scorns an aged *m,*
31: 1 The advice which his *m* gave him:
Sg 3: 4 I should bring him to the home of my *m,*
3:11 crown with which his *m* has crowned him
8: 2 lead you, bring you in to the home of my *m.*
8: 5 it was there that your *m* conceived you,
Wis 7:12 I had not known that she is the *m* of these.
Sir 3: 4 he stores up riches who reveres his *m.*
3: 6 obeys the LORD who brings comfort to his *m.*
3:16 of his Creator, he who angers his *m.*
4:10 and help their *m* as a husband would;
4:10 and he will be more tender to you than a *m.*
23:14 *m* in mind when you sit among the mighty,
40: 1 day he returns to the *m* of all the living,
41:15 father and *m* be ashamed of immorality,
Is 8: 4 knows how to call his father or *m* by name,
49:15 Can a *m* forget her infant,
50: 1 of divorce with which I dismissed your *m?*
50: 1 for your crimes that your *m* was dismissed.
66: 9 Shall I bring a *m* to the point of birth,
66:13 As a *m* comforts her son,
Jer 4:31 the anguish of a *m* with her first child
13:18 Say to the king and to the queen *m:*
15: 8 the *m* of youths the spoiler at midday;
15: 9 The *m* of seven swoons away,
15:10 Woe to me, *m,* that you gave me birth!
16: 7 to drink over the death of father or *m.*
20:14 day my *m* gave me birth never be blessed!
20:17 Then my *m* would have been my grave,
22:26 cast you out, you and the *m* who bore you,
29: 2 was after King Jeconiah and the queen *m,*

50:12 Your *m* shall be sorely put to shame,
Ez 16: 3 father was an Amorite and your *m* a Hittite.
16:44 fond of proverbs will say of you, 'Like *m*,
16:45 the *m* who spurned her husband and children,
16:45 *m* was a Hittite and your father an Amorite.
19: 2 What a lioness was your *m*,
19:10 *m* was like a vine planted by the water;
22: 7 Within you, father and *m* are despised;
23: 2 were two women, daughters of the same *m*,
44:25 dead person, unless it be their father, *m*,
Hos 2: 4 Protest against your *m*, protest!
2: 7 Yes, their *m* has played the harlot;
4: 5 I will destroy your *m*.
Mi 7: 6 the daughter rises up against her *m*,
Zec 13: 3 prophesies, his parents, father and *m*,
13: 3 he prophesies, his parents, father and *m*,
Mt 1: 3 of Perez and Zerah, whose *m* was Tamar.
1: 5 was the father of Boaz, whose *m* was Rahab,
1: 5 was the father of Obed, whose *m* was Ruth.
1: 6 whose *m* had been the wife of Uriah.
1:18 When his *m* Mary was engaged to Joseph,
2:11 the house, found the child with Mary his *m*.
2:13 "Get up, take the child and his *m*,
2:14 and his *m* and left that night for Egypt.
2:20 "Get up, take the child and his *m*,
2:21 He got up, took the child and his *m*,
10:35 with his father, a daughter with her *m*,
10:37 Whoever loves father or *m*,
12:46 his *m* and his brothers appeared outside
12:47 "Your *m* and your brothers are standing
12:48 to the one who had told him, "Who is my *m*?
12:50 he said, "There are my *m* and my brothers.
12:50 Father is brother and sister and *m* to me."
13:55 Isn't Mary known to be his *m* and James,
14: 8 Prompted by her *m* she said,
14:11 given to the girl, who took it to her *m*.
15: 4 has said, 'Honor your father and your *m*,'
15: 4 curses father or *m* shall be put to death.'
15: 5 'Whoever says to his father or his *m*,
15: 6 to God, need not honor his father or his *m*.'
19: 5 his father and *m* and cling to his wife,
19:19 'Honor your father and your *m*';
19:29 up home, brothers or sisters, father or *m*,
20:20 The *m* of Zebedee's sons came up to him
23:37 a *m* bird gathers her young under her wings,
27:56 *m* of James and Joseph, and the mother of
Mk 3:31 His *m* and his brothers arrived,
3:32 "Your *m* and your brothers and sisters are
3:33 in reply, "Who are my *m* and my brothers?"
3:34 "These are my *m* and my brothers.
3:35 of God is brother and sister and *m* to me."
5:40 Jesus took the child's father and *m* and
6:24 She went out and said to her *m*,
6:24 The *m* answered, "The head of John
6:28 to the girl, and the girl gave it to her *m*.
7:10 Moses said, 'Honor your father and your *m*';
7:10 curses father or *m* shall be put to death.'
7:11 'If a person says to his father or *m*,
7:12 him to do nothing more for his father or *m*.
10: 7 and *m* and the two shall become as one.
10:19 Honor your father and your *m*.'"
10:29 up home, brothers or sisters, *m* or father,
15:40 Mary the *m* of James the younger and Joses,
15:47 *m* of Joses observed where he had been laid.
16: 1 over, Mary Magdalene, Mary the *m* of James,
Lk 1:43 I that the *m* of my Lord should come to me?
1:60 At this his *m* intervened,
2:33 The child's father and *m* were marveling at
2:34 Simeon blessed them and said to Mary his *m*:
2:48 were astonished, and his *m* said to him:
2:51 His *m* meanwhile kept all these things in
7:12 carried out, the only son of a widowed *m*.
7:15 Then Jesus gave him back to his *m*.
8:19 His *m* and brothers came to be with him,
8:20 "Your *m* and your brothers are standing
8:21 "My *m* and my brothers are those who hear
12:53 *m* against daughter and daughter against *m*,
13:34 *m* bird collects her young under her wings,
14:26 turning his back on his father and *m*,
18:20 Honor your father and your *m*.'"
24:10 Magdala, Joanna, and Mary the *m* of James.
Jn 2: 1 in Galilee, and the *m* of Jesus was there.
2: 3 the wine ran out, and Jesus' *m* told him,
2: 5 His *m* instructed those waiting on table,
2:12 along with his *m* and brothers [and his
6:42 Do we not know his father and *m*?
19:25 Near the cross of Jesus there stood his *m*,
19:26 *m* there with the disciple whom he loved,
19:26 whom he loved, Jesus said to his *m*,
19:27 he said to the disciple, "There is your *m*."
Acts 1:14 in their company, and Mary the *m* of Jesus,
12:12 Mary the *m* of John (also known as Mark),
16: 1 Timothy, whose *m* was Jewish and a believer,
Rom 16:13 a chosen servant of the Lord, and to his *m*,
16:13 his mother, who has been a *m* to me as well.
Gal 4:26 is freeborn, and it is she who is our *m*.
4:31 of a slave girl but of a *m* who is free.
Eph 5:31 reason a man shall leave his father and *m*,
6: 2 "Honor your father and *m*" is the first
1Thes 2: 7 as any nursing *m* fondling her little ones.
2Tm 1: 5 your grandmother Lois and to your *m* Eunice,
Heb 7: 3 Without father, *m* or ancestry,
Rv 17: 5 "Babylon the great, *m* of harlots and all

MOTHER-IN-LAW (19)

Dt 27:23 'Cursed be he who has relations with his *m*!'
Ru 1:14 and Orpah kissed her *m* good-bye,
2:11 done for your *m* after your husband's death;
2:18 she took into the city and showed to her *m*.
2:19 So her *m* said to her,
2:19 she told her *m* with whom she had worked.
3: 1 When she was back with her *m*,
3: 6 and did just as her *m* had instructed her.
3:16 Ruth went home to her *m*,
3:17 wish me to come back to my *m* empty-handed!"
Tb 10:12 honor your father-in-law and your *m*,
14:13 care of his aging father-in-law and *m*;
Mi 7: 6 mother, The daughter-in-law against her *m*,
Mt 8:14 and found Peter's *m* in bed with a fever.
10:35 her mother, a daughter-in-law with her *m*:
Mk 1:30 Simon's *m* lay ill with a fever,
Lk 4:38 *m* was in the grip of a severe fever,
12:53 against mother, *m* against daughter-in-law,
12:53 daughter-in-law, daughter-in-law against *m*."

MOTHER-OF-PEARL (1)

Est 1: 6 pavement, which was of porphyry, marble, *m*,

MOTHERLIKE (1)

Sir 15: 2 *M* she will meet him, like a young bride

MOTHERS—MOTHER'S (77)

Gn 20:12 but only my father's daughter, not my *m*;
24:28 ran off and told her *m* household about it.
27:29 and may your *m* sons bow down to you.
28: 2 to the home of your *m* father Bethuel,
32:12 strike me down and slay the *m* and children.
Ex 23:19 "You shall not boil a kid in its *m* milk.
34:26 "You shall not boil a kid in its *m* milk."
Lv 18: 9 your father's daughter or your *m* daughter,
18:13 your *m* sister, since she is your *m* relative.
20:19 with your *m* sister or your father's sister;
Nm 12:12 its *m* womb with its flesh half consumed."
Dt 14:21 "You shall not boil a kid in its *m* milk.
Jgs 8:19 "They were my brothers, my *m* sons,"
9: 1 went to his *m* kinsmen in Shechem,
9: 1 whole clan to which his *m* family belonged,
9: 3 When his *m* kin repeated these words to
16:17 been consecrated to God from my *m* womb.
Ru 1: 8 "Go back, each of you, to your *m* house!
1Sm 20:30 and to the disclosure of your *m* shame,
1Kgs 15: 2 His *m* name was Maacah,
22:42 His *m* name was Azubah, daughter of Shilhi.
2Kgs 8:26 His *m* name was Athaliah;
15:33 His *m* name was Jerusha, daughter of Zadok.
18: 2 His *m* name was Abi, daughter of Zechariah.
21: 1 His *m* name was Hephzibah.
21:19 His *m* name was Meshullemeth,
22: 1 His *m* name was Jedidah,
23:36 His *m* name was Zebidah,
24: 8 His *m* name was Nehushta,
24:18 His *m* name was Hamutal,
Jdt 8:26 tending the flocks of Laban, his *m* brother.
16:12 the supposed sons of rebel *m* cut them down;
Jb 1:21 said, "Naked I came forth from my *m* womb,
31:18 guiding me even from my *m* womb
Ps(s) 22:10 first formed, my security at my *m* breast.
22:11 at birth, From my *m* womb you are my God.
50:20 against your *m* son you spread rumors.
69: 9 to my brothers, a stranger to my *m* sons,
71: 6 from my *m* womb you are my strength;
109:14 let not his *m* sin be blotted out;
131: 2 Like a weaned child on its *m* lap,
139:13 you knit me in my *m* womb.
Prv 1: 8 and reject not your *m* teaching;
6:20 bidding, and reject not your *m* teaching;
Eccl 5:14 As he came forth from his *m* womb,
11: 5 fashions the human frame in the *m* womb,
Sg 6: 9 is my dove, my perfect one, her *m* chosen,
8: 1 were my brother, nursed at my *m* breasts!
Wis 7: 1 And in my *m* womb I was molded into flesh
Sir 3: 2 a *m* authority he confirms over her sons.
3: 9 but a *m* curse uproots the growing plant.
3:11 disgrace for her children, a *m* shame.
7:27 your *m* birthpangs forget not.
40: 1 From the day one leaves his *m* womb to the
46:13 to his Maker, dedicated from his *m* womb,
50:22 Who fosters men's growth from their *m* womb,
Is 49: 1 from my *m* womb he gave me my name.
Jer 6:24 hold of us, throes like a *m* in childbirth.
16: 3 this place, the *m* who will give them birth,
17:11 A partridge that *m* a brood not her own is
31: 8 in their midst, The *m* and those with child;
50:43 seizes him, throes like a *m* in childbirth.
52: 1 His *m* name was Hamutal,
Lam 2:12 They ask their *m*, "Where is the cereal?"
2:12 And breathe their last in their *m*' arms.
5: 3 widowed are our *m*.
Hos 10:14 time of war, smashing *m* and their children.
14: 1 their expectant *m* shall be ripped open.
Am 1:13 they ripped open expectant *m* in Gilead,
Mt 24:19 on pregnant or nursing *m* in those days.
Mk 10:30 as many homes, brothers and sisters, *m*,
Lk 1:15 with the Holy Spirit from his *m* womb.
Jn 3: 4 to his *m* womb and be born over again?"
19:25 Jesus there stood his mother, his *m* sister,
1Tm 1: 9 godless, men who kill their fathers or *m*,
5: 2 younger men as brothers, older women as *m*,

MOTHS (4)

Sir 42:13 For just as *m* come from garments,
Is 51: 8 They shall be like a garment eaten by *m*,
Mt 6:19 *M* and rust corrode;
6:20 which neither *m* nor rust corrode nor

MOTION (1)

Wis 7:24 For Wisdom is mobile beyond all *m*,

MOTIONED (4)

Acts 12:17 He *m* to them to be quiet,
13:16 So Paul arose, *m* to them for silence,
19:33 He *m* for silence,
21:40 on the steps and *m* the people to silence.

MOTIONLESS (3)

Jos 3:17 *m* on dry ground in the bed of the Jordan
4: 3 where the priests have been standing *m*.
Ezr 9: 4 I remained *m* until the evening sacrifice.

MOTIONS (1)

2Mc 7:26 went through the *m* of persuading her son.

MOTIVATION (1)

2Cor 2:17 We speak in Christ's name, pure in *m*,

MOTIVES (5)

1Cor 15:32 those beasts at Ephesus for purely human *m*,
Phil 1:15 preach Christ from *m* of envy and rivalry,
1:17 from pure *m* but as an intrigue against me,
1:18 whether from specious *m* or genuine ones,
1Thes 2: 3 deceit or impure *m* or any sort of trickery;

MOTLEY (2)

Jdt 1:16 with all his numerous, *m* horde of warriors;
Jer 50:37 A sword upon her *m* throng,

MOTTLED (2)

Gn 31:10 that were streaked, speckled and *m*.
31:12 they mate, are streaked, speckled and *m*,

MOUND (17)

Gn 31:46 a *m*; and they had a meal there at the *m*.
31:48 "This *m*," said Laban, "shall be a witness
31:51 "Here is this *m*, and here is the memorial
31:52 This *m* shall be witness,
31:52 I pass beyond this *m* into your territory,
Ex 15: 8 up, the flowing waters stood like a *m*,
Jos 8:28 reducing it to an everlasting *m* of ruins,
1Sm 20:19 other occasion and wait near the *m* there.
20:41 David rose from beside the *m* and
2Sm 18:17 large *m* of stones was erected over him.
20:15 They threw up a *m* against the city,
Jb 21:33 and over him the funeral *m* keeps watch,
Ps(s) 78:13 and he made the waters stand as in a *m*.
Sir 21: 8 is collecting stones for his funeral *m*.
Jer 6: 6 throw up a siege *m* against Jerusalem.
49: 2 She shall become a *m* of ruins,

MOUNDS (2)

Jb 13:12 maxims, your fabrications are *m* of clay.
27:16 like dust and store away *m* of clothing,

MOUNT (174)

Gn 31:25 also pitched his tents there, on *M* Gilead.
Ex 19:11 *M* Sinai before the eyes of all the people.
19:18 *M* Sinai was all wrapped in smoke,
19:20 the LORD came down to the top of *M* Sinai,
19:23 LORD, "The people cannot go up to *M* Sinai,
24:16 The glory of the LORD settled upon *M* Sinai.
28:17 you shall *m* four rows of precious stones:
31:18 had finished speaking to Moses on *M* Sinai,
33: 6 So, from *M* Horeb onward,
34: 2 when you are to go up *M* Sinai and there
34: 4 up *M* Sinai as the LORD had commanded him,
34:29 As Moses came down from *M* Sinai with the
34:32 all that the LORD had told him on *M* Sinai.
Lv 7:38 the LORD enjoined on Moses at *M* Sinai
25: 1 The LORD said to Moses on *M* Sinai,
26:46 LORD had Moses promulgate on *M* Sinai
27:34 gave Moses on *M* Sinai for the Israelites.
Nm 3: 1 that the LORD spoke to Moses on *M* Sinai.
20:22 whole Israelite community came to *M* Hor.
20:23 *M* Hor, on the border of the land of Edom,
20:25 his son Eleazar and bring them up on *M* Hor.
20:27 *M* Hor in view of the whole community,
21: 4 *M* Hor they set out on the Red Sea road,
21: 8 Moses, "Make a saraph and *m* it on a pole,
28: 6 holocaust that was offered at *M* Sinai
33:23 from Kehelathah, they camped at *M* Shepher.
33:24 Setting out from *M* Shepher,
33:32 from Bene-jaakan, they camped at *M* Gidgad.
33:33 Setting out from *M* Gidgad,

MOUNT (cont.)

33:37 at *M* Hor on the border of the land of Edom.
33:38 ascended *M* Hor at the LORD's command,
33:39 years old when he died on *M* Hor.
33:41 Setting out from *M* Hor,—They camped
34: 7 Great Sea you shall draw a line to *M* Hor,
34: 8 from *M* Hor to Labo in the land of Hamath,
Dt 3: 8 from the Wadi Arnon to *M* Hermon
4:48 on the edge of the Wadi Arnon to *M* Sion
11:29 on Mount Gerizim, the curse on *M* Ebal.
27: 4 besides setting up on *M* Ebal these stones
27:12 Benjamin shall stand on *M* Gerizim
27:13 shall stand on *M* Ebal to pronounce curses.
28:13 you will always *m* higher and not decline,
32:49 the LORD said to Moses, "Go up on *M* Nebo,
32:50 on *M* Hor and there was taken to his people;
33: 2 *M* Paran and advanced from Meribath-kadesh.
34: 1 went up from the plains of Moab to *M* Nebo,
Jos 8:30 to the LORD, the God of Israel, on *M* Ebal,
8:33 were facing *M* Gerizim and half Mount Ebal,
11:17 from *M* Halak that rises toward Seir as far
11:17 the Lebanon valley at the foot of *M* Hermon.
12: 1 Jordan, from the River Arnon to *M* Hermon,
12: 5 He ruled over *M* Hermon,
12: 7 valley to *M* Halak which rises toward Seir,
13: 5 of *M* Hermon to Labo in the land of Hamath.
13:11 Geshurites and Maacathites, all *M* Hermon,
15: 9 extended to the cities of *M* Ephron,
15:10 the boundary curved westward to *M* Seir
15:10 north of the ridge of *M* Jearim
15:11 through Shikkeron, and across to *M* Baalah,
24:30 region of Ephraim north of *M* Gaash.
Jgs 2: 9 region of Ephraim north of *M* Gaash.
4: 6 "go, march on *M* Tabor,
4:12 son of Abinoam, had gone up to *M* Tabor.
4:14 So Barak went down *M* Tabor,
9: 7 him, Jotham went to the top of *M* Gerizim,
9:48 he went up *M* Zalmon with all his soldiers,
1Sm 31: 1 and falling mortally wounded on *M* Gilboa,
31: 8 Saul and his three sons lying on *M* Gilboa.
2Sm 1: 6 *M* Gilboa and saw Saul leaning on his spear,
15:17 opposite the ascent of the *M* of Olives,
15:23 on ahead of him by way of the *M* of Olives,
15:30 As David went up the *M* of Olives,
24: 6 Gilead and to the district below *M* Hermon.
1Kgs 1:33 *M* my son Solomon upon my own mule and
12:18 to *m* his chariot to flee to Jerusalem,
18:19 Now summon all Israel to me on *M* Carmel,
18:20 and had the prophets assemble on *M* Carmel.
20:33 out to him, the king had him *m* his chariot.
2Kgs 2:25 From there he went to *M* Carmel,
4:25 she reached the man of God on *M* Carmel.
19:31 shall come a remnant, and from *M* Zion,
23:13 of Jerusalem, south of the *M* of Misconduct,
1Chr 4:42 to *M* Seir under the leadership of Pelatiah,
5:23 as far as Baal-hermon, Senir, and *M* Hermon.
10: 1 a number of them fell, slain on *M* Gilboa.
10: 8 his sons where they had fallen on *M* Gilboa.
2Chr 3: 1 house of the LORD in Jerusalem on *M* Moriah,
10:18 to *m* his chariot and flee to Jerusalem.
13: 4 Abijah stood on *M* Zemariam,
20:10 and those of *M* Seir whom you did not allow
20:22 of *M* Seir who were coming against Judah,
20:23 of *M* Seir and completely exterminated them.
33:15 the *m* of the LORD's house and in Jerusalem,
Neh 2:12 and with no other animals but my own *m*.
2:14 room here for my *m* to pass with me astride,
9:13 On *M* Sinai you came down,
12:31 I had the princes of Judah *m* the wall,
Jdt 9:13 your covenant, your holy temple, *M* Zion,
1Mc 4:37 army assembled, and went up to *M* Zion.
4:60 high walls and strong towers around *M* Zion,
5:54 They ascended *M* Zion in joy and gladness
6:48 established camps in Judea and at *M* Zion.
6:62 *M* Zion and saw how the place was fortified,
7:33 After this, Nicanor went up to *M* Zion.
10:11 build the walls and encircle *M* Zion
14:26 which they affixed to pillars on *M* Zion.
16:20 to seize Jerusalem and the *m* of the temple.
2Mc 5:23 the man who appointed him; at *M* Gerizim,
6: 2 that on *M* Gerizim to Zeus the Hospitable,
Jb 20: 6 Though his pride *m* up to the heavens and
Ps(s) 42: 7 of the Jordan and of Hermon, from *M* Mizar.
48: 3 *M* Zion, "the recesses of the North,"
48:12 let *M* Zion be glad,
74: 2 *M* Zion, where you took up
78:68 the tribe of Judah, *M* Zion which he loved.
125: 1 They who trust in the LORD are like *M* Zion,
Sir 24:13 raised aloft, like a cypress on *M* Hermon,
Is 4: 5 of *M* Zion and over her place of assembly,
8:18 the LORD of hosts who dwells on *M* Zion.
10:12 all his work on *M* Zion and in Jerusalem,
10:32 shake his fist at the *m* of daughter Zion,
14:13 I will take my seat on the *M* of Assembly,
16: 1 the desert, to the *m* of daughter Zion.
18: 7 to *M* Zion where dwells the name of the
24:23 will reign on *M* Zion and in Jerusalem,
28:21 For the LORD shall rise up as on *M* Perazim,
37:32 shall come a remnant, and from *M* Zion,
Jer 4:15 from *M* Ephraim they announce destruction:
26:18 of ruins, and the temple *m* a forest ridge.
31: 6 the watchmen will call out on *M* Ephraim:
31:12 Shouting, they shall *m* the heights of Zion,
46: 4 Harness the horses, *m*, charioteers!
50:19 and Bashan, And on *M* Ephraim and Gilead,
Lam 5:18 That *M* Zion should be desolate,
Ez 35: 2 Son of man, set your face against *M* Seir,
35: 3 I am coming at you, *M* Seir.
35: 7 I will make *M* Seir a desolate waste,
35:15 A waste shall you be, *M* Seir,
Hos 14: 4 save us, nor shall we have horses to *m*;
Jl 3: 5 For on *M* Zion there shall be a remnant,
Am 6: 1 to the overconfident on the *m* of Samaria,
Ob 1: 8 Edom, and understanding from the *m* of Esau?
1: 9 crushed, till all on *M* Esau are destroyed.
1:17 on *M* Zion there shall be a portion saved;
1:19 They shall occupy the Negeb, the *m* of Esau,
1:21 ascend *M* Zion to rule the mount of Esau,
Mi 3:12 And the *m* of the temple to a forest ridge.
4: 1 In days to come the *m* of the LORD's house
4: 2 "Come, let us climb the *m* of the LORD,
4: 7 the LORD shall be king over them on *M* Zion,
Hb 3: 3 from Teman, the Holy One from *M* Paran.
Zec 14: 4 his feet shall rest upon the *M* of Olives,
14: 4 The *M* of Olives shall be cleft in two from
Mt 21: 1 entering Bethphage on the *M* of Olives,
24: 3 While he was seated on the *M* of Olives,
26:30 praise, they walked out to the *M* of olives.
Mk 11: 1 Bethphage and Bethany on the *M* of Olives,
13: 3 on the *M* of Olives facing the temple,
14:26 praise, they walked out to the *M* of Olives.
Lk 19:29 and Bethany on the *m* called Olivet,
19:35 laying their cloaks on it, helped him *m*.
19:37 his approach to the descent from *M* Olivet,
21:37 city to spend the night on the *M* of Olives.
22:39 way, as was his custom, to the *M* of Olives;
Jn 8: 1 while Jesus went out to the *M* of Olives.
Acts 1:12 from the *m* called Olivet near Jerusalem
7:30 appeared to him in the desert near *M* Sinai
7:38 the angel on *M* Sinai and with our fathers;
Gal 4:24 One is from *M* Sinai, and brought forth
Heb 12:22 to *M* Zion and the city of the living God,
Rv 14: 1 He was standing on *M* Zion,

MOUNTAIN (247)

Gn 22:14 now say, "On the *m* the LORD will see."
31:54 He then offered a sacrifice on the *m* and
31:54 had eaten, they passed the night on the *m*.
Ex 3: 1 the desert, he came to Horeb, the *m* of God.
3:12 Egypt, you will worship God on this very *m*."
4:27 he went, and when they met at the *m* of God,
15:17 planted them on the *m* of your inheritance
18: 5 where he was encamped near the *m* of God,
19: 2 Israel was encamped here in front of the *m*,
19: 3 the mountain, Moses went up the *m* to God.
19:12 Set limits for the people all around the *m*,
19:12 Take care not to go up the *m*,
19:12 If anyone touches the *m*, he must be put
19:13 horn resounds may they go up to the *m*."
19:14 Then Moses came down from the *m* to the
19:16 lightning, and a heavy cloud over the *m*,
19:17 stationed themselves at the foot of the *m*.
19:18 and the whole *m* trembled violently.
19:20 he summoned Moses to the top of the *m*,
19:23 set limits around the *m* to make it sacred."
20:18 the trumpet blast and the *m* smoking,
24: 4 he erected at the foot of the *m* an altar
24:12 to Moses, "Come up to me on the *m* and,
24:13 his aide, and went up to the *m* of God.
24:15 Moses had gone up, a cloud covered the *m*.
24:18 midst of the cloud as he went up on the *m*;
25:40 to the pattern shown you on the *m*.
26:30 to the pattern shown you on the *m*.
27: 8 box, just as it was shown you on the *m*.
32: 1 of Moses' delay in coming down from the *m*,
32:15 Moses then turned and came down the *m* with
32:19 down and broke them on the base of the *m*.
34: 2 present yourself to me on the top of the *m*.
34: 3 is even to be seen on any part of the *m*;
34: 3 herds are not to go grazing toward this *m*."
Nm 10:33 They moved on from the *m* of the LORD,
20:28 Then Aaron died there on top of the *m*.
20:28 Moses and Eleazar came down from the *m*,
Dt 1: 6 'You have stayed long enough at this *m*.
4:11 came near and stood at the foot of the *m*,
5: 4 face on the *m* from the midst of the fire.
5: 5 of the fire and would not go up the *m*,
5:22 voice to your entire assembly on the *m*
5:23 darkness, while the *m* was ablaze with fire,
9: 9 when I had gone up the *m* to receive the
9: 9 Meanwhile I stayed on the *m* forty days and
9:10 LORD spoke to you on the *m*
9:15 come down again from the blazing, fiery *m*,
10: 1 then come up the *m* to me.
10: 3 and went up the *m* carrying the two tablets.
10: 4 which he spoke to you on the *m*
10: 5 them to me, I turned and came down the *m*,
10:10 forty days and forty nights on the *m*,
14: 5 ibex, the addax, the oryx, and the *m* sheep.
32:50 you shall die on the *m* you have climbed,
Jos 9: 1 in the *m* regions and in the foothills,
10: 6 *m* country have joined forces against us."
10:40 the *m* regions, the Negeb, the foothills,
10:40 the Negeb, the foothills, and the *m* slopes,
11: 2 to the northern kings in the *m* regions
11: 3 Perizzites and Jebusites in the *m* regions,
11:16 the *m* regions,
11:16 as the *m* regions and foothills of Israel,
11:21 At that time Joshua penetrated the *m*
11:21 Debir, Anab, the entire *m* region of Judah,
11:21 Judah, and the entire *m* region of Israel.
12: 8 It included the *m* regions and foothills,
13: 6 the Sidonian inhabitants of the *m* regions
14:12 this *m* region which the LORD promised me
15: 8 the boundary rose to the top of the *m*
15: 9 From the top of the *m* it ran to the
15:48 In the *m* regions: Shamir, Jattir,
17:15 the *m* regions of Ephraim are so narrow."
17:16 "Our *m* regions are not enough for us;
17:18 for the *m* region which is now forest shall
18:16 *m* on the north of the Valley of Rephaim,
19:50 Timnah-serah in the *m* region of Ephraim.
20: 7 in Galilee in the *m* region of Naphtali,
20: 7 Shechem in the *m* region of Ephraim,
20: 7 (that is, Hebron) in the *m* region of Judah.
21:11 that is, Hebron, in the *m* region of Judah,
21:21 at Shechem in the *m* region of Ephraim;
24: 4 the *m* region of Seir in which to settle,
24:30 *m* region of Ephraim north of Mount Gaash.
24:33 son Phinehas in the *m* region of Ephraim.
Jgs 1: 9 the Canaanites who lived in the *m* region,
1:19 he gained possession of the *m* region.
1:34 hemmed in the Danites in the *m* region,
2: 9 *m* region of Ephraim north of Mount Gaash.
3: 3 Hivites who dwell in the *m* region
3:27 the horn in the *m* region of Ephraim,
4: 5 and Bethel in the *m* region of Ephraim,
7: 3 Gideon put them to this test on the *m*,
7:24 throughout the *m* region of Ephraim to say,
10: 1 of Shamir in the *m* region of Ephraim.
12:15 land of Ephraim on the *m* of the Amalekites.
17: 1 *m* region of Ephraim whose name was Micah.
17: 8 house of Micah in the *m* region of Ephraim.
18: 2 house of Micah in the *m* region of Ephraim,
18:13 From there they went on to the *m* region of
19: 1 residing in remote parts of the *m* region
19:16 he was from the *m* region of Ephraim,
19:18 Judah far up into the *m* region of Ephraim,
1Sm 25:20 down through a *m* defile riding on an ass,
2Sm 21: 6 before the LORD in Gibeon, on the LORD's *m*.
21: 9 dismembered them on the *m* before the LORD.
1Kgs 5:29 and eighty thousand stonecutters in the *m*.
18:44 and leave the *m* before the rain stops you.'"
19: 8 days and forty nights to the *m* of God,
19:11 outside and stand on the *m* before the LORD;
2Kgs 2:16 carried him away to some *m* or some valley."
4:27 when she reached the man of God on the *m*,
19:23 my many chariots I climbed the *m* heights,
1Chr 6:52 Shechem in the *m* region of Ephraim,
Jdt 1: 6 all the inhabitants of the *m* region,
2:22 chariots, and marched into the *m* region.
3: 9 to the main ridge of the Judean *m*,
4: 7 them to keep firm hold of the *m* passes,
5: 1 for battle, and had blocked the *m* passes,
5: 5 near you [that inhabits this *m* region];
5:15 and took possession of the whole *m* region.
5:19 again in the *m* region which was unoccupied.
6: 7 will now conduct you to the *m* region,
6:11 From there they led him into the *m* region
6:13 So they took cover below the *m*,
6:13 and left him lying at the foot of the *m*;
7: 1 move against Bethulia, seize the *m* passes,
7:12 water that flows out at the base of the *m*,
7:18 encamped in the *m* region opposite Dothan;
10:10 she went down the *m* and crossed the valley;
10:13 take possession of the whole *m* district
11: 2 your people who dwell in the *m* region,
13:10 the ravine, reached Bethulia on the *m*.
14:11 their arms and went to the slopes of the *m*.
15: 3 *m* district around Bethulia took to flight.
15: 5 the rest of the *m* region took part in this,
1Mc 4:18 Gorgias and his army are near us on the *m*.
4:19 appeared, looking down from the *m*.
4:38 in the courts as in a forest or on some *m*,
9:15 and pursued them as far as the *m* slopes.
9:38 up and hid themselves under cover of the *m*.
9:40 and after the survivors fled toward the *m*,
2Mc 2: 4 he went off to the *m* which Moses climbed
Jb 14:18 But as a *m* falls at last and its rock is
39: 1 Do you know about the birth of the *m* goats,
Ps(s) 2: 6 have set up my king on Zion, my holy *m*."
3: 5 to the LORD, he answers me from his holy *m*.
11: 1 you say to me, "Flee to the *m* like a bird!
15: 1 Who shall dwell on your holy *m*?
24: 3 Who can ascend the *m* of the LORD?
43: 3 lead me on And bring me to your holy *m*,
48: 2 His holy *m*,
68:17 at the *m* God has chosen for his throne,
99: 9 LORD, our God, and worship at his holy *m*;
Prv 27:25 appears, and the *m* greens are gathered in,
Sg 4: 6 lengthen, I will go to the *m* of myrrh,
Wis 9: 8 bid me build a temple on your holy *m*
Sir 43:22 When the *m* growth is scorched with heat,
Is 2: 2 The *m* of the LORD's house shall be
2: 2 the highest *m* and raised above the hills.
2: 3 "Come, let us climb the LORD's *m*,
11: 9 shall be no harm or ruin on all my holy *m*;
18: 3 earth, When the signal is raised on the *m*,

18: 6 shall all be left to the *m* birds of prey,
25: 6 On this *m* the LORD of hosts will provide
25: 7 On this *m* he will destroy the veil that
25:10 the hand of the LORD will rest on this *m*,
27:13 come and worship the LORD on the holy *m*,
30:25 Upon every high *m* and lofty hill there
30:29 with a flute Toward the *m* of the LORD,
31: 4 to wage war upon the *m* and hill of Zion.
37:24 my many chariots I climbed the *m* heights,
40: 4 in, every *m* and hill shall be made low;
40: 9 Go up onto a high *m*,
56: 7 *m* and make joyful in my house of prayer;
57: 7 Upon a high and lofty *m* you made your bed,
57:13 inherit the land, and possess my holy *m*.
65:11 forsake the LORD, forgetting my holy *m*,
65:25 shall hurt or destroy on all my holy *m*,
66:20 and dromedaries, to Jerusalem, my holy *m*,
Jer 3: 6 She has gone up every high *m*,
16:16 hunters to hunt them out from every *m*
31:23 "May the LORD bless you, holy *m*,
50: 6 From *m* to hill they wandered,
51:25 I am against you, destroying *m*,
51:25 over the cliffs, and make you a burnt *m*:
Bar 5: 7 commanded that every lofty *m* be made low,
Ez 11:23 on the *m* which is to the east of the city.
17:22 shoot, And plant it on a high and lofty *m*;
17:23 the *m* heights of Israel I will plant it.
20:40 my holy *m*, on the mountain height
28:14 you were on the holy *m* of God,
28:16 Then I banned you from the *m* of God;
34:14 and on the *m* heights of Israel shall be
40: 2 where he set me down on a very high *m*.
43:12 area on the *m* top shall be most sacred.
Dn 2:34 from a *m* without a hand being put to it,
2:35 a great *m* and filled the whole earth.
2:45 from the *m* without a hand being put to it,
9:16 away from your city Jerusalem, your holy *m*.
9:20 the LORD, my God, on behalf of his holy *m*—
11:45 between the sea and the glorious holy *m*,
Jl 2: 1 in Zion, sound the alarm on my holy *m*!
4:17 am your God, dwelling on Zion, my holy *m*;
Am 3: 9 Gather about the *m* Samaria
4: 1 Hear this word, women of the *m* of Samaria,
Ob 1:16 As you have drunk upon my holy *m*,
1:17 the *m* shall be holy,
Mi 7:12 from sea to sea, and from *m* to mountain;
Zep 3:11 no longer exalt yourself on my holy *m*.
Zec 4: 7 What are you, O great *m*?
8: 3 *m* of the LORD of hosts, the holy mountain.
14: 4 the *m* shall move to the north
14: 5 And the valley of the LORD's *m* shall be
Mt 4: 8 The devil then took him up a very high *m*
8: 1 When he came down from the *m*,
14:23 he went up on the *m* by himself to pray,
17: 1 and led them up on a high *m* by themselves.
17:20 seed, you would be able to say to this *m*,
21:21 to the fig tree, but if you say to this *m*,
28:16 to the *m* to which Jesus had summoned them.
Mk 3:13 He then went up the *m* and summoned the men
5:11 was feeding there on the slope of the *m*.
6:46 of them, he went off to the *m* to pray.
9: 2 with him and led them up a high *m*.
9: 9 As they were coming down the *m*,
11:23 assure you, whoever says to this *m*,
Lk 3: 5 And every *m* and hill shall be leveled.
6:12 Then he went out to the *m* to pray,
6:17 Coming down the *m* with them,
9:28 and James, and went up onto a *m* to pray.
9:37 down from the *m* and a large crowd met them.
Jn 4:20 Our ancestors worshiped on this *m*,
4:21 Father neither on this *m* nor in Jerusalem.
6: 3 *m* and sat down there with his disciples.
6:15 him king, so he fled back to the *m* alone.
Gal 4:25 The *m* Sinai [Hagar] is in Arabia and
Heb 8: 5 to the pattern shown you on the *m*."
12:18 to an untouchable *m* and a blazing fire,
12:20 "If even an animal touches the *m*,
2Pt 1:18 while we were in his company on the holy *m*.
Rv 6:14 *m* and island was uprooted from its base.
6:15 all hid themselves in caves and *m* crags.
8: 8 huge *m* all in flames was cast into the sea.
21:10 in spirit to the top of a very high *m*

MOUNTAINS (200)

Gn 7:19 the highest *m* everywhere were submerged,
7:20 fifteen cubits higher than the submerged *m*.
8: 4 the ark came to rest on the *m* of Ararat.
8: 5 the tenth month the tops of the *m* appeared.
14:10 into these, while the rest fled to the *m*.
49:26 The blessings of the everlasting *m*,
Ex 32:12 that he might kill them in the *m* and
Nm 23: 7 me here, Moab's king, from the Eastern *M*:
27:12 "Go up here into the Abarim *M* and view
33:47 they camped in the Abarim *M* opposite Nebo.
33:48 Setting out from the Abarim *M*,
Dt 1: 7 of the Canaanites in the Arabah, the *m*,
12: 2 without fail every place on the high *m*,
32:22 licking with flames the roots of the *m*,
32:49 here in the Abarim *M* [it is in the land of
33:15 *m* and the best from the timeless hills;
33:19 tribes to the *m* where feasts are duly held,
Jos 18:12 flank of Jericho, up westward into the *m*,
Jgs 3:27 down from the *m* with him as their leader.
5: 5 *M* trembled in the presence of the LORD,
6: 2 established the fire signals on the *m*,
11:37 that I may go off down the *m* to mourn my
11:38 and mourned her virginity on the *m*.
1Sm 26:20 as if he were hunting partridge in the *m*."
2Sm 1:21 *M* of Gilboa, may there be neither dew
1Kgs 19:11 the *m* and crushing rocks before the LORD
20:23 "Their gods are gods of *m*.
20:28 Aram has said the LORD is a god of *m*,
22:17 "I see all Israel scattered on the *m*,
1Chr 12: 9 and were as swift as the gazelles on the *m*.
2Chr 2: 1 eighty thousand to cut the stone in the *m*,
2:17 and eighty thousand cutters in the *m*,
18:16 "I see all Israel scattered on the *m*,
21:11 also set up high places in the *m* of Judah;
Tb 1: 5 offer sacrifice on all the *m* of Galilee
1:21 who then escaped into the *m* of Ararat.
5: 6 to Rages, for Rages is situated at the *m*,
5:10 to Media and crossed all its plains and *m*;
Jdt 1:15 himself he overtook in the *m* of Ragae,
2:21 near the *m* to the north of Upper Cilicia.
4: 5 guards on all the summits of the high *m*,
5: 3 of people is this that dwells in the *m*?
5:16 and they lived in these *m* a long time.
6: 4 and the *m* shall be drunk with their blood,
7: 4 Neither the high *m* nor the valleys and
7:10 on the height of the *m* where they dwell;
7:10 is not easy to reach the summit of their *m*.
7:13 will go up to the summits of the nearby *m*,
15: 2 road, both through the valley and in the *m*.
15: 7 till the towns and villages in the *m*
16: 3 Assyrian came from the *m* of the north,
16:15 The *m* to their bases, and the seas are
1Mc 2:28 Thereupon he fled to the *m* with his sons,
4: 5 so he began to hunt for them in the *m*,
6:39 the *m* gleamed with their brightness and
10:70 you displaying power against us in the *m*?
11:68 detached an ambush against him in the *m*.
2Mc 9:28 miserable death in the *m* of a foreign land.
10: 6 like wild animals in caves on the *m*.
Jb 9: 5 He removes the *m* before they know it;
24: 8 They are drenched with the rain of the *m*,
28: 9 and overturns the *m* at their foundations.
39: 8 He ranges the *m* for pasture,
40:20 For the produce of the *m* is brought to him,
Ps(s) 18: 8 the foundations of the *m* trembled and
36: 7 Your justice is like the *m* of God;
46: 3 and *m* plunge into the depths of the sea.
46: 4 and foam and the *m* quake at its surging.
50:10 forests, beasts by the thousand on my *m*.
65: 7 You set the *m* in place by your power,
68:16 *m* of Bashan; rugged the *m* of Bashan.
68:17 Why look you jealously, you rugged *m*,
72: 3 The *m* shall yield peace for the people,
72:16 the *m* the crops shall rustle like Lebanon;
75: 7 neither from the desert nor from the *m*—
76: 5 O powerful One, from the everlasting *m*.
78:54 holy land, to the *m* his right hand had won.
80:11 The *m* were hidden in its shadow;
83:15 a forest, as a flame setting the *m* ablaze,
87: 1 His foundation upon the holy *m*
90: 2 Before the *m* were begotten and the earth
95: 4 the earth, and the tops of the *m* are his.
97: 5 The *m* melt like wax before the LORD,
98: 8 the *m* shout with them for joy
104: 6 above the *m* the waters stood.
104: 8 As the *m* rose, they went down the valleys
104:10 the watercourses that wind among the *m*,
104:13 You water the *m* from your palace;
104:18 The high *m* are for wild goats;
104:32 who touches the *m*,
114: 4 The *m* skipped like rams,
114: 6 You *m*, that you skip like rams?
121: 1 I lift up my eyes toward the *m*;
125: 2 *M* are round about Jerusalem;
133: 3 Hermon, which come down upon the *m* of Zion;
144: 5 touch the *m*, and they shall smoke;
147: 8 Who makes grass sprout on the *m*
148: 9 You *m* and all you hills,
Prv 8:25 Before the *m* were settled into place,
Sg 2: 8 here he comes springing across the *m*,
2:17 or a young stag upon the *m* of Bether.
4: 1 of goats streaming down the *m* of Gilead.
4: 8 the haunts of lions, from the leopards' *m*.
8:14 gazelle or a young stag on the *m* of spices!
Sir 16:17 The roots of the *m*, the earth's foundations,
39:28 which in their fury can dislodge *m*;
43: 4 metal, it sets the *m* aflame with its rays;
43:16 before his might the *m* quake.
Is 2:14 all the lofty *m* and all the high hills,
5:25 When the *m* quake,
13: 2 Upon the bare *m* set up a signal;
13: 4 Listen! the rumble on the *m*,
14:25 in my land and trample him on my *m*;
17:13 Windswept, like chaff on the *m*,
22: 5 Walls crash; they cry for help to the *m*.
34: 3 The *m* shall run with their blood,
40:12 the *m* in scales and the hills in a balance?
41:15 To thresh the *m* and crush them,
42:11 exult, and shout from the top of the *m*.
42:15 I will lay waste *m* and hills,
44:23 Break forth, you *m*, into song, you forest,
45: 2 I will go before you and level the *m*;
49:11 I will cut a road through all my *m*,
49:13 O earth, break forth into song, you *m*.
52: 7 How beautiful upon the *m* are the feet of
54:10 Though the *m* leave their place and the
55:12 *M* and hills shall break out in song before
63:19 with the *m* quaking before you
65: 7 Since they burned incense on the *m*,
65: 9 from Judah, those who are to inherit my *m*;
Jer 3:23 indeed are the hills, the thronging *m*;
4:24 I looked at the *m*, and they were trembling,
9: 9 Over the *m*, break out in cries
13:16 Before your feet stumble on darkening *m*;
18:14 waters dry up that flow fresh down the *m*?
31: 5 shall plant vineyards on the *m* of Samaria;
46:18 Like Tabor among the *m* he shall come,
50: 6 mislead them, straggling on the *m*;
Lam 4:19 us on the *m* and waylaid us in the desert.
Bar 6:38 statues are like stones from the *m*;
6:62 on high to burn up the *m* and the forests,
Ez 6: 2 Son of man, turn toward the *m* of Israel,
6: 3 *M* of Israel, hear the word of the Lord
6: 3 Thus says the Lord GOD [to the *m* and hills,
7:16 to the *m* like the doves of the valleys
18: 6 and just, if he does not eat on the *m*,
18:11 none of them), a son who eats on the *m*,
18:15 a son who does not eat on the *m*,
19: 9 would not be heard on the *m* of Israel.
22: 9 within you are those who feast on the *m*;
31:12 nations, cut it down and left it on the *m*.
32: 5 I will leave your flesh on the *m*,
33:25 You eat on the *m*,
33:28 and the *m* of Israel shall be so desolate
34: 6 and wandered over all the *m* and high hills;
34:13 pasture them upon the *m* of Israel
34:14 shall they be pastured on the *m* of Israel.
35:12 you have uttered against the *m* of Israel:
36: 1 son of man, prophesy to the *m* of Israel:
36: 1 *M* of Israel, hear the word of the LORD!
36: 4 *m* of Israel, hear the word of the LORD:
36: 4 [Thus says the Lord GOD to the *m* and hills,
36: 6 land of Israel, and say to the *m* and hills,
36: 8 As for you, *m* of Israel,
37:22 nation upon the land, in the *m* of Israel,
38: 8 the *m* of Israel which were long a ruin],
38:20 *M* shall be overturned,
39: 2 I will lead you against the *m* of Israel.
39: 4 Upon the *m* of Israel you shall fall,
39:17 you, a great slaughter on the *m* of Israel:
Dn 3:75 *M* and hills, bless the Lord:
Hos 10: 8 Then they shall cry out to the *m*,
Jl 2: 2 Like dawn spreading over the *m*,
4:18 on that day, the *m* shall drip new wine,
Am 4:13 Him who formed the *m*,
9:13 The juice of grapes shall drip down the *m*,
Jon 2: 7 Down I went to the roots of the *m*;
Mi 1: 4 The *m* melt under him and the valleys split
4: 1 Shall be established higher than the *m*;
6: 1 Arise, present your plea before the *m*,
6: 2 Hear, O *m*, the plea of the LORD,
Na 1: 5 The *m* quake before him,
2: 1 *m* there advances the bearer of good news,
3:18 Your people are scattered upon the *m*,
Hb 3: 6 The eternal *m* are shattered,
3:10 at sight of you the *m* tremble.
Hg 1:11 a drought upon the land and upon the *m*;
Zec 6: 1 between two *m*; and the *m* were of bronze.
14: 5 the valley of those two *m* reaches its edge;
Mal 1: 3 I made his *m* a waste,
Mt 24:16 those in Judea must flee to the *m*.
Mk 13:14 in Judea must flee to the *m*.
Lk 21:21 in Judea at the time must flee to the *m*;
23:30 Then they will begin saying to the *m*,
1Cor 13: 2 if I have faith great enough to move *m*,
Heb 11:38 They wandered about in deserts and on *m*,
Rv 6:16 They cried out to the *m* and rocks,
16:20 Every island fled and *m* disappeared.

MOUNTAINSIDE (8)

Dt 9:21 I threw into the wadi that went down the *m*.
2Sm 13:34 down the *m* from the direction of Bahurim.
2Kgs 6:17 so that he saw the *m* filled with horses
23:16 turned and saw the graves there on the *m*,
Is 7:25 *m* which used to be hoed with the mattock:
Mt 5: 1 When he saw the crowds he went up on the *m*.
15:29 He went up onto the *m* and sat down there.
17: 9 coming down the *m* Jesus commanded them,

MOUNTAINTOP (5)

Ex 24:17 LORD was seen as a consuming fire on the *m*.
Jos 18:13 on the *m* south of Lower Beth-horon.
18:14 the boundary line swung south from the *m*
Is 30:17 you are left like a flagstaff on the *m*,
Ez 6:13 their altars, on every high hill and *m*,

MOUNTAINTOPS (4)

Jgs 9:25 then set men in ambush for him on the *m*,
2Mc 9: 8 he could weigh the *m* in his scales,
Hos 4:13 On the *m* they offer sacrifice and on the
Jl 2: 5 the rumble of chariots they leap on the *m*;

MOUNTED (30)

Gn 24:61 they *m* their camels and followed the man.
Ex 28:11 of Israel and then *m* in gold filigree work.
28:20 stones are to be *m* in gold filigree work,
39: 6 were prepared and *m* in gold filigree work;
39:10 Four rows of precious stones were *m* on it:
39:13 They were *m* in gold filigree work.
Nm 21: 9 made a bronze serpent and *m* it on a pole,
1Sm 25:42 She got up immediately, *m* an ass,
30:17 young men, who *m* their camels and fled.
2Sm 13:29 all the other princes rose, *m* their mules,
18: 9 He was *m* on a mule,
18:24 and a lookout *m* to the roof of the gate
22:11 He *m* a cherub and flew,
1Kgs 1:44 and they *m* him upon the king's own mule.
13:13 it, he *m* and followed the man of God,
18:45 Ahab *m* his chariot and made for Jezreel.
2Kgs 9:16 Jehu *m* his chariot and drove to Jezreel,
12:18 of Aram *m* a siege against Gath.
Jdt 2:15 commanded, and twelve thousand *m* archers,
Est 8:10 he sent by *m* couriers riding thoroughbred
8:14 Couriers *m* on royal steeds sped forth in
2Mc 3:25 caparisoned horse, *m* by a dreadful rider.
Ps(s) 18:11 He *m* a cherub and flew,
107:26 They *m* up to heaven;
Jer 22: 4 palace, riding in chariots or *m* on horses,
Ez 23: 6 attractive young men, knights *m* on horses.
23:12 impeccably clothed, knights *m* on horses,
38:15 and many peoples with you, all *m* on horses,
Mt 21: 7 and laid their cloaks on them, and he *m*.
Jn 12:14 Jesus found a donkey and *m* it;

MOUNTING (7)

Ex 25: 7 for *m* on the ephod and the breastpiece.
31: 5 bronze, in cutting and *m* precious stones,
35: 9 for *m* on the ephod and on the breastpiece.
35:27 for *m* on the ephod and on the breastpiece;
35:33 bronze, in cutting and *m* precious stones,
1Kgs 1:38 down, and *m* Solomon on King David's mule,
Sir 32: 6 Like a gold *m* with an emerald seal is

MOUNTS (3)

Jb 17: 2 indeed mocked, and, as their provocation *m*,
Ps(s) 47: 6 God *m* his throne amid shouts of joy;
Is 22: 6 takes up the quivers, Aram *m* the horses,

MOURN (42)

Lv 10: 6 shall *m* for those whom the LORD's fire has
Jgs 11:37 to *m* my virginity with my companions."
11:40 go yearly to *m* the daughter of Jephthah
1Sm 25: 1 died, and all Israel gathered to *m* him;
2Sm 3:31 with sackcloth, and *m* over Abner."
13:39 during all that time to *m* over his son;
1Kgs 13:29 to the city to *m* over it and to bury it.
14:13 and all Israel will *m* him and bury him,
Jb 5:11 lowly, and those who *m* he exalts to safety.
Eccl 3: 4 a time to *m*,
Sir 7:34 those who weep, but *m* with those who mourn;
Is 3:26 Her gates will lament and *m*,
19: 8 The fishermen shall *m* and lament,
22:12 of hosts, called on you To weep and *m*,
57:18 to them and to those who *m* for them,
61: 2 by our God, to comfort all who *m*;
61: 3 who *m* in Zion a diadem instead of ashes,
Jer 4: 8 gird yourselves with sackcloth, *m* and wail:
4:28 Because of this the earth shall *m*,
6:26 *M* as for an only child with bitter wailing,
12: 4 How long must the earth *m*,
22:10 not for him who is dead, *m* not for him!
25:33 None will *m* them,
48:17 *M* for him, all you his neighbors,
49: 3 Put on sackcloth and *m*,
Lam 1: 4 *m* for lack of pilgrims going to her feasts;
Ez 7:12 not the buyer rejoice nor the seller *m*,
24:16 but do not *m* or weep or shed any tears.
24:23 You shall not *m* or weep,
Dn 14:40 seventh day the king came to *m* for Daniel.
Hos 10: 5 *m* for it and its priests wail over it,
Am 8: 8 of this, and all who dwell in it *m*,
8:10 I will make them *m* as for an only son,
9: 5 my touch, so that all who dwell on it *m*,
Zec 7: 3 "Must I *m* and abstain in the fifth month
12:10 *m* for him as one mourns for an only son,
12:12 And the land shall *m*, each family apart;
Jn 16:20 will weep and *m* while the world rejoices;
2Cor 12:21 and I may have to *m* over the many who
Jas 4: 9 Begin to lament, to *m*, and to weep;
Rv 18:11 of the world will weep and *m* over her too,

MOURNED (21)

Gn 37:34 on his loins, and *m* his son many days.
50: 3 and the Egyptians *m* him for seventy days.
Nm 20:29 days the whole house of Israel *m* him.
Dt 21:13 *m* her father and mother for a full month,
Jgs 11:38 and *m* her virginity on the mountains.
1Sm 28: 3 had died and, after being *m* by all Israel,
2Sm 1:12 They *m* and wept and fasted until evening
11:26 that her husband had died, she *m* her lord.
1Kgs 13:30 body in his own grave, and they *m* over it:
1Chr 7:22 Their father Ephraim *m* a long time,
2Chr 35:24 and all Judah and Jerusalem *m* him.
Jdt 16:24 the house of Israel *m* her for seven days.
1Mc 1:27 she who sat in the bridal chamber *m*,
2:14 garments, put on sackcloth, and *m* bitterly.
2:39 heard of it, they *m* deeply for them.
2:70 in Modein, and all Israel *m* him greatly.
9:20 They *m* for him many days,
12:52 They *m* over Jonathan and his men,
Jb 27:15 no burial, and their widows shall not be *m*.
Dn 10: 2 those days, I, Daniel, *m* three full weeks.
Zec 7: 5 When you fasted and *m* in the fifth and in

MOURNER (1)

Dt 26:14 I have not eaten any of the tithe as a *m*;

MOURNERS (6)

Jb 29:25 *m* took comfort from my cheerful glance.
Eccl 12: 5 lasting home, and *m* go about the streets;
Sir 48:24 into the future and consoled the *m* of Zion;
Lam 4:10 To serve them as *m'* food in the downfall
Hos 9: 4 Theirs will be like *m'* bread,
Am 5:16 to wail and professional *m* to lament,

MOURNFUL (1)

Jer 12:11 desert waste, They have made it a *m* waste,

MOURNING (79)

Gn 23: 2 performed the customary *m* rites for her.
27:41 "When the time of *m* for my father comes,
37:35 go down *m* to my son in the nether world."
38:12 After Judah completed the period of *m*,
50: 4 When that period of *m* was over,
50:10 observed seven days of *m* for his father.
50:11 the land saw the *m* at Goren-ha-atad,
Ex 33: 4 heard this bad news, they went into *m*,
Dt 34: 8 the period of grief and *m* for Moses.
1Sm 6:19 The people went into *m* at this great
2Sm 11:27 But once the *m* was over,
14: 2 "Pretend to be in *m*.
14: 2 who has been long in *m* for a departed one.
14: 2 Put on *m* apparel and do not anoint
19: 2 the king was weeping and *m* for Absalom;
19: 3 that day's victory was turned into *m*
1Kgs 14:18 He was buried with all Israel *m* him,
Ezr 10: 6 was in *m* over the betrayal by the exiles.
Neh 1: 4 to weep and continued *m* for several days;
Tb 2: 6 "Your festivals shall be turned into *m*,
Est 4: 3 reached, the Jews went into deep *m*,
C:13 she put on garments of distress and *m*.
9:22 sorrow into joy, from *m* into festivity.
1Mc 1:25 And there was great *m* for Israel,
1:39 her feasts were turned into *m*,
1:40 been, and her exalation was turned into *m*.
3:51 and your priests are in *m* and humiliation.
9:41 Thus the wedding was turned into *m*,
12:52 fear, and all Israel fell into deep *m*.
13:26 lamentation, *m* over him for many days.
Jb 30:31 My harp is turned to *m*,
Ps(s) 30:12 You changed my *m* into dancing;
35:14 bewailing a mother, I was bowed down in *m*.
38: 7 all the day I go in *m*,
42:10 Why must I go about in *m*,
43: 2 Why must I go about in *m*,
Eccl 7: 2 house of *m* than to the house of feasting,
7: 4 heart of the wise is in the house of *m*,
Wis 14:15 For a father, afflicted with untimely *m*,
18:10 wail of *m* for children was borne to them.
19: 3 and were *m* at the burials of the dead,
Sir 22: 6 a song in time of *m* is inopportune talk,
22:11 Seven days of *m* for the dead,
26: 6 A jealous wife is heartache and *m* and a
38:17 Weeping bitterly, *m* fully,
Is 29: 2 distress upon Ariel, with *m* and grief.
33: 9 The country languishes in *m*,
35:10 joy and gladness, sorrow and *m* will flee.
50: 3 I clothe the heavens in *m*,
51:11 joy and gladness, sorrow and *m* will flee.
60:20 and the days of your *m* shall be at an end.
61: 3 give them oil of gladness in place of *m*,
66:10 with her, all you who were *m* over her!
Jer 14: 2 Her people sink down in *m*:
16: 5 Go not into a house of *m*,
31:13 I will turn their *m* into joy,
31:16 Cease your cries of *m*, wipe the tears from
48:38 of Moab and in all his squares there is *m*;
Lam 5:15 has ceased, our dance has turned into *m*;
Bar 4: 9 God has brought great *m* upon me,
4:11 but with *m* and lament I let them go.
4:23 With *m* and lament I sent you forth,
4:34 and her exultation shall be turned to *m*:
5: 1 take off your robe of *m* and misery;
Ez 26:16 They shall be clothed in *m* and,
27:32 In their *m* they utter a lament over you;
Jl 1: 9 In *m* are the priests,
2:12 heart, with fasting, and weeping, and *m*;
Am 8:10 *m* and all your songs into lamentations.
Mi 1: 8 like the jackals, and *m* like the ostriches.
Zec 12:11 On that day the *m* in Jerusalem shall be as
12:11 *m* of Hadadrimmon in the plain of Megiddo.
Mt 9:15 go in *m* so long as the groom is with them?
Jas 4: 9 be turned into *m* and your joy into sorrow.
Rv 18: 7 No widow am I, and never will I go into *m*!'
18: 8 come all at once, death and *m* and famine.
18:15 Weeping and *m*, they cry out:
18:19 their heads and cried out, weeping and *m*:
21: 4 and there shall be no more death or *m*,

MOURNS (8)

Is 24: 4 The earth *m* and fades,
24: 7 The wine *m*, the vine languishes,
Jer 14: 2 Judah *m*, her gates are lifeless;
23:10 on their account the land *m*,
31:15 Rachel *m* her children,
Hos 4: 3 Therefore the land *m*, and everything that
Jl 1:10 The field is ravaged, the earth *m*,
Zec 12:10 mourn for him as one *m* for an only son,

MOUSE (1)

Lv 11:29 the rat, the *m*, the various kinds of lizards,

MOUTH (266)

Gn 4:11 be banned from the soil that opened its *m*
29: 2 A large stone covered the *m* of the well.
29: 3 the *m* of the well and water the flocks.
29: 3 stone back again over the *m* of the well.
29: 8 roll the stone away from the *m* of the well;
29:10 the stone away from the *m* of the well,
42:27 to see his money in the *m* of his bag.
43:21 was each man's money in the *m* of his bag
44: 1 put each man's money in the *m* of his bag.
44: 2 In the *m* of the youngest one's bag put
Ex 4:15 to him, then, and put the words in his *m*.
Nm 16:30 and the ground opens its *m* and swallows
16:32 and the earth opened its *m* and swallowed
22:28 But now the LORD opened the *m* of the ass,
22:38 I can speak only what God puts in my *m*."
23: 5 he had put an utterance in Balaam's *m*,
23:12 puts in my *m* that I must repeat with care?"
23:16 and having put an utterance in his *m*,
26:10 The earth opened its *m* and swallowed them
Dt 8: 3 that comes forth from the *m* of the LORD.
11: 6 when the ground opened its *m* and swallowed
18:18 kinsmen, and will put my words into his *m*;
32: 1 let the earth hearken to the words of my *m*!
Jos 10:18 "Roll large stones to the *m* of the cave
10:22 "Open the *m* of the cave and bring out
10:27 the *m* of the cave large stones were placed,
15: 5 the Salt Sea as far as the *m* of the Jordan.
Jgs 18:19 put your hand over your *m*.
1Sm 1:12 prayer before the LORD, Eli watched her *m*,
14:26 no one would raise a hand to his *m* from it,
14:27 he raised it to his *m* and his eyes lit up.
17:35 attack it and rescue the prey from its *m*.
2Sm 22: 9 nostrils, and a devouring fire from his *m*;
1Kgs 8:15 who with his own *m* made a promise to my
17:24 word of the LORD comes truly from your *m*."
2Kgs 4:34 bed, placing his *m* upon the child's mouth,
19:28 my hook in your nose and my bit in your *m*,
2Chr 6: 4 who with his own *m* made a promise to my
6:15 With your own *m* you spoke it,
35:22 words of Neco that came from the *m* of God,
36:22 kingdom, both by word of *m* and in writing:
Ezr 1: 1 kingdom, both by word of *m* and in writing:
Est C:24 Put in my *m* persuasive words in the
1Mc 9:55 his *m* was closed and he was paralyzed,
2Mc 6:18 was being forced to open his *m* to eat pork.
Jb 3: 1 this, Job opened his *m* and cursed his day.
5:16 have hope, and iniquity closes her *m*.
8: 2 words from your *m* are like a mighty wind!
8:21 more will he fill your *m* with laughter,
9:20 I were right, my own *m* might condemn me;
12:11 the ear judge words as the *m* tastes food?
15: 5 Because your wickedness instructs your *m*,
15: 6 Your own *m* condemns you,
15:13 God and let such words escape your *m*!
20:12 Though wickedness is sweet in his *m*,
20:13 let it go but keeps it still within his *m*.
22:22 Receive instruction from his *m*,
23: 4 before him, and fill my *m* with arguments;
23:12 of his *m* I have treasured in my heart.
31:30 Even though I had not suffered my *m* to sin
33: 2 Behold, now I open my *m*;
35:16 Yet Job to no purpose opens his *m*,
37: 2 angry voice as it rumbles forth from his *m*!
40: 4 I put my hand over my *m*.
40:23 though the torrent surges about his *m*.
41: 6 Who can force open the doors of his *m*,
41:11 Out of his *m* go forth firebrands;
41:13 a flame pours from his *m*.
42: 5 I had heard of you by word of *m*,
Ps(s) 5:10 For in their *m* there is no sincerity;
10: 7 His *m* is full of cursing,
17: 4 My *m* has not transgressed after the manner
18: 9 from his *m* that kindled coals into flame.
19:15 Let the words of my *m* and the thought of
22:22 Save me from the lion's *m*;
33: 6 by the breath of his *m* all their host.
34: 2 his praise shall be ever in my *m*.
36: 4 The words of his *m* are empty and false;
37:30 The *m* of the just man tells of wisdom and
38:14 not, like a dumb man who opens not his *m*.
38:15 neither hears nor has in his *m* a retort.

39: 2 I will set a curb on my *m*.”
39:10 I was speechless and opened not my *m*,
40: 4 And he put a new song into my *m*,
49: 4 My *m* shall speak wisdom;
50:16 and profess my covenant with your *m*,
50:19 To your *m* you give free rein for evil,
51:17 lips, and my *m* shall proclaim your praise.
54: 4 hearken to the words of my *m*.
63: 6 with exultant lips my *m* shall praise you.
69:16 me up, nor the pit close its *m* over me.
71: 8 My *m* shall be filled with your praise,
71:15 My *m* shall declare your justice,
78: 1 incline your ears to the words of my *m*.
78: 2 I will open my *m* in a parable,
81:11 open wide your *m*,
89: 2 my *m* shall proclaim your faithfulness.
107:42 rejoice, and all wickedness closes its *m*.
119:13 I declare all the ordinances of your *m*.
119:43 Take not the word of truth from my *m*,
119:72 The law of your *m* is to me more precious
119:88 that I may keep the decrees of your *m*.
119:103 your promises, sweeter than honey to my *m!*
119:108 Accept, O LORD, the free homage of my *m*,
119:131 open *m* in my yearning for your commands.
126: 2 Then our *m* was filled with laughter,
138: 1 [for you have heard the words of my *m*
138: 4 LORD, when they hear the words of your *m;*
141: 3 O LORD, set a watch before my *m*,
145:21 May my *m* speak the praise of the LORD,
Prv 2: 6 his *m* come knowledge and understanding;
5: 3 with honey, and her *m* is smoother than oil;
5: 7 me, go not astray from the words of my *m*.
6: 2 your lips, caught by the words of your *m;*
7:24 to me, be attentive to the words of my *m!*
8: 7 Yes, the truth my *m* recounts,
8: 8 Sincere are all the words of my *m*,
8:13 the evil way, and the perverse *m* I hate.
10:11 fountain of life is the *m* of the just, but the *m*
10:13 the *m* of the wicked conceals violence].
10:14 but the *m* of a fool is imminent ruin.
10:31 The *m* of the just yields wisdom,
10:32 how to please, but the *m* of the wicked,
11: 9 *m* the impious man would ruin his neighbor,
11:11 the *m* of the wicked it is overthrown.
13: 3 He who guards his *m* protects his life;
14: 3 In the *m* of the fool is a rod for his back,
15: 2 but the *m* of fools spurts forth folly.
15:14 but the *m* of fools feeds on folly.
15:28 but the *m* of the wicked pours out evil.
16:26 labors for him, for his *m* urges him on.
18: 4 The words from a man's *m* are deep waters,
18: 6 into strife, and his *m* provokes a beating.
18: 7 The fool's *m* is his ruin;
18:20 From the fruit of his *m* a man has his fill;
19:24 he will not even lift it to his *m*.
19:28 and the *m* of the wicked pours out iniquity.
20:17 afterward his *m* will be filled with gravel.
21:23 He who guards his *m* and his tongue keeps
22:14 The *m* of the adulteress is a deep pit;
24: 7 not to open his *m* at the gate.
26: 7 A proverb in the *m* of a fool hangs limp,
26: 9 a drunkard is a proverb in the *m* of fools.
26:15 he is too weary to lift it to his *m*.
26:28 enemy, and the flattering *m* works ruin.
27: 2 Let another praise you—not your own *m;*
30:20 she eats, wipes her *m*,
30:32 put your hand on your *m;*
31: 8 Open your *m* in behalf of the dumb,
31: 9 Open your *m*, decree what is just,
31:26 She opens her *m* in wisdom,
Eccl 6: 7 All man's toil is for his *m*,
10:12 Words from the wise man's *m* win favor,
Sg 1: 2 Let him kiss me with kisses of his *m!*
2: 3 shadow, and his fruit is sweet to my *m*.
4: 3 your *m* is lovely.
5:16 His *m* is sweetness itself;
7:10 apples, And your *m* like an excellent wine
Wis 1:11 unpunished, and a lying *m* slays the soul.
Sir 5:14 if not, put your hand over your *m*.
6: 5 A kind *m* multiplies friends,
14: 1 Happy the man whose *m* brings him no grief,
20:28 a muzzle over the *m* they silence reproof.
22:27 Who will set a guard over my *m*,
23: 9 Let not your *m* form the habit of swearing,
23:13 Let not your *m* become used to coarse talk,
24: 2 assembly of the Most High she opens her *m*,
24: 3 “From the *m* of the Most High I came forth,
26:12 *m* drinks from any water that he finds,
28:12 yet both you do with your *m!*
28:24 with thorns, set barred doors over your *m;*
29:24 for as a guest you dare not open your *m*.
34: 8 is found in the *m* of the faithful man.
40:30 *m* of the shameless man begging is sweet,
51:25 I open my *m* and speak of her:
Is 1:20 for the *m* of the LORD has spoken!
6: 7 He touched my *m* with it.
9:11 on the west devour Israel with open *m*.
9:16 sinful, and every *m* gives vent to folly.
10:14 No one fluttered a wing, or opened a *m*,
11: 4 strike the ruthless with the rod of his *m*,
34:16 For the *m* of the LORD has ordered it,
37:29 my hook in your nose and my bit in your *m*,
40: 5 for the *m* of the LORD has spoken.
48: 3 long ago, they went forth from my *m*,
51:16 I have put my words into your *m* and
53: 7 he submitted and opened not his *m;*
53: 7 he was silent and opened not his *m*.
55:11 my word be that goes forth from my *m;*
57: 4 sport, at whom do you open wide your *m*,
58:14 father, for the *m* of the LORD has spoken.
59:21 into your *m* Shall never leave your mouth,
62: 2 a new name pronounced by the *m* of the LORD.
Jer 1: 9 LORD extended his hand and touched my *m*,
1: 9 saying, See, I place my words in your *m!*
5:14 Behold, I make my words in your *m*,
9: 7 arrow is his tongue, his *m* utters deceit;
9:11 the *m* of the LORD has spoken make it known:
23:16 they speak, not from the *m* of the LORD.
Lam 3:29 Let him put his *m* to the dust;
3:38 it proceeds from the *m* of the Most High,
4: 4 cleaves to the roof of its *m* in thirst;
Ez 2: 8 open your *m* and eat what I shall give you.
3: 2 my *m* and he gave me the scroll to eat.
3: 3 it, and it was as sweet as honey in my *m*.
3:17 When you hear a word from my *m*,
3:27 Only when I speak with you and open your *m*,
4:14 never has any unclean meat entered my *m*.”
24:27 that day your *m* shall be opened and you
33:22 and he opened my *m* when the fugitive
33:22 My *m* was opened, and I was dumb no longer.
Dn 7: 5 among the teeth in its *m* were three tusks.
7: 8 like a man, and a *m* that spoke arrogantly.
7:20 the eyes and the *m* that spoke arrogantly,
10:16 opened my *m* and said to the one facing me,
14:27 He put them into the *m* of the dragon,
Hos 2:19 I remove from her *m* the names of the Baals,
6: 5 I slew them by the words of my *m;*
Am 3:12 As the shepherd snatches from the *m* of the
Mi 3: 5 when one fails to put something in their *m*,
4: 4 for the *m* of the LORD of hosts has spoken.
7: 5 in your bosom guard the portals of your *m*.
Na 3:12 That fall, when shaken, into the hungry *m*.
Zec 9: 7 and take from his *m* his bloody meat,
Mal 2: 6 True doctrine was in his *m*,
2: 7 instruction is to be sought from his *m*,
Mt 4: 4 utterance that comes from the *m* of God.’ ”
12:34 The *m* speaks whatever fills the mind.
13:35 “I will open my *m* in parables,
15:11 goes into a man's *m* that makes him impure;
15:11 it is what comes out of his *m*.”
15:17 enters the *m* passes into the stomach
15:18 comes out of the *m* originates in the mind?
17:27 Open its *m* and you will discover there a
Mk 9:18 *m* and grinds his teeth and becomes rigid.
9:20 he began to roll around and foam at the *m*.
Lk 1:64 his *m* was opened and his tongue loosed,
9:39 a convulsion and makes him foam at the *m*,
22:71 We have heard it from his own *m*.”
Acts 1:16 Holy Spirit through the *m* of David
8:32 shearer he was silent and opened not his *m*.
11: 8 unclean or impure has ever entered my *m!*’
15:27 who will convey this message by word of *m:*
23: 2 his attendants to strike Paul on the *m*.
Rom 3:19 This means that every *m* is silenced and
2Thes 2: 8 destroy him with the breath of his *m*
Jas 3:10 Blessing and curse come out of the same *m*.
1Pt 2:22 no deceit was found in his *m*.
Rv 1:16 sharp, two-edged sword came out of his *m*,
2:16 fight against them with the sword of my *m*.
3:16 hot nor cold, I will spew you out of my *m!*
10: 9 in your *m* it will taste as sweet as honey.”
10:10 In my *m* it tasted as sweet as honey,
12:15 spewed a torrent of water out of his *m*
12:16 opening its *m* and swallowing the flood
12:16 flood which the dragon spewed out of his *m*.
13: 2 had paws like a bear and the *m* of a lion.
13: 5 The beast was given a *m* for uttering proud
16:13 *m* of the dragon, from the *m* of the beast,
16:13 beast, and from the *m* of the false prophet;
19:15 Out of his *m* came a sharp sword for
19:21 of the *m* of the One who rode the horse,

MOUTHFUL (1)

Jn 6: 7 buy loaves enough to give each of them a *m!*”

MOUTHING (1)

Ps(s) 94: 4 the wicked glory, *M* insolent speeches,

MOUTHINGS (1)

Ps(s) 73: 9 They set their *m* in place of heaven,

MOUTHPIECE (1)

Jer 15:19 without the vile, you shall be my *m*.

MOUTHS (55)

Gn 43:12 that was put back in the *m* of your bags;
44: 8 money that we found in the *m* of our bags.
Dt 30:14 you, already in your *m* and in your hearts;
Jgs 7: 6 to their *m* by hand numbered three hundred,
1Sm 2: 3 nor let arrogance issue from your *m*.
1Kgs 22:22 lying spirit in the *m* of all his prophets.’
22:23 in the *m* of all these prophets of yours,
2Chr 18:21 lying spirit in the *m* of all his prophets.’
18:22 spirit in the *m* of these your prophets,
Neh 9:20 manna you did not withhold from their *m*,
Est C:20 to close the *m* of those who praise you,
C:21 to open the *m* of the heathen to acclaim
Jb 16:10 their *m* are agape to bite me.
21: 5 be astonished, put your hands over your *m*.
29: 9 and covered their *m* with their hands;
29:10 tongues stuck to the roofs of their *m*.
32: 5 was no reply in the *m* of the three men,
Ps(s) 8: 3 Out of the *m* of babes and sucklings you
17:10 their cruel hearts, their *m* speak proudly.
22:14 They open their *m* against me like ravening
35:21 And they open wide their *m* against me,
58: 7 O God, smash their teeth in their *m;*
59: 8 Though they bay with their *m*,
59:13 By the sin of their *m* and the word of
62: 5 They bless with their *m*,
63:12 but the *m* of those who speak falsely
78:30 and their food was still in their *m*,
78:36 their *m* and lied to him with their tongues,
109: 2 opened wicked and treacherous *m* against me.
115: 5 They have *m* but speak not;
135:16 They have *m* but speak not;
135:17 hear not, nor is there breath in their *m*.
144: 8 Whose *m* swear false promises while their
144:11 Whose *m* swear false promises while their
Wis 8:12 they would place their hands upon their *m*.
10:21 Because Wisdom opened the *m* of the dumb,
Sir 21:26 Fools' thoughts are in their *m*,
Is 59:21 nor the *m* of your children Nor the mouths
Lam 2:16 All your enemies open their *m* against you;
3:46 our enemies have opened their *m* against us;
Ez 34:10 they may no longer be food for their *m*.
Dn 3:33 Now we cannot open our *m;*
6:23 the lions' *m* so that they have not hurt me.
Jl 1: 5 of the grape will be withheld from your *m*.
Mi 7:16 They shall put their hands over their *m;*
Zep 3:13 be found in their *m* a deceitful tongue;
Zec 14:12 and their tongues shall rot in their *m*.
Lk 1:70 he promised through the *m* of his holy ones,
Rom 3:14 Their *m* are full of curses and bitterness.
Jas 3: 3 into the *m* of horses to make them obey us,
Rv 9:17 of their *m* came fire and sulphur and smoke.
9:18 sulphur and fire which shot out of their *m*—
9:19 was not only in their *m* but in their tails;
11: 5 fire will come out of the *m* of these

MOVABLE (1)

Ez 41:24 Each door had two *m* leaves;

MOVE (42)

Gn 1:28 all the living things that *m* on the earth.”
9: 2 upon all the creatures that *m* about on the
34:10 you can settle and *m* about freely in it,
34:21 in the land and *m* about in it freely;
41:44 *m* hand or foot in all the land of Egypt.”
42:34 and you may *m* about freely in the land.’ ”
Ex 10:23 nor could they *m* from where they were,
33:11 son of Nun, would not *m* out of the tent.
Lv 11:46 the creatures that *m* about in the water
Nm 1:51 When the Dwelling is to *m* on,
9:19 obeyed the LORD and would not *m* on;
22:26 to *m* either to the right or to the left.
Dt 19:14 “You shall not *m* your neighbor's
31: 2 and am no longer able to *m* about freely;
Jgs 19: 7 The man still made a *m* to go,
1Sm 5: 8 “Let them *m* the ark of the God of Israel
1Kgs 17: 9 *M* on to Zarephath of Sidon and stay there.
2Kgs 5:11 God, and would *m* his hand over the spot,
23:18 be,” he said, “let no one *m* his bones.”
Jdt 7: 1 come to his support, to *m* against Bethulia,
1Mc 15:39 He ordered him to *m* his troops against
Ps(s) 31: 9 enemy but enabling me to *m* about at large.
104:26 And where ships *m* about with Leviathan,
Eccl 4:15 I saw all those who are to live and *m*
Sir 12:15 While you stand firm, he makes no bold *m;*
Is 46: 7 it stays, and does not *m* from the spot.
Jer 49:14 Gather together, *m* against her,
Bar 6:26 *m* of themselves if one sets them upright,
Ez 1:17 *m* in any of the four directions they faced,
Zec 14: 4 the mountain shall *m* to the north
Dn 11:31 Armed forces shall *m* at his command and
Hos 5:10 become like those that *m* a boundary line;
Mt 12:45 They *m* in and settle there.
17:20 ‘Move from here to there,’ and it would *m*.
Mk 1:38 “Let us *m* on to the neighboring villages
Lk 10: 7 Do not *m* from house to house.
15:16 but no one made a *m* to give him anything.
Jn 19: 1 *m* was to take Jesus and have him scourged.
Acts 7: 4 God made him *m* from there to this land
14: 5 A *m* was made by Gentiles and Jews,
17:28 ‘In him we live and *m* and have our being,’
1Cor 13: 2 I have faith great enough to *m* mountains,

MOVED (86)

Gn 12: 8 he *m* on to the hill country east of Bethel,
13:18 Abram *m* his tents and went on to settle
26:22 When he had *m* on from there,
27:22 So Jacob *m* up closer to his father.
35:21 Israel *m* on and pitched his tent beyond
37:17 man told him, “They have *m* on from here;

MOVED (cont.)

Ex 2: 6 She was *m* with pity for him and said,
14:19 camp, now *m* and went around behind them.
36: 2 *m* them to come and take part in the work.
Nm 9:18 bidding of the LORD the Israelites *m* on,
9:22 but when it lifted, they *m* on.
10:12 *m* on from the desert of Sinai by stages,
10:33 They *m* on from the mountain of the LORD,
21:10 The Israelites *m* on and encamped in Oboth.
22: 1 Then the Israelites *m* on and encamped in
Jos 3: 1 Joshua *m* with all the Israelites from
Jgs 20:18 battle, *m* on to Bethel and consulted God.
1Sm 5: 9 *m* the ark of the God of Israel to Gath!
17:48 then *m* to meet David at close quarters,
23:26 As Saul *m* along one rim of the gorge,
24: 5 So David *m* up and stealthily cut off an
2Sm 17:22 all his people *m* on and crossed the Jordan.
2Kgs 16: 9 who listened to him and *m* against Damascus,
24: 1 king of Babylon, *m* against him,
1Chr 16:30 he has made the world firm, not to be *m*.
2Chr 14: 8 Zerah the Ethiopian *m* against them with a
Jdt 7:17 Thereupon the Moabites *m* camp,
8:16 is not man that he should be *m* by threats,
1Mc 2:24 heart was *m* and his just fury was aroused;
3:57 Then the army *m* off,
5:36 From there he *m* on and took Chaspho,
6:32 citadel and *m* his camp to Beth-zechariah,
6:33 *m* his force hastily along the road to
6:36 it moved, they *m* too and never left it.
9:11 Then the army of Bacchides *m* out of camp
13:12 Then Trypho *m* from Ptolemais with a large
13:20 *m* along opposite him everywhere he went.
2Mc 10:16 *m* quickly against the strongholds of the
12:27 of these, he *m* his army to Ephron,
Jb 14:18 at last and its rock is *m* from its place,
15:19 was given, when no foreigner *m* among them.
18: 4 [or the rock be *m* out of its place]?
Ps(s) 93: 1 he has made the world firm, not to be *m*.
96:10 He has made the world firm, not to be *m*;
104: 5 upon its foundation, not to be *m* forever;
112: 6 He shall never be *m*;
Is 10:13 I have *m* the boundaries of peoples,
Jer 2:31 Why do my people say, "We have *m* on.
Bar 3:38 she has appeared on earth, and *m* among men.
Ez 1: 9 they did not turn when they *m*,
1:12 they did not turn when they *m*
1:17 they faced, without veering as they *m*.
1:19 creatures moved, the wheels *m* with them;
1:24 When they *m*, the sound of the tumult
10:11 When they *m*, they went in any one
10:11 four directions without veering as they *m*;
10:11 towards it without veering as they *m*.
10:16 When the cherubim *m*,
Zec 1:14 *m* for the sake of Jerusalem and Zion,
Mt 9: 9 As he *m* on, Jesus saw a man
9:27 As Jesus *m* on from there,
9:36 of the crowds, his heart was *m* with pity.
13:53 these parables, he *m* on from that district.
14:14 the vast throng, his heart was *m* with pity,
15:32 "My heart is *m* with pity for the crowd.
18:27 *M* with pity, the master let the official go
20:34 *M* with compassion,
Mk 1:41 *M* with pity, Jesus stretched out his hand
2:14 As he *m* on he saw Levi the son of Alphaeus
8: 2 "My heart is *m* with pity for the crowd.
10: 1 From there he *m* on to the districts of
10:28 Peter was *m* to say to him,
Lk 7:13 The Lord was *m* with pity upon seeing her
10:33 came on him and was *m* to pity at the sight.
15:20 caught sight of him and was deeply *m*.
19:36 their cloaks on the roadway as he *m* along;
Jn 7: 1 After this, Jesus *m* about within Galilee.
11:33 in spirit, *m* by the deepest emotions.
11:54 no longer *m* about freely in Jewish circles.
20: 1 She saw that the stone had been *m* away,
Acts 1:21 company while the Lord Jesus *m* among us,
8:36 *m* along the road they came to some water,
27: 8 Again with difficulty we *m* along the coast
Col 1: 4 *m* as you are by the hope held in store

MOVEMENT (2)

2Sm 20: 8 that could be drawn with a downward *m*.
Jn 5: 4 disabled][waiting for the *m* of the water].

MOVES (4)

Dt 27:17 be he who *m* his neighbor's landmarks!'
Ps(s) 69:35 him, the seas and whatever *m* in them!"
102:15 servants, and her dust *m* them to pity.
Eccl 10: 9 He who *m* stones may be hurt by them,

MOVING (11)

Gn 3: 8 they heard the sound of the LORD God *m*
7: 4 earth every *m* creature that I have made."
19: 9 Lot, *m* in closer to break down the door.
1Sm 1:13 though her lips were *m*,
13: 5 *M* up against Israel, they encamped in
2Sm 15:23 all the soldiers *m* on ahead of him
Ez 1:13 *m* to and fro among the living creatures.
Mt 14:29 began to walk on the water, *m* toward Jesus.
Acts 3: 9 people saw him *m* and giving praise to God,
9:28 *m* freely about Jerusalem and expressing
27:17 *m* the ship and the ship was carried along.

MOWED (2)

Ex 17:13 And Joshua *m* down Amalek and his people
Is 14:12 to the ground, you who *m* down the nations!

MOWING (1)

Am 7: 1 up (the late growth after the king's *m*).

MOWN (1)

Na 1:12 still they shall be *m* down and disappear.

MOZA (5)

1Chr 2:46 Ephah, Caleb's concubine, bore Haran, *M*,
8:36 Zimri became the father of *M*.
8:37 *M* became the father of Binea,
9:42 Zimri became the father of *M*.
9:43 *M* became the father of Binea,

MOZAH (1)

Jos 18:26 Ramah, Beeroth, Mizpeh, Chephirah, *M*,

MUCH (253)

Gn 14:23 that I would not take so *m* as a thread or
16: 6 her so *m* that Hagar ran away from her.
25:22 jostled each other so *m* that she exclaimed,
29: 7 "There is still *m* daylight left;
30:30 had before I came has grown into very *m*,
32: 8 Jacob was very *m* frightened.
37: 4 so *m* that they would not even greet him.
44: 1 bags with as *m* food as they can carry,
47:20 with the famine too *m* for them to bear,
48: 5 mine as *m* as Reuben and Simeon are mine.
Ex 16: 5 as *m* as they gather on the other days."
16:18 a large amount did not have too *m*,
16:22 sixth day they gathered twice as *m* food,
20:18 position *m* farther away and said to Moses,
21:22 as *m* as the woman's husband demands of him,
36: 5 "The people are bringing *m* more than is
Lv 14:21 "If a man is poor and cannot afford so *m*,
25:16 are many, the price shall be so *m* the more;
25:16 are few, the price shall be so *m* the less.
26:10 So *m* of the old crops will you have stored
Dt 2: 5 not give you so *m* as a foot of their land,
12:15 your heart's desire as *m* as meat as the LORD,
14:24 the journey is too *m* for you and you are
16:17 but each of you with as *m* as he can give,
28:38 "Though you spend *m* seed on your field,
29:14 it is just as *m* with those who are not
31:27 How *m* more, then after I am dead!
Jos 18: 3 "How *m* longer will you put off taking
1Sm 17:24 all retreated before him, very *m* afraid.
19: 4 but has helped you very *m* by his deeds.
21:13 remarks and became very *m* afraid of Achish,
23: 3 How *m* more so if we go to Keilah against
2Sm 2:26 How *m* longer will you refrain from
3:22 expedition, bringing *m* plunder with them.
4:11 How *m* more now,
16:11 how *m* more might this Benjaminite do so!
19:35 "How *m* longer have I to live,
1Kgs 1:40 playing flutes and rejoicing so *m* as to
8:27 how *m* less this temple which I have built!
2Kgs 3: 2 though not as *m* as his father and mother.
21: 6 He did *m* evil in the LORD's sight and
21:16 shedding so *m* innocent blood as to fill
1Chr 5: 9 they had *m* livestock in the land of Gilead.
22: 3 so *m* bronze that it could not be weighed,
22: 8 'You have shed *m* blood,
22: 8 too *m* blood upon the earth in my sight.
2Chr 6:18 how *m* less this temple which I have built!
9: 1 and by camels bearing spices, *m* gold,
14:13 the cities, for there was *m* booty in them.
20:25 so *m* that they were unable to carry it all;
24:11 and they saw that it contained *m* money,
25: 9 "The LORD can give you *m* more than that."
25:13 of the inhabitants and took away *m* booty.
27: 3 *m* construction done on the wall of Ophel.
28: 8 they also took from them *m* plunder,
31:10 eaten to the full and have had *m* left over,
32:15 how *m* the less shall your god save you
Neh 2:10 they were very *m* displeased that someone
3:33 his anger and he became very *m* incensed.
6:16 lost *m* face in the eyes of the nations,
13: 8 This displeased me very *m*,
Tb 3: 6 to die than to endure so *m* misery in life,
10:12 from now on they are as *m* your parents
12: 2 "Father, how *m* shall I pay him?
12: 3 How *m* of a bonus should I give him?"
Jdt 2:18 *m* gold and silver from the royal palace.
10: 7 *m* astounded at her beauty and said to her,
12:18 I ever enjoyed life as *m* as I do today."
1Mc 1: 9 years, causing *m* distress over the earth.
1:24 with great arrogance and shed *m* blood.
4:23 and his men collected *m* gold and silver,
6: 8 he was struck with fear and very *m* shaken.
6:54 home, for the famine was too *m* for them.
9: 6 of the troops, they were very *m* afraid,
9:39 tambourines and musicians and *m* equipment.
10:87 returned to Jerusalem, laden with *m* booty.
11:51 they returned to Jerusalem with *m* spoil.
11:53 received from him, he caused him *m* trouble.
12:44 to so *m* trouble when we are not at war?
13:17 of provoking *m* hostility among the people,
13:32 Thus he brought *m* evil on the land.
15:26 with gold and silver and *m* equipment.
16:11 of Jericho, and he had *m* silver and gold,
2Mc 9:20 are going as you wish, I thank God very *m*,
15:11 not so *m* with the safety of shield and
15:18 They were not so *m* concerned about their
Jb 4:19 How *m* more with those that dwell in houses
7:17 What is man, that you make *m* of him,
9:14 How *m* less shall I give him any answer,
15:16 his sight, How *m* less so is the abominable,
25: 6 How *m* less man,
42:10 gave to Job twice as *m* as he had before.
Ps(s) 119:14 decrees I rejoice, as *m* as in all riches.
119:107 I am very *m* afflicted;
129: 1 *M* have they oppressed me from my youth,
129: 2 *M* have they oppressed me from my youth;
Prv 11:31 how *m* more the wicked and the sinner!
14:29 The patient man shows *m* good sense,
15:11 how *m* more the hearts of men!
16:16 How *m* better to acquire wisdom than gold!
17: 7 how *m* more, lying words in a noble!
19: 7 how *m* more do his friends shun him!
19:10 *m* less should a slave rule over princes.
25:27 To eat too *m* honey is not good;
Eccl 1:18 For in *m* wisdom there is much sorrow,
2:13 *m* as light has the advantage over darkness.
5:11 laboring man, whether he eats little or *m*,
8:17 However *m* man toils in searching,
9:18 and a single slip can ruin *m* that is good."
12:12 *m* study there is weariness for the flesh.
Sg 4:10 *m* more delightful is your love than wine,
Wis 12:18 and with *m* lenience you govern us;
13: 4 how *m* more powerful is he who made them.
Sir 3:22 With what is too *m* for you meddle not,
10:30 in poverty, how *m* more so in wealth!
10:30 in wealth, in poverty how *m* the more!
20: 2 It is *m* better to admonish than to lose
20: 7 He who talks too *m* is detested;
20:11 A man may buy *m* for little,
27:24 There is nothing that I hate so *m*,
29:19 who undertakes too *m* falls into lawsuits.
29:23 little or *m* be content with what you have,
31:12 Nor cry out, "How *m* food there is here!"
31:21 If perforce you have eaten too *m*,
32: 8 Be brief, but say *m* in those few words,
34:11 I have seen *m* in my travels,
42: 5 Of acquiring *m* or little,
43:20 He scatters frost like so *m* salt;
47:18 Gold you gathered like so *m* iron,
51:27 labored only a little, but have found *m*.
Is 21:11 Seir, "Watchman, how *m* longer the night?
21:11 Watchman, how *m* longer the night?"
Jer 2:22 you scour it with soap, and use *m* lye,
Bar 6:58 *m* better to be a king displaying his valor,
Ez 15: 5 how *m* less, when the fire has devoured
20:16 *m* were their hearts devoted to their idols,
23:32 drink, so wide and deep, which holds so *m*,
31: 9 I made it beautiful, with *m* foliage,
38:13 away cattle and goods, to seize *m* plunder?"
46: 7 ram, for the lambs as *m* as he has at hand,
46:11 ram, but for the lambs as *m* as one pleases,
Dn 4:33 kingdom, and became *m* greater than before.
7: 5 was given the order, "Up, devour *m* flesh."
13:27 old men, the servants felt very *m* ashamed,
14: 6 not see how *m* he eats and drinks every day?"
Hg 1: 6 You have sown *m*, but have brought in little;
1: 9 You expected *m*, but it came to little;
Mt 5:18 Of this *m* I assure you:
5:46 Do not tax collectors do as *m*?
5:47 Do not pagans do as *m*?
6: 2 You can be sure of this *m*,
6:30 will he not provide *m* more for you,
7:11 how *m* more will your heavenly Father give
8:10 I have never found this *m* faith in Israel.
10:25 how *m* more the members of his household!
12:12 think how *m* more precious a human being is
13:57 They found him altogether too *m* for them.
14: 6 the court which delighted Herod so *m*
19:29 times as *m* and inherit everlasting life.
27:14 count, *m* to the procurator's surprise.
Mk 5:19 *m* the Lord in his mercy has done for you."
6: 3 They found him too *m* for them.
6: 6 so *m* did their lack of faith distress him.
6:20 he heard him speak he was very *m* disturbed;
6:31 it impossible for them to so *m* as eat.
8:31 them that the Son of Man had to suffer *m*,
9:12 Man that he must suffer *m* and be despised?
12:27 You are very *m* mistaken."
Lk 2: 9 around them, and they were very *m* afraid.
6:33 Sinners do as *m*.
7: 9 found so *m* faith among the Israelites."
10:20 do not rejoice so *m* in the fact that the
11: 8 persistence, and give him as *m* as he needs.
11:13 how *m* more will the heavenly Father give
12:24 *m* more important you are than the birds!
12:28 how *m* more will he provide for you,
12:48 *m* has been given a man, *m* will be required
15:29 yet you never gave me so *m* as a kid goat
16: 5 to the first, 'How *m* do you owe my master?'
16: 7 he said to a second, 'How *m* do you owe?'

17:25 *m* and be rejected by the present age.
17:28 It was *m* the same in the days of Lot:
22:69 This *m* only will I say:
Jn 1:50 You will see *m* greater things than that."
6:11 with the dried fish, as *m* as they wanted,
7: 5 even his brothers had *m* confidence in him.)
7:12 there was *m* guarded debate about him.
8:26 I could say *m* about you in condemnation,
9:25 "I know this *m*: I was blind before;
11: 5 Martha and her sister and Lazarus very *m*.
11:36 Jews to remark, "See how *m* he loved him!"
12:24 But if it dies, it produces *m* fruit.
12:44 not so *m* in me as in him who sent me;
13:33 children, I am not to be with you *m* longer.
14:25 This *m* have I told you while I was still
15: 8 bearing *m* fruit and becoming my disciples.
15:20 your words as *m* as they respected mine.
16: 7 It is *m* better for you that I go.
16:12 I have *m* more to tell you,
Acts 2: 6 They were *m* confused because each one
2:13 a sneer, "They have had too *m* new wine!"
9:16 how *m* he will have to suffer for my name."
13:11 be blind, unable so *m* as to see the sun."
15: 2 This created dissension and *m* controversy
15: 7 After *m* discussion, Peter took the floor
19: 2 so *m* as heard that there is a Holy Spirit."
26:29 replied, "Whether little more or *m* more,
27: 9 *M* time had now gone by.
28:10 They paid us *m* honor,
Rom 3: 2 The answer is, *m* in every respect.
5:15 *m* more did the grace of God and the
5:17 *m* more shall those who receive the
9:22 with *m* patience vessels fit for wrath,
11:12 world, how *m* more their full number!
11:24 so *m* the more will they who belong to it
1Cor 2: 3 and in fear, and with *m* trepidation.
2: 9 nor has it so *m* as dawned on man what God
3: 3 being still very *m* in a natural condition.
9:11 is it too *m* to expect a material harvest
14: 5 tongues, but I *m* prefer that you prophesy.
2Cor 1: 5 have shared *m* in the suffering of Christ,
3: 8 how *m* greater will be the glory of the
5: 8 would *m* rather be away from the body
7: 4 with utter frankness and boast *m* about you.
8:15 "He who gathered *m* had no excess and he
9: 6 Let me say this *m*:
9:12 but also overflows in *m* gratitude to God.
10: 7 may belong to Christ but just as *m* do we.
12:15 If I love you too *m*,
Phil 1: 6 I am sure of this *m*:
1: 8 God himself can testify how *m* I long for
1:21 hence dying is so *m* gain.
1Thes 3: 7 we have been *m* consoled by your faith
3: 8 so *m* so that we shall continue to flourish
2Thes 1: 4 so *m* so that in God's communities we can
1Tm 1: 7 *m* less the matters they discuss with such
3:13 *m* assurance in their faith in Christ Jesus.
Phlm 1:16 and how *m* more to you,
Heb 5:11 About this we have *m* to say,
9:14 how *m* more will the blood of Christ,
10:29 Do you not suppose that a *m* worse
12:25 how *m* greater punishment will be ours if
1Pt 3: 7 as *m* as you to the gracious gift of life.
1Jn 5: 9 The testimony of God is *m* greater:
2Jn 1:12 there is *m* more that I could write you,
3Jn 1:13 is *m* more that I had in mind to write you,
Jude 1:11 So *m* the worse for them!
1:23 abhor so *m* as their flesh-stained clothing.
Rv 2: 6 But you have this *m* in your favor:
14:20 and so *m* blood poured out of the winepress

MUCH-VAUNTED (1)

2Cor 11:12 chance to say that in their *m* ministry

MUD (15)

2Sm 22:43 the *m* in the streets I trampled them down.
Ps(s) 18:43 the *m* in the streets I trampled them down.
40: 3 of destruction, out of the *m* of the swamp;
Sir 22: 1 The sluggard is like a stone in the *m*;
Is 10: 6 tread them down like the *m* of the streets.
57:20 calmed, And its waters cast up *m* and filth.
Jer 38: 6 only mud, and Jeremiah sank into the *m*.
38:22 Now that your feet are stuck in the *m*,
Na 3:14 Go down into the *m* and tread the clay,
Jn 9: 6 spat on the ground, made *m* with his saliva,
9: 6 and smeared the man's eyes with the *m*.
9:11 Jesus made *m* and smeared it on my eyes,
9:14 had made the *m* paste and opened his eyes.)
9:15 He told them, "He put *m* on my eyes.

MUDDY (1)

2Mc 1:21 could not find any fire, but only *m* water,

MUFFLE (1)

Lv 13:45 and his head bare, and shall *m* his beard;

MULBERRIES (1)

1Mc 6:34 of grapes and *m* to provoke them to fight.

MULBERRY (1)

Is 40:20 *M* wood, the choice portion which a

MULE (6)

2Sm 18: 9 He was mounted on a *m*, and, as the *m* passed
18: 9 as the *m* passed under the branches of a
1Kgs 1:33 Mount my son Solomon upon my own *m*
1:38 and mounting Solomon on King David's *m*,
1:44 and they mounted him upon the king's own *m*.

MULE-LOADS (1)

2Kgs 5:17 let me, your servant, have two *m* of earth,

MULES (13)

2Sm 13:29 the other princes rose, mounted their *m*,
1Kgs 10:25 garments, weapons, spices, horses and *m*.
18: 5 may find grass and save the horses and *m*,
1Chr 12:41 came bringing food on asses, camels, *m*,
2Chr 9:24 garments, weapons, spices, horses and *m*.
Ezr 2:66 their *m* two hundred and forty-five,
Neh 7:67 their *m* two hundred and forty-five,
Jdt 2:17 of camels, asses, and *m* for their baggage;
15:11 She harnessed her *m*,
Ps(s) 32: 9 Be not senseless like horses or *m*:
Is 66:20 chariots, in carts, upon *m* and dromedaries,
Ez 27:14 and *m* were exchanged for your wares.
Zec 14:15 shall be the plague upon the horses, *m*,

MULTIPLICATION (1)

Mt 6: 7 win a hearing by the sheer *m* of words.

MULTIPLIED (8)

Ex 1:12 were oppressed, the more they *m* and spread.
11: 9 my wonders may be *m* in the land of Egypt."
Dt 1:10 has so *m* you that you are now as numerous
Jgs 16:24 of our land, the one who has *m* our slain."
Prv 9:11 be *m* and the years of your life increased."
Sir 23: 3 my failings increase, and my sins be *m*;
Is 57: 9 king with scented oil, and *m* your perfumes;
Lam 2: 5 Judah he has *m* moaning and groaning.

MULTIPLIES (4)

Jb 35:16 his mouth, and without knowledge *m* words.
Eccl 10:14 yet the fool *m* words.
Sir 6: 5 A kind mouth *m* friends,
31:30 it lessens his strength and *m* his wounds.

MULTIPLY (37)

Gn 1:22 God blessed them, saying, "Be fertile, *m*,
1:22 and let the birds *m* on the earth."
1:28 "Be fertile and *m*; fill the earth and subdue
6: 1 *m* on earth and daughters were born to them,
9: 1 "Be fertile and *m* and fill the earth.
9: 7 Be fertile, then, and *m*;
17: 2 my covenant, and I will *m* you exceedingly."
17:20 him fertile and will *m* him exceedingly.
26:24 I will bless you and *m* your descendants
28: 3 *m* you that you may become an assembly of
35:11 "I am God Almighty; be fruitful and *m*.
Ex 23:29 that the wild beasts will *m* against you.
Lv 26:21 me, I will *m* my blows another sevenfold,
Dt 7:13 He will love and bless and *m* you;
13:18 *m* you as he promised your fathers on oath;
1Chr 27:23 to *m* Israel like the stars of the heavens.
Jb 9:17 me, and *m* my wounds without cause;
10:17 upon me and *m* your harassment of me;
29:18 I shall *m* years like the phoenix.
Ps(s) 16: 4 They *m* their sorrows who court other gods.
Eccl 6:11 there are many sayings that *m* vanity,
Sir 23:16 Two types of men *m* sins,
Jer 3:16 When you *m* and become fruitful in the land,
23: 3 there they shall increase and *m*.
33:22 I will *m* the descendants of my servant
46:11 No use to *m* remedies;
Ez 36:11 and beasts upon you, to *m* and be fruitful.
36:37 to *m* them like sheep.
37:26 covenant with them, and I will *m* them,
47: 9 of living creature that can *m* shall live,
Dn 3:36 *m* their offspring like the stars of heaven,
Na 3:15 *M* like the grasshoppers, *m* like the locusts!
2Cor 9: 8 God can *m* his favors among you so that you
9:10 he will *m* the seed you sow and increase
Col 1:10 You will *m* good works of every sort and
Heb 6:14 said, "I will indeed bless you, and *m* you."

MULTIPLYING (1)

Gn 8:17 abound on the earth, breeding and *m* on it."

MULTITUDE (25)

Gn 48:19 descendants shall become a *m* of nations."
Jos 11: 4 and with a *m* of horses and chariots.
1Sm 17:47 All this *m*, too, shall learn
2Sm 6:19 and each woman in the entire *m* of Israel,
2Chr 13: 8 simply because you are a huge *m* and have
14:10 in your name we have come against this *m*.
20: 2 "A great *m* is coming against you from
20:12 before this vast *m* that comes against us.
20:15 or lose heart at the sight of this vast *m*,
Jdt 5:10 and grew into such a great *m* that the
1Mc 5:30 ahead and saw a countless *m* of people,
Jb 31:34 *m* and the scorn of the tribes terrified me
Ps(s) 42: 5 thanksgiving, with the *m* keeping festival.
Wis 6: 2 the *m* and lord it over throngs of peoples!
18: 5 reproof you carried off their *m* of sons
18:20 and in the desert a plague struck the *m*;
Sir 33:19 Listen, to me, O leaders of the *m*;
Is 16:14 shall be degraded despite all its great *m*;
Dn 10: 6 and his voice sounded like the roar of a *m*.
Zec 2: 8 of the *m* of men and beasts in her midst.
Mk 3: 8 an equally great *m* came to him from Judea,
Lk 2:13 with the angel a *m* of the heavenly host,
11:53 and to make him speak on a *m* of questions,
Jas 5:20 his soul from death and cancel a *m* of sins.
1Pt 4: 8 be constant, for love covers a *m* of sins.

MULTITUDES (1)

Gn 48:16 they may become teeming *m* upon the earth!"

MUNIFICENCE (1)

Est 1: 7 flowed freely, as befitted the king's *m*.

MURDER (20)

2Chr 24:25 of the *m* of the son of Jehoiada the priest.
2Mc 4:35 and angry over the unjust *m* of the man.
4:36 went to see him about the *m* of Onias.
Ps(s) 94: 6 stranger they slay, the fatherless they *m*,
Wis 14:25 blood and *m*, theft and guile, corruption,
Jer 7: 9 Are you to steal and *m*,
41: 4 The second day after the *m* of Gedaliah,
Hos 4: 2 False swearing, lying, *m*,
Mt 5:21 forefathers, 'You shall not commit *m*;
15:19 From the mind stem evil designs *m*,
Mk 7:21 acts of fornication, theft, *m*,
15: 7 rebels who had committed *m* in the uprising.
Lk 23:19 causing an uprising in the city, and for *m*.
23:25 thrown in prison for insurrection and *m*,
Acts 23:27 whom the Jews seized and were about to *m*.
26:21 me in the temple court and tried to *m* me.
Rom 1:29 maliciousness, greed, ill will, envy, *m*,
13: 9 you shall not *m*;
Jas 2:11 do not commit adultery but do commit *m*,
4: 2 you do not obtain, and so you resort to *m*.

MURDERED (7)

Jgs 20: 4 and the Levite, the husband of the *m* woman,
2Kgs 14: 5 he slew the officials who had *m* the king,
2Chr 21:13 and also because you have *m* your brothers
Tb 2: 3 "Father, one of our people has been *m*!
1Mc 2: 9 Her infants have been *m* in her streets,
Mt 23:35 whom you *m* between the temple building and
Lk 11:47 but it was your fathers who *m* them.

MURDERER (20)

Nm 35:16 death, he is a *m* and shall be put to death.
35:17 death, he is a *m* and shall be put to death.
35:18 death, he is a *m* and shall be put to death.
35:19 The avenger of blood may execute the *m*,
35:21 his death, he shall be put to death as a *m*.
35:21 of blood may execute the *m* on sight.
35:30 is required for the execution of the *m*.
35:31 life of a *m* who deserves the death penalty;
2Sm 16: 8 now you suffer ruin because you are a *m*."
2Kgs 6:32 a *m* is sending someone to cut off my head?
9:31 "Is all well, Zimri, *m* of your master?"
2Mc 4:38 and there he put the *m* to death.
9:28 So this *m* and blasphemer,
Jb 24:14 When there is no light the *m* rises,
Ez 18:10 if he begets a son who is a thief, a *m*,
Mt 5:21 every *m* shall be liable to judgment.
Acts 3:14 instead to be granted the release of a *m*.
28: 4 another, "This man must really be a *m* if,
1Pt 4:15 it that none of you suffers for being a *m*,
1Jn 3:15 Anyone who hates his brother is a *m*,

MURDERERS (11)

2Kgs 14: 6 children of the *m* he did not put to death,
2Mc 12: 6 he marched against the *m* of his kinsmen.
Wis 12: 5 These merciless *m* of children,
Is 1:21 used to lodge within her, but now, *m*.
Ez 28: 9 when you face your *m*?
Mt 22: 7 to destroy those *m* and burn their city.
23:31 that you are the sons of the prophets' *m*.
Acts 7:52 your turn have become his betrayers and *m*.
1Tm 1: 9 men who kill their fathers or mothers, *m*,
Rv 21: 8 traitors to the faith, the depraved and *m*,
22:15 dogs and sorcerers, the fornicators and *m*,

MURDERESS (1)

Mt 23:37 *m* of prophets and stoner of those who were

MURDERESSES (2)

Ez 16:38 you the sentence of adulteresses and *m*;
23:45 sentence meted out to adulteresses and *m*,

MURDERING (3)

1Kgs 18: 4 Jezebel was *m* the prophets of the LORD,
18:13 Jezebel was *m* the prophets of the LORD

MURDERING (cont.)
21:19 After *m*, do you also take possession?

MURDEROUS (3)
2Sm 16: 7 "Away, away, you *m* and wicked man!
Jer 9: 7 A *m* arrow is his tongue,
Acts 9: 1 *m* threats against the Lord's disciples,

MURDERS (6)
Dt 22:26 rises up against his neighbor and *m* him:
2Mc 4: 3 such a point that *m* were being committed
Ps(s) 10: 8 in hiding he *m* the innocent;
Lk 11:48 committed the *m* and you erect the tombs.
1Jn 3:15 that eternal life abides in no *m* heart.
Rv 9:21 they repent of their *m* or their sorcery,

MURKY (1)
Jude 1: 6 shrouded in *m* darkness against the

MURMUR (2)
Lk 19: 7 this was observed, everyone began to *m*,
Jn 6:41 started to *m* in protest because he claimed,

MURMURED (3)
Jdt 5:22 people standing round about the tent *m*;
Ps(s) 106:25 They *m* in their tents,
Lk 15: 2 at which the Pharisees and the scribes *m*,

MURMURING (3)
Dt 1:27 LORD, your God, you set to *m* in your tents,
Jn 6:43 "Stop your *m*," Jesus told them.
6:61 were *m* in protest at what he had said.

MURMURINGS (1)
Lam 3:62 against me], The whispered *m* of my foes,

MUSCLE (2)
Gn 32:33 the sciatic *m* that is on the hip socket,
32:33 hip socket was struck at the sciatic *m*.

MUSHI (8)
Ex 6:19 The sons of Merari were Mahli and *M*.
Nm 3:20 of Merari, by clans, were Mahli and *M*.
1Chr 6: 4 The sons of Merari were Mahli and *M*.
6:32 son of Shemer, son of Mahli, son of *M*,
23:21 The sons of Merari: Mahli and *M*.
23:23 The sons of *M*: Mahli, Eden.
24:26 The descendants of Merari were Mahli, *M*,
24:30 The descendants of *M* were Mahli,

MUSHITES (2)
Nm 3:33 the clans of the Mahlites and the *M*;
26:58 clan of the Mahlites, the clan of the *M*,

MUSIC (19)
1Chr 13: 8 enthusiasm, amid songs and *m* on lyres,
15:28 and cymbals, and the *m* of harps and lyres.
Neh 12:27 thanksgiving hymns and the *m* of cymbals,
1Mc 9:41 and the sound of *m* into lamentation.
13:51 the *m* of harps and cymbals and lyres,
Ps(s) 45: 9 from ivory palaces string *m* brings you joy.
49: 5 set forth my riddle to the *m* of the harp.
71:22 will I give you thanks with *m* on the lyre,
Wis 19:18 while the flow of *m* steadily persists.
Sir 32: 6 seal is string *m* with delicious wine.
39:15 With *m* on the harp and all stringed
40:20 Wine and *m* delight the soul,
47: 9 each year With string *m* before the altar,
49: 1 honey to the taste, like *m* at a banquet.
Is 14:11 your pomp is brought, the *m* of your harps.
Lam 5:14 abandoned the gate, the young men their *m*.
Am 6: 5 Improvising to the *m* of the harp,
Lk 15:25 home, he heard the sound of *m* and dancing.
15:26 him the reason for the dancing and the *m*.

MUSICAL (10)
1Chr 15:16 as chanters, to play on *m* instruments,
2Chr 5:13 *m* instruments to "give thanks to the LORD,
7: 6 with the *m* instruments of the LORD which
23:13 *m* instruments were leading the acclaim.
34:12 who were skillful with *m* instruments
Neh 12:36 Hanani, with the *m* instruments of David,
Dn 3: 4 bagpipe, and all the other *m* instruments,
3: 7 bagpipe, and all the other *m* instruments,
3:10 and all the other *m* instruments should
3:15 bagpipe, and all the other *m* instruments;

MUSICIANS (2)
1Kgs 5:11 or Heman, Chalcol, and Darda, the *m*—
1Mc 9:39 with tambourines and *m* and much equipment.

MUST (691)
Gn 3:22 he *m* not be allowed to put out his hand to
4:14 and I *m* avoid your presence and become a
15:14 bring judgment on the nation they *m* serve,
17: 9 you *m* keep my covenant throughout the ages.
17:10 your descendants after you that you *m* keep:
17:13 those acquired with money *m* be circumcised.
18:21 that I *m* go down and see whether or not
26: 9 "She *m* certainly be your wife!
27:33 Now he *m* remain blessed!"
27:45 *M* I lose both of you in a single day?"
30:15 you *m* now take my son's mandrakes too?"
37:21 "We *m* not take his life.
42:20 But you *m* come back to me with your
42:36 *M* you make me childless?
42:36 Why *m* such things always happen to me?"
42:38 befall him on the journey you *m* make,
43:11 "If it *m* be so, then do this:
43:12 for you *m* return the amount that was put
43:18 "It *m* be," they thought, "on account of
43:23 *m* have put treasures in your bags for you.
44:28 *m* have been torn to pieces by wild beasts;
45:28 I *m* go and see him before I die."
46:34 asks what your occupation is, you *m* answer,
47:24 is in, you *m* give a fifth of it to Pharaoh,
50:25 you *m* bring my bones up with you from this
Ex 2:14 thought, "The affair *m* certainly be known."
3: 3 *m* go over to look at this remarkable sight,
5:11 Yet there *m* not be the slightest reduction
5:18 you *m* still deliver your quota of bricks."
8:23 We *m* go a three days' journey in the
8:25 *m* not play false again by refusing to let
10: 7 to him, "How long *m* he be a menace to us?
10: 9 "Young and old *m* go with us,"
10: 9 as our flocks and herds *m* accompany us.
10:24 But your flocks and herds *m* remain."
10:25 "You *m* also grant us sacrifices and
10:26 Hence, our livestock also *m* go with us.
10:26 Not an animal *m* be left behind.
10:26 of them we *m* sacrifice to the LORD our God,
10:26 shall not know which ones we *m* sacrifice
12: 3 your families *m* procure for itself a lamb,
12: 5 *m* be a year-old male and without blemish.
12:10 of it *m* be kept beyond the next morning;
12:15 For seven days you *m* eat unleavened bread.
12:17 you *m* celebrate this day throughout your
12:25 you *m* also observe this rite when you have
12:42 night all the Israelites *m* keep a vigil
12:46 It *m* be eaten in one and the same house;
12:47 community of Israel *m* keep this feast.
12:48 males among them *m* first be circumcised,
13: 3 Nothing made with leaven *m* be eaten.
13: 5 this month that you *m* celebrate this rite,
13:13 Every first-born son you *m* redeem.
19: 6 That is what you *m* tell the Israelites."
19:12 touches the mountain, he *m* be put to death.
19:13 *m* be stoned to death or killed with arrows.
19:13 man or beast, *m* not be allowed to live.
19:22 approach the LORD *m* sanctify themselves;
19:24 *m* not break through to come up to the LORD;
20:26 on which you *m* not be indecently uncovered.
21:12 a man a mortal blow *m* be put to death.
21:14 you *m* take him even from my altar and put
21:19 he *m* compensate him for his enforced
21:28 or a woman to death, the ox *m* be stoned;
21:29 or a woman, not only *m* the ox be stoned,
21:29 but its owner also *m* be put to death.
21:30 he *m* pay in ransom for his life whatever
21:32 he *m* pay the owner of the slave thirty
21:32 shekels of silver, and the ox *m* be stoned.
21:34 the owner of the cistern *m* make good by
21:36 not keep it in, he *m* make full restitution,
22: 2 He *m* make full restitution.
22: 4 he *m* make restitution with the best
22: 5 started the fire *m* make full restitution.
22: 6 if caught, *m* make twofold restitution.
22: 8 *m* make twofold restitution to the other.
22:10 the owner *m* accept the oath,
22:11 theft, he *m* make restitution to the owner.
22:13 is not present, the man *m* make restitution.
22:16 he *m* still pay him the customary marriage
22:29 You *m* do the same with your oxen and your
22:29 but on the eighth day you *m* give it to me.
23:12 work, but on the seventh day you *m* rest,
23:15 you *m* eat unleavened bread for seven days
23:24 you *m* demolish them and smash their sacred
23:33 They *m* not abide in your land,
25:15 they *m* remain in the rings of the ark and
25:38 shears and trays, *m* be of pure gold.
27:18 *m* be used, and the pedestals *m* be of bronze.
27:19 the tent pegs of the court, *m* be of bronze.
28:38 this plate *m* always be over his forehead,
28:42 You *m* also make linen drawers for them,
29:14 the bullock you *m* burn up outside the camp,
29:34 the next day, this remnant *m* be burned up;
30:13 the registered group *m* pay a half-shekel,
30:14 group *m* give this contribution to the LORD.
30:20 the meeting tent, they *m* wash with water,
30:21 the LORD they *m* wash their hands and feet,
30:37 you *m* treat it as sacred to the LORD.
31:13 to Moses, "You *m* also tell the Israelites:
31:14 you *m* keep the sabbath as something sacred.
31:14 that day, he *m* be rooted out of his people.
34:11 *m* keep the commandments I am giving you
34:20 you do not redeem it, you *m* break its neck.
34:21 on that day you *m* rest even during the
Lv 1: 2 *m* be from the herd or from the flock.
1: 3 the herd, it *m* be a male without blemish.
1:10 a goat, he *m* bring a male without blemish.
2: 1 LORD, his offering *m* consist of fine flour.
2: 4 it *m* be in the form of unleavened cakes
2: 5 it *m* be of fine flour mixed with oil and
2: 6 *m* be broken into pieces, and oil *m* be poured
2: 7 prepared in a pot, it *m* be of fine flour,
3: 1 female animal, but it *m* be without blemish.
3: 6 female animal, but it *m* be without blemish.
3: 9 tail, which he *m* sever close to the spine,
3:10 liver, which he *m* sever above the kidneys.
3:15 and the lobe of the liver, which he *m* sever
4: 9 liver, which he *m* sever above the kidneys.
4:12 of the ash heap, there it *m* be burned.
4:21 This bullock *m* also be brought outside the
5:17 that he incurs guilt for which he *m* answer,
5:19 penalty of the guilt *m* be paid to the LORD."
6: 5 it *m* not go out.
6: 6 it *m* not go out.
6: 9 but it *m* be eaten in the form of
6:19 but it *m* be eaten in a sacred place,
6:20 stained part *m* be washed in a sacred place.
6:23 an offering *m* be burned up in the fire.
7: 4 which *m* be severed above the kidneys.
7: 6 but it *m* be eaten in a sacred place,
7:17 third day, it *m* be burned up in the fire.
8:35 Hence you *m* remain at the entrance of the
10:10 You *m* be able to distinguish between what
10:11 you *m* teach the Israelites all the laws
10:13 sacred, you *m* eat it in a sacred place.
11:32 *m* be put in water and remain unclean until
11:33 unclean, and the vessel itself you *m* break.
11:35 or a jar-stand, this *m* be broken to pieces;
13:49 with leprosy and *m* be shown to the priest.
13:52 leprosy, it *m* be destroyed by fire.
16:22 region, it *m* be sent away into the desert.
16:31 for you, on which you *m* mortify yourselves.
18:26 *m* keep my statutes and decrees forbidding
19: 6 it *m* be eaten on the very day of your
20:25 You, too, *m* set apart,
21: 6 the food of their God, they *m* be holy.
22:16 they bring down guilt that *m* be punished;
22:19 that he offers *m* be an unblemished male.
22:21 is to find acceptance, it *m* be unblemished;
22:30 it *m*, therefore, be eaten on the same day;
22:32 I, the LORD, *m* be held as sacred.
24: 9 his sons, who *m* eat it in a sacred place,
24:16 alien and native alike *m* be put to death
25:24 you *m* permit the land to be redeemed.
25:28 when it *m* be released and returned to its
25:31 and in the jubilee they *m* be released.
25:34 *m* always remain their hereditary property.
26:43 But the land *m* first be rid of them,
27: 8 sum, the person *m* be set before the priest,
27:11 sacrifice, it *m* be set before the priest,
27:29 they *m* be put to death.
Nm 4:19 each of them his task and what he *m* carry;
4:24 what they *m* do and what they must carry:
4:27 to what they *m* do and what they must carry;
13:33 and so we *m* have seemed to them."
14:33 your children *m* wander for forty years,
15:31 broken his commandment, he *m* be cut off.
15:38 they and their descendants *m* put tassels
16:13 the desert, that you *m* now lord it over us?
18:15 but you *m* let the first-born of man,
18:17 *m* splash on the altar of their fat you *m* burn
23:12 puts in my mouth that I *m* repeat with care?"
23:26 you that I *m* do all that the LORD tells me?"
24:13 Whatever the LORD says I *m* repeat.
30: 3 but *m* fulfill exactly the promise he has
31:23 it *m* also be purified with lustral water.
35: 6 the six cities of asylum which you *m*
35:31 he *m* be put to death.
Dt 1:22 we must follow and the cities we *m* take.'
1:33 in the fire, to show the way you *m* go.
3:18 But all you troops equipped for battle *m*
4:39 This is why you *m* now know,
4:40 You *m* keep his statutes and commandments
5:31 the statutes and decrees you *m* teach them,
7: 5 "But this is how you *m* deal with them:
8: 5 So you *m* realize that the LORD,
8:10 have eaten your fill, you *m* bless the LORD,
10:19 So you too *m* befriend the alien,
11: 2 but you yourselves who *m* now understand
12: 1 decrees which you *m* be careful to observe
12:16 but *m* pour it out on the ground like water.
12:18 These you *m* eat before the LORD,
12:27 and there you *m* offer both the flesh and
12:27 sacrifices the blood indeed *m* be poured
13:15 you *m* inquire carefully into the matter
14:21 "You *m* not eat any animal that has died
15: 2 he *m* not press his neighbor,
15:18 You *m* not be reluctant to let your slave
15:23 *m* be poured out on the ground like water.
16:19 you *m* be impartial.
17:15 you set over you as king *m* be your kinsman;
17:16 that you *m* never go back that way again.
18:13 *m* be altogether sincere toward the LORD,
20:17 You *m* doom them all
20:19 fruit, but you *m* not cut down the trees.
21: 5 or violence *m* be settled by their decision.
21:12 she *m* shave her head and pare her nails
23:15 enemies at your mercy, your camp *m* be holy;
23:24 But you *m* keep your solemn word and
28:34 driven mad by what your eyes *m* look upon.

28:67 *m* feel and the sight that your eyes *m* see.
30: 8 *m* again heed the LORD's voice and carry
31: 5 you *m* deal with them exactly as I have
31: 7 for you *m* bring this people into the land
31: 7 *m* put them in possession of their heritage.
31:13 do not know it yet, *m* hear it and learn it,
31:23 for it is you who *m* bring the Israelites
32:46 and which you *m* impress on your children,
Jos 1:14 But all the warriors among you *m* cross
1:14 you *m* help them until the LORD
3: 3 carry, you *m* also break camp and follow it,
7:12 enemies, but *m* turn their back to them,
7:14 morning you *m* present yourselves by tribes.
11: 6 You *m* hamstring their horses and burn
20: 4 who *m* receive him and assign him a place
22:18 *m* you now add to it?
23: 7 You *m* not invoke their gods,
23: 8 them, but you *m* remain loyal to the LORD,
Jgs 3:24 *m* be easing himself in the cool chamber."
5:30 "They *m* be dividing the spoil they took:
5:30 there *m* be a damsel or two for each man,
7: 4 man is to go with you, he *m* go with you.
7: 4 But no one is to go if I tell you he *m* not."
7:17 of the camp, and as I do, you *m* do also.
7:18 you too *m* blow horns all around the camp
8:23 The LORD *m* rule over you."
9: 2 You *m* remember that I am your own flesh
9: 9 answered them, *M* I give up my rich oil,
9:11 *M* I give up my sweetness and my good fruit,
9:13 *M* I give up my wine that cheers gods and
13:14 She *m* not eat anything that comes from the
14: 3 that you *m* go and take a wife from the
14:13 you *m* give me thirty tunics and thirty
14:16 his wife wept and said, "You *m* hate me;
14:16 my father or my mother, *m* I tell it to you?"
15:18 *M* I now die of thirst or fall into the
18:14 Now decide what you *m* do!"
19:24 the man you *m* not commit this wanton crime."
21:17 of Benjamin who survive *m* have heirs,
Ru 3: 1 *m* seek a home for you that will please you.
4: 5 Naomi, you *m* take also Ruth the Moabite,
1Sm 2:24 No, my sons, you *m* not do these things!
5: 7 of the God of Israel *m* not remain with us,
6: 3 Israel, you must not send it alone, but *m*,
8:19 There *m* be a king over us.
8:20 We too *m* be like other nations,
10: 8 I shall then tell you what you *m* do."
10:19 'Not so, but you *m* appoint a king over us.'
11: 2 I *m* gouge out every man's right eye,
12:12 said to me, 'Not so, but a king *m* rule us,'
12:20 *m* not turn from the LORD, but *m* worship
12:20 but *m* worship him with your whole heart.
12:24 But you *m* fear the LORD and worship him
14:34 but you *m* not sin against the LORD by
14:38 We *m* investigate and find out how this sin
14:45 This *m* not be!
20: 3 *m* not know of this lest he be grieved.'
20:16 The name of Jonathan *m* never be allowed by
20:26 "He *m* have become unclean by accident,
22:23 that seeks your life *m* seek my life also.
25:11 *M* I take my bread, my wine, my meat
25:17 for you *m* realize that otherwise evil is
26:10 *m* be the LORD himself who will strike him,
27:12 "He *m* certainly be detested by his people
28: 1 *m* go out on campaign with me to Jezreel."
29: 4 He *m* not go down into battle with us,
30:23 "You *m* not do this,
2Sm 2:22 Why *m* I strike you to the ground?
2:26 *M* the sword destroy to the utmost?
3:13 You *m* not appear before me unless you
3:38 "You *m* recognize that a great general has
4:11 *m* I hold you responsible for his death and
5: 8 *m* strike at them through the water shaft.
5:23 "You *m* not attack frontally,
9:10 sons and servants *m* till the land for him.
12:14 deed, the child born to you *m* surely die."
14: 7 We *m* put him to death for the life of his
14: 7 we *m* extinguish the heir also.'
14:14 We *m* indeed die; we are then like water
14:16 For the king *m* surely consent to free his
18: 3 "You *m* not come out with us.
19:22 "Shimei *m* be put to death for this.
21: 3 "What *m* I do for you and how must I make
21:17 "You *m* not go out to battle with us again
23: 7 He who wishes to touch them *m* arm himself
23: 7 of a spear, and they *m* be consumed by fire."
24:13 decide what I *m* reply to him who sent me."
24:24 to Araunah, "No, I *m* pay you for it,
1Kgs 1:42 are a man of worth and *m* bring good news."
2: 6 you *m* not allow him to go down to the
2: 9 But you *m* not let him go unpunished.
8:61 You *m* be wholly devoted to the LORD,
12:10 "This is what you *m* say to this people
12:24 You *m* not march out to fight against your
14: 5 This is what you *m* tell her.
18:27 Perhaps he is asleep and *m* be awakened."
20:24 This is what you *m* do:
22:16 "How many times *m* I adjure you to tell me
22:32 cried out, "That *m* be the king of Israel!"
2Kgs 4:22 I *m* go quickly to the man of God,
5:18 *m* bow down in the temple of Rimmon.
6:22 "You *m* not kill them," replied Elisha.
11: 5 "This is what you *m* do:
12: 6 they *m* make whatever repairs on the temple
12: 8 *m* no longer take funds from your clients,
16:15 You *m* also sprinkle on it all the blood of
17:12 LORD had told them, "You *m* not do this."
17:35 "You *m* not venerate other gods,
17:37 You *m* be careful to observe forever the
17:37 for you, and you *m* not venerate other gods.
17:38 you *m* not forget; you *m* not venerate
17:39 But the LORD, your God, you *m* venerate;
1Chr 15:12 *m* sanctify yourselves along with your
17:11 been completed and you *m* join your fathers,
19:12 too strong for me, you *m* come to my help;
22: 5 for the LORD *m* be made so magnificent
22:14 up wood and stones, to which you *m* add.
23:30 They *m* be present every morning to offer
23:31 they *m* always be present before the LORD.
2Chr 2: 4 And the house I intend to build *m* be large,
2: 8 I intend to build *m* be lofty and wonderful.
11: 4 You *m* not march out to fight against your
18:15 "How many times *m* I adjure you to tell me
18:31 exclaimed, "That *m* be the king of Israel!"
23: 3 "Here is the king's son who *m* reign,
23: 4 This is what you *m* do:
23: 4 in on the sabbath *m* guard the thresholds,
23: 5 another third *m* be at the king's palace
23: 6 *m* observe the prescriptions of the LORD.
23: 7 tries to enter the house *m* be slain.
23:14 "you *m* not put her to death in the LORD's
24: 5 You *m* hasten this affair."
Ezr 4: 3 God, but we alone *m* build it for the LORD,
7:17 You *m* take care,
Neh 2: 2 If you are not sick, you *m* be sad at heart."
6: 7 like these *m* reach the ear of the king,
8:10 rejoicing in the LORD *m* be your strength!"
8:11 today is holy, and you *m* not be saddened."]
8:14 that the Israelites *m* dwell in booths
9:12 the way in which they *m* travel.
13:27 *M* it also be heard of you that you have
Tb 5:10 God's sunlight, but *m* remain in darkness,
6:11 "Tonight we *m* stay with Raguel,
6:13 tonight we *m* speak for the girl,
8:10 to dig a grave, for he said, "I *m* do this,
14: 9 you *m* tell your children to do what is
Jdt 8:34 You *m* not inquire into what I am doing,
Est 6: 9 *m* clothe the man the king wishes to reward,
E: 8 We *m* provide for the future,
E:22 you too *m* celebrate this memorable day
9:12 What *m* they have done in the other royal
1Mc 5:42 all *m* go into battle."
6:43 armor, and he thought the king *m* be on it.
2Mc 2:29 *m* give attention to the whole structure,
3:13 *m* be confiscated for the royal treasury.
6:17 further ado we *m* go on with our story.
Jb 9:29 If I *m* be accounted guilty,
11: 2 *m* the garrulous man necessarily be right?
17:14 If I *m* call corruption "my father,"
32:16 *M* I wait? Now that they speak no more
34:33 Would you then say that God *m* punish,
34:33 It is you who *m* choose,
39: 2 Number the months that they *m* fulfill,
Ps(s) 32: 9 bit and bridle their temper *m* be curbed,
42:10 Why *m* I go about in mourning,
43: 2 Why *m* I go about in mourning,
45:12 for he is your lord, and you *m* worship him.
65: 2 To you *m* vows be fulfilled,
65: 3 To you all flesh *m* come
69: 5 *M* I restore what I did not steal?
Prv 1:31 they *m* eat the fruit of their own way,
6:31 if he be caught he *m* pay back sevenfold;
13:13 He who despises the word *m* pay for it,
14:19 Evil men *m* bow down before the good,
19:15 deep sleep, and the sluggard *m* go hungry.
24:14 Such, you *m* know,
Eccl 2:18 because I *m* leave them to a man who is to
2:21 labored over it, he *m* leave his property.
10:10 easy progress, he *m* increase his efforts;
Wis 12:19 deeds, that those who are just *m* be kind;
15:12 "For one *m*," says he, "make profit
16:28 one *m* give you thanks before the sunrise,
Sir 8:13 think any pledge a debt you *m* pay.
14:17 All *m* die.
16:28 of life which *m* return into it again.
18:29 trained in her words *m* show their wisdom,
19:14 every story you *m* not believe.
20: 9 no good, and some *m* be paid back double.
32:14 He who would find God *m* accept discipline:
39:28 When destruction *m* be,
42:17 Yet even God's holy ones *m* fail in
Is 7:13 you to weary men, *m* you also weary my God?
27: 5 He *m* make peace with me;
38:10 said, "In the noontime of life I *m* depart!
46: 1 They *m* be borne up on shoulders,
48: 6 look at all this; *m* you not admit it?
Jer 2:25 these strangers, and after them I *m* go."
4:14 How long *m* your pernicious thoughts lodge
4:21 How long *m* I see that signal,
9:18 We *m* leave the land,
10: 5 They *m* be carried about,
12: 1 even so, I *m* discuss the case with you.
12: 4 How long *m* the earth mourn,
18:20 *M* good be repaid with evil that they
20: 8 Whenever I speak, I *m* cry out,
22:15 *M* you prove your rank among kings by
25:28 You *m* drink!
26: 8 of him, crying, "You *m* be put to death!
27: 9 however, *m* not listen to your prophets,
27:15 name, with the result that I *m* banish you,
29: 6 There you *m* increase in number,
31:20 My heart stirs for him, I *m* show him mercy,
31:22 woman *m* encompass the man with devotion.
32:32 so that I *m* put it out of my sight for all
36:16 *m* certainly tell the king all these things."
49:12 not sentenced to drink the cup *m* drink it!
51:49 Babylon, too, *m* fall,
Lam 2:20 *M* women eat their offspring,
5: 4 we must buy, for our own wood we *m* pay.
Bar 4:18 He who has brought this evil upon you *m*
6:26 the ground, the worshipers *m* raise them up.
Ez 4:12 For your food you *m* bake barley loaves
8: 6 here, so that I *m* depart from my sanctuary?
8:17 now they *m* also put the branch to my nose?
16:58 you *m* bear it all,
18:26 of the iniquity he committed that he *m* die.
20:11 them my ordinances, which everyone *m* keep,
22:19 I *m* gather you together within Jerusalem.
44: 3 He *m* enter by way of the vestibule of the
44:26 he *m* wait an additional seven days,
Dn 9: 2 of Jerusalem seventy years *m* be fulfilled.
10:20 Soon I *m* fight the prince of Persia again.
11:36 ready, for what is determined *m* take place.
Hos 4:14 So *m* a people without understanding come
Jl 1:10 the grain is ravaged, the *m* has failed,
Am 6:10 no one *m* mention the name of the Lord
Mi 1:15 Yet *m* I bring to you the conqueror,
Hb 1: 3 why *m* I look at misery?
Zec 7: 3 *M* I mourn and abstain in the fifth month
Mal 2:15 You *m* then safeguard life that is your own,
2:16 You *m* then safeguard life that is your own,
3: 7 Yet you say, "How *m* we return?"
3:15 Rather *m* we call the proud blessed;
Mt 3:15 We *m* do this if we would fulfill all of
5:16 your light *m* shine before men so that they
5:31 wife, he *m* give her a decree of divorce.'
5:48 you *m* be made perfect as your heavenly
10:16 You *m* be clever as snakes and innocent as
12:26 Satan, he *m* be torn by dissension.
16:21 to his disciples that he *m* go to Jerusalem
16:24 to come after me, he *m* deny his very self,
17:10 the scribes claim that Elijah *m* come first?"
17:17 How long *m* I remain with you?
18:21 wrongs me, how often *m* I forgive him?
19:16 good *m* I do to possess everlasting life?"
20:26 who aspires to greatness *m* serve the rest,
20:27 first among you *m* serve the needs of all.
22: 9 That is why you *m* go out into the byroads
22:24 his brother *m* take the wife and produce
24:16 those in Judea *m* flee to the mountains.
24:17 he *m* not come down to get anything out of
24:18 he *m* not turn back to pick up his cloak.
24:44 You *m* be prepared in the same way.
26:27 "All of you *m* drink from it,"
26:54 fulfilled which say it *m* happen this way?"
Mk 8:34 to come after me, he *m* deny his very self,
9:11 the scribes claim that Elijah *m* come first?"
9:12 Man that he *m* suffer much and be despised?
9:19 How long *m* I remain with you?
9:35 he *m* remain the last one of all and the
10:17 what *m* I do to share in everlasting life?"
10:21 him, "There is one thing more you *m* do.
10:43 who aspires to greatness *m* serve the rest;
10:44 first among you *m* serve the needs of all.
12:19 his brother *m* take the wife and produce
13:10 *m* first be proclaimed to all the Gentiles.
13:14 in Judea *m* flee to the mountains.
13:15 he *m* not come down or enter his house to
13:16 he *m* not turn back to pick up his cloak.
Lk 4:43 "To other towns I *m* announce the good
9:22 he said, *m* first endure many sufferings,
9:23 to be my follower *m* deny his very self,
9:41 How long *m* I remain with you?
9:44 Man *m* be delivered into the hands of men."
10:25 what *m* I do to inherit everlasting life?"
13:33 For all that, I *m* proceed on course today,
14:18 some land and *m* go out and inspect it.
17:25 he *m* suffer much and be rejected by the
18:18 what *m* I do to share in everlasting life?"
18:22 "There is one thing further you *m* do.
18:31 "We *m* now go up to Jerusalem so that all
21: 9 Neither *m* you be perturbed when you hear
21:21 Judea at the time *m* flee to the mountains;
21:21 those in the heart of the city *m* escape it;
21:21 those in the country *m* not return.
21:22 when all that is written *m* be fulfilled.
22:32 You in turn *m* strengthen your brothers."
22:36 the man who has a purse *m* carry it;
22:36 a sword *m* sell his coat and buy one.
22:37 I tell you, *m* come to be fulfilled in me.
24: 7 that the Son of Man *m* be delivered into
24:46 is written that the Messiah *m* suffer and rise
Jn 3: 7 tell you you *m* all be begotten from above.
3:14 desert, so *m* the Son of Man be lifted up,
3:30 He *m* increase, while I must decrease.
3:36 see life, but *m* endure the wrath of God."
4:24 worship him *m* worship in Spirit and truth."
6:28 "What *m* we do to perform the works of
7:40 began to say, "This *m* be the Prophet."

MUST (cont.)

9: 4 We *m* do the deeds of him who sent me while
10:16 I *m* lead them, too, and they shall hear
12:34 claim that the Son of Man *m* be lifted up?
13:14 then you *m* wash each other's feet.
13:15 as I have done, so you *m* do.
13:34 for you, so *m* your love be for each other.
14:31 He has no hold on me but the world *m* know
15:16 Your fruit *m* endure,
15:27 You *m* bear witness as well,
19: 7 he *m* die because he made himself God's Son.
Acts 1:15 there *m* have been a hundred and twenty
2:15 You *m* realize that these men are not drunk,
2:38 "You *m* reform and be baptized,
3:21 Jesus *m* remain in heaven until the time of
4: 9 If we *m* answer today for a good deed done
4:10 all the people of Israel *m* realize
4:17 we *m* give them a stern warning
9:15 "You *m* go!
10:28 "You *m* know that it is not proper for a
12:15 they could say was, "It *m* be his angel."
13:38 You *m* realize, my brothers, that it is
14:22 "We *m* undergo many trials if we are to
16:30 and said, "Men, what *m* I do to be saved?"
17:32 *m* hear you on this topic some other time."
18:15 your own law, you *m* see to it yourselves.
19:21 there," he said, "I *m* visit Rome too."
19:36 *m* calm yourselves and not do anything rash.
20:35 by such hard work that you *m* help the weak.
22:10 'What is it I *m* do, sir?'
22:18 'You *m* make haste,' he said.
23:11 me here in Jerusalem, so *m* you do in Rome."
23:15 you *m* suggest to the commander that he
24: 3 Therefore we *m* always and everywhere
25:10 that is where I *m* be tried.
26:23 namely, that the Messiah *m* suffer,
28: 4 "This man *m* really be a murderer if,
28:28 Now you *m* realize that this salvation of
Rom 3: 4 God *m* be proved true even though every man
3: 7 glory, why *m* I be condemned as a sinner?
6:11 you *m* consider yourselves dead to sin but
6:16 You *m* realize that,
12: 9 Your love *m* be sincere.
13: 5 You *m* obey, then, not only to escape
14: 3 The man who will eat anything *m* not
14: 3 *m* not sit in judgment on him who eats.
14:13 *m* no longer pass judgment on one another.
14:15 You *m* not let the food you eat bring to
15: 1 we *m* not be selfish.
1Cor 2:14 it *m* be appraised in a spiritual way.
3:10 however, *m* be careful how he builds.
5:11 clear that you *m* not eat with such a man.
5:12 not those inside the community you *m* judge?
6: 6 *M* brother drag brother into court,
6:19 You *m* know that your body is a temple of
7:10 a wife *m* not separate from her husband.
7:11 she *m* either remain single or become
7:11 a husband *m* not divorce his wife.
7:12 to live with him, he *m* not divorce her.
7:13 to live with her, she *m* not divorce him.
15:25 Christ *m* reign until God has put all
15:53 body *m* be clothed with incorruptibility,
2Cor 1:11 But you *m* help us with your prayers,
9: 7 Everyone *m* give according to what he has
10: 8 If I find I *m* make a few further claims
11: 1 You *m* endure little of my folly.
11:21 To my shame I *m* confess that we have been
11:30 If I *m* boast, I will make a point of my
12: 1 I *m* go on boasting,
13:11 And now, brothers, I *m* say good-bye.
Gal 1: 7 the gospel of Christ *m* have confused you.
Eph 4:17 you *m* no longer live as the pagans do
4:22 that you *m* lay aside your former way of
4:24 You *m* put on that new man created in God's
4:26 The sun *m* not go down on your wrath;
4:28 who has been stealing *m* steal no longer;
6:13 You *m* put on the armor of God if you are
Phil 2: 5 Your attitude *m* be that of Christ:
2:10 name every knee *m* bend in the heavens,
2:25 too, that I *m* send you Epaphroditus,
3:15 spiritually mature *m* have this attitude.
Col 1:23 But you *m* hold fast to faith,
3: 8 You *m* put that aside now:
3:15 Christ's peace *m* reign in your hearts,
4: 4 Pray that I may speak it clearly, as I *m*.
1Thes 2: 9 You *m* recall, brothers, our efforts
4: 1 you *m* learn to make still greater progress.
5: 8 We who live by day *m* be alert,
2Thes 3:13 *m* never grow weary of doing what is right,
1Tm 2: 9 the women *m* deport themselves properly.
2:11 A woman *m* listen in silence and be
2:12 she *m* be quiet.
3: 2 A bishop *m* be irreproachable,
3: 3 He *m* not be addicted to drink.
3: 4 *m* be a good manager of his own household,
3: 7 He *m* also be well thought of by those
3: 8 In the same way, deacons *m* be serious,
3: 9 They *m* hold fast to the divinely revealed
3:12 Deacons may be married but once and *m* be
4:11 Such are the things you *m* urge and teach.
5: 9 She *m* have been married only once.
5:16 who are widows, she *m* assist them.
6: 1 All under the yoke of slavery *m* regard
6: 2 brothers in the faith *m* not take liberties
6: 2 *m* perform their tasks even more faithfully,
6: 2 are the things you *m* teach and preach.
2Tm 2: 1 *m* be strong in the grace which is ours in
2: 2 you *m* hand on to trustworthy men
2:24 *m* not be quarrelsome but *m* be kindly
2:24 He *m* be an apt teacher,
3:14 *m* remain faithful to what you have learned
Ti 1: 6 you, a presbyter *m* be irreproachable,
1: 7 The bishop as God's steward *m* be blameless.
1: 9 he *m* hold fast to the authentic message,
1:11 These *m* be silenced.
2: 2 the older men that they *m* be temperate,
2: 3 the older women *m* behave in ways that
2: 3 They *m* not be slanderous gossips or slaves
2: 4 By their good example they *m* teach the
2: 7 teaching *m* have the integrity of serious,
3: 2 They *m* be forbearing and display a perfect
3:11 You *m* recognize such a person as perverted
Heb 2: 1 we *m* attend all the more to what we have
4:13 eyes of him to whom we *m* render an account.
5: 3 and so *m* make sin offerings for himself
10:23 We *m* consider how to rouse
11: 6 who comes to God *m* believe that he exists,
12:20 the mountain, it *m* be stoned to death."
13:17 over you as men who *m* render an account.
13:23 I *m* let you know that our brother Timothy
Jas 1: 6 Yet he *m* ask in faith, never doubting,
1: 7 *m* not expect to receive anything from the
2: 1 Jesus Christ *m* not allow of favoritism.
2:24 You *m* perceive that a person is justified
5: 8 You, too, *m* be patient.
5:12 else, my brothers, you *m* not swear an oath,
5:13 among you is suffering hardship, he *m* pray.
1Pt 2:15 You *m* silence the ignorant talk of foolish
2:17 You *m* esteem the person of every man.
3: 1 You married women *m* obey your husbands,
3: 7 *m* show consideration for those who share
3:10 *m* keep his tongue from evil and his lips
3:11 He *m* turn from evil and do good,
4:17 what *m* be the end for those who refuse
5: 5 younger men *m* be obedient to your elders.
2Pt 1:14 how close is the day when I *m* fold my tent.
1:20 First you *m* understand this:
3: 8 This point *m* not be overlooked,
3:11 in this way, what sort of men *m* you not be!
1Jn 3:16 too *m* lay down our lives for our brothers.
4:11 we *m* have the same love for one another.
4:21 whoever loves God *m* also love his brother.
2Jn 1: 8 you *m* receive your reward in full.
Jude 1:22 the others you *m* rescue,
Rv 1: 1 show his servants what *m* happen very soon.
4: 1 show you what *m* take place in time to come."
10:11 "You *m* prophesy again for many peoples
22: 6 show his servants what *m* happen very soon."
22:11 The virtuous *m* live on in their virtue and

MUSTACHE (1)

2Sm 19:25 trimmed his *m* nor washed his clothes

MUSTARD (5)

Mt 13:31 "The reign of God is like a *m* seed which
17:20 you, if you had faith the size of a *m* seed,
Mk 4:31 It is like *m* seed which, when planted
Lk 13:19 It is like *m* seed which a man took and
17: 6 "If you had faith the size of a *m* seed,

MUSTER (3)

1Chr 12:24 This is the *m* of the detachments of armed
1Mc 3:27 a *m* of all the forces of his kingdom,
Rv 20: 8 and *m* for war the troops of Gog and Magog,

MUSTERED (27)

Gn 14:14 he *m* three hundred and eighteen of his
Ex 14: 6 made his chariots ready and *m* his soldiers
Nm 21:23 but *m* all his forces and advanced into the
Jos 8:10 *m* the army and went up to Ai at its head,
Jgs 6:33 Midian and Amalek and the Kedemites *m*
20:17 *m* four hundred thousand swordsmen ready
1Sm 28: 1 In those days the Philistines *m* their
28: 4 Saul, too, *m* all Israel;
29: 1 had *m* all their forces in Aphek,
1Kgs 20:15 them he *m* all the Israelite soldiery,
2Kgs 3: 6 Joram as king *m* all Israel,
6:24 *m* his whole army and laid siege to Samaria.
25:19 commander, who *m* the people of the land,
2Chr 25: 5 Amaziah *m* Judah and placed them,
26:11 *m* by Jeiel the scribe and Maaseiah
Jdt 2:15 He *m* a hundred and twenty thousand picked
Est 9: 2 The Jews *m* in their cities throughout the
9:15 and the Jews in Susa *m* again on the
9:16 provinces, also *m* and defended themselves,
9:18 *m* on the thirteenth and fourteenth of the
1Mc 10: 2 he *m* a very large army and marched out to
13:10 So Simon *m* all the men able to fight,
16: 4 John then *m* in the land twenty thousand
2Mc 11: 2 *m* about eighty thousand infantry and all
Jer 52:25 commander who *m* the people of the land,
Ez 38: 8 After many days you will be *m* [in the last
Rv 19:19 and the armies they had *m* to do battle

MUSTERING (5)

2Sm 10:15 defeat by Israel with a full *m* of troops;
18: 1 After *m* the troops he had with him,
2Chr 17:14 *m* according to their ancestral houses.
Is 13: 4 The LORD of hosts is *m* an army for battle.
Na 2: 4 steel are the chariots on the day of his *m*.

MUTE (14)

Wis 17: 4 and *m* phantoms with somber looks appeared.
Bar 6:40 for when they see a deaf *m*,
Mt 9:32 him a *m* who was possessed by a demon.
9:33 demon was expelled the *m* began to speak,
12:22 who was brought to him was blind and *m*.
15:30 cripples, the deformed, the blind, the *m*,
15:31 the crowds as they beheld the *m* speaking,
Mk 7:37 He makes the deaf hear and the *m* speak!"
9:17 you because he is possessed by a *m* spirit.
9:25 spirit by saying to him, *M* and deaf spirit,
Lk 1:20 But now you will be *m*—
11:14 Jesus was casting out a devil which was *m*,
1Cor 12: 2 were pagans you were led astray to *m* idols,
2Pt 2:16 A *m* beast spoke with a human voice to

MUTILATE (1)

Phil 3: 2 Be on guard against those who *m*.

MUTINY (1)

Mk 3:26 *m* in his ranks and is torn by dissension,

MUTTER (1)

Is 8:19 fortunetellers (who chirp and *m*!);

MUTTONS (1)

Neh 5:18 one beef, six choice *m*,

MUTUAL (7)

Sir 25: 1 and the *m* love of husband and wife.
Acts 5:12 By *m* agreement they used to meet in
Rom 1:24 in the *m* degradation of their bodies,
1Cor 7: 5 unless perhaps by *m* consent for a time,
Gal 5:15 You will end up in *m* destruction!
Phil 4: 2 come to some *m* understanding in the Lord.
2Thes 1: 3 grows apace and your *m* love increases;

MUTUALLY (4)

Rom 1:12 may be *m* encouraged by our common faith.
Eph 4:32 another, compassionate, and *m* forgiving,
Col 2:19 *m* supported and upheld by joints and
1Pt 4: 9 Be *m* hospitable without complaining.

MUZZLE (4)

Dt 25: 4 not *m* an ox when it is treading out grain.
Sir 20:28 a *m* over the mouth they silence reproof.
1Cor 9: 8 not *m* an ox while it treads out grain."
1Tm 5:18 *m* on an ox when he is threshing the grain,"

MYNDOS (1)

1Mc 15:23 Sampsames, Sparta, Delos, *M*,

MYRA (1)

Acts 27: 5 and Pamphylia, and came to *M* in Lycia.

MYRIAD (2)

Ps(s) 68:18 The chariots of God are *m*,
Mi 6: 7 thousands of rams, with *m* streams of oil?

MYRIADS (9)

Gn 24:60 may you grow into thousands of *m*;
Dt 33:17 [These are the *m* of Ephraim,
Jdt 16: 3 north, with the *m* of his forces he came;
2Mc 11: 4 confidence in his *m* of foot soldiers,
Ps(s) 3: 7 I fear not the *m* of people arrayed against
144:13 and increase to *m* in our meadows;
Dn 7:10 to him, and *m* upon myriads attended him.
Heb 12:22 to *m* of angels in festal gathering,

MYRRH (17)

Ex 30:23 five hundred shekels of free-flowing *m*;
Est 2:12 six months were spent with oil of *m*,
Ps(s) 45: 9 With *m* and aloes and cassia your robes are
Prv 7:17 I have sprinkled my bed with *m*,
Sg 1:13 for me a sachet of *m* to rest in my bosom.
3: 6 like a column of smoke Laden with *m*,
4: 6 lengthen, I will go to the mountain of *m*,
4:14 *M* and aloes,
5: 1 I gather my *m* and my spices,
5: 5 to my lover, with my hands dripping *m*:
5: 5 choice *m* upon the fittings of the lock.
5:13 lips are red blossom; they drip choice *m*.
Sir 24:15 cinnamon, or fragrant balm, or precious *m*,
Mt 2:11 with gifts of gold, frankincense, and *m*.
Mk 15:23 they tried to give him wine drugged with *m*,
Jn 19:39 bringing a mixture of *m* and aloes which
Rv 18:13 and amomum, perfumes, *m* and frankincense;

MYRTLE (6)

Neh 8:15 in branches of olive trees, oleasters, *m,*
Is 41:19 plant in the desert the cedar, acacia, *m,*
55:13 shall grow, instead of nettles, the *m,*
Zec 1: 8 standing among *m* trees in a shady place,
1:10 among the *m* trees spoke up and said,
1:11 was standing among the *m* trees and said,

MYRTLES (1)

Lv 23:40 and boughs of *m* and of valley poplars,

MYSELF (170)

Gn 3:10 afraid, because I was naked, so I hid *m."*
16: 5 I *m* gave my maid to your embrace;
22:16 "I swear by *m,* declares the LORD,
24:27 As for *m* also, the LORD has led me
24:45 scarcely finished saying this prayer to *m*
27:12 bring on *m* a curse instead of a blessing."
31:39 I made good the loss *m.*
43: 9 I *m* will stand surety for him.
46:30 have seen for *m* that Joseph is still alive."
Ex 19: 4 on eagle wings and brought you here to *m.*
33: 3 But I *m* will not go up in your company,
33:14 "I *m,"* the LORD answered, "will go
Lv 16: 2 reveal *m* in a cloud above the propitiatory,
17:10 I will set *m* against that one who partakes
20: 3 I *m* will turn against such a man and cut
20: 5 I *m* will set my face against that man and
Nm 8:16 I have taken them for *m* in place of every
8:17 I consecrated them to *m* on the day I slew
11:14 I cannot carry all this people by *m,*
12: 6 you, in visions will I reveal *m* to him,
18: 8 "I *m* have given you charge of the
Dt 4:22 I *m* shall die in this country without
18:19 my name, I *m* will make him answer for it.
31:23 I *m* will be with you."
Jgs 16:28 avenge *m* once and for all on the Philistines."
19:19 for the woman and *m* and for our servant;
Ru 3:13 you, as the LORD lives, I will claim you *m.*
1Sm 2:27 'I went so far as to reveal *m* to your
13:12 assembled at Michmash, I said to *m,*
14:24 before I am able to avenge *m* on my enemies."
16: 3 and I *m* will tell you what to do;
25:33 blood and from avenging *m* personally.
2Sm 1: 6 "It was by chance that I found *m* on Mount
6:22 the LORD, but I will demean *m* even more.
18: 2 soldiers, "I intend to go out with you *m."*
1Kgs 17:12 in and prepare something for *m* and my son;
18:15 I serve, I will present *m* to him today."
22:30 "I will disguise *m* and go into battle,
2Kgs 20: 3 I conducted *m* in your presence,
1Chr 22: 7 build a house *m* for the honor of the LORD,
28: 2 *m* for the ark of the covenant of the LORD,
2Chr 34:21 "On behalf of *m* and those who are left in
Neh 5:10 I *m,* my kinsmen, and my attendants
12:38 followed by *m* and the other half of the
Tb 2: 5 I washed *m* and ate my food in sorrow.
3:10 It is far better for me not to hang *m,*
Est F: 4 The two dragons are *m* and Haman.
1Mc 3:14 "I will make a name for *m* and win glory
6:11 I said to *m:* "Into what tribulation
2Mc 6:27 now, I will prove *m* worthy of my old age,
Jb 9:21 Though I am innocent, I *m* cannot know it;
9:30 *m* with snow and cleanse my hands with lye,
9:32 For he is not a man like *m,*
10: 1 I will give *m* up to complaint;
19:27 Whom I *m* shall see:
31:37 a prince I should present *m* before him.
Ps(s) 2: 6 "I *m* have set up my king on Zion,
35:13 I afflicted *m* with fasting and poured
69:11 I humbled *m* with fasting,
131: 1 I busy not *m* with great things,
Eccl 1:16 Though I said to *m,*
2: 1 I said to *m,*
2: 4 I built *m* houses and planted vineyards;
2: 6 And I constructed for *m* reservoirs to
2: 8 I amassed for *m* silver and gold,
2: 8 I got for *m* male and female singers and
2:10 deny them, nor did I deprive *m* of any joy,
2:15 So I said to *m,*
3:17 And I said to *m,*
3:18 I said to *m:* As for the children
4: 8 do I toil and deprive *m* of good things?"
Wis 8:17 Thinking thus within *m,*
Sir 24:29 the waters into a garden, Said to *m,*
33:18 you that not for *m* only have I toiled,
Is 38: 3 I conducted *m* in your presence,
42:14 silence, I have said nothing, holding *m* in;
43:21 to drink, The people whom I formed for *m,*
45:23 By *m* I swear, uttering my just decree
48:15 I *m* have spoken, I have called him,
57:17 angry, and struck them, hiding *m* in wrath,
59:21 the covenant with them which I *m* have made,
Jer 4:12 And I *m* now pronounce sentence upon them.
20: 7 You duped me, O LORD, and I let *m* be duped;
20: 9 I say to *m,* I will not mention him,
21: 5 and I *m* will fight against you with
22: 5 do not obey these commands, I swear by *m,*
22:14 says, "I will build *m* a spacious house,
23: 3 I *m* will gather the remnant of my flock
31:19 I turn in repentance; I have come to *m,*
31:32 covenant, and I had to show *m* their master,
49:10 So I *m* will strip Esau;
Lam 3:18 I tell *m* my future is lost,
Ez 14: 3 should I allow *m* to be consulted by them?
20: 3 I will not allow *m* to be consulted by you,
20: 5 of Egypt I revealed *m* to them and swore:
20: 9 whose presence I had made *m* known to them,
20:31 Shall I let *m* be consulted by you,
20:31 swear I will not let *m* be consulted by you.
22:16 In you I will allow *m* to be profaned in
34:11 I *m* will look after and tend my sheep.
34:15 I *m* will pasture my sheep; I *m* will give
35:11 make *m* known among you when I judge you,
38:23 make *m* known in the sight of many nations;
Dn 7:28 face blanched, but I kept the matter to *m.*
8: 2 In my vision I saw *m* in the fortress of
10: 3 did not anoint *m* at all until the end
Hos 2:25 I will sow him for *m* in the land,
10:11 I *m* laid a yoke upon her fair neck;
Hb 2: 1 guard post, and station *m* upon the rampart,
Zec 9:13 Judah as my bow, I will arm *m* with Ephraim;
Mt 8: 9 *m* and I have troops assigned to me.
Lk 7: 7 is why I did not presume to come to you *m.*
12:19 Then I will say to *m:*
Jn 1:34 Now I have seen for *m* and have testified,
5:30 I cannot do anything of *m.*
5:34 (Not that I *m* accept such human testimony
6:35 "I *m* am the bread of life.
6:51 I *m* am the living bread come down from
6:70 "Did I not choose the Twelve of you *m?*
7:28 The truth is, I have not come of *m.*
8:28 that I AM and that I do nothing by *m.*
8:50 I seek no glory for *m:*
8:54 "If I glorify *m,* that glory comes to nothing.
12:32 will draw all men to *m."*
14:10 The words I speak are not spoken of *m;*
14:21 I too will love him and reveal *m* to him."
15:26 and whom I *m* will send from the Father
17:19 I consecrate *m* for their sakes now,
18:38 "Speaking for *m,* I find no case
Acts 9:16 I *m* shall indicate to him how much he will
10:26 I am only a man *m."*
23: 6 I find *m* on trial now because of my hope
26: 2 I count *m* fortunate to be able to make my
Rom 10:20 who were not looking for me I revealed *m."*
11: 1 I *m* am an Israelite,
11: 4 "I have left for *m* seven thousand men who
16: 2 has been of help to many, including *m.*
1Cor 2: 1 As for *m,* brothers, when I came to you
4: 3 I do not even pass judgment on *m.*
4: 4 not mean that I am declaring *m* innocent.
4: 6 I have applied all this to *m* and Apollos
6:12 I will not let *m* be enslaved by anything.
7: 8 they remain as they are, even as I do *m;*
9: 6 Is it only *m* and Barnabas who are forced
9:19 I made *m* the slave of all so as to win
9:22 I have made *m* all things to all men in
9:27 preached to others I *m* should be rejected.
15: 3 on to you first of all what I *m* received,
16: 4 If it seems fitting that I should go *m,*
2Cor 3: 1 Am I beginning to speak well of *m* again?
7: 5 quarrels with others and fears within *m.*
11: 5 I consider *m* inferior to the
11: 7 humbling *m* with a view to exalting you?
11: 9 I kept *m* from being burdensome to you,
12: 5 about *m* unless it be about my weaknesses.
12:15 gladly spend *m* and be spent for your sakes.
12:19 this recital that I am defending *m* to you?
Gal 1:10 this how I seek to ingratiate *m* with men?
Phil 1:27 whether I come and see you *m* or hear about
2:24 in the Lord that I *m* will be coming soon.
3:13 of *m* as having reached the finish line.
4:11 *m* in I have learned to be self-sufficient.
1Tm 1:15 Of these I *m* am the worst.
2Tm 1: 5 I find *m* thinking of your sincere faith
Rv 1: 9 found *m* on the island called Patmos
2:24 And now I address *m* to you others in
3:21 as I *m* won the victory and took my seat
9:16 a number I heard *m.*
22:18 I *m* give witness to all who hear the

MYSIA (3)

1Mc 8: 8 give hostages and a section of Lycia, *M,*
Acts 16: 7 to *M* they tried to go on into Bithynia,
16: 8 Crossing through *M* instead,

MYSIAN (1)

1Mc 1:29 the *M* commander to the cities of Judah,

MYSIANS (1)

2Mc 5:24 king sent Appollonius, commander of the *M,*

MYSTERIES (13)

Jgs 13:19 on the rock to the LORD, whose works are *m.*
Ps(s) 78: 2 in a parable, I will utter *m* from of old.
Wis 14:15 down to his subjects *m* and sacrifices.
14:23 child-slaying sacrifices or clandestine *m,*
Sir 39: 7 his counsel, as he meditates upon his *m.*
Dn 2:28 there is a God in heaven who reveals *m,*
2:29 he who reveals *m* showed you what is to be.
2:47 and Lord of kings and a revealer of *m;*
Mt 13:11 a knowledge of the *m* of the reign of God,
Lk 8:10 *m* of the reign of God have been confided,
1Cor 4: 1 Christ and administrators of the *m* of God.
13: 2 with full knowledge, comprehend all *m,*
14: 2 him, because he utters *m* in the Spirit.

MYSTERIOUS (5)

Dt 30:11 you today is not too *m* and remote for you.
Jgs 13:18 him, "Why do you ask my name, which is *m*
1Cor 2: 7 a *m,* a hidden wisdom.
Eph 3: 9 *m* design which for ages was hidden in God,
Rv 10: 7 to blow his trumpet, the *m* plan of God,

MYSTERY (21)

Dn 2:18 of the God of heaven in regard to this *m,*
2:19 the *m* was revealed to Daniel in a vision,
2:27 "The *m* about which the king has inquired,
2:30 To me also this *m* has been revealed;
2:47 that is why you were able to reveal this *m."*
4: 6 in you and no *m* is too difficult for you;
Mk 4:11 *m* of the reign of God has been confided.
Rom 11:25 ignorant of this *m* lest you be conceited;
16:25 the gospel which reveals the *m* hidden for
1Cor 2: 8 of the rulers of this age knew the *m;*
15:51 Now I am going to tell you a *m.*
Eph 1: 9 us the wisdom to understand fully the *m,*
3: 4 about in speaking of the *m* of Christ,
6:19 make known the *m* of the gospel
6:20 *m* for which I am an ambassador in chains.
Col 1:26 that *m* hidden from ages and generations
1:27 *m* brings to the Gentiles—the *m* of Christ
2: 2 by their knowledge of the *m* of God
4: 3 an opening to proclaim the *m* of Christ,
1Tm 3:16 Wonderful, indeed, is the *m* of our faith,

MYTHS (4)

1Tm 1: 4 with interminable *m* and genealogies,
4: 7 to do with profane *m* or old wives' tales.
Ti 1:14 and unaffected by Jewish *m* or rules
2Pt 1:16 It was not by way of cleverly concocted *m*

N

NAAM (1)

1Chr 4:15 son of Jephunneh, were Ir, Elah, and *N.*

NAAMAH (5)

Gn 4:22 The sister of Tubalcain was *N.*
Jos 15:41 Gederoth, Beth-dagon, *N* and Makkedah;
1Kgs 14:21 His mother was the Ammonite named *N.*
14:31 His mother was the Ammonite named *N.*
2Chr 12:13 Rehoboam's mother was named *N,*

NAAMAN (20)

Gn 46:21 Bela, Becher, Ashbel, Gera, *N,*
Nm 26:40 The descendants of Bela were Arad and *N:*
26:40 through *N* the clan of the Naamanites.
2Kgs 5: 1 *N,* the army commander of the king of Aram,
5: 4 *N* went and told his lord just what the
5: 5 *N* set out, taking along ten silver talents
5: 6 letter I am sending my servant *N* to you,
5: 9 *N* came with his horses and chariots and
5:11 But *N* went away angry, saying, "I thought
5:14 So *N* went down and plunged into the Jordan
5:17 *N* said: "If you will not accept,
5:19 *N* had gone some distance when Gehazi,
5:20 master was too easy with this Aramean *N,*
5:21 So Gehazi hurried after *N.*
5:21 *N* alighted from his chariot to wait for
5:23 "Please take two talents," *N* said,
5:27 The leprosy of *N* shall cling to you and
1Chr 8: 4 The sons of Ehud were Abishua, *N,*
8: 7 Also *N,* Ahijah, and Gera.
Lk 4:27 yet not one was cured except *N* the Syrian."

NAAMANITES (1)

Nm 26:40 Aradites, through Naaman the clan of the *N.*

NAAMAN'S (2)

2Kgs 5: 2 girl, who became the servant of *N* wife.
5:16 and despite *N* urging,

NAAMATH (1)

Jb 2:11 Bildad from Shuh, and Zophar from *N.*

NAAMATHITE (3)

Jb 11: 1 And Zophar the *N* spoke out and said:
20: 1 Then Zophar the *N* spoke and said:
42: 9 and Bildad the Shuhite, and Zophar the *N,*

NAARAH (4)

Jos 16: 7 from there it descended to Ataroth and *N,*
1Chr 4: 5 of Tekoa, had two wives, Helah and *N.*
4: 6 *N* bore him Ahuzzam,
4: 6 These were the descendants of *N.*

NAARAI (1)

1Chr 11:37 N, the son of Ezbai;

NAARAN (1)

1Chr 7:28 N to the east,

NABAL (20)

1Sm 25: 3 The man was named N, his wife Abigail.
25: 3 but N himself, a Calebite, was harsh
25: 4 the desert that N was shearing his flock,
25: 5 Pay N a visit and greet him in my name.
25: 9 this message fully to N in David's name,
25:10 But N answered the servants of David:
25:19 But she did not tell her husband N.
25:25 lord pay attention to that worthless man N,
25:26 those who seek to harm my lord become as N!
25:34 by dawn N would not have had a single man
25:36 When Abigail came to N,
25:36 and N was merry because he was very drunk.
25:37 But then, when N had become sober,
25:39 On hearing that N was dead, David said:
25:39 the insult I received at the hand of N,
25:39 but has punished N for his own evil deeds."
27: 3 and Abigail, the widow of N from Carmel.
30: 5 and Abigail, the widow of N from Carmel,
2Sm 2: 2 and Abigail, the widow of N of Carmel.
3: 3 of Abigail the widow of N of Carmel;

NABAL'S (1)

1Sm 25:14 But N wife Abigail was informed of this by

NABATEANS (2)

1Mc 5:25 There they met some N,
9:35 to ask permission of his friends, the N,

NABOTH (21)

1Kgs 21: 1 as N the Jezreelite had a vineyard in
21: 2 of Ahab, king of Samaria, Ahab said to N,
21: 3 N answered him,
21: 4 answer N the Jezreelite had made to him:
21: 6 spoke to N the Jezreelite and said to him,
21: 7 the vineyard of N the Jezreelite for you."
21: 8 nobles who lived in the same city with N.
21: 9 a fast and set N at the head of the people.
21:12 and placed N at the head of the people.
21:13 the accusation, N has cursed God and king."
21:14 to Jezebel that N had been stoned to death.
21:15 learned that N had been stoned to death,
21:15 take possession of the vineyard of N the
21:15 to sell you, because N is not alive,
21:16 On hearing that N was dead,
21:16 down to the vineyard of N the Jezreelite,
21:18 He will be in the vineyard of N,
21:19 where the dogs licked up the blood of N,
2Kgs 9:21 him near the field of N the Jezreelite.
9:25 him into the field of N the Jezreelite.
9:26 the blood of N and the blood of his sons,'

NADAB (26)

Ex 6:23 the sister of Nahshon; she bore him N,
24: 1 up to the LORD, you and Aaron, with N,
24: 9 Moses then went up with Aaron, N,
28: 1 brother Aaron, together with his sons N,
Lv 10: 1 sons N and Abihu took their censers and,
Nm 3: 2 The sons of Aaron were N his first-born,
3: 4 But when N and Abihu offered profane fire
26:60 To Aaron were born N and Abihu,
26:61 But N and Abihu died when they offered
1Kgs 14:20 and his son N succeeded him as king.
15:25 the second year of Asa, king of Judah, N,
15:27 which N and all Israel were besieging.
15:31 The rest of the acts of N,
16: 7 and because he killed N
1Chr 2:28 The sons of Shammai were N and Abishur.
2:30 The sons of N were Seled and Appaim.
5:29 The sons of Aaron were N, Abihu, Eleazar,
8:30 son, Abdon, and Zur, Kish, Baal, Ner, N,
9:36 then came Zur, Kish, Baal, Ner, N,
24: 1 The sons of Aaron were N, Abihu, Eleazar,
24: 2 N and Abihu died before their father,
Tb 11:18 nephew N also came to rejoice with Tobit.
14:10 Think, my son, of all that N did to Ahiqar,
14:10 but N went into the everlasting darkness,
14:10 from the deadly trap N had set for him.
14:10 But N himself fell into the deadly trap,

NADABATH (1)

1Mc 9:37 of the great princes of Canaan, from N."

NADAB'S (1)

Tb 14:10 N disgraceful crime rebound against him.

NAG (1)

Col 3:21 not n your children lest they lose heart.

NAGGAI (1)

Lk 3:25 Amos, son of Nahum, son of Esli, son of N,

NAGGING (1)

Prv 19:13 and the n of a wife is a persistent leak.

NAHALAL (2)

Jos 19:15 Thus, with Kattah, N,
21:35 lands, and N with its pasture lands;

NAHALE-GAASH (1)

2Sm 23:30 Hiddai from N;

NAHALIEL (2)

Nm 21:19 they went to Mattanah, from Mattanah to N,
21:19 Mattanah to Nahaliel, from N to Bamoth,

NAHALOL (1)

Jgs 1:30 the inhabitants of Kitron or those of N;

NAHAM (1)

1Chr 4:19 sons of his Jewish wife, the sister of N,

NAHAMANI (1)

Neh 7: 7 Jeshua, Nehemiah, Azariah, Raamiah, N,

NAHARAI (2)

2Sm 23:37 N from Beeroth, armor-bearer of Joab
1Chr 11:39 N, from Beeroth, the armor-bearer of Joab,

NAHARAIM (4)

Gn 24:10 his way to the city of Nahor in Aram N.
Dt 23: 5 son of Beor, from Pethor in Aram N,
Jgs 3: 8 power of Cushan-rishathaim, king of Aram N,
1Chr 19: 6 to hire chariots and horsemen from Aram N,

NAHASH (10)

1Sm 11: 1 N the Ammonite went up and laid siege to
11: 1 All the men of Jabesh begged N,
11: 2 But N the Ammonite replied,
11:10 Jabesh, who were jubilant, and said to N,
12:12 Yet, when you saw N,
2Sm 10: 2 "I will be kind to Hanun, son of N,
17:27 son of N from Rabbah of the Ammonites,
1Chr 4:12 and Tehinnah, the father of the city of N.
19: 1 Afterward N, king of the Ammonites,
19: 2 will show kindness to Hanun, the son of N,

NAHATH (5)

Gn 36:13 The sons of Reuel were N, Zerah, Shammah,
36:17 the clans of N, Zerah, Shammah, and Mizzah
1Chr 1:37 The sons of Reuel were N,
6:11 whose son was Zophai, whose son was N,
2Chr 31:13 Jehiel, Azaziah, N,

NAHBI

Nm 13:14 N, son of Vophsi

NAHOR (19)

Gn 11:22 years old, he became the father of N.
11:23 two hundred years after the birth of N,
11:24 When N was twenty-nine years old,
11:25 N lived one hundred and nineteen years
11:26 he became the father of Abram, N and Haran.
11:27 Terah became the father of Abram, N,
11:29 Abram and N took wives;
22:20 too has borne sons, to your brother N:
22:23 eight Milcah bore to Abraham's brother N.
24:10 his way to the city of N in Aram Naharaim.
24:15 Milcah, the wife of Abraham's brother N)
24:24 the son of Milcah, whom she bore to N.
24:47 son of Nahor, borne to N by Milcah.'
29: 5 asked them, "Do you know Laban, son of N?"
31:53 May the God of Abraham and the god of N
Jos 24: 2 down to Terah, father of Abraham and N,
1Chr 1:26 Shelah, Eber, Peleg, Reu, Serug, N,
Lk 3:34 son of Abraham, son of Terah, son of N,

NAHOR'S (1)

Gn 11:29 Sarai, and the name of N wife was Milcah,

NAHSHON (13)

Ex 6:23 daughter, Elisheba, the sister of N;
Nm 1: 7 N, son of Amminadab; from Issachar:
2: 3 [The prince of the Judahites was N,
7:12 his offering on the first day was N,
7:17 This was the offering of N,
10:14 N, son of Amminadab,
Ru 4:20 Amminadab, Amminadab was the father of N,
4:20 of Nahshon, N was the father of Salmon,
1Chr 2:10 and Amminadab became the father of N,
2:11 N became the father of Salma.
Mt 1: 4 father of Nahshon, N the father of Salmon.
Lk 3:32 Obed, son of Boaz, son of Sala, son of N,

NAHUM (3)

Tb 14: 4 which was spoken by N against Nineveh.
Na 1: 1 The book of the vision of N of Elkosh.
Lk 3:25 son of Mattathias, son of Amos, son of N,

NAIL (4)

1Sm 18:11 the spear, thinking to n David to the wall,
19:10 to n David to the wall with the spear,
26: 8 Let me n him to the ground with one thrust
Wis 13:15 puts it on the wall, fastening it with a n.

NAILING (1)

Col 2:14 snatching it up and n it to the cross.

NAILMARKS (1)

Jn 20:25 finger in the n and my hand into his side."

NAILPRINTS (1)

Jn 20:25 it without probing the n in his hands,

NAILS (6)

Dt 21:12 her n and lay aside her captive's garb.
1Chr 22: 3 iron to make n for the doors of the gates,
2Chr 3: 9 The weight of the n was fifty gold shekels.
Is 41: 7 and he fastens it with n to steady it.
Jer 10: 4 With n and hammers they are fastened,
Dn 4:30 eagle, and his n like the claws of a bird.

NAIM (1)

Lk 7:11 Soon afterward he went to a town called N,

NAKED (42)

Gn 2:25 The man and his wife were both n,
3: 7 and they realized that they were n;
3:10 but I was afraid, because I was n,
3:11 he asked, "Who told you that you were n?
9:21 he became drunk and lay n inside his tent.
Ex 28:42 n flesh from their loins to their thighs.
1Sm 19:24 all that day and night he lay n.
1Chr 21:16 with a n sword in his hand stretched out
2Chr 28:15 who were n they clothed from the booty;
Tb 1:17 to the hungry and my clothing to the n.
4:16 bread, and to the n some of your clothing.
Jb 1:21 said, N I came forth from my mother's womb,
1:21 mother's womb, and n shall I go back again.
22: 6 left them stripped n of their clothing.
24: 7 They pass the night n,
26: 6 N before him is the nether world,
Eccl 5:14 so again shall he depart, n as he came,
Is 20: 2 This he did, walking n and barefoot.
20: 3 Just as my servant Isaiah has gone n and
20: 4 Ethiopia, young and old, n and barefoot,
58: 7 Clothing the n when you see them,
Lam 4:21 you shall become drunk and n.
Ez 16: 7 hair had grown, but you were still stark n.
16:22 girl, stark n and weltering in your blood.
16:37 all sides and expose you n for them to see.
16:39 splendid ornaments, leaving you stark n.
18: 7 food to the hungry and clothes the n;
18:16 his food to the hungry and clothes the n;
23:29 have worked for and leaving you stark n,
Hos 2: 5 her breasts, Or I will strip her n,
Am 2:16 of warriors shall flee n on that day,
Mi 1: 8 I lament and wail, I go barefoot and n;
Mt 25:36 and you welcomed me, n and you clothed me.
25:43 no welcome, n and you gave me no clothing.
25:44 away from home or n or ill or in prison
Mk 14:52 him he left the cloth behind and ran off n.
Acts 19:16 they fled from his house n and bruised.
2Cor 5: 3 provided we are found clothed and not n.
5: 4 because we do not wish to be stripped n
Rv 3:17 how pitiable and poor, how blind and n!
16:15 fear of going n and exposed for all to see!)
17:16 will strip off her finery and leave her n;

NAKEDNESS (20)

Gn 9:22 the father of Canaan, saw his father's n,
9:23 backward and covered their father's n;
9:23 way, they did not see their father's n.
42: 9 You have come to see the n of the land."
42:12 You have come to see the n of the land."
Dt 28:48 hunger and thirst, in n and utter poverty,
Is 47: 3 Your n shall be uncovered and your shame
Lam 1: 8 her think her vile now that they see her n;
Ez 16: 8 of my cloak over you to cover your n;
16:36 revealed your n in your harlotry
22:10 those who uncover the n of their fathers,
23:10 They exposed her n,
23:29 naked, so that your indecent n is exposed.
Hos 2:11 and my flax, with which she covers her n.
Na 3: 5 I will show your n to the nations,
Hb 2:15 and make them drunk, till their n is seen!
Mt 25:38 you away from home or clothe you in your n?
Rom 8:35 distress, or persecution, or hunger, or n,
2Cor 11:27 in cold and n.
Rv 3:18 if the shame of your n is to be covered.

NAME (753)

Gn	2:11	The *n* of the first is the Pishon;
	2:13	The *n* of the second river is the Gihon;
	2:14	The *n* of the third river is the Tigris;
	2:19	the man called each of them would be its *n*.
	4:19	*n* of the first was Adah, and the *n* of the
	4:21	His brother's *n* was Jubal;
	4:26	time men began to invoke the LORD by *n*.
	10:25	the *n* of the first was Peleg,
	10:25	and the *n* of his brother was Joktan.
	11: 4	in the sky, and so make a *n* for ourselves;
	11:29	*n* of Abram's wife was Sarai, and the *n*
	12: 2	I will make your *n* great,
	12: 8	to the LORD and invoked the LORD by *n*.
	13: 4	and there he invoked the LORD by *n*.
	16:11	you shall *n* him Ishmael,
	16:13	To the LORD who spoke to her she gave a *n*,
	17: 5	your *n* shall be Abraham,
	17:15	her *n* shall be Sarah.
	21: 3	Abraham gave the *n* Isaac to this son of
	21:12	Isaac that descendants shall bear your *n*.
	21:33	and there he invoked by *n* the LORD,
	22:24	His concubine, whose *n* was Reumah,
	25: 1	married another wife, whose *n* was Keturah.
	26:25	an altar there and invoked the LORD by *n*.
	26:33	hence the *n* of the city,
	28:19	the former *n* of the town had been Luz.
	32:28	"What is your *n*?"
	32:30	Jacob then asked him, "Do tell me your *n*,
	32:30	"Why should you want to know my *n*?"
	35:10	*n* is Jacob shall no longer be called Jacob,
	35:10	called Jacob, but Israel shall be your *n*."
	36:32	the *n* of his city was Dinhabah.
	36:34	the *n* of his city was Avith.
	36:39	the *n* of his city was Pau.
	36:39	(His wife's *n* was Mehetabel;
	41:45	the *n* of Zaphenath-paneah on Joseph,
	48:16	these boys That in them my *n* be recalled,
Ex	3:13	me to you,' if they ask me, 'What is his *n*?'
	3:15	"This is my *n* forever;
	5:23	I went to Pharaoh to speak in your *n*,
	6: 3	to Abraham, Isaac and Jacob, but my *n*,
	9:16	to make my *n* resound throughout the earth!
	15: 3	The LORD is a warrior, LORD is his *n*!
	20: 7	"You shall not take the *n* of the LORD,
	20: 7	unpunished him who takes his *n* in vain.
	20:24	of my *n* I will come to you and bless you.
	23:13	"Never mention the *n* of any other god;
	28:21	with the *n* of one of the twelve tribes.
	33:19	in your presence I will pronounce my *n*,
	34: 5	stood with him there and proclaimed his *n*,
	39:14	with the *n* of one of the twelve tribes.
Lv	18:21	Molech, thus profaning the *n* of your God.
	19:12	my name, thus profaning the *n* of your God.
	20: 3	my sanctuary and profaned my holy *n*.
	21: 6	shall be sacred, and not profane his *n*;
	22: 2	else they will profane my holy *n*.
	22:32	give you, and do not profane my holy *n*;
	24:11	and cursed and blasphemed the LORD'S *n*.
	24:16	the *n* of the LORD shall be put to death.
	24:16	put to death for blaspheming the LORD'S *n*.
	25:26	means to buy it back in his own *n*,
Nm	1:18	his *n* and lineage according to clan
	6:27	shall they invoke my *n* upon the Israelites,
	13: 4	among the Israelites, by *n* they were:
	17:17	Mark each man's *n* on his staff;
	17:18	and mark Aaron's *n* on Levi's staff,
	26:46	The *n* of Asher's daughter was Serah.
	27: 4	But why should our father's *n* be withdrawn
	32:42	and called it Nobah after his own *n*.
Dt	2:25	*n* they will quake and tremble before you.'
	3:14	*n* Bashan Havvothjair, the *n* it bears today.]
	5:11	'You shall not take the *n* of the LORD,
	5:11	unpunished him who takes his *n* in vain.
	6:13	you serve, and by his *n* shall you swear.
	9:14	blot out their *n* from under the heavens.
	10: 8	to him, and to give blessings in his *n*,
	10:20	hold fast to him and swear by his *n*.
	12:11	chooses as the dwelling place for his *n*
	12:21	chooses for the abode of his *n* is too far,
	14:23	chooses as the dwelling place of his *n*
	14:24	for the abode of his *n* is too far for you,
	16: 2	he chooses as the dwelling place of his *n*.
	16: 6	he chooses as the dwelling place of his *n*,
	16:11	chooses as the dwelling place of his *n*,
	18: 5	to minister in the *n* of the LORD.
	18: 7	he may minister there in the *n* of the LORD,
	18:19	listen to my words which he speaks in my *n*,
	18:20	if a prophet presumes to speak in my *n*
	18:20	to speak, or speaks in the *n* of other gods,
	18:22	a prophet speaks in the *n* of the LORD,
	21: 5	to him and to give blessings in his *n*,
	25: 6	his *n* may not be blotted out from Israel.
	25: 7	to perpetuate his brother's *n* in Israel.'
	26: 2	chooses for the dwelling place of his *n*.
	28:10	earth see you bearing the *n* of the LORD,
	28:58	the glorious and awesome *n* of the LORD,
	29:19	The LORD will blot out his *n* from under
	32:26	and blot out their *n* from men's memories,'
Jos	7: 9	around us and efface our *n* from the earth.
	7: 9	What will you do for your great *n*?"
	22:34	and the Gadites gave the altar its *n*
Jgs	13: 2	clan of the Danites, whose *n* was Manoah.
	13: 6	he came from, nor did he tell me his *n*.
	13:17	Manoah said to him, "What is your *n*,
	13:18	LORD answered him, "Why do you ask my *n*,
	16: 4	in the Wadi Sorek whose *n* was Delilah.
	17: 1	region of Ephraim whose *n* was Micah.
	18:29	the *n* of the city was formerly Laish.
Ru	4: 1	spoken come along, he called to him by *n*,
	4:10	so that the *n* of the departed may not
	4:17	And the neighbor women gave him his *n*,
1Sm	1: 1	certain man from Ramathaim, Elkanah by *n*,
	12:22	*n* the LORD will not abandon his people,
	14:50	The *n* of his general was Abner,
	17:23	Philistine champion, by *n* Goliath of Gath,
	17:45	against you in the *n* of the LORD of hosts,
	20:16	The *n* of Jonathan must never be allowed by
	20:42	we two have sworn by the *n* of the LORD:
	21: 8	his *n* was Doeg the Edomite,
	24:22	that you will not blot out my *n* and family."
	25: 5	Pay Nabal a visit and greet him in my *n*.
	25: 9	this message fully to Nabal in David's *n*,
	25:25	man Nabal, for he is just like his *n*.
	25:25	Fool is his *n*, and he acts the fool.
2Sm	6: 2	which bears the *n* of the LORD of hosts
	6:18	the people in the *n* of the LORD of hosts.
	7:13	It is he who shall build a house for my *n*.
	7:26	Your *n* will be forever great,
	9:12	had a young son whose *n* was Mica;
	12:25	sent the prophet Nathan to *n* him Jedidiah,
	14: 7	neither *n* nor posterity upon the earth."
	15: 3	is no one to hear you in the king's *n*."
	18:18	said, "I have no son to perpetuate my *n*."
	22:50	nations, and I will sing praise to your *n*,
1Kgs	3: 2	temple had been built to the *n* of the LORD.
	8:33	if then they return to you, praise your *n*,
	8:35	and pray, and praise your *n* in this place,
	8:42	(since men will learn of your great *n*
	8:43	the peoples of the earth may know your *n*,
	9: 3	I confer my *n* upon it forever,
	13: 2	born to the house of David, Josiah by *n*,
	15: 2	His mother's *n* was Maacah,
	15:10	His grandmother's *n* was Maacah,
	18:31	LORD had said, "Your *n* shall be Israel."
	21: 8	So she wrote letters in Ahab's *n* and,
	22:16	nothing but the truth in the *n* of the LORD?
	22:42	His mother's *n* was Azubah,
2Kgs	2:24	and he cursed them in the *n* of the LORD.
	8:26	His mother's *n* was Athaliah;
	14: 2	His mother, whose *n* was Jehoaddin,
	14: 7	it Joktheel, the *n* it has to this day.
	14:27	not determined to blot out the *n* of Israel
	15: 2	His mother, whose *n* was Jecholiah,
	15:33	His mother's *n* was Jerusha,
	18: 2	His mother's *n* was Abi,
	21: 1	His mother's *n* was Hephzibah.
	21: 4	"I will establish my *n* in Jerusalem"
	21: 7	of Israel, I shall place my *n* forever.
	21:19	His mother's *n* was Meshullemeth,
	22: 1	His mother's *n* was Jedidah,
	23:27	of which I said, 'There shall my *n* be.'"
	23:31	His mother, whose *n* was Hamutal,
	23:34	he changed his *n* to Jehoiakim.
	23:36	His mother's *n* was Zebidah,
	24: 8	His mother's *n* was Nehushta,
	24:17	king, and changed his *n* to Zedekiah.
	24:18	His mother's *n* was Hamutal,
1Chr	1:43	of Beor, the *n* of whose city was Dinhabah.
	1:46	plateau, and the *n* of his city was Avith.
	1:50	*n* of his city was Pai, and his wife's *n* was
	2:26	also had another wife, Atarah by *n*,
	4:41	by *n* set out during the reign of Hezekiah,
	6:50	designating them by *n* and assigning them
	7:15	Machir took a wife whose *n* was Maacah;
	7:15	his sister's *n* was Molecheth.
	8:29	of Gibeon whose wife's *n* was Maacah;
	9:35	of Gibeon, whose wife's *n* was Maacah.
	12:32	by *n* to come and make David king.
	13: 6	the *n* "LORD enthroned upon the cherubim."
	16: 2	blessed the people in the *n* of the LORD,
	16: 8	Give thanks to the LORD, invoke his *n*;
	16:10	Glory in his holy *n*;
	16:29	Give to the LORD the glory due his *n*!
	16:35	to your holy *n* and glory in praising you."
	16:41	designated by *n* to give thanks to the LORD,
	17: 8	I will make your *n* great like that of the
	17:21	You won for yourself a *n* for great and
	21:19	Gad's command, given in the *n* of the LORD.
	22: 9	For Solomon shall be his *n*,
	23:13	to him, and to bless his *n* forever.
	29:13	thanks and we praise the majesty of your *n*."
	29:16	*n* comes from you and is entirely yours.
2Chr	6:24	afterward they return and praise your *n*,
	6:26	pray toward this place and praise your *n*,
	6:32	from a distant land to honor your great *n*,
	6:33	the peoples of the earth may know your *n*,
	7:14	people, upon whom my *n* has been pronounced,
	7:16	this house that my *n* may be there forever;
	14:10	your *n* we have come against this multitude.
	18:15	nothing but the truth in the *n* of the LORD?"
	19: 8	of Israel to judge in the *n* of the LORD
	20: 9	before you, for your *n* is in this house,
	28: 9	was a prophet of the LORD by the *n* of Oded.
	31:19	designated by *n* to distribute portions
	33: 4	"In Jerusalem shall my *n* be forever":
	33: 7	of Israel I shall place my *n* forever.
	33:18	who spoke to him in the *n* of the LORD,
	36: 4	Jerusalem, and changed his *n* to Jehoiakim.
Ezr	2:61	the Gileadite and became known by his *n*).
	5: 1	Jerusalem in the *n* of the God of Israel.
	6:12	And may the God who causes his *n* to dwell
	8:20	All these men were enrolled by *n*.
	10:16	each family, all of them designated by *n*.
Neh	1: 9	have chosen as the dwelling place for my *n*.'
	1:11	your willing servants who revere your *n*.
	7:63	the Gileadite and became known by his *n*).
	9: 5	blessing, "Blessed is your glorious *n*,
	9:10	you made for yourself a *n* even to this day.
Tb	3:15	never defiled my own *n* or my father's *n*
	5:12	son you are, brother, and what your *n* is."
	8: 5	praised be your *n* forever and ever.
	11:14	be God, and praised be his great *n*,
	11:14	holy *n* be praised throughout all the ages,
	12: 6	by blessing and extolling his *n* in song.
	13:11	drawn to you by the *n* of the Lord God,
	13:18	you they shall praise his holy *n* forever.
	14: 9	*n* sincerely and with all their strength.
Jdt	9: 8	Lord is your *n*.'
	9: 8	the tent where your glorious *n* resides,
	16: 1	to him a new song, exalt and acclaim his *n*.
Est	2:14	pleased with her and had her summoned by *n*.
	3:12	It was written in the *n* of King Ahasuerus
	C:10	we shall live to sing praise to your *n*,
	8: 8	you in turn may write in the king's *n*
	8: 8	For whatever is written in the *n* of the
	8:10	which he wrote in the *n* of King Ahasuerus
	F: 5	who assembled to destroy the *n* of the Jews,
1Mc	2:51	shall win great glory and an everlasting *n*.
	3:14	"I will make a *n* for myself and win glory
	4:33	all who know your *n* may hymn your praise."
	5:57	"Let us also make a *n* for ourselves by
	5:63	the Gentiles, wherever their *n* was heard;
	6:44	and win an everlasting *n* for himself.
	7:37	have chosen this house to bear your *n*,
	14:10	glorious *n* reached the ends of the earth.
	14:43	in the country shall be dated by his *n*.
2Mc	8: 4	and the blasphemies uttered against his *n*;
	8:15	they themselves bore his holy, glorious *n*.
	9:23	in the hinterland, would *n* his successor,
Jb	1:21	blessed be the *n* of the LORD!"
	18:17	the land, and he has no *n* on the earth.
Ps(s)	5:12	may be the joy of those who love your *n*.
	7:18	sing praise to the *n* of the LORD Most High.
	8: 2	how glorious is your *n* over all the earth!
	8:10	how glorious is your *n* over all the earth!
	9: 3	I will sing praise to your *n*,
	9: 6	their *n* you blotted out forever and ever.
	9:11	They trust in you who cherish your *n*,
	18:50	nations, and I will sing praise to your *n*,
	20: 2	the *n* of the God of Jacob defend you!
	20: 6	raise the standards in the *n* of our God.
	20: 8	but we are strong in the *n* of the LORD,
	22:23	I will proclaim your *n* to my brethren;
	29: 2	Give to the LORD the glory due his *n*;
	30: 5	ones, and give thanks to his holy *n*.
	33:21	in his holy *n* we trust.
	34: 4	LORD with me, let us together extol his *n*.
	41: 6	'When will he die and his *n* perish?'
	44: 6	your *n* we trampled down our adversaries.
	44: 9	your *n* we praised always.
	44:21	If we had forgotten the *n* of our God and
	45:18	your *n* memorable through all generations;
	48:11	As your *n*, O God, so also your praise
	52:11	of your *n* before your faithful ones.
	54: 3	O God, by your *n* save me,
	54: 8	I will praise your *n*, O LORD,
	61: 6	me the heritage of those who fear your *n*.
	61: 9	will I sing the praises of your *n* forever,
	63: 5	up my hands, I will call upon your *n*.
	66: 2	earth, sing praise to the glory of his *n*;
	66: 4	sing praise to you, sing praise to your *n*!"
	68: 5	Sing to God, chant praise to his *n*,
	68: 5	upon the clouds, Whose *n* is the LORD;
	69:31	I will praise the *n* of God in song,
	69:37	and those who love his *n* shall inhabit it.
	72:17	*n* be blessed forever; as long as the sun his *n*
	72:19	And blessed forever be his glorious *n*;
	74: 7	your *n* abides they have razed and profaned.
	74:10	Shall the enemy revile your *n* forever?
	74:18	and how a stupid people has reviled your *n*.
	74:21	the afflicted and the poor praise your *n*.
	75: 2	and we invoke your *n*;
	76: 2	in Judah, in Israel great is his *n*.
	79: 6	the kingdoms that call not upon your *n*;
	79: 9	savior, because of the glory of your *n*;
	80:19	us new life, and we will call upon your *n*.
	83: 5	let the *n* of Israel be remembered no more!"
	83:17	with disgrace, that men may seek your *n*,
	86: 9	worship you, O Lord, and glorify your *n*.
	86:11	direct my heart that it may fear your *n*.
	86:12	heart, and I will glorify your *n* forever.
	89:13	Tabor and Hermon rejoice at your *n*.
	89:17	At your *n* they rejoice all the day,
	89:25	and through my *n* shall his horn be exalted.
	91:14	him on high because he acknowledges my *n*.
	92: 2	to the LORD, to sing praise to your *n*,
	96: 2	Sing to the LORD; bless his *n*;

NAME (cont.)
96: 8 give to the LORD the glory due his *n!*
97:12 you just, and give thanks to his holy *n.*
99: 3 Let them praise your great and awesome *n;*
99: 6 Samuel, among those who called upon his *n;*
100: 4 Give thanks to him; bless his *n,*
102:13 and your *n* through all generations.
102:16 And the nations shall revere your *n,*
102:22 the *n* of the LORD may be declared in Zion;
103: 1 and all my being, bless his holy *n.*
105: 1 Give thanks to the LORD, invoke his *n;*
105: 3 Glory in his holy *n;*
106:47 to your holy *n* and glory in praising you.
109:13 next generation may their *n* be blotted out.
111: 9 holy and awesome is his *n.*
113: 1 of the LORD, praise the *n* of the LORD.
113: 2 be the *n* of the LORD both now and forever.
113: 3 the sun is the *n* of the LORD to be praised.
115: 1 your *n* give glory because of your kindness,
116: 4 And I called upon the *n* of the LORD,
116:13 up, and I will call upon the *n* of the LORD;
116:17 and I will call upon the *n* of the LORD.
118:10 in the *n* of the LORD I crushed them.
118:11 in the *n* of the LORD I crushed them.
118:12 in the *n* of the LORD I crushed them.
118:26 is he who comes in the *n* of the LORD;
119:55 By night I remember your *n,* O LORD,
119:132 pity as you turn to those who love your *n.*
122: 4 to give thanks to the *n* of the LORD.
124: 8 Our help is in the *n* of the LORD,
129: 8 We bless you in the *n* of the LORD!"
135: 3 sing praise to his *n,* which we love;
135:13 Your *n,* O LORD, endures forever;
138: 2 holy temple and give thanks to your *n,*
138: 2 above all things your *n* and your promise.
139:20 Wickedly they invoke your *n;*
140:14 the just shall give thanks to your *n:*
142: 8 prison, that I may give thanks to your *n.*
145: 1 and I will bless your *n* forever and ever.
145: 2 and I will praise your *n* forever and ever.
145:21 flesh bless his holy *n* forever and ever.
147: 4 number of the stars; he calls each by *n.*
148: 5 Let them praise the *n* of the LORD,
148:13 Praise the *n* of the LORD, for his *n* alone
149: 3 Let them praise his *n* in the festive dance,
Prv 10: 7 blessed, but the *n* of the wicked will rot.
18:10 The *n* of the LORD is a strong tower;
21:24 Arrogant is the *n* for the man of
22: 1 good *n* is more desirable than great riches,
30: 4 What is his name, what is his son's *n,*
30: 9 want, I steal, and profane the *n* of my God.
Eccl 6: 4 and its *n* is enveloped in darkness;
6:10 Whatever is, was long ago given its *n,*
7: 1 A good *n* is better than good ointment,
Sg 1: 3 Your *n* spoken is a spreading perfume
Wis 2: 4 Even our *n* will be forgotten in time,
10:20 your holy *n* and praised in unison your
14:21 the incommunicable *N* on stocks and stones.
Sir 6: 1 A bad *n* and disgrace will you acquire:
6:23 For discipline is like her *n,*
15: 6 he will find, an everlasting *n* inherit.
17: 8 wonders of his deeds and praise his holy *n.*
22:14 than lead, and what is its *n* but "Fool"?
23: 9 or becoming too familiar with the Holy *N.*
23:10 the Holy *N* will not remain free from sin.
36:11 Show mercy to the people called by your *n;*
36:14 fulfill the prophecies spoken in your *n,*
37: 1 are friends who are friends in *n* only.
37:25 of glory, and his *n* endures forever.
39: 9 through all generations his *n* will live;
39:15 Proclaim the greatness of his *n,*
39:35 proclaim and bless the *n* of the Holy One.
40:18 A child or a city will preserve one's *n,*
41:11 but a virtuous *n* will never be annihilated.
41:12 Have a care for your *n,*
41:13 of life is for limited days, but a good *n,*
43: 8 As its *n* says,
44: 8 *n* and men recount their praiseworthy deeds;
44:14 laid away, but their *n* lives on and on.
45:15 priesthood and bless his people in his *n.*
46: 1 office, Formed to be, as his *n* implies,
47:10 psalms So that when the Holy *N* was praised,
47:13 He built a house to the *n* of God,
47:18 glorious *n* which was conferred upon Israel.
49: 1 The *n* JOSIAH is like blended incense,
50:20 lips, the *n* of the LORD would be his glory.
51: 1 I will make known your *n,*
51:11 *n* and be constant in my prayers to you.
51:12 I bless the *n* of the LORD.
Is 4: 1 Only let your *n* be given us,
7:14 and bear a son, and shall *n* him Immanuel.
8: 3 *N* him Maher-shalal-hash-baz,
8: 4 how to call his father or mother by *n,*
9: 5 They *n* him Wonder-Counselor,
12: 4 Give thanks to the LORD, acclaim his *n;*
12: 4 his deeds, proclaim how exalted is his *n.*
14:22 and cut off from Babylon *n* and remnant,
18: 7 where dwells the *n* of the LORD of hosts.
24:15 of the sea, to the *n* of the LORD,
25: 1 God, I will extol you and praise your *n;*
26: 8 Your *n* and your title are the desire of
26:13 from you only that we can call upon your *n.*
29:23 in his midst, They shall keep my *n* holy;
30:27 See the *n* of the LORD coming from afar in
40:26 and numbers them, calling them all by *n.*
41:25 from the east I summon him by *n;*
42: 8 I am the LORD, this is my *n;*
43: 1 I have called you by *n:*
45: 3 the God of Israel, who calls you by your *n.*
45: 4 chosen one, I have called you by your *n,*
47: 4 redeemer, Whose *n* is the LORD of hosts,
48: 1 O house of Jacob called by the *n* of Israel,
48: 1 You who swear by the *n* of the LORD and
48: 2 of Israel, whose *n* is the LORD of hosts.
48: 9 For the sake of my *n* I restrain my anger,
48:19 Their *n* never cut off or blotted out from
49: 1 from my mother's womb he gave me my *n.*
49:16 palms of my hands I have written your *n;*
50:10 the *n* of the LORD and relying on his God?
51:15 the LORD of hosts by *n.*
52: 5 all the day my *n* is constantly reviled.
54: 5 his *n* is the LORD of hosts;
56: 5 and a *n* Better than sons and daughters;
56: 5 eternal, imperishable *n* will I give them.
56: 6 to him, Loving the *n* of the LORD, and
57:15 living eternally, whose *n* is the Holy One:
59:19 in the west shall fear the *n* of the LORD,
60: 9 silver and gold, In the *n* of the LORD,
62: 2 new *n* pronounced by the mouth of the LORD.
63:14 led your people, bringing glory to your *n.*
63:19 you do not rule, who do not bear your *n.*
64: 1 Thus your *n* would be made known to your
64: 6 There is none who calls upon your *n,*
65: 1 To a nation that did not call upon my *n.*
65:15 and the *n* you leave Shall be used by my
65:15 my servants shall be called by another *n*
66: 5 Your brethren who, because of my *n,*
66:22 LORD, so shall your race and your *n* endure.
Jer 3:17 to honor the *n* of the LORD at Jerusalem,
4: 2 shall the nations use his *n* in blessing,
7:10 before me in this house which bears my *n,*
7:11 my *n* become in your eyes a den of thieves?
7:12 dwelling place of my *n* in the beginning.
7:30 have defiled the house which bears my *n*
10: 6 great are you great and mighty is your *n.*
10:16 his very own tribe, LORD of hosts is his *n.*
10:25 on the tribes that call not upon your *n;*
11:19 so that his *n* will be spoken no more."
11:21 "Do not prophesy in the *n* of the LORD;
12:16 my people's custom of swearing by my *n,*
14: 7 action, O LORD, for the honor of your *n*—
14: 9 are in our midst, O LORD, your *n* we bear:
14:14 Lies these prophets utter in my *n,*
14:15 the prophets who prophesy in my *n,*
15:16 of my heart, Because I bore your *n,*
16:21 they shall know that my *n* is LORD.
20: 3 the LORD will *n* you "Terror on every side."
20: 9 mention him, I will speak in his *n* no more.
23: 6 This is the *n* they give him:
23:25 the prophets who prophesy lies in my *n* say,
23:26 Is my *n* in the hearts of the prophets who
23:27 as their fathers forgot my *n*
23:27 to make my people forget my *n*
25:29 with this city, which is called by my *n,*
26: 9 Why do you prophesy in the *n* of the LORD:
26:16 it is in the *n* of the LORD,
26:20 man who prophesied in the *n* of the LORD,
27:15 Lord, but they prophesy falsely in my *n,*
29: 9 For they prophesy lies to you in my *n;*
29:21 those who prophesy lies to you in my *n,*
29:23 alleging in my *n* things I did not command.
31:35 its waves roar, whose *n* is LORD of hosts;
32:18 great and mighty, whose *n* is LORD of hosts,
33: 2 gave it form and firmness, whose *n* is LORD:
34:16 you changed your mind and profaned my *n*
44:16 to what you say in the *n* of the LORD.
44:26 I swear by my own great *n,*
44:26 shall henceforth pronounce my *n* saying,
46:17 the *n* "The noise that let its time go by."
46:18 says the King whose *n* is LORD of hosts,
48:15 says the King, the LORD of hosts by *n.*
50:34 is their avenger, whose *n* is LORD of hosts;
51:19 his very own tribe, LORD of hosts is his *n.*
51:57 the King, whose *n* is the LORD of hosts.
52: 1 His mother's *n* was Hamutal,
Lam 3:55 I called upon your *n,*
Bar 2:11 made for yourself a *n* till the present day:
2:15 Israel and his descendants bear your *n.*
2:26 which bears your *n* to what it is today,
2:32 of their captivity, and shall invoke my *n.*
3: 5 of our fathers, but your own hand and *n:*
3: 7 that we may call upon your *n,*
4:30 who gave you your *n* is your encouragement.
5: 2 that displays the glory of the eternal *n.*
Ez 10:13 I heard the wheels given the *n* "wheelwork."
20:39 my holy *n* with your gifts and your idols.
23: 4 Oholah was the *n* of the elder,
23: 4 and the *n* of her sister was Oholibah.
36:20 came], they served to profane my holy *n,*
36:21 So I have relented because of my holy *n*
36:22 of Israel, but for the sake of my holy *n,*
36:23 I will prove the holiness of my great *n,*
39: 7 my holy *n* known among my people Israel;
39: 7 no longer allow my holy *n* to be profaned.
39:16 [Also the *n* of the city shall be Hamonah.]
39:25 and I will be jealous for my holy *n.*
43: 7 they and their kings profane my holy *n*
43: 8 my holy *n* by their abominable deeds;
48:35 The *n* of the City shall henceforth be
Dn 2:20 "Blessed be the *n* of God forever and ever,
2:26 asked Daniel, whose *n* was Belteshazzar,
3:26 fathers, and glorious forever is your *n,*
3:43 by your wonders, and bring glory to your *n,*
3:52 And blessed is your holy and glorious *n,*
4: 5 *n* is Belteshazzar after the name of my god,
4:16 Then Daniel, whose *n* was Belteshazzar,
9: 6 prophets, who spoke in your *n* to our kings,
9:15 and made a *n* for yourself even to this day,
9:18 our ruins and the city which bears your *n.*
9:19 this city and your people bear your *n!"*
Hos 1: 4 Give him the *n* Jezreel,
1: 6 Give her the *n* Lo-ruhama;
1: 9 Give him the *n* Lo-ammi,
12: 6 LORD, the God of hosts, the LORD is his *n!*
Jl 2:26 filled, and shall praise the *n* of the LORD,
3: 5 be rescued who calls on the *n* of the LORD;
Am 2: 7 the same prostitute, profaning my holy *n.*
4:13 The LORD, The God of hosts by *n.*
5: 9 whose *n* is LORD.
5:27 say I, the LORD, the God of hosts by *n.*
6:10 for no one must mention the *n* of the LORD.
9: 6 the surface of the earth, I, the LORD by *n.*
9:12 Edom and all the nations shall bear my *n,*
Mi 4: 5 *n* of its god, But we will walk in the *n* of the
5: 3 of the LORD, in the majestic *n* of the LORD,
6: 9 [It is wisdom to fear your *n*
Na 1:14 no descendant shall come to bear your *n;*
Zep 3: 9 they all may call upon the *n* of the LORD,
3:12 Who shall take refuge in the *n* of the LORD;
Zec 5: 4 of him who perjures himself with my *n;*
6:12 Here is a man whose *n* is Shoot,
10:12 in the LORD, and they shall walk in his *n,*
13: 3 you have spoken a lie in the *n* of the LORD."
13: 9 They shall call upon my *n,*
14: 9 be the only one, and his *n* the only one.
Mal 1: 6 hosts to you, O priests, who despise his *n.*
1: 6 But you ask, "How have we despised your *n?"*
1:11 setting, my *n* is great among the nations;
1:11 everywhere they bring sacrifice to my *n,*
1:11 For great is my *n* among the nations,
1:14 and my *n* will be feared among the nations.
2: 2 lay it to heart, to give glory to my *n,*
2: 5 and he feared me, and stood in awe of my *n.*
3:16 those who fear the LORD and trust in his *n.*
3:20 But for you who fear my *n,*
Mt 1:21 She is to have a son and you are to *n* him
1:23 a *n* which means "God is with us."
6: 9 'Our Father in heaven, hallowed be your *n,*
7:22 Lord, have we not prophesied in your *n?*
7:22 we not do many miracles in your *n* as well?'
10:41 *n* of prophet receives a prophet's reward;
12:21 In his *n,* the Gentiles will find hope."
18:20 Where two or three are gathered in my *n,*
21: 9 is he who comes in the *n* of the Lord!
23:39 is he who comes in the *n* of the Lord!' "
26: 3 of the high priest, whose *n* was Caiaphas.
26:14 Then one of the Twelve whose *n* was Judas
27:33 Golgotha (a *n* which means Skull Place),
27:57 man from Arimathea arrived, Joseph by *n.*
28:19 Baptize them in the *n* of the Father,
Mk 3:17 Simon to whom he gave the *n* Peter;
3:17 James (he gave these two the *n* Boanerges,
5: 7 I implore you in God's *n,*
5: 9 "What is your *n?"* "Legion is my *n,*
9:38 we saw a man using your *n* to expel demons
9:39 my *n* can at the same time speak ill of me.
11: 9 is he who comes in the *n* of the Lord!
13:13 Because of my *n,* you will be hated by
16:17 they will use my *n* to expel demons,
Lk 1:13 shall bear a son whom you shall *n* John.
1:27 The virgin's *n* was Mary.
1:31 and bear a son and give him the *n* Jesus.
1:49 done great things for me, holy is his *n;*
1:59 to *n* him after his father Zechariah.
1:61 her, "None of your relatives has this *n."*
1:63 and wrote the words, "His *n* is John."
2:21 *n* Jesus was given the child, the *n* the angel
2:36 was also a certain prophetess, Anna by *n,*
6:14 Simon, to whom he gave the *n* Peter,
6:22 your *n* as evil because of the Son of Man.
8:30 "What is your *n?"*
9:49 we saw a man using your *n* to expel demons,
10:17 the demons are subject to us in your *n."*
11: 2 "Father, hallowed be your *n,*
13:35 is he who comes in the *n* of the Lord.' "
19:38 he who comes as king in the *n* of the Lord!
21: 8 Many will come in my *n* saying,
21:12 kings and governors, all because of my *n.*
24:18 distress, and one of them, Cleopas by *n,*
24:47 In his *n,* penance for the remission of sins
Jn 1:12 These are they who believe in his *n*—
1:42 your *n* shall be Cephas
2:23 Passover festival, many believed in his *n,*
3:18 not believing in the *n* of God's only Son.
5: 2 is a place with the Hebrew *n* Bethesda.
5:43 I have come in my Father's *n,*
5:43 But let someone come in his own *n,*
9: 7 (This *n* means "One who has been sent.")
10: 3 he calls his own by *n* and leads them out.

10:25 in my Father's *n* give witness in my favor,
11:16 Then Thomas (the *n* means "Twin") said to
12:13 is he who comes in the *n* of the Lord!
12:28 Father, glorify your *n!*"
14:13 and whatever you ask in my *n* I will do,
14:14 Anything you ask me in my *n* I will do,
14:26 Spirit whom the Father will send in my *n,*
15:16 ask the Father in my *n* he will give you.
15:21 this they will do to you because of my *n,*
16:23 ask the Father, he will give you in my *n.*
16:24 you have not asked for anything in my *n.*
16:26 On that day you will ask in my *n* and I do
17: 6 I have made your *n* known to those you gave
17:11 protect them with your *n* which you have
17:12 guarded them with your *n* which you gave me.
17:26 To them I have revealed your *n,*
18:10 (The slave's *n* was Malchus.)
20:24 the Twelve, Thomas (the *n* means "Twin"),
20:31 this faith you may have life in his *n.*
Acts 2:21 be saved who calls on the *n* of the Lord.'
2:38 each one of you, in the *n* of Jesus Christ,
3: 6 In the *n* of Jesus Christ,
3:16 It is his name, and trust in this *n,*
4: 7 whose *n* have men of your stripe done this?"
4:10 that it was done in the *n* of Jesus Christ
4:10 In the power of that *n* this man stands
4:12 for there is no other *n* in the whole world
4:17 to mention that man's *n* to anyone again."
4:18 to speak the *n* of Jesus or teach about him.
4:30 and wonders to be worked in the *n* of Jesus,
4:36 to whom the apostles gave the *n* Barnabas
5:28 strict orders not to teach about that *n,*
5:40 not to speak again about the *n* of Jesus,
5:41 of ill-treatment for the sake of the *N.*
8:12 kingdom of God and the *n* of Jesus Christ,
8:16 been baptized in the *n* of the Lord Jesus.
8:27 (a *n* meaning queen) of the Ethiopians,
9:14 priests to arrest any who invoke your *n.*"
9:15 have chosen to bring my *n* to the Gentiles,
9:16 how much he will have to suffer for my *n.*"
9:21 in Jerusalem among those who invoke this *n?*
9:27 fearlessly in the *n* of Jesus at Damascus.
9:28 himself quite openly in the *n* of the Lord.
10:43 him has forgiveness of sins through his *n.*"
10:48 they be baptized in the *n* of Jesus Christ.
13: 8 magician," for that is what his *n* means
15:14 among the Gentiles a people to bear his *n.*
15:17 that bear my *n* may seek out the Lord.
16:18 "In the *n* of Jesus Christ I command you,
19: 5 were baptized in the *n* of the Lord Jesus.
19:13 tried to invoke the *n* of the Lord Jesus
19:17 and the *n* of the Lord Jesus came to be
21:13 For the *n* of the Lord Jesus I am prepared,
22:16 wash away your sins as you call upon his *n.*'
26: 9 to oppose the *n* of Jesus the Nazorean
Rom 1: 5 that we may spread his *n* and bring to
2:17 Let us suppose you bear the *n* of "Jew"
2:24 "On your account the *n* of God is held in
9:17 and my *n* might be proclaimed throughout
10:13 calls on the *n* of the Lord will be saved."
15: 9 the Gentiles and I will sing to your *n.*"
15:20 places where Christ's *n* was already known,
1Cor 1: 2 be, call on the *n* of our Lord Jesus Christ,
1:10 in the *n* of our Lord Jesus Christ,
1:13 Was it in Paul's *n* that you were baptized?
1:15 who can say that you were baptized in my *n.*
4: 7 *N* something you have that you have not
5: 3 sentence in the *n* of our Lord Jesus Christ
6:11 justified in the *n* of our Lord Jesus
15: 9 church of God, I do not even deserve the *n.*
2Cor 2:17 We speak in Christ's *n,*
5:20 We implore you, in Christ's *n:*
Gal 4: 1 in *n* he is master of all his possessions;
Eph 1:21 and every *n* that can be given in this age
3:15 family in heaven and on earth takes its *n;*
5:20 in the *n* of our Lord Jesus Christ.
Phil 2: 1 In the *n* of the encouragement you owe me
2: 1 in the *n* of the solace that love can give,
2: 9 on him the *n* above every other name,
2:10 *n* every knee must bend in the heavens,
Col 3:17 action, do it in the *n* of the Lord Jesus.
2Thes 1:12 In this way the *n* of our Lord Jesus may be
3: 6 in the *n* of the Lord Jesus Christ,
1Tm 6: 1 otherwise the *n* of God and the church's
2Tm 2:19 professes the *n* of the Lord abandon evil."
Phlm 1: 9 done, I prefer to appeal in the *n* of love.
Heb 1: 4 *n* he has inherited is superior to theirs.
2:12 "I will announce your *n* to my brothers,
7: 2 His *n* means "king of justice";
13:15 of lips which acknowledge his *n.*
Jas 2: 7 that noble *n* which has made you God's own.
5:10 prophets who spoke in the *n* of the Lord.
5:14 him with oil in the *N* [of the Lord].
1Pt 4:16 rather glorify God in virtue of that *n.*
1Jn 2:12 through his *N* your sins have been forgiven.
3:23 we are to believe in the *n* of his Son,
5:13 you who believe in the *n* of the Son of God.
3Jn 1: 7 for the sake of the *N* that they set out,
1:15 greet the beloved there, each by *n.*
Rv 2:13 and I know you hold fast to my *n* and have
2:17 stone upon which is inscribed a new *n,*
3: 5 erase his *n* from the book of the living,
3: 8 fast to my word and have not denied my *n.*
3:12 I will inscribe on him the *n* of my God and
3:12 of my God and the *n* of the city of my God,
3:12 from heaven, and my own *n* which is new.
8:11 The star's *n* was "Wormwood" because a
9:11 whose *n* in Hebrew is Abaddon and in Greek
11: 8 has the symbolic *n* "Sodom" or "Egypt,"
13:17 was first marked with the *n* of the beast
13:17 or with the number that stood for its *n.*
14: 1 who had his *n* and the name of his Father
14:11 or its image or accept the mark of its *n.*"
15: 2 and also the number that signified its *n.*
15: 4 refuse you honor, or the glory due your *n,*
16: 9 intense heat blasphemed the *n* of God
17: 5 On her forehead was written a symbolic *n,*
19:12 person was a *n* known to no one but himself.
19:13 in blood, and his *n* was the Word of God.
19:16 A *n* was written on the part of the cloak
20:15 anyone whose *n* was not found inscribed in
22: 4 to face and bear his *n* on their foreheads.

NAMED (198)

Gn 4:17 of a city, which he *n* after his son Enoch.
4:26 turn, a son was born, and he *n* him Enosh.
5: 2 created, he blessed them and *n* them "man."
5: 3 and he *n* him Seth.
5:29 years old, he begot a son and *n* him Noah,
7:13 On the precise day *n,* Noah and his sons
16: 1 however, an Egyptian maidservant *n* Hagar.
16:15 *n* the son whom Hagar bore him Ishmael.
19:37 one gave birth to a son whom she *n* Moab,
19:38 gave birth to a son, and she *n* him Ammon,
22:14 Abraham *n* the site Yahweh-yireh;
24:29 Now Rebekah had a brother *n* Laban.
25:25 so they *n* him Esau.
25:26 so they *n* him Jacob.
27:36 Esau exclaimed, "He has been well *n* Jacob!
29:32 and bore a son, and she *n* him Reuben;
29:33 so she *n* him Simeon.
29:34 that is why she *n* him Levi.
29:35 therefore she *n* him Judah.
30: 6 Therefore she *n* him Dan.
30: 8 So she *n* him Naphtali.
30:11 So she *n* him Gad.
30:13 So she *n* him Asher.
30:18 so she *n* him Issachar.
30:20 so she *n* him Zebulun.
30:21 birth to a daughter, and she *n* her Dinah.
30:24 So she *n* him Joseph meaning,
31:47 it Jegar-sahadutha, but Jacob *n* it Galeed.
31:48 That is why it was *n* Galeed
32: 3 So he *n* that place Mahanaim.
32:31 Jacob *n* the place Peniel,
35: 7 he built an altar and *n* the place Bethel,
35:10 Thus he was *n* Israel.
35:15 Jacob *n* the site Bethel,
35:18 his father, however, *n* him Benjamin.
38: 1 his tent near a certain Adullamite *n* Hirah.
38: 2 he met the daughter of a Canaanite *n* Shua,
38: 3 conceived and bore a son, whom she *n* Er.
38: 4 conceived and bore a son, whom she *n* Onan.
38: 5 bore still another son, whom she *n* Shelah.
38: 6 got a wife *n* Tamar for his first-born,
41:51 He *n* his first-born Manasseh,
41:52 and the second he *n* Ephraim,
50:11 That is why the place was *n* Abel-mizraim.
Ex 2:22 She bore him a son, whom he *n* Gershom;
Nm 3:17 The sons of Levi were *n* Gershon,
3:18 Gershon, by clans, were *n* Libni and Shimei.
11:26 two men, one *n* Eldad and the other Medad,
11:34 So that place was *n* Kibroth-hattaavah,
21: 3 Hence that place was *n* Hormah.
26:59 was Amram, whose wife was *n* Jochebed.
27: 1 son of Joseph, had daughters *n* Mahlah,
Jos 2: 1 went into the house of a harlot *n* Rahab,
Jgs 8:31 also bore him a son, whom he *n* Abimelech.
13:24 The woman bore a son and *n* him Samson.
15:17 and so that place was *n* Ramath-lehi.
18:29 They *n* it Dan after their ancestor Dan,
Ru 1: 2 The man was *n* Elimelech,
1: 4 who married Moabite women, one *n* Orpah,
2: 1 Naomi had a prominent kinsman *n* Boaz,
2:19 at whose place I worked today is *n* Boaz,"
1Sm 1: 2 He had two wives, one *n* Hannah,
4:21 [She *n* the child Ichabod,
7:12 he *n* it Ebenezer,
8: 2 His first-born was *n* Joel,
9: 1 was a stalwart man from Benjamin *n* Kish,
9: 2 He had a son *n* Saul,
14:49 his two daughters were *n,*
14:50 Saul's wife, who was *n* Ahinoam,
17: 4 A champion *n* Goliath of Gath came out from
17:12 was the son of an Ephrathite *n* Jesse,
17:13 three sons who had gone off to war were *n,*
22:20 of Ahimelech, son of Ahitub, *n* Abiathar,
25: 3 The man was *n* Nabal, his wife Abigail.
2Sm 2:16 is in Gideon, was *n* the Field of the Sides.
4: 2 two company leaders *n* Baanah and Rechab,
4: 4 had a son *n* Meribbaal with crippled feet.
9: 2 was a servant of the family of Saul *n* Ziba.
12:24 and bore him a son, who was *n* Solomon.
13: 1 son Absalom had a beautiful sister *n* Tamar,
13: 3 Now Amnon had a friend *n* Jonadab,
14:27 born to him, besides a daughter *n* Tamar,
16: 5 was approaching Bahurim, a man *n* Shimei,
17:25 Amasa was the son of an Ishamelite *n* Ithra,
18:18 The pillar which he *n* for himself is
20: 1 individual from Benjamin *n* Sheba,
20:21 A man *n* Sheba,
1Kgs 14:21 His mother was the Ammonite *n* Naamah.
14:31 His mother was the Ammonite *n* Naamah.
2Kgs 12: 2 His mother, who was *n* Zibiah,
17:34 descendants of Jacob, whom he had *n* Israel.
1Chr 1:19 the first was *n* Peleg (for in his time the
2:29 Abishur's wife, who was *n* Abihail,
2:34 daughters, had an Egyptian slave *n* Jarha.
4: 3 their sister was *n* Hazzelelponi.
4: 9 His mother had *n* him Jabez,
4:38 these just *n* were princes in their clans,
6: 2 sons of Gershon were *n* Libni and Shimei.
7:15 Manasseh's second son was *n* Zelophehad,
7:16 wife, bore a son whom she *n* Peresh.
7:16 He had a brother *n* Sheresh,
7:23 conceived and bore a son whom he *n* Beriah,
9: 9 *n* were heads of their ancestral houses.
2Chr 12:13 Rehoboam's mother was *n* Naamah,
13: 2 His mother was *n* Michaiah,
20:31 His mother was *n* Azubah,
22: 2 His mother was *n* Athaliah,
24: 1 His mother, *n* Zibiah, was from Beer-sheba.
25: 1 His mother, *n* Jehoaddan,
26: 3 His mother, *n* Jecoliah,
27: 1 His mother was *n* Jerusa,
28:15 men just *n* proceeded to help the captives.
29: 1 His mother was *n* Abia,
Ezr 5:14 a certain Sheshbazzar, whom he *n* governor.
Neh 9: 7 from Ur of the Chaldees, and *n* him Abraham.
Tb 1: 9 By her I had a son whom I *n* Tobiah.
6:11 He has a daughter *n* Sarah,
Est 2: 5 of Susa a certain Jew *n* Mordecai,
9:26 days have been *n* Purim after the word pur.
2Mc 1:36 purification, but most people *n* it naphtha.
Jb 1: 1 was a blameless and upright man *n* Job,
Sir 36:11 Israel, whom you *n* your first-born.
Is 14:20 Let him not be *n* forever,
43: 7 Everyone who is *n* as mine,
44: 5 LORD's," another shall be *n* after Jacob,
48: 2 Though you are *n* after the holy city and
48:12 Listen to me, Jacob Israel, whom I *n!*
61: 6 yourselves shall be *n* priests of the LORD,
63:16 our father, our redeemer you are *n* forever.
Jer 7:14 you, I will do to this house *n* after me,
11:16 tree, goodly to behold, the LORD has *n* you;
32:34 They defiled the house *n* after me by the
34:15 before me in the house that is *n* after me.
37:13 the captain of the guard, a man *n* Irijah,
Bar 5: 4 be *n* by God forever the peace of justice,
Ez 39:11 and it shall be *n* "Valley of Hamon-gog."
48:30 of which are *n* after the tribes of Israel.
Dn 5:12 this Daniel, whom the king *n* Belteshazzar.
10: 1 to Daniel, who had been *n* Belteshazzar.
13: 1 In Babylon there lived a man *n* Joakim,
13:45 up the holy spirit of a young boy *n* Daniel,
Mt 1:25 before she bore a son, whom he *n* Jesus.
9: 9 Jesus saw a man *n* Matthew at his post
27:16 the time a notorious prisoner *n* Barabbas.
27:32 their way out they met a Cyrenian *n* Simon.
Mk 3:14 He *n* twelve as his companions whom he
5:22 officials of the synagogue, a man *n* Jairus,
14:32 They went then to a place *n* Gethsemane.
15: 7 There was a prisoner *n* Barabbas jailed
15:21 A man *n* Simon of Cyrene,
Lk 1: 5 there was a priest *n* Zechariah of the
1: 5 wife was a descendant of Aaron *n* Elizabeth.
1:26 from God to a town of Galilee *n* Nazareth,
1:27 to a virgin betrothed to a man *n* Joseph,
2:25 at the time a certain man *n* Simeon.
5:27 *n* Levi sitting at his customs post.
8:41 A man *n* Jairus,
10:38 a woman *n* Martha welcomed him to her
10:39 She had a sister *n* Mary,
16:20 *n* Lazarus who was covered with sores.
19: 2 There was a man there *n* Zacchaeus,
22:47 a crowd came, led by the man *n* Judas,
23:50 There was a man *n* Joseph,
24:13 making their way to a village *n* Emmaus
Jn 1: 6 There was a man *n* John sent by God,
3: 1 A certain Pharisee *n* Nicodemus,
4: 5 Samaritan town *n* Shechem
11: 1 was a certain man *n* Lazarus who was sick.
11:49 One of their number *n* Caiaphas,
Acts 1:19 who *n* the property Field of Blood
1:22 *n* as witness with us to his resurrection."
4:36 was a certain Levite from Cyprus *n* Joseph,
5: 1 Another man *n* Ananias and his wife
5:34 Sanhedrin stood up, a Pharisee *n* Gamaliel,
7:58 cloaks at the feet of a young man *n* Saul.
8: 9 A certain man *n* Simon had been practicing
9:10 There was a disciple in Damascus *n* Ananias
9:12 (Saul saw in a vision a man *n* Ananias
9:33 There he found a man *n* Aeneas,
9:36 woman convert *n* Tabitha (in Greek Dorcas,
10: 1 Caesarea there was a centurion *n* Cornelius,
11:28 One of them *n* Agabus was inspired to stand
12:13 door and a maid *n* Rhoda came to answer it.
13: 6 *n* Bar-Jesus who posed as a prophet.

NAMED (cont.)
14:12 They *n* Barnabas Zeus;
16: 1 where there was a disciple *n* Timothy,
16:14 One who listened was a woman *n* Lydia,
17:34 court of the Areopagus, a woman *n* Damaris,
18: 2 There he found a Jew *n* Aquila,
18: 7 to the house of a Gentile *n* Titus Justus,
18:24 A Jew *n* Apollos,
19:24 There was a silversmith *n* Demetrius who
20: 9 and a certain young lad *n* Eutychus who was
21:10 a prophet *n* Agabus arrived from Judea.
24: 1 of the elders and an attorney *n* Tertullus.
27: 1 *n* Julius from the cohort known as Augusta.
27:16 the lee of a small island *n* Cauda
Rv 6: 8 Its rider was *n* Death,

NAMELESS (1)
Jb 30: 8 Irresponsible, *n* men,

NAMELY (15)
Gn 32:20 others who followed behind the droves, *n:*
Jos 15:13 among the Judahites, *n,* Kiriath-arba
Ezr 8:18 son of Levi, son of Israel, *n* Sherebiah,
Jn 5:36 I have testimony greater than John's, *n,*
7:17 *n,* whether it comes from God
12:48 has his judge, *n,* the word I have spoken
Acts 10:30 ago at this very hour, *n* three o'clock,
15:29 strictly necessary, *n,* to abstain from meat
26:23 *n,* that the Messiah must suffer,
1Cor 3:11 the one that has been laid, *n* Jesus Christ.
11:23 from the Lord what I handed on to you, *n,*
2Cor 8:20 *n* any blame over my handling of this
Eph 1:10 *n,* to bring all things in the heavens and
4:22 *n,* that you must lay aside your former way
Col 2: 2 knowledge of the mystery of God *n* Christ

NAMES (74)
Gn 2:20 The man gave *n* to all the cattle,
25:13 These are the *n* of Ishmael's sons,
25:16 their *n* by their villages and encampments;
26:18 the same *n* that his father had given them.)
36:10 These are the *n* of Esau's sons;
36:40 following are the *n* of the clans of Esau
46: 8 These are the *n* of the Israelites,
48: 6 be recorded in the *n* of their two brothers.
48:16 and the *n* of my fathers Abraham and Isaac,
Ex 1: 1 These are the *n* of the sons of Israel who,
6:16 The *n* of the sons of Levi,
28: 9 on them the *n* of the sons of Israel;
28:10 six of their *n* on one stone,
28:11 engraved with the *n* of the sons of Israel
28:12 Thus Aaron shall bear their *n* on his
28:21 them to match the *n* of the sons of Israel,
28:29 he will thus bear the *n* of the sons of
39: 6 with the *n* of the sons of Israel.
39:14 to match the *n* of the sons of Israel,
Nm 1: 5 are the *n* of those who are to assist you:
3: 3 These are the *n* of the sons of Aaron,
13:16 These are the *n* of the men whom Moses sent
26:33 but only daughters whose *n* were Mahlah,
32:38 Nebo, Baal-meon *n* to be changed!],
32:38 they rebuilt, they called by their old *n.*
34:17 "These are the *n* of the men who shall
Dt 7:24 make their *n* perish from under the heavens.
Jos 17: 3 but only daughters, whose *n* were Mahlah,
2Sm 5:14 These are the *n* of those who were born to
23: 8 These are the *n* of David's warriors.
1Kgs 4: 8 Their *n* were: the son of Hur
1Chr 8:38 Azel had six sons, whose *n* were Azrikam,
9:44 Azel had six sons, whose *n* were Azrikam,
14: 4 These are the *n* of those who were born to
23:24 enrolled one by one according to their *n.*
Ezr 2:62 their *n* could not be found written there;
5: 4 What are the *n* of the men who are building
5:10 We also asked them their *n,*
8:13 younger sons, whose *n* were Eliphelet,
Neh 7:64 their *n* could not be found written there;
10: 1 document appear the *n* of our princes,
Ps(s) 16: 4 out, nor will I take their *n* upon my lips.
23: 3 He guides me in right paths for his *n* sake.
25:11 For your *n* sake,
31: 4 for your *n* sake you will lead and guide me.
49:12 though they have called lands by their *n.*
79: 9 us and pardon our sins for your *n* sake.
106: 8 Yet he saved them for his *n* sake,
109:21 Lord, deal kindly with me for your *n* sake;
143:11 For your *n* sake, O LORD, preserve me;
Wis 18:25 To these *n* the destroyer yielded,
Sir 46:12 *n* receive fresh luster in their children!
Jer 14:21 For your *n* sake spurn us not,
Ez 20: 9 but I acted for my *n* sake,
20:14 an end to them, but I acted for my *n* sake,
20:22 but I stayed my hand, acting for my *n* sake,
20:44 when I deal with you thus, for my *n* sake,
23: 4 [As for their *n:* Samaria is Oholah,
Dn 1: 7 The chief chamberlain changed their *n:*
3:34 For your *n* sake, do not deliver us up
Hos 2:19 I remove from her mouth the *n* of the Baals,
Zep 1: 4 vestige of Baal, the very *n* of his priests.
Zec 13: 2 destroy the *n* of the idols from the land,
Mt 10: 2 The *n* of the twelve apostles are these:
Lk 10:20 you as that your *n* are inscribed in heaven."
Phil 4: 3 with me, whose *n* are in the book of life.
Rv 13: 1 ten diadems and on its heads blasphemous *n.*
13: 8 their *n* written at the world's beginning
17: 3 beast which was covered with blasphemous *n.*
17: 8 All the men of the earth whose *n* have not
21:12 names were written on the gates, the *n*
21:14 the *n* of the twelve apostles of the Lamb.
21:27 Only those shall enter whose *n* are

NAMING (1)
1Kgs 16:24 *n* the city he built Samaria after Shemer,

NANAEON (1)
2Mc 1:15 of the *N* had displayed the treasures,

NANEA (1)
2Mc 1:13 to pieces in the temple of the goddess *N*

NANEA'S (1)
2Mc 1:13 deceitful stratagem employed by *N* priests.

NAOMI (23)
Ru 1: 2 The man was named Elimelech, his wife *N,*
1: 3 plateau, Elimelech, the husband of *N,*
1: 8 Judah, *N* said to her two daughters-in-law,
1:11 "Go back, my daughters!" said *N.*
1:18 *N* then ceased to urge her,
1:19 them, and the women asked, "Can this be *N*
1:20 But she said to them, "Do not call me *N.*
1:21 Why should you call me *N,*
1:22 Thus it was that *N* returned with the
2: 1 *N* had a prominent kinsman named Boaz,
2: 2 Ruth the Moabite said to *N,*
2: 2 *N* said to her, "Go, my daughter,"
2: 6 returned from the plateau of Moab with *N.*
2:20 to the living and to the dead," *N* exclaimed
2:22 "You would do well, my dear," *N* rejoined,
3: 1 with her mother-in-law, *N* said to her,
3:18 *N* then said, "Wait here, my daughter,
4: 3 *N,* who has come back from the Moabite
4: 5 "Once you acquire the field from *N,*
4: 9 from *N* all the holdings of Elimelech,
4:14 Then the women said to *N,*
4:16 *N* took the child,
4:17 news that a grandson had been born to *N.*

NAPHATH-DOR (4)
Jos 11: 2 in the foothills, and in *N* to the west.
12:23 Jokneam (at Carmel), and Dor (in *N*),
17:11 and its towns and natives [the third is *N.*
1Kgs 4:11 Solomon's daughter Taphath, in all the *N;*

NAPHISH (3)
Gn 25:15 Dumah, Massa, Hadad, Tema, Jetur, *N,*
1Chr 1:31 Dumah, Massa, Hadad, Tema, Jetur, *N,*
5:19 against the Hagrites and against Jetur, *N,*

NAPHTALI (52)
Gn 30: 8 So she named him *N.*
35:25 Dan and *N;* the sons of Leah's maid Zilpah:
46:24 The sons of *N:* Jahzeel, Guni,
49:21 *N* is a hind let loose which brings forth
Ex 1: 4 Dan and *N;*
Nm 1:15 Eliasaph, son of Reuel; from *N:*
1:42 Of the descendants of *N,*
1:43 hundred were enrolled in the tribe of *N.*
2:29 and next the tribe of *N.*
10:27 of Enan, over the host of the tribe of *N.*
13:14 son of Vophsi, of the tribe of *N*
26:50 These were the clans of *N,*
34:28 the tribe of *N:*
Dt 27:13 Dan and *N* shall stand on Mount Ebal to
33:23 Of *N* he said: *N* is enriched with favors
34: 2 Gilead, and as far as Dan, all *N,*
Jos 20: 7 in Galilee in the mountain region of *N,*
21: 6 the tribe of Asher, from the tribe of *N,*
21:32 and from the tribe of *N,*
Jgs 1:33 *N* did not drive out the inhabitants of
4: 6 Barak, son of Abinoam, from Kedesh of *N.*
4:10 Barak summoned Zebulun and *N* to Kedesh,
5:18 *N,* too, on the open heights!
6:35 through Asher, Zebulun and *N,*
7:23 The Israelites were called to arms from *N,*
1Kgs 4:15 another daughter of Solomon, in *N;*
7:14 the son of a widow from the tribe of *N;*
15:20 all Chinnereth, besides all the land of *N.*
2Kgs 15:29 Kedesh, Hazor, all the territory of *N,*
1Chr 2: 2 Zebulun, Dan, Joseph, Benjamin, *N,*
6:47 from the tribes of Issachar, Asher, and *N,*
6:61 From the tribe of *N:* Kedesh in Galilee
7:13 The sons of *N* were Jahziel,
12:35 From *N:* one thousand captains,
12:41 Zebulun, and *N* came bringing food on asses,
27:19 for *N,* Jeremoth, son of Azriel
2Chr 16: 4 Abel-maim, and all the store cities of *N.*
34: 6 of the surrounding country as far as *N;*
Tb 1: 1 of the family of Asiel, of the tribe of *N,*
1: 2 is south of Kedesh *N* in upper Galilee,
1: 4 tribe of my forefather *N* had broken away
1: 5 the rest of the tribe of my forefather *N,*
7: 3 "We are of the exiles from *N* at Nineveh."
Ps(s) 68:28 the princes of Zebulun, the princes of *N.*
Is 8:23 the land of Zebulun and the land of *N;*
Ez 48: 2 to the western boundary. *N:*
48: 4 on the frontier of *N,*
48:34 Gad, the gate of Asher, and the gate of *N.*
Mt 4:13 sea near the territory of Zebulun and *N,*
4:15 land of *N* along the sea beyond the Jordan,
Rv 7: 6 twelve thousand from the tribe of *N,*

NAPHTALITES (6)
Nm 7:78 of Ahira, son of Enan, prince of the *N.*
26:48 The *N* by clans were:
Jos 19:32 The sixth lot fell to the *N.*
19:32 of the clans of the *N* extended from Heleph,
19:39 of the clans of the tribe of the *N.*
Jgs 4: 6 with you ten thousand *N* and Zebulunites.

NAPHTHA (1)
2Mc 1:36 purification, but most people named it *n.*

NAPHTUHIM (2)
Gn 10:13 the Ludim, the Anamim, the Lehabim, the *N,*
1Chr 1:11 father of the Ludim, Anamim, Lehabim, *N,*

NARCISSUS (1)
Rom 16:11 of the household of *N* who are in the Lord.

NARD (4)
Sg 1:12 banquet my *n* gives forth its fragrance.
4:14 *N* and saffron, calamus and cinnamon
Mk 14: 3 of perfume made from expensive aromatic *n.*
Jn 12: 3 perfume made from genuine aromatic *n,*

NARRATIVE (1)
Lk 1: 1 Many have undertaken to compile a *n* of the

NARRATIVES (1)
2Mc 2:24 *n* where the material is abundant,

NARROW (9)
Nm 22:24 angel of the LORD took his stand in a *n* lane
22:26 and stopped next in a passage so *n* that
Jos 17:15 the mountain regions of Ephraim are so *n.*"
Prv 23:27 a deep ditch, and the adulteress a *n* pit;
Is 28:20 out in, and the cover too *n* to wrap in.
Mt 7:13 "Enter through the *n* gate.
7:14 But how *n* is the gate that leads to life,
Lk 13:24 "Try to come in through the *n* door.
Acts 12:10 emerged and made their way down a *n* alley,

NARROWLY (1)
Lam 1: 3 come upon her where she is *n* confined.

NARROWNESS (1)
2Cor 6:12 the *n* is in you.

NATHAN (43)
2Sm 5:14 Shammua, Shobab, *N,*
7: 2 on every side, he said to *N* the prophet,
7: 3 *N* answered the king, "Go do whatever
7: 4 that night the LORD spoke to *N* and said:
7:17 *N* reported all these words and this entire
12: 1 The LORD sent *N* to David,
12: 5 very angry with that man and said to *N:*
12: 7 Then *N* said to David: "You are the man!
12:13 Then David said to *N,* "I have sinned
12:13 *N* answered David: "I have sinned
12:15 Then *N* returned to his house.
12:25 sent the prophet *N* to name him Jedidiah,
23:36 Igal, son of *N,*
1Kgs 1: 8 Benaiah, son of Jehoiada, *N* the prophet,
1:10 But he did not invite the prophet *N,*
1:11 Then *N* said to Bathsheba,
1:22 to the king, the prophet *N* came in.
1:24 Then *N* said: "Have you decided;
1:32 summoned Zadok the priest, *N* the prophet,
1:34 There Zadok the priest and *N* the prophet
1:38 So Zadok the priest, *N* the prophet,
1:44 with him Zadok the priest, *N* the prophet,
1:45 *N* the prophet anointed him king at Gihon,
4: 5 Azariah, son of *N,*
4: 5 Zabud, son of *N,* companion to the king;
1Chr 2:36 Attai became the father of *N.*
2:36 *N* became the father of Zabad.
3: 5 Shimea, Shobab, *N,*
11:38 Joel, brother of *N,* from Rehob,
14: 4 Shammua, Shobab, *N,*
17: 1 in his house, he said to *N* the prophet,
17: 2 *N* replied to David, "Do, therefore,
17: 3 that same night the word of God came to *N:*
17:15 whole vision *N* related exactly to David.
29:29 the seer, the history of *N* the prophet,
2Chr 9:29 well known, in the acts of *N* the prophet,

29:25 Gad the king's seer, and of *N* the prophet;
Ezr 8:16 Ariel, Shemaiah, Jarib, Elnathan, *N*,
10:39 Shimei, Shelemiah, *N*,
Sir 47: 1 came *N* who served in the presence of David.
Zec 12:12 the family of the house of *N*,
Lk 3:31 son of Menna, son of Mattatha, son of *N*,

NATHAN-MELECH (1)

2Kgs 23:11 the LORD, near the chamber of *N* the eunuch,

NATHANAEL (6)

Jdt 8: 1 son of Hilkiah, son of Eliab, son of *N*,
Jn 1:45 Philip sought out *N* and told him,
1:47 When Jesus saw *N* coming toward him,
1:48 "How do you know me? *N* asked him.
1:49 "Rabbi," said *N*, "you are the Son of God;
21: 2 (the "Twin"), *N* (from Cana in Galilee),

NATHANAEL'S (1)

Jn 1:46 *N* response to that was,

NATHANIAH (1)

Tb 5:14 I knew Hananiah and *N*,

NATION (196)

Gn 12: 2 "I will make of you a great *n*,
15:14 bring judgment on the *n* they must serve,
17:20 and I will make of him a great *n*.
18:18 he is to become a great and populous *n*,
21:13 woman, I will make a great *n* of him also,
21:18 for I will make of him a great *n*."
35:11 A *n*, indeed an assembly of nations,
46: 3 Egypt, for there I will make you a great *n*.
Ex 9:18 day the *n* was founded up to the present.
9:24 seen in the land since Egypt became a *n*.
19: 6 be to me a kingdom of priests, a holy *n*.
23:27 I will throw into panic every *n* you reach.
32:10 Then I will make of you a great *n*."
33:13 Then, too, this *n* is,
34:10 been wrought in any *n* anywhere on earth,
Nm 14:12 of you a *n* greater and mightier then they."
32:15 will bring about the ruin of this whole *n*."
Dt 2:25 of you into every *n* under the heavens,
4: 6 *n* is truly a wise and intelligent people.'
4: 7 For what great *n* is there that has gods so
4: 8 Or what great *n* has statutes and decrees
4:34 Or did any god venture to go and take a *n*
4:34 for himself from the midst of another *n*,
9:14 of you a *n* mightier and greater than they.'
26: 5 But there he became a *n* great,
28:32 daughters will be given to a foreign *n*
28:36 to a *n* which you and your fathers have not
28:49 will raise up against you a *n* from afar,
28:49 a *n* whose tongue you do not understand,
28:50 you do not understand, a *n* of stern visage,
32:21 with a foolish *n* I will anger them.
33:29 Where else is a *n* victorious in the LORD?
Jos 3:17 the whole *n* had completed the passage.
4: 1 After the entire *n* had crossed the Jordan,
5: 2 the Israelite *n* for the second time."
5: 8 whole *n* remained in camp where they were,
10:13 while the *n* took vengeance on its foes.
Jgs 2:20 "Inasmuch as this *n* has violated my
2Sm 7:23 What other *n* on earth is there like your
8:11 he had taken from every *n* he had conquered;
1Kgs 18:10 there is no *n* or kingdom where my master
18:10 and *n* swear they could not find you.
1Chr 16:20 there, Wandering from nation to *n*,
17:21 another *n* on earth whom a god went to
2Chr 15: 6 *N* crushed nation and city crushed city,
32:15 Since no other god of any other *n* or
Tb 4:19 For no pagan *n* possesses good counsel,
13: 6 show his power and majesty to a sinful *n*.
Jdt 3: 8 every *n* might worship Nebuchadnezzar alone,
5:21 But if they are not a guilty *n*,
9:14 Let your whole *n* and all the tribes know
14: 7 and in every foreign *n*, all who hear of you
Est A: 6 and at their cry every *n* prepared for war,
8:11 any *n* or province which should attack them,
1Mc 2:10 *n* has not taken its share of her realm,
3:59 the ruin of our *n* and our sanctuary.
6:58 and make peace with them and all their *n*.
8:23 the Jewish *n* at sea
8:25 the Jewish *n* will help them wholeheartedly,
8:27 way, if war is made first on the Jewish *n*,
9:29 and those who are hostile to our *n*.
10: 5 have done to him, his brothers, and his *n*."
10:20 you today to be high priest of your *n*;
10:25 Demetrius sends greetings to the Jewish *n*.
11:21 of the law, enemies of their own *n*,
11:25 of his own *n* brought charges against him,
11:30 his brother Jonathan and to the Jewish *n*.
11:33 to bestow benefits on the Jewish *n*,
11:42 will not only do this for you and your *n*,
11:42 you and your *n* when I find the opportunity.
12: 6 the high priest, the senate of the *n*,
13: 6 will I avenge my *n* and the sanctuary,
14: 4 of Simon, who sought the good of his *n*.
14: 6 of his *n* and gained control of the country.
14:28 of priests, people, rulers of the *n*,
14:29 and resisted the enemies of their *n*,
14:29 have thus brought great glory to their *n*.
14:30 rallied his *n* and become their high priest,
14:32 Simon rose up and fought for his *n*,
14:35 the glory he planned to bring to his *n*,
14:35 the loyalty and justice he had shown his *n*.
15: 1 of the Jews, and to all the *n*.
15: 2 priest and ethnarch, and to the Jewish *n*.
15: 9 honor you and your *n* and the temple,
16: 3 brother's, and go out and fight for our *n*;
2Mc 5:22 But he left governors to harass the *n*:
6:12 the ruin but for the correction of our *n*.
6:31 not only for the young but for the whole *n*.
7:16 do not think that our *n* is forsaken by God.
7:37 imploring God to show mercy soon to our *n*,
7:38 that has justly fallen on our whole *n*."
10: 8 *n* should celebrate these days every year.
13:11 and not to allow this *n*,
14: 8 since our entire *n* is suffering great
14:34 unfailing defender of our *n* in these words:
Ps(s) 33:12 Happy the *n* whose God is the LORD,
83: 5 They say, "Come, let us destroy their *n*;
105:13 Wandering from *n* to nation and from one
147:20 He has not done thus for any other *n*;
Prv 14:34 Virtue exalts a *n*,
Wis 10:15 them from the *n* that oppressed them.
17: 2 the lawless thought to enslave the holy *n*,
19: 8 crossed the whole *n* sheltered by your hand,
Sir 17:14 Over every *n* he places a ruler,
24: 6 land, over every people and *n* I held sway.
46:14 By the law of the LORD he judged the *n*,
49: 5 their glory to a foolish foreign *n*
Is 1: 4 sinful *n*, people laden with wickedness,
2: 4 One *n* shall not raise the sword against
5:26 He will give a signal to a far-off *n*,
7: 8 Ephraim shall be crushed, no longer a *n*.
10: 6 Against an impious *n* I send him,
14:32 will one answer the messengers of the *n*?
18: 2 swift messengers, to a *n* tall and bronzed,
18: 2 near and far, a *n* strong and conquering,
18: 7 near and far, a *n* strong and conquering,
26: 2 up the gates to let in a *n* that is just,
26: 3 A *n* of firm purpose you keep in peace;
26:15 *n*, O LORD, increased the nation to your
55: 5 So shall you summon a *n* you knew not,
58: 2 Like a *n* that has done what is just and
60:22 a thousand, the youngest, a mighty *n*;
65: 1 To a *n* that did not call upon my name.
66: 8 one day, or a *n* be born in a single moment?
Jer 2:11 Does any other *n* change its gods?—
5: 9 *n* such as this shall I not take vengeance?
5:15 I will bring against you a *n* from afar,
5:15 A long-lived nation, an ancient *n*,
6:22 from the land of the north, a great *n*,
7:27 This is the *n* which does not listen to the
9: 8 *n* such as this shall I not take vengeance?
12:17 I will uproot and destroy that *n* entirely,
18: 7 and tear down and destroy a *n* or a kingdom.
18: 8 But if that *n* which I have threatened
18: 9 to build up and plant a *n* or a kingdom.
18:10 But if that *n* does what is evil in my eyes,
25:12 *n* and the land of Babylon and the land
25:32 calamity stalks from *n* to nation;
27: 8 *n* or kingdom will not serve Nebuchadnezzar,
27: 8 Babylon, I will punish that *n* with sword,
27:13 *n* that will not serve the king of Babylon?
31:36 of Israel cease as a *n* before me forever.
33:24 as if it were no longer a *n* in their eyes.
49:31 set out against a *n* that is at peace,
49:36 till there is no *n* to which the outcasts
50:41 a people comes from the north, a great *n*,
Lam 4:17 we watched for a *n* that could not save us.
Bar 4:15 He has brought against them a *n* from afar,
4:15 afar, a *n* ruthless and of alien speech,
Ez 37:22 I will make them one *n* upon the land,
38: 8 against a *n* which has survived the sword,
Dn 3:37 are reduced, O Lord, beyond any other *n*,
8:22 four kingdoms that will issue from his *n*,
Jl 4: 8 sell them to the Sabeans, a *n* far off.
Am 6: 1 Leaders of a *n* favored from the first,
6:14 A *n* that shall oppress you from Labo of
Mi 4: 3 One *n* shall not raise the sword against
4: 7 and of those driven far off a strong *n*;
Zep 2: 1 yourselves together, O *n* without shame!
2: 9 the survivors of my *n* dispossess them.
Hg 2:14 this people, and so is this *n* in my sight,
Mal 3: 9 are indeed accursed, for you, the whole *n*,
Mt 21:43 to a *n* that will yield a rich harvest.
24: 7 *N* will rise against nation,
Mk 13: 8 *N* will rise against nation,
Lk 21:10 *N* will rise against nation and kingdom
23: 2 "We found this man subverting our *n*,
Jn 11:48 in and sweep away our sanctuary and our *n*."
11:50 people] than to have the whole *n* destroyed?"
11:51 prophesied that Jesus would die for the *n*—
11:52 and not for this *n* only,
Acts 2: 5 were devout Jews of every *n* under heaven.
7: 7 But I will judge that *n* which they serve,
10:35 the man of any *n* who fears God and acts
17:26 From one stock he made every *n* of mankind
24: 2 made in this *n* through your provident care.
24:10 been a judge over this *n* for many years.
Rom 4:17 I have made you father of many *n*
4:18 became the father of many *n*
10:19 even a *n*; with a senseless nation I will
1Pt 2: 9 chosen race, a royal priesthood, a holy *n*,
Rv 1: 6 who has made us a royal *n* of priests in
5: 9 race and tongue, of every people and *n*.
7: 9 no one could count from every *n* and race,
11: 9 every people and race, language and *n*.
13: 7 over every race and people, language and *n*.
14: 6 to the whole world, to every *n* and race,

NATIONALITIES (1)

2Mc 12:27 city inhabited by people of many *n*.

NATIONALITY (4)

Est 2:10 Esther did not reveal her *n* or family,
2:20 Esther had not revealed her family or *n*,
3: 6 Since they had told Haman of Mordecai's *n*,
Zec 8:23 In those days ten men of every *n*,

NATIONS (549)

Gn 10: 5 and from them sprang the maritime *n*,
10: 5 by their clans within their *n*.
10:20 clans and languages, by their lands and *n*.
10:31 clans and languages by their lands and *n*.
10:32 according to their origins and by their *n*.
10:32 From these the other *n* of the earth
17: 4 are to become the father of a host of *n*.
17: 5 I am making you the father of a host of *n*.
17: 6 I will make *n* of you;
17:16 he shall give rise to *n*,
18:18 *n* of the earth are to find blessing in him?
22:18 all the *n* of the earth shall find blessing
25:23 "Two *n* are in your womb,
26: 4 all the *n* of the earth shall find blessing
27:29 peoples serve you, and *n* pay you homage;
28:14 all the *n* of the earth shall find blessing.
35:11 A nation, indeed an assembly of *n*,
48:19 descendants shall become a multitude of *n*."
Ex 15:14 The *n* heard and quaked;
34:24 *n* before you to give you a large territory,
Lv 18:24 by which the *n* whom I am driving out
18:28 just as it vomited out the *n* before you.
20:23 of the *n* whom I am driving out of your way,
20:24 who has set you apart from the other *n*.
20:26 you apart from the other *n* to be my own.
25:44 you buy them from among the neighboring *n*.
26:33 among the *n* at the point of my drawn sword,
Nm 14:15 the *n* who have heard such reports of you
23: 9 and does not reckon itself among the *n*.
24: 8 He shall devour the *n* like grass,
Dt 4: 6 of your wisdom and intelligence to the *n*,
4:19 to the lot of all other *n* under the heaven;
4:27 The LORD will scatter you among the *n*,
4:27 the *n* to which the LORD will lead you.
4:38 your way *n* greater and mightier than you,
6:14 gods, such as those of the surrounding *n*,
7: 1 occupy, and dislodges great *n* before you
7: 1 *n* more numerous and powerful than you
7: 6 he has chosen you from all the *n* on the
7: 7 not because you are the largest of all *n*
7: 7 for you are really the smallest of all *n*.
7:16 shall consume all the *n* which the LORD,
7:17 yourselves, 'These *n* are greater than we.
7:19 do to all the *n* of whom you are now afraid.
7:22 these *n* before you little by little.
8:20 the *n* which the LORD destroys before you,
9: 1 *n* greater and stronger than yourselves,
9: 4 because of the wickedness of these *n*
9: 5 is driving these *n* out before you on
11:23 will drive all these *n* out of your way,
11:23 *n* greater and mightier than yourselves.
12: 2 *n* you are to dispossess worship their gods.
12:29 removes the *n* from your way as you advance
12:30 gods, 'How did these *n* worship their gods?
13: 8 have not known, gods of any other *n*,
14: 2 who has chosen you from all the *n* on the
15: 6 on you today, you will lend to many *n*,
15: 6 you will rule over many *n*,
17:14 king over you like all the surrounding *n*,
18:12 God, is driving these *n* out of your way.
18:14 Though these *n* whom you are to dispossess
19: 1 removes the *n* whose land he is giving you,
20:16 in the cities of those *n* which the LORD,
26:19 and glory above all other *n* he has made,
28: 1 you high above all the *n* of the earth.
28:10 when all the *n* of the earth see you
28:12 will lend to many *n* and borrow from none.
28:37 all the *n* to which the LORD will lead you.
28:64 *n* from one end of the earth to the other,
28:65 Among these *n* you will find no repose,
29:15 what we passed by in the *n* we traversed,
29:23 furious wrath they and all the *n* will ask,
30: 1 and from among whatever *n* the LORD,
30: 3 all the *n* wherein he has scattered you.
31: 3 he will destroy these *n* before you,
32: 8 Most High assigned the *n* their heritage,
33: 2 forth and his wrath devastated the *n*.
33:17 of the wild ox With which to gore the *n*,
Jos 23: 3 God, has done for you against all these *n*;
23: 4 as their heritage the *n* that survive
23: 7 with these *n* while they survive among you.
23: 9 LORD has driven out large and strong *n*,

NATIONS (cont.)

23:12 of these n while they survive among you,
23:13 no longer drive these n out of your way.
Jgs 2:12 other gods of the various n around them,
2:21 of the n which Joshua left when he died."
2:22 Through these n the Israelites were to be
3: 1 are the n which the LORD allowed to remain,
1Sm 8: 5 appoint a king over us, as other n have,
8:20 We too must be like other n,
2Sm 7:23 cleared n and their gods out of the way
22:44 you made me head over n.
22:50 will I proclaim you, O LORD, among the n,
1Kgs 5:11 fame spread throughout the neighboring n.
5:14 came to hear Solomon's wisdom from all n,
9: 7 become a proverb and a byword among all n,
11: 2 from n with which the LORD had forbidden
14:24 all the abominable practices of the n
2Kgs 16: 3 with the abominable practice of the n
17: 8 They followed the rites of the n whom the
17:11 they burned incense like the n whom the
17:15 they followed the surrounding n whom the
17:26 "The n whom you deported and settled in
17:33 n from among whom they had been deported.
17:41 Thus these n venerated the LORD,
18:33 Has any of the gods of the n ever rescued
19:12 the n whom my fathers destroyed save them?
19:17 have laid waste the n and their lands,
21: 2 n whom the LORD had cleared out
21: 9 into doing even greater evil than the n
1Chr 14:17 land, and the LORD made all the n fear him.
16: 8 make known among the n his deeds.
16:24 day after day Tell his glory among the n;
16:26 all the gods of the n are things of nought,
16:28 Give to the LORD, you families of n,
16:31 let them say among the n:
16:35 gather us and deliver us from the n,
17:21 by driving out the n before your people.
18:11 and gold that he had taken from the n:
2Chr 20: 6 not rule over all the kingdoms of the n?
28: 3 n which the LORD had cleared out
32:13 Were the gods of the n in those lands able
32:14 Who among all the gods of those n which my
32:17 "As the gods of the n in other lands have
32:23 was exalted in the eyes of all the n.
33: 2 n whom the LORD had cleared out
33: 9 into doing even greater evil than the n
36:14 practicing all the abominations of the n
Neh 1: 8 faithless, I will scatter you among the n;
5:17 who came to us from the n round about,
6: 6 "Among the n it has been reported
6:16 all the n round about had taken note of it,
6:16 lost much face in the eyes of the n,
13:26 the many n there was no king like him,
Tb 3: 4 in all the n among whom you scattered us.
13:11 many n shall come to you from afar,
14: 6 All the n of the world shall be converted
Jdt 1: 6 Thus many n came together to resist the
4: 1 king of the Assyrians, had done to the n,
4:12 and mocked for the n to gloat over.
8:22 Wherever we shall be enslaved among the n,
16:17 "Woe to the n that rise against my people!
Est 3: 8 n throughout the provinces of your kingdom,
F: 5 The n are those who assembled to destroy
F: 6 such as have not occurred among the n.
F: 7 of God, the second for all the other n.
F: 8 of judgment before God and among all the n.
1Mc 1: 3 the earth, gathering plunder from many n;
1: 4 strong army and conquered provinces, n,
2:66 your army and direct the war against the n.
11:38 he had hired from the islands of the n.
12:21 both n descended from Abraham.
12:53 the n round about sought to destroy them.
13: 6 for all the n out of hatred have united to
14:32 n armed forces and giving them their pay.
2Mc 4:35 Jews, but many people of other n as well,
6:14 Thus, in dealing with other n, the Lord
8: 9 n to wipe out the entire Jewish race.
11: 3 he did on the sanctuaries of the other n;
Jb 12:23 He makes n great and he destroys them;
36:31 For by these he nourishes the n,
Ps(s) 2: 1 do the n rage and the peoples utter folly?
2: 8 Ask of me and I will give you the n for
7: 9 [The LORD judges the n
9: 6 You rebuked the n and destroyed the wicked;
9:12 proclaim among the n his deeds;
9:16 The n are sunk in the pit they have made;
9:18 shall turn back, all the n that forget God.
9:20 let the n be judged in your presence.
9:21 let the n know that they are but men.
10:16 the n have perished out of his land.
18:44 you made me head over n;
18:50 will I proclaim you, O LORD, among the n,
22:28 of the n shall bow down before him.
22:29 dominion is the LORD's, and he rules the n.
33:10 The LORD brings to nought the plans of n;
44: 3 hand you rooted out the n and planted them;
44:12 among the n you scattered us.
44:15 You made us a byword among the n,
45:18 shall n praise you forever and ever.
46: 7 Though n are in turmoil,
46:11 confess that I am God, exalted among the n,
47: 4 peoples under us; n under our feet.
47: 9 God reigns over the n,
57:10 I will chant your praise among the n,
59: 6 Arise; punish all the n;
59: 9 you deride all the n.
66: 7 his eyes watch the n;
67: 3 among all n,
67: 5 May the n be glad and exult because
67: 5 the n on the earth you guide.
68:31 of strong bulls and the bullocks, the n.
72:11 pay him homage, all n shall serve him.
72:17 all the n shall proclaim his happiness.
78:55 And he drove out n before them;
79: 1 God, the n have come into your inheritance;
79: 6 wrath upon the n that acknowledge you not,
79:10 Why should the n say,
79:10 Let it be known among the n in our sight
80: 9 you drove away the n and planted it.
82: 8 judge the earth, for yours are all the n.
86: 9 n you have made shall come and worship you,
89:51 the n With which your enemies have reviled,
94:10 Shall he who instructs n not chastise,
96: 3 Tell his glory among the n;
96: 5 all the gods of the n are things of nought,
96: 7 Give to the LORD, you families of n,
96:10 before him, all the earth; say among the n:
98: 2 sight of the n he has revealed his justice.
102:16 And the n shall revere your name,
105: 1 make known among the n his deeds.
105:44 And he gave them the lands of the n,
106:27 To scatter their descendants among the n,
106:35 mingled with the n and learned their works.
106:41 He gave them over into the hands of the n,
106:47 our God, and gather us from among the n,
108: 4 I will chant your praise among the n,
110: 6 He will do judgment on the n,
111: 6 giving them the inheritance of the n.
113: 4 High above all n is the LORD;
117: 1 Praise the LORD, all you n;
118:10 All the n encompassed me;
126: 2 Then they said among the n,
135:10 He smote many n and slew mighty kings:
135:15 The idols of the n are silver and gold,
149: 7 to execute vengeance on the n,
Wis 3: 8 They shall judge n and rule over peoples,
8:14 govern peoples, and n would be my subjects
10: 5 the n were sunk in universal wickedness,
14:11 the idols of the n shall a visitation come,
15:15 they esteemed all the idols of the n gods,
Sir 4:15 He who obeys her judges n;
36: 1 and put all the n in dread of you!
39:23 n and turns fertile land into a salt marsh.
44:21 in his descendants the n would be blessed,
46: 6 That all the doomed n might know that the
47:17 and with your answers, you astounded the n.
50:25 My whole being loathes two n,
Is 2: 2 All n shall stream toward it;
2: 4 He shall judge between the n,
10: 7 to destroy, to make an end of n not a few.
10:14 has seized like a nest the riches of n;
11:10 of Jesse, set up as a signal for the n,
11:12 to the n and gather the outcasts of Israel;
12: 4 among the n make known his deeds,
13: 4 the noise of kingdoms, n assembled!
14: 6 That beat down the n in anger,
14: 9 the kings of all n rise from their thrones.
14:12 to the ground, you who mowed down the n!
14:18 All the kings of the n lie in glory,
14:26 and this the hand outstretched over all n.
16: 8 Whose clusters overpowered the lords of n,
17:12 The surging of n that surge like the
23: 3 her revenue, and she the merchant among n.
25: 3 will honor you, fierce n will fear you.
25: 7 peoples, The web that is woven over all n;
29: 7 Shall be the horde of all the n who war
29: 8 dry, So shall the horde of all the n be,
30:28 winnow the n with a destructive winnowing,
33: 3 you rise in your majesty, n are scattered.
34: 1 Come near, O n, and hear, be attentive,
34: 2 n and is wrathful against all their host;
36:18 Has any of the gods of the n ever rescued
37:12 the n whom my fathers destroyed save them?
37:18 have laid waste all the n and their lands,
40:15 the n count as a drop in the bucket,
40:17 Before him all the n are as nought,
41: 2 he delivers the n and subdues the kings;
42: 1 he shall bring forth justice to the n,
42: 6 covenant of the people, a light for the n,
43: 9 Let all the n gather together,
45: 1 right hand I grasp, Subduing n before him,
49: 6 I will make you a light to the n,
49: 7 To the one despised, whom the n abhor,
49:22 See, I will lift up my hand to the n,
51: 5 go forth [and my arm shall judge the n;
52:10 his holy arm in the sight of all the n;
52:15 So shall he startle many n,
54: 3 the n and shall people the desolate cities.
55: 4 the peoples, a leader and commander of n,
55: 5 and n that knew you not shall run to you,
60: 3 N shall walk by your light,
60: 5 the wealth of n shall be brought to you.
60:11 But shall admit to you the wealth of n,
60:12 those n shall be utterly destroyed.
60:16 You shall suck the milk of n,
61: 6 of the n and boast of riches from them.
61: 9 descendants shall be renowned among the n,
61:11 and praise spring up before all the n.
62: 2 N shall behold your vindication,
62:10 of stones, raise up a standard over the n.
64: 1 enemies and the n would tremble before you,
66:12 of the n like an overflowing torrent.
66:18 I come to gather n of every language;
66:19 from them I will send fugitives to the n:
66:19 they shall proclaim my glory among the n.
66:20 from all the n as an offering to the LORD,
Jer 1: 5 you, a prophet to the n I appointed you.
1:10 day I set you over n and over kingdoms.
3:17 there all n will be gathered together to
3:19 a heritage most beautiful among the n!
4: 2 Then shall the n use his name in blessing,
4: 7 his lair, the destroyer of n has set out,
4:16 "Make this known to the n,
5:29 n such as this shall I not take vengeance?
6:18 Therefore hear, O n,
9:15 I will scatter them among n whom neither
9:25 For all these n,
10: 2 Learn not the customs of the n,
10: 2 of the heavens, though the n fear them.
10: 3 For the cult idols of the n are nothing,
10: 7 Who would not fear you, King of the n,
10: 7 Among all the wisest of the n,
10:10 quakes, whose wrath the n cannot endure:
10:25 out your wrath on the n that know you not,
14:22 the n' idols is there any that gives rain?
16:19 will the n come from the ends of the earth,
18:13 Ask among the n—
25: 9 and against all these neighboring n.
25:11 n shall be enslaved to the king of Babylon;
25:13 Jeremiah prophesied against all the n.
25:14 be enslaved to great n and mighty kings,
25:15 all the n to whom I will send you drink it.
25:17 to all the n to which the LORD sent me:
25:31 the LORD has an indictment against the n,
26: 6 city which all the n of the earth shall refer
27: 7 All n shall serve him and his son and his
27: 7 turn shall serve great n and mighty kings.
28:11 of Babylon, from off the neck of all the n.'"
28:14 of all these n serving Nebuchadnezzar,
29:14 I will gather you together from all the n
29:18 all the n among which I will banish them.
30:11 all the n among which I have scattered you;
31: 7 joy for Jacob, exult at the head of the n;
31:10 Hear the word of the LORD, O n,
33: 9 my glory, before all the n of the earth,
36: 2 you against Israel, Judah, and all the n,
43: 5 Judah that had been dispersed among the n
44: 8 a disgrace among all the n of the earth?
46: 1 came to the prophet Jeremiah against the n.
46:12 The n hear of your shame,
46:28 of all the n to which I have driven you,
49:14 a herald has been sent among the n:
49:15 Small will I make you among the n
50: 2 Announce and publish it among the n;
50: 9 Babylon a band of great n from the north;
50:12 See, the last of the n, a desert, dry and
50:23 of horror Babylon has become among the n!
50:46 the outcry is heard among the n.
51: 7 The n drank its wine,
51:20 With you I shatter n,
51:27 the earth, blow the trumpet among the n;
51:41 What a horror has Babylon become among n:
51:58 The toil of the n is for nothing;
Lam 1: 1 Widowed is she who was mistress over n;
1: 3 among the n she finds no place to rest:
1:10 She has seen those n enter her sanctuary
3:14 I have become a laughingstock for all n,
3:45 us offscourings and refuse among the n.
4:15 If they left and wandered among the n,
4:20 we thought we could live on among the n.
Bar 2: 4 horror among all the n round about
2:13 among the n to which you scattered us.
2:29 among the n to which I will scatter them.
3:16 Where are the rulers of the n,
4: 6 sold to the n not for your destruction;
6:66 They show the n no signs in the heavens,
Ez 4:13 unclean among the n where I scatter them.
5: 5 In the midst of the n I placed her,
5: 6 my ordinances more wickedly than the n,
5: 7 more rebellious than the n surrounding you,
5: 7 to the ordinances of the surrounding n;
5: 8 in your midst while the n look on.
5:14 a reproach among the n that surround you,
5:15 warning to the n that surround you.
6: 8 have escaped to other n from the sword,
6: 9 among the n to which they have been exiled,
7:24 I will bring in the worst of the n,
11:12 to the ordinances of the n around you.
11:16 I have removed them far among the n
11:17 I will gather you from the n and assemble
12:15 the n and scatter them over foreign lands.
12:16 among the n to which they will come;
16:14 were renowned among the n for your beauty,
19: 4 Then n raised cries against him in their
19: 8 N laid out against him snares all about him;
20: 9 in the sight of the n among whom they were,
20:14 n in whose presence I had brought them out.
20:22 n in whose presence I brought them out.
20:23 the n and scatter them over foreign lands;

20:32 "We shall be like the n,
20:34 I will bring you out from the n and gather
20:41 I have brought you from among the n
20:41 manifest my holiness in the sight of the n.
22: 4 n and a laughingstock to all foreign lands.
22:15 the n and scatter you over foreign lands,
22:16 to be profaned in the eyes of the n;
23:30 n by defiling yourself with their idols.
25: 7 I will make you plunder for the n,
25: 8 the house of Judah is like all other n,"
26: 3 I will churn up against you many n,
26: 5 and she shall be booty for the n.
28: 7 you foreigners, the most barbarous of n.
28:25 through them in the sight of the n.
29:12 the n and strew them over foreign lands.
29:15 never more to set itself above the n.
29:15 them few, that they may not dominate the n.
30: 3 of clouds, doomsday for the n shall it be.
30:11 people with him, the most ruthless of n,
30:23 the n and strew them over foreign lands.
30:26 the n and strew them over foreign lands.]
31:11 handed it over to the mightiest of the n,
31:12 Foreigners, the most ruthless of the n,
31:16 At the crash of his fall I made the n rock,
31:17 in his shade are dispersed among the n.
32: 2 Lion of the n, you are destroyed.
32: 3 my net over you [with a host of many n,
32: 9 when I lead you captive among the n,
32:12 all of them the most ruthless of the n;
32:16 the daughters of the n shall chant it;
32:18 for the mighty n have thrust them down to
34:28 the n or devoured by beasts of the earth,
34:29 the land, or bear the reproaches of the n.
35:10 two n and the two lands have become mine;
36: 3 become a possession for the rest of the n,
36: 4 and mockery of the remaining n round about;
36: 5 I speak against the rest of the n
36: 6 you have borne the reproach of the n.
36: 7 n shall bear their own reproach.
36:15 I permit you to hear the reproach of n,
36:19 I scattered them among the n,
36:20 they came among the n [wherever they came],
36:21 profaned among the n where they came.
36:22 you profaned among the n to which you came.
36:23 of my great name, profaned among the n,
36:23 Thus the n shall know that I am the LORD,
36:24 For I will take you away from among the n,
36:30 bear among the n the reproach of famine.
36:36 n that remain shall know that I,
37:21 from among the n to which they have come,
37:22 Never again shall they be two n,
37:28 Thus the n shall know that it is I,
38:12 and against a people gathered from the n,
38:16 against my land, that the n may know of me,
38:23 make myself known in the sight of many n;
39: 7 Thus the n shall know that I am the LORD,
39:21 among the nations, and all the n shall see
39:23 The n shall know that because of its sins
39:27 through them in the sight of many n.
39:28 God, since I who exiled them among the n,
Dn 3: 4 N and peoples of every language,
3: 7 the n and peoples of every language all
3:96 Therefore I decree for n and peoples of
3:98 to the n and peoples of every language,
5:19 the n and peoples of every language
6:26 to the n and peoples of every language,
7:14 n and peoples of every language serve him.
11:33 The n wise men shall instruct the many;
12: 1 in distress since n began until that time.
Hos 7: 8 Ephraim mingles with the n,
8: 8 he is now among the n a thing of no value.
8:10 Even though they bargain with the n,
9: 1 not, O Israel, exult not like the n!
9:17 they shall be wanderers among the n.
Jl 2:17 a reproach, with the n ruling over them!
2:19 will I make you a reproach among the n.
4: 2 I will assemble all the n and bring them
4: 2 they have scattered them among the n,
4: 9 Declare this among the n:
4:12 Let the n bestir themselves and come up to
4:12 sit in judgment upon all the neighboring n.
Am 9: 9 to sift the house of Israel among all n,
9:12 of Edom and all the n shall bear my name,
Ob 1: 1 and a herald has been sent among the n:
1: 2 See, I make you small among the n;
1:15 near is the day of the LORD for all the n!
1:16 so shall all the n drink continually.
Mi 4: 2 Many n shall come,
4: 3 and impose terms on strong and distant n;
4:11 How many n are gathered against you!
5: 7 the remnant of Jacob shall be among the n,
5:14 wrath upon the n that have not hearkened.
6:16 and you shall bear the reproach of the n.
7:16 The n shall behold and be put to shame,
Na 3: 4 Who enslaved n with her harlotries,
3: 5 I will show your nakedness to the n,
Hb 1: 5 Look over the n and see,
2: 5 death, Who gathers to himself all the n,
2: 8 all the rest of the n shall despoil you;
2:13 the flames, and n grow weary for nought!
3: 6 his look makes the n tremble.
3:12 the earth, in fury you trample the n.
Zep 2:11 the coastlands of the n shall adore him.
3: 6 I have destroyed n,
3: 8 is my decision to gather together the n,
Hg 2: 7 I will shake all the n,
2: 7 the treasures of all the n will come in,
2:22 destroy the power of the kingdoms of the n.
Zec 1:15 exceedingly angry with the complacent n;
2: 4 to cast down the horns of the n that
2:12 concerning the n that have plundered you:
2:15 Many n shall join themselves to the LORD
7:14 among all the n that they did not know.
8:13 Just as you were a curse among the n,
8:22 Many people and strong n shall come to
9:10 and he shall proclaim peace to the n.
10: 9 I sowed them among the n,
12: 3 and all the n of the earth shall be
12: 9 of all n that come against Jerusalem.
14: 2 all the n against Jerusalem for battle:
14: 3 shall go forth and fight against those n,
14:12 all n that have fought against Jerusalem:
14:14 surrounding n shall be gathered together,
14:16 All who are left of all the n that came
14:18 inflict upon all the n that do not come up
14:19 and the punishment of all the n that do
Mal 1:11 its setting, my name is great among the n;
1:11 For great is my name among the n,
1:14 and my name will be feared among the n.
3:12 Then all n will call you blessed,
Mt 24:10 you will be hated by all n on my account.
24:14 the world as a witness to all the n.
25:32 and all the n will be assembled before him.
28:19 therefore, and make disciples of all the n.
Lk 21:25 On the earth, n will be in anguish,
24:47 of sins is to be preached to all the n,
Acts 13:19 then he destroyed seven n in the land of
13:47 'I have made you a light to the n,
15:17 n that bear my name may seek out the Lord.
26:17 you from this people and from the n,
Gal 3: 8 "All n shall be blessed in you."
1Tm 2: 7 the teacher of the n in the true faith.
2Tm 4:17 and all the n might hear the gospel.
Rv 2:26 the end, I will give authority over the n—
10:11 must prophesy again for many peoples and n,
11:18 The n have raged in anger,
12: 5 to shepherd all the n with an iron rod.
14: 8 n drink the poisoned wine of her lewdness!"
15: 3 and true are your ways, O King of the n!
15: 4 n shall come and worship in your presence.
17:15 large numbers of peoples and n and tongues.
18: 3 n drink the poisoned wine of her lewdness.
18:23 you led all n astray by your sorcery.
19:15 came a sharp sword for striking down the n.
20: 3 n astray until the thousand years are over.
20: 8 the n in all four corners of the earth,
21:24 The n shall walk by its light;
21:26 and wealth of the n shall be brought there,
22: 2 their leaves serve as medicine for the n.

NATIVE (27)

Gn 11:28 before his father Terah, in his n land,
27:46 marry a Hittite woman, a n of the land,
Ex 12:19 Anyone, be he a resident alien or a n,
12:49 same forthe resident alien as for the n."
Lv 16:29 of you, whether a n or a resident alien,
17:15 "Everyone, whether a n or an alien,
23:42 During this week every n Israelite among
24:16 alien and n alike must be put to death for
24:22 have but one rule, for alien and n alike.
Nm 9:14 resident alien as for the n of the land."
15:29 n Israelite or an alien residing with you.
15:30 defiantly, whether he be a n or an alien,
Jos 8:33 And all Israel, stranger and n alike,
2Kgs 17:23 into exile from their n soil to Assyria,
Jdt 8: 3 of this illness in Bethulia, his n city.
2Mc 7:27 to her son and said in their n language:
15:29 n tongue in praise of the divine Sovereign.
Jer 25:19 all the people under him, n and foreign;
Ez 47:22 latter shall be to you like n Israelites;
Mt 13:54 Jesus next went to his n place and spent
13:57 is without honor except in his n place,
Mk 6: 4 is without honor except in his n place,
Lk 4:24 prophet gains acceptance in his n place.
Jn 8:44 Lying speech is his n tongue;
Acts 2: 8 that each of us hears them in his n tongue?
18: 2 a n of Pontus recently arrived from Italy
18:24 a n of Alexandria and a man of eloquence,

NATIVE-BORN (1)

Nm 15:13 "All the n shall make these offerings in

NATIVES (17)

Ex 12:48 may join in its observance just like the n.
Lv 18:26 You, however, whether n or resident aliens,
19:34 no differently than the n born among you;
Nm 32:17 fortified towns, safe from attack by the n.
Jos 17: 7 southward to include the n of En-Tappuah,
17:11 natives there, Endor and its towns and n,
17:11 natives, and Megiddo and its towns and n
Jgs 1:32 live among the Canaanite n of the land,
1:33 live among the Canaanite n of the land.
1Chr 5:25 after the gods of the n of the land,
11: 4 the n of the land were called Jebusites.
2Mc 9: 2 n and forced to beat a shameful retreat.
Ez 23:15 of Babylonians, n of Chaldea
Acts 28: 2 The n showed us extraordinary kindness by
28: 4 from his hand, the n said to one another,

NATURAL (18)

Lv 7:24 fat of an animal that has died a n death
Jgs 18: 7 trusting, with no lack of any n resources.
18:10 a place where no n resource is lacking."
Wis 19: 6 being made over anew, serving its n laws,
Jer 31:36 ever these n laws give way in spite of me,
Ez 11:19 bodies, and replace it with a n heart,
36:26 your stony hearts and giving you n hearts.
Mt 8:12 while the n heirs of the kingdom will be
Rom 1:26 exchanged n intercourse for unnatural,
1:27 and the men gave up n intercourse with
11:21 If God did not spare the n branches,
11:24 you were cut off from the n wild olive and,
1Cor 2:14 The n man does not accept what is taught
3: 3 being still very much in a n condition.
15:44 A n body is put down and a spiritual body
15:44 If there is a n body,
15:46 came the n and after that the spiritual.
Gal 4: 9 n elements to which you seem willing to

NATURALLY (3)

Nm 19:16 he was slain by the sword or died n,
Jn 7:11 During the festival, n,
13:28 N, none of those reclining at table

NATURE (22)

Dt 23:14 with it, when you go outside to ease n,
1Sm 18:24 reported to him the n of David's answer,
24: 4 found a cave, which he entered to ease n.
Eccl 6:10 given its name, and the n of man is known,
Wis 2:23 the image of his own n he made him.
8:19 child, and I came by a noble n;
13: 1 by n foolish who were in ignorance of God,
17:11 For wickedness, of its n cowardly,
19:20 and water forgot its quenching n;
Mt 26:41 The spirit is willing but n is weak."
Mk 14:38 The spirit is willing but n is weak."
Jn 2:25 no one to give him testimony about human n.
Rom 6:19 human affairs because of your weak human n.)
11:24 the natural wild olive and, contrary to n,
11:24 by n be grafted into their own olive tree.
1Cor 11:14 Does not n itself teach you that it is
15:39 Not all bodily n is the same.
Gal 4:23 girl had been begotten in the course of n,
Eph 2: 3 so by n deserved God's wrath like the rest.
Col 3: 5 whatever in your n is rooted in earth;
1Pt 2:11 By their n they wage war on the soul.
2Pt 1: 4 lust might become sharers of the divine n.

NATURES (2)

Wis 7:20 positions of the stars, n of animals,
Gal 4:29 son born in n course persecuted the one

NAVE (19)

1Kgs 6: 3 side to side, along the width of the n,
6: 5 which enclosed the n and the sanctuary,
6:17 The n, or part of the temple in front
6:33 same was done at the entrance to the n,
7:50 and for the doors of the outer room, the n.
2Chr 3: 4 the porch which lay before the n along the
3: 5 The n he overlaid with cypress wood which
3:13 upon their own feet, facing toward the n.
3:17 up the columns to correspond with the n,
4: 7 was prescribed, and placed them in the n,
4: 8 made ten tables and had them set in the n,
4:22 of holies, as well as the doors to the n,
Ez 41: 1 me to the n and measured the pilasters,
41: 2 He measured the length of the n,
41: 4 He measured the space beyond the n,
41:15 The inner n and the outer vestibule were
41:21 The way into the n was a square doorframe.
41:23 " The n had a double door,
41:25 doors of the n were cherubim and palmtrees,

NAVEL (3)

Sg 7: 3 Your n is a round bowl that should never
Ez 16: 4 day you were born your n cord was not cut;
38:12 and goods, who dwell at the n of the earth."

NAVIGABLE (1)

2Mc 5:21 the land n and the sea passable on foot,

NAVIGATOR (1)

Rv 18:17 Every captain and n,

NAY (9)

Dt 15: 4 N, more! since the Lord, your God,
Jb 5: 2 N, impatience kills the fool and
9:12 he seize me forcibly, who can say him n?
11:10 to judgment, who then can say him n?
21:30 N, the evil man is spared calamity when it
23:13 But he had decided, and who can say him n?
37:21 N, rather, it is as the light which men see
Ps(s) 58: 3 N, you willingly commit crimes;

NAY (cont.)
131: 2 *N* rather, I have stilled and quieted my

NAZARETH (19)

Mt 2:23 There he settled in a town called *N.*
4:13 He left *N* and went down to live in
21:11 is the prophet Jesus from *N* in Galilee."
Mk 1: 9 Jesus came from *N* in Galilee and was
1:24 "What do you want of us, Jesus of *N?*
10:47 On hearing that it was Jesus of *N,*
14:67 and said, "You too were with Jesus of *N.*"
16: 6 You are looking for Jesus of *N,*
Lk 1:26 from God to a town of Galilee named *N,*
2: 4 from the town of *N* in Galilee to Judea,
2:39 to Galilee and their own town of *N.*
2:51 went down with them then, and came to *N,*
4:16 He came to *N* where he had been reared,
4:34 What do you want of us, Jesus of *N?*
18:37 answer came that Jesus of *N* was passing by.
24:19 those that had to do with Jesus of *N,*
Jn 1:45 Jesus, son of Joseph, from *N.*"
1:46 that was, "Can anything good come from *N?*"
Acts 10:37 reported all over Judea about Jesus of *N,*

NAZIRITE (12)

Nm 6: 2 the *n* vow to dedicate himself to the LORD,
6: 4 As long as he is a *n* he shall not eat
6: 5 While he is under the *n* vow,
6: 8 long as he is a *n* he is sacred to the LORD.
6:12 of his dedication to the LORD as a *n,*
6:13 "This is the ritual for the *n:*
6:18 tent the *n* shall shave his dedicated head,
6:19 the *n* has shaved off his dedicated hair,
6:19 and shall place them in the hands of the *n.*
6:20 Only after this may the *n* drink wine.
6:21 "This, then, is the law for the *n;*
1Sm 1:22 I will offer him as a perpetual *n.*"

NAZIRITES (3)

1Mc 3:49 and they brought forward the *n,*
Am 2:11 your sons, and *n* among your young men.
2:12 But you gave the *n* wine to drink,

NAZOREAN (12)

Mt 2: 3 "He shall be called a *N.*"
2:23 He shall be called a *N.*
26:71 nearby, "This man was with Jesus the *N.*"
Jn 18: 5 "Jesus the *N,*" they replied.
18: 7 "Jesus the *N,*" they repeated.
19:19 read JESUS THE *N* THE KING OF THE JEWS
Acts 2:22 Jesus the *N* was a man whom God sent to you
3: 6 In the name of Jesus Christ, the *N,*
4:10 done in the name of Jesus Christ the *N*
6:14 We have heard him claim that Jesus the *N*
22: 8 'I am Jesus the *N* whom you are persecuting.'
26: 9 name of Jesus the *N* in every way possible.

NAZOREANS (1)

Acts 24: 5 He is a ringleader of the sect of *N.*

NEAH (1)

Jos 19:13 extended to Rimmon, and turned to *N.*

NEAPOLIS (1)

Acts 16:11 for Samothrace, and the next day on to *N;*

NEAR (278)

Gn 10:19 from Sidon all the way to Gerar, *n* Gaza,
10:19 Gomorrah, Admah and Zeboiim, *n* Lasha.
13:12 of the Plain, pitching his tents *n* Sodom.
13:18 went on to settle *n* the terebinth of Mamre,
19:20 this town ahead is *n* enough to escape to.
24:11 *N* evening, at the time when women go
25:11 Isaac, who made his home *n* Beerlahai-roi.
29: 2 with three droves of sheep huddled *n* it,
38: 1 tent *n* a certain Adullamite named Hirah.
39:10 to lie beside her, or even stay *n* her.
45:10 region of Goshen, where you will be *n* me
Ex 13:20 camped at Etham *n* the edge of the desert.
14:10 Pharaoh was already *n* when the Israelites
15:27 trees, and they camped there *n* the water.
18: 5 he was encamped *n* the mountain of God,
24: 2 the others shall not come too *n,*
32:19 As he drew *n* the camp,
33:21 "is a place *n* me where you shall station
34:30 had become, they were afraid to come *n* him.
Lv 3: 4 kidneys, with the fat on them *n* the loins,
3:10 kidneys, with the fat on them *n* the loins,
3:15 kidneys, with the fat on them *n* the loins,
4: 9 kidneys, with the fat on them *n* the loins,
7: 4 kidneys with the fat on them *n* the loins,
21:11 nor shall he go *n* any dead person.
21:21 *n* to offer up to oblations of the LORD;
21:21 not draw *n* to offer up the food of his God.
22: 3 to draw *n* the sacred offerings which the
Nm 1:51 who comes *n* it shall be put to death.
3:10 layman who comes *n* shall be put to death."
3:38 layman who came *n* was to be put to death.
5:25 before the LORD, shall put it *n* the altar,
8:19 should they come *n* the sanctuary."
16: 5 one and whom he will have draw *n* to him!
16: 5 Whom he chooses, he will have draw *n* him.
16: 9 to have you draw *n* him for the service of
16:34 Israelites *n* them fled at their shrieks,
18: 3 not come *n* the sacred vessels or the altar,
18: 4 But no layman shall come *n* you.
18: 7 layman who draws *n* shall be put to death."
24:17 I behold him, though not *n:*
33: 6 camped at Etham *n* the edge of the desert.
Dt 4:11 *n* and stood at the foot of the mountain,
5:31 Then you wait here *n* me and I will give
13: 8 any other nations, *n* at hand or far away,
15: 9 year, the year of relaxation, is *n,*
22: 2 If this kinsman does not live *n* you,
30:14 No, it is something very *n* to you,
Jos 5:13 While Joshua was *n* Jericho,
7: 2 Ai, which is *n* Bethel on its eastern side,
10:34 encamping *n* it,
11: 2 regions and in the Arabah *n* Chinneroth,
12: 9 kings of Jericho, Ai (which is *n* Bethel),
17: 7 From Michmethath *n* Shechem,
19:11 Dabbesheth and the wadi that is *n* Jokneam.
19:28 Rehob, Hammon and Kanah, *n* Greater Sidon.
Jgs 3:19 from where the idols are, *n* Gilgal,
4:11 terebinth of Zaanannim, which was *n* Kedesh.
6:28 destroyed, the sacred pole *n* it cut down,
6:30 has cut down the sacred pole that was *n* it."
7:22 *n* the border of Abelmeholah at Tabbath.
15:15 *N* him was the fresh jawbone of an ass;
18: 3 *N* the house of Micah,
18:12 and camped in Judah, up *n* Kiriath-jearim;
18:22 when those in the houses *n* that of Micah
19:11 they were *n* Jebus with the day far gone,
Ru 2:14 Then as she sat *n* the reapers,
4: 3 had done this, he said to the *n* relative:
4: 6 The *n* relative replied, "I cannot exercise
4: 8 So the *n* relative, in saying to Boaz,
1Sm 1: 9 chair *n* the doorpost of the LORD's temple.
1:26 lord, I am the woman who stood *n* you here,
4:14 the outcry of the men standing *n* him,
10: 2 you will meet two men *n* Rachel's tomb at
14: 2 pomegranate tree *n* the threshing floor
19:19 told that David was in the sheds *n* Ramah,
19:22 and was told, "At the sheds *n* Ramah."
19:23 At the sheds *n* Ramah he,
20: 1 David fled from the sheds *n* Ramah,
20:19 other occasion and wait *n* the mound there.
23:14 or in the barren hill country *n* Ziph.
23:15 he was at Horesh in the barrens *n* Ziph,
24: 2 told that David was in the desert *n* Engedi.
25:16 time we were pasturing the sheep *n* them.
29: 1 encamped at the spring of Harod *n* Jezreel.
2Sm 2: 3 and they dwelt in the cities *n* Hebron.
2:24 of the valley toward the desert *n* Geba.
4:12 feet, hanging them up *n* the pool in Hebron.
11:20 'Why did you go *n* the city to fight?
11:21 Why did you go *n* the wall?'
13:23 had shearers in Baal-hazor *n* Ephraim,
15:28 I shall be waiting at the fords *n* the desert
17:16 spend the night at the fords *n* the desert,
18: 6 battle was fought in the forest *n* Mahanaim.
20: 8 which was slung, in its sheath *n* his thigh,
20:17 When Joab had come *n* her,
24: 5 Crossing the Jordan, they began *n* Aroer,
1Kgs 1: 9 fatlings at the stone Zoheleth, *n* En-rogel,
2: 1 When the time of David's death drew *n,*
8:46 deport them to a hostile land, far or *n,*
9:26 which is *n* Elath on the shore of the shore
19:15 the road back to the desert *n* Damascus,"
2Kgs 4:27 Gehazi came *n* to push her away,
9:21 him *n* the field of Naboth the Jezreelite.
9:27 he rode through the pass of Gur *n* Ibleam.
11:14 and the captains and trumpeters *n* him,
23:11 *n* the chamber of Nathan-melech the eunuch,
23:19 on the high places *n* the cities of Samaria
25: 4 two walls which was *n* the king's garden.
25: 5 and overtook him in the desert *n* Jericho,
1Chr 23: 1 grown old and was *n* the end of his days,
2Chr 6:36 deport them to another land, far or *n,*
14: 9 in the valley of Zephathah, *n* Mareshah.
Neh 3:15 *n* the king's garden as far as the steps
4: 6 When the Jews who lived *n* them had come
4: 7 behind the wall, *n* the exposed points,
Tb 6: 7 on together till they were *n* Media.
6:18 flee and never again show himself *n* her.
11: 1 When they were *n* Kaserin,
Jdt 2:21 they next encamped *n* the mountains
4: 6 to Esdraelon, facing the plain *n* Dothan,
5: 5 *n* you [that inhabits this mountain region];
7: 3 at the spring in the valley *n* Bethulia,
7:18 and to the east opposite Egrebel, *n* Chusi,
13: 6 to the bedpost *n* the head of Holofernes,
Est D:11 Come *n!*"
9:20 letters to all the Jews, both *n* and far,
1Mc 3:40 pitched their camp *n* Emmaus in the plain.
3:46 assembled and went to Mizpah *n* Jerusalem,
4:18 and his army are *n* us on the mountain.
5:26 imprisoned in Bozrah, in Bosor *n* Alema,
7:31 he went out to fight Judas *n* Caphar-salama.
7:45 a day's journey, from Adasa to *n* Gazara,
8:12 They had conquered kings both far and *n,*
10:75 He pitched camp *n* Joppa,
11:67 their camp *n* the waters of Gennesaret,
2Mc 4:33 inviolable sanctuary at Daphne, *n* Antioch.
4:42 thief himself they slew *n* the treasury.
7:14 When he was *n* death, he said, "It is my
11: 8 while they were still *n* Jerusalem,
13:14 government, he pitched his camp *n* Modein.
15:20 The enemy were already drawing *n* with
Jb 9:11 Should he come *n* me,
33:22 His soul draws *n* to the pit,
Ps(s) 1: 3 He is like a tree planted *n* running water,
10: 8 He lurks in ambush *n* the villages;
22:12 be *n,* for I have no one to help me.
32: 9 be curbed, else they will not come *n* you.
38:18 For I am very *n* to falling,
73:28 But for me, to be *n* God is my good;
85:10 *N* indeed is his salvation to those who
88: 4 and my life draws *n* to the nether world.
91: 7 your right side, *n* you it shall not come.
91:10 you, nor shall affliction come *n* your tent,
107:18 so that they were *n* the gates of death.
119:151 You, O LORD, are *n,*
145:18 The LORD is *n* to all who call upon him,
Prv 7: 8 sense, Going along the street *n* the corner,
27:10 neighbor *n* at hand than a brother far away.
Sg 1: 8 the young ones *n* the shepherds' camps.
Sir 12:12 Let him not stand *n* you, lest he oust you
12:13 bitten, or anyone who goes *n* a wild beast?
14:24 Who encamps *n* her house,
21: 2 that will bite you if you go *n* it;
38:28 So with the smith standing *n* his anvil,
39:13 like roses planted *n* running waters;
Is 13: 6 Howl, for the day of the LORD is *n;*
13:22 Her time is *n* at hand and her days shall
18: 2 and bronzed, To a people dreaded *n* and far,
18: 7 bronzed, from a people dreaded *n* and far,
19:19 a sacred pillar to the LORD *n* the boundary.
29:13 Since this people draws *n* with words only
33:13 you who are *n,*
34: 1 Come *n,* O nations, and hear,
41: 1 Let them draw *n* and speak;
41: 5 these things are *n,* they come to pass.
41:22 Let them come *n* and foretell to us what it
48:16 Come *n* to me and hear this!
50: 8 He is *n* who upholds my right;
54:14 where destruction cannot come *n* you.
55: 6 he may be found, call him while he is *n.*
57: 3 But you, draw *n,* you sons of a sorceress,
57:19 Peace, peace to the far and the *n,*
Jer 2:23 A frenzied she-camel, coursing *n* and far,
23:23 Am I a God *n* at hand only,
25:26 all the kings of the north, *n* and far,
39: 5 captured Zedekiah in the desert *n* Jericho.
41:17 the lodging place of Chimham *n* Bethlehem,
48:16 *N* at hand is Moab's ruin,
48:24 on all the cities of Moab, far and *n.*
52: 7 two walls which was *n* the king's garden.
52: 8 overtook Zedekiah in the desert *n* Jericho,
Lam 4:15 cried to them, "Away, away, do not draw *n!*"
4:18 Our end drew *n,* and came; our time had
Ez 6:12 he that is *n* shall fall by the sword,
7: 7 The time has come, *n* is the day:
22: 5 Those *n* you and those far off shall deride
30: 3 near is the day, *n* is the day of the LORD;
40:40 outside, *n* the entrance of the north gate,
40:46 who may come *n* to minister to the LORD.
42:13 here the priests who draw *n* to the LORD
43:19 of Zadok, who draw *n* me to minister to me,
44:13 no longer draw *n* me to serve as my priests,
44:15 me, they shall draw *n* me to minister to me,
44:25 unclean by coming *n* any dead person,
45: 4 who draw *n* to minister to the LORD;
Dn 6:21 As he drew *n,* he cried out to Daniel
8:17 When he came *n* where I was standing,
9: 7 of Jerusalem, and all Israel, *n* and far,
13: 4 he had a garden *n* his house,
Jl 1:15 for *n* is the day of the LORD,
2: 2 day of the LORD is coming; Yes, it is *n,*
4:14 For *n* is the day of the LORD in the valley
Ob 1:15 *n* is the day of the LORD for all the nations!
Zep 1: 7 for *n* is the day of the LORD,
1:14 *N* is the great day of the LORD, near and
3: 2 trusted, to her God she has not drawn *n.*
Mal 3: 5 I will draw *n* to you for judgment,
Mt 4:13 *n* the territory of Zebulun and Naphtali,
13:10 When the disciples got *n* him,
21: 1 As they drew *n* Jerusalem,
24:32 leaves, you realize that summer is *n.*
24:33 happening, you will know that he is *n,*
26:18 Teacher says, My appointed time draws *n.*
Mk 5:22 the synagogue, a man named Jairus, came *n.*
11: 4 a colt tethered out on the street *n* a gate,
13:28 sprout leaves, you know that summer is *n.*
13:29 happening, you will know that he is *n,*
14:42 My betrayer is *n.*"
Lk 4:26 sent, but to a widow of Zarephath *n* Sidon.
10:11 But know that the reign of God is *n.*'
12:33 no thief comes *n* nor any moth destroys.
18:35 As he drew *n* Jericho a blind man sat at
19:11 because he was *n* Jerusalem where they
21:20 soldiers, know that its devastation is *n.*
21:28 high, for your deliverance is *n* at hand."
21:30 and know for yourselves that summer is *n.*
21:31 I speak, know that the reign of God is *n.*
22: 1 Bread known as the Passover was drawing *n,*

24:28 *n* the village to which they were going,
24:50 Then he led them out *n* Bethany,
Jn 2:13 As the Jewish Passover was *n*,
3:20 *n* it for fear his deeds will be exposed.
3:23 at Aenon *n* Salim where water was plentiful,
4: 5 town named Shechem *n* the plot of land
4:47 restore health to his son, who was *n* death.
6: 4 The Jewish feast of Passover was *n*;
6:23 Then some boats came out from Tiberias *n*
7: 2 as the Jewish feast of Booths drew *n*,
11:54 called Ephraim in the region *n* the desert,
11:55 The Jewish Passover was *n*,
19:20 where Jesus was crucified was *n* the city.
19:25 *N* the cross of Jesus there stood his mother,
Acts 1:12 from the mount called Olivet *n* Jerusalem
7:17 "When the time drew *n* for the fulfillment
7:30 appeared to him in the desert *n* Mount Sinai
7:31 As he drew *n* to observe it carefully,
9:38 Since Lydda was *n* Joppa,
27: 8 called Fair Havens, *n* the town of Lasea.
27:27 sailors began to suspect that land was *n*.
Rom 10: 8 "The word is *n* you, on your lips and in
13:12 The night is far spent; the day draws *n*.
Eph 2:13 been brought *n* through the blood of Christ.
2:17 were far off, and to those who were *n*";
3:12 to God, drawing *n* him with confidence.
Phil 2:30 *n* to death for the sake of Christ's work.
4: 5 The Lord is *n*.
2Tm 4: 6 The time of my dissolution is *n*.
Heb 7:19 and through it we draw *n* to God.
10:22 let us draw *n* in utter sincerity and
10:25 more because you see that the Day draws *n*.
11:22 By faith Joseph, *n* the end of his life,
12:18 You have not drawn *n* to an untouchable
12:22 you have drawn *n* to Mount Zion and the
Rv 1: 3 written in it, for the appointed time is *n*!
22:10 of this book, for the appointed time is *n*!

NEARBY (15)

Gn 18: 2 Looking up, he saw three men standing *n*.
26:25 there, his servants began to dig a well *n*.
Jos 9:16 learned that these people were from *n*,
Ru 4: 2 elders of the city and asked them to sit *n*.
1Sm 19: 9 in hand and David was playing the harp *n*.
1Chr 8:12 who built Ono and Lod with its *n* towns,
2Chr 32: 4 also the running stream in the valley *n*.
Jdt 7:13 go up to the summits of the *n* mountains,
2Mc 6:11 *n* caves to observe the sabbath in secret,
Dn 3:48 and spread out, burning the Chaldeans *n*.
Mt 26:71 another girl saw him and said to those *n*,
Mk 4: 1 while the crowd remained on the shore *n*.
Lk 8:32 of swine was feeding *n* on the hillside,
Jn 18:22 *n* gave Jesus a sharp blow on the face.
Acts 12: 7 Lord stood *n* and light shone in the cell.

NEARED (2)

Mk 11: 1 as they *n* Bethphage and Bethany on the
Lk 15:25 As he *n* the house on his way home,

NEARER (4)

Gn 18:23 Then Abraham drew *n* to him and said:
Ex 3: 5 God said, "Come no *n*!
Jos 3: 4 Do not come *n* to it."
2Sm 18:25 As he kept coming *n*,

NEAREST (9)

Ex 12: 4 it shall join the *n* household in procuring
13:17 Philistines' land, though this was the *n*;
Lv 21: 2 his people, except for his *n* relatives,
Nm 27:11 his heritage to his *n* relative in his clan,
Dt 21: 3 is established which city is *n* the corpse,
21: 6 Then all the elders of that city *n* the
2Chr 5: 9 part of the holy place *n* the sanctuary;
Jer 32: 7 in Anathoth, since you, as *n* relative,
32: 8 as *n* relative, you have the first claim

NEARIAH (3)

1Chr 3:22 were Shemiah, Hattush, Igal, Bariah, *N*,
3:23 The sons of *N* were Elioenai,
4:42 Seir under the leadership of Pelatiah, *N*,

NEARING (3)

1Sm 30:21 On *n* them David greeted them.
Sir 51: 6 soul was *n* the depths of the nether world;
Acts 21:27 The seven-day period was *n* completion

NEARLY (5)

2Mc 5: 2 that all over the city, for *n* forty days,
Mt 26:38 them, "My heart is *n* broken with sorrow.
Lk 5: 7 filled the two boats until they *n* sank.
24:29 It is *n* evening the day is practically
Rom 4:19 as dead (for he was *n* a hundred years old),

NEATLY (1)

Mk 6:40 and fifties, *n* arranged like flower beds.

NEBAI (1)

Neh 10:20 Hashum, Bezai, Hariph, Anathoth, *N*,

NEBAIOTH (5)

Gn 25:13 *N* (Ishmael's first-born),
28: 9 of Abraham's son Ishmael and sister of *N*.
36: 3 daughter of Ishmael and sister of *N*.
1Chr 1:29 *N*, the first-born of Ishmael,
Is 60: 7 the rams of *N* shall be your sacrifices;

NEBALLAT (1)

Neh 11:34 Hazor, Ramah, Gittaim, Hadid, Zeboim, *N*,

NEBAT (25)

1Kgs 11:26 Solomon's servant Jeroboam, son of *N*,
12: 2 Jeroboam, son of *N*, who was still in Egypt,
12:15 he had uttered to Jeroboam, son of *N*,
15: 1 year of King Jeroboam, son of *N*,
16: 3 your house like that of Jeroboam, son of *N*.
16:26 the sinful conduct of Jeroboam, son of *N*,
16:31 to imitate the sins of Jeroboam, son of *N*.
21:22 house like that of Jeroboam, son of *N*,
22:53 father, his mother, and Jeroboam, son of *N*,
2Kgs 3: 3 to the sin to which Jeroboam, son of *N*,
9: 9 with the house of Jeroboam, son of *N*,
10:29 from the sins which Jeroboam, son of *N*,
13: 2 himself like Jeroboam, son of *N*,
13:11 any of the sins which Jeroboam, son of *N*,
14:24 any of the sins which Jeroboam, son of *N*,
15: 9 from the sins which Jeroboam, son of *N*,
15:18 from the sins which Jeroboam, son of *N*,
15:24 from the sins which Jeroboam, son of *N*,
15:28 from the sins which Jeroboam, son of *N*,
17:21 of David, they made Jeroboam, son of *N*,
23:15 high place built by Jeroboam, son of *N*,
2Chr 9:29 the seer which concern Jeroboam, son of *N*.
10: 2 When Jeroboam, son of *N*, heard of this
10:15 LORD had uttered to Jeroboam, the son of *N*,
13: 6 Yet Jeroboam, son of *N*, the servant of

NEBO (13)

Nm 32: 3 Heshbon, Elealeh, Sebam, *N* and Baal-meon,
32:38 rebuilt Heshbon, Elealeh, Kiriathaim, *N*,
33:47 camped in the Abarim Mountains opposite *N*.
Dt 32:49 LORD said to Moses, "Go up on Mount *N*,
34: 1 up from the plains of Moab to Mount *N*,
1Chr 5: 8 in Aroer and as far as *N* and Baal-meon;
Ezr 2:29 sons of *N*, fifty-two; sons of Magbish,
10:43 Shallum, Amariah, Joseph, of the sons of *N*:
Neh 7:33 men of *N*, fifty-two; sons of another Elam,
Is 15: 2 Over *N* and over Medeba Moab wails.
46: 1 Bel bows down, *N* stoops,
Jer 48: 1 Woe to *N*, it is laid waste;
48:22 Holon, Jahzah, and Mephaath, on Dibon, *N*,

NEBUCHADNEZZAR (111)

2Kgs 24: 1 *N*, king of Babylon, moved against him,
24:10 At that time the officials of *N*,
24:11 *N*, king of Babylon, himself arrived
25: 1 *N*, king of Babylon, and his whole army
25: 8 (this was in the nineteenth year of *N*,
25:22 allowed to remain in the land of Judah, *N*,
1Chr 5:41 inflicted on Judah and Jerusalem through *N*.
2Chr 36: 6 *N*, king of Babylon, came up against him
36: 7 *N* also carried away to Babylon some of the
36:10 King *N* sent for him and had him brought to
36:13 He also rebelled against King *N*,
Ezr 1: 7 which *N* had taken away from Jerusalem
2: 1 from the captivity of the exiles, whom *N*,
5:12 them into the power of the Chaldean, *N*,
5:14 which *N* had taken from the temple
6: 5 which *N* took from the temple of Jerusalem
Neh 7: 6 from the captivity of the exiles whom *N*,
Jdt 1: 1 It was the twelfth year of the reign of *N*,
1: 5 Then King *N* waged war against King
1: 7 Now *N*, king of the Assyrians,
1:11 that land disregarded the summons of *N*,
1:12 Then *N* fell into a violent rage against
2: 1 there was a discussion in the palace of *N*,
2: 4 When he had completed his plan, *N*,
2:19 on their expedition in advance of King *N*,
3: 2 "We, the servants of *N* the great king,
3: 8 so that every nation might worship *N* alone,
4: 1 that Holofernes, commander in chief of *N*,
6: 2 What god is there beside *N*?
6: 3 but we, the servants of *N*,
6: 4 they shall utterly perish, says King *N*,
11: 1 have I harmed anyone who chose to serve *N*,
11: 4 as are all the servants of my lord, King *N*."
11: 7 By the life of *N*, king of all the earth,
11: 7 will live for *N* and his whole house.
11:23 you shall dwell in the palace of King *N*,
12:13 Assyrian women who live in the palace of *N*.
14:18 brought disgrace on the house of King *N*.
Est 0: 3 court, and one of the captives whom *N*,
2: 6 with Jeconiah, king of Judah, whom *N*,
Jer 21: 2 Inquire for us of the LORD, because *N*,
21: 7 sword, and famine, into the hand of *N*,
22:25 those whom you fear; the hands of *N*,
24: 1 This was after *N*, king of Babylon, had
25: 1 Josiah, king of Judah (the first year of *N*,
25: 9 says the LORD (and I will send to *N*,
27: 6 given all these lands into the hand of *N*,
27: 8 if any nation or kingdom will not serve *N*,
27:20 vessels that remain in this city, which *N*,
28: 3 vessels of the temple of the LORD which *N*,
28:11 two years I will break the yoke of *N*,
28:14 the necks of all these nations serving *N*,
29: 1 exiled by *N* from Jerusalem to Babylon.
29:21 I am handing them over to *N*,
32: 1 king of Judah, the eighteenth year of *N*.
32:28 over this city to the Chaldeans, for *N*,
34: 1 came to Jeremiah from the LORD while *N*,
35:11 But when *N*, king of Babylon, invaded this
37: 1 was made king over the land of Judah by *N*,
39: 1 ninth year of Zedekiah, king of Judah, *N*,
39: 5 to Riblah, in the land of Hamath, where *N*,
39:11 Concerning Jeremiah, *N*, king of Babylon,
43:10 I will send for my servant *N*,
44:30 of Judah, to his enemy and mortal foe, *N*,
46: 2 at Carchemish on the Euphrates by *N*,
46:13 Jeremiah concerning the advance of *N*,
46:26 over to those who seek their lives, to *N*,
49:28 and the kingdoms of Hazor, defeated by *N*,
49:30 you, a plan has been formed against you *N*,
50:17 her, now *N* of Babylon gnaws her bones.
51:34 He has consumed me, routed me, *N*,
52: 4 reign, on the tenth day of the month, *N*,
52:12 (this was in the nineteenth year of *N*,
52:28 of the people whom *N* led away captive:
52:29 in the eighteenth year of *N*,
52:30 in the twenty-third year of *N*, Nebuzaradan,
Bar 1: 9 king of Judah, had had made after *N*,
1:11 Lord our God, and pray for the life of *N*,
1:12 may live under the protective shadow of *N*,
6: 1 you are being led captive to Babylon by *N*,
Ez 26: 7 Tyre from the north *N* the king of Babylon,
29:18 Son of man, *N*, the king of Babylon,
29:19 I am now giving the land of Egypt to *N*,
30:10 to the throngs of Egypt by the hand of *N*,
Dn 1: 1 King *N* of Babylon came and laid siege to
1:18 chief chamberlain brought them before *N*.
2: 1 King *N* had a dream which left his spirit
2:28 King *N* what is to happen in days to come;
2:46 Then King *N* fell down and worshiped Daniel
3: 1 King *N* had a golden statue made,
3: 3 before the statue which King *N* had set up.
3: 5 the golden statue which King *N* has set up.
3: 7 the golden statue which King *N* had set up.
3: 9 came and accused the Jews to King *N*:
3:13 *N* flew into a rage and sent for Shadrach,
3:14 King *N* questioned them:
3:16 Meshach, and Abednego answered King *N*,
3:91 *N* rose in haste and asked his nobles,
3:93 Then *N* came to the opening of the
3:95 *N* exclaimed, "Blessed be the God
3:98 King *N* to the nations and peoples of every
4: 1 I, *N*, was at home in my palace,
4:15 "This is the dream that I, King *N*, had.
4:25 All this happened to King *N*.
4:28 "It has been decreed for you, King *N*,
4:30 *N* was cast out from among men,
4:31 When this period was over, I, *N*,
4:34 Therefore, I, *N*, now praise and exalt
5: 2 the gold and silver vessels which *N*,
5:11 King *N*, your father, made him chief
5:18 *N* a great kingdom and glorious majesty.

NEBUCHADNEZZAR'S (1)

Dn 3:19 *N* face became livid with utter rage

NEBUSHAZBAN (2)

Jer 39: 3 of Simmagir, the chief officer, *N*,
39:13 chief of the bodyguard, and *N*,

NEBUZARADAN (16)

2Kgs 25: 8 of Nebuchadnezzar, king of Babylon), *N*,
25:11 Then *N*, captain of the guard,
25:12 But some of the country's poor, *N*,
25:20 The captain of the guard, *N*, arrested these
Jer 39: 9 *N*, chief of the bodyguard, deported to
39:10 were left in the land of Judah by *N*,
39:11 gave the following orders through *N*,
39:13 Thereupon *N*, chief of the bodyguard,
40: 1 came to Jeremiah from the LORD, after *N*,
41:10 left in Mizpah and the princesses, whom *N*,
43: 6 the princesses and everyone whom *N*,
52:12 of Nebuchadnezzar, king of Babylon), *N*,
52:15 Then *N*, captain of the guard,
52:16 But some of the country's poor, *N*,
52:26 The captain of the guard, *N*,
52:30 twenty-third year of Nebuchadnezzar, *N*,

NECESSARILY (2)

Jb 11: 2 or must the garrulous man *n* be right?
Heb 7:12 of priesthood, there is *n* a change of law.

NECESSARY (17)

Ex 31: 6 endowed all the experts with the *n* skill
Nm 4:26 ropes and all other objects *n* in their use.
2Kgs 12: 6 whatever repairs on the temple may prove *n*."
12:13 expenses that were *n* to repair the temple.
2Chr 25:16 Why should it be *n* to kill you?"

NECESSARY (cont.)

Tb 8:12 so that if *n* we may bury him without
1Mc 10:39 for the *n* expenses of the sanctuary.
14:34 with all that was *n* for their restoration.
2Mc 3:3 expenses *n* for the sacrificial services.
9:21 so I thought it *n* to form plans for the
10:18 containing everything *n* to sustain a siege,
Sir 32:7 Young man, speak only when *n*,
Acts 15:28 burden beyond that which is strictly *n*,
2Cor 9:5 I have thought it *n* to exhort the brothers
Heb 9:16 it is *n* that the death of the testator be
9:23 It was *n* that the copies of the heavenly
2Pt 1:3 everything *n* for a life of genuine piety,

NECESSITIES (1)

Wis 16:3 be turned from even the craving of *n*,

NECESSITY (3)

2Mc 6:7 birthday the Jews had, from bitter *n*,
Lk 18:1 *n* of praying always and not losing heart:
Heb 8:3 *n* for this one to have something to offer.

NECK (49)

Gn 27:16 his hands and the hairless parts of his *n*.
27:40 you shall throw off his yoke from your *n*."
33:4 him, and flinging himself on his *n*,
41:42 linen and put a gold chain about his *n*.
45:14 on the *n* of his brother Benjamin and wept,
46:29 on his *n* and wept a long time in his arms.
49:8 your hand on the *n* of your enemies;
Ex 13:13 do not redeem it, you shall break its *n*.
34:20 you do not redeem it, you must break its *n*.
Lv 5:8 Snapping its head loose at the *n*,
Dt 28:48 He will put an iron yoke on your *n*,
1Sm 4:18 old man and heavy, he died of a broken *n*.
Jdt 13:8 him twice in the *n* and cut off his head.
16:9 The sword cut through his *n*.
Est D:12 golden scepter, he touched her *n* with it,
Jb 16:12 seized me by the *n* and dashed me to pieces.
39:19 strength, and endow his *n* with splendor?
41:14 Strength abides in his *n*,
Prv 1:9 a torque for your *n*.
3:3 bind them around your *n*;
3:22 to your soul, and an adornment for your *n*.
6:21 your heart always, put them around your *n*;
Sg 1:10 lovely in pendants, your *n* in jewels.
4:4 Your *n* is like David's tower girt with
7:5 Your *n* is like a tower of ivory.
Sir 6:25 her fetters, and your *n* under her yoke.
51:26 Submit your *n* to her yoke,
Is 8:8 up to the *n* it shall reach;
10:27 and his yoke shattered from your *n*.
30:28 a ravine that reaches suddenly to the *n*,
48:4 *n* is an iron sinew and your forehead bronze,
52:2 Loose the bonds from your *n*,
66:3 a lamb, like breaking a dog's *n*;
Jer 27:8 *n* under the yoke of the king of Babylon,
27:11 The people that submits its *n* to the yoke
28:10 yoke from the *n* of the prophet Jeremiah,
28:11 Babylon, from off the *n* of all the nations.'"
28:12 from off the *n* of the prophet Jeremiah,
Lam 1:14 They have settled about my *n*,
Ez 16:11 on your arms, a necklace about your *n*,
Dn 5:7 purple, wear a golden collar about his *n*,
5:16 purple, wear a golden collar about your *n*,
5:29 in purple, with a gold collar about his *n*,
Hos 10:11 I myself laid a yoke upon her fair *n*;
Hb 3:13 wicked, you lay bare their bases at the *n*.
Mt 18:6 to be drowned by a millstone around his *n*,
Mk 9:42 a great millstone fastened around his *n*.
Lk 15:20 to meet him, threw his arms around his *n*,
17:2 the sea with a millstone around his *n*

NECKLACE (5)

Nm 31:50 a bracelet, a ring, an earring, or a *n*."
Ps(s) 73:6 So pride adorns them as a *n*;
Prv 25:12 Like a golden earring, or a *n* of fine gold,
Sg 4:9 of your eyes, with one bead of your *n*.
Ez 16:11 on your arms, a *n* about your neck,

NECKLACES (1)

Ex 35:22 rings, *n* and various other gold articles.

NECKS (20)

Jos 10:24 and put your feet on the *n* of these kings."
10:24 forward and put their feet upon their *n*.
Jgs 8:21 that were on the *n* of their camels.
8:26 that were on the *n* of their camels.
Neh 9:16 they held their *n* stiff and would not obey
9:17 They stiffened their *n* and turned their
9:29 turned stubborn backs, stiffened their *n*,
1Mc 1:61 decree, with the babies hung from their *n*;
Sir 7:23 bend their *n* from childhood.
Is 3:16 and walk with *n* outstretched Ogling and
Jer 7:26 their *n* and done worse than their fathers.
17:23 *n* so as not to hear or take correction.
19:15 their *n* and have not obeyed my words.
27:12 your *n* to the yoke of the king of Babylon;
28:14 A yoke of iron I will place on the *n* of
30:8 yoke from off your *n* and snap your bonds."
Lam 5:5 On our *n* is the yoke of those who drive us;
Bar 4:25 their destruction and trample upon their *n*.
Ez 21:34 lay it on the *n* of depraved and wicked men
Mi 2:3 from which you shall not withdraw your *n*;

NECO (9)

2Kgs 23:29 In his time Pharaoh *N*, king of Egypt,
23:33 Pharaoh *N* took him prisoner at Riblah in
23:34 Pharaoh *N* then appointed Eliakim,
23:35 each proportionately, to pay Pharaoh *N*.
2Chr 35:20 *N*, king of Egypt, came up to fight
35:21 *N* sent messengers to him, saying:
35:22 words of *N* that came from the mouth of
36:4 *N* took his brother Jehoahaz away and
Jer 46:2 Against the army of Pharaoh *N*,

NECROMANCER (1)

1Chr 10:13 because he had sought counsel of a *n*,

NECROMANCERS (1)

2Chr 33:6 and appointed *n* and diviners of spirits,

NEDABIAH (1)

1Chr 3:18 Pedaiah, Shenazzar, Jekamiah, Shama, and *N*.

NEED (139)

Gn 26:24 You have no *n* to fear,
42:19 your brothers *n* be confined in this prison,
43:23 "you have no *n* to fear.
Ex 9:28 you *n* stay no longer."
22:12 and he *n* not make restitution for the
22:14 is present, he *n* not make restitution.
30:15 The rich *n* not give more,
Lv 13:36 on the skin he *n* not look for yellow hair;
26:26 ten women will *n* but one oven for baking
Nm 11:15 so that I *n* no longer face this distress."
14:9 *n* not be afraid of the people of that land;
Dt 15:4 there should be no one of you in *n*.
15:7 is in *n* in the land which the LORD,
15:7 heart nor close your hand to him in his *n*.
15:8 and freely lend him enough to meet his *n*.
24:5 he *n* not go out on a military expedition,
Jos 7:3 you *n* not call for an effort from all the
Jgs 19:19 there is nothing else we *n*."
1Sm 26:8 I will not *n* a second thrust!"
2Sm 3:29 falling by the sword, or one in *n* of bread!"
2Kgs 1:15 you *n* not be afraid of him."
1Chr 23:26 Henceforth the Levites *n* not carry the
2Chr 2:15 cut trees on Lebanon, as many as you *n*,
35:15 was no *n* for them to leave their stations,
Tb 3:10 I *n* no longer live to hear such insults."
5:7 for I *n* you to make the journey with me.
5:12 Do you *n* a tribe and a family?
5:17 prepare whatever you *n* for the journey,
10:1 time Tobiah would *n* to go and to return.
12:17 "No *n* to fear; you are safe.
Jdt 6:9 then there is no *n* for you to be downcast.
1Mc 12:9 Though we have no *n* of these things,
2Mc 2:15 If you *n* them, send messengers
14:35 of all, though you are in *n* of nothing,
Jb 5:22 the beasts of the earth you *n* not dread.
9:18 He *n* not suffer me to draw breath,
13:20 me, then from your presence I *n* not hide:
40:32 him, no *n* to recall any other conflict!
41:1 to do so *n* only see him to be overthrown.
41:4 I *n* hardly mention his limbs,
Prv 3:24 When you lie down, you *n* not be afraid,
25:16 If you find honey, eat only what you *n*,
30:8 [provide me only with the food I *n*
31:5 and violate the rights of all who are in *n*.
Wis 11:5 punished they in their *n* were benefited.
12:13 you *n* show you have not unjustly condemned;
Sir 1:20 A patient man *n* stand firm but for a time,
8:9 the knowledge how to answer in time of *n*,
10:25 affairs, and boast not in your time of *n*.
11:23 "What do I *n*?
15:12 for he has no *n* of wicked man.
22:25 in *n* of support no one need hide in shame;
29:2 Lend to your neighbor in his hour of *n*,
29:3 him and you will always come by what you *n*.
29:27 for my brother's visit I *n* the room!"
32:19 counsel, and then you *n* have no regrets.
33:32 a brother, for you *n* him as you need
38:12 for you *n* him too.
38:32 and wherever they stay, they *n* not hunger.
39:16 in its own time every *n* is supplied.
39:21 Everything is chosen to satisfy a *n*.
39:33 every *n* when it comes he fills.
40:26 he who has it *n* seek no other support:
42:22 no *n* of a counselor for him!
42:24 to meet each *n*,
43:28 More than this we *n* not add;
Is 30:20 you *n* and the water for which you thirst.
54:4 you *n* not blush,
Jer 2:24 No beasts *n* tire themselves seeking her;
14:8 of Israel, O LORD, our savior in time of *n*!
23:4 so that they *n* no longer fear and tremble;
27:9 you, "You *n* not serve the king of Babylon."
27:14 say, "You *n* not serve the king of Babylon,"
31:34 No longer will they have *n* to teach their
40:4 you to come to Babylon, you *n* not come.
44:18 we are in *n* of everything and are being
Lam 5:6 and to Assyria, to fill our *n* of bread.
Ez 17:9 [No *n* of a mighty arm or many people to do
39:12 Israel shall *n* seven months to bury them.
Dn 3:16 "There is no *n* for us to defend ourselves
Zep 3:11 day You *n* not be ashamed of all your deeds,
Mt 6:8 Father knows what you *n* before you ask him.
6:32 Your heavenly Father knows all that you *n*.
8:4 That should be the proof they *n*."
9:12 who are in good health do not *n* a doctor;
14:16 "There is no *n* for them to disperse.
15:6 God, *n* not honor his father or his mother.'
19:20 what do I *n* to do further?"
24:45 of his household to dispense food at *n*?
26:65 What further *n* have we of witnesses?
Mk 2:17 "People who are healthy do not *n* a doctor;
2:25 he was in *n* and he and his men were hungry?
6:12 went off, preaching the *n* of repentance.
14:63 "What further *n* do we have of witnesses?
16:6 "You *n* not be amazed!
Lk 5:31 to them, "The healthy do not *n* a doctor;
9:11 and he healed all who were in *n* of healing.
12:30 Your Father knows that you *n* such things.
15:7 righteous people who have no *n* to repent.
15:14 out in that country and he was in dire *n*.
19:31 say, 'The Master has *n* of it.'"
22:35 bag or sandals, were you in *n* of anything?"
22:71 They said, "What *n* have we of witnesses?
Jn 5:28 no *n* for you to be surprised at this,
13:10 has no *n* to wash [except for his feet];
16:30 is no *n* for anyone to ask you questions.
Acts 2:45 everything on the basis of each one's *n*.
4:35 distributed to everyone according to his *n*.
8:24 *n* the prayers of all of you to the Lord,
17:25 man's service as if he were in *n* of it.
20:35 You *n* to recall the words of the Lord
Rom 15:26 those in *n* among the saints in Jerusalem.
1Cor 12:21 cannot say to the hand, "I do not *n* you,"
12:21 head can say to the feet, "I do not *n* you."
16:6 with what I *n* for the rest of my journey.
2Cor 3:1 Or do I *n* letters of recommendation to you
8:14 should supply their *n* so that their surplus
8:14 their surplus may one day supply your *n*,
9:1 There is really no *n* for me to write you
Eph 4:28 have something to share with those in *n*.
4:29 say only the good things men *n* to hear,
1Thes 4:9 love, there is no *n* for me to write you.
5:1 brothers, we do not *n* to write you;
1Tm 5:16 help to the widows who are really in *n*.
6:8 food and clothing we have all that we *n*.
Ti 3:13 to it that they have everything they *n*.
Heb 4:16 and favor and to find help in time of *n*.
5:12 you *n* to have someone teach you again the
5:12 you *n* milk,
7:11 what *n* would there have been to appoint a
7:27 has no *n* to offer sacrifice day after day,
10:36 You *n* patience to do God's will and
1Jn 2:27 you have no *n* for anyone to teach you.
3:13 No *n*, then, brothers, to be surprised
3:17 heart to his brother when he sees him in *n*.
Rv 21:23 The city had no *n* of sun or moon,
22:5 They will *n* no light from lamps or the sun,

NEEDED (13)

Ex 36:5 people are bringing much more than is *n*
2Kgs 12:7 had not made *n* repairs on the temple.
2Mc 2:29 himself with what is *n* for ornamentation,
10:19 off to places where he was more urgently *n*.
Wis 16:4 but these *n* only be shown how their
16:25 according to what they *n* and desired;
Mk 5:36 What is *n* is trust."
Lk 8:50 is *n* is trust and her life will be spared."
19:34 They explained that the Master *n* it.
Jn 2:25 He *n* no one to give him testimony about
13:29 him to buy what was *n* for the feast,
Col 1:11 endowed with the strength *n* to stand fast,
Rv 13:18 A certain wisdom is *n* here;

NEEDLE'S (3)

Mt 19:24 easier for a camel to pass through a *n* eye
Mk 10:25 easier for a camel to pass through a *n* eye
Lk 18:25 is easier for a camel to go through a *n* eye

NEEDLESS (1)

1Thes 1:8 makes it *n* for us to say anything more.

NEEDLESSLY (1)

Sir 20:22 out of shame, and has him for his enemy *n*.

NEEDS (34)

Ex 12:16 except to prepare the food that everyone *n*.
Jgs 19:20 him, "but let me provide for all your *n*,
Ezr 7:20 supply for the *n* of the house of your God,
Neh 12:47 their portions, according to their daily *n*.
Tb 1:13 I became purchasing agent for all his *n*.
1Mc 16:14 of the country and providing for their *n*,
Jb 20:26 which shall consume him *n* not to be fanned.
Wis 13:16 for, truly, it is an image and *n* help.
Sir 13:6 he *n* something from you he will cajole you,

29:21 Life's prime *n* are water,
39:26 of all *n* for human life are water and fire,
Mt 20:27 first among you must serve the *n* of all.
21: 3 a word to you, say, 'The Master *n* them.'
25:44 or in prison and not attend you in your *n*?'
27:55 Jesus from Galilee to attend to his *n*.
Mk 10:44 first among you must serve the *n* of all.
11: 3 *n* it but he will send it back here at once.' "
15:41 he was in Galilee and attended to his *n*.
Lk 11: 7 I cannot get up to look after your *n*—
11: 8 persistence, and give him as much as he *n*.
Acts 20:34 both my *n* and those of my companions.
27: 3 to visit some friends who cared for his *n*.
28:10 sail they brought us provisions for our *n*.
Rom 12:13 Look on the *n* of the saints as your own;
15:27 contribute to their temporal *n* in return.
16: 2 If she *n* help in anything,
2Cor 9:12 not only supplies the *n* of the members
11: 9 who came from Macedonia supplied my *n*.
Phil 2:25 arms, whom you sent to take care of my *n*.
4: 6 Present your *n* to God in every form of
4:16 Thessalonica you sent something for my *n*,
4:19 My God in turn will supply your *n* fully,
Ti 3:14 work in order to take care of their *n*,
Jas 2:16 well fed," but do not meet their bodily *n*,

NEEDY (40)

Ex 23: 6 *n* fellow men his rights in his lawsuit.
Dt 15: 9 to your *n* kinsman and give him nothing;
15:11 The *n* will never be lacking in the land;
15:11 to your poor and *n* kinsman in your country.
24:14 not defraud a poor and *n* hired servant,
1Sm 2: 8 He raises the *n* from the dust;
Jb 24: 4 They force the *n* off the road;
24:14 the murderer rises, to kill the poor and *n*.
29:16 I was a father to the *n*;
Ps(s) 9:19 For the *n* shall not always be forgotten,
12: 6 they rob the afflicted, and the *n* sigh,
35:10 afflicted and the *n* from their despoilers?"
68:11 O God, you provided it for the *n*.
107:41 Lifted up the *n* out of misery and made the
Prv 14:31 but he who is kind to the *n* glorifies him.
22:22 they are poor, nor crush the *n* at the gate;
30:14 are knives, Devouring the *n* from the earth,
31: 9 what is just, defend the *n* and the poor!
31:20 to the poor, and extends her arms to the *n*.
Wis 2:10 Let us oppress the *n* just man;
Sir 4: 1 force not the eyes of the *n* to turn away.
4: 2 A hungry man grieve not, a *n* man anger not;
4: 3 delay not to give to the *n*.
4: 5 From the *n* turn not your eyes,
29: 9 Because of the precept, help the *n*,
34:21 bread of charity is life itself for the *n*;
Is 10: 2 Depriving the *n* of judgment and robbing my
14:30 shall eat, and the *n* lie down in safety;
25: 4 to the poor, a refuge to the *n* in distress;
26: 6 It is trampled underfoot by the *n*,
32: 7 lies, and the *n* when they plead their case.
41:17 The afflicted and the *n* seek water in vain,
Ez 16:49 and they gave no help to the poor and *n*.
18:12 of his neighbor, oppresses the poor and *n*,
22:29 they afflict the poor and the *n*,
Am 4: 1 You who oppress the weak and abuse the *n*;
5:12 bribes, repelling the *n* at the gate!
8: 4 the *n* and destroy the poor of the land!
Acts 4:34 nor was there anyone *n* among them,
Heb 11:37 garbed in the skins of sheep or goats, *n*,

NEER-DO-WELL (1)

1Sm 1:16 Do not think your handmaid a *n*;

NEGATE (1)

2Tm 3: 5 a pretense of religion but *n* its power.

NEGEB (39)

Gn 12: 9 Then Abram journeyed on by stages to the *N*.
13: 1 From Egypt Abram went up to the *N* with his
13: 3 the *N* he traveled by stages toward Bethel,
20: 1 journeyed on to the region of the *N*,
24:62 and was living in the region of the *N*.
Nm 13:17 Moses said to them, "Go up here in the *N*,
13:22 Going up by way of *N*, they reached Hebron,
13:29 Amalekites live in the region of the *N*;
21: 1 king of Arad, who lived in the *N*,
33:40 who lived in the *N* in the land of Canaan,
Dt 1: 7 the foothills, the *N* and the seacoast;
34: 3 of Judah as far as the Western Sea, the *N*,
34:12 the *N*, the circuit of the Jordan
Jos 10:40 the mountain regions, the *N*,
11:16 the entire *N* all the land of Goshen,
12: 8 Arabah, the slopes, the desert, and the *N*,
15: 1 of Edom, the desert of Zin in the *N*.
15:19 you have assigned to me land in the *N*,
Jgs 1: 9 who lived in the mountain region, in the *N*,
1:15 you have assigned land in the *N* to me,
1:16 to the desert at Arad [which is in the *N*.
1Sm 27:10 And David answered, "The *N* of Judah,"
27:10 *N* of Jerahmeel," or "The *N* of the Kenites.
30: 1 the Amalekites had raided the *N* and Ziklag,
30:14 We raided the *N* of the Cherethites,
30:14 the territory of Judah, and the *N* of Caleb;
2Sm 24: 7 ending up at Beer-sheba in the *N* of Judah.
2Chr 28:18 cities of the foothills and *N* of Judah
Is 21: 1 sweeping in waves through the *N*,
30: 6 [Oracle on the Beasts of the *N* Through
Jer 13:19 The cities of the *N* are besieged,
17:26 from the hill country and the *N*,
32:44 the cities of the foothills and of the *N*,
33:13 country, of the foothills, and of the *N*,
Ob 1:19 They shall occupy the *N*,
1:20 Sepharad shall occupy the cities of the *N*.
Zec 7: 7 the *N* and the foothills were inhabited?
14:10 And from Geba to Rimmon in the *N*,

NEGLECT (17)

Dt 12:19 that you do not *n* the Levite as long as
14:27 But do not *n* the Levite who belongs to
Ezr 4:22 Take care that you do not *n* this matter,
Neh 10:40 We will not *n* the house of our God.
Jb 19:14 My kinsfolk and companions *n* me,
Wis 14:26 Disturbance of good men, *n* of gratitude,
Sir 7:10 in prayers, and *n* not the giving of alms.
7:35 *N* not to visit the sick
18:21 sins, *n* it not till you are in distress.
32:18 The thoughtful man will not *n* direction;
37: 6 *n* him not when you distribute your spoils.
38: 4 herbs which the prudent man should not *n*;
Dn 6: 5 of *n* or misconduct was to be found in him.
Acts 6: 2 "It is not right for us to *n* the word of
1Tm 4:14 Do not *n* the gift you received when,
Heb 13: 2 Do not *n* to show hospitality,
13:16 Do not *n* good deeds and generosity;

NEGLECTED (7)

Jb 18: 4 shall the earth be *n* on your account [or
Wis 3:10 since they *n* justice and forsook the Lord.
Mt 25:45 you *n* to do it to one of these least ones,
25:45 of these least ones, you *n* to do it to me.'
Lk 12: 6 Yet not one of them is *n* by God.
Acts 6: 1 being *n* in the daily distribution of food,
1Tm 1: 6 Some people have *n* these and instead have

NEGLECTING (5)

Dt 8:11 by *n* his commandments and decrees and
2Mc 4:14 Disdaining the temple and *n* the sacrifices,
Mt 23:23 while *n* the weightier matters of the law,
23:23 have practiced, without *n* the others.
Lk 11:42 while *n* justice and the love of God.

NEGLECTS (1)

Sir 23:11 if he *n* his obligation,

NEGLIGENCE (1)

Gn 41: 9 "On this occasion I am reminded of my *n*.

NEGLIGENT (1)

2Chr 29:11 My sons, be not *n* any longer,

NEGOTIATING (1)

2Mc 13:22 attempt by *n* with the men of Beth-zur.

NEHELAMITE (3)

Jer 29:24 Say this to Shemaiah, the *N*:
29:31 says the LORD concerning Shemaiah, the *N*:
29:32 I will therefore punish Shemaiah, the *N*,

NEHEMIAH (16)

Ezr 2: 2 who returned with Zerubbabel, Jeshua, *N*,
Neh 1: 1 The words of *N*, the son of Hacaliah.
3:16 the work and repair was carried out by *N*,
7: 7 who returned with Zerubbabel, Jeshua, *N*,
8: 9 Then *N*, that is, His Excellency,
10: 2 His Excellency *N*,
12:26 and in the time of *N* the governor
12:47 days of Zerubbabel [and in the days of *N*,
2Mc 1:18 and of the fire that appeared when *N*,
1:20 years later, when it so pleased God, *N*,
1:21 *N* ordered the priests to sprinkle with the
1:23 leading and the rest responding with *N*.
1:31 *N* ordered the rest of the liquid to be
1:33 a liquid was found with which *N* and his
1:36 *N* and his companions called the liquid
Sir 49:13 Extolled be the memory of *N*!

NEHEMIAH'S (2)

Neh 5:14 from the time that *N* Lack of Self-interest
2Mc 2:13 it is also told in the records and in *N*

NEHUM (1)

Neh 7: 7 Mordecai, Bilshan, Mispereth, Bigvai, *N*,

NEHUSHTA (1)

2Kgs 24: 8 His mother's name was *N*,

NEHUSHTAN (1)

2Kgs 18: 4 cut down the sacred *N* which Moses had

NEIEL (1)

Jos 19:27 then north of Beth-emek and *N*,

NEIGHBOR (103)

Ex 3:22 Every woman shall ask her *n* and her house
11: 2 people that every man is to ask his *n*,
11: 2 ask his neighbor, and every woman her *n*,
20:16 not bear false witness against your *n*.
22:13 "When a man borrows an animal from his *n*,
Lv 5:21 against the LORD by denying his *n* a deposit
19:13 "You shall not defraud or rob your *n*.
19:18 You shall love your *n* as yourself.
24:19 on his *n* shall receive the same in return.
25:14 any land to your *n* or buy any from him,
Dt 4:42 there if he unwittingly killed his *n*
5:20 not bear dishonest witness against your *n*.
15: 2 his claim on what he has loaned his *n*;
15: 2 his neighbor; he must not press his *n*,
19: 4 when someone unwittingly kills his *n* to
19: 5 he goes with his *n* to a forest to cut wood,
19: 5 the handle and hits his *n* a mortal blow,
19:11 in wait for his *n* out of hatred for him,
22:26 rises up against his *n* and murders him:
24:10 you make a loan of any kind to your *n*,
27:24 'Cursed be he who slays his *n* in secret!'
Ru 4:17 And the *n* women gave him his name,
1Sm 15:28 this day, and has given it to a *n* of yours,
28:16 LORD has abandoned you and is with your *n*?
28:17 grasp and has given it to your *n* David.
2Sm 12:11 to see it, and will give them to your *n*.
1Kgs 8:31 "If a man sins against his *n* and is
2Chr 6:22 "When any man sins against his *n* and is
Jb 16:21 and decide between a man and his *n*.
Ps(s) 12: 3 Everyone speaks falsehood to his *n*;
15: 3 nor takes up a reproach against his *n*;
24: 4 is vain, nor swears deceitfully to his *n*.
88:19 and *n* you have taken away from me;
101: 5 Whoever slanders his *n* in secret,
Prv 3:28 Say not to your *n*, "Go, and come again,
3:29 Plot no evil against your *n*,
6: 1 son, if you have become surety to your *n*,
6: 3 Go, hurry, stir up your *n*!
11: 9 mouth the impious man would ruin his *n*,
11:12 He who reviles his *n* has no sense,
12:26 The just man surpasses his *n*,
14:20 Even by his *n* the poor man is hated,
16:29 A lawless man allures his *n*,
17:18 in pledge, who becomes surety for his *n*.
21:10 his *n* finds no pity in his eyes.
24:28 witness against your *n* without just cause,
25: 8 do later on when your *n* puts you to shame?
25: 9 Discuss your case with your *n*,
25:18 man who bears false witness against his *n*.
26:19 arrows Is the man who deceives his *n*,
27:10 a *n* near at hand than a brother far away.
27:14 When one greets his *n* with a loud voice in
29: 5 his *n* is spreading a net under his feet.
Wis 14:24 but each either waylays and kills his *n*,
Sir 5:14 If you have the knowledge, answer your *n*;
5:17 reproach of his *n* for the doubletongued.
10: 6 matter the wrong, do no violence to your *n*,
14: 9 refuses his *n* and brings ruin on himself.
14:25 beside her, and lives as her welcome *n*;
16:26 Not one should ever crowd its *n*,
19:13 Admonish your *n*—
19:16 Admonish your *n* before you break with him;
28: 7 of the commandments, hate not your *n*,
29: 1 He does a kindness who lends to his *n*,
29: 2 Lend to your *n* in his hour of need,
29:14 A good man goes surety for his *n*,
29:20 surety for your *n* according to your means,
31:15 Recognize that your *n* feels as you do,
31:31 Rebuke not your *n* when wine is served,
34:22 slays his *n* who deprives him of his living:
40:23 A friend, a *n*, are timely guides,
Is 3: 5 oppress one another, yes, every man his *n*.
9:18 brother, each devours the flesh of his *n*.
19: 2 war against brother, *N* against neighbor,
Jer 7: 5 if each of you deals justly with his *n*;
9: 3 Be on your guard, everyone against his *n*;
22:13 Who works his *n* without pay,
Bar 6:43 *n* who has not been dignified as she has,
Ez 18:11 the mountains, defiles the wife of his *n*,
Dn 13:61 they had plotted to impose on their *n*:
Zec 8:10 enemy, for I set every man against his *n*.
11: 6 each of them into the power of his *n*,
14:13 every man shall seize the hand of his *n*,
14:13 each shall be raised against that of his *n*.
Mt 19:19 and 'Love your *n* as yourself.' "
22:39 'You shall love your *n* as yourself.'
Mk 12:31 second, 'You shall love your *n* as yourself.'
12:33 and to love our *n* as ourselves' is worth
Lk 10:27 and your *n* as yourself."
10:29 he said to Jesus, "And who is my *n*?"
10:36 *n* to the man who fell in with the robbers?"
Acts 7:27 who was wronging his *n* pushed Moses aside.
Rom 13: 8 He who loves his *n* has fulfilled the law.
13: 9 this, "You shall love your *n* as yourself."
13:10 Love never wrongs the *n*,
15: 2 Each should please his *n* so as to do him
1Cor 10:24 his own interest but rather that of his *n*.
Gal 5:14 "You shall love your *n* as yourself."

NEIGHBOR (cont.)

Eph 4:25 let everyone speak the truth to his *n*,
Jas 2: 8 it, "You shall love your *n* as yourself."
4:12 Who then are you to judge your *n?*

NEIGHBORHOOD (13)

Ex 7:24 in the *n* of the river for drinking water,
Dt 21: 2 the cities that are in the *n* of the corpse.
1Kgs 7:46 king had them cast in the *n* of the Jordan,
Jdt 3: 9 reached Esdraelon in the *n* of Dothan,
Jer 17:26 the cities of Judah and the *n* of Jerusalem,
Mt 8:34 of him, they begged him to leave their *n.*
16:13 Jesus came to the *n* of Caesarea Philippi,
Mk 3: 8 Transjordan, and the *n* of Tyre and Sidon,
5:10 Jesus not to drive them away from that *n.*
8:10 his disciples to go to the *n* of Dalmanutha.
Lk 1:65 Fear descended on all in the *n;*
8:37 territory asked Jesus to leave their *n,*
9:12 the *n* and find themselves lodging and food,

NEIGHBORING (14)

Lv 25:44 you buy them from among the *n* nations.
1Kgs 5:11 his fame spread throughout the *n* nations.
1Mc 10:84 and plundered Azotus with its *n* towns,
12:33 as far as Ashkalon and its *n* strongholds.
2Mc 4:32 other vessels in Tyre and in the *n* cities.
6: 8 decree was issued ordering the *n* Greek cities
9:25 am also bearing in mind that the *n* rulers,
Jer 25: 9 and against all these *n* nations.
Ez 36: 7 *n* nations shall bear their own reproach.
36:36 *n* nations that remain shall know that I,
Jl 4:11 Hasten and come, all you *n* peoples,
4:12 sit in judgment upon all the *n* nations.
Mk 1:38 "Let us move on to the *n* villages so that
6: 6 made the rounds of the *n* villages instead,

NEIGHBORS-NEIGHBOR'S (78)

Ex 20:17 "You shall not covet your *n* house.
20:17 You shall not covet your *n* wife,
22: 7 did not lay hands on his *n* property.
22:10 he did not lay hands on his *n* property;
22:24 to one of your poor *n* among my people,
22:25 If you take your *n* cloak as a pledge,
32:27 slay your own kinsmen, your friends and *n!"*
Lv 5:21 otherwise retaining his *n* goods unjustly,
18:20 not have carnal relations with your *n* wife,
19:16 stand by idly when your *n* life is at stake.
20:10 If a man commits adultery with his *n* wife,
Dt 5:21 'You shall not covet your *n* wife.
5:21 shall not desire your *n* house or field,
19:14 "You shall not move your *n* landmarks
22:24 and the man because he violated his *n* wife.
23:25 "When you go through your *n* vineyard,
23:26 When you go through your *n* grainfield,
23:26 but do not put a sickle to your *n* grain.
27:17 'Cursed be he who moves his *n* landmarks!'
2Kgs 4: 3 he said, "borrow vessels from all your *n*—
1Chr 12:41 Moreover, their *n* from as far as Issachar,
Ezr 1: 6 All their *n* gave them help in every way,
Tb 2: 8 The *n* mocked me, saying to one another:
Jb 12: 4 I have become the sport of my *n:*
31: 9 and I have lain in wait at my *n* door;
Ps(s) 28: 3 to their *n* though evil is in their hearts.
31:12 of reproach, a laughingstock to my *n,*
38:12 my *n* stand afar off.
44:14 You made us the reproach of our *n,*
79: 4 We have become the reproach of our *n,*
79:12 And repay our *n* sevenfold into their
80: 7 have left us to be fought over by our *n,*
89:42 he is made the reproach of his *n.*
Prv 6: 3 since you have fallen into your *n* power:
6:24 To keep you from your *n* wife,
6:29 So with him who goes in to his *n* wife
25:17 Let your foot be seldom in your *n* house,
Sir 9:14 As best you can, take your *n'* measure,
16: 8 *n* of Lot whom he detested for their pride;
21:28 besmirches himself, and is hated by his *n.*
25: 1 among brethren, friendship among *n,*
25:17 When her husband sits among his *n,*
27:18 a man, you have killed your *n* friendship.
28: 2 Forgive your *n* injustice;
40:29 His *n* delicacies bring revulsion of spirit
Is 11: 7 The cow and the bear shall be *n,*
Jer 6:21 and sons alike, *n* and friends shall perish.
12:14 Thus says the LORD against all my evil *n*
29:23 committing adultery with their *n'* wives,
34:17 me by proclaiming your *n* and kinsmen free.
46:14 the sword has already devoured your *n.*
48:17 Mourn for him, all you his *n,*
48:39 a laughingstock and a horror to all his *n!*
49:10 sons, and brothers, and *n,*
49:18 Gomorrah, and their *n* were overthrown,
50:40 Sodom and Gomorrah, with their *n,*
Lam 1:17 against Jacob for his *n* to be his foes;
Bar 4: 9 "Hear you *n* of Zion!
4:14 "Let Zion's *n* come,
4:24 As Zion's *n* lately saw you taken captive,
Ez 16:26 harlot with the Egyptians, your lustful *n,*
16:57 reproached by the Edomites and all your *n,*
18: 6 if he does not defile his *n* wife,
18:15 the house of Israel, or defile his *n* wife;
22:11 things with the wives of their *n,*
22:12 you despoil your *n* violently;
28:26 on all their *n* who despised them;
33:26 things, each one of you defiles his *n* wife
Dn 9:16 have become the reproach of all our *n.*
Hb 2:15 give your *n* a flood of your wrath to drink,
Mt 13:56 Aren't his sisters our *n?*
Mk 6: 3 Are not his sisters our *n* here?"
Lk 1:58 Her *n* and relatives, upon hearing that
14:12 or brothers or relatives or wealthy *n.*
15: 6 invites friends and *n* in and says to them,
15: 9 it, she calls in her friends and *n* to say,
Jn 9: 8 His *n* and the people who had been
1Cor 10:29 not your own conscience but your *n.*

NEIGHING (1)

Jer 8:16 *n* of his stallions shakes the whole land.

NEIGHINGS (1)

Jer 13:27 Your adulteries, your *n,*

NEIGHS (2)

Sir 33: 6 fickle friend is like the stallion that *n,*
Jer 5: 8 they are, each *n* after another's wife.

NEITHER (208)

Gn 31:52 *n* may I pass beyond this mound into your
Ex 4:10 I have never been eloquent, *n* in the past,
13:22 *N* the column of cloud by day nor the
20:23 *n* gods of silver nor gods of gold shall
23: 2 *N* shall you allege the example of the many
34:16 *N* shall you take their daughters as wives
36: 6 "Let *n* man nor woman make any more
Lv 19:15 Show *n* partiality to the weak nor
22:10 *N* a lay person nor a priest's tenant or
22:24 You shall *n* do this in your own land nor
25: 4 *n* sow your field nor prune your vineyard.
25:37 *n* money at interest nor food at a profit.
27:28 field, shall be *n* sold nor ransomed;
Nm 6: 3 he may *n* drink wine vinegar,
14:44 even though *n* the ark of the covenant of
20: 5 wretched place which has *n* grain nor figs
Dt 2:37 *n* the region bordering on the Wadi Jabbok,
4:28 and stone, gods which can *n* see nor hear,
4:28 can neither see nor hear, *n* eat nor smell.
7: 3 *n* giving your daughters to their sons nor
13: 1 *n* adding to it nor subtracting from it.
17:17 *N* shall he have a great number of wives,
20: 3 be *n* alarmed nor frightened by them.
28:50 that shows *n* respect for the aged nor pity
Jos 5:14 He replied, "*N.* I am the captain of the host
Jgs 1:27 *N* did he dislodge the inhabitants of Dor
6: 5 *n* they nor their camels could be numbered,
11:34 he had *n* son nor daughter besides her.
13: 7 So take *n* wine nor strong drink,
Ru 1: 5 left with *n* her two sons nor her husband.
1Sm 1:11 *n* wine nor liquor shall he drink,
1:15 I have had *n* wine nor liquor;
2:12 they had respect *n* for the LORD nor for
4:20 Yet she *n* answered nor paid any attention.
5: 5 *n* the priests of Dagon nor any others who
12: 4 They replied, "You have *n* cheated us,
12:21 idols which can *n* profit nor save;
13:22 And so on the day of battle *n* sword nor
15:29 The Glory of Israel *n* retracts nor repents,
21: 9 I brought along *n* my sword nor my weapons,
25: 7 *n* did they miss anything all the while
25:15 *n* did we miss anything all the while we
2Sm 1:21 may there be *n* dew nor rain upon you,
1:23 separated *n* in life nor in death,
2:19 turning *n* right nor left in his pursuit.
7:10 *N* shall the wicked continue to afflict
14: 7 *n* name nor posterity upon the earth."
17:12 survive *n* he nor any of his followers.
1Kgs 3:26 said, "It shall be *n* mine nor yours.
13:17 LORD *n* to eat bread nor drink water here,
13:22 in the place where he told you to do *n,*
2Kgs 3:14 should *n* look at you nor notice you at all.
3:17 says, 'Though you will see *n* wind nor rain,
4:23 "It is *n* the new moon nor the sabbath."
12: 9 So the priests agreed that they would *n*
14:26 where there was *n* slave nor freeman,
18: 5 and *n* before him nor after him was there
2Chr 32:17 *n* shall Hezekiah's god save his people
36:17 sparing neither young man nor maiden, *n*
Ezr 9: 1 *N* the Israelite laymen nor the priests nor
10: 6 the night *n* eating food nor drinking water,
Neh 2:16 nothing to the Jews, *n* to the priests,
2:20 but for you there is to be *n* share nor
4:17 *N* I, nor my kinsmen,
5:14 during these twelve years *n* I nor my
Jdt 7: 4 *N* the high mountains nor the valleys and
1Mc 2:36 they *n* threw stones,
10:30 *N* now nor in the future will I collect
10:46 words, they *n* believed nor accepted them,
Jb 8:20 *n* will he take the hand of the wicked.
18:19 He has *n* son nor grandson among his people,
28:18 *N* coral nor jasper should be thought of;
34:19 Who *n* favors the person of princes,
Ps(s) 37:25 *N* in my youth,
38:15 who *n* hears nor has in his mouth a retort.
75: 7 For *n* from the east nor from the west,
75: 7 *n* from the desert nor from the mountains
82: 5 "They know not, *n* do they understand;
121: 4 Indeed he *n* slumbers nor sleeps,
Prv 4:27 Turn *n* to right nor to left,
30: 3 *N* have I learned wisdom,
30: 8 far from me, give me *n* poverty nor riches;
Eccl 2:16 *N* of the wise man nor of the fool will
4: 8 with *n* son nor brother.
8:17 even though *n* by day nor by night do his
Wis 2: 1 *n* is there any remedy for man's dying,
2:10 let us *n* spare the widow nor revere the
2:22 *n* did they count on recompense of holiness
6:23 *N* shall I admit consuming jealousy to my
12:11 *N* out of fear for anyone did you grant
12:13 For *n* is there any god besides you who
15: 4 For *n* did the evil creation of men's fancy
16:12 indeed, *n* herb nor application cured them,
19:21 *n* consumed the flesh of the perishable
Sir 22:16 *N* is a resolve constructed with careful
22:18 *N* can a timid resolve based on foolish
30:19 to an idol that can *n* taste nor smell?
33:20 neither son nor wife, *n* brother nor friend,
37:28 *n* become a glutton for choice foods,
Is 30: 5 that gain them nothing, *N* help nor benefit,
31: 4 Is *n* frightened by their shouts nor
38:18 *N* do those who go down into the pit await
44: 9 their shame, they *n* see nor know anything;
44:18 The idols have *n* knowledge nor reason;
48: 8 You *n* heard nor knew,
Jer 5:12 befall us, *n* sword nor famine shall we see.
9:15 whom *n* they nor their fathers have known;
10: 5 no harm, *n* is it in their power to do good.
15:10 I *n* borrow nor lend, yet all curse me.
16:13 that *n* you nor your fathers have known;
19: 4 gods which *n* they nor their fathers knew;
19: 5 such a thing as I *n* commanded nor spoke of,
22:27 *N* of them shall come back to the land for
32: 4 *N* shall Zedekiah, king of Judah, escape
34: 3 *N* shall you escape his hand;
35: 6 *N* you nor your children shall ever drink
35: 7 *n* plant nor own a vineyard.
35: 8 All our lives we have not drunk wine, *n* we,
37: 2 *N* he, nor his ministers,
44: 3 sacrificing to them, gods which *n* they,
51:62 so that *n* man nor beast should dwell in it,
Bar 1:18 We have *n* heeded the voice of the Lord,
4:15 That has *n* reverence for age nor
6:26 They *n* move of themselves if one sets them
6:33 they can *n* set up a king nor remove him.
6:35 They *n* save a man from death,
6:37 *n* pity the widow nor benefit the orphan.
6:53 They *n* vindicate their own rights,
6:56 They are safe from *n* thieves nor bandits,
6:63 They can *n* execute judgment,
6:65 Kings they *n* curse nor bless.
Ez 2: 6 fear *n* them nor their words when they
2: 6 *N* fear their words nor be dismayed at
14:16 swear they could save *n* sons nor daughters;
14:20 that they could save *n* son nor daughter;
16: 4 you were *n* washed with water nor anointed,
29:18 but *n* he nor his army received any wages
31: 8 *N* were the plane trees like it for
33:12 *n* will the wickedness that a man has done
38:11 without walls, having *n* bars nor gates,
Dn 5:23 that *n* see nor hear nor have intelligence.
6:23 *n* to you have I done any harm,
Hos 2: 1 sea, which can be *n* measured nor counted.
Jon 3: 7 *N* man nor beast, neither cattle nor sheep,
Zep 1:12 hearts, *N* good nor evil can the LORD do."
1:18 *N* their silver nor their gold shall be
Zec 13: 4 *n* shall he assume the hairy mantle to
Mal 1:10 *n* will I accept any sacrifice from your
3:19 on fire, leaving them *n* root nor branch,
3:24 on fire, leaving them *n* root nor branch,
Mt 6:15 others, *n* will your Father forgive you.
6:20 which *n* moths nor rust corrode nor thieves
10: 9 *n* gold nor silver nor copper in your belts;
11:18 words, John appeared *n* eating nor drinking,
21:27 "Then *n* will I tell you on what authority
22:30 they *n* marry nor are given in marriage but
23:13 *n* entering yourselves nor admitting those
24:36 it, *n* the angels in heaven nor the Son,
Mk 11:33 "Then *n* will I tell you on what authority
12:25 they *n* marry nor are given in marriage but
13:32 *n* the angels in heaven nor even the Son,
Lk 7:33 came *n* eating bread nor drinking wine,
7:42 Since *n* was able to repay,
9: 3 journey, *n* walking staff nor traveling bag;
12:24 do not reap, they have *n* cellar nor barn
14:35 is fit for *n* the soil nor the manure heap;
17:21 *N* is it a matter of reporting that it is
17:31 *n* should the man in the field return home.
18: 2 a certain city who respected *n* God nor man.
20: 8 *n* will I tell you by whose authority I act."
21: 9 *N* must you be perturbed when you hear of
23:15 *N* has Herod, who therefore has sent him
Jn 4:21 Father *n* on this mountain nor in Jerusalem.
5:38 *n* do you have his word abiding in your
6:24 that *n* Jesus nor his disciples were there,
8:14 you know *n* the one nor the other.
8:19 "You know *n* me nor my Father.
9: 3 *N*," answered Jesus: "It was no sin

14:17 since it *n* sees him nor recognizes him;
16: 3 you] because they knew *n* the Father nor me.
Acts 3: 6 "I have *n* silver nor gold,
9: 9 during which time he *n* ate nor drank.
15:10 *n* we nor our fathers were able to bear?
23: 8 and that there are *n* angels nor spirits,
24:12 *N* in the temple area,
27:20 *n* the sun nor the stars were to be seen,
Rom 8:38 *n* death nor life, neither angels nor
8:38 *n* the present nor the future,
8:39 *n* height nor depth nor any other creature,
9:11 yet unborn and had done *n* good nor evil,
14:16 *n* may you allow your privilege to become
1Cor 3: 7 This means that *n* he who plants nor he who
7:28 *N* does a virgin commit sin if she marries.
11: 9 *N* was man created for woman but woman for
11:16 remember that *n* we nor the churches of God
13: 5 *n* does it brood over injuries.
Gal 5: 6 In Christ Jesus *n* circumcision nor the
Eph 2: 9 *n* is it a reward for anything you have
1Thes 2: 6 *N* did we seek glory from men,
5: 5 We belong *n* to darkness nor to night;
Heb 10: 8 offerings, you *n* desired nor delighted in."
Rv 3:15 I know you are *n* hot nor cold.
3:16 because you are lukewarm, *n* hot nor cold,
9:21 *N* did they repent of their murders or

NEKODA (4)

Ezr 2:48 sons of Reaiah, sons of Rezin, sons of *N*,
2:60 sons of Delaiah, sons of Tobiah, sons of *N*,
Neh 7:50 sons of Reaiah, sons of Rezin, sons of *N*,
7:62 sons of Delaiah, sons of Tobiah, sons of *N*,

NEMUEL (3)

Gn 46:10 *N*, Jamin, Ohad, Jachin, Zohar,
Nm 26:12 through *N* the clan of the Nemuelites,
1Chr 4:24 The sons of Simeon were *N*,

NEMUELITES (1)

Nm 26:12 through Nemuel the clan of the *N*,

NEPHEG (4)

Ex 6:21 The sons of Izhar were Korah, *N*,
2Sm 5:15 Nathan, Solomon, Ibhar, Elishua, *N*,
1Chr 3: 7 Ibhar, Elishua, Eliphelet, Nogah, *N*,
14: 6 Ibhar, Elishua, Elpelet, Nogah, *N*,

NEPHEW (5)

Gn 14:12 their way, taking with them Abram's *n* Lot,
14:14 Abram heard that his *n* had been captured,
Tb 1:22 He was a close relative—in fact, my *n*.
11:18 *n* Nadab also came to rejoice with Tobit.
Est 2:15 and adopted daughter of his *n* Mordecai,

NEPHEW'S (1)

2Chr 22: 8 the *n* of Ahaziah who were his attendants,

NEPHILIM (1)

Gn 6: 4 the *N* appeared on earth (as well as later),

NEPHTHAR (1)

2Mc 1:36 and his companions called the liquid *n*,

NEPHTOAH (2)

Jos 15: 9 it ran to the fountain of waters of *N*,
18:15 and projected to the spring at *N*.

NEPHUSITES (2)

Ezr 2:50 sons of the Meunites, sons of the *N*,
Neh 7:52 sons of the Meunites, sons of the *N*,

NER (16)

1Sm 14:50 son of Saul's uncle, *N*;
14:51 Kish, Saul's father, and *N*,
26: 5 the spot where Saul and Abner, son of *N*,
26:13 at a great distance from Abner, son of *N*,
2Sm 2: 8 Abner, son of *N*, Saul's general, took
2:12 Now Abner, son of *N*,
3:23 he was informed, "Abner, son of *N*,
3:29 for the death of Abner, son of *N*,
3:37 no part in the killing of Abner, son of *N*.
1Kgs 2: 5 of Israel's armies, Abner, son of *N*,
2:32 Abner, son of *N*, general of Israel's army,
1Chr 8:30 son, Abdon, and Zur, Kish, Baal, *N*,
8:33 *N* became the father of Kish,
9:36 then came Zur, Kish, Baal, *N*,
9:39 *N* became the father of Kish,
26:28 seer, Saul, son of Kish, Abner, son of *N*,

NEREUS (1)

Rom 16:15 Philologus and Julia, to *N* and his sister,

NERGAL (1)

2Kgs 17:30 the men of Cuth made *N*;

NERGAL-SHAREZER (2)

Jer 39: 3 *N*, of Simmagir,
39:13 Nebushazban, the high dignitary, and *N*,

NERI (1)

Lk 3:27 of Zerubbabel, son of Shealtiel, son of *N*,

NERIAH (11)

Jer 32:12 of purchase I gave to Baruch, son of *N*,
32:16 the deed of purchase to Baruch, son of *N*,
36: 4 So Jeremiah called Baruch, son of *N*,
36: 8 Baruch, son of *N*, did everything the
36:14 Scroll in hand, Baruch, son of *N*,
36:32 it to his secretary, Baruch, son of *N*;
43: 3 It is Baruch, son of *N*, who stirs you up
43: 6 the prophet, and Baruch, son of *N*.
45: 1 prophet Jeremiah gave to Baruch, son of *N*,
51:59 the prophet Jeremiah to Seraiah, son of *N*,
Bar 1: 1 of the scroll which Baruch, son of *N*,

NEST (16)

Nm 24:21 O smith, and your *n* is set on a cliff;
Dt 22: 6 a bird's *n* with young birds or eggs in it,
Jb 29:18 "In my own *n* I shall grow old;
39:27 up at your command to build his *n* aloft?
Ps(s) 84: 4 swallow a *n* in which she puts her young
Prv 27: 8 its *n* is a man who is far from his home.
Sir 14:26 Who builds his *n* in her leafage,
27: 9 Birds *n* with their own kind,
36:27 Or a man who has no *n*,
Is 10:14 has seized like a *n* the riches of nations;
34:15 There the hoot owl shall *n* and lay eggs,
Jer 22:23 who dwell on Lebanon, who *n* in the cedars,
49:16 Though you build your *n* high as the eagle,
Ob 1: 4 eagle, and your *n* be set among the stars,
Hb 2: 9 setting his *n* on high to escape the reach
Mt 23:33 Vipers' *n!* Brood of serpents'

NESTED (3)

Ez 31: 6 In its boughs *n* all the birds of the air,
Dn 4: 9 in its branches the birds of the air *n*;
Lk 13:19 and the birds of the air *n* in its branches."

NESTLINGS (2)

Dt 32:11 its *n* forth by hovering over its brood,
Is 16: 2 Like flushed birds, like startled *n*,

NESTS (6)

Ps(s) 104:17 In them the birds build their *n*;
Jer 48:28 that *n* out of reach on the edge of a chasm.
Mt 8:20 have lairs, the birds in the sky have *n*,
13:32 sky come and build their *n* in its branches."
Mk 4:32 birds of the sky to build *n* in its shade."
Lk 9:58 have lairs, the birds of the sky have *n*,

NET (30)

1Sm 19:13 putting a *n* of goat's hair at its head and
19:16 bed, with the *n* of goat's hair at its head.
Jb 18: 8 For he rushes headlong into a *n*,
19: 6 me, and compassed me round with his *n*.
Ps(s) 10: 9 the afflicted and drags them off in his *n*.
57: 7 They have prepared a *n* for my feet;
69:23 before them, and a *n* for their friends.
140: 6 They have spread cords for a *n*;
141:10 all the wicked fall, each into his own *n*,
Prv 1:17 a *n* is spread before the eyes of any bird
7:22 Like a stag that minces toward the *n*,
29: 5 neighbor is spreading a *n* under his feet.
Eccl 9:12 own time than fish taken in the fatal *n*,
Sir 9:13 stepping among snares and walking over a *n*.
Is 51:20 every street corner like antelopes in a *n*.
Lam 1:13 He spread a *n* for my feet,
Ez 12:13 But I will spread my *n* over him,
17:20 I will spread my *n* over him,
19: 8 They spread their *n* to take him,
32: 3 *n* over you [with a host of many nations],
Hos 5: 1 snare at Mizpah, and a *n* spread over Tabor.
7:12 as they go I will spread my *n* around them,
Hb 1:15 his hook, he hauls them away with his *n*,
1:16 Therefore he sacrifices to his *n*,
Mt 4:18 brother Andrew, casting a *n* into the sea.
Jn 21: 6 "Cast your *n* off to the starboard side,"
21: 6 so many fish they could not haul the *n* in.
21: 8 in the boat, towing the *n* full of fish.
21:11 ashore the *n* loaded with sizable fish
21:11 of the great number, the *n* was not torn.

NETAIM (1)

1Chr 4:23 potters and inhabitants of *N* and Gederah,

NETHANEL (14)

Nm 1: 8 *N*, son of Zuar; from Zebulun:
2: 5 the tribe of Issachar [Their prince was *N*,
7:18 On the second day *N*,
7:23 This was the offering of *N*, son of Zuar.
10:15 of Amminadab, was over their host, and *N*,
1Chr 2:14 the second son, Shimea, the third, *N*,
15:24 The priests, Shebaniah, Joshaphat, *N*,
24: 6 The scribe Shemaiah, son of *N*,
26: 4 Joah, the third, Sachar, the fourth, *N*,
2Chr 17: 7 Obadiah, Zechariah, *N* and Micaiah,
35: 9 Conaniah and his brothers Shemaiah, *N*,
Ezr 10:22 Elioenai, Maaseiah, Ishmael, *N*,
Neh 12:21 for Jedaiah, *N*.
12:36 Azarel, Milalai, Gilalai, Maai, *N*,

NETHANIAH (21)

2Kgs 25:23 Ishmael, son of *N*, Johanan, son of
25:25 in the seventh month Ishmael, son of *N*,
1Chr 25: 2 Zaccur, Joseph, *N*, and Asharelah, sons
25:12 The fifth was *N*, his sons, and his brethren:
2Chr 17: 8 them he sent the Levites, Shemaiah, *N*,
Jer 36:14 the princes sent Jehudi, son of *N*,
40: 8 Ishmael, son of *N*; Johanan, son of Kareah;
40:14 the Ammonites, had sent Ishmael, son of *N*,
40:15 "Let me go and kill Ishmael, son of *N*;
41: 1 In the seventh month Ishmael, son of *N*,
41: 2 at table in Mizpah, Ishmael, son of *N*,
41: 6 Ishmael son of *N*, went out from Mizpah
41: 7 once inside the city, Ishmael, son of *N*,
41: 9 this cistern Ishmael, son of *N*,
41:10 Ishmael, son of *N*, led away the remnant
41:10 With these captives, Ishmael, son of *N*,
41:11 heard of the crimes Ishmael, son of *N*,
41:12 and set out to attack Ishmael, son of *N*.
41:15 But Ishmael, son of *N*,
41:16 their guardians, whom Ishmael, son of *N*,
41:18 the Chaldeans, because Ishmael, son of *N*,

NETHER (93)

Gn 37:35 go down mourning to my son in the *n* world.
42:38 my white head down to the *n* world in grief."
44:29 my white head down to the *n* world in grief.'
44:31 of our father down to the *n* world in grief.
Nm 16:30 swallows them alive down into the *n* world,
16:33 to the *n* world with all belonging to them;
Dt 32:22 shall rage to the depths of the *n* world,
1Sm 2: 6 he casts down to the *n* world;
2Sm 22: 6 The cords of the *n* world enmeshed me,
Tb 3:10 go down to the *n* world laden with sorrow.
4:19 to the deepest recesses of the *n* world.
13: 2 he casts down to the depths of the *n* world,
Est B: 7 *n* world by a violent death on a single day,
Jb 7: 9 down to the *n* world shall come up no more.
11: 8 It is deeper than the *n* world;
14:13 that you would hide me in the *n* world and
17:13 If I look for the *n* world as my dwelling,
17:16 Will they descend with me into the *n* world?
21:13 and tranquilly go down to the *n* world.
26: 6 Naked before him is the *n* world,
Ps(s) 6: 6 in the *n* world who gives you thanks?
9:18 To the *n* world the wicked shall turn back,
16:10 will not abandon my soul to the *n* world,
18: 6 The cords of the *n* world enmeshed me,
30: 4 LORD, you brought me up from the *n* world;
31:18 them be reduced to silence in the *n* world.
49:15 sheep they are herded into the *n* world;
49:15 the *n* world is their palace.
49:16 the power of the *n* world by receiving me.
55:16 let them go down alive to the *n* world,
86:13 rescued me from the depths of the *n* world.
88: 4 and my life draws near to the *n* world.
89:49 himself from the power of the *n* world?
116: 3 the snares of the *n* world seized upon me;
139: 8 if I sink to the *n* world,
141: 7 are strewn by the edge of the *n* world.
Prv 1:12 us swallow them up, as the *n* world does,
5: 5 to death, to the *n* world her steps attain;
7:27 house is made up of ways to the *n* world,
9:18 the depths of the *n* world are her guests!
15:11 The *n* world and the abyss lie open before
15:24 that he may avoid the *n* world below.
23:14 and you will save him from the *n* world.
27:20 *n* world and the abyss are never satisfied;
30:16 The *n* world, and the barren womb;
Eccl 9:10 wisdom in the *n* world where you are going.
Sg 8: 6 relentless as the *n* world is devotion;
Wis 1:14 nor any domain of the *n* world on earth,
2: 1 known to have come back from the *n* world.
16:13 you lead down to the gates of the *n* world,
17:14 from the recesses of a powerless *n* world,
Sir 14:16 in the *n* world there are no joys to seek.
17:22 Who in the *n* world can glorify the Most
21:10 that end in the depths of the *n* world.
28:21 besides which even the *n* world is a gain;
41: 4 in the *n* world he has no claim on life.
48: 5 a dead man back to life from the *n* world,
51: 2 of the *n* world you have snatched my feet;
51: 5 fire, from the deep belly of the *n* world;
51: 6 soul was nearing the depths of the *n* world;
51: 9 very earth, from the gates of the *n* world,
Is 5:14 Therefore the *n* world enlarges its throat
7:11 let it be deep as the *n* world,
14: 9 The *n* world below is all astir preparing
14:11 Down to the *n* world your pomp is brought,
14:15 *n* world you go to the recesses of the pit!
28:15 and with the *n* world we have made a pact;
28:18 your pact with the *n* world shall not stand.
38:10 To the gates of the *n* world I shall be
38:18 is not the *n* world that gives you thanks,
57: 9 far away, down even to the *n* world.
Bar 2:17 it is not the dead in the *n* world,
3:11 with those destined for the *n* world?

NETHER (cont.)

3:19 They have vanished down into the *n* world,
Ez 26:20 and I will make you dwell in the *n* lands,
31:15 *n* world I made the abyss close up over him;
31:16 when I cast him down to the *n* world with
31:17 too have come down with him to the *n* world,
32:20 Then from the midst of the *n* world,
32:27 to the *n* world with their weapons of war,
Dn 3:88 For he has delivered us from the *n* world,
Hos 13:14 deliver them from the power of the *n* world?
13:14 where is your sting, O *n* world!
Am 9: 2 Though they break through to the *n* world,
Jon 2: 3 the midst of the *n* world I cried for help,
2: 7 the *n* world were closing behind me forever,
Hb 2: 5 who opens wide his throat like the *n* world,
Acts 2:27 will not abandon my soul to the *n* world,
2:31 that he was not abandoned to the *n* world,
Rv 1:18 I hold the keys of death and the *n* world.
6: 8 Death, and the *n* world was in his train.
20:13 death and the *n* world gave up their dead.
20:14 *n* world were hurled into the pool of fire,

NETOPHA (1)

Jer 40: 8 the sons of Ephai of *N*;

NETOPHAH (7)

2Sm 23:28 Maharai from *N*;
23:29 Heled, son of Baanah, from *N*;
1Chr 11:30 *N*; Heled, son of Baanah, from Netophah;
27:13 for the tenth month, was Maharai from *N*,
Ezr 2:22 men of *N*, fifty-six;
Neh 7:26 men of Bethlehem and *N*,

NETOPHATHITE (2)

2Kgs 25:23 of Kareah, Seraiah, son of Tanhumeth the *N*,
1Chr 27:15 for the twelfth month, was Heldai the *N*,

NETOPHATHITES (3)

1Chr 2:54 of Salma were Bethlehem, the *N*,
9:16 family lived in the villages of the *N*.
Neh 12:28 Jerusalem, from the villages of the *N*,

NETS (13)

Is 19: 8 their *n* in the water shall pine away.
Ez 26: 5 drying place for *n* in the midst of the sea.
26:14 a drying place for *n* shall you be.
47:10 to En-eglaim, spreading their *n* there.
Mt 4:20 abandoned their *n* and became his followers.
4:21 getting their *n* in order with their father,
Mk 1:16 Andrew casting their *n* into the sea;
1:18 abandoned their *n* and became his followers.
1:19 in their boat putting their *n* in order.
Lk 5: 2 had disembarked and were washing their *n*.
5: 4 deep water and lower your *n* for a catch."
5: 5 but if you say so, I will lower the *n*."
5: 6 that their *n* were at the breaking point.

NETTED (1)

Lk 19:18 'Your investment, my lord, has *n* you five.'

NETTING (1)

Jdt 10:21 a canopy with a *n* of crimson and gold,

NETTLES (4)

Jb 30: 7 under the *n* they huddled together.
Prv 24:31 its surface was covered with *n*,
Is 55:13 the cypress shall grow, instead of *n*,
Zep 2: 9 of *n* and a salt pit and a waste forever.

NETWORK (13)

Ex 27: 4 Make a grating of bronze *n* for it;
27: 5 This *n* is to be half as high as the altar.
38: 4 A grating of bronze *n* was made for the
1Kgs 7:17 Two pieces of *n* with a chainlike mesh were
7:18 the piece of *n* on each of the two capitals.
7:20 level of the nodes and their enveloping *n*.
7:41 two pieces of *n* covering the nodes for the
7:42 both pieces of *n* that covered the two nodes
2Kgs 25:17 *n* with pomegranates encircled the capital,
25:17 so for the other pillar, as regards the *n*.
2Chr 4:13 with two rows of pomegranates to each *n*,
Jer 52:22 *n* with pomegranates encircled the capital,
52:23 a hundred pomegranates, all around the *n*.

NETWORKS (2)

2Chr 4:12 and two *n* covering the nodes of the
4:13 four hundred pomegranates for the two *n*,

NEVER (383)

Gn 8:21 *N* again will I doom the earth because of
9:11 that *n* again shall all bodily creatures be
9:15 so that the waters shall *n* again become a
19: 8 who have *n* had intercourse with men.
21:26 "In fact, you *n* told me about it,
24: 6 *N* take my son back there for any reason,"
24: 8 But *n* take my son back there!"
28:15 I will *n* leave you until I have done what
31:38 I have *n* feasted on a ram of your flock.
31:39 I *n* brought you an animal torn by wild
38:21 has *n* been a temple prostitute here."
41:19 *N* have I seen such ugly specimens as these
42:11 your servants have *n* been spies."
42:31 we have *n* been spies.
48:11 "I *n* expected to see your face again,
49:10 The scepter shall *n* depart from Judah,
Ex 4:10 you please, Lord, I have *n* been eloquent,
9:18 such fierce hail as there has *n* been in Egypt
9:24 such fierce hail as had *n* been seen in the
10:14 *N* before had there been such a fierce
10:29 I will *n* appear before you again."
11: 6 the land of Egypt, such as has *n* been,
14:13 whom you see today you will *n* see again.
23: 8 *N* take a bribe,
23:13 *N* mention the name of any other god;
25:15 in the rings of the ark and *n* be withdrawn.
34:10 work such marvels as have *n* been wrought
Nm 16:15 I have *n* taken a single ass from them,
Dt 2: 7 been with you, and you have *n* been in want.'
13:12 *n* again do such evil as this in your midst.
13:17 a heap of ruins forever, *n* to be rebuilt.
15:11 The needy will *n* be lacking in the land;
17:13 it, shall fear, and *n* again be so insolent.
17:16 that you must *n* go back that way again.
19:20 and *n* again do a thing so evil among you.
20: 6 a vineyard and *n* yet enjoyed its fruits?
21: 3 take a heifer that has *n* been put to work
23: 7 *N* promote their peace and prosperity as
28:66 day and night, *n* sure of your existence.
28:68 I told you that you were *n* to see again;
29:19 the LORD will *n* consent to pardon him.
31: 6 he will *n* fail you or forsake you."
31: 8 you and will *n* fail you or forsake you.
32:17 of whom their fathers had *n* stood in awe.
Jos 10:14 *N* before or since was there a day like this,
Jgs 2: 1 that I would *n* break my covenant with you,
1Sm 2:32 there shall *n* be an old man in your family.
4: 7 This has *n* happened before.
4:20 standing around her said to her, *N* fear!
7:13 *n* again to enter the territory of Israel,
15:35 *N* again, as long as he lived, did Samuel
17:39 however, since he had *n* tried armor before.
17:39 these, because I have *n* tried them before."
20:15 *n* withdraw your kindness from my house.
20:16 The name of Jonathan must *n* be allowed by
2Sm 3:29 May the men of Joab's family *n* be without
12:10 the sword shall *n* depart from your house,
1Kgs 1: 6 Yet his father *n* rebuked him or asked why
3:12 there has *n* been anyone like you up to now,
10:10 *N* again did anyone bring such an abundance
2Kgs 2:21 *N* again shall death or miscarriage spring
18: 6 the LORD, Hezekiah *n* turned away from him,
25:16 the house of the LORD, was *n* calculated.
1Chr 17: 5 For I have *n* dwelt in a house,
2Chr 1:12 and glory, such as kings before you *n* had,
7:18 'There shall *n* be lacking someone of yours
Ezr 9:12 *N* promote their peace and prosperity;
Neh 2: 1 As I had *n* before been sad in his presence,
4: 4 *N* shall we be able the wall to rebuild."
6: 9 in the work, and it will *n* be completed."
Tb 2: 8 "Will this man *n* learn!
3: 9 May we *n* see a son or daughter of yours!"
3:13 the earth, *n* again to hear such insults.
3:15 And that I have *n* defiled my own name or
3:15 *n* again let me hear these insults!"
4:19 and *n* let them be erased from your heart.
6:18 flee and *n* again show himself near her.
10:13 *N* cause her grief at any time in your life.
Jdt 8:13 will you *n* understand anything?
11: 1 *N* have I harmed anyone who chose to serve
13:19 Your deed of hope will *n* be forgotten by
Est C:28 have *n* eaten at the table of Haman,
9:28 were *n* to fall into disuse among the Jews,
1Mc 6:36 it moved, they moved too and *n* left it.
9:71 He swore an oath to him that he would *n*
9:72 and *n* came into their territory again.
12:11 have *n* ceased to remember you in the
2Mc 1: 5 and *n* forsake you in time of adversity.
6:16 He *n* withdraws his mercy from us.
6:26 I avoid the punishment of men, I shall *n*,
7: 8 language of his forefathers, he said, *N!*"
10: 4 might *n* again fall into such misfortunes,
15:36 decreed *n* to let this day pass unobserved,
Jb 3:16 like babes that have *n* seen the light?
8:18 "I have *n* seen you!"
10:19 I should be as though I had *n* lived;
21:25 of soul, having *n* tasted happiness.
Ps(s) 1: 3 in due season, and whose leaves *n* fade.
10:11 he hides his face, he *n* sees."
14: 4 Will all these evildoers *n* learn,
15: 5 who does these things shall *n* be disturbed.
30: 7 security, I said, "I shall *n* be disturbed."
31: 2 let me *n* be put to shame.
49: 9 he would *n* have enough to remain alive
49:20 his forebears who shall *n* more see light.
53: 5 Will all these evildoers *n* learn,
55:12 and fraud *n* depart from its streets.
55:23 *n* will he permit the just man to be
58: 9 like an untimely birth that *n* sees the sun.
71: 1 let me *n* be put to shame.
112: 6 He shall *n* be moved;
119:93 *N* will I forget your precepts,
140:11 he cast them into the depths, *n* to rise.
Prv 3:23 your foot will *n* stumble;
4:13 Hold fast to instruction, *n* let her go;
10:30 The just man will *n* be disturbed,
12: 3 the root of the just will *n* be disturbed.
17:12 of her cubs, but *n* a fool in his folly!
25:14 who boastfully promises what he *n* gives.
27:20 nether world and the abyss are *n* satisfied;
28:21 To show partiality is *n* good:
30:15 things are never satisfied, four *n* say,
30:16 never saturated with water, and fire, that *n*
Eccl 1: 7 to the sea, yet *n* does the sea become full.
5: 9 The covetous man is *n* satisfied with money,
7:20 on earth so just as to do good and *n* sin.
9: 6 They will *n* again have part in anything
11: 4 and one who watches the clouds will *n* reap.
Sg 7: 3 bowl that should *n* lack for mixed wine.
Wis 7:10 the splendor of her *n* yields to sleep.
10: 7 desert, Plants bearing fruit that *n* ripens,
12:10 And that their dispositions would *n* change;
15:17 he at least lives, but *n* they.
Sir 4:25 *N* gainsay the truth,
7:13 lie after lie, for it *n* results in good.
7:36 your last days, and you will *n* sin.
11:10 you run after it, you will *n* overtake it;
12:10 *N* trust your enemy,
12:16 he will *n* have enough of your blood.
13:13 take care *n* to accompany men of violence.
17:23 give praise than those who have *n* lived;
19: 6 *N* repeat gossip,
21:12 He can *n* be taught who is not shrewd,
23:11 the scourge will *n* be far from his house.
23:12 may they *n* be heard among Jacob's heirs.
23:14 By wishing you had *n* been born or cursing
23:15 *n* mature in character as long as he lives.
23:16 who *n* stops until the fire breaks forth;
23:17 is sweet and who is *n* through till he dies;
23:26 her disgrace will *n* be blotted out.
24:21 put to shame, he who serves me will *n* fail."
24:26 first man *n* finished comprehending wisdom,
27:16 trusted, he will *n* find an intimate friend.
33:30 But *n* lord it over any human being,
34:10 One *n* put to the proof knows little,
34:14 fears the LORD is never alarmed, *n* afraid;
39: 9 his fame can *n* be effaced;
40:17 But goodness will *n* be cut off,
41:11 but a virtuous name will *n* be annihilated.
43:10 their place and *n* relax in their vigils.
44:13 endure, their glory will *n* be blotted out;
44:18 him, that *n* should all flesh be destroyed.
51:19 burned with desire for her, *n* turning back.
51:19 with her, *n* weary of extolling her.
51:20 such that I will *n* forsake her.
Is 13:20 She shall *n* be inhabited,
14:20 you will *n* be one with them in the grave."
24:20 it down, until it falls, *n* to rise again."
33: 1 destroyer *n* destroyed, O traitor never
33:20 be struck, Whose pegs will *n* be pulled up,
34:10 *n* again shall anyone pass through her.
43:17 they lie prostrate together, *n* to rise,
44:21 O Israel, by me you shall *n* be forgotten:
45:17 You shall *n* be put to shame or disgrace in
47: 8 I shall *n* be a widow,
48:19 *n* cut off or blotted out from my presence.
49:15 should she forget, I will *n* forget you.
49:23 who hope in me shall *n* be disappointed.
51: 6 forever and my justice shall *n* be dismayed.
54: 9 of Noah should *n* again deluge the earth;
54:10 My love shall *n* leave you nor my covenant
57:10 worn out by your many misdeeds, you *n* said,
58:11 garden, like a spring whose water *n* fails.
59:21 into your mouth Shall *n* leave your mouth,
62: 6 *N*, by day or by night, shall they be
66:19 coastlands that have *n* heard of my fame,
Jer 3:19 I thought, and *n* cease following me.
7:31 a thing as I *n* commanded or had in mind.
20:14 day my mother gave me birth *n* be blessed!
22:10 *n* again will he see the land of his birth.
22:11 He has left this place *n* to return.
22:30 who will *n* thrive in his lifetime!
25:27 fall, *n* to rise,
31:12 gardens, *n* again shall they languish.
31:40 *N* again shall the city be rooted up or
32:35 this I *n* commanded them,
32:40 covenant, *n* to cease doing good to them;
32:40 fear of me, that they may *n* depart from me.
33:17 *N* shall David lack a successor on the
35:19 *N* shall there fail to be a descendant of
42:18 and you shall *n* see this place again.
42:19 can *n* say that I did not warn you this day.
46:28 You, my servant Jacob, *n* fear,
50: 5 covenant everlasting, *n* to be forgotten."
50:39 *N* again shall it be peopled,
51:39 overcome with perpetual sleep, *n* to awaken,
51:57 they sleep an eternal sleep, *n* to awaken,
51:64 *N* shall she rise,
Ez 4:14 *N* have I been made unclean,
4:14 *n* have I eaten carrion flesh or that torn
4:14 *n* has any unclean meat entered my mouth."
5: 9 *n* done before, the like of which I will *n*
12:23 they shall *n* quote it again in Israel.
16:41 and you shall *n* again give payment.
20:32 What you are thinking of shall *n* happen:

20:39 and *n* again profane my holy name with your
26:14 *N* shall you be rebuilt,
26:20 so that you may *n* return to take your
26:21 you shall be sought, but *n* again found,
29:15 *n* more to set itself above the nations.
35: 5 *n* let die your hatred for the Israelites,
36:12 *N* again shall you rob them of their
36:14 *n* again shall you devour men or rob your
37:22 *N* again shall they be two nations, and *n*
43: 7 *N* again shall they and their kings profane
Dn 2:10 *n* has any king,
2:44 set up a kingdom that shall *n* be destroyed
11:24 which his fathers or grandfathers *n* did;
13:27 for *n* had any such thing been said about
14: 7 it has *n* taken any food or drink."
14:35 answered, "Babylon, sir, I have *n* seen,
Hos 2:18 me "My husband," and *n* again "My baal."
Am 7:12 but *n* again prophesy in Bethel;
8: 7 *N* will I forget a thing they have done!
8:14 those shall fall, *n* to rise again.
9:15 *n* again shall they be plucked From the
Na 1: 3 the LORD *n* leaves the guilty unpunished.
3: 1 full of plunder, whose looting *n* stops!
Hb 1: 4 is benumbed, and judgment is *n* rendered:
Zec 10: 6 shall be as though I had *n* cast them off,
14:11 *N* again shall she be doomed;
Mt 4: 6 you that you may *n* stumble on a stone.'"
7:16 or figs from prickly plants? *N!*
7:23 declare to them solemnly, 'I *n* knew you.
8:10 I have *n* found this much faith in Israel.
18:10 you *n* despise one of these little ones.
21:16 Did you *n* read this:
21:19 to it, *N* again shall you produce fruit!";
21:29 but he *n* went.
21:42 them, "Did you *n* read in the Scriptures,
26:24 Better for him if he had *n* been born."
26:33 in you shaken, mine will *n* be shaken!"
26:35 have to die with you, I will *n* disown you."
26:55 temple precincts, yet you *n* arrested me.
Mk 2:12 "We have *n* seen anything like this!"
2:25 "Have you *n* read what David did when he
3:29 against the Holy Spirit will *n* be forgiven.
7: 3 *n* eat without scrupulously washing
7: 4 they *n* eat anything from the market
9:25 Get out of him and *n* enter him again!"
9:48 dies not and the fire is *n* extinguished.'
11:14 *N* again shall anyone eat of your fruit!"
14:21 It were better for him had he *n* been born."
14:25 I will *n* again drink of the fruit of the
14:49 temple precincts, yet you *n* arrested me.
Lk 1:15 He will *n* drink wine or strong drink,
4:11 you, that you may *n* stumble on a stone.'"
7: 9 *n* found so much faith among the Israelites."
12:10 the Holy Spirit will *n* be forgiven.
15:29 *n* disobeyed one of your orders, yet you *n*
19:21 You withdraw what you *n* deposited.
19:21 You reap what you *n* sowed.'
19:22 I never deposited, reaping what I *n* sowed!
22:32 prayed for you that your faith may *n* fail.
22:53 the temple you *n* raised a hand against me.
23:29 never bore and the breasts that *n* nursed.'
Jn 4:14 the water I give him will *n* be thirsty;
5:37 have never heard, his form you have *n* seen,
6:50 from heaven for a man to eat and *n* die.
8:33 *N* have we been slaves to anyone.
8:44 and has *n* based himself on truth;
8:51 is true to my word he shall *n* see death."
8:52 man shall *n* know death if he keeps my word.'
9:33 God, he could *n* have done such a thing."
10:28 them eternal life, and they shall *n* perish.
10:41 "John may *n* have performed a sign,"
11:21 been here, my brother would *n* have died.
11:26 is alive and believes in me will *n* die.
11:32 had been here my brother would *n* have died.
13: 8 Peter replied, "You shall *n* wash my feet!"
16: 7 to go, the Paraclete will *n* come to you,
16:32 (Yet I can *n* be alone;
20:25 "I will *n* believe it without probing the
21:23 Jesus *n* told him, as a matter of fact,
Acts 4:17 give them a stern warning *n* to mention
5:42 they *n* stopped teaching and proclaiming
6:13 "This man *n* stops making statements
8:24 what you have just said may *n* happen to me."
10:14 I have *n* eaten anything unclean or impure
13:10 Will you *n* stop trying to make crooked the
13:34 dead would *n* again see the decay of death,
13:38 *n* be acquitted of under the law of Moses.
13:41 which you *n* would have believed
14: 8 sit crippled, *n* having walked in his life.
20:20 *N* did I shrink from telling you what was
20:27 for I have *n* shrunk from announcing to you
20:31 I *n* ceased warning you individually even
20:33 *N* did I set my heart on anyone's silver or
20:38 hear that they would *n* see his face again.
28:26 listen carefully yet you will *n* understand;
28:26 you may look intently yet you will *n* see.
Rom 4:20 he *n* questioned or doubted God's promise;
6: 9 raised from the dead, will *n* die again;
7: 7 I should *n* have known what evil desire was
12:17 *N* repay injury with injury.
13:10 Love *n* wrongs the neighbor,
15:20 It has been a point of honor with me *n* to
15:21 and they who have *n* heard will understand."
1Cor 2: 8 would *n* have crucified the Lord of glory.
7:18 come to another who had *n* been circumsized?
8: 2 means he has *n* really known it as he ought.
8:13 my brother to sin I will *n* eat meat again,
13: 5 Love is *n* rude,
13: 8 Love *n* fails.
2Cor 1:10 hope in him who will *n* cease to deliver us.
1:13 We *n* write anything that you cannot read
1:19 he was *n* anything but "yes."
4: 8 full of doubts, we *n* despair.
4: 9 *n* abandoned; we are struck down but *n*
Gal 4:30 for the slave girl's son shall *n* be an heir
5:26 Let us *n* be boastful, or challenging,
6:14 May I *n* boast of anything but the cross of
Eph 1:16 I have *n* stopped thanking God for you and
4:29 *N* let evil talk pass your lips;
Phil 1:20 I shall *n* be put to shame for my hopes;
2: 3 *N* act out of rivalry or conceit;
Col 2: 1 others who have *n* seen me in the flesh.
1Thes 5:17 Rejoice always, *n* cease praying,
2Thes 3:13 must *n* grow weary of doing what is right,
1Tm 5: 1 *N* censure an older man, but appeal to him
5:22 *N* lay hands hastily on anyone,
2Tm 1: 8 *n* be ashamed of your testimony to our Lord,
3: 7 *n* able to reach a knowledge of the truth.
4: 2 constantly teaching and *n* losing patience.
Heb 3:10 of erring heart, and have *n* known my ways.'
3:11 my anger, 'They shall *n* enter into my rest.'"
4: 3 They shall *n* enter into my rest.'"
4: 5 says, "They shall *n* enter into my rest."
4:15 in every way that we are, yet *n* sinned.
9: 9 sacrifices are offered that can *n* make perfect
10: 1 it was *n* able to perfect the worshipers by
10:11 same sacrifices which can *n* take away sins.
13: 5 for God has said, "I will *n* desert you,
Jas 1: 6 Yet he must ask in faith, *n* doubting,
1:17 cannot change and who is *n* shadowed over.
1Pt 1: 8 Although you have *n* seen him,
2Pt 1:10 surely those who do so will *n* be lost.
1:21 has *n* been put forward by man's willing it.
1Jn 1:10 If we say, "We have *n* sinned,"
3: 1 us is that it *n* recognized the Son.
3Jn 1:11 whoever does what is evil has *n* seen God.
Rv 2:11 shall *n* be harmed by the second death.'
3: 5 I will *n* erase his name from the book of
3:12 temple of my God and he shall *n* leave it.
7:16 *N* again shall they know hunger or thirst,
14: 4 *n* been defiled by immorality with women.
16:18 Such was its violence that there has *n*
18: 7 widow am I, and *n* will I go into mourning!'
18:14 you shall *n* find them again!"
20: 4 those who had *n* worshiped the beast or its
21:25 During the day its gates shall *n* be shut,

NEVER-ENDING (1)

2Pt 2:14 for a woman, theirs is a *n* search for sin.

NEVER-FAILING (3)

2Mc 7:36 enduring brief pain, have drunk of *n* life,
Jb 12:19 and lets their *n* waters flow away.
Lk 12:33 a *n* treasure with the Lord which no thief

NEVERMORE (5)

Ps(s) 77: 8 the Lord reject forever and *n* be favorable?
Jl 2:26 my people shall *n* be put to shame.
2:27 my people shall *n* be put to shame.
Na 2: 1 *n* shall you be invaded by the scoundrel;
Rv 18:21 like this, with violence, and *n* be found!

NEVERTHELESS (27)

Gn 17:19 *N*, your wife Sarah is to bear you a son,
48:19 *N*, his younger brother shall surpass him,
Lv 25:54 not thus redeemed, he shall *n* be released,
Nm 14:22 and who *n* have put me to the test ten
1Sm 20: 3 *N*, as the LORD lives and as you live,
1Kgs 22:44 *N*, the high places did not disappear,
2Kgs 12: 7 *N*, as late as the twenty-third year of the
13: 6 *N*, they did not desist from the sins which
15:35 *N* the high places did not disappear and
1Chr 11: 5 David *n* captured the fortress of Zion,
2Chr 30:11 *N*, some from Asher,
30:18 *N* they ate the Passover,
32:31 *N*, in respect to the ambassadors [princes]
Jdt 3: 8 *N*, he devastated their whole territory and
2Mc 9:23 *N*, I know that my father,
15: 5 *N* he did not succeed in carrying out his
Jer 3: 8 *n* her traitor sister Judah was not
40:16 *N*, Gedaliah, son of Ahikam,
Ez 20:15 *N* I swore to them in the desert not to
20:23 *N* I swore to them in the desert that I
Dn 1:10 the chief chamberlain, he *n* said to Daniel,
Lk 10:20 *N*, do not rejoice so much in the fact that
Acts 5:14 *N* more and more believers,
8:39 *N* the man went on his way rejoicing.
Gal 2:16 *N*, knowing that a man is not justified by
Rv 2:14 *N*, I hold a few matters against you:
2:20 *N* I hold this against you:

NEW (193)

Ex 1: 8 Then a *n* king,
Lv 2:14 the form of fresh grits of *n* ears of grain,
14:42 Then *n* stones shall be brought and put in
14:42 and *n* mortar shall be made and plastered
23:16 present the *n* cereal offering to the LORD.
26:10 to discard them to make room for the *n*.
Nm 16:30 But if the LORD does something entirely *n*,
18:12 the new oil and of the *n* wine and grain
18:27 threshing floor or *n* wine from the press.
28:14 *n* moon holocaust for every new moon
28:26 present to the LORD the *n* cereal offering,
29: 6 *n* moon holocaust with its cereal offering,
Dt 20: 5 *n* house and not yet had the house-warming?
22: 8 "When you build a *n* house,
Jos 9:13 which were *n* when we filled them,
Jgs 5: 8 mother in Israel, *N* gods were their choice;
15:13 *n* ropes and brought him up from the cliff.
16:11 "If they bind me tight with *n* ropes,
16:12 took *n* ropes and bound him with them.
1Sm 6: 7 So now set to work and make a *n* cart.
20: 5 "Tomorrow is the *n* moon,
20:18 "Tomorrow is the *n* moon;
20:24 On the day of the *n* moon,
2Sm 6: 3 The ark of God was placed on a *n* cart and
21:16 with a *n* sword and planned to kill David,
1Kgs 11:29 and the prophet was wearing a *n* cloak.
11:30 Ahijah took off his *n* cloak,
2Kgs 2:20 "Bring me a *n* bowl,"
4:23 "It is neither the *n* moon nor the sabbath."
16:14 the *n* altar and the temple of the LORD
1Chr 13: 7 God on a *n* cart from the house of Abinadab;
23:31 to the LORD on sabbaths, *n* moons,
2Chr 2: 3 and evening, and for the sabbaths, *n* moons,
8:13 particular on the sabbaths, at the *n* moons,
20: 5 the house of the LORD before the *n* court,
31: 3 those on sabbaths, *n* moons and festivals,
34:22 she dwelt in Jerusalem, in the *n* quarter.
Ezr 3: 5 the sacrifices prescribed for the *n* moons
9: 9 Thus he has given us a *n* life to raise
Neh 3: 6 *N* City Gate was repaired by Joiada,
10:34 daily holocaust, for the sabbaths, *n* moons,
12:39 past the Ephraim Gate [the *N* City Gate],
Jdt 8: 6 and sabbaths, *n* moon eves and new moons,
16: 1 Sing to him a *n* song,
16:13 "A *n* hymn I will sing to my God.
1Mc 4:47 and built a *n* altar like the former one.
4:49 *n* sacred vessels and brought the lampstand,
4:53 *n* altar of holocausts that they had made.
10:34 all feast days, sabbaths, *n* moon festivals,
10:88 events, he accorded *n* honors to Jonathan.
2Mc 2:29 As the architect of a *n* house must give
10: 3 purifying the temple, they made a *n* altar.
Jb 7:18 each *n* day and try him at every moment!
32:19 Like a *n* wineskin with wine under pressure,
Ps(s) 33: 3 Sing to him a *n* song;
40: 4 And he put a *n* song into my mouth,
73:14 day and chastisement with each *n* dawn.
80:19 give us *n* life,
81: 4 Blow the trumpet at the *n* moon,
96: 1 Sing to the LORD a *n* song;
98: 1 Sing to the LORD a *n* song,
144: 9 O God, I will sing a *n* song to you;
149: 1 Sing to the LORD a *n* song of praise in
Prv 3:10 grain, with *n* wine your vats will overflow.
Eccl 1: 9 Nothing is *n* under the sun.
1:10 thing of which we say, "See, this is *n!*"
Wis 19:11 later they saw also a *n* kind of bird when,
19:18 like strings of the harp, produce *n* melody,
Sir 9:10 old friend, for the *n* one cannot equal him.
9:10 A *n* friend is like new wine which you
24:23 the Tigris in the days of the *n* fruits.
36: 5 Give *n* signs and work new wonders;
49:10 Gave *n* strength to Jacob and saved him by
Is 1:13 *N* moon and sabbath,
1:14 Your *n* moons and festivals I detest;
15: 6 The grass is withered, *n* growth is gone,
41:15 make of you a threshing sledge, sharp, *n*,
42: 9 have come to pass, *n* ones I now foretell;
42:10 Sing to the LORD a *n* song,
43:19 See, I am doing something *n!*
47:13 at each *n* moon what would happen to you.
48: 6 From now on I announce *n* things to you,
57:10 *N* strength you found,
62: 2 *n* name pronounced by the mouth of the
65:17 about to create *n* heavens and a new earth;
66:22 As the new heavens and the *n* earth which I
66:23 From one *n* moon to another,
Jer 8:22 Why grows not *n* flesh over the wound of
26:10 at the *N* Gate of the house of the LORD.
31:22 LORD has created a *n* thing upon the earth:
31:31 when I will make a *n* covenant with the
36:10 at the entrance of the *N* Temple-Gate,
Ez 11:19 a *n* heart and put a new spirit within them;
18:31 for yourselves a *n* heart and a new spirit.
36:26 *n* heart and place a new spirit within you,
45:17 and libations on the feasts, *n* moons,
46: 1 on the day of the *n* moon it shall be open.
46: 3 of this gate on the sabbaths and *n* moons.
46: 6 On the day of the *n* moon he shall provide
Hos 2:13 to all her joy, her feasts, her *n* moons,
4:11 and *n* deprive my people of understanding.
5: 7 Now shall the *n* moon devour them together
9: 2 nourish them, the *n* wine shall fail them.
10:12 Break up for yourselves a *n* field,

NEW (cont.)

Jl 4:18 that day, the mountains shall drip *n* wine,
Am 8: 5 "When will the *n* moon be over,"
Zep 1:10 the Fish Gate, a wail from the *N* Quarter,
Zec 9:17 that makes the youths flourish, and *n* wine,
Mt 9:17 do not pour *n* wine into old wineskins.
9:17 No, they pour *n* wine into new wineskins,
13:52 from his storeroom both the *n* and the old."
19:28 in the *n* age when the Son of Man takes his
26:29 drink it *n* with you in my Father's reign."
27:60 in fresh linen and laid it in his own *n* tomb
Mk 1:27 *n* teaching in a spirit of authority!
2:21 the *n* from the old
2:22 no man pours *n* wine into old wineskins.
2:22 No, new wine is poured into *n* skins."
14:25 day when I drink it *n* in the reign of God."
16:17 they will speak entirely *n* languages,
Lk 5:36 a piece from a *n* coat to patch an old one.
5:36 If he does, he will only tear the *n* coat,
5:37 no one pours *n* wine into old wineskins.
5:37 do so, the *n* wine will burst the old skins,
5:38 *N* wine should be poured into fresh skins.
5:39 No one, after drinking old wine, wants *n*.
22:20 "This cup is the *n* covenant in my blood,
Jn 13:34 I give you a *n* commandment:
19:41 and in the garden a *n* tomb in which no one
Acts 2:13 a sneer, "They have had too much *n* wine!"
5:20 preach to the people all about this *n* life."
7:18 until a *n* king came to power in Egypt,
9: 2 or woman, living according to the *n* way.
17:19 what this *n* teaching is that you propose.
17:21 to tell about or listen to something *n*.)
18:25 and instructed in the *n* way of the Lord.
18:26 to him God's *n* way in greater detail.
19: 9 the *n* way in the presence of the assembly,
19:23 disturbance broke out concerning the *n* way.
22: 4 this *n* way to the point of death.
24:14 to you that it is according to the *n* way
24:22 was rather well informed about the *n* way,
27:36 This gave them *n* courage,
Rom 6: 4 of the Father, we too might live a *n* life.
7: 6 and we serve in the *n* spirit,
1Cor 11:25 "This cup is the *n* covenant in my blood.
2Cor 3: 6 us qualified ministers of a *n* covenant,
5:17 if anyone is in Christ, he is a *n* creation.
5:17 old order has passed away; now all is *n*!
Eph 2:15 to create in himself one *n* man from us who
4:24 put on that *n* man created in God's image,
Phil 3:21 He will give a *n* form to this lowly body
Col 2:13 God gave you *n* life in company with Christ.
3:10 with its past deeds and put on a *n* man,
1Tm 3: 6 He should not be a *n* convert,
2Tm 1:16 me *n* heart and has not been ashamed of me,
Ti 3: 5 of *n* birth and renewal by the Holy Spirit.
Heb
8: 8 when I will make a *n* covenant with the
8:13 When he says, "a *n* covenant,"
9:10 imposed until the time of the *n* order.
9:15 This is why he is mediator of a *n* covenant:
10:20 by the *n* and living path he has opened up
12:24 to Jesus, the mediator of a *n* covenant,
1Pt 1: 3 he who in his great mercy gave us *n* birth;
2Pt 3: 2 as well as the *n* command of the Lord and
3:13 await are *n* heavens and a new earth where,
1Jn 2: 7 it is no *n* commandment that I write to you,
2: 8 the commandment that I write you is *n*,
2Jn 1: 5 if I were writing you some *n* commandment;
Rv 2:17 stone upon which is inscribed a *n* name,
3:12 the *n* Jerusalem which he will send down
3:12 from heaven, and my own name which is *n*.
5: 9 This is the *n* hymn they sang:
14: 3 were singing a *n* hymn before the throne,
21: 1 Then I saw *n* heavens and a new earth.
21: 2 I also saw a *n* Jerusalem,
21: 5 said to me, "See, I make all things *n*!"

NEW-CREATED (1)

Wis 11:18 drove of bears or fierce lions, Or *n*,

NEWBORN (2)

Mt 2: 2 "Where is the *n* king of the Jews?
1Pt 2: 2 Be as eager for milk as *n* babies

NEWCOMERS (1)

Dt 32:17 had not known before, To *n* just arrived,

NEWER (1)

Dn 8: 3 horns, the one larger and *n* than the other.

NEWFOUND (1)

Acts 16:34 with his whole family his *n* faith in God.

NEWLY (2)

Dt 24: 5 "When a man is *n* wed,
Lk 14:20 said, 'I am *n* married and so I cannot come.'

NEWMOON (1)

Nm 10:10 your festivals, and your *n* feasts,

NEWS (109)

Gn 14:13 brought the *n* to Abram the Hebrew,
22:20 afterward, the *n* came to Abraham:
26:32 him *n* about the well they had been digging;
27:42 *n* of what her older son Esau had in mind,
29:13 heard the *n* about his sister's son Jacob,
34: 7 When they heard the *n*,
45: 2 him, and so the *n* reached Pharaoh's palace.
45:16 When the *n* reached Pharaoh's palace that
Ex 33: 4 When the people heard this bad *n*,
Jos 9: 1 the *n* reached the kings west of the Jordan,
Jgs 9:30 At the *n* of what Gaal,
Ru 4:17 *n* that a grandson had been born to Naomi.
1Sm 4:13 went into the city to divulge his *n*,
4:19 When she heard the *n* concerning the
11: 4 of Saul, they related the *n* to the people,
31: 9 and then sent the good *n* throughout the
2Sm 4: 4 He was five years old when the *n* about
4:10 *n* for which I ought to give him a reward.
10:17 On receiving this *n*,
18:19 "Let me run to take the good *n* to the
18:20 "You are not the man to bring the *n* today.
18:20 On some other day you may take the good *n*,
18:20 but today you would not be bringing good *n*,
18:25 "If he is alone, he has good *n* to report."
18:26 responded, "He, too, is bringing good *n*."
18:27 he comes with good *n*."
18:31 "Let my lord the king receive the good *n*
1Kgs 1:42 are a man of worth and must bring good *n*."
2:28 When the *n* came to Joab,
13:25 *n* to the city where the old prophet lived.
14: 6 been commissioned to give you bitter *n*.
2Kgs 7: 9 This is a day of good *n*,
1Chr 10: 9 the good *n* to their idols and their people.
Tb 10: 8 Tobit, and they will give him *n* of you."
Jdt 10:18 *n* of her arrival spread among the tents,
1Mc 6: 5 a messenger brought him *n* that the armies
6: 8 When the king heard this *n*,
11:15 When Alexander heard the *n*,
2Mc 9:24 happened or any unwelcome *n* came,
Prv 15:30 good *n* invigorates the bones.
25:25 from thirst is good *n* from a far country.
Is 23: 1 the land of the Kittim the *n* reaches them.
23: 5 they shall be in anguish at the *n* of Tyre.
40: 9 of your voice, Jerusalem, herald of good *n*!
41:27 one heard you say, "The first *n* for Zion:
52: 7 tidings, Announcing peace, bearing good *n*,
Jer 20:15 be the man who brought the *n* to my father,
49:23 covered with shame, they have heard bad *n*;
50:43 The king of Babylon hears *n* of them,
Dn 6:15 *n* and he made up his mind to save Daniel;
11:44 When *n* from the east and the north
Jon 3: 6 When the *N* reached the king of Nineveh,
Na 2: 1 there advances the bearer of good *n*,
3:19 this *n* of you clap their hands over you;
Mt 2: 3 this *n* King Herod became greatly disturbed,
4:23 proclaimed the good *n* of the kingdom,
9:26 *N* of this circulated throughout the
9:35 he proclaimed the good *n* of God's reign,
11: 5 the poor have the good *n* preached to them.
24:14 This good *n* of the kingdom will be
26:13 good *n* is proclaimed throughout the world,
28: 8 ran to carry the good *n* to his disciples.
28:10 Go and carry the *n* to my brothers that
Mk 1:14 in Galilee proclaiming the good *n* of God:
1:38 that I may proclaim the good *n* there also.
1:39 preaching the good *n* and expelling demons
3:14 whom he would send to preach the good *n*;
5:14 off and brought the *n* to field and village,
13:10 But the good *n* must first be proclaimed to
14: 9 good *n* is proclaimed throughout the world,
16:10 to announce the good *n* to his followers,
16:13 and announced the good *n* to the others;
16:15 and proclaim the good *n* to all creation.
Lk 1:19 to speak to you and bring you this good *n*.
2:10 I come to proclaim good *n* to you
3:18 sort, he preached the good *n* to the people.
4:43 announce the good *n* of the reign of God,
7:22 the poor have the good *n* preached to them.
8: 1 the good *n* of the kingdom of God.
8:34 the *n* to the town and country roundabout.
9: 6 the good *n* everywhere and curing diseases.
16:16 *n* of God's kingdom has been proclaimed,
20: 1 in the temple and proclaiming the good *n*,
24:22 have just brought us some astonishing *n*.
Jn 4:51 with the *n* that his boy was going to live.
9:30 "Well, this is *n*!
Acts 5:42 the good *n* of Jesus the Messiah.
8:12 believe in the good *n* that Philip preached
8:25 *n* to many villages of Samaria on the way.
8:35 point, telling him the good *n* of Jesus.
8:40 he went about announcing the good *n*
10:36 the good *n* of peace proclaimed through
11:20 the good *n* of the Lord Jesus to them.
11:22 *N* of this eventually reached the ears of
13:32 "We ourselves announce to you the good *n*
14: 7 they continued to proclaim the good *n*.
14:15 We are bringing you the good *n* that will
14:21 *n* in that town and made numerous disciples,
16:10 summoned us to proclaim the good *n* there.
Rom 10:15 are the feet of those who announce good *n*!"
Gal 3: 8 faith, it foretold this good *n* to Abraham:
Eph 2:17 good *n* of peace to you who were far off,
6:22 *n* about me for your hearts' consolation.
Col 4: 7 the Lord, will give you all the *n* about me.
1Thes 3: 6 the good *n* of your faith and love,
2Thes 1: 8 nor heed" the good *n* of our Lord Jesus.
2:14 through our preaching of the good *n*
Heb 4: 2 We have indeed heard the good *n*,
Rv 14: 6 of everlasting good *n* to the whole world,

NEWSMONGER (2)

Prv 11:13 A *n* reveals secrets, but a trustworthy
20:19 A *n* reveals secrets; so have nothing to do

NEXT (199)

Gn 4: 2 *N* she bore his brother Abel.
17:21 shall bear to you by this time *n* year."
18:10 return to you about this time *n* year,
18:14 the appointed time, about this time *n* year,
19:27 Early the *n* morning Abra-ham went to the
19:34 *N* day the older one said to the younger:
20: 8 Early the *n* morning Abimelech called all
21:14 Early the *n* morning Abraham got some bread
22: 3 the *n* morning Abraham saddled his donkey,
22: 9 *N* he tied up his son Isaac,
24:54 When they were up the *n* morning,
25:10 there he was buried *n* to his wife Sarah.
25:26 His brother came out *n*,
26:31 Early the *n* morning they exchanged oaths.
28:18 Early the *n* morning Jacob took the stone
32: 1 Early the *n* morning,
32:17 keep a space between one drove and the *n*."
33: 2 children first, Leah and her children *n*,
33: 7 *n*, Leah and her children came forward
41: 8 *N* morning his spirit was agitated.
Ex 2:13 The *n* day he went out again,
9: 6 And on the *n* day the LORD did so.
12:10 of it must be kept beyond the *n* morning;
18:13 *n* day Moses sat in judgment for the people,
23:18 my feast be kept overnight till the *n* day.
24: 4 of the LORD and, rising early the *n* day,
28:27 *n* to where they join the ephod in front,
29:34 of the bread remains over on the *n* day,
32: 6 Early the *n* day the people offered
32:30 On the *n* day Moses said to the people,
34: 4 and early the *n* morning he went up Mount
34:25 feast be kept overnight for the *n* day.
39:20 *n* to where they joined the ephod in front,
Lv 6: 2 of the altar all night until the *n* morning,
7:15 none of it may be kept till the *n* day.
7:16 is left over may be eaten on the *n* day.
8:18 He *n* brought forward the holocaust ram,
16: 4 tunic, with the linen drawers *n* his flesh,
19: 6 of it shall be left over until the *n* day.
27:18 of years left until the *n* jubilee year,
27:23 to the number of years until the *n* jubilee,
Nm 2:14 and *n* the tribe of Gad.
2:29 and *n* the tribe of Naphtali.
5: 8 if the latter has no *n* of kin to whom
10:18 in companies, was the *n* to set out,
10:22 The camp of the Ephraimites *n* set out,
11:32 the *n* day the people gathered in the quail.
14:40 Early the *n* morning they started up into
17: 6 The *n* day the whole Israelite community
17:23 The *n* day, when Moses entered the tent
22:13 The *n* morning Balaam arose and told the
22:21 So the *n* morning when Balaam arose,
22:26 and stopped *n* in a passage so narrow that
22:41 The *n* morning Balak took Balaam up on
Dt 16: 4 day shall be kept overnight for the *n* day.
Jos 3: 1 Early the *n* morning, Joshua moved
6:12 *n* morning, Joshua had the priests
7: 2 Joshua *n* sent men from Jericho to Ai,
7:16 Early the *n* morning Joshua had Israel come
8:10 Early the *n* morning Joshua mustered the
10:31 Joshua *n* passed on with all Israel from
Jgs 6:28 Early the *n* morning the townspeople found
6:38 *n* morning he wrung the dew from the fleece,
7: 1 Early the *n* morning Jerubbaal (that is,
9:42 The *n* day, when the people were
20:19 The *n* day the Israelites advanced on
21: 4 Early the *n* day the people built an altar
Ru 2:18 *N* she brought out and gave her what she
2:20 is a relative of ours, one of our *n* of kin."
3: 9 cloak over me, for you are my *n* of kin."
4: 4 it if you wish to acquire it as *n* of kin.
4: 4 has a prior claim to yours, and mine is *n*."
1Sm 1:19 *n* morning they worshiped before the LORD,
1:21 The *n* time her husband Elkanah was going
5: 3 people of Ashdod rose early the *n* morning,
5: 4 But the *n* morning early,
5:10 The ark of God was *n* sent to Ekron;
6: 8 You shall *n* take the ark of the LORD and
10:21 *N* he had the tribe of Benjamin come
10:25 Samuel *n* explained to the people the law
16: 9 *N* Jesse presented Shammah,
17:20 Early the *n* morning,
18:10 [The *n* day an evil spirit from God came
20:27 the *n* day, the second day of the month,
20:35 The *n* morning Jonathan went out into the
22:18 to the *n* and killed the priests himself,
25:36 at all before daybreak the *n* morning.
2Sm 11:14 The *n* morning David wrote a letter to Joab

18:15 *N,* ten of Joab's young armor-bearers
23: 9 *N* to him, among the Three warriors,
23:11 *N* to him was Shammah,
1Kgs 1: 6 and *n* in age to Absalom by the same mother.
10:19 *N* to each arm stood a lion;
21: 1 in Jezreel *n* to the palace of Ahab,
21: 2 since it is close by, *n* to my house.
21:10 *N,* get two scoundrels to face him and
2Kgs 4:16 *n* year you will be fondling a baby son."
6:15 Early the *n* morning, when the attendant
6:29 The *n* day I said to her, 'Now give up
6:30 sackcloth underneath, *n* to his skin.
8:15 The *n* day, however, Hazael took a cloth,
19:29 year you shall eat the aftergrowth, *n* year,
19:35 Early the *n* morning,
1Chr 11:12 *N* to him Eleazar,
2Chr 17:15 *N* to him, Jehohanan the commander,
17:16 *N* to him, Amasiah, son of Zichri,
17:18 *N* to him, Jozabad, and with him
Ezr 8:24 *N* I selected twelve of the priestly
Neh 3: 2 were rebuilding, and *n* to them was Zaccur,
3: 4 *n* to him was Meshullam,
3: 4 and *n* to him was Zadok,
3: 5 *N* to him the Tekoites carried out the work
3: 8 *N* to them the work of repair was carried
3: 9 *N* to them the work of repair was carried
3:10 *N* to him Hattush,
3:17 *N* to him, for his own district,
3:19 *n* to him Ezer,
Tb 2: 9 to sleep *n* to the wall of my courtyard.
11:12 *N* he smeared the medicine on his eyes,
14:10 The day you bury your mother *n* to me,
14:12 mother died, he buried her *n* to his father.
Jdt 2:21 and from Bectileth they *n* encamped near
Est 10: 3 Mordecai was *n* in rank to King Ahasuerus,
1Mc 13:20 *N* he began to invade and ravage the country.
13:29 and *n* to the armor he placed carved ships,
2Mc 3:37 a suitable man to be sent to Jerusalem *n,*
7:15 They *n* brought forward the fifth brother
13:23 *N* he heard that Philip,
Jb 41: 8 so close to the *n* that no space intervenes;
Ps(s) 90: 5 the *n* morning they are like the changing
109:13 *n* generation may their name be blotted out.
Wis 17:21 the darkness that *n* should come upon them;
Sir 14:24 and fastens his tent pegs *n* to her walls;
31:20 slumber and a clear mind *n* day on rising.
Is 17:11 make your sprouts blossom on the *n* morning,
37:30 year you shall eat the aftergrowth, *n* year,
37:36 Early the *n* morning,
Jer 20: 3 The *n* morning,
35: 4 the man of God, *n* to the princes' room,
Ez 24:18 *n* morning I did as I had been commanded.
43: 8 my threshold and their doorpost *n* to mine,
48:12 domain, *n* to the territory of the Levites.
Dn 6:20 *n* morning and hastened to the lions' den.
13:28 came to her husband Joakim the *n* day,
14:16 Early the *n* morning,
Jl 1: 3 and their children to the *n* generation.
Jon 4: 7 But the *n* morning at dawn God sent a worm
Mt 4: 5 *N* the devil took him to the holy city,
10:23 persecute you in one town, flee to the *n.*
10:29 Are not two sparrows sold for *n* to nothing?
13:54 Jesus *n* went to his native place and spent
27:62 The *n* day, the one following the Day of
Mk 1:35 Rising early the *n* morning,
10:46 They came to Jericho *n,*
11:12 The *n* day when they were leaving Bethany
11:20 Early *n* morning, as they were walking
12:13 They *n* sent some Pharisees and Herodians
Lk 4:42 The *n* morning he left the town and set out
10:35 The *n* day he took out two silver pieces
11:26 *N* it goes out and returns with seven other
16: 3 thought to himself, 'What shall I do *n?*
20:31 *N,* the second brother married the widow,
Jn 1:29 *n* day, when John caught sight of Jesus
1:35 Testimony of JohnThe *n* day John was there
1:43 The *n* day he wanted to set out for Galilee,
6:22 The *n* day they realized that there had
9:13 *N,* they took the man who had been born
12:12 The *n* day the great crowd that had come
18:24 Annas *n* sent him, bound, to the high
19: 1 Pilate's *n* move was to take Jesus and have
Acts 4: 5 scribes assembled the *n* day in Jerusalem,
5:37 *N* came Judas the Galilean at the time of
7:26 *n* day while some of them were fighting,
7:45 *n* generation of our fathers inherited it.
8:40 Philip found himself at Azotus *n,*
9:41 The *n* thing he did was to call in those
10: 9 About noontime the *n* day,
10:23 The *n* day he went off with them,
14:20 The *n* day he left with Barnabas for Derbe.
16: 1 *n* he came to Lystra,
16: 6 They *n* traveled through Phrygia and
16:11 Samothrace, and the *n* day on to Neapolis;
18: 7 his house was *n* door to the synagogue.
20: 7 Because he intended to leave the *n* day,
20:15 From there we took off the *n* day,
21: 8 *n* day we pushed on and came to Caesarea.
21:18 The *n* day, Paul and the rest of us
21:26 rite of purification with them the *n* day.
22:14 The *n* thing he said was,
22:30 The *n* day the commander released Paul from
23:32 The *n* day they returned to headquarters,
25:17 The very *n* day I took my seat on the bench
25:23 So the *n* day Agrippa and Bernice came with
27:18 by the storm so violently that the *n* day
1Cor 15: 7 *N* he was seen by James;
2Cor 1:17 I change my mind from one minute to the *n?*
1:18 is not "yes" one minute and "no" the *n.*
Rv 19:17 *N* I saw an angel standing on the sun.
20:11 *N* I saw a large white throne and the One

NEZIAH (2)

Ezr 2:54 sons of Sisera, sons of Temah, sons of *N,*
Neh 7:56 sons of Sisera, sons of Temah, sons of *N,*

NEZIB (1)

Jos 15:43 Libnah, Ether, Ashan, Iphtah, Ashnah, *N,*

NIBHAZ (1)

2Kgs 17:31 Ashima, the men of Avva made *N* and Tartak;

NIBSHAN (1)

Jos 15:62 Beth-arabah, Middin, Secacah, *N,*

NICANOR (36)

1Mc 3:38 son of Dorymenes, and *N* and Gorgias,
7:26 Then the king sent *N,*
7:27 *N* came to Jerusalem with a large force and
7:30 *N* had come to him with treachery in mind,
7:31 *N* saw that his plan had been discovered,
7:33 After this, *N* went up to Mount Zion.
7:39 *N* left Jerusalem and pitched his camp at
7:42 *N* spoke wickedly against your sanctuary;
7:44 When his army saw that *N* was dead,
9: 1 that *N* and his army had fallen in battle,
2Mc 8: 9 Ptolemy promptly selected *N,*
8:10 *N* planned to raise the two thousand
8:14 *N* had sold before even meeting them.
8:23 first division and joined in battle with *N.*
8:34 The accursed *N,*
9: 3 had happened to *N* and to Timothy's forces.
12: 2 and Demophon, to say nothing of *N,*
14:12 The king immediately chose *N,*
14:14 have banished Judas, came flocking to *N,*
14:17 Judas' brother Simon had engaged *N,*
14:18 *N* heard of the valor of Judas and his men,
14:23 *N* stayed on in Jerusalem,
14:26 said that *N* was plotting against the state,
14:27 wrote to *N,* stating that he was displeased
14:28 this message reached *N* he was dismayed,
14:30 But Maccabeus noticed that *N* was becoming
14:30 of his men, and went into hiding from *N.*
14:31 When *N* realized that he had been
14:37 Jerusalem, was denounced to *N* as a patriot.
14:39 *N,* to show his detestation of the Jews,
15: 1 When *N* learned that Judas and his
15: 6 In his utter boastfulness and arrogance *N*
15:25 *N* and his men advanced to the sound of
15:28 discovered *N* lying there in all his armor,
15:33 He cut out the tongue of the godless *N,*
Acts 6: 5 and the Holy Spirit; Philip, Prochorus, *N,*

NICANOR'S (10)

1Mc 7:32 About five hundred men of *N* army fell;
7:43 *N* army was crushed,
7:47 they cut off *N* head and his right arm,
2Mc 8:12 When Judas learned of *N* advance and
8:24 and disabled the greater part of *N* army,
14:15 When the Jews heard of *N* coming,
15:30 ordered *N* head and whole right arm to be
15:32 He showed them the vile *N* head and the
15:35 hung up *N* head on the wall of the citadel,
15:37 Since *N* doings ended in this way,

NICODEMUS (5)

Jn 3: 1 A certain Pharisee named *N,*
3: 4 be born again once he is old?" retorted *N.*
3: 9 "How can such a thing happen?" asked *N.*
7:50 number, *N* (the man who had come to him),
19:39 *N* (the man who had first come to Jesus at

NICOLAITANS (2)

Rv 2: 6 you detest the practices of the *N,*
2:15 you who hold to the teaching of the *N.*

NICOLAUS (1)

Acts 6: 5 Nicanor, Timon, Parmenas, and *N* of Antioch,

NICOPOLIS (1)

Ti 3:12 or perhaps Tychicus, hurry to me at *N;*

NIGER (1)

Acts 13: 1 Barnabas, Symeon known as *N,*

NIGHT (347)

Gn 1: 5 "day," and the darkness he called *n.*"
1:14 dome of the sky, to separate day from *n.*
1:16 day, and the lesser one to govern the *n;*
1:18 the earth, to govern the day and the *n,*
8:22 and winter, and day and *n* shall not cease."
14:15 and his party deployed against them at *n,*
19: 2 aside into your servant's house for the *n,*
19: 2 we shall pass the *n* in the town square."
19:33 that *n* they plied their father with wine,
19:34 "Last *n* it was I who lay with my father.
19:35 So that *n,* too, they plied their father
20: 3 Abimelech in a dream one *n* and said to him,
24:23 your father's house for us to spend the *n?"*
24:25 she added, "and room to spend the *n.*"
24:54 eaten and drunk, they spent the *n* there.
26:24 same *n* the LORD appeared to him and said:
28:11 already set, he stopped there for the *n.*
30:16 So that *n* he slept with her,
31:24 But that *n* God appeared to Laban the
31:29 last *n* the God of your father said to me,
31:39 for anything stolen by day or *n.*
31:40 heat ravaged me by day, and the frost by *n,*
31:42 of my toil, and last *n* he gave judgment."
31:54 eaten, they passed the *n* on the mountain.
32:14 After passing the *n* there,
32:22 of him, while he stayed that *n* in the camp.
32:23 In the course of that *n,* however, Jacob
40: 5 in the jail both had dreams on the same *n,*
41:11 Later, we both had dreams on the same *n,*
42:27 At the *n* encampment,
46: 2 God, speaking to Israel in a vision by *n,*
Ex 4:24 at a place where they spent the *n,*
10:13 over the land all that day and all that *n.*
12: 8 That same *n* they shall eat its roasted
12:12 For on this same *n* I will go through Egypt,
12:30 Pharaoh arose in the *n,*
12:31 During the *n* Pharaoh summoned Moses and
12:42 This was a *n* of vigil for the LORD,
12:42 so on this same *n* all the Israelites must
13:21 and at *n* by means of a column of fire to
13:21 Thus they could travel both day and *n.*
13:22 cloud by day nor the column of fire by *n*
14:20 and thus the *n* passed without the rival
14:20 coming any closer together all *n* long.
14:21 the *n* and so turned it into dry land.
14:24 In the *n* watch just before dawn the LORD
40:38 whereas at *n,*
Lv 6: 2 of the altar all *n* until the next morning,
8:35 the meeting tent day and *n* for seven days,
Nm 9:16 which at *n* had the appearance of fire.
9:21 cloud lifted during the day, or even at *n,*
11: 9 At *n,* when the dew fell upon the camp,
11:32 All that day, all *n,*
14: 1 cries, and even in the *n* the people wailed.
14:14 of cloud and by *n* in a column of fire.
22:20 That *n* God came to Balaam and said to him,
Dt 1:33 by day in the cloud, and by *n* in the fire,
16: 1 Abib that he brought you by *n* out of Egypt.
28:66 suspense and stand in dread both day and *n,*
Jos 1: 8 Recite it by day and by *n,*
2: 2 had come there that *n* to spy out the land.
6:11 which they returned to camp for the *n.*
8: 3 sent them off by *n* with these orders:
8: 9 Joshua, however, spent that *n* in the plain.
Jgs 6:25 That same *n* the LORD said to him,
6:27 he would not do it by day, but did it at *n.*
6:40 That *n* God did so;
7: 9 That *n* the LORD said to Gideon,
9:34 During the *n* Abimelech advanced with all
16: 2 with an ambush at the city gate all *n* long.
16: 2 And all the *n* they waited,
18: 2 region of Ephraim, where they passed the *n.*
19: 4 and drinking and passing the *n* there.
19: 6 to spend the *n* here and enjoy yourself?"
19: 7 him he went back and spent the *n* there.
19: 9 Stay for the *n.*
19: 9 Spend the *n* here and enjoy yourself.
19:10 man, however, refused to stay another *n;*
19:11 of the Jebusites and spend the *n* in it."
19:13 either Gibeah or Ramah, to spend the *n.*"
19:15 they turned off to enter Gibeah for the *n.*
19:15 them the shelter of his home for the *n.*
19:20 do not spend the *n* in the public square."
19:25 abused her all *n* until the following dawn,
20: 4 I went into Gibeah of Benjamin for the *n.*
20: 5 *n* and surrounded the house in which I was.
Ru 3: 8 In the middle of the *n,* however, the man
1Sm 14:36 down in pursuit of the Philistines by *n,*
15:11 grew angry and cried out to the LORD all *n.*
15:16 tell you what the LORD said to me last *n.*"
19:11 The same *n,* Saul sent messengers
19:24 all that day and *n* he lay naked.
25:16 For us they were like a rampart *n* and day
26: 7 Abishai went among Saul's soldiers by *n*
28: 8 They came to the woman by *n,*
28:20 he had eaten nothing all that day and *n.*
28:25 Then they stood up and left the same *n.*
31:12 out, and after marching throughout the *n,*
2Sm 2:29 men marched all *n* long through the Arabah
4: 7 traveled on the Arabah road all *n* long.
7: 4 that *n* the LORD spoke to Nathan and said:
12:16 retiring for the *n* to lie on the ground
17: 8 he will not spend the *n* with the people.
17:16 spend the *n* at the fords near the desert,
21:10 on them by day, and the wild animals by *n.*
1Kgs 3: 5 LORD appeared to Solomon in a dream at *n.*
3:19 This woman's son died during the *n;*

NIGHT (cont.)

3:20 *n* she got up and took my son from my side,
8:29 your eyes watch *n* and day over this temple,
8:59 our God, be present to him day and *n*,
2Kgs 6:14 They arrived by *n* and surrounded the city.
7:12 Though it was *n*, the king got up;
8:21 He arose by *n* and broke through the
19:35 That *n* the angel of the LORD went forth
25: 4 all the soldiers left the city by *n*
1Chr 9:27 At *n* they lodged about the house of God,
9:33 day and *n* they had to be ready for service.
17: 3 that same *n* the word of God came to Nathan:
2Chr 1: 7 *n* God appeared to Solomon and said to him,
6:20 your eyes watch day and *n* over this temple,
7:12 to Solomon during the *n* and said to him:
21: 9 He arose by *n* and broke through the
35:14 holocausts and the fatty portions until *n*;
Ezr 10: 6 *n* neither eating food nor drinking water,
Neh 1: 6 day and *n* for your servants the Israelites,
2:12 Then I set out by *n* with only a few other
2:13 I rode out at *n* by the Valley Gate,
2:15 I continued on foot up the wadi by *n*,
4: 3 day and *n* for fear of what they might do.
4:16 as a guard by *n* and a working force by day.
6:10 by *n* they are coming to kill you."
9:12 by day, and by *n* with a column of fire,
9:19 nor did the column of fire by *n* cease to
13:20 the *n* once or twice outside Jerusalem,
13:21 do you spend the *n* alongside the wall?
Tb 2: 9 That same *n* I bathed,
6:14 On the very *n* they approached her,
7:11 all died on the very *n* they approached her.
8: 9 and went to bed for the *n*.
10: 7 home to wail and cry the whole *n* through,
Jdt 6:21 That whole *n* they called upon the God of
7: 5 bastions, and kept watch throughout the *n*.
11: 5 I will tell no lie to my lord this *n*,
11:17 woman, serving the God of heaven *n* and day.
11:17 but each *n* your handmaid will go out to
12: 5 In the *n* watch just before dawn,
12: 7 *n* she went out to the ravine of Bethulia,
13:14 our enemies by my hand this very *n*."
Est A:11 in mind, and tried in every way, until *n*,
4:16 of you, not eating or drinking, *n* or day,
6: 1 That *n* the king, unable to sleep,
1Mc 4: 1 and this detachment set out at *n* in order
4: 5 the *n* Gorgias came into the camp of Judas,
5:29 He led his army from that place by *n*,
5:50 he assaulted the city all that day and *n*,
9:58 he will capture all of them in a single *n*."
11: 6 greeted each other and spent the *n* there.
12:26 made ready to attack the Jews that very *n*.
12:27 armed, ready for combat, throughout the *n*.
13:22 go, there was a heavy fall of snow that *n*,
16: 4 Cendebeus, they spent the *n* at Modein,
2Mc 12: 6 In a *n* attack he set the harbor on fire,
12: 9 he attacked the Jamnian populace by *n*,
13:10 the people to call upon the LORD *n* and day,
13:15 he made a *n* attack on the king's pavilion
Jb 3: 3 on which I was born, the *n* when they said,
3: 5 upon it, the blackness of *n* affright it!
3: 7 May that *n* be barren;
4:13 In my thoughts during visions of the *n*,
5:14 at noonday they grope as though it were *n*,
7: 4 then the *n* drags on;
17:12 Such men change the *n* into day;
20: 8 he fades away like a vision of the *n*.
24: 6 they harvest at *n* in the untilled land.
24: 7 They pass the *n* naked,
24:15 In the *n* the thief roams about,
27:20 at *n* the tempest carries him off.
29:19 the dew rests by *n* on my branches.
30:17 My frame takes no rest by *n*;
33:15 In a dream, in a vision of the *n*,
34:25 he turns at *n* and crushes them.
35:10 my Maker, who has given visions in the *n*,
39:28 On the cliff he dwells and spends the *n*,
Ps(s) 1: 2 LORD and meditates on his law day and *n*.
6: 7 every *n* I flood my bed with weeping;
16: 7 even in the *n* my heart exhorts me.
17: 3 you test my heart, searching it in the *n*,
19: 3 to day, and *n* to night imparts knowledge;
22: 3 by *n*, and there is no relief for me.
32: 4 For day and *n* your hand was heavy upon me;
42: 4 My tears are my food day and *n*,
42: 9 his grace, and at *n* I have his song,
55:11 day and *n* they prowl about upon its walls.
74:16 Yours is the day, and yours the *n*;
77: 3 By *n* my hands are stretched out without
77: 7 In the *n* I meditate in my heart;
78:14 by day, and all *n* with a glow of fire.
88: 2 at *n* I clamor in your presence.
90: 4 that it is past, or as a watch of the *n*.
91: 5 of the *n* nor the arrow that flies by day;
92: 3 and your faithfulness throughout the *n*,
104:20 You bring darkness, and it is *n*;
105:39 them and fire to give them light by *n*.
119:55 By *n* I remember your name,
119:148 the *n* watches in meditation on your promise.
121: 6 not harm you by day, nor the moon by *n*.
134: 1 house of the LORD during the hours of *n*.
136: 9 The moon and the stars to rule over the *n*,
139:11 shall hide me, and *n* shall be my light"
139:12 is not dark, and *n* shines as the day.
Prv 7: 9 dusk of day, at the time of the dark of *n*.
31:15 She rises while it is still *n*,
31:18 at *n* her lamp is undimmed.
Eccl 2:23 even at *n* his mind is not at rest.
8:17 nor by *n* do his eyes find rest in sleep.
Sg 3: 1 bed at *n* I sought him whom my heart loves
3: 8 against danger in the watches of the *n*.
5: 2 dew, my locks with the moisture of the *n*."
7:12 fields and spend the *n* among the villages.
Wis 7:30 for that, indeed, *n* supplants,
10:17 for them by day and a starry flame by *n*.
17: 2 with darkness, fettered by the long *n*,
17: 5 stars succeed in lighting up that gloomy *n*.
17:14 So they, during that *n*, powerless though it
17:21 Over them alone was spread oppressive *n*,
18: 6 That *n* was known beforehand to our fathers,
18:14 the *n* in its swift course was half spent,
Sir 36:27 no nest, but lodges where *n* overtakes him?
38:27 and designer who, laboring *n* and day,
40: 5 to rest, his cares at *n* disturb his sleep.
Is 4: 5 by day and a light of flaming fire by *n*.
5:11 linger into the *n* while wine inflames them!
10:29 "We will spend the *n* at Geba."
15: 1 Laid waste in a *n*,
15: 1 Laid waste in a *n*,
16: 3 high noon let your shadow be like the *n*,
21: 8 my post through all the watches of the *n*.
21:11 Seir, "Watchman, how much longer the *n*?
21:11 Watchman, how much longer the *n*?"
21:12 replies, "Morning has come, and again *n*.
21:13 thicket in the nomad country spend the *n*,
26: 9 My soul yearns for you in the *n*,
27: 3 Lest anyone harm it, *n* and day I guard it.
28:19 morning it shall pass, By day and by *n*;
29: 7 Then like a dream, a vision in the *n*,
30:29 sing as on a *n* when a feast is observed,
34:10 *N* and day it shall not be quenched,
38:12 Day and *n* you give me over to torment;
38:13 [day and *n* you give me over to torment].
60:11 day and *n* they shall not be closed But
60:19 of the moon shine upon you at *n*;
62: 6 Never, by day or by *n*,
65: 4 the graves and spending the *n* in caverns,
Jer 6: 5 let us rush upon her by *n*,
8:23 That I might weep day and *n* over the slain
14: 8 a traveler who has stopped but for a *n*?
14:17 Let my eyes stream with tears day and *n*,
16:13 there you can serve strange gods day and *n*,
31:35 the day, moon and stars to light the *n*;
33:20 with night, so that day and *n* no longer
33:25 When I have no covenant with day and *n*,
36:30 to the heat of day, to the cold of *n*.
39: 4 them, he and all his warriors fled by *n*,
49: 9 If thieves by *n*,
52: 7 took to flight and left the city by *n*
Lam 1: 2 Bitterly she weeps at *n*,
2:18 your tears flow like a torrent day and *n*;
2:19 Rise up, shrill in the *n*,
Bar 2:25 to the heat of day and the frost of *n*.
Dn 2:19 During the *n* the mystery was revealed to
5:30 The same *n* Belshazzar
6:19 the king returned to his palace for the *n*;
7: 2 In the vision I saw during the *n*,
7: 7 visions of the *n* I saw the fourth beast,
7:13 As the visions during the *n* continued,
14:15 The priests entered that *n* as usual,
Hos 4: 5 the prophets shall stumble with you at *n*;
7: 6 All the *n* their anger sleeps;
Jl 1:13 Come, spend the *n* in sackcloth,
Am 5: 8 into dawn, and darkens day into *n*;
Ob 1: 5 If thieves came to you, if robbers by *n*,
Jon 4:10 up in one night and in one *n* it perished.
Mi 3: 6 Therefore you shall have *n*,
Zep 3: 3 Her judges are wolves of the *n* that have
Zec 1: 8 I had a vision during the *n*.
14: 7 day, known to the LORD, not day and *n*,
Mt 2:14 and his mother and left that *n* for Egypt.
16: 2 ["In the evening you say, 'Red sky at *n*,
21:17 the city to Bethany, where he spent the *n*.
22:13 out into the *n* to wail and grind his teeth.'
28:13 the *n* and stole him while we were asleep.'
Mk 5: 5 Uninterruptedly *n* and day,
14:30 this very *n* before the cock crows twice,
Lk 2: 8 keeping *n* watch by turns over their flocks.
2:37 worshiping day and *n* in fasting and prayer.
5: 5 at it all *n* long and have caught nothing;
6:12 pray, spending the *n* in communion with God.
11: 5 him in the middle of the *n* and says to him,
12:20 very *n* your life shall be required of you.
17:34 on that *n* there will be two men in one bed;
18: 7 his chosen who call out to him day and *n*?
21:37 city to spend the *n* on the Mount of Olives.
Jn 3: 2 of the Jewish Sanhedrin, came to him at *n*.
9: 4 The *n* comes on when no one can work.
11:10 But if he goes walking at *n* he will
13:30 It was *n*.
18:18 Now the *n* was cold, and the servants
19:39 first come to Jesus at *n*) likewise came,
21: 3 All through the *n* they caught nothing.
Acts 4: 3 them and put them in jail for the *n*.
5:19 During the *n*, however, an angel of the
9:24 and *n* in an attempt to do away with him.
9:25 wall one *n* and lowered him to the ground,
12: 6 *n* before Herod was to bring him to trial,
16: 9 There one *n* Paul had a vision.
16:33 *n* he took them in and bathed their wounds;
17:10 As soon as it was *n*,
18: 9 One *n* in a vision the Lord said to Paul:
20:31 not forget that for three years, *n* and day,
23:11 That *n* the Lord appeared at Paul's side
23:31 escorted him that *n* as far as Antipatris.
26: 7 people fervently worship God day and *n*
27:23 Last *n* a messenger of the God whose man I
27:27 It was the fourteenth *n* of the storm,
Rom 13:12 The *n* is far spent; the day draws near.
1Cor 11:23 the *n* in which he was betrayed took bread,
2Cor 11:25 I passed a day and *n* on the sea.
1Thes 2: 9 how we worked day and *n* all the time we
3:10 as we ask him fervently *n* and day that we
5: 2 the Lord is coming like a thief in the *n*.
5: 5 We belong neither to darkness nor to *n*;
5: 7 sleep by *n* and drunkards drink by night.
2Thes 3: 8 Rather, we worked day and *n*,
1Tm 5: 5 *n* and day in supplications and prayers.
2Tm 1: 3 as indeed I do constantly, *n* and day.
Rv 4: 8 Day and *n*, without pause, they sang:
7:15 and *n* they minister to him in his temple;
8:12 lost a third of its light, as did the *n*.
12:10 who *n* and day accused them before our God.
14:11 There shall be no relief day or *n* for
20:10 There they will be tortured day and *n*,
21:25 never be shut, and there shall be no *n*.
22: 5 The *n* shall be no more.

NIGHTFALL (3)

Gn 29:23 At *n* he took his daughter Leah and brought
Tb 6: 2 The travelers walked till *n*,
Ps(s) 30: 6 At *n*, weeping enters in,

NIGHTJAR (2)

Lv 11:16 species of crows, the ostrich, the *n*,
Dt 14:15 species of crows, the ostrich, the *n*,

NIGHTMARES (1)

Eccl 5: 2 For *n* come with many cares,

NIGHTS (25)

Gn 7: 4 on the earth for forty days and forty *n*,
7:12 *n* heavy rain poured down on the earth.
43:21 at a *n* encampment and opened our bags,
Ex 24:18 there he stayed for forty days and forty *n*.
34:28 with the LORD for forty days and forty *n*,
Dt 9: 9 and forty *n* without eating or drinking,
9:11 at the end of the forty days and forty *n*,
9:18 and forty *n* without eating or drinking,
9:25 "Those forty days, then, and forty *n*,
10:10 forty days and forty *n* on the mountain,
1Sm 30:12 nor drunk water for three days and three *n*.
1Kgs 19: 8 days and forty *n* to the mountain of God,
Neh 4:16 the people to spend the *n* inside Jerusalem,
2Mc 2:26 easy, is one of sweat and of sleepless *n*,
8: 7 He preferred the *n* as being especially
Jb 2:13 ground with him seven days and seven *n*,
7: 3 and troubled *n* have been told off for me.
39: 9 you, and to pass the *n* by your manger?
Dn 3:71 *N* and days, bless the Lord;
Jon 2: 1 belly of the fish three days and three *n*.
Mt 4: 2 He fasted forty days and forty *n*,
12:40 days and three *n* in the belly of the whale,
12:40 and three *n* in the bowels of the earth.
2Cor 6: 5 men familiar with hard work, sleepless *n*,
11:27 labor, hardship, many sleepless *n*;

NIGHT-WATCHES (1)

Ps(s) 63: 7 and through the *n* I will meditate on you

NILE (19)

Gn 41: 1 He saw himself standing by the *N*,
41: 2 Nile, when up out of the *N* came seven cows,
41: 3 *N*; and standing on the bank of the Nile
41:17 I was standing on the bank of the *N*,
41:18 Nile, when up from the *N* came seven cows,
Sir 24:25 It sparkles like the *N* with knowledge,
39:22 His blessing overflows like the *N*;
47:14 with instruction, like the *N* in flood!
Is 19: 7 the Nile; All the sown land along the *N*
19: 8 and lament, all who cast hook in the *N*;
23: 3 The grain of Shihor, the harvest of the *N*,
Jer 2:18 go to Egypt, to drink the waters of the *N*?
46: 7 Who is this that surges forward like the *N*,
46: 8 Egypt surges like the *N*,
Am 8: 8 While it rises up and tosses like the *N*,
9: 5 on it mourn, While it rises up like the *N*,
Zec 10:11 all the depths of the *N* shall be dried up.

NILES (9)

Ez 29: 3 Great crouching monster amidst your *N*:
29: 3 Who say, "The *N* are mine;
29: 4 the fish of your *N* stick to your scales,
29: 4 your *N* along with all the fish of your Niles
29: 5 desert, you and all the fish of your *N*;
29: 9 Because you said, "The *N* are mine;

29:10 I am coming at you and against your *N;*
30:12 I will turn the *N* into dry land and sell

NIMBLE (1)

Ps(s) 45: 2 is *n* as the pen of a skillful scribe.

NIMRAH (1)

Nm 32: 3 "The region of Ataroth, Dibon, Jazer, *N,*

NIMRIM (2)

Is 15: 6 The waters of *N* have become a waste;
Jer 48:34 even the waters of *N* turn into a desert.

NIMROD (4)

Gn 10: 8 Cush became the father of *N,*
10: 9 hence the saying, "Like *N,*
1Chr 1:10 Cush became the father of *N,*
Mi 5: 5 and the land of *N* with the drawn sword;

NIMSHI (5)

1Kgs 19:16 shall anoint Jehu, son of *N,*
2Kgs 9: 2 for Jehu, son of Jehoshaphat, son of *N.*
9:14 Thus Jehu, son of Jehoshaphat, son of *N,*
9:20 The driving is like that of Jehu, son of *N,*
2Chr 22: 7 Jehu, son of *N*

NINE (36)

Gn 5: 5 of Adam was *n* hundred and thirty years;
5: 8 of Seth was *n* hundred and twelve years;
5:11 of Enosh was *n* hundred and five years;
5:14 of Kenan was *n* hundred and ten years;
5:20 of Jared was *n* hundred and sixty-two years;
5:27 was *n* hundred and sixty-nine years;
9:29 of Noah was *n* hundred and fifty years;
11:19 hundred and *n* years after the birth of Reu,
Nm 29:26 the fifth day you shall offer *n* bullocks,
34:13 to be given to the *n* and one half tribes.
Dt 3:11 iron, *n* regular cubits long and four wide,
Jos 13: 7 apportion among the *n* tribes and the
14: 2 the remaining *n* and a half tribes.
15:44 *n* cities and their villages.
15:54 *n* cities and their villages.
21:16 *n* cities from the two tribes mentioned.
Jgs 4: 3 for with his *n* hundred iron chariots he
4:13 all *n* hundred of his iron chariots
2Sm 24:8 again after *n* months and twenty days.
1Chr 3: 8 Japhia, Elishama, Eliada, and Eliphelet *n.*
9: 9 families were *n* hundred and fifty-six.
Ezr 2: 8 sons of Zattu, *n* hundred and forty-five;
2:36 of Jeshua, *n* hundred and seventy-three;
Neh 7:38 three thousand *n* hundred and thirty.
7:39 of Jeshua, *n* hundred and seventy-three;
11: 1 the other *n* would remain in other cities.
11: 8 *n* hundred and twenty-eight in number.
2Mc 5:27 about *n* others withdrew to the wilderness,
7:27 who carried you in my womb for *n* months,
8:24 killed more than *n* thousand of the enemy,
10:18 When at least *n* thousand took refuge in
Sir 25: 7 There are *n* who come to my mind as blessed,
Mk 15:25 *n* in the morning when they crucified him.
Lk 17:17 Where are the other *n?*
Acts 2:15 It is only *n* in the morning!
23:23 to leave for Caesarea by *n* o'clock tonight,

NINE-YEAR (1)

2Kgs 17: 1 began his *n* reign over Israel in Samaria.

NINETEEN (3)

Gn 11:25 and *n* years after the birth of Terah,
Jos 19:38 *n* cities and their villages,
2Sm 2:30 *n* other servants of David were missing.

NINETEENTH (4)

2Kgs 25: 8 (this was in the *n* year of Nebuchadnezzar,
1Chr 24:16 to Happizzez, the *n* to Pethahiah,
25:26 The *n* fell to Mallothi, his sons, and his
Jer 52:12 (was in the *n* year of Nebuchadnezzar,

NINETY (9)

Gn 5: 9 When Enosh was *n* years old,
17:17 Or can Sarah give birth at *n?"*
1Chr 9: 6 and six hundred and *n* of their brethren.
2Mc 8:11 promising to deliver *n* slaves for a talent
12:17 When they had gone on some *n* miles,
Ez 4: 5 same number of days, three hundred and *n,*
4: 9 lie upon your side, three hundred and *n.*
41:12 and it measured *n* cubits from side to side.
Dn 12:11 be one thousand two hundred and *n* days.

NINETY-EIGHT (3)

1Sm 4:15 (Eli was *n* years old,
Ezr 2:16 of Ater, who were sons of Hezekiah, *n;*
Neh 7:21 sons of Ater who were sons of Hezekiah, *n;*

NINETY-FIVE (4)

Gn 5:17 of Mahalalel was eight hundred and *n* years;
5:30 and *n* years after the birth of Noah,
Ezr 2:20 sons of Gibeon, *n;*
Neh 7:25 sons of Gibeon, *n;*

NINETY-NINE (6)

Gn 17: 1 When Abram was *n* years old,
17:24 Abraham was *n* years old when the flesh of
Mt 18:12 will he not leave the *n* out on the hills
18:13 than about the *n* that did not wander away.
Lk 15: 4 does not leave the *n* in the wasteland and
15: 7 over one repentant sinner than over *n*

NINETY-SIX (2)

Ezr 8:35 Israel twelve bulls for all Israel, *n* rams,
Jer 52:23 there were *n* pomegranates.

NINETY-TWO (2)

Ezr 2:58 slaves of Solomon was three hundred and *n.*
Neh 7:60 slaves of Solomon was three hundred and *n.*

NINETY-YEAR-OLD (1)

2Mc 6:24 men would think the *n* Eleazar had gone

NINEVEH (39)

Gn 10:11 he went forth to Asshur, where he built *N,*
10:12 as well as Resen, between *N* and Calah,
2Kgs 19:36 broke camp, and went back home to *N.*
Tb 1: 3 people who had been deported with me to *N,*
1:10 Now, after I had been deported to *N,*
1:17 and been thrown outside the walls of *N,*
1:19 But a certain citizen of *N* informed the
1:22 my behalf, and I was able to return to *N.*
2: 2 from among our kinsmen exiled here in *N.*
7: 3 "We are of the exiles from Naphtali at *N."*
11: 1 When they were near Kaserin, just before *N,*
11:15 for she was approaching the gate of *N.*
11:16 the gate of *N* to meet his daughter-in-law.
11:16 people of *N* saw him walking along briskly,
11:17 was joy for all the Jews who lived in *N.*
14: 1 and received an honorable burial in *N.*
14: 4 word which was spoken by Nahum against *N.*
14: 4 happen, and shall overtake Assyria and *N;*
14: 8 "Now, as for you, my son, depart from *N;*
14:15 the destruction of *N* and saw its effects.
14:15 done against the citizens of *N* and Assyria.
Jdt 1: 1 of the Assyrians in the great city of *N.*
2:21 After a three-day march from *N,*
Is 37:37 broke camp and went back home to *N.*
Jon 1: 2 "Set out for the great city of *N,*
3: 2 "Set out for the great city of *N,*
3: 3 So Jonah made ready and went to *N,*
3: 3 Now *N* was an enormously large city;
3: 4 "Forty days more and *N* shall be destroyed,"
3: 5 when the people of *N* believed God;
3: 6 When the News reached the king of *N,*
3: 7 Then he had this proclaimed throughout *N,*
4:11 And should I not be concerned over *N,*
Na 1: 1 Oracle about *N.*
2: 9 *N* is like a pool whose waters escape;
3: 7 you runs from you, saying, *N* is destroyed;
Zep 2:13 He will make *N* a waste,
Mt 12:41 the citizens of *N* will rise with the
Lk 11:32 the citizens of *N* will rise along with the

NINEVEH'S (1)

Tb 14:15 dying he rejoiced over *N* destruction,

NINEVITES (1)

Lk 11:30 Just as Jonah was a sign for the *N,*

NINTH (25)

Lv 23:32 on the evening of the *n* of the month,
25:22 and even into the *n* year,
Nm 7:60 On the *n* day it was the turn of Abidon,
2Kgs 17: 6 In the *n* year of Hoshea,
18:10 year of Hezekiah, the *n* year of
25: 1 month of the *n* year of Zedekiah's reign,
25: 3 On the *n* day of the fourth month,
1Chr 12:13 Eliel seventh, Johanan eighth, Elzabad *n,*
24:11 the eighth to Abijah, the *n* to Jeshua,
25:16 The *n* was Mattaniah, his sons, and his
27:12 *N,* for the ninth month,
Ezr 10: 9 it was in the *n* month,
1Mc 4:52 on the twenty-fifth day of the *n* month,
Jer 36: 9 In the *n* month, in the fifth year
36:22 his winter house, since it was the *n* month,
39: 1 the tenth month of the *n* year of Zedekiah,
39: 2 On the *n* day of the fourth month,
52: 4 the tenth month of the *n* year of his reign,
52: 6 On the *n* day of the fourth month,
Ez 24: 1 day of the tenth month, in the *n* year,
Hg 2:10 On the twenty-fourth day of the *n* month,
2:18 from the twenty-fourth day of the *n* month.
Zec 7: 1 on the fourth day of Chislev, the *n* month,
Rv 21:20 chrysolite, the eighth beryl, the *n* topaz,

NISAN (3)

Neh 2: 1 *N* of the twentieth year of King Artaxerxes,
Est 0: 1 King Ahasuerus, on the first day of *N,*
3: 7 In the first month, *N,* in the twelfth year

NISROCH (2)

2Kgs 19:37 was worshiping in the temple of his god *N,*
Is 37:38 was worshiping in the temple of his god *N,*

NO-AMON (1)

Na 3: 8 than *N* that was set among the streams,

NO-GOD (1)

Dt 32:21 *n'* and angered me with their vain idols,

NO-GODS (4)

Dt 32:17 They offered sacrifice to demons, to *n,"*
2Chr 13: 9 bull and seven rams becomes a priest of *n.*
Bar 4: 7 Maker with sacrifices to demons, to *n;*
6:49 then can one not know that these are *n,*

NO-PEOPLE (1)

Dt 32:21 vain idols, I will provoke them with a *n';*

NOADIAH (2)

Ezr 8:33 the Levites Jozabad, son of Jeshua, and *N,*
Neh 6:14 keep in mind as well *N* the prophetess and

NOAH (50)

Gn 5:29 years old, he begot a son and named him *N,*
5:30 and ninety-five years after the birth of *N,*
5:32 When *N* was five hundred years old,
6: 8 But *N* found favor with the LORD.
6: 9 These are the descendants of *N.*
6: 9 *N,* a good man and blameless in that age,
6:13 led depraved lives on earth, he said to *N:*
6:22 This *N* did;
7: 1 LORD said to *N:* "Go into the ark,
7: 5 *N* did just as the LORD had commanded him.
7: 6 *N* was six hundred years old when the flood
7: 7 *N* went into the ark because of the waters
7: 9 male and female entered the ark with *N,*
7:13 the precise day named, *N* and his sons Shem,
7:15 the breath of life entered the ark with *N.*
7:16 species they came, as God had commanded *N.*
7:23 *N* and those with him in the ark were left.
8: 1 then God remembered *N* and all the animals,
8: 6 *N* opened the hatch he had made in the ark,
8:11 So *N* knew that the waters had lessened on
8:13 *N* then removed the covering of the ark and
8:15 Then God said to *N:* "Go out of the ark,
8:18 So *N* came out,
8:20 Then *N* built an altar to the LORD,
9: 1 blessed *N* and his sons and said to them:
9: 8 God said to *N* and to his sons with him:
9:17 God told *N:* "This is the sign
9:18 of *N* who came out of the ark were Shem,
9:19 These three were the sons of *N,*
9:20 Now *N,* a man of the soil,
9:24 When *N* woke up from his drunkenness and
9:28 *N* lived three hundred and fifty years
9:29 of *N* was nine hundred and fifty years;
Nm 26:33 only daughters whose names were Mahlah, *N,*
27: 1 of Joseph, had daughters named Mahlah, *N,*
36:11 Mahlah, Tirzah, Hoglah, Milcah and *N,*
Jos 17: 3 only daughters, whose names were Mahlah, *N,*
1Chr 1: 4 Jared, Enoch, Methuselah, Lamech, *N,*
Tb 4:12 My boy, keep in mind *N,* Abraham, Isaac,
Sir 44:17 *N,* found just and perfect,
Is 54: 9 *N,* when I swore that the waters of Noah
Ez 14:14 and even if these three men were in it, *N,*
14:20 off from it man and beast, even if *N,*
Mt 24:38 right up to the day *N* entered the ark.
Lk 3:36 son of Arphaxad, son of Shem, son of *N,*
17:26 As it was in the days of *N,*
17:27 right up to the day *N* entered the ark
Heb 11: 7 By faith *N,* warned about things not yet
2Pt 2: 5 he preserved *N* as a preacher of holiness,

NOAH'S (8)

Gn 7:11 In the six hundredth year of *N* life,
7:13 *N* wife, and the three wives of Noah's sons
8:13 the six hundred and first year of *N* life,
10: 1 These are the descendants of *N* sons,
10:32 These are the groupings of *N* sons,
Mt 24:37 of Man will repeat what happened in *N* time.
1Pt 3:20 They had disobeyed as long ago as *N* day,

NOB (6)

1Sm 21: 2 David went to Ahimelech, the priest of *N,*
22: 9 come to Ahimelech, son of Ahitub, in *N.*
22:11 to all his family who were priests in *N;*
22:19 put the priestly city of *N* to the sword,
Neh 11:32 Bethel and its dependencies, Anathoth, *N,*
Is 10:32 Even today he will halt at *N,*

NOBAH (3)

Nm 32:42 *N* also campaigned against Kenath,
32:42 and called it *N* after his own name.
Jgs 8:11 route of the nomads east of *N* and Jogbehah,

NOBILITY (4)

Wis 8: 3 *n* the splendor of companionship with God;

NOBILITY (cont.)

Is 5:14 Down go their *n* and their masses,
Dn 1: 3 Israelites of royal blood and of the *n*,
Rv 18:23 Because your merchants were the world's *n*,

NOBLE (38)

Jgs 5: 2 *n* deeds by the people who bless the LORD,
Tb 5:14 are a kinsman, and from a *n* and good line!
7: 7 You are the son of a *n* and good father.
8: 7 not because of lust, but for a *n* purpose.
9: 6 noble and good child, son of a *n* and good,
2Mc 4:37 the prudence and *n* conduct of the deceased.
6:18 a man of advanced age and *n* appearance,
6:23 But he made up his mind in a *n* manner,
6:28 and I will leave to the young a *n* example
7:11 out his hands, as he spoke these *n* words:
7:21 Filled with a *n* spirit that stirred her
12:42 The *n* Judas warned the soldiers to keep
12:43 he acted in a very excellent and *n* way,
14:42 suffer outrages unworthy of his *n* birth.
15:11 spear as with the encouragement of *n* words,
15:17 Encouraged by Judas' *n* words,
Prv 8: 6 for *n* things I speak;
17: 7 how much more, lying words in a *n!*
19: 6 Many curry favor with a *n;*
Eccl 10:17 are you, O land, whose king is of *n* birth,
Wis 3:15 the fruit of *n* struggles is a glorious one;
8:15 in the assembly I should appear *n*,
8:19 child, and I came by a *n* nature;
8:20 or rather, being *n*,
Sir 45:23 And, at the prompting of his *n* heart,
Is 9:14 [The elder and the *n* are the head,
32: 5 No more will the fool be called *n*,
32: 8 *n* man plans noble things, and by noble
Lam 4: 1 is the gold, how changed the *n* metal;
Lk 19:12 "A man of *n* birth went to a faraway
1Tm 3: 1 wants to be a bishop aspires to a *n* task.
6:12 you made your *n* profession of faith.
6:13 his *n* profession before Pontius Pilate,
2Tm 2:21 of the house and ready for every *n* service.
Jas 2: 7 that *n* name which has made you God's own.

NOBLEMAN (2)

1Mc 3:32 He left Lysias, a *n* of royal blood,
Is 3: 3 and elder, The captain of fifty and the *n*,

NOBLER (1)

Wis 18:12 instant their *n* offspring were destroyed.

NOBLES (45)

Nm 21:18 princes sank, that the *n* of the people dug,
Jgs 5: 9 Israel, *n* of the people who bless the LORD;
1Sm 2: 8 To seat them with *n* and make a glorious
1Kgs 21: 8 *n* who lived in the same city with Naboth.
21:11 the elders and the *n* who dwelt in his city
2Chr 23:20 Then he took the captains, the *n*,
Neh 2:16 neither to the priests, nor to the *n*,
4: 8 then addressed these words to the *n*,
4:13 stood beside me, for I had said to the *n*,
5: 7 I called the *n* and magistrates to account,
6:17 were going to Tobiah from the *n* of Judah,
7: 5 it into my mind to gather together the *n*,
13:17 I took the *n* of Judah to task,
Jdt 2: 2 He summoned all his ministers and *n*,
Est A:10 lowly were exalted and they devoured the *n*.
1: 3 the Persian and Median aristocracy, the *n*,
1Mc 1: 6 He therefore summoned his officers, the *n*,
2Mc 4:31 affair, leaving Andronicus, one of his *n*,
Jb 34:18 and to *n*, "You are wicked!"
34:20 He brings on *n*,
Ps(s) 68:32 Let *n* come from Egypt;
83:12 Make their *n* like Oreb and Zeeb;
149: 8 with chains, their *n* with fetters of iron;
Prv 8:16 By me princes govern, and *n;*
Sir 48: 6 You sent kings down to destruction, and *n*,
Is 5:13 Their *n* die of hunger,
34:12 Her *n* shall be no more,
Jer 14: 3 The *n* send their servants for water,
27:20 with all the *n* of Judah and Jerusalem
39: 6 Babylon, who slew also all the *n* of Judah.
39:13 and all the *n* of the king of Babylon,
41: 1 of royal descent, one of the king's *n*,
Bar 1: 4 the *n*, the kings' sons, the elders,
1: 9 and the skilled workers, and the *n*,
Ez 17:13 oath, while removing the *n* of the land,
22:27 Her *n* within her are like wolves that tear
Dn 3:91 rose in haste and asked his *n*,
3:94 governors, and *n* of the king came together,
4:33 My *n* and lords sought me out;
5:23 before you, so that you and your *n*,
6: 8 of the kingdom, the prefects, satraps, *n*,
Jon 3: 7 Nineveh, by decree of the king and his *n:*
Na 3:10 For her *n* they cast lots,
3:18 king of Assyria, your *n* have gone to rest;
Rv 6:15 of the earth, the *n* and those in command,

NOBLEST (2)

Est 6: 9 to one of the *n* of the king's officials,
2Mc 4:12 the *n* young men to wear the Greek hat.

NOBLY (3)

2Mc 13:14 followers to fight *n* to death for the laws,
14:42 preferring to die *n* rather than fall into
Rom 14:21 acting *n* if you abstained from eating meat,

NOBODIES (1)

2Cor 6: 9 *n* who in fact are well known

NOBODY (3)

Dn 13:16 *N* else was there except the two elders,
Mt 9:16 *N* sews a piece of unshrunken cloth on an
1Cor 12: 3 That is why I tell you that *n* who speaks

NOCTURNAL (1)

Dt 23:11 becomes unclean because of a *n* emission,

NOD (5)

Gn 4:16 presence and settled in the land of *N*,
2Mc 8:18 *n* destroy not only those who attack us,
Ps(s) 64: 9 all who see them *n* their heads.
Sir 12:18 Then he will *n* his head and clap his hands
Mt 25: 5 delayed his coming, so they all began to *n*,

NODAB (1)

1Chr 5:19 and against Jetur, Naphish, and *N*,

NODAN (1)

2Sm 6: 6 they came to the threshing floor of *N*,

NODES (8)

1Kgs 7:17 *n* of the) capitals on top of the columns,
7:20 of the *n* and their enveloping network.
7:41 *n* for the capitals on top of the columns,
7:42 that covered the two *n* of the capitals
2Chr 4:12 two *n* for the capitals topping these two
4:12 the *n* of the capitals topping the columns;
4:13 two *n* of the capitals topping the columns.

NOGAH (2)

1Chr 3: 7 Ibhar, Elishua, Eliphelet, *N*,
14: 6 Solomon, Ibhar, Elishua, Elpelet, *N*,

NOHAH (1)

1Chr 8: 2 the second son, Aharah, the third, *N*,

NOISE (28)

Ex 32:17 Joshua heard the *n* of the people shouting,
Jos 6:10 any *n* or outcry until he gave the word:
1Sm 4: 6 The Philistines, hearing the *n* of shouting,
1Kgs 1:45 That is the *n* you heard.
2Kgs 11:13 Athaliah heard the *n* made by the people,
Jdt 6: 1 When the *n* of the crowd surrounding the
Est A: 4 There was *n* and tumult,
1Mc 5:31 *n* of the battle was resounding to heaven
6:41 All who heard the *n* of their numbers,
9:13 The earth shook with the *n* of the armies,
Is 13: 4 the *n* of kingdoms, nations assembled!
22: 2 the housetops, O city full of *n* and chaos,
29: 6 With thunder, earthquake, and great *n*,
31: 4 by their shouts nor disturbed by their *n*,
Jer 10:22 a *n!* it comes closer,
46:17 the name "The *n* that let its time go by."
49:21 At the *n* of their fall the earth quakes,
Bar 6:40 forward Bel and ask the god to make *n*,
Ez 3:12 and I heard behind me the *n* of a loud
3:13 the *n* made by the wings of the living
10: 5 The *n* of the wings of the cherubim could
19: 7 in it were appalled at the *n* of his roar.
26:10 cover you with dust, amid the *n* of steeds,
26:13 I will put an end to the *n* of your songs,
26:15 At the *n* of your fall, at the groaning of
37: 7 and even as I was prophesying I heard a *n;*
Mk 5:38 Jesus was struck by the *n* of people
Acts 2: 2 up in the sky there came a *n* like a strong,

NOISEMAKERS (1)

Jer 48:45 the brow of Moab, the skull of the *n*.

NOISOME (1)

Ps(s) 38: 6 *N* and festering are my sores because of

NOISY (6)

1Mc 9:39 and suddenly saw a *n* crowd with baggage;
Jb 31:34 Because I feared the *n* multitude
Is 28:28 crush it with his *n* cartwheels and horses.
32:14 will be forsaken, the *n* city deserted;
Am 5:23 Away with your *n* songs!
1Cor 13: 1 well, but do not have love, I am a *n* gong,

NOMAD (2)

Wis 5:14 memory of the *n* camping for a single day.
Is 21:13 thicket in the *n* country spend the night,

NOMADS (2)

Jgs 8:11 route of the *n* east of Nobah and Jogbehah,
2Mc 12:11 The defeated *n* begged Judas to make

NOMINATED (1)

Acts 1:23 they *n* two, Joseph (called Barsabbas,

NON-GREEKS (1)

Rom 1:14 I am under obligation to Greeks and *n*,

NON-ISRAELITE (1)

1Kgs 9:20 All the *n* people who remained in the land,

NON-OBSERVERS (1)

Lk 5:30 drink with tax collectors and *n* of the law?"

NONE (192)

Gn 2:20 but *n* proved to be the suitable partner
23: 6 *N* of us would deny you his burial ground
39:11 and *n* of the household servants were then
41:24 but *n* of them can give me an explanation."
Ex 8: 6 may learn that there is *n* like the LORD,
9: 4 *n* belonging to the Israelites will die."
9:14 that there is *n* like me anywhere on earth.
12:10 *N* of it must be kept beyond the next
12:22 *n* of you shall go outdoors until morning.
16:26 day, the sabbath, *n* of it will be there."
Lv 7:15 *n* of it may be kept till the next day.
18: 6 *N* of you shall approach a close relative
21: 1 *N* of you shall make himself unclean for
21:17 *N* of your descendants,
22:30 *n* of it shall be left over until the next
Nm 7: 9 He gave *n* to the Kohathites,
14:23 *N* of these who have spurned me shall see it.
32:11 *n* of these men of twenty years or more who
Dt 3: 4 his cities, *n* of them eluding our grasp,
11:25 *N* shall stand up against you;
15: 6 *n;* you will rule over many nations, and *n*
16: 4 and *n* of the meat which you sacrificed on
28:12 lend to many nations and borrow from *n*.
Jos 5: 5 *n* of those born in the desert during the
11:11 there to the sword, till *n* was left alive.
11:14 the last of them, leaving *n* alive.
Jgs 2:19 relinquishing *n* of their evil practices or
20: 8 *N* of us is to leave for his tent or return
21: 1 sworn at Mizpah that *n* of them would give
21: 8 they found that *n* of the men of
21: 9 army established that *n* of the inhabitants
1Sm 10:24 There is *n* like him among all the people!"
14:24 So *n* of the people tasted food.
14:39 But *n* of the people answered him.
21:10 "There is *n* to match it.
22: 8 *N* of you shows sympathy for me or
30:17 *n* escaped except four hundred young men,
2Sm 7:22 is *n* like you and there is no God but you,
15:14 or *n* of us will escape from Absalom.
17:12 *N* shall survive
1Kgs 9:22 But Solomon enslaved *n* of the Israelites,
12:20 *N* remained loyal to David's house except
14: 2 *n* will recognize you as Jeroboam's wife.
18:40 Let *n* of them escape!"
2Kgs 4: 6 "There is *n* left," he answered her.
12:14 *N* of the funds brought to the temple of
24:14 *N* were left among the people of the land
2Chr 14:10 there is *n* like you to help the powerless
Neh 7: 4 and *n* of the houses had been rebuilt.
13:15 I warned them to sell *n* of these victuals.
13:24 and *n* of them knew how to speak Jewish;
Jdt 12: 3 *N* of your people are with us."
Est 5:13 Yet *n* of this satisfies me as long as I
1Mc 2:61 *n* who hope in him shall fail in strength.
8:14 *n* of them put on a crown or wore purple as
11:36 Henceforth *n* of these provisions shall
2Mc 11:31 and *n* of the Jews shall be molested in any
Jb 2:13 nights, but *n* of them spoke a word to him;
3: 9 may it look for daylight, but have *n*,
10: 7 and that *n* can deliver me out of your hand?
11:19 you shall take your rest with *n* to disturb.
14: 4 There is *n*, however short his days.
24:16 *n* of them know the light,
30:13 me, they attack with *n* to stay them;
32:12 behold, there is *n* who has convicted Job,
34:27 away from him and heeded *n* of his ways,
37:24 men revere him, though *n* can see him,
Ps(s) 40: 6 your plans for us there is *n* to equal you;
49:18 For when he dies, he shall take *n* of it;
69:21 was none; for comforters, and I found *n*.
78:38 his anger and let *n* of his wrath be roused.
86: 8 There is *n* like you among the gods,
Prv 2:19 *N* who enter thereon come back again,
3:15 and *n* of your choice pos-sessions can
3:31 the lawless man and choose *n* of his ways:
6:29 *n* who touches her shall go unpunished.
20: 1 *n* who goes astray for it is wise.
28:17 to flee to the grave, *n* should support him.
Eccl 4: 1 of the victims with *n* to comfort them!
4: 1 violence, and there is *n* to comfort them!
6: 2 he lacks *n* of all the things he craves;
8: 8 it, and *n* has mastery of the day of death.
Sg 4: 2 big with twins, *n* of them thin and barren.
6: 6 big with twins, *n* of them thin and barren.
8: 1 I would kiss you and *n* would taunt me.
Wis 5:12 so that *n* discerns the way it went through
16:15 But your hand *n* can escape.

Sir 10:23 but *n* is greater than he who fears God.
11: 5 some that *n* would consider wear a crown.
14: 6 *N* is more stingy than he who is stingy
15:20 sin, to *n* does he give strength for lies.
40: 6 So short is his rest it seems like *n*,
42:25 another, yet *n* of them has he made in vain,
Is 1:31 and there shall be *n* to quench the flames.
5:27 *N* of them will stumble with weariness,
5:27 none will slumber and *n* will sleep.
5:27 *N* will have his waist belt loose,
5:29 they carry it off and *n* will rescue it.
14: 8 to rest, there will be *n* to cut us down."
34:15 assemble, *n* shall be missing its mate.
43:10 was formed, and after me there shall be *n*.
43:13 There is *n* who can deliver from my hand.
45: 6 men may know that there is *n* besides me.
46: 9 is no other, I am God, there is *n* like me.
47:15 wanders his own way, with *n* to save you.
59:16 was appalled that there was *n* to intervene;
64: 6 There is *n* who calls upon your name,
65:25 *N* shall hurt or destroy on all my holy
Jer 4: 4 like fire, and burn till *n* can quench it,
10: 7 in all their domain, there is *n* like you.
11:23 *N* shall be spared among them,
23: 4 and *n* shall be missing,
25:33 *N* will mourn them, none will gather them
29:32 *N* of them shall survive among this people
30: 7 How mighty is that day— *n* like it!
30:13 There is *n* to plead your cause,
31: 9 on a level road, so that *n* shall stumble.
44:13 *N* of the remnant of Judah that have come
44:14 *N* shall return to the land of Judah though
50: 9 *n* shall return without effect.
Bar 3:31 *N* knows the way to her,
6:13 but *n* does away with those that offend
Ez 7:25 they shall seek peace, but there will be *n*.
12:28 *N* of my words shall be delayed any longer;
14:15 traversed by *n* because of the wild beasts,
18:11 things (though the father does *n* of them),
18:22 *N* of the crimes he committed shall be
18:24 *N* of his virtuous deeds shall be remembered,
20: 8 *n* of them threw away the detestable things
33:13 *n* of his virtuous deeds shall be
33:16 *N* of the sins he committed shall be held
44: 9 *n* of the foreigners who live among the
46:18 so that *n* of my people will be driven from
Dn 1:19 all of them, *n* was found equal to Daniel,
4: 4 but *n* of them could tell me its meaning.
4:15 Although *n* of the wise men in my kingdom
5: 8 *n* of them could either read the writing or
11:45 shall come to his end with *n* to help him.
12:10 *n* of them shall have understanding,
13:43 though I have done *n* of the things with
Hos 7: 7 *n* of them calls upon me.
Am 5: 6 *n* to quench it for the house of Israel:
Ob 1:18 Then *n* shall survive of the house of Esau,
Mi 5: 7 and tears, and there is *n* to deliver.
Na 2: 9 but *n* turns back.
3:18 upon the mountains, with *n* to gather them.
Zep 3:13 couch their flocks with *n* to disturb them.
3:18 you, so that *n* may recount your disgrace.
Zec 8:17 and let *n* of you plot evil against another
9: 8 as a guard that *n* may pass to and fro;
Mt 7:21 *N* of those who cry out,
12:43 for a place of rest and finding *n*.
18:30 But he would hear *n* of it.
26:60 They discovered *n*, despite the many false
Mk 8:14 one loaf they had *n* with them in the boat.
12:22 *n* of the seven left any children behind.
13:18 praying that *n* of this happens in winter.
Lk 1:61 to her, *N* of your relatives has this name."
3:11 man with two coats give to him who has *n*.
4:26 It was to *n* of these that Elijah was sent,
13: 7 of fruit on this fig tree and found *n*.
14:33 *n* of you can be my disciple if he does not
18:19 *N* is good but God alone.
21:15 wisdom which *n* of your adversaries can take
Jn 13:28 *n* of those reclining at table understood
17:12 *n* but him who was destined to be lost
19:36 "Break *n* of his bones."
21: 4 *n* of the disciples knew it was Jesus.
Acts 4:32 *N* of them ever claimed anything as his own;
11:19 making the message known to *n* but Jews.
20:25 I know as I speak these words that *n* of
25: 7 him, *n* of which they were able to prove.
26:26 I am convinced that *n* of this escapes him
27:22 *N* among you will be lost—only the ship.
27:42 so that *n* might swim away and escape;
Rom 14: 7 *N* of us lives as his own master and none
1Cor 1:14 baptized *n* of you except Crispus and Gaius,
1:15 so there are *n* who can say that you were
2: 4 My message and my preaching had *n* of the
2: 8 *N* of the rulers of this age knew the
4: 6 so that *n* of you will grow self-important
7:29 wives should live as though they had *n*;
2Cor 11: 9 and in want I was a burden to *n* of you,
Heb 7:13 *n* of whose members ever officiated at the
1Pt 4:15 that *n* of you suffers for being a murderer,
2Pt 3: 9 *n* to perish but all to come to repentance.
1Jn 2:19 served to show that *n* of them was ours.

NONENTITIES (1)

Jer 8:19 with their foreign *n*

NONETHELESS (11)

Mt 18: 7 *N*, woe to that man through whom scandal
26:56 *N*, all this has happened in fulfillment of
Mk 13:13 *N*, the man who holds out till the end is
Lk 12:48 who *n* deserved to be flogged will get off
Jn 6:58 Unlike your ancestors who ate and died *n*,
8:14 My testimony is valid *n*,
8:37 *N*, you are trying to kill me because my
Acts 13:46 Paul and Barnabas spoke out fearlessly, *n*:
1Cor 9:17 I am *n* entrusted with a charge.
2Cor 9: 3 I *n* send the brothers so that our claims
1Pt 2: 4 stone, rejected by men but approved, *n*,

NONSENSE (4)

2Mc 2:32 it would be *n* to write a long preface to a
Zec 10: 2 For the teraphim speak *n*,
Lk 24:11 like *n* and they refused to believe them.
3Jn 1:10 he is doing in spreading evil *n* about us.

NONSENSICAL (1)

1Cor 15:36 A *n* question!

NOON (18)

Gn 43:16 for they are to dine with me at *n*."
43:25 gifts to await Joseph's arrival at *n*,
1Kgs 18:26 it and called on Baal from morning to *n*,
18:27 When it was *n*, Elijah taunted them:
18:29 *N* passed and they remained in a prophetic
20:16 They marched out at *n*,
2Kgs 4:20 he stayed with her until *n*,
Ps(s) 55:18 In the evening, and at dawn, and at *n*,
91: 6 darkness nor the devastating plague at *n*.
Sir 43: 3 At *n* it seethes the surface of the earth,
Is 16: 3 high *n* let your shadow be like the night,
Dn 13: 7 When the people left at *n*, Susanna used
Mt 20: 5 around *n* and midafternoon and did the same.
27:45 From *n* onward, there was darkness
Mk 15:33 When *n* came, darkness fell on the whole
Jn 4: 6 The hour was about *n*.
19:14 Day for Passover, and the hour was about *n*.)
Acts 22: 6 along, approaching Damascus around *n*,

NOONDAY (5)

Jb 5:14 at *n* they grope as though it were night,
11:17 your life shall be brighter than the *n*;
Ps(s) 37: 6 bright as the *n* shall be your vindication.
Sir 34:16 from the heat, a shade from the *n* sun,
Jer 20:16 cries in the morning, battle alarms at *n*,

NOONTIME (2)

Is 38:10 I said, "In the *n* of life I must depart!
Acts 10: 9 About *n* the next day, as the men were

NOOSE (1)

Jb 18:10 A *n* for him is hid on the ground,

NOR (728)

Gn 8:21 *n* will I ever again strike down all living
21:26 it, *n* did I ever hear of it until now."
31:52 *n* may you pass beyond it into mine.
Ex 4: 1 will not believe me, *n* listen to my plea?
4: 8 you, *n* heed the message of the first sign,
4: 9 even these two signs, *n* heed your plea,
4:10 nor recently, *n* now that you have
10:14 swarm of locusts, *n* will there ever be.
10:23 *n* could they move from where they were,
11: 6 as has never been, *n* will ever be again.
13:22 Neither the column of cloud by day *n* the
20:17 nor his male or female slave, *n* his ox
20:17 ass, *n* anything else that belongs to him."
20:23 neither gods of silver *n* gods of gold
22:27 God, *n* curse a prince of your people.
23: 2 as an excuse for doing wrong, *n* shall you,
23: 7 to death, *n* shall you acquit the guilty.
23:18 *n* shall the fat of my feast be kept
23:24 gods, *n* shall you make anything like them;
30: 9 *n* shall you pour out a libation upon it.
30:15 not give more, *n* shall the poor give less,
30:32 *n* may you make any other oil of a like
32:18 *n* does it sound like cries of defeat;
34:25 *n* shall the sacrifice of the Passover
36: 6 "Let neither man *n* woman make any more
Lv 7:18 him *n* shall it be reckoned to his credit;
12: 4 touch anything sacred *n* enter the sanctuary
13: 4 the skin, *n* has the hair turned white,
18: 3 *n* shall you do as they do in the land of
18:17 *n* shall you marry and have intercourse
18:23 *n* shall a woman set herself in front of an
19: 4 idols, *n* make molten gods for yourselves.
19: 9 *n* shall you glean the stray ears of grain.
19:10 *n* gather up the grapes that have fallen.
19:15 to the weak *n* deference to the mighty,
19:16 *n* shall you stand by idly when your
19:27 temples, *n* trim the edges of your beard.
21: 5 *n* shave the edges of the beard, nor lacerate
21: 7 *n* a woman who has been divorced by her
21:11 *n* shall he go near any dead person.
21:23 he may not approach the veil *n* go up to
22:10 "Neither a lay person *n* a priest's tenant
22:16 *n* in the eating of the sacred offering
22:25 *n* receive from a foreigner any such animals
23:22 *n* shall you glean the stray ears of your
25: 4 sow your field *n* prune your vineyard.
25: 5 *n* shall you pick the grapes of your
25:11 *n* shall you reap the aftergrowth or pick
25:30 *n* shall it be released in the jubilee.
25:37 money at interest *n* food at a profit.
26: 1 *n* shall you set up a stone figure for
27:28 field, shall be neither sold *n* ransomed;
Nm 1:49 shall not enroll *n* include in the census
5:15 pour oil on it *n* put frankincense over it,
6: 3 juice, *n* eat either fresh or dried grapes.
9:12 till morning, *n* breaking any of its bones,
14:44 covenant of the LORD *n* Moses left the camp.
16:15 them, *n* have I wronged any one of them."
18:20 Israelites *n* hold any portion among them;
20: 5 grain *n* figs nor vines nor pomegranates?
20:17 or vineyards, *n* drink of any well water,
21:22 vineyard, *n* will we drink any well water,
23:19 man that he should speak falsely, *n* human,
23:21 observed in Jacob, *n* misery seen in Israel.
23:23 against Jacob, *n* omen against Israel.
35:23 he was not his enemy *n* seeking to harm him:
35:32 *N* shall you accept indemnity to allow a
Dt 2:37 Wadi Jabbok, *n* the cities of the highlands.
4: 2 to what I command you *n* subtract from it.
4: 9 *n* let them slip from your memory as long
4:21 not cross the Jordan *n* enter the good land
4:28 neither see *n* hear, neither eat nor smell.
4:31 *n* forget the covenant which under oath he
5:21 house or field, *n* his male or female slave,
5:21 *n* his ox or ass, nor anything that belongs
7: 3 *n* taking their daughters for your sons.
7:14 childless *n* shall your livestock be barren.
7:25 or gold on them, *n* take it for yourselves,
8: 4 *n* did your feet swell these forty years.
9:27 people *n* upon their wickedness and sin,
13: 1 neither adding to it *n* subtracting from it.
13: 9 listen to him, *n* look with pity upon him,
14: 1 You shall not gash yourselves *n* shave the
15: 7 heart *n* close your hand to him in his need.
15:19 *n* shear the firstlings of your flock.
16:22 *n* shall you erect a sacred pillar,
17:16 *n* shall he make his people go back again
17:17 *n* shall he accumulate a vast amount of
17:20 *n* turn aside to the right or to the left
18:10 or daughter in the fire, *n* a fortuneteller,
18:11 *n* one who consults ghosts and spirits or
18:16 our God, *n* see this great fire any more,
20: 3 be neither alarmed *n* frightened by them.
22: 5 man, *n* shall a man put on a woman's dress;
23: 1 wife, *n* shall he dishonor his father's bed.
23: 3 *n* any descendant of his even to the tenth
23: 4 *n* any descendants of theirs even to the
23: 8 since he is your brother, *n* the Egyptian,
23:18 *n* a temple prostitute among the Israelite
24: 5 *n* shall any public duty be imposed on him.
24:16 children, *n* children for their fathers;
24:17 *n* take the clothing of a widow as a pledge.
25:14 *n* shall you keep two different measures in
28:45 *n* keep the commandments and statutes he
28:50 respect for the aged *n* pity for the young.
29: 4 in tatters *n* your sandals from your feet;
29: 5 not your food, *n* wine or beer your drink.
30:13 *N* is it across the sea,
Jos 1: 5 I will not leave you *n* forsake you.
1: 9 Do not fear *n* be dismayed,
22:19 against the LORD *n* involve us in rebellion,
Jgs 1:31 *N* did Asher drive out the inhabitants of
5: 8 Not a shield could be seen, *n* a lance,
6: 4 leaving no sustenance in Israel, *n* sheep,
6: 5 they *n* their camels could be numbered,
7:12 *N* could their camels be counted,
8:23 over you, *n* shall my son rule over you.
8:35 *N* were they grateful to the family of
11:34 he had neither son *n* daughter besides her.
13: 6 he came from, *n* did he tell me his name.
13: 7 So take neither wine *n* strong drink,
13:14 *n* take wine or strong drink, nor eat
13:23 *N* would he have let us see all this just
Ru 1: 5 with neither her two sons *n* her husband.
1Sm 1:11 neither wine *n* liquor shall he drink,
1:15 I have had neither wine *n* liquor;
2: 3 *n* let arrogance issue from your mouths.
2:13 neither for the LORD *n* for the priests' duties
4:20 she neither answered *n* paid any attention.
5: 5 neither the priests of Dagon *n* any others
12: 4 nor oppressed us, *n* accepted anything
12:21 idols which can neither profit *n* save;
13:22 neither sword *n* spear could be found
14: 3 *N* did the soldiers know that Jonathan had
15:29 Glory of Israel neither retracts *n* repents,
21: 9 along neither my sword *n* my weapons,
30:12 he had not taken food *n* drunk water for
2Sm 1:21 dew *n* rain upon you, nor upsurgings
1:23 separated neither in life *n* in death,
2:19 neither right *n* left in his pursuit.
3:34 with chains, *n* your feet placed in fetters;
12:17 would not, *n* would he take food with them.

NOR (cont.)

14: 7 neither name *n* posterity upon the earth.”
17:12 neither he *n* any of his followers.
19:25 feet nor trimmed his mustache *n* washed
20: 1 in David, *n* any share in the son of Jesse.
21: 4 *n* is it our place to put any man to death
22:38 *n* did I turn again till I made an end
1Kgs 1:26 *n* Zadok the priest, nor Benaiah,
1:26 son of Jehoiada, *n* your servant Solomon.
3:11 *n* for riches, nor for the life
3:26 said, “It shall be neither mine *n* yours.
8:57 and may he not forsake us *n* cast us off.
11:13 *N* will I take away the whole kingdom.
13: 8 *n* eat bread or drink water in this place.
13:17 neither to eat bread *n* drink water here,
13:28 not eaten the body *n* had it harmed the ass.
17:14 not go empty, *n* the jug of oil run dry,
17:16 did not go empty, *n* the jug of oil run dry,
2Kgs 3:14 neither look at you *n* notice you at all.
3:17 ‘Though you will see neither wind *n* rain,
4:23 “It is neither the new moon *n* the sabbath.”
12: 9 people *n* make the repairs on the temple.
14: 6 *n* shall children be put to death for their
14:26 where there was neither slave *n* freeman,
17:22 committed, *n* would they desist from them.
17:34 *n* observe the statutes and regulations,
17:35 nor worship them, nor serve them, *n*
18: 5 and neither before him *n* after him was
19:32 *n* shoot an arrow at it, nor come before
19:32 a shield, *n* cast up siege-works against it.
22:13 book, *n* fulfill our written obligations.”
23:25 *n* could any after him compare with him.
1Chr 17: 9 *n* shall wicked men ever again oppress them,
21:24 *n* offer up holocausts that cost me nothing.”
2Chr 1:11 *n* for the life of those who hate you, nor
1:12 *n* will those have them who come after you.”
6: 5 *n* have I chosen any man to be commander of
20:33 *n* as yet had the people fixed their hearts
21:12 path of your father Jehoshaphat, *n* of Asa,
25: 4 children, *n* children for their fathers;
35:18 *n* had any king of Israel kept a Passover
36:17 *n* maiden, neither the aged *n* the decrepit;
Ezr 9: 1 nor the priests *n* the Levites have kept
10: 6 night neither eating food *n* drinking water,
Neh 2:16 *n* to the nobles, nor to the magistrates,
2:16 *n* to the others who would be concerned
2:20 share *n* claim nor memorial in Jerusalem.”
4:17 nor any of my attendants, *n* any of the
5:14 twelve years neither I *n* my brethren lived
9:19 *n* did the column of fire by night cease to
9:35 *n* did they turn away from their evil deeds.
13:25 *n* take any of their daughters for your sons
Tb 3: 3 *n* for my inadvertent offenses, nor
3: 5 *n* have we trodden the paths of truth
3:15 *N* does he have a close kinsman or other
4:15 *n* let drunkenness accompany you on your
5: 2 since he does not know me *n* do I know him?
Jdt 7: 4 Neither the high mountains *n* the valleys
8:16 he should be moved by threats, *n* human,
8:18 generations, *n* does there exist today,
8:27 try their hearts, *n* has he done so with us.
9:11 *n* does your power depend upon stalwart men;
11: 2 *N* would I have raised my spear against
11:10 *n* does the sword prevail against them,
16: 6 *n* did titans bring him low, *n* huge giants
Est C:28 *n* have I graced the banquet of the king or
9:28 *n* into oblivion among their descendants.
1Mc 2:22 We will not obey the words of the king *n*
2:34 *n* will we obey the king's command to
2:36 *n* blocked up their own hiding places.
8:26 war they shall not give *n* provide grain,
10:30 Neither now *n* in the future will I collect
10:46 they neither believed *n* accepted them,
2Mc 6: 6 feasts, *n* even admit that he was a Jew.
7:22 *n* was it I who set in order the elements
8:16 *n* to fear the large number of the Gentiles
Jb 1:22 *n* did he say anything disrespectful of God.
3: 4 above call for it, *n* light shine upon it!
3: 6 year, *n* enter into the count of the months!
3: 9 have none, *n* gaze on the eyes of the dawn,
3:26 I have no peace *n* ease;
5: 6 *n* does trouble spring out of the ground;
14:12 not awake, *n* be roused out of their sleep.
16:18 not my blood, *n* let my outcry come to rest!
18:19 son *n* grandson among his people, nor any
20: 9 *n* shall his dwelling again behold him.
21: 9 fear, *n* is the scourge of God upon them.
27: 4 speak falsehood, *n* my tongue utter deceit!
28: 7 knows, *n* has the hawk's eye seen that path.
28: 8 trodden it, *n* has the lion gone that way.
28:13 *n* is it to be had in the land of the
28:15 it, *n* can its price be paid with silver.
28:17 it, *n* can golden vessels reach its worth.
28:18 coral *n* jasper should be thought of;
32: 9 wise, *n* the aged who understand the right.
32:21 to anyone, *n* give flattering titles to any.
33: 7 *n* should my presence weigh heavily upon
34:19 *n* respects the rich more than the poor?
35:15 *n* does he show concern that a man will die.
41:18 nor will the spear, nor the dart, *n* the
Ps(s) 1: 1 Nor walks in the way of sinners, *n* sits
1: 5 wicked shall not stand, *n* shall sinners,
6: 2 your anger, *n* chastise me in your wrath.
9:19 *n* shall the hope of the afflicted forever
15: 3 *n* takes up a reproach against his neighbor;
16: 4 *n* will I take their names upon my lips.
16:10 *n* will you suffer your faithful one to
18:38 *n* did I turn again till I made an end of
19: 4 *n* a discourse whose voice is not heard;
22:25 *n* disdained the wretched man in his misery,
22:25 *N* did he turn his face away from him,
24: 4 vain, *n* swears deceitfully to his neighbor.
26: 4 men, *n* do I consort with hypocrites.
26: 9 of sinners, *n* with men of blood my life.
28: 5 deeds of the LORD *n* the work of his hands,
33:16 *n* is a warrior delivered by great strength.
36:12 me *n* the hand of the wicked disquiet me.
37: 1 evildoers, *n* jealous of those who do wrong;
37:25 Neither in my youth, *n* now that I am old,
37:25 forsaken *n* his descendants begging bread.
37:33 *n* let him be condemned when he is on trial.
38:15 neither hears *n* has in his mouth a retort.
44: 4 *n* did their own arm make them victorious,
44: 7 my bow did I trust, *n* did my sword save me;
44:18 *n* have we been disloyal to your covenant;
44:19 *n* our steps turned aside from your path,
55:20 is not in them, *n* do they fear God.
69:16 nor the abyss swallow me up, *n* the pit
75: 7 *n* from the west, neither from the desert *n*
78: 8 steadfast *n* its spirit faithful toward God.
78:22 believed not God *n* trusted in his help.
78:37 him, *n* were they faithful to his covenant.
78:42 *n* the day he delivered them from the foe,
81:10 you *n* shall you worship any alien god.
86:14 life, *n* do they set you before their eyes.
89:23 him, *n* shall the wicked afflict him.
89:34 from him, *n* will I belie my faithfulness.
91: 5 of the night *n* the arrow that flies by day;
91: 6 darkness *n* the devastating plague at noon.
91:10 *n* shall affliction come near your tent,
92: 7 knows not, *n* does a fool understand this.
94:14 off his people, *n* abandon his inheritance;
103: 9 chide, *n* does he keep his wrath forever.
103:10 *n* does he requite us according to our
104: 9 pass, *n* shall they cover the earth again.
107:38 *n* did he suffer their cattle to decrease.
109:12 a kindness, *n* anyone to pity his orphans.
115:17 the LORD, *n* those who go down into silence;
121: 4 Indeed he neither slumbers *n* sleeps,
121: 6 not harm you by day, *n* the moon by night.
129: 7 hand, *n* the gatherer of sheaves his arms;
131: 1 heart is not proud, *n* are my eyes haughty;
131: 1 things, *n* with things too sublime for me.
132: 3 live in, *n* lie on the couch where I sleep;
135:17 not, *n* is there breath in their mouths.
139:15 *n* was my frame unknown to you When I was
147:10 *n* is he pleased with the fleetness of men.
Prv 4:27 Turn neither to right *n* to left,
5:13 *n* to my instructors incline my ear!
6: 4 to your eyes, *n* slumber to your eyelids;
6:35 *n* be satisfied with the greatest gifts.
8:26 not made, *n* the first clods of the world.
22:22 are poor, *n* crush the needy at the gate;
22:24 man, *n* the companion of a wrathful man,
23:10 landmark, *n* invade the fields of orphans;
23:20 *n* with those who eat meat to excess;
24:19 with evildoers, *n* envious of the wicked;
25: 6 presence, *n* occupy the place of great men;
25:27 *n* to seek honor after honor.
27:24 forever, *n* even a crown from age to age.
30: 3 *n* have I the knowledge of the Holy One.
30: 8 from me, give me neither poverty *n* riches;
31: 3 *n* your strength to those who ruin kings.
Eccl 1: 8 seeing *n* is the ear filled with hearing.
1:11 *n* of those to come will there be any
2:10 them, *n* did I deprive myself of any joy,
2:16 Neither of the wise man *n* of the fool will
4: 8 with neither son *n* brother.
8: 8 *n* are the wicked saved by their wickedness.
8:17 *n* by night do his eyes find rest in sleep.
9:10 nor reason, *n* knowledge, nor wisdom
9:11 nor the battle by the valiant, *n* a
9:11 nor riches by the shrewd, *n* favor by
10:20 *n* in the privacy of your bedroom revile
Sg 8: 7 quench love, *n* floods sweep it away.
Wis 1: 4 *n* dwells she in a body under debt of sin.
1: 8 *n* will chastising condemnation pass him by.
1:12 *n* draw to yourselves destruction by the
1:13 *n* does he rejoice in the destruction of
1:14 *n* any domain of the nether world on earth,
2: 1 *n* is anyone known to have come back from
2:10 let us neither spare the widow *n* revere
2:22 *n* discern the innocent souls' reward.
3:18 no hope *n* comfort in the day of scrutiny;
4: 3 not strike deep root *n* take firm hold.
4: 8 *n* can it be measured in terms of years.
4:14 *n* did they take this into account.
6: 4 law, *n* walk according to the will of God,
6: 7 no partiality, *n* does he fear greatness,
6:22 of her, *n* shall I diverge from the truth.
7: 9 *n* did I liken any priceless gem to her;
12:14 *N* can any king or prince confront you on
14:13 were not, *n* shall they continue forever;
15: 4 us, *n* the fruitless labor of painters,
15: 9 is to die *n* that his span of life is brief;
15:15 for vision, *n* nostrils to snuff the air,
15:15 *N* ears to hear, nor fingers
15:19 *N* for their looks are they good or
16:12 neither herb *n* application cured them,
16:14 *n* can he bring back the soul once it is
17: 5 *n* did the flaming brilliance of the stars
19:21 went about in them, *n* melted the icelike,
Sir 1:25 *n* approach it with duplicity of heart.
4:27 man, *n* refuse to do so before rulers.
4:29 speech, *n* lazy and slack in your deeds.
4:30 lion at home, *n* sly and suspicious at work.
7: 4 *n* from the king a place of honor.
7: 7 *n* disgrace yourself before the assembly.
7:12 *n* against your friend and companion.
7:15 Hate not laborious tasks, *n* farming,
7:18 *n* a dear brother for the gold of Ophir.
7:20 *n* a laborer who devotes himself to his
8:16 man, *n* ride with him through the desert;
10:18 man, *n* stubborn anger to one born of woman.
10:22 but poor, *n* proper to honor any sinner.
12: 3 *n* is it an act of mercy that he does.
14:12 *n* have you been told the grave's appointed
16: 1 children, *n* rejoice in wicked offspring.
16: 9 *N* did he spare the doomed people who were
16:10 *N* the six hundred thousand foot soldiers
16:25 nor grow weary, *n* ever cease from
16:26 *n* should they ever disobey his word.
18: 4 *n* increase, nor penetrate the wonders
18:14 reproach, *n* spoil any gift by harsh words.
19:18 *n* is there prudence in the counsel of
20:15 no friends, *n* thanks for his generosity;
23: 2 spared, *n* the sins of my heart overlooked;
24:26 *n* will the last succeed in fathoming her.
25:20 woman's beauty, *n* be greedy for her wealth;
26:20 upright, *n* a shopkeeper free from sin:
28:16 it has no rest, *n* can he dwell in peace.
28:19 its yoke *n* been fettered with its chain;
28:22 among the just *n* scorch them in its flame,
30:19 to an idol that can neither taste *n* smell?
30:23 *n* is there aught to be gained from
31:12 a greedy gullet to his table, *N* cry out,
31:14 *n* reach when he does for the same dish.
31:31 *n* put him to shame while he is merry;
33:20 *n* wife, neither brother nor friend,
34:19 *n* for their many sacrifices does he
35: 6 most pleasing, *n* will it ever be forgotten.
35:14 *n* to the widow when she pours out her
35:18 *N* will it withdraw till the Most High
37:11 about her rival, *n* to a coward about war,
37:27 *n* is everything suited to every taste.
38:33 *n* are they prominent in the assembly;
38:33 *n* are they found among the rulers;
41:14 *n* is it always the proper thing to blush:
45:13 *n* may they ever be worn by any Except his
45:22 people *n* shares with them their heritage;
47:22 *n* permit even one of his promises to fail.
47:22 one, *n* destroy the offspring of his friend.
48:12 *n* was any man able to intimidate his will.
48:15 not repent, *n* did they give up their sins,
Is 2: 4 another, *n* shall they train for war again.
5:27 loose, *n* the thong of his sandal broken.
8:12 fear not, *n* stand in awe of what they fear.
9:12 who struck them, *n* seek the LORD of hosts.
10: 7 he intends, *n* does he have this in mind;
11: 3 he judge, *n* by hearsay shall he decide,
13:18 *n* shall they have eyes of pity for
13:20 She shall never be inhabited, *n* dwelt in,
13:20 tent there, *n* shepherds couch their flocks.
17: 8 *n* shall he regard what his fingers have
22: 2 slain with the sword, *n* killed in battle.
22:11 *n* did you consider him who built it long
23: 4 *n* given birth, nor raised young men, nor
25: 2 is a city no more, *n* ever to be rebuilt.
27:11 *n* shall he who formed them have mercy on
28:27 sledge, *n* does a cartwheel roll over cumin.
28:28 *n* does he crush it with his noisy
29:22 be ashamed of, *n* shall his face grow pale.
30: 5 gain them nothing, Neither help *n* benefit,
31: 1 to the Holy One of Israel *n* seek the LORD!
31: 4 by their shouts *n* disturbed by their noise,
32: 5 *n* the trickster be considered honorable.
33:20 be pulled up, *n* any of its ropes severed.
33:23 mast in place, *n* keep the sail spread out.
34:12 no more, *n* shall kings be proclaimed there;
35: 8 may pass over it, *n* fools go astray on it.
35: 9 *n* beast of prey go up to be met upon it.
37:33 *n* shoot an arrow at it, nor come
37:33 a shield, *n* cast up siegeworks against it.
38:18 gives you thanks, *n* death that praises you;
40:16 *n* its animals be enough for holocausts.
40:28 He does not faint *n* grow weary,
42: 8 I give to no other, *n* my praise to idols.
43:23 *n* honor me with your sacrifices.
43:23 of offerings, *n* weary you for frankincense.
43:24 *n* fill me with the fat of your sacrifices;
44: 9 shame, they neither see *n* know anything;
44:18 The idols have neither knowledge *n* reason;
44:19 *n* have the intelligence and sense to say,
45:19 hiding *n* from some dark place of the earth,
48: 8 You neither heard *n* knew,
49:10 *n* shall the scorching wind or the sun
51:14 into the pit, *n* shall they want for bread.
52:12 you come out, *n* leave in headlong flight,
53: 2 *n* appearance that would attract us to him.

53: 9 had done no wrong *n* spoken any falsehood.
54:10 leave you *n* my covenant of peace be shaken,
55: 8 not your thoughts, *n* are your ways my ways,
56: 3 *N* let the eunuch say,
57:13 you cry out, *n* save you in your distress.
57:16 will not accuse forever, *n* always be angry;
59: 1 short to save, *n* his ear too dull to hear.
59: 6 *n* can they cover themselves with their
59:21 *n* the mouths of your children Nor the
59:21 *N* the mouths of your children's children,
60:19 *N* the brightness of the moon shine upon
62: 8 *N* shall foreigners drink your wine,
63:16 not to know us, *n* Israel to acknowledge us,
65:23 *n* beget children for sudden destruction;
66:24 not die, *n* their fire be extinguished,
Jer 5:12 us, neither sword *n* famine shall we see.
7:24 But they obeyed not, *n* did they pay heed.
7:26 Yet they have not obeyed me *n* paid heed;
9:15 neither they *n* their fathers have known;
9:22 *n* the strong man glory in his strength,
9:22 *n* the rich man glory in his riches;
10:23 choice, *n* is it for him to direct his step.
11:14 of this people, *n* utter a plea for them.
14:14 gave them no command *n* did I speak to them.
15:10 I neither borrow *n* lend, yet all curse me.
16:13 neither you *n* your fathers have known;
16:17 from me, *n* does their guilt escape my view.
18:18 the priests, *n* of counsel from the wise,
18:18 the wise, *n* of messages from the prophets.
19: 4 which neither they *n* their fathers knew;
19: 5 nor spoke of, *n* did it ever enter my mine.
32:35 *n* did it even enter my mind that they
33:18 *n* shall priests of Levi ever be lacking,
35: 6 you *n* your children shall ever drink wine.
35: 7 neither plant *n* own a vineyard.
35: 8 *n* our wives, *n* our sons, *n* our daughters.
35: 8 our wives, nor our sons, *n* our daughters.
37: 2 Neither he, *n* his ministers, *n* the people
38:16 *n* will I hand you over to these men who
42:14 alarm no longer, *n* hunger for bread;
44: 3 neither they, nor you, *n* your fathers knew.
46: 6 The swift cannot flee, *n* the hero escape:
51:62 neither man *n* beast should dwell in it,
Lam 4:12 believe, *n* any of the world's inhabitants,
4:16 with favor, *n* show kindness to the elders.
Bar 1:18 *n* followed the precepts which the Lord set
3:22 been heard of in Canaan, *n* seen in Teman.
3:23 to wisdom, *n* have they her paths in mind.
3:27 *n* did he give them the way of
3:31 way to her, *n* has any understood her paths.
4:13 *n* did they tread the disciplined paths of
4:15 for age *n* tenderness for childhood;
6:23 *n* did they feel anything when they were
6:26 them upright, *n* come upright if they fall;
6:33 can neither set up a king *n* remove him.
6:35 death, *n* deliver the weak from the strong.
6:36 *n* do they save any man in an emergency.
6:37 pity the widow *n* benefit the orphan.
6:52 over the land, *n* do they give men rain.
6:53 *n* do they recover what is unjustly taken,
6:56 are safe from neither thieves *n* bandits,
6:63 neither execute judgment, *n* benefit man.
6:65 Kings they neither curse *n* bless.
6:66 *n* are they brilliant like the sun, *n* shining
Ez 2: 6 fear neither them *n* their words when they
2: 6 their words *n* be dismayed at their looks,
3: 6 *n* to the many peoples [with difficult
3: 9 them not, *n* be dismayed at their looks,
3:19 from his evil *n* from his wicked conduct,
5: 7 by my statutes *n* fulfilling my ordinances,
5:11 not look upon you with pity *n* have mercy.
7: 4 not look upon you with pity *n* have mercy;
7: 9 not look upon you with pity *n* have mercy;
7:11 not be long in coming, *n* shall it delay.
7:12 not the buyer rejoice *n* the seller mourn,
8:18 upon them with pity *n* will I show mercy.
9: 5 look on them with pity *n* show any mercy!
9:10 look upon them with pity, *n* show any mercy.
11:11 for you, *n* shall you be the meat within it.
13: 5 *n* did you build a wall about the house of
13: 9 *n* be recorded in the register of the house
13: 9 of Israel, *n* enter the land of Israel;
13:15 be no wall, *n* shall there be whitewashers
14:16 they could save neither sons *n* daughters;
14:20 they could save neither son *n* daughter;
16: 4 water *n* anointed, *n* were you rubbed
16: 4 with salt, *n* swathed in swaddling clothes.
18: 6 *n* raise his eyes to the idols of the house
18: 6 *n* have relations with a woman in her
18: 8 he does not lend at interest *n* exact usury;
18:20 *n* shall the father be charged with the
22:26 *n* teach the difference between the unclean
23:27 it, *n* shall you remember Egypt again.
24:14 I will not have pity *n* repent.
24:22 your beards *n* eating the customary bread.
29:18 but neither he *n* his army received any
31: 8 *n* could the fir trees match its boughs,
32:13 *n* shall the hoof of beast disturb them.
33:12 from his wickedness *n* can the virtuous man,
34: 4 *n* heal the sick nor bind up the injured.
34: 4 not bring back the strayed *n* seek the lost,
38:11 without walls, having neither bars *n* gates,
44:13 *n* shall they touch any of my sacred things,
44:20 their heads *n* let their hair hang loose,
47:12 leaves shall not fade, *n* their fruit fail.
Dn 3:30 *n* have we done as you ordered us for our
3:94 been singed, *n* were their garments altered;
5:10 Be not troubled in mind, *n* look so pale!
5:23 neither see nor hear *n* have intelligence.
Hos 2: 1 which can be neither measured *n* counted.
4:15 Come not to Gilgal, *n* up to Beth-aven,
5:13 he cannot heal you *n* take away your sore.
7:10 return to the LORD, their God, *n* seek him,
14: 4 save us, *n* shall we have horses to mount;
Jl 2: 2 been from of old, *n* will it be after them,
Am 2:15 his life, *n* the bowman stand his ground;
2:15 not escape, *n* the horseman save his life.
5:22 *n* consider your stall-fed peace offerings.
7:14 *n* have I belonged to a company of prophets;
Jon 3: 7 man nor beast, neither cattle *n* sheep,
3: 7 shall not eat, *n* shall they drink water.
Mi 2: 3 *N* shall you walk with head high,
4: 3 another, *n* shall they train for war again.
4:12 of the LORD, *n* understand his counsel,
5: 6 for no man, *n* tarry for the sons of men.
Hb 3:17 tree blossom not *n* fruit be on the vines,
Zep 1:12 "Neither good *n* evil can the LORD do."
1:18 Neither their silver *n* their gold shall be
3:13 *N* shall there be found in their mouths a
Hg 2:19 the seed has not sprouted, *n* have the vine,
Zec 4: 6 Not by an army, *n* by might,
8:17 another in his heart, *n* love a false oath.
11: 6 *N* shall I spare the inhabitants of the
11:16 *n* seek the strays, *n* heal the injured, *n* feed
Mal 2:13 *n* accepts it favorably from your hand;
3: 6 change, *n* do you cease to be sons of Jacob.
3:19 fire, leaving them neither root *n* branch,
3:24 fire, leaving them neither root *n* branch,
Mt 5:35 *n* by the earth (it is his footstool),
5:35 *n* by Jerusalem (it is the city of the
6:20 which neither moths *n* rust corrode nor
10: 9 gold *n* silver nor copper in your belts;
11:18 John appeared neither eating *n* drinking,
12:19 *n* will his voice be heard in the streets.
22:30 they neither marry *n* are given in marriage
23:13 *n* admitting those who are trying to enter.
24:36 it, neither the angels in heaven *n* the Son,
Mk 12:25 they neither marry *n* are given in marriage
13:32 the angels in heaven *n* even the Son,
14:40 open, *n* did they know what to say to him.
Lk 6:44 thornbushes, *n* grapes picked from brambles.
7:33 came neither eating bread *n* drinking wine,
9: 3 neither walking staff *n* traveling bag;
12:24 not reap, they have neither cellar *n* barn
12:33 no thief comes near *n* any moth destroys.
14:35 fit for neither the soil *n* the manure heap;
16:26 *n* can anyone cross from your side to us.'
18: 2 city who respected neither God *n* man.
Jn 1:13 *n* by carnal desire, nor by man's willing
1:25 Messiah, *n* Elijah, nor the Prophet,
4:21 neither on this mountain *n* in Jerusalem.
6:24 neither Jesus *n* his disciples were there,
8:11 Jesus said, *N* do I condemn you.
8:14 you know neither the one *n* the other.
8:19 "You know neither me *n* my Father.
10:12 who is no shepherd *n* owner of the sheep
14:17 since it neither sees him *n* recognizes him;
16: 3 because they knew neither the Father *n* me.
Acts 2:27 *n* will you suffer your faithful one to
2:31 world, *n* did his body undergo corruption,
3: 6 "I have neither silver *n* gold,
4:34 *n* was there anyone needy among them,
9: 9 during which time he neither ate *n* drank.
15:10 neither we *n* our fathers were able to bear?
17:25 *n* does he receive man's service as if he
23: 8 that there are neither angels *n* spirits,
24:12 *n* in the synagogue, *n* anywhere else in
27:20 the sun *n* the stars were to be seen,
28:21 *n* have any of the brothers arrived with a
Rom 8:38 *n* life, neither angels nor principalities,
8:38 present *n* the future, nor powers,
8:39 height nor depth *n* any other creature,
9: 7 are true Israelites *n* are all Abraham's
9:11 unborn and had done neither good *n* evil,
1Cor 2: 9 *n* has it so much as dawned on man what God
3: 7 *n* he who waters is of any special account,
9:15 *n* do I write this now to see to it that
10:10 *N* are you to grumble as some of them did,
11:11 of man *n* man independent of woman.
11:16 remember that neither we *n* the churches of
2Cor 12:20 to my liking, *n* may you find me to yours.
Gal 1:12 it from any man, *n* was I schooled in it.
3:17 years later, *n* is its promise nullified.
5: 6 *n* the lack of it counts for anything;
Eph 5: 4 *N* should there be any obscene,
1Thes 5: 5 We belong neither to darkness *n* to night;
2Thes 1: 8 *n* heed" the good news of our Lord Jesus.
2: 3 *n* the man of lawlessness been revealed
3: 8 among you, *n* depend on anyone for food.
1Tm 3: 3 *N* can he be someone who loves money.
6: 7 *n* have we the power to take anything out.
2Tm 1: 8 of your testimony to our Lord, *n* of me,
Ti 2: 7 completely under control *n* may you
2:10 contradicting them *n* stealing from them,
Heb 10: 8 you neither desired *n* delighted in."
12: 5 the Lord *n* lose heart when he reproves you;
12:18 *n* gloomy darkness and storm and trumpet
12:19 *n* a voice speaking words such that those
13: 5 never desert you, *n* will I forsake you."
2Pt 2: 5 *N* did he spare the ancient world
1Jn 2:15 world, *n* the things that the world affords.
3:10 *n* anyone who fails to love his brother.
Rv 3:15 I know you are neither hot *n* cold.
3:16 you are lukewarm, neither hot *n* cold,
7:16 *n* shall the sun or its heat beat down on
20: 4 beast or its image *n* accepted its mark
21:27 *n* anyone who is a liar or has done a

NORM (2)

Nm 27:11 This is the legal *n* for the Israelites,
Wis 2:11 But let our strength be our *n* of justice;

NORMAL (4)

Ex 14:27 at dawn the sea flowed back to its *n* depth.
1Kgs 13: 6 the king recovered the *n* use of his hand.
Tb 5:15 you are away I will give you the *n* wages,
1Cor 15: 8 by me, as one born out of the *n* course.

NORMS (2)

Nm 35:24 of blood in accordance with these *n*,
35:29 be *n* for you and all your descendants,

NORTH (150)

Gn 13:14 where you are, gaze to the *n* and south,
14:15 as far as Hobah, which is *n* of Damascus.
28:14 spread out east and west, *n* and south.
Ex 26:20 the other side of the Dwelling, the *n* side,
26:35 table, which is to be put on the *n* side.
27:11 the *n* side there shall be similar hangings,
36:25 the other side of the Dwelling, the *n* side,
38:11 On the *n* side there were similar hangings,
40:22 tent, on the *n* side of the Dwelling,
Lv 1:11 before the LORD at the *n* side of the altar.
Nm 2:25 *n* side shall be the divisional camp of Dan,
3:35 They camped at the *n* side of the Dwelling.
10: 6 those encamped on the *n* side shall set out.
34: 7 following shall be your boundary on the *n*:
35: 5 east, south, west and *n*—
Dt 2: 3 turn and go *n*.
3:27 and look out to the west, and to the *n*,
Jos 8:11 before the city, they pitched camp *n* of Ai,
8:13 *n* of the city and the ambush west of it,
13: 3 in the *n* is reckoned Canaanite territory,
15: 6 up to Beth-hoglah, and ran *n* of Betharabah,
15: 7 climbed to Debir, *n* of the vale of Achor,
15:10 *n* of the ridge of Mount Jearim (that is,
16: 6 From Michmethath on the *n*,
17: 9 ran *n* of the wadi and ended at the sea.
17:10 to Ephraim and that on the *n* to Manasseh;
17:10 Asher on the *n* and Issachar on the east.
18: 5 house of Joseph its territory in the *n*.
18:16 mountain on the *n* of the Valley of Rephaim,
18:17 Inclining to the *n*,
19:14 Skirting *n* of Hannathon,
19:27 then *n* of Beth-emek and Neiel,
24:30 region of Ephraim *n* of Mount Gaash.
Jgs 2: 9 region of Ephraim *n* of Mount Gaash.
7: 1 was in the valley *n* of Gibeath-hammoreh.
21:19 feast of the LORD at Shiloh, *n* of Bethel,
1Sm 14: 5 One crag was to the *n*,
1Kgs 7:25 rested on twelve oxen, three facing *n*,
7:39 south side of the temple and five on the *n*.
2Kgs 16:14 and set it on the *n* side of his altar.
1Chr 9:24 four sides, to the east, the west, the *n*,
26:14 counselor, and the *n* side fell to his lot.
26:17 the east, six watched each day, on the *n*,
2Chr 4: 4 It rested on twelve oxen, three facing *n*,
Tb 1: 2 and to the west of Asser, *n* of Phogor.
Jdt 2:21 the mountains to the *n* of Upper Cilicia.
16: 3 Assyrian came from the mountains of the *n*,
Jb 23: 9 Where the *n* enfolds him,
26: 7 He stretches out the *N* over empty space,
37: 9 from the *n* winds,
37:22 From the *N* the splendor comes,
Ps(s) 48: 3 Mount Zion, "the recesses of the *N*,"
89:13 *N* and south you created;
107: 3 and the west, from the *n* and the south.
Prv 25:23 The *n* wind brings rain,
27:16 he cannot tell *n* from south.
Eccl 1: 6 now toward the south, then toward the *n*,
11: 3 a tree falls to the south or to the *n*,
Sg 4:16 Arise, *n* wind!
Sir 43:17 drives on the south wind, the angry *n* wind,
Is 14:13 of Assembly, in the recesses of the *N*.
14:31 For there comes a smoke from the *n*,
41:25 I have stirred up one from the *n*,
43: 6 I will say to the *n*:
49:12 from afar, others from the *n* and the west,
Jer 1:13 I replied, "that appears from the *n*."
1:14 And from the *n*, said the LORD to me,
1:15 I am summoning all the kingdoms of the *n*,
3:12 Go, proclaim these words toward the *n*,
3:18 come from the land of the *n* to the land
4: 6 Evil I bring from the *n*,
6: 1 For evil threatens from the *n*,
6:22 a people comes from the land of the *n*,
13:20 up your eyes and see men coming from the *n*.

NORTH (cont.)

16:15 Israelites out of the land of the *n*
23: 8 house of Israel up from the land of the *n*—
25: 9 for and fetch all the tribes of the *n*,
25:26 all the kings of the *n*,
31: 8 bring them back from the land of the *n*;
46: 6 There in the *n*, on the Euphrates' bank,
46:20 from the *n* a horsefly lights upon her.
46:24 Egypt, handed over to the people of the *n*.
47: 2 waters are rising from the *n*,
50: 3 A people from the *n* advances against her
50: 9 a band of great nations from the *n*;
50:41 a people comes from the *n*,
51:48 the destroyers come against her from the *n*,
Ez 1: 4 As I looked, a stormwind came from the *N*,
8: 3 Jerusalem, to the entrance of the *n* gate,
8: 5 Son of man, look toward the *n*!
8: 5 I looked toward the *n* and saw northward of
8:14 the entrance of the *n* gate of the temple,
9: 2 of the upper gate which faces the *n*,
16:46 with her daughters, living to the *n* of you;
21: 3 to *n* every face shall be scorched by it.
21: 9 sheath against everyone from south to *n*,
23:24 They shall come against you from the *n*
26: 7 the *n* Nebuchadnezzar the king of Babylon,
32:30 the princes of the *n* and all the Sidonians,
38: 6 the recesses of the *n* with all its troops,
38:15 from your home in the recesses of the *n*,
39: 2 you come up from the recesses of the *n*;
40:19 Then he proceeded *n*,
40:20 the outer court, there was a gate facing *n*,
40:23 court had a gate opposite the *n* gate,
40:35 Then he brought me to the *n* gate,
40:40 outside, near the entrance of the *n* gate,
40:44 were two chambers, one beside the *n* gate,
40:44 the other beside the south gate, facing *n*.
40:46 and the chamber which faces *n* is for the
41:11 entrance on the *n* and another on the south.
42: 1 Then he led me *n* to the outer court,
42: 1 bringing me to some chambers on the *n*
42: 2 length was a hundred cubits on the *n* side,
42: 4 entrances of the chambers were on the *n*.
42:11 These looked like the chambers to the *n*,
42:13 "The *n* and south chambers which border on
42:17 Then he turned and measured the *n* side:
44: 4 of the *n* gate to the façade of the temple,
46: 9 *n* gate they shall leave by the south gate,
46: 9 south gate they shall leave by the *n* gate;
46:19 reserved to the priests] which face the *n*.
47: 2 He led me outside by the *n* gate,
47:15 is the boundary of the land on the *n* side:
47:17 frontier of Hamath and Damascus to the *n*.
48: 8 thousand cubits from *n* to south,
48: 9 across by twenty thousand *n* and south.
48:10 have twenty-five thousand cubits on the *n*,
48:13 across and twenty thousand *n* and south.
48:16 the *n* side, forty-five hundred cubits;
48:17 extend *n* two hundred and fifty cubits,
48:30 On the *n* side,
Dn 8: 4 I saw the ram butting toward the west, *n*,
11: 6 the king of the *n* in the interest of peace.
11: 7 enter the stronghold of the king of the *n*,
11: 8 have nothing to do with the king of the *n*.
11:11 go out to fight against the king of the *n*,
11:13 the king of the *n* shall raise another army,
11:15 When the king of the *n* comes,
11:40 but the king of the *n* shall overwhelm him
11:44 news from the east and the *n* terrifies him,
Am 8:12 sea to sea and rove from the *n* to the east
Zep 2:13 will stretch out his hand against the *n*,
3:10 and as far as the recesses of the *N*,
Zec 2:10 Flee from the land of the *n*,
6: 6 was turning toward the land of the *n*,
6: 8 they that go forth to the land of the *n*
6: 8 make my spirit rest in the land of the *n*."
Lk 13:29 and the west, from the *n* and the south,
Rv 21:13 were three gates facing east, three *n*,

NORTHEASTER (1)

Acts 27:14 a hurricane struck, the kind called a *n*."

NORTHERLY (1)

Ez 48: 1 Hazar-enon, on the *n* border with Damascus,

NORTHERN (16)

Nm 34: 9 This shall be your *n* boundary.
Jos 11: 2 and to the *n* kings in the mountain regions
15: 6 The *n* boundary climbed from the bay where
15: 8 at the *n* end of the Valley of Rephaim,
15:11 then extended along the *n* flank of Ekron,
18:12 Their *n* boundary began at the Jordan and
18:12 and went over the *n* flank of Jericho,
18:18 across the *n* flank of the Arabah overlook,
18:19 boundary continued across the *n* flank
18:19 and extended to the *n* tip of the Salt Sea,
2Kgs 11:11 southern to the *n* limit of the enclosure,
2Chr 23:10 to the *n* extremity of the enclosure,
Sir 43:21 Cold *n* blasts he sends that turn the ponds
Jer 10:22 closer, a great uproar from the *n* land:
Ez 47:17 This is the *n* boundary.
48: 1 at the *n* extremity,

NORTHERNER (1)

Jl 2:20 No, the *n* I will remove far from you,

NORTHLAND (1)

Jer 46:10 of hosts holds a slaughter feast in the *n*,

NORTHWARD (2)

Jos 12: 2 and the land *n* through half of Gilead to
Ez 8: 5 I looked toward the north and saw *n* of the

NORTHWEST (1)

Acts 27:12 port exposed on the southwest and the *n*.

NOSE (11)

Gn 24:22 half a shekel, which he fastened on her *n*,
24:47 on her *n* and the bracelets on her wrists.
2Kgs 19:28 my hook in your *n* and my bit in your
Jb 40:24 by his eyes, or pierce his *n* with a trap?
40:26 Can you put a rope into his *n*,
Sg 7: 5 Your *n* is like the tower on Lebanon that
Is 3:21 the signet rings, and the *n* rings;
37:29 my hook in your *n* and my bit in your mouth,
Ez 8:17 now they must also put the branch to my *n*?
16:12 about your neck, a ring in your *n*,
23:25 you in fury, cutting off your *n* and ears;

NOSES (1)

Ps(s) 115: 6 they have *n* but smell not;

NOSTRILS (12)

Gn 2: 7 and blew into his *n* the breath of life,
7:22 faintest breath of life in its *n* died out.
Nm 11:20 your very *n* and becomes loathsome to you.
Dt 33:10 bring the smoke of sacrifice to your *n*,
2Sm 22: 9 Smoke rose from his *n*,
Jb 27: 3 in me and the breath of God is in my *n*,
41:12 From his *n* issues steam,
Ps(s) 18: 9 Smoke rose from his *n*,
Wis 2: 2 Because the breath in our *n* is a smoke and
15:15 eyes for vision, nor *n* to snuff the air,
Is 2:22 let man alone, in whose *n* is but a breath;
Am 4:10 your *n* I brought the stench of your camps;

NOTABLE (2)

1Chr 17:17 on me as henceforth the most *n* of men,
Est 6: 1 the chronicle of *n* events be brought in.

NOTABLY (1)

Ez 19:11 *N* tall was she with her many clusters.

NOTE (29)

Gn 21: 1 took *n* of Sarah as he had said he would;
31:12 *N* well. All the he-goats in the flock
38:28 hand, to *n* that this one came out first.
Ex 16:29 Take *n*! The LORD has given you
Lv 27:26 *N* that a first-born animal,
27:28 *N*, also, that any one of his possessions
Nm 16: 2 members of the council and men of *n*.
Jgs 19:30 Take *n* of it, and state what you propose
Ru 3: 4 down, take *n* of the place where he does so.
1Sm 21:13 David took *n* of these remarks and became
23:22 Take *n* of the place where he sets foot"
2Kgs 5: 7 Take *n*! You can see he is only looking
Neh 3:36 Take *n*, O our God, how we were mocked!
6:16 the nations round about had taken *n* of it,
Tb 14:11 my children, *n* well what almsgiving does,
Ps(s) 87: 6 shall *n*, when the peoples are enrolled:
Sir 1: 7 her, has seen her and taken *n* of her.
Is 42:20 You see many things without taking *n*;
58: 3 afflict ourselves, and you take no *n* of it?"
Jer 2:31 generation, take *n* of the word of the Lord:
18:18 let us carefully *n* his every word."
Bar 4:14 to take *n* of the captivity of my sons and
Zec 11:16 who will take no *n* of those that perish,
Mt 24:15 on holy ground (let the reader take *n*!),
Mk 13:14 let the reader take *n*—
Jn 9:14 *N* that it was on a sabbath that Jesus had
Acts 17:22 I *n* that in every respect you are
1Cor 15:46 Take *n*, the spiritual was not first;
2Pt 3: 3 *N* this first of all: in the last days,

NOTED (5)

Gn 28: 6 Esau *n* that Isaac had blessed Jacob when
Ex 3: 9 *n* that the Egyptians are oppressing them.
2Sm 3:36 All the people *n* this with approval,
Est B: 5 "Having *n*,
Acts 23: 6 Paul, it should be *n*,

NOTES (1)

1Cor 14: 7 if there is no distinction among the *n*?

NOTHING (330)

Gn 11: 6 *n* will later stop them from doing whatever
14:24 *N* for me except what my servants have used
24:50 can say *n* to you either for or against it.
28:17 This is *n* else but an abode of God,
29:15 *n* just because you are a relative of mine?
32:11 the Jordan here with *n* but my staff,
39: 9 and he has withheld from me *n* but yourself,
47:18 there is *n* left to put at my lord's
Ex 1: 8 Then a new king, who knew *n* of Joseph,
5:23 yours, and you have done *n* to rescue them."
10:15 *N* green was left on any tree or plant
12:20 *N* leavened may you eat;
13: 3 *N* made with leaven must be eaten.
13: 7 no leaven and *n* leavened may be found in
22: 2 If he has *n*,
Lv 10: 3 But Aaron said *n*.
Nm 11: 6 we see *n* before us but this manna."
30: 5 bound herself and says *n* to her about it,
30: 8 of it, yet says *n* to her that day about it,
30:12 says *n* to express to her his disapproval,
30:15 after day, says *n* at all to her about them,
30:15 of them he said *n* to her about them.
Dt 3: 5 *n* of the great number of unwalled towns.
5:22 "These words, and *n* more,
8: 9 without stint and where you will lack *n*,
9: 3 them to *n* and subdue them before you,
15: 9 help to your needy kinsman and give him *n*;
16: 4 *N* leavened may be found in all your
22:26 You shall do *n* to the maiden,
28:55 using for food when *n* else is left him
29:22 all its soil being *n* but sulphur and salt,
32:27 the LORD had *n* to do with it.'"
Jos 11:15 He left *n* undone that the LORD had
Jgs 11: 2 him, "You shall inherit *n* in our family,
13: 4 wine or strong drink and to eat *n* unclean.
13: 7 wine nor strong drink, and eat *n* unclean.
19:19 there is *n* else we need."
19:30 *N* like this has been done or seen from the
1Sm 3:17 Hide *n* from me!
3:18 told him everything, and held *n* back.
10:16 But he mentioned *n* to him of what Samuel
12: 5 that you have found *n* in my possession."
12:21 they are *n*.
20: 2 My father does *n*,
20:21 As the LORD lives, there will be *n* to fear.
20:26 Saul, however, said *n* that day,
20:39 The boy knew *n*;
22:15 Your servant knows *n* at all,
22:23 Fear *n*;
25:21 in the desert so that he missed *n*.
25:36 *n* at all before daybreak the next morning.
28:20 he had eaten *n* all that day and night.
29: 6 for I have found *n* wrong with you from the
29: 7 and do *n* that might displease the
30:19 *N* was missing,
2Sm 12: 3 But the poor man had *n* at all except one
13:22 Absalom, moreover, said *n* at all to Amnon,
15:11 went in good faith, knowing *n* of the plan.
17:19 on the cover so that *n* could be noticed.
19: 7 that officers and servants mean *n* to you.
24:24 to the LORD my God holocausts that cost *n*."
1Kgs 5: 7 They left *n* unprovided.
8: 9 There was *n* in the ark but the two stone
10: 3 and there remained *n* hidden from him that
10:20 *N* like this was produced in any other
11:22 *N*," he said, "but please let me go!"
17:12 lives," she answered, "I have *n* baked;
18:43 up and looked, but reported, "There is *n*."
22: 3 doing *n* to take it from the king of Aram?"
22:16 me *n* but the truth in the name of the LORD?
2Kgs 4: 2 yours has *n* in the house but a jug of oil,"
9:35 her, they found *n* of her but the skull,
20:13 there was *n* in his house or in all his
20:15 "There is *n* in my storerooms that I did
20:17 *n* shall be left,
1Chr 21:24 nor offer up holocausts that cost me *n*."
2Chr 5:10 There was *n* in it but the two tablets
9: 2 and there remained *n* hidden from Solomon
9:19 *N* like this had ever been produced in any
18:15 me *n* but the truth in the name of the LORD
28:21 to the king of Assyria, it availed him *n*.
Neh 2:16 *n* of where I had gone or what I was doing,
2:16 for as yet I had disclosed *n* to the Jews,
5: 5 Yet we can do *n* about it,
5:12 everything and exact *n* further from them.
6: 8 *N* of what you report has taken place;
8:10 allot portions to those who had *n* prepared;
8:17 *n* of this sort from the days of Jeshua,
Tb 1:20 I was left with *n*.
7:11 *n* until you set aside what belongs to me."
8:14 was alive, and that there was *n* wrong.
10: 7 the road her son had taken, and she ate *n*.
12:11 I will conceal *n* at all from you.
Jdt 9: 1 her head, and wearing *n* over her sackcloth.
Est 6: 3 attendants replied, *N* was done for him."
1Mc 11: 5 but the king said *n*.
2Mc 4:25 but with *n* that made him worthy of the
7:12 because he regarded his sufferings as *n*.
11:26 they may have *n* to worry about but may
12: 2 and Demophon, to say *n* of Nicanor,
14:23 in Jerusalem, where he did *n* out of place.
14:35 of all, though you are in need of *n*,
Jb 1: 9 "Is it for *n* that Job is God-fearing?
2:10 Through all this, Job said *n* sinful.
5:24 stock of your household, you shall miss *n*.
26: 7 and suspends the earth over *n* at all;
27:19 he opens his eyes and *n* remains to him.
28:13 Man knows *n* to equal it,

Ps(s) 19: 7 *n* escapes its heat.
Prv 9:13 Folly is fickle, she is inane, and knows *n*.
10: 2 Ill-gotten treasures profit *n*,
13: 7 One man pretends to be rich, yet has *n*;
20:19 so have *n* to do with a babbler!
23:29 Who have wounds for *n*?
24:21 *n* to do with those who rebel against them;
28: 5 Evil men understand *n* of justice,
29:24 himself put under a curse, yet discloses *n*.
30: 6 Add *n* to his words,
30:30 of beasts, who retreats before *n*;
Eccl 1: 8 there is *n* man can say.
1: 9 *N* is new under the sun.
2:10 *N* that my eyes desired did I deny them,
2:11 after wind, with *n* gained under the sun.
2:24 There is *n* better for man than to eat and
3:12 I recognized that there is *n* better than
3:22 And I saw that there is *n* better for a man
5:14 having *n* from his labor that he can carry
8:15 because there is *n* good for man under the
Wis 4: 5 useless, unripe for eating, and fit for *n*.
7: 8 And deemed riches *n* in comparison with her,
8: 7 and *n* in life is more useful for men than
11:24 that are and loathe *n* that you have made;
Sir 6: 1 Say *n* harmful,
8:16 For bloodshed is *n* to him;
8:17 with a fool, for he can keep *n* to himself.
8:18 a stranger do *n* that should be kept secret,
12: 4 the downtrodden, give *n* to the proud man.
18:22 *n* prevent the prompt payment of your vows;
18:33 and a winebibber with *n* in your purse.
19: 7 Tell *n* to friend or foe;
20: 5 One man is silent because he has *n* to say;
23:27 That *n* is better than the fear of the LORD,
23:27 *n* more salutary than to obey his
27:24 There is *n* that I hate so much,
32:18 proud and insolent man is deterred by *n*.
32:19 Do *n* without counsel,
33:30 it over any human being, and do *n* unjust.
39:18 *n* can limit his achievement.
39:20 to him there is *n* unexpected.
40: 7 up astonished that there was *n* to fear.
40:26 Fear of the LORD leaves *n* wanting;
42:22 the same, With nothing added, *n* taken away;
48:13 *N* was beyond his power;
Is 6: 9 Look intently, but you shall know *n*!
13:17 *n* of silver and take no delight in gold.
15: 6 withered, new growth is gone, *n* is green.
16:12 to pray, but it shall avail him *n*.
24:12 In the city *n* remains but ruin;
29:22 Now Jacob shall have *n* to be ashamed of,
30: 5 be ashamed of a people that gain them *n*,
30: 6 humps of camels To a people good for *n*,
39: 2 there was *n* in his house or in his whole
39: 4 there is *n* in my storerooms that I did not
39: 6 *n* shall be left,
40:17 as nought, as *n* and void he accounts them.
40:23 and makes the rulers of the earth as *n*.
41:12 be as *n* at all who do battle with you.
41:24 Why, you are *n* and your work is nought!
41:29 Ah, all of them are *n*,
42:14 away, and kept silence, I have said *n*,
44: 9 Idol makers all amount to *n*,
49: 4 I thought I had toiled in vain, and for *n*,
52: 3 You were sold for *n*,
52:11 come forth from there, touch *n* unclean!
59: 8 there is *n* that is right in their paths;
Jer 10: 3 For the cult idols of the nations are *n*,
13: 7 But it was rotted, good for *n*!
13:10 be like this loincloth which is good for *n*.
22:17 heart are set on *n* except on your own gain,
26: 2 I command you, tell them, and omit *n*.
32:17 *n* is impossible to you.
32:30 the Israelites did *n* but provoke me with
38: 5 for the king could do *n* with them.
38:14 "hide *n* from me."
38:27 for *n* had been heard of the earlier
40:16 of Kareah, "You shall do *n* of the kind;
42: 4 I will withhold *n* from you.
42:21 in *n* that he has commissioned me to make
51:58 The toil of the nations is for *n*;
Bar 6:45 and they are *n* else than what these
Ez 15: 5 even when it was whole it was good for *n*;
16:22 you remembered *n* of when you were a girl,
21:31 *N* shall be as it was!
Dn 4:32 who live on the earth are counted as *n*;
11: 8 have *n* to do with the king of the north.
14:32 But now they were given *n*,
Hos 10: 4 *N* but make promises,
Am 3: 7 the Lord GOD does *n* without revealing his
Hg 2: 3 Does it not seem like *n* in your eyes?
Mt 5:13 Then it is good for *n* but to be thrown out
6:26 not sow or reap, they gather *n* into barns;
9:33 *N* like this has ever been seen in Israel!"
10:26 *N* is concealed that will not be revealed,
10:26 and *n* hidden that will not become known.
10:29 Are not two sparrows sold for next to *n*?
14:17 "We have *n* here,"
15:32 been with me three days, and have *n* to eat.
17:20 *N* would be impossible for you.
21:19 to it, but found *n* there except leaves.
22:12 The man had *n* to say.
23:16 'If a man swears by the temple it means *n*,
23:18 'If a man swears by the altar it means *n*,
Mk 6: 8 *n* on their journey but a walking stick
7:12 him to do *n* more for his father or mother.
7:15 *N* that enters a man from outside can make
7:18 "Do you not see that *n* that enters a man
7:20 that and *N* else is what makes him impure.
8: 2 been with me three days and have *n* to eat.
10:49 they did so, "You have *n* to fear from him!
11:13 When he reached it he found *n* but leaves;
14:51 him who was covered by *n* but a linen cloth.
16: 8 of their great fear, they said *n* to anyone.
Lk 1:37 sixth month, for *n* is impossible with God."
2:10 "You have *n* to fear!
3:13 "Exact *n* over and above your fixed amount."
4: 2 During that time he ate *n*,
5: 5 at it all night long and have caught *n*;
8:17 There is *n* hidden that will not be exposed,
8:17 *n* concealed that will not be known and
9: 3 "Take *n* for the journey,
9:13 "We have *n* but five loaves and two fish.
9:36 telling *n* of what they had seen at that
10:19 of the enemy, and *n* shall ever injure you.
11: 6 from a journey and I have *n* to offer him';
12: 2 is *n* concealed that will not be revealed,
12: 2 *n* hidden that will not be made known.
12: 7 Fear *n*, then.
18:34 They understood *n* of this.
23:15 this man has done *n* that calls for death.
23:41 we've done, but this man has done *n* wrong.
24:12 down but could see *n* but the wrappings.
Jn 1: 3 being, and apart from him *n* came to be.
4: 9 that Jews have *n* to do with Samaritans.)
6:12 are left over so that *n* will go to waste."
6:39 I should lose *n* of what he has given me;
7:49 Only this lot, that knows *n* about the law
8:28 that I AM and that I do *n* by myself.
8:40 Abraham did *n* like that.
8:54 I glorify myself, that glory comes to *n*.
12:19 one another, "See, there is *n* you can do!
15: 5 abundantly, for apart from me you can do *n*.
15:21 name, for they know *n* of him who sent me.
18:20 There was *n* secret about anything I said.
21: 3 All through the night they caught *n*.
Acts 2:12 could make *n* at all of what had happened.
4:14 with them, they could think of *n* to say,
5:36 In the end it came to *n*.
5:38 is that you have *n* to do with these men.
11: 8 *N* unclean or impure has ever entered my
17:21 love *n* more than to tell about or listen
19:27 the great goddess Artemis will count for *n*.
21:14 not be dissuaded, we said *n* further except,
21:24 is *n* in what they have been told about you,
25:11 But if there is *n* to the charges these men
25:26 I have *n* definite to write about him to
26:22 *N* that I say differs from what the
26:31 *n* that deserves death or imprisonment."
27:33 eaten *n*.
28: 6 and seeing *n* unusual happen to him,
28:17 I have done *n* against our people or our
28:18 they found *n* against me deserving of death.
Rom 3:20 law does *n* but point out what is sinful.
4: 5 But when a man does *n*,
8:18 *n* compared with the glory to be revealed
11:15 *N* less than life from the dead!
14:14 the Lord Jesus that *n* is unclean in itself;
1Cor 1:28 those who count for *n*, to reduce to *n*
2: 2 of *n* but Jesus Christ and him crucified.
4: 4 Mind you, I have *n* on my conscience.
7:12 although I know of *n* the Lord has said,
7:19 Circumcision counts for *n*,
7:30 conduct themselves as though they owned *n*,
8: 4 we know that an idol is really *n*,
11:22 of God, and embarrass those who have *n*?
13: 2 move mountains, but have not love, I am *n*.
13: 3 to be burned, but have not love, I gain *n*.
14:14 is at prayer but my mind contributes *n*.
2Cor 6:10 We seem to have *n*, yet everything is ours!
6:17 'and touch *n* unclean.
9: 4 to say *n* for you
11: 5 inferior to the "super-apostles" in *n*.
12:11 Even though I am *n*,
Gal 2: 6 God plays no favorites), made me add *n*.
6: 3 amounts to something, when in fact he is *n*,
6:15 means *n* whether one is circumcised or not.
Eph 4:30 Do *n* to sadden the Holy Spirit with whom
5: 7 therefore have *n* to do with them.
1Thes 3: 5 and all our labor might have gone for *n*.
4:12 good example to outsiders and want for *n*.
1Tm 3:10 then, if there is *n* against them,
4: 4 *n* is to be rejected when it is received
4: 7 Have *n* to do with profane myths or old
6: 7 We brought *n* into this world,
2Tm 2:23 Have *n* to do with senseless,
Ti 1:15 to those defiled unbelievers *n* is clean.
3:10 after that, have *n* to do with him.
Heb 2: 8 all things to him, God left *n* unsubjected.
4:13 *N* is concealed from him;
7:14 regarding which Moses said *n* about priests.
7:19 for the law brought *n* to perfection.
Jas 1: 4 you may be fully mature and lacking in *n*.
2:15 has *n* to wear and no food for the day,
2:17 is with the faith that does *n* in practice.
1Pt 3: 7 *n* will keep your prayers from being
1Jn 2:10 there is *n* in him to cause a fall.
2:16 for *n* that the world affords comes from
3: 5 in him there is *n* sinful.
3:21 our consciences have *n* to charge us with,
4: 8 The man without love has known *n* of God,
3Jn 1: 4 *N* delights me more than to hear that my
1: 7 and they are accepting *n* from the pagans.
Rv 1:17 "There is *n* to fear.
2: 2 self-styled apostles who are *n* of the sort,
2: 9 *n* other than members of Satan's assembly.
2:24 *n* of the so-called "deep secrets" of Satan;
3:17 am so rich and secure that I want for *n*."
21:27 there, but *n* profane shall enter it,
22: 3 *N* deserving a curse shall be found there.

NOTHINGNESS (2)

Jer 10:15 *N* are they,
51:18 *N* are they,

NOTICE (16)

Ex 23: 5 When you *n* the ass of one who hates you
Ru 2:10 I, a foreigner, be favored with your *n*?"
2:19 May he who took *n* of you be blessed!"
1Sm 20: 6 him go on short *n* to his city Bethlehem,
2Sm 18:27 "I *n* that the first one runs like Ahimaaz,
2Kgs 3:14 neither look at you nor *n* you at all.
Jb 35:13 hear or that the Almighty does not take *n*.
Ps(s) 144: 3 LORD, what is man, that you *n* him;
Prv 1:24 I extended my hand and no one took *n*;
Hos 7: 9 his strength, but he takes no *n* of it;
7: 9 is a sprinkling, but he takes no *n* of it.
Mt 26:53 *n* more than twelve legions of angels?
Mk 7:24 however, he could not escape *n*.
Lk 21:29 *N* the fig tree, or any other tree.
Acts 21:26 he entered the temple precincts to give *n*
Jas 2: 3 to take *n* of the well-dressed man and say,

NOTICED (22)

Gn 21: 9 Sarah *n* the son whom Hagar the Egyptian
24:63 around, he *n* that camels were approaching.
31: 5 "I have *n* that your father's attitude
37:18 They *n* him from a distance,
40: 6 morning, he *n* that they looked disturbed.
Ex 34:30 *n* how radiant the skin of his face had
Jgs 19:17 When he *n* the traveler in the public
2Sm 12:19 But David *n* his servants whispering among
17:19 on the cover so that nothing could be *n*.
20:12 man *n* that all the soldiers were stopping.
24:20 Now Aaaunah looked down and *n* the king
2Kgs 12:11 When they *n* that there was a large amount
2Mc 14:30 But Maccabeus *n* that Nicanor was becoming
Jb 1: 8 said to Satan, "Have you *n* my servant Job,
2: 3 said to Satan, "Have you *n* my servant Job,
Jer 33:24 you not *n* what these people are saying:
Mt 6: 5 or on street corners in order to be *n*.
Mk 10:14 indignant when he *n* it and said to them:
14:67 When she *n* Peter warming himself,
Jn 1:38 turned around and *n* them following him,
21:20 and *n* that the disciple whom Jesus loved
Rv 13: 3 I *n* that one of the beast's heads seemed

NOTICING (3)

Ex 2: 5 *N* the basket among the reeds,
Nm 32: 1 *N* that the land of Jazer and of Gilead was
Lk 14: 7 *n* how they were trying to get the places

NOTIFIED (2)

Jdt 14:12 Assyrians saw them, they *n* their captains;
15: 5 for they too had been *n* of the happenings

NOTIFY (1)

Jl 2:16 Gather the people, *n* the congregation;

NOTIONS (1)

Jb 15:12 Why do your *n* carry you away,

NOTORIOUS (2)

2Mc 13: 6 A man guilty of sacrilege or *n* for certain
Mt 27:16 at the time a *n* prisoner named Barabbas.

NOTWITHSTANDING (1)

Jb 34: 6 *N* my right I am set at nought;

NOUGHT (46)

Dt 16:15 you shall do *n* but make merry.
1Chr 16:26 the gods of the nations are things of *n*,
Jdt 13:17 brought to *n* the enemies of your people."
Est C:22 your scepter to those that are *n*.
1Mc 9:68 the enterprise he had planned came to *n*,
Jb 20:22 straits, and *n* shall be left of his goods.
24:25 confute me, and reduce my argument to *n*?
30: 2 Such strength as they had, to me meant *n*;
32:22 For I know *n* of flattery;
34: 6 Notwithstanding my right I am set at *n*;
34: 9 a man *n* that he is pleasing to God."
39:16 young and ruthlessly makes *n* of her brood;
Ps(s) 10: 3 covetous blasphemes, sets the LORD at *n*.
33:10 The LORD brings to *n* the plans of nations;

NOUGHT (cont.)
34:10 for *n* is lacking to those who fear him.
39: 6 my days, and my life is as *n* before you;
73:20 when you arise, set at *n* these phantoms.
96: 5 the gods of the nations are things of *n*,
97: 7 put to shame, who glory in the things of *n*;
143:12 bring to *n* all my foes,
Prv 10:28 the expectation of the wicked comes to *n*.
11: 7 what is expected from strength comes to *n*.
Wis 5: 1 his oppressors who set at *n* his labors.
5:13 to *n* and held no sign of virtue to display,
7:25 *n* that is sullied enters into her.
7:28 For there is *n* God loves,
17:12 For fear is *n* but the surrender of the
Sir 41:10 Whatever is of nought returns to *n*,
Is 19: 3 them, and I will bring to *n* their counsel;
40:17 Before him all the nations are as *n*,
40:23 He brings princes to *n* and makes the
41:11 perish and come to *n* who offer resistance.
41:24 Why, you are nothing and your work is *n*!
41:29 all of them are nothing, their works are *n*,
44:25 It is I who bring to *n* the omens of liars,
45:14 the gods are *n*.
52: 4 Assyria, too, oppressed them for *n*.
Jer 6: 6 *n* but oppression within her!
6:14 They would repair, as though it were *n*,
8:11 They would repair, as though it were *n*,
Hos 12:12 Gilead is falsehood, they have come to *n*,
Am 5: 5 led into exile, and Bethel shall become *n*.
Hb 2:13 the flames, and nations grow weary for *n*!
Zec 9: 5 Ekron, too, for her hope shall come to *n*.
Mt 10:39 himself to *n* for me discovers who he is.

NOURISH (7)
Prv 10:21 The just man's lips *n* many,
Wis 16:26 not the various kinds of fruits that *n* man,
Sir 15: 3 *N* him with the bread of understanding,
28: 3 Should a man *n* anger against his fellows
Is 58:14 I will *n* you with the heritage of Jacob,
Hos 9: 2 floor and wine press shall not *n* them,
1Cor 9: 7 not *n* himself with the milk of his flock?

NOURISHED (6)
2Sm 12: 3 He *n* her,
Jb 21:24 His figure is full and *n*,
Wis 16:20 you *n* your people with food of angels and
16:23 fire, again, that the just might be *n*,
Bar 4: 8 You forsook the Eternal God who *n* you,
Col 1:21 you *n* hostility in your hearts because of

NOURISHES (2)
Jb 36:31 For by these he *n* the nations,
Eph 5:29 he *n* it and takes care of it as Christ

NOURISHMENT (6)
2Sm 13: 6 my eyes, that I may take *n* from her hand."
13: 7 brother Amnon and prepare some *n* for him."
13:10 to Tamar, "Bring the *n* into the bedroom,
Jb 33:20 and his senses reject the choicest *n*.
38:41 Who provides *n* for the ravens when their
Hb 3:17 olive fail and the terraces produce no *n*,

NOVEL (2)
Wis 16: 2 you benefited your people with a *n* dish,
16: 3 period of privation, partook of a *n* dish.

NOWADAYS (1)
1Sm 25:10 *N* there are many servants who run away

NOWHERE (6)
Prv 26: 2 its flight, a curse uncalled-for arrives *n*.
Wis 17:10 face even the air that they could *n* escape.
Is 45:14 "With you only is God, and *n* else;
Lam 4:15 among the nations, *n* could they remain.
Mt 8:20 but the Son of Man has *n* to lay his head."
Lk 9:58 but the Son of Man has *n* to lay his head."

NOXIOUS (1)
Jb 31:40 of wheat and *n* weeds instead of barley!

NULL (3)
Nm 30: 6 any pledge she has made becomes *n* and void;
30:13 vow or in her pledge becomes *n* and void;
30:14 allow to remain valid or render *n* and void.

NULLIFIED (2)
Mt 15: 6 of your tradition you have *n* God's word.
Gal 3:17 thirty years later, nor is its promise *n*.

NULLIFY (2)
1Mc 14:44 or priests to *n* any of these decisions,
Mk 7:13 That is the way you *n* God's word in favor

NUMBED (2)
Ps(s) 38: 9 I am *n* and severely crushed;
Jn 12:40 has blinded their eyes, and *n* their hearts,

NUMBER (171)
Gn 42:16 So send one of your *n* to get your brother,
47: 2 whom he had selected from their full *n*.
Ex 1: 5 The total *n* of the direct descendants of
12: 4 to the *n* of persons who partake of it.
38:26 the *n* of these was six hundred and three
Lv 25:15 On the basis of the *n* of years since the
25:15 on the basis of the *n* of years for crops,
25:16 is really the *n* of crops that he sells you.
25:27 to the *n* of years since the sale,
27:18 its money value according to the *n* of years
27:23 to the *n* of years until the next jubilee,
Nm 1:45 The total *n* of the Israelites of twenty
2: 9 The total *n* of those registered by
2:16 The total *n* of those registered by
2:24 The total *n* of those registered by
2:31 The total *n* of those registered by
2:32 The total *n* of those registered by
3:39 The total *n* of male Levites a month old or
3:40 old or more, and compute their total *n*.
3:48 and his sons as ransom for the extra *n*."
4:48 the total *n* registered was eight thousand
15:12 Whatever the *n* you offer,
26:53 with the *n* of individuals in each group.
26:54 to the *n* of men registered in it.
26:62 *n* of male Levites one month or more of age,
29:18 rams and lambs in proportion to their *n*,
29:21 rams and lambs in proportion to their *n*,
29:24 rams and lambs in proportion to their *n*,
29:27 rams and lambs in proportion to their *n*,
29:30 rams and lambs in proportion to their *n*,
29:33 rams and lambs in proportion to their *n*,
29:37 rams and lambs in proportion to their *n*,
32: 1 Gadites had a very large *n* of livestock.
Dt 1:23 proposal, I chose twelve men from your *n*,
3: 5 nothing of the great *n* of unwalled towns.
3:19 of which I know you have a large *n*,
17:16 But he shall not have a great *n* of horses;
17:17 Neither shall he have a great *n* of wives,
25: 2 the *n* of stripes his guilt deserves.
32: 8 the peoples after the *n* of the sons of God;
Jos 4: 5 equal in *n* the tribes of the Israelites.
21:41 Thus the total *n* of cities within the
Jgs 20:15 The *n* of the Benjaminite swordsmen from
1Sm 6: 4 to correspond to the *n* of Philistine lords,
6:18 corresponded to the *n* of all the cities of
23:13 David and his men, about six hundred in *n*,
2Sm 6: 1 picked men of Israel, thirty thousand in *n*.
24: 1 by prompting him to *n* Israel and Judah.
24: 2 the people, that I may know their *n*."
24: 3 "May the LORD your God increase the *n* of
24: 9 to the king the *n* of people registered:
1Kgs 8: 5 ark sheep and oxen too many to *n* or count.
18:31 for the *n* of tribes of the sons of Jacob,
2Kgs 10:14 They were taken alive, forty-two in *n*,
17:25 among them that killed some of their *n*.
17:32 from their *n* priests for the high places,
24:14 and men of the army, ten thousand in *n*,
1Chr 4:27 clans did not equal the *n* of the Judahites.
10: 1 the Philistines, and a *n* of them fell,
12: 4 of the Thirty, and in addition to their *n*;
16:19 When they were few in *n*,
21: 2 *n* of the Israelites from Beer-sheba to Dan,
21: 2 report back to me that I may know their *n*."
22: 4 not be weighed, and cedar trees without *n*.
23: 3 and their total *n* was found to be
25: 7 Their *n*, together with that of their
27:24 Therefore the *n* did not enter into the
2Chr 2:16 who were found to *n* one hundred
4:18 so many in *n* that the weight of the bronze
14:14 carried off a great *n* of sheep and camels.
18: 5 gathered his prophets, four hundred in *n*,
23: 4 a third of your *n*,
26:11 divided into bands according to the *n*
26:12 The entire *n* of family heads over these
28: 5 away captive a large *n* of his people,
29:32 The *n* of holocausts that the assembly
29:34 Since the priests were too few in *n* to be
32: 5 a great *n* of spears and shields prepared.
35: 7 of lambs and kids, thirty thousand in *n*,
Ezr 3: 4 in the proper *n* required for each day.
6:17 keeping with the *n* of the tribes of Israel.
8:34 was in order as to *n* and weight,
Neh 11: 8 nine hundred and twenty-eight in *n*.
11:19 one hundred and seventy-two in *n*.
Tb 10: 1 When the *n* of days was reached and his son
Jdt 2:17 He took along a very large *n* of camels,
5:10 the *n* of their race could not be counted.
Est 5:11 of his riches, the large *n* of his sons,
9:11 when the *n* of those killed in the
1Mc 2:38 cattle, to the *n* of a thousand persons.
9: 6 When his men saw the great *n* of the troops,
10:77 had such a large *n* of horsemen to rely on.
15: 3 I have recruited a large *n* of mercenary
2Mc 4:39 a large *n* of gold vessels had been stolen,
5:14 and the same *n* being sold into slavery.
5:26 armed men, he cut down a large *n* of people.
8: 6 and put to flight a large *n* of the enemy.
8:16 *n* of the Gentiles attacking them unjustly,
10:20 they allowed a *n* of them to escape.
10:24 collected a large *n* of cavalry from Asia;
14:30 he gathered together a large *n* of his men,
Jb 1: 3 she-asses, and a great *n* of work animals,
14: 5 You know the *n* of his months;
21:21 him, when the *n* of his months is finished?
31: 4 he not see my ways, and *n* all my steps?
36:26 the *n* of his years is past searching out.
38:21 them, and the *n* of your years is great!
39: 2 hinds, *N* the months that they must fulfill,
Ps(s) 39: 5 LORD, my end and what is the *n* of my days,
90:12 Teach us to *n* our days aright,
104:25 *n* of living things both small and great,
105:12 When they were few in *n*,
105:34 came locusts and grasshoppers without *n*;
147: 4 He tells the *n* of the stars;
Sgs 6: 8 maidens without *n*
Wis 6:24 *n* of wise men is the safety of the world,
11:20 all things by measure and *n* and weight.
Sir 1: 2 who can *n* these?
37:23 but the life of Israel is days without *n*.
41:13 days, but a good name, for days without *n*.
Is 1:11 What care I for the *n* of your sacrifices?
31: 1 trust in chariots because of their *n*,
47: 9 sorceries and the great *n* of your spells;
Jer 2:32 my people have forgotten me days without *n*.
29: 6 There you must increase in *n*,
44:28 to the land of Judah shall be few in *n*.
52:28 This is the *n* of the people whom
Bar 2:13 for we are left few in *n* among the nations
Ez 4: 5 their sins I allot you the same *n* of days,
5: 3 *n* and tie them in the hem of your garment.
20:37 the staff and bring back but a small *n*.
33: 2 select one of their *n* to be their watchman,
40:17 were on the pavement, were thirty in *n*.
Hos 2: 1 The *n* of the Israelites shall be like the
Jl 1: 6 has invaded my land, mighty and without *n*;
Mt 1:17 Thus the total *n* of generations is:
Mk 2:15 The *n* of those who followed him was large.
6:38 When they learned the *n* they answered,
13: 6 *n* will come attempting to impersonate me.
Lk 5: 6 they caught such a great *n* of fish
13:23 are they few in *n* who are to be saved?"
24:24 Some of our *n* went to the tomb and found
Jn 7:50 One of their own *n*,
11:49 One of their *n* named Caiaphas,
21:11 In spite of the great *n*,
Acts 1:17 He was one of our *n* and he had been given
2:47 to their *n* those who were being saved.
4: 4 *n* of the men came to about five thousand.
6: 1 In those days, as the *n* of disciples grew,
6: 3 Look around among your own *n*,
6: 7 while at the same time a *n* of the
11:21 great *n* of them believed and were converted
14: 1 as to convince a good *n* of Jews and Greeks.
15: 7 God selected me from your *n* to be the one
15:22 from among their *n* and sent to Antioch
15:24 We have heard that some of our *n* without
17: 4 a great *n* of Greeks sympathetic to Judaism,
19:19 A *n* who had been dealing in magic even
20:30 From your own *n*,
Rom 9:27 "Though the *n* of the Israelites should be
11:12 Gentile world, how much more their full *n*!
11:25 until the full *n* of Gentiles enter in,
Rv 5:11 They were countless in *n*,
7: 4 I heard the *n* of those who were so marked
9:16 two hundred million in *n*— a *n* I heard
13:17 or with the *n* that stood for its name.
13:18 calculate the *n* of the beast, for it is a *n*
13:18 The man's *n* is six hundred sixty-six.
15: 2 and also the *n* that signified its name.

NUMBERED (36)
Gn 46:26 of Jacob's sons *n* sixty-six persons in all.
Nm 3:22 they *n* seven thousand five hundred.
3:28 they *n* eight thousand three hundred.
3:34 they *n* six thousand two hundred.
3:43 they *n* twenty-two thousand two hundred and
4:36 *n* two thousand seven hundred and fifty.
4:40 they *n* two thousand six hundred and thirty.
4:44 clans, they *n* three thousand two hundred.
23:10 Jacob, or *n* Israel's wind-borne particles?
Jgs 6: 5 neither they nor their camels could be *n*,
7: 6 to their mouths by hand *n* three hundred,
1Sm 13:15 Saul then *n* the soldiers he had with him,
14: 2 those with him *n* about six hundred men.
2Sm 24:10 David regretted having *n* the people,
1Kgs 3: 8 so vast that it cannot be *n* or counted.
5:12 and his songs *n* a thousand and five.
7: 3 these beams *n* forty-five,
9:23 in the work *n* five hundred and fifty.
20:15 Israelite soldiery, who *n* seven thousand.
1Chr 7: 2 Their kindred *n* twenty-two thousand six
7: 4 *n* thirty-six thousand men in organized
7:11 They *n* seventeen thousand two hundred men
7:40 Their family records *n* twenty-six thousand
2Chr 5: 6 that they could not be counted or *n*.
Jdt 7: 2 Their forces *n* a hundred and seventy
1Mc 2:18 sons shall be *n* among the King's Friends,
6:30 army *n* a hundred thousand foot-soldiers,
Jb 16:22 For my years are *n* now,
Ps(s) 88: 5 I am *n* with those who go down into the pit;
Is 22:10 You *n* the houses of Jerusalem,
Jer 33:22 Like the host of heaven which cannot be *n*,
Dn 5:26 has *n* your kingdom and put an end to it;

Mt 15:38 The people who were fed *n* four thousand,
Mk 6:44 had eaten the loaves *n* five thousand men.
8: 9 Those who had eaten *n* about four thousand.
Jn 6:10 Even though the men *n* about five thousand,

NUMBERING (4)

1Mc 10:63 The king also honored him by *n* him among
2Mc 12:10 *n* at least five thousand foot soldiers,
Jb 25: 3 Is there any *n* of his troops?
Sir 42: 7 Of *n* every deposit,

NUMBERS (31)

Nm 22: 3 the Israelites greatly because of their *n*,
2Sm 12: 2 rich man had flocks and herds in great *n*.
15:12 and the people with Absalom increased in *n*.
1Kgs 1:19 oxen, fatlings, and sheep in great *n*;
1:25 oxen, fatlings, and sheep in great *n*;
8:65 *n* from Labo of Hamath to the Wadi of Egypt,
1Chr 23:31 feast days, in such *n* as are prescribed,
2Chr 7: 8 who had assembled in very large *n* from
16: 8 with great *n* of chariots and drivers?
30: 3 not sanctified themselves in sufficient *n*,
30:24 priests sanctified themselves in great *n*,
32:29 and he acquired sheep and oxen in great *n*,
Jdt 9:11 "Your strength is not in *n*,
16: 3 Their *n* blocked the torrents,
1Mc 4: 8 be afraid of their *n* or dread their attack.
4:35 so as to return to Judea with greater *n*.
6:41 All who heard the noise of their *n*,
2Mc 10:19 his men, in sufficient *n* to besiege them,
Is 40:26 He leads out their army and *n* them,
Mt 24:11 will rise in great *n* to mislead many.
Mk 1: 5 of Jerusalem went out to him in great *n*.
2: 2 At that they began to gather in great *n*.
3: 9 In view of their *n*,
6:31 People were coming and going in great *n*,
Acts 5:14 more believers, men and women in great *n*,
11:24 Thereby large *n* were added to the Lord.
11:26 met with the church and instructed great *n*.
16: 5 stronger in faith and daily increased in *n*.
19:26 great *n* of people to change their religion.
28:23 him and came to his lodgings in great *n*.
Rv 17:15 large *n* of peoples and nations and tongues.

NUMENIUS (4)

1Mc 12:16 So we have chosen *N*,
14:22 Since *N*, son of Antiochus,
14:24 Simon sent *N* to Rome with a great gold
15:15 *N* and his companions left Rome with

NUMEROUS (82)

Gn 16:10 I will make your descendants so *n*,"
26: 4 I will make your descendants as *n* as the
26:16 you have become far too *n* for us."
32:13 sands of the sea, which are too *n* to count.'"
48: 4 *n* and raise you into an assembly of tribes,
Ex 1: 7 They became so *n* and strong that the land
1: 9 "Look how *n* and powerful the Israelite
5: 5 how *n* the people of the land are already,"
12:38 their livestock, very *n* flocks and herds.
23:30 *n* enough to take possession of the land.
32:13 descendants as *n* as the stars in the sky;
Lv 26: 9 upon you, and make you fruitful and *n*,
Nm 22:15 *n* and more distinguished than the others.
Dt 1:10 you are now as *n* as the stars in the sky.
2:10 strong and *n* and tall like the Anakim;
2:21 strong and *n* and tall like the Anakim.
7: 1 seven nations more *n* and powerful than you
7:22 lest the wild beasts become too *n* for you.
10:22 has made you as *n* as the stars of the sky.
26: 5 he became a nation great, strong and *n*.
28:62 Of you who were *n* as the stars in the sky,
30: 5 more prosperous and *n* than your fathers.
30:16 and decrees, you will live and grow *n*,
Jos 11: 4 an army *n* as the sands on the seashore,
17:17 "You are a *n* people and very strong.
22: 8 with great wealth, with very *n* livestock,
24: 3 I made his descendants *n*,
Jgs 6: 5 their tents would become as *n* as locusts;
7:12 lay in the valley, as *n* as locusts.
1Sm 13: 5 soldiers as *n* as the sands of the seashore.
2Sm 17:11 who are as *n* as the sands by the sea,
1Kgs 4:20 Israel were as *n* as the sands by the sea;
5:21 David a wise son to rule this *n* people."
7:47 all the articles because they were so *n*;
10: 2 arrived in Jerusalem with a very *n* retinue,
10:27 as *n* as the sycamores of the foothills.
1Chr 5:23 The *n* members of the half-tribe of
23:17 sons, but the sons of Rehabiah were very *n*.
24: 4 found to be more *n* than those of Ithamar,
2Chr 1: 9 a people as *n* as the dust of the earth.
1:15 as *n* as the sycamores of the foothills.
5: 6 oxen so *n* that they could not be counted
9: 1 *n* retinue and by camels bearing spices,
9:27 as *n* as the sycamores of the foothills.
18: 2 Ahab offered *n* sheep and oxen for him and
21: 3 Their father gave them *n* gifts of silver,
26:10 towers in the desert and dug *n* cisterns,
Ezr 10:13 people are *n* and it is the rainy season,
Neh 9:23 children as *n* as the stars of the heavens,
Jdt 1:16 Then he returned home with all his *n*,
1Mc 11: 1 forces, as *n* as the sands of the seashore,
16: 7 them, for the enemy's horsemen were very *n*.
Jb 21:11 These folk have infants *n* as lambs,
Ps(s) 40: 6 How *n* have you made,
40:13 They are more *n* than the hairs of my head,
107:41 misery and made the families *n* like flocks.
Prv 7:26 many are those she has struck down dead, *n*,
Wis 4: 3 But the *n* progeny of the wicked shall be
Sir 44:21 he would make him *n* as the grains of dust,
Is 54: 1 For more *n* are the children of the
Jer 2:28 For as *n* as your cities are your gods,
5: 6 their many crimes and their *n* rebellions.
11:13 For as *n* as your cities are your gods,
15: 8 more *n* before me than the sands of the sea.
30:15 Because of your great guilt, your *n* sins,
46:23 More *n* than locusts,
51:14 I will fill you with men as *n* as locusts,
Bar 2:29 surely this great and *n* throng will
Ez 17:17 by Pharaoh with a great army and *n* troops.
31: 6 in its shade dwelt *n* peoples of every race.
47:10 be like those of the Great Sea, very *n*.
Jl 2: 2 over the mountains, a people *n* and mighty!
Na 3:16 Make your couriers more *n* than the stars,
Zec 10: 8 I redeem them they will be as *n* as before.
Acts 7:17 our people in Egypt grew more and more *n*,
9:32 Once when Peter was making *n* journeys,
14:21 news in that town and made *n* disciples,
17: 4 to Judaism, and *n* prominent women.
17:12 as did *n* influential Greek women and men.
Rom 4:18 him, *N* as this shall your de-scendants be."
Heb 11:12 descendants as *n* as the stars in the the
Rv 20: 8 Gog and Magog, *n* as the sands of the sea.

NUMSKULL (1)

Prv 17:21 the father of a *n* has no joy.

NUN (31)

Ex 33:11 but his young assistant, Joshua, son of *N*,
Nm 11:28 in the camp," Joshua, son of *N*,
13: 8 son of *N*,
13:16 But Hoshea, son of *N*, Moses called Joshua.
14: 6 while Joshua, son of *N*,
14:30 son of Jephunneh, and Joshua, son of *N*.
14:38 the land, only Joshua, son of *N*,
26:65 son of Jephunneh, and Joshua, son of *N*.
27:18 replied to Moses, "Take Joshua, son of *N*,
32:12 son of Jephunneh, and Joshua, son of *N*,
32:28 the priest Eleazar, to Joshua, son of *N*,
34:17 Eleazar the priest, and Joshua, son of *N*,
Dt 1:38 there, but your aide Joshua, son of *N*,
31:23 the LORD commissioned Joshua, son of *N*,
32:44 So Moses, together with Joshua, son of *N*,
34: 9 Now Joshua, son of *N*,
Jos 1: 1 LORD said to Moses' aide Joshua, son of *N*:
2: 1 Then Joshua, son of *N*,
2:23 crossed the Jordan to Joshua, son of *N*,
6: 6 Summoning the priests, Joshua, son of *N*,
14: 1 Eleazar the priest, Joshua, son of *N*,
17: 4 Eleazar the priest, to Joshua, son of *N*,
19:49 in their midst to Joshua, son of *N*.
19:51 Eleazar the priest, Joshua, son of *N*,
21: 1 Eleazar the priest, to Joshua, son of *N*,
24:29 After these events, Joshua, son of *N*,
Jgs 2: 8 had done for Israel, Joshua, son of *N*,
1Kgs 16:34 LORD had foretold through Joshua, son of *N*.
1Chr 7:27 whose son was Elishama, whose son was *N*,
Neh 8:17 sort from the days of Jeshua, son of *N*,
Sir 46: 1 Valiant leader was JOSHUA, son of *N*,

NURSE (13)

Gn 21: 7 she added, "that Sarah would *n* children!
24:59 sister Rebekah and her *n* to take leave,
35: 8 Death came to Rebekah's *n* Deborah;
Ex 2: 7 of the Hebrew women to *n* the child for you?"
2: 9 to her, "Take this child and *n* it for me,
Ru 4:16 placed him on her lap, and became his *n*.
2Sm 4: 4 Jezreel, and his *n* took him up and fled.
1Kgs 1: 2 to attend you, lord king, and to *n* you.
3:21 I rose in the morning to *n* my child,
2Kgs 11: 2 and spirited him away, along with his *n*,
2Chr 22:11 slain, and put him and his *n* in a bedroom.
Is 66:11 may *n* with delight at her abundant breasts!
Jas 3:14 Should you instead *n* bitter jealousy and

NURSED (8)

Ex 2: 9 woman therefore took the child and *n* it.
1Sm 1:23 and *n* her son until she had weaned him.
1Kgs 1: 4 beautiful, *n* the king and cared for him,
2Mc 7:27 for nine months, *n* you for three years,
Sg 8: 1 were my brother, *n* at my mother's breasts!
Is 60:16 milk of nations, and be *n* at royal breasts;
Lk 11:27 that bore you and the breasts that *n* you!"
23:29 never bore and the breasts that never *n*.'

NURSES (2)

Is 49:23 foster fathers, their princesses your *n*;
60: 4 and your daughters in the arms of their *n*.

NURSING (6)

Gn 50:15 "Suppose Joseph has been *n* a grudge
Dt 32:25 the *n* babe as well as the hoary old man.
Mt 24:19 on pregnant or *n* mothers in those days.
Mk 13:17 with pregnant and *n* women in those days.
Lk 21:23 "The women who are pregnant or *n* at the
1Thes 2: 7 as any *n* mother fondling her little ones.

NURSLING (1)

Jer 44: 7 out from Judah man and wife, child and *n*,

NURSLINGS (1)

Is 66:12 As *n*, you shall be carried in her arms,

NURTURED (1)

Wis 7: 4 clothes and with constant care I was *n*.

NUT (1)

Sg 6:11 I came down to the *n* garden to look at

NYMPHAS (1)

Col 4:15 *N* and the assembly that meets at his house.

O

OAK (10)

Gn 35: 8 she was buried under the *o* below Bethel,
Jos 19:33 Heleph, from the *o* at Zaanannim to Lakkum,
24:26 *o* that was in the sanctuary of the LORD.
1Chr 10:12 buried their bones under the *o* of Jabesh,
Is 6:13 As with a terebinth or an *o* whose trunk
44:14 He cuts down cedars, takes a holm or an *o*,
Ez 6:13 beneath every green tree and leafy *o*,
Dn 13:59 "Under an *o*," he said.
Hos 4:13 Beneath *o* and poplar and terebinth,
Am 2: 9 the cedars, and as strong as the *o* trees.

OAKS (5)

Ps(s) 29: 9 LORD twists the *o* and strips the forests,
Is 2:13 cedars of Lebanon and all the *o* of Bashan,
61: 3 They will be called *o* of justice,
Ez 27: 6 highest *o* of Bashan they made your oars;
Zec 11: 2 Wail, you *o* of Bashan,

OAR (1)

Ez 27:29 from their ships come all who ply the *o*;

OARS (1)

Ez 27: 6 highest oaks of Bashan they made your *o*;

OARSMEN (2)

Ez 27: 8 of Sidon and Arvad served as your *o*;
27:26 the deep waters your *o* brought you home,

OATH (111)

Gn 21:31 the two took an *o* there.
24: 7 by *o* the promise he then made to me,
24: 8 you, you will be released from this *o*.
24:37 My master put me under *o*, saying:
25:33 So he sold Jacob his birthright under *o*.
26: 3 the *o* that I swore to your father Abraham.
31:53 took the *o* by the Awesome One of Isaac.
50: 5 made me promise on *o* to bury him in the
50: 6 your father, as he made you promise on *o*."
50:24 the land that he promised on *o* to Abraham,
50:25 Then, putting the sons of Israel under *o*,
Ex 22:10 the owner must accept the *o*,
Lv 5: 4 it, rashly utters an *o* to do good or evil,
5: 4 recognizes that he is guilty of such an *o*;
Nm 5:21 the woman with this *o* of imprecation
11:12 you have promised under *o* to their fathers?
14:23 which I promised on *o* to their fathers.
30: 3 himself under *o* to a pledge of abstinence,
30:11 a vow or binds herself under *o* to a pledge,
30:14 that she makes under *o* to mortify herself,
32:11 under *o* to Abraham and Isaac and Jacob.
Dt 4:31 which under *o* he made with your fathers.
6:18 the LORD promised on *o* to your fathers,
6:23 the land he promised on *o* to our fathers,
7: 8 to the *o* he had sworn to your fathers,
7:12 which he promised on *o* to your fathers.
8: 1 the LORD promised on *o* to your fathers.
9: 5 promise which he made on *o* to your fathers,
13:18 you as he promised your fathers on *o*;
26:15 which you promised on *o* to our fathers.'
31:20 which I promised on *o* to their fathers,
31:21 which I promised on *o* to their fathers."
31:23 into the land which I promised them on *o*.
Jos 2:17 how we will fulfill the *o* you made us take:
2:20 be quit of the *o* you have made us take."
6:26 On that occasion Joshua imposed the *o*:
9:15 princes of the community sealed with an *o*.
9:20 punished for the *o* we have sworn to them."
14: 9 On that occasion Moses swore this *o*,
Jgs 2: 1 land which I promised on *o* to your fathers.
21: 5 For they had taken a solemn *o* that anyone
1Sm 14:24 And Saul swore a very rash *o* that day,
14:26 from it, because the people feared the *o*.

OATH (cont.)

14:27 his father had put the people under *o*,
14:28 father put the people under a strict *o*,
20:17 for David, Jonathan renewed his *o* to him,
24:23 gave Saul his *o* and Saul returned home,
2Sm 19:24 And the king gave him his *o*.
21: 2 the Israelites had given them their *o*,
21: 7 because of the LORD's *o* that formed a bond
1Kgs 1:30 fulfill the *o* I swore to you by the LORD,
2:43 have you not kept the *o* of the LORD and
8:31 to take an *o* sanctioned by a curse,
8:31 the *o* before your altar in this temple,
2Kgs 25:24 gave the commanders and their men his *o*.
1Chr 16:16 into with Abraham and by his *o* to Isaac;
2Chr 6:22 to take an *o* of execration against himself,
6:22 for the *o* before your altar in this temple,
15:15 All Judah rejoiced over the *o*,
Ezr 10: 5 an *o* from the chiefs of the priests,
Neh 5:12 had them administer an *o* to these men
10:30 take this *o* to follow the law of God
Tb 8:20 Tobiah and made an *o* in his presence,
9: 3 You witnessed the *o* that Raguel has sworn;
9: 3 I cannot violate his *o*."
Jdt 8:11 God and yourselves this *o* which you took.
8:30 ourselves by an *o* that we cannot break.
1Mc 6:61 king and the leaders swore an *o* to them,
6:62 he broke the *o* he had sworn and gave
7:18 the agreement and the *o* that they swore."
9:71 He swore an *o* to him that he would never
2Mc 7:24 with mere words, but with promises on *o*,
14:32 As they declared under *o* that they did not
14:33 hand toward the temple and swore this *o*:
Ps(s) 59:13 for the lies they have told under *o*.
105: 9 into with Abraham and by his *o* to Isaac;
Eccl 8: 2 of the king, and in view of your *o* to God,
9: 2 rashly, so it is for him who fears an *o*.
Sir 41:17 and of breaking an *o* or agreement.
44:21 God promised him with an *o* that in his
Is 65:16 He who takes an *o* in the land shall swear
Jer 11: 5 the *o* which I swore to your fathers,
32:22 as you had promised their fathers under *o*,
Bar 2:34 with my *o* I promised to their fathers,
Ez 16: 8 I swore an *o* to you and entered into a
16:59 you have done, you who despised your *o*,
17:13 he made a covenant, binding him under *o*,
17:16 who set him up to rule, whose *o* he spurned,
17:18 He spurned his *o*, breaking his covenant.
17:19 As I live, my *o* which he spurned,
44:12 therefore I have sworn an *o* against them,
Zec 8:17 another in his heart, nor love a false *o*.
Mt 5:33 your forefathers, 'Do not take a false *o*;
14: 9 but because of his *o* and the guests who
26:63 "I order you to tell us under *o* before
26:72 Again he denied it with an *o*:
Mk 6:26 of his *o* and the presence of the guests,
14:56 under *o* but their testimony did not agree.
Lk 1:73 The *o* he swore to Abraham our father he
Acts 23:12 bound themselves by *o* not to eat or drink
23:13 than forty of them who took the *o* together.)
23:14 by *o* to touch no food until we kill Paul.
23:21 *o* not to eat or drink until they kill him.
Heb 6:16 an *o* gives firmness to a promise and puts
6:17 would not change, guaranteed it by *o*,
7:20 This has been confirmed by an *o*.
7:20 old covenant became priests without an *o*,
7:28 but the word of the *o* which came after the
Jas 5:12 you must not swear an oath, any *o* at all,
Rv 10: 6 an *o* by the One who lives forever and ever,

OATH-FILLED (1)

Sir 27:14 Their *o* talk makes the hair stand on end,

OATHS (8)

Gn 26:31 Early the next morning they exchanged *o*.
Lv 5:22 the sinful *o* that men make in such cases,
2Mc 15:10 of the Gentiles and their violation of *o*.
Ps(s) 139:20 your foes swear faithless *o*.
Wis 14:30 deliberately swore false *o* despising piety.
18: 6 of the *o* in which they put their faith,
Ez 21:28 they are bound by the *o* they have sworn,
Hos 10: 4 Nothing but make promises, swear false *o*,

OBADIAH (21)

1Kgs 18: 4 was bitter, and Ahab had summoned *O*,
18: 4 of the LORD, *O* took a hundred prophets,
18: 5 Ahab said to *O*,
18: 6 way by himself, *O* another way by himself.
18: 7 As *O* was on his way, Elijah met him.
18: 7 him, *O* fell prostrate and asked,
18: 9 But *O* said, "What sin have I committed,
18:16 So *O* went to meet Ahab and informed him.
1Chr 3:21 Pelatiah, Jeshaiah, Rephaiah, Arnan, *O*,
7: 3 The sons of Izarahiah were Michael, *O*,
8:38 first-born, Ishmael, Sheariah, Azariah, *O*,
9:16 *O*,
9:44 first-born, Ishmael, Sheariah, Azariah, *O*,
12:10 Ezer was their chief, *O* was second,
27:19 for Zebulun, Ishmaiah, son of *O*;
2Chr 17: 7 he sent his leading men, Ben-hail, *O*,
34:12 their overseers were Jahath and *O*,
Ezr 8: 9 of the sons of Joab, *O*,
Neh 10: 6 Shebaniah, Malluch, Harim, Meremoth, *O*,
12:25 the other, were Mattaniah, Bakbukiah, *O*.
Ob 1: 1 The vision of *O*.

OBAL (1)

Gn 10:28 Jerah, Hadoram, Uzal, Diklah, *O*,

OBDURATE (7)

Ex 7:14 is *o* in refusing to let the people go.
8:11 he became *o* and would not listen to them
8:28 became *o* and would not let the people go.
9: 7 remained *o* and would not let the people go.
9:34 he with his servants became *o*,
10: 1 his servants *o* in order that I may perform
Rom 9:18 he wishes, and whom he wishes he makes *o*.

OBED (13)

Ru 4:17 They called him *O*.
4:21 father of Boaz, Boaz was the father of *O*,
4:22 *O* was the father of Jesse,
1Chr 2:12 Boaz became the father of *O*.
2:12 *O* became the father of Jesse.
2:37 Ephlal became the father of *O*.
2:38 *O* became the father of Jehu.
11:47 Eliel, *O*,
26: 7 sons of Shemaiah were Othni, Rephael, *O*,
2Chr 23: 1 Azariah, son of *O*;
Mt 1: 5 mother was Rahab, Boaz was the father of *O*,
1: 5 *O* was the father of Jesse,
Lk 3:32 son of David, son of Jesse, son of *O*,

OBED-EDOM (18)

2Sm 6:10 diverted it to the house of *O* the Gittite.
6:11 house of *O* the Gittite for three months,
6:11 and the Lord blessed *O* and his whole house
6:12 family of *O* and all that belonged to him,
6:12 *O* into the City of David amid festivities.
1Chr 13:13 it instead to the house of *O* the Gittite.
13:14 of *O* with his family for three months,
15:18 Mattithiah, Eliphelehu, Mikneiah, *O*,
15:21 But Mattithiah, Eliphelehu, Mikneiah, *O*,
15:24 *O* and Jeiel were also gatekeepers before
15:25 of the LORD with joy from the house of *O*.
16: 5 Jehiel, Mattithiah, Eliab, Benaiah, *O*
16:38 there *O* and sixty-eight of his brethren,
16:38 sixty-eight of his brethren, including *O*,
26: 8 All these were the sons of *O*,
26: 8 Of *O*, sixty-two.
26:15 To *O* fell the south side,
2Chr 25:24 he found in the house of God with *O*,

OBED-EDOM'S (2)

1Chr 13:14 *O* household and all that he possessed.
26: 4 *O* sons: Shemaiah, the first-born,

OBEDIENCE (24)

Dt 1:19 "Then, in *o* to the command of the LORD,
2:37 However, in *o* to the command of the LORD,
34: 9 and so the Israelites gave him their *o*,
Jos 8: 8 set it afire in *o* to the LORD's command.
17: 4 So in *o* to the command of the LORD a
19:50 In *o* to the command of the LORD,
21: 3 heritage, in *o* to this command of the LORD,
21: 8 in *o* to the LORD's command through Moses.
Jgs 2:17 of *o* to the commandments of the LORD.
1Sm 15:22 as in *o* to the command of the LORD?
15:22 *O* is better than sacrifice,
Ps(s) 40: 7 not, but ears open to *o* you gave me.
Eccl 4:17 Let your approach be *o*,
Rom 5:19 through one man's *o* all shall become just.
6:16 of sin, which leads to death, or of *o*,
15:18 to win the Gentiles to *o* by word and deed,
16:19 Your *o* is known to all,
2Cor 7:15 he recalls the *o* you showed to God
10: 6 in anyone else once your own *o* is perfect.
Heb 5: 8 he was, he learned *o* from what he suffered;
1Pt 1: 2 to a life of *o* to Jesus Christ and purification
1:22 By *o* to the truth you have purified
2:15 Such *o* is the will of God.
4:17 those who refuse *o* to the gospel of God?

OBEDIENT (15)

1Sm 12:14 if you are *o* to him and do not rebel
Prv 25:12 fine gold, is a wise reprover to an *o* ear.
Jer 13: 5 *O* to the LORD's command,
Bar 6:59 *o* in the service for which they are sent.
Lk 2:51 and came to Nazareth, and was *o* to them.
Rom 1: 5 name and bring to *o* faith all the Gentiles,
6:16 offer yourselves to someone as *o* slaves,
2Cor 2: 9 and learn whether you are *o* in all matters.
9:13 for your *o* faith in the gospel of Christ,
10: 5 into captivity to make it *o* to Christ.
Phil 2:12 dearly beloved, *o* as always to my urging,
1Pt 1:14 As *o* sons,
2:13 the Lord, be *o* to every human institution,
3: 5 reliant on God and *o* to their husbands
5: 5 you younger men must be *o* to your elders.

OBEDIENTLY (3)

Jos 10:23 *O*, they brought out to him from the cave
Jer 35:10 we *o* do everything our father Jonadab
Phil 2: 8 he humbled himself, *o* accepting even death,

OBELISKS (1)

Jer 43:13 He shall smash the *o* of the temple of the

OBEY (96)

Lv 26:15 refusing to *o* all my commandments and
26:18 "If even after this you do not *o* me,
26:21 defiant in your unwillingness to *o* me,
Nm 27:20 the whole Israelite community may *o* him.
Dt 5:27 we will listen and *o*.'
9:23 your God, and would not trust or *o* him.
11:28 you do not *o* the commandments of the LORD,
21:18 not *o* them even though they chastise him,
28:13 long as you *o* the commandments of the LORD,
30:16 If you *o* the commandments of the LORD,
Jos 1:16 *o* you as completely as we obeyed Moses.
1:18 and does not *o* every command you give him,
24:24 serve the LORD, our God, and *o* his voice."
Jgs 3: 4 to determine whether they would *o* the
6:10 But you did not *o* me."
1Sm 12:15 But if you do not *o* the LORD and if you
15:20 "I did indeed *o* the LORD and fulfill the
1Kgs 2:42 And you answered, "I accept and *o*.'
6:12 my ordinances, keep and *o* all my commands,
20:36 you did not *o* the voice of the LORD,
2Kgs 10: 6 "If you are on my side and will *o* me,
22:13 did not *o* the stipulations of this book,
Ezr 7:26 Whoever does not *o* the law of your God and
Neh 9:16 stiff and would not *o* your commandments.
9:17 They refused to *o* and no longer remembered
9:29 insolent and would not *o* your commandments;
9:29 stiffened their necks, and would not *o*.
Est 3: 8 They do not *o* the laws of the king,
1Mc 2:18 now, be the first to *o* the king's command,
2:19 all the Gentiles in the king's realm *o* him,
2:22 We will not *o* the words of the king nor
2:33 "Come out and *o* the king's command,
2:34 nor will we *o* the king's command to
6:23 and to follow his orders and *o* his edicts.
10:38 *o* no other authority than the high priest.
12:43 soldiers to *o* him as they would himself.
2Mc 7:30 I will not *o* the king's command.
7:30 I *o* the command of the law given to our
Jb 36:11 If they *o* and serve him,
36:12 But if they *o* not,
Sir 23:27 more salutary than to *o* his commandments.
Is 1:19 If you are willing, and *o*,
30: 9 who refuse to *o* the law of the LORD.
Jer 11: 6 Hear the words of this covenant and *o* them.
11: 7 I warned your fathers to *o* my voice,
11:10 forefathers who refused to *o* my words.
12:17 But if they do not *o*,
13:10 wicked people who refuse to *o* my words,
17:24 If you *o* me wholeheartedly,
17:27 you do not *o* me and keep holy the sabbath,
18:10 is evil in my eyes, refusing to *o* my voice,
22: 5 But if you do not *o* these commands,
26: 5 you constantly though you do not *o* them,
34: 4 But if you *o* the word of the LORD,
34:14 fathers, however, did not heed me or *o* me.
34:17 You did not *o* me by proclaiming your
35:13 you not take correction and *o* my words?
35:15 but you did not heed me or *o* me.
35:16 but this people does not *o* me!
35:17 because when I spoke they did not *o*,
38:20 Please *o* the voice of the LORD and do as I
40: 3 against the LORD and did not *o* his voice,
42: 6 we will *o* the command of the LORD,
42:21 message, but you *o* the voice of the LORD,
43: 4 the people did not *o* the LORD's command
Ez 2: 8 you, son of man, *o* me when I speak to you:
17:14 and would keep his covenant and *o* him.
33:31 hear your words, but they will not *o* them,
33:32 to your words, but they will not *o* them.
Dn 7:27 all dominions shall serve and *o* him."
Mt 8:27 "that even the winds and the sea *o* him?"
Mk 1:27 gives orders to unclean spirits and they *o*!"
4:41 this be that the wind and the sea *o* him?"
Lk 8:25 even the winds and the sea and they *o* him?"
17: 6 into the sea,' and it would *o* you.
Jn 14:15 you love me and *o* the commands I give you,
Acts 4:19 sight for us to *o* you rather than God.
5:29 "Better for us to *o* God than men!
5:32 whom God has given to those that *o* him."
7:39 He it was whom our fathers would not *o*;
Rom 2: 8 disobey the truth and *o* wickedness.
6:12 your mortal body and make you *o* its lusts;
6:16 you are the slaves of the one you *o*,
13: 1 *o* the authorities that are over him,
13: 5 You must *o*,
16:26 the Gentiles that they may believe and *o*—
Eph 6: 1 Children, *o* your parents in the Lord,
6: 5 *o* your human masters with the reverence,
Col 3:20 *o* your parents in everything as the
3:22 I say, *o* your human masters perfectly,
2Thes 3:14 If anyone will not *o* our injunction,
Ti 3: 1 and its officials, to *o* the laws,

Heb 5: 9 of eternal salvation for all who *o* him,
Jas 3: 3 the mouths of horses to make them *o* us,
1Pt 2:18 slaves, *o* your masters with all deference,
3: 1 You married women must *o* your husbands,

OBEYED (37)

Gn 22:18 all this because you *o* my command."
26: 5 this because Abraham *o* me,
28: 7 and that Jacob had *o* his father and mother
Nm 5: 4 The Israelites *o* the command that the
9:19 *o* the LORD and would not move on;
36:10 The daughters of Zelophehad *o* the command
Jos 1:16 will obey you as completely as we *o* Moses.
5: 6 they had not *o* the command of the LORD.
5:15 And Joshua *o*.
10:14 this, when the LORD *o* the voice of a man;
22: 2 you, and have *o* every command I gave you.
Jgs 2: 2 Yet you have not *o* me.
6:35 Manasseh, which also *o* his summons;
1Sm 28:21 "Remember, your maidservant *o* you:
2Sm 5:25 David *o* the LORD's command and routed the
22:45 as soon as they heard me, they *o*.
1Kgs 3: 3 and *o* the statutes of his father David;
11:10 strange gods, Solomon had not *o* him).
14: 4 The wife of Jeroboam *o*.
1Chr 29:23 he prospered, and all Israel *o* him.
2Chr 11: 4 They *o* this message of the LORD and gave
Est 2: 8 the king's order and decree had been *o*
1Mc 5:61 they had not *o* Judas and his brothers,
8:16 entire country, and they all *o* that one,
14:43 and strongholds, he shall be *o* by all.
Ps(s) 18:45 as soon as they heard me they *o*.
81:12 heard not my voice, and Israel *o* me not;
106:25 tents, and *o* not the voice of the LORD.
Jer 7:24 But they *o* not, nor did they pay heed.
7:26 Yet they have not *o* me nor paid heed;
19:15 their necks and have not *o* my words.
35:14 they *o* their father's command.
35:14 Me, however, you have not *o*,
35:18 Since you have *o* the command of Jonadab,
Dn 9: 6 We have not *o* your servants the prophets,
Rom 6:17 you sincerely *o* that rule of teaching
Heb 11: 8 By faith Abraham *o* when he was called,

OBEYING (6)

Nm 17:12 *O* the orders of Moses,
Dt 11:27 for *o* the commandments of the LORD,
2Kgs 14: 6 *o* the LORD's command written in the book
Ps(s) 103:20 who do his bidding, *o* his spoken word.
Jer 42: 6 well with us for *o* the command of the LORD,
44:23 the LORD, not *o* the voice of the LORD,

OBEYS (9)

Prv 1:33 But he who *o* me dwells in security,
8:33 Happy the man who *o* me,
29:19 for he understands what is said, but *o* not.
Sir 3: 6 he *o* the LORD who brings comfort to his
4:15 He who *o* her judges nations;
24:21 He who *o* me will not be put to shame,
Bar 3:33 departs, calls it, and it *o* him trembling;
Jn 9:31 that if someone is devout and *o* his will,
14:21 He who *o* the commandments he has from me

OBIL (1)

1Chr 27:30 over the camels was *O* the Ishmaelite;

OBJECT (37)

Gn 31:37 a single *o* taken from your belongings?
Lv 11:35 *o* on which one of their dead bodies falls,
27:16 "If the *o* which someone dedicates to the
Nm 35:22 in wait for him he throws some *o* at him,
Dt 9:21 taking the calf, the sinful *o* you had made,
1Kgs 15:13 she had made an outrageous *o* for Asherah.
15:13 this *o* and burned it in the Kidron Valley.
2Chr 15:16 she had made an outrageous *o* for Asherah;
29: 8 he has made them an *o* of terror,
Neh 2:17 that we may no longer be an *o* of derision!"
Tb 3: 4 exile, and death, till we were an *o* lesson,
Jb 7:12 Why have you set me up as an *o* of attack;
17: 6 their *o* lesson I have become.
Ps(s) 31:12 For all my foes I am an *o* of reproach,
Sir 42:11 an *o* of derision in public gatherings.
Jer 6:10 the LORD has become for them an *o* of scorn,
15: 4 And I will make them an *o* of horror to all
18: 4 Whenever the *o* of clay which he was making
18: 4 clay another *o* of whatever sort he pleased.
18:16 into a desert, an *o* of lasting ridicule:
19: 8 this city an *o* of amazement and derision.
20: 7 All the day I am an *o* of laughter;
24: 9 I will make them an *o* of horror to all the
25: 9 will doom them, making them an *o* of horror,
25:18 and a desert, an *o* of ridicule and cursing,
29:18 and make them an *o* of horror to all the
34:17 I will make you an *o* of horror to all the
49:13 shall become an *o* of horror and a disgrace,
49:17 Edom shall become an *o* of horror.
50:23 What an *o* of horror Babylon has become
Ez 5:15 you shall be a reproach and an *o* of scorn,
20:26 so as to make them an *o* of horror.
22: 4 Therefore I make you an *o* of scorn to the
Acts 10:11 *o* come down that looked like a big canvas.
10:16 then the *o* was snatched up into the sky.
11: 5 An *o* like a big canvas came down;
Rom 8:24 But hope is not hope if its *o* is seen;

OBJECTED (8)

Ex 4: 1 "But," *o* Moses,
2Kgs 4:43 But his servant *o*,
Tb 6:14 Tobiah *o*, however:
Jn 8:57 At this the Jews *o*:
9:16 Others *o*,
11:12 At this the disciples *o*,
12:34 The crowd *o* to his words:
Acts 28:19 When the Jews *o*,

OBJECTING (1)

Acts 11:18 When they heard this they stopped *o*,

OBJECTION (4)

Mt 9:14 John's disciples came to him with the *o*,
Mk 2:18 People came to Jesus with the *o*,
Jn 7:41 But an *o* was raised:
Acts 10:29 to your summons without raising any *o*.

OBJECTS (18)

Gn 24:53 he brought out *o* of silver and gold
Nm 4: 4 meeting tent concerns the most sacred *o*.
4:15 *o* and all their utensils on breaking camp,
4:15 But they shall not touch the sacred *o*;
4:15 are the *o* in the meeting tent that the
4:16 the sacred *o* and utensils that are in it."
4:19 die when they approach the most sacred *o*,
4:20 shall not go in to look upon the sacred *o*,
4:26 and all other *o* necessary in their use.
4:32 them all the *o* connected with his service,
7: 9 the sacred *o* which were their charge.
10:21 carrying the sacred *o* for the Dwelling,
2Kgs 7:15 other *o* that the Arameans had thrown away
23: 4 LORD all the *o* that had been made for Baal,
2Chr 21: 3 gifts of silver, gold and precious *o*,
32:23 and costly *o* for King Hezekiah of Judah,
36:19 afire, and destroyed all its precious *o*.
36:23 and destroyed all its precious *o*.

OBLATION (56)

Ex 29:18 holocaust, a sweet smelling *o* to the LORD.
29:25 altar as a sweet-smelling *o* to the LORD.
29:41 this as a sweet-smelling *o* to the LORD.
30:20 to offer an *o* to the LORD they must wash
Lv 1: 9 holocaust, a sweet-smelling *o* to the LORD.
1:13 holocaust, a sweet-smelling *o* to the LORD.
1:17 holocaust, a sweet-smelling *o* to the LORD.
2: 2 offering, a sweet-smelling *o* to the LORD.
2: 3 It is a most sacred *o* to the LORD.
2: 9 altar as a sweet-smelling *o* to the LORD.
2:10 It is a most sacred *o* to the LORD.
2:11 any leaven or honey as an *o* to the LORD.
2:16 all the frankincense, as an *o* to the LORD.
3: 3 he shall offer as an *o* to the LORD
3: 5 fire, as a sweet-smelling *o* to the LORD.
3: 9 As an *o* to the LORD he shall present the
3:11 on the altar as the food of the LORD's *o*.
3:14 From it he shall offer as an *o* to the LORD
3:16 altar as the food of the sweet-smelling *o*.
6: 8 offering, a sweet-smelling *o* to the LORD.
6:14 it as a sweet-smelling *o* to the LORD.
7: 5 burn on the altar as an *o* to the LORD.
7:25 animal from which an *o* is made to the LORD,
8:21 holocaust, a sweet-smelling *o* to the LORD,
8:28 offering, a sweet-smelling *o* to the LORD.
22:22 an animal on the altar as an *o* to the LORD.
22:27 to be offered as an *o* to the LORD.
23: 8 days you shall offer an *o* to the LORD.
23:13 oil, as a sweet-smelling *o* to the LORD;
23:18 as a sweet-smelling *o* to the LORD.
23:25 work, and you shall offer an *o* to the LORD."
23:27 yourselves and offer an *o* to the LORD.
23:36 days you shall offer an *o* to the LORD,
23:36 sacred assembly and offer an *o* to the LORD.
23:37 and offer as an *o* to the LORD holocausts
24: 7 which shall serve as an *o* to the LORD,
Nm 15: 3 *o* from the herd or from the flock,
15:10 of wine, as a sweet-smelling *o* to the LORD.
15:13 present a sweet-smelling *o* to the LORD.
15:14 presents a sweet-smelling *o* to the LORD,
15:24 a sweet-smelling *o* pleasing to the LORD,
15:25 their holocaust as an *o* to the LORD.
18:17 burn as a sweet-smelling *o* to the LORD,
28: 3 is the *o* which you shall offer to the LORD:
28: 6 Sinai as a sweet-smelling *o* to the LORD.
28: 8 morning, as a sweet-smelling *o* to the LORD.
28:13 may be a sweet-smelling *o* to the LORD.
28:19 *o* you shall offer a holocaust to the LORD,
28:24 for a sweet-smelling *o* to the LORD.
29: 6 them, as a sweet-smelling *o* to the LORD.
29:36 a sweet-smelling *o* to the LORD one bullock,
Ps(s) 40: 7 Sacrifice or *o* you wished not,
Sir 35: 1 To keep the law is a great *o*,
38:11 Offer your sweet-smelling *o*, and petition,
Dn 3:38 or leader, no holocaust, sacrifice, *o*,
9:27 the week he shall abolish sacrifice and *o*;

OBLATIONS (19)

Lv 4:35 on the altar with the other *o* of the LORD.
5:12 on the altar with the other *o* of the Lord.
6:10 as their portion from the *o* of the LORD;
6:11 their rightful share in the *o* of the LORD
6:11 Whatever touches the *o* becomes sacred."
7:30 in with his own hands the *o* to the LORD.
7:35 the priestly share from the *o* of the LORD,
10:12 offering left over from the *o* of the LORD,
10:13 This is your due from the *o* of the LORD,
10:15 shall first be brought in with the *o*,
21: 6 since they offer up the *o* of the LORD,
21:21 may draw near to offer up the *o* of the LORD;
24: 9 sacred among the various *o* to the LORD,
Nm 18: 9 to share in the *o* that are most sacred,
28: 2 that are offered to me as sweet-smelling *o*.
Dt 18: 1 *o* of the LORD and the portions due to him.
1Sm 2:28 and I assigned all the *o* of the Israelites
Sir 45:21 The *o* of the LORD are his food,
Is 19:21 they shall offer sacrifices and *o*,

OBLIGATED (2)

Mt 23:16 swears by the gold of the temple he is *o*.'
23:18 he swears by the gift on the altar he is *o*.'

OBLIGATION (6)

Nm 32:22 quit of every *o* to the LORD and to Israel,
2Chr 2: 3 such is Israel's perpetual *o*.
Est 9:27 the inviolable *o* of celebrating these two
Sir 23:11 if he neglects his *o*,
Rom 1:14 I am under *o* to Greeks and non-Greeks,
15:27 own accord, yet they are also under *o*.

OBLIGATIONS (9)

Nm 3: 7 They shall discharge his *o* and those of
3:38 the *o* of the sanctuary for the Israelites.
2Kgs 22:13 of this book, nor fulfill our written *o*."
Neh 9:34 and the *o* of which you reminded them.
1Mc 8:26 their *o* without receiving any recompense.
8:28 shall fulfill their *o* without deception.
11:33 our friends and who observe their *o* to us.
Sir 23:11 A man who often swears heaps up *o*;
1Cor 7: 3 fulfill his conjugal *o* toward his wife,

OBLIGATORY (7)

Nm 4: 3 to undertake *o* tasks in the meeting tent.
4:23 to undertake *o* tasks in the meeting tent.
4:30 to undertake *o* tasks in the meeting tent.
4:35 to undertake *o* tasks in the meeting tent,
4:39 to undertake *o* tasks in the meeting tent,
4:43 to undertake *o* tasks in the meeting tent,
2Chr 35:25 These have been made *o* for Israel,

OBLIGE (1)

2Mc 6: 8 *o* them to partake of the sacrifices,

OBLIGED (4)

2Chr 34:33 *o* all who were in Israel to serve the LORD,
1Mc 8: 7 They had taken him alive and *o* him and the
2Mc 8:26 *o* to return by reason of the late hour,
Jude 1: 3 But now I feel *o* to write and encourage

OBLIVION (3)

Est 9:28 Jews, nor into *o* among their descendants.
Ps(s) 88:13 darkness, or your justice in the land of *o*?
Wis 17: 3 of *o* Were scattered in fearful trembling,

OBNOXIOUS (2)

Wis 2:12 beset the just one, because he is *o* to us;
Jer 2:21 How could you turn out *o* to me,

OBOTH (4)

Nm 21:10 The Israelites moved on and encamped in *O*.
21:11 Setting out from *O*,
33:43 Setting out from Punon, they camped at *O*.
33:44 out from *O*, they camped at Iye-abarim

OBSCENE (1)

Eph 5: 4 Nor should there be any *o*,

OBSCENELY (1)

Ez 16:25 a dais for yourself to use your beauty *o*,

OBSCURE (5)

Prv 22:29 he will not stand in the presence of *o* men.
Sir 17:26 How *o* then the thoughts of flesh and blood!
39: 3 He studies *o* parables,
Is 33:19 will look no more, the people of *o* speech,
Lk 18:34 His utterance remained *o* to them,

OBSCURED (1)

Jb 37:21 men see not while it is *o* among the clouds,

OBSCURES (2)

Jb 38: 2 *o* divine plans with words of ignorance?
Wis 4:12 For the witchery of paltry things *o* what

OBSCURITY (3)

Jb 3: 6 May *o* seize that day;
Sir 20:10 while from *o* a man can lift up his head.
32:16 out of *o* he draws forth a clear plan.

OBSERVANCE (19)

Ex 12:48 may join in its *o* just like the natives.
Dt 4: 2 In your *o* of the commandments of the LORD,
Est 9:23 for the future this *o* which they instituted
2Mc 15: 4 who commanded the *o* of the sabbath day,
Wis 14:18 this *o* among those to whom it was strange,
Is 29:13 become routine *o* of the precepts of men,
Acts 16: 4 transmitted to the people for *o* the decisions
21:24 you follow the law yourself with due *o*.
Rom 3:20 in God's sight through *o* of the law;
3:28 justified by faith apart from *o* of the law.
Gal 1:14 *o* far beyond most of my contemporaries,
2:16 by legal *o* but by faith in Jesus Christ,
2:16 by faith in Christ, not by *o* of the law;
3: 2 Was it through *o* of the law or through
3:10 All who depend on *o* of the law,
4:10 keep the ceremonial *o* of days and months,
6:13 that they may boast about your bodily *o*.
Phil 3: 5 in legal *o* I was a Pharisee,
3: 9 justice of my own based on *o* of the law.

OBSERVANCES (1)

1Mc 1:49 forget the law ancd change all their *o*.

OBSERVE (120)

Ex 12:24 "You shall *o* this as a perpetual
12:25 you must also *o* this rite when you have
31:16 So shall the Israelites *o* the sabbath,
Lv 19:37 then, to *o* all my statutes and decrees.
20: 8 Be careful, therefore, to *o* what I,
20:22 to *o* all my statutes and all my decrees;
22:31 "Be careful to *o* the commandments which I,
25:18 *O* my precepts and be careful to keep my
26: 3 and are careful to *o* my commandments,
Nm 9:14 he too shall *o* the rules and regulations
Dt 4: 1 and decrees which I am teaching you to *o*,
4: 5 that you may *o* them in the land you are
4: 6 *O* them carefully,
4:14 you are to *o* over in the land you will occupy.
5: 1 you may learn them and take care to *o* them.
5:15 has commanded you to *o* the sabbath day.
5:31 that they may *o* them in the land which I
6: 1 has ordered that you be taught to *o* in the
6: 3 then, Israel, and be careful to *o* them,
6:24 *o* all these statutes in fear of the LORD,
7:11 therefore carefully *o* the commandments,
8: 1 "Be careful to *o* all the commandments I
11:22 *o* all these commandments I enjoin on you,
11:32 be careful to *o* all the statutes and
12: 1 be careful to *o* in the land which the LORD,
13: 1 enjoin on you, you shall be careful to *o*,
13: 5 his commandment shall you *o*,
15: 5 and carefully *o* all these commandments
16: 1 *O* the month of Abib by keeping the
19: 9 you carefully *o* all these commandments
24: 8 of leprosy you shall be careful to *o* exactly
24:18 that is why I command you to *o* this rule.
24:22 that is why I command you to *o* this rule.
26:16 you to *o* these statutes and decrees.
26:16 to *o* them with all your heart and with all
26:17 are to walk in his ways and *o* his statutes,
28: 1 and are careful to *o* all his commandments
28:13 which I order you today to *o* carefully,
28:15 and are not careful to *o* all his
28:58 "If you are not careful to *o* every word
31:12 and carefully *o* all the words of this law.
Jos 1: 7 taking care to *o* the entire law which my
1: 8 may *o* carefully all that is written in it;
22: 5 to *o* the precept and law which Moses,
23: 6 Therefore strive hard to *o* and carry out
Jgs 13:14 Let her *o* all that I have commanded her."
1Kgs 6:12 if you *o* my statutes,
2Kgs 10:31 to *o* wholeheartedly the law of the LORD,
17:34 LORD nor *o* the statutes and regulations,
17:37 to *o* forever the statutes and regulations,
21: 8 are careful to *o* all I have commanded them,
23: 3 they would follow him and *o* his ordinances,
23:21 the people to *o* the Passover of the LORD,
1Chr 22:13 if you are careful to *o* the precepts and
23:32 They shall *o* what is prescribed for them
2Chr 13:11 for we *o* our duties to the LORD,
14: 3 fathers, and to *o* the law and its commands.
23: 6 must *o* the prescriptions of the LORD.
33: 8 are careful to *o* all that I commanded them,
Neh 10:30 and to *o* carefully all the commandments of
Est E:24 that does not *o* this decree shall be
9:22 to *o* these days with feasting and gladness,
1Mc 2:67 also gather about you all who *o* the law,
2:68 deserve, and *o* the precepts of the law."
11:33 friends and who *o* their obligations to us.
2Mc 6:11 in nearby caves to *o* the sabbath in secret,
11:31 to *o* their dietary laws and other laws,
13:23 their terms, and swore to *o* their rights.
Jb 7:18 You *o* him with each new day and try him at
Ps(s) 105:45 might keep his statutes and *o* his laws.
106: 3 Happy are they who *o* what is right,
107:43 Who is wise enough to *o* these things and
119: 2 Happy are they who *o* his decrees,
119:22 and contempt, for I *o* your decrees.
119:33 your statutes, that I may exactly *o* them.
119:34 *o* your law and keep it with all my heart.
119:69 with all my heart I will *o* your precepts.
119:100 than the elders, because I *o* your precepts.
119:115 and I will *o* the commands of my God.
119:129 therefore I *o* them.
119:145 I will *o* your statutes.
Prv 6:20 *O*, my son, your father's bidding,
Eccl 8: 2 *O* the precept of the king,
8:16 know wisdom and to *o* what is done on earth,
Wis 6:18 To *o* her laws is the basis for
Sir 23:19 *O* every step a man takes and peer into
Is 41:20 all may see and know, *o* and understand,
56: 1 *O* what is right,
56: 4 To the eunuchs who *o* my sabbaths and
Jer 5: 1 streets of Jerusalem, look about and *o*,
8: 7 swallow and thrush *o* their time of return,
11: 3 who does not *o* the terms of this covenant,
11: 8 they had failed to *o* as I commanded them.
34:18 did not *o* the terms of the agreement
Ez 11:20 and *o* and carry out my ordinances;
18: 9 statutes and is careful to *o* my ordinances,
18:19 and has been careful to *o* all my statutes,
20:13 They did not *o* my statutes,
20:18 Do not *o* the statutes of your parents or
20:19 *o* my statutes and be careful to keep my
20:21 they did not *o* my statutes or keep my
20:21 that bring life to those who *o* them,
36:27 by my statutes, careful to *o* my decrees.
37:24 by my statutes and carefully *o* my decrees.
43:11 may carefully *o* all its laws and statutes.
44:24 *o* my laws and statutes on all my festivals,
45:21 you shall *o* the feast of the Passover;
Dn 9: 4 those who love you and *o* your commandments!
Mt 23: 3 everything and *o* everything they tell you.
Mk 7: 4 There are many other traditions they *o*—
12:43 "I want you to *o* that this poor widow
Lk 21:30 You *o* them when they are budding,
Jn 19: 4 *O* what I do.
Acts 3:16 him perfect health, as all of you can *o*.
7:31 As he drew near to *o* it carefully,
Rom 2:25 to be sure, has value if you *o* the law,
4:14 If only those who *o* the law are heirs,
Gal 3: 5 Is it because you *o* the law or because you
Eph 5:29 *O* that no one ever hates his own flesh;
1Pt 3: 2 *o* the reverent purity of your way of life.

OBSERVED (52)

Gn 50:10 *o* seven days of mourning for his father.
Lv 18:30 customs that have been *o* before you.
Nm 23:21 Misfortune is not *o* in Jacob,
Dt 15: 2 of debts, which shall be *o* as follows.
Jos 6:21 They *o* the ban by putting to the sword all
1Sm 16:18 "I have *o* that one of the sons of Jesse
2Sm 14: 1 *o* how the king felt toward Absalom,
2Kgs 18: 6 but *o* the commandments which the LORD had
23:22 No Passover such as this had been *o* during
2Chr 17: 4 the God of his father and *o* his commands,
35:18 No such Passover had been *o* in Israel
35:19 of Josiah's reign that this Passover was *o*.
Ezr 10: 3 Let the law be *o*!
Jdt 4:13 For the people *o* a fast of many days'
Est 3: 5 When Haman *o* that Mordecai would not kneel
1Mc 1:57 of the covenant, and whoever *o* the law,
4:59 dedication of the altar should be *o* with joy
7:48 and *o* that day as a great festival.
7:49 be *o* every year on the thirteenth of Adar.
13:48 impure, he settled there men who *o* the law.
2Mc 3: 1 laws were strictly *o* because of the piety
8:27 then *o* the sabbath with fervent praise
Ps(s) 119:56 I have had, that I have *o* your precepts.
Prv 7: 7 the simple ones, I *o* among the young men,
Wis 14:16 practice gained strength and was *o* as law,
Sir 19:23 and feigns not to hear, but when not *o*,
44:20 He *o* the precepts of the Most High,
Is 30:29 will sing as on a night when a feast is *o*,
Jer 16:11 have forsaken, and my law they have not *o*.
35:16 *o* the command which their father laid on
Dn 3:30 Your commandments we have not heeded or *o*,
Zep 2: 3 humble of the earth, who have *o* his law;
Mt 2: 2 We *o* his star at its rising and have come
2: 9 The star which they had *o* at its rising
17:26 he replied, "From foreigners," Jesus *o*:
21:15 when they *o* the wonders he worked,
Mk 1:16 he *o* Simon and his brother Andrew casting
7: 2 They had *o* a few of his disciples eating
12:41 he *o* the crowd putting money into the
14: 1 Bread were to be *o* in two days' time,
15:47 mother of Joses *o* where he had been laid.
Lk 14: 1 the leading Pharisees, they *o* him closely.
18:24 When Jesus *o* this he said:
19: 7 When this was *o*,
23:56 They *o* the sabbath as a day of rest,
Jn 20: 6 He *o* the wrappings on the ground and saw
Acts 7:53 the ministry of angels have not *o* it."
8:18 Simon *o* that it was through the laying on
22:28 The commander then *o*,
1Cor 14:34 rule *o* in all the assemblies of believers,
Gal 2:14 As soon as I *o* that they were not being
2Tm 3:10 You have *o* my resolution,

OBSERVER (3)

Wis 1: 6 the sure *o* of his heart and the listener
Acts 22:12 a devout *o* of the law and well spoken of
Jas 4:11 you judge the law you are no *o* of the law,

OBSERVES (3)

Sir 35: 1 and he who *o* the commandments sacrifices a
10: 5 The one who *o* the law
Rom 14: 6 who *o* the day does so to honor the Lord.

OBSERVING (14)

Lv 13:15 on *o* the raw flesh,
18:30 not to defile yourselves by *o* the
Nm 9: 3 it, *o* all its rules and regulations."
9:12 bones, but *o* all the rules of the Passover.
Dt 6:25 is to consist in carefully *o* all these
7:12 heeding these decrees and *o* them carefully,
1Kgs 2: 3 God, following his ways and *o* his statutes,
8:61 *o* his statutes and keeping his
2Chr 34:31 thus *o* the terms of the covenant written
Neh 2:13 *o* how the walls of Jerusalem lay in ruins
Mt 27: 6 The chief priests picked up the silver, *o*,
Mk 11:13 *O* a fig tree some distance off,
Acts 4:13 *O* the self-assurance of Peter and John,
1Pt 2:12 By *o* your good works they may give glory

OBSOLETE (2)

Heb 8:13 covenant," he declares the first one *o*.
8:13 And what has become *o* and has grown old is

OBSTACLE (3)

Is 8:14 an *o* and a stumbling stone to both the
1Cor 9:12 any *o* in the way of the gospel of Christ.
1Pt 2: 8 is likewise "an *o* and a stumbling stone."

OBSTACLES (1)

Jer 6:21 before this people *o* to bring them down;

OBSTINACY (2)

Ex 9:35 his *o* he would not let the Israelites go,
Acts 19: 9 When some in their *o* would not believe,

OBSTINATE (18)

Ex 4:21 I will make him *o*,
7: 3 Yet I will make Pharaoh so *o* that,
7:13 was *o* and would not listen to them,
7:22 *o* and would not listen to Moses and Aaron,
8:15 remained *o* and would not listen to them,
9:12 But the LORD made Pharaoh *o*,
10:20 of Egypt, the LORD made Pharaoh *o*,
10:27 But the LORD made Pharaoh *o*,
11:10 presence, the LORD made Pharaoh *o*,
14: 4 make Pharaoh so *o* that he will pursue them.
14: 8 So *o* had the LORD made Pharaoh that he
14:17 so *o* that they will go in after them.
Dt 2:30 made him stubborn in mind and *o* in heart
2Chr 30: 8 Be not *o*,
Jb 36: 5 Behold, God rejects the *o* in heart;
Jer 8: 5 do these people rebel with *o* resistance?
Ez 2: 4 Hard of face and *o* of heart are they to
3: 7 Israel is stubborn of brow and *o* in heart.

OBTAIN (22)

Gn 24: 7 and you will *o* a wife for my son there.
24:48 to *o* the daughter of my master's kinsman
41:57 world came to Joseph to *o* rations of grain,
1Kgs 21: 7 I will *o* the vineyard of Naboth the
Tb 5: 2 shall I be able to *o* the money from him,
1Mc 9:70 him and to *o* the release of the prisoners.
14: 1 to *o* help so that he could fight Trypho.
2Mc 4:23 to *o* decisions on some important matters.
Jb 32:20 Let me speak and *o* relief;
Sir 8: 9 From it you will *o* the knowledge how to
Ez 17:15 to Egypt to *o* horses and a great army.
Mt 21:34 the tenants to *o* his share of the grapes.
26:59 were busy trying to *o* false testimony
Mk 12: 2 tenants to *o* from them his share of produce
Acts 26:18 they may *o* the forgiveness of their sins
Rom 11: 7 Israel did not *o* what she was seeking,
2Tm 2:10 in order that they may *o* the salvation to
Heb 11:13 They did not *o* what had been promised but
11:35 in order to *o* a better resurrection.
11:39 they did not *o* what had been promised.
Jas 4: 2 What you desire you do not *o*,
4: 2 You do not *o* because you do not ask.

OBTAINED (28)

Dt 8:17 my own hand that has *o* for me this wealth.'
Jos 17: 1 who had already *o* Gilead and Bashan,
19: 9 the Simeonites *o* their heritage within it.
21: 4 Aaron the priest *o* thirteen cities by lot
21: 5 The rest of the Kohathites *o* ten cities by

21: 6 The Gershonites *o* thirteen cities by lot
21: 7 *o* twelve cities from the tribes of Reuben,
21:17 From the tribe of Benjamin they *o* the four
21:20 Kohathite clans among the Levites *o* by lot,
21:23 From the tribe of Dan they *o* the four
21:28 From the tribe of Issachar they *o* the four
2Sm 21:12 he went and *o* the bones of Saul and of his
1Chr 6:16 the ark had *o* a permanent resting place.
6:46 The other Kohathites *o* ten cities by lot
6:47 The clans of the Gershonites *o* thirteen
6:48 The clans of the Merarites *o* twelve cities
6:51 *o* cities by lot from the tribe of Ephraim.
Est B: 5 that stability of government cannot be *o*,
4:14 like this that you *o* the royal dignity?"
9:16 themselves, and *o* rest from their enemies.
9:22 Jews *o* rest from their enemies
2Mc 4: 7 *o* the high priesthood by corrupt means:
4:27 Although Menelaus had *o* the office,
Jb 28:12 But whence can wisdom be *o*,
Ps(s) 107:37 vineyards, And they *o* a fruitful yield.
Heb 6:15 waiting, Abraham *o* what God had promised.
8: 6 Jesus has *o* a more excellent ministry now,
11:33 did what was just, *o* the promises;

OBTAINS (4)

Prv 28:13 he who confesses and forsakes them *o* mercy.
29:23 but he who is humble of spirit *o* honor.
31:13 She *o* wool and flax and makes cloth with
Sir 32:14 he who seeks him *o* his request.

OBTUSE (1)

Mk 7:22 envy, blasphemy, arrogance, an *o* spirit.

OBVIOUS (5)

1Mc 8:18 for it was *o* that the kingdom of the
2Mc 6: 9 It was *o*, therefore, that disaster impended.
Jn 18:21 be *o* that they will know what I said."
Gal 3:11 It should be *o* that no one is justified in
5:19 It is *o* what proceeds from the flesh:

OBVIOUSLY (1)

Lk 23:15 *o* this man has done nothing that calls for

OCCASION (55)

Gn 15:18 *o* that the LORD made a covenant with Abram,
41: 9 "On this *o* I am reminded of my negligence.
Ex 2:11 On one *o*, after Moses had grown up,
18:11 for he took *o* of their being dealt with
Nm 7:84 of Israel on the *o* of its anointing:
Jos 5: 2 On this *o* the LORD said to Joshua,
6:26 On that *o* Joshua imposed the oath:
8:33 of the people of Israel on this first *o*.
14: 9 On that *o* Moses swore this oath,
Jgs 3:29 *o* they slew about ten thousand Moabites,
20:15 cities on that *o* was twenty-six thousand,
1Sm 11:15 Israelites celebrated the *o* with great joy.
14:37 But he received no answer on this *o*.
20:19 the other *o* and wait near the mound there.
2Sm 21:18 On that *o* Sibbecai,
1Kgs 8: 5 present for the *o* sacrificed before the ark
8:65 On this *o* Solomon and all the Israelites,
2Chr 7: 8 On this *o* Solomon and with him all Israel,
13:18 The Israelites were subdued on that *o* and
35:17 The Israelites who were present on that *o*
Ezr 6:20 of whom had purified himself for the *o*,
Neh 8: 4 platform that had been made for the *o*;
8:17 days of Jeshua, son of Nun, until this *o*;
Jdt 12: 2 partake of them, lest it be an *o* of sin;
1Mc 8:25 them wholeheartedly, as the *o* shall demand;
8:27 help them willingly, as the *o* shall demand,
2Mc 14: 4 On that *o* he kept quiet.
Ez 7:19 for this has been the *o* of their sin.
14: 3 they keep the *o* of their sin before them.
14: 4 and keeping the *o* of his sin before him,
14: 7 and keeps the *o* of his sin before him,
44:12 became an *o* of sin to the house of Israel,
Dn 13:14 for an *o* when they could meet her alone.
Mt 11:25 On one *o* Jesus spoke thus:
14: 1 On one *o* Herod the tetrarch,
27: 9 that *o*, what was said through Jeremiah
27:15 Now on the *o* of a festival the procurator
Mk 4: 1 *o* he began to teach beside the lake.
15: 6 Now on the *o* of a festival he would
Lk 5:12 On one *o* in a certain town,
10:25 On one *o* a lawyer stood up to pose him
14:25 On one *o* when a great crowd was with him,
17:17 Jesus took the *o* to say,
Jn 4:45 that he had done in Jerusalem on that *o*.
5: 1 Later, on the *o* of a Jewish feast,
Acts 1: 4 On one *o* when he met with them,
13: 2 On one *o*, while they were engaged
14: 9 one *o* he was listening to Paul preaching,
26:12 "On one such *o* I was traveling toward
Rom 3:27 What *o* is there then for boasting?
14:16 privilege to become an *o* for blasphemy.
14:21 your brother an *o* for stumbling or scandal,
1Cor 8: 9 right you become an *o* of sin to the weak.
8:13 so that I may not be an *o* of sin to him.
1Tm 5:14 give our enemies no *o* to speak ill of us.

OCCASIONED (1)

Gal 4:13 that first *o* my bringing you the gospel.

OCCASIONS (5)

Jgs 20:30 line of battle at Gibeah as on other *o*.
20:31 in the open field, just as on the other *o*.
1Sm 21: 6 segregated from women as on previous *o*.
Hos 8:11 to expiate sin, his altars became *o* of sin.
Zec 8:19 months shall become *o* of joy and gladness,

OCCUPANTS (2)

1Chr 22:18 delivered the *o* of the land into my power,
1Mc 13:11 drove out the *o* and remained there.

OCCUPATION (5)

Gn 46:33 summons you and asks what your *o* is,
47: 3 When Pharaoh asked them what their *o* was,
Dt 2:24 Begin the *o*; engage him in battle.
2:31 you Sihon and his land, begin the actual *o*.'
Eccl 2:23 All his days sorrow and grief are his *o*;

OCCUPIED (30)

Dt 3:12 "When we *o* the land at that time,
4:47 They *o* his land and the land of Og,
17:14 you, and have *o* it and settled in it,
26: 1 heritage, and have *o* it and settled in it,
30: 5 into the land which your fathers once *o*,
Jos 12: 1 conquered and whose lands they *o*,
13:12 Moses conquered and *o* these territories,
21:43 Once they had conquered and *o* it,
22:33 and Gadites or ravaging the land they *o*.
Jgs 9:41 his kinsmen from Shechem, which they had *o*.
11:21 who defeated them and *o* all the land of
11:26 when Israel *o* Heshbon and its villages,
21:23 where they rebuilt and *o* the cities.
2Kgs 13:13 his ancestors, and Jeroboam *o* the throne.
16: 6 which they have *o* until the present.
17: 5 then *o* the whole land and attacked Samaria,
1Chr 5:10 they had defeated them they *o* their tents
10: 7 thereupon the Philistines came and *o* them.
2Chr 28:18 and Gimzo and its dependencies, and *o* them.
Jdt 5:18 and their cities were *o* by their enemies.
1Mc 11:56 captured the elephants and *o* Antioch.
12:33 He then turned to Joppa and *o* it,
14:34 Azotus, a place previously *o* by the enemy;
2Mc 3:11 Tobias, a man who *o* a very high position.
14: 2 and a fleet, and that he had *o* the country,
Jer 39: 3 king of Babylon came and *o* the middle gate:
40:10 jars, and to settle in the cities they *o*.
Dn 9:20 I was still *o* with my prayer,
9:21 I was still *o* with this prayer,
1Cor 7:33 demands and *o* with pleasing his wife.

OCCUPIES (1)

Sir 39: 1 of old and *o* himself with the prophecies;

OCCUPY (49)

Lv 14:34 infection on any house of the land you *o*,
25:24 in every part of the country that you *o*,
Dt 1: 8 now and *o* the land I swore to your fathers,
1:21 Go up and *o* it,
1:39 them I will give it, and they shall *o* it.
4: 5 them in the land you are entering to *o*.
4:14 are to observe over in the land you will *o*.
4:26 which you will *o* when you cross the Jordan.
5:33 long life in the land which you are to *o*.
7: 1 the land which you are to enter and *o*,
10:11 that they may enter in and *o* the land
11:10 to enter and *o* is not like the land of Egypt
11:29 the land which you are to enter and *o*,
11:31 to enter and *o* the land which the LORD,
12: 1 God of your fathers, has given you to *o*,
15: 4 he will give you to *o* as your heritage,
19: 2 the LORD, your God, is giving you to *o*.
19:14 the LORD, your God, is giving you to *o*.
21: 1 the LORD, your God, is giving you to *o*,
23:21 on the land you are to enter and *o*.
25:19 he is giving you to *o* as your heritage,
28:21 you from the land you are entering to *o*.
28:63 out of the land you are now entering to *o*.
30: 5 once occupied, that you too may *o* it,
30:16 you in the land you are entering to *o*.
30:18 you are crossing the Jordan to enter and *o*.
31:13 land which you will cross the Jordan to *o*."
32:47 land which you will cross the Jordan to *o*."
Jos 1:15 you may return and *o* your own land,
Jgs 1:18 however, did not *o* Gaza with its territory,
Neh 2: 8 the city wall and the house that I shall *o*."
9:15 You bade them enter and *o* the land which
Jdt 2:11 and plunder in each country you *o*.
1Mc 15: 7 and now *o* shall remain in your possession.
Prv 25: 6 presence, nor *o* the place of great men;
Wis 13:13 he takes and carves to *o* his spare time.
Sir 38:33 They do not *o* the judge's bench,
Is 44:13 in appearance and dignity, to *o* a shrine.
Jer 50:39 dwell there, and ostriches shall *o* it;
Ez 28: 2 *o* a godly throne in the heart of the sea!—"
Am 2:10 forty years, to *o* the land of the Amorites:
Ob 1:19 They shall *o* the Negeb,
1:19 And they shall *o* the lands of Ephraim and
1:19 of Samaria, And Benjamin shall *o* Gilead.
1:20 *o* the Canaanite land as far as Zarephath,
1:20 Sepharad shall *o* the cities of the Negeb.
Zec 9: 6 inhabited, and the baseborn shall *o* Ashdod.
14:11 the king's wine presses, they shall *o* her.

OCCUPYING (5)

Gn 13: 7 and the Perizzites were *o* the land.)
1Sm 13:16 had with them were now *o* Geba of Benjamin,
24: 4 men were *o* the inmost recesses of the cave.
Est 1: 2 while he was *o* the royal throne in the
1Mc 15:28 "You are *o* Joppa and Gazara and the

OCCUR (6)

Tb 14: 4 prophets, whom God commissioned, shall *o*.
Jb 3: 6 let it not *o* among the days of the year,
Mt 18: 7 It is inevitable that scandal should *o*.
24: 3 "Tell us, when will all this *o*?
Mk 13: 4 "Tell us, when will this *o*?
Acts 11:28 did in fact *o* while Claudius was emperor.)

OCCURRED (15)

Gn 26: 1 one that had *o* in the days of Abraham),
Jgs 11: 5 When this *o* the elders of Gilead went to
20:12 "What is this evil which has *o* among you?
2Sm 13: 1 Some time later the following incident *o*.
2Chr 11: 4 home, for what has *o* I have brought about.'"
32:31 the sign that had *o* in the land,
Est 6: 2 the passage *o* in which Mordecai reported
F: 6 such as have not *o* among the nations.
1Mc 4:26 went and told Lysias all that had *o*.
Dn 9:12 calamity that has ever *o* under heaven.
Lk 10:13 in your midst had *o* in Tyre and Sidon,
24:12 went away full of amazement at what had *o*.
Acts 5:12 many signs and wonders *o* among the people.
8:13 the signs and the great miracles as they *o*,
2Thes 2: 3 Since the mass apostasy has not yet *o* nor

OCCURRENCE (1)

Acts 2: 7 The whole *o* astonished them.

OCCURRING (1)

1Pt 4:12 that a trial by fire is *o* in your midst.

OCCURS (4)

Jos 8: 6 When this *o*,
Eccl 8:14 This is a vanity which *o* on earth:
Wis 1: 5 and when injustice *o* it is rebuked.
Mt 13:21 or persecution involving the message *o*,

OCEAN (3)

Ps(s) 104: 6 With the *o*,
Hb 3:10 the *o* gives forth its roar.
Jude 1:13 They are wild *o* waves,

OCHRAN (5)

Nm 1:13 Pagiel, son of *O* from Gad:
2:27 Asher [Their prince was Pagiel, son of *O*,
7:72 day it was the turn of Pagiel, son of *O*,
7:77 This was the offering of Pagiel, son of *O*.
10:26 over their host, and Pagiel, son of *O*,

OCINA (1)

Jdt 2:28 and Tyre, and those who dwelt in Sur and *O*,

O'CLOCK (3)

Acts 3: 1 the temple for prayer at the three *o* hour,
10:30 ago at this very hour, namely three *o*,
23:23 to leave for Caesarea by nine *o* tonight,

OCTAVES (1)

Is 1:13 calling of assemblies, *o* with wickedness:

ODDS (1)

Mt 10:35 come to set a man at *o* with his father,

ODE (1)

Ps(s) 45: 2 as I sing my *o* to the king,

ODED (3)

2Chr 15: 1 Upon Azariah, son of *O*,
15: 8 words and the prophecy *O* the prophet],
28: 9 was a prophet of the LORD by the name of *O*.

ODIOUS (9)

2Sm 16:21 *o* you have made yourself to your father,
Prv 30:23 Under an *o* woman when she is wed,
Wis 12: 4 land, whom you hated for deeds most *o*—
14: 9 Equally *o* to God are the evildoer and his
Sir 7:26 you have a wife, let her not seem *o* to you;
10: 7 *O* to the LORD and to men is arrogance.
13:21 though what he says is *o*,
Jer 6:15 They are *o*;
8:12 They are *o*;

ODOMERA (1)

1Mc 9:66 He struck down *O* and his kinsmen and the

ODOR (19)

Gn 8:21 When the LORD smelled the sweet *o,*
Ex 5:21 You have brought us into bad *o* with
Lv 2:12 to be placed on the altar for a pleasing *o.*
Lv 4:31 on the altar for an *o* pleasing to the LORD.
Lv 17:6 burn the fat for an *o* pleasing to the LORD.
1Chr 19:6 had put themselves in bad *o* with David,
Ezr 6:10 offer sacrifices of pleasing *o* to the God
Tb 6:18 as the demon smells the *o* they give off,
Tb 8:3 The demon, repelled by the *o* of the fish,
Jdt 16:16 the sweet *o* of every sacrifice is a trifle,
Sir 24:15 like the *o* of incense in the holy place.
Sir 35:5 rises as a sweet *o* before the Most High.
Sir 39:14 Send up the sweet *o* of incense,
Sir 39:14 Send up the sweet *o* of your hymn of praise;
Sir 45:16 burn sacrifices of sweet *o* for a memorial,
Sir 50:15 a sweet-smelling *o* to the Most High God,
Ez 16:19 you, you set before them as an appeasing *o.*
Ez 20:41 As a pleasing *o* I will accept you,
2Cor 2:16 to the latter an *o* dealing death,

ODORS (2)

Ez 6:13 offered appeasing *o* to any of their gods.
Ez 20:28 there they sent up appeasing *o,*

OFF (583)

Gn 8:7 until the waters dried *o* from the earth.
Gn 17:14 such a one shall be cut *o* from his people;
Gn 19:17 Get *o* to the hills at once,
Gn 24:28 *o* and told her mother's household about it.
Gn 27:35 here by a ruse and carried *o* your blessing,"
Gn 27:40 you shall throw *o* his yoke from your neck."
Gn 29:26 *o* a younger daughter before an older one.
Gn 30:37 peeling *o* the bark down to the white core
Gn 31:18 and he drove *o* with all his livestock and
Gn 31:26 carrying *o* my daughters like war captives?
Gn 31:27 and I would have sent you *o* with merry
Gn 34:29 They carried *o* all their wealth,
Gn 37:14 So he sent him *o* from the valley of Hebron.
Gn 38:14 his sheep, she took *o* her widow's garb,
Gn 38:19 she took *o* her shawl and put on her
Gn 41:42 Pharaoh took *o* his signet ring and put it
Gn 43:8 that we may be *o* and on our way if you and
Gn 43:13 too, and be *o* on your way back to the man.
Gn 43:15 were *o* on their way down to Egypt to
Gn 44:3 the men and their donkeys were sent *o.*
Gn 45:18 where you will live *o* the fat of the land.'
Gn 47:22 *o* the allowance Pharaoh had granted them,
Ex 4:25 of flint and cut *o* her son's foreskin and,
Ex 5:4 *O* to your labor!
Ex 5:18 ' *O* to work, then!
Ex 8:9 houses and courtyards and fields died *o.*
Ex 9:20 their servants and livestock *o* to shelter.
Ex 12:15 to the seventh shall be cut *o* from Israel.
Ex 12:19 be cut *o* from the community of Israel.
Ex 18:27 who went *o* to his own country.
Ex 30:33 a layman, shall be cut *o* from his kinsmen."
Ex 30:38 fragrance, shall be cut *o* from his kinsmen."
Ex 32:2 *o* the golden earrings they are wearing,
Ex 32:3 *o* their earrings and brought them to Aaron,
Ex 32:24 'Let anyone who has gold jewelry take it *o.*'
Ex 33:5 Take *o* your ornaments,
Ex 40:3 in it, and screen *o* the ark with the veil.
Ex 40:21 screening *o* the ark of the commandments,
Lv 5:8 neck, yet without breaking it *o* completely,
Lv 6:4 *o* these garments and put on other garments,
Lv 7:20 the person shall be cut *o* from his people.
Lv 7:21 too, shall be cut *o* from his people."
Lv 7:25 such a one shall be cut *o* from his people.
Lv 7:27 any blood shall be cut *o* from his people."
Lv 14:8 shave *o* all his hair and bathe in water;
Lv 14:9 again shave *o* all the hair of his head,
Lv 14:41 that has been scraped *o* shall be dumped
Lv 15:3 whether the flow drains *o* or is blocked up;
Lv 16:10 by sending it *o* to Azazel in the desert.
Lv 16:22 *o* their iniquities to an isolated region,
Lv 16:23 he shall strip *o* and leave in the
Lv 17:4 a man shall be cut *o* from among his people.
Lv 17:9 the LORD, shall be cut *o* from his kinsmen.
Lv 17:10 and will cut him *o* from among his people.
Lv 17:14 anyone who partakes of it shall be cut *o.*
Lv 18:29 shall be cut *o* from among his people.
Lv 19:8 Such a one shall be cut *o* from his people.
Lv 20:3 and cut him *o* from the body of his people;
Lv 20:5 his family and will cut *o* from their people
Lv 20:6 such a one and cut him *o* from his people.
Lv 20:17 they shall be publicly cut *o* from their
Lv 20:18 of them shall be cut *o* from their people,
Lv 22:3 such a one shall be cut *o* from my presence.
Lv 22:24 or cut *o* you shall not offer to the LORD.
Lv 23:29 on this day shall be cut *o* from his people,
Lv 26:26 And as I cut *o* your supply of bread,
Nm 5:23 then wash them *o* into the bitter water,
Nm 6:19 nazirite has shaved *o* his dedicated hair,
Nm 9:13 Passover, shall be cut *o* from his people,
Nm 11:18 Oh, how well *o* we were in Egypt!'
Nm 15:30 and shall be cut *o* from among his people.
Nm 15:31 broken his commandment, he must be cut *o.*
Nm 19:13 of the LORD and shall be cut *o* from Israel.
Nm 19:20 purified shall be cut *o* from the community,
Nm 22:21 ass, and went *o* with the princes of Moab.
Nm 22:23 turned *o* the road and went into the field,
Nm 24:11 Be *o* at once, then, to your home.
Dt 1:43 arrogantly marched *o* into the hill country.
Dt 16:9 "You shall count *o* seven weeks,
Dt 19:5 its head flies *o* the handle and hits his
Dt 22:8 otherwise, if someone falls *o,*
Dt 23:2 whose penis has been cut *o* may be admitted
Dt 25:12 you shall chop *o* her hand without pity.
Dt 25:18 *o* at the rear all those who lagged behind.
Dt 28:26 the field, with no one to frighten them *o.*
Dt 28:40 for your olives will drop *o* unripe.
Dt 32:13 land and live *o* the products of its fields,
Jos 5:6 people that came forth from Egypt died *o*
Jos 7:24 and led them *o* to the Valley of Achor.
Jos 8:3 sent them *o* by night with these orders:
Jos 18:3 How much longer will you put *o* taking steps
Jos 22:7 *o* to their tents with his blessing was,
Jgs 1:6 him, cut *o* his thumbs and his big toes.
Jgs 1:7 with their thumbs and big toes cut *o,*
Jgs 3:18 went *o* with the tribute bearers.
Jgs 4:14 Deborah then said to Barak, "Be *o,*
Jgs 6:19 So Gideon went *o* and prepared a kid and an
Jgs 11:37 that I may go *o* down the mountains to
Jgs 14:19 Then he went *o* to his own family in anger,
Jgs 16:12 But he snapped them *o* his arms like thread.
Jgs 16:19 a man who shaved *o* his seven locks of hair.
Jgs 16:22 began to grow as soon as it was shaved *o.*
Jgs 18:20 idol and went *o* in the midst of the band.
Jgs 18:24 and have gone *o* with my priest as well,"
Jgs 19:11 let us turn *o* to this city of the
Jgs 19:12 will not turn *o* to a city of foreigners,
Jgs 19:15 turned *o* to enter Gibeah for the night.
Jgs 20:31 and in the beginning they killed *o* about
Jgs 20:39 killing *o* some thirty of the men of Israel,
Jgs 20:45 picked *o* five thousand men among them,
Jgs 21:6 one of the tribes of Israel has been cut *o.*
Jgs 21:23 they carried *o* a wife for each of them
Ru 3:15 her, "Take *o* your cloak and hold it out."
Ru 4:7 take *o* his sandal and give it to the other.
Ru 4:8 it for yourself," drew *o* his sandal.
1Sm 5:4 hands broken *o* and lying on the threshold,
1Sm 9:3 of Saul's father, Kish, had wandered *o.*
1Sm 14:13 followed him and finished them *o.*
1Sm 14:36 them until daybreak and to kill them all *o.*"
1Sm 15:27 a loose end of his mantle, and it tore *o.*
1Sm 17:13 sons who had gone *o* to war were named,
1Sm 17:34 came to carry *o* a sheep from the flock,
1Sm 17:39 So he took them *o.*
1Sm 17:46 I will strike you down and cut *o* your head.
1Sm 17:51 he dispatched him and cut *o* his head.
1Sm 23:5 He drove *o* their cattle and inflicted a
1Sm 23:24 So they went *o* to Ziph ahead of Saul.
1Sm 24:5 stealthily cut *o* an end of Saul's mantle.
1Sm 24:6 that he had cut *o* an end of Saul's mantle.
1Sm 24:12 Since I cut *o* an end of your mantle and
1Sm 26:2 So Saul went *o* down to the desert of Ziph
1Sm 27:9 or woman alive, but would carry *o* sheep,
1Sm 30:2 they had carried them *o* when they left.
1Sm 30:5 had also been carried *o* with the rest.
1Sm 30:9 So David went *o* with his six hundred men
1Sm 31:9 They cut *o* Saul's head and stripped him of
2Sm 1:9 'Stand up to me, please, and finish me *o,*
2Sm 2:15 So they rose and were counted *o:*
2Sm 4:6 the house had dozed *o* while sifting wheat,
2Sm 4:7 struck and killed him, and cut *o* his head.
2Sm 4:12 killed them and cut *o* their hands and feet,
2Sm 8:2 told *o* two lengths of line for execution,
2Sm 10:4 after shaving *o* half their beards and
2Sm 14:23 Joab then went *o* to Geshur and brought
2Sm 14:24 So Absalom went *o* to his house and did not
2Sm 14:32 I would be better *o* if I were still there!'
2Sm 15:9 a safe journey, and he went *o* to Hebron.
2Sm 16:9 Let me go over, please, and lop *o* his head."
2Sm 17:1 men, and be *o* in pursuit of David tonight.
2Sm 18:9 while the mule he had been riding ran *o.*
2Sm 18:23 Ahimaaz sped *o* by way of the Jordan plain
2Sm 20:22 advice, and they cut *o* the head of Sheba,
2Sm 21:2 Saul had attempted to kill them *o* in his
2Sm 21:10 fending *o* the birds of the sky from
2Sm 21:12 who had carried them *o* secretly from the
1Kgs 6:16 was set *o* by cedar partitions from the floor
1Kgs 6:36 The inner court was walled *o* by means of
1Kgs 7:39 The sea was placed *o* to the southeast from
1Kgs 8:57 and may he not forsake us nor cast us *o.*
1Kgs 9:7 I will cut *o* Israel from the land I gave
1Kgs 11:16 until they had killed *o* every male in Edom.
1Kgs 11:30 Ahijah took *o* his new cloak,
1Kgs 12:16 So Israel went *o* to their tents,
1Kgs 13:28 he went *o* and found the body lying in the
1Kgs 13:34 to be cut *o* and destroyed from the earth.
1Kgs 14:10 I will cut *o* every male in Jeroboam's line,
1Kgs 15:21 heard of it, he left *o* fortifying Ramah,
1Kgs 15:29 he killed *o* the entire house of Jeroboam,
1Kgs 16:11 he killed *o* the whole house of Baasha,
1Kgs 20:11 to boast as though he were taking it *o.*'"
1Kgs 20:43 Israel went *o* homeward and entered Samaria.
1Kgs 21:16 Ahab started *o* on his way down to the
1Kgs 21:21 and will cut *o* every male in Ahab's line,
2Kgs 4:7 and sell the oil to pay *o* your creditor;
2Kgs 4:29 Gehazi, "take my staff with you and be *o;*
2Kgs 6:6 out to the spot, Elisha cut *o* a stick,
2Kgs 6:32 is sending someone to cut *o* my head?
2Kgs 7:13 *o* than all the throng that has perished,
2Kgs 9:8 I will cut *o* every male in Ahab's line,
2Kgs 11:1 she began to kill *o* the whole royal family.
2Kgs 11:7 The two of your divisions who are going *o*
2Kgs 11:9 sabbath and those going *o* duty that week,
2Kgs 13:21 the grave of Elisha, and everyone went *o.*
2Kgs 20:17 this day, shall be carried *o* to Babylon;
2Kgs 21:8 be driven *o* the land I gave their fathers,
2Kgs 21:14 I will cast *o* the survivors of my
2Kgs 24:13 He carried *o* all the treasures of the
2Kgs 25:15 the captain of the guard also carried *o.*
2Kgs 25:29 Jehoiachin took *o* his prison garb and ate
1Chr 10:9 They stripped him, cut *o* his head,
1Chr 19:4 their garments cut *o* half-way at the hips.
1Chr 28:9 abandon him, he will cast you *o* forever:
2Chr 4:10 The sea was placed *o* to the southeast from
2Chr 10:16 So all Israel went *o* to their tents.
2Chr 12:9 attacked Jerusalem and carried *o* the
2Chr 14:14 *o* a great number of sheep and camels.
2Chr 16:5 heard of it, he left *o* fortifying Ramah;
2Chr 22:10 she proceeded to kill *o* all the royal
2Chr 28:11 have carried *o* from among your brethren,
2Chr 28:17 attacked Judah, and carried *o* captives.
Ezr 3:13 a mighty clamor which was heard afar *o.*
Ezr 5:14 and carried *o* to the temple in Babylon,
Neh 4:17 that accompanied me took *o* his clothes;
Neh 12:43 at Jerusalem could be heard from afar *o.*
Tb 3:8 the wicked demon Asmodeus killed them *o*
Tb 6:18 as the demon smells the odor they give *o,*
Tb 11:8 cataracts shrink and peel *o* from his eyes;
Tb 11:13 used both hands to peel *o* the cataracts.
Jdt 4:7 be easy to ward *o* the attacking forces,
Jdt 7:13 Then thirst will begin to carry them *o,*
Jdt 7:27 we would be better *o* to become their prey.
Jdt 10:3 She took *o* the sackcloth she had on,
Jdt 13:1 They went *o* to their beds,
Jdt 13:8 him twice in the neck and cut *o* his head.
Jdt 13:9 She rolled his body *o* the bed and took the
Jdt 13:10 and the two went *o* together as they were
Jdt 16:7 She took *o* her widow's garb to raise up
Est 4:4 on, so that he might take *o* his sackcloth;
Est C:13 Taking *o* her splendid garments,
Est D:1 she took *o* her penitential garments and
Est 6:14 Haman *o* to the banquet Esther had prepared.
1Mc 1:22 He stripped *o* everything,
1Mc 2:9 ornaments have been carried *o* as spoils,
1Mc 3:57 Then the army moved *o,*
1Mc 7:47 cut *o* Nicanor's head and his right arm,
1Mc 9:36 and carried *o* John and everything he had.
1Mc 11:17 *o* Alexander's head and sent it to Ptolemy.
2Mc 1:16 cut *o* their heads and tossed them to the
2Mc 1:34 fenced the place *o* and declared it sacred.
2Mc 2:4 how he went *o* to the mountain which Moses
2Mc 4:31 went *o* in haste to settle the affair,
2Mc 4:38 his purple robe, tore *o* his other garments,
2Mc 5:21 *o* eighteen hundred talents from the temple,
2Mc 7:4 to scalp him and cut *o* his hands and feet,
2Mc 7:7 tearing *o* the skin and hair of his head,
2Mc 9:9 in hideous torments, his flesh rotted *o,*
2Mc 10:19 while he himself went *o* to places where he
2Mc 12:35 and cut *o* his arm at the shoulder.
2Mc 14:12 him *o* with orders to put Judas to death,
2Mc 15:30 arm to be cut *o* and taken to Jerusalem.
Jb 1:15 and the Sabeans carried them *o* in a raid.
Jb 1:17 seized the camels, carried them *o,*
Jb 1:20 began to tear his cloak and cut *o* his hair.
Jb 6:9 he would put forth his hand and cut me *o!*
Jb 7:3 troubled nights have been told *o* for me.
Jb 11:20 Escape shall be cut *o* from them,
Jb 15:33 and like an olive tree casting *o* its bloom.
Jb 16:6 if I leave *o,*
Jb 18:14 and marches him *o* to the king of terrors.
Jb 20:28 that run *o* in the day of God's anger.
Jb 24:4 They force the needy *o* the road;
Jb 27:8 the impious man expect when he is cut *o,*
Jb 27:20 at night the tempest carries him *o.*
Jb 30:11 and have thrown *o* restraint in my presence.
Jb 30:15 My dignity is borne *o* on the wind,
Jb 30:20 you stand *o* and look at me,
Jb 34:37 his sin by brushing *o* our arguments
Jb 39:29 his eyes behold it afar *o.*
Jb 41:3 Who has assailed him and come *o* safe
Jb 41:5 Who can strip *o* his outer garment,
Ps(s) 10:9 the afflicted and drags them *o* in his net.
Ps(s) 27:9 cast me not *o;*
Ps(s) 30:12 you took *o* my sackcloth and clothed me
Ps(s) 31:23 my anguish, "I am cut *o* from your sight";
Ps(s) 37:9 For evildoers shall be cut *o,*
Ps(s) 37:22 land, while those he curses shall be cut *o.*
Ps(s) 37:28 and the posterity of the wicked is cut *o.*
Ps(s) 37:38 the future of the wicked shall be cut *o.*
Ps(s) 38:12 my neighbors stand afar *o.*
Ps(s) 44:10 you have cast us *o* and put us in disgrace,
Ps(s) 44:24 Cast us not *o* forever!
Ps(s) 58:8 Let them vanish like water flowing *o;*
Ps(s) 60:8 and measure *o* the valley of Succoth.
Ps(s) 71:9 Cast me not *o* in my old age;
Ps(s) 74:1 Why, O God, have you cast us *o* forever?
Ps(s) 75:11 I will break *o* the horns of all the wicked;
Ps(s) 88:6 no longer and who are cut *o* from your care.
Ps(s) 88:17 your terrors have cut me *o.*

94:14 For the LORD will not cast *o* his people,
108: 8 and measure *o* the valley of Succoth;
127: 2 for you to rise early, or put *o* your rest,
Prv 2:22 But the wicked will be cut *o* from the land,
10:31 but the perverse tongue will be cut *o*.
23:18 a future, and your hope will not be cut *o*.
24:14 a future, and your hope will not be cut *o*.
26: 6 He cuts *o* his feet,
Eccl 4: 3 And better *o* than both is the yet unborn,
9: 4 a live dog is better *o* than a dead lion.
11:10 Ward *o* grief from your heart and put away
Sg 5: 3 I have taken *o* my robe,
Wis 4: 5 Their twigs shall be broken *o* untimely,
11:11 afar *o* and those close by were afflicted:
13:11 tree and skillfully scrape *o* all its bark,
16:29 wintry frost and runs *o* like useless water.
18: 5 As a reproof you carried *o* their multitude
18:23 the anger, and cut *o* the way to the living.
Sir 5: 8 to the LORD, put it not *o* from day to day;
5:11 wind, and start not *o* in every direction.
14:18 one falls *o* and another sprouts
23: 5 ward *o* passion from my heart,
24:30 like the dawn, to become known afar *o*.
27:22 plots mischief and no one can ward him *o*;
31:10 he has been tested by gold and come *o* safe,
32:11 be *o* for home!
37: 4 but in time of trouble he stands afar *o*.
40:17 But goodness will never be cut *o*,
43:15 its power and breaks *o* the hailstones.
Is 5:29 they carry it *o* and none will rescue it.
7:20 It shall also shave *o* the beard.
8: 4 shall be carried *o* by the king of Assyria.
10: 6 I order him To seize plunder, carry *o* loot,
10:33 lops *o* the boughs with terrible violence;
14:22 and cut *o* from Babylon name and remnant,
15: 2 head is shaved, every beard sheared *o*.
20: 2 and take *o* the sackcloth from your waist,
22: 3 leaders fled away together, fled afar *o*;
22:25 sure spot shall give way, break *o* and fall,
27: 8 them *o* with my cruel wind in time of storm.
27:11 branches shall wither and be broken *o*,
29:20 who are alert to do evil will be cut *o*,
33:13 Hear, you who are far *o*,
33:23 spoils and the lame will carry *o* the loot.
34:17 his hands he marks *o* their shares of her;
39: 6 this day, shall be carried *o* to Babylon;
40:12 sea, and marked *o* the heavens with a span?
41: 9 whom I have chosen and will not cast *o*—
41:16 them *o* and the storm shall scatter them.
44:13 a plane and measures it *o* with a compass,
46:13 bringing on my justice, it is not far *o*,
47: 2 Strip *o* your train,
48:19 cut *o* or blotted out from my presence.
52: 2 Shake *o* the dust,
53: 8 he was cut *o* from the land of the living,
54: 6 A wife married in youth and then cast *o*,
57:13 All these the wind shall carry *o*,
59:14 is repelled, and justice stands far *o*;
Jer 2:20 you broke your yoke, you tore *o* your bonds.
3: 8 she too went *o* and played the harlot.
5: 5 had broken the yoke, torn *o* the harness.
6:29 refined, the wicked are not drawn *o*.
7:29 *o* your dedicated hair and throw it away!
7:29 *o* the generation that draws down his wrath.
11:19 us cut him *o* from the land of the living,
12: 7 I abandon my house, cast *o* my heritage;
13:26 I now will strip *o* your skirts from you,
14:19 Have you cast Judah *o* completely?
18: 2 Rise up, be *o* to the potter's house;
23:23 only, says the LORD, and not a God far *o*?
23:33 "You are the burden, and I cast you *o*,
28:11 from *o* the neck of all the nations.' "
28:12 from *o* the neck of the prophet Jeremiah,
30: 8 yoke from *o* your necks and snap your bonds."
31:37 Then will I cast *o* the whole race of
36:23 cut *o* the piece with a scribe's knife
41: 5 of it, eighty men with beards shaved *o*,
43:12 gods, and burn the gods or carry them *o*.
44:17 had enough food to eat and we were well *o*;
47: 4 And cut *o* from Tyre and Sidon the last of
49:19 So I, in an instant, will drive men *o*;
49:29 camels they shall carry *o* for themselves,
50:16 Cut *o* from Babylon the sower and him who
50:44 So I, in one instant, will drive them *o*,
51:13 come, the term at which you shall be cut *o*!
52:19 too the captain of the guard carried *o*,
52:33 Jehoiachin took *o* his prison garb and ate
Lam 1: 6 *o* without strength before their captors.
2: 3 He broke *o*,
Bar 1: 9 king of Babylon, carried *o* Jeconiah,
1:22 but each one of us went *o* after the
4:20 I have taken *o* the garment of peace,
4:26 *o* by their enemies like sheep in a raid.
5: 1 take *o* your robe of mourning and misery;
6:17 bolts, lest they be carried *o* by robbers.
6:57 seize them strip *o* the gold and the silver,
Ez 3:14 me, and I went *o* spiritually stirred,
6:12 He that is far *o* shall die of pestilence,
12:27 "The vision he sees is a long way *o*;
13:21 I will tear *o* your veils and rescue my
14: 8 will cut him *o* from the midst of my people.
14:13 it and cut *o* from it both man and beast;
14:17 the land cutting *o* from it man and beast,
14:19 fury, cutting *o* from it man and beast,
14:21 pestilence, to cut *o* from it man and beast,
17: 4 tearing *o* its topmost branch,
17: 9 it out by the roots and strip *o* its fruit,
17:22 its topmost branches tear *o* a tender shoot,
18: 8 if he holds *o* from evildoing,
18:17 who holds *o* from evildoing,
19:12 withered her up, her fruit was torn *o*;
21: 8 cut *o* from you the virtuous and the wicked.
21:31 *O* with the turban and away with the crown!
22: 5 Those near you and those far *o* shall
23:25 you in fury, cutting *o* your nose and ears;
23:26 They shall strip *o* your clothes and seize
25: 7 nations, I will cut you *o* from the peoples,
25:13 Edom and cut *o* from it man and beast.
25:16 I will cut *o* the Cherethites and wipe out
26:16 and strip *o* their embroidered garments.
29: 8 you, and cut *o* from you both man and beast.
29:19 He shall carry *o* its riches,
34: 3 You have fed *o* their milk,
34:29 longer be carried *o* by famine in the land,
35: 7 waste, and cut *o* from it any traveler.
37:11 up, our hope is lost, and we are cut *o*."
38:13 your horde, to carry *o* silver and gold,
40:38 opening *o* the vestibule of the gate,
44:19 they shall take *o* the garments in which
45: 3 Also from this sector measure *o* a strip,
47: 3 Then when he had walked *o* to the east with
47: 3 he measured *o* a thousand cubits and had me
47: 4 He measured *o* another thousand and once
47: 4 he measured *o* a thousand and had me wade;
47: 5 Once more he measured *o* a thousand,
Dn 1: 2 which he carried *o* to the land of Shinar,
4:11 lop *o* its branches, strip *o* its leaves
11:11 be given into his hand and be carried *o*.
13:13 said to each other, "Let us be *o* for home,
13:39 he opened the doors and ran *o*.
Hos 8: 9 a wild ass *o* on its own
Jl 1: 7 He has stripped it, sheared *o* its bark;
1:16 our very eyes has not the food been cut *o*;
4: 8 sell them to the Sabeans, a nation far *o*.
Am 3:14 shall be broken *o* and fall to the ground.
6: 3 You would put *o* the evil day,
7:12 *O* with you,
9: 1 you break them *o* on the heads of them all!
Ob 1:11 day when aliens carried *o* his possessions,
Jon 4: 8 "I would be better *o* dead than alive."
Mi 2: 8 you have stripped *o* the mantle covering
2:10 Be *o*, this is no place to rest";
4: 7 and of those driven far *o* a strong nation;
Na 1:13 Now will I break his yoke from *o* you,
Hb 2:10 for your household, cutting *o* many peoples,
Zec 3: 4 before him, "Take *o* his filthy garments,
10: 6 be as though I had never cast them *o*,
11:10 breaking *o* the covenant which I had made
11:11 that day it was broken *o*.
11:14 *o* the brotherhood between Judah and Israel.
11:16 of the fat ones and tear *o* their hoofs!
13: 8 *o* and perish and one third shall be left.
Mal 2: 3 feasts, and you will be carried *o* with it.
2:12 May the LORD cut *o* from the man who does
Mt 5:30 your trouble, cut it *o* and throw it away!
8: 9 one man the order, 'Dismissed,' *o* he goes.
9:31 But they went *o* and spread word of him
11: 7 As the messengers set *o*,
12: 1 to pull *o* the heads of grain and eat them.
12:29 make *o* with his property unless he first ties
12:45 *O* it goes again to bring back with it this
13:22 anxiety and the lure of money choke it *o*.
13:25 weeds through his wheat, and then made *o*.
18: 8 undoing, cut it *o* and throw it from you!
18:27 let the official go and wrote *o* the debt.
21: 1 sent *o* two disciples with the instructions:
21: 6 went *o* and did what Jesus had ordered;
22:15 Then the Pharisees went *o* and began to
22:22 by this reply, they went *o* and left him.
25:10 they went *o* to buy it the groom arrived,
25:18 *o* instead and dug a hole in the ground,
25:25 so out of fear I went *o* and buried your
25:46 These will go *o* to eternal punishment and
26:14 went *o* to the chief priests and said,
26:51 high priest's servant, cutting *o* his ear.
26:57 led him *o* to Caiaphas the high priest,
27: 5 He went *o* and hanged himself.
27:28 They stripped *o* his clothes and wrapped
27:31 own clothes, and led him *o* to crucifixion.
27:40 down *o* that cross if you are God's Son!"
27:48 one of them ran *o* and got a sponge.
Mk 1:20 the hired men, and went *o* in his company.
1:35 he went *o* to a lonely place in the desert;
1:44 "Go *o* and present yourself to the priest
1:45 The man went *o* and began to proclaim the
2:23 pull *o* heads of grain as they went along.
4: 7 thorns, which grew up and choked it *o*,
4:15 comes to carry *o* what was sown in them.
4:19 of other sorts come to choke it *o*;
4:39 The wind fell *o* and everything grew calm.
5:14 The swineherds ran *o* and brought the news
5:20 At that the man went *o* and began to
5:24 went *o* together and a large crowd followed,
6:12 With that they went *o*,
6:16 exclaimed, "John, whose head I had cut *o*,
6:32 So Jesus and the apostles went *o* in the
6:46 of them, he went *o* to the mountain to pray.
7:24 went *o* to the territory of Tyre and Sidon.
7:29 said to her, "For such a reply, be *o* now!
7:33 took him *o* by himself away from the crowd.
8:13 boat again, and went *o* to the other shore.
9: 2 and John *o* by themselves with him and led
9:43 your hand is your difficulty, cut it *o*!
9:45 If your foot is your undoing, cut it *o*!
11: 1 he sent *o* two of his disciples with the
11: 4 So they went *o*,
11:13 Observing a fig tree some distance *o*,
12: 3 him, beat him, and sent him *o* empty-handed.
12:12 Finally they left him and went *o*.
13:11 When men take you *o* into custody,
14:10 went *o* to the chief priests to hand Jesus
14:16 The disciples went *o*.
14:47 the high priest's slave, cutting *o* his ear.
14:52 he left the cloth behind and ran *o* naked.
14:53 Then they led Jesus *o* to the high priest,
15:36 Someone ran *o*,
Lk 6: 1 His disciples were pulling *o* grain-heads,
7: 8 I say to one, 'On your way,' and *o* he goes;
7:24 When the messengers of John had set *o*,
7:42 was able to repay, he wrote *o* both debts.
9:56 Then they set *o* for another town.
10:30 him, and then went *o* leaving him half-dead.
11:22 such a one carries *o* the arms on which he
12:48 be flogged will get *o* with fewer stripes.
15:13 belongings and went *o* to a distant land,
15:20 With that he set *o* for his father's house.
15:20 While he was still a long way *o*,
16:23 he raised his eyes and saw Abraham afar *o*,
16:25 that you were well *o* in your lifetime,
17: 2 He would be better *o* thrown into the sea
18:16 Do not shut them *o*.
22: 4 He went *o* to confer with the chief priests
22: 8 sent Peter and John *o* with the instruction,
22:13 *o* and found everything just as he had said;
22:50 priest's servant and cut *o* his right ear.
Jn 4: 8 had gone *o* to the town to buy provisions.)
4:28 her water jar and went *o* into the town.
5:15 The man went *o* and informed the Jews that
6:15 come and carry him *o* to make him king,
7:35 going *o* to the Diaspora among the Greeks,
8:53 [Then each went *o* to his own house,
9: 7 So the man went *o* and washed,
9:15 I washed it *o*, and now I can see."
13: 4 rose from the meal and took *o* his cloak.
20: 2 so she ran *o* to Simon Peter and the other
20:15 if you are the one who carried him *o*,
21: 3 replied, and went *o* to get into their boat.
21: 6 "Cast your net *o* to the starboard side,"
21:18 you fast and carry you *o* against your will."
Acts 2:39 still far *o* whom the Lord our God calls."
3:23 shall be ruthlessly cut *o* from the people.'
5:26 went *o* with the guard and brought them in,
5:36 to pass himself *o* as someone of importance.
6:12 seized him, and led him *o* to the Sanhedrin.
8: 9 himself *o* as someone of great importance.
9:30 down to Caesarea and sent him *o* to Tarsus.
10:23 The next day he went *o* with them,
11:25 Barnabas went *o* to Tarsus to look for Saul;
12:17 then left them to go *o* to another place.
13: 3 they imposed hands on them and sent them *o*.
15: 3 The church saw them *o* and they made their
17:10 brothers sent Paul and Silas *o* to Beroea.
17:14 sent Paul *o* directly on his way to the sea,
17:19 Then they led him *o* the Areopagus,
20:15 From there we took *o* the next day,
21: 2 for Phoenicia, we boarded it and sailed *o*.
21: 5 came out of the city to see us *o*,
27: 5 sea *o* the coast of Cilicia and Pamphylia,
28: 5 But Paul shook the snake *o* into the fire
Rom 11:17 If some of the branches were cut *o* and you,
11:19 were cut *o* that I might be grafted in."
11:20 They were cut *o* because of unbelief and
11:22 if you do not, you too will be cut *o*.
11:24 were cut *o* from the natural wild olive and,
13:12 Let us cast *o* deeds of darkness and put on
1Cor 7: 1 better *o* having no relations with a woman.
7:21 better *o* making the most of your slavery.
11: 6 wear a veil, she ought to cut *o* her hair.
11: 6 to have her hair cut *o* or her head shaved,
2Cor 2:13 good-bye to them and went *o* to Macedonia.
Gal 1:17 apostles before me, I went *o* to Arabia;
Eph 2:13 who once were far *o* have been brought near
2:17 good news of peace to you who were far *o*,
Col 2:11 which strips *o* the carnal body completely.
2:15 show of them, and leading them *o* captive,
1Thes 5: 4 that the day should catch you *o* guard,
2Tm 4: 4 to the truth and will wander *o* to fables.
Jas 1:24 *o* and promptly forgets what he looked like.
4:13 there, trade, and come *o* with a profit!"
1Pt 4:12 you, but it should not catch you *o* guard.
2Pt 2:15 and wander *o* on the path taken by Balaam,
Rv 12:14 she could fly *o* to her place in the desert,
12:17 *o* to make war on the rest of her offspring,
17:16 strip *o* her finery and leave her naked;

OFF-SPRING (1)

Lv 21:15 he will have base *o* among his people.

OFFAL (5)

Ex 29:14 But the flesh and hide and *o* of the
Lv 4:11 with its head, legs, inner organs, and *o*,
8:17 *o* he burned in the fire outside the camp,
16:27 flesh and *o* shall be burned up in the fire.
Nm 19: 5 with its hide and flesh, its blood and *o*;

OFFEND (4)

Jb 34:31 I will *o* no more.
Sir 9:13 But if you approach him, *o* him not,
Bar 6:13 does away with those that *o* against it.
1Tm 5:20 so that the rest may fear to *o*.

OFFENDED (14)

Gn 31:35 feel *o* that I cannot rise in your presence;
35:22 When Israel heard of it, he was greatly *o*.
38: 7 Er, Judah's first-born, greatly *o* the LORD;
38:10 What he did greatly *o* the LORD,
Jgs 2:11 Israelites *o* the LORD by serving the Baals.
3: 7 had *o* the LORD by forgetting the LORD,
3:12 Again the Israelites *o* the LORD,
4: 1 however, the Israelites again *o* the LORD.
6: 1 The Israelites *o* the LORD,
10: 6 The Israelites again *o* the LORD,
13: 1 The Israelites again *o* the LORD,
1Chr 5:25 they *o* the God of their fathers by lusting
Neh 1: 7 Grievously have we *o* you,
2Cor 7:12 had given the offense or for the one *o*,

OFFENDER (1)

1Cor 5: 2 of grieving, and getting rid of the *o*!

OFFENDERS (2)

Wis 12: 2 Therefore you rebuke *o* little by little,
Mk 2:16 with tax collectors and *o* against the law,

OFFENDS (1)

Rom 14:20 man to eat when the food *o* his conscience.

OFFENSE (29)

Gn 31:36 "What crime or *o* have I committed,"
40: 1 cupbearer and baker gave *o* to their lord,
Nm 25:11 to the Israelites for the *o* to my honor.
Dt 19:15 crime or any *o* of which he may be guilty;
21:22 "If a man guilty of a capital *o* is put to
22:26 since she is not guilty of a capital *o*.
Jgs 3:12 who because of this *o* strengthened Eglon,
1Sm 19: 4 for he has committed no *o* against you,
20: 1 "What crime or what *o* does your father
2Sm 10: 6 In view of the *o* they had given to David,
Ezr 6:11 is to be reduced to rubble for this *o*.
Jdt 5:20 God, and if we verify this *o* of theirs,
Jb 7:21 Why do you not pardon my *o*,
Ps(s) 51: 3 greatness of your compassion wipe out my *o*.
51: 5 For I acknowledge my *o*,
59: 4 Not for any *o* or sin of mine,
Prv 19:11 and it is his glory to overlook an *o*.
Sir 21: 3 Every *o* is a two-edged sword;
31:17 gorge not yourself, lest you give *o*.
Mk 15:26 The inscription proclaiming his *o* read,
Rom 5:15 But the gift is not like the *o*.
5:15 For if by the *o* of the one man all died,
5:16 upon one *o* and brought condemnation,
5:17 reign through one man because of his *o*,
5:18 a single *o* brought condemnation to all men,
1Cor 10:32 *o* to Jew or Greek or to the church of God,
2Cor 2: 5 anyone has given *o* he has hurt not only me,
6: 3 We avoid giving anyone *o*,
7:12 had given the *o* or for the one offended,

OFFENSES (16)

1Kgs 8:50 all the *o* they have committed against you,
Tb 3: 3 not for my sins, nor for my inadvertent *o*,
Jb 35: 6 Even if your *o* are many,
Prv 10:12 stirs up disputes, but love covers all *o*.
Eccl 10: 4 for mildness abates great *o*.
Sir 17:20 up sin, pray to him and make your *o* few.
Is 43:25 I, who wipe out, for my own sake, your *o*;
44:22 I have brushed away your *o* like a cloud,
53: 5 But he was pierced for our *o*,
53:12 sins of many, and win pardon for their *o*.
59:12 For our *o* before you are many,
59:12 Yes, our *o* are present to us,
Jer 33: 8 all their *o* by which they sinned and
Rom 5:16 came after many *o* and brought acquittal.
5:20 The law came in order to increase *o*;
Eph 2: 1 You were dead because of your sins and *o*,

OFFENSIVE (3)

Dt 23:10 shall keep yourselves from everything *o*.
Sir 27:13 The conversation of the wicked is *o*,
Ez 20:28 [there they brought their *o* offerings],

OFFER (262)

Gn 22: 2 There you shall *o* him up as a holocaust on
30:20 This time my husband will *o* me presents,
Ex 3:18 that we may *o* sacrifice to the LORD,
5: 3 that we may *o* sacrifice to the LORD,
5: 8 'Let us go to *o* sacrifice to our God.'
5:17 'Let us go and *o* sacrifice to the LORD.
8: 4 the people go to *o* sacrifice to the LORD.
8:21 and *o* sacrifice to your God in this land."
8:22 do so, for the sacrifices we *o* to the LORD,
8:22 If before their very eyes we *o* sacrifices
8:23 in the desert to *o* sacrifice to the LORD,
8:24 you go to *o* sacrifice to the LORD your God,
8:25 the people go to *o* sacrifice to the LORD.
10:25 and holocausts to *o* up to the LORD,
23:18 "You shall not *o* the blood of my
24: 5 to *o* holocausts and sacrifice young bulls
29:38 this is what you shall *o* on the altar:
29:41 lamb you shall *o* at the evening twilight,
29:41 You shall *o* this as a sweet-smelling
30: 9 you shall not *o* up any profane incense,
30:20 to *o* an oblation to the LORD they must
34:25 "You shall not *o* me the blood of
Lv 1: 5 shall *o* up its blood by splashing it on
1:13 The priest shall *o* them up and then burn
2:13 On every offering you shall *o* salt.
2:14 you shall *o* it in the form of fresh grits
3: 1 he may *o* before the LORD either a male or
3: 3 From the peace offering he shall *o* as an
3: 6 he may *o* either a male or a female animal,
3:14 From it he shall *o* as an oblation to the
5: 8 shall *o* the one for the sin offering first.
7:12 he shall *o* unleavened cakes mixed with oil,
9: 2 blemish, and *o* them before the LORD.
9: 7 "and *o* your sin offering and your
12: 7 The priest shall *o* them up before the LORD
14:20 priest slaughter the holocaust and *o* it,
14:31 the priest shall *o* up one as a sin
15:15 them to the priest, who shall *o* them up,
15:30 The priest shall *o* up one of them as a sin
16: 9 shall bring in and *o* up as a sin offering.
16:11 "Thus shall Aaron *o* up the bullock,
16:24 and *o* his own and the people's holocaust,
17: 5 to *o* up in the open field the Israelites
17: 5 Israelites shall henceforth *o* to the LORD,
17: 7 No longer shall they *o* their sacrifices to
17: 9 of the meeting tent to *o* it to the LORD,
18:21 You shall not *o* any of your offspring to
21: 6 since they *o* up the oblations of the LORD,
21:17 come forward to *o* up the food of his God.
21:21 draw near to *o* up the oblations of the LORD;
21:21 not draw near to *o* up the food of his God.
22:18 in Israel, who wishes to *o* a sacrifice,
22:20 You shall not *o* one that has any defect,
22:22 or ringworm, you shall not *o* to the LORD;
22:24 out or cut off you shall not *o* to the LORD.
22:25 animals to *o* up as the food of your God;
22:29 you *o* a thanksgiving sacrifice to the LORD,
22:29 so *o* it that it may be acceptable for you;
23: 8 days you shall *o* an oblation to the LORD.
23:12 you shall *o* to the LORD for a holocaust an
23:18 you shall *o* to the LORD a holocaust of
23:25 and you shall *o* an oblation to the LORD."
23:27 yourselves and *o* an oblation to the LORD.
23:36 days you shall *o* an oblation to the LORD,
23:36 assembly and *o* an oblation to the LORD.
23:37 and *o* as an oblation to the LORD
27:10 to *o* one animal in place of another,
Nm 6:11 The priest shall *o* up the one as a sin
6:16 and shall *o* up the sin offering and the
6:17 He shall then *o* up the ram as a peace
8:11 Let Aaron then *o* the Levites before the
8:15 purify them and *o* them as a wave offering;
15:12 Whatever the number you *o*,
15:19 you shall *o* the LORD a contribution
15:20 You shall *o* it just as you offer a
15:24 the whole community shall *o* the holocaust
16:17 put incense in it, and *o* it to the LORD;
17: 5 the altar to *o* incense before the LORD,
18: 9 in whatever they *o* me as cereal offerings
28: 3 the oblation which you shall *o* to the LORD:
28: 8 you shall *o* with the same cereal offering
28: 9 you shall *o* two unblemished yearling lambs,
28:11 "On the first of each month you shall *o*
28:19 you shall *o* a holocaust to the LORD,
28:22 and *o* one goat as a sin offering in
28:27 You shall *o* as a sweet-smelling holocaust
29: 2 You shall *o* as a sweet-smelling holocaust
29: 8 You shall *o* as a sweet-smelling holocaust
29:13 You shall *o* as a sweet-smelling holocaust
29:17 the second day you shall *o* twelve bullocks,
29:20 the third day you shall *o* eleven bullocks,
29:23 the fourth day you shall *o* ten bullocks,
29:26 the fifth day you shall *o* nine bullocks,
29:29 the sixth day you shall *o* eight bullocks,
29:32 the seventh day you shall *o* seven bullocks,
29:36 You shall *o* up in holocaust as a
Dt 2:26 king of Heshbon, with this *o* of peace:
12:13 Take care not to *o* up your holocausts in
12:14 but *o* them up in the place which the LORD
12:27 and there you must *o* both the flesh and
16: 2 You shall *o* the Passover sacrifice from
20:10 attack a city, first *o* it terms of peace.
23:19 You shall not *o* a harlot's fee or a dog's
27: 6 and shall *o* on it holocausts to the LORD,
28:68 and there you will *o* yourselves for sale
Jos 22:23 secede from the LORD, or to *o* holocausts,
Jgs 6:26 Then take the spare bullock and *o* it as a
11:31 I shall *o* him up as a holocaust."
13:16 will, you may *o* a holocaust to the LORD.
16:23 Philistines assembled to *o* a great sacrifice
Ru 1:12 And even if I could *o* any hopes,
1Sm 1: 4 the day came for Elkanah to *o* sacrifice,
1:21 to *o* the customary sacrifice to the LORD
1:22 I will *o* him as a perpetual nazirite."
2:19 her husband to *o* the customary sacrifice.
9: 7 servant, "If we go, what can we *o* the man?
10: 4 you and *o* you two wave offerings of bread,
10: 8 to *o* holocausts and to sacrifice peace
18:21 *o* her to him to become a snare for him,
18:26 When the servants reported this *o* to David,
2Sm 15:12 for the sacrifices he was about to *o*.
16:20 *O* your counsel on what we should do."
24:12 I *o* you three alternatives;
24:22 king take and *o* up whatever he may wish.
24:24 for I cannot *o* to the LORD my God
1Kgs 8:29 which I, your servant, *o* in this place.
8:30 people Israel which they *o* in this place.
9:25 Three times a year Solomon used to *o*
12:27 If now this people go up to *o* sacrifices
12:33 he was going to *o* sacrifice.
13: 1 was standing at the altar to *o* sacrifice.
13: 2 the high places who *o* sacrifice upon you,
2Kgs 5:17 for I will no longer *o* holocaust or
10:24 proceeded to *o* sacrifices and holocausts.
17:35 nor serve them, nor *o* sacrifice to them.
1Chr 16:40 to *o* holocausts to the LORD on the altar
21:10 I *o* you three alternatives;
21:24 nor *o* up holocausts that cost me nothing."
21:28 he continued to *o* sacrifices there.
23:13 forever, to *o* sacrifice before the LORD,
23:30 morning to *o* thanks and to praise the LORD,
2Chr 2: 5 unless it be to *o* incense in his presence?
6:20 which I your servant *o* toward this place.
28:25 high places to *o* sacrifice to other gods.
29: 7 and refused to burn incense and *o*
29:11 him, to be his ministers and to *o* incense."
29:21 to *o* them on the altar of the LORD.
32:12 only, and on it alone you shall *o* incense'?
35:12 of the common people to *o* to the LORD,
Ezr 3: 2 in order to *o* on it the holocausts prescribed
3: 5 might *o* as a free-will gift to the LORD.
3: 6 they began to *o* holocausts to the LORD,
6:10 that they may continue to *o* sacrifices of
7:17 and to *o* them on the altar of the house of
Neh 1: 6 now *o* in your presence day and night for
Tb 1: 4 *o* sacrifice in the place where the temple,
1: 5 used to *o* sacrifice on all the mountains
14: 6 be converted and shall *o* God true worship;
1Mc 1:51 the cities of Judah to *o* sacrifices,
2:23 to *o* sacrifice on the altar in Modein
10:24 words and *o* dignities and gifts,
11:34 all those who *o* sacrifices for us in Jerusalem
12:11 *o* on our feasts and other appropriate days,
12:42 large army he was afraid to *o* him violence.
2Mc 7:37 I *o* up my body and my life for our
Jb 6:22 to *o* a gift for me from your possessions,
17: 3 me one to *o* you a pledge on my behalf:
21: 2 and let that be the consolation you *o*.
21:34 How then can you *o* me vain comfort,
26: 3 how profuse is the advice you *o*!
42: 8 Job, and *o* up a holocaust for yourselves;
Ps(s) 4: 6 *O* just sacrifices, and trust in the LORD.
27: 6 And I will *o* in his tent sacrifices with
50:14 *O* to God praise as your sacrifice and
51:18 should I *o* a holocaust,
51:21 shall they *o* up bullocks on your altar.
54: 8 Freely will I *o* you sacrifice:
66:15 Holocausts of fatlings I will *o* you,
72:10 of Tarshish and the Isles shall *o* gifts;
116:17 To you will I *o* sacrifice of thanksgiving,
Prv 17: 8 has a bribe to *o* rates it a magic stone;
21:27 so when they *o* it with a bad intention.
Sg 8: 7 Were one to *o* all he owns to purchase love,
Sir 17:22 in place of the living who *o* their praise?
20:18 the unruly are always ready to *o* it.
35: 4 you *o* is in fulfillment of the precepts.
35:11 But *o* no bribes, these he does not accept!
38:11 *O* your sweet-smelling oblation and
40:21 The flute and the harp *o* sweet melody,
45:16 to *o* holocausts and choice offerings,
50:15 hand for the cup, to *o* blood of the grape,
Is 16: 3 *O* counsel, take their part:
19:21 they shall *o* sacrifices and oblations,
41:11 perish and come to nought who *o* resistance.
57: 7 bed, and there you went up to *o* sacrifice.
Jer 14:12 If they *o* holocausts or cereal offerings,
16: 5 go not there to lament or *o* sympathy.
32: 7 uncle Shallum, will come to you with the *o*:
33:18 ever be lacking, to *o* holocausts before me,
42: 9 to whom you sent me to *o* your prayer:
48:35 LORD, to *o* a holocaust on the high place,
Lam 3:30 Let him *o* his cheek to be struck,
Bar 1:10 *o* these on the altar of the Lord our God,
Ez 43:24 them and *o* them to the LORD as holocausts.
43:25 you shall *o* a he-goat as a sin offering,
43:27 the priests shall *o* your holocausts and
44:15 stand before me to *o* me fat and blood,
45:17 He shall *o* the sin offerings,
45:22 day the prince shall *o* on his own behalf,
45:23 he shall *o* as a holocaust to the LORD

45:23 offering he shall *o* one male goat each day.
45:24 As a cereal offering he shall *o* one ephah
45:24 he shall *o* one hin of oil for each ephah.
46: 2 *o* his holocausts and peace offerings,
46:12 and he shall *o* his holocausts or his peace
46:13 He shall *o* as a daily holocaust to the
46:13 this he shall *o* every morning.
Dn 3:38 or incense, no place to *o* first fruits,
Hos 4:13 On the mountaintops they *o* sacrifice and
4:14 and with prostitutes you *o* sacrifice!
8:13 Though they *o* sacrifice,
13: 2 "To these," they say, *o* sacrifice."
Am 5:23 But if you would *o* me holocausts,
Hg 2:14 and what they *o* there is unclean.
Zec 10: 2 dreams they tell, empty comfort they *o*.
Mal 1: 8 When you *o* a blind animal for sacrifice,
1: 8 When you *o* the lame or the sick,
2:12 anyone to *o* sacrifice to the LORD of hosts!
3: 3 that they may *o* due sacrifice to the LORD.
Mt 2: 8 me so that I may go and *o* him homage too."
5:24 brother, and then come and *o* your gift.
5:39 *o* no resistance to injury.
5:39 the right cheek, turn and *o* him the other.
8: 4 the priest and *o* the gift Moses prescribed.
11:25 of heaven and earth, to you I *o* praise;
16:26 can a man *o* in exchange for his very self?
Mk 1:44 and *o* for your cure what Moses prescribed.
8:37 What can a man *o* in exchange for his life?
Lk 1: 9 the sanctuary of the Lord and *o* incense.
2:24 They came to *o* in sacrifice "a pair of
5:14 *O* for your healing what Moses prescribed;
5:33 disciples fast frequently and *o* prayers;
10:21 "I *o* you praise,
11: 6 a journey and I have nothing to *o* him';
23:36 to *o* him their sour wine and saying,
Acts 8:18 made them an *o* of money with the request,
14:13 to *o* sacrifice to them with the crowds.
Rom 6:13 no more shall you *o* the members of your
6:13 *o* yourselves to God as men who have come
6:16 *o* yourselves to someone as obedient slaves,
12: 1 to *o* your bodies as a living sacrifice holy
1Cor 9:18 that when preaching I *o* the gospel free of
1Tm 2: 8 *o* prayers with blameless hands held aloft,
Heb 5: 1 God, to *o* gifts and sacrifices for sins.
7:27 has no need to *o* sacrifice day after day,
8: 3 is appointed to *o* gifts and sacrifices;
8: 3 for this one to have something to *o*.
8: 5 They *o* worship in a sanctuary which is
9:25 he might *o* himself there again and again,
12:28 through which we may *o* worship acceptable
13:15 us continually *o* God a sacrifice of praise,

OFFERED (152)

Gn 8:20 clean bird, he *o* holocausts on the altar.
22:13 *o* it up as a holocaust in place of his son.
31:54 He then *o* a sacrifice on the mountain and
46: 1 he *o* sacrifices to the God of his father
Ex 29:42 holocaust shall be *o* before the LORD
32: 6 *o* holocausts and brought peace offerings.
35:24 of silver or bronze *o* it to the LORD;
40:29 *o* holocausts and cereal offerings on it,
Lv 5:10 shall be *o* as a holocaust in the usual way.
7: 3 of its fat shall be taken from it and *o* up:
7: 8 the hide of the holocaust that he has *o*.
7:10 offerings that are *o* up dry or mixed with oil
7:15 shall be eaten on the day it is *o*;
7:16 be eaten on the day the sacrifice is *o*,
9:15 it and *o* it up for sin as before.
9:16 holocaust, and *o* it in the usual manner.
10: 1 they *o* up before the LORD profane fire,
14:19 Only after he has *o* the sin offering in
22:27 to be *o* as an oblation to the LORD.
24: 8 *o* on the part of the Israelites by an
Nm 3: 4 But when Nadab and Abihu *o* profane fire
8:13 to be *o* as a wave offering to the LORD;
8:21 *o* them as a wave offering before the LORD,
17:12 as he *o* the incense and made atonement for
18:15 of beast, such as are to be *o* to the LORD,
23: 2 and have *o* a bullock and a ram on each."
23:14 and *o* a bullock and a ram on each of them.
26:61 when they *o* profane fire before the LORD.
28: 2 are *o* to me as sweet-smelling oblations.
28: 6 holocaust that was *o* at Mount Sinai
28: 8 lamb, to be *o* during the evening twilight,
28:15 These are to be *o* in addition to the
28:30 one goat shall be *o* as a sin offering in
29: 5 one goat shall be *o* as a sin offering in
29: 6 *o* in addition to the ordinary new moon
29:11 *o* in addition to the atonement sin offering,
29:16 *o* in addition to the established holocaust
Dt 12:31 because they *o* to their gods every
26:14 I have not *o* any of it to the dead.
32:17 They *o* sacrifice to demons,
Jos 8:31 On this altar they *o* holocausts and peace
Jgs 2: 5 They *o* sacrifice there to the LORD.
5:25 in a princely bowl she *o* curds.
6:28 bullock *o* on the altar that was built.
13:19 offering and *o* it on the rock to the LORD,
19:15 but no one *o* them the shelter of his home
19:18 no one has *o* us the shelter of his house.
21: 4 there and *o* holocausts and peace offerings.
1Sm 2:13 When someone *o* a sacrifice,
6:14 the cows were *o* as a holocaust to the LORD.
6:15 The men of Beth-shemesh also *o* other
7: 9 and *o* it entire as a holocaust to the LORD.
13: 9 offerings," and he *o* up the holocaust.
13:12 So in my anxiety I *o* up the holocaust."
30:12 of pressed raisins were also *o* to him.
2Sm 6:17 Then David *o* holocausts and peace
24:25 LORD, and *o* holocausts and peace offerings.
1Kgs 3: 3 yet he *o* sacrifice and burned incense on
3: 4 its altar Solomon *o* a thousand holocausts.
3:15 the Lord, *o* holocausts and peace offerings,
8:59 May this prayer I have *o* to the LORD,
8:62 with him *o* sacrifices before the LORD.
8:63 Solomon *o* as peace offerings to the LORD
8:64 he *o* there the holocausts,
9: 3 of petition which you *o* in my presence.
10: 5 holocausts he *o* in the temple of the LORD,
2Kgs 3:27 and *o* him as a holocaust upon the wall.
16:12 then went up to it and *o* sacrifice on it,
23: 8 the high places where they had *o* incense.
1Chr 16: 1 *o* up holocausts and peace offerings to God.
21:26 and *o* up holocausts and peace offerings.
29:21 *o* sacrifices and holocausts to the LORD,
2Chr 1: 6 and Solomon *o* sacrifice in the LORD's
1: 6 he *o* a thousand holocausts upon it.
7: 5 *o* as sacrifice twenty-two thousand oxen,
7: 7 there he *o* the holocausts and the fat of
8:12 In those times Solomon *o* holocausts to the
9: 4 holocausts he *o* in the house of the LORD,
17:16 son of Zichri, who *o* himself to the LORD,
18: 2 Ahab *o* numerous sheep and oxen for him and
24:14 They *o* holocausts in the LORD's temple
25:14 down before them and *o* sacrifice to them.
28: 3 he *o* sacrifice in the Valley of Ben-hinnom,
28: 4 *o* sacrifice and incense on the high places,
29:24 The priests then slaughtered them and *o*
33:22 Amon *o* sacrifice to all the idols which
34:25 me and have *o* incense to other gods,
35:16 the holocausts *o* on the altar of the LORD,
Ezr 3: 3 and *o* holocausts to the LORD on it,
3: 4 and they *o* the daily holocausts in the
3: 5 they *o* the established holocaust,
6:17 house of God, they *o* one hundred bulls,
8:25 *o* for the house of our God by the king,
8:35 *o* as holocausts to the God of Israel
Neh 2: 1 charge, I took some and *o* it to the king.
12:43 Great sacrifices were *o* on that day,
Jdt 4: 7 passes, since these *o* access to Judea.
4:14 sackcloth as they *o* the daily holocaust,
9: 1 While the incense was being *o* in the
16:18 were purified, they *o* their holocausts,
1Mc 4:53 they arose and *o* sacrifice according to
4:56 *o* holocausts and sacrifices of deliverance
5:54 Zion in joy and gladness and *o* holocausts,
7:33 holocaust that was being *o* for the king.
2Mc 1: 8 we *o* sacrifices and fine flour;
1:18 of the temple and the altar, *o* sacrifices.
2: 9 Solomon in his wisdom *o* a sacrifice
3:32 *o* a sacrifice for the man's recovery.
3:35 After Heliodorus had *o* a sacrifice to the
10: 3 they *o* sacrifice for the first time in two
13:23 come to this agreement, he *o* a sacrifice,
Sir 15:10 But praise is *o* by the wise man's tongue;
18:16 both are *o* by a kindly man.
46:16 called upon God, and *o* him a suckling lamb;
47: 8 every deed he *o* thanks to God Most High,
Is 51:23 you, While you *o* your back like the ground,
Jer 35: 5 of wine and *o* them cups to drink the wine.
Ez 6:13 *o* appeasing odors to any of their gods.
16:20 and *o* as sacrifices to be devoured by them!
20:28 there they *o* their sacrifices [there they
43:25 all unblemished, shall be *o* for seven days.
44: 7 sanctuary to profane it when you *o* me food,
46:15 and the oil are to be *o* every morning as
Dn 2:46 and ordered sacrifice and incense *o* to him.
Jon 1:16 the men *o* sacrifice and made vows to him.
Mt 13:33 He *o* them still another image:
Mk 16:20 They *o* this excuse:
Lk 22:17 a cup he *o* a blessing in thanks and said:
Acts 7:41 the calf and *o* sacrifice to the idol,
24:26 he hoped he would be *o* a bribe by Paul,
Rom 15:16 may be *o* up as a pleasing sacrifice,
1Cor 8: 1 Now about meats that have been *o* to idols.
8: 4 of eating meats that have been *o* to idols:
10:19 that meat *o* to an idol is really offered
10:28 say to you, "This was *o* in idol worship,"
2Cor 9:11 through us it results in thanks *o* to God.
1Tm 2: 1 and thanksgiving be *o* for all men,
Heb 5: 7 he *o* prayers and supplications with loud
7:27 he did that once for all when he *o* himself.
9: 7 with the blood which he *o* for himself and
9: 9 in which gifts and sacrifices are *o* that
9:14 spirit *o* himself up umblemished to God,
9:28 *o* up once to take away the sins of many;
10: 1 sacrifices *o* continually year after year.
10: 8 (These are *o* according to the
10:12 But Jesus *o* one sacrifice for sins and
11: 4 Abel *o* God a sacrifice greater than Cain's.
11:17 Abraham, when put to the test, *o* up Issac;
Jas 2:21 works when he *o* his son Isaac on the altar?

OFFERER (5)

Lv 1: 9 however, the *o* shall first wash with water.
1:12 When the *o* has cut it up into pieces,
1:13 however, the *o* shall first wash with water.
27:10 The *o* shall not present a substitute for
27:13 If the *o* wishes to redeem the animal,

OFFERING (480)

Gn 4: 3 In the course of time Cain brought an *o* to
4: 4 LORD looked with favor on Abel and his *o*,
4: 5 offering, but on Cain and his *o* he did not.
Ex 22:28 delay the *o* of your harvest and your press.
29:14 up outside the camp, since this is a sin *o*.
29:24 may wave them as a wave *o* before the LORD.
29:26 and wave it as a wave *o* before the LORD;
29:27 the breast of whatever wave *o* is waved,
29:27 thigh of whatever raised *o* is raised up,
29:36 sacrificing a bullock each day as a sin *o*,
29:41 cereal *o* and libation as in the morning.
30: 8 the established incense *o* before the LORD.
30: 9 incense, or any holocaust or cereal *o*;
30:10 a year with the blood of the atoning sin *o*.
32: 4 them to Aaron, who accepted their *o*,
35:22 could presented an *o* of gold to the LORD.
38:24 having previously been given as an *o*,
38:29 The bronze, given as an *o*,
Lv 1: 2 animal *o* to the LORD, such an *o* must
1: 3 "If his holocaust *o* is from the herd,
1: 9 the whole *o* on the altar as a holocaust,
1:10 "If his holocaust *o* is from the flock,
1:13 the whole *o* on the altar as a holocaust,
1:14 choose a turtledove or a pigeon as his *o*.
2: 1 cereal *o* to the LORD, his *o* must consist
2: 2 he shall burn on the altar as a token *o*,
2: 3 the cereal *o* belongs to Aaron and his sons.
2: 4 cereal *o* you present is baked in an oven,
2: 5 a cereal *o* that is fried on a griddle,
2: 6 Such a cereal *o* must be broken into pieces,
2: 7 a cereal *o* that is prepared in a pot,
2: 8 A cereal *o* that is made in any of these
2: 8 bring to the LORD, *o* it to the priest,
2: 9 Its token *o* the priest shall then lift
2: 9 lift from the cereal *o* and burn on the altar
2:10 the cereal *o* belongs to Aaron and his sons.
2:11 "Every cereal *o* that you present to the
2:12 to the LORD in the *o* of first fruits,
2:13 every cereal *o* that you present to the
2:13 of your God be lacking from your cereal *o*.
2:13 On every *o* you shall offer salt.
2:14 a cereal *o* of first fruits to the LORD,
2:15 *o* you shall put oil and frankincense.
2:16 For its token *o* the priest shall then burn
3: 1 a peace *o* makes his offering from the herd,
3: 2 shall lay his hand on the head of his *o*,
3: 3 From the peace *o* he shall offer as an
3: 6 "If the peace *o* he presents to the LORD
3: 7 If he presents a lamb as his *o*,
3: 8 laying his hand on the head of his *o*,
3: 9 he shall present the fat of the peace *o*:
4: 3 bull as a sin *o* for the sin he committed.
4:10 as is removed from the ox of the peace *o*;
4:14 shall present a young bull as a sin *o*.
4:21 This is the sin *o* for the community.
4:23 bring as his *o* an unblemished male goat.
4:24 the goat as a sin *o* before the LORD,
4:25 then take some of the blood of the sin *o*
4:26 on the altar like the fat of the peace *o*.
4:28 unblemished she-goat as the *o* for his sin.
4:29 laid his hand on the head of the sin *o*,
4:31 as the fat is removed from the peace *o*,
4:32 however, for his sin *o* he presents a lamb,
4:33 he shall slaughter this sin *o* in the place
4:34 blood of the sin *o* on his finger and put it
5: 6 as his sin *o* for the sin he has committed
5: 7 he shall bring to the LORD as the sin *o*
5: 7 for a sin *o* and the other for a holocaust.
5: 8 shall offer the one for the sin *o* first.
5: 9 of the sin *o* against the side of the altar.
5: 9 Such is the *o* for sin.
5:11 he shall present as a sin *o* for his sin
5:11 frankincense on it, because it is a sin *o*.
5:12 take a handful of this flour as a token *o*,
5:12 he shall burn as a sin *o* on the altar
5:15 guilt *o* an unblemished ram from the flock,
5:18 he shall bring as a guilt *o* to the priest
5:19 Such is the *o* for guilt;
5:24 on the day of his guilt *o* he shall make
5:25 As his guilt *o* he shall bring to the LORD
5:25 this as his guilt *o* to the priest,
6: 7 "This is the ritual of the cereal *o*.
6: 8 he shall burn on the altar as its token *o*,
6:10 like the sin *o* and the guilt offering.
6:13 "This is the *o* that Aaron and his sons
6:13 fine flour for the established cereal *o*,
6:14 Having broken the *o* into pieces,
6:15 for the LORD the whole *o* shall be burned.
6:16 *o* of a priest shall be a whole burnt *o*;
6:18 the LORD, shall the sin *o* be slaughtered.
6:19 who presents the sin *o* may partake of it;
6:22 the priestly line may partake of the sin *o*,
6:23 But no one may partake of any sin *o* of
6:23 such an *o* must be burned up in the fire.

OFFERING (cont.)

7: 2 also shall the guilt *o* be slaughtered.
7: 5 This is the guilt *o.*
7: 7 the sin *o* and the guilt offering are alike,
7: 7 the guilt *o* likewise belongs to the priest
7: 9 every cereal *o* that is baked in an oven or
7:12 anyone makes a peace *o* in thanksgiving,
7:13 His *o* shall also include loaves of
7:13 the victim of his peace *o* for thanksgiving.
7:14 who splashes the blood of the peace *o.*
7:16 sacrifice is a votive or a freewill *o,*
7:18 of the peace *o* is eaten on the third day,
7:20 flesh of a peace *o* belonging to the LORD,
7:21 eats of a peace *o* belonging to the LORD,
7:29 He who presents a peace *o* to the LORD
7:29 bring a part of it as his special *o* to him,
7:30 is to be waved as a wave *o* before the LORD.
7:32 from your peace *o* you shall give to the
7:32 to the priest the right leg as a raised *o.*
7:33 *o* shall have the right leg as his portion,
8: 2 anointing oil, the bullock for a sin *o,*
8:14 brought forward the bullock for a sin *o,*
8:27 had wave them as a wave *o* before the LORD.
8:28 holocaust on the altar as the ordination *o,*
8:29 and waved it as a wave *o* before the LORD;
8:31 that is in the basket of the ordination *o,*
9: 2 calf for a sin *o* and a ram for a holocaust,
9: 3 Take a he-goat for a sin *o,*
9: 4 and an ox and a ram for a peace *o,*
9: 4 LORD, along with a cereal *o* mixed with oil;
9: 7 "and offer your sin *o* and your holocaust
9: 7 the *o* of the people in atonement for them,
9: 8 the calf that was his own sin *o.*
9:10 the liver that were taken from the sin *o,*
9:15 Thereupon he had the people's *o* brought up.
9:15 the goat that was for the people's sin *o,*
9:17 He then presented the cereal *o;*
9:18 ox and the ram, the peace *o* of the people.
9:21 the right legs as a wave *o* before the LORD,
9:22 *o* the sin *o* and holocaust and peace
10:12 *o* left over from the oblations of the LORD,
10:14 wave *o* and the leg of the raised offering,
10:14 wave offering and the leg of the raised *o,*
10:15 of the raised *o* and the breast of the wave *o*
10:15 to be waved as a wave *o* before the LORD.
10:16 inquired about the goat of the sin *o,*
10:17 you not eat the sin *o* in the sacred place,
10:18 have eaten the *o* in the sanctuary,
10:19 sin *o* and holocaust before the LORD today,
10:19 Had I then eaten of the sin *o* today,
12: 6 and a pigeon or a turtledove for a sin *o.*
12: 8 for a holocaust and the other for a sin *o.*
14:10 fine flour mixed with oil for a cereal *o,*
14:12 the priest shall present it as a guilt *o,*
14:12 waving them as a wave *o* before the LORD.
14:13 sin *o* and the holocaust are slaughtered;
14:13 like the sin *o,* the guilt *o* belongs
14:14 take some of the blood of the guilt *o*
14:17 right foot, over the blood of the guilt *o.*
14:19 Only after he has offered the sin *o* in
14:20 and offer it, together with the cereal *o,*
14:21 lamb for a guilt *o,* to be used as a wave *o*
14:21 fine flour mixed with oil for a cereal *o,*
14:22 as a sin *o* and the other as a holocaust.
14:24 wave them as a wave *o* before the LORD.
14:28 right foot, over the blood of the guilt *o.*
14:31 as a sin *o* and the other as a holocaust,
14:31 as a holocaust, along with the cereal *o.*
15:15 as a sin *o* and the other as a holocaust.
15:30 as a sin *o* and the other as a holocaust.
16: 3 for a sin *o* and a ram for a holocaust.
16: 5 for a sin *o* and one ram for a holocaust.
16: 6 his sin *o* to atone for himself and for his
16: 9 shall bring in and offer up as a sin *o.*
16:11 Aaron offer up the bullock, his sin *o,*
16:25 burn the fat of the sin *o* on the altar.
17: 4 an *o* to the LORD in front of his Dwelling,
19: 5 you sacrifice your peace *o* to the LORD,
19:21 tent a ram as his guilt *o* to the LORD.
22:10 or hired servant may eat of any sacred *o.*
22:14 eats of a sacred *o* through inadvertence,
22:14 to the priest for the sacred *o,*
22:16 nor in the eating of the sacred *o*
22:18 *o* or as a freewill offering to the LORD,
22:18 offering or as a freewill *o* to the LORD,
22:21 When anyone presents a peace *o* to the LORD
22:21 fulfillment of a vow, or as a freewill *o,*
22:23 you may indeed present as a freewill *o,*
22:23 it will not be acceptable as a votive *o.*
23:13 Its cereal *o* shall be two tenths of an
23:14 this day, when you bring your God this *o,*
23:16 shall present the new cereal *o* to the LORD.
23:17 wave *o* of your first fruits to the LORD,
23:18 along with their cereal *o* and libations,
23:19 male goat shall be sacrificed as a sin *o,*
23:19 and two yearling lambs as a peace *o.*
23:20 the two lambs as a wave *o* before the LORD;
24: 7 to the LORD, a token *o* for the bread.
27: 2 a vow of *o* one or more persons to the LORD,
27: 9 "If the *o* vowed to the LORD is an animal
Nm 4: 7 bread *o* shall remain on the table.
4:16 fragrant incense, the established cereal *o,*
5:15 priest and shall take along as an *o* for her
5:15 *o* of jealousy, a cereal *o* for an appeal
5:18 cereal *o* of her appeal, that is, the cereal *o*
5:25 cereal *o* of jealousy from the woman's hand,
5:25 and having waved this *o* before the LORD,
5:26 cereal *o* as its token *o* and burn it
6:11 as a sin *o* and the other as a holocaust,
6:12 bringing a yearling lamb as a guilt *o.*
6:14 bringing as his *o* to the LORD one
6:14 unblemished yearling ewe lamb for a sin *o,*
6:14 one unblemished ram as a peace *o,*
6:16 up the sin *o* and the holocaust for him.
6:17 as a peace *o* to the LORD, with its cereal *o*
6:18 it in the fire that is under the peace *o.*
6:20 wave them as a wave *o* before the LORD.
6:20 wave *o* and the leg of the raised offering.
6:20 wave offering and the leg of the raised *o.*
6:21 this is the *o* to the LORD which is
7: 2 an *o* was made by the princes of Israel,
7: 3 The *o* they brought before the LORD
7: 3 presented as their *o* before the Dwelling.
7: 5 LORD then said to Moses, "Accept their *o,*
7:11 his *o* for the dedication of the altar."
7:12 his *o* on the first day was Nahshon,
7:13 His *o* consisted of one silver plate
7:13 fine flour mixed with oil for a cereal *o;*
7:16 one goat for a sin *o;*
7:17 and five yearling lambs for a peace *o.*
7:17 This was the *o* of Nahshon,
7:18 of Zuar, prince of Issachar, made his *o.*
7:19 He presented as his *o* one silver plate
7:19 fine flour mixed with oil for cereal *o;*
7:22 one goat for a sin *o;*
7:23 and five yearling lambs for a peace *o.*
7:23 This was the *o* of Nethanel, son of Zuar.
7:25 His *o* consisted of one silver plate
7:25 fine flour mixed with oil for a cereal *o;*
7:28 one goat for a sin *o;*
7:29 and five yearling lambs for a peace *o.*
7:29 This was the *o* of Eliab, son of Helon.
7:31 His *o* consisted of one silver plate
7:31 fine flour mixed with oil for a cereal *o;*
7:34 one goat for a sin *o;*
7:35 and five yearling lambs for a peace *o.*
7:35 This was the *o* of Elizur, son of Shedeur.
7:37 His *o* consisted of one silver plate
7:37 fine flour mixed with oil for a cereal *o;*
7:40 one goat for a sin *o;*
7:41 and five yearling lambs for a peace *o.*
7:41 This was the *o* of Shelumiel,
7:43 His *o* consisted of one silver plate
7:43 fine flour mixed with oil for a cereal *o;*
7:46 one goat for a sin *o;*
7:47 and five yearling lambs for a peace *o.*
7:47 This was the *o* of Eliasaph, son of Reuel.
7:49 His *o* consisted of one silver plate
7:49 fine flour mixed with oil for a cereal *o;*
7:52 one goat for a sin *o;*
7:53 and five yearling lambs for a peace *o.*
7:53 This was the *o* of Elishama,
7:55 His *o* consisted of one silver plate
7:55 fine flour mixed with oil for a cereal *o;*
7:58 one goat for a sin *o;*
7:59 and five yearling lambs for a peace *o.*
7:59 This was the *o* of Gamaliel,
7:61 His *o* consisted of one silver plate
7:61 fine flour mixed with oil for a cereal *o;*
7:64 one goat for a sin *o;*
7:65 and five yearling lambs for a peace *o.*
7:65 This was the *o* of Abidan, son of Gideoni.
7:67 His *o* consisted of one silver plate
7:67 fine flour mixed with oil for a cereal *o;*
7:70 one goat for a sin *o;*
7:71 and five yearling lambs for a peace *o.*
7:71 This was the *o* of Ahiezer,
7:73 His *o* consisted of one silver plate
7:73 fine flour mixed with oil for a cereal *o;*
7:76 one goat for a sin *o;*
7:77 and five yearling lambs for a peace *o.*
7:77 This was the *o* of Pagiel, son of Ochran.
7:79 His *o* consisted of one silver plate
7:79 fine flour mixed with oil for a cereal *o;*
7:82 one goat for a sin *o;*
7:83 and five yearling lambs for a peace *o.*
7:83 This was the *o* of Ahira, son of Enan.
8: 8 its cereal *o* of fine flour mixed with oil;
8: 8 shall take another young bull for a sin *o.*
8:11 the LORD as a wave *o* from the Israelites,
8:12 *o* and the other as a holocaust to the LORD,
8:13 to be offered as a wave *o* to the LORD;
8:15 purify them and offer them as a wave *o;*
8:21 offered them as a wave *o* before the LORD,
9: 7 we be deprived of presenting the LORD's *o*
9:13 the LORD's *o* at the prescribed time.
15: 3 fulfillment of a vow, or as a freewill *o,*
15: 4 shall also present to the LORD a cereal *o*
15: 6 you shall present a cereal *o* of two tenths
15: 7 thus making a sweet-smelling *o* to the LORD.
15: 8 of a vow, or as a peace *o* to the LORD,
15: 9 you shall present a cereal *o* of three tenths
15:24 with its prescribed cereal *o* and libation,
15:24 as well as one he-goat as a sin *o.*
15:27 bring a yearling she-goat as a sin *o,*
16:15 said to the LORD, "Pay no heed to their *o.*
16:35 and fifty men who were *o* the incense.
17: 4 *o* hammered into a covering for the altar,
18:11 the gift in every wave *o* of the Israelites;
18:18 the right leg of the wave *o* belong to you.
19: 9 The heifer is a sin *o.*
19:17 from the sin *o* shall be put in a vessel,
23: 2 *o* a bullock and a ram on each altar.
23:30 *o* a bullock and a ram on each altar.
28: 4 *o* one lamb in the morning and the other
28: 5 each with a cereal *o* of one tenth of an
28: 8 *o* and the same libation as in the morning,
28: 9 yearling lambs, with their cereal *o,*
28:12 with oil as the cereal *o* for each bullock,
28:12 mixed with oil as the cereal *o* for the ram,
28:13 with oil as the cereal *o* for each lamb,
28:15 shall be sacrificed as a sin *o* to the LORD.
28:20 *o* three tenths of an ephah for each
28:22 as a sin *o* in atonement for yourselves.
28:26 you present to the LORD the new cereal *o,*
28:28 *o* three tenths of an ephah for each
28:30 as a sin *o* in atonement for yourselves.
28:31 established holocaust with its cereal *o.*
29: 3 *o* three tenths of an ephah for the
29: 5 as a sin *o* in atonement for yourselves.
29: 6 new moon holocaust with its cereal *o,*
29: 6 established holocaust with its cereal *o,*
29: 9 *o* three tenths of an ephah for the
29:11 one goat shall be sacrificed as a sin *o.*
29:11 in addition to the atonement sin *o,*
29:11 established holocaust with its cereal *o,*
29:14 *o* three tenths of an ephah for each of the
29:16 one goat shall be sacrificed as a sin *o.*
29:16 holocaust with its cereal *o* and libation.
29:19 number, as well as one goat for a sin *o,*
29:19 holocaust with its cereal *o* and libation.
29:22 number, as well as one goat for a sin *o,*
29:22 holocaust with its cereal *o* and libation.
29:25 number, as well as one goat for a sin *o,*
29:25 holocaust with its cereal *o* and libation.
29:28 number, as well as one goat for a sin *o,*
29:28 holocaust with its cereal *o* and libation.
29:31 number, as well as one goat for a sin *o,*
29:31 holocaust with its cereal *o* and libation.
29:34 number, as well as one goat for a sin *o,*
29:34 holocaust with its cereal *o* and libation.
29:38 number, as well as one goat for a sin *o,*
29:38 holocaust with its cereal *o* and libation.
31:50 each of us will bring as an *o* to the LORD
Dt 12:11 every special *o* you have vowed to the LORD.
12:17 herd or flock, of any *o* you have vowed,
13:17 its spoils as a whole burnt *o* to the LORD,
16:10 measure of your own freewill *o* shall be
18: 3 from those who are *o* a sacrifice,
23:19 kind of votive *o* in the house of the LORD,
23:24 *o* you have freely promised to the LORD.
Jos 22:29 building an altar for holocaust, grain *o,*
Jgs 6:18 and bring out my *o* and set it before you."
13:19 *o* and offered it on the rock to the LORD,
13:23 a holocaust and cereal *o* from our hands!
20:26 besides *o* holocausts and peace offerings
21:13 at the rock Rimmon, *o* them peace.
1Sm 2:15 come and say to the man *o* the sacrifice,
2:29 part of every *o* of my people Israel?'
3:14 sacrifice or *o* will ever expiate its crime."
6: 3 make amends to him through a guilt *o.*
6: 4 "What guilt *o* should be our amends to him?",
6: 8 it the golden articles that you are *o,*
6:17 as a guilt *o* to the LORD were as follows:
7:10 While Samuel was *o* the holocaust,
13:10 just finished this *o* when Samuel arrived.
26:19 you against me, let an *o* appease him;
2Sm 24:23 "May the LORD your God accept your *o.*"
1Kgs 8:54 When Solomon finished *o* this entire prayer
18:29 state until the time for *o* sacrifice.
18:36 At the time for *o* sacrifice,
2Kgs 10:25 As soon as he finished *o* the holocaust,
1Chr 16: 2 *o* up the holocausts and peace offerings,
21:23 the wood, and the wheat for the cereal *o.*
23:29 of the fine flour for the cereal *o,*
23:31 *o* of holocausts to the LORD on sabbaths,
2Chr 7: 4 people were *o* sacrifices before the LORD.
23:18 temple for *o* the holocausts of the LORD,
26:16 LORD to make an *o* on the altar of incense.
29:21 were brought for a sin *o* for the kingdom,
29:23 Then the he-goats for the sin *o* were led
29:24 for "The holocaust and the sin *o,*"
35:14 were busy *o* holocausts and the fatty
Ezr 6: 3 *o* sacrifices and bringing burnt offerings.
8:28 and the gold are a freewill *o* to the LORD,
Neh 10:34 for the showbread, for the daily cereal *o,*
12:47 made their consecrated *o* to the Levites,
Tb 1: 8 third year I would bring them this *o,*
4:11 Alms are a worthy *o* in the sight of the
Jdt 16:19 Judith dedicated, as a votive *o* to God,
1Mc 1:22 light with all its fixtures, the *o* table,
2Mc 2:11 not been eaten, the sin *o* was burned up."
3:33 priest was *o* the sacrifice of atonement,
14:31 priests were *o* the customary sacrifices,
Jb 1: 5 and *o* holocausts for every one of them.
13: 4 over falsehoods and *o* vain remedies,
Eccl 4:17 rather than the fools' *o* of sacrifice;
Wis 18: 9 holy children of the good were *o* sacrifice
Sir 3:14 not be forgotten, it will serve as a sin *o*—

30:19 What good is an *o* to an idol that can
35: 1 the commandments sacrifices a peace *o*.
35: 5 The just man's *o* enriches the altar and
38:11 petition, a rich *o* according to your means.
45:14 His cereal *o* is wholly burnt with the
Is 53:10 If he gives his life as an *o* for sin,
65: 3 *O* sacrifices in the groves and burning
66: 3 a cereal offering, like *o* swine's blood;
66:20 from all the nations as an *o* to the LORD,
66:20 bring their *o* to the house of the LORD
Jer 11:12 the gods to which they have been *o* incense.
11:13 are the altars for *o* sacrifice to Baal.
Ez 20:31 By *o* your gifts,
43:18 altar when it is set up for the *o* of holocausts
43:19 a young bull as a sin *o* to the priests,
43:21 Then take the bull of the sin *o*,
43:22 present an unblemished he-goat as a sin *o*,
43:25 days you shall offer a he-goat as a sin *o*,
44:27 the sanctuary, he shall present his sin *o*,
44:29 eat the cereal *o*, the sin *o*, and the guilt *o*
45:16 bound to this *o* [for the prince in Israel].
45:19 take some of the blood from the sin *o*
45:22 the people of the land, a bull as a sin *o*.
45:23 *o* he shall offer one male goat each day.
45:24 As a cereal *o* he shall offer one ephah for
46: 5 with a cereal *o* of one ephah for the ram,
46: 7 with a cereal *o* of one ephah for the bull
46:11 the cereal *o* shall be an ephah for a bull,
46:12 the prince makes a freewill *o* to the LORD,
46:14 as a cereal *o* one sixth of an ephah,
46:14 This cereal *o* to the LORD is mandatory
46:15 The lamb, the cereal *o*,
Hos 10: 6 to Assyria, as an *o* to the great king.
Jl 1: 9 *o* and libation from the house of the LORD;
1:13 of your God is deprived of *o* and libation.
Zec 6:14 The crown itself shall be a memorial *o* in
Mal 1: 7 By *o* polluted food on my altar!
1:11 bring sacrifice to my name, and a pure *o*;
1:12 the LORD's table and its *o* may be polluted,
Mt 23:19 *o* or the altar which makes the *o* sacred?
Mk 12:33 worth more than any burnt *o* or sacrifice."
Acts 14:18 stop the crowds from *o* sacrifice to them.
21:26 time the *o* was to be made for each of them.
Rom 8: 3 the likeness of sinful flesh as a sin *o*,
12:13 be generous in *o* hospitality.
16: 5 he is the first *o* that Asia made to Christ.
Eph 5: 2 He gave himself for us as an *o* to God,
Phil 4:18 you through Epaphroditus, a fragrant *o*,
Ti 2:11 God has appeared, *o* salvation to all men.
Heb 8: 4 *o* the gifts which the law prescribes.
10: 2 the priests would have stopped *o* them,
10: 5 "Sacrifice and *o* you did not desire,
10:10 *o* of the body of Jesus Christ once for all.
10:11 and *o* again and again those same
10:14 By one *o* he has forever perfected those
10:18 forgiven, there is no further *o* for sin.
13:11 as a sin *o* are burned outside the camp.
1Pt 2: 5 *o* spiritual sacrifices acceptable to God
1Jn 2: 2 He is an *o* for our sins,
4:10 and has sent his Son as an *o* for our sins.

OFFERINGS (216)

Ex 20:24 sacrifice your holocausts and peace *o*,
24: 5 young bulls as peace *o* to the LORD,
29:28 From their peace *o*,
32: 6 offered holocausts and brought peace *o*.
35:29 LORD such voluntary *o* as they thought best,
36: 3 to bring their voluntary *o* to Moses.
36: 6 So the people stopped bringing their *o*;
40:29 and offered holocausts and cereal *o* on it,
Lv 5:13 The rest of the flour, like the cereal *o*,
6: 5 holocaust and burn the fat of the peace *o*.
6:18 This is the ritual for sin *o*.
7: 1 "This is the ritual for guilt *o*,
7:10 whereas all cereal *o* that are offered up
7:11 the peace *o* that are presented to the LORD.
7:14 From each of his *o* he shall present one
7:34 for from the peace *o* of the Israelites I
7:37 cereal *o*, sin *o*, guilt *o*, [ordination *o*
7:37 [ordination offerings] and peace *o*,
7:38 of Sinai to bring their *o* to the LORD.
10:14 due from the peace *o* of the Israelites.
14:11 is being purified, as well as all these *o*,
17: 5 them there as peace *o* to the LORD.
22: 2 *o* which the Israelites consecrate to me;
22: 3 to draw near the sacred *o* which the
22: 4 from a flow, may eat of these sacred *o*,
22: 7 he eat of the sacred *o* which are his food.
22:15 The sacred *o* which the Israelites
23:37 to the LORD holocausts and cereal *o*,
23:38 your various votive *o* and the freewill *o*
26:31 refusing to accept your sweet-smelling *o*.
Nm 6:14 along with their cereal *o* and libations,
7:10 the princes brought *o* before the altar on
7:84 were the *o* for the dedication of the altar,
7:87 yearling lambs, with their cereal *o*;
7:87 those for the sin *o* were twelve goats.
7:88 The animals for the peace *o* were,
7:88 were the *o* for the dedication of the altar
10:10 over your holocausts and your peace *o*;
15:13 shall make these *o* in the same way,
18: 8 in the various sacred *o* of the Israelites;
18: 9 cereal *o* or sin offerings or guilt offerings;
28: 2 be careful to present to me the food *o*
28:20 cereal *o* of fine flour mixed with oil;
28:23 These *o* you shall make in addition to the
28:24 same *o* each day for seven days as food *o*
28:28 cereal *o* of fine flour mixed ed with oil;
28:31 You shall make these *o*,
29: 3 cereal *o* of fine flour mixed with oil;
29: 9 cereal *o* of fine flour mixed with oil;
29:14 cereal *o* of fine flour mixed with oil;
29:18 with their cereal *o* and libations as
29:21 with their cereal *o* and libations as
29:24 with their cereal *o* and libations as
29:27 with their cereal *o* and libations as
29:30 with their cereal *o* and libations as
29:33 with their cereal *o* and libations as
29:37 with their cereal *o* and libations as
29:39 "These are the *o* you shall make to the
29:39 holocausts, cereal *o*, libations, and peace *o*
29:39 you present as your votive or freewill *o*."
Dt 12: 6 contributions, your votive and freewill *o*,
12:11 you shall bring all the *o* I command you:
12:14 shall make whatever *o* I enjoin upon you.
12:17 you have vowed, of your freewill *o*,
12:26 sacred gifts or votive *o* that you may have,
18: 8 along with his monetary *o* and heirlooms.
20:18 abominable *o* as they make to their gods,
27: 7 also sacrifice peace *o* and eat them there,
33:10 your nostrils, and burnt *o* to your altar.
Jos 8:31 offered holocausts and peace *o* to the LORD.
22:23 grain *o* or peace offerings upon it,
22:27 our holocausts, sacrifices, and peace *o*.
Jgs 20:26 holocausts and peace *o* before the LORD.
21: 4 there and offered holocausts and peace *o*.
1Sm 2:17 treated the *o* to the LORD with disdain.
2:29 and on the *o* which I have prescribed?
10: 4 you and offer you two wave *o* of bread,
10: 8 offer holocausts and to sacrifice peace *o*.
11:15 sacrificed peace *o* there before the LORD,
13: 9 said, "Bring me the holocaust and peace *o*,"
2Sm 6:17 holocausts and peace *o* before the LORD.
6:18 When he finished making these *o*,
24:25 LORD, and offered holocausts and peace *o*.
1Kgs 3:15 the Lord, offered holocausts and peace *o*,
7:51 in the dedicated *o* of his father David,
8:63 Solomon offered as peace *o* to the LORD
8:64 the cereal *o*, and the fat of the peace *o*
8:64 the LORD was too small to hold these *o*.
9:25 peace *o* on the altar which he had built
15:15 father's and his own votive *o* of silver,
2Kgs 12:19 the dedicated *o* presented by his forebears,
1Chr 6:34 Aaron and his descendants who burnt the *o*
16: 1 offered up holocausts and peace *o* to God.
16: 2 offering up the holocausts and peace *o*,
21:26 and offered up holocausts and peace *o*.
26:20 house of God and the stores of votive *o*.
26:26 of the votive *o* dedicated by King David,
28:12 of God and the stores of the votive *o*,
29: 9 people rejoiced over these freewill *o*,
2Chr 5: 1 in the dedicated *o* of his father David,
7: 7 the holocausts and the fat of the peace *o*,
7: 7 the holocausts, the cereal *o* and the fat.
15:18 of God his father's votive *o* and his own:
29:31 and thank *o* for the house of the LORD.
29:31 forward the sacrifices and thank *o*
29:31 all the holocausts which were freewill *o*.
29:35 *o* and the libations for the holocausts.
30:22 peace *o* and singing praises to the LORD,
31: 2 in regard to holocausts or peace *o*,
31:10 to bring the *o* to the house of the LORD,
31:12 When this had been done, the *o*,
31:14 he distributed the *o* made to the LORD and
33:16 on it peace *o* and thank offerings,
Ezr 1: 4 *o* for the house of God in Jerusalem.'"
1: 6 gifts besides all their freewill *o*.
2:68 made freewill *o* for the house of God,
6: 3 offering sacrifices and bringing burnt *o*.
7:16 together with the freewill *o* which the
7:17 the cereal *o* and libations proper to these,
Neh 10:34 holy *o*, for sin *o* to make atonement
10:38 and our *o* of the fruit of every tree,
10:40 and Levites bring the *o* of grain,
12:44 over the chambers set aside for stores, *o*,
13: 5 had previously been stored the cereal *o*,
13: 5 and gatekeepers, and the *o* due the priests.
13: 9 utensils of the house of God, the cereal *o*,
Jdt 4:14 votive *o* and the freewill *o* of the people.
16:18 they offered their holocausts, freewill *o*,
2Mc 2:13 and the royal letters about sacred *o*
5:16 *o* made by other kings for the advancement,
6: 5 with abominable *o* prohibited by the laws.
9:16 he would adorn with the finest *o* the holy
Ps(s) 20: 4 *o* and graciously accept your holocaust.
51:21 due sacrifices, burnt *o* and holocausts;
56:13 your thank *o* I will fulfill.
66:15 I will offer you, with burnt *o* of rams;
107:22 *o* and declare his works with shouts of joy.
Prv 7:14 "I owed peace *o*,
Wis 3: 6 as sacrificial *o* he took them to himself.
Sir 7: 9 the Most High will accept my *o*."
7:31 contributions, due sacrifices and holy *o*.
30:18 eat are like the *o* placed before a tomb.
45:16 mankind to offer holocausts and choice *o*,
45:20 The sacred *o* he allotted to him,
47: 2 Like the choice fat of the sacred *o*,
50:13 With the *o* to the LORD in their hands,
Is 1:13 Bring no more worthless *o*;
43:23 I did not exact from you the service of *o*,
57: 6 you poured out libations, and brought *o*.
60: 7 They will be acceptable *o* on my altar,
Jer 14:12 If they offer holocausts or cereal *o*,
17:26 cereal *o* and incense and thank offerings
33:11 who bring thank *o* to the house of the LORD,
33:18 holocausts before me, to burn cereal *o*,
41: 5 *o* and incense for the house of the LORD.
Bar 1:10 you are to procure holocausts, sin *o*,
1:10 and frankincense, and to prepare cereal *o*;
6:29 For women bring the *o* to these gods of
Ez 20:28 [there they brought their offensive *o*,
20:40 tributes and the first fruits of your *o*,
40:39 slaughtered the sin offerings and guilt *o*.
42:13 and here they shall keep the most sacred *o*:
42:13 cereal *o*, sin *o*, and guilt *o*;
43:27 your holocausts and peace *o* on the altar.
44:30 and all the best of your *o* of every kind,
45:13 These are the *o* you shall make:
45:15 and peace *o* and atonement sacrifices,
45:17 to provide the holocausts, cereal *o*,
45:17 sin *o*, cereal *o*, holocausts, and peace *o*
45:25 the same rites, making the same sin *o*,
45:25 the same cereal *o* and offerings of oil.
45:25 the same cereal offerings and *o* of oil.
46: 2 priests offer his holocausts and peace *o*,
46:12 the LORD, whether holocausts or peace *o*,
46:12 or his peace *o* as on the sabbath;
46:20 cook the guilt *o* and the sin offerings,
46:20 the sin offerings, and bake the cereal *o*,
Hos 14: 3 render as *o* the bullocks from our stalls.
Jl 2:14 *O* and libations for the LORD, your God.
Am 4: 5 proclaim publicly your freewill *o*,
5:22 Your cereal *o* I will not accept,
5:22 nor consider your stall-fed peace *o*.
5:25 and *o* for forty years in the desert,
Zep 3:10 of the North, they shall bring me *o*.
Mal 3: 8 In tithes and in *o*!
Lk 21: 1 the rich putting their *o* into the treasury,
21: 5 adorned with precious stones and votive *o*.
Acts 7:42 and *o* for forty years in the desert,
24:17 alms to my own people and to make my *o*.
Rom 15:31 and that the *o* I bring to Jerusalem may be
1Cor 9:13 at the altar share the *o* of the altar?
11: 3 Idol *O* head of every man is Christ;
Heb 5: 3 *o* for himself as well as for the people.
10: 6 and sin *o* you took no delight in.
10: 8 "Sacrifices and *o*, holocausts and sin *o*

OFFERS (19)

Lv 1:14 he *o* a bird as a holocaust to the LORD,
7: 8 the priest who *o* a holocaust for someone
7: 9 shall belong to the priest who *o* it,
7:33 The descendant of Aaron who *o* up the blood
17: 8 who *o* a holocaust or sacrifice without
21: 8 as sacred who *o* up the food of your God;
22:19 goat that he *o* must be an unblemished male.
Dt 20:12 peace with you and instead *o* you battle,
1Kgs 8:38 conscience and *o* some prayer or petition,
2Chr 6:29 people *o* a prayer or petition of any kind,
Ps(s) 50:23 that *o* praise as a sacrifice glorifies me;
Eccl 9: 2 him who *o* sacrifice and him who does not.
Sir 23:22 and *o* as heir her son by a stranger.
29:15 backer, for he *o* his very life for you.
34:18 gifts who *o* in sacrifice ill-gotten goods!
34:20 he who *o* sacrifice from the possessions
35: 2 In works of charity one *o* fine flour,
Dn 6:14 three times a day he *o* his prayer."
Rom 14:21 or anything else that *o* your brother an

OFFICE (25)

Gn 40:21 He restored the chief cupbearer to his *o*,
Dt 10: 6 Eleazar succeeding him in the priestly *o*.
17: 9 or to the judge who is in *o* at that time.
19:17 of the priests or judges in *o* at that time;
26: 3 priest in *o* at that time and say to him,
Jos 20: 6 of the high priest who is in *o* at the time.
1Kgs 2:27 Abiathar from his *o* of priest of the LORD,
1Chr 23:11 as a single family, fulfilling a single *o*.
1Mc 11:63 in Galilee, intending to remove him from *o*.
2Mc 4:10 the king's approval and came into *o*,
4:27 Although Menelaus had obtained the *o*,
4:50 of the men in power, remained in *o*,
7:24 him his Friend and entrust him with high *o*.
10:13 not command the respect due to his high *o*,
13: 3 but in the hope of being established in *o*.
Ps(s) 109: 8 may another take his *o*.
Wis 18:21 bearing the weapon of his special *o*,
Sir 45: 7 He made him perpetual in his *o* when he
46: 1 assistant to Moses in the prophetic *o*,
Is 22:19 your *o* and pull you down from your station.
Lk 20:20 to the *o* and authority of the procurator.
Jn 3:10 "You hold the *o* of teacher of Israel and
Acts 1:20 And again, 'May another take his *o*.'
Heb 5: 5 glorify himself with the *o* of high priest;
7:23 prevented by death from remaining in *o*;

OFFICER (11)

1Sm 17:18 take these ten cheeses for the field o.
18:13 his presence by appointing him a field o.
22: 7 you an o over a thousand or a hundred men,
29: 3 "Why, that is David, the o of Saul,
2Kgs 7:17 of the gate the o who was his adjutant;
Jer 20: 1 of Immer, chief o in the house of the LORD.
39: 3 Nergal-sharezer, of Simmagir, the chief o,
39:13 and Nergal-sharezer, the chief o,
Dn 2:15 "O o of the king,"
Zec 10: 4 chief, from him warrior's bow and every o.
2Tm 2: 4 this in order to please his commanding o.

OFFICERS (74)

Ex 15: 4 of his o were submerged in the Red Sea.
18:21 and set them as o over groups of thousands,
18:25 the people as o over groups of thousands,
Nm 31:14 Moses became angry with the o of the army,
31:48 Then the o who had been clan and company
Dt 1:15 fifties and over tens, and other tribal o.
20: 9 o shall be appointed over the army.
Jos 1:10 So Joshua commanded the o of the people:
3: 2 Three days later the o went through the
8:33 alike, with their elders, o and judges,
23: 2 leaders, judges and o) and said to them:
24: 1 their leaders, their judges and their o.
1Sm 14:38 then said, "Come here, all o of the army.
18: 5 even to Saul's own o
18:22 is fond of you, and all his o love you.
18:30 against them than any other of Saul's o,
22: 9 who was standing with the o of Saul,
2Sm 11: 1 along with his o and the army of Israel,
11: 9 royal palace with the other o of his lord,
11:17 against Joab, some o of David's army fell,
15:15 The king's o answered him,
15:17 the city, with all his o accompanying him,
16: 6 stones at David and at all the king's o,
18: 1 David placed o in command of groups of a
19: 7 that o and servants mean nothing to you.
1Kgs 9:22 commanders, adjutants, chariot o,
14:27 which he entrusted to the o of the guard
2Kgs 3:11 One of the o of the king of Israel replied,
6:11 the king of Aram called together his o.
6:12 one, my lord king," answered one of the o.
10:25 holocaust, Jehu said to the guards and o,
10:25 o put them to the sword and cast them out.
24:12 with his mother, his ministers, o,
24:14 all the o and men of the army,
1Chr 24: 5 o of the holy place, and o of the divine
26:30 one thousand seven hundred police o,
26:31 them outstanding o at Jazer of Gilead.
26:32 His brethren were also police o,
27: 1 and other o who served the king in all
2Chr 12:10 which he entrusted to the o of the guard
21: 9 with his o and all the chariots he had.
23:13 the o and the trumpeters around him,
33:14 o in all the fortified cities of Judah.
Neh 2: 9 king also sent with me army o and cavalry.
Jdt 2:14 the generals and o of the Assyrian army.
5:22 and the o of Holofernes and all the
6:17 of all his own words among the Assyrian o,
12:10 to which he did not invite any of the o.
Est 1: 3 over a feast for all his o and ministers:
1Mc 1: 6 He therefore summoned his o,
1: 8 So his o took over his kingdom,
2:15 The o of the king in charge of enforcing
2:17 the o of the king addressed Mattathias:
2:31 It was reported to the o and soldiers of
2:38 So the o and soldiers attacked them on the
3:55 this Judas appointed o among the people,
5:40 stream, Timothy said to the o of his army:
5:42 he stationed the o of the people beside
6:28 all his Friends, the o of his army,
7:26 king sent Nicanor, one of his famous o,
16:19 To the army o he sent letters inviting
Jer 26:21 o and princes were informed of his words,
29:26 may be police o in the house of the LORD,
51:27 Appoint recruiting o against her,
Ez 23: 6 dressed in purple, governors and o,
23:12 after the Assyrians, governors and o,
23:23 young men, all of them governors and o,
Mk 6:21 dinner for his court circle, military o,
14:65 while the o manhandled him.
Lk 22: 4 and o about a way to hand him over to them.
Acts 16:35 o with orders to let these men go.
16:38 The o reported this to the magistrates,
25:23 military o and prominent men of the city.

OFFICES (3)

2Chr 13:10 Aaron, and the Levites also have their o.
31:17 according to their various o and classes.
1Mc 13:15 in connection with the o that he held.

OFFICIAL (14)

1Kgs 22: 9 king of Israel called an o and said to him,
2Kgs 8: 6 that the king placed an o at her disposal,
2Chr 18: 8 So the king of Israel called an o,
1Mc 13:37 to our o to grant you release from tribute.
14:44 in royal purple or wear an o gold brooch.
Eccl 5: 7 for the high o has another higher than he
Is 22:15 Up, go to that o,
Mt 18:26 o prostrated himself in homage and said,
18:27 master let the o go and wrote off the debt.
18:28 But when that same o went out he met a
Mk 5:36 that had been brought and said to the o:
Jn 4:46 happened to be a royal o whose son was ill.
4:49 "Sir," the royal o pleaded with him,
Acts 8:27 a court o in charge of the entire treasury

OFFICIALS (60)

Gn 20: 8 called all his court o and informed them
41:37 This advice pleased Pharaoh and all his o.
41:38 another like him," Pharaoh asked his o,
50: 7 with him went all of Pharaoh's o
Nm 22:18 But Balaam replied to Balak's o,
Dt 1:15 them your leaders as o over thousands,
16:18 "You shall appoint judges and o
20: 5 "Then the o shall say to the soldiers,
20: 8 In fine, the o shall say to the soldiers,
20: 9 o have finished speaking to the soldiers,
29: 9 chiefs and judges, your elders and o,
31:28 your tribal elders and your o before me,
1Sm 8:14 and olive groves, and give them to his o.
1Kgs 1: 9 king's sons, and all the royal o of Judah.
4: 2 and these were the o he had in his service:
2Kgs 12:21 Certain of his o entered into a plot
12:22 son of Shomer, were the o who killed him.
14: 5 he slew the o who had murdered the king,
24:10 At that time the o of Nebuchadnezzar,
25:24 "Do not be afraid of the Chaldean o,"
1Chr 23: 4 LORD, six thousand were to be o and judges,
26:29 of Israel's civil affairs as o and judges.
2Chr 19:11 and the Levites will be your o.
24:11 the chest was brought to the royal o
26:11 command of Hananiah, one of the king's o.
32: 9 he sent his o to Jerusalem with this
32:16 His o said still more against the LORD God
34:13 Levites were scribes, o and gatekeepers.
Ezr 4: 7 and the rest of his fellow o to Artaxerxes,
4: 9 the scribe, and their fellow judges, o,
4:17 and their fellow o living in Samaria and
4:23 Shimshai, the scribe, and their fellow o,
5: 3 and Shethar-bozenai, and their fellow o,
5: 6 and their fellow o from West-of-Euphrates;
6: 6 you, their fellow o in West-of-Euphrates,
6:13 and their fellow o carried out fully the
7:28 and with all the most influential royal o.
8:25 our God by the king, his counselors, his o,
Est 1:11 her beauty to the populace and the o,
1:14 the seven Persian and Median o who were in
1:16 In the presence of the king and of the o,
1:16 but all the o and the populace throughout
1:18 conduct will rebel against all the royal o,
1:21 found acceptance with the king and the o,
2:18 honor of Esther to all his o and ministers,
3: 1 rank, seating him above all his fellow o.
3:12 every province, and the o of every people,
5:11 placed him above the o and royal servants.
6: 9 to one of the noblest of the king's o,
8: 9 and o of the hundred and twenty-seven
9: 3 Moreover, all the o of the provinces,
1Mc 10:41 All the additional funds that the o did
12:45 and their garrisons, as well as the o,
Sir 32: 9 forward, and with o be not too insistent.
Dn 3: 2 magistrates and all the o of the provinces
3: 3 magistrates and all the o of the provinces,
Mt 18:23 who decided to settle accounts with his o.
Mk 5:22 One of the o of the synagogue,
5:35 people from the o house arrived saying,
Ti 3: 1 subject to the government and its o,

OFFICIATED (2)

2Kgs 17:32 who o for them in the shrines on the high
Heb 7:13 none of whose members ever o at the altar.

OFFICIATES (1)

Dt 17:12 who o there in the ministry of the LORD,

OFFSCOURINGS (1)

Lam 3:45 made us o and refuse among the nations.

OFFSETS (2)

1Kgs 6: 6 because there were o along the outside of
Ez 41: 6 and there were o in the outside wall of

OFFSHOOT (3)

1Mc 1:10 There sprang from these a sinful o,
Sir 3:27 he is the o of an evil plant.
40:15 The o of violence will not flourish,

OFFSHOOTS (1)

Wis 4: 3 their spurious o shall not strike deep

OFFSPRING (62)

Gn 3:15 and the woman, and between your o and hers;
4:25 has granted me more o in place of Abel,"
15: 3 continued, "See, you have given me no o,
19:32 with him, that we may have o by our father."
19:34 him, that we may both have o by our father."
21:13 nation of him also, since he too is your o."
30: 3 on my knees, so that I too may have o,
38: 9 to avoid contributing o for his brother.
Lv 18:21 any of your o to be immolated to Molech,
20: 2 of his o to Molech shall be put to death.
20: 3 for in giving his o to Molech,
20: 4 a man's crime of giving his o to Molech,
Dt 28: 4 of your soil and the o of your livestock,
28:11 of your womb, the o of your livestock,
28:18 of your soil and the o of your livestock,
28:51 They will consume the o of your livestock
30: 9 of your womb, the o of your livestock,
Ru 4:12 o the LORD will give you from this girl,
2Kgs 10: 3 best and the fittest of your master's o,
1Chr 17:11 I will raise up your o after you who will
2Chr 22:10 off all the royal o of the house of Judah.
32:21 own o struck him down there with the sword.
Tb 13:16 Happy for me if a remnant of my o survive
1Mc 1:38 She became a stranger to her own o,
Jb 5:25 many, and your o as the grass of the earth.
21: 8 see before them their kinsfolk and their o.
27:14 His o shall not be filled with bread.
39: 4 When their o thrive and grow,
Ps(s) 132:11 "Your own o I will set upon your throne;
Wis 18:12 instant their nobler o were destroyed.
Sir 10:19 Whose o can be in honor?
10:19 Which o are in honor?
10:19 Whose o can be in disgrace?
10:19 Which o are in disgrace?
16: 1 children, nor rejoice in wicked o.
41: 5 witless o are in the homes of the wicked.
47:22 one, nor destroy the o of his friend.
Is 6:13 [Holy o is the trunk.]
14:22 Babylon name and remnant, progeny and o,
22:24 descendants and o,
41: 8 o of Abraham my friend
44: 3 I will pour out my spirit upon your o,
61: 9 the nations, and their o among the peoples;
65: 9 From Jacob I will save o,
65:23 blessed by the LORD are they and their o.
Jer 7:15 all your brethren, all the o of Ephraim.
14: 5 deserts her o because there is no grass.
29:32 punish Shemaiah, the Nehelamite, and his o.
Lam 2:20 Must women eat their o,
Bar 3:21 their o were far from the way to her.
Dn 3:36 multiply their o like the stars of heaven,
13:56 O of Canaan,
Mal 2:15 and what does that one require but godly o?
Mt 22:24 the wife and produce o for his brother.'
Mk 12:19 the wife and produce o for his brother.'
Lk 1:35 o to be born will be called Son of God.
Acts 3:25 when he said to Abraham, 'In your o,
17:28 poets have put it, 'for we too are his o.'
17:29 If we are in fact God's o,
Gal 3:19 o came to whom the promise had been given.
Rv 12:17 went off to make war on the rest of her o,
22:16 I am the Root and O of David,

OFTEN (36)

Gn 31:40 How o the scorching heat ravaged me by day,
1Kgs 5:28 Lebanon each month in relays o thousand,
2Kgs 4: 9 Since he visits us o,
2Chr 36:15 Early and o did the LORD,
Tb 1: 6 would o make the pilgrimage alone to
5: 6 I have o traveled to Media;
5:10 I have o traveled to Media and crossed all
Est E: 5 O, too, the fair speech of friends
1Mc 14:29 there have o been wars in our country,
2Mc 9:25 whom I have o before entrusted and
Jb 21:17 How o is the lamp of the wicked put out?
21:17 How o does destruction come upon them,
Ps(s) 78:38 O he turned back his anger and let none of
78:40 IV How o they rebelled against him in the
Sir 11: 5 The oppressed o rise to a throne,
11: 6 The exalted o fall into utter disgrace;
19:14 Admonish your friend o it may be slander;
20:14 He gives little and criticizes o,
23:11 A man who o swears heaps up obligations;
30: 1 He who loves his son chastises him o,
34:12 O I was in danger of death,
Jer 31:20 O as I threaten him,
Dn 13: 4 and the Jews had recourse to him o because
Mt 17:15 he o falls into the fire and frequently
18:21 wrongs me, how o must I forgive him?
23:37 o have I yearned to gather your children,
25:40 as o as you did it for one of my least
25:45 as o as you neglected to do it to one of
Mk 9:22 O it throws him into fire and into water.
Lk 5:16 He o retired to deserted places and prayed.
13:34 How o have I wanted to gather your
Jn 18: 2 Jesus had o met there with his disciples.
Rom 1:13 I want you to know that I have o planned
15:22 have so o been hindered from visiting you.
Phil 3:18 I have o said this to you before;
2Tm 1:16 because he has o given me new heart and

OG (22)

Nm 21:33 But O, king of Bashan,
32:33 of the Amorites, and the kingdom of O,
Dt 1: 4 the Amorites, who lived in Heshbon, and O,
3: 1 But O, king of Bashan,
3: 3 LORD, our God, delivered into our hands O,
3: 4 of Argob, the kingdom of O in Bashan:

3:10 of *O* in Bashan including Salecah and Edrei.
3:11 *O,* king of Bashan,
3:13 and all of Bashan, the kingdom of *O,*
4:47 They occupied his land and the land of *O,*
29: 6 this place, Sihon, king of Heshbon, and *O,*
31: 4 them just as he dealt with Sihon and *O,*
Jos 2:10 Egypt, and how you dealt with Sihon and *O,*
9:10 the Jordan, Sihon, king of Heshbon, and *O,*
12: 4 Secondly, *O,* king of Bashan, a survivor
13:12 the entire kingdom in Bashan of *O,*
13:30 all of Bashan, the entire kingdom of *O,*
13:31 once the royal cities of *O* in Bashan,
1Kgs 4:19 of Sihon, king of the Amorites, and of *O,*
Neh 9:22 Sihon, king of Heshbon, and the land of *O,*
Ps(s) 135:11 Sihon, king of the Amorites, and *O,*
136:20 And *O,* king of Bashan,

OGLING (1)

Is 3:16 outstretched *O* and mincing as they go,

OHAD (2)

Gn 46:10 Nemuel, Jamin, *O,*
Ex 6:15 The sons of Simeon were Jenuel, Jamin, *O,*

OHEL (1)

1Chr 3:20 The sons of Meshullam were Hashubah, *O,*

OHOLAH (5)

Ez 23: 4 *O* was the name of the elder,
23: 4 Samaria is *O,* and Jerusalem is Oholibah.]
23: 5 *O* became a harlot faithless to me;
23:36 Son of man, would you judge *O*
23:44 Thus they came to *O* and Oholibah,

OHOLIAB (5)

Ex 31: 6 As his assistant I have appointed *O,*
35:34 He has also given both him and *O,*
36: 1 will set to work with *O* and with all the
36: 2 Moses then called Bezalel and *O* and all
38:23 commanded Moses, and he was assisted by *O,*

OHOLIBAH (6)

Ez 23: 4 elder, and the name of her sister was *O.*
23: 4 Samaria is Oholah, and Jerusalem is *O*
23:11 Though her sister *O* saw all this,
23:22 Therefore, *O,* thus says the Lord GOD:
23:36 Son of man, would you judge Oholah and *O?*
23:44 Thus they came to Oholah and *O,*

OHOLIBAMAH (8)

Gn 36: 2 *O,* granddaughter through Anah of Zibeon
36: 5 and *O* bore Jeush,
36:14 The descendants of Esau's wife *O*—
36:18 The descendants of Esau's wife *O:*
36:18 These are the clans of Esau's wife *O,*
36:25 The descendants of Anah were Dishon and *O,*
36:41 the clans of Timna, Alvah, Jetheth, *O,*
1Chr 1:52 the chiefs of Timna, Aliah, Jetheth, *O,*

OIL (217)

Gn 28:18 memorial stone, and poured *o* on top of it.
35:14 it he made a libation and poured out *o.*
Ex 25: 6 *o* for the light;
25: 6 anointing *o* and for the fragrant incense;
27:20 to bring you clear *o* of crushed olives,
29: 2 flour make unleavened cakes mixed with *o,*
29: 2 oil, and unleavened wafers spread with *o,*
29: 7 the anointing *o* and anoint him with it,
29:21 together with some of the anointing *o,*
29:23 of bread, one of the cakes made with *o,*
29:40 fourth of a hin of *o* of crushed olives and,
30:24 together with a hin of olive *o;*
30:25 and blend them into sacred anointing *o,*
30:26 With this sacred anointing *o* you shall
30:31 As sacred anointing *o* this shall belong to
30:32 may you make any other *o* of a like mixture.
31:11 sons in their ministry, the anointing *o,*
35: 8 *o* for light;
35: 8 anointing *o* and for the fragrant incense;
35:14 the lamps, and the *o* for the light;
35:15 the anointing *o,*
35:28 as well as spices, and *o* for the light,
35:28 spices, and oil for the light, anointing *o,*
37:29 The sacred anointing *o* and the fragrant
39:37 all its appurtenances, the *o* for the light,
39:38 light, the golden altar, the anointing *o,*
40: 9 "Take the anointing *o* and anoint the
Lv 2: 1 pour *o* on it and put frankincense over it.
2: 2 take a handful of this fine flour and *o,*
2: 4 oil, or of unleavened wafers spread with *o.*
2: 5 of fine flour mixed with *o* and unleavened.
2: 6 into pieces, and *o* must be poured over it.
2: 7 it must be of fine flour, deep-fried in *o.*
2:15 offering you shall put *o* and frankincense.
2:16 shall then burn some of the grits and *o,*
5:11 He shall not put *o* or frankincense on it,
6: 8 from it a handful of its fine flour and *o,*
6:14 in *o* on a griddle when you bring it in.
7:10 that are offered up dry or mixed with *o*
7:12 with oil, unleavened wafers spread with *o,*
7:12 fine flour mixed with *o* and well kneaded.
8: 2 with the vestments, the anointing *o,*
8:10 Taking the anointing *o,*
8:11 some of this *o* seven times on the altar,
8:12 some of the anointing *o* on Aaron's head,
8:26 cake, one loaf of bread made with *o,*
8:30 Taking some of the anointing *o* and some of
9: 4 along with a cereal offering mixed with *o;*
10: 7 the anointing *o* of the LORD is upon you."
14:10 flour mixed with *o* for a cereal offering,
14:10 for a cereal offering, and one log of *o.*
14:12 a guilt offering, along with the log of *o,*
14:15 The priest shall also take a log of *o* and
14:17 Of the *o* left in his hand the priest shall
14:18 The rest of the *o* in his hand the priest
14:21 oil for a cereal offering, a log of *o,*
14:24 lamb, along with the log of *o,*
14:26 The priest shall then pour some of the *o*
14:28 Some of the *o* in his hand the priest shall
14:29 The rest of the *o* in his hand the priest
21:10 upon whose head the anointing *o* has been
21:12 his God, for with the anointing *o* upon him,
23:13 of an ephah of fine flour mixed with *o,*
24: 2 clear *o* of crushed olives for the light,
Nm 4: 9 containers of *o* from which it is supplied.
4:16 shall be in charge of the *o* for the light,
4:16 cereal offering, and the anointing *o.*
5:15 pour *o* on it nor put frankincense over it,
6:15 *o* and of unleavened wafers spread with oil.
7:13 flour mixed with *o* for a cereal offering;
7:19 flour mixed with *o* for cereal offering;
7:25 flour mixed with *o* for a cereal offering;
7:31 flour mixed with *o* for a cereal offering;
7:37 flour mixed with *o* for a cereal offering;
7:43 flour mixed with *o* for a cereal offering;
7:49 flour mixed with *o* for a cereal offering;
7:55 flour mixed with *o* for a cereal offering;
7:61 flour mixed with *o* for a cereal offering;
7:67 flour mixed with *o* for a cereal offering;
7:73 flour mixed with *o* for a cereal offering;
7:79 flour mixed with *o* for a cereal offering;
8: 8 offering of fine flour mixed with *o;*
11: 8 which tasted like cakes made with *o.*
15: 4 flour mixed with a fourth of a hin of *o,*
15: 6 flour mixed with a third of a hin of *o,*
15: 9 of fine flour mixed with half a hin of *o,*
18:12 assigned to you all the best of the new *o*
28: 5 a fourth of a hin of *o* of crushed olives.
28: 9 of an ephah of fine flour mixed with *o,*
28:12 *o* as the cereal offering for each bullock,
28:12 with *o* as the cereal offering for the ram,
28:13 *o* as the cereal offering for each lamb,
28:20 offerings of fine flour mixed with *o;*
28:28 offerings of fine flour mixed with *o;*
29: 3 offerings of fine flour mixed with *o;*
29: 9 offerings of fine flour mixed with *o;*
29:14 offerings of fine flour mixed with *o;*
35:25 priest who has been anointed with sacred *o.*
Dt 7:13 of your soil, your grain and wine and *o,*
11:14 have your grain, wine and *o* to gather in;
12:17 of your tithe of grain or wine or *o,*
14:23 your tithe of the grain, wine and *o,*
18: 4 first fruits of your grain and wine and *o,*
28:40 country, you will have no *o* for ointment,
28:51 they will leave you no grain or wine or *o,*
32:13 from its rocks and olive *o* from its hard,
33:24 *o* of his olive trees runs over his feet!
Jgs 9: 9 answered them, 'Must I give up my rich *o,*
1Sm 10: 1 Samuel poured *o* on Saul's head;
16: 1 Fill your horn with *o,* and be on your way.
16:13 Then Samuel, with the horn of *o* in hand,
2Sm 1:21 shield of Saul, no longer anointed with *o.*
14: 2 apparel and do not anoint yourself with *o,*
1Kgs 1:39 of *o* from the tent and anointed Solomon.
5:25 and twenty thousand measures of pure *o.*
17:12 flour in my jar and a little *o* in my jug.
17:14 not go empty, nor the jug of *o* run dry,
17:16 did not go empty, nor the jug of *o* run dry,
2Kgs 4: 2 has nothing in the house but a jug of *o,*"
4: 4 pour the *o* into all the vessels,
4: 5 her the vessels, she would pour in *o.*
4: 6 And then the *o* stopped.
4: 7 and sell the *o* to pay off your creditor;
9: 1 your loins, take this flask of *o* with you,
9: 3 the flask you have, pour *o* on his head,
9: 6 man poured the *o* on his head and said,
18:32 and orchards, of olives, *o* and fruit syrup.
20:13 his silver, gold, spices and fine *o,*
1Chr 9:29 as well as the fine flour, the wine, the *o,*
12:41 of meal, pressed figs, raisins, wine, *o,*
27:28 and over the stores of *o* was Joash.
2Chr 2: 9 of wine, and twenty thousand measures of *o.*"
2:14 barley, *o* and wine which he has promised.
11:11 in them, with supplies of food, *o* and wine.
31: 5 the best of their grain, wine, *o* and honey,
32:28 for the harvest of grain, for wine and *o,*
Ezr 3: 7 and sent food and drink and *o* to the
6: 9 God of heaven, wheat, salt, wine, and *o,*
7:22 *o,*
Neh 5:11 wine, and the *o* that you have lent them."
10:38 the fruit of every tree, of wine and of *o,*
10:40 bring the offerings of grain, wine, and *o;*
13: 5 grain, wine, and *o* allotted to the Levites,
13:12 of grain, wine, and *o* to the storerooms;
Tb 1: 7 give the tithe of grain, wine, olive *o,*
Jdt 10: 5 a leather flask of wine and a cruse of *o.*
11:13 wine and *o* which they had sanctified
16: 7 She anointed her face with fragrant *o;*
Est 2:12 six months were spent with *o* of myrrh,
Jb 20:17 He shall see no streams of *o,*
24:11 Between the rows they press out the *o;*
29: 6 and the rock flowed with streams of *o;*
Ps(s) 23: 5 You anoint my head with *o;*
45: 8 the *o* of gladness above your fellow kings.
55:22 His words are smoother than *o,*
89:21 with my holy *o* I have anointed him,
92:11 you have anointed me with rich *o.*
104:15 hearts, So that their faces gleam with *o,*
109:18 like water and like *o* into his bones;
141: 5 it is *o* for the head,
Prv 5: 3 honey, and her mouth is smoother than *o;*
Eccl 10:19 Bread and *o* call forth merriment and wine
Sir 39:26 and honey, the blood of the grape, and *o,*
45:15 him and anointed him with the holy *o,*
Is 21: 5 Rise up, O princes, *o* the shield!
39: 2 silver and gold, the spices and fine *o,*
57: 9 you approached the king with scented *o,*
61: 3 them *o* of gladness in place of mourning,
Jer 31:12 The grain, the wine, and the *o,*
40:10 to collect the wine, the fruit and the *o,*
41: 8 wheat and barley, *o* and honey."
Ez 16: 9 away your blood, and anointed you with *o.*
16:13 Fine flour, honey, and *o* were your food.
16:18 my *o* and my incense you set before them;
16:19 I had given you, the fine flour, the *o,*
23:41 it, on which you had set my incense and *o.*
27:17 exchanging Minnith wheat, figs, honey, *o,*
32:14 clear, and their streams flow like *o,*
45:14 The regulation for *o:*
45:14 for every measure of *o,*
45:24 he shall offer one hin of *o* for each ephah.
45:25 same cereal offerings and offerings of *o.*
46: 5 the lambs, and a hin of *o* for each ephah.
46: 7 has at hand, and for each ephah a hin of *o.*
46:11 pleases, and a hin of *o* with each ephah.
46:14 of a hin of *o* to moisten the fine flour.
46:15 and the *o* are to be offered every morning
Dn 13:17 "Bring me *o* and soap,"
Hos 2: 7 my wool and my flax, my *o* and my drink."
2:10 gave her the grain, the wine, and the *o,*
2:24 respond to the grain, and wine, and *o,*
12: 2 terms with Assyria, and carries *o* to Egypt.
Jl 1:10 the must has failed, the *o* languishes.
2:19 I will send you grain, and wine, and *o,*
2:24 the vats shall overflow with wine and *o.*
Mi 6: 7 of rams, with myriad streams of *o?*
6:15 reap, tread out the olive, yet pour no *o,*
Hg 1:11 grain, and upon the wine, and upon the *o,*
2:12 touches bread, or pottage, or wine, or *o,*
Zec 4:12 fresh *o* through the two golden channels?"
Mt 25: 3 taking their torches, brought no *o* along,
25: 4 took flasks of *o* as well as their torches.
25: 8 to the sensible, 'Give us some of your *o,*
Mk 6:13 many demons, anointed the sick with *o,*
Lk 7:37 *o* and stood behind him at his feet,
7:38 kissing them and perfuming them with the *o.*
7:46 You did not anoint my head with *o,*
10:34 dressed his wounds, pouring in *o* and wine.
16: 6 The man replied, 'A hundred jars of *o.*'
Heb 1: 9 the *o* of gladness above your fellow kings."
Jas 5:14 him with *o* in the Name [of the Lord].
Rv 6: 6 But spare the olive *o* and the wine!"
18:13 wine and olive *o,*

OILS (3)

Am 6: 6 and anoint themselves with the best *o;*
Mk 16: 1 and Salome bought perfumed *o* with which
Jn 19:40 up in wrappings of cloth with perfumed *o.*

OINTMENT (8)

Ex 30:25 oil, perfumed *o* expertly prepared.
Dt 28:40 your country, you will have no oil for *o,*
2Chr 16:14 kinds of aromatics compounded into an *o.*
Jdt 10: 3 with water, and anointed it with rich *o.*
Ps(s) 133: 2 *o* upon the head runs down over the beard,
Eccl 7: 1 A good name is better than good *o,*
9:18 fly that dies can spoil the perfumer's *o,*
Rv 3:18 Buy *o* to smear on your eyes,

OINTMENT-MAKERS (1)

1Sm 8:13 He will use your daughters as *o,*

OINTMENTS (4)

1Chr 9:30 priests, however, who mixed the spiced *o.*
Est C:12 *o* she covered her head with dirt and ashes.
Sg 4:10 the fragrance of your *o* than all spices!
Jn 12: 3 the house was filled with the *o* fragrance.

OLD (337)

Gn 5: 3 *o* when he begot a son in his likeness,
5: 6 When Seth was one hundred and five years *o,*
5: 9 When Enosh was ninety years *o,*

OLD (cont.)

5:12 When Kenan was seventy years o,
5:15 When Mahalalel was sixty-five years o,
5:18 was one hundred and sixty-two years o,
5:21 When Enoch was sixty-five years o,
5:25 was one hundred and eighty-seven years o,
5:28 was one hundred and eighty-two years o,
5:32 When Noah was five hundred years o,
6: 4 They were the heroes of o,
7: 6 Noah was six hundred years o when the
11:10 When Shem was one hundred years o,
11:12 When Arpachshad was thirty-five years o,
11:14 When Shelah was thirty years o,
11:16 When Eber was thirty-four years o,
11:18 When Peleg was thirty years o,
11:20 When Reu was thirty-two years o,
11:22 When Serug was thirty years o,
11:24 When Nahor was twenty-nine years o,
11:26 When Terah was seventy years o,
12: 4 seventy-five years o when he left Haran.
15:15 you shall be buried at a contented o age.
16:16 years o when Hagar bore him Ishmael.
17: 1 When Abram was ninety-nine years o,
17:12 male among you, when he is eight days o,
17:17 be born to a man who is a hundred years o?
17:24 Abraham was ninety-nine years o when the
17:25 his son Ishmael was thirteen years o
18:11 Now Abraham and Sarah were o,
18:12 I am so withered and my husband is so o,
18:13 'Shall I really bear a child, as o as I am?'
19: 4 the townsmen of Sodom, both young and o—
19:31 "Our father is getting o,
21: 2 and bore Abraham a son in his o age,
21: 4 When his son Isaac was eight days o,
21: 5 years o when his son Isaac was born to him.
21: 7 Yet I have borne him a son in his o age."
24: 1 Abraham had now reached a ripe o age,
24:36 Sarah bore a son to my master in her o age,
25: 8 a ripe old age, grown o after a full life;
25:20 was forty years o when he married Rebekah,
25:26 was sixty years o when they were born.
26:34 When Esau was forty years o,
27: 1 was so o that his eyesight had failed him,
27: 2 I am so o that I may now die at any time.
35:29 as an o man and was taken to his kinsmen.
37: 2 When Joseph was seventeen years o,
37: 3 sons, for he was the child of his o age;
41:46 o when he entered the service of Pharaoh,
44:20 a young brother, the child of his o age.

Ex 7: 7 Moses was eighty years o and Aaron
10: 9 "Young and o must go with us,"

Lv 14:42 and put in the place of the o stones,
19:32 of the aged, and show respect for the o;
25:22 you will continue to eat from the o crop;
25:22 in, you will still have the o to eat from.
26:10 So much of the o crops will you have

Nm 3:39 total number of male Levites a month o
3:40 males of the Israelites a month o or more,
8:25 When he is fifty years o,
18:16 a boy is to be paid when he is a month o;
32:38 they rebuilt, they called by their o names.
33:39 years o when he died on Mount Hor.

Dt 4:25 and have grown o in the land,
4:32 "Ask now of the days of o,
31: 2 I am now one hundred and twenty years o
32: 7 Think back on the days of o,
32:25 nursing babe as well as the hoary o man.
34: 7 hundred and twenty years o when he died,

Jos 6:21 men and women, young and o,
9: 4 old sacks for their asses, and o wineskins,
9: 5 They wore o,
13: 1 When Joshua was o and advanced in years,
13: 1 now you are o and advanced in years,
14: 7 forty years o when the servant of the LORD,
14:10 and although I am now eighty-five years o,
23: 1 when Joshua was o and advanced in years,
23: 2 "I am o and advanced in years.

Jgs 2: 8 was a hundred and ten years o when he died;
8:32 At a good o age Gideon,
19:16 an o man came from his work in the field;
19:17 city, the o man asked where he was going,
19:20 "You are welcome," the o man said to him,
19:22 They said to the o man whose house it was,

Ru 1:12 Go, for I am too o to marry again.
4:15 your comfort and the support of your o age,

1Sm 2:22 When Eli was very o,
2:31 no man in your family shall reach o age.
2:32 shall never be an o man in your family.
4:15 (Eli was ninety-eight years o,
4:18 since he was an o man and heavy,
5: 9 he afflicted its inhabitants, young and o,
8: 1 In his o age Samuel appointed his sons
8: 5 and said to him, "Now that you are o,
12: 2 As for me, I am o and gray,
13: 1 o when he became king and he reigned . . .
17:12 days of Saul was o and well on in years.
24:14 The o proverb says,
28:14 replied, "It is an o man who is rising,
30: 2 and all who were in the city, young and o,

2Sm 2:10 years o when he became king over Israel,
4: 4 He was five years o when the news about
5: 4 was thirty years o when he became king,
7:10 continue to afflict them as they did of o,
19:33 o man of eighty and very wealthy besides,
19:34 for your o age as my guest in Jerusalem."
19:36 I am now eighty years o.

1Kgs 1: 1 King David was o and advanced in years,
2: 6 to go down to the grave in peaceful o age.
11: 4 When Solomon was o his wives had turned
13:11 There was an o prophet living in the city,
13:25 news to the city where the o prophet lived.
14:21 was forty-one years o when he became king,
15:23 In his o age, Asa had an infirmity
22:42 thirty-five years o when he began to reign,

2Kgs 4:18 The day came when the child was o enough
8:17 thirty-two years o when he began to reign,
8:26 twenty-two years o when he began his reign,
12: 1 was seven years o when he became king.
14: 2 twenty-five years o when he became king,
15: 2 was sixteen years o when he began to reign,
15:33 twenty-five years o when he became king,
16: 2 was twenty years o when he became king,
16:15 But the o bronze altar shall be mine for
18: 2 twenty-five years o when he became king,
19:25 I prepared it, From days of o I planned it.
21: 1 was twelve years o when he began to reign,
21:19 twenty-two years o when he began to reign,
22: 1 was eight years o when he began to reign,
23:31 years o when he began to reign,
23:36 twenty-five years o when he began to reign,
24: 8 eighteen years o when he began to reign,
24:18 was twenty-one years o when he became king,

1Chr 2:21 married her when he was sixty years o.
4:22 [These are events of o
23: 1 grown o and was near the end of his days,
23: 3 thirty years o and above were counted,
23:27 from the time they were twenty years o.
25: 8 for their functions equally, young and o,
29:28 He died at a ripe o age,

2Chr 3: 3 sixty cubits according to the o measure,
12:13 was forty-one years o when he became king,
20:31 thirty-five years o when he became king,
21: 5 was thirty-two years o when he became king,
21:20 was thirty-two years o when he became king,
22: 2 was twenty-two years o when he became king,
24: 1 was seven years o when he became king,
24:15 ripe o age; he was a hundred and thirty years o
25: 1 twenty-five years o when he became king,
26: 3 was sixteen years o when he became king,
27: 1 twenty-five years o when he became king,
27: 8 twenty-five years o when he became king,
28: 1 was twenty years o when he became king,
29: 1 twenty-five years o when he became king,
33: 1 was twelve years o when he became king,
33:21 was twenty-two years o when he became king,
34: 1 was eight years o when he became king,
36: 2 twentythree years o when he became king,
36: 5 twenty-five years o when he became king,
36: 9 was eighteen years o when he became king,
36:11 was twenty-one years o when he became king,

Ezr 3:12 the o men who had seen the former house,

Neh 8: 2 and those children o enough to understand.
8: 3 and those children o enough to understand;
12:46 the days of David and Asaph my father in times of o.

Tb 3:10 And thus would I cause my father in his o
4:12 Isaac, and Jacob, our fathers from of o:
8: 7 allow us to live together to a happy o age."
14: 2 years o when he lost his eyesight,

Jdt 16:23 to be very o in the house of her husband,

Est 3:13 provinces, that all the Jews, young and o,

1Mc 3:29 laws which had been in effect from of o.
14: 9 O men sat in the squares,
16: 3 I have now grown o,

2Mc 5:13 There was a massacre of young and o,
6:22 because of their o friendship with him.
6:25 would bring shame and dishonor on my o age.
6:27 I will prove myself worthy of my o age,

Jb 4:11 The o lion perishes for lack of prey,
12:12 So with o age is wisdom,
14: 8 Even though its root grow o in the earth,
15:10 There are gray-haired o men among us more
21: 7 Why do the wicked surive, grow o,
29:18 "In my own nest I shall grow o;
32: 6 I am young and you are very o;
42:17 Then Job died, o and full of years.

Ps(s) 25: 6 O LORD, and your kindness are from of o.
37:25 Neither in my youth, nor now that I am o,
44: 2 deeds you did in their days, in days of o:
71: 9 Cast me not off in my o age;
71:18 And now that I am o and gray,
74: 2 your flock which you built up of o,
74:12 Yet, O God, my king from of o,
77: 6 I consider the days of o;
77:12 yes, I remember your wonders of o.
78: 2 parable, I will utter mysteries from of o.
92:15 They shall bear fruit even in o age;
93: 2 Your throne stands firm from of o;
102:26 Of o you established the earth,
102:27 though all of them grow o like a garment.
119:52 I remember your ordinances of o,
119:152 Of o I know from your decrees,
139:24 is crooked, and lead me in the way of o.
143: 5 I remember the days of o;
148:12 Young men too, and maidens, o men and boys,

Prv 8:23 From of o I was poured forth,
17: 6 Grandchildren are the crown of o men,
20:29 and the dignity of o men is gray hair.
22: 6 even when he is o,
23:22 and despise not your mother when she is o.

Eccl 1:11 There is no remembrance of the men of o;
4:13 Better is a poor but wise youth than an o

Wis 2:10 o man for his hair grown white with time.
3:17 and dishonored will their o age be at last;
4: 9 an unsullied life, the attainment of o age.
4:16 the many years of the wicked man grown o.
8: 8 learning, she knows the things of o,
9: 8 which you had established from of o.
11:14 Him who of o had been cast out in exposure
14: 6 For of o, when the proud giants

Sir 1:13 devoted men was she created from of o,
3:12 son, take care of your father when he is o;
8: 6 is old, for some of us, too, will grow o.
8: 9 Reject not the tradition of o men which
9:10 Discard not an o friend,
11:16 birth, and evil grows o with evildoers.
11:20 with it, grow o while doing your task.
14:17 All flesh grows o,
16: 7 of o who rebelled long ago in their might;
25: 2 and an o man lecherous in his dotage.
25: 3 youth, how will you acquire in your o age?
25: 6 The crown of o men is wide experience;
30:24 life, worry brings on premature o age.
36:10 that they may inherit the land as of o,
36:14 Give evidence of your deeds of o;
39: 1 o and occupies himself with the prophecies;
42:18 sees from of o the things that are to come:
44: 2 portion, his own part, since the days of o.
46: 9 Caleb remained with him even in his o age

Is 20: 4 and exiles from Ethiopia, young and o,
22:11 the two walls for the water of the o pool.
23: 7 your wanton city, whose origin is from o,
25: 1 have fulfilled your wonderful plans of o,
37:26 I prepared it, From days of o I planned it,
44: 7 Who of o announced future events?
45:21 the beginning and foretold it from of o?
46: 4 Even to your o age I am the same,
47: 6 And upon o men you laid a very heavy yoke.
48: 5 bronze, I foretold them to you of o;
51: 9 Awake as in the days of o,
63: 9 them and carrying them all the days of o.
63:11 they remembered the days of o and Moses,
64: 3 such as they had not heard of from of o.
65:20 or an o man who does not round out his

Jer 6:16 the pathways of o Which is the way to good,
18:15 stumble out of their ways, the paths of o,
25: 5 and your fathers, from of o and forever.
28: 8 of o, the prophets who were before you
30:20 His sons shall be as of o,
31:13 and dance, and young men and o as well.
33: 7 lot of Israel, and rebuild them as of o.
33:11 For I will restore this country as of o,
38:11 in the palace, from which he took some o,
38:12 "Put the o, tattered rags
51:22 and wife, with you I shatter o and young,
52: 1 was twenty-one years o when he became king,

Lam 2:10 in silence sit the o men of duaghter Zion;
2:17 the threat He set forth from days of o;
2:21 the dust of the streets lie young and o,
5:14 The o men have abandoned the gate,
5:21 give us anew such days as we had of o.

Bar 3:10 of your foes, grown o in a foreign land,

Ez 9: 6 O men, youths and maidens,
16: 8 saw that you were now o enough for love.
32:27 not lie with the mighty men fallen of o,

Dn 13: 8 o men saw her enter every day for her walk,
13:19 the two o men got up and hurried to her.
13:24 and the o men also shouted at her,
13:27 At the accusations by the o men,
13:50 God has given you the prestige of o age."

Hos 4:11 O wine and new deprive my people of

Jl 2: 2 Their like has not been from of o,
3: 1 prophesy, your o men shall dream dreams,

Am 9:11 ruins, and rebuild it as in the days of o,

Mi 5: 1 Whose origin is from of o,
6: 6 him with holocausts, with calves a year o?
7:14 in Bashan and Gilead, as in the days of o;
7:20 have sworn to our fathers from days of o.

Zec 8: 4 O men and old women,
8: 4 each with staff in hand because of o age,

Mt 2:16 o and under in Bethlehem and its environs,
5:30 The O Law and the New"It was also said,
9:16 a piece of unshrunken cloth on an o cloak;
9:17 do not pour new wine into o wineskins.
13:52 from his storeroom both the new and the o."

Mk 2:21 a patch of unshrunken cloth on an o cloak.
2:21 the new from the o—
2:22 no man pours new wine into o wineskins.

Lk 1:18 I am an o man;
1:36 kinswoman has conceived a son in her o age;
5:36 a piece from a new coat to patch an o one.
5:36 piece taken from it will not match the o.
5:37 no one pours new wine into o wineskins.
5:37 do so, the new wine will burst the o skins,
5:39 No one, after drinking o wine, wants new.
5:39 He says, 'I find the o wine better.' "
9: 8 "One of the prophets of o has risen."
9:19 prophets of o has returned from the dead."

Jn 3: 4 "How can a man be born again once he is o?"
9:21 He is o enough to speak for himself."

Acts 2:17 visions and your *o* men shall dream dreams.
15:18 these things known to him from of *o*.'
Rom 4:19 dead (for he was nearly a hundred years *o*),
6: 6 our *o* self was crucified with him so that
1Cor 5: 7 *o* yeast to make of yourselves fresh dough,
5: 8 celebrate the feast not with the *o* yeast,
2Cor 3:14 when the *o* covenant is read the veil
5:17 The *o* order has passed away;
Eph 4:22 the *o* self which deteriorates through illusion
Col 3: 9 What you have done is put aside your *o*
1Tm 4: 7 to do with profane myths or *o* wives' tales.
Heb 1:10 "Lord, of *o* you established the earth,
1:11 all of them will grow *o* like a garment.
7:20 *o* covenant became priests without an oath,
7:23 Under the *o* covenant there were many
8: 6 *O* and New Covenant If that first covenant
8:13 and has grown *o* is close to disappearing.
11: 2 of faith the men of *o* were approved by God.
2Pt 3: 5 that of *o* there were heavens and an earth
1Jn 2: 7 but an *o* one which you had from the start.
2: 7 The commandment, now *o*,

OLDEN (2)

2Sm 13:18 is how maiden princesses dressed in *o* days.
Jb 20: 4 Do you not know this from *o* time,

OLDER (21)

Gn 19:31 The *o* one said to the younger:
19:33 the *o* one went in and lay with her father;
19:34 Next day the *o* one said to the younger:
19:37 The *o* one gave birth to a son whom she
25:23 other, and the *o* shall serve the younger."
27: 1 he called his *o* son Esau and said to him,
27:15 her *o* son Esau that she had in the house,
27:42 news of what her *o* son Esau had in mind,
29:16 the *o* was called Leah,
29:26 off a younger daughter before an *o* one.
1Sm 18:17 said to David, "There is my *o* daughter,
2Chr 22: 1 since all the *o* sons had been slain by the
Jb 32: 4 But since these men were *o* than he,
Sir 32: 3 Being *o*,
Ez 16:61 your sisters, those *o* and younger than you,
Jn 21:18 you are *o* you will stretch out your hands,
Rom 9:12 to her, "The *o* shall serve the younger."
1Tm 5: 1 Never censure an *o* man,
5: 2 men as brothers, *o* women as mothers,
Ti 2: 2 Tell the *o* men that they must be temperate,
2: 3 the *o* women must behave in ways that befit

OLDEST (7)

Gn 10:21 Japheth's *o* brother and the ancestor of
43:33 to their age, from the *o* to the youngest,
44:12 with the *o* and ending with the youngest,
1Sm 17:13 *o* sons of Jesse had followed Saul to war;
17:14 While the three *o* had joined Saul.
17:28 When Eliab, his *o* brother,
1Mc 16: 2 Simon called his two *o* sons,

OLEASTERS (1)

Neh 8:15 and bring in branches of olive trees, *o*,

OLIVE (51)

Gn 8:11 there in its bill was a plucked-off *o* leaf!
Ex 23:11 regard to your vineyard and your *o* grove.
30:24 together with a hin of *o* oil;
Dt 6:11 and *o* groves that you did not plant;
8: 8 of *o* trees and of honey
24:20 you knock down the fruit of your *o* trees,
28:40 you have *o* trees throughout your country,
32:13 from its rocks and *o* oil from its hard,
33:24 the oil of his *o* trees runs over his feet!
Jos 24:13 and *o* groves which you did not plant.
Jgs 9: 8 So they said to the *o* tree,
9: 9 But the *o* tree answered them,
15: 5 and the vineyards and *o* orchards as well.
1Sm 8:14 of your fields, vineyards, and *o* groves,
1Kgs 6:23 each ten cubits high, made of *o* wood.
6:31 the sanctuary, doors of *o* wood were made;
6:32 The two doors were of *o* wood,
6:33 the doorposts of *o* wood were rectangular.
2Kgs 5:26 to take garments, *o* orchards or vineyards,
1Chr 27:28 Over the *o* trees and sycamores of the
Neh 5:11 fields, their vineyards, their *o* groves,
8:15 country and bring in branches of *o* trees,
9:25 cisterns already dug, vineyards, *o* groves,
Tb 1: 7 would give the tithe of grain, wine, *o* oil,
Jdt 15:13 themselves with garlands of *o* leaves.
2Mc 14: 4 the customary *o* branches from the temple.
Jb 15:33 and like an *o* tree casting off its bloom.
Ps(s) 52:10 I, like a green *o* tree in the house of God,
128: 3 children like *o* plants around your table.
Sir 24:14 Jericho, Like a fair *o* tree in the field,
50:10 Like a luxuriant *o* tree thick with fruit,
Is 17: 6 As when an *o* tree has been beaten,
24:13 As with an *o* tree after it is beaten,
41:19 desert the cedar, acacia, myrtle, and *o*;
Jer 11:16 A spreading *o* tree,
Hos 14: 7 His splendor shall be like the *o* tree and
Am 4: 9 fig trees and *o* trees the locust devoured;
Mi 6:15 shall sow, yet not reap, tread out the *o*,
Hb 3:17 Though the yield of the *o* fail and the
Hg 2:19 the pomegranate and the *o* tree yet borne.
Zec 4: 3 their tubes, and beside it are two *o* trees,
4:11 two *o* trees at each side of the lampstand?"
4:12 "What are the two *o* tufts which freely
Rom 11:17 off and you, a branch of the wild *o* tree,
11:17 come to share in the rich root of the *o*,
11:24 were cut off from the natural wild *o* and,
11:24 were grafted into the cultivated *o*,
11:24 by nature be grafted into their own *o* tree.
Rv 6: 6 But spare the *o* oil and the wine!"
11: 4 These are the two *o* trees and the two
18:13 wine and *o* oil,

OLIVES (22)

Ex 27:20 to bring you clear oil of crushed *o*,
29:40 a fourth of a hin of oil of crushed *o* and,
Lv 24: 2 you clear oil of crushed *o* for the light,
Nm 28: 5 with a fourth of a hin of oil of crushed *o*.
Dt 28:40 ointment, for your *o* will drop off unripe.
2Sm 15:17 opposite the ascent of the Mount of *O*,
15:23 on ahead of him by way of the Mount of *O*,
15:30 As David went up the Mount of *O*,
2Kgs 18:32 and wine, of bread and orchards, of *o*,
Is 17: 6 Two or three *o* remain at the very top,
Zec 14: 4 his feet shall rest upon the Mount of *O*,
14: 4 The Mount of *O* shall be cleft in two from
Mt 21: 1 entering Bethphage on the Mount of *O*,
24: 3 While he was seated on the Mount of *O*,
26:30 praise, they walked out to the Mount of *o*.
Mk 11: 1 Bethphage and Bethany on the Mount of *O*,
13: 3 seated on the Mount of *O* facing the temple,
14:26 praise, they walked out to the Mount of *O*.
Lk 21:37 city to spend the night on the Mount of *O*.
22:39 way, as was his custom, to the Mount of *O*;
Jn 8: 1 while Jesus went out to the Mount of *O*.
Jas 3:12 A fig tree, brothers, cannot produce *o*,

OLIVET (3)

Lk 19:29 and Bethany on the mount called *O*,
19:37 his approach to the descent from Mount *O*,
Acts 1:12 from the mount called *O* near Jerusalem

OLYMPAS (1)

Rom 16:15 and Julia, to Nereus and his sister, to *O*,

OLYMPIAN (1)

2Mc 6: 2 in Jerusalem and dedicate it to *O* Zeus,

OMAR (3)

Gn 36:11 The sons of Eliphaz were Teman, *O*,
36:15 the clans of Teman, *O*,
1Chr 1:36 The sons of Eliphaz were Teman, *O*,

OMEGA (3)

Rv 1: 8 Lord God says, "I am the Alpha and the *O*,
21: 6 I am the Alpha and the *O*,
22:13 I am the Alpha and the *O*,

OMEN (4)

Nm 23:23 against Jacob, nor *o* against Israel.
1Kgs 20:33 is my brother," Hearing this as a good *o*,
2Mc 5: 4 prayed that this vision might be a good *o*.
Zec 3: 8 who sit before you are men of good *o*.

OMENS (4)

Nm 24: 1 did not go aside as before to seek *o*,
Sir 34: 5 Divination, *o* and dreams all are unreal;
Is 44:25 It is I who bring to nought the *o* of liars,
Lk 21:11 and in the sky fearful *o* and great signs.

OMER (4)

Ex 16:16 has enough to eat, an *o* for each person,
16:18 But when they measured it out by the *o*,
16:33 "Take an urn and put an *o* of manna in it.
16:36 [An *o* is one tenth of an ephah.]

OMERFUL (1)

Ex 16:32 Keep an *o* of manna for your descendants,

OMERS (1)

Ex 16:22 twice as much food, two *o* for each person.

OMIT (3)

Est 6:10 Do not *o* anything you proposed."
2Mc 2:31 and to *o* detailed treatment of the matter.
Jer 26: 2 I command you, tell them, and *o* nothing.

OMITTING (1)

Lk 11:42 you should practice, without *o* the others.

OMRI (17)

1Kgs 16:16 day in the camp all Israel proclaimed *O*,
16:17 *O* marched up from Gibbethon,
16:21 Ginath, to make him king, and half for *O*.
16:22 of *O* prevailed over those of Tibni,
16:22 Tibni died and *O* became king.
16:23 year of Asa, king of Judah, *O* became king;
16:25 But *O* did evil in the LORD's sight beyond
16:27 The rest of the acts of *O*,
16:28 *O* rested with his ancestors;
16:29 year of Asa, king of Judah, Ahab son of *O*,
16:30 Ahab, son of *O*,
2Kgs 8:26 she was daughter of *O*,
1Chr 7: 8 were Zemirah, Joash, Eliezer, Elioenai, *O*,
9: 4 was Uthai, son of Ammihud, son of *O*,
27:18 for Issachar, *O*,
2Chr 22: 2 mother was named Athaliah, daughter of
Mi 6:16 You have kept the decrees of *O*,

ONAM (4)

Gn 36:23 were Alvan, Mahanath, Ebal, Shepho, and *O*.
1Chr 1:40 were Alian, Manahath, Ebal, Shephi, and *O*.
2:26 Atarah by name, who was the mother of *O*.
2:28 The sons of *O* were Shammai and Jada.

ONAN (7)

Gn 38: 4 conceived and bore a son, whom she named *O*
38: 8 Then Judah said to *O*,
38: 9 *O*, however, knew that the descendants
46:12 Er, *O*, Shelah, Perez, and Zerah—but Er
Nm 26:19 died in the land of Canaan were Er and *O*.
1Chr 2: 3 Er, *O*, and Shelah;

ONCE (320)

Gn 8:12 days and then released the dove *o* more;
19:17 Get off to the hills at *o*,
25:29 *O*, when Jacob was cooking a stew,
27:43 flee at *o* to my brother Laban in Haran,
29:35 *O* more she conceived and bore a son,
31:10 *O*, in the breeding season,
31:21 *O* he was across the Euphrates,
35:12 The land I *o* gave to Abraham and Isaac I
37: 5 *O* Joseph had a dream,
41:10 *O*, when Pharaoh was angry,
43:20 came down here *o* before to procure food.
44: 4 "Go at *o* after the men!
45: 4 brother Joseph, whom you *o* sold into Egypt.
Ex 8:28 But *o* more Pharaoh became obdurate and
10:17 But now, do forgive me my sin *o* more,
12:31 and Aaron and said, "Leave my people at *o*,
22:20 *o* aliens yourselves in the land of Egypt.
23: 9 *o* aliens yourselves in the land of Egypt.
30:10 *O* a year Aaron shall perform the atonement
30:10 this atonement is to be made *o* a year
32: 7 to Moses, "Go down at *o* to your people,
34: 8 at *o* bowed down to the ground in worship.
Lv 13: 6 and *o* more examine him on the seventh day.
13: 7 he shall *o* more show himself to the priest.
14:43 "If the infection breaks out *o* more after
16:34 *o* a year atonement shall be made for all
18: 3 do in the land of Egypt, where you *o* lived,
19:34 you too were *o* aliens in the land of Egypt.
Nm 5:27 *O* she has done so,
11:15 please do me the favor of killing me at *o*,
12: 4 So at *o* the LORD said to Moses and Aaron
16:21 this band, that I may consume them at *o*."
17:10 community, that I may consume them at *o*."
18:30 *O* you have made your contribution from the
24:11 Be off at *o*, then, to your home.
32:19 heritage with them *o* we cross the Jordan,
Dt 2:23 who *o* dwelt in villages as far as Gaza,
3:13 Bashan was *o* called a land of the Rephaim.
5:15 that you too were *o* slaves in Egypt,
6:21 son, 'We were *o* slaves of Pharaoh in Egypt,
7:22 You cannot exterminate them all at *o*,
9:19 Yet *o* again the LORD listened to me.
10:10 and the LORD had *o* again heard me and
10:19 *o* aliens yourselves in the land of Egypt.
12:29 *o* they have been wiped out before you and
15:15 you too were *o* slaves in the land of Egypt,
16:12 that you too were *o* slaves in Egypt,
24:18 For, remember, you were *o* slaves in Egypt,
24:22 remember that you were *o* slaves in Egypt;
28:63 "Just as the LORD *o* took delight in
30: 5 the land which your fathers *o* occupied,
Jos 2: 7 fords of the Jordan, and *o* they had left,
6: 3 circle the city, marching *o* around it.
6:11 LORD circle the city, going *o* around it,
6:14 around the city *o* before returning to camp;
10:20 *O* Joshua and the Israelites had finally
13:31 Edrei, *o* the royal cities of Og in Bashan,
14:12 *O* they had taken possession of Leshem,
20: 6 *O* he has stood judgment before the
21:43 *O* they had conquered and occupied it,
22: 3 now you have not *o* abandoned your kinsmen,
24:11 *O* you crossed the Jordan and came to
Jgs 2:10 But *o* the rest of that generation were
6:39 not be angry with me if I speak *o* more.
9: 8 *O* the trees went to anoint a king over
9:28 Zebul *o* subject to the men of Hamor,
16: 1 *O* Samson went to Gaza,
16:28 myself *o* and for all on the Philistines."
20:25 *o* again the Benjaminites who came out of
Ru 1: 1 *O* in the time of the judges there was a
4: 5 *O* you acquire the field from Naomi,
1Sm 1:22 to her husband, *O* the child is weaned,
1:24 *O* he was weaned,
3:13 I am condemning his family *o* and for all,

ONCE (cont.)

23:22 Go now and make sure *o* more!
2Sm 2:22 *O* more Abner said to Asahel:
11:27 But *o* the mourning was over,
17:21 Cross the water at *o*,
1Kgs 10:22 *O* every three years the fleet of Tarshish
15:29 *O* he was king,
16:11 *O* he was seated on the royal throne,
22: 5 Israel, "Seek the word of the LORD at *o*."
22: 9 to him, "Get Micaiah, son of Imlah, at *o*."
2Kgs 2:19 *O* the inhabitants of the city complained
4:35 and then *o* more lay down upon the boy,
4:38 *O*, when the guild prophets were seated
6: 1 The guild prophets *o* said to Elisha:
8: 1 Elisha *o* said to the woman whose son he
9:13 At *o* each took his garment,
13:21 *O* some people were burying a man,
1Chr 14:13 *O* again the Philistines raided the valley;
20: 5 *O* again there was war with the Philistines,
21:28 *O* David saw that the LORD had heard him on
2Chr 9:21 *O* every three years the fleet of Tarshish
18: 4 Israel, "Seek the word of the LORD at *o*."
18: 8 he said, "Get Micaiah, son of Imlah, at *o*."
Ezr 4:20 Powerful kings were *o* in Jerusalem who
Neh 2:15 till I *o* more reached the Valley Gate,
13:12 *o* more brought in the tithes of grain,
13:18 Israel by *o* more profaning the sabbath?"
13:20 the night *o* or twice outside Jerusalem,
Tb 2: 8 *O* before he was hunted down for execution
Jdt 13:11 *O* more he has made manifest his strength
1Mc 1:10 son of King Antiochus, *o* a hostage at Rome.
2:35 Then the enemy attacked them at *o*;
3:30 feared that, as had happened more than *o*,
5:12 Come at *o* and rescue us from them,
7:35 and his army are not delivered to me at *o*,
2Mc 5: 7 and *o* again took refuge in the country of
5:20 *o* the great Sovereign became reconciled.
6:23 to send him at *o* to the abode of the dead,
7:10 put out his tongue at *o* when told to do so,
8: 5 *O* Maccabeus got his men organized,
14:16 they set out at *o* and came upon the enemy
Jb 2: 1 *O* again the sons of God came to present
6:17 snow heaped upon them, Yet *o* they flow,
8:21 *O* more will he fill your mouth with
9: 3 could not answer him *o* in a thousand times.
14:20 *o* for all against him and he passes on;
18:19 people, nor any survivor where *o* he dwelt.
23: 7 I should *o* and for all preserve my rights.
29:22 *O* I spoke,
33:14 For God does speak, perhaps *o*,
33:21 cannot be seen, and his bones, *o* invisible,
40: 5 Though I have spoken *o*,
40:32 *O* you but lay a hand upon him,
Ps(s) 30: 7 *O*, in my security,
31:23 *O* I said in my anguish,
41: 5 *O* I said, "O LORD, have pity on me;
48: 6 They also see, and at *o* are stunned,
71:20 of the earth you will *o* more raise me.
80:15 *O* again, O LORD of hosts,
89:20 *O* you spoke in a vision,
89:36 *O*, by my holiness,
Prv 3:28 I will give," when you can give at *o*.
20:14 but *o* he has gone his way,
20:25 trap for a man, or to regret a vow *o* made.
23:35 When shall I awake to seek wine *o* again?"
Eccl 12: 7 the dust returns to the earth as it *o* was,
Wis 5: 3 "This is he whom *o* we held as a
5:13 Even so we, *o* born,
11: 8 *o* you had shown by the thirst they then
12: 9 or wiped out at *o* by terrible beasts or by
16:14 he bring back the soul *o* it is confined.
18: 5 them perish all at *o* in the mighty water.
Sir 21: 5 from a poor man's lips is heard at *o*,
31:21 too much, *o* you have emptied your stomach,
32: 7 when they have asked you more than *o*;
38:23 rally your courage, *o* the soul has left.
39:12 *O* more I will set forth my theme to shine
40:14 the stones, but suddenly, *o* and for all,
50:14 *O* he had completed the services at the
Is 28: 4 man sees it, he picks and swallows it at *o*.
38:10 *O* I said, "In the noontime of life
48:13 When I call them, they stand forth at *o*.
60:15 *O* you were forsaken,
65: 7 I will at *o* pour out in full measure their
Jer 16:18 I will at *o* repay them double for their
31:28 As I *o* watched over them to uproot and
34:16 you forced them *o* more into slavery.
37:17 *O* King Zedekiah had him brought to his
38:14 *O* King Zedekiah summoned the prophet
41: 7 When they were *o* inside the city,
42: 2 We are now few who *o* were many,
50:18 land, as *o* I punished the king of Assyria;
Lam 1: 1 How lonely she is now, the *o* crowded city!
Bar 4:37 Here come your sons whom you *o* let go,
Ez 26:17 *O* she was mighty on the sea,
40: 3 all at *o* I saw a man whose appearance was
42:14 When the priests have *o* entered,
47: 4 and *o* more had me wade through the water,
47: 5 *O* more he measured off a thousand,
Dn 2:35 silver, and gold all crumbled at *o*,
4:23 *o* you have learned it is heaven that rules.
4:30 At *o* this was fulfilled.
11:30 who forsake it he shall *o* more single out.
14:39 *o* brought Habakkuk back to his own place.
Hos 7: 4 *o* the dough is kneaded until it has risen.
Mt 2:16 *O* Herod realized that he had been deceived
8:15 She got up at *o* and began to wait on him.
9: 2 There the people at *o* brought to him a
9:33 *O* the demon was expelled the mute began to
10:14 *o* outside it shake its dust from your feet.
12: 1 *O* on a sabbath Jesus walked through the
13: 5 sprouted at *o* since the soil had no depth,
14:31 at *o* stretched out his hand and caught him.
14:32 *O* they had climbed into the boat,
21: 3 Then he will let them go at *o*."
22: 1 to address them, *o* more using parables.
22:25 *O* there were seven brothers.
23:15 but *o* he is converted you make a devil of
26:43 *O* more, on his return,
27:50 *O* again Jesus cried out in a loud voice,
Mk 4:32 of all the earth's seeds, yet *o* it is sown,
5:30 *o* that healing power had gone out from him.
6:25 "I want you to give me, at *o*,
7:35 At *o*, the man's ears were opened;
9:33 to Capernaum and Jesus, *o* inside the house,
10: 1 *O* more crowds gathered around him,
10:32 Taking the Twelve aside *o* more,
11: 3 it but he will send it back here at *o*.'"
11:27 They returned *o* more to Jerusalem.
12: 1 began to address them *o* more in parables:
13:28 *O* the sap of its branches runs high and it
14:40 *O* again he found them asleep on his return.
14:61 *O* again the high priest interrogated him:
14:70 *O* again he denied it.
14:70 later the bystanders said to Peter *o* more,
Lk 1: 8 *O*, when it was the turn of Zechariah's
2:17 *o* they saw,
5:25 At *o* the man stood erect before them.
6: 1 *O* on a sabbath Jesus was walking through
8:51 *O* he had arrived at the house,
13:25 When *o* the master of the house has risen
15: 6 *O* arrived home,
16:19 *O* there was a rich man who dressed in
17:20 *O*, on being asked by the Pharisees when
18: 2 *O* there was a judge in a certain city who
22:66 *O* they had brought him before their council,
23:16 release him, *o* I have taught him a lesson."
Jn 3: 4 "How can a man be born again *o* he is old?"
4:46 He went to Cana in Galilee *o* more,
5: 7 the pool *o* the water has been stirred up.
6:24 *O* the crowd saw that neither Jesus nor his
7:10 *o* his brothers had gone up to the festival
8:12 Jesus spoke to them *o* again.
9:27 "I have told you *o*
10:19 the Jews were sharply divided *o* more.
11:38 *O* again troubled in spirit,
12:32 out, and I *o* I am lifted up from earth
13:12 cloak back on and reclined at table *o* more.
13:17 *O* you know all these things,
13:31 *O* Judas had left, Jesus said:
13:33 I say to you now what I *o* said to the Jews:
20:26 the disciples were *o* more in the room,
21: 1 showed himself to the disciples *o* again].
Acts 3: 1 *O*, when Peter and John were going up to
8:12 but *o* they began to believe in the good
9:11 said to him, "Go at *o* to Straight Street,
9:32 *O* when Peter was making numerous journeys,
9:34 The man got up at *o*.
11:26 *o* he had found him,
12:23 angel of the Lord struck Herod down at *o*
13:11 At *o* a misty darkness came over him,
13:17 of the people Israel *o* chose our fathers.
13:29 *O* they had thus brought about all that had
16:13 *O*, on the sabbath,
16:40 *O* outside the prison,
19:13 Some itinerant Jewish exorcists *o* tried to
19:21 *O* I have been there,"
22:16 Be baptized at *o* and wash away your sins
22:18 'Leave Jerusalem at *o* because they will
23:30 life, I decided at *o* to send him to you.
26: 9 I *o* thought it my duty to oppose the name
28: 1 *O* on shore,
Rom 4:18 many nations, just as it was *o* told him,
6: 9 know that Christ, *o* raised from the dead,
6:10 His death was death to sin, *o* for all;
6:17 be to God, though *o* you were slaves of sin,
8:20 own accord but by him who *o* subjected it;
11:30 Just as you were *o* disobedient to God and
15:12 *O* more, Isaiah says, "The root of Jesse
1Cor 15: 6 he was seen by five hundred brothers at *o*,
2Cor 7: 8 you grief for a time), I am happy *o* again;
10: 6 else *o* your own obedience is perfect.
11:25 I was stoned *o*,
Gal 3:15 or set it aside *o* it is legally validated.
4: 9 seem willing to enslave yourselves *o* more?
5: 3 I point out *o* more to all who receive
Eph 2: 3 All of us were *o* of their company;
2:13 But now in Christ Jesus you who *o* were far
Phil 1:26 My being with you *o* again should make you
4:10 that your concern for me bore fruit *o* more.
4:16 something for my needs, not *o* but twice.
Col 1:21 You yourselves were *o* alienated from him;
3: 7 Your own conduct was *o* of this sort,
4:16 *O* this letter has been read to you,
1Thes 2:18 I, Paul, tried more than *o*—
4: 6 as we *o* indicated to you by our testimony.
1Tm 1:13 I was *o* a blasphemer,
3: 2 must be irreproachable, married only *o*,
3: 6 the punishment *o* meted out to the devil.
3:12 Deacons may be married but *o* and must be
5: 9 She must have been married only *o*.
Ti 1: 6 must be irreproachable, married only *o*,
3: 3 We ourselves were *o* foolish,
3:10 Warn a heretic *o* and then a second time;
Heb 4: 7 because of unbelief, God *o* more set a day,
6: 4 For when men have *o* been enlightened and
7:27 did that *o* for all when he offered himself.
9: 7 into the inner one, and that but *o* a year,
9:11 he entered *o* for all into the sanctuary,
9:26 take away sins *o* for all by his sacrifice.
9:27 Just as it is appointed that men die *o*,
9:28 offered up *o* to take away the sins of many;
10: 2 them, for the worshipers, *o* cleansed,
10:10 of the body of Jesus Christ *o* for all.
10:18 *O* these have been forgiven,
12:26 *o* more shake not only earth but heaven!"
12:27 And that *o* more" shows that shaken,
Jas 1:12 *O* he has been proved,
1:15 *O* passion has conceived,
1Pt 1:14 that *o* shaped you in your ignorance.
2:10 *O* you were no people,
2:10 *o* there was no mercy for you,
3:18 reason why Christ died for sins *o* for all,
2Pt 2:20 caught up and overcome in pollution *o* more,
2:21 law handed on to them, *o* they had known it.
Jude 1: 3 faith delivered *o* for all to the saints.
Rv 1:18 *O* I was dead but now I live
2: 8 who *o* died but now lives has this to say:
3:18 on your eyes, if you would see *o* more.
4: 2 At *o* I was caught up in ecstasy.
17: 8 you saw existed *o* but now exists no longer.
17: 8 abyss *o* more before going to final ruin.
17: 8 for it existed *o* and now exists no longer,
17:11 which existed *o* but now exists no longer,
18: 8 Therefore her plagues will come all at *o*,
19: 3 *O* more they sang "Alleluia!"
22: 2 fruit twelve times a year, *o* each month;

ONES (216)

Gn 30:42 go to Laban, but the sturdy *o* to Jacob.
42:25 grain, their money replaced in each *o* sack,
42:35 there in each *o* sack was his moneybag!
44: 2 youngest *o* bag put also my silver goblet,
44:20 This *o* full brother is dead,
49:24 But each *o* bow remained stiff,
Ex 6:27 These are the *o* who spoke to Pharaoh,
10:10 "if I ever let your little *o* go with you!
10:24 Your little *o*, too, may go with you.
10:26 shall not know which *o* we must sacrifice
Lv 11: 2 land animals these are the *o* you may eat:
27:33 whether good *o* or bad ones are thus chosen,
Nm 14: 3 wives and little *o* will be taken as booty.
14:31 Your little *o*,
16:27 with their wives and sons and little *o*,
25: 4 execution of the guilty *o* before the LORD,
31: 9 Midianites with their little *o* as captives,
31:16 they are the very *o* who on Balaam's advice
Dt 1:39 Your little *o*,
33: 3 But all his holy *o* were in his hand;
Jgs 11: 7 "Are you not the *o* who hated me and drove
18:21 to depart, they placed their little *o*,
1Sm 2: 9 guard the footsteps of his faithful *o*,
2Sm 7: 9 you famous like the great *o* of the earth.
1Chr 16:13 his servants, sons of Jacob, his chosen *o*!
2Chr 6:41 may your faithful *o* rejoice in good things.
20:13 before the LORD, with their little *o*,
31:18 in the family records, for their little *o*,
Tb 8:15 Let all your chosen *o* praise you;
10:12 as the *o* who brought you into the world.
Jdt 7:27 and not have to behold our little *o* dying
16:11 When my lowly *o* shouted,
2Mc 5: 6 *o* own kindred was the greatest failure,
9:12 God, and not to think *o* mortal self divine."
Jb 5: 1 To which of the holy *o* will you appeal?
38:41 ravens when their young *o* cry out to God,
39:30 His young *o* greedily drink blood;
42:12 latter days of Job more than his earlier *o*.
Ps(s) 16: 3 me cherish the holy *o* who are in his land!
17:14 bequeath their abundance to their little *o*.
30: 5 praise to the LORD, you his faithful *o*,
31:24 Love the LORD, all you his faithful *o*!
34:10 Fear the LORD, you his holy *o*,
37:28 is right, and forsakes not his faithful *o*.
49: 9 Too high is the price to redeem *o* life;
50: 5 "Gather my faithful *o* before me,
52:11 of your name before your faithful *o*.
60: 7 of bowshot That your loved *o* may escape;
69:33 "See you lowly *o*,
72: 2 justice and your afflicted *o* with judgment.
74:19 unmindful of the lives of your afflicted *o*.
76: 6 the hands of all the mighty *o* have failed.
79: 2 your faithful *o* to the beasts of the earth.
85: 9 peace To his people, and to his faithful *o*.
89: 6 in the assembly of the holy *o*.
89: 8 is terrible in the council of the holy *o*;
89:20 a vision, and to your faithful *o* you said:
94: 8 you senseless *o* among the people;
97:10 he guards the lives of his faithful *o*;

105: 6 his servants, sons of Jacob, his chosen o!
105:43 with shouts of joy, his chosen o.
106: 5 I may see the prosperity of your chosen o,
108: 7 That your loved o may escape,
116: 6 The LORD keeps the little o;
116:15 of the LORD is the death of his faithful o.
127: 4 hand of a warrior are the sons of o youth.
132: 9 let your faithful o shout merrily for joy.
132:16 her faithful o shall shout merrily for joy.
137: 9 and smash your little o against the rock!
145:10 O LORD, and let your faithful o bless you.
148:14 this his praise from all his faithful o,
Prv 1:22 "How long, you simple o,
2: 8 justice, protecting the way of his pious o.
7: 7 And I saw among the simple o,
8: 5 You simple o,
13: 3 to open wide o lips brings downfall.
14:26 even for o children he will be a refuge.
18: 8 morsels that sink into o inmost being.
26:22 morsels that sink into o inmost being.
Sg 1: 8 the young o near the shepherds' camps.
Wis 3: 9 grace and mercy are with his holy o,
10:17 the holy o the recompense of their labors,
11:12 the remembrance of the o who had departed.
17:13 more o expectation is of itself uncertain,
18: 1 But your holy o had very great light;
18: 5 to put to death the infants of the holy o,
18: 9 That your holy o should share alike the
Sir 20: 2 better to admonish than to lose o temper,
25:13 of all sufferings is that from o foes,
25:13 of all vengeance is that of o enemies:
27:14 on end, their brawls make one stop o ears.
29:22 man's fare under the shadow of o own roof
30:24 Envy and anger shorten o life,
31: 2 Concern for o livelihood banishes slumber;
38:19 extremity and heartache destroy o health.
40:18 A child or a city will preserve o name,
40:25 Gold and silver make o way secure,
42:17 Yet even God's holy o must fail in
46: 1 the great savior of God's chosen o,
Is 1:27 judgment, and her repentant o by justice.
5: 9 houses shall be in ruins, large o and fine,
10:16 hosts, will send among his fat o leanness,
10:33 are felled, and the lofty o brought low;
32:10 a year you overconfident o will be shaken;
42: 9 have come to pass, new o I now foretell;
65: 9 My chosen o shall inherit the land,
65:15 Shall be used by my chosen o for cursing;
65:22 and my chosen o shall long enjoy the
Jer 5: 5 will go to the great o and speak with them;
24: 3 ones are very good, but the bad o very bad,
Lam 1: 2 not one to console her of all her dear o;
1: 5 Her little o have gone away,
1:15 o in my midst the LORD has cast away;
2:19 to him for the lives of your little o
Bar 6:15 useless as o broken tools are their gods,
Ez 6: 4 cast down your slain o before your idols;
30:13 I will put an end to the great o of
36:12 are the o whom I will have walk upon you;
Dn 4:14 is this decided, by order of the holy o,
7:18 But the holy o of the Most High shall
7:21 that horn made war against the holy o
7:22 in favor of the holy o of the Most High,
7:22 came when the holy o possessed the kingdom.
7:25 and oppress the holy o of the Most High,
8:25 his cunning shall be against the holy o,
Hos 14: 1 their little o shall be dashed to pieces,
Na 3:10 even her little o were dashed to pieces at
Zec 6: 6 o went toward the land of the south.
11:16 of the fat o and tear off their hoofs!
13: 6 I was wounded in the house of my dear o."
13: 7 I will turn my hand against the little o.
14: 5 shall come, and all his holy o with him.
Mal 2:16 And covering o garment with injustice,
Mt 10:42 cup of cold water to one of these lowly o
12:27 Let them be the o to judge you.
12:41 generation and be the o to condemn it.
18: 6 one of these little o who believe in me,
18:10 you never despise one of these little o.
18:14 of these little o shall ever come to grief.
19:18 "Which o?"
20:25 their great o make their importance felt.
22:16 You court no o favor and do not act out of
23:35 all the blood of the just o shed on earth,
25: 3 The foolish o,
25: 4 but the sensible o took flasks of oil as
25: 8 The foolish o said to the sensible,
25: 9 But the sensible o replied,
25:10 and the o who were ready went in to the
25:45 neglected to do it to one of these least o,
Mk 4:15 Those on the path are the o to whom,
4:20 good soil are the o who listen to the word,
10:42 their great o make their importance felt.
Lk 1:70 promised through the mouths of his holy o,
8:13 Those on the rocky ground are the o who,
12:18 pull down my grain bins and build larger o.
17: 2 giving scandal to one of these little o.
20:27 Some Sadducees came forward (the o who
22:28 You are the o who have stood loyally by me
Jn 6:64 of course, the o who refused to believe,
15: 2 o he trims clean to increase their yield.
15:13 to lay down o life for one's friends.
Acts 2:45 everything on the basis of each o need.
6: 1 the o who spoke Greek complained that
24:19 province of Asia are the o who found me.
Rom 8:33 bring a charge against God's chosen o?
12: 6 O gift may be prophecy;
14:23 does not accord with o belief is sinful.
1Cor 3:12 o build on this foundation with gold,
4:10 We are the weak o, you the strong!
9: 8 I am giving you are merely human o,
14:30 the first o should then keep quiet.
14:36 Are you the only o to whom it has come?
2Cor 1: 1 holy o of the church who live in Achaia.
2: 2 make me happy again but the o I grieved?
8:12 to give should accord with o means,
10: 2 o who accuse us of weak human behavior.
12:11 the o who should have been commending me.
12:19 done everything to build you up, my dear o.
13:12 All the holy o send greetings to you.
Gal 3:18 if o inheritance comes through the law,
6:13 The very o who accept circumcision do not
Eph 1: 1 Jesus Christ, to the holy o [at Ephesus],
3:18 able to grasp fully, with all the holy o,
Phil 1: 1 Jesus, to all the holy o at Philippi,
1:18 whether from specious motives or genuine o,
4: 1 my joy and my crown, continue, my dear o,
Col 1: 2 our brother, to the holy o at Colossae,
1:26 past but now revealed to his holy o.
3:12 Because you are God's chosen o,
4:11 These are the only circumcised o among
1Thes 2: 7 any nursing mother fondling her little o.
3:13 of our Lord Jesus with all his holy o.
2Thes 1:10 holy o and adored by all who have believed
1Tm 5:14 I should like to see the younger o marry,
5:20 The o who do commit sin,
5:25 inconspicuous o cannot be hidden forever.
Jas 2: 6 They are the o who hale you into the
4: 4 O you unfaithful o,
1Pt 2:18 reasonable o but even those who are harsh.
3:17 to do so for good deeds than for evil o.
1Jn 2: 1 My little o,
2:12 Little o, I address you,
2:28 Remain in him now, little o,
3: 7 Little o, let no one deceive you;
4: 4 You are of God, you little o,
Jude 1:14 o about him to pass judgment on all men,
Rv 7:14 "These are the o who have survived the
8: 3 with the prayers of all God's holy o.
11:18 the prophets and the holy o who revere you,
14:12 This is what sustains the holy o
17: 6 was drunk with the blood of God's holy o
17:14 the o who were called:
22:11 virtue and the holy o in their holiness!

ONESELF (1)

Jas 1:27 keeping o unspotted by the world

ONESIMUS (2)

Col 4: 6 With him is O, our dear and faithful
Phlm 1:11 He has become in truth O [Useful],

ONESIPHORUS (2)

2Tm 1:16 the Lord have mercy on the family of O,
2Tm 4:19 Prisca and Aquila and the family of O.

ONIAS (19)

1Mc 12: 7 was sent to the high priest O from Arius,
12: 8 O welcomed the envoy with honor and
12:19 is a copy of the letter that was sent to O:
12:20 sends greetings to O the high priest.
2Mc 3: 1 the high priest O and his hatred of evil,
3: 5 Since he could not prevail against O,
3:31 begged O to invoke the Most High,
3:33 "Be very grateful to the high priest O,"
3:35 had spared his life, he bade O farewell,
4: 1 false accusation that it was O who threatened
4: 4 O saw that the opposition was serious and
4: 7 O' brother Jason obtained the high
4:33 When O had clear evidence of the facts,
4:34 privately and asked him to lay hands on O.
4:34 So Andronicus went to O,
4:36 went to see him about the murder of O.
4:38 he had committed the outrage against O;
15:12 O, the former high priest,
15:14 O then said of him,

ONION (1)

2Kgs 6:25 a kab of wild o for five pieces of silver.

ONIONS (1)

Nm 11: 5 cucumbers, the melons, the leeks, the o,

ONLOOKERS (3)

Jb 20: 7 like the fuel of his fire, and the o say,
Dn 13:33 All her relatives and the o were weeping.
Acts 7:57 The o were shouting aloud,

ONLY (555)

Gn 3: 3 it is o about the fruit of the tree in the
6: 7 men whom I have created, and not o the men,
7:23 O Noah and those with him in the ark were
9: 4 O flesh with its lifeblood still in it you
18:29 saying, "What if o forty are found there?"
18:30 What if o thirty are found there?"
19:20 It's o a small place.
20:12 my sister, but o my father's daughter,
22: 2 "Take your son Isaac, your o one,
23:13 "Ah, if o you would please listen to me!
24:44 she answers, Not o may you have a drink,
27:38 his father, "Have you o that one blessing,
29: 3 O when all the shepherds were assembled
29: 8 o then can we water the flocks."
30:32 O such animals shall be my wages.
30:43 and he came to own, not o large flocks,
31:15 He not o sold us;
34:12 o give me the maiden in marriage."
34:15 We will agree with you o on this condition,
34:22 kindred people with us o on this condition,
41: 7 Pharaoh woke up, to find it was o a dream.
41:40 O in respect to the throne shall I outrank
42: 4 It was o Joseph's full brother Benjamin
42:19 o one of your brothers need be confined in
42:38 full brother is dead, he is the o one left.
44:10 o the one who is found to have it shall
44:17 O the one in whose possession the goblet
44:20 he is the o one by that mother who is left,
44:26 o if our youngest brother is with us can
45:15 and o then were his brothers able to talk
46: 4 Not o will I go down to Egypt with you;
47:19 o give us seed,
47:22 O the priests' lands Joseph did not take
47:26 O the land of the priests did not pass
50: 8 o their children and their flocks and
Ex 8: 5 and your houses and be left o in the river."
8: 7 o in the river shall they be left."
9:26 O in the land of Goshen,
11: 8 O then will I depart."
12:20 you dwell you may eat o unleavened bread."
13: 7 O unleavened bread may be eaten during the
14:14 you have o to keep still."
18:18 o yourself but also these people with you.
19:13 O when the ram's horn resounds may they go
20:20 o to test you and put his fear upon you,
21:29 or a woman, not o must the ox be stoned,
22:26 his is the o covering he has for his body.
32:32 If you would o forgive their sin!
32:33 "Him o who has sinned against me will I
34:31 O after Moses called to them did Aaron and
40:37 o when it lifted did they go forward.
Lv 10: 6 lest you bring not o death on yourselves
11: 4 that only chew the cud or o have hoofs:
13:28 clean, since it is o the scar of the burn.
13:39 o tetter that has broken out on the skin,
14: 8 o when he is thus made clean may he come
14:19 O after he has offered the sin offering in
14:36 O after this is he to go in to examine the
15:28 days, and o then is she to be purified.
16: 3 O in this way may Aaron enter the sanctuary.
16:26 o then may he enter the camp.
16:28 o then may he enter the camp.
21:23 O, he may not approach the veil nor go up
22: 7 O then may he eat of the sacred offerings
22:27 o from the eighth day onward will it be
Nm 3: 4 Thereafter o Eleazar and Ithamar performed
3:10 But o Aaron and his descendants shall you
4:15 O after Aaron and his sons have finished
5:26 O then shall he have the woman drink the
6:20 O after this may the nazirite drink wine.
8:15 O then shall the Levites enter upon their
8:22 O then did they enter upon their service
9:20 was over the Dwelling o for a few days.
9:21 there o from evening until morning;
10: 4 when one of them is blown, o the princes,
12:14 o then may she be brought back."
14: 3 this land o to have us fall by the sword?
14:38 had gone to reconnoiter the land, o Joshua,
15:26 Not o the whole Israelite community,
15:31 He has o himself to blame."
17:23 had sprouted and put forth not o shoots,
18: 7 But o you and your sons are to have charge
18:23 O the Levites are to perform the service
19: 7 and o afterward may he return to the camp.
20: 5 o to bring us to this wretched place which
20:19 "We want o to go up along the highway.
22:20 yet o on the condition that you do exactly
22:35 but you may say o what I tell you."
22:38 I can speak o what God puts in my mouth."
23:13 you can see o some and not all of them,
25: 9 but o after twenty-four thousand had died.
26:33 but o daughters whose names were Mahlah,
32:16 o to build sheepfolds here for our flocks,
35:15 asylum shall serve not o the Israelites
35:28 O after the death of the high priest may
Dt 2:28 O let me march through,
2:35 Our o booty was the livestock and the loot
3:19 O your wives and children,
4:12 there was o a voice.
12:16 O you shall not partake of the blood,
14: 7 only chew the cud or o have cloven hoofs:
15:23 O, you shall not partake of its blood,
16: 3 you shall eat with it o unleavened bread,
16: 6 o at the place which he chooses as the
17: 6 to death on the testimony of o one witness.
19:15 fact shall be established o on the testimony

ONLY (cont.)
24:16 *o* for his own guilt shall a man be put to
28:62 the stars in the sky, *o* a few will be left,
30:10 if *o* you heed the voice of the LORD,
30:14 you have *o* to carry it out.
31:18 *o* because of all the evil they have done
Jos 6:10 *o* then were they to shout.
6:15 on that day *o* did they march around the
6:17 *O* the harlot Rahab and all who are in the
7: 3 if *o* about two or three thousand go up,
17: 3 Manasseh, had had no sons, but *o* daughters,
17:14 us *o* one lot and one share as our heritage?
Jgs 3: 2 those generations *o* of the Israelites who
7:14 can *o* be the sword of the Israelite Gideon,
9: 5 *O* the youngest son of Jerubbaal,
10:15 *O* save us this day."
11:34 She was an *o* child:
15:13 *o* bind you and deliver you over to them."
1Sm 1:15 was *o* pouring out my troubles to the LORD.
1:23 *O*, may the LORD bring your resolve to
2:15 accept boiled meat from you, *o* raw meat."
9:13 *o* after he blesses the sacrifice will the
13:22 *O* Saul and his son Jonathan had them.
14:43 "I *o* tasted a little honey from the end
15: 9 *o* what was worthless and of no account.
17:29 was *o* talking."
17:33 and fight with him, for you are *o* a youth;
18: 8 David ten thousands, but *o* thousands to me.
19:10 Saul, so that the spear struck *o* the wall,
20:14 *O* this: if I am still alive,
20:39 *o* Jonathan and David knew what was meant.
21: 5 no ordinary bread on hand, *o* holy bread;
2Sm 6:21 not *o* will I make merry before the LORD,
8: 4 preserving *o* enough for a hundred chariots.
15: 4 *o* I could be appointed judge in the land!
15:20 You came *o* yesterday,
17: 3 is the death of *o* one man you are seeking;
19: 1 If *o* I had died instead of you,
19:29 deserved *o* death from my lord the king,
23:10 after Eleazar, but *o* to strip the slain.
1Kgs 8:25 provided *o* that your descendants look to
11:17 Meanwhile, Hadad, who was *o* a boy,
14: 8 his whole heart, doing *o* what pleased me.
17:12 there is *o* a handful of flour in my jar
18:22 "I am the *o* surviving prophet of the LORD,
2Kgs 3:25 Finally *o* Kirhareseth was left behind its
5: 3 "If *o* my master would present himself to
5: 7 see he is *o* looking for a quarrel with me!"
7:10 voice, *o* the horses and asses tethered,
10:23 here with you, but *o* worshipers of Baal."
13:19 Now, you will defeat Aram *o* three times."
17:18 *O* the tribe of Judah was left.
1Chr 2:34 Sheshan, who had no sons, *o* daughters,
7:15 but to Zelophehad *o* daughters were born.
22:13 *O* then shall you succeed,
23:22 Eleazar died leaving no sons, *o* daughters;
24: 2 *o* Eleazar and Ithamar served as priests.
29:14 *o* give you what we have received from you.
29:15 we are *o* your guests,
2Chr 6:16 provided *o* that your descendants look to
10:17 reigned over *o* those Israelites who lived
16:12 not seek the LORD, but *o* the physicians.
18:17 he prophesies no good about me, but *o* evil?"
20:24 they saw *o* corpses fallen on the ground,
21:17 there was left to him *o* one son,
25: 4 but *o* for his own guilt shall a man be put
28:23 they *o* caused further disaster to him and
32: 8 For he has *o* an arm of flesh,
32:12 prostrate yourselves before one altar *o*,
33:23 the contrary, Amon *o* increased his guilt.
Ezr 4:13 thus it can *o* result in harm to the throne.
10:15 *O* Jonathan,
Neh 2:12 Then I set out by night with *o* a few other
4:10 *o* half my able men took a hand in the work,
9: 6 "It is you, O LORD, you are the *o* one;
Tb 3:10 'You had *o* one beloved daughter,
3:15 "I am my father's *o* daughter,
4: 6 works will bring success, not *o* to you,
6:15 I am my father's *o* child.
8:17 you were merciful toward two *o* children.
12: 4 Tobit answered, "It is *o* fair,
Jdt 4: 3 and *o* recently had all the people of Judea
4: 7 defile was *o* wide enough for two abreast.
8:29 Not today *o* is your wisdom made evident,
10: 2 she used *o* on sabbaths and feast days.
11: 7 not *o* do men serve him through you;
Est E: 3 *o* do they seek to do harm to our subjects;
E: 4 Not *o* do they drive out gratitude from
1Mc 5:48 we will *o* march through."
6:25 have acted aggressively not *o* against us,
9: 6 camp, until *o* eight hundred men remained.
9:54 But he *o* began to tear it down.
10:14 *O* in Beth-zur did some remain of those who
10:70 "You are the *o* one who resists us.
11:34 not *o* of the territory of Judea,
11:42 will not *o* do this for you and your nation,
2Mc 1:21 could not find any fire, but *o* muddy water,
1:24 and merciful, the *o* king and benefactor,
2: 1 not *o* that Jeremiah the prophet ordered
2:28 our efforts to giving *o* a summary outline.
2:29 the frescoes has *o* to concern himself
4:35 As a result, not *o* the Jews,
5: 7 end received *o* disgrace for his treachery,
6:30 I am not *o* enduring terrible pain in my
6:31 *o* for the young but for the whole nation.
7:17 *O* wait, and you will see how his great
8:18 mere nod destroy not *o* those who attack us,
8:20 when *o* eight thousand Jews fought along
9:15 but fit *o* to be thrown out with their
10:28 not *o* their valor but also their reliance
11: 9 that they were ready to assault not *o* men,
11:12 himself escaped *o* by shameful flight.
Jb 1:12 *o* do not lay a hand upon his person."
2: 6 "He is in your power; *o* spare his life."
10:22 land where darkness is the *o* light.
13:20 These things *o* do not use against me,
14:22 *O* his own flesh pains him,
22: 8 and *o* the privileged were to dwell in it.
25: 6 a maggot, the son of man, who is *o* a worm?
28:22 Death say, *O* by rumor have we heard of it."
35: 8 *o* a man like yourself; and your justice *o*
41: 1 to do so need *o* see him to be overthrown.
Ps(s) 23: 6 *O* goodness and kindness follow me all the
35:17 from the lions, my *o* life.
37: 8 be not vexed, it will *o* harm you.
39: 6 *o* a breath is any human existence.
39: 7 *o*, man goes his way; like vapor only
39:12 *o* a breath is any man.
51: 6 "Against you *o* have I sinned,
62: 2 *O* in God is my soul at rest;
62: 3 He *o* is my rock and my salvation,
62: 6 *O* in God be at rest,
62: 7 He *o* is my rock and my salvation,
62:10 *O* a breath are mortal men;
68: 7 *o* rebels remain in the parched land.
81:14 If *o* my people would hear me,
88:19 my *o* friend is darkness.
102:11 for you lifted me up *o* to cast me down.
139:19 If *o* you would destroy the wicked,
Prv 11:23 The desire of the just ends *o* in good;
12:19 forever, the lying tongue, for *o* a moment.
14:23 is profit, but mere talk tends *o* to penury.
25:16 If you find honey, eat *o* what you need,
26:19 neighbor, and then says, "I was *o* joking."
30: 8 [provide me *o* with the food I need;]
Eccl 7:29 Behold, *o* this have I found out:
Wis 11: 9 had been tried, though *o* mildly chastised,
11:19 Not *o* could these attack and completely
16: 4 but these needed *o* be shown how their
17: 6 But *o* intermittent,
17:18 And were it *o* the whistling wind,
19:13 came upon the sinners *o* after forewarnings
19:15 And not that *o*; but what punishment
Sir 9:10 you drink with pleasure *o* when it has aged.
11:33 Avoid a wicked man, for he breeds *o* evil,
16:21 men, which *o* the foolish knave will think.
18: 5 When a man ends he is *o* beginning,
18:17 *O* a fool upbraids before giving;
21:18 stupid man knows it *o* as inscrutable words.
23:19 is not mindful, fearing *o* the eyes of men;
29:14 and *o* the shameless would play him false;
31: 3 wealth, and his *o* rest is wanton pleasure;
32: 3 that is *o* your right,
32: 7 Young man, speak *o* when necessary,
33:18 you that not for myself *o* have I toiled,
37: 1 are friends who are friends in name *o*.
38:16 As is *o* proper,
41: 9 you will beget them *o* for groaning.
41:14 judge of disgrace *o* according to my rules,
43:34 *o* a few of his works have we seen.
46: 8 they were the *o* two spared from the six
51:27 I have labored *o* a little,
Is 4: 1 *O* let your name be given us,
10:22 the sea, *O* a remnant of them will return;
10:25 For *o* a brief moment more,
17: 6 *O* a scattering of grapes shall be left!
26:13 from you *o* that we can call upon your name.
29:13 *o* and honors me with their lips alone,
30: 5 help nor benefit, but *o* shame and reproach.
32:11 bare, with *o* a loincloth to cover you.
45:14 "With you *o* is God,
45:24 *O* in the LORD are just deeds and power.
51:12 you then fear mortal man, who is human *o*,
Jer 3:13 *O* know your guilt:
4:10 say, "You *o* deceived us When you said:
5: 4 It is *o* the lowly,
6:26 as for an *o* child with bitter wailing,
7: 5 *O* if you thoroughly reform your ways and
17:11 in the end he is *o* a fool.
23:23 Am I a God near at hand *o*,
28: 9 LORD *o* when his prophetic prediction is
29:10 *O* after seventy years have elapsed for
29:19 the prophets, *o* to have them go unheeded,
31:30 through his own fault *o* shall anyone die:
32:30 youth have done *o* what is evil in my eyes;
37:10 attacking you, and *o* the wounded remained,
38: 6 There was no water in the cistern, *o* mud,
44:14 *O* scattered refugees shall return.
Bar 1:19 and *o* too ready to disregard his voice.
Ez 3:27 *O* when I speak with you and open your mouth,
11:16 and was for a while their *o* sanctuary in
14:14 could save *o* themselves by their virtue,
14:20 would save *o* themselves by their virtue.
16:47 Yet not *o* in their ways did you walk,
18: 4 *o* the one who sins shall die.
18:18 *O* the father,
18:20 *O* the one who sins shall die.
20:24 with eyes *o* for the idols of their fathers.
22: 6 by family, are in you *o* for bloodshed.
33:32 For them you are *o* a ballad singer,
40:46 the *o* Levites who may come near to
43: 8 to mine, so that *o* a wall was between us,
44: 3 *O* the prince may sit down in it to eat his
44:22 women, but *o* virgins of the race of Israel;
46:17 to the latter *o* until the year of release,
46:17 *O* the inheritance given to his sons is
47:11 *O* its marshes and swamps shall not be made
Dn 11:24 but *o* for a time.
11:36 shall prosper *o* till divine wrath is ready,
13:15 the garden as usual, with two maids *o*.
14: 4 but Daniel adored *o* his God.
14: 5 but *o* the living God who made heaven and
14: 7 "it is *o* clay inside and bronze outside;
Hos 4:19 they shall have *o* shame from their altars.
Am 6:10 *O* a few shall be left to carry the dead
8:10 I will make them mourn as for an *o* son,
Mi 6: 8 *O* to do right and to love goodness,
Zec 8:19 *o* love faithfulness and peace.
12:10 mourn for him as one mourns for an *o* son,
14: 9 be the only one, and his name the *o* one.
Mt 5:47 And if you greet your brothers *o*,
7:21 *o* the one who does the will of my Father
9:16 hole will pull, and the rip *o* get worse.
9:21 "If *o* I can touch his cloak,"
10:39 who seeks *o* himself brings himself to ruin,
12:24 expel demons *o* with the help of Beelzebul,
12:29 *O* then can he rob his house.
13:21 he has no roots, so he lasts *o* for a time.
13:34 He spoke to them in parables *o*,
15:24 *o* to the lost sheep of the house of Israel,"
16: 7 and Sadducees," they could think *o*,
19:11 *o* those to whom it is given to do so.
19:23 *o* with difficulty will a rich man enter
20:12 'This last group did *o* an hour's work,
20:31 to silence, but they *o* shouted the louder,
21:21 *o* will you do what I did to the fig tree,
23: 9 *O* one is your father, the One in heaven.
23:10 *O* one is your teacher, the Messiah.
24:14 *O* after that will the end come.
24:36 in heaven nor the Son, but the Father *o*.
27:23 But they *o* shouted the louder,
Mk 2:26 which *o* the priests were permitted to eat?
3:27 *O* then can he plunder his house.
4:17 Being rootless, they last *o* a while.
4:22 hidden *o* to be revealed at a later time;
4:34 To them he spoke *o* by way of parable,
5:26 on the contrary, she *o* grew worse.
7:15 that which comes out of him, and *o* that,
7:19 his stomach *o* and passes into the latrine."
9: 8 no longer saw anyone with them *o* Jesus.
9:29 "This kind you can drive out *o* by prayer."
10:24 The disciples could *o* marvel at his words.
13:32 heaven nor even the Son, but *o* the Father.
15:14 They *o* shouted the louder,
Lk 5:36 If he does, he will *o* tear the new coat,
6: 4 though *o* priests are allowed to eat it?"
7: 6 he was *o* a short distance from the house,
7:12 carried out, the *o* son of a widowed mother.
8:42 he come to his home because his *o* daughter,
9:38 he is my *o* child.
9:55 He turned toward them *o* to reprimand them.
10:42 one thing *o* is required.
16:30 someone would *o* go to them from the dead,
17: 9 servant who was *o* carrying out his orders?
19:42 *o* you had known the path to peace this day;
22:45 to his disciples, *o* to find them asleep,
22:69 This much *o* will I say:
23:41 are *o* paying the price for what we've done,
24:18 "Are you the *o* resident of Jerusalem who
Jn 1: 8 but *o* to testify to the light,
1:14 glory of an *o* Son coming from the Father,
1:18 It is God the *o* Son,
2: 9 *o* the waiters knew,
2:12 but they stayed there *o* a few days.
2:22 *O* after Jesus had been raised from the
3:16 so loved the world that he gave his *o* Son,
3:18 not believing in the name of God's *o* Son.
4:10 "If *o* you recognized God's gift,
5:18 that he not *o* was breaking the sabbath but,
5:19 he can do *o* what he sees the Father doing.
5:34 refer to these things *o* for your salvation.)
6:22 they realized that there had been *o* one boat
6:46 *o* the one who is from God has seen the
7:12 he is *o* misleading the crowd!"
7:33 *O* a little while longer am I to be with you,
7:49 *O* this lot,
8:26 I *o* tell the world what I have heard from
8:28 I say *o* what the Father has taught me.
10:10 comes *o* to steal and slaughter and destroy,
10:33 who are *o* a man are making yourself God."
11: 8 the Jews *o* recently trying to stone you,
11:52 and not for this nation *o*,
12: 9 *o* because of Jesus but also to see Lazarus,
12:35 "The light is among you *o* a little longer.
13: 9 Peter said to him, "then not *o* my feet,
15:25 this *o* fulfills the text in their law:
16: 2 Not *o* will they expel you from synagogues;
16:13 on his own, but will speak *o* what he hears,
17: 3 to know you, the *o* true God,

Acts 2:15 It is *o* nine in the morning!
8:16 since they had *o* been baptized in the name
10:26 I am *o* a man myself."
10:40 *o* to have God raise him up on the third
10:41 but *o* by such witnesses as had been chosen
14:15 "We are *o* men, human like you.
16: 3 that it was *o* his father who was Greek.
17: 5 This *o* aroused the resentment of the Jews,
18:25 although he knew *o* of John's baptism.
19:26 not *o* at Ephesus but throughout most of
19:27 not *o* that our trade will be discredited,
20:24 I put no value on my life if *o* I can
21:13 I am prepared, not *o* for imprisonment,
23:21 all ready now, waiting *o* for your consent."
23:34 came from, *o* to learn he was from Cilicia.
26:29 I would to God that not *o* you but all who
27: 7 arriving at Cnidus *o* with difficulty.
27:10 and heavy loss, not *o* to ship and cargo,
27:16 *o* with difficulty were we able to gain
27:22 None among you will be lost *o* the ship.
Rom 1:32 not *o* do them but approve them in others.
4: 9 blessedness apply *o* to the circumcised,
4:14 If *o* those who observe the law are heirs,
4:15 the law serves *o* to bring down wrath,
4:16 not *o* for those who have the law but for
5: 3 But not *o* that
5:11 Not *o* that;
7: 1 has power over a man *o* so long as he lives?
7: 7 *o* through the law that I came to know sin.
8:17 if *o* we suffer with him so as to be
8:23 Not *o* that, but we ourselves,
9:10 Not *o* that, for when Rebekah
9:24 whom he called, not *o* from among the Jews,
9:27 of the sea, *o* the remnant will be saved,
13: 3 is right but *o* when his conduct is evil.
13: 4 *O* if you do wrong ought you to be afraid.
13: 5 not *o* to escape punishment but also for
14: 2 one who is weak in faith eats *o* vegetables.
14:14 it is *o* when a man thinks something
15:24 *o* after I have had the joy of being with you
16: 4 Not *o* I but all the churches of the
1Cor 3: 1 you as spiritual men but *o* as men of flesh,
3: 5 of them doing *o* what the Lord assigned him.
3: 7 waters is of any special account, *o* God,
3:15 saved, but *o* as one fleeing through fire.
4:15 guardians in Christ, you have *o* one father.
9: 6 Is it *o* myself and Barnabas who are forced
10: 9 of them did, *o* to be destroyed by snakes.
11:28 *o* then should he eat of the bread and
14:28 each one speaking *o* to himself and to God.
14:36 Are you the *o* ones to whom it has come?
15:19 hopes in Christ are limited to this life *o*,
2Cor 2: 5 has given offense he has hurt not *o* me,
3:14 it is *o* in Christ that it is taken away.
4: 3 it is such *o* for those who are headed
7: 7 not *o* by his arrival but by the
8:10 work last year, not *o* to carry it through,
8:17 Not *o* did he welcome our appeal,
8:21 We are concerned not *o* for God's approval
9:12 this public benefit not *o* supplies the needs
10:12 they *o* demonstrate their ignorance.
12: 2 his body I cannot say, *o* God can say
12: 6 me because I would *o* be telling the truth.
12:14 I do not want what you have, I *o* want you.
13: 1 "A judicial fact shall be established *o*
13: 8 the truth, but *o* for the sake of the truth.
Gal 1:23 they had *o* heard that "he who was
2:10 The *o* stipulation was that we should be
3: 2 I want to learn *o* one thing from you:
3:16 to many, but as if it applied *o* to one,
3:19 it was to be valid *o* until that descendant
3:20 no mediator when *o* one person is involved;
4:18 and not *o* when I happen to be with you.
4:20 If *o* I could be with you now and speak to
5: 5 we hope for, and *o* faith can yield it.
5: 6 *o* faith,
6: 3 he is nothing, he is *o* deceiving himself.
6: 7 A man will reap *o* what he sows.
6:13 They want you to be circumcised *o* that
Eph 4:29 say *o* the good things men need to hear,
6: 6 service for appearance *o* and to please men,
Phil 1: 7 It is *o* right that I should entertain such
1:29 not *o* to believe in him but also to suffer
2:12 not *o* when I happen to be with you but all
Col 2:12 In baptism you were not *o* buried with him
4:11 These are the *o* circumcised ones among
1Thes 1: 8 This is true not *o* in Macedonia and Achaia;
2: 8 not *o* God's tidings but our very lives,
3: 8 flourish *o* if you stand firm in the Lord!
1Tm 1:17 the immortal, the invisible, the *o* God,
3: 2 must be irreproachable, married *o* once,
5: 9 She must have been married *o* once.
5:13 becoming not *o* time-wasters but gossips
5:23 Stop drinking water *o*.
5:24 while other men's sins will appear *o* later.
6: 5 religion *o* as a means of personal gain.
6:15 He is the blessed and *o* ruler,
2Tm 2:20 there are vessels not *o* of gold and silver
2:23 As you well know, they *o* breed quarrels,
4: 8 and not *o* to me,
Ti 1: 6 must be irreproachable, married *o* once,
Heb 3:14 We have become part-ners of Christ if *o* we
5: 4 but *o* when called by God as Aaron was.
8: 5 is *o* a copy and shadow of the heavenly one,
9: 7 *o* the high priest went into the inner one,
9:10 but can *o* cleanse in matters of food and
9:17 comes into force *o* in the case of death;
10: 1 had *o* a shadow of the good things to come,
10: 3 there came *o* a yearly recalling of sins,
10:27 sacrifice for sin *o* a fearful expectation
11:17 promises was ready to sacrifice his *o* son,
12:26 once more shake not *o* earth but heaven!"
12:27 so that *o* what is unshaken may remain.
Jas 5:17 Elijah was *o* a man like us,
1Pt 2:18 not *o* the good and reasonable ones but
3: 2 They have *o* to observe the reverent purity
4:18 if the just man is saved *o* with difficulty,
1Jn 2: 2 for our sins, and not for our sins *o*,
2:19 It *o* served to show that none of them was
4: 9 he sent his *o* Son to the world that we
5: 6 not in water *o*,
5:16 is *o* for those whose sin is not deadly.
2Jn 1: 1 and not *o* I but also all those who have
3Jn 1:10 Not *o* does he refuse to welcome the
Jude 1: 4 deny Jesus Christ, our *o* master and Lord.
1:10 not *o* revile what they have no knowledge
1:12 without shame and *o* look after themselves.
1:25 Glory be to this *o* God our savior,
Rv 2:17 name, to be known *o* by him who receives it.'
9: 4 but *o* to those men who had not the seal
9: 5 them but *o* to torture them for five months;
9:19 not *o* in their mouths but in their tails;
13: 5 it received was to last *o* forty-two months.
17:10 does come he will remain *o* a short while.
17:12 along with the beast, but *o* for an hour.
21:27 *O* those shall enter whose names are

ONO (5)

1Chr 8:12 who built *O* and Lod with its nearby towns,
Ezr 2:33 sons of Lod, Hadid, and *O*,
Neh 6: 2 together at Caphirim in the plain of *O*."
7:37 sons of Lod, Hadid, and *O*,
11:35 Gittaim, Hadid, Zeboim, Neballat, Lod, *O*,

ONRUSH (1)

Is 33: 4 they rush upon it like the *o* of locusts.

ONSET (2)

Hb 1: 9 Their combined *o* is that of a stormwind
Mk 13: 8 This is but the *o* of the pains of labor.

ONSLAUGHT (1)

1Mc 1:30 attacked the city suddenly, in a great *o*,

ONTO (11)

Gn 24:18 and quickly lowering the jug *o* her hand,
Ex 7:28 and into your bedroom and *o* your bed,
Jgs 20:32 them away from the city *o* the highways.
20:32 drawn away from the city *o* the highways,
1Sm 21:14 doors of the gate and drooling *o* his beard.
2Kgs 3:25 each of them cast stones *o* every fertile
Sir 46: 9 he won his way *o* the summits of the land;
Is 40: 9 Go up *o* a high mountain,
Mt 15:29 up *o* the mountainside and sat down there.
Lk 9:28 James, and went up *o* a mountain to pray.
Rv 9: 3 Out of the smoke, *o* the land,

ONWARD (9)

Ex 33: 6 So, from Mount Horeb *o*,
Lv 22:27 the eighth day *o* will it be acceptable,
Nm 8:24 Each from his twenty-fifth year *o* shall
1Chr 17: 5 house, from the time when I led Israel *o*,
Dn 13:64 And from that day *o* Daniel was greatly
Mt 27:45 From noon *o*,
Jn 11:53 day *o* there was a plan afoot to kill him.
19:27 From that hour *o*,
Acts 3:24 prophets who have spoken, from Samuel *o*,

ONYCHA (2)

Ex 30:34 storax and *o* and galbanum, these are pure
Sir 24:15 Like galbanum and *o* and sweet spices,

ONYX (10)

Ex 25: 7 *o* stones and other gems for mounting on
28: 9 "Get two *o* stones and engrave on them the
28:20 row, a chrysolite, an *o* and a jasper.
35: 9 *o* stones and other gems for mounting on
35:27 The princes brought *o* stones and other
39: 6 The *o* stones were prepared and mounted in
39:13 fourth row a chrysolite, an *o* and a jasper.
1Chr 29: 2 of wood, *o* stones and settings for them,
Jb 28:16 Ophir, with the precious *o* or the sapphire.
Ez 28:13 topaz, and beryl, chrysolite, *o*,

OPEN (197)

Gn 25:27 skillful hunter, a man who lived in the *o*;
25:29 cooking a stew, Esau came in from the *o*,
29: 2 about, he saw a well in the *o* country,
34:10 The land is *o* before you;
Ex 9:19 whatever else you have in the *o* fields
9:25 was in the *o* throughout the land of Egypt;
Lv 17: 5 as they used to offer up in the *o* field
Nm 13:19 towns in which they dwell *o* or fortified?
16:31 this than the ground beneath them split *o*,
19:15 likewise, every vessel that is *o*,
19:16 who in the *o* country touches a dead person,
Dt 15: 8 you shall *o* your hand to him and freely
15:11 that is why I command you to *o* your hand
21: 1 lying in the *o* on the land which the LORD,
22:25 it is in the *o* fields that a man comes
22:27 was in the *o* fields that he came upon her,
28:12 The LORD will *o* up for you his rich
Jos 8:17 and the city was *o* and unprotected.
8:24 were slain by the sword there in the *o*,
10:22 *O* the mouth of the cave and bring out
20: 8 on the *o* tableland in the tribe of Reuben,
21:12 although the *o* country and villages
Jgs 3:25 he did not *o* the doors of the upper room,
5:18 Naphtali, too, on the *o* heights!
20:31 of the Israelite soldiers in the *o* field,
1Sm 6:18 including fortified cities and *o* villages.
20: 5 go and hide in the *o* country until evening.
20:11 they were out in the *o* country together,
20:24 So David hid in the *o* country.
25:15 them during our stay in the *o* country.
30:11 in the *o* country and brought to David.
2Sm 2:18 fleet of foot as a gazelle in the *o* field,
10: 8 and Maacah remained apart in the *o* country.
11:11 servants are encamped in the *o* field.
11:23 and came out into the *o* against us,
22:20 He set me free in the *o*.
1Kgs 1:40 to split *o* the earth with their shouting.
6:18 carved in the form of gourds and *o* flowers;
6:29 of cherubim, palm trees, and *o* flowers.
6:32 of cherubim, palm trees, and *o* flowers.
6:35 carved cherubim, palm trees, and *o* flowers,
8:52 "Thus may your eyes be *o* to the petition
2Kgs 6:17 Then he prayed, "O LORD, *o* his eyes,
8:12 you will rip *o* their pregnant women."
9: 3 Then *o* the door and flee without delay."
13:17 and said, *O* the window toward the east."
15:16 even to ripping *o* all the pregnant women.
19:16 *O* your eyes, O LORD, and see!
1Chr 6:41 although the *o* country and the villages
19: 9 their help remained apart in the *o* field.
2Chr 6:40 may your eyes be *o* and your ears attentive
7:15 Now my eyes shall be *o* and my ears
29: 4 gathered them in the *o* space to the east,
32: 6 together in his presence in the *o* space
Ezr 10: 9 in the *o* place before the house of God,
Neh 1: 6 your ear be attentive, and your eyes *o*,
8: 1 man in the *o* space before the Water Gate,
8: 3 the *o* place that was before the Water Gate,
8:16 and in the *o* spaces of the Water Gate and
Tb 6: 5 "Cut the fish *o* and take out its gall,
6: 6 After the lad had cut the fish *o*,
Jdt 10: 9 to *o* the gate for her as she requested.
13:11 *O*! *O* the gate!
Est C:21 to *o* the mouths of the heathen to acclaim
1Mc 5:48 But they would not *o* to him.
11:12 their enmity became *o*.
11:68 This army attacked him in the *o*,
2Mc 1: 4 May he *o* your heart to his law and his
6:18 being forced to *o* his mouth to eat pork.
15:19 were about the battle in the *o* country.
Jb 11: 5 would speak, and *o* his lips against you,
32:20 let me *o* my lips,
33: 2 Behold, now I *o* my mouth;
41: 6 Who can force *o* the doors of his mouth,
Ps(s) 5:10 Their throat is an *o* grave;
18:20 He set me free in the *o*,
22:14 They *o* their mouths against me like
35:21 And they *o* wide their mouths against me,
40: 7 not, but ears *o* to obedience you gave me.
51:17 O Lord, *o* my lips,
60: 4 have rocked the country and split it *o*;
78: 2 I will *o* my mouth in a parable,
81:11 *o* wide your mouth,
104:28 when you *o* your hand,
118:19 *O* to me the gates of justice;
119:18 *O* my eyes,
119:131 *o* mouth in my yearning for your commands.
145:16 You *o* your hand and satisfy the desire of
Prv 1:20 in the *o* squares she raises her voice;
3:20 By his knowledge the depths break *o*,
7:12 is in the streets, now in the *o* squares,
13: 3 to *o* wide one's lips brings downfall.
15:11 world and the abyss lie *o* before the LORD;
20:13 eyes wide *o* mean abundant food.
24: 7 not to *o* his mouth at the gate.
25:28 Like an *o* city with no defenses is the man
27: 5 *o* rebuke than a love that remains hidden.
31: 8 *O* your mouth in behalf of the dumb,
31: 9 *O* your mouth,
Sg 5: 2 *O* to me,
5: 5 I rose to *o* to my lover,
Sir 4:31 Let not your hand be *o* to receive and
8:19 *O* your heart to no man,
22:18 Small stones lying on an *o* height will not
29:24 for as a guest you dare not *o* your mouth.
39: 6 the Most High, To *o* his lips in prayer,
39:13 *o* up your petals,
51:25 I *o* my mouth and speak of her:
Is 9:11 on the west devour Israel with *o* mouth.
22:18 like a ball into an *o* land To perish there,

OPEN (cont.)
22:22 shall shut, when he shuts, no one shall *o.*
26: 2 *O* up the gates to let in a nation that is
37:17 *O* your eyes, O LORD and see!
41:18 I will *o* up rivers on the bare heights,
42: 7 the nations, To *o* the eyes of the blind,
42:20 your ears are *o,*
45: 8 Let the earth *o* and salvation bud forth;
57: 4 sport, at whom do you *o* wide your mouth,
60:11 Your gates shall stand *o* constantly;
63:13 the depths like horses in the *o* country,
Jer 5:16 Their quivers are like *o* graves;
32:11 title and conditions, and the *o* one.
32:14 both the sealed and the *o* deed of purchase,
32:19 whose eyes are *o* to all the ways of men,
50:26 upon her from every side, *o* her granaries,
Lam 2:11 faint away in the *o* spaces of the town.
2:16 your enemies *o* their mouths against you;
Ez 2: 8 *o* your mouth and eat what I shall give you.
3:27 when I speak with you and *o* your mouth,
29: 5 You shall fall upon the *o* field,
32: 4 on the *o* field I will cast you.
33:27 those who are in the *o* field I have given
37:12 *o* your graves and have you rise from them,
37:13 *o* your graves and have you rise from them,
38:11 "I will go up against a land of *o*
39: 5 On the *o* field you shall fall,
41:10 chambers of the court was an *o* space
41:11 side chambers had entrances to the *o* space,
41:11 surrounding the *o* space was five cubits.
46: 1 on the day of the new moon it shall be *o.*
Dn 3:33 Now we cannot *o* our mouths;
6:11 a day, with the windows *o* toward Jerusalem.
9:18 *o* your eyes and see our ruins and the city
13:25 as one of them ran to *o* the garden doors.
Hos 14: 1 their expectant mothers shall be ripped *o.*
Am 1:13 they ripped *o* expectant mothers in Gilead,
Mi 1: 4 melt under him and the valleys split *o,*
2:13 burst *o* the gate and go out through it;
Na 3:13 foes the gates of your land are *o* wide,
Zec 2: 8 live in Jerusalem as though in *o* country,
11: 1 *O* your doors,
12: 4 upon the house of Judah I will *o* my eyes,
13: 1 On that day there shall be *o* to the house
Mal 3:10 I not *o* for you the floodgates of heaven,
Mt 13:35 "I will *o* my mouth in parables,
17:27 *O* its mouth and you will discover there a
20:33 "Lord," they told him, *o* our eyes!"
25:11 *O* the door for us.'
25:13 keep your eyes *o*
26:43 they could not keep their eyes *o.*
Mk 2: 4 so they began to *o* up the roof over the
4:22 covered so as to be brought out into the *o.*
8:15 he instructed them, "Keep your eyes *o!*
14:40 They could not keep their eyes *o,*
Lk 4:42 the town and set out into the *o* country.
12:36 knocks, you will *o* for him without delay.
13:25 knocking and saying, 'Sir, *o* for us,'
Jn 4:35 *O* your eyes and see!
9:26 How did he *o* your eyes?"
10:21 a devil cannot *o* the eyes of the blind!"
Acts 1:18 His body burst wide *o,*
9: 8 unable to see, even though his eyes were *o.*
10:11 He saw the sky *o* and an object come down
12:14 that she did not stop to *o* the door,
16:26 *o* and everyone's chains were pulled loose.
16:27 woke up to see the prison gates wide *o.*
26:18 to *o* the eyes of those to whom I am
27: 5 We crossed the *o* sea off the coast of
Rom 3:13 Their throats are *o* tombs;
2Cor 6:13 to his children), *o* wide your hearts!
Rv 3: 7 one can close, who closes and no one can *o,*
3: 8 *o* door before you which no one can close.
4: 1 above me there was an *o* door to heaven,
5: 2 worthy to *o* the scroll and break its seals?"
5: 3 to *o* the scroll or examine its contents.
5: 4 be found worthy to *o* or examine the scroll.
5: 5 to *o* the scroll with the seven seals."
5: 9 receive the scroll and break *o* its seals,
6: 1 Lamb broke *o* the first of the seven seals,
6: 3 When the Lamb broke *o* the second seal,
6: 5 When the Lamb broke *o* the third seal,
6: 7 When the Lamb broke *o* the fourth seal,
6: 9 When the Lamb broke *o* the fifth seal,
6:12 When I saw the Lamb break *o* the sixth seal,
8: 1 When the Lamb broke *o* the seventh seal,
10: 8 take the *o* scroll from the hand of the

OPEN-HEARTED (1)

Gal 4:15 What has happened to your *o* spirit?

OPENED (105)

Gn 3: 5 moment you eat of it your eyes will be *o*
3: 7 Then the eyes of both of them were *o,*
4:11 you shall be banned from the soil that *o*
7:11 and the floodgates of the sky were *o.*
8: 6 Noah *o* the hatch he had made in the ark,
21:19 Then God *o* her eyes,
41:56 Joseph *o* all the cities that had grain and
42:27 *o* his bag to give his donkey some fodder,
43:21 at a night's encampment and *o* our bags,
44:11 lowered his bag to the ground and *o* it,
Nm 16:32 and the earth *o* its mouth and swallowed
22:28 But now the LORD *o* the mouth of the ass,
26:10 The earth *o* its mouth and swallowed them
Dt 11: 6 when the ground *o* its mouth and swallowed
Jgs 3:25 upper room, they took the key and *o* them.
4:19 But she *o* a jug of milk for him to drink,
16:18 up this time, for he has *o* his heart to me."
19:27 When her husband rose that day and *o* the
1Sm 3:15 and *o* the doors of the temple of the LORD.
2Kgs 4:35 who now sneezed seven times and *o* his eyes.
6:17 And the LORD *o* the eyes of the servant,
6:20 "O LORD, *o* their eyes that they may see."
6:20 The LORD, *o* their eyes,
9:10 Then he *o* the door and fled.
13:17 He *o* it.
2Chr 29: 3 *o* the doors of the LORD's house and
Neh 7: 3 are not to be *o* until the sun is hot,
8: 5 Ezra *o* the scroll so that all the people
8: 5 and, as he *o* it,
Tb 8:13 maid, who lit a lamp, *o* the bedroom door,
11: 7 "I am certain that his eyes will be *o.*
Jdt 10: 9 "Order the gate of the city *o* for me,
13:13 *o* the gate and welcomed the two women.
1Mc 3:28 He *o* his treasure chests,
10:76 of the city became afraid and *o* the gates,
11: 2 in the cities *o* their gates to welcome him,
2Mc 1:16 they *o* a hidden trapdoor in the ceiling,
Jb 3: 1 this, Job *o* his mouth and cursed his day.
31:32 the street, but I *o* my door to wayfarers
Ps(s) 7:16 He has *o* a hole,
39:10 I was speechless and *o* not my mouth,
78:23 skies above and the doors of heaven he *o;*
106:17 The earth *o* and swallowed up Dathan,
109: 2 *o* wicked and treacherous mouths against me.
Sg 5: 6 I *o* to my lover
7:13 have *o* if the pomegranates have blossomed;
Wis 10:21 Because Wisdom *o* the mouths of the dumb,
Sir 43:14 At it, the storehouse is *o,*
51:19 *o* her gate and I came to know her secrets.
Is 10:14 No one fluttered a wing, or *o* a mouth,
24:18 For the windows on high will be *o,*
35: 5 Then will the eyes of the blind be *o,*
53: 7 treated, he submitted and *o* not his mouth;
53: 7 he was silent and *o* not his mouth.
Jer 31:26 Upon this I awoke and *o* my eyes;
Lam 3:46 our enemies have *o* their mouths against us;
Ez 1: 1 exiles by the river Chebar, the heavens *o,*
3: 2 So I *o* my mouth and he gave me the
24:27 shall be *o* and you shall be dumb no longer.
33:22 and he *o* my mouth when the fugitive
33:22 My mouth was *o,* and I was dumb no longer.
44: 2 is not to be *o* for anyone to enter by it;
46:12 the eastern gate shall be *o* for him,
Dn 7:11 court was convened, and the books were *o.*
10:16 I *o* my mouth and said to the one facing me,
13:39 he *o* the doors and ran off.
14:18 As soon as he had *o* the door,
Na 2: 7 The river gates are *o,*
Mt 2:11 Then they *o* their coffers and presented
3:16 Suddenly the sky *o* and he saw the Spirit
7: 7 Knock, and it will be *o* to you.
27:52 The earth quaked, boulders split, tombs *o.*
Mk 7:34 (that is, "Be *o!*")
7:35 At once, the man's ears were *o;*
8:24 The man *o* his eyes and said,
Lk 1:64 his mouth was *o* and his tongue loosed,
3:21 the skies *o* and the Holy Spirit descended
11: 9 knock and it shall be *o* to you.'
24:31 their eyes were *o* and they recognized him;
24:45 Then he *o* their minds to the understanding
Jn 1:51 you shall see the sky *o* and the angels of
9:10 said to him then, "How were your eyes *o?*"
9:14 had made the mud paste and *o* his eyes.)
9:17 "Since it was your eyes he *o,*
9:21 But how he can see now, or who *o* his eyes,
9:30 know where he comes from, yet he *o* my eyes.
11:37 said, "He *o* the eyes of that blind man.
Acts 5:19 angel of the Lord *o* the gates of the jail,
5:23 but when we *o* it we found no one inside."
8:32 shearer he was silent and *o* not his mouth.
9:40 She *o* her eyes,
12:10 to the city, which *o* for them of itself.
12:16 *o* the door and were astonished to see him.
14:27 he had *o* the door of faith to the Gentiles.
16:14 *o* her heart to accept what Paul was saying.
1Cor 16: 9 A door has been *o* wide for my work,
2Cor 2:12 opportunity was *o* wide for me by the Lord.
2Thes 2:10 they have not *o* their hearts to the truth
Heb 10:20 new and living path he has *o* up for us
Rv 9: 2 he *o* it and smoke poured out of the shaft
10: 2 he held a little scroll which had been *o.*
11:19 Then God's temple in heaven *o* and in the
15: 5 which is the tent of witness *o* up,
19:11 The heavens were *o,*
20:12 the scrolls, the book of the living was *o.*

OPENING (26)

Gn 6:16 Make an *o* for daylight in the ark,
Ex 2: 6 On *o* it,
28:32 shall have an *o* for the head in the center,
28:32 and around this *o* there shall be a selvage,
28:32 be a selvage, woven as at the *o* of a shirt,
39:23 with an *o* in its center like the opening
39:23 around the *o* to keep it from being torn.
1Kgs 7:31 within which was a rounded *o* to provide
7:31 There was carved work at the *o,*
1Chr 9:27 and they had the duty of *o* it each morning.
Jdt 1: 4 with an *o* forty cubits wide for the
2Mc 14:44 as they quickly drew back and left an *o,*
Prv 17:14 The start of strife is like the *o* of a dam;
Sg 5: 4 My lover put his hand through the *o;*
Is 45: 1 *O* doors before him and leaving the gates
Ez 40:12 cubits on either side, from *o* to opening.
40:38 a chamber *o* off the vestibule of the gate,
Dn 3:93 Then Nebuchadnezzar came to the *o* of the
6:18 had been brought to block the *o* of the den.
Zec 5: 8 pushing the leaden cover into the *o.*
Acts 7:56 he exclaimed, "I see an *o* in the sky,
2Cor 6:11 to you frankly, *o* our hearts wide to you.
Col 4: 3 an *o* to proclaim the mystery of Christ,
Rv 12:16 by *o* its mouth and swallowing the flood

OPENLY (10)

2Mc 7: 6 when he protested *o* with the words,
Jb 13:10 He will *o* rebuke you if even in secret you
16: 8 up my traducer, speaking *o* against me;
Jer 5:11 For they have *o* rebelled against me,
Mk 1:45 possible for Jesus to enter a town *o.*
8:32 He said these things quite *o.*
Jn 7:13 No one dared talk *o* about him,
Acts 9:28 himself quite *o* in the name of the Lord.
19:18 and *o* confessed their former practices.
2Cor 4: 2 We proclaim the truth *o* and commend

OPENNESS (1)

Lk 8:15 those who hear the word in a spirit of *o,*

OPENS (28)

Ex 13: 2 that *o* the womb among the Israelites,
13:12 to the LORD every son that *o* the womb;
13:15 everything of the male sex that *o* the womb,
34:19 that *o* the womb among all your livestock,
Nm 3:12 that *o* the womb among the Israelites.
8:16 that *o* the womb among the Israelites.
16:30 and the ground *o* its mouth and swallows
18:15 Every living thing that *o* the womb,
Dt 20:11 your terms of peace and *o* its gates to you,
2Chr 20:16 wadi which *o* on the wilderness of Jeruel.
Jb 27:19 he *o* his eyes and nothing remains to him.
33:16 *o* the ears of men and as a warning to them,
35:16 Yet Job to no purpose *o* his mouth,
36:10 He *o* their ears to correction and exhorts
Ps(s) 38:14 not, like a dumb man who *o* not his mouth.
Prv 8: 6 honesty *o* my lips.
31:26 She *o* her mouth in wisdom,
Sir 24: 2 assembly of the Most High she *o* her mouth,
26:12 tent peg and *o* her quiver for every arrow.
Is 5:14 its throat and *o* its maw without limit;
22:22 when he *o,*
43:16 who *o* a way in the sea and a path in the
50: 4 after morning he *o* my ear that I may hear;
Jer 50:25 The LORD *o* his armory and brings forth the
Hb 2: 5 *o* wide his throat like the nether world,
Jn 10: 3 the keeper *o* the gate for him.
Rv 3: 7 David's key, who *o* and no one can close,
3:20 If anyone hears me calling and *o* the door,

OPHEL (5)

2Chr 27: 3 much construction done on the wall of *O.*
33:14 to the Fish Gate and encircling *O;*
Neh 3:27 *O* [the temple slaves were dwelling on *O.*
11:21 The temple slaves lived on *O.*

OPHIR (14)

1Kgs 9:28 They went to *O,* and brought back four
10:11 fleet, which used to bring gold from *O,*
22:49 made Tarshish ships to go to *O* for gold;
1Chr 1:23 Uzal, Diklah, Ebal, Abimael, Sheba, *O,*
29: 4 three thousand talents of *O* gold,
2Chr 8:18 who accompanied Solomon's servants to *O*
9:10 of Solomon who brought gold from *O*
Tb 13:17 be paved with rubies and stones of *O;*
Jb 22:24 fine gold of *O* as pebbles from the brook,
28:16 It cannot be bought with gold of *O,*
Ps(s) 45:10 her place at your right hand in gold of *O.*
Sir 7:18 nor a dear brother for the gold of *O.*
Is 13:12 rare than pure gold, men, than gold of *O.*
Jer 10: 9 brought from Tarshish, and gold from *O,*

OPHNI (1)

Jos 18:24 Ophrah, Chephar-ammoni, *O* and Geba;

OPHRAH (8)

Jos 18:23 Bethel, Avvim, Parah, *O,*
Jgs 6:11 in *O* that belonged to Joash the Abiezrite.
6:24 day it is still in *O* of the Abiezrites.
8:27 of the gold and placed it in his city *O.*
8:32 of his father Joash in *O* of the Abiezrites.
9: 5 He then went to his ancestral house in *O,*

1Sm 13:17 the *O* road toward the district of Shual;
1Chr 4:14 Meonothai became the father of *O*.

OPINION (10)

Sir 3:23 Their own *o* has misled many,
14: 8 In the miser's *o* his share is too small;
Mt 17:25 "What is your *o*, Simon?
22:17 Give us your *o*, then, in this case.
22:42 "What is your *o* about the Messiah?
Mk 12:14 truthful man, unconcerned about anyone's *o*.
Lk 10:36 "Which of these three, in your *o*,
12:42 said, "Who in your *o* is that faithful,
1Cor 7:25 but I give my *o* as one who is trustworthy,
7:40 She will be happier, though, in my *o*,

OPINIONS (1)

Jb 15: 2 Should a wise man answer with airy *o*,

OPPONENT (10)

Dt 25:11 save her husband from the blows of his *o*,
Prv 18:17 then his *o* comes and puts him to the test.
25: 8 seen bring not forth hastily against an *o*;
Ez 18: 8 judges fairly between a man and his *o*;
Mt 5:25 your *o* while on your way to court with him.
5:25 your *o* may hand you over to the judge,
Lk 12:58 with your *o* to appear before a magistrate,
18: 3 saying, 'Give me my rights against my *o*.'
Ti 2: 8 no *o* will be able to find anything bad to
1Pt 5: 8 Your *o* the devil is prowling like a

OPPONENTS (5)

2Sm 2:16 *o* head and thrust his sword into his *o*
Na 1: 8 He makes an end of his *o*,
Lk 13:17 words, his *o* were covered with confusion;
Phil 1:28 be intimidated by your *o* in any situation.

OPPORTUNE (1)

Mk 14:11 kept looking for an *o* way to hand him over.

OPPORTUNITIES (1)

2Mc 9:25 for *o* and waiting to see what will happen.

OPPORTUNITY (26)

Ex 12:39 no *o* even to prepare food for the journey.
Jgs 14: 4 was providing an *o* against the Philistines;
1Mc 11:42 you and your nation when I find the *o*.
15:34 Now that we have the *o*,
2Mc 4:32 Then Menelaus, thinking this a good *o*,
10:14 troops and used every *o* to attack the Jews.
14: 5 But he found an *o* to further his mad
14:29 *o* to carry out this order by a stratagem.
Wis 12:20 granting time and *o* to abandon wickedness,
Sir 19:24 him from sinning, when he finds the *o*,
26:10 over an unruly wife, lest, finding an *o*,
Mt 26:16 he kept looking for an *o* to hand him over.
Lk 4:13 tempting he left him, to await another *o*.
22: 6 then kept looking for an *o* to hand him
Rom 7: 8 Sin seized that *o*;
7:11 Sin found its *o* and used the commandment:
2Cor 2:12 of *o* was opened wide for me by the Lord.
5:12 but we are giving you an *o* to boast about
Gal 6:10 While we have the *o*,
Eph 5:16 Make the most of the present *o*,
6:18 At every *o* pray in the Spirit,
Phil 1:16 provide an *o* to defend the gospel's cause;
4:10 of course, but lacked the *o* to show it.
Col 4: 5 make the most of every *o*.
Heb 11:15 would have had the *o* of returning there.
12:17 because he had no *o* to alter his choice,

OPPOSE (17)

Nm 14:34 you will realize what it means to *o* me.
22:34 that you stood against me to *o* my journey.
Jgs 2: 3 they shall *o* you and their gods shall
1Chr 19:11 Abishai, then lined up to *o* the Ammonites.
Est C: 2 one to *o* you in your will to save Israel.
1Mc 7:25 and realized that he could not *o* them,
9:29 has been no one like him to *o* our enemies,
9:51 In each he put a garrison to *o* Israel.
Jb 10: 2 Let me know why you *o* me.
Ps(s) 55:19 against me, for many there are who *o* me.
Wis 12:12 or who can *o* your decree?
Is 49:25 Those who *o* you I will oppose,
50: 8 if anyone wishes to *o* me,
Acts 26: 9 I once thought it my duty to *o* the name of
Rom 9:19 For who can *o* his will?"
2Tm 3: 8 Moses, so these men also *o* the truth;

OPPOSED (19)

Gn 49:23 Harrying and attacking, the archers *o* him;
Nm 22:32 rash journey of yours is directly *o* to me.
2Chr 26:18 They *o* King Uzziah, saying to him:
Jdt 1:11 him as a lone individual *o* to them,
Est B: 4 which by its laws is *o* to every other
1Mc 8: 5 and the others who *o* them in battle had
8:11 *o* them they destroyed and enslaved;
2Mc 4:21 that the king was *o* to his policies;
10:17 the walls, and cut down those who *o* them,
12:33 who *o* them with three thousand foot
Sir 46: 7 Jephunneh, when they *o* the rebel assembly,
Lk 2:34 of many in Israel, a sign that will be *o*—
Acts 13: 8 that is what his name means *o* them
18: 6 When they *o* him and insulted him,
27:43 was anxious to save Paul, he *o* their plan.
1Cor 16: 9 but at the same time there are many *o*.
Gal 3:21 that the law is *o* to the promises [of God]?
5:17 the two are directly *o*.
2Tm 3: 8 Just as Jannes and Jambres *o* Moses,

OPPOSES (1)

Rom 13: 2 the man who *o* authority rebels against the

OPPOSING (3)

2Mc 14:29 However, there was no way of *o* the king,
Lk 23: 2 nation, *o* the payment of taxes to Caesar,
Acts 7:51 you are always *o* the Holy Spirit just as

OPPOSITE (73)

Gn 15:10 in two, and placed each half *o* the other;
21:16 a shrub, and then went and sat down *o* him,
21:16 As she sat *o* him, he began to cry.
Ex 14: 2 shall camp in front of Baal-zephon, just *o*,
25:12 rings on one side and two on the *o* side.
25:27 on two *o* sides of the frame as holders for
25:33 on the *o* branch there are to be three cups,
26: 5 that the loops are directly *o* each other.
26:35 south side of the Dwelling, *o* the table,
30: 4 two on one side and two on the *o* side,
36:12 set, with the loops directly *o* each other.
37: 3 rings for one side and two for the *o* side.
37:19 on the *o* branch there were three cups,
37:27 two on one side and two on the *o* side,
40:24 lampstand in the meeting tent, *o* the table,
Nm 22: 5 of the earth and are settling down *o* us!
33: 7 opposite Baal-zephon, and they camped *o*
33:47 they camped in the Abarim Mountains *o* Nebo.
Dt 1: 1 [in the desert, in the Arabah, *o* Suph,
2:19 As you come *o* the Ammonites,
3:29 while we were in the ravine *o* Beth-peor.
4:46 the Jordan in the ravine *o* Beth-peor,
11:30 *o* the Gilgal beside the terebinth of
34: 6 the ravine *o* Beth-peor in the land of Moab,
Jos 3:16 Thus the people crossed over *o* Jericho.
18:14 south from the mountaintop *o* Beth-horon
18:17 thence to Geliloth, *o* the pass of Adummim.
19:34 In the *o* direction,
Jgs 6: 4 the Kedemites would come up, encamp *o* them,
16: 3 them to the top of the ridge *o* Hebron.
19:10 asses, and traveled till they came *o* Jebus,
1Sm 17: 3 one hill and the Israelites on an *o* hill,
17:21 drew up *o* each other in battle array.
25:20 were also coming down from the *o* direction.
26:13 Going across to an *o* slope,
2Sm 2:13 of the pool and the other on the *o* side.
15:17 halted *o* the ascent of the Mount of Olives,
1Kgs 11: 7 of the Ammonites, on the hill *o* Jerusalem.
20:27 The Israelites, encamped *o* them,
20:29 were encamped *o* each other for seven days.
1Chr 8:32 in Jerusalem, *o* their fellow tribesmen.
9:38 dwelt *o* their brethren in Jerusalem.
Neh 3:10 of Harumaph, who repaired *o* his own house.
3:16 Beth-zur, to a place *o* the tombs of David,
3:19 the Corner, *o* the ascent to the arsenal.
3:25 carried out the work of repair *o* the
3:26 to a point *o* the Water Gate on the east,
3:27 sector *o* the great projecting tower,
3:30 repaired the place *o* his own lodging.
12: 9 their brethren ministered *o* them by turns.
12:24 Their brethren who stood *o* them to sing
12:24 the man of God, one section *o* the other,
Jdt 7:18 encamped in the mountain region *o* Dothan;
7:18 men to the south and to the east *o* Egrebel,
1Mc 2:32 camped *o* and prepared to attack them on
5:37 assembled another army and camped *o* Raphon,
5:55 his brother was in Galilee *o* Ptolemais,
9: 2 and camping *o* the ascent at Arbela,
10:48 a large army and encamped *o* Demetrius.
13:20 army moved along *o* him everywhere he went.
2Mc 15:33 the other wages of his folly *o* the temple.
Sir 33:15 come in pairs, the one the *o* of the other.
Jer 1:15 Opposite her walls all around and *o* all
Ez 40:13 to the back wall of the cell on the *o* side:
40:23 inner court had a gate *o* the north gate,
46: 9 entered, but he shall leave by the *o* gate.
Dn 5: 5 Suddenly, *o* the lampstand,
Zec 14: 4 Olives, which is *o* Jerusalem to the east.
Mk 12:41 Taking a seat *o* the treasury,
Lk 8:26 of the Gerasenes, which is *o* Galilee.
Acts 20:15 the next day, and reached a point *o* Chios;

OPPOSITES (1)

Wis 15: 7 that serve for clean purposes and their *o*,

OPPOSITION (8)

Gn 16:12 In *o* to all his kin shall he encamp."
25:18 pitched camp in *o* to his various kinsmen.
2Chr 28:12 *o* to those who had returned from the war.
1Mc 11:38 under his rule and that he had no *o*,
2Mc 4: 4 that the *o* was serious and that Apollonius,
Phil 1:28 Their *o* foreshadows downfall for them,
1Thes 2: 2 good tidings to you in the face of great *o*.
Heb 12: 3 Remember how he endured the *o* of sinners;

OPPRESS (24)

Ex 1:11 the Israelites to *o* them with forced labor.
22:20 "You shall not molest or *o* an alien,
23: 9 You shall not *o* an alien;
Jgs 10:12 the Amalekites, and the Midianites *o* you?
1Chr 16:21 He let no one *o* them,
17: 9 nor shall wicked men ever again *o* them,
2Chr 28:20 him, but to *o* him rather than to help him.
Jb 10: 3 Is it a pleasure for you to *o*,
Ps(s) 105:14 to another people, He let no man *o* them,
119:122 let not the proud *o* me.
Prv 28:16 prudent the prince, the more his deeds *o*.
Wis 2:10 Let us *o* the needy just man;
Is 3: 5 them, And the people shall *o* one another,
Jer 7: 6 if you no longer *o* the resident
22: 3 Do not wrong or *o* the resident alien,
Ez 18:16 who does not *o* anyone,
22: 7 within you, they *o* orphans and widows.
22:29 and *o* the resident alien without justice.
45: 8 of Israel will no longer *o* my people,
Dn 7:25 High and *o* the holy ones of the Most High,
Am 4: 1 You who *o* the weak and abuse the needy;
6:14 A nation that shall *o* you from Labo of
Zep 3:19 that time I will deal with all who *o* you;
Zec 7:10 Do not *o* the widow or the orphan,

OPPRESSED (47)

Gn 15:13 be enslaved and *o* for four hundred years.
Ex 1:12 Yet the more they were *o*,
Dt 26: 6 When the Egyptians maltreated and *o* us,
28:29 "You will be *o* and robbed continually,
28:33 and you will be *o* and crushed at all times
Jgs 4: 3 sorely *o* the Israelites for twenty years.
10: 8 afflicted and *o* the Israelites in Bashan,
1Sm 10:18 the power of all the kingdoms that *o* you.'
12: 3 Whom have I *o*?
12: 4 "You have neither cheated us, nor *o* us,
12: 8 went to Egypt and the Egyptians *o* them,
2Kgs 13:22 King Hazael of Aram *o* Israel during the
2Chr 16:10 Asa also *o* some of his people at this time.
Neh 5:15 then too, their men *o* the people.
9:27 the power of their enemies, who *o* them.
Jdt 5:11 labor at brickmaking, *o* and enslaved them.
9:11 the God of the lowly, the helper of the *o*,
13:20 your life when your people were being *o*,
2Mc 8: 2 his people, who were being *o* on all sides;
Jb 20:19 Because he has *o* the poor,
36: 6 rights, but grants vindication to the *o*,
Ps(s) 9:10 The LORD is a stronghold for the *o*,
10:18 the defense of the fatherless and the *o*,
103: 6 justice and the rights of all the *o*.
106:42 Their enemies *o* them,
129: 1 Much have they *o* me from my youth,
129: 2 say, Much have they *o* me from my youth;
146: 7 faith forever, secures justice for the *o*,
Wis 10:15 delivered them from the nation that *o* them.
19:16 *o* with awful toils those who now shared
Sir 4: 9 the *o* from the hand of the oppressor;
11: 5 The *o* often rise to a throne,
35:13 the weak, yet he hears the cry of the *o*.
Is 23:12 exult no more, he says, you who are now *o*,
26:16 O LORD, *o* by your punishment,
51:14 The *o* shall soon be released;
52: 4 Assyria, too, *o* them for nought.
53: 8 *O* and condemned,
58: 6 Setting free the *o*,
58: 7 hungry, sheltering the *o* and the homeless;
Jer 21:12 the *o* from the hand of the oppressor,
50:33 *O* are the men of Israel,
Acts 7: 6 to slavery and *o* four hundred years.
7:19 dealt craftily with our people and *o* them.
2Pt 2: 7 a just man *o* by the conduct of men

OPPRESSES (5)

Prv 14:31 He who *o* the poor blasphemes his Maker,
22:16 He who *o* the poor to enrich himself will
28: 3 A rich man who *o* the poor is like a
Ez 18: 7 if he *o* no one,
18:12 wife of his neighbor, *o* the poor and needy,

OPPRESSING (6)

Ex 3: 9 truly noted that the Egyptians are *o* them.
Est 7: 6 "The enemy *o* us is this wicked Haman."
Ps(s) 42:10 go about in mourning, with the enemy *o* me?"
43: 2 go about in mourning, with the enemy *o* me?
119:78 proud be put to shame for *o* me unjustly;
Am 5:12 *O* the just,

OPPRESSION (22)

Dt 26: 7 and saw our affliction, our toil and our *o*.
2Kgs 13: 4 since he saw the *o* to which the king of
Neh 9:27 time of their *o* they would cry out to you,
Jb 35: 9 In great *o* men cry out;
Ps(s) 44:25 forgetting our woe and our *o*?
55:12 *o* and fraud never depart from its streets.
107:39 dwindled and were brought low through *o*,

OPPRESSION (cont.)
119:134 Redeem me from the *o* of men,
Prv 21: 7 The *o* of the wicked will sweep them away,
Eccl 5: 7 If you see *o* of the poor,
7: 7 For *o* can make a fool of a wise man,
Sir 10: 7 and the sin of *o* they both hate.
Is 14: 6 the nations in anger, with *o* unchecked.
33:15 honestly, who spurns what is gained by *o*,
54:14 be established, far from the fear of *o*,
58: 9 If you remove from your midst *o*,
Jer 6: 6 nought but *o* within her!
22:17 blood, on practicing *o* and extortion.
Lam 1: 3 fled into exile from *o* and cruel slavery;
Bar 4:21 who will deliver you from *o* at enemy hands.
Ez 45: 9 Put away violence and *o*,
Am 3: 9 disorders within her, the *o* in her midst."

OPPRESSIONS (1)
Eccl 4: 1 all the *o* that take place under the sun:

OPPRESSIVE (2)
Wis 17:21 Over them alone was spread *o* night,
Is 10: 1 unjust statutes and who write *o* decrees,

OPPRESSOR (9)
Jb 27:13 an *o* receives from the Almighty:
Ps(s) 72: 4 the children of the poor, and crush the *o*.
Prv 29:13 The poor and the *o* have a common bond:
Sir 4: 9 the oppressed from the hand of the *o*;
Is 14: 4 How the *o* has reached his end!
51:13 in constant dread of the fury of the *o*;
Jer 21:12 the oppressed from the hand of the *o*,
22: 3 Rescue the victim from the hand of his *o*.
Zec 9: 8 No *o* shall pass over them again,

OPPRESSORS (16)
Jgs 2:18 cries of affliction under their *o*.
6: 9 the power of Egypt and of all your other *o*.
2Mc 4:16 in every thing, became their enemies and *o*.
Jb 6:23 me from the enemy, or to redeem me from *o*?
Ps(s) 119:121 leave me not to my *o*.
Eccl 4: 1 From the hand of their *o* comes violence,
Wis 5: 1 his *o* who set at nought his labors.
10:14 of royalty and authority over his *o*,
16: 4 For upon those *o*,
Sir 36: 8 and your people's *o* meet destruction.
Is 14: 2 of its captors and ruling over its *o*.
19:20 they cry out to the LORD against their *o*,
49:26 I will make your *o* eat their own flesh,
51:13 to destroy, what is there of the *o* fury?
60:14 The children of your *o* shall come,
Jer 30:20 I will punish all his *o*.

OPPROBRIOUS (1)
2Pt 2:11 pass no *o* sentence in the Lord's presence.

OPPROBRIUM (2)
Prv 9: 7 and he who reproves a wicked man incurs *o*.
Bar 6:47 have left frauds and *o* to their successors.

ORACLE (35)
Nm 23: 7 Then Balaam gave voice to his *o*:
23:18 Balaam gave voice to his *o*:
24: 3 came upon him, and he gave voice to his *o*:
24:15 Then Balaam gave voice to his *o*:
24:20 seeing Amalek, Balaam gave voice to his *o*:
24:21 seeing the Kenites, he gave voice to his *o*:
24:23 he gave voice to his *o*:
Dt 18:20 *o* that I have not commanded him to speak,
18:21 recognize an *o* which the LORD has spoken?',
18:22 oracle is not fulfilled or verified, it is an *o*
1Sm 2:30 This, therefore, is the *o* of the LORD,
2Kgs 9:25 the LORD delivered this *o* against him:
Tb 2: 6 I was reminded of the *o* pronounced by the
Prv 16:10 The king's lips are an *o*;
Sir 33: 3 law is dependable for him as a divine *o*.
Is 13: 1 An *o* concerning Babylon;
14:28 that King Ahaz died, there came this *o*:
15: 1 *O* on Moab;
17: 1 *O* on Damascus:
19: 1 *O* on Egypt:
21: 1 *O* on the wastelands by the sea:
21:11 *O* on Edom:
21:13 *O* on Arabia:
22: 1 *O* of the Valley of Vision:
23: 1 *O* on Tyre:
30: 6 *O* on the Beasts of the Negeb] Through the
Ez 12:10 This *o* concerns Jerusalem and the whole
21:28 In their eyes this is but a lying *o*;
Na 1: 1 *O* about Nineveh.
Hb 1: 1 The *o* which Habakkuk the prophet received
2:18 Or the molten image and lying *o*,
Zec 9: 1 An *o*: The word of the LORD
12: 1 An *o*: the word of the LORD
Mal 1: 1 An *o*. The word of the LORD

ORACLES (6)
Dt 18:11 and spirits or seeks *o* from the dead.
Tb 14: 4 one of all the *o* shall remain unfulfilled,
Jer 23:31 LORD, who borrow speeches to pronounce *o*.
Hb 2:19 Can such a thing give *o*?
Acts 7:38 received the *o* of life to pass on to you.
Heb 5:12 again the basic elements of the *o* of God;

ORACULAR (1)
2Thes 2: 2 or terrified, whether by an *o* utterance,

ORB (1)
Sir 43: 2 The *o* of the sun, resplendent at its rising:

ORCHARD (5)
Is 29:17 orchard, and the *o* be regarded as a forest!
32:15 orchard and the *o* be regarded as a forest.
32:16 in the desert and justice abide in the *o*.

ORCHARDS (6)
Jgs 15: 5 and the vineyards and olive *o* as well.
2Kgs 5:26 or to take garments, olive *o* or vineyards,
18:32 a land of grain and wine, of bread and *o*,
Sir 40:19 Sheepfolds and *o* bring flourishing health;
Is 10:18 His splendid forests and *o*.
16:10 the *o* are taken away joy and gladness,

ORDAIN (3)
Ex 28:41 Anoint and *o* them,
29: 9 and thus shall you *o* Aaron and his sons.
Dt 11:28 turn aside from the way I *o* for you today,

ORDAINED (12)
Ex 29:29 that in them they may be anointed and *o*.
Lv 16:32 by the priest who has been anointed and *o*
21:10 has been *o* to wear the special vestments,
Nm 3: 3 who were *o* to exercise the priesthood.
1Chr 6:34 as Moses, the servant of God, had *o*.
12:24 to him Saul's kingdom, as the LORD had *o*.
15:15 had *o* according to the word of the LORD.
2Chr 10:15 divinely *o* to fulfill the prophecy the LORD
Sir 7:15 nor farming, which was *o* by the Most High.
41: 4 Thus God has *o* for all flesh;
42:15 they do his will as he has *o* for them.
45:15 *o* him and anointed him with the holy oil,

ORDAINING (1)
Ex 29:35 "Seven days you shall spend in *o* them,

ORDAINS (2)
Nm 31:21 law, as prescribed by the LORD to Moses, *o*:
Lam 3:37 it comes to pass, except the Lord *o* it;

ORDER (178)
Gn 2:16 The LORD God gave man this *o*:
25:13 sons, listed in the *o* of their birth:
43:31 and, now in control of himself, gave the *o*,
46:34 in *o* that you may stay in the region of
47: 4 continued, "in *o* to stay in this country,
Ex 5: 6 and foremen of the people this *o*:
6:16 the sons of Levi, in their genealogical *o*,
6:19 the clans of Levi in their genealogical *o*.
9:19 *o* all your livestock and whatever else you
10: 1 servants obdurate in *o* that I may perform
19:21 through toward the LORD in *o* to see him;
27:20 "You shall *o* the Israelites to bring you
28:10 the other stone, in the *o* of their birth.
29:36 you shall anoint it in *o* to consecrate it.
Lv 10: 4 sons of Aaron's uncle Uzziel, with the *o*,
14: 4 he shall *o* the man who is to be purified,
14: 5 The priest shall then *o* him to slay one of
14:36 The priest shall then *o* the house to be
14:40 he shall *o* the infected stones to be
24: 2 *O* the Israelites to bring you clear oil of
Nm 5: 2 *O* the Israelites to expel from camp every
10:28 was the *o* of departure for the Israelites,
20: 8 presence *o* the rock to yield its waters.
27:14 you both rebelled against my *o* to manifest
32:28 *o* in their regard to the priest Eleazar,
34: 2 to Moses, "Give the Israelites this *o*:
34:13 Moses also gave this *o* to the Israelites:
36: 8 in *o* that all the Israelites may remain in
Dt 2: 4 Give this *o* to the people:
8: 3 in *o* to show you that not by bread alone
9: 5 in *o* to keep the promise which he made
13: 6 in *o* to lead you astray from the way which
19: 7 is why I *o* you to set apart three cities.
24: 7 Israelite in *o* to enslave him and sell him,
27: 1 elders of Israel, gave the people this *o*:
27:11 That same day Moses gave the people this *o*:
28:13 which I *o* you today to observe carefully,
28:14 in *o* to follow other gods and serve them.
31:10 the elders of Israel, giving them this *o*:
31:25 the ark of the covenant of the LORD this *o*:
Jos 2: 3 So the king of Jericho sent Rahab the *o*,
4:24 in *o* that all the peoples of the earth may
6: 8 At this *o* they proceeded,
Ru 4:10 in *o* to raise up a family for her late
1Sm 16:16 If your lordship will *o* it,
23: 8 in *o* to go down to Keilah and besiege
23:26 David and his men in *o* to capture them,
2Sm 13:28 be afraid, for it is I who *o* you to do it.
17:14 in *o* thus to bring Absalom to ruin.
24: 3 my lord the king to *o* a thing of this kind?"
24: 4 in *o* to register the people of Israel.
1Kgs 1:27 Was this done by my royal master's *o*
2:29 sent Benaiah, son of Jehoiada, with the *o*,
2:46 The king then gave the *o* to Benaiah,
5:31 By *o* of the king,
8: 1 At the *o* of Solomon,
9:15 in *o* to build the temple of the LORD,
22:27 king's son, and say, 'This is the king's *o*:
22:31 his thirty-two chariot commanders the *o*,
2Kgs 17:27 The king of Assyria gave the *o*,
20: 1 'Put your house in *o*,
1Chr 6:17 their services in an *o* prescribed for them.
11:10 in his reign in *o* to make him true king,
12:39 All these soldiers, drawn up in battle *o*,
24:19 This was the appointed *o* of their service
2Chr 1:11 knowledge in *o* to rule my people
2: 8 My servants will labor with yours in *o* to
5: 2 At Solomon's *o* the elders of Israel and
18:26 king's son, and say, 'This is the king's *o*:
18:30 had given his chariot commanders the *o*,
24:21 and at the king's *o* they stoned him to
31: 5 As soon as the *o* was promulgated,
31:16 their service in the *o* of their classes.
34: 8 in *o* to cleanse the temple as well as the
36:22 in *o* to fulfill the word of the LORD
Ezr 1: 1 in *o* to fulfill the word of the LORD
3: 2 in *o* to offer on it the holocausts prescribed
5: 5 *o* be sent back concerning this matter.
6: 1 Thereupon King Darius issued an *o* to
8:17 in *o* to procure for us ministers for the
8:34 was in *o* as to number and weight,
Neh 5: 2 in *o* to get grain to eat that we may live."
9:26 them in *o* to bring them back to you,
9:29 them, in *o* to bring them back to your law.
Tb 12:13 your dinner in *o* to go and bury the dead,
Jdt 2: 3 refused to comply with the *o* he had issued.
2: 6 they did not comply with the *o* I issued.
10: 9 them, *O* the gate of the city opened for me,
Est 1:12 at the royal *o* issued through the eunuchs.
1:15 for disobeying the *o* of King Ahasuerus
2: 8 When the king's *o* and decree had been
3: 3 "Why do you disobey the king's *o*?"
3:12 of Haman, an *o* to the royal satraps,
8:14 sped forth in haste at the king's *o*,
8:17 every city, wherever the king's *o* arrived,
9: 1 When the day arrived on which the *o*
9:14 The king then gave an *o* to this effect,
1Mc 2:23 altar in Modein according to the king's *o*.
2:31 certain men who had flouted the king's *o*
4: 2 in *o* to attack the camp of the Jews
5:42 beside the stream and gave them this *o*:
5:48 cross your territory in *o* to reach our own;
6:26 citadel in Jerusalem in *o* to capture it,
6:40 marched forward steadily and in good *o*.
2Mc 6:15 in *o* that he may not have to punish us
7:22 nor was it I who set in *o* the elements of
11:10 *o* with the aid of their heavenly ally.
14:29 to carry out this *o* by a stratagem.
Ps(s) 110: 4 forever, according to the *o* of Melchizedek."
Is 10: 6 under my wrath I *o* him To seize plunder,
38: 1 Put your house in *o*,
45:12 I gave the *o* to all their host.
Jer 7:18 poured out to strange gods in *o* to hurt me.
27:10 you, in *o* to drive you far from your land,
36:14 son of Cushi, to Baruch with the *o*:
39: 6 at Riblah by *o* of the king of Babylon,
Bar 6:61 across the whole world, fulfill the *o*;
Ez 21:27 bidding him to give the *o* for slaying,
36:29 I will *o* the grain to be abundant,
Dn 2:15 the reason for this harsh *o* from the king?"
2:30 but in *o* that its meaning may be made
3:22 garments, for the king's *o* was urgent.
4:14 is this decided, by *o* of the holy ones,
5:29 Then by *o* of Belshazzar they clothed
6:24 At his *o* Daniel was removed from the den,
7: 5 It was given the *o*,
11:17 in marriage in *o* to destroy the kingdom,
Zep 3: 8 In *o* to pour out upon them my wrath,
Mt 4:21 getting their nets in *o* with their father,
6: 5 or on street corners in *o* to be noticed.
8: 8 Just give an *o* and my boy will get better.
8: 9 If I give one man the *o*,
13:30 at harvest time I will *o* the harvesters,
14:10 sent the *o* to have John beheaded in prison.
26:63 "I *o* you to tell us under oath before the
27:58 Pilate issued an *o* for its release.
27:64 You should issue an *o* having the tomb kept
Mk 1:19 were in their boat putting their nets in *o*.
14:15 room, spacious, furnished, and all in *o*.
Lk 7: 7 give the *o* and my servant will be cured.
7: 8 too am a man who knows the meaning of an *o*,
8:31 with him not to *o* them back to the abyss.
19: 4 was along Jesus' route, in *o* to see him.
Acts 6: 2 the word of God in *o* to wait on tables.
23:22 commander sent the boy away with the *o*,
Rom 1:13 in *o* to do some fruitful work among you,
5:20 The law came in *o* to increase offenses;
7:13 sin, in *o* to be seen clearly as sin,
9:11 in *o* that God's decree might stand fast
9:23 and in *o* to make known the riches of his
1Cor 9:20 a Jew to the Jews in *o* to win the Jews.

9:22 all men in *o* to save at least some of them.
14:40 that everything is done properly and in *o.*
15:23 to life again, but each one in proper *o:*
2Cor 5:17 The old *o* has passed away; now all is new!
8: 8 I am not giving an *o* but simply testing
11: 8 support from them in *o* to minister to you.
11:32 close watch on the city in *o* to arrest me,
12: 7 in *o* that I might not become conceited I
13: 7 not in *o* that we may appear approved but
Gal 2:16 in *o* to be justified by faith in Christ,
Col 2: 5 happy to see good *o* among you and the
1Thes 2: 9 you in *o* not to impose on you in any way.
2Thes 1: 5 in *o* to be found worthy of his kingdom
2:10 their hearts to the truth in *o* to be saved.
1Tm 1: 3 stay on in Ephesus in *o* to warn certain
2Tm 2: 4 this in *o* to please his commanding officer.
2:10 in *o* that they may obtain the salvation to
Ti 3:14 work in *o* to take care of their needs,
Heb 5: 6 forever, according to the *o* of Melchizedek."
5:10 priest according to the *o* of Melchizedek.
6:20 forever according to the *o* of Melchizedek.
7:11 a priest according to the *o* of Melchizedek,
7:11 a priest according to the *o* of Aaron?
7:17 forever according to the *o* of Melchizedek."
7:21 forever, according to the *o* of Melchizedek.' "
9:10 flesh, imposed until the time of the new *o.*
11:35 in *o* to obtain a better resurrection.

ORDERED (152)

Gn 43:17 Doing as Joseph had *o,*
45:21 gave them the wagons, as Pharaoh had *o,*
47:11 As Pharaoh had *o,*
50: 2 Then he *o* the physicians in his service to
Ex 1:17 did not do as the king of Egypt had *o* them,
19: 7 all that the LORD had *o* him to tell them,
31: 6 make all the things I have *o* you to make:
36: 6 *o* a proclamation to be made throughout the
Lv 7:36 he anointed them the LORD *o* the Israelites
8: 5 told them what the LORD had *o* to be done.
9: 5 So they brought what Moses had *o.*
Nm 13: 3 the desert of Paran, as the LORD had *o.*
18:24 That is why I have *o* that they are not to
20: 9 its place before the LORD, as he was *o.*
23: 2 So he did as Balaam had *o,*
23:30 And Balak did as Balaam had *o,*
30: 1 instructions, just as the LORD had *o* him.
31:47 share, Moses, as the LORD had *o,*
Dt 6: 1 has *o* that you be taught to observe in the
28:69 covenant which the LORD *o* Moses to make
31: 5 deal with them exactly as I have *o* you.
Jos 4:12 vanguard of the Israelites, as Moses had *o.*
6: 6 then *o* them to take up the ark of the
6: 7 And he *o* the people to proceed in a circle
8:29 then at sunset Joshua *o* the body removed
Jgs 7: 8 and Gideon *o* the rest of the Israelites to
1Sm 18:22 Saul then *o* his servants to speak to David
1Kgs 19: 5 touched him and *o* him to get up and eat.
19: 7 back a second time, touched him, and *o,*
21:11 did as Jezebel had *o* them in writing,
22:34 He *o* his charioteer,
2Kgs 1: 9 "Man of God," he *o,*
7:14 "Go and find out," he *o.*
9:33 "Throw her down," he *o.*
10: 8 entrance of the city until morning," he *o.*
10:14 "Take them alive," Jehu *o.*
18:16 he himself had *o* to be overlaid with gold,
18:36 for the king had *o* them not to answer him.
20: 7 Isaiah then *o* a poultice of figs to be
23:16 he *o* the bones taken from the graves and
1Chr 14:12 gods there, and David *o* them to be burnt.
21:17 it not I who *o* the census of the people?
22: 2 David then *o* that all the aliens who lived
2Chr 18:33 He *o* his charioteer,
29:15 then they came as the king had *o,*
29:21 and for Judah, and he *o* the sons of Aaron,
29:27 Then Hezekiah *o* the holocaust to be
Ezr 2:63 and His Excellency *o* them not to partake
5:14 King Cyrus *o* to be removed from the temple
7:23 Let everything that is *o* by the God of
Neh 7:65 and His Excellency *o* them not to partake
13:19 I *o* the doors to be closed and forbade
13:22 Then I *o* the Levites to purify themselves
Tb 8:19 and four rams which he *o* to be slaughtered.
Jdt 6:10 Then Holofernes *o* the servants who were
7: 1 following day Holofernes *o* his whole army,
7:16 and he *o* their proposal to be carried out.
10: 9 So they *o* the youths to open the gate for
12: 1 Then he *o* them to lead her into the room
12: 7 *o* his bodyguard not to hinder her.
13: 3 She had *o* her maid to stand outside the
Est 3: 2 that is what the king had *o* in his regard.
5: 5 And the king *o,*
9:21 He *o* them to celebrate every year both the
9:25 the king *o* in writing that the wicked plan
1Mc 1:51 *o* the cities of Judah to offer sacrifices,
3:27 so he *o* a muster of all the forces of his
4:27 out as he intended and as the king had *o.*
5:49 So Judas *o* a proclamation to be made in
9:54 Alcimus *o* the wall of the inner court of
10: 6 and he *o* that the hostages in the citadel
10:11 He *o* the workmen to build the walls and
10:62 He *o* Jonathan to be divested of his
11: 2 him, as King Alexander had *o* them to do,
11:23 this, Jonathan *o* the siege to continue.
12:17 also *o* them to come to you and greet you,
12:27 Jonathan *o* his men to be on guard and to
12:43 He also *o* his friends and soldiers to obey
15:39 He *o* him to move his troops against Judea
15:41 As the king *o,*
2Mc 1:21 he *o* them to scoop some out and bring it.
1:21 Nehemiah *o* the priests to sprinkle with
1:31 Nehemiah *o* the rest of the liquid to be
2: 1 Jeremiah the prophet *o* the deportees
2: 4 *o* that the tent and the ark should
5:12 He *o* his soldiers to cut down without
5:25 work, he *o* his men to parade fully armed.
7: 5 the king *o* them to carry him to the fire
9: 4 Therefore he *o* his charioteer to drive
13: 4 he *o* him to be taken to Beroea and
14:31 sacrifices, and *o* them to surrender Judas.
15:30 *o* Nicanor's head and whole right arm to be
Ps(s) 78: 9 The sons of Ephraim, *o* ranks of bowmen,
Sir 10: 1 the government of a prudent man is well *o.*
16:25 He *o* for all time what they were to do and
48:22 As *o* by the illustrious prophet Isaiah,
Is 23:11 *o* the destruction of Canaan's strongholds.
34:16 For the mouth of the LORD has *o* it,
36:21 for the king had *o* them not to answer him.
38:21 Isaiah then *o* a poultice of figs to be
51:23 tormentors, those who *o* you to bow down,
Jer 37:21 King Zedekiah *o* that Jeremiah be confined
38:10 Then the king *o* Ebed-melech the Cushite to
Bar 2:28 the day you *o* him to write down your law
Ez 8: 8 Son of man, he *o,* dig through the wall.
9:11 "I have done as you *o.*"
Dn 2: 2 So he *o* that the magicians,
2:12 *o* all the wise men of Babylon to be put to
2:46 and *o* sacrifice and incense offered to him.
3: 2 He then *o* the satraps,
3: 5 you are *o* to fall down and worship the
3:19 He *o* the furnace to be heated seven times
3:30 nor have we done as you *o* us for our good.
5: 2 he *o* the gold and silver vessels which
6:17 So the king *o* Daniel to be brought and
6:25 king then *o* the men who had accused Daniel,
13:18 by the side gate to fetch what she had *o,*
13:28 Before all the people they *o:*
13:32 but those wicked men *o* her to uncover her
13:56 one side, he *o* the other one to be brought.
14:14 Daniel *o* his servants to bring some ashes,
Mt 2:16 He *o* the massacre of all the boys two
12:16 *o* them not to make public what he had done.
14:19 he *o* the crowds to sit down on the grass.
16:20 Then he strictly *o* his disciples not to
18:25 of paying it, his master *o* him to be sold,
21: 6 went off and did what Jesus had *o;*
26:19 The disciples then did as Jesus had *o,*
Mk 6:17 Herod was the one who had *o* John arrested,
7:36 but the more he *o* them not to,
Lk 8:56 but he *o* them not to tell anyone what had
18:39 in the lead sternly *o* him to be quiet,
18:40 halted and *o* that he be brought to him.
Jn 2: 7 "Fill those jars with water," Jesus *o,*
8: 5 the law, Moses *o* such women to be stoned.
Acts 4:15 so they *o* them out of the court while they
5:34 accused *o* out of court for a few minutes,
5:40 They *o* them not to speak again about the
8:38 He *o* the carriage stopped,
16:22 stripped them and *o* them to be flogged.
18: 2 of Claudius had *o* all Jews to leave Rome.
21:34 he *o* Paul to be led away to headquarters.
23: 2 the high priest Ananias *o* his attendants
23:10 He therefore *o* his troops to go down and
23:35 Then he *o* Paul to be kept under guard in
25: 6 on the bench and *o* Paul to be brought in.
25:17 seat on the bench and *o* the man brought in.
27: 6 vessel bound for Italy, and he *o* us aboard.
27:43 he *o* those who could swim to jump
1Cor 9:14 Likewise the Lord himself *o* that those who
2Cor 4:15 Indeed, everything is *o* to your benefit,
Gal 2: 3 was with me, was *o* to undergo circumcision,

ORDERING (10)

2Sm 2:26 How much longer will you refrain from *o*
1Mc 1:44 *o* them to follow customs foreign to their
2Mc 6: 8 a decree was issued *o* the neighboring
14:27 and *o* him to send Maccabeus as a prisoner
Mk 3:12 *o* them sternly not to reveal who he was.
6:27 *o* him to bring back the Baptizer's head.
Lk 2: 1 a decree *o* a census of the whole world.
8:29 By now Jesus was *o* the unclean spirit to
Acts 7:44 *o* him to make it according to the pattern
23: 3 the law yourself by *o* me to be struck!"

ORDERS (73)

Gn 12:20 Then Pharaoh gave men *o* concerning him,
19: 9 an immigrant, and now he dares to give *o!*
42:25 Then Joseph gave *o* to have their
Ex 6:13 gave them his *o* regarding both the Israelites
18:23 you *o* you will be able to stand the strain,
29:35 Carry out all these *o* in regard to Aaron
Lv 9: 6 said, "This is what the LORD *o* you to do,
13:54 he shall give *o* to have the infected
Nm 14:41 are you again disobeying the LORD's *o?*
17: 5 in keeping with the *o* which the LORD had
17:12 Obeying the *o* of Moses,
Jos 1:18 If anyone rebels against your *o* and does
8: 4 Joshua sent them off by night with these *o:*
8: 8 These are my *o* to you."
Jgs 21:10 sent twelve thousand warriors with *o* to go
1Sm 7: 5 Samuel then gave *o,*
2Sm 17:23 Then, having left *o* concerning his family,
1Kgs 5:20 Give *o,* then, to have cedars from
2Kgs 11: 5 He gave them these *o:*
11:15 He had given *o* that she should not be
22: 3 with *o* to go to the high priest Hilkiah
1Chr 21:27 Then the LORD gave *o* to the angel to
23:27 for David's final *o* were to enlist the
2Chr 1:18 Solomon gave *o* for the building of a house
31:11 Hezekiah then gave *o* that chambers be
Ezr 4:21 Give *o,*
8:36 the *o* of the king were presented to the
Neh 13: 9 Then I gave *o* to purify the chambers,
Tb 6:16 "Do you not remember your father's *o?*
Jdt 2:13 disobey a single one of the *o* of your lord;
4: 8 carried out the *o* given them by Joakim,
12: 6 sent this message to Holofernes, "Give *o,*
1Mc 1:51 the *o* he published throughout his kingdom.
2:19 his fathers and consents to the king's *o,*
3:39 and ravage it according to the king's *o.*
3:42 they knew of the *o* which the king had
5:58 They gave *o* to the men of their army who
6:12 and for no cause gave *o* that the
6:23 and to follow his *o* and obey his edicts.
6:62 *o* for the encircling wall to be destroyed.
7: 9 with *o* to take revenge on the Israelites.
7:26 of Israel, with *o* to destroy the people.
9:55 a word to give *o* concerning his house.
12:23 given *o* that you should be told of this."
13:17 he gave *o* to get the money and the boys,
14:44 or to contradict the *o* given by him,
2Mc 3:13 But because of the *o* he had from the king,
5:24 with *o* to kill all the grown men and sell
7: 3 gave *o* to have pans and caldrons heated.
9: 7 the Jews, he gave *o* to drive even faster.
14:13 sent him off with *o* to put Judas to death,
15: 5 and my *o* are that you take up arms and
15:10 he gave his *o* and pointed out at the same
Sir 43: 5 made it, at whose *o* it urges on its steeds.
Jer 39:11 gave the following *o* through Nebuzaradan,
Lam 1:17 The LORD gave *o* against Jacob for his
Mt 8:18 Jesus gave *o* to cross to the other shore.
14: 9 he gave *o* that the request be granted.
Mk 1:27 gives *o* to unclean spirits and they obey!"
8:30 them strict *o* not to tell anyone about him.
13:34 and he *o* the man at the gate to watch with
Lk 14:22 some time, 'Your *o* have been carried out,
15:29 I never disobeyed one of your *o,*
17: 9 servant who was only carrying out his *o?*
Jn 11:57 priests and the Pharisees had given *o*
Acts 5:28 you strict *o* not to teach about that name,
10:48 So he gave *o* that they be baptized in the
16:35 officers with *o* to let these men go.
16:36 have sent *o* that you are to be released.
22:24 He issued *o* that he be examined under the
23:31 According to their *o,*
24:23 He gave *o* to the centurion that Paul was
25:21 so I issued *o* that he be kept in custody

ORDINANCE (29)

Ex 12:24 *o* for yourselves and your descendants.
27:21 This shall be a perpetual *o* for the
28:43 *o* for him and for his descendants.
29:28 by a perpetual *o* as a contribution.
30:21 This shall be a perpetual *o* for him and
Lv 3:17 This shall be a perpetual *o* for your
6:15 This is a perpetual *o:*
7:34 *o* as a contribution from the Israelites."
7:36 a perpetual *o* throughout their generations.
10: 9 a perpetual *o* throughout your generations,
10:15 to you and your children by a perpetual *o,*
16:29 "This shall be an everlasting *o* for you:
16:31 by everlasting *o* it shall be a most solemn
16:34 then, shall be an everlasting *o* for you:
17: 7 *o* for them and their descendants.
Nm 18: 8 by perpetual *o* I have assigned them to you
18:11 by perpetual *o* I have assigned it to you
18:19 By perpetual *o* I have assigned to you and
18:23 is a perpetual *o* for all your generations.
19:10 This is a perpetual *o,*
19:21 This shall be a perpetual *o* for you.
2Chr 8:14 And according to the *o* of his father David
Est 1: 8 *o* of the king the drinking was unstinted,
Ps(s) 81: 5 in Israel, an *o* of the God of Jacob,
119:137 are just, O LORD, and your *o* is right.
119:149 according to your *o* give me life.
Sir 44:20 In his own flesh he incised the *o,*
Jer 8: 7 my people do not know the *o* of the LORD.
Rom 13: 2 authority rebels against the *o* of God;

ORDINANCES (63)

Gn 26: 5 my mandate (my commandments, my *o,*
Ex 24: 3 related all the words and *o* of the LORD,
Dt 4:45 These are the *o,*
6:17 the *o* and statutes he has enjoined on you.
6:20 on, when your son asks you what these *o,*

ORDINANCES (cont.)

Jos 24:25 made statutes and *o* for them at Shechem,
2Sm 22:23 For his *o* were all present to me,
1Kgs 2: 3 and observing his statutes, commands, *o*,
6:12 you observe my statutes, carry out my *o*,
8:58 and *o* which he enjoined on our fathers.
2Kgs 23: 3 they would follow him and observe his *o*,
2Chr 7:17 you and keeping my statutes and *o*,
33: 8 and the statutes and the *o* given by Moses."
Ezr 7:10 and on teaching statutes and *o* in Israel.
Neh 1: 7 and the *o* which you committed to your
9:13 You gave them just *o*,
9:29 they sinned against your *o*,
10:30 the LORD, our LORD, his *o* and his statutes.
Jb 38:33 Do you know the *o* of the heavens;
Ps(s) 18:23 For his *o* were all present to me,
19:10 The *o* of the LORD are true,
89:31 my law and walk not according to my *o*,
119: 7 heart, when I have learned your just *o*.
119:13 my lips I declare all the *o* of your mouth.
119:20 with longing for your *o* at all times.
119:30 I have set your *o* before me.
119:39 which I dread, for your *o* are good.
119:43 from my mouth, for in your *o* is my hope;
119:52 I remember your *o* of old,
119:62 to give you thanks because of your just *o*.
119:75 I know, O LORD, that your *o* are just,
119:91 According to your *o* they still stand firm:
119:102 From your *o* I turn not away,
119:106 I resolve and swear to keep your just *o*.
119:120 with dread of you, and I fear your *o*.
119:121 I have fulfilled just *o*;
119:156 according to your *o* give me life.
119:160 each of your just *o* is everlasting.
119:164 times a day I praise you for your just *o*.
119:175 live to praise you, and may your *o* help me.
147:19 to Jacob, his statutes and his *o* to Israel.
147:20 his *o* he has not made known to them.
Ez 5: 6 my *o* more wickedly than the nations,
5: 6 my *o* and has not lived by my statutes.
5: 7 ordinances, but acting according to the *o*
11:12 not lived, and whose *o* you have not kept;
11:12 to the *o* of the nations around you.
11:20 statutes, and observe and carry out my *o*;
18: 9 statutes and is careful to observe my *o*,
18:17 but keeps my *o* and lives by my statutes
20:11 my statutes and made known to them my *o*,
20:13 *o* that bring life to those who keep them.
20:16 despised my *o* and desecrated my sabbaths.
20:18 statutes of your parents or keep their *o*;
20:19 my statutes and be careful to keep my *o*;
20:21 did not observe my statutes or keep my *o*
20:24 for they did not keep my *o*,
20:25 and *o* through which they could not live.
23:25 and they will judge you by their own *o*.
Hos 8:12 Though I write for him my many *o*,
Mal 3:22 Horeb, The statutes and *o* for all Israel.
Lk 1: 6 all the commandments and *o* of the Lord.

ORDINARILY (1)

Dt 18: 6 anywhere in Israel in which he *o* resides,

ORDINARY (16)

Ex 18:22 decisions for the people in all *o* cases.
18:26 decisions for the people in all *o* cases.
30:32 not be used in any *o* anointing of the body,
Lv 15:25 her flow continues beyond the *o* period,
Nm 10: 7 an assembly you are to blow an *o* blast,
16:29 if these men die an *o* death,
29: 6 in addition to the *o* new moon holocaust
Jos 14:11 less vigor whether for war or for *o* tasks.
1Sm 21: 5 to David, "I have no *o* bread on hand,
1Mc 10:62 Jonathan to be divested of his *o* garments
2Mc 14:23 of *o* people who gathered around him;
Sir 33: 9 sanctifies, and others he lists as *o* days.
Is 8: 1 and inscribe on it in *o* letters:
Acts 17:17 in the public square with *o* passers-by.
1Cor 3: 3 And is not your behavior that of *o* men?
Heb 10:29 by which he was sanctified to be *o*,

ORDINATION (13)

Ex 29:22 its right thigh, since this is the *o* ram,
29:26 take the breast of Aaron's *o* ram and wave
29:27 whether this be the *o* ram or anything else
29:31 of the *o* ram and boil it in the holy place.
29:33 was made at their *o* and consecration;
29:34 If some of the flesh of the *o* sacrifice or
Lv 7:37 *o* offerings] and peace offerings,
8:22 brought forward the second ram, the *o* ram,
8:28 holocaust on the altar as the *o* offering,
8:29 this was Moses' own portion of the *o* ram.
8:31 that is in the basket of the *o* offering,
8:33 *o* are completed; for your ordination is

OREB (7)

Jgs 7:25 *O* and Zeeb, killing Oreb at the rock of *O*
7:25 of *O* and Zeeb to Gideon beyond the Jordan.
8: 3 the princes of Midian, *O* and Zeeb.
Ps(s) 83:12 Make their nobles like *O* and Zeeb;
Is 10:26 such as struck Midian at the rock of *O*;

OREN (1)

1Chr 2:25 were Ram, the first-born, then Bunah, *O*,

ORGANIZATION (1)

Wis 7:17 that I might know the *o* of the universe

ORGANIZE (1)

1Mc 2:15 to the city of Modein to *o* the sacrifices.

ORGANIZED (2)

1Chr 7: 4 thousand men in *o* military troops,
2Mc 8: 5 Once Maccabeus got his men *o*,

ORGANS (17)

Ex 12: 9 with its head and shanks and inner *o*.
29:13 All the fat that covers its inner *o*,
29:17 inner *o* and shanks you shall first wash,
29:22 tail, the fat that covers its inner *o*,
Lv 1: 9 The inner *o* and the shanks,
1:13 The inner *o* and the shanks,
3: 3 LORD the fatty membrane over the inner *o*,
3: 9 the fatty membrane over the inner *o*,
3:14 LORD the fatty membrane over the inner *o*,
4: 8 the fatty membrane over the inner *o*,
4:11 its flesh, with its head, legs, inner *o*,
7: 3 tail, the fatty membrane over the inner *o*,
8:16 all the fat that was over the inner *o*,
8:21 the inner *o* and the shanks with water,
8:25 tail and all the fat over the inner *o*,
9:14 Having washed the inner *o* and the shanks,
9:19 tail, the fatty membrane over the inner *o*,

ORGIES (2)

Gal 5:21 factions, envy, drunkenness, *o*,
1Pt 4: 3 debauchery, evil desires, drunkenness, *o*,

ORIGIN (15)

Lv 7:21 *o* or from some loathsome crawling creature,
2Mc 7:23 as he brings about the *o* of everything,
Wis 7: 5 For no king has any different *o* or birth,
Is 23: 7 this your wanton city, whose *o* is from old,
Ez 16: 3 *o* and birth you are of the land of Canaan;
21:35 you were created, in the land of your *o*,
29:14 the land of Pathros, the land of their *o*,
Mi 5: 1 Whose *o* is from of old,
Mt 21:25 What was the *o* of John's baptism?
Mk 11:30 baptism of divine *o* or merely from men?"
Acts 15:23 to the brothers of Gentile *o* in Antioch,
Gal 2:15 Jews by birth, not sinners of Gentile *o*.
Eph 4: 3 as its *o* and peace as its binding force.
Phil 3: 9 It has its *o* in God and is based on faith.

ORIGINAL (9)

Gn 36:20 the Horite, the *o* settlers in the land:
Lv 25:28 be released and returned to its *o* owner.
27:10 both the *o* and its substitute shall be
27:33 both the *o* animal and its substitute shall
2Chr 24:13 the house of God according to its *o* form,
2Mc 2:28 for exact details to the *o* author,
Wis 13: 3 for the *o* source of beauty fashioned them.
13: 5 beauty of created things their *o* author,
Lk 1: 2 *o* eyewitnesses and ministers of the word.

ORIGINATE (3)

Jn 7:22 not *o* with Moses but with the patriarchs).
1Cor 14:36 Did the preaching of God's word *o* with you?
Jas 4: 1 do the conflicts and disputes among you *o*?

ORIGINATES (2)

Mt 15:18 what comes out of the mouth *o* in the mind?
Eph 4:14 wind of doctrine that *o* in human trickery

ORIGINS (6)

Gn 10:32 according to their *o* and by their nations.
Jn 7:27 comes, no one is supposed to know his *o*."
7:28 "So you know me, and you know my *o*?
Acts 5:38 purpose or activity is human in its *o*,
Rom 9: 5 came the Messiah (I speak of his human *o*).
Phil 3: 5 tribe of Benjamin, a Hebrew of Hebrew *o*;

ORION (3)

Jb 9: 9 He made the Bear and *O*,
38:31 the Pleiades, or loosened the bonds of *O*?
Am 5: 8 He who made the Pleiades and *O*,

ORNAMENT (3)

1Mc 1:22 the golden *o* on the façade of the temple.
Prv 20:15 of corals, wise lips are a precious *o*.
Bar 6: 8 bring gold, as to a maiden in love with *o*,

ORNAMENTATION (1)

2Mc 2:29 concern himself with what is needed for *o*,

ORNAMENTED (1)

1Mc 4:57 They *o* the façade of the temple with gold

ORNAMENTS (15)

Ex 33: 4 went into mourning, and no one wore his *o*.
33: 5 Take off your *o*,
33: 6 onward, the Israelites laid aside their *o*.
2Sm 1:24 who decked your attire with *o* of gold.
1Mc 2: 9 glorious *o* have been carried off as spoils,
14:43 the right to wear royal purple and gold *o*.
2Mc 2: 2 the gold and silver idols and their *o*.
5: 3 flights of arrows and flashes of gold *o*,
Sg 1:11 pendants of gold for you and silver *o*.
Ez 7:20 the beauty of their *o* they put their pride:
16:17 You took the splendid gold and silver *o*
16:39 garments and take away your splendid *o*,
23:26 off your clothes and seize your splendid *o*.
23:40 yourself, painted your eyes, and put on *o*.
1Tm 2: 9 decked out in fancy hair styles, gold *o*,

ORNAN (9)

1Chr 21:15 by the threshing floor of *O* the Jebusite.
21:18 on the threshing floor of *O* the Jebusite.
21:20 While *O* was threshing wheat,
21:22 David said to *O*:
21:23 But *O* said to David:
21:24 But King David replied to *O*:
21:25 So David paid *O* six hundred shekels of
21:28 on the threshing floor of *O* the Jebusite,
2Chr 3: 1 the threshing floor of *O* the Jebusite.

ORNATE (3)

Ex 39:28 the *o* turbans of fine linen;
Jgs 5:30 an *o* shawl or two for me in the spoil."
Rv 21:19 was *o* with precious stones of every sort:

ORPAH (2)

Ru 1: 4 who married Moabite women, one named *O*,
1:14 and *O* kissed her mother-in-law good-by,

ORPHAN (20)

Ex 22:21 You shall not wrong any widow or *o*.
Dt 10:18 executes justice for the *o* and the widow,
14:29 the *o* and the widow who belong to your
16:11 the alien, the *o* and the widow among you.
16:14 the *o* and the widow who belong to your
24:17 the rights of the alien or of the *o*,
24:19 it be for the alien, the *o* or the widow,
24:20 be for the alien, the *o* and the widow.
24:21 let what remains be for the alien, the *o*,
26:12 the Levite, the alien, the *o* and the widow,
26:13 the Levite, the alien, the *o* and the widow,
27:19 rights of the alien, the *o* or the widow!'
Tb 1: 8 for when my father died, he left me an *o*.
Jb 6:27 You would even cast lots for the *o*,
Sir 35:14 He is not deaf to the wail of the *o*,
Jer 7: 6 oppress the residential alien, the *o*,
22: 3 or oppress the resident alien, the *o*,
Bar 6:37 neither pity the widow nor benefit the *o*.
Hos 14: 4 for in you the *o* finds compassion."
Zec 7:10 Do not oppress the widow or the *o*,

ORPHANED (2)

Jn 14:18 I will not leave you *o*;
1Thes 2:17 were *o* by separation from you for a time

ORPHANS (19)

Ex 22:23 wives will be widows, and your children *o*.
Tb 1: 8 The third tithe I gave to *o* and widows,
2Mc 3:10 money was a care fund for widows and *o*,
8:28 to the persecuted and to widows and *o*;
8:30 and the rest to the persecuted, to *o*,
Jb 22: 9 and the resources of *o* you have destroyed.
24: 3 The asses of *o* they drive away;
29:12 the poor who cried out for help, the *o*,
Ps(s) 68: 6 The father of *o* and the defender of widows
109:12 him a kindness, nor anyone to pity his *o*.
Prv 23:10 landmark, nor invade the fields of *o*;
Is 1:17 redress the wronged, hear the *o* plea,
9:16 and their *o* and widows he does not pity;
10: 2 widows their plunder, and *o* their prey!
Jer 49:11 Leave your *o* behind,
Lam 5: 3 We have become *o*,
Ez 22: 7 within you, they oppress *o* and widows.
Mal 3: 5 Against those who defraud widows and *o*;
Jas 1:27 Looking after *o* and widows in their

ORTHOSIA (1)

1Mc 15:37 had gotten aboard a ship and escaped to *O*.

ORYX (1)

Dt 14: 5 the roe deer, the ibex, the addax, the *o*,

OSPREY (2)

Lv 11:13 the eagle, the vulture, the *o*, the kite,
Dt 14:12 the eagle, the vulture, the *o*, the various

OSTENSIBLY (1)

2Mc 3: 8 set out on his journey *o* to visit the cities

OSTRACIZE (1)

Lk 6:22 when they *o* you and insult you and

OSTRACIZED (1)

2Thes 3:14 be *o* that he may be ashamed of his conduct.

OSTRICH (5)

Lv 11:16 the various species of crows, the *o*,
Dt 14:15 all the various species of crows, the *o*,
Jb 30:29 the brother of jackals, companion to the *o*.
39:13 The wings of the *o* beat idly;
Lam 4: 3 has become as cruel as the *o* in the desert.

OSTRICHES (5)

Is 13:21 There *o* shall dwell,
34:13 an abode for jackals and a haunt for *o*.
43:20 Wild beasts honor me, jackals and *o*,
Jer 50:39 shall dwell there, and *o* shall occupy it;
Mi 1: 8 like the jackals, and mourning like the *o*.

OTHER (683)

Gn 1: 6 to separate one body of water from the *o*."
5: 4 of Seth, and he had *o* sons and daughters.
5: 7 of Enosh, and he had *o* sons and daughters.
5:10 of Kenan, and he had *o* sons and daughters.
5:13 Mahalalel, and he had *o* sons and daughters.
5:16 of Jared, and he had *o* sons and daughters.
5:19 of Enoch, and he had *o* sons and daughters.
5:22 and he had *o* sons and daughters.
5:26 of Lamech, and he had *o* sons and daughters.
5:30 of Noah, and he had *o* sons and daughters.
6:19 Of all *o* living creatures you shall bring
9:23 since their faces were turned the *o* way,
10:32 From these the *o* nations of the earth
11:11 and he had *o* sons and daughters.
11:13 of Shelah, and he had *o* sons and daughters.
11:15 of Eber, and he had *o* sons and daughters.
11:17 of Peleg, and he had *o* sons and daughters.
11:19 of Reu, and he had *o* sons and daughters.
11:21 of Serug, and he had *o* sons and daughters.
11:23 of Nahor, and he had *o* sons and daughters.
11:25 of Terah, and he had *o* sons and daughters.
13:11 Thus they separated from each *o*;
14:16 along with the women and the *o* captives.
15:10 two, and placed each half opposite the *o*;
25:22 jostled each *o* so much that she exclaimed,
25:23 But one shall surpass the *o*,
29:27 one, and then I will give you the *o* too,
30:40 The sheep, on the *o* hand,
31:50 or take *o* wives besides my daughters,
34:27 Then the *o* sons of Jacob followed up the
41: 3 Behind them seven *o* cows,
41:13 to my post, but the *o* man was impaled."
41:19 Behind them came seven *o* cows,
41:54 there was famine in all the *o* countries,
42:13 with our father, and the *o* one is gone."
43:14 you, so that he may let your *o* brother go,
43:22 have brought *o* money to procure food with.
45:23 and bread and *o* provisions for his journey.
47:21 from one end of Egypt's territory to the *o*.
48:18 the *o* one is the first-born;
49:16 for his kindred like any *o* tribe of Israel.
50: 7 court and all the *o* dignitaries of Egypt,
Ex 1:15 of whom was called Shiphrah and the *o* Puah,
14: 7 chariots and all the *o* chariots of Egypt,
16: 5 twice as much as they gather on the *o* days."
16:26 On the *o* six days you can gather it,
17:12 hands, one on one side and one on the *o*,
18: 4 The *o* was called Eliezer;
18: 7 Having greeted each *o*,
18:11 the LORD is a deity great beyond any *o*;
18:12 a holocaust and *o* sacrifices to God,
19: 5 possession, dearer to me than all *o* people,
20: 3 You shall not have *o* gods besides me.
21:18 the *o* with a stone or with his fist,
21:19 provided the *o* can get up and walk around
22: 8 must make twofold restitution to the *o*.
22: 9 or any *o* animal to another for safekeeping,
23:13 "Never mention the name of any *o* god;
24: 6 the *o* half he splashed on the altar.
25: 7 onyx stones and *o* gems for mounting on the
25:20 they shall be turned toward each *o*,
25:32 branches on one side, and three on the *o*.
26: 3 and the same for the *o* five.
26: 4 the edge of the end sheet in the *o* set.
26: 5 the loops are directly opposite each *o*.
26: 9 set, and the *o* six sheets into another set.
26:20 boards on the *o* side of the Dwelling,
26:27 the Dwelling, five for those on the *o* side,
27:15 on the *o* side there shall be hangings to
28:10 stone, and the other six on the *o* stone,
28:25 the *o* two ends of the cords being fastened
28:26 Make two *o* rings of gold and put them on
29:19 "After this take the *o* ram,
29:39 and the *o* lamb at the evening twilight.
29:41 The *o* lamb you shall offer at the evening
30:32 may you make any *o* oil of a like mixture.
33:16 out from every *o* people on the earth."
34:14 You shall not worship any *o* god,
34:30 and the *o* Israelites saw Moses and noticed
35: 9 onyx stones and *o* gems for mounting on the
35:22 necklaces and various *o* gold articles.
35:27 The princes brought onyx stones and *o* gems
35:33 in carving wood, and in every *o* craft.
35:35 thread, weaving, and all *o* arts and crafts.
36: 2 Bezalel and Oholiab and all the *o* experts
36:10 and the same for the *o* five.
36:12 loops on the inner sheet in the *o* set,
36:12 with the loops directly opposite each *o*.
36:16 and the *o* six sheets into another set.
36:17 of the corresponding sheet in the *o* set.
36:25 boards on the *o* side of the Dwelling,
36:32 the Dwelling, five for those on the *o* side,
37: 8 at one end, the *o* at the other end,
37: 9 They were turned toward each *o*,
37:18 branches on one side and three on the *o*.
38:14 toward the *o* side,
39:18 The *o* two ends of the two chains were
39:19 Two *o* gold rings were made and put on the
Lv 4:20 as he did with the *o* sin-offering bullock.
4:21 just as has been prescribed for the *o* one.
4:35 the altar with the *o* oblations of the LORD.
5: 7 a sin offering and the *o* for a holocaust.
5:10 The *o* bird shall be offered as a holocaust
5:12 the altar with the *o* oblations of the Lord.
6: 4 off these garments and put on *o* garments,
7:24 by wild beasts may be put to any *o* use,
9:16 holocaust, *o* than the morning holocaust,
11:23 All *o* winged insects that have four legs
12: 8 a holocaust and the *o* for a sin offering.
14: 9 his eyebrows, and any *o* hair he may have,
14:22 as a sin offering and the *o* as a holocaust.
14:31 as a sin offering and the *o* as a holocaust,
15:15 as a sin offering and the *o* as a holocaust.
15:30 as a sin offering and the *o* as a holocaust.
20:24 who has set you apart from the *o* nations.
20:26 you apart from the *o* nations to be my own.
25:49 or by some *o* relative or fellow clansman;
Nm 1:49 in the census along with the *o* Israelites.
1:52 the *o* Israelites shall camp by companies,
2:33 were not registered with the *o* Israelites,
4:26 and all *o* objects necessary in their use.
5:19 'If no *o* man has had intercourse with you,
5:20 by letting a man *o* than your husband
6: 3 may neither drink wine vinegar, *o* vinegar,
6:11 as a sin offering and the *o* as a holocaust,
8:12 and the *o* as a holocaust to the LORD,
9: 7 proper time along with the *o* Israelites?"
11:26 two men, one named Eldad and the *o* Medad,
18: 1 You and your sons as well as the *o* members
18: 2 also your *o* kinsmen of the tribe of Levi,
19:18 a bone, a slain person or *o* dead body,
21:13 they encamped on the *o* side of the Arnon,
22: 1 *o* side of the Jericho stretch of the Jordan.
26:62 were not registered with the *o* Israelites,
28: 4 and the *o* during the evening twilight,
28: 8 The *o* lamb,
31:42 The half for the *o* Israelites,
32:26 *o* livestock remain in the towns of Gilead,
35: 3 serve their herds and flocks and *o* animals.
35: 6 refuge, and in addition forty-two *o* cities
36: 1 the ancestral houses of the *o* Israelites.
36: 3 marry into one of the *o* Israelite tribes,
Dt 1:15 and over tens, and *o* tribal officers.
3:20 will give them on the *o* side of the Jordan.
4:19 the lot of all *o* nations under the heaven;
4:32 ask from one end of the sky to the *o*:
4:35 know the LORD is God and there is no *o*.
4:39 and on earth below, and that there is no *o*.
5: 7 You shall not have *o* gods besides me.
6:14 You shall not follow *o* gods,
7: 4 sons from following me to serving *o* gods,
8:19 the LORD, your God, and follow *o* gods,
10:10 "After I had spent these *o* forty days and
10:15 in preference to all *o* peoples,
11:16 that you serve *o* gods and worship them.
11:28 I ordain for you today, to follow *o* gods,
11:30 on the *o* side of the western road in the
13: 3 or wonder, urging you to follow *o* gods,
13: 7 entices you secretly to serve *o* gods,
13: 8 have not known, gods of any *o* nations,
13: 8 away, from one end of the earth to the *o*:
13:14 to serve *o* gods whom you have not known,
15:21 lame or blind or has any *o* serious defect,
17: 3 his covenant, by serving *o* gods,
18:20 to speak, or speaks in the name of *o* gods,
21:15 two wives loves one and dislikes the *o*;
25:13 in your bag, one large and the *o* small;
25:14 in your house, one large and the *o* small.
26:19 and glory above all *o* nations he has made,
28:14 in order to follow *o* gods and serve them.
28:64 from one end of the earth to the *o*,
29:25 went and served *o* gods and adored them,
30:17 are led astray and adore and serve *o* gods,
31:18 evil they have done in turning to *o* gods.
31:20 fat, if they turn to *o* gods and serve them,
33:24 "More blessed than the *o* sons be Asher!
Jos 4:11 and when all had reached the *o* side,
7: 7 to dwell on the *o* side of the Jordan.
7: 9 the *o* inhabitants of the land hear of it,
8:11 north of Ai, on the *o* side of the ravine.
13: 8 Now the *o* half of the tribe of Manasseh as
13:21 and the *o* cities of the tableland and,
13:27 Zaphon, the *o* part of the kingdom of Sihon,
17: 2 now made to the *o* descendants of Manasseh,
17: 2 Shemida, the *o* male children of Manasseh,
17:16 on the *o* hand,
19:27 In the *o* direction,
21: 1 the *o* tribes of the Israelites at Shiloh
22: 7 and to the *o* half Joshua had given a
22: 9 Manasseh left the *o* Israelites at Shiloh
22:11 The *o* Israelites heard the report that the
23:16 on you, serve *o* gods and worship them,
24: 2 dwelt beyond the River and served *o* gods.
24:16 forsake the LORD for the service of *o* gods.
Jgs 2:12 *o* gods of the various nations around them,
2:17 themselves to the worship of *o* gods.
2:19 following *o* gods in service and worship,
6: 9 of Egypt and of all your *o* oppressors.
7: 5 to the *o*, everyone who kneels down
7: 7 So let all the *o* soldiers go home."
7:14 Gideon, son of Joash," the *o* replied.
9:44 while the *o* two companies rushed upon all
10:13 you still forsook me and worshiped *o* gods.
13:10 came to me the *o* day has appeared to me,"
16: 7 her, "I shall be as weak as any *o* man."
16:11 her, "I shall be as weak as any *o* man."
16:13 the pin, I shall be as weak as any *o* man."
16:17 me, and I shall be as weak as any *o* man."
16:29 one at his right hand, the *o* at his left.
17: 9 my way to find some *o* place of residence."
18: 7 Sidonians and had no contact with *o* people.
18:28 and they had no contact with *o* people.
19:13 servant, "let us make for some *o* place,
20:14 assembled from their *o* cities to Gibeah,
20:15 Benjaminite swordsmen from the *o* cities
20:17 Meanwhile the *o* Israelites who,
20:30 line of battle at Gibeah as on *o* occasions.
20:31 the open field, just as on the *o* occasions.
20:32 the one led to Bethel, the *o* to Gibeon.
20:38 the *o* Israelites had agreed with the men
Ru 1: 4 women, one named Orpah, the *o* Ruth.
1:11 Have I *o* sons in my womb who may become
4: 7 take off his sandal and give it to the *o*.
1Sm 1: 2 wives, one named Hannah, the *o* Peninnah;
6:15 The men of Beth-shemesh also offered *o*
8: 5 appoint a king over us, as *o* nations have,
8:20 We too must be like *o* nations,
9: 2 was no *o* Israelite handsomer than Saul;
12:19 our *o* sins the evil of asking for a king."
13: 7 and *o* Hebrews passed over the Jordan into
14: 1 to the Philistine outpost on the *o* side."
14: 4 each side, one called Bozez, the *o* Seneh.
14: 5 north, toward Michmash, the *o* to the south,
14:40 I and my son Jonathan will stand on the *o*."
17:21 drew up opposite each *o* in battle array.
18:10 attendance, playing the harp as at *o* times,
18:16 on the *o* hand,
18:25 "The king desires no *o* price for the
18:30 against them than any *o* of Saul's officers,
19:21 Informed of this, Saul sent *o* messengers,
20:19 *o* occasion and wait near the mound there.
20:41 They kissed each *o* and wept aloud together.
21: 7 for no *o* bread was on hand except the
23:26 the gorge, David and his men took to the *o*.
26:19 'Go serve *o* gods!'
28: 8 disguised himself, putting on *o* clothes,
2Sm 2:13 of the pool and the *o* on the opposite side.
2:30 nineteen *o* servants of David were missing.
7:23 What *o* nation on earth is there like your
11: 9 palace with the *o* officers of his lord,
12: 1 there were two men, one rich, the *o* poor.
13:27 sent Amnon and all the *o* princes with him.
13:29 had commanded, all the *o* princes rose,
17: 9 in one of the caves or in some *o* place.
18:20 On some *o* day you may take the good news,
20:10 guard against the sword in Joab's *o* hand,
1Kgs 3:22 The *o* woman answered, "It is not so!
3:23 The *o* answers, 'No!
3:25 give half to one woman and half to the *o*."
3:26 The *o*,
5:11 He was wiser than all *o* men
6:27 touched a side wall while the *o* wing,
7: 5 rectangular, and the doorways faced each *o*,
7:21 called Jachin, and the *o* to the left,
7:51 and *o* articles in the treasuries of the
8:60 may know the LORD is God and there is no *o*.
10:20 and twelve *o* lions stood on the steps,
10:20 like this was produced in any *o* kingdom.
12:29 And he put one in Bethel, the *o* in Dan.
18:23 prepare the *o* and place it on the wood,
20:23 On the *o* hand,
20:29 encamped opposite each *o* for seven days.
22: 7 "Is there no *o* prophet of the LORD here
22: 8 *o* through whom we might consult the LORD,
22:12 *o* prophets prophesied in a similar vein,
2Kgs 2:15 in Jericho, who were on the *o* side,
5:17 sacrifice to any *o* god except to the LORD.
7:15 was strewn with garments and *o* objects
9: 7 the *o* servants of the LORD shed by Jezebel,
11:17 and the king and the people as the *o*,
12: 8 the priest Jehoiada and the *o* priests.
12:13 and for any *o* expenses that were necessary
17: 7 Egypt, and because they venerated *o* gods.
17:35 "You must not venerate *o* gods,
17:37 for you, and you must not venerate *o* gods.

OTHER (cont.)
17:38 you must not venerate *o* gods.
19:11 of Assyria have done to all *o* countries:
22:17 me and have burned incense to *o* gods,
23:24 all the *o* horrors to be seen in the land
25:17 and so for the *o* pillar,
25:28 the *o* kings who were with him in Babylon.
1Chr 3: 9 David, in addition to *o* sons by concubines;
6:33 Levites were appointed to all the *o* services
6:46 The *o* Kohathites obtained ten cities by
12:38 From the *o* side of the Jordan,
14: 3 David took *o* wives in Jerusalem and became
19:16 the Arameans from the *o* side of the River,
21: 2 to Joab and to the *o* generals of the army,
23:17 Eliezer had no *o* sons,
27: 1 and *o* officers who served the king in all
29: 2 stones, every *o* kind of precious stone,
29:21 and many *o* sacrifices for all Israel;
29:24 and also all the *o* sons of King David,
2Chr 2: 4 for our God is greater than all *o* gods.
3:12 a wall of the building, while the *o* wing,
3:17 for the right side and the *o* for the left,
5: 1 the gold and all the *o* articles in the
5:13 cymbals and *o* musical instruments to
9: 9 There was no *o* spice like that which the
9:19 Twelve *o* lions stood there,
9:19 had ever been produced in any *o* kingdom.
9:22 Thus King Solomon surpassed all the *o*
11:21 than all his *o* wives and sixty concubines;
18: 6 "Is there no *o* prophet of the LORD here
18:11 The *o* prophets prophesied in the same vein,
20:23 of Seir, they began to destroy each *o*.
23: 6 but all the *o* people must observe the
24:14 and basins and *o* gold and silver utensils.
25:17 "Come, let us meet each *o* face to face."
26:17 and with him eighty *o* priests of the LORD,
26:20 priest and all the *o* priests examined him,
28:25 high places to offer sacrifice to *o* gods.
31: 6 Israelites and Judahites living in *o*
32:13 I have done to all the peoples of *o* lands?
32:15 Since no *o* god of any other nation or
32:17 "As the gods of the nations in *o* lands
32:19 of the gods of the *o* peoples of the earth,
32:22 king of Assyria, as from every *o* power;
32:27 jewels, and *o* precious things of all kinds;
34:13 Some of the *o* Levites were scribes,
34:22 Then Hilkiah and the *o* men from the king
34:25 me and have offered incense to *o* gods,
Ezr 1:10 *o* ware,
2:31 sons of the *o* Elam,
4:10 and the *o* peoples whom the great and
6:16 Levites, and the *o* returned exiles
7:24 or any *o* servant of that house of God.
9:11 from one end to the *o* in their uncleanness.
10:25 Among the *o* Israelites:
Neh 1: 2 of my brothers, came with *o* men from Judah.
2:12 Then I set out by night with only a few *o*
2:12 and with no *o* animals but my own mount.
4:10 took a hand in the work, while the *o* half,
4:11 with one hand and held a weapon with the *o*.
6: 1 and our *o* enemies that I had rebuilt the
6:14 *o* prophets who were trying to frighten me.
8:15 oleasters, myrtle, palm and *o* leafy trees,
10:32 them on the sabbath or on any *o* holyday.
11: 1 other nine would remain in the *o* cities.
11:20 Levites, were in all the *o* cities of Judah,
12:24 the man of God, one section opposite the *o*,
12:38 the *o* half of the princes of the people,
13:15 grapes, figs, and every *o* kind of burden,
13:16 every *o* kind of merchandise and selling it
13:24 to the languages of the various *o* peoples.
Tb 1: 7 oil, pomegranates, figs, and *o* fruits.
3:15 and he has no *o* child to make his heir,
3:15 *o* relative whom I might bide my time
3:17 before any *o* who might wish to marry her.
5: 6 The *o* replied: "Yes, I have been there
6:12 has a daughter named Sarah, but no *o* child.
6:12 all *o* men have the right to marry her.
6:13 that it is your right, before all *o* men,
6:15 And they have no *o* son to bury them!"
7:15 the *o* bedroom and bring the girl there."
8:21 the *o* half will be yours when I and my
Jdt 5: 4 with all the *o* inhabitants of the West?"
8:20 since we acknowledge no *o* god but the Lord,
9:14 and that there is no *o* who protects the
10: 4 rings, earrings, and all her *o* jewelry.
10:21 and gold, emeralds and *o* precious stones.
11:21 "No *o* woman from one end of the world to
11:21 woman from one end of the world to the *o*
13: 3 the bedroom and wait, as on the *o* days,
14: 4 Then you and all the *o* inhabitants of the
14:12 leaders and all their *o* commanders.
15:13 and she and the *o* women crowned themselves
Est 2:12 *o* six months with perfumes and cosmetics.
2:17 king loved Esther more than all *o* women,
3: 8 differing from those of every *o* people.
B: 4 by its laws is opposed to every *o* people
D: 4 while the *o* followed her, bearing her train.
9:12 they have done in the *o* royal provinces!
9:16 The *o* Jews,
F: 7 of God, the second for all the *o* nations.
1Mc 5:14 reading this letter, suddenly *o* messengers,
5:27 have been imprisoned in *o* cities of Gilead.
5:36 Maked, Bosor, and the *o* cities of Gilead.
5:37 Raphon, on the *o* side of the stream.
5:41 and camps on the *o* side of the river,
6:20 he constructed catapults and *o* devices.
6:29 Mercenary forces also came to him from *o*
6:38 one or the *o* of the two flanks of the army,
8:11 All the *o* kingdoms and islands that had
9:22 The *o* acts of Judas,
9:45 on one side, marsh and thickets on the *o*,
9:48 the Jordan and swam across to the *o* side,
10:38 obey no *o* authority than the high priest.
10:43 he owes the king, or because of any *o* debt,
10:54 us now establish friendship with each *o*.
10:56 in Ptolemais, so that we may see each *o*,
11: 6 greeted each *o* and spent the night there.
11: 9 "Come, let us make a pact with each *o*;
11:24 silver, gold apparel, and many *o* presents,
11:35 release from payment of all *o* things
11:41 of Jerusalem and from the *o* strongholds,
12: 2 Sparta and *o* places for the same purpose.
12:11 offer on our feasts and *o* appropriate days,
12:45 with *o* strongholds and their garrisons,
13:39 Any *o* tax that may have been collected in
15: 5 *o* privileges they conferred on you.
16:19 sent *o* men to Gazara to do away with John.
16:23 and his *o* achievements these things are
2Mc 2: 3 With *o* similar words he urged them not to
3:26 Then two *o* young men,
4:19 but should be used for some *o* purpose.
4:32 he had already sold some *o* vessels in Tyre
4:35 Jews, but many people of *o* nations as well,
4:38 his purple robe, tore off his *o* garments,
5:16 made by *o* kings for the advancement,
6:14 Thus, in dealing with *o* nations,
10:28 *o* taking fury as their leader in the fight.
11: 3 he did on the sanctuaries of the *o* nations;
11:31 to observe their dietary laws and *o* laws,
12:11 cattle and to help them in every *o* way.
13: 6 of sacrilege or notorious for certain *o* crimes
14:11 the *o* Friends who were hostile to Judas
14:26 Alcimus saw their friendship for each *o*,
15: 2 has exalted with holiness above all *o* days."
15:33 *o* wages of his folly opposite the temple.
Jb 40:32 upon him, no need to recall any *o* conflict!
42:15 In all the land no *o* women were as
Ps(s) 16: 4 multiply their sorrows who court *o* gods.
19: 7 forth, and its course is to their *o* end;
55:14 But you, my *o* self,
147:20 He has not done thus for any *o* nation;
Prv 28:28 the wicked gain pre-eminence, *o* men hide;
Eccl 3:19 the one dies as well as the *o*.
4:10 falls, the *o* will lift up his companion.
4:11 two sleep together, they keep each *o* warm.
7:14 Both the one and the *o* God has made,
9:13 *o* hand I saw this wise deed under the sun,
Sg 5: 9 How does your lover differ from any *o*,
5: 9 How does your lover differ from any *o*,
Wis 2:15 us, Because his life is not like *o* men's,
Sir 6:11 When things go well, he is your *o* self,
26: 6 and a scourging tongue like the *o* three.
33:15 in pairs, the one the opposite of the *o*.
40:16 riverbank, withered before all *o* plants;
40:26 he who has it need seek no *o* support:
45:18 of *o* families were inflamed against him,
Is 6: 3 they cried one to the *o*.
13: 8 They look aghast at each *o*,
26:13 our God, *o* lords than you have ruled us;
41: 6 One man helps another, one says to the *o*,
42: 8 my glory I give to no *o*,
44:14 and lays hold of *o* trees of the forest,
45: 5 I am the LORD and there is no *o*,
45: 6 I am the LORD, there is no *o*;
45:18 I am the LORD, and there is no *o*.
45:21 the LORD, besides whom there is no *o* God?
45:22 there is no *o*!
46: 9 I am God, there is no *o*,
Jer 2:11 Does any *o* nation change its gods?—
9: 4 Each one deceives the *o*,
9:19 this dirge, and each *o* this lament.
13:14 I will dash them against each *o*,
17:19 and leave, and at the *o* gates of Jerusalem.
23:27 their dreams which they recount to each *o*,
23:30 the LORD, who steal my words from each *o*.
24: 2 But the *o* basket contained very bad figs,
25:26 the north, near and far, one after the *o*;
25:33 strewn from one end of the earth to the *o*.
32:20 day, both in Israel and among all *o* men,
34: 1 subject to him, as well as the *o* peoples,
36:12 son of Hananiah, and the *o* princes.
39: 3 all the *o* princes of the king of Babylon.
40:11 and those in all *o* lands heard that the
41:11 and the *o* army leaders with him heard of
41:13 son of Kareah, and the *o* army leaders,
44: 2 on Jerusalem and the *o* cities of Judah.
52:22 and so for the *o* pillar.
52:32 the *o* kings who were with him in Babylon.
Bar 1:22 of our own wicked hearts, served *o* gods,
3:36 no *o* is to be compared to him:
Ez 1:11 the *o* two wings of each covered his body.
1:23 wings were stretched out, one toward the *o*.
3:19 If, on the *o* hand,
3:21 When, on the *o* hand,
4: 8 you cannot turn from one side to the *o*
6: 8 have escaped to *o* nations from the sword,
8:15 You shall see *o* abominations,
15: 2 wood of the vine better than any *o* wood?
16:34 you were different from all *o* women.
18:14 On the *o* hand,
21:19 prophesy, brushing one hand against the *o*:
21:22 one hand against the *o* and wreak my fury.
22:13 I am brushing one hand against the *o*
25: 8 the house of Judah is like all *o* nations,"
31: 5 grew taller than every *o* tree of the field,
40:23 one hundred cubits from one gate to the *o*.
40:25 windows on both sides, like the *o* windows.
40:40 and on the *o* side of the vestibule of the
40:44 south, and the *o* beside the south gate,
41: 6 built one above the *o* in three stories,
41:19 face looking at a palmtree on the *o*;
41:24 were on one doorjamb and two on the *o*.
42:14 They shall put on *o* garments,
44:19 of the sanctuary, putting on *o* garments;
47:18 side, and the land of Israel on the *o* side,
Dn 1:10 with the *o* young men of your age,
1:13 *o* young men who eat from the royal table,
2:30 that I am wiser than any *o* living person,
3: 4 bagpipe, and all the *o* musical instruments,
3: 7 bagpipe, and all the *o* musical instruments,
3:10 and all the *o* musical instruments should
3:15 bagpipe, and all the *o* musical instruments;
3:21 their coats, hats, shoes and *o* garments,
3:37 are reduced, O Lord, beyond any *o* nation,
3:96 there is no *o* God who can rescue like this."
7:12 The *o* beasts,
7:20 on its head, and the *o* one that sprang up,
8: 3 horns, the one larger and newer than the *o*.
11:38 silver, precious stones, and *o* treasures.
13:10 they did not tell each *o* their trouble,
13:13 One day they said to each *o*,
13:14 met again, they asked each *o* the reason.
13:52 After they were separated one from the *o*,
13:56 side, he ordered the *o* one to be brought.
14:41 of Daniel, and there is no *o* besides you!"
Hos 2: 2 one head and come up from *o* lands,
3: 1 to *o* gods and are fond of raisin cakes.
Jl 2:27 am the LORD, your God, and there is no *o*;
Mi 7: 2 to shed blood, each one ensnares the *o*.
Zep 2:15 That told herself, "There is no *o* than I!"
Hg 2:12 or pottage, or wine, or oil, or any *o* food,
Zec 4: 3 one on the right and the *o* on the left."
7: 9 show kindness and compassion toward each *o*.
11: 7 one of which I called "Favor," and the *o*,
11:14 Then I snapped asunder my *o* staff,
Mal 2:10 Why then do we break faith with each *o*,
Mt 4:21 farther and caught sight of two *o* brothers,
5:39 the right cheek, turn and offer him the *o*.
6:24 *o* or be attentive to one and despise the *o*.
8:18 Jesus gave orders to cross to the *o* shore.
11:18 In *o* words,
12: 4 him and his men or anyone *o* than priests?
12:13 it became as sound as the *o*.
12:33 rotten and its fruit rotten, one or the *o*,
14:22 the boat and precede him to the *o* side.
16: 5 discovered when they arrived at the *o* side
18: 6 On the *o* hand,
20: 3 came out about midmorning and saw *o* men
20:21 at your right hand and the *o* at your left,
20:24 The *o* ten,
22: 4 A second time he sent *o* servants, saying:
23: 4 hard to carry, to lay on *o* men's shoulders,
24:31 from one end of the heavens to the *o*.'
25: 2 foolish, while the *o* five were sensible.
25:11 Later the *o* bridesmaids came back.
26:35 And all the *o* disciples said the same.
27:61 and the *o* Mary remained sitting there,
28: 1 came with the *o* Mary to inspect the tomb.
Mk 4:13 you going to understand *o* figures like it?
4:19 cravings of *o* sorts come to choke it off;
4:36 sitting, while the *o* boats accompanied him.
5: 1 territory on the *o* side of the lake.
5:21 back to the *o* side again in the boat,
6:45 precede him to the *o* side toward Bethsaida,
7: 4 There are many *o* traditions they observe
7:13 And you have many *o* such practices besides."
8:13 boat again, and went off to the *o* shore.
10:37 one at your right and the *o* at your left,
10:41 The *o* ten,
12:31 is no *o* commandment greater than these."
12:32 'He is the One, there is no *o* than he.'
16:20 but *o* terrible things are imminent.
Lk 3:19 brother's wife, and for all his *o* crimes.
4:43 "To *o* towns I must announce the good news
5: 7 mates in the *o* boat to come and help them.
6:29 you on one cheek, turn and give him the *o*;
6:49 On the *o* hand,
7:30 Pharisees and the lawyers, on the *o* hand,
7:41 a total of five hundred coins, the *o* fifty.
11:26 with seven *o* spirits far worse than itself,
16:13 he will hate the one and love the *o*
16:13 be attentive to the one and despise the *o*.
17:17 Where are the *o* nine?
17:24 flashes from one end of the sky to the *o*.
17:34 one will be taken and the *o* left.
17:35 one will be taken and the *o* left."
18:10 one was a Pharisee, the *o* a tax collector.
18:13 The *o* man,

18:14 the temple justified but the *o* did not.
20: 2 In *o* words, who has authorized you?"
21:29 "Notice the fig tree, or any *o* tree.
22:65 directed many *o* insulting words at him.
23:12 who had previously been set against each *o*,
23:33 one on his right and the *o* on his left.
23:40 But the *o* one rebuked him:
24:10 *o* women with them also told the apostles,
Jn 6:22 crowd remained on the *o* side of the lake.
6:25 they found him on the *o* side of the lake,
8:14 you know neither the one nor the *o*.
8:18 my behalf, the Father who sent me is the *o*."
10: 1 in some *o* way is a thief and a marauder.
10:16 *o* sheep that do not belong to this fold.
11:56 in the temple vicinity saying to each *o*,
13:34 for you, so must your love be for each *o*.
19:24 They said to each *o*,
19:32 Jesus, first of the one, then of the *o*.
20: 2 she ran off to Simon Peter and the *o* disciple
20: 3 Peter and the *o* disciple started out on
20: 4 but then the *o* disciple outran Peter and
20:12 One was seated at the head and the *o* at
20:25 The *o* disciples kept telling him:
20:30 performed many *o* signs as well
21: 2 Zebedee's sons, and two *o* disciples.
21: 8 Meanwhile the *o* disciples came in the boat,
21:25 are still many *o* things that Jesus did,
Acts 2:37 They asked Peter and the *o* apostles,
2:40 of his testimony he used many *o* arguments,
4:12 for there is no *o* name in the whole world
5:39 If, on the *o* hand,
7:26 Why are you trying to hurt each *o*?'
9:32 among *o* places
17:32 must hear you on this topic some *o* time."
19:25 these men and *o* workers in the same craft.
27: 1 Paul and some *o* prisoners were handed over
27:44 on planks, or on *o* debris from the ship.
Rom 1:13 among you, as I have among the *o* Gentiles.
7: 4 to that *O* who was raised from the dead,
8:39 height nor depth nor any *o* creature,
9:18 In *o* words,
12:10 Anticipate each *o* in showing respect.
13: 9 and any *o* commandment there may be are all
1Cor 2:15 The spiritual man, on the *o* hand,
3:11 *o* than the one that has been laid,
6:18 *o* sin a man commits is outside his body,
7:12 As for the *o* matters,
7:34 The married woman, on the *o* hand,
11: 7 A man, on the *o* hand,
11:16 the churches of God recognize any *o* usage.
11:34 As for *o* matters,
14: 3 The prophet, on the *o* hand,
14:17 indeed, but the *o* man will not be helped.
15:37 but a kernel of wheat or some *o* grain.
2Cor 11: 4 or a gospel *o* than the gospel you accepted,
11: 8 I robbed *o* churches,
11:28 Leaving *o* sufferings unmentioned,
12:13 inferior to the *o* churches except in this,
12:18 to you, and I sent the *o* brother with him.
Gal 1: 7 But there is no *o*.
1: 9 gospel to you *o* than the one you received,
1:19 I did not meet any *o* apostles except James,
3:10 on observance of the law, on the *o* hand,
3:24 In *o* words,
4:22 slave girl, and the *o* by his freeborn wife.
Phil 1:22 If, on the *o* hand,
2: 9 on him the name above every *o* name,
1Thes 5:15 See that no one returns evil to any *o*;
1Tm 1:10 and those who in *o* ways flout the sound
5:24 while *o* men's sins will appear only later.
6: 3 Whoever teaches in any *o* way,
Heb 7:27 Unlike the *o* high priests,
10: 9 In *o* words,
10:11 *o* priest stands ministering day by day,
10:23 each *o* to love and good deeds.
10:33 at *o* times you associated yourselves with
Jas 1:25 There is, on the *o* hand,
3Jn 1: 2 in all *o* ways as you do in the spirit.
Rv 2: 9 nothing *o* than members of Satan's assembly.
3:15 How I wish you were one or the *o*—
4: 4 this throne were twenty-four *o* thrones
8:13 the *o* three angels are about to blow!"
16:19 parts, and the *o* Gentile cities also fell.
17: 4 adorned with gold and pearls and *o* jewels.

OTHER-WORLDLY (1)

Lk 16: 8 worldly take more initiative than the *o*

OTHERS (208)

Gn 15:16 time-span the *o* shall come back here;
31:49 you and me when we are out of each *o* sight.
32:20 all the *o* who followed behind the droves,
35: 2 his family and all the *o* who were with him:
41: 3 on the bank of the Nile beside the *o*,
Ex 9:21 *O*, however, did not take the warning
24: 2 the *o* shall not come too near,
35:34 the tribe of Dan, the ability to teach *o*.
Lv 19:19 animals with *o* of a different species;
Nm 1:47 registered by ancestral tribe with the *o*.
22:15 numerous and more distinguished than the *o*.
Jgs 6:35 and these tribes advanced to meet the *o*.
20:47 But six hundred *o* who turned and fled
1Sm 5: 5 nor any *o* who enter the temple of Dagon
1Chr 9:29 *O* were appointed to take care of the
16:41 Jeduthun and the *o* who were chosen
26:28 son of Zeruiah, and all *o* had consecrated,
Ezr 3:12 Many *o*, however, lifted up their voices
Neh 2:16 *o* who would be concerned about the matter.
5: 3 *O* said: "We are forced to pawn
5: 4 Still *o* said: "To pay the king's tax
5: 5 our fields and our vineyards belong to *o*."
7: 3 watch posts, and *o* before their own houses."
10:29 and all *o* who have separated themselves
1Mc 6:43 any of the *o* and covered with royal armor,
8: 5 and the *o* who opposed them in battle had
10:71 and let us test each *o* strength there;
10:72 I am and who the *o* are who are helping me.
15:33 what we took is not the property of *o*,
16:20 He also sent *o* to seize Jerusalem and the
2Mc 2:27 one who thus seeks to give enjoyment to *o*.
3:19 to the walls, *o* peered through the windows,
5:23 his fellow citizens worse than the *o* did.
5:27 about nine *o* withdrew to the wilderness,
6:11 *O*, who had assembled in nearby caves to
7: 2 One of the brothers, speaking for the *o*,
7: 4 of the one who had spoken for the *o*,
7:39 and treated him even worse than the *o*,
8: 1 *o* who remained faithful to Judaism,
8:14 But the *o* sold everything they had left,
9: 6 bowels of *o* with many barbarous torments.
9:28 sufferings such as he had inflicted on *o*,
10:36 *O* who climbed up the same way swung around
10:36 Still *o* broke down the gates and let in
11: 7 and he exhorted the *o* to join him in
Jb 21:33 and the countless *o* who have gone before.
24:24 they are laid low and, like all *o*,
30:25 Or have I not wept for the hardships of *o*;
31:10 for another, and may *o* cohabit with her!
34:24 the mighty, and sets *o* in their stead,
Ps(s) 49:11 pass away, leaving to *o* their wealth.
Prv 5: 9 her house, Lest you give your honor to *o*,
11:25 who refreshes *o* will himself be refreshed.
Eccl 2: 9 up more than all *o* before me in Jerusalem;
5: 7 him and above these are *o* higher still
7:22 that you have many times spoken ill of *o*.
Wis 11:13 own torments was a benefit to these *o*,
16: 3 That those *o*,
18: 1 And those *o*,
19: 5 while those *o* met an extraordinary death.
19:14 *o* did not receive unfamiliar visitors,
19:17 *o* had been at the portals of the just
Sir 11:19 will be till he dies and leaves them to *o*.
14: 4 What he denies himself he collects for *o*,
14:15 Will you not leave your riches to *o*,
31:31 and distress him not in the presence of *o*.
33: 9 and *o* he lists as ordinary days.
33:12 *O* he curses and brings low,
36:18 yet some foods are more agreeable than *o*;
44: 9 But of *o* there is no memory,
48:16 was right, but *o* were extremely sinful.
49: 5 So he gave over their power to *o*,
Is 49:12 from afar, *o* from the north and the west,
56: 8 *O* will I gather to him besides those
65:22 *o* to live in, or plant for others to eat.
Jer 26:22 and *o* with him into Egypt to bring Uriah
34:10 All the princes and the *o* who entered the
36:32 and many *o* of the same kind in addition.
Bar 3:19 world, and *o* have risen up in their stead.
6:31 their gods as *o* do at a funeral banquet.
Ez 9: 5 To the *o* I heard him say:
28:24 than all the *o* about them who despise them;
39:15 until *o* have buried it in the Valley of
40:24 they were the same size as the *o*.
40:28 Its dimensions were the same as the *o*;
40:29 its vestibule were the same size as the *o*.
40:33 its vestibule were the same size as the *o*;
Dn 2:40 break in pieces and subdue all these *o*,
7: 3 immense beasts, each different from the *o*.
7: 7 fourth beast, different from all the *o*,
7:19 so very terrible and different from the *o*,
7:23 on earth, different from all the *o*;
8: 8 shattered, and in its place came up four *o*,
11: 4 torn to pieces and belong to *o* than they.
12: 2 *o* shall be an everlasting horror and
12: 5 I, Daniel, looked and saw two *o*,
Na 3: 9 her strength, and Egypt, and *o* without end;
Mt 5:19 of these commands and teaches *o* to do so
6:14 "If you forgive the faults of *o*,
6:15 If you do not forgive *o*,
6:16 faces so that *o* may see they are fasting.
7: 2 on *o* will be the verdict passed on you.
7:12 *o* the way you would have them treat you:
10:17 Be on your guard with respect to *o*.
13:11 of God, but it has not been given to the *o*.
13:41 his kingdom all who draw *o* to apostasy,
15:30 the blind, the mute, and many *o* besides.
16:14 *o* Elijah, still others Jeremiah or one
20: 6 afternoon he found still *o* standing around.
20:28 Man who has come, not to be served by *o*,
21:41 lease his vineyard out to *o* who will see to it
23:23 have practiced, without neglecting the *o*.
23:34 *o* you will flog in your synagogues and
26:67 *O* slapped him, saying:
27:42 "He saved *o* but he cannot save himself!
Mk 4:11 *o* outside it is all presented in parables,
6:15 *O* were saying, "He is Elijah"; still others,
8:28 John the Baptizer, others, Elijah, still *o*,
11: 8 while *o* spread reeds which they had cut in
12: 5 So too with many *o*;
12: 9 tenants and turn his vineyard over to *o*.
12:43 than all the *o* who donated to the treasury.
15:31 "He saved *o* but he cannot save himself!
15:41 *o* who had come up with him to Jerusalem.
16:13 good news to the *o*; but the others put no
Lk 5:29 crowd of tax collectors and *o* at dinner.
6:31 to *o* what you would have them do to you.
8: 3 and many *o* who were assisting them out of
9: 8 from the dead"; *o*, "Elijah has appeared
9: 8 and still *o*,
9:19 while *o* claim that one of the prophets of
9:34 disciples grew fearful as the *o* entered it.
11:16 *O*, to test him,
11:42 should practice, without omitting the *o*.
20:16 tenant farmers and give the vineyard to *o*."
23:32 Two *o* who were criminals were led along
23:35 kept jeering at him, saying, "He saved *o*;
24: 9 all these things to the Eleven and the *o*.
Jn 2:14 and doves, and *o* seated changing coins.
4:38 *O* have done the labor,
7:12 "He is a good man," while *o* kept saying,
7:41 *O* were claiming, "He is the Messiah."
9: 9 *o* maintained it was not but someone who
9:16 *O* objected,
10:21 *O* maintained: "These are not the words
11:46 Some *o*,
12:29 *O* maintained,
13:14 then you must wash each *o* feet.
18:34 own, or have *o* been telling you about me?"
19:18 they crucified him, and two *o* with him;
Acts 8: 7 Many *o* were paralytics or cripples,
12:12 where many *o* were gathered in prayer.
13:16 Israelites and you *o* who reverence our God,
13:26 of Abraham and you *o* who reverence our God,
14: 4 with the Jews and *o* with the apostles.
15: 2 and some *o* should go up to see the
15:35 continued in Antioch, along with many *o*,
17: 9 they released Jason and the *o* on bail.
17:18 *O* commented,
17:32 of the dead, some sneered, while *o* said,
17:34 a woman named Damaris, and a few *o*.
28:24 *o* would not believe.
28:31 *o* would not believe.
Rom 1:32 not only do them but approve them in *o*.
2: 3 these things in *o* yet do them yourself?
2:21 Now then, teacher of *o*,
11:17 have been grafted in among the *o* and have
1Cor 5:13 God will judge the *o*.
9: 2 Although I may not be an apostle for *o*,
9:12 If *o* have this right over you,
9:27 preached to *o* I myself should be rejected.
14:19 *o* than ten thousand words in a tongue.
15:10 I have worked harder than all the *o*,
2Cor 3: 1 to you or from you as *o* might?
7: 5 quarrels with *o* and fears within myself.
8: 8 love against the concern which *o* show.
8:13 relief of *o* ought not to impoverish you;
10:15 not boast immoderately of the work of *o*;
Gal 2:12 Gentiles before *o* came who were from James.
Phil 1:13 the praetorium here, and to *o* as well;
1:15 and rivalry, but *o* do so out of good will.
1:17 *o* promote Christ,
2: 3 humbly of *o* as superior to themselves.
2: 4 to *o*' interests rather than to his own.
4: 3 Clement and the *o* who have labored with me,
Col 2: 1 many *o* who have never seen me in the flesh.
1Thes 2: 6 did we seek glory from men, you or any *o*,
2Thes 3: 1 may make progress and be hailed by many *o*,
1Tm 5:22 or you may be sharing in the misdeeds of *o*.
2Tm 2: 2 men who will be able to teach *o*.
2:20 for distinguished and *o* for common use.
3:13 will go from bad to worse, deceiving *o*,
Phlm 1: 6 sharing of the faith with *o* may enable you
Heb 5:12 by this time you should be teaching *o*,
11:35 *O* were tortured and would not receive
11:36 Still *o* endured mockery,
2Pt 2: 5 as a preacher of holiness, with seven *o*,
1Jn 4: 5 Those *o* belong to the world;
Jude 1:22 the *o* you must rescue,
Rv 2:24 And now I address myself to you *o* in
14: 9 followed the *o* and said in a loud voice:
18: 6 Pay her back as she has paid *o*;
20: 5 The *o* who were dead did not come to life

OTHERWISE (60)

Gn 11: 4 *o* we shall be scattered all over the
32:12 *O* I fear that when he comes he will strike
38:23 *o* we shall become a laughingstock.
Ex 1:10 *o*, in time of war they too may join
5: 3 *o* he will punish us with pestilence or the
12:33 they thought that *o* they would all die.
19:21 *o* many of them will be struck down.
33: 3 *o* I might exterminate you on the way."
34:16 *o*, when their daughters render their
Lv 5:21 *o* retaining his neighbor's goods unjustly,
8:35 *o*, you shall die;
11:39 one of the animals that you could *o* eat,
16: 2 *o*, when I reveal myself in a cloud

OTHERWISE (cont.)

18:28 *o* the land will vomit you out also for
20:22 *o* the land where I am bringing you to
21:12 *o* he will profane the sanctuary of his God,
21:15 *o* he will have base off-spring among his
Nm 1:53 *O* God's wrath will strike the Israelite
15: 5 each lamb sacrificed in holocaust or *o*.
16:26 *o* you too will be swept away because of
Dt 8:17 *O*, you might say to yourselves,
12:29 *O*, once they have been wiped out before
21:23 *o*, since God's curse rests on him
22: 8 *o*, if someone falls off,
23:15 *o*,
23:22 *o* you will be held guilty,
24:15 *O* he will cry to the LORD against you,
Jgs 9:15 *O*, let fire come from the buckthorn and
1Sm 4: 9 *o* you will become slaves to the Hebrews,
13:19 *O* the Hebrews will make swords or spears."
25:17 for you must realize that *o* evil is in
25:34 *O*, as the LORD,
2Sm 14:19 just as your majesty has said, and not *o*.
17:16 *O* the king and all the people with him
2Kgs 2:10 *o* not."
2Chr 1:10 for *o* who could rule this great people of
25: 8 *o* the LORD will defeat you in the face of
35:21 who is with me, as *o* he will destroy you."
Tb 4:19 but if he should decide *o*,
Jdt 5:21 *o* their Lord and God will shield them,
1Mc 14:45 Whoever acts *o* or violates any of these
Jb 35:15 But now that you have done *o*,
Eccl 3:15 and God restores what would *o* be displaced.
Wis 8:21 could not *o* possess her except God gave it
Dn 3:15 *o*,
6: 8 *o* he shall be cast into a den of lions.
6:13 *o* he shall be cast into a den of lions?"
14:12 *o* Daniel shall die for his lies against
Mt 2:13 Stay there until I tell you *o*.
5:25 *O* your opponent may hand you over to the
6: 1 *O* expect no recompense from your heavenly
13:15 *o* they might see with their eyes,
27:64 *O* his disciples may go and steal him and
Jn 14: 2 *o*,
Rom 11: 6 of their works *o* grace would not be grace.
1Cor 7:14 If it were *o*,
15: 2 *O* you have believed in vain.
1Thes 4:13 *o* you might yield to grief,
1Tm 6: 1 *o* the name of God and the church's
Heb 10: 2 Were matters *o*,

OTHNI (1)

1Chr 26: 7 The sons of Shemaiah were *O*,

OTHNIEL (9)

Jos 15:17 *O*, son of Caleb's brother Kenaz,
15:18 On the day of her marriage to *O*,
Jgs 1:13 *O*, son of Caleb's younger brother Kenaz,
1:14 On the day of her marriage to *O* she
3: 9 LORD, he raised up for them a savior, *O*,
3:11 then was at rest for forty years, until *O*,
1Chr 4:13 The sons of Kenaz were *O* and Seraiah.
4:13 The sons of *O* were Hathath and Meonothai;
27:15 the Netophathite, of the family of *O*,

OURSELVES (62)

Gn 11: 4 let us build *o* a city and a tower with its
11: 4 top in the sky, and so make a name for *o*;
37:27 instead of doing away with him *o*.
43: 7 man kept asking about *o* and our family:
Ex 1: 9 people are growing, more so than we *o*!
10:26 but we *o* shall not know which ones we must
Nm 31:50 to make atonement for *o* before the LORD,
32:17 But we *o* will march as troops in the van
32:19 for *o* on this eastern side of the Jordan."
32:32 We *o* will go across into the land of
Dt 1:41 We will go up *o* and fight,
3: 7 loot of each city we took as booty for *o*.
Jos 22:27 for you on behalf of *o* and our descendants,
1Sm 14: 8 go over to those men and show *o* to them.
1Kgs 20:31 us, therefore, to garb *o* in sackcloth,
2Kgs 6: 2 beam apiece we can build *o* a place to live."
1Chr 19:13 Hold steadfast and let us show *o*
Ezr 8:21 that we might humble *o* before our God to
8:21 to petition from him a safe journey for *o*,
Neh 10:33 We impose these commandments on *o*:
Jdt 8:30 to bind *o* by an oath that we cannot break.
1Mc 5:57 "Let us also make a name for *o* by going
8:20 to enroll *o* among your allies and friends."
2Mc 2:26 upon *o* the labor of making this digest,
Jb 34: 4 Let us discern for *o* what is right;
Ps(s) 83:13 us take for *o* the dwelling place of God."
Wis 2: 8 us crown *o* with rosebuds ere they wither.
Is 58: 3 afflict *o*, and you take no note of it?"
Jer 50: 5 *o* to the LORD with covenant everlasting,
Dn 3:16 us to defend *o* before you in this matter.
Am 6:13 by our own strength, seized for *o* Karnaim?"
Mk 12:33 and to love our neighbor as *o*' is worth
Lk 9:13 we *o* go and buy food for all these people?"
Jn 4:42 We have heard for *o*,
Acts 13:32 "We *o* announce to you the good news that
20: 6 We *o* set sail from Philippi as soon as the
20:13 We *o* went on ahead to the ship and set
21:12 both we *o* and the people of Caesarea urged
23:14 "We have bound *o* by oath to touch no food
Rom 3: 9 do we find *o* in a position of superiority?
8:23 Not only that, but we *o*,
1Cor 11:31 If we were to examine *o*,
15:30 why are we continually putting *o* in danger?
2Cor 1: 9 to death so that we might trust, not in *o*,
3: 5 entitled of *o* to take credit for anything.
4: 2 *o* to every man's conscience before God.
4: 5 not *o* we preach but Christ Jesus as Lord,
4: 5 and *o* as your servants for Jesus' sake.
5:12 not begin to recommend *o* to you again,
5:13 Indeed, if we are ever caught up out of *o*,
6: 4 we strive to present *o* as ministers of God,
6: 6 conducting *o* with innocence,
7: 1 let us purify *o* from every defilement of
10:12 as to classify or compare *o* with certain
10:14 We are not overreaching *o*,
2Thes 3: 9 present *o* as an example for you to imitate.
Ti 3: 3 We *o* were once foolish,
3: 3 and envy, hateful *o* and hating one another.
Heb 10:25 We should not absent *o* from the assembly,
2Pt 1:18 We *o* heard this said from heaven while we
1Jn 1: 8 free of the guilt of sin," we deceive *o*;
4:14 We have seen for *o*,

OUST (1)

Sir 12:12 you, lest he *o* you and take your place.

OUSTED (1)

Dt 2:21 Ammonites, who *o* them and took their place.

OUT-OF-DOORS (1)

Ezr 10:13 rainy season, so that we cannot remain *o*;

OUT-OF-THE-WAY (2)

Mk 6:31 yourselves to an *o* place and rest a little."
Lk 9:12 and food, for this is certainly an *o* place."

OUTBIDDING (1)

2Mc 4:24 *o* Jason by three hundred talents of silver.

OUTBURST (2)

Dt 29:23 Why this fierce *o* of wrath?'
Is 54: 8 In an *o* of wrath,

OUTBURSTS (2)

2Cor 12:20 I may find discord, jealousy, *o* of anger,
Gal 5:20 bickering, jealousy, *o* of rage,

OUTCAST (2)

Ps(s) 69: 9 I have become an *o* to my brothers,
Jer 30:17 "The *o*" they have called you,

OUTCASTS (8)

Neh 1: 9 even though your *o* have been driven to the
Is 11:12 to the nations and gather the *o* of Israel;
16: 3 shadow be like the night, To hide the *o*,
16: 4 Let the *o* of Moab live with you,
27:13 *o* in the land of Egypt Shall come
Jer 49:36 to which the *o* of Elam shall not come.
Mi 4: 6 gather the lame, And I will assemble the *o*,
Zep 3:19 I will save the lame, and assemble the *o*;

OUTCOME (6)

2Mc 13:14 Leaving the *o* to the Creator of the world,
Wis 8: 8 in advance and the *o* of times and ages.
Is 41:22 we may reflect on them And know their *o*;
46:10 At the beginning I foretell the *o*;
47: 7 things to heart, you disregarded their *o*.
Mt 26:58 he sat down with the guards to see the *o*.

OUTCRY (18)

Gn 18:20 *o* against Sodom and Gomorrah is so great,
19:13 for the *o* reaching the LORD against those
Jos 6:10 make any noise or *o* until he gave the word:
1Sm 4:14 Hearing the *o* of the men standing near him,
5:12 the *o* from the city went up to the heavens.
Neh 5: 1 Then there rose a great *o* of the common
Jb 3: 7 let no joyful *o* greet it!
16:18 not my blood, nor let my *o* come to rest!
30: 5 men, with an *o* like that against a thief
Ps(s) 17: 1 attend to my *o*;
144:14 the walls, no exile, no *o* in our streets.
Sir 30: 7 and will quake inwardly at every *o*.
Is 5: 7 for justice, but hark, the *o*!
Jer 48: 4 Moab is crushed, their *o* is heard in Zoar.
49:21 quakes, to the Red Sea the *o* is heard!
50:46 the *o* is heard among the nations.
Mt 25: 7 At the *o* all the virgins woke up and got
Acts 22:24 out why they made such an *o* against him.

OUTDID (2)

Jer 38:22 "They betrayed you, *o* you,
Ez 23:11 her sister's, and she *o* her in harlotry.

OUTDOOR (1)

Prv 24:27 Complete your *o* tasks,

OUTDOORS (1)

Ex 12:22 But none of you shall go *o* until morning.

OUTER (32)

Nm 4:25 covering and the *o* wrapping of tahash skin,
1Kgs 6:29 the *o* rooms had carved figures of cherubim,
6:30 and the *o* rooms was overlaid with gold.
7:50 of holies, and for the doors of the *o* room,
2Kgs 16:18 a throne, and the *o* entrance for the king.
2Chr 33:14 Afterward he built an *o* wall for the City
Est 6: 4 Now Haman had entered the *o* court of the
2Mc 14:41 were forcing the *o* gate and calling for
Jb 41: 5 Who can strip off his *o* garment,
Ez 10: 5 could be heard as far as the *o* court;
40: 5 [Then I saw an *o* wall that completely
40:17 Then he brought me to the *o* court,
40:20 he proceeded north, where, on the *o* court,
40:31 But its vestibule was toward the *o* court;
40:34 But its vestibule was toward the *o* court;
40:37 Its vestibule was toward the *o* court;
41:15 The inner nave and the *o* vestibule were
41:17 inner and *o* rooms were carved the figures
42: 1 Then he led me north to the *o* court,
42: 3 court and the pavement of the *o* court,
42: 7 parallel to the chambers along the *o* court;
42: 8 belonging to the *o* court was fifty cubits,
42: 9 *o* court where the wall of the court began.
42:14 not leave the holy place for the *o* court
44: 1 me back to the *o* gate of the sanctuary,
44:19 are to go out to the people in the *o* court,
46:20 do not have to take them into the *o* court
46:21 Then he led me into the *o* court and had me
47: 2 and around to the *o* gate facing the east,
Heb 9: 2 a tabernacle was constructed, the *o* one,
9: 6 to go into the *o* tabernacle constantly,
Rv 11: 2 Exclude the *o* court of the temple,

OUTERMOST (1)

Ez 42: 5 The *o* chambers were the lowest,

OUTFITTED (1)

Ez 38: 4 army, horses and riders all handsomely *o*,

OUTFLANK (1)

1Sm 23:26 his men were attempting to *o* David

OUTFLOW (1)

2Chr 32:30 This same Hezekiah stopped the upper *o* of

OUTLAWS (1)

Dn 11:14 and *o* of your people shall rise up in

OUTLAY (1)

Lk 14:28 calculate the *o* to see if he has enough money

OUTLET (2)

Sir 25:24 Allow water no *o*,
Jas 3:11 forth fresh water and foul from the same *o*?

OUTLINE (2)

2Mc 2:28 our efforts to giving only a summary *o*.
Is 44:13 and marks with a stylus the *o* of an idol.

OUTLINES (1)

Jb 26:14 Lo, these are but the *o* of his ways,

OUTLIVED (2)

Jos 24:31 who *o* Joshua and knew all that the LORD
Jgs 2: 7 and of those elders who *o* Joshua and who

OUTLOOK (2)

1Cor 14:20 Brothers, do not be childish in your *o*.
2Pt 3: 1 as reminders urging you to sincerity of *o*.

OUTLYING (2)

1Chr 4:33 with all their *o* villages as far as Baal.
2Mc 9:25 I made hurried visits to the *o* provinces.

OUTNUMBER (3)

Nm 3:46 of the Israelites who *o* the Levites,
Ps(s) 69: 5 Those *o* the hairs of my head who hate me
139:18 I to recount them, they would *o* the sands:

OUTNUMBERS (1)

2Kgs 6:16 "Our side *o* theirs."

OUTPOST (8)

1Sm 13:23 An *o* of the Philistines had pushed forward
14: 1 over to the Philistine *o* on the other side."
14: 4 *o* there was a rocky crag on each side,
14: 6 us go over to that *o* of the uncircumcised.
14:11 appeared before the *o* of the Philistines,

14:12 *o* called to Jonathan and his armor-bearer.
14:15 including the *o* and the raiding parties,
Jdt 10:11 valley, they encountered the Assyrian *o*.

OUTPOSTS (3)

Jgs 7:11 with his aide Purah to the *o* of the camp.
1Mc 12:27 He also set *o* all around the camp.
Is 29: 3 with *o* and set up siege works against you.

OUTRAGE (9)

Gn 16: 5 are responsible for this *o* against me.
34: 7 What Shechem had done was an *o* in Israel;
2Mc 4:38 where he had committed the *o* against Onias;
8:17 keeping before their eyes the lawless *o*
12: 3 Some people of Joppa also committed this *o*:
Ps(s) 73: 8 *o* from on high they threaten.
Is 59:13 from following our God, Threatening *o*,
Jer 20: 8 must cry out, violence and *o* is my message;
Hos 12:15 upon him and repay him for his *o*.

OUTRAGED (1)

Lk 18:32 He will be mocked and *o* and spat upon.

OUTRAGEOUS (4)

1Kgs 15:13 she had made an *o* object for Asherah.
2Chr 15:16 she had made an *o* object for Asherah;
2Mc 4:13 through the *o* wickedness of the ungodly
10:34 kept repeating *o* blasphemies and uttering

OUTRAGES (1)

2Mc 14:42 and suffer *o* unworthy of his noble birth.

OUTRAN (2)

2Sm 18:23 way of the Jordan plain and *o* the Cushite.
Jn 20: 4 *o* Peter and reached the tomb first.

OUTRANK (1)

Gn 41:40 in respect to the throne shall I *o* you.

OUTRANKS (2)

Mt 10:24 "No pupil *o* his teacher,
Jn 13:16 no messenger *o* the one who sent him.

OUTRIGHT (2)

Gn 30:31 "You do not have to pay me anything *o*.
37:22 but don't kill him *o*."

OUTS (1)

2Sm 3:25 the ins and *o* of all that you are doing?"

OUTSET (2)

Prv 20:21 at the *o* will in the end not be blessed.
Mk 4:16 to the word accept it joyfully at the *o*.

OUTSHONE (1)

Dn 6: 4 Daniel *o* all the supervisors and satraps

OUTSIDE (138)

Gn 9:22 and he told his two brothers *o* about it.
15: 5 He took him *o* and said:
19:16 and led them to safety *o* the city.
19:17 As soon as they had been brought *o*,
24:11 the camels kneel by the well *o* the city.
24:30 Laban rushed *o* to the man at the spring.
24:31 *o* when I have made the house ready for you,
39:12 her hand, he got away from her and ran *o*.
39:13 left his cloak in her hand as he fled *o*,
39:15 he left his cloak beside me and ran away *o*."
39:18 he left his cloak beside me and fled *o*."
Ex 12:46 may not take any of its flesh *o* the house.
25:11 Plate it inside and *o* with pure gold,
26:35 *O* the veil you shall place the table and
27:21 *o* the veil which hangs in front of the
29:14 of the bullock you must burn up *o* the camp,
33: 7 to pitch at some distance away, *o* the camp.
33: 7 would go to this meeting tent *o* the camp.
37: 2 The inside and *o* were plated with gold,
40:22 the north side of the Dwelling, *o* the veil,
Lv 4:12 shall be brought *o* the camp to a clean
4:21 must also be brought *o* the camp and burned,
6: 4 the ashes to a clean place *o* the camp.
8:17 and offal he burned in the fire *o* the camp,
9:11 hide he burned up in the fire *o* the camp.
10: 4 and carry them to a place *o* the camp."
10: 5 and took them, in their tunics, *o* the camp,
13:46 dwell apart, making his abode *o* the camp.
14: 3 who is to go *o* the camp to examine him.
14: 8 still remain *o* his tent for seven days.
14:40 and cast in an unclean place *o* the city.
14:41 be dumped in an unclean place *o* the city.
14:45 hauled away to an unclean place *o* the city.
14:53 fly away over the countryside *o* the city.
15:25 for several days *o* her menstrual period,
16:27 make atonement, shall be taken *o* the camp,
17: 3 or goat, whether in the camp or *o* of it,
24: 3 *o* the veil that hangs in front of the
24:14 to Moses, "Take the blasphemer *o* the camp,
24:23 the blasphemer *o* the camp and stoned him;
Nm 12:14 her be confined *o* the camp for seven days;
12:15 was confined *o* the camp for seven days,
15:35 the whole community stone him *o* the camp."
15:36 led him *o* the camp and stoned him to death,
19: 3 *o* the camp and slaughtered in his presence.
19: 9 deposit them in a clean place *o* the camp.
31:13 community, went *o* the camp to meet them,
31:19 you shall stay *o* the camp for seven days,
35: 5 thousand cubits *o* the city along each side
Dt 23:11 nocturnal emission, he shall go *o* the camp,
23:13 *O* the camp you shall have a place set
23:14 and with it, when you go *o* to ease nature,
24:11 but shall wait *o* until the man to whom you
24:11 making the loan brings his pledge *o* to you.
25: 5 shall not marry anyone *o* the family;
Jos 2:19 any of them pass *o* the doors of your house,
6:23 forth and placed them *o* the camp of Israel.
Jgs 12: 9 had thirty daughters married *o* the family,
12: 9 sons thirty young women from *o* the family.
19:25 his concubine and thrust her *o* to them.
1Sm 9:26 and he and Samuel went *o* the city together.
2Sm 13:17 was his attendant and said, "Put her *o*,
1Kgs 6: 6 there were offsets along the *o* of the temple
6:10 was built all along the *o* of the temple,
19:11 "Go *o* and stand on the mountain before
2Kgs 10:24 stationed eighty men *o* with this warning,
11:15 "Bring her *o* through the ranks.
23: 4 He had these burned *o* Jerusalem on the
23: 6 pole, to the Kidron Valley, *o* Jerusalem;
2Chr 23:14 "Take her *o* through the ranks,
24: 8 they put *o* the gate of the LORD's temple.
32: 3 stop the waters of the springs *o* the city.
32: 5 towers upon it, and built another wall *o*.
33:15 in Jerusalem, and he cast them *o* the city.
Neh 13: 8 household goods thrown *o* the chamber.
13:20 spent the night once or twice *o* Jerusalem,
Tb 1:17 and been thrown *o* the walls of Nineveh,
Jdt 10:18 her as she waited *o* the tent of Holofernes,
13: 1 Bagoas closed the tent from the *o* and
13: 3 her maid to stand *o* the bedroom and wait,
1Mc 15:30 tribute money of the districts *o* the territory
2Mc 1:16 heads and tossed them to the people *o*.
Ps(s) 41: 7 when he leaves he gives voice to it *o*.
Prv 22:13 The sluggard says, "A lion is *o*;
Sir 21:22 house, while the well-bred man remains *o*;
Jer 21: 4 the Chaldeans who besiege you *o* the walls.
Ez 7:15 The sword is *o*;
40:40 Along the wall of the vestibule, but *o*,
41: 6 and there were offsets in the *o* wall of
41: 9 The width of the *o* wall which enclosed
41:17 interior part of the temple as well as *o*,
41:25 the vestibule *o* was a wooden lattice.
43:21 part of the temple, *o* the sanctuary.
46: 2 The prince shall enter from *o* by way of
47: 2 He led me *o* by the north gate,
Dn 14: 7 "it is only clay inside and bronze *o*;
14:14 Then they went *o*,
Mt 10:14 once *o* it shake its dust from your feet.
11:19 of tax collectors and those *o* the law!'
12:14 When the Pharisees were *o* they began to
12:46 his brothers appeared *o* to speak with him.
21:39 seized him, dragged him *o* the vineyard,
23:25 You cleanse the *o* of cup and dish,
23:26 of the cup so that its *o* may be clean.
23:27 beautiful to look at on the *o* but inside
25:30 worthless servant into the darkness *o*,
Mk 1:33 the whole town was gathered *o* the door.
2:12 mat and went *o* in the sight of everyone.
3: 6 When the Pharisees went *o*,
3:31 stood *o* they sent word to him to come out.
3:32 brothers and sisters are *o* asking for you."
4:11 others *o* it is all presented in parables,
7:15 enters a man from *o* can make him impure;
7:18 enters a man from *o* can make him impure?
8:23 blind man's hand and led him *o* the village.
12: 8 killed him and dragged him *o* the vineyard.
Lk 1:10 people was praying *o* at the incense hour,
8:20 are standing *o* and they wish to see you."
11:39 You cleanse the *o* of cup and dish,
11:40 not he who made the *o* make the inside too?
13:25 door and you stand *o* knocking and saying,
20:15 dragged him *o* the vineyard and killed him.
Jn 19:13 then brought Jesus *o* and took a seat on a
Acts 5:23 and the guards at their posts *o* the gates,
9:40 Peter first made everyone go *o*;
12:14 but ran in and announced that Peter was *o*.
14:13 the temple of Zeus, which stood *o* the town,
16:13 *o* the city gate to the bank of the river,
16:40 Once *o* the prison,
21:30 They seized Paul, dragged him *o* the temple,
1Cor 6:18 other sin a man commits is *o* his body,
2Cor 12: 2 he was in or *o* his body I cannot say,
12: 3 whether in or *o* his body I do not know,
1Tm 3: 7 be well thought of by those *o* the church,
Heb 13:11 as a sin offering are burned *o* the camp.
13:12 Therefore Jesus died *o* the gate,
13:13 Let us go to him *o* the camp,
Rv 14:20 The winepress was trodden *o* the city,
22:15 *O* are the dogs and sorcerers,

OUTSIDER (1)

Gn 29:19 to give her to you rather than to an *o*.

OUTSIDERS (4)

Gn 31:15 Are we not regarded by him as *o*?
1Cor 5:12 What business is it of mine to judge *o*?
Col 4: 5 Be prudent in dealing with *o*;
1Thes 4:12 good example to *o* and want for nothing.

OUTSKIRTS (3)

Nm 11: 1 among them and consumed the *o* of the camp.
Jgs 6: 4 of the land as far as the *o* of Gaza,
1Sm 14: 2 near the threshing floor on the *o* of Geba;

OUTSTANDING (5)

Dt 1:15 So I took *o* men of your tribes,
1Chr 26:31 among them *o* officers at Jazer of Gilead.
Neh 3: 5 some of their *o* men would not submit to
Est B: 3 who is *o* for constant devotion and
Rom 16: 7 they are *o* apostles,

OUTSTRETCHED (29)

Ex 6: 1 compelled by my *o* arm,
6: 6 my *o* arm and with mighty acts of judgment.
14:16 your staff and, with hand *o* over the sea,
Dt 4:34 by war, with his strong hand and *o* arm,
5:15 from there with his strong hand and *o* arm.
7:19 strong hand and *o* arm with which the LORD,
9:29 by your great power and with your *o* arm.
11: 2 his majesty, his strong hand and *o* arm;
26: 8 of Egypt with his strong hand and *o* arm,
1Kgs 8:42 name and your mighty hand and your *o* arm),
8:54 kneeling with his hands *o* toward heaven.
2Kgs 17:36 land of Egypt with great power and *o* arm:
2Chr 6:32 name, your mighty power, and your *o* arm,
2Mc 15:12 with *o* arms for the whole Jewish community.
Ps(s) 136:12 With a mighty hand and an *o* arm,
Is 3:16 with necks *o* Ogling and mincing as they go,
5:25 not turned back, and his hand is still *o*.
9:11 not turned back, and his hand is still *o*!
9:16 is not turned back, his hand is still *o*!
9:20 is not turned back, his hand is still *o*!
10: 4 is not turned back, his hand is still *o*!
14:26 and this the hand *o* over all nations.
Jer 21: 5 against you with *o* hand and mighty arm,
27: 5 earth, by my great power, with my *o* arm;
32:17 earth by your great might, with your *o* arm;
32:21 With strong hand and *o* arm you brought
Ez 20:33 the Lord GOD, with a mighty hand and *o* arm,
20:34 With a mighty hand and *o* arm,
Acts 13:17 and with an *o* arm he led them out of it.

OUTWEIGH (1)

Jb 6: 3 They would now *o* the sands of the sea!

OUTWITTED (1)

2Mc 14:31 he had been disgracefully *o* by the man,

OUTWITTING (1)

2Cor 2:11 from *o* us.

OUTWORKS (1)

2Sm 20:16 the city stood on the *o* and called out,

OVEN (9)

Lv 2: 4 offering you present is baked in an *o*,
7: 9 offering that is baked in an *o* or deep-fried
11:35 if it is an *o* or a jar-stand,
26:26 ten women will need but one *o* for baking
Neh 3:11 adjoining sector, as far as the *O* Tower,
12:38 past the *O* Tower as far as the Broad Wall,
Sir 22:24 Before flames burst forth an *o* smokes;
Hos 7: 4 are all kindled to wrath like a blazing *o*,
Mal 3:19 lo, the day is coming, blazing like an *o*,

OVENS (3)

Ex 7:28 even into your *o* and your kneading bowls.
Hos 7: 6 the plotters approach with hearts like *o*.
7: 7 They are all heated like *o*,

OVERAWE (2)

Is 2:19 his majesty, when he arises to *o* the earth.
2:21 his majesty, when he arises to *o* the earth.

OVERBEARING (2)

Prv 21:24 *o* pride who acts with scornful effrontery.
30:13 how *o* their glance!

OVERBOARD (3)

Acts 27:19 deliberately threw even the ship's gear *o*.
27:38 the ship further by throwing the wheat *o*.
27:43 swim to jump *o* first and make for land.

OVERCAME (8)

1Sm 13: 3 Now Jonathan *o* the Philistine garrison
17:50 *o* the Philistine with sling and stone;

OVERCAME (cont.)

2Chr 13: 7 men, scoundrels, joined him and *o* Rehoboam,
1Mc 5: 3 them heavily, *o* and despoiled them.
Wis 16:10 fangs of poisonous reptiles *o* your sons,
18:22 he *o* the bitterness not by bodily strength,
18:22 But by word he *o* the smiter,
Mk 4:41 A great awe *o* them at this.

OVERCHARGE (1)

Prv 28: 8 increases his wealth by interest and *o*

OVERCOME (33)

Gn 43:30 for he was so *o* with affection for his
44:34 to see the anguish that would *o* my father."
Nm 5:14 or if a man is *o* by a feeling of jealousy
24:19 do valiantly, and Jacob shall *o* his foes.
Jos 2: 9 of the land are *o* with fear of you.
2:24 of the land are *o* with fear of us."
7: 3 two or three thousand go up, they can *o* Ai.
Jgs 16: 5 *o* and bind him so as to keep him helpless.
1Sm 13: 4 Thus all Israel learned that Saul had *o*
2Kgs 10: 4 They were *o* with fright and said,
Jdt 15: 2 were amazed, and *o* with fear and trembling.
1Mc 3:18 "It is easy for many to be *o* by a few;
2Mc 9: 4 *O* with anger,
Ps(s) 13: 5 lest my enemy say, "I have *o* him";
40:13 my sins so *o* me that I cannot see;
65: 4 We are *o* by our sins;
78:65 as wakes from sleep a champion *o* with wine;
Eccl 4:12 Where a lone man may be *o*,
Jer 23: 2 I am like a man who is drunk, *o* by wine,
51:39 that they may be *o* with perpetual sleep,
Hos 7: 5 the princes are *o* with the heat of wine.
Zec 9:15 *o* sling stones and trample them underfoot;
Mt 17: 6 fell forward on the ground, *o* with fear.
Mk 9: 6 what to say, for they were all *o* with awe.
9:15 of Jesus, the whole crowd was *o* with awe.
Lk 1:12 disturbed upon seeing him, and *o* by fear.
9: 1 to *o* all demons and to cure diseases.
Jn 1: 5 in darkness, a darkness that did not *o* it.
16: 6 this to say to you, you are *o* with grief.
16:33 I have *o* the world."
Acts 19:28 they were *o* with fury and began to shout,
2Pt 2:19 the slave of that by which he has been *o*.
2:20 are caught up and *o* in pollution once more,

OVERCONFIDENT (5)

Sir 5: 5 Of forgiveness be not *o*,
Is 32: 9 ladies, rise up and hear my voice, *o* women,
32:10 more than a year you *o* ones will be shaken;
32:11 Shudder, you who are *o*!
Am 6: 1 in Zion, to the *o* on the mount of Samaria,

OVERDRIVEN (1)

Gn 33:13 if *o* for a single day,

OVEREATING (1)

Sir 37:29 choice foods, For sickness comes with *o*,

OVERFLOW (13)

Ps(s) 32: 6 Though deep waters *o*,
65:12 and your paths *o* with a rich harvest;
65:13 The untilled meadows *o* with it,
73: 7 their fancies *o* their hearts.
Prv 3:10 with grain, with new wine your vats will *o*.
Wis 5:22 them and the streams shall abruptly *o*;
Is 8: 7 all its channels, and *o* all its banks;
60: 5 you see, your heart shall throb and *o*,
Jl 2:24 and the vats shall *o* with wine and oil.
4:13 The vats *o*,
Zec 1:17 My cities shall again *o* with prosperity;
2Cor 10:15 influence may also grow among you and *o*.
1Thes 3:12 *o* with love for one another and for all,

OVERFLOWED (2)

Jos 4:18 their course and as before *o* all its banks.
Ps(s) 78:20 waters gushed forth, and the streams *o*;

OVERFLOWING (9)

1Chr 12:16 it was *o* both its banks in the first month,
Jb 20:22 When he abounds to *o*,
Sir 47:14 when you were young, *o* with instruction,
Is 28: 2 storm, Like a flood of water, great and *o*,
66:12 wealth of the nations like an *o* torrent.
Rom 5:17 who receive the *o* grace and gift of justice
2Cor 8: 2 In the midst of severe trial their *o* joy
Col 2: 7 as you were taught, and *o* with gratitude.
1Tm 1:14 our Lord has been granted me in *o* measure,

OVERFLOWS (6)

Jos 3:15 which *o* all its banks during the entire
Ps(s) 23: 5 my cup *o*.
45: 2 I My heart *o* with a goodly theme;
Sir 24:23 It *o* like the Pishon,
39:22 His blessing *o* like the Nile;
2Cor 9:12 church but also *o* in much gratitude to God.

OVERGROW (2)

Hos 9: 6 Weeds shall *o* their silver treasures,
10: 8 thorns and thistles shall *o* their altars.

OVERGROWN (4)

Prv 24:31 it was all *o* with thistles;
Is 5: 6 or hoed, but *o* with thorns and briers;
32:13 of my people, *o* with thorns and briers;
34:13 Her castles shall be *o* with thorns,

OVERHEARD (5)

Gn 27: 6 I *o* your father tell your brother Esau,
1Sm 17:31 had spoken were *o* and reported to Saul,
Tb 7:10 Raguel *o* the words; so he said to the boy:
Est A:13 He *o* them plotting,
Jn 7:32 *o* this debate about him among the crowd,

OVERHEARING (2)

Mt 9:12 *O* the remark, he said:
Mk 2:17 *O* the remark,

OVERINDULGE (1)

1Tm 3: 8 may not *o* in drink or give in to greed.

OVERJOYED (3)

Mt 2:10 They were *o* at seeing the star,
Jn 3:29 for him and is *o* to hear his voice.
Acts 12:14 *o* that she did not stop to open the door,

OVERLAID (21)

Jgs 17: 3 made of them a carved idol *o* with silver.
17: 4 son, by making a carved idol *o* with silver."
18:14 idols, and a carved idol *o* with silver?
18:18 idols, and the carved idol *o* with silver,
1Kgs 6:21 Solomon *o* the interior of the temple with
6:21 sanctuary a cedar altar, *o* it with gold,
6:22 The entire temple was *o* with gold so that
6:22 before the sanctuary was also *o* with gold.
6:28 The cherubim, too, were *o* with gold.
6:30 inner and the outer rooms was *o* with gold.
6:32 The doors were *o* with gold,
10:18 throne made, and *o* it with refined gold.
2Kgs 18:16 he himself had ordered to be *o* with gold,
2Chr 3: 4 He *o* its interior with pure gold.
3: 5 The nave he *o* with cypress wood which he
3: 7 as its walls and its doors, he *o* with gold,
3: 8 He *o* it with fine gold to the amount of
3:10 workmanship, which were then *o* with gold.
4: 9 the gates he *o* with bronze.
9:17 ivory throne which he *o* with fine gold.
Hb 2:19 See, it is *o* with gold and silver,

OVERLAND (1)

Acts 20:13 had made, since his plan was to travel *o*.

OVERLAYING (1)

1Chr 29: 4 silver, for *o* the walls of the rooms,

OVERLOOK (5)

Dt 24:19 harvest in your field and *o* a sheaf there,
Jos 18:18 across the northern flank of the Arabah *o*,
Prv 19:11 anger, and it is his glory to *o* an offense.
Wis 11:23 you *o* the sins of men that they may repent.
Sir 28: 7 of the Most High's covenant, and *o* faults.

OVERLOOKED (4)

1Sm 12: 3 have I accepted a bribe and *o* his guilt?
Sir 23: 2 not be spared, nor the sins of my heart *o*;
Acts 17:30 *o* bygone periods when men did not know him;
2Pt 3: 8 This point must not be *o*, dear friends.

OVERLOOKS (4)

Nm 21:20 at the headland of Pisgah that *o* Jeshimon.
23:28 Balaam to the top of Peor, that *o* Jeshimon.
1Sm 13:18 that *o* the Valley of the Hyenas toward
Sir 42:11 place that *o* the approaches to the house.

OVERLORD (1)

2Kgs 17: 4 pay the annual tribute to his Assyrian *o*.

OVERNIGHT (12)

Ex 23:18 of my feast be kept *o* till the next day.
34:25 Passover feast be kept *o* for the next day.
Lv 19:13 withhold *o* the wages of your day laborer.
Nm 22: 8 he said to them in reply, "Stay here *o*,
22:19 But, you too shall stay here *o*,
Dt 16: 4 first day shall be kept *o* for the next day.
21:23 a tree, it shall not remain on the tree *o*.
Jos 8:13 it, and Joshua waited *o* among his troops.
2Sm 19: 8 not a single man will remain with you *o*,
2Kgs 4:11 Elisha arrived and stayed in the room *o*.
Tb 4:14 *o* the wages of any man who works for you,
14:10 stay *o* within the confines of the city.

OVERPOWER (3)

Jb 15:24 distress and anguish *o* him.
31:23 will be upon me, and his majesty will *o* me.
Ob 1: 7 They deceive you, they *o* you

OVERPOWERED (8)

2Sm 13:14 Not heeding her plea, he *o* her;
1Mc 10:49 Alexander pursued him, and *o* his soldiers.
Wis 2: 4 by the sun's rays and *o* by its heat.
Is 16: 8 Whose clusters *o* the lords of nations,
28: 7 stagger from strong drink, *o* by wine;
Dn 6:25 lions *o* them and crushed all their bones.
Acts 19:16 evil spirit sprang at them and *o* them all.
Rv 12: 8 they were *o* and lost their place in heaven.

OVERPOWERS (1)

Lk 11:22 someone stronger than he comes and *o* him,

OVERRAN (4)

Jgs 20:37 made a sudden dash into Gibeah, *o* it,
1Sm 5: 6 swarmed in their ships and *o* their fields.
2Sm 5:18 came and *o* the valley of Rephaim.
5:22 came up again and *o* the valley of Rephaim.

OVERREACHING (2)

2Cor 10:14 We are not *o* ourselves,
1Thes 4: 6 and that each refrain from *o* or cheating

OVERRULED (1)

2Sm 24: 4 *o* Joab and the leaders of the army,

OVERRUN (3)

Ex 8: 1 pools, to make frogs *o* the land of Egypt."
8: 3 They, too, made frogs *o* the land of Egypt.
Sir 36:25 A vineyard with no hedge will be *o*;

OVERSEER (4)

Ru 2: 5 Boaz asked the *o* of his harvesters,
2: 6 The *o* of the harvesters answered,
2Chr 24:11 scribe and an *o* for the high priest came,
31:12 *o* of these things was Conaniah the Levite,

OVERSEERS (10)

Gn 41:34 should also take action to appoint *o*,
1Kgs 5:30 to three thousand three hundred *o*,
1Chr 27:31 were the *o* of King David's possessions.
28: 1 the *o* of all the king's estates and
29: 6 and the *o* of the king's affairs came
2Chr 2: 1 he placed three thousand six hundred *o*.
2:17 six hundred *o* to keep the people working.
8:10 and fifty *o* who had charge of the people.
34:12 their *o* were Jahath and Obadiah,
34:17 handed it over to the *o* and the workmen."

OVERSHADOW (1)

Lk 1:35 and the power of the Most High will *o* you;

OVERSHADOWED (5)

Wis 19: 7 The cloud *o* their camp;
Bar 5: 8 of tree have *o* Israel at God's command;
Mt 4:16 On those who inhabit a land *o* by death,
17: 5 when suddenly a bright cloud *o* them.
Lk 9:34 he was speaking, a cloud came and *o* them,

OVERSHADOWING (2)

Mk 9: 7 A cloud came, *o* them,
Heb 9: 5 cherubim of glory *o* the place of expiation.

OVERSIGHTS (1)

1Mc 13:39 any *o* and defaults incurred up to now,

OVERSTEP (1)

Jer 5:22 which by eternal decree it may not *o*.

OVERTAKE (23)

Gn 44: 4 When you *o* them,
Ex 15: 9 enemy boasted, "I will pursue and *o* them;
Dt 19: 6 the homicide and *o* him and strike him dead,
Jos 2: 5 have to pursue them immediately to *o* them."
Jgs 20:32 that disaster was about to *o* them.
1Sm 30: 8 Can I *o* them?"
30: 8 shall surely *o* them and effect a rescue."
2Sm 15:14 Leave quickly, lest he hurry and *o* us,
Tb 14: 4 happen, and shall *o* Assyria and Nineveh;
Jdt 11:11 repulsed and fail, but death will *o* them.
1Mc 12:30 pursued them, but he could not *o* them,
Ps(s) 7: 6 Let the enemy pursue and *o* me;
36:12 Let not the foot of the proud *o* me nor the
69:25 let the fury of your anger *o* them.
Wis 14:30 But on both counts shall justice *o* them:
Sir 7: 1 Do no evil, and evil will not *o* you;
11:10 if you run after it, you will never *o* it;
Jer 23:17 hardness of heart, "No evil shall *o* you,"
Hos 2: 9 after her lovers, she shall not *o* them;
Am 9:10 who say, "Evil will not reach or *o* us."
9:13 LORD, When the plowman shall *o* the reaper,
Zec 1: 6 the prophets, did not these *o* your fathers?
Jn 5:14 sins so that something worse may not *o* you."

OVERTAKEN (4)

Jgs 20:41 they realized the disaster that had *o* them.
1Mc 6:13 that this is why these evils have *o* me;
Jb 30:27 days of affliction have *o* me.
Mt 12:28 demons, then the reign of God has *o* you.

OVERTAKES (5)

Jb 3:25 For what I fear *o* me,
Prv 1:26 I will mock when terror *o* you;
Sir 36:27 has no nest, but lodges where night *o* him?
Mt 23:35 until retribution *o* you for all the blood
Mk 4:17 or persecution *o* them because of the word,

OVERTAKING (2)

Gn 19:19 the hills to keep the disaster from *o* me,
1Thes 5: 3 the suddenness of pains *o* a woman in labor,

OVERTHREW (9)

Gn 19:25 He *o* those cities and the whole Plain,
19:29 God *o* the cities where Lot had been living.
Ex 15: 7 your great majesty you *o* your adversaries;
Dt 29:22 which the LORD *o* in his furious wrath they
1Chr 1:46 He *o* the Midianites on the Moabite plateau,
2Mc 12:15 *o* Jericho without battering-ram or siege
Jer 20:16 the cities which the LORD relentlessly *o*;
Lam 1:13 He spread a net for my feet, and *o* me.
Am 4:11 upheaval as when God *o* Sodom and

OVERTHROW (11)

Gn 19:21 I will not *o* the town you speak of.
Lv 26:30 your high places, *o* your incense stands,
2Sm 10: 3 the city, to spy on it, and to *o* it,
1Chr 19: 3 explore the land, spying it out for its *o*?"
Ezr 6:12 *o* every king or people who may undertake
Tb 13:12 *o* your towers and set fire to your homes;
Jdt 9: 8 and to *o* with iron the horns of your altar.
1Mc 4:18 stand firm against our enemies and *o* them.
Zep 1: 3 I will *o* the wicked;
Hg 2:22 I will *o* the thrones of kingdoms,
2:22 I will *o* the chariots and their riders,

OVERTHROWN (14)

Jb 41: 1 hope to do so need only see him to be *o*.
Ps(s) 9: 4 turned back, *o* and destroyed before you.
11: 3 When the pillars are *o*,
Prv 10: 8 commands, but a prating fool will be *o*.
11:11 through the mouth of the wicked it is *o*.
12: 7 The wicked are *o* and are no more,
14:32 The wicked man is *o* by his wickedness,
Wis 17:19 water, or the rude crash of *o* rocks,
Is 1: 7 strangers devour [a waste, like Sodom *o*—
13:19 be *o* by God like Sodom and like Gomorrah.
Jer 48: 1 Disgraced and *o* is the stronghold:
49:18 Gomorrah, and their neighbors were *o*,
Lam 4: 6 Which was *o* in an instant without the
Ez 30: 4 are seized and her foundations are *o*.

OVERTHROWS (2)

Prv 21:22 and *o* the stronghold in which it trusts.
Sir 28:14 walled cities, and *o* powerful dynasties.

OVERTOOK (14)

Gn 31:25 When Laban *o* Jacob,
44: 6 *o* them and repeated these words to them,
Jgs 9:57 curse of Jotham, son of Jerubbaal, *o* them.
18:22 near that of Micah took up arms and *o* them.
2Sm 22: 6 enmeshed me, the snares of death *o* me.
2Kgs 25: 5 king and *o* him in the desert near Jericho,
Jdt 1:15 himself he *o* in the mountains of Ragae,
2Mc 1: 7 during the trouble and violence that *o* us
Ps(s) 18: 6 enmeshed me, the snares of death *o* me.
18:38 I pursued my enemies and *o* them,
Jer 39: 5 and *o* and captured Zedekiah in the desert
41:12 They *o* him at the Great Waters in Gibeon.
52: 8 and *o* Zedekiah in the desert near Jericho,
Acts 2:43 A reverent fear *o* them all,

OVERTURN (1)

Wis 5:23 and evildoing *o* the thrones of potentates.

OVERTURNED (4)

Jer 50:40 As when God *o* Sodom and Gomorrah,
Ez 38:20 Mountains shall be *o*,
Mt 21:12 He *o* the money-changers' tables and the
Mk 11:15 He *o* the money-changers' tables and the

OVERTURNS (4)

Jb 9: 5 he *o* them in his anger.
28: 9 and *o* the mountains at their foundations.
Prv 15:25 The LORD *o* the house of the proud,
Sir 10:14 *o* and establishes the lowly in their stead.

OVERWHELM (10)

Gn 32: 9 "If Esau should attack and *o* one camp,"
Dt 28: 2 blessings will come upon you and *o* you:
28:15 these curses shall come upon you and *o* you:
Jdt 6: 4 We will *o* them with it,
Jb 9:17 With a tempest he might *o* me,
12:15 he sends them forth and they *o* the land.
Ps(s) 69:16 Let not the flood-waters *o* me,
88: 8 heavy, and with all your billows you *o* me.
140:10 the mischief which they threaten *o* them.
Dn 11:40 but the king of the north shall *o* him with

OVERWHELMED (24)

2Sm 22: 5 the floods of perdition *o* me;
Tb 3: 6 insulting calumnies, and I am *o* with grief.
Jdt 15: 3 Then all the Israelite warriors *o* them.
Est 4: 4 *O* with anguish,
1Mc 6: 9 There he remained many days, *o* with sorrow,
8: 5 them in battle had been *o* and subjugated.
10:82 the phalanx, *o* it and put it to flight.
11:72 so *o* the enemy that they took to flight.
2Mc 12:22 the enemy was *o* with fear and terror at
Ps(s) 18: 5 round about me, the destroying floods *o* me;
38: 5 of my sin, For my iniquities have *o* me;
124: 4 us, then would the waters have *o* us;
Prv 12:21 just, but the wicked are *o* with misfortune.
Wis 10:19 But their enemies she *o*,
Sir 21:24 man would be *o* by the disgrace of it.
Jer 51:42 sea rises, she is *o* by the roaring waves!
Dn 11:22 shall be completely *o* by him and crushed,
11:26 seek to destroy him, his army shall be *o*,
Hos 11: 8 My heart is *o*, my pity is stirred.
Na 3:19 For who has not been *o*,
Mt 17:23 At these words they were *o* with grief.
19:25 heard this they were completely *o*,
Mk 10:26 They were completely *o* at this,
2Pt 3: 6 it was *o* by the deluge.

OVERWHELMING (6)

Dt 28:45 will come upon you, pursuing you and *o* you,
1Mc 12:31 called Zabadeans, *o* and plundering them.
Prv 27: 4 Anger is relentless, and wrath *o*—
Is 10:22 is decreed as *o* justice demands.
28:15 When the *o* scourge passes,
28:18 When the *o* scourge passes,

OVERWHELMS (3)

Ps(s) 55: 6 and horror *o* me,
69: 3 the flood *o* me.
Jer 14:17 which *o* the virgin daughter of my people,

OVERWISE (1)

Eccl 7:16 "Be not just to excess, and be not *o*,

OWE (10)

1Mc 13:39 now, as well as the crown tax that you *o*.
Ps(s) 65: 2 I To you we *o* our hymn of praise,
Mt 18:28 'Pay back what you *o*,' he demanded.
Lk 16: 5 to the first, 'How much do you *o* my master?'
16: 7 he said to a second, 'How much do you *o*?'
Rom 13: 8 *O* no debt to anyone except the debt that
Eph 6: 5 the awe, and the sincerity you *o* to Christ.
Phil 2: 1 of the encouragement you *o* me in Christ,
Phlm 1:19 to mention that you *o* me your very self!
3Jn 1: 8 we *o* it to such men to support them and

OWED (10)

1Mc 13:15 money that he *o* the royal treasury
2Mc 8:10 tribute *o* by the king to the Romans
Prv 7:14 "I *o* peace offerings,
Mt 18:24 one was brought in who *o* him a huge amount.
18:28 fellow servant who *o* him a mere fraction
18:28 him a mere fraction of what he himself *o*.
18:30 put in jail until he paid back what he *o*.
18:34 torturers until he paid back all that he *o*.
Lk 7:41 men *o* money to a certain money-lender;
7:41 one *o* a total of five hundred coins,

OWES (4)

1Mc 10:43 precincts, because of money he *o* the king,
Jb 6:14 A friend *o* kindness to one in despair,
37:23 his great justice *o* no one an accounting.
Phlm 1:18 has done you an injury or *o* you anything,

OWING (2)

Ez 4:17 that, *o* to the scarcity of bread and water,
Eph 2: 8 it is *o* to his favor that salvation is

OWL (15)

Lv 11:17 gull, the various species of hawks, the *o*,
11:17 the owl, the cormorant, the screech *o*,
11:18 cormorant, the screech owl, the barn *o*,
11:18 screech owl, the barn owl, the desert *o*,
Dt 14:16 gull, the various species of hawks, the *o*,
14:16 species of hawks, the owl, the screech *o*,
14:17 the screech owl, the ibis, the desert *o*,
Ps(s) 102: 7 desert owl; I have become like an *o*
Is 34:11 desert *o* and hoot owl shall possess her,
34:11 the screech *o* and raven shall dwell in her.
34:15 There the hoot *o* shall nest and lay eggs,
Zep 2:14 The screech *o* and the desert owl shall

OWLS (2)

Is 13:21 rest there and *o* shall fill the houses;
14:23 make it a haunt of hoot *o* and a marshland;

OWN (866)

Gn 9: 5 For your *o* lifeblood,
10: 5 each with its *o* language
13:10 as far as Zoar, like the LORD's *o* garden,
15: 4 your *o* issue shall be your heir."
15:13 shall be aliens in a land not their *o*,
22:12 not withhold from me your *o* beloved son."
24: 4 but that you will go to my *o* land and to
24:38 go to my father's house, to my *o* relatives,
24:40 son from my *o* kindred of my father's house.
30:30 do something for my *o* household as well."
30:40 Thus he produced special flocks of his *o*,
30:43 increasingly prosperous, and he came to *o*,
32: 2 home, while Jacob continued on his *o* way.
32: 6 I *o* cattle,
37:27 After all, he is our brother, our *o* flesh."
40: 5 same night, each dream with its *o* meaning.
41:11 and each of our dreams had its *o* meaning.
42: 7 But he concealed his *o* identity from them
42:37 *o* two sons if I do not return him to you."
45:10 and herds, and everything that you *o*.
46:32 herds, as well as everything else they *o*.
47: 1 and herds and everything else they *o*;
47: 5 may put them in charge of my *o* livestock."
Ex 2: 8 went and called the child's *o* mother.
2:11 striking a Hebrew, one of his *o* kinsmen.
6: 7 I will take you as my *o* people,
6: 8 I will give it to you as your *o* possession
15:16 the people you had made your *o* passed over.
16:16 each man providing for those of his *o* tent."
18:27 who went off to his *o* country.
21:21 since the slave is his *o* property.
22: 4 best produce of his *o* field or vineyard.
22:23 then your *o* wives will be widows,
29:26 this is to be your *o* portion.
30:38 this for his *o* enjoyment of its fragrance,
31:18 stone tablets inscribed by God's *o* finger.
32:11 your wrath blaze up against your *o* people,
32:13 and how you swore to them by your *o* self,
32:27 from gate to gate, and slay your *o* kinsmen,
32:29 you were against your *o* sons and kinsmen,
33: 8 and stand at the entrance of their *o* tents,
33:10 worship at the entrance of their *o* tents.
33:13 this nation is, after all, your *o* people."
34: 9 and sins, and receive us as your *o*."
Lv 7:30 with his *o* hands the oblations to the LORD.
8:29 was Moses' *o* portion of the ordination ram.
9: 8 the calf that was his *o* sin offering.
14:15 of it into the palm of his *o* left hand;
14:26 oil into the palm of his *o* left hand
16:24 and offer his *o* and the people's holocaust,
17:11 may thereby be made for your *o* lives,
18: 7 Besides, since she is your *o* mother,
18: 9 born in your *o* household or born elsewhere.
18:10 that would be a disgrace to your *o* family.
20:17 having had intercourse with his *o* sister.
20:24 I am giving it to you as your *o*,
20:26 apart from the other nations to be my *o*.
21: 3 his *o* family while she remains unmarried;
21:14 but a virgin, taken from his *o* people,
22:24 You shall neither do this in your *o* land
25:10 own property, every one to his *o* family
25:13 one of you shall return to his *o* property.
25:26 means to buy it back in his *o* name,
25:27 so that he may thus regain his *o* property.
25:45 Such slaves you may *o* as chattels,
25:48 may be redeemed by one of his *o* brothers,
26:29 eat the flesh of your *o* sons and daughters.
26:39 away for their *o* and their fathers' guilt.
Nm 1:52 each in his *o* division of the camp,
2: 2 shall camp, each in his *o* division,
2:17 in his proper place, with his *o* division.
2:34 the march they were in their *o* divisions,
5:10 may dispose of his *o* sacred contributions;
10: 9 When in your *o* land you go to war against
10:14 its *o* standard and arranged in companies,
10:18 its *o* standard and arranged in companies,
10:22 its *o* standard and arranged in companies,
10:25 its *o* standard and arranged in companies,
10:30 to my own country and to my *o* kindred."
16:17 fifty followers shall take his *o* censer,
16:17 and you and Aaron, each with his *o* censer,
17:24 prince identified his *o* staff and took it,
18:29 to the LORD your *o* full contribution.
22:13 of Balak, "Go back to your *o* country,
22:30 said to Balaam, "Am I not your *o* beast,
24:13 I could not of my *o* accord to anything,
24:14 now that I am about to go to my *o* people,
27: 3 for his *o* sin without leaving any sons.
27:20 Invest him with some of your *o* dignity,
32:42 and called it Nobah after his *o* name.
35: 8 Levites in proportion to its *o* heritage."
35:26 If the homicide of his *o* accord leaves the
35:28 may the homicide return to his *o* district.
36: 7 will retain their *o* ancestral heritage.
36: 8 to a clan of her *o* ancestral tribe,
36: 8 possession of their *o* ancestral heritage.
36: 9 will retain their *o* ancestral heritage."

OWN (cont.)

Dt 2: 9 Ar to the descendants of lot as their *o*.
2:19 it to the descendants of Lot as their *o*.
3:14 it after his *o* name Bashan Havvothjair,
3:18 God, has given you this land as your *o*.
4: 3 your *o* eyes what the LORD did at Baal-peor:
4: 9 the things which your *o* eyes have seen,
4:20 Egypt, that you might be his very *o* people,
7: 6 the earth to be a people peculiarly his *o*.
7:19 great testings which your *o* eyes have seen,
8:17 own power and the strength of my *o* hand
9:10 of stone inscribed, by God's *o* finger,
10:13 I enjoin on you today for your *o* good?
10:21 things which your *o* eyes have seen.
11: 7 With your *o* eyes you have seen all these
12:12 but has no share of his *o* in your heritage.
12:17 you shall not, in your *o* communities,
12:21 to your heart's desire in your *o* community.
13: 7 "If your *o* full brother,
14: 2 the earth to be a people peculiarly his *o*.
15:22 but in your *o* communities you may eat it,
16:10 and the measure of your *o* freewill
17: 8 "If in your *o* community there is a case
18:15 raise up for you from among your *o* kinsmen;
19:12 the elders of his *o* city shall send for
20: 1 chariots and an army greater than your *o*,
21:17 double share of whatever he happens to *o*,
22: 2 take it to your *o* place and keep it with
24:14 whether he be one of your *o* countrymen or
24:16 his *o* guilt shall a man be put to death.
26:12 may eat their fill in your *o* community,
26:18 you are to be a people peculiarly his *o*,
28:53 of your *o* sons and daughters whom the LORD,
29: 2 the great testings your *o* eyes have seen,
29:21 *o* descendants who will rise up after you,
32: 9 While the LORD's *o* portion was Jacob,
32:27 boast, 'Our *o* hand won the victory;
33: 7 His *o* hands defend his cause and you will
33: 9 and his *o* children he refused to recognize.
Jos 1:15 you may return and occupy your *o* land,
2:19 he will be responsible for his *o* death,
9: 4 Gibeon put into effect a device of their *o*.
20: 6 back home to his *o* city from which he fled."
21: 3 Out of their *o* heritage,
22: 4 to your *o* land,
22: 6 them and sent them away to their *o* tents.
22: 8 to your *o* tents with great wealth,
22: 9 to the land of Gilead, their *o* property,
22:16 against him by building an altar of your *o*!
22:19 *o* in addition to the altar of the LORD,
22:23 an altar of our *o* to secede from the LORD,
22:26 interests by building this altar of our *o*:
24:22 "You are your *o* witnesses that you have
24:28 the people, each to his *o* heritage.
Jgs 2: 6 take possession of his *o* hereditary land.
3: 6 *o* daughters to their sons in marriage,
4:11 had detached himself from his *o* people,
7: 2 say, 'My *o* power brought me the victory.'
9: 2 remember that I am your *o* flesh and bone."
11:19 me pass through your land to my *o* place.'
12: 3 in my *o* hand and went on to the Ammonites,
14:19 Then he went off to his *o* family in anger,
17:11 to whom he became as one of his *o* sons.
21:23 and went back to their *o* territory,
21:24 his *o* heritage in his own clan and tribe.
Ru 4: 6 my claim lest I depreciate my *o* estate.
1Sm 4:10 every man fled to his *o* tent.
5:11 Let it return to its *o* place,
6: 9 along the route to his *o* territory,
8:22 of Israel, "Each of you go to his *o* city."
10:25 dismissed the people, each to his *o* place.
12:22 For the sake of his *o* great name the LORD
13:14 The LORD has sought out a man after his *o*
13:15 set out from Gilgal and went his *o* way;
14:46 who returned to their *o* territory.
15:12 where he erected a trophy in his *o* honor,
15:17 "Though little in your *o* esteem,
17:38 Then Saul clothed David in his *o* tunic,
17:51 with the Philistine's *o* sword [which he
17:54 but he kept Goliath's armor in his *o* tent.
18: 5 the whole army, even to Saul's *o* officers.]
18:28 besides, his *o* daughter Michal loved David.
20:30 to your *o* shame and to the disclosure of
22:14 bodyguard, and honored in your *o* house?
25:11 that I have slaughtered for my *o* shearers,
25:39 has punished Nabal for his *o* evil deeds."
25:43 David's wife Michal, Saul's *o* daughter,
31: 4 So Saul took his *o* sword and fell upon it.
2Sm 1:16 "You are responsible for your *o* death,
3:19 and then went to make his *o* report to
6:20 When David returned to bless his *o* family,
11: 9 lord, and did not go down to his *o* house.
12: 4 but he would not take from his *o* flocks
12: 8 house and your lord's wives for your *o*.
12: 9 you took his wife as your *o*,
12:11 bring evil upon you out of your *o* house.
12:20 He returned to his *o* house,
14:13 for not bringing back his *o* banished son.
14:24 the king said, "Let him go to his *o* house;
15:19 you, too, are an exile from your *o* country.
15:27 your sons with you, your *o* son Ahimaaz,
16:11 "If my *o* son,
17:23 departed, going to his home in his *o* city.
18:17 all the Israelites fled to their *o* tents.
19:38 let your servant go back to die in his *o* city
19:40 Godspeed as he returned to his *o* district.
20:22 scattered from the city to their *o* tents,
23:21 hand, then killed him with his *o* spear.
24: 3 royal majesty to see it with his *o* eyes.
1Kgs 1:33 my *o* mule and escort him down to Gihon.
1:44 they mounted him upon the king's *o* mule.
1:47 you and exalt his throne more than your *o*!'
1:48 my throne, so that I see it with my *o* eyes.' "
1:49 left in terror, each going his *o* way.
2:32 will hold him responsible for his *o* blood,
2:37 You shall be responsible for your *o* blood."
2:44 LORD requites you for your *o* wickedness.
4:19 one prefect besides, in the king's *o* land.
7: 1 His *o* palace Solomon completed after
8:15 who with his *o* mouth made a promise to my
8:24 promise, have this day, by your *o* power,
9:27 In this fleet Hiram placed his *o* expert
10: 7 report until I came and saw with my *o* eyes,
10:13 with her servants to her *o* country.
11:19 the sister of Queen Tahpenes, his *o* wife.
11:20 where he then lived with Pharaoh's *o* sons.
11:21 "Give me leave to return to my *o* country."
11:22 are seeking to return to your *o* country?"
12:16 Now look to your *o* house, David."
13:30 He laid the man's body in his *o* grave,
15:15 and his *o* votive offerings of silver,
17:19 he was staying, and laid him on his *o* bed.
22:30 into battle, but you put on your *o* clothes,"
2Kgs 2:12 gripped his *o* garment and tore it in two.
3:27 up the siege and returned to their *o* land.
4:13 replied, "I am living among my *o* people."
7: 2 "You shall see it with your *o* eyes,"
7:19 "You shall see it with your *o* eyes,
8:20 of Judah and chose a king of its *o*.
9:21 of Judah, set out, each in his *o* chariot,
10:16 And he took him along in his *o* chariot.
12: 6 for themselves, each from his *o* clients.
12:19 Ahaziah, kings of Judah, as well as his *o*,
13: 5 Aram, dwelt in their *o* homes as formerly.
14: 6 each one shall die for his *o* sin."
17:29 But these peoples began to make their *o*
17:33 the LORD they served their *o* gods,
18:27 their *o* excrement and drink their urine?"
18:31 eat of his *o* vine and of his own fig-tree,
18:31 and drink the water of his *o* cistern,
18:32 I come to take you to a land like your *o*,
19: 7 report, he will return to his *o* land,
19:34 shield and save this city for my *o* sake,
20: 6 be a shield to this city for my *o* sake,
20:18 Some of your *o* bodily descendants shall be
21:26 in his *o* grave in the garden of Uzza,
23:30 where they buried him in his *o* grave.
24: 7 of Egypt did not again leave his *o* land,
25:27 in the inaugural year of his *o* reign,
1Chr 9:25 Their kinsmen who had lived in their *o*
10: 4 So Saul took his *o* sword and fell on it;
11:23 hand, and killed him with his *o* spear.
16:43 the people departed, each to his *o* home,
17:11 after you who will be one of your *o* sons,
17:22 You made your people Israel your *o* forever,
20: 2 stones, which David wore on his *o* head.
21:12 or three days of the LORD'S *o* sword,
21:23 "Take it as your *o*,
2Chr 1:18 and also of a house for his *o* royal estate.
3:13 They stood upon their *o* feet,
6: 4 who with his *o* mouth made a promise to my
6: 4 by his *o* hands brought it to fulfillment.
6:15 *o* mouth you spoke it, and by your own
7:11 to the house of the LORD and his *o* house.
8: 1 the house of the LORD and his *o* house,
9: 6 report until I came and saw with my *o* eyes.
9:12 to her *o* country with her servants.
10:16 Now look to your *o* house, David!"
15:18 his father's votive offerings and his *o*:
18:29 disguised, but you put on your *o* clothes."
21: 8 they chose a king of their *o*.
22: 4 To his *o* destruction,
25: 4 his *o* guilt shall a man be put to death."
25: 8 Instead, go on your *o*,
25:14 of Seir, which he set up as his *o* gods;
25:15 not save their *o* people from your hand?"
25:16 let you take counsel to your *o* destruction,
26:16 he became proud to his *o* destruction and
28:19 who let Judah go its *o* way and proved
29: 8 and mockery, as you see with your *o* eyes.
31: 1 various cities, each to his *o* possession.
31: 3 From his *o* wealth the king allotted a
32:21 had to return shamefaced to his *o* country.
32:21 some of his *o* offspring struck him down
33:20 ancestors and was buried in his *o* palace.
33:24 him and put him to death in his *o* house.
35:24 servants removed him from his *o* chariot,
36:17 young men in their *o* sanctuary building,
Ezr 2: 1 each man in his *o* city (those who returned
4:16 no longer *o* any part of West-of-Euphrates."
Neh 2:12 and with no other animals but my *o* mount.
3:10 who repaired opposite his *o* house.
3:17 Next to him, for his *o* district,
3:28 work of repair, each before his *o* house.
3:30 repaired the place opposite his *o* lodging.
3:36 Turn back their derision upon their *o*
4: 9 went back, each to his *o* task at the wall.
4:16 Jerusalem, each man with his *o* attendant,
5: 5 And though these are our *o* kinsmen and our
5: 7 are exacting interest from your *o* kinsmen!"
5: 8 you, however, are selling your *o* brothers,
5:16 though I had acquired no land of my *o*,
6: 8 rather, it is the invention of your *o* mind."
7: 3 posts, and others before their *o* houses."
7: 6 each man to his *o* city (those who returned
11: 3 man on the property he owned in his *o* city.)
13:10 had deserted, each man to his *o* field.
13:19 I posted some of my *o* men at the gates so
Tb 1: 4 I lived as a young man in my *o* country,
1: 9 I married Anna, a woman of our *o* lineage.
2: 5 Returning to my *o* quarters,
3:15 And that I have never defiled my *o* name or
4: 8 Son, give alms in proportion to what you *o*.
4:12 all of them took wives from among their *o*
5: 9 man who is one of our *o* Israelite kinsmen!"
5:13 Hananiah the elder, one of your *o* kinsmen."
5:21 Your *o* eyes will see the day when he
6:16 you to marry a woman from your *o* family.
6:18 his kinswoman, of his *o* family's lineage,
8:21 half of whatever I *o* when you go back in
10: 6 trustworthy, and is one of our *o* kinsmen.
12:10 guilty of sin are their *o* worst enemies.
Jdt 6:17 his *o* words among the Assyrian officers,
8: 2 husband, Manasseh, of her *o* tribe and clan,
9: 3 had felt the shame of their *o* deceiving.
12: 1 with his *o* delicacies to eat and his own wine
15:10 With your *o* hand you have done all this;
16:24 husband, Manasseh, and to her *o* relatives;
Est 1:22 its *o* script and to each people in its own
1:22 every man should be lord in his *o* home.
2: 7 Mordecai had taken her as his *o* daughter.
3:12 its *o* script and to each people in its own
C:22 but turn their *o* counsel against them and
7: 8 queen while she is with me in my *o* house!"
8: 9 *o* script and to each people in its own
8: 9 to the Jews in their *o* script and language.
E: 3 begin plotting against their *o* benefactors.
E:19 that the Jews may follow their *o* laws,
1Mc 1: 8 over his kingdom, each in his *o* territory,
1:24 all this, he went back to his *o* country,
1:38 She became a stranger to her *o* offspring,
2:36 nor blocked up their *o* hiding places.
3:33 of his son Antiochus until his *o* return.
4:32 let them tremble at their *o* destruction.
5:48 your territory in order to reach our *o*;
6:52 by setting up machines of their *o*,
6:54 the rest scattered each to his *o* home,
6:59 live according to their *o* laws as formerly;
8: 4 although it was very remote from their *o*.
9:69 and resolved to return to his *o* country
9:72 He returned to his *o* country and never
10:13 his place and returned to his *o* country.
10:37 them, and let them follow their *o* laws,
10:72 were twice put to flight in their *o* land.
11: 1 Alexander's kingdom and add it to his *o*.
11:21 of the law, enemies of their *o* nation,
11:25 his *o* nation brought charges against him,
11:73 in Kadesh, where they pitched their *o* camp.
13: 5 to save my *o* life in any time of distress,
13:24 Then Trypho returned to his *o* country.
14:32 spending large sums of his *o* money to
15: 6 I authorize you to coin your *o* money,
2Mc 3: 3 defrayed from his *o* revenues all the
3:36 high God that he had seen with his *o* eyes.
4: 1 about the funds against his *o* country,
4:21 so he took measures for his *o* security.
4:26 who had cheated his *o* brother and now saw
5: 6 one's *o* kindred was the greatest failure,
6:16 he does not abandon his *o* people.
6:19 his *o* accord to the instrument of torture,
6:21 urged him to bring meat of his *o* providing,
7:18 We suffer these things on our *o* account,
8:35 successful in destroying his *o* army.
9:12 When he could no longer bear his *o* stench,
9:16 and would provide from his *o* revenues the
10: 7 about the purification of his *o* Place.
10:30 and shielding him with their *o* armor,
11:23 undisturbed in conducting their *o* affairs.
11:24 customs but prefer their *o* way of life.
11:24 us to let them retain their *o* customs.
11:26 may contentedly go about their *o* business."
11:29 return home and attend to your *o* affairs.
12:22 pierced by the swords of their *o* men.
12:42 for they had seen with their *o* eyes what
14: 8 out of consideration for my *o* countrymen,
15:34 be he who has kept his *o* Place undefiled!"
15:37 I will bring my *o* story to an end here too.
Jb 2:11 they set out each one from his *o* place:
5:13 He catches the wise in their *o* ruses,
7:11 My *o* utterance I will not restrain;
9:20 I were right, my *o* mouth might condemn me;
12:18 a waistcloth to bind the king's *o* loins.
14:22 Only his *o* flesh pains him,
15: 6 own mouth condemns you, not I; you *o*
18: 7 in, and his *o* counsel casts him down.
19:27 my *o* eyes,
21:16 If their happiness is not in their *o* hands
21:20 feels it, Let his *o* eyes see the calamity,
29:18 "In my *o* nest I shall grow old;

32: 1 because he was righteous in his *o* eyes.
40:14 that your *o* right hand can save you.
Ps(s) 5:11 let them fall by their *o* devices;
7:17 His mischief shall recoil upon his *o* head;
9:17 are trapped by the work of their *o* hands.
12: 5 our lips are our *o*;
33:12 people he has chosen for his *o* inheritance.
35:21 We saw him with our *o* eyes!"
37:15 their swords shall pierce their *o* hearts,
44: 3 How with your *o* hand you rooted out the
44: 4 their *o* sword did they conquer the land,
44: 4 nor did their *o* arm make them victorious,
49: 8 redeem himself, or pay his *o* ransom to God;
64: 9 He brings them down by their *o* tongues;
69:23 Let their *o* table be a snare before them,
69:34 and his *o* who are in bonds he spurns not.
69:36 They shall dwell in the land and *o* it,
81:13 they walked according to their *o* counsels.
113: 8 princes, with the princes of his *o* people.
132:11 *o* offspring I will set upon your throne;
135: 4 for himself, Israel for his *o* possession.
141:10 all the wicked fall, each into his *o* net,
Prv 1:18 *o* blood, they set a trap for their own
1:31 *o* way, and with their own devices be
3: 5 heart, on your *o* intelligence rely not;
3: 7 Be not wise in your *o* eyes.
5:15 own cistern, running water from your *o*
5:22 *o* iniquities the wicked man will be caught,
5:22 meshes of his *o* sin he will be held fast;
9:12 If you are wise, it is to your *o* advantage;
11: 6 faithless are caught in their *o* intrigue.
12:11 He who tills his *o* land has food in plenty,
12:15 way of the fool seems right in his *o* eyes,
14: 1 but Folly tears hers down with her *o* hands.
14:10 The heart knows its *o* bitterness,
15:27 greedy of gain brings ruin on his *o* house,
15:32 who rejects admonition despises his *o* soul,
16: 2 ways of a man may be pure in his *o* eyes,
16: 4 LORD has made everything for his *o* ends,
18: 9 is *o* brother to the man who is destructive.
19: 3 A man's *o* folly upsets his way,
19: 8 gains intelligence is his *o* best friend;
21: 2 ways of a man may be right in his *o* eyes,
23:15 be wise, my *o* heart also will rejoice;
26: 5 folly, lest he become wise in his *o* eyes.
26:12 You see a man wise in his *o* eyes?
26:17 is he who meddles in a quarrel not his *o*.
27: 2 *o* mouth; Someone else—not your own
27:10 Your *o* friend and your father's friend
28:10 evil way will himself fall into his *o* pit.
28:11 The rich man is wise in his *o* eyes,
29:24 The accomplice of a thief is his *o* enemy:
30:12 is a group that is pure in its *o* eyes,
31:22 She makes her *o* coverlets;
Eccl 4: 5 folds his arms and consumes his *o* flesh"
9:12 *o* time than fish taken in the fatal net,
Sg 1: 6 my *o* vineyard I have not cared for.
2: 7 do not stir up love before its *o* time.
3: 5 do not stir up love before its *o* time.
8: 4 do not stir up love, before its *o* time.
8:12 My vineyard is at my *o* disposal;
Wis 2:20 for according to his *o* words,
2:23 the image of his *o* nature he made him.
6:16 Because she makes her *o* rounds,
8:18 I went about seeking to take her for my *o*.
11:13 *o* torments was a benefit to these others,
12: 6 took with their *o* hands defenseless lives,
12:23 you tormented through their *o* abominations.
17: 2 they lay confined beneath their *o* roofs as
17:11 cowardly, testifies in its *o* condemnation,
19:13 they justly suffered for their *o* misdeeds,
19:17 each sought the entrance of his *o* gate.
19:20 Fire in water maintained its *o* strength,
Sir 3:23 Their *o* opinion has misled many,
4:22 Show no favoritism to your *o* discredit;
4:22 no one intimidate you to your *o* downfall.
7:21 wise servant be dear to you as your *o* self;
8:15 For he will go his *o* way straight,
11:34 make a stranger of you to your *o* household.
13:14 Every living thing loves its *o* kind,
13:15 its own kind; with his *o* kind every man
14: 5 himself and does not enjoy what is his *o*?
14: 6 he punishes his *o* miserliness.
14:10 bread, but on his *o* table he sets it stale.
15:14 he made him subject to his *o* free choice.
17: 1 man, and in his *o* image he made him.
17: 3 He endows man with a strength of his *o*,
17:14 ruler, but the LORD's *o* portion is Israel.
19: 4 strays after them sins against his *o* life.
21: 7 but the wise man knows his *o* faults.
24: 1 sings her *o* praises, before her own people
27: 9 Birds nest with their *o* kind,
28: 2 you pray, your *o* sins will be forgiven.
28: 4 fellows, yet seek pardon for his *o* sins?
29:22 man's fare under the shadow of one's *o* roof
30:11 Give him not his *o* way in his youth,
31:15 you do, and keep in mind your *o* dislikes:
37: 7 a way, but some counsel ways of their *o*;
37:13 Then, too, heed your *o* heart's counsel;
37:21 When a man is wise to his *o* advantage,
37:21 of his knowledge are seen in his *o* person;
38:31 hands, each one an expert at his *o* task;
39:16 in its *o* time every need is supplied.
44: 1 men, our ancestors, each in his *o* time:
44: 2 of the Most High's portion, his *o* part,
44: 6 and at peace in their *o* estates
44:20 In his *o* flesh he incised the ordinance,
47: 7 and shattered their power till our *o* day.
47:22 remnant, to David a root from his *o* family.
51:30 his *o* time God will give you your reward.
Is 3: 7 my *o* house there is no bread or clothing!
4: 1 eat our *o* food and wear our own clothing;
5:21 own sight, and prudent in their *o* esteem!
7: 6 tear Judah asunder, make it our *o* by force,
10:13 "By my *o* power I have done it,
13:14 turn to his kindred and flee to his *o* land.
14: 1 Israel and settles them on their *o* soil,
14:18 nations lie in glory, each in his *o* tomb;
23:10 Cross to your *o* land,
26:15 LORD, increased the nation to your *o* glory,
30:20 your *o* eyes you shall see your Teacher,
36:12 *o* excrement and drink their own urine?"
36:16 eat of hisown vine and of his *o* fig tree,
36:16 tree, and drink the water of his *o* cistern,
36:17 I come to take you to a land like your *o*,
37: 7 report, he will return to his *o* land,
37:35 shield and save this city for my *o* sake,
39: 7 Some of your *o* bodily descendants shall be
43:25 It is I, I, who wipe out, for my *o* sake,
47:15 Each wanders his *o* way,
48:11 For my sake, for my *o* sake,
49:26 make your oppressors eat their *o* flesh,
49:26 *o* blood as with the juice of the grape.
50:11 *o* fire and by the flares you have burnt!
53: 6 like sheep, each following his *o* way;
56:11 *o* way, every one of them to his own gain:
57:17 wrath, as they went their *o* rebellious way.
58: 3 fast day you carry out your *o* pursuits,
58: 7 them, and not turning your back on your *o*.
58:13 following your *o* pursuits on my holy day;
58:13 your ways, seeking your *o* interests,
59:16 So his *o* arm brought about the victory,
63: 5 *o* arm brought about the victory and my *o*
65: 2 in evil paths and follow their *o* thoughts,
66: 3 *o* ways and taken pleasure in their own
Jer 1:16 gods and adoring their *o* handiwork.
2:19 own wickedness chastises you, your *o*
3:15 over you shepherds after my *o* heart,
5:19 me to serve strange gods in your *o* land,
5:19 you serve strangers in a land not your *o*."
6:19 this people, the fruit of their *o* schemes,
7: 6 or follow strange gods to your *o* harm,
7: 8 trust in deceitful words to your *o* loss!
7:19 rather themselves, to their *o* confusion?
10:16 Israel is his very *o* tribe,
12: 6 For even your *o* brothers,
12:14 which I gave my people Israel as their *o*:
14:14 divination, dreams of their *o* imagination,
14:16 will pour out upon them their *o* wickedness.
17:11 *o* is the man who acquires wealth unjustly:
18:12 We will follow our *o* devices;
18:18 And so, let us destroy him by his *o* tongue;
20: 4 Your *o* eyes shall see them fall by the
22:17 are set on nothing except on your *o* gain,
23: 8 they shall again live on their *o* land.
23:16 Visions of their *o* fancy they speak,
23:26 lies and their *o* deceitful fancies?
23:36 For each man his *o* word becomes the burden
25: 7 me with your handiwork to your *o* harm.
25:14 own deeds and according to their *o*
26:11 city, as you have heard with your *o* ears."
26:19 this great evil to our *o* undoing."
27:11 him I will leave in peace on its *o* land,
29: 7 LORD, for upon its welfare depends your *o*.
29:25 *o* authority to all the people of Jerusalem,
30:21 His leader shall be one of his *o*,
31:17 Your sons shall return to their *o* borders.
31:30 through his *o* fault only shall anyone die:
32:39 to their *o* good and that of their children
35: 7 neither plant nor *o* a vineyard.
35: 9 we *o* no vineyards or fields or crops,
37: 7 out to help you will return to its *o* land,
40: 9 the king of Babylon, for their *o* welfare;
44:26 I swear by my *o* great name,
46:16 let us return to our *o* people,
49:13 By my *o* self I have sworn, says the LORD:
49:20 *o* pasture shall be aghast because of them.
50:16 to his *o* people, everyone flees to his own
50:45 *o* pasture shall be aghast because of them.
51: 9 Leave her, let us go, each to his *o* land."
51:19 Israel is his very *o* tribe,
51:24 to Zion, as you shall see with your *o* eyes,
Lam 4:10 women boiled their *o* children,
5: 4 we must buy, for our *o* wood we must pay.
Bar 1:22 after the devices of our *o* wicked hearts,
2:14 and deliver us for your *o* sake:
3: 5 of our fathers, but your *o* hand and name:
4:33 so shall she grieve over her *o* desolation.
6:27 their sacrifices for their *o* advantage.
6:53 They neither vindicate their *o* rights,
Ez 3:21 warning, and you shall save your *o* life.
7:16 them all to death, each one for his *o* sins.
13: 2 Say to those who prophesy their *o* thought:
13: 3 their *o* spirit and have seen no vision.
13:17 your people who prophesy their *o* thoughts;
16:15 But you were captivated by your *o* beauty,
16:15 on every passer-by, whose *o* you became.
18:13 his death shall be his *o* fault.
18:20 The virtuous man's virtue shall be his *o*,
22: 3 which has made idols for her *o* defilement.
22:11 sisters, the daughters of his *o* fathers.
23:25 they will judge you by their *o* ordinances.
32:10 shall continuously tremble for his *o* life.
33: 4 him, shall be responsible for his *o* death.
33: 5 he is responsible for his *o* death,
33: 6 that person is taken because of his *o* sin.
34:13 I will bring them back to their *o* country
34:27 they shall dwell securely on their *o* soil.
36: 7 nations shall bear their *o* reproach.
36:24 lands, and bring you back to your *o* land.
45:22 day the prince shall offer on his *o* behalf,
46:18 for his sons from his *o* property,
48:12 tract of land their *o* most sacred domain,
Dn 2:30 may understand the thoughts in your *o* mind.
3:95 or worship any god except their *o* God.
6:18 the king sealed with his *o* ring and the
9:17 and for your *o* sake,
9:19 and act without delay, for your *o* sake,
11: 9 of the south, and return to his *o* country.
11:19 turn to the strongholds of his *o* land,
13:61 for by their *o* words Daniel had convicted
14:39 once brought Habakkuk back to his *o* place.
Hos 8: 4 for themselves, to their *o* destruction.
8: 9 a wild ass off on its *o*—
11: 6 repent, their *o* counsels shall devour them.
Jl 2: 7 They advance, each in his *o* lane,
2: 8 another, each advances in his *o* track;
4: 4 I will return your deed upon your *o* head.
4: 6 removing them far from their *o* country!
4: 7 I will return your deed upon your *o* head.
Am 4:12 So now I will deal with you in my *o* way,
6: 5 David, they devise their *o* accompaniment.
6:13 and say, "Have we not, by our *o* strength,
9:15 I will plant them upon their *o* ground;
Ob 1:15 deed shall come back upon your *o* head
Jon 4: 2 I said while I was still in my *o* country?
Mi 4: 4 under his *o* vine or under his own fig tree,
Hb 1: 6 of the land to take dwellings not his *o*.
1:11 culprit who makes his *o* strength his god!
2:10 off many peoples, forfeiting your *o* life:
Zep 2:11 Then, each from its *o* place,
Hg 1: 4 for you to dwell in your *o* paneled houses,
1: 9 while each of you hurries to his *o* house.
Zec 11: 5 their *o* shepherds do not feel for them.
12: 6 Jerusalem shall not abide on its *o* site.
Mal 1: 5 Your *o* eyes shall see it,
2:15 must then safeguard life that is your *o*,
2:16 must then safeguard life that is your *o*,
3:17 the LORD of hosts, my *o* special possession,
Mt 2:12 back to their *o* country by another route.
6:34 Today has troubles enough of its *o*.
7: 3 eye when you miss the plank in your *o*?
7: 4 all the time the plank remains in your *o*?
7: 5 Remove the plank from your *o* eye first;
9: 1 the crossing, and came back to his *o* town.
10:36 a man's enemies those of his *o* household.
13:57 in his native place, indeed in his *o* house."
20:28 give his *o* life as a ransom for the many."
27:31 of the cloak, dressed him in his *o* clothes,
27:60 in fresh linen and laid it in his *o* new tomb
Mk 5:40 his *o* companions and entered the room
6: 1 returned to his *o* part of the country
6: 4 among his own kindred, and in his *o* house."
6:22 Herodias' *o* daughter came in at one point
13:34 servants in charge, each with his *o* task;
15:20 the purple, dressed him in his *o* clothes,
Lk 2: 3 went to register, each to his *o* town.
2:39 to Galilee and their *o* town of Nazareth.
4:23 'Do here in your *o* country the things we
6:41 eye when you miss the plank in your *o*?
6:42 yourself to see the plank lodged in your *o*?
6:42 remove the plank from your *o* eye first;
10:34 on his *o* beast and brought him to an inn,
16: 8 when it comes to dealing with their *o* kind.
16:12 money, who will give you what is your *o*?
18: 9 who believed in their *o* self-righteousness
18:28 left all we *o* to become your followers."
19:22 I intend to judge you on your *o* evidence.
22:71 We have heard it from his *o* mouth."
Jn 1:11 own he came, yet his *o* did not accept him.
4:41 his *o* spoken word many more came to faith.
4:44 no one esteems a prophet in his *o* country.)
5:18 still, was speaking of God as his *o* Father,
5:30 my *o* will but the will of him who sent me.
5:31 "If I witness on my *o* behalf,
5:43 But let someone come in his *o* name,
6:38 *o* will that I have come down from heaven,
7:16 "My doctrine is not my *o*;
7:17 comes from God or is simply spoken on my *o*.
7:18 on his *o* is bent on self-glorification.
7:50 One of their *o* number,
8:13 "You are your *o* witness.
8:14 "What if I am my *o* witness?
8:42 I did not come of my *o* will;
8:53 [Then each went off to his *o* house,
10: 3 he calls his *o* by name and leads them out.
11:51 (He did not say this on his *o*.
12:49 For I have not spoken on my *o*;
13: 1 He had loved his *o* in this world,

OWN (cont.)

15:19 to the world, it would love you as its o;
16:13 He will not speak on his o,
18:34 answered, "Are you saying this on your o,
18:35 "It is your o people and the chief
Acts 1:19 'Akeldama' in their o language.
2: 6 heard these men speaking his o language.
2:11 speaking in his o tongue about the marvels
3:12 walk by some power or holiness of our o?
3:22 prophet like me from among your o kinsmen:
4:23 the two went back to their o people and
4:32 of them ever claimed anything as his o;
6: 3 Look around among your o number,
7:21 him and brought him up as her o son.
7:41 over the product of their o hands.
13:22 my o heart who will fulfill my every wish.'
17:28 as some of your o poets have put it,
18: 6 "Your blood be on your o heads.
18:15 terminology and titles and your o law,
20:20 from telling you what was for your o good,
20:28 has acquired at the price of his o blood.
20:30 From your o number,
21:11 belt, tied his o hands and feet with it.
23:29 he was accused in matters of their o law
24:17 alms to my o people and to make
25:19 with him over issues in their o religion,
26: 4 and the life I have led among my o people
27:10 ship and cargo, but to our o lives as well."
28:16 was allowed to take a lodging of his o,
28:19 to make accusations against my o people.
Rom 1:27 o persons the penalty for their perversity.
1:28 o depraved sense to do what is unseemly.
3:25 He did so to manifest his o justice,
4:19 weak in faith he thought of his o body,
7:15 I cannot even understand my o actions.
7:16 When I act against my o will,
8:20 o accord but by him who once subjected it;
8:32 did not spare his o Son but handed him over
10: 3 justice and seeking to establish their o,
11:24 nature be grafted into their o olive tree.
12:13 Look on the needs of the saints as your o;
12:16 Do not be wise in your o estimation.
14: 5 Each should be certain of his o conscience.
14: 7 o master and none of us dies as his o master.
15:27 They did so of their o accord,
16:18 not Christ our Lord, but their o bellies,
1Cor 2:11 self but the man's o spirit within him?
4: 7 why are you boasting as if it were your o?
6: 8 injure and cheat your very o brothers.
6:18 but the fornicator sins against his o body.
6:19 You are not your o.
7: 2 his o wife and every woman her own husband.
7: 7 Still, each one has his o gift from God,
7:35 going into this with you for your o good.
9:27 I do is discipline my o body and master it,
10:24 o interest but rather that of his neighbor.
10:29 not your o conscience but your neighbor's.
10:33 way I can by seeking, not my o advantage,
11:21 everyone is in haste to eat his o supper.
15:10 not on my o but through the favor of God.
15:38 to each seed its o fruition.
15:41 The sun has a splendor of its o,
16:21 who send you this greeting in my o hand.
2Cor 10: 6 else once your o obedience is perfect.
10:12 people like that are their o appraisers,
11:26 endangered by floods, robbers, my o people,
Gal 2:20 and the life I live now is not my o;
6: 5 Everyone should bear his o responsibility.
6:11 I write to you in my o large handwriting!
Eph 1:14 redemption of a people God has made his o,
2: 8 This is not your o doing,
2:15 In his o flesh he abolished the law with
5:28 love their wives as they do their o bodies.
5:29 that no one ever hates his o flesh;
Phil 2: 4 to others' interests rather than to his o.
2:21 Everyone is busy seeking his o interests
2:28 him, and my o anxieties may be lessened.
3: 9 of my o based on observance of the law.
4: 7 Then God's o peace,
Col 1:24 In my o flesh I fill up what is lacking in
2:18 a one takes his stand on his o experience;
3: 7 Your o conduct was once of this sort,
4:18 This greeting is from Paul— in my o hand!
1Thes 2: 7 on our o importance as apostles of Christ.
4:11 at peace and attend to your o affairs.
2Thes 2: 6 until he shall be revealed in his o time.
2: 8 him by manifesting his o presence.
3:17 This greeting is in my o hand—Paul's.
1Tm 1: 2 hope, to Timothy, my o true child in faith.
3: 4 must be a good manager of his o household,
3: 5 does not know how to manage his o house,
5: 8 If anyone does not provide for his o
2Tm 1: 9 of ours but according to his o design
4: 3 doctrine, but, following their o desires,
Ti 1: 3 manifested in his o good time as his word,
1: 4 Titus, my o true child in our common faith:
1:12 A man of Crete, one of their o prophets,
2:14 to cleanse for himself a people of his o,
Phlm 1:19 I, Paul, write this in my o hand:
Heb 4:10 rests from his o work as God did from his.
5: 4 not take this honor on his o initiative,
7:27 o sins and then for those of the people;
9:12 of goats and calves, but with his o blood,
9:25 sanctuary with blood that is not his o;
13:12 to sanctify the people by his o blood.
Jas 1:14 and lure of his o passion tempt every man.
2: 7 that noble name which has made you God's o.
1Pt 2: 9 a people he claims for his o to proclaim
2:24 o body he brought your sins to the cross,
4:17 begun, and begun with God's o household.
2Pt 1: 3 him who called us by his o glory and power.
1: 8 like these, made increasingly your o,
2: 1 the Master who acquired them for his o,
3:16 do the rest of Scripture) to their o ruin.
1Jn 3:12 Because his o deeds were wicked while his
5: 9 God has given on his o Son's behalf.
5:10 he has given on his o Son's behalf.
Jude 1: 6 too, who did not keep to their o domain,
Rv 1: 5 and freed us from our sins by his o blood,
3:12 from heaven, and my o name which is new.
13: 2 The dragon gave it his o power and throne,

OWNED (8)

Gn 25: 5 everything that he o to his son Isaac.
39: 5 the LORD's blessing was on everything he o,
39: 6 left everything he o in Joseph's charge,
Neh 11: 3 man on the property he o in his own city.)
Zec 13: 5 the soil, for I have o land since my youth."
Acts 4:34 for all who o property or houses sold them
4:37 that he o and made a donation of the money,
1Cor 7:30 themselves as though they o nothing,

OWNER (40)

Ex 21:28 The o of the ox,
21:29 in the habit of goring people and its o,
21:29 but its o also must be put to death.
21:32 o of the slave thirty shekels of silver,
21:34 the o of the cistern must make good by
21:34 restoring the value of the animal to its o;
21:36 of goring and its o would not keep it in,
22: 7 the o of the house shall be brought to God,
22:10 the o must accept the oath,
22:11 theft, he must make restitution to the o.
22:13 maimed or dies while the o is not present,
22:14 But if the o is present,
Lv 5:24 give the o one fifth of its value.
14:35 the o of the house shall come and report
25:28 be released and returned to its original o.
27:24 shall revert to the hereditary o of this land
Jgs 19:23 o of the house went out to them and said,
1Kgs 16:24 built Samaria after Shemer, the former o.
Eccl 5:10 to the o except to feast his eyes upon?
5:12 riches kept by their o to his hurt.
7:12 is that wisdom preserves the life of its o.
Sir 6: 4 o and makes him the sport of his enemies.
19: 3 for contumacious desire destroys its o.
Is 1: 3 An ox knows its o,
Bar 6:58 a handy tool in a house, the joy of its o,
Mi 2: 2 They cheat an o of his house,
Mt 20: 1 God is like the case of the o of an estate
20: 8 the o of the vineyard said to his foreman,
20:11 Thereupon they complained to the o.
21:33 was a property o who planted a vineyard,
21:40 What do you suppose the o of the vineyard
24:43 if the o of the house knew when the thief
Mk 12: 9 you suppose the o of the vineyard will do?
14:14 Whatever house he enters, say to the o,
Lk 16: 8 "The o then gave his devious employee
20:13 The o of the vineyard asked himself,
20:15 o of the vineyard has in store for them?
22:10 into the house he enters, and say to the o,
Jn 10:12 who is no shepherd nor o of the sheep
Acts 21:11 bind the o of this belt and hand him over

OWNERS (9)

Tb 2:12 When she sent back the goods to their o,
2:12 the cloth and sent it back to the o.
2:13 Give it back to its o,
2:14 her, and told her to give it back to its o.
Prv 26:28 The lying tongue is its o enemy,
Ez 13:18 every size of head so as to entrap their o.
Mt 13:27 The o slaves came to him and said,
Lk 19:33 As they untied the ass, its o said to them,
Col 4: 1 You slave o,

OWNERSHIP (1)

Ps(s) 37:34 He will promote you to o of the land;

OWNING (1)

1Sm 25: 2 o three thousand sheep and a thousand

OWNS (5)

Gn 23: 9 to sell me the cave of Machpelah that he o;
24:36 age, and he has given him everything he o.
39: 8 house, but has entrusted to me all he o.
Sg 8: 7 one to offer all he o to purchase love,
Mt 18:12 A man o a hundred sheep and one of them

OX (75)

Ex 20:17 his male or female slave, nor his o or ass,
21:28 an o gores a man or a woman to death,
21:28 or a woman to death, the o must be stoned;
21:28 The owner of the o,
21:29 But if an o was previously in the habit of
21:29 or a woman, not only must the o be stoned,
21:31 if it is a boy or a girl that the o gores.
21:32 of silver, and the o must be stoned.
21:33 again, should an o or an ass fall into it,
21:35 o hurts another's ox so badly that it dies,
21:35 they shall sell the live o and divide
21:36 But if it was known that the o was
21:36 must make full restitution, an o for an ox;
21:37 an o or a sheep and slaughters or sells it,
21:37 he shall restore five oxen for the one o,
22: 3 found alive in his possession, be it an o,
22: 8 appropriation, whether it be about an o,
22: 9 "When a man gives an ass, or an o,
23: 4 upon your enemy's o or ass going astray,
23:12 your o and your ass may also have rest,
Lv 4:10 removed from the o of the peace offering;
7:23 not eat the fat of any o or sheep or goat.
9: 4 and an o and a ram for a peace offering,
9:18 Finally he slaughtered the o and the ram,
9:19 of fat from the o and from the ram,
17: 3 who slaughters an o or a sheep or goat,
22:19 the o or sheep or goat that he offers must
22:23 An o or a sheep that is in any way
22:27 "When an o or a lamb or a goat is born,
22:28 You shall not slaughter an o or a sheep on
27:26 If it is an o or a sheep,
Nm 7: 3 two princes, and an o for every prince.
15: 8 When you sacrifice an o as a holocaust,
15:11 The same is to be done for each o,
22: 4 us as an o devours the grass of the field."
Dt 5:14 or your o or ass or any of your beasts,
5:21 his male or female slave, nor his o or ass,
14: 4 the o, the sheep, the goat, the red deer,
22: 1 "You shall not see your kinsman's o or
22: 4 You shall not see your kinsman's ass or o
22:10 with an o and an ass harnessed together.
25: 4 muzzle an o when it is treading out grain.
28:31 o will be slaughtered before your eyes,
33:17 the wild o With which to gore the nations,
Jos 7:24 and with his sons and daughters, his o,
1Sm 12: 3 Whose o have I taken?
14:34 of them to bring his o or his sheep to me.
14:34 to the LORD whatever o he had seized,
2Sm 6:13 steps, he sacrificed an o and a fatling.
Jb 6: 5 Does the o low over his fodder?
24: 3 they take the widow's o for a pledge.
39: 9 Will the wild o consent to serve you,
40:15 Behemoth, that feeds on grass like an o.
Prv 7:22 like an o that is led to slaughter;
15:17 love is than a fatted o and hatred with it.
Sir 25: 8 plows not like a donkey yoked with an o.
38:25 Who guides the o and urges on the bullock,
Is 1: 3 An o knows its owner,
11: 7 the lion shall eat hay like the o.
32:20 and let the o and the ass go freely!
65:25 o [but the serpent's food shall be dust].
66: 3 slaughtering an o is like slaying a man;
Ez 1:10 and on the left side the face of an o,
10:14 the first face was that of an o,
Dn 4:22 an o and be bathed with the dew of heaven;
4:29 you shall be given grass to eat like an o,
4:30 from among men, he ate grass like an o,
5:21 with wild asses, and ate grass like an o;
Lk 13:15 Which of you does not let his o or ass out
14: 5 has a son or an o and he falls into a pit,
1Cor 9: 8 not muzzle an o while it treads out grain."
1Tm 5:18 on an o when he is threshing the grain,"
Rv 4: 7 resembled a lion, the second an o;

OXEN (102)

Gn 49: 6 men, in their willfulness they maimed o.
Ex 20:24 and peace offerings, your sheep and your o.
21:37 it, he shall restore five o for the one ox,
22:29 do the same with your o and your sheep;
Nm 7: 3 of six baggage wagons and twelve o,
7: 6 So Moses accepted the wagons and o,
7: 7 He gave two wagons and four o to the
7: 8 and four wagons and eight o to the
7:17 for a sin offering; and two o,
7:23 for a sin offering; and two o,
7:29 for a sin offering; and two o,
7:35 for a sin offering; and two o,
7:41 for a sin offering; and two o,
7:47 for a sin offering; and two o,
7:53 for a sin offering; and two o,
7:59 for a sin offering; and two o,
7:65 for a sin offering; and two o,
7:71 for a sin offering; and two o,
7:77 for a sin offering; and two o,
7:83 for a sin offering; and two o,
7:88 offerings were, in all, twenty-four o,
22:40 Here Balak slaughtered o and sheep,
31:28 one out of every five hundred persons, o,
31:30 and the same from the different beasts, o,
31:33 thousand sheep, seventy-two thousand o,
31:38 thirty-six thousand o,
31:44 five hundred sheep, thirty-six thousand o,
Dt 14:26 money for whatever you desire, o or sheep,
Jos 6:21 men and women, young and old, as well as o,
Jgs 6: 4 in Israel, nor sheep, o or asses.
1Sm 8:16 as well as your best o and your asses,

11: 5 Saul came in from the field, behind his *o.*
11: 7 Taking a yoke of *o,*
11: 7 the same as this will be done to his *o!*"
14:32 the spoil and took sheep, *o* and calves,
15: 3 women, children and infants, *o* and sheep,
15: 9 Agag and the best of the fat sheep and *o,*
15:14 my ears, and the lowing of *o* that I hear?"
15:15 best sheep and *o* to sacrifice to the LORD,
15:21 from the spoil the men took sheep and *o,*
22:19 men and women, children and infants, and *o,*
27: 9 woman alive, but would carry off sheep, *o,*
30:20 Moreover, David took all the sheep and *o,*
2Sm 6: 6 steadied it, for the *o* were making it tip.
24:22 Here are *o* for holocausts,
24:22 sledges and the yokes of the *o* for wood.
24:24 floor and the *o* for fifty silver shekels.
1Kgs 1: 9 When he slaughtered sheep, *o,*
1:19 He has slaughtered *o,*
1:25 He went down today and slaughtered *o,*
5: 3 ten fatted *o,* twenty pasture-fed *o*
7:25 This rested on twelve *o,*
7:29 between the frames there were lions, *o,*
7:29 likewise, above and below the lions and *o,*
7:44 one sea, twelve *o* supporting the sea,
8: 5 sheep and *o* too many to number or count.
8:63 *o* and one hundred twenty thousand sheep.
19:19 as he was plowing with twelve yoke of *o;*
19:20 Elisha left the *o,*
19:21 Elisha left him and, taking the yoke of *o,*
2Kgs 16:17 sea from the bronze *o* that supported it,
1Chr 12:41 food on asses, camels, mules, and *o*—
12:41 meal, pressed figs, raisins, wine oil, *o,*
13: 9 the ark, for the *o* were upsetting it.
21:23 I also give you the *o* for the holocausts,
2Chr 4: 3 a ring of figures of *o* encircled the sea,
4: 4 It rested on twelve *o,*
4:15 one sea, and the twelve *o* under it;
5: 6 were sacrificing sheep and *o* so numerous
7: 5 offered as sacrifice twenty-two thousand *o,*
15:11 to the LORD at the time seven hundred *o*
18: 2 and *o* for him and the people with him,
29:32 assembly brought forward was seventy *o,*
29:33 six hundred *o* and three thousand sheep.
31: 6 of Judah also brought in tithes of *o,*
32:29 he acquired sheep and *o* in great numbers,
35: 7 were present, and also three thousand *o;*
35: 8 victims together with three hundred *o.*
35: 9 victims, together with five hundred *o.*
35:12 They did the same with the *o.*
Tb 10:10 male and female slaves, *o* and sheep,
Jb 1: 3 thousand camels, five hundred yoke of *o,*
1:14 "The *o* were plowing and the asses grazing
42:12 six thousand camels, a thousand yoke of *o,*
Ps(s) 8: 8 All sheep and *o,*
66:15 I will sacrifice *o* and goats.
69:32 This will please the LORD more than *o*
144:14 may our *o* be well laden.
Prv 14: 4 Where there are no *o,*
Is 22:13 you slaughter *o* and butcher sheep,
30:24 The *o* and the asses that till the ground
34: 7 Wild *o* shall be struck down with fatlings,
Jer 31:12 wine, and the oil, the sheep and the *o;*
50:27 Slay all her *o,* let them go down to
52:20 and the twelve *o* of bronze under the sea,
Am 6:12 or can one plow the sea with *o?*
Lk 14:19 yoke of *o* and I am going out to test them.
Jn 2:14 he came upon people engaged in selling *o,*
2:15 sheep and *o* alike out of the temple area,
Acts 14:13 brought *o* and garlands to the gates
1Cor 9: 9 Is God concerned here for *o,*

OXGOAD (1)

Jgs 3:31 who slew six hundred Philistines with an *o.*

OXGOADS (1)

1Sm 13:21 sharpening the axes and for setting the *o.*

OZEM (2)

1Chr 2:15 Nethanel, the fourth, Raddai, the fifth, *O,*
2:25 the first-born, then Bunah, Oren, and *O,*

OZIEL (1)

Jdt 8: 1 of Merari, son of Joseph, son of *O,*

OZNI (1)

Nm 26:16 through *O* the clan of the Oznites,

OZNITES (1)

Nm 26:16 Shunites, through Ozni the clan of the *O,*

P

PAARAI (1)

2Sm 23:35 *P* the Arbite;

PACE (3)

Gn 33:14 while I proceed more slowly at the *p* of
33:14 before me and at the *p* of my children,
Ps(s) 50:18 When you see a thief, you keep *p* with him,

PACED (1)

2Kgs 4:35 He arose, *p* up and down the room,

PACIFY (1)

Prv 16:14 of death, but a wise man can *p* it.

PACK (3)

2Kgs 3:17 your livestock and your *p* animals to drink.'
Ps(s) 22:17 me, a *p* of evildoers closes in upon me;
Jer 46:19 *P* your baggage for exile,

PACT (19)

Gn 17: 7 throughout the ages as an everlasting *p,*
17:13 shall be in your flesh as an everlasting *p.*
17:19 my covenant with him as an everlasting *p,*
21:27 them to Abimelech and the two made a *p.*
21:32 they had thus made the *p* in Beer-sheba,
26:28 Let us make a *p* with you:
31:44 Come, then, we will make a *p,*
Lv 26:46 the *p* between himself and the Israelites.
Jgs 2: 2 make a *p* with the inhabitants of this land,
Neh 10: 1 of all this, we are entering into a firm *p,*
1Mc 11: 9 "Come, let us make a *p* with each other;
Ps(s) 55:21 on his associates, and violates his *p.*
Prv 2:17 her youth and forgets the *p* with her God;
Is 28:15 with the nether world we have made a *p;*
28:18 *p* with the nether world shall not stand.
Am 1: 9 and did not remember the *p* of brotherhood,
Hg 2: 5 This is the *p* that I made with you when

PADDAN (1)

Gn 48: 7 this because, when I was returning from *P,*

PADDAN-ARAM (10)

Gn 25:20 of *P* and the sister of Laban the Aramean.
28: 2 Go now to *P,*
28: 5 he went to *P,*
28: 6 sent him to *P* to get himself a wife there,
28: 7 obeyed his father and mother and gone to *P.*
31:18 and all the property he had acquired in *P,*
33:18 Having thus come from *P,*
35: 9 On Jacob's arrival from *P,*
35:26 sons of Jacob who were born to him in *P.*
46:15 the sons whom Leah bore to Jacob in *P,*

PADDING (1)

Jb 15:27 with his crassness, *p* his loins with fat,

PADON (2)

Ezr 2:44 sons of Keros, sons of Siaha, sons of *P,*
Neh 7:47 sons of Keros, sons of Sia, sons of *P,*

PAGAN (7)

Dt 29:17 our God, to go and serve these *p* gods!
Tb 4:19 For no *p* nation possesses good counsel,
1Mc 1:47 to build *p* altars and temples and shrines,
1:54 cities of Judah they built *p* altars.
2:45 went about and tore down the *p* altars;
Is 17:10 though you plant your *p* plants and set out
Mt 10: 5 "Do not visit *p* territory and do not

PAGANS (13)

Est C:26 You know that I hate the glory of the *p,*
Ps(s) 115: 2 Why should the *p* say,
Lam 2: 9 Her king and her princes are among the *p;*
Bar 6: 3 gold and wood, which cast fear upon the *p.*
Mt 5:47 Do not *p* do as much?
6: 7 In your prayer do not rattle on like the *p.*
Acts 2:23 even made use of *p* to crucify and kill him.
1Cor 5: 1 you of a kind not even found among the *p*—
12: 2 were *p* you were led astray to mute idols,
Eph 4:17 that you must no longer live as the *p* do
1Pt 2:12 the *p* may slander you as troublemakers,
4: 3 devoted enough time to what the *p* enjoy,
3Jn 1: 7 and they are accepting nothing from the *p.*

PAGIEL (5)

Nm 1:13 *P,* son of Ochran; from Gad:
2:27 the tribe of Asher [Their prince was *P,*
7:72 On the eleventh day it was the turn of *P,*
7:77 This was the offering of *P,* son of Ochran.
10:26 of Ammishaddai, over their host, and *P,*

PAHATH-MOAB (6)

Ezr 2: 6 sons of *P,*
8: 4 of the sons of *P,*
10:30 of the sons of *P:*
Neh 3:11 Malchijah, son of Harim, and Hasshub, of *P.*
7:11 sons of *P* who were sons of Jeshua and Joab,
10:15 Parosh, *P,* Elam, Zattu,

PAI (1)

1Chr 1:50 The name of his city was *P,*

PAID (59)

Gn 30:16 I have *p* for you with my son's mandrakes."
42:21 when he pleaded with us, yet we *p* no heed;
47: 7 After Jacob had *p* his respects to Pharaoh,
Ex 30:16 the LORD, of the forfeit *p* for their lives."
Lv 5:19 penalty of the guilt must be *p* to the LORD."
Nm 18:16 a boy is to be *p* when he is a month old;
Dt 2:28 give me to drink, you shall be *p* in silver.
Jgs 8:27 all Israel *p* idolatrous homage to it there,
11:28 *p* no heed to the message Jephthah sent him.
1Sm 4:20 she neither answered nor *p* any attention.
2Sm 18:28 ground he *p* homage to the king and said,
24:20 So he went out and *p* homage to the king,
1Kgs 1:47 went in and *p* their respects to our lord,
1:53 and he came and *p* homage to the king.
2:19 king stood up to meet her and *p* her homage.
5: 1 they *p* Solomon tribute and were his
2Kgs 17: 3 Hoshea became his vassal and *p* him tribute.
18:15 Hezekiah *p* him all the funds there were in
1Chr 21:25 So David *p* Ornan six hundred shekels of
2Chr 24:17 of Judah came and *p* homage to the king,
25: 9 talents that I *p* for the troops of Israel?"
26: 8 The Ammonites *p* tribute to Uzziah and his
27: 5 *p* him one hundred talents of silver,
32:33 of Jerusalem *p* him honor at his death.
33:10 and his people, but they *p* no attention.
Ezr 4:20 taxes, tributes, and tolls were *p* to them.
Neh 9:34 they *p* no attention to your commandments
Tb 2:12 They *p* her the full salary,
1Mc 7:11 But these *p* no attention to their words,
8: 4 and the rest *p* tribute to them every year.
10:61 accuse him, but the king *p* no heed to them.
10:64 saw the honor *p* to him in the proclamation,
2Mc 7:25 the youth *p* no attention to him at all,
Jb 4:20 with no heed *p* to it,
28:15 it, nor can its price be *p* with silver.
Sir 13:21 he speaks wisely and no attention is *p* him.
20: 9 no good, and some must be *p* back double.
51:16 In the short time I *p* heed,
Is 65: 6 I will not be quiet until I have *p* in full
Jer 7:26 Yet they have not obeyed me nor *p* heed;
Dn 3:12 men, O king, have *p* no attention to you;
6:14 Jewish exile, has *p* no attention to you,
9:10 against you and *p* no heed to your command,
Jon 1: 3 found a ship going to Tarshish, *p* the fare,
Mt 5:26 released until you have *p* the last penny.
18:30 put in jail until he *p* back what he owed.
18:34 torturers until he *p* back all that he owed.
26:15 They *p* him thirty pieces of silver,
27:10 and they *p* it out for the potter's field
Lk 12:59 from there until you have *p* the last penny."
Acts 4:33 Jesus, and great respect was *p* to them all;
18:17 but Gallio *p* no attention to it.
18:22 up and *p* his respects to the congregation,
21:18 Paul and the rest of us *p* a visit to James
25:13 in Caesarea and *p* Festus a courtesy call.
28:10 They *p* us much honor,
Phil 4:18 says that I have been fully *p* and more.
1Tm 5:17 do well as leaders deserve to be *p* double,
Rv 18: 6 Pay her back as she has *p* others;

PAILS (1)

Ex 7:19 blood, even in the wooden *p* and stone jars."

PAIN (39)

Gn 3:16 in *p* shall you bring forth children.
34:25 the third day, while they were still in *p,*
Lv 10: 9 your sons are forbidden under *p* of death,
1Chr 4: 9 him Jabez, saying, "I bore him with *p.*"
4:10 and make me free of misfortune, without *p!*"
2Chr 6:29 and in awareness of his affliction and *p,*
21:19 of the disease and he died in great *p.*
2Mc 3:17 who saw him the *p* that lodged in his heart.
6:30 terrible *p* in my body from this scourging,
7:36 My brothers, after enduring brief *p,*
9:11 God, for he was racked with *p* unceasingly.
Jb 6:10 and could exult through unremitting *p,*
16: 6 I speak, this *p* I have will not be checked;
33:19 *p* and unceasing suffering within his frame,
Ps(s) 69:27 and added to the *p* of him you wounded.
69:30 But I am afflicted and in *p;*
73: 4 For they are in no *p;*
Sir 27:29 and *p* will consume them before they die;
38: 7 *p* and the druggist prepares his medicines;
Is 26:18 We conceived and writhed in *p,*
50:11 you shall lie down in a place of *p.*
Jer 15:18 Why is my *p* continuous,
20:18 forth from the womb, to see sorrow and *p,*
30:15 your *p* is without relief.
45: 3 the LORD adds grief to my *p;*
Lam 1:13 He left me desolate, in *p* all the day.
Dn 3:50 way touched them or caused them *p* or harm.
Mi 4:10 Writhe in *p,* grow faint, O daughter Zion,
Mt 4:24 with various diseases and racked with *p:*
Mk 10:38 or be baptized in the same bath of *p* as I?"
Jn 16:21 she no longer remembers her *p* for joy that
Rom 9: 2 is great grief and constant *p* in my heart.
2Cor 2: 2 For if I cause you *p,* who can make me
1Tm 6:10 faith, and have come to grief amid great *p.*
Rv 2:22 I mean to cast her down on a bed of *p;*
9: 5 the *p* they inflicted was like that of a

PAIN (cont.)

12: 2 aloud in *p* as she labored to give birth.
16:10 men bit their tongues in *p* and blasphemed
21: 4 more death or mourning, crying out or *p*,

PAINED (1)

Prv 23:35 "They struck me, but it *p* me not;

PAINFUL (3)

Sir 27:15 in bloodshed, their cursing is *p* to hear.
29:28 *P* things to a sensitive man are abuse at
2Cor 2: 1 not to visit you again in *p* circumstances.

PAINFULLY (1)

Mt 8: 6 is at home in bed paralyzed, suffering *p*."

PAINS (16)

2Chr 21:15 severe *p* from a disease in your bowels,
1Mc 7:21 no *p* to maintain his high priesthood,
2Mc 9: 5 *p* in his bowels and sharp internal torment,
Jb 7:15 prefer choking and death rather than my *p*.
9:28 cheer, Then I am in dread of all my *p*;
14:22 Only his own flesh *p* him,
Ps(s) 38: 8 For my loins are filled with burning *p*;
Eccl 2:11 to the toil at which I had taken such *p*,
Is 26:17 give birth writhes and cries out in her *p*,
66: 7 Before the *p* come upon her,
Jer 22:23 How you shall groan when *p* come upon you,
Mi 4: 9 are seized with *p* like a woman in travail?
Mk 13: 8 This is but the onset of the *p* of labor.
Gal 4:19 in labor *p* until Christ is formed in you.
4:27 song, you stranger to the *p* of childbirth!
1Thes 5: 3 of *p* overtaking a woman in labor,

PAINTED (1)

Ez 23:40 for them you bathed yourself, *p* your eyes,

PAINTERS (2)

Wis 15: 4 deceive us, nor the fruitless labor of *p*,
Sir 51: 5 From deceiving lips and *p* of lies,

PAINTS (1)

Jer 22:14 it with cedar, and *p* it with vermillion.

PAIR (17)

Gn 7: 2 and of the unclean animals, one *p*,
7: 3 and of all the unclean birds, one *p*,
Ex 28: 7 It shall have a *p* of shoulder straps
Nm 25: 8 his retreat where be pierced the *p* of them,
Jgs 15: 4 he tied between each *p* of tails one of the
19: 3 set out with his servant and a *p* of asses,
19:10 set out with a *p* of saddled asses,
Is 21: 7 If he sees a chariot, a *p* of horses,
21: 9 a single chariot, a *p* of horses;
Am 2: 6 and the poor man for a *p* of sandals.
3:12 from the mouth of the lion a *p* of legs
8: 6 and the poor man for a *p* of sandals;
Lk 2:24 "a *p* of turtledoves or two young pigeons,"
2:39 When the *p* had fulfilled all the
Acts 8:17 The *p* upon arriving imposed hands on them
18: 2 Paul went to visit the *p*,
Rv 6: 5 of which held a *p* of scales in his hand.

PAIRS (7)

Gn 7: 2 every clean animal, take with you seven *p*,
7: 3 of every clean bird of the air, seven *p*,
7:15 *P* of all creatures in which there was the
Ex 25:35 knob below each of the three *p* of branches
37:21 knob below each of the three *p* of branches
Sir 33:15 come in *p*, the one the opposite of the other
Lk 10: 1 sent them in *p* before him to every town

PALACE (130)

Gn 12:15 So she was taken into Pharaoh's *p*.
41:40 You shall be in charge of my *p*,
45: 2 him, and so the news reached Pharaoh's *p*.
45:16 *p* that Joseph's brothers had come,
47:14 and Canaan, and he put it in Pharaoh's *p*.
Ex 7:28 *p* and into your bedroom and onto your bed,
2Sm 5: 8 blind and the lame shall not enter the *p*."
5: 9 he built up the area from Millo to the *p*.
5:11 and masons, who built a *p* for David.
7: 1 King David was settled in his *p*,
11: 2 and strolled about on the roof of the *p*.
11: 8 Uriah left the *p*,
11: 9 *p* with the other officers of his lord,
15:16 whom he left behind to take care of the *p*.
15:35 If you hear anything from the royal *p*,
16:21 whom he left behind to take care of the *p*.
19:11 silent about restoring the king to his *p*?"
19:12 you be last to restore the king to his *p*?
19:31 lord the king has returned safely to his *p*."
20: 3 When King David came to his *p* in Jerusalem,
20: 3 of the *p* and placed them in confinement.
1Kgs 3: 1 until he should finish building his *p*,
4: 6 Ahishar, major-domo of the *p*;
7: 1 His own *p* Solomon completed after thirteen
7: 8 A *p* like this tribunal was built for
9: 1 the temple of the LORD, the royal *p*,
9:10 temple of the LORD and the *p* of the king
9:15 to build the temple of the LORD, his *p*,
9:24 went up from the City of David to her *p*,
10: 4 Solomon's great wisdom, the *p* he had built,
10:12 of the LORD and for the *p* of the king,
11:20 the queen kept him in Pharaoh's *p*,
14:26 of the LORD and those of the royal *p*,
14:27 on duty at the entrance of the royal *p*.
15:18 the temple of the LORD and of the royal *p*.
16: 9 of Arza, superintendent of his *p* in Tirzah,
16:18 *p* and burned down the palace over him.
21: 1 vineyard in Jezreel next to the *p* of Ahab,
22:39 the ivory *p* and all the cities he built,
2Kgs 7: 9 Come, let us go and inform the *p*."
7:11 this and it was reported within the *p*.
11: 5 on the sabbath shall guard the king's *p*;
11:16 forcibly to the horse gate of the royal *p*,
11:19 LORD through the guards' gate to the *p*,
11:20 been slain with the sword at the royal *p*.
12:19 in the treasuries of the temple and the *p*,
14:14 of the LORD and the treasuries of the *p*,
15:25 him within the *p* stronghold in Samaria,
16: 8 *p* treasuries and sent them as a present
18:15 temple of the LORD and in the *p* treasuries.
18:18 son of Hilkiah, the master of the *p*;
18:37 Then the master of the *p*,
19: 2 He sent Eliakim, the master of the *p*,
20:18 servants in the *p* of the king of Babylon."
21:18 ancestors and was buried in his *p* garden,
21:23 against him and slew the king in his *p*,
24:13 the temple of the LORD and those of the *p*,
25: 9 the house of the LORD, the *p* of the king,
2Chr 7:11 the house of the LORD and the royal *p*;
8:11 David to the *p* which he had built for her,
9: 3 Solomon's wisdom, the *p* he had built,
9:11 temple of the LORD and the *p* of the king;
12: 9 of the temple of the LORD and of the king's *p*.
12:10 on duty at the entrance of the royal *p*.
16: 2 of the royal *p* and sent them to Ben-hadad,
21:17 away all the wealth found in the king's *p*,
23: 5 another third must be at the king's *p*
23:15 at the entrance to the Horse Gate of the *p*,
25:24 together with the treasures of the *p*,
26:21 of the *p* and ruled the people of the land.
28: 7 son, and Azrikam, the master of the *p*,
33:20 his ancestors and was buried in his own *p*.
36: 7 the LORD and put them in his *p* in Babylon.
Ezr 4:14 since we partake of the salt of the *p*,
6: 4 The costs are to be borne by the royal *p*.
Neh 3:25 the Upper *P* at the quarters of the guard.
Tb 1:20 All that I had was taken to the king's *p*,
Jdt 2: 1 a discussion in the *p* of Nebuchadnezzar,
2:18 and much gold and silver from the royal *p*.
11:23 dwell in the *p* of King Nebuchadnezzar,
12:13 women who live in the *p* of Nebuchadnezzar."
Est 1: 5 court of the royal *p* for all the people,
1: 9 women inside the royal *p* of King Ahasuerus.
2: 8 in to the royal *p* under the care of Hegai,
2: 9 out seven maids for her from the royal *p*,
2:13 harem to the royal *p* whatever she chose.
2:16 King Ahasuerus in his *p* in the tenth month,
4:13 that because you are in the king's *p*,
5: 1 courtyard, looking toward the royal *p*,
5: 1 the audience chamber, facing the *p* doorway.
6: 4 entered the outer court of the king's *p*
7: 7 anger and went into the garden of the *p*,
7: 8 the garden of the *p* to the banquet hall,
9: 4 for Mordecai was powerful in the royal *p*,
1Mc 7: 2 to enter the royal *p* of his ancestors,
11:46 But he took refuge in the *p*,
Ps(s) 45:16 they enter the *p* of the king.
49:15 the nether world is their *p*.
104: 3 have constructed your *p* upon the waters.
104:13 You water the mountains from your *p*;
Is 22:15 to that official, Shebna, master of the *p*,
36: 3 there came out to him the master of the *p*,
36:22 Then the master of the *p*,
37: 2 He sent Eliakim, the master of the *p*,
39: 7 servants in the *p* of the king of Babylon."
63:15 your holy and glorious *p*!
Jer 22: 1 Go down to the *p* of the king of Judah and
22: 4 continue to enter the gates of this *p*,
22: 5 this *p* shall become rubble.
22: 6 LORD concerning the *p* of the king of Judah:
26:10 they came up from the king's *p* to the
27:18 *p* of the king of Judah and in Jerusalem
27:21 of the LORD, in the *p* of the king of Judah,
30:18 upon hill, and *p* restored as it was.
32: 2 the quarters of the guard, at the king's *p*.
36:12 So he went down to the king's *p*,
37:17 King Zedekiah had him brought to his *p*
38: 7 a Cushite, a courtier in the king's *p*,
38: 8 went there from the *p* and said to him,
38:11 went first to the linen closet in the *p*,
39: 8 the king's *p* and the houses of the people,
52:13 the house of the LORD, the *p* of the king,
Bar 6:58 or a wooden post in a *p*,
Dn 1: 4 as could take their place in the king's *p*;
4: 1 I, Nebuchadnezzar, was at home in my *p*,
4:26 on the roof of the royal *p* in Babylon,
5: 5 on the plaster of the wall in the king's *p*.
6:19 the king returned to his *p* for the night;
Na 2: 7 The river gates are opened, the *p* shudders.
Mt 26: 3 were assembled in the *p* of the high priest,

PALACES (13)

2Chr 36:19 walls of Jerusalem, set all its *p* afire,
Ps(s) 45: 9 from ivory *p* string music brings you joy.
Prv 30:28 yet they find their way into king's *p*.
Is 13:22 castles, and jackals in her luxurious *p*.
Jer 6: 5 us rush upon her by night, destroy her *p*!"
9:20 up through our windows, has entered our *p*;
17:27 which will consume the *p* of Jerusalem.
19:13 And the houses of Jerusalem and the *p* of
33: 4 of this city and the *p* of Judah's kings,
49:27 and it shall devour the *p* of Ben-hadad.
Hos 8:14 Israel has forgotten his maker and built *p*.
Mt 11: 8 luxuriously are to be found in royal *p*.
Lk 7:25 eat in splendor are to be found in royal *p*.

PALAL (1)

Neh 3:25 After him *P*, son of Uzai, carried out

PALATE (4)

Ps(s) 119:103 How sweet to my *p* are your promises,
137: 6 cleave to my *p* if I remember you not,
Sir 36:19 As the *p* tests meat by its savor,
Ez 3:26 I will make your tongue stick to your *p* so

PALE (7)

Is 19: 9 the combers and weavers shall turn *p*;
24: 6 Therefore they who dwell on earth turn *p*,
24:23 the moon will blush and the sun grow *p*,
29:22 be ashamed of, nor shall his face grow *p*.
Jer 30: 6 Why have all their faces turned deathly *p*?
Dn 5:10 Be not troubled in mind, nor look so *p*!
Rv 9:17 were fiery red, deep blue, and *p* yellow.

PALLU (6)

Gn 46: 9 Hanoch, *P*, Hezron, and Carmi.
Ex 6:14 the first-born of Israel, were Hanoch, *P*,
Nm 16: 1 and Abiram, sons of Eliab, son of *P*,
26: 5 through *P* the clan of the Palluites,
26: 8 From *P* descended Eliab.
1Chr 5: 3 the first-born of Israel, were Hanoch, *P*,

PALLUITES (1)

Nm 26: 5 through Pallu the clan of the *P*,

PALM (25)

Ex 15:27 springs of water and seventy *p* trees,
Lv 14:15 some of it into the *p* of his own left hand;
14:26 oil into the *p* of his own left hand
Nm 33: 9 springs of water and seventy *p* trees,
Jgs 4: 5 She used to sit under Deborah's *p* tree,
1Kgs 6:29 had carved figures of cherubim, *p* trees,
6:32 with carved figures of cherubim, *p* trees,
6:32 molded to the cherubim and the *p* trees.
6:35 and back, and had carved cherubim, *p* trees,
7:36 cherubim, lions, and *p* trees were carved,
Neh 8:15 oleasters, myrtle, *p* and other leafy trees,
1Mc 13:37 gold crown and the *p* branch that you sent.
13:51 shouts of jubilation, waving of *p* branches,
2Mc 14: 4 him with a gold crown and a *p* branch,
Ps(s) 92:13 just man shall flourish like the *p* tree,
Sg 5:11 his locks are *p* fronds,
7: 8 Your very figure is like a *p* tree.
7: 9 I will climb the *p* tree,
Sir 24:14 on Mount Hermon, Like a *p* tree in Engedi,
Is 9:13 and tail, *p* branch and reed in one day.
19:15 to do for head or tail, *p* branch or reed.
Ez 40:22 and its *p* decorations were of the same
Jl 1:12 The pomegranate, the date *p* also,
Jn 12:13 got *p* branches and came out to meet him.
Rv 7: 9 and holding *p* branches in their hands.

PALMS (16)

Lv 23:40 branches of *p* and boughs of myrtles and of
Nm 24:10 Balak beat his *p* together in a blaze of
Dt 34: 3 with the lowlands at Jericho, city of *p*,
34:12 with the lowlands at Jericho, city of *p*,
Jgs 1:16 Judahites from the city of *p* to the desert
3:13 Israel, taking possession of the city of *p*.
14: 9 out into his *p* and ate it as he went along.
2Chr 3: 5 fine gold, embossing on it *p* and chains.
28:15 brought them to Jericho, the city of *p*,
2Mc 10: 7 with leaves, green branches and *p*,
Is 49:16 the *p* of my hands I have written your name;
Ez 40:16 The pilasters were decorated with *p*.
40:26 with *p* here and there on its pilasters.
40:31 *p* were on its pilasters,
40:34 *p* were on its pilasters here and there,
40:37 *p* were on its pilasters here and there,

PALMTREE (3)

Ez 41:18 a *p* between every two cherubim.
41:19 a man's face looking at a *p* on one side,
41:19 a lion's face looking at a *p* on the other;

PALMTREES (4)

Ez 41:18 were carved the figures of cherubim and *p:*
41:20 cherubim and *p* were carved on the walls.
41:25 the doors of the nave] were cherubim and *p,*
41:26 [and *p* on both side walls of the vestibule,

PALTI (2)

1Sm 25:43 wife Michal, Saul's own daughter, to *P,*
1Chr 11:27 Helez, from *P;*

PALTIEL (2)

Nm 34:26 *P,* son of Azzan;from the tribe of Asher:
2Sm 3:15 her and took her away from her husband *P,*

PALTRY (1)

Wis 4:12 For the witchery of *p* things obscures what

PAMPER (1)

Sir 30: 9 *P* your child and he will be a terror for

PAMPERED (1)

Bar 4:26 My *p* children have trodden rough roads,

PAMPERS (1)

Prv 29:21 If a man *p* his servant from childhood,

PAMPHYLIA (6)

1Mc 15:23 Delos, Myndos, Sicyon, Caria, Samos, *P,*
Acts 2:10 the province of Asia, Phrygia, and *P,*
13:13 put out to sea and sailed to Perga in *P.*
14:24 they passed through Pisidia and came to *P.*
15:38 that, as he had deserted them at *P,*
27: 5 open sea off the coast of Cilicia and *P,*

PAN (2)

2Sm 13: 9 the *p* and set out the cakes before him.
2Mc 7: 5 As a cloud of smoke spread from the *p,*

PANELED (3)

1Kgs 7: 7 *p* with cedar from floor to ceiling beams.
Ez 41:16 were *p* with precious wood all around,
Hg 1: 4 time for you to dwell in your own *p* houses,

PANELING (3)

1Kgs 6:15 from floor to ceiling beams with cedar *p,*
7:32 The four wheels were below the *p,*
Ps(s) 74: 6 chisel and hammer they hack at all its *p.*

PANELS (7)

1Kgs 7:28 *p* were set within the framework.
7:29 the *p* between the frames there were lions,
7:31 at the opening, on *p* that were angular,
7:35 with supports and *p* which were of one
7:36 the surfaces of the supports and on the *p,*
2Kgs 18:16 He broke up the door *p* and the uprights of
Jer 22:14 cuts out windows for it, *p* it with cedar,

PANGS (13)

Gn 3:16 will intensify the *p* of your childbearing;
35:17 When her *p* were most severe,
1Sm 4:19 she was seized with the *p* of labor,
Jb 39: 1 goats, watch for the birth *p* of the hinds,
Is 13: 8 *p* and sorrows take hold of them,
21: 3 *p* have seized me like those of a woman in
Jer 13:21 Will not *p* seize you like those of a woman
22:23 upon you, like the *p* of a woman in travail!
49:24 Distress and *p* take hold of her,
Dn 10:16 with *p* at the vision and I was powerless.
Hos 13:13 The birth *p* shall come for him,
Mt 24: 8 These are the early stages of the birth *p.*
Acts 2:24 God freed him from death's bitter *p,*

PANIC (16)

Ex 14:24 force a glance that threw it into a *p;*
23:27 I will throw into *p* every nation you reach.
Dt 28:28 strike you with madness, blindness and *p.*
Jgs 8:12 captive, throwing the entire army into *p.*
1Sm 5:11 A deadly *p* had seized the whole city,
14:15 Then *p* spread to the army and to the
14:15 so that the *p* was beyond human endurance.
2Sm 17: 2 weary and discouraged, I shall cause him *p.*
Jdt 14: 3 and do not find him, *p* will seize them,
Is 22: 5 It is a day of *p,*
31: 9 He shall rush past his crag in *p,*
Jer 49:24 she turns to flee, *p* has seized her.
51:32 set on fire, while warriors are in *p.*
Mi 2:12 they shall not be thrown into *p* by men.
Mk 13: 7 wars and threats of war, do not yield to *p.*
Lk 24:37 In their *p* and fright they thought they

PANIC-STRICKEN (3)

1Mc 9: 7 he was *p*
2Mc 3:24 were *p* at God's power and fainted away
8:16 exhorted them not be *p* before the enemy,

PANS (10)

Ex 27: 3 well as shovels, basins, forks and fire *p,*
38: 3 pots, shovels, basins, forks and fire *p,*
Nm 4:14 the fire *p,* forks, shovels, basins,
1Kgs 7:50 bowls, cups, and fire *p* of pure gold;
2Kgs 25:14 the *p* and all the bronze vessels used for
2Chr 35:13 the sacred meals in pots, caldrons and *p,*
1Mc 11:35 of the tax on the salt *p* and the crown tax.
2Mc 7: 3 gave orders to have *p* and caldrons heated.
Jer 52:18 shovels, the snuffers, the bowls, the *p,*
52:19 bowls, the pots, the lampstands, the *p,*

PANTHER (2)

Sir 28:23 like a *p,* it will tear them to pieces.
Hos 13: 7 like a *p* by the road I will keep watch.

PANTING (1)

Is 42:14 cry out as a woman in labor, gasping and *p.*

PAPER (1)

2Jn 1:12 you, I do not intend to put it down on *p;*

PAPHOS (2)

Acts 13: 6 over the whole island as far as *P,*
13:13 From *P,* Paul and his companions

PAPYRUS (4)

Ex 2: 3 hide him no longer, she took a *p* basket,
Jb 8:11 Can the *p* grow up without mire?
Is 18: 2 by sea, in *p* boats on the waters!
35: 7 lurk will be a marsh for the reed and *p.*

PAR (1)

Lk 6:40 studies will be on a *p* with his teacher.

PARABLE (27)

Ps(s) 78: 2 I will open my mouth in a *p,*
Prv 1: 6 That he may comprehend proverb and *p,*
Ez 24: 3 Propose this *p* to the rebellious house:
Mt 13:18 "Mark well, then, the *p* of the sower.
13:24 He proposed to them another *p:*
13:31 He proposed still another *p:*
13:36 to us the *p* of the weeds in the field."
15:15 spoke up to say, "Explain the *p* to us."
21:33 "Listen to another *p.*
Mk 4: 9 Having spoken this *p,* he added:
4:13 "You do not understand this *p?*
4:34 To them he spoke only by way of *p,*
12:12 well enough that he meant the *p* for them.)
Lk 8: 4 He spoke to them in a *p:*
8: 9 him what the meaning of this *p* might be.
8:11 This is the meaning of the *p.*
12:16 He told them a *p* in these words:
12:41 Peter said, "Do you intend this *p* for us,
13: 6 Jesus spoke this *p:*
14: 7 He went on to address a *p* to the guests,
15: 3 Then he addressed this *p* to them:
18: 1 He told them a *p* on the necessity of
18: 9 He then spoke this *p* addressed to those
19:11 to these things he went on to tell a *p,*
20: 9 began to tell the people the following *p:*
20:19 that he had told the *p* with them in mind.
21:29 Then he told them a *p:*

PARABLES (17)

Sir 39: 3 He studies obscure *p,*
Ez 21: 5 not this the one who is forever spinning *p?'* "
Mt 13: 3 He addressed them at length in *p,*
13:10 asked him, "Why do you speak to them in *p?"*
13:13 "I use *p* when I speak to them because
13:34 Jesus taught the crowds in the form of *p.*
13:34 He spoke to them in *p* only,
13:35 "I will open my mouth in *p,*
13:53 When Jesus had finished these *p,*
21:45 priests and the Pharisees heard these *p,*
22: 1 began to address them, once more using *p.*
Mk 4: 2 them at great length, by the use of *p,*
4:10 with the Twelve questioned him about the *p.*
4:11 others outside it is all presented in *p,*
4:33 By means of many such *p* he taught them the
12: 1 He began to address them once more in *p:*
Lk 8:10 been confided, but to the rest in *p* that,

PARACLETE (4)

Jn 14:16 the Father and he will give you another *P—*
14:26 the *P,*
15:26 When the *P* comes,
16: 7 I fail to go, the *P* will never come to you,

PARADE (5)

2Mc 5:25 work, he ordered his men to *p* fully armed.
Sir 7: 5 *P* not your justice before the Lord,
42:12 Let her not *p* her charms before men,
Mk 12:38 who like to *p* around in their robes and
Lk 20:46 who like to *p* around in their robes,

PARADED (1)

2Mc 6:10 their children were publicly *p* about the city

PARADISE (3)

Sir 40:27 The fear of God is a *p* of blessings;
Lk 23:43 this day you will be with me in *p."*
2Cor 12: 4 to *P* to hear words which cannot be uttered,

PARAGON (1)

Sir 1:22 wisdom's treasures is the *p* of prudence;

PARAH (1)

Jos 18:23 Beth-arabah, Zemaraim, Bethel, Avvim, *P,*

PARALLEL (5)

Ez 42: 3 three *p* rows of them on different levels.
42: 7 *p* to the chambers along the outer court;
45: 6 thousand long, *p* to the sacred tract;
47:20 boundary up to a point *p* to Labo of Hamath.
48:21 *p* with the tribal portions for the prince.

PARALYTIC (5)

Mt 9: 2 Jesus saw their faith he said to the *p,*
Mk 2: 4 let down the mat on which the *p* was lying.
2: 9 Which is easier, to say to the *p,*
Lk 5:18 Some men came along carrying a *p* on a mat.
Acts 9:33 a *p* who had been bedridden for eight years.

PARALYTICS (1)

Acts 8: 7 Many others were *p* or cripples,

PARALYZED (11)

1Mc 9:55 his mouth was closed and he was *p,*
Wis 17:19 these sounds, inspiring terror, *p* them.
Mt 4:24 the possessed, the lunatics, the *p.*
8: 6 "Sir, my serving boy is at home in bed *p,*
9: 2 brought to him a *p* man lying on a mat.
9: 6 he then said to the *p* man
28: 4 The guards grew *p* with fear of him and
Mk 2: 3 people arrived bringing a *p* man to him.
2: 5 saw their faith, he said to the *p* man,
2:10 to forgive sins" (he said to the *p* man),
Lk 5:24 he then addressed the *p* man:

PARAMOUR (1)

Hos 3: 1 Give your love to a woman beloved of a *p,*

PARAN (9)

Gn 21:21 with his home in the wilderness of *P.*
Nm 10:12 the cloud came to rest in the desert of *P.*
12:16 Hazeroth and encamped in the desert of *P.*
13: 3 Moses dispatched them from the desert of *P,*
13:26 Israelites in the desert of *P* at Kadesh,
Dt 1: 1 opposite Suph, between *P* and Tophel,
33: 2 Mount *P* and advanced from Meribath-kadesh.
1Kgs 11:18 They left Midian and passing through *P,*
Hb 3: 3 from Teman, the Holy One from Mount *P.*

PARAPET (5)

Dt 22: 8 build a new house, put a *p* around the roof;
Jdt 14: 1 head and hang it on the *p* of your wall.
Sg 8: 9 a wall, we will build upon it a silver *p;*
Mt 4: 5 holy city, set him on the *p* of the temple,
Lk 4: 9 Jerusalem, set him on the *p* of the temple,

PARATH (4)

Jer 13: 4 and are wearing, and go now to the *P;*
13: 5 I went to the *P* and buried the loincloth.
13: 6 Go now to the *P* and fetch the loincloth
13: 7 Again I went to the *P,*

PARCELED (1)

Dt 32: 8 when he *p* out the descendants of Adam,

PARCHED (18)

Dt 8:15 and scorpions, its *p* and waterless ground;
29:18 both the watered soil and the *p* ground,
Jos 5:11 the form of unleavened cakes and *p* grain.
Jb 30: 3 lot, they who fled to the *p* wastelands:
Ps(s) 63: 2 and my soul thirsts like the earth, *p,*
68: 7 only rebels remain in the *p* land.
69: 4 I am wearied with calling, my throat is *p;*
143: 6 my soul thirsts for you like *p* land.
Sir 43:23 and the scattered dew enriches the *p* land.
Is 5:13 hunger, and their masses are *p* with thirst.
32: 2 like the shade of a great rock in a *p* land.
35: 1 The desert and the *p* land will exult;
41:17 in vain, their tongues are *p* with thirst.
53: 2 before him, like a shoot from the *p* earth;
58:11 and give you plenty even on the *p* land.
Jer 51:39 When they are *p,* I will set a drink
51:43 desert, *p* and arid land Where no man lives,
Ez 19:13 in the desert, in a land dry and *p,*

PARCHES (2)

Jb 14:11 a lake fail, or a stream grows dry and *p,*

PARCHES (cont.)

Jas 1:11 up with its scorching heat it *p* the meadow,

PARCHING (2)

Is 4: 6 shade from the *p* heat of day,
Jer 2:25 wearing out your shoes and *p* your throat!

PARCHMENTS (1)

2Tm 4:13 Carpus, and the books, especially the *p*.

PARDON (23)

Ex 34: 9 yet *p* our wickedness and sins,
Nm 14:19 *P*, then, the wickedness of this people
14:20 "I *p* them as you have asked.
Dt 29:19 the LORD will never consent to *p* him.
1Sm 1:26 *P*, my lord! As you live,
1Kgs 8:30 from your heavenly dwelling and grant *p*.
2Chr 6:21 dwelling, and when you have heard, *p*.
7:14 and *p* their sins and revive their land.
30:18 *p* to everyone who has resolved to seek God,
Jb 7:21 Why do you not *p* my offense,
Ps(s) 25:11 name's sake, O LORD, you will *p* my guilt,
65: 4 it is you who *p* them.
79: 9 us and *p* our sins for your name's sake.
Sir 28: 4 his fellows, yet seek *p* for his own sins?
39: 6 his lips in prayer, to ask *p* for his sins.
Is 2: 9 [Do not *p* them!]
53:12 sins of many, and win *p* for their offenses.
Jer 5: 1 and seeks to be faithful, and I will *p* her!
5: 7 Why should I *p* you these things?
Ez 16:63 shame when I *p* you for all you have done,
Dn 9:19 O Lord, hear! O Lord, *p*!
Lk 6:37 *P*, and you shall be pardoned.
Acts 8:22 may *p* you for thinking the way you have.

PARDONABLE (1)

Wis 13: 8 But again, not even these are *p*.

PARDONED (5)

Wis 6: 6 For the lowly may be *p* out of mercy but
Sir 20:27 he who pleases the great is *p* his faults.
Is 22:14 not be *p* this wickedness till you die,
Lk 6:37 Pardon, and you shall be *p*.
Col 2:13 He *p* all our sins.

PARDONS (3)

Neh 9:17 But you are a God of *p*,
Ps(s) 103: 3 He *p* all your iniquities,
Mi 7:18 *p* sin for the remnant of his inheritance;

PARE (1)

Dt 21:12 she must shave her head and *p* her nails

PARENT (4)

Prv 17:21 To be a fool's *p* is grief for a man;
Sg 3: 4 home of my mother, to the room of my *p*.
6: 9 mother's chosen, the dear one of her *p*.
8: 5 you, it was there that your *p* conceived.

PARENTAGE (1)

Prv 17: 6 men, and the glory of children is their *p*.

PARENTS (41)

Tb 8: 1 drinking, the girl's *p* wanted to retire.
8: 4 When the girl's *p* left the bedroom and
8:14 told the girl's *p* that Tobiah was alive,
10:12 now on they are as much your *p* as the ones
1Mc 10: 9 Jonathan, and he gave them back to their *p*.
2Mc 12:24 power the *p* and relatives of many of them,
Ps(s) 109:15 the memory of these *p* from the earth,
Prv 19:14 and possessions are an inheritance from *p*,
Wis 4: 6 give evidence of the wickedness of their *p*,
12: 6 and *p* who took with their own hands
Sir 3: 7 his father, and serves his *p* as rulers.
7:28 Remember, of these *p* you were born;
Ez 20:18 of your *p* or keep their ordinances;
Dn 13: 3 her pious *p* had trained their daughter
13:39 When she was sent for, she came with her *p*,
Zec 13: 3 If a man still prophesies, his *p*,
13: 3 When he prophesies, his *p*,
Mt 10:21 turn against *p* and have them put to death.
Mk 13:12 against their *p* and have them put to death.
Lk 2:27 and when the *p* brought in the child Jesus
2:41 His *p* used to go every year to Jerusalem
2:43 Jesus remained behind unknown to his *p*.
2:48 When his *p* saw him they were astonished,
8:51 Peter, John, James, and the child's *p*.
8:56 Her *p* were astounded,
18:29 home or wife or brothers, *p* or children,
21:16 You will be delivered up even by your *p*,
Jn 9: 2 of his *p* that caused him to be born blind?"
9: 3 was no sin, either of this man or of his *p*.
9:18 the *p* of this man who now could see.
9:20 The *p* answered: "We know this is our son,
9:22 (His *p* answered in this fashion because
9:23 That was why his *p* said,
Rom 1:30 wrongdoing and rebellious toward their *p*.
2Cor 12:14 not save up for their *p*, but *p* for children.
Eph 6: 1 Children, obey your *p* in the Lord,
Col 3:20 obey your *p* in everything as the
1Tm 5: 4 fittingly support their *p* and grandparents;
2Tm 3: 2 arrogant, abusive, disobedient to their *p*,
Heb 11:23 *p* hid him for three months after his birth,

PARK (4)

2Kgs 19:23 reached the remotest heights, its forest *p*.
Neh 2: 8 for Asaph, the keeper of the royal *p*,
Sg 4:13 You are a *p* that puts forth pomegranates,
Is 37:24 reached the remotest heights, its forest *p*.

PARKS (1)

Eccl 2: 5 I made gardens and *p*,

PARLEYED (1)

2Mc 13:23 Dismayed, he *p* with the Jews,

PARMASHTA (1)

Est 9: 9 Aspatha, Porathai, Adalia, Aridatha, *P*,

PARMENAS (1)

Acts 6: 5 Philip, Prochorus, Nicanor, Timon, *P*,

PARNACH (1)

Nm 34:25 Elizaphan, son of *P*

PAROSH (6)

Ezr 2: 3 sons of *P*,
8: 3 of the sons of *P*,
10:25 Of the sons of *P*:
Neh 3:25 After him, Pedaiah, son of *P*,
7: 8 sons of *P*, two thousand one hundred
10:15 *P*, Pahath-moab,

PARSHANDATHA (1)

Est 9: 7 They also killed *P*,

PART (144)

Gn 4: 4 fruit of the soil, while Abel, for his *p*,
4:22 Zillah, on her *p*,
6:17 I, on my *p*, am about to bring the flood
17: 9 "On your *p*, you and your descendants
28:22 I will faithfully return a tenth *p* to you."
Ex 10:14 of Egypt and settled down on every *p* of it.
16:20 a *p* of it over until the following morning,
34: 3 even to be seen on any *p* of the mountain;
34:11 But you, on your *p*, must keep
35:24 to have acacia wood for any *p* of the work,
36: 2 moved them to come and take *p* in the work.
Lv 6:20 stained *p* must be washed in a sacred place.
7:29 a *p* of it as his special offering to him,
10:18 brought into the inmost *p* of the sanctuary,
11:25 and everyone who picks up any *p* of their
13:43 skin leprosy of the fleshy *p* of the body,
13:56 tear the infected *p* out of the garment,
16:14 his finger on the fore *p* of the propitiatory
24: 8 offered on the *p* of the Israelites by an
25:24 in every *p* of the country that you occupy,
27:22 and not a *p* of his hereditary property,
Nm 18:28 priest the *p* to be contributed to the LORD.
18:30 made your contribution from the best *p*,
18:32 as you make a contribution of the best *p*.
31:27 active *p* in the war by going out to combat,
Dt 1:30 took your *p* before your very eyes in Egypt,
Jos 13: 1 a very large *p* of the land still remains
13:27 the other *p* of the kingdom of Sihon,
Jgs 2:21 I for my *p* will not clear away for them
9:53 *p* of a millstone down on Abimelech's head,
20: 6 through every *p* of the territory of Israel,
1Sm 2:29 *p* of every offering of my people Israel?'
24:16 May he see this, and take my *p*,
30:26 sent *p* of the spoil to the elders of Judah,
2Sm 3:37 the king had no *p* in the killing of Abner,
12:13 "The LORD on his *p* has forgiven your sin:
14: 6 There being no one to *p* them,
18: 2 *p* of the soldiers under Joab's command,
18:31 that this day the LORD has taken your *p*,
1Kgs 5:23 for your *p*, shall furnish the provisions
6:17 *p* of the temple in front of the sanctuary,
6:19 In the innermost *p* of the temple was
6:27 were placed in the inmost *p* of the temple,
8: 8 could be seen from that *p* of the holy place
13:34 This was a sin on the *p* of the house of
1Chr 21:12 destroying angel in every *p* of Israel?
23:14 were counted as *p* of the tribe of Levi.
23:28 take *p* in the service of the house of God.
2Chr 2:15 For our *p*, we will cut trees on Lebanon,
5: 9 *p* of the holy place nearest the sanctuary;
7: 7 Then Solomon consecrated the middle *p* of
26:18 faith and no longer have a *p* in the glory
30:18 The greater *p* of the people,
36:23 among you belongs to any *p* of his people,
Ezr 1: 3 among you belongs to any *p* of his people,
4:16 no longer own any *p* of West-of-Euphrates."
9: 2 have taken a leading *p* in this apostasy!"
Neh 5:16 own, I did my *p* in this work on the wall,
9: 3 LORD their God, for a fourth *p* of the day,
9: 3 and during another fourth *p* they made
Tb 1: 6 for my *p*, would often make the pilgrimage
6: 6 Then he broiled and ate *p* of the fish;
12:18 to you it was not out of any favor on my *p*,
Jdt 15: 5 rest of the mountain region took *p* in this,
1Mc 6:40 *P* of the king's army extended over the
6:48 A *p* of the king's army went up to
9:23 raised their heads in every *p* of Israel,
10:33 land of Judah into any *p* of my kingdom
12:11 We, on our *p*, have never ceased
12:23 We, on our *p*, are informing you
12:37 for *p* of the east wall above the ravine
13:33 Simon, on his *p*,
2Mc 3:10 explained that *p* of the money was a care
3:11 and a *p* was the property of Hyrcanus,
4:14 to take *p* in the unlawful exercises on the
8:24 disabled the greater *p* of Nicanor's army,
9: 7 and every *p* of his body was racked by the
11:15 and the king, on his *p*,
15: 5 of the sabbath day, he said, "I, on my *p*,
Jb 32:17 to make reply, I too will speak my *p*;
Ps(s) 68:29 power, O God, with which you took our *p*;
119:57 O LORD, that my *p* is to keep your words.
Eccl 9: 6 *p* in anything that is done under the sun.
Sir 11: 9 in the strife of the arrogant take no *p*.
43:25 who go down to the sea tell *p* of its story,
44: 2 of the Most High's portion, his own *p*,
Is 6:13 If there be still a tenth *p* in it,
16: 3 Offer counsel, take their *p*;
44:15 With a *p* of their wood he warms himself,
44:15 another *p* he makes a god which he adores,
Jer 37:12 to take *p* with his family in the division
Bar 6:10 give *p* of it to the harlots on the terrace.
Ez 41:17 *p* of the temple as well as outside,
43:21 be burnt in a designated *p* of the temple,
45: 4 *p* of the land belonging to the priests,
46:16 of *p* of his inheritance to any of his sons,
46:17 But if he makes a gift of *p* of his
46:18 The prince shall not seize any *p* of the
48:14 or alienate this, the best *p* of the land,
Dn 11:41 Edom, Moab, and the chief *p* of Ammon,
13:46 will have no *p* in the death of this woman."
Mt 5:18 of the law, not the smallest *p* of a letter,
5:29 Better to lose *p* of your body than to have
5:30 Better to lose *p* of your body than to have
13: 4 *P* of what he sowed landed on a footpath,
13: 5 *P* of it fell on rocky ground,
13: 7 Again, *p* of the seed fell among thorns,
13: 8 *P* of it, finally, landed on good soil
15: 3 "Why do you for your *p* act contrary to
16:18 I for my *p* declare to you,
18:14 it is no *p* of your heavenly Father's plan
Mk 6: 1 *p* of the country followed by his disciples.
10:15 like a little child shall not take *p* in it."
14:11 He for his *p* kept looking for an opportune
Lk 2:52 Jesus, for his *p*, progressed steadily
22:29 I for my *p* assign to you the dominion my
Jn 2:24 For his *p*, Jesus would not trust himself
15: 7 you live in me, and my words stay *p* of you,
Acts 5: 2 put aside a *p* of the proceeds for himself;
5:41 The apostles for their *p* left the
8: 1 Saul, for his *p*, concurred in the act
9:22 Saul for his *p* grew steadily more powerful,
9:29 their *p* responded by trying to kill him.
14: 3 He for his *p* confirmed the message with
15:40 Paul, for his *p*,
26: 9 "For my *p*, I once thought it my duty
28:22 For our *p*, we are anxious to hear you
Rom 11:25 blindness has come upon *p* of Israel until
1Cor 9:24 runners in the stadium take *p* in the race,
Eph 1:15 For my *p*, from the time I first heard
2:12 you had no *p* in Christ and were excluded
5:11 Take no *p* in vain deeds done in darkness;
5:33 for her *p* showing respect for her husband.
Phil 1:29 your special privilege to take Christ's *p*—
2Thes 2: 9 will appear as *p* of the workings of Satan,
2Tm 2: 5 if one takes *p* in an athletic contest,
3:14 You, for your *p*, must remain faithful
4: 6 I for my *p* am already being poured out
4:16 of my case in court, no one took my *p*.
Heb 12: 1 since we for our *p* are surrounded by this
1Jn 4:19 We, for our *p*, love because he first loved
Rv 8:11 *p* of all the water turned to wormwood.
9:20 That *p* of mankind which escaped the
19:16 the *p* of the cloak that covered his thigh:

PARTAKE (42)

Ex 12: 4 to the number of persons who *p* of it.
12: 7 of every house in which they *p* of the lamb.
12:43 No foreigner may *p* of it.
12:44 who has been bought for money may *p* of it,
12:45 alien or hired servant may *p* of it.
12:48 no man who is uncircumcised may *p* of it.
34:15 invite you and you may *p* of his sacrifice.
Lv 3:17 You shall not *p* of any fat or any blood."
6:11 All the male descendants of Aaron may *p* of
6:19 who presents the sin offering may *p* of it;
6:22 priestly line may *p* of the sin offering,
6:23 But no one may *p* of any sin offering of
7: 6 the males of the priestly line may *p* of it;
7:19 "All who are clean may *p* of this flesh.
7:26 you dwell, you shall not *p* of any blood,
17:12 not even a resident alien, may *p* of blood.

17:14 You shall not *p* of the blood of any meat.
21:22 He may, however, *p* of the food of his God:
Nm 18:10 every male among you may *p* of them.
18:11 in your family who are clean may *p* of it.
18:13 of your family who are clean may *p* of them.
Dt 12:16 Only you shall not *p* of the blood,
12:17 *p* of your tithe of grain or wine or oil,
12:23 make sure that you do not *p* of the blood;
12:24 Do not *p* of the blood,
14:26 *p* of it and make merry with your family.
15:23 Only, you shall not *p* of its blood,
Jgs 13:16 you press me, I will not *p* of your food.
Ezr 2:63 His Excellency ordered them not to *p*
4:14 Now, since we *p* of the salt of the palace,
Neh 7:65 ordered them not to *p* of the most holy foods
Jdt 12: 2 But Judith said, "I will not *p* of them,
2Mc 6: 7 bitter necessity, to *p* of the sacrifices,
6: 8 oblige them to *p* of the sacrifices,
Ps(s) 141: 4 and let me not *p* of their dainties.
Eccl 5:18 property, and grants power to *p* of them,
6: 2 God does not grant him power to *p* of them,
Is 24: 9 drink is bitter to those who *p* of it.
Jer 2: 3 Should anyone presume to *p* of them,
1Cor 10:17 are one body, for we all *p* of the one loaf.
10:21 You cannot *p* of the table of the Lord and
10:30 And why is it, if I *p* thankfully,

PARTAKES (4)

Lv 7:27 Every person who *p* of any blood shall be
17:10 aliens residing among them, *p* of any blood,
17:10 set myself against that one who *p* of blood
17:14 blood, anyone who *p* of it shall be cut off.

PARTED (9)

Gn 38: 1 About that time Judah *p* from his brothers
1Kgs 20:36 When they *p* company,
Jdt 14:15 As no one answered, he *p* the curtains,
Jb 41: 9 that they hold fast and cannot be *p*.
Ps(s) 22: 8 they mock me with *p* lips,
Wis 5:12 the *p* air straightway flows together again
Dn 13:13 So they went out and *p*;
Acts 2: 3 which *p* and came to rest on each of them.
2Tm 1: 4 Recalling your tears when we *p*,

PARTHIANS (1)

Acts 2: 9 We are *P*, Medes, and Elamites.

PARTIAL (3)

Jb 32:21 I would not be *p* to anyone,
Prv 18: 5 It is not good to be *p* to the guilty,
Sir 35:13 Though not unduly *p* toward the weak,

PARTIALITY (9)

Lv 19:15 *p* to the weak nor deference to the mighty,
2Chr 19: 7 our God there is no injustice, no *p*,
Jb 13: 8 Is it for him that you show *p*?
13:10 rebuke you if even in secret you show *p*.
Prv 24:23 To show *p* in judgment is not good.
28:21 To show *p* is never good:
Wis 6: 7 For the Lord of all shows no *p*,
Mal 2: 9 keep my ways, but show *p* in your decisions.
Acts 10:34 to see how true it is that God shows no *p*.

PARTICIPANTS (1)

2Kgs 23: 3 all the people stood as *p* in the covenant.

PARTICIPATE (1)

Ex 18:12 came with all the elders of Israel to *p*

PARTICIPATED (1)

2Mc 5:20 afterward *p* in their good fortune;

PARTICLES (1)

Nm 23:10 Jacob, or numbered Israel's wind-borne *p*?

PARTICULAR (8)

Jos 17:16 in *p* those in Beth-shean and its towns,
2Kgs 6: 8 with his servants to attack a *p* place.
2Chr 8:13 command of Moses, and in *p* on the sabbaths,
24:16 in *p* with respect to God and his temple.
1Mc 1:42 one people, each abandoning his *p* customs.
2Mc 4: 5 the general and *p* good of all the people.
Acts 25:26 him before all of you, and in *p* before you,
1Cor 2: 1 testimony with any *p* eloquence or "wisdom."

PARTICULARLY (1)

Phil 4:22 who believe, *p* those in Caesar's service.

PARTICULARS (2)

1Kgs 6:38 year, and it was completed in all *p*,
1Chr 29:30 together with the *p* of his reign and valor,

PARTIES (9)

Ex 22: 8 both *p* shall present their case before God;
Dt 1:16 to both *p* even if one of them is an alien.
19:17 the two *p* in the dispute shall appear
1Sm 14:15 including the outpost and the raiding *p*,
1Kgs 5:26 and Solomon, since they were *p* to a treaty.
1Mc 8:30 But if both *p* hereafter decide to add or
Mk 6:39 sit down on the green grass in groups or *p*.
Acts 19:38 Let the *p* argue their case.
Phil 2: 3 let all *p* think humbly of others as

PARTING (3)

Gn 31:28 a *p* kiss to my daughters and grandchildren!
Jb 38:24 Which way to the *p* of the winds,
Mi 1:14 you shall give *p* gifts to Moresheth-gath;

PARTISANS (2)

2Sm 16:21 your father, all your *p* will take courage."
1Kgs 16:22 *p* of Omri prevailed over those of Tibni,

PARTITIONS (1)

1Kgs 6:16 by cedar *p* from the floor to the rafters,

PARTLY (11)

Wis 17:15 Were *p* smitten by fearsome apparitions and
17:15 and *p* stricken by their soul's surrender;
Dn 2:33 legs iron, its feet partly iron and *p* tile.
2:41 saw, *p* of potter's tile and partly of iron,
2:42 tile, and the toes *p* iron and partly tile,
2:42 shall be *p* strong and partly fragile.
Lk 11:36 body is lighted up and not *p* in darkness,

PARTNER (5)

Gn 2:18 I will make a suitable *p* for him."
2:20 proved to be the suitable *p* for the man.
Tb 8: 6 let us make him a *p* like himself,'
Prv 28:24 and calls it no sin, is a *p* of the brigand.
Phlm 1:17 If then you regard me as a *p*,

PARTNERS (2)

Lk 5:10 Zebedee's sons, who were *p* with Simon.
Heb 3:14 We have become *p* of Christ

PARTOOK (6)

Gn 43:32 and to the Egyptians who *p* of his board.
Jos 9:14 Israelite princes *p* of their provisions,
Ezr 6:21 returned from the exile *p* of it together
Ps(s) 41:10 friend who had my trust and *p* of my bread,
Wis 16: 3 period of privation, *p* of a novel dish.
Jn 13:18 'He who *p* of bread with me has raised his

PARTRIDGE (2)

1Sm 26:20 as if he were hunting *p* in the mountains."
Jer 17:11 A *p* that mothers a brood not her own is

PARTS (21)

Gn 27:16 his hands and the hairless *p* of his neck.
Ex 30:34 these are pure frankincense in equal *p*;
Lv 8:21 *p* of the ram on the altar as a holocaust,
15: 2 flow from his private *p* is thereby unclean.
Nm 18:29 that you receive, and from the best *p*,
Dt 25:11 and seizes the latter by his private *p*,
Jos 18: 5 to me you shall divide it into seven *p*.
Jgs 19: 1 Levite residing in remote *p* of the mountain
2Chr 11:13 themselves to him from all *p* of their land,
Tb 5: 3 I divided it into two *p*,
13:11 light will shine to all *p* of the earth;
Jb 30:17 my inward *p* seethe and will not be stilled.
Jer 34:18 in two, between those two *p* they passed.
34:19 who passed between the *p* of the calf,
Bar 6:27 Even their wives cure *p* of the meat,
Rom 15:15 in *p* of this letter by way of reminder.
1Cor 1:13 Has Christ, then, been divided into *p*?
Eph 1:23 of him who fills the universe in all its *p*.
1Thes 1: 9 The people of those *p* are reporting what
Rv 5: 6 spirits of God, sent to all *p* of the world.
16:19 The great city was split into three *p*,

PARTY (25)

Gn 14:15 and his *p* deployed against them at night,
Nm 14: 6 had been in the *p* that scouted the land,
Dt 25: 1 innocent *p* and condemning the guilty party,
Ru 4: 7 one *p* would take off his sandal and give
1Sm 25:36 *p* in his house like that of a king,
30:15 "Will you lead me down to this raiding *p*?"
30:15 and I will lead you to the raiding *p*."
2Kgs 11:17 made a covenant between the LORD as one *p*
Tb 11: 3 the rest of the *p* are still on the way."
1Mc 9:39 had come out to meet the bride's *p*
11:39 had previously belonged to Alexander's *p*,
Is 19:24 shall be a third *p* with Egypt and Assyria,
Dn 11:23 treacherously rise to power with a small *p*.
Mt 10: 4 Simon the Zealot *P* member,
Mk 2:16 scribes who belonged to the Pharisee *p*
3:18 Thaddaeus, Simon of the Zealot *P*,
Lk 2:44 Thinking he was in the *p*,
5:30 scribes of their *p* said to his disciples,
14: 8 you are invited by someone to a wedding *p*,
14:15 At these words one in the *p* said to him,
Acts 1:13 Simon, the Zealot *p* member,
5:17 (that is, the *p* of the Sadducees),
18:28 his public refutation of the Jewish *p*
23: 9 Pharisee *p* arose and declared emphatically:

PARUAH (1)

1Kgs 4:17 Jehoshaphat, son of *P*,

PARVAIM (1)

2Chr 3: 7 (The gold was from *P*.)

PAS-DAMMIM (1)

1Chr 11:13 He was with David at *P*,

PASACH (1)

1Chr 7:33 The sons of Japhlet were *P*,

PASCHAL (2)

Mk 14:12 it was customary to sacrifice the *p* lamb,
Lk 22: 7 it was appointed to sacrifice the *p* lamb.

PASEAH (4)

1Chr 4:12 Eshton became the father of Bethrapha, *P*,
Ezr 2:49 sons of Gazzam, sons of Uzza, sons of *P*,
Neh 3: 6 Gate was repaired by Joiada, son of *P*;
7:51 sons of Gazzam, sons of Uzza, sons of *P*,

PASHHUR (13)

1Chr 9:12 Adaiah, son of Jeroham, son of *P*,
Ezr 2:38 sons of *P*, one thousand two hundred
10:22 of the sons of *P*:
Neh 7:40 sons of *P*,
10: 4 Seraiah, Azariah, Jeremiah, *P*,
11:12 son of Amzi, son of Zechariah, son of *P*,
Jer 20: 1 prophesying these things by the priest *P*,
20: 3 *P* had released Jeremiah from the stocks,
20: 3 Instead of *P*, the LORD will name you
20: 6 You *P*, and all the members of your
21: 1 the LORD when King Zedekiah sent him *P*,
38: 1 son of *P*, Jucal, son of Shelemiah, and *P*

PASS (171)

Gn 19: 2 we shall *p* the night in the town square."
19:29 Thus it came to *p*:
31:52 I *p* beyond this mound into your territory,
31:52 nor may you *p* beyond it into mine.
47:26 of the priests did not *p* over to Pharaoh.
Ex 12:13 Seeing the blood, I will *p* over you;
12:23 the LORD will *p* over that door and not let
14:16 Israelites may *p* through it on dry land.
33:19 "I will make all my beauty *p* before you,
Nm 20:17 Kindly let us *p* through your country.
20:18 him, "You shall not *p* through here;
20:20 still said, "No, you shall not *p* through,"
20:21 to let them *p* through
21:22 message, "Let us *p* through your country.
21:23 not let Israel *p* through his territory,
27: 7 their father's heritage *p* on to them.
27: 8 let his heritage *p* on to his daughter;
34: 4 Sea, and turning south of the Akrabbim *P*,
36: 7 will *p* from one tribe to another,
36: 9 heritage can *p* from one tribe to another,
Dt 2: 4 to *p* through the territory of your kinsmen,
2:27 me *p* through your country by the highway;
2:30 refused to let us *p* through his land,
13: 3 or wonder he has foretold you comes to *p*,
Jos 2:19 of them *p* outside the doors of your house,
7: 7 allow this people to *p* over the Jordan,
15: 3 Sea, southward below the *p* of
15: 7 of the Gilgal that faces the *p* of Adummim,
18:17 to Geliloth, opposite the *p* of Adummim.
Jgs 1:36 from the Akrabim *p* to Sela and beyond.
8:13 returned from battle by the *p* of Heres.
11:17 Edom saying, 'Let me *p* through your land.'
11:19 me *p* through your land to my own place.'
11:20 to let Israel *p* through his territory.
12: 5 the fleeing Ephraimites said, "Let me *p*,"
21: 3 why has it come to *p* in Israel that today
1Sm 10: 9 That very day all these signs came to *p*. . . .
13:23 had pushed forward to the *p* of Michmash.
1Kgs 8:32 action and *p* judgment on your servants.
13:32 of Samaria shall certainly come to *p*."
2Kgs 6: 9 Do not *p* by this place,
9:27 he rode through the *p* of Gur near Ibleam.
19:25 Now I have brought it to *p*:
2Chr 6:23 action and *p* judgment on your servants,
20:12 O our God, will you not *p* judgment
Neh 2:14 here for my mount to *p* with me astride,
Jdt 7:31 if those days *p* without help coming to us,
8:33 tonight to let me *p* through with my maid;
2Mc 15:36 never to let this day *p* unobserved,
Jb 9:11 should he *p* by, I am not aware of him;
14: 5 you have fixed the limit which he cannot *p*.
19: 8 He has barred my way and I cannot *p*;
24: 7 They *p* the night naked,
39: 9 you, and to *p* the nights by your manger?
42: 7 And it came to *p* after the LORD had spoken
Ps(s) 42: 8 your breakers and your billows *p* over me.
49:11 the senseless and the stupid *p* away,
57: 2 your wings I take refuge, till harm *p* by.
73:10 to such a *p* that they have not even water!"
84: 7 When they *p* through the valley of the
89:42 All who *p* by the way have plundered him;
90:10 toil, for they *p* quickly and we drift away.

PASS (cont.)
104: 9 You set a limit they may not p.
105:19 p and the word of the LORD proved him true.
109:23 Like a lengthening shadow I p away;
129: 8 And those that p by say not,
148: 6 he gave them a duty which shall not p away.
Prv 4:15 cross it not, turn aside from it, and p on.
26:10 who p by is he who hires a drunken fool.
Wis 1: 8 nor will chastising condemnation p him by.
2: 4 will p away like the traces of a cloud,
2: 7 and let no springtime blossom p us by;
Sir 13: 7 When later he sees you he will p you by,
42: 9 Lest she p her prime unmarried,
Is 5:19 let it come to p, that we may know it!"
8: 8 It shall p into Judah,
8:21 shall p through it hard-pressed and hungry,
11:13 The envy of Ephraim shall p away,
23: 6 P over to Tarshish,
23:12 Arise, p over to the Kittim,
28:19 morning after morning it shall p,
34:10 never again shall anyone p through her.
35: 8 No one unclean may p over it,
37:26 I planned it, now I have brought it to p:
41: 5 these things are near, they come to p.
42: 9 See, the earlier things have come to p,
43: 2 When you p through the water,
47: 2 bare your legs, p through the streams.
48:16 At the time it comes to p,
51:10 sea into a way for the redeemed to p over?
62:10 Pass through, p through the gates,
Jer 2:10 P over to the coasts of the Kittim and see,
5:22 though its billows roar, they cannot p.
6: 9 P your hand,
17:15 Let it come to p!"
22: 8 will p by this city and ask one another:
25:31 he is to p judgment upon all mankind:
33:13 flocks will again p under the hands of the
Lam 1:12 "Come, all you who p by the way,
2:15 All who p by clap their hands at you;
3:37 Who commands so that it comes to p,
Ez 9: 4 P through the city [through Jerusalem] and
9: 5 P through the city after him and strike!
12: 5 dig a hole in the wall and p through it;
14:17 commanding the sword to p through the land
16:21 to them, making them p through fire.
20:31 by making your children p through the fire,
29:11 beast shall p through it; they shall not p
39:14 Men shall be permanently employed to p
39:15 When they p through,
41: 7 one could p from the lowest to the middle
46:21 me p around the four corners of the court,
Dn 4:13 of a beast, till seven years p over him.
4:20 wild beasts till seven years p over him'
4:22 seven years shall p over you,
4:29 an ox, and seven years shall p over you,
Jl 4:17 and strangers shall p through her no more.
Am 5:17 be lamentation when I p through your midst,
6: 2 P over to Calneh and see,
Mi 1: 5 the crime of Jacob all this comes to p,
1:11 P by, you who dwell in Shaphir!
Zec 9: 8 none may p to and fro; No oppressor shall p
Mt 5:18 until heaven and earth p away,
15:28 Your wish will come to p."
19:24 it is easier for a camel to p through a
24:34 will not p away until all this takes place.
24:35 will p away but my words will not pass.
26:39 if it is possible, let this cup p me by.
26:42 this cannot p me by without my drinking it,
Mk 6:48 He meant to p them by.
10:25 It is easier for a camel to p through a
13:30 p away until all these things take place.
13:31 will p away but my words will not pass.
14:35 it were possible this hour might p him by.
Lk 16:17 for the heavens and the earth to p away
16:17 single stroke of a letter of the law to p.
21:32 will not p away until all this takes place.
21:33 will pass away, but my words will not p.
Jn 4: 4 He had to p through Samaria,
5:27 to p judgment because he is Son of Man;
8:15 p judgment according to appearances but I p
13: 1 for him to p from this world to the Father.
18:31 p judgment on him according to your law?"
Acts 2:17 'It shall come to p in the last days,
5:36 to p himself off as someone of importance.
7:38 the oracles of life to p on to you.
27:12 the harbor was not fit to p the winter in,
Rom 2:16 God will p judgment on the secrets of men
2:27 the law, he will p judgment on you who,
14: 4 are you to p judgment on another's servant?
14:13 must no longer p judgment on one another.
1Cor 4: 3 you or any human court p judgment on me.
4: 3 I do not even p judgment on myself.
13: 8 will be silent, knowledge will p away.
13:10 perfect comes, the imperfect will p away.
2Cor 3:11 was destined to p away was given in glory,
Eph 4:29 Never let evil talk p your lips;
Col 2:16 to p judgment on you in terms of what you
1Tm 6:15 God will bring to p at his chosen time.
Heb 7:24 has a priesthood which does not p away.
12:27 that shaken, created things will p away,
2Pt 2:11 p no opprobrious sentence in the Lord's
Jude 1:15 ones about him to p judgment on all men,
Rv 20: 4 on them were empowered to p judgment.

PASSABLE (1)
2Mc 5:21 the land navigable and the sea p on foot,

PASSAGE (18)
Nm 22:26 and stopped next in a p so narrow that
Jos 3:17 until the whole nation had completed the p.
Jdt 1: 4 cubits wide for the p of his chariot forces
Est 6: 2 the p occurred in which Mordecai reported
Wis 5:11 afterward no mark of p can be found in it.
Ez 40:11 of the gate's p itself was thirteen cubits.
42:11 were also chambers, before which was a p.
Mk 12:10 you not familiar with this p of Scripture:
12:26 of Moses, in the p about the burning bush,
Lk 4:17 and found the p where it was written:
4:21 Scripture p is fulfilled in your hearing."
9:31 They appeared in glory and spoke of his p,
20:37 Moses in the p about the bush showed that
24:27 every p of Scripture which referred to him.
Jn 19:37 is still another Scripture p which says:
Acts 8:32 This was the p of Scripture he was reading:
8:35 this Scripture p as his starting point,
Heb 2: 6 this is testified to, in the p that says:

PASSAGES (1)
2Pt 3:16 are certain p in them hard to understand.

PASSAGEWAY (1)
Ez 41: 7 p that led upward to the side chambers,

PASSAGEWAYS (1)
Ps(s) 68:21 the LORD, my Lord, controls the p of death.

PASSED (102)
Gn 12: 6 Abram p through the land as far as the
15:17 torch, which p between those pieces.
31:54 eaten, they p the night on the mountain.
37:28 Some Midianite traders p by,
38:12 Years p, and Judah's wife,
47:20 so the land p over to Pharaoh,
Ex 2:23 A long time p, during which the king
7:25 days p after the LORD had struck the river.
12:27 who p over the houses of the Israelites in
14:20 and thus the night p without the rival
15:16 stone, while your people, O LORD, p over,
15:16 the people you had made your own p over.
24:18 But Moses p into the midst of the cloud as
29:29 Aaron shall be p down to his descendants,
33:22 cover you with my hand until I have p by.
34: 6 Thus the LORD p before him and cried out,
Nm 20:17 until we have p through your territory."
20:29 community understood that Aaron had p away;
21:22 until we have p through your territory."
Dt 29:15 what we p by in the nations we traversed,
Jos 4:13 thousand troops equipped for battle p over
10:29 Joshua then p on with all Israel from
10:31 Joshua next p on with all Israel from
10:34 Joshua p on with all Israel to Eglon;
15:10 p north of the ridge of Mount Jearim
24:17 among all the peoples through whom we p.
Jgs 9:25 these robbed all who p them on the road.
11:26 Three hundred years have p;
11:29 He p through Gilead and Manasseh,
18: 2 region of Ephraim, where they p the night.
1Sm 13: 7 and other Hebrews p over the Jordan into
15:12 return he had p on and gone down to Gilgal.
2Sm 18: 9 p under the branches of a large terebinth,
20:14 Sheba p through all the tribes of Israel
1Kgs 18:29 Noon p and they remained in a prophetic
22: 1 p without war between Aram and Israel.
2Kgs 4: 8 Afterward, whenever he p by,
14: 9 p by and trampled the thistle underfoot.
2Chr 20:10 they p them by and did not destroy them.
25:18 Lebanon p by and trampled the thistle down.
30:10 So the couriers p from city to city in the
Ezr 10:17 they had p judgment on all the men
Neh 2:13 by the Valley Gate, p by the Dragon Spring,
2:14 Then I p over to the Spring Gate and to
9:11 ground they p through the midst of the sea;
Tb 5: 3 already p since I deposited that money!
Jdt 13:10 They p through the camp,
Est D: 6 She p through all the portals till she
1Mc 5:51 the city, and p through it over the slain.
5:66 of the Philistines and p through Marisa.
6:31 They p through Idumea and camped before
12:10 a long time has p since your mission to us.
2Mc 11:36 p judgment should be submitted to the king.
Jb 4:15 Then a spirit p before me,
17:11 My days are p away,
Ps(s) 37:36 Yet as I p by, lo!
66: 6 through the river they p on foot;
90: 9 our days have p away in your indignation;
106:33 spirit, and the rash utterance p his lips.
Prv 24:30 I p by the field of the sluggard,
Eccl 5:16 days of his life are p in gloom and sorrow,
Wis 5: 9 p like a shadow and like a fleeting rumor;
5:10 heaving water, of which, when it has p,
Sir 42: 2 or of the sentence to be p upon the sinful;
Is 10:28 he has reached Aiath, p through Migron,
Jer 8:20 "The harvest has p,
17:16 You know what p my lips;
34:18 cut in two, between those two parts they p.
34:19 who p between the parts of the calf,
42: 7 Ten days p before the word of the LORD
Lam 4:21 land of Uz, To you also shall the cup be p;
Ez 16: 6 I p by and saw you weltering in your blood.
16: 8 Again I p by you and saw that you were now
Dn 4:21 the Most High has p upon my lord king:
Jon 2: 4 your breakers and your billows p over me.
Mt 7: 2 on others will be the verdict p on you.
15:29 that place and p along the Sea of Galilee.
Mk 14:23 took a cup, gave thanks and p it to them,
Lk 17:11 p along the borders of Samaria and Galilee.
19: 1 Entering Jericho, he p through the city.
Jn 5:24 condemnation, but has p from death to life.
6:11 and p them around to those reclining there;
Acts 5:15 so that when Peter p by at least his
8: 9 He p himself off as someone of great
9:23 After quite some time has p,
12:10 They p the first guard,
14:24 p through Pisidia and came to Pamphylia.
19: 1 Paul p through the interior of the country
21: 3 We caught sight of Cyprus but p it by on
24:11 Not more than twelve days have p since I
24:27 Two years p, following which Felix
27:16 We p under the lee of a small island named
28:11 ship which had p the winter at the island.
1Cor 5: 3 and have already p sentence in the name of
10: 1 under the cloud and all p through the sea;
16: 5 to you after I have p through Macedonia.
2Cor 5:17 The old order has p away; now all is new!
11:25 I p a day and night on the sea.
Heb 4:14 high priest who has p through the heavens,
1Jn 3:14 That we have p from death to life we know
Rv 21: 1 heavens and the former earth had p away,
21: 4 or pain, for the former world has p away."

PASSER-BY (9)
Ps(s) 80:13 walls, so that every p plucks its fruit,
1Kgs 9: 8 p shall catch his breath in amazement,
Jer 19: 8 p will be amazed and will catch his breath.
49:17 Every p shall be appalled and catch his
Bar 6:43 is drawn aside by some p who lies with her,
Ez 5:14 that surround you, which every p may see.
16:15 and you lavished your harlotry on every p,
16:25 obscenely, spreading your legs for every p,
36:34 a wasteland exposed to the gaze of every p.

PASSERS-BY (4)
1Kgs 13:25 Some p saw the body lying in the road,
Prv 9:15 to p as they go on their straight way:
Jer 18:16 All p will be amazed,
Acts 17:17 in the public square with ordinary p.

PASSES (22)
Ex 33:22 When my glory p I will set you in the
Jdt 4: 7 them to keep firm hold of the mountain p,
5: 1 battle, and had blocked the mountain p,
7: 1 against Bethulia, seize the mountain p,
Jb 14:20 once for all against him and he p on;
Prv 10:25 When the tempest p,
12:16 anger, but the shrewd man p over an insult.
Eccl 1: 4 One generation p and another comes,
Sir 26:19 And the man who p from justice to sin,
Is 28:15 When the overwhelming scourge p,
28:18 When the overwhelming scourge p,
28:19 Whenever it p, it shall take you;
33:21 boat is rowed, where no majestic ship p,
Jer 50:13 Everyone who p by Babylon will be appalled
51:43 Where no man lives, and no one p through.
Hos 6: 4 cloud, like the dew that early p away.
13: 3 cloud or like the dew that early p away,
Mi 5: 7 When it p through,
Zep 2: 2 you are driven away, like chaff that p on;
2:15 Whoever p by her hisses,
Mt 15:17 enters the mouth p into the stomach
Mk 7:19 his stomach only and p into the latrine."

PASSING (43)
Gn 32:14 After p the night there,
Jgs 3:26 Ehud made good his escape and, p the idols,
19: 4 eating and drinking and p the night there.
1Sm 7:16 He made a yearly journey, p through Bethel,
2Sm 15:18 city, were p in review before the king,
1Kgs 11:18 They left Midian and p through Paran,
19:11 the LORD will be p by."
20:39 As the king was p,
2Chr 7:21 everyone p by it will be amazed and ask:
Est 2:19 Mordecai was p his time at the king's gate,
Jb 33:18 the pit and his life from p to the grave.
33:28 He delivered my soul from p to the pit,
Ps(s) 9:17 In p sentence,
78:39 were flesh, a p breath that returns not.
144: 4 his days, like a p shadow.
Prv 26:17 Like the man who seizes a p dog by the
Wis 2: 5 For our lifetime is the p of a shadow;
3: 2 and their p away was thought an affliction
4: 8 is honorable comes not with the p of time,
5:14 and like the p memory of the nomad camping

7:27 And *p* into holy souls from age to age,
17: 9 *p* of insects and the hissing of reptiles,
Is 41: 3 He pursues them, *p* on without loss,
Ez 5: 1 razor, *p* it over your head and beard.
26:18 isles in the sea are terrified at your *p*.
Dn 11:40 *p* through the countries like a flood.
13:53 *p* unjust sentences,
Zep 3: 6 streets deserted, with no one *p* through;
Mt 7: 1 want to avoid judgment, stop *p* judgment.
20:30 roadside, who heard that Jesus was *p* by,
Lk 9:52 town to prepare for his *p* through,
18:37 came that Jesus of Nazareth was *p* by.
Acts 15:33 After *p* some time there,
Rom 15:24 set out for Spain, I hope to see you in *p*;
15:28 for Spain, *p* through your midst on the way.
1Cor 4: 5 *p* judgment before the time of his return.
7:31 it, for the world as we know it is *p* away.
16: 7 I do not want to see you just in *p*.
Heb 9:11 *p* through the greater and more perfect
1Pt 1: 7 than the *p* splendor of fire-tried gold,
1Jn 2:17 And the world with its seductions is *p*
Rv 16: 5 One who is and who was, in *p* this sentence!
19:11 standard in *p* judgment and in waging war.

PASSION (9)

Sir 23: 5 ward off *p* from my heart,
23:16 For burning *p* is a blazing fire,
Eph 4:31 Get rid of all bitterness, all *p* and anger,
Col 3: 5 fornication, uncleanness, *p*,
1Tm 6: 4 man in his *p* for polemics and controversy.
6:10 their *p* for it have strayed from the faith,
Jas 1:14 tug and lure of his own *p* tempt every man.
1:15 Once *p* has conceived,
2Pt 2:18 bombast while baiting their hooks with *p*,

PASSIONATE (1)

1Thes 4: 5 not in *p* desire as do the Gentiles who

PASSIONS (9)

Rom 1:26 delivered them up to disgraceful *p*.
7: 5 the sinful *p* roused by the law worked in
Gal 5:24 their flesh with its *p* and desires.
1Tm 5:11 for when their *p* estrange them from Christ
2Tm 2:22 turn from youthful *p* and pursue integrity,
Ti 3: 3 of our *p* and of pleasures of various kinds.
2Pt 3: 3 ruled by their *p* will arrive on the scene.
Jude 1:16 They live by their *p*, uttering bombast.
1:18 be impostors living by their godless *p*."

PASSOVER (79)

Ex 12:11 It is the *P* of the LORD.
12:21 families, and slaughter them as *P* victims.
12:27 'This is the *P* sacrifice of the LORD,
12:43 "These are the regulations for the *P*.
12:48 you wish to celebrate the *P* of the LORD,
34:25 *P* feast be kept overnight for the next day.
Lv 23: 5 The *P* of the LORD falls on the fourteenth
Nm 9: 2 to celebrate the *P* at the prescribed time.
9: 4 told the Israelites to celebrate the *P*.
9: 5 celebrating the *P* in the desert of Sinai
9: 6 and so could not keep the *P* that day.
9:10 a journey, he may still keep the LORD's *P*.
9:12 but observing all the rules of the *P*.
9:13 on a journey, who yet fails to keep the *P*,
9:14 among you wishes to keep the LORD's *P*,
9:14 the rules and regulations for the *P*.
28:16 of the first month falls the *P* of the LORD,
33: 3 On the *P* morrow the Israelites went forth
Dt 16: 1 month of Abib by keeping the *P* of the LORD,
16: 2 You shall offer the *P* sacrifice from your
16: 5 *P* in any of the communities which the LORD,
16: 6 from Egypt, shall you sacrifice the *P*.
Jos 5:10 they celebrated the *P* on the evening of
5:11 On the day after the *P* they ate of the
5:12 On that same day after the *P* on which they
2Kgs 23:21 the people to observe the *P* of the LORD,
23:22 No *P* such as this had been observed during
23:23 this *P* of the LORD was kept in Jerusalem.
2Chr 30: 1 to celebrate the *P* in honor of the LORD,
30: 2 to celebrate the *P* during the second month,
30: 5 to celebrate the *P* in honor of the LORD,
30:15 They slaughtered the *P* on the fourteenth
30:17 were in charge of slaughtering the *P* victims
30:18 Nevertheless they ate the *P*,
35: 1 Jerusalem a *P* to honor the Lord; the *P*
35: 6 Slay the *P* sacrifice,
35: 7 as a *P* victim for any who were present,
35: 8 *P* victims together with three hundred oxen.
35: 9 to the Levites five thousand *P* victims,
35:11 The *P* sacrifice was slaughtered,
35:13 cooked the *P* on the fire as prescribed,
35:14 the *P* for themselves and for the priests.
35:16 so that the *P* could be celebrated
35:17 were present on that occasion kept the *P*
35:18 No such *P* had been observed in Israel
35:18 of Israel kept a *P* like that of Josiah,
35:19 of Josiah's reign that this *P* was observed.
Ezr 6:19 *P* on the fourteenth day of the first month.
6:20 the *P* for the rest of the exiles,
Ez 45:21 you shall observe the feast of the *P*;
Mt 26: 2 know that in two days' time it will be *P*,
26:17 wish us to prepare the *P* supper for you?"
26:18 the *P* with my disciples in your house.' "
26:19 had ordered, and prepared the *P* supper.
Mk 14: 1 The feasts of *P* and Unleavened Bread were
14:12 us to go to prepare the *P* supper for you?"
14:14 where I may eat the *P* with my disciples?'
14:16 told them, and they prepared the *P* supper.
Lk 2:41 year to Jerusalem for the feast of the *P*,
22: 1 Bread known as the *P* was drawing near,
22: 8 "Go and prepare our *P* supper for us."
22:11 where I may eat the *P* with my disciples?'
22:13 and accordingly they prepared the *P* supper.
22:15 to eat this *P* with you before I suffer.
Jn 2:13 As the Jewish *P* was near,
2:23 he was in Jerusalem during the *P* festival,
6: 4 The Jewish feast of *P* was near;
11:55 The Jewish *P* was near,
11:55 went up to Jerusalem for *P* purification.
12: 1 Six days before *P* Jesus came to Bethany,
13: 1 Before the feast of *P*,
18:28 impurity if they were to eat the *P* supper.
18:39 whereby I release someone to you at *P* time.
19:14 (It was the Preparation Day for *P*,
Acts 12: 4 to bring him before the people after the *P*.
1Cor 5: 7 Christ our *P* has been sacrificed.
Heb 11:28 kept the *P* and sprinkled the lamb's blood,

PAST (56)

Gn 18: 3 favor, please do not go on *p* your servant.
31: 5 toward me is not as it was in the *p*;
Ex 4:10 never been eloquent, neither in the *p*,
Jos 24: 2 In times *p* your fathers,
1Sm 2:30 'I said in the *p* that your family and your
14:23 The battle continued *p* Beth-horon;
2Sm 4: 6 Rechab and his brother Baanah slipped *p*
5: 2 In days *p*, when Saul was our king,
15:18 while the whole army marched *p* him.
1Chr 9:20 Eleazar, had been their chief in times *p*—
Neh 12:38 *p* the Oven Tower as far as the Broad Wall,
12:39 *p* the Ephraim Gate [the New City Gate],
2Mc 15: 8 they had received from heaven in the *p*,
Jb 9:10 He does great things *p* finding out,
14:13 keep me sheltered till your wrath is *p*;
29: 2 Oh, that I were as in the months *p*!
36:26 the number of his years is *p* searching out.
37: 5 wonders *p* our searching out.
Ps(s) 77: 6 the years long *p* I remember.
79: 8 not against us the iniquities of the *p*;
90: 4 sight are as yesterday, now that it is *p*,
Sg 2:11 "For see, the winter is *p*,
Sir 2:10 the generations long *p* and understand;
11:27 brings forgetfulness of *p* delights;
21: 1 and for your *p* sins pray to be forgiven.
42:19 He makes known the *p* and the future,
51: 8 of the LORD, his kindness through ages *p*;
Is 16:13 of the LORD spoke against Moab in times *p*.
26:20 for a brief moment, until the wrath is *p*.
31: 9 He shall rush *p* his crag in panic,
43:18 Remember not the events of the *p*,
48: 3 Things of the *p* I foretold long ago,
58:12 foundations from ages *p* you shall raise up;
65:16 the hardships of the *p* shall be forgotten,
65:17 *p* shall not be remembered or come to mind.
Jer 46:26 shall be inhabited again, as in times *p*,
Ez 36:11 I will repeople you as in the *p*,
47:15 the direction of Hethlon, *p* Labo of Hamath,
Dn 2: 9 to present me with till the crisis is *p*.
13:52 Now have your *p* sins come to term:
Lk 24:18 things that went on there these *p* few days?"
Acts 14:16 In *p* ages he let the Gentiles go their way.
20:16 *p* Ephesus so as not to lose time in Asia,
Rom 3:25 sake of remitting sins committed in the *p*—
Gal 4: 8 In the *p*, when you did not acknowledge
Col 1:26 *p* but now revealed to his holy ones.
3: 9 self with its *p* deeds and put on a new man,
Ti 1: 2 who cannot lie, promised in endless ages *p*.
Heb 1: 1 In times *p*, God spoke in fragmentary
6:10 shown him by your service, *p* and present,
11:11 power to conceive though she was *p* the age,
1Pt 3: 5 The holy women of *p* ages used to adorn
2Pt 2: 1 In times *p* there were false prophets among
Jude 1:25 too, be his, might and power from ages *p*,
Rv 9:12 The first woe is *p*, but beware!
11:14 The second woe is *p*, but beware!

PASTE (1)

Jn 9:14 had made the mud *p* and opened his eyes.)

PASTORS (1)

Eph 4:11 *p* and teachers in roles of service for

PASTURAGE (2)

Ez 45:15 for every two hundred from the *p* of Israel,
Jl 1:18 Because they have no *p*,

PASTURE (159)

Gn 30:31 I will again *p* and tend your flock,
30:36 continued to *p* the rest of Laban's flock.
37:12 gone to *p* their father's flocks at Shechem,
47: 4 for there is no *p* for your servants'
Lv 25:34 the *p* land belonging to their cities shall
Nm 35: 2 as well as *p* lands around the cities.
35: 3 and the *p* lands shall serve their herds
35: 4 The *p* lands of the cities to be assigned
35: 5 serve them as the *p* lands of their cities.
35: 7 their *p* lands to be assigned the Levites.
Jos 14: 4 their *p* lands for the cattle and flocks.
21: 2 dwell in, with *p* lands for our livestock."
21: 3 the following cities with their *p* lands.
21: 8 These cities with their *p* lands the
21:11 region of Judah, with the adjacent *p* lands,
21:13 with its *p* lands; also, Libnah with its *p*
21:14 Jattir with its *p* lands, Eshtemoa with its *p*
21:15 Holon with its *p* lands, Debir with its *p*
21:16 Ashan with its *p* lands, Juttah with its *p*
21:16 lands, and Beth-shemesh with its *p* lands:
21:17 Gibeon with its *p* lands, Geba with its *p*
21:18 pasture lands, Anathoth with its *p* lands,
21:18 pasture lands, and Almon with its *p* lands.
21:19 These cities which with their *p* lands
21:21 They were assigned, with its *p* lands,
21:21 also Gezer with its *p* lands,
21:22 pasture lands, Kibzaim with its *p* lands.
21:22 Beth-horon with its *p* land.
21:23 Elteke with its *p* lands, Gibbethon with its *p*
21:24 pasture lands, Aijalon with its *p* lands,
21:24 lands, and Gath-rimmon with its *p* lands.
21:25 *p* lands and Ibleam with its pasture lands.
21:26 These cities which with their *p* lands
21:27 for homicides at Golan, with its *p* lands;
21:28 Kishion with its *p* lands, Daberath with its *p*
21:29 pasture lands, Jarmuth with its *p* lands,
21:29 lands, and En-gannim with its *p* lands;
21:30 Mishal with its *p* lands, Abdon with its *p*
21:31 pasture lands, Helkath with its *p* lands,
21:31 pasture lands, and Rehob with its *p* lands;
21:32 at Kedesh in Galilee, with its *p* lands;
21:32 *p* lands and Rakkath with its pasture lands.
21:33 These cities which with their *p* lands
21:34 Jokneam with its *p* lands, Kartah with its *p*
21:35 its pasture lands, Rimmon with its *p* lands,
21:35 lands, and Nahalal with its *p* lands;
21:36 Bezer with its *p* lands, Jahaz with its *p*
21:37 pasture lands, Kedemoth with its *p* lands,
21:37 lands, and Mephaath with its *p* lands:
21:38 at Ramoth in Gilead with its *p* lands,
21:38 lands, also Mahanaim with its *p* lands,
21:39 Heshbon with its *p* lands, and Jazer with its *p*
21:41 the Israelites which, with their *p* lands,
21:42 cities went the *p* lands round about it.
2Sm 7: 8 It was I who took you from the *p* and from
1Chr 4:39 of the valley, seeking *p* for their flocks.
4:41 they found *p* there for their flocks.
5:16 all the *p* lands of Sirion to the borders.
6:40 its adjacent *p* lands in the land of Judah,
6:42 a city of asylum, Libnah with its *p* lands,
6:42 its pasture land, Jattir with its *p* lands,
6:42 pasture lands, Eshtemoa with its *p* lands,
6:43 Holon with its *p* lands, Debir with its *p*
6:44 Ashan with its *p* lands, Jetta with its *p*
6:44 lands, and Beth-shemesh with its *p* lands.
6:45 Gibeon with its *p* lands, Geba with its *p*
6:45 Almon with its *p* lands, Anathoth with its *p*
6:45 had thirteen cities with their *p* lands.
6:49 cities with their *p* lands to the Levites,
6:52 its pasture lands, Gezer with its *p* lands,
6:53 pasture lands, Kibzaim with its *p* lands,
6:53 lands, and Beth-horon with its *p* lands.
6:54 Elteke with its *p* lands, Gibbethon with its *p*
6:54 pasture lands, Aijalon with its *p* lands,
6:54 lands, and Gath-rimmon with its *p* lands.
6:55 *p* lands and Ibleam with its pasture lands.
6:56 Golan in Bashan with its *p* lands and
6:56 lands and Ashtaroth with its *p* lands.
6:57 Kedesh with its *p* lands, Daberath with its *p*
6:58 its pasture lands, Ramoth with its *p* lands,
6:58 lands, and Engannim with its *p* lands.
6:59 Mashal with its *p* lands, Abdon with its *p*
6:60 Hilkath with its *p* lands, and Rehob with its *p*
6:61 Kedesh in Galilee with its *p* lands,
6:61 its pasture lands, Hammon with its *p* lands,
6:61 lands, and Kiriathaim with its *p* lands.
6:62 Jokneam with its *p* lands, Kartah with its *p*
6:62 its pasture lands, Rimmon with its *p* lands,
6:62 pasture lands, and Tabor with its *p* lands.
6:63 Bezer in the desert with its *p* lands,
6:63 its pasture lands, Jahzah with its *p* lands,
6:64 pasture lands, Kedemoth with its *p* lands,
6:64 lands, and Mephaath with its *p* lands.
6:65 Ramoth in Gilead with its *p* lands,
6:65 pasture lands, Mahanaim with its *p* lands,
6:66 pasture lands, Heshbon with its *p* lands,
6:66 pasture lands, and Jazer with its *p* lands.
13: 2 the Levites from their cities with *p* lands,
17: 7 I took you from the *p*,
2Chr 11:14 left their assigned *p* lands and their holdings
Jb 24: 2 they steal away herds and *p* them.
39: 8 He ranges the mountains for *p*,
Ps(s) 74: 1 anger smolder against the sheep of your *p*?
79:13 we, your people and the sheep of your *p*,
Sg 1: 7 my heart loves, where you *p* your flock,
1: 8 *p* the young ones near the shepherds' camps.
Is 5:17 Lambs shall graze there at *p*,
27:10 city shall be desolate, an abandoned *p*,

PASTURE (cont.)
32:19 wild asses to frolic in, and flocks to p,
49: 9 Along the ways they shall find p,
61: 5 shall stand ready to p your flocks,
65:10 Sharon shall be a p for the flocks and the
Jer 9: 9 in cries of lamentation, over the p lands,
23: 1 who mislead and scatter the flock of my p,
23:10 the land mourns, the p ranges are seared.
49:20 own p shall be aghast because of them.
50:45 own p shall be aghast because of them.
Lam 1: 6 Her princes, like rams that find no p,
Ez 25: 5 I will make Rabbah a p for camels,
34: 2 Should not shepherds, rather, p sheep?
34: 8 pastured themselves and did not p my sheep;
34:10 so that they may no longer p themselves.
34:13 them back to their own country and p them
34:14 In good pastures will I p them,
34:15 I myself will p my sheep;
34:18 not enough for you to graze on the best p,
34:23 appoint one shepherd over them to p them,
34:23 he shall p them and be their shepherd.
34:31 [You, my sheep, you are the sheep of my p,
45: 4 their homes and p land for their cattle.
48:15 assigned to the City for dwellings and p;
48:17 The p lands of the City shall extend north
Zep 2: 7 by the sea they shall p.
3:13 They shall p and couch their flocks with
Jn 10: 9 He will go in and out, and find p.

PASTURE-FED (1)
1Kgs 5: 3 of meal, ten fatted oxen, twenty p oxen,

PASTURED (3)
Ez 34: 3 the fatlings, but the sheep you have not p.
34: 8 p themselves and did not pasture my sheep;
34:14 shall they be p on the mountains of Israel.

PASTURES (14)
1Chr 4:40 They found abundant and good p,
Ps(s) 23: 2 In verdant p he gives me repose;
Is 7:19 clefts, on all thornbushes and in all p.
14:30 In my p the poor shall eat,
49: 9 on every bare height shall their p be.
Jer 25:37 place, desolate lie the peaceful p;
Ez 34:14 In good p will I pasture them,
34:14 and in rich p shall they be pastured on
34:18 trample the rest of your p with your feet?
Hos 4:16 them broad p as though they were lambs?
Jl 1:19 for fire has devoured the p of the plain,
1:20 and fire has devoured the p of the plain.
2:22 for the p of the plain are green;
Am 1: 2 The p of the shepherds will languish,

PASTURING (4)
Gn 29: 7 the flocks now, and then continue p them?"
36:24 he was p the asses of his father Zibeon.)
1Sm 25:16 whole time we were p the sheep near them.
Ez 34: 2 of Israel who have been p themselves!

PATARA (1)
Acts 21: 1 came to Rhodes and went on from there to P.

PATCH (5)
Jb 39: 8 pasture, and seeks out every p of green.
Is 1: 8 in a vineyard, Like a shed in a melon p,
Bar 6:69 For like a scarecrow in a cucumber p,
Mk 2:21 a p of unshrunken cloth on an old cloak.
Lk 5:36 a piece from a new coat to p an old one.

PATCHED (1)
Jos 9: 5 wore old, p sandals and shabby garments;

PATCHES (1)
Mt 13:20 The seed that fell on p of rock is the man

PATH (74)
Gn 49:17 by the roadside, a horned viper by the p,
2Kgs 21:21 followed exactly the p his father had trod,
21:22 and did not follow the p of the LORD.
2Chr 20:32 the p of his father Asa unswervingly,
21:12 followed the p of your father Jehoshaphat,
34: 2 following the p of his ancestor David.
Tb 5:14 No, they did not stray from the right p;
Jdt 13:16 has protected me in the p I have followed,
2Mc 2: 6 him came up intending to mark the p,
Jb 3:23 Men whose p is hidden from them,
19: 8 he has veiled my p in darkness;
28: 7 The p to it no bird of prey knows,
28: 7 knows, nor has the hawk's eye seen that p.
28:26 for the rain and a p for the thunderbolts,
38:25 a p To bring rain to no man's land,
41:24 Behind him he leaves a shining p;
Ps(s) 16:11 You will show me the p to life,
27:11 O LORD, your way, and lead me on a level p,
37: 7 p of the man who does malicious deeds.
37:14 poor, to slaughter those whose p is right.
44:19 nor our steps turned aside from your p,
77:20 way, and your p through the deep waters,
119:35 Lead me in the p of your commands,
119:105 to my feet is your word, a light to my p.
142: 4 spirit is faint within me, you know my p.
Prv 1:15 them, hold back your foot from their p!
2: 9 and justice, honesty, every good p;
2:18 For her p sinks down to death,
4:14 The p of the wicked enter not,
4:18 the p of the just is like shining light,
4:26 Survey the p for your feet,
10:17 A p to life is his who heeds admonition,
12:28 In the p of justice there is life,
15:19 but the p of the diligent is a highway.
15:24 The p of life leads the prudent man upward,
16:17 The p of the upright avoids misfortune;
22: 5 and snares are on the p of the crooked;
Wis 5:10 be found, no p of its keel in the waves.
14: 3 a road, and through the waves a steady p,
Sir 2:12 hands, to the sinner who treads a double p!
10: 6 and do not walk the p of arrogance.
21: 6 who hates correction walks the sinner's p,
21:10 The p of sinners is smooth stones that end
37:15 to God to set your feet in the p of truth.
43:13 rebuke marks out the p for the lightning,
49: 9 JOB, who always persevered in the right p.
51:15 My feet kept to the level p because from
Is 26: 7 the p of the just you make level.
30:11 Out of our p!
40:14 Who taught him the p of judgment,
41: 3 loss, by a p his feet do not even tread.
43:16 in the sea and a p in the mighty waters,
57:14 the stumbling blocks from my people's p.
Ez 18:24 turns from p of the virtue to do evil,
23:13 Both had gone down the same p,
23:31 you followed in the p of your sister,
Mi 2:13 With a leader to break the p they shall
Na 1: 3 In hurricane and tempest is his p,
Mt 13:19 The seed along the p is the man who hears
21: 8 from the trees and lay them along his p.
Mk 1: 3 way of the Lord, clear him a straight p.' "
4:15 Those on the p are the ones to whom,
Lk 3: 4 way of the Lord, Clear him a straight p.
19:42 only you had known the p to peace this day;
Rom 3:17 The p of peace is unknown to them;
4:12 follow the p of faith which Abraham walked
Gal 5: 7 who diverted you from the p of truth?
1Thes 3:11 Jesus make our p to you a straight one!
2Thes 3: 6 brother who wanders from the straight p
Heb 10:20 the sanctuary by the new and living p
2Pt 2:15 and wander off on the p taken by Balaam,
2Jn 1: 4 of your children walking in the p of truth,
3Jn 1: 3 to how truly you walk in the p of truth.
1: 4 that my children are walking in this p.

PATHROS (3)
Is 11:11 that is left from Assyria and Egypt, P,
Ez 29:14 bringing them back to the land of P,
30:13 into the land of Egypt, and devastate P.

PATHRUSIM (2)
Gn 10:14 Anamim, the Lehabim, the Naphtuhim, the P,
1Chr 1:12 the Ludim, Anamim, Lehabim, Naphtuhim, P,

PATHS (58)
Jgs 5: 6 traveled the roads went by roundabout p.
Tb 1: 3 life on the p of truth and righteousness.
3: 5 have we trodden the p of truth before you.
4: 5 life, and do not tread the p of wrongdoing.
4:19 and ask him to make all your p straight
Jb 13:27 all my p and trace out all my footsteps.
24:13 they abide not in its p.
30:12 To subvert my p they rise up;
38:20 and set them on their homeward p?
Ps(s) 8: 9 sea, and whatever swims the p of the seas.
17: 5 My steps have been steadfast in your p,
23: 3 guides me in right p for his name's sake.
25: 4 teach me your p,
25:10 All the p of the LORD are kindness and
65:12 and your p overflow with a rich harvest;
Prv 2: 8 walk honestly, Guarding the p of justice,
2:13 straight p to walk in the way of darkness,
2:15 ways are crooked, and devious their p;
2:19 come back again, or gain the p of life.
2:20 of good men, and keep to the p of the just.
3: 6 of him, and he will make straight your p.
3:17 are pleasant ways, and all her p are peace;
4:11 you, I lead you on straightforward p.
5: 6 you the road to life, her p will ramble,
5:21 all their p he surveys;
7:25 turn to her ways, go not astray in her p;
8:20 way of duty I walk, along the p of justice,
14:14 and the good man reaps the fruit of his p.
Wis 2:16 aloof from our p as from things impure.
9:18 were the p of those on earth made straight,
12:24 For they went far astray in the p of error,
Sir 11:15 love and virtuous p are from the LORD.
14:21 ways in his heart, and understands her p;
32:22 smooth roads, be careful on all your p.
33:11 in different p he has them walk.
39:24 For the virtuous his p are level,
48:22 was right and held fast to the p of David,
Is 2: 3 us in his ways, and we may walk in his p."
3:12 they destroy the p you should follow.
33: 8 are desolate, travelers have quit the p,
42:16 by p unknown I will guide them.
59: 8 there is nothing that is right in their p;
65: 2 in evil p and follow their own thoughts,
Jer 18:15 stumble out of their ways, the p of old,
Lam 3: 9 with fitted stones, and turned my p aside.
Bar 3:21 not known, they have not perceived her p,
3:23 way to wisdom, nor have they her p in mind.
3:31 way to her, nor has any understood her p.
4:13 tread the disciplined p of his justice.
Hos 2: 8 against her, so that she cannot find her p.
14:10 Straight are the p of the LORD,
Jl 2: 7 own lane, without swerving from their p.
Mi 4: 2 us in his ways, that we may walk in his p."
Mt 3: 3 the way of the Lord, make straight his p.' "
Lk 1:76 the Lord to prepare straight p for him,
Acts 2:28 You have shown me the p of life;
13:10 to make crooked the straight p of the Lord?
Heb 12:13 Make straight the p you walk on,

PATHWAYS (1)
Jer 6:16 ask the p of old Which is the way to good,

PATIENCE (20)
Nm 21: 4 But with their p worn out by the journey,
Prv 25:15 By p is a ruler persuaded,
Wis 2:19 have proof of his gentleness and try his p.
Dn 12:12 Blessed is the man who has p and
Mi 2: 7 O house of Jacob, "Is the LORD short of p,
Rom 9:22 endured with much p vessels fit for wrath,
15: 4 might derive hope from the lessons of p
15: 5 God, the source of all p and encouragement,
2Cor 6: 6 with innocence, knowledge, and p,
12:12 great p the signs that show the apostle,
Eph 4: 2 with perfect humility, meekness, and p,
Col 3:12 with kindness, humility, meekness, and p.
1Tm 1:16 Jesus Christ might display all his p,
2Tm 3:10 have observed my resolution, fidelity, p,
4: 2 constantly teaching and never losing p.
Heb 6:12 but imitate those who, through faith and p,
10:36 You need p to do God's will and receive
Jas 5:10 models in suffering hardship and in p,
2Pt 3: 9 Rather, he shows you generous p,
3:15 our Lord's p is directed toward salvation.

PATIENT (26)
Neh 9:30 You were p with them for many years,
Jb 6:11 and what is my limit that I should be p?
Prv 14:29 The p man shows much good sense,
15:18 up strife, but a p man allays discord.
16:32 A p man is better than a warrior,
Eccl 7: 8 is the p spirit than the lofty spirit.
Sir 1:20 A p man need stand firm but for a time,
2: 4 befalls you, in crushing misfortune be p;
18: 9 p with men and showers upon them his mercy.
Mt 18:26 p with me and I will pay you back in full.'
Lk 21:19 By p endurance you will save your lives.
Acts 18:14 give you Jews a p and reasonable hearing.
Rom 8:25 see means awaiting it with p endurance.
12:12 Rejoice in hope, be p under trial,
15: 1 We who are strong in faith should be p
1Cor 13: 4 Love is p; love is kind.
2Cor 6: 4 God, acting with p endurance amid trials,
Gal 5:22 spirit is love, joy, peace, p endurance,
1Thes 5:14 be p toward all.
Heb 6:15 And so, after p waiting,
Jas 5: 7 Be p, therefore, my brothers,
5: 8 You, too, must be p.
Rv 2: 2 deeds, your labors, and your p endurance.
2: 3 You are p and endure hardship for my cause.
2:19 as well as your p endurance;
6:11 and they were told to be p a little while

PATIENTLY (10)
2Mc 6:14 the Lord p waits until they reach the full
Bar 4:25 bear p the anger that has come from God
Acts 26: 3 I beg you to listen to me p.
Rom 2: 7 honor, and immortality by p doing right;
1Cor 4:12 Persecution comes our way; we bear it p.
2Cor 1: 6 may endure p the same sufferings we endure.
2Tm 2:24 p and gently correcting those who
Heb 5: 2 He is able to deal p with erring sinners,
Jas 5: 7 He looks forward to it p while the soil
1Pt 3:20 while God p waited until the ark was built.

PATMOS (1)
Rv 1: 9 found myself on the island called P

PATRIARCH (1)
Heb 7: 4 Abraham the p gave one tenth of his booty!

PATRIARCHS (6)
Jn 7:22 not originate with Moses but with the p).
Acts 7: 8 same for Jacob, and Jacob for the twelve p.
7: 9 the p sold Joseph into slavery in Egypt,
Rom 9: 5 theirs were the p,
11:28 they are beloved by him because of the p.
15: 8 in fulfilling the promises to the p,

PATRIMONY (1)
Jb 20:19 poor, and stolen a *p* he had not built up,

PATRIOT (1)
2Mc 14:37 Jerusalem, was denounced to Nicanor as a *p*.

PATROBAS (1)
Rom 16:14 to Asyncritus, Phlegon, Hermes, *P*,

PATROCLUS (1)
2Mc 8: 9 promptly selected Nicanor, son of *P*,

PATROL (3)
1Mc 15:41 they could go out and *p* the roads of Judea.
Zec 1:10 they whom the LORD has sent to *p* the earth."
6: 7 the earth, he said, "Go, *p* the earth!"

PATROLLED (2)
Zec 1:11 trees and said, "We have *p* the earth;
6: 7 Then, as they *p* the earth,

PATROLLING (3)
Jb 1: 7 and said, "From roaming the earth an *p* it."
2: 2 said, "From roaming the earth and *p* it."
Zec 6: 7 emerged, eager to set about *p* the earth,

PATRONS (1)
Est E: 2 the bountiful generosity of their *p*.

PATTERN (16)
Ex 25: 9 to the *p* that I will now show you.
25:40 to the *p* shown you on the mountain.
26:30 to the *p* shown you on the mountain.
39: 3 into an embroidered *p* on the fine linen.
Nm 8: 4 to the *p* which the LORD had shown Moses.
1Kgs 7:19 columns were finished wholly in a lotus *p*
1Chr 28:11 Then David gave to his son Solomon the *p*
28:12 He provided also the *p* for all else that
28:19 writing the exact specifications of the *p*,
Sir 38:27 seals, and whose concern is to vary the *p*.
Jer 29:22 Judah in Babylon will *p* a curse after them:
Acts 7:44 to make it according to the *p* he had seen.
Rom 2:20 at hand a clear *p* of knowledge and truth.
Phil 3:10 by being formed into the *p* of his death.
3:21 according to the *p* of his glorified body,
Heb 8: 5 to the *p* shown you on the mountain."

PATTERNS (1)
Wis 13:13 and *p* it on the image of a man or makes

PAU (1)
Gn 36:39 the name of his city was *P*.

PAUL (195)
Acts 13: 9 as *P*) was filled with the Holy Spirit;
13:13 *P* and his companions put out to sea and
13:16 So *P* arose, motioned to them for silence,
13:43 Jewish converts followed *P* and Barnabas,
13:45 with violent abuse whatever *P* said.
13:46 *P* and Barnabas spoke out fearlessly,
13:50 persecution started against *P* and Barnabas.
14: 3 *P* and Barnabas spent considerable time
14: 6 When *P* and Barnabas learned of this,
14: 9 and *P* looked
14:11 When the crowds saw what *P* had done,
14:12 *P* they called Hermes,
14:14 the apostles Barnabas and *P* heard of this,
14:19 stoned *P* and dragged him out of the town,
15: 2 between them and *P* and Barnabas.
15: 2 Finally it was decided that *P*,
15:12 They listened to Barnabas and *P* as the two
15:22 sent to Antioch along with *P* and Barnabas.
15:25 along with our beloved Barnabas and *P*,
15:35 *P* and Barnabas continued in Antioch,
15:36 After a certain time *P* said to Barnabas,
15:38 But *P* insisted that,
15:40 *P*, for his part, chose Silas
16: 1 *P* arrived first at Derbe;
16: 3 *P* was anxious to have him come along on
16: 3 *P* had him circumcised because of the Jews
16: 9 There one night *P* had a vision.
16:14 her heart to accept what *P* was saying.
16:17 to follow *P* and the rest of us shouting,
16:18 days until finally *P* became annoyed,
16:19 they seized *P* and Silas and dragged them
16:25 while *P* and Silas were praying and singing
16:28 but *P* shouted to him:
16:29 fell trembling at the feet of *P* and Silas.
16:36 The jailer conveyed this information to *P*:
17: 1 *P* and Silas took the road through
17: 2 *P* joined the people there and conducted
17: 4 and threw in their lot with *P* and Silas.
17: 5 *P* and Silas before the people's assembly.
17:10 brothers sent *P* and Silas off to Beroea.
17:13 had been proclaimed by *P* in Beroea also,
17:14 sent *P* off directly on his way to the sea,
17:15 *P* was taken as far as Athens by his escort,
17:16 While *P* was waiting for them in Athens,
17:22 Then *P* stood up in the Areopagus and
17:33 At this point, *P* left them.
18: 1 that, *P* left Athens and went to Corinth.
18: 2 *P* went to visit the pair,
18: 4 *P* led discussions in which he persuaded
18: 5 *P* was absorbed in preaching and giving
18: 7 *P* withdrew and went to the house of a
18: 8 who heard *P* believed and were baptized.
18: 9 One night in a vision the Lord said to *P*:
18:11 *P* ended by settling there for a year and a
18:12 against *P* and brought him before the bench.
18:14 *P* was about to speak in self-defense when
18:18 *P* stayed on in Corinth for quite a while;
19: 1 *P* passed through the interior of the
19: 4 *P* then explained, "John's baptism was
19: 6 As *P* laid his hands on them,
19: 8 *P* entered the synagogue,
19: 9 of the assembly, *P* simply left them.
19:11 extraordinary miracles at the hands of *P*.
19:13 adjure you by the Jesus whom *P* preaches."
19:15 answered, "Jesus I recognize, *P* I know;
19:21 *P* made up his mind to travel through
19:26 this *P* has persuaded great numbers of
19:30 *P* wanted to go before this gathering but
19:31 friends of *P* sent word to him advising him
20: 1 *P* brought his disciples together to
20: 7 the breaking of bread, *P* preached to them.
20: 8 *P* talked on and on,
20:10 *P* hurried down immediately and threw
20:11 Afterward *P* went upstairs again,
20:13 sail for Assos, where we were to pick *P* up.
20:16 *P* had decided to sail past Ephesus so as
20:17 *P* sent word from Miletus to Ephesus,
20:36 *P* knelt down with them all and prayed.
21: 4 *P* that he should not go up to Jerusalem;
21:12 urged *P* not to proceed to Jerusalem.
21:18 *P* and the rest of us paid a visit to James
21:19 *P* first greeted them,
21:20 heard it they praised God, and said to *P*:
21:26 *P* gathered the men together and went
21:27 recognized *P* in the temple precincts
21:29 that *P* had brought him into the temple.
21:30 They seized *P*,
21:32 the soldiers, they stopped assaulting *P*.
21:33 *P* and had him bound with double irons.
21:34 ordered *P* to be led away to headquarters.
21:35 When *P* reached the steps,
21:37 Just as *P* was about to be led into the
21:39 *P* replied, "I am a Jew, a citizen of Tarsus
21:40 With his permission *P* then stood on the
22:22 speech the crowd had been listening to *P*,
22:24 *P* to be brought inside the headquarters.
22:25 No sooner had they bound *P* than he said to
22:27 The commander rushed in and asked *P*,
22:27 "I am," *P* answered.
22:28 "Ah," said *P*, "but I am a citizen
22:29 *P* he had restrained a citizen of Rome.
22:30 day the commander released *P* from prison,
22:30 *P* down and made him stand before them.
23: 1 *P* gazed intently at the Sanhedrin.
23: 2 his attendants to strike *P* on the mouth.
23: 3 *P* said to him in rebuttal:
23: 5 *P* answered: "My brothers, I did not know
23: 6 *P*, it should be noted,
23:10 feared they would tear *P* to pieces.
23:10 rescue *P* from their midst and take him back
23:12 to eat or drink until they had killed *P*.
23:14 by oath to touch no food until we kill *P*.
23:15 have *P* brought down to you on the pretext
23:16 him to enter, and he told *P* about it.
23:17 *P* then called for one of the centurions,
23:18 "The prisoner *P* called me and asked me to
23:20 to have *P* brought down to the Sanhedrin,
23:31 the infantry took *P* and escorted him that
23:33 to the governor and brought *P* before him.
23:34 letter, asked *P* what province he came from,
23:35 Then he ordered *P* to be kept under guard
24: 1 their case against *P* to the governor.
24:10 The governor then gestured to *P*,
24:23 He gave orders to the centurion that *P* was
24:24 and sent for *P* to hear him speak about
24:25 As *P* talked on about uprightness,
24:26 he hoped he would be offered a bribe by *P*,
24:27 with the Jews, so he left *P* in prison.
25: 2 presented him with their case against *P*,
25: 3 that he favor them rather than *P*,
25: 4 *P* was being kept in custody at Caesarea,
25: 6 the bench and ordered *P* to be brought in.
25: 7 When *P* appeared,
25: 9 to please the Jewish people, asked *P*,
25:10 *P* answered: "I stand before the imperial
25:19 who had died but who *P* claimed is alive.
25:21 *P* appealed to be kept here until there
25:23 At Festus' command *P* was brought in.
26: 1 Agrippa now spoke to *P*:
26: 1 So *P* stretched out his hand and began his
26:24 As *P* went on defending himself in this way,
26:24 way, Festus interrupted with a shout, *P*,
26:25 "No, Your Excellency," answered *P*,
26:28 At this, Agrippa said, "A little more, *P*,
26:29 *P* replied, "Whether little more
27: 1 *P* and some other prisoners were handed
27: 3 where Julius kindly allowed *P* to visit
27: 9 It was then that *P* uttered this warning:
27:11 pilot and the shipowner to listening to *P*.
27:21 time when *P* stood up among them and said:
27:24 'Do not be afraid, *P*,' he said.
27:31 *P* alerted the centurion and the soldiers
27:33 *P* urged all on board to take some food:
27:43 the centurion was anxious to save *P*,
28: 3 *P* had just fed the fire with a bundle of
28: 5 But *P* shook the snake off into the fire
28: 8 *P* went in to see the man and praying,
28: 9 to come to *P* and they too were healed.
28:15 When *P* saw them,
28:16 *P* was allowed to take a lodging of his own,
28:17 Three days later *P* invited the prominent
28:25 Then *P* added one final word:
28:30 years *P* stayed on in his rented lodgings,
Rom 1: 1 Greetings from *P*,
1Cor 1: 1 *P*, called by God's will to be an apostle
1:12 One of you will say, "I belong to *P*,"
1:13 Was it *P* who was crucified for you?
3: 4 When someone says, "I belong to *P*,"
3: 5 And who is *P*?
3:22 All things are yours, whether it be *P*,
16:21 It is I, *P*, who send you this greeting
2Cor 1: 1 *P*, by God's will an apostle of Jesus Christ,
10: 1 I, *P*, exhort you by the meekness
Gal 1: 1 *P*, an apostle sent not by men or by any man,
5: 2 Pay close attention to me, *P*,
Eph 1: 1 *P*, by the will of God an apostle of Jesus
3: 1 That is why to me, *P*,
Phil 1: 1 *P* and Timothy, servants of Christ Jesus,
Col 1: 1 *P*, an apostle of Christ Jesus by the will
1:23 to every creature under heaven, and I, *P*,
4:18 This greeting is from *P*— in my own hand!
1Thes 1: 1 *P*, Silvanus,
2:18 I, *P*, tried more than once
2Thes 1: 1 *P*, Silvanus,
1Tm 1: 1 *P*, an apostle of Christ Jesus by command
2Tm 1: 1 *P*, by the will of God an apostle of Christ
Ti 1: 1 *P*, a servant of God,
1: 4 *P* to Titus, my own true child
Phlm 1: 1 *P*, a prisoner of Christ Jesus,
1: 9 Yes, I, *P*, ambassador of Christ
1:19 I, *P*, write this in my own hand:
2Pt 3:15 *P*, our beloved brother,

PAUL'S (11)
Acts 16:37 *P* response to this was,
19:29 *P* traveling companions from Macedonia.
21:11 He came up to us, and taking *P* belt,
23:11 night the Lord appeared at *P* side and said:
23:16 The son of *P* sister heard about the plot,
23:24 Also provide horses for *P* journey,
24: 2 Following *P* summons to the bar,
25: 8 *P* defense was,
25:14 there, Festus referred *P* case to the king.
1Cor 1:13 Was it in *P* name that you were baptized?
2Thes 3:17 This greeting is in my own hand *P*.

PAULUS (1)
Acts 13: 7 of the proconsular governor Sergius *P*,

PAUPER (2)
Sir 10:21 Be it tenant or wayfarer, alien or *p*,
25: 2 A proud *p*, a rich dissembler,

PAUSE (1)
Rv 4: 8 Day and night, without *p*, they sang:

PAUSED (1)
Jb 4:16 It *p*, but its likeness I could not discern;

PAUSES (1)
Hb 3: 6 He *p* to survey the earth;

PAVED (1)
Tb 13:17 shall be *p* with rubies and stones of Ophir;

PAVEMENT (12)
2Kgs 16:17 that supported it, and set it on a stone *p*.
2Chr 7: 3 *p* with their faces to the earth and adored,
Est 1: 6 Gold and silver couches were on the *p*,
Is 14:19 Going down to the *p* of the pit,
Ez 40:17 court, where there were chambers and a *p*.
40:17 The *p* was laid all around the court,
40:17 and the chambers, which were on the *p*,
40:18 The *p* lay alongside the gates,
40:18 this was the lower *p*.
41: 8 was a raised *p* completely enclosing it
42: 3 inner court and the *p* of the outer court,
Jn 19:13 bench at the place called the Stone *P*—

PAVEMENTS (1)
Is 54:11 and unconsoled, I lay your *p* in carnelians,

PAVILION (3)
1Chr 17: 5 but I have been lodging in tent or *p* as

PAVILION (cont.)

2Mc 13:15 he made a night attack on the king's *p*
Dn 11:45 He shall pitch the tents of his royal *p*

PAVILIONS (3)

1Kgs 20:12 *p* with the kings when he heard this reply.
20:16 Ben-hadad was drinking heavily in the *p*
Hb 3: 7 trembling are the *p* of the land of Midian.

PAWN (3)

Neh 5: 2 "We are forced to *p* our sons and
5: 3 'We are forced to *p* our fields,
Jb 22: 6 unjustly kept your kinsmen's goods in *p*,

PAWS (3)

Lv 11:27 those that walk on *p* are unclean for you;
Jb 39:21 He jubilantly *p* the plain and rushes in
Rv 13: 2 had *p* like a bear and the mouth of a lion.

PAY (148)

Gn 23:13 I will *p* you the price of the field.
27:29 serve you, and nations *p* you homage;
30:28 wages you want from me, and I will *p* them.
30:31 "What should I *p* you?"
30:31 do not have to *p* me anything outright.
34:11 and I will *p* whatever you demand of me.
34:12 price, I will *p* you whatever you ask;
38:16 "What will you *p* me for letting you have
50:15 plans to *p* us back in full for all the wrong
Ex 5: 9 on it and *p* no attention to lying words."
21:22 he shall *p* in the presence of the judges.
21:30 he must *p* in ransom for his life whatever
21:32 he must *p* the owner of the slave thirty
22: 2 he shall be sold to *p* for his theft.
22:15 shall *p* her marriage price and marry her.
22:16 he must still *p* him the customary marriage
30:13 the registered group must *p* a half-shekel,
30:15 the LORD to *p* the forfeit for their lives.
Lv 19: 8 whoever eats of it then shall *p* the
20:17 the man shall *p* the penalty of having had
20:19 does so shall *p* the penalty of incest.
20:20 shall *p* the penalty by dying childless.
25:27 and then *p* back the balance to the one to
25:51 the sale price he shall *p* back as ransom;
25:52 his years of service shall he *p* his ransom.
27:13 shall *p* one fifth more than this valuation.
27:15 he shall *p* one fifth more than the price
27:19 he shall *p* one fifth more than the price
27:31 he shall *p* one fifth more than their value.
Nm 16:15 to the LORD, *P* no heed to their offering.
20:19 drink any of your water, we will *p* for it.
Dt 7:10 a one, but makes him personally *p* for it.
13: 4 *p* no attention to the words of that
22:29 shall *p* the girl's father fifty silver shekels
24:15 You shall *p* him each day's wages before
1Sm 25: 5 *P* Nabal a visit and greet him in my name.
25:25 *p* attention to that worthless man Nabal,
2Sm 9: 8 should *p* attention to a dead dog like me?"
16: 4 "I *p* you homage, my lord the king.
24:24 to Araunah, "No, I must *p* you for it,
1Kgs 5:20 and I will *p* you whatever you say for your
20:39 *p* for his life with your life or *p* out a talent
20:42 your life shall *p* for his life,
2Kgs 3: 4 used to *p* the king of Israel as tribute a
4: 7 and sell the oil to *p* off your creditor;
10:24 into your hands, he shall *p* life for life."
17: 4 and for failure to *p* the annual tribute to
18:14 I will *p* whatever tribute you impose on me."
22: 5 should then *p* them out to the carpenters,
23:35 each proportionately, to *p* Pharaoh Neco.
2Chr 34:10 and these in turn used it to *p* the workmen
Ezr 4:13 up again, they will no longer *p* taxes,
Neh 5: 4 "To *p* the king's tax we have borrowed
Tb 2:12 goods to their owners, they would *p* her.
4:14 who works for you, but *p* him immediately.
5: 7 I will, of course, *p* you."
5:10 I will of course *p* you, brother."
12: 2 "Father, how much shall I *p* him?
Jdt 8:21 and God will make us *p* for its profanation
Est 4: 7 had promised to *p* to the royal treasury
1Mc 2:68 *P* back the Gentiles what they deserve,
3:28 chests, gave his soldiers a year's *p*,
8: 2 them and forcing them to *p* tribute.
8: 7 who succeeded him to *p* a heavy tribute,
10: 3 written in peaceful terms, to *p* him honor;
14:32 armed forces and giving them their *p*.
15:31 *p* me five hundred talents of silver for
15:35 *p* you a hundred talents for these cities."
2Mc 4: 9 he agreed to *p* a hundred and fifty more,
Jb 7:17 you make much of him, or *p* him any heed?
13:17 *P* careful heed to my speech,
Ps(s) 2:12 with trembling *p* homage to him,
10:17 you *p* heed To the defense of the
34:22 the enemies of the just *p* for their guilt.
49: 8 redeem himself, or *p* his own ransom to God;
72:11 All kings shall *p* him homage,
116:14 I will *p* in the presence of all his people.
116:18 I will *p* in the presence of all his people,
119:95 destroy me, but I *p* heed to your decrees.
Prv 6:31 if he be caught he must *p* back sevenfold;
13:13 He who despises the word must *p* for it,
22:27 For if you have not the means to *p*,
30:10 curse you, and you have to *p* the penalty.
Sg 8:11 would have to *p* a thousand silver pieces.
Sir 3: 1 Children, *p* heed to a father's right;
8: 2 lest he *p* out the price of your downfall;
8:13 think any pledge a debt you must *p*.
20:11 for little, but *p* for it seven times over.
29: 2 *p* back your neighbor when a loan falls due;
29:23 and *p* no heed to him who would disparage
35: 7 In generous spirit *p* homage to the LORD,
35: 8 and *p* your tithes in a spirit of joy.
37:11 *p* no attention to any advice they give.
38:17 mourning fully, *p* your tribute of sorrow,
Is 21: 7 riding a camel, Then let him *p* heed,
24: 6 and its inhabitants *p* for their guilt;
28:23 *p* attention and listen to what I say:
Jer 5:21 *P* attention to this,
7:24 But they obeyed not, nor did they *p* heed.
22:13 Who works his neighbor without *p*,
25: 4 Though you refused to listen or *p* heed,
Lam 5: 4 we must buy, for our own wood we must *p*.
Ez 22:26 they *p* no attention to my sabbaths,
23:49 and you shall *p* for your sins of idolatry.
40: 4 and *p* strict attention to all that I will
44: 5 Son of man, *p* strict attention,
Hos 5: 1 Hear this, O priests, *P* attention,
5:15 *p* for their guilt and seek my presence.
10: 2 heart is false, now they *p* for their guilt;
Jl 1: 2 *P* attention,
Jon 2:10 What I have vowed I will *p*:
Mi 6: 2 the plea of the LORD, *p* attention,
Zec 1: 4 they would not listen or *p* attention to me,
Mt 2: 2 its rising and have come to *p* him homage."
17:24 "Does your master not *p* the temple tax?"
18:26 with me and I will *p* you back in full.'
18:28 *P* back what you owe,' he demanded.
18:29 give me time and I will *p* you back in full.'
20: 4 vineyard and I will *p* you whatever is fair.'
20: 8 'Call the workmen and give them their *p*,
20: 9 came up they received a full day's *p*,
20:14 Take your *p* and go home.
20:14 man who was hired last the same *p* as you.
22:17 lawful to *p* tax to the emperor or not?"
23:23 You *p* tithes on mint and herbs and seeds
Mk 12:14 lawful to *p* the tax to the emperor or not?
12:14 Are we to *p* or not to pay?"
15:19 before him and pretended to *p* him homage.
Lk 3:14 Be content with your *p*."
9:44 *P* close attention to what I tell you:
11:42 You *p* tithes on mint and rue and all the
18:12 I *p* tithes on all I possess.'
19: 8 anyone in the least, I *p* him back fourfold."
20:22 May we *p* tax to the emperor or not?"
Jn 10:13 That is because he works for *p*;
10:20 Why *p* any attention to him?"
Acts 21:24 *p* the fee for the shaving of their heads.
Rom 13: 5 You *p* taxes for the same reason,
13: 7 *P* each one his due:
Gal 5: 2 *P* close attention to me,
1Tm 5:19 *P* no attention to an accusation against a
Phlm 1:19 I agree to *p*—
Jude 1:11 themselves to Balaam's error for *p*,
Rv 6: 6 "A day's *p* for a ration of wheat and the
18: 6 *P* her back as she has paid others; *p* her

PAYING (11)

Lv 27:27 by *p* one fifth more than its fixed value.
2Sm 3:14 by *p* a hundred Philistine foreskins."
1Chr 18: 2 Moabites became his subjects, *p* tribute.
18: 6 Arameans became his subjects, *p* tribute.
1Mc 11:34 instead of *p* the royal taxes that formerly
Is 55: 1 Come, without *p* and without cost,
66: 3 burning incense, like *p* homage to an idol.
Jer 32: 9 from my cousin Hanamel, *p* him the money,
Mt 18:25 As he had no way of *p* it,
Lk 23:41 are only *p* the price for what we've done,
Acts 8:10 rank of society were *p* attention to him.

PAYMENT (19)

Gn 47:14 as *p* for the rations that were being
Ex 30:13 This *p* of a half-shekel is a contribution
Dt 27:25 who accepts *p* for slaying an innocent man!'
2Chr 28:21 princes to make *p* to the king of Assyria,
1Mc 10:35 Let no man have authority to exact *p* from
11:35 grant them release from *p* of all other things
Jb 31:39 *p* and grieved the hearts of its tenants;
Sir 18:22 nothing prevent the prompt *p* of your vows;
29: 5 But when *p* is due he disappoints him and
Ez 16:31 unlike a prostitute, since you disdained *p*.
16:32 wife receives, instead of her husband, *p*.
16:34 Since you gave *p* instead of receiving it,
16:41 harlotry, and you shall never again give *p*.
27:15 tusks and ebony wood they gave you for *p*.
29:20 as *p* for his toil I have given him the
Mt 18:25 and all his property, in *p* of the debt.
Lk 23: 2 nation, opposing the *p* of taxes to Caesar,
2Cor 1:22 sealed us, thereby depositing the first *p*,
Eph 1:14 the first *p* against the full redemption of

PAYMENTS (1)

2Mc 4:27 *p* of the money he had promised to the king,

PAYS (12)

Jgs 18: 4 "He *p* me a salary and I am his priest."
Ps(s) 142: 5 to see, but there is no one who *p* me heed.
Prv 16:17 *p* attention to his way safeguards his life.
19:19 The man of violent temper *p* the penalty;
21:29 but the upright man *p* heed to his ways.
Eccl 11: 4 One who *p* heed to the wind will not sow,
Sir 29: 6 curses and insults the borrower *p* him back,
Is 42:23 listens and *p* heed for the time to come?
Jer 51: 6 vengeance for the LORD, he *p* her her due.
Mt 15: 8 'This people *p* me lip service but their
Mk 7: 6 'This people *p* me lip service but their
1Cor 9: 6 soldier in the field *p* for his rations?

PEACE (390)

Gn 15:15 however, shall join your forefathers in *p*;
26:29 toward you and have let you depart in *p*.
26:31 farewell, and they departed from him in *p*.
34: 5 he held his *p* until they came home.
Ex 4:18 Jethro replied, "Go in *p*."
20:24 sacrifice your holocausts and *p* offerings,
24: 5 young bulls as *p* offerings to the LORD,
29:28 From their *p* offerings,
32: 6 offered holocausts and brought *p* offerings.
Lv 3: 1 "If someone in presenting a *p* offering
3: 3 From the *p* offering he shall offer as an
3: 6 "If the *p* offering he presents to the
3: 9 he shall present the fat of the *p* offering:
4:10 is removed from the ox of the *p* offering;
4:26 the altar like the fat of the *p* offering.
4:31 as the fat is removed from the *p* offering,
6: 5 and burn the fat of the *p* offerings.
7:11 *p* offerings that are presented to the LORD.
7:12 anyone makes a *p* offering in thanksgiving,
7:13 victim of his *p* offering for thanksgiving.
7:14 who splashes the blood of the *p* offering.
7:18 the *p* offering is eaten on the third day,
7:20 of a *p* offering belonging to the LORD,
7:21 eats of a *p* offering belonging to the LORD,
7:29 He who presents a *p* offering to the LORD
7:32 from your *p* offering you shall give to
7:33 offers up the blood and fat of the *p* offering
7:34 for from the *p* offerings of the Israelites
7:37 [ordination offerings] and *p* offerings,
9: 4 and an ox and a ram for a *p* offering,
9:18 and the ram, the *p* offering of the people.
9:22 sin offering and holocaust and *p* offering,
10:14 due from the *p* offerings of the Israelites.
17: 5 them there as *p* offerings to the LORD.
19: 5 you sacrifice your *p* offering to the LORD,
22:21 When anyone presents a *p* offering to the
23:19 and two yearling lambs as a *p* offering.
26: 6 I will establish *p* in the land,
Nm 6:14 one unblemished ram as a *p* offering,
6:17 up the ram as a *p* offering to the LORD,
6:18 in the fire that is under the *p* offering.
6:26 LORD look upon you kindly and give you *p*!
7:17 and five yearling lambs for a *p* offering.
7:23 and five yearling lambs for a *p* offering.
7:29 and five yearling lambs for a *p* offering.
7:35 and five yearling lambs for a *p* offering.
7:41 and five yearling lambs for a *p* offering.
7:47 and five yearling lambs for a *p* offering.
7:53 and five yearling lambs for a *p* offering.
7:59 and five yearling lambs for a *p* offering.
7:65 and five yearling lambs for a *p* offering.
7:71 and five yearling lambs for a *p* offering.
7:77 and five yearling lambs for a *p* offering.
7:83 and five yearling lambs for a *p* offering.
7:88 The animals for the *p* offerings were,
10:10 over your holocausts and your *p* offerings;
15: 8 of a vow, or as a *p* offering to the LORD,
29:39 and *p* offerings you present as your votive
Dt 2:26 king of Heshbon, with this offer of *p*:
20:10 attack a city, first offer it terms of *p*.
20:11 your terms of *p* and opens its gates to you,
20:12 *p* with you and instead offers you battle,
23: 7 their *p* and prosperity as long as you live.
27: 7 sacrifice *p* offerings and eat them there,
Jos 8:31 holocausts and *p* offerings to the LORD.
10: 1 of Gibeon had made their *p* with Israel,
10: 4 concluded *p* with Joshua and the Israelites.
11:19 Gibeon, no city made *p* with the Israelites;
11:23 And the land enjoyed *p*.
14:15 And the land enjoyed *p*.
21:44 it, the LORD gave them *p* on every side,
22:23 grain offerings or *p* offerings upon it,
22:27 holocausts, sacrifices, and *p* offerings.
Jgs 4:17 Kenite Heber were at *p* with one another.
20:26 holocausts and *p* offerings before the LORD.
21: 4 and offered holocausts and *p* offerings.
21:13 at the rock Rimmon, offering them *p*.
1Sm 1:17 Eli said, "Go in *p*,
7:14 was *p* between Israel and the Amorites.
10: 8 holocausts and to sacrifice *p* offerings.
11:15 *p* offerings there before the LORD,
13: 9 "Bring me the holocaust and *p* offerings,"
20:13 you of it and send you on your way in *p*.
20:42 length Jonathan said to David, "Go in *p*,
25: 6 Say to him, *P* be with you,
25:35 "Go up to your home in *p*!
2Sm 3:21 bade Abner farewell, and he went away in *p*.

3:22 him in Hebron but had gone his way in *p*.
3:23 he has been sent on his way in *p*."
6:17 holocausts and *p* offerings before the LORD.
10:19 then made *p* with the Israelites and became
15:27 you and Abiathar return to the city in *p*,
17: 3 then all the people will be at *p*."
24:25 and offered holocausts and *p* offerings.
1Kgs 2: 5 for the blood of war in a time of *p*,
2:33 be the *p* of the LORD forever for David,
3:15 Lord, offered holocausts and *p* offerings,
5: 4 he had *p* on all his borders round about.
5:18 LORD, my God, has given me *p* on all sides.
5:26 and there was *p* between Hiram and Solomon,
8:63 Solomon offered as *p* offerings to the LORD
8:64 offerings, and the fat of the *p* offerings,
9:25 *p* offerings on the altar which he had built
20:18 they have come out for *p* or for war,
22:17 Let each of them go back home in *p*.'"
22:45 also made *p* with the king of Israel.
2Kgs 5:19 "Go in *p*," Elisha said to him.
18:31 Make *p* with me and surrender!
20:19 will be *p* and security in my lifetime."
22:20 you shall go to your grave in *p*,
1Chr 12:19 *P*, *p* to you, and *p* to him who helps you;
16: 1 up holocausts and *p* offerings to God.
16: 2 offering up the holocausts and *p* offerings,
19:19 made *p* with David and became his subjects.
21:26 and offered up holocausts and *p* offerings.
22: 9 I will bestow *p* and tranquillity on Israel.
2Chr 7: 7 holocausts and the fat of the *p* offerings,
13:23 time, ten years of *p* began in the land.
14: 4 of Judah, and under him the kingdom had *p*.
14: 5 for the land had *p* and no war was waged
14: 5 years, because the LORD had given him *p*.
15: 5 there was no *p* for anyone to go or come,
18:16 Let each of them go back home in *p*.'"
20:30 Jehoshaphat's kingdom enjoyed *p*,
29:35 along with the fat of the *p* offerings and
30:22 slaying *p* offerings and singing praises to
31: 2 in regard to holocausts or *p* offerings,
33:16 on it *p* offerings and thank offerings,
34:28 and you shall be taken to your grave in *p*.
Ezr 9:12 Never promote their *p* and prosperity;
Tb 7:11 May he grant you mercy and *p*."
7:12 heaven grant both of you *p* and prosperity."
10:12 Go in *p*, my daughter;
10:13 Go in *p*, my child.
10:13 kissed them both and sent them away in *p*.
12: 5 that you have brought back, and go in *p*."
Jdt 3: 1 to him to sue for *p* in these words:
7:24 in not making *p* with the Assyrians.
8:35 and the rulers said to her, "Go in *p*,
Est B: 2 to restore the *p* desired by all men.
9:30 Mordecai sent documents concerning *p*
10: 3 and the herald of *p* for his whole race.
1Mc 6:49 He made *p* with the men of Beth-zur,
6:58 and make *p* with them and all their nation.
6:61 he sent *p* terms to the Jews,
7:13 among the Israelites to seek *p* with them,
8:22 the Jews as a record of *p* and alliance:
9:58 companions are living in *p* and security.
9:70 sent ambassadors to make *p* with him
10: 4 first to make *p* with him
10: 4 before he makes *p* with Alexander
10:66 returned in *p* and happiness to Jerusalem.
11:50 So they threw down their arms and made *p*.
11:62 to him for mercy, and he granted them *p*.
11:66 When they sued for *p*,
13:40 Let there be *p* between us."
13:45 loud voices, begging Simon to grant them *p*.
13:50 out to Simon for peace, and he gave them *p*.
14: 8 The people cultivated their land in *p*;
14:11 He brought *p* to the land,
16:10 He then returned to Judea in *p*.
2Mc 1: 1 the Jews in Egypt, and wish them true *p*!
1: 4 law and his commandments and grant you *p*.
3: 1 While the holy city lived in perfect *p* and
12: 2 would not allow them to live in *p*.
12:12 respects, Judas agreed to make *p* with them.
13:25 of that city were angered by the *p* treaty;
14: 6 keep the kingdom from enjoying *p* and quiet.
14:10 it is impossible for the state to enjoy *p*."
Jb 3:26 I have no *p* nor ease;
5:23 and the wild beasts shall be at *p* with you.
16:12 I was in *p*, but he dislodged me;
22:21 Come to terms with him to be at *p*.
Ps(s) 29:11 may the LORD bless his people with *p*!
34:15 seek *p*,
37:11 land, they shall delight in abounding *p*.
37:37 for there is a future for the man of *p*.
55:19 and *p* from those who war against me,
72: 3 The mountains shall yield *p* for the people,
72: 7 shall flower in his days, and profound *p*,
85: 9 for he proclaims *p* To his people,
85:11 justice and *p* shall kiss.
119:165 Those who love your law have great *p*,
120: 6 long have I dwelt with those who hate *p*.
120: 7 When I speak of *p*, they are ready for war.
122: 6 Pray for the *p* of Jerusalem!
122: 7 May *p* be within your walls,
122: 8 and friends I will say, *P* be within you!"
125: 5 *P* be upon Israel!
128: 6 *P* be upon Israel!
147:14 He has granted *p* in your borders;
Prv 1:33 he who obeys me dwells in security, in *p*,
3: 2 For many days, and years of life, and *p*,
3:17 pleasant ways, and all her paths are *p*;
3:29 against him who lives at *p* with you.
7:14 "I owed *p* offerings,
10:10 but he who frankly reproves promotes *p*.
12:20 evil, but those who counsel *p* have joy.
14:17 of himself, but the prudent man is at *p*.
16: 7 he makes even his enemies be at *p* with him.
17: 1 Better a dry crust with *p* than a house
29: 9 he may rage or laugh but can have no *p*.
Eccl 3: 8 a time of war, and a time of *p*.
Wis 3: 3 But they are in *p*.
14:22 war of ignorance, they call such evils *p*.
Sir 1:16 with blossoms of *p* and perfect health.
13:17 there be *p* between the hyena and the dog?
13:17 the rich and the poor can there be *p*?
20: 1 and a man may be wise to hold his *p*.
28: 9 and sows discord among those at *p*.
28:13 for they destroy the *p* of many.
28:16 it has no rest, nor can he dwell in *p*.
35: 1 the commandments sacrifices a *p* offering.
41: 1 you for the man at *p* amid his possessions,
44: 6 established and at *p* in their own estates
47:13 SOLOMON reigned during an era of *p*,
50:23 you joy of heart and may *p* abide among you;
Is 9: 5 God-Hero, Father-Forever, Prince of *P*.
26: 3 you keep in *p*; in peace, for its trust in you
26:12 O LORD, you mete out *p* to us,
27: 5 He must make *p* with me; *p* shall he make
32:17 Justice will bring about *p*;
36:16 'Make *p* with me and surrender!
38:17 thus is my bitterness transformed into *p*.
39: 8 will be *p* and security in my lifetime."
48:22 [There is no *p* for the wicked,
52: 7 him who brings glad tidings, Announcing *p*,
54:10 leave you nor my covenant of *p* be shaken,
54:13 and great shall be the *p* of your children.
55:12 depart, in *p* you shall be brought back;
57: 2 of evil, the just man enters into *p*;
57:19 *P*, peace to the far and the near,
57:21 No *p* for the wicked!
59: 8 The way of *p* they know not,
59: 8 crooked, whoever treads them knows no *p*.
60:17 I will appoint *p* your governor,
Jer 4:10 *P* shall be yours;
6:14 *P*, *p*!" they say, though there is no *p*.
8:11 *P*, *p*!" they say, though there is no *p*.
8:15 We wait for *p* to no avail;
12: 5 And if in a land of *p* you fall headlong,
12:12 no *p* for all mankind.
14:13 I will give you lasting *p* in this place."
14:19 We wait for *p*, to no avail;
23:17 the word of the LORD, *P* shall be yours";
27:11 him I will leave in *p* on its own land,
28: 9 But the prophet who prophesies *p* is
30: 5 fear reigns, not *p*.
33: 6 reveal to them an abundance of lasting *p*.
34: 5 You shall die in *p*,
49:31 set out against a nation that is at *p*,
Lam 3:17 My soul is deprived of *p*,
Bar 3:13 of God, you would have dwelt in enduring *p*.
3:14 and life, where light of the eyes, and *p*.
4:20 I have taken off the garment of *p*,
5: 4 be named by God forever the *p* of justice,
6: 2 I will bring you back from there in *p*.
Ez 7:25 When anguish comes they shall seek *p*,
13:10 saying, *P*!" when there was no *p*,
13:16 it visions of *p* when there was no peace,
34:25 I will make a covenant of *p* with them,
37:26 I will make with them a covenant of *p*;
43:27 holocausts and *p* offerings on the altar.
45:15 and *p* offerings and atonement sacrifices,
45:17 offerings, holocausts, and *p* offerings,
46: 2 offer his holocausts and *p* offerings,
46:12 LORD, whether holocausts or *p* offerings,
46:12 or his *p* offerings as on the sabbath;
Dn 3:98 they dwell on earth: abundant *p*!
6:26 "All *p* to you!
11: 6 the king of the north in the interest of *p*.
Am 5:22 nor consider your stall-fed *p* offerings.
Ob 1: 7 those at *p* with you;
Mi 3: 5 teeth have something to bite, announce *p*,
5: 4 he shall be *p*.
Na 2: 1 the bearer of good news, announcing *p*!
Hg 2: 9 And in this place I will give you *p*,
Zec 7: 7 cities were inhabited and at *p*,
8:12 LORD of hosts, for it is the seedtime of *p*:
8:16 and *p* in the judgments at your gates,
8:19 only love faithfulness and *p*.
9:10 and he shall proclaim *p* to the nations.
Mal 2: 5 covenant with him was one of life and *p*;
Mt 10:34 that my mission on earth is to spread *p*.
10:34 My mission is to spread, not *p*,
26:49 went over to Jesus, said to him, *P*,
28: 9 Jesus stood before them and said, *P*!"
Mk 5:34 Go in *p* and be free of this illness."
9:50 and you will be at *p* with one another."
Lk 1:79 death, to guide our feet into the way of *p*."
2:14 *p* on earth to those on whom his favor
2:29 Master, you can dismiss your servant in *p*;
7:50 Now go in *p*."
8:48 Now go in *p*."
10: 5 any house, first say, *P* to this house.'
10: 6 man there, your *p* will rest on him;
12:51 I have come to establish *p* on the earth?
14:32 still at a distance, asking for terms of *p*.
19:38 *P* in heaven and glory in the highest!"
19:42 only you had known the path to *p* this day;
24:36 in their midst [and said to them, *P* to you."]
Jn 14:27 *P*' is my farewell to you, my *p* is my gift
14:27 do not give it to you as the world gives *p*.
16:33 you all this that in me you may find *p*.
20:19 *P* be with you," he said.
20:21 *P* be with you," he said again.
20:26 *P* be with you,"
Acts 9:31 Galilee, and Samaria the church was at *p*.
10:36 the good news of *p* proclaimed through
15:24 discussions and disturbed your *p* of mind.
16:20 are agitators disturbing the *p* of our city!
24: 2 through your efforts we enjoy great *p*.
Rom 1: 7 grace and *p* from God our Father and the
2:10 and *p* for everyone who has done good,
3:17 The path of *p* is unknown to them;
5: 1 *p* with God through our Lord Jesus Christ.
8: 6 but that of the spirit toward life and *p*.
14:17 of eating or drinking, but of justice, *p*,
14:19 work for *p* and to strengthen one another.
15:13 fill you with all joy and *p* in believing
15:33 May the God of *p* be with you all.
16:20 *p* will quickly crush Satan under your feet.
1Cor 1: 3 Grace and *p* from God our Father and the
7:15 God has called you to live in *p*.
14:33 God is a God, not of confusion, but of *p*.
16:11 come to me by sending him on his way in *p*.
2Cor 1: 2 Grace and *p* from God our Father and the
13:11 harmony and *p*, and the God of love and *p*
Gal 1: 3 We wish you the favor and *p* of God our
5:22 the fruit of the spirit is love, joy, *p*,
6:16 *P* and mercy on all who follow this rule of
Eph 1: 2 Grace and *p* to you from God our Father and
2:14 It is he who is our *p*,
2:15 from us who had been two and to make *p*,
2:17 the good news of *p* to you who were far off,
4: 3 as its origin and *p* as its binding force.
6:15 propagate the gospel of *p* as your footgear.
6:23 grant the brothers *p* and love and faith.
Phil 1: 2 Grace and *p* be yours from God our Father
4: 7 Then God's own *p*,
4: 9 Then will the God of *p* be with you.
Col 1: 2 May God our Father give you grace and *p*.
1:20 making *p* through the blood of his cross.
3:15 Christ's *p* must reign in your hearts,
3:15 one body you have been called to that *p*.
1Thes 1: 1 Grace and *p* be yours.
4:11 remain at *p* and attend to your own affairs.
5: 3 when people are saying, *P* and security,"
5:13 Remain at *p* with one another.
5:23 the God of *p* make you perfect in holiness.
2Thes 1: 2 Grace and *p* be yours from God the Father
3:16 who is the Lord of *p* give you continued *p*
1Tm 1: 2 and *p* be yours from God the Father and
3: 3 but, rather, gentle, a man of *p*.
2Tm 1: 2 and *p* from God the Father and from Christ
2:22 and pursue integrity, faith, love, and *p*,
Ti 1: 4 May grace and *p* from God our Father,
Phlm 1: 3 Grace to you and *p* from God our Father and
Heb 7: 2 also king of Salem, that is, "king of *p*."
12:11 it brings forth the fruit of *p* and justice
12:14 Strive for *p* with all men,
13:20 May the God of *p*,
Jas 3:18 is sown in *p* for those who cultivate peace.
1Pt 1: 2 Favor and *p* be yours in abundance.
3:11 and do good, seek *p* and follow after it,
5:14 *P* to all of you who are in Christ.
2Pt 1: 2 may grace be yours and *p* in abundance
3:14 stain or defilement, and at *p* in his sight.
1Jn 3:19 are at *p* before him no matter
2Jn 1: 3 and *p* from God the Father and from Jesus
3Jn 1:15 *P* be with you.
Jude 1: 2 May mercy, *p*,
Rv 1: 4 John wishes you grace and *p*—
6: 4 *p* by allowing men to slaughter one another.

PEACE-OFFERING (1)

Lv 4:35 just as the fat is removed from the *p* lamb,

PEACE-OFFERINGS (1)

2Kgs 16:13 sprinkling the blood of his *p* on the altar.

PEACEABLE (3)

1Mc 7:27 to Judas and his brothers this *p* message:
Lk 10: 6 If there is a *p* man there,
Jas 3:17 It is also *p*, lenient, docile,

PEACEABLY (8)

Jgs 11:13 Now restore the same *p*."
1Sm 29: 7 Withdraw *p*, now, and do nothing
1Mc 7:28 I will come with a few men to meet you *p*."
7:29 to Judas, and they greeted one another *p*.
7:33 people came out to greet him *p*
10:47 he had been the first to address them *p*,
Sir 12:11 though he acts humbly and *p* toward you,

PEACEABLY (cont.)

Rom 12:18 If possible, live *p* with everyone.

PEACEFUL (25)

1Sm 16: 4 meet him and inquired, "Is your visit *p*,
1Kgs 2: 6 him to go down to the grave in *p* old age.
1Chr 4:40 and the land was spacious, quiet, and *p*.
22: 9 He will be a *p* man,
Est E: 8 the kingdom undisturbed and *p* for all men,
1Mc 1:30 He spoke to them deceitfully in *p* terms,
5:48 Then Judas sent them this *p* message:
7:10 to Judas and his brothers in *p* terms.
8:20 us to you to make a *p* alliance with you,
10: 3 a letter to Jonathan written in *p* terms,
11: 2 He entered Syria with *p* words,
11:38 King Demetrius saw that the land was *p*
11:52 throne, and the land was *p* under his rule,
13:37 We are willing to be on most *p* terms with
2Mc 4: 6 would be impossible to have a *p* government,
10:12 endeavored to have *p* relations with them.
Ps(s) 35:20 but against the *p* in the land they
Wis 18:14 For when *p* stillness compassed everything
Sir 26: 2 joy to her husband, *p* and full is his life.
Is 9: 6 His dominion is vast and forever *p*,
32:18 My people will live in *p* country,
Jer 25:37 place, desolate lie the *p* pastures;
33: 9 over all the *p* benefits I will give her.
Ez 34:29 prepare for them *p* fields for planting;
38:11 the *p* people who are living in security,

PEACEFULLY (11)

2Sm 3:24 Why did you let him go *p* on his way?
1Chr 12:18 "If you come *p*,
Tb 14: 1 died *p* at the age of a hundred and twelve,
Jdt 7:15 rebellion and their refusal to meet you *p*."
1Mc 5:25 who received them *p* and told them all that
7:15 He spoke with them *p* and swore to them,
2Mc 5:25 he pretended to be *p* disposed and waited
Ps(s) 4: 9 As soon as I lie down, I fall *p* asleep,
Sir 44:14 Their bodies are *p* laid away,
Is 14: 7 The whole earth rests *p*,
Heb 11:31 for she had *p* received the spies.

PEACEMAKERS (1)

Mt 5: 9 Blest too the *p*;

PEAK (1)

Jer 22: 6 to me like Gilead, like the *p* of Lebanon,

PEAKS (2)

Jdt 5: 1 fortified the summits of all the higher *p*,
Jer 17: 3 on the high hills, the *p* in the highland.]

PEALS (8)

Ex 9:23 the LORD sent forth hail and *p* of thunder.
19:16 day there were *p* of thunder and lightning,
Rv 4: 5 came flashes of lightning and *p* of thunder;
8: 5 *P* of thunder and flashes of lightning
11:19 were flashes of lightning and *p* of thunder,
14: 2 roaring of the deep, or loud *p* of thunder;
16:18 lightning flashes and *p* of thunder,
19: 6 of the deep, or mighty *p* of thunder,

PEARL (2)

Mt 13:46 When he found one really valuable *p*,
Rv 21:21 twelve pearls, each made of a single *p*;

PEARLS (9)

Jb 28:18 it surpasses *p* and Arabian topaz.
Prv 31:10 a worthy wife, her value is far beyond *p*.
Mt 7: 6 holy to dogs or toss your *p* before swine.
13:45 is like a merchant's search for fine *p*.
1Tm 2: 9 in fancy hair styles, gold ornaments, *p*,
Rv 17: 4 adorned with gold and *p* and other jewels.
18:12 of gold and silver, precious stones and *p*;
18:16 Adorned all in gold and jewels and *p*!
21:21 The twelve gates were twelve *p*,

PEBBLE (3)

2Sm 17:13 so that not even a *p* of it can be found."
1Mc 10:73 is not a stone or a *p* or a place to flee."
Am 9: 9 a sieve, letting no *p* fall to the ground.

PEBBLES (1)

Jb 22:24 the fine gold of Ophir as *p* from the brook,

PECKING (2)

Gn 40:17 *p* at them out of the basket on my head."
40:19 birds will be *p* the flesh from your body."

PECULIARLY (3)

Dt 7: 6 face of the earth to be a people *p* his own.
14: 2 face of the earth to be a people *p* his own.
26:18 you are to be a people *p* his own,

PEDAHEL (1)

Nm 34:28 *P*, son of Ammihud."

PEDAHZUR (5)

Nm 1:10 Gamaliel, son of *P*,
2:20 [Their prince was Gamaliel, son of *P*,
7:54 day it was the turn of Gamaliel, son of *P*,
7:59 was the offering of Gamaliel, son of *P*.
10:23 over their host, and Gamaliel, son of *P*,

PEDAIAH (8)

2Kgs 23:36 mother's name was Zebidah, daughter of *P*,
1Chr 3:18 Shealtiel, Malchiram, *P*,
3:19 The sons of *P* were Zerubbabel and Shimei.
27:20 half-tribe of Manasseh, Joel, son of *P*;
Neh 3:25 After him, *P*,
8: 4 Hilkiah, and Maaseiah, and on his left *P*,
11: 7 son of Joed, son of *P*
13:13 priest Shelemiah, Zadok the scribe, and *P*,

PEDDLES (1)

Prv 13:16 but the fool *p* folly.

PEDESTAL (1)

Ex 38:27 of the veil, one talent for each *p*,

PEDESTALS (45)

Ex 26:19 forty silver *p* under the twenty boards,
26:19 so that there are two *p* under each board,
26:21 the north side, with their forty silver *p*,
26:25 sixteen silver *p*, two *p* under each board.
26:32 of gold and shall rest on four silver *p*.
26:37 and cast five bronze *p* for them.
27:10 with twenty columns and twenty *p* of bronze;
27:11 with twenty columns and twenty *p* of bronze;
27:12 cubits long, with ten columns and ten *p*.
27:14 cubits, with three columns and three *p*;
27:15 cubits, with three columns and three *p*.
27:16 It shall have four columns and four *p*.
27:17 bands and hooks of silver, and *p* of bronze.
27:18 must be used, and the *p* must be of bronze.
35:11 boards, its bars, its columns and its *p*;
35:17 of the court, with their columns and *p*;
36:24 forty silver *p* under the twenty boards,
36:24 so that there were two *p* under each board,
36:26 the north side, with their forty silver *p*,
36:30 sixteen silver *p*, two *p* under each board.
36:36 it, and four silver *p* were cast for them.
36:38 their five *p* were of bronze.
38:10 with twenty columns and twenty *p* of bronze,
38:11 with twenty columns and twenty *p* of bronze,
38:12 cubits long, with ten columns and ten *p*,
38:14 cubits, with three columns and three *p*;
38:15 cubits, with three columns and three *p*.
38:17 The *p* of the columns were of bronze,
38:19 four columns and four *p* of bronze for it,
38:27 *p* of the sanctuary and the *p* of the veil,
38:27 one hundred talents for the one hundred *p*.
38:30 the *p* at the entrance of the meeting tent,
38:31 *p* around the court, the *p* at the entrance
39:33 the boards, the bars, the columns, the *p*,
39:40 of the court with their columns and *p*,
40:18 He placed its *p*,
Nm 3:36 of the Dwelling, its bars, columns, *p*,
3:37 of the surrounding court with their *p*,
4:31 the Dwelling with its bars, columns and *p*,
4:32 of the surrounding court with their *p*,
Jb 38: 6 Into what were its *p* sunk,

PEEL (2)

Tb 11: 8 cataracts shrink and *p* off from his eyes;
11:13 used both hands to *p* off the cataracts.

PEELED (1)

Gn 30:38 The rods that he had thus *p* he then set

PEELING (1)

Gn 30:37 made white stripes in them by *p* off the bark

PEEPS (2)

Sir 14:23 Who *p* through her windows,
21:23 A boor *p* through the doorway of a house,

PEER (3)

Sir 23:19 step a man takes and *p* into hidden corners.
Jn 20: 5 He did not enter but bent down to *p* in,
20:11 Even as she wept, she stooped to *p* inside,

PEERED (2)

Jgs 5:28 *p* down and wailed the mother of Sisera,
2Mc 3:19 to the walls, others *p* through the windows,

PEERING (1)

Sg 2: 9 the windows, *p* through the lattices.

PEERS (1)

Jas 1:25 the man who *p* into freedom's ideal law and

PEG (9)

Jgs 4:21 got a tent *p* and took a mallet in her hand.
4:21 *p* through his temple down into the ground,
4:22 dead, with the tent *p* through his temple.
5:26 With her left hand she reached for the *p*,
Sir 26:12 *p* and opens her quiver for every arrow.
27: 2 Like a *p* driven between fitted stones,
Is 22:23 I will fix him like a *p* in a sure spot,
22:25 the *p* fixed in a sure spot shall give way,
Ez 15: 3 Can you make even a *p* from it,

PEGS (11)

Ex 27:19 tent *p* and all the tent pegs of the court,
35:18 tent *p* for the Dwelling and for the court,
38:20 All the tent *p* for the Dwelling and for
38:31 and all the tent *p* for the Dwelling and
39:40 of the court with its ropes and tent *p*,
Nm 3:37 court with their pedestals, *p* and ropes.
4:32 court with their pedestals, *p* and ropes.
Jb 4:21 The *p* of their tent are plucked up;
Sir 14:24 and fastens his tent *p* next to her walls;
Is 33:20 be struck, Whose *p* will never be pulled up,

PEKAH (11)

2Kgs 15:25 His adjutant *P*, son of Remaliah,
15:27 year of Azariah, king of Judah, *P*,
15:29 During the reign of *P*,
15:30 Hoshea, son of Elah, conspired against *P*,
15:31 son of Uzziah] The rest of the acts of *P*,
15:32 In the second year of *P*,
15:37 first loosed Rezin, king of Aram, and *P*,
16: 1 In the seventeenth year of *P*,
16: 5 Then Rezin, king of Aram, and *P*,
2Chr 28: 6 For *P*, son of Remaliah,
Is 7: 1 son of Uzziah, Rezin, king of Aram, and *P*,

PEKAHIAH (3)

2Kgs 15:22 and his son *P* succeeded him as king.
15:23 year of Azariah, king of Judah, *P*,
15:26 The rest of the acts of *P*,

PEKOD (2)

Jer 50:21 of Merathaim, and those who live in *P*;
Ez 23:23 the men of Babylon and all of Chaldea, *P*,

PELAIAH (3)

1Chr 3:24 of Elioenai were Hodaviah, Eliashib, *P*,
Neh 8: 7 and *P* explained the law to the people,
10:11 brethren Shebaniah, Hodiah, Kelita, *P*,

PELALIAH (1)

Neh 11:12 Adaiah, son of Jeroham, son of *P*,

PELATIAH (5)

1Chr 3:21 The sons of Hananiah were *P*,
4:42 to Mount Seir under the leadership of *P*,
Neh 10:23 Hezir, Meshezabel, Zadok, Jaddua, *P*,
Ez 11: 1 whom were Jaazaniah, son of Azzur, and *P*,
11:13 While I was prophesying, *P*,

PELEG (8)

Gn 10:25 the name of the first was *P*,
11:16 years old, he became the father of *P*.
11:17 and thirty years after the birth of *P*,
11:18 When *P* was thirty years old,
11:19 *P* lived two hundred and nine years after
1Chr 1:19 *P* (for in his time the world was divided),
1:25 Shem, Arpachshad, Shelah, Eber, *P*,
Lk 3:35 Nahor, son of Serug, son of Reu, son of *P*,

PELET (2)

1Chr 2:47 of Jahdai were Regem, Jotham, Geshan, *P*,
12: 3 also Jeziel and *P*,

PELETH (1)

1Chr 2:33 The sons of Jonathan were *P* and Zaza.

PELETHITES (7)

2Sm 8:18 was in command of the Cherethites and *P*.
15:18 As all the Cherethites and *P*,
20: 7 So Joab and the Cherethites and *P* and all
20:23 was in command of the Cherethites and *P*.
1Kgs 1:38 and the Cherethites and *P* went down,
1:44 of Jehoiada, and the Cherethites and *P*,
1Chr 18:17 in command of the Cherethites and the *P*;

PELUSIUM (1)

Ez 30:15 I will pour out my wrath on *P*,

PEN (3)

Ps(s) 45: 2 is nimble as the *p* of a skillful scribe.
Jer 8: 8 falsehood by the lying *p* of the scribes!
3Jn 1:13 do not wish to write it out with *p* and ink.

PENALTY (23)

Lv 5:19 *p* of the guilt must be paid to the LORD."

19: 8 whoever eats of it then shall pay the *p*
20:17 the man shall pay the *p* of having had
20:19 whoever does so shall pay the *p* of incest.
20:20 aunt shall pay the *p* by dying childless.
24:15 curses his God shall bear the *p* of his sin;
Nm 35:31 of a murderer who deserves the death *p*;
Jos 22:23 upon it, the LORD himself will exact the *p*.
Est 4:11 summoned, suffers the automatic *p* of death,
2Mc 6:22 in this way he would escape the death *p*,
Prv 19:19 The man of violent temper pays the *p*;
22: 3 simpletons continue on and suffer the *p*.
27:12 simpletons continue on and suffer the *p*.
30:10 he curse you, and you have to pay the *p*.
Lam 4: 6 my people is greater than the *p* of Sodom,
Ez 16:58 *p* of your lewdness and your abominations
23:35 bear the *p* of your lewdness and harlotry.
23:49 inflict on you the *p* of your lewdness,
Dn 13:61 they inflicted on them the *p* they had
Lk 23:22 about him that calls for the death *p*.
Acts 25:11 death, I do not seek to escape that *p*.
Rom 1:27 own persons the *p* for their perversity.
2Thes 1: 9 Such as these will suffer the *p* of eternal

PENANCE (3)

Jdt 4: 9 cried to God with great fervor and did *p*—
Is 58: 5 of fasting I wish, of keeping a day of *p*:
Lk 24:47 *p* for the remission of sins is to be

PENDANT (3)

Ex 13:16 on your hand and as a *p* on your forehead:
Dt 6: 8 and let them be as a *p* on your forehead.
11:18 sign, and let them be a *p* on your forehead.

PENDANTS (6)

Jgs 8:26 in addition to the crescents and *p*,
Sg 1:10 Your cheeks lovely in *p*,
1:11 *p* of gold for you and silver ornaments.
Is 3:19 the *p*,
Ez 16:12 neck, a ring in your nose, *p* in your ears,
28:13 Of gold your *p* and jewels were made,

PENETRATE (7)

Jb 11: 7 Can you *p* the designs of God?
41: 5 outer garment, or *p* his double corselet?
Ps(s) 109:18 may it *p* into his entrails like water and
Sir 18: 4 increase, nor *p* the wonders of the LORD.
Jer 21:13 will attack us, who can *p* our retreats?"
Dn 11:17 to *p* the entire strength of his kingdom.
Mk 7:19 It does not *p* his being,

PENETRATED (8)

Lv 13: 3 itself shows that it has *p* below the skin,
13: 4 but does not seem to have *p* below the skin,
13:25 and this seems to have *p* below the skin,
13:30 find that the sore has *p* below the skin
13:31 finds that it has not *p* below the skin,
13:32 and does not seem to have *p* below the skin,
13:34 skin and that it has not *p* below the skin,
Jos 11:21 At that time Joshua *p* the mountain regions

PENETRATES (4)

Jb 28: 3 to the farthest confines he *p*.
Wis 7:24 and she *p* and pervades all things by
Sir 42:18 He plumbs the depths and *p* the heart;
Heb 4:12 It *p* and divides soul and spirit,

PENIEL (1)

Gn 32:31 Jacob named the place *P*,

PENINNAH (4)

1Sm 1: 2 two wives, one named Hannah, the other *P*;
1: 2 *P* had children,
1: 4 wife *P* and to all her sons and daughters,
1: 7 of the LORD, *P* would approach her,

PENIS (1)

Dt 23: 2 been crushed or whose *p* has been cut off

PENITENT (1)

Sir 17:19 But to the *p* he provides a way back,

PENITENTIAL (2)

Est D: 1 she took off her *p* garments and arrayed
Mal 3:14 in *p* dress in awe of the LORD of hosts?

PENNIES (1)

Lk 12: 6 Are not five sparrows sold for a few *p*?

PENNY (3)

Mt 5:26 be released until you have paid the last *p*.
Lk 12:59 from there until you have paid the last *p*."
21: 4 every *p* she had to live on."

PENT-UP (1)

Is 59:19 For it shall come like a *p* river which the

PENTAPOLIS (1)

Wis 10: 6 when he fled as fire descended upon *P*—

PENTECOST (5)

Tb 2: 1 Then on our festival of *P*,
2Mc 12:32 After this feast called *P*,
Acts 2: 1 *P* came it found them gathered in one place.
20:16 by the feast of *P* if at all possible.
1Cor 16: 8 I intend to stay in Ephesus until *P*.

PENUEL (8)

Gn 32:32 At sunrise, as he left *P*,
Jgs 8: 8 to *P* and made the same request of them,
8: 8 *P* answered him as had the men of Succoth.
8: 9 So to the men of *P*,
8:17 tower of *P* and slew the men of the city.
1Kgs 12:25 Then he left it and built up *P*.
1Chr 4: 4 *P* was the father of Gedor,
8:25 Iphdeiah, and *P* were the sons of Shashak.

PENURY (1)

Prv 14:23 is profit, but mere talk tends only to *p*.

PEOPLE (1976)

Gn 11: 6 "If now, while they are one *p*,
14:21 of Sodom said to Abram, "Give me the *p*;
17:14 such a one shall be cut off from his *p*;
18:24 there were fifty innocent *p* in the city;
18:24 the sake of the fifty innocent *p* within it?
18:26 find fifty innocent *p* in the city of Sodom,
18:28 there are five less than fifty innocent *p*?
19: 4 all the *p* to the last man
22:14 hence *p* now say,
32: 8 he divided the *p* who were with him,
34:16 you and become one kindred *p* with you.
34:22 kindred *p* with us only on this condition,
34:30 if these *p* unite against me and attack me,
35: 6 Thus Jacob and all the *p* who were with him
41:40 and all my *p* shall dart at your command.
41:55 Egypt and the *p* cried to Pharaoh for bread,
42: 6 who dispensed the rations to all the *p*.
46:26 Jacob's *p* who migrated to Egypt
46:27 all the *p* comprising Jacob's family who
47:21 Pharaoh, and the *p* were reduced to slavery,
47:23 Joseph told the *p*:
48:20 shall the *p* of Israel pronounce blessings;
50:20 his present end, the survival of many *p*.
Ex 1: 9 and powerful the Israelite *p* are growing,
1:20 The *p* too, increased and grew strong.
3: 7 "I have witnessed the affliction of my *p*
3:10 I will send you to Pharaoh to lead my *p*,
3:12 when you bring my *p* out of Egypt,
3:21 so well-disposed toward this *p* that,
4:16 He shall speak to the *p* for you:
4:21 however, so that he will not let the *p* go.
4:30 and he performed the signs before the *p*.
4:31 The *p* believed, and when they heard
5: 1 Let my *p* go, that they may celebrate
5: 4 by taking the *p* away from their work?
5: 5 how numerous the *p* of the land are already,"
5: 6 and foremen of the *p* this order:
5: 7 "You shall no longer supply the *p* with
5:10 foremen of the *p* went out and told them,
5:12 The *p*, then, scattered throughout the land
5:22 "Lord, why do you treat this *p* so badly?
5:23 name, he has maltreated this *p* of yours,
6: 7 I will take you as my own *p*,
7: 4 judgment I will bring the hosts of my *p*,
7:14 is obdurate in refusing to let the *p* go.
7:16 Let my *p* go to worship me in the desert.
7:26 Let my *p* go to worship me,
8: 4 the *p* go to offer sacrifice to the LORD.
8:16 Let my *p* go to worship me.
8:17 If you will not let my *p* go,
8:18 there shall be no flies where my *p* dwell,
8:19 distinction between my *p* and your people.
8:25 the *p* go to offer sacrifice to the LORD.
8:28 became obdurate and would not let the *p* go.
9: 1 Let my *p* go to worship me.
9: 7 obdurate and would not let the *p* go.
9:13 Let my *p* go to worship me,
9:17 way for my *p* by refusing to let them go?
10: 3 Let my *p* go to worship me.
10: 4 If you refuse to let my *p* go,
11: 2 *p* that every man is to ask his neighbor,
11: 3 the Egyptians well-disposed toward the *p*;
11: 3 servants and the *p* in the land of Egypt.
12:27 Then the *p* bowed down in worship,
12:31 and Aaron and said, "Leave my *p* at once,
12:33 The Egyptians likewise urged the *p* on,
12:34 The *p*, therefore, took their dough
12:36 Egyptians so well-disposed toward the *p*
13: 3 Moses said to the *p*,
13:17 Now, when Pharaoh let the *p* go,
13:17 the *p* see that they would have to fight,
13:22 ever left its place in front of the *p*.
14: 5 to the king of Egypt that the *p* had fled,
14:13 But Moses answered the *p*, "Fear not!
15:13 In your mercy you led the *p* you redeemed;
15:16 they were frozen like stone, while your *p*,
15:16 the *p* you had made your own passed over.
15:24 As the *p* grumbled against Moses,
16: 4 Each day the *p* are to go out and gather
16:27 day some of the *p* went out to gather it,
16:30 After that the *p* rested on the seventh day.
17: 1 Here there was no water for the *p* to drink.
17: 3 for water, the *p* grumbled against Moses,
17: 4 to the LORD, "What shall I do with this *p*?
17: 5 Moses, "Go over there in front of the *p*,
17: 6 water will flow from it for the *p* to drink."
17:13 and his *p* with the edge of the sword.
18: 1 had done for Moses and for his *p* Israel:
18:10 "who has rescued his *p* from the hands of
18:11 the *p* from the power of the Egyptians."
18:13 next day Moses sat in judgment for the *p*,
18:14 saw all that he was doing for the *p*,
18:14 thing is this that you are doing for the *p*?
18:14 Why do you sit alone while all the *p* have
18:15 "The *p* come to me to consult God.
18:18 only yourself but also these *p* with you.
18:21 all the *p* for able and God-fearing men,
18:22 decisions for the *p* in all ordinary cases.
18:23 and all these *p* will go home satisfied."
18:25 the *p* as officers over groups of thousands,
18:26 decisions for the *p* in all ordinary cases.
19: 5 possession, dearer to me than all other *p*,
19: 7 went and summoned the elders of the *p*.
19: 8 to tell them, the *p* all answered together,
19: 8 back to the LORD the response of the *p*.
19: 9 that when the *p* hear me speaking with you,
19: 9 to the LORD the response of the *p*,
19:10 "Go to the *p* and have them sanctify
19:11 Mount Sinai before the eyes of all the *p*.
19:12 limits for the *p* all around the mountain,
19:14 came down from the mountain to the *p*
19:16 so that all the *p* in the camp trembled.
19:17 led the *p* out of the camp to meet God,
19:21 "Go down and warn the *p* not to break
19:23 LORD, "The *p* cannot go up to Mount Sinai,
19:24 But the priests and the *p* must not break
19:25 went down to the *p* and told them this.
20:18 the *p* witnessed the thunder and lightning,
20:20 Moses answered the *p*,
20:21 Still the *p* remained at a distance,
21:29 in the habit of goring *p* and its owner,
22:24 to one of your poor neighbors among my *p*,
22:27 revile God, nor curse a prince of your *p*.
24: 2 the *p* shall not come up at all with Moses."
24: 3 When Moses came to the *p* and related all
24: 7 the covenant, he read it aloud to the *p*,
24: 8 took the blood and sprinkled it on the *p*,
31:14 that day, he must be rooted out of his *p*.
32: 1 When the *p* became aware of Moses' delay in
32: 3 So all the *p* took off their earrings and
32: 6 Early the next day the *p* offered
32: 7 to Moses, "Go down at once to your *p*,
32: 9 I see how stiffnecked this *p* is,"
32:11 your wrath blaze up against your own *p*,
32:12 relent in punishing your *p*.
32:14 he had threatened to inflict on his *p*.
32:17 Joshua heard the noise of the *p* shouting,
32:21 "What did this *p* ever do to you that you
32:22 well enough how prone the *p* are to evil.
32:25 their foes, Aaron had let the *p* run wild,
32:28 there fell about three thousand of the *p*.
32:30 On the next day Moses said to the *p*,
32:31 this *p* has indeed committed a grave sin in
32:34 go and lead the *p* whither I have told you.
32:35 Thus the LORD smote the *p* for having had
33: 1 "You and the *p* whom you have brought up
33: 3 company, because you are a stiff-necked *p*;
33: 4 When the *p* heard this bad news,
33: 5 You are a stiff-necked *p*.
33: 8 the *p* would all rise and stand at the
33:10 all the *p* would rise and worship at the
33:12 indeed, are telling me to lead this *p* on;
33:13 too, this nation is, after all, your own *p*."
33:16 how can it be known that we, your *p* and I,
33:16 Then we, your *p* and I,
33:16 out from every other *p* on the earth."
34: 9 This is indeed a stiff-necked *p*;
34:10 Before the eyes of all your *p* I will work
34:10 so that this *p* among whom you live may see
36: 3 morning after morning the *p* continued to
36: 5 "The *p* are bringing much more than is
36: 6 So the *p* stopped bringing their offerings;
Lv 4: 3 and thereby makes the *p* also become guilty,
7:20 the person shall be cut off from his *p*.
7:21 person, too, shall be cut off from his *p*."
7:25 such a one shall be cut off from his *p*.
7:27 of any blood shall be cut off from his *p*."
9: 7 offering of the *p* in atonement for them,
9:18 and the ram, the peace offering of the *p*.
9:22 his hands over the *p* and blessed them.
9:23 On coming out they again blessed the *p*.
9:23 of the LORD was revealed to all the *p*.
9:24 all the *p* cried out and fell prostrate.
10: 3 sight of all the *p* I will reveal my glory."
16:24 in atonement for himself and for the *p*,
16:33 the priests and all the *p* of the community.
17: 4 a man shall be cut off from among his *p*.
17:10 and will cut him off from among his *p*.
18:29 shall be cut off from among his *p*.

PEOPLE (cont.)

19: 8 Such a one shall be cut off from his *p.*
20: 3 and cut him off from the body of his *p;*
20: 5 will cut off from their *p* both him and all
20: 6 such a one and cut him off from his *p.*
20:17 off from their *p* for this shameful deed;
20:18 of them shall be cut off from their *p,*
21: 1 unclean for any dead person among his *p,*
21:14 but a virgin, taken from his own *p,*
21:15 he will have base off-spring among his *p.*
23:29 on this day shall be cut off from his *p,*
23:30 I will remove him from the midst of his *p.*
24:11 So the *p* brought him to Moses,
26:12 I will be your God, and you will be my *p;*
Nm 5:21 malediction and imprecation among your *p*
5:27 an example of imprecation among her *p.*
9:13 the Passover, shall be cut off from his *p,*
11: 1 *p* complained in the hearing of the LORD;
11: 2 But when the *p* cried out to Moses,
11: 8 the *p* would grind it between millstones or
11:10 When Moses heard the *p,*
11:11 that you burden me with all this *p?*
11:12 Was it I who conceived all this *p?*
11:13 Where can I get meat to give to all this *p?*
11:14 I cannot carry all this *p* by myself,
11:16 true elders and authorities among the *p,*
11:17 may share the burden of the *p* with you.
11:18 "To the *p,* however, you shall say:
11:21 "The *p* around me include six hundred
11:24 out and told the *p* what the LORD had said.
11:24 Gathering seventy elders of the *p,*
11:29 that all the *p* of the LORD were prophets!
11:32 the next day the *p* gathered in the quail.
11:33 the LORD's wrath flared up against the *p,*
11:34 it was there that the greedy *p* were buried.
11:35 the *p* set out for Hazeroth.
12:15 and the *p* did not start out again until
12:16 After that the *p* set out from Hazeroth and
13:18 Are the *p* living there strong or weak,
13:28 *p* who are living in the land are fierce,
13:30 however, to quiet the *p* toward Moses,
13:31 with him said, "We cannot attack these *p;*
13:32 And all the *p* we saw there are huge men,
14: 1 cries, and even in the night the *p* wailed.
14: 9 need not be afraid of the *p* of that land;
14:11 to Moses, "How long will this *p* spurn me?
14:13 you brought out this *p* from among them.
14:14 you, O LORD, are in the midst of this *p;*
14:15 If now you slay this whole *p,*
14:16 this *p* into the land he swore to give them;
14:19 this *p* in keeping with your great kindness,
14:39 the Israelites, the *p* felt great remorse.
15:26 fault of inadvertence affects all the *p.*
15:30 and shall be cut off from among his *p.*
17: 6 "It is you who have slain the LORD's *p.*"
17:12 the blow was already falling on the *p.*
17:12 the incense and made atonement for the *p,*
20: 1 first month, and the *p* settled at Kadesh.
20: 3 The *p* contended with Moses,
20:24 "Aaron is about to be taken to his *p,*
21: 2 "If you deliver this *p* into my hand,
21: 5 the *p* complained against God and Moses,
21: 6 among the *p* saraph serpents, which bit the *p*
21: 7 Then the *p* came to Moses and said,
21: 7 So Moses prayed for the *p,*
21:16 LORD said to Moses, "Bring the *p* together,
21:18 princes sank, that the nobles of the *p* dug,
21:29 You are ruined, O *p* of Chemosh!
21:33 with all his *p* to give battle at Edrei.
21:34 deliver him with all his *p* and his land.
21:35 him down with his sons and all his *p,*
22: 5 "A *p* has come here from Egypt who now
22: 6 Please come and curse this *p*
22:11 'This *p* that came here from Egypt now
22:12 not go with them and do not curse this *p,*
22:17 come and lay a curse on this *p* for me."
23: 9 Here is a *p* that lives apart and does not
23:24 Here is a *p* that springs up like a lioness,
24:14 now that I am about to go to my own *p,*
24:14 what this *p* will do to your *p* in the days
24:24 deliver his *p* from the hands of the Kittim?
25: 1 the *p* degraded themselves by having
25: 2 *p* to the sacrifices of their god, and the *p*
25: 4 Moses, "Gather all the leaders of the *p,*
27:13 it, you too shall be taken to your *p,*
31: 2 and then you shall be taken to your *p.*"
31: 3 So Moses told the *p,*
31:11 with the *p* and beasts they had captured,
33:14 there was no water for the *p* to drink.
Dt 1:28 that the *p* are stronger and taller than we
2: 4 Give this order to the *p:*
2:10 a *p* strong and numerous and tall like the
2:16 an end to all the soldiers among the *p,*
2:21 a *p* strong and numerous and tall like the
2:32 So Sihon and all his *p* advanced against us
2:33 we defeated him and his sons and all his *p.*
3: 1 us with all his *p* to give battle at Edrei.
3: 2 into your hand with all his *p* and his land.
3: 3 hands Og, king of Bashan, with all his *p.*
3:28 he shall cross at the head of this *p*
4: 6 nation is truly a wise and intelligent *p.*'
4:10 and he said to me, 'Assemble the *p* for me;
4:20 Egypt, that you might be his very own *p,*
4:33 Did a *p* ever hear the voice of God
5:28 heard the words these *p* have spoken to you,
7: 6 For you are a *p* sacred to the LORD,
7: 6 of the earth to be a *p* peculiarly his own.
9: 2 to the sky, the Anakim, a *p* great and tall.
9: 6 to possess, for you are a stiff-necked *p.*
9:12 for your *p* whom you have brought out of
9:13 I have seen now how stiff-necked this *p* is,'
9:26 O Lord GOD, destroy not your *p,*
9:27 this *p* nor upon their wickedness and sin,
9:28 *p* from whose land you have brought us say,
9:29 are, after all, your *p* and your heritage,
10:11 now and set out at the head of your *p,*
13:10 the rest of the *p* shall join in with you.
14: 2 For you are a *p* sacred to the LORD,
14: 2 of the earth to be a *p* peculiarly his own.
14:21 itself, for you are a *p* sacred to the LORD,
16:18 *p* in all the communities which the LORD,
17: 7 afterward all the *p* are to join in.
17:13 And all the *p,* on hearing of it,
17:16 *p* go back again to Egypt to acquire them,
18: 3 a right to the following things from the *p:*
20:11 all the *p* to be found in it shall serve
21: 8 Absolve, O LORD, your *p* Israel,
21: 8 blood remain in the midst of your *p* Israel.'
26:15 and bless your *p* Israel and the soil you
26:18 you are to be a *p* peculiarly his own,
26:19 and you will be a *p* sacred to the LORD,
27: 1 elders of Israel, gave the *p* this order:
27: 9 This day you have become the *p* of the LORD,
27:11 That same day Moses gave the *p* this order:
27:12 Gerizim to pronounce blessings over the *p,*
27:15 And all the *p* shall answer, 'Amen!'
27:16 And all the *p* shall answer, 'Amen!'
27:17 And all the *p* shall answer, 'Amen!'
27:18 And all the *p* shall answer, 'Amen!'
27:19 And all the *p* shall answer, 'Amen!'
27:20 And all the *p* shall answer, 'Amen!'
27:21 And all the *p* shall answer, 'Amen!'
27:22 And all the *p* shall answer, 'Amen!'
27:23 And all the *p* shall answer, 'Amen!'
27:24 And all the *p* shall answer, 'Amen!'
27:25 And all the *p* shall answer, 'Amen!'
27:26 And all the *p* shall answer, 'Amen!'
28: 9 establish you as a *p* sacred to himself,
28:33 A *p* whom you do not know will consume the
29:12 you as his *p* and he may be your God,
31: 7 for you must bring this *p* into the land
31:12 Assemble the *p*— men, women
31:16 and then this *p* will take to rendering
32: 6 thus repaid by you, O stupid and foolish *p?*
32:28 For they are a *p* devoid of reason,
32:36 the LORD shall do justice for his *p:*
32:44 the words of this song for the *p* to hear.
32:50 climbed, and shall be taken to your *p,*
32:50 on Mount Hor and there was taken to his *p;*
33: 2 from Sinai and dawned on his *p* from Seir;
33: 5 When the chiefs of the *p* assembled and the
33: 7 you will bring him to his *p.*
33:21 while the heads of the *p* were gathered.
Jos 1: 2 *p* into the land I will give the Israelites.
1: 6 so that you may give this *p* possession of
1:10 So Joshua commanded the officers of the *p:*
1:11 "Go through the camp and instruct the *p,*
3: 3 and issued these instructions to the *p:*
3: 5 Joshua also said to the *p,*
3: 6 of the covenant and go on ahead of the *p;*
3:14 *p* struck their tents to cross the Jordan,
3:16 Thus the *p* crossed over opposite Jericho.
4: 2 to Joshua, "Choose twelve men from the *p,*
4:10 LORD had commanded Joshua to tell the *p.*
4:10 The *p* crossed over quickly,
4:19 The *p* came up from the Jordan on the tenth
5: 4 Of all the *p* who came out of Egypt,
5: 6 *p* that came forth from Egypt died off
6: 5 that signal, all the *p* shall shout aloud.
6: 7 *p* to proceed in a circle around the city,
6:10 But the *p* had been commanded by Joshua not
6:16 blew the horns and Joshua said to the *p,*
6:20 As the horns blew, the *p* began to shout.
6:20 and the *p* stormed the city in a frontal
7: 3 and advised, "Do not send all the *p* up;
7: 3 need not call for an effort from all the *p.*"
7: 4 three thousand of the *p* made the attack,
7: 5 confidence of the *p* melted away like water.
7: 7 ever allow this *p* to pass over the Jordan,
7:13 Rise, sanctify the *p.*
8: 1 the king of Ai into your power, with his *p,*
8: 5 of the *p* and I will come up to the city,
8:13 Thus the *p* took up their stations,
8:33 of the *p* of Israel on this first occasion.
9:16 learned that these *p* were from nearby,
9:19 these all remonstrated with the *p,*
10:33 Lachish, but Joshua defeated him and his *p,*
11:14 but the *p* they put to the sword,
14: 8 who went up with me discouraged the *p,*
17:14 Our *p* are too many,
17:17 "You are a numerous *p* and very strong.
24: 2 before God, Joshua addressed all the *p:*
24: 7 darkness between your *p* and the Egyptians,
24:16 But the *p* answered,
24:19 Joshua in turn said to the *p,*
24:21 But the *p* answered Joshua,
24:22 Joshua therefore said to the *p,*
24:24 Then the *p* promised Joshua,
24:25 So Joshua made a covenant with the *p* that
24:27 And Joshua said to all the *p,*
24:28 Then Joshua dismissed the *p,*
Jgs 2: 4 to all the Israelites, the *p* wept aloud,
2: 6 When Joshua dismissed the *p,*
2: 7 The *p* served the LORD during the entire
4:11 Heber had detached himself from his own *p,*
5: 2 of noble deeds by the *p* who bless the LORD,
5: 9 Israel, nobles of the *p* who bless the LORD;
5:13 *p* of the LORD came down for me as warriors.
5:18 Zebulun is the *p* defying death;
9:29 that this *p* were entrusted to my command!
9:42 next day, when the *p* were taking the field,
9:43 watched till he saw the *p* leave the city,
10:18 And among the *p* the princes of Gilead
11:11 the *p* made him their leader and commander.
11:23 the Amorites out of the way of his *p,*
14: 3 among your kinsfolk or among all our *p,*
16:24 When the *p* saw him,
16:30 the lords and all the *p* who were in it.
18: 7 They saw that the *p* dwelling there lived
18: 7 Sidonians and had no contact with other *p.*
18:10 Those against whom you go are a trusting *p,*
18:27 attacked Laish, a quiet and trusting *p;*
18:28 Sidon and they had no contact with other *p.*
20: 2 all the *p* and all the tribesmen of Israel,
20: 2 themselves in the assembly of the *p* of God.
20: 8 All the *p* rose as one man to say,
21: 2 So the *p* went to Bethel and remained there
21: 4 Early the next day the *p* built an altar
21:15 The *p* were still disconsolate over
Ru 1: 6 LORD had visited his *p* and given them food.
1:10 her they would return with her to her *p.*
1:15 has gone back to her *p* and her god.
1:16 I will lodge, your *p* shall be my people,
2:11 to a *p* whom you did not know previously.
4: 4 present, including the elders of my *p,*
4: 9 then said to the elders and to all the *p,*
1Sm 2:13 nor for the priests' duties toward the *p.*
2:24 hear the *p* of the LORD spreading about you.
2:29 part of every offering of my *p* Israel?'
4: 4 So the *p* sent to Shiloh and brought from
5: 3 *p* of Ashdod rose early the next morning,
5: 6 LORD dealt severely with the *p* of Ashdod.
5:10 entered that city, the *p* there cried out,
6:13 The *p* of Beth-shemesh were harvesting the
6:19 The *p* went into mourning at this great
8:19 The *p,* however, refused to listen
8:21 had listened to all the *p* had to say,
9: 2 he stood head and shoulders above the *p.*
9:12 *p* have a sacrifice today on the high place.
9:13 The *p* will not eat until he arrives;
9:16 are to anoint as commander of my *p* Israel.
9:16 my *p* from the clutches of the Philistines,
9:17 he is to govern my *p.*"
10: 1 You are to govern the LORD's *p* Israel,
10:17 Samuel called the *p* together to the LORD
10:23 and when he stood among the *p,*
10:24 Samuel said to all the *p,*
10:24 There is none like him among all the *p!*"
10:24 Then all the *p* shouted,
10:25 Samuel next explained to the *p* the law of
10:25 This done, Samuel dismissed the *p,*
11: 4 of Saul, they related the news to the *p,*
11: 5 "Why are the *p* weeping?"
11: 7 of the LORD, the *p* turned out to a man.
11:12 The *p* then said to Samuel:
11:14 Samuel said to the *p,*
11:15 So all the *p* went to Gilgal,
12: 6 Continuing, Samuel said to the *p:*
12:18 all the *p* dreaded the LORD and Samuel.
12:22 name the LORD will not abandon his *p,*
12:22 the LORD himself chose to make you his *p.*
13: 2 sent the rest of the *p* back to their tents.
13:14 and has appointed him commander of his *p,*
13:15 *p* went up after Saul to meet the soldiers,
14:24 the whole *p,* about ten thousand
14:24 that day, putting the *p* under this ban:
14:24 So none of the *p* tasted food.
14:26 from it, because the *p* feared the oath.
14:27 that his father had put the *p* under oath,
14:28 father put the *p* under a strict oath,
14:28 As a result the *p* are weak."
14:30 if the *p* had eaten freely today of their
14:31 Aijalon, the *p* were completely exhausted.
14:33 Informed that the *p* were sinning against
14:34 "Mingle with the *p* and tell each of them
14:39 But none of the *p* answered him.
14:40 *p* responded, "Do what you think best."
14:41 but if this guilt is in your *p* Israel,
14:41 Saul were designated, and the *p* went free.
15: 1 sent to anoint you king over his *p* Israel.
15: 8 but on the rest of the *p* he put into
15:24 In my fear of the *p,* I did what they said.
15:30 the elders of my *p* and before Israel.
18:13 led the *p* on their military expeditions,
23: 8 Saul then called all the *p* to war,
26:16 you *p* deserve death because you have not
27:12 must certainly be detested by his *p* Israel.
31: 9 Philistines to their idols and to the *p.*
2Sm 2:26 *p* to stop the pursuit of their brothers?"

3:18 'By my servant David I will save my *p* Israel
3:31 to Joab and to all the *p* who were with him,
3:32 at the grave of Abner, and the *p* also wept.
3:34 And all the *p* continued to weep for him.
3:36 All the *p* noted this with approval,
3:37 So on that day all the *p* and all Israel
5: 2 *p* Israel and shall be commander of Israel.' "
5:12 his rule for the sake of his *p* Israel.
6: 2 Then David and all the *p* who were with him
6:18 the *p* in the name of the LORD of hosts.
6:19 He then distributed among all the *p*,
6:19 With this, all the *p* left for their homes.
6:21 he appointed me commander of the LORD's *p*,
7: 7 judges whom I charged to tend my *p* Israel,
7: 8 the flock to be commander of my *p* Israel.
7:10 I will fix a place for my *p* Israel;
7:11 I first appointed judges over my *p* Israel.
7:23 on earth is there like your *p* Israel,
7:23 which God has led, redeeming it as his *p*;
7:23 and their gods out of the way of your *p*,
7:24 yourself your *p* Israel as yours forever,
8:15 and administering justice to all his *p*.
10:12 sake of our *p* and the cities of our God;
14:13 same kind of thing against the *p* of God?
14:15 because the *p* have given me cause to fear.
15:12 the *p* with Absalom increased in numbers.
16:18 and all this *p* and all Israel have chosen,
17: 2 When all the *p* with him flee,
17: 3 I can bring back the rest of the *p* to you,
17: 3 then all the *p* will be at peace."
17: 8 he will not spend the night with the *p*.
17:16 and all the *p* with him will be destroyed."
17:22 all his *p* moved on and crossed the Jordan.
17:29 "The *p* have been hungry and tired and
19: 9 When all the *p* were informed that the king
19:10 all the *p* were arguing among themselves,
19:40 Then all the *p* crossed over the Jordan but
19:41 All the *p* of Judah and half of the *p* of Israel
20:22 She went to all the *p* with her advice,
22:28 You save lowly *p*,
22:44 "You rescued me from the strife of my *p*;
22:44 A *p* I had not known became my slaves;
24: 2 from Dan to Beer-sheba and register the *p*,
24: 3 God increase the number of *p* a hundredfold
24: 4 in order to register the *p* of Israel.
24: 9 to the king the number of *p* registered:
24:10 David regretted having numbered the *p*,
24:15 when the plague broke out among the *p*.
24:15 of the *p* from Dan to Beer-sheba died.]
24:16 angel causing the destruction among the *p*,
24:17 David saw the angel who was striking the *p*,
24:21 that the plague may be checked among the *p*."
1Kgs 1:39 They blew the horn and all the *p* shouted,
1:40 Then all the *p* went up after him,
3: 2 the *p* were sacrificing on the high places,
3: 8 *p* whom you have chosen, a *p* so vast
3: 9 your *p* and to distinguish right from wrong.
3: 9 who is able to govern this vast *p* of yours?"
5:21 David a wise son to rule this numerous *p*."
5:30 work, directing the *p* engaged in the work.
6:13 and will not forsake my *p* Israel."
8:16 the day I brought my *p* Israel out of Egypt,
8:16 but I choose David to rule my *p* Israel.'
8:30 *p* Israel which they offer in this place.
8:33 "If your *p* Israel sin against you and are
8:34 and forgive the sin of your *p* Israel,
8:36 sin of your servant and of your *p* Israel,
8:36 you have given to your *p* as their heritage.
8:37 *p* besieges them in one of their cities;
8:38 if then any one [of your entire *p* Israel]
8:41 likewise, who is not of your *p* Israel,
8:43 name, may fear you as do your *p* Israel,
8:44 your *p* forth to war against their enemies,
8:50 Forgive your *p* their sins and all the
8:51 For they are your *p* and your inheritance,
8:52 and to the petition of your *p* Israel.
8:56 LORD who has given rest to his *p* Israel,
8:59 and of his *p* Israel as each day requires,
8:66 On the eighth day he dismissed the *p*,
8:66 to his servant David and to his *p* Israel.
9:20 non-Israelite *p* who remained in the land,
9:23 policed the *p* engaged in the work numbered
12: 5 When the *p* had departed,
12: 6 answer do you advise me to give this *p*?"
12: 7 the servant of this *p* and submit to them,
12: 9 answer do you advise me to give this *p*,
12:10 "This is what you must say to this *p*
12:13 him, the king gave the *p* a harsh answer.
12:15 The king did not listen to the *p*,
12:16 listen to them, the *p* answered the king:
12:23 and to Benjamin, and to the rest of the *p*:
12:27 If now this *p* go up to offer sacrifices in
12:27 of this *p* will return to their master,
12:28 made two calves of gold and said to the *p*:
12:30 because the *p* frequented these calves in
12:31 from among the *p* who were not Levites.
13:33 the high places from among the common *p*.
14: 2 was he who predicted my reign over this *p*.
14: 7 I exalted you from among the *p*
14: 7 and made you ruler of my *p* Israel.
16: 2 the dust and made you ruler of my *p* Israel,
16: 2 and have caused my *p* Israel to sin,
16:21 At that time the *p* of Israel were divided,

18:21 Elijah appealed to all the *p* and said,
18:21 The *p*, however, did not answer him.
18:22 So Elijah said to the *p*,
18:24 All the *p* answered, "Agreed!"
18:30 Then Elijah said to all the *p*,
18:37 Answer me, that this *p* may know that you,
18:39 this, all the *p* fell prostrate and said,
19:21 their flesh, and gave it to his *p* to eat.
20: 8 All the elders and all the *p* said to him,
20:42 pay for his life, your *p* for his people.' "
21: 9 a fast and set Naboth at the head of the *p*.
21:12 and placed Naboth at the head of the *p*.
22: 4 and I are as one, and your *p* and my people,
22:44 and the *p* continued to sacrifice and to
2Kgs 3: 7 and I shall be as one, your *p* and mine,
4:13 She replied, "I am living among my own *p*."
4:41 pot and said, "Serve it to the *p* to eat."
4:42 "Give it to the *p* to eat," Elisha said.
4:43 "Give it to the *p* to eat,"
6:18 prayed to the LORD, "Strike this *p* blind,
6:30 the *p* saw that he was wearing sackcloth
7:16 The *p* went out and plundered the camp of
7:17 the *p* trampled him to death at the gate,
7:20 the *p* trampled him to death at the gate.
9: 6 'I anoint you king over the *p* of the LORD,
10: 9 morning, he stopped and said to all the *p*:
10:18 all the *p* together and said to them:
11:13 Athaliah heard the noise made by the *p*,
11:14 with all the *p* of the land rejoicing and
11:17 party and the king and the *p* as the other,
11:17 by which they would be the LORD's *p*;
11:17 covenant, between the king and the *p*.
11:18 Thereupon all the *p* of the land went to
11:19 the guards, and all the *p* of the land,
11:20 All the *p* of the land rejoiced and the
12: 4 the *p* continued to sacrifice and to burn
12: 9 the *p* nor make the repairs on the temple.
13:21 Once some *p* were burying a man,
14: 4 but the *p* continued to sacrifice and to
14:21 Thereupon all the *p* of Judah took the
15: 4 the *p* continued to sacrifice and to burn
15: 5 vizier and regent for the *p* of the land.
15:35 *p* continued to sacrifice and to burn incense
16:15 cereal-offerings, and libations of the *p*.
17:19 Even the *p* of Judah,
17:24 The king of Assyria brought *p* from Babylon,
17:29 the Samarians had made, each *p* set up gods.
18:26 earshot of the *p* who are on the wall."
18:36 But the *p* remained silent and did not
20: 5 back and tell Hezekiah, the leader of my *p*:
21:24 but the *p* of the land then slew all who
22: 4 the doorkeepers had collected from the *p*.
22:13 "Go, consult the LORD for me, for the *p*,
23: 2 priests, prophets, and all the *p*,
23: 3 *p* stood as participants in the covenant.
23:21 the *p* to observe the Passover of the LORD,
23:30 Then the *p* of the land took Jehoahaz,
23:35 the silver and gold from the *p* of the land,
24:14 among the *p* of the land except the poor.
25: 3 the city, and the *p* had no more bread,
25:11 the last of the *p* remaining in the city,
25:19 *p* of the land, and sixty of the common *p*
25:22 As for the *p* whom he had allowed to remain
25:26 all the *p*, great and small, left
1Chr 2:53 the *p* of Zorah and the Eshtaolites derived.
10: 9 the good news to their idols and their *p*.
11: 2 my *p* Israel and be ruler over them.' "
13: 4 for the idea was pleasing to all the *p*.
14: 2 exalted for the sake of his *p* Israel.
16: 2 he blessed the *p* in the name of the LORD,
16:20 to nation, from one kingdom to another *p*.
16:36 Let all the *p* say, Amen!
16:43 Then all the *p* departed,
17: 6 of Israel whom I commanded to guide my *p*,
17: 7 you might become ruler over my *p* Israel.
17: 9 I will assign a place for my *p* Israel and
17:10 when I appointed judges over my *p* Israel.
17:21 "Is there, like your *p* Israel,
17:21 earth whom a god went to redeem as his *p*?
17:21 by driving out the nations before your *p*.
17:22 You made your *p* Israel your own forever,
18:14 dispensed justice and right to all his *p*.
19:13 the sake of our *p* and the cities of our God;
20: 3 He deported the *p* of the city and set them
21: 3 the LORD increase his *p* a hundredfold!
21:17 it not I who ordered the census of the *p*?
21:17 but do not afflict your *p* with this plague!"
21:22 that the plague may be stayed from the *p*."
22:18 land is subdued before the LORD and his *p*.
23:25 God of Israel, has given rest to his *p*,
28: 2 "Hear me, my brethren and my *p*.
28:21 the *p* will do everything that you command."
29: 9 *p* rejoiced over these freewill offerings,
29:14 "But who am I, and who are my *p*,
29:17 I have seen your *p* here present also giving
29:18 in the hearts and minds of your *p* forever,
2Chr 1: 9 a *p* as numerous as the dust of the earth.
1:10 wisdom and knowledge to lead this *p*,
1:10 who could rule this great *p* of yours?"
1:11 rule my *p* over whom I have made you king,
2:10 "Because the LORD loves his *p*,
2:17 hundred overseers to keep the *p* working.
6: 5 I brought my *p* out of the land of Egypt,

6: 5 any man to be commander of my *p* Israel;
6: 6 and I choose David to rule my *p* Israel.'
6:21 petitions of your servant and of your *p* Israel
6:24 When your *p* Israel have sinned against you
6:25 and forgive the sin of your *p* Israel,
6:27 sin of your servants and of your *p* Israel.
6:27 which you gave your *p* as their heritage.
6:29 *p* offers a prayer or petition of any kind,
6:32 the foreigner, too, who is not of your *p*,
6:33 your name, fearing you as do your *p* Israel,
6:34 *p* go forth to war against their enemies,
6:39 Forgive your *p* who have sinned against you.
7: 4 The king and all the *p* were offering
7: 6 and all the *p* dedicated the house of God.
7:10 month he sent the *p* back to their tents,
7:10 David, for Solomon, and for his *p* Israel.
7:13 the land, if I send pestilence among my *p*,
7:14 pestilence among my people, and if my *p*,
7:20 uproot the *p* from the land I gave them;
8: 7 All the *p* that remained of the Hittites,
8:10 fifty overseers who had charge of the *p*.
10: 5 When the *p* had departed,
10: 6 answer do you advise me to give this *p*?"
10: 7 kindly with this *p* and give in to them,
10: 9 answer do you advise me to give this *p*,
10:10 should give to this *p* who have said to you,
10:12 Jeroboam and all the *p* came back to King
10:15 The king would not listen to the *p*,
10:16 listen to them, the *p* answered the king.
13:17 his *p* inflicted a severe defeat upon them;
16:10 also oppressed some of his *p* at this time.
17: 9 the cities of Judah and taught among the *p*.
18: 2 sheep and oxen for him and the *p* with him,
18: 3 "your *p* and my people as well.
19: 4 went out again among the *p* from Beer-sheba
20: 7 inhabitants of this land before your *p* Israel
20:21 After consulting with the *p*,
20:25 Jehoshaphat and his *p* came to take plunder,
20:33 nor as yet had the *p* fixed their hearts on
21:14 than you, the LORD will strike your *p*,
21:19 His *p* did not made a pyre for him like
23: 5 when all the *p* will be in the courts of
23: 6 but all the other *p* must observe the
23:10 He stationed all the *p*,
23:12 of the *p* running and acclaiming the king,
23:12 went to the *p* in the temple of the LORD.
23:13 and all the *p* of the land rejoicing and
23:16 between himself and all the *p* and the king,
23:16 the king, that they should be the LORD's *p*.
23:17 And all the *p* went to the temple of Baal
23:20 the people, and all the *p* of the land,
23:21 All the *p* of the land rejoiced and the
24:10 All the princes and the *p* rejoiced;
24:19 the *p* would not listen to their warnings.
24:20 his stand above the *p* and said to them:
24:23 did away with all the princes of the *p*,
25:14 back with him the gods of the *p* of Seir,
25:15 could not save their own *p* from your hand?"
26: 1 All the *p* of Judah chose Uzziah,
26:21 of the palace and ruled the *p* of the land.
27: 2 the *p*, however, continued to act sinfully
28: 5 away captive a large number of his *p*,
29:36 Hezekiah and all the *p* rejoiced over what
29:36 over what God had reestablished for the *p*,
30: 3 and the *p* were not gathered at Jerusalem.
30:12 brought it about that the *p* were of one mind
30:13 Thus many *p* gathered in Jerusalem to
30:18 The greater part of the *p*,
30:20 The LORD heard Hezekiah and spared the *p*.
30:27 levitical priests rose and blessed the *p*;
31: 4 He also commanded the *p* living in
31: 8 they blessed the LORD and his *p* Israel.
31:10 left over, for the LORD has blessed his *p*.
32: 6 he appointed army commanders over the *p*.
32: 8 And the *p* took confidence from the words
32:14 ban was able to save his *p* from my hand?
32:15 *p* from my hand or the hands of my fathers,
32:17 lands have not saved their *p* from my hand,
32:17 Hezekiah's god save his *p* from my hand."
32:18 to the *p* of Jerusalem who were on the wall,
33:10 The LORD spoke to Manasseh and his *p*,
33:17 Though the *p* continued to sacrifice on the
33:25 But the *p* of the land slew all those who
33:25 Amon, and then they, the *p* of the land,
34:30 the priests, the Levites, and all the *p*,
35: 3 now the LORD, your God, and his *p* Israel.
35: 5 houses of your brethren, the common *p*,
35: 7 to the common *p* a flock of lambs and kids,
35: 8 also gave a freewill gift to the *p*,
35:12 of the common *p* to offer to the LORD,
35:13 brought them quickly to all the common *p*.
36: 1 The *p* of the land took Jehoahaz,
36:14 and the *p* added infidelity to infidelity,
36:15 compassion on his *p* and his dwelling place.
36:16 *p* was so inflamed that there was no remedy.
36:23 among you belongs to any part of his *p*,
Ezr 1: 3 among you belongs to any part of his *p*,
1: 4 by the *p* of that place with silver,
2:70 common *p* took up residence in Jerusalem;
3: 1 the *p* gathered at Jerusalem as one man.
3:11 and all the *p* raised a great shout of joy,
3:13 for the *p* raised a mighty clamor which was
4: 4 Thereupon the *p* of the land set out to

PEOPLE (cont.)

4: 4 intimidate and dishearten the *p* of Judah
5:12 house and led the *p* captive to Babylon.
6:12 every king or *p* who may undertake to alter
7:13 in my kingdom belonging to the *p* of Israel,
7:16 offerings which the *p* and priests freely
7:25 justice to all the *p* in West-of-Euphrates,
8:36 support to the *p* and to the house of God.
10: 1 and the *p* wept profusely.
10: 9 All the *p*, standing in the open place
10:13 *p* are numerous and it is the rainy season,

Neh 1:10 They are your servants, your *p*,
3:38 The *p* worked with a will.
4: 8 the magistrates, and the rest of the *p*:
4:13 the magistrates, and the rest of the *p*:
4:16 the *p* to spend the nights inside Jerusalem,
5: 1 there rose a great outcry of the common *p*
5:10 lent the *p* money and grain without charge.
5:13 Then the *p* did as they had promised.
5:15 had laid a heavy burden on the *p*,
5:15 then too, their men oppressed the *p*.
5:18 for the labor lay heavy upon this *p*.
5:19 God, in my favor all that I did for this *p*.
7: 5 the nobles, the magistrates, and the common *p*,
7:71 The contributions of the rest of the *p*
8: 1 the whole *p* gathered as one man in the
8: 3 and all the *p* listened attentively to the
8: 5 Ezra opened the scroll so that all the *p*
8: 5 was standing higher up than any of the *p*);
8: 5 and, as he opened it, all the *p* rose.
8: 6 the LORD, the great God, and all the *p*,
8: 7 and Pelaiah explained the law to the *p*,
8: 9 instructing the *p* said to all the people:
8: 9 for all the *p* were weeping as they heard
8:11 [And the Levites quieted all the *p* saying,
8:12 Then all the *p* went to eat and drink,
8:13 the family heads of the whole *p* and also
8:16 The *p* went out and brought in branches
9:10 all his servants and the *p* of his land,
9:32 prophets, our fathers, and your entire *p*,
10:15 The leaders of the *p*:
10:29 The rest of the *p*,
10:35 We, priests, Levites, and *p*,
11: 1 of the *p* took up residence in Jerusalem,
11: 1 and the rest of the *p* cast lots to bring
11: 2 The *p* applauded all those men who
11:24 deputy in all affairs that concerned the *p*.
12:30 themselves, then they purified the *p*,
12:38 the other half of the princes of the *p*,
13: 1 the book of Moses in the hearing of the *p*,

Tb 1: 3 *p* who had been deported with me to Nineveh,
1:16 charitable works for my kinsmen and my *p*.
1:17 If I saw one of my *p* who had died and been
2: 3 "Father, one of our *p* has been murdered!
3:10 *P* would level this insult against my father:
4:13 kinsmen the sons and daughters of your *p*,
11:16 *p* of Nineveh saw him walking along briskly,
14:10 For I see that *p* here shamelessly commit

Jdt 1: 6 came together to resist the *p* of Cheleoud.
3: 7 The *p* of these cities and all the
3: 8 and every *p* and tribe invoke him as a god.
4: 3 all the *p* of Judea been gathered together,
4: 5 The *p* there posted guards on all the
4: 8 and the senate of the whole *p* of Israel,
4:13 For the *p* observed a fast of many days
4:14 and the freewill offerings of the *p*.
5: 3 of *p* is this that dwells in the mountains?
5: 5 I will tell you the truth about this *p*
5: 6 "These *p* are descendants of the Chaldeans.
5:20 lord and master, if these *p* are at fault,
5:22 *p* standing round about the tent murmured;
5:23 they said, "for they are a powerless *p*,
6: 5 taken revenge on this race of *p* from Egypt.
6:18 the *p* fell prostrate and worshiped God;
6:19 Have pity on the lowliness of our *p*,
7:23 All the *p*, therefore, including youths,
8: 9 heard of the harsh words which the *p*,
8:11 to me, you rulers of the *p* of Bethulia.
8:11 What you said to the *p* today is not proper.
8:20 he will not disdain us or any of our *p*.
8:29 all the *p* have recognized your prudence,
8:30 The *p*, however, were so tortured
9:14 who protects the *p* of Israel but you alone."
10:12 and asked her, "To what *p* do you belong?
10:19 this *p* that has such women among them?
11: 2 your *p* who dwell in the mountain region,
11:10 For our *p* are not punished,
11:16 such deeds that *p* throughout the world
11:22 done well in sending you ahead of your *p*,
12: 3 None of your *p* are with us."
12: 8 to direct her way for the triumph of his *p*.
13:13 All the *p*, from the least to the greatest,
13:17 All the *p* were greatly astonished.
13:17 brought to nought the enemies of your *p*."
13:20 your life when your *p* were being oppressed,
13:20 And all the *p* answered, "Amen!
14: 6 of one of the men in the assembly of the *p*,
14: 8 Judith told him, in the presence of the *p*,
14: 9 finished her account, the *p* cheered loudly,
15: 9 You are the splendid boast of our *p*.
15:10 And all the *p* answered, "Amen!"
15:13 At the head of all the *p*,
15:14 and the *p* swelled this hymn of praise:
16: 2 and sets his encampment among his *p*;
16:17 to the nations that rise against my *p*!
16:18 *p* then went to Jerusalem to worship God;
16:19 of Holofernes that the *p* had given her,
16:20 For three months the *p* continued their

Est A:17 *p* because of the two eunuchs of the king.
1: 5 court of the royal palace for all the *p*,
1:22 script and to each *p* in its own language,
3: 6 to destroy all the Jews, Mordecai's *p*,
3: 7 of Mordecai's *p* on a single day,
3: 8 kingdom, there is a certain *p* living apart,
3: 8 laws differing from those of every other *p*.
3:11 king said to Haman, "but as for this *p*,
3:12 province, and the officials of every *p*,
3:12 script and to each *p* in its own language.
B: 4 the world, there is one *p* of bad will,
B: 4 by its laws is opposed to every other *p*
B: 5 *p* is continually at variance with all men,
B: 7 so that when these *p*,
4: 8 and intercede with him in behalf of her *p*.
4:11 "All the servants of the king and the *p*
C: 8 God, King, God of Abraham, spare your *p*,
C:16 *p* of the land of my forefathers that you,
7: 3 and I beg that you spare the lives of my *p*.
7: 4 *p* and I have been delivered to destruction,
8: 6 I witness the evil that is to befall my *p*,
8: 9 script and to each *p* in its own language,
F: 6 the name of the Jews, but my *p* is Israel,
F: 6 *p* and delivered us from all these evils.
F: 7 one for the *p* of God,
F: 9 *p* and rendered justice to his inheritance.
F:10 all future generations of his *p* Israel."

1Mc 1:11 of the law, and they seduced many *p*,
1:13 from among the *p* promptly went to the king,
1:30 and destroyed many of the *p* in Israel.
1:41 whole kingdom that all should be one *p*,
1:51 He appointed inspectors over all the *p*,
1:52 Many of the *p*, those who abandoned
2: 7 ruin of my *p* and the ruin of the holy city,
2:67 and you shall avenge the wrongs of your *p*.
3: 3 He spread abroad the glory of his *p*,
3: 5 who troubled his *p* he destroyed by fire.
3:42 to destroy and utterly wipe out the *p*.
3:43 *p* from their ruined estate, and fight for our *p*
3:55 this Judas appointed officers among the *p*,
4:17 from the pursuit, he said to the *p*:
4:31 this army into the hands of your *p* Israel;
4:55 All the *p* prostrated themselves and adored
4:58 There was great joy among the *p* now that
4:61 *p* might have a stronghold facing Idumea.
5: 2 they began to massacre and persecute the *p*.
5: 4 to the *p* by ambushing them along the roads.
5: 6 body of *p* with Timothy as their leader.
5:16 When Judas and the *p* heard this,
5:18 of Zechariah, and Azariah, leader of the *p*,
5:19 "Take charge of these *p*,"
5:27 seize and destroy all these *p* in one day."
5:30 ahead and saw a countless multitude of *p*,
5:30 and beginning to attack the *p* within.
5:42 *p* beside the stream and gave them this order:
5:43 to the attack, with all the *p* behind him,
5:45 and their goods, a great crowd of *p*,
5:53 and encouraging the *p* the whole way,
5:61 It was a bad defeat for the *p*,
6: 3 because his plan became known to the *p*
6:19 called all the *p* together to besiege them.
6:24 the sons of our *p* have become our enemies;
6:44 *p* and win an everlasting name for himself.
7: 6 this accusation to the king against the *p*:
7:18 fear and dread of them came upon all the *p*,
7:22 were disturbing their *p* gathered about him.
7:26 of Israel, with orders to destroy the *p*.
7:33 *p* came out to greet him peaceably
7:37 a house of prayer and petition for your *p*.
7:46 of Judea *p* came out and closed in on them.
7:48 The *p* rejoiced greatly,
8:15 that concerned the *p* and their well-being.
8:20 and his brothers, with the Jewish *p*,
8:29 have made an agreement with the Jewish *p*.
9: 2 Arbela, they captured it and killed many *p*.
9:27 time prophets ceased to appear among the *p*.
9:73 *p* and he destroyed the impious in Israel.
10: 7 Jerusalem and read the letter to all the *p*.
10:46 When Jonathan and the *p* heard these words,
10:86 and the *p* of that city came out to meet
11: 2 and the *p* in the cities opened their gates
11:14 because the *p* of that region had revolted.
11:61 *p* of Gaza locked their gates against him.
11:62 the *p* of Gaza appealed to him for mercy,
12: 3 Jonathan and the Jewish *p* have sent us
12: 6 and the rest of the Jewish *p* send
12:35 he assembled the elders of the *p*,
12:37 The *p* therefore worked together on
13: 2 saw that the *p* were in dread and terror,
13: 2 the *p* and exhorted them in these words:
13: 7 As the *p* heard these words,
13:17 of provoking much hostility among the *p*,
13:36 kings, and to the elders and the Jewish *p*.
13:42 and the *p* began to write in their records
14: 4 His *p* were delighted with his power and
14: 8 The *p* cultivated their land in peace;
14:14 among his *p* and was zealous for the law;
14:16 When *p* heard in Rome and even in Sparta
14:20 the priests, and the rest of the Jewish *p*,
14:21 *p* have informed us of your glory and fame,
14:23 *p* have voted to receive the men with honor,
14:23 the *p* of Sparta may have a record of them.
14:25 When the *p* heard of these things,
14:28 in a great assembly of priests, *p*,
14:35 When the Jewish *p* saw Simon's loyalty and
14:35 In every way he sought to exalt his *p*.
14:41 " 'The Jewish *p* and their priest have,
14:44 It shall not be lawful for any of the *p* or
14:46 " 'All the *p* approved of granting Simon
14:47 and ethnarch of the Jewish *p* and priests
15:17 by Simon the high priest and the Jewish *p*,
15:35 harm to our *p* and laying waste our country;
15:39 could launch attacks against the Jewish *p*.
15:40 the *p* and to make incursions into Judea,
15:40 where he took *p* captive or massacred them.

2Mc 1:10 The *p* of Jerusalem and Judea,
1:16 heads and tossed them to the *p* outside.
1:26 this sacrifice on behalf of all your *p* Israel
1:27 Gather together our scattered *p*,
1:29 Plant your *p* in your holy place,
1:33 and his *p* had burned the sacrifices,
1:36 purification, but most *p* named it naphtha.
2: 7 his *p* together again and shows them mercy.
2:17 It is God who has saved all his *p* and has
3:18 *P* rushed out of their houses in crowds to
4: 5 general and particular good of all the *p*.
4:16 very *p* whose manner of life they emulated,
4:22 great pomp by Jason and the *p* of the city,
4:30 the *p* of Tarsus and Mallus rose in revolt,
4:35 Jews, but many *p* of other nations as well,
4:39 *p* assembled in protest against Lysimachus.
4:41 the *p* picked up stones or pieces of wood
4:48 the case for the city, for the *p*,
5:19 not chosen the *p* for the sake of the Place,
5:19 Place, but the Place for the sake of the *p*.
5:26 armed men, he cut down a large number of *p*.
6:16 misfortunes, he does not abandon his own *p*.
8: 2 the Lord to look kindly upon his *p*,
8:36 by the capture of the *p* of Jerusalem testified
9: 2 Thereupon the *p* had swift recourse to arms,
9:24 the *p* throughout the realm would know to
10:21 he assembled the rulers of the *p* and accused
11: 6 they and all the *p* begged the Lord with
11:16 "Lysias sends greetings to the Jewish *p*.
11:25 that this *p* too should be undisturbed,
11:27 The king's letter to the *p* was as follows:
11:34 the Romans, send greetings to the Jewish *p*.
12: 3 *p* of Joppa also committed this outrage:
12: 4 the *p* of Joppa took them out to sea and
12:26 where he killed twenty-five thousand *p*.
12:27 city inhabited by *p* of many nationalities.
12:28 twenty-five thousand of the *p* in it.
13:10 the *p* to call upon the LORD night and day,
13:25 the *p* of that city were angered by the
14: 8 conduct of the *p* just mentioned.
14: 9 its hard-pressed *p* with the same gracious
14:15 to him who established his *p* forever,
14:23 of ordinary *p* who gathered around him;
15:14 prays for his *p* and their holy city."
15:24 blasphemously come against your holy *p*!"

Jb 1:19 It fell upon the young *p* and they are dead;
17: 6 as evil, and I am made a byword of the *p*;
18:19 has neither son nor grandson among his *p*,

Ps(s) 3: 7 of *p* arrayed against me on every side.
3: 9 Upon your *p* be your blessing.
14: 4 who eat up my *p* just as they eat bread?
14: 7 the LORD restores the well-being of his *p*,
18:28 *p* you save but haughty eyes you bring low;
18:44 You rescued me from the strife of the *p*,
18:44 A *p* I had not known became my slaves;
22: 7 the scorn of men, despised by the *p*.
22:32 *p* yet to be born the justice he has shown.
28: 8 The LORD is the strength of his *p*,
28: 9 Save your *p*,
29:11 strength to his *p*; may the LORD bless his *p*
33:12 *p* he has chosen for his own inheritance.
43: 1 and fight my fight against a faithless *p*;
44:13 You sold your *p* for no great price;
45:11 ear, forget your *p* and your father's house.
45:13 the rich among the *p* seek your favor.
47:10 together with the *p* of the God of Abraham.
50: 4 and the earth, to the trial of his *p*:
50: 7 "Hear, my *p*, and I will speak;
53: 5 who eat up my *p* just as they eat bread,
53: 7 When God restores the well-being of his *p*,
59:12 O God, slay them, lest they beguile my *p*;
60: 5 You have made your *p* feel hardships;
62: 9 Trust in him at all times, O my *p*!
68: 8 you went forth at the head of your *p*,
68:36 he gives power and strength to his *p*.
72: 2 He shall govern your *p* with justice and
72: 3 The mountains shall yield peace for the *p*,
72: 4 He shall defend the afflicted among the *p*,
73:10 "So he brings his *p* to such a pass that
74:18 and how a stupid *p* has reviled your name.
77:16 With your strong arm you redeemed your *p*,
77:21 You led your *p* like a flock under the care
78: 1 Hearken, my *p*, to my teaching;
78:20 also give bread and provide meat for his *p*?"
78:52 But his *p* he led forth like sheep and
78:62 He abandoned his *p* to the sword and was

78:71 he brought him to shepherd Jacob, his *p*,
79:13 we, your *p* and the sheep of your pasture,
80: 5 will you burn with anger while your *p* pray?
81: 9 Hear, my *p*,
81:12 "But my *p* heard not my voice,
81:14 If only my *p* would hear me,
83: 4 Against your *p* they plot craftily;
83: 7 the Ishmaelites, Moab and the *p* of Hagar,
85: 3 You have forgiven the guilt of your *p*;
85: 7 and shall not your *p* rejoice in you?
85: 9 for he proclaims peace To his *p*,
89:16 Happy the *p* who know the joyful shout;
89:20 over the *p* I have set a youth.
94: 5 Your *p*, O LORD, they trample down
94: 8 Understand, you senseless ones among the *p*;
94:14 For the LORD will not cast off his *p*,
95: 7 is our God, and we are the *p* he shepherds,
95:10 They are a *p* of erring heart,
100: 3 his *p*,
105:13 nation and from one kingdom to another *p*,
105:24 *p* and made them stronger than their foes,
105:25 he changed, so that they hated his *p*,
105:43 And he led forth his *p* with joy;
106: 4 Remember me, O LORD, as you favor your *p*;
106: 5 chosen ones, rejoice in the joy of your *p*,
106:40 And the LORD grew angry with his *p*,
106:48 Let all the *p* say, Amen!
107:32 extol him in the assembly of the *p* and praise
111: 6 made known to his *p* the power of his works,
111: 9 He has sent deliverance to his *p*;
113: 8 princes, with the princes of his own *p*.
114: 1 house of Jacob from a *p* of alien tongue,
116:14 I will pay in the presence of all his *p*.
116:18 I will pay in the presence of all his *p*,
125: 2 so the LORD is round about his *p*,
135:12 a heritage, the heritage of Israel his *p*.
135:14 generations, For the LORD defends his *p*,
136:16 Who led his *p* through the wilderness,
144:15 Happy the *p* for whom things are thus;
144:15 happy the *p* whose God is the LORD.
148:14 and he has lifted up the horn of his *p*.
148:14 the children of Israel, the *p* close to him.
149: 4 For the LORD loves his *p*,
Prv 11:14 For lack of guidance a *p* falls;
11:26 Him who monopolizes grain, the *p* curse
14:28 but if his *p* are few,
24:24 men will curse him, *p* will denounce him;
28:12 when the wicked gain pre-eminence, *p* hide.
28:15 bear is a wicked ruler over a poor *p*.
29: 2 When the just prevail, the *p* rejoice;
29: 2 but when the wicked rule, the *p* groan.
29:18 Without prophecy the *p* become demoralized;
30:11 is a group of *p* that curses its father,
30:31 he-goat, and the king at the head of his *p*.
Eccl 4:16 There is no end to all these *p*,
12: 9 wise, Qoheleth taught the *p* knowledge,
Wis 4:14 But the *p* saw and did not understand,
6:24 a prudent king, the stability of his *p*;
9: 7 You have chosen me king over your *p* and
9:12 and I shall judge your *p* justly and be
10:15 The holy *p* and blameless race
12:19 And you taught your *p*,
15:14 the enemies of your *p* who enslaved them.
16: 2 you benefited your *p* with a novel dish,
16:20 you nourished your *p* with food of angels
18: 7 Your *p* awaited the salvation of the just
18:13 they acknowledged that the *p* was God's son.
19: 5 and your *p* might experience a glorious
19:22 you magnified and glorified your *p*;
Sir 9:17 but the ruler of his *p* is the skilled sage.
10: 1 wise magistrate lends stability to his *p*,
10: 3 A wanton king destroys his *p*,
10: 8 Dominion is transferred from one *p* to
10:20 he who fears God is in honor among his *p*.
16: 6 upon a godless *p* wrath flames out.
16: 9 *p* who were uprooted because of their sin;
16:15 Among so many *p* I cannot be known;
24: 1 before her own *p* she proclaims her glory;
24: 6 land, over every *p* and nation I held sway.
24:12 I have struck root among the glorious *p*,
26: 5 charges in public, trial before all the *p*,
35:23 Till he defends the cause of his *p*,
36:11 Show mercy to the *p* called by your name;
36:16 for you are ever gracious to your *p*;
37:25 wise for his *p* wins a heritage of glory,
41:18 of theft from the *p* where you settle,
42:11 in the city, a reproach among the *p*,
45: 3 He gave him the commandments for his *p*,
45: 7 bestowed on him the priesthood of his *p*;
45:15 his priesthood and bless his *p* in his name.
45:16 memorial, and to atone for the *p* of Israel.
45:17 To teach the precepts to his *p*,
45:22 the *p* nor shares with them their heritage;
45:23 God of all, he met the crisis of his *p* And,
45:26 wisdom of heart to govern his *p* in justice,
46: 7 the *p* and suppressed the wicked complaint
46: 8 To lead the *p* into their inheritance,
46:10 That all the *p* of Jacob might know how
46:13 Beloved of his *p*, dear to his Maker,
46:13 kingdom and anointed princes to rule the *p*.
47: 5 warrior and raise up the might of his *p*,
47:23 who by his policy made the *p* rebel;
48:15 Despite all this the *p* did not repent,
48:15 But Judah remained, a tiny *p*,
50: 1 among his brethren, the glory of his *p*,
50: 4 He protected his *p* against brigands and
50:17 Then all the *p* with one accord would
50:19 All the *p* of the land would shout for joy,
50:21 Then again the *p* would lie prostrate to
50:25 two nations, the third is not even a *p*:
Is 1: 3 does not know, my *p* has not understood.
1: 4 sinful nation, *p* laden with wickedness,
1:10 the instruction of our God, *p* of Gomorrah!
2: 6 You have abandoned your *p*,
3: 5 them, And the *p* shall oppress one another,
3: 7 You shall not make me ruler of the *p*."
3:12 My *p*— a babe in arms will be their tyrant,
3:12 O my *p*, your leaders mislead,
3:13 rises to accuse, standing to try his *p*.
3:15 What do you mean by crushing my *p*,
5:13 Therefore my *p* go into exile,
5:25 wrath of the LORD blazes against his *p*,
6: 5 lips, living among a *p* of unclean lips;
6: 9 Go and say to this *p*: Listen carefully,
6:10 are to make the heart of this *p* sluggish,
7: 2 of the king and heart of the *p* trembled,
7:17 The LORD shall bring upon you and your *p*
8: 6 Because this *p* has rejected the waters of
8:11 warning me not to walk in the way of this *p*:
8:12 not alliance what this *p* calls alliance,
8:19 should not a *p* inquire of their gods,
9: 1 The *p* who walked in darkness have seen a
9: 8 falls upon Israel, And all the *p* know it,
9:12 The *p* do not turn to him who struck them,
9:15 The leaders of this *p* mislead them and
9:18 quakes, and the *p* are like fuel for fire;
10: 6 and against a *p* under my wrath I order him
10:22 For though your *p*, O Israel,
10:24 O my *p*, who dwell in Zion,
11:11 his *p* that is left from Assyria and Egypt,
11:16 remnant of his *p* that is left from Assyria,
14:20 ruined your land, you have slain your *p*!
14:32 in her the afflicted of his *p* find refuge."
18: 2 and bronzed, To a *p* dreaded near and far,
18: 7 hosts from a *p* tall and bronzed, from a *p*
19:25 "Blessed be my *p* Egypt,
21:10 O my *p* who have been threshed,
22: 4 me for the ruin of the daughter of my *p*.
22:16 you doing here, and what *p* have you here,
23:13 [This *p* is the land of the Chaldeans,
25: 3 Therefore a strong *p* will honor you,
25: 8 his *p* he will remove from the whole earth;
26:11 shamed when they see your zeal for your *p*:
26:20 Go, my *p*, enter your chambers
27:11 This is not an understanding *p*;
28: 5 brilliant diadem to the remnant of his *p*,
28:11 he will speak to this *p* to whom he said:
28:14 you arrogant, who rule this *p* in Jerusalem:
29:13 Since this *p* draws near with words only
29:14 this *p* in surprising and wondrous fashion:
30: 5 be ashamed of a *p* that gain them nothing,
30: 6 humps of camels To a *p* good for nothing,
30: 9 This is a rebellious *p*,
30:19 O *p* of Zion,
30:26 day the LORD binds up the wounds of his *p*,
32:13 the fruitful vine, And the soil of my *p*,
32:18 My *p* will live in peaceful country,
33:19 *p* of alien tongue you will look no more,
33:19 will look no more, the *p* of obscure speech,
33:24 the *p* who live there will be forgiven
34: 5 in judgment upon Edom, a *p* I have doomed.
36:11 earshot of the *p* who are on the wall."
40: 1 Comfort, give comfort to my *p*,
40: 7 [So then, the *p* is the grass.]
42: 5 its *p* and spirit to those who walk on it:
42: 6 you, and set you as a covenant of the *p*,
42:22 This is a *p* despoiled and plundered,
43: 8 the *p* who are blind though they have eyes,
43:20 in the wasteland for my chosen *p* to drink,
43:21 to drink, The *p* whom I formed for myself,
47: 6 Angry at my *p*,
49:13 his *p* and shows mercy to his afflicted.
51: 4 Be attentive to me, my *p*;
51: 7 you *p* who have my teaching at heart:
51:16 to Zion: You are my *p*.
51:22 your Master, your God, who defends his *p*:
52: 4 To Egypt in the beginning my *p* went down,
52: 5 My *p* have been taken away without redress;
52: 6 on that day my *p* shall know my renown,
52: 9 For the Lord comforts his *p*,
53: 8 living, and smitten for the sin of his *p*,
54: 3 nations and shall *p* the desolate cities.
56: 3 LORD will surely exclude me from his *p*";
58: 1 Tell my *p* their wickedness,
59:10 wall, like *p* without eyes we feel our way.
60:12 For the *p* or kingdom shall perish that
60:21 Your *p* shall all be just,
62:10 the gates, prepare the way for the *p*;
62:12 They shall be called the holy *p*,
63: 3 and of my *p* there was no one with me.
63: 8 They are indeed my *p*,
63:14 Thus you led your *p*,
64: 8 look upon us, who are all your *p*.
65: 2 my hands all the day to a rebellious *p*,
65: 3 own thoughts, *P* who provoke me continually,
65:10 for the cattle of my *p* who have sought me.
65:18 to be a joy and its *p* to be a delight;
65:19 rejoice in Jerusalem and exult in my *p*.
65:22 the years of a tree, so the years of my *p*;
Jer 1:18 and princes, against its priests and *p*.
2:11 But my *p* have changed their glory for
2:13 Two evils have my *p* done:
2:16 the *p* of Memphis and Tahpanhes shave the
2:31 Why do my *p* say, "We have moved on.
2:32 my *p* have forgotten me days without number.
4:11 it will be said of this *p* and of Jerusalem,
4:11 a wind comes toward the daughter of my *p*."
4:22 Fools my *p* are,
5:14 this *p* is the wood that it shall devour!—
5:15 nation, a *p* whose language you know not,
5:21 and senseless *p* Who have eyes and see not,
5:26 For there are among my *p* criminals;
5:31 Yet my *p* will have it so;
6:14 though it were nought, the injury to my *p*:
6:19 See, I bring evil upon this *p*,
6:21 before this *p* obstacles to bring them down;
6:22 See, a *p* comes from the land of the north,
6:26 O daughter of my *p*,
6:27 A tester among my *p* I have appointed you,
7:12 because of the wickedness of my *p* Israel.
7:16 You, now, do not intercede for this *p*;
7:23 I will be your God and you shall be my *p*.
7:30 The *p* of Judah have done what is evil in
7:33 The corpses of this *p* will be food for the
8: 5 do these *p* rebel with obstinate resistance?
8: 7 my *p* do not know the ordinance of the LORD.
8:11 the injury to the daughter of my *p*:
8:19 the cry of the daughter of my *p*,
8:21 broken by the ruin of the daughter of my *p*.
8:22 over the wound of the daughter of my *p*?
8:23 over the slain of the daughter of my *p*!
9: 1 I might leave my *p* and depart from them.
9:20 in the street, young *p* in the squares.
11: 4 Then you shall be my *p*,
11:14 Do not intercede on behalf of this *p*,
12:14 which I gave my *p* Israel as their own:
12:16 they who formerly taught my *p* to swear by
12:16 shall be built up in the midst of my *p*.
13:10 This wicked *p* who refuse to obey my words,
13:11 to be my *p*,
14: 2 Her *p* sink down in mourning:
14:10 Thus says the LORD of this *p*:
14:11 Do not intercede for this *p*.
14:16 The *p* to whom they prophesy shall be cast
14:17 overwhelms the virgin daughter of my *p*,
15: 1 me, my heart would not turn toward this *p*.
15: 7 I destroyed my *p* through bereavement;
15:20 you toward this *p* a solid wall of brass.
16: 5 have withdrawn my friendship from this *p*,
16: 8 Enter not a house where *p* are celebrating,
16:10 all these words to this *p* and they ask you:
17:26 To it *p* will come from the cities of Judah
18:15 Yet my *p* have forgotten me:
19: 1 of the elders of the *p* and of the priests,
19:11 Thus will I smash this *p* and this city,
19:14 of the house of God and said to all the *p*:
21: 7 the *p* in this city who survive pestilence,
21: 8 And to this *p* you shall say:
22: 2 and your *p* that enter by these gates!
22: 4 horses, with their ministers, and their *p*.
22: 8 Many *p* will pass by this city and ask one
23: 2 against the shepherds who shepherd my *p*:
23:13 by Baal and led my *p* Israel astray.
23:22 and did they but proclaim to my *p* my words,
23:27 think to make my *p* forget my name for Baal.
23:32 and who lead my *p* astray by recounting
23:32 command, and they do this *p* no good at all,
23:33 And when this *p*,
24: 7 They shall be my *p* and I will be their God,
25: 1 to Jeremiah concerning all the *p* of Judah,
25: 2 prophet Jeremiah spoke to all the *p* of Judah
25:19 servants, his princes, all the *p* under him,
26: 2 speak to the *p* of all the cities of Judah
26: 7 and all the *p* heard Jeremiah speak these
26: 8 that the LORD bade him speak to all the *p*,
26: 9 And all the *p* gathered about Jeremiah in
26:11 said to the princes and to all the *p*,
26:12 this answer to the princes and all the *p*:
26:16 the *p* said to the priests and the prophets,
26:17 forward and said to all the *p* assembled,
26:18 of Judah, and he told all the *p* of Judah:
26:24 handed over to the *p* to be put to death.
27:11 The *p* that submits its neck to the yoke of
27:12 serve him and his *p*,
27:13 Why should you and your *p* die by the sword,
27:16 and to all the *p* I spoke as follows:
28: 1 the presence of the priests and all the *p*:
28: 5 the *p* assembled in the house of the LORD,
28: 7 your hearing and the hearing of all the *p*.
28:11 and said in the presence of all the *p*:
28:15 you have raised false confidence in this *p*.
29: 1 and all the *p* who were exiled by
29:16 and all the *p* who remain in this city,
29:25 own authority to all the *p* of Jerusalem,
29:32 *p* to see the good I will do to this people,
30: 3 the lot of my *p* (of Israel and Judah,
30:22 You shall be my *p*, and I will be your God.
31: 1 tribes of Israel, and they shall be my *p*.
31: 2 The *p* that escaped the sword have found

PEOPLE (cont.)
31: 7 The LORD has delivered his *p*,
31:14 and my *p* shall be filled with my blessings,
31:33 will be their God, and they shall be my *p*.
32:21 outstretched arm you brought your *p* Israel
32:38 They shall be my *p*,
32:42 I brought upon this *p* all this great evil,
33:24 you not noticed what these *p* are saying:
33:24 They spurn my *p* as if it were no longer a
34: 8 agreement with all the *p* in Jerusalem
34:19 courtiers, the priests, and the common *p*,
35:16 but this *p* does not obey me!
36: 7 with which the LORD has threatened this *p*.
36: 9 the LORD was proclaimed for all the *p*
36:14 you the scroll you read publicly to the *p*."
37: 2 nor the *p* of the land would listen to the
37: 4 he still came and went freely among the *p*.
37:18 wronged you, or your ministers, or this *p*,
38: 1 Jeremiah speaking these words to all the *p*:
38: 4 who are left in this city, and all the *p*,
38: 4 is not interested in the welfare of our *p*,
39: 8 the king's palace and the houses of the *p*,
39: 9 Babylon the rest of the *p* left in the city,
39:14 And so he remained among the *p*.
40: 5 stay with him among the *p*,
40: 6 with him among the *p* left in the land.
40:11 When the *p* of Judah in Moab,
41:10 of the *p* left in Mizpah and the princesses,
41:13 the *p* who were Ishmael's captives rejoiced.
41:16 took charge of the remnant of the *p*,
42: 1 Azariah, son of Hoshaiah, and all the *p*,
42: 8 of Kareah, his army leaders, and all the *p*,
43: 1 to the *p* all these words of the LORD,
43: 4 *p* did not obey the LORD's command to stay
44: 1 the *p* of Judah who were living in Egypt,
44:15 the *p* who lived in Lower and Upper Egypt,
44:20 To all the *p*, men and women,
44:21 kings and princes, and the *p* generally?
44:24 Jeremiah said further to all the *p*,
44:26 LORD, all you *p* of Judah who live in Egypt;
46: 8 the earth, destroying the city and its *p*.
46:16 let us return to our own *p*,
46:24 Egypt, handed over to the *p* of the north.
47: 2 all that is in it, the cities and their *p*.
47: 2 All the *p* of the land set up a wailing cry.
48: 2 "Come, let us put an end to her as a *p*."
48:42 Moab shall be destroyed, no more a *p*,
48:43 pit, and trap be upon you, *p* of Moab,
48:46 O Moab, you are ruined, O *p* of Chemosh!
49: 1 why have his *p* settled in Gad's cities?
50: 3 A *p* from the north advances against her to
50: 6 Lost sheep were my *p*,
50:16 sword, each of them turns to his own *p*,
50:35 Chaldeans, says the LORD, upon Babylon's *p*,
50:41 a *p* comes from the north,
51:35 My blood upon the *p* of Chaldea,
51:45 Leave her, my *p*,
52: 6 the city and the *p* had no more bread,
52:15 exile the rest of the *p* left in the city,
52:25 *p* of the land, and sixty of the common *p*
52:28 the *p* whom Nebuchadnezzar led away captive:
52:28 three thousand and twenty-three *p* of Judah;
52:30 seven hundred and forty-five *p* of Judah:
Lam 1: 7 When her *p* fell into enemy hands,
1:11 All her *p* groan, searching for bread;
2:11 of the downfall of the daughter of my *p*,
3:48 over the downfall of the daughter of my *p*.
4: 3 The daughter of my *p* has become as cruel
4: 6 my *p* is greater than the penalty of Sodom,
4:10 in the downfall of the daughter of my *p*.
4:14 that *p* could not touch even their garments:
Bar 1: 3 well as all the *p* who came to the reading:
1: 4 kings' sons, the elders, and the whole *p*,
1: 7 the whole *p* who were with him in Jerusalem.
1: 9 and the *p* of the land from Jerusalem,
2:11 you who led your *p* out of the land of
2:30 heed me, because they are a stiff-necked *p*.
2:35 be my *p*; and I will not again remove my *p*
4: 5 Fear not, my *p*!
6: 8 *P* bring gold, as to a maiden in love
Ez 3: 5 Not to a *p* with difficult speech and
5:10 that remain of your *p* in every direction.
5:12 A third of your *p* shall die of pestilence
6: 8 When some of your *p* have escaped to other
7:27 the hands of the common *p* shall tremble.
11: 1 Pelatiah, son of Benaiah, princes of the *p*.
11:20 they shall be my *p* and I will be their God.
12:19 Then say to the *p* of the land:
13: 9 shall not belong to the community of my *p*,
13:10 the very reason that they led my *p* astray,
13:17 of your *p* who prophesy their own thoughts;
13:18 Do you think to entrap the lives of my *p*,
13:19 You dishonor me before my *p* with handfuls
13:19 lying to my *p* who willingly hear lies.
13:21 your veils and rescue my *p* from your power,
13:23 but I will rescue my *p* from your power.
14: 8 I will cut him off from the midst of my *p*.
14: 9 him and root him out of my *p* Israel.
14:11 Thus they shall be my *p*,
17: 9 need of a mighty arm or many *p* to do this.]
18:18 and did what was not good among his *p*,
21:17 son of man, for it is destined for my *p*;
21:17 of Israel, victims of the sword with my *p*.
22:25 they devour *p*,
22:29 The *p* of the land practice extortion and
24:19 Then the *p* asked me,
24:19 I therefore spoke to the *p* that morning,
25:14 upon Edom I will entrust to my *p* Israel,
26:11 Your *p* he shall slay by the sword;
30: 5 and *p* of the allied territory shall fall
30:11 He and his *p* with him,
33: 2 and the *p* of this country select one of
33: 3 country, blows the trumpet to warn the *p*,
33:10 You *p* say, "Our crimes and our sins
33:31 My *p* come to you as people always do;
34:30 LORD, am their God, and they are my *p*,
36: 8 branches and bear fruit for my *p* Israel,
36:12 [My *p* Israel are the ones whom I will have
36:13 and you rob your *p* of their children";
36:14 devour men or rob your *p* of their children,
36:15 peoples, or rob your *p* of their children,
36:20 "These are the *p* of the LORD,
36:28 you shall be my *p*,
37:12 O my *p*, I will open your graves
37:13 graves and have you rise from them, O my *p*!
37:23 they may be my *p* and I may be their God.
37:27 will be their God, and they shall be my *p*.
38:11 the peaceful *p* who are living in security,
38:12 *p* gathered from the nations, a *p* concerned
38:14 When my *p* Israel are dwelling in security,
38:16 my *p* Israel like a cloud covering the land.
39: 7 make my holy name known among my *p* Israel;
39:13 All the *p* of the land shall bury them and
42:14 then approach the place destined for the *p*."
44:11 holocausts and the sacrifices for the *p*,
44:11 stand before the *p* to minister for them.
44:19 are to go out to the *p* in the outer court,
44:19 holiness to the *p* with their garments.
44:23 They shall teach my *p* to distinguish
45: 8 of Israel will no longer oppress my *p*,
45: 9 Stop evicting my *p*!
45:16 All the *p* of the land shall be bound to
45:22 and on behalf of all the *p* of the land,
46: 3 The *p* of the land shall worship before the
46: 9 When the *p* of the land enter the presence
46:18 the *p* by evicting them from their property.
46:18 of my *p* will be driven from their property.
46:20 the risk of transmitting holiness to the *p*."
46:24 ministers cook the sacrifices of the *p*."
Dn 2:44 be destroyed or delivered up to another *p*;
7:27 be given to the holy *p* of the Most High,
9: 6 our fathers, and all the *p* of the land.
9:15 who led your *p* out of the land of Egypt
9:16 Jerusalem and your *p* have become the
9:19 this city and your *p* bear your name!"
9:20 my sin and the sin of my *p* Israel,
9:24 decreed for your *p* and for your holy city:
9:26 And the *p* of a leader who will come shall
10:14 shall happen to your *p* in the days to come;
11:14 *p* shall rise up in fulfillment of vision,
11:34 When they fall, few *p* shall help them,
11:39 he shall station a *p* of a foreign god.
12: 1 the great prince, guardian of your *p*;
12: 1 At that time your *p* shall escape,
12: 7 of the holy *p* was brought to an end,
13: 5 two elders of the *p* were appointed judges,
13: 5 elders who were to govern the *p* as judges."
13: 7 When the *p* left at noon,
13:26 When the *p* in the house heard the cries
13:28 *p* came to her husband Joakim the next day,
13:28 Before all the *p* they ordered:
13:34 In the midst of the *p* the two elders rose
13:41 since they were elders and judges of the *p*,
13:47 All the *p* turned and asked him,
13:50 Then all the *p* returned in haste.
13:64 Daniel was greatly esteemed by the *p*.
Hos 1: 9 the name Lo-ammi, for you are not my *p*,
2: 2 Then the *p* of Judah and of Israel shall
2:25 I will say to Lo-ammi, "You are my *p*,"
3: 1 Even as the LORD loves the *p* of Israel,
3: 4 For the *p* of Israel shall remain many days
3: 5 Then the *p* of Israel shall turn back and
4: 1 Hear the word of the LORD, O *p* of Israel,
4: 6 My *p* perish for want of knowledge!
4: 8 They feed on the sin of my *p*,
4: 9 priests shall fare no better than the *p*:
4:11 wine and new deprive my *p* of understanding.
4:14 a *p* without understanding come to ruin.
7: 1 would bring about the restoration of my *p*,
10: 5 The *p* mourn for it and its priests wail
10:10 the wanton *p* I came and I chastised them;
11: 7 *p* are in suspense about returning to him;
Jl 1: 6 For a *p* has invaded my land,
2: 2 the mountains, a *p* numerous and mighty!
2: 5 Like a mighty *p* arrayed for battle.
2:16 Gather the *p*,
2:17 weep, And say, "Spare, O LORD, your *p*,
2:18 for his land and took pity on his *p*.
2:19 The LORD answered and said to his *p*:
2:26 my *p* shall nevermore be put to shame.
2:27 my *p* shall nevermore be put to shame.
4: 2 there on behalf of my *p* and my inheritance,
4: 3 Over my *p* they have cast lots;
4: 6 the *p* of Judah and Jerusalem to the Greeks,
4: 8 sons and your daughters to the *p* of Judah,
4:16 quake, but the LORD is a refuge to his *p*,
4:19 Because of violence done to the *p* of Judah,
Am 1: 5 the *p* of Aram shall be exiled to Kir,
3: 6 in a city, will the *p* not be frightened?
6: 1 to whom the *p* of Israel have recourse!
7: 8 the plummet in the midst of my *p* Israel;
7:15 said to me, Go, prophesy to my *p* Israel.
8: 2 time is ripe to have done with my *p* Israel;
9:10 the sword shall all sinners among my *p* die,
9:14 bring about the restoration of my *p* Israel;
Ob 1:13 gate of my *p* on the day of their calamity;
Jon 1: 8 your country, and to what *p* do you belong?"
3: 5 when the *p* of Nineveh believed God;
Mi 1: 9 to Judah, It reaches to the gate of my *p*,
2: 4 The fields of my *p* are measured out,
2: 8 But of late my *p* has risen up as an enemy:
2: 9 *p* you drive out from their pleasant houses;
2:11 then he would be the prophet of this *p*.
3: 3 They eat the flesh of my *p*,
3: 5 the prophets who lead my *p* astray;
6: 2 For the LORD has a plea against his *p*,
6: 3 O my *p*, what have I done to you,
6: 5 My *p*, remember what Moab's King Balak
7:14 Shepherd your *p* with your staff,
Na 3:18 Your *p* are scattered upon the mountains,
Hb 1: 6 up Chaldea, that bitter and unruly *p*,
3:13 You come forth to save your *p*,
3:16 that will come upon the *p* who attack us.
Zep 2: 8 *p* and made boasts against their territory.
2: 9 The remnant of my *p* shall plunder them,
2:10 boasted against the *p* of the LORD of hosts.
3:12 remnant in your midst a *p* humble and lowly,
Hg 1: 2 This *p* says: "Not now has the Time come
1:12 of the *p* listened to the voice of the LORD,
1:12 him, and the *p* feared because of the LORD.
1:13 to the *p* as the message of the LORD:
1:14 the spirit of all the remnant of the *p*,
2: 2 of Jehozadak, and to the remnant of the *p*:
2: 4 all you *p* of the land says the LORD,
2:14 So is this *p*, and so is this nation
Zec 2: 8 *P* will live in Jerusalem as though in open
2:15 LORD on that day, and they shall be his *p*,
7: 5 all the *p* of the land and to the priests:
8: 6 in the eyes of the remnant of this *p*,
8: 7 my *p* from the land of the rising sun,
8: 8 They shall be my *p*,
8:11 the remnant of this *p* as in former days,
8:12 I will have the remnant of the *p* possess.
8:22 Many *p* and strong nations shall come to
9:16 God, shall save them on that day, his *p*,
13: 9 I will say, "They are my *p*,"
14: 2 the *p* shall not be removed from the city.
Mal 1: 4 the *p* with whom the LORD is angry forever.
2: 9 contemptible and base before all the *p*,
Mt 1:21 because he will save his *p* from their sins."
2: 4 of the chief priests and scribes of the *p*,
2: 6 a ruler who is to shepherd my *p* Israel.'"
4:16 a *p* living in darkness has seen a great
4:23 cured the *p* of every disease and illness.
6: 1 performing religious acts for *p* to see.
8:18 Seeing the *p* crowd around him,
9: 2 There the *p* at once brought to him a
9:12 *P* who are in good health do not need a
9:12 health do not need a doctor; sick *p* do.
9:17 *P* do not pour new wine into old wineskins.
9:32 suddenly some *p* brought him a mute who was
11:18 neither eating nor drinking, and *p* say,
12:15 Many *p* followed him and he cured them all,
12:27 help, by whose help do your *p* expel them?
12:36 on judgment day *p* will be held accountable
14: 5 to kill John but was afraid of the *p*,
14:19 disciples, who in turn gave them to the *p*.
14:35 *P* brought him all the afflicted,
15: 8 'This *p* pays me lip service but their
15:30 *p* came to him bringing with them cripples,
15:38 The *p* who were fed numbered four thousand,
16:13 "Who do *p* say that the Son of Man is?"
21:23 elders of the *p* came up to him and said:
21:26 human,' we shall have reason to fear the *p*,
22:30 When *p* rise from the dead,
24:38 the flood *p* were eating and drinking,
26: 3 the chief priests and elders of the *p*
26: 5 festival, for fear of a riot among the *p*."
26:47 by the chief priests and elders of the *p*.
27: 1 the chief priests and the elders of the *p*
27:25 The whole *p* said in reply,
27:39 *P* going by kept insulting him,
27:64 may go and steal him and tell the *p*,
Mk 1: 5 All the Judean countryside and the *p* of
1:22 The *p* were spellbound by his teaching
1:45 yet *p* kept coming to him from all sides.
2: 3 *p* arrived bringing a paralyzed man to him.
2:13 *p* kept coming to him in crowds and he
2:17 *P* who are healthy do not need a doctor;
2:17 healthy do not need a doctor; sick *p* do.
2:18 *P* came to Jesus with the objection,
4:16 those sown on rocky ground are *p*
5:14 and the *p* came to see what had happened.
5:35 *p* from the official's house arrived saying,
5:38 *p* wailing and crying loudly on all sides.
6:14 had become widespread and *p* were saying,
6:31 *P* were coming and going in great numbers,
6:33 *P* saw them leaving,
6:33 *P* from all the towns hastened on foot to

6:39 He told them to make the *p* sit down on the
6:40 The *p* took their places in hundreds and
6:54 the boat *p* immediately recognized him.
7: 6 'This *p* pays me lip service but their
7:32 Some *p* brought him a deaf man who had a
8: 4 *p* sufficient bread in this deserted spot?"
8: 8 The *p* in the crowd ate until they had
8:22 some *p* brought him a blind man and begged
8:24 can see *p* but they look like walking trees!"
8:27 "Who do *p* say that I am?"
10:13 *P* were bringing their little children to
10:48 *p* were scolding him to make him keep quiet,
11: 8 Many *p* spread their cloaks on the road,
11:32 (They had reason to fear the *p*,
12:25 When *p* rise from the dead,
14: 2 during the festival, or the *p* may riot."
14:43 these *p* had been sent by the chief priests,
15:29 *P* going by kept insulting him,
Lk 1:10 *p* was praying outside at the incense hour,
1:17 to prepare for the Lord a *p* well-disposed."
1:21 the *p* were waiting for Zechariah,
1:68 because he has visited and ransomed his *p*.
1:77 Giving his *p* a knowledge of salvation in
2:10 of great joy to be shared by the whole *p*.
2:32 the Gentiles, the glory of your *p* Israel."
3:15 The *p* were full of anticipation,
3:18 sort, he preached the good news to the *p*.
3:21 When all the *p* were baptized,
4:40 all who had *p* sick with a variety of
5:31 sick *p* do.
6:17 a large crowd of *p* was with them from all
6:18 *p* who came to hear him and be healed of
7: 1 this discourse in the hearing of the *p*,
7: 5 you," they said, "because he loves our *p*,
7:16 and, "God has visited his *p*."
8: 4 with *p* resorting to him from one town
8:12 Those on the footpath are *p* who hear,
8:35 The *p* went out to see for themselves what
9: 5 When *p* will not receive you,
9:13 ourselves go and buy food for all these *p*?"
9:61 first let me take leave of my *p* at home."
10:10 *p* of any town you enter do not welcome you,
11:19 Beelzebul, by whom do your *p* cast them out?
13:29 *P* will come from the east and the west,
15: 7 righteous *p* who have no need to repent.
16: 4 Here is a way to make sure that *p* will
16:16 *p* of every sort are forcing their way in.
18:43 All the *p* witnessed it and they too gave
19:47 destroy him, as were the leaders of the *p*,
20: 1 One day when he was teaching the *p* in the
20: 6 if we say, 'From men,' the *p* will stone us,
20: 9 began to tell the *p* the following parable:
20:19 on him, but they were afraid of the *p*.
20:45 In the hearing of all the *p*,
21:23 and the wrath against this *p* will be great.
21:24 The *p* will fall before the sword:
21:38 all the *p* came to hear him in the temple.
22: 2 but they were afraid of the *p*.
22:25 "Earthly kings lord it over their *p*.
22:66 At daybreak, the elders of the *p*,
23: 5 "He stirs up the *p* by his teaching
23:13 chief priests, the ruling class, and the *p*,
23:14 man before me as one who subverts the *p*.
23:27 A great crowd of *p* followed him,
23:35 The *p* stood there watching,
24:19 and deed in the eyes of God and all the *p*;
Jn 2:10 *P* usually serve the choice wine first;
2:14 he came upon *p* engaged in selling oxen,
3:23 and *p* kept coming to be baptized.
4:20 but you *p* claim that Jerusalem is the
4:22 You *p* worship what you do not understand,
4:28 She said to the *p*:
4:45 in Galilee, the *p* there welcomed him.
4:48 "Unless you *p* see signs and wonders,
5: 3 were crowded with sick *p* lying there blind,
5:44 How can *p* like you believe,
6: 5 shall we buy bread for these *p* to eat?"
6:10 Jesus said, "Get the *p* to recline."
6:14 When the *p* saw the sign he had performed
7:25 led some of the *p* of Jerusalem to remark:
8: 2 and when the *p* started coming to him,
9: 8 His neighbors and the *p* who had been
10:41 while he stayed there many *p* came to him.
11:19 and many Jewish *p* had come out to console
11:50 *p* than to have the whole nation destroyed?"
11:55 which meant that many *p* from the country
11:56 various *p* in the temple vicinity saying to
12:16 that the *p* had done to him precisely
18:14 advantage of having one man die for the *p*.)
18:35 "It is your own *p* and the chief priests
Acts 2:47 God and winning the approval of all the *p*.
3: 2 to beg from the *p* as they entered.
3: 9 *p* saw him moving and giving praise to God,
3:12 saw this, he addressed the *p* as follows:
3:23 shall be ruthlessly cut off from the *p*.'
4: 2 angry because they were teaching the *p*
4: 8 "Leaders of the *p*!
4:10 then you and all the *p* of Israel must
4:17 this from spreading further among the *p*
4:21 no way to punish them because of the *p*,
4:23 the two went back to their own *p*
5:12 signs and wonders occurred among the *p*.
5:13 fact that the *p* held them in great esteem.
5:15 The *p* carried the sick into the streets
5:20 preach to the *p* all about this new life."
5:25 over there in the temple, teaching the *p*."
5:34 of the law highly regarded by all the *p*.
6: 8 worked great wonders and signs among the *p*.
6:12 God, and in this way they incited the *p*,
7:17 our *p* in Egypt grew more and more numerous,
7:19 craftily with our *p* and oppressed them.
7:19 exposure so that the *p* would not survive.
7:34 *p* in Egypt and have heard their groaning,
7:51 "You stiff-necked *p*,
8:10 *P* from every rank of society were paying
8:15 The two went down to these *p* and prayed
9:13 he has done to your holy *p* in Jerusalem.
9:15 and their kings and to the *p* of Israel.
9:21 *p* and bring them before the chief priests?"
9:32 to God's holy *p* living in Lydda.
10: 2 to the *p* and he constantly prayed to God.
10:27 He found many *p* assembled there,
10:42 He commissioned us to preach to the *p* and
10:47 these *p* who have received the Holy Spirit,
12: 4 bring him before the *p* after the Passover.
12:20 been infuriated by the *p* of Tyre and Sidon,
13:15 have any exhortation to address to the *p*,
13:17 God of the *p* Israel once chose our fathers.
13:17 He made this *p* great during their sojourn
13:24 of repentance to all the *p* of Israel.
13:31 These are his witnesses now before the *p*.
13:42 the *p* invited them to speak on this
14:19 and Iconium arrived and won the *p* over.
15:14 among the Gentiles a *p* to bear his name.
16: 4 they transmitted to the *p* for observance
17: 2 Paul joined the *p* there and conducted
18:10 There are many of my *p* in this city."
18:13 "is influencing *p* to worship God in ways
19: 4 He used to tell the *p* about the one who
19:26 numbers of *p* to change their religion.
19:29 *P* rushed together to the theater and
19:32 *p* were shouting all sorts of things,
20:12 To the great comfort of the *p*,
21:12 both we ourselves and the *p* of Caesarea
21:28 his teaching everywhere against our *p*,
21:30 *P* came running from all sides.
21:34 but different *p* in the crowd shouted out
21:36 A crowd of *p* was following along shouting,
21:39 I beg you, let me address these *p*."
21:40 on the steps and motioned the *p* to silence.
23: 5 'You shall not curse a prince of your *p*!'"
24:17 alms to my own *p* and to make my offerings.
25: 9 Festus, wishing to please the Jewish *p*,
26: 4 and the life I have led among my own *p*
26: 7 The twelve tribes of our *p* fervently
26:10 I sent many of God's holy *p* to prison.
26:17 you from this *p* and from the nations,
26:18 of their sins and a portion among God's *p*.'
26:20 *p* of Damascus, then to the *p* of Jerusalem
26:23 light to our *p* and to the Gentiles."
28:17 against our *p* or our ancestral customs;
28:19 cause to make accusations against my own *p*.
28:26 'Go to this *p* and say:
28:27 The mind of this *p* has grown sluggish.
Rom 9:25 who were not my *p* I will call 'my people,'
9:26 it was said to them, 'You are not my *p*,'
10:21 hands to an unbelieving and contentious *p*."
11: 1 I ask, then, has God rejected his *p*?
11: 2 has not rejected his *p* whom he foreknew.
15:10 Again, "Rejoice, O Gentiles, with his *p*."
1Cor 1: 2 Christ Jesus and called to be a holy *p*,
5:10 association with immoral *p* in this world,
6: 1 to the wicked and not to God's holy *p*?
7:28 But such *p* will have trials in this life,
10: 7 says, "The *p* sat down to eat and drink,
10:15 I address you as one addresses sensible *p*.
14:21 in alien speech I will speak to this *p*,
2Cor 6:16 I will be their God and they shall be my *p*.
10:11 Well, let such *p* give this some thought,
10:12 with certain *p* who recommend themselves.
10:12 Since *p* like that are their own appraisers,
11:26 endangered by floods, robbers, my own *p*,
Gal 4:17 The *p* I have referred to are not courting
Eph 1:14 redemption of a *p* God has made his own,
5:12 mention the things these *p* do in secret;
1Thes 1: 9 The *p* of those parts are reporting what
5: 3 Just when *p* are saying,
1Tm 1: 3 Ephesus in order to warn certain *p*
1: 6 Some *p* have neglected these and instead
2Tm 2:14 Keep reminding *p* of these things and
4: 3 when *p* will not tolerate sound doctrine,
Ti 2:14 and to cleanse for himself a *p* of his own,
3: 1 Remind *p* to be loyally subject to the
3:14 Let our *p* devote themselves to honest work
Phlm 1: 5 toward the Lord Jesus and all God's *p*.
1: 7 the hearts of God's *p* have been refreshed.
Heb 2:17 their behalf, to expiate the sins of the *p*.
4: 9 rest still remains for the *p* of God.
5: 3 offerings for himself as well as for the *p*.
6:10 service, past and present, to his holy *p*.
7: 5 of Levi should receive tithes from the *p*,
7:11 the basis of which the *p* received the law),
7:27 his own sins and then for those of the *p*;
8:10 will be their God and they shall be my *p*.
9: 7 for himself and for the sins of the *p*.
9:19 all the commandments of the law to the *p*,
9:19 and sprinkled the book and all the *p*,
10:30 repay," and "The Lord will judge his *p*."
11:25 to be ill-treated along with God's *p*
13:12 gate, to sanctify the *p* by his own blood.
13:24 all your leaders and to all the *p* of God.
1Pt 2: 9 a *p* he claims for his own to proclaim the
2:10 were no people, but now you are God's *p*;
3:14 do not stand in awe of what this *p* fears."
2Pt 2: 1 there were false prophets among God's *p*,
Jude 1: 5 The Lord first rescued his *p* from the land
1:10 These *p*, however, not only revile
Rv 5: 8 which were the prayers of God's holy *p*.
5: 9 race and tongue, of every *p* and nation.
7: 9 from every nation and race, *p* and tongue.
7:13 me, "Who are these *p* all dressed in white?
8: 4 God, and with it the prayers of God's *p*.
8:11 Many *p* died from this polluted water.
11: 9 Men from every *p* and race,
13: 7 wage war against God's *p* and conquer them.
13: 7 granted authority over every race and *p*,
13:10 endurance that distinguishes God's holy *p*.
14: 6 to every nation and race, language and *p*.
18: 4 "Depart from her, my *p*,
20: 9 beloved city where God's *p* were encamped;
21: 3 dwell with them and they shall be his *p*

PEOPLED (3)

Gn 9:19 Noah, and from them the whole earth was *p*.
Sir 16: 4 Through one wise man can a city be *p*;
Jer 50:39 Never again shall it be *p*,

PEOPLES (227)

Gn 17:16 and rulers of *p* shall issue from him."
25:23 *p* are quarreling while still within you;
27:29 "Let *p* serve you,
28: 3 you that you may become an assembly of *p*.
49:10 to him, and he receives the *p*' homage.
Ex 18:19 Act as the *p* representative before God,
Lv 9:15 Thereupon he had the *p* offering brought up.
9:15 the goat that was for the *p* sin offering,
16:15 he shall slaughter the *p* sin-offering goat,
16:24 out and offer his own and the *p* holocaust,
Nm 24:20 First of the *p* was Amalek,
Dt 7:14 You will be blessed above all *p*;
10:15 descendants, in preference to all other *p*,
18: 9 to imitate the abominations of the *p* there.
20:15 does not belong to the *p* of this land.
32: 8 the *p* after the number of the sons of God;
32:43 of his servants and purges his *p* land.
Jos 4:24 in order that all the *p* of the earth may
24:17 and among all the *p* through whom we passed.
24:18 approach the LORD drove out [all the *p*,
1Sm 8: 7 "Grant the *p* every request.
27: 8 *p* living in the land between Telam,
2Sm 22:48 who made *p* subject to me and helped me
1Kgs 8:43 all the *p* of the earth may know your name,
8:53 the *p* of the earth for your inheritance,
8:60 that all the *p* of the earth may know the
2Kgs 17:29 But these *p* began to make their own gods
1Chr 16:24 his glory among the nations; among all *p*,
2Chr 6:33 all the *p* of the earth may know your name,
7:20 make it a proverb and a byword among all *p*.
13: 9 priests like the *p* of foreign lands?
18:27 And he said, "Hear, O *p*, all of you!"
25:15 "Why have you had recourse to this *p* gods
32:13 I have done to all the *p* of other lands?
32:19 of the gods of the other *p* of the earth,
Ezr 3: 3 Despite their fear of the *p* of the land,
4:10 and the other *p* whom the great and
6:21 from the uncleanness of the *p* of the land
9: 1 aloof from the *p* of the land
9: 2 the holy race with the *p* of the land.
9:11 with the filth of the *p* of the land,
9:14 by intermarrying with these abominable *p*?
10: 2 foreign women of the *p* of the land.
10:11 *p* of the land and from these foreign women."
Neh 9:22 You gave them kingdoms and *p*,
9:24 their kings as well as the *p* of the land,
9:30 over into the power of the *p* of the lands.
10:29 *p* of the lands in favor of the law of God,
10:31 marry our daughters to the *p* of the land,
10:32 When the *p* of the land bring in
13:24 to the languages of the various other *p*.
Jdt 1: 8 along the seacoast, to the *p* of Carmel,
6: 1 of the whole throng of coastland *p*,
Est B: 2 *p* and to hold sway over the whole world,
3:14 every province was published to all the *p*.
C:16 O Lord, chose Israel from among all *p*,
E:11 the good will which we have toward all *p*
8:13 province was published among all the *p*,
8:17 many of the *p* of the land embraced Judaism,
9: 2 but all *p* were seized with a fear of them.
10: 3 as the promoter of his *p* welfare and the
2Mc 5:20 itself, having shared in the *p* misfortunes,
Jb 12:23 he spreads *p* abroad and he abandons them.
Ps(s) 2: 1 do the nations rage and the *p* utter folly?
7: 8 Let the assembly of the *p* surround you;
9: 9 he governs the *p* with equity.
18:48 who made *p* subject to me and preserved me
33:10 he foils the designs of *p*.
44: 3 you smashed the *p*,
44:15 the nations, a laughingstock among the *p*.

PEOPLES (cont.)

45: 6 p are subject to you;
47: 2 All you p, clap your hands, shout to God
47: 4 He brings p under us;
47:10 The princes of the p are gathered together
49: 2 Hear this, all you p;
56: 8 in your wrath bring down the p, O God.
57:10 I will give thanks to you among the p,
65: 8 of their waves and the tumult of the p.
66: 8 Bless our God, you p,
67: 4 May the p praise you, O God; may all the p
67: 5 exult because you rule the p in equity;
67: 6 p praise you, O God; may all the p
68:31 scatter the p who delight in war.
77:15 the p you have made known your power.
87: 6 They shall note, when the p are enrolled:
96: 3 among all p, his wondrous deeds.
96:10 he governs the p with equity.
96:13 with justice and the p with his constancy.
97: 6 his justice, and all p see his glory.
98: 9 world with justice and the p with equity.
99: 1 The LORD is king; the p tremble;
99: 2 Zion is great, he is high above all the p.
102:23 in Jerusalem, When the p gather together,
105:20 him, the ruler of the p set him free.
105:44 and they took what the p had toiled for,
106:34 They did not exterminate the p,
108: 4 I will give thanks to you among the p,
117: 1 glorify him, all you p!
144: 2 in whom I trust, who subdues p under me.
148:11 Let the kings of the earth and all p,
149: 7 on the nations, punishments on the p;
Prv 14:34 exalts a nation, but sin is a p disgrace.
Wis 3: 8 They shall judge nations and rule over p,
6: 2 multitude and lord it over throngs of p!
6:21 throne and scepter, you princes of the p,
8:14 I should govern p, and nations would be
12:12 Or when p perish,
Sir 10: 2 As the p judge, so are his ministers;
28:14 many, and makes them refugees among the p;
36: 8 and your p oppressors meet destruction.
37:22 When a man is wise to his p advantage,
39: 5 He travels among the p of foreign lands to
39:10 P will speak of his wisdom,
44:19 ABRAHAM, father of many p,
46: 6 the LORD was watching over his p battles.
47: 4 the giant and wiped out the p disgrace,
47:16 coasts, and their p came to hear you;
48:19 The p hearts melted within them,
Is 2: 3 many p shall come and say:
2: 4 the nations, and impose terms on many p.
3:14 judgment with his p elders and princes:
8: 9 Know, O p, and be appalled!
10: 2 and robbing my p poor of their rights,
10:13 I have moved the boundaries of p,
14: 6 struck the p in wrath relentless blows;
17:12 many p that roar like the roar of the seas!
24:13 it is within the land, and among the p,
25: 6 p A feast of rich food and choice wines,
25: 7 he will destroy the veil that veils all p,
30:28 on the jaws of the p to send them astray].
33: 3 At the roaring sound, p flee;
33:12 The p shall be as in a limekiln,
34: 1 O nations, and hear, be attentive, O p!
41: 1 you p, wait for my words!
43: 4 for you and p in exchange for your life.
43: 9 gather together, let the p assemble!
49: 1 Hear me, O coastlands, listen, O distant p.
49:22 the nations, and raise my signal to the p;
51: 4 and my judgment, as the light of the p.
55: 4 As I made him a witness to the p,
56: 7 be called a house of prayer for all p.
57:14 remove the stumbling blocks from my p path.
60: 2 the earth, and thick clouds cover the p;
61: 9 nations, and their offspring among the p;
63: 6 I trampled down the p in my anger,
Jer 5:23 this p heart is stubborn and rebellious;
12:16 learn my p custom of swearing by my name,
34: 1 subject to him, as well as the other p,
51:27 Dedicate p to war against her,
51:28 Dedicate p to war against her:
51:44 p shall stream to him no more.
51:58 for the flames the p weary themselves.
Lam 1:18 Listen, all you p,
Bar 6:50 To all p and kings it will be clear that
Ez 3: 6 nor to the many p [with difficult speech
20:32 the nations, like the p of foreign lands,
20:35 I will lead you to the desert of the p,
23:24 north with chariots and wagons and many p.
25: 7 the nations, I will cut you off from the p,
25:10 that she may not be remembered among the p.
26: 2 it is broken, the gateway to the p;
27: 3 the trade of the p to many a coastland:
27:33 you drew from the seas you filled many p;
27:36 The traders among the p now hiss at you;
28:19 Among the p, all who knew you stand
28:25 from the p among whom they are scattered,
29:13 from the p among whom they are scattered,
31: 6 its shade dwelt numerous p of every race.
31:12 the p of the land withdrew from its shade,
32: 9 I will grieve the hearts of many p when I
32:10 Many p shall be appalled at you,
34:13 p and gather them from the foreign lands;
36:15 of nations, or bear insults from p,
38: 6 north with all its troops, many p with you.
38: 8 which has been assembled from many p
38: 8 p and all of whom now dwell in security.
38: 9 all your troops and the many p with you.
38:15 of the north, you and many p with you,
38:22 his troops, and upon the many p with him.
39: 4 all your troops and the p who are with you.
39:27 When I bring them back from among the p,
Dn 3: 4 "Nations and p of every language,
3: 7 the nations and p of every language all
3:96 Therefore I decree for nations and p of
3:98 to the nations and p of every language,
5:19 p of every language dreaded and feared him.
6:26 to the nations and p of every language,
7:14 nations and p of every language serve him.
8:24 He shall destroy powerful p;
Jl 2: 6 Before them p are in torment,
2:17 Why should they say among the p,
4:11 Hasten and come, all you neighboring p,
Mi 1: 2 Hear, O p, all of you, give heed,
4: 1 above the hills, And p shall stream to it:
4: 3 He shall judge between many p and impose
4: 5 all the p walk each in the name of its god,
4:13 hoofs bronze, that you may crush many p;
5: 6 of Jacob shall be in the midst of many p,
5: 7 among the nations, in the midst of many p,
Na 3: 4 her harlotries, and p by her witchcraft:
Hb 1:17 his sword to slay p without mercy?
2: 5 nations, and rallies to himself all the p—
2: 8 Because you despoiled many p all the rest
2:10 for your household, cutting off many p,
2:13 p toil for the flames,
Zep 3: 9 will change and purify the lips of the p,
3:20 and praise, among all the p of the earth,
Zec 8:20 There shall yet come p,
11:10 the covenant which I had made with all p;
12: 2 a bowl to stupefy all p round about.
12: 3 make Jerusalem a weighty stone for all p.
12: 4 will strike blind all the horses of the p,
12: 6 right and left all the surrounding p;
Mt 13:15 Sluggish indeed is this p heart.
Mk 11:17 be called a house of prayer for all p—
Lk 2:31 saving deed displayed for all the p to see:
Acts 4:25 the Gentiles rage, the p conspire in folly?
4:27 with the Gentiles and the p of Israel.
7:45 the land during the conquest of those p
17: 5 bring Paul and Silas before the p assembly.
Rom 15:11 you Gentiles and sing his glory, all you p."
2Tm 2:18 They are upsetting some p faith.
Rv 1: 7 p of the earth shall lament him bitterly.
10:11 must prophesy again for many p and nations,
17:15 large numbers of p and nations and tongues.

PEOR (10)

Nm 23:28 So he took Balaam to the top of P,
25: 3 thus submitted to the rites of Baal of P,
25: 5 have submitted to the rites of Baal of P."
25:18 P and as regards their kinswoman Cozbi,
25:18 at the time of the slaughter because of P."
31:16 Israelites toward the LORD in the P affair,
Dt 4: 3 everyone that followed the Baal of P;
Jos 15:59 Tekoa, Ephrathah (that is, Bethlehem), P,
22:17 For the sin of P, a plague came upon the
Ps(s) 106:28 of P and ate the sacrifices of dead gods.

PERAZIM (1)

Is 28:21 For the LORD shall rise up as on Mount P,

PERCEIVE (7)

Jb 23: 8 or to the west, I cannot p him;
33:14 once, or even twice, though one p it not.
Prv 24:12 does not he who tests hearts p it?
Is 43:19 Now it springs forth, do you not p it?
Lk 8:10 in parables that, 'Seeing they may not p,
Heb 11: 3 Through faith we p that the worlds were
Jas 2:24 You must p that a person is justified by

PERCEIVED (9)

Gn 31: 2 Jacob p, too, that Laban's attitude
Ezr 8:15 There I p that both laymen and priests
Neh 13:15 In those days I p that men in Judah were
1Mc 5:31 When Judas p that the struggle had begun
Jb 13: 1 my ear has heard and p it.
Wis 6:12 and she is readily p by those who love her,
19:18 p exactly from a review of what took place.
Bar 3:21 have not known, they have not p her paths,
Mt 14:30 But when he p how strong the wind was,

PERCEIVES (3)

Ps(s) 94: 7 the God of Jacob p not."
Prv 22: 3 The shrewd man p evil and hides,
27:12 The shrewd man p evil and hides;

PERCH (1)

Gn 8: 9 dove could find no place to alight and p,

PERCHED (1)

Tb 2:10 there were birds p on the wall above me,

PERCHES (1)

Bar 6:70 in a garden on which p every kind of bird,

PERDITION (2)

2Sm 22: 5 the floods of p overwhelmed me;
2Thes 2: 3 that son of p and adversary who exalts

PERDURING (1)

Wis 7:27 and renews everything while herself p;

PERENNIAL (2)

Wis 11: 6 when the p river was troubled with impure
Sir 42:21 P is his almighty wisdom;

PERES (2)

Dn 5:25 MENE, TEKEL, and P.
5:28 P,

PERESH (1)

1Chr 7:16 Machir's wife, bore a son whom she named P.

PEREZ (17)

Gn 38:29 So he was called P.
46:12 Er, Onan, Shelah, P,
46:12 and the sons of P were Hezron and Hamul.
Nm 26:20 through P the clan of the Perezites,
Ru 4:12 may your house become like the house of P,
4:18 These are the descendants of P:
4:18 P was the father of Hezron,
1Chr 2: 4 daughter-in-law Tamar bore him P and Zerah,
2: 5 The sons of P were Hezron and Hamul.
4: 1 P, Hezron, Carmi, Hur, and Shobal.
9: 4 son of Bani, one of the descendants of P,
27: 3 a descendant of P,
Neh 11: 4 son of Mehallalel, of the sons of P;
11: 6 The total of the sons of P who dwelt in
Mt 1: 3 Jesus Judah was the father of P and Zerah,
1: 3 P was the father of Hezron,
Lk 3:33 son of Arni, son of Hezron, son of P,

PEREZ-UZZA (1)

1Chr 13:11 place has been called P even to this day.

PEREZ-UZZAH (1)

2Sm 6: 8 has been called P down to the present day.)

PEREZITES (2)

Nm 26:20 through Perez the clan of the P,
26:21 The P were:

PERFECT (54)

1Chr 28: 9 him with a p heart and a willing soul,
2Mc 3: 1 While the holy city lived in p peace and
9:15 p equality with the Athenians all the Jews,
Jb 12: 4 he calls upon him, the just, the p man,"
22: 3 it a gain to him if you make your ways p?
36: 4 the one p in knowledge I set before you.
37:16 wondrous work of him who is p in knowledge?
Ps(s) 19: 8 The law of the LORD is p,
50: 2 From Zion, p in beauty, God shines forth.
119:80 Let my heart be p in your statutes,
119:138 decrees in justice and in p faithfulness.
Prv 4:18 light, that grows in brilliance till p day.
Sg 5: 2 my sister, my beloved, my dove, my p one!
6: 9 One alone is my dove, my p one,
Wis 4:13 Having become p in a short while,
9: 6 though one be p among the sons of men,
Sir 1:16 LORD, with blossoms of peace and p health.
19:17 p wisdom is the fulfillment of the law.
21:11 he who is p in fear of the LORD has wisdom.
34: 8 and p wisdom is found in the mouth of the
44:17 NOAH, found just and p,
Ez 16:14 the nations for your beauty, p as it was,
27: 3 Tyre, you said, "I am a ship, p in beauty."
27:11 on your walls, and made p your beauty.
28:12 of complete wisdom and p beauty,
40:47 long and a hundred cubits wide, a p square.
48:20 as a p square you shall set apart the
Mt 5:48 made p as your heavenly Father is perfect.
Lk 7:10 house, they found the servant in p health.
Acts 3:16 Such faith has given him p health,
Rom 12: 2 God's will, what is good, pleasing and p.
15: 5 enable you to live in p harmony with one
1Cor 13:10 When the p comes,
2Cor 10: 6 anyone else once your own obedience is p.
Eph 4: 2 calling you have received, with p humility,
4:13 p man who is Christ come to full stature.
Col 1: 9 through p wisdom and spiritual insight.
3:14 binds the rest together and makes them p.
3:16 In wisdom made p,
4:12 that you be p and have full conviction
1Thes 5:23 the God of peace make you p in holiness.
1Tm 2: 2 and tranquil lives in p piety and dignity.
Ti 3: 2 and display a p courtesy toward all men.
Heb 2:10 the work of salvation p through suffering.
7:28 appoints as priest the Son, made p forever.
9: 9 make p the conscience of the worshiper,
9:11 and more p tabernacle not made by hands,

10: 1 it was never able to *p* the worshipers by
11:40 Without us, they were not to be made *p.*
12:23 of all, to the spirits of just men made *p,*
1Jn 2: 5 has the love of God been made *p* in him.
4:18 rather, *p* love casts out all fear.
4:18 love is not yet *p* in one who is afraid.

PERFECTED (3)

Ez 27: 4 your builders placed you, *p* your beauty.
Heb 5: 9 and when *p,* he became the source
10:14 forever *p* those who are being sanctified.

PERFECTION (12)

Est D: 5 She glowed with the *p* of her beauty and
Jb 11: 7 Dare you vie with the *p* of the Almighty?
Wis 6:15 taking thought of her is the *p* of prudence,
12:17 when the *p* of your power is disbelieved;
Ez 28:12 You were stamped with the seal of *p,*
Mt 19:21 Jesus told him, "If you seek *p,*
2Cor 12: 9 for you, for in weakness power reaches *p.*"
Heb 7:11 *p* had been achieved through the levitical
7:19 for the law brought nothing to *p.*
Jas 1: 4 Let endurance come to its *p* so that you
1Jn 4:12 in us, and his love is brought to *p* in us.
4:17 Our love is brought to *p* in this,

PERFECTLY (11)

2Chr 4: 2 It was *p* round,
Prv 25: 4 from silver, and it comes forth *p* purified;
Mt 12:13 He did so, and it was *p* restored;
Mk 3: 5 The man did so and his hand was *p* restored.
5:15 by Legion sitting fully clothed and *p* sane,
8:25 laid hands on his eyes, and he saw *p;*
Lk 6:10 The man did so and his hand was *p* restored.
Acts 4:10 name this man stands before you *p* sound.
2Cor 7: 1 God strive to fulfill our consecration *p.*
Col 3:22 slaves I say, obey your human masters *p,*
Rv 21:16 The city is *p* square,

PERFECTS (2)

Sir 38:28 and he keeps watch till he *p* it in detail.
Heb 12: 2 on Jesus, who inspires and *p* our faith.

PERFIDY (2)

2Mc 15:10 the *p* of the Gentiles and their violation
Jb 21:34 comfort, while in your answers *p* remains?

PERFORCE (1)

Sir 31:21 If *p* you have eaten too much,

PERFORM (35)

Ex 4:17 with it you are to *p* the signs."
4:21 see that you *p* before Pharaoh all the
10: 1 I may *p* these signs of mine among them
29: 1 shall *p* in consecrating them as my priests.
30:10 shall *p* the atonement rite on its horns.
Nm 8:24 *p* the required service in the meeting tent.
18:21 for the service they *p* in the meeting tent.
18:23 are to *p* the service of the meeting tent,
27:21 as a whole shall *p* all their actions."
Dt 3:24 or on earth can *p* deeds as mighty as yours?
25: 5 *p* the duty of a brother-in-law
25: 7 does not intend to *p* his duty toward me
34:11 signs and wonders the LORD sent him to *p*
Jos 3: 5 tomorrow the LORD will *p* wonders among
2Sm 2:14 "Let the young men rise and *p* for us."
Tb 4: 5 *P* good works all the days of your life,
Jdt 11:16 God has sent me to *p* with you such deeds
1Mc 10:42 belong to the priests who *p* the services.
Is 28:21 his work, his singular work, to *p* his deed,
Ez 45:25 for seven days, he shall *p* the same rites,
Lk 2:27 *p* for him the customary ritual of the law,
6: 7 see if he would *p* a cure on the sabbath
13:32 and tomorrow I cast out devils and *p* cures,
Jn 3: 2 for no man can *p* signs and wonders such as
3: 2 such as you *p* unless God is with him."
5:36 These very works which I *p* testify on my
6:28 "What must we do to *p* the works of God?"
6:30 sign are you going to *p* for us to see?
7:31 be expected to *p* more signs than this man?"
9:16 is a sinner, how can he *p* signs like these?"
10:37 If I do not *p* my Father's works,
10:38 But if I do *p* them,
1Tm 6: 2 must *p* their tasks even more faithfully,
2Tm 4: 5 hardship, *p* your work as an evangelist,
Rv 13:14 to *p* by authority of the first beast,

PERFORMED (44)

Gn 23: 2 *p* the customary mourning rites for her.
32:11 that you have loyally *p* for your servant:
Ex 4:30 and he *p* the signs before the people.
11:10 although Moses and Aaron *p* these various
Nm 3: 4 Thereafter only Eleazar and Ithamar *p* the
14:11 despite all the signs I have *p* among them?
Jos 5: 8 When the rite had been *p,*
24:17 He *p* those great miracles before our very
1Sm 26:16 This is no creditable service you have *p.*
2Sm 23:22 Such were the deeds *p* by Benaiah,
1Chr 6:17 and they *p* their services in an order
6:18 Those who so *p* are the following,
11:19 Such deeds as these the Three warriors *p.*
23:24 They *p* the work of the service of the
25: 1 is the list of those who *p* this service:
2Chr 34:25 me by every deed that they have *p,*
Ezr 10:13 that can be *p* in a single day or even two,
Tb 1: 3 I *p* many charitable works for my kinsmen
1:16 During Shalmaneser's reign I *p* many
Jdt 15:12 blessed her and *p* a dance in her honor.
1Mc 8: 2 deeds that they had *p* against the Gauls,
9:22 Judas, his battles, the brave deeds he *p,*
16:23 John, his wars and the brave deeds he *p,*
Sir 48:14 In life he *p* wonders,
Is 41: 4 Who has *p* these deeds?
Mt 12:12 good deeds may be *p* on the sabbath."
14: 6 Herodias' daughter *p* a dance
23: 5 All their works are *p* to be seen.
Mk 6:22 *p* a dance which delighted Herod
Lk 11:38 *p* the ablutions prescribed before eating.
Jn 2:11 Jesus *p* this first of his signs at Cana in
4:54 Jesus *p* on returning from Judea to Galilee.
6:14 saw the sign he had *p* they began to say,
7:21 "I have *p* a single work and you profess
10:41 "John may never have *p* a sign,"
12:18 him because they heard he had *p* this sign.
12:37 Despite his many signs *p* in their presence,
15:24 Had I not *p* such works among them as no
20:30 Jesus *p* many other signs as well
Acts 2:43 wonders and signs were *p* by the apostles.
8: 6 *p* attended closely to what he had to say.
2Cor 12:12 I have *p* among you with great patience the
2Tm 1:18 And the many services he has *p* for Christ
Rv 13:13 It *p* great prodigies;
19:20 false prophet who *p* in its presence

PERFORMER (1)

Sir 49: 1 incense, made lasting by a skilled *p.*

PERFORMING (13)

Ex 39:26 which was to be worn in *p* the ministry
Nm 18: 7 have charge of *p* the priestly functions
Ez 22:28 that are false and *p* lying divinations,
Mt 6: 1 against *p* religious acts for people to see.
11: 2 prison heard about the works Christ was *p,*
24:24 *p* signs and wonders so great as to mislead
Mk 13:22 will appear *p* signs and wonders to mislead,
Jn 2:23 for they could see the signs he was *p.*
6: 2 they saw the signs he was *p* for the sick.
7: 3 there may see the works you are *p.*
11:47 said, "with this man *p* all sorts of signs?
Acts 7:36 *p* wonders and signs in the land of Egypt,
Heb 9: 6 In *p* their service the priests used to go

PERFORMS (3)

Lv 14:11 The priest who *p* the purification ceremony
Mk 9:39 No man who *p* a miracle using my name can
Rom 12: 8 *p* works of mercy should do so cheerfully.

PERFUME (19)

Ex 30:33 Whoever prepares a *p* like this,
Jb 41:23 the sea he churns like *p* in a kettle.
Prv 21:17 he who loves wine and *p* will not be rich.
27: 9 *P* and incense gladden the heart,
Eccl 9: 8 white, and spare not the *p* for your head.
Sg 1: 3 Your name spoken is a spreading *p*—
3: 6 and with the *p* of every exotic dust?
Sir 24:15 balm, or precious myrrh, I give forth *p;*
Is 3:20 headdresses, bangles, cinctures, *p* boxes,
3:24 Instead of *p* there will be stench,
Mt 26: 7 a woman carrying a jar of costly *p* came up
26:12 By pouring this *p* on my body,
Mk 14: 3 jar of *p* made from expensive aromatic nard.
14: 3 jar, she began to pour the *p* on his head.
14: 4 the point of this extravagant waste of *p?*
Lk 7:46 oil, but she has anointed my feet with *p.*
Jn 11: 2 with *p* and dried his feet with her hair.)
12: 3 costly *p* made from genuine aromatic nard,
12: 5 "Why was not this *p* sold?

PERFUMED (4)

Ex 30:25 oil, *p* ointment expertly prepared.
Mk 16: 1 and Salome bought *p* oils with which they
Lk 7:37 of *p* oil and stood behind him at his feet,
Jn 19:40 it up in wrappings of cloth with *p* oils.

PERFUMER (1)

Ex 37:29 were prepared in their pure form by a *p.*

PERFUMERS (2)

Neh 3: 8 his side was Hananiah, one of the *p'* guild.
Eccl 9:18 "A fly that dies can spoil the *p* ointment,

PERFUMES (6)

Est 2:12 the other six months with *p* and cosmetics.
Sg 4:16 my garden that its *p* may spread abroad.
Wis 2: 7 Let us have our fill of costly wine and *p,*
Is 57: 9 with scented oil, and multiplied your *p;*
Lk 23:56 they went home to prepare spices and *p.*
Rv 18:13 cinnamon and amomum, *p,*

PERFUMING (2)

Mk 14: 8 By *p* my body she is anticipating its
Lk 7:38 hair, kissing them and *p* them with the oil.

PERGA (3)

Acts 13:13 out to sea and sailed to *P* in Pamphylia.
13:14 on from *P* and came to Antioch in Pisidia.
14:25 After preaching the message in *P,*

PERGAMUM (2)

Rv 1:11 to Ephesus, Smyrna, *P,*
2:12 the presiding spirit of the church in *P,*

PERHAPS (47)

Gn 16: 2 *p* I shall have sons through her."
32:21 when I face him, *p* he will forgive me."
Ex 32:30 *p* I may be able to make atonement for your
Nm 23: 3 *P* the LORD will meet me,
23:27 *p* God will approve of your cursing them
Dt 7:17 *P* you will say to yourselves,
1Sm 6: 5 *P* then he will cease to afflict you,
9: 6 *P* he can tell us how to accomplish our
14: 6 *P* the LORD will help us,
23:22 *p* they are playing some trick on me).
2Sm 12:22 *P* the LORD will grant me the child's life.'
14:15 *P* he will grant the petition of his
16:12 *P* the LORD will look upon my affliction
1Kgs 18:27 *P* he is asleep and must be awakened."
20:31 *P* he will spare your life."
2Kgs 2:16 *P* the spirit of the LORD has carried him
19: 4 *P* the LORD, your God, will hear
Tb 2:13 *P* it was stolen!
10: 2 *P* he has been detained there; or *p* Gabael
13: 6 *p* he may look with favor upon you and show
1Mc 9: 8 *p* we can put up a good fight against them."
Jb 33:14 For God does speak, *p* once,
Wis 13: 6 For they indeed have gone astray *p,*
Is 37: 4 *P* the LORD, your God, will hear
47:12 *P* you can make them avail, *p* you can
Jer 20:10 *P* he will be trapped;
21: 2 *P* the LORD will deal with us according to
26: 3 *P* they will listen and turn back,
36: 3 *P,* when the house of Judah hears all the
36: 7 *P* they will lay their supplication before
Ez 12: 3 *p* they will see that they are a rebellious
Jl 2:14 *P* he will again relent and leave behind
Jon 1: 6 *P* God will be mindful of us so that we may
Zep 2: 3 *p* you may be sheltered on the day of the
Mt 7: 6 at best, and *p* even tear you to shreds.
Mk 4:12 lest *p* they repent and be forgiven."
Lk 13: 9 then *p* it will bear fruit.
20:13 *P* if I send the son I love,
Jn 7:26 *P* even the authorities have decided that
Acts 17:27 grope for him and *p* eventually to find him
1Cor 7: 5 unless *p* by mutual consent for a time,
15:35 *P* someone will say,
2Cor 13: 5 *P* you yourselves do not realize that
Ti 3:12 I send Artemas to you, or *p* Tychicus,
Phlm 1:15 *P* he was separated from you for a while

PERIDA (1)

Neh 7:57 of Sotai, sons of Sophereth, sons of *P,*

PERIL (1)

Lam 5: 9 *p* of our lives we bring in our sustenance,

PERILS (2)

2Mc 2:18 us from great *p* and has purified his Place.
Eccl 12: 5 And one fears heights, and *p* in the street;

PERIMETER (1)

Ez 48:35 *p* of the City is eighteen thousand cubits.

PERIOD (46)

Gn 31:35 a woman's *p* is upon me."
38:12 After Judah completed the *p* of mourning,
50: 3 at it, for that is the full *p* of embalming;
50: 4 When that *p* of mourning was over,
Lv 12: 2 the same uncleanness as at her menstrual *p.*
15:25 for several days outside her menstrual *p,*
15:25 her flow continues beyond the ordinary *p,*
15:25 be unclean, just as during her menstrual *p.*
15:33 as for the woman who has her menstrual *p,*
20:18 with a woman during her menstrual *p,*
27:17 is made at the beginning of a jubilee *p,*
Nm 6: 5 *p* of his dedication to the LORD is over,
6:12 *p* of his dedication to the LORD
6:12 The previous *p* is not valid,
6:13 On the day he completes the *p* of his
Dt 15: 1 *p* you shall have a relaxation of debts,
31:10 comes at the end of every seven-year *p,*
34: 8 the *p* of grief and mourning for Moses.
2Sm 11: 4 she was just purified after her monthly *p.*
13:23 *p* of two years, Absalom had shearers
15: 7 *p* of four years, Absalom said to the king:
2Kgs 23:22 during the *p* when the Judges ruled Israel,
23:22 or during the entire *p* of the kings of
2Chr 21:19 went on until a *p* of two years had elapsed,
Ezr 10: 9 in Jerusalem within the three-day *p:*

PERIOD (cont.)

Neh 7: 5 those who had returned in the earliest p.
Est 2:12 Of this p of beautifying treatment,
2Mc 4:17 laws of God, as the following p will show.
Wis 7: 2 was molded into flesh in a ten-months' p—
16. 3 While these, after a brief p of privation,
Bar 6: 2 many years, a p seven generations long;
Ez 18: 6 relations with a woman in her menstrual p;
22:10 who coerce women in their menstrual p.
Dn 4:31 When this p was over,
8:19 is to happen later in the p of wrath;
Mt 24:22 Indeed, if the p had not been shortened,
24:29 "Immediately after the stress of that p,
Mk 13:20 Indeed, had the Lord not shortened the p,
13:24 "During that p after trials of every sort
Acts 8:11 the spell of his magic over a long p;
12: 1 During that p, King Herod
19: 8 synagogue, and over a p of three months,
21:26 when the p of purification would be over,
21:27 The seven-day p was nearing completion
Rv 2:10 you will be tried over a p of ten days.
7:14 who have survived the great p of trial;

PERIODS (3)

Gn 18:11 and Sarah had stopped having her womanly p.
1Chr 9:25 turns in assisting them for seven-day p,
Acts 17:30 bygone p when men did not know him;

PERISH (115)

Gn 6:17 everything on earth shall p.
41:36 so that the land may not p in the famine."
47:15 us food or we shall p under your eyes;
47:19 we and our land p before your very eyes?
47:19 us seed, that we may survive and not p,
Nm 4:18 clans p from the body of the Levites.
16:13 milk and honey, to make us p in the desert,
17:28 Are we to p to the last man?"
24:20 was Amalek, but this end is to p forever.
24:24 and conquered Eber, He too shall p forever.
Dt 4:26 that you shall all quickly p from the land
7:24 make their names p from under the heavens.
8:19 you this day that you will p utterly.
8:20 p for not heeding the voice of the LORD,
11:17 soon p from the good land he is giving you.
28:20 p for the evil you have done
28:22 wind, that will plague you until you p.
30:18 I tell you now that you will certainly p;
Jos 22:20 man, he did not p alone for his guilt!"
23:13 you p from this good land which the LORD,
23:16 you will quickly p from the good land
Jgs 5:31 May all your enemies p thus, O LORD!
Ru 4:10 p among his kinsmen and fellow citizens.
1Sm 2: 9 but the wicked shall p in the darkness.
12:25 to do evil, both you and your king shall p."
27: 1 "I shall p some day at the hand of Saul.
Jdt 6: 4 they shall utterly p,
Est 4:14 but you and your father's house will p.
4:16 If I p, I perish?"
C:24 and those who are in league with him may p.
2Mc 7:20 who saw her seven sons p in a single day,
Jb 3: 3 P the day on which I was born,
3:11 Why did I not p at birth,
4: 9 By the breath of God they p,
4:20 with no heed paid to it, they p forever.
6:18 they go into the desert and p.
8:13 and so shall the hope of the godless man p.
34:15 his breath, All flesh would p together,
36:12 But if they obey not, they p;
36:14 expire in youth, and p among the reprobate.
Ps(s) 2:12 Lest he be angry and you p from the way,
9:19 shall the hope of the afflicted forever p.
37:20 But the wicked p,
41: 6 'When will he die and his name p?'
49:13 he resembles the beasts that p.
49:21 not prudence, resembles the beasts that p.
68: 3 the fire, so the wicked p before God.
73:27 For indeed, they who withdraw from you p;
80:17 or cut it down p before you at your rebuke.
83:18 let them be confounded and p,
92:10 O LORD, for behold, your enemies shall p;
102:27 They shall p, but you remain though all
104:29 breath, they p and return to their dust.
106:26 against them to let them p in the desert,
112:10 the desire of the wicked shall p.
146: 4 on that day his plans p.
Prv 11:10 and when the wicked p,
13:23 but some men p for lack of a law court.
19: 9 unpunished, and he who utters lies will p.
21:28 The false witness will p,
Wis 4:19 shall be in grief and their memory shall p.
12:12 Or when peoples p,
18: 5 them p all at once in the mighty water.
18:19 they p unaware of why they suffered ill.
Sir 3:25 end, and he who loves danger will p in it.
8:15 and through his folly you will p with him.
9: 8 Through woman's beauty many p,
14:19 All man's works will p in decay,
20:21 shame, and p through a fool's intimidation.
29:10 and hide it not under a stone to p;
Is 2:18 The idols will p forever.
22:18 like a ball into an open land To p there,
29:14 The wisdom of its wise men shall p and the
31: 3 fall, and both of them shall p together.
41:11 p and come to nought who offer resistance.
60:12 or kingdom shall p that does not serve you;
66:17 all p with their deeds and their thoughts,
Jer 6:21 sons alike, neighbors and friends shall p.
8:14 and enter the walled cities, to p there;
10:11 not make heaven and earth p from the earth,
10:15 they will p in their time of punishment.
27:10 to make me banish you so that you will p.
27:15 that I must banish you, and you will p,
40:15 dispersed and the remnant of Judah will p."
44:27 All the men of Judah in Egypt shall p by
50:30 all her warriors shall p on that day,
51: 6 one save his life, p not for her guilt;
51:18 that will p in their time of punishment.
Lam 4: 5 accustomed to dainty food p in the streets;
4: 9 Better for those who p by the sword than
Ez 5:12 of pestilence and p of hunger within you;
6:12 and he that is besieged shall p by famine;
32:13 her animals p beside her abundant waters;
Dn 2:18 p with the rest of the wise men of Babylon.
Hos 4: 3 of the air, and even the fish of the sea p.
4: 6 My people p for want of knowledge!
10:15 At dawn the king of Israel shall p utterly.
Am 1: 8 and the last of the Philistines shall p,
2:14 Flight shall p from the swift,
Jon 1: 6 will be mindful of us so that we may not p."
1:14 let us not p for taking this man's life;
3: 9 his blazing wrath, so that we shall not p."
Zep 2: 5 and leave you to p without an inhabitant!
Zec 11: 9 what is to perish, let it p,
11:16 who will take no note of those that p,
13: 8 cut off and p and one third shall be left.
Jn 10:28 them eternal life, and they shall never p.
Rom 2:12 the law will p without reference to it;
Col 2:22 deal with things that p in their use.
Heb 1:11 They will p, but you remain;
10:39 are not among those who draw back and p,
2Pt 3: 9 none to p but all to come to repentance.
Jude 1:11 pay, and like Korah they p in rebellion.

PERISHABLE (2)

Wis 19:21 of the p animals that went about in them,
Jn 6:27 You should not be working for p food but

PERISHED (38)

Gn 7:21 All creatures that stirred on earth p:
Nm 16:33 over them, and they p from the community.
20: 3 p with our kinsmen in the LORD's presence!
Dt 2:14 generation of soldiers had p from the camp,
Jgs 4:21 into the ground, so that he p in death.
9:49 about a thousand men and women, p.
2Sm 1:27 have fallen, the weapons of war have p!"
2Kgs 7:13 better off than all the throng that has p,
Tb 10: 4 has p and is no longer among the living!"
10: 7 My child has p!"
Jdt 16:12 they p before the ranks of my Lord.
1Mc 2:63 to his dust, and his schemes have p.
13: 4 of Israel, that all my brothers have p,
13:18 who might say that Jonathan p because
16:10 and about two thousand of the enemy p.
16:21 that his father and his brothers had p,
2Mc 5: 9 so many from their country p in exile;
Ps(s) 9: 7 of the cities you uprooted has p.
10:16 the nations have p out of his land.
83:11 at the torrent Kishon, Who p at Endor;
88:12 your faithfulness among those who have p?
119:92 delight, I should have p in my affliction.
Eccl 9: 6 and hatred and rivalry have long since p.
Wis 10: 3 anger, he p through his fratricidal wrath.
17:10 the hissing of reptiles, And p trembling,
Sir 16:10 who p for the impiety of their hearts.
34: 7 and those who believed in them have p.
Jer 48:36 the wealth they acquired has p.
49: 7 in Teman, has counsel p from the prudent,
Lam 1:19 My priests and my elders p in the city;
Bar 3:28 p for lack of prudence, p through their folly.
Ez 26:17 How have you p,
Jl 1:11 because the harvest of the field has p.
1:18 pasturage, even the flocks of sheep have p.
Jon 4:10 came up in one night and in one night it p.
Mi 4: 9 Or has your counselor p,
1Cor 10: 8 so that in one day twenty-three thousand p.

PERISHES (8)

1Sm 26:10 him to die, or he goes out and p in battle.
Jb 4: 7 Reflect now, what innocent person p?
4:11 The old lion p for lack of prey,
18:17 His memory p from the land,
20: 7 Yet he p forever like the fuel of his fire,
Prv 11: 7 When a wicked man dies his hope p,
Is 57: 1 The just man p,
1Cor 8:11 of your "knowledge" the weak one p,

PERISHING (5)

Nm 17:27 Israelites cried out to Moses, "We are p;
1Mc 3: 9 he gathered together those who were p.
Prv 31: 6 Give strong drink to one who is p,
Eccl 7:15 a just man p in his justice,
Bar 3: 3 enthroned forever, while we are p forever.

PERIZZITES (24)

Gn 13: 7 and the P were occupying the land.)
15:20 the Kadmonites, the Hittites, the P,
34:30 of the land, the Canaanites and the P.
Ex 3: 8 of the Canaanites, Hittites, Amorites, P,
3:17 of the Canaanites, Hittites, Amorites, P,
23:23 bring you to the Amorites, Hittites, P,
33: 2 out the Canaanites, Amorites, Hittites, P,
34:11 you the Amorites, Canaanites, Hittites, P,
Dt 7: 1 Girgashites, Amorites, Canaanites, P,
20:17 the Hittites, Amorites, Canaanites, P,
Jos 3:10 the Canaanites, Hittites, Hivites, P,
9: 1 Hittites, Amorites, Canaanites, P,
11: 3 P and Jebusites in the mountain regions,
12: 8 to the Hittites, Amorites, Canaanites, P,
17:15 there in the land of the P and Rephaim,
24:12 of you which drove them [the Amorites, P,
Jgs 1: 4 the Canaanites and P into their power,
1: 5 When they defeated the Canaanites and P,
3: 5 the Canaanites, Hittites, Amorites, P,
1Kgs 9:20 descendants of the Amorites, Hittites, P,
2Chr 8: 7 remained of the Hittites, Amorites, P,
Ezr 9: 1 abominations [Canaanites, Hittites, P,
Neh 9: 8 of the Canaanites, Hittites, Amorites, P,
Jdt 5:16 They expelled the Canaanites, the P,

PERJURER (1)

Zec 5: 3 it shall every p be expelled from here.

PERJURERS (2)

Mal 3: 5 Against the sorcerers, adulterers, and p
1Tm 1:10 sexual perverts, kidnapers, liars, p,

PERJURES (1)

Zec 5: 4 house of him who p himself with my name;

PERJURY (5)

Ps(s) 144: 8 while their right hands are raised in p.
144:11 while their right hands are raised in p.
Wis 14:25 corruption, faithlessness, turmoil, p,
Jer 7: 9 steal and murder, commit adultery and p,
Dn 13:61 own words Daniel had convicted them of p.

PERMANENT (16)

Gn 17: 8 whole land of Canaan, as a p possession;
48: 4 descendants after you as a p possession.'
Lv 25:47 has a p or a temporary residence among you,
1Sm 28: 2 "I shall appoint you my p bodyguard."
1Chr 6:16 the ark had obtained a p resting place.
1Mc 14:41 Simon shall be their p leader and high
Ps(s) 119:142 is everlasting justice, and your law is p.
119:151 are near, and all your commands are p.
Sir 45:15 and with his family, as p as the heavens,
Jer 49:19 of Jordan to the p feeding grounds,
50:44 Jordan's thicket to the p feeding grounds,
Ez 33:24 have as p possession the land that has
46:17 the inheritance given to his sons is p.
Jn 8:35 (No slave has a p place in the family,
Heb 10:34 that you had better and more p possessions.
2Pt 1:10 to make your call and election p,

PERMANENTLY (4)

Nm 15:14 alien residing with you p or for a time,
36: 4 heritage of these women will be p added
2Sm 19:14 not become my general p in place of Joab.'"
Ez 39:14 Men shall be p employed to pass through

PERMEATE (1)

Dt 32: 2 the rain, and my discourse p like the dew,

PERMISSIBLE (1)

Mk 10: 2 it was p for a husband to divorce his wife.

PERMISSION (8)

1Mc 9:35 of the convoy to ask p of his friends,
2Mc 11:30 full p to observe their dietary laws
Dn 14:26 Give me p, O king, and I will kill this
14:26 "I give you p," the king said.
Mt 17: 4 With your p I will erect three booths here,
Jn 19:38 asked Pilate's p to remove Jesus' body.
Acts 21:40 With his p Paul then stood on the steps
26: 1 "You have p to state your case."

PERMIT (21)

Ex 3:18 P us, then, to go a three days' journey
Lv 25:24 occupy, you must p the land to be redeemed.
Dt 18:14 LORD, your God, will not p you to do so.
Jos 1:13 God, will p you to settle in this land.'
1Sm 2:33 I will p some of your family to remain at
24: 8 men and would not p them to attack Saul.
2Sm 15:25 me back and p me to see it and its lodging.
18:22 may, p me also to run after the Cushite."
1Mc 12:40 was afraid that Jonathan would not p him,
Ps(s) 55:23 will he p the just man to be disturbed.
Wis 12:19 that you would p repentance for their sins.
Sir 23: 1 of my life, p me not to fall by them!
47:22 nor p even one of his promises to fail.
Ez 36:15 I p you to hear the reproach of nations,

Mk 1:34 But he would not *p* the demons to speak,
5:37 not *p* anyone to follow him except Peter,
11:16 he would not *p* anyone to carry things
Lk 8:32 asked him to *p* them to enter the swine.
Acts 6: 4 This will *p* us to concentrate on prayer
27: 7 would not *p* us to continue our course,
1Tm 2:12 I do not *p* a woman to act as teacher,

PERMITS (2)

Prv 10: 3 The LORD *p* not the just to hunger,
1Cor 16: 7 to spend some time with you, if the Lord *p.*

PERMITTED (11)

1Sm 4: 3 "Why has the LORD *p* us to be defeated
Ezr 7:24 you that it is not *p* to impose taxes,
Est 9:13 let the Jews in Susa be *p* again tomorrow
Sir 45: 5 He *p* him to hear his voice,
Mt 12: 2 are doing what is not *p* on the sabbath."
Mk 2:24 do they do a thing not *p* on the sabbath?"
2:26 bread which only the priests were *p* to eat?
3: 4 "Is it *p* to do a good deed on the sabbath
10: 4 "Moses *p* divorce and the writing of a
Lk 8:51 he *p* no one to enter with him except Peter,
Rv 13:15 then *p* to give life to the beast's image,

PERMITTING (5)

Jgs 1:34 not *p* them to go down into the plain.
3:28 Jordan leading to Moab, *p* no one to cross.
1Sm 3:19 not *p* any word of his to be without effect.
1Kgs 15: 4 son after him and *p* Jersualem to endure;
Heb 6: 3 And, God *p,* we shall advance!

PERNICIOUS (2)

Jer 4:14 long must your *p* thoughts lodge within you?
2Pt 2: 1 teachers who will smuggle in *p* heresies.

PERPETRATED (3)

Est E: 7 when one considers the wicked deeds *p*
2Mc 8:17 lawless outrage *p* by the Gentiles
12: 5 barbarous deed *p* against his countrymen,

PERPETUAL (43)

Ex 12:14 pilgrimage to the LORD, as a *p* institution.
12:17 your generations as a *p* institution.
12:24 "You shall observe this as a *p* ordinance
27:21 This shall be a *p* ordinance for the
28:43 This shall be a *p* ordinance for him and
29: 9 shall the priesthood be theirs by *p* law,
29:28 by a *p* ordinance as a contribution.
30:21 This shall be a *p* ordinance for him and
31:16 their generations as a *p* covenant.
32:13 give your descendants as their *p* heritage.'"
40:15 they shall receive a *p* priesthood
Lv 3:17 This shall be a *p* ordinance for your
6:15 This is a *p* ordinance:
7:34 and to his sons by a *p* ordinance as a
7:36 a *p* ordinance throughout their generations.
10: 9 a *p* ordinance throughout your generations,
10:15 to you and your children by a *p* ordinance,
23:14 This shall be a *p* statute for you and your
23:21 be a *p* statute for you wherever you dwell.
23:31 This is a *p* statute for you and your
23:41 By *p* statute for you and your descendants
24: 3 a *p* statute for you and your descendants,
24: 9 to the LORD, it is his by *p* right."
25:46 hereditary property, making them *p* slaves.
Nm 10: 8 by *p* statute for you and your descendants.
15:15 a *p* rule for all your descendants.
18: 8 by *p* ordinance I have assigned them to you
18:11 by *p* ordinance I have assigned it to you
18:19 By *p* ordinance I have assigned to you and
18:23 is a *p* ordinance for all your generations.
19:10 This is a *p* ordinance,
19:21 This shall be a *p* ordinance for you.
Jos 4: 7 to serve as a *p* memorial to the Israelites."
1Sm 1:22 I will offer him as a *p* nazirite."
2Kgs 25:30 granted him by the king was a *p* allowance,
2Chr 2: 3 for the *p* display of the showbread,
2: 3 such is Israel's *p* obligation.
Tb 1: 6 is prescribed for all Israel by *p* decree.
1Mc 13:29 he carved suits of armor as a *p* memorial,
Sir 45: 7 He made him *p* in his office when he
Jer 51:39 that they may be overcome with *p* sleep,
52:34 by the king of Babylon was a *p* allowance,
Jude 1: 6 These the Lord has kept in *p* bondage,

PERPETUALLY (1)

Lv 6:11 of the LORD *p* throughout your generations.

PERPETUATE (2)

Dt 25: 7 refuses to *p* his brother's name in Israel.'
2Sm 18:18 for he said, "I have no son to *p* my name."

PERPETUITY (2)

Lv 25:23 "The land shall not be sold in *p;*
25:30 in *p* to the purchaser and his descendants;

PERPLEXED (3)

1Mc 3:31 Greatly *p,* he decided to go to Persia
Sir 13:25 withdrawn and *p* is the laborious schemer.
Lk 9: 7 heard of all that was happening and was *p,*

PERSECUTE (14)

1Mc 5: 2 they began to massacre and *p* the people.
Jb 19:28 But you who say, "How shall we *p* him,
Ps(s) 55: 4 down evil upon me, and with fury they *p* me.
119:86 they *p* me wrongfully;
119:161 Princes *p* me without cause
Mt 5:11 Blest are you when they insult you and *p*
10:23 When they *p* you in one town,
Lk 11:49 and some of these they will *p* and kill';
21:12 any of this, they will manhandle and *p* you,
Jn 5:16 on the sabbath that they began to *p* him.
Acts 7:52 any prophet whom your fathers did not *p?*
9: 4 saying, "Saul, Saul, why do you *p* me?"
22: 7 say to me, 'Saul, Saul, why do you *p* me?'
26:14 me in Hebrew, 'Saul, Saul, why do you *p* me?

PERSECUTED (14)

Dt 30: 7 to your enemies and the foes who *p* you.
2Mc 8:28 booty to the *p* and to widows and orphans;
8:30 half to themselves and the rest to the *p,*
Ps(s) 109:16 but *p* the wretched and poor and the
Bar 4:25 Your enemies have *p* you,
Mt 5:10 Blest are those *p* for holiness' sake;
5:12 they *p* the prophets before you in the very
Acts 22: 4 I *p* this new way to the point of death.
1Cor 15: 9 in fact, because I *p* the church of God,
2Cor 4: 9 We are *p* but never abandoned;
Gal 4:29 son born in nature's course *p* the one
Phil 3: 6 and so zealous that I *p* the church.
1Thes 2:15 the Lord Jesus and the prophets, and *p* us.
2Tm 3:12 life in Christ Jesus can expect to be *p.*

PERSECUTING (5)

Acts 9: 5 answered, "I am Jesus, the one you are *p.*
22: 8 'I am Jesus the Nazorean whom you are *p.*'
26:15 'I am that Jesus whom you are *p.*
Gal 1:13 You know that I went to extremes in *p* the
1:23 formerly *p* us is now preaching the faith

PERSECUTION (10)

Mt 13:21 setback or *p* involving the message occurs,
Mk 4:17 or *p* overtakes them because of the word,
10:30 and *p* besides
Acts 8: 1 of a great *p* of the church in Jerusalem.
11:19 *p* that arose because of Stephen
13:50 got a *p* started against Paul and Barnabas.
Rom 8:35 Trial, or distress, or *p,*
1Cor 4:12 *P* comes our way; we bear it patiently.
Gal 6:12 eye to escaping *p* for the cross of Christ.
2Thes 1: 4 constancy and your faith in *p* and trial.

PERSECUTIONS (3)

2Cor 12:10 *p* and difficulties for the sake of Christ;
2Tm 3:11 through *p* and sufferings in Antioch,
3:11 You know what *p* I have had to bear,

PERSECUTOR (1)

1Tm 1:13 I was once a blasphemer, a *p,*

PERSECUTORS (11)

Ps(s) 31:16 from the clutches of my enemies and my *p.*
119:84 When will you do judgment on my *p?*
119:150 by malicious *p* who are far from your law.
119:157 Though my *p* and my foes are many,
142: 7 Rescue me from my *p,*
Jer 15:15 me, LORD, visit me, and avenge me on my *p.*
17:18 Let my *p,* not me, be confounded;
20:11 my *p* will stumble, they will not triumph.
Lam 1: 3 All her *p* come upon her where she is
Mt 5:44 love your enemies, pray for your *p.*
Rom 12:14 Bless your *p;* bless and do not curse them.

PERSEPOLIS (1)

2Mc 9: 2 He had entered the city called *P* and

PERSEUS (1)

1Mc 8: 5 Philip and *P,*

PERSEVERANCE (3)

Lk 8:15 retain it, and bear fruit through *p.*
2Pt 1: 6 lead to perseverance, and *p* to piety,

PERSEVERE (7)

Ps(s) 101: 2 I will *p* in the way of integrity;
Acts 14:22 to *p* in the faith with this instruction:
Rom 12:12 hope, be patient under trial, *p* in prayer.
Phil 1:25 I will stay with you, and *p* with you all,
1Tm 4:16 *P* at both tasks.
Heb 12: 1 and *p* in running the race which lies ahead;
Jude 1:21 *P* in God's love,

PERSEVERED (3)

Sir 2:10 Has anyone *p* in his fear and been forsaken?
49: 9 to JOB, who always *p* in the right path.
Heb 11:27 for he *p* as if he were looking on the

PERSEVERES (2)

1Chr 28: 7 if he *p* in keeping my commandments and
Dn 12:12 Blessed is the man who has patience and *p*

PERSEVERING (1)

1Cor 15:58 Be steadfast and *p,*

PERSEVERINGLY (1)

Col 4: 2 Pray *p,* be attentive to prayer

PERSIA (36)

2Chr 36:22 In the first year of Cyrus, king of *P,*
36:22 the LORD inspired King Cyrus of *P*
36:23 "Thus says Cyrus, king of *P:*
Ezr 1: 1 In the first year of Cyrus, king of *P,*
1: 1 the LORD inspired King Cyrus of *P*
1: 2 "Thus says Cyrus, king of *P:*
1: 8 Cyrus, king of *P,*
3: 7 to the port of Joppa, as Cyrus, king of *P,*
4: 3 as King Cyrus of *P* has commanded us."
4: 5 the remaining years of Cyrus, king of *P,*
4: 5 and until the reign of Darius, king of *P.*
4: 7 fellow officials to Artaxerxes, king of *P.*
4:24 year of the reign of Darius, king of *P.*
6:14 and Darius [and of Artaxerxes, king of *P.*
7: 1 during the reign of Artaxerxes, king of *P,*
9: 9 the good will of the kings of *P* toward us.
Jdt 1: 7 messengers to all the inhabitants of *P,*
Est 10: 2 chronicles of the kings of Media and *P.*
1Mc 3:31 to *P* and levy tribute on those provinces,
6: 1 that in *P* there was a city called Elymais,
6: 5 While he was in *P,*
6:16 *P* in the year one hundred and forty-nine.
6:56 had returned from *P* and Media with the
14: 2 When Arsaces, king of *P* and Media,
2Mc 1:13 in *P* with his seemingly irresistible army,
1:19 When our fathers were being exiled to *P,*
1:20 Nehemiah, commissioned by the king of *P,*
9: 1 retreated in disgrace from the region of *P.*
9:21 On returning from the regions of *P,*
Ez 27:10 *P* and Lud and Put were in your army as
38: 5 *P,* Cush, and Put with them
Dn 10: 1 In the third year of Cyrus, king of *P,*
10:13 of *P* stood in my way for twenty-one days,
10:13 there with the prince of the kings of *P,*
10:20 Soon I must fight the prince of *P* again.
11: 2 "Three kings of *P* are yet to come;

PERSIAN (11)

Ezr 4: 9 officials, and agents from among the *P,*
Neh 12:22 up until the reign of Darius the *P.*
Est 1: 3 the *P* and Median aristocracy,
1:14 the seven *P* and Median officials who were
1:18 This very day the *P* and Median ladies who
E:10 a Macedonian, certainly not of *P* blood,
Dn 6: 9 and irrevocable under Mede and *P* law."
6:13 irrevocable under the Mede and *P* law."
6:16 "that under the Mede and *P* law every
6:29 of Darius and the reign of Cyrus the *P.*
14: 1 Cyrus the *P* succeeded to his kingdom.

PERSIANS (9)

2Chr 36:20 until the kingdom of the *P* came to power.
Jdt 16:10 "The *P* were dismayed at her daring,
Est 1:19 among the laws of the *P* and Medes,
E:14 the rule of the *P* to the Macedonians.
E:23 future it may be, for us and for loyal *P,*
1Mc 1: 1 defeated Darius, king of the *P* and Medes,
2Mc 1:33 known and the king of the *P* was told that,
Dn 5:28 been divided and given to the Medes and *P.*"
8:20 represents the kings of the Medes and *P.*

PERSIS (1)

Rom 16:12 and also to dear *P,*

PERSIST (7)

Ex 9: 2 to let them go and *p* in holding them,
Lv 26:27 you still *p* in disobeying and defying me,
Dt 28:21 bring a pestilence upon you that will *p*
28:60 which you dread, and they will *p* among you.
29:18 can safely *p* in his stubbornness of heart,
Mi 7:18 Who does not *p* in anger forever,
Jn 20:27 Do not *p* in your unbelief, but believe!"

PERSISTED (10)

Gn 18:29 Abraham *p,* saying, "What if only forty
18:32 But he still *p:* "Please let not my Lord
42:14 "It is just as I said," Joseph *p;*
Jos 17:12 cities, the Canaanites *p* in this region.
2Kgs 13: 6 had caused Israel to commit, but *p* in them.
13:11 had caused Israel to commit, but *p* in them.
Am 1:11 Because he *p* in his anger and kept his
Jn 8: 7 When they *p* in their questioning,

PERSISTED (cont.)

9:26 They *p:* "Just what did he do to you?
Acts 19: 3 how were you baptised?" he *p.*

PERSISTENCE (3)

1Mc 8: 4 and *p* had conquered the whole country,
Prv 18: 1 with all *p* he picks a quarrel.
Lk 11: 8 friendship, he will do so because of his *p.*

PERSISTENT (2)

Prv 19:13 and the nagging of a wife is a *p* leak.
27:15 For a *p* leak on a rainy day the match is a

PERSISTENTLY (1)

Sir 51:18 the good I *p* strove for.

PERSISTS (2)

Dt 25: 8 If he *p* in saying,
Wis 19:18 melody, while the flow of music steadily *p.*

PERSON (84)

Ex 4:25 her son's foreskin and, touching his *p,*
16:16 has enough to eat, an omer for each *p,*
16:22 twice as much food, two omers for each *p.*
Lv 4: 2 When a *p* inadvertently commits a sin
4:27 "If a private *p* commits a sin
5: 1 *p* refuses to give the information which,
7:20 the *p* shall be cut off from his people.
7:21 offering belonging to the LORD, that *p,*
7:27 Every *p* who partakes of any blood shall be
13:30 it, the priest shall declare the *p* unclean,
13:31 the *p* with scall sore for seven days,
13:39 on the skin, and the *p* therefore is clean.
21: 1 unclean for any dead *p* among his people,
21:11 garments, nor shall he go near any dead *p.*
22: 4 if anyone touches a *p* who has become
22:10 "Neither a lay *p* nor a priest's tenant or
27: 8 sum, the *p* must be set before the priest,
Nm 6: 6 LORD, he shall not enter where a dead *p* is.
6:11 he has committed by reason of the dead *p.*
19:13 after touching the body of any deceased *p,*
19:16 who in the open country touches a dead *p,*
19:18 a bone, a slain *p* or other dead body,
19:22 unclean *p* touches becomes unclean itself,
35:30 is not sufficient for putting a *p* to death.
Dt 1:17 judgment, do not consider who a *p* is;
5:23 the *p* of all your tribal heads and elders,
7:10 with destruction the *p* who hates him;
17: 6 is required for putting a *p* to death;
29:18 If any such *p,*
Jos 10:28 city, on its king, and on every *p* in it,
10:30 He put it to the sword with every *p* there,
10:32 and put it to the sword with every *p* in it,
10:35 the doom that day on every *p* in it,
10:37 its king, all its towns, and every *p* there,
10:37 the doom on it and on every *p* there.
10:39 and fulfilled the doom on every *p* there,
11:11 doom by putting every *p* there to the sword,
20: 9 who had killed a *p* accidentally
2Kgs 8: 5 his master had restored a dead *p* to life,
Jb 1:12 only do not lay a hand upon his *p.*"
4: 7 Reflect now, what innocent *p* perishes?
34:19 Who neither favors the *p* of princes,
Sir 26:15 is a modest wife, priceless her chaste *p.*
37:21 of his knowledge are seen in his own *p;*
Ez 14: 4 his answer in *p* because of his many idols.
14: 7 him, I, the LORD, will be his answer in *p.*
33: 6 that *p* is taken because of his own sin.
44:25 unclean by coming near any dead *p,*
Dn 2:30 that I am wiser than any other living *p,*
11:21 shall rise in his place a despicable *p,*
Hg 2:13 If a *p* unclean from contact with a corpse
Mt 5:39 When a *p* strikes you on the right cheek,
10:11 "Look for a worthy *p* in every town or
14: 2 it is he in *p,* raised from the dead;
Mk 7:11 'If a *p* says to his father or mother,
13:20 the period, not a *p* would be saved.
Jn 5:12 *p* who told you to pick it up and walk,"
9:32 ever gave sight to a *p* blind from birth.
Acts 4: 2 resurrection of the dead in the *p* of Jesus.
Rom 2:26 *p* keeps the precepts of the law,
1Cor 4: 6 association with one *p* rather than another.
5:11 covetous, an idolater, an abusive *p,*
7:26 good to me for a *p* to continue as he is.
9:22 a weak *p* with a view to winning the weak.
11:21 One *p* goes hungry while another gets drunk.
12: 7 To each *p* the manifestation of the Spirit
2Cor 10:10 but when he is here in *p* he is
Gal 3:20 be no mediator when only one *p* is involved;
Eph 5: 5 no fornicator, no unclean or lustful *p*
Col 1:20 of him, to reconcile everything in his *p,*
2:15 off captive, triumphed in the *p* of Christ.
2Tm 2:21 The lesson is that if a *p* will but cleanse
Ti 3:11 recognize such a *p* as perverted and sinful;
Heb 7: 7 that a lesser *p* is blessed by a greater.
7: 9 so to speak, tithed in the *p* of his father,
12:16 you no fornicator or godless *p* like Esau,
Jas 2:18 To such a *p* one might say,
2:24 You must perceive that a *p* is justified by
3: 2 If a *p* is without fault in speech he is a
5:13 If a *p* is in good spirits,
5:20 the *p* who brings a sinner back from his
1Pt 2:17 You must esteem the *p* of every man.
Rv 19:12 *p* was a name known to no one but himself.
20:13 Each *p* was judged according to his conduct.

PERSONAL (18)

Gn 39: 4 to Joseph and made him his *p* attendant;
Dt 12: 6 your tithes and *p* contributions,
12:11 your tithes and *p* contributions,
12:17 offerings, or of your *p* contributions.
17: 8 or of civil rights or of *p* injury,
1Sm 25:35 I have granted your request as a *p* favor."
2Sm 5: 8 the blind shall be the *p* enemies of David."
2Kgs 12: 5 the census tax, *p* redemption money,
25:19 five men in the *p* service of the king who
1Chr 29: 3 of my God my *p* fortune in gold and silver:
2Chr 20:25 an abundance of cattle and *p* property,
Est 1:14 who were in the king's *p* service
2: 2 Then the king's *p* attendants suggested:
1Mc 10:40 I make a yearly *p* grant of fifteen
Jer 52:25 and seven men in the *p* service of the king
1Tm 6: 5 value religion only as a means of *p* gain.
2Pt 1:20 in Scripture which is a *p* interpretation.

PERSONALLY (6)

Dt 4:37 *p* led you out of Egypt by his great power,
7:10 such a one, but makes him *p* pay for it.
1Sm 25:26 blood and from avenging yourself *p.*
25:31 for having avenged yourself *p.*
25:33 shedding blood and from avenging myself *p.*
2Sm 3:19 Abner also spoke *p* to Benjamin,

PERSONS (36)

Gn 12: 5 and the *p* they had acquired in Haran,
46:15 thirty-three *p* in all,
46:18 these she bore to Jacob—sixteen *p* in all.
46:22 Rachel bore to Jacob—fourteen *p* in all.
46:25 these she bore to Jacob—seven *p* in all.
46:26 numbered sixty-six *p* in all.
46:27 who were born to him in Egypt— two *p*—
46:27 come to Egypt amounted to seventy *p* in all.
Ex 12: 4 to the number of *p* who partake of it.
Lv 27: 2 vow of offering one or more *p* to the LORD,
27: 3 for *p* between the ages of twenty and sixty,
27: 5 for *p* between the ages of five and twenty,
27: 6 for *p* between the ages of one month and
27: 7 for *p* of sixty or more,
Nm 18: 3 shall look after your *p* and the whole tent;
19:18 on all the vessels and *p* that were in it,
31:28 one out of every five hundred *p,*
31:30 you shall take one out of every fifty *p,*
31:40 and sixteen thousand *p,*
31:46 five hundred asses, and sixteen thousand *p.*
31:47 of every fifty, both of *p* and of beasts,
Neh 5:17 I set my table for a hundred and fifty *p,*
1Mc 2:38 cattle, to the number of a thousand *p.*
5: 5 the towers along with all the *p* in them.
Jer 52:29 hundred and thirty-two *p* from Jerusalem;
52:30 four thousand six hundred *p* in all.
Ez 33: 6 the watchman responsible for that *p* death,
Jon 4:11 *p* who cannot distinguish their right hand
Lk 20:21 of *p* but teach the way of God in truth.
Jn 8:17 law that evidence given by two *p* is valid.
Acts 7:14 all his kinsfolk—seventy-five *p* in all.
Rom 1:27 own *p* the penalty for their perversity.
1Cor 5: 9 my letter not to associate with immoral *p.*
1Pt 3:20 few *p,* eight in all, escaped in the ark
Rv 3: 4 a few *p* who have not soiled their garments;
11:13 *p* were killed during the earthquake;

PERSUADE (4)

Jgs 13:15 angel of the LORD, "Can we *p* you to stay,
Jdt 12:11 "Go and *p* this Hebrew woman in your care
2Mc 11:14 terms, and promising to *p* the king also,
2Cor 5:11 in awe of the Lord we try to *p* men,

PERSUADED (12)

2Chr 18: 2 and *p* him to go up against Ramoth-gilead.
2Mc 4:34 pledges with right hands joined, *p* him,
4:46 fresh air, and *p* him to change his mind.
Prv 25:15 By patience is a ruler *p,*
Ez 36:37 I will be *p* to do for the house of Israel:
Acts 5:39 This speech *p* them.
6:11 They *p* some men to make the charge that
18: 4 in which he *p* certain Jews and Greeks.
19:26 this Paul has *p* great numbers of people to
Rom 4:21 fully *p* that God could do whatever
1Cor 7:40 *p* that in this I have the Spirit of God.
Heb 6: 9 we are *p* of better things in your regard,

PERSUADING (2)

2Mc 7:26 she went through the motions of *p* her son.
11:14 *p* them to settle everything on just terms,

PERSUASION (1)

2Mc 13:26 as well as he could and won them over by *p.*

PERSUASIVE (3)

Est C:24 mouth *p* words in the presence of the lion,
Acts 19: 8 debated fearlessly, with *p* arguments,
1Cor 2: 4 of the *p* force of "wise" argumentation,

PERSUASIVENESS (2)

Prv 16:21 yet pleasing speech increases his *p.*
16:23 eloquent, and augments the *p* of his lips.

PERTAINED (5)

Nm 3:25 had charge of whatever *p* to the Dwelling,
3:31 They had charge of whatever *p* to the ark,
3:36 whatever *p* to the boards of the Dwelling,
1Chr 26:25 His associate *p* to Eliezer,
27: 1 the king in all that *p* to the divisions,

PERTAINING (1)

1Chr 26:32 in everything *p* to God and to the king.

PERTAINS (5)

2Chr 19:11 over you in everything that *p* to the LORD,
19:11 house of Judah in all that *p* to the king;
Col 3: 1 set your heart on what *p* to higher realms
4:12 conviction about whatever *p* to God's will.
1Tm 1:11 that *p* to the glorious gospel of God

PERTURBED (5)

Prv 28:22 The avaricious man is *p* about his wealth,
Wis 18:17 *p* them and unexpected fears assailed them;
Dn 14:13 They were not *p,*
Lk 21: 9 *p* when you hear of wars and insurrections.
1Pt 4: 7 Therefore do not be *p;*

PERUDA (1)

Ezr 2:55 of Sotai, sons of Hassophereth, sons of *P,*

PERVADES (1)

Wis 7:24 and *p* all things by reason of her purity.

PERVADING (1)

Wis 7:23 all-seeing, And *p* all spirits,

PERVERSE (16)

Dt 32: 5 degenerate children, a *p* and crooked race!
1Mc 1:34 There they installed a sinful race, *p* men,
Ps(s) 14: 3 they have become *p;*
53: 4 they have become *p;*
Prv 2:12 the way of evil men, from men of *p* speech,
3:32 To the LORD the *p* man is an abomination,
8:13 the evil way, and the *p* mouth I hate.
10:31 wisdom, but the *p* tongue will be cut off.
15: 4 of life, but a *p* one crushes the spirit.
17:20 He who is *p* in heart finds no good,
Wis 1: 3 For *p* counsels separate a man from God,
Jer 9: 4 their tongues to lying, and are *p,*
Mt 17:17 "What an unbelieving and *p* lot you are!
Lk 9:41 "What an unbelieving and *p* lot you are!
Rom 1:18 the irreligious and *p* spirit of men who,
2Thes 2:11 Therefore God is sending upon them a *p*

PERVERSELY (3)

Ps(s) 101: 3 I hate him who does *p;*
Is 26:10 in an upright land he acts *p,*
32: 6 do wickedness, to speak *p* against the LORD,

PERVERSITY (10)

Jdt 6: 5 for saying these things in a moment of *p*
Prv 2:14 Who delight in doing evil, rejoice in *p;*
6:14 He has *p* in his heart,
Is 5:18 to those who tug at guilt with cords of *p,*
29:16 Your *p* is as though the potter were taken
Ez 22: 5 of your foul reputation and your great *p.*
Hos 5: 2 In their *p* they have sunk into wickedness,
10:13 you have cultivated wickedness, reaped *p,*
Rom 1:18 spirit of men who, in this *p* of theirs,
1:27 their own persons the penalty for their *p.*

PERVERT (7)

Jb 8: 3 Does God *p* judgment,
Prv 10:32 but the mouth of the wicked, how to *p.*
17:23 concealed bribe to *p* the course of justice.
Wis 4:11 *p* his mind or deceit beguile his soul;
Jer 23:36 so that you *p* the words of the living God,
Mi 3: 9 what is just, and *p* all that is right;
Jude 1: 4 They *p* the gracious gift of our God to

PERVERTED (6)

Ps(s) 58: 4 From the womb the wicked are *p;*
Prv 15: 7 knowledge, but the heart of fools is *p.*
Jer 3:21 have *p* their ways and forgotten the LORD,
Hb 1: 4 this is why judgment comes forth *p.*
2Tm 3: 8 with *p* minds they falsify the faith.
Ti 3:11 recognize such a person as *p* and sinful;

PERVERTING (2)

Ex 23: 2 a lawsuit, side with the many in *p* justice.

1Sm 8: 3 gain and accepted bribes, *p* justice.

PERVERTS (3)

Prv 19:28 An unprincipled witness *p* justice,
Sir 8: 2 many, and *p* the character of princes.
1Tm 1:10 mothers, murderers, fornicators, sexual *p*,

PEST (1)

Ex 10:17 to take at least this deadly *p* from me."

PESTILENCE (50)

Ex 5: 3 he will punish us with *p* or the sword."
9: 3 with a very severe *p*.
9:15 such *p* as would wipe you from the earth.
Lv 26:25 walled cities, I will send in *p* among you,
Nm 14:12 will strike them with *p* and wipe them out.
Dt 28:21 The LORD will bring a *p* upon you that will
1Sm 4: 8 Egyptians with various plagues and with *p*.
2Sm 24:13 or to have a three days' *p* in your land?
24:15 Thus David chose the *p*.
24:15 The LORD then sent a *p* over Israel from
1Kgs 8:37 "If there is famine in the land or *p*;
1Chr 21:12 of the LORD's own sword, a *p* in the land,
21:14 Therefore the LORD sent *p* upon Israel,
2Chr 6:28 is famine in the land, when there is *p*,
7:13 the land, if I send *p* among my people,
20: 9 upon us, the sword of judgment, or *p*,
Ps(s) 91: 3 snare of the fowler, from the destroying *p*,
91: 6 Not the *p* that roams in darkness nor the
Jer 14:12 destroy them with the sword, famine, and *p*.
18:21 let their men die of *p*,
21: 6 they shall die in a great *p*.
21: 7 and the people in this city who survive *p*,
21: 9 city shall die by the sword or famine or *p*.
24:10 send upon them the sword, famine, and *p*,
27: 8 that nation with sword, famine, and *p*,
27:13 people die by the sword, famine, and *p*,
28: 8 *p* against many lands and mighty kingdoms.
29:17 sending against them sword, famine and *p*.
29:18 pursue them with sword, famine, and *p*,
32:24 attacking it, amid sword, famine, and *p*.
32:36 king of Babylon amid sword, famine, and *p*:
34:17 the LORD, for the sword, famine, and *p*.
38: 2 city shall die by sword, or famine, or *p*;
42:17 shall die by the sword, famine, and *p*;
42:22 and *p* in the place where you wish to go
44:13 Jerusalem with sword, hunger, and *p*.
Ez 5:12 die of *p* and perish of hunger within you;
5:17 *P* and bloodshed shall stalk through you,
6:11 fall by the sword, by famine, and by *p*.
6:12 He that is far off shall die of *p*,
7:15 *p* and hunger are within.
7:15 *p* and famine shall devour those in the
12:16 of them to escape the sword, famine and *p*,
14:19 Or if I were to send *p* into this land,
14:21 the sword, famine, wild beasts, and *p*,
28:23 Into it I will send *p*,
38:21 hold judgment with him in *p* and bloodshed;
Am 4:10 I sent upon you a *p* like that of Egypt,
Hb 3: 5 Before him goes *p*,
Mt 24: 7 and *p* and earthquakes in many places.

PESTILENT (1)

1Mc 10:61 Some *p* Israelites,

PESTILENTIAL (1)

Est E: 7 in your midst by the *p* influence

PESTLE (1)

Prv 27:22 should pound the fool to bits with the *p*,

PETALS (9)

Ex 25:31 and knobs and *p* springing directly from it.
25:33 almond blossoms, each with its knob and *p*;
25:34 almond blossoms, with their knobs and *p*,
37:17 and knobs and *p* springing directly from it.
37:19 almond blossoms, each with its knob and *p*;
37:20 almond blossoms, with their knobs and *p*,
Sir 39:13 open up your *p*, like roses planted near

PETER (162)

Mt 4:18 two brothers, Simon now known as *P*,
10: 2 first Simon, now known as *P*,
14:28 *P* spoke up and said,
14:29 So *P* got out of the boat and began to walk
15:15 Then *P* spoke up to say,
16:16 "You are the Messiah," Simon *P* answered,
16:22 *P* took him aside and began to remonstrate
16:23 Jesus turned on *P* and said,
17: 1 Six days later Jesus took *P*,
17: 4 Then *P* said to Jesus,
17:24 of the temple tax approached *P* and said,
17:25 "Of course he does," *P* replied.
18:21 Then *P* came up and asked him,
26:33 *P* responded, "Though all may have
26:35 *P* replied, "Even though I have to die
26:37 He took along *P* and Zebedee's two sons,
26:40 He said to *P*, "So you could not stay awake
26:58 *P* kept following him at a distance as far
26:69 *P* was sitting in the courtyard when one of
26:73 some bystanders came over to *P* and said,
26:75 *P* remembered the prediction Jesus had made:
Mk 3:17 Simon to whom he gave the name *P*;
5:37 not permit anyone to follow him except *P*,
8:29 *P* answered him, "You are the Messiah!"
8:32 *P* then took him aside and began to
8:33 and, eyeing the disciples, reprimanded *P*:
9: 2 Six days later, Jesus took *P*,
9: 5 Then *P* spoke to Jesus:
10:28 *P* was moved to say to him,
11:21 *P* remembered and said to him,
13: 3 the Mount of Olives facing the temple, *P*,
14:29 *P* said to him,
14:31 But *P* kept reasserting vehemently,
14:33 at the same time he took along with him *P*,
14:37 He said to *P*, "Asleep, Simon?
14:54 *P* followed him at a distance right into
14:66 While *P* was down in the courtyard,
14:67 When she noticed *P* warming himself,
14:70 later the bystanders said to *P* once more,
14:72 *P* recalled the prediction Jesus had made
16: 7 Go now and tell his disciples and *P*,
16:20 They promptly reported to *P* and his
Lk 5: 8 Simon *P* fell at the knees of Jesus saying,
6:14 Simon, to whom he gave the name *P*,
8:45 Everyone disclaimed doing it, while *P* said,
8:51 no one to enter with him except *P*,
9:20 *P* said in reply, "The Messiah of God."
9:28 eight days after saying this he took *P*,
9:32 *P* and those with him had fallen into a
9:33 When these were leaving, *P* said to Jesus:
12:41 *P* said, "Do you intend this parable
18:28 *P* said, "We have left all we own
22: 8 sent *P* and John off with the instruction,
22:34 "I tell you, *P*, the cock will not crow
22:54 priest, while *P* followed at a distance.
22:55 sitting beside it, and *P* sat among them.
22:58 But *P* said, "No, sir, not I!"
22:60 *P* responded, "My friend, I do not know
22:61 Lord turned around and looked at *P*, and *P*
24:12 *P*, however, got up and ran to the tomb.
Jn 1:42 name shall be Cephas (which is rendered *P*)."
1:44 Bethsaida, the same town as Andrew and *P*.
6:68 Simon *P* answered him,
13: 6 Thus he came to Simon *P*,
13: 8 *P* replied, "You shall never wash my feet!"
13: 9 "Lord," Simon *P* said to him,
13:24 *P* signaled him to ask Jesus whom he meant.
13:36 "Lord," Simon *P* said to him,
13:37 "Lord," *P* said to him,
18:10 Then Simon *P*, who had a sword, drew it
18:11 Jesus said to *P*, "Put your sword back
18:15 Simon *P*, in company with another
18:16 while *P* was left standing at the gate.
18:16 woman at the gate, and then brought *P* in.
18:17 servant girl who kept the gate said to *P*,
18:18 *P* joined them and stood there warming
18:25 *P* had been standing there warming himself.
18:26 of the man whose ear *P* had severed.
18:27 *P* denied it again.
20: 2 so she ran off to Simon *P* and the other
20: 3 *P* and the other disciple started out on
20: 4 outran *P* and reached the tomb first.
20: 6 Simon *P* came along behind him and entered
21: 2 Assembled were Simon *P*,
21: 3 Simon *P* said to them,
21: 7 the disciple Jesus loved cried out to *P*,
21: 7 the Lord, Simon *P* threw on some clothes
21:11 Simon *P* went aboard and hauled ashore the
21:15 eaten their meal, Jesus said to Simon *P*,
21:16 "Yes, Lord," *P* said,
21:17 *P* was hurt because he had asked a third
21:19 of death by which *P* was to glorify God.)
21:20 *P* turned around at that,
21:21 Seeing him, *P* was prompted to ask Jesus,
Acts 1:13 *P* and John and James and Andrew;
1:15 *P* stood up in the center of the brothers;
2:14 *P* stood up with the Eleven,
2:37 They asked *P* and the other apostles,
2:38 *P* answered: "You must reform
3: 1 when *P* and John were going up to the
3: 3 When he saw *P* and John on their way in,
3: 4 *P* fixed his gaze on the man; so did John.
3: 4 "Look at us!" *P* said.
3: 6 Then *P* said: "I have neither silver
3: 7 Then *P* took him by the right hand and
3:11 the man stood there clinging to *P* and John,
3:12 When *P* saw this,
4: 1 *P* and John were still addressing the crowd,
4: 7 They brought *P* and John before them and
4: 8 Then *P*, filled with the Holy Spirit,
4:13 Observing the self-assurance of *P* and John,
4:19 *P* and John answered,
5: 3 *P* exclaimed: "Ananias, why have you let
5: 8 *P* said to her, "Tell me, did you sell
5: 9 *P* replied, "How could you two scheme
5:15 so that when *P* passed by at least his
5:29 To this, *P* and the apostles replied:
8:14 word of God, they sent *P* and John to them.
8:20 *P* said in answer: "May you and your money
9:32 Once when *P* was making numerous journeys,
9:34 *P* said to him, "Aeneas, Jesus Christ cures
9:38 the disciples who had heard that *P* was
9:39 *P* set out with them as they asked.
9:40 *P* first made everyone go outside;
9:40 her eyes, then looked at *P* and sat up.
9:43 Thus it happened that *P* stayed on in Joppa
10: 5 and summon a certain Simon, known as *P*.
10: 9 *P* went up to the roof terrace to pray.
10:13 "Get up, *P*! Slaughter, then eat."
10:17 While *P* was trying to make out the meaning
10:18 inquire whether Simon *P* was a guest there.
10:19 *P* was still pondering the vision when the
10:21 *P* went down to the men and said,
10:23 *P* invited them in and treated them as
10:25 As *P* entered, Cornelius went to meet
10:26 *P* said as he helped him to his feet,
10:27 *P* then went in,
10:32 to invite Simon known as *P* to come here.
10:34 *P* proceeded to address them in these words:
10:44 *P* had not finished these words when the
10:45 believers who had accompanied *P*
10:46 *P* put the question at that point:
11: 2 when *P* went up to Jerusalem some among the
11: 4 *P* then explained the whole affair to them
11: 7 listened as a voice said to me, 'Get up, *P*!
11:13 to Joppa and fetch Simon, known also as *P*.
12: 3 of the Jews, he took *P* into custody too.
12: 5 *P* was thus detained in prison,
12: 6 trial, *P* was sleeping between two soldiers,
12: 7 He tapped *P* on the side and woke him.
12: 9 *P* followed him out,
12:11 *P* had recovered his senses by this time,
12:13 *P* knocked at the door and a maid named
12:14 ran in and announced that *P* was outside.
12:16 Through all this, *P* kept on knocking.
12:18 who did not know what had happened to *P*.
15: 7 *P* took the floor and said to them:
Gal 2: 7 just as *P* was for the circumcised (for he
2: 8 (for he who worked through *P*
1Pt 1: 1 *P*, an apostle of Jesus Christ,
2Pt 1: 1 Simeon *P*, servant and apostle

PETER'S (8)

Mt 8:14 entered *P* house and found *P* mother-in-law
19:27 Then it was *P* turn to say to him:
Jn 1:40 hearing John was Simon *P* brother Andrew.
6: 8 Jesus' disciples, Andrew, Simon *P* brother,
Acts 10:44 upon all who were listening to *P* message.
12: 7 that, the chains dropped from *P* wrists.

PETHAHIAH (4)

1Chr 24:16 to Happizzez, the nineteenth to *P*,
Ezr 10:23 Shimei, Kelaiah (also called Kelita), *P*,
Neh 9: 5 Sherebiah, Hodiah, Shebaniah, and *P* said,
11:24 *P*, son of Meshezabel,

PETHOR (2)

Nm 22: 5 Balaam, son of Beor, at *P* on the Euphrates,
Dt 23: 5 son of Beor, from *P* in Aram Naharaim,

PETHUEL (1)

Jl 1: 1 the LORD which came to Joel, the son of *P*.

PETITION (31)

2Sm 14:15 he will grant the *p* of his maidservant.
1Kgs 8:28 kindly on the prayer and *p* of your servant,
8:38 of conscience and offers some prayer or *p*,
8:45 listen in heaven to their prayer and *p*,
8:52 *p* of your servant and to the *p* of your people
8:54 this entire prayer of *p* to the LORD,
9: 3 of *p* which you offered in my presence.
2Chr 6:19 kindly on the prayer and *p* of your servant,
6:29 people offers a prayer or *p* of any kind,
6:35 listen from heaven to their prayer and *p*,
Ezr 8:21 to *p* from him a safe journey for ourselves,
8:23 to our God for this, and our *p* was granted.
Est 5: 7 "This is my *p* and request:
5: 8 majesty to grant my *p* and honor my request,
1Mc 7:37 be a house of prayer and *p* for your people.
Sir 35:16 his *p* reaches the heavens.
38:11 Offer your sweet-smelling oblation and *p*,
39: 6 the LORD, his Maker, to *p* the Most High,
Jer 37:20 Hear now, my lord king, and grant my *p*:
42: 2 prophet Jeremiah and said, "Grant our *p*;
Dn 6: 8 any *p* to god or man for thirty days,
6:13 address a *p* to god or man for thirty days,
9:17 O God, the prayer and *p* of your servant;
9:18 when we present our *p* before you,
9:20 people Israel, presenting my *p* to the LORD,
9:23 When you began your *p*,
Zec 12:10 of Jerusalem a spirit of grace and *p*;
Jn 16:26 not say that I will *p* the Father for you.
Jas 5:16 fervent *p* of a holy man is powerful indeed.
1Jn 5:16 if the sin is not deadly, should *p* God,

PETITIONED (2)

Jer 38:26 'I *p* the king not to send me back to
Lk 7: 4 approaching Jesus they *p* him earnestly.

PETITIONING (1)

2Mc 11:24 *p* us to let them retain their own customs.

PETITIONS (6)

1Kgs 8:30 Listen to the *p* of your servant and of
2Chr 6:21 Listen to the *p* of your servant and of
6:39 dwelling place, hear their prayer and *p*,
Eph 6:18 Spirit, using prayers and *p* of every sort.
Phil 4: 6 form of prayer and in *p* full of gratitude.
1Tm 2: 1 First of all, I urge that *p*,

PEULLETHAI (1)

1Chr 26: 5 the sixth, Issachar, the seventh, *P*,

PHALANX (3)

1Mc 6:45 He dashed up to it in the middle of the *p*,
9:12 the *p* attacked as they blew their trumpets.
10:82 were exhausted, Simon attacked the *p*,

PHALANXES (2)

1Mc 6:35 The beasts were distributed along the *p*,
6:38 the enemy and to be protected from the *p*.

PHANTOM (1)

Ps(s) 39: 7 A *p* only, man goes his ways;

PHANTOMS (2)

Ps(s) 73:20 you, when you arise, set at nought these *p*.
Wis 17: 4 and mute *p* with somber looks appeared.

PHANUEL (1)

Lk 2:36 name, daughter of *P* of the tribe of Asher.

PHARAOH (219)

Gn 12:15 courtiers saw her, they praised her to *P*.
12:17 But the LORD struck *P* and his household
12:18 Then *P* summoned Abram and said to him:
12:20 Then *P* gave men orders concerning him,
37:36 a courtier of *P* and his chief steward.
39: 1 a courtier of *P* and his chief steward)
40: 2 *P* was angry with his two courtiers,
40:13 within three days *P* will lift up your head
40:13 You will be handing *P* his cup as you
40:14 do me the favor of mentioning me to *P*,
40:17 were all kinds of bakery products for *P*,
40:19 within three days *P* will lift up your head
40:21 so that he again handed the cup to *P*;
41: 1 After a lapse of two years, *P* had a dream.
41: 4 Then *P* woke up.
41: 7 Then *P* woke up,
41: 9 the chief cupbearer spoke up and said to *P*:
41:10 Once, when *P* was angry,
41:14 *P* therefore had Joseph summoned,
41:15 *P* then said to him: "I had certain dreams
41:16 Joseph replied to *P*, "but God who will give *P*
41:17 Then *P* said to Joseph: "In my dream
41:25 Joseph said to *P*: "Both of Pharaoh' dreams
41:25 thus foretold to *P* what he is about to do.
41:28 It is just as I told *P*:
41:28 has revealed to *P* what he is about to do.
41:32 That *P* had the same dream twice means that
41:33 let *P* seek out a wise and discerning man
41:34 *P* should also take action to appoint
41:37 advice pleased *P* and all his officials.
41:38 another like him," *P* asked his officials,
41:39 So *P* said to Joseph:
41:41 Herewith," *P* told Joseph,
41:42 *P* took off his signet ring and put it on
41:44 "I, *P*, proclaim,"
41:45 *P* also bestowed the name of
41:46 years old when he entered the service of *P*,
41:55 cried to *P* for bread, *P* directed all
42:15 life of *P* that you shall not leave here.
42:16 if they are untrue, as *P* lives,
44:18 your servant, for you are the equal of *P*.
45: 8 and he has made of me a father to *P*,
45:16 had come, *P* and his courtiers were pleased.
45:17 *P* told Joseph: "Say to your brothers:
45:21 gave them the wagons, as *P* had ordered,
46: 5 wagons that *P* had sent for his transport.
46:31 "I will go and inform *P*, telling him:
46:33 So when *P* summons you and asks what your
47: 1 Joseph went and told *P*,
47: 2 He then presented to *P* five of his
47: 3 *P* asked them what their occupation was,
47: 5 *P* said to Joseph, "They may settle
47: 5 *P*, king of Egypt, heard about it, *P*
47: 7 his father Jacob and presented him to *P*.
47: 7 After Jacob had paid his respects to *P*,
47: 8 paid his respects to Pharaoh, *P* asked him,
47:10 *P* farewell and withdrew from his presence.
47:11 As *P* had ordered, Joseph settled
47:20 acquired all the farm land of Egypt for *P*,
47:20 so the land passed over to *P*,
47:22 *P* and lived off the allowance *P* had
47:23 I have acquired you and your land for *P*,
47:24 is in, you must give a fifth of it to *P*,
47:26 that a fifth of its produce should go to *P*.
47:26 land of the priests did not pass over to *P*.
50: 4 "and convey to *P* this request of mine.
50: 6 *P* replied, "Go and bury your father,
Ex 1:11 *P* the supply cities of Pithom and Raamses.
1:19 The midwives answered *P*,
1:22 *P* then commanded all his subjects,
2:15 *P*, too, heard of the affair
3:10 I will send you to *P* to lead my people,
3:11 to *P* and lead the Israelites out of Egypt?"
4:21 *P* all the wonders I have put in your power.
4:22 you shall say to *P*: Thus says the Lord:
5: 1 that, Moses and Aaron went to *P* and said,
5: 2 *P* answered, "Who is the LORD,
5: 5 of the land are already," continued *P*,
5: 6 That very day *P* gave the taskmasters and
5:10 went out and told them, "Thus says *P*:
5:14 the taskmasters of *P* had placed over them,
5:15 foremen came and made this appeal to *P*:
5:17 *P* answered,
5:20 they left *P* and came upon Moses and Aaron,
5:21 You have brought us into bad odor with *P*
5:23 since I went to *P* to speak in your name,
6: 1 "Now you shall see what I will do to *P*.
6:11 the LORD said to Moses, "Go and tell *P*,
6:12 me, how can it be that *P* will listen to me,
6:13 orders regarding both the Israelites and *P*,
6:27 These are the ones who spoke to *P*,
6:29 Repeat to *P*,
6:30 how can it be that *P* will listen to me?"
7: 1 I have made you as God to *P*,
7: 2 *P* to let the Israelites leave his land.
7: 3 Yet I will make *P* so obstinate that,
7: 7 Aaron eighty-three when they spoke to *P*.
7: 9 *P* demands that you work a sign or wonder,
7: 9 your staff and throw it down before *P*,
7:10 to *P* and did as the LORD had commanded.
7:10 his staff down before *P* and his servants,
7:11 *P*, in turn, summoned wise men
7:13 *P*, however, was obstinate
7:14 *P* is obdurate in refusing to let the
7:20 river in full view of *P* and his servants,
7:22 So *P* remained obstinate and would not
7:26 LORD said to Moses, "Go to *P* and tell him:
8: 4 Then *P* summoned Moses and Aaron
8: 5 Moses answered *P*,
8: 6 "Tomorrow," said *P*.
8: 8 promise he had made to *P* about the frogs;
8:11 But when *P* saw that there was a respite,
8:15 man and beast, the magicians said to *P*,
8:15 Yet *P* remained obstinate and would not
8:16 to *P* when he goes forth to the water,
8:20 house of *P* and the houses of his servants;
8:21 Then *P* summoned Moses and Aaron and said
8:24 "Well, then," said *P*,
8:25 from *P* and his servants and his subjects.
8:25 *P*, however, must not play false again
8:27 flies from *P* and his servants and subjects.
8:28 But once more *P* became obdurate and would
9: 1 LORD said to Moses, "Go to *P* and tell him:
9: 8 of *P* let Moses scatter it toward the sky.
9:10 a furnace and stood in the presence of *P*.
9:12 But the LORD made *P* obstinate,
9:13 present yourself to *P* and say to him:
9:27 Then *P* summoned Moses and Aaron and said
9:34 But *P*, seeing that the rain and hail
10: 1 Then the LORD said to Moses, "Go to *P*,
10: 3 So Moses and Aaron went to *P* and told him,
10: 6 With that he turned and left *P*.
10: 8 So Moses and Aaron were brought back to *P*,
10:10 "The LORD help you," *P* replied,
10:16 *P* summoned Moses and Aaron and said,
10:18 When Moses left the presence of *P*,
10:20 of Egypt, the LORD made *P* obstinate,
10:24 *P* then summoned Moses and Aaron and said,
10:27 But the LORD made *P* obstinate,
10:28 "Leave my presence," *P* said to him,
11: 1 plague will I bring upon *P* and upon Egypt.
11: 5 from the first-born of *P* on the throne to
11: 9 *P* refuses to listen to you that my wonders
11:10 presence, the LORD made *P* obstinate,
12:29 from the first-born of *P* on the throne to
12:30 *P* arose in the night,
12:31 night *P* summoned Moses and Aaron and said,
13:15 When *P* stubbornly refused to let us go,
13:17 Now, when *P* let the people go,
14: 3 *P* will then say, 'The Israelites are
14: 4 *P* so obstinate that he will pursue them.
14: 4 receive glory through *P* and all his army,
14: 5 *P* and his servants changed their minds
14: 6 So *P* made his chariots ready and mustered
14: 8 So obstinate had the LORD made *P* that he
14:10 *P* was already near when the Israelites
14:17 receive glory through *P* and all his army,
14:18 through *P* and his chariots and charioteers."
18: 8 *P* and the Egyptians for the sake of Israel,
18:10 from the hands of *P* and the Egyptians.
Dt 6:21 son, 'We were once slaves of *P* in Egypt,
6:22 Egypt and against *P* and his whole house.
7: 8 and ransomed you from the hand of *P*,
7:18 LORD, your God, did to *P* and to all Egypt:
11: 3 he wrought among the Egyptians, on *P*,
29: 1 *P* and all his servants and to all his land;
34:11 to perform in the land of Egypt against *P*
1Sm 2:27 were in Egypt as slaves to the house of *P*.
6: 6 as the Egyptians and *P* were stubborn?
1Kgs 3: 1 Solomon allied himself by marriage with *P*,
3: 1 The daughter of *P*,
9:16 *P*, king of Egypt, had come up
11: 1 women besides the daughter of *P* (Moabites,
11:18 additional men, they went into Egypt to *P*,
11:19 Hadad won great favor with *P*,
11:21 of the army, was dead, he said to *P*,
11:22 *P* said to him, "What do you lack
2Kgs 17: 7 of Egypt, from under the domination of *P*,
18:21 That is what *P*,
23:29 In his time *P* Neco,
23:33 *P* Neco took him prisoner at Riblah in the
23:34 *P* Neco then appointed Eliakim,
23:35 Jehoiakim gave the silver and gold to *P*,
23:35 the land to raise the amount *P* demanded.
23:35 from each proportionately, to pay *P* Neco.
1Chr 4:18 the sons of Bithiah, the daughter of *P*,
2Chr 8:11 Solomon brought the daughter of *P* up from
Neh 9:10 You worked signs and wonders against *P*,
1Mc 4: 9 Red Sea, when *P* pursued them with an army.
Ps(s) 135: 9 against *P* and against all his servants.
136:15 But swept *P* and his army into the Red Sea
Is 19:11 How can you say to *P*,
36: 6 That is what *P*, king of Egypt, is to all
Jer 25:19 cursing, as they are today;] *P*,
37:11 Jerusalem at the threat of the army of *P*,
44:30 I will hand over *P* Hophra,
46: 2 Against the army of *P* Neco,
46:17 Call *P*, king of Egypt, by the name
46:25 and Egypt, her gods and her kings, *P*,
47: 1 the Philistines, before *P* attacked Gaza:
Ez 17:17 by *P* with a great army and numerous troops.
29: 2 Son of man, set your face against *P*,
29: 3 I am coming at you, *P*,
30:21 Son of man, I have broken the arm of *P*,
30:22 I am coming at *P*, the king of Egypt.
30:25 strong, but the arms of *P* shall drop.]
31: 2 Son of man, say to *P*,
31:18 Such are *P* and all his hordes,
32: 2 Son of man, utter a lament over *P*,
32:31 When *P* sees these, he shall be comforted
32:31 slain by the sword *P* and all his army,
32:32 slain by the sword *P* and all his hordes,
Acts 7:10 favor and wisdom in the court of the *P*,
7:13 and his family ties became known to the *P*.
Rom 9:17 Scripture says to *P*,

PHARAOH'S (50)

Gn 12:14 and when *P* courtiers saw her,
12:15 So she was taken into *P* palace.
40: 7 So he asked *P* courtiers who were with him
40:11 *P* cup was in my hand;
40:11 out into his cup, and put it in *P* hand."
40:20 on the third day, which was *P* birthday,
41:14 his clothes, he came into *P* presence.
41:25 "Both of *P* dreams have the same meaning.
41:35 collecting the grain under *P* authority,
41:46 After Joseph left *P* presence,
45: 2 him, and so the news reached *P* palace.
45:16 *P* palace that Joseph's brothers had come,
47:14 and Canaan, and he put it in *P* palace.
47:19 become *P* slaves and our land his property;
47:25 to my lord that we can be *P* slaves."
50: 4 was over, Joseph spoke to *P* courtiers.
50: 7 and with him went all of *P* officials who
Ex 2: 5 *P* daughter came down to the river to bathe,
2: 7 Then his sister asked *P* daughter,
2: 9 *P* daughter said to her,
2:10 child grew, she brought him to *P* daughter,
8: 8 After Moses and Aaron left *P* presence,
8:26 When Moses left *P* presence,
9: 7 But though *P* messengers informed him that
9:20 Some of *P* servants feared the warning of
9:33 *P* presence and had gone out of the city,
10: 7 But *P* servants said to him,
10:11 With that they were driven from *P* presence.
11: 3 was very highly regarded by *P* servants
11: 8 With that he left *P* presence in hot anger.
11:10 these various wonders in *P* presence,
14: 9 *P* whole army,
14:23 all *P* horses and chariots and charioteers
14:28 charioteers of *P* whole army
15: 4 *P* chariots and army he hurled into the sea;
15:19 They sang thus because *P* horses and
18: 4 he has rescued me from *P* sword."
1Kgs 7: 8 this tribunal was built for *P* daughter,
9:24 As soon as *P* daughter went up from the
11:20 in *P* palace, where he then lived with *P*
Sg 1: 9 steeds of *P* chariots would I liken you,
Is 19:11 wisest of *P* advisers give stupid counsel.
30: 2 They find their strength in *P* protection
30: 3 *P* protection shall be your shame,
Jer 37: 5 Also, *P* army had set out from Egypt,
37: 7 *P* army which has set out to help you will
Acts 7:10 of Egypt and of the *P* entire household.
7:21 and *P* daughter adopted him and brought him
Heb 11:24 to be known as the son of *P* daughter;

PHARATHON (1)

1Mc 9:50 as Emmaus, Beth-horon, Bethel, Timnath, *P*,

PHARISEE (15)

Mt 23:26 Blind *P!* First cleanse the inside
Mk 2:16 When the scribes who belonged to the *P*
Lk 7:36 *P* who invited Jesus to dine with him.
7:39 When his host, the *P,*
11:37 a *P* invited him to dine at his house.
11:38 the *P* was surprised that he had not first
18:10 one was a *P,*
18:11 *P* with head unbowed prayed in this fashion:
Jn 3:1 A certain *P* named Nicodemus,
Acts 5:34 Sanhedrin stood up, a *P* named Gamaliel,
23:6 I am a Pharisee and was born a *P.*
23:9 *P* party arose and declared emphatically:
26:5 if they wish, to my life lived as a *P,*
Phil 3:5 in legal observance I was a *P,*

PHARISEES (85)

Mt 3:7 When he saw that many of the *P* and
5:20 *P* you shall not enter the kingdom of God.
9:11 *P* saw this and complained to his disciples,
9:14 "Why is it that while we and the *P* fast,
9:34 the *P* were saying, "He casts out demons
12:2 When the *P* spied this, they protested:
12:14 When the *P* were outside they began to plot
12:21 Blasphemy of the *P.*
12:24 When the *P* heard this, they charged.
12:38 Some of the scribes and *P* then spoke up,
15:1 *P* and scribes from Jerusalem approached
15:12 "Do you realize the *P* were scandalized
16:1 The *P* and Sadducees came along,
16:6 against the yeast of the *P* and Sadducees,"
16:11 but warning you against the yeast of the *P?*"
16:12 but against the *P'* and Sadducees' teaching.
19:3 Some *P* came up to him and said,
21:45 priests and the *P* heard these parables,
22:15 Then the *P* went off and began to plot how
22:34 *P* heard that he had silenced the Sadducees,
22:41 Jesus put a question to the assembled *P,*
23:2 and the *P* have succeeded Moses as teachers;
23:13 "Woe to you scribes and *P,* you frauds!
23:15 Woe to you scribes and *P,* you frauds!
23:23 Woe to you scribes and *P,* you frauds!
23:25 Woe to you scribes and *P,* you frauds!
23:27 Woe to you scribes and *P,* you frauds!
23:29 Woe to you scribes and *P,* you frauds!
27:62 and the *P* called at Pilate's residence.
Mk 2:18 and the *P* were accustomed to fast.
2:18 and those of the *P* fast while yours do not?"
2:24 At this the *P* protested:
3:6 When the *P* went outside,
7:1 The *P* and some of the experts in the law
7:3 The *P,* and in fact all Jews,
7:5 So the *P* and the scribes questioned him:
8:11 *P* came forward and began to argue with him.
8:15 the yeast of the *P* and the yeast of Herod,"
10:2 Then some *P* came up and as a test began to
12:13 They next sent some *P* and Herodians after
Lk 5:17 Sitting close by were *P* and teachers of
5:21 The scribes and the *P* began a discussion,
5:30 The *P* and the scribes of their party said
5:33 the disciples of the *P* do the same.
6:2 Some of the *P* asked,
6:7 The scribes and *P* were on the watch to see
7:30 The *P* and the lawyers,
7:36 went to the *P* home and reclined to eat.
7:37 learned that he was dining in the *P* home.
11:39 The Lord said to him: "You *P!*
11:42 Woe to you *P!*
11:43 Woe to you *P!*
11:53 the scribes and *P* began to manifest fierce
12:1 "Be on guard against the yeast of the *P,*
13:31 It was then that certain *P* came to him.
14:1 meal in the house of one of the leading *P,*
14:3 Jesus asked the lawyers and the *P,*
15:2 at which the *P* and the scribes murmured,
16:14 The *P,* who were avaricious men,
17:20 by the *P* when the reign of God would come,
19:39 Some of the *P* in the crowd said to him,
20:1 the good news, the high priests and *P,*
Jn 1:24 Those whom the *P* had sent proceeded to
4:1 Now when Jesus learned that the *P* had
7:32 The *P* overheard this debate about him
7:32 and the chief priests and *P* together sent
7:45 back, the chief priests and *P* asked them,
7:47 you too have been taken in! the *P* retorted.
7:48 Or the *P?* believing in him, do you
8:3 The scribes and the *P* led a woman forward
8:13 This caused the *P* to break in with:
9:13 the man who had been born blind to the *P.*
9:15 The *P,* in turn, began to inquire
9:16 This prompted some of the *P* to assert,
9:40 Some of the *P* around him picked this up,
11:46 to the *P* and reported what Jesus had done.
11:47 the *P* called a meeting of the Sanhedrin.
11:57 (The chief priests and the *P* had given
12:19 The *P* remarked to one another,
12:42 they refused to admit it because of the *P,*
18:3 supplied by the chief priests and the *P,*
Acts 15:5 Some of the converted *P* then got up and
23:6 some of them were Sadducees and some *P.*
23:7 a dispute arose between *P* and Sadducees
23:8 while the *P* believe in all these things.)

PHARPAR (1)

2Kgs 5:12 rivers of Damascus, the Abana and the *P,*

PHASELIS (1)

1Mc 15:23 Lycia, Halicarnassus, Rhodes, *P,*

PHASIRON (1)

1Mc 9:66 and the sons of *P* in their encampment;

PHICOL (3)

Gn 21:22 that time Abimelech, accompanied by *P,*
21:32 in Beer-sheba, Abimelech along with *P,*
26:26 by Ahuzzath, his councilor, and *P,*

PHILADELPHIA (2)

Rv 1:11 Smyrna, Pergamum, Thyatira, Sardis, *P,*
3:7 the presiding spirit of the church in *P,*

PHILEMON (1)

Phlm 1:1 to our beloved friend and fellow worker *P,*

PHILETUS (1)

2Tm 2:17 This is the case with Hymenaeus and *P,*

PHILIP (46)

1Mc 6:2 weapons left there by Alexander, son of *P,*
6:14 Then he summoned *P,*
6:55 Lysias heard that *P,*
6:63 where he found *P* in possession of the city.
8:5 *P* and Perseus, king of the Macedonians,
2Mc 5:22 at Jerusalem, *P,* a Phrygian by birth,
6:11 were betrayed to *P* and all burned to death.
8:8 When *P* saw that Judas was gaining ground
9:29 His foster brother *P* brought the body home;
13:23 Next he heard that *P,*
Mt 10:3 *P* and Bartholomew,
14:3 of Herodias, the wife of his brother *P.*
Mk 3:18 Andrew, *P,*
6:17 of Herodias, the wife of his brother *P,*
Lk 3:1 *P* his brother tetrarch of the region of
6:14 brother, James and John, *P* and Bartholomew,
Jn 1:43 out for Galilee, but first he came upon *P.*
1:44 Now *P* was from Bethsaida,
1:45 *P* sought out Nathanael and told him,
1:46 and *P* replied, "Come, see for yourself."
1:48 "Before *P* called you," Jesus answered,
6:5 crowd coming toward him, he said to *P,*
6:7 *P* replied, "Not even with two hundred
12:21 They approached *P,*
12:22 *P* went to tell Andrew; *P* and Andrew
14:8 "Lord," *P* said to him,
14:9 *P,*" Jesus replied, "after I have been with
Acts 1:13 *P* and Thomas,
6:5 *P,*
8:5 *P,* for example, went down to the town
8:6 the crowds that heard *P* and saw the
8:12 believe in the good news that *P* preached
8:13 rest and became a devoted follower of *P.*
8:26 of the Lord then addressed himself to *P:*
8:26 *P* began the journey.
8:29 The Spirit said to *P,*
8:30 *P* ran ahead and heard the man reading the
8:31 *P* to get in and sit down beside him.
8:34 The eunuch said to *P,*
8:35 *P* launched out with this Scripture passage
8:38 and *P* went down into the water with the
8:39 *P* away and the eunuch saw him no more.
8:40 *P* found himself at Azotus next,
21:8 we entered the home of *P* the evangelist,

PHILIPPI (6)

Mt 16:13 came to the neighborhood of Caesarea *P,*
Mk 8:27 set out for the villages around Caesarea *P.*
Acts 16:12 from there we went to *P,*
20:6 We ourselves set sail from *P* as soon as
Phil 1:1 Christ Jesus, to all the holy ones at *P,*
1Thes 2:2 from the humiliation we had suffered at *P*—

PHILIPPIANS (1)

Phil 4:15 You yourselves know, my dear *P,*

PHILIP'S (2)

1Mc 1:1 After Alexander the Macedonian, *P* son,
Jn 6:6 to do but he asked this to test *P* response.)

PHILISTIA (11)

Ex 15:14 anguish gripped the dwellers in *P.*
2Chr 26:6 cities in the district of Ashdod and in *P.*
1Mc 3:41 A force from Idumea and from *P* joined with
Ps(s) 60:10 I will triumph over *P.*"
83:8 and Amalek, *P* with the inhabitants of Tyre;
87:4 Of *P,*
108:10 I will triumph over *P.*"
Sir 50:26 Those who live in Seir and *P,*
Is 14:29 Rejoice not, O *P,*
14:31 *P,* all of you melts away!
Jl 4:4 Tyre and Sidon, and all the regions of *P?*

PHILISTINE (56)

Jgs 14:1 to Timnah and saw there one of the *P* women.
14:2 "There is a *P* woman I saw in Timnah whom
1Sm 5:8 all the *P* lords and inquired of them,
5:11 a summons to all the *P* lords and pleaded:
6:4 to correspond to the number of *P* lords,
6:12 The *P* lords followed them as far as the
6:16 *P* lords returned to Ekron the same day.
13:3 the *P* garrison which was in Gibeah,
14:1 go over to the *P* outpost on the other side."
14:4 intended to get over to the *P* outpost
14:19 the tumult in the *P* camp kept increasing.
17:4 Goliath of Gath came out from the *P* camp;
17:8 I am a *P,* and you are Saul's servants.
17:10 The *P* continued: "I defy the ranks
17:11 when they heard this challenge of the *P,*
17:16 [Meanwhile the *P* came forward and took his
17:23 he was talking with them, the *P* champion,
17:26 this *P* and frees Israel of the disgrace?
17:26 Who is this uncircumcised *P* in any case,
17:32 am at your service to go and fight this *P.*"
17:33 go up against this *P* and fight with him,
17:36 uncircumcised *P* will be as one of them,
17:37 keep me safe from the clutches of this *P.*"
17:40 also ready to hand, he approached the *P.*
17:41 *P* also advanced closer and closer to David.
17:43 The *P* said to David, "Am I a dog
17:43 *P* cursed David by his gods and said to him,
17:46 the corpses of the *P* army
17:48 The *P* then moved to meet David at close
17:48 the battle line in the direction of the *P.*
17:49 the sling and struck the *P* on the forehead.
17:50 David overcame the *P* with sling and stone;
17:50 he struck the *P* mortally,
17:54 head of the *P* and brought it to Jerusalem;
17:55 [When Saul saw David go out to meet the *P,*
17:57 So when David returned from slaying the *P,*
18:6 (on David's return after slaying the *P),*
18:30 [The *P* chiefs continued to make forays,
19:5 took his life in his hands and slew the *P,*
21:10 "The sword of Goliath the *P,*
22:10 and the sword of Goliath the *P* as well."
28:4 *P* levies advanced to Shunem and encamped.
29:2 As the *P* lords were marching their groups
29:3 The *P* chiefs asked,
29:4 But the *P* chiefs were angered at this and
29:7 nothing that might displease the *P* lords."
29:9 But the *P* chiefs have determined you are
2Sm 1:20 of Ashkelon, Lest the *P* maidens rejoice,
3:14 I espoused by paying a hundred *P* foreskins."
21:17 his assistance and struck and killed the *P.*
23:13 *P* clan was encamped in the Vale of Rephaim.
23:16 So the Three warriors broke through the *P*
1Chr 11:16 and a *P* garrison was at Bethlehem.
14:16 routed the *P* army from Gibeon to Gezer.
1Mc 4:22 to attack, they all fled to *P* territory.
Zec 9:6 I will destroy the pride of the *P*

PHILISTINES (222)

Gn 10:14 and the Caphtorim from whom the *P* sprang.
21:32 left and returned to the land of the *P.*
21:34 in the land of the *P* for many years.
26:1 down to Abimelech, king of the *P* in Gerar.
26:8 for a long time, Abimelech, king of the *P,*
26:14 animals, that the *P* became envious of him.
26:15 (The *P* had stopped up and filled with
26:18 the *P* had stopped up after Abraham's death;
Ex 13:17 did not lead them by way of the *P'* land,
23:31 from the Red Sea to the sea of the *P,*
Jos 13:2 all Geshur and all the districts of the *P*
13:3 held by the five lords of the *P* in Gaza,
Jgs 3:3 the five lords of the *P;*
3:31 who slew six hundred *P* with an oxgoad.
10:6 of the Ammonites, and the gods of the *P.*
10:7 the power of [the *P* and] the Ammonites.
10:11 the Amorites, the Ammonites, the *P,*
13:1 into the power of the *P* for forty years.
13:5 of Israel from the power of the *P.*"
14:3 and take a wife from the uncircumcised *P?*"
14:4 providing an opportunity against the *P;*
15:3 time the *P* cannot blame me if I harm them."
15:5 loose in the standing grain of the *P,*
15:6 When the *P* asked who had done this,
15:6 So the *P* went up and destroyed her and her
15:9 The *P* went up and, from a camp in Judah,
15:11 you not know that the *P* are our rulers?
15:12 you prisoner, to deliver you over to the *P.*"
15:14 Lehi, and the *P* came shouting to meet him,
15:20 for twenty years in the days of the *P.*
16:5 The lords of the *P* came to her and said,
16:8 So the lords of the *P* brought her seven
16:9 so she said to him, "The *P* are upon you,
16:12 "The *P* are upon you, Samson!"
16:14 Then she said, "The *P* are upon you,
16:18 she summoned the lords of the *P,*
16:18 *P* came and brought up the money with them.
16:20 When she said, "The *P* are upon you,
16:21 The *P* seized him and gouged out his eyes.
16:23 The lords of the *P* assembled to offer a
16:27 all the lords of the *P* were there,
16:28 avenge myself once and for all on the *P.*"
16:30 And Samson said, "Let me die with the *P!*"

PHILISTINES (cont.)

1Sm 4: 1 the P gathered for an attack on Israel.
4: 1 at Ebenezer, while the P camped at Aphek.
4: 2 The P then drew up in battle formation
4: 2 struggle Israel was defeated by the P,
4: 3 permitted us to be defeated today by the P?
4: 6 The P, hearing the noise of shouting, asked,
4: 7 come into the camp, the P were frightened.
4: 9 Take courage and be manly, P;
4:10 The P fought and Israel was defeated;
4:17 "Israel fled from the P;
5: 1 The P, having captured the ark of God,
6: 1 LORD had been in the land of the P
6:17 The golden hemorrhoids the P sent back
6:18 of the P belonging to the five lords,
6:21 "The P have returned the ark of the LORD;
7: 3 will deliver you from the power of the P."
7: 7 When the P heard that the Israelites had
7: 7 became afraid of the P and said to Samuel,
7: 8 us, to save us from the clutches of the P."
7:10 the P advanced to join battle with Israel.
7:10 the LORD thundered loudly against the P,
7:11 forth from Mizpah and pursued the P,
7:13 Thus were the P subdued,
7:14 The cities from Ekron to Gath which the P
7:14 of these cities from the dominion of the P.
9:16 save my people from the clutches of the P,
10: 5 where there is a garrison of the P.
12: 9 king of Hazor, into the grasp of the P,
13: 3 in Gibeah, and P got word of it
13: 4 Saul had overcome the garrison of the P
13: 4 Israel had brought disgrace upon the P;
13: 5 The P also assembled for battle,
13:11 time, and with the P assembled at Michmash,
13:12 the P will come down against me at Gilgal,
13:16 and the P were encamped at Michmash.
13:17 left the camp of the P in three bands.
13:19 whole land of Israel, for the P had said,
13:20 down to the P to sharpen their plowshares,
13:23 An outpost of the P had pushed forward to
14:11 them appeared before the outpost of the P,
14:13 as the P turned to flee him,
14:20 and rushed into the fight, where the P,
14:21 P and had gone up with them to the camp,
14:22 on hearing that the P were fleeing,
14:30 the P by now have been the greater for it?"
14:31 After the P were routed that day from
14:36 us go down in pursuit of the P by night,
14:37 "Shall I go down in pursuit of the P?
14:46 that Saul gave up the pursuit of the P,
14:47 Beth-rehob, the king of Zobah, and the P.
14:52 waged against the P during Saul's lifetime.
17: 1 The P rallied their forces for battle at
17: 2 drawing up their battle line to meet the P.
17: 3 The P were stationed on one hill and the
17:19 against the P in the Vale of the Terebinth."
17:21 The Israelites and the P drew up opposite
17:23 ranks of the P and spoke as before
17:51 with the P own sword [which he drew from
17:51 their hero was dead, the P took to flight.
17:52 went in pursuit of the P to the approaches
17:52 and P fell wounded along the road from
17:53 On their return from the pursuit of the P,
17:57 David was still holding the P head.
18:17 let the P strike him."
18:21 for him, so that the P may strike him."
18:25 bride than the foreskins of one hundred P,
18:25 to bring about David's death through the P.
18:27 forth with his men and slew two hundred P.
19: 8 P and inflicted a great defeat upon them,
23: 1 David received information that the P were
23: 2 inquiring, "Shall I go and defeat these P?"
23: 2 you will defeat the P and rescue Keilah."
23: 3 go to Keilah against the forces of the P!"
23: 4 for I will deliver the P into your power."
23: 5 his men to Keilah and fought with the P.
23:27 because the P have invaded the land."
23:28 pursuit of David and went to meet the P.
24: 2 Saul returned from the pursuit of the P,
27: 1 choice but to escape to the land of the P;
27: 7 and four months in the country of the P.
27:11 long as he lived in the country of the P.
28: 1 In those days the P mustered their
28: 5 When Saul saw the camp of the P,
28:15 for the P are waging war against me and
28:19 you as well, into the clutches of the P.
28:19 the army of Israel into the hands of the P."
29: 1 P had mustered all their forces in Aphek,
29:11 the morning to return to the land of the P.
29:11 The P, however, went on up to Jezreel.
30:16 land of the P and from the land of Judah.
31: 2 the P pursued Saul and his sons closely,
31: 7 Then the P came and lived in those cities.
31: 8 the battle the P came to strip the slain,
31: 9 of the P to their idols and to the people.
31:11 heard what the P had done to Saul,
2Sm 3:18 Israel from the grasp of the P
5:17 When the P heard that David
5:18 P came and overran the valley of Rephaim.
5:19 of the LORD, "Shall I attack the P—
5:19 I will surely deliver the P into your grip."
5:22 But the P came up again and overran the
5:24 before you to attack the camp of the P."
5:25 routed the P from Gibeon as far as Gezer.
8: 1 David attacked the P and conquered them,
8:12 and Moab, from the Ammonites, from the P,
19:10 he who rescued us from the grip of the P.
21:12 where the P had hanged them at the time
21:15 another battle between the P and Israel.
21:15 down with his servants and fought the P,
21:18 there was another battle with the P in Gob.
21:19 There was another battle with the P in Gob,
23: 9 when the P assembled there for battle.
23:10 stood his ground and fought the P
23:11 The P had assembled at Lehi,
23:11 When the soldiers fled from the P,
23:12 He slew the P, and the LORD brought
23:14 and there was a garrison of P in Bethlehem.
1Kgs 5: 1 from the River to the land of the P,
15:27 and struck him down at Gibbethon of the P,
16:15 The army was besieging Gibbethon of the P
2Kgs 8: 2 in the land of the P for seven years.
8: 3 woman returned from the land of the P
18: 8 the watchtowers and walled cities of the P,
1Chr 1:12 and Caphtorim, from whom the P sprang.
10: 1 Now the P were at war with Israel;
10: 1 the Israelites fled before the P,
10: 2 The P pressed hard after Saul and his sons.
10: 2 When the P had killed Jonathan,
10: 7 thereupon the P came and occupied them.
10: 8 day, when the P came to strip the slain,
10: 9 land of the P to convey the good news
10:11 had heard what the P had done to Saul,
11:13 where the P had massed for battle.
11:13 its defenders were retreating before the P.
11:14 ground, kept it safe, and cut down the P.
11:15 P were encamped in the valley of Rephaim.
11:18 broke through the encampment of the P,
12:20 he came with the P to battle against Saul.
12:20 However, he did not help the P,
14: 8 When the P had heard that David was
14: 9 Meanwhile the P had come and raided the
14:10 of God, "Shall I advance against the P,
14:12 The P had left their gods there,
14:13 Once again the P raided the valley;
14:15 before you to strike the army of the P."
18: 1 David defeated the P and subdued them;
18: 1 its towns away from the control of the P.
18:11 from Edom, Moab, the Ammonites, the P,
20: 4 there was another battle with the P,
20: 4 of the Raphaim, and the P were subdued.
20: 5 Once again there was war with the P,
2Chr 9:26 of the P and down to the border of Egypt.
17:11 Some of the P brought Jehoshaphat gifts
21:16 animosity of the P and of the Arabs
26: 6 fought the P and razed the walls of Gath,
26: 7 God helped him against the P,
28:18 The P too had raided the cities of the
1Mc 3:24 and the rest fled to the country of the P.
4:30 camp of the P into the hand of Jonathan,
5:66 land of the P and passed through Marisa.
5:68 turned toward Azotus in the land of the P.
Ps(s) 56: 1 of David, when the P held him in Gath.
Sir 46:18 enemy and destroyed all the lords of the P.
47: 7 He destroyed the hostile P and shattered
Is 2: 6 fortunetellers and soothsayers, like the P;
9:11 Aram on the east and the P on the west
11:14 down on the foothills of the P to the west,
Jer 25:20 all the kings of the land of the P:
47: 1 to the prophet Jeremiah concerning the P,
47: 4 the day which has come to ruin all the P,
47: 4 Yes, the LORD is destroying the P,
Ez 16:27 over to the will of your enemies, the P,
16:57 neighbors, despised on all sides by the P.
25:15 Because the P have acted revengefully,
25:16 I am stretching out my hand against the P;
Am 1: 8 Ekron, and the last of the P shall perish,
6: 2 the great, and down to Gath of the P!
9: 7 P from Caphtor and the Arameans from Kir?
Ob 1:19 mount of Esau, and the foothills of the P;
Zep 2: 5 you, I will humble you, land of the P,

PHILOLOGUS (1)

Rom 16:15 to P and Julia,

PHILOMETOR (3)

2Mc 4:21 to Egypt for the coronation of King P,
9:29 he later withdrew into Egypt, to Ptolemy P.
10:13 Cyprus, which P had entrusted to him,

PHILOSOPHERS (1)

Acts 17:18 Epicurean and Stoic p disputed with him,

PHILOSOPHY (2)

Col 2: 8 p that follows mere human traditions,
2: 8 a p based on cosmic powers rather than on

PHINEHAS (28)

Ex 6:25 one of Putiel's daughters, who bore him P.
Nm 25: 7 When P, son of Eleazar,
25:11 Then the LORD said to Moses, P,
31: 6 a thousand from each tribe, with P,
Jos 22:13 land of Gilead an embassy consisting of P,
22:30 When P the priest and the princes of the
22:31 P, son of Eleazar the priest,
22:32 P, son of Eleazar the priest,
24:33 son P in the mountain region of Ephraim.
Jgs 20:28 of God was there in those days, and P,
1Sm 1: 3 where the two sons of Eli, Hophni and P,
2:34 will happen to your two sons, Hophni and P:
4: 4 The two sons of Eli, Hophni and P,
4:11 and Eli's two sons, Hophni and P,
4:17 Your two sons, Hophni and P,
4:19 His daughter-in-law, the wife of P,
14: 3 brother of Ichabod, who was the son of P,
1Chr 5:30 Eleazar became the father of P.
5:30 P became the father of Abishua.
6:35 his son Eleazar, whose son was P,
9:20 P, son of Eleazar,
Ezr 7: 5 son of Bukki, son of Abishua, son of P,
8: 2 Of the sons of P,
8:33 who was assisted by Eleazar, son of P;
1Mc 2:26 zeal for the law, just as P did with Zimri,
2:54 P our father,
Ps(s) 106:30 Then P stood forth in judgment and the
Sir 45:23 P too, the son of Eleazar,

PHLEGON (1)

Rom 16:14 Greetings to Asyncritus, P,

PHOEBE (1)

Rom 16: 1 I commend to you our sister P,

PHOENICIA (9)

2Mc 3: 5 time was governor of Coelesyria and P,
3: 8 to visit the cities of Coelesyria and P,
4: 4 the governor of Coelesyria and P,
4:22 following this, he led his army into P.
8: 8 to Ptolemy, governor of Coelesyria and P,
10:11 as commander-in-chief of Coelesyria and P.
Acts 11:19 arose because of Stephen went as far as P,
15: 3 they made their way through P and Samaria,
21: 2 When we found a ship bound for P,

PHOENIX (2)

Jb 29:18 I shall multiply years like the p.
Acts 27:12 of making P and spending the winter there.

PHOGOR (1)

Tb 1: 2 above and to the west of Asser, north of P.

PHRASE (1)

Jer 23:38 Because you use this p,

PHRASEMAKERS (1)

Bar 3:23 Midian and Teman, the p seeking knowledge,

PHRASES (1)

Wis 8: 8 turns of p and the solutions of riddles;

PHRYGIA (3)

Acts 2:10 Pontus, the province of Asia, P,
16: 6 They next traveled through P and Galatian
18:23 and P to reassure all his disciples.

PHRYGIAN (1)

2Mc 5:22 at Jerusalem, Philip, a P by birth,

PHYGELUS (1)

2Tm 1:15 in Asia, including even P and Hermogenes,

PHYLACTERIES (1)

Mt 23: 5 They widen their p and wear huge tassels.

PHYSICAL (4)

Gal 4:14 My p condition was a challenge which you
1Tm 4: 8 p training is to some extent valuable,
Heb 7:16 in a commandment concerning p descent,
1Pt 3:21 This baptism is no removal of p stain,

PHYSICIAN (4)

Sir 38: 1 Hold the p in honor,
Jer 8:22 Is there no balm in Gilead, no p there?
Lk 4:23 the proverb, P, heal yourself,'
Col 4:14 Luke, our dear p, sends you greetings.

PHYSICIANS (2)

Gn 50: 2 the p in his service to embalm his father.
2Chr 16:12 he did not seek the LORD, but only the p.

PI-HAHIROTH (4)

Ex 14: 2 Israelites to turn about and camp before P,
14: 9 them as they lay encamped by the sea, at P,
Nm 33: 7 out from Etham, they turned back to P,
33: 8 Setting out from P,

PIBESETH (1)

Ez 30:17 men of On and of P shall fall by the sword,

PICK (28)

Gn 47: 6 father and brothers in the *p* of the land."
47:11 holdings in Egypt on the *p* of the land,
Ex 17: 9 said to Joshua, *P* out certain men,
Lv 19:10 you shall not *p* your vineyard bare,
25: 5 nor shall you *p* the grapes of your
25:11 or *p* the grapes from the untrimmed vines.
Dt 24:21 When you *p* your grapes,
Jgs 1: 7 off, used to *p* up scraps under my table.
1Sm 20:21 *p* it up,' come, for you are safe.
1Kgs 1: 8 and his companions, the *p* of David's army,
1:10 Nathan, or Benaiah, or the *p* of the army,
2Kgs 6: 7 *P* it up," he said.
1Mc 12:45 *P* out a few men to stay with you,
Sir 11:30 like a spy he will *p* out the weak spots.
Is 41:27 I will *p* out a bearer of the glad tidings."
Jer 2:33 How well you *p* your way when seeking love!
12: 3 *P* them out like sheep for the slaughter,
Ez 24: 5 joints taken from the *p* of the flock.
Jon 1:12 to them, *P* me up and throw me into the sea,
Mt 7:16 Do you ever *p* grapes from thornbushes,
24:18 he must not turn back to *p* up his cloak.
Mk 2: 9 or to say, 'Stand up, *p* up your mat,
2:11 *P* up your mat and go home."
13:16 he must not turn back to *p* up his cloak.
Jn 5: 8 *P* up your mat and walk!"
5:11 me who told me, *P* up your mat and walk.' "
5:12 person who told you to *p* it up and walk,"
Acts 20:13 sail for Assos, where we were to *p* Paul up.

PICKED (53)

Gn 18: 7 He ran to the herd, *p* out a tender,
Ex 18:25 He *p* out able men from all Israel and put
Nm 31:50 to the LORD some gold article he has *p* up,
Jos 6: 7 with the *p* troops marching ahead of the
6: 9 with the horns marched the *p* troops;
6:13 Ahead of these marched the *p* troops,
10: 7 his *p* troops and the rest of his soldiers.
Jgs 20:16 seven hundred *p* men who were left-handed,
20:34 Gibeah, ten thousand *p* men from all Israel,
20:45 *p* off five thousand men among them,
Ru 4: 2 Then Boaz *p* out ten of the elders of the
1Sm 5: 3 So they *p* Dagon up and replaced him.
20:38 Jonathan's boy *p* up the arrow and brought
24: 3 So Saul took three thousand *p* men from all
26: 2 Ziph with three thousand *p* men of Israel,
29: 4 him return to the place you *p* out for him.
29:10 with you, go to the place I *p* out for you.
2Sm 6: 1 again assembled all the *p* men of Israel,
10: 9 he made a selection from all the *p* troops
13:10 So Tamar *p* up the cakes she had prepared
1Kgs 11:18 Paran, where they *p* up additional men,
2Kgs 2:13 Then he *p* up Elijah's mantle which had
4:20 *p* him up and carried him to his mother;
4:39 from which he *p* a clothful of wild gourds.
2Chr 13: 3 force of four hundred thousand *p* warriors,
13: 3 hundred thousand *p* and valiant warriors.
13:17 thousand *p* men of Israel fell slain.
25: 5 three hundred thousand *p* men fit for war,
Tb 8:19 *p* out two steers and four rams
Jdt 2:15 a hundred and twenty thousand *p* troops,
3: 6 them he impressed *p* troops as auxiliaries.
1Mc 4: 1 thousand infantry and a thousand *p* cavalry,
4:28 thousand *p* men and five thousand cavalry,
6:35 bronze helmets, and five hundred *p* cavalry.
9: 5 Judas, with three thousand *p* men,
12:41 *p* fighting men and came to Beth-shan.
2Mc 3:27 Men *p* him up and laid him on a stretcher.
4:41 the people *p* up stones or pieces of wood
13:15 attack on the king's pavilion with a *p* force
Dn 11:15 *p* troops shall have the strength to resist.
Na 2: 6 His *p* troops are called,
Mt 16: 9 and how many baskets-full you *p* up?
27: 6 The chief priests *p* up the silver,
Mk 2:12 The man stood and *p* up his mat and went
Lk 5:25 He *p* up the mat he had been lying on and
6:44 thornbushes, nor grapes *p* from brambles.
Jn 5: 9 he *p* up his mat and began to walk.
8:59 At that they *p* up rocks to throw at Jesus,
9:40 Some of the Pharisees around him *p* this up,
13: 4 He *p* up a towel and tied it around himself.
15: 6 *p* up to be thrown in the fire and burnt.
Acts 20: 9 When they *p* him up he was dead.
Rv 18:21 A powerful angel *p* up a stone like a huge

PICKING (2)

Jos 8: 3 *P* out thirty thousand warriors,
Est 2: 9 Then *p* out seven maids for her from the

PICKS (8)

Lv 11:25 and everyone who *p* up any part of their
11:28 and everyone who *p* up their dead bodies
2Sm 12:31 he assigned to work with saws, iron *p*,
1Chr 20: 3 and set them to work with saws, iron *p*,
Prv 18: 1 with all persistence he *p* a quarrel.
31:16 She *p* out a field to purchase;
Is 28: 4 man sees it, he *p* and swallows it at once.
40:20 a skilled craftsman *p* out for himself,

PICTURED (1)

Ez 8:10 upon the wall were *p* the figures

PIECE (32)

Gn 23: 4 a *p* of property for a burial ground,
23:15 A *p* of land worth four hundred shekels of
Ex 4:25 But Zipporah took a *p* of flint and cut off
15:25 who pointed out to him a certain *p* of wood.
25:36 form but a single *p* of pure beaten gold.
37:22 formed but a single *p* of pure beaten gold.
Lv 15: 4 and any *p* of furniture on which he sits,
15: 6 Whoever sits on a *p* of furniture on which
15:17 Any *p* of cloth or leather with seed on it
27:16 to the LORD is a *p* of his hereditary land,
Ru 4: 3 is putting up for sale the *p* of land that
1Sm 2:36 him for a *p* of silver or a loaf of bread,
1Kgs 7:18 *p* of network on each of the two capitals.
7:32 of the wheels and the stand were of one *p*.
7:34 each stand, were of one *p* with the stand.
7:35 were of one *p* with the top of the stand.
1Chr 16: 3 every woman, a loaf of bread, a *p* of meat,
Jb 42:11 one gave him a *p* of money and a gold ring.
Jer 2:27 They who say to a *p* of wood,
36:23 four columns the king would cut off the *p*
Hos 4:12 They consult their *p* of wood,
Am 3:12 with the corner of a couch or a *p* of a cot.
Mt 9:16 a *p* of unshrunken cloth on an old cloak;
Lk 5:36 a *p* from a new coat to patch an old one.
5:36 the *p* taken from it will not match the old.
15: 9 I have found the silver *p* I lost.'
24:42 They gave him a *p* of cooked fish,
Jn 19:23 one *p* from top to bottom and had no seam.
20: 7 *p* of cloth which had covered the head
Acts 1:18 bought a *p* of land with his unjust gains,
5: 1 Sapphira likewise sold a *p* of property.
5: 8 *p* of property for such and such an amount?"

PIECEMEAL (1)

2Mc 15:33 saying he would feed it *p* to the birds and

PIECES (89)

Gn 15:17 torch, which passed between those *p*.
33:19 *p* of bullion from the descendants of Hamor,
37:28 to the Ishmaelites for twenty *p* of silver.
37:33 Joseph has been torn to *p*!"
44:28 he must have been torn to *p* by wild beasts;
Ex 22:30 torn to *p* in the field you shall not eat;
29:17 Cut the ram into *p*;
29:17 then put them with the *p* and with the head.
Lv 1: 6 skin the holocaust and cut it up into *p*.
1: 8 wood on them, they shall lay the *p* of meat,
1:12 When the offerer has cut it up into *p*,
2: 6 a cereal offering must be broken into *p*,
6:14 Having broken the offering into *p*,
8:20 After cutting up the ram into *p*,
8:20 burned the head, the cut-up *p* and the suet,
9:13 him the *p* and the head of the holocaust,
11:35 or a jar-stand, this must be broken to *p*;
Jos 24:32 of Shechem, for a hundred *p* of money.
Jgs 14: 6 he tore the lion in *p* as one tears a kid.
19:29 of his concubine, cut her into twelve *p*,
1Sm 11: 7 Taking a yoke of oxen, he cut them into *p*,
2Sm 18:11 to give you fifty *p* of silver and a belt."
18:12 a thousand *p* of silver in my two hands,
1Kgs 7:17 Two *p* of network with a chainlike mesh
7:41 two *p* of network covering the nodes for
7:42 pomegranates in double rows on both *p*
11:30 off his new cloak, tore it into twelve *p*,
11:31 "Take ten *p* for yourself;
18:23 Let them choose one, cut it into *p*,
2Kgs 2:24 and tore forty-two of the children to *p*.
5: 5 ten silver talents, six thousand gold *p*,
6:25 an ass's head sold for eighty *p* of silver,
6:25 a kab of wild onion for five *p* of silver.
8:12 you will dash their little children to *p*,
23:14 He broke to *p* the pillars,
25:13 of the LORD, the Chaldeans broke into *p*;
2Chr 14: 2 places, breaking to *p* the sacred pillars,
28:24 of God's house and broke them in *p*.
Ezr 1:10 other ware, one thousand *p*.
1:11 five thousand four hundred *p*.
Jdt 5:22 of Moab alike said he should be cut to *p*.
2Mc 1:13 they were cut to *p* in the temple of the
4:41 the people picked up stones or *p* of wood
Jb 16:12 seized me by the neck and dashed me to *p*.
Ps(s) 7: 3 like the lion's prey, to be torn to *p*,
119:72 than thousands of gold and silver *p*.
Sg 8:11 one would have to pay a thousand silver *p*.
8:12 the thousand *p* are for you,
Sir 28:23 like a panther, it will tear them to *p*.
Is 7:23 vines, worth a thousand *p* of silver,
13:16 shall be dashed to *p* in their sight;
27: 9 the stones of the altars like *p* of chalk;
Jer 5: 6 all who come out are torn to *p* For their
52:17 of the LORD, the Chaldeans broke into *p*;
Ez 23:47 them and hack them to *p* with their swords.
24: 4 Put in it *p* of meat, all good pieces:
24: 5 boil these *p* and the joints that are in it.
24: 6 Take out its *p*,
Dn 2: 5 be cut to *p* and your houses destroyed.
2:34 its iron and tile feet, breaking them in *p*.
2:40 break in *p* and subdue all these others,
2:40 breaks in *p* and crushes everything else.
2:44 it shall break in *p* all these kingdoms and
2:45 being put to it, which broke in *p* the tile,
3:96 shall be cut to *p* and his house destroyed.
11: 4 torn to *p* and belong to others than they
Hos 3: 2 So I bought her for fifteen *p* of silver
14: 1 their little ones shall be dashed to *p*,
Mi 1: 7 All her idols shall be broken to *p*,
3: 3 They chop them in *p* like flesh in a kettle,
Na 3:10 dashed to *p* at the corner of every street;
Zec 11:12 counted out my wages, thirty *p* of silver.
11:13 So I took the thirty *p* of silver and threw
Mt 25:15 one he disbursed five thousand silver *p*,
25:25 your thousand silver *p* in the ground.
26:15 They paid him thirty *p* of silver,
27: 3 He took the thirty *p* of silver back to the
27: 9 "They took the thirty *p* of silver,
Mk 14: 5 silver *p* and the money given to the poor."
Lk 10:35 The next day he took out two silver *p* and
15: 8 if she has ten silver *p* and loses one,
20:18 falls on that stone will be smashed to *p*.
Jn 6:13 gathered twelve baskets full of *p* left over
12: 5 could have brought three hundred silver *p*,
Acts 19:19 it came to fifty thousand silver *p*.
23:10 commander feared they would tear Paul to *p*.
Gal 5:15 go on biting and tearing one another to *p*,
Rv 18:12 of ivory *p* and expensive wooden furniture;

PIERCE (9)

Ex 21: 6 doorpost, he shall *p* his ear with an awl,
Jdt 6: 6 the spear of my servants will *p* your sides,
Jb 6: 4 For the arrows of the Almighty *p* me,
20:24 the bow of bronze shall *p* him through;
40:24 him by his eyes, or *p* his nose with a trap?
40:26 nose, or *p* through his cheek with a gaff?
Ps(s) 37:15 But their swords shall *p* their own hearts,
Lam 3:44 in a cloud which prayer could not *p*.
Hb 3:14 You *p* with your shafts the heads of their

PIERCED (15)

Nm 25: 8 his retreat where be *p* the pair of them,
1Sm 31: 3 he was *p* through the abdomen.
2Kgs 9:27 And they *p* him as he rode through the pass
Jdt 16:12 Sons of slave girls *p* them through;
2Mc 3:16 of the high priest was *p* to the heart,
12:22 another, *p* by the swords of their own men.
Ps(s) 22:17 They have *p* my hands and my feet;
73:21 my heart was embittered and my soul was *p*,
109:22 and poor, and my heart is *p* within me.
Is 51: 9 who crushed Rahab, you who *p* the dragon?
53: 5 But he was *p* for our offenses,
Lam 4: 9 Who waste away, as though *p* through,
Lk 2:35 and you yourself shall be *p* with a sword
Jn 19:37 "They shall look on him whom they have *p*."
Rv 1: 7 eye shall see him, even of those who *p* him.

PIERCES (9)

2Kgs 18:21 which *p* the hand of anyone who leans on it.
Jb 16:13 directions, He *p* my sides without mercy,
16:14 He *p* me with thrust upon thrust;
27:22 His hand *p* the fugitive dragon as from his
Prv 7:23 toward the net, till an arrow *p* its liver;
Sir 22:19 he who *p* the heart bares its feelings.
35:17 The prayer of the lowly *p* the clouds;
Is 36: 6 which *p* the hand of anyone who leans on it.
Lam 3:13 He *p* my sides with shafts from his quiver.

PIERCING (1)

Rv 1:10 me a *p* voice like the sound of a trumpet,

PIETY (18)

1Mc 2:57 David, for his *p*, received as a heritage
2Mc 3: 1 because of the *p* of the high priest Onias
Jb 4: 6 Is not your *p* a source of confidence,
15: 4 You in fact do away with *p*,
22: 4 it because of your *p* that he reproves you
Prv 16: 6 By kindness and *p* guilt is expiated,
20:28 Kindness and *p* safeguard the king,
Wis 14:30 deliberately swore false oaths despising *p*.
Hos 6: 4 Your *p* is like a morning cloud,
10:12 yourselves justice, reap the fruit of *p*;
Col 2:23 show of wisdom in their affected *p*,
1Tm 2: 2 tranquil lives in perfect *p* and dignity.
4: 7 Train yourself for the life of *p*,
5: 4 let these learn that *p* begins at home and
6:11 Instead, seek after integrity, *p*,
2Pt 1: 3 necessary for a life of genuine *p*,
1: 6 to perseverance, and perseverance to *p*,
1: 7 to piety, and *p* to care for your brother,

PIG (2)

Lv 11: 6 is therefore unclean for you; and the *p*,
Dt 14: 8 and the *p*, which indeed has hoofs and is

PIGEON (3)

Gn 15: 9 ram, a turtledove, and a young *p*."
Lv 1:14 choose a turtledove or a *p* as his offering.
12: 6 and a *p* or a turtledove for a sin offering.

PIGEONS (9)

Lv 5: 7 for his sin two turtledoves or two *p*,
5:11 to afford even two turtledoves or two *p*,
12: 8 she may take two turtledoves or two *p*,
14:22 a log of oil, and two turtledoves or *p*,
14:30 Then, of the turtledoves or *p*,
15:14 he shall take two turtledoves or two *p*,
15:29 she shall take two turtledoves or two *p*
Nm 6:10 he shall bring two turtledoves or two *p*
Lk 2:24 "a pair of turtledoves or two young *p*,"

PIGS (2)

Lk 15:15 sent him to his farm to take care of the *p*.
15:16 with the husks that were fodder for the *p*,

PIKES (1)

2Sm 18:14 And taking three *p* in hand,

PILASTERS (19)

Ez 40: 7 *p* between the cells measured five cubits.
40: 9 gate, which was eight cubits, and its *p*,
40:10 *p* on either side were also of equal size.
40:14 The *p* adjoining the court on either side
40:16 let into the cells [and into their *p*;
40:16 The *p* were decorated with palms.
40:21 Its cells, three on either side, its *p*,
40:24 there was a southern gate, whose cells, *p*,
40:26 with palms here and there on its *p*.
40:29 its cells, its *p*, and its vestibule were
40:31 toward the outer court; palms were on its *p*,
40:33 Its cells, its *p*, and its vestibule were
40:34 palms were on its *p* here and there,
40:36 the dimensions of its cells, its *p*,
40:37 palms were on its *p* here and there,
40:48 the temple and measured the *p* on each side,
40:49 up to it, and there were columns by the *p*,
41: 1 brought me to the nave and measured the *p*,
41: 3 and measured the *p* flanking that entrance,

PILATE (54)

Mt 27: 2 away to be handed over to the procurator *P*.
27:13 Then *P* said to him,
27:17 *P* said to them, "Which one do you wish
27:22 *P* said to them, "Then what am I to do
27:24 *P* finally realized that he was making no
27:58 *P* issued an order for its release.
27:65 *P* told them, "You have a guard.
Mk 15: 1 led him away, and handed him over to *P*.
15: 2 *P* interrogated him:
15: 4 *P* interrogated him again:
15: 9 that he honor the custom, *P* rejoined,
15:12 *P* again asked them,
15:14 *P* protested, "Why?
15:15 So *P*, who wished to satisfy the crowd,
15:43 *P* and urgently requested the body of Jesus.
15:44 *P* was surprised that Jesus should have
15:45 was dead, *P* released the corpse to Joseph.
Lk 3: 1 when Pontius *P* was procurator of Judea,
13: 1 blood *P* had mixed with their sacrifices.
23: 1 assembly rose up and led him before *P*.
23: 3 *P* asked him, "Are you the king
23: 4 *P* reported to the chief priests and the
23: 6 this *P* asked if the man was a Galilean;
23:11 robe on him and sent him back to *P*.
23:12 Herod and *P*,
23:13 *P* then called together the chief priests,
23:20 *P* addressed them again,
23:24 *P* then decreed that what they demanded
23:52 *P* with a request for Jesus' body.
Jn 18:29 *P* came out to them.
18:31 *P* said, "Why do you not take him
18:33 *P* went back into the praetorium and
18:35 "I am no Jew!" *P* retorted.
18:37 At this *P* said to him,
18:38 "Truth!" said *P*.
18:38 *P* went out again to the Jews and said to
19: 4 *P* went out a second time and said to the
19: 5 and the purple cloak, *P* said to them,
19: 6 *P* said,
19: 8 When *P* heard this kind of talk,
19:10 *P* asked him. Do you not know that I have
19:12 After this, *P* was eager to release him,
19:13 *P* heard what they were saying,
19:15 *P* exclaimed. "Shall I crucify your king!"
19:16 end, *P* handed Jesus over to be crucified.
19:19 *P* had an inscription placed on the cross
19:21 chief priests of the Jews tried to tell *P*,
19:22 to be King of the Jews' " *P* answered,
19:31 They asked *P* that the legs be broken and
19:38 *P* granted it, so they came and took the
Acts 3:13 presence when *P* was ready to release him.
4:27 Herod and Pontius *P* in league with the
13:28 death, they begged *P* to have him executed.
1Tm 6:13 his noble profession before Pontius *P*,

PILATE'S (5)

Mt 27:62 and the Pharisees called at *P* residence.
Mk 15: 5 But greatly to *P* surprise,
Jn 19: 1 *P* next move was to take Jesus and have him
19:38 asked *P* permission to remove Jesus' body.
Acts 3:13 handed over and disowned in *P* presence

PILDASH (1)

Gn 22:22 (the father of Aram), Chesed, Hazo, *P*,

PILE (7)

Lv 24: 6 shall place in two piles, six in each *p*,
24: 7 On each *p* put some pure frankincense,
2Kgs 10: 8 *P* them in two heaps at the entrance of the
Sir 31: 3 The rich man labors to *p* up wealth,
Jer 21: 4 I will *p* up in the midst of this city,
50:26 *P* up her goods in heaps and doom it,
Ez 24: 5 Then *p* the wood beneath it;

PILED (6)

Ex 15: 8 At a breath of your anger the waters *p* up,
Jos 7:26 and *p* a great heap of stones over him,
8:29 a great heap of stones was *p* up over it,
Jgs 15:16 jawbone of an ass I have *p* them in a heap;
Is 30:33 is *p* with dry grass and wood in abundance,
Rv 18: 5 For her sins have *p* up as high as heaven,

PILED-UP (1)

Lk 12:20 To whom will all this *p* wealth of yours go?'

PILES (1)

Lv 24: 6 These you shall place in two *p*,

PILGRIM (5)

Ex 23:14 a year you shall celebrate a *p* feast to me.
Lv 23:39 a *p* feast of the LORD for a whole week.
23:41 descendants you shall keep this *p* feast
Dt 16:15 this *p* feast in honor of the LORD,
Ps(s) 39:13 before you, a *p* like all my fathers.

PILGRIMAGE (10)

Ex 12:14 shall celebrate with *p* to the LORD,
Nm 28:17 fifteenth day of this month is the *p* feast.
29:12 you shall celebrate a *p* feast to the LORD.
1Sm 1: 3 This man regularly went on *p* from his city
1: 7 made their *p* to the sanctuary of the LORD,
1Kgs 12:32 duplicate in Bethel the *p* feast of Judah,
Tb 1: 6 would often make the *p* alone to Jerusalem
5:14 me they used to make the *p* to Jerusalem,
Ps(s) 84: 6 their hearts are set upon the *p*:
Acts 8:27 on a *p* to Jerusalem and was returning home.

PILGRIMS (1)

Lam 1: 4 mourn for lack of *p* going to her feasts;

PILHA (1)

Neh 10:25 Hoshea, Hananiah, Hasshub, Hallohesh, *P*,

PILING (2)

Ez 24:10 bonfire, *p* on wood and kindling the fire,
Acts 7:58 The witnesses meanwhile were *p* their

PILLAGE (14)

Ezr 9: 7 lands, to the sword, to captivity, to *p*,
Jdt 8:19 were handed over to the sword and to *p*,
1Mc 6: 3 and tried to capture and *p* the city.
Jer 30:16 all who pillage you I will hand over to *p*,
Bar 6:14 but it cannot save itself from war or *p*.
Ez 30:24 against Egypt so as to plunder and *p* it.
34: 8 my sheep have been given over to *p*,
36: 4 *p* and mockery of the remaining nations
38:12 neither bars nor gates, to plunder and *p*,
38:13 it for *p* that you have summoned your horde,
39:10 them and *p* those who pillaged them,
Am 3:11 you of your strength, and *p* your castles,
Zep 1:13 given to *p* and their houses to devastation;

PILLAGED (3)

Is 10:13 of peoples, their treasures I have *p*,
Ez 26:12 shall be plundered, your merchandise *p*;
39:10 them and pillage those who *p* them,

PILLAGING (1)

Ez 29:19 and *p* it for the wages of his soldiers,

PILLAR (22)

Gn 19:26 back, and she was turned into a *p* of salt.
Lv 26: 1 erect an idol or a sacred *p* for yourselves,
Dt 16:22 nor shall you erect a sacred *p*,
Jgs 9: 6 the terebinth at the memorial *p* in Shechem.
2Sm 18:18 During his lifetime Absalom had taken a *p*
18:18 The *p* which he named for himself is called
2Kgs 3: 2 He did away with the *p* of Baal,
11:14 When she saw the king standing by the *p*,
25:17 five cubits high surmounted each *p*,
25:17 and so for the other *p*,
2Chr 23:13 king standing beside his *p* at the entrance,
Ps(s) 99: 7 From the *p* of cloud he spoke to them;
Wis 10: 7 a disbelieving soul, a standing *p* of salt.
18: 3 *p* which was a guide on the unknown way,
Sir 24: 4 did I dwell, my throne on a *p* of cloud.
Is 19:19 a sacred *p* to the LORD near the boundary.
Jer 1:18 made you a fortified city, A *p* of iron,
52:22 five cubits high surmounted the one *p*,
52:22 and so for the other *p*.
Hos 3: 4 or prince, Without sacrifice or sacred *p*,
1Tm 3:15 the living God, the *p* and bulwark of truth.
Rv 3:12 " 'I will make the victor a *p* in the

PILLARS (32)

Ex 23:24 demolish them and smash their sacred *p*.
24: 4 twelve *p* for the twelve tribes of Israel.
34:13 smash their sacred *p*,
Dt 7: 5 down their altars, smash their sacred *p*,
12: 3 down their altars, smash their sacred *p*,
1Sm 2: 8 For the *p* of the earth are the LORD's,
1Kgs 14:23 too, built for themselves high places, *p*,
2Kgs 17:10 They set up *p* and sacred poles for
18: 4 removed the high places, shattered the *p*,
23:14 He broke to pieces the *p*,
25:13 *p* that belonged to the house of the LORD,
25:16 The weight in bronze of the two *p*,
25:17 Each of the *p* was eighteen cubits high;
1Chr 18: 8 sea and the *p* and the vessels of bronze.
2Chr 14: 2 places, breaking to pieces the sacred *p*,
31: 1 cities of Judah and smashed the sacred *p*,
Est 1: 6 byssus from silver rings on marble *p*.
1Mc 14:26 which they affixed to *p* on Mount Zion.
Jb 9: 6 of its place, and the *p* beneath it tremble.
26:11 The *p* of the heavens tremble and are
Ps(s) 11: 3 When the *p* are overthrown,
75: 4 dwell in it quake, I have set firm its *p*.
Jer 27:19 says the LORD of hosts concerning the *p*,
52:17 *p* that belonged to the house of the LORD,
52:20 guard carried off, as well as the two *p*,
52:21 Each of the *p* was eighteen cubits high and
Ez 26:11 your mighty *p* he shall pull to the ground.
Hos 10: 1 his land, the more sacred *p* he set up.
10: 2 their altars and destroy their sacred *p*.
Mi 5:12 images and the sacred *p* from your midst;
Gal 2: 9 on me, those who were the acknowledged *p*,
Rv 10: 1 like the sun and his legs like *p* of fire.

PILLORY (1)

Jer 29:26 by putting them into the stocks or the *p*.

PILOT (1)

Acts 27:11 *p* and the shipowner to listening to Paul.

PILOTING (1)

Wis 10: 4 saved it, *p* the just man on frailest wood.

PILTAI (1)

Neh 12:17 for Maadiah, *P*; for Bilgah, Shammua;

PIN (3)

Jgs 16:13 into the web and fasten them with the *p*,
16:14 the web, and fastened them in with the *p*.
16:14 pulled out both the weaver's *p* and the web.

PINE (4)

Ps(s) 112:10 he shall gnash his teeth and *p* away;
Is 19: 8 their nets in the water shall *p* away.
41:19 together with the plane tree and the *p*,
60:13 the cypress, the plane and the *p*,

PINED (1)

Wis 1:16 considered it a friend, and *p* for it,

PINES (3)

Ps(s) 63: 2 *p* and my soul thirsts like the earth,
84: 3 yearns and *p* for the courts of the LORD.
119:81 My soul *p* for your salvation;

PINIONS (8)

Dt 32:11 to receive them and bore them up on his *p*.
33: 3 at his feet and he bore them up on his *p*.
Jb 39:13 her plumage is lacking in *p*.
Ps(s) 68:14 with silver, and her *p* with a golden hue.
91: 4 With his *p* he will cover you,
Wis 5:11 the fluid air, lashed by the beat of *p*,
Ez 17: 3 eagle, with great wings, with long *p*,
Hos 4:19 The wind has bound them up in its *p*;

PINK (4)

Lv 13:19 the boil have a white scab or a *p* blotch,
13:24 the burn now becomes a *p* or a white blotch,
13:42 *p* sore on his bald crown or bald forehead,
13:43 same *p* appearance as that of skin leprosy

PINON (2)

Gn 36:41 Alvah, Jetheth, Oholibamah, Elah, *P*,
1Chr 1:52 Aliah, Jetheth, Oholibamah, Elah, *P*,

PIOUS (6)

2Chr 32:32 of Hezekiah's acts, including his *p* works,
35:26 his *p* deeds in regard to what is written
2Mc 12:45 in godliness, it was a holy and *p* thought.
Prv 2: 8 justice, protecting the way of his *p* ones.

Dn 13: 3 her *p* parents had trained their daughter
Lk 2:25 He was just and *p*,

PIPE (3)

Gn 4:21 of all who play the lyre and the *p*.
Jb 30:31 and my reed *p* to sounds of weeping.
Ps(s) 150: 4 and dance, praise him with strings and *p*.

PIPED (2)

Mt 11:17 'We *p* you a tune but you did not dance!
Lk 7:32 'We *p* you a tune but you did not dance,

PIRAM (1)

Jos 10: 3 sent for Hoham, king of Hebron, *P*,

PIRATHON (3)

Jgs 12:15 died and was buried in *P* in the land of
2Sm 23:30 Benaiah from *P*;
1Chr 11:31 Benaiah, from *P*;

PIRATHONITE (3)

Jgs 12:13 After him the *P* Abdon,
12:15 Israel for eight years, the *P* Abdon,
1Chr 27:14 for the eleventh month, was Benaiah the *P*,

PISGAH (8)

Nm 21:20 the headland of *P* that overlooks Jeshimon.
23:14 him to the lookout field on the top of *P*,
Dt 3:17 Sea of the Arabah, under the slopes of *P*.
3:27 to the top of *P* and look out to the west,
4:49 as the Arabah Sea under the slopes of *P*.
34: 1 the headland of *P* which faces Jericho,
Jos 12: 3 to a point under the slopes of *P*.
13:20 the valley, Beth-peor, the slopes of *P*,

PISHON (2)

Gn 2:11 The name of the first is the *P*;
Sir 24:23 It overflows like the *P*,

PISIDIA (2)

Acts 13:14 on from Perga and came to Antioch in *P*.
14:24 passed through *P* and came to Pamphylia.

PISPA (1)

1Chr 7:38 The sons of Jether were Jephunneh, *P*,

PISTACHIOS (1)

Gn 43:11 honey, gum and resin, and *p* and almonds.

PIT (66)

2Sm 18:17 up and cast into a deep *p* in the forest,
2Kgs 10:14 number, then slain at the *p* of Beth-eked.
1Mc 7:19 to him, throwing them into the great *p*.
Jb 33:18 *p* and his life from passing to the grave.
33:22 His soul draws near to the *p*,
33:24 "Deliver him from going down to the *p*;
33:28 He delivered my soul from passing to the *p*,
33:30 back his soul from the *p* to the light,
Ps(s) 7:16 but he falls into the *p* which he has made.
9:16 nations are sunk in the *p* they have made;
28: 1 become one of those going down into the *p*.
30: 4 me from among those going down into the *p*.
35: 7 without cause they dug a *p* against my life.
35: 8 into the *p* they have dug let them fall.
40: 3 He drew me out of the *p* of destruction,
55:24 bring them down into the *p* of destruction;
57: 7 They have dug a *p* before me,
69:16 me up, nor the *p* close its mouth over me.
88: 5 numbered with those who go down into the *p*;
88: 7 have plunged me into the bottom of the *p*,
94:13 days, till the *p* be dug for the wicked.
143: 7 I become like those who go down into the *p*.
Prv 1:12 of life, like those who go down to the *p*!
22:14 The mouth of the adulteress is a deep *p*;
23:27 deep ditch, and the adulteress a narrow *p*;
26:27 He who digs a *p* falls into it;
28:10 evil way will himself fall into his own *p*.
28:18 he whose ways are crooked falls into the *p*.
Eccl 10: 8 He who digs a *p* may fall into it,
Sir 27:26 As he who digs a *p* falls into it,
51: 2 death, and kept back my body from the *p*,
Is 14:15 world you go to the recesses of the *p*!
14:19 Going down to the pavement of the *p*,
24:17 Terror, *p*, and trap are upon you,
24:18 fall into the *p*; He who climbs out of the *p*
24:22 gathered together like prisoners into a *p*;
38:17 my life from the *p* of destruction,
38:18 who go down into the *p* await your kindness.
51: 1 to the *p* from which you were quarried;
51:14 they shall not die and go down into the *p*,
Jer 18:20 that they should dig a *p* to take my life?
18:22 For they have dug a *p* to capture me,
48:43 Terror, *p*, and trap be upon you,
48:44 falls into the *p*; He who climbs from the *p*
Lam 3:47 Terror and the *p* have been our lot.
3:53 They struck me down alive in the *p*,
3:55 name, O LORD, from the bottom of the *p*;
Ez 19: 4 cries against him in their *p* he was caught;
19: 8 net to take him, in their *p* he was caught.
26:20 down with those who descend into the *p*,
26:20 ruins, with those who go down in the *p*,
28: 8 They shall thrust you down to the *p*,
31:14 of mortals, those who go down into the *p*.
31:16 world with those who go down into the *p*.
32:18 earth, with those who go down into the *p*.
32:23 have been made in the recesses of the *p*;
32:24 with those who go down into the *p*;
32:29 lie, and with those who go down into the *p*.
32:30 disgrace with those who go down to the *p*.
Jon 2: 7 But you brought my life up from the *p*,
Zep 2: 9 nettles and a salt *p* and a waste forever.
Mt 12:11 sheep and it falls into a *p* on the sabbath.
15:14 man leads another, both will end in a *p*."
Lk 14: 5 has a son or an ox and he falls into a *p*,

PITCH (19)

Gn 6:14 in it, and cover it inside and out with *p*.
Ex 2: 3 basket, daubed it with bitumen and *p*,
33: 7 Moses used to *p* at some distance away,
Nm 9:17 the cloud came to rest, they would *p* camp.
1Mc 5:42 "Do not allow any man to *p* a tent;
2Mc 4:13 and foreign customs reached such a *p*,
Sir 13: 1 He who touches *p* blackens his hand;
28:11 *P* and resin make fire flare up,
Is 13:20 The Arab shall not *p* his tent there,
34: 9 changed into *p* and her earth into sulphur,
34: 9 and her land shall become burning *p*;
Jer 6: 3 all around, they *p* their tents,
10:20 no one to *p* my tent,
Ez 4: 2 build a tower, lay out a ramp, *p* camps,
25: 4 encampments among you and *p* their tents;
Dn 3:46 to stoke the furnace with brimstone, *p*,
11:45 He shall *p* the tents of his royal pavilion
14:27 Then Daniel took some *p*,
Acts 8: 8 The rejoicing in that town rose to fever *p*.

PITCHED (28)

Gn 25:18 and each of them *p* camp in opposition to
26:25 After he had *p* his tent there,
31:25 Jacob's tents were *p* in the highlands;
31:25 Laban also *p* his tents there,
33:19 The plot of ground on which he had *p* his
35:21 moved on and *p* his tent beyond Migdal-eder.
38: 1 parted from his brothers and *p* his tent
Ex 19: 2 to the desert of Sinai, they *p* camp.
Nm 1:51 when the Dwelling is to be *p*,
Jos 8:11 before the city, they *p* camp north of Ai,
Jgs 4:11 *p* his tent by the terebinth of Zaanannim,
2Sm 6:17 place within the tent David had *p* for it.
16:22 So a tent was *p* on the roof for Absalom,
1Chr 16: 1 within the tent which David had *p* for it.
2Chr 1: 4 had provided a place and *p* a tent for it.)
1Mc 3:40 and *p* their camp near Emmaus in the plain.
7:19 Jerusalem and *p* his camp in Beth-zaith.
7:39 Jerusalem and *p* his camp at Beth-horon,
9:64 He came and *p* his camp before Bethbasi,
10:69 army, Apollonius *p* his camp at Jamnia.
10:75 He *p* camp near Joppa,
10:86 left there and *p* his camp at Ashkalon,
11:67 *p* their camp near the waters of Gennesaret,
11:73 in Kadesh, where they *p* their own camp.
13:13 But Simon *p* his camp at Adida,
2Mc 13:14 the government, he *p* his camp near Modein.
Ps(s) 19: 5 He has *p* a tent there for the sun,
Wis 11: 2 and in solitudes they *p* their tents;

PITCHER (1)

Eccl 12: 6 And the *p* is shattered at the spring,

PITCHERS (4)

Ex 25:29 as its *p* and bowls for pouring libations.
37:16 as its *p* and bowls for pouring libations,
Nm 4: 7 as well as the bowls and *p* for libations;
1Chr 28:16 pure gold to be used for the forks and *p*,

PITCHES (1)

Sir 14:25 Who *p* his tent beside her,

PITCHFORK (1)

Is 30:24 silage tossed to them with shovel and *p*.

PITCHING (3)

Gn 12: 8 *p* his tent with Bethel to the west and Ai
13:12 of the Plain, *p* his tents near Sodom.
1Chr 15: 1 for the ark of God, *p* a tent for it there.

PITEOUS (1)

Wis 18:10 and the *p* wail of mourning for children

PITFALL (1)

Jb 18: 8 into a net, and he wanders into a *p*.

PITFALLS (1)

Sir 27:29 The trap seizes those who rejoice in *p*,

PITHOM (1)

Ex 1:11 Pharaoh the supply cities of *P* and Raamses.

PITHON (2)

1Chr 8:35 The sons of Micah were *P*,
9:41 The sons of Micah were *P*,

PITIABLE (2)

1Cor 15:19 this life only, we are the most *p* of men.
Rv 3:17 how wretched you are, how *p* and poor,

PITIED (1)

Mk 6:34 He *p* them, for they were like sheep

PITIES (2)

Sir 12:13 Who *p* a snake charmer when he is bitten,
Is 49:10 For he who *p* them leads them and guides

PITIFUL (1)

2Mc 3:21 It was *p* to see the populace variously

PITILESS (2)

Jer 6:23 cruel and *p* are they.
50:42 javelin they wield, cruel and *p* are they;

PITS (3)

Gn 14:10 Valley of Siddim was full of bitumen *p*;
Ps(s) 119:85 The proud have dug *p* for me;
2Pt 2: 4 consigned them to *p* of darkness,

PITY (121)

Ex 2: 6 She was moved with *p* for him and said,
Dt 7:16 You are not to look on them with *p*,
13: 9 or listen to him, nor look with *p* upon him,
19:13 Do not look on him with *p*,
19:21 Do not look on such a man with *p*.
25:12 you shall chop off her hand without *p*.
28:50 respect for the aged nor *p* for the young.
30: 3 and taking *p* on you,
32:36 on his servants he shall have *p*.
Jgs 2:18 it was thus the LORD took *p* on their
1Sm 1:11 look with *p* on the misery of your handmaid,
24:11 killing you, but I took *p* on you instead.
2Sm 12: 6 because he has done this and has had no *p*."
Tb 3:15 look favorably upon me and have *p* on me;
13: 9 will again *p* the children of the righteous.
Jdt 6:19 Have *p* on the lowliness of our people,
Est 3:13 of their enemies, without any *p* or mercy,
4:16 have *p* on your inheritance and turn our
2Mc 4:37 was deeply grieved and full of *p*;
7: 6 words, 'And he will have *p* on his servants.'"
7:27 "Son, have *p* on me,
8: 2 to have *p* on the temple,
Jb 19:21 *P* me, pity me, O you my friends
33:24 to justice, He will take *p* on him and say,
Ps(s) 4: 2 Have *p* on me, and hear my prayer!
6: 3 Have *p* on me, O LORD,
9:14 Have *p* on me, O LORD;
25:16 Look toward me, and have *p* on me,
26:11 redeem me, and have *p* on me.
27: 7 have *p* on me, and answer me.
30:11 Hear, O LORD, and have *p* on me;
31:10 Have *p* on me, O LORD,
41: 5 Once I said, "O LORD, have *p* on me;
41:11 But you, O LORD, have *p* on me,
56: 2 Have *p* on me, O God,
57: 2 Have *p* on me, O God; have pity on me,
59: 6 have no *p* on any worthless traitors.
67: 2 May God have *p* on us and bless us;
72:13 He shall have *p* for the lowly and the poor;
77:10 Has God forgotten *p*?
86: 3 You are my God; have *p* on me,
86:16 Turn toward me, and have *p* on me;
90:13 Have *p* on your servants!
102:14 mercy on Zion, for it is time to *p* her,
102:15 servants, and her dust moves them to *p*.
109:12 a kindness, nor anyone to *p* his orphans.
119:58 have *p* on me according to your promise.
119:132 *p* as you turn to those who love your name.
123: 2 on the LORD, our God, till he have *p* on us.
123: 3 Have *p* on us, O LORD, have pity on us,
Prv 6:34 he will have no *p* on the day of vengeance;
21:10 his neighbor finds no *p* in his eyes.
Wis 10: 5 him resolute against *p* for his child.
Sir 36:12 Take *p* on your holy city,
Is 9:16 their orphans and widows he does not *p*;
13:18 nor shall they have eyes of *p* for children.
14: 1 When the LORD has *p* on Jacob and again
30:18 to show you favor, and he rises to *p* you;
33: 2 O LORD, have *p* on us, for you we wait.
51: 3 comfort Zion and have *p* on all her ruins;
54: 8 But with enduring love I take *p* on you,
63: 9 of his love and *p* he redeemed them himself,
63:15 your might, your surge of *p* and your mercy?
Jer 12:15 I will *p* them again and bring them back,
13:14 show no compassion, I will not spare or *p*,
15: 5 Who will *p* you, Jerusalem,
16: 5 says the LORD, my kindness and my *p*.
21: 7 sword, without quarter, without *p* or mercy.

PITY (cont.)
30:18 tents of Jacob, his dwellings I will *p;*
Lam 2: 2 without *p* all the dwellings of Jacob;
2:17 he has destroyed and had no *p,*
2:21 day of your wrath, slaughtered without *p.*
3:32 Though he punishes, he takes *p,*
3:43 and pursued us, you slew us and took no *p;*
Bar 6:37 neither *p* the widow nor benefit the orphan.
Ez 5:11 not look upon you with *p* nor have mercy.
7: 4 not look upon you with *p* nor have mercy;
7: 9 not look upon you with *p* nor have mercy;
8:18 upon them with *p* nor will I show mercy.
9: 5 not look on them with *p* nor show any mercy!
9:10 I, however, will not look upon them with *p,*
16: 5 No one looked on you with *p* or compassion
20:17 But I looked on them with *p,*
24:14 I will not have *p* nor repent.
39:25 and have *p* on the whole house of Israel,
Hos 1: 6 I no longer feel *p* for the house of Israel;
1: 7 Yet for the house of Judah I feel *p;*
2: 6 I will have no *p* on her children,
2:25 the land, and I will have *p* on Lo-ruhama.
11: 8 My heart is overwhelmed, my *p* is stirred.
Jl 2:18 for his land and took *p* on his people.
Am 1:11 brother with the sword, choking up all *p;*
5:15 will have *p* on the remnant of Joseph.
Na 3: 7 "Nineveh is destroyed; who can *p* her?
Mt 9:27 crying out, "Son of David, have *p* on us!"
9:36 of the crowds, his heart was moved with *p.*
14:14 vast throng, his heart was moved with *p,*
15:22 to him, "Lord, Son of David, have *p* on me!
15:32 "My heart is moved with *p* for the crowd.
17:15 "Lord," he said, "take *p* on my son,
18:27 Moved with *p,* the master let the official
20:30 shout, "Lord, Son of David, have *p* on us!"
20:31 louder, "Lord, Son of David, have *p* on us!"
Mk 1:41 Moved with *p,* Jesus stretched
8: 2 "My heart is moved with *p* for the crowd.
10:47 out, "Jesus, Son of David, have *p* on me!"
10:48 the louder, "Son of David, have *p* on me!"
Lk 7:13 with *p* upon seeing her and said to her,
10:33 on him and was moved to *p* at the sight.
16:24 called out, 'Father Abraham, have *p* on me.
17:13 and said, "Jesus, Master, have *p* on us!"
18:38 out, "Jesus, Son of David, have *p* on me!"
18:39 all the more, "Son of David, have *p* on me!"
Rom 1:31 loyalty, without affection, without *p.*
9:15 I will have *p* on whomever I wish."
Phil 2: 1 of fellowship in spirit, compassion, and *p,*
2:27 the point of death, but God took *p* on him;
Jude 1:23 Even with those you *p,* be on your guard;

PLACATE (2)

Jer 36: 9 king of Judah a fast to *p* the LORD was
Acts 12:20 chamberlain Blastus and attempted to *p* him,

PLACE (823)

Gn 2:21 of his ribs and closed up its *p* with flesh.
4:25 has granted me more offspring in *p* of Abel,"
8: 9 dove could find no *p* to alight and perch,
11: 9 It was from that *p* that he scattered them
12: 6 the land as far as the sacred *p* at Shechem,
13: 3 to the *p* between Bethel and Ai where his
18:24 would you wipe out the *p,*
18:26 I will spare the whole *p* for their sake."
19: 3 aside to his *p* and entered his house.
19:13 We are about to destroy this *p,*
19:14 "Get up and leave this *p,*"
19:20 It's only a small *p.*
19:20 it's a small *p,*
19:27 the next morning Abraham went to the *p*
20:11 would surely be no fear of God in this *p,*
20:13 In whatever *p* we come to,
21:23 swear to me by God at this *p* that you will
21:31 This is why the *p* is called Beer-sheba;
22: 3 out for the *p* of which God had told him.
22: 4 day Abraham got sight of the *p* from afar.
22: 9 came to the *p* of which God had told him,
22:13 it up as a holocaust in *p* of his son.
23: 9 at its full price, for a burial *p.*"
23:20 from the Hittites to Abraham as a burial *p.*
24:25 is plenty of straw and fodder at our *p,*"
24:31 for you, as well as a *p* for the camels?"
26: 7 of the *p* asked questions about his wife,
26: 7 the *p* would kill him on account of Rebekah,
30: 2 Jacob retorted, "Can I take the *p* of God,
32: 3 So he named that *p* Mahanaim.
32:31 Jacob named the *p* Peniel,
33:17 That is why the *p* was called Succoth.
35: 7 he built an altar and named the *p* Bethel,
38:21 So he asked the men of the *p,*
38:22 the men of the *p* said there was no temple
40:14 me to Pharaoh, to get me out of this *p.*
41:41 *p* you in charge of the whole land of Egypt."
44:33 in *p* of the boy as the slave of my lord,
47:30 out of Egypt and buried in their burial *p.*"
50:11 That is why the *p* was named Abel-mizraim.
50:19 Can I take the *p* of God?
50:25 bring my bones up with you from this *p.*"
Ex 3: 5 for the *p* where you stand is holy ground.
4: 5 will take *p* so that they may believe,"
4:24 journey, at a *p* where they spent the night,
8:19 This sign shall take *p* tomorrow."
9:19 open fields to be brought to a *p* of safety.
10:26 to him until we arrive at the *p* itself."
13: 3 you came out of Egypt, that *p* of slavery.
13:14 brought us out of Egypt, that *p* of slavery.
13:22 ever left its *p* in front of the people.
14:19 the front, took up its *p* behind them,
15:17 the *p* where you made your seat,
15:23 Hence this *p* was called Marah.
16:33 Then *p* it before the LORD for safekeeping
17: 7 The *p* was called Massah and Meribah,
17:12 so they put a rock in *p* for him to sit on.
20: 2 of the land of Egypt, that *p* of slavery.
20:24 In whatever *p* I choose for the remembrance
21:13 *p* which I will set apart for this purpose.
23:20 way and bring you to the *p* I have prepared.
25:21 you shall then *p* on top of the ark.
26:33 divides the holy *p* from the holy of holies.
26:35 you shall *p* the table and the lampstand,
29:31 ordination ram and boil it in the holy *p.*
30: 6 This altar you are to *p* in front of the
30:18 *P* it between the meeting tent and the altar,
33:21 "is a *p* near me where you shall station
40: 7 *P* the laver between the meeting tent and
Lv 4:12 be brought outside the camp to a clean *p*
4:12 At the *p* of the ash heap,
4:24 the *p* where the holocausts are slaughtered.
4:29 slaughter it at the *p* of the holocausts.
4:33 the *p* where the holocausts are slaughtered.
6: 4 the ashes to a clean *p* outside the camp.
6: 9 of unleavened cakes and in a sacred *p:*
6:18 At the *p* where holocausts are slaughtered,
6:19 but it must be eaten in a sacred *p,*
6:20 stained part must be washed in a sacred *p.*
7: 2 the *p* where the holocausts are slaughtered,
7: 6 but it must be eaten in a sacred *p,*
10: 4 and carry them to a *p* outside the camp."
10:13 most sacred, you must eat it in a sacred *p.*
10:14 leg of the raised offering, in a clean *p;*
10:17 not eat the sin offering in the sacred *p,*
13:19 should now in the *p* of the boil have a
13:23 blotch remains in its *p* without spreading,
13:28 But if the blotch remains in its *p* without
13:37 its *p* and that black hair has grown on it,
14:11 shall *p* the man who is being purified,
14:13 lamb he shall slaughter in the sacred *p*
14:40 and cast in an unclean *p* outside the city.
14:41 be dumped in an unclean *p* outside the city.
14:42 brought and put in the *p* of the old stones,
14:45 away to an unclean *p* outside the city.
16:24 bathing his body with water in a sacred *p,*
24: 6 These you shall *p* in two piles,
24: 9 his sons, who must eat it in a sacred *p,*
27:10 to offer one animal in *p* of another,
Nm 2:17 march, every man shall be in his proper *p,*
3:12 in *p* of every first-born
3:41 *p* of all the first-born of the Israelites,
3:41 as well as their cattle in *p* of all the
3:45 *p* of all the first-born of the Israelites,
3:45 the Levites' cattle in *p* of their cattle,
4: 6 They shall then put the poles in *p.*
4: 8 They shall then put the poles in *p.*
4:10 covering of tahash skin, and *p* on a litter.
4:11 They shall then put the poles in *p.*
4:12 They shall then *p* them on a litter.
4:14 skin over this, and put the poles in *p.*
5:18 *p* in her hands the cereal offering
6:19 shall *p* them in the hands of the nazirite.
8:16 I have taken them for myself in *p* of
8:18 But in *p* of all the first-born Israelites
10:29 *p* which the LORD has promised to give us.
10:33 *p* went the three days' journey with them.
11: 3 Hence that *p* was called Taberah,
11:16 When they are in *p* beside you,
11:23 or not what I have promised you takes *p.*"
11:34 So that *p* was named Kibroth-hattaavah,
13:24 there that they called the *p* Wadi Eshcol.
14:40 to go up to the *p* that the LORD spoke of:
16: 7 *p* incense in them before the LORD tomorrow.
19: 9 deposit them in a clean *p* outside the camp.
20: 5 only to bring us to this wretched *p*
20: 9 took the staff from its *p* before the LORD,
21: 3 Hence that *p* was named Hormah.
23:13 "Please come with me to another *p* from
23:27 "Come, let me bring you to another *p;*
32:14 rising up in your fathers' *p* to add still
35:31 "You shall not accept indemnity in *p* of
Dt 1:31 your journey until you arrived at this *p.*'
1:33 before you to find you a resting *p*—
2:12 them out of the way and taking their *p,*
2:21 who ousted them and took their *p.*
2:22 have taken their *p* down to the present.
2:23 and took their *p*
5: 6 of the land of Egypt, that *p* of slavery.
6:12 of the land of Egypt, that *p* of slavery.
7: 8 with his strong hand from the *p* of slavery,
8:14 of the land of Egypt, that *p* of slavery;
9: 7 land of Egypt until you arrived in this *p,*
10: 2 you broke, and you shall *p* them in the ark.'
11: 5 in the desert until you arrived in this *p;*
11:24 Every *p* where you set foot shall be yours:
12: 2 without fail every *p* on the high mountains,
12: 3 out the remembrance of them in any such *p.*
12: 5 you shall resort to the *p* which the LORD,
12: 9 you have not yet reached your resting *p,*
12:11 in security, then to the *p* which the LORD,
12:11 chooses as the dwelling *p* for his name you
12:13 up your holocausts in any *p* you fancy,
12:14 but offer them up in the *p* which the LORD
12:18 the LORD, your God, in the *p* he chooses,
12:21 and if the *p* which the LORD,
12:26 with you to the *p* which the LORD chooses,
13: 6 and ransomed you from that *p* of slavery.
13:11 of the land of Egypt, that *p* of slavery.
14:23 then in the *p* which the LORD,
14:23 chooses as the dwelling *p* of his name you
14:24 your tithe, because the *p* which the LORD,
14:25 money in hand, go to the *p* which the LORD,
15:20 the LORD, your God, in the *p* he chooses.
16: 2 in the *p* which he chooses as the dwelling
16: 2 he chooses as the dwelling *p* of his name.
16: 6 the *p* which he chooses as the dwelling *p*
16: 7 shall cook and eat it at the *p* the LORD,
16:11 In the *p* which the LORD,
16:11 God, chooses as the dwelling *p* of his name,
16:15 LORD, your God, in the *p* which he chooses;
16:16 LORD, your God, in the *p* which he chooses:
17: 8 shall then go up to the *p* which the LORD,
17:10 give you in the *p* which the LORD chooses,
18: 6 may desire, the *p* which the LORD chooses,
19: 1 and you have taken their *p* and are settled
19: 4 take refuge in such a *p* to save his life:
21: 4 at a *p* that has not been plowed or sown,
22: 2 *p* and keep it with you until he claims it;
23:13 have a *p* set aside to be used as a latrine.
26: 2 you shall go to the *p* which the LORD,
26: 2 chooses for the dwelling *p* of his name.
29: 6 When we came to this *p,*
31:11 LORD, your God, in the *p* which he chooses,
34: 6 this day no one knows the *p* of his burial.
Jos 1: 3 deliver to you every *p* where you set foot.
4: 3 and *p* them where you are to stay tonight."
4:11 also crossed to its *p* in front of them.
5: 9 the *p* is called Gilgal to the present day.
5:15 the *p* on which you are standing is holy."
7:26 That is why the *p* is called the Valley of
8: 9 They went to the *p* of ambush,
8:28 Then Joshua destroyed the *p* by fire,
9:27 of the LORD, in the *p* of the LORD's choice.
17:15 clear out a *p* for yourselves there
20: 4 assign him a *p* in which to live among them.
Jgs 2: 5 and so that *p* came to be called Bochim.
6: 8 I brought you out of the *p* of slavery.
6:38 That is what took *p.*
7:21 all remained standing in *p* around the camp,
9:35 his soldiers rose from their *p* of ambush,
11:19 'Let me pass through your land to my own *p.*'
15:17 and so that *p* was named Ramath-lehi.
17: 8 he set out to find another *p* of residence.
17: 9 my way to find some other *p* of residence."
18:10 a *p* where no natural resource is lacking."
18:12 hence to this day the *p,*
19:13 servant, "let us make for some other *p,*
20: 3 to be told how the crime had taken *p,*
20:23 in the same *p* as on the previous day,
20:33 ambush rushed from their *p* west of Gibeah,
Ru 1: 7 left the *p* where they had been living.
2:19 at whose *p* I worked today is named Boaz,"
3: 4 down, take note of the *p* where he does so.
3: 4 Then go, uncover a *p* at his feet,
3: 7 she stole up, uncovered a *p* at his feet,
1Sm 3: 2 One day Eli was asleep in his usual *p.*
3: 9 When Samuel went to sleep in his *p,*
5:11 Let it return to its own *p,*
6: 8 the ark of the LORD and *p* it on the cart,
8:18 When this takes *p,*
9:12 have a sacrifice today on the high *p.*
9:13 him before he goes up to the high *p* to eat.
9:14 toward them on his way to the high *p.*
9:19 of me to the high *p* and eat with me today.
9:25 came down from the high *p* into the city,
10: 5 down from the high *p* preceded by lyres,
10:25 dismissed the people, each to his own *p.*
12: 8 Egypt, and he gave them this *p* to live in.
20:18 be missed, since your *p* will be vacant.
20:25 dine, taking his usual *p* against the wall,
20:25 the king's side, and David's *p* was vacant.
20:27 day of the month, David's *p* was vacant.
21: 3 I have arranged a meeting *p* with my men.
22: 6 under a tamarisk tree on the high *p,*
23:13 left Keilah and wandered from *p* to place.
23:22 Take note of the *p* where he sets foot"
23:28 *p* came to be called the Gorge of Divisions.
26: 5 David himself then went to the *p*
26:12 the water jug from their *p* at Saul's head,
27: 5 a *p* to live in one of the country towns.
29: 4 him return to the *p* you picked out for him.
29:10 with you, go to the *p* I picked out for you.
2Sm 2:16 And so that *p,* which is in Gideon,
2:23 to the *p* where Asahel had fallen and died,
5:20 That is why the *p* is called Baal-perazim.
6: 8 (The *p* has been called Perez-uzzah down to
6:17 *p* within the tent David had pitched for it.
7:10 I will fix a *p* for my people Israel;
7:10 in their *p* without further disturbance.
11:15 *P* Uriah up front,

11:16 *p* where he knew the defenders were strong.
14:17 of my lord the king provide a resting *p;*
16: 5 as Saul's family, was coming out of the *p,*
17: 9 in one of the caves or in some other *p.*
17:25 Amasa in command of the army in Joab's *p.*
18:26 From his *p* atop the gate he cried out,
19:14 become my general permanently in *p* of Joab.' "
21: 4 it our *p* to put any man to death in Israel."
21: 5 have no *p* in all the territory of Israel,
1Kgs 1:30 me and should sit upon my throne in my *p.*"
1:35 and sit upon my throne and reign in my *p.*
2:35 son of Jehoiada, over the army in his *p,*
2:35 and put Zadok the priest in *p* of Abiathar.
3: 4 because that was the most renowned high *p.*
5: 8 of barley and straw to the required *p.*
5:15 had been anointed king in *p* of his father,
5:19 *p* who shall build the temple in my honor.'
7:16 cast in bronze, to *p* on top of the columns,
8: 6 ark of the covenant of the LORD to its *p*
8: 7 wings spread out over the *p* of the ark,
8: 8 part of the holy *p* adjoining the sanctuary;
8:10 When the priests left the holy *p,*
8:21 I have provided in it a *p* for the ark in
8:29 the *p* where you have decreed you shall be
8:29 which I, your servant, offer in this *p.*
8:30 people Israel which they offer in this *p.*
8:35 and pray, and praise your name in this *p,*
8:39 from your heavenly dwelling *p* and forgive.
10: 9 pleased to *p* you on the throne of Israel.
11: 7 Solomon then built a high *p* to Chemosh,
13: 8 nor eat bread or drink water in this *p.*
13:16 bread or drink water with you in this *p,*"
13:22 in the *p* where he told you to do neither,
16:10 Asa, king of Judah, and reigned in his *p.*
18:12 will carry you to some *p* I do not know,
18:23 into pieces, and *p* it on the wood,
18:23 prepare the other and *p* it on the wood,
21:19 In the *p* where the dogs licked up the
2Kgs 6: 2 apiece we can build ourselves a *p* to live."
6: 8 with his servants to attack a particular *p.*
6: 9 Do not pass by this *p,*
6:10 the *p* which the man of God had indicated,
10: 3 offspring, *p* him on his father's throne,
15:10 killed him at Ibleam, and reigned in his *p.*
15:14 son of Jabesh, and reigned in his *p.*
15:25 in Samaria, and reigned in his *p.*
15:30 in his *p* [in the twentieth year of Jotham,
17:24 of Samaria in *p* of the Israelites.
18:25 will that I have come up to destroy this *p?*
21: 7 of Israel, I shall *p* my name forever.
22:16 I will bring upon this *p* and upon its
22:17 this *p* and it cannot be extinguished.'
22:19 my threats that this *p* and its inhabitants
22:20 see all the evil I will bring upon this *p.*' "
23: 8 tore down the high *p* of the satyrs
23:15 at Bethel, the high *p* built by Jeroboam,
23:15 this same altar and high *p* he tore down,
23:34 of Josiah, king in *p* of his father Josiah;
24:17 In *p* of Jehoiachin,
1Chr 4:41 is still in force and dwelt in their *p*
5:22 dwelling *p* until the time of the exile.
6:16 the ark had obtained a permanent resting *p.*
13:11 Therefore that *p* has been called
14:11 Therefore that *p* was called Baal-perazim.
15: 1 David and prepared a *p* for the ark of God,
15: 3 LORD to the *p* which he had prepared for it.
15:12 to the *p* which I have prepared for it.
16:27 praise and joy are in his holy *p.*
16:39 of the LORD on the high *p* at Gibeon,
17: 9 I will assign a *p* for my people Israel and
21:25 six hundred shekels of gold for the *p.*
21:29 were at that time on the high *p* at Gibeon.
24: 5 for there were officers of the holy *p,*
29:23 the LORD as king in *p* of his father David;
2Chr 1: 3 assembly, he went to the high *p* at Gibeon,
1: 4 had provided a *p* and pitched a tent for it.)
1: 5 front of the LORD's Dwelling on the high *p.*
1:13 to Jerusalem from the high *p* at Gibeon,
5: 7 ark of the covenant of the LORD to its *p*
5: 8 wings spread out over the *p* of the ark,
5: 9 part of the holy *p* nearest the sanctuary;
5:11 When the priests came out of the holy *p*
6:12 Solomon then took his *p* before the altar
6:20 the *p* where you have decreed you shall be
6:20 which I your servant offer toward this *p.*
6:21 Israel which they direct toward this *p.*
6:26 pray toward this *p* and praise your name,
6:30 listen from your heavenly dwelling *p,*
6:33 listen from your heavenly dwelling *p,*
6:39 listen from your heavenly dwelling *p,*
6:40 ears attentive to the prayer of this *p.*
6:41 "Advance, LORD God, to your resting *p,*
7:12 chosen this *p* for my house of sacrifice.
7:15 my ears attentive to the prayer of this *p.*
9: 8 *p* you on his throne as king for the LORD,
11:15 In their *p,* he himself appointed priests
20:26 therefore that *p* has ever since been
24:11 then took it back and returned it to its *p.*
33: 7 tribes of Israel I shall *p* my name forever.
34:24 evil upon this *p* and upon its inhabitants,
34:25 against this *p* and cannot be extinguished.'
34:27 spoken against this *p* and its inhabitants;
34:28 bring upon this *p* and upon its inhabitants.' "
36:15 on his people and his dwelling *p.*
Ezr 1: 4 survived, in whatever *p* he may have dwelt,
1: 4 by the people of that *p* with silver,
2:68 the house of God, to rebuild it in its *p.*
6: 3 The house is to be rebuilt as a *p* for
6: 5 to be returned to their *p* in the temple of
6: 6 do not interfere in that *p.*
8:17 for Iddo, the leader in the *p* Casiphia,
9: 8 remnant and gave us a stake in his holy *p;*
10: 6 Then Ezra retired from his *p* before the
10: 9 in the open *p* before the house of God,
Neh 1: 9 *p* which I have chosen as the dwelling *p*
3:16 to a *p* opposite the tombs of David,
3:30 repaired the *p* opposite his own lodging.
4: 6 had come to us from one *p* after another,
6: 8 "Nothing of what you report has taken *p;*
8: 3 the open *p* that was before the Water Gate,
Tb 1: 4 offer sacrifice in the *p* where the temple,
2: 3 the market *p* where he was just strangled!"
5: 6 know the *p* well and I know all the routes.
6:17 and *p* them on the embers for the incense.
6:18 who will take the *p* of brothers for you.
7:17 of heaven grant you joy in *p* of your grief.
14: 4 shall take *p* in the time appointed for it.
Jdt 6:16 gathered in haste at the *p* of assembly.
8:12 in the *p* of God in human affairs?
Est 2: 4 the king shall reign in *p* of Vashti."
2: 9 and her maids to the best *p* in the harem.
2:17 her head and made her queen in *p* of Vashti.
C: 7 to *p* the honor of man above that of God.
C:13 In *p* of her precious ointments she covered
E:19 a copy of this letter publicly in every *p,*
1Mc 1: 1 and Medes, he became king in his *p,*
1:25 for Israel, in every *p* where they dwelt,
3: 1 who was called Maccabeus, took his *p.*
3:46 at Mizpah a *p* of prayer for Israel.
4:43 stones of the Abomination to an unclean *p.*
4:46 stones in a suitable *p* on the temple hill,
5:29 He led his army from that *p* by night,
5:35 all the male population, plundered the *p,*
5:49 make an attack from the *p* where he was.
6:17 had reared as a child, to be king in his *p;*
6:57 scanty, the *p* we are besieging is strong,
6:62 Mount Zion and saw how the *p* was fortified,
9:30 today to be our ruler and leader in his *p,*
9:31 and took the *p* of Judas his brother.
10:13 left his *p* and returned to his own country.
10:14 for they used it as a *p* of refuge.
10:73 is not a stone or a pebble or a *p* to flee."
11:37 in a conspicuous *p* on the holy hill.' "
11:40 he might make him king in his father's *p.*
13: 8 in *p* of your brothers Judas and Jonathan.
13:32 him and assumed the kingship in his *p,*
14:17 Simon had been made high priest in his *p*
14:34 a *p* previously occupied by the enemy;
14:48 *p* in the precincts of the temple,
16: 3 Take my *p* and my brother's,
2Mc 1:14 with his Friends had come to the *p*
1:19 sure that the *p* would be unknown to anyone.
1:29 Plant your people in your holy *p,*
1:33 in the very *p* where the exiled priests had
1:34 fenced the *p* off and declared it sacred.
2: 7 "The *p* is to remain unknown until God
2: 8 that the *P* might be gloriously sanctified."
2:18 under the heavens to his holy *P,*
2:18 from great perils and has purified his *P.*
3: 2 the kings themselves honored the *P* and
3:12 their trust in the sanctity of the *P*
3:18 the *P* was in danger of being profaned.
3:30 who had marvelously glorified his holy *P;*
3:38 some special divine power about the *P.*
3:39 heaven watches over that *P* and protects it,
4:30 While these things were taking *p,*
4:38 *p* where he had committed the outrage
5:10 kind or any *p* in the tomb of his ancestors.
5:16 the glory, and the honor of the *P.*
5:17 while and hence disregarded the holy *P.*
5:19 people for the sake of the *P,* but the Place
5:20 Therefore, the *P* itself,
6: 2 as the inhabitants of the *p* requested.
8:17 by the Gentiles against the holy *P*
9:17 *p* to proclaim there the power of God.
10: 5 the purification of the temple took *p.*
10: 7 about the purification of his own *P.*
10:34 inside, relying on the strength of the *p,*
11: 5 *p* about twenty miles from Jerusalem,
11:23 our father has taken his *p* among the gods,
12:18 behind in one *p* a very strong garrison.
12:21 well as the baggage, to a *p* called Karnion,
13: 5 at that *p* a tower seventy-five feet high,
14:21 came forward and thrones were set in *p.*
14:23 Jerusalem, where he did nothing out of *p.*
14:35 of a temple for your dwelling *p* among us.
15:34 be he who has kept his own *P* undefiled!"
Jb 2:11 him, they set out each one from his own *p:*
5: 8 In your *p,* I would appeal to God,
6:17 in the heat, they disappear from their *p.*
7:10 his *p* shall know him no more.
7:12 of the deep, that you *p* a watch over me?
8:18 Yet if one tears him from his *p,*
9: 6 He shakes the earth out of its *p,*
14:18 at last and its rock is moved from its *p,*
16: 4 could talk as you do, were you in my *p.*
18: 4 [or the rock be moved out of its *p?*
18:21 and such is the *p* of him who knows not God!
21:28 and where the dwelling *p* of the wicked?"
27:21 it sweeps him out of his *p.*
28: 1 silver, and a *p* for gold which men refine.
28:12 and where is the *p* of understanding?
28:20 and where is the *p* of understanding?
28:23 it is he who is familiar with its *p.*
29:25 I took a king's *p* in the armed forces.
30:23 death to the destined *p* of everyone alive.
33:22 to the pit, his life to the *p* of the dead.
34:13 or who else set all the land in its *p?*
37: 1 my heart trembles and leaps out of its *p.*
38:12 the morning and shown the dawn its *p*
38:19 is the way to the dwelling *p* of light,
Ps(s) 8: 4 the moon and the stars which you set in *p*—
11: 2 they *p* the arrow on the string to shoot
12: 9 strut and in high *p* are the basest of men.
22: 4 Yet you are enthroned in the holy *p,*
24: 3 or who may stand in his holy *p?*
37:10 though you mark his *p* he will not be there.
44:20 Though you thrust us down into a *p* of
45:10 her *p* at your right hand in gold of Ophir.
45:17 The *p* of your fathers your sons shall have;
62: 5 from my *p* on high they plan to dislodge me;
65: 7 You set the mountains in *p* by your power,
73: 9 They set their mouthings in *p* of heaven,
74: 7 the *p* where your name abides they have
83:13 take for ourselves the dwelling *p* of God."
84: 2 How lovely is your dwelling *p,*
103:16 he is gone, and his *p* knows him no more.
104: 8 valleys to the *p* you had fixed for them.
119:54 the theme of my song in the *p* of my exile.
132: 5 no rest, Till I find a *p* for the LORD,
132: 8 resting *p* you and the ark of your majesty.
132:14 "Zion is my resting *p* forever;
132:17 I will *p* a lamp for my anointed.
137: 6 not, If I *p* not Jerusalem ahead of my joy.
Prv 8:25 Before the mountains were settled into *p,*
15: 3 The eyes of the LORD are in every *p,*
17: 7 Fine words are out of *p* in a fool;
24:15 the just man, ravage not his dwelling *p;*
25: 6 presence, nor occupy the *p* of great men;
26: 1 in harvest, honor for a fool is out of *p.*
Eccl 1: 5 then it presses on to the *p* where it rises.
1: 7 To the *p* where they go,
3:16 the sun in the judgment *p* I saw wickedness,
3:20 Both go to the same *p;*
4: 1 the oppressions that take *p* under the sun:
4:15 heir apparent who will succeed to his *p.*
6: 6 his goods, do not both go to the same *p?*
8:10 and as they left the sacred *p,*
10: 4 ruler burst upon you, forsake not your *p;*
Wis 8:12 they would *p* their hands upon their mouths.
9: 8 altar in the city that is your dwelling *p.*
18:16 he alighted, he filled every *p* with death;
19:18 exactly from a review of what took *p.*
Sir 7: 4 authority, nor from the king a *p* of honor.
10:15 plucks up, to plant the humble in their *p:*
12:12 near you, lest he oust you and take your *p.*
17:22 in *p* of the living who offer their praise?
24: 7 Among all these I sought a resting *p;*
24:15 like the odor of incense in the holy *p.*
32: 2 fulfilled your duty, then take your *p,*
33:12 brings low, and expels them from their *p.*
36:12 your holy city, Jerusalem, your dwelling *p.*
38:12 Then give the doctor his *p* lest he leave;
42:11 no *p* that overlooks the approaches to the
43:10 their *p* and never relax in their vigils.
46:12 bones return to life from their resting *p,*
49:10 bones return to life from their resting *p*—
Is 4: 5 of Mount Zion and over her *p* of assembly,
7:23 *p* where there used to be a thousand vines,
13:13 and the earth shall be shaken from its *p,*
14: 2 take them and bring them along to its *p,*
22:22 I will *p* the key of the House of David on
22:23 spot, to be a *p* of honor for his family;
26:21 See, the LORD goes forth from his *p,*
28: 8 with filthy vomit, with no *p* left clean.
28:12 This is the resting *p,*
28:15 and in falsehood we have found a hiding *p*—
28:17 lies, and waters shall flood the hiding *p.*
33:21 In a *p* of rivers and wide streams on which
33:23 it cannot hold the mast in *p,*
34:14 repose, and find for herself a *p* to rest.
45:19 hiding nor from some dark *p* of the earth,
46: 7 when they set it in *p* again,
48: 5 before they took *p* I let you hear of them,
49:20 say to you, "This *p* is too small for me,
50:11 you shall lie down in a *p* of pain.
53: 9 the wicked and a burial *p* with evildoers,
54:10 leave their *p* and the hills be shaken,
55:13 In *p* of the thornbush,
60:13 and glory to the *p* where I set my feet.
60:17 In *p* of bronze I will bring gold,
60:17 In *p* of wood, bronze,
61: 3 To *p* on those who mourn in Zion a diadem
61: 3 give them oil of gladness in *p* of mourning,
63:18 Why have the wicked invaded your holy *p,*
65:10 and the valley of Achor a resting *p*
66: 1 what is to be my resting *p?*
Jer 1: 9 saying, See, I *p* my words in your mouth!
4: 7 of nations has set out, has left his *p,*

PLACE (cont.)

6:21 I will *p* before this people obstacles to
6:23 they ride forth on steeds, Each in his *p*,
7: 3 so that I may remain with you in this *p*.
7: 6 no longer shed innocent blood in this *p*,
7: 7 harm, will I remain with you in this *p*,
7:12 the dwelling *p* of my name in the beginning.
7:14 *p* which I gave to you and your fathers,
7:20 and my wrath will pour out upon this *p*,
7:31 they have built the high *p* of Topheth
7:32 lack of space, Topheth will be a burial *p*.
13: 7 loincloth from the *p* where I had hid it.
13:21 What will you say when they *p* as rulers
14:13 I will give you lasting peace in this *p*."
16: 2 not have sons or daughters in this *p*,
16: 3 and daughters who will be born in this *p*,
16: 9 *p* the cry of joy and the cry of gladness,
17:12 from the beginning, such is our holy *p*.
19: 3 I am going to bring such evil upon this *p*
19: 4 have forsaken me and alienated this *p*
19: 4 this *p* with the blood of the innocent.
19: 6 this *p* will no longer be called Topheth,
19: 7 In this *p* I will foil the plan of Judah
19:11 Topheth shall be a burial *p*, for lack of *p*
19:12 I will do to this *p* and to its inhabitants,
19:13 shall be defiled like the *p* of Topheth,
22: 3 and do not shed innocent blood in this *p*.
22:11 He has left this *p* never to return.
22:12 shall die in the *p* where they exiled him;
24: 5 from this *p* into the land of the Chaldeans.
25:36 For the LORD lays waste their grazing *p*,
27:22 bring them back and restore them to this *p*.
28: 3 Within two years I will restore to this *p*
28: 3 Babylon, took away from this *p* to Babylon.
28: 4 And I will bring back to this *p* Jeconiah,
28: 6 all the exiles back from Babylon to this *p*!
28:14 A yoke of iron I will *p* on the necks of
29:10 you my promise to bring you back to this *p*.
29:14 back to the *p* from which I have exiled you.
29:26 you priest in *p* of the priest Jehoiada,
31:33 I will *p* my law within them,
32:37 to this *p* and settle them here in safety.
33:10 In this *p* of which you say,
33:12 In this *p*, now desolate, without man
34:13 Egypt, out of the *p* where they were slaves,
40: 2 LORD your God, foretold the ruin of this *p*.
41:17 to the lodging *p* of Chimham near Bethlehem,
42:18 and you shall never see this *p* again.
42:22 in the *p* where you wish to go and settle.
44:29 the LORD, that I will punish you in this *p*.
48:35 LORD, to offer a holocaust on the high *p*,
50:42 Each in his *p* for battle against you,
51:37 A *p* of horror and ridicule,
51:62 you yourself threatened to destroy this *p*,
Lam 1: 3 among the nations she finds no *p* to rest:
Bar 3:15 Who has found the *p* of wisdom,
6:44 that takes *p* around these gods is a fraud:
Ez 3:12 as the glory of the LORD rose from its *p*:
3:20 when I *p* a stumbling block before him,
3:23 that the glory of the LORD was in that *p*,
4: 4 *p* the sins of the house of Israel upon you.
4:15 cow's dung in *p* of human excrement;
5: 2 *p* another third around the city and strike
12: 3 migrate from where you live to another *p*;
16:24 a platform and a dais in every public *p*.
16:31 and erecting your dais in every public *p* !
20:29 sort of high *p* do you betake yourselves?—and
20:29 call it a high *p* even to the present day.
21:35 In the *p* where you were created,
25: 5 of the Ammonites a resting *p* for flocks.
26: 5 drying *p* for nets in the midst of the sea.
26: 8 He shall *p* a siege tower against you,
26:14 a drying *p* for nets shall you be.
26:20 to take your *p* in the land of the living.
32:20 and *p* shall be made with them for all
34:12 I will rescue them from every *p* where they
34:26 I will *p* them about my hill,
36:26 a new heart and *p* a new spirit within you,
39:11 Gog for his tomb a well-known *p* in Israel,
41:21 In front of the holy *p* was something that
41:23 and also the holy *p* had a double door.
42:13 for it is a holy *p*.
42:14 they shall not leave the holy *p* for the
42:14 approach the *p* destined for the people."
45: 4 it shall be a *p* for their homes and
46:19 There, at their west end, I saw a *p*,
Dn 1: 4 as could take their *p* in the king's palace;
2:39 Another kingdom shall take your *p*,
3:38 or incense, no *p* to offer first fruits,
8: 8 and in its *p* came up four others,
8:22 The four that rose in its *p* when it was
11:21 shall rise in his *p* a despicable person,
11:36 ready, for what is determined must take *p*.
14:39 at once brought Habakkuk back to his own *p*.
Hos 5:15 I will go back to my *p* until they pay for
Jl 4: 7 from the *p* into which you have sold them,
Jon 4: 5 left the city for a *p* to the east of it,
Mi 1: 3 For see, the LORD comes forth from his *p*,
1: 6 in the field, a *p* to plant for vineyards;
2:10 Be off, this is no *p* to rest";
6: 4 from the *p* of slavery I released you;
Zep 1: 4 from this *p* the last vestige of Baal,
2:11 Then, each from its own *p*,
Hg 2: 9 And in this *p* I will give you peace,
Zec 1: 8 standing among myrtle trees in a shady *p*,
5:11 ready, they will deposit it there in its *p*."
6:11 *p* it on the head of [Joshua,
9: 1 of Hadrach, and Damascus is its resting *p*,
14:10 Jerusalem shall remain exalted in its *p*.
14:10 of Benjamin to the *p* of the First Gate,
Mt 2: 9 standstill over the *p* where the child was.
8:11 the west and will find a *p* at the banquet
11:21 in you had taken *p* in Tyre and Sidon,
11:23 worked in you had taken *p* in Sodom,
12: 9 left that *p* and went into their synagogue.
12:15 of this, and so he withdrew from that *p*.
12:43 searching for a *p* of rest and finding none.
13:54 Jesus next went to his native *p* and spent
13:57 is without honor except in his native *p*,
14:13 boat from there to a deserted *p* by himself.
14:15 is a deserted *p* and it is already late.
14:35 and when the men of that *p* recognized him
15:21 Then Jesus left that *p* and withdrew to the
15:29 that *p* and passed along the Sea of Galilee.
19:13 he could *p* his hands on them in prayer.
19:15 hands on their heads before he left that *p*.
24:34 will not pass away until all this takes *p*.
25:33 The sheep he will *p* on his right hand,
26:36 went with them to a *p* called Gethsemane.
27:33 Golgotha (a name which means Skull *P*),
28: 6 Come and see the *p* where he was laid.
Mk 1:35 he went off to a lonely *p* in the desert;
6: 4 is without honor except in his native *p*,
6:11 If any *p* will not receive you or hear you,
6:31 to an out-of-the-way *p* and rest a little."
6:32 in the boat by themselves to a deserted *p*.
6:33 all the towns hastened on foot to the *p*,
6:35 is a deserted *p* and it is already late.
6:55 bedrolls to the *p* where they heard he was.
7:10 and in another *p*, 'Whoever curses father
7:24 From that *p* he went off to the territory
9:50 Salt is excellent in its *p*;
10:46 *p* with his disciples and a sizable crowd,
13:30 pass away until all these things take *p*.
14:15 That is the *p* you are to get ready for us."
14:32 They went then to a *p* named Gethsemane.
15:22 site of Golgotha (which means "Skull *P*"),
16: 6 See the *p* where they laid him.
Lk 1:20 until the day these things take *p*,
2: 2 *p* while Quirinius was governor of Syria.
2: 7 for them in the *p* where travelers lodged.
4:24 prophet gains acceptance in his native *p*.
9:12 for this is certainly an out-of-the-way *p*."
10: 1 to every town and *p* he intended to visit.
11: 1 One day he was praying in a certain *p*.
12:17 'I have no *p* to store my harvest.
13:29 their *p* at the feast in the kingdom of God.
13:31 "Leave this *p*!
14: 8 do not sit in the *p* of honor in case some
14: 9 to proceed shamefacedly to the lowest *p*.
14:10 invited is go and sit in the lowest *p*,
15:15 to one of the propertied class of the *p*,
15:17 my father's *p* have more than enough to eat,
16:28 that they may not end in this *p* of torment.'
17:23 you he is to be found in this *p* or that.
20:35 but those judged worthy of a *p* in the age
21:32 will not pass away until all this takes *p*.
22:14 the hour arrived, he took his *p* at table,
22:40 On reaching the *p* he said to them,
23: 5 Galilee, where he began, to this very *p*."
23:33 When they came to Skull *P*,
Jn 4:20 is the *p* where men ought to worship God."
5: 2 there is a *p* with the Hebrew name Bethesda.
5:13 The crowd in that *p* was so great that
6:10 grass for them to find a *p* on the ground.
6:23 boats came out from Tiberias near the *p*
8:35 (No slave has a permanent *p* in the family,
8:35 family, but the son has a *p* there forever.)
10:40 *p* where John had been baptizing earlier,
10:42 In that *p*, many came to believe in him.
11:32 When Mary came to the *p* where Jesus was,
13:19 before it takes *p*, so that when it takes *p*
14: 2 that I was going to prepare a *p* for you?
14: 3 I am indeed going to prepare a *p* for you,
14:23 to him and make our dwelling *p* with him.
14:29 before it takes *p*, so that when it takes *p*
18: 2 The *p* was familiar to Judas as well (the
19:13 bench at the *p* called the Stone Pavement
19:17 is called the *P* of the Skull (in Hebrew,
19:20 since the *p* where Jesus was crucified was
19:36 took *p* for the fulfillment of Scripture:
19:41 In the *p* where he had been crucified there
20: 7 wrappings, but rolled up in a *p* by itself.
20:12 foot of the *p* where Jesus' body had lain.
20:19 the *p* where they were for fear of the Jews,
21: 1 This is how the appearance took *p*.
Acts 2: 1 came it found them gathered in one *p*.
4:16 show of power took *p* through them.
4:31 The *p* where they were gathered shook as
5:20 "Go out now and take your *p* in the temple
6:13 statements against the holy *p* and the law."
6:14 Jesus the Nazorean will destroy this *p*
7: 7 after that they will worship me in this *p*.
7:33 for the *p* where you stand is holy ground.
7:46 find a dwelling *p* for the house of Jacob.
7:49 What is my resting *p* to be like?
8:19 so that if I *p* my hands on anyone he will
12: 9 this was taking *p* through the angel's help.
12:17 then left them to go off to another *p*.
13:35 That is why he said in still another *p*,
15:10 *p* on the shoulders of these converts
16:13 we thought there would be a *p* of prayer.
16:16 we were on our way out to the *p* of prayer
16:26 a severe earthquake suddenly shook the *p*,
17: 6 been creating a disturbance all over the *p*.
21:28 area and thus profaned this sacred *p*."
26:26 all, it did not take *p* in a dark corner!
27: 8 along the coast to a *p* called Fair Havens,
28: 7 of that *p* was the estate of Publius,
Rom 9:26 in the very *p* where it was said to them,
1Cor 7:35 I have no desire to *p* restrictions on you,
9:12 *p* any obstacle in the way of the gospel
12:18 of the body in the *p* he wanted it to be.
2Cor 4:14 and *p* both us and you in his presence.
Gal 5:13 *p* yourselves at one another's service.
Eph 2: 6 us up and gave us a *p* in the heavens,
2:22 become a dwelling *p* for God in the Spirit.
4:32 In *p* of these, be kind to one another,
5: 4 all that is out of *p*.
1Tm 2: 8 that in every *p* the men shall offer
3:13 who serve well as deacons gain a worthy *p*
2Tm 2:18 that the resurrection has already taken *p*.
Phlm 1:13 your *p* while I am in prison for the gospel;
Heb 4: 5 and again, in the *p* we have referred to,
4: 8 if Joshua had led them into the *p* of rest,
5: 6 just as he says in another *p*,
8: 7 would have been no *p* for a second one.
8:10 I will *p* my laws in their minds and I will
9: 2 this was called the holy *p*.
9: 5 of glory overshadowing the *p* of expiation.
9:15 since his death has taken *p* for
11: 8 to the *p* he was to receive as a heritage;
11:15 back to the *p* from which they had come,
2Pt 1:19 you would on a lamp shining in a dark *p*
1Jn 1:10 him a liar and his word finds no *p* in us.
2:15 world, the Father's love has no *p* in him,
Jude 1: 6 own domain, who deserted their dwelling *p*.
Rv 2: 5 you and remove your lampstand from its *p*.
2:13 the very *p* where Satan's throne is erected;
2:24 on you I *p* no further burden.
4: 1 show you what must take *p* in time to come."
8: 3 He took his *p* at the altar of incense and
12: 6 special *p* had been prepared for her by God;
12: 8 overpowered and lost their *p* in heaven.
12:14 she could fly off to her *p* in the desert,
16:16 kings in a *p* called in Hebrew "Armageddon."
17: 3 to a desolate *p* where I saw a woman seated
18: 2 She has become a dwelling *p* for demons.

PLACED (118)

Gn 2: 8 and he *p* there the man whom he had formed.
15:10 in two, and *p* each half opposite the other;
48:20 Manasseh,'" he *p* Ephraim before Manasseh.
Ex 2: 3 it, *p* it among the reeds on the river bank.
5:14 the taskmasters of Pharaoh had *p* over them,
16:34 So Aaron *p* it in front of the commandments
26: 5 and so *p* that the loops are directly
37:27 Underneath the molding gold rings were *p*,
38: 4 was made for the altar and *p* round it,
40:18 He *p* its pedestals,
40:20 he *p* poles alongside the ark and set the
40:24 He *p* the lampstand in the meeting tent,
40:26 He *p* the golden altar in the meeting tent,
40:30 He *p* the laver between the meeting tent
Lv 2:12 to be *p* on the altar for a pleasing odor.
8: 7 him with the robe, *p* the ephod on him,
8:26 these he *p* on top of the portions of fat
9:20 he *p* on top of the breasts and burned them
Dt 10: 5 and *p* the tablets in the ark I had made.
Jos 4: 8 along to the camp site, where they *p* them,
6:23 and *p* them outside the camp of Israel.
6:24 *p* in the treasury of the house of the LORD.
10:27 the mouth of the cave large stones were *p*,
22:25 For the LORD has *p* the Jordan as a
Jgs 8:27 of the gold and *p* it in his city Ophrah.
9:49 Abimelech, *p* it against the crypt.
18:21 turned to depart, they *p* their little ones,
19:28 So the man *p* her on an ass and started out
Ru 4:16 Naomi took the child, *p* him on her lap,
1Sm 6:11 they *p* the ark of the LORD on the cart,
6:15 were, and had *p* them on the great stone.
6:18 which the ark of the LORD was *p* is still
7:12 stone and *p* it between Mizpah and Jeshanah;
9:22 where he *p* them at the head of the guests,
9:24 what went with it, and *p* it before Saul.
10:25 which he *p* in the presence of the LORD.
2Sm 3:34 with chains, nor your feet *p* in fetters;
6: 3 The ark of God was *p* on a new cart and
8: 6 David then *p* garrisons in Aram of Damascus,
8:14 after which he *p* garrisons in Edom.
10:10 He *p* the rest of the soldiers under the
12:30 it was *p* on David's head.
18: 1 David *p* officers in command of groups of a
19:29 yet you *p* your servant among the guests at
20: 3 of the palace and *p* them in confinement.
20:12 road to the field and *p* a garment over him,
1Kgs 6:27 were *p* in the inmost part of the temple,
7:39 The stands were *p*,

7:39 The sea was *p* off to the southeast from
9:27 In this fleet Hiram *p* his own expert
21:12 and *p* Naboth at the head of the people.
2Kgs 8: 6 the king *p* an official at her disposal,
13:16 *p* his hands over the king's hands and said,
1Chr 12:15 the lesser *p* over hundreds and the greater
12:19 and *p* them among the leaders of his troops.
19:11 *p* under the command of his brother Abishai,
2Chr 2: 1 he *p* three thousand six hundred overseers.
2:10 his people, he has *p* you over them as king."
4: 7 as was prescribed, and *p* them in the nave,
4:10 The sea was *p* off to the southeast from
6:11 And I have *p* there the ark,
6:13 he had *p* in the middle of the courtyard.
7:19 statutes and commands which I *p* before you,
17: 2 He *p* armed forces in all the fortified
17:19 the king had *p* in the fortified cities
25: 5 Amaziah mustered Judah and *p* them,
33: 7 He *p* an idol that he had carved in the
35:24 *p* him in another he had in reserve,
Ezr 1: 7 Jerusalem and *p* in the house of his god.
Neh 7: 2 Over Jerusalem I *p* Hanani,
11:16 levitical chiefs who were *p* over the
13: 4 who had been *p* in charge of the chambers
Tb 1:21 who succeeded him as king, *p* Ahiqar,
2: 2 were *p* before me I said to my son Tobiah:
8: 2 and *p* them on the embers for the incense.
9: 5 moneybags, and they *p* them on the camels.
Jdt 5: 1 peaks, and *p* roadblocks in the plains.
6:16 They *p* Achior in the center of the throng,
Est 2:17 So he *p* the royal diadem on her head and
4: 5 eunuchs whom he had *p* at her service,
5:11 *p* him above the officials
6: 8 when the royal crown was *p* on his head.
8:12 many *p* in authority to become accomplices
1Mc 4:61 also *p* a garrison there to protect it,
13:29 and next to the armor he *p* carved ships,
2Mc 3:12 *p* their trust in the sanctity of the Place
3:22 secure for those who had *p* them in trust,
15:20 their elephants *p* in strategic positions,
Jb 20: 4 olden time, since man was *p* upon the earth,
Ps(s) 21: 4 you *p* on his head a crown of pure gold.
89:20 "On a champion I have *p* a crown;
Sir 30:18 are like the offerings *p* before a tomb.
42: 6 or of a lock *p* where there are many hands;
Is 57: 8 the doorpost you *p* your indecent symbol.
Jer 20: 2 So he had the prophet scourged and *p* in
24: 1 of figs *p* before the temple of the LORD.
26: 4 not living according to the law I *p* before
Ez 5: 5 In the midst of the nations I *p* her,
11: 7 Your slain whom you have *p* within it,
17: 5 by plentiful waters, like a willow he *p* it,
27: 4 the midst of the sea your builders *p* you,
28:14 With the Cherub I *p* you;
32:25 in the midst of the slain they are *p*.
32:27 whose swords were *p* under their heads and
32:29 have been *p* with those slain by the sword;
43: 8 When they *p* their threshold against my
Dn 1: 2 and *p* in the temple treasury of his god.
8:13 the desolating sin which is *p* there,
Zec 3: 9 at the stone that I have *p* before Joshua,
Lk 9:47 took a little child and *p* it beside him,
Jn 19:19 an inscription *p* on the cross which read, JESUS
Acts 7:16 *p* in the tomb which Abraham had bought
1Cor 10:27 want to go, eat whatever is *p* before you,
15:27 that God "has *p* all things under his feet."
Heb 3: 6 was faithful as the Son *p* over God's house.
6:18 to seize the hope which is *p* before us.
10:13 until his enemies are *p* beneath his feet.
Rv 10: 2 He *p* his right foot on the sea and his

PLACES (126)

Ex 14:11 "Were there no burial *p* in Egypt that you
Lv 26:30 I will demolish your high *p*,
Nm 21:28 and swallowed up the high *p* of the Arnon.
33: 2 the starting *p* of the various stages.
33: 2 starting *p* of the successive stages were:
33:52 images, and demolish all their high *p*.
35: 6 as *p* where a homicide can take refuge,
35:12 as *p* of asylum from the avenger of blood,
Jgs 20:33 all the men of Israel rose from their *p*.
1Sm 23:23 the various hiding *p* he is holding out.
30:31 all the *p* frequented by David and his men.
1Kgs 3: 2 the people were sacrificing on the high *p*,
3: 3 sacrifice and burned incense on the high *p*.
12:31 He also built temples on the high *p* and
12:32 Bethel priests of the high *p* he had built.
13: 2 of the high *p* who offer sacrifice upon you,
13:32 on the high *p* in the cities of Samaria
13:33 the high *p* from among the common people.
13:33 and became a priest of the high *p*.
14:23 They, too, built for themselves high *p*,
15:14 The high *p* did not disappear;
20:24 their posts and put prefects in their *p*.
22:44 Nevertheless, the high *p* did not disappear,
22:44 and to burn incense on the high *p*.
2Kgs 12: 4 Still, the high *p* did not disappear;
14: 4 Thus the high *p* did not disappear,
15: 4 Yet the high *p* did not disappear;
15:35 Nevertheless the high *p* did not disappear
16: 4 and burned incense on the high *p*,
17: 9 They built high *p* in all their settlements,
17:11 There, on all the high *p*,
17:29 on the high *p* which the Samaritans had made,
17:32 from their number priests for the high *p*,
17:32 for them in the shrines on the high *p*.
18: 4 It was he who removed the high *p*,
18:22 high *p* and altars Hezekiah has removed,
21: 3 *p* which his father Hezekiah had destroyed.
23: 5 on the high *p* in the cities of Judah
23: 8 the high *p* where they had offered incense.
23: 8 He also tore down the high *p* of the satyrs,
23: 9 The priests of the high *p* could not
23:13 king defiled the high *p* east of Jerusalem,
23:14 the *p* where they had been with human bones.
23:19 on the high *p* near the cities of Samaria
23:20 of the high *p* that were at the shrines,
1Chr 6:39 *p* to which their encampment was limited.
2Chr 8:11 for the *p* where the ark of the LORD has
11:15 high *p* and satyrs and calves he had made.
14: 2 the heathen altars and the high *p*,
14: 4 He removed the high *p* and incense stands
15:17 the high *p* did not disappear from Israel,
17: 6 the high *p* and the sacred poles from Judah.
20:17 Take your *p*, stand firm,
20:33 But the high *p* were not removed,
21:11 set up high *p* in the mountains of Judah;
28: 4 sacrifice and incense on the high *p*,
28:25 up high *p* to offer sacrifice to other gods.
30:16 They stood in the *p* prescribed for them
31: 1 the high *p* and altars throughout Judah,
32:12 Hezekiah removed his high *p* and altars
33: 3 *p* which his father Hezekiah had torn down,
33:17 continued to sacrifice on the high *p*,
33:19 the sites where he built high *p*
34: 3 purge Judah and Jerusalem of the high *p*,
35:10 been arranged, the priests took their *p*,
Neh 8: 7 who remained in their *p*
9: 3 When they had taken their *p*,
1Mc 1:53 wherever *p* of refuge could be found.
2:31 had gone out to the hiding *p* in the desert.
2:36 stones, nor blocked up their own hiding *p*.
2:41 die as our kinsmen died in the hiding *p*."
10:40 of the royal revenues, from appropriate *p*.
11:69 out of their *p* and joined in the battle.
12: 2 to Sparta and other *p* for the same purpose.
12: 4 to the authorities in the various *p*,
2Mc 8:31 and carefully stored them in suitable *p*;
10:17 vigorously, they gained control of the *p*,
10:19 off to *p* where he was more urgently needed.
Jb 15:15 If in his holy one God *p* no confidence,
Ps(s) 74:20 for the hiding *p* in the land and the
78:58 *p* and with their idols roused his jealousy.
Eccl 10: 6 position while the rich sit in lowly *p*.
Sir 17:14 Over every nation he *p* a ruler,
Is 15: 2 goes daughter Dibon to the high *p* to weep;
16:12 When Moab grows weary on the high *p*,
26: 5 He humbles those in high *p*,
32:18 in secure dwellings and quiet resting *p*.
36: 7 whose high *p* and altars Hezekiah removed,
41: 9 the earth and summoned from its far-off *p*,
Jer 5: 1 and observe, Search through her public *p*,
8: 3 in any of the *p* to which I banish them,
19: 5 They have built high *p* for Baal to
24: 9 in all the *p* to which I will drive them.
29:14 and all the *p* to which I have banished you,
32:35 high *p* to Baal in the Valley of Ben-hinnom,
40:12 from the *p* to which they had scattered.
51:51 the holy *p* of the house of the LORD.
Bar 2:24 fathers brought out from their burial *p*.
Ez 6: 3 you, and I will destroy your high *p*.
6: 6 In all your dwelling *p* cities shall be
6: 6 be made desolate and high *p* laid waste,
16:16 gowns and made for yourself gaudy high *p*,
34:13 the land's ravines and all its inhabited *p*.
43: 7 the corpses of their kings [their high *p*.
Hos 10: 8 The high *p* of Aven shall be destroyed,
Am 7: 9 The high *p* of Isaac shall be laid waste,
Ob 1: 6 they search Esau, seek out his hiding *p*!
Mt 19:28 take your *p* on twelve thrones to judge
23: 6 They are fond of *p* of honor at banquets
24: 7 and pestilence and earthquakes in many *p*.
Mk 1:45 He stayed in desert *p*;
6:40 took their *p* in hundreds and fifties,
6:56 they laid the sick in the market *p*
8: 6 the crowd to take their *p* on the ground.
12:39 the synagogues, and *p* of honor at banquets.
13: 8 in various *p* and there will be famine.
13:34 leaves home and *p* his servants in charge,
Lk 1:52 thrones and raised the lowly to high *p*.
5:16 He often retired to deserted *p* and prayed.
8:29 demon would drive him into *p* of solitude.
14: 7 trying to get the *p* of honor at the table:
20:46 in synagogues, and *p* of honor at banquets.
21:11 plagues and famines in various *p*—
Jn 14: 2 Father's house there are many dwelling *p*;
Acts 9:32 among other *p*—
Rom 15:20 in *p* where Christ's name was already known,

PLACING (9)

Gn 21:14 Then, *p* the child on her back,
41:48 *p* in each town the crops of the fields
1Sm 5: 2 the temple of Dagon, *p* it beside Dagon.
2Kgs 4:34 bed, *p* his mouth upon the child's mouth,
2Chr 4: 6 *p* five of them to the right and five to
2Mc 8:22 divided his army into four, *p* his brothers,
Mk 10:16 them and blessed them, *p* his hands on them.
Acts 9:12 Ananias coming to him and *p* his hands
Rom 9:33 I am *p* in Zion a stone to make men stumble

PLAGUE (38)

Ex 7:27 send a *p* of frogs over all your territory.
11: 1 *p* will I bring upon Pharaoh and upon Egypt.
30:12 *p* may come upon them for being registered.
Nm 8:19 so that no *p* may strike among the
11:33 and he struck them with a very great *p*.
Dt 28:22 wind, that will *p* you until you perish.
Jos 22:17 a *p* came upon the community of the LORD.
1Sm 5: 6 great and deadly *p* of mice that swarmed
6: 4 *p* has struck all of you and your lords.
2Sm 24:15 when the *p* broke out among the people.
24:21 that the *p* may be checked among the people."
24:25 country, and the *p* was checked in Israel.
1Kgs 8:37 whatever *p* or sickness there may be,
1Chr 21:17 but do not afflict your people with this *p*!"
21:22 that the *p* may be stayed from the people."
2Chr 6:28 there is a *p* or sickness of any kind;
21:14 and all that is yours with a great *p*;
Ps(s) 78:50 death, and delivered their beasts to the *p*.
91: 6 in darkness nor the devastating *p* at noon.
106:29 him by their deeds, and a *p* attacked them.
106:30 forth in judgment and the *p* was checked;
Eccl 6: 2 This is vanity and a dire *p*.
Wis 16: 3 creatures sent to *p* them were so loathsome,
18:20 and in the desert a *p* struck the multitude;
Sir 40: 9 *P* and bloodshed,
48:21 of the Assyrians and routed them with a *p*.
Bar 2:25 anguish, by hunger and the sword and *p*.
Ez 33:27 fastnesses and in caves shall die by the *p*.
Hb 3: 5 pestilence, and the *p* follows in his steps.
Zec 14:12 And this shall be the *p* with which the
14:15 this *p* shall be the plague upon the horses,
14:18 upon them shall fall the *p* which the LORD
2Tm 2:17 of their talk will spread like the *p*.
Rv 6: 8 and *p* and the wild beasts of the earth.
11: 6 the earth at will with any kind of *p*.
16:21 *p* of hailstones, because this *p* was so severe.

PLAGUES (15)

Gn 12:17 severe *p* because of Abram's wife Sarai.
1Sm 4: 8 with various *p* and with pestilence.
Jdt 5:12 Egypt with *p* for which there was no remedy.
Hos 13:14 Where are your *p*, O death!
Lk 21:11 *p* and famines in various places
Rv 9:18 By these three *p*—
9:20 That part of mankind which escaped the *p*
15: 1 seven angels holding the seven final *p*
15: 6 came the seven angels holding the seven *p*.
15: 8 *p* of the seven angels had come to an end.
16: 9 name of God who had power to send these *p*,
18: 4 her and sharing the *p* inflicted on her!
18: 8 Therefore her *p* will come all at once,
21: 9 with the seven last *p* came and said to me,
22:18 visit him with all the *p* described herein!

PLAIN (68)

Gn 13:10 the whole Jordan *P* was as far as Zoar,
13:11 the whole Jordan *P* and set out eastward.
13:12 Lot settled among the cities of the *P*,
19:17 Don't look back or stop anywhere on the *P*.
19:25 He overthrew those cities and the whole *P*,
19:28 Gomorrah and the whole region of the *P*,
19:29 when God destroyed the Cities of the *P*,
Jos 8: 9 Joshua, however, spent that night in the *p*.
Jgs 1:19 not dislodge those who lived on the *p*,
1:34 not permitting them to go down into the *p*.
2Sm 18:23 way of the Jordan *p* and outran the Cushite.
2Chr 35:22 but went out to fight in the *p* of Megiddo.
Neh 6: 2 together at Caphirim in the *p* of Ono."
6:12 it was *p* to me that God had not sent him;
Jdt 1: 5 war against King Arphaxad in the vast *p*,
1: 6 and King Arioch of the Elamites, in the *p*.
1: 8 Upper Galilee, and the vast *p* of Esdraelon,
2:21 Nineveh, they reached the *p* of Bectileth,
2:27 Descending to the *p* of Damascus at the
4: 6 way to Esdraelon, facing the *p* near Dothan,
6:11 and brought him out of the camp into the *p*.
7:18 of the Assyrian army was encamped in the *p*,
14: 2 into the *p* against the advance guard
15: 7 villages in the mountains and on the *p*
1Mc 3:24 down the descent of Beth-horon into the *p*.
3:40 pitched their camp near Emmaus in the *p*.
4: 6 appeared in the *p* with three thousand men,
4:14 were defeated and fled toward the *p*.
4:21 the army of Judas in the *p* ready to attack,
5:52 to the great *p* in front of Beth-shan,
10:71 your forces, come down now to us in the *p*,
10:73 cavalry and such a force as this in the *p*,
10:77 at the same time he advanced into the *p*,
10:83 The horsemen too were scattered over the *p*.
11:67 at daybreak they went to the *p* of Hazor.
11:68 There, in front of him on the *p*,
12:49 the Great *P* to destroy all Jonathan's men.
13:13 pitched his camp at Adida, facing the *p*.

PLAIN (cont.)
16: 5 Modein, rose early, and marched into the *p.*
16:10 refuge in the towers on the *p* of Azotus,
16:11 appointed governor of the *p* of Jericho,
Jb 39:21 He jubilantly paws the *p* and rushes in his
Ps(s) 78:12 in the land of Egypt, in the *p* of Zoan.
78:43 in Egypt and his marvels in the *p* of Zoan,
Prv 5:21 each man's ways are *p* to the LORD's sight;
8: 9 of them are *p* to the man of intelligence,
Wis 7:21 as are hidden I learned and such as are *p;*
19: 7 and a grassy *p* out of the mighty flood.
Is 40: 4 The rugged land shall be made a *p,*
63:14 country, Like cattle going down into the *p,*
Jer 21:13 am against you, Valley-site, Rock of the *P,*
48: 8 Ruined is the valley, wasted the *p,*
Ez 3:22 Get up and go out into the *p,*
3:23 So I got up and went out into the *p,*
8: 4 like the vision I had seen in the *p.*
37: 1 the LORD and set me in the center of the *p,*
37: 2 how many they were on the surface of the *p.*
Dn 3: 1 the *p* of Dura in the province of Babylon.
Jl 1:19 fire has devoured the pastures of the *p,*
1:20 fire has devoured the pastures of the *p.*
2:22 for the pastures of the *p* are green;
Zec 4: 7 Before Zerubbabel you are but a *p.*
12:11 of Hadadrimmon in the *p* of Megiddo.
14:10 Negeb, all the land shall turn into a *p;*
Jn 10:24 are the Messiah, tell us so in *p* words."
16:25 tell you about the Father in *p* speech.
2Cor 7:12 but to make *p* in the sight of God the
2Tm 3: 9 of these will be *p* for all to see.

PLAINLY (7)
Nm 12: 8 face I speak to him, *p* and not in riddles.
14:14 you, LORD, who *p* reveal yourself!
Ezr 4:18 you sent us has been read *p* in my presence.
Neh 8: 8 read *p* from the book of the law of God,
Mk 7:35 from the impediment, and began to speak *p.*
Jn 11:14 Finally Jesus said *p:*
16:29 "At last you are speaking *p,*"

PLAINS (27)
Nm 22: 1 *p* of Moab on the other side of the Jericho
26: 3 So on the *p* of Moab along the Jericho
26:63 *p* of Moab along the Jericho stretch
31:12 community at their camp on the *p* of Moab,
33:48 they camped on the *p* of Moab along the
33:49 camp along the Jordan on the *p* of Moab
33:50 The LORD spoke to Moses on the *p* of Moab
35: 1 instructions to Moses on the *p* of Moab
36:13 on the *p* of Moab beside the Jericho
Dt 34: 1 went up from the *p* of Moab to Mount Nebo,
34: 8 Israelites wept for Moses in the *p* of Moab,
Jos 4:13 over before the LORD to the *p* of Jericho.
5:10 encamped at Gilgal on the *p* of Jericho,
13:32 Moses gave when he was in the *p* of Moab,
1Kgs 20:28 is a god of mountains, not a god of *p,*
1Chr 16:32 let the *p* rejoice and all that is in them!
2Chr 26:10 He had plowmen in the foothills and the *p,*
Neh 12:29 and from the *p* of Geba and Azmaveth (for
Tb 5:10 Media and crossed all its *p* and mountains;
Jdt 2:27 despoiled their cities, devastated their *p,*
5: 1 peaks, and placed roadblocks in the *p.*
6: 4 and their *p* filled with their corpses.
1Mc 4:15 as far as Gazara and the *p* of Judea,
Ps(s) 50:11 of the air, and whatever stirs in the *p,*
74:20 in the land and the *p* are full of violence.
96:12 the *p* be joyful and all that is in them!
Sir 43:22 and the flowering *p* as though by flames,

PLAINTIVE (4)
Jer 3:21 the *p* weeping of Israel's children,
Mi 2: 4 over you, and there shall be a *p* chant:
Hb 3: 1 To a *p* tune.

PLAITED (1)
Lam 1:14 by his hand they have been *p:*

PLAN (60)
1Sm 24:12 that I *p* no harm and no rebellion.
26:18 What evil do I *p?*
2Sm 15:11 in good faith, knowing nothing of the *p.*
16: 2 to Ziba, "What do you *p* to do with these?"
17: 4 This *p* was agreeable to Absalom and to all
1Kgs 6:38 all particulars, exactly according to *p,*
Neh 4: 9 warned and that God had upset their *p,*
Jdt 2: 2 and nobles, laid before them his secret *p,*
2: 4 When he had completed his *p,*
8:14 discern his mind, and understand his *p?*
8:34 tell you until my *p* has been accomplished."
9: 9 a widow, the strong hand to execute my *p.*
Est 4:16 for our enemies *p* our ruin and are bent
8: 3 and the *p* he had devised against the Jews.
9:25 wicked *p* Haman had devised
1Mc 5:27 Tomorrow their enemies *p* to attack the
6: 3 because his *p* became known to the people
7:31 Nicanor saw that his *p* had been discovered,
2Mc 3:23 in trust, Heliodorus went on with his *p.*
11: 2 *p* was to make Jerusalem a Greek settlement;
14:22 suddenly carry out some treacherous *p.*
15: 5 not succeed in carrying out his cruel *p.*
Jb 10: 3 hands, and smile on the *p* of the wicked?
38:33 you put into effect their *p* on the earth?
Ps(s) 20: 5 is in your heart and fulfill your every *p.*
33:11 But the *p* of the LORD stands forever;
62: 5 my place on high they *p* to dislodge me;
64: 6 They resolve on their wicked *p;*
140: 5 from violent men Who *p* to trip up my feet
Wis 19: 3 dead, They adopted another senseless *p;*
Sir 32:16 out of obscurity he draws forth a clear *p.*
43:24 His is the *p* that calms the deep,
Is 5:19 On with the *p* of the Holy One of Israel!
8:10 Form a *p,* and it shall be thwarted;
14:26 This is the *p* proposed for the whole earth,
19:17 *p* which the LORD of hosts has in mind
44:26 carry out the *p* announced by my messengers;
46:10 I say that my *p* shall stand,
46:11 from a distant land, one to carry out my *p.*
Jer 18:11 fashioning evil against you and making a *p.*
19: 7 I will foil the *p* of Judah and Jerusalem;
48: 2 Evil they *p* against Heshbon:
49:30 a *p* has been formed against you
51:29 LORD's *p* against Babylon is carried out,
Ez 42:11 with the same exits and *p* and entrances.
Am 3: 7 without revealing his *p* to his servants,
Mi 2: 1 Woe to those who *p* iniquity,
Mt 18:14 it is no part of your heavenly Father's *p*
Lk 7:30 baptism defeated God's *p* in their regard.
23:51 associated with their *p* or their action.
Jn 11:53 day onward there was a *p* afoot to kill him.
Acts 2:23 up by the set purpose and *p* of God;
20:13 made, since his *p* was to travel overland.
27:43 anxious to save Paul, he opposed their *p.*
Eph 1: 9 the *p* he was pleased to decree in Christ,
3: 3 God's secret *p* as I have briefly described
Heb 11:40 made a better plan, a *p* which included us.
Rv 10: 7 blow his trumpet, the mysterious *p* of God,
17:17 it into their minds to carry out his *p,*

PLANE (7)
Gn 30:37 fresh shoots of poplar, almond and *p* trees,
Sir 24:14 like a *p* tree growing beside the water.
Is 41:19 together with the *p* tree and the pine,
44:13 a *p* and measures it off with a compass,
60:13 the cypress, the *p* and the pine,
Ez 31: 8 were the *p* trees like it for branches;
Jn 3:31 is earthly, and he speaks on an earthly *p.*

PLANK (7)
Sg 8: 9 door, we will reinforce it with a cedar *p.*"
Mt 7: 3 eye when you miss the *p* in your own?
7: 4 all the time the *p* remains in your own?
7: 5 Remove the *p* from your own eye first;
Lk 6:41 eye when you miss the *p* in your own?
6:42 yourself to see the *p* lodged in your own?
6:42 remove the *p* from your own eye first;

PLANKING (1)
1Kgs 6:15 and its floor was laid with fir *p.*

PLANKS (1)
Acts 27:44 The rest were to follow, on *p,*

PLANNED (36)
Nm 16:28 have done, and that it was not I who *p* it:
Dt 19:19 do to him as he *p* to do to his kinsman.
Jgs 20:32 had *p* the flight so as to draw them away
1Sm 20: 7 angry, you can be sure he has *p* some harm.
2Sm 21:16 girt with a new sword and *p* to kill David,
1Kgs 9: 1 palace, and everything else that he had *p,*
2Kgs 19:25 ago I prepared it, From days of old I *p* it.
2Chr 7:11 accomplished everything he had *p*
Jdt 9: 5 present, also, and the future you have *p.*
9:13 have *p* dire things against your covenant,
Est 9:24 had *p* to destroy them and had cast the pur,
1Mc 3: 3 he *p* battles and protected the camp with
6:19 But Judas *p* to destroy them,
8: 9 of Greece had *p* to come and destroy them,
9:68 the enterprise he had *p* came to nought,
14:35 and the glory he *p* to bring to his nation,
2Mc 5:21 In his arrogance he *p* to make the land
8:10 Nicanor *p* to raise the two thousand
9: 4 he *p* to make the Jews suffer for the
12: 8 On hearing that the men of Jamnia *p* to
Is 14:27 The LORD of hosts has *p;*
19:12 What the LORD of hosts has *p* against Egypt.
23: 8 Who has *p* such a thing against Tyre,
23: 9 The LORD of hosts has *p* it,
37:26 ago I prepared it, From days of old I *p* it,
46:11 I have *p* it, and I will do it.
Jer 26: 3 so that I may repent of the evil I have *p*
51:12 For the LORD has *p* and he will carry out
Ez 21:34 because you *p* with false visions and lying
Mi 6: 5 people, remember what Moab's King Balak *p,*
Jn 12:10 the chief priests *p* to kill Lazarus too,
Acts 4:28 in your powerful providence you *p* long ago.
27:39 so they *p* to run the ship aground on it if
Rom 1:13 that I have often *p* to visit you
1Cor 2: 7 God *p* it before all ages for our glory.
2Cor 1:16 I *p* to visit you,

PLANNER (1)
Na 1:11 evil against the LORD, the scoundrel *p.*

PLANNING (9)
1Sm 23: 9 found out that Saul was *p* to harm him,
2Chr 28:10 And now you are *p* to make the children of
Neh 6: 2 They were *p* to do me harm.
6: 6 that you and the Jews are *p* a rebellion;
1Mc 8: 4 and by *p* and persistence had conquered the
Is 32: 6 fool speaks foolishly, *p* evil in his heart:
32: 7 trickster uses wicked trickery, *p* crimes:
Ez 11: 2 these are the men who are *p* evil and
Mi 2: 3 I am *p* against this race an evil from

PLANS (46)
Gn 50:15 *p* to pay us back in full for all the wrong
1Sm 23:10 a report that Saul *p* to come to Keilah,
2Kgs 6: 8 he would make *p* with his servants to
16:11 *p* which King Ahaz sent him from Damascus,
1Chr 29:19 that he may carry out all these *p*
Ezr 4: 5 *p* during the remaining years of Cyrus,
Tb 4:19 grant success to all your endeavors and *p.*
Jdt 8:16 the Lord our God give surety for his *p.*
Est 0:13 them plotting, investigated their *p,*
1Mc 12:35 made *p* for building strongholds in Judea,
16:13 *p* to do away with Simon and his sons.
2Mc 9:21 to form *p* for the general welfare of all.
13: 9 his mind full of savage *p* for inflicting
Jb 5:12 He frustrates the *p* of the cunning,
17:11 days are passed away, my *p* are at an end,
37:12 changes their rounds, according to his *p,*
38: 2 obscures divine *p* with words of ignorance?
Ps(s) 14: 6 You would confound the *p* of the afflicted,
33:10 The LORD brings to nought the *p* of nations;
36: 5 He *p* wickedness in his bed;
40: 6 your *p* for us there is none to equal you;
140: 9 further not their *p.*
146: 4 on that day his *p* perish.
Prv 12: 5 The *p* of the just are legitimate;
15:22 *P* fail when there is no counsel,
16: 1 Man may make *p* in his heart,
16: 3 works to the LORD, and your *p* will succeed.
16: 9 In his mind a man *p* his course,
16:20 He who *p* a thing will be successful;
19:21 Many are the *p* in a man's heart,
20:18 *P* made after advice succeed;
21: 5 The *p* of the diligent are sure of profit,
Wis 9:14 of mortals are timid, and unsure are our *p.*
Sir 22:18 on foolish *p* withstand fear of any kind.
Is 25: 1 you have fulfilled your wonderful *p* of old,
29:15 would hide their *p* too deep for the LORD!
30: 1 LORD, Who carry out *p* that are not mine,
32: 8 But the noble man *p* noble things,
Jer 18:23 you, O LORD, know all their *p* to slay me.
29:11 I know well the *p* I have in mind for you,
29:11 for you, says the LORD, *p* for your welfare,
29:11 *p* to give you a future full of hope.
49:20 Hear the *p* he has made against those that
50:45 Hear the *p* he has made against the land of
2Cor 1:17 in making those *p* I was acting insincerely?
1:17 Or that my *p* are so determined by

PLANT (56)
Gn 1:11 every kind of *p* that bears seed and every
1:12 the earth brought forth every kind of *p*
1:29 I give you every seed-bearing *p* all over
9:20 of the soil, was the first to *p* a vineyard.
Ex 10:15 any tree or *p* throughout the land of Egypt.
Lv 19:23 into the land and *p* any fruit tree there,
Dt 6:11 and olive groves that you did not *p;*
16:21 "You shall not *p* a sacred pole of any
28:30 Though you *p* a vineyard,
28:39 Though you *p* and cultivate vineyards,
Jos 24:13 and olive groves which you did not *p.*
2Sm 7:10 I will *p* them so that they may dwell in
2Kgs 19:29 and reap, *p* vineyards and eat their fruit!
1Chr 17: 9 *p* them in it to dwell there henceforth
2Mc 1:29 *P* your people in your holy place,
Jb 14: 9 and put forth branches like a young *p.*
30: 4 the roots of the broom *p* were their food.
Ps(s) 105:35 they devoured every *p* throughout the land;
Eccl 3: 2 a time to *p,* and a time to uproot
3: 2 time to plant, and a time to uproot the *p.*
Sir 3: 9 but a mother's curse uproots the growing *p.*
3:27 he is the offshoot of an evil *p.*
10:15 plucks up, to *p* the humble in their place:
49: 7 and destroy, and then to build and to *p.*
Is 5: 7 and the men of Judah are his cherished *p;*
17:10 though you *p* your pagan plants and set out
17:11 you make them grow the day you *p* them
37:30 and reap, *p* vineyards and eat their fruit!
41:19 of water, I will *p* in the desert the cedar,
65:21 and eat the fruit of the vineyards they *p;*
65:22 others to live in, or *p* for others to eat.
Jer 1:10 destroy and to demolish, to build and to *p.*
18: 9 to build up and *p* a nation or a kingdom.
24: 6 to *p* them, not to pluck them out.
29: 5 *p* gardens, and eat their fruits.
29:28 *p* gardens and eat their fruits. . . ."
31: 5 *p* vineyards on the mountains of Samaria;
31: 5 those who *p* them shall enjoy the fruits.

31:28 I will watch over them to build and to *p*.
35: 7 neither *p* nor own a vineyard.
42:10 I will *p* you,
Ez 16: 7 your blood and grow like a *p* in the field.
17:22 And *p* it on a high and lofty mountain;
17:23 the mountain heights of Israel I will *p* it.
Am 9:14 cities, *P* vineyards and drink the wine,
9:15 I will *p* them upon their own ground;
Jon 4: 6 And when the LORD God provided a gourd *p*,
4: 6 Jonah was very happy over the *p*.
4: 7 dawn God sent a worm which attacked the *p*,
4: 9 "Have you reason to be angry over the *p*?"
4:10 "You are concerned over the *p* which cost
Mi 1: 6 in the field, a place to *p* for vineyards;
Zep 1:13 but shall not dwell in them, *p* vineyards,
1Cor 15:37 you sow, you do not sow the full-blown *p*,
Rv 8: 7 a third of the trees and every green *p*.
9: 4 harm to the grass in the land or to any *p*

PLANTED (40)

Gn 2: 8 Then the LORD God *p* a garden in Eden,
21:33 Abraham *p* a tamarisk at Beer-sheba,
Ex 15:17 *p* them on the mountain of your inheritance
Nm 24: 6 a stream, like the cedars *p* by the LORD.
Dt 20: 6 Is there anyone who has *p* a vineyard and
1Chr 11:13 The plow-land was fully *p* with barley,
Ps(s) 1: 3 He is like a tree *p* near running water,
44: 3 hand you rooted out the nations and *p* them;
80: 9 you drove away the nations and *p* it.
80:16 and protect what your right hand has *p*
92:14 They that are *p* in the house of the LORD
104:16 LORD, the cedars of Lebanon, which he *p*;
107:37 They sowed fields and *p* vineyards,
Eccl 2: 4 I built myself houses and *p* vineyards;
Sir 39:13 petals, like roses *p* near running waters;
Is 5: 2 it of stones, and *p* the choicest vines;
40:24 Scarcely are they *p* or sown,
44:14 which the Lord had *p* and the rain made
61: 3 justice, *p* by the LORD to show his glory.
Jer 2:21 I had *p* you, a choice vine
11:17 The LORD of hosts who *p* you has decreed
12: 2 You *p* them; they have taken root,
17: 8 He is like a tree *p* beside the waters that
45: 4 what I have *p*, I am uprooting:
Ez 17: 5 seed of the land, and *p* it in a seedbed;
17: 7 it more freely than the bed where it was *p*.
17: 8 field by plentiful waters it was *p*,
17:10 True, it is *p*, but will it prosper?
19:10 Your mother was like a vine *p* by the water;
19:13 So now she is *p* in the desert,
31: 4 sending its rivers round where it was *p*,
Hos 9:13 saw, was like Tyre, *p* in a beauteous spot;
Am 5:11 Though you have *p* choice vineyards,
Mt 21:33 was a property owner who *p* a vineyard,
Mk 4:31 mustard seed which, when *p* in the soil,
12: 1 "A man *p* a vineyard, put a hedge
Lk 13:19 seed which a man took and *p* in his garden.
17:28 they bought and sold, they built and *p*.
20: 9 "A man *p* a vineyard, leased it
1Cor 3: 6 I *p* the seed and Apollos watered it,

PLANTING (7)

1Mc 3:56 or were just married, or were *p* vineyards,
Jb 31: 8 eat of it, or may my *p* be rooted up!
Is 28:24 loosening and harrowing his land for *p*?
60:21 possess the land, They, the bud of my *p*,
Ez 28:26 security, building houses and *p* vineyards.
34:29 prepare for them peaceful fields for *p*;
Mt 15:13 "Every *p* not put down by my heavenly

PLANTS (22)

Gn 1:30 ground, I give all the green *p* for food."
3:18 to you, as you eat of the *p* of the field.
9: 3 give them all to you as I did the green *p*.
1Kgs 5:13 He discussed *p*, from the cedar on Lebanon
2Kgs 19:26 ashamed, Becoming like the *p* of the field,
Ps(s) 128: 3 children like olive *p* around your table.
144:12 be like *p* well-nurtured in their youth,
Prv 31:16 out of her earnings she *p* a vineyard.
Wis 7:20 of men, uses of *p* and virtues of roots
10: 7 desert, *P* bearing fruit that never ripens,
Sir 24:29 Said to myself, "I will water my *p*,
40:16 riverbank, withered before all other *p*;
43:24 the deep, and *p* the islands in the sea.
Is 17:10 *p* and set out your foreign vine slips,
37:27 ashamed, Becoming like the *p* of the field,
61:11 As the earth brings forth its *p*,
Mt 7:16 from thornbushes, or figs from prickly *p*?
13:32 yet when full-grown it is the largest of *p*.
Lk 11:42 on mint and rue and all the garden *p*,
1Cor 3: 7 This means that neither he who *p* nor he
3: 8 *p* and he who waters work to the same end.
9: 7 *p* a vineyard and does not eat of its yield?

PLASTER (3)

Dt 27: 2 up some large stones and coat them with *p*.
27: 4 you today, and coating them with *p*,
Dn 5: 5 on the *p* of the wall in the king's palace.

PLASTERED (1)

Lv 14:42 mortar shall be made and *p* on the house.

PLASTERING (1)

Lv 14:48 has in fact not spread after the *p*,

PLATE (29)

Ex 25:11 *P* it inside and outside with pure gold,
25:13 poles of acacia wood and *p* them with gold.
25:24 *P* it with pure gold and make a molding of
25:28 shall make of acacia wood and *p* with gold.
26:29 *P* the boards with gold,
27: 2 You shall then *p* it with bronze.
27: 6 wood for the altar, and *p* them with bronze.
28:36 make a *p* of pure gold and engrave on it,
28:37 This *p* is to be tied over the miter with a
28:38 this *p* must always be over his forehead,
30: 3 and its horns you shall *p* with pure gold.
30: 5 too, of acacia wood and *p* them with gold.
39:30 The *p* of the sacred diadem was made of
Lv 8: 9 miter on his head, attaching the gold *p*,
Nm 7:13 His offering consisted of one silver *p*
7:19 *p* weighing a hundred and thirty shekels
7:25 His offering consisted of one silver *p*
7:31 His offering consisted of one silver *p*
7:37 His offering consisted of one silver *p*
7:43 His offering consisted of one silver *p*
7:49 His offering consisted of one silver *p*
7:55 His offering consisted of one silver *p*
7:61 His offering consisted of one silver *p*
7:67 His offering consisted of one silver *p*
7:73 His offering consisted of one silver *p*
7:79 His offering consisted of one silver *p*
7:85 *p* weighed a hundred and thirty shekels,
1Mc 15:32 the gold and silver *p* on the sideboard,
Sir 45:12 *p* wrought with the insignia of holiness,

PLATEAU (13)

Nm 21:20 from Bamoth to the cleft in the *p* of Moab
Dt 3:10 comprising all the cities of the *p*
4:43 in the desert, in the region of the *p*,
Ru 1: 1 and two sons to reside on the *p* of Moab.
1: 2 time after their arrival on the Moabite *p*,
1: 6 She then made ready to go back from the *p*
1:22 accompanied her back from the *p* of Moab.
2: 6 who returned from the *p* of Moab with Naomi.
4: 3 who has come back from the Moabite *p*,
1Chr 1:46 overthrew the Midianites on the Moabite *p*,
8: 8 became a father on the Moabite *p*
Tb 5: 6 at the mountains, Ecbatana out on the *p*."
Jer 48:21 For judgment has come on the land of the *p*:

PLATED (13)

Ex 26:29 the bars, which are also to be *p* with gold.
26:37 have them *p* with gold,
36:34 The boards were *p* with gold,
36:34 for the bars, which were also *p* with gold.
36:38 their capitals and bands, were *p* with gold;
37: 2 The inside and outside were *p* with gold,
37: 4 of acacia wood were made and *p* with gold;
37:11 It was *p* with pure gold,
37:15 were made of acacia wood and *p* with gold.
37:26 sides, and its horns were *p* with pure gold;
37:28 were made of acacia wood and *p* with gold.
38: 2 The whole was *p* with bronze.
38: 6 were made of acacia wood and *p* with bronze.

PLATES (6)

Ex 25:29 Of pure gold you shall make its *p* and cups,
37:16 that were set on the table, its *p* and cups,
Nm 4: 7 violet cloth and put on it the *p* and cups,
7:84 twelve silver *p*,
17: 3 them hammered into *p* to cover the altar,
Is 40:19 *p* with gold and fits with silver chains?

PLATFORM (7)

2Chr 6:13 He had made a bronze *p* five cubits long,
Neh 8: 4 *p* that had been made for the occasion;
9: 4 on the *p* of the Levites were Jeshua,
2Mc 13:26 But Lysias took the *p*,
Ez 16:24 a *p* and a dais in every public place.
16:31 building your *p* at every street corner and
16:39 to tear down your *p* and demolish your dais;

PLATING (1)

Ex 38:28 hooks on the columns, for *p* the capitals,

PLATTER (4)

Mt 14: 8 me the head of John the Baptizer on a *p*."
14:11 brought in on a *p* and given to the girl,
Mk 6:25 once, the head of John the Baptizer on a *p*."
6:28 in the head on a *p* and gave it to the girl,

PLAUSIBLE (1)

1Tm 4: 2 things taught by demons through *p* liars

PLAY (24)

Gn 4:21 of all who *p* the lyre and the pipe.
Ex 8:25 must not *p* false again by refusing to let
1Sm 16:16 you, he will *p* and you will feel better."
16:23 Saul, David would take the harp and *p*,
19:17 "Why did you *p* this trick on me?
1Chr 15:16 as chanters, to *p* on musical instruments,
16: 5 These were to *p* on harps and lyres,
2Mc 3:32 some foul *p* at the hands of the Jews,
Jb 13: 8 Do you *p* advocate on behalf of God?
40:29 Can you *p* with him, as with a bird?
Ps(s) 68:26 in their midst the maidens *p* on timbrels.
Prv 24: 2 violence, and their lips speak of foul *p*.
Wis 12:26 of punishment which was but child's *p*
Sir 1:26 *P* not the hypocrite before men;
29:14 and only the shameless would *p* him false;
Is 11: 8 The baby shall *p* by the cobra's den,
Hos 3: 3 not *p* the harlot Or belong to any man;
4:10 they shall *p* the harlot but not increase,
4:13 That is why your daughters *p* the harlot,
4:15 Though you *p* the harlot,
Mt 26:68 *P* the prophet for us, Messiah!
Mk 14:65 him and hit him, saying, *P* the prophet!"
Lk 22:64 *P* the prophet; which one struck you?"
Gal 6:12 are making a *p* for human approval

PLAYED (18)

Gn 38:24 daughter-in-law Tamar had *p* the harlot
Jgs 16:25 prison, and he *p* the buffoon before them.
1Sm 18: 7 The women *p* and sang:
2Kgs 3:15 When the minstrel *p*,
1Chr 15:20 and Benaiah, *p* on harps set to "Alamoth."
Jer 3: 6 every green tree she has *p* the harlot.
3: 8 she too went off and *p* the harlot.
Ez 16:16 gaudy high places, where you *p* the harlot. . . .
16:17 images, with which also you *p* the harlot.
16:26 You *p* the harlot with the Egyptians,
16:28 You also *p* the harlot with the Assyrians,
16:29 Again and again you *p* the harlot,
23: 3 even as young girls *p* the harlot in Egypt.
23:19 But she *p* the harlot all the more,
23:30 because you *p* the harlot with the nations
Hos 2: 7 Yes, their mother has *p* the harlot;
5: 3 Now Ephraim has *p* the harlot,
1Cor 14: 7 how will anyone know what is being *p*

PLAYERS (1)

Mt 9:23 *p* and the crowd who were making a din,

PLAYING (13)

Gn 21: 9 had borne to Abraham *p* with her son Isaac;
Jgs 11:34 came forth, *p* the tambourines and dancing.
1Sm 16:16 will look for a man skilled in *p* the harp.
18:10 attendance, *p* the harp as at other times,
19: 9 in hand and David was *p* the harp nearby.
23:22 perhaps they are *p* some trick on me).
1Kgs 1:40 *p* flutes and rejoicing so much as to split
Prv 8:30 day by day, *P* before him all the while,
8:31 the while, *p* on the surface of his earth;
Ez 16:25 passer-by, *p* the harlot countless times.
16:28 and after *p* the harlot with them,
Zec 8: 5 with boys and girls *p* in her streets.
Rv 14: 2 the melody of harpists *p* on their harps.

PLAYMATES (2)

Mt 11:16 in the town squares, calling to their *p*:
Lk 7:32 the city squares and calling to their *p*,

PLAYS (2)

Gal 2: 6 God *p* no favorites),
Eph 6: 9 have a Master in heaven who *p* no favorites.

PLAYTHING (1)

Wis 15:12 Instead, he esteemed our life a *p*,

PLEA (29)

Gn 30: 6 he has heeded my *p* and given me a son."
Ex 4: 1 will not believe me, nor listen to my *p*?
4: 9 even these two signs, nor heed your *p*,
5: 2 that I should heed his *p* to let Israel go?
Nm 27: 7 "The *p* of Zelophehad's daughters is just;
36: 1 came up and laid this *p* before Moses and
1Sm 19: 6 Saul heeded Jonathan's *p* and swore,
2Sm 13:14 Not heeding her *p*,
2Kgs 16: 7 king of Assyria, with the *p*:
2Chr 6:42 God, reject not the *p* of your anointed,
Jb 5: 8 to God, and to God I would state my *p*.
31:37 This is my final *p*;
34:28 so that he heard the *p* of the afflicted.
37:19 we cannot, for the darkness, make our *p*.
Ps(s) 5: 4 dawn I bring my *p* expectantly before you.
6:10 The LORD has heard my *p*;
109: 7 forth condemned, and may his *p* be in vain.
132:10 servant, reject not the *p* of your anointed.
Is 1:17 redress the wronged, hear the orphan's *p*,
1:23 not, and the widow's *p* does not reach them.
Jer 11:14 of this people, nor utter a *p* for them.
44: 4 with the *p* not to commit this horrible
Bar 2:19 do we base our *p* for mercy in your sight,
Mi 6: 1 Arise, present your *p* before the mountains,
6: 2 Hear, O mountains, the *p* of the LORD,
6: 2 For the LORD has a *p* against his people,

PLEA (cont.)

Mt 14:36 with the *p* that he let them do no more
15:25 forward then and did him homage with the *p*,
Rv 3:10 Because you have kept my *p* to stand fast,

PLEAD (17)

Gn 44:16 can we *p* or how try to prove our innocence?
Jos 20: 4 he shall *p* his case before the elders,
Est 4: 8 she was to *p* and intercede with him in
Jb 19:16 answer, though in my speech I *p* with him.
40:27 Will he then *p* with you,
Sir 33:21 wealth, lest then you have to *p* with him;
33:22 Far better that your children *p* with you
Is 32: 7 lies, and the needy when they *p* their case.
Jer 2:29 How dare you still *p* with me?
30:13 There is none to *p* your cause,
Bar 2: 8 and we did not *p* before the Lord,
Mt 7:22 When that day comes, many will *p* with me,
18:29 to his knees and began to *p* with him,
Lk 15:28 father came out and began to *p* with him.
Eph 4: 1 I *p* with you,
Phil 1: 4 rejoicing, as I *p* on your behalf,
4: 2 I *p* with Evodia just as I do with Syntyche:

PLEADED (15)

Gn 27:36 Then he *p*, "Haven't you saved a blessing
42:21 the anguish of his heart when he *p* with us,
1Sm 5:11 summons to all the Philistine lords and *p*:
2Mc 4:47 if they had *p* their case before Scythians.
15: 2 The Jews who were forced to follow him *p*,
Ps(s) 30: 9 with the LORD I *p*:
Wis 7: 7 I *p* and the spirit of Wisdom came to me.
18: 2 them, they thanked them, and *p* with them,
Jer 41: 8 were ten among them who *p* with Ishmael:
Mt 18:32 your entire debt when you *p* with me.
Mk 5:10 He *p* hard with Jesus not to drive them
Lk 8:31 They *p* with him not to order them back to
Jn 4:49 "Sir," the royal official *p* with him,
Rom 11: 2 Elijah, how he *p* with God against Israel?
1Thes 2:12 how we encouraged and *p* with you to make

PLEADING (15)

Gn 47:15 all the Egyptians came to Joseph, *p*,
2Kgs 1:13 to his knees before Elijah, *p* with him.
Ps(s) 28: 2 Hear the sound of my *p*,
28: 6 LORD, for he has heard the sound of my *p*;
31:23 the sound of my *p* when I cried out to you.
55: 2 turn not away from my *p*;
86: 6 my prayer and attend to the sound of my *p*.
143: 1 hearken to my *p* in your faithfulness;
Wis 12:20 punished them with such solicitude and *p*,
Jer 7:16 raise not in their behalf a *p* prayer!
31:18 I hear, I hear Ephraim *p*:
Dn 6:12 found Daniel praying and *p* before his God.
9: 3 to the Lord God, *p* in earnest prayer,
Rom 1:10 always *p* that somehow by God's will I may
Col 4:12 *p* earnestly in prayer that you stand firm,

PLEADS (3)

1Kgs 20:32 "Your servant Ben-hadad *p* for his life,"
Prv 18:17 *p* his case first seems to be in the right;
Is 59: 4 brings suit justly, no one *p* truthfully;

PLEASANT (17)

Gn 49:15 a settled life was, and how *p* the country,
2Mc 15:38 a more *p* drink that increases delight,
Ps(s) 16: 6 the measuring lines have fallen on *p* sites;
81: 3 sound the timbrel, the *p* harp and the lyre.
133: 1 Behold, how good it is, and how *p*,
141: 6 crag, and they heard how *p* were my words.
Prv 3:17 Her ways are *p* ways,
Eccl 11: 7 and it is *p* for the eyes to see the sun.
Wis 19:11 prompted by desire, they asked for *p* foods;
Is 27: 2 The *p* vineyard,
32:12 Beat your breasts for the *p* fields,
Jer 3:19 treat you as sons, And give you a *p* land,
42: 6 Whether it is *p* or difficult,
Ez 33:32 singer, with a *p* voice and a clever touch.
Hos 4:13 and terebinth, because of their *p* shade.
Mi 2: 9 people you drive out from their *p* houses;
Zec 7:14 they made the *p* land into a desert.

PLEASE (156)

Gn 12:13 *P* say, therefore, that you are my sister,
13: 9 *P* separate from me.
16: 6 Do to her whatever you *p*."
18: 3 favor, *p* do not go on past your servant.
18:32 *P*, let not my Lord grow angry if I speak
19: 2 with his face to the ground, he said, *P*,
19: 8 to you, and you may do to them as you *p*.
20:15 settle wherever you *p*."
23: 5 *P*, sir, listen to us!
23:11 *P*, sir, listen to me!
23:13 "Ah, if only you would *p* listen to me!
23:14 Ephron replied to Abraham, *P*.
24:14 if I say to a girl, *P* lower your jug,
24:17 *P* give me a sip of water from your jug."
24:23 Tell me, *p*, And is there room
24:43 *P* give me a little water from your jug,
24:45 I said to her, *P* let me have a drink.'
27:19 *P* sit up and eat some of my game,
27:31 and bringing it to his father, he said, *P*,
30:14 *P* let me have some of your son's mandrakes."
30:27 "If you will *p*. . . .
32:30 then asked him, "Do tell me your name, *p*."
33:10 me the favor, *p* accept this gift from me,
33:15 *P* indulge me in this, my lord."
34: 8 *P* give her to him in marriage.
37:16 "Could you *p* tell me where they are
38:25 *P* verify," she added, "whose seal
40: 8 *P* tell the dreams to me."
40:14 *p* do me the favor of mentioning me to
43:20 "If you *p*, sir," they said, "we came down
47: 4 *P*, therefore, let your servants settle
47:29 "If you really wish to *p* me,
50: 4 *P* do me this favor,"
50:17 *P* therefore, forgive the crime
Ex 4:10 however, said to the LORD, "If you *p*,
4:13 Yet he insisted, "If you *p*, Lord, send
4:18 and said to him, "Let me go back, *p*,
16:23 either bake or boil the manna, as you *p*;
Nm 10:31 Moses said, *P*, do not leave us;
11:15 *p* do me the favor of killing me at once,
12:11 *p* do not charge us with the sin that we
12:13 Then Moses cried to the LORD, *P*, not this!
22: 6 *P* come and curse this people for us;
22:11 *P* come and lay a curse on them for us;
22:16 *P* do not refuse to come to me.
22:17 *P* come and lay a curse on this people for
23:13 *P* come with me to another place from which
36: 6 They may marry anyone they *p*,
Jos 24:15 If it does not *p* you to serve the LORD,
Jgs 4:19 to her, *P* give me a little water to drink.
6:15 But he answered him, *P*, my lord,
10:15 Do to us whatever you *p*.
Ru 3: 1 I must seek a home for you that will *p* you.
1Sm 9:18 and said, *P* tell me where the seer lives."
11:10 you, and you may do whatever you *p* with us."
16:15 *P*! An evil spirit from God is tormenting
19: 2 *p* be on your guard tomorrow morning;
20:13 *p* my father to bring any injury upon you,
20:29 *P* let me go,' he begged, 'for we are
25: 8 *P* give your servants and your son David
25:24 *P* let your handmaid speak to you,
25:28 *P* forgive the transgression of your
26:19 *P*, now, let my lord the king listen
28:22 you, in turn, *p* listen to your maidservant.
2Sm 1: 9 Then he said to me, 'Stand up to me, *p*,
13: 5 *P* let my sister Tamar come and encourage
13: 6 *P* let my sister Tamar come and prepare
13: 7 *P* go to the house of your brother Amnon
13:13 So *p*, speak to the king; he will not keep
13:24 *P*, your majesty, come with all
13:26 *p* let my brother Amnon come to us."
14:11 But she went on to say, *P*, your majesty,
14:12 *P* let your servant say still another word
16: 9 Let me go over, *p*, and lop off his head."
17: 1 *P* let me choose twelve thousand men,
19:38 *P* let your servant go back to die in his
24: 3 But why does it *p* my lord the king to
1Kgs 2:17 he said, *P* ask King Solomon,
3:26 *P*, my lord, give her the living child— *p*
11:22 "Nothing," he said, "but *p* let me go!"
11:38 and *p* me by keeping my statutes and my
17:10 *P* bring me a small cupful of water to
17:11 after her, *P* bring along a bit of bread."
19:20 the oxen, ran after Elijah, and said, *P*,
2Kgs 2: 2 "Stay here, *p*," Elijah said to Elisha.
2: 4 Then Elijah said to him, "Stay here, *p*,
2: 6 Elijah said to Elisha, *P* stay here;
4:16 *P*, my lord," she protested, "you are a man
5:15 *P* accept a gift from your servant."
5:17 "If you will not accept, *p* let me,
5:22 *P* give them a talent of silver and two
5:23 *P* take two talents,"
6: 3 *P* agree to accompany your servants,"
16: 2 He did not *p* the LORD,
18:26 *P* speak to your servants in Aramaic;
2Chr 28: 1 He did not *p* the LORD as his forefather
Ezr 5:17 Now, if it *p* the king, let a search be made
Neh 2: 5 "If it *p* the king, and if your servant
2: 7 "If it *p* the king, let the letters be given
9:37 over our bodies and our cattle as they *p*.
Tb 3: 6 "So now, deal with me as you *p*,
3:15 But if it *p* you, Lord, not to slay me,
5:11 Tobit asked, "Brother, tell me, *p*,
10: 7 *P* let me go, for I know that my father
Jdt 3: 3 make use of them as you *p*.
9:12 *P*, please, God of my forefather,
Est 1:19 If it *p* the king, let an irrevocable royal
3: 9 If it *p* the king, let a decree be issued
3:11 this people, do with them whatever you *p*."
5: 4 "If it *p* your majesty," Esther replied,
2Mc 2:16 you also to *p* celebrate the feast.
2:25 aimed to *p* those who prefer simple reading,
7:16 men, mortal though you are, do what you *p*.
11:26 *p* send them messengers to give them our
Ps(s) 69:32 This will *p* the LORD more than oxen or
Prv 2:10 your heart, knowledge will *p* your soul,
10:32 The lips of the just know how to *p*,
Wis 14:19 mayhap in his determination to *p* the ruler,
Sir 2:16 Those who fear the LORD seek to *p* him,
Is 36:11 *P* speak to your servants in Aramaic;
Jer 6:20 no favor with me, your sacrifices *p* me not.
32: 8 guard and said, *P* buy my field in Anathoth,
36:17 "Tell us, *p*, how you came to write down
38:20 *P* obey the voice of the LORD and do as I
40: 4 if it does not *p* you to come to Babylon,
40: 5 him among the people, or go wherever you *p*."
Ez 16:37 all your lovers whom you tried to *p*,
Dn 1:12 Azariah, *P* test your servants for ten days.
Jon 4: 3 And now, LORD, *p* take my life from me;
Mt 9:18 *P* come and lay your hand on her and she
15:27 *P*, Lord," she insisted, "even the dogs eat
20:15 I am free to do as I *p* with my money,
Mk 5:23 *P* come and lay your hands on her so that
7:28 *P*, Lord," she replied, "even the dogs
9:22 heart you can do anything to help us, *p* do!"
Lk 14:18 *P* excuse me.'
14:19 *P* excuse me.'
Acts 9:38 request, *P* come over to us without delay."
13:15 to address to the people, *p* speak up."
21:23 *P* do as we tell you.
25: 9 But Festus, wishing to *p* the Jewish people,
Rom 8: 8 those who are in the flesh cannot *p* God.
15: 2 Each should *p* his neighbor so as to do him
15: 3 with Scripture, Christ did not *p* himself:
16: 2 *P* welcome her in the Lord,
1Cor 10:33 I try to *p* all in any way I can by seeking,
2Cor 5: 9 we make it our aim to *p* him whether we are
Gal 1:10 you say I am trying to *p* at this point
Eph 6: 6 service for appearance only and to *p* men,
1Thes 2: 4 we speak like those who strive to *p* God,
2Tm 2: 4 this in order to *p* his commanding officer.
Ti 2: 9 They should try to *p* them in every way,
Heb 11: 6 without faith, it is impossible to *p* him.
Jas 2: 3 man and say, "Sit right here, *p*,"

PLEASED (70)

Gn 41:37 advice *p* Pharaoh and all his officials.
45:16 had come, Pharaoh and his courtiers were *p*.
Nm 14: 8 If the LORD is *p* with us,
24: 1 that the LORD was *p* to bless Israel,
Jgs 14: 8 he returned to marry the woman who *p* him,
1Sm 18:20 it was reported to Saul, who was *p* at this,
18:26 he was *p* with the prospect of becoming the
29: 6 *p* to have you active with me in the camp,
2Sm 3:36 were *p* with everything that the king did.
15:26 But if he should say, 'I am not *p* with you,'
1Kgs 3:10 Lord was *p* that Solomon made this request.
5:21 the words of Solomon, Hiram was *p* and said,
10: 9 has *p* to place you on the throne of Israel.
14: 8 with his whole heart, doing only what *p* me.
15: 5 because David had *p* the LORD and did not
15:11 Asa *p* the LORD like his forefather David,
2Kgs 14: 3 He *p* the LORD, yet not like his forefather
15: 3 He *p* the LORD just as his father Amaziah
15:34 He *p* the LORD, just as his father Uzziah
18: 3 He *p* the LORD, just as his forefather
20:13 Hezekiah was *p* at this,
22: 2 He *p* the LORD and conducted himself
1Chr 28: 4 it *p* him to make me king over all Israel.
2Chr 9: 8 who has been so *p* with you as to place you
26: 4 He *p* the LORD, just as his father
27: 2 He *p* the LORD just as his father Uzziah
29: 2 He *p* the LORD just as his forefather David
34: 2 He *p* the LORD, following the path
Jdt 7:16 words *p* Holofernes and all his ministers,
11:20 words *p* Holofernes and all his servants;
15:10 and God is *p* with what you have wrought.
Est 2: 4 This suggestion *p* the king,
2: 9 The girl *p* him and won his favor.
2:14 *p* with her and had her summoned by name.
5:14 This suggestion *p* Haman,
9: 5 they did to their enemies as they *p*.
1Mc 8:21 The proposal *p* the Romans,
2Mc 1:20 Many years later, when it so *p* God,
Ps(s) 51: 8 Behold, you are *p* with sincerity of heart,
51:18 For you are not *p* with sacrifices;
51:21 Then shall you be *p* with due sacrifices,
147:10 not, nor is he *p* with the fleetness of men.
147:11 The LORD is *p* with those who fear him,
Prv 16: 7 When the LORD is *p* with a man's ways,
Wis 4:10 He who *p* God was loved;
Is 39: 2 Hezekiah was *p* at this,
42: 1 I uphold, my chosen one with whom I am *p*,
42:21 Though it *p* the LORD in his justice to
53:10 the LORD was *p* to crush him in infirmity.]
58: 2 what is due them, *p* to gain access to God.
Jer 9:23 For with such am I *p*,
18: 4 clay another object of whatever sort he *p*.
49: 9 by night, they would destroy as they *p*.
Dn 8: 4 it did what it *p* and became very powerful.
Hos 8:13 and eat it, the LORD is not *p* with them.
Mi 6: 7 Will the LORD be *p* with thousands of rams,
Mal 2:17 sight of the LORD, And he is *p* with him";
Mt 17:12 him and they did as they *p* with him.
Mk 9:13 They did entirely as they *p* with him,
Lk 12:32 has *p* your Father to give you the kingdom.
14:14 You should be *p* that they cannot repay you,
23: 8 Herod was extremely *p* to see Jesus.
Jn 21:18 your belt and went about as you *p*;
Acts 12: 3 he saw that this *p* certain of the Jews,
1Cor 1:21 it *p* God to save those who believe through
10: 5 know that God was not *p* with most of them,

Eph 1: 9 the plan he was *p* to decree in Christ,
Col 1:19 It *p* God to make absolute fullness reside
1Tm 2: 3 is good, and God our savior is *p* with it,
Heb 13:16 God is *p* by sacrifices of that kind.

PLEASES (30)

Lv 16: 2 to come whenever he *p* into the sanctuary,
Dt 23:17 in any one of your communities that *p* him.
Jgs 14: 3 his father, "Get her for me, for she *p* me."
Tb 4: 3 Do whatever *p* her,
Jdt 8:15 power to protect us at such time as he *p*,
Est 2: 4 *p* the king shall reign in place of Vashti."
5: 8 if it *p* your majesty to grant my petition
7: 3 with you, O king, and if it *p* your majesty,
8: 5 it *p* your majesty and seems proper to you,
9:13 So Esther said, "If it *p* your majesty,
Prv 21: 1 wherever it *p* him,
Eccl 8: 3 a base plot, for he does whatever he *p*,
Sir 20:26 by his words, a prudent man *p* the great.
20:27 he who *p* the great is pardoned his faults.
35: 3 To refrain from evil *p* the LORD,
39: 6 Then, if it *p* the LORD Almighty,
Is 56: 4 what *p* me and hold fast to my covenant,
Bar 4: 4 for what *p* God is known to us!
Ez 46: 5 for the ram, whatever he *p* for the lambs,
46:11 a ram, but for the lambs as much as one *p*,
Dn 4:32 he does as he *p* with the powers of heaven
11: 3 and rule with great might, doing as he *p*.
11:16 He shall attack him and do as he *p*,
11:36 "The king shall do as he *p*,
Mi 7: 3 for a price, The great man speaks as he *p*,
Jn 8:29 deserted me since I always do what *p* him."
Rom 14:18 this way *p* God and wins the esteem of men.
1Cor 15:38 God gives body to it as he *p*—
Eph 5:10 in your judgment of what *p* the Lord.
3Jn 1: 6 do a good thing if, in a way that *p* God,

PLEASING (46)

Gn 3: 6 the tree was good for food, *p* to the eyes,
Lv 2:12 not to be placed on the altar for a *p* odor.
4:31 it on the altar for an odor *p* to the LORD.
10:19 today, would it have been *p* to the LORD?"
17: 6 burn the fat for an odor *p* to the LORD.
Nm 15:24 a sweet-smelling oblation *p* to the LORD,
1Kgs 11:33 what is *p* to me according to my statutes
14:13 house has something *p* to the LORD,
2Kgs 12: 3 what was *p* to the LORD as long as he lived,
20: 3 in your presence, doing what was *p* to you!"
1Chr 13: 4 this, for the idea was *p* to all the people.
2Chr 14: 1 Asa did what was good and *p* to the LORD,
24: 2 Joash did what was *p* to the LORD as long
25: 2 He did what was *p* in the sight of the LORD,
Ezr 6:10 to offer sacrifices of *p* odor to the God
Jdt 12:14 Whatever is *p* to him I will promptly do.
Jb 34: 9 profits a man nought that he is *p* to God."
Ps(s) 104:34 *P* to him be my theme;
Prv 9:17 is sweet, and bread gotten secretly is *p!*"
15:26 LORD, but the pure speak what is *p* to him.
16:21 yet *p* speech increases his persuasiveness.
16:24 *P* words are a honeycomb,
24: 4 with every precious and *p* possession.
Eccl 7:26 He who is *p* to God will escape her,
12:10 Qoheleth sought to find *p* sayings,
Sg 7: 7 How beautiful you are, how *p*,
Wis 4:14 for his soul was *p* to the Lord,
9: 9 Who understands what is *p* in your eyes and
Sir 25: 1 for they are *p* to the LORD and to men:
35: 6 The just man's sacrifice is most *p*,
45: 9 through whose *p* sound at each step He
Is 38: 3 in your presence, doing what was *p* to you!"
Ez 20:41 As a *p* odor I will accept you,
Rom 12: 2 is God's will, what is good, *p* and perfect.
15:16 may be offered up as a *p* sacrifice,
1Cor 7:32 Lord's affairs, concerned with *p* the Lord;
7:33 demands and occupied with *p* his wife.
7:34 her and is concerned with *p* her husband.
Eph 5: 2 an offering to God, a gift of *p* fragrance.
Phil 4:18 a sacrifice acceptable and *p* to God.
Col 1:10 of the Lord and *p* to him in every way.
3:22 purpose of attracting attention and *p* men
1Thes 4: 1 to conduct yourselves in a way *p* to God
Heb 11: 5 before he was taken up, he was *p* to God
13:21 he carry out in you all that is *p* to him.
1Jn 3:22 and doing what is *p* in his sight.

PLEASURE (32)

Gn 18:12 is so old, am I still to have sexual *p?*"
1Chr 29:17 test and that you take *p* in uprightness.
Ezr 5:17 *p* in this matter be communicated to us."
Jdt 8:17 he will hear our cry if it is his good *p*.
Est 1: 8 to comply with the good *p* of everyone.
Jb 10: 3 Is it a *p* for you to oppress,
Prv 21:17 He who loves *p* will suffer want;
Eccl 2: 1 with *p* and the enjoyment of good things."
5: 3 For God has no *p* in fools;
12: 1 of which you will say, I have no *p* in them;
Wis 6:21 If, then, you find *p* in throne and scepter,
7: 2 man, and the *p* that accompanies marriage.
8:18 with Wisdom, and good *p* in her friendship,
9:10 with me, that I may know what is your *p*.
9:18 straight, and men learned what was your *p*,
Sir 9:10 you drink with *p* only when it has aged.
11:23 What further *p* can be mine?"
31: 3 up wealth, and his only rest is wanton *p*;
33:13 a potter, to be molded according to his *p*,
Is 1:11 of calves, lambs and goats I find no *p*.
66: 3 ways and taken *p* in their own abominations,
Jer 14:10 The LORD has no *p* in them;
Ez 18:23 derive any *p* from the death of the wicked?
18:32 have no *p* in the death of anyone who dies,
33:11 I take no *p* in the death of the wicked man,
Am 5:21 feasts, I take no *p* in your solemnities;
Hg 1: 8 I may take *p* in it and receive my glory,
Mal 1:10 I have no *p* in you,
1Cor 10: 7 eat and drink, and arose to take their *p*."
Eph 1: 5 such was his will and *p*—
2Tm 3: 4 lovers of *p* rather than of God as they
Heb 10:38 and if he draws back I take no *p* in him.

PLEASURES (5)

Sir 18:32 Have no joy in the *p* of a moment which
41: 1 successful, who still can enjoy life's *p*.
Lk 8:14 and *p* of life and they do not mature.
Ti 3: 3 of our passions and of *p* of various kinds.
Jas 4: 3 to squandering what you receive on your *p*.

PLEBEIAN (1)

Wis 18:11 even the *p* suffered the same as the king.

PLEDGE (50)

Gn 38:17 "provided you leave a *p* until you send it."
38:18 Judah asked, "What *p* am I to give to you?"
38:20 Adullamite to recover the *p* from the woman;
Ex 22:25 If you take your neighbor's cloak as a *p*,
Lv 5:21 a deposit or a *p* or a stolen article,
Nm 25:12 that I hereby give him my *p* of friendship,
25:13 him the *p* of an everlasting priesthood,
30: 3 himself under oath to a *p* of abstinence,
30: 4 vow to the LORD, or binds herself to a *p*,
30: 5 the *p* to which she bound herself
30: 5 vow or any *p* she has made remains valid.
30: 6 any *p* she has made becomes null and void;
30: 7 under a rash *p* to which she bound herself,
30: 8 the vow or *p* she had made remains valid.
30: 9 the rash *p* to which she had bound herself,
30:10 any *p* to which such a woman binds herself,
30:11 a vow or binds herself under oath to a *p*,
30:12 vow or any *p* she had made remains valid.
30:13 her vow or in her *p* becomes null and void;
30:14 "Any vow or any *p* that she makes under
30:15 as valid any vow or any *p* she has made;
Dt 24: 6 or even its upper stone as a *p* for debt,
24: 6 be taking the debtor's sustenance as a *p*.
24:10 enter his house to receive a *p* from him,
24:11 the loan brings his *p* outside to you.
24:12 not sleep in the mantle he gives as a *p*,
24:17 nor take the clothing of a widow as a *p*.
Jos 2:14 "We *p* our lives for yours,"
2Mc 10:28 the one having as *p* of success and victory
12:12 the *p* of friendship had been exchanged,
12:25 his solemn *p* to restore them unharmed,
13:22 giving them his *p* and receiving theirs,
Jb 17: 3 Grant me one to offer you a *p* on my behalf:
24: 3 they take the widow's ox for a *p*.
Prv 6: 1 neighbor, given your hand in *p* to another,
17:18 is the man who gives his hand in *p*,
20:25 to *p* a sacred gift is a trap for a man,
22:26 not one of those who give their hand in *p*,
Sir 8:13 think any *p* a debt you must pay.
29:16 turn a *p* on their behalf into misfortune,
Ez 17:18 Though he gave his hand in *p*,
18: 7 one, gives back the *p* received for a debt,
18:12 commits robbery, does not give back a *p*,
18:16 who does not oppress anyone, or exact a *p*,
Am 2: 8 in *p* they recline beside any altar;
Mi 2:10 For any trifle you exact a crippling *p*.
2Cor 5: 5 and has given us the Spirit as a *p* of it.
Eph 1:14 He is the *p* of our inheritance,
1Tm 5:12 condemnation for breaking their first *p*.
1Pt 3:21 but the *p* to God of an irreproachable

PLEDGED (4)

2Chr 32: 3 When they had *p* him their support,
Ezr 10:19 They *p* themselves to dismiss their wives,
Ps(s) 15: 4 it be to his loss, changes not his *p* word;
89:50 which you *p* to David by your faithfulness?

PLEDGES (4)

2Mc 4:34 through sworn *p* with right hands joined,
Prv 11:15 another, but he who hates giving *p* is safe.
Ez 33:15 what is right and just, giving back *p*,
Mt 5:33 rather, make good to the Lord all your *p*.'

PLEIADES (3)

Jb 9: 9 the *P* and the constellations of the south;
38:31 Have you fitted a curb to the *P*,
Am 5: 8 He who made the *P* and Orion,

PLENTEOUS (1)

Ps(s) 130: 7 is kindness and with him is *p* redemption;

PLENTIFUL (5)

Gn 28:14 shall be as *p* as the dust of the earth,
Ez 17: 5 A shoot by *p* waters,
17: 8 a fertile field by *p* waters it was planted,
Lk 18:30 who will not receive a *p* return in this age
Jn 3:23 at Aenon near Salim where water was *p*,

PLENTY (12)

Gn 24:25 is *p* of straw and fodder at our place,"
33: 9 "I have *p*," replied Esau; "you should keep
41:47 During the seven years of *p*,
41:48 these years of *p* that the land of Egypt
Ps(s) 37:19 in days of famine they have *p*.
Prv 12:11 He who tills his own land has food in *p*,
28:19 cultivates his land will have *p* of food,
Sir 10:26 Better the worker who has *p* of everything
18:25 the time of hunger in the time of *p*,
Is 58:11 and give you *p* even on the parched land.
Jn 6:10 there was *p* of grass for them to find a
2Cor 8:14 Your *p* at the present time should supply

PLIED (2)

Gn 19:33 that night they *p* their father with wine,
19:35 night, too, they *p* their father with wine,

PLIGHT (5)

Gn 21:17 has heard the boy's cry in this *p* of his.
31:42 But God saw my *p* and the fruits of my toil,
Ex 5:19 foremen knew they were in a sorry *p*,
Neh 2:17 "You see the evil *p* in which we stand:
Ps(s) 107:26 their hearts melted away in their *p*.

PLOT (34)

Gn 33:19 The *p* of ground on which he had pitched
Jos 24:32 were buried in Shechem in the *p* of ground
2Sm 23:11 there was a *p* of land full of lentils.
23:12 in the middle of the *p* and defended it.
2Kgs 9:26 repay you for it in that very *p* of ground,
9:26 So now take him into this *p* of ground,
12:21 *p* against him and killed him at Beth-millo.
Est 2:22 When the *p* became known to Mordecai,
E:23 who *p* against us a reminder of destruction.
1Mc 3:52 You know what they *p* against us.
9:60 however, because their *p* became known.
Ps(s) 35: 4 back and confounded who *p* evil against me.
52: 4 All the day you *p* harm;
83: 4 Against your people they *p* craftily;
Prv 3:29 *P* no evil against your neighbor,
12:20 Deceit is in the hands of those who *p* evil,
14:22 Do not those who *p* evil go astray?
24: 2 For their hearts *p* violence,
Eccl 8: 3 do not join in with a base *p*,
Sir 7: 8 Do not *p* to repeat a sin;
7:12 *P* no mischief against your brother,
Jer 18:18 "let us contrive a *p* against Jeremiah.
Ez 45: 2 Of this land a square *p*,
Zec 7:10 *p* evil against one another in your hearts.
8:17 of you *p* evil against another in his heart,
Mt 12:14 *p* against him to find a way to destroy him.
22:15 to *p* how they might trap Jesus in speech.
Mk 3: 6 they immediately began to *p* with the
Jn 4: 5 *p* of land which Jacob had given to his son
Acts 9:24 Saul, but their *p* came to his attention.
20: 3 *p* was hatched against him by certain Jews;
23:16 son of Paul's sister heard about the *p*,
23:30 be informed of a *p* against this man's life,
25: 3 Their *p* was to kill him on the way.

PLOTS (15)

Ps(s) 21:12 they intend evil against you, devising *p*,
37:12 The wicked man *p* against the just and
52: 9 wealth, and his strength in harmful *p*."
Prv 6:18 A heart that *p* wicked schemes,
24: 8 He who *p* evil doing
Wis 1: 4 into a soul that *p* evil wisdom enters not,
Sir 11:32 and *p* against your choicest possessions.
27:22 *p* mischief and no one can ward him off;
Is 7: 5 and the son of Remaliah] *p* against you,
Jer 11:15 in my house, while she prepares her *p?*
11:19 that they were hatching *p* against me:
Lam 3:60 vindictiveness, all their *p* against me.
3:61 insults, O LORD, [all their *p* against me],
Dn 11:24 and devise *p* against their strongholds;
11:25 because of the *p* devised against him.

PLOTTED (7)

Gn 37:18 he came up to them, they *p* to kill him.
1Kgs 15:27 *p* against him and struck him down at
16: 9 of half his chariots, *p* against him.
Neh 4: 2 Thereupon they all *p* together to come and
Est 2:21 *p* in anger to lay hands on King Ahasuerus.
Dn 13:61 they had *p* to impose on their neighbor:
Mt 26: 4 They *p* to arrest Jesus by some trick and

PLOTTER (3)

2Mc 3:38 an enemy or a *p* against the government,
4: 2 He dared to brand as a *p* against the
4:50 the chief *p* against his fellow citizens.

PLOTTERS (1)
Hos 7: 6 the *p* approach with hearts like ovens.

PLOTTING (8)
Est A:13 He overheard them *p*,
E: 3 even begin *p* against their own benefactors.
1Mc 11: 8 *P* evil against Alexander,
2Mc 14:26 said that Nicanor was *p* against the state,
Ps(s) 31:14 together against me, *p* to take my life.
Prv 6:14 perversity in his heart, is always *p* evil,
16:30 He who winks his eye is *p* trickery;
Ez 11: 5 of Israel, and what you are *p* I well know.

PLOTTINGS (2)
Ps(s) 31:21 shelter of your presence from the *p* of men;
Acts 20:19 came my way from the *p* of certain Jews.

PLOW (7)
Dt 22:10 *p* with an ox and an ass harnessed together.
Jb 4: 8 those who *p* for mischief and sow trouble,
Sir 38:25 can he become learned who guides the *p*,
Hos 10:11 was to be harnessed, Judah was to *p*,
Am 6:12 or can one *p* the sea with oxen?
Lk 9:62 "Whoever puts his hand to the *p* but keeps
1Cor 9:10 for the plowman should *p* in hope and the

PLOW-LAND (1)
1Chr 11:13 The *p* was fully planted with barley,

PLOWED (6)
Dt 21: 4 at a place that has not been *p* or sown,
Jgs 14:18 to them, "If you had not *p* with my heifer,
Ps(s) 129: 3 Upon my back the plowers *p*;
Jer 26:18 Zion shall become a *p* field,
Hos 10: 4 grows wild like wormwood in a *p* field!
Mi 3:12 of you, Zion shall be *p* like a field,

PLOWERS (1)
Ps(s) 129: 3 Upon my back the *p* plowed;

PLOWING (9)
Ex 34:21 during the seasons of *p* and harvesting.
1Sm 8:12 set them to do his *p* and his harvesting,
1Kgs 19:19 as he was *p* with twelve yoke of oxen;
19:21 *p* equipment for fuel to boil their flesh,
Jb 1:14 were *p* and the asses grazing beside them,
Sir 6:19 As though *p* and sowing,
38:26 His care is for *p* furrows,
Is 28:24 Is the plowman forever *p*,
Lk 17: 7 "If one of you had a servant *p* or herding

PLOWLAND (1)
Nm 21:30 Their *p* is ruined from Heshbon to Dibon;

PLOWMAN (4)
Ps(s) 141: 7 As when a *p* breaks furrows in the field,
Is 28:24 Is the *p* forever plowing,
Am 9:13 LORD, When the *p* shall overtake the reaper,
1Cor 9:10 for the *p* should plow in hope and the

PLOWMEN (1)
2Chr 26:10 He had *p* in the foothills and the plains,

PLOWS (2)
Prv 20: 4 In seedtime the sluggard *p* not;
Sir 25: 8 who *p* not like a donkey yoked with an ox.

PLOWSHARES (5)
1Sm 13:20 down to the Philistines to sharpen their *p*,
13:21 *p* and mattocks was two-thirds of a shekel,
Is 2: 4 into *p* and their spears into pruning hooks;
Jl 4:10 Beat your *p* into swords,
Mi 4: 3 They shall beat their swords into *p*,

PLUCK (9)
Dt 23:26 you may *p* some of the ears with your hand,
1Kgs 14:15 will *p* out Israel from this good land
Ps(s) 33: 3 *p* the strings skillfully,
52: 7 He shall *p* you from your tent,
Is 23:16 *P* the strings skillfully,
Jer 12:14 See, I will *p* them up from their land;
12:14 house of Judah I will *p* up in their midst.
24: 6 to plant them, not to *p* them out.
Mi 1:16 Make yourself bald, *p* out your hair,

PLUCKED (12)
Dt 28:63 and you will be *p* out of the land you are
Ezr 9: 3 my mantle, *p* hair from my head and beard,
Jb 4:21 The pegs of their tent are *p* up;
18:14 He is *p* from the security of his tent;
30: 4 They *p* saltwort and shrubs;
Ps(s) 129: 6 housetops, which withers before it is *p*;
Prv 30:17 Will be *p* out by the ravens in the valley;
Is 50: 6 beat me, my cheeks to those who *p* my beard;
Dn 7: 4 While I watched, the wings were *p*;
Am 4:11 you were like a brand *p* from the fire;
9:15 they be *p* From the land I have given them,
Gal 4:15 have *p* out your eyes and given them to me.

PLUCKED-OFF (1)
Gn 8:11 and there in its bill was a *p* olive leaf!

PLUCKING (1)
Jer 12:15 But after *p* them up,

PLUCKS (2)
Ps(s) 80:13 walls, so that every passer-by *p* its fruit,
Sir 10:15 The roots of the proud God *p* up,

PLUMAGE (3)
Jb 39:13 her *p* is lacking in pinions.
Ez 17: 3 wings, with long pinions, with thick *p*,
17: 7 great eagle, great of wing, rich in *p*;

PLUMB (1)
Jdt 8:14 You cannot *p* the depths of the human heart

PLUMBS (1)
Sir 42:18 He *p* the depths and penetrates the heart;

PLUMMET (5)
2Kgs 21:13 with the *p* I used for the house of Ahab.
Is 34:11 The LORD will measure her with line and *p*
Am 7: 7 he was standing by a wall, *p* in hand.
7: 8 And when I answered, "A *p*,"
7: 8 lay the *p* in the midst of my people Israel;

PLUNDER (52)
Dt 20:14 use this *p* of your enemies which the LORD,
1Sm 14:36 to *p* among them until daybreak and to kill
2Sm 3:22 an expedition, bringing much *p* with them.
8:12 Amalekites, and from the *p* of Hadadezer,
2Chr 20:25 Jehoshaphat and his people came to take *p*,
28: 8 they also took from them much *p*,
28:14 soldiers left their captives and the *p*
Jdt 2:11 slaughter and *p* in each country you occupy.
9: 4 Their wives you handed over to *p*,
Est 9:16 of their foes, without engaging in *p*,
1Mc 1: 3 the earth, gathering *p* from many nations;
1:35 the *p* they had collected from Jerusalem.
4:17 "Do not be greedy for the *p*,
4:18 Afterward you can freely take the *p*."
4:23 Then Judas went back to *p* the camp,
13:34 for all that Trypho did was to *p* the land.
2Mc 8:30 They divided the enormous *p*,
Ps(s) 62:11 in *p* take no empty pride;
109:11 and strangers *p* the fruit of his labors.
Prv 16:19 the meek than to share *p* with the proud.
22:23 will *p* the lives of those who plunder them.
Sir 16:13 A criminal does not escape with his *p*;
40: 9 wrath and the sword, *p* and ruin,
Is 10: 2 of their rights, Making widows their *p*,
10: 6 under my wrath I order him To seize *p*,
11:14 west, together they shall *p* the Kedemites;
17:14 who despoil us, the lot of those who *p* us.
59: 7 thoughts, *p* and ruin are on their highways.
60:18 land, or *p* and ruin within your boundaries.
Jer 12:14 all my evil neighbors who *p* the heritage
20: 5 will give as *p* into the hand of their foes,
30:16 All who *p* you shall be plundered,
50:10 Chaldea shall be their *p*,
50:11 rejoice and exult, you that *p* my portion;
Ez 23:46 and deliver them over to terror and *p*.
25: 7 I will make you *p* for the nations,
30:24 against Egypt so as to *p* and pillage it.
36: 5 their possession to be delivered over to *p*.
38:12 neither bars nor gates, to *p* and pillage,
38:13 "Is it for *p* that you have come?
38:13 away cattle and goods, to seize much *p*?"
39:10 Thus they shall *p* those who plundered them
Dn 11:33 of the sword, of flames, exile, and *p*.
Hos 7: 1 thieves break in, bandits *p* abroad.
Na 2:10 "Plunder the silver, *p* the gold!"
2:13 his dens with prey, and his caves with *p*.
3: 1 to the bloody city, all lies, full of *p*,
Zep 2: 9 The remnant of my people shall *p* them,
Zec 2:13 they become *p* for their slaves.
Mk 3:27 Only then can he *p* his house.

PLUNDERED (27)
2Kgs 7:16 went out and *p* the camp of the Arameans;
2Chr 28:21 Though Ahaz *p* the LORD's house and the
Jdt 2:23 and *p* all the Rassisites and the
2:26 burned their tents, and *p* their sheepfolds.
8:21 Judea will fall, our sanctuary will be *p*,
15: 6 down on the camp of the Assyrians, *p* it,
15:11 thirty days the whole populace *p* the camp,
1Mc 1:19 and Antiochus *p* the land of Egypt.
1:31 He *p* the city and set fire to it,
5:35 all the male population, *p* the place,
5:51 every male, razed and *p* the city,
6:24 as they could find and have *p* our estates.
8:10 They *p* them,
10:84 and *p* Azotus with its neighboring towns,
11:48 they set on fire and *p* on a large scale.
11:61 besieged it and burned and *p* its suburbs.
Ps(s) 44:11 those who hated us *p* us at will,
89:42 All who pass by the way have *p* him;
Is 13:16 houses shall be *p* and their wives ravished.
42:22 This is a people despoiled and *p*,
42:24 Who was it that gave Jacob to be *p*,
Jer 30:16 All who plunder you shall be *p*,
50:37 upon her treasures, that they may be *p*;
Ez 26:12 Your wealth shall be *p*,
39:10 *p* them and pillage those who pillaged them,
Zec 2:12 me) concerning the nations that have *p* you:
14: 2 the city shall be taken, houses *p*,

PLUNDERERS (4)
Jgs 2:14 them over to *p* who despoiled them.
2Kgs 17:20 them and delivered them over to *p*,
Jer 18:22 when suddenly you send *p* against them.
50:10 plunder, and all her *p* shall be enriched,

PLUNDERING (9)
Dt 20:14 that is worth *p* you may take as your booty,
1Sm 14:48 from the hands of those who were *p* them.
23: 1 Keilah and *p* the threshing floors.
Tb 3: 4 So you handed us over to *p*,
Est 9:10 However, they did not engage in *p*.
9:15 However, they did not engage in *p*.
1Mc 5:68 and after *p* their cities he returned to
12:31 called Zabadeans, overwhelming and *p* them.
Ez 29:19 *p* and pillaging it for the wages of his

PLUNGE (7)
2Mc 2:24 who wish to *p* into historical narratives
Jb 9:31 with lye, Yet you would *p* me in the ditch,
Ps(s) 46: 3 and mountains *p* into the depths of the sea.
Sir 12:16 heart he schemes to *p* you into the abyss.
Jn 5: 7 "I do not have anyone to *p* me into the
1Pt 4: 4 when you do not *p* into the same swamp
Rv 2:22 her companions in sin I will *p* into

PLUNGED (5)
2Kgs 5:14 So Naaman went down and *p* into the Jordan
Ps(s) 88: 7 You have *p* me into the bottom of the pit,
Mk 9:42 to be *p* in the sea with a great millstone
Rv 8:12 were hit hard enough to be *p* into darkness.
16:10 Its kingdom was *p* into darkness;

PLUNGES (2)
Prv 19:15 Laziness *p* a man into deep sleep,
Sir 1:19 anger *p* a man to his downfall.

PLUS (3)
Tb 5:15 wages, *p* expenses for you and for my son.
Ez 43:13 in cubits of one cubit *p* a handbreadth.
45:12 *p* fifteen shekels shall be your mina.

PLY (4)
Gn 19:32 let us *p* our father with wine and then lie
19:34 Let us *p* him with wine again tonight,
Prv 31:19 the distaff, and her fingers *p* the spindle.
Ez 27:29 from their ships come all who *p* the oar;

PLYING (1)
Wis 13:11 off all its bark, And deftly *p* his art,

POCHERETH-HAZZEBAIM (2)
Ezr 2:57 of Shephatiah, sons of Hattil, sons of *P*,
Neh 7:59 of Shephatiah, sons of Hattil, sons of *P*,

POCKET (1)
1Sm 17:40 put them in the *p* of his shepherd's bag.

POCKETED (1)
Mt 28:15 The soldiers *p* the money and did as they

POETS (2)
Nm 21:27 That is why the *p* say:
Acts 17:28 being,' as some of your own *p* have put it,

POINT (79)
Gn 22: 2 on a height that I will *p* out to you."
25:32 said Esau, "I'm on the *p* of dying.
35:18 for she was at the *p* of death
50: 5 Since my father, at the *p* of death,
Lv 26:33 the nations at the *p* of my drawn sword,
Nm 21:24 Israel defeated him at the *p* of the sword,
Jos 12: 3 to a *p* under the slopes of Pisgah.
15: 3 Zin, up to a *p* south of Kadesh-barnea,
Jgs 20:43 and were now pursued to a *p* east of Gibeah,
1Sm 4:19 with child and at the *p* of giving birth.
7:12 explaining, "To this *p* the LORD helped us."
16: 3 to anoint for me the one I *p* out to you."
2Sm 7:18 house, that you have brought me to this *p*?
2Kgs 19: 3 Children are at the *p* of birth,
1Chr 21:15 but as he was on the *p* of destroying it,
Neh 3:26 to a *p* opposite the Water Gate on the east,
Tb 8: 2 At this *p* Tobiah,
Est A: 8 them, and were at the *p* of destruction.

2Mc 4: 3 When Simon's hostility reached such a *p*
7: 9 At the *p* of death he said:
14:41 troops, on the *p* of capturing the tower,
15:38 If it is well written and to the *p*,
Sir 51: 6 I was at the *p* of death,
Is 37: 3 Children are at the *p* of birth,
66: 9 Shall I bring a mother to the *p* of birth,
Jer 17: 1 Engraved with a diamond *p*
26:19 But we are on the *p* of committing this
Ez 47:20 up to a *p* parallel to Labo of Hamath.
Dn 3: 8 At that *p*, some of the Chaldeans came
Jon 1: 4 arose the ship was on the *p* of breaking up.
Mt 17:19 Jesus at that *p* and asked him privately,
18:15 wrong against you, go and *p* out his fault,
19:13 At one *p*, children were brought to him
26: 8 "What is the *p* of such extravagance?
Mk 1:12 At that *p* the Spirit sent him out toward
1:28 From that *p* on his reputation spread
6:22 Herodias' own daughter came in at one *p*
14: 4 the *p* of this extravagant waste of perfume?
14:34 is filled with sorrow to the *p* of death.
Lk 5: 6 that their nets were at the breaking *p*.
7: 2 was at that moment sick to the *p* of death.
Jn 2: 3 At a certain *p* the wine ran out,
4:27 His disciples, returning at this *p*,
11:49 priest that year, addressed them at this *p*:
14: 7 From this *p* on you know him;
Acts 1:15 At one *p* during those days, Peter stood
4:21 At that *p* they were dismissed with further
8:35 this Scripture passage as his starting *p*,
10:46 Peter put the question at that *p*:
14:19 Just at that *p*, some Jews from Antioch
17:33 At this *p*, Paul left them.
20: 3 As he was on the *p* of embarking for Syria,
20:15 next day, and reached a *p* opposite Chios;
20:31 you individually even to the *p* of tears.
22: 4 persecuted this new way to the *p* of death.
22: 5 "On this *p* the high priest and the whole
22:22 Up to this *p* in his speech the crowd had
Rom 3:20 law does nothing but *p* out what is sinful.
15:20 It has been a *p* of honor with me never to
1Cor 8:10 to the *p* that he eats the idol-offering?
14:15 What is my *p* here?
2Cor 1: 8 even to the *p* of despairing of life.
11:30 boast, I will make a *p* of my weaknesses.
Gal 1:10 you say I am trying to please at this *p*—
3:17 My *p* is this:
4:30 What does Scripture say on the *p*?
5: 3 I *p* out once more to all who receive
5:16 My *p* is that you should live in accord
Phil 2:27 He was, in fact, sick to the *p* of death,
1Thes 4:11 Make it a *p* of honor to remain at peace
2Thes 3: 8 laboring to the *p* of exhaustion so as not
2Tm 2: 9 even to the *p* of being thrown into chains
Ti 3: 9 They are useless and have no *p*.
Heb 8: 1 The main *p* in what we are saying is this:
11:37 sawed in two, put to death at sword's *p*;
12: 4 yet resisted to the *p* of shedding blood.
Jas 2:10 Whoever falls into sin on one *p* of the law,
2:25 Rahab the harlot will illustrate the *p*.
2Pt 1: 9 is shortsighted to the *p* of blindness.
3: 8 This *p* must not be overlooked,

POINTED (13)

Ex 15:25 who *p* out to him a certain piece of wood.
32: 8 turned aside from the way I *p* out to them,
Dt 9:12 already turned aside from the way I *p* out
9:16 the way which the LORD had *p* out to you
Jgs 13:23 But his wife *p* out to him,
1Kgs 13:12 And his sons *p* out to him the road taken
2Kgs 6: 6 When he *p* out to the spot,
2Chr 3: 1 which had been *p* out to his father David,
2Mc 15:10 he gave his orders and *p* out at the same
Mt 24: 1 and his disciples came up and *p* out to him
Mk 14: 2 Yet they *p* out, "Not during the festival,
Lk 1:61 They *p* out to her, "None of your relatives
Acts 20:35 I have always *p* out to you that it is by

POINTING (4)

1Kgs 6:27 wing, *p* toward the middle of the room,
Acts 5:25 Someone then came up to them, *p* out,
Heb 6: 9 in your regard, things *p* to your salvation.
1Pt 1:11 the Spirit of Christ within them was *p* to,

POINTLESS (2)

Gal 2:21 I will not treat God's gracious gift as *p*.
Jas 1:26 his worship is *p*.

POINTS (5)

Lv 27:14 value in keeping with its good or bad *p*,
Neh 4: 7 behind the wall, near the exposed *p*,
2Mc 14:22 armed men in readiness at suitable *p*
Sir 37: 7 Every counselor *p* out a way,
Rom 2:18 able to make sound judgments on disputed *p*.

POISED (3)

1Sm 18:11 Saul *p* the spear,
Est 0: 5 great dragons came on, both *p* for combat.
Rv 9:19 were like snakes with heads *p* to strike.

POISON (14)

Dt 29:17 would bear such *p* and wormwood among you.
32:33 venom of dragons and the cruel *p* of cobras.
2Kgs 4:40 "Man of God, there is *p* in the pot!"
2Mc 10:13 high office, he ended his life by taking *p*.
Jb 6: 4 me, and my spirit drinks in their *p*;
20:16 The *p* of asps he shall drink in;
Ps(s) 58: 5 Theirs is *p* like a serpent's,
Sir 25:14 No *p* worse than that of a serpent,
Jer 8:14 destruction, he has given us *p* to drink,
9:14 give them wormwood to eat and *p* to drink.
23:15 give them wormwood to eat, and *p* to drink;
Mk 16:18 be able to drink deadly *p* without harm,
16:20 be able to drink deadly *p* without harm,
Jas 3: 8 It is a restless evil, full of deadly *p*.

POISONED (4)

Acts 8:23 *p* with gall and caught in the grip of sin."
14: 2 and *p* their minds against the brothers.
Rv 14: 8 nations drink the *p* wine of her lewdness!"
18: 3 nations drink the *p* wine of her lewdness.

POISONOUS (6)

Dt 32:32 *P* are their grapes and bitter their
Prv 23:32 it bites like a serpent, or like a *p* adder.
Wis 16:10 the fangs of *p* reptiles overcame your sons,
Jer 8:17 Yes, I will send against you *p* snakes,
Mt 7:10 loaf, or a *p* snake when he asks for a fish?
Acts 28: 3 brushwood he had collected, when a *p* snake,

POLE (14)

Nm 13:23 on it, which two of them carried on a *p*,
21: 8 "Make a saraph and mount it on a *p*,
21: 9 a bronze serpent and mounted it on a *p*,
Dt 16:21 "You shall not plant a sacred *p* of any
Jgs 6:25 and cut down the sacred *p* that is by it.
6:26 wood from the sacred *p* you have cut down."
6:28 destroyed, the sacred *p* near it cut down,
6:30 has cut down the sacred *p* that was near it."
1Kgs 16:33 built in Samaria, and also made a sacred *p*.
2Kgs 13: 6 sacred *p* also remained standing in Samaria.
17:16 *p* and worshiped all the host of heaven,
21: 3 altars to Baal, and also set up a sacred *p*,
23: 6 of the LORD he also removed the sacred *p*,
Is 9: 3 burdened them, the *p* on their shoulder,

POLEMICS (1)

1Tm 6: 4 man in his passion for *p* and controversy.

POLES (53)

Ex 25:13 *p* of acacia wood and plate them with gold.
25:14 These *p* you are to put through the rings
25:27 as holders for the *p* to carry the table.
25:28 These *p* for carrying the table you shall
27: 6 also make *p* of acacia wood for the altar,
27: 7 These *p* are to be put through the rings,
30: 4 as holders for the *p* used in carrying it.
30: 5 Make the *p*, too, of acacia wood
34:13 pillars, and cut down their sacred *p*.
35:12 the ark, with its *p*,
35:13 with its *p* and all its appurtenances,
35:15 the altar of incense, with its *p*;
35:16 with its bronze grating, its *p*,
37: 4 *P* of acacia wood were made and plated with
37:14 as holders for the *p* to carry the table.
37:15 These *p* were made of acacia wood and
37:27 side, as holders for the *p* to carry it.
37:28 The *p*, too, were made of acacia wood
38: 5 the bronze grating, as holders for the *p*,
38: 7 The *p* were put through the rings on the
39:35 the ark of the commandments with its *p*,
39:39 grating, its *p* and all its appurtenances,
40:20 he placed *p* alongside the ark and set the
Nm 4: 6 They shall then put the *p* in place.
4: 8 They shall then put the *p* in place.
4:11 They shall then put the *p* in place.
4:14 skin over this, and put the *p* in place.
Dt 7: 5 sacred pillars, chop down their sacred *p*,
12: 3 pillars, destroy by fire their sacred *p*,
1Kgs 8: 7 sheltering the ark and its *p* from above.
8: 8 The *p* were so long that their ends could
14:15 because they made sacred *p* for themselves
14:23 high places, pillars, and sacred *p*,
2Kgs 17:10 They set up pillars and sacred *p* for
18: 4 pillars, and cut down the sacred *p*
23:14 pieces the pillars, cut down the sacred *p*,
1Chr 15:15 the ark of God on their shoulders with *p*,
2Chr 5: 8 sheltering the ark and its *p* from above.
5: 9 The *p* were long enough so that their ends
14: 2 pillars, and cutting down the sacred *p*.
17: 6 high places and the sacred *p* from Judah.
19: 3 since you have removed the sacred *p* from
24:18 began to serve the sacred *p* and the idols;
31: 1 the sacred pillars, cut down the sacred *p*,
33: 3 altars for the Baals, made sacred *p*,
33:19 he built high places and erected sacred *p*
34: 3 sacred *p* and the carved and molten images.
34: 4 the sacred *p* and the carved and molten
34: 7 broke up the sacred *p* and carved images
Is 10:19 will be so few, Like *p* set up for signals,
17: 8 the sacred *p* or the incense stands.
27: 9 no sacred *p* or incense altars shall stand.
Jer 17: 2 remember their altars and their sacred *p*,
Mi 5:13 will tear out the sacred *p* from your midst,

POLICE (3)

1Chr 26:30 one thousand seven hundred *p* officers,
26:32 His brethren were also *p* officers,
Jer 29:26 may be *p* officers in the house of the LORD,

POLICED (1)

1Kgs 9:23 The supervisors of Solomon's works who *p*

POLICIES (1)

2Mc 4:21 that the king was opposed to his *p*;

POLICY (3)

2Mc 9:27 I am confident that, following my *p*,
11:24 our father's *p* concerning Greek customs
Sir 47:23 who by his *p* made the people rebel;

POLISH (1)

Jer 46: 4 *p* your spears,

POLISHED (7)

2Chr 4:16 from *p* bronze for the house of the LORD.
Ezr 8:27 two vases of excellent *p* bronze,
1Mc 13:27 a monument of stones, *p* front and back,
Sir 22:17 is like the *p* surface of a smooth wall.
Is 49: 2 He made me a *p* arrow,
Rv 1:15 gleamed like *p* brass refined in a furnace,
2:18 fire and whose feet gleam like *p* brass,

POLISHES (1)

Sir 12:11 Rub him as one *p* a brazen mirror,

POLLED (12)

Nm 1:20 who were fit for military service were *p*,
1:22 who were fit for military service were *p*,
1:24 who were fit for military service were *p*,
1:26 who were fit for military service were *p*,
1:28 who were fit for military service were *p*,
1:30 who were fit for military service were *p*,
1:32 who were fit for military service were *p*,
1:34 who were fit for military service were *p*,
1:36 who were fit for military service were *p*,
1:38 who were fit for military service were *p*,
1:40 who were fit for military service were *p*,
1:42 who were fit for military service were *p*,

POLLUTE (1)

Jude 1: 8 Similarly, these visionaries *p* the flesh;

POLLUTED (13)

Ex 7:18 and the river itself shall become so *p*
7:21 and the river itself became so *p* that the
Est C:27 abhor it like a *p* rag,
Prv 25:26 Like a troubled fountain or a *p* spring is
Is 24: 5 The earth is *p* because of its inhabitants,
64: 5 men, all our good deeds are like *p* rags;
Jer 3: 9 Eager to sin, she *p* the land,
Zep 3: 1 Woe to the city, rebellious and *p*,
Mal 1: 7 By offering *p* food on my altar!
1: 7 Then you ask, "How have we *p* it?"
1:12 the LORD's table and its offering may be *p*,
2Pt 2:20 When men have fled a *p* world by
Rv 8:11 Many people died from this *p* water.

POLLUTING (1)

2Chr 36:14 *p* the LORD's temple

POLLUTION (1)

2Pt 2:20 are caught up and overcome in *p* once more,

POMEGRANATE (6)

Ex 28:34 first a gold bell, then a *p*,
39:26 first a bell, then a *p*,
1Sm 14: 2 (Saul's command post was under the *p* tree
Sg 8: 2 give you spiced wine to drink and *p* juice.
Jl 1:12 The *p*, the date palm also, and the apple,
Hg 2:19 fig, the *p* and the olive tree yet borne.

POMEGRANATES (21)

Ex 28:33 the hem at the bottom you shall make *p*,
39:24 the hem of the robe *p* were made of violet,
39:25 the *p* all around the hem of the robe:
Nm 13:23 on a pole, as well as some *p* and figs.
20: 5 has neither grain nor figs nor vines nor *p*?
Dt 8: 8 and barley, of vines and fig trees and *p*,
1Kgs 7:18 Four hundred *p* were also cast;
7:42 four hundred *p* in double rows on both
2Kgs 25:17 and a network with *p* encircled the capital,
2Chr 3:16 a hundred *p* which he set on the chains.
4:13 also four hundred *p* for the two networks,
4:13 with two rows of *p* to each network,
Tb 1: 7 the tithe of grain, wine, olive oil, *p*,
Sg 4:13 You are a park that puts forth *p*,

POMEGRANATES (cont.)

6:11 if the *p* had blossomed.
7:13 buds have opened if the *p* have blossomed;
Sir 45: 8 and tunic and robe with *p* around the hem,
Jer 52:22 and a network with *p* encircled the capital,
52:22 The *p* . . .
52:23 there were ninety-six *p*.
52:23 There were a hundred *p*,

POMP (7)

1Mc 10:60 So he went with *p* to Ptolemais,
10:86 city came out to meet him with great *p*.
11: 6 Jonathan met the king with *p* at Joppa,
11:60 Ashkalon, the citizens welcomed him with *p*.
2Mc 4:22 *p* by Jason and the people of the city,
Is 14:11 Down to the nether world your *p* is brought,
Acts 25:23 Agrippa and Bernice came with great *p*

POMPOUS (1)

2Tm 3: 4 They will be treacherous, reckless, *p*,

PONDER (8)

Dt 30: 1 dispersed you, you *p* them in your heart:
Ps(s) 48:10 God, we *p* your kindness within your temple.
64:10 the work of God, and *p* what he has done.
77: 4 when I *p*, my spirit grows faint.
77: 7 I *p*, and my spirit broods:
77:13 your exploits I *p*.
143: 5 your doings, the works of your hands I *p*.
Is 52:15 see, those who have not heard shall *p* it.

PONDERED (1)

Gn 37:11 up against him but his father *p* the matter.

PONDERING (2)

Is 14:16 they see you they will stare, *p* over you:
Acts 10:19 *p* the vision when the Spirit said to him:

PONDERS (1)

Sir 14:21 Who *p* her ways in his heart,

PONDS (1)

Sir 43:21 he sends that turn the *p* to lumps of ice.

PONTIFICATE (1)

1Mc 16:24 are recorded in the chronicle of his *p*,

PONTIUS (3)

Lk 3: 1 when *P* Pilate was procurator of Judea,
Acts 4:27 Herod and *P* Pilate in league with the
1Tm 6:13 made his noble profession before *P* Pilate,

PONTUS (3)

Acts 2: 9 in Mesopotamia, Judea and Cappadocia, *P*,
18: 2 a native of *P* recently arrived from Italy
1Pt 1: 1 live as strangers scattered throughout *P*,

POOL (27)

Jgs 1:15 Caleb gave her the upper and the lower *p*.
2Sm 2:13 set out and met them at the *p* of Gibeon.
2:13 the *p* and the other on the opposite side.
4:12 feet, hanging them up near the *p* in Hebron.
1Kgs 22:38 the chariot was washed at the *p* of Samaria,
2Kgs 18:17 *p* on the highway of the fuller's field.
20:20 and his construction of the *p* and conduit
Neh 2:14 to the Spring Gate and to the King's *P*.
3:15 also repaired the wall of the Aqueduct *P*
3:16 far as the artificial *p* and the barracks.
1Mc 9:33 camped by the waters of the *p* of Asphar.
2Mc 12:16 slaughter on it that the adjacent *p*,
Sir 43:21 and clothes each *p* with a coat of mail.
50: 3 dug, the *p* with a vastness like the sea's.
Is 7: 3 at the end of the conduit of the upper *p*,
22: 9 you collected the water of the lower *p*.
22:11 the two walls for the water of the old *p*.
36: 2 he stopped at the conduit of the upper *p*,
Na 2: 9 Nineveh is like a *p* whose waters escape;
Jn 5: 2 Now in Jerusalem by the Sheep *P* there is a
5: 7 the *p* once the water has been stirred up.
9: 7 he told him, "Go, wash in the *p* of Siloam."
Rv 19:20 alive into the fiery *p* of burning sulphur.
20:10 was hurled into the *p* of burning sulphur,
20:14 world were hurled into the *p* of fire,
20:15 the living was hurled into this *p* of fire.
21: 8 lot is the fiery *p* of burning sulphur,

POOLS (9)

Ex 7:19 their streams and canals and *p*,
8: 1 staff over the streams and canals and *p*,
Jos 15:19 land in the Negeb, give me also *p* of water."
15:19 So he gave her the upper and the lower *p*.
Jgs 1:15 the Negeb to me, give me also *p* of water."
Ps(s) 107:35 He changed the desert into *p* of water,
114: 8 Jacob, Who turned the rock into *p* of water,
Sg 7: 5 *p* in Heshbon by the gate of Bath-rabbim.
Is 35: 7 The burning sands will become *p*,

POOR (179)

Ex 6:12 will listen to me, *p* speaker that I am!"
6:30 to the LORD, "Since I am a *p* speaker,
22:24 to one of your *p* neighbors among my people,
23: 3 You shall not favor a *p* man in his lawsuit.
23:11 that the *p* among you may eat of it and the
23:11 of the field may eat what the *p* leave.
30:15 not give more, nor shall the *p* give less,
Lv 14:21 "If a man is *p* and cannot afford so much,
19:10 you shall leave for the *p* and the alien.
23:22 you shall leave for the *p* and the alien.
27: 8 the vow is too *p* to meet the fixed sum,
Dt 15:11 your *p* and needy kinsman in your country.
24:12 If he is a *p* man, you shall not sleep
24:14 not defraud a *p* and needy hired servant,
24:15 since he is *p* and looks forward to them.
Ru 3:10 after the young men, whether *p* or rich.
1Sm 2: 7 The LORD makes *p* and makes rich,
2: 8 from the ash heap he lifts up the *p*,
18:23 I am *p* and insignificant."
2Sm 12: 1 there were two men, one rich, the other *p*.
12: 3 But the *p* man had nothing at all except
12: 4 Instead he took the *p* man's ewe lamb and
2Kgs 24:14 among the people of the land except the *p*.
25:12 But some of the country's *p*,
Tb 2: 2 go out and try to find a *p* man from among
2: 3 out to look for some *p* kinsman of ours.
4: 7 not turn your face away from any of the *p*,
Est 9:22 food to one another and gifts to the *p*.
2Mc 4:47 while he condemned to death those *p* men
Jb 5:15 But the *p* from the edge of the sword and
20:19 Because he has oppressed the *p*,
24: 4 the *p* of the land are driven into hiding.
24:14 murderer rises, to kill the *p* and needy.
29:12 For I rescued the *p* who cried out for help,
31:16 If I have denied anything to the *p*,
31:19 clothing, or a *p* man without covering,
34:19 nor respects the rich more than the *p*?
34:28 But caused the cries of the *p* to reach him,
Ps(s) 34:11 The great grow *p* and hungry;
37:14 bow to bring down the afflicted and the *p*,
40:18 Though I am afflicted and *p*,
41: 2 he who has regard for the lowly and the *p*;
49: 3 birth or high degree, rich and *p* alike.
69:34 For the LORD hears the *p*,
70: 6 But I am afflicted and *p*;
72: 4 the people, save the children of the *p*,
72:12 shall rescue the *p* man when he cries out,
72:13 for the lowly and the *p*; the lives of the *p*
74:21 the afflicted and the *p* praise your name.
82: 4 Rescue the lowly and the *p*;
86: 1 answer me, for I am afflicted and *p*.
109:16 the wretched and *p* and the brokenhearted,
109:22 For I am wretched and *p*,
109:31 he stood at the right hand of the *p* man,
112: 9 Lavishly he gives to the *p*;
113: 7 lifts up the *p* To seat them with princes,
132:15 provision, her *p* I will fill with bread.
140:13 to the afflicted, judgment to the *p*.
Prv 13: 7 another pretends to be *p*,
13: 8 his life, but the *p* man heeds no rebuke.
13:23 A lawsuit devours the tillage of the *p*,
14:20 Even by his neighbor the *p* man is hated,
14:21 but happy is he who is kind to the *p*!
14:31 who oppresses the *p* blasphemes his Maker,
17: 5 He who mocks the *p* blasphemes his Maker;
18:23 The *p* man implores, but the rich man
19: 1 Better a *p* man who walks in his integrity
19: 4 but the friend of the *p* man deserts him.
19: 7 All the *p* man's brothers hate him;
19:17 has compassion on the *p* lends to the LORD,
19:22 rather be a *p* man than a liar.
21:13 *p* will himself also call and not be heard.
22: 2 Rich and *p* have a common bond:
22: 7 The rich rule over the *p*,
22: 9 for he gives of his sustenance to the *p*.
22:16 He who oppresses the *p* to enrich himself
22:22 Injure not the poor because they are *p*,
28: 3 A rich man who oppresses the *p* is like a
28: 6 Better a *p* man who walks in his integrity
28: 8 gathers it for him who is kind to the *p*.
28:11 *p* man who is intelligent sees through him.
28:15 bear is a wicked ruler over a *p* people.
28:27 He who gives to the *p* suffers no want,
29: 7 man has a care for the rights of the *p*;
29:13 *p* and the oppressor have a common bond:
29:14 a king is zealous for the rights of the *p*,
30:14 from the earth, and the *p* from among men.
31: 9 what is just, defend the needy and the *p*!
31:20 She reaches out her hands to the *p*,
Eccl 4:13 Better is a *p* but wise youth than an old
4:14 even in his royalty he was *p* at birth.
5: 7 If you see oppression of the *p*,
6: 8 or what advantage has the *p* man in
9:15 But in the city lived a man who, though *p*,
9:15 Yet no one remembered this *p* man.
9:16 yet the wisdom of the *p* man is despised
Sir 4: 1 son, rob not the *p* man of his livelihood;
4: 4 avert not your face from the *p*.
4: 8 Give a hearing to the *p* man,
7:32 To the *p* man also extend your hand,
10:22 just to despise a man who is wise but *p*,
10:29 The *p* man is honored for his wisdom as the
11: 1 The *p* man's wisdom lifts his head high and
11:21 in an instant, to make a *p* man rich.
13: 3 the *p* man is wronged and begs forgiveness.
13:17 the rich and the *p* can there be peace?
13:18 too the *p* are feeding grounds for the rich.
13:19 so does the rich man abhor the *p*.
13:20 *p* man trips he is pushed down by a friend.
13:21 When a *p* man speaks they make sport of him;
13:22 A *p* man speaks and they say:
21: 5 from a *p* man's lips is heard at once,
22:23 fast friends with a man while he is *p*;
26: 4 Be he rich or *p*, his heart is content,
29: 8 To a *p* man, however, be generous;
29:22 Better a *p* man's fare under the shadow of
30:14 Better a *p* man strong and robust,
31: 4 The *p* man toils for a meager subsistence,
34:20 sacrifice from the possessions of the *p*.
Is 3:14 loot wrested from the *p* is in your house.
3:15 grinding down the *p* when they look to you?
10: 2 and robbing my people's *p* of their rights,
11: 4 But he shall judge the *p* with justice,
14:30 In my pastures the *p* shall eat,
25: 4 For you are a refuge to the *p*,
26: 6 by the needy, by the footsteps of the *p*.
29:19 the *p* rejoice in the Holy One of Israel.
32: 7 How to ruin the *p* with lies,
Jer 5:28 fatherless or judging the cause of the *p*.
20:13 life of the *p* from the power of the wicked!
22:16 he dispensed justice to the weak and the *p*,
39:10 But some of the *p* who had no property were
40: 7 *p* who had not been led captive to Babylon,
52:16 But some of the country's *p*,
Bar 6:27 do not share it with the *p* and the weak;
Ez 16:49 and they gave no help to the *p* and needy.
18:12 of his neighbor, oppresses the *p* and needy,
22:29 they afflict the *p* and the needy,
Dn 4:24 and for your misdeeds by kindness to the *p*;
Am 2: 6 and the *p* man for a pair of sandals.
8: 4 the needy and destroy the *p* of the land!
8: 6 and the *p* man for a pair of sandals;
Zec 7:10 widow or the orphan, the alien or the *p*;
Mt 5: 3 "How blest are the *p* in spirit:
11: 5 the *p* have the good news preached to them.
19:21 sell your possessions, and give to the *p*.
26: 9 a good price and the money given to the *p*."
26:11 The *p* you will always have with you but
Mk 10:21 and sell what you have and give to the *p*;
12:42 but one *p* widow came and put in two small
12:43 "I want you to observe that this *p* widow
14: 5 silver pieces and the money given to the *p*."
14: 7 The *p* you will always have with you and
Lk 4:18 sent me to bring glad tidings to the *p*,
6:20 "Blest are you *p*;
7:22 the *p* have the good news preached to them.
14:21 town and bring in the *p* and the crippled,
18:22 Sell all you have and give to the *p*.
19: 8 give half my belongings, Lord, to the *p*.
21: 2 also a *p* widow putting in two copper coins.
21: 3 *p* widow has put in more than all the rest.
Jn 12: 5 and the money have been given to the *p*."
12: 6 did not say this out of concern for the *p*,
12: 8 The *p* you always have with you,
13:29 the feast, or to give something to the *p*.)
1Cor 13: 3 the *p* and hand over my body to be burned,
2Cor 6:10 *p*, yet we enrich many.
8: 9 sake he made himself *p* though he was rich,
8:10 some advice on this matter of rich and *p*.
9: 9 "He scattered abroad and gave to the *p*,
Gal 2:10 was that we should be mindful of the *p*—
Jas 2: 2 at the same time a *p* man in shabby clothes.
2: 3 whereas you were to say to the *p* man,
2: 5 Did not God choose those who are *p* in the
2: 6 Yet you treated this *p* man shamefully.
Rv 3:17 how wretched you are, how pitiable and *p*,
13:16 all men, small and great, rich and *p*,

POORER (1)

Prv 11:24 another is too sparing, yet is the *p*.

POORLY (2)

2Mc 15:38 if it is *p* done and mediocre,
1Cor 4:11 very hour we go hungry and thirsty, *p* clad,

POPLAR (2)

Gn 30:37 however, got some fresh shoots of *p*,
Hos 4:13 incense, Beneath oak and *p* and terebinth,

POPLARS (5)

Lv 23:40 and boughs of myrtles and of valley *p*,
Jb 40:22 all about him are the *p* on the bank.
Sir 50:13 their dignity clustered around him like *p*,
Is 15: 7 away they carry across the Gorge of the *P*,
44: 4 verdure like *p* beside the flowing waters.

POPULACE (11)

Jdt 15:11 thirty days the whole *p* plundered the camp,
Est 1:11 her beauty to the *p* and the officials,
1:16 but all the officials and the *p* throughout
1Mc 11:45 delighted over their arrival, for the *p*,

11:46 while the *p* gained control of the main
11:49 When the *p* saw that the Jews held the city
2Mc 3:21 It was pitiful to see the *p* variously
12: 9 them, he attacked the Jamnian *p* by night,
Sir 7: 7 Be guilty of no evil before the city's *p*,
Lk 7:29 The entire *p* that had heard Jesus,
19:48 for indeed the entire *p* was listening to

POPULAR (2)

Sir 20:12 A wise man makes himself *p* by a few words,
Ez 36: 3 and have become a byword and a *p* jeer;

POPULATION (9)

Lv 26:22 till your *p* dwindles away and your roads
Jos 8:25 thousand men and women, the entire *p* of Ai.
1Sm 7: 2 the whole Israelite *p* turned to the LORD.
Neh 7: 4 wide and spacious but its *p* was small,
1Mc 5:28 He slaughtered all the male *p*,
5:35 he killed all the male *p*,
2Mc 12: 7 later and wipe out the entire *p* of Joppa.
12:13 and inhabited by a mixed *p* of Gentiles.
Lk 8:37 the entire *p* of the Gerasene territory

POPULOUS (1)

Gn 18:18 that he is to become a great and *p* nation,

PORATHAI (1)

Est 9: 8 killed Parshandatha, Dalphon, Aspatha, *P*,

PORCH (8)

1Kgs 6: 3 The *p* in front of the temple was twenty
7: 6 The *p* of the columned hall he made fifty
7: 6 *p* extended the width of the columned hall,
7:12 of the temple of the LORD and the temple *p*.
7:21 erected adjacent to the *p* of the temple,
2Chr 3: 4 the *p* which lay before the nave along the
8:12 LORD which he had built in front of the *p*,
Jl 2:17 the *p* and the altar let the priests,

PORCIUS (1)

Acts 24:27 which Felix was succeeded by *P* Festus.

PORK (3)

2Mc 6:18 being forced to open his mouth to eat *p*.
7: 1 them to eat *p* in violation of God's law.
7: 7 "Will you eat the *p* rather than have your

PORPHYRY (1)

Est 1: 6 were on the pavement, which was of *p*,

PORT (8)

2Chr 2:15 float them down to you at the *p* of Joppa,
Ezr 3: 7 trees from the Lebanon to the *p* of Joppa,
1Mc 14: 5 As his crowning glory he captured the *p* of
2Mc 14: 1 had sailed into the *p* of Tripolis with a
Is 23: 1 ships of Tarshish, for your *p* is destroyed;
Acts 13: 4 went down to the *p* of Seleucia and set
18:18 At the *p* of Cenchreae he shaved his head
27:12 This was a Cretan *p* exposed on the

PORTALS (5)

Est D: 6 She passed through all the *p* till she
Ps(s) 24: 7 reach up, you ancient *p*,
24: 9 reach up, you ancient *p*,
Wis 19:17 those others had been at the *p* of the just
Mi 7: 5 in your bosom guard the *p* of your mouth.

PORTENT (2)

Ps(s) 71: 7 A *p* am I to many,
Is 20: 3 as a sign and *p* against Egypt and Ethiopia,

PORTENTS (6)

1Chr 16:12 deeds that he has wrought, his *p*,
Ps(s) 105: 5 wondrous deeds that he has wrought, his *p*,
Wis 10:16 withstood fearsome kings with signs and *p*;
Is 8:18 we are signs and *p* in Israel from the LORD
Lam 2:14 for you in vision false and misleading *p*.
Lk 12:56 you can interpret the *p* of earth and sky,

PORTICO (4)

1Chr 28:11 of the *p* and of the building itself,
Jn 10:23 in the temple area, in Solomon's *P*,
Acts 3:11 over to them excitedly in Solomon's *P*.
5:12 agreement they used to meet in Solomon's *P*.

PORTICOES (1)

Jn 5: 2 Its five *p* were crowded with sick people

PORTION (65)

Gn 31:14 we still an heir's *p* in our father's house?
43:34 *p* was five times as large as anyone else's.
Ex 16: 4 are to go out and gather their daily *p*;
29:26 this is to be your own *p*.
Lv 6:10 as their *p* from the oblations of the LORD;
7:24 one *p* as a contribution to the LORD
7:33 shall have the right leg as his *p*,
8:29 was Moses' own *p* of the ordination ram.
Nm 18:20 hold any *p* among them; I will be your *p*
Dt 26:13 sacred *p* and I have given it to the Levite,
32: 9 While the LORD's own *p* was Jacob,
33:21 be his when the princely *p* was assigned,
Jos 15:13 son of Jephunneh, a *p* among the Judahites,
17: 6 Manasseh received each a *p* among his sons.
19: 9 the *p* of the latter was too large for them,
22: 7 to the other half Joshua had given a *p*
1Sm 1: 4 he used to give a *p* each to his wife
1: 5 a double *p* to Hannah because he loved her,
9:23 the *p* I gave you and told you to put aside."
9:24 a reserved *p* that has been set before you.
2Sm 11: 8 and a *p* was sent out after him from the
20: 1 and cried out, "We have no *p* in David,
2Kgs 2: 9 "May I receive a double *p* of your spirit."
2Chr 31: 3 the king allotted a *p* for holocausts,
Est C: 9 Do not spurn your *p*,
Jb 20:29 This is the *p* of a wicked man,
21:17 upon them, the *p* he allots in his anger?
24:18 Their *p* in the land is accursed,
27:13 This is the *p* of a wicked man from God,
31:17 widow to languish While I ate my *p* alone,
Ps(s) 16: 5 O LORD, my allotted *p* and my cup,
17:14 men whose *p* in life is in this world,
73:26 is the rock of my heart and my *p* forever.
142: 6 my refuge, my *p* in the land of the living."
Wis 2: 9 tokens of our rejoicing, for this our *p* is,
Sir 7:31 give him his *p* as you have been commanded:
14:14 good things, let no choice *p* escape you.
17:14 a ruler, but the LORD's own *p* is Israel.
24:12 the glorious people, in the *p* of the LORD,
44: 2 The abounding glory of the Most High's *p*,
45:20 to him, with the showbread as his *p*;
45:22 For the LORD himself is his *p*,
48:12 filled with a twofold *p* of his spirit,
Is 17:14 Such is the *p* of those who despoil us,
40:20 the choice *p* which a skilled craftsman
53:12 I will give him his *p* among the great,
57: 6 the smooth stones of the wadi is your *p*,
61: 7 and disgrace and spittle were their *p*,
Jer 6: 3 pitch their tents, each one grazes his *p*.
10:16 Not like these is the *p* of Jacob:
12:10 The *p* that delighted me they have turned
13:25 lot, the *p* measured out to you from me,
50:11 rejoice and exult, you that plunder my *p*;
51:19 Not like these is the *p* of Jacob,
Lam 3:24 My *p* is the LORD,
Ez 47:14 All of you shall have a like *p* in this
Dn 1: 5 *p* of food and wine from the royal table.
Ob 1:17 But on Mount Zion there shall be a *p* saved;
Hb 1:16 For thanks to them his *p* is generous,
Zec 2:16 possess Judah as his *p* of the holy land,
Lk 10:42 *p* and she shall not be deprived of it."
Acts 2:17 pour out a *p* of my spirit on all mankind:
2:18 pour out a *p* of my spirit in those days,
8:21 You can have no *p* or lot in this affair.
26:18 of their sins and a *p* among God's people.'

PORTIONED (1)

Mi 2: 4 our fields are *p* out among our captors,

PORTIONS (28)

Gn 43:34 *p* were brought to them from Joseph's table,
Lv 8:26 on top of the *p* of fat and the right leg.
9:19 The *p* of fat from the ox and from the ram,
10:15 in with the oblations, the fatty *p*,
22: 6 sacred *p* until he has first bathed his body
Nm 22:40 and sent *p* to Balaam and to the princes
Dt 18: 1 oblations of the LORD and the *p* due to him.
18: 8 then receive the same *p* to eat as the rest,
Jos 13:32 These are the *p* which Moses gave when he
14: 1 Here follow the *p* which the Israelites
19:49 the *p* of the land they were to inherit,
19:51 the final *p* into which Eleazar the priest,
2Sm 19:43 Or have *p* from his table been given to us?"
2Chr 31:19 men designated by name to distribute *p*
35:14 holocausts and the fatty *p* until night;
Neh 8:10 allot *p* to those who had nothing prepared;
8:12 went to eat and drink, to distribute *p*,
12:44 the *p* legally assigned to the priests
12:47 the singers and the gatekeepers their *p*,
13:10 that the *p* due the Levites were no longer
Eccl 11: 2 Make seven or eight *p*;
Jer 31:14 I will lavish choice *p* upon the priests,
Ez 45: 7 in length to one of the tribal *p*
47:13 tribes of Israel [Joseph having two *p*.
48: 8 *p* from the eastern to the western boundary.
48:21 parallel with the tribal *p* for the prince.
48:22 the territory between the *p* of Judah and
48:29 tribes of Israel, and these are their *p*,

PORTRAITS (1)

Ez 23:15 chariot warriors, the *p* of Babylonians,

PORTRESS (1)

2Sm 4: 6 The *p* of the house had dozed off while

PORTS (1)

Acts 27: 2 bound for *p* in the province of Asia,

POSE (3)

Jer 29:26 all madmen and those who *p* as prophets,
Lk 10:25 a lawyer stood up to *p* him this problem:
20:28 no resurrection) to *p* this problem to him:

POSED (1)

Acts 13: 6 named Bar-Jesus who *p* as a prophet.

POSES (1)

Jer 29:27 of Anathoth who *p* as a prophet among you?

POSIDONIUS (1)

2Mc 14:19 So he sent *P*,

POSING (1)

Jn 8: 6 (They were *p* this question to trap him,

POSITION (17)

Gn 37: 7 suddenly my sheaf rose to an upright *p*,
45:13 my high *p* in Egypt and what you have seen.
Ex 20:18 up a *p* much farther away and said to Moses,
Jos 8: 9 taking up their *p* to the west of Ai,
8:11 he led were drawn up in *p* before the city,
1Kgs 15:13 Maacah from her *p* as queen mother,
1Chr 9:22 had established them in their *p* of trust.
Neh 12:40 two choirs took up a *p* in the house of God;
1Mc 9:11 out of camp and took its *p* for combat.
16: 6 and his men took their *p* against the enemy.
2Mc 3:11 Tobias, a man who occupied a very high *p*.
14: 3 his *p* and regain access to the holy altar.
Eccl 10: 6 lofty *p* while the rich sit in lowly places.
Acts 24:11 you, since you are in a *p* to understand.
Rom 3: 9 do we find ourselves in a *p* of superiority?
Ti 3:14 they may be in *p* to live fruitful lives.
Rv 12:17 He took up his *p* by the shore of the sea.

POSITIONS (9)

Jos 10: 5 against Gibeon, where they took up siege *p*.
2Kgs 12:16 the workmen, because they held *p* of trust.
22: 7 to them, because they held *p* of trust.
1Mc 5:50 When the men of the army took up their *p*,
10:37 *p* of trust in the affairs of the kingdom.
2Mc 8: 6 He captured strategic *p*,
13:18 tried to take their *p* by a stratagem.
15:20 their elephants placed in strategic *p*,
Wis 7:19 Cycles of years, *p* of the stars,

POSSESS (63)

Gn 15: 8 "How am I to know that I shall *p* it?"
Lv 14:34 of Canaan, which I am giving you to *p*,
25:44 male and female, you may indeed *p*,
Nm 14:24 just been, and his descendants shall *p* it.
Dt 3:20 they too *p* the land which the LORD,
5:31 in the land which I am giving them to *p*.'
6:18 and may enter in and *p* the good land which
8: 1 and may enter in and *p* the land which the
9: 4 the LORD has brought me in to *p* this land';
9: 6 God, is giving you this good land to *p*,
16:20 life and may *p* the land which the LORD,
29:16 and stone, of gold and silver, that they *p*.
Jos 1:15 they like you *p* the land which the LORD,
18: 3 taking steps to *p* the land which the LORD,
22:19 If you consider the land you now *p* unclean,
Jgs 11:24 Should you not *p* that which your god
11:24 Chemosh gave you to *p*, and should we not *p*
18: 9 beginning your expedition to *p* the land.
1Kgs 2: 6 Act with the wisdom you *p*;
1Chr 28: 8 that you may continue to *p* this good land
Neh 9:23 had commanded their fathers to enter and *p*.
Jdt 12:16 He was burning with the desire to *p* her,
Ps(s) 37: 9 who wait for the LORD shall *p* the land.
37:11 But the meek shall *p* the land,
37:22 But those whom he blesses shall *p* the land,
37:29 shall *p* the land and dwell in it forever.
Wis 8:21 not otherwise *p* her except God gave it
Sir 1:17 she heightens the glory of those who *p* her.
4:16 If one trusts her, he will *p* her;
14:13 friend, and give him a share in what you *p*.
19: 3 Rottenness and worms will *p* him,
45:24 should *p* the high priesthood forever.
Is 14: 2 and *p* them as male and female slaves on
14:21 Lest they rise and *p* the earth,
34:11 the desert owl and hoot owl shall *p* her,
34:17 They shall *p* her forever,
57:13 inherit the land, and *p* my holy mountain.
60:21 all be just, they shall always *p* the land,
Jer 32: 8 relative, you have the first claim to *p* it;
Ez 35:10 we shall *p* them—although the LORD
Dn 5:14 that you *p* brilliant knowledge and
7:18 the kingship, to *p* it forever and ever."
9:26 be cut down when he does not *p* the city;
Zec 2:16 *p* Judah as his portion of the holy land,
8:12 I will have the remnant of the people *p*.
Mt 19:16 what good must I do to *p* everlasting life?"
Lk 18:12 I pay tithes on all I *p*.'
Jn 5:40 are unwilling to come to me to *p* that life.
8:12 no, he shall *p* the light of life."
1Cor 8: 7 Not all, of course, *p* this "knowledge."
2Cor 4: 1 we *p* this ministry through God's mercy,

POSSESS (cont.)

4: 7 This treasure we p in earthen vessels,
10: 4 They p God's power for the destruction of
Phil 3: 9 The justice I p is that which comes
Phlm 1:15 that you might p him forever,
2Pt 1:12 and are firmly rooted in the truth you p.
1:19 we p the prophetic message as something
1Jn 5:12 not p the Son of God does not possess life.
5:13 make you realize that you p eternal life
2Jn 1: 9 in the teaching of Christ does not p God,
Rv 17:12 p royal authority along with the beast,

POSSESSED (30)

Ex 35:26 thread, All the women who p the skill,
Jgs 10: 4 and p thirty cities in the land of Gilead;
1Chr 2:22 who p twenty-three cities in the land of
13:14 Obed-edom's household and all that he p.
2Chr 24:20 Then the spirit of God p Zechariah,
32:27 Hezekiah p very great wealth and glory.
Neh 9:22 They p the land of Sihon,
Dn 5:12 of the extraordinary mind p by this Daniel,
7:22 time came when the holy ones p the kingdom.
Mt 4:24 the p, the lunatics, the paralyzed.
8:16 drew on, they brought him many who were p.
8:28 They were p by demons and were so savage
8:33 including the story about the two p men.
9:32 brought him a mute who was p by a demon.
12:22 A p man who was brought to him was blind
Mk 1:32 all who were ill, and those p by demons.
3:22 Jerusalem asserted, "He is p by Beelzebul,"
3:30 had said, "He is p by an unclean spirit."
5:15 sight of the man who had been p by Legion
5:16 explained what had happened to the p man,
5:18 had been p was pressing to accompany him.
9:17 to you because he is p by a mute spirit.
Lk 8:27 by a man from the town who was p by demons.
8:36 by witnesses how the p man had been cured.
13:11 p by a spirit which drained her strength.
Jn 8:48 saying you are a Samaritan, and p besides?"
8:49 "I am not p.
8:52 "Now we are sure you are p,"
10:20 "He is p by a devil—out of his mind!
Acts 19:13 over those who were p by evil spirits,

POSSESSES (11)

Jos 22:19 cross over to the land the LORD p,
Tb 4:19 For no pagan nation p good counsel,
1Mc 10:43 with all the goods he p in my kingdom.
Sir 42:18 The Most High p all knowledge,
Jn 5:24 faith in him who sent me p eternal life.
5:26 just as the Father p life in himself,
1Jn 5:10 of God p that testimony within his heart.
5:12 Whoever possesses the Son p life;
2Jn 1: 9 the teaching p both the Father and the Son.
Rv 17: 9 Here is the clue for one who p wisdom!

POSSESSING (1)

Phil 2: 2 by your unanimity, p the one love,

POSSESSION (119)

Gn 15: 7 the Chaldeans to give you this land as a p."
17: 8 the whole land of Canaan, as a permanent p;
22:17 shall take p of the gates of their enemies,
24:60 gain p of the gates of their enemies!"
28: 4 gain p of the land where you are staying,
30:33 p that is not a speckled or spotted goat,
35: 4 to Jacob all the foreign gods in their p
44:16 the one in whose p the goblet was found."
44:17 "Only the one in whose p the goblet was
48: 4 descendants after you as a permanent p.'
Ex 6: 8 I will give it to you as your own p—
19: 5 my covenant, you shall be my special p,
22: 3 If what he stole is found alive in his p,
23:30 numerous enough to take p of the land.
Lv 20:24 Their land shall be your p,
25:28 the p of the purchaser until the jubilee,
Nm 21:24 and took p of his land from the Arnon to
21:35 left to him, and they took p of his land.
27:11 in his clan, who shall then take p of it."
32:18 Israelites has taken p of his heritage,
32:22 region shall be your p before the LORD.
33:53 shall take p of the land and settle in it,
36: 8 in p of their own ancestral heritage.
Dt 2: 5 given Esau p of the highlands of Seir.
2: 9 I will not give you p of any of their land,
2:19 give you p of any land of the Ammonites,
3:28 put them in p of the land you are to see.'
4: 1 in and take p of the land which the LORD,
4:22 cross over and take p of that good land.
9: 5 you are going in to take p of their land;
9:23 to take p of the land he was giving you,
11: 8 p of the land into which you are crossing,
11:31 you take p of it and settle there,
31: 7 you must put them in p of their heritage.
32:49 I am giving to the Israelites as their p.
33:23 The lake and south of it are his p!"
Jos 1: 6 p of the land which I swore to their fathers
1:11 in and take p of the land which the LORD,
8: 7 rise from ambush and take p of the city,
19:47 Once they had taken p of Leshem,
23: 5 you will take p of their land as the LORD,
24: 8 You took p of their land,
Jgs 1:19 Judah, he gained p of the mountain region.
1:27 Manasseh did not take p of Beth-shean
1:31 or those of Sidon, or take p of Mahaleb,
2: 6 went to take p of his own hereditary land.
3:13 Israel, taking p of the city of palms.
8: 6 of Zebah and Zalmunna already in your p,
8:15 of Zebah and Zalmunna already in your p,
17: 2 when they were taken from you, are in my p.
1Sm 12: 5 well, that you have found nothing in my p."
13:22 in the p of any of the soldiers with Saul
24:21 over Israel shall come into your p,
1Kgs 21:15 take p of the vineyard of Naboth the
21:16 of Naboth the Jezreelite, to take p of it.
21:18 of Naboth, of which he has come to take p.
21:19 After murdering, do you also take p?
2Kgs 17:24 took p of Samaria and dwelt in its cities.
1Chr 7:29 however, had p of Beth-shean and its towns,
2Chr 20:11 to drive us out of the p you have given us.
31: 1 to their various cities, each to his own p.
Ezr 7:14 of the law of your God which is in your p,
7:25 the wisdom of your God which is in your p,
9:11 entering to take as your p is a land unclean
Neh 9:24 The sons went in to take p of the land,
9:25 p of houses filled with all good things,
Jdt 1:14 all his chariots, and took p of his cities.
2:10 and take p of all their territories for me.
5:15 and took p of the whole mountain region.
10:13 take p of the whole mountain district
15: 7 from the slaughter took p of what was left,
1Mc 6:63 where he found Philip in p of the city.
7:22 They took p of the land of Judah and
8: 3 p of the silver and gold mines in Spain,
8:10 They plundered them, took p of their land,
10:76 the gates, and so Jonathan took p of Joppa.
10:89 him Ekron and all its territory as a p.
11: 8 King Ptolemy took p of the cities along
11:34 Therefore we confirm their p,
11:66 expelled them from the city, took p of it,
12: 9 the sacred books that are in our p,
15: 7 and now occupy shall remain in your p.
15:29 and taken p of many districts in my realm.
15:30 of Judea of which you have taken p;
2Mc 2:14 of the war, and we now have them in our p.
2:22 regained p of the world-famous temple,
10:36 rest of the troops, who took p of the city.
12:28 got p of the city and slaughtered
13:13 could invade Judea and take p of the city,
15:37 in p of the Hebrews from that time on,
Ps(s) 2: 8 and the ends of the earth for your p.
135: 4 Jacob for himself, Israel for his own p.
Prv 3:35 Honor is the p of wise men,
24: 4 filled with every precious and pleasing p.
Wis 1:16 it, Because they deserve to be in its p.
2:24 and they who are in his p experience it.
8: 5 And if riches be a desirable p in life,
Sir 51:21 therefore I have made her my prize p.
Jer 30: 3 they shall have it as their p.
32:23 They entered and took p of it,
Ez 7:24 nations, who shall take p of their houses.
11:15 the land of Israel has been given as our p."
25: 4 deliver you into the p of the Easterners.
25:10 Ammonites, into the p of the Easterners,
33:24 single individual, received p of the land;
33:24 p the land that has been given to us."
33:25 yet you would keep p of the land?
33:26 yet you would keep p of the land?
36: 2 our p" [therefore prophesy in these words:
36: 3 become a p for the rest of the nations,
36: 5 their p to be delivered over to plunder.
36:12 they shall take p of you,
48: 1 with his p reaching from the eastern to
Ob 1:17 take p of those that dispossessed them.
Mal 3:17 says the LORD of hosts, my own special p,
Lk 9:39 A spirit takes p of him and with a sudden
22: 3 Then Satan took p of Judas,
Acts 7: 5 him and his descendants after him as a p—

POSSESSIONS (56)

Gn 12: 5 Lot, all the p that they had accumulated,
13: 6 their p were so great that they could not
14:11 The victors seized all the p and food
14:12 had been living in Sodom, as well as his p.
14:16 He recovered all the p,
14:16 bringing back his kinsman Lot and his p,
24: 2 his household, who had charge of all his p:
32:24 the stream and had brought over all his p,
36: 7 Their p had become too great for them to
39: 4 household and entrusted to him all his p.
39: 5 in charge of his household and all his p,
46: 6 p they had acquired in the land of Canaan.
Lv 27:28 p which a man vows as doomed to the LORD,
Nm 16:32 [and all of Korah's men] and all their p.
Dt 3:20 may all return to the p I have given you.'
33:11 his p and accept the ministry of his hands.
Jos 7:24 and his sheep, his tent, and all his p,
1Sm 25:21 p in the desert so that he missed nothing.
1Chr 27:31 these were the overseers of King David's p.
28: 1 overseers of all the king's estates and p,
Ezr 8:21 for ourselves, our children, and all our p.
10: 8 suffer the confiscation of all his p,
Tb 4: 7 "Give alms from your p.
1Mc 2:10 of her realm, and laid its hand on her p?
2:28 leaving behind in the city all their p.
3:12 Their p were seized and the sword of
5:28 all the male population, took all their p,
6: 6 p taken from the armies they had destroyed;
12:23 you that your cattle and your p are ours,
Jb 6:22 to offer a gift for me from your p,
15:29 not be rich, and his p shall not endure;
31:12 till it consumed all my p to the roots.
Ps(s) 105:21 lord of his house and ruler of all his p,
Prv 3:15 none of your choice p can compare with her.
8:11 and no choice p can compare with her.]
19:14 Home and p are an inheritance from parents,
20:21 P gained hastily at the outset will in the
Eccl 2:26 p to be given to whatever man God sees fit.
Sir 11:19 have found rest, now I will feast on my p,"
11:32 blood, and plots against your choicest p.
14: 4 others, and in his p a stranger will revel.
31:11 but would not, So that his p are secure,
34:20 offers sacrifice from the p of the poor.
41: 1 of you for the man at peace amid his p,
Is 11:14 Edom and Moab shall be their p,
Bar 3:17 of whose p there was no end?
Ob 1:11 on the day when aliens carried off his p,
1:13 upon his p on the day of his calamity!
Zec 9: 4 Lo, the LORD will strip her of her p,
Mt 19:21 "If you seek perfection, go, sell your p,
19:22 man went away sad, for his p were many.
Mk 10:22 He went away sad, for he had many p.
Lk 11:21 guards his courtyard, his p go undisturbed.
12:15 but his p do not guarantee him life."
14:33 disciple if he does not renounce all his p.
Gal 4: 1 though in name he is master of all his p;
Heb 10:34 that you had better and more permanent p.

POSSESSOR (2)

Prv 16:22 Good sense is a fountain of life to its p,
Sir 25:11 its p is beyond compare.

POSSIBLE (29)

1Mc 11:22 for a conference at Ptolemais as soon as p.
2Mc 3: 6 and that it would be p to bring it all
Mt 19:26 but for God all things are p."
24:24 to mislead even the chosen if that were p.
26:39 "My Father, if it is p,
Mk 1:45 longer p for Jesus to enter a town openly.
9:23 Everything is p to a man who trusts."
10:27 With God all things are p."
13:22 signs and wonders to mislead, if it were p,
14:35 if it were p this hour might pass him by.
Lk 18:27 that are impossible for men are p for God."
Acts 17:15 Silas and Timothy to join him as soon as p.
20:16 by the feast of Pentecost if at all p.
26: 9 name of Jesus the Nazorean in every way p.
27:39 planned to run the ship aground on it if p.
Rom 5: 7 though it is barely p that for a good man
8:24 is it p for one to hope for what he sees?
8:32 Is it p that he who did not spare his own
12:18 If p, live peaceably with everyone.
1Cor 9:19 of all so as to win over as many as p.
16: 6 If it is at all p, I should like to remain
2Cor 4: 8 We are afflicted in every way p,
11: 9 In every way p I kept myself from being
Gal 3:14 thereby making it p for us to receive the
4:15 if it were p you would have plucked out
Phil 3:12 but I am racing to grasp the prize if p,
2Thes 3:16 give you continued peace in every p way.
1Tm 5:10 has she been eager to do every p good work?
Ti 2:10 every way p the doctrine of God our Savior.

POSSIBLY (2)

Jer 25:29 to inflict evil, how can you p be spared?
52:34 p as a sequel to the murder of Gedaliah,

POST (15)

Gn 40:13 up your head and restore you to your p.
41:13 I was restored to my p,
Jos 8:19 so, the men in ambush rose from their p,
10:18 the cave and p men over it to guard them.
1Sm 14: 2 (Saul's command p was under the
2Chr 34:31 Standing at his p, the king made a covenant
Is 21: 8 my p through all the watches of the night.
Jer 51:12 make strong the watch; P sentries,
Bar 6:58 or a wooden p in a palace,
Ez 21:27 cry, to p battering-rams at the gates,
Dn 2:48 He advanced Daniel to a high p,
Hb 2: 1 I will stand at my guard p,
Mt 9: 9 at his p where taxes were collected.
Mk 2:14 son of Alphaeus at his tax collector's p,
Lk 5:27 named Levi sitting at his customs p.

POSTED (5)

Neh 4: 3 We prayed to our God and p a watch against
13:19 I p some of my own men at the gates so
Jdt 4: 5 The people there p guards on all the
2Mc 14:22 Judas had p armed men in readiness at
Is 22: 7 chariots, and horses are p at the gates,

POSTERITY (23)

Gn 18:19 that he may direct his sons and his p

21:23 falsely with me or with my progeny and *p*,
1Sm 20:42 me, and between your *p* and mine forever."
2Sm 4: 8 avenged my lord the king on Saul and his *p*."
14: 7 husband neither name nor *p* upon the earth."
22:51 to David and his *p* forever."
Neh 9: 8 him and his *p* the land of the Canaanites,
Tb 4:12 that their *p* shall inherit the land.
Ps(s) 18:51 your anointed, to David and his *p* forever.
21:11 from the earth and their *p* from among men.
37:28 and the *p* of the wicked is cut off.
89: 5 Forever will I confirm your *p* and
89:30 I will make his *p* endure forever and his
89:37 His *p* shall continue forever,
102:29 their *p* shall continue in your presence.
109:13 May his *p* meet with destruction;
112: 2 His *p* shall be mighty upon the earth;
Sir 44:12 with them their family endures, their *p*,
44:21 of dust, and exalt his *p* like the stars;
47:22 He does not uproot the *p* of his chosen one,
Lk 20:28 marry the widow and raise *p* to his brother.
Acts 7: 6 *p* will be strangers in a foreign land,
8:33 of justice, Who will ever speak of his *p*,

POSTING (1)

Jgs 7:19 watch, just after the *p* of the guards.

POSTS (11)

1Kgs 6:31 the doorframes had beveled *p*.
7: 5 The *p* of all the doorways were rectangular,
20:24 their *p* and put prefects in their places.
2Chr 35:15 were at their *p* as prescribed by David:
Neh 7: 3 of Jerusalem, some at their watch *p*,
Jdt 7:32 Then he dispersed the men to their *p*,
8:36 from the tent and returned to their *p*.
2Mc 12:27 took up their *p* in defense of the walls,
Jer 50:14 Take your *p* encircling Babylon,
Bar 3:34 the stars at their *p* shine and rejoice;
Acts 5:23 the guards at their *p* outside the gates,

POT (22)

Lv 2: 7 a cereal offering that is prepared in a *p*,
7: 9 is baked in an oven or deep-fried in a *p*
Nm 11: 8 cook it in a *p* and make it into loaves,
Jgs 6:19 the meat in a basket and the broth in a *p*,
1Sm 2:14 it into the basin, kettle, caldron, or *p*.
2Kgs 4:38 said to his servant, "Put the large *p* on,
4:39 On his return he cut them up into the *p* of
4:40 "Man of God, there is poison in the *p*!"
4:41 He threw it into the *p* and said,
4:41 was no longer anything harmful in the *p*.
Jb 41:12 issues steam, as from a seething *p* or bowl.
41:23 He makes the depths boil like a *p*;
Eccl 7: 6 For as the crackling of thorns under a *p*,
Sir 13: 2 the earthen *p* go with the metal cauldron?
13: 2 they knock together, the *p* will be smashed:
22: 7 Teaching a fool is like gluing a broken *p*,
Jer 19:11 a clay *p* so that it cannot be repaired.
48:38 shattered Moab like a *p* that no one wants,
Ez 24: 3 Set up the *p*,
24: 6 to the bloody city, a *p* containing rust,
24:11 Then I will set the *p* empty on the coals
Zec 14:21 And every *p* in Jerusalem and in Judah

POTENTATE (1)

Gn 10: 8 of Nimrod, who was the first *p* on earth.

POTENTATES (1)

Wis 5:23 and evildoing overturn the thrones of *p*.

POTIPHAR (2)

Gn 37:36 meanwhile, sold Joseph in Egypt to *P*,
39: 1 taken down to Egypt, a certain Egyptian *P*,

POTIPHERA (3)

Gn 41:45 him in marriage Asenath, the daughter of *P*,
41:50 borne to him by Asenath, daughter of *P*,
46:20 and Ephraim, whom Asenath, daughter of *P*,

POTS (11)

Ex 27: 3 Make *p* for removing the ashes,
38: 3 All the utensils of the altar, the *p*,
1Kgs 7:40 When Hiram made the *p*,
7:45 one sea, twelve oxen supporting the sea, *p*,
2Kgs 25:14 They took also the *p*,
2Chr 4:11 Huram also made the *p*,
4:16 likewise the *p*, the shovels and the forks
35:13 and also cooked the sacred meals in *p*,
Jer 52:18 They took also the *p*,
52:19 also, the fire holders, the bowls, the *p*,
Zec 14:20 The *p* in the house of the LORD shall be as

POTSHERD (3)

Jb 2: 8 And he took a *p* to scrape himself,
Is 45: 9 a *p* among potsherds of the earth!
Jer 19: 2 Ben-hinnom, at the entrance of the *P* Gate;

POTSHERDS (1)

Is 45: 9 a potsherd among *p* of the earth!

POTTAGE (1)

Hg 2:12 garment and the fold touches bread, or *p*,

POTTER (12)

Wis 15: 7 For truly the *p*, laboriously working
Sir 27: 5 test of what the *p* molds is in the furnace,
33:13 Like clay in the hands of a *p*,
38:29 So with the *p* sitting at his labor,
Is 29:16 as though the *p* were taken to be the clay:
29:16 Or the vessel should say of the *p*,
41:25 like red earth, as the *p* treads the clay.
64: 7 we are the clay and you the *p*:
Jer 18: 6 you, house of Israel, as this *p* has done?
18: 6 Indeed, like clay in the hand of the *p*,
Lam 4: 2 than earthen jars made by the hands of a *p*!
Rom 9:21 Does not a *p* have the right to make from

POTTERS (8)

1Chr 4:23 *p* and inhabitants of Netaim and Gederah,
Is 30:14 crashes like a *p* jar smashed beyond rescue,
Jer 18: 2 Rise up, be off to the *p* house;
18: 3 went down to the *p* house and there he was,
19: 1 Go, buy a *p* earthen flask.
Dn 2:41 saw, partly of *p* tile and partly of iron,
Mt 27: 7 the *p* field as a cemetery for foreigners.
27:10 *p* field just as the Lord had commanded me."

POTTERY (1)

Jb 41:22 His belly is sharp as *p* fragments;

POUCH (3)

Jdt 13:10 to her maid, who put it into her food *p*;
13:15 Then she took the head out of the *p*,
Jb 14:17 My misdeeds would be sealed up in a *p*,

POUCHES (1)

Tb 1:14 I also deposited several *p* containing a

POULTICE (2)

2Kgs 20: 7 Isaiah then ordered a *p* of figs to be
Is 38:21 Isaiah then ordered a *p* of figs to be

POULTRY (1)

Neh 5:18 one beef, six choice muttons, *p*—

POUNCED (3)

1Sm 14:32 So they *p* upon the spoil and took sheep,
15:19 You have *p* on the spoil,
Acts 18:17 Then they all *p* on Sosthenes,

POUND (4)

Nm 11: 8 it between millstones or *p* it in a mortar,
Prv 27:22 should *p* the fool to bits with the pestle,
Ez 26: 9 He shall *p* your walls with battering-rams
Jn 12: 3 Mary brought a *p* of costly perfume made

POUNDED (2)

Jgs 5:22 Then the hoofs of the horses *p*,
Acts 27:18 We were being *p* by the storm so violently

POUNDING (1)

Acts 27:41 stern was shattered by the *p* of the sea.

POUNDS (1)

Jn 19:39 and aloes which weighed about a hundred *p*.

POUR (75)

Ex 4: 9 from the river and *p* it on the dry land.
29:12 you shall *p* out at the base of the altar.
30: 9 nor shall you *p* out a libation upon it.
Lv 2: 1 *p* oil on it and put frankincense over it.
4: 7 rest of the bullock's blood he shall *p* out
4:18 The rest of the blood he shall *p* out at
4:25 he shall *p* out at the base of this altar.
4:30 he shall *p* out at the base of the altar.
4:34 he shall *p* out at the base of the altar.
14:15 priest shall also take a log of oil and *p*
14:26 The priest shall then *p* some of the oil
17:13 *p* out its blood and cover it with earth.
Nm 5:15 *p* oil on it nor put frankincense over it,
28: 7 you shall *p* out to the LORD in the
Dt 12:16 but must *p* it out on the ground like water.
12:24 but *p* it out on the ground like water.
Jgs 6:20 then *p* out the broth."
1Kgs 18:34 "and *p* it over the holocaust and over the
2Kgs 4: 4 *p* the oil into all the vessels,
4: 5 handed her the vessels, she would *p* in oil.
9: 3 From the flask you have, *p* oil on his head,
Jb 10:10 Did you not *p* me out as milk,
Ps(s) 16: 4 Blood libations to them I will not *p* out,
42: 5 now that I *p* out my soul within me,
62: 9 *P* out your hearts before him;
69:25 *P* out your wrath upon them;
79: 6 *P* out your wrath upon the nations that
119:171 My lips *p* forth your praise,
142: 3 My complaint I *p* out before him;
Prv 1:23 I will *p* out to you my spirit,
Eccl 11: 3 are full, they *p* out rain upon the earth.
Wis 11:18 forth fiery breath, Or *p* out roaring smoke,
Sir 20:12 fools *p* forth their blandishments in vain.
24:31 Thus do I *p* out instruction like prophecy
32: 4 wine is present, do not *p* out discourse,
36: 6 Rouse your anger, *p* out wrath,
39: 6 He will *p* forth his words of wisdom and in
Is 44: 3 I will *p* out water upon the thirsty ground,
44: 3 I will *p* out my spirit upon your offspring,
46: 6 There are those who *p* out gold from a
65: 7 I will at once *p* out in full measure their
Jer 6:11 will *p* it out upon the child in the street,
7:20 and my wrath will *p* out upon this place,
10:25 *P* out your wrath on the nations that know
14:16 will *p* out upon them their own wickedness.
44:17 queen of heaven and *p* out libations to her,
44:25 of heaven and to *p* out libations to her."
Lam 2:19 *P* out your heart like water in the
Ez 7: 8 Soon now I will *p* out my fury upon you and
9: 8 when you *p* out your fury on Jerusalem?"
21:36 I will *p* out my indignation upon you;
24: 3 the pot, set it up, then *p* in some water.
24: 7 she did not *p* it out on the earth,
30:15 I will *p* out my wrath on Pelusium,
Hos 5:10 Upon them I will *p* out my wrath like water.
9: 4 shall not *p* libations of wine to the LORD,
Jl 3: 1 I will *p* out my spirit upon all mankind.
3: 1 in those days, I will *p* out my spirit.
Am 9: 6 and *p* them upon the surface of the earth,
Mi 2:11 *p* you wine and strong drink as my prophecy,"
6:15 reap, tread out the olive, yet *p* no oil,
Zep 3: 8 In order to *p* out upon them my wrath,
Zec 4:12 two olive tufts which freely *p* out fresh oil
12:10 I will *p* out on the house of David and on
Mal 3:10 *p* down blessing upon you without measure?
Mt 9:17 do not *p* new wine into old wineskins.
9:17 No, they *p* new wine into new wineskins,
26: 7 him at table and began to *p* it on his head.
Mk 14: 3 she began to *p* the perfume on his head.
Lk 6:38 will they *p* into the fold of your garment.
Acts 2:17 that I will *p* out a portion of my spirit
2:18 *p* out a portion of my spirit in those days,
2Pt 2:12 These men *p* abuse on things of which they
Rv 16: 1 "Go and *p* out upon the earth the seven
18: 6 *P* into her cup twice the amount she

POURED (82)

Gn 7:12 nights heavy rain *p* down on the earth.
28:18 a memorial stone, and *p* oil on top of it.
35:14 upon it he made a libation and *p* out oil.
Ex 9:33 the rain no longer *p* down upon the earth.
Lv 2: 6 into pieces, and oil must be *p* over it.
8:12 He also *p* some of the anointing oil on
9: 9 blood he *p* out at the base of the altar.
21:10 whose head the anointing oil has been *p*
Nm 19:17 and spring water shall be *p* on them.
Dt 12:27 be *p* out against the altar of the LORD,
15:23 must be *p* out on the ground like water.
Ru 3:15 did so, he *p* out six measures of barley,
1Sm 7: 6 and *p* it out on the ground before the LORD,
10: 1 Samuel *p* oil on Saul's head;
2Sm 14:14 we are then like water that is *p* out on
23:16 drink it, and instead *p* it out to the LORD,
2Kgs 3:11 who *p* water on the hands of Elijah,
4:40 The stew was *p* out for the men to eat,
9: 6 young man *p* the oil on his head and said,
1Chr 11:18 he *p* it out as a libation to the LORD,
2Chr 12: 7 be *p* out upon Jerusalem through Shishak.
Tb 3:11 and facing the window, *p* out this prayer:
2Mc 1:31 of the liquid to be *p* upon large stones.
Ps(s) 22:15 I am like water *p* out;
35:13 and *p* forth prayers within my bosom.
45: 3 grace is *p* out upon your lips;
77:18 The clouds *p* down water;
79: 3 They have *p* out their blood like water
Prv 8:23 From of old I was *p* forth,
Wis 2: 3 will be *p* abroad like unresisting air.
Sir 1: 8 He has *p* her forth upon all his works,
50:15 And *p* it out at the foot of the altar,
Is 29:10 has *p* out on you a spirit of deep sleep.
32:15 the spirit from on high is *p* out on us.
42:25 So he *p* out wrath upon them,
57: 6 To these you *p* out libations,
Jer 7:18 *p* out to strange gods in order to hurt me.
19:13 heaven and *p* out libations to strange gods.
32:29 libations were *p* out to strange gods
42:18 was *p* out upon the citizens of Jerusalem,
42:18 anger be *p* out on you when you reach Egypt.
44: 6 Therefore the fury of my anger *p* forth in
44:19 queen of heaven and *p* out libations to her,
44:19 in her image and *p* out libations to her?
48:11 He was not *p* from one flask to another,
Lam 2: 4 daughter Zion he *p* out his wrath like fire.
2:11 My gall is *p* out on the ground because of
4:11 spent his anger, *p* out his blazing wrath;
Ez 16:36 Because you *p* out your lust and revealed
20:28 and there they *p* out their libations.
22:22 I, the LORD, have *p* out my fury on you.
22:31 Therefore I have *p* out my fury upon them;
24: 7 she *p* it on the bare rock;
36:18 Therefore I *p* out my fury upon them

POURED (cont.)

36:18 the blood which they *p* out on the ground,
39:29 *p* out my spirit upon the house of Israel,
Dn 9:11 of God, was *p* out over us for our sins.
9:27 that is decreed is *p* out upon the horror."
Mi 1: 4 before the fire, like water *p* down a slope.
Na 1: 6 His fury is *p* out like fire,
Zep 1:17 And their blood shall be *p* out like dust,
Mt 26:28 to be *p* out in behalf of many for the
Mk 2:22 No, new wine is *p* into new skins."
14:24 covenant, to be *p* out on behalf of many.
Lk 5:38 New wine should be *p* into fresh skins.
Jn 13: 5 Then he *p* water into a basin and began to
Acts 2:33 the Father, then *p* this Spirit out on us.
10:45 have been *p* out on the Gentiles also,
Rom 5: 5 love of God has been *p* out in our hearts
Phil 2:17 Even if my life is to be *p* out as a
2Tm 4: 6 am already being *p* out like a libation.
Rv 9: 2 he opened it and smoke *p* out of the shaft
14:10 *p* full strength into the cup of his anger.
14:20 and so much blood *p* out of the winepress
16: 2 and when he *p* out his bowl on the earth,
16: 3 The second angel *p* out his bowl on the sea.
16: 4 *p* out his bowl on the rivers and springs.
16: 8 The fourth angel *p* out his bowl on the sun.
16:10 *p* out his bowl on the throne of the beast.
16:12 The sixth angel *p* out his bowl on the
16:17 angel *p* out his bowl upon the empty air.
18:19 They *p* dust on their heads and cried out,

POURED-OUT (2)

Ez 20:33 hand and outstretched arm, with *p* wrath,
20:34 hand and outstretched arm, with *p* wrath,

POURING (15)

Ex 25:29 as its pitchers and bowls for *p* libations.
29: 7 and anoint him with it, *p* it on his head.
37:16 as its pitchers and bowls for *p* libations,
Lv 8:15 atonement for the altar by *p* out the blood
1Sm 1:15 I was only *p* out my troubles to the LORD.
2Kgs 16:13 and cereal-offering, *p* out his libation,
Jer 44:18 queen of heaven and *p* out libations to her,
Ez 14:19 land, *p* out upon it my bloodthirsty fury,
20: 8 Then I thought of *p* out my fury on them
20:13 Then I thought of *p* out my fury on them in
20:21 Then I thought of *p* out my fury on them,
23: 8 breasts and *p* out their impurities on her.
Zec 10: 1 And sends men the *p* rain;
Mt 26:12 By *p* this perfume on my body,
Lk 10:34 and dressed his wounds, *p* in oil and wine.

POURS (13)

Jb 16:13 mercy, he *p* out my gall upon the ground.
41:13 a flame *p* from his mouth.
Ps(s) 19: 3 Day *p* out the word to day,
75: 9 and foaming wine, And he *p* out from it;
107:40 But he who *p* out contempt upon princes,
Prv 15: 2 The tongue of the wise *p* out knowledge,
15:28 but the mouth of the wicked *p* out evil.
19:28 and the mouth of the wicked *p* out iniquity.
Sir 35:14 to the widow when she *p* out her complaint;
Am 5: 8 *p* them out upon the surface of the earth;
Mk 2:22 no man *p* new wine into old wineskins.
Lk 5:37 no one *p* new wine into old wineskins.

POVERTY (28)

Lv 25:25 to *p* and has to sell some of his property,
25:35 to *p* and is unable to hold out beside you,
25:47 is reduced to such *p* that he sells himself
Dt 28:48 and thirst, in nakedness and utter *p*,
Jgs 14:15 Did you invite us here to reduce us to *p*?"
Tb 4:13 worthlessness there is decay and dire *p*,
4:21 be discouraged, my child, because of our *p*.
Prv 6:11 will *p* come upon you like a highway man,
10:15 the ruination of the lowly is their *p*.
13:18 *P* and shame befall the man who disregards
20:13 Love not sleep, lest you be reduced to *p*;
21: 5 but all rash haste leads certainly to *p*.
23:21 For the drunkard and the glutton come to *p*,
24:34 will *p* come upon you like a highwayman,
28:19 from idle pursuits a man has his fill of *p*.
30: 8 far from me, give me neither *p* nor riches;
Sir 10:30 Honored in *p*, how much more so in wealth!
10:30 in wealth, in *p* how much the more!
11:14 and evil, life and death, *p* and riches,
13:23 *p* is evil by the standards of the proud.
18:25 of plenty, *p* and want in the day of wealth.
18:32 of a moment which bring on *p* redoubled;
22: 3 if it be a daughter she brings him to *p*.
Lam 3: 5 beset me round about with *p* and weariness;
3:19 of my homeless *p* is wormwood and gall;
2Cor 8: 2 *p* have produced an abundant generosity.
8: 9 so that you might become rich by his *p*.
Rv 2: 9 I know of your tribulation and your *p*,

POWDER (5)

Ex 30:35 This fragrant *p*,
32:20 in the fire and then ground it down to *p*,
Dt 9:21 I ground it down to *p* as fine as dust,
2Kgs 23:15 up the stones and grinding them to *p*,
Is 40:15 the coastlands weigh no more than *p*.

POWDERY (1)

Dt 28:24 rain the LORD will give your land *p* dust,

POWER (426)

Gn 9: 2 into your *p* they are delivered.
16: 6 "Your maid is in your *p*.
31:29 I have it in my *p* to harm all of you;
49: 3 excelling in rank and excelling in *p*!
49:24 By the *p* of the Mighty One of Jacob,
Ex 1: 8 knew nothing of Joseph, came to *p* in Egypt.
4:21 all the wonders I have put in your *p*.
9:16 to show you my *p* and to make my name
14:30 on that day from the *p* of the Egyptians.
14:31 the great *p* that the LORD had shown
15: 6 O LORD, magnificent in *p* your right hand,
18:11 the people from the *p* of the Egyptians."
32:11 such great *p* and with so strong a hand?
Nm 14:13 For by your *p* you brought out this people
14:17 *p* of my LORD be displayed in its greatness,
22:38 But what *p* have I to say anything?
Dt 4:37 led you out of Egypt by his great *p*,
8:17 'It is my own *p* and the strength of my own
8:18 God, who gives you the *p* to acquire wealth,
9:29 great *p* and with your outstretched arm.
26: 8 and outstretched arm, with terrifying *p*,
33:26 darling, who rides the heavens in his *p*,
34:12 and the terrifying *p* that Moses exhibited
Jos 2:24 has delivered all this land into our *p*;
6: 2 delivered Jericho and its king into your *p*.
7: 7 delivering us into the *p* of the Amorites,
8: 1 have delivered the king of Ai into your *p*,
8: 7 LORD, your God, will deliver into your *p*.
8:18 Ai, for I will deliver it into your *p*."
9:25 And now that we are in your *p*,
10: 8 for I have delivered them into your *p*.
10:19 your God, has delivered them into your *p*."
10:30 the LORD delivered into the *p* of Israel.
10:32 delivered Lachish into the *p* of Israel,
11: 8 them into the *p* of the Israelites,
21:44 brought all their enemies under their *p*.
24: 8 you, but I delivered them into your *p*.
24:11 you, but I delivered them also into your *p*.
Jgs 1: 2 I have delivered the land into his *p*."
1: 4 Canaanites and Perizzites into their *p*,
2:14 He allowed them to fall into the *p* of
2:16 them from the *p* of their despoilers,
2:18 save them from the *p* of their enemies
2:23 or delivering them into the *p* of Israel.
3: 8 to fall into the *p* of Cushan-rishathaim,
3:10 king of Aram, into his *p*,
3:28 your enemies the Moabites into your *p*."
3:30 brought under the *p* of Israel at that time;
4: 2 to fall into the *p* of the Canaanite king,
4: 7 troops, and will deliver them into your *p*."
4: 9 have Sisera fall into the *p* of a woman."
4:14 the LORD has delivered Sisera into your *p*.
4:24 their *p* weighed ever heavier upon him,
6: 1 them into the *p* of Midian for seven years,
6: 9 I rescued you from the *p* of Egypt and of
6:13 and has delivered us into the *p* of Midian."
6:14 have and save Israel from the *p* of Midian.
7: 2 you for me to deliver Midian into their *p*,
7: 2 and say, 'My own *p* brought me the victory.'
7: 7 you and will deliver Midian into your *p*.
7:14 Midian and all the camp into his *p*."
7:15 delivered the camp of Midian into your *p*."
8: 3 your *p* God delivered the princes of Midian,
8: 7 delivered Zebah and Zalmunna into my *p*,
8:22 for you rescued us from the *p* of Midian."
8:34 the *p* of their enemies all around them.
9:17 when he saved you from the *p* of Midian;
10: 7 *p* of [the Philistines and] the Ammonites.
11:21 Sihon and all his men into the *p* of Israel,
11:30 "If you deliver the Ammonites into my *p*,"
11:32 and the LORD delivered them into his *p*,
12: 2 but you did not rescue me from their *p*.
12: 3 and the LORD delivered them into my *p*.
13: 1 the *p* of the Philistines for forty years.
13: 5 of Israel from the *p* of the Philistines."
16:23 has delivered into our *p* Samson our enemy."
16:24 god has delivered into our *p* our enemy,
18:10 God has indeed given it into your *p*:
20:28 tomorrow I will deliver him into your *p*."
1Sm 4: 8 deliver us from the *p* of these mighty gods?
7: 3 deliver you from the *p* of the Philistines."
10:18 *p* of the Egyptians and from the *p* of all
12:10 deliver us now from the *p* of our enemies,
12:11 from the *p* of your enemies on every side,
14:37 Will you deliver them into the *p* of Israel?"
23: 4 I will deliver the Philistines into your *p*."
2Sm 3: 6 Abner was gaining *p* in the house of Saul.
1Kgs 3: 1 With the royal *p* firmly in his grasp,
8:24 that promise, have this day, by your own *p*,
2Kgs 3:15 the *p* of the LORD came upon Elisha and he
5: 7 "Am I a god with *p* over life and death,
13: 3 a long time left them in the *p* of Hazael,
13: 5 the Israelites, freed from the *p* of Aram,
17:36 of Egypt with great *p* and outstretched arm:
17:39 deliver you from the *p* of all your enemies."
19:19 our God, save us from the *p* of this man,
19:26 While their inhabitants, shorn of *p*,
1Chr 14:10 and will you deliver them into my *p*?"
14:10 for I will deliver them into your *p*."
22:18 the occupants of the land into my *p*,
29:11 "Yours, O LORD, are grandeur and *p*,
29:12 In your hand are *p* and might;
2Chr 6:32 to honor your great name, your mighty *p*,
12: 5 I have abandoned you to the *p* of Shishak.'"
12:13 his *p* in Jerusalem and continued to rule;
13:20 did not regain *p* during the time of Abijah;
16: 8 on the LORD, he delivered them into your *p*.
18:14 they will be delivered into your *p*."
20: 6 In your hand is *p* and might,
21: 4 kingdom and had consolidated his *p*,
24:24 a very large force into their *p*,
25: 8 who has the *p* to reinforce or to defeat."
26:15 and his *p* was ascribed to the marvelous
28: 5 him into the *p* of the king of Aram.
28: 5 delivered into the *p* of the king of Israel,
30:12 the *p* of God brought it about that the
32:22 king of Assyria, as from every other *p*;
36:20 the kingdom of the Persians came to *p*.
Ezr 5:12 delivered them into the *p* of the Chaldean,
Neh 9:24 land and delivered them over into their *p*,
9:27 them into the *p* of their enemies,
9:27 deliver them from the *p* of their enemies.
9:28 abandoned them to the *p* of their enemies,
9:30 into the *p* of the peoples of the lands.
Tb 13: 6 show his *p* and majesty to a sinful nation.
Jdt 2:12 I have spoken I will accomplish by my *p*.
5: 3 In what does their *p* and strength consist?
7:25 God has sold us into their *p* by laying us
8:15 *p* to protect us at such time as he pleases,
9: 7 rider, boasting of the *p* of their infantry,
9:11 nor does your *p* depend upon stalwart men;
9:14 that you are the god of all *p* and might,
11: 7 and by the *p* of him who has sent you to
13:11 in Israel and his *p* against our enemies;
16:13 wonderful in *p* and unsurpassable.
Est 3:13 to be carried away with the sense of *p*,
4:16 almighty King, all things are in your *p*,
4:23 King of gods and Ruler of every *p*.
4:25 Save us by your *p*, and help me, who am
4:30 Save us from the *p* of the wicked,
9: 4 that he was continually growing in *p*.
10: 2 All the acts of his *p* and valor,
1Mc 1:58 So they used their *p* against Israel,
3:35 to crush and destroy the *p* of Israel
10:70 displaying *p* against us in the mountains?
14: 4 His people were delighted with his *p* and
2Mc 3:24 Lord of spirits who holds all *p* manifested
3:24 at God's *p* and fainted away in terror.
3:28 clearly experienced the sovereign *p* of God.
3:29 all hope of aid, due to an act of God's *p*,
3:34 proclaim to all men the majesty of God's *p*."
3:38 some special divine *p* about the Place.
4:50 to the covetousness of the men in *p*,
7:16 "Since you have *p* among men,
7:17 *p* will torment you and your descendants."
9: 8 clearly manifesting to all the *p* of God.
9:17 place to proclaim there the *p* of God.
11: 4 did not take God's *p* into account at all,
12:24 because he had in his *p* the parents and
15:17 which had *p* to instill valor and stir
15:27 greatly over this manifestation of God's *p*.
15:34 the LORD who manifests his divine *p*,
Jb 1:12 "Behold, all that he has is in your *p*;
2: 6 "He is in your *p*; only spare his life."
10:16 you show your wondrous *p* against me,
21: 7 surive, grow old, become mighty in *p*?
23: 6 he contend against me with his great *p*,
26:12 By his *p* he stirs up the sea,
30:18 One with great *p* lays hold of my clothing;
35: 9 for help because of the *p* of the mighty,
36:22 Behold, God is sublime in his *p*.
37:23 him, pre-eminent in *p* and judgment;
Ps(s) 37:17 For the *p* of the wicked shall be broken,
37:33 The LORD will not leave him in his *p* nor
49:16 the *p* of the nether world by receiving me.
59:12 beguile my people; shake them by your *p*,
62:12 that *p* belongs to God,
63: 3 sanctuary to see your *p* and your glory,
65: 7 You set the mountains in place by your *p*,
68:29 Show forth, O God, your *p*.
68:29 the *p*, O God, with which you took
68:34 Behold, his voice resounds, the voice of *p*:
68:35 "Confess the *p* of God!"
68:35 his *p* is in the skies.
68:36 he gives *p* and strength to his people.
71:19 Your *p* and your justice,
77:15 the peoples you have made known your *p*.
78:26 and by his *p* brought on the south wind.
79:11 your great *p* free those doomed to death.
80: 3 Rouse your *p*, and come to save us.
89:49 himself from the *p* of the nether world?
106: 8 for his name's sake, to make known his *p*.
106:42 them, and they were humbled under their *p*.
110: 2 *p* the LORD will stretch forth from Zion:
110: 3 is princely *p* in the day of your birth,
111: 6 known to his people the *p* of his works,
118:15 right hand of the LORD has struck with *p*:
118:16 right hand of the LORD has struck with *p*."
145: 6 They discourse of the *p* of your terrible

147: 5 Great is our Lord and mighty in *p:*
Prv 3:27 when it is in your *p* to do it for him.
6: 3 you have fallen into your neighbor's *p:*
18:21 Death and life are in the *p* of the tongue;
Eccl 5:18 property, and grants *p* to partake of them,
6: 2 does not grant him *p* to partake of them,
9:10 turn your hand to, do with what *p* you have;
Wis 1: 3 separate a man from God, and his *p,*
6: 2 you who are in *p* over the multitude and
6: 8 for those in *p* a rigorous scrutiny impends.
7:26 light, the spotless mirror of the *p* of God,
10: 2 fall, and gave him *p* to rule all things.
12: 9 Not that you were without *p* to have the
12:15 *p* to punish one who has incurred no blame.
12:17 the perfection of your *p* is disbelieved;
12:18 for *p,* whenever you will, attends you.
Sir 3:19 For great is the *p* of God;
5: 1 say not: "I have the *p.*"
8: 1 influential man, lest you fall into his *p.*
9: 2 *p* over you to trample upon your dignity.
9:13 Keep far from the man who has *p* to kill,
15:18 he is mighty in *p,*
17: 3 and with *p* over all things else on earth.
18: 3 Who can measure his majestic *p,*
28:10 the sterner his anger, the greater his *p,*
33:20 have *p* over you as long as you live.
36: 2 the heathen, that they may realize your *p.*
38: 5 by a twig that men might learn his *p?*
43:15 storm its *p* and breaks off the hailstones.
43:30 the LORD's majesty, and wonderful is his *p.*
43:31 though he is still beyond your *p* to praise;
46: 4 Did he not by his *p* stop the sun,
46: 5 to him in hailstones of tremendous *p,*
47: 7 and shattered their *p* till our own day.
48:13 Nothing was beyond his *p;*
49: 5 So he gave over their *p* to others,
51: 3 and from the *p* of those who sought my life;
Is 8: 7 mighty [the king of Assyria and all his *p.*
10:13 "By my own *p* I have done it,
19: 4 deliver Egypt into the *p* of a cruel master,
31: 1 in horsemen because of their combined *p,*
37:27 While their inhabitants, shorn of *p,*
40:10 Here comes with *p* the Lord GOD,
40:14 *P* of the Creator Behold,
40:26 of his *p* not one of them is missing!
45:24 "Only in the LORD are just deeds and *p.*
66:14 LORD's *p* shall be known to his servants,
Jer 10: 5 harm, neither is it in their *p* to do good.
10:12 He who made the earth by his *p,*
16:21 them in no doubt Of my strength and my *p:*
20:13 life of the poor from the *p* of the wicked!
21:10 It shall be given into the *p* of the king
23:10 is an evil course, theirs is unjust *p.*
27: 5 on the face of the earth, by my great *p,*
38: 5 "He is in your *p*";
42:11 you to save you, to rescue you from his *p.*
51:15 He has sworn who made the earth by his *p,*
Bar 6:62 their equal, whether in beauty or in *p;*
Ez 13:21 veils and rescue my people from your *p,*
13:23 but I will rescue my people from your *p.*
30:12 sell the land over to the *p* of the wicked.
34:27 them from the *p* of those who enslaved them.
35: 5 delivered over to the *p* of the sword
Dn 2:20 forever and ever, for wisdom and *p* are his.
2:23 because you have given me wisdom and *p.*
2:37 given dominion and strength, *p* and glory;
3:88 world, and saved us from the *p* of death;
3:94 had had no *p* over the bodies of these men;
6:28 and he delivered Daniel from the lions' *p.*"
7:26 and his *p* is taken away by final and
8: 4 withstand it or be rescued from its *p;*
8: 7 and no one could rescue it from its *p.*
8: 8 of its *p* the great horn was shattered,
8:10 Its *p* extended to the host of heaven,
11: 6 But her bid for *p* shall fail:
11:15 The *p* of the south shall not withstand him,
11:23 treacherously rise to *p* with a small party.
11:41 of Ammon, which shall escape from his *p.*
11:42 He shall extend his *p* over the countries,
12: 7 when the *p* of the destroyer of the holy
13:22 if I refuse, I cannot escape your *p.*
13:23 Yet it is better for me to fall in your *p*
Hos 13:14 them from the *p* of the nether world?
Mi 2: 1 accomplish it when it lies within their *p.*
3: 8 But as for me, I am filled with *p,*
Na 1: 3 The LORD is slow to anger, yet great in *p,*
Hb 3: 4 from beside him, where his *p* is concealed.
Hg 2:22 the *p* of the kingdoms of the nations.
Zec 9: 4 possessions, and smite her *p* on the sea,
11: 6 *p* of his neighbor, or into the *p* of his king;
11: 6 and I will not deliver it out of their *p.)*
Mt 1:18 child through the *p* of the Holy Spirit.
7:22 Have we not exorcised demons by its *p?*
21:23 Who has given you this *p?*"
22:29 understand the Scriptures and the *p* of God.
24:30 clouds of heaven' with *p* and great glory.
26:45 is to be handed over to the *p* of evil men.
26:64 the *P* and coming on the clouds of heaven."
Mk 5:30 once that healing *p* had gone out from him.
9: 1 they see the reign of God established in *p.*"
11:28 Who has given you the *p* to do them?"
12:24 understand the Scriptures or the *p* of God.
13:26 in the clouds with great *p* and glory.
14:36 Father), you have the *p* to do all things.
14:62 the *P* and coming with the clouds of heaven."
16:20 by spirits to grasp the true *p* of God.
16:20 the years of Satan's *p* has been fulfilled,
Lk 1:17 before him, in the spirit and *p* of Elijah,
1:35 the *p* of the Most High will overshadow you;
4: 6 all this *p* and the glory of these kingdoms;
4: 6 the *p* has been given to me and I give it
4:14 returned in the *p* of the Spirit to Galilee,
4:36 the unclean spirits with authority and *p,*
5:17 and the *p* of the Lord made him heal.
6:19 *p* went out from him which cured all.
8:46 I know that *p* has gone forth from me."
9: 1 *p* and authority to overcome all demons
10:19 I have given you *p* to tread on snakes and
12: 5 *p* to cast into Gehenna after he has killed.
12:26 If the smallest things are beyond your *p,*
19:37 loudly for the display of *p* they had seen,
21:27 coming on a cloud with great *p* and glory.
22:69 his seat at the right hand of the *P* of God.'"
24:49 until you are clothed with *p* from on high."
Jn 5:27 The Father has given over to him *p* to pass
10:18 I have *p* to lay it down, and I have *p*
19:10 have the *p* to release you and the *p* to crucify
19:11 "You would have no *p* over me whatever
Acts 1: 8 *p* when the Holy Spirit comes down on you;
3:12 man walk by some *p* or holiness of our own?
4: 7 "By what *p* or in whose name have men of
4:10 In the *p* of that name this man stands
4:16 show of *p* took place through them.
4:33 With *p* the apostles bore witness to the
6: 8 of was a man filled with grace and *p,*
7:18 until a new king came to *p* in Egypt,
8:10 "He is the *p* of the great God,"
8:19 with the request, "Give me that *p* too,
10:38 anointed him with the Holy Spirit and *p.*
19:20 continue to spread with influence and *p.*
Rom 1: 4 in *p* according to the spirit of holiness,
1:16 It is the *p* of God leading everyone who
1:20 realities, God's eternal *p* and divinity,
6: 9 death has no more *p* over him.
6:14 Sin will no longer have *p* over you;
7: 1 has *p* over a man only so long as he lives?
7:18 desire to do right is there but not the *p.*
7:24 me from this body under the *p* of death?
9:17 that through you I might show my *p,*
9:22 to show his wrath and make known his *p,*
12: 8 with the *p* of exhortation should exhort.
15:13 the *p* of the Holy Spirit you may have hope
15:19 and marvels, by the *p* of God's Spirit.
1Cor 1:18 experiencing salvation it is the *p* of God.
1:24 Christ the *p* of God and the wisdom of God.
2: 4 but the convincing *p* of the Spirit.
2: 5 on the wisdom of men but on the *p* of God.
4:20 of God does not consist in talk but in *p.*
6:14 up the Lord, will raise us also by his *p.*
12: 8 to another the *p* to express knowledge.
12:10 *p* to distinguish one spirit from another.
13: 7 to its trust, its hope, its *p* to endure.
15:24 every sovereignty, authority, and *p,*
15:56 is sin, and sin gets its *p* from the law.
2Cor 4: 7 *p* comes from God and not from us.
6: 7 with the message of truth and the *p* of God;
10: 4 God's *p* for the destruction of strongholds.
10: 8 claims about the *p* the Lord has given us
12: 9 you, for in weakness *p* reaches perfection."
12: 9 that the *p* of Christ may rest upon me.
12:12 apostle, signs and wonders and deeds of *p.*
13: 4 of weakness, but he lives by the *p* of God.
13: 4 him, but we live with him by God's *p* in us.
Gal 3:13 Christ has delivered us from the *p* of the
Eph 1:19 scope of his *p* in us who believe.
1:21 heaven, high above every principality, *p,*
3: 7 bestowed on me by the exercise of his *p,*
3:20 To him whose *p* now at work in us can do
5:26 in the bath of water by the *p* of the word,
6:10 strength from the Lord and his mighty *p.*
Phil 3:10 and the *p* flowing from his resurrection;
3:21 by his *p* to subject everything to himself.
Col 1:13 He rescued us from the *p* of darkness and
2:10 is the head of every principality and *p.*
2:12 the *p* of God who raised him from the dead.
1Thes 1: 5 mere matter of words for you but one of *p;*
2Thes 1: 8 when "with flaming *p* he will inflict
1:11 *p* every honest intention and work of faith.
2: 9 accompanied by all the *p* and signs and
1Tm 6: 7 nor have we the *p* to take anything out.
2Tm 1:10 He has robbed death of its *p* and has
3: 5 a pretense of religion but negate its *p.*
4: 1 and by his appearing and his kingly *p,*
Heb 2: 4 it by signs, miracles, varied acts of *p,*
2:14 the devil, the prince of death, of his *p,*
7:16 the *p* of a life which cannot be destroyed.
11:11 *p* to conceive though she was past the age,
Jas 1:21 taken root in you, with its *p* to save you.
2:14 Such faith has no *p* to save one, has it?
1Pt 1: 5 who are guarded with God's *p* through faith;
1:12 the *p* of the Holy Spirit sent from heaven.
2Pt 1: 1 *p* of our God and Savior Jesus Christ;
1: 3 That divine *p* of his has freely bestowed
1: 3 him who called us by his own glory and *p.*
1:16 the coming in *p* of our Lord Jesus Christ,
2:11 though greater than men in strength and *p,*
1Jn 5: 4 and the *p* that has conquered the world is
Jude 1:25 too, be his, might and *p* from ages past,
Rv 1: 6 to him be glory and *p* forever and ever!
4:11 worthy to receive glory and honor and *p!*
5:12 that was slain to receive *p* and riches,
6: 4 Its rider was given *p* to rob the earth of
7: 2 given *p* to ravage the land and the sea,
7:12 and thanksgiving and honor, *p* and might,
9:19 The deadly *p* of the horses was not only in
11: 6 These witnesses have *p* to close up the sky
11: 6 They also have *p* to turn water into blood
11:17 You have assumed your great *p,*
12:10 "Now have salvation and *p* come,
13: 2 The dragon gave it his own *p* and throne,
13:15 so that the image had the *p* of speech and
16: 9 of God who had *p* to send these plagues,
17:13 bestow their *p* and authority on the beast.

POWERFUL (49)

Ex 1: 9 and *p* the Israelite people are growing,
Dt 7: 1 seven nations more numerous and *p* than you
2Sm 5:10 David grew steadily more *p,*
22:18 enemy, from my foes, who were too *p* for me.
2Kgs 10:11 Jezreel, as well as all his *p* supporters,
1Chr 5: 2 in fact, became *p* among his brothers,
11: 9 David became more and more *p,*
2Chr 12: 1 consolidated his rule and had become *p,*
22: 9 no one *p* enough to wield the kingship.
Ezr 4:20 *P* kings were once in Jerusalem who ruled
Est C:30 O God, more *p* than all,
9: 4 for Mordecai was *p* in the royal palace,
2Mc 12:35 a *p* horseman and one of Bacenor's men,
14: 1 port of Tripolis with a *p* army and a fleet,
Jb 34:20 removing the *p* without lifting a hand;
Ps(s) 18:18 and from my foes, who were too *p* for me.
76: 5 Resplendent you came, O *p* One,
93: 4 More *p* than the roar of many waters,
93: 4 more *p* than the breakers of the sea
93: 4 *p* on high is the LORD.
136:18 And slew *p* kings, for his mercy endures
Prv 24: 5 A wise man is more *p* than a strong man,
Wis 13: 4 how much more *p* is he who made them.
Sir 8:12 Lend not to one more *p* than yourself;
28:14 walled cities, and overthrows *p* dynasties.
48:24 By his *p* spirit he looked into the future
50: 2 with *p* turrets for the temple precincts;
Is 43:17 leads out chariots and horsemen, a *p* army,
Jer 5:27 Therefore they grow *p* and rich,
Dn 8: 4 it did what it pleased and became very *p.*
8: 8 The he-goat became very *p,*
8:24 He shall be strong and *p,*
8:24 He shall destroy *p* peoples;
11: 3 But a *p* king shall appear and rule with
Mt 3:11 one who will follow me is more *p* than I.
Mk 1: 7 "One more *p* than I is to come after me.
Lk 24:19 a prophet *p* in word and deed in the eyes
Acts 4:28 in your *p* providence you planned long ago.
7:22 He was a man *p* in word and deed.
9:22 Saul for his part grew steadily more *p,*
1Cor 1:25 than men, and his weakness more *p* than men.
2Cor 13: 3 weak in dealing with you, but is *p* in you.
Col 1:29 of his which is so *p* a force within me.
Heb 1: 3 and he sustains all things by his *p* word.
11:34 though weak they were made *p,*
Jas 5:16 fervent petition of a holy man is *p* indeed.
Rv 6:15 and those in command, the wealthy and *p,*
9: 3 locusts as *p* as scorpions in their sting.
18:21 A *p* angel picked up a stone like a huge

POWERLESS (14)

2Chr 14:10 like you to help the *p* against the strong.
20:12 We are *p* before this vast multitude that
Jdt 5:23 they said, "for they are a *p* people,
Jb 26: 2 What help you give to the *p,*
Wis 13:17 And for vigor he invokes the *p;*
17:14 they, during that night, *p* though it was,
17:14 them from the recesses of a *p* nether world,
Dn 3:44 Let them be shamed and *p,*
10: 8 I turned the color of death and was *p.*
10:16 with pangs at the vision and I was *p.*
Rom 5: 6 the appointed time, when we were still *p,*
8: 3 *p* because of its weakening by the flesh.
2Cor 12:10 for when I am *p,*
Gal 4: 9 how can you return to those *p,*

POWERS (16)

Wis 7:20 beasts, *P* of the winds and thoughts of men,
Sir 45: 2 the Lord strengthened him with fearful *p;*
Dn 4:32 he does as he pleases with the *p* of heaven
Mt 13:54 this man get such wisdom and miraculous *p?*
14: 2 why such miraculous *p* are at work in him!"
Mk 6:14 why such miraculous *p* are at work in him."
Lk 21:26 The *p* in the heavens will be shaken.
Rom 8:38 neither the present nor the future, nor *p,*
1Cor 12:10 of healing, and still another miraculous *p.*
Eph 3:10 to the principalities and *p* of heaven,
6:12 but against the principalities and *p,*
Col 1:16 or dominations, principalities or *p;*
2: 8 based on cosmic *p* rather than on Christ.
2:15 did God disarm the principalities and *p.*
Heb 6: 5 word of God and the *p* of the age to come,

POWERS (cont.)

1Pt 3:22 with angelic rulers and *p* subjected to him.

PRACTICALLY (1)

Lk 24:29 It is nearly evening—the day is *p* over."

PRACTICE (35)

Lv 19:26 Do not *p* divination or soothsaying.
2Kgs 16: 3 in accordance with the abominable *p* of the
2Chr 28: 3 to the abominable *p* of the nations
Ezr 7:10 Ezra had set his heart on the study and *p*
Neh 9:29 from which men draw life when they *p* them.
2Mc 15:12 from childhood in every virtuous *p*,
Prv 21:15 To *p* justice is a joy for the just,
Wis 14:16 *p* gained strength and was observed as law,
Sir 50:29 If he puts them into *p*,
Jer 6:13 prophet and priest, all *p* fraud.
8:10 for gain, prophet and priest, all *p* fraud.
32:35 mind that they should *p* such abominations.
Ez 13:23 longer see false visions and *p* divination,
22:29 of the land *p* extortion and commit robbery;
Hos 4:11 have abandoned the LORD to *p* harlotry.
7: 1 They *p* falsehood,
Mt 6:20 *p* instead to store up heavenly treasure,
7:24 who hears my words and puts them into *p*
7:26 my words but does not put them into *p*
Lk 6:46 Lord,' and not put into *p* what I teach you?
6:47 me will hear my words and put them into *p*.
6:49 heard my words but not put them into *p*
11:42 These are the things you should *p*,
Jn 13:17 blest will you be if you put them into *p*.
Acts 15: 1 you are circumcised according to Mosaic *p*,
16:21 are not lawful for us Romans to adopt or *p*."
25:16 I replied that it was not the Roman *p* to
2Cor 11:13 They *p* deceit in their disguise as
Heb 5:14 trained by *p* to distinguish good from evil.
Jas 1:23 to God's word but does not put it into *p*
1:25 but one who carries out the law in *p*.
2:17 is with the faith that does nothing in *p*.
3:13 let him show this in *p* through a humility
Rv 2:14 sacrificed to idols and to *p* fornication.
2:20 my servants by teaching them to *p* lewdness

PRACTICED (15)

2Kgs 17:17 by fire, *p* fortune-telling and divination,
17:19 God, but followed the rites *p* by Israel.
21: 6 He *p* soothsaying and divination,
21:11 has *p* these abominations and has done
2Chr 33: 6 He *p* augury,
Ps(s) 52: 4 is like a sharpened razor, you *p* deceiver!
Sir 15: 1 he who is *p* in the law will come to wisdom.
49: 3 and, though times were evil, he *p* virtue.
Ez 9: 4 all the abominations that are *p* within it.
18:13 Because he *p* all these abominations,
18:22 shall live because of the virtue he has *p*.
33:12 The virtue which a man has *p* will not save
Mt 23:23 It is these you should have *p*,
2Cor 12:21 fornication, and sensuality they *p*.
Jude 1: 7 they *p* unnatural vice.

PRACTICES (14)

Jgs 2:19 none of their evil *p* or stubborn conduct.
1Kgs 14:24 Judah imitated all the abominable *p* of the
2Kgs 17: 9 They adopted unlawful *p* toward the LORD,
21: 2 following the abominable *p* of the nations
2Chr 17: 4 his commands, and not the *p* of Israel.
33: 2 following the abominable *p* of the nations
Ps(s) 101: 7 not dwell within my house who *p* deceit.
Is 33:15 He who *p* virtue and speaks honestly,
Mk 7:13 And you have many other such *p* besides."
Jn 3:20 Everyone who *p* evil hates the light;
Acts 19:18 and openly confessed their former *p*.
Rom 1:24 them up in their lusts to unclean *p*;
2Cor 4: 2 we repudiate shameful, underhanded *p*.
Rv 2: 6 you detest the *p* of the Nicolaitans,

PRACTICING (6)

2Chr 36:14 *p* all the abominations of the nations and
Jer 22:17 blood, on *p* oppression and extortion.
Ez 8: 6 that the house of Israel is *p* here,
8:13 still greater abominations that they are *p*.
Acts 8: 9 A certain man named Simon had been *p* magic
Jas 2:14 good is it to profess faith without *p* it?

PRAETORIUM (8)

Mt 27:27 soldiers took Jesus inside the *p*
Mk 15:16 Jesus away into the hall known as the *p*;
Jn 18:28 they brought Jesus from Caiaphas to the *p*.
18:28 They did not enter the *p* themselves,
18:33 went back into the *p* and summoned Jesus.
19: 9 Going back into the *p*,
Acts 23:35 Paul to be kept under guard in Herod's *p*.
Phil 1:13 become well known throughout the *p* here,

PRAISE (314)

Gn 29:35 time I will give grateful *p* to the LORD";
49: 8 "You, Judah, shall your brothers *p*
Ex 15: 2 He is my God, I *p* him;
Dt 26:19 he will then raise you high in *p* and renown
2Sm 22:50 nations, and I will sing *p* to your name,
1Kgs 8:33 if then they return to you, *p* your name,
8:35 and pray, and *p* your name in this place,
1Chr 16: 4 LORD, to celebrate, thank, and *p* the LORD,
16: 9 Sing to him, sing his *p*,
16:27 *p* and joy are in his holy place.
16:28 of nations, give to the LORD glory and *p*;
23: 5 and four thousand were to *p* the LORD with
23: 5 instruments which David had devised for *p*.
23:30 morning to offer thanks and to *p* the LORD,
25: 3 a lyre, to give thanks and *p* to the LORD.
29:13 thanks and we *p* the majesty of your name."
2Chr 6:24 but afterward they return and *p* your name,
6:26 pray toward this place and *p* your name,
8:14 of *p* and ministry alongside the priests,
20:21 and some to *p* the holy Appearance
31: 2 or peace offerings, thanksgiving or *p*,
Ezr 3:10 the cymbals to *p* the LORD in the manner
3:11 in songs of *p* and thanksgiving to the LORD,
10:11 But now, give *p* to the LORD,
Neh 6:19 Thus they would *p* his good deeds in my
9: 5 name, and exalted above all blessing and *p*."
12:46 hymns of *p* and thanksgiving to God
Tb 8: 5 and all your creation *p* you forever.
8:15 Let all your chosen ones *p* you;
12: 6 Give him the *p* and the glory.
12: 7 *P* them with due honor.
12:18 *p* him with song.
12:20 So now get up from the ground and *p* God.
13: 3 *P* him, you Israelites, before the Gentiles,
13: 6 done for you, and *p* him with full voice.
13: 6 In the land of my exile I *p* him,
13:10 *P* the Lord for his goodness,
13:11 generation shall give joyful *p* in you,
13:16 see your glory and to *p* the King of heaven!
13:18 in you they shall *p* his holy name forever.
Jdt 13:14 "Praise God, *p* him! *P* God,
15:14 and the people swelled this hymn of *p*:
Est C:10 thus we shall live to sing *p* to your name,
C:10 Do not silence those who *p* you."
4:20 to close the mouths of those who *p* you,
1Mc 4:33 all who know your name may hymn your *p*."
4:56 and sacrifices of deliverance and *p*.
13:47 entered the city with hymns and songs of *p*.
2Mc 8:27 then observed the sabbath with fervent *p*
10: 7 they sang hymns of grateful *p* to him who
10:38 they blessed, with hymns of grateful *p*,
15:29 native tongue in *p* of the divine Sovereign.
Ps(s) 7:18 sing *p* to the name of the LORD Most High.
8: 3 you have fashioned *p* because of your foes,
9: 3 I will sing *p* to your name,
9:12 Sing *p* to the LORD enthroned in Zion;
18:50 nations, and I will sing *p* to your name,
21:14 We will sing, chant the *p* of your might.
22:23 in the midst of the assembly I will *p* you:
22:24 "You who fear the Lord, *p* him;
22:26 gift will I utter *p* in the vast assembly;
22:27 they who seek the LORD shall *p* him:
27: 6 I will sing and chant *p* to the LORD.
29: 1 sons of God, give to the LORD glory and *p*,
30: 5 Sing *p* to the LORD, you his faithful ones,
30:13 soul might sing *p* to you without ceasing;
33: 1 in the LORD, *p* from the upright is fitting.
34: 2 his *p* shall be ever in my mouth.
35:18 in the mighty throng I will *p* you.
35:28 tongue shall recount your justice, your *p*,
45:18 shall nations *p* you forever and ever.
47: 7 *p* to God, sing *p*; sing *p* to our king, sing *p*
47: 8 sing hymns of *p*.
48:11 your *p* reaches to the ends of the earth.
49:19 will *p* you for doing well for yourself,"
50:14 Offer to God *p* as your sacrifice and
50:23 that offers *p* as a sacrifice glorifies me;
51:17 lips, and my mouth shall proclaim your *p*.
54: 8 I will *p* your name,
57: 8 I will sing and chant *p*.
57:10 I will chant your *p* among the nations,
59:18 your *p* will I sing;
63: 6 with exultant lips my mouth shall *p* you.
65: 2 To you we owe our hymn of *p*,
66: 2 on earth, sing *p* to the glory of his name;
66: 2 proclaim his glorious *p*.
66: 4 sing praise to you, sing *p* to your name!"
66: 8 our God, you peoples, loudly sound his *p*;
66:17 in words, *p* was on the tip of my tongue.
67: 4 *p* you, O God; may all the peoples praise
67: 6 *p* you, O God; may all the peoples praise
68: 5 Sing to God, chant *p* to his name,
68:33 earth, sing to God, chant *p* to the Lord.
69:31 I will *p* the name of God in song,
69:35 Let the heavens and the earth *p* him,
71: 8 My mouth shall be filled with your *p*,
71:14 always hope and *p* you ever more and more.
74:21 may the afflicted and the poor *p* your name.
75:10 I will sing *p* to the God of Jacob.
79:13 all generations we will declare your *p*.
84: 5 continually they *p* you.
92: 2 thanks to the LORD, to sing *p* to your name,
96: 6 *p* and grandeur are in his sanctuary.
96: 7 of nations, give to the LORD glory and *p*;
98: 4 all you lands; break into song; sing *p*.
98: 5 Sing *p* to the LORD with the harp,
99: 3 Let them *p* your great and awesome name;
100: 4 with thanksgiving, his courts with *p*;
101: 1 to you, O LORD, I will sing *p*.
102:19 and let his future creatures *p* the LORD:
102:22 and his *p*, in Jerusalem, When the peoples
104:33 I will sing *p* to my God while I live.
105: 2 Sing to him, sing his *p*,
107:32 and *p* him in the council of the elders.
108: 2 I will sing and chant *p*.
108: 4 I will chant your *p* among the nations,
109: 1 O God, whom I *p*, be not silent,
109:30 in the midst of the throng I will *p* him,
111:10 His *p* endures forever.
113: 1 *P*, you servants of the LORD, praise
115:17 It is not the dead who *p* the LORD,
117: 1 *P* the LORD, all you nations; glorify him,
119:164 a day I *p* you for your just ordinances.
119:171 My lips pour forth your *p*,
119:175 Let my soul live to *p* you,
135: 3 *P* the LORD, for the LORD is good; sing *p*
138: 1 presence of the angels I will sing your *p*;
144: 9 a ten-stringed lyre I will chant your *p*,
145: 2 and I will *p* your name forever and ever.
145:21 May my mouth speak the *p* of the LORD,
146: 1 *P* the LORD, O my soul;
146: 2 I will *p* the LORD all my life; I will sing *p*
147: 1 *P* the LORD, for he is good; sing *p*
147: 1 it is fitting to *p* him.
147: 7 sing *p* with the harp to our God,
147:12 *p* your God,
148: 1 *P* the LORD from the heavens, *p* him
148: 2 *P* him, all you his angels, praise him,
148: 3 *P* him, sun and moon; praise him,
148: 4 *P* him, you highest heavens,
148: 5 Let them *p* the name of the LORD,
148: 7 *P* the LORD from the earth,
148:13 old men and boys, *P* the name of the LORD,
148:14 Be this his *p* from all his faithful ones,
149: 1 song of *p* in the assembly of the faithful.
149: 3 Let them *p* his name in the festive dance,
149: 3 them sing *p* to him with timbrel and harp.
150: 1 *P* the LORD in his sanctuary, *p* him
150: 2 *P* him for his mighty deeds, *p* him for
150: 3 *P* him with the blast of the trumpet, *p* him
150: 4 *P* him with timbrel and dance, *p* him
150: 5 *P* him with sounding cymbals, *p* him
150: 6 Let everything that has breath *p* the LORD!
Prv 27: 2 Let another *p* you—not your own mouth;
27:21 so a man is tested by the *p* he receives.
28: 4 Those who abandon the law *p* the wicked man
31:28 Her children rise up and *p* her;
31:31 and let her works *p* her at the city gates.
Sir 11: 2 *P* not a man for his looks.
15: 9 Unseemly is *p* on a sinner's lips,
15:10 But *p* is offered by the wise man's tongue;
17: 8 wonders of his deeds and *p* his holy name.
17:22 in place of the living who offer their *p*?
17:23 give *p* than those who have never lived;
18:28 who attains to her should declare her *p*;
27: 7 *P* no man before he speaks,
31: 9 Who is he, that we may *p* him?
32: 2 their joy and win *p* for your hospitality.
32:13 Above all, give *p* to your Creator,
35: 2 gives alms he presents his sacrifice of *p*.
37:24 full enjoyment, and all who see him *p* him;
39: 9 Many will *p* his understanding;
39:14 Send up the sweet odor of your hymn of *p*;
43:29 Let us *p* him the more,
43:31 though he is still beyond your power to *p*;
43:33 or who can *p* him as he is?
44: 1 Now will I *p* those godly men,
44:15 retold, and the assembly proclaims their *p*.
47: 8 thanks to God Most High, in words of *p*.
49:11 How can we fittingly *p* ZERUBBABEL,
50:18 over the throng sweet strains of *p* resound.
51: 1 I *p* you, O God my savior!
51:11 I will ever *p* your name and be constant in
51:12 For this reason I thank him and I *p* him;
51:17 I will give my teacher grateful *p*.
51:29 of God, and be not ashamed to give him *p*.
Is 12: 5 *p* to the LORD for his glorious achievement;
25: 1 my God, I will extol you and *p* your name;
42: 8 I give to no other, nor my *p* to idols.
42:10 new song, his *p* from the end of the earth:
42:12 LORD, and utter his *p* in the coastlands.
43:21 for myself, that they might announce my *p*.
60:18 your walls "Salvation" and your gates *P*."
61:11 and *p* spring up before all the nations.
62: 9 shall eat it, and you shall *p* the LORD;
Jer 13:11 to be my people, my renown, my *p*,
17:14 I may be saved, for it is you whom I *p*.
20:13 Sing to the LORD, *p* the LORD,
30:19 From them will resound songs of *p*,
31: 7 proclaim your *p* and say:
33: 9 Then Jerusalem shall be my joy, my *p*,
Bar 2:32 shall *p* me in the land of their captivity,
3: 6 and you O Lord, we will *p*!
3: 7 upon your name, and *p* you in our captivity,
Dn 2:23 O God of my fathers, I give thanks and *p*,
3:57 Lord, *p* and exalt him above all forever.
3:58 Lord, *p* and exalt him above all forever.
3:59 Lord, *p* and exalt him above all forever.
3:60 Lord, *p* and exalt him above all forever.
3:61 *p* and exalt him above all forever.
3:62 *p* and exalt him above all forever.

3:63 *p* and exalt him above all forever.
3:64 *p* and exalt him above all forever.
3:65 *p* and exalt him above all forever.
3:66 *p* and exalt him above all forever.
3:67 *p* and exalt him above all forever.
3:68 *p* and exalt him above all forever.]
3:69 *p* and exalt him above all forever.
3:70 *p* and exalt him above all forever.
3:71 *p* and exalt him above all forever.
3:72 *p* and exalt him above all forever.
3:73 *p* and exalt him above all forever.
3:74 Lord, *p* and exalt him above all forever.
3:75 *p* and exalt him above all forever.
3:76 *p* and exalt him above all forever.
3:77 *p* and exalt him above all forever.
3:78 *p* and exalt him above all forever.
3:79 Lord, *p* and exalt him above all forever.
3:80 *p* and exalt him above all forever.
3:81 *p* and exalt him above all forever.
3:82 *p* and exalt him above all forever.
3:83 *p* and exalt him above all forever.
3:84 *p* and exalt him above all forever.
3:85 *p* and exalt him above all forever.
3:86 *p* and exalt him above all forever.
3:87 *p* and exalt him above all forever.
3:88 *p* and exalt him above all forever.
3:90 *p* him and give him thanks,
4:34 *p* and exalt and glorify the King of heaven,
Jl 2:26 filled, and shall *p* the name of the LORD,
Jon 2:10 But I, with resounding *p*,
Hb 3: 3 glory, and with his *p* the earth is filled.
Zep 3:19 give them *p* and renown in all the earth,
3:20 For I will give you renown and *p*,
Mt 5:16 acts and give *p* to your heavenly Father.
11:25 of heaven and earth, to you I offer *p*;
21:16 and children you have framed a hymn of *p*'?"
26:30 Then, after singing songs of *p*,
Mk 2:12 all gave *p* to God,
14:26 After singing songs of *p*,
Lk 1:64 loosed, and he began to speak in *p* of God.
4:15 synagogues, and all were loud in his *p*.
5:26 Full of awe, they gave *p* to God,
7:16 seized them all and they began to *p* God.
7:29 even the tax collectors, gave *p* to God,
10:21 "I offer you *p*,
18:43 witnessed it and they too gave *p* to God.
19:37 disciples began to rejoice and *p* God loudly
Jn 5:41 "It is not that I accept human *p*—
5:44 when you accept *p* from one another yet do
12:43 preferred the *p* of men to the glory of God.
Acts 3: 9 people saw him moving and giving *p* to God,
13:48 responded to the word of the Lord with *p*.
Rom 2:29 Such a one receives his *p*,
7:25 All *p* to God, through Jesus Christ
14:11 me and every tongue shall give *p* to God."
15: 9 "Therefore I will *p* you among the
15:11 And, *P* the Lord, all you Gentiles
1Cor 4: 5 time, everyone will receive his *p* from God.
11: 2 I *p* you because you always remember me and
11:17 What I now have to say is not said in *p*,
11:22 Shall I *p* you?
14:16 If your *p* of God is solely with the spirit,
14:17 You will be uttering *p* very well indeed,
2Cor 8:18 churches *p* for his preaching of the gospel.
Eph 1: 6 that all might *p* the glorious favor he has
1:12 we were predestined to *p* his glory by
1:14 God has made his own, to *p* his glory.
5:19 Sing *p* to the Lord with all your hearts.
Phil 1:11 ripened in you, to the glory and *p* of God.
4: 8 decent, virtuous, or worthy of *p*.
Heb 2:12 sing your *p* in the midst of the assembly";
13:15 us continually offer God a sacrifice of *p*,
Jas 5:13 good spirits, he should sing a hymn of *p*.
1Pt 1: 7 gold, may by its genuineness lead to *p*,
2Pt 1:17 He received glory and *p* from God the
Rv 4: 9 and *p* to the One seated on the throne,
5:12 wisdom and strength, honor and glory and *p*!"
5:13 throne, and to the Lamb, be *p* and honor,
7:12 *P* and glory, wisdom and thanksgiving
11:17 "We *p* you, the Lord God Almighty
19: 5 *P* our God, all you his servants,

PRAISED (40)

Gn 12:15 courtiers saw her, they *p* her to Pharaoh.
Jgs 16:24 When the people saw him, they *p* their god.
2Sm 14:25 could so be *p* for his beauty as Absalom,
22: 4 *P* be the LORD,'
1Chr 16:25 For great is the LORD and highly to be *p*;
Neh 5:13 answered, "Amen," and *p* the LORD.
Tb 8: 5 *p* be your name forever and ever.
8:15 Raguel *p* the God of heaven in these words:
11:14 "Blessed be God, and *p* be his great name,
11:14 his holy name be *p* throughout all the ages,
14:15 Tobiah *p* God for all that he had done
Jdt 6:20 they reassured Achior and *p* him highly.
1Mc 4:55 themselves and adored and *p* Heaven,
5:64 and men gathered about them and *p* them.
2Mc 3:30 the Jews *p* the Lord who had marvelously
12:41 They all therefore *p* the ways of the Lord,
15:34 *p* the LORD who manifests his divine power,
Jb 36:24 extol his work, which men have *p* in song.
Ps(s) 18: 4 *P* be the LORD,
44: 9 your name we *p* always.
48: 2 and wholly to be *p* in the city of our God.
96: 4 For great is the LORD and highly to be *p*;
113: 3 of the sun is the name of the LORD to be *p*.
145: 3 Great is the LORD and highly to be *p*;
Prv 12: 8 According to his good sense a man is *p*,
31:30 the woman who fears the LORD is to be *p*.
Eccl 8:10 were *p* in the city for what they had done.
Wis 10:20 name and *p* in unison your conquering hand
Sir 47:10 psalms So that when the Holy Name was *p*,
Is 64:10 fathers *p* you Has been burned with fire;
Dn 4:31 I *p* and glorified him who lives forever:
5: 4 them, they *p* their gods of gold and silver,
5:23 and you *p* the gods of silver and gold,
13:63 his wife *p* God for their daughter Susanna,
Mt 9: 8 *p* God for giving such authority to men.
Acts 21:20 When they heard it they *p* God,
2Cor 1: 3 *P* be God,
Eph 1: 3 *P* be the God and Father of our Lord Jesus
Jas 3: 9 use it to say, *P* be the Lord and Father";
1Pt 1: 3 *P* be the God and Father of our Lord Jesus

PRAISES (31)

1Chr 16: 7 for the first time these *p* of the LORD:
2Chr 20:19 Korahites rose to sing the *p* of the LORD,
29:30 then commanded the Levites to sing the *p*
29:30 They sang *p* till their joy was full,
30:21 the Levites and the priests sang the *p*
30:22 peace offerings and singing *p* to the LORD,
Neh 12:24 who stood opposite them to sing *p*
Tb 12:22 They kept thanking God and singing his *p*;
13: 8 his majesty, and sing his *p* in Jerusalem."
Ps(s) 9:15 death, That I may declare all your *p* and,
33: 2 with the ten-stringed lyre chant his *p*.
61: 9 So will I sing the *p* of your name forever,
71:22 I will sing your *p* with the harp,
71:23 lips shall shout for joy as I sing your *p*;
106: 2 deeds of the LORD, or proclaim all his *p*?
106:12 they believed his words and sang his *p*.
145: 4 *p* your works and proclaims your might.
149: 6 let the high *p* of God be in their throats.
Sg 6: 9 and concubines, and they sang her *p*;
Wis 18: 9 previously sung the *p* of the fathers.
Sir 24: 1 Wisdom sings her own *p*,
31:11 secure, and the assembly recounts his *p*.
39:10 of his wisdom, and in assembly sing his *p*.
39:15 greatness of his name, loudly sing his *p*,
47: 6 *p* and ascribed to him tens of thousands.
47: 8 loved his Maker and daily had his *p* sung;
51:22 a reward, and my tongue will declare his *p*.
Is 38:18 gives you thanks, nor death that *p* you;
60: 6 and proclaiming the *p* of the LORD,
Lk 17:16 face at the feet of Jesus and spoke his *p*.
24:53 temple constantly, speaking the *p* of God.

PRAISEWORTHY (10)

Sir 44: 8 a name and men recount their *p* deeds;
Dn 3:26 "Blessed are you, and *p*,
3:52 fathers, *p* and exalted above all forever;
3:52 name, *p* and exalted above all for all ages.
3:53 glory, *p* and glorious above all forever.
3:54 kingdom, *p* and exalted above all forever.
3:55 cherubim, *p* and exalted above all forever.
3:56 of heaven, *p* and glorious forever.
Mt 5:47 brothers only, what is so *p* about that?
2Cor 9:13 Because of your *p* service they are

PRAISING (18)

1Chr 16:35 to your holy name and glory in *p* you."
2Chr 5:13 voice *p* and giving thanks to the LORD,
7: 3 faces to the earth and adored, *p* the LORD,
7: 6 which King David had made for *p* the LORD,
Ezr 3:11 *p* the LORD because the foundation of the
Tb 11:15 in, rejoicing and *p* God with full voice.
11:16 Rejoicing and *p* God, Tobit went out
12: 6 God's deeds, and do not be slack in *p* him.
14: 2 blessing God and *p* the divine Majesty.
Ps(s) 106:47 to your holy name and glory in *p* you.
Wis 19: 9 and bounded about like lambs, *p* you,
Lk 2:13 of the heavenly host, *p* God and saying,
2:20 and *p* God for all they had heard and seen,
5:25 he had been lying on and went home *p* God.
17:15 cured, came back *p* God in a loud voice.
Acts 2:47 *p* God and winning the approval of all the
3: 8 walking, jumping about, and *p* God.
4:21 of whom were *p* God for what had happened.

PRANCE (1)

Hb 1: 8 His horses *p*, his horsemen come from afar:

PRATING (2)

Prv 10: 8 commands, but a *p* fool will be overthrown.
12:18 The *p* of some men is like sword thrusts,

PRAY (122)

Gn 32:12 Save me, I *p*, from the hand of my brother
Ex 8: 4 *P* the LORD to remove the frogs from me and
8: 5 appointing the time when I am to *p* for you
8:24 not go too far away and that you *p* for me."
8:25 *p* to the LORD that the flies may depart
9:28 *P* to the LORD, for we have had enough
10:17 me my sin once more, and *p* the LORD,
Nm 12:13 *P*, heal her!"
21: 7 *P* the LORD to take the serpents from us."
Jos 7: 8 *P*, Lord, what can I say, now
Jgs 6:18 Do not depart from here, I *p* you,
1Sm 7: 5 Mizpah, that I may *p* to the LORD for you."
12:19 to Samuel, *P* to the LORD your God for us,
12:23 to sin against the LORD by ceasing to *p* for
1Kgs 8:33 return to you, praise your name, *p* to you,
8:35 if then they repent of their sin, and *p*,
8:44 against their enemies, if they *p* to you,
8:48 *p* to you toward the land you gave their
2Kgs 6:18 LORD, "Strike this people blind, I *p* you."
1Chr 17:25 your servant has made bold to *p* before you.
2Chr 6:24 *p* to you and entreat you in this temple,
6:26 *p* toward this place and praise your name,
6:34 and *p* to you in the direction of this city
6:38 when they *p* in the direction of their land
7:14 been pronounced, humble themselves and *p*,
Ezr 6:10 *p* for the life of the king and his sons.
Neh 1: 8 But remember, I *p*,
Tb 3: 1 Then with sobs I began to *p*:
6:18 with her, both of you first rise up to *p*.
8: 4 Let us *p* and beg our LORD to have mercy on
8: 5 *p* and beg that deliverance might be theirs.
Jdt 8:31 *p* for us that the Lord may send rain to
11:17 will go out to the ravine and *p* to God.
1Mc 3:44 and to *p* and implore mercy and compassion.
2Mc 12:44 useless and foolish to *p* for them in death.
Jb 21:15 And what gain shall we have if we *p* to him?"
33:26 He shall *p* and God will favor him;
42: 8 and let my servant Job *p* for you;
Ps(s) 5: 3 To you I *p*,
32: 6 faithful man *p* to you in time of stress.
69:14 But I *p* to you, O LORD,
80: 5 you burn with anger while your people *p*?
122: 6 *P* for the peace of Jerusalem!
122: 9 the LORD, our God, I will *p* for your good.
141: 5 but I will still *p* under these afflictions.
Sir 17:20 sin, *p* to him and make your offenses few.
21: 1 and for your past sins *p* to be forgiven.
28: 2 then when you *p*, your own sins will be
37:15 *p* to God to set your feet in the path of
38: 9 when you are ill, delay not, but *p* to God,
Is 1:15 Though you *p* the more,
16:12 places, he shall enter his sanctuary to *p*,
45:20 idols and *p* to gods that cannot save.
Jer 29: 7 *p* for it to the LORD,
29:12 When you call me, when you go to *p* to me,
37: 3 *P* to the LORD, our God, for us."
42: 2 *p* for us to the LORD,
42: 4 I will *p* to the LORD,
42:20 your God, saying, *P* for us to the LORD,
Bar 1:11 God, and *p* for the life of Nebuchadnezzar,
1:13 *P* for us also to the Lord,
Dn 3:41 whole heart, we fear you and we *p* to you.
Mt 5:44 love your enemies, *p* for your persecutors.
6: 5 the hypocrites who love to stand and *p*
6: 6 Whenever you *p*, go to your room,
6: 6 your door, and *p* to your Father in private.
6: 9 This is how you are to *p*:
14:23 went up on the mountain by himself to *p*,
18:19 on earth to *p* for anything whatever,
21:22 You will receive all that you *p* for,
26:36 "Stay here while I go over there and *p*."
26:41 and *p* that you may not undergo the test.
26:42 Withdrawing a second time, he began to *p*:
26:44 somewhat, and began to *p* a third time,
Mk 6:46 of them, he went off to the mountain to *p*.
11:25 When you stand to *p*, forgive anyone
14:32 "Sit down here while I *p*."
14:38 and *p* that you may not be put to the test.
14:39 back again he began to *p* in the same words.
Lk 6:12 Then he went out to the mountain to *p*,
6:28 curse you and *p* for those who maltreat you.
9:28 James, and went up onto a mountain to *p*.
11: 1 disciples asked him, "Lord, teach us to *p*,
11: 2 He said to them, "When you *p*, say:
18:10 "Two men went up to the temple to *p*;
21:36 *P* constantly for the strength to escape
22:40 *P* that you may not be put to the test."
22:46 and *p* that you may not be subjected to the
Jn 17: 9 "For these I *p*— not for the world
17:20 "I do not *p* for them alone.
17:20 I *p* also for those who will believe in me
17:21 I *p* that they may be [one] in us,
Acts 8:22 *P* that the Lord may pardon you for
10: 9 Peter went up to the roof terrace to *p*.
Rom 8:26 for we do not know how to *p* as we ought;
15:31 *P* that I may be kept safe from the
1Cor 11:13 it proper for a woman to *p* to God unveiled?
14:13 should *p* for the gift of interpretation.
14:14 If I *p* in a tongue my spirit is at prayer
14:15 I want to *p* with my spirit, and also to *p*
2Cor 9:14 They *p* for you longingly because of the
13: 7 We *p* God that you may do no evil
Eph 3:16 and I *p* that he will bestow on you gifts
6:18 At every opportunity *p* in the Spirit,
6:18 *P* constantly and attentively for all in
6:19 *P* for me that God may put his word on my
6:20 *P* that I may have courage to proclaim it
Col 4: 2 *P* perseveringly, be attentive to prayer, and *p*

PRAY (cont.)

4: 3 P for us, too, that God may provide us
4: 4 P that I may speak it clearly, as I must.
1Thes 5:25 Brothers, p for us too.
2Thes 1:11 We p for you always that our God may make
3: 1 p for us that the word of the Lord may
3: 2 P that we may be delivered from confused
Heb 13:18 P for us;
Jas 5:13 among you is suffering hardship, he must p.
5:14 They in turn are to p over him,
5:16 sins to one another, and p for one another,
1Pt 4: 7 remain calm so that you will be able to p.
1Jn 5:16 I do not say that one should p about that.

PRAYED (77)

Gn 24:12 Then he p: "LORD, God of my master
24:42 "When I came to the spring today, I p:
32:10 Then he p: "O God of my father Abraham
Ex 8:26 left Pharaoh's presence, he p to the LORD;
10:18 the presence of Pharaoh, he p to the LORD,
Nm 11: 2 he p to the LORD and the fire died out.
21: 7 So Moses p for the people,
Dt 9:20 him had I not p for him also at that time.
Jos 7: 7 "Alas, O Lord GOD," Joshua p,
10:12 to the Israelites, Joshua p to the LORD,
Jgs 13: 8 Manoah then p to the LORD.
1Sm 1:10 In her bitterness she p to the LORD,
1:27 I p for this child,
8: 6 He p to the LORD,
1Kgs 19: 4 He p for death:
2Kgs 4:33 the door on them both, and p to the LORD.
6:17 Then he p, "O LORD, open his eyes,
6:18 came down to get him, Elisha p to the LORD,
6:20 When they entered Samaria, Elisha p,
19:15 before him, he p in the LORD's presence:
20: 2 his face to the wall and p to the LORD:
1Chr 4:10 Jabez p to the God of Israel:
21:17 face to the ground, and David p to God:
2Chr 6:14 Thus he p: "LORD, God of Israel,
30:18 for Hezekiah p for them,
32:20 son of Amos, p and called out to heaven.
32:24 He p to the LORD,
33:13 before the God of his fathers and p to him.
Ezr 8:23 So we fasted, and p to our God for this,
10: 1 While Ezra p and acknowledged their guilt,
Neh 1: 4 I fasted and p before the God of heaven.
1: 5 I p: "O LORD, God of heaven,
2: 4 I p to the God of heaven and then answered
4: 3 We p to our God and posted a watch against
Tb 12:12 you that when you, Tobit, and Sarah p,
Jdt 9: 1 Judith p to the Lord with a loud voice:
Est C: 1 the Lord had done, he p to him and said:
C:14 Then she p to the Lord,
1Mc 4:30 Seeing that the army was strong, he p thus:
11:71 clothes, threw earth on his head, and p.
2Mc 1: 8 But we p to the Lord,
2: 8 in the time of Moses and when Solomon p
2:10 Just as Moses p to the Lord and fire
2:10 so Solomon also p and fire came down and
5: 4 p that this vision might be a good omen.
12:42 they p that the sinful deed might be fully
14:15 p to him who established his people forever,
15:22 He p to him thus: "You, O LORD, sent
Jb 42:10 of Job, after he had p for his friends;
Ps(s) 72:15 of Arabia, and to be p for continually;
109: 4 for my love they slandered me, but I p.
Wis 7: 7 Therefore I p, and prudence was given me;
Is 37:15 it out before him, he p to the LORD:
38: 2 his face to the wall and p to the LORD:
Jer 32:16 son of Neriah, I p thus to the LORD.
Bar 1: 5 They wept and fasted and p before the Lord,
Dn 3:25 In the fire Azariah stood up and p aloud:
9: 4 I p to the LORD, my God, and confessed,
Jon 4: 2 "I beseech you, LORD," he p,
Lk 5:16 He often retired to deserted places and p.
18:11 with head unbowed p in this fashion:
22:32 p for you that your faith may never fail.
22:41 down on his knees and p in these words:
22:44 he p with all the greater intensity,
Acts 1:24 Then they p: "O LORD, you read the hearts
4:31 where they were gathered shook as they p.
6: 6 p over them and then imposed hands on them.
8:15 p that they might receive the Holy Spirit.
9:40 then he knelt down and p.
10: 2 to the people and he constantly p to God.
12: 5 church p fervently to God on his behalf.
13: 3 Then, after they had fasted and p,
20:36 Paul knelt down with them all and p.
21: 5 off, and we knelt down on the beach and p.
27:29 anchors from the stern and p for daylight.
Jas 5:17 yet he p earnestly that it would not rain
5:18 When he p again, the sky burst forth with

PRAYER (165)

Gn 24:45 "I had scarcely finished saying this p to
30:17 he slept with her, and God heard her p;
30:22 he heard her p and made her fruitful.
Nm 21: 3 Israel's p and delivered up the Canaanites,
Dt 9:26 This was my p to him:
Jgs 13: 9 God heard the p of Manoah,
1Sm 1:12 As she remained long at p before the LORD,
1:16 my p has been prompted by my deep sorrow
2Sm 7:27 finds the courage to make this p to you.
1Kgs 8:28 on the p and petition of your servant,
8:29 may you heed the p which I,
8:38 conscience and offers some p or petition,
8:45 listen in heaven to their p and petition,
8:54 this entire p of petition to the LORD,
8:59 May this p I have offered to the LORD,
9: 3 "I have heard the p of petition which you
17:22 The LORD heard the p of Elijah;
2Kgs 6:18 the prophet's p the LORD struck them blind.
19: 4 send up a p for the remnant that is here.'"
19:20 to your p for help against Sennacherib,
20: 5 I have heard your p and seen your tears.
1Chr 4:10 And God granted his p.
2Chr 6:19 on the p and petition of your servant,
6:20 may you heed the p which I your servant
6:29 people offers a p or petition of any kind,
6:32 arm, when they come in p to this temple,
6:35 listen from heaven to their p and petition,
6:39 dwelling place, hear their p and petitions,
6:40 your ears attentive to the p of this place.
7: 1 When Solomon had ended his p,
7:12 "I have heard your p,
7:15 my ears attentive to the p of this place.
30:27 voice was heard and their p reached heaven,
33:13 he heard his p and restored him to his
33:18 of the acts of Manasseh, his p to his God,
33:19 His p and how his supplication was heard,
Neh 1: 6 and your eyes open, to heed the p which I,
1:11 may your ear be attentive to my p and that
11:17 the psalms, who led the thanksgiving at p;
Tb 3:11 and facing the window, poured out this p:
3:16 the p of these two suppliants was heard in
12: 8 P and fasting are good,
12:12 of your p before the Glory of the Lord;
13: 1 Then Tobit composed this joyful p:
Jdt 9:12 King of all you have created, hear my p!
12: 6 my lord, to let your handmaid go out for p."
13: 3 she said she would be going out for her p.
13:10 as they were accustomed to do for p.
Est C:10 Hear my p; have pity on your inheritance
1Mc 3:46 formerly at Mizpah a place of p for Israel.
5:33 blowing their trumpets and shouting in p.
7:37 a house of p and petition for your people.
7:40 Here Judas uttered this p:
2Mc 1: 8 we prayed to the Lord, and our p was heard;
1:23 was being burned, the priests recited a p,
1:24 The p was as follows:
3:21 the populace variously prostrated in p
10:27 After the p, they took up their arms
15:24 With this he ended his p.
Jb 16:17 free from violence, and my p is sincere.
42: 8 for his p I will accept,
Ps(s) 4: 2 Have pity on me, and hear my p!
6:10 the LORD has accepted my p.
17: 1 hearken to my p from lips without deceit.
22: 2 why have you forsaken me, far from my p,
39:13 Hear my p, O LORD; to my cry give ear;
42: 9 I have his song, a p to my living God.
54: 4 O God, hear my p;
55: 2 Hearken, O God, to my p;
61: 2 Hear, O God, my cry; listen to my p!
66:19 he has hearkened to the sound of my p.
66:20 who refused me not my p or his kindness!
84: 9 O LORD of hosts, hear my p;
86: 6 p and attend to the sound of my pleading.
88: 3 Let my p come before you;
88:14 with my morning p I wait upon you.
102: 2 O LORD, hear my p, amd let my cry come
102:18 he has regarded the p of the destitute,
102:18 the destitute, and not despised their p.
141: 2 Let my p come like incense before you;
142: 1 A p when he was in the cave.
143: 1 O LORD, hear my p;
Prv 15: 8 but the p of the upright is his delight.
15:29 the wicked, but the p of the just he hears.
28: 9 the law, even his p is an abomination.
Wis 18:21 office, p and the propitiation of incense;
Sir 4: 6 he curse you, his Creator will hear his p.
7:14 and repeat not the words of your p.
21: 5 P from a poor man's lips is heard at once,
34:26 Who will hear his p,
35:17 The p of the lowly pierces the clouds;
36:16 Hear the p of your servants,
39: 6 the Most High, To open his lips in p,
39: 6 of wisdom and in p give thanks to the LORD,
48:20 He heard the p they uttered and saved them
Is 37: 4 Send up a p for the remnant that is here.'"
37:21 to your p for help against Sennacherib,
38: 5 I have heard your p and seen your tears.
45:14 you they shall fall prostrate, saying in p:
56: 7 mountain and make joyful in my house of p;
56: 7 be called a house of p for all peoples.
Jer 7:16 raise not in their behalf a pleading p!
42: 9 to whom you sent me to offer your p:
Lam 3: 8 when I cry out for help, he stops my p;
3:44 in a cloud which p could not pierce.
Bar 2:14 Hear, O Lord, our p of supplication,
3: 4 God of Israel, hear the p of Israel's few,
4:20 put on sackcloth for my p of supplication,
Dn 6:11 his custom of going home to kneel in p
6:14 three times a day he offers his p."
9: 3 to the Lord God, pleading in earnest p,
9:17 O God, the p and petition of your servant;
9:20 I was still occupied with my p,
9:21 I was still occupied with this p,
10:12 yourself before God, your p was heard.
13:44 The Lord heard her p.
Jon 2: 2 of the fish Jonah said this p to the LORD,
2: 8 My p reached you in your holy temple.
Mt 6: 7 In your p do not rattle on like the pagans.
17:21 kind does not leave but by p and fasting.]"
19:13 that he could place his hands on them in p.
21:13 'My house shall be called a house of p,'
26:39 advanced a little and fell prostrate in p.
Mk 1:35 there he was absorbed in p.
9:29 "This kind you can drive out only by p."
11:17 be called a house of p for all peoples'
11:24 you will receive whatever you ask for in p,
Lk 1:13 your p has been heard.
2:37 worshiping day and night in fasting and p.
3:21 was at p after likewise being baptized,
19:46 'My house is meant for a house of p' but
22:45 he rose from p and came to his disciples,
Acts 1:14 they devoted themselves to constant p.
3: 1 the temple for p at the three o'clock hour,
4:24 voices in p to God on hearing the story:
6: 4 on p and the ministry of the word."
10:31 'your p has been heard and your generosity
11: 5 "I was at p in the city of Joppa when,
12:12 where many others were gathered in p.
14:23 presbyters and, with p and fasting,
16:13 we thought there would be a place of p.
16:16 we were on our way out to the place of p
Rom 1: 9 that I constantly mention you in p,
10: 1 desire, my p to God for the Israelites,
12:12 be patient under trial, persevere in p.
1Cor 7: 5 for a time, to devote yourselves to p.
14:14 is at p but my mind contributes nothing.
2Cor 13: 9 Our p is that you may be built up to
Phil 1: 4 which is constantly, in every p I utter
1: 9 My p is that your love may more and more
4: 6 of p and in petitions full of gratitude.
Col 4: 2 Pray perseveringly, be attentive to p,
4:12 earnestly in p that you stand firm,
1Tm 2: 3 P of this kind is good,
4: 5 for it is made holy by God's word and by p.
Jas 5:15 This p uttered in faith will reclaim the
1Pt 1:17 In p you call upon a Father who judges
Jude 1:20 holy faith through p in the Holy Spirit.

PRAYERS (37)

Est D: 1 the third day, putting an end to her p,
1Mc 12:11 sacrifices and p that we offer on our feasts
2Mc 1: 5 May he hear your p,
10:16 after public p asking God to be their ally,
15:26 men met the army with supplication and p.
Ps(s) 35:13 fasting and poured forth p within my bosom.
65: 2 must vows be fulfilled, you who hear p.
72:20 The p of David the son of Jesse are ended.
Sir 7:10 Be not impatient in p,
51:11 your name and be constant in my p to you.
Mk 12:40 and recite long p for appearance sake;
Lk 5:33 disciples fast frequently and offer p;
20:47 they recite long p to keep up appearances.
Acts 2:42 life, to the breaking of bread and the p.
8:24 "I need the p of all of you to the Lord,
10: 4 "Your p and your generosity have risen in
Rom 15:30 the struggle by your p to God on my behalf.
2Cor 1:11 But you must help us with your p,
1:11 gift granted us through the p of so many.
Eph 1:16 God for you and recommending you in my p.
6:18 using p and petitions of every sort.
Phil 1:19 thanks to your p and the support I receive
Col 1: 3 in our p for you because we have heard of
1Thes 1: 2 all of you and we remember you in our p,
1Tm 2: 1 First of all, I urge that petitions, p,
2: 8 offer p with blameless hands held aloft,
5: 5 night and day in supplications and p.
2Tm 1: 3 whenever I remember you in my p—
Phlm 1: 4 my brother, as I commend you in my p,
1: 6 And my p is that your sharing of the faith
1:22 through your p I shall be restored to you.
Heb 5: 7 he offered p and supplications with loud
13:19 p that I may be restored to you very soon.
1Pt 3: 7 will keep your p from being answered.
Rv 5: 8 which were the p of God's holy people.
8: 3 together with the p of all God's holy ones.
8: 4 God, and with it the p of God's people.

PRAYING (27)

1Sm 1:13 her mouth, for Hannah was p silently;
1:26 who stood near you here, p to the LORD.
1Chr 29:10 of the whole assembly, p in these words:
2Chr 14:10 Asa called upon the LORD, his God, p:
2Mc 1: 6 Even now we are p for you here.
3:31 p that the life of the man who was about
15:12 was p with outstretched arms for the whole
15:27 their hands and p to God with their hearts,
Sir 50:19 would shout for joy, p to the Merciful One,
Dn 6:12 found Daniel p and pleading before his God.
Mt 6: 5 "When you are p,
24:20 Keep p that you will not have to flee in
Mk 13:18 Keep p that none of this happens in winter.
14:35 p that if it were possible this hour might

Lk 1:10 people was *p* outside at the incense hour,
9:18 One day when Jesus was *p* in seclusion and
9:29 While he was *p*, his face changed
11: 1 One day he was *p* in a certain place.
18: 1 necessity of *p* always and not losing heart:
Acts 7:59 was being stoned he could be heard *p*,
9:12 He is there *p*."
10:30 I was *p* at home when a man in dazzling
16:25 while Paul and Silas were *p* and singing
22:17 I was *p* in the court of the temple,
28: 8 Paul went in to see the man and *p*,
Col 1: 9 Ever since we heard this we have been *p*
1Thes 5:17 Rejoice always, never cease *p*,

PRAYS (8)

1Kgs 8:42 when he comes and *p* toward this temple,
2Mc 15:14 *p* for his people and their holy city."
Prv 27: 6 the greetings of an enemy one *p* against.
Wis 13:17 *p* about his goods or marriage or children,
Sir 3: 5 by children, and when he *p* he is heard.
34:24 If one man *p* and another curses,
1Cor 11: 4 Any man who *p* or prophesies with his head
11: 5 any woman who *p* or prophesies with her

PRE-EMINENCE (2)

Prv 28:12 but when the wicked gain *p*,
28:28 When the wicked gain *p*,

PRE-EMINENT (1)

Jb 37:23 discover him, *p* in power and judgment;

PREACH (38)

Ez 21: 2 of man, look southward, *p* toward the south,
21: 7 Jerusalem, *p* against their sanctuary,
Am 7:16 Israel, *p* not against the house of Isaac.
Jon 1: 2 great city of Nineveh, and *p* against it;
Mi 2: 6 *P* not," they preach, "let them not preach
Mt 11: 1 locality to teach and *p* in their towns.
Mk 3:14 whom he would send to *p* the good news;
Lk 4:44 continued to *p* in the synagogues of Judea.
Acts 5:20 *p* to the people all about this new life."
10:42 He commissioned us to *p* to the people and
Rom 1:15 to *p* the gospel to you Romans as well.
2:16 when, in accordance with the gospel I *p*,
2:21 You who *p* against stealing, do you steal?
10: 8 (that is, the word of faith which we *p*).
10:14 can they hear unless there is someone to *p*?
10:15 And how can men *p* unless they are sent?
15:20 point of honor with me never to *p* in places
16:25 which I proclaim when I *p* Jesus Christ,
1Cor 1:17 send me to baptize, but to *p* the gospel
1:23 for "wisdom," but we *p* Christ crucified
9:14 who *p* the gospel should live by the gospel.
9:16 I am ruined if I do not *p* it!
15:11 is what we *p* and this is what you believed.
2Cor 2:12 I came to Troas to *p* the gospel of Christ,
4: 5 ourselves we *p* but Christ Jesus as Lord,
10:16 we hope to *p* the gospel even beyond your
Gal 1: 8 should *p* to you a gospel not in accord
Eph 3: 8 was given the grace to *p* to the Gentiles
Phil 1:15 *p* Christ from motives of envy and rivalry,
Col 1:25 me to *p* among you his word in its fullness,
1Thes 2: 2 we drew courage from our God to *p* his good
1Tm 6: 2 These are the things you must teach and *p*.
2Tm 2: 8 This is the gospel I *p*;
4: 2 kingly power, I charge you to *p* the word,
1Pt 1:12 to you by those who *p* the gospel to you,
3:19 that he went to *p* to the spirits in prison.

PREACHED (26)

Dt 13: 6 to take, he has *p* apostasy from the LORD,
Jer 28:16 you have *p* rebellion against the LORD.
29:32 because he *p* rebellion against the LORD.
Mt 11: 5 and the poor have the good news *p* to them.
Mk 16:20 The Eleven went forth and *p* everywhere.
Lk 3:18 sort, he *p* the good news to the people.
7:22 and the poor have the good news *p* to them.
24:47 of sins is to be *p* to all the nations,
Acts 8:12 to believe in the good news that Philip *p*
10:37 in Galilee with the baptism John *p*;
20: 7 for the breaking of bread, Paul *p* to them.
26:20 I *p* a message of reform and of conversion
28:31 he *p* the reign of God and taught about the
1Cor 9:27 *p* to others I myself should be rejected.
15: 1 to remind you of the gospel I *p* to you,
15: 2 if you hold fast to it as I *p* it to you.
15:12 me, if Christ is *p* as raised from the dead,
2Cor 1:19 Timothy, and I *p* to you as Son of God,
11: 4 preaching another Jesus than the one we *p*,
11: 7 *p* the gospel of God to you free of charge,
Eph 4:21 that he has been *p* and taught to you in
1Thes 2: 9 all the time we *p* God's good tidings to you
1Tm 3:16 *p* among the Gentiles,
1Pt 1:25 "word" is the gospel which was *p* to you.
4: 6 the gospel was *p* even to the dead was that,
2Pt 3: 2 Lord and Savior *p* to you by the apostles.

PREACHER (3)

Mt 3: 1 appearance as a *p* in the desert of Judea,
2Tm 1:11 been appointed *p* and apostle and teacher,
2Pt 2: 5 he preserved Noah as a *p* of holiness,

PREACHES (2)

Acts 19:13 "I adjure you by the Jesus whom Paul *p*."
Gal 1: 9 if anyone *p* a gospel to you other than the

PREACHING (41)

Mt 12:41 the *p* of Jonah they reformed their lives;
21:32 When John came *p* a way of holiness,
Mk 1: 7 The theme of his *p* was:
1:39 So he went into their synagogues *p* the
6:12 they went off, *p* the need of repentance.
Lk 8: 1 he journeyed through towns and villages *p*
11:32 For at the *p* of Jonah they reformed,
Acts 8: 4 had been dispersed went about *p* the word.
14: 9 one occasion he was listening to Paul *p*,
14:25 After *p* the message in Perga,
15:35 teaching and *p* the word of the Lord.
16: 6 from *p* the message in the province of Asia.
18: 5 Paul was absorbed in *p* and giving evidence
20:25 *p* the kingdom will ever see my face again.
Rom 1: 9 The God I worship in the spirit by *p* the
15:16 with the priestly duty of *p* the gospel of
15:19 I have completed *p* the gospel of Christ
1Cor 1:21 the absurdity of the *p* of the gospel.
2: 4 My message and my *p* had none of the
4:15 in Christ Jesus through my *p* of the gospel.
9:16 *p* the gospel is not the subject of a boast;
9:18 that when *p* I offer the gospel free of
14:36 Did the *p* of God's word originate with you?
15:14 our *p* is void of content and your faith is
2Cor 8:18 churches praise for his *p* of the gospel.
11: 4 *p* another Jesus than the one we preached,
Gal 1:23 us is now *p* the faith he tried to destroy,"
5:11 me, brothers, if I am still *p* circumcision,
Eph 3: 6 of the promise through the *p* of the gospel.
1Thes 1: 5 Our *p* of the gospel proved not a mere
2:16 keep us from *p* salvation to the Gentiles.
3: 2 fellow worker in *p* the gospel of Christ,
2Thes 2:14 He called you through our *p* of the good
1Tm 4:13 reading of Scripture, to *p* and teaching.
5:17 those whose work is *p* and teaching.
2Tm 2: 9 in *p* it I suffer as a criminal,
2:15 following a straight course in *p* the truth.
4:15 guard, for he has strongly resisted our *p*.
4:17 so that through me the *p* task might be
Ti 1: 3 in the *p* entrusted to me by the command
1Pt 3: 1 of the gospel may be won over apart from *p*,

PRECAUTION (1)

Mk 14:44 him and lead him away, taking every *p*."

PRECEDE (6)

Gn 32:21 I first appease him with gifts that *p* me,
Ex 23:27 "I will have the fear of me *p* you,
Jos 3:11 the whole earth will *p* you into the Jordan.
1Mc 10:34 and the three days that *p* each feast day,
Mt 14:22 into the boat and *p* him to the other side.
Mk 6:45 *p* him to the other side toward Bethsaida,

PRECEDED (8)

Ex 13:21 The LORD *p* them, in the daytime
1Sm 10: 5 coming down from the high place *p* by lyres,
1Kgs 14: 9 You have done worse than all who *p* you:
1Chr 17:13 him as I withdrew it from him who *p* you;
Jdt 9: 5 events and of what *p* and followed them.
10:22 out to the antechamber, *p* by silver lamps;
Eccl 1:10 has already existed in the ages that *p* us.
Jer 34: 5 the kings who *p* you from the first;

PRECEDENCE (2)

Eccl 4:16 these people, to all over whom he takes *p*;
Wis 7:29 Compared to light, she takes *p*;

PRECEDING (3)

1Mc 3:30 with a more liberal hand than the *p* kings.
Mt 21: 9 The groups *p* him as well as those
Mk 11: 9 Those *p* him as well as those who followed

PRECEIVING (1)

Nm 24: 1 *p* that the LORD was pleased to bless

PRECEPT (6)

Jos 22: 5 to observe the *p* and law which Moses,
Prv 19:16 He who keeps the *p* keeps his life,
Eccl 8: 2 Observe the *p* of the king,
Wis 16: 6 to remind them of the *p* of your Law.
Sir 29: 9 Because of the *p*, help the needy,
Rom 5:14 had not sinned by breaking a *p* as did Adam,

PRECEPTS (54)

Ex 15:26 heed his commandments and keep all his *p*,
Lv 25:18 my *p* and be careful to keep my regulations,
26: 3 "If you live in accordance with my *p* and
26:15 if you reject my *p* and spurn my decrees,
26:43 spurned my *p* and abhorred my statutes.
26:46 These are the *p*, decrees and laws
1Chr 22:13 *p* and decrees which the LORD gave Moses
24:19 in keeping with the *p* given them by Aaron,
29:19 desire to keep your commandments, *p*,
1Mc 2:68 they deserve, and observe the *p* of the law."
Ps(s) 19: 9 The *p* of the LORD are right,
103:18 his covenant and remember to fulfill his *p*.
111: 7 sure are all his *p*,
119: 4 commanded that your *p* be deligently kept.
119:15 meditate on your *p* and consider your ways.
119:27 Make me understand the way of your *p*,
119:40 Behold, I long for your *p*;
119:45 walk at liberty, because I seek your *p*.
119:56 I have had, that I have observed your *p*.
119:63 of all who fear you and keep your *p*.
119:69 with all my heart I will observe your *p*.
119:78 I will meditate on your *p*.
119:87 the earth, but I have not forsaken your *p*.
119:93 Never will I forget your *p*,
119:94 save me, for I have sought your *p*.
119:100 than the elders, because I observe your *p*.
119:104 Through your *p* I gain discernment;
119:110 for me, but from your *p* I have not strayed.
119:128 For in all your *p* I go forward;
119:134 oppression of men, that I may keep your *p*.
119:141 but your *p* I have not forgotten.
119:159 See how I love *p*,
119:168 I keep your *p* and your decrees,
119:173 ready to help me, for I have chosen your *p*.
Wis 6:10 the holy *p* hallowed shall be found holy,
Sir 4:17 With her *p* she puts him to the proof,
6:37 Reflect on the *p* of the LORD,
17:12 of them he gives *p* about his fellow men.
18:13 his guidance, who are diligent in his *p*.
29: 1 the *p* who holds out a helping hand.
35: 4 that you offer is in fulfillment of the *p*.
42: 2 Of the law of the Most High and his *p*,
44:20 He observed the *p* of the Most High,
45: 5 That he might teach his *p* to Jacob,
45:17 To teach the *p* to his people,
Is 29:13 become routine observance of the *p* of men,
Bar 1:18 the *p* which the Lord set before us.
2:10 the *p* of the Lord which he set before us.
4: 1 She is the book of the *p* of God,
Mt 15: 9 reverence, making dogmas out of human *p*.' "
Mk 7: 7 because they teach as dogmas mere human *p*.'
Rom 2:26 person keeps the *p* of the law,
Eph 2:15 abolished the law with its commands and *p*,
Col 2:22 are based on merely human *p* and doctrines.

PRECINCTS (20)

1Mc 10:43 temple of Jerusalem or in any of its *p*,
14:48 a conspicuous place in the *p* of the temple,
2Mc 1:15 with a few attendants came to the temple *p*.
Sir 50: 2 with powerful turrets for the temple *p*;
Mt 21:12 Jesus entered the temple *p* and drove out
21:15 children were shouting out in the temple *p*,
21:23 After Jesus had entered the temple *p*,
24: 1 Jesus left the temple *p* then,
26:55 day to day I sat teaching in the temple *p*,
Mk 11:11 Jerusalem and went into the temple *p*.
11:15 he entered the temple *p* and began to drive
11:27 walking in the temple *p* the chief priests,
12:35 teaching in the temple *p* he went on to say:
14:49 your reach daily, teaching in the temple *p*,
Jn 2:14 In the temple *p* he came upon people
5:14 found him in the temple *p* and said to him:
8:59 himself and slipped out of the temple *p*.
Acts 5:20 take your place in the temple *p* and preach
21:26 Then he entered the temple *p* to give
21:27 of Asia recognized Paul in the temple *p*

PRECIOUS (83)

Gn 30:20 she said, "God has brought me a *p* gift.
Ex 28:17 it you shall mount four rows of *p* stones:
31: 5 bronze, in cutting and mounting *p* stones,
35:33 bronze, in cutting and mounting *p* stones,
39:10 Four rows of *p* stones were mounted on it:
1Sm 26:21 because you have held my life *p* today.
2Sm 1:26 More *p* have I held love for you than love
12:30 It weighed a talent, of gold and *p* stones;
1Kgs 10: 2 a large amount of gold, and *p* stones.
10:10 large quantity of spices, and *p* stones.
10:11 quantity of cabinet wood and *p* stones.
2Kgs 22: 4 and have him smelt down the *p* metals
1Chr 20: 2 and it contained *p* stones,
29: 2 mosaic stones, every other kind of *p* stone,
29: 8 Those who had *p* stones gave them into the
2Chr 3: 6 also decorated the building with *p* stones.
9: 1 bearing spices, much gold, and *p* stones.
9: 9 quantity of spices, as well as *p* stones.
9:10 also brought cabinet wood and *p* stones.
20:25 personal property, garments and *p* vessels.
21: 3 gifts of silver, gold and *p* objects,
32:27 gold, *p* stones, spices, jewels, and other *p*
36:10 with *p* vessels from the temple of the LORD.
36:19 afire, and destroyed all its *p* objects.
36:23 , and destroyed all its *p* objects.
Ezr 1: 6 and with many *p* gifts besides all their
8:27 of excellent polished bronze, as *p* as gold.
Tb 13:16 emerald, and all your walls with *p* stones,
Jdt 10:21 and gold, emeralds and other *p* stones.
Est 4:16 In place of her *p* ointments she covered
4:30 state, and covered with gold and *p* stones,

PRECIOUS (cont.)

1Mc 1:23 away the gold and silver and the *p* vessels;
Jb 28:10 his eyes behold all that is *p*.
28:16 of Ophir, with the *p* onyx or the sapphire.
Ps(s) 19:11 They are more *p* than gold,
36: 8 How *p* is your kindness, O God!
72:14 and *p* shall their blood be in his sight.
116:15 *P* in the eyes of the LORD is the death of
119:72 *p* than thousands of gold and silver pieces.
133: 2 It is as when the *p* ointment upon the head
Prv 1:13 All kinds of *p* wealth shall we gain,
3:15 She is more *p* than corals,
6:26 is married, she is a trap for your *p* life.
20:15 of corals, wise lips are a *p* ornament.
21:20 *P* treasure remains in the house of the wise,
24: 4 with every *p* and pleasing possession.
Sir 7:19 a gracious wife is more *p* than corals.
24:15 cinnamon, or fragrant balm, or *p* myrrh,
30:15 More *p* than gold is health and well-being,
41:12 better than *p* treasures in the thousands;
45:11 *P* stones with seal engravings in golden
49: 1 *P* is his memory,
50: 9 of beaten gold, studded with *p* stones;
Is 28:16 A *p* cornerstone as a sure foundation;
43: 4 Because you are *p* in my eyes and glorious,
44: 9 nothing, and their *p* works are of no avail,
54:12 carbuncles, and all your walls of *p* stones.
Jer 15:19 If you bring forth the *p* without the vile,
Lam 4: 2 Zion's *p* sons,
4: 7 ruddy than coral, more *p* than sapphire.
Ez 22:25 people, seizing their wealth and *p* things,
26:12 be torn down, your *p* houses demolished;
27:22 choicest spices, all kinds of *p* stones,
28:13 every *p* stone was your covering [carnelian,
41:16 were paneled with *p* wood all around,
Dn 11: 8 and their *p* vessels of silver and gold,
11:38 shall glorify with gold, silver, *p* stones,
Hos 13:15 It shall loot his land of every *p* thing.
Jl 4: 5 brought my *p* treasures into your temples!
Na 2:10 to their wealth in *p* things of every kind!
Mt 12:12 much more *p* a human being is than a sheep.
Lk 21: 5 adorned with *p* stones and votive offerings.
1Cor 3:12 foundation with gold, silver, *p* stones,
Jas 5: 7 the farmer awaits the *p* yield of the soil.
1Pt 1: 7 which is more *p* than the passing splendor
2: 4 approved, nonetheless, and *p* in God's eyes.
2: 6 in Zion, an approved stone, and *p*.
3: 4 This is *p* in God's eyes.
2Pt 1: 4 on us the great and *p* things he promised,
Rv 18:12 of gold and silver, *p* stones and pearls;
21:11 of a *p* jewel that sparkled like a diamond.
21:19 was ornate with *p* stones of every sort:

PRECISE (1)

Gn 7:13 On the *p* day named,

PRECISELY (5)

2Mc 4:16 *P* because of this,
Lk 1: 2 *p* as those events were transmitted to us
Jn 12:16 to him *p* what had been written about him.)
Rom 5: 8 *p* in this that God proves his love for us:
Rv 9:15 this was *p* the hour,

PRECISION (1)

Eccl 12:10 and to write down true sayings with *p*.

PREDECESSOR (1)

2Sm 7:15 from him as I withdrew it from your *p* Saul,

PREDECESSORS (5)

1Kgs 16:25 in the LORD'S sight beyond any of his *p*.
16:30 sight of the LORD more than any of his *p*.
Neh 5:15 The earlier governors, my *p*,
1Mc 11:26 the king treated him just as his *p* had
11:38 who had served under his *p* hated him.

PREDESTINED (4)

Rom 8:29 he *p* to share the image of his Son,
8:30 Those he *p* he likewise called;
Eph 1: 5 he likewise *p* us through Christ Jesus to
1:11 we were *p* to praise his glory by being the

PREDICT (4)

1Kgs 22:13 be the same as any of theirs; *p* good."
2Chr 18:12 prophets unanimously *p* good for the king,
18:12 let your word, like each of theirs, *p* good."
Is 47:11 shall come evil you will not know how to *p*:

PREDICTED (8)

Gn 41:54 of famine set in, just as Joseph had *p*.
1Kgs 5:19 the LORD *p* to my father David when he said:
13:26 and killed him, as the LORD *p* to him."
14: 2 It was he who *p* my reign over this people.
2Kgs 7:17 man of God had *p* when the king visited him.
23:17 man of God who came from Judah and *p*
Rom 9:29 It is just as Isaiah *p*:
1Pt 1:11 for he *p* the sufferings destined for

PREDICTING (1)

1Kgs 22:13 are unanimously *p* good for the king.

PREDICTION (4)

Ps(s) 105:19 Till his *p* came to pass and the word of
Jer 28: 9 only when his prophetic *p* is fulfilled.
Mt 26:75 and Peter remembered the *p* Jesus had made:
Mk 14:72 Peter recalled the *p* Jesus had made to him,

PREFACE (1)

2Mc 2:32 be nonsense to write a long *p* to a story

PREFECT (6)

1Kgs 4:19 There was one *p* besides,
22:26 and take him back to Amon, *p* of the city,
2Chr 18:25 and take him back to Amon, *p* of the city,
31:13 and of Azariah, the *p* of the house of God.
Neh 11:22 The *p* of the Levites in Jerusalem was Uzzi,
Dn 2:48 chief *p* over all the wise men of Babylon.

PREFECTS (10)

1Kgs 5:30 answerable to Solomon's *p* for the work,
20:24 from their posts and put *p* in their places.
2Chr 35: 8 and Jehiel, *p* of the house of God,
Jer 51:23 his team, with you I shatter satraps and *p*.
51:28 king of Media, Its governors and all its *p*,
51:57 her wise men drunk, her governors, her *p*,
Dn 3: 2 He then ordered the satraps, *p*,
3: 3 The satraps, *p*,
3:94 When the satraps, *p*,
6: 8 All the supervisors of the kingdom, the *p*,

PREFER (15)

Gn 13: 9 If you *p* the left, I will go to the right;
13: 9 if you *p* the right, I will go to the left."
29:19 "I *p* to give her to you rather than to an
1Kgs 21: 2 better vineyard in exchange, or, if you *p*,
21: 6 'Sell me your vineyard, or, if you *p*,
1Chr 21:13 But I *p* to fall into the hand of the LORD,
2Mc 2:25 aimed to please those who *p* simple reading,
11:24 Greek customs but *p* their own way of life.
Jb 7:15 *p* choking and death rather than my pains.
Ps(s) 132:14 in her will I dwell, for I *p* her.
1Cor 4:21 Which do you *p*,
14: 5 in tongues, but I much *p* that you prophesy.
2Cor 1:24 I *p* to work with you toward your happiness.
Phil 1:22 and I do not know which to *p*.
Phlm 1: 9 be done, I *p* to appeal in the name of love.

PREFERABLE (1)

Sir 30:17 *P* is death to a bitter life,

PREFERENCE (5)

Dt 10:15 descendants, in *p* to all other peoples,
21:16 wife he loves, in *p* to his true first-born,
1Sm 2:29 And why do you honor your sons in *p* to me,
Prv 8:10 Receive my instruction in *p* to silver,
1Cor 7: 7 Given my *p*, I should like you to be as I

PREFERRED (14)

Gn 25:28 Isaac *p* Esau,
25:28 but Rebekah *p* Jacob.
2Sm 6:21 who *p* me to your father and his whole
1Mc 1:63 they *p* to die rather than to be defiled
2Mc 8: 7 He *p* the nights as being especially
Jb 36:21 for you have *p* carousal to affliction.
Prv 1:30 And in their arrogance they *p* arrogance.
Wis 7: 8 I *p* her to scepter and throne,
Is 65:12 my sight and *p* things which displease me,
Jer 8: 3 Death will be *p* to life by all the
Jn 12:43 *p* the praise of men to the glory of God.
Acts 3:14 You disowned the Holy and Just One and *p*
27:11 the centurion *p* listening to the pilot and
27:12 the majority *p* to put out to sea in the

PREFERRING (2)

2Mc 6:19 *p* a glorious death to a life of defilement,
14:42 *p* to die nobly rather than fall into the

PREFERS (1)

Ps(s) 132:13 he *p* her for his dwelling.

PREGNANCY (2)

Gn 16: 4 When she became aware of her *p*,
16: 5 but ever since she became aware of her *p*,

PREGNANT (12)

Gn 16: 4 had intercourse with her, and she became *p*.
16:11 "You are now *p* and shall bear a son;
19:36 Lot's daughters became *p* by their father.
21: 2 *p* and bore Abraham a son in his old age,
25:21 heard his entreaty, and Rebekah became *p*.
Ex 21:22 "When men have a fight and hurt a *p* woman,
2Kgs 8:12 pieces, you will rip open their *p* women."
15:16 them even to ripping open all the *p* women.
Ps(s) 7:15 conceived iniquity and was *p* with mischief,
Mt 24:19 hard on *p* or nursing mothers in those days.
Mk 13:17 with *p* and nursing women in those days.
Lk 21:23 "The women who are *p* or nursing at the

PREJUDICE (2)

1Mc 11: 5 To *p* the king against Jonathan,
1Tm 5:21 apply these rules without *p*,

PREMATURE (1)

Sir 30:24 one's life, worry brings on *p* old age.

PREOCCUPIED (1)

Sir 51:19 I became *p* with her,

PREPARATION (13)

1Chr 29:19 build the castle for which I have made *p*."
Jdt 4: 5 stored up provisions in *p* for war.
Est 2:12 the twelve months' *p* decreed for the women.
2Mc 2:27 just as the *p* of a festive banquet is no
Dn 1:18 time the king had specified for their *p*,
Mt 26:12 she has contributed toward my burial *p*.
27:62 next day, the one following the Day of *P*,
Mk 14: 8 body she is anticipating its *p* for burial.
15:42 As it grew dark (it was *P* Day,
Lk 23:54 That was the Day of *P*,
Jn 19:14 (It was the *P* Day for Passover,
19:31 Since it was the *P* Day the Jews did not
19:42 the Jewish *P* Day they buried Jesus there,

PREPARATIONS (3)

1Sm 18:27 David made *p* and sallied forth with his
1Chr 22: 5 Therefore I will make *p* for it."
Neh 5:18 though the daily *p* were made at my expense

PREPARE (69)

Gn 27: 4 your catch *p* an appetizing dish for me,
27: 7 with it *p* an appetizing dish for me to eat,
27: 9 will *p* an appetizing dish for your father,
Ex 12:16 except to *p* the food that everyone needs.
12:39 opportunity even to *p* food for the journey.
16: 5 however, when they *p* what they bring in,
Nm 23: 1 and *p* seven bullocks and seven rams for
23:29 *p* for me seven bullocks and seven rams."
Jos 1: 2 So *p* to cross the Jordan here,
1:11 and instruct the people, *P* your provisions,
8: 1 all the army with you and *p* to attack Ai.
18: 8 to survey the land, *p* a description of it,
Jgs 13:15 you to stay, while we *p* a kid for you?"
2Sm 12: 4 and herds to *p* a meal for the wayfarer
13: 6 come and *p* some fried cakes before my eyes,
13: 7 Amnon and *p* some nourishment for him."
1Kgs 17:12 in and *p* something for myself and my son;
17:13 can *p* something for yourself and your son.
18:23 shall *p* the other and place it on the wood,
18:25 "Choose one young bull and *p* it first,
20:12 *P* the assault,"
2Kgs 9:21 *P* my chariot," said Joram.
2Chr 2: 8 order to *p* for me a great quantity of wood,
35: 4 *P* yourselves in your ancestral houses and
Tb 5:17 son, *p* whatever you need for the journey,
7:15 *p* the other bedroom and bring the girl
8:19 So the servants began to *p* the feast.
11: 3 Let us hurry on ahead of your wife to *p*
Est 5: 8 to a banquet which I shall *p* for you;
1Mc 3:44 The assembly gathered together to *p* for
Ps(s) 7:14 bow, *P* his deadly weapons against them,
Sir 2: 1 to serve the LORD, *p* yourself for trials.
2:17 Those who fear the LORD *p* their hearts and
18:18 before sickness *p* the cure.
33: 4 *P* your words and you will be listened to;
38:16 As is only proper, *p* the body,
Is 40: 3 In the desert *p* the way of the LORD!
57:14 Build up, build up, *p* the way,
62:10 the gates, *p* the way for the people;
Jer 6: 4 *P* for war against her, Up!
46: 3 *P* shield and buckler!
46:14 Take your stand, *p* yourselves,
Bar 1:10 frankincense, and to *p* cereal offerings;
Ez 12: 3 on, *p* your baggage as though for exile,
34:29 *p* for them peaceful fields for planting;
38: 7 *P* yourself, be ready, you and all your
Dn 11:10 shall *p* and assemble a great armed host,
11:25 the king of the south shall *p* for battle
14:11 O king, set out the food and *p* the wine;
Am 4:12 deal thus with you, *p* to meet your God,
Mal 3: 1 my messenger to *p* the way before me;
Mt 3: 3 *P* the way of the Lord,
11:10 ahead of you, to *p* your way before you.'
26:17 wish us to *p* the Passover supper for you?"
Mk 14:12 us to go to *p* the Passover supper for you?"
Lk 1:17 to *p* for the Lord a people well-disposed."
1:76 the Lord to *p* straight paths for him,
7:27 ahead of you to *p* your way before you.'
9:52 town to *p* for his passing through,
12:47 knew his master's wishes but did not *p*
17: 8 Would you not rather say, *P* my supper.
22: 8 "Go and *p* our Passover supper for us."
22:12 It is there you are to *p*."
23:56 they went home to *p* spices and perfumes.
Jn 12: 7 it against the day they *p* me for burial.
14: 2 you that I was going to *p* a place for you?

14: 3 I am indeed going to *p* a place for you,
Heb 12:10 to *p* us for the short span of mortal life;
Rv 16:12 up to *p* the way for the kings of the East.

PREPARED (91)

Gn 18: 7 and gave it to a servant, who quickly *p* it.
18: 8 as well as the steer that had been *p*,
19: 3 He *p* a meal for them,
27:14 and with them she *p* an appetizing dish,
27:17 appetizing dish and the bread she had *p*.
27:31 he too *p* an appetizing dish with his game,
43:16 and have an animal slaughtered and *p*,
50: 5 he had *p* for himself in the land of Canaan,
Ex 23:20 way and bring you to the place I have *p*.
30:25 oil, perfumed ointment expertly *p*.
30:35 This fragrant powder, expertly *p*,
37:29 were *p* in their pure form by a perfumer.
39: 6 were *p* and mounted in gold filigree work;
Lv 2: 7 a cereal offering that is *p* in a pot,
Jos 8: 3 Joshua and all the soldiers *p* to attack Ai.
24: 9 king of Moab, *p* to war against Israel.
Jgs 6:19 So Gideon went off and *p* a kid and an
19: 5 rose early in the morning and he *p* to go.
2Sm 3:20 David *p* a feast for Abner and for the men
13:10 So Tamar picked up the cakes she had *p* and
13:27 Absalom *p* a banquet fit for royalty.
1Kgs 5:32 and *p* the wood and stones for building the
18:26 they *p* it and called on Baal from morning
18:26 they hopped around the altar they had *p*.
2Kgs 10: 1 *p* letters and sent them to the city rulers,
19:25 Long ago I *p* it,
1Chr 12:40 for their brethren had *p* for them.
15: 1 of David and *p* a place for the ark of God,
15: 3 LORD to the place which he had *p* for it.
15:12 Israel, to the place which I have *p* for it.
2Chr 25: 8 on your own, strongly *p* for the conflict;
26: 5 *p* to seek God as long as Zechariah lived,
32: 5 had a great number of spears and shields *p*.
34:24 I am *p* to bring evil upon this place and
35:14 Afterward they *p* the Passover for
35:14 *p* for themselves and for the priests,
35:15 their brethren, the Levites, *p* for them.
Ezr 1: 5 whom God had inspired to do so *p* to go up
4: 6 of Ahashuerus they *p* a written accusation
Neh 8:10 allot portions to those who had nothing *p*;
Tb 2: 1 feast of Weeks, a fine dinner was *p* for me,
Jdt 12:19 She then took the things her maid had *p*,
Est A: 6 and at their cry every nation *p* for war,
3:14 peoples, that they might be *p* for that day.
4:16 Thus *p*, I will go to the king,
5: 4 today with Haman to a banquet I have *p*."
5: 5 with Haman to the banquet Esther had *p*.
6:14 Haman off to the banquet Esther had *p*.
7: 9 Haman *p* it for Mordecai,
8:13 so that the Jews might be *p* on that day to
1Mc 2:32 and *p* to attack them on the sabbath.
3:28 and commanded them to be *p* for anything.
6:33 and the armies *p* for battle,
7:29 But Judas' enemies were *p* to seize him.
15: 7 All the weapons you have *p*
2Mc 1:21 material for the sacrifices had been *p*,
Jb 13:18 Behold, I have *p* my case,
15:26 his shield, like a king *p* for the charge.
Ps(s) 57: 7 They have *p* a net for my feet;
65:10 you have *p* the grain.
65:11 Thus have you *p* the land:
Prv 19:29 Rods are *p* for the arrogant,
Is 19:14 has *p* among them a spirit of dizziness,
26:11 the fire *p* for your enemies consume them.
30:33 pyre has long been ready, *p* for the king;
37:26 Long ago I *p* it,
Ez 23:41 You sat on a couch *p* for them,
Zep 1: 7 Yes, the LORD has *p* a slaughter feast,
Mt 11:14 If you are *p* to accept it,
22: 4 who were invited, See, I have my dinner *p*!
24:44 You must be *p* in the same way.
25:34 *p* for you from the creation of the world.
25:41 fire *p* for the devil and his angels!
26:19 had ordered, and *p* the Passover supper.
Mk 14:16 told them, and they *p* the Passover supper.
Lk 12:38 midnight or before sunrise and find them *p*,
22:13 and accordingly they *p* the Passover supper.
22:33 am *p* to face imprisonment and death itself."
24: 1 to the tomb bringing the spices they had *p*.
Acts 10:10 while it was being *p* he fell into a trance.
21:13 For the name of the Lord Jesus I am *p*,
23:15 We are *p* to kill him before he gets there."
Rom 9:23 objects of mercy, and which he *p* for glory
1Cor 2: 9 man what God has *p* for those who love him."
Eph 2:10 good deeds which God *p* for us in advance.
Heb 10: 5 not desire, but a body you have *p* for me;
11:16 their God, for he has *p* a city for them.
Rv 9:15 and the year for which they had been *p*,
12: 6 a special place had been *p* for her by God;
19: 7 his bride has *p* herself for the wedding.
19:17 for the great feast God has *p* for you!
21: 2 beautiful as a bride *p* to meet her husband.

PREPARES (5)

Ex 30: 7 Morning after morning, when he *p* the lamps,
30:33 Whoever *p* a perfume like this,
2Sm 13: 5 she *p* something appetizing in my presence,
Sir 38: 7 pain and the druggist *p* his medicines;
Jer 11:15 beloved in my house, while she *p* her plots?

PREPARING (9)

Nm 19: 9 There they are to be kept for *p* lustral
1Chr 9:31 Koreite, was entrusted with *p* the cakes.
28: 2 and I was *p* to build it.
Est A:13 they were *p* to lay hands on King Ahasuerus.
1Mc 5:11 and they are *p* to come and seize this
7: 2 As he was *p* to enter the royal palace of
Wis 13:12 refuse from his handiwork in *p* his food,
14: 1 one *p* for a voyage and about to traverse
Is 14: 9 world below is all astir *p* for your coming;

PRESBYTER (3)

1Tm 5:19 no attention to an accusation against a *p*
Ti 1: 4 Qualities of a *P*.
1: 6 instructed you, a *p* must be irreproachable,

PRESBYTERS (14)

Acts 11:30 to the *p* in the care of Barnabas and Saul.
14:23 In each church they installed *p* and,
15: 2 and *p* in Jerusalem about this question.
15: 4 as well as by the apostles and the *p*,
15: 6 The apostles and the *p* accordingly
15:22 It was resolved by the apostles and the *p*
15:23 "The apostles and the *p*,
16: 4 the apostles and *p* had made in Jerusalem.
20:17 to Ephesus, summoning the *p* of that church.
21:18 to James in the presence of all the *p*.
1Tm 4:14 of prophecy, the *p* laid their hands on you.
5:17 *P* who do well as leaders deserve to be
Ti 1: 5 the appointment of *p* in every town.
Jas 5:14 He should ask for the *p* of the church.

PRESCRIBE (2)

Sir 45:17 his laws, and authority to *p* and to judge:
Is 45:11 children, or *p* the work of my hands for me!

PRESCRIBED (61)

Ex 5:14 *p* amount of bricks yesterday and today,
13:10 you shall keep this *p* rite at its
16:23 he told them, "That is what the LORD *p*.
23:15 days at the *p* time in the month of Abib,
34:18 For seven days at the *p* time in the month
Lv 4:21 just as has been *p* for the other one.
20: 8 I, the LORD, who make you holy, have *p*.
23:37 and libations, as *p* for each day,
Nm 9: 2 to celebrate the Passover at the *p* time.
9: 3 is the *p* time when you shall celebrate it,
9:13 present the LORD's offering at the *p* time.
10: 8 and the use of them is *p* by perpetual
15:24 with its *p* cereal offering and libation,
29: 6 together with the libations *p* for them,
29:18 and libations as *p* for the bullocks,
29:21 and libations as *p* for the bullocks,
29:24 and libations as *p* for the bullocks,
29:27 and libations as *p* for the bullocks,
29:30 and libations as *p* for the bullocks,
29:33 and libations as *p* for the bullocks,
29:37 and libations as *p* for the bullocks,
30:17 These are the statutes which the LORD *p*
31:21 is what the law, as *p* by the LORD to Moses,
36:13 LORD *p* for the Israelites through Moses,
Dt 5:33 exactly the way *p* for you by the LORD,
31:10 at the *p* time in the year of relaxation
1Sm 2:29 and on the offerings which I have *p*?
2Kgs 23:21 as it was *p* in that book of the covenant.
1Chr 6:17 their services in an order *p* for them.
23:31 and feast days, in such numbers as are *p*,
23:32 is *p* for them concerning the meeting tent,
2Chr 4: 7 lampstands of gold, ten of them as was *p*,
30: 5 for not many had kept it in the manner *p*.
30:16 *p* for them according to the law of Moses,
31: 3 and festivals, as *p* in the law of the LORD.
35:12 to the LORD, as is *p* in the book of Moses.
35:13 They cooked the Passover on the fire as *p*.
35:15 Asaph, were at their posts as *p* by David:
Ezr 3: 2 on it the holocausts *p* in the law of Moses,
3: 4 kept the feast of Booths in the manner *p*,
3: 5 the sacrifices *p* for the new moons and all
6:18 in Jerusalem, as is *p* in the book of Moses.
Neh 8: 1 law of Moses which the LORD *p* for Israel.
8:14 They found it written in the law *p* by the
9:14 statutes, and law you *p* for them,
10:37 also as is *p* in the law,
Tb 1: 6 as is *p* for all Israel by perpetual decree.
3: 8 intercourse with her, as it is *p* for wives.
Jdt 5:18 they deviated from the way he *p* for them,
Est 9:27 every year in the manner *p* by this letter,
2Mc 6:21 of the meat of the sacrifice *p* by the king,
10: 8 By public edict and decree they *p*
15: 3 who *p* the keeping of the sabbath day.
Ps(s) 40: 8 in the written scroll it is *p* for me,
Mt 8: 4 to the priest and offer the gift Moses *p*.
Mk 1:44 and offer for your cure what Moses *p*.
Lk 5:14 Offer for your healing what Moses *p*;
11:38 performed the ablutions *p* before eating.
20:28 Moses *p* that if a man's brother dies
Jn 2: 6 As *p* for Jewish ceremonial washings,
Acts 7:44 tent as God *p* it when he spoke to Moses,

PRESCRIBES (5)

Nm 19: 2 the regulation which the law of the LORD *p*.
Neh 8:15 leafy trees, to make booths, as the law *p*."
10:35 altar of the LORD, our God, as the law *p*.
Jb 36:23 Who *p* for him his conduct,
Heb 8: 4 already offering the gifts which the law *p*.

PRESCRIPTION (2)

2Chr 4:20 burn according to *p* before the sanctuary,
30:18 they ate the Passover, contrary to the *p*;

PRESCRIPTIONS (11)

Lv 8:35 seven days, carrying out the *p* of the LORD;
2Chr 23: 6 people must observe the *p* of the LORD.
29:25 and lyres according to the *p* of David,
29:25 *p* were from the LORD through his prophets.
35: 4 classes according to the *p* of King David
Neh 12:45 with the *p* of David and of Solomon,
Est 9:32 *p* for Purim and was recorded in the book.
1Mc 14:45 of these *p* shall be liable to punishment.
Lk 2:39 fulfilled all the *p* of the law of the Lord,
Col 2:22 Such *p* deal with things that perish in
Heb 10: 8 are offered according to the *p* of the law.)

PRESECUTORS (1)

Jdt 16: 2 he snatched me from the hands of my *p*.

PRESENCE (283)

Gn 4:14 and I must avoid your *p* and become a
4:16 LORD's *p* and settled in the land of Nod,
17: 1 Walk in my *p* and be blameless.
19:27 place where he had stood in the LORD's *p*.
23: 9 Let him sell it to me in your *p*,
23:11 in the *p* of my kinsmen I make this gift.
23:18 by purchase in the *p* of all the Hittites
24:40 'The LORD, in whose *p* I have always walked,
31:35 feel offended that I cannot rise in your *p*;
33:10 since to come into your *p* is for me like
33:10 is for me like coming into the *p* of God,
41:14 his clothes, he came into Pharaoh's *p*.
41:46 After Joseph left Pharaoh's *p*,
43: 3 in my *p* unless your brother is with you.'
43: 5 in my *p* unless your brother is with you.'"
43: 9 to bring him back, to set him in your *p*,
44:23 you, you shall not come into my *p* again.'
45: 1 himself in the *p* of all his attendants,
47:10 Pharaoh farewell and withdrew from his *p*.
Ex 8: 8 After Moses and Aaron left Pharaoh's *p*,
8:25 "As soon as I leave your *p* I will pray to
8:26 When Moses left Pharaoh's *p*,
9: 8 and in the *p* of Pharaoh let Moses scatter
9:10 a furnace and stood in the *p* of Pharaoh.
9:11 The magicians could not stand in Moses' *p*,
9:33 Pharaoh's *p* and had gone out of the city,
10:11 that they were driven from Pharaoh's *p*.
10:18 When Moses left the *p* of Pharaoh,
10:28 "Leave my *p*," Pharaoh said to him,
11: 8 With that he left Pharaoh's *p* in hot anger.
11:10 these various wonders in Pharaoh's *p*,
17: 6 did, in the *p* of the elders of Israel.
21:22 and he shall pay in the *p* of the judges.
28:30 heart whenever he enters the *p* of the LORD.
28:30 Israelites over his heart in the LORD's *p*.
28:35 and leaves the LORD's *p* in the sanctuary;
33:19 and in your *p* I will pronounce my name,
34:34 the *p* of the LORD to converse with him,
35:20 whole Israelite community left Moses' *p*,
Lv 9:24 Fire came forth from the LORD's *p* and
10: 2 forth from the LORD's *p* and consumed them,
10: 2 consumed them, so that they died in his *p*.
16: 1 died when they approached the LORD's *p*,
19:32 "Stand up in the *p* of the aged,
22: 3 such a one shall be cut off from my *p*.
Nm 3: 4 Sinai, they met death in the *p* of the LORD,
4: 7 On the table of the *P* they shall spread a
6: 9 "If someone dies very suddenly in his *p*,
11:20 your midst, and in his *p* you have wailed,
12: 8 The *p* of the LORD he beholds.
17:20 my *p* the Israelites' grumbling against you."
17:24 staffs from the LORD's *p* to the Israelites.
19: 3 outside the camp and slaughtered in his *p*.
20: 3 perished with our kinsmen in the LORD's *p*!
20: 8 their *p* order the rock to yield its waters.
27: 2 forward, and standing in the *p* of Moses,
27:19 Have him stand in the *p* of the priest
27:21 the decisions of the Urim in the LORD's *p*;
27:22 him stand in the *p* of the priest Eleazar
Dt 14:23 shall eat in his *p* your tithe of the grain,
16:11 his *p* together with your son and daughter,
19:17 before the LORD in the *p* of the priests
25: 2 and in his *p* receive the number of stripes
25: 9 his sister-in-law, in the *p* of the elders,
26:10 your God, you shall bow down in his *p*.
28:31 Your ass will be stolen in your *p*,
31: 7 and in the *p* of all Israel said to him,
31:11 read this law aloud in the *p* of all Israel.
Jos 6: 1 siege because of the *p* of the Israelites,
8:32 There, in the *p* of the Israelites,

PRESENCE (cont.)

10:12 to the LORD, and said in the *p* of Israel:
19:51 the land by lot in the *p* of the LORD,
22:27 the LORD in his *p* with our holocausts,
Jgs 3:19 when all his attendants had left his *p*,
5: 5 Mountains trembled in the *p* of the LORD,
5: 5 the One of Sinai, in the *p* of the LORD,
1Sm 2:17 men sinned grievously in the *p* of the LORD;
2:18 apron, was serving in the *p* of the LORD.
2:30 family should minister in my *p* forever.
2:35 function in the *p* of my anointed forever.
3:10 place, the LORD came and revealed his *p*,
6:20 "Who can stand in the *p* of this Holy One?
10:25 book, which he placed in the *p* of the LORD.
11:15 went to Gilgal, where in the *p* of the LORD,
12: 3 in the *p* of the LORD and of his anointed.
18:13 his *p* by appointing him a field officer.
19:24 in the prophetic state in the *p* of Samuel;
20:29 our city, and my brothers insist on my *p*.
21: 7 which had been removed from the LORD's *p*
21:16 you bring in this one to carry on in my *p*?
26:20 to the ground far from the *p* of the LORD.
2Sm 7:15 predecessor Saul, whom I removed from my *p*.
12:12 will bring it about in the *p* of all Israel,
13: 5 she prepares something appetizing in my *p*,
19: 9 sitting at the gate, they came into his *p*.
22:13 of his *p* coals were kindled to flame.
24: 4 so they left the king's *p* in order to
1Kgs 1:23 the prophet entered the king's *p* and,
1:28 the king's *p* and stood before him,
1:32 When they had entered the king's *p*,
8:22 in the *p* of the whole community of Israel,
8:25 in my presence, as you have lived in my *p*.'
9: 3 of petition which you offered in my *p*.
9: 4 live in my *p* as your father David lived,
2Kgs 8:19 him a lamp in the LORD's *p* for all time.
13:23 them or to cast them out from his *p*.
19:15 out before him, he prayed in the LORD's *p*:
20: 3 I conducted myself in your *p*,
24:20 and Judah till he cast them out from his *p*.
1Chr 11: 3 a covenant with them in the *p* of the LORD;
13:10 he died there in God's *p*,
16:29 Bring gifts, and enter his *p*;
17:16 Then David came in and sat in the LORD'S *p*,
17:24 your servant, is established in your *p*.
24: 5 holy place, and officers of the divine *p*,
24: 6 made a record of it in the *p* of the king,
24:31 of Aaron, cast lots in the *p* of King David,
28: 8 Therefore, in the *p* of all Israel,
29:10 the LORD in the *p* of the whole assembly,
29:22 drank in the LORD'S *p* with great rejoicing.
2Chr 1: 6 *p* on the bronze altar at the meeting tent;
2: 3 the burning of fragrant incense in his *p*,
2: 5 unless it be to offer incense in his *p*?
6:12 in the *p* of the whole community of Israel
6:13 Solomon knelt in the *p* of the whole of
6:16 to my law, even as you have lived in my *p*.'
7:14 seek my *p* and turn from their evil ways,
7:17 you live in my *p* as your father David did,
27: 6 he lived resolutely in the *p* of the LORD,
32: 6 He gathered them together in his *p* in the
34: 4 In his *p*, the altars of the Baals were
Ezr 4:18 you sent us has been read plainly in my *p*.
8:29 in the *p* of the chief priests and Levites
9:15 all this, we can no longer stand in your *p*."
Neh 1: 6 now offer in your *p* day and night for your
2: 1 As I had never before been sad in his *p*,
3:34 saying in the *p* of his brethren and the
6:19 in my *p* and relate to him whatever I said;
8: 3 daybreak till midday, in the *p* of the men,
13:28 I drove him from my *p*.
Tb 3:16 heard in the glorious *p* of Almighty God.
8:20 summoned Tobiah and made an oath in his *p*,
Jdt 2: 5 Go forth from my *p*,
2:14 So Holofernes left the *p* of his lord,
5: 8 expelled them from the *p* of their gods.
6: 1 *p* of the whole throng of coastland peoples,
11: 5 and let your handmaid speak in your *p*!
11:13 minister in the *p* of our God in Jerusalem:
12:13 So Bagoas left the *p* of Holofernes,
12:19 had prepared, and ate and drank in his *p*.
13: 1 the attendants from their master's *p*.
14: 8 So Judith told him, in the *p* of the people,
Est 1:11 Vashti into his *p* wearing the royal crown,
1:16 In the *p* of the king and of the officials,
1:17 that Queen Vashti be ushered into his *p*,
1:19 to come into the *p* of King Ahasuerus
3: 7 was cast in Haman's *p* to determine the day
C:24 persuasive words in the *p* of the lion,
8: 1 and Mordecai was admitted to the king's *p*,
8: 4 So she rose and, standing in his *p*, said:
8:15 Mordecai left the king's *p* clothed in a
9:25 Yet, when Esther entered the royal *p*,
1Mc 1:18 Ptolemy was frightened at his *p* and fled,
11:26 great honor in the *p* of all his Friends.
2Mc 3: 9 given, and explained the reason for his *p*,
4:18 were held at Tyre in the *p* of the king,
Jb 1:12 So Satan went forth from the *p* of the LORD.
2: 7 So Satan went forth from the *p* of the LORD
13:16 that no impious man can come into his *p*.
13:20 me, then from your *p* I need not hide:
16:21 he may do justice for a mortal in his *p*
30:11 me, and have thrown off restraint in my *p*.
33: 7 nor should my *p* weigh heavily upon you.
Ps(s) 9:20 let the nations be judged in your *p*.
16:11 of life, fullness of joys in your *p*,
17:15 on waking, I shall be content in your *p*.
18:13 of his *p* coals were kindled to flame.
21: 7 you gladdened him with the joy of your *p*.
27: 8 your *p*, O LORD, I seek.
31:21 of your *p* from the plottings of men;
42: 6 him, in the *p* of my savior and my God.
42:12 him, in the *p* of my savior and my God.
43: 5 him, in the *p* of my savior and my God.
44:17 and in the *p* of the enemy and the avenger.
51:13 Cast me not out from your *p*,
68: 9 it rained from heaven at the *p* of God,
68: 9 at the presence of God, at the *p* of God,
73:22 I was like a brute beast in your *p*.
88: 2 at night I clamor in your *p*.
102:29 their posterity shall continue in your *p*.
116:14 LORD I will pay in the *p* of all his people.
116:18 LORD I will pay in the *p* of all his people,
138: 1 *p* of the angels I will sing your praise;
139: 7 from your *p* where can I flee?
140:14 the upright shall dwell in your *p*.
Prv 22:29 *p* of kings; he will not stand in the *p*
25: 5 Remove the wicked from the *p* of the king,
25: 6 Claim no honor in the king's *p*,
Eccl 5: 1 be quick to make a promise in God's *p*.
11:10 heart and put away trouble from your *p*,
Wis 12:12 into your *p* as vindicator of unjust men?
14:17 that they could not honor him in his *p*
Sir 8: 8 the training to serve in the *p* of princes.
23:14 Lest in their *p* you commit a blunder and
24: 2 the *p* of his hosts she declares her worth:
27:23 In your *p* he uses honeyed talk,
31:31 and distress him not in the *p* of others.
34:20 the man who slays a son in his father's *p*
45: 3 words and sustained him in the king's *p*.
47: 1 came NATHAN who served in the *p* of David.
50:13 in the *p* of the whole assembly of Israel.
Is 26:17 out in her pains, so were we in your *p*,
38: 3 I conducted myself in your *p*,
48:19 never cut off or blotted out from my *p*.
51: 4 For law shall go forth from my *p*,
57: 1 Though he is taken away from the *p* of evil,
Jer 15:19 I restore you, in my *p* you shall stand;
23:39 lift you on high and cast you from my *p*,
28: 1 in the *p* of the priests and all the people:
28: 5 prophet Hananiah in the *p* of the priests
28:11 and said in the *p* of all the people:
32:12 in the *p* of my cousin Hanamel and of
32:13 In their *p* I gave Baruch this charge:
52: 3 the LORD that he cast them out from his *p*.
Lam 2:19 your heart like water in the *p* of the Lord;
Bar 2:14 grant us favor in the *p* of our captors,
2:28 down your law in the *p* of the Israelites:
Ez 16:50 and committed abominable crimes in my *p*;
20: 9 in whose *p* I had made myself known to them,
20:14 nations in whose *p* I had brought them out.
20:22 the nations in whose *p* I brought them out.
44: 3 in it to eat his meal in the *p* of the LORD.
46: 9 *p* of the LORD to worship on the festivals,
Dn 2:27 In the king's *p* Daniel made this reply:
2:36 we shall also give in the king's *p*.
3:40 your *p* today as we follow you unreservedly;
5:13 Daniel was brought into the *p* of the king.
Hos 5:15 they pay for their guilt and seek my *p*.
6: 2 day he will raise us up, to live in his *p*.
Zep 1: 7 Silence in the *p* of the Lord GOD!
Zec 2:17 Silence, all mankind, in the *p* of the LORD!
Mk 6:25 back to the king's *p* and made her request:
6:26 of his oath and the *p* of the guests,
13:14 *p* standing where it should not be
Lk 12: 9 in the *p* of men will be disowned in the *p*
19:27 king, bring them in and slay them in my *p*.'"
23:14 I have examined him in your *p* and have no
24:43 fish, which he took and ate in their *p*.
Jn 1: 1 the Word was in God's *p*,
8:38 you what I have seen in the Father's *p*;
12:37 his many signs performed in their *p*,
20:30 in the *p* of his disciples.
Acts 2:28 you will fill me with joy in your *p*.'
3:13 *p* when Pilate was ready to release him.
10:31 and your generosity remembered in God's *p*.
19: 9 of the new way in the *p* of the assembly,
21:18 to James in the *p* of all the presbyters.
24:21 what I called out as I stood in their *p*:
26: 2 able to make my defense today in your *p*,
2Cor 2:17 been sent by God and of standing in his *p*.
4:14 Jesus and place both us and you in his *p*.
Gal 2:14 had this to say to Cephas in the *p* of all
1Thes 3: 9 the joy we feel in his *p* because of you,
2Thes 1: 9 eternal ruin apart from the *p* of the Lord
2: 8 annihilate him by manifesting his own *p*.
1Tm 6:12 called when, in the *p* of many witnesses,
2Tm 4: 1 In the *p* of God and of Christ Jesus,
1Pt 2:19 hardship through his awareness of God's *p*,
2Pt 2:11 no opprobrious sentence in the Lord's *p*.
1Jn 2: 1 sin, we have, in the *p* of the Father,
Jude 1:24 and exultant in the *p* of his glory.
Rv 3: 5 him in the *p* of my Father and his angels.
8: 2 in God's *p* were given seven trumpets.
9:13 the horns of the altar of gold in God's *p*.
11: 4 stand in the *p* of the Lord of the earth.
11:16 God's *p* fell down to worship God and said:
14: 3 in the *p* of the four living creatures and
15: 4 nations shall come and worship in your *p*.
19:20 in its *p* the prodigies that led men astray,
20:11 his *p* until they could no longer be seen.

PRESENT (221)

Gn 23:10 Now Ephron was *p* with the Hittites.
33:11 Do accept the *p* I have brought you;
42:13 the youngest one is at *p* with our father,
42:32 at *p* with our father in the land of Canaan.'
43:15 down to Egypt to *p* themselves to Joseph.
50:20 meant it for good, to achieve his *p* end,
Ex 7:15 water, go and *p* yourself by the river bank,
8:16 "Early tomorrow morning *p* yourself to
9:13 *p* yourself to Pharaoh and say to him:
9:18 day the nation was founded up to the *p*.
10: 6 first settled on this soil up to the *p* day."
12: 6 then, with the whole assembly of Israel *p*,
16: 9 *P* yourselves before the LORD,
22: 8 both parties shall *p* their case before God;
22:13 is maimed or dies while the owner is not *p*,
22:14 But if the owner is *p*,
34: 2 Mount Sinai and there *p* yourself to me
Lv 2: 4 cereal offering you *p* is baked in an oven,
2: 5 If you *p* a cereal offering that is fried
2: 7 If you *p* a cereal offering that is
2:11 that you *p* to the LORD shall be unleavened,
2:12 Such you may indeed *p* to the LORD in the
2:13 *p* to the LORD shall be seasoned with salt.
2:14 "If you *p* a cereal offering of first
3: 9 he shall *p* the fat of the peace offering:
4: 3 guilty, he shall *p* to the LORD a young,
4:14 shall *p* a young bull as a sin offering.
5:11 he shall *p* as a sin offering for his sin
6: 7 sons shall first *p* it before the LORD,
6:13 *p* to the LORD [on the day he is anointed]:
6:14 you shall *p* it as a sweet-smelling
7:14 From each of his offerings he shall *p* one
9: 7 then *p* the offering of the people in
14:12 the priest shall *p* it as a guilt offering,
17: 4 to *p* it as an offering to the LORD
22:23 you may indeed *p* as a freewill offering,
23:16 *p* the new cereal offering to the LORD.
23:38 freewill offerings that you *p* to the LORD.
26:12 Ever *p* in your midst,
27:10 The offerer shall not *p* a substitute for
Nm 3: 6 of Levi and *p* them to Aaron the priest,
6:16 The priest shall *p* them before the LORD,
7:11 "Let one prince a day *p* his offering for
8:10 While the Levites are *p* before the LORD,
9:13 because he did not *p* the LORD's offering
15: 4 whoever does so shall also *p* to the LORD a
15: 6 With each sacrifice of a ram you shall *p* a
15: 9 with it you shall *p* a cereal offering of
15:13 *p* a sweet-smelling oblation to the LORD.
27:21 He shall *p* himself to the priest Eleazar,
28: 2 you shall be careful to *p* to me the food
28:26 you *p* to the LORD the new cereal offering,
29:39 you *p* as your votive or freewill offerings."
Dt 2:22 Esau have taken their place down to the *p*.
21: 5 the descendants of Levi, shall also be *p*,
29: 3 But not even at the *p* day has the LORD yet
29:14 of us who are now here *p* before the LORD,
31:14 and *p* yourselves at the meeting tent that
31:21 they are inclined to do even at the *p* time,
Jos 5: 9 the place is called Gilgal to the *p* day.
7:14 morning you must *p* yourselves by tribes.
7:26 over him, which remains to the *p* day.
8:29 up over it, which remains to the *p* day.
14:14 Caleb, son of Jephunneh, to the *p* day,
15:63 beside the Judahites to the *p* day.]
16:10 who live on within Ephraim to the *p* day,
Jgs 1:21 beside the Benjaminites to the *p* day.
10: 4 these are called Havvoth-jair to the *p* day.
21: 9 of the inhabitants of that city were *p*.
Ru 4: 4 you, bidding you before those here *p*,
1Sm 6:18 of Joshua the Beth-shemite at the *p* time.
9: 7 and we have no *p* to give the man of God.
10:27 They despised him and brought him no *p*.
12: 2 lived with you from my youth to the *p* day.
25: 2 *p* for the shearing of his flock in Carmel.
25:27 Accept this *p*,
27: 6 to the kings of Judah up to the *p* time.
29: 3 the day he came over to me until the *p*."
2Sm 3: 8 At *p* I am doing a kindness to the house of
3:13 when you come to *p* yourself to me."
6: 8 been called Perez-uzzah down to the *p* day.)
7: 6 led the Israelites out of Egypt to the *p*,
18:18 himself is called Yadabshalom to the *p* day.
20: 4 Then *p* yourself here."
22:23 For his ordinances were all *p* to me,
1Kgs 3:17 I gave birth in the house while she was *p*.
8: 5 *p* for the occasion sacrificed before the ark
8:59 LORD, our God, be *p* to him day and night,
10:12 such wood was brought or seen to the *p* day.
13: 7 the man of God, "and I will give you a *p*."
15:19 I am sending you a *p* of silver and gold.
18: 1 spoke to Elijah, "Go, *p* yourself to Ahab,"
18: 2 So Elijah went to *p* himself to Ahab.
18:15 whom I serve, I will *p* myself to him today."
2Kgs 5: 3 would *p* himself to the prophet in Samaria,"

5:26 "Was I not *p* in spirit when the man
8: 9 Hazael went to visit him, carrying a *p*,
16: 6 which they have occupied until the *p*.
16: 8 sent them as a *p* to the king of Assyria,
17:23 soil to Assyria, an exile lasting to the *p*.
1Chr 4:43 and have resided there to the *p* day.
23:30 They must be *p* every morning to offer
23:31 they must always be *p* before the LORD.
29:17 here *p* also giving to you generously.
2Chr 5:11 (all the priests who were *p* had purified
15: 2 and if you seek him he will be *p* to you;
15: 4 Israel, and sought him, he was *p* to them.
15:15 complete desire, so that he was *p* to them.
21:10 sovereignty of Judah down to the *p* time.
31: 1 those Israelites who had been *p* went forth
35: 7 as a Passover victim for any who were *p*,
35:17 The Israelites who were *p* on that occasion
35:18 all of Judah and Israel that were *p*,
Ezr 3:12 the foundation of the *p* house being laid.
8:15 that both laymen and priests were *p*,
Tb 1: 7 to Jerusalem and *p* them to the priests,
Jdt 9: 5 The *p*, also, and the future you have
10:15 our men will accompany you to *p* you to him.
14:10 with the house of Israel to the *p* day.
Est B: 7 whose *p* ill will is of long standing,
1Mc 10:39 Ptolemais and its confines I give as a *p*
13:30 he built at Modein is there to the *p* day.
15: 8 All debts, *p* or future,
16:19 to him so that he might *p* them with silver,
2Mc 1:23 a prayer, and all *p* joined in with them,
7: 9 fiend, you are depriving us of this *p* life,
7:27 educated and supported you to your *p* age.
11:36 so that we may *p* them to your advantage,
Jb 1: 6 God came to *p* themselves before the LORD,
2: 1 God came to *p* themselves before the LORD,
31:37 like a prince I should *p* myself before him.
Ps(s) 18:23 For his ordinances were all *p* to me,
71:17 till the *p* I proclaim your wondrous deeds;
139: 8 sink to the nether world, you are *p* there.
Prv 21:14 gift allays anger, and a concealed *p*,
Wis 4: 2 When it is *p* men imitate it,
9: 9 works and was *p* when you made the world;
14:17 to flatter him when absent, as though *p*.
Sir 14:14 Deprive not yourself of *p* good things,
32: 4 When wine is *p*,
39:19 The works of all mankind are *p* to him;
Is 41:21 *P* your case, says the LORD;
48:16 At the time it comes to pass, I am *p*:
59:12 Yes, our offenses are *p* to us,
Jer 17:16 what passed my lips; it is *p* before you.
34:21 Babylon who have at *p* withdrawn from you,
44:15 the women who were *p* in the immense crowd,
44:23 this evil has befallen you at the *p* day.
52:25 service of the king who were *p* in the city,
Bar 1:13 yet been withdrawn from us at the *p* day.
1:19 out of the land of Egypt until the *p* day,
2:11 made for yourself a name till the *p* day:
Ez 20:29 call it a high place even to the *p* day.
43:22 *p* an unblemished he-goat as a sin offering,
43:24 from the flock, and *p* them before the LORD;
44:27 the sanctuary, he shall *p* his sin offering,
Dn 2: 9 to *p* me with till the crisis is past.
7:16 I approached one of those *p* and asked him
9:18 when we *p* our petition before you,
14:14 the king alone was *p*.
Hos 7: 2 their crimes surround them, *p* to my sight.
11: 9 God and not man, the Holy One *p* among you;
13:13 not *p* himself where children break forth.
Mi 6: 1 Arise, *p* your plea before the mountains,
Mal 1: 8 *P* it to your governor; see if he will accept
Mt 12:41 *p* generation and be the ones to condemn it.
12:42 *p* generation and be the one to condemn it.
14: 9 the guests who were *p* he gave orders
14:20 All those *p* ate their fill.
23:28 Thus you *p* to view a holy exterior while
23:36 you, will be the fate of the *p* generation.
24:34 the *p* generation will not pass away until
27:55 women were *p* looking on from a distance.
Mk 1:44 "Go off and *p* yourself to the priest and
4:10 those *p* with the Twelve questioned him
4:30 What image will help to *p* it?
10:30 this *p* age a hundred times as many homes,
15:40 also women *p* looking on from a distance.
Lk 4:22 All who were *p* spoke favorably of him;
11:30 the Son of Man be a sign for the *p* age.
11:32 will rise along with the *p* generation,
12:56 sky, why can you not interpret the *p* time?
13: 1 some were *p* who told him about the
17:25 suffer much and be rejected by the *p* age.
21:32 the *p* generation will not pass away until
Jn 1: 2 He was *p* to God in the beginning.
12:17 The crowd that was *p* when he called
Acts 5:38 The *p* case is similar.
20:30 men will *p* themselves distorting the truth
25:24 Agrippa and all you who are here *p* with us,
28:22 we are anxious to hear you *p* your views.
Rom 3:26 to manifest his justice in the *p*,
8:18 I consider the sufferings of the *p* to be
8:38 neither the *p* nor the future,
11: 5 in the *p* time there is a remnant chosen by
1Cor 3:22 or the world, or life, or death, or the *p*,
4:13 that is the *p* state of affairs.
5: 3 me, though absent in body I am *p* in spirit,
7:26 In the *p* time of stress it seems good to
2Cor 4: 4 have been blinded by the god of the *p* age
4:17 The *p* burden of our trial is light enough,
5: 4 While we live in our *p* tent we groan;
6: 4 strive to *p* ourselves as ministers of God,
8:14 Your plenty at the *p* time should supply
10: 1 (you say) when *p* in your midst am lowly,
10:11 that we mean to be in action when we are *p*.
Gal 1: 4 our sins, to rescue us from the *p* evil age,
2: 2 the gospel as I *p* it to the Gentiles
Eph 2: 2 to the *p* age and to the prince of the air,
5:16 Make the most of the *p* opportunity,
5:27 word, to *p* to himself a glorious church,
Phil 4: 6 *P* your needs to God in every form of
Col 1:22 body by dying, so as to *p* you to God holy,
2Thes 3: 9 but that we might *p* ourselves as an
2Tm 1:12 and for its sake I undergo *p* hardships.
4:10 soon, for Demas, enamored of the *p* world,
Heb 2: 8 At *p* we do not see all things thus subject,
6:10 have shown him by your service, past and *p*,
9: 9 This is a symbol of the *p* time,
2Pt 3: 7 The *p* heavens and earth are reserved by
1Jn 1: 1 *p* to the Father and became visible to us.)

PRESENTABLE (2)

1Cor 12:24 less *p* a propriety which the more *p*

PRESENTATION (2)

Jgs 3:18 the *p* went off with the tribute bearers.
Acts 15:13 When they concluded their *p*,

PRESENTED (50)

Gn 24:53 articles of clothing and *p* them to Rebekah;
34:20 thus *p* the matter to their fellow townsmen:
43:26 they *p* him with the gifts they had brought
47: 2 He then *p* to Pharaoh five of his brothers
47: 7 his father Jacob and *p* him to Pharaoh.
Ex 35:22 could *p* an offering of gold to the LORD.
Lv 5:25 *p* this as his guilt offering to the priest,
7:11 the peace offerings that are *p* to the LORD.
9: 9 When his sons *p* the blood to him,
9:17 He then *p* the cereal offering;
10:19 "Even though they *p* their sin offering
Nm 7: 3 *p* as their offering before the Dwelling.
7:12 The one who *p* his offering on the first
7:19 He *p* as his offering one silver plate
17: 3 *p* before the LORD they have become sacred.
Dt 31:14 went and *p* themselves at the meeting tent.
Jos 17: 4 These *p* themselves to Eleazar the priest,
Jgs 3:17 He *p* the tribute to Eglon,
6:19 out to him under the terebinth and *p* them.
20: 2 *p* themselves in the assembly of the people
1Sm 1: 9 at Shiloh, and *p* herself before the LORD;
1:24 *p* him at the temple of the LORD in Shiloh.
16: 8 called Abinadab and *p* him before Samuel,
16: 9 Next Jesse *p* Shammah,
16:10 same way Jesse *p* seven sons before Samuel,
17:57 Abner took him and *p* him to Saul.
1Kgs 22:21 came forth and *p* himself to the LORD,
2Kgs 12:19 the dedicated offerings *p* by his forebears,
2Chr 11:13 and Levites throughout Israel *p* themselves
18:20 came forward and *p* himself to the LORD,
Ezr 8:36 the orders of the king were *p* to the
Neh 2: 9 and *p* the king's letters to them.
Tb 12:12 it was I who *p* and read the record of your
2Mc 4:32 from the temple and *p* them to Andronicus;
4:44 senate *p* to him the justice of their cause.
11:17 have *p* your signed communication and asked
14: 4 *p* him with a gold crown and a palm branch,
15:15 hand, Jeremiah *p* a gold sword to Judas.
Dn 2: 2 they came and *p* themselves to the king,
7:13 the Ancient One and was *p* before him,
Mt 2:11 their coffers and *p* him with gifts of gold,
14:12 Later his disciples *p* themselves to carry
15:22 woman living in that locality *p* herself,
Mk 4:11 the others outside it is all *p* in parables,
Lk 2:22 so that he could be *p* to the Lord,
19:16 The first *p* himself and said,
Acts 6: 6 They *p* these men to the apostles,
24: 1 *p* their case against Paul to the governor.
25: 2 leaders *p* him with their case against Paul,
25:15 of the Jews *p* their case against this man

PRESENTING (5)

Lv 3: 1 "If someone in *p* a peace offering makes
Nm 9: 7 why should we be deprived of *p* the LORD's
Sir 50:19 at the altar by *p* to God the sacrifice due;
Dn 9:20 people Israel, *p* my petition to the LORD,
2Cor 11: 2 *p* you as a chaste virgin to Christ.

PRESENTLY (1)

Jn 20: 6 *P*, Simon Peter came along behind him and

PRESENTS (20)

Gn 24:53 gave costly *p* to her brother and mother
30:20 This time my husband will offer me *p*,
32:14 him the following *p* for his brother Esau:
Lv 3: 6 he *p* to the LORD is from the flock,
3: 7 If he *p* a lamb as his offering,
3:12 "If he *p* a goat,
4:32 however, for his sin offering he *p* a lamb,
6:19 who *p* the sin offering may partake of it;
7:29 He who *p* a peace offering to the LORD
22:21 When anyone *p* a peace offering to the LORD
Nm 15:14 *p* a sweet-smelling oblation to the LORD,
1Kgs 10:13 besides such *p* as were given her from
1Mc 11:24 him silver, gold apparel, and many other *p*,
12:43 him to all his friends, and gave him *p*.
Sir 34:18 *p* from the lawless win not God's favor.
35: 2 he gives alms he *p* his sacrifice of praise.
Ez 46: 4 The holocausts which the prince *p* to the
Dn 2: 6 from me gifts and *p* and great honors.
2:48 to a high post, gave him many generous *p*,
5:17 your gifts, or give your *p* to someone else;

PRESERVATION (2)

1Chr 23:28 the chambers, and the *p* of everything holy:
2Mc 3:40 and the *p* of the treasury turned out.

PRESERVE (32)

Gn 38: 8 and thus *p* your brother's line."
Neh 1: 5 you who *p* your covenant of mercy toward
9:32 God, you who in your mercy *p* the covenant,
1Mc 10:20 after our interests and *p* amity with us."
2Mc 14:36 holiness, *p* forever undefiled this house,
Jb 23: 7 and I should once and for all *p* my rights.
Ps(s) 12: 8 us and *p* us always from this generation,
25:20 *P* my life, and rescue me;
25:21 Let integrity and uprightness *p* me,
32: 7 from distress you will *p* me;
33:19 from death and *p* them in spite of famine.
40:12 may your kindness and your truth ever *p* me.
41: 3 The LORD will keep and *p* him;
61: 8 bid kindness and faithfulness *p* him.
64: 2 from the dread enemy *p* my life.
138: 7 Though I walk amid distress, you *p* me;
140: 2 *p* me from violent men,
140: 5 *p* me from violent men Who plan to trip up
143:11 For your name's sake, O LORD, *p* me;
Prv 4: 6 Forsake her not, and she will *p* you;
14: 3 his back, but the lips of the wise *p* them.
Sir 40:18 A child or a city will *p* one's name,
Jer 50:20 for I will forgive the remnant I *p*.
Ez 7:13 of his sins, no one shall *p* his life.
18:27 is right and just, he shall *p* his life;
Mk 3: 4 To *p* life—or destroy it?"
8:35 Whoever would *p* his life will lose it,
8:35 for my sake and the gospel's will *p* it.
Lk 6: 9 To *p* life—or destroy it?"
17:33 Whoever tries to *p* his life will lose it;
Eph 4: 3 Make every effort to *p* the unity which has
1Thes 5:23 May he *p* you whole and entire,

PRESERVED (20)

Gn 20:16 your honor has been *p* with everyone."
Dt 3:11 is still *p* in Rabbah of the Ammonites.]
32:34 "Is not this *p* in my treasury,
Jos 14:10 the LORD has *p* me while Israel was
Neh 1: 2 Jews, the remnant *p* after the captivity,
1Mc 14:26 They have thus *p* its liberty."
Jb 10:12 me, and your providence has *p* my spirit.
Ps(s) 18:49 subject to me and *p* me from my enemies,
30: 4 you *p* me from among those going down into
Wis 10: 1 She *p* the first-formed father of the world
10: 5 *p* him resolute against pity for his child.
10:12 She *p* him from foes,
11:25 or be *p*, had it not been called forth
19: 6 that your children might be *p* unharmed.
Sir 42:24 to meet each need, each creature is *p*.
51:12 of every kind and *p* me in time of trouble.
Is 38:17 have *p* my life from the pit of destruction,
Dn 4:23 means that your kingdom shall be *p* for you,
Mt 9:17 new wineskins, and in that way both are *p*."
2Pt 2: 5 though he *p* Noah as a preacher of holiness,

PRESERVES (7)

1Kgs 14: 3 ten loaves, some cakes, and a jar of *p*,
Jb 36: 5 he *p* not the life of the wicked.
Prv 15:25 but he *p* intact the widow's landmark.
Eccl 7:12 is that wisdom *p* the life of its owner.
Wis 16:26 is your word that *p* those who believe you!
Sir 32:24 He who keeps the law *p* himself;
Jn 12:25 life in this world *p* it to life eternal.

PRESERVING (1)

2Sm 8: 4 *p* only enough for a hundred chariots.

PRESIDE (1)

Sir 32: 1 If you are chosen to *p* at dinner,

PRESIDED (3)

1Sm 19:20 saw the band of prophets, *p* over by Samuel,
Est 1: 3 he *p* over a feast for all his officers
Jb 29:25 I chose out their way and *p*;

PRESIDING (9)

Mt 27:19 While he was still *p* on the bench,
Rv 1:20 are the *p* spirits of the seven churches,
2: 1 "To the *p* spirit of the church in Ephesus,

PRESIDING (cont.)

2: 8 "To the *p* spirit of the church in Smyrna,
2:12 the *p* spirit of the church in Pergamum,
2:18 the *p* spirit of the church in Thyatira,
3: 1 "To the *p* spirit of the church in Sardis,
3: 7 the *p* spirit of the church in Philadelphia,
3:14 the *p* spirit of the church in Laodicea,

PRESS (23)

Ex 22:28 the offering of your harvest and your *p.*
Nm 18:27 the threshing floor or new wine from the *p.*
18:30 of the threshing floor or of the wine *p.*
Dt 15: 2 he must not *p* his neighbor,
15: 3 You may *p* a foreigner,
15:14 your flock and threshing floor and wine *p,*
16:13 from your threshing floor and wine *p.*
Jgs 6:11 the wine *p* to save it from the Midianites,
7:25 of Oreb and Zeeb at the wine *p* of Zeeb.
13:16 LORD answered Manoah, "Although you *p* me,
Jb 24:11 Between the rows they *p* out the oil;
Ps(s) 56: 2 all the day they *p* their attack against me.
Is 5: 2 built a watchtower, and hewed out a wine *p.*
63: 3 "The wine *p* I have trodden alone,
Jer 17:16 Yet I did not *p* you to send calamity;
Lam 1:15 in the wine *p* virgin daughter Judah.
Hos 9: 2 floor and wine *p* shall not nourish them,
Jl 4:13 Come and tread, for the wine *p* is full;
Mt 5:41 anyone *p* you into service for one mile,
Mk 3: 9 could avoid the *p* of the crowd against him.
15: 8 to *p* their demand that he honor the custom,
Lk 19:43 hem you in, and *p* you hard from every side.
2Pt 1:15 I shall *p* to have you recall these things

PRESSED (31)

Gn 19: 9 With that, they *p* hard against Lot,
40:11 I took the grapes, *p* them out into his cup,
Jos 7: 5 They *p* them back across the clearing in
Jgs 19: 7 but when his father-in-law *p* him he went
20:42 with the fight being *p* against them.
1Sm 25:18 *p* raisins, and two hundred cakes of *p* figs,
30:12 a cake of *p* figs and two cakes of pressed
31: 1 As they *p* their attack on Israel,
2Sm 16: 1 of bread, an ephah of cakes of *p* raisins,
2Kgs 5:23 Naaman said, and *p* them upon him.
1Chr 10: 2 Philistines *p* hard after Saul and his sons.
12:41 in great quantity of meal, *p* figs,
Jdt 1:14 He *p* on to Ecbatana and took its towers,
1Mc 2:30 because misfortunes *p* so hard on them.
10:50 He *p* the battle hard until sunset,
2Mc 8:20 yet when the Macedonians were hard *p,*
12:23 Judas *p* the pursuit vigorously,
Ps(s) 44:26 to the dust, our bodies are *p* to the earth.
118:13 I was hard *p* and was falling,
Is 59: 5 their eggs will die, if one of them is *p,*
65: 8 When the juice is *p* from grapes,
Lam 3:16 teeth with gravel, *p* my face in the dust;
Mt 27:32 man they *p* into service to carry the cross.
Mk 15:21 they *p* him into service to carry the cross.
Lk 5: 1 crowd *p* in on him to hear the word of God,
6:38 Good measure *p* down,
11:29 While the crowds *p* around him he began to
24:29 But they *p* him: "Stay with us.
Jn 8:19 They *p* him: "And where is this 'Father'

PRESSER (1)

Is 63: 2 and your garments like those of the wine *p?*

PRESSES (6)

Jb 24:11 They tread the wine *p,* yet suffer thirst,
Eccl 1: 5 then it *p* on to the place where it rises.
Is 16:10 In the wine *p* no one treads grapes,
Lam 3:36 the Most High, When he *p* a crooked claim,
Hb 2: 3 still has its time, *p* on to fulfillment,
Zec 14:10 the Tower of Hananel to the king's wine *p,*

PRESSING (3)

Mk 5:18 had been possessed was *p* to accompany him.
Lk 8:45 the crowds are milling and *p* around you!"
2Cor 11:28 there is that daily tension *p* on me,

PRESSURE (2)

Jb 32:19 Like a new wineskin with wine under *p,*
Mk 4:17 When some *p* or persecution overtakes them

PRESTIGE (2)

1Chr 25: 5 to enhance his *p,* God gave Heman
Dn 13:50 since God has given you the *p* of old age."

PRESTILENCE (1)

Dt 32:24 hunger and consuming fever and bitter *p,*

PRESUME (5)

Gn 11: 6 stop them from doing whatever they *p* to do.
Jer 2: 3 Should anyone *p* to partake of them,
Lk 7: 7 is why I did not *p* to come to you myself.
7:43 Simon answered, "He, I *p,*
Rom 2: 4 do you *p* on his kindness and forbearance?

PRESUMED (2)

2Sm 14:15 *p* to speak of this matter to your majesty,
Jn 21:12 Not one of the disciples *p* to inquire,

PRESUMES (2)

Dt 18:20 But if a prophet *p* to speak in my name an
Ez 33:13 if he then *p* on his virtue and does wrong,

PRESUMING (2)

Gn 18:27 "See how I am *p* to speak to my Lord,
Jdt 14:14 tent, *p* that he was sleeping with Judith.

PRESUMPTION (4)

1Sm 15:23 rebellion, and *p* is the crime of idolatry.
1Mc 3:20 With great *p* and lawlessness they come
2Mc 9: 8 he who previously, in his superhuman *p,*
Jer 49:16 spread beguiled you, and your *p* of heart;

PRESUMPTUOUS (3)

2Mc 5:18 from his *p* action as soon as he approached.
Prv 30:32 If you have foolishly been proud or *p*—
Sir 13: 8 Guard against being *p;*

PRESUMPTUOUSLY (1)

Dt 18:22 The prophet has spoken it *p,*

PRETEND (5)

2Sm 13: 5 "Lie down on your bed and *p* to be sick.
14: 2 *P* to be in mourning.
2Mc 6:21 and to *p* to be eating some of the meat of
Jn 4:12 *p* to be greater than our ancestor Jacob,
8:53 *p* to be greater than our father Abraham,

PRETENDED (3)

2Sm 13: 6 So Amnon lay down and *p* to be sick.
2Mc 5:25 he *p* to be peacefully disposed and waited
Mk 15:19 before him and *p* to pay him homage.

PRETENDING (2)

Ez 22:28 *p* to visions that are false and performing
Acts 27:30 *P* that they were going to run out anchors

PRETENDS (4)

Prv 13: 7 man *p* to be rich, yet has nothing; another *p*
26:24 With his lips an enemy *p,*
Sir 20: 7 he who *p* to authority is hated.

PRETENSE (3)

2Mc 6:24 it would be unbecoming to make such a *p;*
Gal 2:13 even Barnabas was swept away by their *p.*
2Tm 3: 5 make a *p* of religion but negate its power.

PRETENSES (1)

1Pt 2: 1 *p,* jealousies, and disparaging remarks

PRETENSION (1)

2Cor 10: 5 We demolish sophistries and every proud *p*

PRETENSIONS (1)

Jas 3: 5 It is a small member, yet it makes great *p.*

PRETENTIOUS (1)

Jas 4:16 you can do is make arrogant and *p* claims.

PRETERNATURAL (1)

1Sm 28:13 "I see a *p* being rising from the earth."

PRETEXT (7)

Gn 43:18 they want to use it as a *p* to attack us
Nm 12: 1 Aaron spoke against Moses on the *p*
2Chr 35:22 he had sought a *p* for fighting with him.
2Mc 1:14 On the *p* of marrying the goddess,
Acts 23:15 Paul brought down to you on the *p*
23:20 on the *p* that they want to question him
1Thes 2: 5 of flattering words or greed under any *p,*

PRETEXTS (2)

Jb 33:10 *p* against me and reckons me as his enemy.
Prv 18: 1 In estrangement one seeks *p:*

PRETTY (1)

Jer 46:20 Egypt is a *p* heifer,

PREVAIL (22)

Gn 32:26 the man saw that he could not *p* over him,
1Sm 2: 9 For not by strength does man *p;*
1Chr 16:14 throughout the earth his judgments *p* He
2Chr 11:17 son of Solomon, *p* for three years;
14:10 let no man *p* against you."
Jdt 11:10 nor does the sword *p* against them,
Est 6:13 Jewish race, you will not *p* against him,
2Mc 3: 5 Since he could not *p* against Onias,
Jb 14:20 You *p* once for all against him and he
Ps(s) 9:20 Rise, O LORD, let not man *p;*
105: 7 throughout the earth his judgments *p.*
Prv 29: 2 When the just *p,* the people rejoice;
29:16 When the wicked *p,* crime increases;
30: 1 I am not God, that I should *p.*
Sir 5: 3 "Who can *p* against me?"
Is 54:17 No weapon fashioned against you shall *p;*
Jer 1:19 will fight against you, but not *p* over you,
15:20 they fight against you, they shall not *p,*
20:10 then we can *p,* and take our vengeance
Am 5:15 love good, and let justice *p* at the gate;
Mt 16:18 the jaws of death shall not *p* against it.
Acts 16:15 She managed to *p* on us.

PREVAILED (6)

Gn 30: 8 a fateful struggle with my sister, and I *p.*"
32:29 with divine and human beings and have *p.*"
1Kgs 16:22 partisans of Omri *p* over those of Tibni,
1Chr 21: 4 However, the king's command *p* over Joab,
Ps(s) 129: 2 yet they have not *p* against me.
Lam 1:16 were reduced to silence when the enemy *p.*"

PREVAILS (1)

Wis 7:30 but wickedness *p* not over Wisdom.

PREVENT (10)

Jos 22:25 would *p* ours from revering the LORD.
1Kgs 15:17 Ramah to *p* communication with Asa,
2Chr 16: 1 Ramah to *p* any communication with Asa,
1Mc 4:60 to *p* the Gentiles from coming and
12:36 *p* its garrison from commerce with the city.
Sir 18:22 nothing *p* the prompt payment of your vows;
38:18 he deserves, One or two days, to *p* gossip;
Jn 7:23 the sabbath to *p* a violation of Mosaic law,
Acts 24:23 to *p* his friends from seeing to his wants.
2Cor 2:11 your sakes and, before Christ, to *p* Satan

PREVENTED (6)

1Sm 25:33 who this day have *p* me from shedding blood
1Mc 13:49 men in the citadel in Jerusalem were *p*
Jer 5:25 Your crimes have *p* these things,
36: 5 I am *p* from doing so.
Acts 16: 6 *p* by the Holy Spirit from preaching
Heb 7:23 were *p* by death from remaining in office;

PREVENTING (2)

1Mc 7:24 *p* them from going out into the country.
15:25 Trypho by *p* anyone from going in or out.

PREVIOUS (8)

Lv 18:27 which the *p* inhabitants defiled the land;
Nm 6:12 The *p* period is not valid,
Jos 20: 5 unintentionally and not out of *p* hatred.
Jgs 3: 2 who would not have had that *p* experience]:
20:23 combat in the same place as on the *p* day,
1Sm 21: 6 segregated from women as on *p* occasions.
2Mc 10:12 of the *p* injustice that had been done them,
Dn 7: 8 *p* horns were torn away to make room for it.

PREVIOUSLY (27)

Gn 31: 2 toward him was not what it had *p* been.
Ex 5: 7 for their brickmaking as you have *p* done.
5: 8 same quota of bricks as they have *p* made.
21:29 But if an ox was *p* in the habit of goring
21:36 But if it was known that the ox was *p* in
38:24 having *p* been given as an offering,
Dt 4:42 neighbor to whom he had *p* borne no malice,
19: 4 neighbor to whom he had *p* borne no malice.
19: 6 he had *p* borne the slain man no malice.
Ru 2:11 come to a people whom you did not know *p.*
1Sm 10:11 When all who had known him *p* saw him in a
14:21 the Hebrews who had *p* sided with the
1Chr 9:18 *P* they had stood guard at the king's gate
Neh 13: 5 had *p* been stored the cereal offerings,
Est 9:31 just as they had *p* enjoined upon
1Mc 3:30 and for the gifts that he had *p* given
9:72 he had *p* taken from the land of Judah.
11:27 and in all the honors he had *p* held,
11:39 who had *p* belonged to Alexander's party,
14:33 where *p* the enemy's arms had been stored.
14:34 of Azotus, a place *p* occupied by the enemy;
15:27 agreements he had *p* made with Simon
2Mc 9: 8 Thus he who *p,* in his superhuman
9:16 the holy temple which he had *p* despoiled;
10:24 who had *p* been defeated by the Jews,
Wis 18: 9 having *p* sung the praises of the fathers.
Lk 23:12 who had *p* been set against each other,

PREY (46)

Gn 15:11 Birds of *p* swooped down on the carcasses,
49: 9 a lion's whelp, you have grown up on *p,*
49:27 mornings he devours the *p,*
Nm 23:24 its *p* and has drunk the blood of the slain.
Dt 31:17 that they will become a *p* to be devoured,
33:20 that has seized the arm and head of the *p.*
1Sm 17:35 attack it and rescue the *p* from its mouth.
2Kgs 21:14 a *p* and a booty for all their enemies,
Jdt 7:27 we would be better off to become their *p.*
10:12 are about to be delivered up to you as *p.*
16: 4 babes to the ground, make my children a *p,*

1Mc 3: 4 a lion, like a young lion roaring for *p*.
Jb 4:11 The old lion perishes for lack of *p*,
9:26 reed, like an eagle swooping upon its *p*.
16: 9 I am the *p* his wrath assails,
19:22 you were divine, and insatiably *p* upon me?
28: 7 The path to it no bird of *p* knows,
29:17 from his teeth I forced the *p*.
38:39 Do you hunt the *p* for the lioness or
39:29 From thence he watches for his *p*;
Ps(s) 7: 3 me, Lest I become like the lion's *p*,
17:12 fix their gaze, Like lions hungry for *p*,
63:11 the sword, and shall be the *p* of jackals.
104:21 for the *p* and seek their food from God.
124: 6 who did not leave us a *p* to their teeth.
Prv 12:27 The slothful man catches not his *p*,
Sir 13:18 Lion's *p* are the wild asses of the desert;
27:10 As a lion crouches in wait for *p*,
Is 5:29 They growl and seize the *p*,
10: 2 widows their plunder, and orphans their *p*!
18: 6 all be left to the mountain birds of *p*,
18: 6 The birds of *p* shall summer on them and on
31: 4 a lion or a lion cub growling over its *p*,
35: 9 nor beast of *p* go up to be met upon it.
46:11 I call from the east a bird of *p*,
Jer 12: 9 My heritage is a *p* for hyenas,
Ez 13:21 they shall no longer be *p* to your hands.
19: 3 He learned to seize *p*,
19: 6 He learned to seize *p*,
22:25 are like roaring lions that tear *p*;
22:27 within her are like wolves that tear *p*,
39: 4 To birds of *p* of every kind and to the
Hos 5:14 It is I who rend the *p* and depart,
Am 3: 4 a lion roar in the forest when it has no *p*?
Na 2:13 He filled his dens with *p*,
Lk 10:30 Jerusalem to Jericho who fell *p* to robbers.

PREYING (1)

Na 2:14 Your *p* on the land I will bring to an end,

PRICE (39)

Gn 23: 9 it to me in your presence, at its full *p*,
23:13 I will pay you the *p* of the field.
34:12 No matter how high you set the bridal *p*,
Ex 22:14 this was covered by the *p* of its hire.
22:15 he shall pay her marriage *p* and marry her.
22:16 him the customary marriage *p* for virgins.
Lv 25:16 are many, the *p* shall be so much the more;
25:16 are few, the *p* shall be so much the less.
25:27 he shall make a deduction from the *p*
25:50 distributing the sale *p* over these years
25:51 of the sale *p* he shall pay back as ransom;
27:15 one fifth more than the *p* thus established,
27:19 one fifth more than the *p* thus established,
27:23 and on the same day the *p* thus established
Dt 23:19 dog's *p* as any kind of votive offering
1Sm 13:21 The *p* for the plowshares and mattocks was
18:25 "The king desires no other *p* for the
1Chr 21:22 Sell it to me at its full *p*,
21:24 buy it from you properly, at its full *p*.
Jb 28:15 it, nor can its *p* be paid with silver.
Ps(s) 44:13 You sold your people for no great *p*;
49: 9 Too high is the *p* to redeem one's life;
Prv 6:26 For the *p* of a loose woman may be scarcely
27:26 and the goats will bring the *p* of a field,
Sir 6:15 A faithful friend is beyond *p*,
8: 2 lest he pay out the *p* of your downfall;
Is 45:13 let my exiles go free Without *p* or ransom,
Bar 6:24 They are bought at any *p*,
Mi 7: 3 makes demands, The judge is had for a *p*,
Zec 11:13 the handsome *p* at which they valued me."
Mt 26: 9 a good *p* and the money given to the poor."
27: 9 with a *p* on his head, a *p* set by the Israelites,
Lk 23:41 are only paying the *p* for what we've done,
Acts 20:28 he has acquired at the *p* of his own blood.
1Cor 6:20 You have been purchased, and at a *p*!
7:23 You have been bought at a *p*!
Col 1:27 to make known to them the glory beyond *p*
1Pt 1:19 gold, but by Christ's blood beyond all *p*:

PRICELESS (2)

Wis 7: 9 her, nor did I liken any *p* gem to her;
Sir 26:15 is a modest wife, *p* her chaste person.

PRICKLY (1)

Mt 7:16 from thornbushes, or figs from *p* plants?

PRIDE (70)

Dt 17:20 estranged from his countrymen through *p*,
2Chr 32:26 then Hezekiah humbled himself for his *p*—
Jdt 9: 9 See their *p*, and send forth your wrath
9:10 crush their *p* by the hand of a woman.
Est C: 5 that it was not out of insolence or *p*
C: 7 It is not out of *p* that I am acting thus.
2Mc 5:21 on foot, so carried away was he with *p*.
Jb 20: 6 Though his *p* mount up to the heavens and
22:29 For he brings down the *p* of the haughty.
33:17 man from evil and keeping *p* away from him,
35:12 he answers not against the *p* of the wicked.
36: 9 have done and their sins of boastful *p*.
38:15 is withheld, and the arm of *p* is shattered.
Ps(s) 31:19 insolence against the just in *p* and scorn.
62:11 in plunder take no empty *p*;
73: 6 So *p* adorns them as a necklace;
76:13 terrible Lord Who checks the *p* of princes,
Prv 8:13 *P*, arrogance, the evil way,
11: 2 When *p* comes, disgrace comes;
16:18 *P* goes before disaster,
21:24 *p* who acts with scornful effrontery.
29:23 Man's *p* causes his humiliation,
Wis 5: 8 What did our *p* avail us?
15: 9 and takes *p* in modeling counterfeits.
Sir 7:17 More and more, humble your *p*;
10:12 *p* is man's stubbornness in withdrawing
10:13 For *p* is the reservoir of sin,
16: 8 of Lot whom he detested for their *p*;
32:12 you wish, but without sin or words of *p*.
47: 4 slingstone that crushed the *p* of Goliath.
48:18 fist at Zion and blasphemed God in his *p*.
Is 2:17 Human *p* will be abased,
9: 8 those who say in arrogance and *p* of heart,
13:11 I will put an end to the *p* of the arrogant,
13:19 kingdoms, the glory and *p* of the Chaldeans,
16: 6 We have heard of the *p* of Moab,
23: 9 planned it, to disgrace all *p* of majesty,
25:11 low their *p* as his hands sweep over them.
60:15 Now I will make you the *p* of the ages,
62: 7 And makes of it the *p* of the earth.
Jer 13: 9 *p* of Judah to rot, the great *p* of Jerusalem.
13:17 If you do not listen to this in your *p*,
48:29 heard of the *p* of Moab, *p* beyond bounds:
48:29 His loftiness, his *p* his scorn, his insolence
Ez 7:20 beauty of their ornaments they put their *p*:
24:21 my sanctuary, the stronghold of your *p*,
24:25 of their soul, and the *p* of their hearts,
30:18 Her haughty *p* shall cease from her,
Dn 4:34 those who walk in *p* he is able to humble.
11:12 In the *p* of his heart, he shall lay low
Am 6: 8 I abhor the *p* of Jacob,
8: 7 The LORD has sworn by the *p* of Jacob:
Ob 1: 3 The *p* of your heart has deceived you;
Na 2: 3 restore the vine of Jacob, the *p* of Israel,
Zep 2:10 Such shall be the requital of their *p*,
Zec 9: 6 I will destroy the *p* of the Philistine
10:11 The *p* of Assyria shall be cast down,
Mt 3: 9 Do not *p* yourselves on the claim,
Rom 2:17 firmly on the law and *p* yourself on God.
2:23 You who *p* yourself on the law,
1Cor 15:31 brothers, by the very *p* you take in me,
2Cor 5:12 those who take *p* in external appearances,
Eph 2: 9 so let no one *p* himself on it.
Col 2:18 he is inflated with empty *p* by his human
2:23 chief effect is that they indulge men's *p*.
Jas 1: 9 brother in humble circumstances take *p*

PRIDING (1)

Jdt 9: 7 force, *p* themselves on horse and rider,

PRIEST (507)

Gn 14:18 and wine, and being a *p* of God Most High,
41:45 the daughter of Potiphera, *p* of Heliopolis.
41:50 daughter of Potiphera, *p* of Heliopolis.
46:20 daughter of Potiphera, *p* of Heliopolis,
Ex 2:16 seven daughters of a *p* of Midian came to
3: 1 his father-in-law Jethro, the *p* of Midian.
18: 1 father-in-law Jethro, the *p* of Midian,
28: 3 him apart for his sacred service as my *p*.
29:30 The descendant who succeeds him as *p* and
31:10 the sacred vestments for Aaron the *p*,
35:19 the sacred vestments for Aaron, the *p*,
38:21 direction of Ithamar, son of Aaron the *p*.
39:41 the sacred vestments for Aaron the *p*,
40:13 anoint him, thus consecrating him as my *p*.
Lv 1: 9 The *p* shall then burn the whole offering
1:12 it up into pieces, the *p* shall lay these,
1:13 The *p* shall offer them up and then burn
1:15 the *p* shall snap its head loose and
1:17 halves, the *p* shall burn it on the altar,
2: 8 bring to the LORD, offering it to the *p*,
2: 9 Its token offering the *p* shall then lift
2:16 For its token offering the *p* shall then
3:11 All this the *p* shall burn on the altar as
3:16 All this the *p* shall burn on the altar as
4: 3 if it is the anointed *p* who thus sins and
4: 5 The anointed *p* shall then take some of the
4: 7 The *p* shall also put some of the blood on
4:10 *p* shall burn it on the altar of holocausts.
4:16 the anointed *p* shall bring some of its
4:20 Thus the *p* shall make atonement for them,
4:25 The *p* shall then take some of the blood of
4:26 Thus the *p* shall make atonement for the
4:30 The *p* shall then take some of its blood on
4:31 and the *p* shall burn it on the altar for
4:31 Thus the *p* shall make atonement for him,
4:34 The *p* shall then take some of the blood of
4:35 and the *p* shall burn it on the altar with
4:35 *p* shall make atonement for the man's sin,
5: 6 *p* shall then make atonement for his sin.
5: 8 He shall bring them to the *p*,
5:10 Thus the *p* shall make atonement for the
5:12 When he has brought it to the *p*,
5:13 Thus the *p* shall make atonement for the
5:13 cereal offerings, shall belong to the *p*."
5:16 This is to be given to the *p*,
5:18 guilt offering to the *p* an unblemished ram
5:18 The *p* shall then make atonement for the
5:25 this as his guilt offering to the *p*,
6: 3 The *p*, clothed in his linen robe
6: 5 morning the *p* shall put firewood on it.
6:15 him as the anointed *p* shall do likewise.
6:16 of a *p* shall be a whole burnt offering;
6:19 The *p* who presents the sin offering may
7: 5 All this the *p* shall burn on the altar as
7: 7 to the *p* who makes atonement with it.
7: 8 the *p* who offers a holocaust for someone
7: 9 shall belong to the *p* who offers it,
7:14 this shall belong to the *p* who splashes
7:31 The *p* shall burn the fat on the altar,
7:32 the *p* the right leg as a raised offering.
7:34 up, and I have given them to Aaron, the *p*,
12: 6 she shall bring to the *p* at the entrance
12: 7 The *p* shall offer them up before the LORD
12: 8 The *p* shall make atonement for her,
13: 2 he shall be brought to Aaron, the *p*,
13: 3 the *p*, on seeing this, shall declare
13: 4 the *p* shall quarantine the stricken man
13: 5 seventh day the *p* shall again examine him.
13: 5 the *p* shall quarantine him for another
13: 6 skin, the *p* shall declare the man clean;
13: 7 himself to the *p* to be declared clean,
13: 7 he shall once more show himself to the *p*.
13: 8 Should the *p*, on examining it,
13: 9 with leprosy, he shall be brought to the *p*.
13:10 Should the *p*, on examining him,
13:11 The *p* shall declare the man unclean
13:12 on the skin and, as far as the *p* can see,
13:13 man from head to foot, should the *p* then,
13:15 raw flesh, the *p* shall declare him unclean,
13:16 turns white, he shall return to the *p*;
13:19 blotch, he shall show himself to the *p*.
13:21 But if the *p*, on examining him, finds
13:21 the *p* shall quarantine him for seven days.
13:22 the skin, the *p* shall declare him unclean;
13:23 the *p* shall therefore declare him clean.
13:25 or a white blotch, the *p* shall examine it.
13:25 the *p* shall therefore declare him unclean
13:26 But if the *p*, on examining it, finds
13:26 the *p* shall quarantine him for seven days.
13:27 Should the *p*, when examining it on
13:28 *p* shall therefore declare the man clean,
13:30 should the *p*, on examining it, find
13:30 it, the *p* shall declare the person unclean,
13:31 But if the *p*, on examining the scall sore,
13:31 the *p* shall quarantine the person with
13:33 Then the *p* shall quarantine him for
13:34 If the *p*, when examining the scall
13:36 clean, the *p* shall again examine it.
13:37 clean, and the *p* shall declare him clean.
13:39 blotches, the *p* shall make an examination.
13:43 The *p* shall examine him; and if the scab
13:44 and the *p* shall declare him unclean by
13:49 with leprosy and must be shown to the *p*.
13:50 the *p* shall quarantine the infected
13:51 the *p* shall again examine the infection.
13:53 But if the *p*, on examining the infection,
13:55 "Then the *p* shall again examine the
13:56 But if the *p*, on examining the infection,
14: 2 He shall be brought to the *p*,
14: 3 If the *p* finds that the sore of leprosy
14: 5 The *p* shall then order him to slay one of
14: 6 the *p* shall dip them all in the blood of
14:11 The *p* who performs the purification
14:12 the *p* shall present it as a guilt offering,
14:13 belongs to the *p* and is most sacred.)
14:14 Then the *p* shall take some of the blood
14:15 The *p* shall also take a log of oil and
14:17 Of the oil left in his hand the *p* shall
14:18 The rest of the oil in his hand the *p*
14:18 *p* make atonement for him before the LORD.
14:19 *p* slaughter the holocaust and offer it,
14:20 When the *p* has thus made atonement for him,
14:23 purification he shall bring them to the *p*,
14:24 the *p* shall wave them as a wave offering
14:26 The *p* shall then pour some of the oil into
14:28 Some of the oil in his hand the *p* shall
14:29 his hand the *p* shall put on the man's head.
14:31 the *p* shall offer up one as a sin offering
14:31 Thus shall the *p* make atonement before the
14:35 the house shall come and report to the *p*,
14:36 The *p* shall then order the house to be
14:37 If the *p*, on examining it, finds that
14:39 *p* shall return to examine the house again.
14:44 and replastered, the *p* shall come again;
14:48 If the *p* finds, when he comes to examine
15:14 meeting tent, he shall give them to the *p*,
15:15 Thus shall the *p* make atonement before the
15:29 the *p* at the entrance of the meeting tent.
15:30 The *p* shall offer up one of them as a sin
15:30 Thus shall the *p* make atonement before the
16:32 "This atonement is to be made by the *p*
17: 5 bringing them to the *p* at the entrance of
17: 6 The *p* shall splash the blood on the altar
19:22 With this ram the *p* shall make atonement
21: 7 "A *p* shall not marry a woman who has been
21: 7 for the *p* is sacred to his God.
21:13 "The *p* shall marry a virgin.

PRIEST (cont.)

21:21 No descendant of Aaron the *p* who has any
22:11 But a slave whom a *p* acquires by purchase
22:14 to the *p* for the sacred offering,
23:10 the first fruits of your harvest to the *p*,
23:11 day after the sabbath the *p* shall do this.
23:20 The *p* shall wave the bread of the first
23:20 be sacred to the LORD and belong to the *p*.
27: 8 sum, the person must be set before the *p*,
27:11 sacrifice, it must be set before the *p*,
27:12 and the value set by the *p* shall stand.
27:14 the *p* shall determine its value in keeping
27:14 and the value set by the *p* shall stand.
27:18 the *p* shall estimate its money value
27:23 the *p* shall compute its value in
Nm 3: 6 of Levi and present them to Aaron the *p*,
3:32 however, was Eleazar, son of Aaron the *p*;
4:16 "Eleazar, son of Aaron the *p*,
4:28 supervision of Ithamar, son of Aaron the *p*.
4:33 supervision of Ithamar, son of Aaron the *p*."
5: 8 be the LORD's and shall fall to the *p*;
5: 8 the *p* makes amends for the guilty man.
5: 9 are bound to make shall fall to the *p*.
5:10 property of the *p* to whom he gives them."
5:15 he shall bring his wife to the *p* and shall
5:16 "The *p* shall first have the woman come
5:18 the *p* shall uncover her head and place in
5:21 the *p* adjure the woman with this oath
5:23 The *p* shall put these imprecations in
5:30 the *p* shall apply this law in full to her.
6:10 the *p* at the entrance of the meeting tent.
6:11 The *p* shall offer up the one as a sin
6:16 The *p* shall present them before the LORD,
6:19 *p* shall take a boiled shoulder of the ram,
6:20 The *p* shall then wave them as a wave
6:20 become sacred and shall belong to the *p*,
7: 8 supervision of Ithamar, son of Aaron the *p*.
15:25 Then the *p* shall make atonement for the
15:28 and the *p* shall make atonement before the
17: 2 Moses, "Tell Eleazar, son of Aaron the *p*,
17: 4 So Eleazar the *p* had the bronze censers of
18:28 *p* the part to be contributed to the LORD.
19: 3 This is to be given to Eleazar the *p*,
19: 4 Eleazar the *p* shall take some of its blood
19: 6 and the *p* shall take some cedar wood,
19: 7 The *p* shall then wash his garments and
25: 7 son of Eleazar, son of Aaron the *p*,
25:11 son of Eleazar, son of Aaron the *p*,
26: 1 to Moses and Eleazar, son of Aaron the *p*,
26: 3 Moses and the *p* Eleazar registered those
26:63 men registered by Moses and the *p* Eleazar
26:64 been registered by Moses and the *p* Aaron
27: 2 in the presence of Moses, the *p* Eleazar,
27:19 the *p* Eleazar and of the whole community,
27:21 He shall present himself to the *p* Eleazar,
27:22 the *p* Eleazar and of the whole community,
31: 6 son of Eleazar, the *p* for the campaign,
31:12 to Moses and the *p* Eleazar and to the
31:13 When Moses and the *p* Eleazar,
31:21 Eleazar the *p* told the soldiers who had
31:26 "With the help of the *p* Eleazar and of
31:29 *p* Eleazar as a contribution to the LORD.
31:31 So Moses and the *p* Eleazar did this,
31:41 to the LORD, Moses gave to the *p* Eleazar,
31:51 the *p* Eleazar accepted this gold from them,
31:54 and the *p* Eleazar accepted the gold from
32: 2 they came to Moses and the *p* Eleazar and
32:28 order in their regard to the *p* Eleazar,
33:38 *p* ascended Mount Hor at the LORD's command,
34:17 Eleazar the *p*,
35:25 *p* who has been anointed with sacred oil.
35:28 of asylum until the death of the high *p*.
35:28 Only after the death of the high *p* may the
35:32 in the land before the death of the high *p*.
36: 1 this plea before Moses and the *p* Eleazar
Dt 17:12 insolence to refuse to listen to the *p*
18: 3 flock, the *p* shall receive the shoulder,
20: 2 the *p* shall come forward and say to the
26: 3 *p* in office at that time and say to him,
26: 4 The *p* shall then receive the basket from
Jos 14: 1 Eleazar the *p*,
17: 4 presented themselves to Eleazar the *p*,
19:51 final portions into which Eleazar the *p*,
20: 6 of the high *p* who is in office at the time.
21: 1 Levite families came up to Eleazar the *p*,
21: 4 the descendants of Aaron the *p*
21:13 Thus to the descendants of Aaron the *p*
22:13 of Phinehas, son of Eleazar the *p*,
22:30 the *p* and the princes of the community,
22:31 Phinehas, son of Eleazar the *p*,
22:32 Phinehas, son of Eleazar the *p*,
Jgs 17: 5 one of his sons, who became his *p*.
17:10 "Be father and *p* to me, and I will give
17:12 the young Levite, who became his *p*,
17:13 me, since the Levite has become my *p*."
18: 4 "He pays me a salary and I am his *p*."
18: 6 The *p* said to them, "Go and prosper:
18:16 of the gate, and the *p* stood there also.
18:18 overlaid with silver, the *p* said to them,
18:19 Come with us and be our father and *p*.
18:19 Is it better for you to be *p* for the
18:19 to be *p* for a tribe and a clan in Israel?"
18:20 The *p*, agreeing, took the ephod,
18:24 made, and have gone off with my *p* as well,"
18:27 what Micah had made, and the *p* he had had,
1Sm 1: 9 Eli the *p* was sitting on a chair near the
2:11 in the service of the LORD under the *p* Eli.
2:14 the fork brought up, the *p* would keep.
2:15 "Give me some meat to roast for the *p*.
2:35 I will choose a faithful *p* who shall do
14: 3 son of Eli, the *p* of the LORD at Shiloh,
14:19 While Saul was speaking to the *p*,
14:19 he said to the *p*, "Withdraw your hand."
14:36 But the *p* said, "Let us consult God."
21: 2 David went to Ahimelech, the *p* of Nob,
21: 3 David answered the *p*: "The king gave
21: 5 But the *p* replied to David,
21: 6 David answered the *p*: "We have indeed
21: 7 So the *p* gave him holy bread,
21:10 The *p* replied: "The sword of Goliath
22:11 king sent a summons to Ahimelech the *p*,
23: 9 to harm him, he said to the *p* Abiathar,
30: 7 his God, David said to Abiathar, the *p*,
2Sm 15:27 The king also said to the *p* Zadok:
20:26 Ira the Jairite was also David's *p*.
1Kgs 1: 7 son of Zeruiah, and with Abiathar the *p*,
1: 8 However, Zadok the *p*,
1:19 all the king's sons, Abiathar the *p*,
1:25 of the army, and Abiathar the *p*,
1:26 nor Zadok the *p*, nor Benaiah,
1:32 Then King David summoned Zadok the *p*,
1:34 There Zadok the *p* and Nathan the prophet
1:38 So Zadok the *p*, Nathan the prophet,
1:39 Then Zadok the *p* took the horn of oil from
1:42 speaking, Jonathan, son of Abiathar the *p*,
1:44 The king sent with him Zadok the *p*,
1:45 Zadok the *p* and Nathan the prophet
2:22 and has with him Abiathar the *p* and Joab,
2:26 The king said to Abiathar the *p*:
2:27 Abiathar from his office of *p* of the LORD,
2:35 and put Zadok the *p* in place of Abiathar.
4: 2 Azariah, son of Zadok, *p*;
13:33 and became a *p* of the high places.
2Kgs 11: 9 did just as Jehoiada the *p* commanded.
11: 9 off duty that week, came to Jehoiada the *p*.
11:15 Then Jehoiada the *p* instructed the
11:18 completely, and slew Mattan, the *p* of Baal,
12: 3 lived, because the *p* Jehoiada guided him.
12: 8 the *p* Jehoiada and the other priests.
12:10 The *p* Jehoiada then took a chest,
12:11 the royal scribe [and the *p* would come up,
16:10 King Ahaz sent to Uriah the *p* a model of
16:11 Uriah the *p* built an altar according to
16:15 altar," King Ahaz commanded Uriah the *p*,
16:16 the *p* did just as King Ahaz had commanded.
22: 4 with orders to go to the high *p* Hilkiah
22: 8 high *p* Hilkiah informed the scribe Shaphan,
22:10 that the *p* Hilkiah had given him a book,
22:12 and issued this command to Hilkiah the *p*,
22:14 So Hilkiah the *p*, Ahikam, Achbor,
23: 4 Then the king commanded the high *p* Hilkiah,
23:24 book that the *p* Hilkiah had found
25:18 Seraiah the high *p*, Zephaniah the second *p*,
1Chr 5:36 *p* in the temple Solomon built in Jerusalem.
16:39 But the *p* Zadok and his priestly brethren
24: 6 king, and of the leaders, of Zadok the *p*,
27: 5 month, was Benaiah, son of Jehoiada the *p*,
29:22 him as the LORD'S prince, and Zadok as *p*.
2Chr 13: 9 bull and seven rams becomes a *p* of no-gods.
19:11 Amariah is high *p* over you in everything
22:11 of Ahaziah, and wife of Jehoiada the *p*,
23: 8 Judah did just as Jehoiada the *p* commanded.
23: 8 *p* had not dismissed any of the divisions.
23: 9 the *p* gave the captains the spears,
23:14 Then Jehoiada the *p* sent out the captains
23:14 For," the *p* continued, "you must not
23:17 and they slew Mattan, the *p* of Baal,
24: 2 the LORD as long as Jehoiada the *p* lived.
24:11 scribe and an overseer for the high *p* came,
24:20 possessed Zechariah, son of Jehoiada the *p*.
24:25 of the murder of the son of Jehoiada the *p*.
26:17 But Azariah the *p*, and with him eighty
26:20 *p* and all the other priests examined him,
31: 2 to each *p* and Levite his proper service,
31:10 concerning the heaps, and the *p* Azariah,
34: 9 They came to Hilkiah the high *p* and turned
34:14 Hilkiah the *p* found the book of the law of
34:18 king, "Hilkiah the *p* has given me a book."
Ezr 2:63 should be a *p* bearing the Urim and Thummim.
7: 5 son of Eleazar, son of the high *p* Aaron
7:12 king of kings, to Ezra the *p*,
7:21 Whatever Ezra the *p*, scribe of the law
7:24 impose taxes, tributes, or tolls on any *p*,
8:30 " The *p* and the Levites then took over
8:33 of our God and consigned to the *p* Meremoth,
10:10 Then Ezra, the *p*, stood up and said
Neh 3: 1 Eliashib the high *p* and his priestly
3:20 of the house of Eliashib, the high *p*.
7:65 should be a *p* bearing the Urim and Thummim.
8: 2 the *p* brought the law before the assembly,
10:39 An Aaronite *p* shall be with the Levites
13: 4 Before this, the *p* Eliashib,
13:13 the storerooms I appointed the *p* Shelemiah,
13:28 of Joiada, son of Eliashib the high *p*,
Jdt 4: 6 who was high *p* in Jerusalem in those days,
4: 8 orders given them by Joakim, the high *p*,
4:14 The high *p* Joakim, and all the priests
15: 8 *p* Joakim and the elders of the Israelites,
1Mc 2: 1 son of Simeon, a *p* of the family of Joarib,
7: 5 led by Alcimus, who desired to be high *p*.
7:14 "A *p* of the line of Aaron has come with
10:20 you today to be high *p* of your nation;
10:32 and I transfer it to the high *p*,
10:38 obey no other authority than the high *p*.
10:69 sent this message to Jonathan the high *p*:
12: 3 "The high *p* Jonathan and the Jewish
12: 6 "Jonathan the high *p*,
12: 7 was sent to the high *p* Onias from Arius,
12:20 sends greetings to Onias the high *p*.
13:36 sends greetings to Simon the high *p*,
13:42 "In the first year of Simon, high *p*,
14:17 his brother Simon had been made high *p*
14:20 Sparta send greetings to Simon the high *p*,
14:23 decree has been made for Simon the high *p*."
14:27 year under Simon the high *p* in Asaramel,
14:29 country, Simon, son of the *p* Mattathias,
14:30 rallied his nation and become their high *p*,
14:35 they made him their leader and high *p*
14:41 " 'The Jewish people and their *p* have,
14:41 and high *p* until a true prophet arises.
14:47 accepted and agreed to act as high *p*,
15: 1 to Simon, the *p* and ethnarch of the Jews,
15: 2 greetings to Simon, the *p* and ethnarch,
15:17 by Simon the high *p* and the Jewish people,
15:21 you, hand them over to Simon the high *p*,
15:24 letter was also sent to Simon the high *p*.
16:12 gold, being the son-in-law of the high *p*.
16:24 that he succeeded his father as high *p*.
2Mc 3: 1 of the high *p* Onias and his hatred of evil,
3: 4 *p* about the supervision of the city market.
3: 9 received by the high *p* of the city,
3:10 The high *p* explained that part
3:16 of the high *p* was pierced to the heart,
3:21 and the high *p* full of dread and anguish.
3:32 the high *p* offered a sacrifice for the
3:33 *p* was offering the sacrifice of atonement,
3:33 "Be very grateful to the high *p* Onias,"
14: 3 A certain Alcimus, a former high *p*,
14:13 up Alcimus as high *p* of the great temple.
15:12 Onias, the former high *p*,
Ps(s) 110: 4 "You are a *p* forever,
Sir 7:31 Honor God and respect the *p*;
46:13 as a prophet, was SAMUEL, the judge and *p*.
50: 1 the glory of his people, was SIMON the *p*,
50:19 As the high *p* completed the services at
Is 8: 2 And I took reliable witnesses, Uriah the *p*,
24: 2 Layman and *p* alike,
28: 7 *P* and prophet stagger from strong drink,
Jer 6:13 prophet and *p*, all practice fraud.
8:10 all are greedy for gain, prophet and *p*,
14:18 and the *p* forage in a land they know not.
20: 1 prophesying these things by the *p* Pashhur,
21: 1 son of Malchiah, and the *p* Zephaniah,
23:11 Both prophet and *p* are godless!
23:33 this people, or a prophet or a *p* asks you,
23:34 If a prophet or a *p* or anyone else
29:25 to all the priests and to Zephaniah, the *p*,
29:26 you priest in place of the *p* Jehoiada,
29:29 When the *p* Zephaniah read this letter to
37: 3 and Zephaniah, son of Maaseiah the *p*,
52:24 the high priest, Zephaniah, the second *p*,
Lam 2: 6 scorned in fierce wrath both king and *p*.
2:20 Are *p* and prophet to be slain in the
Bar 1: 7 son of Hilkiah, son of Shallum, the *p*,
Ez 1: 3 the word of the LORD came to the *p* Ezekiel,
7:26 instruction shall be lacking to the *p*,
44:21 No *p* shall drink wine when he is to enter
44:26 After a *p* has been cleansed,
45:19 Then the *p* shall take some of the blood
Am 7:10 Amaziah, the *p* of Bethel,
Hg 1: 1 son of Shealtiel, and to the high *p* Joshua,
1:12 son of Shealtiel, and the high *p* Joshua,
1:14 and the spirit of the high *p* Joshua,
2: 2 son of Shealtiel, and to the high *p* Joshua,
2: 4 LORD, and take courage, Joshua, high *p*,
Zec 3: 1 *p* standing before the angel of the LORD,
3: 8 Listen, O Joshua, high *p*!
6:11 son of Jehozadak, the high *p* Zerubbabel.
6:13 The *p* shall be put at his right hand,
Mal 2: 7 the lips of the *p* are to keep knowledge,
Mt 8: 4 the *p* and offer the gift Moses prescribed.
26: 3 were assembled in the palace of the high *p*,
26:57 Jesus led him off to Caiaphas the high *p*,
26:62 high *p* rose to his feet and addressed him:
26:63 The high *p* then said to him:
26:65 At this the high *p* tore his robes:
Mk 1:44 "Go off and present yourself to the *p* and
2:26 in the days of Abiathar the high *p*
14:53 Then they led Jesus off to the high *p*,
14:60 The high *p* rose to his feet before the
14:61 Once again the high *p* interrogated him:
14:63 At that the high *p* tore his robes and said:
14:66 the servant girls of the high *p* came along.
Lk 1: 5 there was a *p* named Zechariah of the
1: 8 fulfilling his functions as a *p* before God,
5:14 no one, but go and show yourself to the *p*.
10:31 *p* happened to be going down the same road;
22:54 and brought him to the house of the high *p*,
Jn 11:49 named Caiaphas, who was high *p* that year,

11:51 It was rather as high *p* for that year that
18:10 drew it and struck the slave of the high *p*,
18:13 of Caiaphas who was high *p* that year.
18:15 disciple, who was known to the high *p*,
18:16 The disciple known to the high *p* came out
18:19 The high *p* questioned Jesus,
18:22 "Is that the way to answer the high *p*?"
18:24 sent him, bound, to the high *p* Caiaphas.
Acts 4: 6 next day in Jerusalem, Annas the high *p*,
5:17 high *p* and all his supporters (that is,
5:21 When the high *p* and his supporters arrived
5:27 high *p* began the interrogation in this way:
7: 1 high *p* asked whether the charges were true.
9: 1 went to the high *p* and asked him for
14:13 Even the *p* of the temple of Zeus,
19:14 the seven sons of Sceva, a Jewish high *p*,
22: 5 "On this point the high *p* and the whole
23: 2 the high *p* Ananias ordered his attendants
23: 4 "How dare you insult God's high *p*?"
23: 5 I did not know that he was the high *p*.
24: 1 the high *p* Ananias came down to Caesarea
Heb 2:17 faithful high *p* before God on their behalf,
3: 1 and high *p* whom we acknowledge in faith,
4:14 high *p* who has passed through the heavens,
4:15 For we do not have a high *p* who is unable
5: 1 Every high *p* is taken from among men and
5: 5 glorify himself with the office of high *p*;
5: 6 in another place, "You are a *p* forever,
5:10 *p* according to the order of Melchizedek.
6:20 being made high *p* forever according to the
7: 1 king of Salem and *p* of the Most High God,
7: 3 like the Son of God he remains a *p* forever.
7:11 a *p* according to the order of Melchizedek,
7:11 a *p* according to the order of Aaron?
7:15 The matter is clearer still if another *p*
7:16 one who has become a *p*,
7:17 "You are a *p* forever according to the
7:21 'You are a *p* forever,
7:26 fitting that we should have such a high *p*:
7:28 came after the law appoints as *p* the Son,
8: 1 we have such a high *p*,
8: 3 Now every high *p* is appointed to offer
8: 4 If he were on earth he would not be a *p*,
9: 7 only the high *p* went into the inner one,
9:11 *p* of the good things which have come to be,
9:25 as the high *p* enters year after year into
10:11 other *p* stands ministering day by day,
10:21 a great *p* who is over the house of God,
13:11 high *p* as a sin offering are burned outside

PRIEST-SCRIBE (3)

Ezr 7:11 which King Artaxerxes gave to Ezra the *p*,
Neh 8: 9 and] Ezra the *p* [and the Levites who were
12:26 of Nehemiah the governor and of Ezra the *p*.

PRIEST-TEACHER (1)

2Chr 15: 3 Israel had no true God, no *p* and no law,

PRIESTHOOD (35)

Ex 29: 9 shall the *p* be theirs by perpetual law,
40:15 *p* throughout all future generations."
Lv 16:32 to the *p* in succession to his father.
Nm 3: 3 who were ordained to exercise the *p*.
16:10 him, and yet you now seek the *p* too.
18: 1 *p* shall rest on you and your sons alone.
18: 7 I give you the *p* as a gift.
25:13 after him the pledge of an everlasting *p*,
Jos 18: 7 the *p* of the LORD is their heritage;
Ezr 2:62 hence they were degraded from the *p*,
Neh 7:64 hence they were degraded from the *p*,
13:29 they defiled the *p* and the covenant of the *p*
1Mc 2:54 received the covenant of an everlasting *p*.
7: 9 Alcimus, to whom he granted the high *p*,
7:21 spared no pains to maintain his high *p*,
11:27 He confirmed him in the high *p* and in all
11:57 "I confirm you in the high *p* and appoint
14:38 Demetrius confirmed him in the high *p*,
2Mc 2:17 them their heritage, the kingdom, the *p*,
4: 7 Jason obtained the high *p* by corrupt means:
4:24 that he secured the high *p* for himself,
4:25 that made him worthy of the high *p*;
4:29 as his substitute in the high *p*,
11: 3 to put the high *p* up for sale every year.
14: 7 dignity, that is to say, the high *p*,
Sir 45: 7 he bestowed on him the *p* of his people;
45:15 in his *p* and bless his people in his name.
45:24 should possess the high *p* forever.
Hos 4: 6 knowledge, I will reject you from my *p*;
Heb 7:11 had been achieved through the levitical *p*
7:12 When there is a change of *p*,
7:24 forever, has a *p* which does not pass away.
1Pt 2: 5 as an edifice of spirit, into a holy *p*,
2: 9 however, are "a chosen race, a royal *p*,

PRIESTLY (31)

Lv 6:22 the *p* line may partake of the sin offering,
7: 6 the males of the *p* line may partake of it;
7:35 the *p* share from the oblations of the LORD,
27:21 that is doomed, it shall become *p* property.
Nm 3: 4 and Ithamar performed the *p* functions
3:10 appoint to have charge of the *p* functions.
18: 7 have charge of performing the *p* functions
18: 8 to you and to your sons as your *p* share.
Dt 10: 6 Eleazar succeeding him in the *p* office.
18: 1 "The whole *p* tribe of Levi shall have no
Jos 3:15 No sooner had these *p* bearers of the ark
21:19 belonged to the *p* descendants of Aaron,
1Sm 2:36 Appoint me, I beg you, to a *p* function,
22:19 also put the *p* city of Nob to the sword,
1Chr 16:39 But the priest Zadok and his *p* brethren he
24: 3 assigned the functions for the *p* service.
24:31 the heads of the *p* and levitical families;
2Chr 31:15 Under him in the *p* cities were Eden,
Ezr 8:24 of the *p* leaders along with Sherebiah,
Neh 3: 1 Eliashib the high priest and his *p*
12: 7 These were the *p* heads and their brethren
12:12 of Joiakim these were the *p* family heads:
1Mc 3:49 They brought with them the *p* vestments,
2Mc 3: 4 a certain Simon, of the *p* course of Bilgah,
3:15 in their *p* robes before the altar,
Jer 1: 1 son of Hilkiah, of a *p* family in Anathoth,
Lam 2: 9 *p* instruction is wanting,
Lk 1: 5 named Zechariah of the *p* class of Abijah;
1: 9 it fell to him by lot according to *p* usage
1:23 Then, when his time of *p* service was over,
Rom 15:16 with the *p* duty of preaching the gospel of

PRIESTS—PRIEST'S (462)

Gn 47:22 Only the *p*' lands Joseph did not take over.
47:22 Since the *p* had a fixed allowance from
47:26 land of the *p* did not pass over to Pharaoh.
Ex 19: 6 You shall be to me a kingdom of *p*,
19:22 The *p*, too, who approach the LORD
19:24 But the *p* and the people must not break
28: 1 brought to you, that they may be my *p*.
28: 4 his sons are to wear in serving as my *p*,
28:41 and ordain them, consecrating them as my *p*.
29: 1 shall perform in consecrating them as my *p*.
29:44 consecrate Aaron and his sons to be my *p*.
30:30 shall also anoint and consecrate as my *p*.
40:15 their father, anoint them also as my *p*.
Lv 1: 5 before the LORD, but Aaron's sons, the *p*,
1: 7 After Aaron's sons, the *p*, have put some
1:11 Then Aaron's sons, the *p*, shall splash its
2: 2 he has brought it to Aaron's sons, the *p*,
3: 2 but Aaron's sons, the *p*, shall splash its
7:35 day he called them to be the *p* of the LORD;
13: 2 or to one of the *p* among his descendants,
16:33 the *p* and all the people of the community.
21: 1 to Moses, "Speak to Aaron's sons, the *p*,
21: 5 "The *p* shall not make bare the crown of
21: 9 "A *p* daughter who loses her honor by
21:10 "The most exalted of the *p*,
22:10 "Neither a lay person nor a *p* tenant or
22:12 A *p* daughter who is married to a layman
22:13 if a *p* daughter is widowed or divorced and,
22:15 LORD the *p* shall not allow to be profaned
Nm 3: 3 the anointed *p* who were ordained to
10: 8 "It is the sons of Aaron, the *p*,
Dt 17: 9 to the levitical *p* or to the judge who is
17:18 that is in the custody of the levitical *p*.
18: 3 The *p* shall have a right to the following
19:17 of the *p* or judges in office at that time;
21: 5 The *p*, the descendents of Levi,
24: 8 out all the directions of the levitical *p*.
27: 9 Moses, with the levitical *p*,
31: 9 he entrusted it to the levitical *p* who
Jos 3: 3 our God, which the levitical *p* will carry,
3: 6 And he directed the *p* to take up the ark
3: 8 Now command the *p* carrying the ark of the
3:13 feet of the *p* carrying the ark of the LORD,
3:14 with the *p* carrying the ark of the
3:17 the *p* carrying the ark of the covenant of
4: 3 where the *p* have been standing motionless.
4: 9 the *p* stood who were carrying the ark
4:10 The *p* carrying the ark remained in the bed
4:11 side, the ark of the LORD, borne by the *p*,
4:16 "Command the *p* carrying the ark of the
4:18 and when the *p* carrying the ark of the
6: 4 *p* carrying ram's horns ahead of the ark.
6: 4 seven times, and have the *p* blow the horns.
6: 6 Summoning the *p*, Joshua, son of Nun,
6: 6 ark of the covenant with seven of the *p*
6: 8 with the seven *p* who carried the ram's
6: 9 *p* with the horns marched the picked troops;
6:12 had the *p* take up the ark of the LORD.
6:13 The seven *p* bearing the ram's horns
6:16 the *p* blew the horns and Joshua said to
8:33 the levitical *p* who were carrying the ark
Jgs 18:30 and his descendants were *p* for the tribe
1Sm 1: 3 were ministering as *p* of the LORD.
2:13 nor for the *p*' duties toward the people.
2:13 the *p* servant would come with a
2:15 the *p* servant would come and say to the
2:28 of all the tribes of Israel to be my *p*,
5: 5 neither the *p* of Dagon nor any others who
6: 2 they summoned *p* and fortune-tellers to ask,
22:11 and to all his family who were *p* in Nob;
22:17 the rounds and kill the *p* of the LORD,
22:17 to lift a hand to strike the *p* of the LORD.
22:18 Doeg, "You make the rounds and kill the *p*!"
22:18 one to the next and killed the *p* himself,
22:21 that Saul had slain the *p* of the LORD,
2Sm 8:17 and Ahimelech, son of Abiathar, were *p*.
8:18 And David's sons were *p*.
15:35 the *p* Zadok and Abiathar there with you.
15:35 report it to the *p* Zadok and Abiathar,
17:15 Hushai said to the *p* Zadok and Abiathar:
19:12 sent word to the *p* Zadok and Abiathar:
20:25 Zadok and Abiathar were *p*.
1Kgs 4: 4 Zadok and Abiathar, *p*
8: 3 Israel had arrived, the *p* took up the ark;
8: 4 (The *p* and Levites carried them.)
8: 6 The *p* brought the ark of the covenant of
8:10 When the *p* left the holy place,
8:11 the *p* could no longer minister because
12:31 made *p* from among the people who
12:32 Bethel *p* of the high places he had built.
13: 2 who shall slaughter upon you the *p* of the
13:33 but again made *p* for the high places from
2Kgs 10:11 his powerful supporters, intimates, and *p*,
10:19 all his worshipers, and all his *p*.
12: 5 For the *p* Joash made this rule:
12: 6 the *p* may take for themselves,
12: 7 the *p* had not made needed repairs on the
12: 8 the priest Jehoiada and the other *p*.
12: 9 So the *p* agreed that they would neither
12:10 The *p* who guarded the entry would put into
12:17 they belonged to the *p*.
17:27 "Send back one of the *p* whom I deported,
17:28 So one of the *p* who had been deported from
17:32 from their number *p* for the high places,
19: 2 the scribe, and the elders of the *p*,
23: 2 *p*, prophets, and all the people
23: 8 in all the *p* from the cities of Judah,
23: 9 The *p* of the high places could not
23:20 He slaughtered upon the altars all the *p*
1Chr 9: 2 there were certain lay Israelites, the *p*,
9:10 Among the *p* were Jedaiah;
9:30 It was the sons of *p*, however, who mixed
13: 2 and also the *p* and the Levites from their
15:11 David summoned the *p* Zadok and Abiathar,
15:14 the *p* and the Levites sanctified
15:24 The *p*, Shebaniah, Joshaphat, Nethanel,
16: 6 and the *p* Benaiah and Jahaziel were to be
18:16 and Ahimelech, son of Abiathar, were *p*;
23: 2 together with the *p* and the Levites.
24: 2 only Eleazar and Ithamar served as *p*.
24: 6 houses of the *p* and of the Levites,
28:13 as for the divisions of the *p* and Levites,
28:21 The classes of the *p* and Levites are ready
2Chr 4: 6 but the sea was for the *p* to wash in.
4: 9 He made the court of the *p* and the great
5: 5 it was the levitical *p* who carried them.
5: 7 The *p* brought the ark of the covenant of
5:11 When the *p* came out of the holy place (all
5:11 (all the *p* who were present had purified
5:12 a hundred and twenty *p* blowing trumpets.
5:14 The *p* could not continue to minister
6:41 May your *p*, LORD God, be clothed with
7: 2 *p* could not enter the house of the LORD,
7: 6 The *p* were standing at their stations,
7: 6 *p* blew the trumpets and all Israel stood.
8:14 various classes of the *p* for their service,
8:14 of praise and ministry alongside the *p*,
8:15 to the *p* and Levites or the treasuries.
11:13 Now the *p* and Levites throughout Israel
11:14 his sons repudiated them as *p* of the LORD.
11:15 he himself appointed *p* for the high places
13: 9 "Have you not expelled the *p* of the LORD,
13: 9 *p* like the peoples of foreign lands?
13:10 The *p* ministering to the LORD are sons of
13:12 and his *p* are here with trumpets to sound
13:14 to the LORD and the *p* sounded the trumpets.
17: 8 together with the *p* Elishama and Jehoram.
19: 8 Jehoshaphat appointed some Levites and *p*
23: 4 a third of your number, both *p* and Levites,
23: 6 *p* and those Levites who are ministering.
23:18 temple into the hands of the levitical *p*,
24: 5 the *p* and Levites and said to them:
26:17 and with him eighty other *p* of the LORD,
26:18 burn incense to the LORD, but for the *p*,
26:19 the moment he showed his anger to the *p*,
26:20 priest and all the other *p* examined him,
29: 4 He summoned the *p* and Levites,
29:16 The *p* entered the interior of the LORD's
29:21 and he ordered the sons of Aaron, the *p*,
29:22 and the *p* collected the blood and cast it
29:24 The *p* then slaughtered them and offered
29:26 of David, and the *p* with the trumpets.
29:34 Since the *p* were too few in number to be
29:34 and the *p* had sanctified themselves;
29:34 willing than the *p* to sanctify themselves.
30: 3 the *p* had not sanctified themselves in
30:15 The *p* and Levites, touched with shame,
30:16 The *p* sprinkled the blood given them by
30:21 and the Levites and the *p* sang the praises
30:24 *p* sanctified themselves in great numbers,
30:25 together with the *p* and Levites and the
30:27 levitical *p* rose and blessed the people;
31: 2 the classes of the *p* and the Levites
31: 4 provide the support of the *p* and Levites,
31: 9 the *p* and the Levites concerning the heaps,
31:16 for all *p* who were eligible to enter the
31:17 The *p* were inscribed in their family

PRIESTS—PRIEST'S (cont.)

31:19 the *p* who lived on the lands attached to
31:19 portions to every male among the *p*
34: 5 bones of the *p* he burned upon their altars.
34:30 and the inhabitants of Jerusalem, the *p*,
35: 2 He reappointed the *p* to their duties and
35: 8 gift to the people, the *p* and the Levites.
35: 8 gave to the *p* two thousand six hundred
35:10 had been arranged, the *p* took their places,
35:11 whereupon the *p* sprinkled some of the
35:14 the Passover for themselves and for the *p*.
35:14 Indeed the *p*, the sons of Aaron,
35:14 prepared for themselves and for the *p*,
35:18 like that of Josiah, the *p* and Levites,
36:14 the *p* and the people added infidelity to
Ezr 1: 5 Judah and Benjamin and the *p* and Levites
2:36 The *p*: sons of Jedaiah,
2:61 Also, of the *p*: sons of Habaiah, sons
2:69 silver, and one hundred garments for the *p*.
2:70 The *p*, the Levites, and some
3: 2 Jozadak, together with his brethren the *p*,
3: 8 the *p* and Levites and all who had come
3:10 vested *p* with the trumpets and the Levites,
3:12 Many of the *p*, Levites, and family heads,
6: 9 requirements of the *p* who are in Jerusalem
6:16 The Israelites *p*, Levites, and the other
6:18 they set up the *p* in their classes and the
6:20 of the exiles, for their brethren the *p*,
7: 7 Some of the Israelites and some *p*,
7:13 to the people of Israel, its *p* or Levites,
7:16 offerings which the people and *p* freely
8:15 that both laymen and *p* were present,
8:29 in the presence of the chief *p* and Levites
9: 1 "Neither the Israelite laymen nor the *p*
9: 7 over, we and our kings and our *p*,
10: 5 demanded an oath from the chiefs of the *p*,
10:18 Among the *p*, the following were found
Neh 2:16 nothing to the Jews, neither to the *p*,
3:22 work of repair was carried out by the *p*,
3:28 Gate the *p* carried out the work of repair,
5:12 Then I called for the *p* and had them
7:39 The *p*: sons of Jedaiah,
7:63 Also, of the *p*: sons of Habaiah, sons of
7:69 gold, fifty basins, thirty garments for *p*,
7:71 of silver, and sixty-seven garments for *p*.
7:72 The *p*, the Levites, the gatekeepers,
8:13 *p* and the Levites gathered around Ezra
9:32 us, our kings, our princes, our *p*,
9:34 Yes, our kings, our princes, our *p*,
10: 1 of our princes, our Levites, and our *p*.
10: 9 these are the *p*.
10:29 The rest of the people, *p*,
10:35 We, *p*, Levites, and people,
10:37 to the *p* who serve in the house of our God,
10:38 wine and of oil, we will bring to the *p*,
10:40 of the sanctuary, and the ministering *p*,
11: 3 cities of Judah dwelt lay Israelites, *p*,
11:10 Among the *p* were:
11:20 rest of Israel, including *p* and Levites,
12: 1 *p* and Levites who returned with Zerubbabel,
12:22 the family heads of the *p* were written
12:30 *p* and Levites first purified themselves,
12:35 and Jeremiah, *p* with the trumpets,
12:41 me half the magistrates, the *p* Eliakim,
12:44 legally assigned to the *p* and Levites.
12:44 For Judah rejoiced in its appointed *p* and
13: 5 gatekeepers, and the offerings due the *p*.
13:30 various functions for the *p* and Levites,
Tb 1: 7 to Jerusalem and present them to the *p*,
Jdt 4:14 and all the *p* in attendance on the Lord
11:13 had sanctified and reserved for the *p*
1Mc 3:51 and your *p* are in mourning and humiliation.
4:38 mountain, and the *p*' chambers demolished.
4:42 He chose blameless *p*, devoted to the law;
4:57 *p*' chambers and furnished them with doors.
5:67 At that time some *p* fell in battle who had
7:33 Some of the *p* from the sanctuary and some
7:36 The *p*, however, went in and stood
10:42 belong to the *p* who perform the services.
11:23 He selected some elders and *p* of Israel
12: 6 priest, the senate of the nation, the *p*,
14:20 Simon the high priest, the elders, the *p*,
14:28 in Asaramel, in a great assembly of *p*,
14:44 or *p* to nullify any of these decisions,
14:47 and ethnarch of the Jewish people and *p*
2Mc 1:10 and member of the family of the anointed *p*,
1:13 deceitful stratagem employed by Nanea's *p*.
1:15 When the *p* of the Nanaeon had displayed
1:15 entered the temple, the *p* locked the doors.
1:19 devout *p* of the time took some of the fire
1:20 *p* who had hidden the fire to look for it.
1:21 Nehemiah ordered the *p* to sprinkle with
1:23 was being burned, the *p* recited a prayer,
1:30 Then the *p* began to sing hymns.
1:33 where the exiled *p* had hidden the fire,
3:15 *P* prostrated themselves in their priestly
4:14 that the *p* no longer cared about the
14:31 *p* were offering the customary sacrifices,
14:34 *p* stretched out their hands toward heaven,
15:31 stationed the *p* before the altar,
Ps(s) 78:64 Their *p* fell by the sword,
99: 6 Moses and Aaron were among his *p*,
132: 9 May your *p* be clothed with justice;
132:16 Her *p* I will clothe with salvation,
Sir 7:29 With all your soul, fear God, revere his *p*.
50:12 received the sundered victims from the *p*
50:16 sons of Aaron would sound a blast, the *p*,
Is 37: 2 the scribe, and the elders of the *p*,
61: 6 yourselves shall be named *p* of the LORD,
66:21 Some of these I will take as *p* and Levites,
Jer 1:18 and princes, against its *p* and people.
2: 8 The *p* asked not, "Where is the LORD?"
2:26 their princes, their *p* and their prophets;
4: 9 the *p* will be amazed,
5:31 falsely, and the *p* teach as they wish;
8: 1 Judah, the bones of the *p* and the prophets,
13:13 to David's throne, the *p* and prophets,
18:18 mean the loss of instruction from the *p*,
19: 1 of the elders of the people and of the *p*,
26: 7 Now the *p*, the prophets, and all
26: 8 the *p* and prophets laid hold of him,
26:11 The *p* and prophets said to the princes and
26:16 the people said to the *p* and the prophets,
27:16 *p* and to all the people I spoke as follows:
28: 1 the presence of the *p* and all the people:
28: 5 prophet Hananiah in the presence of the *p*
29: 1 elders among the exiles, to the *p*,
29:25 Jerusalem, to all the *p* and to Zephaniah,
31:14 I will lavish choice portions upon the *p*,
32:32 their princes, their *p* and their prophets,
33:18 nor shall *p* of Levi ever be lacking,
33:21 with the *p* of Levi who minister to me.
34:19 and of Jerusalem, the courtiers, the *p*,
48: 7 go into exile, his *p* and princes with him.
49: 3 into exile along with his *p* and captains.
Lam 1: 4 All her gateways are deserted, her *p* groan,
1:19 My *p* and my elders perished in the city;
4:13 of her prophets and the crimes of her *p*,
4:16 He does not receive the *p* with favor,
Bar 1: 7 and to the *p* and the whole people who were
1:16 our kings and rulers and *p* and prophets,
6: 9 Then sometimes the *p* take the silver and
6:17 the *p* reinforce their houses with gates
6:27 Their *p* resell their sacrifices for their
6:30 and in their temples the *p* squat with torn
6:32 The *p* take some of their clothing and put
6:48 the *p* deliberate among themselves where
6:54 gods, though the *p* flee and are safe,
Ez 22:26 Her *p* violate my law and profane what is
40:45 is for the *p* who have charge of the temple,
40:46 is for the *p* who have charge of the altar.
42:13 here the *p* who draw near to the LORD shall
42:14 When the *p* have once entered,
43:19 a young bull as a sin offering to the *p*,
43:24 the *p* shall strew salt on them and offer
43:27 the *p* shall offer your holocausts and
44:13 no longer draw near me to serve as my *p*,
44:15 As for the Levitical *p*,
44:22 may marry women who are the widows of *p*.
44:30 of every kind, shall belong to the *p*;
44:30 *p* to bring a blessing down upon your house.
44:31 The *p* shall not eat anything,
45: 4 part of the land belonging to the *p*,
46: 2 *p* offer his holocausts and peace offerings,
46:19 reserved to the *p* which face the north.
46:20 "Here the *p* cook the guilt offerings and
48:10 In this sacred tract the *p* shall have
48:11 The consecrated *p*, the Zadokites,
48:13 territory corresponding to that of the *p*,
Dn 3:84 *P* of the Lord, bless the Lord;
14: 8 the king called his *p* and said to them,
14:10 There were seventy *p* of Bel,
14:11 into the temple of Bel, the *p* of Bel said,
14:15 The *p* entered that night as usual,
14:21 The angry king arrested the *p*,
14:28 killed the dragon, and put the *p* to death."
Hos 4: 4 with you is my grievance, O *p*!
4: 9 The *p* shall fare no better than the people:
5: 1 Hear this, O *p*, Pay attention,
6: 9 a band of *p* slay on the way to Shechem,
10: 5 people mourn for it and its *p* wail over it,
Jl 1: 9 In mourning are the *p*,
1:13 Gird yourselves and weep, O *p*!
2:17 Between the porch and the altar let the *p*,
Mi 3:11 a bribe, her *p* give decisions for a salary,
Zep 1: 4 vestige of Baal, the very names of his *p*.
3: 4 Her *p* profane what is holy,
Hg 2:11 Ask the *p* for a decision:
2:12 "No," the *p* answered.
2:13 The *p* answered, "They become unclean."
Zec 7: 3 the *p* of the house of the LORD of hosts,
7: 5 to all the people of the land and to the *p*:
Mal 1: 6 So says the LORD of hosts to you, O *p*,
2: 1 And now, O *p*, this commandment is for you:
Mt 2: 4 of the chief *p* and scribes of the people,
12: 4 to him and his men or anyone other than *p*?
12: 5 Have you not read in the law how the *p* on
16:21 at the hands of the elders, the chief *p*,
20:18 be handed over to the chief *p* and scribes,
21:15 The chief *p* and the scribes became
21:23 the chief *p* and elders of the people came
21:45 *p* and the Pharisees heard these parables,
26: 3 At that time the chief *p* and elders of the
26:14 Iscariot went off to the chief *p* and said,
26:47 by the chief *p* and elders of the people.
26:51 drew it, and slashed at the high *p* servant,
26:58 a distance as far as the high *p* residence.
26:59 The chief *p*, with the whole Sanhedrin,
27: 1 At daybreak all the chief *p* and the elders
27: 3 back to the chief *p* and elders and said,
27: 6 The chief *p* picked up the silver,
27:12 he was accused by the chief *p* and elders,
27:20 the chief *p* and elders convinced the
27:41 The chief *p*, the scribes, and the elders
27:62 the chief *p* and the Pharisees called at
28:11 to the chief *p* all that had happened.
Mk 2:26 which only the *p* were permitted to eat?
8:31 be rejected by the elders, the chief *p*,
10:33 handed over to the chief *p* and the scribes.
11:18 The chief *p* and the scribes heard of this
11:27 in the temple precincts the chief *p*,
14: 1 and therefore the chief *p* and scribes
14:10 to the chief *p* to hand Jesus over to them.
14:43 these people had been sent by the chief *p*,
14:47 drew his sword and struck the high *p* slave,
14:53 to the high priest, and all the chief *p*,
14:54 a distance right into the high *p* courtyard,
14:55 The chief *p* with the whole Sanhedrin were
15: 1 As soon as it was daybreak the chief *p*,
15: 3 The chief *p*, meanwhile, brought many
15:10 that the chief *p* had handed him over.
15:11 the chief *p* incited the crowd to have him
15:31 The chief *p* and the scribes also joined in
Lk 6: 4 even though only *p* are allowed to eat it?"
9:22 by the elders, the high *p* and the scribes,
17:14 "Go and show yourselves to the *p*."
19:47 The chief *p* and scribes meanwhile were
20: 1 the good news, the high *p* and Pharisees,
20:19 and high *p* tried to get their hands on him,
22: 2 and the high *p* and scribes began to look
22: 4 He went off to confer with the chief *p* and
22:50 high *p* servant and cut off his right ear.
22:52 the chief *p*, the chiefs of the temple guard,
22:66 the elders of the people, the chief *p*,
23: 4 reported to the chief *p* and the crowds,
23:10 The chief *p* and scribes were at hand to
23:13 Pilate then called together the chief *p*,
24:20 how our chief *p* and leaders delivered him
Jn 1:19 sent *p* and Levites from Jerusalem to ask,
7:32 and the chief *p* and Pharisees together
7:45 back, the chief *p* and Pharisees asked them,
11:47 The result was that the chief *p* and the
11:57 (The chief *p* and the Pharisees had given
12:10 the chief *p* planned to kill Lazarus too,
18: 3 supplied by the chief *p* and the Pharisees,
18:15 with Jesus as far as the high *p*' courtyard,
18:26 insisted one of the high *p* slaves
18:35 the chief *p* who have handed you over to me.
19: 6 As soon as the chief *p* and the temple
19:15 The chief *p* replied, "We have no king
19:21 chief *p* of the Jews tried to tell Pilate,
Acts 4: 1 were still addressing the crowd, the *p*,
4:23 told them what the *p* and elders had said.
5:24 *p* did not know what to make of the affair.
6: 7 many *p* among those who embraced the faith.
9:14 chief *p* to arrest any who invoke your name."
9:21 people and bring them before the chief *p*?"
22:30 *p* and the whole Sanhedrin to a meeting;
23:14 to the chief *p* and the elders and said:
25: 2 There the Jewish chief *p* and the leaders
25:15 While I was in Jerusalem the chief *p* and
26:10 the authority I received from the chief *p*,
26:12 authority and commission of the chief *p*.
Heb 7: 5 The law provides that the *p* of the tribe
7:14 regarding which Moses said nothing about *p*.
7:20 The *p* of the old covenant became priests
7:23 Under the old covenant there were many *p*
7:27 Unlike the other high *p*,
7:28 the law sets up as high *p* men who are weak,
8: 4 for there are *p* already offering the gifts
9: 6 In performing their service the *p* used to
10: 2 the *p* would have stopped offering them,
Rv 1: 6 of *p* in the service of his God and Father
5:10 of them a kingdom, and *p* to serve our God,
20: 6 they shall serve God and Christ as *p*,

PRIMACY (1)

Col 1:18 dead, so that *p* may be his in everything.

PRIME (5)

Ps(s) 36: 9 their fill of the *p* gifts of your house;
Prv 1:12 nether world does, alive, in the *p* of life,
Sir 29:21 Life's *p* needs are water,
42: 9 Lest she pass her *p* unmarried,
Hos 9:10 the first fruits of the fig tree in its *p*,

PRIMEVAL (2)

Dt 33:27 He spread out the *p* tent;
Ps(s) 74:15 you brought dry land out of the *p* waters.

PRINCE (106)

Gn 49:26 on the brow of the *p* among his brothers.
Ex 22:27 revile God, nor curse a *p* of your people.
Lv 4:22 "Should a *p* commit a sin inadvertently by
Nm 2: 3 [The *p* of the Judahites was Nahshon,
2: 5 tribe of Issachar [Their *p* was Nethanel,
2: 7 [Their *p* was Eliab,

2:10 [Their *p* was Elizur,
2:12 the tribe of Simeon [Their *p* was Shelumiel,
2:14 [Their *p* was Eliasaph,
2:18 [Their *p* was Elishama,
2:20 tribe of Manasseh [Their *p* was Gamaliel,
2:22 [Their *p* was Abidan,
2:25 [Their *p* was Ahiezer,
2:27 the tribe of Asher [Their *p* was Pagiel,
2:29 [Their *p* was Ahira,
3:24 *p* of their ancestral house was Eliasaph,
3:30 *p* of their ancestral house was Elizaphan,
3:32 The chief *p* of the Levites,
3:35 The *p* of the ancestral house of the clans
7: 3 every two princes, and an ox for every *p*.
7:11 "Let one *p* a day present his offering for
7:12 son of Amminadab, *p* of the tribe of Judah.
7:18 day Nethanel, son of Zuar, *p* of Issachar,
7:24 Eliab, son of Helon, *p* of the Zebulunites.
7:30 son of Shedeur, *p* of the Reubenites.
7:36 son of Zurishaddai, *p* of the Simeonites.
7:42 Eliasaph, son of Reuel, *p* of the Gadites.
7:48 son of Ammihud, *p* of the Ephraimites.
7:54 son of Pedahzur, *p* of the Manassehites.
7:60 son of Gideoni, *p* of the Benjamites.
7:66 son of Ammishaddai, *p* of the Danites.
7:72 Pagiel, son of Ochran, *p* of the Asherites.
7:78 Ahira, son of Enan, *p* of the Naphtalites.
17:21 twelve in all, one from each tribal *p*;
17:24 *p* identified his own staff and took it,
25:14 *p* of an ancestral house of the Simeonites.
25:18 Cozbi, the daughter of a Midianite *p*,
34:18 and one *p* from each of the tribes whom you
Dt 33:16 upon the brow of the *p* among his brothers,
Jos 22:14 each one being both *p* and military leader
2Sm 13: 4 He asked him, *P*, why are you so dejected
1Kgs 11:34 but will keep him a *p* as long as he lives
1Chr 2:10 father of Nahshon, a *p* of the Judahites.
5: 6 he was a *p* of the Reubenites.
29:22 and they anointed him as the LORD'S *p*,
Ezr 1: 8 counted out to Sheshbazzar, the *p* of Judah.
Jb 31:37 a *p* I should present myself before him.
Ps(s) 82: 7 men you shall die, and fall like any *p*."
Prv 25: 7 than that you be humbled before the *p*.
28:16 The less prudent the *p*,
Wis 12:14 Nor can any king or *p* confront you on
Sir 10:23 The *p*, the ruler, the judge are in honor;
41:16 Before *p* and ruler, of flattery;
46:19 before the LORD and his anointed *p*,
Is 9: 5 God-Hero, Father-Forever, *P* of Peace.
Jer 36:26 them, but commanded Jerahmeel, a royal *p*,
38: 6 threw him into the cistern of *P* Malchiah,
Ez 7:27 while the *p* shall be enveloped in terror,
12:12 The *p* who is among them shall shoulder his
19: 1 raise a lamentation over the *p* of Israel:
21:30 for you, depraved and wicked *p* of Israel,
28: 2 Son of man, say to the *p* of Tyre:
34:24 and my servant David shall be *p* among them.
37:22 and there shall be one *p* for them all.
37:24 My servant David shall be *p* over them,
37:25 with my servant David their *p* forever.
38: 2 Magog], the chief *p* of Meshech and Tubal,
38: 3 at you, Gog, chief *p* of Meshech and Tubal.
39: 1 at you, Gog, chief *p* of Meshech and Tubal.
44: 3 Only the *p* may sit down in it to eat his
45: 7 The *p* shall have a section bordering on
45:16 to this offering [for the *p* in Israel].
45:17 duty of the *p* to provide the holocausts,
45:22 day the *p* shall offer on his own behalf,
46: 2 The *p* shall enter from outside by way of
46: 4 The holocausts which the *p* presents to the
46: 8 The *p* shall always enter and depart by the
46:10 *p* shall be in their midst when they enter,
46:12 *p* makes a freewill offering to the LORD,
46:16 If the *p* makes a gift of part of his
46:17 of release, when it shall revert to the *p*.
46:18 The *p* shall not seize any part of the
48:21 The remainder shall belong to the *p*:
48:21 with the tribal portions for the *p*.
48:22 and of Benjamin shall belong to the *p*.
Dn 3:38 We have in our day no *p*,
8:11 It boasted even against the *p* of the host,
8:25 But when he rises against the *p* of princes,
10:13 but the *p* of the kingdom of Persia stood
10:13 there with the *p* of the kings of Persia,
10:20 Soon I must fight the *p* of Persia again.
10:20 When I leave, the *p* of Greece will come;
10:21 except Michael, your *p*,
11:22 crushed, and even the *p* of the covenant.
12: 1 there shall arise Michael, the great *p*,
Hos 3: 4 shall remain many days without king or *p*,
Mi 7: 3 the *p* makes demands,
Mt 9:34 casts out demons through the *p* of demons."
12:24 the help of Beelzebul, the *p* of demons."
Mk 3:22 demons with the help of the *p* of demons."
Lk 11:15 "It is by Beelzebul, the *p* of devils,
Jn 12:31 now will this world's *p* be driven out,
14:30 the *P* of this world is at hand.
16:11 for the *p* of this world has been condemned.
Acts 23: 5 'You shall not curse a *p* of your people!' "
Eph 2: 2 to the present age and to the *p* of the air,
Heb 2:14 he might rob the devil, the *p* of death,

PRINCELY (7)

Dt 33:21 be his when the *p* portion was assigned,
Jgs 5:25 in a *p* bowl she offered curds.
1Kgs 8:13 I have truly built you a *p* house,
11: 3 of *p* rank and three hundred concubines,
2Chr 6: 2 truly built you a *p* house and dwelling,
Ps(s) 110: 3 Yours is *p* power in the day of your birth,
Wis 14:16 graven things were worshiped by *p* decrees.

PRINCES (241)

Ex 15:15 Then were the *p* of Edom dismayed;
35:27 The *p* brought onyx stones and other gems
Lv 4:26 priest shall make atonement for the *p* sin,
Nm 1:16 the community, *p* of their ancestral tribes,
1:44 Moses and Aaron and the twelve *p* of Israel.
4:34 So Moses and Aaron and the *p* of the
4:46 when Moses and Aaron and the Israelites *p*
7: 2 an offering was made by the *p* of Israel,
7: 2 *p* of the tribes who supervised the census.
7: 3 oxen, that is, a wagon for every two *p*,
7:10 the *p* brought offerings before the altar
7:84 given by the *p* of Israel on the occasion
10: 4 but when one of them is blown, only the *p*,
13: 2 from each ancestral tribe, all of them *p*."
17:17 in all, one from each of their tribal *p*.
17:21 Israelites, and their *p* gave him staffs,
21:18 The well that was the *p* sank,
22: 8 So the *p* of Moab lodged with Balaam.
22:13 Balaam arose and told the *p* of Balak,
22:14 So the *p* of Moab went back to Balak with
22:15 Balak again sent *p*,
22:21 his ass, and went off with the *p* of Moab.
22:35 So Balaam went on with the *p* of Balak.
22:40 to Balaam and to the *p* who were with him.
23: 6 holocaust together with all the *p* of Moab.
23:17 his holocaust together with the *p* of Moab.
27: 2 of Moses, the priest Eleazar, the *p*,
31:13 Eleazar, with all the *p* of the community,
32: 2 and to the *p* of the community and said,
36: 1 and before the *p* who were the heads
Jos 9:14 Israelite *p* partook of their provisions,
9:15 the *p* of the community sealed with an oath.
9:18 because the *p* of the community had sworn
9:18 entire community grumbled against the *p*,
9:21 the *p* recommended that they be let live,
9:21 the community did as the *p* advised them.
13:21 killed, with his vassals, the *p* of Midian,
17: 4 to Joshua, son of Nun, and to the *p*,
22:14 son of Eleazar the priest, and ten *p*,
22:30 the priest and the *p* of the community,
22:32 and the *p* returned from the Reubenites and
Jgs 5: 3 Give ear, O *p*!
5:14 From Ephraim, *p* were in the valley;
5:15 With Deborah were the *p* of Issachar;
7:25 They captured the two *p* of Midian,
8: 3 your power God delivered the *p* of Midian,
8: 6 But the *p* of Succoth replied,
8:14 the seventy-seven *p* and elders of Succoth.
8:18 "They appeared to be *p*."
10:18 the *p* of Gilead said to one another,
2Sm 10: 3 the Ammonite *p* said to their lord Hanun:
13:23 near Ephraim, and he invited all the *p*.
13:27 he sent Amnon and all the other *p* with him.
13:29 had commanded, all the other *p* rose,
13:30 *p* and that not one of them had survived.
13:32 that all the young *p* have been killed!
13:33 in the report that all the *p* are dead.
13:35 The *p* have come.
13:36 he finished speaking than the *p* came in,
1Kgs 8: 1 the *p* in the ancestral houses of the
2Kgs 10: 6 [The seventy *p* were in the care of
10: 7 took the *p* and slew all seventy of them,
10: 8 "They have brought the heads of the *p*,"
10:13 the *p* and the family of the queen mother."
11: 2 bedroom where the *p* were about to be slain.
1Chr 4:38 these just named were *p* in their clans,
7:40 men, warriors, and chiefs among the *p*.
12:29 with twenty-two *p* of his father's house.
19: 3 Hanun, the Ammonite *p* said to Hanun,
2Chr 1: 2 hundreds, the judges, the *p* of all Israel,
5: 2 the *p* of the Israelite ancestral houses,
21: 4 brothers and also some of the *p* of Israel.
22: 8 he also encountered the *p* of Judah and the
24:10 All the *p* and the people rejoiced;
24:17 the *p* of Judah came and paid homage to the
24:23 did away with all the *p* of the people,
28:14 before the *p* and the whole assembly.
28:21 *p* to make payment to the king of Assyria,
29:20 King Hezekiah hastened to convoke the *p*
29:30 King Hezekiah and the *p* then commanded
30: 2 The king, his *p*, and the entire assembly
30: 6 the letters written by the king and his *p*,
30:12 *p* in accordance with the word of the LORD.
30:24 and the *p* had contributed to the assembly
31: 8 and the *p* had come and seen the heaps,
32: 3 decided in counsel with his *p* and warriors
32:31 ambassadors *p* sent to him from Babylon
35: 8 *p* also gave a freewill gift to the people,
36:14 Likewise all the *p* of Judah,
36:18 the LORD's house and of the king and his *p*,
Ezr 8:20 and the *p* appointed to serve the Levites)
Neh 9:32 that have befallen us, our kings, our *p*,
9:34 Yes, our kings, our *p*,
10: 1 sealed document appear the names of our *p*,
10:30 join with their brethren who are their *p*,
12:31 I had the *p* of Judah mount the wall,
12:32 by Hoshaiah and half the *p* of Judah,
12:38 and the other half of the *p* of the people,
Jdt 2:14 of his lord, and summoned all the *p*,
9: 3 smote the slaves together with their *p*,
9: 3 and the *p* together with their servants.
1Mc 9:37 daughter of one of the great *p* of Canaan,
Jb 3:15 with *p* who had gold and filled their houses
29:10 The voice of the *p* was silenced,
34:19 Who neither favors the person of *p*,
Ps(s) 2: 2 and the *p* conspire together against the
45:17 you shall make them *p* through all the land.
47:10 The *p* of the peoples are gathered together
68:28 *p* of Judah in a body, the *p* of Zebulun, the *p*
76:13 terrible Lord Who checks the pride of *p*,
105:22 That he might train his *p* to be like him
107:40 But he who pours out contempt upon *p*,
113: 8 with princes, with the *p* of his own people.
118: 9 take refuge in the LORD than to trust in *p*.
119:23 Though *p* meet and talk against me,
119:161 *P* persecute me without cause
146: 3 Put not your trust in *p*, in man,
148:11 the *p* and all the judges of the earth,
Prv 8:16 By me *p* govern, and nobles;
14:28 if his people are few, it is the *p* ruin.
17:26 man, but beyond reason to scourge *p*.
19:10 much less should a slave rule over *p*.
28: 2 a land is rebellious, its *p* will be many;
31: 4 strong drink is not for *p*!
Eccl 7:19 wise man than would be ten *p* in the city,
10: 7 while *p* walked on the ground like slaves.
10:16 a servant, and whose *p* dine in the morning!
10:17 and whose *p* dine at the right time (for
Sg 7: 2 are your feet in sandals, O *p* daughter!
Wis 6: 9 To you, therefore, O *p*, are my words
6:21 throne and scepter, you *p* of the peoples,
8:15 terrible *p*, hearing of me, would be afraid;
Sir 7:14 not yourself into the deliberations of *p*,
8: 2 many, and perverts the character of *p*.
8: 8 the training to serve in the presence of *p*.
10: 3 a city grows through the wisdom of its *p*.
11: 1 lifts his head high and sets him among *p*.
44: 4 Resolute *p* of the folk,
46:13 kingdom and anointed *p* to rule the people.
Is 1:10 Hear the word of the LORD, *p* of Sodom!
1:23 Your *p* are rebels and comrades of thieves;
3: 4 I will make striplings their *p*;
3:14 judgment with his people's elders and *p*:
19:11 Utter fools are the *p* of Zoan!
19:13 *p* of Zoan have become fools, the *p* of
21: 5 Rise up, O *p*, oil the shield!
23: 8 bestower of crowns, Whose merchants are *p*,
30: 4 When their *p* are at Zoan and their
31: 9 *p* shall flee in terror from his standard,
32: 1 will reign justly and *p* will rule rightly.
34:12 all her *p* are gone.
40:23 He brings *p* to nought and makes the rulers
49: 7 and *p* shall prostrate themselves Because
Jer 1:18 Against Judah's kings and *p*,
2:26 They, their kings and their *p*,
4: 9 LORD, The king will lose heart, and the *p*;
8: 1 the bones of the kings and *p* of Judah,
17:25 or upon their horses, along with their *p*,
24: 1 king of Judah, and the *p* of Judah,
24: 8 treat Zedekiah, king of Judah, and his *p*,
25:18 the cities of Judah, her kings and her *p*,
25:19 king of Egypt, and his servants, his *p*,
26:10 *p* of Judah were informed of these things,
26:11 said to the *p* and to all the people,
26:12 this answer to the *p* and all the people:
26:16 Thereupon the *p* and all the people said to
26:21 officers and *p* were informed of his words,
29: 2 courtiers, the *p* of Judah and Jerusalem,
32:32 and Judeans, with their kings and their *p*,
34:10 All the *p* and the others who entered the
34:19 The *p* of Judah and of Jerusalem,
34:21 Zedekiah, too, king of Judah, and his *p*,
35: 4 the man of God, next to the *p*' room,
36:12 where the *p* were just then in session:
36:12 Zedekiah, son of Hananiah, and the other *p*.
36:14 Thereupon the *p* sent Jehudi,
36:19 At this the *p* said to Baruch,
36:21 the *p* who were in attendance on the king.
37:14 in custody and brought him to the *p*.
37:15 The *p* were enraged, and had Jeremiah
38: 4 be put to death," the *p* said to the king;
38:17 you surrender to the *p* of Babylon's king,
38:18 not surrender to the *p* of Babylon's king,
38:22 be brought out to the *p* of Babylon's king,
38:25 If the *p* hear I spoke to you,
38:27 When all the *p* came to Jeremiah,
39: 3 All the *p* of the king of Babylon came and
39: 3 and all the other *p* of the king of Babylon.
44:17 our kings and *p* have done in the cities of
44:21 you, your fathers, your kings and *p*,
48: 7 go into exile, his priests and *p* with him.
49:38 in Elam and destroy from there king and *p*,
50:35 upon Babylon's people, her *p* and wise men!
51:57 I will make her *p* and her wise men drunk,
52:10 as well as all the *p* of Judah at Riblah.

PRINCES (cont.)

Lam 1: 6 Her *p,* like rams that find no pasture,
2: 2 the ground in dishonor her king and her *p.*
2: 9 Her king and her *p* are among the pagans;
4: 7 Brighter than snow were her *p,*
5:12 *P* were gibbeted by them,
Bar 1: 9 Babylon, carried off Jeconiah, and the *p,*
2: 1 governed Israel, against our kings and *p,*
Ez 11: 1 Pelatiah, son of Benaiah, *p* of the people.
17:12 away its king and *p* with him to Babylon.
21:17 It is for all the *p* of Israel,
22: 6 the *p* of Israel, family by family,
22:25 *p* are like roaring lions that tear prey;
26:16 All the *p* of the sea shall step down from
30:13 of Memphis and the *p* of the land of Egypt,
32:29 There are Edom, her kings, and all her *p,*
32:30 the *p* of the north and all the Sidonians,
39:18 drink the blood of the *p* of the land [rams,
45: 8 so that the *p* of Israel will no longer
45: 9 Enough, you *p* of Israel!
48:22 which lie in the midst of the *p* property,
Dn 8:25 But when he rises against the prince of *p,*
9: 6 spoke in your name to our kings, our *p,*
9: 8 we are shamefaced, like our kings, our *p,*
10:13 until finally Michael, one of the chief *p,*
11: 5 but one of his *p* shall grow stronger still
Hos 5:10 The *p* of Judah have become like those that
7: 3 wickedness they regale the king, the *p* too,
7: 5 the *p* are overcome with the heat of wine.
7:16 Their *p* shall fall by the sword because of
8: 4 they established *p,* but without my
8:10 *p* shall shortly succumb under the burden.
9:15 all their *p* are rebels.
13:10 of whom you said, "Give me a king and *p*"?
Am 1:15 go into captivity, he and his *p* with him,
2: 3 her midst, and her *p* I will slay with him,
Hb 1:10 at kings, and *p* are his laughingstock;
3:14 the heads of their *p* whose boast would
Zep 1: 8 slaughter feast I will punish the *p,*
3: 3 Her *p* in her midst are roaring lions;
Zec 12: 5 and the *p* of Judah shall say to themselves,
12: 6 On that day I will make the *p* of Judah
Mt 2: 6 are by no means least among the *p* of Judah,
Acts 4:26 the *p* gathered together against the Lord

PRINCESS (2)

2Chr 22:11 But Jehosheba, a royal *p,*
Lam 1: 1 The *p* among the provinces has been made a

PRINCESSES (5)

Jgs 5:29 The wisest of her *p* answers her,
2Sm 13:18 that is how maiden *p* dressed in olden days.
Is 49:23 your foster fathers, their *p* your nurses;
Jer 41:10 of the people left in Mizpah and the *p,*
43: 6 the *p* and everyone whom Nebuzaradan,

PRINCIPAL (2)

Gn 10:12 and Calah, the latter being the *p* city.
1Mc 10:37 be stationed in the king's *p* strongholds

PRINCIPALITIES (5)

Rom 8:38 death nor life, neither angels nor *p,*
Eph 3:10 made known to the *p* and powers of heaven,
6:12 human forces but against the *p* and powers,
Col 1:16 thrones or dominations, *p* or powers;
2:15 Thus did God disarm the *p* and powers.

PRINCIPALITY (2)

Eph 1:21 right hand in heaven, high above every *p,*
Col 2:10 him who is the head of every *p* and power.

PRIOR (1)

Ru 4: 4 for no one has a *p* claim to yours,

PRISCA (3)

Rom 16: 3 Give my greetings to *P* and Aquila;
1Cor 16:19 Aquila and *P,*
2Tm 4:19 *P* and Aquila and the family of Onesiphorus.

PRISCILLA (4)

Acts 18: 2 arrived from Italy with his wife *P.*
18:18 for Syria, in the company of *P* and Aquila.
18:19 he left *P* and Aquila behind and entered
18:26 When *P* and Aquila heard him,

PRISON (50)

Gn 39:20 But even while he was in *p,*
42:19 your brothers need be confined in this *p,*
Jgs 16:21 and he was put to grinding in the *p.*
16:25 So they called Samson from the *p,*
1Kgs 22:27 Put this man in *p* and feed him scanty
2Kgs 25:27 up Jehoiachin, king of Judah, from *p.*
25:29 Jehoiachin took off his *p* garb and ate at
2Chr 18:26 Put this man in *p* and feed him scanty
Neh 12:39 [and they came to a halt at the *P* Gate].
1Mc 14: 3 brought him to Arsaces, who put him in *p.*
Ps(s) 142: 8 Lead me forth from *p,* that I may give
Eccl 4:14 for from a *p* house one comes forth to rule,
7:26 is a snare and whose hands are *p* bonds.
Wis 17:16 into that unbarred *p* and was kept confined.
Jer 37: 4 time Jeremiah had not yet been put into *p;*
37:15 into *p* in the house of Jonathan the scribe,
37:18 this people, that you should put me in *p?*
52:11 and kept in *p* until the day of his death.
52:31 king of Judah, and released him from *p.*
52:33 Jehoiachin took off his *p* garb and ate at
Mt 5:25 to the guard, who will throw you into *p.*
11: 2 Now John in *p* heard about the works Christ
14:10 sent the order to have John beheaded in *p.*
25:36 me, in *p* and you came to visit me.'
25:39 did we visit you when you were ill or in *p?*'
25:43 in *p* and you did not come to comfort me.'
25:44 or in *p* and not attend you in your needs?'
Mk 6:28 The man went and beheaded John in the *p.*
Lk 3:20 to his guilt by shutting John up in *p.*
12:58 jailer, and the jailer throw you into *p.*
23:19 in *p* for causing an uprising in the city,
23:25 thrown in *p* for insurrection and murder,
Jn 3:24 of course, had not yet been thrown into *p.)*
Acts 12: 4 he had him arrested and thrown into *p,*
12: 5 Peter was thus detained in *p,*
12:17 how the Lord had brought him out of *p.*
16:23 many lashes they were thrown into *p,*
16:26 place, rocking the *p* to its foundations.
16:27 woke up to see the *p* gates wide open.
16:37 Let them come into the *p* and escort us out."
16:40 Once outside the *p,* however, the two first
22:30 day the commander released Paul from *p,*
24:27 with the Jews, so he left Paul in *p.*
26:10 I sent many of God's holy people to *p.*
Phil 1: 7 of my gracious lot when I lie in *p*
Phlm 1:13 your place while I am in *p* for the gospel;
Heb 10:34 in the sufferings of those who were in *p*
1Pt 3:19 that he went to preach to the spirits in *p.*
Rv 2:10 some of you into *p* to put you to the test;
20: 7 are over, Satan will be released from his *p.*

PRISONER (26)

Ex 12:29 to the first-born of the *p* in the dungeon,
Jgs 15:10 they answered, "To take Samson *p;*
15:12 said to him, "We have come to take you *p,*
2Kgs 23:33 him *p* at Riblah in the land of Hamath,
1Mc 13:12 Judah, bringing Jonathan with him as a *p.*
2Mc 14:27 Maccabeus as a *p* to Antioch without delay.
14:33 you do not hand Judas over to me as *p,*
Jer 40: 1 where he had found him a *p* in chains,
Mt 27:15 procurator was accustomed to release one *p,*
27:16 at the time a notorious *p* named Barabbas.
Mk 15: 6 a festival he would release for them one *p—*
15: 7 There was a *p* named Barabbas jailed along
Acts 23:18 "The *p* Paul called me and asked me to
25:14 "There is a *p* here,"
25:20 I asked whether the *p* was willing to go to
25:27 send on a *p* without indicating the charges
28:17 I was handed over to the Romans as a *p.*
Rom 7:23 me the *p* of the law of sin in my members.
Eph 3: 1 a *p* for Christ Jesus on behalf of you
4: 1 plead with you, then, as a *p* for the Lord,
Col 4: 3 the mystery of Christ, for which I am a *p.*
4:10 Aristarchus, who is a *p* along with me,
2Tm 1: 8 to our Lord, nor of me, a *p* for his sake;
Phlm 1: 1 Paul, a *p* of Christ Jesus,
1: 9 ambassador of Christ and now a *p* for him,
1:23 Epaphras, my fellow *p* in Christ Jesus,

PRISONERS (24)

Gn 39:20 the jail where the royal *p* were confined.
39:22 Joseph in charge of all the *p* in the jail,
1Mc 9:70 him and to obtain the release of the *p.*
9:72 and he released the *p* he had previously
14: 7 *p* of war and made himself master of Gazara,
Ps(s) 68: 7 he leads forth *p* to prosperity;
79:11 Let the *p'* sighing come before you;
102:21 the earth, To hear the groaning of the *p,*
Is 24:22 be gathered together like *p* into a pit;
42: 7 the blind, to bring out *p* from confinement,
49: 9 the desolate heritages, Saying to the *p:*
61: 1 to the captives and release to the *p,*
Lam 3:34 tramples underfoot all the *p* in the land.
Zec 9:11 I will bring forth your *p* from the dungeon.
9:12 return to the fortress of the waiting *p,*
Lk 4:18 of sight to the blind and release to *p,*
Acts 5:21 the jail that the *p* were to be brought in.
16:25 hymns to God as their fellow *p* listened,
16:27 Thinking that the *p* had escaped,
22: 5 the *p* I would arrest back to Jerusalem
27: 1 Paul and some other *p* were handed over to
27:42 *p* so that none might swim away and escape;
Rom 16: 7 and Junias, my kinsmen and fellow *p;*
Heb 13: 3 Be as mindful of *p* as if you were sharing

PRISONS (2)

Is 42:22 of them trapped in holes, hidden away in *p.*
Lk 21:12 you, summoning you to synagogues and *p,*

PRIVACY (2)

Eccl 10:20 in the *p* of your bedroom revile the rich.
Sir 29:21 and clothing, a house, too, for decent *p.*

PRIVATE (12)

Gn 43:30 He went into a *p* room and wept there.
Lv 4:27 If a *p* person commits a sin
15: 2 flow from his *p* parts is thereby unclean.
Dt 25:11 hand and seizes the latter by his *p* parts,
Jgs 3:19 and said, "I have a *p* message for you,
15: 1 he said, "Let me be with my wife in *p,*"
Est C:27 a polluted rag, and do not wear it in *p.*
2Mc 13:13 After a *p* meeting with the elders,
Mt 6: 6 your door, and pray to your Father in *p.*
10:27 What you hear in *p,* proclaim from
Acts 20:20 or from teaching you in public or in *p.*
Gal 2: 2 all this in *p* conference with the leaders,

PRIVATELY (12)

1Sm 18:22 servants to speak to David *p* and to say:
2Sm 3:27 city gate as though to speak with him *p.*
Tb 12: 6 the two men aside *p* and said to them:
2Mc 4:34 *p* and asked him to lay hands on Onias.
6:21 unlawful ritual meal took the man aside *p,*
Mt 17:19 Jesus at that point and asked him *p,*
24: 3 his disciples came up to him *p* and said:
Mk 4:34 kept explaining things *p* to his disciples.
9:28 house his disciples began to ask him *p,*
13: 3 John, and Andrew began to question him *p.*
Lk 10:23 Turning to his disciples he said to them *p:*
Acts 23:19 by the hand and drew him aside to ask *p,*

PRIVATION (1)

Wis 16: 3 While these, after a brief period of *p,*

PRIVILEGE (3)

Rom 14:16 your *p* to become an occasion for blasphemy.
Gal 3:18 of promise that God granted Abraham his *p.*
Phil 1:29 it is your special *p* to take Christ's part

PRIVILEGED (1)

Jb 22: 8 might, and only the *p* were to dwell in it.

PRIVILEGES (3)

Lv 25:35 to him the *p* of an alien or a tenant,
1Mc 15: 5 and whatever other *p* they conferred on you.
Bar 4: 3 glory to another, your *p* to an alien race.

PRIVY (1)

Jb 15: 8 Are you *p* to the counsels of God,

PRIZE (7)

Prv 31:11 his heart to her, has an unfailing *p.*
Wis 10:12 And she gave him the *p* for his stern
Sir 10:27 *p* yourself as you deserve.
51:21 therefore I have made her my *p* possession.
Phil 3:12 but I am racing to grasp the *p* if possible,
3:14 I run toward the *p* to which God calls me
Col 2:18 Let no one rob you of your *p* by insisting

PRIZED (3)

2Mc 4:15 highly *p* what the Greeks esteemed as glory.
Is 1:29 be ashamed of the terebinths which you *p,*
Ez 26:17 perished, gone from the seas, city most *p!*

PROBABLY (2)

Tb 10: 6 *P* they have to take care of some
Est 6: 6 the king more *p* wish to reward than me?"

PROBATION (1)

1Tm 3:10 They should be put on *p* first;

PROBE (6)

Ps(s) 139:23 *P* me, O God, and know my heart;
Wis 6: 3 *p* your works and scrutinize your counsels!
Sir 13:11 test you, and though smiling he will *p* you.
18: 2 his works, and who can *p* his mighty deeds?
Jer 17:10 LORD, alone *p* the mind and test the heart,
20:12 who test the just, who *p* mind and heart,

PROBED (4)

Ps(s) 139: 1 O LORD, you have *p* me and you know me;
Eccl 7:22 All these things I *p* in wisdom.
Wis 11:10 former as a stern king you *p* and condemned.
Bar 3:32 he has *p* her by his knowledge

PROBES (2)

Jb 28:11 He *p* the wellsprings of the streams,
Sir 31:26 As the furnace *p* the work of the smith,

PROBING (1)

Jn 20:25 it without *p* the nailprints in his hands,

PROBLEM (3)

Lk 10:25 a lawyer stood up to pose him this *p:*
20:21 They put to him this *p:*
20:28 is no resurrection) to pose this *p* to him:

PROCEDURE (1)

Acts 25:27 It seems to me a senseless *p* to send on a

PROCEED (20)

Gn 24:49 I can then *p* accordingly."
33:14 while I *p* more slowly at the pace of the
Dt 1:40 and *p* into the desert on the Red Sea road.'
2: 1 and *p* into the desert on the Red Sea road,
Jos 2:16 then you may *p* on your way."
6: 7 people to *p* in a circle around the city,
Jgs 20: 9 We will *p* against it by lot,
1Kgs 9: 6 and *p* to venerate and worship strange gods,
1Chr 22:19 *P* to build the sanctuary of the LORD God,
2Chr 7:19 you *p* to venerate and worship strange gods,
Jdt 2: 6 and *p* against all the land of the West,
5: 9 their abode and *p* to the land of Canaan.
Jer 18:23 *p* against them in the time of your anger.
Bar 6:61 by God to *p* across the whole world,
Lk 9: 4 whatever house you enter and *p* from there.
9:51 he firmly resolved to *p* toward Jerusalem,
12:37 seat them at table, and *p* to wait on them.
13:33 For all that, I must *p* on course today,
14: 9 have to *p* shamefacedly to the lowest place.
Acts 21:12 Caesarea urged Paul not to *p* to Jerusalem.

PROCEEDED (30)

Gn 28:10 from Beer-sheba and *p* toward Haran.
31:17 *p* to put his children and wives on camels,
50:18 Then his brothers *p* to fling themselves
Dt 3: 1 "Then we turned and *p* toward Bashan.
Jos 6: 8 At this order they *p*, with the seven priests
Jgs 9: 6 *p* to make Abimelech king by the terebinth
9:50 Abimelech *p* to Thebez,
2Sm 24: 6 Then they *p* to Dan;
1Kgs 20: 1 chariotry, *p* to invest and attack Samaria.
2Kgs 10:24 they *p* to offer sacrifices and holocausts.
2Chr 22:10 she *p* to kill off all the royal offspring
25:11 They *p* to the Valley of Salt,
28:15 the men just named *p* to help the captives.
30:14 They *p* to take down the altars that were
35:11 blood and the Levites *p* to the skinning.
Neh 2: 9 Thus I *p* to the governors of
12:31 The first of these *p* to the right,
12:38 The second choir *p* to the left,
Jdt 1:13 he *p* with his army against King Arphaxad,
2:19 Then he and his whole army *p* on their
2:25 he *p* to the southern borders of Japheth,
12:15 Thereupon she *p* to put on her festive
2Mc 4:22 After going to Joppa, he *p* to Jerusalem.
Jb 35: 1 Then Elihu *p* and said:
36: 1 Elihu *p* further and said:
Ez 40:19 Then he *p* north,
Jn 1:25 had sent *p* to question him further:
Acts 10:34 Peter *p* to address them in these words:
16:32 They *p* to announce the word of God to him
27:13 looking for, so they weighed anchor and *p*,

PROCEEDING (2)

Mk 1:19 *P* a little farther along,
Lk 1:39 *p* in haste into the hill country to a

PROCEEDS (6)

Eccl 10: 5 evil, like a mistake that *p* from the ruler:
Lam 3:38 it *p* from the mouth of the Most High,
Acts 4:34 or houses sold them and donated the *p*.
5: 2 he put aside a part of the *p* for himself;
5: 3 for yourself some of the *p* from that field?
Gal 5:19 It is obvious what *p* from the flesh:

PROCESS (4)

Mt 16:26 whole world and destroy himself in the *p*?
Mk 5:26 sort and exhausted her savings in the *p*,
8:36 whole world and destroys himself in the *p*?
Lk 9:25 whole world and destroys himself in the *p*?

PROCESSION (4)

2Mc 6: 7 compelled to march in his *p*
Ps(s) 42: 5 and led them in *p* to the house of God,
55:15 side I walked in *p* in the house of God!
118:27 Join in *p* with leafy boughs up to the

PROCHORUS (1)

Acts 6: 5 Philip, *P*, Nicanor, Timon, Parmenas,

PROCLAIM (101)

Gn 41:44 "I, Pharaoh, *p*," he told Joseph,
Lv 23:37 on which you shall *p* a sacred assembly,
Dt 5: 1 decrees which I *p* in your hearing this day,
27:14 shall *p* aloud to all the men of Israel:
32: 3 Oh, *p* the greatness of our God.
Jgs 7: 3 Now *p* to all the soldiers,
2Sm 22:50 Therefore will I *p* you, O LORD, among
1Kgs 12: 1 where all Israel had come to *p* him king.
21: 9 *P* a fast and set Naboth at the head of the
2Kgs 10: 5 We will *p* no one king; do whatever you
10:20 *P* a solemn assembly in honor of Baal."
1Chr 16: 9 sing his praise, *p* all his wondrous deeds.
2Chr 10: 1 Israel had come to Shechem to *p* him king.
Neh 6: 7 in Jerusalem to *p* you king of Judah.
Tb 12: 6 Before all men, honor and *p* God's deeds,
2Mc 3:34 *p* to all men the majesty of God's power."
9:17 place to *p* there the power of God.
Ps(s) 2: 7 I will *p* the decree of the LORD:
9:12 *p* among the nations his deeds;
18:50 Therefore will I *p* you, O LORD, among
22:23 I will *p* your name to my brethren;
22:32 they may *p* to a people yet to be born
30:10 give you thanks or *p* your faithfulness?
50: 6 And for the heavens *p* his justice;
51:17 my lips, and my mouth shall *p* your praise.
52:11 and *p* the goodness of your name before
64:10 And all men fear and *p* the work of God,
66: 2 *p* his glorious praise.
71:17 till the present I *p* your wondrous deeds;
71:18 forsake me not Till I *p* your strength to
72:17 all the nations shall *p* his happiness.
89: 2 my mouth shall *p* your faithfulness.
89: 6 The heavens *p* your wonders, O LORD,
92: 3 To *p* your kindness at dawn and your
97: 6 The heavens *p* his justice,
105: 2 sing his praise, *p* all his wondrous deeds.
106: 2 deeds of the LORD, or *p* all his praises?
Eccl 6: 3 of this man I *p* that the child born dead
Sir 15:10 its rightful steward will *p* it.
19:26 and his gait, *p* him for what he is.
39:15 *P* the greatness of his name,
39:15 sing out with joy as you *p*:
39:35 heart *p* and bless the name of the Holy One.
Is 12: 4 known his deeds, *p* how exalted is his name.
24:14 the sea they *p* the majesty of the LORD:
40: 2 and *p* to her that her service is at an end,
48:20 With shouts of joy *p* this, make it known;
61: 1 To *p* liberty to the captives and release
66:19 they shall *p* my glory among the nations.
Jer 3:12 Go, *p* these words toward the north,
4: 5 *P* it in Judah, make it heard in Jerusalem;
4:15 They *p* it from Dan,
5:20 this to the house of Jacob, *p* it in Judah:
7: 2 of the LORD, and there *p* this message:
11: 6 *P* all these words in the cities of Judah
16:10 When you *p* all these words to this people
19: 2 *p* the words which I will speak to you:
23:22 and did they but *p* to my people my words,
31: 7 *p* your praise and say:
31:10 LORD, O nations, *p* it on distant coasts,
34:17 I now *p* you free, says the LORD,
42:21 Today I *p* his message,
46:14 in Migdol, *p* it in Memphis and Tahpanhes!
Jl 1:14 *P* a fast, call an assembly; Gather the
2:15 *p* a fast, call an assembly; Gather the
4: 9 *p* a war, rouse the warriors to arms!
Am 3: 9 *P* this in the castles of Ashdod,
4: 5 *p* publicly your freewill offerings,
Mi 3: 5 in their mouth, *p* war against him.
Zec 1:14 the angel who spoke with me said to me, *P*:
1:17 *P* further: Thus says the Lord of Hosts
9:10 and he shall *p* peace to the nations.
Mt 4:17 that time on Jesus began to *p* this theme:
10:27 you hear in private, *p* from the housetops.
12:18 and he will *p* justice to the Gentiles.
Mk 1:38 so that I may *p* the good news there also.
1:45 off and began to *p* the whole matter freely,
5:20 At that the man went off and began to *p*
16:15 world and *p* the good news to all creation.
Lk 2:10 I come to *p* good news to you
4:18 to the poor, to *p* liberty to captives,
9: 2 *p* the reign of God and heal the afflicted.
9:60 come away and *p* the kingdom of God."
Acts 9:20 and soon began to *p* in the synagogues that
11:28 *p* that there was going to be a severe famine
14: 7 where they continued to *p* the good news.
16:10 had summoned us to *p* the good news there.
26:23 *p* light to our people and to the Gentiles."
26:25 The message I *p* is the sober truth.
Rom 1: 1 apostle and set apart to *p* the gospel of God
16:25 which I *p* when I preach Jesus Christ,
1Cor 11:26 you *p* the death of the Lord until he comes!
2Cor 4: 2 We *p* the truth openly and commend
Eph 6:20 that I may have courage to *p* it as I ought.
Phil 2:11 tongue *p* to the glory of God the Father:
Col 1:28 This is the Christ we *p* while we admonish
4: 3 with an opening to *p* the mystery of Christ,
2Tm 1: 1 sent to *p* the promise of life in him,
1Pt 2: 9 to *p* the glorious works" of the One
1Jn 1: 1 and we *p* to you the eternal life that was
1: 3 What we have seen and heard we *p* in turn

PROCLAIMED (58)

Ex 32: 5 Aaron built an altar before the calf and *p*,
34: 5 LORD stood with him there and *p* his name,
Dt 4:13 He *p* to you his covenant,
4:45 statutes and decrees which he *p* to them
15: 2 relaxation in honor of the LORD has been *p*.
1Kgs 13:32 For the word of the LORD which he *p*
16:16 So that day in the camp all Israel *p* Omri,
21:12 They *p* a fast and placed Naboth at the
2Kgs 11:12 They *p* him king and anointed him,
14:21 *p* him king to succeed his father Amaziah.
21:24 and *p* his son Josiah king in his stead.
23:16 which the man of God had *p* as Jeroboam
23:16 of the man of God who had *p* these words,
23:30 him, and *p* him king to succeed his father.
1Chr 29:22 time they *p* David's son Solomon king,
2Chr 20: 3 He *p* a fast for all Judah
24: 9 They had it *p* throughout Judah and
26: 1 *p* him king to succeed his father Amaziah.
30: 5 they issued a decree to be *p* throughout
Ezr 8:21 Then I *p* a fast, there by the river
Neh 9:18 they made themselves a molten calf, and *p*,
Tb 11:17 Before them all Tobit *p* how God had
Est E:11 peoples that he was *p* 'father of the king,'
1Mc 3:56 He *p* that those who were building houses,
Ps(s) 147:19 He has *p* his word to Jacob,
Wis 18:19 that disturbed them had *p* this beforehand,
Is 34:12 be no more, nor shall kings be *p* there;
Jer 36: 9 a fast to placate the LORD was *p* for all
Lam 1:21 Bring on the day you have *p*,
Dn 4:20 sentinel that came down from heaven and *p*:
5:29 and *p* him third in the government of the
Jon 3: 5 they *p* a fast and all of them,
3: 7 Then he had this *p* throughout Nineveh,
Hg 1:13 *p* to the people as the message of the
Mt 4:23 synagogues, *p* the good news of the kingdom,
9:35 he *p* the good news of God's reign,
24:14 This good news of the kingdom will be *p*
26:13 the good news is *p* throughout the world,
Mk 7:36 he ordered them not to, the more they *p* it.
13:10 news must first be *p* to all the Gentiles.
14: 9 the good news is *p* throughout the world,
Lk 12: 3 locked rooms will be *p* from the rooftops.
16:16 the good news of God's kingdom has been *p*,
Jn 12:44 Jesus *p* aloud: "Whoever puts faith in me
Acts 8: 5 town of Samaria and there *p* the Messiah.
10:36 *p* through Jesus Christ who is Lord of all.
13: 5 *p* the word of God in the Jewish synagogues,
13:38 the forgiveness of sins is being *p* to you,
14:21 After they had *p* the good news in that
15:21 for generations now Moses has been *p* in
15:36 the towns where we *p* the word of the Lord."
17:13 of God had been *p* by Paul in Beroea also,
Rom 9:17 name might be *p* throughout all the earth."
Gal 1:11 I *p* to you is no mere human invention.
Phil 1:18 motives or genuine ones, Christ is being *p*!
1Pt 1:12 what has now been *p* to you by those who
Rv 1: 9 I *p* God's word and bore witness to Jesus.
5: 2 I saw a mighty angel who *p* in a loud voice:

PROCLAIMING (17)

Lv 25:10 year you shall make sacred by *p* liberty
Is 60: 6 and *p* the praises of the LORD,
Jer 34:15 by *p* the emancipation of your brethren
34:17 me by *p* your neighbors and kinsmen free.
Mk 1: 4 *p* a baptism of repentance which led to the
1:14 appeared in Galilee *p* the good news of God:
15:26 The inscription *p* his offense read,
Lk 3: 3 Jordan *p* a baptism of repentance
8: 1 and *p* the good news of the kingdom of God.
20: 1 people in the temple and *p* the good news,
Jn 1:15 John testified to him by *p*:
Acts 2:31 thus *p* beforehand the resurrection of the
4: 2 and *p* the resurrection of the dead
5:42 and *p* the good news of Jesus the Messiah.
8:25 their testimony and *p* the word of the Lord,
13:24 John heralded the coming of Jesus by *p* a
1Cor 2: 1 I did not come *p* God's testimony with any

PROCLAIMS (9)

Ps(s) 19: 2 of God, and the firmament *p* his handiwork.
85: 9 I will hear what God *p*; the LORD—for he *p*
145: 4 praises your works and *p* your might.
Sir 24: 1 before her own people she *p* her glory;
25: 7 mind as blessed, a tenth whom my tongue *p*:
44:15 is retold, and the assembly *p* their praise.
Is 62:11 See, the LORD *p* to the ends of the earth:
Lk 1:25 "My being *p* the greatness of the Lord,

PROCLAMATION (12)

Ex 36: 6 ordered a *p* to be made throughout the camp:
Lv 23:21 day you shall by *p* have a sacred assembly,
1Sm 13: 3 the horn throughout the land, with a *p*,
2Chr 36:22 to issue this *p* throughout his kingdom,
Ezr 1: 1 to issue this *p* throughout his kingdom,
10: 7 A *p* was made throughout Judah and
Neh 8:15 and that they should have this *p* made
1Mc 5:49 So Judas ordered a *p* to be made in the
10:63 make a *p* that no one is to bring charges
10:64 saw the honor paid to him in the *p*,
14:28 of the country, the following *p* was made:
Mk 16:20 sacred and immortal *p* of eternal salvation.

PROCLAMATIONS (1)

Acts 2: 4 make bold *p* as the Spirit prompted them.

PROCONSULAR (1)

Acts 13: 7 the court of the *p* governor Sergius Paulus,

PROCONSULS (1)

Acts 19:38 There are *p*.

PROCONSULSHIP (1)

Acts 18:12 During Gallio's *p* in Achaia,

PROCURATOR (7)

Mt 27: 2 him away to be handed over to the *p* Pilate.
27:11 Jesus was arraigned before the *p*,
27:15 *p* was accustomed to release one prisoner,
27:21 So when the *p* asked them,
28:14 If any word of this gets to the *p*,
Lk 3: 1 Caesar, when Pontius Pilate was *p* of Judea,
20:20 over to the office and authority of the *p*.

PROCURATORS (4)

Est 3: 9 and I will deliver to the *p* ten thousand
9: 3 *p* supported the Jews from fear of Mordecai;
Mt 27:14 on a single count, much to the *p* surprise.
27:27 The *p* soldiers took Jesus inside the

PROCURE (16)

Gn 24: 3 that you will not *p* a wife for my son from
24:37 'You shall not *p* a wife for my son among
42: 5 were among those who came to *p* rations.
42: 7 "From the land of Canaan, to *p* food."
42:10 your servants have come to *p* food.
43: 2 "Go back and *p* us a little more food."
43: 4 with us, we will go down to *p* food for you.
43:20 "we came down here once before to *p* food.
43:22 We have brought other money to *p* food with.
Ex 12: 3 of your families must *p* for itself a lamb,
12:21 them, "Go and *p* lambs for your families,
29: 1 *P* a young bull and two unblemished rams.
Nm 19: 2 Tell the Israelites to *p* for you a red
Ezr 8:17 to *p* for us ministers for the house of God.
1Mc 10: 6 to gather an army and *p* arms as his ally;
Bar 1:10 funds, with which you are to *p* holocausts,

PROCURED (1)

1Mc 10:21 and he gathered an army and *p* many arms.

PROCUREMENT (2)

Neh 10:35 determined by lot concerning the *p* of wood:
13:31 I also provided for the *p* of wood at

PROCURES (1)

Prv 6: 8 or ruler, She *p* her food in the summer,

PROCURING (2)

Ex 12: 4 in *p* one and shall share in the lamb
Jgs 20:10 and *p* supplies for the soldiers who will

PRODIGIES (6)

Jos 24: 5 with the *p* which I wrought in her midst.
Prv 8:22 ways, the forerunner of his *p* of long ago;
Rv 13:13 It performed great *p*;
13:14 Because of the *p* it was allowed to perform
16:14 these spirits were devils who worked *p*.
19:20 in its presence the *p* that led men astray,

PRODUCE (62)

Gn 4:12 soil, it shall no longer give you its *p*.
19:25 of the cities and the *p* of the soil.
31:37 so, *p* it here before your kinsmen and mine,
47:26 that a fifth of its *p* should go to Pharaoh.
49:20 "Asher's *p* is rich,
Ex 22: 4 the best *p* of his own field or vineyard.
23:10 you may sow your land and gather in its *p*.
23:16 when you gather in the *p* from the fields.
Lv 23:39 you have gathered in the *p* of the land,
25: 3 prune your vineyard, gathering in their *p*.
25: 6 all its *p* will be food equally for you
25:12 sacred for you, you may not eat of its *p*,
Nm 6: 4 not eat anything of the *p* of the vine;
18:30 Levites as if it were *p* of the threshing floor
Dt 7:13 fruit of your womb and the *p* of your soil,
14:22 *p* that grows in the field you have sown;
14:28 shall bring out all the tithes of your *p*
16:13 *p* from your threshing floor and wine press.
22: 9 if you do, its *p* shall become forfeit,
26:12 all the tithes of your *p* in the third year,
28: 4 the *p* of your soil and the offspring of
28:11 of your livestock, and the *p* of your soil,
28:18 the *p* of your soil and the offspring of
28:51 of your livestock and the *p* of your soil,
30: 9 of your livestock, and the *p* of your soil;
33:14 With the best of the *p* of the year,
Jos 5:11 the Passover they ate of the *p* of the land
5:12 on which they ate of the *p* of the land,
Jgs 6: 4 and destroy the *p* of the land as far as
2Sm 9:10 You shall bring in the *p*,
1Kgs 7:14 knowledge of how to *p* any work in bronze.
1Chr 27:27 and over their *p* for the wine cellars was
2Chr 31: 5 oil and honey, and all the *p* of the fields;
Ezr 9:12 will grow strong, enjoy the *p* of the land,
Neh 9:37 Its rich *p* goes to the kings whom you set
1Mc 11:34 *p* of the soil and the fruit of the trees.
14: 8 *p* and the trees of the field their fruit.
Jb 31:39 If I have eaten its *p* without payment and
40:20 the *p* of the mountains is brought to him,
Prv 3: 9 wealth, with first fruits of all your *p*;
Wis 13:11 his art, *p* something fit for daily use,
16:19 so as to consume the *p* of the wicked land.
19:18 like strings of the harp, *p* new melody,
Sir 34: 4 Can the unclean *p* the clean?
38:27 His care is to *p* a vivid impression,
Is 32:17 right will *p* calm and security.
43: 9 them *p* witnesses to prove themselves right,
65:22 ones shall long enjoy the *p* of their hands.
Bar 6:46 Even those who *p* them are not long-lived;
Ez 48:18 whose *p* shall provide food for the workers
Hb 3:17 fail and the terraces *p* no nourishment,
Mt 21:19 to it, "Never again shall you *p* fruit!";
22:24 the wife and *p* offspring for his brother.'
Mk 4: 8 grain that sprang up to *p* at a rate of thirty-
12: 2 from them his share of *p* from the vineyard.
12:19 the wife and *p* offspring for his brother.'
Lk 6:43 "A good tree does not *p* decayed fruit any
Jn 15: 5 in me and I am him, will *p* abundantly,
18:23 "If I said anything wrong *p* the evidence,
1Cor 14: 7 case of lifeless things which *p* a sound,
Jas 3:12 A fig tree, brothers, cannot *p* olives,
Rv 22: 2 of life which *p* fruit twelve times a year,

PRODUCED (15)

Gn 4: 1 "I have *p* a man with the help of the LORD."
30:40 Thus he *p* special flocks of his own,
41:47 of plenty, when the land *p* abundant crops,
1Kgs 10:20 like this was *p* in any other kingdom.
2Kgs 8: 6 *p* from the day she left the land until now."
2Chr 9:19 this had ever been *p* in any other kingdom.
Wis 9: 2 man to rule the creatures *p* by you,
14: 2 this latter, and Wisdom the artificer *p* it.
14: 8 he for having *p* it, and it, because though
Bar 6:45 They are *p* by woodworkers and goldsmiths,
6:47 how then can what they have *p* be gods?
Ez 17: 6 a vine, *p* branches and put forth shoots.
Hg 1:11 beasts, and upon all that is *p* by hand.
2Cor 8: 2 poverty have *p* an abundant generosity.
Jas 5:18 forth with rain and the land *p* its crop.

PRODUCES (15)

Wis 7:27 to age, she *p* friends of God and prophets.
8: 5 is more rich than Wisdom, who *p* all things?
Is 30:23 that the soil *p* will be rich and abundant.
34: 1 fills it listen, the world and all it *p*.
Mt 12:35 good man *p* good from his store of goodness;
12:35 an evil man *p* evil from his evil store.
13:22 Such a one *p* no yield.
Mk 4:28 The soil *p* of itself first the blade,
Lk 6:43 any more than a decayed tree *p* good fruit.
6:45 man *p* goodness from the good in his heart;
6:45 evil man *p* evil out of his store of evil.
Jn 12:24 But if it dies, it *p* much fruit.
1Cor 12:11 and the same Spirit who *p* all these gifts,
2Cor 7:10 God's sake *p* a repentance without regrets,
Eph 5: 9 Light *p* every kind of goodness and justice

PRODUCING (1)

Ps(s) 104:14 for men's use, *P* bread from the earth,

PRODUCT (4)

Dt 27:15 to the LORD, the *p* of a craftsman's hands
Wis 13:10 Gold and silver, the *p* of art,
Acts 7:41 celebration over the *p* of their own hands.
17:29 or stone, a *p* of man's genius and his art.

PRODUCTION (2)

Ex 31: 4 in the *p* of embroidery,
35:32 in the *p* of embroidery,

PRODUCTIVE (2)

Hos 10: 1 The more *p* his land,
Phil 1:22 in the flesh, that means *p* toil for me

PRODUCTS (10)

Gn 40:17 one were all kinds of bakery *p* for Pharaoh,
43:11 Put some of the land's best *p* in your
45:23 jackasses loaded with the finest *p* of Egypt
Nm 18:13 the first *p* that they bring in to the LORD
Dt 26: 2 take some first fruits of the various *p*
26:10 fruits of the *p* of the soil which you,
32:13 the land and live off the *p* of its fields,
Wis 14: 5 will that the *p* of your Wisdom be not idle;
Sir 38:29 He is always concerned for his *p*,
Ez 27:16 Edom traded with you, so many were your *p*,

PROFANATION (7)

Lv 21: 4 this would be a *p*.
22: 9 else they will die for their *p*.
Jdt 4: 3 altar, and the temple been purified from *p*.
8:21 us pay for its *p* with our life's blood.
Is 48:11 why should I suffer *p*?
56: 2 Who keeps the sabbath free from *p*,
56: 6 free from *p* and hold to my covenant,

PROFANE (32)

Ex 30: 9 altar you shall not offer up any *p* incense,
Lv 10: 1 they offered up before the LORD *p* fire,
10:10 between what is sacred and what is *p*,
21: 6 they shall be sacred, and not *p* his name;
21:12 he will *p* the sanctuary of his God,
21:23 not *p* these things that are sacred to me,
22: 2 else they will *p* my holy name.
22:32 LORD, give you, and do not *p* my holy name;
Nm 3: 4 But when Nadab and Abihu offered *p* fire
18:32 Do not *p* the sacred gifts of the
26:61 when they offered *p* fire before the LORD.
Jdt 9: 8 for they have resolved to *p* your sanctuary,
1Mc 1:45 to *p* the sabbaths and feast days,
1:63 unclean food or to *p* the holy covenant;
2:34 obey the king's command to *p* the sabbath."
2Mc 5:16 with *p* hands the votive offerings made
6: 2 also to *p* the temple in Jerusalem and
Prv 30: 9 in want, I steal, and *p* the name of my God.
Ez 7:22 robbers shall enter and *p* it.
20:39 and never again *p* my holy name with your
22:26 violate my law and *p* what is holy to me;
22:26 distinguish between the sacred and the *p*,
36:20 they came], they served to *p* my holy name,
42:20 a wall, to separate the sacred from the *p*.
43: 7 Never again shall they and their kings *p*
44: 7 sanctuary to *p* it when you offered me food,
44:23 distinguish between the sacred and the *p*,
48:15 twenty-five-thousand-cubit line are *p* land,
Zep 3: 4 Her priests *p* what is holy,
1Tm 4: 7 to do with *p* myths or old wives' tales.
2Tm 3: 2 to their parents, ungrateful, *p*,
Rv 21:27 there, but nothing *p* shall enter it,

PROFANED (30)

Lv 19: 8 for having *p* what is sacred to the LORD.
20: 3 defiled my sanctuary and *p* my holy name.
22:15 LORD the priests shall not allow to be *p*
Jdt 4:12 *p* and mocked for the nations to gloat over.
1Mc 1:43 they sacrificed to idols and *p* the sabbath.
3:51 your sanctuary has been trampled on and *p*,
2Mc 3:18 because the Place was in danger of being *p*.
8: 2 on the temple, which was *p* by godless men;
10: 5 the temple had been *p* by the Gentiles,
Ps(s) 74: 7 your name abides they have razed and *p*.
Is 9:16 They are wholly *p* and sinful,
47: 6 Angry at my people, I *p* my inheritance,
Jer 34:16 But then you changed your mind and *p* my
Ez 7:22 face from them, and my treasure shall be *p*:
7:24 strength, and their sanctuaries shall be *p*.
20: 9 that it should not be *p* in the sight of
20:14 that it should not be *p* in the sight of
20:22 lest it be *p* in the sight of the nations
22:16 myself to be *p* in the eyes of the nations;
22:26 so that I have been *p* in their midst.
28:18 sinful trade, I have *p* your sanctuaries,
36:21 Israel *p* among the nations where they came.
36:22 you *p* among the nations to which you came.
36:23 of my great name, *p* among the nations,
36:23 the nations, in whose midst you have *p* it.
39: 7 will no longer allow my holy name to be *p*.
43: 8 *p* my holy name by their abominable deeds;
Mi 4:11 They say, "Let her be *p*,
Mal 2:11 has *p* the temple which the LORD loves,
Acts 21:28 temple area and thus *p* this sacred place."

PROFANELY (1)

Mal 1:12 But you behave *p* toward me by thinking the

PROFANING (6)

Lv 18:21 to Molech, thus *p* the name of your God.
19:12 by my name, thus *p* the name of your God.
Neh 13:17 that you are doing, *p* the sabbath day?
13:18 against Israel by once more *p* the sabbath?"
Jer 16:18 of *p* my land with their detestable corpses
Am 2: 7 go to the same prostitute, *p* my holy name.

PROFANITY (1)

2Mc 12:14 them and even uttering blasphemies and *p*.

PROFESS (5)

Ps(s) 50:16 and *p* my covenant with your mouth,
Jn 7:21 single work and you *p* astonishment over it.
Eph 4:15 let us *p* the truth in love and the
1Tm 2:10 as becomes women who *p* to be religious,
Jas 2:14 is it to *p* faith without practicing it?

PROFESSED (1)

Mk 16:17 accompany those who have *p* their faith:

PROFESSES (2)

Wis 2:13 He *p* to have knowledge of God and styles
2Tm 2:19 who *p* the name of the Lord abandon evil."

PROFESSING (2)

Phil 1:26 Courage in *P* the Faith.
1Tm 3:16 mystery of our faith, as we say in *p* it:

PROFESSION (6)

Sir 38: 1 you, and God it was who established his *p*.
38:24 The scribe's *p* increases his wisdom;
1Tm 6:12 witnesses, you made your noble *p* of faith.
6:13 made his noble *p* before Pontius Pilate,
Heb 4:14 of God, let us hold fast to our *p* of faith.
10:23 unswervingly to our *p* which gives us hope,

PROFESSIONAL (3)

2Mc 2:30 all sides is the task of the *p* historian;
8: 9 associated Gorgias, a *p* military commander,
Am 5:16 farmers to wail and *p* mourners to lament,

PROFFER (1)

Hos 9: 4 the LORD, or *p* their sacrifices before him.

PROFFERS (1)

Sir 37: 8 Be on the alert when one *p* advice,

PROFICIENCY (1)

Dn 1:17 and *p* in all literature and science,

PROFIT (34)

Lv 25:37 neither money at interest nor food at a *p*.
1Sm 12:21 idols which can neither *p* nor save;
Jb 15: 3 not avail, and in words which are to no *p*?
35: 3 To say, "What does it *p* me;
Ps(s) 44:13 you made no *p* from the sale of them.
Prv 3:14 For her *p* is better than profit in silver,
10: 2 Ill-gotten treasures *p* nothing,
14:23 In all labor there is *p*,
21: 5 The plans of the diligent are sure of *p*,
Eccl 1: 3 What *p* has man from all the labor which he
2:15 Where is the *p* for me?
2:22 For what *p* comes to a man from all the
5:15 What then does it *p* him to toil for wind?
6:11 multiply vanity, what *p* is there for a man?
Wis 6:25 take instruction from my words, to your *p*.
13:19 And for *p* in business and success with his
15:12 one must," says he, "make *p* every way,
Sir 27: 1 For the sake of *p* many sin,
29:11 for that will *p* you more than the gold.
37: 8 why should the *p* fall to him?
Mal 3:14 and what do we *p* by keeping his command,
Mt 16:26 What *p* would a man show if he were to gain
Mk 8:36 What *p* does a man show who gains the whole
Lk 9:25 What *p* does he show who gains the whole
19:15 the money, to learn what *p* each had made.
Acts 16:16 *p* to her masters by fortune-telling.
16:19 saw that their source of *p* was gone,
1Cor 15:32 human motives, what *p* was there for me?
1Tm 6: 2 since those who will *p* from their work are
Heb 4: 2 the word which they heard did not *p* them,
12:10 but God does so for our true *p*,
Jas 4:13 a year there, trade, and come off with a *p*!"
1Pt 5: 2 and not for shameful *p* either,

PROFITABLE (4)

Jb 22: 2 Can a man be *p* to God?
22: 2 Though to himself a wise man be *p*!
1Cor 11:17 your meetings are not *p* but harmful.
Rv 18:19 grew rich from their *p* trade with her!

PROFITED (1)

Sir 51:17 Since in this way I have *p*,

PROFITLESS (1)

Wis 1:11 Therefore guard against *p* grumbling,

PROFITS (4)

Jb 34: 9 *p* a man nought that he is pleasing to God."
Prv 11:18 The wicked man makes empty *p*,
Wis 14: 2 For the urge for *p* devised this latter,
Ez 22:13 *p* you have made and because of the bloodshed

PROFLIGACY (1)

1Pt 4: 4 plunge into the same swamp of *p* as they.

PROFOUND (1)

Ps(s) 72: 7 shall flower in his days, and *p* peace,

PROFOUNDLY (1)

Ps(s) 38: 7 my folly, I am stooped and bowed down *p*;

PROFUSE (1)

Jb 26: 3 how *p* is the advice you offer!

PROFUSELY (1)

Ezr 10: 1 and the people wept *p*.

PROFUSION (1)

Jdt 7:18 equipment was spread out in *p* everywhere.

PROGENY (9)

Gn 21:23 falsely with me or with my *p* and posterity,
48: 6 *P* born to you after them shall remain yours;
Jb 21: 8 Their *p* is secure in their sight;
39: 3 they deliver their *p* in the desert.
Wis 3:16 and the *p* of an unlawful bed will
4: 3 *p* of the wicked shall be of no avail;
Sir 44:13 And for all time their *p* will endure,
Is 14:22 Babylon name and remnant, *p* and offspring,
48:14 will against Babylon and the *p* of Chaldea.

PROGRESS (15)

Ezr 5: 8 and is making good *p* under their hands.
6:14 Jews continued to make *p* in the building,
Jb 31:26 or the moon in the splendor of its *p*,
Ps(s) 68:25 view your progress, O God, the *p* of my God,
Eccl 10:10 dull, though at first he made easy *p*,
Sir 33:17 by the LORD's blessing I have made *p*
Lk 8:14 but their *p* is stifled by the cares and
Acts 9:31 making steady *p* in the fear of the Lord;
Gal 1:14 I made *p* in Jewish observance far beyond
Phil 1:25 all, for your joy and your *p* in the faith.
1Thes 4: 1 so you must learn to make still greater *p*.
4:10 Yet we exhort you to even greater *p*,
2Thes 3: 1 may make *p* and be hailed by many others,
1Tm 4:15 you, so that everyone may see your *p*.

PROGRESSED (2)

2Chr 24:13 task of restoration *p* under their hands.
Lk 2:52 *p* steadily in wisdom and age and grace

PROGRESSING (2)

Neh 4: 1 of the walls of Jerusalem was *p*—
Gal 5: 7 You were *p* so very well;

PROGRESSIVE (1)

2Jn 1: 9 Anyone who is so *p*" that he does not

PROHIBIT (1)

1Mc 1:45 to *p* holocausts, sacrifices, and libations

PROHIBITED (2)

2Mc 6: 5 with abominable offerings *p* by the laws.
Lk 6: 2 are you doing what is *p* on the sabbath?"

PROHIBITION (5)

Dn 6: 8 *p* ought to be put in force by royal decree:
6: 9 O king, issue the *p* over your signature,
6:10 King Darius signed the *p* and made it law.
6:13 they went to remind the king about the *p*:
6:16 law every royal *p* or decree is irrevocable."

PROHIBITIONS (1)

Jer 35: 8 Rechab's son, our father, in all his *p*.

PROJECT (1)

Lk 14:28 if he has enough money to complete the *p*?

PROJECTED (1)

Jos 18:15 and *p* to the spring at Nephtoah.

PROJECTING (3)

Neh 3:25 and the tower *p* from the Upper Palace
3:26 Water Gate on the east, and the *p* tower.
3:27 sector opposite the great *p* tower,

PROJECTS (2)

Prv 22:12 but he defeats the *p* of the faithless.
Jas 1:11 the rich man wither away amid his many *p*.

PROLIFIC (1)

Ex 1: 7 But the Israelites were fruitful and *p*.

PROLONG (2)

Eccl 8:13 man, and he shall not *p* his shadowy days,
Lam 4:22 O daughter Zion, he will not *p* your exile;

PROLONGATION (1)

Dn 7:12 a *p* of life for a time and a season.

PROLONGED (4)

Jdt 13: 1 for they were all tired from the *p* banquet.
Sir 13:11 For by *p* talk he will test you,
48:23 back the sun and *p* the life of the king.
Is 13:22 near at hand and her days shall not be *p*.

PROLONGING (1)

Ps(s) 85: 6 with us, *p* your anger to all generations?

PROLONGS (4)

Prv 10:27 The fear of the LORD *p* life,
28:16 He who hates ill-gotten gain *p* his days.
Sir 30:22 very life of man, cheerfulness *p* his days.
37:30 died, but the abstemious man *p* his life.

PROMINENCE (1)

Sir 29:18 Has exiled men of *p* and sent them

PROMINENT (10)

Ru 2: 1 Naomi had a *p* kinsman named Boaz,
2Kgs 10: 6 were in the care of *p* men of the city,
Est A: 2 a *p* man who served at the king's court,
Prv 31:23 Her husband is *p* at the city gates as he
Sir 38:33 bench, nor are they *p* in the assembly;
Dn 8: 5 a he-goat with a *p* horn on its forehead
Acts 17: 4 to Judaism, and numerous *p* women.
25:23 of military officers and *p* men of the city.
28:17 *p* men of the Jewish community to visit him.
Gal 2: 6 makes no difference to me how *p* they were

PROMISCUOUSNESS (1)

Eph 5: 3 for lewd conduct or *p* or lust of any sort,

PROMISE (112)

Gn 24: 7 confirmed by oath the *p* he then made to me,
50: 5 made me *p* on oath to bury him in the tomb
50: 6 bury your father, as he made you *p* on oath."
Ex 8: 8 *p* he had made to Pharaoh about the frogs;
Nm 30: 3 must fulfill exactly the *p* he has uttered.
32:24 flocks, but also fulfill your express *p*."
Dt 6: 3 more, in keeping with the *p* of the LORD,
9: 5 *p* which he made on oath to your fathers,
Jos 21:45 Not a single *p* that the LORD made to the
23:14 Every *p* has been fulfilled for you,
23:15 But just as every *p* the LORD,
1Sm 25:30 *p* of success he has made concerning you,
2Sm 7:28 have made this generous *p* to your servant.
22:31 the *p* of the LORD is fire-tried;
1Kgs 2: 4 the *p* he made on my behalf when he said,
6:12 you the *p* I made to your father David.
8:15 who with his own mouth made a *p* to my
8:20 the LORD has fulfilled the *p* that he made:
8:24 kept the *p* you made to my father David,
8:24 You who spoke that *p*, have this day,
8:25 the further *p* you made to my father David,
8:26 this *p* which you made to my father David,
8:56 *p* he made through his servant Moses.
2Kgs 15:12 Thus the LORD's *p* to Jehu,
1Chr 17:17 For you have made a *p* regarding your
17:23 may the *p* that you have uttered concerning
2Chr 1: 9 may your *p* to my father David be fulfilled,
6: 4 who with his own mouth made a *p* to my
6:10 the LORD has fulfilled the *p* that he made.
6:15 kept the *p* you made to my father David,
6:16 the further *p* you made to my father David,
6:17 may this *p* which you made to your servant
21: 7 of his *p* to give him and his sons a lamp
Neh 1: 8 I pray, the *p* which you gave through Moses,
5:13 every man who fails to keep this *p*,
1Mc 13:19 broke his *p* and would not let Jonathan go.
Ps(s) 18:31 unerring, the *p* of the LORD is fire-tried;
56: 5 In God, in whose *p* I glory,
56:11 In God, in whose *p* I glory,
77: 9 cease, his *p* fail for all generations?
89:35 the *p* of my lips I will not alter.
119:11 Within my heart I treasure your *p*,
119:38 your servant your *p* to those who fear you.
119:41 O LORD, your salvation according to your *p*.
119:50 my affliction is that your *p* gives me life.
119:58 heart, have pity on me according to your *p*.
119:67 I went astray, but now I hold to your *p*.
119:76 me according to your *p* to your servants.
119:82 My eyes strain after your *p*;
119:123 after your salvation and your just *p*.
119:133 Steady my footsteps according to your *p*,
119:140 Your *p* is very sure,
119:148 the night watches in meditation on your *p*.
119:154 for the sake of your *p* give me life.
119:158 loathing, because they kept not to your *p*.
119:162 I rejoice at your *p*, as one who has found
119:170 rescue me according to your *p*.
119:172 May my tongue sing of your *p*,
132:11 a firm *p* from which he will not withdraw:
138: 2 above all things your name and your *p*.
Eccl 5: 1 be quick to make a *p* in God's presence.
Sir 20:22 A man makes a *p* to a friend out of shame,
29: 3 Keep your *p*, be honest with him and you
44:22 he renewed the same *p* because of Abraham,
Is 45:19 I, the LORD, *p* justice,
Jer 18: 9 I *p* to build up and plant a nation or a
29:10 you my *p* to bring you back to this place.
32:42 will bring upon them all the good I *p* them.
33:14 *p* I made to the house of Israel and Judah.
34: 5 it is I who make this *p*, says the LORD.
Mi 2: 7 my words *p* good to him who walks uprightly?
Mt 10:42 And I *p* you that whoever gives a cup of
20:21 *P* me that these sons of mine will sit,
Lk 24:49 I send down upon you the *p* of my Father.
Acts 1: 4 for the fulfillment of my Father's *p*,
2:39 you and your children that the *p* was made,
7:17 of the *p* made by God to Abraham,
13:23 "According to his *p*, God has brought
18:21 As he said goodbye he gave them his *p*,
26: 6 hope in the *p* made by God to our fathers.
26: 7 hope that they will see that *p* fulfilled.
Rom 4:13 Certainly the *p* made to Abraham and his
4:14 an empty word and the *p* loses its meaning.
4:16 *p* holds true for all Abraham's descendants,
4:20 he never questioned or doubted God's *p*;
9: 8 the *p* who are to be considered descendants.
9: 9 And this was the *p*: "I will return
1Cor 10:13 Besides, God keeps his *p*.
Gal 3:17 thirty years later, nor is its *p* nullified.
3:18 is no longer conferred in virtue of the *p*.
3:18 *p* that God granted Abraham his privilege.
3:19 came to whom the *p* had been given.
3:22 *p* might be fulfilled in those who believe,

PROMISE (cont.)

4:23 of the free woman was the fruit of the *p.*
4:28 You, my brothers, are children of the *p,*
Eph 2:12 were strangers to the covenant and its *p;*
3: 6 the *p* through the preaching of the gospel.
6: 2 the first commandment to carry a *p* with it
1Tm 4: 8 so, with its *p* of life here and hereafter.
2Tm 1: 1 sent to proclaim the *p* of life in him,
Heb 4: 1 *p* of entrance into his rest still holds,
6:13 When God made his *p* to Abraham,
6:16 to a *p* and puts an end to all argument.
6:17 wishing to give the heirs of his *p* even
10:23 the *p* deserves our trust
11: 9 with Isaac and Jacob, heirs of the same *p;*
11:11 One who had made the *p* was worthy of trust.
2Pt 2:19 They *p* them freedom though they themselves
3: 9 The Lord does not delay in keeping his *p*—
3:13 and a new earth where, according to his *p,*
1Jn 2:25 a promise and the *p* is no less than this:

PROMISED (116)

Gn 21: 1 he did for her as he had *p.*
28:15 leave you until I have done what I *p* you."
50:24 to the land that he *p* on oath to Abraham,
Ex 12:25 land which the LORD will give you as he *p.*
32:13 and all this land that I *p,* I will give your
Nm 10:29 the place which the LORD has *p* to give us.
10:29 for the LORD has *p* prosperity to Israel."
11:12 you have *p* under oath to their fathers?
11:23 or not what I have *p* you takes place."
14:23 land which I *p* on oath to their fathers.
24:11 I *p* to reward you richly, but the LORD
30:13 then whatever she has expressly *p* in her
32:11 see this country I *p* under oath to Abraham
Dt 1:11 thousand times over, and bless you as he *p!*
6:18 which the LORD *p* on oath to your fathers,
6:23 into the land he *p* on oath to our fathers,
7:12 which he *p* on oath to your fathers.
8: 1 which the LORD *p* on oath to your fathers.
9: 3 destroy them quickly, as the LORD *p* you.
9:28 to bring them into the land he *p* them';
11:25 any land where you set foot, as he *p* you.
12:20 has enlarged your territory, as he *p* you,
13:18 multiply you as he *p* your fathers on oath;
15: 6 the LORD, your God, will bless you as he *p.*
19: 8 and gives you all the land he *p* your
23:24 offering you have freely *p* to the LORD.
26:15 honey which you *p* on oath to our fathers.'
26:18 a people peculiarly his own, as he *p* you;
26:19 sacred to the LORD, your God, as he *p.*"
27: 3 of your fathers, is giving you as he *p* you.
29:12 as he *p* you and as he swore to your
31: 3 who will cross before you, as the LORD *p*
31:20 honey which I *p* on oath to their fathers,
31:21 land which I *p* on oath to their fathers."
31:23 into the land which I *p* them on oath.
Jos 1: 3 As I *p* Moses, I will deliver to you every
5: 6 he had *p* their fathers he would give us.
13:14 no heritage since, as the LORD had *p* them,
13:33 God of Israel, is their heritage, as he *p.*
14:10 Now, as he *p,* the LORD has preserved me
14:12 region which the LORD *p* me that day,
14:12 be able to drive them out, as the LORD *p.*"
21:44 every side, just as he had *p* their fathers.
22: 4 God, has settled your kinsmen as he *p* them,
23: 5 of their land as the LORD, your God, *p* you.
23:10 himself who fights for you, as he *p* you.
24:24 Then the people *p* Joshua, "We will serve
Jgs 2: 1 the land which I *p* on oath to your fathers.
6:36 going to save Israel through me, as you *p,*
6:37 you will save Israel through me, as you *p.*"
2Sm 7:25 and his house, and do as you have *p.*
7:29 for you, Lord GOD, have *p,* and by your
1Kgs 2:24 David and made of me a dynasty as he *p,*
5:26 moreover, gave Solomon wisdom as he *p* him,
8:56 rest to his people Israel, just as he *p.*
9: 5 as I *p* your father David when I said,
2Kgs 4:16 Elisha *p,* "This time next you will be
4:17 had given birth to a son, as Elisha had *p.*
8:19 For he had *p* David that he would leave him
20: 9 the LORD that he will do what he has *p:*
1Chr 17:23 Bring about what you have *p,*
17:26 and have *p* this good thing to your servant,
27:23 for the LORD had *p* to multiply Israel like
2Chr 2:14 wheat, barley, oil and wine which he has *p.*
23: 3 as the LORD *p* concerning the sons of David.
Neh 5:12 these men that they would do as they had *p.*
5:13 Then the people did as they had *p.*
Jdt 8:11 When you *p* to hand over the city to our
Est 4: 7 the exact amount of silver Haman had *p*
2Mc 1:29 your people in your holy place, as Moses *p.*"
2:18 the sacred rites, as he *p* through the law.
4: 8 he *p* the king three hundred and sixty
4:27 payments of the money he had *p* to the king,
4:45 himself on the losing side, *p* Ptolemy,
8:36 So he who had *p* to provide tribute for the
12:11 and *p* to supply the Jews with cattle
Ps(s) 60: 8 God *p* in his sanctuary:
66:14 uttered and my words *p* in my distress.
108: 8 God *p* in his sanctuary:
119:116 Sustain me as you have *p,* that I may live;
Sir 44:21 God *p* him with an oath that in his
Is 38: 7 the LORD that he will do what he has *p:*
Jer 18:10 of the good with which I *p* to bless it.
32:22 as you had *p* their fathers under oath,
Bar 2:34 which with my oath I *p* to their fathers,
Ez 36:36 I, the LORD, have *p,* and I will do it.
37:14 I have *p,* and I will do it, says the LORD.
Dn 3:36 To whom you *p* to multiply their offspring
Mt 28: 6 He has been raised, exactly as he *p.*
Mk 14:11 they were jubilant and *p* to give him money.
Lk 1:55 Even as he *p* our fathers, *p* Abraham
1:70 he *p* through the mouths of his holy ones,
Acts 2:33 received the *p* Holy Spirit from the Father,
7: 5 but he *p* to give it to him and his
13:32 God *p* our fathers he has fulfilled for us,
Rom 1: 2 which he *p* long ago through his prophets,
4:21 that God could do whatever he had *p.*
2Cor 9: 5 for the bountiful gift you have already *p.*
Gal 3:14 us to receive the *p* Spirit through faith.
3:29 which means you inherit all that was *p.*
Eph 1:13 sealed with the Holy Spirit who had been *p.*
Col 1:23 hope *p* you by the gospel you have heard.
Ti 1: 2 who cannot lie, *p* in endless ages past.
Heb 6:15 waiting, Abraham obtained what God had *p.*
9:15 may receive the *p* eternal inheritance.
10:36 to do God's will and receive what he has *p.*
11: 9 in the *p* land as in a foreign country,
11:13 been *p* but saw and saluted it from afar.
11:39 faith, they did not obtain what had been *p.*
12:26 then shook the earth, but now he has *p,*
Jas 1:12 life the Lord has *p* to those who love him.
2: 5 of the kingdom he *p* to those who love him?
2Pt 1: 4 on us the great and precious things he *p,*
3: 4 "Where is that *p* coming of his?

PROMISES (27)

Gn 18:19 effect for Abraham the *p* he made about him."
Dt 13: 2 or a dreamer who *p* you a sign or wonder,
Jos 23:14 soul that not one of all the *p* the LORD,
Neh 9: 8 These *p* of yours you fulfilled,
Est C:16 and that you fulfilled all your *p* to them.
1Mc 10:15 the *p* that Demetrius had made to Jonathan;
11:53 his *p* and became estranged from Jonathan.
2Mc 7:24 not with mere words, but with *p* on oath,
Ps(s) 12: 7 The *p* of the LORD are sure, like tried
119:103 How sweet to my palate are your *p,*
144: 8 Whose mouths swear false *p* while their
144:11 Whose mouths swear false *p* while their
Prv 25:14 man who boastfully *p* what he never gives.
Wis 12:21 you gave the sworn covenants of goodly *p!*
Sir 47:22 nor permit even one of his *p* to fail.
Hos 10: 4 Nothing but make *p,* swear false oaths,
Rom 9: 4 the lawgiving, the worship, and the *p;*
15: 8 in fulfilling the *p* to the patriarchs,
2Cor 1:20 *p* God has made have been fulfilled in him;
7: 1 Since we have these *p,* beloved, let us
Gal 3:16 There were *p* spoken to Abraham and to his
3:21 that the law is opposed to the *p* [of God]?
Heb 6:12 faith and patience, are inheriting the *p.*
7: 6 and blessed him who had received God's *p.*
8: 6 of a better covenant, founded on better *p.*
11:17 the *p* was ready to sacrifice his only son,
11:33 did what was just, obtained the *p;*

PROMISING (6)

1Sm 1:11 weeping copiously, and she made a vow, *p:*
1Kgs 20: 3 and your wives and your *p* sons are mine.'"
1Mc 11:28 *p* him in return three hundred talents.
2Mc 8:11 Jewish slaves and *p* to deliver ninety slaves
11:14 terms, and *p* to persuade the king also,
Mt 4: 8 of the world in their magnificence, *p,*

PROMOTE (11)

Dt 23: 7 Never *p* their peace and prosperity as long
Ezr 9:12 Never *p* their peace and prosperity;
Ps(s) 37:34 He will *p* you to ownership of the land;
Wis 14:18 And to *p* this observance among those to
Jer 29: 7 *P* the welfare of the city to which I have
1Cor 7:35 on you, but I do want to *p* what is good,
Phil 1: 5 *p* the gospel from the very first day.
1:17 others *p* Christ, not from pure motives
1Tm 1: 4 which *p* idle speculations rather than that
Ti 1: 1 and to *p* their knowledge of the truth as
Rv 13:12 authority of the first beast to *p* its interests

PROMOTED (3)

Est 5:11 and just how the king had *p* him and placed
10: 2 greatness of Mordecai, whom the king *p,*
Dn 3:97 Then the king *p* Shadrach, Meshach,

PROMOTER (2)

Est 10: 3 as the *p* of his people's welfare and the
Acts 17:18 "He sounds like a *p* of foreign gods,"

PROMOTES (2)

Prv 10:10 but he who frankly reproves *p* peace.
Rom 3: 7 to light God's truth and thus *p* his glory,

PROMOTING (1)

Phil 4: 3 have struggled at my side in *p* the gospel,

PROMPT (5)

Ps(s) 119:60 I was *p* and did not hesitate in keeping
Sir 6: 5 and gracious lips *p* friendly greetings.
18:22 nothing prevent the *p* payment of your vows;
Is 16: 5 judge upholding right and *p* to do justice.
2Pt 1:13 as I live, to *p* you with this reminder.

PROMPTED (12)

Ex 35:21 as his heart suggested and his spirit *p,*
35:22 and the women, all as their heart *p* them,
Nm 31:16 Balaam's advice *p* the unfaithfulness of the
1Sm 1:16 has been *p* by my deep sorrow and misery."
1Kgs 20:35 was *p* by the LORD to say to his companion,
Wis 19:11 also a new kind of bird when, *p* by desire,
Mt 14: 8 *P* by her mother she said, "Bring me the
Jn 9:16 This *p* some of the Pharisees to assert,
21:21 Seeing him, Peter was *p* to ask Jesus,
Acts 2: 4 bold proclamations as the Spirit *p* them.
2Cor 1:12 this has been *p,* not by debased human
Gal 2: 2 I went *p* by a revelation,

PROMPTING (3)

2Sm 24: 1 by *p* him to number Israel and Judah.
Sir 45:23 people And, at the *p* of his noble heart,
Acts 21: 4 Under the Spirit's *p,* they tried to tell Paul

PROMPTLY (17)

Dt 4:26 length of time but shall be *p* wiped out.
Jgs 9:33 *P* at sunrise tomorrow morning,
1Sm 25:34 you, if you had not come so *p* to meet me,
Tb 9: 5 Gabael *p* checked over the sealed moneybags,
10:10 *p* handed over to Tobiah Sarah his wife,
Jdt 10:15 "By coming down thus *p* to see our master,
12:14 Whatever is pleasing to him I will *p* do.
Est 2: 9 So he *p* furnished her with cosmetics and
1Mc 1:13 from among the people *p* went to the king,
2Mc 6:13 *p* instead of letting them go for long.
8: 9 Ptolemy *p* selected Nicanor,
Eccl 8:11 against evildoers is not *p* executed,
Is 5:26 speedily and *p* will they come.
Dn 3:13 who were *p* brought before the king.
Mk 6:27 He *p* dispatched an executioner,
16:20 They *p* reported to Peter and his
Jas 1:24 goes off and *p* forgets what he looked like.

PROMPTS (2)

Ex 25: 2 contribution that his heart *p* him to give
35: 5 Everyone, as his heart *p* him,

PROMULGATE (2)

Lv 26:46 and laws which the LORD had Moses *p*
Dt 33:10 They *p* your decisions to Jacob and your

PROMULGATED (7)

2Chr 31: 5 As soon as the order was *p,* the Israelites
Est 3:14 A copy of the decree to be *p* as law in
3:15 the decree was *p* in the stronghold of Susa.
4: 8 their destruction which had been *p* in Susa,
8:13 A copy of the letter to be *p* as law in
8:14 the decree was *p* in the stronghold of Susa.
Gal 3:19 in view of transgressions and *p* by angels,

PROMULGATION (1)

Mt 19: 7 divorce and the *p* of a divorce decree?"

PRONE (10)

Ex 32:22 well enough how *p* the people are to evil.
1Sm 5: 3 *p* on the ground before the ark of the LORD.
5: 4 *p* on the ground before the ark of the LORD,
Ps(s) 10:10 He stoops and lies *p* till by his violence
Ez 3:23 I fell *p,* but then spirit entered into me
9: 8 I fell *p,* crying out, Alas, Lord GOD!
11:13 I fell *p* and cried out in a loud voice;
43: 3 I fell *p* as the glory of the LORD entered
44: 4 filling the LORD's temple, and I fell *p.*
1Cor 13: 5 is not self-seeking, it is not *p* to anger;

PRONOUNCE (13)

Gn 48:20 you shall the people of Israel *p* blessings;
Ex 33:19 you, and in your presence I will *p* my name,
Nm 23:20 It is a blessing I have been given to *p;*
Dt 11:29 you shall *p* the blessing on Mount Gerizim,
17:11 give you and the verdict they *p* for you,
27:12 Gerizim to *p* blessings over the people,
27:13 shall stand on Mount Ebal to *p* curses.
Ps(s) 58: 2 like gods *p* justice and judge fairly,
Sir 23: 7 my children, to the instruction that I *p,*
Jer 1:16 I will *p* my sentence against them for all
4:12 And I myself now *p* sentence upon them.
23:31 the LORD, who borrow speeches to *p* oracles.
44:26 of Judah shall henceforth *p* my name saying,

PRONOUNCED (21)

Dt 33: 1 God, *p* upon the Israelites before he died.
Jgs 17: 2 shekels of silver over which you *p* a curse
Ru 1:21 since the LORD has *p* against me and the
2Sm 17:14 Then Absalom and all the Israelites *p* the
1Kgs 15:29 which the LORD had *p* through his servant,

2Kgs 9:36 *p* through his servant Elijah the Tishbite:
25: 6 the king of Babylon, who *p* sentence on him.
1Chr 4:41 They *p* against them the ban that is still
2Chr 7:14 my people, upon whom my name has been *p*,
Tb 2: 6 *p* by the prophet Amos against Bethel:
Est C:20 to do away with the decree you have *p*,
Ps(s) 119:138 You have *p* your decrees in justice and in
133: 3 For there the LORD has *p* his blessing,
Is 62: 2 by a new name *p* by the mouth of the LORD.
Jer 16:10 LORD *p* all these great evils against us?
39: 5 king of Babylon *p* sentence upon him.
52: 9 the king of Babylon, who *p* sentence on him.
Dn 7:22 judgment was *p* in favor of the holy ones
Mk 6:41 raised his eyes to heaven, *p* a blessing,
Lk 9:16 his eyes to heaven, *p* a blessing over them,
24:30 them to eat, he took bread, *p* the blessing,

PRONOUNCEMENT (3)

Jb 29:22 no more, but received my *p* drop by drop.
Prv 30: 1 The *p* of mortal man: "I am not God:
Mt 15:12 were scandalized when they heard your *p*?"

PRONOUNCEMENTS (2)

Ps(s) 73: 9 of heaven, and their *p* roam the earth:
Hos 4:12 of wood, and their wand makes *p* for them,

PRONOUNCES (2)

Prv 16:10 no judgment he *p* is false.
Am 3: 1 O men of Israel, that the LORD *p* over you,

PRONOUNCING (1)

2Sm 14:13 In *p* as he has, the king shows himself

PRONUNCIATION (1)

Jgs 12: 6 not being able to give the proper *p*,

PROOF (19)

Ex 3:12 be your *p* that it is I who have sent you:
2Mc 15:35 and evident *p* to all of the LORD's help.
Jb 6:26 Do you consider your words as *p*,
Ps(s) 86:17 Grant me a *p* of your favor,
Wis 1: 3 man from God, and his power, put to the *p*,
2:19 *p* of his gentleness and try his patience.
Sir 4:17 With her precepts she puts him to the *p*,
31:25 wine-drinking be the *p* of your strength,
34:10 One never put to the *p* knows little,
Mt 8: 4 That should be the *p* they need."
Mk 1:44 That should be a *p* for them."
Lk 5:14 that should be a *p* for them."
Acts 13:34 As a *p* that the one whom he raised from
Rom 3: 5 our wrongdoing provides *p* of God's justice,
2Cor 8:24 show these men the *p* of your love,
13: 3 for a *p* of the Christ who speaks in me.
Gal 4: 6 The *p* that you are sons is the fact that
Jas 2:20 Do you want *p*, you ignoramus, that
2:22 There you see *p* that faith was both

PROOFS (1)

Acts 9:22 with his *p* that this Jesus was the Messiah.

PROP (1)

Is 3: 1 and *p* [all supplies of bread and water]:

PROPAGATE (1)

Eph 6:15 to *p* the gospel of peace as your footgear.

PROPENSITY (1)

Prv 21:25 The sluggard's *p* slays him,

PROPER (37)

Lv 23: 4 at their *p* time with a sacred assembly.
Nm 2:17 march, every man shall be in his *p* place,
9: 7 its *p* time along with the other Israelites?"
Dt 22: 5 woman shall not wear an article *p* to a man,
Jgs 6:26 instead, the *p* kind of altar to the LORD,
12: 6 not being able to give the *p* pronunciation,
2Chr 31: 2 to each priest and Levite his *p* service,
Ezr 3: 4 in the *p* number required for each day.
7:17 cereal offerings and libations *p* to these,
Jdt 8:11 What you said to the people today is not *p*.
Est 3: 8 it is not *p* for the king to tolerate them.
8: 5 it pleases your majesty and seems *p* to you,
1Mc 12:11 as it is right and *p* to remember brothers.
2Mc 14:22 But the conference was held in the *p* way.
Prv 25:11 settings are words spoken at the *p* time.
Wis 16:23 be nourished, forgot even its *p* strength;
Sir 4:23 Refrain not from speaking at the *p* time,
10:22 wise but poor, nor *p* to honor any sinner.
20: 6 but a boasting fool ignores the *p* time.
20:19 for he does not utter it at the *p* time.
31:28 are wine drunk freely at the *p* time.
38:16 As is only *p*, prepare the body, absent not
38:30 His care is for *p* coloring,
39:29 In his treasury also, kept for the *p* time,
39:34 for each shows its worth at the *p* time.
41:14 nor is it always the *p* thing to blush:
Jer 40: 4 go wherever you think good and *p*";
Ez 41: 6 were no supports in the temple wall *p*.
Dn 3:27 your ways right, and all your judgments *p*.
3:28 You have executed *p* judgments in all that
3:28 By a *p* judgment you have done all this
3:31 done to us, you have done by a *p* judgment.
Acts 10:28 "You must know that it is not *p* for a Jew
1Cor 11:13 it *p* for a woman to pray to God unveiled?
15:23 to life again, but each one in *p* order:
Eph 4:16 and with the *p* functioning of the members
1Tm 6: 3 Christ and the teaching *p* to true religion,

PROPERLY (6)

1Chr 21:24 I will buy it from you *p*, at its full price.
Mt 22:11 of a man not *p* dressed for a wedding feast.
22:12 'how is it you came in here not *p* dressed?'
1Cor 14:40 that everything is done *p* and in order.
Col 4: 6 strive to respond *p* to all who address you.
1Tm 2: 9 the women must deport themselves *p*.

PROPERTIED (1)

Lk 15:15 himself to one of the *p* class of the place,

PROPERTY (88)

Gn 23: 4 holdings a piece of *p* for a burial ground,
31: 1 this wealth of his by using our father's *p*."
31:18 all the *p* he had acquired in Paddan-aram,
34:10 freely in it, and acquire landed *p* here."
36: 6 *p* he had acquired in the land of Canaan,
47:19 Pharaoh's slaves and our land his *p*;
47:27 There they acquired *p*, were fertile,
Ex 21: 4 master's *p* and the man shall leave alone.
21:21 be punished, since the slave is his own *p*.
22: 7 did not lay hands on his neighbor's *p*.
22:10 he did not lay hands on his neighbor's *p*;
Lv 25:10 every one of you shall return to his own *p*,
25:13 every one of you shall return to his own *p*,
25:25 to poverty and has to sell some of his *p*,
25:27 it, so that he may thus regain his own *p*.
25:32 to redeem the town houses that are their *p*.
25:33 *p* in the midst of the Israelites.
25:34 it must always remain their hereditary *p*.
25:41 his kindred and to the *p* of his ancestors.
25:46 leave to your sons as their hereditary *p*,
27:21 that is doomed, it shall become priestly *p*.
27:22 and not a part of his hereditary *p*,
Nm 5:10 the *p* of the priest to whom he gives them."
27: 4 have *p* among our father's kinsmen."
27: 7 hereditary *p* among their father's kinsmen,
32: 5 land be given to your servants as their *p*.
32:29 you shall give them Gilead as their *p*
32:30 their *p* with you in the land of Canaan."
32:32 hereditary *p* on this side of the Jordan."
33:53 for I have given you the land as your *p*.
33:54 there shall his *p* be within the heritage
35: 2 Israelites that out of their hereditary *p*
35: 8 the cities from the *p* of the Israelites,
36: 8 every daughter who inherits *p* in any of
Dt 8:13 your silver and gold, and all your *p*,
21:16 when he comes to bequeath his *p* to his
Jos 12: 6 and the half-tribe of Manasseh, as their *p*.
21:12 given to Caleb, son of Jephunneh, as his *p*.
22: 9 to the land of Gilead, their own *p*,
1Sm 25: 2 was a man of Maon who had *p* in Carmel;
2Sm 19:30 I say, 'You and Ziba shall divide the *p*.'"
2Kgs 8: 6 saying, "Restore all her *p* to her,
1Chr 4:22 and Joash and Saraph, who held *p* in Moab,
7:28 Their *p* and their dwellings were in Bethel
2Chr 20:25 an abundance of cattle and personal *p*,
35: 7 these were from the king's *p*.
Neh 11: 3 each man on the *p* he owned in his own city.)
Tb 1:20 Afterward, all my *p* was confiscated;
10:10 his wife, together with half of all his *p*:
1Mc 15:33 what we took is not the *p* of others,
2Mc 3:11 orphans, and a part was the *p* of Hyrcanus,
Eccl 2:21 not labored over it, he must leave his *p*.
5:18 Any man to whom God gives riches and *p*,
6: 2 to whom God gives riches and *p* and honor,
Sir 42: 3 or of dividing an inheritance or *p*;
Jer 39:10 But some of the poor who had no *p* were
Ez 44:28 no property in Israel, for I am their *p*.
45: 5 and ten thousand wide as *p* for the Levites,
45: 6 As *p* of the City you shall designate a
45: 7 of the combined sacred tract and City *p*,
45: 8 This shall be his *p* in Israel,
46:16 that *p* is theirs by inheritance.
46:18 the people by evicting them from their *p*.
46:18 inheritance for his sons from his own *p*,
46:18 of my people will be driven from their *p*.
48:20 the sacred tract together with the City *p*.
48:21 sides of the sacred tract and the City *p*,
48:22 the *p* of the Levites and the City property,
48:22 which lie in the midst of the prince's *p*,
Mt 12:29 his *p* unless he first ties him securely?
18:25 with his wife, his children, and all his *p*,
19:29 wife or children or *p* for my sake will
21:33 There was a *p* owner who planted a vineyard,
24:47 he will put him in charge of all his *p*.
Mk 3:27 a strong man's house and despoil his *p*
10:29 sisters, mother or father, children or *p*,
10:30 and sisters, mothers, children and *p*—
Lk 12:44 master will put him in charge of all his *p*.
15:12 So the father divided up the *p*.
15:30 gone through your *p* with loose women,
16: 1 was reported to him for dissipating his *p*.
Acts 1:19 Jerusalem, who named the *p* Field of Blood
2:45 they would sell their *p* and goods,
4:34 for all who owned *p* or houses sold them
5: 1 wife Sapphira likewise sold a piece of *p*.
5: 8 piece of *p* for such and such an amount?"

PROPHECIES (10)

Tb 14: 4 a single word of the *p* shall prove false.
Sir 36:14 fulfill the *p* spoken in your name,
39: 1 of old and occupies himself with the *p*;
Jer 45: 1 when he wrote in a book the *p* that
Acts 19: 6 began to speak in tongues and to utter *p*.
1Cor 13: 8 *P* will cease, tongues will be silent,
14:31 You can all speak your *p*, but one by one,
1Thes 5:20 Do not despise *p*.
1Tm 1:18 accordance with the *p* made in your regard,
1:19 so that under the inspiration of these *p*

PROPHECY (30)

2Sm 7:25 confirm for all time the *p* you have made
1Kgs 2:27 thus fulfilling the *p* with the LORD had
12:15 fulfill the *p* he had uttered to Jeroboam,
2Kgs 1:17 of the *p* of the LORD spoken by Elijah.
7:18 the *p* of the man of God to the king,
10:17 the *p* which the LORD had spoken to Elijah.
2Chr 9:29 prophet, in the *p* of Ahijah the Shilonite,
10:15 the *p* the LORD had uttered to Jeroboam,
15: 8 these words and the *p* [Oded the prophet],
Neh 6:12 he voiced this *p* concerning me that I
Prv 29:18 Without *p* the people become demoralized;
Sir 24:31 *p* and bestow it on generations to come.
44: 3 prudence, or seers of all things in *p*;
Ez 30: 2 Son of man, speak this *p*:
Dn 9:24 will be introduced, vision and *p* ratified,
Mi 2:11 pour you wine and strong drink as my *p*,"
Mt 13:14 Isaiah's *p* is fulfilled in them which says:
Lk 1:67 with the Holy Spirit, uttered this *p*:
Acts 21: 9 had four unmarried daughters gifted with *p*.
Rom 12: 6 One's gift may be *p*; its use should be in
1Cor 12:10 *P* is given to one; to another power to
13: 2 If I have the gift of *p* and,
14: 1 on spiritual gifts— above all, the gift of *p*.
14: 6 have some revelation, or knowledge, or *p*,
14:22 while *p* is not for those who are without
14:24 enters while all are uttering *p*,
14:39 Set your hearts on *p*,
1Tm 4:14 gift you received when, as a result of *p*,
2Pt 1:20 there is no *p* contained in Scripture which
1:21 *P* has never been put forward by man's

PROPHESIED (30)

Nm 11:25 as the spirit came to rest on them, they *p*.
11:26 rest on them also, and they *p* in the camp.
1Kgs 14:18 *p* through his servant the prophet Ahijah.
16:12 had *p* to Baasha through the prophet Jehu,
22:12 The other prophets *p* in a similar vein,
22:38 harlots bathed there, as the LORD had *p*.
2Kgs 2:22 pure even to this day, just as Elisha *p*.
14:25 God of Israel, had *p* through his servant,
2Chr 18:11 The other prophets *p* in the same vein,
20:37 from Mareshah, *p* against Jehosphaphat,
Jer 2: 8 The prophets *p* by Baal,
20: 6 be buried, because you have *p* lies to them.
23:13 *p* by Baal and led my people Israel astray.
23:21 I did not speak to them, yet they *p*.
25:13 which Jeremiah *p* against all the nations].
26:11 he has *p* against this city,
26:20 another man who *p* in the name of the LORD,
26:20 he *p* the same things against this city and
28: 6 May he fulfill the things you have *p* by
28: 8 prophets who were before you and me *p* war,
37:20 who *p* to you that the king of Babylon
Ez 13:16 prophets of Israel who *p* to Jerusalem
37: 7 I *p* as I had been told,
37:10 I *p* as he told me, and the spirit came
38:17 who *p* in those days that I would bring you
Mt 7:22 'Lord, Lord, have we not *p* in your name?
Mk 7: 6 *p* about you hypocrites when he wrote,
Jn 11:51 he *p* that Jesus would die for the nation
1Pt 1:10 They *p* the divine favor that was destined
Jude 1:14 descended from Adam, *p* when he said,

PROPHESIES (12)

1Kgs 22: 8 because he *p* not good but evil about me."
22:18 tell you he *p* not good but evil about me?"
2Chr 18: 7 for he *p* not good but always evil about me.
18:17 I not tell you that he *p* no good about me,
Jer 28: 9 But the prophet who *p* peace is recognized
29:31 *p* to you without a mission from me,
Ez 12:27 he *p* of the distant future!"
Zec 13: 3 If a man still *p*, his parents, father
13: 3 When he *p*, his parents, father and
1Cor 11: 4 Any man who prays or *p* with his head
11: 5 any woman who prays or *p* with her head
14: 4 himself, but he who *p* builds up the church.

PROPHESY (66)

Ezr 5: 1 began to *p* to the Jews in Judah and

PROPHESY (cont.)

Jdt 6: 2 to p among us as you have done today,
Wis 14:28 either go mad with enjoyment, or p lies,
Jer 5:31 The prophets p falsely, and the priests
11:21 saying, "Do not p in the name of the LORD;
14:14 of their own imagination, they p to you.
14:15 Concerning the prophets who p in my name,
14:16 The people to whom they p shall be cast
19:14 Topheth, where the LORD had sent him to p,
23:25 the prophets who p lies in my name say,
23:26 who p lies and their own deceitful fancies?
23:32 am against the prophets who p lying dreams,
26: 9 Why do you p in the name of the LORD:
26:12 "It was the LORD who sent me to p against
26:18 used to p in the days of Hezekiah,
27:10 For they p lies to you, in order to drive
27:14 king of Babylon," for they p lies to you.
27:15 the Lord, but they p falsely in my name,
27:16 to the words of your prophets who p to you:
27:16 Babylon soon now," for they p lies to you.
29: 9 For they p lies to you in my name;
29:21 about those who p lies to you in my name,
32: 3 "How dare you p: Thus says the LORD:
Ez 4: 7 with bared arm you shall p against it.
6: 2 mountains of Israel, and p against them:
11: 4 Therefore p against them, son of man, p!
13: 2 of man, p against the prophets of Israel,
13: 2 prophesy against the prophets of Israel, p!
13: 2 Say to those who p their own thought:
13:17 their own thoughts; against these, p:
21: 2 p against the forest of the southern land.
21: 7 and p against the land of Israel,
21:14 Son of man, p!
21:19 As for you, son of man, p,
21:33 As for you, son of man, p:
25: 2 toward the Ammonites and p against them.
28:21 man, look toward Sidon, and p against it:
29: 2 and p against him and against all Egypt.
34: 2 of man, p against the shepherds of Israel,
34: 2 these words p to them [to the shepherds]:
35: 2 face against Mount Seir, and p against it.
36: 1 son of man, p to the mountains of Israel:
36: 3 possession" [therefore p in these words:
36: 6 p concerning the land of Israel,
37: 4 P over these bones, and say to them:
37: 9 P to the spirit, prophesy, son of man,
37:12 Therefore, p and say to them:
38: 2 of Meshech and Tubal, and p against him:
38:14 Therefore p, son of man, and say to Gog:
39: 1 son of man, p against Gog in these words:
Jl 3: 1 Your sons and daughters shall p,
Am 2:12 drink, and commanded the prophets not to p.
3: 8 The Lord GOD speaks— who will not p!
7:12 prophesying, but never again p in Bethel;
7:15 and said to me, Go, p to my people Israel.
7:16 p not against Israel,
Zec 13: 4 prophet shall be ashamed to p his vision,
Mt 15: 7 did Isaiah p about you when he said:
Acts 2:17 Your sons and daughters shall p,
2:18 my spirit in those days, and they shall p.
1Cor 14: 5 in tongues, but I much prefer that you p.
Rv 10:11 must p again for many peoples and nations,
11: 3 p for those twelve hundred and sixty days,

PROPHESYING (9)

Nm 11:27 Moses, "Eldad and Medad are p in the camp,"
1Kgs 22:10 and all the prophets were p before them.
2Chr 18: 9 and all the prophets were p before them.
Jer 20: 1 heard p these things by the priest Pashhur,
27:15 you and the prophets who are p to you.
Ez 11:13 While I was p, Pelatiah, the son
37: 7 told, and even as I was p I heard a noise;
Am 7:12 There earn your bread by p,
1Cor 13: 9 is imperfect and our p is imperfect.

PROPHET (256)

Ex 7: 1 and Aaron your brother shall act as your p.
Nm 12: 6 Should there be a p among you,
Dt 13: 2 "If there arises among you a p or a
13: 4 to the words of that p or that dreamer;
13: 6 p or that dreamer shall be put to death,
18:15 "A p like me will the LORD,
18:18 them a p like you from among their kinsmen,
18:20 But if a p presumes to speak in my name an
18:22 though a p speaks in the name of the LORD,
18:22 The p has spoken it presumptuously,
34:10 then no p has arisen in Israel like Moses,
Jgs 6: 8 a p to the Israelites who said to them,
1Sm 3:20 Samuel was an accredited p of the LORD.
9: 9 is now called p was formerly called seer.)
22: 5 But the p Gad said to David:
2Sm 7: 2 on every side, he said to Nathan the p,
12:25 and sent the p Nathan to name him Jedidiah,
24:11 morning, the LORD had spoken to the p Gad,
1Kgs 1: 8 Benaiah, son of Jehoiada, Nathan the p,
1:10 But he did not invite the p Nathan,
1:22 speaking to the king, the p Nathan came in.
1:23 the p entered the king's presence and,
1:32 summoned Zadok the priest, Nathan the p,
1:34 the p are to anoint him king of Israel,
1:38 So Zadok the priest, Nathan the p,
1:44 with him Zadok the priest, Nathan the p,
1:45 Nathan the p anointed him king at Gihon,
11:29 p Ahijah the Shilonite met him on the road.
11:29 area, and the p was wearing a new cloak.
13:11 There was an old p living in the city,
13:18 he said to him, "I, too, am a p like you,
13:20 spoke to the p who had brought him back,
13:25 the news to the city where the old p lived.
13:26 the p who had brought him back from his
13:29 The p lifted up the body of the man of God
14: 2 Shiloh, where you will find the p Ahijah.
14:18 through his servant the p Ahijah.
16: 7 [Through the p Jehu,
16:12 prophesied to Baasha through the p Jehu,
18:22 "I am the only surviving p of the LORD,
18:36 the p Elijah came forward and said,
19:16 of Abel-meholah, as p to succeed you.
20:13 Then a p came up to Ahab,
20:22 Then the p went up to the king of Israel
20:37 The p met another man and said,
20:38 The p went on and waited for the king on
22: 7 p of the LORD here whom we may consult?"
2Kgs 1: 9 The p was seated on a hilltop when he
2:24 The p turned and saw them,
3:11 "Is there no p of the LORD here through
5: 3 would present himself to the p in Samaria,"
5: 8 and find out that there is a p in Israel."
5:10 The p sent him the message:
5:13 "if the p had told you to do something
6:12 "The Israelite p Elisha can tell the king
8: 9 arrival, he stood before the p and said,
9: 1 The p Elisha called one of the guild
9: 4 man (the guild p) went to Ramoth-gilead.
13:17 The p exclaimed, "The LORD's arrow
14:25 through his servant, the p Jonah,
17:13 Israel and Judah by every p and seer,
19: 2 wrapped in sackcloth, to tell the p Isaiah,
20: 1 Hezekiah was mortally ill, the p Isaiah,
20:11 So the p Isaiah invoked the LORD,
20:14 the p came to King Hezekiah and asked him:
20:15 the p asked.
23:18 bones of the p who had come from Samaria.
1Chr 17: 1 in his house, he said to Nathan the p,
29:29 the seer, the history of Nathan the p,
2Chr 9:29 well known, in the acts of Nathan the p,
12: 5 Then Shemaiah the p came to Rehoboam and
12:15 in the history of Shemaiah the p and of
13:22 are written in the midrash of the p Iddo.
15: 8 these words and the prophecy [Oded the p,
18: 6 p of the LORD here whom we may consult?"
21:12 letter from the p Elijah with this message:
25:15 Amaziah, and he sent a p to him who said:
25:16 Therefore the p desisted.
26:22 The p Isaiah, son of Amos, wrote the rest
28: 9 was a p of the LORD by the name of Oded.
29:25 Gad the king's seer, and of Nathan the p;
32:20 of this, King Hezekiah and the p Isaiah,
32:32 written in the Vision of the P Isaiah,
35:18 in Israel since the time of the p Samuel,
36:12 not humble himself before the p Jeremiah,
Tb 2: 6 pronounced by the p Amos against Bethel:
1Mc 4:46 until a p should come and decide what to
14:41 and high priest until a true p arises.
2Mc 2: 1 not only that Jeremiah the p ordered the
2: 2 fire with them, but also that the p,
2: 4 The same document also tells how the p,
15:14 said of him, "This is God's p Jeremiah,
Ps(s) 74: 9 there is no p now, and no one of us knows
Wis 11: 1 their affairs prosper through the holy p.
Sir 46:13 womb, Consecrated to the LORD as a p,
46:15 As a trustworthy p he was sought out and
46:20 from the grave he raised his voice as a p,
48: 1 p whose words were as a flaming furnace.
48: 8 vengeance, and a p as your successor.
48:22 As ordered by the illustrious p Isaiah,
49: 7 who even in the womb had been made a p,
Is 3: 2 Hero and warrior, judge and p,
9:14 the p who teaches falsehood is the tail.]
28: 7 Priest and p stagger from strong drink,
37: 2 wrapped in sackcloth, to tell the p Isaiah,
38: 1 Hezekiah was mortally ill, the p Isaiah,
39: 3 the p came to King Hezekiah and asked him,
Jer 1: 5 you, a p to the nations I appointed you.
6:13 p and priest, all practice fraud.
8:10 all are greedy for gain, p and priest,
14:18 Even the p and the priest forage in a land
20: 2 So he had the p scourged and placed in the
20: 3 from the stocks, the p said to him:
23:11 Both p and priest are godless!
23:28 the p who has a dream recount his dream;
23:33 this people, or a p or a priest asks you,
23:34 If a p or a priest or anyone else mentions
23:37 Thus shall you ask the p, "What answer
25: 2 This word the p Jeremiah spoke to all the
28: 1 month of the fourth year, the p Hananiah,
28: 5 The prophet Jeremiah answered the p
28: 9 But the p who prophesies peace is
28:10 Thereupon the p Hananiah took the yoke
28:10 the yoke from the neck of the p Jeremiah,
28:11 At that, the p Jeremiah went away.
28:12 Some time after the p Hananiah had broken
28:12 yoke from off the neck of the p Jeremiah,
28:15 the prophet Hananiah the p Jeremiah said:
28:17 in the seventh month, Hananiah the p died.
29: 1 contents of the letter which the p Jeremiah
29:27 of Anathoth who poses as a p among you?
29:29 priest Zephaniah read this letter to the p,
32: 2 and the p Jeremiah was imprisoned in the
34: 6 The p Jeremiah told all these things to
36: 8 did everything the p Jeremiah commanded;
36:26 Baruch, the secretary, and the p Jeremiah.
37: 2 words of the LORD spoken by Jeremiah the p.
37: 3 to the p Jeremiah with this request:
37: 6 of the LORD then came to the p Jeremiah:
37:13 he seized the p Jeremiah,
38: 9 in all they have done to the p Jeremiah,
38:10 and draw the p Jeremiah out of the cistern
38:14 Once King Zedekiah summoned the p Jeremiah
42: 1 low, approached the p Jeremiah and said,
42: 4 the p Jeremiah answered them:
43: 6 also Jeremiah, the p, and Baruch,
45: 1 message that the p Jeremiah gave to Baruch,
46: 1 came to the p Jeremiah against the nations.
46:13 The message which the LORD gave to the p
47: 1 the p Jeremiah concerning the Philistines,
49:34 came to the p Jeremiah at the beginning
50: 1 of the Chaldeans, through the p Jeremiah:
51:59 errand given by the p Jeremiah to Seraiah,
Lam 2:20 p to be slain in the sanctuary of the LORD?
Ez 2: 5 shall know that a p has been among them.
14: 4 of his sin before him, has recourse to a p.
14: 7 him, yet asks a p to consult me for him,
14: 9 As for the p, if he is beguiled
14: 9 I, the LORD, shall have beguiled that p;
14:10 inquirer and the p shall be punished alike,
33:33 shall know that there was a p among them.
Dn 3:38 We have in our day no prince, p,
9: 2 of which the LORD spoke to the p Jeremiah:
14:33 In Judea there was a p, Habakkuk;
Hos 9: 7 "The p is a fool, the man of the spirit
9: 8 A p is Ephraim's watchman with God,
12:14 a p the LORD brought Israel out of Egypt,
12:14 of Egypt, and by a p they were protected.
Am 7:14 Amos answered Amaziah, "I was no p,
Mi 2:11 then he would be the p of this people.
Hb 1: 1 which Habakkuk the p received in vision.
3: 1 Prayer of Habakkuk, the p.
Hg 1: 1 the p Haggai to the governor of Judah,
1: 3 of the LORD came through Haggai, the p:)
1:12 God, and to the words of the p Haggai,
2: 1 word of the LORD came through the p Haggai:
2:10 the word of the LORD came to the p Haggai:
Zec 1: 1 word of the LORD came to the p Zechariah,
1: 7 word of the LORD came to the p Zechariah,
13: 4 p shall be ashamed to prophesy his vision,
13: 5 mislead, but he shall say, "I am no p,
Mal 3:23 Lo, I will send you Elijah, the p,
3:24 Lo, I will send you Elijah, the p,
Mt 1:22 what the Lord had said through the p:
2: 5 "Here is what the p has written:
2:15 what the Lord had said through the p:
2:17 through Jeremiah the p was then fulfilled:
3: 3 that the p Isaiah had spoken when he said:
4:14 what had been said through Isaiah the p:
8:17 what had been said through Isaiah the p:
10:41 He who welcomes a p because he bears the
10:41 the name of p receives a prophet's reward;
11: 9 Why then did you go out—to see a p?
11: 9 A p indeed, and something more!
12:17 what had been said through Isaiah the p:
12:39 will be given it but that of the p Jonah.
13:17 many a p and many a saint longed to see
13:35 fulfill what had been said through the p:
13:57 "No p is without honor except in his
14: 5 of the people, who regarded him as a p.
21: 4 to fulfill what was said through the p:
21:11 is the p Jesus from Nazareth in Galilee."
21:26 the people, who all regard John as a p."
21:46 to fear the crowds who regarded him as a p.
24:15 and destructive thing which the p Daniel
26:68 "Play the p for us, Messiah!
27: 9 said through Jeremiah the p was fulfilled:
Mk 1: 2 In Isaiah the p it is written:
6: 4 "No p is without honor except in his
6:15 "He is a p equal to any of the prophets."
11:32 people, who all regarded John as a true p.)
14:65 him and hit him, saying, "Play the p!"
Lk 1:76 child, shall be called p of the Most High;
3: 4 in the book of the words of Isaiah the p:
4:17 the book of the p Isaiah was handed him,
4:24 p gains acceptance in his native place.
4:27 in Israel in the time of Elisha the p;
7:16 "A great p has risen among us,"
7:26 Then what did you go out to see—a p?
7:39 said to himself, "If this man were a p,
13:33 since no p can be allowed to die anywhere
20: 6 so convinced are they that John was a p."
22:64 "Play the p; which one struck you?"
24:19 a p powerful in word and deed in the eyes
Jn 1:21 "Are you the P?"
1:23 He said, quoting the p Isaiah,
1:25 are not the Messiah, nor Elijah, nor the P,
4:19 the woman, "I can see you are a p.
4:44 that no one esteems a p in his own country.)
6:14 the P who is to come into the world."
7:40 words began to say, "This must be the P."
7:52 will not find the P coming from Galilee."

9:17 "He is a *p*," he replied.
12:38 was to fulfill the word of the *p* Isaiah:
Acts 2:16 No, it is what Joel the *p* spoke of:
2:30 He was a *p* and knew that God had sworn to
3:22 a *p* like me from among your own kinsmen:
3:23 Anyone who does not listen to that *p* shall
7:37 you from among your kinsmen a *p* like me.'
7:48 made by human hands, for as the *p* says:
7:52 any *p* whom your fathers did not persecute?
8:28 in his carriage reading the *p* Isaiah.
8:30 and heard the man reading the *p* Isaiah.
8:34 me, if you will, of whom the *p* says this
13: 6 magician named Bar-Jesus who posed as a *p*.
13:20 rule them until the time of the *p* Samuel.
21:10 stay, a *p* named Agabus arrived from Judea.
28:25 said to your fathers through the *p* Isaiah:
1Cor 14: 3 The *p*, on the other hand, speaks to men
14: 5 The *p* is greater than one who speaks in
14:37 thinks he is a *p* or a man of the Spirit,
Rv 16:13 beast, and from the mouth of the false *p*;
19:20 beast was captured along with the false *p*
20:10 beast and the false *p* had also been thrown.

PROPHETESS (8)

Ex 15:20 The *p* Miriam,
Jgs 4: 4 At this time the *p* Deborah,
2Kgs 22:14 in Jerusalem, where the *p* Huldah resided.
2Chr 34:22 men from the king went to the *p* Huldah,
Neh 6:14 keep in mind as well Noadiah the *p* and
Is 8: 3 to the *p* and she conceived and bore a son.
Lk 2:36 There was also a certain *p*, Anna by name,
Rv 2:20 that self-styled *p* who seduces my servants

PROPHETIC (24)

1Sm 10: 5 will meet a band of prophets, in a *p* state,
10: 6 and you will join them in their *p* state
10:10 so that he joined them in their *p* state.
10:11 saw him in a *p* state among the prophets,
10:13 When he came out of the *p* state,
19:20 Samuel, in a *p* frenzy, they too fell into the *p*
19:21 messengers, who also fell into the *p* state.
19:21 but they too fell into the *p* state.
19:23 in a *p* condition until he reached the spot.
19:24 in the *p* state in the presence of Samuel;
1Kgs 18:29 *p* state until time for offering sacrifice.
Sir 46: 1 of Nun, assistant to Moses in the *p* office,
Jer 28: 9 only when his *p* prediction is fulfilled.
Ez 7:26 *P* vision shall fade;
2Pt 1:19 *p* message as something altogether reliable.
Jude 1:17 the *p* words of the apostles of our Lord
Rv 1: 3 Happy is the man who reads this *p* message,
19:10 The *p* spirit proves itself by witnessing
22: 6 the Lord, the God of *p* spirits,
22: 7 man who heeds the *p* message of this book!"
22:10 "Do not seal up the *p* words of this book,
22:18 to all who hear the *p* words of this book.
22:19 anyone takes from the words of this *p* book,

PROPHETICALLY (1)

Mt 11:13 as well as the law spoke *p* until John.

PROPHETS (257)

Nm 11:29 that all the people of the LORD were *p*!
1Sm 10: 5 that city, you will meet a band of *p*,
10:10 from there to Gibeah, a band of *p* met him,
10:11 saw him in a prophetic state among the *p*,
10:11 Is Saul also among the *p*?"
10:12 proverb arose, "Is Saul also among the *p*?"
19:20 But when they saw the band of *p*,
19:24 why they say, "Is Saul also among the *p*?"
28: 6 in dreams or by the Urim or through *p*.
28:15 longer answers me through *p* or in dreams,
1Kgs 18: 4 Jezebel was murdering the *p* of the LORD,
18: 4 of the LORD, Obadiah took a hundred *p*,
18:13 Jezebel was murdering the *p* of the LORD
18:13 that I hid a hundred of the *p* of the LORD,
18:19 *p* of Baal and the four hundred *p* of Asherah
18:20 and had the *p* assemble on Mount Carmel.
18:22 there are four hundred and fifty *p* of Baal.
18:25 Elijah then said to the *p* of Baal,
18:40 Elijah said to them, "Seize the *p* of Baal.
19: 1 that he had put all the *p* to the sword.
19:10 your altars, and put your *p* to the sword.
19:14 your altars, and put your *p* to the sword.
20:35 One of the guild *p* was prompted by the
20:41 of Israel recognized him as one of the *p*.
22: 6 king of Israel gathered together the *p*,
22:10 and all the *p* were prophesying before them.
22:12 The other *p* prophesied in a similar vein,
22:13 the *p* are unanimously predicting good for
22:22 a lying spirit in the mouths of all his *p*.'
22:23 in the mouths of all these *p* of yours,
2Kgs 2: 3 guild *p* went out to Elisha and asked him,
2: 5 guild *p* approached Elisha and asked him.
2: 7 Fifty of the guild *p* followed,
2:15 The guild *p* in Jericho,
3:13 "Go to the *p* of your father and to the *p*
4: 1 woman, the widow of one of the guild *p*,
4:38 when the guild *p* were seated before him,
4:38 make some vegetable stew for the guild *p*."
5:22 guild *p* from the hill country of Ephraim.
6: 1 The guild *p* once said to Elisha:
6:18 to the *p* prayer the LORD struck them blind.
9: 1 called one of the guild *p* and said to him:
9: 7 I avenge the blood of my servants the *p*,
10:19 Now summon for me all Baal's *p*,
17:13 and which I sent you by my servants the *p*,"
17:23 foretold through all his servants, the *p*;
21:10 the LORD spoke through his servants the *p*:
23: 2 priests, *p*, and all the people, small
24: 2 had threatened through his servants the *p*.
1Chr 16:22 not my anointed, and to my *p* do no harm."
2Chr 18: 5 The king of Israel gathered his *p*,
18: 9 and all the *p* were prophesying before them.
18:11 The other *p* prophesied in the same vein,
18:12 *p* unanimously predict good for the king,
18:21 a lying spirit in the mouths of all his *p*.'
18:22 spirit in the mouths of these your *p*,
20:20 Trust in his *p* and you will succeed."
24:19 Although *p* were sent to them to convert
29:25 were from the LORD through his *p*.
36:16 his warnings, and scoffed at his *p*,
Ezr 5: 1 Then the *p* Haggai and Zechariah,
5: 2 with the *p* of God giving them support.
6:14 supported by the message of the *p*,
9:11 which you gave through your servants the *p*:
Neh 6: 7 that you have set up *p* in Jerusalem to
6:14 the other *p* who were trying to frighten me.
9:26 they slew your *p* who bore witness against
9:30 through your spirit, by means of your *p*;
9:32 kings, our princes, our priests, our *p*,
Tb 4:12 tribe, because we are sons of the *p*.
14: 4 indeed, whatever was said by Israel's *p*,
14: 5 come, just as the *p* of Israel said of her.
1Mc 9:27 time *p* ceased to appear among the people.
9:54 down, thus destroying the work of the *p*.
2Mc 2:13 kings, the writings of the *p* and of David,
15: 9 them with words from the law and the *p*,
Ps(s) 105:15 not my anointed, and to my *p* do no harm."
Wis 7:27 to age, she produces friends of God and *p*.
Sir 36:15 in you, and let your *p* be proved true.
49:10 Then, too, the TWELVE *P*—
Is 29:10 [the *p* and covered your heads [the seers].
30:10 to the *p*, "Do not descry for us what is
Jer 2: 8 The *p* prophesied by Baal,
2:26 their princes, their priests and their *p*;
2:30 sword devoured your *p* like a ravening lion.
4: 9 priests will be amazed, and the *p* stunned.
5:13 The *p* have become wind,
5:31 The *p* prophesy falsely,
7:25 sent you untiringly all my servants the *p*.
8: 1 Judah, the bones of the priests and the *p*,
13:13 to David's throne, the priests and *p*,
14:13 I replied, it is the *p* who say to them,
14:14 Lies these *p* utter in my name,
14:15 Concerning the *p* who prophesy in my name,
14:15 and famine shall these *p* meet their end.
18:18 from the wise, nor of messages from the *p*.
23: 9 Concerning the *p*:
23:13 Among Samaria's *p* I saw unseemly deeds:
23:14 *p* I saw deeds still more shocking:
23:15 thus says the LORD of hosts against the *p*:
23:15 For from Jerusalem's *p* ungodliness has
23:16 Listen not to the words of your *p*,
23:21 I did not send these *p*,
23:25 the *p* who prophesy lies in my name say,
23:26 Is my name in the hearts of the *p* who
23:30 Therefore I am against the *p*,
23:31 Yes, I am against the *p*, says the LORD,
23:32 am against the *p* who prophesy lying dreams,
25: 4 all his servants the *p* with this message:
26: 5 to the words of my servants the *p*,
26: 7 Now the priests, the *p*,
26: 8 people, the priests and *p* laid hold of him,
26:11 The priests and *p* said to the princes and
26:16 the people said to the priests and the *p*,
27: 9 You, however, must not listen to your *p*,
27:14 not listen to the words of those *p* who say,
27:15 you and the *p* who are prophesying to you.
27:16 to the words of your *p* who prophesy to you:
27:18 If they were *p*, if the word of the LORD
28: 8 the *p* who were before you and me
29: 1 among the exiles, to the priests, the *p*,
29: 8 by the *p* and diviners who are among you;
29:15 has raised up for us *p* here in Babylon"
29:19 I kept sending them my servants the *p*,
29:26 all madmen and those who pose as *p*,
32:32 their princes, their priests and their *p*,
35:15 I kept sending you all my servants the *p*,
37:19 And where are your *p* now,
44: 4 kept sending to you all my servants the *p*,
Lam 2: 9 And her *p* have not received any vision
2:14 *p* had for you false and specious visions;
4:13 of her *p* and the crimes of her priests,
Bar 1:16 our kings and rulers and priests and *p*,
1:21 in all the words of the *p* whom he sent us,
2:20 had warned us through your servants the *p*:
2:24 you had made through your servants the *p*,
Ez 13: 2 of man, prophesy against the *p* of Israel,
13: 3 Woe to those *p* who are fools,
13: 4 Like foxes among ruins are your *p*,
13: 9 I will stretch out my hand against the *p*
13:16 those *p* of Israel who prophesied to
22:28 Her *p* cover them with whitewash,
38:17 times through my servants, the *p* of Israel,
Dn 9: 6 We have not obeyed your servants the *p*,
9:10 you gave us through your servants the *p*.
Hos 4: 5 and the *p* shall stumble with you at night;
6: 5 this reason I smote them through the *p*.
12:11 I granted many visions and spoke to the *p*,
Am 2:11 I who raised up *p* among your sons,
2:12 drink, and commanded the *p* not to prophesy.
3: 7 revealing his plan to his servants, the *p*.
7:14 nor have I belonged to a company of *p*;
Mi 3: 5 regarding the *p* who lead my people astray;
3: 6 The sun shall go down upon the *p*,
3:11 for a salary, her *p* divine for money,
Zep 3: 4 Her *p* are insolent, treacherous men;
Zec 1: 4 like your fathers whom the former *p* warned:
1: 5 And the *p*, can they live forever?
1: 6 which I entrusted to my servants the *p*,
7: 3 the house of the LORD of hosts, and the *p*,
7: 7 which the LORD spoke through the former *p*,
7:12 sent by his spirit through the former *p*.
8: 9 hear these words spoken by the *p*
13: 2 I will also take away the *p* and the spirit
Mt 2:23 what was said through the *p* was fulfilled:
5:12 the *p* before you in the very same way.
5:17 I have come to abolish the law and the *p*.
7:12 this sums up the law and the *p*.
7:15 "Be on your guard against false *p*,
10:41 the name of prophet receives a *p* reward;
11:13 All the *p* as well as the law spoke
16:14 still others Jeremiah or one of the *p*."
22:40 the whole law is based, and the *p* as well."
23:29 *p* and decorate the monuments of the saints.
23:30 have joined them in shedding the *p*' blood.'
23:31 that you are the sons of the *p*' murderers.
23:34 shall send you *p* and wise men and scribes.
23:37 *p* and stoner of those who were sent to you!
24:11 False *p* will rise in great numbers to
24:24 False messiahs and false *p* will appear,
26:56 in fulfillment of the writings of the *p*."
Mk 6:15 "He is a prophet equal to any of the *p*."
8:28 others, Elijah, still others, one of the *p*."
13:22 False messiahs and false *p* will appear
Lk 1:70 of his holy ones, the *p* of ancient times:
6:23 it was that their fathers treated the *p*.
6:26 treated the false *p* in just this way.
9: 8 others, "One of the *p* of old has risen."
9:19 of the *p* of old has returned from the dead."
10:24 many *p* and kings wished to see what you
11:47 You build the tombs of the *p*,
11:49 has said, 'I will send them *p* and apostles,
11:50 *p* shed since the foundation of the world.
13:28 and all the *p* safe in the kingdom of God,
13:34 the *p* and stone those who are sent to you!
16:16 law and the *p* were in force until John.
16:29 answered, 'They have Moses and the *p*.
16:31 'If they do not listen to Moses and the *p*,
18:31 written by the *p* concerning the Son of Man
24:25 to believe all that the *p* have announced!
24:27 Beginning, then, with Moses and all the *p*,
24:44 and the *p* and psalms had to be fulfilled."
Jn 1:45 the *p* too—Jesus, son of Joseph,
6:45 It is written in the *p*:
8:52 The *p* are dead.
8:53 Or the *p*, who died!
Acts 3:18 he announced long ago through all the *p*:
3:21 God spoke of long ago through his holy *p*.
3:24 "Moreover, all the *p* who have spoken,
3:25 You are the children of those *p*,
7:42 So we find it written in the Book of the *P*:
10:43 To him all the *p* testify,
11:27 *p* came down from Jerusalem to Antioch.
13: 1 church at Antioch certain *p* and teachers:
13:15 After the reading of the law and of the *p*,
13:27 the *p* which we read sabbath after sabbath.
13:40 what was said by the *p* be realized in you:
15:15 The words of the *p* agree with this,
15:32 Judas and Silas, who were themselves *p*,
24:14 all that is written in the law and the *p*,
26:22 differs from what the *p* and Moses foretold:
26:27 Do you believe the *p*, King Agrippa?
28:23 appealing to the law of Moses and the *p*.
Rom 1: 2 which he promised long ago through his *p*,
3:21 though both law and *p* bear witness to it
11: 3 "Lord, they have killed your *p*,
16:26 manifested through the writings of the *p*,
1Cor 12:28 up in the church first apostles, second *p*,
12:29 Are all *p*?
14:29 Let no more than two or three *p* speak,
14:32 of the prophets are under the *p*' control,
Eph 2:20 on the foundation of the apostles and *p*,
3: 5 by the Spirit to the holy apostles and *p*.
4:11 It is he who gave apostles, *p*,
1Thes 2:15 Jews who killed the Lord Jesus and the *p*,
Ti 1:12 A man of Crete, one of their own *p*,
Heb 1: 1 varied ways to our fathers through the *p*;
11:32 Jephthah, of David and Samuel and the *p*,
Jas 5:10 the *p* who spoke in the name of the Lord.
1Pt 1:10 the *p* carefully searched out and examined.
2Pt 2: 1 past there were false *p* among God's people,
2:16 a human voice to restrain the *p* madness.
3: 2 teaching delivered long ago by the holy *p*,
1Jn 4: 1 many false *p* have appeared in the world.
4: 4 and thus you have conquered the false *p*.

PROPHETS (cont.)

Rv 10: 7 which he announced to his servants the *p*,
11:10 these two *p* harassed everyone on earth.
11:12 The two *p* heard a loud voice from heaven
11:18 the *p* and the holy ones who revere you,
16: 6 those who shed the blood of saints and *p*,
18:20 you heavens, you saints, apostles and *p!*
18:24 "In her was found the blood of *p* and
22: 9 the *p* and those who heed the message

PROPITIATION (1)

Wis 18:21 office, prayer and the *p* of incense;

PROPITIATORY (24)

Ex 25:17 "You shall then make a *p* of pure gold,
25:18 of beaten gold for the two ends of the *p*,
25:20 spread out above, covering the *p* with them;
25:20 but with their faces looking toward the *p*.
25:21 *p* you shall then place on top of the ark.
25:22 will meet you and there, from above the *p*,
26:34 Set the *p* on the ark of the commandments
31: 7 the commandments with the *p* on top of it,
35:12 the ark, with its poles, the *p*,
37: 6 The *p* was made of pure gold,
37: 7 gold were made for the two ends of the *p*,
37: 8 directly from the *p* at its two ends.
37: 9 spread out above, covering the *p* with them.
37: 9 but with their faces looking toward the *p*.
39:35 of the commandments with its poles, the *p*,
40:20 alongside the ark and set the *p* upon it.
Lv 16: 2 the veil, in front of the *p* of the ark;
16: 2 I reveal myself in a cloud above the *p*,
16:13 may cover the *p* over the commandments;
16:14 with his finger on the fore part of the *p*
16:14 his finger seven times in front of the *p*.
16:15 sprinkling it on the *p* and before it.
Nm 7:89 above the *p* on the ark of the commandments,
1Chr 28:11 inner chambers, and the room with the *p*.

PROPORTION (24)

Ex 12: 4 shall share in the lamb in *p* to the number
Lv 25:27 in *p* to the number of years since the sale,
25:52 in *p* to his years of service shall he pay
27:23 its value in *p* to the number of years
Nm 7: 5 Levites, to each group in *p* to its duties."
7: 7 to the Gershonites in *p* to their duties,
7: 8 oxen to the Merarites in *p* to their duties,
26:54 in *p* to the number of men registered in it.
29:18 rams and lambs in *p* to their number,
29:21 rams and lambs in *p* to their number,
29:24 rams and lambs in *p* to their number,
29:27 rams and lambs in *p* to their number,
29:30 rams and lambs in *p* to their number,
29:33 rams and lambs in *p* to their number,
29:37 rams and lambs in *p* to their number,
35: 8 to the Levites in *p* to its own heritage."
Dt 15:14 wine press, in *p* to the blessing the LORD,
16:10 shall be in *p* to the blessing the LORD,
16:17 give, in *p* to the blessings which the LORD,
Tb 4: 8 Son, give alms in *p* to what you own.
2Mc 3: 6 out of all *p* to the cost of the sacrifices,
Rom 12: 6 its use should be in *p* to his faith.
1Cor 3: 8 will receive his wages in *p* to his toil.
Rv 18: 7 In *p* to her boasting and sensuality,

PROPORTIONATELY (1)

2Kgs 23:35 from the people of the land, from each *p*,

PROPORTIONS (1)

Ez 40:22 *p* as those of the gate facing the east.

PROPOSAL (15)

Gn 34:18 *p* seemed fair to Hamor and his son Shechem.
Dt 1:23 Agreeing with the *p*, I chose twelve men
1Sm 25:39 David then sent a *p* of marriage to Abigail.
30:24 Who could agree with this *p* of yours?
2Sm 17: 6 Shall we follow his *p?*
1Kgs 5:22 to Solomon, "I agree to the *p* you sent me,
2Chr 30: 4 When this *p* had been approved by the king
Ezr 10:15 son of Tikvah, were against this *p*,
Neh 6: 4 Four times they sent me this same *p*,
Jdt 7:16 and he ordered their *p* to be carried out.
Est 1:21 This *p* found acceptance with the king and
1Mc 1:12 The *p* was agreeable;
6:60 The *p* found favor with the king and the
8:21 The *p* pleased the Romans,
Acts 6: 5 The *p* was unanimously accepted by the

PROPOSE (17)

Gn 26:28 so we *p* that there be a sworn agreement
44:10 "Even though it ought to be as you *p*,
Jos 9: 6 to *p* that you make an alliance with us."
9:11 we *p* that you make an alliance with us.'
Jgs 14:12 said to them, "Let me *p* a riddle to you.
14:13 *P* your riddle,"
19:30 note of it, and state what you *p* to do."
20: 7 here, O Israelites, state what you *p* to do."
2Sm 21: 4 said, "I will do for you whatever you *p*."
1Kgs 17:13 "Go and do as you *p*.
2Chr 28:13 for what you *p* will make us guilty before
Sir 16:23 to my words, While I *p* measured wisdom,
Ez 17: 2 Son of man, *p* a riddle,
24: 3 *P* this parable to the rebellious house:
Lk 7:40 "Simon, I have something to *p* to you."
Acts 17:19 know what this new teaching is that you *p*.
1Cor 14:26 What do we *p*, brothers?

PROPOSED (20)

Dt 1:14 answered me, 'We agree to do as you have *p*.'
Jgs 14:16 for you have *p* a riddle to my countrymen,
2Sm 17: 6 "This is what Ahithophel *p*.
1Kgs 2:23 has not *p* this at the cost of his life.
2Chr 32: 1 cities, and *p* to take them by storm.
Ezr 10: 5 Israel that they would do as had been *p*;
Jdt 7:28 of our forefathers, to do as we have *p*,
Est 6:10 Take the robe and horse as you have *p*,
6:10 Do not omit anything you *p*."
1Mc 1:16 Antiochus *p* to become king of Egypt,
10:56 become your father-in-law as you have *p*."
2Mc 11:15 common good, agreed to all that Lysias *p*;
Is 14:24 As I have *p*, so shall it stand:
14:26 This is the plan *p* for the whole earth,
Jer 44:17 will we continue doing what we had *p*;
Mt 13:24 He *p* to them another parable:
13:31 He *p* still another parable:
Lk 5:36 He then *p* to them this figure:
Jn 18:14 (It was Caiaphas who had *p* to the Jews the
2Thes 2: 4 above every so-called god *p* for worship,

PROPOSING (1)

Eph 4:14 in human trickery and skill in *p* error.

PROPPED (1)

1Kgs 22:35 *p* up in his chariot facing the Arameans,

PROPRIETY (1)

1Cor 12:24 *p* which the more presentable already have.

PROSCRIBE (1)

Lk 6:22 and insult you and *p* your name as evil

PROSECUTE (1)

Acts 25: 5 this man is at fault, they can *p* him there."

PROSECUTED (1)

2Mc 4:48 those who had *p* the case for the city,

PROSECUTION (2)

Lk 23: 2 They started his *p* by saying,
Acts 24: 2 Tertullus began his *p* by addressing Felix:

PROSPECT (2)

1Sm 18:26 the *p* of becoming the king's son-in-law.
Lk 21:36 the strength to escape whatever is in *p*,

PROSPER (31)

Dt 4:40 you and your children after you may *p*,
5:29 and their descendants would *p* forever.
5:33 LORD, your God, that you may live and *p*,
6: 3 them, that you may grow and *p* the more,
6:18 that you may, according to his word, *p*,
12:25 may *p* for doing what is right in the sight
12:28 may always *p* for doing what is good
19:13 of shedding innocent blood, that you may *p*.
21: 9 that you may *p* for doing what is right in
28:63 took delight in making you grow and *p*,
Jgs 17:13 said, "Now I know that the LORD will *p* me,
18: 6 The priest said to them, "Go and *p*:
2Chr 24:20 the LORD's commands, so that you cannot *p?*
26: 5 long as he sought the LORD, God made him *p*.
Tb 7:11 son, may the Lord of heaven *p* you both.
Ps(s) 73: 3 when I saw them *p* though they were wicked.
90:17 *p* the work of our hands for us!
90:17 *P* the work of our hands!]
122: 6 May those who love you *p!*
Prv 11:10 When the just *p*, the city rejoices;
28:25 but he who trusts in the LORD will *p*.
Wis 11: 1 their affairs *p* through the holy prophet.
Is 52:13 See, my servant shall *p*,
Jer 7:23 ways that I command you, so that you may *p*.
12: 1 Why does the way of the godless *p*,
Ez 17: 9 Can it *p?*
17:10 True, it is planted, but will it *p?*
17:15 Can he *p?*
Dn 11:36 He shall *p* only till divine wrath is ready,
Hos 14: 9 I have humbled him, but I will *p* him.
Mal 3:15 for indeed evildoers *p*, and even tempt

PROSPERED (9)

1Sm 18:14 expeditions, and *p* in all his enterprises,
2Kgs 18: 7 him, and he *p* in all that he set out to do.
1Chr 29:23 he *p*, and all Israel obeyed him.
2Chr 14: 6 So they built and *p*.
31:21 He did this wholeheartedly, and he *p*.
32:30 Hezekiah *p* in all his undertakings.
Jdt 5:17 not sin in the sight of their God, they *p*,
1Mc 2:47 arrogant, and the work *p* in their hands.
Wis 10:10 She *p* him in his labors and made abundant

PROSPERITY (39)

Nm 10:29 you, for the LORD has promised *p* to Israel."
10:32 with you the *p* the LORD will bestow on us."
Dt 5:16 long life and *p* in the land which the LORD,
22: 7 thus that you shall have *p* and a long life.
23: 7 their peace and *p* as long as you live.
30: 9 God, will again take delight in your *p*,
30:15 I have today set before you life and *p*,
1Kgs 10: 7 wisdom and *p* surpass the report I heard.
Ezr 9:12 Never promote their peace and *p*;
Tb 7:12 of heaven grant both of you peace and *p*."
10:11 grant *p* to you and to your wife Sarah.
13:14 you, and happy those who rejoice in your *p*.
14: 2 and after he recovered it he lived in *p*,
2Mc 14:14 of the Jews would mean *p* for themselves.
Jb 17:15 and my *p*, who shall see?
20:21 built up, Therefore his *p* shall not endure,
21:13 They live out their days in *p*,
36:11 and serve him, they spend their days in *p*,
42:10 Also, the LORD restored the *p* of Job,
Ps(s) 25:13 He abides in *p*, and his descendants inherit
35:27 he wills the *p* of his servant!"
68: 7 he leads forth prisoners to *p*;
106: 5 That I may see the *p* of your chosen ones,
118:25 O LORD, grant *p!*
122: 7 be within your walls, *p* in your buildings.
128: 5 *p* of Jerusalem all the days of your life;
Prv 8:18 riches and honor, enduring wealth and *p*.
24:25 and on them will come the blessing of *p*.
28:10 [And blameless men will gain *p*
Sir 11:25 The day of *p* makes one forget adversity;
11:25 the day of adversity makes one forget *p*.
12: 8 In our *p* we cannot know our friends;
22:23 thus will you enjoy his *p* with him.
Is 48:18 commandments, your *p* would be like a river,
66:12 Lo, I will spread *p* over her like a river,
Ez 16:49 sated with food, complacent in their *p*,
Dn 4:24 then your *p* will be long."
Zec 1:17 My cities shall again overflow with *p*;
Acts 19:25 "you know that our *p* depends on this work.

PROSPEROUS (12)

Gn 30:43 Thus the man grew increasingly *p*,
Dt 6:24 as *p* and happy a life as we have today;
8:16 test you, but also make you *p* in the end.
30: 5 you more *p* and numerous than your fathers.
Tb 10:13 all of us be *p* all the days of our lives."
Jb 12: 6 Yet the tents of robbers are *p*,
15:21 when all is *p*, the spoiler comes upon him.
Ps(s) 34:13 desires life, and takes delight in *p* days?
Sir 29:17 Going surety has ruined many *p* men and
Dn 4: 1 was at home in my palace, content and *p*.
11:24 By stealth he shall enter *p* provinces and
1Pt 3:10 who cares for life and wants to see *p* days

PROSPERS (2)

Ps(s) 1: 3 [Whatever he does, *p*
Prv 28:13 He who conceals his sins *p* not,

PROSTITUTE (12)

Gn 38:21 men of the place, "Where is the temple *p*,
38:21 "There has never been a temple *p* here."
38:22 the place said there was no temple *p* there."
Lv 19:29 degrade your daughter by making a *p* of her;
21: 7 who has been a *p* or has lost her honor,
21:14 or a woman who has lost her honor as a *p*,
Dt 23:18 nor a temple *p* among the Israelite men.
Ez 16:30 these things, acting like a shameless *p*,
16:31 Yet you were unlike a *p*,
Am 2: 7 Son and father go to the same *p*,
1Cor 6:15 members and make them the members of a *p?*
6:16 is joined to a *p* becomes one body with her?

PROSTITUTES (8)

1Kgs 14:24 There were also cult *p* in the land.
15:12 banishing the temple *p* from the land and
22:47 the rest of the cult *p* who had remained
2Kgs 23: 7 *p* which were in the temple of the LORD,
2Mc 6: 4 they amused themselves with *p* and had
Hos 4:14 harlots, and with *p* you offer sacrifice!
Mt 21:31 and *p* are entering the kingdom of God
21:32 collectors and the *p* did believe in him.

PROSTITUTION (1)

Ez 16:34 No one sought you out for *p*.

PROSTITUTIONS (1)

Jer 13:27 your neighings, your shameless *p*:

PROSTRATE (52)

Ex 11: 8 then come down to me, and *p* before me,
23: 5 one who hates you lying *p* under its burden,
Lv 9:24 this, all the people cried out and fell *p*.
Nm 14: 5 But Moses and Aaron fell *p* before the
16: 4 When Moses heard this, he fell *p*.
16:22 But they fell *p* and cried out,
17:10 But they fell *p*.
20: 6 of the meeting tent, where they fell *p*.
Dt 9:18 I lay *p* before the LORD for forty days and

9:25 and forty nights, I lay *p* before the LORD,
Jos 5:14 Joshua fell *p* to the ground in worship,
7: 6 *p* before the ark of the LORD until evening;
7:10 Why are you lying *p*?
Jgs 13:20 wife saw this, they fell *p* to the ground;
Ru 2:10 Casting herself *p* upon the ground,
1Sm 17:49 in his brow, and he fell *p* on the ground.
25:23 and, falling *p* on the ground before David,
2Sm 9: 6 Saul, came to David, he fell *p* in homage.
14: 4 king and fell *p* to the ground in homage,
14:22 Falling *p* to the ground in homage and
1Kgs 18: 7 Recognizing him, Obadiah fell *p* and asked,
18:39 this, all the people fell *p* and said,
2Chr 32:12 shall *p* yourselves before one altar only,
Ezr 10: 1 weeping and *p* before the house of God,
Jdt 3: 2 the great king, lie *p* before you,
6:18 this the people fell *p* and worshiped God;
7:25 sold us into their power by laying us *p*
9: 1 Judith threw herself down *p*,
10:23 She threw herself down *p* before him,
13: 2 tent with Holofernes, who lay *p* on his bed,
2Mc 10:26 Lying *p* at the foot of the altar,
Jb 1:20 He cast himself *p* upon the ground,
Ps(s) 37:24 Though he fall, he does not lie *p*,
57: 5 *p* in the midst of lions which devour men;
68:31 Let them *p* themselves with bars of silver;
97: 7 all gods are *p* before him.
119:25 I lie *p* in the dust; give me life according
Wis 4:19 and *p* and rock them to their foundations;
Sir 50:17 quickly fall *p* to the ground In adoration
50:21 Then again the people would lie *p* to
Is 29: 4 *P* you shall speak from the earth,
43:17 a powerful army, Till they lie *p* together,
44:17 god, his idol, and *p* before it in worship,
45:14 Before you they shall fall *p*,
49: 7 and princes shall *p* themselves Because of
60:14 who despised you shall fall *p* at your feet.
Dn 8:17 where I was standing, I fell *p* in terror.
Mt 4: 9 you if you *p* yourself in homage before me."
9:36 They were lying *p* from exhaustion,
26:39 He advanced a little and fell *p* in prayer.
Lk 4: 7 *P* yourself in homage before me,
1Cor 14:25 Falling *p*, he will worship God, crying out,

PROSTRATED (18)

Gn 17: 3 When Abram *p* himself, God continued
17:17 Abraham *p* himself and laughed as he said
Jgs 7:15 and explanation of the dream, he *p* himself.
1Sm 20:41 David rose from beside the mound and *p*
1Chr 21:16 sackcloth, *p* themselves face to the ground,
2Chr 29:28 The entire assembly *p* itself,
29:29 who were with him knelt and *p* themselves.
29:30 was full, then fell down and *p* themselves.
33: 3 and *p* himself before the whole host of
Neh 8: 6 down and *p* themselves before the LORD,
9: 3 and *p* themselves before the LORD their God.
Jdt 4:11 *p* themselves in front of the temple building,
1Mc 4:55 *p* themselves and adored and praised Heaven,
2Mc 3:15 Priests *p* themselves in their priestly
3:21 to see the populace variously *p* in prayer
10: 4 they *p* themselves and begged the Lord that
Mt 2:11 They *p* themselves and did him homage.
18:26 the official *p* himself in homage and said,

PROSTRATING (1)

1Chr 29:20 bowing down and *p* themselves before the

PROSTRATIONS (1)

2Mc 13:12 weeping and fasting and *p* for three days,

PROTECT (17)

Gn 28:15 I will *p* you wherever you go,
28:20 to *p* me on this journey I am making and to
Ex 26:13 on either side of the Dwelling to *p* it.
2Sm 18:12 to *p* the youth Absalom for his sake.
Ezr 8:22 to *p* us against enemies along the way,
Tb 5:17 May God in heaven *p* you on the way and
Jdt 8:15 power to *p* us at such time as he pleases,
1Mc 4:61 Judas also placed a garrison there to *p* it,
Ps(s) 5:12 *P* them, that you may be the joy of those
69:30 let your saving help, O God, *p* me.
80:16 and *p* what your right hand has planted
83: 4 they conspire against those whom you *p*.
Wis 5:16 his right hand, and *p* them with his arm.
Is 26: 1 he sets up walls and ramparts to *p* us.
31: 5 shall shield Jerusalem, To *p* and deliver,
Jn 17:11 *p* them with your name which you have given
Jude 1:24 There is One who can *p* you from a fall and

PROTECTED (10)

Dt 32:36 their *p* and unprotected alike disappearing,
Jos 24:17 great miracles before our very eyes and *p* us
1Sm 30:23 He has *p* us and delivered into our grip
Ezr 8:31 and he *p* us from enemies and bandits along
Jdt 13:16 who has *p* me in the path I have followed,
1Mc 3: 3 battles and *p* the camp with his sword.
6:38 the enemy and to be *p* from the phalanxes.
Sir 50: 4 He *p* his people against brigands and
Jer 26:24 But Ahikam, son of Shaphan, *p* Jeremiah,
Hos 12:14 out of Egypt, and by a prophet they were *p*.

PROTECTING (1)

Prv 2: 8 of justice, *p* the way of his pious ones.

PROTECTION (12)

Dt 32:38 Let them be your *p*!
1Sm 22:23 You are under my *p*."
1Mc 11:16 Alexander fled to Arabia to seek *p*.
2Mc 5: 9 find *p* because of his relations with them.
13:17 with the help and *p* of the LORD.
Jb 1:10 his family and all that he has with your *p*?
Eccl 7:12 protection of wisdom is as the *p* of money;
Is 4: 6 over all, his glory will be shelter and *p*:
30: 2 *p* and take refuge in Egypt's shadow;
30: 3 Pharaoh's *p* shall be your shame,
Bar 6:69 in a cucumber patch, that is no *p*,

PROTECTIVE (1)

Bar 1:12 live under the *p* shadow of Nebuchadnezzar,

PROTECTOR (3)

Jdt 9:11 of the weak, the *p* of the forsaken,
2Mc 4: 2 of the city, a *p* of his compatriots,
Sir 29:16 and the ingrate abandons his *p*;

PROTECTS (7)

Jdt 6: 2 the Israelites because their God *p* them?
9:14 who *p* the people of Israel but you alone."
2Mc 3:39 in heaven watches over that Place and *p* it,
Ps(s) 146: 9 The LORD *p* strangers; the fatherless
Prv 13: 3 He who guards his mouth *p* his life;
Is 38:16 Those live whom the LORD *p*; yours . . .
1Jn 5:18 rather, God *p* the one begotten by him,

PROTEST (10)

2Mc 4:33 evidence of the facts, he made a public *p*,
4:39 people assembled in *p* against Lysimachus.
Hos 2: 4 Protest against your mother, *p*!
4: 4 But let no one *p*, let no one complain;
Mt 3:14 John tried to refuse him with the *p*,
Jn 6:41 started to murmur in *p* because he claimed,
6:61 were murmuring in *p* at what he had said.
Acts 13:51 their feet in *p* and went on to Iconium.
18: 6 out his garments in *p* and say to them:

PROTESTED (14)

Ex 6:12 But Moses *p* to the LORD,
6:30 But Moses *p* to the LORD, "Since I am
1Sm 2:16 And if the man *p* to him, "Let the fat be
2Kgs 4:16 "Please, my lord," she *p*, "you are a man
2Mc 7: 6 canticle, when he *p* openly with the words,
Ez 4:14 "Oh no, LORD GOD!" I *p*.
Mt 12: 2 When the Pharisees spied this, they *p*:
Mk 2:24 At this the Pharisees *p*: "Look! Why do
15:14 Pilate *p*, "Why? What crime has he
Jn 10:32 for rocks to stone him, Jesus *p* to them,
11: 8 "Rabbi," *p* the disciples, "with the Jews
12: 4 (the one about to hand him over), *p*:
Acts 9:13 But Ananias *p*: "Lord, I have heard
23: 4 At this, the attendants *p*,

PROTESTING (1)

Mt 26: 8 disciples saw this they grew indignant, *p*:

PROTRUDED (1)

2Sm 2:23 javelin, and the weapon *p* from his back.

PROUD (65)

Lv 13:24 and the *p* flesh of the burn now becomes a
2Chr 25:19 and thus ambition makes you *p*.
26:16 he became *p* to his own destruction and
32:25 his debt of gratitude, for he had become *p*.
Est 4:16 thus in not bowing down to the *p* Haman.
1Mc 1: 3 him, and his heart became *p* and arrogant.
Jb 28: 8 The *p* beasts have not trodden it,
38:11 and here shall your *p* waves be stilled!
41:26 he is king over all *p* beasts.
Ps(s) 36:12 Let not the foot of the *p* overtake me nor
94: 2 render their deserts to the *p*.
119:21 You rebuke the accursed *p*,
119:51 Though the *p* scoff bitterly at me,
119:69 Though the *p* forge lies against me,
119:78 Let the *p* be put to shame for oppressing
119:85 The *p* have dug pits for me;
119:122 let not the *p* oppress me.
123: 4 the arrogant, with the contempt of the *p*.
131: 1 O LORD, my heart is not *p*,
138: 6 he sees, and the *p* he knows from afar.
140: 6 the *p* who have hidden a trap for me;
Prv 15:25 The LORD overturns the house of the *p*,
16: 5 Every *p* man is an abomination to the LORD;
16:19 the meek than to share plunder with the *p*.
21: 4 Haughty eyes and a *p* heart
30:32 you have foolishly been *p* or presumptuous
Wis 14: 6 when the *p* giants were being destroyed,
Sir 3:27 affliction of the *p* man there is no cure;
9:12 Rejoice not at a *p* man's success;
10: 9 Why are dust and ashes *p*?
10:15 The roots of the *p* God plucks up,
10:17 The traces of the *p* God sweeps away and
12: 4 the downtrodden, give nothing to the *p* man.
12:14 So is it with the companion of the *p* man,
13:19 A *p* man abhors lowliness;
13:23 poverty is evil by the standards of the *p*.
21: 4 so too a *p* man's home is destroyed.
25: 2 A *p* pauper, a rich dissembler,
27:28 and abuse will be the lot of the *p*,
32:18 *p* and insolent man is deterred by nothing.
35:20 merciless and wreaks vengeance upon the *p*;
Is 2:12 his day against all that is *p* and arrogant,
10:12 utterance of the king of Assyria's *p* heart,
16: 6 of the pride of Moab, how very *p* he is,
Ez 7:24 I will put an end to their *p* strength,
16:49 she and her daughters were *p*,
16:56 repute by you while you felt *p* of yourself,
30: 6 fall, and down shall come her *p* strength;
31:10 because it became *p* in heart at its height,
33:28 so that its *p* strength will come to an end,
Dn 5:20 *p* and his spirit hardened by insolence,
8:25 be *p* of heart and destroy many by stealth.
Hos 13: 6 they became *p* of heart and forgot me.
Hb 2: 4 the *p*, unstable man—
Zep 3:11 I remove from your midst the *p* braggarts,
Mal 3:15 Rather must we call the *p* blessed;
3:19 the *p* and all evildoers will be stubble,
Lk 1:51 confused the *p* in their inmost thoughts.
2Cor 10: 5 We demolish sophistries and every *p*
12: 7 to beat me and keep me from getting *p*.
1Tm 6:17 rich in this world's goods not to be *p*,
2Tm 3: 2 will be lovers of self and of money, *p*,
Jas 1:10 and the rich man be *p* of his lowliness,
4: 6 the *p* but bestows his favor on the lowly."
Rv 13: 5 for uttering *p* boasts and blasphemies,

PROUDER (1)

Phil 1:26 should make you even *p* of me in Christ.

PROUDHEARTED (1)

Tb 4:13 Do not be so *p* toward your kinsmen the

PROUDLY (3)

Ps(s) 10: 2 *P* the wicked harass the afflicted,
17:10 their cruel hearts, their mouths speak *p*.
31:24 who act *p* Take courage and be stouthearted,

PROVE (34)

Gn 44:16 can we plead or how try to *p* our innocence?
Jgs 2:22 the Israelites were to be made to *p* whether
Ru 2:13 said, "May I *p* worthy of your kindness,
2Sm 2: 7 therefore, and *p* yourselves valiant men,
10:12 let us *p* our valor for the sake of our
2Kgs 12: 6 repairs on the temple may *p* necessary."
1Chr 19:12 "If the Arameans *p* too strong for me,
19:12 and if the Ammonites *p* too strong for you,
Ezr 2:59 and Immer were unable to *p* that their
Neh 1: 8 'Should you *p* faithless, I will scatter you
7:61 and Immer were unable to *p* that their
Tb 14: 4 word of the prophecies shall *p* false.
Jdt 6: 9 my words shall not *p* false in any respect."
2Mc 6:27 now, I will *p* myself worthy of my old age,
Jb 6:24 *p* to me wherein I have erred.
Ps(s) 62:10 In a balance they *p* lighter, all together,
Sir 42:10 or, as a wife, lest she *p* unfaithful;
Is 43: 9 produce witnesses to *p* themselves right,
43:26 Speak up, *p* your innocence!
50: 9 GOD is my help; who will *p* me wrong?
54:17 every tongue you shall *p* false that
Jer 22:15 Must you *p* your rank among kings by
Ez 36:23 I will *p* the holiness of my great name,
36:23 in their sight I *p* my holiness through you.
38:16 in their sight I *p* my holiness through you,
38:23 I will *p* my greatness and holiness and
39:27 and will *p* my holiness through them in the
Dn 12:10 and tested, but the wicked shall *p* wicked;
Mt 5:45 This will *p* that you are sons of your
11:19 Yet time will *p* where wisdom lies."
Jn 16: 8 comes, he will *p* the world wrong about sin,
Acts 25: 7 him, none of which they were able to *p*.
1Cor 4: 2 an administrator is that he *p* trustworthy.
Phil 2:15 *p* yourselves innocent and straightforward,

PROVED (26)

Gn 2:20 *p* to be the suitable partner for the man.
Jgs 21:14 but these *p* to be not enough for them.
2Chr 28:19 way and *p* utterly faithless to the LORD.
30: 7 your brethren who *p* faithless to the LORD,
32: 1 after he had *p* his fidelity by such deeds,
Ezr 4:15 which has *p* fatal to kings and provinces,
Neh 9:16 "But they, our fathers, *p* to be insolent;
Jb 23:10 if he *p* me, I should come forth as gold.
Ps(s) 105:19 pass and the word of the LORD *p* him true.
Wis 3: 6 As gold in the furnace, he *p* them,
11:14 their thirst *p* unlike that of the just.
Sir 36:15 in you, and let your prophets be *p* true.
46:15 out and his words *p* him true as a seer.
Mk 5: 4 No one had *p* strong enough to tame him.
Acts 6:10 but they *p* no match for the wisdom and
7:20 He *p* to be an exceedingly handsome child.
12:19 When it *p* unsuccessful, he had the guards

PROVED (cont.)

Rom 3: 4 p true even though every man be p a liar,
16:10 Apelles, who p himself in Christ's service,
1Cor 15:10 favor of his to me has not p fruitless.
2Cor 7:14 boasting to Titus has been p equally true.
8:22 eagerness has been p to us in many ways.
1Thes 1: 5 Our preaching of the gospel p not a mere
1: 5 as well as we do what we p to be like when,
Jas 1:12 Once he has been p, he will receive the

PROVEN (2)

Jdt 2: 5 my presence, take with you men of p valor,
Prv 31:29 "Many are the women of p worth,

PROVERB (17)

1Sm 10:12 Thus the p arose, "Is Saul also among
24:14 The old p says, 'From the wicked comes
1Kgs 9: 7 become a p and a byword among all nations,
2Chr 7:20 make it a p and a byword among all peoples.
Ps(s) 49: 5 My ear is intent upon a p; I will set forth
Prv 1: 6 That he may comprehend p and parable,
26: 7 A p in the mouth of a fool hangs limp,
26: 9 of a drunkard is a p in the mouth of fools.
Sir 20:19 A p when spoken by a fool is unwelcome,
Ez 12:22 this p that you have in the land of Israel:
12:23 I will put an end to this p;
17: 2 and speak this p to the house of Israel:
18: 2 p that you recite in the land of Israel:
18: 3 among you who will repeat this p in Israel.
Mk 7:17 his disciples questioned him about the p.
Lk 4:23 them, "You will doubtless quote me the p,
2Pt 2:22 How well the p fits them:

PROVERBS (10)

1Kgs 5:12 Solomon also uttered three thousand p,
Prv 1: 1 The P of Solomon, the son of David,
10: 1 The P of Solomon:
25: 1 These also are p of Solomon.
Eccl 12: 9 weighed, scrutinized and arranged many p.
Sir 3:28 The mind of a sage appreciates p,
8: 8 wise, but acquaint yourself with their p;
18:29 dispensing sound p like life-giving waters.
50:27 Wise instruction, appropriate p, I have
Ez 16:44 everyone who is fond of p will say of you,

PROVES (7)

Dt 17: 8 which p too complicated for you to decide,
1Kgs 1:52 Solomon answered, "If he p himself worthy,
Prv 16: 2 eyes, but it is the LORD who p the spirit.
21: 2 own eyes, but it is the LORD who p hearts.
Wis 2:11 for weakness p itself useless.
Rom 5: 8 in this that God p his love for us:
Rv 19:10 spirit p itself by witnessing to Jesus."

PROVIDE (54)

Gn 6:21 you are to p yourself with all the food
22: 8 himself will p the sheep for the holocaust."
45:11 still lie ahead, I will p for you there,
50:21 I will p for you and for your children."
Ex 5:10 I will not p you with straw.
21:19 idleness and p for his complete cure.
Jgs 19:20 to him, "but let me p for all your needs,
Ru 4:14 has not failed to p you today with an heir!
2Sm 14:17 word of my lord the king p a resting place;
19:34 and I will p for your old age as my guest
1Kgs 4: 7 each having to p for one month in the year.
5:22 p all the cedars and fir trees you wish.
5:24 So Hiram continued to p Solomon with all
5:25 kors of wheat to p for his household,
7:31 p a receptacle a cubit and a half in depth.
17: 9 have designated a widow there to p for you."
2Kgs 3:16 the LORD, P many catch basins in this wadi.'
2Chr 31: 4 p the support of the priests and Levites,
Jdt 12: 3 shall we get more of the same to p for you?
Est B: 2 to p for my subjects a life of complete
E: 8 We must p for the future,
1Mc 8:26 wage war they shall not give nor p grain,
12: 4 requesting them to p the envoys with safe
2Mc 8:36 So he who had promised to p tribute for
9:16 and would p from his own revenues the
12:43 Jerusalem to p for an expiatory sacrifice.
Jb 20: 2 So now my thoughts p me with an answer,
Ps(s) 33:17 thought its strength, it cannot p escape.
78:20 also give bread and p meat for his people?"
Prv 27:26 in, The lambs will p you with clothing,
30: 8 p me only with the food I need;]
Eccl 2:24 p himself with good things by his labors.
Sir 45:24 of friendship, to p for the sanctuary,
Is 25: 6 will p for all peoples A feast of rich food
Ez 39:17 for the slaughter I am about to p for you,
39:19 From the slaughter which I will p for you,
45:17 the duty of the prince to p the holocausts,
46: 6 moon he shall p an unblemished young bull,
46:14 With it every morning he shall p as a
46:18 He shall p an inheritance for his sons
48:18 shall p food for the workers of the City.
Dn 11:39 him he shall p with abundant honor;
Mt 6:30 tomorrow, will he not p much more for you,
10: 9 P yourselves with neither gold nor silver
26:53 I can call on my Father to p at a moment's
Lk 12:28 tomorrow, how much more will he p for you,
Jn 4:14 within him, leaping up to p eternal life."
Acts 23:24 Also p horses for Paul's journey,
1Cor 16: 6 that you may p me with what I need for the
2Cor 9:10 bread for the eater will p in abundance;
Phil 1:16 aware that my circumstances p an
Col 4: 3 that God may p us with an opening to
2Thes 1: 7 will p relief to you who are sorely tired,
1Tm 5: 8 If anyone does not p for his own relatives

PROVIDED (53)

Gn 24:32 being unloaded and p with straw and fodder,
38:17 p you leave a pledge until you send it."
Ex 5:18 Straw shall not be p for you,
8:24 p that you do not go too far away and that
12:44 of it, p you have first circumcised him.
21:19 p the other can get up and walk around
Lv 11: 3 p it is cloven-footed and chews the cud.
25:44 p you buy them from among the neighboring
Nm 36: 6 p they marry into a clan of their
Dt 14: 6 p it is cloven-footed and chews the cud.
26:18 and p you keep all his commandments,
28: 9 P that you keep the commandments of the
30: 2 p that you and your children return to the
Jgs 7:16 and p them all with horns and with empty
16:27 and women looked on as Samson p amusement.
19:21 to his house and p fodder for the asses.
1Sm 30:11 He was p with food, which he ate,
2Sm 15: 1 After this Absalom p himself with chariots,
20: 3 He p for them, but had no further
1Kgs 2:19 and a throne was p for the king's mother,
5: 7 p food for King Solomon and for all the
8:21 I have p in it a place for the ark in
8:25 p only that your descendants look to their
2Kgs 12:16 p with the funds to give to the workmen,
21: 8 p that they are careful to observe all I
24:13 of Israel, had p in the temple of the LORD,
1Chr 28:12 He p also the pattern for all else that he
2Chr 1: 4 he had p a place and pitched a tent for it.)
6:16 p only that your descendants look to their
23:18 with rejoicing and song, as David had p.
24: 3 Jehoiada p him with two wives,
26:14 Uzziah p for them—for the entire army
33: 8 p they are careful to observe all that I
Neh 13:31 I also p for the procurement of wood at
2Mc 4:49 crime and p sumptuously for their burial.
12: 3 to embark on boats which they had p.
Ps(s) 68:11 goodness, O God, you p it for the needy.
Wis 14:18 the artisan's ambition p a stimulus.
Sir 39:25 for the good he p from the beginning,
49:15 Even his dead body was p for.
Dn 14: 3 they p for it six barrels of fine flour,
Jon 4: 6 And when the LORD God p a gourd plant,
Mt 21:22 all that you pray for, p you have faith."
Lk 7:44 and you p me with no water for my feet.
Rom 11:22 toward you, p you remain in his kindness;
2Cor 5: 1 we have a dwelling p for us by God,
5: 3 will, p we are found clothed and not naked.
Phil 4:12 go hungry, to be well p for or do without.
1Tm 1: 8 p one uses it in the way law is supposed
2:15 p she continues in faith and love and
6: 6 p one is content with a sufficiency.
1Pt 4:11 is to do it with the strength p by God.
2Pt 1:11 Savior Jesus Christ will be richly p for.

PROVIDENCE (4)

Jb 10:12 me, and your p has preserved my spirit.
Wis 14: 3 But your p, O Father!
17: 2 own roofs as exiles from the eternal p.
Acts 4:28 in your powerful p you planned long ago.

PROVIDENT (1)

Acts 24: 2 made in this nation through your p care.

PROVIDES (10)

Jb 24: 5 The steppe p food for the young among them;
38:41 Who p nourishment for the ravens when
Ps(s) 147: 8 with clouds, who p rain for the earth;
Wis 6: 7 well as the small, and he p for all alike;
13:16 Thus lest it fall down he p for it,
Sir 17:19 But to the penitent he p a way back,
38: 2 wisdom, and the king p for his sustenance.
Rom 3: 5 if our wrongdoing p proof of God's justice,
1Tm 6:17 p us richly with all things for our use.
Heb 7: 5 The law p that the priests of the tribe of

PROVIDING (11)

Ex 16:16 are, each man p for those of his own tent."
Jgs 14: 4 p an opportunity against the Philistines;
1Mc 12:38 by p them with gates and bars.
16:14 of the country and p for their needs,
2Mc 6:21 and urged him to bring meat of his own p,
Wis 16: 2 they craved, by p quail for their food;
Sir 47: 9 p sweet melody for the psalms So that when
Dn 4: 9 and its fruit abundant, p food for all.
4:18 foliage and abundant fruit, p food for all,
Acts 20: 2 p as he went many words of encouragement
1Pt 1:12 They knew by revelation that they were p,

PROVINCE (44)

Ezr 2: 1 These are the inhabitants of the p who
4:10 and elsewhere in the p West-of-Euphrates,
4:17 and elsewhere in the p West-of-Euphrates,
5: 8 p of Judah and the house of the great God:
6: 2 Ecbatana, the stronghold in the p of Media,
7:16 may receive throughout the p of Babylon,
Neh 1: 3 p are in great distress and under reproach.
7: 6 These are the inhabitants of the p who
11: 3 the p who took up residence in Jerusalem.
Est 1:22 to each p in its own script and to each
3:12 royal satraps, the governors of every p,
3:12 to each p in its own script and to each
3:14 every p was published to all the peoples,
8: 9 to each p in its own script and to each
8:11 any nation or p which should attack them,
E: 24 "Every city and p, without exception, that
8:13 p was published among all the peoples,
8:17 and every p and in each and every city,
9:28 generation, by every clan, in every p,
1Mc 3:29 moreover the income from the p was small,
7:20 he handed the p over to Alcimus,
9:69 men who had advised him to invade the p.
10:38 added to Judea from the p of Samaria
10:63 military commander and governor of the p.
11:62 traveled on through the p as far as Damascus.
11:64 them, leaving his brother Simon in the p.
12:25 them, giving them no time to enter his p.
Dn 2:48 made him ruler of the whole p of Babylon
2:49 administrators of the p of Babylon,
3: 1 in the plain of Dura in the p of Babylon.
3:12 made administrators of the p of Babylon:
3:97 Meshach, and Abednego in the p of Babylon.
8: 2 in the fortress of Susa in the p of Elam;
Acts 2: 9 and Cappadocia, Pontus, the p of Asia,
16: 6 preaching the message in the p of Asia.
19:10 that all the inhabitants of the p of Asia,
19:26 but throughout most of the p of Asia,
20:18 the first day I set foot in the p of Asia
21:27 Jews from the p of Asia recognized Paul
23:34 the letter, asked Paul what p he came from,
24:19 the p of Asia are the ones who found me.
25: 1 days after Festus had arrived in the p,
27: 2 bound for ports in the p of Asia,
Rv 1: 4 To the seven churches in the p of Asia;

PROVINCES (37)

1Kgs 20:14 the retainers of the governors of the p.'"
20:15 up the retainers of the governors of the p,
20:17 the governors of the p marched out first,
20:19 of the p with the army following them
Ezr 4:15 which has proved fatal to kings and p,
Est 1: 1 and twenty-seven p from India to Ethiopia
1: 3 the nobles, and the governors of the p.
1:16 throughout the p of King Ahasuerus.
1:22 He sent letters to all the royal p,
2: 3 king appoint commissaries in all the p
2:18 p and bestowing gifts with royal bounty.
3: 8 nations throughout the p of your kingdom,
3:13 were sent by couriers to all the royal p,
B: 1 and twenty-seven p from India to Ethiopia,
4: 3 (Likewise in each of the p,
4:11 of the king and the people of his p know
8: 5 destruction of the Jews in all the royal p.
8: 9 and twenty-seven p from India to Ethiopia:
8:12 spoil throughout the p of King Ahasuerus;
E: 1 to the governors of the p in the hundred
9: 2 cities throughout the p of King Ahasuerus
9: 3 Moreover, all the officials of the p,
9: 4 p that he was continually growing in power.
9:12 must they have done in the other royal p!
9:16 The other Jews, who dwelt in the royal p,
9:20 and far, in all the p of King Ahasuerus.
9:30 and twenty-seven p of Ahasuerus' kingdom.
1Mc 1: 4 a very strong army and conquered p,
3:31 go to Persia and levy tribute on those p,
6: 1 Antiochus was traversing the inland p,
8: 8 Mysia, and Lydia from among their best p.
2Mc 9:25 I made hurried visits to the outlying p
Eccl 2: 8 and gold, and the wealth of kings and p.
Lam 1: 1 among the p has been made a toiling slave.
Dn 3: 2 all the officials of the p to be summoned
3: 3 and all the officials of the p,
11:24 By stealth he shall enter prosperous p and

PROVING (1)

1Thes 1: 3 and Father of the way you are p your faith,

PROVISION (2)

Ps(s) 132:15 I will bless her with abundant p,
Rom 13:14 and make no p for the desires of the flesh.

PROVISIONED (1)

2Sm 19:33 had p the king during his stay in Mahanaim.

PROVISIONS (36)

Gn 6:21 it may serve as p for you and for them."
42:19 and take home p for your starving families.
42:25 sack, and p given them for their journey.
45:21 he supplied them with p for the journey.

45:23 and bread and other *p* for his journey.
Dt 27:26 fails to fulfill any of the *p* of this law!'
Jos 1:11 and instruct the people, 'Prepare your *p,*
9: 4 They chose *p* for a journey, making use
9:11 *p* for the journey and go to meet them.
9:12 home as *p* the day we left to come to you,
9:14 the Israelite princes partook of their *p,*
1Kgs 5:23 furnish the *p* I desire for my household."
20:27 were called to arms and supplied with *p;*
1Chr 12:41 and oxen *p* in great quantity of meal,
2Chr 11:23 and he furnished them with copious *p*
Jdt 2:18 abundant *p* for each man, and much gold
4: 5 stored up *p* in preparation for war.
10: 5 all these *p* she wrapped up and gave to the
12: 3 "But if your *p* give out, where shall we
Est 2: 9 furnished her with cosmetics and *p.*
1Mc 1:35 inside it, storing up weapons and *p,*
6:53 But there were no *p* in the storerooms,
6:53 and the tide-over *p* had been eaten up by
6:57 growing weaker every day, our *p* are scanty,
9:52 and put soldiers in them and stores of *p.*
11:36 none of these *p* shall ever be revoked.
13:21 by way of the desert, and to send them *p.*
13:33 bars, and he stored up *p* in the fortresses.
2Mc 12:14 of their walls and their supply of *p,*
13:25 indignant that they wanted to annul its *p.*
Ps(s) 78:25 even a surfeit of *p* he sent them.
Prv 6: 8 the summer, stores up her *p* in the harvest.
31:14 ships, she secures her *p* from afar.
Dn 14: 8 tell me who it is that consumes these *p,*
Jn 4: 8 had gone off to the town to buy *p.)*
Acts 28:10 set sail they brought us *p* for our needs.

PROVOCATION (6)

1Kgs 2: 5 and put bloodshed without *p* on the belt
2:31 family the blood which Joab shed without *p.*
Jb 17: 2 I am indeed mocked, and, as their *p* mounts,
Prv 27: 3 but a fool's *p* is heavier than both.
Is 3: 8 the LORD, a *p* in the sight of his majesty.
Jer 32:29 poured out to strange gods as a *p* to me.

PROVOCATIONS (1)

2Kgs 23:26 of all the *p* that Manasseh had given,

PROVOKE (17)

Dt 4:25 by this evil done in his sight *p* the LORD,
9:18 LORD and the evil you had done to *p* him.
32:21 idols, I will *p* them with a 'no-people';
1Kgs 14: 9 strange gods and molten images to *p* me;
16:26 causing Israel to sin and to *p* to the LORD,
1Mc 6:34 grapes and mulberries to *p* them to fight.
Jb 12: 6 prosperous, and those who *p* God are secure.
Sir 8:16 *P* no quarrel with a quick-tempered man,
28:11 up, and insistent quarrels *p* bloodshed.
Is 65: 3 own thoughts, People who *p* me continually,
Jer 8:19 [Why do they *p* me with their idols,
25: 6 them, lest you *p* me with your handiwork,
32:30 but *p* me with the works of their hands,
32:32 citizens of Jerusalem, have done to *p* me.
44: 3 because of the evil they did to *p* me,
1Cor 10:22 Do we mean to *p* the Lord to jealous anger?
Col 3: 6 These are the sins which *p* God's wrath.

PROVOKED (25)

Dt 9: 8 At Horeb you so *p* the LORD that he was
9:22 likewise, you *p* the LORD to anger.
31:29 the LORD's sight, and *p* him by your deeds."
32:16 They *p* him with strange gods and angered
32:21 "Since they have *p* me with their 'no-god'
Jgs 2:12 by their worship of these gods *p* the LORD.
1Kgs 14:15 poles for themselves and thus *p* the LORD.
15:30 Israel to commit, by which he *p* the LORD,
21:22 you have *p* me by leading Israel into sin."
2Kgs 17:11 They did evil things that *p* the LORD,
21: 6 in the LORD's sight and *p* him to anger.
21:15 they have done evil in my sight and *p* me
2Chr 33: 6 so that he *p* the LORD with the great evil
Ezr 5:12 fathers *p* the wrath of the God of heaven,
Tb 5:14 Do not be *p* with me, brother, for wanting
Ps(s) 78:41 tempted God and *p* the Holy One of Israel.
106:29 They *p* him by their deeds, and a plague
Prv 24:19 Be not *p* with evildoers, nor envious
Jer 11:17 of Judah, who *p* me by sacrificing to Baal.
25: 7 *p* me with your handiwork to your own harm.
Bar 4: 7 you *p* your Maker with sacrifices to demons,
Ez 8:17 and again and again they have *p* me
16:26 so many times that I was *p* to anger.
Dn 11:11 the stronghold, the king of the south, *p,*
Zec 8:14 harm you when your fathers *p* me to wrath,

PROVOKES (1)

Prv 18: 6 him into strife, and his mouth *p* a beating.

PROVOKING (10)

1Kgs 16: 2 Israel to sin, *p* me to anger by their sins,
16: 7 the LORD, *p* him to anger by his evil deeds,
16:13 and caused Israel to commit, *p* the LORD,
22:54 served and worshiped Baal, thus *p* the LORD,
2Kgs 17:17 evil doing in the LORD's sight, *p* him till,
22:17 *p* me by everything to which they turn
23:19 of Israel had erected, thereby *p* the LORD;
2Chr 34:25 *p* me by every deed that they have
1Mc 13:17 fear of *p* much hostility among the people,
Jer 44: 8 you go on *p* me by the works of your hands,

PROWESS (1)

1Kgs 22:46 of the acts of Jehoshaphat, with his *p,*

PROWL (5)

Ps(s) 55:11 day and night they *p* about upon its walls.
59: 7 snarl like dogs and *p* about the city.
59:15 snarl like dogs and *p* about the city;
Ez 14:15 I were to cause wild beasts to *p* the land,
Mt 7:15 but underneath are wolves on the *p.*

PROWLED (1)

Ez 19: 6 He *p* among the lions,

PROWLING (1)

1Pt 5: 8 Your opponent the devil is *p* like a

PRUDENCE (24)

1Chr 22:12 May the LORD give you *p* and discernment
Jdt 8:29 all the people have recognized your *p,*
2Mc 4:37 the *p* and noble conduct of the deceased.
Jb 12:16 With him are strength and *p;*
Ps(s) 49: 4 *p* shall be the utterance of my heart.
49:21 for all his splendor, if he have not *p,*
Prv 13:16 The shrewd man does everything with *p.*
Wis 6:15 thought of her is the perfection of *p,*
7: 7 Therefore I prayed, and *p* was given me;
7:16 as well as all *p* and knowledge of crafts.
8: 6 And if *p* renders service, who in the world
8: 7 For she teaches moderation and *p,*
8:18 in frequenting her society there is *p,*
8:21 and this, too, was *p,* to know whose is
Sir 1:22 wisdom's treasures is the paragon of *p;*
6:36 If you see a man of *p,* seek him out;
19:18 nor is there *p* in the counsel of sinners.
25: 5 understanding and *p* to the venerable!
44: 3 for their might, Or counselors in their *p,*
Jer 9:23 glory in this, that in his *p* he knows me,
Bar 3: 9 listen and know *p!*
3:14 Learn where *p* is, where strength, where
3:28 They perished for lack of *p,*
Dn 1:20 of wisdom or *p* which the king put to them,

PRUDENT (31)

1Kgs 2: 9 You are a *p* man and will know how to deal
1Chr 26:14 lots for his son Zechariah, a *p* counselor,
Tb 12: 7 A king's secret it is *p* to keep,
12:11 to you, 'A king's secret it is *p* to keep,
Ps(s) 111:10 *p* are all who live by it.
Prv 14:17 fool of himself, but the *p* man is at peace.
15: 5 admonition, but *p* is he who heeds reproof.
15:24 The path of life leads the *p* man upward,
19:14 parents, but a *p* wife is from the LORD.
28: 2 but with a *p* man it knows security.
28:16 The less *p* the prince, the more his deeds
Wis 6:24 is the safety of the world, and a *p* king,
Sir 1: 4 and *p* understanding, from eternity.
10: 1 the government of a *p* man is well ordered.
10:24 When free men serve a *p* slave,
20:26 by his words, a *p* man pleases the great.
21:17 views of a *p* man are sought in an assembly,
21:20 but the *p* man at the most smiles gently.
21:25 the words of the *p* are carefully weighed.
22:17 A resolve that is backed by *p*
33: 3 The *p* man trusts in the word of the LORD,
38: 4 herbs which the *p* man should not neglect;
40:23 guides, but better than either, a *p* wife.
Is 5:21 their own sight, and *p* in their own esteem!
29:14 and the understanding of its *p* men be hid.
Jer 49: 7 in Teman, has counsel perished from the *p,*
Dn 1: 4 wise, quick to learn, and *p* in judgment,
Hos 14:10 let him who is *p* know them.
Am 5:13 Therefore the *p* man is silent at this time,
Acts 6: 3 acknowledged to be deeply spiritual and *p,*
Col 4: 5 Be *p* in dealing with outsiders;

PRUDENTLY (3)

2Chr 11:23 He acted *p,* distributing various of his
Jer 3:15 heart, who will shepherd you wisely and *p.*
Dn 2:14 Then Daniel *p* took counsel with Arioch,

PRUNE (2)

Lv 25: 3 field, and for six years *p* your vineyard,
25: 4 neither sow your field nor *p* your vineyard.

PRUNED (1)

Is 5: 6 it shall not be *p* or hoed, but overgrown

PRUNES (1)

Jn 15: 2 He *p* away every barren branch,

PRUNING (5)

Sg 2:12 earth, the time of *p* the vines has come,
Is 2: 4 plowshares and their spears into *p* hooks;
18: 5 comes the cutting of branches with *p* hooks
Jl 4:10 into swords, and your *p* hooks into spears;
Mi 4: 3 plowshares, and their spears into *p* hooks;

PSALM (2)

Acts 13:33 to what is written in the second *p,*
1Cor 14:26 When you assemble, one has a *p,*

PSALMS (9)

Neh 11:17 of Zabdi, son of Asaph, director of the *p,*
Ps(s) 95: 2 let us joyfully sing *p* to him.
Sir 44: 5 Composers of melodious *p,* or discoursers
47: 9 providing sweet melody for the *p*
Lk 20:42 Does not David himself say in the *p,*
24:44 and the prophets and *p* had to be fulfilled."
Acts 1:20 "It is written in the Book of *P.*
Eph 5:19 another in *p* and hymns and inspired songs.
Col 3:16 gratefully to God from your hearts in *p,*

PSALTERY (4)

Dn 3: 4 of the trumpet, flute, lyre, harp, *p,*
3: 7 of the trumpet, flute, lyre, harp, *p,*
3:10 of the trumpet, flute, lyre, harp, *p,*
3:15 of the trumpet, flute, lyre, harp, *p,*

PSEUDO-HIGH-PRIEST (1)

2Mc 4:13 wickedness of the ungodly *p* Jason,

PSEUDO-PRIESTS (1)

2Kgs 23: 5 He also put an end to the *p* whom the kings

PTOLEMAIS (19)

1Mc 5:15 that the inhabitants of *P,* Tyre, and Sidon,
5:22 and he pursued them to the very gate of *P.*
5:55 his brother was in Galilee opposite *P,*
10: 1 son of Antiochus, came up and took *P.*
10:39 *P* and its confines I give as a present to
10:56 but meet me in *P,* so that we may see
10:57 to *P* in the year one hundred and sixty-two.
10:58 Their wedding was celebrated at *P* with
10:60 So he went with pomp to *P,*
11:22 was furious, and set out immediately for *P.*
11:22 for a conference at *P* as soon as possible.
11:24 to danger by going to the king at *P.*
12:45 rest back home, and then come with me to *P.*
12:48 Then as soon as Jonathan had entered *P,*
13:12 Then Trypho moved from *P* with a large army
2Mc 6: 8 At the suggestion of the citizens of *P,*
13:24 from *P* to the region of the Gerrenes.
13:25 When he came to *P*
Acts 21: 7 our voyage from Tyre we put in at *P,*

PTOLEMY (29)

1Mc 1:18 and with a large fleet, to make war on *P,*
1:18 *P* was frightened at his presence and fled,
3:38 Lysias chose *P,* son of Dorymenes,
10:51 Alexander sent ambassadors to *P,*
10:55 King *P* answered in these words:
10:57 So *P* with his daughter Cleopatra set out
10:58 and *P* gave him his daughter Cleopatra in
11: 2 them to do, since *P* was his father-in-law.
11: 3 But when *P* entered the cities,
11: 8 King *P* took possession of the cities along
11:12 her to Demetrius, *P* broke with Alexander;
11:13 Then *P* entered Antioch and assumed the
11:15 the news, he came to challenge *P* in battle.
11:15 *P* marched out and met him with a strong
11:17 cut off Alexander's head and sent it to *P.*
11:18 But three days later King *P* himself died,
15:16 of the Romans, sends greetings to King *P.*
16:11 *P,* son of Abubus, had been appointed
16:16 had drunk freely, *P* and his men sprang up,
16:18 Then *P* wrote an account of this and sent
16:21 and that *P* had sent men to kill him also.
2Mc 1:10 counselor of King *P* and member of the
4:45 himself on the losing side, promised *P,*
4:46 *P* retired with the king under a colonnade,
8: 8 becoming more frequent, he wrote to *P,*
8: 9 *P* promptly selected Nicanor,
9:29 later withdrew into Egypt, to *P* Philometor.
10: 8 Death of *P.*
10:12 *P,* surnamed Macron, had taken the lead

PTOLEMY'S (1)

1Mc 11:16 King *P* triumph was complete when the Arab

PUAH (4)

Gn 46:13 Tola, *P,* Jashub, and Shimron.
Ex 1:15 whom was called Shiphrah and the other *P,*
Jgs 10: 1 Israel the Issacharite Tola, son of *P,*
1Chr 7: 1 The sons of Issachar were Tola, *P,*

PUBERTY (1)

Ez 16: 7 and developed, you came to the age of *p;*

PUBLIC (49)

Nm 25: 4 and hold a *p* execution of the guilty ones
Dt 24: 5 nor shall any *p* duty be imposed on him.

PUBLIC (cont.)

Jgs 19:15 in the *p* square of the city he had entered,
19:17 the traveler in the *p* square of the city,
19:20 and do not spend the night in the *p* square."
2Sm 21:12 secretly from the *p* square of Beth-shan,
Neh 3: 8 as far as the wall of the *p* square.
Est 4: 6 in the *p* square in front of the royal gate,
C: 27 which rests on my head when I appear in *p*;
6: 9 on the horse in the *p* square of the city,
6:11 had him ride in the *p* square of the city,
1Mc 14:22 recorded the following in the *p* decrees:
14:23 a copy of their words in the *p* archives,
2Mc 3:18 houses in crowds to make *p* supplication,
4:33 evidence of the facts, he made a *p* protest,
10: 8 By *p* edict and decree they prescribed
10:16 *p* prayers asking God to be their ally,
12: 4 this was done by *p* vote of the city.
15: 6 erect a *p* monument of victory over Judas
15:36 By *p* vote it was unanimously decreed never
Jb 30:28 I rise up in *p* to voice my grief.
Prv 5:14 to utter ruin, condemned by the *p* assembly!"
Wis 14:17 made a *p* image of him they wished to honor,
Sir 26: 5 Though false charges in *p*, trial before all
31:24 is miserly with food is denounced in *p*,
41:16 before the *p* assembly, of crime;
42:11 an object of derision in *p* gatherings.
Is 59:14 For truth stumbles in the *p* square,
Jer 5: 1 and observe, Search through her *p* places,
Ez 16:24 a platform and a dais in every *p* place.
16:31 and erecting your dais in every *p* place!
Mt 12:16 them not to make *p* what he had done.
23: 7 of respect in *p* and of being called 'Rabbi.'
Mk 1:45 whole matter freely, making the story *p*.
12:38 robes and accept marks of respect in *p*,
Lk 1:80 when he made his *p* appearance in Israel.
8:39 town making *p* what Jesus had done for him.
11:43 in synagogues and marks of respect in *p*.
20:46 robes, and love marks of respect in *p*,
Jn 7:26 in *p* and they don't say a word to him!
Acts 5:18 apostles and threw them into the *p* jail.
16:37 flogged us in *p* without even a trial,
17: 5 who engaged loafers from the *p* square to
17:17 in the *p* square with ordinary passers-by.
18:28 He was vigorous in his *p* refutation of the
19:19 collected their books and burned them in *p*.
20:20 or from teaching you in *p* or in private.
2Cor 9:12 The administering of this *p* benefit not
Col 2:15 He made a *p* show of them,

PUBLICLY (19)

Lv 20:17 they shall be *p* cut off from their people
24:11 This man quarreled *p* with another
Dt 25: 9 his foot and spit in his face, saying *p*,
Est E: 19 a copy of this letter *p* in every place,
2Mc 6:10 circumcised their children were *p* paraded
Sir 1:28 reveal your secrets and *p* cast you down,
Jer 36: 6 Do you go on the fast day and read *p* in
36:10 *p* read the words of Jeremiah from his book.
36:13 he had heard Baruch read *p* from his book.
36:14 you the scroll you read *p* to the people."
Bar 1:14 read out *p* this scroll which we send you,
Am 4: 5 proclaim *p* your freewill offerings,
Lk 20:26 They were unable to trap him *p* in speech.
Jn 7: 4 to be known *p* keeps his actions hidden.
18:20 "I have spoken *p* to any who would listen.
Acts 12:21 seat on the rostrum and *p* addressed them.
1Tm 5:20 sin, however, are to be *p* reprimanded,
Heb 10:33 you were *p* exposed to insult and trial;
3Jn 1:10 if I come I will speak *p* of what he is

PUBLISH (8)

Ps(s) 145: 7 They *p* the fame of your abundant goodness
Is 48:20 *P* it to the ends of the earth,
Jer 46:14 Announce it in Egypt, *p* it in Migdol,
48:20 *P* it at the Arnon, Moab is ruined!
50: 2 *p* it among the nations; *p* it, hide it not,
Dn 3:99 It has seemed good to me to *p* the signs
Mi 1:10 *P* it not in Gath, weep not at all;

PUBLISHED (6)

Est 1:20 king will issue is *p* throughout his realm,
3:14 in every province was *p* to all the peoples,
8:13 every province was *p* among all the peoples,
9:14 this effect, and the decree was *p* in Susa.
1Mc 1:51 the orders he *p* throughout his kingdom.
Lk 2: 1 In those days Caesar Augustus *p* a decree

PUBLIUS (2)

Acts 28: 7 vicinity of that place was the estate of *P*,
28: 8 It happened that *P*' father was sick in bed,

PUDENS (1)

2Tm 4:21 Eubulus, *P*, Linus, Claudia,

PUFF (1)

Jb 15: 2 airy opinions, or *p* himself up with wind?

PUFFED (2)

2Mc 5:17 *P* up in spirit, Antiochus did not realize
Sir 32: 1 chosen to preside at dinner, be not *p* up,

PUFFED-UP (1)

Ps(s) 101: 5 haughty eyes and *p* heart I will not endure.

PUL (2)

2Kgs 15:19 During his reign, *P*, king of Assyria,
1Chr 5:26 incited against them the anger of *P*,

PULL (16)

Jgs 2: 2 land, and you were to *p* down their altars.
2Sm 11:15 Then *p* back and leave him to be struck
Tb 13:12 all who destroy you and *p* down your walls,
Sir 49: 7 been made a prophet, To root out, *p* down,
Is 22:19 office and *p* you down from your station.
Jer 31:28 watched over them to uproot and *p* down,
Ez 26:11 mighty pillars he shall *p* to the ground.
Mt 9:16 thing he has used to cover the hole will *p*,
12: 1 to *p* off the heads of grain and eat them.
12:11 Will he not take hold of it and *p* it out?
13:28 'Do you want us to go out and *p* them up?'
13:29 *p* up the weeds and you might take the
Mk 2:21 he has used to cover the hole would *p* away
2:23 to *p* off heads of grain as they went along.
Lk 5: 3 to *p* out a short distance from the shore;
12:18 *p* down my grain bins and build larger ones.

PULLED (12)

Gn 19:10 out their hands, *p* Lot inside with them,
37:28 and they *p* Joseph up out of the cistern
Lv 14:40 shall order the infected stones to be *p* out
14:43 once more after the stones have been *p* out
14:45 It shall be *p* down, and all its stones,
Jgs 16:14 he *p* out both the weaver's pin and the web.
Neh 13:25 some of them beaten and their hair *p* out;
1Mc 6: 7 that they had *p* down the Abomination which
Is 33:20 be struck, Whose pegs will never be *p* up,
Mk 5: 4 *p* the chains apart and smashed the fetters.
Acts 3: 7 took him by the right hand and *p* him up.
16:26 open and everyone's chains were *p* loose.

PULLEY (1)

Eccl 12: 6 and the broken *p* falls into the well,

PULLING (1)

Lk 6: 1 His disciples were *p* off grain-heads,

PULLS (1)

Ez 17: 9 will wither when he *p* it up by the roots?

PULVERIZE (1)

Is 27: 9 He shall *p* all the stones of the altars

PULVERIZED (1)

2Kgs 23:12 He *p* them and threw the dust into the

PUNISH (80)

Ex 5: 3 he will *p* us with pestilence or the sword."
32:34 me to punish, I will *p* them for their sin."
Lv 26:16 I will *p* you with terrible woes
1Sm 15: 2 'I will *p* what Amalek did to Israel when
2Sm 24:17 *P* me and my kindred."
1Kgs 8:32 the wicked and *p* him for his conduct,
11:39 I will *p* David's line for this, but not
1Chr 12:18 may the God of our fathers see and *p* you."
21: 7 displeased God, who began to *p* Israel.
Tb 3: 3 *P* me not for my sins, nor for my
Jdt 16:17 in the day of judgment he will *p* them:
1Mc 7: 7 let him *p* them and all their supporters."
15:21 that he may *p* them according to their law."
2Mc 1:28 *P* those who tyrannize over us and
6:13 a sign of great kindness to *p* sinners
6:15 he may not have to *p* us more severely later,
Jb 13:26 me, and *p* in me the faults of my youth.
34:33 more," Would you then say that God must *p*,
42: 8 I will accept, not to *p* you severely.
Ps(s) 5:11 *P* them, O God; let them fall by their own
10:15 *p* their wickedness; let them not survive.
38: 2 O LORD, in your anger *p* me not,
59: 6 Arise; *p* all the nations; have no pity
89:33 I will *p* their crime with a rod and their
Wis 12:15 power to *p* one who has incurred no blame.
12:22 our enemies with a thousand blows you *p*,
Sir 39:28 There are storm winds created to *p*,
46: 1 To *p* the enemy and to win the inheritance
Is 10:12 I will *p* the utterance of the king of
13:11 Thus I will *p* the world for its evil and
24:21 *p* the host of the heavens in the heavens,
26:21 to *p* the wickedness of the earth's
27: 1 LORD will *p* with his sword that is cruel,
57: 6 Should I decide not to *p* these things?
Jer 2:19 chastises you, your own infidelities *p* you.
5: 9 Shall I not *p* them for these things?
5:29 Shall I not *p* these things?
9: 8 things, says the LORD, shall I not *p* them?
10:24 *P* us, O LORD, but with equity, not in
11:22 I am going to *p* them.
14:10 their guilt, and will *p* their sins.
21:14 I will *p* you, says the LORD, as your
23: 2 but I will take care to *p* your evil deeds.
23:34 LORD," I will *p* that man and his house.
25:12 I will *p* the king of Babylon and the
27: 8 Babylon, I will *p* that nation with sword,
29:32 says the LORD, I will therefore *p* Shemaiah,
30:20 I will *p* all his oppressors.
36:31 I will *p* him and his descendants and his
44:13 Thus will I *p* those who live in Egypt,
44:29 the LORD, that I will *p* you in this place.
46:25 I will *p* Amon of Thebes,
49: 8 destruction upon Esau when I come to *p* him.
50:18 I will *p* the king of Babylon and his land,
50:31 day has come, the time for me to *p* you.
51:44 I will *p* Bel in Babylon, and make him
51:47 coming when I will *p* the idols of Babylon;
51:52 says the LORD, when I will *p* her idols,
Lam 4:22 wickedness, O daughter Edom, he will *p*,
Ez 23:45 But just men shall *p* them with the
Hos 1: 4 for in a little while I will *p* the house
2:15 I will *p* her for the days of the Baals,
4: 9 I will *p* them for their ways,
4:14 Am I then to *p* your daughters for harlotry,
8:13 remember their guilt and *p* their sins;
9: 9 remember their iniquity and *p* their sins.
12: 3 he shall *p* Jacob for his conduct,
Am 3: 2 Therefore I will *p* you for all your crimes.
3:14 On the day when I *p* Israel for his crimes,
Jon 4: 2 to anger, rich in clemency, loathe to *p*.
Zep 1: 8 slaughter feast I will *p* the princes,
1: 9 I will *p*, on that day, all who leap over
1:12 I will *p* the men who thicken on their lees,
Zec 10: 3 the shepherds, and I will *p* the leaders;
Mt 24:51 He will *p* him severely and settle with him
Lk 12:46 He will *p* him severely and rank him among
Acts 4:21 no way to *p* them because of the people,
2Cor 10: 6 We are ready to *p* disobedience in anyone
Jude 1: 9 He simply said, "May the Lord *p* you."

PUNISHED (37)

Gn 42:21 we are being *p* because of our brother.
Ex 21:20 slave dies under his hand, he shall be *p*.
21:21 for a day or two, he is not to be *p*,
Lv 19:20 they shall be *p* but not put to death,
22:16 they bring down guilt that must be *p*;
Jos 9:20 be *p* for the oath we have sworn to them."
1Sm 25:39 but has *p* Nabal for his own evil deeds."
2Kgs 15:16 At that time, Menahem *p* Tappuah,
15:16 He *p* them even to ripping open all the
Jdt 11:10 For our people are not *p*, nor does
1Mc 9:26 them to Bacchides, who *p* and derided them.
2Mc 1:17 be our God, who has thus *p* the wicked!
Jb 33:27 did wrong, yet he has not *p* me accordingly.
Prv 11:31 If the just man is *p* on earth, how much
21:11 When the arrogant man is *p*, the simple
Wis 3: 4 For if before men, indeed, they be *p*,
11: 5 were *p* they in their need were benefited.
11: 8 they then had how you *p* their adversaries.
11:16 *p* by the very things through which he sins.
12:14 confront you on behalf of those you have *p*.
12:20 *p* them with such solicitude and pleading,
14:10 thing made shall be *p* with its contriver.
16: 1 they were fittingly *p* by similar creatures,
16: 9 they deserved to be *p* by such means;
16:16 know you were *p* by the might of your arm,
18: 8 For when you *p* our adversaries,
Sir 23:21 a man will be *p* in the streets of the city;
Is 24:22 and after many days they will be *p*.
26:14 For you have *p* and destroyed them,
Jer 30:14 as an enemy would strike, *p* you cruelly;
44:13 in Egypt, just as I *p* Jerusalem with sword,
50:18 his land, as once I *p* the king of Assyria;
51: 5 of guilt to be *p* by the Holy One of Israel.
Lam 1: 5 The LORD has *p* her for her many sins.
Ez 14:10 inquirer and the prophet shall be *p* alike,
23:10 for women, for they *p* her grievously.
2Cor 6: 9 *p*, but not put to death; sorrowful,

PUNISHES (5)

2Mc 6:14 measure of their sins before he *p* them;
Jb 35:15 you have done otherwise, God's anger *p*,
Ps(s) 7:12 just judge is God, a God who *p* day by day.
Sir 14: 6 he *p* his own miserliness.
Lam 3:32 Though he *p*, he takes pity,

PUNISHING (6)

Ex 32:12 relent in *p* your people.
34: 7 but *p* children and grandchildren to the
Lv 18:25 defiled, I am *p* it for its wickedness,
Nm 14:18 but *p* children to the third and fourth
Jdt 7:28 who is *p* us for our sins and those of our
Ez 25:17 of vengeance on them, *p* them furiously.

PUNISHMENT (73)

Gn 4:13 "My *p* is too great to bear.
19:15 will be swept away in the *p* of the city."
Ex 20: 5 inflicting *p* for their fathers' wickedness
32:14 So the LORD relented in the *p* he had
Lv 26:28 you with sevenfold fiercer *p* for your sins,
Nm 21: 6 In *p* the LORD sent among the people saraph
Jos 22:31 the Israelites free from *p* by the LORD."
2Chr 24:24 So *p* was meted out to Joash.
Ezr 7:26 upon him, whether death or corporal *p*,

Jdt 2:10 guard them for me till the day of their *p*.
7:15 Thus you will render them dire *p* for their
Est E: 18 who governs all, brought just *p* upon him.
1Mc 14:45 these prescriptions shall be liable to *p*.
2Mc 4:38 the Lord rendered him the *p* he deserved.
4:48 sacred vessels, quickly suffered unjust *p*.
6:26 for the time being, I avoid the *p* of men,
8:11 little did he dream of the *p* that was to
9: 6 a fit *p* for him who had tortured the
9:18 But since God's *p* had justly come upon him,
Jb 37:13 of the earth, whether for *p* or mercy,
Prv 15:10 *p* is in store for the man who goes astray;
Wis 3:10 shall receive a *p* to match their thoughts,
12:26 But they who took no heed of *p* which was
16: 2 Instead of this *p*, you benefited
16:24 grows tense for *p* against the wicked,
19: 4 might fill out the torments of their *p*,
19:15 but what *p* was to be theirs since they
Sir 5: 3 for the LORD will exact the *p*.
16:12 Great as his mercy is his *p*;
23:24 and her *p* will extend to her children;
33:27 and for a wicked slave, *p* in the stocks.
Is 10: 3 What will you do on the day of *p*,
26:16 O LORD, oppressed by your *p*,
30:32 the LORD will bring down on him in *p*,
66:15 burning heat and his *p* with fiery flames.
Jer 6: 6 Woe to the city marked for *p*;
6:15 in their time of *p* they shall go down,
8:12 in their time of *p* they shall go down,
10:15 they will perish in their time of *p*.
11:23 the men of Anathoth, the year of their *p*.
17: 1 Sin and *P* upon the tablets of their hearts.
23:12 the year of their *p*, says the LORD.
44:29 my threats of *p* for you shall be fulfilled,
46:21 ruin comes upon them, the time of their *p*.
48:44 things upon Moab in the year of their *p*,
50:27 their day has come, the time of their *p*.
51:18 work, that will perish in their time of *p*.
Lam 4: 6 The *p* of the daughter of my people is
Ez 14:10 Each shall receive *p* for his sin,
Hos 9: 7 They have come, the days of *p*!
Jl 2:13 rich in kindness, and relenting in *p*.
Mi 7: 4 your *p* has come;
Hb 1:12 O Rock, you have readied him for *p*!
Zec 14:19 This shall be the *p* of Egypt,
14:19 and the *p* of all the nations that do not
Mt 25:46 to eternal *p* and the just to eternal life."
Acts 22: 5 I would arrest back to Jerusalem for *p*.
Rom 3: 5 "Is not God unjust when he inflicts *p*?"
13: 5 to escape *p* but also for conscience' sake.
2Cor 2: 6 The *p* already inflicted by the majority on
2Thes 1: 8 "with flaming power he will inflict *p*
1Tm 3: 6 incur the *p* once meted out to the devil.
Heb 2: 2 and disobedience received its due *p*,
10:29 Do you not suppose that a much worse *p* is
12:25 For if the Israelites did not escape *p*
12:25 how much greater *p* will be ours if we turn
1Pt 2:14 he commissions for the *p* of criminals
2Pt 2: 9 *p* of the wicked up to the day of judgment.
1Jn 4:18 And since fear has to do with *p*.
Jude 1: 7 us, as they undergo a *p* of eternal fire.
Rv 18:10 for fear of the *p* inflicted on her,
18:15 for fear of the *p* inflicted on her.
18:20 God has exacted *p* from her on your account.

PUNISHMENTS (13)

Dt 5: 9 inflicting *p* for their fathers' wickedness
2Mc 7:36 shall receive just *p* for your arrogance.
Ps(s) 149: 7 vengeance on the nations, *p* on the peoples;
Wis 19:13 And the *p* came upon the sinners only after
Ez 5: 8 *p* in your midst while the nations look on.
5:10 I will inflict *p* upon you and scatter all
11: 9 over to foreigners, and inflict *p* upon you.
14:21 though I send Jerusalem my four cruel *p*,
16:41 inflict *p* on you while many women look on.
28:22 when I inflict *p* upon it and use it to
28:26 They shall dwell secure while I inflict *p*
30:14 set fire to Zoan, and inflict *p* on Thebes.
30:19 Thus will I inflict *p* on Egypt,

PUNON (2)

Nm 33:42 out from Zalmonah, they camped at *P*.
33:43 Setting out from *P*, they camped at Oboth.

PUPIL (4)

1Chr 25: 8 equally, young and old, master and *p* alike.
Sir 3:24 Where the *p* of the eye is missing,
Mt 10:24 "No *p* outranks his teacher,
10:25 The *p* should be glad to become like his

PUR (3)

Est 3: 7 the twelfth year of King Ahasuerus, the *p*,
9:24 to destroy them and had cast the *p*,
9:26 have been named Purim after the word *p*.

PURAH (2)

Jgs 7:10 go down to the camp with your aide *P*.
7:11 his aide *P* to the outposts of the camp.

PURCHASE (17)

Gn 23:18 was conveyed to Abraham by *p* in the
Ex 21: 2 When you *p* a Hebrew slave,
Lv 22:11 But a slave whom a priest acquires by *p* or
25:15 last jubilee shall you *p* the land from him;
Dt 2: 6 You shall *p* from them with silver the food
2Kgs 12:13 and for the *p* of the wood and hewn stone
22: 6 and for the *p* of wood and hewn stone for
2Chr 1:16 would acquire them by *p* from Cilicia,
1Mc 13:49 the country and back for the *p* of food;
Jb 28:15 Solid gold cannot *p* it,
Prv 31:16 She picks out a field to *p*;
Sg 8: 7 Were one to offer all he owns to *p* love,
Jer 32: 7 relative, have the first right of *p*."
32:11 on the scales, I accepted the deed of *p*,
32:12 This deed of *p* I gave to Baruch,
32:14 both the sealed and the open deed of *p*,
32:16 After giving the deed of *p* to Baruch,

PURCHASED (6)

Gn 49:32 in it that had been *p* from the Hittites."
Lv 27:22 one he had *p* and not a part
27:24 owner of this land from whom it had been *p*.
1Kgs 10:28 Cilicia, where the king's agents *p* them.
1Cor 6:20 You have been *p*, and at a price!
Rv 5: 9 you *p* for God men of every race and tongue,

PURCHASER (3)

Lv 25:28 the possession of the *p* until the jubilee,
25:30 in perpetuity to the *p* and his descendants;
25:50 With his *p* he shall compute the years from

PURCHASING (1)

Tb 1:13 so that I became *p* agent for all his needs.

PURE (80)

Ex 25:11 Plate it inside and outside with *p* gold,
25:17 shall then make a propitiatory of *p* gold,
25:24 Plate it with *p* gold and make a molding of
25:29 *p* gold you shall make its plates and cups,
25:31 shall make a lampstand of *p* beaten gold
25:36 form but a single piece of *p* beaten gold.
25:38 shears and trays, must be of *p* gold.
25:39 Use a talent of *p* gold for the lampstand
28:14 of gold, as well as two chains of *p* gold,
28:22 "when the chains of *p* gold,
28:36 make a plate of *p* gold and engrave on it,
30: 3 and its horns you shall plate with *p* gold.
30:34 these are *p* frankincense in equal parts;
30:35 is to be salted and so kept *p* and sacred.
31: 8 the *p* gold lampstand with all its
37: 6 The propitiatory was made of *p* gold,
37:11 It was plated with *p* gold,
37:16 for pouring libations, were of *p* gold.
37:17 The lampstand was made of *p* beaten gold
37:22 formed but a single piece of *p* beaten gold.
37:23 shears and trays, were made of *p* gold.
37:24 A talent of *p* gold was used for the
37:26 and its horns were plated with *p* gold;
37:29 prepared in their *p* form by a perfumer.
39:15 Chains of *p* gold,
39:25 bells of *p* gold were also made and put
39:30 diadem was made of *p* gold and inscribed,
39:37 the *p* gold lampstand with its lamps set up
Lv 24: 4 shall be set up on the *p* gold lampstand,
24: 6 pile, on the *p* gold table before the LORD.
24: 7 On each pile put some *p* frankincense,
Nm 5:28 has not defiled herself, but is still *p*,
1Kgs 5:25 and twenty thousand measures of *p* oil.
6:21 the interior of the temple with *p* gold.
7:49 the lampstands of *p* gold,
7:50 bowls, cups, and fire pans of *p* gold;
10:21 of the Forest of Lebanon were of *p* gold.
2Kgs 2:22 the water has stayed *p* even to this day,
1Chr 28:16 the *p* gold to be used for the forks and
2Chr 3: 4 He overlaid its interior with *p* gold.
4:20 the lampstands and their lamps of *p* gold
4:22 bowls, cups and firepans of *p* gold.
9:20 of the Forest of Lebanon were of *p* gold;
13:11 they display the showbread on the *p* table,
Tb 8:15 you, O God, with every holy and *p* blessing!
13:16 gold, and their battlements with *p* gold.
2Mc 13: 8 altar with its *p* fire and ashes
Jb 11: 4 "My teaching is *p*,
Ps(s) 19:10 The fear of the LORD is *p*,
21: 4 you placed on his head a crown of *p* gold.
Prv 8:19 is better than gold, yes, than *p* gold,
15:26 but the *p* speak what is pleasing to him.
16: 2 the ways of a man may be *p* in his own eyes,
22:11 The LORD loves the *p* of heart;
30:12 There is a group that is *p* in its own eyes,
Sg 5:11 His head is *p* gold;
Wis 7:23 they be intelligent, *p* and very subtle.
7:25 a *p* effusion of the glory of the Almighty:
14:24 longer safeguard either lives or *p* wedlock;
Is 13:12 I will make mortals more rare than *p* gold,
25: 6 and choice wines, juicy, rich food and *p*,
Dn 2:32 The head of the statue was *p* gold,
Hb 1:13 Too *p* are your eyes to look upon evil,
Mal 1:11 sacrifice to my name, and a *p* offering;
2Cor 2:17 speak in Christ's name, *p* in motivation,
Phil 1:17 *p* motives but as an intrigue against me,
4: 8 deserves respect, all that is honest, *p*,
1Tm 1: 5 is the love that springs from a *p* heart,
5:22 Keep yourself *p*.
Heb 10:22 and our bodies washed in *p* water.
Jas 1: 2 count it *p* joy when you are involved in
1:27 make for *p* worship without stain
1Pt 2: 2 Be as eager for milk as newborn babies *p*
1Jn 3: 3 on him keeps himself pure, as he is *p*.
Rv 14: 4 are *p* and follow the Lamb wherever he goes.
15: 6 The angels were dressed in *p* white linen,
19:14 and dressed in fine linen, *p* and white.
21:18 the city was of *p* gold,
21:21 and the streets of the city were of *p* gold,

PUREBRED (1)

Gn 49:11 the vine, his *p* ass to the choicest stem.

PURELY (1)

1Cor 15:32 beasts at Ephesus for *p* human motives,

PUREST (2)

2Chr 4:21 lamps and gold tongs [this was the *p* gold],
Ps(s) 19:11 precious than gold, than a heap of *p* gold;

PURGE (15)

Ex 29:36 you *p* the altar in making atonement for it;
Dt 13: 6 Thus shall you *p* the evil from your midst.
17: 7 Thus shall you *p* the evil from your midst.
17:12 Thus shall you *p* the evil from your midst.
19:13 but *p* from Israel the stain of shedding
19:19 Thus shall you *p* the evil from your midst.
21: 9 and you shall *p* from your midst the guilt
21:21 Thus shall you *p* the evil from your midst,
22:21 Thus shall you *p* the evil from your midst.
22:22 Thus shall you *p* the evil from your midst.
22:24 Thus shall you *p* the evil from your midst.
24: 7 Thus shall you *p* the evil from your midst.
Jgs 20:13 to death and thus *p* the evil from Israel."
2Chr 34: 3 *p* Judah and Jerusalem of the high places,
Ez 22:15 lands, so that I may *p* your uncleanness.

PURGED (5)

Lv 16:19 *p* of the defilements of the Israelites.
Dt 26:13 'I have *p* my house of the sacred portion
2Chr 34: 5 Thus he *p* Judah and Jerusalem.
Prv 30:12 in its own eyes, yet is not *p* of its filth.
Is 6: 7 your wickedness is removed, your sin *p*."

PURGES (2)

Dt 32:43 of his servants and *p* his people's land.
Is 4: 4 And *p* Jerusalem's blood from her midst

PURIFICATION (24)

Lv 12: 4 till the days of her *p* are fulfilled.
12: 6 "When the days of her *p* for a son or for
14: 2 the victim of leprosy at the time of his *p*.
14:11 The priest who performs the *p* ceremony
14:23 of his *p* he shall bring them to the priest,
14:32 who has insufficient means for his *p*."
15:13 he shall wait seven days for his *p*.
Nm 6: 9 shall shave his head on the day of his *p*,
Neh 12:45 ministry of *p* (as did the singers
2Mc 1:18 We shall be celebrating the *p* of the
1:36 called the liquid nephthar, meaning *p*,
2:16 celebrate the feast of the *p* of the temple,
2:19 his brothers, of the *p* of the great temple,
10: 5 Chislev, the *p* of the temple took place.
10: 7 had brought about the *p* of his own Place.
Sir 34:25 he has bathed, what did he gain by the *p*?
Ez 43:23 When you have finished the *p*,
Jn 3:25 A controversy about *p* arose between John's
11:55 went up to Jerusalem for Passover *p*.
Acts 21:24 you and join with them in their rite of *p*;
21:26 the rite of *p* with them the next day.
21:26 the day when the period of *p* would be over,
24:18 completing the rites of *p* without any crowd
1Pt 1: 2 to Jesus Christ and *p* with his blood.

PURIFIED (48)

Lv 12: 4 days more in becoming *p* of her blood;
12: 5 sixty-six days in becoming *p* of her blood.
14: 4 he shall order the man who is to be *p*,
14: 7 times the man to be *p* from his leprosy.
14: 7 When he has thus *p* him,
14: 8 The man being *p* shall then wash his
14:11 shall place the man who is being *p*,
14:18 shall put on the head of the man being *p*.
14:25 tip of the right ear of the man being *p*,
14:31 before the LORD for the man who is to be *p*.
15:28 seven days, and only then is she to be *p*.
Nm 19:19 thus *p* on the seventh day,
19:20 *p* shall be cut off from the community,
31:23 it must also be *p* with lustral water.
2Sm 11: 4 she was just *p* after her monthly period.
2Kgs 2:21 "Thus says the LORD, 'I have *p* this water.
2Chr 5:11 priest who were present had *p* themselves
Ezr 6:20 one of whom had *p* himself for the occasion,

PURIFIED (cont.)

Neh 12:30 Levites first *p* themselves, then they *p*
Jdt 4: 3 and the temple been *p* from profanation.
12: 9 Then she returned *p* to the tent,
16:18 when they were *p*,
1Mc 4:41 in the citadel, while he *p* the sanctuary.
4:43 these *p* the sanctuary and carried away the
4:48 interior of the temple and *p* the courts.
13:47 he *p* the houses in which there were idols.
2Mc 2:18 us from great perils and has *p* his Place.
12:38 they *p* themselves according to custom and
14:36 this house, which has been so recently *p*."
Ps(s) 51: 9 me of sin with hyssop, that I may be *p*;
Prv 25: 4 silver, and it comes forth perfectly *p*;
Sir 51:20 *p* my hands in cleanness I attained to her.
Ez 24:13 I would have *p* you, and you refused to be *p*
24:13 not be *p* until I wreak my fury on you.
39:16 Thus the land shall be *p*.
43:26 the altar, and it shall be *p* and dedicated.
Dn 8:14 then the sanctuary shall be *p*."
11:35 the rest may be tested, refined, and *p*,
12:10 Many shall be refined, *p*,
Mk 7: 2 disciples eating meals without having *p*—
Acts 10:15 God has *p* you are not to call unclean."
11: 9 God has *p* you are not to call unclean.'
15: 9 but *p* their hearts by means of faith also.
Heb 9:22 to the law almost everything is *p* by blood,
9:23 of the heavenly models be *p* in this way,
1Pt 1:22 By obedience to the truth you have *p*

PURIFY (30)

Gn 35: 2 then *p* yourselves and put on fresh clothes.
Lv 14:49 To *p* the house,
14:52 Thus shall he *p* the house with the bird's
Nm 8: 6 from among the Israelites and *p* them.
8: 7 is what you shall do to them to *p* them.
8: 7 wash their clothes, and so *p* themselves.
8:15 *p* them and offer them as a wave offering;
8:21 and made atonement for them to *p* them.
19:12 he shall *p* himself with the water on the
19:12 But if he fails to *p* himself on the third
19:13 Everyone who fails to *p* himself after
31:19 *p* yourselves on the third
31:20 You shall also *p* every article of cloth,
Neh 13: 9 Then I gave orders to *p* the chambers,
13:22 *p* themselves and to go and watch the gates,
1Mc 4:36 go up to *p* the sanctuary and rededicate it."
Is 52:11 *P* yourselves,
66:17 and *p* themselves to go to the groves,
Ez 36:33 When I *p* you from all your crimes,
39:12 To *p* the land,
39:14 who lie unburied, so as to *p* the land.
43:20 you shall *p* it and make atonement for it.
43:22 to *p* the altar as was done with the bull.
45:18 bull as a sacrifice to *p* the sanctuary.
Zep 3: 9 will change and *p* the lips of the peoples,
Zec 13: 1 a fountain to *p* from sin and uncleanness.
Mal 3: 3 [silver], and he will *p* the sons of Levi,
Lk 2:22 to *p* them according to the law of Moses,
2Cor 7: 1 let us *p* ourselves from every defilement
Jas 4: 8 *p* your hearts,

PURIFYING (5)

Lv 8:15 horns around the altar, thus *p* the altar.
2Mc 10: 3 After *p* the temple, they made a new altar.
Mal 3: 3 He will sit refining and *p* [silver],
Mk 7: 5 instead take food without *p* their hands?"
Eph 5:26 *p* her in the bath of water by the power of

PURIM (5)

Est 9:26 days have been named *P* after the word pur.
9:28 These days of *P* were never to fall into
9:29 full authority this second letter about *P*,
9:31 these days of *P* which Mordecai the Jew and
9:32 for *P* and was recorded in the book.

PURITY (6)

1Mc 14:36 temple and inflict grave injury on its *p*.
Wis 7:24 and pervades all things by reason of her *p*.
1Tm 4:12 example of love, faith, and *p* to believers.
5: 2 younger women as sisters, with absolute *p*.
2Tm 2:22 those who call on the Lord in *p* of heart.
1Pt 3: 2 observe the reverent *p* of your way of life.

PURPLE (63)

Ex 25: 4 violet, *p* and scarlet yarn;
26: 1 twined and of violet, *p* and scarlet yarn,
26:31 a veil woven of violet, *p* and scarlet yarn,
26:36 *p* and scarlet yarn and of fine linen
27:16 *p* and scarlet yarn and of fine linen
28: 5 violet, *p* and scarlet yarn and fine linen.
28: 6 thread and of violet, *p* and scarlet yarn,
28: 8 gold thread, of violet, *p* and scarlet yarn,
28:15 *p* and scarlet yarn on cloth of fine linen
28:33 *p* and scarlet yarn and fine linen twined,
35: 6 violet, *p* and scarlet yarn;
35:23 happened to have violet, *p* or scarlet yarn,
35:25 *p* and scarlet yarn and fine linen thread,
35:35 *p* and scarlet yarn and fine linen thread,
36: 8 on them with violet, *p* and scarlet yarn.
36:35 was woven of violet, *p* and scarlet yarn,
36:37 was made of violet, *p* and scarlet yarn,
38:18 *p* and scarlet yarn and of fine linen
38:23 *p* and scarlet yarn and of fine linen.
39: 1 *p* and scarlet yarn were woven the service
39: 2 *p* and scarlet yarn and of fine linen
39: 3 *p* and scarlet yarn into an embroidered
39: 5 gold thread, of violet, *p* and scarlet yarn,
39: 8 *p* and scarlet yarn on cloth of fine linen
39:24 *p* and scarlet yarn and of fine linen
39:29 twined and of violet, *p* and scarlet yarn,
Nm 4:13 ashes, they shall spread a *p* cloth over it.
Jgs 8:26 the *p* garments worn by the kings of Midian,
2Chr 2: 6 in gold, silver, bronze and iron, in *p*,
2:13 and iron, with stone and wood, with *p*,
3:14 He made the veil of violet, *p*,
1Mc 8:14 a crown or wore *p* as a display of grandeur.
10:20 also sent him a *p* robe and a crown of gold.
10:62 garments and to be clothed in royal *p*;
10:64 and the *p* with which he was clothed,
11:58 drink from gold cups, to dress in royal *p*,
14:43 right to wear royal *p* and gold ornaments.
14:44 in royal *p* or wear an official gold brooch.
2Mc 4:38 stripped Andronicus of his *p* robe,
Prv 31:22 fine linen and *p* are her clothing.
Sg 3:10 its roof of gold, Its seat of *p* cloth.
7: 6 your hair is like draperies of *p*;
Sir 6:30 her bonds, your *p* cord.
Jer 4:30 doomed, what do you mean by putting on *p*,
10: 9 of the smelter, Clothed with violet and *p*—
Lam 4: 5 brought up in *p* now cling to the ash heaps.
Bar 6:11 but though they are wrapped in *p* clothing,
6:71 rotting of the *p* and the linen upon them,
Ez 23: 6 the Assyrians, warriors dressed in *p*,
27: 7 *P* and scarlet from the coasts of Elishah
27:16 were your products, exchanging garnets, *p*,
Dn 5: 7 men of Babylon, "shall be clothed in *p*,
5:16 what it means, you shall be clothed in *p*,
5:29 of Belshazzar they clothed Daniel in *p*,
Mk 15:17 They dressed him in royal *p*,
15:20 mocking him, they stripped him of the *p*,
Lk 16:19 rich man who dressed in *p* and linen
Jn 19: 2 around his shoulders a cloak of royal *p*.
19: 5 the crown of thorns and the *p* cloak,
Acts 16:14 in *p* goods from the town of Thyatira.
Rv 17: 4 The woman was dressed in *p* and scarlet and
18:12 fine linen and *p* garments,
18:16 dressed in fine linen and *p* and scarlet,

PURPOSE (48)

Gn 21:29 "What is the *p* of these seven ewe lambs
37:22 His *p* was to rescue him from their hands
Ex 21:13 a place which I will set apart for this *p*.
1Kgs 5:19 I *p* to build a temple in honor of the LORD,
1Chr 12:34 thousand men rallying with a single *p*.
17:19 servant's sake and in keeping with your *p*,
22: 7 it was my *p* to build a house myself for
28: 2 It was my *p* to build a house of repose
2Chr 26:18 who have been consecrated for this *p*.
Tb 8: 7 not because of lust, but for a noble *p*.
Est F: 7 For this *p* he arranged two lots:
1Mc 6:20 for which *p* he constructed catapults and
12: 2 to Sparta and other places for the same *p*.
2Mc 3: 8 but in reality to carry out the king's *p*.
4:19 right, but should be used for some other *p*.
Jb 10:13 I know that they are your *p*:
35:16 Yet Job to no *p* opens his mouth,
42: 2 and that no *p* of yours can be hindered.
Sir 13: 7 While it serves his *p* he will beguile you,
32:17 reproof and distorts the law to suit his *p*.
39:21 "What is the *p* of this?"
Is 26: 3 A nation of firm *p* you keep in peace;
44:10 who forms a god, or casts an idol to no *p*,
46:10 plan shall stand, I accomplish my every *p*.
Jer 12:13 they have tired themselves out to no *p*;
Lk 13:32 and on the third day my *p* is accomplished.
Jn 13:18 my *p* here is the fulfillment of Scripture:
19:24 (The *p* of this was to have the Scripture
Acts 2:23 delivered up by the set *p* and plan of God;
5:38 *p* or activity is human in its origins,
21: 5 but to no *p*.
Rom 1:21 themselves through speculating to no *p*,
9:21 for a lofty *p* and another for a humble one?
13: 4 without *p* that the ruler carries the sword;
1Cor 14:26 everything is done with a constructive *p*.
2Cor 1:24 Domineering over your faith is not my *p*.
Gal 2:21 through the law, then Christ died to no *p*!
3: 4 such remarkable experiences all to no *p*—
3: 4 if indeed they were to no *p*?
Eph 3:11 of heaven, in accord with his age-old *p*,
6:22 I have sent him to you for the very *p* of
Phil 2:16 not run the race in vain or work to no *p*.
Col 3:22 not with the *p* of attracting attention and
4: 8 I am sending him to you for this *p*,
Ti 1: 5 My *p* in leaving you in Crete was that you
Heb 6:17 evidence that his *p* would not change,
Jas 4: 5 suppose it is to no *p* that Scripture says,
1Jn 1: 4 our *p* in writing you this is that our joy

PURPOSELY (1)

Acts 9:21 Did he not come here *p* to apprehend such

PURPOSES (4)

Jos 18: 4 they shall describe for *p* of inheritance.
2Kgs 12: 5 "All the funds for sacred *p* that are
Jb 17:11 are at an end, the cherished *p* of my heart.
Wis 15: 7 that serve for clean *p* and their opposites,

PURSE (8)

Dt 14:25 for money and, with the *p* of money in hand,
Prv 1:14 your lot with us, we shall all have one *p*—
Sir 18:33 and a winebibber with nothing in your *p*.
Is 46: 6 a *p* and weigh out silver on the scales;
Lk 22:35 without *p* or traveling bag or sandals,
22:36 however, the man who has a *p* must carry it;
Jn 12: 6 He held the *p*,
13:29 idea that, since Judas held the common *p*,

PURSES (3)

Is 3:22 the court dresses, wraps, cloaks, and *p*;
Mk 6: 8 bag, not a coin in the *p* in their belts.
Lk 12:33 Get *p* for yourselves that do not wear out,

PURSUE (30)

Ex 14: 4 Pharaoh so obstinate that he will *p* them.
15: 9 boasted, "I will *p* and overtake them;
Dt 19: 6 *p* the homicide and overtake him
Jos 2: 5 to *p* them immediately to overtake them."
8:16 in the city had been called out to *p* them.
10:19 *P* your enemies,
1Sm 25:29 rises to *p* you and to seek your life,
26:18 "Why does my lord *p* his servant?
30: 8 of the LORD, "Shall I *p* these raiders?
2Sm 20: 6 Take your lord's servants and *p* him,
1Chr 14:14 "Do not try to *p* them,
Jdt 14: 4 whole territory of Israel will *p* them
1Mc 9:48 enemy did not *p* them across the Jordan.
Jb 13:25 a wind-driven leaf, or *p* a withered straw?
Ps(s) 7: 6 Let the enemy *p* and overtake me;
71:11 *p* and seize him,
83:16 So *p* them with your tempest and rout them
Wis 19: 2 their way, they would regret it and *p* them.
Is 51: 1 Listen to me, you who *p* justice,
Jer 9:15 I will send the sword to *p* them until I
29:18 I will *p* them with sword,
49:37 I will send the sword to *p* them until I
Lam 3:66 *P* them in wrath and destroy them from
Ez 5: 2 strew in the wind, and *p* it with the sword.
5:12 and I will *p* them with the sword.
12:14 every direction, and *p* them with the sword.
35: 6 of blood, and blood, I swear, shall *p* you.
44:10 Israel strayed from me to *p* their idols,
Hos 8: 3 the enemy shall *p* them.
2Tm 2:22 from youthful passions and *p* integrity,

PURSUED (59)

Gn 14:15 defeated them, and *p* them as far as Hobah,
31:23 he *p* him for seven days until he caught up
35: 5 about, so that no one *p* the sons of Jacob.
Ex 14: 8 made Pharaoh that he *p* the Israelites
14: 9 The Egyptians, then, *p* them;
Dt 11: 4 in the water of the Red Sea as they *p* you,
Jos 8:24 All the inhabitants of Ai who had *p* the
10:10 and *p* them down the Beth-horon slope,
11: 8 defeated them and *p* them to Greater Sidon,
24: 6 the Egyptians *p* your fathers to the Red
Jgs 4:16 *p* the chariots and the army as far as
7:23 and from all Manasseh and they *p* Midian.
7:25 Then they *p* Midian and carried the heads
8:12 He *p* them and took the two kings of Midian,
20:43 and were now *p* to a point east of Gibeah,
1Sm 7:11 forth from Mizpah and *p* the Philistines,
14:22 were fleeing, *p* them in the rout.
23:25 and *p* David into the desert below Maon.
31: 2 Philistines *p* Saul and his sons closely,
2Sm 20:10 Then Joab and his brother Abishai *p* Sheba,
22:38 I *p* my enemies and destroyed them,
2Kgs 9:27 Jehu *p* him, shouting, "Kill him too!"
14:19 But he was *p* to Lachish and killed there.
17:15 The vanity they *p*, they themselves became:
25: 5 But the Chaldean army *p* the king and
2Chr 13:19 Abijah *p* Jeroboam and took cities from him:
14:12 and those with him *p* them as far as Gerar,
17: 3 the ways his father had *p* in the beginning,
25:27 But they *p* him to Lachish and put him to
Tb 8: 3 *p* him there and bound him hand and foot.
1Mc 3: 5 He *p* the wicked,
3:24 He *p* Seron down the descent of Beth-horon
4: 9 Red Sea, when Pharaoh *p* them with an army.
4:15 *p* as far as Gazara and the plains of Judea,
5:22 he *p* them to the very gate of Ptolemais.
5:60 and were *p* to the frontiers of Judea,
7:45 The Jews *p* them a day's journey,
9:15 and *p* them as far as the mountain slopes.
10:49 army of Demetrius fled, Alexander *p* him,
11:73 *p* the enemy as far as their camp in Kadesh,
12:30 Then Jonathan *p* them,
15:11 *P* by Antiochus,
16: 9 John *p* them until Cendebeus reached Kedron,
2Mc 8:25 When they had *p* the enemy for some time,
Ps(s) 18:38 I *p* my enemies and overtook them,
Eccl 7:25 I sought and *p* wisdom and reason,

Wis 2: 4 dispersed like a mist *P* by the sun's rays
11:20 *p* by retribution and winnowed out by your
16:16 *P* by unwonted rains and hailstorms and
19: 3 away with entreaty, they *p* as fugitives.
Sir 40: 6 mind's eye sees, like a fugitive being *p*;
Jer 39: 5 the Arabah, but the Chaldean army *p* them,
50:17 A stray sheep was Israel that lions *p*;
52: 8 But the Chaldean army *p* the king and
Lam 3:43 You veiled yourself in wrath and *p* us,
Am 1:11 Because he *p* his brother with the sword,
Acts 26:11 them that I *p* them even to foreign cities.
Gal 2: 2 sure the course I was pursuing, or had *p*,
Rv 12:13 *p* the woman who had given birth to the boy.

PURSUERS (11)

Jos 2: 7 But the *p* set out along the way to the
2:16 to them, "that your *p* may not find you.
2:22 they stayed three days until their *p*,
8:20 toward the desert now turned on their *p*;
Neh 9:11 Their *p* you hurled into the depths,
1Mc 2:33 the *p* said to them.
12:51 As their *p* saw that they were ready to
Ps(s) 7: 2 save me from all my *p* and rescue me,
35: 3 and block the way in the face of my *p*;
Is 30:16 —Not so swift as your *p*.
Lam 4:19 Our *p* were swifter than eagles in the air,

PURSUES (16)

Lv 26:17 will take to flight though no one *p* you.
26:36 as if from the sword, though no one *p* them;
Jos 20: 5 Though the avenger of blood *p* him,
2Sm 24:13 your enemy three months while he *p* you,
Ps(s) 143: 3 For the enemy *p* me;
Prv 11:19 but he who *p* evil does so to his death.
11:27 he who *p* evil will have evil befall him.
13:21 Misfortune *p* sinners,
15: 9 LORD, but he loves the man who *p* virtue.
21:21 He who *p* justice and kindness will find
28: 1 The wicked man flees although no one *p* him;
Sir 14:22 Who *p* her like a scout,
31: 5 for he who *p* wealth is led astray by it.
Is 41: 3 He *p* them,
Na 1: 8 and his enemies he *p* with darkness.
Hb 2: 9 to him who *p* evil gain for his household,

PURSUING (10)

Dt 28:45 come upon you, *p* you and overwhelming you,
Jgs 8: 5 exhausted, and I am *p* Zebah and Zalmunna,
1Sm 24:15 Whom are you *p*?
2Sm 2:22 "Stop *p* me!
2:28 *p* Israel no farther and fighting no more.
1Kgs 20:20 The Arameans fled with Israel *p* them,
Ps(s) 35: 6 with the angel of the LORD *p* them.
38:21 repay evil for good harass me for *p* good.
Hos 12: 2 Ephraim chases the wind, ever *p* the gale.
Gal 2: 2 leaders, to make sure the course I was *p*,

PURSUIT (33)

Gn 14:14 in his house, and went in *p* as far as Dan.
Ex 14:10 Egyptians were on the march in *p* of them.
14:23 of Egyptians23The Egyptians followed in *p*;
Jos 8:17 in this *p* of Joshua and the Israelites,
Jgs 1: 6 They set out in *p*,
4:22 Then when Barak came in *p* of Sisera,
1Sm 14:36 go down in *p* of the Philistines by night,
14:37 "Shall I go down in *p* of the Philistines?
14:46 that Saul gave up the *p* of the Philistines,
17:52 went in *p* of the Philistines to the
17:53 their return from the *p* of the Philistines,
23:28 Saul interrupted his *p* of David and went
24: 2 returned from the *p* of the Philistines,
30: 8 The LORD answered him, "Go in *p*,
30:10 continued the *p* with four hundred men,
2Sm 2:19 turning neither right nor left in his *p*.
2:21 But Asahel would not desist from his *p*.
2:24 Abishai, however, continued the *p* of Abner.
2:26 the people to stop the *p* of their brothers?"
2:27 from the *p* of their brothers until morning."
2:30 Joab, after interrupting the *p* of Abner,
17: 1 men, and be off in *p* of David tonight.
18:16 turned back from the *p* of the Israelites,
20: 7 from Jerusalem to campaign in *p* of Sheba,
20:13 everyone went on after Joab in *p* of Sheba,
1Kgs 22:33 not the king of Israel, gave up *p* of him.
2Chr 18:32 king of Israel and gave up their *p* of him.
1Mc 4:16 Judas and the army returned from the *p*,
15:39 Meanwhile the king went in *p* of Trypho.
2Mc 8:26 that reason they could not continue the *p*.
12:20 over each cohort, and went in *p* of Timothy;
12:23 Judas pressed the *p* vigorously,
1Cor 7:34 Lord, in *p* of holiness in body and spirit.

PURSUITS (6)

Dt 33:18 "Rejoice, O Zebulun, in your *p*,
Ps(s) 39: 7 like vapor only are his restless *p*;
Prv 12:11 but he who follows idle *p* is a fool.
28:19 from idle *p* a man has his fill of poverty.
Is 58: 3 on your fast day you carry out your own *p*,
58:13 from following your own *p* on my holy day;

PUSH (3)

2Kgs 4:27 Gehazi came near to *p* her away,
Ez 34:21 Because you *p* with side and shoulder,
Phil 3:13 what lies behind but *p* on to what is ahead.

PUSHED (8)

Jgs 16:30 He *p* hard,
1Sm 13:23 had *p* forward to the pass of Michmash.
2Sm 11:23 but we *p* them back to the entrance of the
1Mc 13:43 a siege machine, *p* it up against the city,
Sir 13:20 a poor man trips he is *p* down by a friend.
Acts 7:27 was wronging his neighbor *p* Moses aside.
19:33 crowd Alexander, as the Jews *p* him forward.
21: 8 The next day we *p* on and came to Caesarea.

PUSHES (2)

Nm 35:20 "If a man *p* another out of hatred,
35:22 if a man *p* another accidentally and not

PUSHING (3)

Zec 5: 8 *p* the leaden cover into the opening.
Mk 3:10 afflictions kept *p* toward him to touch him.
5:24 a large crowd followed, *p* against Jesus.

PUSTULE (1)

Lv 13: 2 has on his skin a scab or *p* or blotch

PUSTULES (1)

Lv 14:56 as well as for scabs, *p* and blotches,

PUT (985)

Gn 3:12 "The woman whom you *p* here with me
3:15 I will *p* enmity between you and the woman,
3:22 he must not be allowed to *p* out his hand
4:15 So the LORD *p* a mark on Cain,
5:29 ground that the LORD has *p* under a curse,
6:13 to *p* an end to all mortals on earth;
6:14 gopherwood, *p* various compartments in it,
6:16 *P* an entrance in the side of the ark,
10: 6 Cush, Mizraim, *P*, and Canaan.
15: 6 Abram *p* his faith in the LORD,
19: 9 But his guests *p* out their hands,
21:15 So she *p* the child down under a shrub,
22: 1 these events, God *p* Abraham to the test.
22: 9 and *p* him on top of the wood on the altar.
24: 2 *P* your hand under my thigh,
24: 9 So the servant *p* his hand under the thigh
24:22 ten shekels, which he *p* on her wrists.
24:37 My master *p* me under oath, saying:
24:47 So I *p* the ring on her nose and the
26:11 or his wife shall forthwith be *p* to death."
28:11 he *p* it under his head and lay down to
28:18 the stone that he had *p* under his head,
29: 3 Then they would *p* the stone back again
30:36 Then he *p* a three days' journey between
30:40 which he did not *p* with Laban's flock.
30:42 animals he would not *p* the rods there.
31: 6 what effort I *p* into serving your father;
31:17 to *p* his children and wives on camels,
31:34 the idols, *p* them inside a camel cushion,
32:17 *p* these animals in charge of his servants,
33:15 "Let me at least *p* at your disposal some
34:26 *p* Hamor and his son Shechem to the sword,
35: 2 purify yourselves and *p* on fresh clothes.
37:34 rent his clothes, *p* sackcloth on his loins,
38:19 her shawl and *p* on her widow's garb again.
38:28 giving birth, one infant *p* out his hand;
39: 4 he *p* him in charge of his household and
39: 5 From the moment that he *p* him in charge of
39:22 The chief jailer *p* Joseph in charge of all
40: 3 and he *p* them in custody in the house of
40:11 into his cup, and *p* it in Pharaoh's hand."
40:15 which I should have been *p* into a dungeon."
41:10 he *p* me and the chief baker in custody in
41:33 and *p* him in charge of the land of Egypt.
41:42 signet ring and *p* it on Joseph's finger.
41:42 linen and *p* a gold chain about his neck.
42:30 "spoke to us sternly and *p* us in custody
42:37 *P* him in my care,
43:11 *P* some of the land's best products in your
43:12 that was *p* back in the mouths of your bags;
43:18 money *p* back in our bags the first time,
43:22 not know who *p* the first money in our bags."
43:23 must have *p* treasures in your bags for you.
44: 1 *p* each man's money in the mouth of his bag.
44: 2 youngest one's bag *p* also my silver goblet,
46: 5 and the sons of Israel *p* their father and
47: 5 may *p* them in charge of my own livestock."
47:14 Canaan, and he *p* it in Pharaoh's palace.
47:18 there is nothing left to *p* at my lord's
47:29 *p* your hand under my thigh as a sign of
48:14 *p* out his right hand and laid it on the
Ex 2:15 of the affair and sought to *p* him to death.
3:22 clothing to *p* on your sons and daughters.
4: 4 "Now *p* out your hand,"
4: 4 So he *p* out his hand and laid hold of it,
4: 6 said to him, *P* your hand in your bosom."
4: 6 He *p* it in his bosom,
4: 7 "Now, *p* your hand back in your bosom."
4: 7 Moses *p* his hand back in his bosom,
4:15 to him, then, and *p* the words in his mouth.
4:21 all the wonders I have *p* in your power.
5:21 have *p* a sword in their hands to slay us."
15:25 regulations for them, *p* them to the test.
16:23 is left *p* away and keep for the morrow."
16:24 When they *p* it away for the morrow,
16:33 "Take an urn and *p* an omer of manna in it.
17: 2 Why do you *p* the LORD to a test?"
17:12 they *p* a rock in place for him to sit on.
18:25 men from all Israel and *p* them in charge
19:12 the mountain, he must be *p* to death.
20:20 only to test you and *p* his fear upon you,
21:12 a man a mortal blow must be *p* to death.
21:14 him even from my altar and *p* him to death.
21:15 his father or mother shall be *p* to death.
21:16 has him when caught, shall be *p* to death.
21:17 his father or mother shall be *p* to death.
21:18 not mortally, but enough to *p* him in bed,
21:29 but its owner also must be *p* to death.
22:18 lies with an animal shall be *p* to death.
23: 7 and the just you shall not *p* to death,
24: 6 half of the blood and *p* it in large bowls;
25:11 *p* a molding of gold around the top of it.
25:14 These poles you are to *p* through the
25:16 *p* the commandments which I will give you.
25:21 *p* the commandments which I will give you.
26:11 bronze clasps and *p* them into the loops,
26:35 table, which is to be *p* on the north side.
27: 5 *P* it down around the altar,
27: 7 These poles are to be *p* through the rings,
28:26 Make two other rings of gold and *p* them on
28:30 decision you shall *p* the Urim and Thummim,
29: 3 spread with oil, and *p* them in a basket.
29: 6 *P* the miter on his head,
29:12 your finger *p* it on the horns of the altar.
29:17 *p* them with the pieces and with the head.
29:20 Some of its blood you shall take and *p* on
29:24 *p* into the hands of Aaron and his sons,
30: 3 *P* a gold molding around it.
30: 4 the molding you shall *p* gold rings,
30:18 tent and the altar, and *p* water in it.
30:36 Grind some of it into fine dust and *p* this
31:14 Whoever desecrates it shall be *p* to death.
31:15 on the sabbath day shall be *p* to death.
32:27 *P* your sword on your hip,
34:33 with them, he *p* a veil over his face.
34:35 so he would again *p* the veil over his face
35: 2 does work on that day shall be *p* to death.
36:12 Fifty loops were thus *p* on one inner sheet,
37: 2 and a molding of gold was *p* around it.
37: 3 rings were cast and *p* on its four supports,
37: 5 these were *p* through the rings on the
37:11 and a molding of gold was *p* around it.
37:12 a handbreadth high was also *p* around it,
37:26 and a molding of gold was *p* around it.
38: 7 The poles were *p* through the rings on the
39:19 *p* on the two lower ends of the breastpiece,
39:25 pure gold were also made and *p* between
40: 3 *P* the ark of the commandments in it,
40: 5 *P* the golden altar of incense in front of
40: 6 *P* the altar of holocausts in front of the
40: 7 tent and the altar, and *p* water in it.
40: 8 *p* the curtain at the entrance of the court.
40:18 set up its boards, *p* in its bars,
40:19 and *p* the covering on top of the tent,
40:20 the commandments and *p* them in the ark;
40:22 He *p* the table in the meeting tent,
40:29 He *p* the altar of holocausts in front of
40:30 and altar, and *p* water in it for washing.
Lv 1: 7 have *p* some burning embers on the altar
2: 1 pour oil on it and *p* frankincense over it.
2:15 offering you shall *p* oil and frankincense.
4: 7 The priest shall also *p* some of the blood
4:18 He shall also *p* some of the blood on the
4:25 offering on his finger and *p* it on the horns
4:30 blood on his finger and *p* it on the horns
4:34 offering on his finger and *p* it on the horns
5:11 He shall not *p* oil or frankincense on it,
6: 4 off these garments and *p* on other garments,
6: 5 morning the priest shall *p* firewood on it.
7:24 by wild beasts may be *p* to any other use,
8: 7 Then he *p* the tunic on Aaron,
8: 9 Thummim in it, and *p* the miter on his head,
8:13 them with sashes, and *p* turbans on them,
8:15 he *p* it on the horns around the altar,
8:23 and *p* it on the tip of Aaron's right ear,
8:24 and he *p* some of the blood on the tips of
8:27 He then *p* all these things into the hands
9: 9 blood and *p* it on the horns of the altar.
10: 1 incense on the fire they had *p* in them,
11:32 must be *p* in water and remain unclean
14:14 and *p* it on the tip of the man's right ear,
14:17 *p* some on the tip of the man's right ear,
14:18 *p* on the head of the man being purified.
14:25 and *p* it on the tip of the right ear of
14:28 also *p* on the tip of the man's right ear,
14:29 hand the priest shall *p* on the man's head.
14:34 if I *p* a leprous infection on any house of
14:42 and *p* in the place of the old stones,
16: 4 the linen sash and *p* on the linen miter.
16: 4 he shall not *p* them on until he has first
16:13 the LORD he shall *p* incense on the fire,

PUT (cont.)

16:18 shall *p* it on the horns around the altar,
16:21 and so *p* them on the goat's head.
16:23 he had *p* on when he entered there.
16:24 sacred place, he shall *p* on his vestments,
17:11 blood, I have made you *p* it on the altar,
19:14 *p* a stumbling block in front of the blind,
19:19 and do not *p* on a garment woven with two
19:20 they shall be punished but not *p* to death,
20: 2 offspring to Molech shall be *p* to death.
20: 4 to Molech, and fail to *p* him to death,
20: 9 his father or mother shall be *p* to death;
20:10 and the adulteress shall be *p* to death.
20:11 man and his stepmother shall be *p* to death;
20:12 both of them shall be *p* to death;
20:13 be *p* to death for their abominable deed;
20:15 an animal, the man shall be *p* to death,
20:16 let them both be *p* to death;
20:27 shall be *p* to death by stoning;
22:22 do not *p* such an animal on the altar as an
24: 7 On each pile *p* some pure frankincense,
24:16 the name of the LORD shall be *p* to death.
24:16 *p* to death for blaspheming the LORD'S name.
24:17 of any human being shall be *p* to death;
24:21 whoever slays a man shall be *p* to death.
26: 8 will *p* a hundred of your foes to flight,
27:29 they must be *p* to death.
Nm 1:51 who comes near it shall be *p* to death.
3:10 layman who comes near shall be *p* to death."
3:38 layman who came near was to be *p* to death.
4: 6 these they shall *p* a cover of tahash skin,
4: 6 They shall then *p* the poles in place.
4: 7 cloth and *p* on it the plates and cups,
4: 8 They shall then *p* the poles in place.
4:11 They shall then *p* the poles in place.
4:14 *p* all the utensils with which it is served:
4:14 skin over this, and *p* the poles in place.
5:15 pour oil on it nor *p* frankincense over it,
5:17 he shall meanwhile *p* some holy water,
5:23 The priest shall *p* these imprecations in
5:25 before the LORD, shall *p* it near the altar,
6:18 and *p* it in the fire that is under the
7: 5 that these things may be *p* to use in the
14:22 and who nevertheless have *p* me to the test
15:35 to Moses, "This man shall be *p* to death;
15:38 *p* tassels on the corners of their garments,
16: 7 *p* fire in them and place incense in them
16:17 shall take his own censer, *p* incense in it,
16:18 incense on the fire they had *p* in them,
17:11 your censer, *p* fire from the altar in it,
17:23 had sprouted and *p* forth not only shoots,
17:25 *P* back Aaron's staff in front of the
18: 7 layman who draws near shall be *p* to death."
19:17 the sin offering shall be *p* in a vessel,
20:26 his garments and *p* them on his son Eleazar;
20:28 his garments and *p* them on his son Eleazar.
23: 5 he had *p* an utterance in Balaam's mouth,
23:16 and having *p* an utterance in his mouth,
25:11 that is why I did not *p* an end to the
31:23 tin and lead, you shall *p* into the fire,
31:23 stand fire you shall *p* into the water.
31:54 and *p* it in the meeting tent as a memorial
35:12 so that a homicide shall not be *p* to death
35:16 he is a murderer and shall be *p* to death.
35:17 he is a murderer and shall be *p* to death.
35:18 he is a murderer and shall be *p* to death.
35:21 he shall be *p* to death as a murderer.
35:31 he must be *p* to death.
Dt 2:16 "When at length death had *p* an end to all
2:25 This day I will begin to *p* a fear and
3:28 shall *p* them in possession of the land
6:16 "You shall not *p* the LORD,
7:24 you, till you have *p* an end to them.
13: 6 or that dreamer shall be *p* to death,
13:16 you shall *p* the inhabitants of that city
16: 9 sickle is first *p* to the standing grain.
17: 6 no one shall be *p* to death on the
18:18 and will *p* my words into his mouth;
20:13 your hand, *p* every male in it to the sword;
21: 3 *p* to work as a draft animal under a yoke,
21:22 *p* to death and his corpse hung on a tree,
22: 5 man, nor shall a man *p* on a woman's dress;
22: 8 a new house, *p* a parapet around the roof;
22:12 "You shall *p* twisted cords on the four
23:15 you and to *p* your enemies at your mercy,
23:25 you wish, but do not *p* them in your basket.
23:26 do not *p* a sickle to your neighbor's grain.
24: 7 sell him, the kidnaper shall be *p* to death.
24:16 shall not be *p* to death for their children,
24:16 his own guilt shall a man be *p* to death.
28:20 "The LORD will *p* a curse on you,
28:48 He will *p* an iron yoke on your neck,
31: 7 *p* them in possession of their heritage.
31:26 "Take this scroll of the law and *p* it
32:30 or two men *p* ten thousand to flight,
33: 8 For you *p* him to the test at Massah and
Jos 1:18 you give him, he shall be *p* to death.
2: 3 *P* out the visitors who have entered your
6:19 shall be *p* in the treasury of the LORD."
7:11 have deceitfully *p* them in their baggage.
8:24 and *p* to the sword those inside the city.
9: 4 Gibeon *p* into effect a device of their own.
10:24 *p* your feet on the necks of these kings."
10:24 forward and *p* their feet upon their necks.
10:28 captured and *p* to the sword at that time.
10:30 *p* it to the sword with every person there,
10:32 *p* it to the sword with every person in it,
10:37 They *p* it to the sword with its king,
10:39 They *p* them to the sword and fulfilled the
11:12 with their cities and *p* them to the sword,
11:14 but the people they *p* to the sword,
11:17 All their kings he captured and *p* to death.
13:22 *p* to the sword also the soothsayer Balaam,
18: 3 "How much longer will you *p* off taking
19:47 which they captured and *p* to the sword.
24: 7 he *p* darkness between your people and the
24:23 *p* away the strange gods that are among you
Jgs 1:25 the city, which they then *p* to the sword;
3: 4 These served to *p* Israel to the test,
4:15 And the LORD *p* Sisera and all his chariots
6:31 for him, he shall be *p* to death by morning.
7: 3 Gideon *p* them to this test on the mountain,
9: 2 *P* this question to all the citizens of
9:23 God *p* bad feelings between Abimelech and
9:26 citizens of Shechem *p* their trust in him,
16:21 and he was *p* to grinding in the prison.
16:26 *P* me where I may touch the columns that
18:19 *p* your hand over your mouth.
18:27 they *p* them to the sword and destroyed
20:13 that we may *p* them to death and thus purge
20:37 it, and *p* the whole city to the sword.
21: 5 Mizpah should be *p* to death without fail.
21:10 and *p* those who lived there to the sword,
21:16 woman in Benjamin has been *p* to death."
Ru 3: 3 then *p* on your best attire and go down to
4: 4 to *p* in your claim for it if you wish to
4: 4 He answered, "I will *p* in my claim."
4: 6 *P* in a claim yourself in my stead,
1Sm 4:13 news, which *p* the whole city in an uproar.
7: 3 *p* away your foreign gods and your
7: 4 *p* away their Baals and Ashtaroth,
9:23 portion I gave you and told you to *p* aside."
11:12 over the men and we will *p* them to death."
11:13 say, "No man is to be *p* to death this day,
14:27 his father had *p* the people under oath,
14:28 father *p* the people under a strict oath,
15: 8 but on the rest of the people he *p* into
15:18 'Go and *p* the sinful Amalekites under a
17:40 *p* them in the pocket of his shepherd's bag.
17:49 David *p* his hand into the bag and took out
18: 5 So Saul *p* him in charge of his soldiers,
22:19 *p* the priestly city of Nob to the sword,
23: 7 "God has *p* him in my grip.
26:12 the LORD had *p* them into a deep slumber.
31:10 They *p* his armor in the temple of Astarte,
2Sm 1:14 afraid to *p* forth your hand to desecrate
4:10 in Ziklag I seized and *p* to death the man
12:31 iron axes, or *p* to work at the brickmold.
13:17 was his attendant and said, *P* her outside,
13:18 *p* her out and barred the door after her,
13:19 Tamar *p* ashes on her head and tore the
13:28 I say to you, 'Kill Amnon,' *p* him to death.
13:33 So let not my lord the king *p* faith in the
14: 2 *P* on mourning apparel and do not anoint
14: 7 We must *p* him to death for the life of his
14:32 If I am guilty, let him *p* me to death."
15:14 upon us and *p* the city to the sword."
17:25 Absalom had *p* Amasa in command of the army
18: 2 David then *p* a third part of the soldiers
19: 6 you have *p* all your servants to shame
19:22 "Shimei must be *p* to death for this.
21: 1 because he *p* the Gibeonites to death."
21: 4 our place to *p* any man to death in Israel."
21: 9 they were *p* to death during the first days
22:15 He sent forth arrows to *p* them to flight;
22:23 to me, and his statutes I *p* not from me;
22:41 My enemies you *p* to flight before me and
23:23 David *p* him in command of his bodyguard.
1Kgs 2: 5 and *p* bloodshed without provocation on the
2: 8 LORD that I would not *p* him to the sword.
2:24 this day shall Adonijah be *p* to death."
2:26 die, I will not *p* you to death this time,
2:35 *p* Zadok the priest in place of Abiathar.
5:17 should *p* these enemies under the soles
5:19 'It is your son whom I will *p* upon your
8: 9 tablets which Moses had *p* there at Horeb,
10:17 and he *p* them in the hall of the Forest
10:24 the wisdom which God had *p* in his heart.
11:15 the slain, *p* to death every male in Edom.
11:28 he *p* him in charge of the entire labor
12: 4 "Your father *p* on us a heavy yoke.
12:10 to lighten the yoke your father *p* on them:
12:11 Whereas my father *p* a heavy yoke on you,
12:14 "My father *p* on you a heavy yoke,
12:29 And he *p* one in Bethel, the other in Dan.
13:29 body of the man of God and *p* it on the ass,
18:42 earth, and *p* his head between his knees.
19: 1 he had *p* all the prophets to the sword.
19:10 altars, and *p* your prophets to the sword.
19:14 altars, and *p* your prophets to the sword.
20:24 their posts and *p* prefects in their places.
21:27 and *p* on sackcloth over his bare flesh.
22:23 the LORD has *p* a lying spirit in the
22:27 *P* this man in prison and feed him scanty
22:30 into battle, but you *p* on your own clothes,"
2Kgs 2:20 bowl," Elisha said, "and *p* salt into it."
3:10 three kings to *p* them in the grasp of Moab."
3:13 together to *p* them in the grasp of Moab."
4:38 he said to his servant, *P* the large pot on,
7:17 The king *p* in charge of the gate the
10: 7 seventy of them, *p* their heads in baskets,
10:25 *p* them to the sword and cast them out.
11:12 and *p* the crown and the insignia upon him.
11:16 the royal palace, where she was *p* to death.
12:10 The priests who guarded the entry would *p*
13:16 the king of Israel, *P* your hand on the bow."
14: 6 of the murderers he did not *p* to death,
14: 6 shall not be *p* to death for their children,
14: 6 children be *p* to death for their fathers;
16: 9 inhabitants to Kir and *p* Rezin to death.
17:18 the LORD *p* them away out of his sight.
17:23 the LORD *p* Israel away out of his sight as
18: 5 He *p* his trust in the LORD,
18:23 horses if you can *p* riders on them.
19: 7 I am about to *p* in him such a spirit that,
19:28 I will *p* my hook in your nose and my bit
20: 1 *P* your house in order,
23: 5 He also *p* an end to the pseudo-priests
23:27 will I *p* out of my sight as I did Israel.
24: 3 inexorably *p* them out of his sight
25:21 them struck down and *p* to death in Riblah,
1Chr 1: 8 descendants of Ham were Cush, Mesraim, *P*,
5:20 them because they had *p* their trust in him.
8: 8 he had *p* away his wives Hushim and Baara.
8:13 they *p* the inhabitants of Gath to flight.
10:10 armor they *p* in the house of their gods,
11:25 David *p* him in charge of his bodyguard.
19: 6 had *p* themselves in bad odor with David,
28:15 use to which each lampstand was to be *p*.
29:17 that you *p* hearts to the test and that you
2Chr 1: 5 he *p* in front of the LORD'S Dwelling on
5:10 two tablets which Moses *p* there on Horeb,
9:16 *p* in the hall of the Forest of Lebanon.
9:23 the wisdom which God had *p* in his heart.
10:11 Whereas my father *p* a heavy yoke on you,
11:11 fortifications and *p* commanders in them,
15:13 the God of Israel, was to be *p* to death,
17: 2 and *p* garrisons in the land of Judah and
18:22 So now the LORD has *p* a lying spirit in
18:26 *P* this man in prison and feed him scanty
18:29 disguised, but you *p* on your own clothes."
21: 4 he *p* to the sword all his brothers and
22: 9 brought him to Jehu, who *p* him to death.
22:11 and *p* him and his nurse in a bedroom.
22:11 sight, so that she did not *p* him to death.
23:14 not *p* her to death in the LORD'S temple."
23:15 of the palace, they *p* her to death there.
23:21 Athaliah had been *p* to death by the sword.
24: 8 *p* outside the gate of the LORD'S temple.
25: 4 but he did not *p* their children to death,
25: 4 shall not be *p* to death for their children,
25: 4 his own guilt shall a man be *p* to death."
25:27 him to Lachish and *p* him to death there.
28:15 they clothed them, *p* sandals on their feet,
32:14 nations which my fathers *p* under the ban
33:24 him and *p* him to death in his own house.
35: 3 *P* the holy ark in the house built by
36: 7 LORD and *p* them in his palace in Babylon.
Neh 4: 5 midst, kill them, and *p* an end to the work."
5: 9 and *p* an end to the derision of our
5:10 Let us *p* an end to this usury!
7: 1 and the Levites] were *p* in charge of them.
7: 5 When my God had *p* it into my mind to
7:69 His Excellency *p* into the treasury one
Tb 1:19 all about me and wanted to *p* me to death,
2: 4 the street and *p* him in one of the rooms,
5: 3 his copy I *p* with the money.
6: 6 had cut the fish open, he *p* aside the gall,
12:14 the dead, I was sent to *p* you to the test.
Jdt 2:23 He devastated *P* and Lud,
2:27 and *p* all their youths to the sword.
8: 5 She *p* sackcloth about her loins and wore
8:12 you should have *p* God to the test this day,
8:27 *p* them in the crucible to try their hearts,
9: 2 You *p* a sword into his hand to take
10: 3 and *p* on the festive attire she had worn
10: 4 sandals for her feet, and *p* on her anklets,
12:15 Thereupon she proceeded to *p* on her
13:10 to her maid, who *p* it into her food pouch;
16: 4 to burn my land, *p* my youths to the sword,
16: 8 and *p* on a linen robe to beguile him.
Est A:14 and, upon their confession, *p* to death.
A:15 Mordecai, too, *p* them into writing.
4: 1 his garments, *p* on sackcloth and ashes,
4: 4 she sent garments for Mordecai to *p* on,
C:13 she *p* on garments of distress and mourning.
C:13 all her festive adornments were *p* aside,
C:24 *P* in my mouth persuasive words in the
5: 1 Esther *p* on her royal garments and stood
8: 2 *p* Mordecai in charge of the house of Haman.
1Mc 1: 2 captured fortresses, and *p* kings to death.
1: 9 after his death they all *p* on royal crowns,
1:50 command of the king should be *p* to death.
1:60 their children circumcised were *p* to death,
2:14 sons tore their garments, *p* on sackcloth,
2:47 They *p* to flight the arrogant,
3: 3 and *p* on his breastplate like a giant.
4:20 They saw that their army had been *p* to
4:51 They also *p* loaves on the table

6: 5 the land of Judah had been *p* to flight;
6:14 and *p* him in charge of his whole kingdom.
6:24 they have *p* to death as many of us as they
8:14 none of them *p* on a crown or wore purple
9: 8 we can *p* up a good fight against them."
9:51 In each he *p* a garrison to oppose Israel.
9:52 and *p* soldiers in them and stores of
9:53 *p* them in custody in the citadel
9:61 in the mischief and *p* them to death.
10:21 Jonathan *p* on the sacred vestments in the
10:32 that he may *p* in it such men as he shall
10:70 laughed at and *p* to shame on your account.
10:72 were twice *p* to flight in their own land.
10:82 phalanx, overwhelmed it and *p* it to flight.
11:15 with a strong force and *p* him to flight.
11:66 possession of it, and *p* a garrison there.
12:44 "Why have you *p* all your soldiers to so
14: 3 him to Arsaces, who *p* him in prison.
14:29 and his brothers have *p* themselves in
16: 7 two corps and *p* his cavalry between them,
16: 8 Cendebeus and his army were *p* to flight;
16:22 him, he had them arrested and *p* to death,
2Mc 2: 5 a room in a cave in which he *p* the tent,
2:21 land, *p* to flight the barbarian hordes,
4:34 for justice, he immediately *p* him to death.
4:38 and there he *p* the murderer to death.
4:42 a few, while they *p* all the rest to flight.
6: 9 and *p* to death those who would not consent
7:10 He *p* out his tongue at once when told to
8: 6 *p* to flight a large number of the enemy.
8:24 army, and *p* all of them to flight.
9: 2 Antiochus was *p* to flight by the natives
9: 4 done by those who had *p* him to flight.
9:15 he would *p* on perfect equality with the
10:11 he *p* a certain Lysias in charge of the
10:22 So he *p* them to death as traitors,
10:36 they *p* the towers to the torch,
11: 3 and to *p* the high priesthood up for sale
11:11 horsemen, and *p* all the rest to flight.
12: 6 and *p* to the sword those who had taken
12:37 were not expecting it and *p* them to flight.
14:13 him off with orders to *p* Judas to death,
Jb 1:11 But now *p* forth your hand and touch
1:15 They *p* the herdsmen to the sword,
1:17 off, and *p* those tending them to the sword,
2: 5 But now *p* forth your hand and touch his
6: 9 he would *p* forth his hand and cut me off!
9:20 I innocent, he might *p* me in the wrong.
10: 2 Do not *p* me in the wrong!
13:27 You *p* my feet in the stocks;
14: 9 and *p* forth branches like a young plant.
18: 2 When will you *p* an end to words?
21: 5 astonished, *p* your hands over your mouths.
21:17 How often is the lamp of the wicked *p* out?
22:23 if you *p* iniquity far from your tent,
23:16 the Almighty has *p* me in dismay.
27:18 or like a booth *p* up by the vine-keeper.
31:24 Had I *p* my trust in gold or called fine
31:36 on my shoulder or *p* it on me like a diadem;
38:33 you *p* into effect their plan on the earth?
40: 4 I *p* my hand over my mouth.
40:26 Can you *p* a rope into his nose,
40:29 Can you *p* him in leash for your maidens?
41:20 The arrow will not *p* him to flight;
Ps(s) 4: 8 You *p* gladness into my heart,
6:11 shall be *p* to shame in utter terror;
18:15 sent forth his arrows to *p* them to flight,
18:23 to me, and his statues I *p* not from me,
18:41 My enemies you *p* to flight before me,
21:13 succeed, For you shall *p* them to flight;
22: 6 they trusted, and they were not *p* to shame.
25: 2 let me not be *p* to shame,
25: 3 No one waits for you shall be *p* to shame;
25: 3 be *p* to shame who heedlessly break faith.
25:18 *P* an end to my affliction and my suffering,
25:20 let me not be *p* to shame,
31: 2 let me never be *p* to shame.
31:18 O LORD, let me not be *p* to shame,
31:18 let the wicked be *p* to shame;
33:22 be upon us who have *p* our hope in you.
35: 4 *p* to shame and disgraced who seek my life;
35:13 But I, when they were ill, *p* on sackcloth;
35:16 they *p* me to the test;
35:26 Let all be *p* to shame and confounded who
37:19 They are not *p* to shame in an evil time;
40: 4 And he *p* a new song into my mouth,
40:15 Let all be *p* to shame and confusion who
44: 8 and those who hated us you *p* to shame.
44:10 you have cast us off and *p* us in disgrace,
52: 9 But *p* his trust in his great wealth,
53: 6 they are *p* to shame,
69: 7 who wait for you be *p* to shame through me,
69:22 Rather they *p* gall in my food,
70: 3 *p* to shame and confounded who seek my life.
71: 1 let me never be *p* to shame.
71:13 *p* to shame and consumed who attack my life;
78: 7 sons that they should *p* their hope in God,
78:66 And he *p* his foes to flight and cast them
80:12 It *p* forth its foliage to the Sea,
83:18 Let them be shamed and *p* to rout forever;
85: 9 and to those who *p* in him their hope.
90: 7 anger, and by your wrath we are *p* to rout.
97: 7 who worship graven things are *p* to shame,
103:12 so far has he *p* our transgressions from us.
109:28 may my adversaries be *p* to shame,
119: 6 *p* to shame when I beheld all your commands.
119:31 O LORD, let me not be *p* to shame.
119:78 be *p* to shame for oppressing me unjustly;
119:80 in your statutes, that I be not *p* to shame.
119:87 have all but *p* an end to me on the earth,
125: 3 the just *p* forth to wickedness their hands.
127: 2 for you to rise early, or *p* off your rest,
127: 5 they shall not be *p* to shame when they
129: 5 be *p* to shame and fall back that hate Zion.
144: 6 forth lightning, and *p* them to flight,
146: 3 *P* not your trust in princes,
Prv 4: 9 She will *p* on your head a graceful diadem;
4:24 *P* away from you dishonest talk,
4:24 talk, deceitful speech *p* far from you.
6:21 your heart always, *p* them around your neck;
23: 2 And *p* a knife to your throat if you have a
24:20 the lamp of the wicked will be *p* out.
29:24 he hears himself *p* under a curse,
30: 8 *P* falsehood and lying far from me,
30:32 or presumptuous *p* your hand on your mouth;
Eccl 3:11 and has *p* the timeless into their hearts,
10: 6 a fool *p* in lofty position while the rich
11:10 and *p* away trouble from your presence,
Sg 5: 3 taken off my robe, am I then to *p* it on?
5: 4 My lover *p* his hand through the opening;
Wis 1: 3 from God, and his power, *p* to the proof,
2:19 With revilement and torture let us *p* him
6: 6 the mighty shall be mightily *p* to the test.
18: 5 to *p* to death the infants of the holy ones,
18: 6 of the oaths in which they *p* their faith,
18:21 the wrath and *p* a stop to the calamity,
Sir 5: 8 to the LORD, *p* it not off from day to day;
5:14 if not, *p* your hand over your mouth.
6:25 *P* your feet into her fetters,
15: 4 he will trust in her and not be *p* to shame.
24:21 He who obeys me will not be *p* to shame,
27: 8 it, and *p* it on like a splendid robe.
31:14 Toward what he eyes, do not *p* out a hand;
31:31 nor *p* him to shame while he is merry;
32:24 trusts in the LORD shall not be *p* to shame.
33:29 *P* him to work,
34:10 One never *p* to the proof knows little,
34:13 for they *p* their hope in their savior;
36: 1 and *p* all the nations in dread of you!
46:20 as a prophet, to *p* an end to wickedness.
48:10 in time to come to *p* an end to wrath
Is 1:16 *P* away your misdeeds from before my eyes;
4: 1 name be given us, *p* an end to our disgrace!"
10:13 like a giant, I have *p* down the enthroned.
13:11 will *p* an end to the pride of the arrogant,
21: 2 I will *p* an end to all groaning!"
22:12 to shave your head and *p* on sackcloth.
28:25 gith and sow cumin, *P* in wheat and barley,
30:12 And *p* your trust in what is crooked and
31: 1 Who *p* their trust in chariots because of
36: 8 horses, if you can *p* riders on them.'
37: 7 I am about to *p* in him such a spirit that,
37:29 I will *p* my hook in your nose and my bit
38: 1 *P* your house in order,
41:11 all shall be *p* to shame and disgrace who
41:23 or evil, that will *p* us in awe and in fear.
42: 1 I am pleased, Upon whom I have *p* my spirit;
43:20 For I *p* water in the desert and rivers in
43:28 the holy gates, *p* Jacob under the ban,
44:10 an idol to no purpose, will be *p* to shame;
45:16 Those are *p* to shame and disgrace who vent
45:17 be *p* to shame or disgrace in future ages."
46:13 I will *p* salvation within Zion,
50: 7 knowing that I shall not be *p* to shame.
51: 9 Awake, awake, *p* on strength,
51:16 I have *p* my words into your mouth and
51:23 *p* it into the hands of your tormentors,
52: 1 *P* on your strength, O Zion:
52: 1 *P* on your glorious garments,
54: 4 Fear not, you shall not be *p* to shame;
57: 4 wide your mouth, and *p* out your tongue?
59:17 He *p* on justice as his breastplate,
59:21 words that I have *p* into your mouth
63:11 is he who *p* his holy spirit in their midst;
65:13 shall rejoice, but you shall be *p* to shame;
66: 5 but they shall be *p* to shame.
66:19 to Tarshish, *P* and Lud,
Jer 3: 8 *p* her away and gave her a bill of divorce,
4: 1 *p* your detestable things out of my sight,
7: 4 *P* not your trust in the deceitful words:
9: 3 *p* no trust in any brother.
10:14 every artisan is *p* to shame by his idol:
13: 1 it on your loins, but do not *p* it in water.
13: 2 as the LORD commanded, and *p* it on.
17:13 The rebels in the land shall be *p* to shame;
20:11 failure they will be *p* to utter shame,
26: 8 of him, crying, "You must be *p* to death!
26:15 if you *p* me to death,
26:24 handed over to the people to be *p* to death.
27: 2 yoke bars and *p* them over your shoulders.
31:21 Set up road markers, *p* up guideposts;
32:14 of purchase, and *p* them in an earthen jar,
32:32 so that I must *p* it out of my sight for
32:40 into their hearts I will *p* the fear of me,
37: 4 Jeremiah had not yet been *p* into prison;
37:18 people, that you should *p* me in prison?
38: 4 "This man ought to be *p* to death,"
38: 7 that they had *p* Jeremiah into the cistern.
38:12 *P* the old, tattered rags between your armpits
46: 4 polish your spears, *p* on your breastplates.
46: 9 Set out, warriors, Cush and *P*,
48: 2 "Come, let us *p* an end to her as a people."
49: 3 *P* on sackcloth and mourn,
50: 2 her images are *p* to shame,
50:12 Your mother shall be sorely *p* to shame,
51:17 every artisan is *p* to shame by his idol:
51:47 her whole land shall be *p* to shame,
52:27 them struck down and *p* to death in Riblah,
Lam 3:29 Let him *p* his mouth to the dust;
Bar 3: 7 you *p* into our hearts the fear of you:
4:20 have *p* on sackcloth for my prayer of
5: 1 *p* on the splendor of glory from God
6:25 worship them are *p* to confusion because,
6:32 and *p* it on their wives and children.
6:38 and their worshipers will be *p* to shame.
Ez 3:25 *p* cords upon you and bind you with them,
4: 9 *p* them in a single vessel and make bread
7:16 I will *p* them all to death,
7:18 They shall *p* on sackcloth,
7:20 of their ornaments they *p* their pride:
7:24 I will *p* an end to their proud strength,
8:17 now they must also *p* the branch to my nose?
10: 7 He took up some of it and *p* it in the
11:19 a new heart and *p* a new spirit within them;
12:23 I will *p* an end to this proverb;
16:10 *p* sandals of fine leather on your feet;
16:11 I *p* bracelets on your arms,
16:41 Thus I will *p* an end to your harlotry,
17: 6 vine, produced branches and *p* forth shoots.
17:23 It shall *p* forth branches and bear fruit,
19: 9 They *p* him in a cage and took him away to
19:11 strong branch she *p* out as a royal scepter.
20:13 on them in the desert to *p* an end to them,
20:17 I did not *p* an end to them in the desert.
21:16 burnished to be *p* in the hand of a slayer.
21:24 Then *p* a signpost at the head of each road,
22:20 you together in my furious wrath, *p* you in,
23:27 I will *p* an end to your lewdness and to
23:40 painted your eyes, and *p* on ornaments.
23:42 who *p* bracelets on the women's arms and
23:48 I will *p* an end to lewdness in the land,
24: 4 *P* in it pieces of meat, all good pieces:
24: 8 she *p* her blood on the bare rock,
24:17 your turban, *p* your sandals on your feet,
26:13 I will *p* an end to the noise of your songs,
27:10 Lud and *P* were in your army as warriors;
27:31 they shave their heads and *p* on sackcloth,
28: 4 *p* gold and silver into your treasuries.
29: 4 I will *p* hooks in your jaws and make the
30: 5 Ethiopia, *P*, Lud, all Arabia, Libya,
30:10 I will *p* an end to the throngs of Egypt by
30:13 I will *p* an end to the great ones of
30:24 of Babylon, and *p* my sword in his hand,
30:25 when I *p* my sword in the hand of the king
34:10 I will claim my sheep from them and *p* a
36:27 I will *p* my spirit within you and make you
37: 6 I will *p* sinews upon you,
37: 6 and *p* spirit in you so that you may come
37:14 will *p* my spirit in you that you may live,
37:26 and *p* my sanctuary among them forever.
38: 5 *P* with them [all with shields and helmets],
39:15 bone, let them *p* up a marker beside it,
42:14 They shall *p* on other garments,
43: 9 From now on they shall *p* far from me their
43:20 and *p* it on the four horns of the altar,
44:17 they shall not *p* on anything woolen when
45: 9 *P* away violence and oppression,
45:19 and *p* it on the doorposts of the temple,
Dn 1:11 chamberlain had *p* in charge of Daniel,
1:20 or prudence which the king *p* to them,
2:12 the wise men of Babylon to be *p* to death.
2:24 not *p* the wise men of Babylon to death.
2:34 a mountain without a hand being *p* to it,
2:44 all these kingdoms and *p* an end to them,
2:45 the mountain without a hand being *p* to it,
3:40 who trust in you cannot be *p* to shame.
3:42 Do not let us be *p* to shame,
5:20 he was *p* down from his royal throne and
5:26 numbered your kingdom and *p* an end to it;
6: 8 ought to be *p* in force by royal decree:
11:18 shall *p* an end to his shameful conduct,
13:28 fully determined to *p* Susanna to death.
13:53 and the just you shall not *p* to death.'
13:62 they *p* them to death.
14:22 He *p* them to death,
14:27 He *p* them into the mouth of the dragon,
14:28 the dragon, and *p* the priests to death."
Hos 14: 7 the Lebanon cedar, and *p* forth his shoots.
Jl 2:26 my people shall nevermore be *p* to shame.
2:27 my people shall nevermore be *p* to shame.
Am 6: 3 You would *p* off the evil day,
Jon 3: 5 of them, great and small, *p* on sackcloth.
Mi 3: 5 one fails to *p* something in their mouth,
3: 7 Then shall the seers be *p* to shame,
7: 5 *P* no trust in a friend,
7: 7 LORD, I will *p* my trust in God my savior;
7:16 The nations shall behold and be *p* to shame,
7:16 They shall *p* their hands over their mouths;
Na 3: 6 upon you, disgrace you and *p* you to shame;

PUT (cont.)

3:9 *P* and the Libyans were her auxiliaries.
3:10 and all her great men were *p* into chains.
Zec 3:5 He also said, *P* a clean miter on his head."
3:5 And they *p* a clean miter on his head and
6:13 The priest shall be *p* at his right hand,
10:5 them, and shall *p* the horsemen to rout.
Mal 2:5 fear I *p* in him,
Mt 4:7 shall not *p* the Lord your God to the test.' "
5:15 a lamp and then *p* it under a bushel basket.
7:26 Anyone who hears my words but does not *p*
9:25 *p* out he entered and took her by the hand,
10:21 against parents and have them *p* to death.
12:10 there, and they *p* this question to Jesus,
13:46 he went back and *p* up for sale all that he
13:48 to *p* what was worthwhile into containers.
14:3 Herod had had John arrested, *p* in chains,
15:4 father or mother shall be *p* to death.'
15:13 "Every planting not *p* down by my heavenly
16:21 and the scribes, and to be *p* to death,
17:10 The disciples *p* this question to him:
17:23 the hands of men, who will *p* him to death,
18:30 *p* in jail until he paid back what he owed.
19:27 we have *p* everything aside to follow you.
20:12 but you have *p* them on the same basis as
21:25 us, 'Then why did you not *p* faith in it?';
21:32 a way of holiness, you *p* no faith in him;
21:33 planted a vineyard, *p* a hedge around it,
22:41 *p* a question to the assembled Pharisees,
24:45 master has *p* in charge of his household
24:47 will *p* him in charge of all his property.
25:21 I will *p* you in charge of larger affairs.
25:23 I will *p* you in charge of larger affairs.
26:51 accompanied Jesus *p* his hand to his sword,
26:52 *P* back your sword where it belongs.
26:59 Jesus so that they might *p* him to death.
27:1 action against Jesus to *p* him to death.
27:20 ask for Barabbas and have Jesus *p* to death.
27:37 had *p* the charge against him in writing:
Mk 1:13 forty days, *p* to the test there by Satan.
3:27 unless he has first *p* him under restraint.
4:21 "Is a lamp acquired to be *p* under a
4:21 Is it not meant to be *p* on a stand?
5:27 in the crowd and *p* her hand to his cloak.
5:40 Then he *p* them all out.
6:56 Wherever he *p* in an appearance,
7:10 father or mother shall be *p* to death.'
7:33 He *p* his fingers into the man's ears and,
8:31 priests, and the scribes, be *p* to death,
9:11 Finally they *p* to him this question:
9:31 the hands of men who will *p* him to death;
10:28 "We have *p* aside everything to follow you!"
11:22 *P* your trust in God.
11:31 ask, 'Then why did you not *p* faith in it?'
12:1 planted a vineyard, *p* a hedge around it,
12:41 Many of the wealthy *p* in sizable amounts;
12:42 but one poor widow came and *p* in two small
13:12 their parents and have them *p* to death.
14:38 and pray that you may not be *p* to the test.
15:17 wove a crown of thorns and *p* it on him,
16:13 but the others *p* no more faith in them
16:14 since they had *p* no faith in those who had
Lk 4:12 shall not *p* the Lord your God to the test.' "
5:4 *P* out into deep water and lower your nets
6:46 and not *p* into practice what I teach you?
6:47 hear my words and *p* them into practice.
6:49 my words but not *p* them into practice
9:18 were with him, he *p* the question to them,
9:22 priests and the scribes, and be *p* to death,
11:33 "One who lights a lamp does not *p* it in
12:37 I tell you, he will *p* on an apron,
12:44 will *p* him in charge of all his property.
15:22 robe and *p* it on him; *p* a ring on his finger
17:8 *P* on your apron and wait on me while I eat
18:33 They will scourge him and *p* him to death,
19:23 then, did you not *p* my money out on loan,
20:3 "Let me *p* a question for you to answer:
20:21 They *p* to him this problem:
21:3 poor widow has *p* in more than all the rest.
21:16 and some of you will be *p* to death.
22:40 "Pray that you may not be *p* to the test."
23:11 after which they *p* a magnificent robe on
23:26 They *p* a crossbeam on Simon's shoulder for
Jn 4:27 No one *p* a question,
4:50 *p* his trust in the word Jesus spoke to him,
6:30 "So that we can *p* faith in you,"
9:15 He told them, "He *p* mud on my eyes.
9:22 Messiah would be *p* out of the synagogue.
10:37 my Father's works, *p* no faith in me.
10:38 put no faith in me, *p* faith in these works,
11:45 what Jesus did, to *p* their faith in him.
12:21 in Galilee, and *p* this request to him:
13:12 he *p* his cloak back on and reclined at
13:17 will you be if you *p* them into practice.
18:7 Jesus *p* the question to them again,
18:11 to Peter, *P* your sword back in its sheath.
18:31 "We may not *p* anyone to death,"
20:2 We don't know where they have *p* him!"
20:13 and I do not know where they have *p* him."
20:27 *P* your hand into my side.
21:16 A second time he *p* his question,
Acts 3:2 They would bring him every day and *p* him
3:15 You *p* to death the Author of life.
4:3 them and *p* them in jail for the night.
5:2 *p* aside a part of the proceeds for himself;
5:9 scheme to *p* the Spirit of the Lord to test?
5:25 Those men you *p* in jail are standing over
5:30 has raised up Jesus whom you *p* to death,
7:52 they *p* to death those who foretold the
10:46 Peter *p* the question at that point:
12:8 angel said, *P* on your belt and your sandals!"
12:8 him, "Now *p* on your cloak and follow me."
13:13 Paul and his companions *p* out to sea and
13:18 years he *p* up with them in the desert:
14:23 to the Lord in whom they had *p* their faith.
15:10 do you *p* God to the test by trying to
16:11 We *p* out to sea from Troas and set
16:24 he *p* them in maximum security,
17:28 as some of your own poets have *p* it,
18:8 whole household, *p* his faith in the Lord.
19:2 some disciples to whom he *p* the question,
20:15 on the day after that we *p* in at Miletus.
20:24 I *p* no value on my life if only I can
21:1 we *p* out to sea and sailed straight to Cos.
21:3 Finally we *p* in at Tyre,
21:7 our voyage from Tyre we *p* in at Ptolemais,
26:10 be *p* to death I cast my vote against them.
27:3 The following day we *p* in at Sidon,
27:12 the majority preferred to *p* out to sea in
28:12 We *p* in at Syracuse and spent three days
Rom 3:3 unbelief *p* an end to God's faithfulness?
8:13 you *p* to death the evil deeds of the body,
9:30 How, then, shall we *p* it?
9:33 who believes in him will not be *p* to shame."
10:11 one who believes in him will be *p* to shame."
10:19 I *p* the question again,
12:16 *P* away ambitious thoughts and associate
13:12 of darkness and *p* on the armor of light.
13:14 *p* on the Lord Jesus Christ and make no
14:13 Instead you should resolve to *p* no
1Cor 4:9 has *p* us apostles at the end of the line,
6:7 Why not *p* up with injustice,
9:12 we *p* up with all sorts of hardships so as
13:4 Love is not jealous, it does not *p* on airs,
13:11 I became a man I *p* childish ways aside.
15:25 until God has *p* all enemies under his feet,
15:44 is *p* down and a spiritual body comes up.
16:2 *p* aside whatever he has been able to save,
16:10 come, be sure to *p* him at ease among you.
2Cor 1:10 We have *p* our hope in him who will never
6:9 punished, but not *p* to death;
7:14 to him about you, I was not *p* to shame.
8:16 who has *p* an equal zeal for you in the
9:4 then I should be *p* to shame
11:1 *P* up with me, I beg you!
11:19 yourselves, you gladly *p* up with fools.
11:20 You even *p* up with those who exploit you,
11:20 you, who impose upon you and *p* on airs,
Gal 4:19 and you *p* me back in labor pains until
Eph 1:22 He has *p* all things under Christ's feet
2:16 his cross, which *p* that enmity to death.
4:24 *p* on that new man created in God's image,
4:25 to it, then, that you *p* an end to lying;
6:11 *P* on the armor of God so that you may be
6:13 You must *p* on the armor of God if you are
6:19 for me that God may *p* his word on my lips,
Phil 1:20 I shall never be *p* to shame for my hopes;
3:4 right to *p* his trust in external evidence,
Col 3:5 *P* to death whatever in your nature is
3:8 You must *p* that aside now:
3:9 What you have done is *p* aside your old
3:10 with its past deeds and *p* on a new man,
3:14 Over all these virtues *p* on love,
1Thes 3:5 fearing that the tempter had *p* you to the
1Tm 3:10 They should be *p* on probation first;
4:6 If you *p* these instructions before the
5:18 "You shall not *p* a muzzle on an ox when
2Tm 4:5 *p* up with hardship,
Heb 2:8 honor, and *p* all things under his feet."
2:13 and "I will *p* my trust in him";
10:16 I will *p* my laws in their hearts and I
10:28 Anyone who rejects the law of Moses is *p*
11:17 By faith Abraham, when *p* to the test,
11:34 the jaws of lions, *p* out raging fires,
11:37 sawed in two, *p* to death at sword's point;
Jas 1:23 God's word but does not *p* it into practice
3:3 When we *p* bits into the mouths of horses
1Pt 2:20 But if you *p* up with suffering for doing
3:18 He was *p* to death insofar as fleshly
4:10 *p* your gifts at the service of one another,
2Pt 1:21 never been *p* forward by man's willing it.
1Jn 4:1 but *p* the spirits to a test to see if they
2Jn 1:12 you, I do not intend to *p* it down on paper;
Rv 2:10 of you into prison to *p* you to the test;
2:23 her, and her children I will *p* to death.
17:17 For God has *p* it into their minds to carry

PUTEOLI (1)

Acts 28:13 which enabled us to reach *P* in two days.

PUTHITES (1)

1Chr 2:53 the Ithrites, the *P*,

PUTIEL'S (1)

Ex 6:25 son, Eleazar, married one of *P* daughters,

PUTS (34)

Ex 30:33 this, or whoever *p* any of this on a layman,
Nm 22:38 I can speak only what God *p* in my mouth."
23:12 *p* in my mouth that I must repeat with care?"
Jos 23:10 One of you *p* to flight a thousand,
1Sm 2:6 "The LORD *p* to death and gives life;
Jb 4:18 Lo, he *p* no trust in his servants,
20:3 A rebuke which *p* me to shame I hear,
24:15 roams about, and he *p* a mask over his face;
33:11 He *p* my feet in the stocks;
38:36 Who *p* wisdom in the heart,
Ps(s) 84:4 swallow a nest in which she *p* her young
Prv 18:17 his opponent comes and *p* him to the test.
18:18 The lot *p* an end to disputes,
25:8 later on when your neighbor *p* you to shame?
31:19 She *p* her hands to the distaff,
Sg 2:13 The fig tree *p* forth its figs,
4:13 You are a park that *p* forth pomegranates,
Wis 13:15 fitting shrine for it and *p* it on the wall,
Sir 4:17 and at first she *p* him to the test;
4:17 With her precepts she *p* him to the proof,
17:4 He *p* the fear of him in all flesh,
26:13 her thoughtfulness *p* flesh on his bones;
50:29 If he *p* them into practice,
Is 28:16 who *p* his faith in it shall not be shaken.
Bar 6:26 one *p* gifts beside them as beside the dead.
Mt 7:24 "Anyone who hears my words and *p* them
Lk 8:16 *p* it under a bushel basket or under a bed;
8:16 he *p* it on a lampstand so that whoever
9:62 "Whoever *p* his hand to the plow but keeps
15:5 it, he *p* it on his shoulders in jubilation.
Jn 12:44 "Whoever *p* faith in me believes not so
16:2 anyone who *p* you to death will claim
Heb 6:16 to a promise and *p* an end to all argument.
1Pt 2:6 who *p* his faith in it shall not be shaken."

PUTTING (54)

Gn 8:9 *P* out his hand,
33:2 *p* the maids and their children first,
50:25 Then, *p* the sons of Israel under oath,
Ex 2:3 bitumen and pitch, and *p* the child in it,
20:25 for by *p* a tool to it you desecrate it.
23:1 Do not join the wicked in *p* your hand,
Nm 35:19 the murderer, *p* him to death on sight.
35:30 is not sufficient for *p* a person to death.
Dt 17:6 is required for *p* a person to death;
20:19 not destroy its trees by *p* an ax to them.
26:2 God, gives you, and *p* them in a basket,
Jos 6:21 They observed the ban by *p* to the sword
10:35 it the same day, *p* it to the sword.
11:11 doom by *p* every person there to the sword,
Jgs 1:8 and captured it, *p* it to the sword;
6:19 *P* the meat in a basket and the broth in a
6:37 I am *p* this woolen fleece on the threshing
20:48 *p* to the sword the inhabitants of the
Ru 4:3 is *p* up for sale the piece of land that
1Sm 6:8 *p* in a box beside it the golden articles
14:24 oath that day, *p* the people under this ban:
17:38 *p* a bronze helmet on his head and arming
19:8 a great defeat upon them, *p* them to flight.
19:13 *p* a net of goat's hair at its head and
28:8 he disguised himself, *p* on other clothes,
30:17 *p* them under the ban so that none escaped
2Sm 13:19 Then, *p* her hands to her head,
1Kgs 7:51 of his father David, *p* the silver,
2Chr 5:1 of his father David, *p* the silver,
Neh 10:1 a firm pact, which we are *p* into writing.
Jdt 8:25 to the Lord our God, for *p* us to the test,
Est D:1 the third day, *p* an end to her prayers,
1Mc 13:32 in his place, *p* on the crown of Asia.
2Mc 7:40 undefiled, *p* all his trust in the Lord.
12:23 *p* the sinners to the sword and destroying
Ps(s) 8:7 of your hands, *p* all things under his feet:
Wis 18:9 offering sacrifice and *p* into effect
Jer 4:30 doomed, what do you mean by *p* on purple,
7:8 *p* your trust in deceitful words to your
29:26 by *p* them into the stocks or the pillory.
Ez 44:19 of the sanctuary, *p* on other garments;
Dn 13:56 *P* him to one side,
Mk 1:19 were in their boat *p* their nets in order.
8:23 *P* spittle on his eyes he laid his hands on
9:36 in their midst, and *p* his arms around him,
12:41 the crowd *p* money into the collection box.
Lk 21:1 rich *p* their offerings into the treasury,
21:2 also a poor widow *p* in two copper coins.
Jn 20:25 without *p* my finger in the nailmarks and
Acts 27:4 Then, *p* out from Sidon,
1Cor 15:30 are we continually *p* ourselves in danger?
Phil 3:3 Jesus rather than *p* our trust in the flesh
1Thes 5:8 *p* on faith and love as a breastplate and
Rv 13:15 power of speech and of *p* to death

PUVAH (1)

Nm 26:23 through *P* the clan of the Puvahites,

PUVAHITES (1)

Nm 26:23 Tolaites, through Puvah the clan of the *P*,

PUZZLED (1)

Jn 13:22 at one another, *p* as to whom he could mean.

PYRAMIDS (2)

1Mc 13:28 He set up seven *p* facing one another for
13:29 the *p* he devised a setting of big columns,

PYRE (3)

2Chr 16:14 also burned a very great funeral *p* for him.
21:19 made a *p* for him like that of his fathers.
Is 30:33 For the *p* has long been ready,

PYRRHUS (1)

Acts 20: 4 Accompanying him were Sopater, son of *P*,

Q

QOHELETH (7)

Eccl 1: 1 The words of David's son, *Q*,
1: 2 Vanity of vanities, says *Q*,
1:12 I, *Q*, was king over Israel in Jerusalem,
7:27 Behold, this have I found, says *Q*,
12: 8 Vanity of vanities, says *Q*,
12: 9 being wise, *Q* taught the people knowledge,
12:10 *Q* sought to find pleasing sayings,

QUADRUPEDS (1)

Lv 11:27 Of the various *q*,

QUAIL (7)

Ex 16:13 the evening *q* came up and covered the camp.
Nm 11:31 that drove in *q* from the sea and brought
11:32 the next day the people gathered in the *q*.
Ps(s) 105:40 They asked, and he brought them *q*,
Wis 16: 2 they craved, by providing *q* for their food;
19:12 appease them *q* came to them from the sea.
Sir 26: 5 my heart quakes, a fourth before which I *q*:

QUAKE (13)

Dt 2:25 name they will *q* and tremble before you.'
Ps(s) 46: 4 foam and the mountains *q* at its surging.
75: 4 Though the earth and all who dwell in it *q*,
Sir 16:17 at his mere glance, quiver and *q*.
30: 7 and will *q* inwardly at every outcry.
43:16 before his might the mountains *q*.
Is 5:25 When the mountains *q*,
14:16 who made the earth tremble, and kingdoms *q*?
Ez 26:15 slays in your midst, shall not the isles *q*?
26:18 this, the day of your fall, the islands *q*!
27:28 of your mariners, the shores begin to *q*.
Jl 4:16 The heavens and the earth *q*,
Na 1: 5 The mountains *q* before him,

QUAKED (7)

Ex 15:14 The nations heard and *q*;
Jgs 5: 4 The earth *q* and the heavens were shaken,
2Sm 22: 8 "The earth swayed and *q*:
Ps(s) 18: 8 The earth swayed and *q*;
68: 9 through the wilderness, The earth *q*;
77:19 the earth quivered and *q*.
Mt 27:52 The earth *q*, boulders split, tombs opened.

QUAKES (8)

Ps(s) 55: 5 My heart *q* within me;
99: 1 the earth *q*.
Sir 26: 5 There are three things at which my heart *q*,
Is 9:18 the wrath of the LORD of hosts the land *q*,
Jer 10:10 King, Before whose anger the earth *q*,
49:21 At the noise of their fall the earth *q*,
50:46 the earth *q*;
51:29 The earth *q* and writhes,

QUAKING (4)

Ps(s) 48: 7 *Q* seizes them there;
Sir 25:22 Feeble hands and *q* knees
Is 63:19 come down, with the mountains *q*
Mi 7:17 They shall come *q* from their fastnesses,

QUALIFIED (4)

Gn 47: 5 and if you know any of them to be *q*,
1Mc 13:40 of you are *q* for enrollment in our service,
2Cor 2:16 such a mission as this, is anyone really *q*?
3: 6 has made us *q* ministers of a new covenant,

QUALITIES (5)

Lv 27:12 value in keeping with its good or bad *q*,
Eccl 12:14 judgment every work, with all its hidden *q*,
Phil 2:22 know from experience what Timothy's *q* are,
2Pt 1: 8 *Q* like these,
1: 9 Any man who lacks these *q* is shortsighted

QUALITY (1)

1Cor 3:13 fire will test the *q* of each man's work.

QUALM (1)

1Sm 25:31 this as a *q* or burden on your conscience,

QUALMS (1)

2Pt 2:10 *q* whatever about reviling celestial beings,

QUANTITIES (5)

Gn 41:49 grain in *q* like the sands of the sea,
1Chr 18: 8 cities of Hadadezer, large *q* of bronze,
22:14 such great *q* that they cannot be weighed.
29: 2 of precious stone, and great *q* of marble.
2Chr 31: 5 the Israelites brought, in great *q*,

QUANTITY (12)

2Sm 8: 8 David removed a very large *q* of bronze.
1Kgs 10:10 gold talents, a very large *q* of spices,
10:11 *q* of cabinet wood and precious stones.
1Chr 12:41 provisions in great *q* of meal,
23:29 mixing, and of all measures of *q* and size.
2Chr 2: 8 order to prepare for me a great *q* of wood,
9: 9 gold talents and a very large *q* of spices,
Jdt 12:20 charmed by her, drank a great *q* of wine,
15: 7 the enormous *q* of booty they had seized.
1Mc 9:35 deposit with them their great *q* of baggage.
2Mc 8:20 thousand and took a great *q* of booty,
Sir 38:29 for his products, and turns them out in *q*.

QUARANTINE (8)

Lv 13: 4 shall *q* the stricken man for seven days.
13: 5 priest shall *q* him for another seven days,
13:21 out, the priest shall *q* him for seven days.
13:26 out, the priest shall *q* him for seven days.
13:31 the priest shall *q* the person with scall
13:33 priest shall *q* him for another seven days.
13:50 *q* the infected article for seven days.
14:38 behind him and *q* the house for seven days.

QUARANTINED (2)

Lv 13:54 washed and then *q* for another seven days.
14:46 it is *q* shall be unclean until evening.

QUARANTINING (1)

Lv 13:11 the man unclean without first *q* him,

QUARREL (16)

Gn 26:22 but over this one they did not *q*.
Ex 17: 2 Moses replied, "Why do you *q* with me?
21:18 "When men *q* and one strikes the other
Jgs 11:25 Did he ever *q* with Israel,
2Kgs 5: 7 can see he is only looking for a *q* with me!"
2Chr 35:21 "What *q* is between us, king of Judah?
2Mc 3: 4 had a *q* with the high priest about the
Prv 3:30 *Q* not with a man without cause.
17:14 therefore, check a *q* before it begins!
18: 1 with all persistence he picks a *q*.
20: 3 shun strife, while every fool starts a *q*.
26:17 ears is he who meddles in a *q* not his own.
Sir 6: 9 an enemy, and tells of the *q* to your shame.
8: 2 *Q* not with a rich man,
8:16 Provoke no *q* with a quick-tempered man,
Jas 4: 2 and you cannot acquire, so you *q* and fight.

QUARRELED (8)

Gn 26:20 shepherds of Gerar *q* with Isaac's servants,
26:21 another well, and they *q* over that one too;
Ex 17: 2 They *q*,
17: 7 the Israelites *q* there and tested the LORD,
Lv 24:11 This man *q* publicly with another Israelite
Jgs 8: 1 And they *q* bitterly with him.
2Sm 14: 6 servant had two sons, who *q* in the field.
Jn 6:52 At this the Jews *q* among themselves,

QUARRELING (4)

Gn 25:23 two peoples are *q* while still within you;
Is 58: 4 Yes, your fast ends in *q* and fighting,
Rom 13:13 excess and lust, not in *q* and jealousy.
1Cor 1:11 household that you are *q* among yourselves.

QUARRELS (7)

Gn 13: 7 There were *q* between the herdsmen of
2Chr 19: 8 *q* among the inhabitants of Jerusalem.
Sir 28:11 up, and insistent *q* provoke bloodshed.
1Cor 3: 3 long as there are jealousy and *q* among you,
2Cor 7: 5 *q* with others and fears within myself.
2Tm 2:23 As you well know, they only breed *q*,
Ti 3: 9 from all controversies and *q* about the law.

QUARRELSOME (7)

Prv 21: 9 than in a roomy house with a *q* woman.
21:19 than with a *q* and vexatious wife.
25:24 than in a roomy house with a *q* woman.
27:15 leak on a rainy day the match is a *q* woman.
Sir 28: 8 be fewer, for a *q* man kindles disputes,
2Tm 2:24 not be *q* but must be kindly toward all.
Ti 3: 2 them not to speak evil of anyone or be *q*.

QUARRIED (2)

1Kgs 5:31 large blocks were *q* to give the temple a
Is 51: 1 hewn, to the pit from which you were *q*;

QUARRY (1)

1Kgs 6: 7 was built of stone dressed at the *q*,

QUARTER (9)

1Sm 9: 8 Saul, "I have a *q* of a silver shekel.
2Kgs 22:14 themselves to the Second *Q* in Jerusalem,
2Chr 34:22 she dwelt in Jerusalem, in the new *q*.
Jdt 2:11 As for those who resist, show them no *q*,
1Mc 12:37 The *q* called Chaphenatha was also repaired.
2Mc 12:16 pool, which was about a *q* of a mile wide,
Jer 21: 7 them with the edge of the sword, without *q*,
Zep 1:10 from the Fish Gate, a wail from the New *Q*,
Rv 6: 8 given authority over one *q* of the earth,

QUARTERMASTER (1)

Jer 51:59 Seraiah was chief *q*.

QUARTERS (19)

1Sm 1:18 She went to her *q*,
17:48 then moved to meet David at close *q*,
26: 5 of Ner, the general, had their sleeping *q*.
1Kgs 7: 8 His living *q* were in another court,
Neh 3:25 the Upper Palace at the *q* of the guard.
3:31 *q* of the temple slaves and the merchants,
Tb 2: 5 Returning to my own *q*,
Jdt 14:17 entered the tent where Judith had her *q*;
Jer 32: 2 was imprisoned in the *q* of the guard,
32: 8 came to me to the *q* of the guard and said,
32:12 who happened to be in the *q* of the guard.
33: 1 was still imprisoned in the *q* of the guard:
37:21 Jeremiah be confined in the *q* of the guard,
37:21 Jeremiah remained in the *q* of the guard.
38: 6 Malchiah, which was in the *q* of the guard,
38:13 Jeremiah remained in the *q* of the guard.
38:28 Thus Jeremiah stayed in the *q* of the guard
39:14 Jeremiah taken out of the *q* of the guard,
39:15 was still imprisoned in the *q* of the guard,

QUARTUS (1)

Rom 16:24 our brother *Q* wish to be remembered to you.

QUEEN (55)

1Kgs 10: 1 The *q* of Sheba,
10: 4 When the *q* of Sheba witnessed Solomon's
10:10 as the *q* of Sheba gave to King Solomon.
10:13 King Solomon gave the *q* of Sheba
11:19 him in marriage the sister of *Q* Tahpenes,
11:20 the *q* kept him in Pharaoh's palace,
15:13 Maacah from her position as *q* mother,
2Kgs 10:13 the princes and the family of the *q* mother."
2Chr 9: 1 the *q* of Sheba heard of Solomon's fame,
9: 3 the *q* of Sheba witnessed Solomon's wisdom,
9: 9 which the *q* of Sheba gave to King Solomon.
9:12 King Solomon gave the *q* of Sheba
15:16 he deposed as *q* mother because she had
Neh 2: 6 Then the king, and the *q* seated beside him,
Est 1: 9 *Q* Vashti also gave a feast for the women
1:11 to bring *Q* Vashti into his presence
1:12 But *Q* Vashti refused to come at the royal
1:15 "What is to be done by law with *Q* Vashti
1:16 *Q* Vashti has not wronged the king alone,
1:17 that *Q* Vashti be ushered into his presence,
2:17 her head and made her *q* in place of Vashti.
2:22 became known to Mordecai, he told *Q* Esther,
4: 4 *Q* Esther's maids and eunuchs came and told
C:12 *Q* Esther, seized with mortal anguish,
D: 7 height of majestic anger, the *q* staggered,
5: 2 He saw *Q* Esther standing in the courtyard,
5: 3 king said to her, "What is it, *Q* Esther?
5:12 *Q* Esther invited no one but me to the
7: 1 Haman went to the banquet with *Q* Esther.
7: 2 to Esther, "Whatever you ask, *Q* Esther,
7: 3 *Q* Esther replied:
7: 5 where," said King Ahasuerus to *Q* Esther,
7: 6 was seized with dread of the king and *q*.
7: 7 Haman stayed to beg *Q* Esther for his life,
7: 8 the *q* while she is with me in my own house!"
8: 1 of Haman, enemy of the Jews, to *Q* Esther;
8: 7 said to *Q* Esther and to the Jew Mordecai:
9:12 reported to the king, he said to *Q* Esther:
9:29 *Q* Esther, daughter of Abihail
9:31 and *Q* Esther had designated for the Jews,
F: 3 Esther, whom the king married and made *q*.
Ps(s) 45:10 the *q* takes her place at your right hand
Jer 7:18 dough to make cakes for the *q* of heaven,
13:18 Say to the king and to the *q* mother:
29: 2 was after King Jeconiah and the *q* mother,
44:17 *q* of heaven and pour out libations to her,
44:18 burning incense to the *q* of heaven
44:19 And when we burned incense to the *q* of
44:25 burn incense to the *q* of heaven
Ez 16:13 beautiful, with the dignity of a *q*.
Dn 5:10 When the *q* heard of the discussion between
Mt 12:42 the *q* of the South will rise with the
Lk 11:31 The *q* of the South will rise at the

QUEEN (cont.)

Acts 8:27 (a name meaning *q*) of the Ethiopians,
Rv 18: 7 said to herself, 'I sit enthroned as a *q*.

QUEENS—QUEEN'S (4)

Est 1:17 For the *q* conduct will become known to all
1:18 who hear of the *q* conduct will rebel
Sg 6: 8 There are sixty *q*,
6: 9 her fortunate, the *q* and concubines,

QUELL (1)

Is 25: 5 even so you *q* the uproar of the wanton.

QUELLED (1)

Is 30: 7 Therefore I call her "Rahab *q*."

QUENCH (10)

2Sm 14: 7 Thus they will *q* my remaining hope and
21:17 us again lest you *q* the lamp of Israel."
Ps(s) 104:11 field, till the wild asses *q* their thirst.
Sg 8: 7 Deep waters cannot *q* love,
Is 1:31 and there shall be none to *q* the flames.
42: 3 and a smoldering wick he shall not *q*,
Jer 4: 4 out like fire, and burn till none can *q* it,
Am 4: 8 city for water that did not *q* their thirst;
5: 6 with none to *q* it for the house of Israel:
Mt 12:20 not *q* until judgment is made victorious.

QUENCHED (8)

Wis 2: 3 beating of our hearts, And when this is *q*,
Sir 23:16 fire, not to be *q* till it burns itself out:
Is 34:10 Night and day it shall not be *q*,
43:17 to rise, snuffed out and *q* like a wick.
Jer 7:20 it will burn without being *q*.
21:12 out like fire which burns without being *q*,
Ez 21: 3 The blazing flame shall not be *q*,
21: 4 have kindled it, and it shall not be *q*.

QUENCHES (2)

Wis 16:17 all expectation, in water which *q* anything,
Sir 3:29 Water *q* a flaming fire,

QUENCHING (1)

Wis 19:20 strength, and water forgot its *q* nature;

QUESTION (60)

Ex 22: 8 In every *q* of dishonest appropriation,
Nm 5:15 offering for an appeal in a *q* of guilt.
Jgs 9: 2 this *q* to all the citizens of Shechem:
1Sm 17:30 from him to another and asked the same *q*;
Ezr 10:14 elders and magistrates of each city in *q*,
Tb 6: 7 The boy asked the angel this *q*:
Jb 9:19 If it be a *q* of strength,
38: 3 I will *q* you,
40: 7 I will *q* you, and you tell me the answers!
Is 41:28 counsel, to make an answer when I *q* them.
45:11 You *q* me about my children,
Jer 1:11 The word of the LORD came to me with the *q*:
1:13 the word of the LORD came to me with the *q*:
38:14 "I have a *q* to ask you,"
Dn 1:20 In any *q* of wisdom or prudence which the
Mt 12:10 to be there, and they put this *q* to Jesus,
15: 1 from Jerusalem approached Jesus with the *q*:
16:13 Philippi, he asked his disciples this *q*:
17:10 The disciples put this *q* to him:
18: 1 the disciples came up to Jesus with the *q*,
19:17 "Why do you *q* me about what is good?
21:24 "I too will ask a *q*.
22:23 is no resurrection, came to him with a *q*:
22:41 Jesus put a *q* to the assembled Pharisees,
Mk 8:27 On the way he asked his disciples this *q*:
9:11 Finally they put to him this *q*:
9:32 his words, they were afraid to *q* him.
10:10 the disciples began to *q* him about this.
11:29 Jesus said to them, "I will ask you a *q*.
12:18 is no resurrection came to him with a *q*:
13: 3 John, and Andrew began to *q* him privately.
Lk 7:20 the Baptizer sends us to you with this *q*:
9:18 were with him, he put the *q* to them,
9:45 they were afraid to *q* him about the matter.
20: 2 by the elders, approached him with the *q*,
20: 3 "Let me put a *q* for you to answer:
22:51 Jesus said in answer to their *q*,
22:68 you will not believe me, and if I *q* you,
Jn 1:25 had sent proceeded to *q* him further:
4:27 No one put a *q*,
8: 6 (They were posing this *q* to trap him,
16:19 Jesus was aware that they wanted to *q* him,
18: 7 Jesus put the *q* to them again,
18:21 Why do you *q* me?
18:21 *Q* those who heard me when I spoke.
21:16 A second time he put his *q*,
Acts 10:46 Peter put the *q* at that point:
15: 2 and presbyters in Jerusalem about this *q*.
19: 2 found some disciples to whom he put the *q*,
19:36 Since this is beyond *q*,
21:13 He answered with a *q*:
23:20 that they want to *q* him more carefully.
24: 8 Feel free now to *q* him about all this and

Rom 3: 7 Another *q*:
9:16 So it is not a *q* of man's willing or doing
10:19 I put the *q* again,
1Cor 10:25 market without raising any *q* of conscience.
10:27 you, without raising any *q* of conscience.
15:36 A nonsensical *q*!
2Thes 2: 1 On the *q* of the coming of our Lord Jesus

QUESTIONED (22)

Jgs 8:14 who upon being *q* listed for him the
1Sm 11:12 "Who *q* whether Saul should rule over us?
2Sm 11: 7 When he came, David *q* him about Joab,
1Kgs 10: 2 She came to Solomon and *q* him on every
2Kgs 8: 6 The king *q* the woman,
2Chr 9: 1 She came to Solomon and *q* him on every
31: 9 Then Hezekiah *q* the priests and the
Ezr 5: 9 We then *q* the elders,
Jdt 6:16 and Uzziah *q* him about what had happened.
Est A:14 and the king had the two eunuchs *q* and,
2Mc 14: 5 invited to the council by Demetrius and *q*
Jer 38:27 the princes came to Jeremiah, they *q* him,
Dn 3:14 King Nebuchadnezzar *q* them:
Mt 27:11 arraigned before the procurator, who *q* him:
Mk 4:10 with the Twelve *q* him about the parables.
7: 5 So the Pharisees and the scribes *q* him:
7:17 his disciples *q* him about the proverb.
9:21 Then Jesus *q* the father:
Lk 23: 9 He *q* Jesus at considerable length,
Jn 1:21 They *q* him further, "Who, then?
18:19 The high priest *q* Jesus,
Rom 4:20 Yet he never *q* or doubted God's promise;

QUESTIONERS (1)

Acts 4:13 men of no standing, the *q* were amazed.

QUESTIONING (2)

2Mc 7: 2 "What do you expect to achieve by *q* us?
Jn 8: 7 When they persisted in their *q*,

QUESTIONS (13)

Gn 26: 7 men of the place asked *q* about his wife,
43: 7 We had to answer his *q*.
1Kgs 10: 1 fame, came to test him with subtle *q*.
2Chr 9: 1 to Jerusalem to test him with subtle *q*,
19:10 whether it concerns bloodguilt or *q* of law,
2Mc 2:30 To enter into *q* and examine them
Mt 6:31 Stop worrying, then, over *q* like,
22:46 dared, from that day on, to ask him any *q*.
Mk 12:34 one had the courage to ask him any more *q*.
Lk 2:46 listening to them and asking them *q*.
11:53 and to make him speak on a multitude of *q*,
Jn 16:23 On that day you will have no *q* to ask me.
16:30 There is no need for anyone to ask you *q*.

QUICK (11)

Gn 18: 6 hastened into the tent and told Sarah, *Q*,
Jgs 2:17 They were *q* to stray from the way their
1Sm 20:38 Again he called to his lad, "Hurry, be *q*,
2Kgs 3:23 *Q*! To the spoils, Moabites
Eccl 5: 1 be *q* to make a promise in God's presence.
Is 59: 7 and they are *q* to shed innocent blood;
Dn 1: 4 handsome, intelligent and wise, *q* to learn,
Lk 15:22 *Q*! bring out the finest robe
Jn 13:27 "Be *q* about what you are to do."
Col 3: 8 all the anger and *q* temper,
Jas 1:19 Let every man be *q* to hear,

QUICK-MELTING (1)

Wis 19:21 the icelike, *q* kind of ambrosial food.

QUICK-TEMPERED (3)

Prv 14:17 The *q* man makes a fool of himself,
14:29 but the *q* man displays folly at its height.
Sir 8:16 Provoke no quarrel with a *q* man,

QUICKENING (1)

Wis 15:11 him, and breathed into him a *q* soul,

QUICKENS (1)

Sir 28:12 If you blow upon a spark, it *q* into flame,

QUICKER (1)

Jb 8:12 and uncut, it withers *q* than any grass.

QUICKLY (61)

Gn 18: 7 gave it to a servant, who *q* prepared it.
24:18 and *q* lowering the jug onto her hand,
24:20 she *q* emptied her jug into the drinking
24:46 She *q* lowered the jug she was carrying and
27:20 Isaac asked, "How did you succeed so *q*,
Nm 11:27 So, when a young man *q* told Moses,
17:11 and bring it *q* to the community to make
Dt 4:26 that you shall all *q* perish from the land
7: 4 flare up against you and *q* destroy you.
9: 3 you can drive them out and destroy them *q*,
9:12 he said to me, 'Go down from here now, *q*,
Jos 4:10 The people crossed over *q*,
10: 6 Come up here *q* and save us.
23:16 you will *q* perish from the good land
1Sm 4:16 The man *q* came up to Eli and said,
17:17 bring them *q* to your brothers in the camp.
17:48 while David ran *q* toward the battle line
23:27 messenger came to Saul, saying, "Come *q*,
25:18 Abigail *q* got together two hundred loaves,
25:23 David, she dismounted *q* from the ass and,
28:24 in the house, which she now *q* slaughtered.
2Sm 15:14 Leave *q*,
1Kgs 20:33 the men *q* took him at his word and said,
2Kgs 4:22 I must go *q* to the man of God,
2Chr 35:13 brought them *q* to all the common people.
Jdt 13: 1 When it grew late, his servants *q* withdrew.
13:12 they *q* descended to their city gate and
1Mc 6:27 Unless you *q* forestall them,
13:10 and *q* completing the walls of Jerusalem,
2Mc 4:12 He *q* established a gymnasium at the very
4:48 vessels, *q* suffered unjust punishment.
7: 4 While they were being *q* heated,
10:16 *q* against the strongholds of the Idumeans.
14:11 *q* added fuel to Demetrius' indignation.
14:44 as they *q* drew back and left an opening,
Ps(s) 37: 2 For like grass they *q* wither,
49:15 *Q* their form is consumed;
78:33 Therefore he *q* ended their days and their
79: 8 may your compassion *q* come to us,
81:15 in my ways, *Q* would I humble their enemies;
90:10 toil, for they pass *q* and we drift away.
Prv 13:11 Wealth *q* gotten dwindles away,
Eccl 7: 9 Do not in spirit become *q* discontented,
Wis 6:15 sake keeps vigil shall *q* be free from care;
13: 9 how did they not more *q* find its Lord?
14:15 an image of the child so *q* taken from him,
Sir 20:17 why the downfall of the wicked comes so *q*.
21: 5 at once, and justice is *q* granted him.
50:17 would *q* fall prostrate to the ground
Is 58: 8 the dawn, and your wound shall *q* be healed;
Jer 9:17 Let them come *q* and intone a dirge for us,
Dn 2:24 *q* brought Daniel to the king and said,
Mt 21:20 "Why did the fig tree wither up so *q*?"
28: 7 Then go *q* and tell the disciples:
Lk 14:21 'Go out *q* into the streets and alleys of
16: 6 said, 'Take your invoice, sit down *q*,
19: 6 He *q* descended,
Jn 11:31 consoling her saw her get up *q* and go out,
Acts 14:20 His disciples *q* formed a circle about him,
Rom 9:28 for *q* and decisively will the Lord execute
16:20 peace will *q* crush Satan under your feet.

QUIET (31)

Nm 13:30 however, to *q* the people toward Moses,
Jgs 18: 7 manner of the Sidonians, *q* and trusting,
18:27 attacked Laish, a *q* and trusting people;
2Kgs 11:20 of the land rejoiced and the city was *q*,
1Chr 4:40 pastures, and the land was spacious, *q*,
2Chr 23:21 of the land rejoiced and the city was *q*,
1Mc 7:50 for a short time the land of Judah was *q*.
9:57 and the land of Judah was *q* for two years.
2Mc 14: 4 On that occasion he kept *q*.
14: 6 keep the kingdom from enjoying peace and *q*.
Jb 20:20 Though he has known no *q* in his greed,
Eccl 9:17 "The *q* words of the wise are better
Sir 25:19 to aged feet is a railing wife to a *q* man.
Is 30:15 in *q* and in trust your strength lies.
32:18 in secure dwellings and *q* resting places.
33:20 let your eyes see Jerusalem as a *q* abode,
62: 1 for Jerusalem's sake I will not be *q*,
65: 6 I will not be *q* until I have paid in full
Ez 16:42 I will be *q* and no longer vexed.
Jon 1:11 asked, "that the sea may *q* down for us?"
1:12 into the sea, that it may *q* down for you;
Mk 1:25 "Be *q*!
4:39 *Q*! Be still!
10:48 were scolding him to make him keep *q*,
Lk 4:35 Jesus said to him sharply, "Be *q*!
9:36 The disciples kept *q*,
18:39 in the lead sternly ordered him to be *q*,
Acts 12:17 He motioned to them to be *q*,
16:39 They came along and tried to *q* them;
1Cor 14:30 the first ones should then keep *q*.
1Tm 2:12 she must be *q*.

QUIETED (3)

Neh 8:11 [And the Levites *q* all the people saying,
Ps(s) 131: 2 stilled and *q* my soul like a weaned child.
Acts 19:35 Finally the town clerk *q* the mob.

QUIETER (1)

Acts 22: 2 them in Hebrew, they grew *q* still.

QUIETLY (6)

Jb 37: 8 take to cover and remain *q* in their dens.
Is 18: 4 I will *q* look on from where I dwell,
Jer 42:10 remain *q* in this land I will build you up,
Mt 1:19 her to the law, decided to divorce her *q*.
2Thes 3:12 to earn the food they eat by working *q*.
1Tm 2: 9 They should dress modestly and *q*,

QUINQUENNIAL (1)

2Mc 4:18 When the *q* games were held at Tyre in the

QUINTUS (1)

2Mc 11:34 *Q* Memmius and Titus Manius,

QUIRINIUS (1)

Lk 2: 2 took place while *Q* was governor of Syria.

QUIT (4)

Nm 32:22 *q* of every obligation to the LORD and to
Jos 2:20 be *q* of the oath you have made us take."
Is 33: 8 are desolate, travelers have *q* the paths,
Jl 2:16 Let the bridegroom *q* his room,

QUITE (20)

1Sm 20: 7 But if he becomes *q* angry,
28:21 and seeing that he was *q* terror-stricken,
2Sm 10: 5 word to them, since the men were *q* ashamed.
Neh 7: 4 Now the city was *q* wide and spacious but
Wis 15:14 but all *q* senseless,
Mk 8:32 He said these things *q* openly.
Lk 13:11 stooped *q* incapable of standing erect.
17:10 It is *q* the same with you who hear me.
Jn 16:32 each will go his way, leaving me *q* alone.
Acts 5:37 He too built up *q* a following,
8:13 as they occurred, and was *q* carried away.
9:23 After *q* some time has passed,
9:28 himself *q* openly in the name of the Lord.
18:18 Paul stayed on in Corinth for *q* a while;
22:28 "It cost me *q* a sum to get my citizenship."
28: 6 After waiting for *q* some time,
1Cor 15:34 Some of you are *q* ignorant of God;
2Cor 11: 4 you accepted, you seem to endure it *q* well.
Phil 2:20 I have no one *q* like him for genuine
Jas 2:19 You are *q* right.

QUIVER (11)

Gn 27: 3 your *q* and bow
Dt 32:41 sword, and my hand shall lay hold of my *q*.
Jb 39:20 Do you make the steed to *q* while his
39:23 Around him rattles the *q*,
Ps(s) 127: 5 Happy the man whose *q* is filled with them;
Sir 16:17 at his mere glance, *q* and quake.
26:12 tent peg and opens her *q* for every arrow.
Is 49: 2 me a polished arrow, in his *q* he hid me.
Lam 3:13 He pierces my sides with shafts from his *q*.
Hb 3: 9 is your bow, filled with arrows is your *q*.
3:16 at the sound, my lips *q*.

QUIVERED (1)

Ps(s) 77:19 the earth *q* and quaked.

QUIVERS (4)

Is 15: 4 of Moab tremble, his soul *q* within him;
22: 6 Elam takes up the *q*,
Jer 5:16 Their *q* are like open graves;
51:11 Sharpen the arrows, fill the *q*;

QUOTA (5)

Ex 5: 8 *q* of bricks as they have previously made.
5:18 you must still deliver your *q* of bricks."
1Kgs 5: 8 each brought his *q* of barley and straw to
1Thes 2:16 have been "filling up their *q* of sins,"
Rv 6:11 the *q* was filled of their fellow servants

QUOTE (2)

Ez 12:23 they shall never *q* it again in Israel.
Lk 4:23 "You will doubtless *q* me the proverb,

QUOTED (1)

Heb 4: 7 he spoke through David the words we have *q*:

QUOTING (1)

Jn 1:23 He said, *q* the prophet Isaiah,

R

RAAMA (2)

1Chr 1: 9 of Cush were Seba, Havilah, Sabta, *R*,
1: 9 The descendants of *R* were Sheba and Dedan.

RAAMAH (3)

Gn 10: 7 Seba, Havilah, Sabtah, *R*, and Sabteca.
10: 7 The descendants of *R*:
Ez 27:22 of Sheba and *R* also traded with you,

RAAMIAH (1)

Neh 7: 7 Zerubbabel, Jeshua, Nehemiah, Azariah, *R*,

RAAMSES (2)

Ex 1:11 Pharaoh the supply cities of Pithom and *R*.
Jdt 1: 9 to Tahpanhes, *R*, all the land of Goshen,

RABBAH (15)

Dt 3:11 is still preserved in *R* of the Ammonites.]
Jos 13:25 as far as Aroer, toward *R* (that is,
15:60 (that is, Kiriath-jearim) and *R*;
2Sm 11: 1 they ravaged the Ammonites and besieged *R*
12:26 Joab fought against *R* of the Ammonites and
12:27 against *R* and have taken the watercity.
12:29 the rest of the soldiers and went to *R*.
17:27 son of Nahash from *R* of the Ammonites,
1Chr 20: 1 the Ammonites, and went on to besiege *R*,
20: 1 When Joab had attacked *R* and destroyed it,
Jer 49: 2 when against *R* of the Ammonites I will
49: 3 ravager approaches, shriek, daughters of *R*!
Ez 21:25 *R* of the Ammonites or to Judah's capital,
25: 5 I will make *R* a pasture for camels,
Am 1:14 I will kindle a fire upon the wall of *R*,

RABBI (15)

Mt 23: 7 of respect in public and of being called *R*.'
23: 8 As to you, avoid the title *R*.'
26:25 "Surely it is not I, *R*?"
26:49 over to Jesus, said to him, "Peace, *R*,"
Mk 9: 5 *R*, how good it is for us to be here!
11:21 Peter remembered and said to him, *R*, look!
14:45 then went directly over to him and said, *R*!"
Jn 1:38 They said to him, *R* (which means Teacher),
1:49 *R*," said Nathanael,
3: 2 *R*," he said, "we know you are a teacher
3:26 So they came to John, saying, *R*,
4:31 Meanwhile the disciples were urging him, *R*,
6:25 side of the lake, they said to him, *R*,
9: 2 His disciples asked him, *R*,
11: 8 *R*," protested the disciples,

RABBITH (1)

Jos 19:20 Shunem, Hapharaim, Shion, Anaharath, *R*,

RABBLE (1)

Jgs 11: 3 A *r* had joined company with him,

RABBONI (1)

Mk 10:51 *R*," the blind man said,

RABBOUNI (1)

Jn 20:16 She turned to him and said [in Hebrew], *R*!"

RACAL (1)

1Sm 30:29 to those in Eshtemoa, to those in *R*,

RACE (57)

Nm 13:33 giants [the Anakim were a *r* of giants];
Dt 32: 5 children, a perverse and crooked *r*!
32:20 What a fickle *r* they are,
2Kgs 17:20 So the LORD rejected the whole *r* of Israel.
Ezr 9: 2 the holy *r* with the peoples of the land.
Tb 8: 6 and from these two the human *r* descended.
Jdt 5:10 the number of their *r* could not be counted.
6: 5 revenge on this *r* of people from Egypt.
8:32 generation among the descendants of our *r*.
Est A: 6 war, to fight against the *r* of the just.
A: 8 The whole *r* of the just were dismayed with
6:13 beginning to decline, is of the Jewish *r*,
8: 6 how can I behold the destruction of my *r*?"
E:13 royal consort, together with their whole *r*.
E:21 of the chosen *r* into one of joy.
9:31 *r* the duty of fasting and supplication.
10: 3 and the herald of peace for his whole *r*.
1Mc 1:34 There they installed a sinful *r*,
2Mc 7:28 same way the human *r* came into existence.
8: 9 nations to wipe out the entire Jewish *r*.
12:31 disposed to their *r* in the future also.
Ps(s) 24: 6 Such is the *r* that seeks for him,
Eccl 9:11 the sun that the *r* is not won by the swift,
Wis 10:15 The holy people and blameless *r*—
12:10 *r* was wicked and their malice ingrained,
12:11 they were a *r* accursed from the beginning.
14: 6 raft, left to the world a future for his *r*,
Sir 44:17 renewed the *r* in the time of devastation.
45: 9 the children of his *r* would be remembered;
Is 1: 4 people laden with wickedness, evil *r*,
14:20 be named forever, that scion of an evil *r*!
57: 3 sons of a sorceress, adulterous, wanton *r*!
57: 4 not rebellious children, a worthless *r*;
61: 9 them as a *r* the LORD has blessed.
65:23 For a *r* blessed by the LORD are they and
66:22 LORD, so shall your *r* and your name endure.
Jer 8: 3 survivors of this wicked *r* who remain
12: 5 wearied you, how will you *r* against horses?
31:36 Then shall the *r* of Israel cease as a
31:37 *r* of Israel because of all they have done,
33:26 descendants rulers for the *r* of Abraham,
Bar 4: 3 to another, your privileges to an alien *r*.
Ez 31: 6 shade dwelt numerous peoples of every *r*.
44:22 women, but only virgins of the *r* of Israel;
Dn 9: 1 son of Ahasuerus, of the *r* of the Medes,
Mi 2: 3 I am planning against this *r* an evil from
Acts 20:24 I can finish my *r* and complete the service
1Cor 9:24 runners in the stadium take part in the *r*,
Phil 2:16 run the *r* in vain or work to no purpose.
2Tm 4: 7 the good fight, I have finished the *r*,
Heb 12: 1 in running the *r* which lies ahead;
1Pt 2: 9 You, however, are "a chosen *r*,
Rv 5: 9 for God men of every *r* and tongue,
7: 9 no one could count from every nation and *r*,
11: 9 Men from every people and *r*,
13: 7 granted authority over every *r* and people,
14: 6 to the whole world, to every nation and *r*,

RACES (1)

Est 3:13 in with all the *r* throughout the world,

RACHEL (40)

Gn 29: 6 here comes his daughter *R* with his flock."
29: 9 them, *R* arrived with her father's sheep;
29:10 As soon as Jacob saw *R*,
29:11 Then Jacob kissed *R* and burst into tears.
29:16 the older was called Leah, the younger *R*.
29:17 eyes, but *R* was well formed and beautiful.
29:18 Since Jacob had fallen in love with *R*,
29:18 seven years for your younger daughter *R*."
29:20 So Jacob served seven years for *R*,
29:25 Was it not for *R* that I served you?
29:28 Laban gave him his daughter *R* in marriage.
29:29 to his daughter *R* as her maidservant.)
29:30 then consummated his marriage with *R* also,
29:31 made her fruitful, while *R* remained barren.
30: 1 When *R* saw that she failed to bear
30: 6 Bilhah conceived and bore a son, *R* said,
30: 8 again and bore a second son, and *R* said,
30:14 *R* asked Leah,
30:15 *R* answered.
30:22 Then God remembered *R*;
30:25 After *R* gave birth to Joseph,
31: 4 So Jacob sent for *R* and Leah to meet him
31:14 *R* and Leah answered him:
31:19 and *R* had meanwhile appropriated her
31:32 had no idea that *R* had stolen the idols.
31:34 Now *R* had taken the idols,
31:35 without finding them, *R* said to her father,
33: 1 among Leah, *R* and the two maidservants,
33: 2 her children next, and *R* and Joseph last.
33: 7 *R* and her children came forward and bowed
35:16 *R* began to be in labor and to suffer great
35:19 Thus *R* died; and she was buried
35:24 the sons of *R*:
46:19 The sons of Jacob's wife *R*:
46:22 These were the sons whom *R* bore to Jacob
46:25 whom Laban had given to his daughter *R*;
48: 7 returning from Paddan, your mother *R* died,
Ru 4:11 wife come into your house like *R* and Leah,
Jer 31:15 *R* mourns her children,
Mt 2:18 *R* bewailing her children;

RACHEL'S (5)

Gn 30: 7 *R* maidservant Bilhah conceived again and
31:33 Leaving Leah's tent, he went into *R*.
35:20 same monument marks *R* grave to this day.
35:25 the sons of *R* maid Bilhah:
1Sm 10: 2 you will meet two men near *R* tomb at

RACING (1)

Phil 3:12 but I am *r* to grasp the prize if possible,

RACKED (4)

2Mc 9: 7 part of his body was *r* by the violent fall.
9:11 of God, for he was *r* with pain unceasingly.
Ps(s) 22:15 all my bones are *r*.
Mt 4:24 with various diseases and *r* with pain:

RADDAI (1)

1Chr 2:14 the third, Nethanel, the fourth, *R*,

RADIANCE (3)

Sir 26:16 of a virtuous wife is the *r* of her home.
Is 60: 3 by your light, and kings by your shining *r*.
Rv 21:11 The city had the *r* of a precious jewel

RADIANT (7)

Ex 34:29 become *r* while he conversed with the LORD.
34:30 how *r* the skin of his face had become,
34:35 see that the skin of Moses' face was *r*;
Ps(s) 34: 6 Look to him that you may be *r* with joy,
Sg 5:10 My lover is *r* and ruddy;
Is 60: 5 Then you shall be *r* at what you see,
Mt 17: 2 as the sun, his clothes as *r* as light.

RAFT (2)

Wis 14: 5 have been safe crossing the surge on a *r*.
14: 6 of the universe, who took refuge on a *r*,

RAFTERS (5)

1Kgs 6: 9 was roofed in with *r* and boards of cedar.
6:16 cedar partitions from the floor to the *r*,
2Chr 34:11 for the tie beams and *r* of the buildings
Eccl 10:18 When hands are lazy, the *r* sag;
Sg 1:17 the beams of our house are cedars, our *r*,

RAFTS (2)

1Kgs 5:23 and I will arrange them into *r* in the sea
5:23 There I will break up the *r*,

RAG (1)

Est C:27 abhor it like a polluted *r*,

RAGAE (2)

Jdt 1: 5 in the vast plain, in the district of *R*.
1:15 himself he overtook in the mountains of *R*,

RAGE (25)

Gn 49: 7 their fury so fierce, and their *r* so cruel!
Dt 32:22 shall *r* to the depths of the nether world,
2Kgs 19:27 you come or go, and also your *r* against me.
19:28 Because of your *r* against me and your fury
Tb 1:18 In his *r* he killed many Israelites,
Jdt 1:12 into a violent *r* against all that land,
1Mc 7:35 In a *r* he swore:
15:36 had seen, the king fell into a violent *r*.
2Mc 4:25 a cruel tyrant and the *r* of a wild beast.
9: 7 Breathing fire in his *r* against the Jews,
Ps(s) 2: 1 the nations *r* and the peoples utter folly?
46: 4 Though its waters *r* and foam and the
102: 9 their *r* against me they make a curse of me.
Prv 29: 9 he may *r* or laugh but can have no peace.
Is 37:28 you come or go, and also your *r* against me.
37:29 Because of your *r* against me and your fury
Jer 21: 5 arm, in anger, and wrath, and great *r*!
32:37 in anger, wrath, and great *r* I banish them;
Dn 3:13 flew into a *r* and sent for Shadrach,
3:19 became livid with utter *r* against Shadrach,
11:30 his *r* and energy against the holy covenant;
Hb 3: 8 the streams, your *r* against the sea,
Acts 4:25 'Why did the Gentiles *r*,
27:20 to be seen, so savagely did the storm *r*.
Gal 5:20 bickering, jealousy, outbursts of *r*,

RAGED (4)

1Sm 18:10 God came over Saul, and he *r* in his house.
31: 3 The battle *r* around Saul,
1Mc 9:13 the battle *r* from morning until evening.
Rv 11:18 The nations have *r* in anger,

RAGES (11)

Tb 1:14 Gabael, son of Gabri, who lived at *R*,
4: 1 he had deposited with Gabael at *R* in Media,
4:20 with Gabri's son Gabael at *R* in Media.
5: 6 kinsman Gabael, who lives at *R* in Media.
5: 6 travel from Ecbatana to *R*, for *R* is situated
6:13 When we return from *R*,
6:13 And when we return from *R*,
9: 2 servants and two camels and travel to *R*.
9: 5 and two camels, traveled to *R* in Media,
Na 1: 8 have recourse to him, when the flood *r*;

RAGING (9)

2Mc 5:11 *R* like a wild animal,
Ps(s) 50: 3 around him is a *r* storm.
83:15 As a fire *r* in a forest,
124: 5 us then would have swept the *r* waters.
Sir 36: 8 Let *r* fire consume the fugitive,
Is 30:30 In *r* fury and flame of consuming fire,
Dn 3:88 the *r* flame and delivered us from the fire.
Jon 1:15 him into the sea, and the sea's *r* abated.
Heb 11:34 broke the jaws of lions, put out *r* fires,

RAGS (6)

Prv 23:21 to poverty, and torpor clothes a man in *r*.
Is 30:22 them away like filthy *r* to which you say,
64: 5 all our good deeds are like polluted *r*;
Jer 38:11 from which he took some old, tattered *r*;
38:12 *r* between your armpits and the ropes."
41: 5 men with beards shaved off, clothes in *r*,

RAGUEL (21)

Tb 6:11 "Tonight we must stay with *R*,
6:13 I know that *R* cannot keep her from you or
7: 1 Azariah, lead me straight to our kinsman *R*."
7: 1 So he brought him to the house of *R*,
7: 6 *R* sprang up and kissed him,
7: 9 *R* slaughtered a ram from the flock and
7: 9 ask *R* to let me marry my kinswoman Sarah."
7:10 *R* overheard the words;
7:11 *R* said to him:
7:12 Then *R* called his daughter Sarah,
7:15 Later *R* called his wife Edna and said,
8: 9 But *R* got up and summoned his servants.
8:11 *R* went back into the house and called his
8:15 *R* praised the God of heaven in these words:
9: 3 You witnessed the oath that *R* has sworn;
10: 7 which *R* had sworn to hold for his daughter,
10: 8 *R* said to Tobiah:
10:10 *R* then promptly handed over to Tobiah
10:14 When Tobiah left *R*,
10:14 he said good-bye to *R* and his wife Edna,
14:12 in Ecbatana with his father-in-law *R*.

RAGUEL'S (6)

Tb 3: 7 it so happened that *R* daughter Sarah also
3:17 *R* daughter Sarah to Tobit's son Tobiah,
3:17 *R* daughter Sarah came downstairs from her
9: 6 When they entered *R* house,
11:15 and that he had married *R* daughter Sarah,
14:13 Then he inherited *R* estate as well as that

RAHAB (14)

Jos 2: 1 went into the house of a harlot named *R*,
2: 3 So the king of Jericho sent *R* the order,
2: 8 *R* came to them on the roof and said:
6:17 Only the harlot *R* and all who are in the
6:23 The spies entered and brought out *R*,
6:25 Because *R* the harlot had hidden the
Jb 9:13 the helpers of *R* bow beneath him.
26:12 up the sea, and by his might he crushes *R*;
Ps(s) 89:11 You have crushed *R* with a mortal blow;
Is 30: 7 Therefore I call her *R* quelled."
51: 9 Was it not you who crushed *R*,
Mt 1: 5 the father of Boaz, whose mother was *R*,
Heb 11:31 By faith *R* the harlot escaped from being
Jas 2:25 *R* the harlot will illustrate the point.

RAHAM (1)

1Chr 2:44 Shema became the father of *R*,

RAID (9)

Gn 49:19 by raiders, but he shall *r* at their heels.
Jgs 9:33 tomorrow morning, make a *r* on the city.
21:23 each of them from their *r* on the dancers,
1Sm 27:10 who asked, "Whom did you *r* this time?"
2Kgs 5: 2 the land of Israel in a *r* a little girl,
13:20 of Moabites used to *r* the land each year.
1Mc 9:36 Jambri from Medaba made a *r* and seized
Jb 1:15 and the Sabeans carried them off in a *r*.
Bar 4:26 off by their enemies like sheep in a *r*.

RAIDED (7)

Gn 49:19 "Gad shall be *r* by raiders,
1Sm 30: 1 the Amalekites had *r* the Negeb and Ziklag,
30:14 We *r* the Negeb of the Cherethites,
1Chr 14: 9 had come and *r* the valley of Rephaim.
14:13 Once again the Philistines *r* the valley;
2Chr 25:13 dismissed from battle service with him *r*
28:18 The Philistines too had *r* the cities of

RAIDERS (4)

Gn 49:19 "Gad shall be raided by *r*,
1Sm 13:17 *r* left the camp of the Philistines in
30: 8 of the LORD, "Shall I pursue these *r*?
2Kgs 6:23 Aramean *r* came into the land of Israel.

RAIDING (4)

1Sm 14:15 including the outpost and the *r* parties,
30:15 "Will you lead me down to this *r* party?"
30:15 master, and I will lead you to the *r* party."
2Kgs 13:21 when suddenly they spied such a *r* band.

RAIDS (2)

Jgs 11: 3 with him, and went out with him on *r*.
1Sm 27: 8 men went up and made *r* on the Geshurites,

RAILED (1)

1Sm 20:34 since his father had *r* against him.

RAILER (1)

Sir 23: 8 the *r* and the arrogant man fall thereby.

RAILING (3)

Sir 8: 3 Dispute not with a man of *r* speech,
9:18 Feared in the city is the man of *r* speech,
25:19 to aged feet is a *r* wife to a quiet man.

RAIMENT (1)

Ps(s) 45:14 her *r* is threaded with spun gold.

RAIN (107)

Gn 2: 5 for the LORD God had sent no *r* upon the
7: 4 Seven days from now I will bring *r* down on
7:12 nights heavy *r* poured down on the earth.
Ex 9:18 tomorrow at this hour I will *r* down such
9:33 the *r* no longer poured down upon the earth.
9:34 that the *r* and hail and thunder had ceased,
16: 4 will now *r* down bread from heaven for you.
Lv 26: 4 I will give you *r* in due season,
Dt 11:11 valleys that drinks in *r* from the heavens,
11:14 *r* to your land, the early *r* and the late *r*,
11:17 up the heavens, so that no *r* will fall,
28:12 heavens, to give your land *r* in due season,
28:24 For *r* the LORD will give your land powdery
32: 2 May my instruction soak in like the *r*,
1Sm 12:17 the LORD, and he will send thunder and *r*.
12:18 and the LORD sent thunder and *r* that day.
2Sm 1:21 may there be neither dew nor *r* upon you,
21:10 until *r* came down on them from the sky,
22:12 with spattering *r* and thickening clouds,
23: 4 making the greensward sparkle after *r*.'
1Kgs 8:35 the sky is closed, so that there is no *r*,
8:36 way to live and sending *r* upon this land
17: 1 shall be no dew or *r* except at my word."
17: 7 dry, because no *r* had fallen in the land.
17:14 day when the LORD sends *r* upon the earth.'"
18: 1 said, "that I may send *r* upon the earth."
18:41 drink, for there is the sound of a heavy *r*."
18:44 leave the mountain before the *r* stops you.'"
18:45 with clouds and wind, and a heavy *r* fell.
2Kgs 3:17 'Though you will see neither wind nor *r*,
2Chr 6:26 the sky is closed so that there is no *r*,
6:27 and send *r* upon your land which you gave
7:13 If I close heaven so that there is no *r*,
Jdt 8:31 Lord may send *r* to fill up our cisterns,
Jb 5:10 He gives *r* upon the earth and sends water
20:23 and *r* down his missiles of war upon him.
24: 8 are drenched with the *r* of the mountains,
28:26 for the *r* and a path for the thunderbolts,
29:23 They waited for me as for the *r*;
36:27 that filter in *r* through his mists,
36:28 them and the showers *r* down on mankind.
37: 6 likewise to his heavy, drenching *r*.
38:26 a path To bring *r* to no man's land,
38:28 Has the *r* a father;
Ps(s) 68:10 A bountiful *r* you showered down,
72: 6 shall be like *r* coming down on the meadow,
84: 7 early *r* clothes it with generous growth.
105:32 For *r* he gave them hail,
135: 7 with the lightning he makes the *r*;
140:11 May he *r* burning coals upon them;
147: 8 with clouds, who provides *r* for the earth;
Prv 16:15 and his favor is like a *r* cloud in spring.
25:14 Like clouds and wind when no *r* follows is
25:23 The north wind brings *r*,
26: 1 Like snow in summer, or *r* in harvest,
28: 3 like a devastating *r* that leaves no food.
Eccl 11: 3 are full, they pour out *r* upon the earth.
12: 2 while the clouds return after the *r*;
Wis 16:22 in the hail and flashed lightning in the *r*.
Sir 1: 2 The sand of the seashore, the drops of *r*,
35:24 of distress as *r* clouds in time of drought.
Is 4: 6 of day, refuge and cover from storm and *r*.
5: 6 command the clouds not to send *r* upon it.
25: 4 Shelter from the *r*,
25: 4 As with the cold *r*,
30:23 *r* for the seed that you sow in the ground,
32: 2 from the wind, a retreat from the *r*.
44:14 and the *r* made grow to serve man for fuel.
45: 8 like gentle *r* let the skies drop it down.
55:10 For just as from the heavens the *r* and
Jer 3: 3 showers were withheld, the spring *r* failed.
5:24 our God, Who gives us *r* early and late,
10:13 He makes the lightning flash in the *r*,
14: 4 no *r* in the land the farmers are ashamed,
14:22 nations' idols is there any that gives *r*?
51:16 He makes the lightning flash in the *r*,
Bar 6:52 king over the land, nor do they give men *r*.
Ez 13:11 I will bring down a flooding *r*,
13:13 of my anger there shall be a flooding *r*,
34:26 about my hill, sending *r* in due season,
38:22 flooding *r* and hailstones,
38:22 fire and brimstone, I will *r* upon him,
Dn 3:68 Dew and *r*,
Hos 6: 3 come to us like the *r*, like spring *r* that waters
10:12 till he come and *r* down justice upon you."
Jl 2:23 *r* come down for you, the early and the late *r*
Am 4: 7 Though I also withheld the *r* from you when
4: 7 sent *r* upon one city but not upon another;
4: 7 by rain, but another without *r* dried up;
Hb 3:10 A torrent of *r* descends;
Zec 10: 1 Ask of the LORD *r* in the spring season!
10: 1 And sends men the pouring *r*;
14:17 LORD of hosts, no *r* shall fall upon them.
Lk 12:54 west, you say immediately that *r* is coming
Acts 14:17 heavens he sends down *r* and rich harvests;
28: 2 for it had began to *r* and was growing cold.
Heb 6: 7 in the *r* falling on it again and again,
Jas 5:17 it would not rain and no *r* fell on the land
5:18 with *r* and the land produced its crop.
Jude 1:12 on the wind like clouds that bring no *r*.
Rv 11: 6 close up the sky so that no *r* will fall during

RAIN-CLOUDS (1)

Ps(s) 18:12 dark, misty *r* his wrap.

RAINBOW (4)

Sir 43:11 firmament by its brilliance, Behold the *r*!
50: 7 like the *r* appearing in the cloudy sky;
Rv 4: 3 the throne was a *r* as brilliant as emerald.
10: 1 in a cloud, with a *r* about his head;

RAINDROPS (1)

Mi 5: 6 coming from the LORD, like *r* on the grass,

RAINED (8)

Gn 19:24 at the same time the LORD *r* down
Ex 9:23 LORD *r* down hail upon the land of Egypt;
Ps(s) 68: 9 it *r* from heaven at the presence of God,
78:24 He *r* manna upon them for food and gave
78:27 And he *r* meat upon them like dust,
Sir 46: 6 Which he *r* down upon the hostile army till
Ez 22:24 [that is, not *r* on] at the time of my fury.
Lk 17:29 *r* down from heaven and destroyed them all.

RAINING (1)

Ezr 10: 9 the matter at hand and because it was *r*.

RAINS (8)

Jb 29:23 they drank in my words like the spring *r*.
Ps(s) 11: 6 He *r* upon the wicked fiery coals and
Sg 2:11 winter is past, the *r* are over and gone.
Wis 16:16 *r* and hailstorms and unremitting downpours,
Ez 34:26 season, *r* that shall be a blessing to them.
Mt 5:45 the good, he *r* on the just and the unjust.
7:27 The *r* fell, the torrents came,
Jas 5: 7 soil receives the winter and the spring *r*.

RAINY (4)

Ezr 10:13 people are numerous and it is the *r* season,
Prv 27:15 a *r* day the match is a quarrelsome woman.
Ez 1:28 *r* day was the splendor that surrounded him.
Mt 7:25 When the *r* season set in,

RAISE (108)

Gn 48: 4 and *r* you into an assembly of tribes,
Ex 23: 5 help him, rather, to *r* it up.
Dt 17: 7 be the first to *r* their hands against him;
18:15 *r* up for you from among your own kinsmen;
18:18 I will *r* up for them a prophet like you
26:19 he will then *r* you high in praise and
28: 1 will *r* you high above all the nations of
28:49 will *r* up against you a nation from afar,
32:40 "To the heavens I *r* my hand and swear:
Ru 4: 5 and *r* up a family for the departed on his
4:10 in order to *r* up a family for her late
1Sm 14:26 no one would *r* a hand to his mouth from it,
24:11 'I will not *r* a hand against my lord,
2Sm 7:12 ancestors, I will *r* up your heir after you,
1Kgs 14:14 the LORD will *r* up for himself a king of
2Kgs 23:35 the land to *r* the amount Pharaoh demanded.
1Chr 17:11 I will *r* up your offspring after you who
Ezr 5: 3 you to build this house and *r* this edifice?
5: 9 you to build this house and *r* this edifice?'
9: 6 ashamed and confounded to *r* my face to you,
9: 9 Thus he has given us a new life to *r* again
Tb 3:12 Lord, to you I turn my face and *r* my eyes.
Jdt 16: 7 garb to *r* up the afflicted in Israel.
1Mc 3:31 provinces, and so *r* a large sum of money.
2Mc 7: 9 world will *r* us up to live again forever.
7:34 *r* your hand against the children of Heaven.
8:10 Nicanor planned to *r* the two thousand
Jb 30:22 You *r* me up and drive me before the wind;
38:34 Can you *r* your voice among the clouds,
Ps(s) 20: 6 and *r* the standards in the name of our God.
41:11 you, O LORD, have pity on me, and *r* me up,
71:20 of the earth you will once more *r* me.
83: 3 For behold, your enemies *r* a tumult,
104:14 You *r* grass for the cattle,
109: 6 *R* up a wicked man against him,
138: 7 the anger of my enemies you *r* your hand;
Prv 2: 3 and to understanding *r* your voice;
8: 1 Wisdom call, and Understanding *r* her voice?
Sir 36: 2 *R* your hand against the heathen,
47: 5 warrior and *r* up the might of his people,
50:20 Then coming down he would *r* his hands over
Is 2: 4 shall not *r* the sword against another,
10:26 Then the LORD of hosts will *r* against them
10:26 and he will *r* his staff over the sea as he
11:12 He shall *r* a signal to the nations and
44:23 *R* a glad cry, you heavens:
44:26 Be rebuilt; I will *r* up their ruins.
49: 6 be my servant, to *r* up the tribes of Jacob,
49:22 nations, and *r* my signal to the peoples;
51: 6 *R* your eyes to the heavens,
52: 8 Your watchmen *r* a cry,
54: 1 *R* a glad cry,
58:12 foundations from ages past you shall *r* up;
60: 4 *R* your eyes and look about;
61: 4 shall *r* up And restore the ruined cities,
62:10 stones, *r* up a standard over the nations.
Jer 6: 1 in Tekoa, *r* a signal over Beth-haccherem;
7:16 *r* not in their behalf a pleading prayer!
10:20 to pitch my tent, no one to *r* its curtains.
23: 5 I will *r* up a righteous shoot to David;
30: 9 their king, whom I will *r* up for them.
33:15 time, I will *r* up for David a just shoot;
50:15 *r* the war cry against her on all sides,
50:32 there is no one to *r* him up.
51:12 Against the walls of Babylon *r* a signal,
51:14 who shall *r* over you the vintage shout!
51:27 *R* a signal on the earth,
Bar 6:26 the ground, the worshipers must *r* them up.
Ez 4: 2 *R* a siege against it:
18: 6 nor *r* his eyes to the idols of the house
18:15 or *r* his eyes to the idols of the house of
19: 1 *r* a lamentation over the prince of Israel:
21:27 slaying, to *r* his voice in the battle cry,
26: 8 about you, and *r* his shields against you.
31:14 in stature or *r* its crest among the clouds;
33:25 mountains, you *r* your eyes to your idols,
Dn 11:13 the king of the north shall *r* another army,
Hos 6: 2 on the third day he will *r* us up,
11: 7 they cry out to him, shall not *r* them up.
14: 8 they shall dwell in his shade and *r* grain;
Am 1: 2 from Zion, and from Jerusalem *r* his voice:
5: 2 upon her land, with no one to *r* her up.
9:11 day I will *r* up the fallen hut of David;
9:11 will wall up its breaches, *r* up its ruins,
Jon 4:10 cost you no labor and which you did not *r*;
Mi 4: 3 shall not *r* the sword against another,
5: 4 We shall *r* against it seven shepherds,
Zec 5: 5 *R* your eyes and see what this is that
11:16 For I will *r* up a shepherd in the land who
Mt 3: 9 God can *r* up children to Abraham from
10: 8 Cure the sick, *r* the dead,
Lk 3: 8 *r* up children to Abraham from these stones.
18:13 not even daring to *r* his eyes to heaven.
20:28 the widow and *r* posterity to his brother.
Jn 2:19 answer, "and in three days I will *r* it up."
2:20 you are going to *r* it up in three days'!"
6:39 that I should *r* it up on the last day.
6:40 Him I will *r* up on the last day."
6:44 I will *r* him up on the last day.
6:54 and I will *r* him up on the last day.
Acts 3:22 " 'The Lord God will *r* up for you a
7:37 'God will *r* up for you from among your
10:40 only to have God *r* him up on the third day
1Cor 6:14 up the Lord, will *r* us also by his power.
15:15 not *r* him up if the dead are not raised.
2Cor 4:14 will *r* us up along with Jesus and place
Heb 11:19 that God was able to *r* from the dead,
Jas 4:10 of the Lord and he will *r* you on high.

RAISED (182)

Ex 7:20 Aaron *r* his staff and struck the waters of
17:11 As long as Moses kept his hands *r* up,
29:27 thigh of whatever raised offering is *r* up,
Lv 7:32 the priest the right leg as a *r* offering.
7:34 that is waved and the leg that is *r* up,
9:22 Aaron then *r* his hands over the people and
10:14 offering and the leg of the *r* offering,
10:15 The leg of the *r* offering and the breast
Nm 6:20 offering and the leg of the *r* offering.
24: 2 When he *r* his eyes and saw Israel encamped,
Dt 13:10 Your hand shall be the first *r* to slay him;
Jos 5: 7 It was the children whom he *r* up in their
5:13 he *r* his eyes and saw one who stood facing
6:20 the signal horn, they *r* a tremendous shout.
11:13 by fire any of the cities built on *r* sites,
Jgs 2:16 Even when the LORD *r* up judges to deliver
2:18 Whenever the LORD *r* up judges for them,
3: 9 out to the LORD, he *r* up for them a savior,
3:15 out to the LORD, he *r* up for them a savior,
7: 6 Those who lapped up the water *r* to their
1Sm 14:27 he *r* it to his mouth and his eyes lit up.
2Sm 23: 1 the utterance of the man God *r* up,
1Kgs 7:35 there was a *r* collar half a cubit high,
11:14 LORD then *r* up an adversary to Solomon:
11:23 God *r* up against Solomon another adversary,
2Kgs 3: 4 Now Mesha, king of Moab, who *r* sheep,
19:22 against whom have you *r* your voice And
25:27 year of his own reign, *r* up Jehoiachin,
1Chr 21:16 When David *r* his eyes,
2Chr 5:13 and when they *r* the sound of the trumpets,
32: 5 where it was broken down, *r* towers upon it,
Ezr 3:11 and all the people *r* a great shout of joy,
3:13 *r* a mighty clamor which was heard afar off.
4:13 is rebuilt and its walls are *r* up again,
4:16 is rebuilt and its walls are *r* up again,
Neh 8: 6 and all the people, their hands *r* high,
Tb 13:18 "Blessed be God who has *r* you up!
Jdt 1: 3 the gates he *r* towers of a hundred cubits,
10:23 before him, but his servants *r* her up.
11: 2 Nor would I have *r* my spear against your
Est 3: 1 After these events King Ahasuerus *r* Haman,
6: 4 be hanged on the gibbet he had *r* for him.
1Mc 9:23 law *r* their heads in every part of Israel,
9:47 Jonathan *r* his arm to strike Bacchides,
13:27 and *r* high enough to be seen at a distance.
14:37 while he also *r* the wall of Jerusalem to a
2Mc 3:20 all of them with hands *r* toward heaven,
14:33 he *r* his right hand toward the temple and
15:29 so they *r* tumultuous shouts in their
Jb 30: 7 Among the bushes they *r* their raucous cry;
31:21 If I have *r* my hand against the innocent
Ps(s) 9:14 who have *r* me up from the gates of death,
41:10 of my bread, has *r* his heel against me.
60: 6 You have *r* for those who fear you a banner
106:26 Then with *r* hand he swore against them to
107:25 His command *r* up a storm wind which tossed
144: 8 while their right hands are *r* in perjury.
144:11 while their right hands are *r* in perjury.
Wis 10: 1 And she *r* him up from his fall,
Sir 24:13 "Like a cedar on Lebanon I am *r* aloft,
45: 6 He *r* up also,
46: 2 What glory was his when he *r* his arm,
46:20 from the grave he *r* his voice as a prophet,
51: 9 So I *r* my voice from the very earth,
Is 1: 2 Sons have I *r* and reared,
2: 2 the highest mountain and *r* above the hills.
18: 3 When the signal is *r* on the mountain,
23: 4 in labor, nor given birth, nor *r* young men,
37:23 against whom have you *r* your voice And
52:13 he shall be *r* high and greatly exalted.
Jer 6:17 When I *r* up watchmen for them:
28:15 you have *r* false confidence in this people.
29:15 has *r* up for us prophets here in Babylon"
Bar 2: 5 We are brought low, not *r* up,
Ez 1:19 *r* from the ground, the wheels also were *r*.
1:20 were *r* together with the living creatures;
16:24 you *r* for yourself a platform and a dais
19: 3 One whelp she *r* up,
19: 4 Then nations *r* cries against him in their
41: 8 was a *r* pavement completely enclosing it
Dn 4:31 I, Nebuchadnezzar, *r* my eyes to heaven;
7: 4 it was *r* from the ground to stand on two
7: 5 it was *r* up on one side,
8:25 he shall be broken without a hand being *r*.
Am 2:11 I who *r* up prophets among your sons,
Zec 2: 1 I *r* my eyes and looked;
2: 4 Judah, so that no man *r* his head any more;
2: 4 nations that *r* their horns to scatter the land
2: 5 Again I *r* my eyes and looked:
5: 1 I *r* my eyes again and saw a scroll flying.
5: 9 Then I *r* my eyes and saw two women coming
6: 1 Again I *r* my eyes and saw four chariots
9:16 jewels in a crown *r* aloft over his land.
14:13 shall be *r* against that of his neighbor.
Mt 11: 5 the deaf hear, dead men are *r* to life,
14: 2 it is he in person, *r* from the dead;
14:24 about in the waves *r* by strong head winds.
16:21 be put to death, and *r* up on the third day.
17:23 and he will be *r* up on the third day."
20:19 But on the third day he will be *r* up."
22:31 As to the fact that the dead are *r*,
26:32 But after I am *r* up,
27:53 of saints who had fallen asleep were *r*.
27:64 the people, 'He has been *r* from the dead!'
28: 6 He has been *r*, exactly as he promised.
28: 7 'He has been *r* from the dead and now goes
Mk 6:14 the Baptizer has been *r* from the dead;
6:16 whose head I had cut off, has been *r* up!"
6:41 the two fish, Jesus *r* his eyes to heaven,
14:28 But after I am *r* up,
16: 6 He has been *r* up; he is not here.
16:14 those who had seen him after he had been *r*.
Lk 1:52 thrones and *r* the lowly to high places.
1:69 He has *r* a horn of saving strength for us
7:22 the deaf hear, dead men are *r* to life,
9: 7 saying, "John has been *r* from the dead";
9:16 the two fish, Jesus *r* his eyes to heaven,
9:22 death, and then be *r* up on the third day."
16:23 he *r* his eyes and saw Abraham afar off,
17:13 distance, they *r* their voices and said,
22:53 the temple you never *r* a hand against me.
24: 6 He is not here; he has been *r* up.
24:34 were greeted with, "The Lord has been *r*!
Jn 2:22 Only after Jesus had been *r* from the dead
7:41 But an objection was *r*:
12: 1 of Lazarus whom Jesus had *r* from the dead.
12: 9 see Lazarus, whom he had *r* from the dead.
12:17 *r* him from the dead kept testifying to it.
13:18 of bread with me has *r* his heel against me.'
19:29 wine on some hyssop and *r* it to his lips.
21:14 the disciples after being *r* from the dead.
Acts 2:14 stood up with the Eleven, *r* his voice,
2:24 bitter pangs, however, and *r* him up again,
2:32 This is the Jesus God has *r* up,
3:15 But God *r* him from the dead,
3:26 When God *r* up his servant,
4:10 you crucified and whom God *r* from the dead.
4:24 All *r* their voices in prayer to God on
5:30 has *r* up Jesus whom you put to death,
13:22 removed him and *r* up David as their king;
13:30 Yet God *r* him from the dead,
13:34 As a proof that the one whom he *r* from the
13:37 God has *r* up did not undergo corruption.
Rom 4:24 in him who *r* Jesus our Lord from the dead,
4:25 our sins and *r* up for our justification.
6: 4 *r* from the dead by the glory of the Father,
6: 9 We know that Christ, once *r* from the dead,
7: 4 to that Other who was *r* from the dead,
8:11 who *r* Jesus from the dead dwells in you,
8:11 then he who *r* Christ from the dead will
8:34 Christ Jesus, who died or rather was *r* up,
9:17 says to Pharaoh, "This is why I *r* you up;
10: 9 in your heart that God *r* him from the dead,
1Cor 3:14 man has *r* on this foundation still stands,
6:14 God, who *r* up the Lord,
15:12 if Christ is preached as *r* from the dead,
15:13 of the dead, Christ himself has not been *r*.
15:14 And if Christ has not been *r*,
15:15 witness before him that he *r* up Christ;
15:15 did not raise him up if the dead are not *r*.
15:16 if the dead are not *r*, then Christ was not *r*;
15:17 and if Christ was not *r*,
15:20 as it is, Christ is now *r* from the dead,
15:29 If the dead are not *r*,
15:32 If the dead are not *r*,
15:35 will say, "How are the dead to be *r* up?
15:52 sound and the dead will be *r* incorruptible,
2Cor 4:14 knowing that he who *r* up the Lord Jesus
5:15 him who for their sakes died and was *r* up.
Gal 1: 1 and God his Father who *r* him from the dead
Eph 2: 6 *r* us up and gave us a place in the heavens,
Col 2:12 not only buried with him but also *r* to life
2:12 the power of God who *r* him from the dead.
3: 1 you have been *r* up in company with Christ,
1Thes 1:10 from heaven the Son he *r* from the dead
2Tm 2: 8 a descendant of David, was *r* from the dead.

RAISED (cont.)

1Pt 1:21 who *r* him from the dead and gave him glory.
Rv 10: 3 the seven thunders *r* their voices too.
10: 5 *r* his right hand to heaven and took

RAISES (26)

1Sm 2: 6 he *r* up again.
2: 8 He *r* the needy from the dust;
Tb 4:19 If the Lord chooses, he *r* a man up;
Ps(s) 113: 7 He *r* up the lowly from the dust;
135: 7 *r* storm clouds from the end of the earth;
145:14 falling and *r* up all who are bowed down.
146: 8 The LORD *r* up those that were bowed down;
Prv 1:20 in the open squares she *r* her voice;
Sir 10: 4 of God, who *r* up on it the man of the hour;
11:12 he *r* him free of the vile dust,
21:20 A fool *r* his voice in laughter,
28:17 A blow from a whip *r* a welt,
Is 5:25 his people, he *r* his hand to strike them;
8: 7 *r* against them the waters of the River,
9:10 But the LORD *r* up their foes against them
10:24 with a rod, and *r* his staff against you.
Jer 25:30 from his holy dwelling he *r* his voice;
29:31 a mission from me, and *r* false confidence,
Ez 18:12 give back a pledge, *r* his eyes to idols,
Hos 11: 4 like one who *r* an infant to his cheeks;
Jl 2:11 LORD *r* his voice at the head of his army;
4:16 from Zion, and from Jerusalem *r* his voice;
Jn 5:21 as the Father *r* the dead and grants life,
Acts 26: 8 to believe that God *r* dead men to life.
2Cor 1: 9 in ourselves, but in God who *r* the dead.
10: 5 that *r* itself against the knowledge of God;

RAISIN (5)

2Sm 6:19 bread, a cut of roast meat, and a *r* cake.
1Chr 16: 3 of bread, a piece of meat, and a *r* cake.
Sg 2: 5 Strengthen me with *r* cakes,
Is 16: 7 For the *r* cakes of Kir-hareseth they sigh,
Hos 3: 1 turn to other gods and are fond of *r* cakes.

RAISING (21)

Nm 20:11 Then, *r* his hand, Moses struck the rock
Dt 9:17 *R* the two tablets with both hands I threw
Jgs 21: 2 evening, *r* their voices in bitter lament.
1Kgs 15: 4 *r* up his son after him and permitting
Ezr 4:12 They are *r* up its walls,
Est D:12 *R* the golden scepter,
2Mc 12:37 *r* a battle cry in his ancestral language,
Ez 31:10 in stature, *r* its crest among the clouds,
Dn 10:10 touched me, *r* me to my hands and knees.
Am 6:14 Beware, I am *r* up against you,
Hb 1: 6 For see, I am *r* up Chaldea,
Mk 12:26 As to the *r* of the dead,
Lk 6:20 Then, *r* his eyes to his disciples,
Acts 10:29 to your summons without *r* any objection.
13:33 for us, their children, in *r* up Jesus,
17:31 in the sight of all by *r* him from the dead."
17:32 When they heard about the *r* of the dead,
1Cor 10:25 without *r* any question of conscience.
10:27 you, without *r* any question of conscience.
15:29 If the *r* of the dead is not a reality,
Eph 1:20 It is like the strength he showed in *r*

RAISINS (4)

1Sm 25:18 grain, a hundred cakes of pressed *r*,
30:12 of pressed *r* were also offered to him.
2Sm 16: 1 of bread, an ephah of cakes of pressed *r*,
1Chr 12:41 in great quantity of meal, pressed figs, *r*,

RAKE (1)

Sir 23:17 The *r* to whom all bread is sweet and who

RAKEM (1)

1Chr 7:16 named Sheresh, whose sons were Ulam and *R*.

RAKKATH (2)

Jos 19:35 cities were Ziddim, Zer, Hammath, *R*,
21:32 pasture lands and *R* with its pasture lands.

RAKKON (1)

Jos 19:46 Bene-berak, Gath-rimmon, Me-jarkon and *R*,

RALLIED (12)

Gn 48: 2 you," he *r* his strength and sat up in bed.
Ex 32:26 All the Levites then *r* to him,
1Sm 17: 1 The Philistines *r* their forces for battle
2Sm 2:25 Here the Benjaminites *r* around Abner,
Jdt 1: 6 To him there *r* all the inhabitants of the
1Mc 5:38 "All the Gentiles around us have *r* to him,
11:47 They all *r* around him and spread out
11:55 soldiers whom Demetrius had discharged *r*
14:30 *r* his nation and become their high priest,
15:10 his ancestors, and all the troops *r* to him,
2Mc 12:38 *r* his army and went to the city of Adullam.
Jer 40:15 All the Jews who have now *r* to you will be

RALLIES (1)

Hb 2: 5 nations, and *r* to himself all the peoples

RALLY (3)

Ps(s) 60: 3 our defenses; you have been angry; *r* us!
Sir 38:23 *r* your courage,
Jer 49: 5 flight, with no one to *r* the fugitives.

RALLYING (3)

1Chr 12:34 fifty thousand men *r* with a single purpose.
1Mc 9:14 with all the most stouthearted *r* to him,
2Mc 14:15 and that the Gentiles were *r* to him,

RAM (91)

Gn 15: 9 she-goat, a three-year-old *r*,
22:13 a *r* caught by its horns in the thicket.
22:13 So he went and took the *r* and offered it
31:38 I have never feasted on a *r* of your flock.
Ex 29:17 Cut the *r* into pieces;
29:18 entire *r* shall then be burned on the altar,
29:19 "After this take the other *r*,
29:22 "Now from this *r* you shall take its fat:
29:22 thigh, since this is the ordination *r*,
29:26 Aaron's ordination *r* and wave it as a wave
29:27 whether this be the ordination *r* or
29:31 ordination *r* and boil it in the holy place.
29:32 the *r* and the bread that is in the basket.
Lv 5:15 offering an unblemished *r* from the flock,
5:16 for him with the guilt-offering *r*,
5:18 *r* of the flock of the established value.
5:25 *r* of the flock of the established value.
8:18 He next brought forward the holocaust *r*,
8:20 After cutting up the *r* into pieces,
8:21 parts of the *r* on the altar as a holocaust,
8:22 forward the second ram, the ordination *r*,
8:29 was Moses' own portion of the ordination *r*.
9: 2 for a sin offering and a *r* for a holocaust,
9: 4 and an ox and a *r* for a peace offering,
9:18 Finally he slaughtered the ox and the *r*,
9:19 of fat from the ox and from the *r*,
16: 3 for a sin offering and a *r* for a holocaust.
16: 5 a sin offering and one *r* for a holocaust.
19:21 tent a *r* as his guilt offering to the LORD.
19:22 With this *r* the priest shall make
Nm 5: 8 from the atonement *r* with which the priest
6:14 one unblemished *r* as a peace offering,
6:17 up the *r* as a peace offering to the LORD,
6:19 shall take a boiled shoulder of the *r*,
7:15 one young bull, one *r*,
7:21 with incense, one young bull, one *r*,
7:27 one young bull, one *r*,
7:33 one young bull, one *r*,
7:39 one young bull, one *r*,
7:45 one young bull, one *r*,
7:51 one young bull, one *r*,
7:57 one young bull, one *r*,
7:63 one young bull, one *r*,
7:69 one young bull, one *r*,
7:75 one young bull, one *r*,
7:81 one young bull, one *r*,
15: 6 With each sacrifice of a *r* you shall
15:11 The same is to be done for each ox, *r*,
23: 2 offering a bullock and a *r* on each altar.
23: 2 and have offered a bullock and a *r* on each."
23:14 offered a bullock and a *r* on each of them.
23:30 offering a bullock and a *r* on each altar.
28:11 to the LORD two bullocks, one *r*,
28:12 with oil as the cereal offering for the *r*,
28:14 each bullock, a third of a hin for the *r*,
28:19 shall consist of two bullocks, one *r*,
28:20 for each bullock, two tenths for the *r*,
28:27 holocaust to the LORD two bullocks, one *r*,
28:28 for each bullock, two tenths for the *r*,
29: 2 holocaust to the LORD one bullock, one *r*,
29: 3 for the bullock, two tenths for the *r*,
29: 8 holocaust to the LORD one bullock, one *r*,
29: 9 for the bullock, two tenths for the *r*,
29:36 oblation to the LORD one bullock, one *r*,
Ru 4:19 of Hezron, Hezron was the father of *R*,
4:19 *R* was the father of Amminadab,
1Chr 2: 9 The sons born to Hezron were Jerahmeel, *R*,
2:10 *R* became the father of Amminadab,
2:25 the first-born of Hezron, were *R*,
2:27 The sons of *R*,
Ezr 10:19 their guilt they gave a *r* from the flock.
Tb 7: 9 Raguel slaughtered a *r* from the flock and
Jb 32: 2 Barachel the Buzite, of the family of *R*,
Ez 43:23 bull and an unblemished *r* from the flock,
43:25 and a young bull and a *r* from the flock,
45:24 for each bull and one ephah for each *r*;
46: 4 unblemished lambs and an unblemished *r*,
46: 5 a cereal offering of one ephah for the *r*,
46: 6 also six lambs and a *r* without blemish,
46: 7 one ephah for the bull and one for the *r*,
46:11 be an ephah for a bull, an ephah for a *r*,
Dn 8: 3 by the river a *r* with two great horns,
8: 4 I saw the *r* butting toward the west,
8: 6 *r* I had seen standing by the river,
8: 7 the *r* with furious blows when they met,
8: 7 It threw the *r*,
8:20 "The two-horned *r* you saw represents the
Mt 1: 3 father of Hezron, Hezron the father of *R*.
1: 4 *R* was the father of Amminadab,
Rv 13:11 horns like a *r* and it spoke like a dragon.

RAMA (1)

2Chr 22: 6 received at *R* in his battle against Hazael,

RAMAH (35)

Jos 18:25 *R*, Beeroth, Mizpeh, Chephirah, Mozah,
19:29 back to *R* and to the fortress city of Tyre;
19:36 Hammath, Rakkath, Chinnereth, Adamah, *R*,
Jgs 4: 5 situated between *R* and Bethel in the
19:13 for some other place, either Gibeah or *R*,
1Sm 1:19 LORD, and then returned to their home in *R*.
2:11 When Elkanah returned home to *R*,
7:17 Then he used to return to *R*,
8: 4 in a body to Samuel at *R* and said to him,
15:34 Samuel departed for *R*,
16:13 When Samuel took his leave, he went to *R*.
19:18 he went to Samuel in *R*,
19:19 told that David was in the sheds near *R*,
19:22 Saul then went to *R* himself.
19:22 and was told, "At the sheds near *R*."
19:23 At the sheds near *R* he,
20: 1 David fled from the sheds near *R*,
25: 1 they buried him at his home in *R*.
28: 3 by all Israel, was buried in his city, *R*.
1Kgs 15:17 *R* to prevent communication with Asa,
15:21 heard of it, he left off fortifying *R*,
15:22 beams with which Baasha was fortifying *R*.
2Kgs 8:29 on him at *R* in his battle against Hazael,
1Chr 27:27 Over the vineyards was Shimei from *R*,
2Chr 16: 1 *R* to prevent any communication with Asa,
16: 5 heard of it, he left off fortifying *R*;
16: 6 with which Baasha had been fortifying *R*,
Ezr 2:26 men of *R* and Geba,
Neh 7:30 men of *R* and Geba,
11:33 Anathoth, Nob, Ananiah, Hazor, *R*,
Is 10:29 *R* is in terror, Gibeah of Saul has fled.
Jer 31:15 In *R* is heard the sound of moaning,
40: 1 of the bodyguard, had released him in *R*,
Hos 5: 8 Blow the horn in Gibeah, the trumpet in *R*!
Mt 2:18 "A cry was heard at *R*,

RAMATH-LEHI (1)

Jgs 15:17 and so that place was named *R*.

RAMATH-MIZPEH (1)

Jos 13:26 (that is, from Heshbon to *R* and Betonim,

RAMATHAIM (2)

1Sm 1: 1 There was a certain man from *R*,
1Mc 11:34 three districts of Aphairema, Lydda, and *R*.

RAMBLE (1)

Prv 5: 6 you the road to life, her paths will *r*,

RAMESES (4)

Gn 47:11 the pick of the land, in the region of *R*.
Ex 12:37 The Israelites set out from *R* for Succoth,
Nm 33: 3 They set out from *R* in the first month,
33: 5 Setting out from *R*,

RAMIAH (1)

Ezr 10:25 *R*, Izziah, Malchijah, Mijamin, Eleazar,

RAMOTH (5)

Dt 4:43 *R* in Gilead for the Gadites;
Jos 20: 8 of Reuben, *R* in Gilead in the tribe of Gad,
21:38 at *R* in Gilead with its pasture lands,
1Chr 6:58 pasture lands, *R* with its pasture lands,
6:65 *R* in Gilead with its pasture lands,

RAMOTH-GILEAD (20)

1Kgs 4:13 the son of Geber in *R*,
22: 3 "Do you not know that *R* is ours and we
22: 4 "Will you come with me to fight against *R*?"
22: 6 I go to attack *R* or shall I refrain?"
22:12 "Go up to *R*; you shall succeed.
22:15 "Micaiah, shall we go to fight against *R*,
22:20 Ahab, so that he will go up and fall at *R*?'
22:29 King Jehoshaphat of Judah went up to *R*,
2Kgs 8:28 battle against Hazael, king of Aram, at *R*,
9: 1 this flask of oil with you, and go to *R*.
9: 4 young man (the guild prophet) went to *R*.
9:14 had been besieging *R* against Hazael,
2Chr 18: 2 him, and persuaded him to go up against *R*.
18: 3 of Judah, "Will you come with me to *R*?"
18: 5 and asked them, "Shall we go to attack *R*,
18:11 "Go up to *R*.
18:14 "Micaiah, shall we go to fight against *R*,
18:19 so that he will go up and fall at *R*?"
18:28 King Jehoshaphat of Judah went up to *R*
22: 5 battle against Hazael, king of Aram, at *R*.

RAMOTH-NEGEB (2)

Jos 19: 8 cities as far as Baalath-beer (that is, *R*)
1Sm 30:27 to those in Bethel, to those in *R*,

RAMP (4)

Ez 4: 2 build a tower, lay out a *r*,

21:27 at the gates, to cast up a *r*,
26: 8 tower against you, cast up a *r* about you,
Hb 1:10 He laughs at any fortress, heaps up a *r*,

RAMPART (7)

1Sm 25:16 For us they were like a *r* night and day
Lam 2: 8 grief on wall and *r* till both succumbed.
Dn 11: 7 and shall come against the *r* and enter the
Na 2: 2 guard the *r*,
3: 8 the flood for her *r* and water her wall?
Hb 2: 1 guard post, and station myself upon the *r*,
Lk 19:43 when your enemies encircle you with a *r*,

RAMPARTS (4)

2Mc 12:13 fortified with earthworks and *r* and
12:15 then they furiously stormed the *r*.
Ps(s) 48:14 Consider her *r*,
Is 26: 1 he sets up walls and *r* to protect us.

RAMPS (1)

Ez 17:17 When *r* are cast up and siege towers are

RAMS (82)

Gn 32:15 two hundred ewes and twenty *r*;
Ex 19:13 Only when the *r* horn resounds may they go
25: 5 *r'* skins dyed red,
26:14 shall make a covering of *r'* skins dyed red,
29: 1 Procure a young bull and two unblemished *r*.
29: 3 them along with the bullock and the two *r*.
29:15 "Then take one of the *r*,
35: 7 *r'* skins dyed red,
35:23 hair, *r'* skins dyed red or tahash skins,
36:19 for the tent was made of *r'* skins dyed red,
39:34 the covering of *r'* skins dyed red,
Lv 8: 2 the bullock for a sin offering, the two *r*,
23:18 yearling lambs, one young bull, and two *r*,
Nm 7:17 and two oxen, five *r*,
7:23 and two oxen, five *r*,
7:29 and two oxen, five *r*,
7:35 and two oxen, five *r*,
7:41 and two oxen, five *r*,
7:47 and two oxen, five *r*,
7:53 and two oxen, five *r*,
7:59 and two oxen, five *r*,
7:65 and two oxen, five *r*,
7:71 and two oxen, five *r*,
7:77 and two oxen, five *r*,
7:83 and two oxen, five *r*,
7:87 in all, twelve young bulls, twelve *r*,
7:88 were, in all, twenty-four oxen, sixty *r*,
23: 1 seven bullocks and seven *r* for me here."
23:29 prepare for me seven bullocks and seven *r*."
29:13 to the LORD thirteen bullocks, two *r*,
29:14 two tenths for each of the two *r*,
29:17 you shall offer twelve bullocks, two *r*,
29:18 *r* and lambs in proportion to their number,
29:20 you shall offer eleven bullocks, two *r*,
29:21 *r* and lambs in proportion to their number,
29:23 day you shall offer ten bullocks, two *r*,
29:24 *r* and lambs in proportion to their number,
29:26 day you shall offer nine bullocks, two *r*,
29:27 *r* and lambs in proportion to their number,
29:29 day you shall offer eight bullocks, two *r*,
29:30 *r* and lambs in proportion to their number,
29:32 day you shall offer seven bullocks, two *r*,
29:33 *r* and lambs in proportion to their number,
29:37 *r* and lambs in proportion to their number,
Dt 32:14 sheep, with the fat of its lambs and *r*;
Jos 6: 4 priests carrying *r* horns ahead of the ark.
6: 5 on the *r* horns and you hear that signal,
6: 6 *r* horns in front of the ark of the LORD.
6: 8 seven priests who carried the *r* horns
6:13 The seven priests bearing the *r* horns
1Sm 15:22 and submission than the fat of *r*.
2Kgs 3: 4 lambs and the wool of a hundred thousand *r*.
1Chr 15:26 seven bulls and seven *r* were sacrificed.
29:21 the LORD, a thousand bulls, a thousand *r*,
2Chr 13: 9 and seven *r* becomes a priest of no-gods.
17:11 flock of seven thousand seven hundred *r*
29:21 Seven bulls, seven *r*,
29:22 the *r* and cast the blood on the altar;
29:32 forward was seventy oxen, one hundred *r*,
Ezr 6: 9 young bulls, *r*, and lambs for holocausts
6:17 offered one hundred bulls, two hundred *r*,
7:17 to use this money to buy bulls, *r*,
8:35 twelve bulls for all Israel, ninety-six *r*,
Tb 8:19 four *r* which he ordered to be slaughtered.
Jb 42: 8 take seven bullocks and seven *r*,
Ps(s) 66:15 will offer you, with burnt offerings of *r*;
114: 4 The mountains skipped like *r*,
114: 6 You mountains, that you skip like *r*?
Is 1:11 of whole-burnt *r* and fat of fatlings;
34: 6 and goats, with the fat of *r'* kidneys;
60: 7 the *r* of Nebaioth shall be your sacrifices;
Jer 25:34 like choice *r* you shall fall.
50: 8 be like the *r* at the head of the flock.
51:40 lambs to the slaughter, like *r* and goats.
Lam 1: 6 Her princes, like *r* that find no pasture,
Ez 4: 2 camps, and set up battering *r* all around.
27:21 they dealt in lambs, *r*,
34:17 one sheep and another, between *r* and goats.
39:18 the blood of the princes of the land *r*,
45:23 seven bulls and seven *r* without blemish,
Dn 3:40 it were holocausts of *r* and bullocks,
Mi 6: 7 the LORD be pleased with thousands of *r*,

RAN (69)

Gn 16: 6 her so much that Hagar *r* away from her.
18: 2 he *r* from the entrance of the tent to
18: 7 He *r* to the herd,
24:17 came up, the servant *r* toward her and said,
24:20 and *r* back to the well to draw more water,
24:28 Then the girl *r* off and told her mother's
29:12 son, and she *r* to tell her father.
33: 4 Esau *r* to meet him,
39:12 hand, he got away from her and *r* outside.
39:15 his cloak beside me and *r* away outside."
Nm 17:12 his censer and *r* in among the community,
Jos 15: 2 The boundary there *r* from the bay that
15: 6 to Beth-hoglah, and *r* north of Betharabah,
15: 9 it *r* to the fountain of waters of Nephtoah,
15:10 to Beth-shemesh, and *r* across to Timnah.
16: 5 Ephraimites *r* from east of Atarothaddar
16: 8 From Tappuah the boundary *r* westward to
17: 7 another boundary *r* southward to include
17: 9 *r* north of the wadi and ended at the sea.
18:13 Then it *r* down to Ataroth-addar,
19:12 it *r* to the district of Chisloth-tabor,
19:27 direction, it *r* eastward of Beth-dagon,
19:34 it *r* through Aznoth-tabor and from there
Jgs 9:54 So his attendant *r* him through and he died.
13:10 the woman *r* in haste and told her husband.
1Sm 3: 5 He *r* to Eli and said, "Here I am.
10:23 They *r* to bring him from there;
17:48 while David *r* quickly toward the battle
17:51 Then David *r* and stood over him;
20:36 And as the boy *r*,
2Sm 18: 9 while the mule he had been riding *r* off.
1Kgs 2:39 two of Shimei's servants *r* away to Achish,
17: 7 After some time, however, the brook *r* dry,
18:46 who girded up his clothing and *r* before
19:20 Elisha left the oxen, *r* after Elijah,
Tb 11: 4 And the dog *r* along behind them.
11: 9 Then Anna *r* up to her son,
Jdt 1:15 of Ragae, *r* him through with spears,
6:12 they seized their weapons and *r* out of the
7:21 of Bethulia, and the cisterns *r* dry,
11:12 food gave out and all their water *r* low,
1Mc 6:46 He *r* right under the elephant and stabbed
16:21 But someone *r* ahead and brought word to
2Mc 3:19 maidens secluded indoors *r* together,
14:43 he gallantly *r* up to the top of the wall
14:45 anger, he got up and *r* through the crowd,
Jer 3:13 How you *r* hither and yon to strangers
23:21 send not send these prophets, yet they *r*;
Dn 13:25 as one of them *r* to open the garden doors.
13:38 garden, saw this crime, we *r* toward them.
13:39 he opened the doors and *r* off.
Mt 27:48 one of them *r* off and got a sponge.
28: 8 *r* to carry the good news to his disciples.
Mk 5: 6 at a distance, he *r* up and did him homage,
5:14 The swineherds *r* off and brought the news
5:29 of her affliction *r* through her whole body.
9:15 They *r* up to greet him.
14:52 he left the cloth behind and *r* off naked.
15:36 Someone *r* off,
Lk 15:20 He *r* out to meet him,
19: 4 He first *r* on in front,
24:12 Peter, however, got up and *r* to the tomb.
Jn 2: 3 At a certain point the wine *r* out,
20: 2 so she *r* off to Simon Peter and the other
Acts 8:30 Philip *r* ahead and heard the man reading
12:14 *r* in and announced that Peter was outside.
22:26 centurion *r* to the commander and demanded,
27:15 into the wind, we yielded and *r* before it.
27:41 but the ship hit a sandbar and *r* aground.

RANCOR (1)

Est 1:18 with corresponding disdain and *r*.

RANDOM (2)

1Kgs 22:34 Someone, however, drew his bow at *r*,
2Chr 18:33 drew his bow at *r* and hit the king of

RANGE (2)

Jer 25:30 Mightily he roars over the *r*,
Zec 4:10 of the LORD that *r* over the whole earth.

RANGED (3)

Gn 25:18 The Ishmaelites *r* from Havilah-by-Shur,
2Kgs 3:24 They *r* through the countryside striking
Wis 19: 9 For they *r* about like horses,

RANGES (2)

Jb 39: 8 He *r* the mountains for pasture,
Jer 23:10 the land mourns, the pasture *r* are seared.

RANK (24)

Gn 49: 3 excelling in *r* and excelling in power
Ex 20:23 Do not make anything to *r* with me;
1Kgs 11: 3 of princely *r* and three hundred concubines,
1Chr 15:18 with these, their brethren of the second *r*:
Neh 11:17 Bakbukiah, second in *r* among his brethren;
Est 1:14 service and held first *r* in the realm,
3: 1 son of Hammedatha the Agagite, to high *r*,
B: 3 who has gained the second *r* in the kingdom,
E:11 attained the *r* second to the royal throne.
10: 3 Mordecai was next in *r* to King Ahasuerus,
Jb 30: 1 disdained to *r* with the dogs of my flock.
Ps(s) 4: 3 Men of *r*, how long will you be dull
58: 2 justice and judge fairly, you men of *r*?
62:10 an illusion are men of *r*;
89: 7 For who in the skies can *r* with the LORD?
Jer 22:15 Must you prove your *r* among kings by
Dn 11: 7 of her line shall succeed to his *r*,
Hos 2:14 *r* growth and wild beasts shall devour them.
Mi 5: 4 it seven shepherds, eight men of royal *r*;
Mt 20:27 and whoever wants to *r* first among you
Mk 9:35 and said, "If anyone wishes to *r* first,
10:44 whoever wants to *r* first among you must
Lk 12:46 and *r* him among those undeserving of trust.
Acts 8:10 *r* of society were paying attention to him.

RANKLES (1)

Jb 34: 6 in my wound the arrow *r*,

RANKS (24)

Ex 12:17 I brought your *r* out of the land of Egypt,
Jos 7: 5 front of the city gate till they broke *r*,
24: 1 When they stood in *r* before God,
Jgs 20:33 They reformed their *r* at Baal-tamar,
1Sm 17: 8 He stood and shouted to the *r* of Israel:
17:10 "I defy the *r* of Israel today.
17:23 came up from the *r* of the Philistines and
1Kgs 22:34 "Rein about and take me out of the *r*,
2Kgs 11:15 "Bring her outside through the *r*.
2Chr 18:33 "Rein about and take me out of the *r*,
23:14 "Take her outside through the *r*,
Jdt 15: 2 No one kept *r* any longer;
16:12 they perished before the *r* of my Lord.
1Mc 4:35 Lysias saw his *r* beginning to give way,
Ps(s) 78: 9 sons of Ephraim, ordered *r* of bowmen,
Is 14:31 the north, without a straggler in the *r*.
Jer 8:14 Let us form *r* and enter the walled cities,
46: 5 With broken *r* They fall back;
46:21 in her *r* are like fatted calves;
Na 2: 6 troops are called, *r* break at their charge;
Mk 3:26 mutiny in his *r* and is torn by dissension,
Jn 1:15 'The one who comes after me *r* ahead of me,
1:30 me is to come a man who *r* ahead of me,
1Jn 2:19 was from our *r* that they took their leave

RANSACK (1)

1Kgs 20: 6 and they shall *r* your house and the houses

RANSACKED (1)

Gn 31:37 Now that you have *r* all my things,

RANSOM (24)

Ex 21:30 he must pay in *r* for his life whatever
Lv 25:51 of the sale price he shall pay back as *r*;
25:52 to his years of service shall he pay his *r*.
27: 8 determine the sum for his *r* in keeping
Nm 3:46 As *r* for the two hundred and seventy-three
3:48 and his sons as *r* for the extra number."
3:49 So Moses took the silver as *r* from those
3:51 gave this *r* silver to Aaron and his sons,
18:16 The *r* for a boy is to be paid when he is a
Tb 5:19 Rather let it be a *r* for our son!
1Mc 10:33 of my kingdom I set at liberty without *r*;
Jb 33:24 I have found him a *r*."
Ps(s) 49: 8 redeem himself, or pay his own *r* to God;
69:19 Come and *r* my life;
Prv 13: 8 A man's riches serve as *r* for his life,
21:18 The wicked man serves as *r* for the just,
Sir 18:19 the time of visitation you will have a *r*.
Is 43: 3 I give Egypt as your *r*,
45:13 let my exiles go free Without price or *r*,
50: 2 Is my hand too short to *r*?
Jer 31:11 The LORD shall *r* Jacob,
Mt 20:28 to give his own life as a *r* for the many."
Mk 10:45 to give his life in *r* for the many."
1Tm 2: 6 Jesus, who gave himself as a *r* for all."

RANSOMED (13)

Lv 27: 2 who are to be *r* at a fixed sum of money,
27:28 field, shall be neither sold nor *r*;
Dt 7: 8 and *r* you from the hand of Pharaoh,
9:26 majesty has *r* and brought out of Egypt
13: 6 Egypt and *r* you from that place of slavery.
15:15 of Egypt, and the LORD, your God, *r* you.
21: 8 LORD, your people Israel, whom you have *r*,
24:18 and the LORD, your God, *r* you from there;
Is 35:10 has *r* will return and enter Zion singing,
51:11 has *r* will return and enter Zion singing,
Lk 1:68 because he has visited and *r* his people.
Rv 14: 3 thousand who had been *r* from the world.
14: 4 They have been *r* as the first fruits of

RAPACIOUS (1)

Sir 14:10 The miser's eye is *r* for bread,

RAPACIOUSNESS (1)

Lk 11:39 but within you are filled with r and evil.

RAPHA (1)

1Chr 8: 2 the third, Nohah, the fourth, and R,

RAPHAEL (28)

Tb 3:17 So R was sent to heal them both:
5: 4 he found the angel R standing before him,
5: 8 R replied,
5:10 When R entered the house,
5:10 R said, "Hearty greetings to you!"
5:10 R said, "Take courage!
5:10 R answered: "Yes, I can go
5:12 R said: "Why? Do you need
5:13 R answered,
5:16 R replied: "I will go with him
6:11 close to Ecbatana, R said to the boy,
6:11 R continued: "Tonight we must stay
6:16 R said to him: "Do you not remember
6:18 heard R say that she was his kinswoman,
7: 9 and reclined to eat, Tobiah said to R,
8: 3 R pursued him there and bound him hand and
8: 3 Then R returned immediately.
9: 1 Then Tobiah called R and said to him:
9: 5 So R, together with the four servants
9: 5 R gave Gabael his bond and told him about
11: 2 near Kaserin, just before Nineveh, R said:
11: 4 both went on ahead and R said to Tobiah,
11: 7 R said to Tobiah before he reached his
12: 5 So Tobiah called R and said,
12: 6 R called the two men aside privately and
12:15 I am R, one of the seven angels
12:17 But R said to them:
12:21 When R ascended they rose to their feet

RAPHAEL'S (1)

Tb 8: 2 point Tobiah, mindful of R instructions,

RAPHAH (1)

1Chr 8:37 the father of Binea, whose son was R,

RAPHAIM (3)

1Chr 20: 4 Sippai, one of the descendants of the R,
20: 6 a giant, also a descendant of the R,
20: 8 These were the descendants of the R of

RAPHAIN (1)

Jdt 8: 1 son of Ananias, son of Gideon, son of R,

RAPHON (1)

1Mc 5:37 another army and camped opposite R,

RAPHU (1)

Nm 13: 9 Palti, son of R, of the tribe

RAPID (1)

Dn 9:21 came to me in r flight at the time of the

RAPIDLY (1)

Mk 9:25 Jesus, on seeing a crowd r gathering,

RAPINE (1)

Hb 1: 9 each comes for the r,

RAPTURE (1)

Jdt 12:16 The heart of Holofernes was in r over her,

RARE (2)

Is 13:12 I will make mortals more r than pure gold,
Rom 5: 7 It is r that anyone should lay down his

RASH (9)

Nm 22:32 hinder you because this r journey of yours
30: 7 a r pledge to which she bound herself,
30: 9 r pledge to which she had bound herself,
1Sm 14:24 And Saul swore a very r oath that day,
Ps(s) 39: 3 I refrained from r speech.
106:33 and the r utterance passed his lips.
Prv 21: 5 but all r haste leads certainly to poverty.
Hb 2: 4 The r man has no integrity;
Acts 19:36 must calm yourselves and not do anything r.

RASHLY (6)

Lv 5: 4 of it, r utters an oath to do good or evil,
5: 4 such as men are accustomed to utter r,
1Mc 5:67 had gone out r to fight in their desire
Prv 20:25 R to pledge a sacred gift is a trap for a
Eccl 9: 2 as it is for him who swears r,
Sir 9:18 speech, and he who talks r is hated.

RASSISITES (1)

Jdt 2:23 and plundered all the R and the

RAT (1)

Lv 11:29 the r, the mouse, the various kinds of lizards,

RATE (2)

Mk 4: 8 r of thirty- and sixty- and a hundredfold."
Phil 3: 8 I have come to r all as loss in the light

RATES (3)

1Kgs 10:29 r to all the Hittite and Aramean kings.
2Chr 1:17 At these r they served as middlemen for
Prv 17: 8 has a bribe to offer r it a magic stone;

RATHER (199)

Gn 18:24 r than spare it for the sake of the fifty
29:19 to give her to you r than to an outsider.
37:27 R, let us sell him to these Ishmaelites,
42: 2 we may stay alive r than die of hunger."
Ex 23: 5 help him, r, to raise it up,
23:24 r, you must demolish them and smash their
Lv 7:18 r, it shall be considered as refuse,
25:40 R, let him be like a hired servant or like
Dt 7:18 R, call to mind what the LORD,
32:47 r, it means your very life,
Jos 22:24 We did it r out of our anxious concern
Jgs 19:24 R let me bring out my maiden daughter or
1Sm 24:18 "You are in the right r than I;
30:24 R, the share of the one who goes down to
2Sm 10: 3 Is it not r to explore the city,
19:44 Also, we are the firstborn r than you.
2Kgs 18:27 it not r to the men sitting on the wall,
20:10 R, let it go back ten steps."
1Chr 10:14 and had not r inquired of the LORD.
19: 3 servants r come to you to explore the land,
23:28 R, their duty shall be to assist the sons
2Chr 6: 9 r, your son whom you will beget
17: 4 R, he sought the God of his father and
28:20 him, but to oppress him r than to help him.
36:13 his heart r than return to the LORD,
Ezr 9: 9 r, he has turned the good will of the kings
Neh 6: 8 r, it is the invention of your own mind."
6:12 r, because Tobiah and Sanballat had bribed
Tb 5:19 R let it be a ransom for our son!
8:16 R you have dealt with us according to your
Jdt 11: 4 R, you will be well treated,
Est E:15 but r are governed by very just laws and
1Mc 1:63 they preferred to die r than to be defiled
13: 6 R will I avenge my nation and the sanctuary,
2Mc 7: 2 We are ready to die r than transgress the
7: 7 "Will you eat the pork r than have your
14:42 preferring to die nobly r than fall into
Jb 3:21 search for it r than for hidden treasures,
7:15 prefer choking and death r than my pains.
9:15 him, but should r beg for what was due me.
32: 2 himself r than God to be in the right.
34:11 R, he requites men for their conduct,
35: 2 it right to say, "I am just r than God?"
35:11 Taught us r than the beasts of the earth,
35:11 us wise r than the birds of the heavens?"
37:21 Nay, r, it is as the light which men see not
Ps(s) 52: 5 evil r than good, falsehood r than honest
69:22 R they put gall in my food,
84:11 I had r one day in your courts than a
84:11 I had r lie at the threshold of the house
91: 8 R with your eyes shall you behold and see
131: 2 Nay r, I have stilled and quieted my soul
Prv 8:10 silver, and knowledge r than choice gold.
18: 2 but r in displaying what he thinks.
19:22 r be a poor man than a liar.
Eccl 4:17 r than the fools' offering of sacrifice;
5: 6 R, fear God!
6: 5 dead child is at rest r than such a man.
Wis 4: 9 R, understanding is the hoary crown for men,
7:10 And I chose to have her r than the light,
8:16 with her no grief, but r joy and gladness.
8:20 or r, being noble, I attained an unsullied
15: 9 R, he vies with goldsmiths
Sir 4:26 guilt, but of your ignorance r be ashamed.
16: 3 r die childless than have godless children!
25:15 would r dwell than live with an evil woman.
38:20 think r of the end.
Is 10: 7 R, it is in his heart to destroy,
36:12 it not r to the men sitting on the wall,
58: 6 This, r, is the fasting that I wish:
59: 2 R, it is your crimes that separate you
Jer 7:19 is it not r themselves,
7:23 This r is what I commanded them:
7:32 called such, but r the Valley of Slaughter.
9:13 but followed r the hardness of their
9:23 But r, let him who glories, glory in this,
14:12 R, I will destroy them with the sword,
16:15 but r, "As the LORD lives,
19: 6 or the Valley of Ben-hinnom, but r,
22:10 Weep r for him who is going away;
22:12 R, he shall die in the place where they
23: 8 out of the land of Egypt"; but r,
26:19 Did they not r fear the LORD and entreat
32: 4 r shall he be handed over to the king of
34: 3 r you will be captured and fall into his
44:17 R will we continue doing what we had
Bar 3:30 her, bearing her away r than choice gold?
6: 5 R, say in your hearts,
6:58 who are within, r than these false gods;
6:58 post in a palace, r than these false gods!
Ez 11:12 you have not kept; r, you have acted
12:23 R, say to them:
16: 5 R, you were thrown out on the ground as
16:33 r bestowed your gifts on all your lovers,
16:50 R, they became haughty and committed
17: 9 Will he not r tear it out by the roots and
17:10 Will it not r wither,
18:23 Do I not r rejoice when he turns from his
18:25 Is it my way that is unfair, or r,
18:29 that is not fair, house of Israel, or r,
33:11 man, but r the wicked man's conversion,
34: 2 Should not shepherds, r, pasture sheep?
Dn 2:44 r, it shall break in pieces all these kingdoms
3:95 yielded their bodies r than serve or worship
Hos 1: 6 r, I abhor them utterly.
6: 6 and knowledge of God r than holocausts.
Mi 1: 9 r, it has come even to Judah,
3: 4 R shall he hide his face from them at that
6:13 R I will begin to strike you with
7:18 anger forever, but delights r in clemency,
Mal 3:15 R must we call the proud blessed;
Mt 5:33 r, make good to the Lord all your pledges.
10:28 R, fear him who can destroy both body and
Lk 11:28 R," he replied, "blest are they who hear
11:33 a bushel basket, but r on a lampstand,
17: 8 Would you not r say, 'Prepare my supper.
Jn 3:19 but men loved darkness r than light
6:22 r, they had set out by themselves.
6:39 r, that I should raise it up on the last
9: 3 R, it was to let God's works show forth in
11: 4 r it is for God's glory,
11:51 It was r as high priest for that year that
20:17 R, go to my brothers and tell them,
Acts 1: 4 "Wait, r, for the fulfillment of my Father's
4:19 God's sight for us to obey you r than God.
4:32 ever claimed anything as his own; r,
7:39 would not obey; r, they thrust him aside
10:35 R, the man of any nation who fears God and
13:25 R, look for the one who comes after me.
15:11 Our belief is r that we are saved by the
17:25 R, it is he who gives to all life and
24:22 was r well informed about the new way,
25: 3 requesting that he favor them r than Paul,
Rom 1:12 r, what I wish is that we may be mutually
1:25 and served the creature r than the Creator
4:20 r, he was strengthened in faith
6:13 R, offer yourselves to God as men who have
7:13 R, sin, in order to be seen clearly as sin,
8:34 Christ Jesus, who died or r was raised up,
11:11 R, by their transgression salvation has
13:14 R, put on the Lord Jesus Christ and make
15:15 Yet I have written to you r boldly in
15:21 but r to fulfill the words of Scripture,
1Cor 1:10 r, be united in mind and judgment.
4: 6 association with one person r than another.
9:10 or does he not r say this for our sakes?
9:15 r die than let anyone rob me of my boast!
10:24 own interest but r that of his neighbor.
14:19 but in the church I would r say five
14:34 R, as the law states,
16:11 R, help him come to me by sending him on
2Cor 4: 2 R, we repudiate shameful,
5: 4 but r to have the heavenly dwelling envelop
5: 8 much r be away from the body and at home
7:14 R, just as everything I ever said to you
13:10 authority to build up r than to destroy.
Gal 2:14 according to Gentile ways r than Jewish,
4: 9 or r, have been known by him
Eph 4:15 R, let us profess the truth in love and
4:28 r, let him work with his hands at honest
5:11 done in darkness; r, condemn them.
6: 7 doing it for the Lord r than men.
Phil 2: 3 r, let all parties think humbly of others
2: 4 to others' interests r than to his own.
2: 7 R, he emptied himself and took the form of
2:21 own interests r than those of Christ Jesus.
3: 3 in Christ Jesus r than putting our trust in
4:17 not that I am eager for the gift; r, my
Col 2: 8 based on cosmic powers r than on Christ.
3: 2 on things above r than on things of earth.
3:11 R, Christ is everything in all of you.
3:23 Do it for the Lord r than for men,
1Thes 2: 4 r, having met the test imposed on us
2: 4 "the tester of our hearts," r than men.
2Thes 3: 8 R, we worked day and night,
3:15 r, correct him as you would a brother.
1Tm 1: 4 speculations r than that training
2:10 r, as becomes women who profess
3: 3 He ought not to be contentious but, r,
2Tm 1: 7 spirit, but r one that makes us strong,
3: 4 lovers of pleasure r than of God as they
Heb 2:16 angels, but r the children of Abraham;
11:25 r than enjoy the fleeting rewards of sin.
13:22 for I have written to you r briefly.
Jas 1:14 R, the tug and lure of his own passion
5:12 R, let it be "yes" if you mean yes and
1Pt 1:15 R, become holy yourselves in every aspect
2: 7 For those without faith, it is r,
3: 4 is r the hidden character of the heart,
4:16 r glorify God in virtue of that name.
2Pt 1:21 It is r that men impelled by the Holy

3: 9 *R,* he shows you generous patience,
3:18 Grow *r* in grace,
1Jn 2:27 *R,* as his anointing teaches you about all
4:18 *r,* perfect love casts out all fear.
5:18 *r,* God protects the one begotten by him,
2Jn 1: 5 *r,* it is a commandment we have had from
3Jn 1:14 *R,* I hope to see you soon,

RATIFIED (3)

Ps(s) 111: 9 he has *r* his covenant forever;
Dn 9:24 will be introduced, vision and prophecy *r,*
Gal 3:17 a covenant formally *r* by God is not set

RATION (3)

Lk 12:42 to dispense their *r* of grain in season?
Jn 3:34 he does not *r* his gift of the Spirit.
Rv 6: 6 "A day's pay for a *r* of wheat and the

RATIONED (2)

Gn 41:56 that had grain and *r* it to the Egyptians,
Jdt 7:21 to drink, but their drinking water was *r.*

RATIONS (15)

Gn 41:57 world came to Joseph to obtain *r* of grain,
42: 1 that grain *r* were available in Egypt,
42: 2 "that *r* of grain are available in Egypt.
42: 5 were among those who came to procure *r.*
42: 6 who dispensed the *r* to all the people.
42:26 their donkeys with the *r* and departed.
42:33 go home with *r* for your starving families.
43: 2 up all the *r* they had brought from Egypt,
44: 2 goblet, together with the money for his *r.*"
47:14 for the *r* that were being dispensed,
Lv 26:26 all the bread they dole out to you in *r*—
1Kgs 11:18 who gave Hadad a house, appointed him *r,*
22:27 feed him scanty *r* of bread and water
2Chr 18:26 in prison and feed him scanty *r* of bread
1Cor 9: 6 What soldier in the field pays for his *r?*

RATTLE (1)

Mt 6: 7 In your prayer do not *r* on like the pagans.

RATTLES (1)

Jb 39:23 Around him *r* the quiver,

RATTLING (2)

Jer 47: 3 hooves of his steeds, the *r* chariot,
Ez 37: 7 it was a *r* as the bones came together,

RAUCOUS (1)

Jb 30: 7 Among the bushes they raised their *r* cry;

RAVAGE (8)

1Mc 3:39 and *r* it according to the king's orders.
13: 1 army to invade and *r* the land of Judah,
13:20 Next he began to invade and *r* the country.
Prv 24:15 of the just man, *r* not his dwelling place;
Jer 5: 6 slay them, wolves of the desert *r* them,
5:10 Climb to her terraces, and *r* them,
49:28 Rise up, attack Kedar, *r* the Easterners.
Rv 7: 2 were given power to *r* the land and the sea,

RAVAGED (14)

Gn 31:40 How often the scorching heat *r* me by day,
41:30 When the famine has *r* the land,
1Sm 5: 6 He *r* and afflicted the city and its
2Sm 11: 1 they *r* the Ammonites and besieged Rabbah.
Tb 13:10 all who were *r* may he cherish within you
Jer 4:20 In an instant my tents are *r;*
9:11 Why is the land *r,*
12:10 Many shepherds have *r* my vineyard,
Ez 19: 7 He *r* their strongholds,
Hos 10:14 fortresses shall be *r* As Salman *r* Beth-arbel
Jl 1:10 The field is *r,* the earth mourns,
1:10 the earth mourns, Because the grain is *r,*
Na 2: 3 have *r* them and ruined the tendrils.

RAVAGER (5)

Jgs 16:24 our power our enemy, the *r* of our land,
Jer 48:15 The *r* of Moab and his cities advances,
48:18 Moab's *r* has come up against you,
48:32 upon your vintage, the *r* has fallen.
49: 3 Howl, Heshbon, for the *r* approaches,

RAVAGERS (1)

Na 2: 3 Though *r* have ravaged them and ruined the

RAVAGING (2)

Jos 22:33 and Gadites or *r* the land they occupied.
Ez 21:36 I will hand you over to *r* men,

RAVEN (3)

Gn 8: 7 had made in the ark, and he sent out a *r,*
Sg 5:11 his locks are palm fronds, black as the *r.*
Is 34:11 the screech owl and *r* shall dwell in her.

RAVENING (2)

Ps(s) 22:14 mouths against me like *r* and roaring lions.
Jer 2:30 sword devoured your prophets like a *r* lion.

RAVENOUS (7)

Gn 49:27 "Benjamin is a *r* wolf;
Lv 26: 6 I will rid the country of *r* beasts,
Ps(s) 17: 9 My *r* enemies beset me; they shut up
Prv 23: 2 to your throat if you have a *r* appetite.
28:15 Like a roaring lion or a *r* bear is a
Sir 39:30 fire and hail, famine, disease, *R* beasts,
Ez 34:25 with them, and rid the country of *r* beasts,

RAVENS (7)

1Kgs 17: 4 and I have commanded *r* to feed you there."
17: 6 *R* brought him bread and meat in the morning,
Jb 38:41 the *r* when their young ones cry out to God,
Ps(s) 147: 9 and to the young *r* when they cry to him.
Prv 30:17 Will be plucked out by the *r* in the valley;
Zep 2:14 the window, the *r* croak from the doorway.
Lk 12:24 Consider the *r:*

RAVINE (11)

Dt 3:29 while we were in the *r* opposite Beth-peor.
4:46 the Jordan in the *r* opposite Beth-peor,
34: 6 *r* opposite Beth-peor in the land of Moab,
Jos 8:11 north of Ai, on the other side of the *r.*
1Sm 14: 4 Flanking the *r* through which Jonathan
Jdt 11:17 will go out to the *r* and pray to God.
12: 7 night she went out to the *r* of Bethulia,
13:10 through the camp, and skirting the *r,*
1Mc 12:37 of the east wall above the *r* had collapsed.
Is 10:29 They cross the *r:*
30:28 in a *r* that reaches suddenly to the neck,

RAVINES (8)

Jdt 2: 8 Their slain shall fill their *r* and wadies,
Is 7:19 in the steep *r* and in the rocky clefts,
Ez 6: 3 mountains and hills, the *r* and valleys]:
31:12 lay broken in all the *r* of the land,
34:13 the land's *r* and all its inhabited places].
35: 8 and all your *r* [in them the slain shall
36: 4 the mountains and hills, the *r* and valleys,
36: 6 the mountains and hills, the *r* and valleys:

RAVISH (1)

Jgs 19:24 *R* them, or do whatever you want with them;

RAVISHED (5)

Sg 4: 9 You have *r* my heart,
4: 9 *r* my heart with one glance of your eyes,
Is 13:16 shall be plundered and their wives *r.*
Lam 5:11 The wives in Zion were *r* by the enemy,
Zec 14: 2 shall be taken, houses plundered, women *r;*

RAW (8)

Ex 12: 9 It shall not be eaten *r* or boiled,
Lv 13:10 hair white and that there is *r* flesh in it,
13:14 But as soon as *r* flesh appears on him,
13:15 on observing the *r* flesh,
13:15 him unclean, because *r* flesh is unclean;
13:16 If, however, the *r* flesh again turns white,
1Sm 2:15 accept boiled meat from you, only *r* meat."
Jb 22:24 from your tent, And treat *r* gold like dust,

RAWBONED (1)

Gn 49:14 "Issachar is a *r* ass,

RAYS (4)

Wis 2: 4 by the sun's *r* and overpowered by its heat.
Sir 43: 4 it sets the mountains aflame with its *r;*
Hb 3: 4 *r* shine forth from beside him,
Mal 3:20 the sun of justice with its healing *r;*

RAZE (4)

Ps(s)
137: 7 "Raze it, *r* it down to its foundations!"
Is 25:12 The high-walled fortress he will *r,*
Ez 26: 4 destroy the walls of Tyre and *r* her towers.

RAZED (5)

2Chr 26: 6 the Philistines and *r* the walls of Gath,
Jdt 5:18 temple of their God was *r* to the ground,
1Mc 5:51 every male, *r* and plundered the city,
Ps(s) 74: 7 your name abides they have *r* and profaned.
Is 14:17 Who made the world a desert, *r* its cities,

RAZIS (2)

2Mc 14:37 A certain *R,* one of the elders of Jerusalem,
14:41 for fire to set the door ablaze, *R,*

RAZOR (7)

Nm 6: 5 nazirite vow, no *r* shall touch his hair.
Jgs 13: 5 and bear, no *r* shall touch his head,
16:17 and told her, "No *r* has touched my head,
1Sm 1:11 drink, and no *r* shall ever touch his head."
Ps(s) 52: 4 your tongue is like a sharpened *r,*
Is 7:20 Lord shall shave with the *r* hired from
Ez 5: 1 a sharp sword and use it like a barber's *r,*

RE-ECHO (2)

Lv 25: 9 trumpet blast shall *r* throughout your land.
Sir 50:18 Then hymns would *r,*

RE-ENTERED (1)

1Kgs 1:28 *r* the king's presence and stood before him,

REACH (68)

Gn 19:11 they were utterly unable to *r* the doorway.
32:20 thus shall you say to Esau, when you *r* him;
Ex 23:27 I will throw into panic every nation you *r.*
26:28 the boards, shall *r* across from end to end.
36:33 was made to *r* across from end to end.
Nm 11:23 Moses, "Is this beyond the LORD's *r?*
21:15 Arnon and the wadi gorges That *r* back
24: 7 waters, he shall have the sea within *r;*
34: 9 *r* to Ziphron and terminate at Hazar-enan.
Jos 3: 8 Jordan when they *r* the edge of the waters."
1Sm 2:31 that no man in your family shall *r* old age.
9:13 you may *r* him before he goes up to the
24:16 part, and grant me justice beyond your *r!*"
27: 1 of Israel, and I shall be out of his *r.*"
2Kgs 19:32 'He shall not *r* this city,
Neh 6: 7 like these must *r* the ear of the king,
Jdt 7:10 easy to *r* the summit of their mountains.
1Mc 5:48 cross your territory in order to *r* our own;
2Mc 6:14 patiently waits until they *r* the full measure
9:10 that he could *r* the stars of heaven,
12:21 hard to besiege and even hard to *r* because
Jb 3:22 and are glad when they *r* the grave:
20: 6 the heavens and his head *r* to the clouds,
28:17 it, nor can golden vessels *r* its worth.
34:28 But caused the cries of the poor to *r* him,
41:18 Should the sword *r* him,
Ps(s) 21: 9 May your hand *r* all your enemies,
21: 9 enemies, may your right hand *r* your foes!
24: 7 *r* up, you ancient portals, that the king
24: 9 Lift, up, O gates, your lintels; *r* up,
32: 6 deep waters overflow, they shall not *r* him.
71:19 power and your justice, O God, *r* to heaven.
107: 7 by a direct way to *r* an inhabited city.
119:170 Let my supplication *r* you;
139:18 did I *r* the end of them,
144: 7 *R* out your hand from on high
Wis 1: 9 the sound of his words shall *r* the Lord,
Sir 9:12 remember he will not *r* death unpunished.
31:14 nor *r* when he does for the same dish.
31:18 be not the first to *r* out your hand.
33:24 When your few days *r* their limit,
43:32 and weary not, though you cannot *r* the end;
Is 1:23 not, and the widow's plea does not *r* them.
8: 8 up to the neck it shall *r;*
15: 5 his fugitives *r* Zoar [Eglath-shelishiyah].
28:15 scourge passes, it will not *r* us;
30: 4 are at Zoan and their messengers *r* Hanes,
37:33 He shall not *r* this city,
48: 8 knew, they did not *r* your ears beforehand.
49: 6 salvation may *r* to the ends of the earth.
59: 9 is far from us and justice does not *r* us.
Jer 33: 3 things great beyond *r* of your knowledge.
42:16 you fear shall *r* you in the land of Egypt.
42:18 be poured out on you when you *r* Egypt.
48:28 that nests out of *r* on the edge of a chasm.
51:53 destroyers from me shall *r* her,
51:61 When you *r* Babylon,
Lam 3:41 us *r* out our hearts toward God in heaven!
Bar 4:22 swiftly *r* you from your eternal savior.
6: 2 you *r* Babylon you will be there many years,
Hos 10: 9 war was not to *r* them in Gibeah.
Am 9:10 who say, "Evil will not *r* or overtake us."
Mi 5: 3 greatness shall *r* to the ends of the earth;
Hb 2: 9 nest on high to escape the *r* of misfortune!
Mk 14:49 I was within your *r* daily,
Lk 8:19 they could not *r* him because of the crowd.
Acts 28:13 which enabled us to *r* Puteoli in two days.
2Tm 3: 7 never able to *r* a knowledge of the truth.

REACHED (139)

Gn 11:31 But when they *r* Haran, they settled there.
15:16 not have *r* its full measure until then."
19: 1 The two angels *r* Sodom in the evening,
22:10 Then he *r* out and took the knife to
24: 1 Abraham had now *r* a ripe old age,
24:30 When he *r* him, he was still standing
26:19 the wadi and *r* spring water in their well,
26:32 they told him, "We have *r* water!"
32: 7 Jacob, they said, "We *r* your brother Esau.
33: 3 ground seven times, until he *r* his brother.
37:14 When Joseph *r* Shechem,
45: 2 him, and so the news *r* Pharaoh's palace.
45:16 When the news *r* Pharaoh's palace that
Ex 3: 9 indeed the cry of the Israelites has *r* me,
16:35 manna until they *r* the borders of Canaan.
Nm 13:22 Going up by way of Negeb, they *r* Hebron,
13:23 They also *r* the Wadi Eshcol,
21:23 When he *r* Jahaz,
Dt 1:19 We had *r* Kadesh-barnea when I said to you,

REACHED (cont.)

12: 9 you have not yet *r* your resting place,
Jos 2: 1 When the two *r* Jericho,
4:11 quickly, and when all had *r* the other side,
9: 1 the news *r* the kings west of the Jordan,
13:16 Their territory *r* from Aroer,
17:10 they *r* Asher on the north and Issachar on
18:12 till it *r* the desert of Beth-aven.
18:14 Beth-horon till it *r* Kiriath-baal (that is,
18:16 flank of the Jebusites, *r* En-rogel.
19:22 The boundary *r* Tabor,
19:26 Amad and Mishal, and *r* Carmel on the west,
19:27 *r* Zebulun and the valley of Iphtahel;
24: 6 you out of Egypt, and when you *r* the sea,
Jgs 5:26 With her left hand she *r* for the peg,
8: 4 When Gideon *r* the Jordan and crossed it
13:11 When he *r* the man he said to him,
15:14 When he *r* Lehi,
15:15 he *r* out, grasped it, and with it killed a
20:47 fled through the desert *r* the rock Rimmon,
Ru 1: 6 plateau of Moab because word *r* her there
1:19 went on together till they *r* Bethlehem.
1Sm 4:12 the battlefield and *r* Shiloh that same day,
17:20 He *r* the barricade of the camp just as the
19:23 a prophetic condition until he *r* the spot.
30: 1 and his men *r* Ziklag on the third day,
2Sm 2: 4 A report *r* David that the men of
6: 6 Uzzah *r* out his hand to the ark of God and
13:30 a report *r* David that Absalom had killed
13:39 but his longing *r* out for Absalom as he
15:32 When David *r* the top,
17:18 They sped on their way and *r* the house of
19:11 When the talk of all Israel *r* the king,
19:16 When the king, on his return, *r* the Jordan,
22: 7 he heard my voice, and my cry *r* his ears.
22:17 "He *r* out from on high and grasped me;
1Kgs 14:17 when she *r* Tirzah and crossed the
2Kgs 3:24 But when they *r* the camp of Israel,
4:25 till she *r* the man of God on Mount Carmel.
4:27 when she *r* the man of God on the mountain,
4:32 When Elisha *r* the house,
5:24 When they *r* the hill,
6: 7 And the man *r* down and grasped it.
7: 5 but when they *r* the edge of the camp,
7: 8 After the lepers *r* the edge of the camp,
9:18 to the king, "The messenger has *r* them,
9:20 reported, "The messenger has *r* them,
9:21 They *r* him near the field of Naboth the
17:26 A report *r* the king of Assyria:
19:23 I *r* the remotest heights,
19:28 me and your fury which has *r* my ears,
1Chr 13: 9 As they *r* the threshing floor of Chidon,
2Chr 28: 9 them with a fury that has *r* up to heaven.
30:27 voice was heard and their prayer *r* heaven,
Neh 2:15 while till I once more *r* the Valley Gate,
Tb 1: 9 When I *r* manhood I married Anna,
10: 1 of days was *r* and his son did not appear,
11: 7 said to Tobiah before he *r* his father:
11:17 When Tobit *r* Sarah,
Jdt 2:21 Nineveh, they *r* the plain of Bectileth,
2:24 along the Wadi Abron, until he *r* the sea.
3: 5 *r* Holofernes and given him this message,
3: 9 *r* Esdraelon in the neighborhood of Dothan,
6:11 till they *r* the springs below Bethulia.
13:10 the ravine, *r* Bethulia on the mountain.
Est 4: 3 wherever the king's legal enactment *r*,
1Mc 3:16 When he *r* the ascent of Beth-horon,
3:26 His fame *r* the king,
5:42 But when Judas *r* the running stream,
5:46 When they *r* Ephron,
5:53 whole way, until he *r* the land of Judah.
11: 4 When he *r* Azotus,
12:40 and kill him, he set out and *r* Beth-shan.
14:10 his glorious name *r* the ends of the earth.
16: 9 John pursued them until Cendebeus *r* Kedron,
2Mc 4: 3 When Simon's hostility *r* such a point that
4:13 and foreign customs *r* such a pitch,
6:15 later, when our sins have *r* their fullness.
8:35 like a runaway slave, until he *r* Antioch.
11: 5 he invaded Judea, and when he *r* Beth-zur,
12:17 gone on some ninety miles, they *r* Charax,
14:28 this message *r* Nicanor he was dismayed,
Ps(s) 18: 7 my voice, and my cry to him *r* his ears.
18:17 He *r* out from on high and grasped me;
69: 3 I have *r* the watery depths;
Wis 4:13 while, he *r* the fullness of a long career;
18:16 he still *r* to heaven,
Sir 47:16 Your fame *r* distant coasts,
Is 10:10 Just as my hand *r* out to idolatrous
10:28 he has *r* Aiath,
14: 4 How the oppressor has *r* his end!
16: 8 While they *r* as far as Jazer and scattered
37:24 I *r* the remotest heights,
37:29 me and your fury which has *r* my ears,
Jer 37:13 But when he *r* the Gate of Benjamin,
Bar 3:21 have not perceived her paths, or *r* her;
Ez 33:22 when the fugitive *r* me in the morning.
Dn 6:25 Before they *r* the bottom of the den,
7:13 When he *r* the Ancient One and was
8:23 reign, when sinners have *r* their measure,
Jon 2: 8 My prayer *r* you in your holy temple.
3: 6 When the News *r* the king of Nineveh,
Mt 14:34 crossing they *r* the shore at Gennesaret;
Mk 11:13 When he *r* it he found nothing but leaves;
11:15 When they *r* Jerusalem he entered the
14:16 When they *r* the city they found it just as
15: 1 is, the whole Sanhedrin), *r* a decision.
Jn 10:31 of the Jews again *r* for rocks to stone him,
12:38 who has believed what has *r* our ears?
20: 4 disciple outran Peter and *r* the tomb first.
Acts 8:40 news in all the towns until he *r* Caesarea.
11:22 *r* the ears of the church in Jerusalem,
20:15 the next day, and *r* a point opposite Chios;
21:31 on his life when a report *r* the commander
21:35 When Paul *r* the steps,
2Cor 5:14 The love of Christ impels us who have *r*
Phil 3:12 It is not that I have *r* it yet,
3:13 of myself as having *r* the finish line.
3:16 our course, no matter what stage we have *r*.
Jas 5: 4 have *r* the ears of the Lord of hosts.
Rv 14:20 around, it *r* as high as a horse's bridle.

REACHES (22)

2Kgs 10: 2 when this letter *r* you decide which is the
Ezr 9: 6 our heads and our guilt *r* up to heaven.
Jdt 11:15 the response *r* them and they act upon it,
Ps(s) 36: 6 O LORD, your kindness *r* to heaven;
48:11 your praise *r* to the ends of the earth.
Prv 31:20 She *r* out her hands to the poor,
Wis 8: 1 she *r* from end to end mightily and
Sir 18: 7 days is great if it *r* a hundred years:
18:11 man, but the LORD's mercy *r* all flesh,
35:16 his petition *r* the heavens.
35:17 it does not rest till it *r* its goal,
40: 7 As he *r* safety, he wakes up astonished
Is 22:14 This *r* the ears of the LORD of hosts
23: 1 the land of the Kittim the news *r* them.
30:28 in a ravine that *r* suddenly to the neck,
65:20 a mere youth who *r* but a hundred years,
Jer 4:18 of yours, how it *r* to your very heart!
51: 9 Her judgment *r* heaven,
Mi 1: 9 to Judah, It *r* to the gate of my people,
Zec 14: 5 valley of those two mountains *r* its edge;
2Cor 12: 9 you, for in weakness power *r* perfection."
Jas 1:15 and when sin *r* maturity it begets death.

REACHING (13)

Gn 19:13 for the outcry *r* the LORD against those in
28:12 the ground, with its top *r* to the heavens;
Jos 19:11 *r* Dabbesheth and the wadi that is near
Jgs 19:29 On *r* home, he took a knife to the body
2Sm 24: 8 *r* Jerusalem again after nine months and
1Chr 17:17 servant's family *r* into the distant future,
Neh 6:17 of Judah, and Tobiah's letters were *r* them,
Jdt 16:23 *r* the advanced age of a hundred and five.
1Mc 12: 3 After *r* Rome,
Ez 48: 1 *r* from the eastern to the western boundary.
Mt 20: 2 After *r* an agreement with them for the
Lk 22:40 On *r* the place he said to them,
Acts 28:25 Without *r* any agreement among themselves,

REACTING (1)

2Mc 4:41 *R* against Lysimachus' attack,

READ (88)

Ex 24: 7 the covenant, he *r* it aloud to the people,
Dt 17:19 He shall keep it with him and *r* it all the
31:11 you shall *r* this law aloud in the presence
Jos 8:34 Then were *r* aloud all the words of the law,
8:35 Joshua *r* aloud to the entire community,
2Kgs 5: 6 of Israel he brought the letter, which *r*:
5: 7 When he *r* the letter,
19:14 from the hand of the messengers and *r* it;
22: 8 Hilkiah gave the book to Shaphan, who *r* it.
22:10 a book, and then *r* it aloud to the king.
22:16 in the book which the king of Judah has *r*.
23: 2 in the temple of the LORD, *r* out to them.
2Chr 34:18 And Shaphan *r* from it before the king.
34:24 that has been *r* before the king of Judah.
34:30 and he had *r* aloud to them the entire text
Ezr 4:18 sent us has been *r* plainly in my presence.
4:23 Artaxerxes' letter had been *r* before Rehum,
Neh 8: 3 he *r* out of the book from daybreak till
8: 8 *r* plainly from the book of the law of God,
8: 8 it so that all could understand what was *r*.
8:18 Ezra *r* from the book of the law of God day
9: 3 they *r* from the book of the law of the
Tb 12:12 it was I who presented and *r* the record of
Est 6: 1 While this was being *r* to him,
1Mc 10: 7 and *r* the letter to all the people.
14:19 were *r* before the assembly in Jerusalem.
15: 2 and to all the nations, which *r* as follows:
2Mc 6:12 Now I beg those who *r* this book not to be
9:18 It *r* thus:
11:22 The king's letter *r* thus:
15:38 delights the ears of those who *r* the work.
Is 29:11 one who can read, with the request, *R* this,"
29:12 When it is handed to one who cannot *r*,
29:12 "Read this," he replies, "I cannot *r*."
34:16 Look in the book of the LORD and *r*:
37:14 from the hand of the messengers and *r* it;
Jer 29: 3 sent to the king of Babylon, the letter *r*:
29:29 Zephaniah *r* this letter to the prophet,
36: 6 Do you go on the fast day and *r* publicly
36: 6 *r* them also to all the men of Judah who
36: 8 he *r* the LORD's words in the LORD's house.
36:10 *r* the words of Jeremiah from his book.
36:11 all the words of the LORD *r* from the book.
36:13 had heard Baruch *r* publicly from his book.
36:14 the scroll you *r* publicly to the people."
36:15 down," they said to him, "and *r* it to us."
36:15 Baruch *r* it to them,
36:21 and *r* it to the king and to all the
51:61 see that you *r* aloud all these words,
Bar 1: 3 *r* the words of this scroll for Jeconiah,
1:14 And *r* out publicly this scroll which we
Dn 5: 8 none of them could either *r* the writing or
5:15 to *r* this writing and tell me its meaning,
5:16 to *r* the writing and tell me what it means,
5:17 but the writing I will *r* for you,
Hb 2: 2 the tablets, so that one can *r* it readily.
Mt 12: 3 "Have you not *r* what David did when he
12: 5 Have you not *r* in the law how the priests
16: 3 sky, can you not *r* the signs of the times?]
19: 4 "Have you not *r* that at the beginning the
21:16 Did you never *r* this:
21:42 them, "Did you never *r* in the Scriptures,
22:31 have you not *r* what God said to you,
Mk 2:25 "Have you never *r* what David did when he
12:26 dead, have you not *r* in the book of Moses,
15:26 The inscription proclaiming his offense *r*,
Lk 6: 3 "Have you not *r* what David did when he
10:26 How do you *r* it?"
20:24 Whose inscription do you *r*?"
Jn 19:19 inscription placed on the cross which *r*
19:20 and Greek, was *r* by many of the Jews,
Acts 1:24 "O Lord, you *r* the hearts of men.
13:27 prophets which we *r* sabbath after sabbath.
15:21 town and has been *r* aloud in the synagogues
15:31 When it was *r* there was great delight at
2Cor 1:13 anything that you cannot *r* and understand.
3: 2 You are my letter, known and *r* by all men,
3:14 covenant is *r* the veil remains unlifted;
3:15 is *r* a veil covers their understanding.
Eph 3: 4 When you *r* what I have said,
5:14 That is why we *r*:
Col 4:16 read to you, see that it is *r* in the assembly
4:16 *r* the letter that is coming from Laodicea.
1Thes 5:27 the Lord that this letter be *r* to them all.
Heb 9:19 When Moses had *r* all the commandments of

READER (2)

Mt 24:15 on holy ground (let the *r* take note!),
Mk 13:14 let the *r* take note!—those

READIED (1)

Hb 1:12 O Rock, you have *r* him for punishment!

READILY (4)

2Mc 1: 3 him and to do his will *r* and generously.
Jb 3:24 For sighing comes more *r* to me than food,
Wis 6:12 she is *r* perceived by those who love her,
Hb 2: 2 the tablets, so that one can read it *r*.

READINESS (4)

Jdt 9: 6 All your ways are in *r*,
2Mc 14:22 Judas had posted armed men in *r* at
Wis 17: 7 And mockeries of the magic art were in *r*,
2Cor 7:11 not to speak of *r* to defend yourselves!

READING (15)

Neh 13: 1 when there was *r* from the book of Moses in
1Mc 5:14 While they were *r* this letter,
2Mc 2:25 aimed to please those who prefer simple *r*,
8:23 After *r* to them from the holy book and
Jer 36:23 Each time Jehudi finished *r* three or four
51:63 When you have finished *r* this book,
Bar 1: 3 well as all the people who came to the *r*:
Lk 4:16 habit of doing, he stood up to do the *r*.
Acts 8:28 in his carriage *r* the prophet Isaiah.
8:30 and heard the man *r* the prophet Isaiah.
8:30 him, "Do you really grasp what you are *r*?"
8:32 This was the passage of Scripture he was *r*:
13:15 After the *r* of the law and of the prophets,
23:34 The governor, upon *r* the letter,
1Tm 4:13 devote yourself to the *r* of Scripture,

READS (5)

Dn 5: 7 *r* this writing and tells me what it means,"
Lk 16:15 in the eyes of men, but God *r* your hearts.
Acts 15: 8 God, who *r* the hearts of men,
1Cor 15:27 Scripture *r* that God "has placed all
Rv 1: 3 is the man who *r* this prophetic message,

READY (110)

Gn 22: 1 *R*!" he replied
24:31 when I have made the house *r* for you,
24:51 Here is Rebekah, *r* for you;
37:13 Get *r*; I will send you to them."
37:13 "I am *r*," Joseph answered.
Ex 14: 6 his chariots *r* and mustered his soldiers
19:11 their garments and be *r* for the third day;
19:15 He warned them, "Be *r* for the third day.
34: 2 Get *r* for tomorrow morning,

Nm 14:40 *r* to go up to the place that the LORD
Dt 2:13 Get *r*, then, to cross the Wadi Zered.'
Jos 18: 8 to map out the land were *r* for the journey,
Jgs 19: 9 was *r* to go with his concubine and servant,
20:17 hundred thousand swordsmen *r* for battle,
Ru 1: 6 She then made *r* to go back from the
1Sm 12:16 stand *r* to witness the great marvel the
17:40 With his sling also *r* to hand,
2Sm 15:15 answered him, "Your servants are *r*,
15:26 say, 'I am not pleased with you,' I am *r*;
1Kgs 14: 2 "Get *r* and disguise yourself so that none
20:12 and they made *r* to storm the city.
2Kgs 8: 1 "Get *r*!
8: 2 woman got *r* and did as the man of God said,
1Chr 9:33 day and night they had to be *r* for service.
28:21 *r* for all the service of the house of God;
Neh 4:15 work, half of the men with spears at the *r*,
Tb 11: 9 I have seen you again, son, I am *r* to die!"
Jdt 2: 7 Tell them to have earth and water *r*,
5: 1 that the Israelites were *r* for battle,
Est 7:10 gibbet which he had made *r* for Mordecai,
1Mc 3:13 him, an assembly of faithful men *r* for war.
3:58 in the morning be *r* to fight these
4:21 the army of Judas in the plain *r* to attack,
4:35 were *r* either to live or to die bravely,
5:39 camped beyond the stream, *r* to attack you."
12:26 made *r* to attack the Jews that very night.
12:27 on guard and to remain armed, *r* for combat,
12:28 Jonathan and his men were *r* for battle,
12:50 and went out in compact body *r* to fight.
12:51 that they were *r* to fight for their lives,
13:22 Trypho got all his cavalry *r* to go,
2Mc 7: 2 We are *r* to die rather than transgress the
8:21 *r* to die for their laws and their country.
10:24 in Judea, *r* to conquer it by force.
11: 9 that they were *r* to assault not only men,
13:12 encouraged them and told them to stand *r*.
Jb 18:12 Disaster is *r* at his side,
32:19 under pressure, my bosom is *r* to burst.
Ps(s) 119:173 Let your hand be *r* to help me,
120: 7 When I speak of peace, they are *r* for war.
Prv 16:30 he who compresses his lips has mischief *r*.
22:18 your bosom, if they all are *r* on your lips.
Wis 6:10 learned in them will have *r* a response.
10:21 of the dumb, and gave *r* speech to infants.
16:20 them bread from heaven, *r* to hand,
Sir 6: 7 first test him, and be not too *r* to trust him
20:18 the unruly are always *r* to offer it.
26:19 sin, for whom the LORD makes *r* the sword.
Is 14:21 Make *r* to slaughter his sons for the guilt
30:33 For the pyre has long been *r*,
61: 5 shall stand *r* to pasture your flocks,
65: 1 was *r* to respond to those who asked me not,
Jer 9: 2 They *r* their tongues like a drawn bow;
Bar 1:19 God, and only too *r* to disregard his voice.
Ez 7:14 sound the trumpet and make everything *r*,
38: 7 Prepare yourself, be *r*,
Dn 3:15 Be *r* now to fall down and worship the
11:36 shall prosper only till divine wrath is *r*,
Jon 1: 3 *r* to flee to Tarshish away from the LORD.
3: 3 So Jonah made *r* and went to Nineveh,
Hb 3: 9 Bared and *r* is your bow,
Zec 5:11 when the temple is *r*,
Mt 22: 4 everything is *r*.
22: 8 'The banquet is *r*,
24:50 when he is not *r* and least expects him.
25: 7 virgins woke up and got their torches *r*.
25:10 who were *r* went in to the wedding with him.
Mk 1: 3 crying, 'Make *r* the way of the Lord,
3: 9 disciples to have a fishing boat *r* for him
4:29 When the crop is *r* he 'wields the sickle,
11:24 if you are *r* to believe that you will
14:15 That is the place you are to get *r* for us."
Lk 3: 4 crying, 'Make *r* the way of the Lord,
12:35 your waists and your lamps be burning *r*.
14:17 invited, 'Come along, everything is *r* now.'
22: 9 him, "Where do you want us to get it *r*?"
Acts 3:13 presence when Pilate was *r* to release him.
5: 9 They stand *r* to carry you out too."
21:15 we got *r* and started up toward Jerusalem.
23:21 They are all *r* now,
23:23 "Get *r* to leave for Caesarea by nine
Rom 7:21 leads to wrongdoing is always *r* at hand.
9:22 vessels fit for wrath, *r* to be destroyed,
1Cor 3: 2 solid food because you were not *r* for it.
3: 2 You are not *r* for it even now,
14: 8 is uncertain, who will get *r* for battle?
2Cor 8:11 so that your *r* resolve may be matched by
9: 2 that Achaia has been *r* since last year.
9: 3 I do so that you may be *r*,
9: 5 It should be *r* as a gracious gift,
10: 6 We are *r* to punish disobedience in anyone
2Tm 2:21 of the house and *r* for every noble service.
Ti 3: 1 to be *r* to take on any honest employment.
Phlm 1:22 And get a room *r* for me;
Heb 11:17 promises was *r* to sacrifice his only son,
1Pt 1: 5 stands *r* to be revealed in the last days.
3:15 for this hope of yours, be ever *r* to reply,
4: 5 stands *r* to judge the living and the dead.
Rv 8: 6 the seven trumpets made *r* to blow them.
12: 4 *r* to devour her child when it should be

REAFFIRM (1)

2Cor 2: 8 I therefore beg you to *r* your love for him.

REAFFIRMED (1)

Gn 41:32 means that the matter has been *r* by God

REAIAH (5)

1Chr 2:52 the father of Kiriath-jearim, were *R*,
4: 2 *R*, the son of Shobal,
5: 5 whose son was Micah, whose son was *R*,
Ezr 2:47 sons of Giddel, sons of Gahar, sons of *R*,
Neh 7:50 sons of Giddel, sons of Gahar, sons of *R*,

REAL (11)

1Mc 11:11 His *r* reason for accusing Alexander,
Wis 2: 6 let us enjoy the good things that are *r*,
Jn 1: 9 The *r* light which gives light to every
6:32 Father who gives you the *r* heavenly bread.
6:55 my flesh is real food and my blood *r* drink.
Rom 2:29 He is a *r* Jew who is one inwardly,
1Tm 5: 3 the claims of widows who are *r* widows
5: 5 The *r* widow, left destitute, is one
Heb 10: 1 things to come, and no *r* image of them,
1Jn 2: 8 is over and the *r* light begins to shine.

REALITIES (2)

Rom 1:20 the creation of the world, invisible *r*,
Heb 9:23 *r* themselves called for better sacrifices.

REALITY (5)

2Mc 3: 8 but in *r* to carry out the king's purpose.
Sir 34: 3 What is seen in dreams is to *r* what the
1Cor 10:19 to that idol, or that an idol is a *r*?
15:29 If the raising of the dead is not a *r*,
Col 2:17 the *r* is the body of Christ.

REALIZATION (1)

Acts 12: 9 but with no clear *r* that this was taking

REALIZE (42)

Ex 10: 7 not yet *r* that Egypt is being destroyed?"
Lv 23:43 booths, that your descendants may *r* that,
Nm 14:34 Thus you will *r* what it means to oppose me.
Dt 8: 5 So you must *r* that the LORD,
Jgs 16:20 he did not *r* that the LORD had left him.
1Sm 25:17 for you must *r* that otherwise evil is in
28: 1 So Achish said to David, "You *r*,
2Sm 19:21 Yet *r* that I have been the first of the
2Chr 2: 7 for I *r* that your servants know how to cut
2Mc 5:17 Antiochus did not *r* that it was because of
11:13 and came to *r* that the Hebrews were
Wis 13: 4 let them from these things *r* how much more
Sir 36: 2 the heathen, that they may *r* your power.
Is 42:25 round about them, yet they did not *r*,
Mt 9: 6 To help you *r* that the Son of Man has
15:12 "Do you *r* the Pharisees were scandalized
24:32 sprouts leaves, you *r* that summer is near.
Jn 8:28 you will come to *r* that I AM and that I do
8:37 I *r* you are one of Abraham's stock.
10:38 so as to *r* what it means that the Father
13: 7 "You may not *r* now what I am doing,
17: 7 *r* that all that you gave me comes from you.
19: 4 you *r* that I find no case [against him]."
Acts 2:15 You must *r* that these men are not drunk,
4:10 must *r* that it was done in the name of Jesus
12:12 After coming to *r* this,
13:38 You must *r*, my brothers, that it is through
22:26 demanded, "Do you *r* what you are doing?
25:10 done the Jews no wrong, as you yourself *r*.
28:28 Now you must *r* that this salvation of God
Rom 6:16 You must *r* that,
1Cor 6: 9 Can you not *r* that the unholy will not
9:13 Do you not *r* that those who work in the
2Cor 2: 4 to help you *r* the great love I bear you.
13: 5 do not *r* that Christ Jesus is in you
Eph 3: 4 you will *r* that I know what I am talking
Jas 1: 3 *R* that when your faith is tested this
3: 1 you should *r* that those of us who do so
1Pt 1:18 *R* that you were delivered from the futile
1Jn 5:13 make you *r* that you possess eternal life
Rv 3: 4 I *r* that you have in Sardis a few persons
3:17 Little do you *r* how wretched you are,

REALIZED (29)

Gn 3: 7 opened, and they *r* that they were naked;
28: 8 Esau *r* how displeasing the Canaanite women
Ex 32:25 When Moses *r* that, to the scornful joy
Jgs 20:41 *r* the disaster that had overtaken them.
2Sm 12:19 themselves and *r* that the child was dead.
2Kgs 12:12 The amount thus *r* they turned over to the
1Chr 19: 6 When the Ammonites *r* that they had put
1Mc 4:21 When they *r* this,
5:34 army of Timothy *r* that it was Maccabeus,
7:25 and *r* that he could not oppose them,
2Mc 14: 3 *r* that there was no way for him to salvage
14:31 When Nicanor *r* that he had been
Eccl 2:24 Even this, I *r*, is from the hand of God.
Jer 12:11 *r* that they were hatching plots against me:
Mt 2:16 Once Herod *r* that he had been deceived by
16:12 They finally *r* he was not issuing a
17:13 The disciples then *r* that he had been
21:45 they *r* he was speaking about them.
27:24 Pilate finally *r* that he was making no
Mk 5:33 to tremble now as she *r* what had happened,
12:28 he *r* how skillfully Jesus answered them.
Lk 1:22 they *r* that he had seen a vision inside.
Jn 4:53 It was at that very hour, the father *r*,
6:15 Jesus *r* that they would come and carry him
6:22 The next day they *r* that there had been
13: 1 Jesus *r* that the hour had come for him to
Acts 13:40 what was said by the prophets be *r* in you:
22:29 The commander became alarmed because he *r*
1Jn 2: 8 you is new, as it is *r* in him and you,

REALIZING (13)

Gn 38:16 and not *r* that she was his daughter-in-law,
Jgs 13:21 *r* that it was the angel of the LORD,
20:32 *r* that disaster was about to overtake them.
1Mc 1: 5 to his bed, *r* that he was going to die.
15:12 *r* what a mass of troubles had come upon
2Mc 5: 6 not *r* that triumph over one's own kindred
12:12 *R* that they could indeed be useful in
Lk 17:15 One of them, *r* that he had been cured,
20:23 *R* their duplicity he said,
Jn 19:28 Jesus, *r* that everything was now finished,
Acts 4:13 and *r* that the speakers were uneducated
Col 4: 1 *r* that you too have a master in heaven.
1Pt 5: 9 *r* that the brotherhood of believers is

REALLY (58)

Gn 3: 1 "Did God *r* tell you not to eat from any
16:13 "Have I *r* seen God and remained alive
18:13 laugh and say, 'Shall I *r* bear a child,
27:21 learn whether you *r* are my son Esau or not."
27:24 he asked him, "Are you *r* my son Esau?"
31:16 father *r* belongs to us and our children.
34: 3 Jacob, indeed was *r* in love with the girl,
37: 8 you *r* going to make yourself king over us?"
45: 5 It was *r* for the sake of saving lives that
45: 8 was not *r* you but God who had me come here;
47:29 "If you *r* wish to please me,
Ex 15:26 "If you *r* listen to the voice of the LORD,
22:11 But if the custodian is *r* guilty of theft,
Lv 25:16 is *r* the number of crops that he sells you.
Dt 7: 7 for you are *r* the smallest of all nations.
9: 4 for it is *r* because of the wickedness of
13: 4 testing you to learn whether you *r* love him
2Chr 2: 5 Yet who is *r* able to build him a house,
Ezr 5:17 to discover whether a decree *r* was issued
Tb 12:19 I did not *r* do so;
2Mc 3: 9 and he asked if these things were *r* true.
Sir 21:27 curses his adversary he *r* curses himself.
31:27 Does he *r* live who lacks the wine which
40:29 another's table, his life is not *r* a life.
Zec 7: 5 years, was it *r* for me that you fasted?
Mt 13:46 When he found one *r* valuable pearl,
14:28 spoke up and said, "Lord, if it is *r* you,
Lk 7:25 What, *r*, did you go out to see—
9:33 (He did not *r* know what he was saying.)
24:39 Look at my hands and my feet; it is *r* I.
Jn 4:42 that this *r* is the Savior of the world."
8:36 if the son frees you, you will *r* be free.
9:18 had *r* been born blind and had begun to see,
10:24 If you *r* are the Messiah,
14: 7 If you *r* knew me,
16:31 "Do you *r* believe?
17: 9 you have given me, for they are *r* yours.
Acts 8:30 him, "Do you *r* grasp what you are reading?"
17:27 though he is not *r* far from any one of us.
28: 4 "This man must *r* be a murderer if,
Rom 10:19 again, did Israel *r* not understand?
1Cor 3:18 In that way he will *r* be wise,
4: 8 Would that you had *r* begun to reign,
5:11 What I *r* wrote about was your not
8: 2 means he has never *r* known it as he ought.
8: 4 we know that an idol is *r* nothing,
10:19 to an idol is *r* offered to that idol,
2Cor 2:16 a mission as this, is anyone *r* qualified?
9: 1 There is *r* no need for me to write you
11:23 Now I am *r* talking like a fool—I am more:
Gal 4: 8 as slaves to gods who are not *r* divine.
4:17 What they *r* want is to exclude you so that
Eph 4:29 need to hear, things that will *r* help them.
Phil 1:10 learn to value the things that *r* matter,
1Tm 5:16 give help to the widows who are *r* in need.
1Jn 2:19 not that they *r* belonged to us;
Rv 3: 9 Jews who are not *r* Jews but frauds,
17:11 is *r* one of the seven and is on its way to

REALM (18)

2Kgs 20:13 all his *r* that Hezekiah did not show them.
Ezr 7:23 come upon the *r* of the king and his sons.
Est 1:14 service and held first rank in the *r*.
1:20 will issue is published throughout his *r*,
2: 3 all the provinces of his *r* to bring together
3: 6 people, throughout the *r* of King Ahasuerus.
1Mc 2:10 nation has not taken its share of her *r*,
2:19 all the Gentiles in the king's *r* obey him,
10:52 "Now that I have returned to my *r*,
15: 4 it and laid waste many cities in my *r*.

REALM (cont.)

15:29 taken possession of many districts in my r.
2Mc 9:24 the people throughout the r would know to
Eccl 5: 7 violation of rights and justice in the r,
Is 39: 2 in his whole r that he did not show them.
Mt 11:23 You shall go down to the r of death!'
Lk 10:15 You shall be hurled down to the r of death!'
Gal 4:29 the one whose birth was in the r of spirit,
1Pt 3:18 but was given life in the r of the spirit.

REALMS (1)

Col 3: 1 on what pertains to higher r where Christ

REAP (30)

Lv 19: 9 "When you r the harvest of your land,
19: 9 that you r the field to its very edge,
23:10 which I am giving you, and r your harvest,
23:22 "When you r the harvest of your land,
23:22 that you r the field to its very edge,
25: 5 of your harvest you shall not r,
25:11 nor shall you r the aftergrowth or pick
25:20 year, if we do not then sow or r our crop?'
Dt 24:19 "When you r the harvest in your field and
2Kgs 19:29 But in the third year, sow and r,
Jb 4: 8 for mischief and sow trouble, r the same.
Ps(s) 126: 5 Those that sow in tears shall r rejoicing.
Eccl 11: 4 one who watches the clouds will never r.
Is 37:30 But in the third year, sow and r,
Hos 8: 7 sow the wind, they shall r the whirlwind;
10:12 yourselves justice, r the fruit of piety;
Mi 6:15 You shall sow, yet not r,
Mt 6:26 They do not sow or r,
25:24 You r where you did not sow and gather
25:26 You know I r where I did not sow and
Lk 12:24 they do not sow, they do not r,
19:21 You r what you never sowed.'
Jn 4:38 sent you to r what you had not worked for.
2Cor 9: 6 He who sows sparingly will r sparingly,
9: 6 he who sows bountifully will r bountifully.
Gal 6: 7 A man will r only what he sows.
6: 8 flesh, he will r a harvest of corruption;
6: 8 is the spirit, he will r everlasting life.
6: 9 in due time we shall r our harvest.
Rv 14:15 down the harvest, for now is the time to r;

REAPED (5)

Gn 26:12 region and r a hundredfold the same year.
Jb 5: 5 What they have r the hungry shall eat up;
Jer 12:13 They have sown wheat and r thorns,
Hos 10:13 have cultivated wickedness, r perversity,
Rv 14:16 all the earth and r the earth's harvest.

REAPER (4)

Ps(s) 129: 7 With which the r fills not his hand,
Am 9:13 When the plowman shall overtake the r,
Jn 4:36 The r already collects his wages and
4:36 that sower and r may rejoice together.

REAPERS (4)

Ru 2:14 Then as she sat near the r,
2Kgs 4:18 enough to go out to his father among the r.
Is 17: 5 Like the r mere armful of stalks when he
Dn 14:33 going to bring it to the r in the field,

REAPING (1)

Lk 19:22 I never deposited, r what I never sowed!

REAPPEARED (2)

Gn 43:31 After washing his face, he r and,
Jn 8: 2 At daybreak he r in the temple area;

REAPPOINTED (2)

2Chr 35: 2 He r the priests to their duties and
Tb 1:22 and Esarhaddon r him.

REAPPRAISED (1)

Phil 3: 7 have now r as loss in the light of Christ.

REAPS (5)

Prv 14:14 and the good man r the fruit of his paths.
22: 8 He who sows iniquity r calamity,
Eccl 5: 9 and the lover of wealth r no fruit from it;
Sir 11: 3 but she r the choicest of all harvests.
Jn 4:37 'One man sows; another r.'

REAR (27)

Ex 26:12 to hang down over the r of the Dwelling.
26:22 six boards for the r of the Dwelling,
26:23 for the corners at the r of the Dwelling.
26:25 Thus, there shall be in the r eight boards,
26:27 other side, and five for those at the r,
36:27 six boards at the r of the Dwelling,
36:28 at the corners in the r of the Dwelling.
36:30 Thus, there were in the r eight boards,
36:32 other side, and five for those at the r,
Nm 10:25 Finally, as r guard for all the camps,
Dt 25:18 off at the r all those who lagged behind.
Jos 6: 9 the r guard followed the ark,
6:13 the r guard followed the ark of the LORD,
8: 4 "See that you ambush the city from the r,
10:19 your enemies, and harry them in the r.
1Sm 29: 2 were marching in the r guard with Achish.
2Sm 5:23 r and meet them before the mastic trees.
10: 9 drawn up against him, both front and r,
1Kgs 6:16 At the r of the temple a space of twenty
2Chr 13:13 go around them to come at them from the r;
1Mc 9:16 Judas and his men, taking them in the r.
2Mc 10:36 defenders, taking the besieged in the r;
Is 52:12 you, and your r guard is the God of Israel.
58: 8 glory of the LORD shall be your r guard.
Ez 19: 2 young lions she couched to r her whelps.
Jl 2:20 sea, and his r toward the western sea;
Zec 10: 9 they shall r their children and return.

REARED (11)

Lv 25:45 children who are born and r in your land.
1Mc 6:17 son Antiochus, whom he had r as a child,
Jb 31:18 like a father God has r me from my youth.
Is 1: 2 Sons have I raised and r,
23: 4 birth, nor raised young men, nor r virgins."
49:21 who has r them?
51:18 her by the hand, of all the sons she r—
Lam 2:22 bore and r my enemy has utterly destroyed."
Lk 4:16 He came to Nazareth where he had been r,
Acts 7:20 months he was r in his father's house,
1Tm 4: 6 r in the words of faith and the sound

REARGUARD (1)

1Mc 4:15 Their whole r fell by the sword,

REARING (1)

2Kgs 10: 6 prominent men of the city, who were r them.]

REASON (92)

Gn 24: 6 "Never take my son back there for any r,"
33:15 But Jacob said, "For what r?
Lv 13:44 him unclean by r of the sore on his head.
Nm 6:11 he has committed by r of the dead person.
Dt 10: 9 For this r, Levi has no share in the heritage
32:28 For they are a people devoid of r,
1Sm 5: 5 For this r, neither the priests of Dagon
21: 3 For that r I have arranged a meeting place
1Chr 29: 2 r I have stored up for the house of my God,
2Chr 19: 2 For this r, wrath is upon you
Ezr 4:15 For that r this city was destroyed.
Neh 6: 6 for this r you are rebuilding the wall;
Est 4: 5 action of Mordecai meant and the r for it.
1Mc 6: 6 they had grown strong by r of the arms,
11:11 His real r for accusing Alexander,
2Mc 3: 9 and explained the r for his presence,
4:28 For this r, both were summoned
4:49 For this r, even some Tyrians
8:26 obliged to return by r of the late hour,
8:26 that r they could not continue the pursuit.
8:36 they were invulnerable for the very r
14: 7 For this r, now that I am deprived
Jb 13: 3 I wish to r with God.
23: 7 There the upright man might r with him,
Prv 17:26 man, but beyond r to scourge princes.
Eccl 7:25 I sought and pursued wisdom and r,
9:10 for there will be no work, nor r,
Wis 2: 2 r is a spark at the beating of our hearts,
7:24 and pervades all things by r of her purity.
14:27 the r and source and extremity of all evil.
17:12 surrender of the helps that come from r;
18:18 each was revealing the r for his dying.
Sir 4: 5 not your eyes, give no man r to curse you;
23:11 swears without r he cannot be found just,
44:21 For this r, God promised him with an oath
51:12 For this r I thank him and I praise him;
Is 9:16 For this r, the Lord does not spare
44:18 The idols have neither knowledge nor r;
Lam 3:21 call this to mind, as my r to have hope:
Ez 7:20 For this r I make them refuse.
13:10 the very r that they led my people astray,
14:23 not without r that I did to it what I did,
33:24 in the ruins on the land of Israel r thus:
Dn 2:15 the r for this harsh order from the king?"
4:31 my r was restored to me,
4:33 At the same time my r returned to me,
13:14 met again, they asked each other the r.
Hos 6: 5 this r I smote them through the prophets,
Jon 4: 4 the LORD asked, "Have you r to be angry?"
4: 9 "Have you r to be angry over the plant?"
4: 9 "I have r to be angry,"
Mi 1: 8 For this r I lament and wail, I go barefoot
Mt 7:29 The r was that he taught with authority
9:11 "What r can the Teacher have for eating
19: 3 a man divorce his wife for any r whatever?"
19: 5 'For this r a man shall leave his father
21:26 human,' we shall have r to fear the people,
21:43 For this r, I tell you, the kingdom of God
21:46 they had r to fear the crowds who regarded
23:34 For this r I shall send you prophets and
25:27 r to deposit my money with the bankers,
Mk 10: 7 for this r a man shall leave his father
11:32 (They had r to fear the people,
12:12 at this, yet they had r to fear the crowd.
Lk 15:26 him the r for the dancing and the music.
Jn 1:31 though the very r I came baptizing with
5:18 The r why the Jews were even more
8:47 The r you do not hear is that you are not
12:39 The r they could not believe was that,
13:11 The r he said, "Not all are washed clean,"
15:19 the r it hates you is that you do not
18:37 The reason I was born, the r why I came
Acts 28:20 This is the r,
Rom 13: 5 You pay taxes for the same r,
1Cor 4: 6 grow self-important by r of his association
11:10 For this r a woman ought to have a sign of
13:11 child, think like a child, r like a child.
15:33 Return to r,
2Cor 2: 9 The r I wrote you was to test you and
5:13 caught up out of ourselves, God is the r;
Gal 6: 4 if he has r to boast of anything,
Eph 5:31 r a man shall leave his father and mother,
2Tm 1: 6 For this r, I remind you to stir into flame
Phlm 1:15 separated from you for a while for this r:
1Pt 3:15 ask you the r for this hope of yours,
3:18 r why Christ died for sins once for all,
4: 6 The r the gospel was preached even to the
2Pt 1: 5 This is r enough for you to make every
1Jn 2:21 My r for having written you is not that
3: 1 The r the world does not recognize us is
3: 5 You know well that the r he revealed

REASONABLE (2)

Acts 18:14 give you Jews a patient and r hearing.
1Pt 2:18 and r ones but even those who are harsh.

REASONED (5)

Gn 32: 9 attack and overwhelm one camp," he r,
32:21 For Jacob r, "If I first appease him
2Kgs 5:13 But his servants came up and r with him.
7: 6 army, and they had r among themselves,
Heb 11:19 r that God was able to raise from the dead,

REASONING (3)

Sir 3:23 and false r unbalanced their judgment.
Mk 2: 8 Jesus was immediately aware of their r,
Lk 5:22 knew their r and answered them by saying:

REASONS (6)

Neh 5: 6 when I heard the r they had for complaint.
Is 41:21 bring forward your r,
1Cor 9: 8 r I am giving you are merely human ones,
10:12 For all these r, let anyone who thinks
Gal 4:18 to be courted for the right r at all times,
Phil 4: 1 For these r, my brothers,

REASSERTING (1)

Mk 14:31 But Peter kept r vehemently,

REASSURANCE (1)

Acts 15:32 and gave them r in a long discourse.

REASSURANCES (1)

Acts 14:22 They gave their disciples r,

REASSURE (4)

2Mc 11:32 I have also sent Menelaus to r you.
Mt 14:27 Jesus hastened to r them:
Mk 6:50 He hastened to r them:
Acts 18:23 country and Phrygia to r all his disciples.

REASSURED (5)

Gn 50:21 By thus speaking kindly to them, he r them.
Tb 5:21 Tobit r her:
Jdt 6:20 Then they r Achior and praised him highly.
Jb 29:24 When I smiled on them they were r;
Mk 16: 6 frightened them thoroughly, but he r them:

REASSURING (2)

Est D: 8 recovered, and comforted her with r words.
2Mc 4:34 and by treacherously r him through sworn

REBA (2)

Nm 31: 8 Evi, Rekem, Zur, Hur and R;
Jos 13:21 Evi, Rekem, Zur, Hur and R;

REBATE (1)

Lv 27:18 with a corresponding r on the valuation.

REBEKAH (29)

Gn 22:23 Bethuel became the father of R.
24:15 words when R (who was born to Bethuel,
24:29 Now R had a brother named Laban.
24:30 bracelets on his sister R and heard her
24:45 when R came out with a jug on her shoulder.
24:51 Here is R, ready for you; take her with you,
24:53 of clothing and presented them to R;
24:58 So they called R and asked her,
24:59 their sister R and her nurse to take leave,
24:60 Invoking a blessing on R, they said:
24:61 Then R and her maids started out;
24:61 So the servant took R and went on his way.

24:64 *R*, too, was looking about,
24:67 Then Isaac took *R* into his tent;
25:20 was forty years old when he married *R*,
25:21 heard his entreaty, and *R* became pregnant.
25:28 but *R* preferred Jacob.
26: 7 the place would kill him on account of *R*,
26: 8 surprised to see Isaac fondling his wife *R*.
26:35 a source of embitterment to Isaac and *R*.
27: 5 *R* had been listening while Isaac was
27: 6 for his father, *R* said to her son Jacob,
27:11 a hairy man," said Jacob to his mother *R*,
27:15 *R* then took the best clothes of her older
27:42 When *R* got news of what her older son Esau
27:46 *R* said to Isaac: "I am disgusted
28: 5 of Bethuel the Aramean, and brother of *R*,
49:31 buried, and so are Isaac and his wife *R*,
Rom 9:10 *R* had conceived twin children by one man

REBEKAH'S (2)

Gn 29:12 that he was her father's relative, *R* son,
35: 8 Death came to *R* nurse Deborah;

REBEL (21)

Ex 23:21 Do not *r* against him,
Nm 14: 9 But do not *r* against the LORD!
Jos 22:19 But do not *r* against the LORD nor involve
22:29 Far be it from us to *r* against the LORD or
1Sm 12:14 and do not *r* against the LORD'S command,
12:15 the LORD and if you *r* against his command,
22:13 he might *r* against me and become my enemy,
2Sm 18:32 all who *r* against you with evil intent
2Kgs 18:20 then, do you rely, that you *r* against me?
Jdt 16:12 supposed sons of *r* mothers cut them down;
Est 1:18 will *r* against all the royal officials,
Ps(s) 74:23 of those who *r* against you
Prv 24:21 to do with those who *r* against them;
Sir 46: 7 when they opposed the *r* assembly,
47:23 who by his policy made the people *r*;
Is 1: 5 yet be struck, you that *r* again and again?
36: 5 then, do you rely, that you *r* against me?
48: 8 a *r* you were called from birth.
Jer 3:11 *R* Israel is inwardly more just than
3:12 Return, *r* Israel,
8: 5 these people *r* with obstinate resistance?

REBELLED (54)

Gn 14: 4 but in the thirteenth year they *r*.
Lv 26:40 *r* against me and of having defied me,
Nm 20:24 because you both *r* against my commandment
26: 9 Korah's band when it *r* against the LORD].
27:14 desert of Zin you both *r* against my order
Dt 9:23 you *r* against this command of the LORD,
Jos 22:16 and *r* against him by building an altar of
Jgs 9:23 of Shechem, who *r* against Abimelech.
2Sm 18:28 up the men who *r* against my lord the king."
18:31 from the grasp of all who *r* against you."
20:21 of Ephraim has *r* against King David.
1Kgs 11:26 mother, Zeruah, also *r* against the king.
11:27 This is why he *r*.
13:21 'Because you *r* against the command of the
13:26 God who *r* against the command of the LORD.
2Kgs 1: 1 After Ahab's death, Moab *r* against Israel.
3: 5 of Moab had *r* against the king of Israel.
18: 7 He *r* against the king of Assyria and did
24: 1 Then Jehoiakim turned and *r* against him.
24:20 Zedekiah *r* against the king of Babylon.
2Chr 13: 6 David, has stood up and *r* against his lord!
36:13 He also *r* against King Nebuchadnezzar,
2Mc 13:23 charge of the government in Antioch had *r*.
Ps(s) 5:11 them out because they have *r* against you.
78:40 How often they *r* against him in the desert
78:56 tempted and *r* against God the Most High,
105:28 it grew dark, but they *r* against his words.
106: 7 but *r* against the Most High at the Red Sea.
107:11 Because they had *r* against the words of
Sir 16: 7 of old who *r* long ago in their might;
Is 43:27 your spokesmen *r* against me Till I
50: 5 And I have not *r*,
63:10 But they *r*, and grieved his holy spirit;
66:24 the corpses of the men who *r* against me;
Jer 2: 8 the shepherds *r* against me.
2:29 You have all *r* against me, says the LORD.
3:13 how you *r* against the LORD,
4:17 surround her, for she has *r* against me,
5:11 For they have openly *r* against me,
33: 8 by which they sinned and *r* against me,
52: 3 Zedekiah *r* against the king of Babylon.
Lam 3:42 We have sinned and *r*;
Ez 2: 3 Israelites, rebels who have *r* against me;
5: 6 But she *r* against my ordinances more
17:15 But this man *r* against him,
20: 8 *r* against me and refused to listen to me;
20:13 house of Israel *r* against me in the desert.
20:21 But their children *r* against me:
20:38 who have *r* and transgressed against me;
Dn 5:23 you have *r* against the Lord of heaven.
9: 5 we have *r* and departed from your
9: 9 Yet we *r* against you and paid no heed to
Hos 7:14 themselves, while they *r* against me.
14: 1 her guilt, for she has *r* against her God.

REBELLING (4)

Jos 22:18 You are *r* against the LORD today and by
Neh 2:19 "Are you *r* against the king?"
Ps(s) 78:17 *r* against the Most High in the wasteland,
Jer 3:22 children, and I will cure you of your *r*.

REBELLION (22)

Nm 27:14 because in the *r* of the community in the
Jos 22:19 against the LORD nor involve us in *r*,
22:22 out of *r* or treachery against the LORD,
1Sm 15:23 For a sin like divination is *r*,
24:12 be convinced that I plan no harm and no *r*.
1Kgs 11:40 for his *r* he escaped to King Shishak,
12:19 into *r* against David's house to this day.
2Kgs 3: 7 "The king of Moab is in *r* against me.
1Chr 9: 1 in captivity to Babylon because of its *r*.
10:13 Thus Saul died because of his *r* against
2Chr 10:19 in *r* against David's house to this day.
Ezr 4:19 *r* and sedition have been fostered there.
Neh 6: 6 you and the Jews are planning a *r*;
Jdt 7:15 render them dire punishment for their *r*
Jb 34:37 For he is adding *r* to his sin by brushing
Prv 17:11 On *r* alone is the wicked man bent,
Is 24:20 Its *r* will weigh it down,
Jer 28:16 you have preached *r* against the LORD.
29:32 because he preached *r* against the LORD.
Lam 1:20 recoils within me from my monstrous *r*.
Ez 2: 8 be not rebellious like this house of *r*,
Jude 1:11 for pay, and like Korah they perish in *r*.

REBELLIONS (2)

Jer 5: 6 For their many crimes and their numerous *r*.
14: 7 Even though our *r* are many,

REBELLIOUS (45)

Nm 17:25 to be kept there as a warning to the *r*,
Dt 9: 7 place, you have been *r* toward the LORD.
31:27 know how *r* and stiff-necked you will be.
1Sm 20:30 "Son of a *r* woman,
2Sm 20: 1 a *r* individual from Benjamin named Sheba,
Ezr 4:12 are now rebuilding this *r* and evil city.
4:15 this city is a *r* city which has proved fatal
Neh 9:26 "But they were contemptuous and *r*:
Ps(s) 78: 8 their fathers, a generation wayward and *r*,
Prv 11:22 is a beautiful woman with a *r* disposition.
28: 2 If a land is *r*, its princes will be many;
Is 30: 1 Woe to the *r* children,
30: 9 This is a *r* people,
57: 4 Are you not *r* children,
57:17 in wrath, as they went their own *r* way.
65: 2 out my hands all the day to a *r* people,
Jer 3: 6 See now what *r* Israel has done!
3: 8 all the adulteries *r* Israel had committed,
3:14 Return, *r* children, says the LORD,
3:22 Return, *r* children, and I will cure you
5:23 But this people's heart is stubborn and *r*;
31:22 will you continue to stray, *r* daughter?
49: 4 strength, your ebbing strength, *r* daughter?
Ez 2: 5 for they are a *r* house
2: 6 at their looks, for they are a *r* house.
2: 7 whether they heed or resist, for they are *r*
2: 8 be not *r* like this house of rebellion,
3: 9 at their looks, for they are a *r* house.
3:26 unable to rebuke them for being a *r* house.
3:27 resist who will, for they are a *r* house.
5: 7 more *r* than the nations surrounding you,
12: 2 of man, you live in the midst of a *r* house;
12: 2 but do not hear, for they are a *r* house.
12: 3 they will see that they are a *r* house.
12: 9 did not the house of Israel, that *r* house,
12:25 In your days, *r* house,
17:12 Son of man, say now to the *r* house:
24: 3 Propose this parable to the *r* house:
44: 6 Say to that *r* house, the house of Israel:
Hos 12: 1 Judah is still *r* against God,
Zep 3: 1 Woe to the city, *r* and polluted,
3:11 all your deeds, your *r* actions against me;
Lk 1:17 and the *r* to the wisdom of the just,
Rom 1:30 wrongdoing and *r* toward their parents.
Eph 2: 2 spirit who is even now at work among the *r*.

REBELS (18)

Nm 20:10 he said to them, "Listen to me, you *r*!
Dt 9:24 you, you have been *r* against the LORD.
31:27 you, you have been *r* against the LORD!
Jos 1:18 If anyone *r* against your orders and does
Jb 24:13 are those who are *r* against the light;
Ps(s) 66: 7 *r* may not exalt themselves.
68: 7 only *r* remain in the parched land.
68:19 received men as gifts—even *r*;
Sir 16: 4 through a clan of *r* it becomes desolate.
Is 1:23 Your princes are *r* and comrades of thieves;
1:28 *R* and sinners alike shall be crushed,
46: 8 and be firm, bear it well in mind, you *r*;
Jer 17:13 The *r* in the land shall be put to shame;
Ez 2: 3 Israelites, *r* who have rebelled against me;
Dn 3:32 to our enemies, lawless and hateful *r*;
Hos 9:15 all their princes are *r*.
Mk 15: 7 *r* who had committed murder in the uprising.

Rom 13: 2 authority *r* against the ordinance of God;

REBIRTH (1)

1Pt 1:23 Your *r* has come,

REBOUND (2)

Tb 14:10 Nadab's disgraceful crime *r* against him.
Ps(s) 7:17 the crown of his head his violence shall *r*.

REBUFFED (3)

Sir 2:10 has anyone called upon him and been *r*?
13:10 Be not bold with him lest you be *r*,
41: 2 failing strength, Tottering and always *r*,

REBUFFING (1)

Sir 41:20 to return a greeting, and of *r* a friend;

REBUILD (22)

Jos 6:26 be the man who attempts to *r* this city,
Ezr 2:68 for the house of God, to *r* it in its place.
6: 7 they are to *r* it on its former site.
Neh 2: 5 the city of my ancestors' graves, to *r* it."
2:17 Come, let us *r* the wall of Jerusalem,
4: 4 Never shall we be able the wall to *r*."
Tb 14: 5 They shall *r* the temple,
14: 5 and they shall *r* Jerusalem with splendor.
Ps(s) 69:36 will save Zion and *r* the cities of Judah.
Is 45:13 He shall *r* my city and let my exiles go
60:10 Foreigners shall *r* your walls,
61: 4 They shall *r* the ancient ruins,
Jer 33: 7 the lot of Israel, and *r* them as of old.
Am 9:11 its ruins, and *r* it as in the days of old,
9:14 shall *r* and inhabit their ruined cities,
Hg 1: 2 the time come to *r* the house of the LORD.
Mal 1: 4 have been crushed but we will *r* the ruins,"
Mt 26:61 God's sanctuary and *r* it in three days.' "
27:40 destroy the temple and *r* it in three days!
Mk 15:29 destroy the temple and *r* it in three days!
Acts 15:16 will return and *r* the fallen hut of David:
15:16 its ruins I will *r* it and set it up again,

REBUILDER (1)

2Mc 1:18 the *r* of the temple and the altar,

REBUILDERS (1)

Is 49:17 Your *r* make haste,

REBUILDING (17)

2Chr 24:27 on him, and of his *r* of the house of God,
Ezr 3: 2 set about *r* the altar of the God of Israel
4:12 are now *r* this rebellious and evil city.
5:11 are *r* the house built here long years ago,
5:13 a decree for the *r* of this house of God.
5:17 the *r* of this house of God in Jerusalem.
6: 8 of the Jews in the *r* of that house of God:
Neh 2:20 We, his servants, shall set about the *r*;
3: 1 took up the task of *r* the Sheep Gate.
3: 1 continued the *r* to the Tower of Hananel.
3: 2 At their side the men of Jericho were *r*,
3:33 Sanballat heard that we were *r* the wall,
6: 6 that for this reason you are *r* the wall;
1Mc 10:44 The cost of *r* and restoring the structures
16:23 deeds he performed, his *r* of the walls,
Jb 12:14 If he breaks a thing down, there is no *r*;
Ps(s) 51:20 your kindness by *r* the walls of Jerusalem;

REBUILDS (1)

Ps(s) 147: 2 The LORD *r* Jerusalem;

REBUILT (51)

Nm 21:27 "Come to Heshbon, let it be *r*,
32:34 The Gadites *r* the fortified towns of Dibon,
32:37 The Reubenites *r* Heshbon,
32:38 These towns, which they *r*,
Dt 13:17 be a heap of ruins forever, never to be *r*.
Jos 19:50 He *r* the city and made it his home.
Jgs 18:28 The Danites then *r* the city,
21:23 where they *r* and occupied the cities.
1Kgs 9:17 Solomon then *r* Gezer),
16:34 his reign, Hiel from Bethel *r* Jericho.
2Kgs 14:22 who *r* Elath and restored it to Judah,
21: 3 He *r* the high places which his father
1Chr 11: 8 He *r* the city on all sides,
2Chr 26: 2 He *r* Elath and restored it to Judah;
32: 5 he *r* the wall where it was broken down,
33: 3 He *r* the high places which his father
Ezr 4:13 is *r* and its walls are raised up again,
4:16 is *r* and its walls are raised up again,
4:21 city may not be *r* until further a decree
5: 8 it is being *r* of cut stone and the walls
5:15 the house of God be *r* on its former site.
6: 3 The house is to be *r* as a place for
Neh 3: 3 Fish Gate was *r* by the sons of Hassenaah;
3:13 they *r* it and set up its doors,
3:14 he *r* it and set up its doors,
3:15 *r* it, roofed it over, and set up its doors,
4:11 whole house of Judah as they *r* the wall.
6: 1 and our other enemies that I had *r* the

REBUILT (cont.)

7: 1 When the wall had been r,
7: 4 small, and none of the houses had been r.
Tb 13:10 so that his tent may be r in you with joy.
13:16 Jerusalem shall be r as his home forever.
14: 5 rebuilt; yes, it will be r for all generations
1Mc 5: 1 r and the sanctuary consecrated as before,
9:62 they r and strengthened its fortifications
Ps(s) 102:17 LORD has r Zion and appeared in his glory;
Sir 49:13 He r our ruined walls,
Is 25: 2 is a city no more, nor ever to be r.
44:26 Be r; I will raise up their ruins.
44:28 He shall say of Jerusalem, "Let her be r,"
58:12 The ancient ruins shall be r for your sake,
Jer 30:18 City shall be r upon hill,
31: 4 I will restore you, and you shall be r,
31:38 when the city shall be r as the LORD's,
Ez 26:14 Never shall you be r,
36:10 cities shall be repeopled, and ruins r.
36:33 the cities, and the ruins shall be r;
36:36 have r what was destroyed and replanted
Dn 9:25 of the word that Jerusalem was to be r
9:25 During sixty-two weeks it shall be r,

REBUKE (37)

2Sm 22:16 earth were laid bare, At the r of the LORD,
2Kgs 19: 3 'This is a day of distress, of r,
19: 4 will r him for the words which the LORD,
Jb 11: 3 and shall you deride and no one give r?
13: 6 Hear now the r I shall utter and listen to
13:10 He will openly r you if even in secret you
20: 3 A r which puts me to shame I hear,
26:11 and are stunned at his thunderous r;
Ps(s) 18:16 were laid bare, At the r of the LORD,
50: 8 Not for your sacrifices do I r you,
68:31 R the wild beast of the reeds,
76: 7 At your r, O God of Jacob,
80:17 or cut it down perish before you at your r.
104: 7 At your r they fled,
119:21 You r the accursed proud,
Prv 13: 1 but the senseless one heeds no r.
13: 8 for his life, but the poor man heeds no r.
19:25 if you r an intelligent man,
27: 5 an open r than a love that remains hidden.
29: 1 r will be crushed suddenly beyond cure.
Eccl 7: 5 r than to hearken to the song of fools;
Wis 11: 7 r to the decree for the slaying of infants,
12: 2 Therefore you r offenders little by little,
12:17 and in those who know you, you r temerity.
Sir 31:31 R not your neighbor when wine is served,
43:13 His r marks out the path for the lightning,
Is 17:13 But God shall r them,
37: 3 'This is a day of distress, of r,
37: 4 will r him for the words which the LORD,
50: 2 Lo, with my r I dry up the sea,
51:20 the wrath of the LORD, the r of your God.
54: 9 not to be angry with you, or to r you.
Jer 29:27 do you not r Jeremiah of Anathoth who
Ez 3:26 to r them for being a rebellious house.
Zec 3: 2 LORD said to Satan, "May the LORD r you,
3: 2 the LORD who has chosen Jerusalem r you!
Lk 19:39 said to him, "Teacher, r your disciples."

REBUKED (15)

Ru 2:16 them for her to glean without being r.
1Kgs 1: 6 never r him or asked why he was doing this.
1Chr 16:21 them, and for their sake he r kings:
Neh 5: 7 I then r them severely, saying to them:
Ps(s) 9: 6 You r the nations and destroyed the wicked;
105:14 them, and for their sake he r kings:
106: 9 He r the Red Sea,
Wis 1: 5 and when injustice occurs it is r.
Mk 1:25 Jesus r him sharply:
4:39 awoke and r the wind and said to the sea:
Lk 4:41 He r them and did not allow them to speak
8:24 and r the wind and the tumultuous waves.
9:42 Jesus then r the unclean spirit,
23:40 But the other one r him:
2Pt 2:16 gain, but he was r for his evildoing.

REBUKES (4)

Ps(s) 39:12 With r for guilt you chasten man;
Prv 28:23 He who r a man gets more thanks in the end
Wis 1: 3 power, put to the proof, r the foolhardy;
Na 1: 4 He r the sea and leaves it dry,

REBUT (1)

Prv 27:11 and I will be able to r him who tuants me.

REBUTTAL (1)

Acts 23: 3 Paul said to him in r: "You are the one

RECAH (1)

1Chr 4:12 These were the men of R.

RECALL (32)

Gn 9:15 I will r the covenant I have made between
9:16 I will see it and r the everlasting
1Chr 16:12 R the wondrous deeds that he has wrought,
Jdt 8:26 R how he dealt with Abraham,
Est F: 2 r the dream I had about these very things,
1Mc 6:12 But I now r the evils I did in Jerusalem,
2Mc 9:21 I r with affection the esteem and good
Jb 11:16 or r it like waters that have ebbed away.
40:32 upon him, no need to r any other conflict!
Ps(s) 42: 5 Those times I r,
105: 5 R the wondrous deeds that he has wrought,
Wis 2: 4 in time, and no one will r our deeds.
Sir 38:20 cease to r him;
38:21 R him not,
42:15 Now will I r God's works;
Is 63: 7 The favors of the LORD I will r,
Jer 2:23 in the Valley, r what you have done:
Ez 20:43 There you shall r your conduct and all the
Mt 5:23 there r that your brother has anything
14: 3 R that Herod had had John arrested,
23:38 R the saying: "You will find your temple
Lk 4:27 R, too, the many lepers in Israel
24:44 R those words I spoke to you when I was
Jn 2:22 did his disciples r that he had said this,
4: 9 R that Jews have nothing to do with
18:39 R your custom whereby I release someone to
Acts 20:35 to r the words of the Lord Jesus himself,
1Thes 2: 9 You must r, brothers, our efforts
Heb 10:32 R the days gone by when,
2Pt 1:12 intend to r these things to you constantly,
1:15 I shall press to have you r these things
3: 2 R the teaching delivered long ago by the

RECALLED (7)

Gn 48:16 these boys That in them my name be r,
2Mc 4:37 he wept as he r the prudence and noble
Sir 3:15 tribulation it will be r to your advantage,
Mt 27:63 "we have r that that imposter while he
Mk 14:72 r the prediction Jesus had made to him,
Jn 2:17 His disciples r the words of Scripture:
12:16 but after Jesus was glorified they r

RECALLING (6)

Est C: 1 R all that the Lord had done,
2Mc 6:17 Let these words suffice for r this truth.
Wis 18:22 r the sworn covenants with their fathers.
Ez 23:19 all the more, r the days of her girlhood,
2Tm 1: 4 R your tears when we parted,
Heb 10: 3 there came only a yearly r of sins,

RECALLS (1)

2Cor 7:15 as he r the obedience you showed to God

RECAPTURE (1)

Sir 27:19 have let your friend go and cannot r him;

RECEDED (1)

Gn 8: 3 Gradually the waters r from the earth.

RECEIPT (2)

Acts 16:24 Upon r of these instruc-tions he put them
Phil 4:18 Herewith is my r,

RECEIVE (135)

Gn 4:11 to r your brother's blood from your hand.
Ex 14: 4 r glory through Pharaoh and all his army,
14:17 r glory through Pharaoh and all his army,
14:18 when I r glory through Pharaoh and his
30:16 r this forfeit money from the Israelites,
34: 9 wickedness and sins, and r us as your own."
40:15 they shall r a perpetual priesthood
Lv 16: 5 From the Israelite community he shall r
22:25 nor r from a foreigner any such animals
24:19 on his neighbor shall r the same in return.
Nm 18:26 When you r from the Israelites the tithes
18:28 all the tithes you r from the Israelites,
18:29 From all the gifts that you r,
32:19 so long as we r a heritage for ourselves
Dt 9: 9 when I had gone up the mountain to r the
18: 3 the flock, the priest shall r the shoulder,
18: 8 r the same portions to eat as the rest,
19:14 heritage you r in the land which the LORD,
24:10 not enter his house to r a pledge from him,
25: 2 r the number of stripes his guilt deserves.
26: 4 The priest shall then r the basket from
32:11 to r them and bore them up on his pinions.
Jos 11:20 doomed in destruction and thus r no mercy,
20: 4 who must r him and assign him a place in
Ru 2:12 May you r a full reward from the LORD,
2Sm 15:28 the desert until I r information from you."
18:22 You will r no reward."
18:31 "Let my lord the king r the good news
2Kgs 2: 9 "May I r a double portion of your spirit."
Ezr 7:16 may r throughout the province of Babylon,
Tb 4:14 as God's servant, you will r your reward.
12: 4 should r half of all that he brought back."
1Mc 14:23 people have voted to r the men with honor,
2Mc 3:38 and you will r him back well-flogged,
7:11 from him I hope to r them again."
7:29 time of mercy I may r you again with them."
7:36 r just punishments for your arrogance.
15: 7 that he would r help from the LORD.
Jb 3:12 Wherefore did the knees r me?
22:22 R instruction from his mouth,
35: 7 give him, or what does he r from your hand?
Ps(s) 24: 5 He shall r a blessing from the LORD,
27:10 mother forsake me, yet will the LORD r me.
73:24 me, and in the end you will r me in glory.
Prv 1: 3 May r training in wise conduct,
2: 1 if you r my words and treasure my commands,
4:10 Hear, my son, and r my words.
8:10 R my instruction in preference to silver,
19:20 Listen to counsel and r instruction,
Wis 3:10 r a punishment to match their thoughts,
5:16 Therefore shall they r the splendid crown,
12: 7 might r a worthy colony of God's children.
19:14 those others did not r unfamiliar visitors,
Sir 4:31 to r and clenched when it is time to give.
46:12 names r fresh luster in their children!
50:21 r from him the blessing of the Most High.
Is 29:24 those who find fault shall r instruction.
55: 1 who have no money, come, r grain and eat;
Jer 9:19 of the LORD, let your ears r his message.
Lam 4:16 He does not r the priests with favor,
Bar 4: 2 Turn, O Jacob, and r her:
Ez 14:10 Each shall r punishment for his sin,
16:33 All harlots r gifts.
47:22 r inheritances among the tribes of Israel.
Dn 1:16 take away the food and wine they were to r,
2: 6 you shall r from me gifts and presents and
7:18 ones of the Most High shall r the kingship,
13:55 "for the angel of God shall r the
Hos 14: 3 "Forgive all iniquity, and r what is good,
Hg 1: 8 I may take pleasure in it and r my glory,
Mt 7: 7 "Ask, and you will r.
10:14 r you or listen to what you have to say,
19:29 for my sake will r many times as much
21:22 You will r all that you pray for,
Mk 4:24 In the measure you give you shall r,
6:11 If any place will not r you or hear you,
10:30 gospel who will not r in this present age
11:24 you will r whatever you ask for in prayer,
12:40 is they who will r the severest sentence."
Lk 7:30 by failing to r his baptism defeated God's
8:13 when they hear the word, r it with joy.
9: 5 When people will not r you,
11: 9 "So I say to you, 'Ask and you shall r;
12:50 I have a baptism to r.
18:30 who will not r a plentiful return in this age
18:42 Jesus said to him, R your sight.
20:10 to r his share of the crop from them;
Jn 7:39 that came to believe in him were to r.
16:24 Ask and you shall r,
20:22 R the Holy Spirit.
Acts 1: 8 You will r power when the Holy Spirit
2:38 you will r the gift of the Holy Spirit.
7:59 heard praying, "Lord Jesus, r my spirit."
8:15 prayed that they might r the Holy Spirit.
8:19 hands on anyone he will r the Holy Spirit."
17:25 nor does he r man's service as if he were
19: 2 "Did you r the Holy Spirit when you
Rom 5:17 much more shall those who r the
8:15 You did not r a spirit of slavery leading
11:31 that they too may r mercy.
1Cor 3: 8 will r his wages in proportion to his toil.
3:14 still stands, he will r his recompense;
4: 5 time, everyone will r his praise from God.
14:30 by, should happen to r a revelation,
2Cor 1:16 I might r your help on my journey to Judea.
5:10 so that each one may r his recompense,
6: 1 beg you not to r the grace of God in vain.
11: 4 or when you r a different spirit than the
Gal 1:12 I did not r it from any man,
3: 2 how did you r the Spirit?
3:14 us to r the promised Spirit through faith.
4: 5 that we might r our status as adopted sons.
5: 3 I point out once more to all who r
Phil 1:19 I r from the Spirit of Jesus Christ.
Col 3:24 r an inheritance from him as your reward.
2Tm 2: 5 he cannot r the winner's crown unless he
Heb 4: 2 them, for they did not r it in faith.
4:16 approach the throne of grace to r mercy
7: 5 of Levi should r tithes from the people,
7: 8 And whereas men subject to death r tithes,
9:15 may r the promised eternal inheritance.
10:36 do God's will and r what he has promised.
11: 8 to the place he was to r as a heritage;
11:35 were tortured and would not r deliverance,
Jas 1: 7 not expect to r anything from the Lord.
1:12 he will r the crown of life the Lord has
4: 3 and you do not r because you ask wrongly,
4: 3 squandering what you r on your pleasures.
1Pt 3: 9 you may r a blessing as your inheritance.
1Jn 3:22 we will r at his hands whatever we ask.
2Jn 1: 8 you must r your reward in full.
1:10 teaching, do not r him into your house;
Rv 4:11 are worthy to r glory and honor and power!
5: 9 to r the scroll and break open its seals,
5:12 Lamb that was slain to r power and riches,

RECEIVED (165)

Gn 12:16 well with Abram, and he r flocks and herds,
33:10 of God, now that you have r me so kindly.
43:23 As for your money, I r it."
Ex 29:25 you have r them back from their hands,
36: 3 They r from Moses all the contributions

38:25 The amount of the silver *r* from the
38:26 was *r* from every man of twenty years or
Lv 8:28 When he had *r* them back,
8:31 in keeping with the command I have *r*:
8:35 for this is the command I have *r*."
10:13 such is the command I have *r*.
10:18 in keeping with the command I had *r*."
Nm 3:50 he *r* in silver one thousand three hundred
34:14 of Manasseh, have already *r* their heritage;
34:15 two and one half tribes have *r* their heritage
Jos 13: 8 Gadites, had *r* their heritage which Moses,
14: 1 the Israelites *r* in the land of Canaan.
14: 4 The Levites themselves *r* no share of the
17: 6 Manasseh *r* each a portion among his sons.
18: 2 Israelites had not yet *r* their heritage.
18: 7 Manasseh have already *r* the heritage
19: 2 For their heritage they *r* Beer-sheba,
19:49 When the last of them had *r* the portions
21:27 The Gershonite clan of the Levites *r* from
21:34 *r* from the tribe of Zebulun the four
22: 9 which they had *r* according to the LORD's
Jgs 18: 1 *r* no heritage among the tribes of Israel.
1Sm 14:37 But he *r* no answer on this occasion.
23: 1 David *r* information that the Philistines
25:39 the insult I *r* at the hand of Nabal,
2Sm 12: 4 Now, the rich man *r* a visitor,
1Kgs 2: 7 For they *r* me kindly when I was fleeing
10:14 The gold that Solomon *r* every year weighed
20:17 Ben-hadad *r* word that some men had marched
1Chr 5:20 they *r* help so that they mastered the
6:56 *r* from the half-tribe of Manasseh:
6:62 the Merarites *r* from the tribe of Zebulun:
6:63 Jordan] they *r* from the tribe of Reuben:
12:19 So David *r* them and placed them among the
29:14 we only give you what we have *r* from you.
2Chr 9:13 The gold that Solomon *r* each year weighed
21:12 He *r* a letter from the prophet Elijah with
22: 6 had *r* at Rama in his battle against Hazael,
26:15 ascribed to the marvelous help he had *r*.
Tb 11:18 for seven happy days, and he *r* many gifts.
14: 1 and *r* an honorable burial in Nineveh.
Jdt 3: 7 all the inhabitants of the countryside *r* him
Est E:10 us in generosity, was hospitably *r* by us.
1Mc 2:54 *r* the covenant of an everlasting
2:56 the assembly, *r* an inheritance in the land.
2:57 *r* as a heritage a throne of everlasting
5:25 who *r* them peacefully and told them all
11:34 taxes that formerly the king *r* from them
11:53 for all the favors he had *r* from him,
12: 8 the envoy with honor and *r* the letter,
12:43 Instead, he *r* him with honor,
13:37 We have *r* the gold crown and the palm
14:40 that they had *r* Simon's envoys with honor.
2Mc 1:35 distributed the large revenues he *r* there.
3: 9 *r* by the high priest of the city,
4:10 *r* the king's approval and came into office,
4:22 There he was *r* with great pomp by Jason
5: 7 the end *r* only disgrace for his treachery,
7:11 "It was from heaven that I *r* these;
8:20 because of the help they *r* from Heaven,
8:33 he *r* the reward his wicked deeds deserved.
9:26 and individual benefits you have *r*,
15: 8 help they had *r* from heaven in the past,
Jb 29:22 more, but *r* my pronouncement drop by drop.
Ps(s) 68:19 on high, taken captives, *r* men as gifts
Wis 16:21 and serving the desire of him who *r* it,
19:15 theirs since they *r* strangers unwillingly!
Sir 42: 7 or of recording all that is given or *r*;
46: 9 his family too *r* an inheritance,
50:12 Son of Jochanan When he *r* the sundered
Is 40: 2 she has *r* from the hand of the LORD double
Jer 44:15 and Upper Egypt, Jeremiah *r* this answer:
Lam 2: 9 have not *r* any vision from the LORD.
Bar 1: 8 [This was when he *r* the vessels of the
Ez 18: 7 no one, gives back the pledge *r* for a debt,
29:18 but neither he nor his army *r* any wages
33:24 individual, *r* possession of the land;
Dn 3:39 heart and humble spirit let us be *r*;
7:14 was presented before him, He *r* dominion,
Am 1: 1 which he *r* in vision concerning Israel,
Mi 1: 1 he *r* concerning Samaria and Jerusalem.
Hb 1: 1 which Habakkuk the prophet *r* in vision.
Mt 1:24 him and *r* her into his home as his wife.
2:12 They *r* a message in a dream not to return
2:22 Instead, because of a warning *r* in a dream,
10: 8 The gift you have *r*, give as a gift.
20: 9 afternoon came up they *r* a full day's pay,
20:11 yet they *r* the same daily wage.
25:16 Immediately the man who *r* the five
25:17 who *r* the two thousand doubled his figure.
25:18 The man who *r* the thousand went off
25:20 The man who had *r* the five thousand came
25:22 *r* the two thousand then stepped forward.
25:24 man who had *r* the thousand stepped forward.
Mk 5:26 She had *r* treatment at the hands of
10:52 Immediately he *r* his sight and started to
Lk 1: 4 reliable the instruction was that you *r*.
7:29 for they had *r* from John the baptismal
9:11 He *r* them and spoke to them of the reign
Jn 10:18 This command I *r* from my Father."
16:14 *r* from me what he will announce to you.
17: 8 message you entrusted to me, and they *r* it.
Acts 2:33 *r* the promised Holy Spirit from the Father,
7:38 *r* the oracles of life to pass on to you.
7:53 You who *r* the law through the ministry of
8:17 hands on them and they *r* the Holy Spirit.
10:47 these people who have *r* the Holy Spirit,
22: 5 *r* letters to our brother Jews in Damascus.
26:10 the authority I *r* from the chief priests,
Rom 1:27 and thus *r* in their own persons the
4:11 he *r* the sign of circumcision as a seal
4:11 attesting to the justice *r* through faith
5:11 through whom we have now *r* reconciliation.
11:30 have *r* mercy through their disobedience,
15:21 "They who *r* no word of him will see him,
15:31 may be well *r* by the saints there;
16:17 contrary to the teaching you have *r*.
1Cor 2:12 The Spirit we have *r* is not the world's
4: 7 something you have that you have not *r*.
4: 7 If, then, you have *r* it,
6:19 the Spirit you have *r* from God.
7:25 I have not *r* any commandment from the Lord,
11:23 I *r* from the Lord what I handed on to you,
15: 1 which you *r* and in which you stand firm.
15: 3 on to you first of all what I myself *r*,
2Cor 1: 4 the same consolation we have *r* from him.
7: 7 reinforcement Titus had already *r* from you,
7:15 God when you *r* him in fear and trembling.
11: 4 different spirit than the one you have *r*,
11:24 of the Jews I *r* forty lashes less one;
Gal 1: 9 a gospel to you other than the one you *r*,
Eph 4: 1 a life worthy of the calling you have *r*,
4: 7 Each of us has *r* God's favor in the
Phil 4:15 by giving me something for what it had *r*.
4:18 of what I *r* from you through Epaphroditus,
Col 2: 6 the Lord, in the spirit in which you *r* him.
4:10 You have *r* instructions about him:
4:17 the ministry you have *r* in the Lord."
2Thes 2:15 Hold fast to the traditions you *r* from us,
3: 6 not follow the tradition you *r* from us.
1Tm 4: 3 to be *r* with thanksgiving by believers
4: 4 be rejected when it is *r* with thanksgiving,
4:14 Do not neglect the gift you *r* when,
Heb 2: 2 and disobedience *r* its due punishment,
5: 5 he *r* it from the One who said to him,
7: 6 *r* tithes of Abraham and blessed him who
7: 6 and blessed him who had *r* God's promises.
7:11 the basis of which the people *r* the law),
11:11 By faith Sarah *r* power to conceive though
11:17 he who had *r* the promises was ready to
11:19 dead, and so he *r* Isaac back as a symbol.
11:31 for she had peacefully *r* the spies.
11:35 *r* back their dead through resurrection.
Jas 2:23 for this he *r* the title "God's friend."
1Pt 4:10 one another, each in the measure he has *r*.
2Pt 1:17 He *r* glory and praise from God the Father
1Jn 2:27 you *r* from him remains in your hearts.
Rv 2:26 the same authority I *r* from my Father.
5: 7 The Lamb came and *r* the scroll from the
13: 5 it *r* was to last only forty-two months.

RECEIVES (20)

Gn 49:10 to him, and he *r* the peoples' homage.
Jb 27:13 an oppressor *r* from the Almighty:
Prv 18:22 it is a favor he *r* from the LORD.
27:21 so a man is tested by the praise he *r*.
Eccl 5:18 so that he *r* his lot and finds joy in the
Sir 16:14 which each *r* according to his deeds.
Ez 16:32 The adulterous wife *r*,
Mt 7: 8 For the one who asks, *r*.
10:41 the name of prophet *r* a prophet's reward;
10:41 is known to be holy *r* a holy man's reward.
13:20 the message and at first *r* it with joy.
Lk 11:10 "For whoever asks, *r*;
Rom 2:29 Such a one *r* his praise,
1Cor 12: 9 Through the Spirit one *r* faith;
12:10 One *r* the gift of tongues,
Heb 6: 7 it is cultivated, *r* the blessing of God.
7: 9 Levi, who *r* tithes,
12: 6 he scourges every son he *r*."
Jas 5: 7 the soil *r* the winter and the spring rains.
Rv 2:17 new name, to be known only by him who *r* it.'

RECEIVING (15)

Nm 26:54 each group *r* its heritage in proportion to
2Sm 10:17 On *r* this news, David assembled all Israel,
20:10 and he died without *r* a second thrust.
1Mc 8:26 their obligations without *r* any recompense.
2Mc 10:20 on *r* seventy thousand drachmas,
13:22 After giving them his pledge and *r* theirs,
Ps(s) 49:16 from the power of the nether world by *r* me.
Ez 16:34 Since you gave payment instead of *r* it,
Acts 16:23 *r* many lashes they were thrown into prison,
20:35 'There is more happiness in giving than *r*.' "
1Thes 1: 6 the Lord, *r* the word despite great trials,
2:13 that in *r* his message from us you took it,
1Tm 6:19 for *r* that life which is life indeed.
Heb 10:26 If we sin willfully after *r* the truth,
12:28 we who are *r* the unshakable kingdom should

RECENT (2)

Jdt 8:18 has not risen among us in *r* generations,
Rv 2:19 efforts of *r* times are greater than ever.

RECENTLY (8)

Ex 4:10 been eloquent, neither in the past, nor *r*,
Jdt 4: 3 and only *r* had all the people of Judea
4: 5 since their fields had *r* been harvested,
2Mc 14:36 this house, which has been so *r* purified."
Jn 11: 8 "with the Jews only *r* trying to stone you,
Acts 18: 2 a native of Pontus *r* arrived from Italy
1Cor 8: 7 Because some were so *r* devoted to idols,
Jude 1: 4 have *r* wormed their way into your midst,

RECEPTACLE (1)

1Kgs 7:31 to provide a *r* a cubit and a half in depth.

RECEPTION (5)

Tb 7: 9 from the flock and gave them a cordial *r*.
Lk 5:29 Levi gave a great *r* for Jesus in his house,
14:13 No, when you have a *r*,
16: 9 they fail you, a lasting *r* will be yours.
1Thes 1: 9 reporting what kind of *r* we had from you,

RECESSES (17)

1Sm 24: 4 were occupying the inmost *r* of the cave.
2Kgs 19:23 the mountain heights, the *r* of Lebanon;
Tb 4:19 down to the deepest *r* of the nether world.
Jb 12:22 The *r* of the darkness he discloses,
Ps(s) 48: 3 Mount Zion, "the *r* of the North,"
128: 3 like a fruitful vine in the *r* of your home;
Sg 2:14 of the rock, in the secret *r* of the cliff,
Wis 17:14 from the *r* of a powerless nether world,
Is 14:13 Mount of Assembly, in the *r* of the North.
14:15 nether world you go to the *r* of the pit!
37:24 the mountain heights, the *r* of Lebanon;
Ez 32:23 graves have been made in the *r* of the pit;
38: 6 the *r* of the north with all its troops,
38:15 come from your home in the *r* of the north,
39: 2 make you come up from the *r* of the north;
Zep 3:10 Ethiopia and as far as the *r* of the North,
Mk 7:21 designs come from the deep *r* of the heart;

RECHAB (7)

2Sm 4: 2 two company leaders named Baanah and *R*,
4: 5 of Rimmon the Beerothite, *R* and Baanah,
4: 6 So *R* and his brother Baanah slipped past
4: 9 David replied to *R* and his brother Baanah,
2Kgs 10:15 left there, Jehu met Jehonadab, son of *R*,
10:23 for them, Jehu, with Jehonadab, son of *R*,
Neh 3:14 Gate was repaired by Malchijah, son of *R*,

RECHABITE (1)

Jer 35: 5 I set before these *R* men bowls full of

RECHABITES (4)

1Chr 2:55 from Hammath of the ancestor of the *R*.
Jer 35: 2 Approach the *R* and speak to them;
35: 3 all his sons, the whole company of the *R*,
35:18 But to the company of the *R* Jeremiah said:

RECHAB'S (5)

Jer 35: 6 "Jonadab, *R* son,
35: 8 Now we have heeded Jonadab, *R* son,
35:14 The advice of Jonadab, *R* son,
35:16 Yes, the children of Jonadab, *R* son,
35:19 fail to be a descendant of Jonadab, *R* son,

RECITAL (1)

2Cor 12:19 this *r* that I am defending myself to you?

RECITE (8)

Ex 17:14 remembered, and *r* it in the ears of Joshua:
Dt 31:19 it to the Israelites and have them *r* it,
31:21 descendants will not have forgotten to *r*,
Jos 1: 8 *R* it by day and by night,
Ps(s) 50:16 "Why do you *r* my statutes,
Ez 18: 2 proverb that you *r* in the land of Israel:
Mk 12:40 and *r* long prayers for appearance sake;
Lk 20:47 they *r* long prayers to keep up appearances.

RECITED (4)

Dt 31:30 Then Moses *r* the words of this song from
32:44 went and *r* all the words of this song for
2Chr 35:25 which is *r* to this day by all the male and
2Mc 1:23 was being burned, the priests *r* a prayer,

RECKLESS (3)

Prv 14:16 the fool is *r* and sure of himself.
Sir 19: 2 and the companion of harlots becomes *r*.
2Tm 3: 4 They will be treacherous, *r*,

RECKON (2)

Ex 12: 2 you shall *r* it the first month of the year.
Nm 23: 9 and does not *r* itself among the nations.

RECKONED (2)

Lv 7:18 for him nor shall it be *r* to his credit;
Jos 13: 3 in the north is *r* Canaanite territory,

RECKONING (5)

Gn 42:22 Now comes the *r* for his blood.”
2Kgs 12:16 no *r* was asked of the men who were
22: 7 No *r* was asked of them regarding the funds
Jb 9:10 finding out, marvelous things beyond *r*.
Ps(s) 40:13 For all about me are evils beyond *r*;

RECKONS (1)

Jb 33:10 pretexts against me and *r* me as his enemy.

RECLAIM (4)

Lv 27:19 the price thus established, and so *r* it.
1Mc 15: 3 kingdom of my ancestors, I intend to *r* it,
Is 11:11 shall again take it in hand to *r* the remnant
Jas 5:15 uttered in faith will *r* the one who is ill,

RECLAIMED (2)

Gn 31: 9 Thus God *r* your father's livestock and
31:16 All the wealth that God *r* from our father

RECLINE (3)

Sir 9: 9 not, *r* not at table to drink by her side,
Am 2: 8 in pledge they *r* beside any altar;
Jn 6:10 Jesus said, “Get the people to *r*.”

RECLINED (9)

Tb 2: 1 dinner was prepared for me, and I *r* to eat.
7: 9 When they had bathed and *r* to eat,
Jdt 12:16 Then Judith came in and *r* on it.
Mt 26:20 it grew dark he *r* at table with the Twelve.
Mk 14:18 They *r* at table,
Lk 7:36 went to the Pharisee's home and *r* to eat.
11:37 He entered and *r* at table.
Jn 13:12 his cloak back on and *r* at table once more.
13:23 Jesus loved, *r* close to him as they ate.

RECLINES (2)

Lk 22:27 who *r* at table or he who serves the meal?
22:27 Is it not the one who *r* at table?

RECLINING (9)

Tb 9: 6 house, they found Tobiah *r* at table.
Jdt 10:21 Now Holofernes was *r* on his bed under a
12:15 for her daily use in *r* at her dinner.
Est 7: 8 on the couch on which Esther was *r*;
Mk 2:15 While Jesus was *r* to eat in Levi's house,
14: 3 *r* at table in the house of Simon the leper,
Jn 6:11 and passed them around to those *r* there;
13:28 none of those *r* at table understood why
1Cor 8:10 *r* at table in the temple of an idol,

RECOGNITION (1)

1Pt 2:14 of criminals and the *r* of the upright.

RECOGNIZE (38)

Gn 42: 8 his brothers, although they did not *r* him,
Dt 18:21 we *r* an oracle which the LORD has spoken?',
21:17 he shall *r* as his first-born the son of
33: 9 and his own children he refused to *r*.
Ru 3:14 but rose before men could *r* one another.
1Sm 18:28 came to *r* that the LORD was with David;
2Sm 3:38 “You must *r* that a great general has
1Kgs 14: 2 so that none will *r* you as Jeroboam's wife.
Tb 5: 2 I show him to make him *r* me and trust me,
Jdt 14: 5 that he may see and *r* the one who despised
Jb 2:12 lifted up their eyes and did not *r* him,
21:29 wayfarers and do you not *r* their monuments?
Eccl 5:17 Here is what I *r* as good:
Wis 11:16 that they might *r* that a man is punished
Sir 31:15 *R* that your neighbor feels as you do,
Jer 9: 5 They refuse to *r* me, says the LORD.
14:20 We *r*, O LORD, our wickedness,
Hos 5: 4 is in them, and they do not *r* the LORD.
Mt 17:12 but they did not *r* him and they did as
Mk 7:24 a certain house and wanted no one to *r* him;
Lk 19:44 failed to *r* the time of your visitation.”
Jn 1:26 There is one among you whom you do not *r*—
1:31 I confess I did not *r* him,
1:33 But I did not *r* him.
10: 4 sheep follow him because they *r* his voice.
10: 5 because they do not *r* a stranger's voice.”
14:17 but you can *r* him because he remains with
Acts 13:27 Jerusalem and their rulers failed to *r* him,
19:15 the evil spirit answered, “Jesus I *r*,
27:39 daylight, they did not *r* the land they saw.
1Cor 2:12 helping us to *r* the gifts he has given us.
11:16 nor the churches of God *r* any other usage.
16:18 You should *r* the worth of such men.
2Cor 1:14 and will *r* that we shall be your boast,
Ti 3:11 *r* such a person as perverted and sinful;
1Jn 3: 1 *r* us is that it never recognized the Son.
4: 2 This is how you can *r* God's Spirit:
5:20 us discernment to *r* the One who is true.

RECOGNIZED (35)

Gn 37:33 He *r* it and exclaimed:
38:26 Judah *r* them and said,
42: 7 ground, he *r* them as soon as he saw them.
42: 8 When Joseph *r* his brothers,
Jgs 18: 3 they *r* the voice of the young Levite and
1Sm 26:17 Saul *r* David's voice and asked,
1Kgs 20:41 of Israel *r* him as one of the prophets.
2Kgs 9:22 When Joram *r* Jehu,
Jdt 8:29 years all the people have *r* your prudence,
Eccl 3:12 I *r* that there is nothing better than to
3:14 I *r* that whatever God does will endure
7:25 and I *r* that wickedness is foolish and
8:17 I *r* that man is unable to find out all
9: 1 All this I have kept in mind and *r*:
Wis 11: 9 mildly chastised, they *r* how the wicked,
11:13 a benefit to these others, they *r* the Lord.
12:27 They saw and *r* the true God whom before
Sir 26: 9 haughty stare an unchaste wife can be *r*.
42: 8 cautious and *r* by all men as discreet.
Jer 28: 9 But the prophet who prophesies peace is *r*
Ez 10:20 river Chebar, whom I now *r* to be cherubim.
Dn 11: 6 and her line shall not be *r*,
Mt 14:35 when the men of that place *r* him
22:18 Jesus *r* their bad faith and said to them,
Mk 6:54 leaving the boat people immediately *r* him.
Lk 24:31 that their eyes were opened and they *r* him;
Jn 4:10 “If only you *r* God's gift,
Acts 3:10 they *r* him as that beggar who used to sit
4:13 they *r* these men as having been with Jesus.
19:34 But when they *r* that he was a Jew,
21:27 some Jews from the province of Asia *r* Paul
Rom 1:20 visible, *r* through the things he has made.
1Tm 6: 4 should be *r* as both conceited and ignorant,
2Pt 2:21 not to have *r* the road to holiness
1Jn 3: 1 recognize us is that it never *r* the Son.

RECOGNIZES (3)

Lv 5: 3 this may be, and then *r* his guilt;
5: 4 then *r* that he is guilty of such an oath;
Jn 14:17 since it neither sees him nor *r* him;

RECOGNIZING (9)

1Kgs 18: 7 *R* him, Obadiah fell prostrate and asked,
1Chr 21:20 sons who were with him, without *r* them.
Dn 9:13 from our wickedness and *r* his constancy,
Lk 24:16 However, they were restrained from *r* him.
Acts 12:14 On *r* his voice she was so overjoyed that
1Cor 11:29 He who eats and drinks without *r* the body
Gal 2: 7 *r* that I had been entrusted with the
2: 9 at work in me for the Gentiles), and *r*,
2Pt 2:20 by *r* the Lord and Savior Jesus Christ,

RECOIL (2)

Ps(s) 7:17 His mischief shall *r* upon his own head;
Jer 12:13 They *r* before their harvest,

RECOILED (1)

Ps(s) 78:57 they *r* like a treacherous bow.

RECOILS (1)

Lam 1:20 *r* within me from my monstrous rebellion.

RECOMMEND (3)

Lk 23:46 “Father, into your hands I *r* my spirit.”
2Cor 5:12 not begin to *r* ourselves to you again,
10:12 with certain people who *r* themselves.

RECOMMENDATION (2)

Jdt 5:22 Now when Achior had concluded his *r*,
2Cor 3: 1 of *r* to you or from you as others might?

RECOMMENDED (1)

Jos 9:21 Thus the princes *r* that they be let live,

RECOMMENDING (1)

Eph 1:16 God for you and *r* you in my prayers.

RECOMMENDS (2)

2Cor 10:18 It is not the man who *r* himself who is
10:18 is approved but the man whom the Lord *r*.

RECOMPENSE (23)

Nm 18:21 in *r* for the service they perform
18:31 are your *r* for service at the meeting tent.
1Mc 8:26 their obligations without receiving any *r*.
Ps(s) 109:20 May this be the *r* from the LORD upon
Prv 10:16 The just man's *r* leads to life,
Eccl 9: 5 There is no further *r* for them,
Wis 2:22 neither did they count on *r* of holiness
5:15 live forever, and in the Lord is their *r*,
10:17 gave the holy ones the *r* of their labors,
Is 35: 4 With divine *r* he comes to save you.
40:10 is his reward with him, his *r* before him.
49: 4 is with the LORD, my *r* is with my God.
61: 8 I will give them their *r* faithfully,
62:11 is his reward with him, his *r* before him.
65: 7 in full measure their *r* into their laps.
Jer 17: 3 In *r* for all your sins throughout your
Hos 9: 7 they have come, the days of *r*!
Mt 6: 1 expect no *r* from your heavenly Father.
Lk 6:35 Then will your *r* be great.
1Cor 3:14 still stands, he will receive his *r*;
9:17 If I do it willingly, I have my *r*;
9:18 And this *r* of mine?
2Cor 5:10 Christ so that each one may receive his *r*,

RECOMPENSED (1)

Prv 13:21 sinners, but the just shall be *r* with good.

RECONCILE (2)

Acts 7:26 fighting, and tried to *r* them by saying:
Col 1:20 of him, to *r* everything in his person,

RECONCILED (12)

2Sm 13:39 as he became *r* to the death of Amnon.
2Mc 1: 5 May he hear your prayers, and be *r* to you,
5:20 glory, once the great Sovereign became *r*.
7:33 he will again be *r* with his servants.
8:29 Lord to be completely *r* with his servants.
Sir 22:22 to a friend, fear not, you can be *r*.
Mt 5:24 altar, go first to be *r* with your brother,
Rom 5:10 we were *r* to him by the death of his Son,
5:10 who have been *r* will be saved by his life.
1Cor 7:11 remain single or become *r* to him again.
2Cor 5:18 who has *r* us to himself through Christ and
5:20 be *r* to God!

RECONCILIATION (5)

Rom 5:11 through whom we have now received *r*.
11:15 their rejection has meant *r* for the world,
2Cor 5:18 Christ and has given us the ministry of *r*.
5:19 he has entrusted the message of *r* to us.
Col 1:22 *r* for you in his mortal body by dying,

RECONCILING (2)

2Cor 5:19 God, in Christ, was *r* the world to himself,
Eph 2:16 *r* both of us to God in one body through

RECONNAISSANCE (1)

Jgs 1:23 The house of Joseph had a *r* made of Bethel,

RECONNOITER (15)

Nm 13: 2 Moses, “Send men to *r* the land of Canaan,
13:16 the men whom Moses sent out to *r* the land.
13:17 In sending them to *r* the land of Canaan,
14:36 men whom Moses had sent to *r* the land
14:38 Of all the men who had gone to *r* the land,
32: 8 them from Kadesh-barnea to *r* the land.
Dt 1:22 'Let us send men ahead to *r* the land for
Jos 2: 1 saying, “Go, *r* the land and Jericho.”
6:25 whom Joshua had sent to *r* Jericho,
7: 2 with instructions to go up and *r* the land.
14: 7 sent me from Kadesh-barnea to *r* the land;
Jgs 18: 2 and Eshtaol, to *r* the land and scout it.
18:14 *r* the land of Laish said to their kinsmen,
18:17 Meanwhile the five men who had gone to *r*
2Kgs 7:14 the king sent them to *r* the Aramean army.

RECONNOITERED (3)

Nm 13:21 So they went up and *r* the land from the
32: 9 went up to the Wadi Eshcol and *r* the land,
Jdt 7: 7 He *r* the approaches to their city and

RECONNOITERING (1)

Nm 13:25 *r* the land for forty days they returned,

RECONSECRATE (1)

Nm 6:11 On the same day he shall *r* his head and

RECONSECRATED (1)

1Mc 4:54 it, on that very day it was *r* with songs,

RECONSIDERED (1)

Tb 3:10 But she *r*, saying to herself:

RECORD (16)

Gn 5: 1 This is the *r* of the descendants of Adam.
11:10 This is the *r* of the descendants of Shem.
11:27 This is the *r* of the descendants of Terah.
1Chr 24: 6 made a *r* of it in the presence of the king,
2Chr 12:15 and of Iddo the seer [his family *r*.
Tb 12:12 presented and read the *r* of your prayer
1Mc 8:22 with the Jews as a *r* of peace and alliance:
14:23 the people of Sparta may have a *r* of them.
Jb 19:23 Would that they were inscribed in a *r*:
Is 8:16 The *r* is to be folded and the sealed
10:19 up for signals, that any boy can *r* them.
30: 8 tablet they can keep, inscribe it in a *r*;
Mal 3:16 And a *r* book was written before him of
Mt 1: 1 A family *r* of Jesus Christ,
Jn 21:25 entire world to hold the books to *r* them.
Rom 1: 2 his prophets, as the holy Scriptures *r*—

RECORDED (42)

Gn 48: 6 be *r* in the names of their two brothers.
Nm 33: 2 By the LORD's command Moses *r* the starting
Jos 8:31 of the LORD, as *r* in the book of the law.
10:13 Is this not *r* in the Book of Jashar?

24:26 which he *r* in the book of the law of God.
2Sm 1:18 Jonathan, which is *r* in the Book of Jashar
1Kgs 11:41 *r* in the book of the chronicles of Solomon.
14:19 are *r* in the book of the chronicles of the
14:29 are *r* in the book of the chronicles of the
22:39 are *r* in the book of the chronicles of the
22:46 are *r* in the book of the chronicles of the
2Kgs 1:18 Ahaziah are *r* in the book of chronicles
8:23 are *r* in the book of the chronicles of the
12:20 are *r* in the book of the chronicles of the
13: 8 are *r* in the book of the chronicles of the
13:12 are *r* in the book of the chronicles of the
14:15 Amaziah, king of Judah, are *r* in the book
14:28 Hamath from Israel, are *r* in the book
15: 6 are *r* in the book of the chronicles of the
15:11 acts of Zechariah are *r* in the book
15:15 are *r* in the book of the chronicles of the
15:21 are *r* in the book of the chronicles of the
15:26 are *r* in the book of the chronicles of the
15:31 are *r* in the book of the chronicles of the
15:36 are *r* in the book of the chronicles of the
16:19 the acts of Ahaz are *r* in the book
1Chr 9: 1 are *r* in the book of the kings of Israel.
2Chr 16:11 can be found *r* in the book of the kings of
Est A:15 Then the king had these things *r*;
9:20 Mordecai *r* these events and sent letters
9:32 for Purim and was *r* in the book.
10: 2 are *r* in the chronicles of the kings of
1Mc 9:22 and his greatness have not been *r*;
14:22 have *r* the following in the public decrees:
16:24 are *r* in the chronicle of his pontificate,
Ps(s) 56: 9 are they not *r* in your book?
69:29 of the living, and not be *r* with the just!
Ez 13: 9 *r* in the register of the house of Israel,
Dn 9:11 sworn malediction, *r* in the law of Moses,
Jn 20:30 signs not *r* here
20:31 But these have been *r* to help you believe
Rv 20:12 to their conduct as *r* on the scrolls.

RECORDER (1)

2Chr 26:11 by Jeiel the scribe and Maaseiah the *r*,

RECORDING (1)

Sir 42: 7 or of *r* all that is given or received;

RECORDS (23)

1Chr 4:33 it was inscribed of them in their family *r*.
5: 1 in the family *r* according to birthright.
5: 7 family *r* according to their descendants,
5:17 in the family *r* in the time of Jotham,
7: 5 thousand warriors in their family *r*.
7: 7 Their family *r* listed twenty-two thousand
7: 9 Their family *r* listed twenty thousand two
7:40 Their family *r* numbered twenty-six
9: 1 all Israel was inscribed in its family *r*
9:22 in the family *r* of their villages.
26:31 their chief according to their family *r*.
2Chr 31:17 *r* according to their ancestral houses,
31:18 to all who were inscribed in the family *r*,
31:19 and to every Levite listed in the family *r*.
Ezr 2:62 These men searched their family *r*,
4:15 made in the historical *r* of your fathers.
4:15 In the historical *r* you can discover and
6: 1 in which the Babylonian *r* were stored away;
Neh 7: 5 people, and to examine their family *r*,
7:64 These men searched their family *r*,
1Mc 13:42 began to write in their *r* and contracts,
2Mc 2: 1 You will find in the *r*,
2:13 it is also told in the *r* and in Nehemiah's

RECOUNT (12)

Ex 10: 2 that you may *r* to your son and grandson
Jgs 5:11 where men *r* the just deeds of the LORD,
1Sm 12: 7 and shall *r* for you all the acts of mercy
Ps(s) 35:28 Then my tongue shall *r* your justice,
40: 6 to tell them, they would be too many to *r*.
139:18 Were I to *r* them,
Sir 44: 8 a name and men *r* their praiseworthy deeds;
Jer 23:27 By their dreams which they *r* to each other,
23:28 the prophet who has a dream *r* his dream;
Zep 3:18 you, so that none may *r* your disgrace.
Lk 8:39 home and *r* all that God has done for you."
Heb 11:32 What more shall I *r*?

RECOUNTED (7)

Gn 24:66 *r* to Isaac all the things he had done.
29:13 then *r* to Laban all that had happened,
41: 8 sages of Egypt and *r* his dreams to them;
45:27 *r* to him all that Joseph had told them,
Est 5:11 He *r* the greatness of his riches,
Lk 1:65 began to be *r* to the last detail.
24:35 Then they *r* what had happened on the road

RECOUNTING (3)

Ps(s) 26: 7 my thanks, and *r* all your wondrous deeds.
Sir 42:17 must fail in *r* the wonders of the LORD,
Jer 23:32 *r* their lies and by their empty boasting.

RECOUNTS (2)

Prv 8: 7 Yes, the truth my mouth *r*,
Sir 31:11 secure, and the assembly *r* his praises.

RECOURSE (13)

Ex 5:22 Moses again had *r* to the LORD and said,
2Sm 21: 1 David had *r* to the LORD,
2Chr 25:15 "Why have you had *r* to this people's gods
25:20 because they had had *r* to the gods of Edom.
Est C:12 mortal anguish, likewise had *r* to the Lord.
2Mc 4: 5 So he had *r* to the king,
9: 2 Thereupon the people had swift *r* to arms,
Jb 8: 5 if you yourself have *r* to God and make
Eccl 7:29 but men have had *r* to many calculations.
Ez 14: 4 of his sin before him, has *r* to a prophet.
Dn 13: 4 and the Jews had *r* to him often because he
Am 6: 1 first, to whom the people of Israel have *r*!
Na 1: 7 He takes care of those who have *r* to him,

RECOVER (26)

Gn 38:20 Adullamite to *r* the pledge from the woman;
Nm 21: 8 who has been bitten looks at it, he will *r*."
Dt 28:31 in your presence, but you will not *r* it.
Jgs 11:26 why did you not *r* them during that time?
1Sm 20:21 send my attendant to go and *r* the arrows.
2Kgs 1: 2 Ekron, whether I shall *r* from this injury."
8: 8 as to whether I shall *r* from this sickness."
8: 9 you whether he will *r* from his sickness."
8:10 Elisha answered, "that he will surely *r*.
8:14 "He told me that you would surely *r*."
20: 1 you shall not *r*.'"
20: 7 and applied to the boil, that he might *r*.
Neh 3:34 Will they *r* these stones,
1Mc 15: 9 When we *r* our kingdom,
Jb 10:20 that I may *r* a little Before I go whence
Sir 29: 6 If the lender is able to *r* barely half,
Is 38: 1 you shall not *r*."
38:21 and applied to the boil, that he might *r*.
Bar 6:53 nor do they *r* what is unjustly taken,
Mt 11: 5 the blind *r* their sight,
Mk 16:18 sick upon whom they lay their hands will *r*."
16:20 sick upon whom they lay their hands will *r*."
Lk 7:22 The blind *r* their sight,
Acts 9:12 hands on him so that he might *r* his sight.)
9:17 to help you *r* your sight and be filled
22:13 'Saul, my brother,' he said, *r* your sight.'

RECOVERED (17)

Gn 14:16 He *r* all the possessions,
Nm 21: 9 serpent looked at the bronze serpent, he *r*.
Jos 5: 8 in camp where they were, until they *r*.
1Sm 30:18 *r* everything the Amalekites had taken,
1Kgs 13: 6 and the king *r* the normal use of his hand.
2Kgs 13:25 times, and thus *r* the cities of Israel.
16: 6 time the king of Edom *r* Elath for Edom,
1Chr 10:12 a man, *r* the bodies of Saul and his sons,
Tb 14: 2 and after he *r* it he lived in prosperity,
Est D: 8 throne, held her in his arms until she *r*,
1Mc 10:53 him and his army, and *r* the royal throne
2Mc 10: 1 leadership, had *r* the temple and the city,
Is 38: 9 had been sick and had *r* from his illness:
39: 1 that Hezekiah had *r* from his sickness,
Mt 9:30 and they *r* their sight.
Jn 9:15 began to inquire how he had *r* his sight.
Acts 12:11 Peter had *r* his senses by this time,

RECOVERING (1)

2Mc 9:22 I have great hopes of *r* from my illness.

RECOVERY (2)

2Mc 3:32 priest offered a sacrifice for the man's *r*.
Lk 4:18 *R* of sight to the blind and release to

RECRIMINATIONS (1)

Gn 45:24 told them, "Let there be no *r* on the way."

RECRUIT (1)

1Mc 4:35 began to *r* mercenaries so as to return

RECRUITED (2)

1Mc 15: 3 I have *r* a large number of mercenary
Jer 12: 6 they have *r* a force against you.

RECRUITING (1)

Jer 51:27 Appoint *r* officers against her,

RECRUITS (1)

Jer 4: 5 the trumpet through the land, summon the *r*!

RECTANGULAR (2)

1Kgs 6:33 where the doorposts of olive wood were *r*.
7: 5 The posts of all the doorways were *r*,

RECTITUDE (2)

Prv 2: 9 Then you will understand *r* and justice,
Wis 5:19 He shall take invincible *r* as a shield

RECUMBENT (1)

Gn 49: 9 He crouches like a lion *r*,

RED (58)

Gn 25:30 "Let me gulp down some of that *r* stuff;
Ex 10:19 the locusts and hurled them into the *R* Sea.
13:18 the *R* Sea by way of the desert road.
15: 4 his officers were submerged in the *R* Sea.
15:22 Moses led Israel forward from the *R* Sea,
23:31 the *R* Sea to the sea of the Philistines,
25: 5 rams' skins dyed *r*,
26:14 make a covering of rams' skins dyed *r*,
35: 7 rams' skins dyed *r*,
35:23 hair, rams' skins dyed *r* or tahash skins,
36:19 the tent was made of rams' skins dyed *r*,
39:34 the covering of rams' skins dyed *r*,
Nm 14:25 set out in the desert on the *R* Sea road."
19: 2 *r* heifer that is free from every blemish
21: 4 Mount Hor they set out on the *R* Sea road,
33:10 from Elim, they camped beside the *R* Sea.
33:11 Setting out from the *R* Sea,
Dt 1:40 proceed into the desert on the *R* Sea road.'
2: 1 proceed into the desert on the *R* Sea road,
11: 4 the water of the *R* Sea as they pursued you,
14: 5 the ox, the sheep, the goat, the *r* deer,
Jos 2:10 LORD dried up the waters of the *R* Sea
4:23 the LORD, your God, had done at the *R* Sea,
24: 6 to the *R* Sea with chariots and horsemen.
Jgs 11:16 the desert to the *R* Sea and came to Kadesh.
1Kgs 9:26 the shore of the *R* Sea in the land of Edom.
2Kgs 3:22 saw the water at a distance as *r* as blood.
Neh 9: 9 in Egypt, you heard their cry by the *R* Sea;
Jdt 5:13 them, God dried up the *R* Sea before them,
1Mc 4: 9 how our fathers were saved in the *R* Sea,
Ps(s) 106: 7 against the Most High at the *R* Sea.
106: 9 He rebuked the *R* Sea,
106:22 land of Ham, terrible things at the *R* Sea.
136:13 Who split the *R* Sea in twain,
136:15 swept Pharaoh and his army into the *R* Sea,
Prv 23:31 Look not on the wine when it is *r*,
Sg 5:13 His lips are *r* blossoms;
Wis 10:18 She took them across the *R* Sea and brought
13:14 *r* and crimsoned its surface with red stain,
19: 7 Out of the *R* Sea an unimpeded road,
Is 1:18 Though they be crimson *r*,
41:25 shall trample the rulers down like *r* earth,
63: 2 Why is your apparel *r*,
Jer 49:21 quakes, to the *R* Sea the outcry is heard!
Ez 24:11 on the coals till its metal glows *r* hot,
Zec 1: 8 There appeared the driver of a *r* horse,
1: 8 in a shady place, and behind him were *r*,
6: 2 The first chariot had *r* horses,
6: 6 the *r* and the white horses went after them,
Mt 16: 2 ["In the evening you say, *R* sky at night,
16: 3 but in the morning, 'Sky *r* and gloomy,
Acts 7:36 signs in the land of Egypt, in the *R* Sea,
Heb 11:29 crossed the *R* Sea as if it were dry land,
Rv 6: 4 Another horse came forth, a *r* one.
6:12 tentcloth and the moon grew *r* as blood.
9:17 The breastplates they wore were fiery *r*,
12: 3 it was a huge dragon, flaming *r*,

REDDISH (3)

Gn 25:25 The first to emerge was *r*,
Lv 13:49 on any leather article is greenish or *r*,
14:37 house consists of greenish or *r* depressions

REDEDICATE (1)

1Mc 4:36 us go up to purify the sanctuary and *r* it."

REDEEM (33)

Ex 13:13 of an ass you shall *r* with a sheep.
13:13 If you do not *r* it,
13:13 Every first-born son you must *r*.
13:15 and why I *r* every first-born of my sons.'
34:20 an ass you shall *r* with one of the flock;
34:20 if you do not *r* it,
34:20 The first-born among your sons you shall *r*.
Lv 25:25 relative, who has the right to *r* it,
25:26 the man has no relative to *r* his land,
25:32 *r* the town houses that are their property.
25:49 if he acquires the means, he may *r* himself.
27:13 If the offerer wishes to *r* the animal,
27:15 one who dedicated his house wishes to *r* it,
27:19 one who dedicated his field wishes to *r* it,
1Chr 17:21 earth whom a god went to *r* as his people?
Jb 6:23 from the enemy, or to *r* me from oppressors?
Ps(s) 25:22 *R* Israel, O God, from all its distress!
26:11 *r* me, and have pity on me.
31: 6 you will *r* me, O LORD, O faithful God.
44:27 *R* us for your kindness' sake.
49: 8 Yet in no way can a man *r* himself,
49: 9 Too high is the price to *r* one's life;
49:16 But God will *r* me from the power of the
69:19 as an answer for my enemies, *r* me.
72:14 From fraud and violence he shall *r* them,
119:154 Plead my cause, and *r* me;
130: 8 he will *r* Israel from all their iniquities.
Jer 31:11 shall *r* him from the hand of his conqueror.
Hos 7:13 Though I wished to *r* them,
13:14 shall I *r* them from death?
Mi 4:10 LORD *r* you from the hand of your enemies.
Zec 10: 8 *r* them they will be as numerous as before.
Ti 2:14 to *r* us from all unrighteousness and to

REDEEMED (37)

Ex 15:13 In your mercy you led the people you *r*;
21: 8 dislikes her, he shall let her be *r*.
Lv 19:20 has not yet been *r* or given her freedom,
25:24 occupy, you must permit the land to be *r*.
25:30 has not been *r* at the end of a full year,
25:31 they may be *r* at any time,
25:33 their cities that had been sold and not *r*,
25:48 he may be *r* by one of his own brothers,
25:54 If he is not thus *r*,
27:20 it to someone else, it may no longer be *r*;
27:27 it may be *r* by paying one fifth more than
27:27 If it is not *r*, it shall be sold
27:29 that are doomed lose the right to be *r*;
Nm 3:49 when the rest had been *r* by the Levites.
18:15 man, as well as of unclean animals, be *r*.
18:17 of cattle, sheep or goats shall not be *r*;
2Sm 7:23 which you *r* for yourself from Egypt?
1Chr 17:21 your people Israel, whom you *r* from Egypt,
Est C: 9 which you *r* for yourself out of Egypt.
Ps(s) 71:23 My soul also, which you have *r*,
74: 2 old, the tribe you *r* as your inheritance,
77:16 With your strong arm you *r* your people,
107: 2 Thus let the *r* of the LORD say,
107: 2 those whom he has *r* from the hand of the
Is 1:27 Zion shall be *r* by judgment,
29:22 God of the house of Jacob, who *r* Abraham:
35: 9 journey to make, and on it the *r* will walk.
43: 1 Fear not, for I have *r* you;
44:22 return to me, for I have *r* you.
44:23 For the LORD has *r* Jacob,
48:20 say, "The LORD has *r* his servant Jacob.
51:10 the sea into a way for the *r* to pass over?
52: 3 nothing, and without money you shall be *r*.
62:12 called the holy people, the *r* of the LORD,
63: 9 of his love and pity he *r* them himself,
Lam 3:58 me in mortal danger, you *r* my life.
Eph 1: 7 that we have been *r* and our sins forgiven,

REDEEMER (16)

Ps(s) 19:15 favor before you, O LORD, my rock and my *r*.
78:35 their rock and the Most High God, their *r*.
Prv 23:11 For their *r* is strong;
Is 41:14 your *r* is the Holy One of Israel.
43:14 Thus says the LORD, your *r*,
44: 6 Thus says the LORD, Israel's King and *r*,
44:24 Thus says the LORD, your *r*,
47: 3 I will yield to no entreaty, says our *r*,
48:17 Thus says the LORD, your *r*,
49: 7 the LORD, the *r* and the Holy One of Israel,
49:26 that I, the LORD, am your savior, your *r*,
54: 5 Your *r* is the Holy One of Israel,
54: 8 I take pity on you, says the LORD, your *r*.
59:20 a *r* to those of Jacob who turn from sin,
60:16 that I, the LORD, am your savior, your *r*,
63:16 our father, our *r* you are named forever.

REDEEMING (3)

Lv 27:20 If, instead of *r* such a field,
2Sm 7:23 which God has led, *r* it as his people;
Is 63: 4 was in my heart, my year for *r* was at hand.

REDEEMS (4)

1Mc 4:11 there is One who *r* and delivers Israel."
Ps(s) 34:23 But the LORD *r* the lives of his servants;
103: 4 He *r* your life from destruction,
Is 52: 9 Lord comforts his people, he *r* Jerusalem.

REDEMPTION (12)

Lv 25:48 his services he still has the right of *r*;
Ru 4: 7 make binding a contract of *r* or exchange,
2Kgs 12: 5 the census tax, personal *r* money,
1Mc 3: 6 By his hand *r* was happily achieved,
Ps(s) 130: 7 is kindness and with him is plenteous *r*;
Rom 3:24 God, through the *r* wrought in Christ Jesus.
8:23 while we await the *r* of our bodies.
1Cor 1:30 our justice, our sanctification, and our *r*.
Eph 1:14 full *r* of a people God has made his own,
4:30 whom you were sealed against the day of *r*.
Col 1:14 Through him we have *r*,
Heb 9:12 with his own blood, and achieved eternal *r*.

REDOUBLED (2)

Neh 6: 9 But instead, I now *r* my efforts.
Sir 18:32 of a moment which bring on poverty *r*;

REDOUND (1)

Jdt 13:20 God make this *r* to your everlasting honor,

REDRESS (3)

Jb 19: 7 I cry for help, but there is no *r*.
Is 1:17 *r* the wronged,
52: 5 My people have been taken away without *r*;

REDUCE (13)

Ex 5: 8 Do not *r* it.
5:19 told not to *r* the daily amount of bricks.
Dt 9: 3 he it is who will *r* them to nothing and
20:20 which to *r* the city that is resisting you.
Jgs 14:15 Did you invite us here to *r* us to poverty?"
2Kgs 19:25 *r* fortified cities into heaps of ruins,
Neh 5: 5 had to *r* our sons and daughters to slavery,
Jb 24:25 confute me, and *r* my argument to nought?
Is 37:26 *r* fortified cities into heaps of ruins,
Hos 2: 5 her like the desert, *r* her to an arid land,
Am 6:11 to bits, and *r* the small house to rubble.
Mt 20:31 them in an effort to *r* them to silence,
1Cor 1:28 to *r* to nothing those who were something;

REDUCED (24)

Gn 47:21 Pharaoh, and the people were *r* to slavery,
Ex 1:13 the Israelites and *r* them to cruel slavery,
Lv 6: 3 the fire has *r* the holocaust on the altar,
25:25 When one of your countrymen is *r* to
25:35 "When one of your fellow countrymen is *r*
25:47 "When one of your countrymen is *r* to such
Jgs 6: 6 Thus was Israel *r* to misery by Midian,
Ezr 6:11 is to be *r* to rubble for this offense.
1Mc 8:10 and *r* them to slavery even to this day.
Ps(s) 31:18 them be *r* to silence in the nether world.
102: 6 insistent sighing I am *r* to skin and bone.
Prv 20:13 Love not sleep, lest you be *r* to poverty;
Sir 26:19 A wealthy man *r* to want;
48: 2 in his zeal he *r* them to straits;
Is 44:11 and stand forth, to be *r* to fear and shame.
Jer 47: 5 is shaved bald, Ashkelon is *r* to silence;
48: 2 You, too, Madmen, shall be *r* to silence;
Lam 1:16 were *r* to silence when the enemy prevailed."
Bar 2:26 And you *r* the house which bears your name
Ez 28:18 I have *r* you to dust on the earth in the
Dn 3:37 we are *r*, O Lord, beyond any other nation,
Mi 3:12 like a field, and Jerusalem *r* to rubble,
Lk 20:26 disconcerted them and *r* them to silence.
Acts 9:22 and *r* the Jewish community of Damascus to

REDUCES (1)

Is 41: 2 With his sword he *r* them to dust,

REDUCING (1)

Jos 8:28 *r* it to an everlasting mound of ruins,

REDUCTION (1)

Ex 5:11 must not be the slightest *r* in your work."

REED (22)

Gn 41: 2 they grazed in the *r* grass.
41:18 they grazed in the *r* grass.
1Kgs 14:15 The LORD will strike Israel like a *r*
2Kgs 18:21 is in fact a broken *r* which pierces the
Jb 8:11 Can the *r* grass flourish without water?
9:26 They shoot by like skiffs of *r*,
30:31 and my *r* pipe to sounds of weeping.
Is 9:13 and tail, palm branch and *r* in one day.
19:15 to do for head or tail, palm branch or *r*.
35: 7 lurk will be a marsh for the *r* and papyrus.
36: 6 is in fact a broken *r* which pierces the
42: 3 A bruised *r* he shall not break,
58: 5 That a man bow his head like a *r*,
Ez 29: 6 been a *r* staff for the house of Israel:
Mt 11: 7 a *r* swaying in the wind?
12:20 The bruised *r* he will not crush;
27:29 his head, and stuck a *r* in his right hand.
27:30 of the *r* and kept striking him on the head.
27:48 it in cheap wine, and sticking it on a *r*,
Mk 15:19 on the head with a *r* and spitting at him,
15:36 stuck it on a *r* to try to make him drink.
Lk 7:24 a *r* swayed by the wind?

REEDS (6)

Ex 2: 3 placed it among the *r* on the river bank.
2: 5 Noticing the basket among the *r*,
Ps(s) 68:31 Rebuke the wild beast of the *r*,
Sir 40:16 Or they are like *r* on the riverbank,
Is 19: 6 *R* and rushes shall wither away,
Mk 11: 8 spread *r* which they had cut in the fields.

REEDY (1)

Jb 40:21 trees he lies, in coverts of the *r* swamp.

REEF (1)

Acts 27:17 they would be driven on the *r* of Syrtis,

REEL (1)

Is 24:20 The earth will *r* like a drunkard,

REELAIAH (1)

Ezr 2: 2 Zerubbabel, Jeshua, Nehemiah, Seraiah, *R*,

REELED (1)

Ps(s) 107:27 They *r* and staggered like drunken men,

REELS (1)

Is 21: 4 My mind *r*,

REENTERED (3)

Gn 44:14 As Judah and his brothers *r* Joseph's house,
1Chr 19:15 before his brother Abishai, and *r* the city.
Mt 9: 1 Then he *r* the boat,

REESTABLISH (3)

2Sm 8: 3 to *r* his dominion at the Euphrates River.
Sir 48:10 and to *r* the tribes of Jacob
Ez 16:62 For I will *r* my covenant with you

REESTABLISHED (4)

2Chr 29:35 the service of the house of the LORD was *r*.
29:36 over what God had *r* for the people,
31: 2 Hezekiah *r* the classes of the priests and
2Mc 2:22 and *r* the laws that were in danger of

REESTABLISHES (1)

Is 62: 2 until he *r* Jerusalem

REFER (6)

Ex 18:22 More important cases they should *r* to you,
24:14 a complaint, let him *r* the matter to them."
Dt 1:17 *R* to me any case that is too hard for you
Jer 26: 6 the earth shall *r* to when cursing another.
Mt 18:17 If he ignores them, *r* it to the church.
Jn 5:34 *r* to these things only for your salvation.)

REFERENCE (4)

1Sm 4:21 with *r* to the capture of the ark of God
2Chr 5:11 purified themselves without *r* to the rotation
Rom 2:12 have the law will perish without *r* to it;
Heb 4: 4 for in *r* to the seventh day Scripture

REFERRED (8)

Ex 18:26 The more difficult cases they *r* to Moses,
1Mc 12: 8 which clearly *r* to alliance and friendship.
2Mc 11:18 be *r* to the king I called to his attention,
Sir 49: 9 He also *r* to JOB,
Lk 24:27 every passage of Scripture which *r* to him.
Acts 25:14 there, Festus *r* Paul's case to the king.
Gal 4:17 The people I have *r* to are not courting
Heb 4: 5 and again, in the place we have *r* to,

REFERRING (2)

Jn 7:39 (Here he was *r* to the Spirit,
Rom 9:27 Isaiah cries out, *r* to Israel,

REFERS (2)

Dn 8:17 of man, that the vision *r* to the end time."
Eph 5:32 I mean that it *r* to Christ and the church.

REFINE (3)

Jb 28: 1 silver, and a place for gold which men *r*.
Is 1:25 you, and *r* your dross in the furnace,
Zec 13: 9 and I will *r* them as silver is refined,

REFINED (14)

Dt 28:54 The most *r* and fastidious man among you
28:56 The most *r* and delicate woman among you,
28:56 so delicate and *r* that she would not
1Kgs 10:18 throne made, and overlaid it with *r* gold.
1Chr 28:18 the *r* gold,
29: 4 and seven thousand talents of *r* silver,
Ps(s) 12: 7 silver, freed from dross, sevenfold *r*.
Is 48:10 See, I have *r* you like silver,
Jer 6:29 In vain has the smelter *r*,
Dn 11:35 fall, so that the rest may be tested, *r*,
12:10 Many shall be *r*, purified, and tested,
Zec 13: 9 and I will refine them as silver is *r*,
Rv 1:15 gleamed like polished brass *r* in a furnace,
3:18 gold *r* by fire if you would be truly rich.

REFINERS (1)

Mal 3: 2 For he is like the *r* fire,

REFINING (2)

Mal 3: 3 He will sit *r* and purifying [silver],
3: 3 *R* them like gold or like silver that they

REFLECT (10)

Dt 32: 7 of old, *r* on the years of age upon age.
Jb 4: 7 *R* now, what innocent person perishes?
18: 2 *R*, and then we can have discussion.
Ps(s) 4: 5 *r*, upon your beds, in silence.
Sir 6:37 *R* on the precepts of the LORD,
Is 41:22 we may *r* on them And know their outcome;
44:19 he does not *r*, nor have the intelligence
Bar 6:41 unable to *r* and abandon these gods,
2Cor 10: 7 he belongs to Christ, let him *r* on this:
2Tm 2: 7 *R* on what I am saying,

REFLECTED (5)

Gn 18:17 The LORD *r*:
2Mc 11:13 He *r* on the defeat he had suffered,
Prv 24:32 And as I gazed at it, I *r*;
Lk 2:19 these things and *r* on them in her heart.
20:14 the tenant farmers saw the son, they *r*.

REFLECTING (2)

Wis 8:17 and *r* in my heart That there is
Dn 8: 5 I was *r*, a he-goat with a prominent horn

REFLECTION (4)

Sir 34: 3 what the *r* of a face is to the face itself.
1Cor 11: 7 is the image of God and the *r* of his glory.
11: 7 Woman, in turn, is the *r* of man's glory.
Heb 1: 3 This Son is the *r* of the Father's glory,

REFLECTIONS (2)

Col 2:18 inflated with empty pride by his human *r*
Heb 4:12 it judges the *r* and thoughts of the heart.

REFLECTS (1)

Sir 14:20 meditates on wisdom, and *r* on knowledge;

REFORM (19)

Jer 7: 3 *R* your ways and your deeds,
7: 5 you thoroughly *r* your ways and your deeds;
18:11 *r* your ways and your deeds.
26:13 Now, therefore, *r* your ways and your deeds;
35:15 to *r* your conduct,
Mt 3: 2 *R* your lives!
3: 8 Give some evidence that you mean to *r*.
3:11 I baptize you in water for the sake of *r*,
4:17 *R* your lives!
11:20 had been worked, with their failure to *r*:
Mk 1:15 *R* your lives and believe in the gospel!"
Lk 3: 8 Give some evidence that you mean to *r*.
13: 3 will all come to the same end unless you *r*.
13: 5 will all come to the same end unless you *r*."
Acts 2:38 "You must *r* and be baptized,
3:19 Therefore, *r* your lives!
8:22 *R* your evil ways.
17:30 on all men everywhere to *r* their lives.
26:20 a message of *r* and of conversion to God,

REFORMED (5)

Jgs 20:33 They *r* their ranks at Baal-tamar
Mt 11:21 have *r* in sackcloth and ashes long ago.
12:41 the preaching of Jonah they *r* their lives;
Lk 10:13 long ago have *r* in sackcloth and ashes.
11:32 For at the preaching of Jonah they *r*,

REFRAIN (14)

Ex 15:21 dancing, and she led them in the *r*:
Dt 23:23 Should you *r* from making a vow,
2Sm 2:26 How much longer will you *r* from ordering
1Kgs 22: 6 I go to attack Ramoth-gilead or shall I *r*?"
22:15 fight against Ramoth-gilead, or shall we *r*?"
2Chr 18: 5 go to attack Ramoth-gilead, or shall I *r*?"
18:14 fight against Ramoth-gilead, or shall I *r*?"
Jb 4: 2 For how can anyone *r* from speaking?
Sir 4:23 *R* not from speaking at the proper time,
13:12 and will not *r* from injury or chains.
35: 3 To *r* from evil pleases the LORD,
2Cor 12: 7 But I *r*, lest anyone think more of me
1Thes 4: 6 and that each *r* from overreaching or
Jas 3:14 at least *r* from arrogant and false claims

REFRAINED (3)

Tb 1:11 but I *r* from eating that kind of food.
Jb 29: 9 The chief men *r* from speaking and covered
Ps(s) 39: 3 I *r* from rash speech.

REFRAINING (1)

2Mc 5:25 then, finding the Jews *r* from work,

REFRESH (7)

Gn 18: 5 a little food, that you may *r* yourselves;
Sg 2: 5 me with raisin cakes, *r* me with apples,
Sir 12: 4 *r* the downtrodden,
Jer 31:25 For I will *r* the weary soul;
Mt 11:28 and find life burdensome, and I will *r* you.
Lk 16:24 tip of his finger in water to *r* my tongue,
Phlm 1:20 *R* this heart of mine in Christ.

REFRESHED (5)

Ex 23:12 of your maidservant and the alien may be *r*.
Prv 11:25 he who refreshes others will himself be *r*.
Rom 15:32 joy and be *r* in spirit by your company.
1Cor 16:18 They have *r* my spirit as they did yours.
Phlm 1: 7 you the hearts of God's people have been *r*.

REFRESHES (3)

Ps(s) 23: 3 he *r* my soul.
Prv 11:25 he who *r* others will himself be refreshed.
25:13 [He *r* the soul of his master.]

REFRESHING (1)

Ps(s) 19: 8 The law of the LORD is perfect, *r* the soul;

REFRESHMENT (3)

1Kgs 13: 7 "Come home with me for some *r*,"
Ps(s) 66:12 and water, but you have led us out to *r*.
Acts 3:20 Thus may a season of *r* be granted you by

REFUGE (109)

Nm 35: 6 as places where a homicide can take *r*,
35:11 killed someone unintentionally may take *r*.
35:15 another unintentionally may take *r* there.
35:25 him to the city of asylum where he took *r*;
35:26 the city of asylum where he has taken *r*,
Dt 4:42 that a homicide might take *r* there if he
19: 3 every homicide will be able to find a *r*.
19: 4 take *r* in such a place to save his life:
19: 5 *r* in one of these cities to save his life.
19:11 and then takes *r* in one of these cities,
23:16 a slave who has taken *r* from him with you.
Jgs 3:26 and, passing the idols, took *r* in Seirah.
6: 2 signals on the mountains, the caves for *r*,
9:15 good faith, come and take *r* in my shadow.
Ru 2:12 under whose wings you have come for *r*."
1Sm 22: 4 him as long as David remained in the *r*.
22: 5 "Do not remain in the *r*.
24:23 while David and his men went up to the *r*.
2Sm 5:17 On hearing this, David went down to the *r*.
22: 3 my God, my rock of *r*!
22: 3 horn of my salvation, my stronghold, my *r*,
22:31 he is a shield to all who take *r* in him."
23:14 At that time David was in the *r*,
1Kgs 20:30 too, fled, and took *r* within the city,
1Mc 1:53 wherever places of *r* could be found.
5: 5 He forced them to take *r* in towers,
10:14 for they used it as a place of *r*.
10:43 Whoever takes *r* in the temple of Jerusalem
10:84 of Dagon and the men who had taken *r* in it.
11:46 But he took *r* in the palace,
15:21 from their country take *r* with you,
16:10 *r* in the towers on the plain of Azotus,
2Mc 5: 5 taken, Menelaus took *r* in the citadel.
5: 7 took *r* in the country of the Ammonites.
5:12 to slay those who took *r* in their houses.
8:33 who had taken *r* in a little house;
10:18 thousand took *r* in two very strong towers,
12: 6 to the sword those who had taken *r* there.
Ps(s) 2:12 Happy are all who take *r* in him!
5:12 take *r* in you be glad and exult forever.
7: 2 O LORD, my God, in you I take *r*;
11: 1 In the LORD I take *r*;
14: 6 of the afflicted, but the LORD is his *r*.
16: 1 Keep me, O God, for in you I take *r*;
17: 7 from their foes to *r* at your right hand.
18: 3 My God, my rock of *r*,
18:31 he is a shield to all who take *r* in him.
25:20 not be put to shame, for I take *r* in you.
28: 8 his people, the saving *r* of his anointed.
31: 2 In you, O LORD, I take *r*;
31: 3 Be my rock of *r*,
31: 5 snare they set for me, for you are my *r*.
31:20 And which, toward those who take *r* in you,
34: 9 happy the man who takes *r* in him.
34:23 no one incurs guilt who takes *r* in him.
36: 8 of men take *r* in the shadow of your wings.
37:39 he is their *r* in time of distress.
37:40 and saves them, because they take *r* in him.
46: 2 God is our *r* and our strength,
57: 2 have pity on me, for in you I take *r*.
57: 2 In the shadow of your wings I take *r*,
59:17 stronghold, my *r* in the day of distress.
61: 4 you will give me rest, for you are my *r*,
61: 5 take *r* in the shelter of your wings!
62: 8 my *r* is in God.
62: 9 God is our *r*!
64:11 man is glad in the LORD and takes *r* in him;
71: 1 In you, O LORD, I take *r*;
71: 3 Be my rock of *r*,
71: 7 am I to many, but you are my strong *r*!
73:28 to make the LORD GOD my *r*.
90: 1 have been our *r* through all generations.
91: 2 Say to the LORD, "My *r* and my fortress,
91: 4 you, and under his wings you shall take *r*;
91: 9 Because you have the LORD for your *r*;
94:22 my stronghold, and my God the rock of my *r*.
104:18 the cliffs are a *r* for rock-badgers.
118: 8 take *r* in the LORD than to trust in man.
118: 9 *r* in the LORD than to trust in princes.
119:114 You are my *r* and my shield;
141: 8 in you I take *r*;
142: 6 I say, "You are my *r*,
144: 2 My *r* and my fortress,
Prv 14:26 even for one's children he will be a *r*.
14:32 but the just man finds a *r* in his honesty.
30: 5 he is a shield to those who take *r* in him.
Wis 14: 6 hope of the universe, who took *r* on a raft,
Sir 51: 1 I will make known your name, *r* of my life;
51: 8 For he saves those who take *r* in him,
Is 4: 6 of day, *r* and cover from storm and rain.
10:31 in flight, the inhabitants of Gebim seek *r*.
14:32 in her the afflicted of his people find *r*."
25: 4 For you are a *r* to the poor, a refuge to
27: 5 Or shall he cling to me for *r*?
28:15 For we have made lies our *r*,
28:17 Hail shall sweep away the *r* of lies,
30: 2 protection and take *r* in Egypt's shadow;
30: 3 and *r* in Egypt's shadow your disgrace.
57:13 who takes *r* in me shall inherit the land,
Jer 4: 6 the standard to Zion, seek *r* without delay!
16:19 my fortress, my *r* in the day of distress!
17:17 ruin, you, my *r* in the day of misfortune.
Jl 4:16 quake, but the LORD is a *r* to his people,
Na 1: 7 LORD is good, a *r* on the day of distress;
3:11 you, too, shall seek a *r* from the foe.
Zep 3:12 Who shall take *r* in the name of the LORD;
Mk 5: 3 The man had taken *r* among the tombs;
Heb 6:18 we who have taken *r* in him might be

REFUGEE (1)

Nm 35:32 allow a *r* to leave his city of asylum

REFUGEES (4)

Sir 28:14 many, and makes them *r* among the peoples;
Jer 44:14 Only scattered *r* shall return.
48:45 shadow stop short the exhausted *r*;
Ob 1:14 Stand not at the crossroads to slay his *r*;

REFUGES (3)

1Sm 23:14 David now lived in the *r* in the desert,
23:19 "David is hiding among us, now in the *r*,
24: 1 there and stayed in the *r* behind Engedi.

REFULGENCE (1)

Wis 7:26 For she is the *r* of eternal light,

REFURBISH (1)

Jdt 3:10 month to *r* all the equipment of his army.

REFUSAL (1)

Jdt 7:15 and their *r* to meet you peacefully."

REFUSE (66)

Gn 24:41 If you visit my kindred and they *r* you,
Ex 4:23 If you *r* to let him go,
7:27 go to worship me, If you *r* to let them go,
9: 2 If you *r* to let them go and persist in
10: 3 How long will you *r* to submit to me?
10: 4 If you *r* to let my people go,
16:28 you *r* to keep my commandments and laws?
Lv 7:18 rather, it shall be considered as *r*,
19: 7 the sacrifice will be unacceptable as *r*,
26:23 you still *r* to be chastened by me and
Nm 14:11 How long will they *r* to believe in me,
22:16 Please do not *r* to come to me.
Dt 17:12 Any man who has the insolence to *r* to
1Sm 1: 7 her, and Hannah would weep and *r* to eat.
1: 8 why do you weep, and why do you *r* to eat?
1Kgs 2:16 Do not *r* me."
2:17 ask King Solomon, who will not *r* you,
2:20 "Do not *r* me."
2:20 king said to her, "for I will not *r* you."
20: 7 my silver and my gold, I did not *r* him."
Tb 3: 6 Lord, *r* me not.
4:13 as to *r* to take a wife for yourself from
Jdt 12:14 She replied, "Who am I to *r* my lord?
Jb 6: 7 I *r* to touch them;
40: 8 Would you *r* to acknowledge my right?
Ps(s) 141: 5 for the head, Which my head shall not *r*,
Prv 3:27 *R* no one the good on which he has a claim
21: 7 away, because they *r* to do what is right.
21:25 slays him, for his hands *r* to work.
Wis 13:12 *r* from his handiwork in preparing his food,
13:13 the good-for-nothing *r* from these remnants,
Sir 4:27 impious man, nor *r* to do so before rulers.
6:24 *r* not my counsel.
7:21 *r* him not his freedom.
12: 4 Give to the good man, *r* the sinner;
28: 4 Should a man *r* mercy to his fellows,
29: 7 Many *r* to lend,
Is 1:20 But if you *r* and resist,
5:25 corpses shall be like *r* in the streets.
30: 9 Children who *r* to obey the law of the LORD.
Jer 8: 5 cling to deceptive idols, *r* to turn back?
9: 5 They *r* to recognize me, says the LORD.
13:10 This wicked people who *r* to obey my words,
25:28 *r* to take the cup from your hand and drink,
38:21 But if you *r* to surrender,
50:33 hold them fast and *r* to let them go.
Lam 3:45 us offscourings and *r* among the nations.
Ez 3: 7 house of Israel will *r* to listen to you,
7:19 and their gold shall be considered *r*.
7:20 For this reason I make them *r*.
Dn 13:21 If you *r*, we will testify against you
13:22 if I *r*, I cannot escape your power.
Am 8: 6 even the *r* of the wheat we will sell!"
Mt 3:14 John tried to *r* him with the protest,
Mk 6:26 of the guests, he did not want to *r* her.
Jn 10:26 *r* to believe because you are not my sheep.
16: 9 in that they *r* to believe in me;
19:10 "Do you *r* to speak to me?"
Acts 18:15 I *r* to judge such matters."
1Cor 4:13 We have become the world's *r*,
1Tm 5:11 *R* to enroll the younger widows,
Heb 12:25 Do not *r* to hear him who speaks.
1Pt 4:17 those who *r* obedience to the gospel of God?
3Jn 1:10 Not only does he *r* to welcome the brothers
Rv 11: 9 three and a half days but *r* to bury them.
15: 4 Who would dare *r* you honor,

REFUSED (74)

Gn 37:35 tried to console him, he *r* all consolation,
39: 8 But he *r*. "As long as I am here."
Ex 13:15 When Pharaoh stubbornly *r* to let us go,
Nm 20:21 *r* to let them pass through her territory,
22:13 for the LORD has *r* to let me go with you."
22:14 the report, "Balaam *r* to come with us."
Dt 1:26 "But you *r* to go up,
2:30 Heshbon, *r* to let us pass through his land,
33: 9 and his own children he *r* to recognize.
Jgs 11:20 *r* to let Israel pass through his territory.
19:10 The man, however, *r* to stay another night;
20:13 But the Benjaminites *r* to accede to the
1Sm 8:19 *r* to listen to Samuel's warning and said,
15: 9 They *r* to carry out the doom on anything
22:17 But the king's servants *r* to lift a hand
28:23 But he *r*, saying, "I will not eat."
31: 4 armor-bearer, badly frightened, *r* to do it.
2Sm 2:23 Still he *r* to stop.
13:25 he *r* to go and began to bid him goodbye.
14:29 summoned him a second time, Joab *r* to come.
23:16 they brought it to David he *r* to drink it,
23:17 So he *r* to drink it.
1Kgs 20:35 But he *r* to strike him.
21: 6 But he *r* to let me have his vineyard."
21:15 the Jezreelite which he *r* to sell you,
2Kgs 5:16 and despite Naaman's urging, he still *r*.
1Chr 10: 4 But the armor-bearer, in great fear, *r*.
11:18 But David *r* to drink it.
11:19 and so he *r* to drink it.
19:19 *r* to come to the aid of the Ammonites.
2Chr 25:16 this thing and have *r* to hear my counsel."
29: 7 and *r* to burn incense and offer holocausts
Neh 9:17 They *r* to obey and no longer remembered
Jdt 2: 3 *r* to comply with the order he had issued.
5: 4 Why have they *r* to come out to meet me
Est 1:12 But Queen Vashti *r* to come at the royal
4: 4 he might take off his sackcloth; but he *r*.
1Mc 1:50 Whoever *r* to act according to the command
15:27 But he *r* to accept the aid;
Jb 31:13 I *r* justice to my manservant or to my maid,
Ps(s) 21: 3 you *r* not the wish of his lips.
66:20 who *r* me not my prayer or his kindness!
Prv 1:24 "Because I called and you *r*,
Wis 12:27 true God whom before they had *r* to know;
16:16 For the wicked who *r* to know you were
Is 42:24 In his ways they *r* to walk,
Jer 3: 3 you have a harlot's brow, you *r* to blush.
5: 3 you laid them low, but they *r* correction;
5: 3 harder than stone, and *r* to return to you.
11:10 their forefathers who *r* to obey my words.
25: 4 Though you *r* to listen or pay heed,
Ez 20: 8 rebelled against me and *r* to listen to me;
24:13 you *r* to be purified of your uncleanness,
33: 5 the trumpet blast yet *r* to take warning;
Dn 6:19 *r* to eat and he dismissed the entertainers.
13:41 the young man was, but she *r* to tell us.
Hos 11: 6 Because they *r* to repent,
Zec 7:11 But they *r* to listen; they stubbornly
Mt 22: 3 guests to the wedding, but they *r* to come.
23:37 her young under her wings, but you *r* me.
27:34 with gall, which he tasted but *r* to drink.
Mk 16:11 had been seen by her, they *r* to believe it.
Lk 13:34 her young under her wings, and you *r* me!
18: 4 For a time he *r*, but finally he thought,
24:11 like nonsense and they *r* to believe them.
Jn 6:64 of course, the ones who *r* to believe,
9:18 The Jews *r* to believe that he had really
12:37 their presence, they *r* to believe in him.
12:42 *r* to admit it because of the Pharisees,
Acts 9:26 even *r* to believe that he was a disciple.
Heb 11:24 *r* to be known as the son of Pharaoh's
12:25 *r* to listen as God spoke to them on earth,
Jude 1: 5 but later destroyed those who *r* to believe.
Rv 13:15 to death anyone who *r* to worship it.

REFUSES (14)

Ex 11: 9 "Pharaoh *r* to listen to you that my
22:16 If her father *r* to give her to him,
Lv 5: 1 any person *r* to give the information which,
Dt 20:12 But if it *r* to make peace with you and
25: 7 *r* to perpetuate his brother's name in Israel.'
Ps(s) 77: 3 my soul *r* comfort.
Sir 14: 9 *r* his neighbor and brings ruin on himself.
Jer 31:15 she *r* to be consoled because her children
Ez 33: 9 his way, and he *r* to turn from his way,
Mk 16:16 who *r* to believe in it will be condemned.
Jn 5:23 He who *r* to honor the Son refuses to honor
1Jn 4: 6 anyone who is not of God *r* to hear us.
Rv 2:21 repent but she *r* to turn from her lewdness.

REFUSING (10)

Ex 7:14 is obdurate in *r* to let the people go.
8:25 must not play false again by *r* to let the
9:17 the way for my people by *r* to let them go?
Lv 26:15 *r* to obey all my commandments and breaking
26:31 *r* to accept your sweet-smelling offerings.
Sir 41:19 Of *r* to give when asked,
Jer 15:18 my wound incurable, *r* to be healed?
18:10 is evil in my eyes, *r* to obey my voice,
Acts 15:38 Pamphylia, *r* to join them on that mission,
1Jn 5:10 *r* to believe in the testimony he has given

REFUTATION (1)

Acts 18:28 He was vigorous in his public *r* of the

REFUTE (4)

Jb 15: 6 you own lips *r* you.
32:12 not one of you who could *r* his statements.
33: 5 If you are able, *r* me;
Ti 1: 9 doctrine and to *r* those who contradict it.

REGAIN (5)

Lv 25:27 it, so that he may thus *r* his own property.
2Chr 13:20 did not *r* power during the time of Abijah;
2Mc 14: 3 position and *r* access to the holy altar.
Ez 7:13 not *r* what he sold as long as he lives,
Jon 1:13 Still the men rowed hard to *r* the land,

REGAINED (4)

Jos 4:18 the soles of their feet *r* the dry ground,
2Mc 2:22 *r* possession of the world-famous temple,
Acts 9:18 fell from his eyes and he *r* his sight.
22:13 instant I *r* my sight and looked at him.

REGALE (1)

Hos 7: 3 In their wickedness they *r* the king,

REGARD (52)

Gn 9: 5 and from man in *r* to his fellow man I
Ex 4:26 of blood," in *r* to the circumcision.
18:20 them in *r* to the decisions and regulations,
23:11 in *r* to your vineyard and your olive grove.
29:35 Carry out all these orders in *r* to Aaron
Nm 4:27 with *r* to what they must do and what they
9: 8 learn what the LORD will command in your *r*."
32:28 order in their *r* to the priest Eleazar,
36: 6 with *r* to the daughters of Zelophehad:
Dt 1: 3 that the LORD had given him in their *r*.
19:15 stand against a man in *r* to any crime
33: 9 He said of his father, 'I *r* him not';
2Sm 17:21 given the following counsel in *r* to you."
18: 5 the various leaders with *r* to Absalom.
2Chr 7:11 planned to do in *r* to the house of the LORD
31: 2 in *r* to holocausts or peace offerings,
35:26 his pious deeds in *r* to what is written in
Ezr 10:13 of us who have sinned in this *r* are many.
Neh 13:24 and so it was in *r* to the languages of the
Jdt 4:13 their cry and had *r* for their distress.
Est 3: 2 that is what the king had ordered in his *r*.
2Mc 4:34 Then, without any *r* for justice,
Jb 24:17 light, for daylight they *r* as darkness.
35: 5 *r* the heavens high above you.
Ps(s) 41: 2 is he who has *r* for the lowly and the poor;
106:44 Yet he had *r* for their affliction when he
Wis 12:15 you *r* it as unworthy of your power to
Is 5:12 But what the LORD does they *r* not,
17: 8 nor shall he *r* what his fingers have made:
63:15 and *r* us from your holy and glorious place!
Jer 24: 5 even so will I *r* with favor Judah's exiles
Ez 44: 5 be attentive in *r* to those who are to be
Dn 2:18 of the God of heaven in *r* to this mystery,
3:99 the most high God has accomplished in my *r*.
11:37 He shall have no *r* for the gods of his
11:37 for no god shall he have *r*,
Zec 9: 8 for now I have *r* for their affliction.
Mt 21:26 the people, who all *r* John as a prophet."
Lk 7: 2 centurion had a servant he held in high *r*,
7:30 his baptism defeated God's plan in their *r*.
Acts 24:16 In this *r* I too always strive to keep my
25:26 I may have something to set down in his *r*.
Rom 16:19 *r* to what is good and innocent of all evil.
1Cor 4: 1 Men should *r* us as servants of Christ and
2Cor 9: 3 for you in this *r* may not be shown empty.
Eph 3: 2 God in his goodness gave me in your *r*.
Phil 1: 7 in your *r* since I hold all of you dear
1Thes 3: 2 encourage you in *r* to your faith
1Tm 1:18 with the prophecies made in your *r*,
6: 1 *r* their masters as worthy of full respect;
Phlm 1:17 If then you *r* me as a partner,
Heb 6: 9 are persuaded of better things in your *r*,

REGARDED (18)

Gn 31:15 Are we not *r* by him as outsiders?
Ex 11: 3 Moses himself was very highly *r* by
Jdt 1:11 *r* him as a lone individual opposed to them,
Est 10: 3 and was *r* with favor by his many brethren,
2Mc 4:15 what their ancestors had *r* as honors,
7:12 because he *r* his sufferings as nothing.
14:37 highly *r*, he was called a father of the Jews
Ps(s) 102:18 When he has *r* the prayer of the destitute,
Is 29:17 orchard, and the orchard be *r* as a forest!
32:15 orchard and the orchard be *r* as a forest.
Mt 14: 5 of the people, who *r* him as a prophet.
21:46 to fear the crowds who *r* him as a prophet.
Mk 11:32 people, who all *r* John as a true prophet.)
Lk 22:24 them about who should be *r* as the greatest.
Acts 5:34 of the law highly *r* by all the people.
Rom 4: 4 wages are not *r* as a favor but as his due.
2Cor 5:16 If at one time we so *r* Christ,
Gal 2: 6 Those who were *r* as important,

REGARDING (11)

Gn 34:17 not comply with our terms *r* circumcision,
Ex 6:13 orders *r* both the Israelites and Pharaoh,
Dt 12:30 Do not inquire *r* their gods,
2Kgs 22: 7 of them *r* the funds consigned to them,
1Chr 17:17 For you have made a promise *r* your
Jdt 10:19 *r* the Israelites with wonder because of
Ez 14:22 their actions and be consoled *r* the evil
Mi 3: 5 *r* the prophets who lead my people astray;
Na 1:14 The LORD has commanded *r* you:
Rom 7: 2 she is released from the law *r* husbands.
Heb 7:14 *r* which Moses said nothing about priests.

REGARDS (15)

Nm 25:18 *r* Peor and as *r* their kinswoman Cozbi,
2Kgs 10:29 *r* the golden calves at Bethel and at Dan.
25:17 so for the other pillar, as *r* the network.
Tb 6: 8 "As *r* the fish's heart and liver,
Jb 41:19 He *r* iron as straw,
Eccl 11: 9 *r* all this God will bring you to judgment.
Sir 37:10 advice from one who *r* you with hostility;
Lam 4:16 has dispersed them, he *r* them no more;
Dn 6: 5 against Daniel as *r* the administration.
Mal 2:13 Because he no longer *r* your sacrifice nor
Rom 14: 5 One man *r* this day as better than that;
2Cor 1:24 As *r* faith, you are standing firm.
1Thes 4: 9 As *r* brotherly love,
5: 1 As *r* specific times and moments,

REGEM (1)

1Chr 2:47 The sons of Jahdai were *R*,

REGEMMELECH (1)

Zec 7: 2 Bethelsarezer sent *R* and his men to

REGENT (3)

1Kgs 22:48 was no king in Edom, but an appointed *r*.
2Kgs 15: 5 vizier and *r* for the people of the land.
2Chr 26:21 Therefore his son Jotham was *r* of the

REGIMENT (1)

Gn 41:34 so as to *r* the land during the seven years

REGION (109)

Gn 19:28 and Gomorrah and the whole *r* of the Plain,
20: 1 Abraham journeyed on to the *r* of the Negeb,
24:62 and was living in the *r* of the Negeb.
26:12 *r* and reaped a hundredfold the same year.
34: 2 Hamor the Hivite, who was chief of the *r*,
35:22 While Israel was encamped in that *r*,
45:10 You will settle in the *r* of Goshen,
46:28 On his arrival in the *r* of Goshen,
46:34 order that you may stay in the *r* of Goshen,
47: 1 and they are now in the *r* of Goshen."
47: 4 your servants settle in the *r* of Goshen."
47: 5 "They may settle in the *r* of Goshen;
47:11 the pick of the land, in the *r* of Rameses.
47:27 in the land of Egypt, in the *r* of Goshen.
50: 8 and herds were left in the *r* of Goshen.
Lv 16:22 off their iniquities to an isolated *r*,
Nm 13:29 Amalekites live in the *r* of the Negeb;
32: 3 the community and said, "The *r* of Ataroth,
32:22 *r* shall be your possession before the LORD.
Dt 2:37 neither the *r* bordering on the Wadi Jabbok,
3: 4 eluding our grasp, the whole *r* of Argob,
3:13 the kingdom of Og, the whole Argob *r*,
3:13 [All this *r* of Bashan was once called a
3:14 took all the *r* of Argob as far as the
4:41 three cities in the *r* east of the Jordan,
4:43 in the desert, in the *r* of the plateau,
4:47 the Amorites in the *r* east of the Jordan:
10: 7 a *r* where there is water in the wadies.]
28:68 to the *r* I told you that you were never to
Jos 11:21 Anab, the entire mountain *r* of Judah,
11:21 Judah, and the entire mountain *r* of Israel.
14:12 *r* which the LORD promised me that day,
17:12 cities, the Canaanites persisted in this *r*.
17:16 in the valley *r* all have iron chariots,
17:18 for the mountain *r* which is now forest
19:50 Timnah-serah in the mountain *r* of Ephraim.
20: 7 in Galilee in the mountain *r* of Naphtali,
20: 7 Shechem in the mountain *r* of Ephraim,
20: 7 is, Hebron) in the mountain *r* of Judah.
21:11 is, Hebron, in the mountain *r* of Judah,
21:21 at Shechem in the mountain *r* of Ephraim;
22:10 the *r* of the Jordan in the land of Canaan,
22:11 *r* of the Jordan facing the land of Canaan,
24: 3 from the *r* beyond the River and led him
24: 4 the mountain *r* of Seir in which to settle,
24:30 mountain *r* of Ephraim north of Mount Gaash.
24:33 son Phinehas in the mountain *r* of Ephraim.
Jgs 1: 9 Canaanites who lived in the mountain *r*,
1:19 he gained possession of the mountain *r*.
1:34 hemmed in the Danites in the mountain *r*,
2: 9 mountain *r* of Ephraim north of Mount Gaash.
3: 3 who dwell in the mountain *r* of Lebanon
3:27 the horn in the mountain *r* of Ephraim,
4: 5 and Bethel in the mountain *r* of Ephraim,

7:24 the mountain *r* of Ephraim to say,
9:37 coming down from the *r* of Tabbur-Haares,
10: 1 of Shamir in the mountain *r* of Ephraim.
11:21 land of the Amorites dwelling in that *r*,
17: 1 mountain *r* of Ephraim whose name was Micah.
17: 8 of Micah in the mountain *r* of Ephraim.
18: 2 of Micah in the mountain *r* of Ephraim,
18:13 From there they went on to the mountain *r*
19: 1 remote parts of the mountain *r* of Ephraim
19:16 he was from the mountain *r* of Ephraim,
19:18 far up into the mountain *r* of Ephraim,
1Sm 23:23 If he is in the *r*, I will search him out
2Sm 5: 6 against the Jebusites who inhabited the *r*.
18: 8 The battle spread out over that entire *r*,
1Kgs 4:10 well as in Socoh and the whole *r* of Hepher;
1Chr 5:10 tents throughout the *r* east of Gilead.
6:52 Shechem in the mountain *r* of Ephraim,
18: 6 set up garrisons in the Damascus *r* of Aram,
2Chr 4:17 The king had them cast in the Jordan *r*,
8: 4 in the desert *r* and all the supply cities,
Ezr 8:25 and all the Israelites of that *r*.
Neh 12:28 together from the *r* about Jerusalem,
Jdt 1: 6 all the inhabitants of the mountain *r*,
2:19 cover all the western *r* with their chariots
2:22 chariots, and marched into the mountain *r*.
4: 4 they sent word to the whole *r* of Samaria,
5: 5 near you [that inhabits this mountain *r*;
5:15 took possession of the whole mountain *r*.
5:19 in the mountain *r* which was unoccupied.
6: 7 will now conduct you to the mountain *r*,
6:11 there they led him into the mountain *r*
7:18 encamped in the mountain *r* opposite Dothan;
11: 2 your people who dwell in the mountain *r*,
15: 5 rest of the mountain *r* took part in this,
1Mc 11:14 because the people of that *r* had revolted.
11:59 governor of the *r* from the Ladder of Tyre
12:32 on to Damascus and traversed that whole *r*.
2Mc 4:36 the king returned from the *r* of Cilicia,
9: 1 retreated in disgrace from the *r* of Persia.
10:14 When Gorgias became governor of the *r*,
12:18 But they did not find Timothy in that *r*,
12:21 because of the difficult terrain of that *r*.
13:24 from Ptolemais to the *r* of the Gerrenes.
Mt 2:22 a dream, Joseph went to the *r* of Galilee.
3: 5 *r* around the Jordan were going out to him.
10:15 it will go easier for the *r* of Sodom and
14:35 him they spread the word throughout the *r*.
Mk 1:28 throughout the surrounding *r* of Galilee.
Lk 2: 8 of JesusThere were shepherds in that *r*,
3: 1 of the *r* of Ituraea and Trachonitis,
3: 3 He went about the entire *r* of the Jordan
4:14 and his reputation spread throughout the *r*.
Jn 11:54 called Ephraim in the *r* near the desert,
Acts 16: 3 circumcised because of the Jews of that *r*,
1Thes 1: 8 every *r* your faith in God is celebrated,

REGIONS (24)

Dt 1: 7 Amorites and to all the surrounding *r*,
19: 3 into three *r* the land which the LORD,
Jos 9: 1 in the mountain *r* and in the foothills,
10:40 the mountain *r*, the Negeb, the foothills,
11: 2 *r* and in the Arabah near Chinneroth,
11: 3 and Jebusites in the mountain *r*,
11:16 the mountain *r*, the entire Negeb
11:16 as the mountain *r* and foothills of Israel,
11:21 *r* and exterminated the Anakim in Hebron,
12: 8 It included the mountain *r* and foothills,
13: 6 *r* between Lebanon and Misrephoth-maim;
15:48 In the mountain *r*: Shamir, Jattir
17:15 the mountain *r* of Ephraim are so narrow."
17:16 "Our mountain *r* are not enough for us;
2Mc 9:21 On returning from the *r* of Persia,
Jl 4: 4 Tyre and Sidon, and all the *r* of Philistia?
Acts 2:10 Egypt, and the *r* of Libya around Cyrene.
17:26 epochs and fixed the boundaries of their *r*.
20: 2 He traveled throughout its *r*,
Rom 15:23 Now I have no more work to do in these *r*,
2Cor 11:10 of mine will not cease in the *r* of Achaia!
Gal 1:21 I entered the *r* of Syria and Cilicia.
Eph 4: 9 descended into the lower *r* of the earth?
6:12 of darkness, the evil spirits in *r* above.

REGISTER (6)

2Sm 24: 2 from Dan to Beer-sheba and *r* the people,
24: 4 in order to *r* the people of Israel.
2Chr 31:16 There was also a *r* by ancestral houses of
Ez 13: 9 recorded in the *r* of the house of Israel,
Lk 2: 3 Everyone went to *r*, each to his own town.
2: 5 to *r* with Mary,

REGISTERED (58)

Ex 30:12 census of the Israelites who are to be *r*,
30:12 no plague may come upon them for being *r*.
30:13 enters the *r* group must pay a half-shekel,
30:14 of twenty years or more who enters the *r*
38:26 years or more who entered the *r* group;
Nm 1:20 first-born of Israel, *r* by lineage in clans
1:22 of Simeon, *r* by lineage in clans
1:24 descendants of Gad, *r* by lineage in clans
1:26 of Judah, *r* by lineage in clans
1:28 of Issachar, *r* by lineage in clans
1:30 Zebulun, *r* by lineage in clans
1:32 of Ephraim, *r* by lineage
1:34 of Manasseh, *r* by lineage in clans
1:36 of Benjamin, *r* by lineage in clans
1:38 of Dan, *r* by lineage in clans
1:40 of Asher, *r* by lineage in clans
1:42 of Naphtali, *r* by lineage in clans
1:44 It was these who were *r*,
1:45 military service, *r* by ancestral houses,
1:47 not *r* by ancestral tribe with the others.
2: 9 *r* by companies in the camp of Judah
2:16 *r* by companies in the camp of Reuben
2:24 *r* by companies in the camp of Ephraim
2:31 *r* by companies in the camp of Dan
2:32 The total number of those *r* by companies
2:33 were not *r* with the other Israelites,
3:22 all their males of a month or more were *r*,
3:28 all their males of a month or more were *r*,
3:34 all their males of a month or more were *r*,
3:39 whom Moses had *r* by clans in keeping
3:43 males of a month or more were *r*,
4:36 tasks in the meeting tent, as *r* by clans,
4:40 tent, as *r* by clans and ancestral houses,
4:44 tasks in the meeting tent, as *r* by clans,
4:48 the total number *r* was eight thousand five
14:29 of twenty years or more, *r* in the census,
26: 3 Eleazar *r* those of twenty years or more,
26: 7 seven hundred and thirty men were *r*.
26:14 twenty-two thousand two hundred men were *r*.
26:18 forty thousand five hundred men were *r*.
26:22 thousand five hundred men were *r*.
26:25 thousand three hundred men were *r*.
26:27 sixty thousand five hundred men were *r*.
26:34 thousand seven hundred men were *r*.
26:37 thousand five hundred men were *r*.
26:41 forty-five thousand six hundred men were *r*.
26:43 thousand four hundred men were *r*.
26:47 thousand four hundred men were *r*.
26:50 thousand four hundred men were *r*.
26:51 and thirty were the Israelites who were *r*.
26:54 in proportion to the number of men *r* in it.
26:57 The Levites *r* by clans were:
26:62 one month or more of age, who were *r*,
26:62 They were not *r* with the other Israelites,
26:63 were the men *r* by Moses and the priest
26:64 a man of those who had been *r* by Moses
2Sm 24: 9 to the king the number of people *r*:
Ezr 8:34 and weight, and the total weight was *r*.

REGISTERING (2)

Nm 1: 2 ancestral houses, *r* each male individually.
3:15 and clans, *r* every male of a month or more."

REGISTRATION (4)

Nm 4:34 community made a *r* among the Kohathites,
4:38 The *r* was then made among the Gershonites,
4:42 Then the *r* was made among the Merarites,
4:46 had completed the *r* among the Levites,

REGRET (10)

1Sm 15:11 "I *r* having made Saul king,
1Mc 11:10 I *r* that I gave him my daughter,
Prv 20:25 a trap for a man, or to *r* a vow once made.
Wis 19: 2 their way, they would *r* it and pursue them.
Sir 12:12 my advice, when you groan with *r*,
13: 6 you, then without *r* he will impoverish you.
30: 5 with joy, and even in death, without *r*:
Jer 42:10 for I *r* the evil I have done you.
Mt 27: 3 condemned, began to *r* his action deeply.
2Cor 7: 8 Or if I did feel some *r* (because I

REGRETS (3)

Sir 32:19 counsel, and then you need have no *r*.
2Cor 7: 8 If I saddened you by my letter I have no *r*.
7:10 sake produces a repentance without *r*,

REGRETTED (7)

Gn 6: 6 he *r* that he had made man on the earth,
1Sm 15:35 the LORD *r* having made him king of Israel.
24: 6 David *r* that he had cut off an end of
2Sm 24:10 David *r* having numbered the people,
24:16 the LORD *r* the calamity and said to the
Mt 21:30 but afterward he *r* it and went.
Mk 6:26 The king bitterly *r* the request;

REGROUP (1)

1Kgs 20:22 "Go, *r* your forces.

REGULAR (5)

Gn 26:17 and made the Wadi Gerar his *r* campsite.
Dt 3:11 of iron, nine *r* cubits long and four wide,
1Chr 16: 6 and Jahaziel were to be the *r* trumpeters
Jdt 2:19 their chariots and cavalry and *r* infantry.
7:11 sir, do not attack them in *r* formation;

REGULARLY (9)

Ex 27:20 so that you may keep lamps burning *r*.
Lv 24: 2 so that you may keep lamps burning *r*.
24: 3 set up the lamps to burn before the LORD *r*,
24: 4 gold lampstand, to burn *r* before the LORD.
24: 8 *R* on each sabbath day this bread shall be
1Sm 1: 3 This man *r* went on pilgrimage from his
1Chr 16:37 the ark *r* according to the daily ritual;
16:40 to the LORD on the altar of holocausts *r*,
Tb 12: 9 who *r* give alms shall enjoy a full life;

REGULATE (1)

Nm 8:26 how you are to *r* the duties of the Levites."

REGULATION (3)

Nm 19: 2 the *r* which the law of the LORD prescribes.
36: 5 So Moses gave this *r* to the Israelites
Ez 45:14 The *r* for oil:

REGULATIONS (12)

Ex 12:43 Aaron, "These are the *r* for the Passover.
15:25 the LORD, in making rules and *r* for them,
18:16 make known to them God's decisions and *r*."
18:20 them in regard to the decisions and *r*,
Lv 25:18 my precepts and be careful to keep my *r*,
Nm 9: 3 it, observing all its rules and *r*."
9:14 observe the rules and *r* for the Passover.
2Kgs 17:34 the LORD nor observe the statutes and *r*,
17:37 to observe forever the statutes and *r*,
1Mc 14:42 to make *r* concerning its functions and
Heb 9: 1 has *r* for worship and an earthly sanctuary.
9:10 *r* concerning the flesh,

REHABIAH (4)

1Chr 23:17 The sons of Eliezer were *R* the chief
23:17 sons, but the sons of *R* were very numerous.
24:21 the chief, of the descendants of *R*;
26:25 pertained to Eliezer, whose son was *R*,

REHEARSE (1)

Jb 21:27 and the arguments you *r* against me.

REHOBOTH-HAN-NAHAR (1)

1Chr 1:48 Samlah died and Shaul from *R* succeeded him.

REHOB (11)

Nm 13:21 as far as where *R* adjoins Labo of Hamath.
Jos 19:28 it extended to Cabul, Mishal, Abdon, *R*,
19:30 Achzib, Ummah, Acco, Aphek and *R*,
21:31 lands, and *R* with its pasture lands;
Jgs 1:31 of Mahaleb, Achzib, Helbah, Aphik or *R*.
2Sm 8: 3 David defeated Hadadezer, son of *R*,
8:12 from the plunder of Hadadezer, son of *R*,
10: 8 while the Arameans of Zobah and *R* and the
1Chr 6:60 lands, and *R* with its pasture lands.
11:38 Joel, brother of Nathan, from *R*,
Neh 10:12 Hodiah, Kelita, Pelaiah, Hanan, Mica, *R*,

REHOBOAM (48)

2Sm 8: 7 when he came to Jerusalem in the days of *R*,
1Kgs 11:43 David, and his son *R* succeeded him as king.
12: 1 *R* went to Shechem,
12: 3 They said to *R*: "Your father put on us
12: 6 King *R* consulted the elders who had been
12:12 third day all Israel came back to King *R*,
12:17 but *R* reigned over the Israelites who
12:18 King *R* then sent out Adoram,
12:18 *R* managed to mount his chariot to flee to
12:21 *R* gathered together all the house of Judah
12:21 of Israel, to restore the kingdom to *R*,
12:23 "Say to *R*, son of Solomon, the king of Judah,
12:27 people will return to their master, *R*,
14:21 *R*, son of Solomon, reigned in Judah.
14:25 In the fifth year of King *R*,
14:27 them, King *R* had bronze shields made,
14:29 The rest of the acts of *R*,
14:30 constant warfare between *R* and Jeroboam.
14:31 *R* rested with his ancestors;
1Chr 3:10 The son of Solomon was *R*,
2Chr 9:31 David, and his son *R* succeeded him as king.
10: 1 *R* went to Shechem,
10: 3 and he and all Israel said to *R*,
10: 6 King *R* consulted the elders who had been
10:12 to King *R* as he had instructed them to do.
10:17 *R*, therefore, reigned over only those
10:18 King *R* then sent out Hadoram,
10:18 *R* himself managed to mount his chariot and
11: 1 On his arrival in Jerusalem *R* gathered
11: 3 "Say to *R*, son of Solomon, king of Judah,
11: 5 *R* took up residence in Jerusalem and built
11:17 the kingdom of Judah and made *R*,
11:18 *R* took to himself as wife Mahalath,
11:21 *R* loved Maacah, daughter of Absalom,
11:22 *R* constituted Abijah,
12: 1 After *R* had consolidated his rule and had
12: 2 happened that in the fifth year of King *R*,
12: 5 Then Shemaiah the prophet came to *R* and
12:10 replace them, King *R* made bronze bucklers,
12:13 King *R* consolidated his power in Jerusalem
12:15 The acts of *R*, first and last, are written
12:15 was war continually between *R* and Jeroboam.
12:16 *R* rested with his ancestors;
13: 7 scoundrels, joined him and overcame *R*,

REHOBOAM (cont.)

13: 7 Solomon, when R was young and unthinking,
Sir 47:23 Expansive in folly, limited in sense, R,
Mt 1: 7 father of Rehoboam, R the father of Abijah,

REHOBOAM'S (1)

2Chr 12:13 R mother was named Naamah, an Ammonite.

REHOBOTH (1)

Gn 26:22 It was called R,

REHOBOTH-IR (1)

Gn 10:11 to Asshur, where he built Nineveh, R,

REHUM (8)

Ezr 2: 2 Mordecai, Bilshan, Mispereth, Bigvai, R,
4: 8 Then R, the governor,
4: 9 R, the governor, Shimshai, the scribe,
4:17 "To R, the governor, Shimshai, the scribe,
4:23 Artaxerxes' letter had been read before R,
Neh 3:17 R, son of Bani.
10:26 Hasshub, Hallohesh, Pilha, Shobek, R,
12: 3 Amariah, Malluch, Hattush, Shecaniah, R,

REIGN (195)

Ex 15:18 The LORD shall r forever and ever.
Dt 17:20 descendants will enjoy a long r in Israel.
Jgs 9: 8 So they said to the olive tree, R over us.'
9:10 you r over us!'
9:12 said to the vine, 'Come you, and r over us.'
9:14 you r over us!'
2Sm 21: 1 During David's r there was a famine for
1Kgs 1:17 r after you and sit upon your throne.
1:24 is to r after you and sit on your throne?
1:30 that your son Solomon should r after me
1:35 and sit upon my throne and r in my place.
2:11 of David's r over Israel was forty years:
6: 1 the fourth year of Solomon's r over Israel,
11:37 you shall r over all that you desire and
14: 2 was he who predicted my r over this people.
14:19 of Jeroboam, with his warfare and his r,
14:20 of Jeroboam's r was twenty-two years.
15: 9 Israel, Asa, king of Judah, began to r;
15:33 twenty-four-year r over Israel in Tirzah.
16: 8 began his two-year r over Israel in Tirzah.
16:34 During his r, Hiel from Bethel rebuilt
21:29 upon his house during the r of his son."
22:41 to r over Judah in the fourth year of Ahab,
22:42 thirty-five years old when he began to r,
22:47 had remained in the r of his father Asa.
22:52 began to r over Israel in Samaria in the
2Kgs 8:17 thirty-two years old when he began to r,
8:20 During Jehoram's r,
8:26 twenty-two years old when he began his r,
10:36 The length of Jehu's r over Israel in
12: 2 began to r in the seventh year of Jehu,
12: 7 twenty-third year of the r of King Joash,
13: 1 seventeen-year r over Israel in Samaria.
13:10 his sixteen-year r over Israel in Samaria.
13:22 Israel during the entire r of Jehoahaz.
14: 1 son of Joash, king of Judah, began to r.
14:23 began his forty-one-year r in Samaria.
15: 2 was sixteen years old when he began to r,
15:17 of Gadi, began his ten year r over Samaria.
15:18 During his r, Pul, king of Assyria,
15:23 his two-year r over Israel in Samaria.
15:27 his twenty-year r over Israel in Samaria.
15:29 During the r of Pekah,
15:32 son of Uzziah, king of Judah, began to r.
16: 1 son of Jotham, king of Judah, began to r.
17: 1 his nine-year r over Israel in Samaria.
18: 1 son of Ahaz, king of Judah, began to r.
21: 1 was twelve years old when he began to r,
21:19 twenty-two years old when he began to r,
22: 1 was eight years old when he began to r,
23:31 twenty-three years old when he began to r,
23:33 of Hamath, thus ending his r in Jerusalem.
23:36 twenty-five years old when he began to r,
24: 1 During his r Nebuchadnezzar,
24: 8 was eighteen years old when he began to r,
24:12 Babylon, who, in the eighth year of his r,
25: 1 month of the ninth year of Zedekiah's r,
25:27 in the inaugural year of his own r,
1Chr 4:31 Until David came to r,
4:41 by name set out during the r of Hezekiah,
5:10 r of Saul they waged war with the Hagrites,
11:10 in his r in order to make him true king,
26:31 fortieth year of David's r search was made,
29:25 giving him a glorious r such as had not
29:30 with the particulars of his r and valor,
2Chr 3: 2 second month of the fourth year of his r.
15:10 month of the fifteenth year of Asa's r,
15:19 war until the thirty-fifth year of Asa's r.
16: 1 In the thirty-sixth year of Asa's r,
16:12 In the thirty-ninth year of his r,
16:13 he died in the forty-first year of his r.
17: 7 year of his r he sent his leading men,
23: 3 "Here is the king's son who must r,
29: 3 first month of the first year of his r,
29:19 r had thrown away because of his apostasy,
34: 3 In the eight year of his r,
34: 8 In the eighteenth year of his r,
35:19 Josiah's r that this Passover was observed.
Ezr 4: 5 king of Persia, and until the r of Darius,
4: 6 Also at the beginning of the r of
4:24 until the second year of the r of Darius,
6:15 in the sixth year of the r of King Darius.
7: 1 these events, during the r of Artaxerxes,
8: 1 Babylon during the r of King Artaxerxes:
Neh 12:22 up until the r of Darius the Persian.
Tb 1: 2 Naphtali, who during the r of Shalmaneser,
1:16 During Shalmaneser's r I performed many
Jdt 1: 1 twelfth year of the r of Nebuchadnezzar,
Est A: 1 year of the r of the great King Ahasuerus,
1: 1 During the r of Ahasuerus
1: 3 in the third year of his r, he presided over
2: 4 the king shall r in place of Vashti."
2:16 Tebeth, in the seventh year of his r.
1Mc 10: 1 He was accepted and began to r there.
11: 9 and you shall r over your father's kingdom.
14: 4 and his magnificence throughout his r.
2Mc 1: 7 In the r of Demetrius,
Ps(s) 146:10 The LORD shall r forever;
Prv 8:15 kings r, and lawgivers establish justice;
Wis 6:21 Wisdom, that you may r as kings forever.
Sir 48:18 During his r Sennacherib led an invasion
Is 24:23 will r on Mount Zion and in Jerusalem,
32: 1 r justly and princes will rule rightly.
Jer 1: 2 of Judah, in the thirteenth year of his r,
1: 3 and continued through the r of Jehoiakim,
23: 5 As king he shall r and govern wisely,
26: 1 In the beginning of the r of Jehoiakim,
27: 1 [In the beginning of the r of Jehoiakim,
28: 1 in [the beginning of] the r of Zedekiah,
49:34 at the beginning of the r of Zedekiah,
51:59 in the fourth year of the r of Zedekiah;
52: 4 tenth month of the ninth year of his r,
52:31 Babylon, in the inaugural year of his r,
Dn 1: 1 In the third year of the r of Jehoiakim,
2: 1 In the second year of his r,
6:29 during the r of Darius and the r of Cyrus
8: 1 the third year of the r of King Belshazzar.
8:23 "After their r, when sinners have reached
9: 2 in the first year of his r I,
Am 6: 3 evil day, yet you hasten the r of violence!
Mt 2: 1 of Judea during the r of King Herod,
3: 2 The r of God is at hand."
5: 3 the r of God is theirs.
5:10 the r of God is theirs.
9:35 he proclaimed the good news of God's r,
10: 7 'The r of God is at hand!'
12:28 then the r of God has overtaken you.
13:11 knowledge of the mysteries of the r of God,
13:19 about God's r without understanding it.
13:24 "The r of God may be likened to a man who
13:31 "The r of God is like a mustard seed
13:33 "The r of God is like yeast which a woman
13:44 "The r of God is like a buried treasure
13:47 "The r of God is also like a dragnet
13:52 scribe who is learned in the r of God
18: 4 of greatest importance in that heavenly r.
18:23 That is why the r of God may be said to be
19:12 renounced sex for the sake of God's r.
20: 1 "The r of God is like the case of the
22: 2 "The r of God may be likened to a king
25: 1 "The r of God can be likened to ten
26:29 I drink it new with you in my Father's r."
Mk 1:15 The r of God is at hand!
4:11 mystery of the r of God has been confided.
4:26 "This is how it is with the r of God.
4:30 comparison shall we use for the r of God?
9: 1 they see the r of God established in power."
10:15 whoever does not accept the r of God
11:10 is the r of our father David to come!
12:34 him, "You are not far from the r of God."
14:25 day when I drink it new in the r of God."
15:43 another who looked forward to the r of God.
Lk 1:33 forever and his r will be without end."
4:43 announce the good news of the r of God,
6:20 the r of God is yours.
8:10 of the r of God have been confided,
9: 2 the r of God and heal the afflicted.
9:11 them and spoke to them of the r of God,
9:27 taste death until they see the r of God."
9:62 looking back is unfit for the r of God."
10: 9 Say to them, 'The r of God is at hand.'
10:11 But know that the r of God is near.'
11:20 out devils, then the r of God is upon you.
13:18 "What does the r of God resemble?
13:20 "To what shall I compare the r of God?
17:20 the Pharisees when the r of God would come,
17:20 watching when the r of God will come.
17:21 The r of God is already in your midst."
18:16 The r of God belongs to such as these.
19:11 that the r of God was about to appear.
21:31 I speak, know that the r of God is near.
22:18 the vine until the coming of the r of God."
23:42 remember me when you enter upon your r."
23:51 and he looked expectantly for the r of God.
Jn 3: 3 no one can see the r of God unless he is
Acts 1: 3 and speaking to them about the r of God.
14:22 if we are to enter into the r of God."
28:23 bearing witness to the r of God among men.
28:31 he preached the r of God and taught about
Rom 5:17 r through one man because of his offense,
5:17 of justice live and r through the one man,
5:21 grace may r by way of justice leading to
1Cor 4: 8 launched upon your r with no help from us.
4: 8 Would that you had really begun to r,
15:25 Christ must r until God has put all
Col 3:15 Christ's peace must r in your hearts,
2Tm 2:12 out to the end we shall also r with him.
Rv 1: 9 r and the endurance we have in Jesus,
5:10 our God, and they shall r on the earth."
11:15 One, and he shall r forever and ever."
11:17 your great power, you have begun your r.
12:10 the r of our God and the authority of his
20: 6 and shall r with him for a thousand years.
22: 5 give them light, and they shall r forever.

REIGNED (90)

Gn 36:31 The following are the kings who r in the
36:31 Edom before any king r over the Israelites.
Jos 13:10 king of the Amorites, who r in Heshbon,
13:12 the Rephaim, who r at Ashtaroth and Edrei.
13:21 This Amorite king, who r in Heshbon,
Jgs 4: 2 the Canaanite king, Jabin, who r in Hazor.
1Sm 13: 1 years old when he became king and he r . . .
2Sm 2:10 king over Israel, and he r for two years.
5: 4 he became king, and he r for forty years:
8:15 David r over all Israel,
1Kgs 2:11 he r seven years in Hebron and
11:42 The time that Solomon r in Jerusalem over
12:17 but Rehoboam r over the Israelites who
14:21 Rehoboam, son of Solomon, r in Judah.
14:21 and he r seventeen years in Jerusalem,
15: 2 He r three years in Jerusalem.
15:10 he r forty-one years in Jerusalem.
15:16 king of Israel, a long as they both r.
15:25 he r over Israel two years.
15:28 of Asa, king of Judah, and r in his stead.
16:10 of Asa, king of Judah, and r in his place.
16:15 of Judah, Zimri r seven days in Tirzah.
16:23 he r over Israel twelve years,
16:29 he r over Israel in Samaria for twenty-two
22:42 and he r twenty-five years in Jerusalem.
22:52 he r two years over Israel.
2Kgs 3: 1 king of Judah, and he r for twelve years].
8:15 And Hazael r in his stead.
8:17 reign, and he r eight years in Jerusalem.
8:26 his reign, and he r one year in Jerusalem.
9:23 Joram r about and fled,
12: 2 of Jehu, and he r forty years in Jerusalem.
14: 2 and he r twenty-nine years in Jerusalem.
15: 2 and he r fifty-two years in Jerusalem.
15:10 killed him at Ibleam, and r in his place.
15:13 he r one month in Samaria.
15:14 Shallum, son of Jabesh, and r in his place.
15:25 stronghold in Samaria, and r in his place.
15:30 and r in his place [in the twentieth year
15:33 king, and he r sixteen years in Jerusalem.
16: 2 king, and he r sixteen years in Jerusalem.
18: 2 and he r twenty-nine years in Jerusalem.
19:37 His son Esarhaddon r in his stead.
21: 1 and he r fifty-five years in Jerusalem.
21:19 to reign, and he r two years in Jerusalem.
22: 1 and he r thirty-one years in Jerusalem.
23:31 reign, and he r three months in Jerusalem.
23:36 reign, and he r eleven years in Jerusalem.
24: 8 reign, and he r three months in Jerusalem.
24:18 king, and he r eleven years in Jerusalem.
1Chr 1:43 The kings who r in the land of Edom before
3: 4 where he r seven years and six months.
3: 4 Then he r thirty-three years in Jerusalem,
18:14 David r over all Israel and dispensed
29:26 the son of Jesse, had r over all Israel.
29:27 time that he r over Israel was forty years:
29:27 in Hebron he r seven years,
2Chr 9:30 Solomon r in Jerusalem over all Israel for
10:17 r over only those Israelites who lived in
12:13 and he r seventeen years in Jerusalem,
13: 2 he r three years in Jerusalem.
20:31 Thus Jehoshaphat r over Judah.
20:31 and he r twenty-five years in Jerusalem.
21: 5 king, and he r eight years in Jerusalem.
21:20 king, and he r eight years in Jerusalem.
22: 1 son of Jehoram, r as the king of Judah.
22: 2 king, and he r one year in Jerusalem.
24: 1 king, and he r forty years in Jerusalem.
25: 1 and he r twenty-nine years in Jerusalem.
26: 3 and he r fifty-two years in Jerusalem.
27: 1 king, and he r sixteen years in Jerusalem.
27: 8 king, and he r sixteen years in Jerusalem.
28: 1 king, and he r sixteen years in Jerusalem.
29: 1 and he r twenty-nine years in Jerusalem.
33: 1 and he r fifty-five years in Jerusalem.
33:21 king, and he r two years in Jerusalem.
34: 1 and he r thirty-one years in Jerusalem.
36: 2 king, and he r three months in Jerusalem.
36: 5 king, and he r eleven years in Jerusalem.
36: 9 r three months [and ten days] in Jerusalem.
36:11 king, and he r eleven years in Jerusalem.
1Mc 1: 7 Alexander had r twelve years when he died.
12: 7 Onias from Arius, who then r over you,
Sir 47:13 SOLOMON r during an era of peace,

Is 37:38 His son Esarhaddon *r* in his stead.
Jer 52: 1 king, and he *r* eleven years in Jerusalem.
Dn 9: 1 Medes, *r* over the kingdom of the Chaldeans;
Rom 5:14 I say, from Adam to Moses death *r*,
5:21 it, so that, as sin *r* through death,
Rv 20: 4 and *r* with Christ for a thousand years.

REIGNING (1)

1Cor 4: 8 to reign, that we might be *r* with you!

REIGNS (2)

Ps(s) 47: 9 God *r* over the nations,
Jer 30: 5 cry of dismay we hear; fear *r*, not peace.

REIN (4)

1Kgs 22:34 *R* about and take me out of the ranks,
2Chr 18:33 *R* about and take me out of the ranks,
Ps(s) 50:19 To your mouth you give free *r* for evil,
Gal 5:13 a freedom that gives free *r* to the flesh.

REINFORCE (3)

2Chr 25: 8 is God who has the power to *r* or to defeat."
Sg 8: 9 is a door, we will *r* it with a cedar plank."
Bar 6:17 the priests *r* their houses with gates and

REINFORCED (3)

2Chr 24:13 according to its original form, and *r* it.
Ezr 5: 8 and the walls are being *r* with timber;
Sir 50: 1 renovated, in whose days the temple was *r*.

REINFORCEMENT (2)

Dn 11: 1 standing as a *r* and a bulwark for me.
2Cor 7: 7 the *r* Titus had already received from you,

REINTRODUCED (1)

2Kgs 21: 6 and *r* the consulting of ghosts and spirits.

REJECT (30)

Lv 26:15 if you *r* my precepts and spurn my decrees,
26:44 enemies' land, I will not *r* or spurn them,
1Sm 8: 7 It is not you they *r*,
2Kgs 23:27 I will *r* this city,
2Chr 6:42 LORD God, *r* not the plea of your anointed,
2Mc 6:20 who have the courage to *r* the food
Jb 5:17 The Almighty's chastening do not *r*.
33:20 and his senses *r* the choicest nourishment.
34:33 must punish, since you *r* what he is doing?
Ps(s) 77: 8 Lord *r* forever and nevermore be favorable?
88:15 Why, O LORD, do you *r* me;
132:10 servant, *r* not the plea of your anointed.
Prv 1: 8 and *r* not your mother's teaching;
6:20 bidding, and *r* not your mother's teaching;
8:33 instruction and wisdom do not *r!*
18: 5 the guilty, and so to *r* a rightful claim.
Wis 9: 4 and *r* me not from among your children;
Sir 4: 4 A beggar in distress do not *r*;
8: 9 *R* not the tradition of old men which they
41: 4 should you *r* the will of the Most High?
Is 7:15 he learns to *r* the bad and choose the good.
7:16 learns to *r* the bad and choose the good,
30:12 Because you *r* this word,
66: 5 who, because of my name, hate and *r* you,
Jer 33:26 then too will I *r* the descendants of Jacob
Ez 2: 6 words when they contradict you and *r* you,
Hos 4: 6 knowledge, I will *r* you from my priesthood;
Jn 6:37 no one who comes will I ever *r*,
Acts 13:46 but since you *r* it and thus convict
Ti 2:12 us to *r* godless ways and worldly desires,

REJECTED (46)

1Sm 10:19 But today you have *r* your God,
15:23 Because you have *r* the command of the LORD,
15:23 of the LORD, he, too, has *r* you as ruler."
15:26 because you *r* the command of the LORD and
16: 1 for Saul, whom I have *r* as king of Israel?
16: 7 his lofty stature, because I have *r* him.
2Kgs 17:15 They *r* his statutes,
17:20 So the LORD *r* the whole race of Israel.
Ps(s) 53: 6 are put to shame, because God has *r* them.
60: 3 God, you have *r* us and broken our defenses;
60:12 Have not you, O God, *r* us,
78:59 heard and was enraged and utterly *r* Israel.
78:67 And he *r* the tent of Joseph,
89:39 Yet you have *r* and spurned and been
108:12 Have not you, O God, *r* us,
118:22 the builders *r* has become the cornerstone.
Wis 11:14 out in exposure they indeed mockingly *r*;
Sir 37:20 are *r* he will be deprived of all enjoyment.
Is 8: 6 *r* the waters of Shiloah that flow gently,
Jer 2:37 For the LORD has *r* those in whom you trust,
6:30 "Silver *r*" they shall be called,
6:30 shall be called, for the LORD has *r* them.
7:29 For the LORD has *r* and cast off the
8: 9 Since they have *r* the word of the LORD,
33:24 has *r* the two tribes which he had chosen"?
Lam 2: 7 has disowned his altar, *r* his sanctuary;
5:22 For now you have indeed *r* us,
Hos 4: 6 Since you have *r* knowledge,
5: 2 into wickedness, and I am *r* by them all.
Mt 21:42 *r* has become the keystone of the structure.
Mk 8:31 Man had to suffer much, be *r* by the elders,
12:10 'The stone *r* by the builders has become
Lk 9:22 endure many sufferings, be *r* by the elders,
13:28 the kingdom of God, and you yourselves *r*.
17:25 suffer much and be *r* by the present age.
20:17 'The stone which the builders *r* has become
Jn 15: 6 live in me is like a withered, *r* branch,
Acts 4:11 This Jesus is 'the stone *r* by you the
7:35 very Moses whom they had *r* with the words,
Rom 11: 1 I ask, then, has God *r* his people?
11: 2 God has not *r* his people whom he foreknew.
1Cor 9:27 preached to others I myself should be *r*.
1Tm 4: 4 be *r* when it is received with thanksgiving,
Heb 12:17 but he was *r* because he had no opportunity
1Pt 2: 4 him, a living stone, *r* by men but approved,
2: 7 the builders *r* that became a cornerstone."

REJECTING (2)

1Sm 8: 7 they reject, they are *r* me as their king.
1Tm 1:19 Some men, by *r* the guidance of conscience,

REJECTION (2)

Lam 3:31 For the Lord's *r* does not last forever;
Rom 11:15 *r* has meant reconciliation for the world,

REJECTS (11)

1Sm 15:26 LORD and the LORD *r* you as king of Israel."
Jb 36: 5 Behold, God *r* the obstinate in heart;
Prv 15:32 He who *r* admonition despises his own soul,
Lk 10:16 He who *r* you, rejects me.
10:16 And he who rejects me, *r* him who sent me."
Jn 12:48 Whoever *r* me and does not accept my words
1Thes 4: 8 whoever *r* these instructions rejects,
4: 8 whoever rejects these instructions *r*,
Heb 10:28 Anyone who *r* the law of Moses is put to

REJOICE (130)

Dt 33:18 *R*, O Zebulun, in your pursuits,
Jgs 9:19 *r* in Abimelech and may he in turn rejoice
1Sm 2: 1 I *r* in my victory.
2Sm 1:20 Ashkelon, Lest the Philistine maidens *r*,
1Chr 16:10 *r*, O hearts that seek the LORD!
16:31 Let the heavens be glad and the earth *r*;
16:32 let the plains *r* and all that is in them!
2Chr 6:41 may your faithful ones *r* in good things.
Tb 11:18 his nephew Nadab also came to *r* with Tobit.
13:13 then, *r* over the children of the righteous,
13:14 and happy those who *r* in your prosperity.
13:14 For they shall *r* in you as they behold all
14: 7 Those who sincerely love God shall *r*,
1Mc 12:12 We likewise *r* in your renown.
Jb 3:22 for hidden treasures, *R* in it exultingly,
20:18 his wealth increases, he shall not *r*.
Ps(s) 2:11 Serve the LORD with fear, and *r* before him;
9:15 the daughter of Zion, *r* in your salvation.
13: 5 Lest my foes *r* at my downfall though I
13: 6 Let my heart *r* in your salvation;
30: 2 clear and did not let my enemies *r* over me.
31: 8 I will *r* and be glad of your kindness,
32:11 Be glad in the LORD and *r*,
33:21 and our shield, For in him our hearts *r*;
35: 9 But I will *r* in the LORD,
35:19 Let not my unprovoked enemies *r* over me;
35:24 my God, let them not *r* over me.
48:12 Zion be glad, Let the cities of Judah *r*,
51:10 the bones you have crushed shall *r*.
63:12 The king, however, shall *r* in God;
66: 6 therefore let us *r* in him.
68: 4 But the just *r* and exult before God;
68: 4 they are glad and *r*.
85: 7 and shall not your people *r* in you?
89:13 Tabor and Hermon *r* at your name.
89:17 At your name they *r* all the day,
92: 5 at the works of your hands I *r*.
96:11 Let the heavens be glad and the earth *r*;
97: 1 The LORD is king; let the earth *r*;
97: 8 of Judah *r* because of your judgments,
105: 3 *r*, O hearts that seek the LORD!
106: 5 chosen ones, *r* in the joy of your people,
107:42 The upright see this and *r*,
109:28 be put to shame, but let your servant *r*.
118:24 let us be glad and *r* in it.
119:14 In the way of your decrees I *r*,
119:162 I *r* at your promise,
149: 2 let the children of Zion *r* in their king.
Prv 2:14 Who delight in doing evil, *r* in perversity;
23:15 heart be wise, my own heart also will *r*;
24:17 *R* not when your enemy falls,
29: 2 When the just prevail, the people *r*;
Eccl 3:22 better for a man than to *r* in his work;
11: 9 *R*, O young man, while you are young
Wis 1:13 does he *r* in the destruction of the living.
Sir 8: 7 *R* not when a man dies;
9:12 *R* not at a proud man's success;
16: 1 children, nor *r* in wicked offspring.
23: 3 succumb to my foes, and my enemy *r* over me?
27:29 The trap seizes those who *r* in pitfalls,
39:31 In doing his bidding they *r*,
51:29 Let your spirits *r* in the mercy of God,
Is 9: 2 As they *r* before you as at the harvest,
14: 8 The very cypresses *r* over you,
14:29 *R* not, O Philistia, not a man of you,
25: 9 let us *r* and be glad that he has saved us!"
29:19 and the poor *r* in the Holy One of Israel.
35: 1 the steppe will *r* and bloom.
35: 2 abundant flowers, and *r* with joyful song.
41:16 But you shall *r* in the LORD,
49:13 Sing out, O heavens, and *r*,
61:10 I *r* heartily in the LORD,
62: 5 in his bride so shall your God *r* in you.
65:13 My servants shall *r*,
65:19 will *r* in Jerusalem and exult in my people.
66:10 *R* with Jerusalem and be glad because of her,
66:14 *r* and your bodies flourish like the grass;
Jer 50:11 Yes, *r* and exult,
Lam 1:21 All my enemies *r* at my misfortune:
4:21 Though you *r* and are glad,
Bar 3:34 whom the stars at their posts shine and *r*;
Ez 7:12 Let not the buyer *r* nor the seller mourn,
18:23 Do I not rather *r* when he turns from his
Hos 9: 1 *R* not,
Jl 2:21 Fear not, O land! exult and *r*
2:23 children of Zion, exult and *r* in the LORD,
Am 6:13 You *r* in Lodebar,
Mi 7: 8 *R* not over me, O my enemy!
Hb 3:18 I *r* in the LORD and exult in my saving God.
Zep 3:17 He will *r* over you with gladness,
Zec 2:14 Sing and *r*, O daughter Zion!
4:10 on that day of small beginnings shall *r*
9: 9 *R* heartily, O daughter Zion, shout for joy,
10: 7 Their hearts shall *r* in the LORD.
Mt 5:12 Be glad and *r*, for your reward is great
Lk 1:14 be yours, and many will *r* at his birth;
1:28 *R*, O highly favored daughter!
6:23 On the day they do so, *r* and exult,
10:20 do not *r* so much in the fact that the
15: 6 *R* with me because I have found my lost
15: 9 friends and neighbors to say, *R* with me!
15:32 But we had to celebrate and *r!*
19:37 disciples began to *r* and praise God loudly
Jn 4:36 life, that sower and reaper may *r* together.
14:28 me you would *r* to have me go to the Father,
16:22 will *r* with a joy no one can take from you.
Rom 12:12 *R* in hope, be patient under trial,
12:15 Rejoice with those who *r*,
15:10 Again, *R*, O Gentiles, with his people."
1Cor 7:30 who *r* as though they were not rejoicing;
13: 6 Love does not *r* in what is wrong but
2Cor 2: 3 be saddened by those who should *r* my heart.
7:16 I *r* because I trust you utterly.
13: 9 even *r* when we are weak and you are strong.
Gal 4:27 *R*, you barren one who bears no children;
Phil 1:18 Indeed, I shall continue to *r*,
2:17 I am glad of it and *r* with all of you.
2:18 be glad on the same score, and *r* with me!
3: 1 For the rest, my brothers, *r* in the Lord.
4: 4 *R* in the Lord always!
4: 4 I say it again. *R!*
1Thes 5:16 *R* always, never cease praying,
1Pt 1: 8 and *r* with inexpressible joy touched with
4:13 *R* instead, in the measure that you share
4:13 glory is revealed, you will *r* exultantly.
Rv 12:12 So *r*, you heavens, and you that dwell
18:20 *R* over her, you heavens, you saints,
19: 7 Let us *r* and be glad, and give him glory!

REJOICED (32)

Ex 18: 9 Jethro *r* over all the goodness that the
2Kgs 11:20 of the land *r* and the city was quiet,
1Chr 29: 9 people *r* over these freewill offerings,
29: 9 King David also *r* greatly.
2Chr 15:15 All Judah *r* over the oath,
23:21 of the land *r* and the city was quiet,
24:10 All the princes and the people *r*;
29:36 Hezekiah and all the people *r* over what
30:25 and the whole assembly of Judah *r*,
Neh 12:44 For Judah *r* in its appointed priests and
Tb 14:15 dying he *r* over Nineveh's destruction,
1Mc 7:48 The people *r* greatly,
2Mc 15:27 and *r* greatly over this manifestation of
Jb 31:25 Or had I *r* that my wealth was great,
31:29 Had I *r* at the destruction of my enemy or
Ps(s) 105:38 Egypt *r* at their going,
107:30 They *r* that they were calmed,
122: 1 I *r* because they said to me,
Eccl 2:10 but my heart *r* in the fruit of all my toil.
Wis 7:12 And I *r* in them all,
Jer 41:13 the people who were Ishmael's captives *r*.
Bar 4:31 who harmed you, who *r* at your downfall;
4:33 As that city *r* at your collapse,
Ez 35:14 you *r* over my land because it was desolate,
Lk 1:58 had extended his mercy to her, *r* with her.
10:21 moment Jesus *r* in the Holy Spirit and said:
13:17 *r* at the marvels Jesus was accomplishing.
Jn 8:56 father Abraham *r* that he might see my day.
20:20 At the sight of the Lord the disciples *r*.
Acts 2:26 heart has been glad and my tongue has *r*,
11:23 he *r* to see the evidence of God's favor.
2Cor 7:13 we have *r* even more at the joy of Titus

REJOICES (8)

Tb 13: 7 God, and my spirit *r* in the King of heaven.

REJOICES (cont.)

Ps(s) 16: 9 Therefore my heart is glad and my soul *r*,
21: 2 in your victory how greatly he *r*!
Prv 11:10 When the just prosper, the city *r*;
Is 62: 5 And as a bridegroom *r* in his bride so
Hb 1:15 and so he *r* and exults.
Jn 16:20 you will weep and mourn while the world *r*;
1Cor 13: 6 in what is wrong but *r* with the truth.

REJOICING (46)

1Sm 6:13 and spied the ark, they greeted it with *r*.
1Kgs 1:40 playing flutes and *r* so much as to split
1:45 at Gihon, and they went up from there *r*,
8:66 *r* and happy over all the blessings the
2Kgs 11:14 people of the land *r* and blowing trumpets,
1Chr 12:41 For there was *r* in Israel.
15:16 and cymbals, to make a loud sound of *r*.
29:22 drank in the LORD'S presence with great *r*.
2Chr 7:10 *r* and glad at heart at the good things the
23:13 people of the land *r* and blowing trumpets,
23:18 in the law of Moses, with *r* and song,
30:21 Bread with great *r* for seven days,
30:26 There was great *r* in Jerusalem,
Neh 8:10 for *r* in the LORD must be your strength!"
12:43 and there was *r* over the great feast of
12:43 and the *r* at Jerusalem could be heard from
Tb 11:15 in, *r* and praising God with full voice.
11:16 *R* and praising God,
Est E:22 among your designated feats with all *r*,
9:17 and made it a day of feasting and *r*.
9:18 and made it a day of feasting and *r*.)
9:19 month of Adar as a day of *r* and feasting,
1Mc 5:23 and brought them to Judea with great *r*.
13:52 should be celebrated every year with *r*,
Jb 8:21 mouth with laughter, and your lips with *r*.
33:26 he shall see God's face with *r*.
Ps(s) 19: 9 of the LORD are right, *r* the heart;
30: 6 weeping enters in, but with the dawn, *r*.
65:13 overflow with it, and *r* clothes the hills.
126: 2 with laughter, and our tongue with *r*.
126: 5 Those that sow in tears shall reap *r*.
126: 6 seed to be sown, They shall come back *r*,
Wis 2: 9 everywhere let us leave tokens of our *r*,
Is 9: 2 brought them abundant joy and great *r*,
65:18 always be *r* and happiness in what I create;
Bar 4:37 of the Holy One, *r* in the glory of God.
5: 5 One, *r* that they are remembered by God.
Ez 7: 7 a time of consternation, not of *r*.
25: 6 *r* most maliciously in your heart over the
Mt 13:44 and *r* at his find went and sold all he had
Acts 8: 8 The *r* in that town rose to fever pitch.
8:39 Nevertheless the man went on his way *r*.
1Cor 7:30 who rejoice as though they were not *r*;
2Cor 6:10 sorrowful, though we are always *r*;
Phil 1: 4 is constantly, in every prayer I utter *r*,
1Pt 1: 6 There is cause for *r* here.

REJOINDER (1)

Sir 4:24 and knowledge through the tongue's *r*.

REJOINED (3)

Ru 2:22 "You would do well, my dear," Naomi *r*,
2Kgs 9:11 When Jehu *r* his master's servants,
Mk 15: 9 demand that he honor the custom, Pilate *r*,

REKEM (5)

Nm 31: 8 *R*, Zur, Hur and Reba;
Jos 13:21 Evi, *R*,
18:27 Beeroth, Mizpeh, Chephirah, Mozah, *R*,
1Chr 2:43 The sons of Hebron were Korah, Tappuah, *R*,
2:44 *R* became the father of Shammai.

REKINDLED (1)

1Mc 13: 7 heard these words, their spirit was *r*.

RELAPSE (1)

Jgs 2:19 would *r* and do worse than their fathers,

RELATE (4)

Neh 6:19 my presence and *r* to him whatever I said;
2Mc 10:10 *r* what happened under Antiochus Eupator,
Jb 15:18 What wise men *r* and have not contradicted
Wis 6:22 is, and how she came to be I shall *r*;

RELATED (13)

Ex 24: 3 *r* all the words and ordinances of the LORD,
Lv 18:17 be shameful, because they are *r* to her.
Ru 3:12 Now, though indeed I am closely *r* to you,
1Sm 11: 4 of Saul, they *r* the news to the people,
2Kgs 8:27 did, since he was *r* to them by marriage.
1Chr 17:15 whole vision Nathan *r* exactly to David.
2Chr 18: 1 but he became *r* to Ahab by marriage.
2Mc 2: 9 It is also *r* how Solomon in his wisdom
Dn 4: 4 had come in, I *r* the dream before them;
Mt 8:33 in the town *r* everything that had happened,
Lk 8:47 she *r* before the whole assemblage why she
9:10 *r* to Jesus all they had accomplished.
Acts 14:27 *r* all that God had helped them accomplish,

RELATING (3)

2Kgs 8: 5 Just as he was *r* to the king how his
2Chr 8:15 in any respect *r* to the priests and Levites
2Mc 15:11 words, he cheered them all by *r* a dream,

RELATION (1)

1Jn 4:17 for our *r* to this world is just like his.

RELATIONS (43)

Gn 4: 1 The man had *r* with his wife Eve,
4:17 Cain had *r* with his wife,
4:25 Adam again had *r* with his wife,
38: 2 Shua, married her, and had *r* with her.
38: 9 whenever he had *r* with his brother's widow,
38:26 But he had no further *r* with her.
Lv 18:20 have carnal *r* with your neighbor's wife,
18:23 You shall not have carnal *r* with an animal,
19:20 "If a man has carnal *r* with a female
20:15 If a man has carnal *r* with an animal,
Nm 25: 1 by having illicit *r* with the Moabite women.
Dt 21:13 for a full month, you may have *r* with her,
22:13 marrying a woman and having *r* with her,
22:14 had *r* with her I did not find her a virgin,'
22:22 *r* with a woman who is married to another,
22:22 the woman with whom he has had *r* shall die.
22:23 who is betrothed, and has *r* with her,
22:25 maiden, seizes her and has *r* with her,
22:28 betrothed, takes her and has *r* with her,
22:29 the man who had *r* with her shall pay the
24: 1 marrying a woman and having *r* with her,
27:20 be he who has *r* with his father's wife,
27:21 'Cursed be he who has *r* with any animal!'
27:22 has *r* with his sister or his half-sister!'
27:23 be he who has *r* with his mother-in-law!'
Jgs 19:25 They had *r* with her and abused her all
21:12 young virgins, who had had no *r* with men,
1Sm 1:19 When Elkanah had *r* with his wife Hannah,
2:22 that they were having *r* with the women
2Sm 11: 4 When she came to him, he had *r* with her,
13:14 he shamed her and had *r* with her.
16:21 "Have *r* with your father's concubines,
20: 3 for them, but had no further *r* with them.
1Kgs 1: 4 the king did not have *r* with herAdonijah,
1Chr 2:21 Hezron had *r* with the daughter of Machir,
2:24 of Hezron, Caleb had *r* with Ephrathah,
2Mc 5: 9 find protection because of his *r* with them.
9:27 mildness and kindness in his *r* with you."
10:12 he endeavored to have peaceful *r* with them.
Ez 18: 6 *r* with a woman in her menstrual period;
Mt 1:25 He had no *r* with her at any time before
1Cor 7: 1 man is better off having no *r* with a woman.
1Pt 5: 5 In your *r* with one another,

RELATIONSHIP (2)

Nm 30:17 the *r* between a husband and his wife,
Est 8: 1 for Esther had revealed his *r* to her.

RELATIVE (26)

Gn 29:12 He told her that he was her father's *r*,
29:15 nothing just because you are a *r* of mine?
Lv 18: 6 *r* to have sexual intercourse with her.
18:12 sister, since she is your father's *r*.
18:13 sister, since she is your mother's *r*.
25:25 sell some of his property, his closest *r*,
25:26 the man has no *r* to redeem his land,
25:49 or by some other *r* or fellow clansman;
Nm 27:11 his heritage to his nearest *r* in his clan,
Ru 2:20 and she continued, "He is a *r* of ours,
3: 2 with whose servants you were, a *r* of ours?
3:12 to you, you have another *r* still closer.
4: 1 closer *r* of whom he had spoken come along,
4: 3 they had done this, he said to the near *r*:
4: 6 The near *r* replied, "I cannot exercise my
4: 8 So the near *r*, in saying to Boaz,
2Sm 19:43 "Because the king is our *r*.
1Kgs 16:11 sparing a single male *r* or friend of his.
Tb 1:22 He was a close *r*— in fact, my nephew.
3:15 other *r* whom I might bide my time to marry.
6:11 must stay with Raguel, who is a *r* of yours.
6:12 Since you are Sarah's closest *r*,
7:10 but you, because you are my closest *r*.
Jer 32: 7 field in Anathoth, since you, as nearest *r*,
32: 8 as nearest *r*, you have the first claim
Jn 18:26 a *r* of the man whose ear Peter had severed.

RELATIVES (22)

Gn 24:38 shall go to my father's house, to my own *r*,
Lv 21: 2 his people, except for his nearest *r*,
Nm 36:11 married *r* on their father's side within
2Kgs 23: 9 but they, along with their *r*,
1Chr 8:32 too, dwelt with their *r* in Jerusalem,
24:31 They too, in the same manner as their *r*,
Tb 1:10 my brothers and *r* ate the food of heathens,
Jdt 16:24 her goods to the *r* of her husband,
16:24 of her husband, Manasseh, and to her own *r*;
2Mc 12:24 power the parents and *r* of many of them,
Ps(s) 122: 8 Because of my *r* and friends I will say,
Dn 13:33 All her *r* and the onlookers were weeping.
13:39 with her parents, children and all her *r*.
13:63 as did Joakim her husband and all her *r*,
Lk 1:58 Her neighbors and *r*,
1:61 out to her, "None of your *r* has this name."
2:44 for him among their *r* and acquaintances.
14:12 or brothers or *r* or wealthy neighbors.
21:16 by your parents, brothers, *r* and friends,
Acts 10:24 had called in his *r* and close friends.
1Tm 5: 8 If anyone does not provide for his own *r*
5:16 a woman church member has *r* who are

RELAX (6)

Dt 15: 2 Every creditor shall *r* his claim on what
15: 3 but you shall *r* the claim on your kinsman
2Chr 15: 7 But as for you, be strong and do not *r*,
Sir 43:10 their place and never *r* in their vigils.
Lk 12:19 *R*! Eat heartily, drink well.
Gal 6: 9 if we do not *r* our efforts,

RELAXATION (4)

Dt 15: 1 period you shall have a *r* of debts,
15: 2 *r* in honor of the LORD has been proclaimed.
15: 9 that the seventh year, the year of *r*,
31:10 at the prescribed time in the year of *r*

RELAXED (2)

Jdt 1:16 and there he and his army *r* and feasted
Wis 16:24 is *r* in benefit for those who trust in you.

RELAYED (1)

2Sm 11:22 and on his arrival he *r* to David all the

RELAYS (1)

1Kgs 5:28 Lebanon each month in *r* of ten thousand,

RELEASE (32)

Ex 2:23 As their cry for *r* went up to God,
Jgs 21:22 to them, *R* them to us as a kindness,
2Kgs 4:30 and as you yourself live, I will not *r* you."
1Mc 9:70 him and to obtain the *r* of the prisoners.
11:35 From this day on we grant them *r* from
13:16 will not revolt against us, we will *r* him."
13:34 that he grant the land a *r* from taxation,
13:37 our official to grant you *r* from tribute.
Jb 12:14 if he imprisons a man, there is no *r*.
Ps(s) 102:21 the prisoners, to *r* those doomed to die"
Is 14:17 its cities, and gave his captives no *r*?
61: 1 to the captives and *r* to the prisoners,
Ez 46:17 to the latter only until the year of *r*,
Mt 27:15 was accustomed to *r* one prisoner,
27:17 "Which one do you wish me to *r* for you,
27:21 "Which one do you wish me to *r* for you?"
27:58 Thereupon Pilate issued an order for its *r*.
Mk 15: 6 festival he would *r* for them one prisoner
15: 9 want me to *r* the king of the Jews for you?"
15:11 the crowd to have him *r* Barabbas instead.
Lk 4:18 of sight to the blind and *r* to prisoners,
23:16 Therefore I mean to *r* him,
23:18 *r* Barabbas for us!"
23:22 I will therefore chastise him and *r* him."
Jn 18:39 I *r* someone to you at Passover time.
18:39 want me to *r* to you the king of the Jews?"
19:10 to *r* you and the power to crucify you?"
19:12 After this, Pilate was eager to *r* him,
Acts 3:13 presence when Pilate was ready to *r* him.
3:14 instead to be granted the *r* of a murderer.
28:18 The Romans tried my case and wanted to *r*
Rv 9:14 *R* the four angels who are tied up on the

RELEASED (42)

Gn 8:12 seven days and then *r* the dove once more;
24: 8 follow you, you will be *r* from this oath.
24:41 Then you shall be *r* from my ban.
24:41 you, then, too, you shall be *r* from my ban.'
Ex 14: 5 "Why, we have *r* Israel from our service!"
Lv 25:28 be *r* and returned to its original owner.
25:30 nor shall it be *r* in the jubilee.
25:31 time, and in the jubilee they must be *r*.
25:33 not redeemed, shall be *r* in the jubilee;
25:41 shall be *r* from your service and return to
25:54 thus redeemed, he shall nevertheless be *r*,
27:21 it shall be *r* as sacred to the LORD;
1Sm 6: 6 that the Israelites were *r* and departed?
1Mc 9:72 and he *r* the prisoners he had previously
10: 6 the hostages in the citadel be *r* to him.
10: 9 They *r* the hostages to Jonathan,
10:43 or because of any other debt, shall be *r*,
Ps(s) 74:15 You *r* the springs and torrents;
105:20 The king sent and *r* him,
Sir 27:19 Like a bird *r* from the hand,
Is 51:14 The oppressed shall soon be *r*;
Jer 20: 3 Pashhur had *r* Jeremiah from the stocks,
40: 1 of the bodyguard, had *r* him in Ramah,
52:31 king of Judah, and *r* him from prison.
Mi 6: 4 Egypt, from the place of slavery I *r* you;
Mt 5:26 be *r* until you have paid the last penny.
27:26 At that, he *r* Barabbas to them.
Mk 15:15 to satisfy the crowd, *r* Barabbas to them;
15:45 he was dead, Pilate *r* the corpse to Joseph.
Lk 12:59 you will not be *r* from there until you
13:16 been *r* from her shackles on the sabbath?"
23:20 for he wanted Jesus to be the one he *r*.

23:25 He *r* the one they asked for,
Acts 4:23 After being *r*, the two went back
16:36 have sent orders that you are to be *r*.
17: 9 story, they *r* Jason and the others on bail.
22:30 next day the commander *r* Paul from prison,
Rom 7: 2 she is *r* from the law regarding husbands.
7: 6 Now we have been *r* from the law
Rv 9:15 So the four angels were *r*;
20: 3 the dragon is to be *r* for a short time.
20: 7 are over, Satan will be *r* from his prison.

RELEASES (5)

Nm 30: 6 and the LORD *r* her from it,
30: 9 bound herself, and the LORD *r* her from it.
30:13 annulled them, the LORD *r* her from them.
Jer 10:13 rain, and *r* stormwinds from their chambers.
51:16 rain, and *r* stormwinds from their chambers.

RELEASING (1)

Is 58: 6 *r* those bound unjustly,

RELENT (7)

Ex 32:12 *r* in punishing your people.
Jb 9:13 He is God and he does not *r*;
Lam 2: 8 his hand brought ruin, yet he did not *r*—
Jl 2:14 again *r* and leave behind him a blessing.
Jon 3: 9 Who knows, God may *r* and forgive,
Zec 8:14 says the LORD of hosts, and I did not *r*,
2Cor 2: 7 you should now *r* and support him so that

RELENTED (4)

Ex 32:14 So the LORD *r* in the punishment he had
Jos 7:26 Then the anger of the LORD *r*.
Ps(s) 106:45 sake he was mindful of his covenant and *r*,
Ez 36:21 So I have *r* because of my holy name which

RELENTING (1)

Jl 2:13 rich in kindness, and *r* in punishment.

RELENTLESS (5)

Jb 41: 2 Is he not *r* when aroused;
Prv 27: 4 Anger is *r*, and wrath overwhelming
Sg 8: 6 is love, *r* as the nether world is devotion;
Is 14: 6 That struck the peoples in wrath *r* blows;
56:11 They are *r* dogs,

RELENTLESSLY (2)

Jb 27:22 he hurls the lightning against them *r*;
Jer 20:16 like the cities which the LORD *r* overthrew;

RELEVANCE (1)

Gal 3:19 What is the *r* of the law, in such case?

RELIABLE (6)

Ps(s) 111: 8 are all his precepts, *R* forever and ever,
Is 8: 2 And I took *r* witnesses,
Mt 25:21 You are an industrious and *r* servant.
25:23 You too are an industrious and *r* servant.
Lk 1: 4 *r* the instruction was that you received.
2Pt 1:19 message as something altogether *r*.

RELIANCE (2)

2Mc 10:28 their valor but also their *r* on the Lord,
Acts 14: 3 out fearlessly, in complete *r* on the Lord.

RELIANT (1)

1Pt 3: 5 *r* on God and obedient to their husbands

RELIED (7)

Dt 32:37 their gods whom they *r* on as their 'rock'?
2Chr 13:18 were victorious because they *r* on the LORD,
16: 7 "Because you *r* on the king of Aram and
16: 8 And yet, because you *r* on the LORD,
1Mc 8:12 friends, however, and those who *r* on them,
Ps(s) 22: 9 "He *r* on the LORD; let him deliver him,
Mt 27:43 He *r* on God; let God rescue him now

RELIEF (18)

Gn 5:29 this one shall bring us *r* from our work
2Sm 21:14 God granted *r* to the land.
24:25 The LORD granted *r* to the country,
1Kgs 7:29 lions and oxen, there were wreaths in *r*.
Ezr 9: 8 our eyes and given us *r* in our servitude.
Neh 9:28 "As soon as they had *r*,
Est 4:14 *r* and deliverance will come to the Jews
Jb 14:14 I would wait, until my *r* should come.
32:20 Let me speak and obtain *r*;
Ps(s) 22: 3 by night, and there is no *r* for me.
Sir 31:21 have emptied your stomach, you will have *r*.
Jer 30:15 your pain is without *r*.
Mk 5:26 savings in the process, yet she got no *r*;
Acts 11:29 the *r* of the brothers who lived in Judea.
12:25 to Jerusalem upon completing the *r* mission,
2Cor 8:13 *r* of others ought not to impoverish you;
2Thes 1: 7 will provide *r* to you who are sorely tried,
Rv 14:11 There shall be no *r* day or night for those

RELIEVE (3)

Ps(s) 4: 2 God, you who *r* me when I am in distress;
25:17 and afflicted *R* the troubles of my heart,
Jer 13:19 Negeb are besieged, with no one to *r* them;

RELIEVED (3)

1Sm 16:23 play, and Saul would be *r* and feel better,
Ps(s) 81: 7 "I *r* his shoulder of the burden;
Jon 4: 6 giving shade that *r* him of any discomfort,

RELIEVES (1)

Is 14: 3 On the day the LORD *r* you of sorrow and

RELIGION (13)

1Mc 1:43 many Israelites were in favor of his *r*;
2:19 so that each forsakes the *r* of his fathers
2:22 depart from our *r* in the slightest degree."
2Mc 6:24 Eleazar had gone over to an alien *r*.
Acts 19:26 great numbers of people to change their *r*.
25:19 with him over issues in their own *r*,
26: 5 as a Pharisee, the strictest sect of our *r*.
1Tm 4: 8 discipline of *r* is incalculably more so,
6: 3 Christ and the teaching proper to true *r*,
6: 5 value *r* only as a means of personal gain.
6: 6 There is, of course, great gain in *r*—
2Tm 3: 5 make a pretense of *r* but negate its power.
Ti 1: 1 of the truth as our *r* embodies it.

RELIGIOUS (6)

1Mc 2:29 according to righteousness and *r* custom
Sir 37:12 Instead, associate with a *r* man,
Mt 6: 1 performing *r* acts for people to see.
Acts 10: 1 cohort Italica, who was *r* and God-fearing.
17:22 in every respect you are scrupulously *r*.
1Tm 2:10 as becomes women who profess to be *r*,

RELINQUISH (3)

Est C:22 *r* your scepter to those that are nought.
Jb 27: 6 My justice I maintain and I will not *r* it;
Jer 17: 4 You will *r* your hold on your heritage

RELINQUISHING (1)

Jgs 2:19 *r* none of their evil practices or stubborn

RELOADED (1)

Gn 44:13 Then, when each man had *r* his donkey,

RELUCTANT (3)

Dt 15:18 must not be *r* to let your slave go free,
Jdt 12:13 *r* to come to my lord to be honored by him,
Wis 17:10 *r* to face even the air that they could

RELY (29)

2Kgs 18:20 On whom, then, do you *r*,
18:21 This Egypt, the staff on which you *r*,
18:21 king of Egypt is to all who *r* on him.
18:22 But if you say to me, We *r* on the LORD,
18:30 not Hezekiah induce you to *r* on the LORD,
19:10 'Do not let your God on whom you *r* deceive
2Chr 14:10 Help us, O LORD, our God, for we *r* on you,
16: 7 the king of Aram and did not *r* on the LORD,
Jdt 7:10 These Israelites do not *r* on their spears,
1Mc 10:77 such a large number of horsemen to *r* on.
Jb 8:15 He shall *r* upon his family,
39:12 Can you *r* on him to thresh out your grain
Prv 3: 5 your heart, on your own intelligence *r* not;
Sir 5: 1 *R* not on your wealth; say not:
5: 2 *R* not on your strength in following the
5:10 *R* not upon deceitful wealth,
Is 36: 5 On whom, then, do you *r*,
36: 6 This Egypt, the staff on which you *r*,
36: 6 king of Egypt, is to all who *r* on him.
36: 7 "We *r* on the LORD,
36: 9 you *r* on Egypt for chariots and horsemen!
36:15 not Hezekiah induce you to *r* on the LORD,
37:10 'Do not let your God on whom you *r* deceive
48: 2 the holy city and *r* on the God of Israel,
Ez 33:26 You *r* on your sword,
Dn 9:18 before you, we *r* not on our just deeds,
Mi 3:11 divine for money, While they *r* on the LORD,
Rom 2:17 *r* firmly on the law and pride yourself on
1Tm 6:17 to *r* on so uncertain a thing as wealth.

RELYING (6)

2Kgs 18:24 *r* as you do on Egypt for chariots and
2Chr 32:10 On what are you *r*,
2Mc 10:34 inside, *r* on the strength of the place,
12:14 *R* on the strength of their walls and their
Is 50:10 in the name of the LORD and *r* on his God?
Lk 11:22 on which he was *r* and divides the spoils.

REMAIN (176)

Gn 6: 3 "My spirit shall not *r* in man forever,
27:33 Now he must *r* blessed!"
31:32 one you find them with shall not *r* alive!
44:33 *r* in place of the boy as the slave of my
48: 6 born to you after them shall *r* yours;
Ex 10:24 But your flocks and herds must *r*."
21: 4 her children shall *r* the master's property
25:15 they must *r* in the rings of the ark and
Lv 6: 2 The holocaust is to *r* on the hearth of the
8:35 Hence you must *r* at the entrance of the
11:32 put in water and *r* unclean until evening,
14: 8 still *r* outside his tent for seven days.
22:27 it shall *r* with its mother for seven days;
25:28 what he has sold shall *r* in the possession
25:34 it must always *r* their hereditary property.
Nm 4: 7 bread offering shall *r* on the table.
30:14 allow to *r* valid or render null and void.
30:15 he has allowed them to *r* valid,
32: 6 then, to engage in war, while you *r* here?
32:17 families can *r* here in the fortified towns,
32:26 other livestock *r* in the towns of Gilead,
33:55 those whom you allow to *r* will become as
36: 8 Israelites may *r* in possession of their own
Dt 3:19 *r* behind in the towns I have given you,
4:27 and there shall *r* but a handful of you
21: 8 blood *r* in the midst of your people Israel.'
21:23 tree, it shall not *r* on the tree overnight.
22:19 Moreover, she shall *r* his wife,
28:41 and daughters, they will not *r* with you,
Jos 1:14 and your livestock shall *r* in the land
7:12 I will not *r* with you unless you remove
10:19 But do not *r* there yourselves.
10:27 were placed, which *r* until this very day.
22: 5 keep his commandments; *r* loyal to him;
23: 8 them, but you must *r* loyal to the LORD,
Jgs 2:23 to *r* instead of expelling them immediately,
3: 1 the nations which the LORD allowed to *r*,
1Sm 1:22 before the LORD and to *r* there forever;
2:33 some of your family to *r* at my altar,
5: 7 of the God of Israel must not *r* with us,
16:22 message, "Allow David to *r* in my service,
19: 2 get out of sight and *r* in hiding.
22: 5 "Do not *r* in the refuge.
26: 9 on the LORD's anointed and *r* unpunished?
30: 9 where those who were to *r* behind halted.
2Sm 18:30 "Step aside and *r* in attendance here."
19: 8 not a single man will *r* with you overnight,
19:11 should you *r* silent about restoring the
1Kgs 2: 4 so conduct themselves that they *r* faithful
11:32 *r* to him for the sake of David my servant,
2Kgs 7: 4 If we *r* here, we shall die too.
15:20 did not *r* in the country but withdrew.
25:22 he had allowed to *r* in the land of Judah,
25:24 *R* in the country and serve the king of
1Chr 17:23 your servant and his house *r* firm forever.
17:27 of your servant, so that it will *r* forever
19: 5 *R* at Jericho,"
2Chr 25:19 *R* at home. Why involve yourself,
32:10 while you *r* under siege in Jerusalem?
Ezr 10:13 season, so that we cannot *r* out-of-doors;
Neh 11: 1 the other nine would *r* in the other cities.
Tb 5:10 see God's sunlight, but must *r* in darkness,
8:20 shall *r* here eating and drinking with me;
14: 4 one of all the oracles shall *r* unfulfilled,
14: 8 do not *r* here.
Jdt 6: 4 and his words shall not *r* unfulfilled.
11:17 Now I will *r* with you,
Est 4:14 Even if you now *r* silent,
7: 4 to be sold into slavery I would *r* silent,
1Mc 8:22 to *r* there with the Jews as a record of
10:14 Only in Beth-zur did some *r* of those who
12:27 his men to be on guard and to *r* armed,
13:38 that you have built shall *r* yours.
15: 7 and now occupy shall *r* in your possession.
2Mc 2: 7 "The place is to *r* unknown until God
Jb 37: 8 take to cover and *r* quietly in their dens.
Ps(s) 49:10 to *r* alive always and not see destruction.
68: 7 only rebels *r* in the parched land.
72:17 as long as the sun his name shall *r*.
83: 2 I O God, do not *r* unmoved;
101: 3 he shall not *r* with me.
102:27 but you *r* though all of them grow old
125: 3 not *r* upon the territory of the just,
Prv 2:21 dwell in the land, the honest will *r* in it;
24:10 If you *r* indifferent in time of adversity,
Wis 3:16 of adulterers will *r* without issue,
10: 7 wickedness, there yet *r* a smoking desert,
11:25 And how could a thing *r*,
Sir 12: 8 in adversity an enemy will not *r* concealed.
22:18 open height will not *r* when the wind blows;
22:23 In time of trouble *r* true to him,
23:10 by the Holy Name will not *r* free from sin.
26:20 A merchant can hardly *r* upright,
Is 7: 4 Take care you *r* tranquil and do not fear;
7:22 shall be the food of all who *r* in the land.
15: 9 from Moab and for those who *r* in the land!
17: 6 Two or three olives *r* at the very top,
21:17 Few of Kedar's stalwart archers shall *r*,
46: 3 of Jacob, all who *r* of the house of Israel,
47: 7 *r* always a sovereign mistress forever!"
51: 6 My salvation shall *r* forever and my
51: 8 justice shall *r* forever and my salvation,
57:11 Was I to *r* silent and unseeing,
64:11 Can you *r* silent,
Jer 3:12 says the LORD, I will not *r* angry with you;
7: 3 so that I may *r* with you in this place.
7: 7 own harm, will I *r* with you in this place,
8: 3 wicked race who *r* in any of the places

REMAIN (cont.)
8:14 Why do we *r* here?
17:25 This city will *r* inhabited forever.
25: 5 then you shall *r* in the land which the
27:18 that the vessels which *r* in the house of
27:19 rest of the vessels that *r* in this city,
27:21 vessels that *r* in the house of the LORD,
27:22 shall be brought, and there they shall *r*,
29:16 and all the people who *r* in this city,
32: 5 There he shall *r*, until I attend to him,
35:15 if you would *r* on the land which I gave
40:10 saying that he himself would *r* in Mizpah,
42:10 *r* quietly in this land I will build you up,
42:13 your God, and decide not to *r* in this land,
51:30 to fight, they *r* in their strongholds;
51:62 it, since it would *r* an everlasting desert."
Lam 4:15 among the nations, nowhere could they *r*.
Ez 5:10 that *r* of your people in every direction.
17:14 so that the kingdom would *r* a modest one,
22:14 Can your heart *r* firm,
24:23 Your turbans shall *r* on your heads,
33:12 the virtuous man, when he sins, *r* alive].
36:36 nations that *r* shall know that I,
44: 2 This gate is to *r* closed;
44: 2 has entered by it, it shall *r* closed.
46: 1 *r* closed throughout the six working days,
46: 2 and *r* standing at the doorpost of the gate;
48:18 shall *r* an area along the sacred tract,
Dn 11:32 but those who *r* loyal to their God shall
Hos 3: 4 shall *r* many days without king or prince,
12: 7 if you *r* loyal and do right and always
Am 6: 9 Should there *r* ten men in a single house,
Mi 5: 3 And they shall *r*, for now his greatness
Zec 14:10 but Jerusalem shall *r* exalted in its place.
Mt 17:17 How long must I *r* with you?
26:38 *R* here and stay awake with me."
Mk 9:19 How long must I *r* with you?
9:35 he must *r* the last one of all and the
14:34 *R* here and stay awake."
Lk 9:41 How long must I *r* with you?
24:49 *R* here in the city until you are clothed
Jn 6:66 and would not *r* in his company any longer.
12:34 the law that the Messiah is to *r* forever.
Acts 3:21 Jesus must *r* in heaven until the time of
11:23 to *r* firm in their commitment to the Lord,
Rom 11:22 toward you, provided you *r* in his kindness;
11:23 And if the Jews do not *r* in their unbelief
1Cor 7: 8 It would be well if they *r* as they are,
7:11 *r* single or become reconciled to him again.
16: 6 I should like to *r* with you for some time
Phil 1:24 more urgent that I *r* alive for your sakes.
1Thes 3: 1 to *r* alone at Athens and send you Timothy.
4:11 *r* at peace and attend to your own affairs.
5:13 *R* at peace with one another.
2Tm 2:13 we are unfaithful he will still *r* faithful,
3:14 must *r* faithful to what you have learned
Heb 1:11 They will perish, but you *r*;
12:27 away, so that only what is unshaken may *r*.
1Pt 4: 7 *r* calm so that you will be able to pray.
1Jn 2:24 heard from the beginning *r* in your hearts.
2:24 from the beginning does *r* in your hearts,
2:24 turn will *r* in the Son and in the Father,
2:27 *r* in him as that anointing taught you.
2:28 *R* in him now,
3:24 his commandments *r* in him and he in them.
4:13 The way we know we *r* in him and he in us
2Jn 1: 9 so "progressive" that he does not *r* rooted
Rv 2:10 *R* faithful until death and I will give you
17:10 he does come he will *r* only a short while.

REMAINDER (4)
Ezr 7:18 to you with the *r* of the silver and gold,
Ez 34:18 that you had to foul the *r* with your feet?
48:21 The *r* shall belong to the prince:
Jas 2:10 the law, even though he keeps the entire *r*,

REMAINED (133)
Gn 16:13 seen God and *r* alive after my vision?"
18:22 Sodom, the LORD *r* standing before Abraham.
29:30 *r* in Laban's service another seven years.
29:31 made her fruitful, while Rachel *r* barren.
39:21 he was in prison, the LORD *r* with Joseph;
49:24 But each one's bow *r* stiff,
50:22 Joseph *r* in Egypt,
Ex 7:22 So Pharaoh *r* obstinate and would not
8:15 *r* obstinate and would not listen to them,
8:27 Not one *r*.
9: 7 *r* obdurate and would not let the people go.
10:19 locust *r* within the confines of Egypt,
17:12 so that his hands *r* steady till sunset.
20:21 Still the people *r* at a distance,
Lv 13: 5 *r* unchanged and has not spread on the skin,
13:37 he judges that the scall has *r* in its
Nm 9:18 stayed over the Dwelling, they *r* in camp.
9:21 *r* there only from evening until morning;
9:22 Israelites *r* in camp and did not depart;
36:12 *r* in the tribe of their father's clan.
Dt 10: 5 they have *r*, in keeping with the command
Jos 3:17 *r* motionless on dry ground in the bed
4:10 The priests carrying the ark *r* in the bed
5: 8 the whole nation *r* in camp where they were,
8:17 not a soldier *r* in Ai [or Bethel],
10:26 trees, where they *r* hanging until evening.
23:14 your God, made to you has *r* unfulfilled.
Jgs 7: 3 of the soldiers left, but ten thousand *r*.
7:21 all *r* standing in place around the camp,
9:21 he *r* for fear of his brother Abimelech.
11:17 So Israel *r* in Kadesh.
15: 8 and *r* in a cavern of the cliff of Etam.
16: 9 and the secret of his strength *r* unknown.
17: 4 It *r* in the house of Micah.
20:26 where they wept and *r* fasting before the
20:47 rock Rimmon, where they *r* for four months.
21: 2 and *r* there before God until evening,
Ru 2: 7 came this morning she has *r* here until now,
1Sm 1:12 As she *r* long at prayer before the LORD,
1:23 And so she *r* at home and nursed her son
2:11 the child *r* in the service of the LORD
13: 2 of whom two thousand *r* with him in
19:24 *r* in the prophetic state in the presence
22: 4 with him as long as David *r* in the refuge.
23:18 before the LORD in Horesh, where David *r*,
25:13 while two hundred *r* with the baggage.
26:12 All *r* asleep, because the LORD had put
30:10 to cross the Wadi Besor and *r* behind.
2Sm 6:11 The ark of the LORD *r* in the house of
10: 8 Tob and Maacah *r* apart in the open country.
11: 1 David, however, *r* in Jerusalem.
11:12 So Uriah *r* in Jerusalem that day.
13:20 But Tamar *r* grief-stricken and forlorn in
15:29 ark of God back to Jerusalem and *r* there.
18:30 So he stepped aside and *r* there.
19:40 crossed over the Jordan but the king *r*;
20: 2 the Judahites *r* loyal to their king.
20: 3 *r* in confinement to the day of their death,
1Kgs 8: 8 (They have *r* there to this day.)
9:20 the non-Israelite people who *r* in the land,
10: 3 and there *r* nothing hidden from him that
11:16 Joab and all Israel *r* there six months
11:40 in Egypt, where he *r* until Solomon's death.
12:20 None *r* loyal to David's house except the
13:24 on the road, and the ass *r* standing by it,
17: 5 He went and *r* by the Wadi Cherith,
18:29 Noon passed and they *r* in a prophetic
22:47 who had *r* in the reign of his father Asa.
2Kgs 10:17 Jehu slew all who *r* there of Ahab's line,
11: 3 he *r* hidden in the temple of the LORD,
13: 6 The sacred pole also *r* standing in Samaria.
18:36 *r* silent and did not answer him one word,
1Chr 5:26 river Gozan, where they have *r* to this day.
12:40 They *r* with David for three days,
13:14 The ark of God *r* in the house of Obed-edom
19: 9 to their help *r* apart in the open field.
20: 1 Rabbah, while David himself *r* in Jerusalem.
2Chr 5: 9 The ark has *r* there to this day.
8: 7 All the people that *r* of the Hittites,
9: 2 and there *r* nothing hidden from Solomon
11:12 Thus Judah and Benjamin *r* his.
22: 9 There *r* in Ahaziah's house no one powerful
22:12 he *r* hidden with them in the house of God,
26:21 Uzziah *r* a leper to the day of his death.
32: 9 himself *r* at Lachish with all his forces,
Ezr 8:31 The hand of our God *r* upon us,
9: 4 I *r* motionless until the evening sacrifice.
Neh 5: 8 They *r* silent,
8: 7 law to the people, who *r* in their places.]
Jdt 8: 4 *r* three years and four months at home,
12: 9 and *r* there until her food was brought to
16:20 the sanctuary, and Judith *r* with them.
16:21 went back to Bethulia and *r* on her estate.
1Mc 6: 9 There he *r* many days,
6:54 Few men *r* in the sanctuary;
9: 6 the camp, until only eight hundred men *r*.
9: 8 his discouragement, he said to those who *r*:
10:47 they *r* his allies for the rest of his life.
13:11 drove out the occupants and *r* there.
2Mc 4:50 of the men in power, *r* in office,
8: 1 enlisting others who *r* faithful to Judaism,
15: 7 But Maccabeus *r* confident,
15:19 who *r* in the city suffered a like agony,
Jb 9: 4 who has withstood him and *r* unscathed?
31:34 then I should have *r* silent,
Sir 46: 9 And the strength he gave to Caleb *r* with
48:15 But Judah *r*, a tiny people, with its rulers
Is 36:21 *r* silent and did not answer him one word,
Jer 37:10 now attacking you, and only the wounded *r*,
37:16 vaulted dungeon, where he *r* a long time.
37:21 Jeremiah *r* in the quarters of the guard.
38:13 Jeremiah *r* in the quarters of the guard.
39:14 And so he *r* among the people.
Dn 1:21 *r* there until the first year of King Cyrus.
2:49 while Daniel himself *r* at the king's court.
10: 8 No strength *r* in me;
14:31 into a lions' den, where he *r* six days.
Jon 2: 1 and he *r* in the belly of the fish three
Mt 26:63 But Jesus *r* silent.
27:61 and the other Mary *r* sitting there,
Mk 3: 4 At this they *r* silent.
4: 1 while the crowd *r* on the shore nearby.
6:43 twelve baskets, besides what *r* of the fish.
14:61 But Jesus *r* silent; he made no reply.
Lk 1:22 making signs to them, for he *r* speechless.
1:56 Mary *r* with Elizabeth about three months
2:43 Jesus *r* behind unknown to his parents.
4:25 days of Elijah when the heavens *r* closed
6: 8 The man rose and *r* standing.
18:34 His utterance *r* obscure to them,
Jn 6:22 The crowd *r* on the other side of the lake.
Acts 5: 4 Was it not yours so long as it *r* unsold?
14: 2 But the Jews who *r* unconvinced stirred up

REMAINING (31)
Gn 32: 9 reasoned, "the *r* camp may still survive."
Ex 38:28 The *r* one thousand seven hundred and
Lv 8:21 he also burned these *r* parts of the ram on
Dt 3:11 was the last *r* survivor of the Rephaim.
Jos 10: 1 *r* among them and that there was great fear
14: 2 concerning the *r* nine and a half tribes.
Jgs 17:12 who became his priest, *r* in his house.
2Sm 14: 7 Thus they will quench my *r* hope and leave
1Kgs 15:18 Asa then took all the silver and gold *r* in
2Kgs 19:30 The *r* survivors of the house of Judah
25:11 exile the last of the people *r* in the city,
25:19 of the common people still *r* in the city.
1Chr 24:20 Of the *r* Levites,
2Chr 8: 8 that is, their descendants *r* in the land,
Ezr 4: 5 their plans during the *r* years of Cyrus,
Jdt 15: 6 The *r* inhabitants of Bethulia swept down
1Mc 3:37 The king took the *r* half of the army and
6:38 The *r* cavalry were stationed on one or the
2Mc 15:37 with the city *r* in possession of the
Is 37:31 The *r* survivors of the house of Judah
Jer 24: 8 the remnant of Jerusalem *r* in this land
29: 1 Jerusalem to the *r* elders among the exiles,
34: 7 Jerusalem and the *r* cities of Judah,
Ez 36: 4 and mockery of the *r* nations round about;
48:15 The *r* five thousand cubits along the
48:23 These are the *r* tribes.
Mt 14:20 The fragments *r*, when gathered up,
14:24 to pray, *r* there alone as evening drew on.
Lk 5: 3 then, *r* seated,
Jn 12:46 who believes in me from *r* in the dark.
Heb 7:23 were prevented by death from *r* in office;

REMAINS (80)
Gn 28:20 "If God *r* with me,
Ex 9:19 Whatever man or beast *r* in the fields and
29:34 some of the bread *r* over on the next day,
Lv 11:36 or a cistern for collecting water *r* clean;
11:37 Any sort of cultivated grain *r* clean even
13:23 blotch *r* in its place without spreading,
13:28 But if the blotch *r* in its place without
15: 3 his uncleanness *r*.
19:23 years, while its fruit *r* uncircumcised,
21: 3 is of his own family while she *r* unmarried;
Nm 5:13 so that her impurity *r* unproved for lack
19: 7 He *r* unclean until the evening,
19:13 not been splashed over him, he *r* unclean:
19:20 not been splashed over him, he *r* unclean.
30: 5 any vow or any pledge she has made *r* valid.
30: 8 the vow or pledge she had made *r* valid.
30:12 any vow or any pledge she has made *r* valid.
Dt 24:20 let what *r* be for the alien,
24:21 let what *r* be for the alien,
Jos 7:26 over him, which *r* to the present day.
8:28 everlasting mound of ruins, as it *r* today.
8:29 up over it, which *r* to the present day.
13: 1 part of the land still *r* to be conquered.
14:14 *r* the heritage of the Kenizzite Caleb,
Jgs 14: 8 he stepped aside to look at the *r* of the
1Sm 18: 8 All that *r* for him is the kingship."
30:24 who *r* with the baggage shall be the same;
1Kgs 13:31 Lay my *r* beside his.
2Kgs 4: 7 with what *r*,
10:27 turned it into a latrine, as it *r* today.
Ezr 10: 2 Yet even now there *r* a hope for Israel.
1Mc 13:25 sent for the *r* of his brother Jonathan,
13:38 we have guaranteed to you *r* in force,
Jb 19: 4 I am at fault and that my fault *r* with me,
21:34 comfort, while in your answers perfidy *r*?
27:19 he opens his eyes and nothing *r* to him.
34:29 If he *r* tranquil, who then can condemn?
Ps(s) 5: 5 no evil man *r* with you;
89:38 Like the moon, which *r* forever
Prv 14: 4 Where there are no oxen, the crib *r* empty;
21:20 treasure *r* in the house of the wise,
27: 5 an open rebuke than a love that *r* hidden.
29: 1 The man who *r* stiff-necked and hates
Sir 1: 1 from the LORD and with him it *r* forever.
11:17 The LORD's gift *r* with the just;
20:25 to dishonor, his shame *r* ever with him.
21:22 a house, while the well-bred man *r* outside;
31:10 and come off safe, and this *r* his glory;
40:12 will be wiped out, but loyalty *r* for ages.
44:11 Their wealth *r* in their families,
Is 4: 3 He who *r* in Zion and he that is left in
5: 8 connect field with field, Till no room *r*,
6:13 whose trunk *r* when its leaves have fallen.
24:12 In the city nothing *r* but ruin;
44:17 Of what *r* he makes a god,
Jer 21: 9 Whoever *r* in this city shall die by the
38: 2 He who *r* in this city shall die by sword,
Ez 11:13 will you utterly wipe out what *r* of Israel?"
Hb 3:11 to rise, the moon *r* in its shelter,
Mt 7: 4 while all the time the plank *r* in your own?
Jn 6:27 food but for food that *r* unto life eternal,
6:56 on my flesh and drinks my blood *r* in me,

9:41 'But we see,' you say, and your sin *r*.
12:24 earth and dies, it *r* just a grain of wheat.
14:17 he *r* with you and will be within you.
Acts 7:16 Their *r* were transferred to Shechem and
2Cor 3:14 old covenant is read the veil *r* unlifted;
Heb 4: 6 Therefore, since it *r* for some to enter,
4: 9 sabbath rest still *r* for the people of God.
7: 3 like the Son of God he *r* a priest forever.
7:24 but Jesus, because he *r* forever,
10:26 *r* for us no further sacrifice for sin
1Pt 4: 2 You are not to spend what *r* of your
1Jn 2:14 are strong, and the word of God *r* in you,
2:27 you received from him *r* in your hearts.
3: 6 The man who *r* in him does not sin.
3: 9 acts sinfully because he *r* of God's stock;
3:24 And this is how we know that he *r* in us:
2Jn 1: 9 while anyone who *r* rooted in the teaching
Rv 3: 2 up, and strengthen what *r* before it dies.

REMAKE (1)

Phil 3:21 this lowly body of ours and *r* it according

REMALIAH (11)

2Kgs 15:25 His adjutant Pekah, son of *R*,
15:27 Azariah, king of Judah, Pekah, son of *R*,
15:30 Elah, conspired against Pekah, son of *R*;
15:32 In the second year of Pekah, son of *R*,
15:37 Rezin, king of Aram, and Pekah, son of *R*,
16: 1 the seventeenth year of Pekah, son of *R*,
16: 5 Rezin, king of Aram, and Pekah, son of *R*,
2Chr 28: 6 For Pekah, son of *R*,
Is 7: 1 Aram, and Pekah, king of Israel, son of *R*,
7: 4 and the Arameans, and of the son of *R*,
7: 5 and the son of *R* plots against you,

REMALIAH'S (2)

Is 7: 8 of Ephraim, and *R* son the head of Samaria.
8: 6 before the loftiness of Rezin and *R* son,

REMAND (1)

Nm 35:25 shall *r* him to the city of asylum

REMARK (6)

Mt 9:12 Overhearing the *r*, he said:
27:47 made some of the bystanders who heard it *r*,
Mk 2:17 Overhearing the *r*, Jesus said to them,
Jn 7:25 led some of the people of Jerusalem to *r*:
11:36 began to weep, which caused the Jews to *r*,
18:38 After this *r*, Pilate went out again

REMARKABLE (3)

Ex 3: 3 "I must go over to look at this *r* sight,
Acts 4:16 a *r* show of power took place through them.
Gal 3: 4 had such *r* experiences all to no purpose

REMARKABLY (1)

2Mc 3:26 Then two other young men, *r* strong,

REMARKED (9)

Mt 8:10 on hearing this and *r* to his followers,
Mk 15:35 A few of the bystanders who heard it *r*,
Jn 1:47 saw Nathanael coming toward him, he *r*:
2:10 charge called the groom over and *r* to him:
6: 8 Andrew, Simon Peter's brother, *r* to him,
6:60 hearing his words, many of his disciples *r*,
12:19 The Pharisees *r* to one another,
Acts 2:12 one another, while a few *r* with a sneer,
26:32 Agrippa further *r* to Festus,

REMARKS (2)

1Sm 21:13 *r* and became very much afraid of Achish,
1Pt 2: 1 jealousies, and disparaging *r* of any kind.

REMEDIES (3)

Jb 13: 4 over falsehoods and offering vain *r*,
Jer 46:11 No use to multiply *r*;
Ez 30:21 bound up with bandages and healing *r*

REMEDY (11)

2Chr 36:16 people was so inflamed that there was no *r*.
Jdt 5:12 with plagues for which there was no *r*.
Prv 13:17 but a trustworthy envoy is a healing *r*.
Wis 2: 1 neither is there any *r* for man's dying,
16: 9 and no *r* was found to save their lives
Sir 6:16 A faithful friend is a life-saving *r*,
Jer 17: 9 than all else is the human heart, beyond *r*;
17:16 the day without *r* I have not desired.
30:13 your cause, no *r* for your running sore,
Mi 1: 9 is no *r* for the blow she has been struck;
1Thes 3:10 face and *r* any shortcomings in your faith?

REMEMBER (178)

Gn 31:50 *r* that even though no one else is about,
40:14 So if you will still *r*,
Ex 13: 3 *R* this day on which you came out of Egypt,
20: 8 *R* to keep holy the sabbath day.
32:13 *R* your servants Abraham,
Lv 26:42 guilt, I will *r* my covenant with Jacob,
26:45 I will *r* them because of the covenant I
Nm 10: 9 will *r* you and save you from your foes.
11: 5 We *r* the fish we used to eat without cost
15:40 Thus you will *r* to keep all my
18: 6 *R*, it is I who have taken your kinsmen,
Dt 5:15 *r* that you too were once slaves in Egypt,
8: 2 *R* how for forty years now the LORD,
8:18 *R* then, it is the LORD, your God,
9:27 *R* your servants, Abraham, Isaac and
15:15 For *r* that you too were once slaves in the
16: 3 that you may *r* as long as you live the day
16:12 *R* that you too were once slaves in Egypt,
24: 9 *R* what the LORD, your God, did to
24:18 For, *r*, you were once slaves in Egypt,
24:22 For *r* that you were once slaves in Egypt;
Jos 1:13 *R* what Moses, the servant of the LORD,
Jgs 9: 2 must *r* that I am your own flesh and bone."
16:28 to the LORD and said, "O Lord GOD, *r* me!
1Sm 1:11 handmaid, if you *r* me and do not forget me,
25:31 benefit on your lordship, *r* your handmaid."
28:21 *R*, your maidservant obeyed you:
2Sm 15:28 *R*, I shall be waiting at the fords near
19:20 and may he not *r* and take to heart the
2Kgs 9:25 For I *r* that when we were driving teams
20: 3 *r* how faithfully and wholeheartedly I
2Chr 6:42 of your anointed, *r* the devotion of David,
Neh 1: 8 But *r*,
13:14 *R* this to my credit, O my God!
13:22 This, too, *r* in my favor,
13:29 *R* against them,
13:31 *R* this in my favor, O my God!
Tb 4: 4 *R*, my son, that she went through many
4:12 *R* that their posterity shall inherit the
6:16 "Do you not *r* your father's orders?
Est B: 8 *R* the days of your lowly estate."
1Mc 2:51 *R* the deeds that our fathers did in their
4: 9 *R* how our fathers were saved in the Red Sea,
4:10 favor us, *r* his covenant with our fathers,
7:38 *R* their blasphemies,
10: 5 will *r* all the wrongs we have done to him,
12:11 have never ceased to *r* you in the
12:11 as it is right and proper to *r* brothers.
2Mc 1: 2 *r* his covenant with his faithful servants,
8: 4 to *r* the criminal slaughter of innocent
9:26 *r* the general and individual benefits you
Jb 7: 7 *R* that my life is like the wind;
10: 9 Oh, *r* that you fashioned me from clay!
14:13 would fix a time for me, and then *r* me!
36:24 *R*, you should extol his work,
Ps(s) 20: 4 May he *r* all your offerings and graciously
22:28 of the earth shall *r* and turn to the LORD;
25: 6 *R* that your compassion,
25: 7 sins of my youth and my frailties *r* not;
25: 7 in your kindness *r* me,
42: 7 so will I *r* you From the land of the
63: 7 I will *r* you upon my couch,
74: 2 *R* your flock which you built up of old,
74:18 *R* how the enemy has blasphemed you,
74:22 *r* how the fool blasphemes you day after
77: 4 When I *r* God, I moan;
77: 7 the years long past I *r*.
77:12 I *r* the deeds of the LORD:
77:12 yes, I *r* your wonders of old.
79: 8 *R* not against us the iniquities of the past;
88: 6 Whom you *r* no longer and who are cut off
89:48 *R* how short my life is;
89:51 *R*, O Lord, the insults to your servants:
103:18 his covenant and *r* to fulfill his precepts.
106: 4 *R* me, O LORD, as you favor your people;
119:52 I *r* your ordinances of old,
119:55 By night I *r* your name,
137: 6 tongue cleave to my palate if I *r* you not,
137: 7 *R*, O LORD, against the children of Edom
143: 5 I *r* the days of old;
Eccl 11: 8 *r* that the days of darkness will be many.
12: 1 *R* your Creator in the days of your youth,
Sir 7:16 *r*,
7:28 *R*, of these parents you were born;
7:36 In whatever you do, *r* your last days,
8: 5 *r*, we all are guilty.
8: 7 *r*, we are all to die.
9:12 *r* he will not reach death unpunished.
14:12 *R* that death does not tarry,
18:25 *R* the time of hunger in the time of plenty,
24:19 You will *r* me as sweeter than honey,
28: 6 *R* your last days,
28: 6 *r* death and decay,
31:13 *R* that gluttony is evil.
38:22 *R* that his fate will also be yours;
41: 3 *r*, it embraces those before you,
Is 19:17 Every time they *r* Judah,
23:16 sing many songs, that they may *r* you.
38: 3 *r* how faithfully and wholeheartedly I
43:18 *R* not the events of the past,
43:25 your sins I *r* no more.
43:26 Would you have me *r*,
44:21 *R* this, O Jacob, you O Israel,
46: 8 *R* this and be firm,
46: 8 *r* the former things,
54: 4 the reproach of your widowhood no longer *r*.
57:11 And did not *r* me or give me any thought?
Jer 2: 2 I *r* the devotion of your youth,
3:16 They will no longer think of it, or *r* it,
14:21 *r* your covenant with us,
15:15 *R* me, LORD, visit me, and avenge me
17: 2 sons *r* their altars and their sacred poles,
18:20 *R* that I stood before you to speak in
31:20 I threaten him, I still *r* him with favor;
31:34 their evildoing and *r* their sin no more.
51:50 *R* the LORD from afar,
Lam 5: 1 *R*, O LORD, what has befallen us,
Bar 2:33 because they shall *r* the fate of their
3: 5 *R* at this time not the misdeeds of our
4: 5 *R*, Israel,
4:27 He who brought this upon you will *r* you.
Ez 6: 9 then those who have escaped will *r* me
16:43 not *r* what happened when you were a girl,
16:60 Yet I will *r* the covenant I made with you
16:61 Then you shall *r* your conduct and be
16:63 you may *r* and be covered with confusion,
23:27 toward it, nor shall you *r* Egypt again.
36:31 Then you shall *r* your evil conduct,
Hos 7: 2 themselves that I *r* all their wickedness.
8:13 still *r* their guilt and punish their sins;
9: 9 *r* their iniquity and punish their sins.
Am 1: 9 and did not *r* the pact of brotherhood,
Mi 6: 5 people, *r* what Moab's King Balak planned,
Hb 3: 2 in your wrath *r* compassion!
Zec 10: 9 nations, yet in distant lands they *r* me;
Mal 3:22 *R* the law of Moses my servant,
Mt 6:21 *R*, where your treasure is,
11: 8 *R*, those who dress luxuriously are to be
16: 9 Do you not *r* the five loaves among five
24:25 *R*, I have told you all about it beforehand;
26:66 *R*, you heard the blasphemy.
Mk 8:19 Do you *r* when I broke the five loaves for
Lk 7:25 *R*, those who dress in luxury and eat in
10: 3 Be on your way, and *r*:
16:25 *r* that you were well off in your lifetime,
17:32 *R* Lot's wife.
20:33 *R*, seven married her."
22:31 *R* that Satan has asked for you,
23:42 *r* me when you enter upon your reign."
24: 6 *R* what he said to you while he was still
Jn 5:14 *R*, now, you have been cured.
15:20 *R* what I told you:
16: 4 comes you may *r* my telling you of them.
20: 9 *R*, as yet they did not understand the
Rom 11:18 boast, *r* that you do not support the root;
16: 5 *R* me also to the congregation that meets
1Cor 10: 1 Brothers, I want you to *r* this:
11: 2 I praise you because you always *r* me and
11:16 *r* that neither we nor the churches of God
Gal 5:13 *r* that you have been called to live in
Eph 2:11 *r* that,
6: 9 *R* that you and they have a Master in
Col 4:18 *R* my chains.
1Thes 1: 2 for all of you and we *r* you in our prayers,
3: 6 and telling us that you constantly *r* us
2Thes 2: 5 do you not *r* how I used to tell you about
2Tm 1: 3 conscience, whenever I *r* you in my prayers
2: 8 *R* that Jesus Christ,
Heb 8:12 evildoing, and their sins I will *r* no more."
10:17 and their transgressions I will *r* no more."
12: 3 *R* how he endured the opposition of sinners;
13: 7 *R* your leaders who spoke the word of God
Jas 5:20 *R* this: the person who brings a sinner back
1Pt 1:16 *r*,
1Jn 3:11 This, *r*, is the message you heard from the
Jude 1:17 *R*, beloved, all of you, the prophetic words
Rv 22: 7 *R*, I am coming soon!
22:12 *R*, I am coming soon!

REMEMBERED (48)

Gn 8: 1 and then God *r* Noah and all the animals,
30:22 Then God *r* Rachel;
Ex 17:14 down in a document as something to be *r*,
1Sm 1:19 with his wife Hannah, the LORD *r* her.
Neh 9:17 *r* the miracles you had worked for them.
Tb 4: 1 That same day Tobit *r* the money he had
Est F: 9 God *r* his people and rendered justice to
1Mc 5: 4 He also *r* the malice of the sons of Baean,
10:46 for they *r* the great evil that Demetrius
Ps(s) 9:13 For the avenger of blood has *r*;
78:39 He *r* that they were flesh,
78:42 They *r* not his hand nor the day he
83: 5 let the name of Israel be *r* no more!"
98: 3 He has *r* his kindness and his faithfulness
105:42 he *r* his holy word to his servant Abraham.
106: 7 They *r* not your abundant kindness,
109:14 the guilt of his fathers be *r* by the LORD;
109:16 earth, Because he *r* not to show kindness,
136:23 Who *r* us in our abjection,
137: 1 of Babylon we sat and wept when we *r* Zion.
Eccl 9:15 Yet no one *r* this poor man.
Sir 3:30 He who does a kindness is *r* afterward;
45: 9 and the children of his race would be *r*;
47:23 Until one arose who should not be *r*,
51: 8 But then I *r* the mercies of the LORD,
Is 17:10 God, your savior, and *r* not the Rock,
63:11 Then they *r* the days of old and Moses,
65:17 of the past shall not be *r* or come to mind.
Jer 44:21 this that the LORD *r* and brought to mind,
Bar 5: 5 Holy One, rejoicing that they are *r* by God.

REMEMBERED (cont.)
Ez 3:20 and his virtuous deeds shall not be *r*;
16:22 you *r* nothing of when you were a girl,
18:22 crimes he committed shall be *r* against him;
18:24 None of his virtuous deeds shall be *r*,
21:37 You shall not be *r*,
25:10 that she may not be *r* among the peoples.
33:13 none of his virtuous deeds shall be *r*;
Dn 14:38 "You have *r* me,
Jon 2: 8 my soul fainted within me, I *r* the LORD;
Mt 26:75 and Peter *r* the prediction Jesus had made:
Mk 11:21 Peter *r* and said to him, "Rabbi, look!
Lk 1:72 fathers and *r* the holy covenant he made,
22:61 *r* the word that the Lord had spoken to him,
Acts 10: 4 sight, and because of them he has *r* you.
10:31 and your generosity *r* in God's presence.
11:16 Then I *r* what the Lord had said:
Rom 16:24 our brother Quartus wish to be *r* to you.
Rv 16:19 God *r* Babylon the great,

REMEMBERING (4)
1Mc 9:38 *R* the blood of John their brother,
2Mc 10: 6 days as on the feast of Booths, *r* how,
Ps(s) 78:35 *R* that God was their rock and the Most
Lam 3:20 *R* it over and over leaves my soul downcast

REMEMBERS (9)
1Chr 16:15 He *r* forever his covenant which he made
Ps(s) 6: 6 For among the dead no one *r* you;
103:14 he *r* that we are dust.
105: 8 He *r* forever his covenant which he
115:12 The LORD *r* us and will bless us:
Sir 16:15 in heaven who *r* me?
28: 1 vengeance, for he *r* their sins in detail.
Jer 14:10 now he *r* their guilt,
Jn 16:21 she no longer *r* her pain for joy that a

REMEMBRANCE (13)
Ex 20:24 In whatever place I choose for the *r* of my
Dt 12: 3 stamp out the *r* of them in any such place.
2Mc 7:20 and worthy of everlasting *r* was the mother,
Ps(s) 9: 7 *r* of the cities you uprooted has perished.
34:17 to destroy *r* of them from the earth.
112: 6 the just man shall be in everlasting *r*.
Eccl 1:11 There is no *r* of the men of old;
1:11 be any *r* among those who come after them.
2:16 of the fool will there be an abiding *r*,
Wis 11:12 at the *r* of the ones who had departed.
Lk 22:19 Do this as a *r* of me."
1Cor 11:24 Do this in *r* of me."
11:25 Do this, whenever you drink it, in *r* of me."

REMETH (1)
Jos 19:21 Anaharath, Rabbith, Kishion, Ebez, *R*,

REMIND (13)
Nm 15:39 let the sight of them *r* you to keep all
Wis 12: 2 and *r* them of the sins they are committing,
16: 6 to *r* them of the precept of your Law.
Is 62: 6 O you who are to *r* the LORD,
Dn 6:13 went to *r* the king about the prohibition:
Hos 7: 2 Yet they do not *r* themselves that I
Lk 4:25 Indeed, let me *r* you,
Jn 14:26 and *r* you of all that I told you.
1Cor 4:17 He will *r* you of my ways in Christ,
15: 1 to *r* you of the gospel I preached to you,
2Tm 1: 6 I *r* you to stir into flame the gift of God
Ti 3: 1 *R* people to be loyally subject to the
Jude 1: 5 I wish to *r* you of certain things,

REMINDED (7)
Gn 41: 9 "On this occasion I am *r* of my negligence.
42: 9 he was *r* of the dreams he had about them.
44:26 So we *r* him, 'We cannot go down there;
Jos 1:12 Joshua *r* the Reubenites,
Neh 9:34 and the obligations of which you *r* them.
Tb 2: 6 I was *r* of the oracle pronounced by the
Est 3: 4 When they had *r* him day after day and he

REMINDER (14)
Ex 13: 9 on your hand and as a *r* on your forehead;
28:12 on his shoulders as a *r* before the LORD.
28:29 his heart as a constant *r* before the LORD.
30:16 may be the Israelites' *r* before the LORD,
Lv 23:24 and with the trumpet blasts as a *r*;
Nm 10:10 will serve as a *r* of you before your God.
17: 5 to be a *r* to the Israelites that no layman,
Est E:23 who plot against us a *r* of destruction.
Wis 16:11 For as a *r* of your injunctions,
Sir 50:16 mightily as a *r* before the Most High.
Ez 29:16 but the living *r* of its guilt for having
Lk 24: 8 With this *r*, his words came back to them.
Rom 15:15 boldly in parts of this letter by way of *r*.
2Pt 1:13 long as I live, to prompt you with this *r*.

REMINDERS (2)
Jb 13:12 Your *r* are ashy maxims,
2Pt 3: 1 as *r* urging you to sincerity of outlook.

REMINDING (3)
2Mc 1: 9 We are now *r* you to celebrate the feast of
15: 9 *r* them of the battles they had already won,
2Tm 2:14 Keep *r* people of these things and charge

REMISSION (3)
Nm 8: 7 Sprinkle them with the water of *r*;
Lk 24:47 penance for the *r* of sins is to be
Acts 13:38 including the *r* of all those charges you

REMISSLY (1)
Jer 48:10 [Cursed be he who does the LORD's work *r*,

REMIT (1)
1Mc 13:39 We *r* any oversights and defaults incurred

REMITS (1)
Sir 16:11 alike are with him who *r* and forgives,

REMITTED (1)
Lk 7:43 I presume, to whom he *r* the larger sum."

REMITTING (1)
Rom 3:25 the sake of *r* sins committed in the past

REMNANT (73)
Gn 45: 7 to ensure for you a *r* on earth and to save
Ex 10: 5 up the *r* you saved unhurt from the hail,
29:34 on the next day, this *r* must be burned up;
Jos 23:12 ally yourselves with the *r* of these nations
2Kgs 19: 4 So send up a prayer for the *r* that is here.' "
19:31 For out of Jerusalem shall come a *r*,
2Chr 30: 6 the *r* left from the hands of the Assyrian
34: 9 Manasseh, Ephraim, and all the *r* of Israel,
Ezr 9: 8 a *r* and gave us a stake in his holy place;
9:14 us as to destroy us without *r* or survivor?
9:15 we have been spared, the *r* we are today.
Neh 1: 2 Jews, the *r* preserved after the captivity,
Tb 13:16 Happy for me if a *r* of my offspring
1Mc 3:35 *r* of Jerusalem and efface their memory
Sir 47:22 So he gave to Jacob a *r*,
Is 1: 9 the LORD of hosts had left us a scanty *r*,
10:19 And the *r* of the trees in his forest will
10:20 On that day The *r* of Israel,
10:21 A *r* will return, the remnant of Jacob
10:22 of the sea, Only a *r* of them will return;
11:11 to reclaim the *r* of his people that is left
11:16 *r* of his people that is left from Assyria,
14:22 hosts, and cut off from Babylon name and *r*,
14:30 with famine that shall slay even your *r*.
16:14 there shall be a *r*,
17: 3 The *r* of Aram shall have the same glory as
28: 5 a brilliant diadem to the *r* of his people,
37: 4 Send up a prayer for the *r* that is here.' "
37:32 For out of Jerusalem shall come a *r*,
Jer 6: 9 Glean, glean like a vine the *r* of Israel;
23: 3 I myself will gather the *r* of my flock
24: 8 the *r* of Jerusalem remaining in this land
25:20 and the *r* of Ashdod
31: 7 has delivered his people, the *r* of Israel.
40:11 the king of Babylon had left a *r* in Judah,
40:15 dispersed and the *r* of Judah will perish."
41:10 led away the *r* of the people left in
41:16 leaders took charge of the *r* of the people,
42: 2 us to the LORD, your God, for all this *r*.
42:15 to the word of the LORD, the *r* of Judah:
42:19 the LORD who has spoken to you, *r* of Judah;
43: 5 leaders took along the whole *r* of Judah
44: 7 and not leave yourselves even a *r*?
44:12 I will take away the *r* of Judah who
44:13 None of the *r* of Judah that have come to
44:28 The whole *r* of Judah who came to settle in
47: 4 the *r* from the coasts of Caphtor.
47: 5 Ashdod, the *r* of their strength,
50:20 for I will forgive the *r* I preserve.
50:26 goods in heaps and doom it, leave not a *r*.
Ez 25:16 and wipe out the *r* on the seacoast.
Jl 3: 5 For on Mount Zion there shall be a *r*,
Am 5:15 hosts, will have pity on the *r* of Joseph.
Mi 2:12 one, I will assemble all the *r* of Israel;
4: 7 I will make of the lame a *r*,
5: 6 The *r* of Jacob shall be in the midst of
5: 7 the *r* of Jacob shall be among the nations,
7:18 pardons sin for the *r* of his inheritance;
Zep 2: 7 belong to the *r* of the house of Judah;
2: 9 The *r* of my people shall plunder them,
3:12 *r* in your midst a people humble and lowly,
3:13 the *r* of Israel.
Hg 1:12 and all the *r* of the people listened to
1:14 and the spirit of all the *r* of the people,
2: 2 of Jehozadak, and to the *r* of the people:
Zec 8: 6 in the eyes of the *r* of this people,
8:11 the *r* of this people as in former days,
8:12 I will have the *r* of the people possess.
9: 7 He also shall become a *r* for our God,
Rom 9:27 sands of the sea, only the *r* will be saved,
9:29 the Lord of hosts had left us a *r*,
11: 5 there is a *r* chosen by the grace of God.

REMNANTS (2)
Lv 9:24 and the *r* of the fat on the altar.
Wis 13:13 the good-for-nothing refuse from these *r*,

REMONSTRATE (2)
Mt 16:22 took him aside and began to *r* with him.
Mk 8:32 took him aside and began to *r* with him.

REMONSTRATED (2)
Gn 44: 7 these words to them, they *r* with him:
Jos 9:19 the princes, these all *r* with the people,

REMONSTRATING (1)
Jer 32: 3 king of Judah, had imprisoned him there, *r*:

REMORSE (6)
Nm 14:39 the Israelites, the people felt great *r*.
1Kgs 8:38 has *r* of conscience and offers some prayer
Sir 14: 1 no grief, who is not stung by *r* for sin.
30:10 when finally your teeth are clenched in *r*.
Rom 14:15 brother feels *r* for the food he has eaten,
Eph 4:19 without *r* they have abandoned themselves

REMOTE (4)
Dt 30:11 today is not too mysterious and *r* for you.
Jgs 19: 1 there was a Levite residing in *r* parts of
1Sm 26:13 a *r* hilltop at a great distance from Abner,
1Mc 8: 4 although it was very *r* from their own.

REMOTEST (2)
2Kgs 19:23 I reached the *r* heights,
Is 37:24 I reached the *r* heights,

REMOVAL (2)
Is 27: 9 this the whole fruit of the *r* of his sin:
1Pt 3:21 This baptism is no *r* of physical stain,

REMOVE (51)
Gn 30:32 go through your whole flock today and *r*
48:17 to *r* it from Ephraim's head to Manasseh's,
Ex 3: 5 *R* the sandals from your feet,
8: 4 to *r* the frogs from me and my subjects,
23:25 and I will *r* all sickness from your midst;
33:23 Then I will *r* my hand,
Lv 4: 8 bullock he shall *r* all the fat:
10: 4 *r* your kinsmen from the sanctuary and
23:30 I will *r* him from the midst of his people.
Nm 17: 2 priest, to *r* the censers from the embers;
Dt 7:15 The LORD will *r* all sickness from you;
Jos 5:15 to Joshua, *R* your sandals from your feet,
7:12 I will not remain with you unless you *r*
7:13 stand up to your enemies until you *r* from
1Kgs 2:31 and you will *r* from me and from my family
2Kgs 23: 4 and the doorkeepers to *r* from the temple
2Chr 15: 8 he was encouraged to *r* the detestable
Tb 3:17 to *r* the cataracts from Tobit's eyes,
1Mc 11:63 in Galilee, intending to *r* him from office.
Jb 11:14 If you *r* all iniquity from your conduct,
24: 2 The wicked *r* landmarks;
Ps(s) 119:29 *R* from me the way of falsehood,
Prv 22:28 *R* not the ancient landmark which your
23:10 *R* not the ancient landmark,
25: 4 *R* the dross from silver,
25: 5 *R* the wicked from the presence of the king,
Is 20: 2 waist, and *r* the sandals from your feet.
25: 8 his people he will *r* from the whole earth;
47: 2 the millstone and grind flour, *r* your veil;
57:14 *r* the stumbling blocks from my people's
58: 9 If you *r* from your midst oppression,
Jer 4: 4 *r* the foreskins of your hearts,
Bar 2:35 and I will not again *r* my people Israel
6:33 they can neither set up a king nor *r* him.
Ez 11:18 *r* from it all its detestable abominations.
11:19 I will *r* the stony heart from their bodies,
25: 7 from the peoples, and *r* you from the lands.
Hos 2: 4 Let her *r* her harlotry from before her,
2:19 I *r* from her mouth the names of the Baals,
Jl 2:20 No, the northerner I will *r* far from you,
Zep 3:11 I *r* from your midst the proud braggarts,
3:18 I will *r* disaster from among you,
Mt 7: 5 *R* the plank from your own eye first;
Lk 1:25 he has seen fit to *r* my reproach among men."
6:42 'Brother, let me *r* the speck from your eye,'
6:42 *r* the plank from your own eye first;
6:42 to *r* the speck from your brother's eye.
Jn 19:38 asked Pilate's permission to *r* Jesus' body.
Acts 7:33 *R* the sandals from your feet,
Rom 11:26 who shall *r* all impiety from Jacob;
Rv 2: 5 to you and *r* your lampstand from its place.

REMOVED (66)
Gn 8:13 Noah then *r* the covering of the ark and
30:23 son, and she said, "God has *r* my disgrace."
30:35 That same day Laban *r* the streaked and
48:12 Joseph *r* them from his father's knees and
Ex 8:27 He *r* the flies from Pharaoh and his
34:34 him, he *r* the veil until he came out again.
Lv 1:16 Its crop and feathers shall be *r* and

4:10 as is r from the ox of the peace offering;
4:31 All the fat shall be r,
4:31 as the fat is r from the peace offering,
4:35 r, just as the fat is r from the peace
Nm 18:11 "You shall also have what is r from the
22:31 Then the LORD r the veil from Balaam's
Jos 5: 9 I have r the reproach of Egypt from you."
8:29 then at sunset Joshua ordered the body r
10:27 At sunset they were r from the trees at
1Sm 18:13 Saul r him from his presence by appointing
21: 7 which had been r from the LORD's presence
31:12 r the bodies of Saul and his sons from the
2Sm 1:10 I r the crown from his head and the armlet
7:15 Saul, whom I r from my presence.
8: 8 David r a very large quantity of bronze.
20:12 So he r Amasa from the road to the field
20:13 When he had been r from the road,
1Kgs 20:41 He immediately r the bandage from his eyes,
22:47 He r from the land the rest of the cult
2Kgs 16:17 from the bases and r the lavers from them;
16:18 In deference to the king of Assyria he r
18: 4 It was he who r the high places,
18:22 high places and altars Hezekiah has r,
23: 6 of the LORD he also r the sacred pole,
23:19 Josiah also r all the shrines on the high
2Chr 14: 4 He r the high places and incense stands
17: 6 and again he r the high places and the
19: 3 since you have r the sacred poles from the
20:33 But the high places were not r,
30:14 also they r all the altars of incense and
32:12 Has not this same Hezekiah r his high
33:15 He r the foreign gods and the idol from
34:33 Josiah r every abominable thing from all
35:24 His servants r him from his own chariot,
Ezr 5:14 King Cyrus ordered to be r from the temple
Est 8: 2 The king r his signet ring from Haman,
1Mc 4:58 that the disgrace of the Gentiles was r.
13:41 the yoke of the Gentiles was r from Israel,
Is 6: 7 touched your lips, your wickedness is r,
11:13 pass away, and the rivalry of Judah be r;
14:25 Then his yoke shall be r from them,
22: 8 at the gates, shelter over Judah is r.
36: 7 whose high places and altars Hezekiah r,
Lam 2: 9 he has r and broken her bars.
Bar 1: 8 the Lord that had been r from the temple,
3: 7 when we have r from our hearts all the
Ez 6: 6 and laid waste, your idols broken and r,
11:16 Though I have r them far among the nations
16:50 then, as you have seen, I r them.
24: 6 containing rust, whose rust has not been r.
24:12 even with fire will its great rust be r.
Dn 6:24 At his order Daniel was r from the den,
8:11 host, from whom it r the daily sacrifice,
Zep 3:15 The LORD has r the judgment against you,
Zec 14: 2 of the people shall not be r from the city.
Lk 5:35 come that the groom is r from their midst,
Acts 13:22 r him and raised up David as their king;
2Cor 3:16 he turns to the Lord, the veil will be r."

REMOVES (6)

Lv 11:40 anyone who r its dead body shall wash his
Dt 12:29 r the nations from your way as you advance
19: 1 r the nations whose land he is giving you,
Jb 9: 5 He r the mountains before they know it;
Is 6:12 Until the LORD r men far away,
Mi 7:18 the God who r guilt and pardons sin for

REMOVING (8)

Ex 27: 3 Make pots for r the ashes,
1Kgs 15:12 and r all the idols his father had made.
2Chr 14: 2 r the heathen altars and the high places,
1Mc 13:48 After r from it everything that was impure,
Jb 34:20 r the powerful without lifting a hand;
Is 1:25 dross in the furnace, r all your alloy.
Ez 17:13 under oath, while r the nobles of the land,
Jl 4: 6 Greeks, r them far from their own country!

RENAMED (3)

Jos 19:47 r the settlement after their ancestor Dan.
Jgs 1:17 the city to destruction, they r it Hormah.
2Kgs 14: 7 He r it Joktheel,

REND (9)

Lv 21:10 shall not bare his head or r his garments,
2Sm 3:31 people who were with him, R your garments,
Ps(s) 50:22 I r you and there be no one to rescue you.
Eccl 3: 7 A time to r, and a time to sew;
Is 63:19 Oh, that you would r the heavens
Jer 36:24 or cause them to r their garments.
Hos 5:14 It is I who r the prey and depart,
13: 8 as though a wild beast were to r them.
Jl 2:13 R your hearts, not your garments,

RENDER (27)

Gn 17: 6 I will r you exceedingly fertile;
Ex 18:22 Let these men r decisions for the people
34:15 when they r their wanton worship to their
34:16 r their wanton worship to their gods,
Lv 16:19 Thus he shall r it clean and holy,
17: 7 whom they used to r their wanton worship.
Nm 30:14 allow to remain valid or r null and void.
2Sm 15: 4 might come to me and I would r him justice."
1Kgs 8:39 r to each one of them according to his
2Chr 6:30 r to everyone according to his conduct,
Jdt 7:15 Thus you will r them dire punishment for
Est E: 8 so as to r the kingdom undisturbed and
Ps(s) 62:13 you r to everyone according to his deeds.
82: 3 r justice to the afflicted and the
94: 2 r their deserts to the proud.
Wis 9: 3 and to r judgment in integrity of heart:
Hos 14: 3 that we may r as offerings the bullocks
Mi 3:11 Her leaders r judgment for a bribe,
Zec 7: 9 R true judgment,
Mk 7:19 Thus did he r all foods clean.
7:23 evils come from within and r a man impure."
Eph 6: 6 Do not r service for appearance only and
Phil 2:30 render me those services you could not r.
1Thes 5:18 never cease praying, r constant thanks;
Heb 4:13 eyes of him to whom we must r an account.
13:17 over you as men who must r an account.

RENDERED (7)

Gn 30:26 very well the service that I have r you."
Ex 18:26 They r decisions for the people in all
Est F: 9 people and r justice to his inheritance.
2Mc 4:38 the Lord r him the punishment he deserved.
Hb 1: 4 law is benumbed, and judgment is never r:
Jn 1:42 name shall be Cephas (which is r Peter)."
1Cor 1:17 cross of Christ be r void of its meaning!

RENDERING (4)

Lv 19:15 shall not act dishonestly in r judgment.
Nm 35:29 wherever you live, for r judgment.
Dt 1:17 In r judgment,
31:16 this people will take to r wanton worship

RENDERS (4)

Ps(s) 140:13 that the LORD r justice to the afflicted,
Wis 8: 6 And if prudence r service,
Zep 3: 5 after morning he r judgment unfailingly,
Jn 5:32 testimony he r me I know can be verified.

RENDING (2)

1Kgs 19:11 A strong and heavy wind was r the
Is 15: 5 On the way to Horonaim they utter r cries.

RENEGADES (1)

1Mc 3:15 And again a large company of r advanced

RENEW (17)

1Mc 12: 1 and r his friendship with the Romans.
12: 3 have sent us to r the earlier friendship
12:16 to r our former friendship and alliance
14:18 inscribed tablets of bronze to r with him
14:22 come to us to r their friendship with us,
15:17 to r their earlier alliance of friendship.
Jb 10:17 You r your attack upon me and
Ps(s) 51:12 O God, and a steadfast spirit r within me.
71:21 R your benefits toward me,
104:30 created, and you r the face of the earth.
Sir 30:23 Distract yourself, r your courage,
Is 40:31 hope in the LORD will r their strength,
55: 3 I will r with you the everlasting covenant,
58:11 He will r your strength,
Dn 11:18 so that he cannot r it against him.
Zep 3:17 you with gladness, and r you in his love,
Phil 2:28 so that you may r your joy on seeing him,

RENEWAL (4)

1Mc 12:10 for the r of brotherhood and friendship,
12:17 our letter about the r of our brotherhood.
Rom 12: 2 but be transformed by the r of your mind,
Ti 3: 5 of new birth and r by the Holy Spirit.

RENEWED (10)

1Sm 20:17 love for David, Jonathan r his oath to him,
30: 6 But with r trust in the LORD his God,
Jb 29:20 within me, and my bow is r in my hand!"
Ps(s) 103: 5 your youth is r like the eagle's.
Sir 43:32 Extol him with r strength,
44:17 r the race in the time of devastation.
44:22 he r the same promise because of Abraham,
Lam 3:23 They are r each morning,
Acts 15:41 giving the churches there r assurance.
2Cor 4:16 because our inner being is r each day even

RENEWS (2)

Wis 7:27 and r everything while herself perduring;
Sir 43: 8 As its name says, each month it r itself;

RENOUNCE (4)

1Mc 10:30 share, I r the right from this day forward:
Jb 27: 5 till I die I will not r my innocence.
Lk 14:33 if he does not r all his possessions.
Acts 21:21 of their children, and to r their customs.

RENOUNCED (2)

Ps(s) 89:40 You have r the covenant with your servant,
Mt 19:12 freely r sex for the sake of God's reign.

RENOUNCING (1)

2Kgs 13: 2 r the sin he had caused Israel to commit.

RENOVATED (1)

Sir 50: 1 In whose time the house of God was r,

RENOWN (22)

Gn 6: 4 They were the heroes of old, the men of r.
Ex 15:11 O terrible in r, worker of wonders,
Dt 26:19 raise you high in praise and r and glory
32: 3 For I will sing the LORD's r.
1Chr 17:24 promised, that your r as LORD of hosts,
1Mc 12:12 We likewise rejoice in your r.
Ps(s) 111: 4 He has won r for his wondrous deeds;
Wis 8:18 and fair r in sharing her discourses,
Sir 39:11 and when he dies his r will not cease.
44: 2 kingly fashion, men of r for their might,
Is 48: 9 the sake of my r I hold it back from you,
52: 6 on that day my people shall know my r,
55:13 the myrtle, This shall be to the LORD's r,
63:12 them, winning for himself eternal r;
Jer 13:11 to be my people, my r,
32:20 all other men, until now you have gained r.
Ez 16:15 you used your r to make yourself a harlot,
39:13 the land shall bury them and gain r for it,
Hb 3: 2 O LORD, I have heard your r,
Zep 3:19 give them praise and r in all the earth,
3:20 For I will give you r and praise,
Lk 4:37 His r kept spreading through the

RENOWNED (16)

2Sm 7:23 yourself r by doing this magnificent deed,
1Kgs 3: 4 because that was the most r high place.
1Chr 12:31 warriors, men r in their ancestral houses.
22: 5 it will be r and glorious in all countries.
2Chr 1: 1 was with him, constantly making him more r.
Jdt 11:23 and shall be r throughout the earth."
16:21 of her life she was r throughout the land.
1Mc 3: 9 Israel and was r to the ends of the earth;
5:63 r in all Israel and among all the Gentiles,
11:51 and they became r throughout his kingdom.
Ps(s) 48: 4 r is he as a stronghold.
76: 2 God is r in Judah,
Sir 45:12 Majestic, glorious, r for splendor,
Is 61: 9 descendants shall be r among the nations,
Bar 3:26 In it were born the giants, r at the first,
Ez 16:14 were r among the nations for your beauty,

RENT (15)

Gn 37:34 Then Jacob r his clothes,
Lv 13:45 keep his garments r and his head bare,
Jos 7: 6 r his garments and lay prostrate before
Jgs 11:35 he saw her, he r his garments and said,
2Sm 1:11 David seized his garments and r them,
13:31 The king stood up, r his garments,
13:31 standing by him also r their garments.
15:32 with r garments and dirt upon his head.
Jdt 14:16 groaning, and howling, and r his garments.
14:19 they r their tunics and were seized with
1Mc 13:45 up on the wall, with their garments r,
Jb 26: 8 yet the cloud is not r by their weight;
Hos 6: 1 to the LORD, For it is he who has r,
Na 1: 6 and the rocks are r asunder before him.
Mk 1:10 he saw the sky r in two and the Spirit

RENTED (1)

Acts 28:30 years Paul stayed on in his r lodgings,

REOPENED (2)

Gn 26:18 (Isaac r the wells which his father's
Neh 13:19 them to be r till after the sabbath.

REPAID (17)

Dt 32: 6 Is the LORD to be thus r by you,
Jgs 1: 7 As I have done, so has God r me."
1Sm 25:21 He has r good with evil.
Ezr 6: 8 let these men be r for their expenses,
1Mc 16:17 vicious act of treason he r good with evil.
Ps(s) 7: 5 my hands, If I have r my friend with evil,
35:12 They have r me evil for good,
109: 5 r me evil for good and hatred for my love.
Is 3:11 with the work of his hands he will be r.
Jer 18:20 Must good be r with evil that they should
Mt 6: 2 be sure of this much, they are already r.
6: 5 I give you my word, they are already r.
6:16 I assure you, they are already r.
Lk 6:34 lend to sinners, expecting to be r in full.
14:14 will be r in the resurrection of the just."
Eph 6: 8 be r by the Lord for whatever good he does.
Col 3:25 will be r for the wrong he has done.

REPAIR (26)

1Kgs 9:25 and he kept the temple in r.
2Kgs 12: 8 "Why do you not r the temple?"
12:13 that were necessary to r the temple.
2Chr 24: 5 may r the house of your God over the years.
24:12 and also iron- and bronze-smiths to r it.

REPAIR (cont.)

Neh 3: 4 son of Hakkoz, carried out the work of r;
3: 5 the Tekoites carried out the work of r;
3: 8 the work of r was carried out by Uzziel,
3: 9 the work of r was carried out by Rephaiah,
3:10 of Hashabneiah, carried out the work of r.
3:12 the work of r was carried out by Shallum,
3:16 the work of r was carried out by Nehemiah,
3:17 him, the Levites carried out the work of r:
3:18 their brethren carried out the work of r:
3:22 work of r was carried out by the priests,
3:23 carried out the r in front of their houses;
3:25 carried out the work of r opposite the
3:25 carried out the work of r to a point
3:28 Gate the priests carried out the work of r,
3:29 Immer, carried out the r before his house,
3:29 him the r was carried out by Shemaiah,
3:31 carried out the work of r as far as the
3:32 the merchants carried out the work of r.
Ps(s) 60: 4 r the cracks in it,
Jer 6:14 They would r, as though it were nought,
8:11 They would r, as though it were nought,

REPAIRED (23)

1Kgs 18:30 he r the altar of the LORD which had been
2Kgs 12:15 with them they r the temple of the LORD.
2Chr 29: 3 the doors of the LORD's house and r them.
Neh 3: 6 The New City Gate was r by Joiada,
3:10 of Harumaph, who r opposite his own house.
3:11 far as the Oven Tower, was r by Malchijah,
3:13 r by Hanun and the inhabitants of Zanoah;
3:13 They also r a thousand cubits of the wall
3:14 The Dung Gate was r by Malchijah,
3:15 The Spring Gate was r by Shallum,
3:15 He also r the wall of the Aqueduct Pool
3:19 of Mizpah, who r the adjoining sector,
3:20 r the adjoining sector from the Corner to
3:21 r the adjoining sector from the entrance
3:24 r the adjoining sector from the house of
3:27 the Tekoites r the adjoining sector
3:30 son of Zalaph, r the adjoining sector;
3:30 son of Berechiah, r the adjoining sector;
3:30 r the place opposite his own lodging.
1Mc 4:48 They also r the sanctuary and the interior
4:57 they r the gates and the priests' chambers
12:37 The quarter called Chaphenatha was also r.
Jer 19:11 smashes a clay pot so that it cannot be r.

REPAIRER (1)

Is 58:12 R of the breach,"

REPAIRING (2)

2Kgs 12:13 wood and hewn stone used in r the breaches,
2Chr 34:10 house who were restoring and r the temple.

REPAIRS (7)

2Kgs 12: 6 r on the temple may prove necessary."
12: 7 had not made needed r on the temple.
12: 8 but you shall turn them over for the r."
12: 9 the people nor make the r on the temple.
22: 5 and lumbermen making r on the temple,
22: 6 of wood and hewn stone for the temple r.
Neh 3:23 Annaniah, made the r alongside his house.

REPAST (1)

Hb 1:16 portion is generous, and his r sumptuous.

REPAY (46)

Gn 44: 4 say to them, 'Why did you r good with evil?
Ex 2: 9 and nurse it for me, and I will r you."
Dt 32:41 r my foes and requite those who hate me.
Jgs 9:24 This was to r the violence done to the
1Sm 2:20 "May the LORD r you with children from
2Kgs 9:26 r you for it in that very plot of ground,
Jb 21:31 and for what he has done who will r him?
Ps(s) 28: 4 R them for their deeds,
28: 4 For the work of their hands r them;
37:21 The wicked man borrows and does not r;
38:21 Those who r evil for good harass me for
41:11 on me, and raise me up, that I may r them."
79:12 And r our neighbors sevenfold into their
137: 8 who shall r you the evil you have done us!
Prv 19:17 LORD, and he will r him for his good deed.
20:22 Say not, "I will r evil!"
24:12 he will r each one according to his deeds.
24:29 I will r the man according to his deeds."
Sir 11:26 of death to r man according to his deeds.
17:18 Later he will rise up and r them,
30: 6 and the one to r his friends with kindness.
Is 1:24 on my foes and fully r my enemies!
Jer 16:18 I will at once r them double for their
25:14 and thus I will r them according to their
32:18 and you r the fathers' guilt,
50:29 R her for her deeds;
51:24 Thus will I r Babylon,
51:56 is a God who requites, he will surely r.
Hos 4: 9 for their ways, and r them for their deeds.
12: 3 his conduct, for his deeds he shall r him.
12:15 upon him and r him for his outrage.
Jl 2:25 And I will r you for the years which the
Mt 6: 4 your Father who sees in secret will r you.
6: 6 who sees what no man sees, will r you.
6:18 Father who sees what is hidden will r you.
16:27 will r each man according to his conduct.
Lk 7:42 Since neither was able to r,
10:35 expense I will r you on my way back.'
14:12 might invite you in return and thus r you.
14:14 should be pleased that they cannot r you,
Rom 2: 6 he will r every man for what he has done:
12:17 Never r injury with injury.
12:19 I will r,'
2Tm 4:14 the Lord will r him according to his deeds.
Heb 10:30 "Vengeance is mine; I will r,"
Rv 18: 7 sensuality, r her in torment and grief!

REPAYING (2)

2Chr 20:11 See how they are now r us by coming to
Is 66: 6 of the LORD r his enemies their deserts!

REPAYMENT (2)

Lk 6:34 you lend to those from whom you expect r,
6:35 lend without expecting r.

REPAYS (4)

Dt 7:10 but who r with destruction the person who
Sir 35:10 For the Lord is one who always r,
35:22 and r men according to their thoughts;
Is 59:18 He r his enemies their deserts,

REPEAT (18)

Ex 6:29 R to Pharaoh, king of Egypt,
23: 1 "You shall not r a false report.
Nm 23:12 puts in my mouth that I must r with care?"
24:13 Whatever the LORD says I must r.
Sir 7: 8 Do not plot to r a sin;
7:14 and r not the words of your prayer.
19: 6 Never r gossip,
Jer 31:23 cities, they shall again r this greeting:
Ez 18: 3 you who will r this proverb in Israel.
45:20 You shall r this on the first day of the
Mt 19:24 I r what I said: it is easier for a camel
24:37 of Man will r what happened in Noah's time.
2Cor 5: 8 I r, we are full of confidence
11:16 I r: let no one think me foolish.
13: 2 and I r it now in my absence
Gal 1: 9 I r what I have just said:
Eph 2: 8 I r, it is owing to his favor that salvation
1Tm 1: 3 Holding to Sound DoctrineI r the

REPEATED (16)

Gn 44: 6 overtook them and r these words to them,
Ex 19:24 The LORD r, "Go down now!
Nm 14:39 Moses r these words to all the Israelites,
Jgs 9: 3 kin r these words to them on his behalf,
15: 8 with r blows, he inflicted a great slaughter
1Sm 8:21 the people had to say, he r it to the LORD,
11: 5 of the inhabitants of Jabesh was r to him.
17:27 They r the same words to him and said,
19: 7 David and r the whole conversation to him.
1Kgs 13:11 When they r to their father the words he
Prv 7:21 She wins him over by her r urging,
Is 30:28 and with r winnowings will he battle
Jer 17:18 misfortune, crush them with r destruction.
Dn 4: 5 I r the dream to him:
Mk 10:24 So Jesus r what he had said:
Jn 18: 7 "Jesus the Nazorean," they r.

REPEATEDLY (6)

1Sm 2:22 he heard r how his sons were treating all
Jb 10:16 r you show your wondrous power against me,
Sir 12:18 nod his head and clap his hands and hiss r,
Jer 6: 9 hand, like a vintager, r over the tendrils.
46:16 he stumbled r, and fell.
Jn 19: 3 R they came up to him and said,

REPEATING (2)

2Mc 10:34 kept r outrageous blasphemies and uttering
Sir 41:23 Of r what you hear,

REPEATS (2)

Prv 26:11 to his vomit, so the fool r his folly.
Sir 19: 5 and he who r an evil report has no sense.

REPEL (1)

Ps(s) 27: 9 do not in anger r your servant.

REPELLED (2)

Tb 8: 3 The demon, r by the odor of the fish,
Is 59:14 Right is r, and justice stands far off;

REPELLING (1)

Am 5:12 accepting bribes, r the needy at the gate!

REPENT (36)

1Sm 15:29 for he is not man that he should r."
1Kgs 8:35 them, and if then they r of their sin,
8:47 may they r in the land of their captivity
2Chr 6:37 when they r in the land where they are
Jb 42: 6 what I have said, and r in dust and ashes.
Ps(s) 110: 4 The LORD has sworn, and he will not r:
Wis 11:23 overlook the sins of men that they may r.
Sir 48:15 Despite all this the people did not r,
Jer 4:28 I have spoken, I will not r,
9: 4 to lying, and are perverse, and cannot r.
15:19 If you r, so that I restore you,
18: 8 r of the evil which I threatened to do.
18:10 I r of the good with which I promised to
26: 3 so that I may r of the evil I have planned
26:13 r of the evil with which he threatens you.
Ez 24:14 I will not have pity nor r.
Hos 11: 6 Because they refused to r,
Mt 21:32 saw that, you did not r and believe in him."
Mk 4:12 lest perhaps they r and be forgiven."
Lk 15: 7 righteous people who have no need to r.
16:30 to them from the dead, then they would r.'
Acts 28:27 ears, understand with their minds, And r;
Rom 2: 4 kindness is an invitation to you to r?
2Tm 2:25 will enable them to r and know the truth.
Heb 6: 6 it is impossible to make them r again,
7:21 "The Lord has sworn, and he will not r:
Rv 2: 5 R, and return to your former deeds.
2: 5 If you do not r I will come to you and
2:16 Therefore r! If you do not,
2:21 I have given her a chance to r but she
2:22 unless they r of their sins with her,
3: 3 keep to it, and r.
3:19 Be earnest about it, therefore. R!
9:20 did not r of the idols they had made.
9:21 they r of their murders or their sorcery,
16: 9 but they did not r or give him due honor.

REPENTANCE (16)

Wis 12:10 them bit by bit, you gave them space for r,
12:19 that you would permit r for their sins.
Sir 18:20 when you have sinned, show r.
Jer 31:19 I turn in r; I have come to myself,
Mk 1: 4 of r which led to the forgiveness of sins.
6:12 they went off, preaching the need of r.
Lk 3: 3 of r which led to the forgiveness of sins,
Acts 5:31 bring r to Israel and forgiveness of sins.
11:18 granted life-giving r even to the Gentiles."
13:24 a baptism of r to all the people of Israel.
19: 4 "John's baptism was a baptism of r.
20:21 I insisted solemnly on r before God
2Cor 7: 9 but because your sadness led to r.
7:10 God's sake produces a r without regrets,
Heb 6: 1 r from dead works,
2Pt 3: 9 wants none to perish but all to come to r.

REPENTANT (4)

Sir 8: 5 Shame not a r sinner;
Is 1:27 by judgment, and her r ones by justice.
Lk 15: 7 more joy in heaven over one r sinner
15:10 before the angels of God over one r sinner."

REPENTED (7)

Jer 26:19 so that he r of the evil with which he had
34:15 Today you indeed r and did what is right
Am 7: 3 And the LORD r of this.
7: 6 The LORD r of this.
Jon 3:10 he r of the evil that he had threatened to
Zec 1: 6 Then they r and admitted:
2Cor 12:21 earlier and have not r of the uncleanness,

REPENTS (4)

1Sm 15:29 Glory of Israel neither retracts nor r,
Sir 21: 6 but he who fears the LORD r in his heart.
Jer 8: 6 No one r of his wickedness,
Lk 17: 3 if he r,

REPEOPLE (2)

Ez 36:11 I will r you as in the past,
36:33 from all your crimes, I will r the cities,

REPEOPLED (3)

Ez 36:10 cities shall be r,
36:35 and destroyed are now r and fortified."
38:12 that were r and against a people gathered

REPHAEL (1)

1Chr 26: 7 The sons of Shemaiah were Othni, R,

REPHAH (1)

1Chr 7:25 Zabad's son was R,

REPHAIAH (5)

1Chr 3:21 of Hananiah were Pelatiah, Jeshaiah, R,
4:42 the leadership of Pelatiah, Neariah, R,
7: 2 The sons of Tola were Uzzi, R,
9:43 the father of Binea, whose son was R,
Neh 3: 9 the work of repair was carried out by R,

REPHAIM (21)

Gn 14: 5 and defeated the R in Ashteroth-karnaim,
15:20 the Hittites, the Perizzites, the R,

Dt 2:11 like them they were considered R.
2:20 of the R from its former inhabitants,
3:11 was the last remaining survivor of the R.
3:13 of Bashan was once called a land of the R.
Jos 12: 4 Og, king of Bashan, a survivor of the R,
13:12 in Bashan of Og, a survivor of the R,
15: 8 at the northern end of the Valley of R,
17:15 there in the land of the Perizzites and R,
18:16 mountain on the north of the Valley of R,
2Sm 5:18 came and overran the valley of R.
5:22 came up again and overran the valley of R.
21:16 Dadu, one of the R,
21:18 from Husha, killed Saph, one of the R.
21:20 He too was one of the R.
21:22 These four were R in Gath,
23:13 clan was encamped in the Vale of R.
1Chr 11:15 were encamped in the valley of R.
14: 9 had come and raided the valley of R.
Is 17: 5 one gleans the ears in the Valley of R.

REPHAN (1)

Acts 7:43 tent of Moloch and the star of the god R,

REPHIDIM (5)

Ex 17: 1 as the LORD directed, and encamped at R.
17: 8 At R, Amalek came and waged war
19: 2 the journey from R to the desert of Sinai,
Nm 33:14 Setting out from Alush, they camped at R,
33:15 from R, they camped in the desert

REPLACE (5)

1Kgs 14:27 To r them, King Rehoboam had bronze
2Chr 12:10 (To r them, King Rehoboam made bronze
Neh 13: 9 r there the utensils of the house of God,
Is 9: 9 are felled, but we will r them with cedars."
Ez 11:19 bodies, and r it with a natural heart,

REPLACED (6)

Gn 42:25 grain, their money r in each one's sack,
Dt 12:29 have r them and are settled in their land,
1Sm 5: 3 So they picked Dagon up and r him.
21: 7 r by fresh bread when it was taken away.
Ezr 3: 3 they r the altar on its foundations and
Dn 8:12 the host, while sin r the daily sacrifice.

REPLACING (1)

Acts 1:25 for this apostolic ministry, r Judas,

REPLANT (1)

Jer 32:41 I will r them firmly in this land,

REPLANTED (1)

Ez 36:36 what was destroyed and r what was desolate.

REPLASTERED (1)

Lv 14:43 out and the house has been scraped and r,

REPLENISH (1)

Jer 31:25 every soul that languishes I will r.

REPLETE (1)

Ps(s) 104:13 earth is r with the fruit of your works.

REPORT (73)

Ex 23: 1 "You shall not repeat a false r.
Lv 14:35 the house shall come and r to the priest,
Nm 13:26 of Paran at Kadesh, made a r to them all,
14:37 men who had given out the bad r
22:14 of Moab went back to Balak with the r,
Dt 1:22 to reconnoiter the land for us and r to us
Jos 2: 2 But a r was brought to the king of Jericho
14: 7 I brought back to him a conscientious r.
22:11 heard the r that the Reubenites,
22:33 The r satisfied the Israelites,
Jgs 18: 8 Zorah and Eshtaol and were asked for a r,
1Sm 2:24 It is not a good r that I hear the people
11: 6 As he listened to this r,
23:10 a r that Saul plans to come to Keilah,
2Sm 2: 4 A r reached David that the men of
3:19 and then went to make his own r to David
11:18 David a r of all the details of the battle,
13:30 a r reached David that Absalom had killed
13:33 in the r that all the princes are dead.
15:13 An informant came to David with the r,
15:35 r it to the priests Zadok and Abiathar,
17:17 in turn were to go and r to King David.
18:25 "If he is alone, he has good news to r."
1Kgs 10: 6 "The r I heard in my country about your
10: 7 r until I came and saw with my own eyes,
10: 7 and prosperity surpass the r I heard.
2Kgs 9:15 one escapes from the city to r in Jezreel."
17:26 A r reached the king of Assyria:
19: 7 a spirit that, when he hears a certain r,
19: 9 king of Assyria heard a r that Tirhakah,
1Chr 21: 2 and r back to me that I may know their
2Chr 9: 6 r until I came and saw with my own eyes.
34:16 same time that he was making his r to him.
Ezr 5: 5 until a r could go to Darius and then a
5: 7 him a r in which was written the following:
5:10 to r them to you in a list of the men who
9: 1 the leaders approached me with this r:
Neh 1: 4 When I heard this r, I began to weep
6: 8 "Nothing of what you r has taken place;
Jdt 10:13 your forces, to give him a trustworthy r;
10:16 give him the r you speak of,
15: 4 country of Israel to r what had happened,
Est 7: 9 who gave the r that benefited the king."
9: 4 and the r was spreading through all the
Ps(s) 112: 7 An evil r he shall not fear;
Prv 22:21 give a dependable r to one who sends you?
Sir 19: 5 and he who repeats an evil r has no sense.
Is 37: 7 a spirit that, when he hears a certain r,
37: 9 king of Assyria heard a r that Tirhakah,
Jer 6:24 We hear the r of them;
21: 3 This is what you shall r to Zedekiah:
37: 5 this r they marched away from the city.
49:14 I have heard a r from the LORD.
Ez 9:11 the writing case at his waist made his r:
21:12 Because of a r; when it comes every heart
Dn 7:28 The r concluded: I, Daniel, was greatly
Jl 4: 9 Let all the soldiers r and march!
Mt 2: 8 r it to me so that I may go and offer him
11: 4 back and r to John what you hear and see:
18:31 to their master to r the whole incident.
Mk 5:36 Jesus disregarded the r that had been
Lk 2:18 at the r given them by the shepherds.
7:17 This was the r that spread about him
7:22 and r to John what you have seen and heard.
Jn 11:57 anyone who knew where he was should r it,
21:23 This is how the r spread among the
Acts 5:23 find them, and hurried back with the r,
5:24 On hearing this r,
12:17 R this to James and the brothers,"
21:31 when a r reached the commander
23:17 he has something to r to him."
23:19 to ask privately, "What do you have to r?"
28:21 with a r or rumor to your discredit.

REPORTED (70)

Gn 44:24 father, we r to him the words of my lord.
Ex 14: 5 When it was r to the king of Egypt that
16:22 of the community came and r this to Moses,
19: 9 r to the LORD the response of the people,
Dt 1:25 land, they brought it down to us and r,
Jos 2:23 of Nun, and r all that had befallen them.
22:32 land of Canaan, and r the matter to them.
Jgs 4:12 It was r to Sisera that Barak,
9: 7 When this was r to him,
9:25 But it was r to Abimelech.
9:42 taking the field, it was r to Abimelech,
9:47 It was r to Abimelech that all the
1Sm 11: 9 and r this to the inhabitants of Jabesh,
17:31 had spoken were overheard and r to Saul,
18:20 Michal loved David, and it was r to Saul,
18:24 r to him the nature of David's answer,
18:26 When the servants r this offer to David,
25:12 return r to him all that had been said.
2Sm 6:12 When it was r to King David that the LORD
7:17 Nathan r all these words and this entire
13:34 He came in and r this,
14:30 garments and r to him what had been done.
14:33 Joab went to the king and r this.
18:10 Someone saw this and r to Joab that he had
24: 9 Joab then r to the king the number of
1Kgs 1:51 It was r to Solomon that Adonijah,
2:30 Benaiah r to the king,
18:43 his servant, who went up and looked, but r,
18:44 And the seventh time the youth r,
20: 9 The couriers left and r this.
2Kgs 7:11 this and it was r within the palace.
9:17 Jezreel saw the troop of Jehu coming and r,
9:18 The watchman r to the king,
9:20 watchman r, "The messenger has reached
18:37 and r to him what the commander had said.
22: 9 the scribe Shaphan went to the king and r,
22:20 This they r to the king.
1Chr 19:17 When this was r to David,
21: 5 Joab r the result of the census to David:
2Chr 34:15 He r this to Shaphan the scribe,
Neh 6: 1 When it had been r to Sanballat,
6: 6 "Among the nations it has been r—
Jdt 5: 1 It was r to Holofernes,
Est 1:17 disdain upon their husbands when it is r,
4:12 When Esther's words were r to Mordecai,
6: 2 in which Mordecai r Bagathan and Teresh,
9:11 the stronghold of Susa was r to the king,
1Mc 2:31 It was r to the officers and soldiers of
5:38 men to spy on the camp, and they r to him:
12:26 r that the enemy had made ready to attack
2Mc 3: 6 and r to him that the treasury in
3: 7 about the riches that had been r to him.
5:11 When these happenings were r to the king,
Is 36:22 and r to him what the commander had said.
Jer 4:20 Ruin after ruin is r;
36:13 To them Micaiah r all that he had heard
Mt 28:11 r to the chief priests all that had happened.
Mk 6:30 The apostles returned to Jesus and r to
16:20 They promptly r to Peter and his
Lk 14:21 servant returning r all this to his master.
14:22 The servant r, after some time,
16: 1 was r to him for dissipating his property.
23: 4 r to the chief priests and the crowds,
Jn 11:46 to the Pharisees and r what Jesus had done.
20:18 Then she r what he had said to her.
Acts 10:37 r all over Judea about Jesus of Nazareth,
15: 4 r all that God had helped them accomplish.
16:38 The officers r this to the magistrates,
1Cor 5: 1 It is actually r that there is lewd
2Cor 7: 7 received from you, for he r your longing,

REPORTING (7)

Dt 1:28 by r that the people are stronger and taller
1Sm 26: 1 Men from Ziph came to Saul in Gibeah r
2Sm 1: 5 David said to the youth who was r to him,
Lk 17:21 a matter of r that it is 'here' or 'there.'
1Thes 1: 9 r what kind of reception we had from you,
3: 6 you r the good news of your faith and love,
Rv 1: 2 who in r all he saw bears witness to the

REPORTS (9)

Gn 37: 2 and he brought his father bad r about them.
Nm 13:32 So they spread discouraging r among the
14:15 who have heard such r of you will say,
14:36 by spreading discouraging r about the land;
Jos 2:11 At these r, we are disheartened;
9: 9 For we have heard r of all that he did in
Tb 10:12 me hear good r about you as long as I live."
Lk 9: 9 is this man about whom I hear all these r?"
23: 8 From the r about him he had wanted for a

REPOSE (8)

Dt 28:65 Among these nations you will find no r,
1Chr 28: 2 It was my purpose to build a house of r
Ps(s) 23: 2 In verdant pastures he gives me r;
Wis 8:16 my dwelling, I should take my r beside her;
Sir 31: 2 more than a serious illness it disturbs r.
Is 28:12 Here is r—
34:14 There shall the lilith r,
Lam 2:18 be no respite for you, no r for your eyes.

REPOSSESSED (1)

Jdt 5:19 they were scattered, and have r Jerusalem,

REPREHENSIBLE (1)

Jas 4:16 All such boasting is r.

REPRESENT (3)

Dt 4:16 by fashioning an idol to r any figure,
Ezr 10:14 Let our leaders r the whole assembly;
Rv 17:12 r ten kings who have not yet been crowned;

REPRESENTATION (1)

Heb 1: 3 glory, the exact r of the Father's being,

REPRESENTATIVE (5)

Ex 18:19 Act as the people's r before God,
2Kgs 25: 8 Jerusalem as the r of the king of Babylon.
Eccl 5: 5 make you guilty, and say not before his r,
Jer 52:12 Jerusalem as the r of the king of Babylon.
Heb 5: 1 from among men and made their r before God,

REPRESENTATIVES (5)

2Mc 4:19 as r of the Antiochians of Jerusalem,
11:20 of these matters I have authorized my r,
Acts 15:22 that r be chosen from among their number
15:25 resolved to choose r and send them to you,
15:30 were the r sent on their way to Antioch;

REPRESENTING (2)

Nm 17:23 tent, Aaron's staff, r the house of Levi,
Rom 1:23 the immortal God for images r mortal man,

REPRESENTS (2)

Dn 8:20 saw r the kings of the Medes and Persians.
Col 1: 7 who r us as a faithful minister of Christ.

REPRIMAND (2)

Prv 17:10 A single r does more for a man of
Lk 9:55 He turned toward them only to r them.

REPRIMANDED (4)

Mt 17:18 Then Jesus r him,
Mk 8:33 around and, eyeing the disciples, r Peter:
9:25 r the unclean spirit by saying to him,
1Tm 5:20 commit sin, however, are to be publicly r,

REPRISAL (1)

Gn 34:27 in r for their sister Dinah's defilement.

REPROACH (58)

Gn 45: 5 not r yourselves for having sold me here.
Dt 28:37 r and barbed scorn from all the nations to
Jos 5: 9 I have removed the r of Egypt from you."
1Sm 1: 6 r to her that the LORD had left her barren.
Neh 1: 3 province are in great distress and under r.
Tb 3: 4 a r in all the nations among whom you

REPROACH (cont.)

Jdt 8:22 mockery and a *r* in the eyes of our masters.
1Mc 2:37 They said, "Let us all die without *r*;
Jb 19: 5 against me and cast up to me any *r*,
27: 6 my heart does not *r* me for any of my days.
Ps(s) 15: 3 man, nor takes up a *r* against his neighbor;
31:12 For all my foes I am an object of *r*,
44:14 You made us the *r* of our neighbors,
57: 4 may he make those a *r* who trample upon me;
69:11 with fasting, and this was made a *r* to me.
69:20 You know my *r*,
79: 4 We have become the *r* of our neighbors,
89:42 he is made the *r* of his neighbors.
119:22 Take away from me *r* and contempt,
119:39 Turn away from me the *r* which I dread,
119:42 shall I have an answer for those who *r* me,
Prv 25:10 Lest, hearing it, he *r* you,
Sir 5:17 *r* of his neighbor for the doubletongued.
14: 2 the man whose conscience does not *r* him,
18:14 My son, to your charity add no *r*,
41: 6 and *r* abides with their descendants.
42:11 A byword in the city, a *r* among the people,
Is 25: 8 The *r* of his people he will remove from
30: 5 help nor benefit, but only shame and *r*.
51: 7 Fear not the *r* of men,
54: 4 the *r* of your widowhood no longer remember.
Jer 20: 8 has brought me derision and *r* all the day.
23:40 And I will bring upon you eternal *r*,
24: 9 kingdoms of the earth, a *r* and a byword,
25: 9 of horror, of ridicule, of everlasting *r*.
29:18 and *r* to all the nations among which I
42:18 malediction and horror, a curse and a *r*.
44:12 of malediction, a horror, a curse and a *r*.
Bar 2: 4 a *r* and a horror among all the nations
3: 8 captivity, where you scattered us, a *r*,
Ez 5:14 a *r* among the nations that surround you,
5:15 you shall be a *r* and an object of scorn,
36: 6 you have borne the *r* of the nations.
36: 7 neighboring nations shall bear their own *r*.
36:15 will I permit you to hear the *r* of nations,
36:30 bear among the nations the *r* of famine.
Dn 3:33 revere you, have become a shame and a *r*.
9:16 have become the *r* of all our neighbors.
Jl 2:17 people, and make not your heritage a *r*,
2:19 more will I make you a *r* among the nations.
Mi 6:16 and you shall bear the *r* of the nations.
Mt 11:20 Christ's Witness to JohnHe began to *r* the
Lk 1:25 he has seen fit to remove my *r* among men."
Phil 2:15 children of God beyond *r* in the midst of a
3: 6 *r* when it came to justice based on the law.
Col 1:22 you to God holy, free of *r* and blame.
1Tm 6:14 *r* until our Lord Jesus Christ shall appear.
Heb 11:26 Moses considered the *r* borne by God's

REPROACHED (2)

Gn 21:25 *r* Abimelech about a well that Abimelech's
Ez 16:57 *r* by the Edomites and all your neighbors,

REPROACHES (3)

Wis 2:12 *R* us for transgressions of the law and
Ez 34:29 in the land, or bear the *r* of the nations.
Rom 15: 3 *r* they uttered against you fell on me."

REPROBATE (3)

Jb 36:14 expire in youth, and perish among the *r*.
Ps(s) 15: 4 By whom the *r* is despised,
Sir 41: 5 A *r* line are the children of sinners,

REPROOF (18)

Jb 13: 6 utter and listen to the *r* from my lips.
Prv 1:23 how long will you turn away at my *r*?
1:25 all my counsel, and my *r* you ignored
1:30 ignored my counsel, they spurned all my *r*;
3:11 spurn not his *r*;
5:12 I hate instruction, and my heart spurn *r*!
10:17 but he who disregards *r* goes astray.
12: 1 knowledge, but he who hates *r* is stupid.
13:18 correction, but he who heeds *r* is honored.
15: 5 admonition, but prudent is he who heeds *r*.
15:10 he who hates *r* will die.
15:31 to salutary *r* will abide among the wise.
15:32 but he who heeds *r* gains understanding.
Wis 17: 7 a jeering *r* of their vaunted shrewdness.
18: 5 As a *r* you carried off their multitude of
Sir 20:28 a muzzle over the mouth they silence *r*.
32:17 *r* and distorts the law to suit his purpose.
2Tm 3:16 for *r*,

REPROOFS (1)

Prv 6:23 and a way to life are the *r* of discipline;

REPROVE (8)

Lv 19:17 Though you may have to *r* your fellow man,
1Sm 3:13 were blaspheming God, he did not *r* them.
Ps(s) 6: 2 O LORD, *r* me not in your anger,
141: 5 let him *r* me;
Prv 9: 8 *R* not an arrogant man,
9: 8 *r* a wise man, and he will love you.
30: 6 Add nothing to his words, lest he *r* you,
Rv 3:19 Whoever is dear to me I *r* and chastise.

REPROVED (3)

Gn 37:10 told it to his father, his father *r* him.
2Mc 2: 7 When Jeremiah heard of this, he *r* them:
Prv 15:12 The senseless man loves not to be *r*;

REPROVER (1)

Prv 25:12 fine gold, is a wise *r* to an obedient ear.

REPROVES (7)

Jb 5:17 Happy is the man whom God *r*!
22: 4 Is it because of your piety that he *r* you
Prv 3:12 For whom the LORD loves he *r*,
9: 7 he who *r* a wicked man incurs opprobrium.
10:10 but he who frankly *r* promotes peace.
Am 5:10 They hate him who *r* at the gate and abhor
Heb 12: 5 of the Lord nor lose heart when he *r* you;

REPROVING (2)

Sir 18:12 but the LORD's mercy reaches all flesh, *R*,
2Tm 4: 2 correcting, *r*, appealing—

REPTILE (1)

Jer 46:22 She sounds like a retreating *r*!

REPTILES (10)

Dt 32:24 with the venom of *r* gliding in the dust.
1Kgs 5:13 wall, and he spoke about beasts, birds, *r*,
Jb 12: 8 Or the *r* on earth to instruct you,
Wis 16:10 fangs of poisonous *r* overcame your sons,
17: 9 passing of insects and the hissing of *r*,
Is 16: 1 Send them forth, hugging the earth like *r*,
Ez 38:20 and all the *r* that crawl upon the ground,
Mi 7:17 like the serpent, like *r* on the ground;
Acts 10:12 creatures and *r* and birds of the sky.
11: 6 creatures of the earth, wild beasts and *r*,

REPUDIATE (3)

Jgs 15: 2 "I thought it certain you wished to *r* her;
1Kgs 9: 7 *r* the temple I have consecrated to my honor.
2Cor 4: 2 Rather, we *r* shameful,

REPUDIATED (3)

2Chr 11:14 and his sons *r* them as priests of the LORD.
Is 43:28 against me Till I *r* the holy gates,
49:21 I was bereft and barren [exiled and *r*;

REPUGNANCE (1)

Ps(s) 36: 5 a way that is not good, with no *r* for evil.

REPUGNANT (2)

1Chr 21: 6 for the king's command was *r* to Joab.
Sir 4: 9 let not justice be *r* to you.

REPULSE (3)

2Kgs 18:24 How then can you *r* even one of the least
2Mc 14:17 of the enemy suffered a slight *r*.
Is 36: 9 How then can you *r* even one of the least

REPULSED (2)

Jdt 11:11 so that my lord will not be *r* and fail,
1Mc 14:26 have stood firm and *r* Israel's enemies.

REPULSIVE (2)

Jb 21:16 if the counsel of the wicked is *r* to God,
33:20 So that to his appetite food becomes *r*,

REPUTATION (12)

1Chr 11:20 Thus he had a *r* like that of the Three.
11:24 gave him a *r* like that of the Three.
1Mc 8: 1 Judas had heard of the *r* of the Romans.
Sir 47:20 You brought dishonor upon your *r*,
Ez 22: 5 of your foul *r* and your great perversity.
Mt 4:24 this, his *r* traveled the length of Syria.
14: 1 the tetrarch, having heard of Jesus' *r*,
Mk 1:28 From that point on his *r* spread throughout
6:14 for his *r* had become widespread and people
Lk 4:14 and his *r* spread throughout the region.
5:15 His *r* spread more and more,
Rv 3: 1 I know the *r* you have of being alive,

REPUTE (2)

Prv 25:10 he reproach you, and your ill *r* cease not.
Ez 16:56 *r* by you while you felt proud of yourself,

REPUTED (1)

1Mc 2:52 trial, and it was *r* to him as uprightness?

REQUEST (51)

Gn 16: 2 Abram heeded Sarai's *r*.
50: 4 "and convey to Pharaoh this *r* of mine.
Ex 33:17 The LORD said to Moses, "This *r*,
Jgs 8: 8 to Penuel and made the same *r* of them,
8:24 to say, "I should like to make a *r* of you.
1Sm 1:27 for this child, and the LORD granted my *r*.
8: 7 "Grant the people's every *r*.
8: 9 Now grant their *r*;
8:22 their *r* and appoint a king to rule them."
12: 1 "I have granted your *r* in every respect,"
25:35 I have granted your *r* as a personal favor."
28:21 hands and fulfilled the *r* you made of me.
2Sm 12:20 where at his *r* food was set before him,
14:21 "I hereby grant this *r*.
14:22 the king has granted the *r* of his servant."
1Kgs 3:10 Lord was pleased that Solomon made this *r*.
2Chr 1: 7 Solomon and said to him, "Make a *r* of me,
10: 7 and give in to them, acceding to their *r*,
16: 4 Ben-hadad agreed to King Asa's *r* and sent
Est 5: 3 What is your *r*?
5: 6 and whatever *r* you make shall be honored,
5: 7 "This is my petition and *r*:
5: 8 to grant my petition and honor my *r*,
7: 2 Whatever *r* you make shall be honored,
9:12 ask, and whatever you *r* shall be honored."
1Mc 11:41 Meanwhile Jonathan sent the *r* to King
13:34 *r* that he grant the land a release
Jb 6: 8 Oh, that I might have my *r*,
Sir 32:14 he who seeks him obtains his *r*.
Is 29:11 is handed to one who can read, with the *r*,
29:12 handed to one who cannot read, with the *r*,
Jer 21: 1 Zephaniah, son of Maaseiah, with this *r*:
37: 3 to the prophet Jeremiah with this *r*:
Dn 1:14 He acceded to this *r*,
2:49 At Daniel's *r* the king made Shadrach,
Mt 8: 5 a centurion approached him with this *r*:
13:36 His disciples came to him with the *r*,
14: 9 he gave orders that the *r* be granted.
27:58 and had gone to *r* the body of Jesus.
Mk 1:40 A leper approached him with a *r*,
5:19 Jesus did not grant his *r*,
6:25 back to the king's presence and made her *r*:
6:26 The king bitterly regretted the *r*;
10:35 they said, "we want you to grant our *r*."
Lk 10:35 and gave them to the innkeeper with the *r*:
23:52 approached Pilate with a *r* for Jesus' body.
Jn 12:21 in Galilee, and put this *r* to him:
Acts 8:19 he made them an offer of money with the *r*,
9:38 sent two men to him with the urgent *r*,
16:39 out with the *r* that they leave the city.
2Jn 1: 5 I would make this *r* of you (not as if I

REQUESTED (9)

Dt 18:16 This is exactly what you *r* of the LORD,
Jos 19:50 LORD, they gave him the city which he *r*,
Jgs 8:26 *r* weighed seventeen hundred gold shekels,
1Kgs 3:12 I do as you *r*.
2Kgs 6: 3 accompany your servants," one of them *r*.
Ezr 7: 6 him, the king granted him all that he *r*.
Jdt 10: 9 youths to open the gate for her as she *r*.
2Mc 6: 2 as the inhabitants of the place *r*.
Mk 15:43 Pilate and urgently *r* the body of Jesus.

REQUESTING (3)

1Mc 12: 4 *r* them to provide the envoys with save
2Mc 2:16 *r* you also to please celebrate the feast.
Acts 25: 3 *r* that he favor them rather than Paul,

REQUESTS (6)

Ezr 7:21 of the law of the God of heaven, *r* of you,
Neh 2: 8 The king granted my *r*,
2Mc 11:15 all the written *r* of Maccabeus to Lysias.
Ps(s) 20: 6 The LORD grant all your *r*!
37: 4 LORD, and he will grant you your heart's *r*.
Jer 39:12 befall him, but treat him as he himself *r*."

REQUIRE (4)

2Sm 3:13 But one thing I *r* of you.
Mal 2:15 what does that one *r* but godly offspring?
2Thes 1: 6 even if strict justice would *r* that God
1Tm 4: 3 *r* abstinence from foods which God created

REQUIRED (19)

Lv 27:16 to the amount of seed *r* to sow it,
Nm 8:24 perform the *r* service in the meeting tent.
8:25 from the *r* service and work no longer.
35:30 is *r* for the execution of the murderer.
Dt 17: 6 is *r* for putting a person to death;
1Kgs 5: 8 quota of barley and straw to the *r* place.
8:31 is *r* to take an oath sanctioned by a curse,
2Chr 6:22 is *r* to take an oath of execration against
8:13 as was *r* day by day according to the
8:14 alongside the priests, as the daily duty *r*.
24: 6 "Why have you not *r* the Levites to bring
Ezr 3: 4 in the proper number *r* for each day.
6: 9 Whatever else is *r*—
7:20 Whatever else you may be *r* to supply for
Neh 8:18 assembly on the eighth day, as was *r*.
2Mc 9:16 revenues the expenses *r* for the sacrifices.
Lk 10:42 one thing only is *r*.
12:20 very night your life shall be *r* of you.
12:48 been given a man, much will be *r* of him.

REQUIREMENT (1)

1Cor 4: 2 The first *r* of an administrator is that he

REQUIREMENTS (1)

Ezr 6: 9 the *r* of the priests who are in Jerusalem

REQUIRES (7)

1Kgs 8:59 and of his people Israel as each day *r*,
2Chr 30:19 though he be not clean as holiness *r*."
Jb 27: 8 when he is cut off, when God *r* his life?
Mi 6: 8 what is good, and what the LORD *r* of you:
Eph 6:13 do all that your duty *r*,
1Tm 1: 4 than that training in faith which God *r*.
1Pt 4:19 as God's will *r* continue in good deeds,

REQUIRING (2)

Dt 23:22 LORD, your God, is strict in *r* it of you.
Rom 4: 6 whom God credits justice without *r* deeds:

REQUITAL (5)

Dt 32:35 Against the day of vengeance and *r*,
Ps(s) 91: 8 you behold and see the *r* of the wicked,
Is 34: 8 vengeance, a year of *r* by Zion's defender.
Bar 3: 8 a *r* for all the misdeeds of our fathers,
Zep 2:10 Such shall be the *r* of their pride,

REQUITE (11)

Dt 32:41 will repay my foes and *r* those who hate me.
Jgs 9:56 Thus did God *r* the evil Abimelech had done
2Sm 3:39 May the LORD *r* the evildoer in accordance
Jdt 16:17 the Lord Almighty will *r* them;
Jb 21:19 him *r* the man himself so that he feels it,
Ps(s) 94:23 And he will *r* them for their evildoing,
103:10 nor does he *r* us according to our crimes.
Wis 5:17 and he shall arm creation to *r* the enemy;
Sir 17:18 and *r* each one of them as they deserve.
Lam 3:64 *R* them as they deserve,
Bar 6:33 well or ill by anyone, they cannot *r* it;

REQUITED (6)

1Sm 25:39 who has *r* the insult I received at the
2Sm 16: 8 The LORD has *r* you for all the bloodshed
22:21 to the cleanness of my hands he *r* me.
22:25 And the LORD *r* me according to my justice,
Ps(s) 18:21 to the cleanness of my hands he *r* me;
18:25 And the LORD *r* me according to my justice,

REQUITES (6)

1Kgs 2:44 the LORD *r* you for your own wickedness.
Jb 34:11 Rather, he *r* men for their conduct,
Ps(s) 31:24 but more than *r* those who act proudly Take
Sir 35:22 Till he *r* mankind according to its deeds,
Is 59:18 their deserts, and *r* his foes with wrath.
Jer 51:56 The LORD is a God who *r*,

REQUITING (2)

2Chr 6:23 *r* the wicked man and holding him
Ps(s) 99: 8 you were to them, though *r* their misdeeds.

REROUTED (1)

Ex 13:18 he *r* them toward the Red Sea by way of

RESCRIPT (1)

Ezr 7:11 This is a copy of the *r* which King

RESCUE (85)

Gn 37:22 His purpose was to *r* him from their hands
Ex 3: 8 Therefore I have come down to *r* them from
5:23 yours, and you have done nothing to *r* them."
6: 6 I will *r* you by my outstretched arm and
18: 8 and how the LORD had come to their *r*.
Dt 32:39 heal them, and from my hand there is no *r*.
Jgs 12: 2 you, but you did not *r* me from their power.
12: 3 When I saw that you would not effect a *r*,
1Sm 14:45 were able to *r* Jonathan from death.
17:35 attack it and *r* the prey from its mouth.
23: 2 will defeat the Philistines and *r* Keilah."
30: 8 shall surely overtake them and effect a *r*."
2Sm 22:49 exalt me and from the violent man you *r* me.
2Kgs 16: 7 Come up and *r* me from the clutches of the
18:32 seduce you by saying, The LORD will *r* us.
18:35 the LORD then *r* Jerusalem from my hand?'"
20: 6 I will *r* you and this city from the hand
Jdt 8:33 enemies, the Lord will *r* Israel by my hand.
1Mc 5:12 Come at once and *r* us from them,
5:17 and go, *r* your kinsmen in Galilee;
Ps(s) 6: 5 *r* me because of your kindness,
7: 2 save me from all my pursuers and *r* me,
7: 3 to be torn to pieces, with no one to *r* me.
17:13 *r* me by your sword from the wicked,
22: 9 let him deliver him, let him *r* him,
22:21 *R* my soul from the sword,
25:20 Preserve my life, and *r* me;
31: 2 In your justice *r* me,
31:16 *r* me from the clutches of my enemies and
40:14 Deign, O LORD, to *r* me;
43: 1 from the deceitful and impious man *r* me.
50:15 I will *r* you,
50:22 I rend you and there be no one to *r* you.
59: 2 *R* me from my enemies,
59: 3 *R* me from evildoers;
69:15 *R* me out of the mire; may I not sink!
70: 2 Deign, O God, to *r* me;
71: 2 In your justice *r* me,
71: 4 O my God, *r* me from the hand of the wicked,
71:11 seize him, for there is no one to *r* him."
72:12 he shall *r* the poor man when he cries out,
82: 4 *R* the lowly and the poor;
91: 3 he will *r* you from the snare of the fowler,
106:43 Many times did he *r* them,
109:21 in your generous kindness *r* me;
119:153 Behold my affliction, and *r* me,
119:170 *r* me according to your promise.
142: 7 *R* me from my persecutors,
143: 9 *R* me from my enemies.
144: 7 Deliver me and *r* me from many waters,
144:11 and *r* me from the hands of aliens,
Prv 19:19 even if you *r* him,
24:11 *R* those who are being dragged to death,
Is 5:29 prey, they carry it off and none will *r* it.
30:14 like a potter's jar smashed beyond *r*,
31: 5 To protect and deliver, to spare and *r* it.
38: 6 I will *r* you and this city from the hand
42:22 are taken as booty, with no one to *r* them,
44:17 before it in worship, he implores it, *R* me,
Jer 15:20 For I am with you, to deliver and *r* you,
15:21 and *r* you from the grasp of the violent.
21:12 *r* the oppressed from the hand of the
22: 3 *R* the victim from the hand of his oppressor.
39:17 But on that day I will *r* you,
42:11 you to save you, to *r* you from his power.
Lam 5: 8 there is no one to *r* us from their hands.
Ez 13:21 your veils and *r* my people from your power,
13:23 but I will *r* my people from your power.
34:12 I will *r* them from every place where they
Dn 3:96 there is no other God who can *r* like this."
6:15 he worked till sunset to *r* him.
8: 7 and no one could *r* it from its power.
Hos 13:10 king, that he may *r* you in all your cities?
Zec 8: 7 I will *r* my people from the land of the
Mt 27:43 let God *r* him now if he wants to.
27:49 Let's see whether Elijah comes to his *r*."
Lk 14: 5 not immediately *r* him on the sabbath day?"
Acts 7:34 groaning, and I have come down to *r* them.
12:11 sent his angel to *r* me from Herod's clutches
23:10 *r* Paul from their midst and take him back
Gal 1: 4 sins, to *r* us from the present evil age,
2Tm 4:18 The Lord will continue to *r* me from all
2Pt 2: 9 knows how to *r* devout men from trial,
Jude 1:22 the others you must *r*,
Rv 12:16 The earth then came to the woman's *r* by

RESCUED (48)

Ex 18: 4 he has *r* me from Pharaoh's sword."
18:10 "who has *r* his people from the hands of
Jgs 3: 9 Caleb's younger brother Kenaz, who *r* them.
3:31 He, too, *r* Israel.
6: 9 I *r* you from the power of Egypt and of all
8:22 for you *r* us from the power of Midian."
1Sm 11: 9 while the sun is hot, they will be *r*."
23: 5 them, and thus *r* the inhabitants of Keilah.
30:18 Amalekites had taken, and *r* his two wives.
2Sm 4: 9 LORD lives, who *r* me from all difficulty,
12: 7 I *r* you from the hand of Saul.
19:10 who *r* us from the grip of the Philistines.
22: 1 song to the LORD when the LORD had *r* him
22:18 He *r* me from my mighty enemy,
22:20 and *r* me, because he loves me.
22:44 "You *r* me from the strife of my people;
2Kgs 18:33 Has any of the gods of the nations ever *r*
18:35 these lands ever *r* his land from my hand?
1Mc 6:53 *r* from the Gentiles and brought to Judea.
2Mc 2:18 for he has *r* us from great perils and has
Jb 29:12 For I *r* the poor who cried out for help,
Ps(s) 18:18 He *r* me from my mighty enemy and from my
18:20 He set me free in the open, and *r* me,
18:44 You *r* me from the strife of the people;
18:49 me and from the violent man you have *r* me.
54: 9 Because from all distress you have *r* me,
56:14 For you have *r* me from death,
69:15 may I be *r* from my foes,
81: 8 In distress you called, and I *r* you;
86:13 *r* me from the depths of the nether world.
107: 6 from their straits he *r* them.
107:13 from their straits he *r* them.
107:19 from their straits he *r* them.
107:28 from their straits he *r* them.
124: 7 were *r* like a bird from the fowlers' snare;
Is 36:18 Has any of the gods of the nations ever *r*
36:20 these lands ever *r* his land from my hand?
49:24 or captives be *r* from a tyrant?
49:25 a warrior, and booty be *r* from a tyrant;
Jer 20:13 For he has *r* the life of the poor from the
Dn 8: 4 could withstand it or be *r* from its power;
Jl 3: 5 be *r* who calls on the name of the LORD;
Mi 4:10 Babylon shall you go, there shall you be *r*.
Acts 7:10 him and *r* him from all his tribulations.
23:27 I intervened with my troops and *r* him.
2Cor 1:10 He *r* us from that danger of death and will
Col 1:13 He *r* us from the power of darkness and
Jude 1: 5 The Lord first *r* his people from the land

RESCUER (2)

Jb 5: 4 shall be crushed at the gate without a *r*.
Ps(s) 35:10 The *r* of the afflicted man from those too

RESCUES (4)

1Sm 11: 3 If no one *r* us,
Ps(s) 34:18 and from all their distress he *r* them.
Sir 40:24 but better than either, charity that *r*.
51: 8 refuge in him, and *r* them from every evil.

RESCUING (1)

Ex 18: 9 in *r* them from the hands of the Egyptians.

RESELL (1)

Bar 6:27 *r* their sacrifices for their own advantage.

RESEMBLE (3)

Wis 13:14 a man or makes it *r* some worthless beast.
Lk 13:18 "What does the reign of God *r*?
1Cor 15:49 Just as we *r* the man from earth,

RESEMBLED (7)

Jgs 8:18 "They all *r* you," they replied.
1Kgs 7:26 thick, and its brim *r* that of a cup,
Ez 1:27 Upward from what *r* his waist I saw what
1:27 *r* his waist I saw what looked like fire;
Mt 28: 3 In appearance he *r* a flash of lightning
Rv 4: 7 The first creature *r* a lion,
14: 2 heaven which *r* the roaring of the deep,

RESEMBLES (2)

Ps(s) 49:13 he *r* the beasts that perish.
49:21 not prudence, *r* the beasts that perish.

RESEMBLING (1)

Ez 1: 5 Within it were figures *r* four living

RESEN (1)

Gn 10:12 Rehoboth-Ir, and Calah, as well as *R*,

RESENTED (3)

Gn 4: 5 Cain greatly *r* this and was crestfallen.
2Mc 7:39 since he bitterly *r* the boy's contempt.
Eccl 8: 1 his face, but an impudent look is *r*.

RESENTFUL (3)

Gn 4: 6 "Why are you so *r* and crestfallen?
1Sm 18: 8 Saul was very angry and *r* of the song,
Prv 19: 3 way, but his heart is *r* against the LORD.

RESENTMENT (5)

2Sm 13:21 not, however, spark the *r* of his son Amnon,
2Chr 25:10 Judah, and returned home blazing with *r*.
Sir 30:23 your courage, drive *r* far away from you;
30:23 nor is there aught to be gained from *r*.
Acts 17: 5 This only aroused the *r* of the Jews,

RESERVE (3)

Gn 41:36 This food will serve as a *r* for the
2Chr 35:24 placed him in another he had in *r*,
Lk 12:19 You have blessings in *r* for years to come.

RESERVED (10)

1Sm 9:24 a *r* portion that has been set before you.
Jdt 11:13 sanctified and *r* for the priests who minister
Jb 38:23 hail Which I have *r* for times of stress,
Ez 46:19 *r* to the priests] which face the north.
Mt 20:23 those to whom it has been *r* by my Father."
Mk 10:40 it is for those to whom it has been *r*."
Acts 1: 7 The Father has *r* that to himself.
2Pt 2:17 The darkest gloom has been *r* for them.
3: 7 and earth are *r* by God's word for fire;
Jude 1:13 thick gloom of darkness has been *r* forever.

RESERVOIR (3)

Sir 10:13 For pride is the *r* of sin,
50: 3 In his time the *r* was dug,
Is 22:11 you made a *r* between the two walls for the

RESERVOIRS (4)

Jdt 7:20 All the *r* of water failed the inhabitants
Eccl 2: 6 myself *r* to water a flourishing woodland.
Sir 39:17 he had but to speak and the *r* were made.
48:17 through the rock and he built *r* for water.

RESETTLE (1)

Hos 11:11 And I will *r* them in their homes,

RESETTLED (1)

1Mc 14:34 these cities he *r* with Jews,

RESHEPH (1)

1Chr 7:25 Zabad's son was Rephah, whose son was *R*,

RESIDE (5)

Lv 25:45 who *r* with you and from their children
Ru 1: 1 and two sons to *r* on the plateau of Moab.
Neh 11: 1 to bring one man in ten to *r* in Jerusalem,
Col 1:19 fullness *r* in him and by means of him,
2Pt 3:13 to his promise, the justice of God will *r*.

RESIDED (4)

Gn 21:34 Abraham *r* in the land of the Philistines
Jgs 17: 7 There was a young Levite who had *r* within
2Kgs 22:14 Jerusalem, where the prophetess Huldah *r*.
1Chr 4:43 and have *r* there to the present day.

RESIDENCE (19)

Lv 25:47 has a permanent or a temporary *r* among you,
Jgs 11: 3 and had taken up *r* in the land of Tob.
17: 8 city he set out to find another place of *r*.
17: 9 am on my way to find some other place of *r*."
2Sm 19: 6 Then Joab went to his *r* and said:
1Chr 11: 7 David took up his *r* in the fortress,
17: 1 After David had taken up *r* in his house,
2Chr 11: 5 Rehoboam took up *r* in Jerusalem and built
Ezr 2:70 the common people took up *r* in Jerusalem;
Neh 7:72 and all Israel took up *r* in their cities.
11: 1 of the people took up *r* in Jerusalem,
11: 2 willingly agreed to take up *r* in Jerusalem.
11: 3 of the province who took up *r* in Jerusalem.
1Mc 13:48 its fortifications and built himself a *r*.
13:53 of all his soldiers, with his *r* in Gazara.
Dn 4:27 as a royal *r* for my splendor and majesty?"
Mt 26:58 a distance as far as the high priest's *r*.
27:62 and the Pharisees called at Pilate's *r*.
Acts 7:29 up his *r* as an alien in the land of Midian,

RESIDENT (21)

Gn 23: 4 "Although I am a *r* alien among you,
Ex 12:19 Anyone, be he a *r* alien or a native,
12:49 the same forthe *r* alien as for the native."
Lv 16:29 of you, whether a native or a *r* alien,
17:12 No one among you, not even a *r* alien,
18:26 You, however, whether natives or *r* aliens,
Nm 9:14 the *r* alien as for the native of the land."
15:15 but one rule for you and for the *r* alien,
35:15 all the *r* or transient aliens among them,
Jgs 10: 1 a *r* of Shamir in the mountain region of
2Sm 4: 3 where they have been *r* aliens to this day.
1Kgs 15:18 son of Hezion, king of Aram, *r* in Damascus.
Neh 13:16 Tyrians who were *r* there were importing fish
Jdt 4:10 All their *r* aliens,
Jer 7: 6 if you no longer oppress the *r* alien,
22: 3 Do not wrong or oppress the *r* alien,
Ez 14: 7 any alien *r* in Israel is estranged from me,
22: 7 your midst, they extort from the *r* alien;
22:29 and oppress the *r* alien without justice.
47:22 for the aliens *r* in your midst who have bred
47:23 In whatever tribe the alien may be *r*,
Lk 24:18 "Are you the only *r* of Jerusalem who does

RESIDENTS (1)

Dn 9: 7 the men of Judah, the *r* of Jerusalem,

RESIDES (8)

Ex 23:21 My authority *r* in him.
Lv 19:33 "When an alien *r* with you in your land,
19:34 You shall treat the alien who *r* with you
Dt 18: 6 in Israel in which he ordinarily *r*,
1Sm 14:41 blame for this *r* in me or my son Jonathan,
Jdt 9: 8 the tent where your glorious name *r*,
Rom 7:17 is not I who do it but sin which *r* in me.
Col 2: 9 the fullness of deity *r* in bodily form.

RESIDING (13)

Lv 17: 8 of Israel or of the aliens *r* among them,
17:10 of Israel or of the aliens *r* among them,
17:13 Israelites or of the aliens *r* among them,
20: 2 an Israelite or an alien *r* in Israel,
22:18 house of Israel, or any alien *r* in Israel,
Nm 15:14 alien *r* with you permanently or for a time,
15:16 the alien *r* among you as for yourselves."
15:26 community, but also the aliens *r* among you,
15:29 a native Israelite or an alien *r* with you.
19:10 Israelites and for the aliens *r* among them.
Dt 28:43 The alien *r* among you will rise higher and
Jgs 19: 1 there was a Levite *r* in remote parts of
Est A: 2 He was a Jew *r* in the city of Susa,

RESIN (3)

Gn 37:25 gum, balm and *r* to be taken down to Egypt.
43:11 some balm and honey, gum and *r*,
Sir 28:11 Pitch and *r* make fire flare up,

RESIST (23)

Jgs 20:39 Israelites wheeled about to *r* as the smoke
2Sm 4: 1 he ceased to *r* and all Israel was alarmed.
Jdt 1: 6 came together to *r* the people of Cheleoud.
2:11 As for those who *r*,
16:14 no one can *r* your word.
Est C: 4 of all, and there is no one who can *r* you,
1Mc 3:53 we be able to *r* them unless you help us?"
5:40 to us first, we shall not be able to *r* him;
Eccl 4:12 man may be overcome, two together can *r*.
Wis 11:21 who can *r* the might of your arm?
Is 1:20 But if you refuse and *r*,
Bar 6:55 They cannot *r* a king, or enemy forces.
Ez 2: 5 And whether they heed or *r*—
2: 7 my words to them, whether they heed or *r*,
3:11 —whether they heed or *r*!
3:27 him heed who will, and let him *r* who will,
Dn 11:14 times many shall *r* the king of the south,
11:15 picked troops shall have the strength to *r*.
Rom 13: 2 those who *r* thus shall draw condemnation
Eph 6:13 of God if you are to *r* on the evil day;
Jas 4: 7 God, *r* the devil and he will take flight.
5: 6 he does not *r* you.
1Pt 5: 9 *R* him, solid in your faith,

RESISTANCE (5)

1Mc 5:44 was subdued, and Judas met with no more *r*.
Is 41:11 perish and come to nought who offer *r*.
Jer 8: 5 Why do these people rebel with obstinate *r*?
Mt 5:39 offer no *r* to injury.
Eph 4:18 because of their ignorance and their *r*;

RESISTED (6)

Gn 48:19 But his father *r*. "I know it, son,"
Jdt 2:25 Cilicia, and cut down everyone who *r* him.
1Mc 14:29 danger and *r* the enemies of their nation,
Gal 2: 5 We *r* so that the truth of the gospel might
2Tm 4:15 guard, for he has strongly *r* our preaching.
Heb 12: 4 not yet *r* to the point of shedding blood.

RESISTING (1)

Dt 20:20 which to reduce the city that is *r* you.

RESISTS (2)

1Mc 10:70 "You are the only one who *r* us.
Jas 4: 6 "God *r* the proud but bestows his favor on

RESOLUTE (4)

2Sm 13:28 Be *r* and act manfully."
1Chr 12:39 came to Hebron with the *r* intention of
Wis 10: 5 preserved him *r* against pity for his child.
Sir 44: 4 *R* princes of the folk,

RESOLUTELY (3)

2Chr 27: 6 he lived *r* in the presence of the LORD,
2Mc 11: 7 Then they *r* set out together.
Sir 51:18 I became *r* devoted to her

RESOLUTION (1)

2Tm 3:10 You have observed my *r*,

RESOLUTIONS (1)

Jer 44:25 keep your vows, carry out your *r*!

RESOLVE (13)

1Sm 1:23 may the LORD bring your *r* to fulfillment!"
14: 7 I will match your *r*."
23:16 David and strengthened his *r* in the LORD.
Ps(s) 64: 6 They *r* on their wicked plan;
119:106 I *r* and swear to keep your just ordinances.
Sir 22:16 Neither is a *r* constructed with careful
22:17 A *r* that is backed by prudent
22:18 Neither can a timid *r* based on foolish
Is 8:10 make a *r*,
Lk 21:14 I bid you *r* not to worry about your
Rom 14:13 Instead you should *r* to put no stumbling
1Cor 7:37 man, however, who stands firm in his *r*,
2Cor 8:11 so that your ready *r* may be matched by

RESOLVED (16)

1Sm 20:33 that his father was *r* to kill David.
2Chr 12:14 for he had not truly *r* to seek the LORD.
30:19 pardon to everyone who has *r* to seek God,
Ezr 7: 9 month he *r* on the journey up from Babylon,
Jdt 9: 8 for they have *r* to profane your sanctuary,
1Mc 1:62 But many in Israel were determined and *r*
6:57 So he hastily *r* to withdraw.
9:69 of them and *r* to return to his own country.
Is 14:24 As I have *r*, so shall it be;
Jer 4:28 I have spoken, I will not repent, I have *r*,
51:11 Babylon he is *r* to destroy.
Dn 1: 8 But Daniel was *r* not to defile himself
11:27 The two kings, *r* on evil,
Lk 9:51 he firmly *r* to proceed toward Jerusalem,
Acts 15:22 It was *r* by the apostles and the
15:25 Therefore we have unanimously *r* to choose

RESORT (5)

Dt 12: 5 you shall *r* to the place which the LORD,
Mk 12: 6 He sent him to them as a last *r*,
2Cor 4: 2 *r* to trickery or falsify the word of God.
Jas 4: 2 you do not obtain, and so you *r* to murder.
Jude 1:16 it is expedient, they *r* to flattery.

RESORTING (1)

Lk 8: 4 *r* to him from one town after another.

RESOUND (13)

Ex 9:16 and to make my name *r* throughout the earth!
Lv 25: 9 of the seventh month let the trumpet *r*;
1Chr 16:32 Let the sea and what fills it *r*;
Ps(s) 65: 9 farthest east and west you make *r* with joy.
96:11 let the sea and what fills it *r*;
98: 7 Let the sea and what fills it *r*,
Sir 47:10 before daybreak the sanctuary would *r*,
50:16 A blast to *r* mightily as a reminder before
50:18 over the throng sweet strains of praise *r*.
Is 42:10 Let the sea and what fills it *r*,
Jer 6: 7 Violence and destruction *r* in her;
30:19 From them will *r* songs of praise,
Zep 2:14 Their call shall *r* from the window,

RESOUNDED (3)

1Sm 4: 5 Israel shouted so loudly that the earth *r*.
Jdt 14: 9 and their city *r* with shouts of joy.
Ps(s) 77:19 Your thunder *r* in the whirlwind;

RESOUNDING (4)

2Chr 20:19 the LORD, the God of Israel, in a *r* chorus.
1Mc 5:31 that the noise of the battle was *r* to heaven
Wis 17:19 Or an echo *r* from the hollow of the hills,
Jon 2:10 But I, with *r* praise, will sacrifice to you;

RESOUNDINGLY (1)

1Thes 1: 8 of the Lord has echoed forth from you *r*.

RESOUNDS (4)

Ex 19:13 horn *r* may they go up to the mountain."
Ps(s) 19: 5 Through all the earth their voice *r*,
46: 7 in turmoil, kingdoms totter, his voice *r*,
68:34 Behold, his voice *r*, the voice of power:

RESOURCE (2)

Jgs 18:10 a place where no natural *r* is lacking."
Prv 8: 5 You simple ones, gain *r*,

RESOURCEFULNESS (3)

Prv 1: 4 That *r* may be imparted to the simple,
14:24 The crown of the wise is *r*;
Sir 34:10 whereas with travel a man adds to his *r*.

RESOURCES (6)

Jgs 18: 7 trusting, with no lack of any natural *r*.
2Chr 24: 7 Baals the dedicated *r* of the LORD's temple.
Jb 22: 9 and the *r* of orphans you have destroyed.
Prv 15: 6 the house of the just there are ample *r*,
Dn 11:13 attack with this large army and great *r*.
2Cor 10: 3 body but we do not wage war with human *r*.

RESPECT (55)

Gn 41:40 in *r* to the throne shall I outrank you.
Lv 19:32 of the aged, and show *r* for the old;
22: 2 "Tell Aaron and his sons to *r* the sacred
Dt 28:50 *r* for the aged nor pity for the young.
1Sm 2:12 they had *r* neither for the LORD nor for
12: 1 "I have granted your request in every *r*,"
2Sm 23:19 and commanded greater *r* than the Thirty,
23:23 and commanded greater *r* than the Thirty.
2Kgs 3:14 were it not that I *r* the king of Judah.
2Chr 8:15 in any *r* relating to the priests and Levites
23:19 that no one unclean in any *r* might enter.
24:16 in particular with *r* to God and his temple.
32:31 in *r* to the ambassadors [princes] sent to
Ezr 7:14 Jerusalem in *r* of the law of your God
Jdt 6: 9 my words shall not prove false in any *r*."
2Mc 6:11 In their *r* for the holiness of that day,
10:13 not command the *r* due to his high office,
15: 2 but show *r* for the day which the
Eccl 5: 8 in every *r* is a king for the arable land.
Sir 4:21 guilt, and a shame that merits honor and *r*.
7:31 Honor God and *r* the priest;
29: 5 and speaks with *r* of his creditor's wealth;
42: 1 not ashamed, lest you sin through human *r*:
Lam 5:12 were gibbeted by them, elders shown no *r*.
Bar 6:40 Chaldeans themselves have no *r* for them;
Mt 10:17 Be on your guard with *r* to others.
21:37 son to them, thinking, 'They will *r* my son.'
22:16 one's favor and do not act out of human *r*.
23: 7 of *r* in public and of being called 'Rabbi.'
Mk 12: 6 thinking, 'They will have to *r* my son.'
12:14 *r* but teach God's way of life sincerely.
12:38 robes and accept marks of *r* in public,
Lk 11:43 in synagogues and marks of *r* in public.
20:13 if I send the son I love, they will *r* him.'
20:46 their robes, and love marks of *r* in public,
Jn 8:49 I revere my Father, while you fail to *r* me.
15:20 They will *r* your words as much as they
Acts 4:33 Jesus, and great *r* was paid to them all;
17:22 in every *r* you are scrupulously religious.
Rom 3: 2 The answer is, much in every *r*.
11:28 In *r* to the gospel, the Jews are enemies
11:28 in *r* to the election, they are beloved

12:10 Anticipate each other in showing *r.*
13: 7 *r* and honor to everyone who deserves them.
1Cor 7:25 With *r* to virgins, I have not received
2Cor 8: 7 that just as you are rich in every *r,*
9: 2 about you to the Macedonians with *r* to it,
Eph 5:33 for her part showing *r* for her husband.
Phil 4: 8 to all that is true, all that deserves *r,*
1Thes 4:10 *r* to all the brothers throughout Macedonia.
5:12 *r* those among you whose task it is to
1Tm 6: 1 regard their masters as worthy of full *r;*
Heb 13:18 as we do, to act rightly in every *r.*
1Pt 2:17 reverence for God, *r* for the emperor.
3: 7 Treat women with *r* as the weaker sex,

RESPECTED (8)

Gn 34:19 more highly *r* than anyone else in his clan.
Jos 4:14 they *r* him as they had respected Moses.
2Kgs 5: 1 was highly esteemed and *r* by his master,
Dn 13: 4 because he was the most *r* of them all.
Lk 18: 2 a certain city who *r* neither God nor man.
Jn 15:20 respect your words as much as they *r* mine.
Heb 12: 9 we *r* our earthly fathers who corrected us,

RESPECTER (1)

Lk 20:21 that you are no *r* of persons but teach the

RESPECTFUL (1)

Tb 14:13 He took *r* care of his aging father-in-law

RESPECTFULLY (2)

Gn 43:28 good health," they said, as they bowed *r.*
1Pt 3:16 ready to reply, but speak gently and *r.*

RESPECTING (1)

Dt 33:21 of the LORD and his decrees *r* Israel."

RESPECTIVE (1)

Gn 10: 5 the maritime nations, in their *r* lands

RESPECTS (6)

Gn 47: 7 After Jacob had paid his *r* to Pharaoh,
1Kgs 1:47 went in and paid their *r* to our lord,
2Mc 12:12 that they could indeed be useful in many *r,*
Jb 34:19 princes, nor *r* the rich more than the poor?
Acts 18:22 went up and paid his *r* to the congregation,
Jas 3: 2 All of us fall short in many *r.*

RESPITE (4)

Ex 8:11 But when Pharaoh saw that there was a *r,*
Ps(s) 39:14 I may find *r* ere I depart and be no more.
Lam 2:18 Let there be no *r* for you,
3:49 eyes flow without ceasing, there is no *r,*

RESPLENDENT (5)

Est 1: 4 and the *r* wealth of his royal estate.
Ps(s) 76: 5 *R* you came, O powerful One,
Sg 6:10 as beautiful as the moon, as *r* as the sun,
Wis 6:12 *R* and unfading is Wisdom,
Sir 43: 2 The orb of the sun, *r* at its rising:

RESPOND (13)

1Sm 14:41 Jonathan, LORD, God of Israel, *r* with Urim;
14:41 is in your people Israel, *r* with Thummim."
Jb 5: 1 Will anyone *r* to you?
13:22 Then call me, and I will *r;*
Is 65: 1 I was ready to *r* to those who asked me not,
Hos 2:17 shall *r* there as in the days of her youth,
2:23 *r* says the LORD; I will *r* to the heavens,
2:23 the heavens, and they shall *r* to the earth;
2:24 The earth shall *r* to the grain,
2:24 and oil, and these shall *r* to Jezreel.
1Cor 4:12 When we are insulted we *r* with a blessing.
Col 4: 6 to *r* properly to all who address you.

RESPONDED (20)

Jgs 14:13 "Propose your riddle," they *r;*
1Sm 14:40 The people *r,* "Do what you think best."
2Sm 10:15 Then the Arameans *r* to their defeat by
18:26 king *r,* "He, too, is bringing good news."
Wis 18:10 But the discordant cry of their enemies *r,*
Mt 21:35 The tenants *r* by seizing the slaves.
26:33 Peter *r,* "Though all may have their faith
27:11 Jesus *r,* "As you say."
Lk 14:16 Jesus *r:* "A man was giving a large dinner
17:14 When he saw them, he *r,*
19:26 He *r* with, 'The moral is:
20:39 Some of the scribes *r,*
22:60 Peter *r,* "My friend, I do not know what
Jn 1:50 Jesus *r:* "Do you believe just because
2:18 Jews *r,* "What sign can you show us
3:10 Jesus *r:* "You hold the office of teacher
19: 7 "We have our law," the Jews *r,*
Acts 8:24 Simon *r,* "I need the prayers of all of you
9:29 for their part *r* by trying to kill him.
13:48 and *r* to the word of the Lord with praise.

RESPONDING (1)

2Mc 1:23 leading and the rest *r* with Nehemiah.

RESPONDS (1)

Sir 35:18 Nor will it withdraw till the Most High *r,*

RESPONSE (20)

Ex 19: 8 back to the LORD the *r* of the people.
19: 9 reported to the LORD the *r* of the people,
1Sm 13:13 Samuel's *r* was: "You have been foolish!
2Kgs 22:18 sent you to consult the LORD, give this *r:*
2Chr 34:26 sent you to consult the LORD, give this *r:*
Jdt 11:15 the *r* reaches them and they act upon it,
Est 4:15 Esther sent back to Mordecai the *r:*
Wis 6:10 those learned in them will have ready a *r.*
Mt 12:11 He said in *r:* "Suppose one of you
15:23 He gave her no word of *r.*
Mk 6: 4 Jesus' *r* to all this was: "No prophet is
10:39 Jesus said in *r,* "From the cup I drink
15: 5 Pilate's surprise, Jesus made no further *r.*
Lk 7:22 Jesus gave this *r:* "Go and report to John
8:50 Jesus heard this, and his *r* was:
Jn 1:46 Nathanael's *r* to that was,
6: 6 to do but he asked this to test Philip's *r.)*
20:28 Thomas said in *r,* "My Lord and my God!"
Acts 10:29 That is why I have come in *r* to your
16:37 Paul's *r* to this was,

RESPONSIBILITIES (1)

Nm 8:26 in sharing their *r* in the meeting tent,

RESPONSIBILITY (6)

Nm 18: 1 but the *r* of the priesthood shall rest on
2Sm 3:29 May the full *r* for the death of Abner,
Ezr 4: 3 *r* to build with us a house for our God,
2Mc 2:28 *r* for exact details to the original author,
Mt 27:24 The *r* is yours."
Gal 6: 5 Everyone should bear his own *r.*

RESPONSIBLE (28)

Gn 16: 5 "You are *r* for this outrage against me.
31:39 me *r* for anything stolen by day or night.
43: 9 You can hold me *r* for him.
Nm 4:27 each man of them *r* for what he is to carry.
4:31 This is what they shall be *r* for carrying,
4:32 service, which he shall be *r* for carrying.
18: 1 house shall be *r* for the sanctuary;
18:23 tent, and they alone shall be held *r;*
30:16 learned of them, he is *r* for her guilt."
Jos 2:19 your house, he will be *r* for his own death,
2:19 But we shall be *r* if anyone in the house
1Sm 22:21 I am *r* for the death of all your family.
2Sm 1:16 to him, "You are *r* for your own death,
4:11 must I hold you *r* for his death and
1Kgs 2:32 The LORD will hold him *r* for his own blood,
2:33 shall be *r* forever for their blood.
2:37 You shall be *r* for your own blood."
2Kgs 10: 9 "You are not *r,* and although I conspired
2Chr 6:23 man and holding him *r* for his conduct,
Est 8:12 Ethiopia, and to those *r* for our interests:
Ez 3:18 sin, but I will hold you *r* for his death.
3:20 *r* for his death if you did not warn him.
33: 4 against him, shall be *r* for his own death.
33: 5 he is *r* for his own death,
33: 6 the watchman *r* for that person's death,
33: 8 guilt, but I will hold you *r* for his death.
Acts 5:28 to make us *r* for that man's blood."
Rom 14: 8 While we live we are *r* to the Lord,

REST (388)

Gn 8: 4 ark came to *r* on the mountains of Ararat.
14:10 these, while the *r* fled to the mountains.
18: 4 feet, and then *r* yourselves under the tree.
30:36 to pasture the *r* of Laban's flock.
31:34 the *r* of her tent without finding them,
42: 4 that Jacob did not send with the *r,*
42:16 while the *r* of you stay here under arrest.
42:19 while the *r* of you may go and take home
42:33 while the *r* of you go home with rations
44: 9 he shall die, and as for the *r* of us,
44:10 and the *r* of you shall be exonerated."
44:16 the *r* of us no less than the one in whose
44:17 the *r* of you may go back safe and sound to
49:26 May they *r* on the head of Joseph.
50:26 and laid to *r* in a coffin in Egypt.
Ex 4: 7 it was again like the *r* of his body.
5: 5 yet you would give them *r* from their labor!"
9:11 no less than on the *r* of the Egyptians.
16:23 Tomorrow is a day of complete *r,*
17:11 of the fight, but when he let his hands *r,*
23:12 *r,* that your ox and your ass may also have *r,*
26:32 gold and shall *r* on four silver pedestals.
29:12 All the *r* of the blood you shall pour out
29:20 Splash the *r* of the blood on all the sides
31:15 seventh day is the sabbath of complete *r,*
33:14 answered, "will go along, to give you *r.*"
34:21 you shall *r;* on that day you must rest
35: 2 as the sabbath of complete *r* to the LORD.
Lv 2: 3 The *r* of the cereal offering belongs to
2:10 The *r* of the cereal offering belongs to
4: 7 The *r* of the bullock's blood he shall pour
4:18 The *r* of the blood he shall pour out at
4:25 The *r* of the blood he shall pour out at
4:30 The *r* of the blood he shall pour out at
4:34 The *r* of the blood he shall pour out at
5: 9 The *r* of the blood shall be squeezed out
5:13 The *r* of the flour,
6: 9 The *r* of it Aaron and his sons may eat;
8:24 The *r* of the blood he splashed on the
9: 9 The *r* of the blood he poured out at the
10: 6 Your kinsmen, the *r* of the house of Israel,
14:18 The *r* of the oil in his hand the priest
14:29 The *r* of the oil in his hand the priest
23: 3 but the seventh day is the sabbath *r,*
23:24 seventh month you shall keep a sabbath *r,*
23:32 of complete *r* and mortify yourselves.
23:39 the eighth day shall be days of complete *r.*
25: 4 year the land shall have complete *r,*
25: 5 in this year of sabbath *r* for the land.
26: 6 that you may lie down to *r* without anxiety.
26:34 then shall the land have *r* and make up for
26:35 enjoying the *r* that you would not let it
Nm 3:49 the *r* had been redeemed by the Levites.
8:14 the Levites from the *r* of the Israelites,
9:17 wherever the cloud came to *r,*
10:12 the cloud came to *r* in the desert of Paran.
10:36 And when it came to *r,*
11:25 and as the spirit came to *r* on them,
11:26 yet the spirit came to *r* on them also,
18: 1 shall *r* on you and your sons alone.
18:30 the *r* of the tithes will be credited to
31:27 combat, and half to the *r* of the community.
Dt 3:13 The *r* of Gilead and all of Bashan,
5:14 male and female slave should *r* as you do.
6: 7 and abroad, whether you are busy or at *r.*
11:19 and abroad, whether you are busy or at *r.*
12:10 when he has given you *r* from all your
13:10 the *r* of the people shall join in with you.
18: 8 receive the same portions to eat as the *r,*
19:20 The *r,* on hearing of it, shall fear,
25:19 gives you *r* from all your enemies round
31:16 "Soon you will be at *r* with your fathers,
Jos 8: 5 The *r* of the people and I will come up to
10: 7 picked troops and the *r* of his soldiers.
13:10 Dibon, with the *r* of the cities of Sihon,
17: 6 Gilead fell to the *r* of the Manassehites.
21: 5 The *r* of the Kohathites obtained ten
21:20 The *r* of the Kohathite clans among the
21:26 *r* of the Kohathite clans were ten in all.
23: 1 *r* from all their enemies round about them,
Jgs 2:10 But once the *r* of that generation were
3:11 The land then was at *r* for forty years,
3:30 and the land had *r* for eighty years.
5:31 And the land was at *r* for forty years.
7: 6 but all the *r* of the soldiers knelt down
7: 8 the *r* of the Israelites to their tents,
8:28 And the land had *r* for forty years,
16:26 support the temple and may *r* against them."
20:45 The *r* turned and fled through the desert
Ru 1: 9 and a home in which you will find *r.*"
2: 7 here until now, with scarcely a moment's *r.*"
3:18 learn what happens, for the man will not *r,*
1Sm 1:21 husband Elkanah was going up with the *r*
2:33 but the *r* of the men of your family shall
7: 2 came to *r* in Kiriath-jearim a long time
13: 2 the *r* of the people back to their tents.
13:15 but the *r* of the people went up after Saul
15: 8 but on the *r* of the people he put into
15:15 but we have carried out the ban on the *r.*"
30: 5 had also been carried off with the *r.*
2Sm 2: 9 Ephraim, Benjamin, and the *r* of Israel.
7: 1 given him *r* from his enemies on every side,
7:11 I will give you *r* from all your enemies.
7:12 time comes and you *r* with your ancestors,
10:10 He placed the *r* of the soldiers under the
12:28 Therefore, assemble the *r* of the soldiers,
12:29 the *r* of the soldiers and went to Rabbah.
16:14 tired out, and stopped there for a *r.*
17: 3 can bring back the *r* of the people to you,
1Kgs 8:56 LORD who has given *r* to his people Israel,
11:41 The *r* of the acts of Solomon,
12:23 to Benjamin, and to the *r* of the people:
14:19 The *r* of the acts of Jeroboam,
14:29 The *r* of the acts of Rehoboam,
15: 7 The *r* of Abijam's acts,
15:23 The *r* of the acts of Asa,
15:31 The *r* of the acts of Nadab,
16: 5 The *r* of the acts of Baasha,
16:14 The *r* of the acts of Elah,
16:20 The *r* of the acts of Zimri,
16:27 The *r* of the acts of Omri,
22:39 The *r* of the acts of Ahab,
22:46 The *r* of the acts of Jehoshaphat,
22:47 He removed from the land the *r* of the cult
2Kgs 1:18 The *r* of the acts of Ahaziah are recorded
8:23 The *r* of the acts of Jehoram,
9: 8 and by all the *r* of the family of Ahab.
10:34 The *r* of the acts of Jehu,
12:20 The *r* of the acts of Joash,
13: 8 The *r* of the acts of Jehoahaz,
13:12 [The *r* of the acts of Joash,
14:15 The *r* of the acts of Jehoash,

REST (cont.)
14:18 The r of the acts of Amaziah are written
14:28 The r of the acts of Jeroboam,
15: 6 The r of the acts of Azariah,
15:11 The r of the acts of Zechariah are
15:15 The r of the acts of Shallum,
15:21 The r of the acts of Menahem,
15:26 The r of the acts of Pekahiah,
15:31 son of Uzziah] The r of the acts of Pekah,
15:36 The r of the acts of Jotham,
16:19 The r of the acts of Ahaz are recorded in
20:20 The r of the acts of Hezekiah,
21:17 The r of the acts of Manasseh,
21:25 The r of the acts that Amon did are
23:28 The r of the acts of Josiah,
24: 5 The r of the acts of Jehoiakim,
1Chr 6:55 belonged to the r of the Kohathite clan.
6:62 The r of the Merarites received from the
11: 8 while Joab restored the r of the city.
12:39 The r of Israel was likewise of one mind
13: 2 let us summon the r of our brethren from
19:11 the r of the army,
22: 9 him r from all his enemies on every side.
22:18 Has he not given you r on every side?
23:25 God of Israel, has given r to his people,
2Chr 9:29 The r of the acts of Solomon,
13:22 The r of Abijah's acts,
14: 6 him, and he has given us r on every side."
15:15 And the LORD gave them r on every side.
20:30 for his God gave him r on every side.
20:34 The r of the acts of Jehoshaphat,
24:14 r of the money to the king and to Jehoiada,
25:26 The r of the acts of Amaziah,
26: 2 Amaziah had gone to r with his ancestors.
26:22 of Amos, wrote the r of the acts of Uzziah,
27: 7 The r of the acts of Jotham,
28:26 The r of his deeds and his activities,
30:25 priests and Levites and the r of the assembly
32:22 he gave them r on every side.
32:32 The r of Hezekiah's acts,
33:18 The r of the acts of Manasseh,
35:26 The r of the chronicle of Josiah,
36: 8 The r of the acts of Jehoiakim,
36:21 have r while seventy years are fulfilled."
Ezr 3: 8 together with the r of their brethren,
4: 3 and the r of the family heads of Israel
4: 7 r of his fellow officials to Artaxerxes,
6:20 the Passover for the r of the exiles,
Neh 4: 8 the magistrates, and the r of the people:
4:13 the magistrates, and the r of the people:
7:71 The contributions of the r of the people
10:29 The r of the people,
11: 1 and the r of the people cast lots to bring
11:20 The r of Israel,
Tb 1: 5 r of the tribe of my forefather Naphtali,
6: 6 the r he salted and kept for the journey.
11: 3 the r of the party are still on the way."
Jdt 7:18 The r of the Assyrian army was encamped in
15: 5 r of the mountain region took part in this,
16:21 For the r of her life she was renowned
Est 9:16 and obtained r from their enemies.
9:22 Jews obtained r from their enemies
1Mc 3:11 Many fell wounded, and the r fled.
3:12 who fought with it the r of his life.
3:24 r fled to the country of the Philistines.
5:18 people, with the r of the army to guard it.
6:54 the r scattered each to his own home,
7:32 the r fled to the City of David.
7:42 and let the r know that Nicanor spoke
8: 4 and the r paid tribute to them every year.
9:18 Then Judas fell, and the r fled.
9:71 try to injure him for the r of his life;
10:47 remained his allies for the r of his life.
12: 6 and the r of the Jewish people send
12:14 r of our allies and friends in these wars;
12:45 men to stay with you, send the r back home,
14: 4 The land was at r all the days of Simon,
14:20 priests, and the r of the Jewish people,
15:32 sideboard, and the r of his rich display,
16: 8 and the r fled toward the stronghold.
16:23 Now the r of the history of John,
2Mc 1:23 leading and the r responding with Nehemiah.
1:31 Nehemiah ordered the r of the liquid to be
4:42 a few, while they put all the r to flight.
7: 4 r of his brothers and his mother looked on.
8:28 the r they divided among themselves and
8:30 to themselves and the r to the persecuted,
8:31 r of the spoils they carried to Jerusalem.
10:36 the gates and let in the r of the troops,
11:11 horsemen, and put all the r to flight.
11:27 the Jewish senate and to the r of the Jews.
12:45 those who had gone to r in godliness,
15: 1 attack them in all safety on the day of r.
Jb 3:13 I should then have been at r With kings
3:17 from troubling, there the weary are at r.
3:26 I have no r, for trouble comes!
11:19 you shall take your r with none to disturb.
16:18 not my blood, nor let my outcry come to r!
30:17 My frame takes no r by night;
Ps(s) 55: 7 like a dove, I would fly away and be at r.
61: 3 you will give me r,
62: 2 Only in God is my soul at r;
62: 6 Only in God be at r, my soul,
73: 5 and are not afflicted like the r of men.
94:13 law you teach, Giving him r from evil days,
95:11 They shall not enter into my r."
127: 2 for you to rise early, or put off your r,
132: 4 give my eyes no sleep my eyelids no r,
139: 3 My journeys and my r you scrutinize,
139: 5 you hem me in and r your hand upon me.
Prv 3:24 down, you need not be afraid, when you r,
4:16 they cannot r unless they have done evil;
6: 9 How long, O sluggard, will you r?
6:10 a little folding of the arms to r—
7:11 and unruly, in her home her feet cannot r;
24:33 a little folding of the arms to r—
Eccl 2:23 even at night his mind is not at r.
6: 5 dead child is at r rather than such a man.
8:17 nor by night do his eyes find r in sleep.
Sg 1: 7 flock, where you give them r at midday,
1:13 for me a sachet of myrrh to r in my bosom.
2: 3 I delight to r in his shadow,
Wis 4: 7 man, though he die early, shall be at r.
7: 1 am a mortal man, the same as all the r,
15:18 as to folly, these are worse than the r,
Sir 6:29 Thus will you afterward find r in her,
11:19 "I have found r,
20:20 sin, yet in this tranquility he cannot r.
22:10 little over the dead man, for he is at r;
22:13 r and not be wearied by his lack of sense.
24:11 Thus in the chosen city he has given me r,
28:16 Whoever heeds it has no r,
31: 1 and the care of wealth drives away r.
31: 3 wealth, and his only r is wanton pleasure;
33:26 a slave work and he will look for his r;
35:17 it does not r till it reaches its goal,
40: 5 Even when he lies on his bed to r,
40: 6 So short is his r it seems like none,
42: 9 wakeful, and worry over her drives away r:
Is 11: 2 The spirit of the LORD shall r upon him:
11: 7 be neighbors, together their young shall r;
13:21 r there and owls shall fill the houses;
14: 8 "Now that you are laid to r,
23:12 the Kittim, even there you shall find no r.
25:10 hand of the LORD will r on this mountain,
28:12 is the resting place, give r to the weary;
34:14 repose, and find for herself a place to r.
38:10 I shall be consigned for the r of my years."
44:19 I then make an abomination out of the r,
57: 2 There is r on his couch for the sincere,
62: 6 who are to remind the LORD, take no r
62: 7 give no r to him, until he re-establishes
Jer 6:16 thus you will find r for your souls.
14:17 with tears day and night, without r,
27:19 r of the vessels that remain in this city,
30:10 Jacob shall again find r,
31: 2 As Israel comes forward to be given his r,
39: 9 the r of the people left in the city,
39: 9 deserted to him, and the r of the workmen.
43: 4 and the r of the leaders and the people
45: 3 weary from groaning, and can find no r":
46:27 Jacob shall again find r,
47: 6 how long till you find r?
47: 7 it find r when the LORD has commanded it?
49:23 they toss like the sea which cannot r.
50:34 with success, and give r to the earth,
52:15 exile the r of the people left in the city,
52:15 king of Babylon, and the r of the artisans.
Lam 1: 3 among the nations she finds no place to r:
5: 5 we are worn out, but allowed no r.
Ez 16:43 lewdness to the r of your abominable deeds?
32:32 is he laid to r among the uncircumcised,
34:15 I myself will give them r,
34:18 the r of your pastures with your feet?
36: 3 a possession for the r of the nations,
36: 5 jealousy I speak against the r of the nations
Dn 2: 1 spirit no r and robbed him of his sleep.
2: 3 my spirit no r until I know what it means."
2:18 with the r of the wise men of Babylon.
11:35 shall fall, so that the r may be tested,
12:13 Go, take your r,
Hos 2:20 I will let them take their r in security.
Am 5:19 he were to r his hand against the wall,
Mi 2:10 Be off, this is no place to r";
5: 2 And the r of his brethren shall return to
Na 3:18 of Assyria, your nobles have gone to r;
Hb 2: 8 all the r of the nations shall despoil you;
Zec 1:11 see, the whole earth is tranquil and at r!"
6: 8 make my spirit r in the land of the north."
12:14 and all the r of the families,
14: 2 but the r of the people shall not be
14: 4 his feet shall r upon the Mount of Olives,
Mt 11:29 Your souls will find r,
12: 5 the sabbath r without incurring guilt?
12:43 for a place of r and finding none.
20:26 who aspires to greatness must serve the r,
22: 6 The r laid hold of his servants,
23: 8 you is your teacher, the r are learners.
23:11 among you will be the one who serves the r.
26:45 Enjoy your r!
27:49 Meanwhile the r said, "Leave him alone.
Mk 6:31 to an out-of-the-way place and r a little."
10:43 who aspires to greatness must serve the r;
Lk 8:10 confided, but to the r in parables that,
10: 6 man there, your peace will r on him;
12:26 your power, why be anxious about the r?
12:31 over you, and the r will follow in turn.
18:11 O God, that I am not like the r of men
21: 3 poor widow has put in more than all the r.
23:56 They observed the sabbath as a day of r,
24:33 Eleven and the r of the company assembled.
Jn 1:32 dove from the sky, and it came to r on him.
1:33 see the Spirit descend and r on someone,
Acts 2: 3 which parted and came to r on each of them.
5: 2 the r he took and laid at the feet of the
8:13 r and became a devoted follower of Philip.
15:17 so that all the r of mankind and all the
16:17 to follow Paul and the r of us shouting,
21:18 Paul and the r of us paid a visit to James
26:30 and Bernice and the r of the company.
27:44 The r were to follow,
28: 9 the r of the sick on the island began to
Rom 11: 8 The r became blind, as Scripture says:
1Cor 9: 5 like the r of the apostles and the brothers
11:32 being condemned with the r of the world.
14:29 let the r judge the worth of what they say.
16: 6 with what I need for the r of my journey.
2Cor 7:13 his mind has been set at r by all of you.
12: 9 that the power of Christ may r upon me.
13: 2 those who sinned before and to all the r,
Gal 2:13 r of the Jews joined in his dissembling,
Eph 2: 3 by nature deserved God's wrath like the r.
Phil 3: 1 For the r, my brothers, rejoice
Col 3:14 the r together and makes them perfect.
1Thes 5: 6 therefore let us not be asleep like the r,
2Thes 3: 1 For the r, brothers, pray for us
1Tm 5:20 so that the r may fear to offend.
Heb 3:11 anger, 'They shall never enter into my r.'"
3:18 swear that they would not enter into his r?
4: 1 promise of entrance into his r still holds,
4: 3 we who have believed who enter into that r,
4: 3 They shall never enter into my r.'"
4: 5 says, "They shall never enter into my r."
4: 8 Joshua had led them into the place of r,
4: 9 r still remains for the people of God.
4:10 And he who enters into God's r,
4:11 Let us strive to enter into that r,
Jas 3: 3 obey us, we guide the r of their bodies.
1Pt 4:14 Spirit in its glory has come to r on you.
2Pt 3: 4 Our forefathers have been laid to r,
3:16 do the r of Scripture) to their own ruin.
Rv 11:13 the r were so terrified that they
12:17 off to make war on the r of her offspring,
14:13 "Yes, they shall find r from their labors,
19:21 The r were slain by the sword which came

RESTED (58)

Gn 2: 2 he r on the seventh day from all the work
2: 3 because on it he r from all the work he
28:12 a stairway r on the ground,
Ex 16:30 After that the people r on the seventh day.
20:11 but on the seventh day he r.
31:17 but on the seventh day he r at his ease."
Jgs 16: 3 Samson r there until midnight.
16:29 temple r and braced himself against them,
1Kgs 2:10 David r with his ancestors and was buried
7:25 This r on twelve oxen,
11:21 David r with his ancestors and that Joab,
11:43 Solomon r with his ancestors;
14:20 He r with his ancestors.
14:31 Rehoboam r with his ancestors;
15: 8 Abijam r with his ancestors;
15:24 He r with his ancestors;
16: 6 Baasha r with his ancestors;
16:28 Omri r with his ancestors;
22:40 Ahab r with his ancestors,
22:51 Jehoshaphat r with his ancestors;
2Kgs 8:24 Jehoram r with his ancestors and was
10:35 Jehu r with his ancestors and was buried
13: 9 Jehoahaz r with his ancestors and was
13:13 Joash r with his ancestors,
14:16 Jehoash r with his ancestors;
14:22 after King Amaziah r with his ancestors.
14:29 Jeroboam r with his ancestors,
15: 7 Azariah r with his ancestors,
15:22 Menahem r with his ancestors,
15:38 Jotham r with his ancestors and was buried
16:20 Ahaz r with his ancestors and was buried
20:21 Hezekiah r with his ancestors and his son
21:18 Manasseh r with his ancestors and was
24: 6 Jehoiakim r with his ancestors,
2Chr 4: 4 It r on twelve oxen,
4: 4 the sea r on their backs.
9:31 He r with his ancestors;
12:16 Rehoboam r with his ancestors;
13:23 Abijah r with his ancestors;
16:13 Asa r with his ancestors;
21: 1 Jehoshaphat r with his ancestors;
26:23 Uzziah r with his ancestors;
27: 9 Jotham r with his ancestors and was buried
28:27 Ahaz r with his ancestors and was buried
32:33 Hezekiah r with his ancestors;
33:20 Manasseh r with his ancestors and was
Ezr 8:32 where we first r for three days.
Neh 2:11 Jerusalem, I first r there for three days.
2:18 the favoring hand of my God had r upon me,
Est 9:17 On the fourteenth of the month they r,
9:18 But on the fifteenth they r,

Ps(s) 68:14 Though you *r* among the sheepfolds,
Sir 44:22 and the blessing *r* upon the head of JACOB.
Jer 48:11 from his youth, has *r* upon his lees;
Ez 3:14 the hand of the LORD *r* heavily upon me.
10:18 of the temple and *r* upon the cherubim.
31:13 fallen trunk *r* all the birds of the air,
Heb 4: 4 *r* from all his work on the seventh day";

RESTFUL (1)

Ps(s) 23: 2 Beside *r* waters he leads me;

RESTING (23)

Nm 10:33 LORD which was to seek out their *r* place
Dt 1:33 journeys before you to find you a *r* place
12: 9 you have not yet reached your *r* place,
Jgs 5:17 dwells along the shore, is *r* in his coves.
2Sm 14:17 word of my lord the king provide a *r* place;
1Kgs 7: 3 of cedar above the beams *r* on the columns;
1Chr 6:16 the ark had obtained a permanent *r* place.
2Chr 6:41 now, "Advance, LORD God, to your *r* place,
Ps(s) 132: 8 *r* place you and the ark of your majesty.
132:14 "Zion is my *r* place forever;
Sg 5:15 are columns of marble *r* on golden bases.
Sir 24: 7 Among all these I sought a *r* place;
46:12 bones return to life from their *r* place,
49:10 bones return to life from their *r* place!—
Is 28:12 This is the *r* place,
32:18 in secure dwellings and quiet *r* places.
65:10 the valley of Achor a *r* place for the cattle
66: 1 what is to be my *r* place?
Ez 25: 5 of the Ammonites a *r* place for flocks.
Zec 9: 1 of Hadrach, and Damascus is its *r* place,
Lk 11:24 arid wastes searching for a *r* place;
16:23 afar off, and Lazarus *r* in his bosom.
Acts 7:49 What is my *r* to be like?

RESTITUTION (17)

Ex 21:36 would not keep it in, he must make full *r*.
22: 2 He must make full *r*.
22: 4 he must make *r* with the best produce of
22: 5 one who started the fire must make full *r*.
22: 6 the thief, if caught, must make twofold *r*.
22: 8 convicts must make twofold *r* to the other.
22:10 accept the oath, and no *r* is to be made.
22:11 of theft, he must make *r* to the owner.
22:12 he need not make *r* for the mangled animal.
22:13 owner is not present, the man must make *r*.
22:14 the owner is present, he need not make *r*.
Lv 5:24 he shall make full *r* of the thing itself,
22:14 *r* to the priest for the sacred offering,
24:18 an animal shall make *r* of another animal.
24:21 Whoever slays an animal shall make *r*,
1Sm 12: 3 I will make *r* to you."
Prv 6:35 He will not consider any *r*,

RESTIVE (1)

Gn 27:40 But when you become *r*,

RESTLESS (6)

Gn 4:12 You shall become a *r* wanderer on the earth."
4:14 and become a *r* wanderer on the earth,
Ps(s) 39: 7 like vapor only are his *r* pursuits;
Sir 31:20 of sleep, and *r* tossing for the glutton!
2Cor 7: 5 arrived in Macedonia I was *r* and exhausted.
Jas 3: 8 It is a *r* evil, full of deadly poison.

RESTLESSNESS (1)

Jb 7: 4 I am filled with *r* until the dawn.

RESTORATION (12)

Nm 5: 8 whom *r* of the ill-gotten goods can be made,
2Chr 24:13 the task of *r* progressed under their hands.
30: 3 not celebrate it at the time of the *r*:
Neh 3:34 Will they complete their *r* in a single day?
4: 1 Ashdodites heard that the *r* of the walls
1Mc 14:34 with all that was necessary for their *r*.
Hos 7: 1 I would bring about the *r* of my people,
Am 9:14 will bring about the *r* of my people Israel;
Zep 2: 7 shall visit them, and bring about their *r*.
3:19 all the earth, when I bring about their *r*.
3:20 I bring about your *r* before your very eyes,
Acts 3:21 in heaven until the time of universal *r*

RESTORE (68)

Gn 37:22 from their hands and *r* him to his father.
40:13 lift up your head and *r* you to your post.
42:34 not spies, I will *r* your brother to you,
48:21 and will *r* you to the land of your fathers.
Ex 21:37 it, he shall *r* five oxen for the one ox,
22: 3 he shall *r* two animals for each one stolen.
Lv 5:16 He shall also *r* what he has sinfully
5:23 *r* the thing that was stolen or unjustly
Nm 5: 7 has done, *r* his ill-gotten goods in full,
Jgs 11:13 Now *r* the same peaceably."
17: 2 so now I will *r* them to you."
2Sm 9: 7 I will *r* to you all the land of your
12: 6 He shall *r* the ewe lamb fourfold because
16: 3 will *r* to me my father's kingdom.'"
19:12 you be last to *r* the king to his palace?
19:13 Why should you be last to *r* the king?'
1Kgs 12:21 of Israel, to *r* the kingdom to Rehoboam,
20:34 "I will *r* the cities which my father took
2Kgs 8: 6 saying, *R* all her property to her,
2Chr 11: 1 against Israel and *r* the kingdom to him.
15: 8 and to *r* the altar of the LORD which was
24: 4 time, Joash decided to *r* the LORD's temple.
24:12 masons and carpenters to *r* the temple,
34: 8 chamberlain, to *r* the house of the LORD,
35:20 Josiah had done all this to *r* the temple,
Ezr 9: 9 again the house of our God and *r* its ruins,
Est B: 2 borders, to *r* the peace desired by all men.
1Mc 3:43 us *r* our people from their ruined estate,
10:10 and began to build and *r* the city.
15: 3 it, that I may *r* it to its former state.
2Mc 9:16 *r* all the sacred vessels many times over;
12:25 his solemn pledge to *r* them unharmed,
Jb 8: 6 awake for you and *r* your rightful domain;
Ps(s) 69: 5 Must I *r* what I did not steal?
80: 4 O LORD of hosts, *r* us;
80: 8 O LORD of hosts, *r* us;
80:20 O LORD of hosts, *r* us;
85: 5 *R* us, O God our savior,
126: 4 *R* our fortunes, O LORD, like the torrents
Sir 43:23 by flames, The dripping clouds *r* them all,
Is 1:26 I will *r* your judges as at first,
49: 6 of Jacob, and *r* the survivors of Israel;
49: 8 To *r* the land and allot the desolate
61: 4 shall raise up And *r* the ruined cities,
Jer 15:19 If you repent, so that I *r* you,
27:22 bring them back and *r* them to this place.
28: 3 Within two years I will *r* to this place
30:17 to pillage, For I will *r* you to health;
30:18 I will *r* the tents of Jacob,
31: 4 Again I will *r* you,
33:11 For I will *r* this country as of old,
Bar 1: 8 the temple, to *r* them to the land of Judah,
6:36 To no blind man do they *r* his sight,
Ez 11:17 and I will *r* to you the land of Israel.
16:53 I will *r* their fortunes,
16:53 I will *r* your fortune along with them],
29:14 scattered, and I will *r* Egypt's fortune,
39:25 Now I will *r* the fortunes of Jacob and
Jl 4: 1 *r* the fortunes of Judah and Jerusalem,
Na 2: 3 The LORD will *r* the vine of Jacob,
Mt 5:13 How can you *r* its flavor?
17:11 is indeed coming, and he will *r* everything.
Mk 9:12 will indeed come first and *r* everything.
Jn 4:47 him to come down and *r* health to his son,
Acts 1: 6 are you going to *r* the rule to Israel now?"
2Cor 7:11 ardent desire to *r* the balance of justice!
Jas 5:15 is ill, and the Lord will *r* him to health.
1Pt 5:10 glory in Christ, will himself *r*,

RESTORED (49)

Gn 20:14 and after he *r* his wife Sarah to him,
20:17 with God, and God *r* health to Abimelech,
40:21 He *r* the chief cupbearer to his office,
41:13 I was *r* to my post,
Nm 5: 8 the goods to be *r* shall be the LORD's
Jgs 17: 3 When he *r* the eleven hundred shekels of
1Sm 7:14 had taken from Israel were *r* to them.
2Kgs 8: 1 to the woman whose son he had *r* to life:
8: 5 how his master had *r* a dead person to life,
8: 5 very woman whose son Elisha had *r* to life
8: 5 is that son of hers whom Elisha *r* to life."
14:22 who rebuilt Elath and *r* it to Judah,
14:25 He *r* the boundaries of Israel from
1Chr 11: 8 around, while Joab *r* the rest of the city.
2Chr 24:13 They *r* the house of God according to its
26: 2 He rebuilt Elath and *r* it to Judah;
29:19 of his apostasy, we have *r* and consecrated,
33:13 and *r* him to his kingdom in Jerusalem.
33:16 He *r* the altar of the LORD,
Neh 3: 8 They *r* Jerusalem as far as the wall of the
Tb 2: 1 wife Anna and my son Tobiah were *r* to me.
6: 9 on the cataracts, his sight will be *r*."
11:17 how God had mercifully *r* sight to his eyes.
2Mc 2:17 and has *r* to all of them their heritage,
5:20 in his anger was *r* in all its glory,
7:14 God-given hope of being *r* to life by him;
11:25 our decision is that their temple be *r*
Jb 22:23 you return to the Almighty, you will be *r*;
42:10 Also, the LORD *r* the prosperity of Job,
Ps(s) 68:10 you *r* the land when it languished;
85: 2 you have *r* the well-being of Jacob.
Sir 49:13 our ruined walls, *R* our shattered defenses,
Jer 30:18 rebuilt upon hill, and palace *r* as it was.
Lam 5:21 us back to you, O LORD, that we may be *r*:
Dn 4:31 my reason was *r* to me,
4:33 I was *r* to my kingdom,
Mi 4: 8 the former dominion shall be *r*,
Mt 9:22 Your faith has *r* you to health."
12:13 He did so, and it was perfectly *r*;
14:36 many as touched it were fully *r* to health.
Mk 3: 5 man did so and his hand was perfectly *r*.
8:25 was *r* and he could see everything clearly.
Lk 6:10 man did so and his hand was perfectly *r*.
7:21 he also *r* sight to many who were blind.)
9:42 cured the boy, and *r* him to his father.
Jn 5:13 been *r* to health had no idea who it was.
Acts 4: 9 cripple and explain how he was *r* to health,
Phlm 1:22 through your prayers I shall be *r* to you.
Heb 13:19 prayers that I may be *r* to you very soon.

RESTORER (1)

Is 58:12 shall call you, *R* of ruined homesteads."

RESTORES (4)

Ps(s) 14: 7 the LORD *r* the well-being of his people,
53: 7 When God *r* the well-being of his people,
Eccl 3:15 God *r* what would otherwise be displaced.
Rom 4:17 the God who *r* the dead to life and calls

RESTORING (8)

Ex 21:34 by *r* the value of the animal to its owner;
2Sm 19:11 silent about *r* the king to his palace?"
19:44 Were we not first to speak of *r* the king?"
2Chr 34:10 house who were *r* and repairing the temple.
1Mc 10:44 The cost of rebuilding and *r* the
Jb 20:18 *R* his gains, he shall not enjoy them;
Is 52: 8 before their eyes, the LORD *r* Zion.
Ez 33:15 just, giving back pledges, *r* stolen goods,

RESTRAIN (7)

Nm 23:20 a blessing which I cannot *r*.
Jb 7:11 My own utterance I will not *r*;
Ps(s) 19:14 From wanton sin especially, *r* your servant;
40:10 I did not *r* my lips,
Is 48: 9 For the sake of my name I *r* my anger,
Jer 2:24 who can *r* her lust?
2Pt 2:16 a human voice to *r* the prophet's madness.

RESTRAINED (7)

1Sm 24: 8 With these words David *r* his men and would
25:34 lives, who has *r* me from harming you,
25:39 and who *r* his servant from doing evil,
Est 5:10 Haman *r* himself,
Mk 5: 3 he could no longer be *r* even with a chain.
Lk 24:16 However, they were *r* from recognizing him.
Acts 22:29 Paul he had *r* a citizen of Rome.

RESTRAINER (1)

2Thes 2: 7 until that *r* shall be taken from the scene.

RESTRAINING (1)

Acts 22:29 *r* Paul he had restrained a citizen of Rome.

RESTRAINS (2)

Prv 10:19 but he who *r* his lips does well.
2Thes 2: 6 You know what *r* him until he shall be

RESTRAINT (4)

Jb 6: 3 Because of this I speak without *r*.
30:11 me, and have thrown off *r* in my presence.
Mk 3:27 unless he has first put him under *r*.
Acts 20:37 They began to weep without *r*,

RESTRICT (1)

Jb 15: 8 of God, and do you *r* wisdom to yourself?

RESTRICTED (1)

1Cor 10:29 liberty be *r* by another man's conscience?

RESTRICTIONS (1)

1Cor 7:35 I have no desire to place *r* on you,

RESTS (20)

Ex 28:37 a way that it *r* on the front of the miter,
Nm 23:24 It *r* not till it has devoured its prey and
Dt 21:23 God's curse *r* on him who hangs on a tree,
Jgs 5:17 Gilead, beyond the Jordan, *r*;
2Kgs 2:15 said, "The spirit of Elijah *r* on Elisha."
Jdt 8:24 the temple, and the altar *r* with us.
Est C:27 which *r* on my head when I appear in public;
Jb 29:19 the dew *r* by night on my branches.
Sir 31: 4 a meager subsistence, and if ever he *r*,
Is 9: 5 upon his shoulder dominion *r*.
14: 7 The whole earth *r* peacefully,
Mt 3:17 My favor *r* on him."
17: 5 is my beloved Son on whom my favor *r*.
Mk 1:11 On you my favor *r*."
Lk 2:14 on earth to those on whom his favor *r*."
3:22 On you my favor *r*."
1Cor 2: 5 your faith *r* not on the wisdom of men but
Phil 1: 7 the solid grounds on which the gospel *r*.
Heb 4:10 *r* from his own work as God did from his.
2Pt 1:17 is my beloved Son, on whom my favor *r*."

RESULT (27)

Jgs 1:21 with the *r* that the Jebusites live in
1Sm 12:18 As a *r*, all the people dreaded the LORD
14:28 As a *r* the people are weak."
18:30 officers, and as a *r* acquired great fame.]
1Chr 4:27 and as a *r* all their clans did not equal
21: 5 Joab reported the *r* of the census to David:
2Chr 17: 5 As a *r*, the LORD made his kingdom

RESULT (cont.)

Ezr 4:13 thus it can only r in harm to the throne.
Neh 13:18 with the r that our God has brought all
2Mc 4:35 As a r, not only the Jews,
4:42 As a r, they wounded many of them
9: 7 As a r he hurtled from the dashing chariot,
10:13 As a r, he was accused before Eupator
Jer 27:15 my name, with the r that I must banish you,
Ez 28:16 in you, the r of your far-flung trade;
Mi 7:13 of its citizens, as a r of their deeds.
Mt 15:31 The r was great astonishment in the crowds
Mk 1:45 As a r of this, it was no longer possible
Lk 11:26 The r is that the last state of the man is
Jn 4:40 r was that, when these Samaritans came
11:47 The r was that the chief priests and the
Acts 11: 2 As a r, when Peter went up to Jerusalem
19:10 with the r that all the inhabitants of the
Rom 15:19 As a r, I have completed preaching
2Cor 8:14 supply your need, with equality as the r.
1Tm 4:14 gift you received when, as a r of prophecy,
Heb 11:12 As a r of this faith,

RESULTING (1)

Acts 11:22 r in Barnabas' being sent to Antioch.

RESULTS (2)

Sir 7:13 lie after lie, for it never r in good.
2Cor 9:11 through us it r in thanks offered to God.

RESUME (3)

Jos 10:13 for a whole day did it r its swift course.
Neh 13:11 together and had them r their stations.
Est 2:19 [To r: From the time the virgins

RESUMED (4)

Gn 29: 1 After Jacob r his journey he came to the
Jos 4:18 the waters of the Jordan r their course
Wis 16:20 Second Example R For this substance of
Acts 5:21 the temple at dawn and r their teaching.

RESUMING (1)

Eccl 1: 6 wind turns again and again, r its rounds.

RESURRECTION (39)

2Mc 7:14 but for you, there will be no r to life."
12:43 as he had the r of the dead in view;
Mt 22:23 day some Sadducees, who hold there is no r,
22:28 At the r, whose wife will she be,
27:53 After Jesus' r they came forth from their
Mk 12:18 there is no r came to him with a question:
12:23 At the r, when they all come back to life,
Lk 14:14 you will be repaid in the r of the just."
20:27 there is no r) to pose this problem to him:
20:33 At the r, whose wife will she be?
20:35 age to come and of r from the dead do not.
20:36 Sons of the r, they are sons of God.
Jn 11:24 Martha replied, "in the r on the last day."
11:25 "I am the r and the life:
Acts 1:22 be named as witness with us to his r."
2:31 beforehand the r of the Messiah.
4: 2 the r of the dead in the person of Jesus.
4:33 bore witness to the r of the Lord Jesus,
17:18 heard to speak of "Jesus" and "the r."
23: 6 because of my hope in the r of the dead."
23: 8 maintain that there is no r and that there
24:15 to be a r of the good and the wicked alike.
24:21 you today because of the r of the dead.'"
Rom 1: 4 spirit of holiness, by his r from the dead:
6: 5 his death, so shall we be through a like r.
1Cor 15:12 some of you say there is no r of the dead?
15:13 If there is no r of the dead,
15:21 the r of the dead comes through a man also.
15:42 So is it with the r of the dead.
Phil 3:10 Christ and the power flowing from his r;
3:11 hope that I may arrive at r from the dead.
2Tm 2:18 saying that the r has already taken place.
Heb 6: 2 and laying-on of hands, r of the dead,
11:35 Women received back their dead through r.
11:35 deliverance, in order to obtain a better r.
1Pt 1: 3 from the r of Jesus Christ from the dead;
3:21 conscience through the r of Jesus Christ.
Rv 20: 5 This is the first r;
20: 6 and holy are they who share in the first r!

RETAIN (11)

Nm 32:32 but we will r our hereditary property on
36: 7 will r their own ancestral heritage.
36: 9 tribes will r their own ancestral heritage."
Dt 13:18 You shall not r anything that is doomed,
Jos 18: 5 Judah is to r its territory in the south,
2Mc 11:24 us to let them r their own customs.
Eccl 8: 8 of the breath of life so as to r it,
Lam 1:11 for food, to r the breath of life.
Am 2:14 the strong man shall not r his strength;
Lk 8:15 the word in a spirit of openness, r it,
1Thes 5:21 Test everything; r what is good.

RETAINED (1)

Lv 5:23 thing that was stolen or unjustly r by him

RETAINERS (5)

Gn 14:14 three hundred and eighteen of his r,
2Sm 13:24 come with all your r to your servant."
1Kgs 20:14 the r of the governors of the provinces.'"
20:15 up the r of the governors of the provinces,
20:17 When the r of the governors of the

RETAINING (1)

Lv 5:21 otherwise r his neighbor's goods unjustly,

RETAINS (1)

Jb 20:13 Though he r it and will not let it go but

RETALIATE (1)

1Mc 2:36 but they did not r;

RETCHES (1)

Jer 48:26 make Moab drunk so that he r and vomits,

RETINUE (6)

Gn 50: 9 it was a very large r.
1Kgs 10: 2 in Jerusalem with a very numerous r,
2Kgs 5:15 with his whole r to the man of God.
2Chr 9: 1 numerous r and by camels bearing spices,
2Mc 3:28 with a great r and his whole bodyguard
Ez 12:14 All his r, his aides, and his troops I will

RETIRE (4)

Nm 8:25 he shall r from the required service and
Tb 8: 1 drinking, the girl's parents wanted to r.
Ps(s) 70: 4 Let them r in their shame who say to me,
74:21 May the humble not r in confusion;

RETIRED (8)

Nm 11:30 Then Moses r to the camp,
1Sm 4: 3 When the troops r to the camp,
1Kgs 18:27 a god and may be meditating, or may have r,
Ezr 10: 6 Then Ezra r from his place before the
2Mc 4:46 Ptolemy r with the king under a colonnade,
Mk 7:24 He r to a certain house and wanted no one
Lk 5:16 He often r to deserted places and prayed.
9:10 with him, he r to a town called Bethsaida,

RETIRES (1)

2Sm 17:13 And if he r into a city,

RETIRING (1)

2Sm 12:16 r for the night to lie on the ground

RETOLD (1)

Sir 44:15 At gatherings their wisdom is r,

RETORT (1)

Ps(s) 38:15 who neither hears nor has in his mouth a r.

RETORTED (15)

Gn 30: 2 Jacob r, "Can I take the place of God,
34:31 But they r, "Should our sister have been
Tb 2:14 So she r: "Where are your charitable deeds
10: 7 But she r, "Stop it, and do not lie to me!
Mt 27: 4 They r, "What is that to us?
Jn 2:20 They r, "This temple took forty-six years
3: 4 r Nicodemus. "Can he return to his mother's
7:20 "You are mad!" the crowd r.
7:47 to have been taken in?" the Pharisees r.
8:39 They r, "Our father is Abraham."
8:52 are sure you are possessed," the Jews r.
9:28 They r scornfully: "You are the one
10:33 that we are stoning you," the Jews r,
18:30 "If he were not a criminal," they r,
18:35 "I am no Jew!" Pilate r.

RETRACED (3)

1Sm 25:12 So David's young men r their steps and on
Mk 16:13 These men r their steps and announced the
Acts 14:21 r their steps to Lystra and Iconium first,

RETRACT (1)

Jgs 11:35 have made a vow to the LORD and I cannot r."

RETRACTS (1)

1Sm 15:29 The Glory of Israel neither r nor repents,

RETREAT (9)

Ex 14:25 the Egyptians sounded the r before Israel,
Nm 25: 8 his r where be pierced the pair of them,
1Kgs 22:25 day when you r into an inside room to hide."
2Kgs 20:11 who made the shadow r the ten steps it had
2Mc 9: 2 natives and forced to beat a shameful r.
Is 32: 2 a shelter from the wind, a r from the rain.
Jer 49: 8 Flee, r, hide in deep holes
Dn 11:30 confront him, he shall lose heart and r.
1Jn 2:28 confident and not r in shame at his coming.

RETREATED (9)

Jgs 20:42 They r before the men of Israel in the
1Sm 17:24 saw the man, they all r before him,
2Sm 23: 9 The Israelites had r,
1Mc 6: 4 So he r and in great dismay withdrew from
6:47 the ardor of its forces, they r from them.
2Mc 9: 1 r in disgrace from the region of Persia.
Ps(s) 78: 9 ranks of bowmen, r in the day of battle.
Jer 41:17 they r to the lodging place of Chimham
Jn 18: 6 they r slightly and fell to the ground.

RETREATING (3)

Jos 8:20 because the Israelites r toward the desert
1Chr 11:13 defenders were r before the Philistines.
Jer 46:22 She sounds like a r reptile!

RETREATS (3)

Prv 30:30 mightiest of beasts, who r before nothing;
Jer 21:13 will attack us, who can penetrate our r?"
49:10 will uncover his r so that he cannot hide.

RETRIBUTION (7)

Wis 11:20 r and winnowed out by your mighty spirit;
14:31 those that are sworn by but the r of sinners
18:11 was smitten with the same r as his master;
Mt 23:35 until r overtakes you for all the blood of
Lk 21:22 These indeed will be days of r,
Rom 2: 5 heart is storing up r for that day of wrath
11: 9 and a trap, a stumbling stone and a r;

RETRIEVE (1)

Lv 26:34 Then shall the land r its lost sabbaths

RETRIEVED (3)

2Chr 36:21 "Until the land has r its lost sabbaths,
Mt 16:10 thousand and how many hampers-full you r?
Lk 15: 8 search until she has r what she lost?

RETURN (301)

Gn 3:19 bread to eat, Until you r to the ground,
3:19 For you are dirt, and to dirt you shall r."
18:10 surely r to you about this time next year,
18:14 about this time next year, I will r to you,
20: 7 Therefore, r the man's wife
20: 7 If you do not r her,
24:54 he said, "Give me leave to r to my master."
28:22 I will faithfully r a tenth part to you."
29:27 in r for another seven years of service
31: 3 to Jacob, R to the land of your fathers,
31:13 this land and r to the land of your birth.'"
42:37 my own two sons if I do not r him to you."
43:12 for you must r the amount that was put
47:16 sell you bread in r for your livestock."
47:17 he sold them food in r for their horses,
Ex 4:21 The LORD said to him, "On your r to Egypt,
13:17 might change their minds and r to Egypt.
22:25 you shall r it to him before sunset;
24:14 him, "Wait here for us until we r to you.
33:11 Moses would then r to the camp,
Lv 13:16 turns white, he shall r to the priest;
14:39 priest shall r to examine the house again.
24:19 his neighbor shall receive the same in r.
24:20 another shall be inflicted on him in r.
25:10 one of you shall r to his own property,
25:13 one of you shall r to his own property.
25:41 r to his kindred and to the property
Nm 10:36 And when it came to rest, he would say, R,
14: 3 it not be better for us to r to Egypt?"
19: 7 and only afterward may he r to the camp.
32:18 We will not r to our homes until every one
32:22 is subdued before him, then you may r here,
35:28 may the homicide r to his own district.
Dt 1:45 On your r you wept before the LORD,
3:20 all r to the possessions I have given you.'
4:30 upon you, you shall finally r to the LORD,
5:30 Go, tell them to r to their tents.
16: 7 in the morning you may r to your tents.
20: 5 Let him r home, lest he die in battle
20: 6 Let him r home,
20: 7 Let him r home,
20: 8 Let him r home,
23:11 shall go outside the camp, and not r until,
24:13 but shall r it to him at sunset that he
30: 2 that you and your children r to the LORD,
30:10 book of the law, when you r to the LORD,
Jos 1:15 you may r and occupy your own land,
2:16 Hide there for three days, until they r;
18: 4 When they r to me you shall divide it into
18: 8 prepare a description of it, and r to him;
22: 4 may now r to your tents beyond the Jordan;
Jgs 6:18 He answered, "I will await your r."
8: 9 too, he said, "When I r in triumph,
11:31 when I r in triumph from the Ammonites
13: 8 r to us to teach us what to do for the boy
14: 2 On his r he told his father and mother,
20: 8 is to leave for his tent or r to his home.
Ru 1:10 her they would r with her to her people.
1Sm 5:11 Let it r to its own place,
7: 3 with your whole heart to r to the LORD,

7:17 Then he used to *r* to Ramah,
15:12 *r* he had passed on and gone down to Gilgal.
15:25 Now forgive my sin, and *r* with me,
15:26 said to Saul, "I will not *r* with you,
15:30 *R* with me that I may worship the LORD your
17:53 *r* from the pursuit of the Philistines,
18: 2 not allow him to *r* to his father's house.
18: 6 David's *r* after slaying the Philistine),
25:12 *r* reported to him all that had been said.
27: 9 On his *r* he brought these to Achish,
29: 4 him *r* to the place you picked out for him.
29:11 to *r* to the land of the Philistines.
2Sm 1:22 back, or the sword of Saul *r* unstained.
8:13 On his *r*, David became famous
12:23 I shall go to him, but he will not *r* to me."
15:20 *R* and take your brothers with you and,
15:27 you and Abiathar *r* to the city in peace,
15:34 if you *r* to the city and say to Absalom,
19:15 man, and so they summoned the king to *r*,
19:16 When the king, on his *r*,
1Kgs 8:33 by an enemy, and if then they *r* to you,
11:21 "Give me leave to *r* to my own country."
11:22 you are seeking to *r* to your own country?"
12:24 Let every man *r* home,
12:26 "The kingdom will *r* to David's house.
12:27 of this people will *r* to their master,
13: 9 drink water and not to *r* by the way I came."
14:28 and then *r* them to the guardroom.
17:21 life breath *r* to the body of this child."
22:27 of bread and water until I *r* in safety.' "
22:28 Micaiah said, "If ever you *r* in safety,
2Kgs 4:39 On his *r* he cut them up into the pot of
19: 7 certain report, he will *r* to his own land,
19: 8 When the commander, on his *r*,
19:28 mouth, and make you *r* the way you came.
19:33 He shall *r* by the same way he came,
1Chr 21:27 to the angel to *r* his sword to its sheath.
2Chr 6:24 but afterward they *r* and praise your name,
9:21 would *r* with a cargo of gold and silver,
11: 4 Let every man *r* home,
12:11 then they would *r* them to the guardroom.)
18:26 of bread and water until I *r* in safety!' "
18:27 Micaiah said, "If ever you *r* in safety,
30: 6 "Israelites, *r* to the LORD,
30: 6 Isaac and Israel, that he may *r* to you,
30: 9 For when you *r* to the LORD,
30: 9 with their captors and *r* to this land;
30: 9 away his face from you if you *r* to him."
32:21 he had to *r* shamefaced to his own country.
36:13 his heart rather than *r* to the LORD,
Ezr 7:28 family heads to make the *r* journey with me.
Neh 1: 9 *r* to me and carefully keep my commandments,
2: 6 my journey would take and when I would *r*.
5:11 you *r* to them this very day their fields,
5:12 "We will *r* everything and exact nothing
9:17 their heads to *r* to their slavery in Egypt.
13:21 time on, they did not *r* on the sabbath.
Tb 1:22 my behalf, and I was able to *r* to Nineveh.
5: 3 of course, give him a salary when you *r*;
5:16 you, and in good health we shall *r* to you,
5:22 will be successful, and he will *r* unharmed."
6: 8 and no demons will ever *r* to him again.
6:13 When we *r* from Rages,
6:13 And when we *r* from Rages,
9: 4 If I should delay my *r* by a single day,
10: 1 the time Tobiah would need to go and to *r*.
11: 1 Then they left and began their *r* journey.
14: 5 all of them shall *r* from their exile,
Jdt 6: 6 Then at my *r*, the sword of my army
13:13 assembled, for her *r* seemed unbelievable.
Est 2:14 She would go in the evening and *r* in the
2:14 She could not *r* to the king unless he was
1Mc 3:33 care of his son Antiochus until his own *r*.
3:56 who were afraid, could each *r* to his home,
4:35 so as to *r* to Judea with greater numbers.
5:19 not fight against the Gentiles until we *r*."
6: 4 dismay withdrew from there to *r* to Babylon.
7:35 when I *r* victorious I will burn this
9:58 Now then, let us have Bacchides *r*,
9:69 them and resolved to *r* to his own country.
10:27 favors in *r* for what you do in our behalf.
11:28 promising him in *r* three hundred talents.
2Mc 8:26 obliged to *r* by reason of the late hour,
11:29 to *r* home and attend to your own affairs.
11:30 those who *r* by the thirtieth of Xanthicus
Jb 7:10 He shall not again *r* to his house;
10:21 little Before I go whence I shall not *r*,
16:22 I am on a journey from which I shall not *r*.
22:23 If you *r* to the Almighty,
34:15 together, and man would *r* to the dust.
39: 4 thrive and grow, they leave and do not *r*.
Ps(s) 6: 5 *R*, O LORD, save my life; rescue me
51:15 your ways, and sinners shall *r* to you.
59: 7 Each evening they *r*, they snarl like dogs
59:15 Each evening they *r*, they snarl like dogs
90: 3 You turn man back to dust, saying, *R*,
90:13 *R*, O LORD! How Long? Have pity
104:29 breath, they perish and *r* to their dust.
109: 4 In *r* for my love they slandered me,
116: 7 *R*, O my soul, to your tranquillity,
116:12 How shall I make a *r* to the LORD for all
Prv 7:20 him, not till the full moon will he *r* home."
Eccl 3:20 from the dust, and to the dust they both *r*.
12: 2 stars, while the clouds *r* after the rain;
Wis 11:15 And in *r* for their senseless,
16:14 the spirit has come away, it does not *r*,
Sir 4: 8 poor man, and *r* his greeting with courtesy;
16:28 manner of life which must *r* into it again.
17: 2 gives him and makes him *r* to earth again.
17:20 *R* to the LORD and give up sin,
17:24 his forgiveness of those who *r* to him!
38:21 him not, for there is no hope of his *r*;
41:20 share, Of failing to *r* a greeting,
46:12 bones *r* to life from their resting place,
49:10 bones *r* to life from their resting place!—
Is 10:21 A remnant will *r*,
10:22 of the sea, Only a remnant of them will *r*;
23:17 She shall *r* to her hire and deal with all
31: 6 *R*, O children of Israel,
35:10 has ransomed will *r* and enter Zion singing,
37: 7 certain report, he will *r* to his own land,
37:29 mouth, and make you *r* the way you came.
37:34 He shall *r* by the same way he came,
42:22 as spoil, with no one to demand their *r*.
43: 3 ransom, Ethiopia and Seba in *r* for you.
43: 4 I give men in *r* for you and peoples in
44:22 *r* to me, for I have redeemed you
51:11 has ransomed will *r* and enter Zion singing,
55:10 *r* there till they have watered the earth,
55:11 It shall not *r* to me void,
63:17 *R* for the sake of your servants,
Jer 3: 1 many lovers, and yet you would *r* to me!
3: 7 she has done all this she will *r* to me.
3: 7 But she did not *r*.
3:10 Judah did not *r* to me whole-heartedly,
3:12 *R*, rebel Israel,
3:14 *R*, rebellious children,
3:22 *R*, rebellious children,
4: 1 return, O Israel, says the LORD, *r* to me.
5: 3 harder than stone, and refused to *r* to you.
8: 7 and thrush observe their time of *r*,
14: 3 They find no water and *r* with empty jars.
18:11 *R*, each of you, from, his evil way;
22:11 He has left this place never to *r*.
24: 7 they shall *r* to me with their whole heart.
31: 8 they shall *r* as an immense throng.
31:16 LORD, they shall *r* from the enemy's land.
31:17 Your sons shall *r* to their own borders.
31:18 If you allow me, I will *r*,
37: 7 set out to help you will *r* to its own land,
37: 8 shall *r* to the fight against this city;
42:12 sorry for you and let you *r* to your land.
44:14 None shall *r* to the land of Judah though
44:14 though they yearn to *r* and live there.
44:14 Only scattered refugees shall *r*.
44:28 Those who escape the sword to *r* from the
46:16 let us *r* to our own people,
47: 6 *R* into your scabbard; stop, be still!
50: 9 none shall *r* without effect.
Lam 3:40 examine our ways that we may *r* to the LORD!
Ez 11:18 They shall *r* to it and remove from it all
14: 6 *R* and be converted from your idols;
16:43 therefore in *r* I am bringing down your
16:55 shall *r* to their former state [you and
16:55 daughters shall *r* to your former state].
18:32 *R* and live!
20:38 but they shall not *r* to the land of Israel.
21:35 *R* it to its sheath!
26:20 so that you may never *r* to take your place
36: 8 my people Israel, for they shall soon *r*.
46: 9 *r* by the gate through which he has entered,
Dn 11: 9 of the south, and *r* to his own country.
11:28 he shall arrange matters and *r* to his land.
13:49 *R* to court, for they have testified falsely
14:12 has eaten it all when you *r* in the morning,
Hos 5: 4 deeds do not allow them to *r* to their God;
6: 1 "Come, let us *r* to the LORD,
7:10 yet they do not *r* to the LORD,
8:13 they shall *r* to Egypt.
9: 3 Ephraim shall *r* to Egypt,
11: 5 He shall *r* to the land of Egypt,
12: 7 You shall *r* by the help of your God,
14: 2 *R*, O Israel, to the LORD, your God;
14: 3 Take with you words, and *r* to the LORD;
Jl 2:12 the LORD, *r* to me with your whole heart,
2:13 not your garments, and *r* to the LORD,
4: 4 I will *r* your deed upon your own head.
4: 7 and I will *r* your deed upon your own head.
Mi 1: 7 and to the wages of a harlot shall they *r*.
5: 2 brethren shall *r* to the children of Israel.)
Hg 2:17 wind, and hail, yet you did not *r* to me,
Zec 1: 3 *R* to me, says the LORD of hosts, and I will *r*
8: 3 I will *r* to Zion,
9:12 *r* to the fortress of the waiting prisoners,
9:12 day, I will *r* you double for your exile.
10: 9 they shall rear their children and *r*.
Mal 3: 7 Return to me, and I will *r* to you,
3: 7 Yet you say, "How must we *r*?"
Mt 2:12 a message in a dream not to *r* to Herod,
10:13 If it is not, your blessing will *r* to you.
24:46 whom his master discovers at work on his *r*!
24:50 that man's master will *r* when he is not
25:27 *r* I could have had it back with interest.
26:43 Once more, on his *r*, he found them asleep;
Mk 14:40 Once again he found them asleep on his *r*.
16:20 they might *r* to the truth and sin no more,
Lk 5:24 your mat with you, and *r* to your house."
8:40 On his *r*, Jesus was welcomed by
9:10 The apostles on their *r* related to Jesus
12:36 awaiting their master's *r* from a wedding,
12:37 whom the master finds wide awake on his *r*.
14:12 might invite you in *r* and thus repay you.
15:18 I will break away and *r* to my father,
17:18 Was there no one to *r* and give thanks to
17:31 neither should the man in the field *r* home.
18:30 of God who will not receive a plentiful *r*
19:12 country to become its king, and then *r*.
19:23 on my *r* I could get it back with interest?'
21:21 those in the country must not *r*.
24: 9 On their *r* from the tomb,
Jn 3: 4 "Can he *r* to his mother's womb and be
4:50 Jesus told him, *R* home.
Acts 1:11 Jesus who has been taken from you will *r*,
7:39 thrust him aside and longed to *r* to Egypt.
15:16 will *r* and rebuild the fallen hut of David:
20: 3 so he decided to *r* by way of Macedonia.
22:17 "Upon my *r* to Jerusalem I was praying in
Rom 9: 9 "I will *r* at this time,
11:35 has given him anything so as to deserve *r*?"
15:27 to contribute to their temporal needs in *r*.
1Cor 4: 5 passing judgment before the time of his *r*.
7: 5 Then *r* to one another,
15:33 *R* to reason, as you ought, and stop
2Cor 1:16 both on my way to Macedonia and on my *r*,
Gal 4: 9 how can you *r* to those powerless,
1Pt 3: 9 not *r* evil for evil or insult for insult.
3: 9 *R* a blessing instead.
Rv 2: 5 Repent, and *r* to your former deeds.

RETURNED (234)

Gn 8: 9 and perch, and it *r* to him in the ark,
14:17 When Abram *r* from his victory over
18:33 speaking with Abraham, and Abraham *r* home.
21:32 left and *r* to the land of the Philistines.
22:19 Abraham then *r* to his servants,
32: 7 When the messengers *r* to Jacob,
42:28 "My money has been *r*!"
44:13 reloaded his donkey, they *r* to the city.
44:24 When we *r* to your servant our father,
50:14 Joseph had buried his father he *r* to Egypt,
Ex 2:18 When they *r* to their father Reuel,
2:18 them, "How is it you have *r* so soon today?"
4:18 After this Moses *r* to his father-in-law
23: 4 astray, see to it that it is *r* to him.
Lv 25:28 be released and *r* to its original owner.
Nm 13:25 the land for forty days they *r*,
17:15 Aaron *r* to Moses at the entrance of the
31:21 told the soldiers who had *r* from combat:
Dt 22: 1 see to it that it is *r* to your kinsman.
Jos 2:22 all along the road without finding them, *r*.
6:11 after which they *r* to camp for the night.
7: 3 explored Ai, they *r* to Joshua and advised,
8:24 Then all Israel *r* and put to the sword
10:15 and all Israel *r* to the camp at Gilgal.]
10:21 all the army *r* safely to Joshua and the
10:43 with all Israel *r* to the camp at Gilgal.
18: 9 and *r* to Joshua in the camp at Shiloh.
22: 9 land of Canaan and *r* to the land of Gilead,
22:32 and the princes *r* from the Reubenites and
Jgs 3:19 He *r*, however, from where the idols are,
8:13 Joash, *r* from battle by the pass of Heres.
9:41 Abimelech *r* to Arumah,
11:34 When Jephthah *r* to his house in Mizpah,
11:39 end of the two months she *r* to her father,
14: 8 he *r* to marry the woman who pleased him,
15:19 drank till his spirit *r* and he revived.
18: 8 When the five *r* to their kinsmen in Zorah
18:26 that they were stronger than he, *r* home.
21:14 When Benjamin *r* at that time,
Ru 1:22 Naomi *r* with the Moabite daughter-in-law,
2: 6 who *r* from the plateau of Moab with Naomi.
1Sm 1:19 LORD, and then *r* to their home in Ramah.
2:11 When Elkanah *r* home to Ramah,
6:16 Philistine lords *r* to Ekron the same day.
6:21 Philistines have *r* the ark of the LORD;
14:46 Philistines, who *r* to their own territory.
15:31 And so Samuel *r* with him,
17:57 when David *r* from slaying the Philistine,
23:18 remained, while Jonathan *r* to his home.
24: 2 Saul *r* from the pursuit of the Philistines,
24:23 David gave Saul his oath and Saul *r* home,
26:25 David went his way, and Saul *r* to his home.
2Sm 1: 1 David *r* from his defeat of the Amalekites
3:27 When Abner *r* to Hebron,
6:20 When David *r* to bless his own family,
10:14 attack on the Ammonites and *r* to Jerusalem.
11: 4 She then *r* to her house.
12:15 Then Nathan *r* to his house.
12:20 He *r* to his own house,
12:31 and all the soldiers then *r* to Jerusalem.
17:20 but found no one, and so *r* to Jerusalem.
19:25 the day the king left until he *r* safely.
19:31 lord the king has *r* safely to his palace."
19:40 him Godspeed as he *r* to his own district.
20:22 while Joab *r* to Jerusalem to the King.
1Kgs 2:41 gone from Jerusalem to Gath, and had *r*,
10:13 she *r* with her servants to her own country.
12: 2 *r* from Egypt as soon as he learned this.

RETURNED (cont.)
12:20 When all Israel heard that Jeroboam had *r,*
13:22 but *r* and ate bread and drank water in the
17:22 *r* to the child's body and he revived.
2Kgs 1: 5 The messengers then *r* to Ahaziah,
1: 5 "Why have you *r?*"
2:18 When they *r* to Elisha in Jericho,
2:25 Mount Carmel, and thence he *r* to Samaria.
3:27 gave up the siege and *r* to their own land.
4:31 He *r* to meet Elisha and informed him that
4:38 When Elisha *r* to Gilgal,
5:15 *r* with his whole retinue to the man of God.
7:15 The messengers *r* and told the king.
8: 3 the woman *r* from the land of the
8:14 Hazael left Elisha and *r* to his master.
8:29 King Joram *r* to Jezreel to be healed of
9:15 but had *r* to Jezreel to be healed of the
9:36 They *r* to Jehu,
14:14 Then he *r* to Samaria.
16:11 it completed by the time the king *r* home.
17:28 from Samaria *r* and settled in Bethel,
23:20 Then he *r* to Jerusalem.
1Chr 4:22 held property in Moab, but *r* to Bethlehem.
16:43 own home, and David *r* to bless his household.
19:15 Joab then *r* to Jerusalem.
20: 3 Then he and his whole army *r* to Jerusalem.
21: 4 all of Israel, and then *r* to Jerusalem.
2Chr 1:13 Solomon *r* to Jerusalem from the high place
9:12 she *r* to her own country with her servants.
10: 2 fled from King Solomon, he *r* from Egypt.
14:14 Then they *r* to Jerusalem.
19: 1 *r* in safety to his house in Jerusalem.
22: 6 He *r* to Jezreel to be healed of the wounds
24:11 then took it back and *r* it to its place.
25:10 Judah, and *r* home blazing with resentment.
25:14 When Amaziah *r* from his conquest of the
25:24 Then he *r* to Samaria.
28:12 opposition to those who had *r* from the war.
28:15 Then they *r* to Samaria.
28:17 The Edomites had *r,*
31: 1 the Israelites *r* to their various cities,
34: 7 Then he *r* to Jerusalem.
Ezr 2: 1 who *r* from the captivity of the exiles,
2: 2 his own city (those who *r* with Zerubbabel,
2:59 The following who *r* from Tel-melah,
6: 5 to be *r* to their place in the temple of
6:16 Levites, and the other *r* exiles
6:21 The Israelites who had *r* from the exile
8: 1 family heads who *r* with me from Babylon
8:35 time, those who had *r* from the captivity,
Neh 7: 5 of those who had *r* in the earliest period.
7: 6 who *r* from the captivity of the exiles
7: 7 his own city (those who *r* with Zerubbabel,
7:61 The following who *r* from Tel-melah,
8:17 the *r* exiles made booths and dwelt in them.
12: 1 priests and Levites who *r* with Zerubbabel,
13: 7 asked leave of the king and *r* to Jerusalem,
Tb 1:18 he *r* as a fugitive from Judea
2: 1 Thus under King Esarhaddon I *r* to my home,
2: 3 When he *r* he exclaimed, "Father!"
3:17 Tobit *r* from the courtyard to his house,
8: 3 Then Raphael *r* immediately.
Jdt 1:16 Then he *r* home with all his numerous,
4: 3 Now, they had lately *r* from exile,
5:19 But now that they have *r* to their God,
6:13 then they *r* to their lord.
7: 7 them, while he himself *r* to his troops.
7:32 they *r* to the walls and towers of the city;
8:36 from the tent and *r* to their posts.
12: 9 Then she *r* purified to the tent,
15: 7 The Israelites who *r* from the slaughter
16:21 were over, each one *r* to his inheritance.
Est 4: 9 Hathach *r* to Esther and told her what
6:12 Mordecai then *r* to the royal gate,
7: 8 When the king *r* from the garden of the
1Mc 1:20 he *r* and went up to Israel and to
2:63 to be found, because he has *r* to his dust,
4:16 When Judas and the army *r* from the pursuit,
4:24 As they *r,* they were singing hymns
5: 8 Jazer and its villages, he *r* to Judea.
5:54 they had *r* in safety.
5:68 their cities he *r* to the land of Judah.
6:56 had *r* from Persia and Media with the army
6:63 Then he departed in haste and *r* to Antioch,
7:20 help him, while he himself *r* to the king.
7:25 he *r* to the king and accused them of grave
9:42 the Jews *r* to the marshes of the Jordan.
9:57 Alcimus was dead, Bacchides *r* to the king,
9:72 He *r* to his own country and never came
10:13 left his place and *r* to his own country.
10:52 "Now that I have *r* to my realm,
10:55 "Happy the day on which you *r* to the land
10:66 *r* in peace and happiness to Jerusalem.
10:68 he was greatly troubled, and *r* to Antioch.
10:87 He and his men then *r* to Jerusalem,
11: 7 called Eleutherus and then *r* to Jerusalem.
11:51 they *r* to Jerusalem with much spoil.
11:54 After this Trypho *r* and brought with him
11:73 who were running away saw it and *r* to him;
11:74 Then Jonathan *r* to Jerusalem.
12:24 generals of Demetrius had *r* to attack him
12:35 When Jonathan *r,* he assembled the elders
12:46 troops, and they *r* to the land of Judah.
13:24 Then Trypho *r* to his own country.
15:36 made no reply, but *r* to the king in anger.
16:10 He then *r* to Judea in peace.
2Mc 3:35 and *r* with his soldiers to the king.
4:25 He *r* with the royal commission,
4:36 When the king *r* from the region of Cilicia,
12: 1 agreements were made, Lysias *r* to the king,
13:26 gaining their good will, he *r* to Antioch.
Is 37: 8 When the commander *r* to Lachish and heard
Jer 11:10 They have *r* to the crimes of their
15: 7 they *r* not from their evil ways.
19:14 When Jeremiah *r* from Topheth,
40:12 they all *r* to the land of Judah from the
43: 5 *r* thence to dwell again in the land of Judah:
Dn 4:33 At the same time my reason *r* to me,
4:33 my majesty and my splendor *r* to me.
6:19 the king *r* to his palace for the night;
13:50 Then all the people *r* in haste.
Am 4: 6 in all your dwellings, Yet you *r* not to me,
4: 8 quench their thirst; Yet you *r* not to me,
4: 9 locust devoured; Yet you *r* not to me,
4:10 of your camps; Yet you *r* not to me,
4:11 from the fire; Yet you *r* not to me,
Zec 4: 1 angel who spoke with me *r* and awakened me,
6:10 Take from the *r* captives Heldai,
Mt 2:21 his mother, and *r* to the land of Israel.
26:40 When he *r* to his disciples,
26:45 he *r* to his disciples and said to them:
Mk 3: 1 He *r* to the synagogue where there was a
3:20 He *r* to the house with them and again the
6: 1 He departed from there and *r* to his own
6:30 The apostles *r* to Jesus and reported to
7:31 *r* by way of Sidon to the Sea of Galilee,
9:33 Teaching They *r* to Capernaum and Jesus,
11:27 They *r* once more to Jerusalem.
14:37 When he *r* he found them asleep.
14:41 He *r* a third time and said to them,
Lk 1:56 about three months and then *r* home.
2:15 When the angels had *r* to heaven,
2:20 shepherds *r,* glorifying and praising God
2:39 they *r* to Galilee and their own town of
2:45 him, they *r* to Jerusalem in search of him.
4: 1 then *r* from the Jordan and was conducted
4:14 *r* in the power of the Spirit to Galilee,
7:10 When the deputation *r* to the house,
8:55 life *r* to her and she got up immediately;
9:19 of the prophets of old has *r* from the dead."
10:17 The seventy-two *r* in jubilation saying,
19:15 He *r,* however, crowned as king.
24:23 but *r* with the tale that they had seen a
24:33 They got up immediately and *r* to Jerusalem,
24:52 then *r* to Jerusalem filled with joy.
Acts 1:12 After that they *r* to Jerusalem from the
9:19 strength *r* to him after he had taken food.
12:25 Barnabas and Saul *r* to Jerusalem upon
13:13 There John left them and *r* to Jerusalem.
17:15 who then *r* with instructions for Silas and
21: 6 we boarded the ship and they *r* home.
23:32 The next day they *r* to headquarters,
Gal 1:17 later I *r* to Damascus.
1Thes 3: 6 since Timothy has *r* to us from you
1Pt 2:23 When he was insulted, he *r* no insult.
2:25 sheep, but now you have *r* to the Shepherd,
Rv 11:11 of life which comes from God *r* to them.

RETURNING (25)

Gn 37:30 he tore his clothes, and *r* to his brothers,
48: 7 do this because, when I was *r* from Paddan,
Nm 14:36 *r* had set the whole community grumbling
31:14 company commanders, who were *r* from
Jos 6:14 around the city once before *r* to camp;
22: 8 are *r* to your own tents with great wealth,
Jgs 7:15 Then *r* to the camp of Israel,
2Kgs 9:18 messenger has reached them, but is not *r.*"
9:20 messenger has reached them, but is not *r.*
1Chr 12:21 As he was *r* to Ziklag,
2Chr 28: 9 the army *r* to Samaria and said to them:
Tb 2: 5 *R* to my own quarters,
1Mc 9:50 On *r* to Jerusalem, Bacchides built strongholds
2Mc 9:21 On *r* from the regions of Persia,
Hos 11: 7 His people are in suspense about *r* to him;
Mt 21:18 At dawn, as Jesus was *r* to the city,
28:11 As the women were *r,* some of the guard went
Lk 2:43 As they were *r* at the end of the feast,
14:21 servant *r* reported all this to his master.
Jn 4:27 His disciples, *r* at this point,
4:54 Jesus performed on *r* from Judea to Galilee.
Acts 8:27 a pilgrimage to Jerusalem and was *r* home.
25: 4 and that he himself would be *r* there soon.
Heb 7: 1 met Abraham *r* from his defeat of the kings
11:15 would have had the opportunity of *r* there.

RETURNS (23)

Lv 22:13 no children, *r* to her father's house,
Dt 30: 9 goodly measure the *r* from all your labors,
2Sm 17: 3 people to you, as a bride *r* to her husband.
Tb 5:21 the day when he *r* to you safe and sound.
Ps(s) 78:39 were flesh, a passing breath that *r* not.
146: 4 When his spirit departs he *r* to his earth;
Prv 17:13 If a man *r* evil for good,
26:11 As the dog *r* to his vomit,
Eccl 12: 7 And the dust *r* to the earth as it once was,
12: 7 and the life breath *r* to God who gave it.
Wis 2: 5 and no one *r.*
Sir 40: 1 day he *r* to the mother of all the living,
40:11 *r* to earth, and what is from above *r* above.
41:10 Whatever is of nought *r* to nought,
Dn 11:10 When it *r* and surges around the stronghold,
Mt 12:44 and *r* to find the dwelling unoccupied,
Lk 11:25 It then *r,* to find the house swept
11:26 Next it goes out and *r* with seven other
12:43 whom his master finds busy when he *r.*
15:30 when this son of yours *r* after having gone
1Thes 5:15 See that no one *r* evil to any other;
2Pt 2:22 "The dog *r* to its vomit,"

REU (6)

Gn 11:18 years old, he became the father of *R.*
11:19 and nine years after the birth of *R,*
11:20 When *R* was thirty-two years old,
11:21 *R* lived two hundred and seven years after
1Chr 1:25 Shem, Arpachshad, Shelah, Eber, Peleg, *R,*
Lk 3:35 son of Nahor, son of Serug, son of *R,*

REUBEN (44)

Gn 29:32 and bore a son, and she named him *R;*
30:14 wheat harvest, when *R* was out in the field,
35:22 in that region, *R* went and lay with Bilhah,
35:23 *R,* Jacob's first-born,
37:21 When *R* heard this, he tried to save him
37:29 When *R* went back to the cistern and saw
42:22 "Didn't I tell you," broke in *R,*
42:37 Then *R* told his father:
46: 8 *R,* Jacob's first-born,
46: 9 Jacob's first-born, and the sons of *R:*
48: 5 be mine as much as *R* and Simeon are mine.
49: 3 "You, *R,* my first-born, my strength
Ex 1: 2 *R,* Simeon, Levi and Judah;
6:14 The sons of *R,* the first-born of Israel,
6:14 these are the clans of *R.*
Nm 1: 5 from *R:* Elizur, son of Shedeur;
1:20 Of the descendants of *R,*
1:21 hundred were enrolled in the tribe of *R.*
2:10 side shall be the divisional camp of *R,*
2:16 registered by companies in the camp of *R*
13: 4 Shammua, son of Zaccur, of the tribe of *R,*
16: 1 son of *R* took two hundred and fifty
26: 5 Of *R,* the first-born of Israel,
34:14 the ancestral houses of the tribe of *R,*
Dt 3:12 I gave *R* and Gad the territory from Aroer,
3:16 and to *R* and Gad the territory from Gilead
27:13 blessings over the people, while *R,*
33: 6 came together "May *R* live and not die out,
Jos 18: 7 while Gad, *R,*
20: 8 on the open tableland in the tribe of *R,*
21: 7 twelve cities from the tribes of *R,*
21:36 across the Jordan, from the tribe of *R,*
22:25 of *R* and Gad have no share in the LORD.
Jgs 5:15 of *R* great were the searchings of heart.
5:16 of *R* great were the searchings of heart!
1Chr 2: 1 *R,* Simeon, Levi, Judah, Issachar,
5: 1 The sons of *R,* the first-born of Israel.
5: 3 The sons of *R,* the first-born of Israel,
6:48 twelve cities by lot from the tribes of *R,*
6:63 Jordan] they received from the tribe of *R:*
11:42 the Reubenite, chief of the tribe of *R;*
Ez 48: 6 *R:* on the frontier of Ephraim;
48: 7 on the frontier of *R,*
48:31 the gate of *R,*
Rv 7: 5 twelve thousand from the tribe of *R,*

REUBENITE (2)

Jos 13:15 What Moses gave to the *R* clans:
1Chr 11:42 to the Thirty, Adina, son of Shiza, the *R,*

REUBENITES (40)

Nm 7:30 of Elizur, son of Shedeur, prince of the *R.*
10:18 The camp of the *R,*
26: 5 first-born of Israel, the *R* by clans were:
26: 7 These were the clans of the *R.*
32: 1 Now the *R* and Gadites had a very large
32: 6 But Moses answered the Gadites and *R:*
32:25 The Gadites and *R* answered Moses,
32:29 If all the Gadites and *R* cross the Jordan
32:31 To this the Gadites and *R* replied,
32:33 So Moses gave them [the Gadites and *R,*
32:37 The *R* rebuilt Heshbon,
Dt 4:43 in the region of the plateau, for the *R;*
11: 6 and what he did to the *R* Dathan and Abiram,
29: 7 we then gave as a heritage to the *R,*
Jos 1:12 Joshua reminded the *R,*
4:12 *R,* Gadites, and half-tribe of Manasseh,
12: 6 them, he assigned their land to the *R,*
13: 8 of Manasseh as well as the *R* and Gadites,
13:23 of the *R* was the bank of the Jordan.
13:23 were the heritage of the clans of the *R.*
22: 1 At that time Joshua summoned the *R,*
22: 9 So the *R,* the Gadites, and the half-tribe
22:10 When the *R,* the Gadites,
22:11 Israelites heard the report that the *R,*
22:13 First however, they sent to the *R,*
22:15 When these came to the *R,*
22:21 The *R,* the Gadites, and the half-tribe

22:30 of the Israelites, heard what the *R*,
22:31 son of Eleazar the priest, said to the *R*,
22:32 and the princes returned from the *R*
22:33 decided against declaring war on the *R*
22:34 The *R* and the Gadites gave the altar its
2Kgs 10:33 of the Gadites, *R* and Manassehites),
1Chr 5: 6 he was a prince of the *R*.
5: 8 The *R* lived in Aroer and as far as Nebo
5:18 The *R*, Gadites, and half-tribe of
5:26 king of Assyria, who deported the *R*,
12:38 the other side of the Jordan, of the *R*,
26:32 them to the administration of the *R*,
27:16 Israel, for the *R* the leader was Eliezer,

REUEL (15)

Gn 36: 4 Basemath bore *R*;
36:10 and *R*,
36:13 The sons of *R* were Nahath,
36:17 The descendants of Esau's son *R*:
36:17 are the clans of *R* in the land of Edom;
Ex 2:18 When they returned to their father *R*,
Nm 1:14 Eliasaph, son of *R* from Naphtali:
2:14 [Their prince was Eliasaph, son of *R*,
7:42 day it was the turn of Eliasaph, son of *R*,
7:47 was the offering of Eliasaph, son of *R*.
10:20 tribe of Simeon, and Eliasaph, son of *R*,
10:29 Hobab, son of *R* the Midianite,
1Chr 1:35 The sons of Esau were Eliphaz, *R*,
1:37 The sons of *R* were Nahath,
9: 8 Meshullam, son of Shephatiah, son of *R*,

REUMAH (1)

Gn 22:24 His concubine, whose name was *R*,

REVEAL (25)

Lv 9: 4 for today the LORD will *r* himself to you."
10: 3 sight of all the people I will *r* my glory."
16: 2 *r* myself in a cloud above the propitiatory,
Nm 12: 6 you, in visions will I *r* myself to him,
14:14 you, LORD, who plainly *r* yourself!
1Sm 2:27 'I went so far as to *r* myself to your
Est 2:10 Esther did not *r* her nationality or family,
Jb 20:27 The heavens shall *r* his guilt,
Sir 1:28 *r* your secrets and publicly cast you down,
4:18 him happiness and *r* her secrets to him.
19: 7 if you have a fault, *r* it not,
Is 26:21 The earth will *r* the blood upon her,
Jer 33: 6 *r* to them an abundance of lasting peace.
Ez 39:13 and gain renown for it, when I *r* my glory,
Dn 2:47 is why you were able to *r* this mystery."
13:11 to *r* their lustful desire to have her.
Mt 11:27 and anyone to whom the Son wishes to *r* him.
Mk 3:12 ordering them sternly not to *r* who he was.
16:20 said to Christ, *r* your just authority now."
Lk 10:22 and anyone to whom the Son wishes to *r* him."
Jn 2:11 Thus did he *r* his glory,
14:21 I too will love him and *r* myself to him."
14:22 will *r* yourself to us and not to the world?"
17:26 and I will continue to *r* it so that your
Gal 1:16 me by his favor chose to *r* his Son to me,

REVEALED (71)

Gn 35: 7 for it was there that God had *r* himself to
41:28 has *r* to Pharaoh what he is about to do.
Lv 9: 6 that the glory of the LORD may be *r* to you.
9:23 glory of the LORD was *r* to all the people.
Nm 20:13 and where he *r* his sanctity among them.
Dt 29:28 *r* concern us and our descendants forever,
1Sm 3: 7 the LORD had not *r* anything to him as yet.
3:10 place, the LORD came and *r* his presence,
1Chr 11: 3 the word of the LORD as *r* through Samuel.
17:25 have *r* to your servant that you will build
Est 2:20 Esther had not *r* her family or nationality,
8: 1 for Esther had *r* his relationship to her.
Ps(s) 98: 2 sight of the nations he has *r* his justice.
Prv 26:26 but his malice will be *r* in the assembly.
Wis 16:21 *r* your sweetness toward your children,
Sir 1: 5 To whom has wisdom's root been *r*?
11:27 when a man dies, his life is *r*.
17:10 them, his commandments he has *r* to them.
45: 3 for his people, and *r* to him his glory.
Is 21: 2 the fearful land, A cruel sight, *r* to me:
40: 5 Then the glory of the LORD shall be *r*,
43: 9 Who among them could have *r* this,
53: 1 To whom has the arm of the LORD been *r*?
56: 1 about to come, my justice, about to be *r*,
Ez 16:36 Because you poured out your lust and *r*
20: 5 land of Egypt I *r* myself to them and swore:
21:29 sinfulness in all your wicked deeds *r*
23:18 was discovered and her shame was *r*,
Dn 2:19 the mystery was *r* to Daniel in a vision,
2:30 To me also this mystery has been *r*;
2:45 *r* to the king what shall be in the future;
Mt 10:26 Nothing is concealed that will not be *r*,
11:25 clever you have *r* to the merest children.
16:17 No mere man has *r* this to you,
Mk 4:22 are hidden only to be *r* at a later time;
16:12 *r* to them completely changed in appearance.
16:14 were at table, Jesus was *r* to the Eleven.
Lk 2:26 It was *r* to him by the Holy Spirit that he
10:21 clever you have *r* to the merest children.
12: 2 is nothing concealed that will not be *r*,
17:30 like that on the day the Son of Man is *r*.
Jn 1:18 ever at the Father's side, who has *r* him.
1:31 water was that he might be *r* to Israel."
12:38 To whom has the might of the Lord been *r*?"
17:26 To them I have *r* your name,
Rom 1:17 For in the gospel is *r* the justice of God
1:18 The wrath of God is being *r* from heaven
2: 5 when the just judgment of God will be *r*,
8:18 compared with the glory to be *r* in us.
10:20 who were not looking for me I *r* myself."
1Cor 2:10 has *r* this wisdom to us through the Spirit.
2Cor 4:10 our bodies the life of Jesus may also be *r*.
4:11 life of Jesus may be *r* in our mortal flesh.
5:10 The lives of all of us are to be *r* before
Gal 3:23 the faith that was coming should be *r*.
Eph 3: 3 plan as I have briefly described it was *r*.
3: 5 now *r* by the Spirit to the holy apostles
Col 1:26 past but now *r* to his holy ones.
2Thes 1: 7 is *r* from heaven with his mighty angels;
2: 3 nor the man of lawlessness been *r*—
2: 6 him until he shall be *r* in his own time.
2: 8 Thereupon the lawless one will be *r*,
1Tm 3: 9 divinely *r* faith with a clear conscience.
Heb 9: 8 way into the sanctuary had not yet been *r*.
1Pt 1: 5 stands ready to be *r* in the last days.
1:20 and *r* for your sake in these last days.
4:13 When his glory is *r*,
5: 1 and sharer in the glory that is to be *r*,
1Jn 3: 5 reason he *r* himself was to take away sins;
3: 8 works that the Son of God *r* himself.
4: 9 God's love was *r* in our midst in this way:

REVEALER (1)

Dn 2:47 and Lord of kings and a *r* of mysteries;

REVEALING (4)

Wis 18:18 there, each was *r* the reason for his dying.
Ez 20: 9 *r* that I would bring them out of the land
Am 3: 7 without *r* his plan to his servants,
Lk 2:32 A *r* light to the Gentiles,

REVEALS (9)

2Sm 7:11 The LORD also *r* to you that he will
Prv 11:13 A newsmonger *r* secrets,
20:19 A newsmonger *r* secrets;
Sir 42:19 and the future, and *r* the deepest secrets.
Dn 2:22 He *r* deep and hidden things and knows what
2:28 there is a God in heaven who *r* mysteries,
2:29 who *r* mysteries showed you what is to be.
Rom 16:25 the gospel which *r* the mystery hidden for
1Jn 2:28 little ones, so that, when he *r* himself,

REVEL (4)

Ex 32: 6 down to eat and drink, and rose up to *r*.
Ps(s) 51:16 then my tongue shall *r* in your justice.
59:17 strength and *r* at dawn in your kindness;
Sir 14: 4 and in his possessions a stranger will *r*.

REVELATION (18)

1Sm 3: 1 a *r* of the LORD was uncommon and vision
9:15 arrival, the LORD had given Samuel the *r*:
2Sm 7:27 of Israel, who said in a *r* to your servant,
16:23 time was as though one had sought divine *r*.
2Mc 2: 4 how the prophet, following a divine *r*,
Ps(s) 119:130 The *r* of your words sheds light,
Is 29:11 For you the *r* of all this has become like
Dn 10: 1 king of Persia, a *r* was given to Daniel,
10: 1 The *r* was certain:
Rom 8:19 eagerly awaits the *r* of the sons of God.
1Cor 1: 7 wait for the *r* of our Lord Jesus Christ.
14: 6 do you if my speech does not have some *r*,
14:26 to give, still another a *r* to share;
14:30 sitting by, should happen to receive a *r*,
Gal 1:12 It came by *r* from Jesus Christ.
2: 2 I went prompted by a *r*,
1Pt 1:12 They knew by *r* that they were providing,
Rv 1: 1 This is the *r* God gave to Jesus Christ,

REVELATIONS (2)

2Cor 12: 1 be, and speak of visions and *r* of the Lord.
12: 7 As to the extraordinary *r*,

REVELRY (5)

Ex 32:18 the sounds that I hear are cries of *r*."
2Mc 6: 4 filled the temple with debauchery and *r*;
Is 5:14 their masses, their throngs and their *r*.
Am 6: 7 and their wanton *r* shall be done away with.
2Pt 2;13 Thinking daytime *r* a delight,

REVENGE (14)

Lv 19:18 Take no *r* and cherish no grudge against
Jgs 15: 7 will not stop until I have taken *r* on you."
2Sm 3:27 *r* for the killing of Joab's brother Asahel.
1Kgs 2: 5 *r* for the blood of war in a time of peace,
Jdt 2: 1 about taking *r* on the whole world,
6: 5 taken *r* on this race of people from Egypt.
9: 2 You put a sword into his hand to take *r*
1Mc 3:15 him to help him take *r* on the Israelites.
7: 9 with orders to take *r* on the Israelites.
7:24 and took *r* on the men who had deserted,
7:38 Take *r* on this man and his army,
9:42 their *r* for the blood of their brother,
15: 4 take *r* on those who have ruined it
Jer 50:15 Take *r* on her, as she has done,

REVENGEFULLY (1)

Ez 25:15 Because the Philistines have acted *r*,

REVENUE (8)

1Sm 8:15 give the *r* to his eunuchs and his slaves.
Ezr 6: 8 royal *r*, the taxes of West-of-Euphrates,
1Mc 10:42 taken from the *r* of the sanctuary every year
10:44 shall be covered out of the royal *r*.
10:45 Judea, shall be donated from the royal *r*."
Prv 3:14 in silver, and better than gold is her *r*;
8:19 pure gold, and my *r* than choice silver.
Is 23: 3 Shihor, the harvest of the Nile, was her *r*,

REVENUES (4)

1Mc 10:40 thousand silver shekels out of the royal *r*,
2Mc 1:35 distributed the large *r* he received there.
3: 3 defrayed from his own *r* all the expenses
9:16 *r* the expenses required for the sacrifices.

REVERE (14)

Lv 19: 3 *R* your mother and father,
Dt 28:58 and to *r* the glorious and awesome name of
Neh 1:11 all your willing servants who *r* your name.
Jb 37:24 Therefore men *r* him,
Ps(s) 22:24 *r* him, all you descendants of Israel!
33: 8 let all who dwell in the world *r* him.
102:16 And the nations shall *r* your name,
Wis 2:10 let us neither spare the widow nor *r* the
Sir 7:29 all your soul, fear God, *r* his priests.
Dn 3:33 we, your servants, who *r* you,
Jn 8:49 However, I *r* my Father,
Acts 19:27 she whom Asia and all the world *r* may soon
Rv 11:18 the prophets and the holy ones who *r* you,
19: 5 the small and the great, who *r* him!"

REVERED (5)

1Kgs 18:12 Your servant has *r* the LORD from his youth.
2Mc 6:28 and generously for the *r* and holy laws."
Ps(s) 130: 4 with you is forgiveness, that you may be *r*.
Eccl 3:14 Thus has God done that he may be *r*.
Heb 11: 7 *r* God and built an ark that his household

REVERENCE (22)

Lv 19:30 Keep my sabbaths, and *r* my sanctuary.
26: 2 Keep my sabbaths, and *r* my sanctuary.
Eccl 8:12 those who fear God, for their *r* toward him:
8:13 shadowy days, for his lack of *r* toward God.
Is 29:13 And their *r* for me has become routine
29:23 they shall *r* the Holy One of Jacob,
Bar 4:15 *r* for age nor tenderness for childhood;
Mal 1: 6 if I am a master, where is the *r* due to me?—
Mt 9:18 a synagogue leader came up, did him *r*,
14:33 Those who were in the boat showed him *r*,
15: 9 They do me empty *r*,
Mk 7: 7 Empty is the *r* they do me because they
Lk 24:52 They fell down to do him *r*,
Acts 13:16 Israelites and you others who *r* our God,
13:26 of Abraham and you others who *r* our God,
19:17 the Lord Jesus came to be held in great *r*.
Eph 5:21 Defer to one another out of *r* for Christ.
6: 5 obey your human masters with the *r*,
Col 3:22 in all sincerity and out of *r* for the Lord.
Heb 5: 7 death, and he was heard because of his *r*.
12:28 worship acceptable to him in *r* and awe.
1Pt 2:17 Foster love for the brothers, *r* for God,

REVERENCED (3)

Dn 6:27 the God of Daniel is to be *r* and feared:
Acts 16:14 She already *r* God,
18: 7 of a Gentile named Titus Justus, who *r* God;

REVERENT (2)

Acts 2:43 A *r* fear overtook them all,
1Pt 3: 2 observe the *r* purity of your way of life.

REVERENTLY (1)

1Pt 1:17 *r* during your sojourn in a strange land.

REVERES (3)

Prv 13:13 he who *r* the commandment will be rewarded.
Sir 3: 4 he stores up riches who *r* his mother.
3: 6 He who *r* his father will live a long life;

REVERING (1)

Jos 22:25 would prevent ours from *r* the LORD.

REVERSED (1)

Est 9: 1 masters of them, the situation was *r*:

REVERT (3)

Lv 27:24 the field shall *r* to the hereditary owner
Ez 46:17 of release, when it shall *r* to the prince.
Hb 2:16 shall *r* the cup from the LORD's right hand,

REVERTS (1)

Ez 26: 2 now that it is ruined, its wealth *r* to me!"

REVIEW (2)

2Sm 15:18 city, were passing in *r* before the king,
Wis 19:18 exactly from a *r* of what took place.

REVIEWED (3)

1Sm 11: 8 When he *r* them in Bezek,
15: 4 and at Telaim *r* two hundred thousand foot
Zec 6: 5 after being *r* by the Lord of all the earth."

REVILE (7)

Ex 22:27 "You shall not *r* God,
Ps(s) 74:10 Shall the enemy *r* your name forever?
102: 9 All the day my enemies *r* me;
Eccl 10:20 in the privacy of your bedroom *r* the rich.
Sir 3:13 *r* him not in the fullness of your strength.
Jude 1: 8 God's dominion and *r* the angelic beings.
1:10 not only *r* what they have no knowledge of

REVILED (9)

Jb 19: 3 These ten times you have *r* me,
Ps(s) 55:13 If an enemy had *r* me,
74:18 and how a stupid people has *r* your name.
89:52 have *r*, O LORD, with which they have *r*
Sir 19: 6 Never repeat gossip, and you will not be *r*.
Is 52: 5 all the day my name is constantly *r*.
Zep 2: 8 when they *r* my people and made boasts
2:10 because they *r* and boasted against the

REVILEMENT (1)

Wis 2:19 With *r* and torture let us put him to the

REVILES (1)

Prv 11:12 He who *r* his neighbor has no sense,

REVILING (2)

2Pt 2:10 qualms whatever about *r* celestial beings,
Rv 13: 6 *r* him and the members of his heavenly

REVILINGS (2)

Is 51: 7 of men, be not dismayed at their *r*.
Zep 2: 8 I have heard the *r* uttered by Moab,

REVIVE (9)

2Chr 7:14 and pardon their sins and *r* their land.
Est 4:30 and all his attendants tried to *r* her.
2Mc 13:11 this nation, which had just begun to *r*,
Ps(s) 71:20 bitter afflictions, you will again *r* me;
Is 57:15 *r* the spirits of the dejected, to *r* the hearts
Lam 1:16 who could console me, any who might *r* me;
Hos 6: 2 He will *r* us after two days;
Hb 3: 2 In the course of the years *r* it,

REVIVED (4)

Gn 45:27 the spirit of their father Jacob *r*.
Jgs 15:19 drank till his spirit returned and he *r*.
1Sm 30:12 When he had eaten, he *r*;
1Kgs 17:22 returned to the child's body and he *r*.

REVIVING (1)

2Kgs 23: 3 thus *r* the terms of the covenant which

REVOKE (10)

Est 8: 3 to *r* the harm done by Haman the Agagite,
8: 5 to *r* the letters which that schemer Haman,
Am 1: 3 and for four, I will not *r* my word;
1: 6 Gaza, and for four, I will not *r* my word;
1: 9 of Tyre, and for four I will not *r* my word;
1:11 Edom, and for four, I will not *r* my word;
1:13 and for four, I will not *r* my word;
2: 1 Moab, and for four, I will not *r* my word;
2: 4 Judah, and for four, I will not *r* my word;
2: 6 Israel, and for four, I will not *r* my word;

REVOKED (3)

Est 8: 8 with the royal signet ring cannot be *r*.
1Mc 11:36 none of these provisions shall ever be *r*.
Ps(s) 85: 4 you have *r* your burning anger.

REVOLT (9)

2Kgs 8:22 has been in *r* against the rule of Judah.
2Chr 21:10 Edom has continued in *r* against the
1Mc 13:16 he is set free he will not *r* against us,
2Mc 4:30 the people of Tarsus and Mallus rose in *r*,
5:11 the king, he thought that Judea was in *r*.
14: 3 incurred defilement at the time of the *r*,
14:38 In the early days of the *r*,
Heb 3: 8 the *r* in the day of testing in the desert,
3:15 voice, harden not your hearts as at the *r*,"

REVOLTED (11)

Nm 26: 9 who *r* against Moses and Aaron [like
2Kgs 8:20 Edom *r* against the sovereignty of Judah
8:22 Libnah also *r* at that time.
2Chr 21: 8 Edom *r* against the sovereignty of Judah;
21:10 Libnah also *r* at that time against
1Mc 11:14 because the people of that region had *r*.
11:43 fight for me, because all my troops have *r*."
2Mc 1: 7 *r* against the holy land and the kingdom,
Ez 2: 3 fathers have *r* against me to this very day.
16:27 Philistines, who *r* at your lewd conduct.
Heb 3:16 those that *r* when they heard that voice?

REVOLVE (1)

Sir 33: 5 his thoughts *r* in circles.

REVOLVING (2)

Gn 3:24 the cherubim and the fiery *r* sword,
Sir 38:29 at his labor, *r* the wheel with his feet.

REVULSION (1)

Sir 40:29 His neighbor's delicacies bring *r* of

REWARD (64)

Gn 15: 1 I will make your *r* very great."
30:18 "God has given me my *r* for having let my
Nm 22:17 I will *r* you very handsomely and will do
22:37 Did you think I could not *r* you?"
24:11 *r* you richly, but the LORD has withheld the *r*
Dt 7:12 "As your *r* for heeding these decrees and
Ru 2:12 May the LORD *r* what you have done!
2:12 May you receive a full *r* from the LORD,
1Sm 24:20 May the LORD *r* you generously for what you
26:23 The LORD will *r* each man for his justice
2Sm 4:10 news for which I ought to give him a *r*.
18:22 You will receive no *r*."
19:37 Why should the king give me this *r*?
Tb 4:14 as God's servant, you will receive your *r*.
Est 6: 3 was done to *r* and honor Mordecai for this?"
6: 6 done for the man whom the king wishes to *r*?"
6: 6 the king more probably wish to *r* than me?"
6: 7 "For the man whom the king wishes to *r*
6: 9 must clothe the man the king wishes to *r*,
6: 9 done for the man whom the king wishes to *r*!'"
6:11 done for the man whom the king wishes to *r*!"
1Mc 10:27 and we will *r* you with favors in return
2Mc 8:33 received the *r* his wicked deeds deserved.
12:45 with a view to the splendid *r* that awaits
Ps(s) 24: 5 from the LORD, a *r* from God his savior.
58:12 say, "Truly there is a *r* for the just;
69:28 guilt, and let them not attain to your *r*.
127: 3 the fruit of the womb is a *r*.
Prv 11:18 but he who sows virtue has a sure *r*.
12:14 the work of his hands comes back to *r* him.
22: 4 The *r* of humility and fear of the LORD is
31:31 Give her a *r* of her labors,
Wis 2:22 holiness nor discern the innocent souls' *r*.
3:14 For he shall be given fidelity's choice *r*
Sir 2: 8 trust him, and your *r* will not be lost.
11:18 a miser's life, and this is his allotted *r*:
12: 2 good to the just man and *r* will be yours,
16:14 Whoever does good has his *r*,
36:15 your name, *R* those who have hoped in you,
51:22 The LORD has granted me my lips as a *r*,
51:30 in his own time God will give you your *r*.
Is 40:10 Here is his *r* with him,
49: 4 my strength, Yet my *r* is with the LORD,
62:11 Here is his *r* with him,
Jer 17:10 heart, To *r* everyone according to his ways,
31:16 sorrow you have shown shall have its *r*,
Dn 11:39 the many and distribute the land as a *r*.
12:13 shall rise for your *r* at the end of days."
Mt 5:12 and rejoice, for your *r* is great in heaven;
10:41 name of prophet receives a prophet's *r*;
10:41 known to be holy receives a holy man's *r*.
10:42 he is a disciple will not want for his *r*."
Mk 9:41 will not, I assure you, go without his *r*.
Lk 6:23 exult, for your *r* shall be great in heaven.
Eph 2: 9 it a *r* for anything you have accomplished,
Col 3:24 receive an inheritance from him as your *r*.
Heb 10:35 it will have great *r*.
11:26 of Egypt, for he was looking to the *r*.
2Pt 2:12 suffering the *r* of their wickedness.
2Jn 1: 8 you must receive your *r* in full.
Rv 11:18 The time to *r* your servants the prophets
22:12 I bring with me the *r* that will be given

REWARDED (6)

1Sm 17:27 is how the man who kills him will be *r*."
2Sm 22:21 "The LORD *r* me according to my justice;
2Chr 15: 7 and do not relax, for your work shall be *r*."
Est A:16 at the court, and *r* him for his actions.
Ps(s) 18:21 The LORD *r* me according to
Prv 13:13 he who reveres the commandment will be *r*.

REWARDING (3)

2Chr 6:23 innocent and *r* him according to his virtue.
Jdt 13:20 everlasting honor, *r* you with blessings,
1Mc 11:53 Instead of *r* Jonathan for all the favors

REWARDS (3)

Ru 4:22 the consequent *r* of which were divine
Heb 11: 6 exists, and that he *r* those who seek him.
11:25 rather than enjoy the fleeting *r* of sin.

REZEPH (2)

2Kgs 19:12 Gozan, Haran, *R*,
Is 37:12 Gozen, Haran, *R*,

REZIN (9)

2Kgs 15:37 at that time that the LORD first loosed *R*,
16: 5 Then *R*, king of Aram,
16: 9 its inhabitants to Kir and put *R* to death.
Ezr 2:48 sons of Gahar, sons of Reaiah, sons of *R*,
Neh 7:50 sons of Gahar, sons of Reaiah, sons of *R*,
Is 7: 1 of Judah, son of Jotham, son of Uzziah, *R*,
7: 4 [the blazing anger of *R* and the Arameans,
7: 8 of Aram, and *R* the head of Damascus;
8: 6 the loftiness of *R* and Remaliah's son,

REZON (2)

1Kgs 11:23 against Solomon another adversary, in *R*,
11:24 *R* gathered men about him and became leader

RHEGIUM (1)

Acts 28:13 we sailed around the toe and arrived at *R*.

RHESA (1)

Lk 3:27 son of Joda, son of Joanan, son of *R*,

RHODA (1)

Acts 12:13 door and a maid named *R* came to answer it.

RHODANITES (1)

Ez 27:15 The *R* trafficked with you;

RHODES (2)

1Mc 15:23 Samos, Pamphylia, Lycia, Halicarnassus, *R*,
Acts 21: 1 came to *R* and went on from there to Patara.

RHODOCUS (1)

2Mc 13:21 sent supplies to the men inside, but *R*,

RIB (1)

Gn 2:22 woman the *r* that he had taken from the man.

RIBAI (2)

2Sm 23:29 Ittai, son of *R*,
1Chr 11:31 Ithai, son of *R*, from Gibeah of Benjamin;

RIBBON (2)

Ex 28:37 to be tied over the miter with a violet *r*
39:31 It was tied over the miter with a violet *r*,

RIBBONS (2)

Ex 28:28 Violet *r* shall bind the rings of the
39:21 Violet *r* bound the rings of the

RIBLAH (11)

2Kgs 23:33 him prisoner at *R* in the land of Hamath,
25: 6 and brought to *R* to the king of Babylon,
25:20 brought them to the king of Babylon at *R*,
25:21 had them struck down and put to death in *R*,
Jer 39: 5 He was brought to *R*,
39: 6 slain at *R* by order of the king of Babylon,
52: 9 therefore, was arrested and brought to *R*,
52:10 as well as all the princes of Judah at *R*.
52:26 brought them to the king of Babylon at *R*,
52:27 had them struck down and put to death in *R*,
Ez 6:14 a desolate waste, from the desert to *R*;

RIBS (1)

Gn 2:21 his *r* and closed up its place with flesh.

RICH (146)

Gn 13: 2 Now Abram was very *r* in livestock,
14:23 lest you should say, 'I made Abram *r*.'
49:20 "Asher's produce is *r*,
Ex 30:15 The *r* need not give more,
34: 6 to anger and *r* in kindness and fidelity,
Nm 14: 7 through and explored is a fine, *r* land.
14:18 LORD is slow to anger and *r* in kindness,
Dt 28:12 you his *r* treasure house of the heavens,
Jgs 9: 9 answered them, 'Must I give up my *r* oil,
Ru 3:10 after the young men, whether poor or *r*.
1Sm 2: 7 The LORD makes poor and makes *r*,
30:16 all the *r* booty they had taken from the land
2Sm 12: 1 a certain town there were two men, one *r*,
12: 2 The *r* man had flocks and herds in great
12: 4 Now, the *r* man received a visitor,
1Chr 29:28 old age, *r* in years and wealth and glory,
Neh 8:10 "Go eat *r* foods and drink sweet drinks,
9:17 slow to anger and *r* in mercy;
9:37 Its *r* produce goes to the kings whom you
Tb 4:21 You will be a *r* man if you fear God,

Jdt 5: 9 Here they settled, and grew very *r* in gold,
10: 3 water, and anointed it with *r* ointment.
11: 8 you alone are competent, *r* in experience,
1Mc 6: 2 and gold, and that its temple was very *r*,
15:32 sideboard, and the rest of his *r* display,
2Mc 7:24 to make him *r* and happy if he would
Jb 15:29 He shall not be *r*,
21:24 nourished, and his bones are *r* in marrow.
27:19 He lies down a *r* man,
34:19 nor respects the *r* more than the poor?
Ps(s) 45:13 the *r* among the people seek your favor.
49: 3 birth or high degree, *r* and poor alike.
49:17 Fear not when a man grows *r*,
65:12 and your paths overflow with a *r* harvest;
92:11 you have anointed me with *r* oil.
119:162 your promise, as one who has found *r* spoil.
Prv 10:15 The *r* man's wealth is his strong city;
13: 7 One man pretends to be *r*,
14:20 hated, but the friends of the *r* are many.
18:11 The *r* man's wealth is his strong city;
18:23 implores, but the *r* man answers harshly.
19: 1 than he who is crooked in his ways and *r*.
21:17 who loves wine and perfume will not be *r*.
22: 2 *R* and poor have a common bond:
22: 7 The *r* rule over the poor,
22:16 yield up his gains to the *r* as sheer loss.
28: 3 A *r* man who oppresses the poor is like a
28: 6 than he who is crooked in his ways and *r*.
28:11 The *r* man is wise in his own eyes,
28:20 in haste to grow *r* will not go unpunished.
Eccl 5:11 the *r* man's abundance allows him no sleep.
10: 6 position while the *r* sit in lowly places.
10:20 the privacy of your bedroom revile the *r*.
Wis 8: 5 in life, what is more *r* than Wisdom,
Sir 8: 2 Quarrel not with a *r* man,
10:29 as the *r* man is honored for his wealth;
11:18 A man may become *r* through a miser's life,
11:21 in an instant, to make a poor man *r*.
13: 3 The *r* man does wrong and boasts of it,
13: 4 the *r* man can use you he will enslave you,
13:17 the *r* and the poor can there be peace?
13:18 too the poor are feeding grounds for the *r*.
13:19 so does the *r* man abhor the poor.
13:20 *r* man stumbles he is supported by a friend;
13:21 the supporters for a *r* man when he speaks;
13:22 A *r* man speaks and all are silent,
24:17 vine, my blossoms become fruit fair and *r*.
25: 2 A proud pauper, a *r* dissembler,
26: 4 Be he *r* or poor,
30:14 robust, than a *r* man with wasted frame.
31: 3 The *r* man labors to pile up wealth,
31: 8 Happy the *r* man found without fault,
38:11 a *r* offering according to your means.
Is 3:24 for the *r* gown,
5:17 and kids shall eat in the ruins of the *r*.
25: 6 feast of *r* food and choice wines, juicy, *r*
30:23 the soil produces will be *r* and abundant.
55: 2 eat well, you shall delight in *r* fare.
Jer 5:27 Therefore they grow powerful and *r*,
9:22 nor the *r* man glory in his riches;
40:12 and had a *r* harvest of wine and fruit.
51:13 who dwell by mighty waters, *r* in treasure,
Ez 17: 7 great eagle, great of wing, *r* in plumage;
27:24 with you, marketing with you *r* garments,
34:14 and in *r* pastures shall they be pastured
Dn 13: 4 Joakim was very *r*;
Hos 12: 9 Though Ephraim says, "How *r* I have become;
Jl 2:13 is he, slow to anger, *r* in kindness,
Jon 4: 2 merciful God, slow to anger, *r* in clemency,
Mi 6:12 You whose *r* men are full of violence,
Zec 11: 5 "Blessed be the LORD, I have become *r*!"
Mt 13:12 has, more will be given until he grows *r*;
19:23 will a *r* man enter into the kingdom of God.
19:24 for a *r* man to enter the kingdom of God."
21:43 to a nation that will yield a *r* harvest.
25:29 who have will get more until they grow *r*,
Mk 10:23 is for the *r* to enter the kingdom of God!"
10:25 for a *r* man to enter the kingdom of God."
Lk 1:53 thing, while the *r* he has sent empty away.
6:24 "But woe to you *r*,
10: 2 "The harvest is *r* but the workers are few;
12:16 "There was a *r* man who had a good harvest.
12:21 grows rich for himself instead of growing *r*
16: 1 "A *r* man had a manager who was reported
16:19 "Once there was a *r* man who dressed in
16:21 scraps that fell from the *r* man's table.
16:22 The *r* man likewise died and was buried.
16:27 I ask you, then,' the *r* man said,
16:30 'No, Father Abraham,' replied the *r* man.
18:23 grew melancholy, for he was a very *r* man.
18:24 be for the *r* to go into the kingdom of God!
18:25 for a *r* man to enter the kingdom of heaven."
21: 1 He glanced up and saw the *r* putting their
Acts 14:17 heavens he sends down rain and *r* harvests;
Rom 10:12 *r* in mercy toward all who call upon him.
11:17 come to share in the *r* root of the olive,
1Cor 4: 8 You have grown *r*!
14:12 to be *r* in those that build up the church.
2Cor 8: 7 that just as you are *r* in every respect,
8: 9 though he was *r*, so that you might become *r*
8:10 some advice on this matter of *r* and poor.
Eph 2: 4 But God is *r* in mercy;
Phil 1:11 It is my wish that you may be found *r* in
Col 3:16 Let the word of Christ, *r* as it is,
1Tm 6: 9 *r* are falling into temptation and a trap.
6:17 *r* in this world's goods not to be proud,
6:18 good, to be *r* in good works and generous,
2Tm 1:14 Guard the *r* deposit of faith with the help
Jas 1:10 and the *r* man be proud of his lowliness,
1:11 *r* man wither away amid his many projects.
2: 5 in the eyes of the world to be *r* in faith
2: 6 Are not the *r* exploiting you?
3:17 *r* in sympathy and the kindly deeds that
5: 1 you *r*, weep and wail over your impending
1Pt 3: 3 or the donning of *r* robes is not for you.
Rv 2: 9 and your poverty, even though you are *r*.
3:17 am so *r* and secure that I want for nothing."
3:18 refined by fire if you would be truly *r*.
13:16 all men, small and great, *r* and poor,
18: 3 grew *r* from her wealth and wantonness."
18:15 who grew *r* from business with the city,
18:19 *r* from their profitable trade with her!

RICHER (4)

Gn 26:13 him, he became *r* and richer all the time,
26:13 him, he became richer and *r* all the time,
Prv 11:24 One man is lavish yet grows still *r*;
Sir 19: 1 He who does so grows no *r*;

RICHES (71)

1Kgs 3:11 for a long life for yourself, nor for *r*,
3:13 such *r* and glory that among kings there is
10:23 in *r* and wisdom all the kings of the earth.
1Chr 29:12 *R* and honor are from you,
2Chr 1:11 your wish and you have not asked for *r*,
1:12 but I will also give you *r*,
9:22 of the earth in *r* as well as in wisdom.
32:29 numbers, for God gave him very great *r*.
Jdt 15: 6 plundered it, and acquired great *r*.
Est 1: 4 he displayed the glorious *r* of his kingdom
5:11 He recounted the greatness of his *r*,
2Mc 3: 6 in Jerusalem was so full of untold *r*
3: 7 about the *r* that had been reported to him.
Jb 20:10 and his hands shall yield up his *r*.
20:15 The *r* he swallowed he shall disgorge;
Ps(s) 49: 7 the abundance of their *r* is their boast.
63: 6 *r* of a banquet shall my soul be satisfied,
112: 3 Wealth and *r* shall be in his house;
119:14 decrees I rejoice, as much as in all *r*.
Prv 3:16 right hand, in her left are *r* and honor;
8:18 With me are *r* and honor,
11:28 He who trusts in his *r* will fall,
13: 8 A man's *r* serve as ransom for his life,
22: 1 good name is more desirable than great *r*,
22: 4 of humility and fear of the LORD is *r*,
30: 8 from me, give me neither poverty nor *r*;
Eccl 4: 8 his toil, and *r* do not satisfy his greed.
5:10 Where there are great *r*,
5:12 *r* kept by their owner to his hurt.
5:13 the *r* be lost through some misfortune,
5:18 Any man to whom God gives *r* and property,
6: 2 to whom God gives *r* and property and honor,
9:11 by the wise, nor *r* by the shrewd,
Wis 7: 8 deemed *r* nothing in comparison with her,
7:11 her company, and countless *r* at her hands;
7:13 her *r* I do not hide away;
8: 5 And if *r* be a desirable possession in life,
8:18 and unfailing *r* in the works of her hands,
Sir 3: 4 he stores up *r* who reveres his mother.
11:14 and evil, life and death, poverty and *r*,
14:15 Will you not leave your *r* to others,
31: 1 Keeping watch over *r* wastes the flesh,
Is 10:14 has seized like a nest the *r* of nations;
30: 6 They carry their *r* on the backs of asses
33: 6 her seasons lasting, the *r* that save her,
45: 3 darkness, and *r* that have been hidden away,
60: 5 For the *r* of the sea shall be emptied out
61: 6 of the nations and boast of *r* from them.
Jer 9:22 strength, nor the rich man glory in his *r*;
Bar 6:34 they cannot give anyone *r* or coppers;
Ez 28: 4 intelligence you have made *r* for yourself;
28: 5 to your trading you have heaped up your *r*;
28: 5 your heart has grown haughty from your *r*—
29:19 He shall carry off its *r*,
30: 4 when her *r* are seized and her foundations
Dn 11: 2 fourth shall acquire the greatest *r* of all.
11: 2 Strengthened by his *r*,
11:24 and *r* among them and devise plots against
11:28 turn back toward his land with great *r*,
11:43 He shall control the *r* of gold and silver
Mi 4:13 and their *r* to the Lord of the whole earth.
Zec 14:14 The *r* of all the surrounding nations shall
Lk 8:14 cares and *r* and pleasures of life
Rom 9:23 order to make known the *r* of his glory
11:12 have meant *r* for the Gentile world,
11:33 *r* and the wisdom and the knowledge of God!
Eph 3: 8 preach to the Gentiles the unfathomable *r*
3:16 gifts in keeping with the *r* of his glory.
Phil 4:19 of his magnificent *r* in Christ Jesus.
Heb 11:26 greater *r* than the treasures of Egypt,
Rv 5:12 that was slain to receive power and *r*,

RICHEST (1)

Sir 36:24 A wife is her husband's *r* treasure,

RICHLY (6)

Nm 24:11 I promised to reward you *r*,
2Mc 3:25 appeared to them a *r* caparisoned horse,
Prv 28:20 The trustworthy man will be *r* blessed;
1Cor 1: 5 in whom you have been *r* endowed with every
1Tm 6:17 provides us *r* with all things for our use.
2Pt 1:11 Savior Jesus Christ will be *r* provided for.

RID (12)

Gn 35: 2 "Get *r* of the foreign gods that you have
Lv 26: 6 I will *r* the country of ravenous beasts,
26:43 But the land must first be *r* of them,
1Mc 8:18 He did this to get *r* of the yoke,
2Mc 14:23 He got *r* of the throngs of ordinary people
Ez 34:25 them, and *r* the country of ravenous beasts,
Mt 15:23 and began to entreat him, "Get *r* of her.
Lk 1:74 *r* of fear and delivered from the enemy,
Acts 22:22 *R* the earth of the likes of him!
1Cor 5: 2 of grieving, and getting *r* of the offender!
5: 7 Get *r* of the old yeast to make of
Eph 4:31 Get *r* of all bitterness,

RIDDEN (3)

Nm 22:30 have you not always *r* upon me until now?
Mk 11: 2 there a colt on which no one has *r*.
Lk 19:30 an ass tied there which no one has yet *r*.

RIDDLE (11)

Jgs 14:12 said to them, "Let me propose a *r* to you.
14:13 "Propose your *r*,"
14:15 After three days' failure to answer the *r*,
14:15 "Coax your husband to answer the *r* for us,
14:16 for you have proposed a *r* to my countrymen,
14:17 and she explained the *r* to her countrymen.
14:18 my heifer, you would not have solved my *r*."
14:19 garments to those who had answered the *r*.
Ps(s) 49: 5 set forth my *r* to the music of the harp.
Sir 47:17 With song and story and *r*,
Ez 17: 2 Son of man, propose a *r*,

RIDDLES (3)

Nm 12: 8 face I speak to him, plainly and not in *r*.
Prv 1: 6 parable, the words of the wise and their *r*.
Wis 8: 8 turns of phrases and the solutions of *r*;

RIDE (15)

Gn 41:43 had him *r* in the chariot of his vizier,
Nm 10:36 O LORD, you who *r* upon the clouds,
Dt 32:13 He had them *r* triumphant over the summits
Jgs 5:10 They who *r* on white asses,
2Sm 16: 2 asses are for the king's household to *r* on.
19:27 that I may *r* on it and go with the king.'
Est 6: 9 have him *r* on the horse in the public
6:11 him *r* in the public square of the city,
Ps(s) 45: 4 In your splendor and your majesty *r* on
66:12 You let men *r* over our heads;
Sir 8:16 man, nor *r* with him through the desert;
Is 30:16 "Upon swift steeds we will *r*."
58:14 make you *r* on the heights of the earth;
Jer 6:23 the roaring sea as they *r* forth on steeds,
50:42 the roaring sea, as they *r* forth on steeds,

RIDER (14)

Gn 49:17 heel, so that the *r* tumbles backward.
Jdt 9: 7 force, priding themselves on horse and *r*,
2Mc 3:25 caparisoned horse, mounted by a dreadful *r*.
3:25 The *r* was seen to be wearing golden armor.
13:15 They also slew the lead elephant and its *r*.
Jb 39:18 she makes sport of the horse and his *r*.
Sir 33: 6 stallion that neighs, no matter who the *r*.
Jer 51:21 With you I shatter horse and *r*,
Zec 12: 4 horse with fright, and its *r* with madness.
Rv 6: 2 its *r* had a bow,
6: 4 Its *r* was given power to rob the earth of
6: 5 the *r* of which held a pair of scales in
6: 8 Its *r* was named Death,
19:11 its *r* was called "The Faithful and True."

RIDERS (8)

2Kgs 18:23 thousand horses if you can put *r* on them.
Is 36: 8 thousand horses, if you can put *r* on them.'
Ez 38: 4 horses and *r* all handsomely outfitted,
39:20 be filled at my table with horses and *r*,
Hg 2:22 their riders, and the *r* with their horses
Rv 9:17 this is how I saw the horses and their *r*.
19:18 and warriors, of horses and their *r*;

RIDES (5)

Lv 15: 9 Any saddle on which the afflicted man *r*,
Dt 33:26 who *r* the heavens in his power, and rides
Ps(s) 68: 5 his name, extol him who *r* upon the clouds,
68:34 *r* on the heights of the ancient heavens.

RIDGE (8)

Nm 34:11 *r* on the east side of Sea of Chinnereth;
Jos 15:10 north of the *r* of Mount Jearim (that is,
16: 2 it crossed the *r* to the border of the
Jgs 16: 3 them to the top of the *r* opposite Hebron.

RIDGE (cont.)

Jdt 3: 9 to the main *r* of the Judean mountain,
6:12 ran out of the city to the crest of the *r*;
Jer 26:18 of ruins, and the temple mount a forest *r*.
Mi 3:12 And the mount of the temple to a forest *r*.

RIDICULE (9)

Tb 8:10 die, we would be subjected to *r* and insult."
Jer 18:16 into a desert, an object of lasting *r*:
25: 9 making them an object of horror, of *r*,
25:18 and a desert, an object of *r* and cursing,
29:18 earth, of malediction, astonishment, *r*,
51:37 A place of horror and *r*,
Mt 9:24 At this they began to *r* him.
Mk 5:40 At this they began to *r* him.
Rom 14: 3 not *r* him who abstains from certain foods;

RIDICULED (5)

Neh 2:19 and Geshem the Arab mocked us and *r* us.
3:33 He *r* the Jews,
1Mc 7:34 But he mocked and *r* them,
2Mc 7:24 in her words, thought he was being *r*.
Ez 36: 3 because you have been *r* and despised on

RIDICULOUS (3)

Wis 17: 8 soul themselves sickened with a *r* fear.
Jer 10:15 Nothingness are they, a *r* work;
51:18 Nothingness are they, a *r* work,

RIDING (15)

Ex 4:20 to the land of Egypt, with them *r* the ass.
Nm 22:22 to hinder him as he was *r* along on his ass,
1Sm 25:20 down through a mountain defile *r* on an ass,
2Sm 18: 9 earth while the mule he had been *r* ran off.
Est 8:10 couriers *r* thoroughbred royal steeds.
2Mc 10:29 majestic men *r* on golden-bridled horses,
Is 19: 1 is *r* on a swift cloud on his way to Egypt;
21: 7 Someone riding an ass, someone *r* a camel,
Jer 17:25 *r* in their chariots or upon their horses,
22: 4 palace, *r* in chariots or mounted on horses,
Ez 27:20 Dedan traded with you for *r* gear.
Zec 9: 9 a just savior is he, Meek, and *r* on an ass,
Rv 19:14 *r* white horses and dressed in fine linen,
19:19 to do battle with the One *r* the horse,

RIFE (1)

Sir 18:27 sin is *r* he keeps himself from wrongdoing.

RIFT (2)

1Kgs 11:25 a *r* in Israel by becoming king over Edom.
Is 30:13 of yours shall be like a descending *r*

RIGGING (1)

Is 33:23 no majestic ship passes, The *r* hangs slack;

RIGHT (450)

Gn 13: 9 the left, I will go to the *r*; if you prefer the *r*
18:19 of the LORD by doing what is *r* and just,
24:48 who had led me on the *r* road to obtain the
32:19 and Jacob himself is *r* behind us.'"
32:21 to add, 'Your servant Jacob is *r* behind us.'"
38:26 and said, "She is more in the *r* than I am,
41:16 God who will give Pharaoh the *r* answer."
48:13 took the two, Ephraim with his *r* hand,
48:13 Manasseh with his left hand, to Israel's *r*,
48:14 *r* hand and laid it on the head of Ephraim,
48:17 had laid his *r* hand on Ephraim's head,
48:18 to Manasseh's, saying, "That is not *r*,
48:18 lay your *r* hand on his head!"
Ex 8:22 But Moses replied, "It is not *r* to do so,
14:22 like a wall to their *r* and to their left.
14:23 after them *r* into the midst of the sea.
14:29 like a wall to their *r* and to their left.
15: 6 power your *r* hand, O LORD, has shattered
15: 6 O LORD, magnificent in power your *r* hand,
15:12 when you stretched out your *r* hand,
15:26 told them, "and do what is *r* in his eyes:
21: 8 He has no *r* to sell her to a foreigner,
28:28 will stay *r* above the embroidered belt
29:20 right ear and on the tips of his sons' *r* ears
29:20 *r* hands and the great toes of their *r* feet
29:22 the fat that is on them, and its *r* thigh,
39:21 so that the breastpiece stayed *r* above the
Lv 7:32 the priest the *r* leg as a raised offering.
7:33 shall have the *r* leg as his portion,
8:23 right ear, on the thumb of his *r* hand,
8:23 hand, and on the big toe of his *r* foot.
8:24 of the blood on the tips of their *r* ears,
8:24 *r* hands, and on the big toes of their *r* feet
8:24 ears, on the thumbs of their right hands,
8:25 with their fat, and likewise the *r* leg;
8:26 top of the portions of fat and the *r* leg.
9:21 *r* legs as a wave offering before the LORD,
14:14 man's right ear, the thumb of his *r* hand,
14:14 and the big toe of his right foot.
14:16 then, dipping his *r* forefinger in it,
14:17 man's *r* ear, the thumb of his right hand,
14:17 hand, and the big toe of his *r* foot,
14:25 tip of the *r* ear of the man being purified,
14:25 *r* hand, and on the big toe of his *r* foot.
14:27 with his *r* forefinger sprinkle it seven times
14:28 man's right ear, the thumb of his *r* hand,
14:28 right hand, and the big toe of his *r* foot,
24: 9 to the LORD, it is his by perpetual *r*."
25:25 relative, who has the *r* to redeem it,
25:29 he has the *r* to buy it back during the
25:32 always have the *r* to redeem the town houses
25:48 services he still has the *r* of redemption;
27:29 that are doomed lose the *r* to be redeemed;
27:33 sacred, without the *r* of being bought back."
Nm 18: 9 You shall have the *r* to share in the
18:18 *r* leg of the wave offering belong to you.
20:17 road without turning to the *r* or the left,
22:26 to move either to the *r* or to the left.
36: 5 of the Josephites are *r* in what they say.
Dt 2:27 without turning aside to the *r* or the left.
5:32 not turning aside to the *r* or to the left,
6:18 is *r* and good in the sight of the LORD,
12: 8 everyone does what seems *r* to himself,
12:25 doing what is *r* in the sight of the LORD.
12:28 is good and *r* in the sight of the LORD,
13:19 on you today, doing what is *r* in his sight.
17:11 without turning aside to the *r* or to the
17:20 *r* or to the left from these commandments.
18: 3 *r* to the following things from the people:
21: 9 doing what is *r* in the sight of the LORD.
28:14 not turning aside to the *r* or to the left
32: 4 how *r* all his ways!
33: 2 While at his *r* hand a fire blazed forth
Jos 1: 7 from it either to the *r* or to the left,
9:25 power, do with us what you think fit and *r*."
22:27 that we have the *r* to worship the LORD in
Jgs 3:16 wore it under his clothes over his *r* thigh.
3:21 left hand drew the dagger from his *r* thigh,
5:26 hand she reached for the peg, with her *r*,
7:20 and in their *r* the horns they were blowing,
9:40 slain *r* up to the entrance of the gate.
16:29 himself against them, one at his *r* hand,
1Sm 6:12 as they went, without turning *r* or left.
9:13 immediately, for you should find him *r* now."
11: 2 I must gouge out every man's *r* eye,
12:23 you and to teach you the good and *r* way.
24:18 "You are in the *r* rather than I;
2Sm 2:14 Joab replied, "All *r*!"
2:19 turning neither *r* nor left in his pursuit.
2:21 Abner said to him, "Turn *r* or left;
16: 6 guard, were on David's *r* and on his left.
19:29 What *r* do I still have to make further
20: 9 With his *r* hand Joab held Amasa's beard as
1Kgs 2:19 for the king's mother, who sat at his *r*.
3: 9 people and to distinguish *r* from wrong.
3:11 so that you may know what is *r*—
6: 8 the annex was at the *r* side of the temple,
7:21 to the porch of the temple, one to the *r*,
7:49 five to the *r* and five to the left before
8:36 teaching them the *r* way to live and
22:19 standing by to his *r* and to his left.
22:43 doing what was *r* in the LORD's sight.
2Kgs 5:21 "Is everything all *r*?"
7: 9 "We are not doing *r*.
10:30 you have done well what I deem *r*,
12:10 *r* as one entered the temple of the LORD.
1Chr 6:24 His brother Asaph stood at his *r* hand.
12: 2 could use either the *r* or the left hand,
18:14 dispensed justice and *r* to all his people.
2Chr 3:17 for the *r* side and the other for the left,
3:17 the *r* Jachin and the one to the left Boaz.
4: 6 five of them to the *r* and five to the left.
4: 7 nave, five to the *r* and five to the left.
4: 8 nave, five to the *r* and five to the left;
4:10 southeast from the *r* side of the temple.
6:27 But teach them the *r* way to live,
9: 8 them as king to administer *r* and justice."
18:18 standing by to his *r* and to his left.
20:32 doing what was *r* in the LORD's sight.
Neh 4:17 everyone kept his weapon at his *r* hand.
8: 4 at his *r* side stood Mattithiah,
12:31 The first of these proceeded to the *r*,
Tb 2:13 owners, we have no *r* to eat stolen food!"
3:17 For Tobiah had the *r* to claim her before
4:21 and do what is *r* before the Lord your God."
5:14 No, they did not stray from the *r* path;
6: 9 blowing into his eyes *r* on the cataracts,
6:12 all other men have the *r* to marry her.
6:13 you have the *r* to marry her listen to me,
6:13 of Moses, and he knows that it is your *r*,
7:10 I have the *r* to give her to anyone but you,
13: 6 all your heart, to do what is *r* before him,
13: 6 do the *r* before him:
14: 9 God faithfully and do what is *r* before him;
1Mc 5:46 *r* or the left; they would have to march *r*
6:45 of the phalanx, killing men *r* and left,
6:46 He ran *r* under the elephant and stabbed it
7:47 they cut off Nicanor's head and his *r* arm,
9: 1 Judah, along with the *r* wing of his army.
9:12 Bacchides was on the *r* wing.
9:14 Seeing that Bacchides was on the *r*,
9:15 drove back the *r* wing and pursued them as
9:16 wing saw that the *r* wing was driven back,
10:30 I renounce the *r* from this day forward:
11:58 gave him the *r* to drink from gold cups,
12:11 as it is *r* and proper to remember brothers.
14:43 *r* to wear royal purple and gold ornaments.
14:46 *r* to act in accord with these decisions,
2Mc 1:18 Chislev, so we thought it *r* to inform you,
4:19 spent on a sacrifice, as that was not *r*,
4:34 through sworn pledges with *r* hands joined,
9:12 he said, "It is *r* to be subject to God,
14:33 he raised his *r* hand toward the temple and
15:15 Stretching out his *r* hand,
15:30 *r* arm to be cut off and taken to Jerusalem.
Jb 6:29 Think it over; I still am *r*.
9:15 Even though I were *r*,
9:20 Though I were *r*, my own mouth might
11: 2 or must the garrulous man necessarily be *r*?
13:18 my case, I know that I am in the *r*.
27: 5 Far be it from me to account you *r*;
32: 2 himself rather than God to be in the *r*.
32: 9 wise, nor the aged who understand the *r*.
33:23 To show him what is *r* for him and bring
34: 4 Let us discern for ourselves what is *r*;
34: 6 Notwithstanding my *r* I am set at nought;
35: 2 Do you think it *r* to say,
36: 3 afar, and to my Maker I will accord the *r*.
40: 8 Would you refuse to acknowledge my *r*?
40:14 that your own *r* hand can save you.
Ps(s) 9: 5 For you upheld my *r* and my cause,
16: 8 him at my *r* hand I shall not be disturbed.
16:11 the delights at your *r* hand forever.
17: 2 your eyes behold what is *r*.
17: 7 from their foes to refuge at your *r* hand.
18:36 your *r* hand has upheld me,
19: 9 The precepts of the LORD are *r*,
20: 7 with the strength of his victorious *r* hand.
21: 9 enemies, may your *r* hand reach your foes!
23: 3 guides me in *r* paths for his name's sake.
26:10 and their *r* hands are full of bribes.
33: 5 He loves justice and *r*;
37:14 poor, to slaughter those whose path is *r*.
37:28 For the LORD loves what is *r*,
37:30 of wisdom and his tongue utters what is *r*.
44: 4 *r* hand and the light of your countenance,
45: 5 may your *r* hand show you wondrous deeds.
45:10 her place at your *r* hand in gold of Ophir.
48:11 Of justice your *r* hand is full;
50:23 the *r* way I will show the salvation of God."
60: 7 help us by your *r* hand,
63: 9 your *r* hand upholds me.
73:23 you have hold of my *r* hand;
74:11 keep your *r* hand idle beneath your cloak?
77:11 the *r* hand of the Most High is changed."
78:54 land, to the mountains his *r* hand had won.
80:16 and protect what your *r* hand has planted
80:18 your help be with the man of your *r* hand,
89:14 strong is your hand, exalted your *r* hand.
89:26 upon the sea, his *r* hand upon the rivers.
89:43 You have exalted the *r* hands of his foes,
91: 7 at your side, ten thousand at your *r* side,
98: 1 His *r* hand has won victory for him,
106: 3 Happy are they who observe what is *r*,
108: 7 ones may escape, help us by your *r* hand,
109: 6 and let the accuser stand at his *r* hand.
109:31 For he stood at the *r* hand of the poor man,
110: 1 "Sit at my *r* hand till I make your
110: 5 The LORD is at your *r* hand;
118:15 *r* hand of the LORD is exalted; the *r* hand
118:16 *r* hand of the LORD has struck with power."
119:137 are just, O LORD, and your ordinance is *r*.
121: 5 he is beside you at your *r* hand.
137: 5 you, Jerusalem, may my *r* hand be forgotten!
138: 7 your *r* hand saves me.
139:10 guide me, and your *r* hand hold me fast.
142: 5 I look to the *r* to see,
144: 8 while their *r* hands are raised in perjury.
144:11 while their *r* hands are raised in perjury.
Prv 1: 3 training in wise conduct, in what is *r*,
3:16 Long life is in her *r* hand,
4:27 Turn neither to *r* nor to left,
8: 9 and *r* to those who attain knowledge.
12:15 way of the fool seems *r* in his own eyes,
14:12 Sometimes a way seems *r* to a man,
16:13 and the man who speaks what is *r* he loves.
16:25 Sometimes a way seems *r* to a man,
18:17 his case first seems to be in the *r*;
20:11 whether his conduct is innocent and *r*.
21: 2 the ways of a man may be *r* in his own eyes,
21: 3 To do what is *r* and just is more
21: 7 away, because they refuse to do what is *r*.
21: 8 but the conduct of the innocent is *r*.
23:16 will exult, when your lips speak what is *r*.
23:19 be wise, and guide your heart in the *r* way.
Eccl 10: 2 man's understanding turns him to his *r*;
10:17 and whose princes dine at the *r* time (for
Sg 2: 6 under my head and his *r* arm embraces me.
8: 3 is under my head and his *r* arm embraces me.
Wis 4:12 of paltry things obscures what is *r*
5:16 For he shall shelter them with his *r* hand,
10: 8 first were bereft of knowledge of the *r*,
Sir 3: 1 Children, pay heed to a father's *r*;
12:12 Let him not sit at your *r* hand,
20: 3 a maiden is he who does *r* under compulsion.
20: 6 A wise man is silent till the *r* time comes,
21:19 to a fool, like a manacle on his *r* hand.
21:21 a wise man, like a bracelet on his *r* arm.
32: 3 that is only your *r*,

35:18 responds, judges justly and affirms the *r*.
36: 5 forth the splendor of your *r* hand and arm;
45:24 on him again God conferred the *r*,
47: 5 who gave strength to his *r* arm To defeat
48:16 Some of these did what was *r*,
48:22 was *r* and held fast to the paths of David,
49: 4 these kings of Judah, *r* to the very end.
49: 9 JOB, who always persevered in the *r* path.
49:11 who was like a signet ring on God's *r* hand,
Is 1:18 Come now, let us set things *r*,
9:19 Though they hack on the *r*,
16: 5 judge upholding *r* and prompt to do justice.
28:17 I will make of *r* a measuring line,
30:10 "Do not descry for us what is *r*;
30:21 you would turn to the *r* or to the left.
32:16 *R* will dwell in the desert and justice
32:17 *r* will produce calm and security.
33: 5 he fills Zion with *r* and justice.
40:27 LORD, and my *r* is disregarded by my God"?
41:10 and uphold you with my *r* hand of justice.
41:13 the LORD, your God, who grasp your *r* hand;
43: 9 produce witnesses to prove themselves *r*,
44:20 "Is not this thing in my *r* hand a fraud?"
45: 1 his anointed, Cyrus, whose *r* hand I grasp,
45:19 promise justice, I foretell what is *r*.
48:13 my *r* hand spread out the heavens.
50: 8 He is near who upholds my *r*;
50: 8 Who disputes my *r*?
54: 3 spread abroad to the *r* and to the left;
56: 1 Observe what is *r*,
59: 8 there is nothing that is *r* in their paths;
59: 9 That is why *r* is far from us and justice
59:11 We look for *r*, but it is not there
59:14 *R* is repelled, and justice stands far off;
61: 8 For I, the LORD, love what is *r*,
62: 8 sworn by his *r* hand and by his mighty arm:
63:12 glorious arm was the guide at Moses' *r*;
64: 4 Would that you might meet us doing *r*,
Jer 11:15 What *r* has my beloved in my house,
12: 1 You would be in the *r*,
22: 3 Do what is *r* and just.
22:15 He did what was *r* and just,
22:24 of Judah, are a signet ring on my *r* hand,
23: 5 he shall do what is just and *r* in the land.
26:14 do with me what you think good and *r*.
32: 7 relative, have the first *r* of purchase."
33:15 he shall do what is *r* and just in the land.
34:15 repented and did what is *r* in my eyes
Lam 2: 3 of his *r* hand when the enemy approached;
2: 4 in his *r* hand He took his stand as a foe,
Bar 6:14 Each has in its *r* hand an axe or dagger,
Ez 1:10 but on the *r* side was the face of a lion,
4: 6 are to lie down again, but on your *r* side,
8: 4 stationed to the *r* of the temple
18: 5 if he does what is *r* and just,
18:19 the son has done what is *r* and just,
18:21 my statutes and does what is *r* and just,
18:27 he has committed, does what is *r* and just,
21:21 Cleave to the *r*!
21:27 In his *r* hand is the divining arrow
33:14 from his sin and does what is *r* and just,
33:16 he has done what is *r* and just,
33:18 turns away from what is *r* and does wrong,
33:19 wickedness and does what is *r* and just,
39: 3 hand, and make the arrows drop from your *r*.
45: 9 and oppression, and do what is *r* and just!
Dn 3:27 your deeds are faultless, all your ways *r*,
4:34 all his works are *r* and his ways just;
12: 7 lifted his *r* and left hands to heaven;
13:15 while they were waiting for the *r* moment,
Hos 2:21 I will espouse you in *r* and in justice,
12: 7 loyal and do *r* and always hope in your God.
Am 3:10 For they know not how to do what is *r*,
Jon 4:11 distinguish their *r* hand from their left,
Mi 3: 1 Is it not your duty to know what is *r*,
3: 9 what is just, and pervert all that is *r*;
6: 8 Only to do *r* and to love goodness,
7: 9 he takes up my cause, and establishes my *r*.
Hb 2:16 revert the cup from the LORD's *r* hand,
Zec 3: 1 Satan stood at his *r* hand to accuse him.
4: 3 one on the *r* and the other on the left."
6:13 The priest shall be put at his *r* hand,
11:17 sword fall upon his arm and upon his *r* eye;
11:17 entirely, and his *r* eye be blind forever!
12: 6 *r* and left all the surrounding peoples;
Mt 5:29 If your *r* eye is your trouble,
5:30 Again, if your *r* hand is your trouble,
5:39 When a person strikes you on the *r* cheek,
6: 3 left hand know what your *r* hand is doing.
14: 4 "It is not *r* for you to live with her."
15:26 "It is not *r* to take the food of sons and
20:21 at your *r* hand and the other at your left,
20:23 my *r* hand or my left is not mine to give.
22:44 Lord said to my lord, Sit at my *r* hand,
24:38 *r* up to the day Noah entered the ark.
25:33 The sheep he will place on his *r* hand,
25:34 The king will say to those on his *r*:
26:64 seated at the *r* hand of the Power
27: 6 "It is not *r* to deposit this in the
27:29 his head, and stuck a reed in his *r* hand.
27:38 with him, one at his *r* and one at his left.
Mk 6:18 *r* for you to live with your brother's wife."
7:27 It is not *r* to take the food of the
10:37 one at your *r* and the other at your left,
10:40 But as for sitting at my *r* or my left,
12:32 You are *r* in saying,
12:36 Sit at my *r* hand until I make your enemies
14:54 *r* into the high priest's courtyard,
14:62 see the Son of Man seated at the *r* hand
15:27 one at his *r* and one at his left.
16: 5 tomb they saw a young man sitting at the *r*,
16:19 heaven and took his seat at God's *r* hand.
Lk 1:11 standing at the *r* of the altar of incense.
6: 6 there was a man whose *r* hand was withered.
7:43 Jesus said to him, "You are *r*."
17:27 *r* up to the day Noah entered the ark
20:42 Sit at my *r* hand while I make your enemies
22:50 priest's servant and cut off his *r* ear.
22:69 his seat at the *r* hand of the Power of God.' "
23:33 one on his *r* and the other on his left.
Jn 4:17 "You are *r* in saying you have no husband!"
5:29 Those who have done *r* shall rise to live;
7: 6 "It is not yet the *r* time for me,
7: 6 me, whereas the time is always *r* for you.
7:28 I was sent by One who has the *r* to send,
8:48 The Jews answered, "Are we not *r*,
18:10 of the high priest, severing his *r* ear.
Acts 2:25 him at my *r* hand I shall not be disturbed.
2:33 Exalted at God's *r* hand,
2:34 Sit at my *r* hand until I make your
3: 7 took him by the *r* hand and pulled him up.
4:19 "Judge for yourselves whether it is *r*
5:31 He whom God has exalted at his *r* hand as
6: 2 "It is not *r* for us to neglect the word
7:55 of God, and Jesus standing at God's *r* hand.
7:56 the Son of Man standing at God's *r* hand."
8:37 said, "Look, there is some water *r* there.
13:10 son of Satan and enemy of all that is *r*!
25:11 me, no one has a *r* to hand me over to them.
Rom 2: 7 and immortality by patiently doing *r*;
7:18 desire to do *r* is there but not the power.
7:21 that even though I want to do what is *r*,
8:34 *r* hand of God and who intercedes for us?
9:21 Does not a potter have the *r* to make from
13: 3 is *r* but only when his conduct is evil.
13: 3 what is *r* and you will gain its approval,
1Cor 8: 9 lest in exercising your *r* you become an
9: 4 Do we not have the *r* to eat and drink?
9: 5 Do we not have the *r* to marry a believing
9:12 right over you, is not our *r* even greater?
9:12 But we have not used this *r*.
2Cor 6: 7 of righteousness with *r* hand and left,
Gal 4:18 be courted for the *r* reasons at all times,
6: 1 by the spirit should gently set him *r*,
Eph 1:20 and seating him at his *r* hand in heaven,
Phil 1: 6 *r* up to the day of Christ Jesus.
1: 7 It is only *r* that I should entertain such
3: 4 a *r* to put his trust in external evidence,
Col 3: 1 where Christ is seated at God's *r* hand.
2Thes 1: 3 *r* that we thank God unceasingly for you,
3:13 must never grow weary of doing what is *r*,
Ti 1:11 by teaching things they have no *r* to teach
2:14 a people of his own, eager to do what is *r*.
3: 8 to God may be careful to do what is *r*.
Phlm 1: 8 I feel that I have every *r* to command you
Heb 1: 3 at the *r* hand of the Majesty in heaven,
1:13 "Sit at my *r* hand till I make your
8: 1 who has taken his seat at the *r* hand of
10:12 took his seat forever at the *r* hand of God;
12: 2 his seat at the *r* of the throne of God.
12:10 They disciplined us as seemed *r* to them,
13:10 who serve the tabernacle have no *r* to eat.
Jas 2: 3 the well-dressed man and say, "Sit *r* here,
2:19 believe that God is one? You are quite *r*.
4:17 knows the *r* thing to do and does not do it,
1Pt 2:20 put up with suffering for doing what is *r*,
3: 6 do what is *r* and let no fears alarm you.
3:13 are committed deeply to doing what is *r*?
3:22 He went to heaven and is at God's *r* hand,
Rv 1:16 In his *r* hand he held seven stars.
1:17 He touched me with his *r* hand and said:
1:20 of the seven stars you saw in my *r* hand,
2: 1 who holds the seven stars in his *r* hand
3:21 victor the *r* to sit with me on my throne,
5: 1 In the *r* hand of the One who sat on the
5: 5 has won the *r* by his victory to open the
5: 7 *r* hand of the One who sat on the throne.
10: 2 He placed his *r* foot on the sea and his
10: 5 raised his *r* hand to heaven and took an oath
13:16 image on their *r* hand or their forehead.

RIGHTEOUS (18)

Tb 3: 2 "You are *r*, O LORD, and all your deeds
7: 7 that such a *r* and charitable man should
13: 9 but will again pity the children of the *r*.
13:13 then, rejoice over the children of the *r*,
Jb 4:17 "Can a man be *r* as against God?
10:15 if *r*, I dare not hold up my head
15:14 one born of woman that he should be *r*?
17: 9 Yet the *r* shall hold to his way,
32: 1 Job, because he was *r* in his own eyes.
35: 7 If you are *r*, what do you give him,
Prv 11:11 the blessing of the *r* the city is exalted,
21:18 the just, and the faithless man for the *r*.
Jer 23: 5 when I will raise up a *r* shoot to David;
Lk 15: 7 *r* people who have no need to repent.
Rom 5:18 *r* act brought all men acquittal and life.
Ti 3: 5 not because of any *r* deeds we had done,
Heb 1: 8 a *r* scepter is the scepter of your kingdom.
Rv 15: 3 *R* and true are your ways,

RIGHTEOUSNESS (11)

Gn 15: 6 who credited it to him as an act of *r*.
Tb 1: 3 of my life on the paths of truth and *r*.
12: 8 than either is almsgiving accompanied by *r*.
12: 8 *r* is better than abundance with wickedness.
13: 6 Bless the Lord of *r*,
14: 7 and shall bless the God of the ages in *r*.
1Mc 2:29 Many who sought to live according to *r* and
Prv 16:12 of wrongdoing, for by *r* the throne endures.
25: 5 and his throne is made firm through *r*.
2Cor 6: 7 the weapons of *r* with right hand and left,
6:14 what do *r* and lawlessness have in common,

RIGHTFUL (4)

Lv 6:11 Aaron may partake of it as their *r* share
Jb 8: 6 awake for you and restore your *r* domain;
Prv 18: 5 to the guilty, and so to reject a *r* claim.
Sir 15:10 its *r* steward will proclaim it.

RIGHTFULLY (1)

Tb 6:12 her father's estate is *r* yours to inherit.

RIGHTLY (10)

Jb 42: 7 for you have not spoken *r* concerning me,
42: 8 For you have not spoken *r* concerning me,
Wis 6: 4 of his kingdom, you judged not *r*,
Sir 41:24 These are the things you should *r* avoid
Is 32: 1 will reign justly and princes will rule *r*.
Ez 34:16 strong I will destroy], shepherding them *r*.
Lk 6:35 You will *r* be called sons of the Most High,
1Cor 7:37 his mind to keep his virgin, also acts *r*.
Heb 13:18 as we do, to act *r* in every respect.
Jas 2: 8 You are acting *r*,

RIGHTS (30)

Ex 21:10 her food, her clothing, or her conjugal *r*.
23: 6 your needy fellow men his *r* in his lawsuit.
Dt 17: 8 or of civil *r* or of personal injury,
21:17 and to him belong the *r* of the first-born.
24:17 the *r* of the alien or of the orphan,
27:19 be he who violates the *r* of the alien,
1Sm 8: 9 of the *r* of the king who will rule them."
8:11 "The *r* of the king who will rule you will
2Mc 13:23 their terms, and swore to observe their *r*.
Jb 23: 7 I should once and for all preserve my *r*.
29:16 the *r* of the stranger I studied,
36: 6 He withholds not the just man's *r*,
Ps(s) 103: 6 justice and the *r* of all the oppressed.
Prv 29: 7 just man has a care for the *r* of the poor;
29:14 If a king is zealous for the *r* of the poor,
29:26 ruler, but the *r* of each are from the LORD.
31: 5 and violate the *r* of all who are in need.
31: 8 the dumb, and for the *r* of the destitute;
Eccl 5: 7 violation of *r* and justice in the realm,
Wis 19:16 those who now shared with them the same *r*.
Sir 47:11 He conferred on him the *r* of royalty and
Is 5:23 bribes, and deprive the just man of his *r*!
10: 2 and robbing my people's poor of their *r*,
Lam 3:35 men's *r* in the very sight of the Most High,
Bar 6:53 They neither vindicate their own *r*,
Ez 18:18 Only the father, since he violated *r*,
Hos 5:11 Is Ephraim maltreated, his *r* violated?
Lk 18: 3 saying, 'Give me my *r* against my opponent.'
1Cor 9:15 As for me, I have not used any of these *r*,
1Pt 4:15 malefactor, or a destroyer of another's *r*.

RIGID (1)

Mk 9:18 mouth and grinds his teeth and becomes *r*.

RIGOROUS (1)

Wis 6: 8 for those in power a *r* scrutiny impends.

RIM (7)

1Sm 23:26 As Saul moved along one *r* of the gorge,
1Kgs 7:23 it was made with a circular *r*,
2Chr 4: 3 below the *r* a ring of figures of oxen
2Mc 13: 5 with a circular *r* sloping down steeply on
Ez 43:13 with a *r* around its edges of one span.
43:17 wide, with a half-cubit *r* surrounding it.
43:20 of the ledge, and on the *r* all around.

RIMMON (13)

Jos 19:13 and to Eth-kazin, extended to *R*,
21:35 pasture lands, *R* with its pasture lands,
Jgs 20:45 and fled through the desert to the rock *R*.
20:47 fled through the desert reached the rock *R*,
21:13 message to the Benjaminites at the rock *R*,
2Sm 4: 2 and Rechab, son of *R* the Beer-othite,
4: 5 The sons of *R* the Beerothite,
4: 9 brother Baanah, sons of *R* the Beerothite:
2Kgs 5:18 enters the temple of *R* to worship there,
5:18 adjutant, must bow down in the temple of *R*.
1Chr 4:32 Etam, also, and Ain, *R*,

RIMMON (cont.)
6:62 pasture lands, *R* with its pasture lands,
Zec 14:10 And from Geba to *R* in the Negeb,

RIMMON-PEREZ (2)
Nm 33:19 Setting out from Rithmah, they camped at *R.*
33:20 Setting out from *R,* they camped at Libnah.

RIMS (3)
Ez 1:18 The four of them had *r,*
1:18 that their *r* were full of eyes all around.
10:12 The *r* of the four wheels were full of eyes

RING (33)
Gn 24:22 took out a gold *r* weighing half a shekel,
24:30 As soon as he saw the *r* and the bracelets
24:47 So I put the *r* on her nose and the
37: 7 a *r* around my sheaf and bowed down to it."
41:42 his signet *r* and put it on Joseph's finger.
Ex 26:24 likewise double at the top, to the first *r.*
36:29 likewise double at the top, to the first *r.*
Nm 31:50 up, such as an anklet, a bracelet, a *r,*
Jgs 8:24 each of you give me a *r* from his booty?"
8:25 which everyone threw a *r* from his booty.
1Sm 3:11 the ears of everyone who hears it to *r.*
2Kgs 21:12 anyone hears of it, his ears shall *r.*
2Chr 4: 3 a *r* of figures of oxen encircled the sea,
Est 3:10 *r* from his hand and gave it to Haman,
3:12 and sealed with the royal signet *r.*
8: 2 The king removed his signet *r* from Haman,
8: 8 seal the letter with the royal signet *r.*"
8: 8 with the royal signet *r* cannot be revoked.
8:10 and sealed with the royal signet *r,*
1Mc 6:15 him his crown, his robe, and his signet *r,*
Jb 42:11 one gave him a piece of money and a gold *r.*
Ps(s) 32: 7 glad cries of freedom you will *r* me round.
49: 6 days when my wicked ensnarers *r* me round?
Prv 11:22 Like a golden *r* in a swine's snout is a
Sir 17:17 goodness God cherishes like a signet *r,*
49:11 was like a signet *r* on God's right hand,
Jer 22:24 of Judah, are a signet *r* on my right hand,
Ez 16:12 necklace about your neck, a *r* in your nose,
Dn 6:18 the king sealed with his own *r* and the
14:11 then shut the door and seal it with your *r.*
14:14 sealed the closed door with the king's *r,*
Hg 2:23 LORD, And I will set you as a signet *r;*
Lk 15:22 a *r* on his finger and shoes on his feet.

RINGED (1)
Sir 50:12 His brethren *r* him about like a garland,

RINGLEADER (1)
Acts 24: 5 He is a *r* of the sect of Nazoreans.

RINGLEADERS (1)
1Mc 9:61 *r* in the mischief and put them to death.

RINGS (42)
Gn 35: 4 and also the *r* they had in their ears.
Ex 25:12 Cast four gold *r* and fasten them on the
25:12 *r* on one side and two on the opposite side.
25:14 put through the *r* on the sides of the ark,
25:15 in the *r* of the ark and never be withdrawn.
25:26 You shall also make four *r* of gold for it
26:29 gold *r* on them as holders for the bars,
27: 4 this to have four bronze *r,*
27: 7 These poles are to be put through the *r,*
28:23 you shall then make two *r* of gold for it
28:24 two *r* at the upper ends of the breastpiece,
28:26 Make two other *r* of gold and put them on
28:27 Then make two more *r* of gold and fasten
28:28 Violet ribbons shall bind the *r* of the
28:28 *r* of the breastpiece to the *r* of the ephod,
30: 4 the molding you shall put gold *r,*
35:22 them, brought brooches, earrings, *r,*
36:34 and gold *r* were made on them as holders
37: 3 *r* were cast and put on its four supports,
37: 3 two *r* for one side and two for the
37: 5 put through the *r* on the sides of the ark,
37:13 *r* of gold were cast for it and fastened,
37:14 The *r* were alongside the frame as holders
37:27 Underneath the molding gold *r* were placed,
38: 5 Four *r* were cast for the four corners of
38: 7 The poles were put through the *r* on the
39:16 two gold filigree rosettes and two gold *r.*
39:16 The two *r* were fastened to the two upper
39:17 the two *r* at the ends of the breastpiece.
39:19 Two other gold *r* were made and put on the
39:20 Two more gold *r* were made and fastened to
39:21 *r* of the breastpiece to the rings
Jgs 8:24 being Ishmaelites, the enemy had gold *r.)*
8:26 The gold *r* that he requested weighed
Jdt 10: 4 feet, and put on her anklets, bracelets, *r,*
Est 1: 6 byssus from silver *r* on marble pillars.
Is 3:21 the signet rings, and the nose *r;*
Dn 6:18 with his own ring and the *r* of the lords
Hos 2:15 herself out with her *r* and her jewels,
Jas 2: 2 dressed, with gold *r* on his fingers,

RINGWORM (2)
Lv 21:20 who is afflicted with eczema, *r* or hernia.
22:22 one that has a running sore or mange or *r,*

RINNAH (1)
1Chr 4:20 The sons of Shimon were Amnon, *R,*

RINSED (3)
Lv 6:21 be scoured afterward and *r* with water.
15:12 every wooden article shall be *r* with water.
Ez 40:38 of the gate, where the holocausts were *r.*

RIOT (6)
2Mc 4:40 now thoroughly enraged, began to *r,*
Mt 26: 5 festival, for fear of a *r* among the people."
27:24 and that a *r* was breaking out instead.
Mk 14: 2 during the festival, or the people may *r.*"
Acts 17: 5 to form a mob and start a *r* in the town.
21:38 Egyptian who caused the *r* some time ago

RIOTERS (1)
Acts 21:32 and centurions and charged down on the *r.*

RIOTING (2)
Acts 19:40 accused of *r* because of today's conduct.
21:31 of the cohort that all Jerusalem was *r.*

RIOTOUS (1)
Prv 20: 1 Wine is arrogant, strong drink is *r;*

RIOTS (1)
2Cor 6: 5 beatings, imprisonments, and *r;*

RIP (2)
2Kgs 8:12 you will *r* open their pregnant women."
Mt 9:16 hole will pull, and the *r* only get worse.

RIPE (14)
Gn 24: 1 Abraham had now reached a *r* old age,
25: 8 he breathed his last, dying at a *r* old age,
Nm 17:23 blossoms as well, and even bore *r* almonds!
1Chr 29:28 He died at a *r* old age,
2Chr 24:15 Jehoiada lived to a *r* old age;
Jl 4:13 Apply the sickle, for the harvest is *r;*
Am 8: 1 a basket of *r* fruit.
8: 2 I answered, "A basket of *r* fruit."
8: 2 is *r* to have done with my people Israel;
Mk 4:28 the ear, finally the *r* wheat in the ear.
4:29 the sickle, for the time is *r* for harvest.'"
Jn 7: 8 because the time is not yet *r* for me."
Rv 14:15 the earth's harvest is fully *r.*"
14:18 vines of the earth, for the clusters are *r.*"

RIPENED (2)
Gn 40:10 came out, and its clusters *r* into grapes.
Phil 1:11 of justice which Jesus Christ has *r* in you,

RIPENING (3)
Sg 5:13 like beds of spice with *r* aromatic herbs.
Sir 51:15 As the blossoms yielded to *r* grapes,
Is 18: 5 and the blooms are succeeded by *r* grapes,

RIPENS (1)
Wis 10: 7 desert, Plants bearing fruit that never *r,*

RIPHATH (2)
Gn 10: 3 Ashkenaz, *R,* and Togarmah.
1Chr 1: 6 The descendants of Gomer were Ashkenaz, *R,*

RIPPED (2)
Hos 14: 1 their expectant mothers shall be *r* open.
Am 1:13 they *r* open expectant mothers in Gilead,

RIPPING (1)
2Kgs 15:16 them even to *r* open all the pregnant women.

RISE (135)
Gn 17:16 he shall give *r* to nations,
31:35 offended that I cannot *r* in your presence;
Ex 33: 8 the people would all *r* and stand at the
33:10 all the people would *r* and worship at the
Nm 24: 7 His king shall *r* higher than .
24:17 Jacob, and a staff shall *r* from Israel,
Dt 28: 7 you the enemies that *r* up against you;
28:43 you will *r* higher and higher above you,
29:21 own descendants who will *r* up after you,
32:38 of your libations *R* up now and help you!
33:11 and of his foes, that they may not *r.*"
Jos 7:13 *R,* sanctify the people.
8: 7 *r* from ambush and take possession of the
Jgs 20:40 signal column began to *r* up from the city.
2Sm 2:14 "Let the young men *r* and perform for us."
12:17 beside him urging him to *r* from the ground:
12:21 the child is dead, you *r* and take food."
15: 2 Absalom used to *r* early and stand
22:39 I smote them and they did not *r;*
Ezr 10: 4 *R,* then, for this is your duty!
Tb 6:18 with her, both of you first *r* up to pray.
Jdt 16:17 to the nations that *r* against my people!
Est 5: 9 that Mordecai at the royal gate did not *r,*
2Mc 12:44 were not expecting the fallen to *r* again,
Jb 14:12 parches, So men lie down and *r* not again.
20:27 and the earth shall *r* up against him.
30:12 To subvert my paths they *r* up;
30:28 I *r* up in public to voice my grief.
Ps(s) 2: 2 The kings of the earth *r* up,
3: 2 Many *r* up against me!
3: 8 *R* up, O LORD!
7: 7 *R* up, O LORD, in your anger; rise against
9:20 O LORD, let no man prevail;
10:12 *R,* O LORD!
17:13 *R,* O LORD, confront them
18:39 I smote them and they could not *r;*
35: 2 shield and buckler, and *r* up in my defense.
36:13 they are thrust down and cannot *r.*
41: 9 'Now that he lies ill, he will not *r* again.'
78: 6 That they too may *r* and declare to their
82: 8 *R,* O God; judge the earth,
94: 2 *R* up, judge of the earth
94:16 Who will *r* up for me against the wicked?
119:62 At midnight I *r* to give you thanks because
127: 2 It is vain for you to *r* early,
139:21 Those who *r* up against you do I not loathe?
140:11 he cast them into the depths, never to *r.*
Prv 6: 9 when will you *r* from your sleep?
31:28 Her children *r* up and praise her;
Sg 3: 2 I will *r* then and go about the city;
Wis 5: 6 shine for us, and the sun did not *r* for us.
Sir 11: 5 The oppressed often *r* to a throne,
17:18 Later he will *r* up and repay them,
Is 5:11 drink as soon as they *r* in the morning,
8: 7 It shall *r* above all its channels,
14: 9 kings of all nations *r* from their thrones.
14:21 Lest they *r* and possess the earth,
14:22 I will *r* up against them,
21: 5 *R* up, O princes, oil the shield!
24:20 it down, until it falls, never to *r* again."
26:14 they have no life, shades that cannot *r;*
26:19 dead shall live, their corpses shall *r;*
28:21 the LORD shall *r* up as on Mount Perazim,
31: 2 He will *r* up against the house of the
32: 9 complacent ladies, *r* up and hear my voice,
33: 3 when you *r* in your majesty,
33:10 Now will I *r* up,
34:10 not be quenched, its smoke shall *r* forever.
43:17 they lie prostrate together, never to *r,*
58:10 Then light shall *r* for you in the darkness,
60: 1 *R* up in splendor!
Jer 2:27 of trouble they cry out, *R* up and save us!"
2:28 Let them *r* up!
8: 4 When someone falls, does he not *r* again?
18: 2 *R* up, be off to the potter's house;
25:27 fall, never to *r,*
31: 6 *R* up, let us go to Zion,
37:10 would *r* up and destroy the city with fire.
49:14 move against her, *r* up for battle.
49:28 *R* up, attack Kedar, ravage the Easterners
49:31 *R* up! set out against a nation
51:64 Never shall she *r,*
Lam 1:14 me into their grip, I am unable to *r.*
2:19 *R* up, shrill in the night,
Ez 10:16 lifted their wings to *r* from the earth,
10:19 wings, and I saw them *r* from the earth,
37:12 open your graves and have you *r* from them,
37:13 open your graves and have you *r* from them,
Dn 7:24 another shall *r* up after them,
11:14 people shall *r* up in fulfillment of vision,
11:21 shall *r* in his place a despicable person,
11:23 *r* to power with a small party.
12:13 shall *r* for your reward at the end of days."
Am 5: 2 She is fallen, to *r* no more,
8:14 those shall fall, never to *r* again.
Jon 1: 6 *R* up, call upon your God!
Mi 4: 1 it shall *r* high above the hills,
Na 1: 9 The enemy shall not *r* a second time;
Hb 2: 7 Shall not your creditors *r* suddenly?
3:10 The sun forgets to *r,*
Mt 12:41 the citizens of Nineveh will *r* with the
12:42 the queen of the South will *r* with the
13:33 the whole mass of dough began to *r.*"
22:30 When people *r* from the dead,
24: 7 Nation will *r* against nation,
24:11 will *r* in great numbers to mislead many.
27:63 made the claim, 'After three days I will *r.*'
Mk 8:31 be put to death, and *r* three days later.
9:10 discuss what "to *r* from the dead" meant.
9:31 three days after his death he will *r.*"
10:34 But three days later he will *r.*"
12:25 When people *r* from the dead,
13: 8 Nation will *r* against nation,
Lk 2:34 the downfall and the *r* of many in Israel,
11:31 The queen of the South will *r* at the
11:32 will *r* along with the present generation,
13:21 until the whole mass of dough began to *r.*"
16:31 even if one should *r* from the dead.'"
18:33 and on the third day he will *r* again."
20:37 dead *r* again when he called the Lord
21:10 "Nation will *r* against nation and kingdom

24: 7 be crucified, and on the third day *r* again."
24:46 and *r* from the dead on the third day.
Jn 5:29 rise to live; the evildoers shall *r* to be
11:23 "Your brother will *r* again,"
11:24 "I know he will *r* again,"
20: 9 that Jesus had to *r* from the dead.)
Acts 17: 3 Messiah had to suffer and *r* from the dead:
26:23 and that, as the first to *r* from the dead,
Rom 15:12 he who will *r* up to rule the Gentiles;
1Thes 4:16 those who have died in Christ will *r* first.
Rv 14:10 of their torment shall *r* forever and ever.
19: 3 smoke began to *r* from her forever and ever,

RISEN (18)

Jgs 9:18 but you have *r* against his family this day
Ezr 4:19 this city has *r* up against kings and that
Jdt 8:18 has not *r* among us in recent generations,
13: 5 shatter the enemies who have *r* against us."
Ps(s) 27:12 for false witnesses have *r* up against me,
35:11 Unjust witnesses have *r* up;
54: 5 For haughty men have *r* up against me,
86:14 O God, the haughty have *r* up against me,
Bar 3:19 world, and others have *r* up in their stead.
Ez 7:11 violence has *r* to support wickedness.
47: 5 for the water had *r* so high it had become
Hos 7: 4 once the dough is kneaded until it has *r*.
Mi 2: 8 But of late my people has *r* up as an enemy:
Mk 9: 9 before the Son of Man had *r* from the dead.
Lk 7:16 "A great prophet has *r* among us,"
9: 8 others, "One of the prophets of old has *r*."
13:25 When once the master of the house has *r* to
Acts 10: 4 and your generosity have *r* in God's sight,

RISES (33)

Gn 2:10 A river *r* in Eden to water the garden;
Dt 22:26 *r* up against his neighbor and murders him:
Jos 11:17 from Mount Halak that *r* toward Seir as far
12: 7 valley to Mount Halak which *r* toward Seir,
1Sm 25:29 *r* to pursue you and to seek your life,
Jdt 14: 2 At daybreak, when the sun *r* on the earth,
Jb 9: 7 He commands the sun, and it *r* not;
16: 8 As a witness there *r* up my traducer,
24:14 When there is no light the murderer *r*,
24:22 To him who *r* without assurance of his
41:17 When he *r* up,
Ps(s) 104:22 When the sun *r*,
Prv 24:16 the just man falls seven times and *r* again,
31:15 She *r* while it is still night,
Eccl 1: 5 The sun *r* and the sun goes down
1: 5 then it presses on to the place where it *r*.
Sg 7: 6 You head *r* like Carmel;
Sir 35: 5 and *r* as a sweet odor before the Most High.
Is 3:13 The LORD *r* to accuse,
13:10 The sun is dark when it *r*,
30:18 to show you favor, and he *r* to pity you;
Jer 51:42 against Babylon the sea *r*,
Dn 8:25 when he *r* against the prince of princes,
Am 8: 8 While it *r* up and tosses like the Nile,
9: 5 on it mourn, While it *r* up like the Nile,
Mi 7: 6 the daughter *r* up against her mother,
Mt 5:45 for his sun *r* on the bad and the good,
17: 9 until the Son of Man *r* from the dead."
1Cor 15:42 subject to decay, what *r* is incorruptible.
15:43 is sown is ignoble, what *r* is glorious.
15:43 Weakness is sown, strength *r* up.
Eph 2:20 You form a building which *r* on the
2Pt 1:19 and the morning star *r* in your hearts.

RISING (33)

Gn 7:20 the crest *r* fifteen cubits higher than the
19:23 *r* over the earth as Lot arrived in Zoar,
19:28 over the land *r* like fumes from a furnace.
Ex 24: 4 of the LORD and, *r* early the next day,
Nm 32:14 *r* up in your fathers' place to add still
Dt 19:11 of hatred for him, and *r* up against him,
Jgs 5:31 your friends be as the sun *r* in its might!
1Sm 25:41 *R* and bowing to the ground,
28:13 see a preternatural being *r* from the earth."
28:14 she replied, "It is an old man who is *r*,
2Sm 12:20 *R* from the ground,
1Kgs 18:44 as small as a man's hand *r* from the sea."
1Mc 6:33 The king, *r* before dawn,
Jb 1: 5 *r* early and offering holocausts for every
Ps(s) 50: 1 from the *r* of the sun to its setting.
113: 3 From the *r* to the setting of the sun is
Sir 26:16 Like the sun *r* in the LORD's heavens,
31:20 slumber and a clear mind next day on *r*.
40:14 lightning and thunder, Which, in its *r*,
42:16 As the *r* sun is clear to all,
43: 2 The orb of the sun, resplendent at its *r*:
Is 45: 6 so that toward the *r* and the setting of
Jer 47: 2 waters are *r* from the north,
Ez 8:11 fragrance of the incense was *r* upward.
10:19 the earth, the wheels *r* along with them.
Dn 7:24 shall be ten kings *r* out of that kingdom;
Hos 13:15 a wind from the LORD, *r* from the desert,
Zec 8: 7 my people from the land of the *r* sun,
Mal 1:11 your hands, For from the *r* of the sun,
Mt 2: 2 at its *r* and have come to pay him homage."
2: 9 The star which they had observed at its *r*
Mk 1:35 *R* early the next morning,

Lk 12:54 "When you see a cloud *r* in the west,

RISK (7)

Jgs 9:17 my father fought for you at the *r* of his life
2Sm 17:17 could not *r* being seen entering the city.
23:17 these men who went at the *r* of their lives?"
1Chr 11:19 at the *r* of their lives they brought it;
Jer 30:21 one take the deadly *r* of approaching me?
Ez 46:20 *r* of transmitting holiness to the people."
Acts 19:40 we run the *r* of being accused of rioting

RISKED (5)

1Chr 11:19 the blood of these men who *r* their lives?"
Jdt 13:20 because you *r* your life when your people
2Mc 14:38 *r* body and life in his ardent zeal for it.
Rom 16: 4 even *r* their lives for the sake of mine.
Phil 2:30 He *r* his life in an effort to render me

RISKING (1)

2Mc 11: 7 him in *r* their lives to help their kinsmen.

RISKS (1)

Mt 5:22 him in contempt he *r* the fires of Gehenna.

RISSAH (2)

Nm 33:21 Setting out from Libnah, they camped at *R*.
33:22 Setting out from *R*,

RITE (11)

Ex 12:25 you must also observe this *r* when you have
12:26 ask you, 'What does this *r* of yours mean?'
13: 5 this month that you must celebrate this *r*,
13:10 *r* at its appointed time from year to year.
29: 1 "This is the *r* you shall perform in
30:10 shall perform the atonement *r* on its horns.
Lv 16:20 the atonement *r* for the sanctuary,
Jos 5: 8 When the *r* had been performed,
Acts 21:24 join with them in their *r* of purification;
21:26 *r* of purification with them the next day.
Eph 2:11 virtue of a hand-executed *r* on their flesh,

RITES (12)

Gn 23: 2 performed the customary mourning *r* for her.
Nm 25: 3 thus submitted to the *r* of Baal of Peor,
25: 5 have submitted to the *r* of Baal of Peor."
2Kgs 17: 8 They followed the *r* of the nations whom
17:19 but followed the *r* practiced by Israel.
17:34 they worship according to their ancient *r*.
2Mc 2:17 kingdom, the priesthood, and the sacred *r*,
Ps(s) 106:28 And they submitted to the *r* of Baal of
Wis 14:23 or frenzied carousals in unheard-of *r*,
19: 3 they were still engaged in funeral *r*
Ez 45:25 seven days, he shall perform the same *r*,
Acts 24:18 temple court completing the *r* of purification

RITHMAH (2)

Nm 33:18 out from Hazeroth, they camped at *R*.
33:19 Setting out from *R*,

RITUAL (14)

Lv 6: 2 This is the *r* for holocausts.
6: 7 "This is the *r* of the cereal offering.
6:18 This is the *r* for sin offerings.
7: 1 "This is the *r* for guilt offerings,
7: 7 are alike, both having the same *r*,
7:11 "This is the *r* for the peace offerings
7:37 This is the *r* for holocausts,
Nm 6:13 "This is the *r* for the nazirite:
1Chr 16:37 ark regularly according to the daily *r*;
2Mc 6:21 Those in charge of that unlawful *r* meal
Sir 45:17 and the *r* to the descendants of Israel.
Lk 2:27 perform for him the customary *r* of the law,
Jn 18:28 for they had to avoid *r* impurity if they
Heb 9:10 of food and drink and various *r* washings:

RIVAL (6)

Ex 14:20 night passed without the *r* camps
Lv 18:18 you shall not marry her sister as her *r*;
1Sm 1: 6 Her *r*, to upset her, turned it
2:32 *r* all the benefits enjoyed by Israel,
Sir 37:11 Speak not to a woman about her *r*,
Jn 19:12 makes himself a king becomes Caesar's *r*."

RIVALRIES (1)

Gal 5:20 jealousy, outbursts of rage, selfish *r*,

RIVALRY (5)

Eccl 4: 4 work is the *r* of one man for another.
9: 6 and hatred and *r* have long since perished.
Is 11:13 pass away, and the *r* of Judah be removed;
Phil 1:15 preach Christ from motives of envy and *r*,
2: 3 Never act out of *r* or conceit;

RIVER (110)

Gn 2:10 A *r* rises in Eden to water the garden;
2:13 The name of the second *r* is the Gihon;
2:14 The name of the third *r* is the Tigris;

2:14 The fourth *r* is the Euphrates.
15:18 of Egypt to the Great *R* [the Euphrates],
Ex 1:22 *r* every boy that is born to the Hebrews,
2: 3 placed it among the reeds on the *r* bank.
2: 5 daughter came down to the *r* to bathe,
2: 5 while her maids walked along the *r* bank.
4: 9 from the *r* and pour it on the dry land.
4: 9 the *r* will become blood on the dry land."
7:15 go and present yourself by the *r* bank,
7:17 the water of the *r* with the staff I hold,
7:18 in the *r* shall die, and the river itself
7:20 struck the waters of the *r* in full view
7:20 the water of the *r* was changed into blood.
7:21 The fish in the river died, and the *r* itself
7:24 neighborhood of the *r* for drinking water,
7:24 they could not drink from the *r* water.
7:25 passed after the LORD had struck the *r*.
7:28 The *r* will teem with frogs.
8: 5 and your houses and be left only in the *r*."
8: 7 only in the *r* shall they be left."
17: 5 go, the staff with which you struck the *r*.
23:31 Philistines, and from the desert to the *R*;
Lv 11: 9 whatever in the seas or in *r* waters has
Dt 1: 7 and as far as the Great *R* [the Euphrates].
11:24 from the Euphrates *R* to the Western Sea,
Jos 1: 4 *r* Euphrates and west to the Great Sea.
12: 1 Jordan, from the *R* Arnon to Mount Hermon,
24: 2 dwelt beyond the *R* and served other gods.
24: 3 region beyond the *R* and led him through
24:14 fathers served beyond the *R* and in Egypt,
24:15 the gods your fathers served beyond the *R*
2Sm 8: 3 his dominion at the Euphrates *R*.
1Kgs 5: 1 from the *R* to the land of the Philistines,
14:15 fathers, scattering them beyond the *R*,
2Kgs 10:33 the *r* Arnon up through Gilead and Bashan.
17: 6 them in Halah, at the Habor, a *r* of Gozan,
18:11 them in Halah, at the Habor, a *r* of Gozan,
23:29 the *r* Euphrates to the king of Assyria.
24: 7 from the Wadi of Egypt to the Euphrates *R*.
1Chr 5: 9 which extends from the Euphrates *R*,
5:26 Halah, Habor, and Hara, and to the *r* Gozan,
18: 3 up his victory stele at the *r* Euphrates.
19:16 the Arameans from the other side of the *R*,
2Chr 9:26 was ruler over all the kings from the *R*
Ezr 8:15 assemble by the *r* that flows toward Ahava,
8:21 proclaimed a fast, there by the *r* of Ahava,
8:31 We set out for Jerusalem from the *r* of
Tb 6: 2 and made camp beside the Tigris *R*.
6: 3 boy went down to wash his feet in the *r*,
Jdt 1: 9 Chelous, Kadesh, and the *R* of Egypt;
Est A: 9 there appeared to come forth a great *r*,
F: 3 tiny spring that grew into a *r*,
F: 3 The *r* is Esther,
1Mc 3:32 the Euphrates *R* to the frontier of Egypt,
3:37 the Euphrates *R* and advanced inland.
5:41 and camps on the other side of the *r*,
11: 7 accompanied the king as far as the *r*
12:30 for they had crossed the *r* Eleutherus.
Jb 40:23 If the *r* grows violent,
Ps(s) 66: 6 through the *r* they passed on foot;
72: 8 and from the *R* to the ends of the earth.
80:12 to the Sea, its shoots as far as the *R*.
Wis 11: 6 when the perennial *r* was troubled with
19:10 fishes the *r* swarmed with countless frogs.
Sir 24:29 suddenly this rivulet of mine became a *r*,
44:21 and from the *R* to the ends of the earth.
Is 7:20 the *R* [with the king of Assyria] the head,
8: 7 raises against them the waters of the *R*,
19: 5 the sea, the *r* shall shrivel and dry up;
48:18 your prosperity would be like a *r*,
59:19 *r* which the breath of the LORD drives on.
66:12 will spread prosperity over her like a *r*,
Bar 1: 4 all who lived in Babylon by the *r* Sud.
Ez 1: 1 I was among the exiles by the *r* Chebar,
1: 3 the land of the Chaldeans by the *r* Chebar.
3:15 who lived at Tel-abib by the *r* Chebar,
3:23 like the glory I had seen by the *r* Chebar.
10:15 creatures I had seen by the *r* Chebar.
10:20 beneath the God of Israel by the *r* Chebar,
10:22 just like those I had seen by the *r* Chebar;
32: 6 the *r* beds shall be filled with your blood.
43: 3 like that which I had seen by the *r* Chebar.
47: 5 was now a *r* through which I could not wade;
47: 5 had become a *r* that could not be crossed
47: 6 Then he brought me to the bank of the *r*,
47: 7 the *r* I saw very many trees on both sides.
47: 9 Wherever the *r* flows, every sort of living
47:12 Along both banks of the *r*,
Dn 8: 2 I was beside the *r* Ulai.
8: 3 by the *r* a ram with two great horns,
8: 6 ram I had seen standing by the *r*,
10: 4 month I was on the bank of the great *r*,
12: 5 one standing on either bank of the *r*.
Am 8: 8 Nile, and settles back like the *r* of Egypt?
9: 5 Nile, and settles back like the *r* of Egypt;
Mi 7:12 and from Egypt, From Tyre even to the *R*,
Na 2: 7 The *r* gates are opened,
Zec 9:10 and from the *R* to the ends of the earth.
Mt 3: 6 the Jordan *R* as they confessed their sins.
Mk 1: 5 the Jordan *R* as they confessed their sins.
Acts 16:13 the city gate to the bank of the *r*,
Rv 9:14 up on the banks of the great *r* Euphrates!"
16:12 out his bowl on the great *r* Euphrates.

RIVER (cont.)

22: 1 then showed me the *r* of life-giving water,
22: 2 On either side of the *r* grew the trees of

RIVERBANK (1)

Sir 40:16 Or they are like reeds on the *r*,

RIVERS (31)

Lv 11:10 the water, whether in the sea or in the *r*,
2Kgs 5:12 Are not the *r* of Damascus,
19:24 the soles of my feet all the *r* of Egypt.
Ps(s) 24: 2 the seas and established it upon the *r*.
78:16 the crag and brought the waters forth in *r*.
89:26 upon the sea, his right hand upon the *r*.
98: 8 Let the *r* clap their hands,
107:33 He changed *r* into desert,
Eccl 1: 7 All *r* go to the sea,
1: 7 place where they go, the *r* keep on going.
Is 18: 1 buzzing insects, beyond the *r* of Ethiopia,
18: 2 and conquering, whose land is washed by *r*.
18: 7 and conquering, whose land is washed by *r*—
33:21 In a place of *r* and wide streams on which
35: 6 forth in the desert, and *r* in the steppe.
37:25 the soles of my feet all the *r* of Egypt.
41:18 I will open up *r* on the bare heights,
42:15 I will turn the *r* into marshes,
43: 2 in the *r* you shall not drown.
43:19 desert I make a way, in the wasteland, *r*.
43:20 *r* in the wasteland for my chosen people
50: 2 I dry up the sea, I turn *r* into a desert;
Jer 46: 7 like the Nile, like *r* of billowing waters?
46: 8 like the Nile, like *r* of billowing waters.
Ez 31: 4 sending its *r* round where it was planted,
Dn 3:78 Seas and *r*, bless the Lord;
Na 1: 4 leaves it dry, and all the *r* he dries up.
Zep 3:10 From beyond the *r* of Ethiopia and as far
Jn 7:38 within him *r* of living water shall flow.' "
Rv 8:10 fell on a third of the *r* and the springs.
16: 4 poured out his bowl on the *r* and springs.

RIVULET (2)

Sir 24:28 Now I, like a *r* from her stream,
24:29 And suddenly this *r* of mine became a river,

RIZIA (1)

1Chr 7:39 sons of Ulla were Arah, Hanniel, and *R*.

RIZPAH (4)

2Sm 3: 7 Now Saul had had a concubine, *R*,
21: 8 that Aiah's daughter *R* had borne to Saul,
21:10 Then *R*, Aiah's daughter, took sackcloth
21:11 When David was informed of what *R*,

ROAD (90)

Gn 16: 7 wilderness, the spring on the *r* to Shur,
24:48 who had led me on the right *r* to obtain
35:19 was buried on the *r* to Ephrath [that is,
Ex 13:18 toward the Red Sea by way of the desert *r*.
Nm 14:25 and set out in the desert on the Red Sea *r*."
20:17 but we will go straight along the royal *r*
21: 4 Mount Hor they set out on the Red Sea *r*,
21:22 royal *r* until we have passed through your
21:33 turned and went up along the *r* to Bashan.
22:22 stationed himself on the *r* to hinder him
22:23 *r* with sword drawn, she turned off the *r*
22:23 had to beat her to bring her back on the *r*.
22:31 LORD standing on the *r* with sword drawn;
Dt 1:22 the land for us and report to us on the *r*
1:40 proceed into the desert on the Red Sea *r*.'
2: 1 proceed into the desert on the Red Sea *r*,
11:30 other side of the western *r* in the country
22: 4 on the *r* without showing concern about it;
Jos 2:22 them all along the *r* without finding them,
3: 4 for you have not gone over this *r* before.
9:17 The third day on the *r*,
Jgs 9:25 these robbed all who passed them on the *r*.
Ru 1: 7 were on the *r* back to the land of Judah,
1Sm 4:13 his chair beside the gate, watching the *r*,
6:12 Beth-shemesh and continued along this *r*,
13:17 the Ophrah *r* toward the district of Shual;
13:18 and the third took the *r* for Geba that
17:52 *r* from Shaaraim as far as Gath and Ekron.
26: 3 beside the *r* on the hill of Hachilah,
2Sm 4: 7 traveled on the Arabah *r* all night long.
13:30 While they were still on the *r*,
15: 2 stand alongside the *r* leading to the gate.
16:13 David and his men continued on the *r*,
20:12 So he removed Amasa from the *r* to the
20:13 When he had been removed from the *r*,
1Kgs 11:29 Ahijah the Shilonite met him on the *r*.
13:10 So he departed by another *r* and did not go
13:12 And his sons pointed out to him the *r*
13:24 But a lion met him on the *r*,
13:24 His corpse lay sprawled on the *r*,
13:25 passers-by saw the body lying in the *r*,
13:28 found the body lying in the *r* with the ass
19:15 the *r* back to the desert near Damascus,"
20:38 went on and waited for the king on the *r*,
2Kgs 6:19 "This is the wrong *r*,
10:15 met Jehonadab, son of Rechab, on the *r*.
Tb 5:10 so I know every *r* well."
10: 7 watch all day at the *r* her son had taken,
11: 5 the *r* by which her son was to come.
Jdt 15: 2 in all directions, and fled along every *r*,
1Mc 6:33 hastily along the *r* to Beth-zechariah;
9: 2 They took the *r* to Galilee,
13:20 went around by the *r* that leads to Adora,
Jb 8:19 There he lies rotting beside the *r*,
19:12 they build up their *r* to attack me,
24: 4 They force the needy off the *r*;
Ps(s) 73:18 You set them, indeed, on a slippery *r*;
Prv 5: 6 Lest you see before you the *r* to life,
8: 2 On the top of the heights along the *r*,
Wis 10:17 labors, Conducted them by a wondrous *r*,
14: 3 you have furnished even in the sea a *r*,
19: 7 Out of the Red Sea an unimpeded *r*,
Is 8:23 in the end he has glorified the seaward *r*,
49:11 I will cut a *r* through all my mountains,
Jer 31: 9 lead them to brooks of water, on a level *r*,
31:21 Set up *r* markers
31:21 to the highway, the *r* by which you went.
39: 4 *R* through the gate between the two walls.
Ez 21:24 Then put a signpost at the head of each *r*,
Hos 13: 7 like a panther by the *r* I will keep watch.
Na 2: 2 guard the rampart, Keep watch on the *r*,
Mt 7:13 leads to damnation is wide, the *r* is clear,
7:14 gate that leads to life, how rough the *r*,
8:28 that no one could travel along that *r*.
20:17 the Twelve aside on the *r* and said to them:
21: 8 huge crowd spread their cloaks on the *r*,
Mk 10:32 were on the *r* going up to Jerusalem,
10:52 sight and started to follow him up the *r*.
11: 8 Many people spread their cloaks on the *r*,
Lk 10:31 happened to be going down the same *r*;
18:35 blind man sat at the side of the *r* begging.
24:32 the *r* and explained the Scriptures to us?"
24:35 they recounted what had happened on the *r*
Acts 8:26 the *r* which goes from Jerusalem to Gaza,
8:36 moved along the *r* they came to some water,
17: 1 Paul and Silas took the *r* through
2Pt 2:15 They have abandoned the straight *r* and
2:21 not to have recognized the *r* to holiness
Jude 1:11 They have taken the *r* Cain took.

ROADBLOCKS (1)

Jdt 5: 1 higher peaks, and placed *r* in the plains.

ROADS (15)

Lv 26:22 dwindles away and your *r* become deserted.
Jgs 5: 6 traveled the *r* went by roundabout paths.
Tb 1:15 him as king, the *r* to Media became unsafe,
5: 2 which *r* to take for the journey into Media!"
5: 4 the *r* who would travel with him to Media.
1Mc 5: 4 the people by ambushing them along the *r*.
15:41 could go out and patrol the *r* of Judea.
Sir 32:21 Be not too sure even of smooth *r*,
Jer 6:16 Stand beside the earliest *r*,
Lam 1: 4 The *r* to Zion mourn for lack of pilgrims
Bar 4:26 My pampered children have trodden rough *r*,
6:42 women, girt with cords, sit by the *r*,
Ez 21:24 make for yourself two *r* over which the
21:24 Both *r* shall lead out from the same land.
21:26 two *r* divide stands the king of Babylon,

ROADSIDE (6)

Gn 38:16 So he went over to her at the *r*,
38:21 prostitute, the one by the *r* in Enaim?"
49:17 Let Dan be a serpent by the *r*,
Mt 20:30 suddenly two blind men sitting by the *r*,
21:19 a fig tree by the *r* he went over to it,
Mk 10:46 ("son of Timaeus") sitting by the *r*.

ROADWAY (1)

Lk 19:36 their cloaks on the *r* as he moved along;

ROAM (5)

2Chr 16: 9 eyes of the LORD *r* over the whole earth,
Ps(s) 73: 9 and their pronouncements *r* the earth:
104:20 then all the beasts of the forest *r* about;
Sg 2:17 cool and the shadows lenghten, *r*,
Jer 5: 1 *R* the streets of Jerusalem,

ROAMED (1)

Gn 21:14 As she *r* aimlessly in the wilderness of

ROAMING (4)

Jb 1: 7 said, "From *r* the earth an patrolling it."
2: 2 said, "From *r* the earth and patrolling it."
Ps(s) 109:10 May his children be *r* vagrants and beggars;
Lam 5:18 should be desolate, with jackals *r* there!

ROAMS (3)

Jb 24:15 In the night the thief *r* about,
Ps(s) 91: 6 Not the pestilence that *r* in darkness nor
Mt 12:43 it *r* through arid wastes searching for a

ROAR (28)

Jb 39:25 the *r* of the chiefs and the shouting.
Ps(s) 38: 9 I *r* with anguish of heart.
42: 8 calls unto deep in the *r* of your cataracts;
74: 4 Your foes *r* triumphantly in your shrine;
93: 4 More powerful than the *r* of many waters,
104:21 Young lions *r* for the prey and seek their
Sir 46:17 the tremendous *r* of his voice was heard.
Is 5:29 Their *r* is that of the lion,
5:29 the lion, like the lion's whelps they *r*;
5:30 [They will *r* over it,
17:12 peoples that roar like the *r* of the seas!
51:15 who stirs up the sea so that its waves *r*;
Jer 2:15 Against him lions *r* full-throated cries.
5:22 though its billows *r*,
10:13 he thunders, the waters in the heavens *r*,
31:35 Who stirs up the sea till its waves *r*,
51:16 he thunders, the waters in the heavens *r*,
51:38 They all *r* like lions,
Ez 19: 7 in it were appalled at the noise of his *r*.
Dn 10: 6 voice sounded like the *r* of a multitude.
Am 1: 2 The LORD will *r* from Zion,
3: 4 a lion *r* in the forest when it has no prey?
Hb 3:10 the ocean gives forth its *r*.
2Pt 3:10 that day the heavens will vanish with a *r*;
Rv 1:15 voice sounded like the *r* of rushing waters.
9: 9 Their wings made a sound like the *r* of
10: 3 then gave a loud cry like the *r* of a lion.

ROARED (1)

Jer 12: 8 Because she has *r* against me,

ROARING (29)

Jgs 14: 5 of Timnah, a young lion came *r* to meet him.
1Mc 3: 4 like a lion, like a young lion *r* for prey.
Ps(s) 22:14 against me like ravening and *r* lions.
35:17 Save me from the *r* beasts;
65: 8 roaring of the seas, the *r* of their waves
Prv 19:12 The king's wrath is like the *r* of a lion,
28:15 Like a *r* lion or a ravenous bear is a
Wis 11:18 forth fiery breath, Or pour out *r* smoke,
17:19 or the *r* cry of the fiercest beasts,
Is 5:30 on that day, with a *r* like that of the sea.]
17:12 the *r* of many peoples that roar like the
30: 6 troubled land of the lioness and *r* lion,
33: 3 At the *r* sound,
66: 6 A sound of *r* from the city,
Jer 6:23 the *r* sea as they ride forth on steeds,
50:42 They sound like the *r* sea,
51:42 rises, she is overwhelmed by the *r* waves!
51:55 Though her waves were *r* like mighty waters,
Ez 1:24 their wings, like the *r* of mighty waters,
22:20 into a furnace and smelted in the *r* flames,
22:25 princes are like *r* lions that tear prey;
43: 2 I heard a sound like the *r* of many waters,
Zep 3: 3 Her princes in her midst are *r* lions;
Zec 11: 3 the *r* of the young lions,
Lk 21:25 at the *r* of the sea and the waves.
1Pt 5: 8 a *r* lion looking for someone to devour.
Rv 14: 2 heaven which resembled the *r* of the deep,
19: 6 of a great crowd, or the *r* of the deep,

ROARS (10)

Jb 4:10 Though the lion *r*,
37: 4 Again his voice *r*—
Prv 20: 2 The dread of the king is as when a lion *r*;
Jer 6:29 The bellows *r*,
25:30 The LORD *r* from on high,
25:30 Mightily he *r* over the range,
Hos 11:10 When he *r*,
Jl 4:16 The LORD *r* from Zion,
Am 3: 8 The lion *r*— who will not be afraid!

ROAST (2)

1Sm 2:15 "Give me some meat to *r* for the priest.
2Sm 6:19 Israel, a loaf of bread, a cut of *r* meat,

ROASTED (12)

Ex 12: 8 That same night they shall eat its *r* flesh
12: 9 not be eaten raw or boiled, but *r* whole,
Lv 2:14 grits of new ears of grain, *r* by fire.
23:14 eat any bread or *r* grain or fresh kernels.
Ru 2:14 he handed her some *r* grain and she ate her
1Sm 17:17 "Take this ephah of *r* grain and these ten
25:18 five dressed sheep, five seahs of *r* grain,
2Sm 17:28 as well as wheat, barley, flour, *r* grain,
Jdt 10: 5 She filled a bag with *r* grain,
Is 44:16 he eats what he has *r* until he is full,
44:19 I baked bread and *r* meat which I ate.
Jer 29:22 whom the king of Babylon *r* in the flames."

ROASTS (1)

Is 44:16 the fire, and on its embers he *r* his meat;

ROB (21)

Lv 19:13 "You shall not defraud or *r* your neighbor.
26:22 to *r* you of your children and wipe out
2Mc 9: 2 *r* the temple and gain control of the city.
Ps(s) 12: 6 "Because they *r* the afflicted,
Sir 4: 1 son, *r* not the poor man of his livelihood;
28:15 and *r* them of the fruit of their toil;
Ez 5:17 beasts that shall *r* you of your children.

36:12 again shall you *r* them of their children.]
36:13 and you *r* your people of their children";
36:14 men or *r* your people of their children,
36:15 or *r* your people of their children,
Mal 3: 8 Dare a man *r* God?
3: 8 And you say, "How do we *r* you?"
3: 9 accursed, for you, the whole nation, *r* me.
Mt 12:29 Only then can he *r* his house.
Rom 2:22 You who abhor idols, do you *r* temples?
1Cor 9:15 die than let anyone *r* me of my boast!
Col 2:18 Let no one *r* you of your prize by
Heb 2:14 that by his death he might *r* the devil,
Rv 3:11 you have lest someone *r* you of your crown.
6: 4 Its rider was given power to *r* the earth

ROBBED (10)

Dt 28:29 "You will be oppressed and *r* continually,
Jgs 9:25 these *r* all who passed them on the road.
2Sm 17: 8 fierce as a bear in the wild *r* of her cubs.
Prv 17:12 Face a bear *r* of her cubs,
Ez 18:18 father, since he violated rights, and *r*,
Dn 2: 1 his spirit no rest and *r* him of his sleep.
Hos 13: 8 attack them like a bear *r* of its young,
Am 3:10 castles what they have extorted and *r*.
2Cor 11: 8 I *r* other churches,
2Tm 1:10 He has *r* death of its power and has

ROBBER (1)

Prv 23:28 Yes, she lies in wait like a *r*,

ROBBERS (8)

Jb 12: 6 Yet the tents of *r* are prosperous,
Bar 6:17 and bolts, lest they be carried off by *r*.
Ez 7:22 *r* shall enter and profane it.
Ob 1: 5 If thieves came to you, if *r* by night,
Lk 10:30 Jerusalem to Jericho who fell prey to *r*.
10:36 neighbor to the man who fell in with the *r*?"
1Cor 6:10 slanderers or *r* will inherit God's kingdom.
2Cor 11:26 continually, endangered by floods, *r*,

ROBBERY (5)

Is 61: 8 love what is right, I hate *r* and injustice;
Ez 18: 7 pledge received for a debt, commits no *r*;
18:12 oppresses the poor and needy, commits *r*,
18:16 anyone, or exact a pledge, or commit *r*;
22:29 the land practice extortion and commit *r*;

ROBBING (2)

Is 10: 2 and *r* my people's poor of their rights,
Mal 3: 8 Yet you are *r* me!

ROBE (40)

Gn 9:23 Shem and Japheth, however, took a *r*,
49:11 his garments, his *r* in the blood of grapes.
Ex 28: 4 a breastpiece, an ephod, a *r*,
28:31 "The *r* of the ephod you shall make
28:34 alternating all around the hem of the *r*.
29: 5 Aaron with the tunic, the *r* of the ephod,
39:22 The *r* of the ephod was woven entirely of
39:24 of the *r* pomegranates were made of violet,
39:25 pomegranates all around the hem of the *r*:
39:26 alternating all around the hem of the *r*
Lv 6: 3 *r* and wearing linen drawers on his body,
8: 7 him with the sash, clothed him with the *r*,
1Chr 15:27 David was clothed in a *r* of fine linen,
Jdt 16: 8 and put on a linen *r* to beguile him.
Est 6: 8 brought the royal *r* which the king wore
6: 9 The *r* and the horse should be consigned to
6:10 Take the *r* and horse as you have proposed,
6:11 So Haman took the *r* and horse,
E:15 in a royal *r* of violet and of white cotton,
1Mc 6:15 He gave him his crown, his *r*,
10:20 sent him a purple *r* and a crown of gold.
2Mc 4:38 stripped Andronicus of his purple *r*,
Jb 29:14 justice was my *r* and my turban.
Ps(s) 73: 6 as a *r* violence enwraps them.
109:18 he be clothed with cursing as with a *r*;
133: 2 till it runs down upon the collar of his *r*.
Sg 5: 3 I have taken off my *r*,
Wis 18:24 on his full-length *r* was the whole world,
Sir 6:31 You will wear her as your *r* of glory,
27: 8 attain it, and put it on like a splendid *r*.
45: 8 and *r* with pomegranates around the hem,
Is 22:21 I will clothe him with your *r*,
61:10 he has clothed me with a *r* of salvation,
Bar 5: 1 take off your *r* of mourning and misery;
Jon 3: 6 he rose from his throne, laid aside his *r*,
Mk 16: 5 sitting at the right, dressed in a white *r*.
Lk 15:22 bring out the finest *r* and put it on him;
23:11 *r* on him and sent him back to Pilate.
Rv 1:13 a Son of Man wearing an ankle-length *r*,
6:11 of the martyrs was given a long white *r*,

ROBED (4)

Ps(s) 93: 1 The LORD is king, in splendor *r*;
93: 1 *r* is the LORD and girt about with strength,
104: 2 and glory, *r* in light as with a cloak.
Prv 7:10 woman comes to meet him, *r* like a harlot,

ROBES (20)

Gn 41:42 He had him dressed in *r* of fine linen and
1Kgs 22:10 clothed in their *r* of state on a threshing
2Chr 18: 9 clothed in their *r* of state on a threshing
Est 4:30 royal throne, clothed in full *r* of state,
2Mc 3:15 in their priestly *r* before the altar,
Ps(s) 45: 9 and aloes and cassia your *r* are fragrant;
Sir 50:11 Vested in his magnificent *r*,
Ez 16:10 you a fine linen sash and silk *r* to wear.
26:16 from their thrones, lay aside their *r*,
Mt 26:65 At this the high priest tore his *r*:
Mk 12:38 *r* and accept marks of respect in public,
14:63 that the high priest tore his *r* and said:
Lk 20:46 who like to parade around in their *r*,
Jn 20:12 and there she saw two angels in dazzling *r*.
Acts 10:30 when a man in dazzling *r* stood before me.
12:21 appointed day Herod, arrayed in royal *r*,
1Pt 3: 3 or the donning of rich *r* is not for you.
Rv 7: 9 *r* and holding palm branches in their hands.
7:14 they have washed their *r* and made them
22:14 Happy are they who wash their *r* so as to

ROBUST (3)

Ex 1:19 They are *r* and give birth before the
2Mc 12:27 *R* young men took up their posts in defense
Sir 30:14 Better a poor man strong and *r*,

ROCK (112)

Gn 49:24 because of the Shepherd, the *R* of Israel,
Ex 17: 6 there in front of you on the *r* in Horeb.
17: 6 Strike the *r*,
17:12 so they put a *r* in place for him to sit on.
33:21 where you shall station yourself on the *r*.
33:22 I will set you in the hollow of the *r*
Lv 11: 5 the *r* badger,
Nm 20: 8 presence order the *r* to yield its waters.
20: 8 From the *r* you shall bring forth water for
20:10 assembled the community in front of the *r*,
20:10 we to bring water for you out of this *r*?"
20:11 Moses struck the *r* twice with his staff,
Dt 8:15 *r* and fed you in the desert with manna,
14: 7 the camel, the hare and the *r* badger,
32: 4 The *R*— how faultless are his deeds.
32:15 who made them and scorned their saving *R*.
32:18 You were unmindful of the *R* that begot you,
32:30 Unless it was because their *R* sold them
32:31 Indeed, their 'rock' is not like our *R*,
32:37 gods whom they relied on as their *r*'?
Jgs 6:20 unleavened cakes and lay them on this *r*;
6:21 Thereupon a fire came up from the *r* which
7:25 killing Oreb at the *r* of Oreb and Zeeb at
13:19 and offered it on the *r* to the LORD,
20:45 fled through the desert to the *r* Rimmon.
20:47 through the desert reached the *r* Rimmon,
21:13 to the Benjaminites at the *r* Rimmon,
1Sm 2: 2 there in no *R* like our God.
2Sm 21:10 and spread it out for herself on the *r*
22: 3 my God, my *r* of refuge!
22:32 Who is a *r* save our God?
22:47 And blessed be my *R*!
22:47 Extolled be my God, *r* of my salvation,
23: 3 of me the *R* of Israel said,
1Chr 11:15 of the Thirty chiefs went down to the *r*,
2Chr 25:12 to the summit of the *R* and then cast down,
Neh 9:15 from a *r* you sent them in their thirst.
2Mc 14:46 Then, standing on a steep *r*,
Jb 14:18 at last and its *r* is moved from its place,
18: 4 [or the *r* be moved out of its place]?
19:24 with lead they were cut in the *r* forever!
24: 8 for want of shelter they cling to the *r*.
28: 9 He sets his hand to the flinty *r*,
29: 6 and the *r* flowed with streams of oil;
Ps(s) 18: 3 you, O LORD, my strength, O LORD, my *r*,
18: 3 My God, my *r* of refuge,
18:32 Who is a *r*, save our God?
18:47 And blessed be my *R*!
19:15 before you, O LORD, my *r* and my redeemer.
27: 5 of his tent, he will set me high upon a *r*.
28: 1 O my *R* be not deaf to me,
31: 3 Be my *r* of refuge,
31: 4 You are my *r* and my fortress;
42:10 I sing to God, my *r*:
55: 3 I *r* with grief,
61: 3 You will set me high upon a *r*;
62: 3 He only is my *r* and my salvation,
62: 7 He only is my *r* and my salvation,
62: 8 and my glory, he is the *r* of my strength;
71: 3 Be my *r* of refuge,
71: 3 safety, for you are my *r* and my fortress.
73:26 the *r* of my heart and my portion forever.
75: 6 speak not haughtily against the *R*.
78:20 For when he struck the *r*,
78:35 that God was their *r* and the Most High God,
81:17 with honey from the *r* I would fill them."
89:27 of me, 'You are my father, my God, the *r*,
92:16 be, Declaring how just is the LORD, my *R*,
94:22 stronghold, and my God the *r* of my refuge.
95: 1 let us acclaim the *R* of our salvation.
105:41 He cleft the *r*,
114: 8 Who turned the *r* into pools of water,
137: 9 and smash your little ones against the *r*!
144: 1 I Blessed be the LORD, my *r*,
Prv 30:19 in the air, the way of a serpent upon a *r*,
Sg 2:14 "O my dove in the clefts of the *r*,
Wis 4:19 prostrate and *r* them to their foundations;
11: 4 and water was given them from the sheer *r*,
Sir 40:15 for the root of the godless is on sheer *r*;
48:17 the *r* and he built reservoirs for water.
Is 10:26 such as struck Midian at the *r* of Oreb;
17:10 God, your savior, and remembered not the *R*,
22:16 on a height and carved his tomb in the *r*:
26: 4 For the LORD is an eternal *R*.
30:29 of the LORD, toward the *R* of Israel,
32: 2 the shade of a great *r* in a parched land.
44: 8 Is there a God or any *R* besides me?
48:21 Water from the *r* he set flowing for them;
48:21 he cleft the *r*,
51: 1 Look to the *r* from which you were hewn,
Jer 13: 4 there hide it in a cleft of the *r*.
21:13 against you, Valley-site, *R* of the Plain,
Ez 24: 7 she poured it on the bare *r*;
24: 8 vengeance, she put her blood on the bare *r*,
26: 4 ground from her and leave her a bare *r*;
26:14 I will make you a bare *r*;
31:16 crash of his fall I made the nations *r*,
Ob 1: 3 you who dwell in the clefts of the *r*,
Hb 1:12 LORD you have marked him for judgment, O *R*,
Mt 7:24 like the wise man who built his house on *r*.
7:25 it had been solidly set on *r*.
13:20 The seed that fell on patches of *r* is the
16:18 you are 'Rock,' and on this *r* I will build
27:60 which had been hewn from a formation of *r*.
Mk 15:46 him in a tomb which had been cut out of *r*.
Lk 6:48 dug deeply and laid the foundation on a *r*.
23:53 and laid it in a tomb hewn out of the *r*,
Rom 9:33 make men stumble and a *r* to make them fall;
1Cor 10: 4 rock that was following them, and the *r*

ROCK-BADGERS (2)

Ps(s) 104:18 the cliffs are a refuge for *r*.
Prv 30:26 *R*— a species not mighty,

ROCKED (2)

Ps(s) 60: 4 You have *r* the country and split it open;
Wis 4: 4 unsteady and shall be *r* by the wind and,

ROCKING (1)

Acts 16:26 the place, *r* the prison to its foundations.

ROCKS (18)

Dt 32:13 from its *r* and olive oil from its hard,
1Sm 13: 6 themselves in caves, in thickets, among *r*,
1Kgs 19:11 mountains and crushing *r* before the LORD
Jdt 16:15 the *r*, like wax, melt before your glance.
Jb 8:17 among the *r* he takes hold.
28:10 He splits channels in the *r*;
Ps(s) 78:15 He cleft the *r* in the desert and gave them
Wis 17:19 water, or the rude crash of overthrown *r*,
Is 2:10 Get behind the *r*, hide in the dust,
2:19 caves in the *r* and into holes in the earth,
2:21 in the *r* and into crevices in the cliffs,
Jer 4:29 shrink into the thickets, they scale the *r*:
16:16 and hill and from the clefts of the *r*.
23:29 says the LORD, like a hammer shattering *r*?
Na 1: 6 and the *r* are rent asunder before him.
Jn 8:59 At that they picked up *r* to throw at Jesus,
10:31 the Jews again reached for *r* to stone him,
Rv 6:16 They cried out to the mountains and *r*,

ROCKY (12)

1Sm 14: 4 outpost there was a *r* crag on each side,
1Kgs 4:16 of Hushai, in Asher and along the *r* coast;
Is 7:19 in the steep ravines and in the *r* clefts,
33:16 his stronghold shall be the *r* fastness,
Jer 18:14 the snow of Lebanon desert the *r* heights?
49:16 You that live in *r* crags,
Mt 13: 5 Part of it fell on *r* ground,
Mk 4: 5 on *r* ground where it had little soil;
4:16 those sown on *r* ground are people who on
Lk 8: 6 Some fell on *r* ground, sprouted up,
8:13 Those on the *r* ground are the ones who,
Acts 27:29 we should be dashed against some *r* coast,

ROD (53)

Ex 21:20 strikes his male or female slave with a *r*
Lv 27:32 as they are counted by the herdsman's *r*.
2Sm 7:14 the *r* of men and with human chastisements;
Jb 9:34 upon us both and withdraw his *r* from me.
Ps(s) 2: 9 You shall rule them with an iron *r*;
23: 4 your *r* and your staff that give me courage.
45: 7 a tempered *r* is your royal scepter.
89:33 with a *r* and their guilt with stripes.
Prv 10: 6 the just, but a *r* for the back of the fool.
13:24 He who spares his *r* hates his son,
14: 3 the mouth of the fool is a *r* for his back,
22: 8 calamity, and the *r* destroys his labors.
22:15 *r* of discipline will drive it far from him.
23:13 if you beat him with the *r*,
23:14 Beat him with the *r*,
26: 3 the ass, and the *r* for the back of fools.
29:15 The *r* of correction gives wisdom,

ROD (cont.)

Sir 23: 2 thoughts, to my mind the *r* of discipline,
33:25 yoke and harness and the *r* of his master.
Is 9: 3 the *r* of their taskmaster you have smashed,
10: 5 My *r* in anger, my staff in wrath.
10:15 As if a *r* could sway him who lifts it,
10:24 Assyrian, though he strikes you with a *r*,
11: 4 the ruthless with the *r* of his mouth,
14: 5 The LORD has broken the *r* of the wicked,
14:29 you, that the *r* which smote you is broken;
28:27 staff, and cumin crushed for food with a *r*.
30:31 be shattered, as he strikes with the *r*;
30:32 While at every sweep of the *r* which the
Jer 48:17 the strong staff is broken, the glorious *r*!
Lam 3: 1 knows affliction from the *r* of his anger,
Ez 21:15 You have spurned the *r* and every judgment!
21:18 Lord GOD, since you have spurned the *r*.
40: 3 holding a linen cord and a measuring *r*.
40: 5 was holding a measuring *r* six cubits long,
40: 5 each of which were found to be one *r*.'
40: 6 threshold, which was found to be a *r* wide.
40: 7 The cells were a *r* long and a rod wide,
40: 7 The cells were a rod long and a *r* wide,
40: 7 the gate toward the inside measured one *r*.
41: 8 a full *r* of six cubits in extent.
42:16 five hundred cubits by his measuring *r*.
42:17 five hundred cubits by the measuring *r*.
42:18 five hundred cubits by the measuring *r*.
42:19 five hundred cubits by the measuring *r*.
Mi 4:14 With the *r* they strike on the cheek the
1Cor 4:21 do you prefer, that I come to you with a *r*,
Heb 9: 4 manna, the *r* of Aaron which had blossomed,
Rv 2:27 a *r* of iron and shatter them like crockery;
11: 1 Someone gave me a measuring *r* and said:
12: 5 to shepherd all the nations with an iron *r*.
19:15 He will shepherd them with an iron *r*;
21:15 me held a *r* of gold for measuring the city,
21:16 He measured the city with the *r* and found

RODANIM (2)

Gn 10: 4 Elishah, Tarshish, the Kittim, and the *R*.
1Chr 1: 7 Elishah, Tarshish, the Kittim, and the *R*.

RODE (11)

Gn 46:29 and *r* to meet his father Israel in Goshen.
Jgs 10: 4 He had thirty sons who *r* on thirty
12:14 grandsons who *r* on seventy saddle-asses.
2Kgs 9:27 he *r* through the pass of Gur near Ibleam.
9:33 Jehu *r* in over her body and,
2Chr 22: 7 his arrival he *r* out with Jehoram to Jehu,
Neh 2:13 I *r* out at night by the Valley Gate,
Est 6: 8 king *r* when the royal crown was placed
2Mc 9: 4 Yet the condemnation of Heaven *r* with him,
Rv 6: 2 He *r* forth victorious, to conquer
19:21 of the mouth of the One who *r* the horse,

RODS (10)

Gn 30:38 The *r* that he had thus peeled he then set
30:39 came to drink, the goats mated by the *r*,
30:41 Jacob would set the *r* in the troughs in
30:41 animals, so that they mated by the *r*;
30:42 animals he would not put the *r* there.
2Mc 10: 7 Carrying *r* entwined with leaves,
Jb 40:18 his frame is like iron *r*.
Prv 19:29 *R* are prepared for the arrogant,
Sg 5:14 are *r* of gold adorned with chrysolites.
2Cor 11:25 three times I was beaten with *r*;

ROE (1)

Dt 14: 5 the red deer, the gazelle, the *r* deer,

ROEBUCKS (1)

1Kgs 5: 3 sheep, not counting harts, gazelles, *r*,

ROGELIM (2)

2Sm 17:27 and Barzillai, the Gileadite from *R*,
19:32 the Gileadite also came down from *R*

ROGUE (1)

Sir 20:13 A gift from a *r* will do you no good,

ROHGAH (1)

1Chr 7:34 The sons of Shomer were Ahi, *R*,

ROLES (1)

Eph 4:12 pastors and teachers in *r* of service for

ROLL (17)

Gn 29: 3 assembled there could they *r* the stone away
29: 8 *r* the stone away from the mouth of the well;
Jos 10:18 *R* large stones to the mouth of the cave
Jgs 21: 9 A *r* call of the army established that none
1Sm 14:33 *R* a large stone here for me."
Is 22:18 He shall grip you firmly And *r* you up and
28:27 sledge, nor does a cartwheel *r* over cumin.
Jer 6:26 people, gird on sackcloth, *r* in the ashes.
25:34 *r* in the dust, leaders of the flock!
36:23 the entire *r* was consumed in the fire.
51:25 against you, *r* you down over the cliffs,
Mi 1:10 In Beth-leaphrah *r* in the dust.
Mt 9: 6 *R* up your mat, and go home."
Mk 9:20 he began to *r* around and foam at the mouth.
16: 3 "Who will *r* back the stone for us from
1Tm 5: 9 To be on the church's *r* of widows,
Heb 1:12 You will *r* them up like a cloak;

ROLLED (12)

Gn 29:10 *r* the stone away from the mouth of the
2Kgs 2: 8 his mantle, *r* it up and struck the water,
Jdt 13: 9 She *r* his body off the bed and took the
Is 9: 4 trampled in battle, every cloak *r* in blood,
34: 4 The heavens shall be *r* up like a scroll,
Mt 27:60 Then he *r* a huge stone across the entrance
28: 2 He came to the stone, *r* it back,
Mk 15:46 *r* a stone across the entrance of the tomb.
16: 4 they found that the stone had been *r* back.
Lk 24: 2 They found the stone *r* back from the tomb;
Jn 20: 7 wrappings, but *r* up in a place by itself.
Rv 6:14 as if it were a scroll being *r* up;

ROLLING (5)

Jgs 7:13 barley bread was *r* into the camp of Midian.
Ez 27:30 dust on their heads, *r* in the ashes.
Mk 15:24 divided up his garments by *r* dice for them
Lk 4:20 *R* up the scroll he gave it back to the
23:34 They divided his garments, *r* dice for them.

ROLLS (4)

Gn 18: 6 Knead it and make *r*."
Jb 30:15 over me *r* the terror.
Prv 26:27 and a stone comes back upon him who *r* it.
Sir 40:14 Which, in its rising, *r* along the stones,

ROMAMTI-EZER (2)

1Chr 25: 4 Hananiah, Hanani, Eliathah, Giddalti, *R*,
25:31 The twenty-fourth fell to *R*

ROMAN (11)

Mt 22:19 When they handed him a small *R* coin,
Acts 6: 9 "Synagogue of *R* Freedmen" (that is,
10: 1 named Cornelius, of the *R* cohort Italica,
16:12 the district of Macedonia and a *R* colony.
16:37 us into jail, although we are *R* citizens!
16:38 alarmed at hearing they were *R* citizens.
22:25 legal to flog a *R* citizen without a trial?"
22:26 This man is a *R* citizen!"
22:27 Are you a *R* citizen?"
23:27 When I learned that he was a *R* citizen,
25:16 I replied that it was not the *R* practice

ROMANS (25)

1Mc 8: 1 Judas had heard of the reputation of the *R*.
8: 8 The *R* took these from him and gave them to
8:10 come and destroy them, the *R* discovered it,
8:10 *R* took their wives and children captive.
8:21 The proposal pleased the *R*,
8:23 "May it be well with the *R* and the Jewish
8:27 nation, the *R* will help them willingly,
8:29 On these terms the *R* have made an
12: 1 and renew his friendship with the *R*.
12: 4 The *R* gave them letters addressed to the
12:16 and we have sent them to the *R* to renew
14:17 But when the *R* heard that his brother
14:24 minas, to confirm the alliance with the *R*.
14:40 the *R* had addressed the Jews as friends,
15:16 "Lucius, Consul of the *R*,
2Mc 4:11 who would later go on an embassy to the *R*
8:10 *R* by selling captured Jews into slavery.
8:36 had promised to provide tribute for the *R*
11:34 The *R* also sent them a letter as follows:
11:34 Memmius and Titus Manius, legates of the *R*,
Jn 11:48 Then the *R* will come in and sweep away our
Acts 16:21 not lawful for us *R* to adopt or practice."
28:17 I was handed over to the *R* as a prisoner.
28:18 The *R* tried my case and wanted to release
Rom 1:15 to preach the gospel to you *R* as well.

ROME (20)

1Mc 1:10 son of King Antiochus, once a hostage at *R*.
7: 1 son of Seleucus, set out from *R*,
8:17 and sent them to *R* to establish an
8:19 After making a very long journey to *R*,
8:24 But if war is first made on *R*,
12: 1 he sent selected men to *R* to confirm and
12: 3 After reaching *R*,
14:16 When people heard in *R* and even in Sparta
14:24 Simon sent Numenius to *R* with a great gold
15:15 his companions left *R* with letters
Acts 2:10 There are even visitors from *R*—
18: 2 Claudius had ordered all Jews to leave *R*.
19:21 there," he said, "I must visit *R* too."
22:29 Paul he had restrained a citizen of *R*.
23:11 me here in Jerusalem, so must you do in *R*."
28:14 This is how we finally came to *R*.
28:15 Certain brothers from *R* who heard about us
28:16 Upon our entry into *R* Paul was allowed to
Rom 1: 7 all in *R*, beloved of God and called to
2Tm 1:17 When he was in *R*, he sought me out

ROME'S (2)

1Mc 8:26 this is *R* decision.
8:28 this is *R* decision.

ROOF (29)

Gn 19: 8 they have come under the shelter of my *r*."
Dt 22: 8 a new house, put a parapet around the *r*;
Jos 2: 6 Now, she had led them to the *r*,
2: 8 Rahab came to them on the *r* and said:
Jgs 9:51 in and going up to the *r* of the tower.
16:27 and from the *r* about three thousand men
1Sm 9:25 a mattress was spread for Saul on the *r*,
9:26 daybreak Samuel called to Saul on the *r*,
2Sm 11: 2 and strolled about on the *r* of the palace.
11: 2 From the *r* he saw a woman bathing,
16:22 So a tent was pitched on the *r* for Absalom,
18:24 to the *r* of the gate above the city wall,
2Kgs 1: 2 *r* terrace at Samaria and had been injured.
4:10 on the *r* and furnish it for him with a bed,
23:12 Judah on the *r* (the roof terrace of Ahaz),
23:12 Judah on the roof (the *r* terrace of Ahaz),
Neh 8:16 for themselves, on the *r* of their houses,
Jdt 8: 5 a tent for herself on the *r* of her house.
Sg 3:10 made its columns of silver, its *r* of gold,
Sir 29:22 fare under the shadow of one's own *r*
Jer 48:38 On every *r* of Moab and in all his squares
Lam 4: 4 cleaves to the *r* of its mouth in thirst;
Dn 4:26 on the *r* of the royal palace in Babylon,
Mt 8: 8 "I am not worthy to have you under my *r*.
24:17 If a man is on the *r* terrace,
Mk 2: 4 up the *r* over the spot where Jesus was.
13:15 If a man is on the *r* terrace,
Lk 5:19 of the crowd, so they went up on the *r*.
Acts 10: 9 Peter went up to the *r* terrace to pray.

ROOFED (2)

1Kgs 6: 9 was *r* in with rafters and boards of cedar.
Neh 3:15 he rebuilt it, *r* it over,

ROOFS (5)

Jb 29:10 tongues stuck to the *r* of their mouths.
Wis 17: 2 *r* as exiles from the eternal providence.
Jer 19:13 all the houses upon whose *r* they burnt
32:29 on the *r* of which incense was burned to
Zep 1: 5 who adore the host of heaven on the *r*,

ROOFTOP (1)

Lk 17:31 the *r* and his belongings are in the house,

ROOFTOPS (2)

Is 15: 3 On the *r* and in the squares everyone wails.
Lk 12: 3 locked rooms will be proclaimed from the *r*.

ROOM (77)

Gn 23: 8 you will allow me *r* for burial of my dead,
24:23 And is there *r* in your father's house for
24:25 she added, "and *r* to spend the night."
26:22 said, "The LORD has now given us ample *r*,
34:21 there is ample *r* in the country for them.
43:30 He went into a private *r* and wept there.
Lv 26:10 have to discard them to make *r* for the new.
Nm 18: 7 the altar and the *r* within the veil.
22:26 there was no *r* to move either to the right or
Jgs 3:20 where he sat alone in his cool upper *r*,
3:23 of the upper *r* on him and locking them.
3:24 that the doors of the upper *r* were locked,
3:25 he did not open the doors of the upper *r*,
1Sm 9:22 and his servant and brought them to the *r*,
2Sm 19: 1 up to the *r* over the city gate to weep.
22:37 You made *r* for my steps;
1Kgs 1:15 So Bathsheba visited the king in his *r*,
6:27 wing, pointing toward the middle of the *r*,
7:50 of gold for the doors of the inner *r*,
7:50 holies, and for the doors of the outer *r*,
17:19 him to the upper *r* where he was staying,
17:23 the upper *r* and gave him to his mother.
20:30 refuge within the city, in an inside *r*.
22:25 when you retreat into an inside *r* to hide."
2Kgs 4:10 let us arrange a little *r* on the roof and
4:11 arrived and stayed in the *r* overnight.
4:35 He arose, paced up and down the *r*,
4:37 then she took her son and left the *r*.
6: 1 *r* for us to continue to live here with you.
1Chr 28:11 chambers, and the *r* with the propitiatory.
2Chr 3: 8 He also made the *r* of the holy of holies.
3:10 For the *r* of the holy of holies he made
Neh 2:14 Since there was no *r* here for my mount to
Tb 3:10 She went in tears to an upstairs *r* in her
3:17 daughter Sarah came downstairs from her *r*.
7:16 She went and made the bed in the *r*,
8: 1 the dining *r* and led him into the bedroom.
Jdt 12: 1 into the *r* where his silverware was kept,
2Mc 2: 5 a *r* in a cave in which he put the tent,
Ps(s) 18:37 You made *r* for my steps;
44: 3 the peoples, but for them you made *r*.
Sg 3: 4 home of my mother, to the *r* of my parent.
Sir 29:27 for my brother's visit I need the *r*!"
42:11 See that there is no lattice in her *r*,
Is 5: 8 field with field, Till no *r* remains,

49:20 too small for me, make *r* for me to live in."
Jer 35: 4 of the LORD, to the *r* of the sons of Hanan,
35: 4 the man of God, next to the princes' *r*,
35: 4 the princes' room, above the *r* of Maaseiah,
36:10 It was in the *r* of Gemariah,
36:20 in the *r* of Elishama the scribe,
36:20 they entered the *r* where the king was.
36:21 it from the *r* of Elishama the scribe,
Ez 8:12 the house of Israel is doing in his idol *r*?
Dn 7: 8 horns were torn away to make *r* for it.
Jl 2:16 Let the bridegroom quit his *r*,
Mt 6: 6 Whenever you pray, go to your *r*,
Mk 2: 2 There was no longer any *r* for them,
5:40 and entered the *r* where the child lay.
14:14 Where is my guest *r* where I may eat the
14:15 Then he will show you an upstairs *r*,
Lk 2: 7 because there was no *r* for them in the
14: 9 come and say to you, 'Make *r* for this man,'
14:22 carried out, my lord, and there is still *r*.'
22:11 Do you have a guest *r* where I may eat the
22:12 That man will show you an upstairs *r*,
Jn 20:26 the disciples were once more in the *r*,
21:25 I doubt there would be *r* enough in the
Acts 1:13 to the upstairs *r* where they were staying:
7:45 God drove out to make *r* for our fathers.
9:37 her body and laid it out in an upstairs *r*.
9:39 arrival they took him upstairs to the *r*.
20: 8 in the upstairs *r* where we were assembled.
2Cor 6:12 There is no lack of *r* for you in us;
7: 2 Make *r* for us in your hearts!
Phlm 1:22 And get a *r* ready for me;
1Jn 4:18 Love has no *r* for fear;

ROOMS (12)

1Kgs 6:29 the outer *r* had carved figures of cherubim,
6:30 and the outer *r* was overlaid with gold.
1Chr 28:11 storerooms, its upper *r* and inner chambers,
29: 4 silver, for overlaying the walls of the *r*,
Tb 2: 4 the street and put him in one of the *r*,
Prv 24: 4 And by knowledge are its *r* filled with
Jer 22:14 myself a spacious house, with airy *r*,"
35: 2 the house of the LORD, to one of the *r*,
Ez 41:17 in both the inner and outer *r* were carved
Am 3:15 ruined, and their many *r* shall be no more,
Mt 24:26 or 'He is in the innermost *r*,'
Lk 12: 3 *r* will be proclaimed from the rooftops.

ROOMY (2)

Prv 21: 9 than in a *r* house with a quarrelsome woman.
25:24 than in a *r* house with a quarrelsome woman.

ROOST (1)

Zep 2:14 and the desert owl shall *r* in her columns;

ROOT (53)

Dt 29:17 Let there be no *r* that would bear such
2Kgs 19:30 shall again strike *r* below and bear fruit
Jb 14: 8 Even though its *r* grow old in the earth,
19:28 that the *r* of the matter is found in him?"
29:19 My *r* is spread out to the waters;
Ps(s) 80:10 for it, and it took *r* and filled the land.
Prv 12: 3 the *r* of the just will never be disturbed.
12:12 but the *r* of the just is enduring.
Wis 3:15 and unfailing is the *r* of understanding.
4: 3 shall not strike deep *r* nor take firm hold.
15: 3 to know your might is the *r* of immortality.
Sir 1: 5 To whom has wisdom's *r* been revealed?
1:18 The *r* of wisdom is fear of the LORD;
3:14 it will take lasting *r*.
7: 6 if you have not strength to *r* out crime,
23:25 Her children will not take *r*;
24:12 I have struck *r* among the glorious people,
35:21 Till he destroys the haughty *r* and branch,
37:17 The *r* of all conduct is the mind;
40:15 for the *r* of the godless is on sheer rock;
47:22 remnant, to David a *r* from his own family.
49: 7 the womb had been made a prophet, To *r* out,
Is 5:24 Even so their *r* shall become rotten and
11:10 On that day, The *r* of Jesse,
14:29 out of the serpent's *r* shall come an adder,
14:30 But I will kill your *r* with famine that
27: 6 In days to come Jacob shall take *r*,
37:31 again strike *r* below and bear fruit above.
Jer 1:10 To *r* up and to tear down,
12: 2 they have taken *r*,
44: 7 Will you *r* out from Judah man and wife,
Ez 14: 9 him and *r* him out of my people Israel.
Hos 9:16 Ephraim is stricken, their *r* is dried up;
14: 6 He shall strike *r* like the Lebanon cedar,
Am 1: 5 *r* out those who live in the Valley of Aven,
1: 8 I will *r* out those who live in Ashdod,
2: 3 I will *r* out the judge from her midst,
Mal 3:19 on fire, leaving them neither *r* nor branch,
3:24 on fire, leaving them neither *r* nor branch,
Mt 3:10 now the ax is laid to the *r* of the tree.
Lk 3: 9 now the ax is laid to the *r* of the tree.
8:13 They have no *r*;
Rom 11:16 mass of dough, and if the *r* is consecrated,
11:17 come to share in the rich *r* of the olive,
11:18 remember that you do not support the *r*;
11:18 the *r* supports you.
15:12 Isaiah says, "The *r* of Jesse will appear,
Eph 3:17 be the *r* and foundation of your life.
1Tm 6:10 The love of money is the *r* of all evil.
Heb 12:15 that no bitter *r* springs up through which
Jas 1:21 welcome the word that has taken *r* in you,
Rv 5: 5 Lion of the tribe of Judah, the *R* of David,
22:16 I am the *R* and Offspring of David,

ROOTED (14)

Ex 31:14 that day, he must be *r* out of his people.
2Kgs 10:28 Jehu *r* out the worship of Baal from Israel.
Jb 31: 8 eat of it, or may my planting be *r* up!
Ps(s) 44: 3 you *r* out the nations and planted them;
Prv 2:22 land, the faithless will be *r* out of it.
Sir 48:15 Until they were *r* out of their land and
Is 40:24 scarcely is their stem *r* in the earth,
Jer 31:40 shall the city be *r* up or thrown down.
44: 8 Will you be *r* out and become a curse and a
Col 2: 7 Be *r* in him and built up in him,
3: 5 whatever in your nature is *r* in earth;
2Pt 1:12 and are firmly *r* in the truth you possess.
2Jn 1: 9 does not remain *r* in the teaching of Christ
1: 9 while anyone who remains *r* in the teaching

ROOTLESS (1)

Mk 4:17 Being *r*, they last only a while.

ROOTS (27)

Dt 32:22 licking with flames the *r* of the mountains,
Jb 5: 3 I have seen a fool spreading his *r*,
8:17 About a heap of stones are his *r* entwined;
18:16 Below, his *r* dry up,
30: 4 the *r* of the broom plant were their food.
31:12 it consumed all my possessions to the *r*.
Wis 7:20 of men, uses of plants and virtues of *r*—
Sir 3: 9 a father's blessing gives a family firm *r*,
10:15 The *r* of the proud God plucks up,
10:16 ground, then digs their *r* from the earth.
16:17 The *r* of the mountains,
Is 11: 1 Jesse, and from his *r* a bud shall blossom.
Jer 17: 8 that stretches out its *r* to the stream:
Ez 17: 6 turned toward him, its *r* lying under him.
17: 7 To him this vine bent its *r*,
17: 9 it out by the *r* and strip off its fruit,
17: 9 will wither when he pulls it up by the *r*?
31: 7 its *r* were turned toward abundant water.
Dn 4:12 But leave in the earth its stump and *r*,
4:20 but leave in the earth its stump and *r*,
4:23 The command that the stump and *r* of the
Am 2: 9 their fruit above, and their *r* beneath.
Jon 2: 7 Down I went to the *r* of the mountains;
Mt 13: 6 it, it began to wither for lack of *r*.
13:21 But he has no *r*,
Mk 4: 6 it, it began to wither for lack of *r*.
11:20 they saw the fig tree withered to its *r*.

ROPE (4)

Jos 2:15 let them down through the window with a *r*;
Jb 39:10 Will a *r* bind him in the furrow,
40:26 Can you put a *r* into his nose,
Is 3:24 be stench, instead of the girdle, a *r*,

ROPES (20)

Ex 35:18 Dwelling and for the court, with their *r*;
39:40 of the court with its *r* and tent pegs,
Nm 3:26 both the Dwelling and the altar, and the *r*.
3:37 court with their pedestals, pegs and *r*.
4:26 together with their *r* and all other
4:32 court with their pedestals, pegs and *r*.
Jgs 15:13 new *r* and brought him up from the cliff.
15:14 the *r* around his arms became as flax that
16:11 "If they bind me tight with new *r*,
16:12 Delilah took new *r* and bound him with them.
2Sm 17:13 all Israel shall bring *r* to that city and
Is 5:18 perversity, and at sin as if with cart *r*!
33:20 be pulled up, nor any of its *r* severed.
54: 2 lengthen your *r* and make firm your stakes.
Jer 38: 6 of the guard, letting him down with *r*.
38:11 down to Jeremiah in the cistern, with *r*.
38:12 rags between your armpits and the *r*."
38:13 drew him up with the *r* out of the cistern.
Acts 9:25 him to the ground, using *r* and a hamper.
27:32 soldiers cut the *r* and let the boat drift.

ROSE (100)

Gn 7:17 the ark, so that it *r* above the earth.
7:19 and higher above the earth *r* the waters,
37: 7 suddenly my sheaf *r* to an upright position,
Ex 19:18 smoke *r* from it as though from a furnace,
32: 6 down to eat and drink, and *r* up to revel.
40:36 Whenever the cloud *r* from the Dwelling,
Nm 9:17 Whenever the cloud *r* from the tent,
9:21 and when it *r* in the morning,
10:11 *r* from the Dwelling of the commandments.
Jos 8:19 so, the men in ambush *r* from their post,
15: 8 the boundary *r* to the top of the mountain
Jgs 3:20 So the king *r* from his chair,
5: 7 When I, Deborah, rose, when I *r*,
9:35 his soldiers *r* from their place of ambush,
9:43 and then *r* against them for the attack.
10: 1 *r* to save Israel the Issacharite Tola,
13:20 as the flame *r* to the sky from the altar,
16: 3 Then he *r*, seized the doors of the city
19: 5 On the fourth day they *r* early in the
19: 8 On the fifth morning he *r* early to depart,
19:27 When her husband *r* that day and opened the
20: 5 But the citizens of Gibeah *r* up against me
20: 8 All the people *r* as one man to say,
20:33 all the men of Israel *r* from their places.
Ru 2:15 She *r* to glean, and Boaz instructed his
3:14 *r* before men could recognize one another.
1Sm 1: 9 Hannah *r* after one such meal at Shiloh,
3: 6 LORD called Samuel, who *r* and went to Eli.
5: 3 people of Ashdod *r* early the next morning,
9:26 Saul *r*, and he and Samuel went outside
20:41 David *r* from beside the mound and
2Sm 2:15 So they *r* and were counted off:
11: 2 One evening David *r* from his siesta and
13:29 had commanded, all the other princes *r*,
22: 9 Smoke *r* from his nostrils,
24:11 When David *r* in the morning,
1Kgs 2:40 So Shimei *r*, saddled his ass, and went
3:21 I *r* in the morning to nurse my child,
8:54 he *r* from before the altar of the LORD,
2Kgs 3:24 Israelites *r* up and attacked the Moabites,
13:21 he came back to life and *r* to his feet.
1Chr 10:12 had done to Saul, its warriors *r* to a man,
21: 1 A satan *r* up against Israel,
28: 2 King David *r* to his feet and said:
2Chr 20:19 *r* to sing the praises of the LORD,
30:27 levitical priests *r* and blessed the people;
Ezr 9: 5 evening sacrifice, I *r* in my wretchedness,
10: 5 Ezra *r* to his feet and demanded an oath
Neh 5: 1 Then there *r* a great outcry of the common
8: 5 and, as he opened it, all the people *r*.
Tb 12:21 When Raphael ascended they *r* to their feet
Jdt 5:11 king of Egypt, however, *r* up against them,
10: 2 the God of Israel, she *r* from the ground.
12: 5 she *r* and sent this message to Holofernes,
Est 8: 4 So she *r* and, standing in his presence,
1Mc 6: 4 of the city who *r* up in battle against him.
9:40 The Jews *r* up against them from their
11:69 Then the men in ambush *r* out of their
14:32 Simon *r* up and fought for his nation,
16: 5 they spent the night at Modein, *r* early,
2Mc 4:30 people of Tarsus and Mallus *r* in revolt,
Jb 29: 8 withdrew, while the elders *r* up and stood;
31:14 me, What then should I do when God *r* up;
Ps(s) 18: 9 Smoke *r* from his nostrils,
78:21 against Jacob, and anger *r* against Israel,
78:31 God *r* against them and slew their best men,
104: 8 As the mountains *r*,
124: 2 When men *r* up against us,
Sg 5: 5 I *r* to open to my lover,
Jer 41: 2 *r* up and attacked with swords Gedaliah,
Ez 3:12 as the glory of the LORD *r* from its place:
10: 4 and the glory of the LORD *r* from over the
10:17 when they *r*, the wheels rose with them
10:17 when they rose, the wheels *r* with them;
11:23 And the glory of the LORD *r* from the city
Dn 3:47 *r* forty-nine cubits above the furnace,
3:91 *r* in haste and asked his nobles,
6:20 the king *r* very early the next morning and
8:22 The four that *r* in its place when it was
13:34 *r* up and laid their hands on her head.
13:61 They *r* up against the two elders,
Jon 3: 6 the king of Nineveh, he *r* from his throne,
Mt 13: 6 depth, but when the sun *r* and scorched it,
26:62 priest *r* to his feet and addressed him:
Mk 4: 6 Then, when the sun *r* and scorched it,
14:60 The high priest *r* to his feet before the
16: 9 Jesus *r* from the dead early on the first
Lk 4:29 They *r* up and expelled him from the town,
6: 8 The man *r* and remained standing.
22:45 he *r* from prayer and came to his disciples,
23: 1 assembly *r* up and led him before Pilate.
Jn 13: 4 him *r* from the meal and took off his cloak.
Acts 8: 8 rejoicing in that town *r* to fever pitch.
10:41 drank with him after he *r* from the dead.
18:12 the Jews *r* in a body against Paul and
26:30 the king *r*, and with him the governor
1Cor 15: 4 with the Scriptures, *r* on the third day;
1Thes 4:14 For if we believe that Jesus died and *r*,
Heb 7:14 that our Lord *r* from the tribe of Judah,

ROSEBUDS (1)

Wis 2: 8 us crown ourselves with *r* ere they wither.

ROSEBUSH (1)

Sir 24:14 a palm tree in Engedi, like a *r* in Jericho,

ROSES (1)

Sir 39:13 petals, like *r* planted near running waters;

ROSETTES (5)

Ex 28:13 Make filigree *r* of gold,
28:14 the cordlike chains to the filigree *r*.
28:25 fastened in front to the two filigree *r*
39:16 two gold filigree *r* and two gold rings.
39:18 fastened in front to the two filigree *r*,

ROSTRUM (1)

Acts 12:21 seat on the *r* and publicly addressed them.

ROT (11)

Prv 10: 7 blessed, but the name of the wicked will *r*.
12: 4 a disgraceful one is like *r* in his bones.
Is 34: 4 their blood, and all the hills shall *r*;
40:20 himself, Choosing timber that will not *r*,
50: 2 Their fish *r* for lack of water,
Jer 13: 9 also I will allow the pride of Judah to *r*,
Ez 24:23 but you shall *r* away because of your sins
Zec 14:12 shall *r* while they stand upon their feet,
14:12 and their eyes shall *r* in their sockets,
14:12 and their tongues shall *r* in their mouths.
Acts 8:20 "May you and your money *r*—

ROTATION (1)

2Chr 5:11 to the *r* of their various classes),

ROTS (1)

Prv 14:30 life to the body, but jealousy *r* the bones.

ROTTED (3)

2Mc 9: 9 alive in hideous torments, his flesh *r* off,
Jer 13: 7 But it was *r*, good for nothing!
Jas 5: 2 Your wealth has *r*,

ROTTEN (7)

Ex 16:20 following morning, it became wormy and *r*.
16:24 commanded, it did not become *r* or wormy.
Jb 41:19 iron as straw, and bronze as *r* wood.
Is 5:24 *r* and their blossom scatter like dust;
Jer 29:17 I will make them like *r* figs,
Mt 12:33 or declare a tree *r* and its fruit rotten,
12:33 or declare a tree rotten and its fruit *r*.

ROTTENNESS (1)

Sir 19: 3 *R* and worms will possess him,

ROTTING (3)

Jb 8:19 There he lies *r* beside the road,
Bar 6:71 *r* of the purple and the linen upon them,
Ez 33:10 we are *r* away because of them.

ROUGH (5)

Is 40: 4 land shall be made a plain, the *r* country,
Bar 4:26 My pampered children have trodden *r* roads,
Mt 7:14 gate that leads to life, how *r* the road,
Lk 3: 5 be made straight And the *r* ways smooth,
Jn 6:18 wind blowing, the sea was becoming *r*.

ROUGHLY (1)

1Cor 4:11 hungry and thirsty, poorly clad, *r* treated,

ROUND (55)

Gn 35: 5 from God fell upon the towns *r* about,
Ex 38: 4 was made for the altar and placed *r* it,
40: 8 Set up the court *r* about,
Nm 10: 3 *r* you at the entrance of the meeting tent;
10: 4 the troops of Israel, shall gather *r* you.
Dt 2: 3 wandered *r* these highlands long enough;
12:10 *r* about and you live there in security,
25:19 from all your enemies *r* about in the land
Jos 21:42 cities went the pasture lands *r* about it.
23: 1 rest from all their enemies *r* about them,
Jgs 2:14 fall into the power of their enemies *r* about
7:13 "that a *r* loaf of barley bread was
1Sm 10: 1 from the grasp of their enemies *r* about.
2Sm 22: 5 "The breakers of death surged *r* about me.
1Kgs 5: 4 he had peace on all his borders *r* about.
10:19 throne had six steps, a back with a *r* top,
2Chr 4: 2 It was perfectly *r*, ten cubits in diameter,
Neh 5:17 who came to us from the nations *r* about,
6:16 the nations *r* about had taken note of it,
Jdt 5:22 people standing *r* about the tent murmured;
1Mc 5: 1 When the Gentiles *r* about heard that the
7:17 blood they have shed *r* about Jerusalem,
12:53 the nations *r* about sought to destroy them.
Jb 11:18 shall look *r* you and lie down in safety,
19: 6 with me, and compassed me *r* with his net.
22:10 Therefore snares are *r* about you,
29: 5 with me, and my children were *r* about me;
Ps(s) 18: 5 The breakers of death surged *r* about me,
32: 7 glad cries of freedom you will ring me *r*.
48:13 Go about Zion, make the *r*;
49: 6 days when my wicked ensnarers ring me *r*?
76:12 let all *r* about him bring gifts to the
78:28 midst of their camp *r* about their tents.
79: 3 their blood like water *r* about Jerusalem,
89: 8 great and awesome beyond all *r* about him.
97: 2 Clouds and darkness are *r* about him,
97: 3 before him and consumes his foes *r* about.
125: 2 Mountains are *r* about Jerusalem;
125: 2 so the LORD is *r* about his people,
Sg 7: 3 Your navel is a *r* bowl that should never
Sir 28:24 As you hedge *r* your vineyard with thorns,
45: 9 the hem, And a rustle of bells *r* about,
Is 15: 8 For the cry has gone *r* the land of Moab;
29: 1 Add year to year, let the feasts come *r*.
42:25 It blazed *r* about them,
65:20 man who does not *r* out his full lifetime;
Jer 5: 6 them, Leopards keep watch *r* their cities:
49: 5 LORD GOD of hosts, from all *r* about you;
Lam 3: 5 me *r* about with poverty and weariness;
Bar 2: 4 us subject to all the kingdoms *r* about us,
2: 4 *r* about to which the Lord has scattered us.
Ez 1: 7 the soles of their feet were *r*.
31: 4 sending its rivers *r* where it was planted,
36: 4 mockery of the remaining nations *r* about;
Zec 12: 2 a bowl to stupefy all peoples *r* about.

ROUNDABOUT (4)

Jgs 5: 6 who traveled the roads went by *r* paths.
2Sm 14:20 did this to come at the issue in a *r* way.
2Kgs 3: 9 After their *r* journey of seven days the
Lk 8:34 brought the news to the town and country *r*.

ROUNDED (3)

1Kgs 7:31 was a *r* opening to provide a receptacle
Sg 7: 2 Your *r* thighs are like jewels,
Mt 22:10 the byroads and *r* up everyone they met,

ROUNDING (1)

1Mc 5:53 and Judas kept *r* up the stragglers and

ROUNDLY (2)

Sg 8: 7 to purchase love, he would be *r* mocked.
Lk 18:15 disciples saw this, they scolded them *r*;

ROUNDS (8)

1Sm 22:17 the *r* and kill the priests of the LORD,
22:18 "You make the *r* and kill the priests!"
Jb 37:12 He it is who changes their *r*,
Eccl 1: 6 wind turns again and again, resuming its *r*.
Sg 3: 3 upon me as they made their *r* of the city:
5: 7 upon me as they made their *r* of the city;
Wis 6:16 Because she makes her own *r*,
Mk 6: 6 the *r* of the neighboring villages instead,

ROUSE (16)

Gn 49: 9 who would dare *r* him?
Jgs 9:32 Now *r* yourself;
Ps(s) 59: 5 *R* yourself to see it, and aid me,
80: 3 *R* your power, and come to save us.
Sir 36: 6 *R* your anger,
Is 19: 2 I will *r* Egypt against Egypt:
50: 4 speak to the weary a word that will *r* them.
Jer 51: 1 I *r* against Babylon,
Dn 11: 2 he shall *r* all the kingdom of Greece.
Jl 4: 7 I will *r* them from the place into which
4: 9 proclaim a war, *r* the warriors to arms!
Mk 14:42 *R* yourselves and come along.
Rom 7: 8 to *r* in me every kind of evil desire.
11:14 trying to *r* my fellow Jews to envy and
Heb 10:23 We must consider how to *r*
Rv 3: 3 If you do not *r* yourselves I will come

ROUSED (8)

Neh 3:33 it *r* his anger and he became very much
1Mc 10:74 heard this message of Apollonius, he was *r*.
Jb 14:12 not awake, nor be *r* out of their sleep.
Ps(s) 78:38 his anger and let none of his wrath be *r*.
78:58 places and with their idols *r* his jealousy.
Jer 6:22 great nation, *r* from the ends of the earth.
50:41 mighty kings *r* from the ends of the earth.
Rom 7: 5 the sinful passions *r* by the law worked in

ROUSES (1)

Is 64: 6 your name, who *r* himself to cling to you;

ROUT (12)

Lv 26: 7 You will *r* your enemies and lay them low
Dt 7:23 *r* them utterly until they are annihilated.
32:30 "How could one man *r* a thousand,
Jgs 4:15 and all his forces to *r* before Barak.
1Sm 14:22 were fleeing, pursued them in the *r*.
1Chr 10: 7 that Saul and his sons had died in the *r*,
Ps(s) 83:16 your tempest and *r* them with your storm.
83:18 Let them be shamed and put to *r* forever;
90: 7 anger, and by your wrath we are put to *r*.
144: 6 to flight, shoot your arrows, and *r* them;
Is 22: 5 It is a day of panic, *r* and confusion,
Zec 10: 5 with them, and shall put the horsemen to *r*.

ROUTE (14)

Dt 2: 8 "Then we left behind us the Arabah *r*,
Jgs 8:11 *r* of the nomads east of Nobah and Jogbehah,
1Sm 6: 9 along the *r* to his own territory,
6:12 The cows went straight for the *r* to
2Kgs 3: 8 They discussed the *r* for their attack,
3: 8 upon the *r* through the desert of Edom.
7:15 and the whole *r* was strewn with garments
Jdt 5:14 along the *r* to Sinai and Kadesh-barnea.
10:13 I will show him the *r* by which he can
1Mc 11: 4 in the war and stacked up along his *r*.
Mt 2:12 back to their own country by another *r*.
Lk 19: 4 a sycamore tree which was along Jesus' *r*,
Acts 8:26 goes from Jerusalem to Gaza, the desert *r*."
Jas 2:25 and sent them out by a different *r*?

ROUTED (19)

Jgs 9:40 But Abimelech *r* him,
1Sm 14:31 were *r* that day from Michmash to Aijalon,
15: 7 Saul *r* Amalek from Havilah to the
2Sm 5:25 David obeyed the LORD's command and *r* the
22:15 he flashed lightning and *r* them.
1Chr 14:16 *r* the Philistine army from Gibeon to Gezer.
Jdt 1:13 He *r* the whole force of Arphaxad,
1Mc 5: 7 He fought many battles with them, *r* them,
11:55 against Demetrius, who was *r* and fled.
2Mc 8:20 the eight thousand *r* one hundred and
9: 2 to arms, and Antiochus' men were *r*,
10:30 and blinded, thrown into confusion and *r*.
Jb 5:13 ruses, and the designs of the crafty are *r*.
Ps(s) 18:15 with frequent lightnings he *r* them.
48: 6 and at once are stunned, terrified, *r*;
Sir 48:21 of the Assyrians and *r* them with a plague.
Jer 46: 5 their heroes are *r*,
51:34 He has consumed me, *r* me,
Dn 3:44 be *r* who inflict evils on your servants;

ROUTES (4)

Dt 19: 3 and so arrange the *r* that every homicide
Tb 5: 6 I know the place well and I know all the *r*.
5:10 I can go with him, for I know all the *r*.
Jb 6:18 Caravans turn aside from their *r*;

ROUTINE (1)

Is 29:13 become *r* observance of the precepts of men,

ROVE (2)

Jb 38:41 out to God, and they *r* abroad without food?
Am 8:12 sea to sea and *r* from the north to the east

ROW (11)

Ex 28:17 in the first *r*, a carnelian, a topaz and
28:18 in the second *r*, a garnet, a sapphire and
28:19 in the third *r*, a jacinth, an agate and
28:20 in the fourth *r*, a chrysolite, an onyx and
39:10 in the first *r* a carnelian,
39:11 in the second *r*, a garnet, a sapphire and
39:12 in the third *r* a jacinth, an agate and
39:13 in the fourth *r* a chrysolite, an onyx and
1Kgs 7: 3 beams numbered forty-five, fifteen to a *r*.
7:18 two hundred of them in a double *r*
Mk 6:48 they tried to *r* with the wind against them,

ROWED (3)

Is 33:21 and wide streams on which no boat is *r*,
Jon 1:13 Still the men *r* hard to regain the land,
Jn 6:19 when they had *r* three or four miles,

ROWS (12)

Ex 28:17 you shall mount four *r* of precious stones:
39:10 *r* of precious stones were mounted on it:
1Kgs 7: 2 was supported by four *r* of cedar columns,
7:24 *r* and were cast in one mold with the sea.
7:42 four hundred pomegranates in double *r*
2Chr 4: 3 there were two *r* of these cast in the same
4:13 with two *r* of pomegranates to each network,
Jb 24:11 Between the *r* they press out the oil;
41: 7 *R* of scales are on his back,
Wis 18:24 were carved in four *r* upon the stones,
Ez 42: 3 parallel *r* of them on different levels.
42: 6 for they were in three *r* and had no

ROYAL (185)

Gn 39:20 jail where the *r* prisoners were confined.
40: 1 the *r* cupbearer and baker gave offense to
Nm 20:17 but we will go straight along the *r* road
21:22 along the *r* road until we have passed
Jos 10: 2 Gibeon was large enough for a *r* city,
13:31 Edrei, once the *r* cities of Og in Bashan,
1Sm 27: 5 your servant live with you in the *r* city?"
2Sm 7:13 And I will make his *r* throne firm forever.
11: 9 But Uriah slept at the entrance of the *r*
12:26 of the Ammonites and captured this *r* city.
14:26 shekels according to the *r* standard.
15:35 If you hear anything from the *r* palace,
16: 6 all the soldiers, including the *r* guard,
24: 3 your *r* majesty to see it with his own eyes.
1Kgs 1: 2 If she sleeps with your *r* majesty,
1: 9 sons, and all the *r* officials of Judah.
1:20 to sit on the throne after your *r* majesty.
1:27 Was this done by my *r* master's order
1:33 "Take with you the *r* attendants.
1:37 As the LORD has been with your *r* majesty,
1:46 Solomon took his seat on the *r* throne,
3: 1 With the *r* power firmly in his grasp,
5: 7 and for all the guests at the *r* table.
9: 1 the temple of the LORD, the *r* palace,
10:13 as were given her from Solomon's *r* bounty.
11:14 the Edomite, who was of the *r* line in Edom.
14:26 of the LORD and those of the *r* palace,
14:27 on duty at the entrance of the *r* palace.
15:18 the temple of the LORD and of the *r* palace.

16:11 Once he was seated on the *r* throne,
16:18 he entered the citadel of the *r* palace and
2Kgs 11: 1 she began to kill off the whole *r* family.
11:16 forcibly to the horse gate of the *r* palace,
11:19 where Joash took his seat on the *r* throne.
11:20 been slain with the sword at the *r* palace.
12:11 *r* scribe [and the priest] would come up,
16:15 the *r* holocaust and cereal-offering,
25:25 Nethaniah, son of Elishama, of *r* descent,
1Chr 28: 5 to sit on the LORD'S *r* throne over Israel.
2Chr 1:18 and also of a house for his own *r* estate.
2:11 the LORD and also a house for his *r* estate.
7:11 the house of the LORD and the *r* palace;
7:18 I will establish your *r* throne as I
12:10 on duty at the entrance of the *r* palace.
16: 2 of the *r* palace and sent them to Ben-hadad,
22:10 all the *r* offspring of the house of Judah.
22:11 But Jehosheba, a *r* princess,
23:20 they seated the king upon the *r* throne.
24:11 Whenever the chest was brought to the *r*
24:11 the *r* scribe and an overseer for the high
26:23 them in the field adjoining the *r* cemetery,
Ezr 5:17 let a search be made in the *r* archives of
6: 4 The costs are to be borne by the *r* palace.
6: 8 From the *r* revenue, the taxes of
7:20 your God, you may draw from the *r* treasury.
7:28 with all the most influential *r* officials.
Neh 2: 8 letter for Asaph, the keeper of the *r* park,
11:23 for they had been appointed by *r* decree,
11:24 was *r* deputy in all affairs that concerned
Jdt 2:18 and much gold and silver from the *r* palace.
Est 1: 2 the *r* throne in the stronghold of Susa,
1: 4 and the resplendent wealth of his *r* estate.
1: 5 court of the *r* palace for all the people,
1: 7 golden cups, and the *r* wine flowed freely,
1: 9 inside the *r* palace of King Ahasuerus.
1:11 into his presence wearing the *r* crown,
1:12 at the *r* order issued through the eunuchs.
1:18 will rebel against all the *r* officials,
1:19 let an irrevocable *r* decree be issued by
1:19 her *r* dignity to one more worthy than she.
1:22 He sent letters to all the *r* provinces,
2: 3 Under the care of the *r* eunuch Hegai,
2: 8 in to the *r* palace under the care of Hegai,
2: 9 out seven maids for her from the *r* palace,
2:13 harem to the *r* palace whatever she chose.
2:14 under the care of the *r* eunuch Shaashgaz,
2:15 for anything but what the *r* eunuch Hegai,
2:17 So he placed the *r* diadem on her head and
2:18 and bestowing gifts with *r* bounty.
2:21 of the *r* eunuchs who guarded the entrance,
3: 2 *r* gate would kneel and bow down to Haman,
3: 3 who were at the *r* gate said to Mordecai,
3: 9 talents for deposit in the *r* treasury."
3:12 So the *r* scribes were summoned;
3:12 of Haman, an order to the *r* satraps,
3:12 and sealed with the *r* signet ring.
3:13 sent by couriers to all the *r* provinces,
4: 2 till he came before the *r* gate,
4: 6 the public square in front of the *r* gate,
4: 7 *r* treasury for the slaughter of the Jews.
B:14 like this that you obtained the *r* dignity?"
D: 1 and arrayed herself in her *r* attire.
D: 6 the king, who was seated on his *r* throne,
5: 1 Esther put on her *r* garments and stood in
5: 1 courtyard, looking toward the *r* palace,
5: 1 on his *r* throne in the audience chamber,
5: 9 that Mordecai at the *r* gate did not rise,
5:11 him above the officials and *r* servants.
5:13 see the Jew Mordecai sitting at the *r* gate."
6: 2 of the *r* eunuchs who guarded the entrance,
6: 8 to reward there should be brought the *r* robe
6: 8 when the *r* crown was placed on his head.
6:10 Jew Mordecai, who is sitting at the *r* gate.
6:12 Mordecai then returned to the *r* gate,
8: 5 of the Jews in all the *r* provinces.
8: 8 and seal the letter with the *r* signet ring."
8: 8 with the *r* signet ring cannot be revoked.
8: 9 month, Sivan, the *r* scribes were summoned.
8:10 and sealed with the *r* signet ring,
8:10 couriers riding thoroughbred *r* steeds.
E:11 attained the rank second to the *r* throne.
E:13 and of Esther, our blameless *r* consort,
8:14 Couriers mounted on *r* steeds sped forth in
8:15 in a *r* robe of violet and of white cotton,
9: 3 and *r* procurators supported the Jews from
9: 4 for Mordecai was powerful in the *r* palace,
9:12 they have done in the other *r* provinces!
9:16 other Jews, who dwelt in the *r* provinces,
9:25 Yet, when Esther entered the *r* presence,
1Mc 1: 9 after his death they all put on *r* crowns,
1:57 law, was condemned to death by *r* decree.
3:32 He left Lysias, a nobleman of *r* blood,
6:43 any of the others and covered with *r* armor,
6:47 of the *r* army and the ardor of its forces,
7: 2 to enter the *r* palace of his ancestors,
7: 4 them, and Demetrius sat on the *r* throne.
10:40 silver shekels out of the *r* revenues,
10:44 shall be covered out of the *r* revenue.
10:45 Judea, shall be donated from the *r* revenue."
10:53 and his army, and recovered the *r* throne
10:55 and took your seat on their *r* throne!
10:62 garments and to be clothed in *r* purple;
11:34 in Jerusalem instead of paying the *r* taxes
11:52 King Demetrius was sure of his *r* throne,
11:54 who became king and wore the *r* crown.
11:58 drink from gold cups, to dress in *r* purple,
13:15 of the money that he owed the *r* treasury
14:43 right to wear *r* purple and gold ornaments.
14:44 *r* purple or wear an official gold brooch.
15: 8 the *r* treasury shall be canceled for you,
2Mc 2:13 and the *r* letters about sacred offerings
3:13 must be confiscated for the *r* treasury.
4:11 He set aside the *r* concessions granted to
4:25 He returned with the *r* commission,
Ps(s) 45: 7 a tempered rod is your *r* scepter.
Wis 18:15 word from heaven's *r* throne bounded,
Sir 47: 6 When he assumed the *r* crown,
Is 60:16 of nations, and be nursed at *r* breasts;
62: 3 of the LORD, a *r* diadem held by your God.
Jer 21:11 To the *r* house of Judah:
36:26 them, but commanded Jerahmeel, a *r* prince,
39: 4 leaving the city on the *R* Garden Road
41: 1 Nethaniah, son of Elishama, of *r* descent,
43: 9 entrance to the *r* building in Tahpanhes,
Bar 5: 6 you borne aloft in glory as on *r* thrones.
Ez 17:13 of the *r* line with whom he made a covenant,
19:11 strong branch she put out as a *r* scepter.
Dn 1: 3 Israelites of *r* blood and of the nobility,
1: 5 portion of food and wine from the *r* table.
1:13 other young men who eat from the *r* table,
1:15 of the young men who ate from the *r* table.
3:95 they disobeyed the *r* command and yielded
4:26 on the roof of the *r* palace in Babylon,
4:27 a *r* residence for my splendor and majesty?"
5:20 his *r* throne and deprived of his glory;
6: 8 ought to be put in force by *r* decree:
6:16 *r* prohibition or decree is irrevocable."
6:27 I decree that throughout my *r* domain the
11:21 to whom the *r* insignia shall not be given.
11:45 He shall pitch the tents of his *r* pavilion
Am 7:13 it is the king's sanctuary and a *r* temple."
Mi 5: 4 it seven shepherds, eight men of *r* rank;
Zec 6:13 of the LORD, and taking up the *r* insignia,
Mt 11: 8 luxuriously are to be found in *r* palaces.
25:31 of heaven, he will sit upon his *r* throne,
Mk 15:17 They dressed him in *r* purple,
Lk 7:25 in splendor are to be found in *r* palaces.
Jn 4:46 to be a *r* official whose son was ill.
4:49 "Sir," the *r* official pleaded with him,
19: 2 around his shoulders a cloak of *r* purple.
Acts 12:20 They won over his *r* chamberlain Blastus
12:21 an appointed day Herod, arrayed in *r* robes,
1Pt 2: 9 are "a chosen race, a *r* priesthood,
Rv 1: 6 who has made us a *r* nation of priests in
17:12 possess *r* authority along with the beast,

ROYALTY (7)

Nm 24: 7 and his *r* shall be exalted.
1Sm 10:25 people the law of *r* and wrote it in a book,
2Sm 13:27 Absalom prepared a banquet fit for *r*.
1Mc 2:57 as a heritage a throne of everlasting *r*.
Eccl 4:14 since even in his *r* he was poor at birth.
Wis 10:14 of *r* and authority over his oppressors,
Sir 47:11 of *r* and established his throne in Israel.

RUB (2)

Tb 6: 9 if you *r* it on the eyes of a man who has
Sir 12:11 *R* him as one polishes a brazen mirror,

RUBBED (1)

Ez 16: 4 nor anointed, nor were you *r* with salt,

RUBBISH (2)

Neh 4: 4 strength, there is no end to the *r*;
Phil 3: 8 I have accounted all else *r* so that Christ

RUBBLE (7)

Ezr 6:11 is to be reduced to *r* for this offense.
Neh 3:35 "It is a *r* heap they are building.
Jer 7:34 for the land will be turned to *r*.
22: 5 this palace shall become *r*.
Am 6:11 to bits, and reduce the small house to *r*.
Mi 3:12 like a field, and Jerusalem reduced to *r*,
Na 3:17 gathered on the *r* fences on a cold day!

RUBIES (3)

Tb 13:17 shall be paved with *r* and stones of Ophir;
Is 54:12 I will make your battlements of *r*,
Ez 27:16 fine linen, coral, and *r* for your wares.

RUDDERS (2)

Acts 27:40 time they untied the guy-ropes of the *r*,
Jas 3: 4 they are directed by very small *r* on

RUDDY (4)

1Sm 16:12 He was *r*, a youth handsome to behold
17:42 up, and seen that he was youthful, and *r*,
Sg 5:10 My lover is radiant and *r*;
Lam 4: 7 whiter than milk, More *r* than coral,

RUDE (3)

Wis 17:19 water, or the *r* crash of overthrown rocks,
Sir 21:24 It is *r* for one to listen at a door;
1Cor 13: 5 Love is never *r*,

RUDENESS (1)

2Mc 14:30 acting with unaccustomed *r* when they met;

RUE (1)

Lk 11:42 on mint and *r* and all the garden plants,

RUEFUL (1)

Wis 5: 3 *r* and groaning through anguish of spirit:

RUFFIANS (1)

Jgs 9: 4 hired shiftless men and *r* as his followers.

RUFFLING (1)

Zec 5: 9 coming forth with a wind *r* their wings,

RUFUS (2)

Mk 15:21 of Cyrene, the father of Alexander and *R*,
Rom 16:13 Greetings to *R*,

RUG (1)

Jgs 4:18 her tent, and she covered him with a *r*.

RUGGED (3)

Ps(s) 68:16 *r* the mountains of Bashan.
68:17 Why look you jealously, you *r* mountains,
Is 40: 4 The *r* land shall be made a plain,

RUGS (1)

Is 21: 5 They set the table, spread out the *r*;

RUHAMA (1)

Hos 2: 3 brothers, "Ammi," and to your sisters, *R*."

RUIN (108)

Nm 32:15 bring about the *r* of this whole nation."
Dt 11: 4 and bringing *r* upon them even to this day;
28:51 until they have brought about your *r*.
Jgs 8:27 and caused the *r* of Gideon and his family.
2Sm 16: 8 you suffer *r* because you are a murderer."
17:14 in order thus to bring Absalom to *r*.
20:20 I do not wish to destroy or to *r* anything.
1Kgs 20: 7 clearly that this man wants to *r* us.
2Kgs 3:19 and *r* every fertile field with stones."
2Chr 34:11 kings of Judah had allowed to fall into *r*.
Tb 4:13 arrogance there is *r* and great disorder.
Jdt 13:16 my face that seduced Holofernes to his *r*,
Est C: 8 for our enemies plan our *r* and are bent
C:22 Let them not gloat over our *r*,
8:12 may help them on the day set for their *r*,
1Mc 2: 7 Why was I born to see the *r* of my people
2: 7 of my people and the *r* of the holy city,
3:59 the *r* of our nation and our sanctuary.
2Mc 6:12 the *r* but for the correction of our nation.
Jb 2: 3 me against him to *r* him without cause."
5:21 hidden, and shall not fear approaching *r*.
30:12 they build their approaches for my *r*.
Ps(s) 35: 8 Let *r* come upon them unawares,
38:13 look to my misfortune, they speak of *r*,
40:15 turned back in disgrace who desire my *r*.
52: 6 You love all that means *r*,
70: 3 be turned back in disgrace who desire my *r*.
73:18 you hurl them down to *r*.
Prv 3:25 of the *r* of the wicked when it comes;
5:14 I have all but come to utter *r*,
6:15 Therefore suddenly *r* comes upon him;
10:14 but the mouth of a fool is imminent *r*.
11: 9 mouth the impious man would *r* his neighbor,
13:15 but the way of the faithless is their *r*.
14:28 his people are few, it is the prince's *r*.
15:27 greedy of gain brings *r* on his own house,
18: 7 The fool's mouth is his *r*;
18:24 Some friends bring *r* on us,
19:13 The foolish son is *r* to his father,
21:12 is one who brings down the wicked to *r*.
24:16 rises again, but the wicked stumble to *r*.
24:22 they send, and the *r* from either one,
26:28 enemy, and the flattering mouth works *r*.
27:10 but if *r* befalls you,
31: 3 nor your strength to those who *r* kings.
Eccl 9:18 and a single slip can *r* much that is good."
Wis 5: 7 our fill of the ways of mischief and of *r*;
Sir 10:13 afflictions and brings men to utter *r*.
14: 9 his neighbor and brings *r* on himself.
27:23 his tone and twists your words to your *r*.
31:25 strength, for wine has been the *r* of many.
40: 9 wrath and the sword, plunder and *r*,
47:23 Who brought *r* to Ephraim and caused them
Is 3: 6 Be our ruler, and take in hand this *r*—
5: 6 Yes, I will make it a *r*:
10: 3 day of punishment, when *r* comes from afar?
11: 9 be no harm or *r* on all my holy mountain;
16: 4 When the struggle is ended, the *r* complete,

RUIN (cont.)

17: 1 shall cease to be a city and become a *r;*
22: 4 me for the *r* of the daughter of my people.
23:13 destroyed, and has been turned into a *r.*
24:12 In the city nothing remains but *r;*
25: 2 the city a heap, the fortified city a *r;*
32: 7 How to *r* the poor with lies,
47:11 come upon you *r* which you will not expect.
59: 7 plunder and *r* are on their highways.
60:18 or plunder and *r* within your boundaries.
Jer 4:20 *R* after ruin is reported;
8:21 by the *r* of the daughter of my people.
17:17 Do not be my *r,* you, my refuge
25:11 This whole land shall be a *r* and a desert.
25:18 her princes, to make them a *r* and a desert,
31:28 to uproot and pull down, to destroy, to *r,*
38: 4 the welfare of our people, but in their *r.*"
40: 2 your God, foretold the *r* of this place.
46:19 Memphis shall become a desert, an empty *r.*
46:21 When the day of their *r* comes upon them,
47: 4 which has come to *r* all the Philistines,
48: 3 from Horonaim of *r* and great destruction!
48:16 Near at hand is Moab's *r,*
49:32 from all sides I will bring *r* upon them,
Lam 1: 7 foes gloated over her, laughed at her *r.*
2: 8 his hand brought *r,* yet he did not relent
Ez 38: 8 mountains of Israel which were long a *r,*
Dn 8:24 strong and powerful, bring about fearful *r,*
9:27 until the *r* that is decreed is poured out
Hos 4:14 a people without understanding come to *r.*
7:13 *R* to them, they have sinned against me!
Jl 1:15 LORD, and it comes as *r* from the Almighty.
Am 5: 9 the strong, and brings *r* upon the fortress;
Ob 1:12 children of Judah on the day of their *r;*
Mi 2: 4 "Our *r* is complete, our fields are portioned
5: 9 horses from your midst and *r* your chariots;
6:16 Therefore I will deliver you up to *r,*
Hb 1: 3 Why do you let me see *r;*
Mt 10:39 seeks only himself brings himself to *r,*
Rom 3:16 *r* and misery strew their course.
14:15 eat bring to *r* him for whom Christ died:
1Cor 1:18 absurdity to those who are headed for *r,*
1Thes 5: 3 *r* will fall on them with the suddenness of
2Thes 1: 9 will suffer the penalty of eternal *r*
2:10 wicked can devise for those destined to *r*
1Tm 6: 9 which drag men down to *r* and destruction.
2Tm 2:14 good and can be the *r* of those who listen.
2Pt 3:16 do the rest of Scripture) to their own *r.*
Rv 17: 8 abyss once more before going to final *r.*
17:11 one of the seven and is on its way to *r.*

RUINATION (1)

Prv 10:15 the *r* of the lowly is their poverty.

RUINED (34)

Ex 9:31 Now the flax and the barley were *r,*
9:32 But the wheat and the spelt were not *r,*
Nm 21:29 You are *r,* O people of Chemosh!
21:30 Their plowland is *r* from Heshbon to Dibon;
2Chr 34: 6 and in the *r* villages of the surrounding
Jdt 4:12 the cities of their inheritance to be *r,*
1Mc 3:43 us restore our people from their *r* estate,
15: 4 and take revenge on those who have *r* it
Ps(s) 9: 7 The enemies are *r* completely forever;
105:16 land and *r* the crop that sustained them,
Prv 11: 3 the faithless are *r* by their duplicity.
Eccl 7:16 excess, and be not overwise, lest you be *r.*
Sir 29:17 Going surety has *r* many prosperous men and
49:13 He rebuilt our *r* walls,
Is 14:20 For you have *r* your land,
58:12 shall call you, "Restorer of *r* homesteads."
61: 4 shall raise up And restore the *r* cities,
Jer 4:13 "Woe to us! we are *r.*"
6: 2 and delicate daughter Zion, you are *r!*
9:18 *R* we are, and greatly ashamed;
10:20 My tent is *r,* all its cords are severed.
48: 8 *R* is the valley,
48:18 up against you, he has *r* your strongholds.
48:20 Publish it at the Arnon, Moab is *r!*
48:46 Woe to you, O Moab, you are *r,*
49:10 He is *r:* sons, and brothers,
Ez 26: 2 now that it is *r,*
Am 3:15 The ivory apartments shall be *r,*
9:14 shall rebuild and inhabit their *r* cities,
Na 2: 3 have ravaged them and *r* the tendrils.
Zec 11: 3 of the shepherds, their glory has been *r.*
Mt 7:27 under all this and was completely *r.*"
9:17 the wine spills out, and the skins are *r.*
1Cor 9:16 I am *r* if I do not preach it!

RUINING (1)

Dt 28:63 now take delight in *r* and destroying you,

RUINOUS (2)

Jb 15:28 loins with fat, He shall dwell in *r* cities,
Jer 44: 6 they became the *r* waste they are today.

RUINS (56)

Dt 13:17 Let it be a heap of *r* forever,
Jos 8:28 reducing it to an everlasting mound of *r,*
1Kgs 9: 8 and this temple shall become a heap of *r.*
2Kgs 19:25 reduce fortified cities into heaps of *r,*
Ezr 9: 9 the house of our God and restore its *r,*
Neh 2: 3 where my ancestors are buried lies in *r,*
2:13 *r* and its gates had been eaten out by fire.
2:17 *r* and its gates have been gutted by fire.
Jb 3:14 the earth who built where now there are *r*
Ps(s) 74: 3 Turn your steps toward the utter *r;*
79: 1 holy temple, they have laid Jerusalem in *r.*
89:41 you have laid his strongholds in *r.*
102: 7 I have become like an owl among the *r.*
109:10 they be cast out of the *r* of their homes.
Prv 29: 4 but he who imposes heavy taxes *r* it.
Sir 21:18 Like a house in *r* is wisdom to a fool;
Is 5: 9 Many houses shall be in *r,*
5:17 and kids shall eat in the *r* of the rich.
37:26 reduce fortified cities into heaps of *r,*
44:26 Be rebuilt; I will raise up their *r.*
49:19 you were waste and desolate, a land of *r,*
51: 3 comfort Zion and have pity on all her *r;*
52: 9 out together in song, O *r* of Jerusalem!
58:12 ancient *r* shall be rebuilt for your sake,
61: 4 They shall rebuild the ancient *r,*
Jer 2:15 his cities are charred *r,*
9:10 I will turn Jerusalem into a heap of *r,*
26:18 a plowed field, Jerusalem a heap of *r,*
27:17 else this city will become a heap of *r.*
44: 2 Today they are *r* and uninhabited,
48: 9 are turned into *r* where no one dwells.
49: 2 She shall become a mound of *r,*
49:13 and all her cities shall become *r* forever.
51:26 *R* forever shall you be,
51:37 Babylon shall become a heap of *r,*
Ez 12:20 Inhabited cities shall be in *r,*
13: 4 Like foxes among *r* are your prophets,
26:20 in the nether lands, in the everlasting *r,*
33:24 in the *r* on the land of Israel reason thus:
33:27 in the *r* I swear shall fall by the sword;
35: 4 Your cities I will turn into *r,*
36: 4 the desolate *r* and abandoned cities,
36:10 cities shall be repeopled, and *r* rebuilt.
36:33 the cities, and the *r* shall be rebuilt;
36:35 "The cities that were in *r,*
36:38 in *r* shall be filled with flocks of men;
38:12 turning my hand against the *r* that were
Dn 9: 2 that for the *r* of Jerusalem seventy years
9:18 our *r* and the city which bears your name.
Hos 9: 6 When they go from the *r,*
Am 9:11 will wall up its breaches, raise up its *r,*
Hg 1: 4 paneled houses, while this house lies in *r?*
1: 9 Because my house lies in *r,*
Mal 1: 4 been crushed but we will rebuild the *r,*"
Acts 15:16 *r* I will rebuild it and set it up again,
Rv 11:13 and a tenth of the city fell in *r.*

RULE (114)

Gn 37: 8 "Or impose your *r* on us?"
Lv 24:22 You shall have but one *r,*
Nm 8:24 "This is the *r* for the Levites.
15:15 one *r* for you and for the resident alien,
15:15 a perpetual *r* for all your descendants.
Dt 15: 6 you will *r* over many nations,
15: 6 many nations, and none will *r* over you,
24:18 is why I command you to observe this *r.*
24:22 is why I command you to observe this *r.*
Jgs 8:22 Israelites then said to Gideon, *R* over us
8:23 answered them, "I will not *r* over you,
8:23 rule over you, nor shall my son *r* over you.
8:23 The LORD must *r* over you."
9: 2 men, or all Jerubbaal's sons, *r* over you,
9: 2 rule over you, or that one man *r* over you?'
1Sm 8: 9 of the rights of the king who will *r* them."
8:11 the king who will *r* you will be as follows:
8:20 with a king to *r* us and to lead us in
8:22 their request and appoint a king to *r* them."
11:12 questioned whether Saul should *r* over us?
12:12 said to me, 'Not so, but a king must *r* us,'
2Sm 3:21 then be king over all whom you wish to *r.*"
5:12 his *r* for the sake of his people Israel.
1Kgs 5:21 David a wise son to *r* this numerous people."
8:16 but I choose David to *r* my people Israel.'
2Kgs 8:22 has been in revolt against the *r* of Judah.
12: 5 For the priests Joash made this *r:*
1Chr 16:33 he comes to *r* the earth.
22:12 when he brings you to *r* over Israel,
2Chr 1:10 who could *r* this great people of yours?"
1:11 *r* my people over whom I have made you king,
6: 6 and I choose David to *r* my people Israel.'
12: 1 consolidated his *r* and had become powerful,
12:13 his power in Jerusalem and continued to *r;*
20: 6 not *r* over all the kingdoms of the nations?
31:16 of the LORD according to the daily *r*
Neh 9:37 who *r* over our bodies and our cattle as
Est B: 2 When I came to *r* many peoples and to hold
E:14 the *r* of the Persians to the Macedonians.
1Mc 1:16 of Egypt, so as to *r* over both kingdoms.
6:12 Yet I was kindly and beloved in my *r.*'
7: 1 city on the seacoast, and began to *r* there.
8:16 every year, to *r* over their entire country,
10:52 and established my *r* by crushing Demetrius
11:38 under his *r* and that he had no opposition,
11:52 and the land was peaceful under his *r,*
Ps(s) 2: 9 You shall *r* them with an iron rod;
8: 7 given him *r* over the works of your hands,
19:14 let it not *r* over me.
49:15 shepherd, and the upright *r* over them.
67: 5 exult because you *r* the peoples in equity;
72: 8 May he *r* from sea to sea,
89:10 You *r* over the surging of the sea;
96:13 for he comes to *r* the earth.
96:13 He shall *r* the world with justice and the
98: 9 for he comes, for he comes to *r* the earth;
98: 9 He will *r* the world with justice and the
110: 2 *R* in the midst of your enemies.
119:133 promise, and let no iniquity *r* over me.
136: 8 The sun to *r* over the day,
136: 9 The moon and the stars to *r* over the night,
Prv 17: 2 servant will *r* over a worthless son,
19:10 much less should a slave *r* over princes.
22: 7 The rich *r* over the poor,
29: 2 but when the wicked *r,*
Eccl 4:14 from a prison house one comes forth to *r,*
7:18 It is good to hold to this *r,*
Wis 3: 8 shall judge nations and *r* over peoples,
9: 2 man to *r* the creatures produced by you,
10: 2 fall, and gave him power to *r* all things.
Sir 17: 4 and gives him *r* over beasts and birds.
46:13 and anointed princes to *r* the people.
Is 3:12 be their tyrant, and women will *r* them!
19: 4 master, A harsh king who shall *r* over them,
28:10 on command, rule on rule, rule on *r,*
28:13 on command, Rule on rule, rule on *r,*
28:14 arrogant, who *r* this people in Jerusalem:
28:26 He has learned this *r,*
32: 1 reign justly and princes will *r* rightly.
63:19 long have we been like those you do not *r,*
Lam 5: 8 Slaves *r* over us;
Bar 2:34 and they shall *r* it.
Ez 17:16 the home of the king who set him up to *r,*
Dn 2:39 bronze, which shall *r* over the whole earth.
4:19 and your *r* extends over the whole earth.
11: 3 king shall appear and *r* with great might,
11: 4 or in keeping with his mighty *r,*
11:39 he shall make them *r* over the many and
Ob 1:21 ascend Mount Zion to *r* the mount of Esau,
Lk 1:32 He will *r* over the house of Jacob forever
3: 1 fifteenth year of the *r* of Tiberius Caesar,
19:14 say, 'We will not have this man *r* over us.'
Acts 1: 6 you going to restore the *r* to Israel now?"
13:20 Later on he set up judges to *r* them until
Rom 6:12 let sin *r* your mortal body and make you
6:17 *r* of teaching which was imparted to you;
14:15 you have ceased to follow the *r* of love.
14:22 have as your *r* of life in the sight of God.
15:12 he who will rise up to *r* the Gentiles;
1Cor 7:17 The general *r* is that each one should lead
7:17 This is the *r* I give in all the churches.
14:34 According to the *r* observed in all the
2Cor 10:16 Following the *r* laid down for us,
Gal 6:16 and mercy on all who follow this *r* of life,
2Thes 3: 5 May the Lord *r* your hearts in the love of
3:10 used to lay down the *r* that anyone who
1Tm 6:16 To him be honor and everlasting *r!*
Rv 2:27 He shall *r* them with a rod of iron and

RULED (18)

Jos 12: 5 He *r* over Mount Hermon,
Jgs 9:22 Abimelech had *r* Israel for three years,
1Kgs 5: 1 Solomon *r* over all the kingdoms from the
5: 4 *r* over all the land west of the Euphrates,
2Kgs 11: 3 of the LORD, while Athaliah *r* the land.
23:22 during the period when the Judges *r* Israel,
1Chr 26: 6 were born sons who *r* over their family,
2Chr 22:12 of God, while Athaliah *r* over the land.
26:21 of the palace and *r* the people of the land.
Ezr 4:20 Jerusalem who *r* over all West-of-Euphrates,
Jdt 1: 1 time Arphaxad *r* over the Medes in Ecbatana.
Est 1: 1 this was the Ahasuerus who *r* over a
1Mc 1: 1 in his place, having first *r* in Greece.
Ps(s) 106:41 of the nations, and their foes *r* over them.
Is 26:13 our God, other lords than you have *r* us;
Acts 13:21 tribe of Benjamin, who *r* for forty years.
Rom 3:27 It is *r* out.
2Pt 3: 3 sneering men who are *r* by their passions

RULER (74)

Gn 45: 8 and *r* over the whole land of Egypt.
45:26 it is he who is *r* of all the land of Egypt,"
Ex 2:14 has appointed you *r* and judge over us?
Jgs 9:30 Ebed, had said, Zebul, the *r* of the city,
1Sm 15:23 the LORD, he, too, has rejected you as *r.*"
1Kgs 1:35 I designate him *r* of Israel and of Judah."
14: 7 people and made you *r* of my people Israel.
16: 2 dust and made you *r* of my people Israel,
21: 7 "A fine *r* over Israel you are indeed!"
2Kgs 10: 5 So the vizier and the *r* of the city,
1Chr 5: 2 his brothers, so that the *r* came from him,
9:11 son of Ahitub, the *r* of the house of God;
11: 2 my people Israel and be *r* over them.'"
17: 7 you might become *r* over my people Israel.
2Chr 7:18 be lacking someone of yours as *r* in Israel.'
9:26 He was *r* over all the kings from the River
34: 8 of Azaliah, Maaseiah, the *r* of the city,
Neh 11:11 son of Ahitub, the *r* of the house of God,

Jdt 8:9 lack of water, had spoken against their r,
9:10 lips, smite the slave together with the r,
9:10 the ruler, the r together with his servant;
Est C:23 King of gods and R of every power.
8:12 For God, the r of all,
1Mc 9:30 today to be our r and leader in his place,
11:57 and appoint you r over the four districts
2Mc 15:3 a r in heaven who prescribed the keeping
15:4 that there was indeed such a r in heaven,
15:5 he said, "I, on my part, am r on earth,
Ps(s) 59:14 men may know that God is the r of Jacob,
105:20 him, the r of the peoples set him free.
105:21 of his house and r of all his possessions,
Prv 6:7 she has no chief, no commander or r,
23:1 When you sit down to dine with a r,
25:15 By patience is a r persuaded,
28:15 bear is a wicked r over a poor people.
29:12 If a r listens to lying words,
29:26 Many curry favor with the r,
Eccl 9:17 heeded than the shout of a r of fools"
10:4 Should the anger of the r burst upon you,
10:5 like a mistake that proceeds from the r:
Wis 14:19 in his determination to please the r,
Sir 4:7 before a r bow your head.
7:6 show favor to the r and mar your integrity.
9:17 the r of his people is the skilled sage.
10:5 of God, who imparts his majesty to the r.
10:23 The prince, the r,
17:14 Over every nation he places a r,
39:4 on the great, and has entrance to the r.
41:16 Before prince and r,
Is 3:6 Be our r, and take in hand this ruin!"—
3:7 You shall not make me r of the people."
60:17 peace your governor, and justice your r.
Jer 22:30 the throne of David as r again over Judah.
40:5 has appointed r over the cities of Judah;
41:2 king of Babylon had made r over the land;
41:18 of Babylon had made r in the land of Judah.
Bar 6:13 a scepter, like the human r of a district;
Dn 2:38 over to you, making you r over them all;
2:48 made him r of the whole province of
Am 1:5 of Aven, And the sceptered r of Beth-eden;
1:8 in Ashdod, and the sceptered r of Ashkelon;
Mi 4:14 they strike on the cheek the r of Israel.
5:1 forth for me one who is to be r in Israel;
Hb 1:14 the sea, like creeping things without a r.
Zec 6:13 he shall sit as r upon his throne.
Mt 2:6 a r who is to shepherd my people Israel.' "
Acts 5:31 God has exalted at his right hand as r
7:27 who has appointed you r and judge over us?'
7:35 words, 'Who has appointed you r and judge?',
7:35 sent to be their r and deliverer.
Rom 13:4 r is God's servant to work for your good.
13:4 purpose that the r carries the sword;
1Tm 6:15 He is the blessed and only r,
Rv 1:5 from the dead and r of the kings of earth.

RULERS (55)

Gn 17:16 and r of peoples shall issue from him."
Ex 34:31 the r of the community come back to him.
Jgs 15:11 not know that the Philistines are our r?
Ru 4:22 fidelity to Yahweh for r and people alike.
2Kgs 10:1 letters and sent them to the city r,
2Chr 23:20 the nobles, the r among the people,
35:9 Jehiel and Jozabad, the r of the Levites,
Ezr 9:2 the leaders and r have taken a leading
Jdt 5:2 he summoned all the r of the Moabites,
6:14 They haled him before the r of the city,
7:23 in a crowd to Uzziah and the r of the city.
8:11 to me, you r of the people of Bethulia.
8:35 Uzziah and the r said to her,
9:3 Therefore you had their r slaughtered;
Est E:6 slander the sincere good will of r.
1Mc 1:4 and conquered provinces, nations, and r,
1:26 dwelt, and the r and the elders groaned.
10:37 and their r be taken from among them,
14:20 "The r and the citizens of Sparta send
14:28 of priests, people, r of the nation,
2Mc 9:25 bearing in mind that the neighboring r,
10:21 assembled the r of the people and accused
Ps(s) 2:10 take warning, you r of the earth.
Prv 8:16 all the r of earth.
Wis 8:11 judgment, and should be a marvel before r.
Sir 3:7 his father, and serves his parents as r.
4:27 impious man, nor refuse to do so before r.
33:19 O r of the assembly,
36:9 crush the heads of the hostile r.
38:33 judgments, nor are they found among the r;
46:18 He brought low the r of the enemy and
48:15 people, with its r from the house of David.
Is 40:23 and makes the r of the earth as nothing.
41:25 He shall trample the r down like red earth,
49:7 whom the nations abhor, the slave of r:
52:5 their r make a boast of it,
Jer 13:21 What will you say when they place as r
30:21 his own, and his r shall come from his kin.
33:26 his descendants r for the race of Abraham,
Bar 1:16 our kings and r and priests and prophets,
3:16 Where are the r of the nations,
Ez 19:14 now without a strong branch, a r scepter.
Hos 7:7 all heated like ovens, and consume their r.
13:10 r, of whom you said, "Give me a king
Mi 3:1 leaders of Jacob, r of the house of Israel!
3:9 of Jacob, you r of the house of Israel!
Mt 10:18 be brought to trial before r and kings,
Lk 8:49 from the r house with the announcement,
12:11 you before synagogues, r and authorities,
Acts 13:27 and their r failed to recognize him,
Rom 13:3 R cause no fear when a man does what is
1Cor 2:6 age, however, not of the r of this age,
2:8 of the r of this age knew the mystery;
Eph 6:12 powers, the r of this world of darkness,
1Pt 3:22 with angelic r and powers subjected to him.

RULES (27)

Ex 15:25 LORD, in making r and regulations for them,
21:1 are the r you shall lay before them.
Nm 9:3 it, observing all its r and regulations."
9:12 but observing all the r of the Passover.
9:14 the r and regulations for the Passover.
1Sm 12:14 king who r you follow the LORD your God
2Sm 23:3 said, 'He that r over men in justice,
23:3 men in justice, that r in the fear of God,
1Kgs 21:18 Ahab, king of Israel, who r in Samaria.
Jb 28:26 When he made r for the rain and a path for
Ps(s) 22:29 is the LORD's, and he r the nations.
66:7 He r by his might forever;
103:19 in heaven, and his kingdom r over all.
Prv 16:32 than a warrior, and he who r his temper,
Sir 41:14 judge of disgrace only according to my r,
Is 40:10 the Lord GOD, who r by his strong arm;
Dn 4:14 the Most High r over the kingdom of men:
4:22 until you know that the Most High r over
4:23 once you have learned it is heaven that r.
4:29 until you learn that the Most High r over
5:21 God r over the kingdom of men and appoints
Rom 12:8 r should exercise his authority with care;
Col 2:20 why should you be bound by r that say,
1Tm 5:7 Make the following r about widows,
5:21 apply these r without prejudice,
2Tm 2:5 winner's crown unless he has kept the r.
Ti 1:14 r invented by men who have swerved from

RULING (4)

Is 14:2 of its captors and r over its oppressors.
Jl 2:17* a reproach, with the nations r over them!
Lk 18:18 One of the r class asked him then,
23:13 together the chief priests, the r class,

RUMAH (1)

2Kgs 23:36 was Zebidah, daughter of Pedaiah, from R.

RUMBLE (2)

Is 13:4 the r on the mountains:
Jl 2:5 As with the r of chariots they leap on the

RUMBLES (1)

Jb 37:2 angry voice as it r forth from his mouth!

RUMBLING (4)

Jer 47:3 steeds, the rattling chariot, the r wheels.
Ez 3:12 I heard behind me the noise of a loud r
3:13 and by the wheels alongside them, a loud r.
Na 3:2 crack of the whip, the r sound of wheels;

RUMMAGED (1)

Gn 31:34 When Laban had r through the rest of her

RUMOR (8)

2Mc 5:5 false r circulated that Antiochus was dead.
Jb 28:22 Death say, "Only by r have we heard of it."
Wis 5:9 like a shadow and like a fleeting r;
Jer 51:46 this year the r comes,
Ez 7:26 be disaster after disaster, r after rumor.
7:26 be disaster after disaster, rumor after r.
Acts 28:21 with a report or r to your discredit.
2Thes 2:2 whether by an oracular utterance, or r,

RUMORS (3)

Ps(s) 50:20 against your mother's son you spread r.
Jer 51:46 for fear of r spread in the land;
Mt 24:6 You will hear of wars and r of wars.

RUN (55)

Ex 32:25 foes, Aaron had let the people r wild,
1Sm 8:11 horses, and they will r before his chariot.
20:36 he said to the boy, R and fetch the arrow."
25:10 servants who r away from their masters.
31:4 "Draw your sword and r me through,
2Sm 18:19 "Let me r to take the good news to the
18:22 may, permit me also to r after the Cushite."
18:22 "Why do you want to r, my son?
18:23 he insisted, "Come what may, I want to r."
22:30 with your aid I r against an armed band,
1Kgs 17:14 not go empty, nor the jug of oil r dry,
17:16 did not go empty, nor the jug of oil r dry,
2Kgs 5:20 r after him and get something out of him."
Jdt 14:3 When they r to the tent of Holofernes and
Jb 1:5 And when each feast had r its course,
6:15 as watercourses that r dry in the wadies;
20:28 that r off in the day of God's anger.
36:28 Till the skies r with them and the showers
Ps(s) 18:30 with your aid I r against an armed band,
119:32 I will r the way of your commands when you
147:18 he lets his breeze blow and the waters r.
Prv 1:16 [For their feet r to evil,
4:12 step will not be impeded, and should you r,
6:18 schemes, feet that r swiftly to evil,
Sir 11:10 Even if you r after it,
Is 13:15 Everyone who is caught shall be r through;
34:3 The mountains shall r with their blood,
40:31 They will r and not grow weary,
45:1 him, and making kings r in his service,
55:5 nations that knew you not shall r to you,
59:7 Their feet r to evil,
63:6 I let their blood r out upon the ground."
Jer 9:17 wet with weeping, our cheeks r with tears.
13:17 will r with tears for the LORD's flock,
49:3 Put on sackcloth and mourn, r to and fro,
Lam 1:16 "At this I weep, my eyes r with tears:
3:48 My eyes r with streams of water over the
Ez 7:17 and all their knees shall r with water.
21:12 daunted, and every knee shall r with water.
28:7 shall r them through your splendid apparel.
Jl 2:4 like steeds they r.
2:7 Like warriors they r,
2:9 assault the city, they r upon the wall,
Am 6:12 Can horses r across a cliff?
9:13 and all the hills shall r with it.
Zec 2:8 came out to meet him, and said to him, R,
Jn 12:19 The whole world has r after him."
Acts 19:40 we r the risk of being accused of rioting
27:30 to r out anchors from the bow of the ship,
27:39 to r the ship aground on it if possible.
Rom 3:15 Swiftly r their feet to shed blood;
1Cor 9:24 In that case, r so as to win!
9:26 I do not r like a man who loses sight of
Phil 2:16 r the race in vain or work to no purpose.
3:14 I r toward the prize to which God calls me

RUNAWAY (1)

2Mc 8:35 fled alone across country like a r slave,

RUNLETS (1)

Ps(s) 46:5 a stream whose r gladden the city of God,

RUNNER (3)

2Sm 18:26 coming nearer, the lookout spied another r.
Jb 9:25 My days are swifter than a r,
Jer 51:31 One r meets another,

RUNNERS (1)

1Cor 9:24 the r in the stadium take part in the race,

RUNNING (33)

Gn 16:8 answered, "I am r away from my mistress,
Lv 22:22 one that has a r sore or mange or ringworm,
Jgs 7:21 camp fell to r and shouting and fleeing.
1Sm 14:16 and were r about in all directions.
2Sm 18:24 he looked about and saw a man r all alone.
18:26 out, "There is another man r by himself."
2Kgs 5:21 Aware that someone was r after him,
2Chr 23:12 of the people r and acclaiming the king,
32:4 and also the r stream in the valley nearby.
1Mc 5:40 and his army were approaching the r stream,
5:42 But when Judas reached the r stream,
11:73 who were r away saw it and returned to him;
2Mc 5:26 and r through the city with armed men,
Ps(s) 1:3 He is like a tree planted near r water,
42:2 I As the hind longs for the r waters,
78:44 their r water,
Prv 5:15 own cistern, r water from your own well.
Sg 5:12 His eyes are like doves beside r waters,
Sir 39:13 petals, like roses planted near r waters;
Is 30:25 hill there will be streams of r water.
Jer 8:6 Everyone keeps on r his course,
12:5 If r against men has wearied you,
30:13 your cause, no remedy for your r sore,
Ez 41:7 temple had a broad way r upward
42:7 On the far side there was a wall r
Mt 6:32 are always r after these things.
Mk 10:17 setting out on a journey a man came r up,
Lk 6:38 pressed down, shaken together, r over,
12:30 this world are always r after these things.
17:23 Do not go r about excitedly.
Jn 20:4 They were r side by side,
Acts 21:30 People came r from all sides.
Heb 12:1 persevere in r the race which lies ahead;

RUNS (16)

Dt 33:24 the oil of his olive trees r over his feet!
2Sm 18:27 notice that the first one r like Ahimaaz,
Ps(s) 19:6 and, like a giant, joyfully r its course.
133:2 upon the head r down over the beard,
133:2 till it r down upon the collar of his robe.
147:15 swiftly r his word!
Prv 18:10 the just man r to it and is safe.
29:6 a snare, but the just man r on joyfully.
Wis 16:29 wintry frost and r off like useless water.
Sir 10:13 of sin, a source which r over with vice;

RUNS (cont)
24:24 It *r* over, like the Euphrates,
33:33 If you mistreat him and he *r* away,
Hos 2: 9 If she *r* after her lovers,
Na 3: 7 Till everyone who sees you *r* from you,
Mk 13:28 *r* high and it begins to sprout leaves,
Jn 10:12 sight of the wolf coming and *r* away,

RURAL (1)
Est 9:19 That is why the *r* Jews,

RUSE (2)
Gn 27:35 here by a *r* and carried off your blessing,"
2Kgs 10:19 This Jehu did as a *r*,

RUSES (1)
Jb 5:13 He catches the wise in their own *r*,

RUSH (10)
1Sm 10: 6 The spirit of the LORD will *r* upon you,
Jdt 14: 2 let all the able-bodied men *r* out of the city
1Mc 4:30 who broke the *r* of the mighty one by the
Jb 15:26 One shall *r* sternly upon him with the
27:20 Terrors *r* upon him by day;
Is 31: 9 He shall *r* past his crag in panic,
33: 4 they *r* upon it like the onrush of locusts.
Jer 6: 4 let us *r* upon her at midday!
6: 5 let us *r* upon her by night,
Na 2: 6 To the wall they *r*,

RUSHED (26)
Gn 24:30 Laban *r* outside to the man at the spring.
Ex 12:39 They had been *r* out of Egypt and had no
Jos 8:19 men in ambush rose from their post, *r* in,
Jgs 9:44 while the other two companies *r* upon all
20:33 ambush *r* from their place west of Gibeah,
1Sm 10:10 met him, and the spirit of God *r* upon him,
11: 6 of God *r* upon him and he became very angry.
14:20 all his men shouted and *r* into the fight,
16:13 on, the spirit of the LORD *r* upon David.
Jdt 14:17 her, he *r* out to the troops and cried:
1Mc 3:23 he *r* suddenly upon Seron and his army,
16:16 in hand, *r* upon Simon in the banquet hall,
2Mc 3:18 People *r* out of their houses in crowds to
12:22 they *r* away in such headlong flight that
14:43 So while the troops *r* in through the doors,
Dn 6:12 So these men *r* in and found Daniel praying
8: 6 river, and *r* toward it with savage force.
13:26 they *r* in by the side gate to see what had
Lk 6:48 floods came the torrent *r* in on that house,
6:49 When the torrent *r* upon it,
Acts 3:11 the whole crowd *r* over to them excitedly
7:57 Then they *r* at him as one man,
14:14 their garments and *r* out into the crowd.
16:29 then *r* in and fell trembling at the feet
19:29 People *r* together to the theater and
22:27 The commander *r* in and asked Paul,

RUSHES (4)
Jb 18: 8 For he *r* headlong into a net,
39:21 and *r* in his might against the weapons.
Prv 7:23 Like a bird that *r* into a snare,
Is 19: 6 Reeds and *r* shall wither away,

RUSHING (7)
Dt 32:35 disaster and their doom is *r* upon them!
Wis 5:11 and cleft by the *r* force Of speeding wings,
17:18 branches, Or the steady sound of *r* water,
Sir 4:25 and struggle not against the *r* stream.
Mt 8:32 The whole herd went *r* down the bluff into
Mk 5:13 went *r* down the bluff into the lake,
Rv 1:15 voice sounded like the roar of *r* waters.

RUST (6)
Ez 24: 6 Woe to the bloody city, a pot containing *r*,
24: 6 rust, whose *r* has not been removed.
24:11 in it melt, and its *r* disappears.
24:12 even with fire will its great *r* be removed.
Mt 6:19 Moths and *r* corrode;
6:20 *r* corrode nor thieves break in and steal.

RUSTLE (3)
Lv 26:36 fainthearted that, if leaves *r* behind them,
Ps(s) 72:16 mountains the crops shall *r* like Lebanon;
Sir 45: 9 the hem, And a *r* of bells round about,

RUTH (14)
Ru 1: 4 women, one named Orpah, the other *R*.
1:14 good-bye, but *R* stayed with her.
1:16 But *R* said, "Do not ask me to abandon
1:22 with the Moabite daughter-in-law, *R*,
2: 2 *R* the Moabite said to Naomi,
2: 8 Boaz said to *R*, "Listen, my daughter!
2:21 "He even told me," added *R* the Moabite,
3: 5 will do whatever you advise," *R* replied.
3: 9 And she replied, "I am your servant *R*.
3:16 *R* went home to her mother-in-law,
4: 5 Naomi, you must take also *R* the Moabite,
4:10 I also take *R* the Moabite,
4:13 Boaz took *R*.
Mt 1: 5 was the father of Obed, whose mother was *R*.

RUTHLESS (8)
2Sm 3:39 men, the sons of Zeruiah, are too *r* for me.
Sir 8:15 Travel not with a *r* man,
Is 11: 4 strike the *r* with the rod of his mouth,
66: 4 I in turn will choose *r* treatment for them
Bar 4:15 from afar, a nation *r* and of alien speech,
Ez 30:11 his people with him, the most *r* of nations,
31:12 Foreigners, the most *r* of the nations,
32:12 all of them the most *r* of the nations;

RUTHLESSLY (5)
Ex 10: 2 how *r* I dealt with the Egyptians
1Sm 6: 6 Was it not after he had dealt *r* with them
Est E:24 shall be *r* destroyed with fire and sword,
Jb 39:16 her young and *r* makes nought of her brood;
Acts 3:23 prophet shall be *r* cut off from the people.'

S

SABACHTHANI (2)
Mt 27:46 out in a loud tone, "Eli, Eli, lema *s*?",
Mk 15:34 in a loud voice, "Eloi, Eloi, lama *s*?"

SABBATH (147)
Ex 16:23 Tomorrow is a day of complete rest, the *s*,
16:25 it today, for today is the *s* of the LORD.
16:26 gather it, but on the seventh day, the *s*,
16:29 The LORD has given you the *s*.
20: 8 "Remember to keep holy the *s* day.
20:10 but the seventh day is the *s* of the LORD,
20:11 has blessed the *s* day and made it holy.
31:14 you must keep the *s* as something sacred.
31:15 the seventh day is the *s* of complete rest,
31:15 work on the *s* day shall be put to death.
31:16 So shall the Israelites observe the *s*,
35: 2 you as the *s* of complete rest to the LORD.
35: 3 fire in any of your dwellings on the *s* day."
Lv 16:31 it shall be a most solemn *s* for you,
23: 3 but the seventh day is the *s* rest,
23: 3 The *s* shall belong to the LORD wherever
23:11 day after the *s* the priest shall do this.
23:15 "Beginning with the day after the *s*,
23:24 the seventh month you shall keep a *s* rest,
23:32 *s* of complete rest and mortify yourselves.
23:32 this *s* of yours from evening to evening."
24: 8 Regularly on each *s* day this bread shall
25: 2 let the land, too, keep a *s* for the LORD.
25: 4 shall have complete rest, a *s* for the LORD,
25: 5 vines in this year of *s* rest for the land.
25: 6 While the land has its *s*,
Nm 15:32 was discovered gathering wood on the *s* day.
28: 9 "On the *s* day you shall offer two
28:10 Each sabbath there shall be the *s*
Dt 5:12 care to keep holy the *s* day as the LORD,
5:14 but the seventh day is the *s* of the LORD,
5:15 has commanded you to observe the *s* day.
2Kgs 4:23 "It is neither the new moon nor the *s*."
11: 5 on the *s* shall guard the king's palace;
11: 9 the *s* and those going off duty that week,
1Chr 9:32 charge of setting out the showbread each *s*.
2Chr 23: 4 come in on the *s* must guard the thresholds,
23: 8 those who were to come in on the *s* as well
23: 8 depart on the *s* since Jehoiada the priest
Neh 9:14 Your holy *s* you made known to them,
10:32 or any kind of grain for sale on the *s* day,
10:32 from them on the *s* or on any other holyday.
13:15 were treading the winepresses on the *s*;
13:15 bringing them to Jerusalem on the *s* day.
13:16 and selling it to the Judahites on the *s*.
13:17 that you are doing, profaning the *s* day?
13:18 Israel by once more profaning the *s*?"
13:19 on the gates of Jerusalem before the *s*,
13:19 them to be reopened till after the *s*.
13:19 so that no burden might enter on the *s* day.
13:21 time on, they did not return on the *s*.
13:22 so that the *s* day might be kept holy.
Jdt 8: 6 her widowhood, except *s* eves and sabbaths,
1Mc 1:43 sacrificed to idols and profaned the *s*.
2:32 and prepared to attack them on the *s*.
2:34 obey the king's command to profane the *s*."
2:38 and soldiers attacked them on the *s*,
2:41 against anyone who attacks us on the *s*,
6:49 a siege, for that was a *s* year in the land.
9:43 he came on the *s* to the banks of the
2Mc 5:25 and waited until the holy day of the *s*;
6: 6 the *s* or celebrate the traditional feasts,
6:11 in nearby caves to observe the *s* in secret,
8:26 late hour, it was the day before the *s*,
8:27 then observed the *s* with fervent praise
8:28 After the *s*, they gave a share of the booty
12:38 according to custom and kept the *s* there.
15: 3 who prescribed the keeping of the *s* day.
15: 4 who commanded the observance of the *s* day,
Is 1:13 New moon and *s*,
56: 2 Who keeps the *s* free from profanation,
56: 6 All who keep the *s* free from profanation
58:13 If you hold back your foot on the *s* from
58:13 If you call the *s* a delight,
66:23 moon to another, and from one *s* to another,
Jer 17:21 care not to carry burdens on the *s* day,
17:22 Bring no burden from your homes on the *s*.
17:22 Do no work whatever, but keep holy the *s*,
17:24 on the sabbath, keeping the *s* holy and
17:27 you do not obey me and keep holy the *s*,
17:27 through the gates of Jerusalem on the *s*,
Lam 2: 6 LORD has made feast and *s* to be forgotten;
Ez 46: 1 but on the *s* and on the day of the new
46: 4 the prince presents to the LORD on the *s*
46:12 or his peace offerings as on the *s*;
Am 8: 5 "that we may sell our grain, and the *s*,
Mt 12: 1 *s* Jesus walked through the standing grain.
12: 2 are doing what is not permitted on the *s*."
12: 5 break the *s* rest without incurring guilt?
12: 8 The Son of Man is indeed Lord of the *s*."
12:10 "Is it lawful to work a cure on the *s*?"
12:11 a sheep and it falls into a pit on the *s*.
12:12 good deeds may be performed on the *s*."
24:20 will not have to flee in winter or on a *s*,
28: 1 After the *s*, as the first day of the week
Mk 1:21 and on the *s* he entered the synagogue and
2:23 walking through standing grain on the *s*,
2:24 do they do a thing not permitted on the *s*?"
2:27 *s* was made for man, not man for the *s*.
2:28 why the Son of Man is lord even of the *s*."
3: 2 to see whether he would heal him on the *s*,
3: 4 it permitted to do a good deed on the *s*—
6: 2 When the *s* came he began to teach in the
15:42 Day, that is, the eve of the *s*),
16: 1 When the *s* was over,
Lk 4:16 on the *s* as he was in the habit of doing,
4:31 he began instructing them on the *s* day.
6: 1 Once on a *s* Jesus was walking through the
6: 2 are you doing what is prohibited on the *s*?"
6: 5 "The Son of Man is Lord even of the *s*."
6: 6 On another *s* he came to teach in a
6: 7 see if he would perform a cure on the *s*
6: 9 ask you, is it lawful to do good on the *s*—
13:10 On a *s* day he was teaching in one of the
13:14 that Jesus should have healed on the *s*,
13:14 on those days to be cured, not on the *s*."
13:15 ass out of the stall on the *s* to water it?
13:16 been released from her shackles on the *s*?"
14: 1 When Jesus came on a *s* to eat a meal in
14: 3 "Is it lawful to cure on the *s* or not?"
14: 5 he not immediately rescue him on the *s* day?"
23:54 Preparation, and the *s* was about to begin.
23:56 They observed the *s* as a day of rest,
Jn 5: 9 The day was a *s*.
5:10 the man who had been cured, "It is the *s*,
5:16 on the *s* that they began to persecute him.
5:18 that he not only was breaking the *s* but,
7:22 And so, even on a *s* you circumcise a man.
7:23 the *s* to prevent a violation of Mosaic law,
7:23 with me for curing a whole man on the *s*?
9:14 (Note that it was on a *s* that Jesus had
9:16 be from God because he does not keep the *s*."
19:31 sabbath, for that *s* was a solemn feast day.
Acts 13:14 On the *s* day they entered the synagogue
13:27 the prophets which we read sabbath after *s*.
13:42 on this subject again on the following *s*.
13:44 following *s*, almost the entire city gathered
15:21 read aloud in the synagogues on every *s*."
16:13 Once, on the *s*, we went outside the city
18: 4 Every *s*, in the synagogue, Paul led
Col 2:16 on yearly or monthly feasts, or on the *s*.
Heb 4: 9 *s* rest still remains for the people of God.

SABBATHS (36)
Ex 31:13 Take care to keep my *s*,
Lv 19: 3 your mother and father, and keep my *s*.
19:30 Keep my *s*, and reverence my sanctuary.
23:38 day, in addition to those of the LORD's *s*,
26: 2 Keep my *s*, and reverence my sanctuary.
26:34 lost *s* during all the time it lies waste,
26:34 the land have rest and make up for its *s*
26:35 let it have on the *s* when you lived there.
26:43 its desolation it may make up its lost *s*,
1Chr 23:31 offering of holocausts to the LORD on *s*,
2Chr 2: 3 morning and evening, and for the *s*,
8:13 of Moses, and in particular on the *s*,
31: 3 of morning and evening and those on *s*,
36:21 "Until the land has retrieved its lost *s*,
Neh 10:34 for the daily holocaust, for the *s*,
Jdt 8: 6 her widowhood, except sabbath eves and *s*,
10: 2 which she used only on *s* and feast days.
1Mc 1:39 were turned into mourning, Her *s* to shame,
1:45 sanctuary, to profane the *s* and feast days,
10:34 Let all feast days, *s*, new moon festivals,
Is 56: 4 To the eunuchs who observe my *s* and choose
Ez 20:12 them my *s* to be a sign between me and them,
20:13 My *s*, too, they desecrated grievously.
20:16 despised my ordinances and desecrated my *s*.
20:20 keep holy my *s*,
20:21 who observe them, and my *s* they desecrated.
20:24 despised my statutes and desecrated my *s*,
22: 8 have spurned, and my *s* you have desecrated.
22:26 they pay no attention to my *s*,

23:38 defiled my sanctuary and desecrated my *s.*
44:24 on all my festivals, and keep my *s* holy.
45:17 libations on the feasts, new moons, and *s,*
46: 3 door of this gate on the *s* and new moons.
Hos 2:13 her joy, her feasts, her new moons, her *s,*
Acts 1:12 a mere *s* journey away.
17: 2 with them about the Scriptures for three *s.*

SABBATICAL (1)

Tb 1: 7 And except for *s* years,

SABEANS (3)

Jb 1:15 them, and the *S* carried them off in a raid.
Is 45:14 of Egypt, the gain of Ethiopia, and the *S,*
Jl 4: 8 of Judah, who shall sell them to the *S,*

SABTA (1)

1Chr 1: 9 descendants of Cush were Seba, Havilah, *S,*

SABTAH (1)

Gn 10: 7 Seba, Havilah, *S,* Raamah, and Sabteca.

SABTECA (2)

Gn 10: 7 Seba, Havilah, Sabtah, Raamah, and *S.*
1Chr 1: 9 were Seba, Havilah, Sabta, Raama, and *S.*

SACHAR (2)

1Chr 11:35 Ahiam, son of *S,*
26: 4 a second son, Joah, the third, *S,*

SACHET (1)

Sg 1:13 for me a *s* of myrrh to rest in my bosom.

SACHIA (1)

1Chr 8:10 of Jobab, Zibia, Mesha, Malcam, Jeuz, *S,*

SACK (2)

Gn 42:25 their money replaced in each one's *s,*
42:35 there in each one's *s* was his moneybag!

SACKCLOTH (58)

Gn 37:34 Jacob rent his clothes, put *s* on his loins,
2Sm 3:31 garments, gird yourselves with *s*
12:16 night to lie on the ground clothed in *s.*
21:10 took *s* and spread it out for herself on
1Kgs 20:31 us, therefore, to garb ourselves in *s,*
20:32 So they dressed in *s* girded at the waist,
21:27 garments and put on *s* over his bare flesh.
21:27 He fasted, slept in the *s,*
2Kgs 6:30 saw that he was wearing *s* underneath,
19: 1 he tore his garments, wrapped himself in *s,*
19: 2 the elders of the priests, wrapped in *s,*
1Chr 21:16 David and the elders, clothed in *s,*
Neh 9: 1 gathered together fasting and in *s,*
Jdt 4:10 and slaves also girded themselves with *s.*
4:11 their *s* covering before the Lord.
4:12 The altar, too, they draped in *s;*
4:14 with *s* as they offered the daily holocaust,
8: 5 *s* about her loins and wore widow's weeds.
9: 1 her head, and wearing nothing over her *s.*
10: 3 She took off the *s* she had on,
Est 4: 1 he tore his garments, put on *s* and ashes,
4: 2 which no one clothed in *s* might enter.
4: 3 they all slept on *s* and ashes.)
4: 4 to put on, so that he might take off his *s;*
1Mc 2:14 and his sons tore their garments, put on *s,*
3:47 That day they fasted and wore *s;*
2Mc 3:19 Women, girded with *s* below their breasts,
10:25 their heads and girding their loins in *s.*
Jb 16:15 I have fastened *s* over my skin,
Ps(s) 30:12 took off my *s* and clothed me with gladness,
35:13 But I, when they were ill, put on *s;*
69:12 I made *s* my garment,
Is 3:24 for the rich gown, a *s* skirt.
15: 3 In the streets they wear *s,*
20: 2 Go and take off the *s* from your waist,
22:12 and mourn, to shave your head and put on *s.*
37: 1 he tore his garments, wrapped himself in *s,*
37: 2 the elders of the priests, wrapped in *s,*
50: 3 in mourning, and make *s* their vesture.
58: 5 head like a reed, and lie in *s* and ashes?
Jer 4: 8 So gird yourselves with *s,* mourn and wail:
6:26 O daughter of my people, gird on *s,*
48:37 and the loins of all are clothed in *s.*
49: 3 Put on *s* and mourn,
Lam 2:10 on their heads and gird themselves with *s;*
Bar 4:20 put on *s* for my prayer of supplication,
Ez 7:18 They shall put on *s,* and horror shall cover
27:31 you they shave their heads and put on *s,*
Dn 9: 3 in earnest prayer, with fasting, *s,*
Jl 1: 8 girt with *s* for the spouse of her youth.
1:13 Come, spend the night in *s,*
Am 8:10 of all with *s* and make every head bald.
Jon 3: 5 and all of them, great and small, put on *s.*
3: 6 aside his robe, covered himself with *s,*
3: 8 be covered with *s* and call loudly to God;
Mt 11:21 have reformed in *s* and ashes long ago.
Lk 10:13 long ago have reformed in *s* and ashes.

Rv 11: 3 hundred and sixty days, dressed in *s.*"

SACKED (2)

Gn 34:27 followed up the slaughter and *s* the city
Jdt 1:14 and took its towers, *s* its marketplaces,

SACKS (4)

Gn 42:35 When they were emptying their *s,*
Jos 9: 4 making use of old *s* for their asses,
Ezr 1: 9 *s* of goldware, thirty; sacks of silverware

SACRED (269)

Gn 12: 6 the land as far as the *s* place at Shechem,
Ex 12:16 the first day you shall hold a *s* assembly,
16:23 complete rest, the sabbath, *s* to the LORD.
19:23 limits around the mountain to make it *s.*"
22:30 "You shall be men *s* to me.
23:24 demolish them and smash their *s* pillars.
28: 2 Aaron you shall have *s* vestments made.
28: 3 him apart for his *s* service as my priest.
28: 4 In making these *s* vestments which your
28:36 it, as on a seal engraving, *S* to the LORD."
28:38 incur in consecrating any of their *s* gifts,
29: 6 on his head, the *s* diadem on the miter.
29:21 that his sons and their vestments may be *s.*
29:29 "The *s* vestments of Aaron shall be passed
29:33 layman may eat of them, since they are *s.*
29:34 it is not to be eaten, since it is *s.*
29:37 *s,* and whatever touches it will become *s*
29:43 hence, it will be made *s* by my glory.
30:10 This altar is most *s* to the LORD."
30:25 and blend them into *s* anointing oil,
30:26 With this *s* anointing oil you shall anoint
30:29 sacred; whatever touches them shall be *s.*
30:31 As *s* anointing oil this shall belong to me
30:32 sacred, and shall be treated as *s* by you.
30:35 is to be salted and so kept pure and *s.*
30:36 incense shall be treated as most *s* by you.
30:37 you must treat it as *s* to the LORD.
31:10 the *s* vestments for Aaron the priest,
31:14 you must keep the sabbath as something *s.*
31:15 sabbath of complete rest, *s* to the LORD.
34:13 sacred pillars, and cut down their *s* poles.
35: 2 but the seventh day shall be *s* to you as
35:19 the *s* vestments for Aaron,
35:21 all its services, and for the *s* vestments.
37:29 The *s* anointing oil and the fragrant
39: 1 as well as the *s* vestments for Aaron,
39:30 The plate of the *s* diadem was made of pure
39:30 *S* to the LORD."
39:41 the *s* vestments for Aaron the priest,
40: 9 all its furnishings, so that it will be *s.*
40:10 consecrating it, so that it will be most *s.*
40:13 Aaron with the *s* vestments and anoint him,
Lv 2: 3 It is a most *s* oblation to the LORD.
2:10 It is a most *s* oblation to the LORD.
5:15 cheating in the LORD's *s* dues,
6: 9 form of unleavened cakes and in a *s* place:
6:10 it is most *s,*
6:11 Whatever touches the oblations becomes *s.*"
6:18 It is most *s.*
6:19 but it must be eaten in a *s* place,
6:20 Whatever touches its flesh shall become *s.*
6:20 stained part must be washed in a *s* place.
6:22 of the sin offering, since it is most *s.*
7: 1 for guilt offerings, which are most *s.*
7: 6 but it must be eaten in a *s* place,
8: 9 attaching the gold plate, the *s* diadem,
10:10 between what is *s* and what is profane,
10:13 most sacred, you must eat it in a *s* place.
10:17 in the sacred place, since it is most *s?*
12: 4 she shall not touch anything *s* nor enter
14:13 (This lamb he shall slaughter in the *s*
14:13 belongs to the priest and is most *s.)*
16: 4 He shall wear the *s* linen tunic,
16: 4 But since these vestments are *s,*
16:24 bathing his body with water in a *s* place,
16:32 wear the linen garments, the *s* vestments,
16:33 and make atonement for the *s* sanctuary,
19: 8 for having profaned what is *s* to the LORD.
19:24 all of its fruit shall be *s* to the LORD as
20:26 you shall be *s;* for I, the LORD, am sacred
21: 6 To their God they shall be *s,*
21: 7 for the priest is *s* to his God.
21: 8 as *s* who offers up the food of your God;
21: 8 treat him as *s,*
21: 8 the LORD, who have consecrated him, am *s.*
21:15 I, the LORD, have made him *s.*"
21:22 is most *s* as well as of what is sacred.
21:23 not profane these things that are *s* to me,
21:23 me, for it is I, the LORD, who make them *s.*"
22: 2 Aaron and his sons to respect the *s* offerings
22: 3 to draw near the *s* offerings which the
22: 4 from a flow, may eat of these *s* offerings,
22: 6 may not eat of the *s* portions until he has
22: 7 eat of the *s* offerings which are his food.
22:10 or hired servant may eat of any *s* offering.
22:12 layman may not eat of the *s* contributions.
22:14 eats of a *s* offering through inadvertence,
22:14 to the priest for the *s* offering,
22:15 The *s* offerings which the Israelites

22:16 profaned nor in the eating of the *s* offering
22:16 it is I, the LORD, who make them *s.*"
22:32 Israelites I, the LORD, must be held as *s.*
22:32 you *s* and led you out of the land of Egypt,
23: 2 you shall celebrate with a *s* assembly.
23: 3 is the sabbath rest, a day for *s* assembly,
23: 4 at their proper time with a *s* assembly.
23: 7 hold a *s* assembly and do no sort of work.
23: 8 hold a *s* assembly and do no sort of work."
23:20 be *s* to the LORD and belong to the priest.
23:21 shall by proclamation have a *s* assembly,
23:24 with a *s* assembly and with the trumpet
23:27 when you shall hold a *s* assembly and
23:35 the first day there shall be a *s* assembly,
23:36 eighth day you shall again hold a *s* assembly
23:37 on which you shall proclaim a *s* assembly,
24: 9 *s* place, since, as something most sacred
25:10 This fiftieth year you shall make *s* by
25:12 is the jubilee, which shall be *s* for you,
26: 1 erect an idol or a *s* pillar for yourselves,
27: 9 animal, when vowed to the LORD, becomes *s.*
27:10 and its substitute shall be treated as *s.*
27:14 dedicates his house as *s* to the LORD,
27:21 it shall be released as *s* to the LORD;
27:23 shall be given as *s* to the LORD;
27:28 is thus doomed becomes most *s* to the LORD.
27:30 the trees, belong to the LORD, as *s* to him.
27:32 be determined by ceding to the LORD as *s*
27:33 and its substitute shall be treated as *s,*
Nm 3:13 made all the first-born in Israel *s* to me,
4: 4 meeting tent concerns the most *s* objects.
4:15 his sons have finished covering the *s* objects
4:15 But they shall not touch the *s* objects;
4:16 the *s* objects and utensils that are in it."
4:19 die when they approach the most *s* objects,
4:20 shall not go in to look upon the *s* objects,
5: 9 every *s* contribution that the Israel-ites
5:10 man may dispose of his own *s* contributions;
6: 5 to the LORD is over, he shall be *s,*
6: 8 as he is a nazirite he is *s* to the LORD.
6:20 become *s* and shall belong to the priest,
7: 9 the *s* objects which were their charge.
10:21 carrying the *s* objects for the Dwelling,
17: 3 before the LORD they have become *s.*
18: 3 not come near the *s* vessels or the altar,
18: 8 the various *s* offerings of the Israelites;
18: 9 to share in the oblations that are most *s,*
18:10 them you shall treat them as most *s;*
18:10 As *s,* they belong to you.
18:17 they are *s.*
18:19 all the contributions from the *s* gifts
18:32 Do not profane the *s* gifts of the
28:18 of these days you shall hold a *s* assembly,
28:25 seventh day you shall hold a *s* assembly,
28:26 offering, you shall hold a *s* assembly,
29: 1 seventh month you shall hold a *s* assembly,
29: 7 seventh month you shall hold a *s* assembly,
29:12 seventh month you shall hold a *s* assembly,
31: 6 who had with him the *s* vessels and the
35:25 priest who has been anointed with *s* oil.
Dt 7: 5 sacred pillars, chop down their *s* poles,
7: 6 For you are a people *s* to the LORD,
12: 3 sacred pillars, destroy by fire their *s* poles,
12:26 any *s* gifts or votive offerings that you
14: 2 For you are a people *s* to the LORD,
14:21 itself, for you are a people *s* to the LORD,
16:21 "You shall not plant a *s* pole of any kind
16:22 nor shall you erect a *s* pillar,
26:13 'I have purged my house of the *s* portion
26:19 and you will be a people *s* to the LORD,
28: 9 establish you as a people *s* to himself,
Jos 6:19 of bronze or iron, are *s* to the LORD.
Jgs 6:25 Baal and cut down the *s* pole that is by it.
6:26 the wood from the *s* pole you have cut down.
6:28 destroyed, the *s* pole near it cut down,
6:30 has cut down the *s* pole that was near it."
1Kgs 8: 4 all the *s* vessels that were in the tent.
14:15 because they made *s* poles for themselves
14:23 high places, pillars, and *s* poles,
16:33 built in Samaria, and also made a *s* pole.
2Kgs 12: 5 "All the funds for *s* purposes that are
13: 6 *s* pole also remained standing in Samaria.
17:10 They set up pillars and *s* poles for
17:16 they also made a *s* pole and worshiped all
18: 4 pillars, and cut down the *s* poles.
21: 3 altars to Baal, and also set up a *s* pole,
23: 6 of the LORD he also removed the *s* pole,
23:14 pieces the pillars, cut down the *s* poles,
1Chr 9:29 care of the utensils and all the *s* vessels,
16:42 and instruments for the *s* chant.
22:19 covenant of the LORD and God's *s* vessels
2Chr 5: 5 all the *s* vessels that were in the tent;
14: 2 sacred pillars, and cutting down the *s*
17: 6 the high places and the *s* poles from Judah.
19: 3 since you have removed the *s* poles from
24:18 began to serve the *s* poles and the idols;
31: 1 the *s* pillars, cut down the sacred poles,
33: 3 erected altars for the Baals, made *s* poles,
33:19 erected *s* poles and carved images before
34: 3 *s* poles and the carved and molten images.
34: 4 the *s* poles and the carved and molten
34: 7 broke up the *s* poles and carved images and
35:13 and also cooked the *s* meals in pots,

SACRED (cont.)

Ezr 3: 5 moons and all the festivals *s* to the LORD,
Jdt 3: 8 territory and cut down their *s* groves,
1Mc 1:46 the sanctuary and the *s* ministers,
4:49 new *s* vessels and brought the lampstand,
10:21 Jonathan put on the *s* vestments in the
10:31 and her tolls, be *s* and free from tax.
12: 9 the *s* books that are in our possession,
2Mc 1:34 fenced the place off and declared it *s.*
2:13 and the royal letters about *s* offerings In
2:17 kingdom, the priesthood, and the *s* rites,
3:12 Place and in the *s* inviolability of a temple
4:48 for the people, and for the *s* vessels,
5:16 He laid his impure hands on the *s* vessels
6: 4 intercourse with women even in the *s* court.
8:33 set fire to the *s* gates and Callisthenes,
9:16 restore all the *s* vessels many times over;
10: 2 in the marketplace and the *s* enclosures.
12:40 found amulets *s* to the idols of Jamnia,
15:17 temple with the *s* vessels were in danger.
Prv 20:25 to pledge a *s* gift is a trap for a man,
Eccl 8:10 and as they left the *s* place,
Sir 45:10 The *s* vestments of gold,
45:20 The *s* offerings he allotted to him,
47: 2 Like the choice fat of the *s* offerings,
Is 17: 8 the *s* poles or the incense stands.
19:19 a *s* pillar to the LORD near the boundary.
23:18 and her hire shall be *s* to the LORD.
27: 9 no *s* poles or incense altars shall stand.
65: 5 I am too *s* for you!"
Jer 2: 3 *S* to the LORD was Israel,
11:15 *s* meat turn away your misfortune from you?
17: 2 remember their altars and their *s* poles,
Lam 4: 1 *s* stones lie strewn at every street corner!
Ez 22:26 distinguish between the *s* and the profane,
42:13 to the LORD shall eat the most *s* meals,
42:13 here they shall keep the most *s* offerings:
42:20 a wall, to separate the *s* from the profane.
43:12 area on the mountain top shall be most *s.*
44:13 of my sacred things, or the most *s* things.
44:23 distinguish between the *s* and the profane,
45: 1 set apart a *s* tract of land for the LORD,
45: 1 its whole area shall be *s.*
45: 4 This shall be the *s* part of the land
45: 6 thousand long, parallel to the *s* tract;
45: 7 of the combined *s* tract and City property,
48:10 In this *s* tract the priests shall have
48:12 this tract of land their own most *s* domain,
48:14 part of the land, for it is *s* to the LORD.
48:18 shall remain an area along the *s* tract,
48:20 *s* tract together with the City property.
48:21 sides of the *s* tract and the City property,
48:21 The *s* tract and the sanctuary of the
Hos 3: 4 or prince, Without sacrifice or *s* pillar,
10: 1 his land, the more *s* pillars he set up.
10: 2 their altars and destroy their *s* pillars.
Mi 5:12 images and the *s* pillars from your midst;
5:13 will tear out the *s* poles from your midst,
Mt 23:17 the gold or the temple which makes it *s?*
23:19 or the altar which makes the offering *s?*
Mk 16:20 *s* and immortal proclamation of eternal
Acts 21:28 temple area and thus profaned this *s* place."
2Tm 3:15 infancy you have known the *s* Scriptures,

SACREDNESS (1)

Lv 10: 3 who approach me I will manifest my *s;*

SACRIFICAL (1)

Phil 2:17 libation over the *s* service of your faith,

SACRIFICE (204)

Gn 31:54 He then offered a *s* on the mountain and
Ex 3:18 desert, that we may offer *s* to the LORD,
5: 3 desert, that we may offer *s* to the LORD,
5: 8 crying, 'Let us go to offer *s* to our God.'
5:17 saying, 'Let us go and offer *s* to the LORD.
8: 4 let the people go to offer *s* to the LORD.
8:21 "Go and offer *s* to your God in this land."
8:23 in the desert to offer *s* to the LORD,
8:24 let you go to offer *s* to the LORD your God,
8:25 let the people go to offer *s* to the LORD.
10:26 Some of them we must *s* to the LORD our God,
10:26 shall not know which ones we must *s* to him
12:27 'This is the Passover *s* of the LORD,
13:15 That is why I *s* to the LORD everything of
20:24 *s* your holocausts and peace offerings,
23:18 the blood of my *s* with leavened bread;
24: 5 *s* young bulls as peace offerings
29:34 If some of the flesh of the ordination *s*
29:38 lambs as the *s* established for each day;
34:15 wanton worship to their gods and *s* to them,
34:15 invite you and you may partake of his *s.*
34:25 me the blood of *s* with leavened bread,
34:25 nor shall the *s* of the Passover feast be
Lv 7:12 together with his thanksgiving *s* he shall offer
7:15 *s* shall be eaten on the day it is offered;
7:16 the *s* is a votive or a freewill offering,
7:16 be eaten on the day the *s* is offered,
7:17 from the *s* be left over on the third day,
9: 4 peace offering, to *s* them before the LORD,
17: 8 who offers a holocaust or *s* without
19: 5 you *s* your peace offering to the LORD,
19: 6 very day of your *s* or on the following day.
19: 7 day, the *s* will be unacceptable as refuse,
22:18 in Israel, who wishes to offer a *s,*
22:29 you offer a thanksgiving *s* to the LORD,
27:11 LORD is unclean and therefore unfit for *s,*
Nm 15: 6 With each *s* of a ram you shall present a
15: 8 When you *s* an ox as a holocaust,
Dt 15:21 defect, you shall not *s* it to the LORD,
16: 2 *s* from your flock or your herd to the LORD,
16: 5 "You may not *s* the Passover in any of the
16: 6 from Egypt, shall you *s* the Passover.
17: 1 "You shall not *s* to the LORD,
18: 3 from those who are offering a *s,*
27: 7 also *s* peace offerings and eat them there,
32:17 They offered *s* to demons,
33:10 They bring the smoke of *s* to your nostrils,
Jos 22:29 or *s* in addition to the altar of the LORD,
Jgs 2: 5 They offered *s* there to the LORD.
16:23 *s* to their god Dagon and to make merry.
1Sm 1: 3 LORD of hosts and to *s* to him at Shiloh,
1: 4 When the day came for Elkanah to offer *s,*
1:21 *s* to the LORD and to fulfill his vows,
2:13 When someone offered a *s,*
2:15 come and say to the man offering the *s,*
2:19 with her husband to offer the customary *s.*
3:14 *s* or offering will ever expiate its crime."
9:12 people have a *s* today on the high place.
9:13 blesses the *s* will the invited guests eat.
10: 8 offer holocausts and to *s* peace offerings.
15:15 the best sheep and oxen to *s* to the LORD,
15:21 to *s* to the LORD their God in Gilgal."
15:22 Obedience is better than *s,*
16: 2 and say, 'I have come to *s* to the LORD.
16: 3 ' Invite Jesse to the *s,*
16: 5 I have come to *s* to the LORD.
16: 5 themselves and invited them to the *s.*
20: 6 whole clan is holding its seasonal *s* there.'
20:29 'for we are to have a clan *s* in our city,
1Kgs 3: 3 *s* and burned incense on the high places.
3: 4 The king went to Gibeon to *s* there,
12:33 he was going to offer *s.*
13: 1 was standing at the altar to offer *s.*
13: 2 of the high places who offer *s* upon you,
18:29 state until the time for offering *s.*
18:36 At the time for offering *s,*
22:44 *s* and to burn incense on the high places.
2Kgs 3:20 In the morning, at the time of the *s,*
5:17 or *s* to any other god except to the LORD.
10:19 is absent, for I have a great *s* for Baal.
12: 4 continued to *s* and to burn incense there.
14: 4 continued to *s* and to burn incense on them.
15: 4 continued to *s* and to burn incense on them.
15:35 continued to *s* and to burn incense on them.
16:12 then went up to it and offered *s* on it,
17:35 them, nor serve them, nor offer *s* to them.
17:36 shall you worship, and to him shall you *s.*
1Chr 23:13 sons forever, to offer *s* before the LORD,
2Chr 1: 6 and Solomon offered *s* in the LORD's
7: 5 offered as *s* twenty-two thousand oxen,
7:12 I have chosen this place for my house of *s.*
11:16 Israel, came to Jerusalem to *s* to the LORD,
25:14 down before them and offered *s* to them.
28: 3 he offered *s* in the Valley of Ben-hinnom,
28: 4 offered *s* and incense on the high places,
28:23 will *s* to them that they may help me also."
28:25 up high places to offer *s* to other gods.
33:17 people continued to *s* on the high places,
33:22 Amon offered *s* to all the idols which his
35: 1 the Passover *s* was slaughtered on the
35: 6 Slay the Passover *s,* sanctify yourselves,
35:11 The Passover *s* was slaughtered,
Ezr 9: 4 I remained motionless until the evening *s.*
9: 5 Then, at the time of the evening *s,*
Tb 1: 4 offer *s* in the place where the temple,
1: 5 used to offer *s* on all the mountains of
Jdt 16:16 the sweet odor of every *s* is a trifle,
1Mc 1:47 shrines, to *s* swine and unclean animals,
2:23 in the sight of all to offer *s* on the altar
2:25 of the king who was forcing them to *s,*
4:53 they arose and offered *s* according to the
2Mc 1:23 While the *s* was being burned,
1:26 accept this *s* on behalf of all your people
1:31 After the *s* was burned, Nehemiah
2: 9 in his wisdom offered a *s* at the dedication
3:32 priest offered a *s* for the man's recovery.
3:33 priest was offering the *s* of atonement,
3:35 After Heliodorus had offered a *s* to the
4:19 silver drachmas for the *s* to Hercules.
4:19 that the money should not be spent on a *s,*
4:20 destined by the sender for the *s* to Hercules
6:21 the meat of the *s* prescribed by the king,
10: 3 offered *s* for the first time in two years,
12:43 to Jerusalem to provide for an expiatory *s.*
13:23 come to this agreement, he offered a *s,*
Ps(s) 40: 7 *S* or oblation you wished not,
50: 5 who have made a covenant with me by *s.*"
50:14 *s* and fulfill your vows to the Most High;
50:23 He that offers praise as a *s* glorifies me;
51:19 My *s,* O God, is a contrite spirit;
54: 8 Freely will I offer you *s:*
66:15 I will *s* oxen and goats.
116:17 To you will I offer *s* of thanksgiving,
141: 2 lifting up of my hands, like the evening *s.*
Prv 15: 8 The *s* of the wicked is an abomination to
21: 3 just is more acceptable to the LORD than *s.*
21:27 The *s* of the wicked is an abomination,
Eccl 4:17 rather than the fools' offering of *s;*
9: 2 for him who offers *s* and him who does not.
Wis 18: 9 holy children of the good were offering *s*
Sir 34:18 his gifts who offers in *s* ill-gotten goods!
34:20 offers *s* from the possessions of the poor.
35: 2 he gives alms he presents his *s* of praise.
35: 6 The just man's *s* is most pleasing,
35:11 Trust not in *s* of the fruits of extortion,
45:14 with the established *s* twice each day;
50: 9 like the fire of incense at the *s;*
50:19 the altar by presenting to God the *s* due;
Is 34: 6 For the LORD has a *s* in Bozrah,
57: 7 your bed, and there you went up to offer *s.*
Jer 7:22 them no command concerning holocaust or *s.*
11:13 are the altars for offering *s* to Baal.
33:18 to burn cereal offerings, and to *s* victims.
Ez 45:15 from the pasturage of Israel, for *s*—
45:18 young bull as a *s* to purify the sanctuary.
Dn 2:46 and ordered *s* and incense offered to him.
3:38 prophet, or leader, no holocaust, *s,*
3:40 So let our *s* be in your presence today as
8:11 host, from whom it removed the daily *s,*
8:12 the host, while sin replaced the daily *s.*
8:13 this vision last concerning the daily *s,*
9:21 rapid flight at the time of the evening *s.*
9:27 the week he shall abolish *s* and oblation;
11:31 *s* and setting up the horrible abomination.
12:11 From the time that the daily *s* is
Hos 3: 4 king or prince, Without *s* or sacred pillar,
4:13 offer *s* and on the hills they burn incense,
4:14 harlots, and with prostitutes you offer *s!*
6: 6 For it is love that I desire, not *s,*
8:13 they offer *s,* immolate flesh and eat it,
12:12 to nought, in Gilgal they *s* to bullocks;
13: 2 "To these," they say, "offer *s.*"
Am 4: 5 Burn leavened food as a thanksgiving *s,*
Jon 1:16 the men offered *s* and made vows to him.
2:10 I, with resounding praise, will *s* to you;
Zec 14:21 come to *s* shall take them and cook in them.
Mal 1: 8 When you offer a blind animal for *s,*
1:10 will I accept any *s* from your hands,
1:11 And everywhere they bring *s* to my name,
1:13 yes, you bring it as a *s.*
2:12 and anyone to offer *s* to the LORD of hosts!
2:13 *s* nor accepts it favorably from your hand;
3: 3 that they may offer due *s* to the LORD.
Mt 9:13 the words, 'It is mercy I desire and not *s.*'
12: 7 the text, 'It is mercy I desire and not *s,*'
Mk 12:33 is worth more than any burnt offering or *s.*"
14:12 it was customary to *s* the paschal lamb,
Lk 2:24 They came to offer in *s* "a pair of
22: 7 it was appointed to *s* the paschal lamb.
Acts 7:41 the calf and offered *s* to the idol,
14:13 wished to offer *s* to them with the crowds.
14:18 stop the crowds from offering *s* to them.
Rom 12: 1 as a living *s* holy and acceptable to God,
15:16 Gentiles may be offered up as a pleasing *s,*
1Cor 10:20 the Gentiles *s* to demons and not to God,
Phil 4:18 a *s* acceptable and pleasing to God.
Heb 7:27 he has no need to offer *s* day after day,
9:26 to take away sins once for all by his *s.*
10: 5 *S* and offering you did not desire,
10:12 But Jesus offered one *s* for sins and took
10:26 there remains for us no further *s* for sin
11: 4 Abel offered God a *s* greater than Cain's.
11:17 the promises was ready to *s* his only son,
13:15 let us continually offer God a *s* of praise,

SACRIFICED (33)

Lv 23:19 One male goat shall be *s* as a sin offering,
27: 9 to the LORD is an animal that may be *s,*
Nm 15: 5 with each lamb *s* in holocaust or otherwise.
28:15 shall be *s* as a sin offering to the LORD.
29:11 one goat shall be *s* as a sin offering.
29:16 one goat shall be *s* as a sin offering.
Dt 16: 4 and none of the meat which you *s* on the
1Sm 1:25 the boy's father had *s* the young bull,
11:15 *s* peace offerings there before the LORD,
2Sm 6:13 six steps, he *s* an ox and a fatling.
1Kgs 8: 5 *s* before the ark sheep and oxen
11: 8 who burned incense and *s* to their gods.
2Kgs 16: 4 he *s* and burned incense on the high places,
1Chr 15:26 LORD, seven bulls and seven rams were *s.*
2Chr 15:11 and *s* to the LORD at that time seven
28:23 He *s* to the gods of Damascus who had
29:27 ordered the holocaust to be *s* on the altar,
33:16 and *s* on it peace offerings and thank
34: 4 over the tombs of those who had *s* to them;
Ezr 4: 2 have *s* to him since the days of Esarhaddon,
6:20 *s* the Passover for the rest of the exiles,
1Mc 1:43 they *s* to idols and profaned the sabbath.
1:59 day of each month they *s* on the altar
Ps(s) 106:37 *s* their sons and their daughters to demons,
106:38 Whom they *s* to the idols of Canaan,
Ez 16:36 *s* the lifeblood of your children to them,
Acts 15:29 namely, to abstain from meat *s* to idols,
21:25 they were merely to avoid meat *s* to idols,
1Cor 5: 7 Christ our Passover has been *s.*

8: 7 eat meat, fully aware that it has been *s*,
Ti 2:14 It was he who *s* himself for us,
Rv 2:14 *s* to idols and to practice fornication.
2:20 lewdness and to eat food *s* to idols.

SACRIFICES (106)

Gn 46: 1 offered *s* to the God of his father Isaac.
Ex 8:22 to do so, for the *s* we offer to the LORD,
8:22 offer *s* which are an abomination to them,
10:25 *s* and holocausts to offer up to the LORD,
18:12 brought a holocaust and other *s* to God,
22:19 "Whoever *s* to any god,
Lv 17: 5 such *s* as they used to offer up in the
17: 7 No longer shall they offer their *s* to the
23:37 and cereal offerings, *s* and libations,
Nm 25: 2 invited the people to the *s* of their god,
25: 2 ate of the *s* and worshiped their god.
Dt 12: 6 you shall bring your holocausts and *s*,
12:11 your holocausts and *s*,
12:27 of your other *s* the blood indeed must be
32:38 Let those who ate the fat of your *s* and
Jos 22:26 not for holocausts or for *s*,
22:27 in his presence with our holocausts, *s*,
22:28 fathers made, not for holocausts or for *s*,
1Sm 2:29 Why do you keep a greedy eye on my *s* and
6:15 holocausts and *s* to the LORD that day.
15:22 so delight in holocausts and *s* as in obedience
2Sm 15:12 Giloh, for the *s* he was about to offer.
1Kgs 8:62 Israel with him offered *s* before the LORD.
12:27 *s* in the temple of the LORD in Jerusalem,
12:32 of Judah, with *s* to the calves he had made;
2Kgs 10:24 they proceeded to offer *s* and holocausts.
16:15 on it all the blood of holocausts and *s*.
1Chr 21:28 Jebusite, he continued to offer *s* there.
29:21 they offered *s* and holocausts to the LORD,
29:21 libations and many other *s* for all Israel;
2Chr 7: 1 and consumed the holocaust and the *s*,
7: 4 people were offering *s* before the LORD.
29:31 and bring forward the *s* and thank
29:31 brought forward the *s* and thank offerings
Ezr 3: 5 the *s* prescribed for the new moons and all
6: 3 offering *s* and bringing burnt offerings.
6:10 that they may continue to offer *s* of
Neh 12:43 Great *s* were offered on that day,
1Mc 1:45 to prohibit holocausts, *s*,
1:51 he ordered the cities of Judah to offer *s*,
2:15 to the city of Modein to organize the *s*.
4:56 holocausts and *s* of deliverance and praise.
11:34 all those who offer *s* for us in Jerusalem
12:11 ceased to remember you in the *s* and prayers
2Mc 1: 8 we offered *s* and fine flour;
1:18 of the temple and the altar, offered *s*.
1:21 the material for the *s* had been prepared,
1:33 Nehemiah and his people had burned the *s*,
2:10 descended from the sky and consumed the *s*,
3: 6 of all proportion to the cost of the *s*,
4:14 the temple and neglecting the *s*,
6: 7 bitter necessity, to partake of the *s*,
6: 8 oblige them to partake of the *s*,
9:16 revenues the expenses required for the *s*.
14:31 the priests were offering the customary *s*,
Ps(s) 4: 6 Offer just *s*, and trust in the LORD.
27: 6 in his tent *s* with shouts of gladness;
50: 8 Not for your *s* do I rebuke you,
51:18 For you are not pleased with *s*;
51:21 Then shall you be pleased with due *s*,
106:28 of Baal of Peor and ate the *s* of dead gods.
Wis 12: 4 Works of witchcraft and impious *s*;
14:15 down to his subjects mysteries and *s*.
14:23 child-slaying *s* or clandestine mysteries,
Sir 7:31 contributions, due *s* and holy offerings.
34:19 their many *s* does he forgive their sins.
35: 1 the commandments *s* a peace offering.
45:16 To burn *s* of sweet odor for a memorial,
50:14 the arranging of the *s* for the Most High,
Is 1:11 What care I for the number of your *s*?
19:21 they shall offer *s* and oblations,
43:23 your holocausts, nor honor me with your *s*.
43:24 money, nor fill me with the fat of your *s*;
56: 7 and *s* will be acceptable on my altar,
60: 7 you, the rams of Nebaioth shall be your *s*;
65: 3 Offering *s* in the groves and burning
Jer 6:20 no favor with me, your *s* please me not.
7:21 Heap your holocausts upon your *s*;
17:26 and the Negeb, to bring holocausts and *s*,
Bar 4: 7 you provoked your Maker with *s* to demons,
6:27 resell their *s* for their own advantage.
6:28 and women in childbed handle their *s*.
Ez 16:20 and offered as *s* to be devoured by them!
20:28 there they offered their *s* [there they
40:41 tables], on which the *s* were slaughtered.
44:11 the holocausts and the *s* for the people,
45:15 and peace offerings and atonement *s*,
46:24 temple ministers cook the *s* of the people."
Hos 9: 4 to the LORD, or proffer their *s* before him.
Am 4: 4 Each morning bring your *s*,
5:25 Did you bring me *s* and offerings for forty
Hb 1:16 Therefore he *s* to his net,
Mal 1:14 but under his vow *s* to the LORD a gelding;
Lk 13: 1 whose blood Pilate had mixed with their *s*.
Acts 7:42 'Did you bring me *s* and offerings for
1Cor 10:18 who eat the *s* do not share in the altar!
Heb 5: 1 before God, to offer gifts and *s* for sins.
8: 3 priest is appointed to offer gifts and *s*;
9: 9 in which gifts and *s* are offered that can
9:23 realities themselves called for better *s*.
10: 1 same *s* offered continually year after year.
10: 3 But through those *s* there came only a
10: 8 First he says, *S* and offerings,
10:11 same *s* which can never take away sins.
13:16 God is pleased by *s* of that kind.
1Pt 2: 5 *s* acceptable to God through Jesus Christ.

SACRIFICIAL (7)

1Sm 16:11 begin the *s* banquet until he arrives here."
2Mc 3: 3 the expenses necessary for the *s* services.
7:42 the *s* meals and the excessive cruelties.
Wis 3: 6 and as *s* offerings he took them to himself.
Sir 50:12 priests while he stood before the *s* wood,
Jer 52:19 the *s* bowls which were of gold or silver,
Ez 36:38 As with *s* sheep, the sheep of Jerusalem

SACRIFICING (12)

Ex 29:36 *s* a bullock each day as a sin offering,
32: 8 and worshiping it, *s* to it and crying out,
Lv 17: 5 tent and *s* them there as peace offerings
1Kgs 3: 2 the people were *s* on the high places,
2Chr 5: 6 before the ark were *s* sheep and oxen
Is 66: 3 *s* a lamb,
Jer 11:17 of Judah, who provoked me by *s* to Baal.
44: 3 strange gods, serving them and *s* to them,
44: 5 away from the evil of *s* to strange gods.
44: 8 by *s* to strange gods here in the land of
Hos 11: 2 *S* to the Baals and burning incense to
1Tm 3: 4 under control without *s* his dignity;

SACRILEGE (1)

2Mc 13: 6 A man guilty of *s* or notorious for certain

SACRILEGES (1)

1Mc 2: 6 When he saw the *s* that were being

SACRILEGIOUS (2)

2Mc 4:39 Many *s* thefts had been committed by
4:42 The *s* thief himself they slew near the

SAD (13)

Gn 40: 7 house, "Why do you look so *s* today?"
Neh 2: 1 I had never before been *s* in his presence,
2: 2 the king asked me, "Why do you look *s*?
2: 2 you are not sick, you must be *s* at heart."
2: 3 How could I not look *s* when the city where
8: 9 Do not be *s*, and do not weep;
Prv 14:13 Even in laughter the heart may be *s*,
Eccl 7: 3 when the face is *s* the heart grows wiser.
Mt 19:22 these words, the young man went away *s*,
Mk 10:22 He went away *s*, for he had many
Jn 16:21 in labor she is *s* that her time has come.
16:22 In the same way, you are *s* for a time,
2Cor 2: 4 not to make you *s* but to help you realize

SADDEN (1)

Eph 4:30 Do nothing to *s* the Holy Spirit with whom

SADDENED (6)

Neh 8:10 Do not be *s* this day,
8:11 and you must not be *s*
Sir 25:22 Depressed mind, *s* face,
2Cor 2: 3 be *s* by those who should rejoice my heart.
7: 8 If I *s* you by my letter I have no regrets.
7: 9 not because you were *s*,

SADDLE (4)

Lv 15: 9 Any *s* on which the afflicted man rides,
2Sm 19:27 who is lame, said to him, *S* the ass for me,
1Kgs 13:13 Then he said to his sons, *S* the ass for me."
13:27 Then he said to his sons, *S* the ass for me."

SADDLE-ASSES (2)

Jgs 10: 4 He had thirty sons who rode on thirty *s*
12:14 and thirty grandsons who rode on seventy *s*.

SADDLEBAGS (1)

Gn 49:14 is a rawboned ass, crouching between the *s*.

SADDLECLOTHS (1)

Jgs 5:10 asses, seated on *s* as they go their way;

SADDLED (10)

Gn 22: 3 the next morning Abraham *s* his donkey,
Nm 22:21 morning when Balaam arose, he *s* his ass,
Jgs 19:10 concubine set out with a pair of *s* asses,
2Sm 16: 1 met him with *s* asses laden with two
17:23 not acted upon, he *s* his ass and departed,
1Kgs 2:40 So Shimei rose, *s* his ass,
13:13 When they had *s* it, he mounted
13:23 and drunk water, the ass was *s* for him,
13:27 When they had *s* it, he went off
2Kgs 4:24 him good-bye, and when the donkey was *s*,

SADDUCEES (13)

Mt 3: 7 and *S* were stepping forward for this bath,
16: 1 The Pharisees and *S* came along,
16: 6 against the yeast of the Pharisees and *S*."
16:12 but against the Pharisees' and *S*' teaching.
22:23 That same day some *S*,
22:34 heard that he had silenced the *S*,
Mk 12:18 Then some *S* who hold there is no
Lk 20:27 Some *S* came forward (the ones who claim
Acts 4: 1 temple guard, and the *S* came up to them,
5:17 supporters (that is, the party of the *S*),
23: 6 some of them were *S* and some Pharisees.
23: 7 and *S* which divided the whole assembly.
23: 8 (The *S*, of course, maintain that there is

SADLY (1)

2Cor 9: 7 not *s*,

SADNESS (3)

Jb 9:27 I will lay aside my *s* and be of good cheer,
Sir 30:21 Do not give in to *s*, torment not yourself
2Cor 7: 9 but because your *s* led to repentance.

SAFE (56)

Gn 28:21 and I come back *s* to my father's house,
44:17 you may go back *s* and sound to your father."
Nm 32:17 towns, *s* from attack by the natives.
1Sm 17:37 me *s* from the clutches of this Philistine."
19:10 struck only the wall, and David got away *s*.
20: 7 If he says, 'Very well,' your servant is *s*.
20:21 pick it up,' come, for you are *s*.
2Sm 15: 9 The king wished him a *s* journey,
18:29 the king asked, "Is the youth Absalom *s*?"
18:32 asked the Cushite, "Is young Absalom *s*?"
22: 3 my savior, from violence you keep me *s*.
22: 4 I exclaim, and I am *s* from my enemies.
1Chr 11:14 made a stand on the sown ground, kept it *s*,
Ezr 8:21 from him a *s* journey for ourselves,
Tb 5:16 we shall return to you, for the way is *s*."
5:17 way and bring you back to me *s* and sound;
5:17 Tobit said to him, "Have a *s* journey."
5:21 the day when he returns to you *s* and sound.
10: 6 he is *s*!
10:11 Have a *s* journey.
12: 3 He led me back *s* and sound;
12:17 "No need to fear; you are *s*.
2Mc 3:15 deposits *s* for those who had made them.
3:22 the almighty Lord to keep the deposits *s*
8:27 and thanks to the Lord who kept them *s*
Jb 21: 9 Their homes are *s* and without fear,
41: 3 Who has assailed him and come off *s*—
Ps(s) 18: 4 I exclaim, and I am *s* from my enemies.
80: 4 face shine upon us, then we shall be *s*.
80: 8 face shine upon us, then we shall be *s*.
80:20 face shine upon us, then we shall be *s*.
119:117 may be *s* and ever delight in your statutes.
Prv 11:15 but he who hates giving pledges is *s*.
18:10 the just man runs to it and is *s*.
28:18 He who walks uprightly is *s*,
28:26 is a fool, but he who walks in wisdom is *s*.
29:25 snare, but he who trusts in the LORD is *s*.
Wis 14: 5 have been *s* crossing the surge on a raft.
Sir 31:10 he has been tested by gold and come off *s*,
33: 1 through trials, again and again he is *s*.
Is 45:22 Turn to me and be *s*,
Jer 7:10 "We are *s*; we can commit all these
8:20 summer is at an end, and yet we are not *s*!"
33:16 be *s* and Jerusalem shall dwell secure;
Bar 6:11 they are not *s* from corrosion or insects.
6:54 gods, though the priests flee and are *s*,
6:56 are *s* from neither thieves nor bandits,
6:58 a house, that keeps *s* those who are within,
Dn 10:19 me, saying, "Fear not, beloved, you are *s*;
Mk 13:13 the end is the one who will come through *s*.
Lk 13:28 all the prophets *s* in the kingdom of God,
Jn 10: 9 Whoever enters through me will be *s*.
Acts 23:24 give him *s* conduct to Felix the governor."
Rom 15:31 be kept *s* from the unbelievers in Judea,
2Tm 4:18 will bring me *s* to his heavenly kingdom.
Rv 3:10 I will keep you *s* in the time of trial

SAFE-CONDUCT (1)

Neh 2: 7 may afford me *s* till I arrive in Judah;

SAFEGUARD (10)

Prv 4: 6 love her, and she will *s* you;
20:28 Kindness and piety *s* the king,
22: 5 he who would *s* his life will shun them.
22:12 The eyes of the LORD *s* knowledge,
Wis 9:11 in my affairs and *s* me by her glory;
14:24 no longer *s* either lives or pure wedlock;
Dn 6: 2 and twenty satraps, to *s* his interests;
Mal 2:15 You must then *s* life that is your own,
2:16 You must then *s* life that is your own,
Phil 3: 1 things no burden, and for you it is a *s*.

SAFEGUARDS (1)

Prv 16:17 who pays attention to his way *s* his life.

SAFEKEEPING (7)

Ex 16:33 before the LORD in *s* for your descendants."
16:34 it in front of the commandments for *s*,
22: 6 *s* and it is stolen from the latter's house,
22: 9 or any other animal to another for *s*,
2Chr 31:12 things were deposited there in *s*.
Jer 36:20 in *s* in the room of Elishama the scribe,
Lk 19:20 is your money, my lord, which I hid for *s*.

SAFELY (13)

Gn 33:18 Jacob arrived *s* at the city of Shechem,
Dt 29:18 can *s* persist in his stubbornness of heart,
Jos 10:21 *s* to Joshua and the camp at Makkedah,
1Sm 19:18 Thus David got *s* away;
2Sm 19:25 the day the king left until he returned *s*.
19:31 lord the king has returned *s* to his palace."
Tb 7:12 Take her and bring her back *s*
10:13 kinsman, may the Lord bring you back *s*,
1Mc 12:52 of Jonathan came *s* into the land of Judah.
Is 66: 7 come upon her, she *s* delivers a male child.
Acts 27:44 In this way all came *s* ashore.
Rom 15:28 *s* handed over this contribution to them,
Jude 1: 1 and have been guarded *s* in Jesus Christ.

SAFER (1)

Tb 14: 4 be *s* in Media than in Assyria or Babylon.

SAFETY (29)

Gn 19:16 and led them to *s* outside the city.
Ex 9:19 open fields to be brought to a place of *s*.
1Sm 19:12 a window, and he made his escape in *s*.
1Kgs 22:27 of bread and water until I return in *s*.' "
22:28 Micaiah said, "If ever you return in *s*,
2Chr 18:26 of bread and water until I return in *s*!' "
18:27 Micaiah said, "If ever you return in *s*,
19: 1 returned in *s* to his house in Jerusalem.
Tb 5:17 and may his angel accompany you for *s*,
Jdt 11: 3 In any case, you have come to *s*.
1Mc 2:44 the survivors fled to the Gentiles for *s*.
5:54 they had returned in *s*.
2Mc 15: 1 to attack them in all *s* on the day of rest.
15:11 not so much with the *s* of shield and spear
Jb 5: 4 His children shall be far from *s*;
5:11 lowly, and those who mourn he exalts to *s*.
11:18 shall look round you and lie down in *s*,
24:23 of his life he gives *s* and support.
Ps(s) 12: 6 "I will grant *s* to him who longs for it."
31: 3 rock of refuge, a stronghold to give me *s*.
33:17 Useless is the horse for *s*;
62: 8 With God is my *s* and my glory,
71: 3 rock of refuge, a stronghold to give me *s*,
Wis 6:24 number of wise men is the *s* of the world,
Sir 40: 7 As he reaches *s*,
Is 14:30 shall eat, and the needy lie down in *s*;
46: 4 continue, and I who will carry you to *s*.
Jer 32:37 to this place and settle them here in *s*.
Acts 27:24 granted *s* to all who are sailing with you.'

SAFFRON (1)

Sg 4:14 Nard and *s*,

SAG (1)

Eccl 10:18 When hands are lazy, the rafters *s*;

SAGACITY (1)

Jdt 11: 8 we have heard of your wisdom and *s*,

SAGE (2)

Sir 3:28 The mind of a *s* appreciates proverbs,
9:17 the ruler of his people is the skilled *s*.

SAGES (2)

Gn 41: 8 So he summoned all the magicians and *s* of
Sir 39: 3 busied with the hidden meanings of the *s*.

SAGGING (1)

Ps(s) 62: 4 beat him down as though he were a *s* fence,

SAIL (14)

2Chr 20:36 him in building ships to *s* to Tarshish;
20:37 wrecked and were unable to *s* to Tarshish.
Is 33:23 mast in place, nor keep the *s* spread out.
Ez 27: 7 became your *s* [to serve you as a banner].
Acts 13: 4 Seleucia and set *s* from there for Cyprus.
18:21 Then he set *s* from Ephesus.
20: 6 We ourselves set *s* from Philippi as soon
20:13 on ahead to the ship and set *s* for Assos,
20:16 Paul had decided to *s* past Ephesus so as
27: 1 it was decided that we were to *s* for Italy,
27: 2 ports in the province of Asia, and set *s*.
27:21 taken my advice and not set *s* from Crete.
28:10 *s* they brought us provisions for our needs.
28:11 Three months later we set *s* in a ship

SAILED (15)

1Mc 13:29 which could be seen by all who *s* the sea.
2Mc 14: 1 had *s* into the port of Tripolis with a
Ps(s) 107:23 They who *s* the sea in ships,
Lk 8:23 So they set out, and as they *s* he slept.
8:26 They *s* to the country of the Gerasenes,
Acts 13:13 put out to sea and *s* to Perga in Pamphylia.
14:26 From there they *s* back to Antioch,
15:39 took Mark along with him and *s* for Cyprus.
18:18 took leave of the brothers and *s* for Syria,
20:14 Assos we took him aboard and *s* to Mitylene.
21: 1 we put out to sea and *s* straight to Cos.
21: 2 for Phoenicia, we boarded it and *s* off.
27: 4 we *s* around the sheltered side of Cyprus
27: 7 we *s* for Salmone and the shelter of Crete.
28:13 we *s* around the toe and arrived at Rhegium.

SAILING (3)

Acts 27: 9 of the year *s* had become hazardous.
27:24 granted safety to all who are *s* with you.'
27:28 after *s* on a short distance they again

SAILOR (1)

Ez 27: 9 *s* on the sea came to you to carry trade.

SAILORS (5)

Ez 27:27 wealth, your goods, your wares, your *s*,
27:29 The *s*,
Acts 27:27 the *s* began to suspect that land was near.
27:30 Then the *s* tried to abandon ship.
Rv 18:17 and navigator, all *s* and seafaring men,

SAINT (1)

Mt 13:17 many a prophet and many a *s* longed to see

SAINTS (22)

1Mc 7:17 "The flesh of your *s* they have strewn,
Wis 5: 5 how his lot is with the *s*!
Mt 13:43 Then the *s* will shine like the sun in
23:29 and decorate the monuments of the *s*.
27:53 of *s* who had fallen asleep were raised.
Rom 8:27 intercedes for the *s* as God himself wills.
12:13 Look on the needs of the *s* as your own;
15:25 for Jerusalem to bring assistance to the *s*.
15:26 for those in need among the *s* in Jerusalem.
15:31 may be well received by the *s* there;
16: 2 welcome her in the Lord, as *s* should.
16:15 Olympas, and all the *s* who are with them.
1Cor 16: 1 About the collection for the *s*,
16:15 and is devoted to the service of the *s*.
Eph 2:19 the *s* and members of the household of God.
Col 1: 4 and the love you bear toward all the *s*—
1:12 worthy to share the lot of the *s* in light.
Jude 1: 3 the faith delivered once for all to the *s*.
Rv 16: 6 those who shed the blood of *s* and prophets,
18:20 Rejoice over her, you heavens, you *s*,
18:24 *s* and of all who were slain on the earth."
19: 8 dress is the virtuous deeds of God's *s*.)

SAIS (1)

2Kgs 17: 4 sending envoys to the king of Egypt at *S*,

SAKE (146)

Gn 12:13 and my life may be spared for your *s*."
18:24 *s* of the fifty innocent people within it?
18:26 I will spare the whole place for their *s*."
18:29 forebear doing it for the *s* of the forty."
18:31 he answered, "for the *s* of the twenty."
18:32 "For the *s* of those ten,"
26:24 for the *s* of my servant Abraham."
39: 5 the Egyptian's house for Joseph's *s*;
45: 5 It was really for the *s* of saving lives
Ex 18: 8 and the Egyptians for the *s* of Israel,
Nm 11:29 answered him, "Are you jealous for my *s*?
Dt 24: 5 for one year for the *s* of his family,
1Sm 12:22 For the *s* of his own great name the LORD
2Sm 5:12 his rule for the *s* of his people Israel.
7:21 servant's *s* and as you have had at heart,
9: 1 I may show kindness for the *s* of Jonathan?"
9: 7 to you for the *s* of your father Jonathan.
10:12 *s* of our people and the cities of our God;
18: 5 "Be gentle with young Absalom for my *s*."
18:12 to protect the youth Absalom for his *s*.
1Kgs 11:12 however, for the *s* of your father David;
11:13 the *s* of my servant David and of Jerusalem,
11:32 to him for the *s* of David my servant,
11:34 as he lives for the *s* of my servant David,
15: 4 Yet for David's *s* the LORD,
2Kgs 19:34 my own *s*, and for the sake of my servant
20: 6 sake, and for the *s* of my servant David.' "
1Chr 14: 2 exalted for the *s* of his people Israel.
16:21 them, and for their *s* he rebuked kings:
17:19 *s* and in keeping with your purpose,
19:13 the *s* of our people and the cities of our God;
Tb 4: 4 for your *s* while you were in her womb.
1Mc 13: 4 for the *s* of these, for the sake of Israel,
2Mc 3:33 his *s* that the Lord has spared your life.
5:19 *s* of the Place, but the Place for the sake
6:25 for the *s* of a brief moment of life,
7:11 for the *s* of his laws I disdain them;
7:23 disregard yourselves for the *s* of his law."
8:15 for their sake, at least for the *s* of the
12:25 him go for the *s* of saving their brethren.
Ps(s) 23: 3 guides me in right paths for his name's *s*.
25:11 For your name's *s*, O LORD, you will
31: 4 your name's *s* you will lead and guide me.
44:23 for your *s* we are being slain all the day,
44:27 Redeem us for your kindness' *s*.
45: 5 cause of truth and for the *s* of justice;
69: 8 of Israel, Since for your *s* I bear insult,
79: 9 us and pardon our sins for your name's *s*.
105:14 them, and for their *s* he rebuked kings:
106: 8 Yet he saved them for his name's *s*,
106:45 And for their *s* he was mindful of his
109:21 deal kindly with me for your name's *s*;
119:154 for the *s* of your promise give me life.
132:10 For the *s* of David your servant,
143:11 For your name's *s*, O LORD, preserve me
Prv 27:13 for another, and for the *s* of a stranger,
Wis 6:15 and he who for her *s* keeps vigil shall
8:10 her *s* I should have glory among the masses,
8:13 For her *s* I should have immortality and
18: 2 for the *s* of the difference between them.
Sir 27: 1 For the *s* of profit many sin,
44:12 endures, their posterity, for their *s*.
Is 37:35 sake, and for the *s* of my servant David.
43:25 It is I, I, who wipe out, for my own *s*,
45: 4 For the *s* of Jacob, my servant,
48: 9 *s* of my name I restrain my anger, for the *s*
48:11 For my sake, for my own *s*,
58:12 ancient ruins shall be rebuilt for your *s*,
62: 1 *s* I will not be silent, for Jerusalem's sake
63:17 Return for the *s* of your servants,
Jer 4: 4 For the *s* of the LORD,
14:21 For your name's *s* spurn us not,
Bar 2:14 and deliver us for your own *s*:
Ez 20: 9 but I acted for my name's *s*,
20:14 end to them, but I acted for my name's *s*,
20:22 I stayed my hand, acting for my name's *s*,
20:44 I deal with you thus, for my name's *s*,
28:17 the *s* of splendor you debased your wisdom.
36:22 of Israel, but for the *s* of my holy name,
Dn 3:34 For your name's *s*, do not deliver us up
3:35 your mercy from us, for the *s* of Abraham,
9:17 for your own *s*, O Lord, let your face shine
9:19 and act without delay, for your own *s*,
Zec 1:14 moved for the *s* of Jerusalem and Zion,
Mal 3:11 For your *s* I will forbid the locust to
Mt 3:11 I baptize you in water for the *s* of reform,
5:10 Blest are those persecuted for holiness' *s*;
15: 3 of God for the *s* of your 'tradition'?
15: 6 This means that for the *s* of your
16:25 loses his life for my *s* will find it.
18: 5 one such child for my *s* welcomes me.
19:12 renounced sex for the *s* of God's reign.
19:29 for my *s* will receive many times as much
24:22 For the *s* of the chosen,
Mk 8:35 for my *s* and the gospel's will preserve it.
9:37 a child such as this for my *s* welcomes me.
12:40 and recite long prayers for appearance *s*;
13:20 But for the *s* of those he has chosen,
16:20 Yet it was for the *s* of sinners that I was
Lk 9:24 loses his life for my *s* will save it.
18:29 for the *s* of the kingdom of God who will
Jn 11:42 I have said this for the *s* of the crowd,
12:30 "That voice did not come for my *s*,
Acts 5:41 of ill-treatment for the *s* of the Name.
Rom 3:25 for the *s* of remitting sins committed in
8:32 for the *s* of us all will not grant us all things
8:36 your *s* we are being slain all the day long;
9: 3 from Christ for the *s* of my brothers,
11:28 the Jews are enemies of God for your *s*;
13: 5 punishment but also for conscience' *s*.
14:20 God's work for the *s* of something to eat.
15:30 for the *s* of our Lord Jesus Christ and the
16: 4 even risked their lives for the *s* of mine.
1Cor 9:23 I do all that I do for the *s* of the gospel
10:28 both for the *s* of the one who called
2Cor 2:15 We are an aroma of Christ for God's *s*,
4: 5 ourselves as your servants for Jesus' *s*.
4:11 being delivered to death for Jesus' *s*,
7:10 *s* produces a repentance without regrets,
8: 9 *s* he made himself poor though he was rich,
12:10 and difficulties for the *s* of Christ;
13: 8 the truth, but only for the *s* of the truth.
Phil 2:30 near to death for the *s* of Christ's work.
3: 8 For his *s* I have forfeited everything;
Col 1:24 sufferings of Christ for the *s* of his body,
2Tm 1: 8 our Lord, nor of me, a prisoner for his *s*;
1:12 and for its *s* I undergo present hardships.
2:10 for the *s* of those whom God has chosen,
Ti 1: 1 apostle of Jesus Christ for the *s* of the faith
Heb 2: 9 he might taste death for the *s* of all men.
12: 2 For the *s* of the joy which lay before him
Jas 4: 6 gift, for the *s* of which it is written,
1Pt 1:20 and revealed for your *s* in these last days.
3:14 you should have to suffer for justice' *s*,
3:18 all, the just man for the *s* of the unjust,
4:14 when you are insulted for the *s* of Christ,
3Jn 1: 7 for the *s* of the Name that they set out,

SAKES (12)

Is 43:14 For your *s* I send to Babylon;
Ez 36:22 Not for your *s* do I act,
36:32 Not for your *s* do I act,

Jn 11:15 For your *s* I am glad I was not there,
17:19 I consecrate myself for their *s* now,
1Cor 9:10 or does he not rather say this for our *s*?
2Cor 2:10 I have done has been for your *s* and,
5:13 back to our senses, it is for your *s*.
5:15 him who for their *s* died and was raised up.
5:21 For our *s* God made him who did not know
12:15 spend myself and be spent for your *s*.
Phil 1:24 more urgent that I remain alive for your *s*.

SAKKUTH (1)

Am 5:26 You will carry away *S*,

SALA (1)

Lk 3:32 son of Obed, son of Boaz, son of *S*,

SALAMIEL (1)

Jdt 8: 1 son of Eliab, son of Nathanael, son of *S*,

SALAMIS (1)

Acts 13: 5 On their arrival in *S* they proclaimed the

SALARY (6)

Dt 15:18 six years was worth twice a hired man's *s*;
Jgs 18: 4 "He pays me a *s* and I am his priest."
1Kgs 5:20 you whatever you say for your servants' *s*."
Tb 2:12 They paid her the full *s*,
5: 3 of course, give him a *s* when you return;
Mi 3:11 bribe, her priests give decisions for a *s*,

SALE (11)

Lv 25:27 to the number of years since the *s*,
25:29 the time of one full year from its *s*.
25:50 *s* to the jubilee, distributing the sale price
25:51 of the *s* price he shall pay back as ransom;
Dt 28:68 and there you will offer yourselves for *s*
Ru 4: 3 is putting up for *s* the piece of land that
Neh 10:32 any kind of grain for *s* on the sabbath day,
2Mc 11: 3 the high priesthood up for *s* every year.
Ps(s) 44:13 you made no profit from the *s* of them.
Mt 13:46 put up for *s* all that he had and bought it.

SALECAH (4)

Dt 3:10 of Og in Bashan including *S* and Edrei.
Jos 12: 5 He ruled over Mount Hermon, *S*,
13:11 Mount Hermon, and all Bashan as far as *S*,
1Chr 5:11 them in the land of Bashan as far as *S*.

SALEM (5)

Gn 14:18 Melchizedek, king of *S*,
Jdt 4: 4 Choba and Aesora, and to the valley of *S*.
Ps(s) 76: 3 In *S* is his abode; his dwelling is in Zion.
Heb 7: 1 king of *S* and priest of the Most High God,
7: 2 he was also king of *S*,

SALIM (1)

Jn 3:23 at Aenon near *S* where water was plentiful,

SALIVA (1)

Jn 9: 6 spat on the ground, made mud with his *s*,

SALLIED (3)

1Sm 7:11 Thereupon the Israelites *s* forth from
18:27 David made preparations and *s* forth with
1Mc 9:67 Simon and his men then *s* forth from the

SALLU (4)

1Chr 9: 7 Among the Benjaminites were *S*,
Neh 11: 7 *S*, son of Meshullam,
12: 7 Bilgah, Shemaiah, and Joiarib, Jedaiah, *S*,
12:20 for *S*,

SALLY (1)

1Mc 14:36 they used to *s* forth to defile the environs

SALMA (5)

1Chr 2:11 Nahshon became the father of *S*
2:11 *S* became the father of Boaz.
2:51 Shobal, the father of Kiriath-jearim, *S*,
2:54 The descendants of *S* were Bethlehem,
Sg 1: 5 the tents of Kedar, as the curtains of *S*.

SALMAN (1)

Hos 10:14 As *S* ravaged Beth-arbel in time of war,

SALMON (4)

Ru 4:20 of Nahshon, Nahshon was the father of *S*,
4:21 father of Salmon, *S* was the father of Boaz,
Mt 1: 4 father of Nahshon, Nahshon the father of *S*.
1: 5 *S* was the father of Boaz,

SALMONE (1)

Acts 27: 7 we sailed for *S* and the shelter of Crete.

SALOME (2)

Mk 15:40 of James the younger and Joses, and *S*.
16: 1 and *S* bought perfumed oils with which they

SALT (49)

Gn 14: 3 the Valley of Siddim (that is, the *S* Sea).
19:26 and she was turned into a pillar of *s*.
Lv 2:13 to the LORD shall be seasoned with *s*.
2:13 Do not let the *s* of the covenant of your
2:13 On every offering you shall offer *s*.
Nm 34: 3 it shall begin at the end of the *S* Sea,
34:12 the Jordan and terminate with the *S* Sea.
Dt 3:17 from Chinnereth to the *S* Sea of the Arabah,
29:22 its soil being nothing but sulphur and *s*,
Jos 3:16 *S* Sea of the Arabah disappeared entirely.
12: 3 eastern side of the *S* Sea of the Arabah
15: 2 that forms the southern end of the *S* Sea,
15: 5 *S* Sea as far as the mouth of the Jordan.
18:19 extended to the northern tip of the *S* Sea,
Jgs 9:45 the city, sowing the site with *s*.
2Sm 8:13 eighteen thousand Edomites in the *S* Valley;
2Kgs 2:20 bowl," Elisha said, "and put *s* into it."
2:21 went out to the spring and threw *s* into it,
14: 7 slew ten thousand Edomites in the *S* Valley,
1Chr 18:12 thousand Edomites in the Valley of *S*.
2Chr 13: 5 and to his sons, by a covenant made in *s*?
25:11 They proceeded to the Valley of *S*,
Ezr 4:14 since we partake of the *s* of the palace,
6: 9 holocausts to the God of heaven, wheat, *s*,
7:22 *s*,
1Mc 10:29 all the Jews, from the tribute, the *s* tax,
11:35 of the tax on the *s* pans and the crown tax.
Jb 6: 6 Can a thing insipid be eaten without *s*?
39: 6 his home and the *s* flats his dwelling.
Ps(s) 107:34 thirsty ground, Fruitful land into *s* marsh,
Wis 10: 7 disbelieving soul, a standing pillar of *s*.
Sir 22:15 Sand and *s* and an iron mass are easier to
39:23 and turns fertile land into a *s* marsh.
39:26 human life are water and fire, iron and *s*,
43:20 He scatters frost like so much *s*;
Jer 17: 6 in a lava waste, a *s* and empty earth.
Ez 16: 4 nor anointed, nor were you rubbed with *s*,
43:24 the priests shall strew *s* on them and
47: 8 and empties into the sea, the *s* waters,
47:11 they shall be left for *s*.
Zep 2: 9 of nettles and a *s* pit and a waste forever.
Mt 5:13 "You are the *s* of the earth.
5:13 But what if *s* goes flat?
Mk 9:50 *S* is excellent in its place; but if salt
9:50 Keep *s* in your hearts and you will be at
Lk 14:34 *S* is good, but if salt loses its flavor

SALTED (3)

Ex 30:35 is to be *s* and so kept pure and sacred.
Tb 6: 6 the rest he *s* and kept for the journey.
Mk 9:49 Everyone will be *s* with fire.

SALTWORT (1)

Jb 30: 4 They plucked *s* and shrubs;

SALU (2)

Nm 25:14 the Midianite woman was Zimri, son of *S*,
1Mc 2:26 just as Phinehas did with Zimri, son of *S*.

SALUTARY (2)

Prv 15:31 to *s* reproof will abide among the wise.
Sir 23:27 more *s* than to obey his commandments.

SALUTE (1)

Mk 15:18 and put it on him, and began to *s* him,

SALUTED (1)

Heb 11:13 been promised but saw and *s* it from afar.

SALVAGE (1)

2Mc 14: 3 there was no way for him to *s* his position

SALVATION (126)

2Sm 22: 3 My shield, the horn of my *s*,
22:47 Extolled be my God, rock of my *s*,
23: 5 to fruition all my *s* and my every desire?
1Chr 16:23 the LORD, all the earth, announce his *s*,
2Chr 6:41 your priests, LORD God, be clothed with *s*,
Jdt 8:17 we wait for the *s* that comes from him,
Est C: 6 the soles of his feet for the *s* of Israel.
1Mc 5:62 whom it was granted to achieve Israel's *s*.
Jb 13:16 And this shall be my *s*,
Ps(s) 3: 3 of me, "There is no *s* for him in God."
3: 9 *S* is the LORD's!
9:15 of the daughter of Zion, rejoice in your *s*.
13: 6 Let my heart rejoice in your *s*;
14: 7 out of Zion would come the *s* of Israel!
18: 3 of refuge, my shield, the horn of my *s*,
35: 3 Say to my soul, "I am your *s*."
35: 9 LORD, I will be joyful because of his *s*.
37:39 The *s* of the just is from the LORD;
38:23 Make haste to help me, O Lord my *s*!
40:11 faithfulness and your *s* I have spoken of;
40:17 And may those who love your *s* say ever,
50:23 the right way I will show the *s* of God."
51:14 Give me back the joy of your *s*,
53: 7 out of Zion would come the *s* of Israel!
62: 2 from him comes my *s*.
62: 3 He only is my rock and my *s*,
62: 7 He only is my rock and my *s*,
67: 3 among all nations, your *s*.
68:20 God, who is our *s*.
70: 5 And may those who love your *s* say ever,
71:15 declare your justice, day by day your *s*,
85: 8 O LORD, your kindness, and grant us your *s*.
85:10 Near indeed is his *s* to those who fear him,
85:14 Justice shall walk before him, and *s*,
91:16 I will gratify him and will show him my *s*.
95: 1 let us acclaim the Rock of our *s*.
96: 2 announce his *s*,
98: 2 The LORD has made his *s* known:
98: 3 of the earth have seen the *s* by our God.
116:13 The cup of *s* I will take up,
118:25 O LORD, grant *s*!
119:41 O LORD, your *s* according to your promise.
119:81 Kaph My soul pines for your *s*;
119:123 strain after your *s* and your just promise.
119:155 Far from sinners is *s*,
119:166 I wait for your *s*, O LORD, and your
119:174 I long for your *s*, O LORD, and your law
132:16 Her priests I will clothe with *s*,
140: 8 O GOD, my Lord, my strength and my *s*;
146: 3 in princes, in man, in whom there is no *s*.
Wis 5: 2 fear, and amazed at the unlooked-for *s*.
16: 6 terrorized, though they had a sign of *s*,
18: 7 Your people awaited the *s* of the just and
Is 12: 3 you will draw water at the fountain of *s*,
26:18 *S* we have not achieved for the earth,
33: 2 every morning, our *s* in time of trouble!
45: 8 Let the earth open and *s* bud forth;
46:13 salvation shall not tarry; I will put *s*
49: 6 my *s* may reach to the ends of the earth.
49: 8 I answer you, on the day of *s* I help you,
51: 5 my *s* shall go forth [and my arm shall
51: 6 My *s* shall remain forever and my justice
51: 8 my justice shall remain forever and my *s*,
52: 7 peace, bearing good news, announcing *s*,
52:10 of the earth will behold the *s* of our God.
56: 1 for my *s* is about to come,
59:11 for *s*,
59:17 He put on justice as his breastplate, *s*,
60:18 your walls "*S*" and your gates "Praise."
61:10 For he has clothed me with a robe of *s*,
Jer 3:23 LORD, our God, alone is the *s* of Israel.
Bar 4:24 so shall they soon see God's *s* come to you,
Mt 24:13 end, however, is the one who will see *s*.
Mk 16:20 and immortal proclamation of eternal *s*.
Lk 1:71 *S* from our enemies and from the hands of
1:77 knowledge of *s* in freedom from their sins,
3: 6 And all mankind shall see the *s* of God.'"
7:50 to the woman, "Your faith has been your *s*.
17:19 your faith has been your *s*."
19: 9 "Today *s* has come to this house,
Jn 4:22 after all, *s* is from the Jews.
5:34 I refer to these things only for your *s*.)
Acts 4:12 There is no *s* in anyone else,
13:26 us that this message of *s* was sent forth.
13:47 a means of *s* to the ends of the earth.'"
16:17 they will make known to you a way of *s*."
28:28 Now you must realize that this *s* of God
Rom 1:16 leading everyone who believes in it to *s*,
10:10 justification, confession on the lips to *s*.
11:11 by their transgression *s* has come to the
13:11 for our *s* is closer than when we first
1Cor 1:18 are experiencing *s* it is the power of God.
2Cor 1: 6 it is for your encouragement and *s*,
6: 2 on a day of *s* I have helped you."
6: 2 Now is the day of *s*!
7:10 a repentance without regrets, leading to *s*,
Eph 1:13 when you heard the glad tidings of *s*,
2: 8 to his favor that *s* is yours through faith.
6:17 helmet of *s* and the sword of the spirit,
Phil 1:19 that this will turn out to my *s*,
1:28 downfall for them, but *s* for you.
2:12 with anxious concern to achieve your *s*,
1Thes 2:16 keep us from preaching *s* to the Gentiles.
5: 8 breastplate and the hope of *s* as a helmet.
5: 9 acquiring *s* through our Lord Jesus Christ.
2Thes 2:13 fruits of those whom God has chosen for *s*,
1Tm 4:16 bring to *s* yourself and all who hear you.
2Tm 2:10 may obtain the *s* to be found in Christ Jesus
3:15 through faith in Jesus Christ leads to *s*.
Ti 2:11 of God has appeared, offering *s* to all men.
Heb 1:14 sent to serve those who are to inherit *s*?
2: 3 escape if we ignore a *s* as great as ours?
2:10 in the work of *s* perfect through suffering.
5: 9 source of eternal *s* for all who obey him,
6: 9 in your regard, things pointing to your *s*.
9:28 to bring *s* to those who eagerly await him.
1Pt 1: 5 a birth to a *s* which stands ready to be
1: 9 you are achieving faith's goal, your *s*.
1:10 This is the *s* which the prophets carefully
2: 2 of the spirit to make you grow into *s*,
2Pt 3:15 our Lord's patience is directed toward *s*.
Jude 1: 3 writing you, beloved, about the *s* we share.
Rv 7:10 out in a loud voice, "*S* is from our God,

SALVATION (cont.)

12:10 "Now have *s* and power come,
19: 1 *S*, glory and might belong to our God,

SALVE (1)

Is 1: 6 not drained, or bandaged, or eased with *s*.

SALVES (1)

Tb 2:10 more they anointed my eyes with various *s*,

SAMARIA (126)

1Kgs 13:32 cities of *S* shall certainly come to pass."
16:24 He then bought the hill of *S* from Shemer
16:24 naming the city he built *S* after Shemer,
16:28 he was buried im *S*,
16:29 over Israel in *S* for twenty-two years.
16:32 in the temple of Baal which he built in *S*,
18: 3 Now the famine in *S* was bitter,
20: 1 proceeded to invest and attack *S*.
20:10 in *S* to make handfuls for all my followers."
20:17 word that some men had marched out of *S*.
20:34 bazaars in Damascus, as my father did in *S*."
20:43 of Israel went off homeward and entered *S*.
21: 1 next to the palace of Ahab, king of *S*,
21:18 meet Ahab, king of Israel, who rules in *S*.
22:10 floor at the entrance of the gate of *S*,
22:37 So they went to *S*,
22:38 the chariot was washed at the pool of *S*,
22:52 *S* in the seventeenth year of Jehoshaphat,
2Kgs 1: 2 his roof terrace at *S* and had been injured.
2:25 Mount Carmel, and thence he returned to *S*.
3: 1 *S* [in the eighteenth year of Jehoshaphat,
3: 6 and when he set out on a campaign from *S*,
5: 3 would present himself to the prophet in *S*,"
6:19 And he led them to *S*.
6:20 When they entered *S*,
6:20 eyes, and they saw that they were inside *S*.
6:24 his whole army and laid siege to *S*.
6:25 Because of the siege the famine in *S* was
7: 1 of barley for a shekel, in the market of *S*.'"
7:18 at this time tomorrow at the gate of *S*."
10: 1 Ahab had seventy descendants in *S*.
10: 1 the guardians of Ahab's descendants in *S*.
10:12 Then he set out for *S*,
10:17 When he arrived in *S*,
10:35 with his ancestors and was buried in *S*.
10:36 over Israel in *S* was twenty-eight years.
13: 1 his seventeen-year reign over Israel in *S*.
13: 6 sacred pole also remained standing in *S*.
13: 9 with his ancestors and was buried in *S*.
13:10 his sixteen-year reign over Israel in *S*.
13:13 Joash was buried with the kings of Israel in *S*
14:14 Then he returned to *S*.
14:16 was buried in *S* with the kings of Israel.
14:23 began his forty-one-year reign in *S*.
15: 8 was king of Israel in *S* for six months.
15:13 he reigned one month in *S*.
15:14 son of Gadi, came up from Tirzah to *S*,
15:17 of Gadi, began his ten year reign over *S*.
15:23 began his two-year reign over Israel in *S*.
15:25 him within the palace stronghold in *S*,
15:27 his twenty-year reign over Israel in *S*.
17: 1 began his nine-year reign over Israel in *S*.
17: 5 occupied the whole land and attacked *S*,
17: 6 of Hoshea, the king of Assyria took *S*,
17:24 cities of *S* in place of the Israelites.
17:24 possession of *S* and dwelt in its cities.
17:26 deported and settled in the cities of *S*
17:28 from *S* returned and settled in Bethel,
18: 9 Shalmaneser, king of Assyria, attacked *S*,
18:10 year of Hosea, king of Israel, *S* was taken.
18:34 Where are the gods of the land of *S*?
21:13 Jerusalem with the same cord as I did *S*,
23:18 bones of the prophet who had come from *S*.
23:19 of *S* which the kings of Israel had erected,
2Chr 18: 2 some years he went down to Ahab at *S*;
18: 9 floor at the entrance of the gate of *S*,
22: 9 he was hiding in *S* and brought him to Jehu,
25:13 the cities of Judah from *S* to Beth-horon.
25:24 Then he returned to *S*.
28: 8 them much plunder, which they brought to *S*.
28: 9 In *S* there was a prophet of the LORD by
28: 9 the army returning to *S* and said to them:
28:15 Then they returned to *S*.
Ezr 4:10 transported and settled in the city of *S*
4:17 and their fellow officials living in *S*
Neh 3:34 of his brethren and the troops of *S*:
Tb 14: 4 even *S* and Jerusalem shall become desolate!
Jdt 1: 9 to all those in *S* and its cities,
4: 4 they sent word to the whole region of *S*,
1Mc 3:10 together with a large army from *S*,
10:30 or from the three districts annexed from *S*.
10:38 added to Judea from the province of *S*
11:28 and the three districts of *S* from tribute,
11:34 were transferred from *S* to Judea in favor
2Mc 15: 1 his companions were in the territory of *S*,
Is 7: 8 *S* is the capital of Ephraim,
7: 8 Ephraim, and Remaliah's son the head of *S*.
8: 4 spoil of *S* shall be carried off by the king
9: 8 know it, Ephraim and those who dwell in *S*,
10: 9 Or Hamath like Arpad, or *S* like Damascus?
10:10 that had more images than Jerusalem and *S*,
10:11 Samaria, Just as I treated *S* and her idols,
36:19 Where are the gods of *S*?
36:19 Have they saved *S* from my hand?
Jer 31: 5 plant vineyards on the mountains of *S*;
41: 5 bodies came from Shechem, Shiloh, and *S*,
Ez 16:46 Your elder sister was *S* with her daughters,
16:51 *S* did not commit half your sins!
16:53 her daughters and of *S* and her daughters
16:55 and her daughters, *S* and her daughters,
23: 4 *S* is Oholah, and Jerusalem is Oholibah.]
Hos 7: 1 Ephraim stands out, the wickedness of *S*;
8: 5 Cast away your calf, O *S*!
8: 6 such is the calf of *S*!
10: 5 of *S* fear for the calf of Beth-aven;
10: 7 The king of *S* shall disappear,
14: 1 *S* shall expiate her guilt,
Am 3: 9 "Gather about the mountain of *S*,
3:12 So the Israelites who dwell in *S* shall
4: 1 this word, women of the mountain of *S*,
6: 1 to the overconfident on the mount of *S*,
8:14 Those who swear by the shameful idol of *S*,
Ob 1:19 the lands of Ephraim and the lands of *S*,
Mi 1: 1 he received concerning *S* and Jerusalem.
1: 5 Is it not *S*?
1: 6 I will make *S* a stone heap in the field,
Lk 17:11 passed along the borders of *S* and Galilee.
Jn 4: 4 He had to pass through *S*.
Acts 1: 8 in Jerusalem, throughout Judea and *S*,
8: 1 throughout the countryside of Judea and *S*.
8: 3 Philip in *S*.
8: 5 town of *S* and there proclaimed the Messiah.
8:14 heard that *S* had accepted the word of God,
8:25 good news to many villages of *S* on the way.
9:31 Galilee, and *S* the church was at peace.
15: 3 made their way through Phoenicia and *S*,

SAMARIANS (1)

2Kgs 17:29 on the high places which the *S* had made,

SAMARIA'S (2)

2Kgs 1: 3 "Go, intercept the messengers of *S* king,
Jer 23:13 Among *S* prophets I saw unseemly deeds:

SAMARITAN (10)

Mt 10: 5 pagan territory and do not enter a *S* town.
Lk 9:50 *S* Inhospitality.
9:52 *S* town to prepare for his passing through,
10:33 But a *S* who was journeying along came on
17:16 This man was a *S*.
Jn 4: 5 and his journey brought him to a *S* town
4: 7 When a *S* woman came to draw water,
4: 9 The *S* woman said to him, "You are a Jew.
4: 9 How can you ask me, a *S* and a woman,
8:48 right, after all, in saying you are a *S*,

SAMARITANS (5)

Lk 9:53 but the *S* would not welcome him because he
Jn 4: 9 that Jews have nothing to do with *S*.)
4:39 Many *S* from that town believed in him on
4:40 result was that, when these *S* came to him,
Acts 8: 9 in the town and holding the *S* spellbound.

SAME (364)

Gn 11: 1 spoke the same language, using the *s* words.
11: 6 one people, all speaking the *s* language,
17:23 the flesh of their foreskins on that *s* day,
17:26 on that *s* day Abraham and his son Ishmael
19:11 at the *s* time they struck the men at the
19:24 at the *s* time the LORD rained down
26:12 region and reaped a hundredfold the *s* year.
26:18 the *s* names that his father had given them.)
26:24 *s* night the LORD appeared to him and said:
26:32 That *s* day Isaac's servants came and
30:35 That *s* day Laban removed the streaked and
33:16 So on the *s* day that Esau began his
35:20 and the *s* monument marks Rachel's grave to
39:17 Then she told him the *s* story:
40: 3 (the *s* jail where Joseph was confined).
40: 5 in the jail both had dreams on the *s* night,
41:11 Later, we both had dreams on the *s* night,
41:25 of Pharaoh's dreams have the *s* meaning.
41:26 the *s* in each dream.
41:32 That Pharaoh had the *s* dream twice means
42:11 All of us are sons of the *s* man.
42:32 of us brothers, sons of the *s* father;
Ex 5: 8 Yet you shall levy upon them the *s* quota
5:13 the *s* daily amount as when your straw was
6:27 the *s* Moses and Aaron.
7:22 magicians did the *s* by their magic arts.
8: 3 magicians did the *s* by their magic arts.
12: 8 That *s* night they shall eat its roasted
12:12 on this *s* night I will go through Egypt,
12:42 so on this *s* night all the Israelites
12:46 It must be eaten in one and the *s* house;
12:49 *s* forthe resident alien as for the native."
12:51 On that *s* day the LORD brought the
22:29 do the *s* with your oxen and your sheep;
26: 2 all the sheets shall be of the *s* size.
26: 3 and the *s* for the other five.
26: 4 and the *s* along the edge of the end sheet
26: 8 all eleven sheets shall be of the *s* size.
29:41 with the *s* cereal offering and libation as
34:16 gods, they will make your sons do the *s*.
36: 9 all the sheets were of the *s* size.
36:10 and the *s* for the other five.
36:11 and the *s* along the edge of the end sheet
36:15 all eleven sheets were the *s* size.
Lv 4:10 This is the *s* as is removed from the ox of
7: 7 are alike, both having the *s* ritual,
12: 2 *s* uncleanness as at her menstrual period.
13:43 bald spot has the *s* pink appearance as
16:16 He shall do the *s* for the meeting tent,
19:34 have the *s* love for him as for yourself;
22:28 sheep on one and the *s* day with its young.
22:30 it must, therefore, be eaten on the *s* day;
23:21 On this *s* day you shall by proclamation
24:19 his neighbor shall receive the *s* in return.
24:20 The *s* injury that a man gives another
27:23 and on the *s* day the price thus
Nm 6:11 On the *s* day he shall reconsecrate his
7: 2 the *s* princes of the tribes who supervised
9: 6 up to Moses and Aaron that *s* day and said,
9:14 You shall have the *s* law for the resident
15:11 The *s* is to be done for each ox,
15:12 you offer, do the *s* for each of them.
15:13 shall make these offerings in the *s* way,
15:16 with the same law and the *s* application of
16:17 each with his own censer, shall do the *s*."
26: 9 the *s* Dathan and Abiram,
28: 8 the *s* cereal offering and the same libation
28:24 you shall make exactly the *s* offerings
31:30 and the *s* from the different beasts,
Dt 2:22 had done the *s* for the descendants of Esau,
7:19 The *s* also will he do to all the nations
12:30 I, too, would do the *s*.'
15:17 slave, also, you shall treat in the *s* way.
18: 8 receive the *s* portions to eat as the rest,
21:23 You shall bury it the *s* day;
22: 3 You shall do the *s* with his ass,
27:11 *s* day Moses gave the people this order:
31:22 So Moses wrote this song that *s* day,
Jos 5:11 On that *s* day after the Passover on which
6:14 and for six days in all they did the *s*.
6:15 the city seven times in the *s* manner;
9:27 the Israelites, at the *s* time he made them,
10:35 they attacked it and captured it the *s* day,
17: 9 This *s* boundary continued down to the Wadi
Jgs 6:25 That *s* night the LORD said to him,
8: 8 to Penuel and made the *s* request of them,
11:13 Now restore the *s* peaceably."
20:23 in the *s* place as on the previous day,
1Sm 2:34 both shall die on the *s* day.
4:12 battlefield and reached Shiloh that *s* day,
6: 4 since the *s* plague has struck all of you
6:16 lords returned to Ekron the *s* day.
8: 9 but at the *s* time,
11: 7 the *s* as this will be done to his oxen!"
16:10 In the *s* way Jesse presented seven sons
17:27 They repeated the *s* words to him and said,
17:30 *s* question; and everyone gave him the *s*
19:11 The *s* night, Saul sent messengers
21:11 That *s* day David took to flight from Saul,
27: 6 That *s* day Achish gave him Ziklag,
28:25 Then they stood up and left the *s* night.
30:24 remains with the baggage shall be the *s*;
31: 6 armor-bearer died together on that *s* day.
2Sm 3:14 *s* time David sent messengers to Ishbaal,
14:13 *s* kind of thing against the people of God?
16: 5 son of Gera of the *s* clan as Saul's family,
24:18 *s* day Gad went to David and said to him,
1Kgs 1: 6 and next in age to Absalom by the *s* mother.
3:17 lord, this woman and I live in the *s* house,
6:33 The *s* was done at the entrance to the nave,
7: 8 the tribunal and of the *s* construction.
7:37 same casting, the same size, the *s* shape.
11: 8 He did the *s* for all his foreign wives who
13: 3 He gave a sign that *s* day and said:
21: 8 nobles who lived in the *s* city with Naboth.
22:13 Let your word be the *s* as any of theirs;
2Kgs 4:17 and by the *s* time the following year she
16: 6 At the *s* time the king of Edom recovered
19:33 He shall return by the *s* way he came,
21:13 Jerusalem with the *s* cord as I did Samaria,
23:15 this *s* altar and high place he tore down,
23:19 very *s* to them as he had done in Bethel.
1Chr 9:19 and his brethren of the *s* ancestral house
11: 1 we are of the *s* bone and flesh as you.
16: 7 on that *s* day, David appointed Asaph
17: 3 *s* night the word of God came to Nathan:
24:31 too, in the *s* manner as their relatives,
24:31 so in the *s* way as the less important one.
26:12 of the LORD, for each group in the *s* way.
2Chr 4: 3 of these cast in the *s* mold with the sea.
18:11 other prophets prophesied in the *s* vein,
27: 5 They brought the *s* to him also in the
28:22 the *s* King Ahaz became even more
29:27 in the *s* instant that the holocaust began,
32:12 Has not this *s* Hezekiah removed his high
32:30 This *s* Hezekiah stopped the upper outflow
34:16 who brought it to the king at the *s* time
35: 5 the Levites and the families may be the *s*.
35:12 They did the *s* with the oxen.

Ezr 5:16 Then this *s* Sheshbazzar came and laid the
8:34 At that *s* time, those who had returned
Neh 4:16 At the *s* time I told the people to spend
6: 4 same proposal, and each time I gave the *s*
6: 5 me the *s* message by one of his servants,
6:17 At that *s* time, however, many letters
13:18 Did not your fathers act in this *s* way,
13:27 that you have done this *s* very great evil,
Tb 2: 9 That *s* night I bathed,
3: 7 On the *s* day, at Ecbatana in Media,
4: 1 That *s* day Tobit remembered the money he
4: 4 she dies, bury her in the *s* grave with me.
12:12 the *s* thing when you used to bury the dead.
12:14 *s* time, however, God commissioned me
Jdt 7: 2 That *s* day all their fighting men went
9: 3 the *s* bed that had felt the shame of their
12: 3 we get more of the *s* to provide for you?
Est 4:16 I and my maids will also fast in the *s* way.
9:11 *s* day, when the number of those killed
1Mc 2:25 At the *s* time, he also killed the messenger
7:42 *s* way, crush this army before us today
8:27 In the *s* way, if war is made first
10:77 at the *s* time he advanced into the plain,
11:48 men in the city, which, at the *s* time,
12: 2 Sparta and other places for the *s* purpose.
2Mc 2: 4 The *s* document also tells how the prophet,
2:12 the feast in the *s* way for eight days.
3:33 the *s* young men in the same clothing again
5:14 and the *s* number being sold into slavery.
6: 8 to act in the *s* way against the Jews:
7: 8 turn suffered the *s* tortures as the first.
7:13 maltreated the fourth brother in the *s* way.
7:28 *s* way the human race came into existence.
8:14 and at the *s* time besought the Lord to
10: 5 the twenty-fifth of the *s* month Chislev,
10:15 At the *s* time the Idumeans,
10:36 up the *s* way swung around on the defenders,
14: 9 people with the *s* gracious consideration
15:10 gave his orders and pointed out at the *s* time
15:13 Then in the *s* way another man appeared,
Jb 3:19 Small and great are there the *s*,
4: 8 for mischief and sow trouble, reap the *s*.
31:15 not the *s* One fashion us before our birth?
33: 6 have been taken from the *s* clay by God.
Ps(s) 102:28 and they are changed, but you are the *s*,
139:12 [Darkness and light are the *s*
Eccl 3:19 Both have the *s* life-breath,
3:20 Both go to the *s* place;
6: 6 his goods, do not both go to the *s* place?
9: 2 vain, in that there is the *s* lot for all,
9: 3 worst, that things turn out the *s* for all.
Wis 7: 1 too am a mortal man, the *s* as all the rest,
7: 6 and in one *s* way they leave it.
17:14 world, while all sleeping the *s* sleep,
18: 9 share alike the *s* good things and dangers,
18:11 with the *s* retribution as his master;
18:11 the plebeian suffered the *s* as the king.
19:16 who now shared with them the *s* rights.
Sir 31:14 nor reach when he does for the *s* dish.
32:20 and let not the *s* thing trip you twice.
42:21 he is from all eternity one and the *s*,
44:22 renewed the *s* promise because of Abraham,
Is 14:10 become weak like us, you are the *s* as we.
17: 3 shall have the *s* glory as the Israelites,
37:34 He shall return by the *s* way he came,
46: 4 Even to your old age I am the *s*,
Jer 26:20 he prophesied the *s* things against this
27:12 king of Judah, I spoke the *s* words:
28: 1 That *s* year, in [the beginning of] the reign
28:17 That *s* year, in the seventh month,
36:32 and many others of the *s* kind in addition.
39:10 given at the *s* time vineyards and farms.
Bar 6:60 and the *s* wind blows over all the land.
Ez 1:16 and all four of them looked the *s*:
4: 5 sins I allot you the *s* number of days,
4:10 each day the *s*.
4:11 each day the *s*.
10:10 All four of them seemed to be made the *s*,
18:24 the *s* kind of abominable things that the
21:24 Both roads shall lead out from the *s* land.
21:32 it shall not be the *s* until he comes who
23: 2 were two women, daughters of the *s* mother,
23:13 Both had gone down the *s* path,
40:21 *s* measurements as those of the first gate;
40:22 palm decorations were of the *s* proportions
40:24 they were the *s* size as the others.
40:28 Its dimensions were the *s* as the others;
40:29 vestibule were the *s* size as the others.
40:32 whose dimensions were found to be the *s*.
40:33 vestibule were the *s* size as the others;
40:36 and its vestibule, and found them the *s*.
42:11 with the *s* exits and plan and entrances.
44: 3 of the gate, and leave by the *s* way.
45:11 the liquid measure shall be of the *s* size:
45:25 seven days, he shall perform the *s* rites,
45:25 same sin offerings, the *s* holocausts, the *s*
46:22 thirty wide, all four of them the *s* size.
Dn 4:33 At the *s* time my reason returned to me,
5:30 The *s* night Belshazzar
Am 2: 7 Son and father go to the *s* prostitute,
Zec 6:10 and go the *s* day to the house of Josiah,
Mt 5:12 the prophets before you in the very *s* way.
5:16 *s* way, your light must shine before men
9:19 followed him, and his disciples did the *s*.
13: 1 That *s* day, on leaving the house, Jesus
17:12 will suffer at their hands in the *s* way."
18:28 But when that *s* official went out he met a
18:35 Father will treat you in exactly the *s* way
20: 5 around noon and midafternoon and did the *s*.
20:11 yet they received the *s* daily wage.
20:12 but you have put them on the *s* basis as us
20:14 man who was hired last the *s* pay as you.
21:30 to his second son and said the *s* thing.
21:36 before, but they treated them the *s* way.
22:23 That *s* day some Sadducees,
22:26 The *s* thing happened to the second,
24:44 You must be prepared in the *s* way.
25:17 In the *s* way, the man who received
26:35 And all the other disciples said the *s*.
26:44 a third time, saying the *s* words as before.
27:44 with him kept taunting him in the *s* way.
Mk 9:39 my name can at the *s* time speak ill of me.
10:38 or be baptized in the *s* bath of pain as I?"
11:18 They were at the *s* time afraid of him
12:21 The *s* thing happened to the third;
13:29 *s* way, when you see these things happening
14:31 They all said the *s*.
14:33 at the *s* time he took along with him Peter,
14:39 back again he began to pray in the *s* words.
15:16 the *s* time they assembled the whole cohort.
Lk 3:11 The man who has food should do the *s*."
5:33 the disciples of the Pharisees do the *s*.
10:31 happened to be going down the *s* road;
10:32 there was a Levite who came the *s* way;
10:37 Jesus said to him, "Then go and do the *s*."
13: 3 all come to the *s* end unless you reform.
13: 5 all come to the *s* end unless you reform."
14:33 In the *s* way,
15:10 there will be the *s* kind of joy before the
17:10 It is quite the *s* with you who hear me.
17:28 It was much the *s* in the days of Lot:
22:20 He did the *s* with the cup after eating,
22:36 the *s* with the traveling bag.
23:40 God, seeing you are under the *s* sentence?
24:13 Two of them that *s* day were making their
Jn 1:44 Bethsaida, the *s* town as Andrew and Peter.
6:11 he did the *s* with the dried fish,
10:15 know me in the *s* way that the Father
16:22 In the *s* way, you are sad for a time,
21:13 it to them, and did the *s* with the fish.
21:24 It is this *s* disciple who is the witness
Acts 6: 7 while at the *s* time a number of the
7: 8 Isaac did the *s* for Jacob,
9: 4 and at the *s* time heard a voice saying,
9:31 at the *s* time it enjoyed the increased
10: 1 The *s* was true of his whole household.
11:17 If God was giving them the *s* gift he gave
19:25 these men and other workers in the *s* craft.
24:14 *s* time, I believe all that is written in
24:15 and I have the *s* hope in God as these men
24:26 *s* time, he hoped he would be offered
27:40 At the *s* time they untied the guy-ropes of
Rom 2: 1 yourself, since you do the very *s* things.
3:30 It is the *s* God who justifies the
6:11 *s* way, you must consider yourselves dead
7: 4 *s* way, my brothers, you died to the law
7: 7 That the law is the *s* as sin?
9:21 make from the *s* lump of clay one vessel
10:12 all have the *s* Lord,
12: 4 not all the members have the *s* function,
12:16 Have the *s* attitude toward all.
13: 5 You pay taxes for the *s* reason,
1Cor 3: 8 plants and he who waters work to the *s* end.
10: 3 All ate the *s* spiritual food.
10: 4 All drank the *s* spiritual drink (they
11:12 In the *s* way that woman was made from man,
11:25 *s* way, after the supper, he took the cup,
12: 4 There are different gifts but the *s* Spirit;
12: 5 are different ministries but the *s* Lord;
12: 6 there are different works but the *s* God
12: 9 by the *s* Spirit another is given the gift
12:11 the *s* Spirit who produces all these gifts,
15:39 Not all bodily nature is the *s*.
16: 9 but at the *s* time there are many opposed.
2Cor 1: 4 *s* consolation we have received from him.
1: 6 patiently the *s* sufferings we endure.
4:16 our body is being destroyed at the *s* time.
10: 9 *s* time, I do not wish to intimidate you
11:12 ministry they work on the *s* terms as we do.
12:18 in the one spirit, walk in the *s* footsteps?
Gal 4: 3 In the *s* way, while we were not yet of age
Eph 3: 6 members of the *s* body and sharers of the
Phil 1:30 Yours is the *s* struggle as mine,
2:18 May you be glad on the *s* score,
1Thes 2:14 You suffered the *s* treatment from your
1Tm 3: 8 In the *s* way, deacons must be serious
Heb 1:12 the *s*, and your years will have no end.
2:11 are consecrated have one and the *s* Father.
6:11 each of you show the *s* zeal till the end,
10: 1 *s* sacrifices offered continually year after
10:11 and offering again and again those *s*
11: 9 Isaac and Jacob, heirs of the *s* promise;
11:29 attempted the *s* thing they were drowned.
13: 8 Jesus Christ is the *s* yesterday,
Jas 2: 2 at the *s* time a poor man in shabby clothes.
3: 4 It is the *s* with ships:
3:10 Blessing and curse come out of the *s* mouth.
3:11 fresh water and foul from the *s* outlet?
1Pt 4: 1 arm yourselves with his *s* mentality.
4: 4 into the *s* swamp of profligacy as they.
5: 5 In the *s* way, you younger men must be
5: 9 the *s* sufferings throughout the world.
1Jn 4:11 we must have the *s* love for one another.
Rv 2:26 the *s* authority I received from my Father.
6: 6 of wheat and the *s* for three of barley!
21:16 its length and its width being the *s*.

SAMLAH (4)

Gn 36:36 When Hadad died, *S*,
36:37 When *S* died,
1Chr 1:47 Hadad died and *S* of Masrekah succeeded him.
1:48 *S* died and Shaul from Rehoboth-han-nahar

SAMOS (2)

1Mc 15:23 Sparta, Delos, Myndos, Sicyon, Caria, *S*,
Acts 20:15 on the second day we crossed to *S*,

SAMOTHRACE (1)

Acts 16:11 Troas and set a course straight for *S*,

SAMPSAMES (1)

1Mc 15:23 to all the countries *S*,

SAMSON (39)

Jgs 13:24 The woman bore a son and named him *S*.
14: 1 *S* went down to Timnah and saw there one of
14: 3 But *S* answered his father,
14: 5 So *S* went down to Timnah with his father
14: 6 But the spirit of the LORD came upon *S*,
14:10 to the woman, and *S* gave a banquet there,
14:12 *S* said to them, "Let me propose a riddle
15: 1 of the wheat harvest, *S* visited his wife,
15: 3 *S* said to them, "This time the Philistines
15: 4 So *S* left and caught three hundred foxes.
15: 6 who had done this, they were told, *S*,
15: 7 *S* said to them, "If this is how you act,
15:10 they answered, "To take *S* prisoner;
15:11 cavern in the cliff of Etam and said to *S*,
15:12 *S* said to them, "Swear to me that you
15:16 Then *S* said, "With the jawbone of an ass
15:19 which *S* drank till his spirit returned and
15:20 *S* judged Israel for twenty years in the
16: 1 Once *S* went to Gaza,
16: 2 Informed that *S* had come there,
16: 3 *S* rested there until midnight.
16: 6 So Delilah said to *S*,
16: 7 which have not dried," *S* answered her,
16: 9 to him, "The Philistines are upon you, *S!*"
16:10 Delilah said to *S*,
16:12 "The Philistines are upon you, *S!*"
16:13 Delilah said to *S* again,
16:14 said, "The Philistines are upon you, *S!*"
16:20 said, "The Philistines are upon you, *S!*",
16:23 has delivered into our power *S* our enemy."
16:25 they said, "Call *S* that he may amuse us."
16:25 So they called *S* from the prison,
16:26 *S* said to the attendant who was holding
16:27 women looked on as *S* provided amusement.
16:28 *S* cried out to the LORD and said,
16:29 *S* grasped the two middle columns on which
16:30 *S* said, "Let me die with the Philistines!"
1Sm 12:11 Barak, Jephthah, and *S*:
Heb 11:32 have no time to tell of Gideon, Barak, *S*,

SAMSON'S (3)

Jgs 14:15 they said on the fourth day to *S* wife,
14:16 At *S* side, his wife wept and said,
14:20 and *S* wife was married to the one who had

SAMUEL (129)

Nm 34:20 *S*, son of Ammihud; from
1Sm 1:20 of her term bore a son whom she called *S*,
2:18 Meanwhile the boy *S*,
2:21 young *S* grew up in the service of the LORD.
2:26 young *S* was growing in stature and in
3: 1 young *S* was minister to the Lord under Eli,
3: 3 and *S* was sleeping in the temple of the
3: 4 The LORD called to *S*,
3: 6 Again the LORD called *S*,
3: 7 that time *S* was not familiar with the LORD,
3: 8 The LORD called *S* again,
3: 9 So he said to *S*, "Go to sleep,
3: 9 When *S* went to sleep in his place,
3:10 calling out as before, "Samuel, *S!*"
3:10 *S* answered, "Speak, for your servant is
3:11 The LORD said to *S*:
3:15 *S* then slept until morning,
3:16 Eli the vision, but Eli called to him, *S*,
3:18 So *S* told him everything,
3:19 *S* grew up, and the LORD was with him,
3:20 *S* was an accredited prophet of the LORD.
4: 1 and *S* spoke to all Israel.
7: 3 *S* said to them: "If you wish with
7: 5 *S* then gave orders,
7: 6 that *S* began to judge the Israelites.
7: 8 afraid of the Philistines and said to *S*,

SAMUEL (cont.)

7: 9 S therefore took an unweaned lamb and
7:10 While S was offering the holocaust,
7:12 S then took a stone and placed it between
7:13 was severe with them as long as S lived.
7:15 S judged Israel as long as he lived.
8: 1 S appointed his sons judges over Israel.
8: 4 in a body to S at Ramah and said to him,
8: 6 S was displeased when they asked for a
8:10 S delivered the message of the LORD in
8:21 When S had listened to all the people had
8:22 S thereupon said to the men of Israel,
9:14 S was coming toward them on his way to the
9:15 the LORD had given S the revelation:
9:17 When S caught sight of Saul,
9:18 Saul met S in the gateway and said,
9:19 S answered Saul: "I am the seer.
9:22 S then took Saul and his servant and
9:24 S said: "This is a reserved portion
9:24 Thus Saul dined with S that day.
9:26 At daybreak S called to Saul on the roof,
9:26 he and S went outside the city together.
9:27 the edge of town, S said to Saul,
10: 1 S poured oil on Saul's head;
10: 9 As Saul turned to leave S,
10:14 When we could not find them, we went to S."
10:15 said, "Tell me, then, what S said to you."
10:16 him of what S had said about the kingship.
10:17 S called the people together to the LORD
10:20 So S had all the tribes of Israel come
10:24 S said to all the people,
10:25 S next explained to the people the law of
10:25 This done, S dismissed the people,
11: 7 does not come out to follow Saul [and S,
11:12 The people then said to S: "Who questioned
11:14 S said to the people,
12: 1 S addressed all Israel: "I have granted
12: 6 Continuing, S said to the people:
12:18 S then called to the LORD,
12:18 all the people dreaded the LORD and S.
12:19 They said to S, "Pray to the LORD your
12:20 "Do not fear," S answered them.
13: 8 the time S had determined.
13: 8 When S did not arrive at Gilgal,
13:10 just finished this offering when S arrived.
13:11 went out to greet him, and S asked him,
13:15 S set out from Gilgal and went his own way;
15: 1 S said to Saul: "It was I the LORD sent
15:10 Then the LORD spoke to S:
15:11 At this S grew angry and cried out to the
15:13 When S came to him, Saul greeted him:
15:14 S asked, "What, then, is the meaning
15:16 S said to Saul: "Stop! Let me tell you
15:17 S then said: "Though little in your own
15:20 Saul answered S: "I did indeed obey
15:22 But S said: "Does the LORD so delight
15:24 Saul replied to S: "I have sinned,
15:26 S said to Saul, "I will not return with you
15:27 S turned to go, Saul seized a loose end
15:28 So S said to him: "The LORD has torn
15:31 And so S returned with him,
15:32 Afterward S commanded,
15:33 S said, "As your sword has made women
15:34 S departed for Ramah,
15:35 again, as long as he lived, did S see Saul.
16: 1 The LORD said to S: "How long will you
16: 2 But S replied: "How can I go?
16: 4 S did as the LORD had commanded him.
16: 7 But the LORD said to S: "Do not judge
16: 8 Abinadab and presented him before S,
16: 9 Next Jesse presented Shammah, but S said,
16:10 sons before Samuel, but S said to Jesse,
16:11 S asked Jesse, "Are these all the sons
16:11 S said to Jesse, "Send for him;
16:13 Then S, with the horn of oil in hand,
16:13 When S took his leave, he went to Ramah.
19:18 he went to S in Ramah,
19:18 Then he and S went to stay in the sheds.
19:20 the band of prophets, presided over by S,
19:22 he inquired, "Where are S and David?",
19:24 the prophetic state in the presence of S;
25: 1 S died, and all Israel gathered to mourn
28: 3 Now S had died and,
28:11 and he answered, S."
28:12 woman saw S, she shrieked at the top of
28:14 Saul knew that it was S,
28:15 S then said to Saul, "Why do you disturb
28:16 To this S said: "But why do you ask me
1Chr 6:12 whose son was Elkanah, whose son was S.
6:13 The sons of S were Joel,
6:18 Heman, the chanter, son of Joel, son of S,
9:22 David and S the seer had established them
11: 3 the word of the LORD as revealed through S.
26:28 Also, whatever S the seer,
29:29 found written in the history of S the seer,
2Chr 35:18 in Israel since the time of the prophet S,
Ps(s) 99: 6 and Aaron were among his priests, and S,
Sir 46:13 to the LORD as a prophet, was S,
46:19 When S approached the end of his life,
Jer 15: 1 Even if Moses and S stood before me,
Acts 3:24 prophets who have spoken, from S onward,
13:20 rule them until the time of the prophet S.
Heb 11:32 Jephthah, of David and S and the prophets,

SAMUEL'S (3)

1Sm 8:19 refused to listen to S warning and said,
13:13 S response was: "You have been foolish!
28:20 for he was badly shaken by S message.

SANBALLAT (10)

Neh 2:10 When S the Horonite and Tobiah the
2:19 On hearing of this, S the Horonite,
3:33 S heard that we were rebuilding the wall,
4: 1 When S, Tobiah, the Arabs,
6: 1 When it had been reported to S,
6: 2 gates), S and Geshem sent me this message:
6: 5 S sent me the same message by one of his
6:12 because Tobiah and S had bribed him,
6:14 Keep in mind Tobiah and S,
13:28 was the son-in-law of S the Horonite!

SANCTIFICATION (3)

Rom 6:19 now the servants of justice for their s.
6:22 is s as you tend toward eternal life.
1Cor 1:30 him our wisdom and also our justice, our s,

SANCTIFIED (15)

1Chr 15:14 Levites s themselves to bring up the ark
2Chr 29:15 their brethren together and s themselves;
29:34 completed and the priests had s themselves;
30: 3 had not s themselves in sufficient numbers,
30:15 s themselves and brought holocausts into
30:17 many in the assembly had not s themselves,
30:24 The priests s themselves in great numbers,
Jdt 11:13 wine and oil which they had s and reserved
2Mc 1:25 evil, who chose our forefathers and s them:
2: 8 that the Place might be gloriously s."
Hg 2:12 If a man carries s flesh in the fold of
2:12 oil, or any other food, do they become s?
Heb 10:10 we have been s through the offering of the
10:14 forever perfected those who are being s.
10:29 by which he was s to be ordinary,

SANCTIFIES (3)

Sir 33: 9 Some he dignifies and s,
33:12 great, some he s and draws to himself.
Heb 5:13 milk alone is ignorant of the word that s,

SANCTIFY (19)

Ex 19:10 have them s themselves today and tomorrow.
19:14 them s themselves and wash their garments.
19:22 who approach the LORD must s themselves;
Lv 20: 7 S yourselves, then, and be holy;
Nm 11:18 S yourselves for tomorrow,
Jos 3: 5 also said to the people, S yourselves,
7:13 Rise, s the people.
7:13 Tell them to s themselves before tomorrow,
1Chr 15:12 must s yourselves along with your brethren
2Chr 29: 5 S yourselves now and sanctify the house of
29:34 willing than the priests to s themselves.
31:18 since they were to s themselves by sharing
35: 6 Slay the Passover sacrifice, s yourselves,
2Mc 1:26 Israel and guard and s your heritage.
Jb 1: 5 course, Job would send for them and s them,
Is 66:17 They who s and purify themselves to go to
Heb 9:13 the sprinkling of a heifer's ashes can s
13:12 the gate, to s the people by his own blood.

SANCTION (3)

Dt 29:11 with you today under this s of a curse,
29:13 this covenant, under this s of a curse;
Neh 10:30 and with the s of a curse take this oath

SANCTIONED (1)

1Kgs 8:31 is required to take an oath s by a curse,

SANCTITY (6)

Nm 20:12 showing forth my s before the Israelites,
20:13 and where he revealed his s among them.
27:14 my s to them by means of the water."
Dt 32:51 to manifest my s among the Israelites.
2Mc 3:12 placed their trust in the s of the Place
1Thes 4: 4 of you guarding his member in s and honor,

SANCTUARIES (7)

Lv 26:31 waste your cities and devastate your s,
1Sm 7:16 and judging Israel at each of these s.
2Mc 11: 3 as he did on the s of the other nations;
Ez 7:24 strength, and their s shall be profaned.
28:18 your sinful trade, I have profaned your s,
Am 7: 9 waste, and the s of Israel made desolate;
Acts 17:24 does not dwell in s made by human hands;

SANCTUARY (233)

Ex 15:17 where you made your seat, O LORD, the s,
25: 8 "They shall make a s for me,
28:29 "Whenever Aaron enters the s,
28:35 and leaves the LORD's presence in the s;
28:43 or approach the altar to minister in the s,
29:30 tent to minister in the s shall be clothed
30:13 according to the standard of the s shekel,
30:24 according to the standard of the s shekel;
31:11 oil, and the fragrant incense for the s.
35:19 the service cloths for use in the s;
36: 1 all the work for the service of the s.
36: 3 for establishing the service of the s.
36: 4 the various kinds of work for the s,
36: 6 make any more contributions for the s."
38:24 used in the entire construction of the s,
38:24 according to the standard of the s shekel;
38:25 according to the standard of the s shekel;
38:26 according to the standard of the s shekel,
38:27 of the s and the pedestals of the veil,
39: 1 woven the service cloths for use in the s,
39:41 the service cloths for use in the s,
Lv 4: 6 before the LORD, toward the veil of the s.
5:15 according to the standard of the s shekel.
5:16 what he has sinfully withheld from the s,
6:23 meeting tent to make atonement in the s;
10: 4 remove your kinsmen from the s and carry
10:18 not brought into the inmost part of the s,
10:18 have eaten the offering in the s,
12: 4 not touch anything sacred nor enter the s
16: 2 to come whenever he pleases into the s,
16: 3 Only in this way may Aaron enter the s.
16:16 Thus he shall make atonement for the s
16:17 the s to make atonement until he departs.
16:20 completed the atonement rite for the s,
16:23 shall strip off and leave in the s the linen
16:27 was brought into the s to make atonement,
16:33 and make atonement for the sacred s,
19:30 Keep my sabbaths, and reverence my s.
20: 3 has defiled my s and profaned my holy name.
21:12 s; otherwise he will profane the sanctuary
26: 2 Keep my sabbaths, and reverence my s.
27: 3 and sixty, the fixed sum, in s shekels,
27:25 according to the standard of the s shekel.
Nm 3:28 They had charge of the s.
3:31 which the ministry of the s was exercised,
3:32 over those who had charge of the s.
3:38 obligations of the s for the Israelites.
3:47 according to the standard of the s shekel,
3:50 shekels according to the s standard.
4:12 Taking the utensils of the s service,
7:13 thirty shekels according to the s standard
7:19 thirty shekels according to the s standard
7:25 thirty shekels according to the s standard
7:31 thirty shekels according to the s standard
7:37 thirty shekels according to the s standard
7:43 thirty shekels according to the s standard
7:49 thirty shekels according to the s standard
7:55 thirty shekels according to the s standard
7:61 thirty shekels according to the s standard
7:67 thirty shekels according to the s standard
7:73 thirty shekels according to the s standard
7:79 thirty shekels according to the s standard
7:85 shekels, according to the s standard.
7:86 apiece, according to the s standard,
8:19 the Israelites should they come near the s."
18: 1 house shall be responsible for the s;
18: 5 have charge of the s and of the altar,
18:16 silver shekels according to the s standard,
19:20 because he defiles the s of the LORD.
28: 7 LORD in the s a fourth of a hin of wine.
Jos 24:26 the oak that was in the s of the LORD.
Jgs 17: 5 Thus the layman Micah had a s.
1Sm 1: 7 made their pilgrimage to the s of the LORD,
2:14 were treated who came to the s at Shiloh.
1Kgs 6: 5 temple, which enclosed the nave and the s,
6:16 the floor to the rafters, enclosing the s,
6:17 or part of the temple in front of the s,
6:19 s to house the ark of the LORD's covenant,
6:21 He made in front of the s a cedar altar,
6:22 before the s was also overlaid with gold.
6:23 In the s were two cherubim,
6:31 At the entrance of the s,
7:49 right and five to the left before the s,
8: 6 beneath the wings of the cherubim in the s,
8: 8 part of the holy place adjoining the s;
1Chr 22:19 Proceed to build the s of the LORD God,
23:32 them concerning the meeting tent, the s,
28:10 has chosen you to build a house as his s.
2Chr 4:20 according to prescription before the s,
5: 7 beneath the wings of the cherubim in the s,
5: 9 that part of the holy place nearest the s;
20: 8 it and they built in it a s to your honor,
26:18 Leave the s, for you have broken faith
29: 5 and clean out the filth from the s.
29: 7 in the s to the honor of the God of Israel.
29:21 a sin offering for the kingdom, for the s,
30: 8 to his s that he has consecrated forever,
35: 5 Stand in the s according to the divisions
36:17 their young men in their own s building,
Neh 10:40 also are housed the utensils of the s,
Jdt 4:12 or the s to be profaned and mocked for the
4:13 the s of the Lord Almighty in Jerusalem.
5:19 repossessed Jerusalem, where their s is,
8:21 Judea will fall, our s will be plundered,
8:24 depend on us, and the defense of the s,
9: 8 for they have resolved to profane your s,
16:20 celebration in Jerusalem before the s,
1Mc 1:21 the s and took away the golden altar,
1:36 citadel became an ambush against the s,
1:37 around the s; they defiled the sanctuary.
1:39 Her s was as desolate as a wilderness;

1:45 sacrifices, and libations in the *s,*
1:46 desecrate the *s* and the sacred ministers,
2: 7 and the *s* into the hands of strangers?
2:12 *s* and our beauty and our glory laid waste,
3:43 estate, and fight for our people and our *s!"*
3:45 The *s* was trampled on,
3:51 your *s* has been trampled on and profaned,
3:58 against us to destroy us and our *s.*
3:59 witness the ruin of our nation and our *s.*
4:36 us go up to purify the *s* and rededicate it."
4:38 They found the *s* desolate,
4:41 in the citadel, while he purified the *s.*
4:43 these purified the *s* and carried away the
4:48 They also repaired the *s* and the interior
5: 1 rebuilt and the *s* consecrated as before,
6: 7 had surrounded with high walls both the *s,*
6:18 were hemming in Israel around the *s,*
6:26 and they have fortified the *s* and Beth-zur.
6:51 For many days he besieged the *s,*
6:54 Few men remained in the *s;*
7:33 Some of the priests from the *s* and some of
7:36 in and stood before the altar and the *s.*
7:42 Nicanor spoke wickedly against your *s;*
9:54 the inner court of the *s* to be torn down,
10:39 I give as a present to the *s* in Jerusalem
10:39 for the necessary expenses of the *s.*
10:42 of the *s* every year shall be canceled,
10:44 structures of the *s* shall be covered
13: 3 house have done for the laws and the *s;*
13: 6 Rather will I avenge my nation and the *s,*
14:29 that their *s* and law might be maintained,
2Mc 4:33 withdrawing to the inviolable *s* at Daphne,
4:34 in spite of his suspicions, to leave the *s.*
15:18 foremost fear was for the consecrated *s.*
Ps(s) 20: 3 May he send you help from the *s,*
60: 8 God promised in his *s:*
63: 3 in the *s* to see your power and your glory,
68:18 the Lord advances from Sinai to the *s.*
68:25 progress of my God, my King, into the *s;*
68:36 Awesome in his *s* is God,
73:17 Till I entered the *s* of God and considered
74: 3 all the damage the enemy has done in the *s.*
74: 7 They set your *s* on fire;
96: 6 praise and grandeur are in his *s.*
108: 8 God promised in his *s:*
114: 2 people of alien tongue, Judah became his *s,*
134: 2 Lift up your hands toward the *s,*
150: 1 Praise the LORD in his *s,*
Sir 45: 9 each step He would be heard within the *s,*
45:24 of friendship, to provide for the *s,*
47:10 before daybreak the *s* would resound,
47:13 name of God, and established a lasting *s.*
50:11 and lent majesty to the court of the *s.*
Is 16:12 high places, he shall enter his *s* to pray,
60:13 and the pine, To bring beauty to my *s,*
62: 9 shall drink the wine in the courts of my *s.*
63:18 why have our enemies trampled your *s?*
Lam 1:10 She has seen those nations enter her *s*
2: 7 has disowned his altar, rejected his *s;*
2:20 prophet to be slain in the *s* of the LORD?
Ez 5:11 my *s* with all your detestable abominations,
8: 6 here, so that I must depart from my *s?*
9: 6 any marked with the X; begin at my *s.*
11:16 *s* in the countries to which they had gone
21: 7 toward Jerusalem, preach against their *s,*
23:38 defiled my *s* and desecrated my sabbaths.
23:39 idols, they entered my *s* to desecrate it.
24:21 I will now desecrate my *s,*
25: 3 out your joy over the desecration of my *s,*
37:26 them, and put my *s* among them forever.
37:28 my *s* shall be set up among them forever.
42:13 border on the free area are the *s* chambers;
43:21 part of the temple, outside the *s.*
44: 1 brought me back to the outer gate of the *s,*
44: 5 those who are to be excluded from the *s.*
44: 7 *s* to profane it when you offered me food,
44: 8 as these to serve me in my *s* in your stead.
44: 9 heart and in flesh, shall ever enter my *s;*
44:11 in my *s* as gatekeepers and temple servants;
44:15 my *s* when the Israelites strayed from me,
44:16 It is they who shall enter my *s,*
44:19 and leave them in the chambers of the *s,*
44:27 the inner court to minister in the *s,*
45: 2 fifty cubits, shall be assigned to the *s.*
45: 3 thousand wide, within which shall be the *s,*
45: 4 to the priests, the ministers of the *s,*
45:18 young bull as a sacrifice to purify the *s.*
46:19 of the gate to the chambers [of the *s,*
47:12 shall be watered by the flow from the *s.*
48: 8 In the center of the tract shall be the *s.*
48:10 the *s* of the LORD shall be in its center.
48:21 the *s* of the temple shall be in the middle.
Dn 8:11 daily sacrifice, and whose *s* it cast down,
8:13 sin which is placed there, the *s,*
8:14 then the *s* shall be purified."
9:17 let your face shine upon your desolate *s.*
9:26 a leader who will come shall destroy the *s.*
11:31 at his command and defile the *s* stronghold,
Am 7:13 for it is the king's *s* and a royal temple."
Mt 26:61 God's *s* and rebuild it in three days.'"
27:51 the *s* was torn in two from top to bottom.
Mk 15:38 the *s* was torn in two from top to bottom.
Lk 1: 9 enter the *s* of the Lord and offer incense.
11:51 met his death between the altar and the *s!*
23:45 The curtain in the *s* was torn in two.
Jn 11:48 in and sweep away our *s* and our nation."
Acts 21:28 against our people, our law, and this *s.*
Heb 8: 2 the *s* and of that true tabernacle set up,
8: 5 They offer worship in a *s* which is only a
9: 1 regulations for worship and an earthly *s.*
9: 8 way into the *s* had not yet been revealed.
9:11 to be, he entered once for all into the *s,*
9:24 did not enter into a *s* made by hands,
9:25 into the *s* with blood that is not his own;
10:19 Jesus assures our entrance into the *s*
13:11 animals whose blood is brought into the *s*
Rv 15: 5 *s* which is the tent of witness opened up,
15: 8 Then the *s* became so filled with the smoke
16: 1 voice from the *s* say to the seven angels,
16:17 in the *s* came a loud voice which said,

SAND (16)

Ex 2:12 he slew the Egyptian and hid him in the *s.*
Dt 33:19 the seas and the hidden treasures of the *s."*
1Kgs 5: 9 as vast as the *s* on the seashore.
Jb 30: 6 of the wadies, in caves of *s* and stone;
39:14 on the ground and deposits them in the *s,*
Ps(s) 78:27 them like dust, and, like the *s* of the sea,
Prv 27: 3 Stone is heavy, and *s* a burden,
Wis 7: 9 all gold, in view of her, is a little *s,*
Sir 1: 2 The *s* of the seashore,
18: 8 a drop of sea water, like a grain of *s,*
22:15 *S* and salt and an iron mass are easier to
Is 10:22 O Israel, were like the *s* of the sea,
48:19 Your descendants would be like the *s,*
Dn 3:36 heaven, or the *s* on the shore of the sea.
Hos 2: 1 Israelites shall be like the *s* of the sea,
Hb 1: 9 a stormwind that heaps up captives like *s.*

SANDAL (10)

Gn 14:23 or a *s* strap from anything that is yours,
Dt 25: 9 his *s* from his foot and spit in his face,
25:10 'the family of the man stripped of his *s.'*
Ru 4: 7 take off his *s* and give it to the other.
4: 8 it for yourself," drew off his *s.*
1Kgs 2: 5 belt about my waist and the *s* on my foot.
Is 5:27 belt loose, nor the thong of his *s* broken.
Mk 1: 7 not fit to stoop and untie his *s* straps.
Lk 3:16 I am not fit to loosen his *s* strap.
Jn 1:27 of whose *s* I am not worthy to unfasten."

SANDALS (25)

Ex 3: 5 Remove the *s* from your feet,
12:11 *s* on your feet and your staff in hand,
Dt 29: 4 you in tatters nor your *s* from your feet;
Jos 5:15 to Joshua, "Remove your *s* from your feet,
9: 5 wore old, patched *s* and shabby garments;
9:13 Look at our garments and *s,*
2Chr 28:15 they clothed them, put *s* on their feet,
Jdt 10: 4 She chose *s* for her feet,
16: 9 Her *s* caught his eyes,
Sg 7: 2 How beautiful are your feet in *s,*
Is 11:15 streamlets, so that it can be crossed in *s.*
20: 2 waist, and remove the *s* from your feet.
Ez 16:10 gown, put *s* of fine leather on your feet;
24:17 on your turban, put your *s* on your feet,
24:23 remain on your heads, your *s* on your feet.
Am 2: 6 silver, and the poor man for a pair of *s.*
8: 6 silver, and the poor man for a pair of *s;*
Mt 3:11 I am not even fit to carry his *s.*
10:10 no traveling bag, no change of shirt, no *s,*
Mk 6: 9 They were, however, to wear *s.*
Lk 10: 4 wear no *s* and greet no one along the way.
22:35 without purse or traveling bag or *s,*
Acts 7:33 'Remove the *s* from your feet,
12: 8 angel said, "Put on your belt and your *s!"*
13:25 not worthy to unfasten the *s* on his feet.'

SANDBAR (1)

Acts 27:41 but the ship hit a *s* and ran aground.

SANDS (17)

Gn 22:17 stars of the sky and the *s* of the seashore;
32:13 your descendants like the *s* of the sea,
41:49 grain in quantities like the *s* of the sea,
Jos 11: 4 an army numerous as the *s* on the seashore,
Jgs 7:12 were as many as the *s* on the seashore.
1Sm 13: 5 as numerous as the *s* of the seashore.
2Sm 17:11 who are as numerous as the *s* by the sea,
1Kgs 4:20 were as numerous as the *s* by the sea;
1Mc 11: 1 as numerous as the *s* of the seashore,
Jb 6: 3 They would now outweigh the *s* of the sea!
Ps(s) 139:18 recount them, they would outnumber the *s:*
Is 35: 7 The burning *s* will become pools,
Jer 15: 8 numerous before me than the *s* of the sea.
33:22 the *s* of the sea which cannot be counted,
Rom 9:27 Israelites should be as the *s* of the sea,
Heb 11:12 in the sky and the *s* of the seashore.
Rv 20: 8 and Magog, numerous as the *s* of the sea.

SANDY (4)

Sir 25:19 Like a *s* hill to aged feet is a railing
Jer 5:22 I made the *s* shore the sea's limit,
Mt 7:26 man who built his house on *s* ground.
Acts 27:39 They could make out a bay with a *s* beach,

SANE (1)

Mk 5:15 sitting fully clothed and perfectly *s,*

SANG (30)

Ex 15: 1 and the Israelites *s* this song to the LORD:
15:19 They *s* thus because Pharaoh's horses and
Nm 21:17 Then it was that Israel *s* this song:
Jgs 5: 1 [and Barak, son of Abinoam,] *s* this song:
1Sm 18: 7 The women played and *s:*
2Sm 1:18 he *s:* "Alas! the glory of Israel
3:33 And the king *s* this elegy over Abner:
22: 1 David *s* the words of this song to the LORD
22: 2 This is what he *s:* "O LORD, my rock,
1Chr 25: 2 under the direction of Aspah who *s*
25: 3 who *s* inspired songs to the accompaniment
2Chr 20:21 They *s:* "Give thanks to the LORD,
29:30 They *s* praises till their joy was full,
30:21 and the Levites and the priests *s* the
2Mc 10: 7 they *s* hymns of grateful praise to him who
Jb 38: 7 While the morning stars *s* in chorus and
Ps(s) 18: 1 who *s* to the Lord the words of this song
78:64 by the sword, and their widows *s* no dirges.
106:12 they believed his words and *s* his praises.
Sg 6: 9 and concubines, and they *s* her praises;
Wis 10:20 and they *s,*
Sir 47: 6 Therefore the women *s* his praises and
Dn 3:51 three in the furnace with one voice *s,*
Mt 11:17 We *s* you a dirge but you did not wail!'
Lk 7:32 We *s* you a dirge but you did not wail.'
Rv 4: 8 Day and night, without pause, they *s:*
5: 9 This is the new hymn they *s:*
15: 3 God, and they *s* the song of Moses,
19: 3 Once more they *s* "Alleluia!"
19: 4 worshiped God seated on the throne and *s,*

SANHEDRIN (25)

Mt 5:22 his brother shall be answerable to the *S,*
26:59 The chief priests, with the whole *S,*
Mk 14:55 The chief priests with the whole *S* were
15: 1 elders and scribes (that is, the whole *S),*
15:43 a distinguished member of the *S.*
Lk 23:50 an upright and holy member of the *S,*
Jn 3: 1 named Nicodemus, a member of the Jewish *S,*
7:48 do not see any of the *S* believing in him,
11:47 the Pharisees called a meeting of the *S.*
12:42 There were many, even among the *S,*
Acts 5:21 supporters arrived they convoked the *S,*
5:27 them in and made them stand before the *S,*
5:33 When the *S* heard this,
5:34 Then a member of the *S* stood up,
5:40 the *S* called in the apostles and had them
5:41 The apostles for their part left the *S*
6:12 him, seized him, and led him off to the *S.*
6:15 the *S* who sat there stared at him intently.
22:30 chief priests and the whole *S* to a meeting;
23: 1 Paul gazed intently at the *S.*
23: 6 Consequently he spoke out before the *S:*
23:15 Now, together with the *S,*
23:20 to have Paul brought down to the *S,*
23:27 I then had him brought before the *S,*
24:20 me guilty of when I stood before the *S,*

SANK (12)

Gn 42:28 At that their hearts *s.*
Ex 15: 5 they *s* into the depths like a stone.
15:10 like lead they *s* in the mighty waters.
Nm 21:18 The well that was the princes *s,*
Jgs 5:27 At her feet he *s* down, fell, lay still;
5:27 feet he *s* and fell; where he sank down
1Mc 12:28 battle, their hearts *s* with fear and dread.
Ps(s) 107:26 they *s* to the depths; their hearts melted
Jer 38: 6 only mud, and Jeremiah *s* into the mud.
Ez 27:27 *S* into the heart of the sea on the day
Lk 5: 7 filled the two boats until they nearly *s.*

SANSANNAH (1)

Jos 15:31 Chesil, Hormah, Ziklag, Madmannah, *S,*

SAP (3)

Lv 26:16 and fever to dim the eyes and *s* the life.
Jb 8:16 He is full of *s* before sunrise,
Mk 13:28 Once the *s* of its branches runs high and

SAPH (1)

2Sm 21:18 occasion Sibbecai, from Husha, killed *S,*

SAPLING (1)

Is 53: 2 He grew up like a *s* before him,

SAPPED (1)

Hos 7: 9 Strangers have *s* his strength,

SAPPHIRA (1)

Acts 5: 1 wife *S* likewise sold a piece of property.

SAPPHIRE (10)

Ex 24:10 his feet there appeared to be s tilework,
28:18 the second row, a garnet, a s and a beryl;
39:11 the second row, a garnet, a s and a beryl;
Tb 13:16 shall be built with s and emerald,
Jb 28:16 of Ophir, with the precious onyx or the s.
Lam 4: 7 ruddy than coral, more precious than s.
Ez 1:26 a throne could be seen, looking like s.
10: 1 the cherubim what appeared to be a s stone;
28:13 beryl, chrysolite, onyx, and jasper, s,
Rv 21:19 course of stones was jasper, the second s,

SAPPHIRES (3)

Jb 28: 6 Its stones are the source of s,
Sg 5:14 His body is a work of ivory covered with s.
Is 54:11 in carnelians, and your foundations in s;

SARAH (55)

Gn 17:15 her name shall be S.
17:17 Or can S give birth at ninety?"
17:19 your wife S is to bear you a son,
17:21 S shall bear to you by this time next year."
18: 6 Abraham hastened into the tent and told S,
18: 9 "Where is your wife S?"
18:10 time next year, and S will then have a son."
18:10 S was listening at the entrance of the tent,
18:11 Now Abraham and S were old,
18:11 S had stopped having her womanly periods.
18:12 So S laughed to herself and said,
18:13 "Why did S laugh and say,
18:14 will return to you, and S will have a son."
18:15 Because she was afraid, S dissembled,
20: 2 he stayed in Gerar, he said of his wife S,
20: 2 Abimelech, king of Gerar, sent and took S.
20:14 and after he restored his wife S to him,
20:16 To S he said: "See, I have given
20:18 household on account of Abraham's wife S.
21: 1 took note of S as he had said he would;
21: 2 S became pregnant and bore Abraham a son
21: 3 Isaac to this son of his whom S bore him.
21: 6 S then said,
21: 7 she added, "that S would nurse children!
21: 9 S noticed the son whom Hagar the Egyptian
21:12 Heed the demands of S,
23:19 S in the cave of the field of Machpelah,
24:36 S bore a son to my master in her old age,
24:67 solace after the death of his mother S.
25:10 there he was buried next to his wife S.
49:31 There Abraham and his wife S are buried,
Tb 3: 7 daughter S also had to listen to abuse,
3:17 Raguel's daughter S to Tobit's son Tobiah,
3:17 daughter S came downstairs from her room.
6:11 He has a daughter named S,
6:16 another thought to this demon, but marry S.
7: 8 and even their daughter S began to weep.
7: 9 ask Raguel to let me marry my kinswoman S."
7:10 entitled to marry my daughter S than you,
7:12 Then Raguel called his daughter S,
7:13 marriage contract stating that he gave S
10:10 promptly handed over to Tobiah S his wife,
10:11 grant prosperity to you and to your wife S.
10:12 he kissed his daughter S and said to her:
10:13 of you and of my daughter S before I die.
10:13 on I am your mother, and S is your beloved.
11:15 that he had married Raguel's daughter S,
11:17 When Tobit reached S,
12:12 you that when you, Tobit, and S prayed,
12:14 me to heal you and your daughter-in-law, S.
Is 51: 2 Look to Abraham, your father, and to S,
Rom 4:19 years old), and of the dead womb of S.
9: 9 at this time, and S shall have a son."
Heb 11:11 By faith S received power to conceive
1Pt 3: 6 for example, S,

SARAH'S (3)

Gn 23: 1 The span of S life was one hundred and
25:12 Ishmael, whom Hagar the Egyptian, S slave,
Tb 6:12 Since you are S closest relative,

SARAI (16)

Gn 11:29 the name of Abram's wife was S,
11:30 S was barren; she had no child.
11:31 son of Haran, and his daughter-in-law S,
12: 5 Abram took his wife S,
12:11 to enter Egypt, he said to his wife S:
12:17 severe plagues because of Abram's wife S.
16: 1 Abram's wife S had borne him no children.
16: 2 S said to Abram: "The LORD has kept me
16: 3 land of Canaan, his wife S took her maid,
16: 5 So S said to Abram: "You are responsible
16: 6 Abram told S: "Your maid is in your power.
16: 6 S then abused her so much that Hagar ran
16: 8 to Shur, and he asked, "Hagar maid of S,
16: 8 "I am running away from my mistress, S."
17:15 for your wife Sarai, do not call her S;

SARAI'S (1)

Gn 16: 2 Abram heeded S request.

SARAPH (6)

Nm 21: 6 the LORD sent among the people s serpents,
21: 8 Moses, "Make a s and mount it on a pole,
Dt 8:15 desert with its s serpents and scorpions,
1Chr 4:22 and Joash and S,
Is 14:29 an adder, its fruit shall be a flying s.
30: 6 roaring lion, of the viper and flying s,

SARASADAI (1)

Jdt 8: 1 of Nathanael, son of Salamiel, son of S,

SARDIS (3)

Rv 1:11 to Ephesus, Smyrna, Pergamum, Thyatira, S,
3: 1 the presiding spirit of the church in S,
3: 4 I realize that you have in S a few persons

SARDONYX (1)

Rv 21:20 the fifth s, the sixth carnelian,

SARGON (1)

Is 20: 1 In the year the general sent by S,

SARID (2)

Jos 19:10 The limit of their heritage was at S.
19:12 From S eastward it ran to the district of

SASH (9)

Ex 28: 4 a robe, a brocaded tunic, a miter and a s.
28:39 The s shall be of variegated work.
Lv 8: 7 the tunic on Aaron, girded him with the s,
16: 4 the linen s and put on the linen miter.
Is 22:21 with your robe, and gird him with your s,
Jer 2:32 virgin forget her jewelry, a bride her s?
Ez 16:10 you a fine linen s and silk robes to wear.
Rv 1:13 robe, with a s of gold about his breast.
15: 6 each with a s of gold about his breast.

SASHES (5)

Ex 28:40 shall have tunics and s and turbans made.
29: 9 them with the tunics, gird them with the s,
39:29 and s of variegated work made of fine
Lv 8:13 them with tunics, girded them with s,
Ez 23:15 with s girded about their waists,

SAT (75)

Gn 18: 1 Mamre, as he s in the entrance of his tent,
21:16 and then went and s down opposite him,
21:16 As she s opposite him, he began to cry.
23:10 of the Hittites who s on his town council:
23:18 Hittites who s on Ephron's town council.
37:25 They then s down to their meal.
38:14 shawl, and s down at the entrance to Enaim,
48: 2 he rallied his strength and s up in bed.
Ex 16: 3 as we s by our fleshpots and ate our fill
18:13 day Moses s in judgment for the people,
32: 6 Then they s down to eat and drink,
Jgs 3:20 where he s alone in his cool upper room,
6:11 Then the angel of the LORD came and s
Ru 2:14 Then as she s near the reapers,
1Sm 20:24 new moon, when the king s at table to dine,
20:25 s facing him, while Abner sat
28:23 got up from the ground, and s on a couch.
2Sm 2:13 And they s down,
7:18 went in and s before the LORD and said,
19: 9 So the king stepped out and s at the gate.
1Kgs 2:19 Then he s down upon his throne,
2:19 for the king's mother, who s at his right.
19: 4 he came to a broom tree and s beneath it.
1Chr 17:16 David came in and s in the LORD'S presence,
29:23 Thereafter Solomon s on the throne of the
Ezr 9: 3 my head and beard, and s there stupefied.
Tb 11: 5 Anna s watching the road by which her son
Est 3:15 The king and Haman then s down to feast,
1Mc 1:27 she who s in the bridal chamber mourned,
7: 4 them, and Demetrius s on the royal throne.
14: 9 Old men s in the squares,
14:12 man s under his vine and his fig tree,
Jb 2: 8 to scrape himself, as he s among the ashes.
2:13 Then they s down upon the ground with him
Ps(s) 137: 1 we s and wept when we remembered Zion.
Jer 15:17 Under the weight of your hand I s alone
Ez 3:15 for seven days I s among them distraught.
8: 1 house, and the elders of Judah s before me,
14: 1 elders of Israel came and s down before me,
20: 1 to consult the LORD and s down before me.
23:41 You s on a couch prepared for them,
Dn 7:10 stream of fire flowed out from where he s;
Jon 3: 6 himself with sackcloth, and s in the ashes.
Mt 5: 1 s down his disciples gathered around him,
13: 1 the house, Jesus s down by the lakeshore.
13:48 they hauled it ashore and s down to put
15:29 up onto the mountainside and s down there.
26:55 day I s teaching in the temple precincts,
26:58 s down with the guards to see the outcome.
27:36 they s down there and kept watch over him.
28: 2 to the stone, rolled it back, and s on it.
Mk 4: 1 that he went and s in a boat on the water,
9:35 So he s down and called the Twelve around
11: 7 cloaks across its back, and he s on it.
Lk 4:20 gave it back to the assistant and s down.
7:15 The dead man s up and began to speak.
18:35 man s at the side of the road begging.
22:55 sitting beside it, and Peter s among them.
Jn 4: 6 tired from his journey, s down at the well.
6: 3 and s down there with his disciples.
8: 2 to him, he s down and began to teach them.
11:20 she went to meet him, while Mary s at home.
Acts 6:15 who s there stared at him intently.
9:40 her eyes, then looked at Peter and s up.
13:14 day they entered the synagogue and s down.
16:13 We s down and spoke to the women who were
22: 3 Here I s at the feet of Gamaliel and was
1Cor 10: 7 says, "The people s down to eat and drink,
Rv 5: 1 the One who s on the throne I saw a scroll.
5: 7 right hand of the One who s on the throne.
14:14 and on the cloud s One like a Son of Man
14:15 voice cried out to him who s on the cloud,
20:11 large white throne and the One who s on it.
21: 5 The One who s on the throne said to me,

SATAN (53)

1Chr 21: 1 A s rose up against Israel,
Jb 1: 6 before the LORD, S also came among them.
1: 7 LORD said to S, "Whence do you come?"
1: 7 Then S answered the LORD and said,
1: 8 LORD said to S, "Have you noticed my
1: 9 But S answered the LORD and said,
1:12 LORD said to S, "Behold, all that he has
1:12 S went forth from the presence of the LORD.
2: 1 before the LORD, and S also came with them.
2: 2 LORD said to S, "Whence do you come?"
2: 2 And S answered the LORD and said,
2: 3 LORD said to S, "Have you noticed my
2: 4 And S answered the LORD and said,
2: 6 And the LORD said to S.
2: 7 So S went forth from the presence of the
Zec 3: 1 S stood at his right hand to accuse him.
3: 2 to Satan, "May the LORD rebuke you, S;
Mt 4:10 Jesus said to him, "Away with you, S!
12:26 If S is expelling Satan,
16:23 and said, "Get out of my sight, you s!
Mk 1:13 forty days, put to the test there by S.
3:23 "How can S expel Satan?
3:26 if S has suffered mutiny in his ranks and
4:15 S comes to carry off what was sown in them.
8:33 "Get out of my sight, you s!
16:20 lawless and faithless age is under S,
Lk 10:18 watched S fall from the sky like lightning.
11:18 If S is divided against himself,
13:16 in the bondage of S for eighteen years
22: 3 Then S took possession of Judas,
22:31 Remember that S has asked for you,
Jn 13:27 Immediately after, S entered his heart.
Acts 5: 3 why have you let S fill your heart so as
13:10 son of S and enemy of all that is right!
26:18 to light and from the dominion of S to God;
Rom 16:20 peace will quickly crush S under your feet.
1Cor 5: 5 over to S for the destruction of his flesh,
7: 5 that S may not tempt you through your lack
2Cor 2:11 sakes and, before Christ, to prevent S—
11:14 S disguises himself as an angel of light.
12: 7 an angel of S to beat me and keep me from
1Thes 2:18 but S blocked the way.
2Thes 2: 9 will appear as part of the workings of S,
1Tm 1:20 S so that they may learn not to blaspheme.
5:15 Already, some have turned away to follow S.
Rv 2:13 martyred in your city where S has his home.
2:24 of the so-called "deep secrets" of S;
12: 9 ancient serpent known as the devil or S,
20: 2 ancient serpent, who is the devil or S,
20: 7 are over, S will be released from his prison.

SATAN'S (4)

Mk 16:20 of the years of S power has been fulfilled,
Rv 2: 9 nothing other than members of S assembly.
2:13 the very place where S throne is erected;
3: 9 I mean to make some of S assembly,

SATE (1)

Dn 13:32 face so as to s themselves with her beauty.

SATED (5)

Ps(s) 123: 3 us, for we are more than s with contempt;
123: 4 than s with the mockery of the arrogant,
Jer 46:10 The sword devours, is s,
Lam 3:15 He has s me with bitter food,
Ez 16:49 and her daughters were proud, s with food,

SATES (1)

Prv 18:20 with the yield of his lips he s himself.

SATIRE (2)

Mi 2: 4 On that day a s shall be sung over you,
Hb 2: 6 him, s and epigrams about him to say:

SATISFIED (24)

Ex 18:23 and all these people will go home s."
Lv 10:20 On hearing this, Moses was s.
Nm 16:13 Are you not s with having led us here away

Jos 22:30 the Manassehites had to say, they were *s.*
22:33 The report *s* the Israelites,
1Kgs 9:12 had given him, but was not *s* with them.
Est C:19 they are not *s* with our bitter servitude,
2Mc 5:15 Not *s* with this,
Ps(s) 63: 6 riches of a banquet shall my soul be *s,*
105:40 and with bread from heaven he *s* them.
107: 9 Because he *s* the longing soul and filled
Prv 6:35 nor be *s* with the greatest gifts.
13: 4 in vain, but the diligent soul is amply *s.*
27:20 The nether world and the abyss are never *s;*
30:15 Three things are never *s,*
Eccl 1: 8 The eye is not *s* with seeing nor is the
5: 9 The covetous man is never *s* with money,
Ez 16:28 the Assyrians, because you were not *s;*
16:28 the harlot with them, you were still not *s.*
16:29 but despite this, you were still not *s.*
Hos 4:10 They shall eat but not be *s,*
Mi 6:14 You shall eat, without being *s,*
Hg 1: 6 you have eaten, but have not been *s;*
1Cor 4: 8 At the moment you are completely *s.*

SATISFIES (1)

Est 5:13 Yet none of this *s* me as long as I

SATISFY (11)

Ps(s) 145:16 and *s* the desire of every living thing.
Prv 6:30 steals to *s* his appetite when he is hungry;
Eccl 4: 8 his toil, and riches do not *s* his greed.
Sir 18:31 If you *s* your lustful appetites they will
39:21 Everything is chosen to *s* a need.
Is 55: 2 your wages for what fails to *s?*
58:10 bread on the hungry and *s* the afflicted;
Ez 7:19 to *s* their craving or fill their bellies,
Mt 15:33 in this deserted spot to *s* such a crowd?"
Mk 7:27 the household *s* themselves at table first.
15:15 So Pilate, who wished to *s* the crowd,

SATRAPIES (1)

Est 8:12 and twenty-seven *s* from India to Ethiopia,

SATRAPS (15)

Ezr 8:36 king were presented to the king's *s*
Jdt 5: 2 all the *s* of the seacoast and said to them:
Est 3:12 of Haman, an order to the royal *s,*
B: 1 great King Ahasuerus writes to the *s*
8: 9 they wrote to the Jews and to the *s,*
9: 3 all the officials of the provinces, the *s,*
Jer 51:23 team, with you I shatter *s* and prefects.
Dn 3: 2 He then ordered the *s,*
3: 3 The *s,* prefects, and governors,
3:94 the *s,* prefects, governors, and nobles
6: 2 entire kingdom one hundred and twenty *s,*
6: 4 Daniel outshone all the supervisors and *s*
6: 5 Therefore the supervisors and *s* tried to
6: 7 So these supervisors and *s* went thronging
6: 8 of the kingdom, the prefects, *s,*

SATURATED (1)

Prv 30:16 the earth, that is never *s* with water,

SATYRS (6)

Lv 17: 7 they offer their sacrifices to the *s*
2Kgs 23: 8 also tore down the high place of the *s,*
2Chr 11:15 high places and *s* and calves he had made.
Is 13:21 ostriches shall dwell, and *s* shall dance.
34:11 to be an empty waste for *s* to dwell in.
34:14 *s* shall call to one another;

SAUCE (1)

Ru 2:14 dip your bread in the *s.*"

SAUL (372)

1Sm 9: 2 He had a son named *S,*
9: 2 was no other Israelite handsomer than *S;*
9: 3 Kish said to his son *S,*
9: 5 *S* said to the servant who was with him,
9: 7 But *S* said to his servant,
9: 8 Again the servant answered *S,*
9:10 *S* then said to his servant, "Well said!
9:17 When Samuel caught sight of *S,*
9:18 *S* met Samuel in the gateway and said,
9:19 Samuel answered *S:* "I am the seer.
9:21 *S* replied: "Am I not a Benjaminite,
9:22 Samuel then took *S* and his servant and
9:24 what went with it, and placed it before *S.*
9:24 Thus *S* dined with Samuel that day.
9:25 a mattress was spread for *S* on the roof,
9:26 At daybreak Samuel called to *S* on the roof,
9:26 *S* rose, and he and Samuel went outside
9:27 the edge of town, Samuel said to *S,*
10: 9 As *S* turned to leave Samuel,
10:11 Is *S* also among the prophets?"
10:12 arose, "Is *S* also among the prophets?"
10:14 *S* replied, "To look for the asses.
10:16 *S* said to his uncle, "He assured us that
10:21 clan of Matri was chosen, and finally *S,*
10:26 *S* also went home to Gibeah,
11: 4 the messengers arrived at Gibeah of *S,*
11: 5 Just then *S* came in from the field,
11: 7 does not come out to follow *S* [and Samuel],
11:11 *S* arranged his troops in three companies
11:12 questioned whether *S* should rule over us?
11:13 *S* broke in to say, "No man is to be put
11:15 the presence of the LORD, they made *S* king.
11:15 and *S* and all the Israelites celebrated
13: 1 *S* was . . . years old
13: 2 *S* chose three thousand men of Israel,
13: 3 *S* sounded the horn throughout the land,
13: 4 Thus all Israel learned that *S* had
13: 4 the soldiers were called up to *S* in Gilgal.
13: 7 *S,* however, held out at Gilgal,
13: 8 Gilgal, the men began to slip away from *S.*
13:10 *S* went out to greet him,
13:11 *S* replied: "When I saw that the men
13:15 went up after *S* to meet the soldiers,
13:15 *S* then numbered the soldiers he had with
13:16 *S,* his son Jonathan, and the soldiers
13:22 of any of the soldiers with *S* or Jonathan.
13:22 Only *S* and his son Jonathan had them.
14: 1 One day Jonathan, son of *S,*
14:16 The lookouts of *S* in Geba of Benjamin saw
14:17 *S* said to those around him,
14:18 *S* then said to Ahijah, "Bring the ephod
14:19 While *S* was speaking to the priest,
14:20 And *S* and all his men shouted and rushed
14:21 join the Israelites under *S* and Jonathan.
14:24 ten thousand combatants, were with *S,*
14:24 And *S* swore a very rash oath that day,
14:33 by eating the flesh with blood, *S* said:
14:35 and *S* built an altar to the LORD
14:36 Then *S* said, "Let us go down in pursuit
14:37 So *S* inquired of God:
14:38 *S* then said, "Come here, all officers of
14:41 And *S* said to the LORD, the God of Israel:
14:41 Jonathan and *S* were designated,
14:42 *S* then said, "Cast lots between me and
14:43 *S* said to Jonathan,
14:44 *S* said, "May God do thus and so to me
14:45 But the army said to *S:*
14:46 *S* gave up the pursuit of the Philistines,
14:47 *S* waged war on all their surrounding
14:49 The sons of *S* were Jonathan,
14:52 When *S* saw any strong or brave man,
15: 1 Samuel said to *S:* "It was I the LORD
15: 4 *S* alerted the soldiers, and at Telaim
15: 5 *S* went to the city of Amalek,
15: 7 *S* routed Amalek from Havilah to the
15:11 "I regret having made *S* king,
15:12 meet Saul, but was informed that *S* had
15:13 When Samuel came to him, *S* greeted him:
15:15 *S* replied: "They were brought from Amalek.
15:16 Samuel said to *S:* "Stop! Let me
15:20 *S* answered Samuel: "I did indeed obey
15:24 *S* replied to Samuel: "I have sinned,
15:26 Samuel said to *S,* "I will not return with
15:27 to go, *S* seized a loose end of his mantle,
15:31 with him, and *S* worshiped the LORD.
15:34 Saul went up to his home in Gibeah of *S.*
15:35 as long as he lived, did Samuel see *S.*
15:35 Yet he grieved over *S,* because the LORD
16: 1 "How long will you grieve for *S,*
16: 2 *S* will hear of it and kill me."
16:14 spirit of the LORD had departed from *S,*
16:15 So the servants of *S* said to him:
16:17 *S* then told his servants,
16:19 *S* dispatched messengers to ask Jesse to
16:20 a kid, and sent them to *S* by his son David.
16:21 David came to *S* and entered his service.
16:21 *S* became very fond of him,
16:23 Whenever the spirit from God seized *S,*
16:23 and *S* would be relieved and feel better,
17: 2 *S* and the Israelites also gathered and
17:11 *S* and all the men of Israel,
17:12 the days of *S* was old and well on in years.
17:13 oldest sons of Jesse had followed *S* to war;
17:14 While the three oldest had joined *S.*
17:15 *S* to tend his father's sheep at Bethlehem.
17:19 *S,* and they, and all Israel are fighting
17:31 spoken were overheard and reported to *S,*
17:32 Then David spoke to *S:* "You cannot go
17:33 But *S* answered David,
17:34 Then David told *S:* "Your servant used
17:37 *S* answered David, "Go!
17:38 Then *S* clothed David in his own tunic,
17:39 He said to *S,* "I cannot go in these,
17:55 *S* saw David go out to meet the Philistine,
17:57 Abner took him and presented him to *S.*
17:58 *S* then asked him, "Whose son are you,
18: 1 the time David finished speaking with *S,*
18: 2 *S* laid claim to David that day and did not
18: 5 every mission on which *S* sent him.
18: 5 So *S* put him in charge of his soldiers,
18: 6 At the approach of *S* and David (on David's
18: 6 of the cities of Israel to meet King *S,*
18: 7 *S* has slain his thousands,
18: 8 *S* was very angry and resentful of the song,
18: 9 from that day on, *S* was jealous of David.
18:10 day an evil spirit from God came over *S,*
18:10 other times, while *S* was holding his spear.
18:11 *S* poised the spear, thinking to nail David
18:12 *S* then began to fear David,
18:12 with him, but had departed from *S* himself.]
18:13 *S* removed him from his presence by
18:15 he was, *S* conceived a fear of David:
18:17 *S* said to David, "There is my older
18:17 " *S* had in mind,
18:18 But David answered *S:* "Who am I?
18:20 loved David, and it was reported to *S,*
18:21 [Thus for the second time *S* said to David,
18:22 *S* then ordered his servants to speak to
18:25 *S* commanded them to say this to David:
18:25 *S* intended in this way to bring about
18:27 *S* gave him his daughter Michal in marriage.
18:28 *S* thus came to recognize that the LORD was
18:29 Therefore *S* feared David all the more [and
19: 1 *S* discussed his intention of killing David
19: 2 "My father *S* is trying to kill you.
19: 4 then spoke well of David to his father *S,*
19: 6 *S* heeded Jonathan's plea and swore,
19: 7 Jonathan then brought David to *S,*
19: 9 an evil spirit from the LORD came upon *S*
19:10 *S* tried to nail David to the wall with the
19:10 wall with the spear, but David eluded *S,*
19:10 *S* sent messengers to David's house to
19:14 When *S* sent messengers to arrest David,
19:15 *S,* however, sent the messengers back
19:17 *S* therefore asked Michal:
19:17 Michal answered *S:*
19:18 him of all that *S* had done to him.
19:19 When *S* was told that David was in the
19:21 Informed of this, *S* sent other messengers,
19:21 For the third time *S* sent messengers,
19:22 *S* then went to Ramah himself.
19:24 they say, "Is *S* also among the prophets?"
20:26 *S,* however, said nothing that day,
20:27 *S* inquired of his son Jonathan,
20:28 Jonathan answered *S:* "David urgently asked
20:30 But *S* was extremely angry with Jonathan
20:32 But Jonathan asked his father *S:*
20:33 this *S* brandished his spear to strike him,
21:11 That same day David took to flight from *S,*
21:12 they not sing, *S* has slain his thousands,
22: 6 Now *S* heard that David and his men had
22: 9 who was standing with the officers of *S,*
22:12 Then *S* said, "Listen, son of Ahitub!"
22:13 *S* asked him, "Why did you conspire
22:19 *S* also put the priestly city of Nob to the
22:21 that *S* had slain the priests of the LORD,
22:21 was there, that he would surely tell *S.*
23: 7 *S* was told that David had entered Keilah,
23: 8 *S* then called all the people to war,
23: 9 found out that *S* was planning to harm him,
23:10 a report that *S* plans to come to Keilah,
23:11 will *S* come down as your servant has heard?
23:12 deliver me and my men into the grasp of *S?*"
23:13 When *S* was informed that David had escaped
23:14 Though *S* sought him continually,
23:15 because *S* had come out to seek his life;
23:17 my father *S* shall not lay a hand to you.
23:17 Even my father *S* knows this."
23:19 Ziphites went up to *S* in Gibeah and said,
23:21 *S* replied: "The LORD bless you
23:24 So they went off to Ziph ahead of *S.*
23:25 When *S* and his men came looking for him,
23:25 *S* heard of this and pursued David into the
23:26 As *S* moved along one rim of the gorge,
23:26 flight to escape *S,* and Saul and his men
23:27 capture them, when a messenger came to *S,*
23:28 *S* interrupted his pursuit of David and
24: 2 And when *S* returned from the pursuit of
24: 3 So *S* took three thousand picked men from
24: 8 men and would not permit them to attack *S.*
24: 8 *S* then left the cave and went on his way.
24: 9 also stepped out of the cave, calling to *S,*
24: 9 When *S* looked back, David bowed
24:10 bowed to the ground in homage and asked *S:*
24:17 saying these things to Saul, *S* answered,
24:18 *S* then said to David:
24:23 gave Saul his oath and *S* returned home,
25:43 but *S* gave David's wife Michal,
26: 1 Men from Ziph came to *S* in Gibeah
26: 2 So *S* went off down to the desert of Ziph
26: 3 *S* camped beside the road on the hill of
26: 3 saw that *S* had come into the desert after
26: 5 to the place where *S* was encamped
26: 5 and examined the spot where *S* and Abner,
26: 6 will go down into the camp with me to *S?*"
26: 7 found *S* lying asleep within the barricade,
26:17 *S* recognized David's voice and asked,
26:21 Then *S* said: "I have done wrong.
26:25 Then *S* said to David: "Blessed are you,
26:25 went his way, and *S* returned to his home.
27: 1 "I shall perish some day at the hand of *S.*
27: 1 then *S* will give up his continual search
27: 4 *S* was told that David had fled to Gath,
28: 3 Meanwhile *S* had driven mediums and
28: 4 *S,* too, mustered all Israel;
28: 5 When *S* saw the camp of the Philistines,
28: 7 Then *S* said to his servants,
28: 8 to the woman by night, and *S* said to her,
28: 9 "You are surely aware of what *S* has done,
28:10 But *S* swore to her by the LORD,
28:12 at the top of her voice and said to *S,*
28:12 You are *S!*"

SAUL (cont.)

28:13 The woman answered S,
28:14 "What does he look like?" asked S.
28:14 S knew that it was Samuel,
28:15 Samuel then said to S,
28:15 S replied: "I am in great straits
28:20 S fell full length on the ground,
28:21 Then the woman came to S,
28:25 She set the meal before S and his servants,
29: 3 "Why, that is David, the officer of S,
29: 5 their dances, S has slain his thousands,
31: 2 Philistines pursued S and his sons closely,
31: 2 Abinadab, and Malchishua, sons of S.
31: 3 The battle raged around S,
31: 4 Then S said to his armor-bearer,
31: 4 So S took his own sword and fell upon it.
31: 5 When the armor-bearer saw that S was dead,
31: 6 Thus S, his three sons, and his
31: 7 had fled and that S and his sons were dead,
31: 8 S and his three sons lying on Mount Gilboa.
31:11 heard what the Philistines had done to S,
31:12 S and his sons from the wall of Beth-shan,
2Sm 1: 1 After the death of S,
1: 4 dead, among them S and his son Jonathan.
1: 5 know that S and his son Jonathan are dead?"
1: 6 Gilboa and saw S leaning on his spear,
1:12 until evening for S and his son Jonathan,
1:17 this elegy for S and his son Jonathan,
1:19 glory of Israel, S, slain upon your heights;
1:21 the warriors' shields, the shield of S,
1:22 back, or the sword of S return unstained.
1:23 S and Jonathan, beloved and cherished,
1:24 Women of Israel, weep over S,
2: 4 that the men of Jabesh-gilead had buried S.
2: 5 kindness to your lord S in burying him.
2: 7 men, for though your lord S is dead,
2: 8 Saul's general, took Ishbaal, son of S,
2:10 Ishbaal, son of S, was forty years old
2:15 of the Benjaminites of Ishbaal, son of S,
3: 1 between the house of S and that of David,
3: 1 grew stronger, but the house of S weaker.
3: 6 between the house of S and that of David,
3: 6 Abner was gaining power in the house of S.
3: 7 Now S had had a concubine,
3: 7 And Ishbaal, son of S, said to Abner,
3: 8 a kindness to the house of your father S,
3:10 take away the kingdom from the house of S
3:14 sent messengers to Ishbaal, son of S,
4: 1 Ishbaal, son of S, heard that Abner
4: 2 Ishbaal, son of S, had two company
4: 4 Jonathan, son of S, had a son named
4: 4 about S and Jonathan came from Jezreel,
4: 8 the head of Ishbaal, son of your enemy S,
4: 8 my lord the king on S and his posterity."
5: 2 In days past, when S was our king,
7:15 as I withdrew it from your predecessor S,
9: 2 a servant of the family of S named Ziba.
9: 6 When Meribbaal, son of Jonathan, son of S,
9: 7 to you all the lands of your grandfather S,
9: 9 that belonged to S and to all his family.
12: 7 I rescued you from the hand of S.
16: 8 for all the bloodshed in the family of S,
19:18 Ziba, too, the servant of the house of S,
19:25 Meribbaal, son of S, also went down to
21: 1 "There is bloodguilt on S and his family
21: 2 S had attempted to kill them off in his
21: 4 against S and his house for silver or gold,
21: 7 Meribbaal, son of Jonathan, son of S,
21: 8 Aiah's daughter Rizpah had borne to S,
21:11 Aiah's daughter, the concubine of S,
21:12 he went and obtained the bones of S and of
21:12 them at the time they killed S on Gilboa.
21:13 the bones of S and of his son Jonathan,
21:14 Then the bones of S and of his son
22: 1 of all his enemies and from the hand of S—
1Chr 5:10 of S they waged war with the Hagrites,
8:33 of Kish, and Kish became the father of S.
8:33 S became the father of Jonathan,
9:39 of Kish, and Kish became the father of S.
9:39 S became the father of Jonathan,
10: 2 pressed hard after S and his sons.
10: 2 Abinadab, and Malchishua, sons of S,
10: 3 the whole fury of the battle descended upon S.
10: 4 S said to his armor-bearer,
10: 4 So S took his own sword and fell on it;
10: 6 Thus, with S and his three sons,
10: 7 that S and his sons had died in the rout,
10: 8 they found S and his sons where they had
10:11 heard what the Philistines had done to S,
10:12 recovered the bodies of S and his sons,
10:13 Thus S died because of his rebellion
11: 2 Even formerly, when S was still the king,
12: 1 he was still under banishment from S,
12:20 with the Philistines to battle against S.
12:20 our heads he will desert to his master S."
12:30 Of the Benjaminites, the brethren of S:
12:30 held their allegiance to the house of S.
13: 3 for in the days of S we did not visit it."
15:29 the City of David, Michal, daughter of S,
26:28 Also, whatever Samuel the seer, S,
1Mc 4:30 into the hand of Jonathan, the son of S,
Is 10:29 Ramah is in terror, Gibeah of S has fled.
Acts 7:58 cloaks at the feet of a young man named S.
8: 1 S, for his part, concurred in the act of
8: 3 After that, S began to harass the church.
9: 1 S, still breathing murderous threats
9: 4 same time heard a voice saying, "Saul, S,
9: 8 S got up from the ground unable to see,
9:11 of Judas ask for a certain S of Tarsus.
9:12 S saw in a vision a man named Ananias
9:17 he laid his hands on Saul and said, S,
9:22 S for his part grew steadily more powerful,
9:23 passed, certain Jews conspired to kill S,
9:27 how on his journey S had seen the Lord,
9:27 and how S had been speaking out fearlessly
9:28 S stayed on with them,
11:25 Barnabas went off to Tarsus to look for S;
11:30 presbyters in the care of Barnabas and S.
12:25 Barnabas and S returned to Jerusalem upon
13: 1 brought up with Herod the tetrarch), and S.
13: 2 "Set apart Barnabas and S for me to do
13: 7 S and was anxious to hear the word of God.
13: 9 S (also known as Paul) was filled with the
13:21 for a king, God gave them S son of Kish,
22: 7 the ground and heard a voice say to me, S,
22: 7 and heard a voice say to me, 'Saul, S,
22:13 S, my brother,' he said, 'recover your sight.'
26:14 a voice saying to me in Hebrew, 'Saul, S,

SAUL'S (45)

1Sm 9: 3 asses of S father, Kish, had wandered off.
9:15 day before S arrival, the LORD had given
10: 1 Samuel poured oil on S head;
10:14 S uncle inquired of him and his servant,
10:15 Then S uncle said, "Tell me, then, what
14: 2 S command post was under the pomegranate
14:50 S wife, who was named Ahinoam,
14:50 of his general was Abner, son of S uncle.
14:51 Kish, S father, and Ner, Abner's father,
14:52 against the Philistines during S lifetime.
17: 8 I am a Philistine, and you are S servants.
17:39 girded himself with S sword over the tunic.
18: 5 to the whole army, even to S own officers.]
18:19 for S daughter Merob to be given to David,
18:20 Now S daughter Michal loved David,
18:23 when S servants mentioned this to David,
18:30 against them than any other of S officers,
19: 1 But S son Jonathan, who was very fond
21: 8 One of S servants was there that day,
21: 8 the Edomite, and he was S chief henchman.
23:16 at Horesh in the barrens near Ziph, S son,
24: 5 and stealthily cut off an end of S mantle.
24: 6 that he had cut off an end of S mantle.
25:43 gave David's wife Michal, S own daughter,
26: 4 who confirmed S arrival David himself then
26: 5 S were within the barricade,
26: 7 So David and Abishai went among S soldiers
26:12 the water jug from their place at S head,
31: 9 off S head and stripped him of his armor,
2Sm 1: 2 On the third day a man came from S camp,
2: 8 Abner, son of Ner, S general,
2:12 of Ner, and the servants of Ishbaal, S son,
3:13 unless you bring back Michal, S daughter,
4:10 death the man who informed me of S death,
6:16 S daughter Michal looked down through the
6:20 S daughter Michal came out to meet him and
6:23 And so S daughter Michal was childless to
9: 1 "Is there any survivor of S house to whom
9: 3 S house to whom I may show God's kindness?"
9: 9 The king then called Ziba, S attendant,
16: 5 son of Gera of the same clan as S family,
21: 7 a bond between David and S son Jonathan.
21: 8 and the five sons of S daughter Merob that
1Chr 12: 2 They were some of S kinsmen,
12:24 at Hebron to transfer to him S kingdom,

SAVAGE (7)

2Mc 10:35 s fury cut down everyone they encountered.
11: 9 not only men, but the most s beasts,
13: 9 his mind full of s plans for inflicting on
15: 2 them in that way, like a s barbarian,
Dn 8: 6 river, and rushed toward it with s force.
Mt 8:28 s that no one could travel along that road.
Acts 20:29 s wolves will come among you who will not

SAVAGELY (1)

Acts 27:20 were to be seen, so s did the storm rage.

SAVE (207)

Gn 19:19 great kindness of intervening to s my life.
32:12 S me, I pray, from the hand
37:21 this, he tried to s him from their hands,
45: 7 a remnant on earth and to s your lives
Nm 10: 9 will remember you and s you from your foes.
Dt 4:42 and that he might s his life by fleeing to
19: 4 take refuge in such a place to s his life:
19: 5 in one of these cities to s his life.
25:11 wife of one intervenes to s her husband
Jos 2:13 and all their kin, and s us from death."
10: 6 Come up here quickly and s us.
Jgs 2:18 he would be with the judge and s them from
6:11 the wine press to s it from the Midianites,
6:14 have and s Israel from the power of Midian.
6:15 him, "Please, my lord, how can I s Israel?
6:36 you are going to s Israel through me,
6:37 know that you will s Israel through me,
7: 7 I will s you and will deliver Midian
10: 1 rose to s Israel the Issacharite Tola,
10:13 Therefore I will s you no more.
10:14 them s you now that you are in distress."
10:15 Only s us this day."
1Sm 4: 3 us and s us from the grasp of our enemies."
7: 8 to s us from the clutches of the
9:16 He shall s my people from the clutches of
10: 1 and to s them from the grasp of their
10:27 men said, "How can this fellow s us?"
12:21 idols which can neither profit nor s;
19:10 him, "Unless you s yourself tonight,
2Sm 3:18 'By my servant David I will s my people
22:28 You s lowly people,
22:32 Who is a rock s our God?
1Kgs 1:12 s your life and that of your son Solomon.
18: 5 may find grass and s the horses and mules,
2Kgs 18:30 LORD, saying, The LORD will surely s us;
19:12 nations whom my fathers destroyed s them?
19:19 our God, s us from the power of this man,
19:34 shield and s this city for my own sake,
1Chr 16:35 And say, S us, O God, our savior,
19:12 prove too strong for you, I will s you.
2Chr 20: 9 in our affliction, and you will hear and s!'
25:15 not s their own people from your hand?"
32:11 will s us from the grasp of the king of
32:13 lands able to s their lands from my hand?
32:14 ban was able to s his people from my hand?
32:14 god, then, be able to s you from my hand?
32:15 s his people from my hand
32:15 the less shall your god s you from my hand!"
32:17 Hezekiah's god s his people from my hand."
Neh 6:11 man like me enter the temple to s his life?
Tb 5:14 God s you, brother!
6:18 You will s her, and she will go with you.
Jdt 6: 2 Their God will not s them;
Est B: 9 s us from death."
C: 2 one to oppose you in your will to s Israel.
4:25 S us by your power, and help me,
4:30 S us from the power of the wicked,
1Mc 6:44 So he gave up his life to s his people and
9: 9 Let us s our lives now,
10:83 the temple of their idol, to s themselves.
12: 4 envoys with s conduct to the land of Judah.
13: 5 to s my own life in any time of distress,
2Mc 7:25 urging her to advise her boy to s his life.
11: 6 and tears to send a good angel to s Israel.
Jb 20:20 his greed, his treasures shall not s him.
40:14 that your own right hand can s you.
Ps(s) 3: 8 S me, my God!
6: 5 Return, O LORD, s my life;
7: 2 s me from all my pursuers and rescue me,
18:28 you s but haughty eyes you bring low;
18:32 Who is a rock, s our God?
22:22 S me from the lion's mouth;
28: 9 S your people, and bless your inheritance;
31:17 s me in your kindness.
35:17 S me from the roaring beasts;
36: 7 man and beast you s,
44: 7 my bow did I trust, nor did my sword s me;
54: 3 O God, by your name s me,
55:17 will call upon God, and the LORD will s me.
57: 4 May he send from heaven and s me;
59: 3 from bloodthirsty men s me.
69: 2 S me, O God, for the waters threaten
69:36 s Zion and rebuild the cities of Judah.
71: 2 incline your ear to me, and s me.
72: 4 the people, s the children of the poor,
72:13 the lives of the poor he shall s.
76:10 to s all the afflicted of the earth.
80: 3 Rouse your power, and come to s us.
86: 2 s your servant who trusts in you.
86:16 servant, and s the son of your handmaid.
106:47 S us, O LORD, our God,
109:26 s me, in your kindness,
109:31 to s him from those who would condemn him.
116: 4 the name of the LORD, "O LORD, s my life!"
119:94 s me, for I have sought your precepts.
119:146 s me, and I will keep your decrees.
140: 5 S me, O LORD, from the hands
Prv 23:14 and you will s him from the nether world.
Wis 14: 4 Showing that you can s from any danger,
16: 9 and no remedy was found to s their lives
Sir 29:12 house, and it will s you from every evil;
Is 25: 9 our God, to whom we looked to s us!
33: 6 her seasons lasting, the riches that s her,
33:22 the LORD our king, he it is who will s us.
35: 4 With divine recompense he comes to s you.
36:15 LORD, saying, "The LORD will surely s us;
36:18 seduce you by saying, "The LORD will s us."
36:20 the LORD then s Jerusalem from my hand?' "
37:12 nations whom my fathers destroyed s them?
37:20 O LORD, our God, s us from his hand,
37:35 shield and s this city for my own sake,
44:20 cannot s itself when the flame consumes it;
45:20 idols and pray to gods that cannot s.
46: 2 unable to s those who bear them,
47:13 Let the astrologers stand forth to s you,
47:14 s themselves from the spreading flames.
47:15 wanders his own way, with none to s you.
49:25 you I will oppose, and your sons I will s.

57:13 you cry out, nor *s* you in your distress.
59: 1 the hand of the LORD is not too short to *s*,
63: 1 announce vindication, I who am mighty to *s*."
65: 9 From Jacob I will *s* offspring,
Jer 2:27 trouble they cry out, "Rise up and *s* us!"
2:28 Will they *s* you in your time of trouble?
14: 9 a man dumbfounded, a champion who cannot *s*?
17:14 *s* me, that I may be saved,
38:17 of Babylon's king, you shall *s* your life;
42:11 says the LORD, for I am with you to *s* you,
47: 3 Fathers turn not to *s* their children;
48: 6 "Flee, *s* your lives,
51: 6 let each one *s* his life,
51:45 let each one *s* himself from the burning
Lam 4:17 watched for a nation that could not *s* us.
Bar 6:14 but it cannot *s* itself from war or pillage.
6:35 They neither *s* a man from death,
6:36 nor do they *s* any man in an emergency.
6:49 which do not *s* themselves either from war
Ez 3:19 die for his sin, but you shall *s* your life.
3:21 the warning, and you shall *s* your own life.
7:19 *s* them on the day of the LORD's wrath.
13:22 turn from his evil conduct and *s* his life;
14:14 could *s* only themselves by their virtue,
14:16 they could *s* neither sons nor daughters;
14:18 be unable to *s* either sons or daughters;
14:20 *s* neither son nor daughter; they would *s*
33: 9 for his guilt, but you shall *s* yourself.
33:12 will not *s* him on the day that he sins;
34:10 I will *s* my sheep,
34:22 I will *s* my sheep so that they may no
36:29 I will *s* you from all your impurities;
Dn 3:17 can *s* us from the white-hot furnace and
3:17 and from your hands, O king, may he *s* us!
6:15 news and he made up his mind to *s* Daniel;
6:17 God, whom you serve so constantly, *s* you."
6:21 been able to *s* you from the lions?"
Hos 1: 7 I will *s* them by the LORD,
1: 7 But I will not *s* them by war,
5:14 carry it away and no one can *s* it from me.
14: 4 Assyria will not *s* us,
Am 2:14 The warrior shall not *s* his life,
2:15 not escape, nor the horseman *s* his life.
Mi 6:14 save; what you do *s*, I will deliver up
Hb 3:13 save your people, to *s* your anointed one.
Zep 1:18 to *s* them on the day of the LORD's wrath,
3:19 I will *s* the lame,
Zec 8:13 so will I *s* you that you may be a blessing;
9:16 LORD, their God, shall *s* them on that day,
10: 6 of Judah, the house of Joseph I will *s*;
12: 7 The LORD shall *s* the tents of Judah first,
Mt 1:21 he will *s* his people from their sins."
8:25 "Lord, *s* us!
14:30 began to sink and cried out, "Lord, *s* me!"
16:25 Whoever would *s* his life will lose it,
27:40 *S* yourself, why don't you?
27:42 "He saved others but he cannot *s* himself!
Mk 15:30 *S* yourself now by coming down from that
15:31 "He saved others but he cannot *s* himself!
Lk 7: 3 him to come and *s* the life of his servant.
9:24 Whoever would *s* his life will lose it,
9:24 loses his life for my sake will *s* it.
19:10 has come to search out and *s* what is lost."
21:19 By patient endurance you will *s* your lives.
23:35 him *s* himself if he is the Messiah of God,
23:37 you are the king of the Jews, *s* yourself."
23:39 Then *s* yourself and us."
Jn 12:27 Father, *s* me from this hour?
12:47 not come to condemn the world but to *s* it.
18:36 to *s* me from being handed over to the Jews.
Acts 2:40 *S* yourselves from this generation which
27:43 the centurion was anxious to *s* Paul,
Rom 11:14 my fellow Jews to envy and *s* some of them.
1Cor 1:21 it pleased God to *s* those who believe
7:16 you know that you will not *s* your husband;
7:16 husband, that you will not *s* your wife?
9:22 men in order to *s* at least some of them.
16: 2 put aside whatever he has been able to *s*,
2Cor 12:14 Children should not *s* up for their parents,
1Tm 1:15 Jesus came into the world to *s* sinners.
Heb 5: 7 to God, who was able to *s* him from death,
7:25 to *s* those who approach God through him,
Jas 1:21 taken root in you, with its power to *s* you.
2:14 Such faith has no power to *s* one, has it?
4:12 and Judge, one who can *s* and destroy.
5:20 will *s* his soul from death

SAVED (114)

Gn 19:20 —that my life may be *s*."
20: 7 that your life may be *s*.
27:36 pleaded, "Haven't you *s* a blessing for me?"
47:25 "You have *s* our lives!"
Ex 2:19 "An Egyptian *s* us from the interference
10: 5 up the remnant you *s* unhurt from the hail,
14:30 Thus the LORD *s* Israel on that day from
Jos 9:26 *s* them from being killed by the Israelites,
24:10 he had to bless you, and I *s* you from him.
Jgs 9:17 when he *s* you from the power of Midian;
10:12 out to me, and I *s* you from their grasp,
1Sm 11:13 this day, for today the LORD has *s* Israel."
14:23 Thus the LORD *s* Israel that day.
2Sm 19: 6 "Though they *s* your life and your sons'
22:42 but no one *s* them;
2Kgs 14:27 the heavens, he *s* them through Jeroboam,
19:11 Will you, then, be *s*?
2Chr 32:17 lands have not *s* their people from my hand,
32:22 Thus the LORD *s* Hezekiah and the
Tb 14: 7 Israelites who are to be *s* in those days
Jdt 10:15 to see our master, you have *s* your life.
Est F: 6 is Israel, who cried to God and was *s*.
F: 6 "The LORD *s* his people and delivered us
1Mc 2:48 They *s* the law from the hands of the
2:59 for their faith, were *s* from the fire.
4: 9 how our fathers were *s* in the Red Sea,
11:48 Thus they *s* the king's life.
12:15 we have been *s* from our enemies
2Mc 1:11 we have been *s* by God from grave dangers,
2:17 It is God who has *s* all his people and has
Ps(s) 18:42 They cried for help— but no one *s* them;
33:16 A king is not *s* by a mighty army,
34: 7 heard, and from all his distress he *s* him.
44: 8 But you *s* us from our foes,
106: 8 Yet he *s* them for his name's sake,
106:10 He *s* them from hostile hands and freed
106:21 They forgot the God who had *s* them,
116: 6 I was brought low, and he *s* me.
Eccl 8: 8 nor are the wicked *s* by their wickedness.
Wis 9:18 was your pleasure, and were *s* by Wisdom.
10: 4 the earth was flooded, Wisdom again *s* it,
16: 7 For he who turned toward it was *s*,
16:11 they were stung, and swiftly they were *s*,
18: 5 a single boy had been cast forth but *s*,
Sir 25: 3 What you have not *s* in your youth,
34:12 of death, but by these attainments I was *s*.
48:20 they uttered and *s* them through ISAIAH.
49:10 to Jacob and *s* him by their faith and hope.
51: 2 You have *s* me from death,
51: 3 From many a danger you have *s* me,
51:12 He *s* me from evil of every kind and
Is 25: 9 us rejoice and be glad that he has *s* us!"
30:15 By waiting and by calm you shall be *s*,
36:19 Have they *s* Samaria from my hand?
37:11 Will you, then, be *s*?
43:12 It is I who foretold, I who *s*;
45:17 *s* by the LORD. *s* forever!
63: 9 or an angel, but he himself who *s* them.
Jer 4:14 of evil, O Jerusalem, that you may be *s*.
17:14 save me, that I may be *s*,
23: 6 In his days Judah shall be *s*,
30: 7 for Jacob, though he shall be *s* from it.
Ez 14:16 they alone would be *s*,
14:18 they alone would be *s*.
17:17 he shall not be *s* in the conflict by
Dn 3:88 world, and *s* us from the power of death;
Ob 1:17 on Mount Zion there shall be a portion *s*;
Mt 19:25 and exclaimed, "Then who can be *s*?"
24:22 shortened, not a human being would be *s*.
27:42 "He *s* others but he cannot save himself!
Mk 10:26 to one another, "Then who can be *s*?"
13:20 the period, not a person would be *s*.
15:31 "He *s* others but he cannot save himself!
16:16 in it and accepts baptism will be *s*;
Lk 8:12 their hearts lest they believe and be *s*.
13:23 are they few in number who are to be *s*?"
18:26 listeners asked him, "Who, then, can be *s*?"
23:35 kept jeering at him, saying, "He *s* others;
Jn 3:17 but that the world might be *s* through him.
11:12 "Lord, if he is asleep his life will be *s*."
Acts 2:21 be *s* who calls on the name of the Lord.'
2:47 to their number those who were being *s*.
4:12 world given to men by which we are to be *s*."
11:14 of what he will tell you, you shall be *s*,
14: 9 him and saw that he had the faith to be *s*.
15: 1 to Mosaic practice, you cannot be *s*."
15:11 Our belief is rather that we are *s* by the
16:30 and said, "Men, what must I do to be *s*?"
16:31 in the Lord Jesus and you will be *s*,
Rom 5: 9 that we shall be *s* by him from God's wrath.
5:10 have been reconciled will be *s* by his life.
8:24 In hope we were *s*.
9:27 of the sea, only the remnant will be *s*,
10: 1 for the Israelites, is that they may be *s*.
10: 9 raised him from the dead, you will be *s*.
10:13 calls on the name of the Lord will be *s*."
11:26 enter in, and then all Israel will be *s*.
1Cor 3:15 He himself will be *s*,
5: 5 his spirit may be *s* on the day of the Lord.
10:33 but that of the many, that they may be *s*.
15: 2 You are being *s* by it at this very moment
2Cor 2:15 *s* and those on the way to destruction;
Eph 2: 5 By this favor you were *s*.
2Thes 2:10 their hearts to the truth in order to be *s*.
1Tm 2: 4 men to be *s* and come to know the truth.
2:15 She will be *s* through childbearing,
2Tm 1: 9 has *s* us and has called us to a holy life,
3:11 you know how the Lord *s* me from them all.
4:17 That is how I was *s* from the lion's jaws.
Ti 3: 5 love of God our savior appeared, he *s* us;
3: 5 He *s* us through baptism of new birth and
Heb 11: 7 built an ark that his household might be *s*.
1Pt 3:21 You are now *s* by a baptismal bath which
4:18 if the just man is *s* only with difficulty,

SAVES (17)

1Sm 17:47 is not by sword or spear that the LORD *s*.
Tb 12: 9 *s* one from death and expiates every sin.
Jb 5:15 and from the hand of the mighty, he *s*.
22:29 but the man of humble mien he *s*.
36:15 *s* the unfortunate through their affliction,
Ps(s) 7:11 me is God, who *s* the upright of heart;
34:19 and those who are crushed in spirit he *s*.
37:40 delivers them from the wicked and *s* them,
138: 7 your right hand *s* me.
145:19 fear him, he hears their cry and *s* them.
Prv 10: 2 profit nothing, but virtue *s* from death.
11: 4 the day of wrath, but virtue *s* from death.
11: 6 The virtue of the upright *s* them,
14:25 The truthful witness *s* lives,
Sir 2:11 he forgives sins, he *s* in time of trouble.
51: 8 For he *s* those who take refuge in him,
Dn 13:60 blessing God who *s* those that hope in him.
Prv 12: 6 speech of the upright *s* them

SAVING (21)

Gn 45: 5 *s* lives that God sent me here ahead of you.
Dt 32:15 god who made them and scorned their *s* Rock.
33:29 The LORD is your *s* shield,
2Sm 22:36 "You have given me your *s* shield,
1Mc 16: 2 and many times we succeeded in *s* Israel.
2Mc 12:25 him go for the sake of *s* their brethren.
Ps(s) 18:36 You have given me your *s* shield;
28: 8 his people, the *s* refuge of his anointed.
51:16 Free me from blood guilt, O God, my *s* God;
68:21 God is a *s* God for us;
69:30 let your *s* help, O God, protect me.
74:12 from of old, you doer of *s* deeds on earth,
106: 4 visit me with your *s* help,
Prv 2:12 *S* you from the way of evil men,
2:16 *S* you from the wife of another,
Is 45:21 There is no just and *s* God but me.
Lam 3:26 hope in silence for the *s* help of the LORD.
Bar 4:29 brought disaster upon you will, in *s* you,
Hb 3:18 rejoice in the LORD and exult in my *s* God.
Lk 1:69 He has raised a horn of *s* strength for us
2:30 For my eyes have witnessed your *s* deed

SAVINGS (3)

Mk 5:26 sort and exhausted her *s* in the process,
12:40 These men devour the *s* of widows and
Lk 20:47 These men are going through the *s* of

SAVIOR (74)

Ex 15: 2 courage is the LORD, and he has been my *s*.
Jgs 3: 9 to the LORD, he raised up for them a *s*,
3:15 to the LORD, he raised up for them a *s*,
2Sm 22: 3 salvation, my stronghold, my refuge, my *s*,
2Kgs 13: 5 So the LORD gave Israel a *s*,
1Chr 16:35 And say, "Save us, O God, our *s*,
Jdt 9:11 the forsaken, the *s* of those without hope.
Est D: 2 after invoking the all-seeing God and *s*,
E:13 of Mordecai, our *s* and constant benefactor,
1Mc 4:30 "Blessed are you, O *S* of Israel,
9:21 the mighty one has fallen, the *s* of Israel!"
2Mc 1:25 and eternal, Israel's *s* from all evil,
Ps(s) 17: 7 O *s* of those who flee from their foes to
18:47 Extolled be God my *s*.
24: 5 from the LORD, a reward from God his *s*.
25: 5 truth and teach me, for you are God my *s*,
27: 9 forsake me not, O God my *s*.
42: 6 him, in the presence of my *s* and my God.
42:12 him, in the presence of my *s* and my God.
43: 5 him, in the presence of my *s* and my God.
65: 6 of justice you answer us, O God our *s*,
79: 9 Help us, O God our *s*,
85: 5 Restore us, O God our *s*,
89:27 'You are my father, my God, the rock, my *s*.'
118:14 courage is the LORD, and he has been my *s*.
118:21 you have answered me and have been my *s*.
Wis 16: 7 by what he saw, but by you, the *s* of all.
Sir 34:13 LORD, for they put their hope in their *s*;
46: 1 implies, the great *s* of God's chosen ones,
51: 1 I praise you, O God my *s*!
51:10 my father, you are my champion and my *s*;
Is 12: 2 God indeed is my *s*;
12: 2 courage is the LORD, and he has been my *s*.
17:10 For you have forgotten God, your *s*,
19:20 sends them a *s* to defend and deliver them.
38:20 The LORD is our *s*;
43: 3 your God, the Holy One of Israel, your *s*.
43:11 It is I, I the LORD; there is no *s* but me.
45:15 God is hidden, the God of Israel, the *s*!
49:26 shall know that I, the LORD, am your *s*,
60:16 shall know that I, the LORD, am your *s*,
62:11 Say to daughter Zion, your *s* comes!
63: 8 So he became their *s*
Jer 14: 8 of Israel, O LORD, our *s* in time of need!
Bar 4:22 will swiftly reach you from your eternal *s*.
Dn 6:28 He is a deliverer and *s*,
Hos 13: 4 God besides me, and there is no *s* but me.
Mi 7: 7 the LORD, I will put my trust in God my *s*;
Zep 3:17 your God, is in your midst, a mighty *s*;
Zec 9: 9 a just *s* is he,
Lk 1:47 Lord, my spirit finds joy in God my *s*,
2:11 in David's city a *s* has been born to you,

SAVIOR (cont.)

Jn 4:42 that this really is the *S* of the world."
Acts 5:31 exalted at his right hand as ruler and *s*
13:23 man's descendants Jesus, a *s* for Israel.
Eph 5:23 of his body the church, as well as its *s*.
Phil 3:20 that we eagerly await the coming of our *S*,
1Tm 1: 1 of God our *s* and Christ Jesus our hope,
2: 3 is good, and God our *s* is pleased with it,
4:10 on the living God who is the *s* of all men,
2Tm 1:10 manifest through the appearance of our *S*.
Ti 1: 3 to me by the command of God our *S*.
1: 4 God our Father, and Christ Jesus our *S*,
2:10 way possible the doctrine of God our *S*.
2:13 of the great God and of our *S* Christ Jesus.
3: 4 kindness and love of God our *s* appeared,
3: 6 lavished on us through Jesus Christ our *S*,
2Pt 1: 1 power of our God and *S* Jesus Christ;
1:11 *S* Jesus Christ will be richly provided for.
2:20 by recognizing the Lord and *S* Jesus Christ,
3: 2 Lord and *S* preached to you by the apostles.
3:18 knowledge of our Lord and *S* Jesus Christ.
1Jn 4:14 Father has sent the Son as *s* of the world.
Jude 1:25 Glory be to this only God our *s*,

SAVIORS (2)

Neh 9:27 great mercy give them *s* to deliver them
Ob 1:21 And *s* shall ascend Mount Zion to rule the

SAVOR (1)

Sir 36:19 As the palate tests meat by its *s*,

SAVORY (1)

Dn 10: 3 I ate no *s* food,

SAWED (1)

Heb 11:37 They were stoned, *s* in two,

SAWS (2)

2Sm 12:31 whom he assigned to work with *s*,
1Chr 20: 3 of the city and set them to work with *s*,

SAYINGS (10)

Jb 6:26 but the *s* of a desperate man as wind?
Prv 4:20 be attentive, to my *s* incline your ear;
22:17 The *s* of the wise:
24:23 These also are *S* of the wise;
Eccl 6:11 there are many *s* that multiply vanity,
12:10 *s*, and to write down true sayings with
12:11 The *s* of the wise are like goads;
Sir 39: 2 men, and goes to the heart of involved *s*;

SCAB (5)

Lv 13: 2 "If someone has on his skin a *s* or
13:10 find that there is a white *s* on the skin
13:19 the boil have a white *s* or a pink blotch,
13:28 dying out, it is merely the *s* of the burn;
13:43 and if the *s* on the sore of the bald spot

SCABBARD (1)

Jer 47: 6 Return into your *s*; stop, be still!

SCABS (3)

Lv 14:56 of garments and houses, as well as for *s*,
Jb 7: 5 My flesh is clothed with worms and *s*;
Is 3:17 the scalps of Zion's daughters with *s*,

SCALE (8)

Lv 19:36 You shall have a true *s* and true weights,
1Sm 17: 5 of *s* armor weighing five thousand shekels,
1Mc 11:48 set on fire and plundered on a large *s*.
Is 14:13 "I will *s* the heavens;
Jer 4:29 shrink into the thickets, they *s* the rocks:
22:20 *S* Lebanon and cry out,
51:53 Though Babylon *s* the heavens,
Jl 2: 7 they run, like soldiers they *s* the wall;

SCALES (25)

Lv 11: 9 waters has both fins and *s* you may eat.
11:10 either fins or *s* are loathsome for you,
11:12 that lacks fins or *s* is loathsome for you.
Dt 14: 9 whatever has both fins and *s* you may eat,
14:10 lack either fins or *s* you shall not eat;
2Mc 9: 8 he could weigh the mountaintops in his *s*,
Jb 6: 2 and my calamity laid with it in the *s*,
31: 6 Let God weigh me in the *s* of justice;
41: 7 Rows of *s* are on his back,
Prv 11: 1 False *s* are an abomination to the LORD,
16:11 Balance and *s* belong to the LORD;
20:23 to the LORD, and false *s* are not good.
Sir 42: 4 Of accuracy of *s* and balances,
Is 40:12 mountains in *s* and the hills in a balance?
40:15 as a drop in the bucket, as dust on the *s*;
46: 6 a purse and weigh out silver on the *s*;
Jer 32:10 and weighed out the silver on the *s*,
Ez 5: 1 set of *s* and divide the hair you have cut.
29: 4 the fish of your Niles stick to your *s*,
29: 4 the fish of your Niles sticking to your *s*.
45:10 You shall have honest *s*,
Dn 5:27 been weighed on the *s* and found wanting;
Am 8: 5 to the shekel, and fix our *s* for cheating!
Acts 9:18 Immediately something like *s* fell from his
Rv 6: 5 of which held a pair of *s* in his hand.

SCALL (9)

Lv 13:30 declare the person unclean, for this is *s*,
13:31 But if the priest, on examining the *s* sore,
13:31 the person with *s* sore for seven days,
13:32 If the *s* has not spread and has no yellow
13:34 when examining the *s* on the seventh day,
13:35 But if the *s* spreads at all on his skin
13:36 If the *s* has indeed spread on the skin he
13:37 he judges that the *s* has remained in its
14:54 law for every kind of human leprosy and *s*,

SCALP (1)

2Mc 7: 4 to *s* him and cut off his hands and feet,

SCALPS (1)

Is 3:17 cover the *s* of Zion's daughters with scabs,

SCANDAL (6)

Mt 18: 7 things will come on the world through *s*!
18: 7 It is inevitable that *s* should occur.
18: 7 woe to that man through whom *s* comes!
Lk 17: 2 than giving *s* to one of these little ones.
Rom 14:21 brother an occasion for stumbling or *s*,
16:17 against those who cause dissension and *s*,

SCANDALIZED (2)

Mt 15:12 were *s* when they heard your pronouncement?"
2Cor 11:29 is *s* that I am not aflame with indignation?

SCANDALS (1)

Lk 17: 1 *S* will inevitably arise,

SCANTY (5)

1Kgs 22:27 Put this man in prison and feed him *s*
2Chr 18:26 Put this man in prison and feed him *s*
1Mc 6:57 weaker every day, our provisions are *s*,
Ps(s) 37:16 Better is the *s* store of the just than the
Is 1: 9 the LORD of hosts had left us a *s* remnant,

SCAR (2)

Lv 13:23 spreading, it is merely the *s* of the boil;
13:28 clean, since it is only the *s* of the burn.

SCARCE (4)

Wis 9:16 And *s* do we guess the things on earth,
Sir 25:18 There is *s* any evil like that in a woman;
Am 4: 6 have made bread *s* in all your dwellings,
Mt 9:37 "The harvest is good but laborers are *s*.

SCARCELY (14)

Gn 24:15 He had *s* finished these words when Rebekah
24:45 "I had *s* finished saying this prayer to
27:30 Jacob had *s* left his father,
Ru 2: 7 here until now, with *s* a moment's rest."
Est 7: 8 *S* had the king spoken when the face of
2Mc 7:30 *s* finished speaking when the youth said:
9: 5 for *s* had he uttered those words when he
Prv 6:26 of a loose woman may be *s* a loaf of bread,
Is 40:24 *S* are they planted or sown, scarcely is
66: 8 Yet Zion is *s* in labor when she gives
Mt 13:15 They have *s* heard with their ears,
Acts 14:18 they could *s* stop the crowds from offering
28:27 They have *s* used their ears to listen;

SCARCITY (1)

Ez 4:17 so that, owing to the *s* of bread and water,

SCARECROW (2)

Jer 10: 5 Like a *s* in a cucumber field are they,
Bar 6:69 For like a *s* in a cucumber patch,

SCARLET (46)

Ex 25: 4 violet, purple and *s* yarn;
26: 1 twined and of violet, purple and *s* yarn,
26:31 a veil woven of violet, purple and *s* yarn,
26:36 purple and *s* yarn and of fine linen twined.
27:16 purple and *s* yarn and of fine linen twined.
28: 5 violet, purple and *s* yarn and fine linen.
28: 6 thread and of violet, purple and *s* yarn,
28: 8 gold thread, of violet, purple and *s* yarn,
28:15 and *s* yarn on cloth of fine linen twined.
28:33 purple and *s* yarn and fine linen twined,
35: 6 violet, purple and *s* yarn;
35:23 happened to have violet, purple or *s* yarn,
35:25 purple and *s* yarn and fine linen thread,
35:35 purple and *s* yarn and fine linen thread,
36: 8 on them with violet, purple and *s* yarn.
36:35 was woven of violet, purple and *s* yarn,
36:37 tent was made of violet, purple and *s* yarn,
38:18 purple and *s* yarn and of fine linen twined,
38:23 purple and *s* yarn and of fine linen.
39: 1 purple and *s* yarn were woven the service
39: 2 purple and *s* yarn and of fine linen twined.
39: 3 purple and *s* yarn into an embroidered
39: 5 gold thread, of violet, purple and *s* yarn,
39: 8 and *s* yarn on cloth of fine linen twined.
39:24 purple and *s* yarn and of fine linen twined;
39:29 twined and of violet, purple and *s* yarn,
Lv 14: 4 birds, as well as some cedar wood, *s* yarn,
14: 6 the cedar wood, the *s* yarn and the hyssop,
14:49 two birds, as well as cedar wood, *s* yarn,
14:51 the cedarwood, the hyssop and the *s* yarn,
14:52 the cedar wood, the hyssop, and the *s* yarn.
Nm 4: 8 Over these they shall spread a *s* cloth and
19: 6 hyssop and *s* yarn and throw them into the
Jos 2:18 tie this *s* cord in the window through
2:21 gone, she tied the *s* cord in the window.
2Sm 1:24 Saul, who clothed you in *s* and in finery,
Sg 4: 3 Your lips are like a *s* strand;
Sir 45:11 the ephod and cincture with *s* yarn,
Is 1:18 Though your sins be like *s*,
Ez 27: 7 Purple and *s* from the coasts of Elishah
Na 2: 4 are crimsoned, the soldiers colored in *s*;
Mt 27:28 and wrapped him in a *s* military cloak.
Rv 17: 3 I saw a woman seated on a *s* beast
17: 4 The woman was dressed in purple and *s* and
18:12 and purple garments, silk and *s* cloth;
18:16 dressed in fine linen and purple and *s*,

SCATTER (40)

Gn 49: 7 I will *s* them in Jacob,
Ex 9: 8 of Pharaoh let Moses *s* it toward the sky.
Lv 26:33 You yourselves I will *s* among the nations
Nm 17: 2 and *s* the fire some distance away,
Dt 4:27 The LORD will *s* you among the nations,
28:64 The LORD will *s* you among all the nations
Neh 1: 8 faithless, I will *s* you among the nations;
Jb 37:11 laden, as they *s* their flashes of light.
Ps(s) 68:31 *s* the peoples who delight in war.
106:27 To *s* their descendants among the nations,
Eccl 3: 5 A time to *s* stones,
Sir 36: 6 out wrath, humble the enemy, *s* the foe.
Is 5:24 rotten and their blossom *s* like dust;
28:25 surface, does he not *s* gith and sow cumin,
41:16 carry them off and the storm shall *s* them.
Jer 9:15 I will *s* them among nations whom neither
13:24 I will *s* them like chaff that flies when
18:17 wind, I will *s* them before their enemies;
23: 1 who mislead and *s* the flock of my pasture,
49:32 I will *s* to the winds those who shave
49:36 I will *s* them to all these winds,
Bar 2:29 among the nations to which I will *s* them.
Ez 4:13 unclean among the nations where I *s* them.
5:10 I will inflict punishments upon you and *s*
5:12 and a third I will *s* in every direction,
6: 5 will *s* their bones all around your altars.
10: 2 the cherubim, then *s* them over the city.
12:14 and his troops I will *s* in every direction,
12:15 the nations and *s* them over foreign lands.
20:23 the nations and *s* them over foreign lands;
22:15 the nations and *s* you over foreign lands,
29:12 and I will *s* the Egyptians among the
30:23 I will *s* the Egyptians among the nations
30:26 [I will *s* the Egyptians among the nations
Dn 4:11 strip off its leaves and *s* its fruit;
Zec 2: 4 raised their horns to *s* the land of Judah."
2:10 for I *s* you to the four winds of heaven,
7:14 but would *s* them with a whirlwind among
Mt 25:24 not sow and gather where you did not *s*,
25:26 I did not sow and gather where I did not *s*.

SCATTERED (77)

Gn 11: 4 otherwise we shall be *s* all over the earth."
11: 8 LORD *s* them from there all over the earth,
11: 9 place that he *s* them all over the earth.
Ex 5:12 *s* throughout the land of Egypt to gather
9:10 Moses *s* it toward the sky,
32:20 which he *s* on the water and made the
Nm 10:35 O LORD, that your enemies may be *s*,
Dt 30: 3 from all the nations wherein he has *s* you.
1Sm 11:11 were so *s* that no two were left together.
14:16 *s* and were running about in all directions.
14:24 and there was *s* fighting in every town in
30:16 were the Amalekites *s* all over the ground,
2Sm 5:20 "The LORD has *s* my enemies before me like
20:22 they *s* from the city to their own tents,
1Kgs 22:17 "I see all Israel *s* on the mountains,
2Kgs 23: 6 which was then *s* over the common graveyard.
2Chr 18:16 "I see all Israel *s* on the mountains,
Neh 4:13 "Our work is *s* and extensive,
Tb 3: 4 in all the nations among whom you *s* us.
13: 3 for though he has *s* you among them,
13: 5 the Gentiles among whom you have been *s*.
14: 4 they shall all be *s* and led away into
Jdt 5:19 from the Dispersion wherein they were *s*,
15: 2 they *s* in all directions,
1Mc 4: 4 forces were still *s* away from the camp.
6:54 the rest *s* each to his own home,
10:83 The horsemen too were *s* over the plain.
2Mc 1:27 Gather together our *s* people,
2:14 books that had been *s* because of the war,
Jb 4:11 of prey, and the cubs of the lioness are *s*.
18:15 over his abode brimstone is *s*.
Ps(s) 44:12 among the nations you *s* us.

53: 6 For God has *s* the bones of your besiegers;
68: 2 his enemies are *s*,
89:11 your strong arm you have *s* your enemies.
92:10 all evildoers shall be *s*.
Wis 5:14 Like smoke *s* by the wind,
17: 3 of oblivion Were *s* in fearful trembling,
Sir 43:23 and the *s* dew enriches the parched land.
48:15 out of their land and *s* all over the earth.
Is 16: 8 as far as Jazer and *s* over the desert,
33: 3 you rise in your majesty, nations are *s*.
Jer 10:21 no success, and all their flocks were *s*.
23: 2 You have *s* my sheep and driven them away.
30:11 all the nations among which I have *s* you;
31:10 He who *s* Israel, now gathers them
40:12 Judah from the places to which they had *s*.
44:14 Only *s* refugees shall return.
49: 5 You shall be *s*,
Bar 2: 4 round about to which the Lord has *s* us.
2:13 number among the nations to which you *s* us.
3: 8 us today in our captivity, where you *s* us,
Ez 6: 8 and have been *s* over the foreign lands,
11:16 nations and *s* them over foreign countries
11:17 the countries over which you have been *s*,
17:21 survivors shall be *s* in every direction.
20:34 from the countries over which you are *s*;
20:41 out of the countries over which you are *s*;
28:25 from the peoples among whom they are *s*,
29:13 from the peoples among whom they are *s*,
34: 5 So they were *s* for lack of a shepherd,
34: 5 My sheep were *s* and wandered over all the
34: 6 my sheep were *s* over the whole earth,
34:12 when he finds himself among his *s* sheep,
34:12 they were *s* when it was cloudy and dark.
36:19 I *s* them among the nations,
Dn 9: 7 all the countries to which you have *s* them
14:14 which they *s* through the whole temple;
Jl 4: 2 Because they have *s* them among the nations,
Na 3:18 Your people are *s* upon the mountains,
Zec 2: 2 that *s* Judah and Israel and Jerusalem."
2: 4 he said, "Here are the horns that *s* Judah,
Jn 10:12 the sheep to be snatched and *s* by the wolf.
16:32 you will be *s* and each will go his way,
Acts 8: 1 All except the apostles *s* throughout the
2Cor 9: 9 "He *s* abroad and gave to the poor,
1Pt 1: 1 who live as strangers *s* throughout Pontus,

SCATTERING (5)

1Kgs 14:15 their fathers, *s* them beyond the River,
2Mc 12:22 *S* in every direction,
Prv 26:18 Like a crazed archer *s* firebrands and
Is 17: 6 Only a *s* of grapes shall be left!
24: 2 he turns it upside down, *s* its inhabitants:

SCATTERS (6)

Jb 26:13 With his angry breath he *s* the waters,
Ps(s) 147:17 He *s* his hail like crumbs;
Sir 43:20 He *s* frost like so much salt;
Mt 12:30 me, and he who does not gather with me *s*.
Mk 4:26 A man *s* seed on the ground.
Lk 11:23 me, and he who does not gather with me *s*.

SCAVENGERS (1)

Ps(s) 59:16 They wander about as *s*;

SCENE (5)

Lk 2:38 Coming on the *s* at this moment,
Acts 5:36 Theudas came on the *s* and tried to pass
21:33 Then, when the commander arrived on the *s*,
2Thes 2: 7 that restrainer shall be taken from the *s*.
2Pt 3: 3 by their passions will arrive on the *s*.

SCENT (1)

Jer 48:11 he kept his taste, and his *s* was not lost.

SCENTED (1)

Is 57: 9 While you approached the king with *s* oil,

SCENTS (1)

Jb 39:25 Even from afar he *s* the battle,

SCEPTER (21)

Gn 49:10 The *s* shall never depart from Judah,
Est 4:11 the king extends to him the golden *s*,
4:22 relinquish your *s* to those that are nought.
4:30 Raising the golden *s*,
8: 4 stretched forth the golden *s* to Esther.
Ps(s) 45: 7 a tempered rod is your royal *s*.
60: 9 Judah, my *s*; Moab shall serve
108: 9 Judah, my *s*; Moab shall serve as my
110: 2 The *s* of your power the LORD will stretch
125: 3 For the *s* of the wicked shall not remain
Wis 6:21 then, you find pleasure in throne and *s*,
7: 8 I preferred her to *s* and throne,
10:14 Until she brought him the *s* of royalty and
Sir 35:21 branch, and smashes the *s* of the wicked;
Bar 6:13 Each has a *s*, like the human ruler
Ez 19:11 One strong branch she put out as a royal *s*.
19:14 now without a strong branch, a ruler's *s*.
30:18 be darkened when I break the *s* of Egypt.
Zec 10:11 cast down, and the *s* of Egypt taken away.
Heb 1: 8 righteous *s* is the scepter of your kingdom.

SCEPTERED (2)

Am 1: 5 of Aven, And the *s* ruler of Beth-eden;
1: 8 in Ashdod, and the *s* ruler of Ashkelon;

SCEPTERS (1)

Nm 21:18 people dug, with their *s* and their staffs."

SCEVA (1)

Acts 19:14 Another time, when the seven sons of *S*,

SCHEDULE (1)

Neh 11:23 and there was a fixed *s* for the singers

SCHEME (6)

2Mc 14: 5 found an opportunity to further his mad *s*
Ps(s) 64: 7 devise a wicked *s*, and conceal the scheme
Ez 38:10 your mind, and you shall devise an evil *s*:
Acts 5: 4 How could you ever concoct such a *s*?
5: 9 *s* to put the Spirit of the Lord to test?

SCHEMED (1)

Bar 3:18 They *s* anxiously for money,

SCHEMER (3)

Est 8: 5 to revoke the letters which that *s* Haman,
Prv 12: 2 the LORD, but the *s* is condemned by him.
Sir 13:25 withdrawn and perplexed is the laborious *s*.

SCHEMES (6)

1Mc 2:63 to his dust, and his *s* have perished.
Prv 6:18 A heart that plots wicked *s*,
15:26 man's *s* are an abomination to the LORD,
Sir 12:16 heart he *s* to plunge you into the abyss.
Jer 6:19 this people, the fruit of their own *s*,
Hos 10: 6 into captivity, Israel be shamed by his *s*.

SCHEMING (1)

Ex 21:14 kills another after maliciously *s* to do so,

SCHOOL (1)

Heb 12:11 justice to those who are trained in its *s*.

SCHOOLED (1)

Gal 1:12 receive it from any man, nor was I *s* in it.

SCHOOLS (1)

Ps(s) 104:25 in which are *s* without number of living

SCIATIC (2)

Gn 32:33 eat the *s* muscle that is on the hip socket,
32:33 hip socket was struck at the *s* muscle.

SCIENCE (1)

Dn 1:17 and proficiency in all literature and *s*,

SCIMITAR (2)

1Sm 17: 6 and had a bronze *s* slung from a baldric.
17:45 against me with sword and spear and *s*,

SCION (1)

Is 14:20 be named forever, that *s* of an evil race!

SCOFF (3)

Ps(s) 22: 8 All who see me *s* at me;
73: 8 They *s* and speak evil;
119:51 Though the proud *s* bitterly at me,

SCOFFED (2)

2Chr 30:10 as Zebulun, but they were derided and *s* at.
36:16 his warnings, and *s* at his prophets,

SCOFFS (2)

Jb 39: 7 He *s* at the uproar of the city,
Hb 1:10 *s* at kings, and princes are his laughingstock;

SCOLD (2)

Mt 19:13 The disciples began to *s* them,
20:31 The crowd began to *s* them in an effort to

SCOLDED (1)

Lk 18:15 disciples saw this, they *s* them roundly;

SCOLDING (3)

Ru 2:15 among the sheaves themselves without *s* her,
Mk 10:13 but the disciples were *s* them for this.
10:48 people were *s* him to make him keep quiet,

SCOOP (2)

2Mc 1:21 he ordered them to *s* some out and bring it.
Is 30:14 fragments cannot be found a sherd to *s* fire

SCOOPED (2)

Jgs 14: 9 So he *s* the honey out into his palms and
14: 9 he had *s* the honey from the lion's carcass.

SCOPE (3)

Jb 28:25 the wind, and fixed the *s* of the waters;
Bar 3:24 of God, how broad the *s* of his dominion:
Eph 1:19 *s* of his power in us who believe.

SCORCH (1)

Sir 28:22 among the just nor *s* them in its flame,

SCORCHED (13)

2Kgs 19:26 growth, like the *s* grass on the housetops.
Prv 6:28 walk on live coals, and his feet not be *s*?
Sir 43:22 When the mountain growth is *s* with heat,
Is 37:27 growth, like the *s* grass on the housetops.
Jer 9: 9 They are *s*, and no man crosses them,
9:11 ravaged, *s* like a wasteland untraversed?
Ez 15: 4 devours both ends and even the middle is *s*,
15: 5 less, when the fire has devoured and *s* it,
21: 3 south to north every face shall be *s* by it.
Mt 13: 6 no depth, but when the sun rose and *s* it,
Mk 4: 6 Then, when the sun rose and *s* it,
Rv 8: 7 A third of the land was *s*,
16: 9 Those who were *s* by the intense heat

SCORCHES (1)

Jb 30:30 the heat *s* my very frame.

SCORCHING (6)

Gn 31:40 How often the *s* heat ravaged me by day,
Dt 28:22 strike you with wasting and fever, with *s*,
Prv 16:27 of evil, and on his lips there is a *s* fire.
Is 49:10 shall the *s* wind or the sun strike them;
Mt 20:12 who have worked a full day in the *s* heat.'
Jas 1:11 up with its *s* heat it parches the meadow,

SCORE (1)

Phil 2:18 May you be glad on the same *s*,

SCORN (21)

Dt 28:37 reproach and barbed *s* from all the nations
2Kgs 19:21 " 'She despises you, laughs you to *s*,
Jdt 12:12 do not entice her, she will laugh us to *s*."
1Mc 2:49 "Arrogance and *s* have now grown strong;
Jb 31:34 and the *s* of the tribes terrified me
Ps(s) 22: 7 the *s* of men, despised by the people.
31:19 insolence against the just in pride and *s*.
44:14 the mockery and the *s* of those around us.
79: 4 the *s* and derision of those around us.
Prv 18: 3 comes contempt, and with disgrace comes *s*.
Wis 4:18 but the Lord laughs them to *s*.
Sir 20:16 How many times they laugh him to *s*!
21:15 them with *s* and casts them behind his back.
31:22 Listen to me, my son, and *s* me not;
Is 37:22 She despises you, laughs you to *s*,
43:28 under the ban, and exposed Israel to *s*.
Jer 6:10 LORD has become for them an object of *s*,
48:29 His loftiness, his pride, his *s*,
Ez 5:15 shall be a reproach and an object of *s*,
22: 4 Therefore I make you an object of *s* to the
Mal 1:13 you *s* it, says the LORD of hosts;

SCORNED (4)

Dt 32:15 god who made them and *s* their saving Rock.
Ps(s) 107:11 of God and *s* the counsel of the Most High.
Is 5:24 and *s* the word of the Holy One of Israel.
Lam 2: 6 has *s* in fierce wrath both king and priest.

SCORNFUL (3)

Ex 32:25 realized that, to the *s* joy of their foes,
Prv 21:24 pride who acts with *s* effrontery.
Zec 4:10 For even they who were *s* on that day of

SCORNFULLY (1)

Jn 9:28 They retorted *s*:

SCORNS (2)

Ps(s) 10: 5 all his foes he *s*.
Prv 30:17 that mocks a father, or *s* an aged mother,

SCORPION (2)

Sir 26: 7 he who marries her seizes a *s*.
Lk 11:12 or hand him a *s* if he asks for an egg?

SCORPIONS (11)

Dt 8:15 desert with its saraph serpents and *s*,
1Kgs 12:11 you with whips, but I will beat you with *s*.'"
12:14 you with whips, but I will beat you with *s*."
2Chr 10:11 you with whips, but I will beat you with *s*!'"
10:14 you with whips, but I will beat you with *s*."
Sir 39:30 hail, famine, disease, Ravenous beasts, *s*,
Ez 2: 6 you and reject you, and when you sit on *s*.
Lk 10:19 and *s* and all the forces of the enemy,
Rv 9: 3 locusts as powerful as *s* in their sting.

SCORPIONS (cont.)

9: 5 they inflicted was like that of a *s* sting.
9:10 They had tails with stingers like *s;*

SCOUNDREL (7)

2Mc 13: 4 the anger of Antiochus against the *s.*
Prv 6:12 A *s,* a villain, is he who deals in crooked
14:14 The *s* suffers the consequences of his ways,
16:27 A *s* is a furnace of evil,
Is 55: 7 Let the *s* forsake his way,
Na 1:11 evil against the LORD, the *s* planner.
2: 1 nevermore shall you be invaded by the *s;*

SCOUNDRELS (4)

Dt 13:14 you hear it said that certain *s* have
1Kgs 21:10 get two *s* to face him and accuse him of
21:13 Two *s* came in and confronted him with the
2Chr 13: 7 Worthless men, *s,* joined him and overcame

SCOUR (1)

Jer 2:22 Though you *s* it with soap,

SCOURED (1)

Lv 6:21 shall be *s* afterward and rinsed with water.

SCOURGE (16)

Nm 17:13 the living and the dead, the *s* was checked.
17:14 thousand seven hundred died from the *s,*
17:15 When the *s* had been checked,
Jos 23:13 *s* for your sides and thorns for your eyes,
2Mc 9:11 some understanding, under the *s* of God,
Jb 5:21 the *s* of the tongue you shall be hidden,
9:23 When the *s* slays suddenly,
21: 9 fear, nor is the *s* of God upon them.
Ps(s) 39:11 Take away your *s* from me;
Prv 17:26 man, but beyond reason to *s* princes.
Sir 23:11 the *s* will never be far from his house.
51: 3 mercy From the *s* of a slanderous tongue,
Is 10:26 will raise against them a *s* such as struck
28:15 When the overwhelming *s* passes,
28:18 When the overwhelming *s* passes,
Jer 15: 3 kinds of *s* I have decreed against them,
Lk 18:33 They will *s* him and put him to death,

SCOURGED (8)

Tb 11:15 all the ages, Because it was he who *s* me,
13: 5 He *s* you for your iniquities,
13: 9 city, he *s* you for the works of your hands,
2Mc 3:34 Since you have been *s* by Heaven,
Jer 20: 2 So he had the prophet *s* and placed in the
Mt 27:26 Jesus, however, he first had *s;*
Mk 15:15 and after he had had Jesus *s,*
Jn 19: 1 next move was to take Jesus and have him *s.*

SCOURGES (4)

Tb 13: 2 For he *s* and then has mercy;
2Mc 7: 1 and tortured with whips and *s* by the king,
Ez 9: 1 Come, you *s* of the city!
Heb 12: 6 he *s* every son he receives."

SCOURGING (4)

2Mc 6:30 terrible pain in my body from this *s,*
Prv 20:30 bloody lashes, and a *s* to the inmost being.
Sir 26: 6 and a *s* tongue like the other three.
Heb 11:36 Still others endured mockery, *s,*

SCOUT (3)

Jgs 18: 2 Eshtaol, to reconnoiter the land and *s* it.
18: 2 their instructions to go and *s* the land,
Sir 14:22 Who pursues her like a *s,*

SCOUTED (3)

Nm 13:32 the Israelites about the land they had *s,*
14: 6 who had been in the party that *s* the land,
Ez 20: 6 land of Egypt to the land I had *s* for them,

SCOUTING (1)

Nm 14:34 Forty days you spent in *s* the land;

SCOUTS (4)

Jos 14: 8 My fellow *s* who went up with me
Jgs 1:24 The *s* saw a man coming out of the city and
1Sm 26: 4 into the desert after him and sent out *s,*
2Kgs 7:13 abandoned horses and send *s* to investigate."

SCRAPE (3)

Jb 2: 8 And he took a potsherd to *s* himself,
Wis 13:11 tree and skillfully *s* off all its bark,
Ez 26: 4 I will *s* the ground from her and leave her

SCRAPED (3)

Lv 14:41 scraped, and the mortar that has been *s*
14:43 and the house has been *s* and replastered,

SCRAPS (2)

Jgs 1: 7 cut off, used to pick up *s* under my table.
Lk 16:21 the *s* that fell from the rich man's table.

SCRATCHES (1)

Ez 28:24 a brier that *s* them more than all the

SCRAWNY (1)

Gn 41:19 Behind them came seven other cows, *s,*

SCREAM (2)

Gn 39:15 When he heard me *s* for help,
Prv 23:29 Who *s?* who shriek?

SCREAMED (3)

Gn 39:14 *s* for her household servants and told them,
39:18 But when I *s* for help,
Mk 5: 5 he *s* and gashed himself with stones.

SCREAMING (2)

1Sm 25:14 to greet our master, but he flew at them *s.*
Jdt 14:19 Loud *s* and howling arose in the camp.

SCREECH (4)

Lv 11:17 hawks, the owl, the cormorant, the *s* owl,
Dt 14:16 species of hawks, the owl, the *s* owl,
Is 34:11 the *s* owl and raven shall dwell in her.
Zep 2:14 The *s* owl and the desert owl shall roost

SCREEN (2)

Ex 40: 3 in it, and *s* off the ark with the veil.
Ps(s) 31:21 You *s* them within your abode from the

SCREENING (2)

Ex 40:21 thus *s* off the ark of the commandments,
Nm 4: 5 sons shall go in and take down the *s* curtain

SCRIBE (48)

2Sm 8:17 Shawsha was *s.*
20:25 Shawsha was the *s.*
2Kgs 12:11 the royal *s* [and the priest] would come up,
18:18 Shebnah the *s;* and the herald Joah,
18:37 Eliakim, son of Hilkiah, Shebnah the *s,*
19: 2 the master of the palace, Shebnah the *s,*
22: 3 year, King Josiah sent the *s* Shaphan,
22: 8 high priest Hilkiah informed the *s* Shaphan,
22: 9 *s* Shaphan went to the king and reported,
22:10 The *s* Shaphan also informed the king that
22:12 Achbor, son of Micaiah, the *s* Shaphan,
25:19 in the city, the *s* of the army commander,
1Chr 18:16 Shavsha was *s;*
24: 6 The *s* Shemaiah, son of Nethanel, a Levite,
27:32 man of intelligence, was counselor and *s;*
2Chr 24:11 the royal *s* and an overseer for the high
26:11 by Jeiel the *s* and Maaseiah the recorder,
34:15 He reported this to Shaphan the *s,*
34:18 Then Shaphan the *s* announced to the king,
34:20 to Abdon, son of Michah, to Shaphan the *s,*
Ezr 4: 8 Rehum, the governor, and Shimshai, the *s,*
4: 9 "Rehum, the governor, Shimshai, the *s,*
4:17 "To Rehum, the governor, Shimshai, the *s,*
4:23 Rehum, the governor, Shimshai, the *s,*
7: 6 He was a *s,* well-versed in the law of Moses
7:11 the *s* of the text of the LORD's
7:12 *s* of the law of the God of heaven (then,
7:21 priest, *s* of the law of the God of heaven,
Neh 8: 1 and they called upon Ezra the *s* to bring
8: 4 Ezra the *s* stood on a wooden platform that
8:13 Levites gathered around Ezra the *s*
12:36 [Ezra the *s* was at their head.]
13:13 the priest Shelemiah, Zadok the *s,*
Ps(s) 45: 2 is nimble as the pen of a skillful *s.*
Is 36: 3 Eliakim, son of Hilkiah, and Shebna the *s,*
36:22 Eliakim, son of Hilkiah, and Shebna the *s,*
37: 2 master of the palace, and Shebna the *s,*
Jer 36:10 the room of Gemariah, son of the *s* Shaphan,
36:12 Elishama, the *s,*
36:20 safekeeping in the room of Elishama the *s,*
36:21 it from the room of Elishama the *s,*
37:15 into prison in the house of Jonathan the *s,*
37:20 me back into the house of Jonathan the *s,*
52:25 and the *s* of the army commander who
Mt 8:19 A *s* approached him and said,
13:52 "Every *s* who is learned in the reign of
Mk 12:32 The *s* said to him:
1Cor 1:20 Where the *s?*

SCRIBES (67)

1Kgs 4: 3 Elihoreph and Ahijah, sons of Shisha, *s:*
2Chr 34:13 Some of the other Levites were *s,*
Est 3:12 So the royal *s* were summoned;
8: 9 month, Sivan, the royal *s* were summoned.
1Mc 7:12 A group of *s,*
2Mc 6:18 Eleazar, one of the foremost *s,*
Sir 38:24 The *s* profession increases his wisdom;
Jer 8: 8 into falsehood by the lying pen of the *s!*
36:12 to the king's palace, into the *s* chamber,
36:23 king would cut off the piece with a *s* knife
Na 3:17 And your *s* as locust swarms gathered on
Mt 2: 4 of the chief priests and *s* of the people,
5:20 surpasses that of the *s* and Pharisees
7:29 taught with authority and not like their *s.*
9: 3 At that some of the *s* said to themselves,
12:38 Some of the *s* and Pharisees then spoke up,
15: 1 Pharisees and *s* from Jerusalem approached
16:21 the elders, the chief priests, and the *s,*
17:10 do the *s* claim that Elijah must come first?"
20:18 be handed over to the chief priests and *s,*
21:15 The chief priests and the *s* became
23: 2 "The *s* and the Pharisees have succeeded
23:13 "Woe to you *s* and Pharisees, you frauds!
23:15 Woe to you *s* and Pharisees, you frauds!
23:23 Woe to you *s* and Pharisees, you frauds!
23:25 Woe to you *s* and Pharisees, you frauds!
23:27 Woe to you *s* and Pharisees, you frauds!
23:29 Woe to you *s* and Pharisees, you frauds!
23:34 shall send you prophets and wise men and *s.*
26:57 where the *s* and elders were convened.
27:41 The chief priests, the *s,*
Mk 1:22 taught with authority, and not like the *s.*
2: 6 the *s* were sitting there asking themselves:
2:16 When the *s* who belonged to the Pharisee
3:22 the *s* who arrived from Jerusalem asserted,
7: 5 So the Pharisees and the *s* questioned him:
8:31 the elders, the chief priests, and the *s,*
9:11 do the *s* claim that Elijah must come first?"
9:14 and *s* in lively discussion with them.
10:33 handed over to the chief priests and the *s.*
11:18 The chief priests and the *s* heard of this
11:27 temple precincts the chief priests, the *s,*
12:28 One of the *s* came up,
12:35 "How can the *s* claim,
12:38 "Be on guard against the *s,*
14: 1 chief priests and *s* began to look for a way
14:43 had been sent by the chief priests, the *s,*
14:53 the elders and the *s* came together.
15: 1 priests, with the elders and *s* (that is,
15:31 and the *s* also joined in and jeered:
Lk 5:21 The *s* and the Pharisees began a discussion,
5:30 the *s* of their party said to his disciples,
6: 7 The *s* and Pharisees were on the watch to
9:22 by the elders, the high priests and the *s,*
11:53 the *s* and Pharisees began to manifest
15: 2 at which the Pharisees and the *s* murmured,
19:47 The chief priests and *s* meanwhile were
20:19 At these words the *s* and high priests
20:39 Some of the *s* responded,
20:46 "Beware of the *s,* who like to parade
22: 2 and the high priests and *s* began to look
22:66 chief priests, and the *s* assembled again.
23:10 *s* were at hand to accuse him vehemently.
Jn 8: 3 The *s* and the Pharisees led a woman
Acts 4: 5 the *s* assembled the next day in Jerusalem,
6:12 incited the people, the elders, and the *s.*
23: 9 some *s* of the Pharisee party arose and

SCRIPT (4)

Est 1:22 *s* and to each people in its own language,
3:12 *s* and to each people in its own language.
8: 9 *s* and to each people in its own language,
8: 9 to the Jews in their own *s* and language.

SCRIPTURE (90)

1Mc 7:16 in one day, according to the text of *S:*
Mt 4: 4 Jesus replied, *S* has it:
4: 6 *S* has it: 'He will bid his angels
4: 7 Jesus answered him, *S* also has it:
4:10 *S* has it: 'You shall do homage
11:10 It is about this man that *S* says,
21:13 *S* has it, 'My house shall be called
26:24 Son of Man is departing, as *S* says of him,
26:31 faith in me will be shaken, for *S* has it:
Mk 9:12 Yet why does *S* say of the Son of Man that
11:17 "Does not *S* have it,
12:10 you not familiar with this passage of *S:*
14:21 of Man is going the way the *S* tells of him.
14:27 faith in me shall be shaken, for *S* has it,
Lk 4: 4 Jesus answered him, *S* has it,
4: 8 In reply, Jesus said to him, *S* has it,
4:10 yourself down from here, for *S* has it,
4:21 *S* passage is fulfilled in your hearing."
7:27 This is the man of whom *S* says,
19:46 *S* has it, 'My house is meant for a house
22:37 It is written in *S,*
24:27 every passage of *S* which referred to him.
Jn 2:17 His disciples recalled the words of *S:*
2:22 believe the *S* and the word he had spoken.
6:31 according to *S,* 'He gave them bread
7:38 *S* has it: 'From within him
7:42 Does not *S* say that the Messiah,
10:35 and *S* cannot lose its force
12:14 donkey and mounted it; in accord with *S:*
13:18 my purpose here is the fulfillment of *S:*
17:12 destined to be lost— in fulfillment of *S.*
19:24 of this was to have the *S* fulfilled:
19:28 was now finished, said to fulfill the *S,*
19:36 events took place for the fulfillment of *S:*
19:37 is still another *S* passage which says:
20: 9 the *S* that Jesus had to rise from the dead.)
Acts 1:16 "the saying in *S* uttered long ago by the
8:32 This was the passage of *S* he was reading:
8:35 with this *S* passage as his starting point,

15:15 agree with this, where it says in *S.*
18:24 He was both an authority on *S* and
23: 5 Indeed, *S* has it, 'You shall not curse
Rom 1:17 as *S* says, "The just man shall live by faith."
2:24 As *S* says, "On your account the name
3: 4 man be proved a liar, so that, as *S* says,
3:10 It is as *S* says: "There is no just man,
4: 3 for what does *S* say?
4:17 is father of us all, which is why *S* says,
8:36 As *S* says: "For your sake
9: 7 descendants his children, but as *S* says,
9:13 It is just as *S* says,
9:17 *S* says to Pharaoh,
9:33 over the stumbling stone, as *S* says:
10:11 *S* says, "No one who believes in him
10:15 *S* says, "How beautiful are the feet
11: 2 Do you not know what *S* says about Elijah,
11: 8 The rest became blind, as *S* says:
11:26 As *S* says: "Out of Zion will come
15: 3 accord with *S,* Christ did not please himself:
15: 9 As *S* has it, "Therefore I will praise you
15:21 but rather to fulfill the words of *S,*
1Cor 1:19 *S* says, "I will destroy the wisdom
3:19 *S* says, "He catches the wise
6:16 *S* says, "The two shall become one flesh."
10: 7 *S* says, "The people sat down to eat
15:27 *S* reads that God "has placed all things
15:45 *S* has it that Adam, the first man,
15:54 then will the saying of *S* be fulfilled:
2Cor 4:13 that spirit of faith of which the *S* says,
Gal 3: 8 Because *S* saw in advance that God's way of
3:16 *S* does not say "and to your descendants,"
3:22 *S* has locked all things in under the
4:27 That is why *S* says:
4:30 What does *S* say on the point?
Eph 4: 8 Thus you find *S* saying:
1Tm 4:13 devote yourself to the reading of *S,*
5:18 The *S* says, "You shall not put a muzzle
2Tm 3:16 All *S* is inspired of God and is useful for
Heb 3:15 When *S* says, "Today, if you should hear
4: 4 to the seventh day *S* somewhere says,
7: 8 tithes, *S* testifies that this man lives on.
7:17 *S* testifies: "You are a priest forever
11: 5 *S* testifies that, before he was taken up,
Jas 2: 8 *S* has it, "You shall love your neighbor
2:23 see how the *S* was fulfilled which says,
4: 5 suppose it is to no purpose that *S* says,
1Pt 1:16 remember, *S* says,
2: 6 For *S* has it: "See, I am laying a cornerstone
2Pt 1:20 in *S* which is a personal interpretation.
3:16 they do the rest of *S)* to their own ruin.

SCRIPTURES (19)

Dn 9: 2 tried to understand in the *S* the counting
Mt 21:42 to them, "Did you never read in the *S,*
22:29 to understand the *S* and the power of God.
26:54 But then how would the *S* be fulfilled
Mk 9:13 they pleased with him, as the *S* say of him."
12:24 to understand the *S* or the power of God.
14:49 But now, so that the *S* may be fulfilled . . ."
Lk 20:17 said, "What do the *S* mean when they say,
24:32 us on the road and explained the *S* to us?"
24:45 their minds to the understanding of the *S.*
Jn 5:39 *S* in which you think you have eternal life
Acts 17: 2 with them about the *S* for three sabbaths.
17:11 the *S* to see whether these things were so.
18:28 from the *S* that Jesus is the Messiah.
Rom 1: 2 through his prophets, as the holy *S* record
15: 4 and the words of encouragement in the *S.*
1Cor 15: 3 for our sins in accordance with the *S;*
15: 4 was buried and, in accordance with the *S,*
2Tm 3:15 your infancy you have known the sacred *S,*

SCROLL (50)

Dt 17:18 law made from the *s* that is in the custody
31:24 a *s* the words of the law in their entirety,
31:26 "Take this *s* of the law and put it beside
Ezr 6: 2 *s* was found containing the following text:
Neh 8: 5 Ezra opened the *s* so that all the people
Tb 7:13 her mother and told her to bring a *s,*
7:13 Her mother brought the *s,*
1Mc 1:57 Whoever was found with a *s* of the covenant,
3:48 They unrolled the *s* of the law,
Ps(s) 40: 8 in the written *s* it is prescribed for me,
Is 29:11 has become like the words of a sealed *s.*
34: 4 The heavens shall be rolled up like a *s,*
Jer 36: 2 Take a *s* and write on it all the words I
36: 4 son of Neriah, who wrote down on a *s,*
36: 6 words from the *s* you wrote at my dictation;
36:14 you the *s* you read publicly to the people."
36:14 *S* in hand, Baruch, son of Neriah,
36:20 Leaving the *s* in safekeeping in the room
36:21 happened, he sent Jehudi to fetch the *s.*
36:25 Gemariah urged the king not to burn the *s,*
36:27 after the king burned the *s* with the text
36:28 *s,* and write on it everything that the first *s*
36:29 You burned that *s,* saying, "Why did you
36:32 Jeremiah took another *s,*
Bar 1: 1 these are the words of the *s* which Baruch,
1: 3 read the words of this *s* for Jeconiah,
1:14 read out publicly this *s* which we send you,
Ez 2: 9 a written *s* which he unrolled before me.
3: 1 eat this *s,* then go, speak to the house
3: 2 my mouth and he gave me the *s* to eat.
3: 3 your stomach with this *s* I am giving you.
Zec 5: 1 I raised my eyes again and saw a *s* flying.
5: 2 I answered, "I see a *s* flying;
Lk 4:17 he unrolled the *s* and found the passage
4:20 Rolling up the *s* he gave it back to the
Rv 1:11 "Write on a *s* what you now see and send
5: 1 of the One who sat on the throne I saw a *s.*
5: 2 worthy to open the *s* and break its seals?"
5: 3 to open the *s* or examine its contents.
5: 4 be found worthy to open or examine the *s.*
5: 5 victory to open the *s* with the seven seals."
5: 7 The Lamb came and received the *s* from the
5: 8 When he had taken the *s,*
5: 9 to receive the *s* and break open its seals,
6:14 as if it were a *s* being rolled up;
10: 2 he held a little *s* which had been opened.
10: 8 take the open *s* from the hand of the angel
10: 9 and said to him, "Give me the little *s.*"
10:10 little *s* from the angel's hand and ate it.

SCROLLS (3)

1Mc 1:56 Any *s* of the law which they found they
Rv 20:12 among the *s,* the book of the living was
20:12 to their conduct as recorded on the *s.*

SCRUPLES (2)

2Mc 6:11 day, they had *s* about defending themselves.
Rom 15: 1 with the *s* of those whose faith is weak;

SCRUPULOUSLY (2)

Mk 7: 3 never eat without *s* washing their hands.
Acts 17:22 that in every respect you are *s* religious.

SCRUTINIZE (2)

Ps(s) 139: 3 My journeys and my rest you *s,*
Wis 6: 3 shall probe your works and *s* your counsels!

SCRUTINIZED (2)

Eccl 12:29 weighed, *s* and arranged many proverbs.
Wis 1: 9 the devices of the wicked man shall be *s,*

SCRUTINIZES (1)

1Cor 2:10 The Spirit *s* all matters,

SCRUTINY (6)

Ps(s) 90: 8 our hidden sins in the light of your *s.*
Wis 3:18 have no hope nor comfort in the day of *s;*
6: 8 for those in power a rigorous *s* impends.
Sir 23:10 under *s* will not be without welts,
Is 40:28 grow weary, and his knowledge is beyond *s.*
Gal 2: 2 and I laid out for their *s* the gospel as I

SCUM (1)

1Cor 4:13 become the world's refuse, the *s* of all;

SCURRIED (1)

Mk 6:55 The crowds *s* about the adjacent area and

SCYTHES (1)

2Mc 13: 2 and three hundred chariots armed with *s.*

SCYTHIAN (1)

Col 3:11 circumcised or uncircumcised, foreigner, *S,*

SCYTHIANS (1)

2Mc 4:47 if they had pleaded their case before *S.*

SCYTHOPOLIS (2)

Jdt 3:10 he set up his camp between Geba and *S,*
2Mc 12:29 set out from there and hastened on to *S,*

SCYTHOPOLITANS (1)

2Mc 12:30 testified to the good will shown by the *S*

SEA (391)

Gn 1:10 the basin of the water he called "the *s.*"
1:21 God created the great *s* monsters and all
1:26 them have dominion over the fish of the *s,*
1:28 Have dominion over the fish of the *s,*
9: 2 on the ground and all the fishes of the *s;*
14: 3 the Valley of Siddim (that is, the Salt *S).*
32:13 your descendants like the sands of the *s,*
41:49 in quantities like the sands of the *s,*
Ex 10:19 the locusts and hurled them into the Red *S.*
13:18 the Red *S* by way of the desert road.
14: 2 Pi-hahiroth, between Migdol and the *s.*
14: 2 of Baal-zephon, just opposite, by the *s.*
14: 9 with them as they lay encamped by the *s,*
14:16 and, with hand outstretched over the *s,*
14:16 over the sea, split the *s* in two,
14:21 over the sea, and the LORD swept the *s*
14:22 into the midst of the *s* on dry land,
14:23 after them right into the midst of the *s.*
14:26 Moses, "Stretch out your hand over the *s,*
14:27 his hand over the *s,* and at dawn the sea
14:27 were fleeing head on toward the *s,*
14:28 had followed the Israelites into the *s.*
14:29 on dry land through the midst of the *s,*
15: 1 horse and chariot he has cast into the *s.*
15: 4 chariots and army he hurled into the *s;*
15: 4 his officers were submerged in the Red *S.*
15: 8 waters congealed in the midst of the *s.*
15:10 When your wind blew, the *s* covered them;
15:19 sea, and the LORD made the waters of the *s*
15:19 on dry land through the midst of the *s.*
15:21 horse and chariot he has cast into the *s.*
15:22 Moses led Israel forward from the Red *S,*
20:11 the earth, the *s* and all that is in them;
23:31 the Red Sea to the *s* of the Philistines,
Lv 11:10 water, whether in the *s* or in the rivers,
Nm 11:22 all the fish of the *s* were caught for them,
11:31 that drove in quail from the *s* and brought
14:25 set out in the desert on the Red *S* road."
21: 4 Mount Hor they set out on the Red *S* road,
24: 7 waters, he shall have the *s* within reach;
33: 8 crossed over through the *s* into the desert,
33:10 from Elim, they camped beside the Red *S.*
33:11 Setting out from the Red *S,*
34: 3 it shall begin at the end of the Salt *S,*
34: 5 Wadi of Egypt, shall terminate at the *S.*
34: 6 you shall have the Great *S* with its coast;
34: 7 Great *S* you shall draw a line to Mount Hor,
34:11 ridge on the east side of *S* of Chinnereth;
34:12 the Jordan and terminate with the Salt *S.*
Dt 1:40 proceed into the desert on the Red *S* road.'
2: 1 proceed into the desert on the Red *S* road,
3:17 Chinnereth to the Salt *S* of the Arabah,
4:49 as the Arabah *S* under the slopes of Pisgah.
11: 4 the water of the Red *S* as they pursued you,
11:24 from the Euphrates River to the Western *S,*
30:13 Nor is it across the *s,*
30:13 the *s* to get it for us and tell us of it,
34: 2 the land of Judah as far as the Western *S,*
Jos 1: 4 river Euphrates and west to the Great *S.*
2:10 *S* before you when you came out of Egypt,
3:16 Salt *S* of the Arabah disappeared entirely.
4:23 the LORD, your God, had done at the Red *S,*
5: 1 Canaanites by the *s* heard that the LORD
9: 1 the coast of the Great *S* as far as Lebanon:
12: 3 the eastern side of the *S* of Chinnereth,
12: 3 eastern side of the Salt *S* of the Arabah
13:27 southeastern tip of the *S* of Chinnereth.
15: 2 that forms the southern end of the Salt *S,*
15: 4 Wadi of Egypt before coming out at the *s.*
15: 5 Salt *S* as far as the mouth of the Jordan.
15: 6 from the bay where the Jordan meets the *s,*
15:11 Jabneel, before it came out at the *s.*
15:12 boundary was the Great *S* and its coast.
15:46 towns and villages, from Ekron to the *s,*
15:47 Wadi of Egypt and the coast of the Great *S.*
16: 3 and to Gezer, ending thence at the *s.*
16: 6 to Upper Beth-horon and thence to the *s.*
16: 8 to the Wadi Kanah and ended at the *s.*
17: 9 ran north of the wadi and ended at the *s.*
17:10 with the *s* as their common boundary,
18:19 extended to the northern tip of the Salt *S,*
19:29 it cut back to Hosah and ended at the *s.*
23: 4 the Jordan and the Great *S* in the west.
24: 6 out of Egypt, and when you reached the *s,*
24: 6 to the Red *S* with chariots and horsemen.
24: 7 he brought the *s* so that it engulfed them.
Jgs 11:16 the desert to the Red *S* and came to Kadesh.
2Sm 17:11 who are as numerous as the sands by the *s,*
22:16 Then the wellsprings of the *s* appeared,
1Kgs 4:20 were as numerous as the sands by the *s;*
5:23 bring them down from the Lebanon to the *s,*
5:23 in the *s* and bring them wherever you say.
7:23 The *s* was then cast;
7:24 rows and were cast in one mold with the *s.*
7:25 the center, where the *s* was set upon them.
7:39 The *s* was placed off to the southeast from
7:44 one sea, twelve oxen supporting the *s,*
9:26 the shore of the Red *S* in the land of Edom.
10:22 of Tarshish ships at *s* with Hiram's fleet.
18:43 "Climb up and look out to *s,*"
18:44 as small as a man's hand rising from the *s.*"
2Kgs 14:25 from Labo of Hamath to the *s* of the Arabah,
16:17 *s* from the bronze oxen that supported it,
25:13 and the bronze *s* in the house of the LORD,
25:16 bronze of the two pillars, the bronze *s,*
1Chr 16:32 Let the *s* and what fills it resound;
18: 8 used to make the bronze *s* and the pillars
2Chr 4: 2 He also made the molten *s.*
4: 3 a ring of figures of oxen encircled the *s,*
4: 3 of these cast in the same mold with the *s.*
4: 4 the *s* rested on their backs.
4: 6 but the *s* was for the priests to wash in.
4:10 The *s* was placed off to the southeast from
4:15 one *s,* and the twelve oxen under it;
8:18 ships and crewmen acquainted with the *s,*
20: 2 is coming against you from across the *s,*
Neh 9: 9 Egypt, you heard their cry by the Red *S;*
9:11 The *s* you divided before them,
9:11 they passed through the midst of the *s;*
Jdt 2:24 the Wadi Abron, until he reached the *s.*
5:13 them, God dried up the Red *S* before them,
Est 10: 1 on the land and on the islands of the *s.*

SEA (cont.)

1Mc 4: 9 how our fathers were saved in the Red *S*,
8:23 Jewish nation at *s* and on land forever;
8:32 justice and make war on you by land and *s*.' "
13:29 could be seen by all who sailed the *s*.
14: 5 made it a gateway to the isles of the *s*.
14:34 the *s* and Gazara on the border of Azotus,
15: 1 letter from the islands of the *s* to Simon,
15:11 Antiochus, Trypho fled to Dor, by the *s*,
15:14 by land and *s* and let no one go in or out.
2Mc 5: 9 Egypt, he crossed the *s* to the Spartans,
5:21 land navigable and the *s* passable on foot,
9: 8 he could command the waves of the *s*,
12: 4 *s* and drowned at least two hundred of them.
Jb 3: 8 Let them curse it who curse the *s*,
6: 3 They would now outweigh the sands of the *s*!
7:12 Am I the *s*, or a monster of the deep,
9: 8 and treads upon the crests of the *s*.
11: 9 earth in measure, and broader than the *s*.
12: 8 you, and the fish of the *s* to inform you.
26:12 By his power he stirs up the *s*,
28:14 and the *s* says, "I have it not."
38: 8 And who shut within doors the *s*,
38:16 you entered into the sources of the *s*,
41:17 the waves of the *s* fall back.
41:23 the *s* he churns like perfume in a kettle.
Ps(s) 8: 9 The birds of the air, the fishes of the *s*,
18:16 Then the bed of the *s* appeared,
33: 7 gathers the waters of the *s* as in a flask;
46: 3 mountains plunge into the depths of the *s*.
66: 6 He has changed the *s* into dry land;
68:23 fetch them back from the depths of the *s*,
72: 8 May he rule from sea to *s*,
74:13 earth, You stirred up the *s* by your might;
77:20 Through the *s* was your way,
78:13 He cleft the *s* and brought them through,
78:27 like dust, and, like the sand of the *s*,
78:53 while he covered their enemies with the *s*.
80:12 It put forth its foliage to the *S*,
89:10 You rule over the surging of the *s*;
89:26 I will set his hand upon the *s*,
93: 4 more powerful than the breakers of the *s*—
95: 5 His is the *s*,
96:11 let the *s* and what fills it resound;
98: 7 Let the *s* and what fills it resound,
104:25 The *s* also, great and wide,
106: 7 against the Most High at the Red *S*.
106: 9 He rebuked the Red *S*,
106:22 land of Ham, terrible things at the Red *S*.
107:23 They who sailed the *s* in ships,
107:29 and the billows of the *s* were stilled;
114: 3 The *s* beheld and fled; Jordan turned back.
114: 5 Why is it, O *s*, that you flee?
136:13 Who split the Red *S* in twain,
136:15 swept Pharaoh and his army into the Red *S*,
139: 9 I settle at the farthest limits of the *s*,
146: 6 and earth, the *s* and all that is in them;
148: 7 the earth, you *s* monsters and all depths;
Prv 8:29 When he set for the *s* its limit,
23:34 like one now lying in the depths of the *s*,
Eccl 1: 7 the sea, yet never does the *s* become full.
Wis 5:22 The water of the *s* shall be enraged
10:18 *S* and brought them through the deep waters
14: 3 you have furnished even in the *s* a road,
19: 7 Out of the Red *S* an unimpeded road,
19:12 appease them quail came to them from the *s*.
Sir 18: 8 Like a drop of *s* water,
24: 6 Over waves of the *s*,
24:27 For deeper than the *s* are her thoughts;
24:29 a river, then this stream of mine, a *s*.
29:17 and tossed them about like waves of the *s*,
43:24 the deep, and plants the islands in the *s*.
43:25 go down to the *s* tell part of its story,
44:21 give them an inheritance from sea to *s*,
47:15 covered the whole earth, and, like a *s*,
Is 5:30 with a roaring like that of the *s*
10:22 O Israel, were like the sand of the *s*
10:26 staff over the *s* as he did against Egypt.
11: 9 of the LORD, as water covers the *s*.
11:11 Shinar, Hamath, and the isles of the *s*.
11:15 shall dry up the tongue of the *S* of Egypt,
16: 8 spread forth and extended over the *s*.
18: 2 of Ethiopia, Sending ambassadors by *s*,
19: 5 The waters shall be drained from the *s*,
21: 1 Oracle on the wastelands by the *s*:
23: 2 crossed the *s* over the deep waters.
23: 4 fortress on the sea, for the *s* has spoken:
23:11 His hand he stretches out over the *s*,
24:14 *s* they proclaim the majesty of the LORD:
24:15 In the coastlands of the *s*,
27: 1 he will slay the dragon that is in the *s*.
40:12 cupped in his hand the waters of the *s*,
42:10 Let the *s* and what fills it resound,
43:16 in the *s* and a path in the mighty waters,
48:18 your vindication like the waves of the *s*;
50: 2 Lo, with my rebuke I dry up the *s*,
51:10 Was it not you who dried up the *s*,
51:10 *s* into a way for the redeemed to pass over?
51:15 who stirs up the *s* so that its waves roar;
57:20 like the tossing *s* which cannot be calmed,
60: 5 of the *s* shall be emptied out before you,
60: 9 All the vessels of the *s* are assembled,
63:11 up out of the *s* the shepherd of his flock?
Jer 6:23 the roaring *s* as they ride forth on steeds,
15: 8 numerous before me than the sands of the *s*.
25:22 of Sidon, and of the shores beyond the *s*;
27:19 concerning the pillars, the bronze *s*,
31:35 Who stirs up the *s* till its waves roar,
33:22 the sands of the *s* which cannot be counted,
46:18 he shall come, like Carmel above the *s*.
48:32 Your tendrils trailed down to the *s*,
49:21 quakes, to the Red *S* the outcry is heard!
49:23 they toss like the *s* which cannot rest.
50:42 They sound like the roaring *s*,
51:36 I will dry up her *s*,
51:42 against Babylon the *s* rises,
52:17 and the bronze *s* in the house of the LORD,
52:20 as well as the two pillars, the one *s*,
52:20 and the twelve oxen of bronze under the *s*,
Lam 2:13 For great as the *s* is your downfall;
Bar 3:30 Who has crossed the *s* and found her,
Ez 26: 3 nations, even as the *s* churns up its waves;
26: 5 place for nets in the midst of the *s*.
26:12 and your clay shall be cast into the *s*.
26:16 the *s* shall step down from their thrones,
26:17 Once she was mighty on the *s*,
26:17 spread terror into all that dwelt by the *s*.
26:18 in the *s* are terrified at your passing.
27: 3 is situated at the approaches of the *s*,
27: 4 midst of the *s* your builders placed you,
27: 9 sailor on the *s* came to you to carry trade.
27:25 and heavily laden in the heart of the *s*.
27:26 wind smashed you in the heart of the *s*.
27:27 of the *s* on the day of your shipwreck.
27:29 The sailors, all the mariners of the *s*,
27:32 destroyed like Tyre in the midst of the *s*?
27:34 Now you are wrecked in the *s*,
28: 2 a godly throne in the heart of the *s*—
28: 8 a bloodied corpse, in the heart of the *s*.
32: 2 You were like a monster in the *s*,
38:20 the fish of the *s* and the birds of the air,
39:11 east of the *s* [it is blocked to travelers].
47: 8 upon the Arabah, and empties into the *s*,
47: 9 this water comes the *s* shall be made fresh.
47:10 of fish shall be like those of the Great *S*,
47:15 the Great *S* in the direction of Hethlon,
47:17 shall extend from the *s* to Hazar-enon,
47:18 down to the eastern *s* as far as Tamar.
47:19 the Wadi of Egypt, and on to the Great *S*.
47:20 the Great *S* forms the boundary up to a
48:28 the Wadi of Egypt, and on to the Great *S*.
Dn 3:36 heaven, or the sand on the shore of the *s*.
7: 2 winds of heaven stirred up the great *s*,
11:45 the *s* and the glorious holy mountain,
Hos 2: 1 shall be like the sand of the *s*,
4: 3 the air, and even the fish of the *s* perish.
Jl 2:20 sea, and his rear toward the western *s*;
Am 5: 8 Who summons the waters of the *s*,
6:12 or can one plow the *s* with oxen?
8:12 Then shall they wander from *s* to sea and
9: 3 hide from my gaze in the bottom of the *s*,
9: 6 I summon the waters of the *s* and pour them
Jon 1: 4 however, hurled a violent wind upon the *s*,
1: 5 they threw its cargo into the *s*.
1: 9 of heaven, who made the *s* and the dry land."
1:11 asked, "that the *s* may quiet down for us?"
1:11 the *s* was growing more and more turbulent.
1:12 "Pick me up and throw me into the *s*,
1:13 not, for the *s* grew ever more turbulent.
1:15 they took Jonah and threw him into the *s*,
2: 4 me into the deep, into the heart of the *s*,
Mi 7:12 Tyre even to the River, from sea to *s*,
7:19 cast into the depths of the *s* all our sins;
Na 1: 4 He rebukes the *s* and leaves it dry,
Hb 1:14 You have made man like the fish of the *s*,
2:14 of the LORD's glory as water covers the *s*.
3: 8 the streams, your rage against the *s*,
3:15 You tread the *s* with your steeds amid the
Zep 1: 3 birds of the sky, and the fishes of the *s*.
2: 7 by the *s* they shall pasture.
Hg 2: 6 and the earth, the *s* and the dry land.
Zec 9: 4 possessions, and smite her power on the *s*,
9:10 His dominion shall be from sea to *s*,
10:11 smite the waves of the *s* and all the depths
14: 8 eastern sea, and half to the western *s*,
Mt 4:13 went down to live in Capernaum by the *s*
4:15 of Naphtali along the *s* beyond the Jordan,
4:18 the *S* of Galilee he watched two brothers,
4:18 brother Andrew, casting a net into the *s*.
8:26 up and took the winds and the *s* to task.
8:27 "that even the winds and the *s* obey him?"
8:32 down the bluff into the *s* and were drowned.
15:29 place and passed along the *S* of Galilee.
18: 6 around his neck, in the depths of the *s*.
21:21 'Be lifted up and thrown into the *s*,'
23:15 over *s* and land to make a single convert,
Mk 1:16 As he made his way along the *S* of Galilee,
1:16 Andrew casting their nets into the *s*;
4:39 and rebuked the wind and said to the *s*:
4:41 this be that the wind and the *s* obey him?"
7:31 by way of Sidon to the *S* of Galilee,
9:42 plunged in the *s* with a great millstone
11:23 'Be lifted up and thrown into the *s*,'
Lk 8:25 even the winds and the *s* and they obey him?"
17: 2 He would be better off thrown into the *s*
17: 6 'Be uprooted and transplanted into the *s*,'
21:25 at the roaring of the *s* and the waves.
Jn 6: 1 *S* of Galilee [to the shore] of Tiberias;
6:18 wind blowing, the *s* was becoming rough.
21: 1 Later, at the *S* of Tiberias,
Acts 4:24 and earth and *s* and all that is in them,
7:36 signs in the land of Egypt, in the Red *S*,
10: 6 leather-tanner whose house stands by the *s*."
10:32 of Simon the leather-tanner, by the *s*.'
13:13 out to *s* and sailed to Perga in Pamphylia.
14:15 earth and the *s* and all that is in them.'
16:11 We put out to *s* from Troas
17:14 sent Paul off directly on his way to the *s*,
21: 1 we put out to *s* and sailed straight to Cos.
27: 5 *s* off the coast of Cilicia and Pamphylia,
27:12 put out to *s* in the hope of making Phoenix
27:27 still being driven across the Ionian *S*,
27:30 they let the ship's boat down into the *s*.
27:40 the anchors and abandoned them to the *s*.
27:41 was shattered by the pounding of the *s*.
28: 4 a murderer if, after his escape from the *s*,
Rom 9:27 should be as the sands of the *s*,
1Cor 10: 1 the cloud and all passed through the *s*;
10: 2 the *s* all of them were baptized into Moses.
2Cor 11:25 I passed a day and night on the *s*.
11:26 in the city, in the desert, at *s*,
Heb 11:29 crossed the Red *S* as if it were dry land,
Rv 4: 6 like a *s* of glass that was crystal-clear.
5:13 on earth and under the earth and in the *s*;
7: 1 wind blew on land or *s* or through any tree.
7: 2 given power to ravage the land and the *s*,
7: 3 "Do no harm to the land or the *s* or the
8: 8 mountain all in flames was cast into the *s*.
8: 8 A third of the *s* turned to blood,
8: 9 of the creatures living in the *s* died,
10: 2 on the *s* and his left foot on the land,
10: 5 angel whom I saw standing on the *s*
10: 6 earth and *s* along with everything in them:
10: 8 angel standing on the *s* and on the land."
12:12 But woe to you, earth and *s*,
12:17 took up his position by the shore of the *s*.
13: 1 of the *s* with ten horns and seven heads;
14: 7 the Creator of the *s* and the springs."
15: 2 like a *s* of glass mingled with fire.
15: 2 On the *s* of glass were standing those who
16: 3 second angel poured out his bowl on the *s*.
16: 3 *s* turned to blood like that of a corpse,
16: 3 and every creature living in the *s* died.
18:21 and hurled it into the *s* and said:
20: 8 and Magog, numerous as the sands of the *s*.
20:13 The *s* gave up its dead;
21: 1 had passed away, and the *s* was no longer.

SEACOAST (12)

Nm 13:29 along the *s* and the banks of the Jordan."
Dt 1: 7 the foothills, the Negeb and the *s*;
Jdt 1: 7 to all who dwelt along the *s*,
3: 6 he went down with his army to the *s*,
5: 2 all the satraps of the *s* and said to them:
5:22 inhabitants of the *s* and of Moab alike
7: 8 together with the generals of the *s*,
1Mc 7: 1 arrived with a few men in a city on the *s*,
11: 8 along the *s* as far as Seleucia-by-the-Sea.
15:38 Cendebeus commander-in-chief of the *s*,
Ez 25:16 and wipe out the remnant on the *s*.
Zep 2: 5 Woe to you who dwell by the *s*,

SEAFARING (1)

Rv 18:17 and navigator, all sailors and *s* men,

SEAH (3)

2Kgs 7: 1 a *s* of fine flour will sell for a shekel,
7:16 and then a *s* of fine flour sold for a
7:18 and one *s* of fine flour for a shekel at

SEAHS (6)

Gn 18: 6 told Sarah, "Quick, three *s* of fine flour!
1Sm 25:18 dressed sheep, five *s* of roasted grain,
1Kgs 18:32 the altar large enough for two *s* of grain.
2Kgs 7: 1 a shekel, and two *s* of barley for a shekel,
7:16 a shekel and two *s* of barley for a shekel,
7:18 "Two *s* of barley will sell for a shekel,

SEAL (40)

Gn 38:18 She answered, "Your *s* and cord,
38:25 *s* and cord and whose staff these are."
Ex 28:11 As a gem-cutter engraves a *s*,
28:21 each stone engraved like a *s* with the name
28:36 and engrave on it, as on a *s* engraving,
39: 6 they were engraved like *s* engravings with
39:14 stone was engraved like a *s* with the name
39:30 gold and inscribed, as on a *s* engraving:
1Kgs 21: 8 name and, having sealed them with his *s*,
Tb 1:22 had been chief cupbearer, keeper of the *s*,
Est 8: 8 *s* the letter with the royal signet ring."
Jb 38:14 The earth is changed as is clay by the *s*,
Sg 8: 6 a seal on your heart, as a *s* on your arm;
Wis 2: 5 be deferred because it is fixed with a *s*;
Sir 22:27 my mouth, and upon my lips an effective *s*,
28:25 As you *s* up your silver and gold,
32: 5 Like a *s* of carnelian in a setting of gold

32: 6 *s* is string music with delicious wine.
42: 6 Of a *s* to keep an erring wife at home,
45:11 with *s* engravings in golden settings,
Ez 28:12 You were stamped with the *s* of perfection,
Dn 2:43 shall *s* their alliances by intermarriage,
12: 4 message and *s* the book until the end time;
14:11 then shut the door and *s* it with your ring.
Mt 27:66 the guard, after fixing a *s* to the stone.
Jn 6:27 on him that God the Father has set his *s*."
Rom 4:11 sign of circumcision as a *s* attesting
1Cor 9: 2 the very *s* of my apostolate in the Lord.
Rv 6: 3 When the Lamb broke open the second *s*,
6: 5 When the Lamb broke open the third *s*,
6: 7 When the Lamb broke open the fourth *s*,
6: 9 When the Lamb broke open the fifth *s*,
6:12 I saw the Lamb break open the sixth *s*,
7: 2 the east holding the *s* of the living God.
7: 3 until we imprint this *s* on the foreheads
8: 1 When the Lamb broke open the seventh *s*,
9: 4 had not the *s* of God on their foreheads.
10: 4 *S* up what the seven thunders have spoken
22:10 not *s* up the prophetic words of this book,

SEALED (28)

Dt 32:34 in my treasury, *s* up in my storehouse,
Jos 9:15 princes of the community *s* with an oath.
1Kgs 21: 8 name and, having *s* them with his seal,
Neh 10: 1 *s* document appear the names of our princes,
10: 2 On the *s* document:
Tb 9: 5 promptly checked over the *s* moneybags,
Est 3:12 Ahasuerus and *s* with the royal signet ring.
8: 8 name of the king and *s* with the royal signet
8:10 Ahasuerus and *s* with the royal signet ring,
Jb 14:17 My misdeeds would be *s* up in a pouch,
41: 7 scales are on his back, tightly *s* together;
Sg 4:12 my bride, an enclosed garden, a fountain *s*.
Is 8:16 the *s* instruction kept among my disciples.
29:11 has become like the words of a *s* scroll.
29:11 he replies, "I cannot; it is *s*."
Jer 32:10 When I had written and *s* the deed,
32:11 the deed of purchase, both the *s* copy,
32:14 both the *s* and the open deed of purchase,
32:44 bought with money, deeds written and *s*,
Lam 3:53 alive in the pit, and *s* me in with a stone.
Dn 6:18 the king *s* with his own ring and the rings
12: 9 to be kept secret and *s* until the end time.
14:14 *s* the closed door with the king's ring,
2Cor 1:22 it is he who anointed us and has *s* us,
Eph 1:13 you were *s* with the Holy Spirit who had
4:30 you were *s* against the day of redemption.
Rv 5: 1 on both sides and was *s* with seven seals.
20: 3 the abyss, which he closed and *s* over him.

SEALS (9)

Tb 7:13 contract, to which they affixed their *s*.
Jb 9: 7 he *s* up the stars.
Sir 38:27 laboring night and day, Fashions carved *s*,
Dn 14:17 "Are the *s* unbroken, Daniel?"
Rv 5: 1 on both sides and was sealed with seven *s*.
5: 2 worthy to open the scroll and break its *s*?"
5: 5 to open the scroll with the seven *s*."
5: 9 to receive the scroll and break open its *s*,
6: 1 Lamb broke open the first of the seven *s*,

SEAM (1)

Jn 19:23 one piece from top to bottom and had no *s*.

SEAMEN (1)

1Kgs 9:27 own expert *s* with the servants of Solomon.

SEAMS (2)

Ez 27: 9 of Gebal were in you to caulk your *s*.
27:27 [the caulkers of your *s*,

SEARCH (52)

Gn 31:35 So, despite his *s*,
44:12 and opened it, and when a *s* was made,
Dt 4:29 shall indeed find him when you *s* after him
Jgs 18: 1 were in *s* of a district to dwell in,
1Sm 23:23 *s* him out among all the families of Judah."
24: 3 men from all Israel and went in *s* of David
26: 2 to *s* for David in the desert of Ziph.
27: 1 *s* for me throughout the land of Israel,
2Sm 5:17 they all took the field in *s* of him.
1Kgs 2:40 to Achish in Gath in *s* of his servants,
18:10 where my master has not sent in *s* of you.
2Kgs 2:16 "Let them go in *s* of your master.
10:23 *S* and be sure that there is no worshiper
1Chr 26:31 fortieth year of David's reign *s* was made,
Ezr 5:17 let a *s* be made in the royal archives of
6: 1 Darius issued an order to *s* the archives
Jb 3:21 *s* for it rather than for hidden treasures,
6:19 The caravans of Tema *s*,
10: 6 seek for guilt in me and *s* after my sins,
13: 9 Will it be well when he shall *s* you out?
Ps(s) 26: 2 in the LORD I trust without wavering, *S* me,
Prv 2: 4 and like hidden treasures *s* her out:
Eccl 1:13 and I applied my mind to *s* and investigate
Wis 6:22 *s* out and bring to light knowledge of her,
9:16 things are in heaven, who can *s* them out?
13: 7 For they *s* busily among his works,
Sir 3:20 into things beyond your strength *s* not.
6:28 *S* her out, discover her; seek her
Jer 5: 1 and observe, *S* through her public places,
6:27 appointed you, to *s* and test their way.
Lam 3:40 Let us *s* and examine our ways that we may
Ez 34: 6 no one to look after them or to *s* for them.
Am 8:12 to the east In *s* of the word of the LORD,
Ob 1: 6 How they *s* Esau,
Mt 13:45 is like a merchant's *s* for fine pearls.
18:12 out on the hills and go in *s* of the stray?
Lk 2:45 they returned to Jerusalem in *s* of him.
2:49 "Why did you *s* for me?
4:42 The crowds went in *s* of him,
12:29 to be in *s* of what you are to eat or drink.
13: 7 *s* of fruit on this fig tree and found none.
15: 8 *s* until she has retrieved what she lost?
19:10 has come to *s* out and save what is lost."
24: 5 do you *s* for the Living One among the dead?
Jn 5:39 *S* the Scriptures in which you think you
Acts 10:19 "There are two men in *s* of you.
12:19 Herod then initiated a *s* for him.
Rom 3:11 no one who understands, no one in *s* of God.
1Cor 7:27 If so, do not go in *s* of one.
1Pt 1:12 Into these matters angels long to *s*.
2Pt 2:14 woman, theirs is a never-ending *s* for sin.
Rv 12:15 to *s* out the woman and sweep her away.

SEARCHED (10)

Gn 31:33 went in and *s* Jacob's tent and Leah's tent,
1Sm 27: 4 had fled to Gath, he no longer *s* for him.
2Sm 17:20 They *s*, but found no one,
2Kgs 2:17 who *s* for three days without finding him.
Ezr 2:62 These men *s* their family records,
Neh 7:64 These men *s* their family records,
Jb 5:27 Lo, this we have *s* out; so it is!
32:12 you attentively as you *s* out what to say;
Ez 22:30 Thus I have *s* among them for someone who
1Pt 1:10 the prophets carefully *s* out and examined.

SEARCHER (3)

Ps(s) 7:10 sustain the just, O *s* of heart and soul,
Jer 11:20 hosts, O just Judge, *s* of mind and heart,
Rv 2:23 know that I am the *s* of hearts and minds,

SEARCHES (4)

1Chr 28: 9 for the LORD *s* all hearts and understands
Ps(s) 11: 5 The LORD *s* the just and the wicked;
Prv 20:27 it *s* through all his inmost being.
Rom 8:27 who *s* hearts knows what the Spirit means,

SEARCHING (12)

Jb 36:26 the number of his years is past *s* out.
37: 5 wonders past our *s* out.
Ps(s) 11: 4 eyes behold, his *s* glance is on mankind.
17: 3 you test my heart, *s* it in the night,
Eccl 8:17 However much man toils in *s*,
Lam 1:11 All her people groan, *s* for bread;
Ez 39:14 For seven months they shall keep *s*.
Mt 2:13 Herod is *s* for the child to destroy him."
12:43 *s* for a place of rest and finding none.
Lk 2:48 father and I have been *s* for you in sorrow."
11:24 through arid wastes *s* for a resting place;
Heb 11:16 But they were *s* for a better,

SEARCHINGS (2)

Jgs 5:15 clans of Reuben great were the *s* of heart.
5:16 clans of Reuben great were the *s* of heart!

SEARED (2)

Jer 23:10 the land mourns, the pasture ranges are *s*.
1Tm 4: 2 men with *s* consciences who forbid marriage

SEARING (5)

Dt 28:22 fiery drought, with blight and *s* wind,
Is 4: 4 her midst with the blast of *s* judgment,
Lam 5:10 by a furnace, with the *s* blasts of famine.
Am 4: 9 I struck you with blight and *s* wind;
Hg 2:17 works of your hands with blight, *s* wind,

SEARS (1)

Sir 38:28 The heat from the fire *s* his flesh,

SEAS (21)

Gn 1:22 multiply, and fill the water of the *s*;
Lv 11: 9 whatever in the *s* or in river waters has
Dt 33:19 the *s* and the hidden treasures of the sand."
Neh 9: 6 is upon it, the *s* and all that is in them.
Jdt 1:12 Egypt as far as the borders of the two *s*.
16:15 The mountains to their bases, and the *s*,
1Mc 6:29 kingdoms and from the islands of the *s*.
Ps(s) 8: 9 and whatever swims the paths of the *s*.
24: 2 the *s* and established it upon the rivers.
65: 6 ends of the earth and of the distant *s*.
65: 8 You still the roaring of the *s*,
69:35 him, the *s* and whatever moves in them!"
135: 6 on earth, in the *s* and in all the deeps.
Prv 30:19 a rock, The way of a ship on the high *s*,
Sir 50: 3 dug, the pool with a vastness like the *s*.
Is 17:12 peoples that roar like the roar of the *s*!
Jer 5:22 I made the sandy shore the *s* limit,
Ez 26:17 How have you perished, gone from the *s*,
27:33 drew from the *s* you filled many peoples;
Dn 3:78 *S* and rivers, bless the Lord;
Jon 1:15 him into the sea, and the *s* raging abated.

SEASHORE (12)

Gn 22:17 stars of the sky and the sands of the *s*;
49:13 by the *s* [This means a shore for ships],
Ex 14:30 saw the Egyptians lying dead on the *s*
Jos 11: 4 an army numerous as the sands on the *s*,
Jgs 7:12 these were as many as the sands on the *s*.
1Sm 13: 5 soldiers as numerous as the sands of the *s*.
1Kgs 5: 9 knowledge, as vast as the sand on the *s*.
2Chr 8:17 and to Elath on the *s* of the land of Edom.
1Mc 11: 1 forces, as numerous as the sands of the *s*,
Sir 1: 2 The sand of the *s*,
Jer 47: 7 Ashkelon and the *s* he has appointed it.
Heb 11:12 in the sky and the sands of the *s*.

SEASON (25)

Gn 31:10 Once, in the breeding *s*,
Lv 26: 4 I will give you rain in due *s*,
Nm 13:20 It was then the *s* for early grapes.
Dt 28:12 heavens, to give your land rain in due *s*,
Jos 3:15 banks during the entire *s* of the harvest,
Jgs 15: 1 some time, in the *s* of the wheat harvest,
Ezr 10:13 people are numerous and it is the rainy *s*,
Jb 5:26 as a shock of grain comes in at its *s*.
38:32 you bring forth the Mazzaroth in their *s*,
Ps(s) 1: 3 water, That yields its fruit in due *s*,
145:15 and you give them their food in due *s*;
Prv 15:23 a word in *s*, how good it is!
Sir 50: 6 like the full moon at the holyday *s*;
51:30 Work at your tasks in due *s*,
Jer 17: 6 in the desert that enjoys no change of *s*,
Ez 34:26 them about my hill, sending rain in due *s*,
Dn 7:12 a prolongation of life for a time and a *s*.
Hos 2:11 grain in its time, and my wine in its *s*;
Zec 10: 1 Ask of the LORD rain in the spring *s*!
Mt 7:25 When the rainy *s* set in,
Mk 9:50 salt becomes tasteless, how can you *s* it?
Lk 1:20 They will all come true in due *s*."
12:42 to dispense their ration of grain in *s*?
Acts 3:20 Thus may a *s* of refreshment be granted you
1Pt 4:17 The *s* of judgment has begun,

SEASONAL (3)

Dt 11:14 soul, I will give the *s* rain to your land,
1Sm 20: 6 clan is holding its *s* sacrifice there.'
Sir 37:11 work, to a *s* laborer about the harvest,

SEASONED (3)

Lv 2:13 present to the LORD shall be *s* with salt.
1Kgs 12:21 a hundred and eighty thousand *s* warriors
2Chr 11: 1 a hundred and eighty thousand *s* warriors,

SEASONING (1)

Lk 14:34 loses its flavor what good is it for *s*?

SEASONS (10)

Ex 34:21 during the *s* of plowing and harvesting.
Ps(s) 104:19 You made the moon to mark the *s*;
Wis 7:18 sun's course and the variations of the *s*.
Sir 33: 8 through him the *s* and feasts come and go.
43: 6 marks the changing times, governing the *s*,
47: 9 feasts and solemnized the *s* of each year
Is 33: 6 That which makes her *s* lasting,
Jer 8: 7 Even the stork in the air knows it *s*;
Dn 2:21 He causes the changes of the times and *s*,
Gal 4:10 observance of days and months, *s* and years!

SEAT (41)

Ex 15:17 the place where you made your *s*,
Lv 15:23 on the bed or on the *s* when he touches it,
17:11 because it is the blood, as the *s* of life,
Dt 12:23 not consume this *s* of life with the flesh.
Ru 4: 1 Boaz went and took a *s* at the gate;
1Sm 2: 8 To *s* them with nobles and make a glorious
1Kgs 1:46 Solomon took his *s* on the royal throne,
10:19 top, and an arm on each side of the *s*.
2Kgs 11:19 where Joash took his *s* on the royal throne.
2Chr 6:10 have taken my *s* on the throne of Israel,
9:18 there was an arm on each side of the *s*,
Jdt 11:19 and there I will set up your judgment *s*.
1Mc 10:52 taken my *s* on the throne of my fathers,
10:55 and took your *s* on their royal throne!
Jb 23: 3 him, that I might come to his judgment *s*!
29: 7 of the city and set up my *s* in the square
Ps(s) 113: 8 lifts up the poor To *s* them with princes,
Prv 9:14 of her house upon a *s* on the city heights,
Eccl 3:16 I saw wickedness, and in the *s* of justice,
Sg 3:10 its roof of gold, Its *s* of purple cloth.
Sir 12:12 right hand, lest he then demand your *s*,
Is 14:13 I will take my *s* on the Mount of Assembly,
Jer 22:30 No descendant of his shall achieve a *s* on
Mt 13: 2 he went and took his *s* in a boat
15:35 the crowd to *s* themselves on the ground.
19:28 his *s* upon a throne befitting his glory,

SEAT (cont.)

Mk 12:41 Taking a *s* opposite the treasury,
14:54 where he found a *s* with the temple guard
16:19 heaven and took his *s* at God's right hand.
Lk 12:37 he will put on an apron, *s* them at table,
22:69 *s* at the right hand of the Power of God.' "
Jn 19:13 took a *s* on a judge's bench at the place
Acts 12:21 took his *s* on the rostrum and publicly
25: 6 On the following day he took his *s* on the
25:17 The very next day I took my *s* on the bench
Rom 14:10 to appear before the judgment *s* of God.
Heb 1: 3 he took his *s* at the right hand of the
8: 1 who has taken his *s* at the right hand of
10:12 his *s* forever at the right hand of God;
12: 2 his *s* at the right of the throne of God.
Rv 3:21 took my *s* beside my Father on his throne.

SEATED (49)

Gn 31:34 a camel cushion, and *s* herself upon them.
43:33 *s* by his directions according to their age,
Ex 2:15 As he was *s* there by a well,
Jgs 5:10 *s* on saddlecloths as they go their way;
1Kgs 1:48 this day *s* one of my sons upon my throne,
2:12 was *s* on the throne of his father David,
2:24 who has *s* me firmly on the throne of my
13:14 of God, whom he found *s* under a terebinth.
16:11 Once he was *s* on the royal throne,
22:10 and King Jehoshaphat of Judah were *s*,
22:19 I saw the LORD *s* on his throne,
2Kgs 1: 9 was *s* on a hilltop when he found him.
4:38 when the guild prophets were *s* before him,
2Chr 18: 9 of Judah were *s* each on his throne,
18:18 I saw the LORD *s* on his throne,
23:20 they *s* the king upon the royal throne.
Neh 2: 6 Then the king, and the queen *s* beside him,
Tb 7: 1 whom they found *s* by his courtyard gate.
Est D: 6 the king, who was *s* on his royal throne,
5: 1 while the king was *s* on his royal throne
1Mc 10:63 The king also had him *s* at his side.
Ps(s) 9: 5 my right and my cause, *s* on your throne,
Prv 20: 8 A king *s* on the throne of judgment dispels
Sir 1: 6 and truly awe-inspiring, *s* upon his throne:
Is 6: 1 saw the Lord *s* on a high and lofty throne,
Ez 1:26 Upon it was *s*,
Mt 23:22 throne and by him who is *s* on that throne.
24: 3 While he was *s* on the Mount of Olives,
26:64 Soon you will see the Son of Man *s* at the
Mk 3:32 The crowd *s* around him told him,
3:34 him at those *s* in the circle he continued,
13: 3 *s* on the Mount of Olives facing the temple,
14:62 and you will see the Son of Man *s* at the
Lk 5: 3 then, remaining *s*, he continued to teach
9:15 his instructions and got them all *s*.
10:39 who *s* herself at the Lord's feet and
24:30 When he had *s* himself with them to eat,
Jn 2:14 and doves, and others *s* changing coins.
20:12 One was *s* at the head and the other at the
Acts 2: 2 all through the house where they were *s*.
Col 3: 1 where Christ is *s* at God's right hand.
Rv 4: 2 and on the throne was *s* One whose
4: 4 upon which were *s* twenty-four elders;
4: 9 and praise to the One *s* on the throne,
4:10 fall down before the One *s* on the throne,
5:13 "To the One *s* on the throne,
7:10 is from our God, who is *s* on the throne,
17: 3 where I saw a woman *s* on a scarlet
19: 4 and worshiped God *s* on the throne and sang,

SEATING (5)

1Kgs 3: 6 even today, *s* a son of his on his throne.
10: 5 food at his table, the *s* of his ministers,
2Chr 9: 4 food at his table, the *s* of his ministers,
Est 3: 1 rank, *s* him above all his fellow officials.
Eph 1:20 dead and *s* him at his right hand in heaven,

SEATS (7)

Ps(s) 122: 5 judgment seats, *s* for the house of David.
Mt 23: 6 at banquets and the front *s* in synagogues,
Mk 12:39 in public, front *s* in the synagogues,
Lk 11:43 You love the front *s* in synagogues and
20:46 respect in public, front *s* in synagogues,
2Thes 2: 4 he who *s* himself in God's temple and even

SEAWARD (1)

Is 8:23 but in the end he has glorified the *s* road,

SEAWEED (1)

Jon 2: 6 *s* clung about my head.

SEBA (4)

Gn 10: 7 *S*, Havilah, Sabtah, Raamah, and Sabteca.
1Chr 1: 9 The descendants of Cush were *S*,
Ps(s) 72:10 kings of Arabia and *S* shall bring tribute.
Is 43: 3 ransom, Ethiopia and *S* in return for you.

SEBAM (1)

Nm 32: 3 Dibon, Jazer, Nimrah, Heshbon, Elealeh, *S*,

SECACAH (1)

Jos 15:61 Beth-arabah, Middin, *S*,

SECEDE (2)

Jos 22:23 an altar of our own to *s* from the LORD,
22:29 us to rebel against the LORD or to *s* now

SECEDED (2)

Jos 22:16 You have *s* from the LORD this day,
Is 7:17 worse than any since Ephraim *s* from Judah.

SECLUDED (1)

2Mc 3:19 maidens *s* indoors ran together,

SECLUSION (2)

Lk 1:24 She went into *s* for five months, saying:
9:18 in *s* and his disciples were with him,

SECOND (186)

Gn 1: 8 morning followed— the *s* day.
2:13 The name of the *s* river is the Gihon;
4:19 was Adah, and the name of the *s* Zillah.
6:16 shall make with bottom, *s* and third decks.
7:11 year of Noah's life, in the *s* month,
8:14 In the *s* month, on the twenty-seventh day
30: 7 Bilhah conceived again and bore a *s* son,
30:12 maidservant Zilpah bore a *s* son to Jacob;
32:20 He gave similar instructions to the *s*
41:52 and the *s* he named Ephraim,
Ex 4: 8 they should believe the message of the *s*.
16: 1 on the fifteenth day of the *s* month after
26: 5 of the corresponding sheet in the *s* set,
26:10 the edge of the end sheet in the *s* set.
28:18 in the *s* row, a garnet, a sapphire
36:11 the edge of the end sheet in the *s* set.
39:11 an emerald; in the *s* row, a garnet,
40:17 of the *s* year the Dwelling was erected.
Lv 8:22 Then he brought forward the *s* ram,
13:58 the thing shall be washed a *s* time,
Nm 1: 1 of Egypt, on the first day of the *s* month,
1:18 community on the first day of the *s* month.
2:16 These shall be *s* on the march.
7:18 On the *s* day Nethanel,
9:11 But he shall keep it in the *s* month,
10: 6 when you sound the *s* alarm,
10:11 *s* year, on the twentieth day of the *s*
29:17 the *s* day you shall offer twelve bullocks,
Dt 24: 3 the wife of another man, and the *s* husband,
24: 3 or if this *s* man who has married her,
24:20 shall not go over the branches a *s* time;
24:21 shall not go over the vineyard a *s* time;
Jos 5: 2 the Israelite nation for the *s* time."
6:14 On this *s* day they again marched around
10:32 so that on the *s* day Joshua captured it
19: 1 The *s* lot fell to Simeon.
Jgs 20:24 they met the Benjaminites for the *s* time,
1Sm 8: 2 His first-born was named Joel, his *s* son,
17:13 the first-born Eliab, the *s* son Abinadab,
18:21 [Thus for the *s* time Saul said to David,
20:27 On the next day, the *s* day of the month,
20:34 and took no food that *s* day of the month,
23:17 be king of Israel and I shall be *s* to you.
26: 8 I will not need a *s* thrust!"
2Sm 3: 3 the *s*, Chileab, of Abigail the widow
14:29 Although he summoned him a *s* time,
20:10 and he died without receiving a *s* thrust.
1Kgs 6: 1 in the month of Ziv, which is the *s* month,
6:27 the corresponding wing of the *s* cherub.
9: 2 planned, the LORD appeared to him a *s* time,
15:25 In the *s* year of Asa,
19: 7 the angel of the LORD came back a *s* time,
2Kgs 1:17 him as king, in the *s* year of Jehoram,
9:19 Joram sent a *s* driver,
10: 6 So Jehu wrote them a *s* letter:
14: 1 In the *s* year of Joash, son of Jehoahaz,
15:32 In the *s* year of Pekah, son of Remaliah,
22:14 themselves to the *S* Quarter in Jerusalem,
25:18 the high priest, Zephaniah the *s* priest,
1Chr 2:13 his first-born, of Abinadab, the *s* son,
3: 1 the *s*, Daniel, by Abigail of Carmel;
3:15 the *s*, Jehoiakim; the third, Zedekiah;
5:12 Joel was chief, Shapham was *s* in command,
6:13 Joel, the first-born, and Abijah, the *s*.
7:15 Manasseh's *s* son was named Zelophehad,
8: 1 of Bela, his first-born, Ashbel, the *s* son,
8:39 Ulam, his first-born, Jeush, the *s* son,
12:10 Ezer was their chief, Obadiah was *s*,
15:18 with these, their brethren of the *s* rank:
16: 5 their chief, and *s* to him were Zechariah,
23:11 was the chief and Zizah was *s* to him;
23:19 Jeriah, the chief, Amariah, the *s*,
23:20 Micah, the chief, and Isshiah, the *s*.
24: 7 lot fell to Jehoiarib, the *s* to Jedaiah,
24:23 were Jeriah, the chief, Amariah, the *s*,
25: 9 Gedaliah was the *s*; he and his brethren
26: 2 the first-born, Jediael, the *s* son,
26: 4 the first-born, Jehozabad, a *s* son,
26:11 father made him chief), Hilkiah, the *s* son,
27: 4 the division of the *s* month was Eleazar,
29:22 Then for a *s* time they proclaimed David's
2Chr 3: 2 *s* month of the fourth year of his reign.
3:12 the corresponding wing of the *s* cherub.
27: 5 to him also in the *s* and in the third year.
28: 7 and also Elkanah, who was *s* to the king.
30: 2 celebrate the Passover during the *s* month,
30:13 feast of Unleavened Bread in the *s* month;
30:15 on the fourteenth day of the *s* month.
31:12 and his brother Shimei was *s* in charge.
Ezr 3: 8 house of God in Jerusalem, in the *s* month,
4:24 until the *s* year of the reign of Darius,
Neh 8:13 On the *s* day, the family heads
11: 9 of Hassenuah, was *s* in charge of the city.
11:17 Bakbukiah, *s* in rank among his brethren;
12:38 The *s* choir proceeded to the left,
Tb 1: 7 years, I used to give a *s* tithe in money,
Jdt 2: 4 of his forces, *s* to himself in command,
7: 6 On the *s* day Holofernes led out all his
Est A: 1 In the *s* year of the reign of the great
2:14 return in the morning to a *s* harem
B: 3 who has gained the *s* rank in the kingdom,
B: 6 the administration and is a *s* father to us,
4: 8 for Haman, who is *s* to the king,
7: 2 Again, on this *s* day,
E:11 he attained the rank *s* to the royal throne.
9:29 full authority this *s* letter about Purim,
F: 7 of God, the *s* for all the other nations.
1Mc 9:54 hundred and fifty-three, in the *s* month,
13:51 On the twenty-third day of the *s* month,
2Mc 5: 1 Antiochus sent his *s* expedition into Egypt.
7: 7 they brought the *s* to be made sport of.
13:22 The king made a *s* attempt by negotiating
Jb 42:14 he called the first Jemimah, the *s* Keziah,
Jer 1:13 A *s* time the word of the LORD came to me
13: 3 A *s* time the word of the LORD came to me
33: 1 The word of the LORD came to Jeremiah a *s*
41: 4 The *s* day after the murder of Gedaliah,
52:24 the high priest, Zephaniah, the *s* priest,
Ez 10:14 was that of an ox, the *s* that of a man,
43:22 On the *s* day present an unblemished
Dn 2: 1 In the *s* year of his reign,
7: 5 The *s* was like a bear;
Jon 3: 1 word of the LORD came to Jonah a *s* time:
Na 1: 9 The enemy shall not rise a *s* time;
Hg 1: 1 sixth month in the *s* year of King Darius,
2:10 ninth month, in the *s* year of King Darius,
2:20 The message of the LORD came a *s* time to
Zec 1: 1 In the *s* year of Darius, in the eight month,
1: 7 In the *s* year of Darius,
6: 2 had red horses, the *s* chariot black horses,
Mt 21:30 came to his *s* son and said the same thing.
21:31 They said, "The *s*."
21:36 A *s* time he dispatched even more slaves
22: 4 A *s* time he sent other servants, saying:
22:26 The same thing happened to the *s*,
22:39 *s* is like it; 'You shall love your neighbor
25:15 silver pieces, to a *s* two thousand,
26:42 Withdrawing a *s* time, he began to pray:
Mk 6: 9 "Do not bring a *s* tunic,"
8:25 Then a *s* time Jesus laid hands on his eyes,
12: 4 The *s* time he sent them another servant;
12:21 The *s* took the woman,
12:31 This is the *s*, 'You shall love your neighbor
14:72 Just then a *s* cock crow was heard and
Lk 16: 7 Then he said to a *s*,
19:18 The *s* came and said,
20:11 He sent a *s* servant whom they also beat.
20:31 Next, the *s* brother married the widow,
Jn 4:54 This was the *s* sign that Jesus performed
8: 8 A *s* time he bent down and wrote on the
9:24 A *s* time they summoned the man who had
19: 4 went out a *s* time and said to the crowd:
21:16 A *s* time he put his question,
Acts 7:13 The *s* time,
10:15 The voice was heard a *s* time:
11: 9 A *s* time the voice from the heavens spoke
12:10 They passed the first guard, then the *s*,
13:33 to what is written in the *s* psalm,
20:15 on the *s* day we crossed to Samos,
Rom 5:16 and brought condemnation, but in the *s*,
1Cor 12:28 in the church first apostles, *s* prophets,
15:47 formed from dust, the *s* is from heaven.
2Cor 13: 2 I said before when I was there the *s* time
Gal 5: 1 on yourselves the yoke of slavery a *s* time!
Ti 3:10 Warn a heretic once and then a *s* time;
Heb 8: 7 there would have been no place for a *s* one.
9: 3 Behind the *s* veil was the tabernacle
9:28 he will appear a *s* time not to take away
10: 9 away the first covenant to establish the *s*.
2Pt 3: 1 I am writing you this *s* letter,
1Jn 2: 8 On *s* thought, the commandment that I
Rv 2:11 shall never be harmed by the *s* death.'
4: 7 creature resembled a lion, the *s* an ox;
6: 3 open the *s* seal, I heard the second living
8: 8 When the *s* angel blew his trumpet,
11:14 The *s* woe is past, but beware!
13:15 The *s* wild beast was then permitted to
14: 8 A *s* angel followed and cried out:
14:18 A *s* angel, who was in charge of the fire
16: 3 The *s* angel poured out his bowl on the sea.
20: 6 The *s* death will have no claim on them;
20:14 the pool of fire, which is the *s* death;
21: 8 fiery pool of burning sulphur, the *s* death!"
21:19 of stones was jasper, the *s* sapphire,

SECONDLY (3)

Jos 12: 4 *S,* Og, king of Bashan, a survivor
2Mc 14: 8 concern for the king's interests, and *s,*
Sir 23:23 *s,* she has wronged her husband;

SECRET (46)

Dt 27:15 and sets it up in *s!'*
27:24 'Cursed be he who slays his neighbor in *s!'*
Jgs 16: 5 and find out the *s* of his great strength,
16: 6 "Tell me the *s* of your great strength and
16: 9 and the *s* of his strength remained unknown.
16:15 not told me the *s* of your great strength!"
2Sm 12:12 You have done this deed in *s,*
Tb 12: 7 A king's *s* it is prudent to keep,
12:11 to you, 'A king's *s* it is prudent to keep,
Jdt 2: 2 and nobles, laid before them his *s* plan,
2Mc 6:11 nearby caves to observe the sabbath in *s,*
Jb 13:10 you if even in *s* you show partiality.
Ps(s) 10: 9 He waits in *s* like a lion in his lair;
40:11 I have made no *s* of your kindness and your
101: 5 Whoever slanders his neighbor in *s,*
139:15 frame unknown to you When I was made in *s,*
Prv 7:10 him, robed like a harlot, with *s* designs
21:14 A *s* gift allays anger,
25: 9 but another man's *s* do not disclose;
Sg 2:14 the rock, in the *s* recesses of the cliff,
Wis 1:10 and discordant grumblings are no *s.*
17: 3 For they who supposed their *s* sins were
18: 9 For in *s* the holy children of the good
Sir 8:18 stranger do nothing that should be kept *s,*
16:19 if all in *s* I am disloyal,
27:16 He who betrays a *s* cannot be trusted,
46:19 bribe or *s* gift have I taken from any man!"
Is 48:16 from the beginning did I speak it in *s;*
Jer 13:17 in your pride, I will weep in *s* many tears;
23:24 Can a man hide in *s* without my seeing him?
Ez 28: 3 Daniel, there is no *s* that is beyond you.
Dn 12: 4 keep *s* the message and seal the book until
12: 9 to be kept *s* and sealed until the end time.
14:13 under the table they had made a *s* entrance
14:21 They showed him the *s* door by which they
Mt 6: 4 mercy *s,* and your Father who sees in *s*
Jn 7:10 up, but as if in *s* and not for all to see.
18:20 There was nothing *s* about anything I said.
19:38 (although a *s* one for fear of the Jews),
Acts 16:37 Now they want to smuggle us out in *s.*
1Cor 14:25 and the *s* of his heart will be laid bare.
Eph 3: 3 God's *s* plan as I have briefly described
5:12 the things these people do in *s*
2Thes 2: 7 *s* force of lawlessness is already at work,
Rv 1:20 This is the *s* meaning of the seven stars

SECRETARY (2)

Jer 36:26 son of Abdeel, to arrest Baruch, the *s,*
36:32 took another scroll, and gave it to his *s,*

SECRETLY (14)

Gn 31:27 Why did you dupe me by stealing away *s?*
Dt 13: 7 friend, entices you *s* to serve other gods,
28:57 brings forth when she *s* uses them for food
Jos 2: 1 of Nun, *s* sent out two spies from Shittim,
2Sm 21:12 off *s* from the public square of Beth-shan,
2Chr 22:11 *s* took Ahaziah's son Joash from among the
1Mc 9:60 sent letters *s* to all his allies in Judea,
2Mc 1:19 hid it *s* in the hollow of a dry cistern,
8: 1 and his companions entered the village *s,*
Jb 31:27 *s* enticed to waft them a kiss with my hand;
Prv 9:17 is sweet, and bread gotten *s* is pleasing!"
Jer 37:17 asked him *s* whether there was any message
38:16 But King Zedekiah swore to Jeremiah *s:*
40:15 of Kareah, said *s* to Gedaliah in Mizpah:

SECRETS (14)

2Mc 13:21 army, betrayed military *s* to the enemy.
Jb 11: 6 the *s* of wisdom are twice as effective:
Ps(s) 44:22 For he knows the *s* of the heart.
Prv 11:13 A newsmonger reveals *s,* but a trustworthy
20:19 A newsmonger reveals *s;* so have nothing to
Wis 6:22 and I shall hide no *s* from you,
Sir 1:28 reveal your *s* and publicly cast you down,
4:18 him happiness and reveal her *s* to him.
27:21 but he who betrays *s* does hopeless damage.
41:23 what you hear, and of betraying *s*—
42:19 and the future, and reveals the deepest *s.*
51:19 opened her gate and I came to know her *s.*
Rom 2:16 on the *s* of men through Christ Jesus.
Rv 2:24 of the so-called "deep *s*" of Satan;

SECT (4)

Acts 24: 5 He is a ringleader of the *s* of Nazoreans.
24:14 which they call a *s*—
26: 5 Pharisee, the strictest *s* of our religion.
28:22 well that this *s* is denounced everywhere."

SECTION (5)

Jos 12: 1 including all the eastern *s* of the Arabah,
Ru 2: 3 happened to be the *s* belonging to Boaz
Neh 12:24 the man of God, one *s* opposite the other,
1Mc 8: 7 tribute, to give hostages and a *s* of Lycia,
Ez 45: 7 The prince shall have a *s* bordering on

SECTIONS (3)

Jos 18: 6 me the description of the land in seven *s.*
18: 9 its cities in writing in seven *s* and returned
Neh 11:36 Some *s* of the Levites from Judah settled

SECTOR (9)

Neh 3:11 The adjoining *s,* as far as the Oven Tower,
3:19 of Mizpah, who repaired the adjoining *s,*
3:20 repaired the adjoining *s* from the Corner
3:21 repaired the adjoining *s* from the entrance
3:24 repaired the adjoining *s* from the house of
3:27 *s* opposite the great projecting tower,
3:30 son of Zalaph, repaired the adjoining *s;*
3:30 of Berechiah, repaired the adjoining *s;*
Ez 45: 3 Also from this *s* measure off a strip,

SECULAR (1)

1Sm 21: 6 even for a *s* journey.

SECUNDUS (1)

Acts 20: 4 Aristarchus and *S* from Thessalonica;

SECURE (27)

Jgs 8:11 and attacked the camp when it felt *s.*
2Chr 17: 5 As a result, the LORD made his kingdom *s,*
1Mc 1:16 When his kingdom seemed *s,*
2Mc 3:22 *s* for those who had placed them in trust,
Jb 5:24 And you shall know that your tent is *s;*
11:18 as the morning, And you shall be *s,*
12: 6 and those who provoke God are *s.*
21: 8 Their progeny is *s* in their sight;
Ps(s) 10: 5 His ways are *s* at all times;
78:53 He led them on *s* and unafraid,
Wis 4:17 intended for him, or why he made him *s.*
7:23 beneficent, kindly, Firm, *s,*
Sir 31:11 would not, So that his possessions are *s,*
40:25 Gold and silver make one's way *s,*
Is 32:18 in *s* dwellings and quiet resting places.
47:10 Because you felt *s* in your wickedness,
Jer 22:21 I spoke to you when you were *s,*
33:16 shall be safe and Jerusalem shall dwell *s;*
49:31 is at peace, that lives *s* says the LORD,
Bar 5: 7 Israel may advance *s* in the glory of God.
Ez 28:26 They shall dwell *s* while I inflict
34:28 by beasts of the earth, but shall dwell *s,*
Zep 2:15 Is this the exultant city that dwelt *s;*
Mt 27:65 Go and *s* the tomb as best you can."
Lk 21:36 and to stand *s* before the Son of Man."
1Tm 6:19 they build a *s* foundation for the future,
Rv 3:17 am so rich and *s* that I want for nothing."

SECURED (5)

2Sm 23: 5 with me, set forth in detail and *s.*
2Kgs 15:20 Menahem *s* the money to give to the king of
2Mc 4:24 that he *s* the high priesthood for himself,
Wis 10:12 him from foes, and *s* him against ambush,
Mk 5: 4 been *s* with handcuffs and chains,

SECURELY (13)

Lv 25:18 for then you will dwell *s* in the land.
26: 5 so that you may dwell *s* in your land.
Dt 33:12 the day while he abides *s* at his breast."
33:28 Israel has dwelt *s,* and the fountain of Jacob
Jgs 18: 7 lived *s* after the manner of the Sidonians,
Prv 3:23 Then you may *s* go your way;
10: 9 He who walks honestly walks *s,*
Is 47: 8 Now hear this voluptuous one, enthroned *s,*
Ez 34:25 *s* in the desert and sleep in the forests.
34:27 and they shall dwell *s* on their own soil.
39: 6 upon those who live *s* in the coastlands;
Mt 12:29 his property unless he first ties him *s?*
Acts 5:23 "We found the jail *s* locked and the

SECURES (3)

Ps(s) 103: 6 The LORD *s* justice and the rights of all
146: 7 faith forever, *s* justice for the oppressed,
Prv 31:14 ships, she *s* her provisions from afar.

SECURITY (32)

Dt 12:10 round about and you live there in *s,*
1Sm 12:11 side, so that you were able to live in *s.*
1Kgs 5: 5 Thus Judah and Israel lived in *s.*
2Kgs 20:19 "There will be peace and *s* in my lifetime."
Tb 14: 7 in *s* shall they dwell forever in the land
Est 9:30 sent documents concerning peace and *s*
1Mc 9:58 his companions are living in peace and *s.*
2Mc 4:21 so he took measures for his own *s.*
Jb 18:14 He is plucked from the *s* of his tent;
31:24 my trust in gold or called fine gold my *s;*
Ps(s) 4: 9 you alone, O LORD, bring *s* to my dwelling.
22:10 first formed, my *s* at my mother's breast.
30: 7 Once, in my *s,*
37: 3 that you may dwell in the land and enjoy *s.*
Prv 1:33 But he who obeys me dwells in *s,*
11:14 *s* lies in many counselors.
28: 2 but with a prudent man it knows *s.*
Sir 47:12 his successor a wise son, who lived in *s:*
Is 32:17 right will produce calm and *s.*
39: 8 "There will be peace and *s* in my lifetime."
Jer 23: 6 shall be saved, Israel shall dwell in *s.*
Ez 28:26 they shall live on it in *s,*
38: 8 the peoples and all of whom now dwell in *s.*
38:11 the peaceful people who are living in *s,*
38:14 When my people Israel are dwelling in *s,*
39:26 when they live in *s* on their land with no
Hos 2:20 and I will let them take their rest in *s.*
Zec 8:10 who came and went had no *s* from the enemy,
14:11 Jerusalem shall abide in *s.*
Acts 16:24 he put them in maximum *s,*
1Thes 5: 3 when people are saying, "Peace and *s,*"
2Pt 3:17 of the wicked, and forfeit the *s* you enjoy.

SEDITION (4)

Ezr 4:15 and that *s* has been fostered there since
4:19 rebellion and *s* have been fostered there.
2Mc 14: 6 who stir up *s* and keep the kingdom from
Acts 24: 5 up *s* among the Jews all over the world.

SEDUCE (5)

2Kgs 18:32 to Hezekiah when he would *s* you by saying,
Jdt 12:16 his time to *s* her from the day he saw her.
Is 36:18 Do not let Hezekiah *s* you by saying,
2Thes 2: 3 Let no one *s* you, no matter how.
Rv 20: 8 He will go out to *s* the nations in all

SEDUCED (6)

2Chr 21:11 of Jerusalem into idolatry and *s* Judah.
Jdt 13:16 was my face that *s* Holofernes to his ruin,
1Mc 1:11 of the law, and they *s* many people,
Sir 42:10 While unmarried, lest she be *s,*
Dn 13:56 Daniel said to him, "beauty has *s* you,
2Cor 11: 3 just as the serpent *s* Eve by his cunning,

SEDUCER (1)

Rv 12: 9 devil or Satan, the *s* of the whole world,

SEDUCES (3)

Ex 22:15 a man *s* a virgin who is not betrothed,
Prv 28:10 He who *s* the upright into an evil way will
Rv 2:20 that self-styled prophetess who *s* my

SEDUCTION (2)

2Thes 2:10 by every *s* the wicked can devise for those
2Pt 2:13 as they share your feasts in a spirit of *s.*

SEDUCTIONS (1)

1Jn 2:17 And the world with its *s* is passing away

SEDUCTIVE (1)

Col 2: 8 *s* philosophy that follows mere human

SEED (63)

Gn 1:11 every kind of plant that bears *s* and every
1:11 on earth that bears fruit with its *s* in it."
1:12 every kind of plant that bears *s*
1:12 on earth that bears fruit with its *s* in it.
38: 9 widow, he wasted his *s* on the ground,
47:19 only give us *s,* that we may survive
47:23 here is your *s* for sowing the land.
47:24 while you keep four-fifths as *s* for your
Ex 16:31 It was like coriander *s,*
Lv 15:16 "When a man has an emission of *s,*
15:17 Any piece of cloth or leather with *s* on it
15:32 chronic flow, or who has an emission of *s,*
19:19 of yours with two different kinds of *s;*
22: 4 or if anyone has had an emission of *s,*
26:16 You will sow your *s* in vain,
27:16 to the amount of *s* required to sow it,
27:16 *s* being valued at fifty silver shekels.
Nm 11: 7 *s* and had the appearance of bdellium.
Dt 11:10 would sow your *s* and then water it by hand,
22: 9 vineyard with two different kinds of *s;*
28:38 "Though you spend much *s* on your field,
Ps(s) 126: 6 forth weeping, carrying the *s* to be sown,
Eccl 11: 6 In the morning sow your *s,*
Wis 7: 2 body and blood, from the *s* of man,
Is 5:10 And a homer of *s* shall yield but an ephah.
30:23 rain for the *s* that you sow in the ground,
55:10 Giving *s* to him who sows and bread to him
Jer 31:27 when I will *s* the house of Israel and the
31:27 with the seed of man and the *s* of beast.
35: 7 Build no house and sow no *s;*
Ez 17: 5 Then he took some *s* of the land,
Jl 1:17 The *s* lies shriveled under its clods;
Am 9:13 and the vintager, him who sows the *s;*
Hg 2:19 Indeed, the *s* has not sprouted,
Mt 13: 7 Again, part of the *s* fell among thorns,
13:19 The *s* along the path is the man who hears
13:20 The *s* that fell on patches of rock is the
13:24 to a man who sowed good *s* in his field.
13:27 'Sir, did you not sow good *s* in your field?
13:31 "The reign of God is like a mustard *s*
13:32 It is the smallest *s* of all,
13:37 farmer sowing good *s* is the Son of Man;
13:38 the good *s* the citizens of the kingdom.
17:20 if you had faith the size of a mustard *s,*

SEED (cont.)
Mk 4: 5 Some of the *s* landed on rocky ground where
4: 8 Some *s*, finally, landed on good soil
4:26 A man scatters *s* on the ground.
4:27 Through it all the *s* sprouts and grows
4:31 It is like mustard *s* which,
Lk 8: 5 "A farmer went out to sow some *s*.
8:11 The *s* is the word of God.
8:14 *s* fallen among briers are those who hear,
8:15 The *s* on good ground are those who hear
13:19 It is like mustard *s* which a man took and
17: 6 you had faith the size of a mustard *s*,
1Cor 3: 6 I planted the *s* and Apollos watered it,
15:36 The *s* you sow does not germinate unless it
15:38 to each *s* its own fruition.
2Cor 9:10 He who supplies *s* for the sower and bread
9:10 *s* you sow and increase your generous yield.
11:22 Are they the *s* of Abraham?
1Pt 1:23 destructible but from an indestructible *s*,

SEED-BEARING (2)
Gn 1:29 I give you every *s* plant all over the
1:29 that has *s* fruit on it to be your food,

SEED-GROUND (1)
Gal 6: 8 but if his *s* is the spirit,

SEEDBED (1)
Ez 17: 5 seed of the land, and planted it in a *s*;

SEEDS (2)
Mt 23:23 You pay tithes on mint and herbs and *s*
Mk 4:31 is the smallest of all the earth's *s*,

SEEDTIME (3)
Gn 8:22 earth lasts cold and heat, *s* and harvest,
Prv 20: 4 In *s* the sluggard plows not;
Zec 8:12 LORD of hosts, for it is the *s* of peace:

SEEK (187)
Gn 41:33 let Pharaoh *s* out a wise and discerning
Nm 10:33 was to *s* out their resting place
16:10 him, and yet you now *s* the priesthood too.
23:15 holocaust, while I *s* a meeting over there."
24: 1 did not go aside as before to *s* omens,
27:21 to have him *s* out for him the decisions of
Dt 4:29 Yet there too you shall *s* the LORD,
Jgs 4:22 him, "Come, I will show you the man you *s*."
Ru 3: 1 must *s* a home for you that will please you.
1Sm 22:23 that seeks your life must *s* my life also.
23:15 because Saul had come out to *s* his life;
25:26 who *s* to harm my lord become as Nabal!
25:29 rises to pursue you and to *s* your life,
26:20 For the king of Israel has come out to *s* a
28: 7 to whom I can go to *s* counsel through her."
2Sm 14:16 one who would *s* to destroy me
1Kgs 19:10 alone am left, and they *s* to take my life."
19:14 alone am left, and they *s* to take my life."
22: 5 of Israel, *S* the word of the LORD at once."
1Chr 14: 8 they went up in unison to *s* him out.
15:13 burst upon us, for we did not *s* him aright."
16:10 rejoice, O hearts that *s* the LORD!
16:11 *s* to serve him constantly.
21: 3 why does my lord *s* to do this thing?
28: 9 If you *s* him, he will let himself be found
2Chr 7:14 and *s* my presence and turn from their evil
11:16 tribes who firmly desired to *s* the LORD,
12:14 he had not truly resolved to *s* the LORD.
14: 3 He commanded Judah to *s* the LORD,
15: 2 if you *s* him he will be present to you;
15:12 They entered into a covenant to *s* the LORD,
15:13 and everyone who would not *s* the LORD,
16:12 even in his sickness he did not *s* the LORD,
18: 4 of Israel, *S* the word of the LORD at once."
19: 3 the land and have been determined to *s* God."
20: 4 Judah gathered to *s* help from the LORD;
20: 4 cities of Judah they came to *s* the LORD.
26: 5 to *s* God as long as Zechariah lived,
30:19 to everyone who has resolved to *s* God,
34: 3 to *s* after the God of his forefather David,
Ezr 4: 2 with you, for we *s* your God just as you do,
8:22 hand of our God is upon all who *s* him,
Neh 2:10 come to *s* the welfare of the Israelites.
Tb 4:18 *S* counsel from every wise man,
Est E: 3 only do they *s* to do harm to our subjects;
1Mc 7:13 among the Israelites to *s* peace with them,
11:16 Alexander fled to Arabia to *s* protection.
Jb 7:21 and should you *s* me I shall then be gone.
10: 6 That you *s* for guilt in me and search
Ps(s) 4: 3 love what is vain and *s* after falsehood?
9:11 name, for you forsake not those who *s* you,
22:27 they who *s* the LORD shall praise him:
27: 4 One thing I ask of the LORD; this I *s*:
27: 8 your presence, O LORD, I *s*.
34:11 who *s* the LORD want for no good thing.
34:15 *s* peace, and follow after it.
35: 4 put to shame and disgraced who *s* my life;
40:15 confusion who *s* to snatch away my life.
40:17 all who *s* you exult and be glad in you,
45:13 the rich among the people *s* your favor.
54: 5 up against me, and fierce men *s* my life;
63: 2 O God, you are my God whom I *s*;
63:10 But they shall be destroyed who *s* my life,
69: 7 Let not those who *s* you blush for me,
69:33 you who *s* God, may your hearts
70: 3 put to shame and confounded who *s* my life.
70: 5 may all who *s* you exult and be glad in you,
71:13 in ignominy and disgrace who *s* to harm me.
77: 3 on the day of my distress I *s* the Lord.
81:16 who hated the LORD would *s* to flatter me,
83:17 with disgrace, that men may *s* your name,
104:21 for the prey and *s* their food from God.
105: 3 rejoice, O hearts that *s* the LORD!
105: 4 *s* to serve him constantly.
119: 2 decrees, who *s* him with all their heart,
119:10 With all my heart I *s* you;
119:45 walk at liberty, because I *s* your precepts.
119:155 because they *s* not your statutes.
119:176 *s* your servant, because your commands
Prv 1:28 they *s* me, but find me not;
2: 4 If you *s* her like silver,
8:17 me I also love, and those who *s* me find me.
23:35 When shall I awake to *s* wine once again?"
25:27 nor to *s* honor after honor.
28: 5 but those who *s* the LORD understand all.
Eccl 3: 6 A time to *s*, and a time to lose;
Sg 3: 2 I will *s* Him whom my heart loves.
6: 1 your lover gone that we may *s* him with you?
Wis 1: 1 goodness, and *s* him in integrity of heart;
6:12 who love her, and found by those who *s* her.
13: 6 though they *s* God and wish to find him.
Sir 2:16 Those who fear the LORD *s* to please him,
3:20 What is too sublime for you, *s* not,
4:11 children and admonishes those who *s* her.
4:12 those who *s* her out win her favor.
6:28 *s* her and you will find her.
6:36 If you see a man of prudence, *s* him out;
7: 4 *S* not from the LORD authority,
7: 6 *S* not to become a judge if you have not
11:10 however you *s* it, you will not find it.
14:16 in the nether world there are no joys to *s*.
18:19 you are judged, *s* merit for yourself,
28: 4 his fellows, yet *s* pardon for his own sins?
33:26 his hands be idle and he will *s* to be free.
37:10 *S* no advice from one who regards you with
39: 6 His care is to *s* the LORD,
40:26 he who has it need *s* no other support:
51:26 For she is close to those who *s* her,
Is 9:12 who struck them, nor *s* the LORD of hosts.
10:31 flight, the inhabitants of Gebim *s* refuge.
11:10 for the nations, The Gentiles shall *s* out,
30: 2 to Egypt, but my counsel they do not *s*.
31: 1 to the Holy One of Israel nor *s* the LORD!
41:12 You shall *s* out, but shall not find,
41:17 afflicted and the needy *s* water in vain,
51: 1 me, you who pursue justice, who *s* the LORD;
55: 6 *S* the LORD while he may be found,
58: 2 They *s* me day after day,
Jer 4: 6 standard to Zion, *s* refuge without delay!
4:30 Your lovers spurn you, they *s* your life.
11:21 the men of Anathoth who *s* your life,
19: 7 by the hand of those that *s* their lives.
19: 9 those who *s* their lives will confine them.
21: 7 their enemies and those who *s* their lives.
22:25 into the hands of those who *s* your life;
29:13 Yes, when you *s* me with all your heart,
30:14 have forgotten you, they do not *s* you.
34:20 their enemies, to those who *s* their lives:
34:21 their enemies, to those who *s* their lives,
38:16 hand you over to these men who *s* your life."
44:30 to his enemies, to those who *s* his life,
45: 5 And do you *s* great things for yourself?
45: 5 *S* them not! I am bringing evil
46:26 hand them over to those who *s* their lives,
49:37 their foes, before those who *s* their life;
50: 4 come, Weeping as they come, to *s* the LORD,
50:20 They shall *s* Israel's guilt,
Bar 3:23 The sons of Hagar who *s* knowledge on earth,
4:28 God, turn now ten times the more to *s* him;
Ez 7:25 When anguish comes they shall *s* peace,
34: 4 not bring back the strayed nor *s* the lost,
34:16 The lost I will *s* out,
Dn 11:26 table companions shall *s* to destroy him,
Hos 3: 5 of Israel shall turn back and *s* the LORD,
5: 6 their herds they shall go to *s* the LORD,
5:15 they pay for their guilt and *s* my presence.
7:10 return to the LORD, their God, nor *s* him,
10:12 a new field, for it is time to *s* the LORD,
Am 5: 4 *S* me, that you may live,
5: 5 that you may live, but do not *s* Bethel;
5: 6 *S* the LORD, that you may live,
5:14 *S* good and not evil,
Ob 1: 6 they search Esau, *s* out his hiding places!
Na 3:11 you, too, shall *s* a refuge from the foe.
Zep 1: 6 the LORD, and those who do not *s* the LORD.
2: 3 *S* the LORD, all you humble of the earth,
2: 3 *S* justice, seek humility;
Zec 8:21 and, "I too will go to *s* the LORD."
8:22 strong nations shall come to *s* the LORD
11:16 of those that perish, nor *s* the strays,
12: 9 On that day I will *s* the destruction of
Mal 3: 1 come to the temple the LORD whom you *s*,
Mt 6:33 *S* first his kingship over you,
7: 7 *S*, and you will find.
19:21 Jesus told him, "If you *s* perfection,
Mk 8:12 he said, "Why does this age *s* a sign?
15:43 He was bold enough to *s* an audience with
Lk 11: 9 *s* and you shall find;
12:31 *S* out instead his kingship over you,
Jn 1:41 was *s* out his brother Simon and tell him,
5:44 *s* the glory that comes from the One [God]?
8:50 I *s* no glory for myself:
Acts 15:17 that bear my name may *s* out the Lord.
17:27 They were to *s* God,
25:11 death, I do not *s* to escape that penalty.
1Cor 7:27 Then do not *s* your freedom.
10:24 No man should *s* his own interest but
14: 1 *S* eagerly after love.
Gal 1:10 this how I *s* to ingratiate myself with men?
5: 4 Any of you who *s* your justification in the
1Thes 2: 6 Neither did we *s* glory from men,
5:15 always *s* one another's good and,
1Tm 6:11 Instead, *s* after integrity,
Heb 11: 6 and that he rewards those who *s* him.
1Pt 3:11 and do good, *s* peace and follow after it,
Rv 9: 6 men will *s* death but will not find it;

SEEKER (1)
Sir 33:18 I toiled, but for every *s* after wisdom.

SEEKING (33)
Nm 35:23 he was not his enemy nor *s* to harm him:
Jos 9:14 without *s* the advice of the LORD.
2Sm 3:17 time you have been *s* David as your king.
16:11 who came forth from my loins, is *s* my life,
17: 3 It is the death of only one man you are *s*;
20:19 You are *s* to beat down a city that is a
1Kgs 11:22 you are *s* to return to your own country?"
1Chr 4:39 of the valley, *s* pasture for their flocks.
22:19 hearts and souls to *s* the LORD your God.
Ezr 6:21 of the land to join them in *s* the LORD,
Est 6: 2 for *s* to lay hands on King Ahasuerus.
1Mc 6:56 that he was *s* to take over the government.
Jb 24: 5 these go forth to their task of *s* food;
Ps(s) 38:13 Men lay snares for me *s* my life;
Wis 6:16 her own rounds, *s* those worthy of her,
8:18 I went about *s* to take her for my own.
Is 58:13 following your ways, *s* your own interests,
Jer 2:24 No beasts need tire themselves *s* her;
2:33 How well you pick your way when *s* love!
Bar 3:23 and Teman, the phrasemakers *s* knowledge,
Jn 5:30 I am not *s* my own will but the will of him
Rom 9:30 That the Gentiles, who were not *s* justice,
9:31 *s* a law from which justice would come,
10: 3 justice and *s* to establish their own,
10:20 "I was found by those who were not *s* me;
11: 3 I alone am left and they are *s* my life."
11: 7 Israel did not obtain what she was *s*,
1Cor 10:33 I try to please all in any way I can by *s*,
Gal 1:16 without *s* human advisers or even going to
2:17 But if, in *s* to be justified in Christ,
Phil 2:21 Everyone is busy *s* his own interests
Heb 11:14 they showed that they were *s* a homeland.
13:14 we are *s* one which is to come.

SEEKS (29)
Dt 18:11 and spirits or *s* oracles from the dead.
1Sm 20: 1 father hold against me that he *s* my life?"
22:23 he that *s* your life must seek my life also.
2Mc 2:27 one who thus *s* to give enjoyment to others.
Jb 39: 8 pasture, and *s* out every patch of green.
Ps(s) 14: 2 see if there be one who is wise and *s* God.
24: 6 race that *s* for him, that seeks the face
27: 8 you my glance *s*; your presence, O LORD,
37:32 man spies on the just, and *s* to slay him.
53: 3 see if there be one who is wise and *s* God.
86:14 and the company of fierce men *s* my life,
Prv 11:27 He who *s* the good commands favor,
14: 6 The senseless man *s* in vain for wisdom,
15:14 mind of the intelligent man *s* knowledge,
18: 1 In estrangement one *s* pretexts:
18:15 and the ear of the wise *s* knowledge.
Eccl 7:28 which my soul still *s* and has not found:
Sir 32:14 he who *s* him obtains his request.
Jer 5: 1 Who lives uprightly and *s* to be faithful,
17: 5 human beings, who *s* his strength in flesh,
Lam 3:25 who waits for him, to the soul that *s* him;
Mt 7: 8 The one who *s*, finds.
10:39 who *s* only himself brings himself to ruin,
Lk 11:10 whoever *s*, finds; whoever knocks,
11:29 It *s* a sign.
Jn 4:23 it is just such worshipers the Father *s*.
7:18 *s* glory for him who sent him is truthful;
8:50 there is one who *s* it,

SEEM (18)
Lv 13: 4 not *s* to have penetrated below the skin,
13:32 not *s* to have penetrated below the skin,
14:37 reddish depressions which *s* to go deeper
Sg 5:12 waters, His teeth would *s* bathed in milk,
Sir 7:26 have a wife, let her not *s* odious to you;
11:30 Though he *s* like a bird confined in a cage,
30: 4 At the father's death, he will *s* not dead,
Is 5:28 The hoofs of their horses *s* like flint,

46:12 you who *s* far from the victory of justice:
Hg 2: 3 Does it not *s* like nothing in your eyes?
Zec 8: 6 Even if this should *s* impossible in the
Mk 10:42 *s* to exercise authority lord it over them;
Acts 2:15 these men are not drunk, as you *s* to think.
1Cor 12:22 *s* less important are in fact indispensable.
2Cor 6:10 We *s* to have nothing,
11: 4 accepted, you *s* to endure it quite well.
13: 7 good, even though we may *s* to have failed.
Gal 4: 9 *s* willing to enslave yourselves once more?

SEEMED (23)

Gn 29:20 yet they *s* to him but a few days because
34:18 *s* fair to Hamor and his son Shechem.
48:17 on Ephraim's head, this *s* wrong to him;
Nm 13:33 and so we must have *s* to them."
1Kgs 20:27 *s* like a couple of small flocks of goats,
Jdt 13:13 assembled, for her return *s* unbelievable.
1Mc 1:16 When his kingdom *s* secure,
2Mc 6:29 what he had said *s* to them utter madness.
12:16 *s* to be filled with the blood that flowed
Ps(s) 73:16 understand this it *s* to me too difficult,
Wis 3: 2 They *s*, in the view of the foolish,
Ez 1:13 they *s* like torches,
8: 2 Downward from what *s* to be his waist,
8: 2 from his waist upward there *s* to be a
10:10 All four of them *s* to be made the same,
40: 2 On it there *s* to be a city being built
Dn 3:99 It has *s* good to me to publish the signs
Lk 24:11 but the story *s* like nonsense and they
Acts 6:15 Stephen's face *s* like that of an angel.
12: 9 The whole thing *s* to him a mirage.
Heb 12:10 They disciplined us as *s* right to them,
Rv 6: 6 I heard what *s* to be a voice coming from
13: 3 heads *s* to have been mortally wounded,

SEEMING (2)

Jos 8:15 fled in *s* defeat toward the desert,
Ez 1:22 could be seen, *s* like glittering crystal,

SEEMINGLY (1)

2Mc 1:13 in Persia with his *s* irresistible army,

SEEMS (19)

Lv 13:25 this *s* to have penetrated below the skin,
Dt 12: 8 everyone does what *s* right to himself,
1Chr 13: 2 "If it *s* good to you,
19:13 then may the LORD do what *s* best to him."
21:23 let my lord the king do what *s* best to him.
Ezr 7:18 You and your brethren may do whatever *s*
Est 8: 5 pleases your majesty and *s* proper to you,
Prv 12:15 way of the fool *s* right in his own eyes,
14:12 Sometimes a way *s* right to a man,
16:25 Sometimes a way *s* right to a man,
18:17 pleads his case first *s* to be in the right;
Sir 40: 6 So short is his rest it *s* like none,
Jer 40: 4 *s* good to you to come with me to Babylon,
Zec 11:12 I said to them, "If it *s* good to you,
Acts 25:27 It *s* to me a senseless procedure to send
1Cor 7:26 In the present time of stress it *s* good to
7:36 and it *s* that something should be done,
16: 4 If it *s* fitting that I should go myself,
Heb 12:11 *s* a cause for grief and not for joy,

SEER (23)

1Sm 9: 9 used to say, "Come, let us go to the *s*."
9: 9 now called prophet was formerly called *s*.)
9:11 and inquired of them, "Is the *s* in town?"
9:18 said, "Please tell me where the *s* lives."
9:19 "I am the *s*.
16: 4 inquired, "Is your visit peaceful, O *s*?"
2Sm 24:11 had spoken to the prophet Gad, David's *s*,
2Kgs 17:13 Israel and Judah by every prophet and *s*,
1Chr 9:22 David and Samuel the *s* had established
21: 9 Then the LORD spoke to Gad, David's *s*,
25: 5 of Heman, the king's *s* in divine matters;
26:28 Also, whatever Samuel the *s*,
29:29 seer, the history of Nathan the prophet,
2Chr 9:29 of Iddo the *s* which concern Jeroboam,
12:15 and of Iddo the *s* [his family record].
16: 7 At that time Hanani the *s* came to Asa,
16:10 the *s* and imprisoned him in the stocks,
19: 2 Jehu the *s*, son of Hanani,
29:25 of David, of Gad the king's *s*,
29:30 in the words of David and of Asaph the *s*.
35:15 Asaph, Heman and Jeduthun, the king's *s*.
Sir 46:15 out and his words proved him true as a *s*.

SEERS (6)

2Chr 33:18 and the words of the *s* who spoke to him in
33:19 found written down in the history of his *s*.
Sir 44: 3 prudence, or *s* of all things in prophecy;
Is 29:10 prophets] and covered your heads [the *s*.
30:10 They say to the *s*,
Mi 3: 7 Then shall the *s* be put to shame,

SEES (60)

Gn 44:30 as soon as he *s* that the boy is missing;
Ex 4:15 When he *s* you, his heart will be glad.
33:20 see, for no man *s* me and still lives.
Lv 13:20 *s* that it is deeper than the skin and that
Nm 24: 4 knows, Of one who sees what the Almighty *s*,
24:16 knows, Of one who *s* what the Almighty sees,
Dt 23:15 if he *s* anything indecent in your midst,
32:36 When he *s* their strength failing,
1Sm 16: 7 Not as man *s* does God see,
2Sm 15:26 let him do to me as he *s* fit."
Jb 7: 8 eye that now *s* me shall no more behold me;
10: 4 Do you see as man *s*?
11:11 the worthlessness of men and *s* iniquity;
28:24 earth and *s* all that is under the heavens.
Ps(s) 10:11 he hides his face, he never *s*."
33:13 he *s* all mankind.
37:13 at him, for he *s* that his day is coming.
58: 9 an untimely birth that never *s* the sun.
58:11 just man shall be glad when he *s* vengeance;
94: 7 murder, And they say, "The LORD *s* not;
97: 4 the earth *s* and trembles.
138: 6 The LORD is exalted, yet the lowly he *s*,
Prv 20:12 The ear that hears, and the eye that *s*—
28:11 poor man who is intelligent *s* through him.
Eccl 2:26 For to whatever man he *s* fit he gives
2:26 to be given to whatever man God *s* fit.
Sir 13: 7 When later he *s* you he will pass you by,
18:10 He *s* and understands that their death is
23:18 no one *s* me; why should I fear sin?"
40: 6 day, Terrified by what his mind's eye *s*,
42:18 *s* from of old the things that are to come:
Is 21: 6 station a watchman, let him tell what he *s*.
21: 7 If he *s* a chariot, a pair of horses,
26:10 and *s* not the majesty of the LORD.
28: 4 when a man *s* it, he picks and swallows
29:15 Who work in the dark, saying, "Who *s* us,
47:10 your wickedness, and said, "No one *s* me."
Lam 3:50 Till the LORD from heaven looks down and *s*.
Ez 12:27 "The vision he *s* is a long way off;
32:31 When Pharaoh *s* these,
33: 6 But if the watchman *s* the sword coming and
Dn 1:10 If he *s* that you look wretched by
Mi 7:10 When my enemy *s* this,
Na 3: 7 Till everyone who *s* you runs from you,
Mt 6: 4 your Father who *s* in secret will repay you.
6: 6 Then your Father, who *s* what no man sees,
6:18 Father who *s* what is hidden will repay you.
Jn 5:19 he can do only what he *s* the Father doing.
11: 9 because he *s* the world bathed in light.
14:17 since it neither *s* him nor recognizes him;
Rom 1:31 One *s* in them men without conscience,
8:24 it possible for one to hope for what he *s*?
1Cor 8:10 If someone *s* you,
2Cor 12: 7 than what he *s* in me or hears from my lips.
1Jn 3:17 heart to his brother when he *s* him in need.
5:16 Anyone who *s* his brother sinning,

SEETHE (1)

Jb 30:17 my inward parts *s* and will not be stilled.

SEETHED (1)

Gn 34: 7 men were shocked and *s* with indignation.

SEETHES (1)

Sir 43: 3 At noon it *s* the surface of the earth,

SEETHING (1)

Jb 41:12 issues steam, as from a *s* pot or bowl.

SEGREGATED (2)

1Sm 21: 6 been *s* from women as on previous occasions.
2Chr 26:21 As a leper he dwelt in a *s* house,

SEGUB (3)

1Kgs 16:34 the foundation, and his youngest son, *S*,
1Chr 2:21 She bore him *S*.
2:22 *S* became the father of Jair,

SEINE (3)

Ez 32: 3 of many nations], and draw you up in my *s*.
Hb 1:15 with his net, He gathers them in his *s*;
1:16 to his net, and burns incense to his *s*;

SEIR (40)

Gn 14: 6 and the Horites in the hill country of *S*,
32: 4 to his brother Esau in the land of *S*,
33:14 of my children, until I join my lord in *S*."
33:16 day that Esau began his journey back to *S*,
36: 6 land of Canaan, and went to the land of *S*,
36: 8 So Esau settled in the highlands of *S*.
36: 9 of the Edomites, in the highlands of *S*.
36:20 are the descendants of *S* the Horite,
36:21 are the Horite clans descended from *S*,
36:30 Horites, clan by clan, in the land of *S*.
Nm 24:18 dispossessed, and no fugitive is left in *S*.
Dt 1: 2 Kadesh-barnea by way of the highlands of *S*.
1:44 cutting you down in *S* as far as Hormah.
2: 1 around the highlands of *S* for a long time.
2: 4 the descendants of Esau, who live in *S*.
2: 5 Esau possession of the highlands of *S*.
2: 8 Arabah route, Elath, Ezion-geber, and *S*,
2:12 In *S*, however, the former inhabitants
2:22 the descendants of Esau, who dwell in *S*,
2:29 the descendants of Esau who dwell in *S*
33: 2 Sinai and dawned on his people from *S*;
Jos 11:17 from Mount Halak that rises toward *S*
12: 7 to Mount Halak which rises toward *S*,
15:10 boundary curved westward to Mount *S*
24: 4 mountain region of *S* in which to settle,
Jgs 5: 4 O LORD, when you went out from *S*,
1Chr 1:38 The descendants of *S* were Lotan,
4:42 Mount *S* under the leadership of Pelatiah,
2Chr 20:10 and those of Mount *S* whom you did not
20:22 of Mount *S* who were coming against Judah,
20:23 Mount *S* and completely exterminated them.
20:23 had finished with the inhabitants of *S*,
25:11 there they killed ten thousand men of *S*.
25:14 back with him the gods of the people of *S*,
Sir 50:26 Those who live in *S* and Philistia,
Is 21:11 They call to me from *S*,
Ez 35: 2 Son of man, set your face against Mount *S*,
35: 3 I am coming at you, Mount *S*.
35: 7 I will make Mount *S* a desolate waste,
35:15 A waste shall you be, Mount *S*,

SEIRAH (1)

Jgs 3:26 and, passing the idols, took refuge in *S*.

SEIZE (48)

Gn 43:18 us and take our donkeys and *s* us as slaves."
Nm 13:30 said, "We ought to go up and *s* the land,
Jgs 7:24 and *s* the water courses against them as
12: 6 they would *s* him and kill him at the fords
21:21 *s* one of the girls of Shiloh for a wife,
1Sm 17:35 If it attacked me, I would *s* it by the jaw,
2Sm 2:21 *s* one of the young men and take what you
1Kgs 13: 4 his hand from the altar and said, *S* him!"
18:40 said to them, *S* the prophets of Baal.
20: 6 They shall *s* and take away whatever they
22:26 said, *S* Micaiah and take him back to Amon,
2Chr 18:25 *S* Micaiah and take him back to Amon,
Jdt 6:10 were standing by in his tent to *s* Achior,
7: 1 against Bethulia, *s* the mountain passes,
14: 2 the earth, let each of you *s* his weapons,
14: 3 They will *s* their armor and hurry to their
14: 3 and do not find him, panic will *s* them,
16: 4 children a prey, and *s* my virgins as spoil.
Est 8:11 and to *s* their goods as spoil throughout
1Mc 5:11 *s* this stronghold to which we have fled.
5:27 *s* and destroy all these people in one day."
7:29 But Judas' enemies were prepared to *s* him.
9:60 them to *s* Jonathan and his companions.
12:40 Looking for a way to *s* and kill him,
16:20 to *s* Jerusalem and the mount of the temple.
Jb 3: 6 May obscurity *s* that day;
9:12 Should he *s* me forcibly,
11:10 If he *s* and imprison or call to judgment,
Ps(s) 71:11 pursue and *s* him,
75: 3 "When I *s* the appointed time,
137: 9 Happy the man who shall *s* and smash your
Sir 41: 9 If you have children, calamity will *s* them;
Is 5:29 They growl and *s* the prey,
10: 6 under my wrath I order him To *s* plunder,
Jer 13:21 *s* you like those of a woman giving birth?
20: 5 shall *s* it and carry it away to Babylon.
Bar 6:57 *s* them strip off the gold and the silver,
Ez 19: 3 He learned to *s* prey,
19: 6 He learned to *s* prey,
23:26 your clothes and *s* your splendid ornaments.
38:13 away cattle and goods, to *s* much plunder?"
46:18 The prince shall not *s* any part of the
Dn 11:21 stealth and fraud he shall *s* the kingdom.
Mi 2: 2 They covet fields, and *s* them;
Zec 14:13 every man shall *s* the hand of his neighbor,
Mal 1:13 You bring in what you *s*,
Jn 7:30 At this they tried to *s* him,
Heb 6:18 to *s* the hope which is placed before us.

SEIZED (100)

Gn 14:11 The victors *s* all the possessions and food
19:16 *s* his hand and the hands of his wife and
21:25 a well that Abimelech's men had *s* by force.
27:33 *s* with a fit of uncontrollable trembling.
34: 2 her, he *s* her and lay with her by force.
34:28 They *s* their flocks,
39:20 He *s* Joseph and threw him into the jail
Ex 15:15 trembling *s* the chieftains of Moab;
Nm 21:25 Israel *s* all the towns here and settled in
21:26 had *s* all his land from Jazer to the Arnon.
Dt 2:34 we *s* all his cities and doomed them all,
33:20 that has *s* the arm and head of the prey.
Jgs 3:28 *s* the fords of the Jordan leading to Moab,
7:24 *s* the water courses as far as Beth-barah,
16: 3 *s* the doors of the city gate and the two
16:21 Philistines *s* him and gouged out his eyes.
19:25 the husband *s* his concubine and thrust her
1Sm 4:19 husband, she was *s* with the pangs of labor,
5:11 A deadly panic had *s* the whole city,
13: 7 all his followers were *s* with fear.
14:34 brought to the LORD whatever ox he had *s*,
15:27 to go, Saul *s* a loose end of his mantle,
16:23 Whenever the spirit from God *s* Saul,
2Sm 1:11 David *s* his garments and rent them,

SEIZED (cont.)

4:10 in Ziklag I *s* and put to death the man who
10: 4 Hanun, therefore, *s* David's servants and,
13:11 to him to eat, he *s* her and said to her,
1Kgs 1:50 he went and *s* the horns of the altar.
1:51 had *s* the horns of the altar and said,
2:28 of the LORD and *s* the horns of the altar.
18:40 They were *s*, and Elijah had them brought
1Chr 19: 4 Thereupon Hanun *s* David's servants and had
2Chr 23:15 So they *s* her, and when she arrived
Neh 2: 2 Though I was *s* with great fear,
Tb 6: 4 *s* the fish and hauled it up on the shore.
Jdt 2:25 He *s* the territory of Cilicia,
4:12 not to allow their children to be *s*,
6:12 they *s* their weapons and ran out of the
7: 5 Yet they all *s* their weapons,
7: 7 their sources of water; these he *s*,
14:19 their tunics and were *s* with consternation.
15: 7 the enormous quantity of booty they had *s*.
Est 3:13 and that their goods should be *s* as spoil.
4:16 Queen Esther, *s* with mortal anguish,
7: 6 was *s* with dread of the king and queen.
8:17 for they were *s* with a fear of the Jews.
9: 2 but all peoples were *s* with a fear of them.
1Mc 1:32 the women and children, and *s* the cattle.
3:12 Their possessions were *s* and the sword of
7: 2 the soldiers *s* Antiochus and Lysias to
9:36 made a raid and *s* and carried off John
9:61 Jonathan's men *s* about fifty of the men of
12:48 men of the city closed the gates and *s* him;
15:30 give up the cities you have *s* and the
15:33 "We have not *s* any foreign land;
2Mc 2:21 few as they were, they *s* the whole land,
8:25 They also *s* the money of those who had
9: 5 he was *s* with excruciating pains
Jb 1:17 formed three columns, *s* the camels,
16:12 *s* me by the neck and dashed me to pieces.
Ps(s) 116: 3 the snares of the nether world *s* upon me;
Is 10:14 has *s* like a nest the riches of nations;
21: 3 have *s* me like those of a woman in labor;
Jer 8:21 I am disconsolate; horror has *s* me.
37:13 he *s* the prophet Jeremiah
48:41 Cities are taken, strongholds *s*:
49:24 she turns to flee, panic has *s* her.
50:24 You were discovered and *s*,
51:32 The fords have been *s*,
51:41 How has she been *s*,
Ez 3:14 The spirit which had lifted me up *s* me,
8: 2 be a hand and *s* me by the hair of my head.
30: 4 are *s* and her foundations are overthrown.
Dn 10: 7 but great fear *s* the men who were with me;
10:16 I was *s* with pangs at the vision and I was
13:40 *s* this one and asked who the young man was,
14:36 The angel of the Lord *s* him by the crown
Am 3: 4 out from its den unless it has *s* something?
6:13 our own strength, *s* for ourselves Karnaim?"
Jon 1:10 men were *s* with great fear and said to him.
Mi 4: 9 are *s* with pains like a woman in travail?
Mt 18:28 He *s* him and throttled him.
21:39 With that they *s* him,
Mk 5:15 perfectly sane, and they were *s* with fear.
12: 3 But they *s* him, beat him, and sent him off
12: 8 Then they *s* and killed him and dragged him
14:51 As they *s* him he left the cloth behind and
Lk 5: 9 they had made *s* him and all his shipmates,
5:26 At this they were all *s* with astonishment.
7:16 *s* them all and they began to praise God.
8:37 neighborhood, for a great fear had *s* them;
Acts 6:12 All together they confronted him, *s* him,
16:19 they *s* Paul and Silas and dragged them
21:27 They *s* him, shouting:
21:30 They *s* Paul, dragged him outside
23:27 whom the Jews *s* and were about to murder.
26:21 That is why the Jews *s* me in the temple
Rom 7: 8 Sin *s* that opportunity;
1Thes 2:17 *s* with the greatest longing to see you.
Rv 20: 2 He *s* the dragon,

SEIZES (15)

Dt 22:25 maiden, *s* her and has relations with her,
25:11 hand and *s* the latter by his private parts,
Jb 18: 9 A trap *s* him by the heel,
27:21 The storm wind *s* him and he disappears;
30:18 by the collar of my tunic he *s* me:
Ps(s) 48: 7 Quaking *s* them there;
119:53 Indignation *s* me because of the wicked who
Prv 7:13 When she *s* him, she kisses him,
26:17 Like the man who *s* a passing dog by the
Sir 26: 7 he who marries her *s* a scorpion.
27:29 The trap *s* those who rejoice in pitfalls,
Is 3: 6 a man *s* his brother in his father's house,
Jer 48:39 one wants, says the LORD How terror *s* Moab,
50:43 Anguish *s* him,
Mk 9:18 Whenever it *s* him it throws him down;

SEIZING (4)

1Mc 5: 8 After *s* Jazer and its villages,
Ez 22:25 people, *s* their wealth and precious things,
23:29 *s* all that you have worked for and leaving
Mt 21:35 The tenants responded by *s* the slaves.

SELA (4)

Jgs 1:36 from the Akrabim pass to *S* and beyond.
2Kgs 14: 7 in the Salt Valley, and took *S* in battle.
Is 16: 1 like reptiles, from *S* across the desert,
42:11 Let the inhabitants of *S* exult,

SELDOM (2)

Prv 25:17 your foot be *s* in your neighbor's house,
Sir 22:12 Speak but *s* with the stupid man,

SELECT (5)

Nm 31: 3 *S* men from your midst and arm them for war,
35:11 *s* for yourselves cities to serve as cities
Ez 33: 2 and the people of this country *s* one of
Zec 4:10 see the *s* stone in the hands of Zerubbabel.
Jas 3: 4 course the steerman's impulse may *s*.

SELECTED (14)

Gn 32:14 Jacob *s* from what he had with him the
47: 2 whom he had *s* from their full number.
Jos 4: 4 whom he had *s* from among the Israelites,
1Sm 17:40 David *s* five smooth stones from the wadi
2Chr 3: 1 David, on the spot which David had *s*,
Ezr 8:24 Next I *s* twelve of the priestly leaders
1Mc 11:23 He *s* some elders and priests of Israel and
12: 1 he sent *s* men to Rome to confirm and renew
2Mc 8: 9 Ptolemy promptly *s* Nicanor,
Sir 45: 4 and meekness God *s* him from all mankind;
Ez 17:13 Then he *s* a man of the royal line with
Lk 6:13 and *s* twelve of them to be his apostles:
Acts 6: 5 Following this they *s* Stephen,
15: 7 God *s* me from your number

SELECTION (1)

2Sm 10: 9 he made a *s* from all the picked troops of

SELECTOR (1)

Wis 8: 4 understanding of God, the *s* of his works.

SELED (2)

1Chr 2:30 The sons of Nadab were *S* and Appaim.
2:30 *S* died without sons.

SELEUCIA (1)

Acts 13: 4 of *S* and set sail from there for Cyprus.

SELEUCIA-BY-THE-SEA (1)

1Mc 11: 8 the cities along the seacoast as far as *S*.

SELEUCUS (5)

1Mc 7: 1 and fifty-one, Demetrius, son of *S*,
2Mc 3: 3 Thus *S*, king of Asia, defrayed from
4: 7 But *S* died, and when Antiochus
5:18 was sent by King *S* to inspect the treasury,
14: 1 his men learned that Demetrius, son of *S*,

SELF (21)

Ex 32:13 and how you swore to them by your own *s*,
1Sm 20:17 because he loved him as his very *s*
2Mc 9:12 and not to think one's mortal *s* divine."
Ps(s) 55:14 But you, my other *s*,
Wis 1: 6 God is the witness of his inmost *s*
Sir 6:11 When things go well, he is your other *s*,
7:21 wise servant be dear to you as your own *s*;
Jer 49:13 By my own *s* I have sworn, says the LORD:
Am 6: 8 The Lord GOD has sworn by his very *s*,
Mt 16:24 to come after me, he must deny his very *s*,
16:26 can a man offer in exchange for his very *s*?
Mk 8:34 to come after me, he must deny his very *s*,
Lk 9:23 to be my follower must deny his very *s*,
14:26 brothers and sisters, indeed his very *s*,
Rom 6: 6 our old *s* was crucified with him so that
7:22 My inner *s* agrees with the law of God,
1Cor 2:11 *s* but the man's own spirit within him?
Eph 4:22 the old *s* which deteriorates through illusion
Col 3: 9 *s* with its past deeds and put on a new man,
2Tm 3: 2 Men will be lovers of *s* and of money,
Phlm 1:19 not to mention that you owe me your very *s*!

SELF-ASSURANCE (1)

Acts 4:13 Observing the *s* of Peter and John,

SELF-ASSURED (1)

2Cor 11:17 What I am about to say in this *s* boasting,

SELF-CONDEMNED (1)

Ti 3:11 he stands *s*.

SELF-CONTROL (5)

Sir 37:30 Through lack of *s* many have died,
1Cor 7: 5 may not tempt you through your lack of *s*.
7: 9 but if they cannot exercise *s*,
2Pt 1: 6 and *s* with discernment
1: 6 *s*, in turn, should lead to perservance,

SELF-CONTROLLED (3)

1Tm 3: 2 married only once, of even temper, *s*,
Ti 1: 8 steady, just, holy, and *s*.
2: 2 must be temperate, serious-minded, and *s*;

SELF-DECEIVED (1)

Jas 1:26 tongue imagines that he is devout, he is *s*;

SELF-DEFENSE (1)

Acts 18:14 to speak in *s* when Gallio said to the Jews:

SELF-ESTEEM (1)

Sir 10:27 My son, with humility have *s*;

SELF-GLORIFICATION (1)

Jn 7:18 Who ever speaks on his own is bent on *s*.

SELF-IMPORTANCE (2)

1Cor 4:18 Some have grown full of *s*,
2Cor 12:20 selfish ambitions, slander and gossip, *s*,

SELF-IMPORTANT (1)

1Cor 4: 6 so that none of you will grow *s* by reason

SELF-INTEREST (1)

2Cor 1:17 Or that my plans are so determined by *s*

SELF-POSSESSED (1)

2Tm 4: 5 As for you, be steady and *s*;

SELF-RIGHTEOUS (3)

Mt 9:13 I have come to call, not the *s*,
Mk 2:17 I have come to call sinners, not the *s*."
Lk 5:32 come to invite the *s* to a change of heart,

SELF-RIGHTEOUSNESS (1)

Lk 18: 9 *s* while holding everyone else in contempt:

SELF-SATISFIED (1)

1Cor 5: 2 Still you continue to be *s*,

SELF-SEEKING (1)

1Cor 13: 5 Love is never rude, it is not *s*,

SELF-STYLED (4)

Rv 2: 2 *s* apostles who are nothing of the sort,
2: 9 I know the slander you endure from *s* Jews
2:20 that *s* prophetess who seduces my servants
3: 9 *s* Jews who are not really Jews but frauds,

SELF-SUFFICIENT (1)

Phil 4:11 I find myself in I have learned to be *s*.

SELF-WILL (1)

Prv 1:32 For the *s* of the simple kills them,

SELF-WILLED (1)

Ti 1: 7 He may not be *s* or arrogant,

SELFISH (5)

Rom 15: 1 we must not be *s*.
2Cor 12:20 jealousy, outbursts of anger, *s* ambitions,
Gal 5:20 jealousy, outbursts of rage, *s* rivalries,
1Tm 5: 6 widow who gives herself up to *s* indulgence,
Jas 3:14 jealousy and *s* ambition in your hearts,

SELFISHLY (1)

Rom 2: 8 *s* disobey the truth and obey wickedness.

SELFSAME (1)

Wis 15: 8 he molds a meaningless god from the *s* clay;

SELL (40)

Gn 23: 4 *s* me from your holdings a piece of
23: 9 to *s* me the cave of Machpelah that he owns;
23: 9 Let him *s* it to me in your presence,
37:27 Rather, let us *s* him to these Ishmaelites,
47:16 *s* you bread in return for your livestock."
47:22 them, they did not have to *s* their land.
Ex 21: 8 He has no right to *s* her to a foreigner,
21:35 they shall *s* the live ox and divide this
Lv 25:14 when you *s* any land to your neighbor or
25:15 of years for crops, shall he *s* it to you.
25:25 poverty and has to *s* some of his property,
Dt 14:21 may eat it, or you may *s* it to a foreigner.
21:14 but you shall not *s* her or enslave her,
24: 7 in order to enslave him and *s* him,
1Kgs 21: 6 and said to him, *S* me your vineyard,
21:15 the Jezreelite which he refused to *s* you,
2Kgs 4: 7 and *s* the oil to pay off your creditor;
7: 1 a seah of fine flour will *s* for a shekel,
7:18 "Two seahs of barley will *s* for a shekel,
1Chr 21:22 *S* me the ground of this threshing floor,

21:22 *S* it to me at its full price,
Neh 13:15 I warned them to *s* none of these victuals.
2Mc 5:24 and *s* the women and young men into slavery.
Prv 23:23 Get the truth, and *s* it not
Ez 30:12 *s* the land over to the power of the wicked.
48:14 may not *s* or exchange or alienate this,
Jl 4: 8 I will *s* your sons and your daughters to
4: 8 of Judah, who shall *s* them to the Sabeans,
Am 2: 6 Because they *s* the just man for silver,
8: 5 over," you ask, "that we may *s* our grain,
8: 6 even the refuse of the wheat we will *s*!"
Zec 11: 5 while those who *s* them say,
Mt 19:21 seek perfection, go, *s* your possessions,
Mk 10:21 and *s* what you have and give to the poor;
Lk 12:33 *S* what you have and give alms.
18:22 *S* all you have and give to the poor.
22:36 a sword must *s* his coat and buy one.
Acts 2:45 they would *s* their property and goods,
5: 8 did you *s* that piece of property for such
Rv 13:16 did not allow a man to buy or *s* anything

SELLER (3)

Is 24: 2 maid as her mistress, the buyer as the *s*,
Ez 7:12 Let not the buyer rejoice nor the *s* mourn,
7:13 The *s* shall not regain what he sold as

SELLERS (1)

Neh 13:20 The merchants and *s* of various kinds of

SELLING (9)

Neh 5: 8 you, however, are *s* your own brothers,
13:16 and *s* it to the Judahites on the sabbath.
2Mc 8:10 the Romans by *s* captured Jews into slavery.
Sir 27: 2 between buying and *s* sin is wedged in.
Mt 21:12 all those engaged there in buying and *s*.
Mk 11:15 out those who were engaged in buying and *s*.
11:15 tables and the stalls of the men *s* doves;
Jn 2:14 he came upon people engaged in *s* oxen,
2:16 He told those who were *s* doves:

SELLS (10)

Ex 21: 7 "When a man *s* his daughter as a slave,
21:16 *s* his victim or still has him when caught,
21:37 an ox or a sheep and slaughters or *s* it,
Lv 25:16 really the number of crops that he *s* you.
25:29 someone *s* a dwelling in a walled town,
25:39 beside you that he *s* you his services,
25:47 he *s* himself to a wealthy alien
27:20 such a field, he *s* it to someone else,
Dt 15:12 a Hebrew man or woman, *s* himself to you,
Prv 31:24 She makes garments and *s* them,

SELVAGE (2)

Ex 28:32 around this opening there shall be a *s*,
39:23 with *s* around the opening to keep it from

SEMACHIAH (1)

1Chr 26: 7 who were men of might, Elihu and *S*.

SEMBLANCE (1)

1Thes 5:22 Avoid any *s* of evil.

SEMEIN (1)

Lk 3:26 son of Maath, son of Mattathias, son of *S*,

SENAAH (2)

Ezr 2:35 sons of *S*, three thousand six hundred
Neh 7:38 sons of *S*, three thousand nine hundred

SENATE (8)

Jdt 4: 8 and the *s* of the whole people of Israel,
1Mc 8:15 They had made for themselves a *s* house,
8:19 envoys entered the *s* and spoke as follows:
12: 3 the men entered the *s* chamber and said,
12: 6 the high priest, the *s* of the nation,
2Mc 1:10 The people of Jerusalem and Judea, the *s*,
4:44 three men sent by the *s* presented to him
11:27 the Jewish *s* and to the rest of the Jews.

SENATOR (1)

2Mc 6: 1 the king sent an Athenian *s* to force

SEND (265)

Gn 24: 7 he will *s* his messenger before you,
24:40 will *s* his messenger with you and make
27:45 Then I will *s* for you and bring you back.
37:13 Get ready; I will *s* you to them."
38:17 "I will *s* you a kid from the flock."
38:17 you leave a pledge until you *s* it."
38:23 After all, I did *s* her the kid,
42: 4 that Jacob did not *s* with the rest,
42:16 *s* one of your number to get your brother,
42:38 you would *s* my white head down to the
44:29 you will *s* my white head down to the
44:31 and your servants will thus *s* the white
Ex 3:10 I will *s* you to Pharaoh to lead my people,
3:20 After that he will *s* you away.
4:13 "If you please, Lord, *s* someone else!"
5:22 And why did you *s* me on such a mission?
6: 1 by my mighty hand, he will *s* them away;
7:27 I will *s* a plague of frogs over all your
23:28 you I will *s* hornets to drive the Hivites,
33: 2 I will *s* an angel before you to the land
33:12 not let me know whom you will *s* with me.
Lv 26:25 cities, I will *s* in pestilence among you,
Nm 13: 2 *S* men to reconnoiter the land of Canaan,
13: 2 shall *s* one man from each ancestral tribe,
31: 4 shall *s* a band of one thousand men to war."
Dt 1:22 'Let us *s* men ahead to reconnoiter the
7:20 LORD, your God, will *s* hornets among them,
15:13 so, you shall not *s* him away empty-handed,
19:12 *s* for him and have him taken from there,
28:48 enemies whom the LORD will *s* against you.
28:68 LORD will *s* you back in galleys to Egypt,
32:24 teeth of wild beasts I will *s* among them,
Jos 1:16 Joshua, "and we will go wherever you *s* us.
7: 3 and advised, "Do not *s* all the people up;
Jgs 6:14 It is I who *s* you."
20:38 signal they were to *s* up from the city.
1Sm 5:11 *S* away the ark of the God of Israel.
6: 2 Tell us what we should *s* back with it."
6: 3 to *s* away the ark of the God of Israel,
6: 3 the God of Israel, you must not *s* it alone,
9:16 "At this time tomorrow I will *s* you a man
11: 3 "Give us seven days to *s* messengers
12:17 the LORD, and he will *s* thunder and rain.
16:11 Samuel said to Jesse, *S* for him;
16:19 to ask Jesse to *s* him his son David,
20:12 David or not, I will *s* you the information.
20:13 you of it and *s* you on your way in peace.
20:21 I will then *s* my attendant to go and
20:31 So *s* for him, and bring him to me,
24:20 his enemy, does he *s* him away unharmed?
29: 4 *S* that man back!
2Sm 11: 6 a message to Joab, *S* me Uriah the Hittite."
14:29 Then he summoned Joab to *s* him to the king,
14:32 here, that I may *s* you to the king to say:
15:36 you shall *s* on to me whatever you hear."
17:16 So *s* a warning to David immediately,
1Kgs 2: 9 to *s* down his hoary head in blood
8:44 *s* your people forth to war
18: 1 said, "that I may *s* rain upon the earth."
20: 6 time tomorrow I will *s* my servants to you,
2Kgs 2:16 "Do not *s* them," he answered.
2:17 until he was embarrassed and said, *S* them."
5: 5 *s* along a letter to the king of Israel."
5: 7 *s* someone to me to be cured of leprosy?
6: 9 of God would *s* word to the king of Israel,
6:10 So the king of Israel would *s* word to the
7:13 horses and *s* scouts to investigate."
9:17 "and *s* him to meet them and to ask
17:27 *S* back one of the priests whom I deported,
19: 4 *s* up a prayer for the remnant that is here.' "
2Chr 2: 6 Now, *s* me men skilled at work in gold,
2: 7 Also *s* me boards of cedar,
2:14 let my lord *s* to his servants the wheat,
6:27 and *s* rain upon your land which you gave
6:34 against their enemies, wherever you *s* them,
7:13 land, if I *s* pestilence among my people,
28:11 *s* back the captives you have carried off
36:15 of their fathers, *s* his messengers to them,
Neh 2: 5 is deserving of your favor, *s* me to Judah,
Tb 5:18 "Why have you decided to *s* my child away?
8:12 *S* one of the maids in to see whether
Jdt 6: 2 He will *s* his force and destroy them from
8:31 Lord may *s* rain to fill up our cisterns,
9: 9 and *s* forth your wrath upon their heads.
16:17 He will *s* fire and worms into their flesh,
Est 9:19 which they *s* gifts of food to one another.
1Mc 3:35 Lysias was to *s* an army against them to
7: 7 *s* a man whom you trust to go and see all
12: 6 *s* greetings to their brothers the Spartans.
12:10 we have ventured to *s* word to you for the
12:18 kindly *s* us an answer on this matter."
12:45 men to stay with you, *s* the rest back home,
13:16 if you *s* us a hundred talents of silver,
13:18 would not *s* Trypho the money and the boys.
13:21 of the desert, and to *s* them provisions.
14:20 *s* greetings to Simon the high priest,
2Mc 1: 1 of Judea *s* greetings to their brethren,
1:10 *s* greetings and good wishes to Aristobulus,
2:15 them, *s* messengers to get them for you.
3:38 against the government, *s* him there,
6:23 to *s* him at once to the abode of the dead,
11: 6 and tears to *s* a good angel to save Israel.
11:26 please *s* them messengers to give them our
11:34 Romans, *s* greetings to the Jewish people.
11:36 *s* someone to us with your decisions so
11:37 to *s* us those who can inform us of your
14:27 and ordering him to *s* Maccabeus as a
15:23 *s* a good angel now to spread fear and
Jb 1: 5 Job would *s* for them and sanctify them,
14:20 with changed appearance you *s* him away.
20:23 God shall *s* against him the fury of his
38:35 you *s* forth the lightnings on their way.
Ps(s) 20: 3 May he *s* you help from the sanctuary,
43: 3 *S* forth your light and your fidelity;
57: 4 May he *s* from heaven and save me;
57: 4 God *s* his kindness and his faithfulness.
104:12 among the branches they *s* forth their song.
104:30 When you *s* forth your spirit,
Prv 24:22 suddenly arises the destruction they *s*,
Wis 9:10 *S* her forth from your holy heavens and
11:17 to *s* upon them a drove of bears or fierce
Sir 24:30 *s* my teachings forth shining like the dawn,
29: 9 their want, do not *s* them away emptyhanded.
39:14 *S* up the sweet odor of incense,
39:14 *S* up the sweet odor of your hymn of praise;
Is 5: 6 command the clouds not to *s* rain upon it.
6: 8 voice of the Lord saying, "Whom shall I *s*?
6: 8 "Here I am," I said; "*s* me!"
10: 6 Against an impious nation I *s* him,
10:16 hosts, will *s* among his fat ones leanness,
13:10 of the heavens *s* forth no light;
16: 1 *S* them forth, hugging the earth
30:28 the jaws of the peoples to *s* them astray].
34: 3 out, their corpses shall *s* up a stench;
37: 4 *S* up a prayer for the remnant that is here.' "
42:19 servant, or deaf like the messenger I *s*?
43:14 For your sakes I *s* to Babylon;
66:19 them I will *s* fugitives to the nations:
Jer 1: 7 To whomever I *s* you,
2:10 and see, *s* to Kedar and carefully inquire:
8:17 Yes, I will *s* against you poisonous snakes,
9:15 I will *s* the sword to pursue them until I
14: 3 The nobles *s* their servants for water,
14:14 I did not *s* them;
14:15 in my name, though I did not *s* them;
14:22 Or can the mere heavens *s* showers?
15: 1 *S* them away from me.
16:16 I will *s* many fishermen,
16:16 I will *s* many hunters to hunt them out
17:16 Yet I did not press you to *s* calamity;
18:22 suddenly you *s* plunderers against them.
22: 7 Against you I will *s* destroyers,
23:21 I did not *s* these prophets,
24:10 I will *s* upon them the sword,
25: 9 I will *s* for and fetch all the tribes of
25: 9 the LORD (and I will *s* to Nebuchadnezzar,
25:15 the nations to whom I will *s* you drink it.
25:16 because of the sword I will *s* among them.
25:27 before the sword that I will *s* among you!
26: 5 whom I *s* you constantly though you do not
27: 3 *S* to the kings of Edom,
27:15 I did not *s* them,
29: 9 I did not *s* them,
29:31 *S* the message to all the exiles:
37:20 do not *s* me back into the house of
38:26 *s* me back to Jonathan's house to die there.' "
42: 5 instructions the LORD, your God, will *s* us.
43:10 I will *s* for my servant Nebuchadnezzar,
48:12 when I will *s* him coopers to turn him over;
49:37 I will *s* the sword to pursue them until I
51: 2 Against Babylon I will *s* winnowers to
51:27 her, *s* up horses like bristling locusts.
Bar 1:10 "We *s* you funds,
1:14 out publicly this scroll which we *s* you,
Ez 3: 6 If I were to *s* you to these,
5:17 I will *s* famine against you,
13: 6 though the LORD did not *s* them;
14:19 if I were to *s* pestilence into this land,
14:21 I *s* Jerusalem my four cruel punishments,
28:23 Into it I will *s* pestilence,
36:29 and I will not *s* famine against you.
39: 6 I will *s* fire upon Magog and upon those
Dn 11:20 In his stead one shall arise who will *s* a
13:29 *S* for Susanna, the daughter of Hilkiah,
Hos 7:12 I will *s* them captive from their land.
8:14 cities, but I will *s* fire upon his cities,
Jl 2:19 See, I will *s* you grain,
Am 1: 4 I will *s* fire upon the house of Hazael,
1: 7 Edom, I will *s* fire upon the wall of Gaza,
1:10 I will *s* fire upon the wall of Tyre,
1:12 wrath to the end, I will *s* fire upon Teman,
2: 2 of Edom's king, I will *s* fire upon Moab,
2: 5 led them astray, I will *s* fire upon Judah,
8:11 GOD, when I will *s* famine upon the land:
Zec 5: 4 I will *s* it forth, says the LORD of hosts,
Mal 2: 2 I will *s* a curse upon you and of your
3:23 Lo, I will *s* you Elijah,
3:24 Lo, I will *s* you Elijah,
Mt 8:31 you expel us, *s* us into the herd of swine."
9:38 to *s* out laborers to gather his harvest."
11:10 says, 'I *s* my messenger ahead of you,
15:32 I do not wish to *s* them away hungry,
23:34 *s* you prophets and wise men and scribes.
Mk 3:14 whom he would *s* to preach the good news;
5:12 *S* us into the swine," they begged him.
6: 7 Twelve and began to *s* them out two by two,
8: 3 If I *s* them home hungry,
11: 3 it but he will *s* it back here at once.' "
12: 6 He still had one to *s*—
Lk 7:27 'I *s* my messenger ahead of you to prepare
10: 2 harvest-master to *s* workers to his harvest.
11:49 said, 'I will *s* them prophets and apostles,
14:32 he will *s* a delegation while the enemy is
16:24 *S* Lazarus to dip the tip of his finger in
16:27 '*s* him to my father's house
20:13 Perhaps if I *s* the son I love,
24:49 I *s* down upon you the promise of my Father.
Jn 3:17 God did not *s* the Son into the world to
7:28 I was sent by One who has the right to *s*,
13:20 you, he who accepts anyone I *s* accepts me,

SEND (cont.)
14:26 Spirit whom the Father will *s* in my name,
15:26 and whom I myself will *s* from the Father
16: 7 you, whereas if I go, I will *s* him to you.
20:21 "As the Father has sent me, so I *s* you."
Acts 7:34 Come now, I will *s* you into Egypt.'
10: 5 *S* some men to Joppa and summon a certain
10:32 *S* someone to Joppa to invite Simon known
11:13 *S* someone to Joppa and fetch Simon,
11:29 and *s* it to the relief of the brothers who
15:23 *s* greetings to the brothers of Gentile
15:25 choose representatives and *s* them to you,
22:21 I mean to *s* you far from here,
23:30 life, I decided at once to *s* him to you.
24:25 I'll *s* for you again when I find the time."
24:26 *s* for him frequently to converse with him.
25: 3 and urging Festus to *s* him to Jerusalem.
25:21 custody until I could *s* him to the emperor."
25:25 the Emperor, I determined to *s* him on.
25:27 It seems to me a senseless procedure to *s*
Rom 15:24 I trust that you will *s* me on my journey
16:16 All the churches of Christ *s* you greetings.
16:22 letter, *s* you my greetings in the Lord.
1Cor 1: 2 *s* greetings to the church of God which is
1:17 For Christ did not *s* me to baptize,
16:19 The churches of Asia *s* you greetings.
16:19 house, *s* you cordial greetings in the Lord.
16:21 who *s* you this greeting in my own hand.
2Cor 9: 3 I nonetheless *s* the brothers so that our
13:12 All the holy ones *s* greetings to you.
Gal 1: 2 me *s* greetings to the churches in Galatia.
Phil 2:19 Lord Jesus, to *s* Timothy to you very soon,
2:23 I hope to *s* him as soon as I see how
2:25 too, that I must *s* you Epaphroditus,
2:28 I have been especially eager to *s* him so
4:21 My brothers here *s* you theirs,
1Thes 3: 2 remain alone at Athens and *s* you Timothy.
2Tm 4:21 Claudia, and all the brothers *s* greetings.
Ti 3:12 When I *s* Artemas to you,
3:15 All who are with me *s* their greetings.
2Jn 1:13 of your elect sister *s* you their greetings.
3Jn 1:15 The beloved here *s* you their greetings;
Rv 1:11 you now see and *s* it to the seven churches:
3:12 Jerusalem which he will *s* down from heaven,
16: 9 of God who had power to *s* these plagues,

SENDER (1)

2Mc 4:20 So the contribution destined by the *s* for

SENDING (49)

Gn 19:29 he was mindful of Abram by *s* Lot away
32: 6 I am *s* my lord this information in the
Ex 4:28 him of all the LORD had said in *s* him,
23:20 "See, I am *s* an angel before you,
Lv 16:10 by *s* it off to Azazel in the desert.
Nm 13:17 *s* them to reconnoiter the land of Canaan,
1Sm 16: 1 I am *s* you to Jesse of Bethlehem,
2Sm 10: 3 your father by *s* men with condolences?
1Kgs 8:36 right way to live and *s* rain upon this land
15:19 I am *s* you a present of silver and gold.
2Kgs 1: 6 that you are *s* to inquire of Baal-zebub,
5: 6 letter I am *s* my servant Naaman to you,
6:32 a murderer is *s* someone to cut off my head?
17: 4 for *s* envoys to the king of Egypt at Sais,
1Chr 19: 3 David is doing this *s* you these consolers
21:26 he answered him by *s* down fire from heaven
2Chr 2: 2 *s* him cedars to build a house for his
2:12 I am now *s* you a craftsman of great skill,
16: 3 See, I am *s* you silver and gold.
Tb 10: 8 I am *s* messengers to your father Tobit,
Jdt 11:22 done well in *s* you ahead of your people,
Est 9:22 *s* food to one another and gifts to the
1Mc 11:31 We are *s* you, for your information
11:43 favor, therefore, of *s* men to fight for me,
Jb 1: 4 *s* invitations to their three sisters to
Is 18: 2 rivers of Ethiopia, *S* ambassadors by sea,
Jer 29:17 I am *s* against them sword,
29:19 I kept *s* them my servants the prophets,
35:15 I kept *s* you all my servants the prophets,
42: 6 of the LORD, our God, to whom we are *s* you,
42:20 you have deceived me, *s* me to the LORD,
44: 4 kept *s* to you all my servants the prophets,
Ez 2: 3 Son of man, I am *s* you to the Israelites,
2: 4 of heart are they to whom I am *s* you.
3: 5 speech and barbarous language am I *s* you,
17:15 *s* envoys to Egypt to obtain horses and a
31: 4 *s* its rivers round where it was planted,
34:26 them about my hill, *s* rain in due season,
Mal 3: 1 I am *s* my messenger to prepare the way
Mt 10:16 doing is *s* you out like sheep among wolves.
Lk 10: 3 I am *s* you as lambs in the midst of wolves.
Acts 15:27 whom we are *s* you are Judas and Silas,
26:18 open the eyes of those to whom I am *s* you,
1Cor 16:11 come to me by *s* him on his way in peace.
Col 4: 8 I am *s* him to you for this purpose,
2Thes 2:11 Therefore God is *s* upon them a perverse
Phlm 1:12 I am *s* to you—and that means I am *s*
Rv 1: 1 known by *s* his angel to his servant John,

SENDS (42)

Jos 22:16 whole community of the LORD *s* this message:
1Sm 20:22 beyond you,' go, for the LORD *s* you away.
1Kgs 17:14 day when the LORD *s* rain upon the earth.' "
1Mc 10:18 *s* greetings to his brother Jonathan.
10:25 Demetrius *s* greetings to the Jewish nation.
11:30 "King Demetrius *s* greetings to his
11:32 *s* greetings to his father Lasthenes.
12:20 *s* greetings to Onias the high priest.
13:36 *s* greetings to Simon the high priest,
15: 2 "King Antiochus *s* greetings to Simon,
15:16 of the Romans, *s* greetings to King Ptolemy.
2Mc 9:19 *s* hearty greetings and best wishes for
11:16 "Lysias *s* greetings to the Jewish people.
11:22 *s* greetings to his brother Lysias.
11:27 "King Antiochus *s* greetings to the Jewish
Jb 5:10 upon the earth and *s* water upon the fields;
12:15 *s* them forth and they overwhelm the land.
12:17 He *s* counselors away barefoot,
37: 3 Everywhere under the heavens he *s* it,
Ps(s) 107:40 *s* them astray through a trackless waste,
147:15 He *s* forth his command to the earth;
147:18 He *s* his word and melts them;
Prv 22:21 give a dependable report to one who *s* you?
25:13 a faithful messenger for the one who *s* him.
26: 6 down violence, who *s* messages by a fool.
Sir 10:13 Because of it God *s* unheard-of afflictions
43:21 he *s* that turn the ponds to lumps of ice.
Is 19:20 *s* them a savior to defend and deliver them.
Jer 3: 1 If man *s* away his wife and,
Zec 10: 1 And *s* men the pouring rain;
Lk 7:20 Baptizer *s* us to you with this question:
Acts 3:20 you by the Lord when he *s* you Jesus,
14:17 heavens he *s* down rain and rich harvests;
23:26 Lysias *s* greetings to His Excellency Felix,
Rom 16:21 my fellow worker, *s* you his greetings;
Col 4:10 a prisoner along with me, *s* you greetings.
4:11 Jesus known also as Justus *s* greetings.
4:12 Epaphras, who is one of you, *s* greetings.
4:14 Luke, our dear physician, *s* you greetings.
1Thes 4: 8 but God who *s* his Holy Spirit upon you.
Jas 1: 1 and of the Lord Jesus Christ, *s* greeting.
1Pt 5:13 chosen together with you, *s* you greeting,

SENEH (1)

1Sm 14: 4 each side, one called Bozez, the other *S.*

SENIOR (2)

Gn 24: 2 said to the *s* servant of his household,
50: 7 Pharaoh's officials who were *s* members

SENIR (4)

Dt 3: 9 by the Sidonians and *S* by the Amorites],
1Chr 5:23 land of Bashan as far as Baal-hermon, *S,*
Sg 4: 8 of Amana, from the top of *S* and Hermon,
Ez 27: 5 *S* they built for you all of your decks;

SENNACHERIB (19)

2Kgs 18:13 the fourteenth year of King Hezekiah, *S,*
19:16 of *S* which he sent to taunt the living God.
19:20 answer to your prayer for help against *S,*
19:36 So *S,* the king of Assyria,
2Chr 32: 1 had proved his fidelity by such deeds, *S,*
32: 2 When Hezekiah saw that *S* was coming with
32: 9 After this, while *S,* king of Assyria,
32:10 "King *S* of Assyria has this to say:
32:22 of Jerusalem from the hand of *S,*
Tb 1:15 died and his son *S* succeeded him as king,
1:18 I also buried anyone whom *S* slew when he
1:18 so when *S* looked for them,
1:22 For under *S,* king of Assyria,
2Mc 8:19 both the time of *S,*
Sir 48:18 *S* led an invasion and sent his adjutant;
Is 36: 1 the fourteenth year of King Hezekiah, *S,*
37:17 letter that *S* sent to taunt the living God.
37:21 answer to your prayer for help against *S,*
37:37 So *S,* the king of Assyria,

SENNACHERIB'S (1)

2Mc 15:22 and eighty-five thousand men of *S* army.

SENSE (35)

Jdt 8:28 that you have said was spoken with good *s,*
Est B: 2 not to be carried away with the *s* of power,
Jb 34:35 intelligence, and his words are without *s.*"
Prv 7: 7 among the young men, a youth with no *s,*
8: 5 ones, gain resource, you fools, gain *s.*
10:21 nourish many, but fools die for want of *s.*
10:23 so is wisdom for the man of *s.*
11:12 He who reviles his neighbor has no *s,*
12: 8 According to his good *s* a man is praised,
13:15 Good *s* brings favor,
14:29 The patient man shows much good *s,*
16:22 *s* is a fountain of life to its possessor,
19:11 It is good *s* in a man to be slow to anger,
21:16 *s* will abide in the assembly of the shades.
24:30 by the vineyard of the man without *s;*
26:16 than seven men who answer with good *s.*
Sir 4:21 There is a *s* of shame laden with guilt,
13: 8 be not as those who lack *s.*
19: 4 He who lightly trusts in them has no *s,*
19: 5 and he who repeats an evil report has no *s.*
22: 9 weep over the fool, for *s* has left him.
22:13 rest and not be wearied by his lack of *s.*
34: 9 a man of experience speaks *s.*
47:23 sons, Expansive in folly, limited in *s,*
Is 44:19 nor have the intelligence and *s* to say,
Bar 6:41 and abandon these gods, for they have no *s.*
Dn 4:13 let him be given the *s* of a beast,
Mk 12:37 him as 'Lord,' in what *s* can he be his son?"
Lk 24:25 "What little *s* you have!
Jn 11:13 thought he meant sleep in the *s* of slumber.
Rom 1:28 own depraved *s* to do what is unseemly.
2Cor 4: 3 gospel can be called "veiled" in any *s,*
1Tm 6: 5 twisted minds who have lost all *s* of truth.
Jas 3: 2 in speech he is a man in the fullest *s,*
3:13 through a humility filled with good *s.*

SENSELESS (29)

Gn 31:28 What you have now done is a *s* thing.
Jb 2:10 even you going to speak as *s* women do?
Ps(s) 32: 9 Be not *s* like horses or mules:
49:11 likewise the *s* and the stupid pass away,
92: 7 A *s* man knows not,
94: 8 Understand, you *s* ones among the people;
Prv 13: 1 correction, but the *s* one heeds no rebuke.
14: 6 The *s* man seeks in vain for wisdom,
15:12 The *s* man loves not to be reproved;
15:21 Folly is joy to the *s* man,
17:18 *S* is the man who gives his hand in pledge,
Wis 1: 5 flees deceit and withdraws from *s* counsels;
11:15 And in return for their *s,*
12:24 among beasts, deceived like *s* infants.
14:11 of men and a trap for the feet of the *s.*
15: 5 of which arouses yearning in the *s* man,
15:14 but all quite *s,* and worse than childish
19: 3 of the dead, They adopted another *s* plan;
Sir 16:21 Such are the thoughts of *s* men,
34: 1 Empty and false are the hopes of the *s,*
Jer 4:22 *S* children they are,
5:21 and *s* people Who have eyes and see not,
10: 8 One and all they are dumb and *s,*
Hos 7:11 Ephraim is like a dove, silly and *s;*
Acts 25:27 It seems to me a *s* procedure to send on a
Rom 1:21 purpose, and their *s* hearts were darkened.
10:19 with a *s* nation I will make you angry."
Gal 3: 1 You *s* Galatians!
2Tm 2:23 Have nothing to do with *s,*

SENSES (8)

1Kgs 18:37 that you have brought them back to their *s.*"
Jb 33:20 and his *s* reject the choicest nourishment.
Eccl 2: 3 I thought of beguiling my *s* with wine,
Ez 14: 5 bring back to their *s* the house of Israel,
Lk 8:35 at his feet dressed and in his full *s;*
15:17 Coming to his *s* at last, he said:
Acts 12:11 Peter had recovered his *s* by this time,
2Cor 5:13 and when we are brought back to our *s,*

SENSIBLE (9)

Tb 6:12 Now the girl is *s,*
Sir 7:19 Dismiss not a *s* wife;
25: 8 Happy is he who dwells with a *s* wife,
Mt 25: 2 were foolish, while the other five were *s.*
25: 4 but the *s* ones took flasks of oil as well
25: 8 The foolish ones said to the *s,*
25: 9 But the *s* ones replied,
1Cor 10:15 I address you as one addresses *s* people.
Ti 2: 5 love their husbands and children, to be *s,*

SENSITIVE (1)

Sir 29:28 Painful things to a *s* man are abuse at

SENSUALISTS (1)

Jude 1:19 These *s,* devoid of the Spirit,

SENSUALITY (4)

Mk 7:22 conduct, greed, maliciousness, deceit, *s,*
2Cor 12:21 fornication, and *s* they practiced.
Rv 18: 7 In proportion to her boasting and *s,*
18: 9 wallowed in her *s* will weep and lament over

SENT (728)

Gn 2: 5 for the LORD God had *s* no rain upon the
8: 7 had made in the ark, and he *s* out a raven,
8: 8 Then he *s* out a dove,
8:10 more and again *s* the dove out from the ark.
12:20 concerning him, and they *s* him on his way,
19:13 is so great that he has *s* us to destroy it."
20: 2 Abimelech, king of Gerar, *s* and took Sarah.
20:13 God *s* me wandering from my father's house,
21:14 the child on her back, he *s* her away.
25: 6 still living, as he *s* them away eastward,
28: 5 Then Isaac *s* Jacob on his way;
28: 6 Isaac had blessed Jacob when he *s* him
31: 4 So Jacob *s* for Rachel and Leah to meet him
31:27 and I would have *s* you off with merry
31:42 you would now have *s* me away empty-handed.
32: 4 Jacob *s* messengers ahead to his brother
32:19 they have been *s* as a gift to my lord Esau;
37:14 So he *s* him off from the valley of Hebron.
37:32 Then they *s* someone to bring the long

38:20 Judah *s* the kid by his friend the
38:25 her out, she *s* word to her father-in-law,
44: 3 the men and their donkeys were *s* off.
45: 5 lives that God *s* me here ahead of you.
45: 7 *s* me on ahead of you to ensure for you a
45:23 what he *s* to his father was ten jackasses
45:24 As he *s* his brothers on their way,
45:27 wagons that Joseph had *s* for his transport,
46: 5 that Pharaoh had *s* for his transport.
46:28 Israel had *s* Judah ahead to Joseph,
Ex 2: 5 the reeds, she *s* her handmaid to fetch it.
3:12 be your proof that it is I who have *s* you:
3:13 'The God of your fathers has *s* me to you,'
3:14 I AM *s* me to you."
3:15 Isaac, the God of Jacob, has *s* me to you.
3:18 the God of the Hebrews, has *s* us word.
5: 3 "The God of the Hebrews has *s* us word.
7:16 the Hebrews, *s* me to you with the message:
9:23 the LORD *s* forth hail and peals of thunder.
10:13 and the LORD *s* an east wind blowing over
18: 2 Moses' wife, whom Moses had *s* back to him,
18: 6 mountain of God, and he *s* word to Moses,
24: 5 having *s* certain young men of the
Lv 16:22 region, it must be *s* away into the desert.
Nm 11:31 There arose a wind *s* by the LORD,
13:16 whom Moses *s* out to reconnoiter the land.
13:27 "We went into the land to which you *s* us.
14:36 Moses had *s* to reconnoiter the land
16:28 the LORD who *s* me to do all I have done,
16:29 mankind, then it was not the LORD who *s* me.
20:14 *s* men to the king of Edom with the message:
20:16 cry and *s* an angel who led us out of Egypt.
21: 6 LORD *s* among the people saraph serpents,
21:21 Now Israel *s* men to Sihon,
21:32 of the Amorites, Moses *s* spies to Jazer;
22: 5 Moab at that time, *s* messengers to Balaam,
22:10 of Zippor, king of Moab, *s* me the message:
22:15 Balak again *s* princes,
22:37 to Balaam, "I *s* an urgent summons to you!
22:40 and *s* portions to Balaam and to the
24:12 warn the very messengers whom you *s* to me.
31: 6 Moses *s* them out on the campaign,
32: 8 I *s* them from Kadesh-barnea
Dt 2:26 "So I *s* messengers from the desert of
9:23 And when he *s* you up from Kadesh-barnea to
34:11 the LORD *s* him to perform in the land
Jos 2: 1 Nun, secretly *s* out two spies from Shittim,
2: 3 So the king of Jericho *s* Rahab the order,
6:17 because she hid the messengers we *s*.
6:25 whom Joshua had *s* to reconnoiter Jericho,
7: 2 Joshua next *s* men from Jericho to Ai,
7:22 The messengers whom Joshua *s* hastened to
8: 3 *s* them off by night with these orders:
8: 9 Then Joshua *s* them away.
10: 3 Adonizedek, king of Jerusalem, *s* for Hoham,
10: 6 the men of Gibeon *s* an appeal to Joshua in
11: 1 learned of this, he *s* a message to Jobab,
14: 7 *s* me from Kadesh-barnea to reconnoiter the
14:11 today as I was the day Moses *s* me forth,
22: 6 them and Joshua *s* them away to their own tents.
22: 7 What Joshua said to them when he *s* them
22:13 First however, they *s* to the Reubenites,
24: 5 "Then I *s* Moses and Aaron,
24:12 And I *s* the hornets ahead of you which
Jgs 3:15 the Israelites *s* their tribute to Eglon,
4: 6 She *s* and summoned Barak,
5: 4 shaken, while the clouds *s* down showers.
6: 8 he *s* a prophet to the Israelites who said
6:35 He *s* messengers,
6:35 he *s* messengers and these tribes advanced
7:24 Gideon also *s* messengers throughout the
9:31 was angry and *s* messengers to Abimelech in
11:12 Then he *s* messengers to the king of the
11:14 *s* messengers to the king of the Ammonites,
11:17 *s* messengers to the king of Edom saying,
11:17 They also *s* to the king of Moab,
11:19 Then Israel *s* messengers to Sihon,
11:28 paid no heed to the message Jephthah *s* him.
11:38 he replied, and *s* her away for two months.
13: 8 he said, "may the man of God whom you *s*,
18: 2 So the Danites *s* from their clan a detail
19:29 *s* them throughout the territory of Israel.
20: 6 cut her up and *s* her through every part
20:12 the tribes of Israel *s* men throughout the
21:10 *s* twelve thousand warriors with orders to
21:13 Then the whole community *s* a message to
1Sm 4: 4 So the people *s* to Shiloh and brought from
5:10 The ark of God was next *s* to Ekron;
5:11 *s* a summons to all the Philistine lords
6:17 golden hemorrhoids the Philistines *s* back
6:21 They then *s* messengers to the inhabitants
11: 7 which he *s* throughout the territory of
12: 8 who *s* Moses and Aaron to bring them out of
12:11 Accordingly, the LORD *s* Jerubbaal.
12:18 and the LORD *s* thunder and rain that day.
13: 2 He *s* the rest of the people back to their
15: 1 "It was I the LORD *s* to anoint you king
15:18 you king of Israel and *s* you on a mission,
15:20 fulfill the mission on which the LORD *s* me.
16:12 *s* and had the young man brought to them.
16:14 tormented by an evil spirit *s* by the LORD.
16:20 a kid, and *s* them to Saul by his son David.
16:22 his armor-bearer, and *s* Jesse the message,
17:31 and reported to Saul, who *s* for him.]
18: 5 every mission on which Saul *s* him.
19:11 *s* messengers to David's house to guard it,
19:14 When Saul *s* messengers to arrest David,
19:15 *s* the messengers back to see David and
19:20 Ramah, he *s* messengers to arrest David.
19:21 Informed of this, Saul *s* other messengers,
19:21 For the third time Saul *s* messengers,
21: 3 which he *s* me or the commission he gave me.
22:11 king *s* a summons to Ahimelech the priest,
25: 5 was shearing his flock, he *s* ten young men,
25:14 "David *s* messengers from the desert to
25:25 did not see the young men whom my lord *s*.
25:32 God of Israel, who *s* you to meet me today.
25:39 then *s* a proposal of marriage to Abigail.
25:40 "David has *s* us to you that he may take
26: 4 into the desert after him and *s* out scouts,
30:26 *s* part of the spoil to the elders of Judah,
31: 9 and then *s* the good news throughout the
2Sm 2: 5 So David *s* messengers to the men of
3:12 Then Abner *s* messengers to David in Telam,
3:14 same time David *s* messengers to Ishbaal,
3:15 Ishbaal *s* for her and took her away from
3:23 he has been *s* on his way in peace."
3:26 David's knowledge *s* messengers after Abner,
5:11 king of Tyre, *s* ambassadors to David;
8:10 he *s* his son Hadoram to King David to
9: 5 So King David *s* for him and had him
10: 2 So David *s* his servants with condolences
10: 3 it, that David has *s* his messengers to you?"
10: 4 garments at the buttocks, *s* them away.
10: 5 told of it, King David *s* out word to them,
10: 6 the Ammonites *s* for and hired twenty
10: 7 David *s* out Joab with the entire levy of
10:16 Hadadezer *s* for and enlisted Arameans from
11: 1 David *s* out Joab along with his officers
11: 4 Then David *s* messengers and took her.
11: 5 conceived, and *s* the information to David,
11: 6 therefore *s* a message to Joab,
11: 6 So Joab *s* Uriah to David.
11: 8 was *s* out after him from the king's table.
11:14 wrote a letter to Joab which he *s* by Uriah.
11:18 Then Joab *s* David a report of all the
11:27 *s* for her and brought her into his house.
12: 1 The LORD *s* Nathan to David,
12:25 *s* the prophet Nathan to name him Jedidiah,
12:27 He *s* messengers to David with the word:
13: 7 David then *s* home a message to Tamar,
13:27 *s* Amnon and all the other princes with him.
14: 2 he *s* to Tekoa and brought from there a
15:10 Then Absalom *s* spies throughout the tribes
15:12 Absalom also *s* to Ahithophel the Gilonite,
18:29 the king's servant Joab *s* your servant on,
19:12 *s* word to the priests Zadok and Abiathar:
22:15 He *s* forth arrows to put them to flight;
24:13 decide what I must reply to him who *s* me."
24:15 [The LORD then *s* a pestilence over Israel
1Kgs 1:44 The king *s* with him Zadok the priest,
1:53 *s* to have him brought down from the altar,
2:25 Then King Solomon *s* Benaiah,
2:29 He *s* Benaiah, son of Jehoiada,
5:14 *s* by all the kings of the earth who had
5:15 of his father, he *s* an embassy to him;
5:16 Solomon *s* back this message to Hiram:
5:22 Hiram then *s* word to Solomon,
5:22 "I agree to the proposal you *s* me,
5:28 He *s* them to the Lebanon each month in
9:14 had *s* king Solomon one hundred and twenty
12:18 King Rehoboam then *s* out Adoram,
15:18 ministers, King Asa *s* them to Ben-hadad,
15:20 Ben-hadad agreed with King Asa and *s* the
18:10 where my master has not *s* in search of you.
18:20 So Ahab *s* to all the Israelites and had
19: 2 then *s* a messenger to Elijah and said,
20: 2 He *s* couriers to Ahab,
20: 5 *s* you word to give me your silver and gold,
20: 7 When he *s* to me for my wives and sons,
20:10 Ben-hadad then *s* him the message,
21: 8 *s* them to the elders and to the nobles who
21:11 through the letters she had *s* them.
21:14 Then they *s* the information to Jezebel
2Kgs 1: 2 he *s* out messengers with the instructions:
1: 6 back to the king who *s* you and tell him:
1: 9 Then the king *s* a captain with his company
1:11 Ahaziah *s* another captain with his company
1:13 *s* a captain with his company of fifty men.
1:16 you *s* messengers to inquire of Baal-zebub,
2: 2 "The LORD has *s* me on to Bethel."
2: 4 for the LORD has *s* me on to Jericho."
2: 6 the LORD has *s* me on to the Jordan."
2:17 So they *s* the fifty men,
3: 7 he *s* the king of Judah the message:
5: 8 torn his garments, he *s* word to the king:
5:10 The prophet *s* him the message:
5:22 replied, "but my master *s* me to say,
5:24 into the house, and *s* the men on their way.
6:14 he *s* there a strong force with horses and
6:23 they had eaten and drunk he *s* them away,
6:32 The king had *s* a man ahead before he
7:14 *s* them to reconnoiter the Aramean army.
8: 9 has *s* me to ask you whether he will
9:19 Joram *s* a second driver,
10: 1 letters and *s* them to the city rulers,
10: 5 and the guardians, *s* this message to Jehu:
10: 7 in baskets, and *s* them to Jehu in Jezreel.
10:21 *s* word of it throughout the land of Israel.
12:19 palace, and *s* them to King Hazael of Aram,
14: 8 Then Amaziah *s* messengers to Jehoash,
14: 9 Israel *s* this reply to the king of Judah:
14: 9 of Lebanon *s* word to the cedar of Lebanon,
16: 7 Ahaz *s* messengers to Tiglath-pileser,
16: 8 *s* them as a present to the king of Assyria,
16:10 King Ahaz *s* to Uriah the priest a model of
16:11 plans which King Ahaz *s* him from Damascus,
17:11 the LORD had *s* into exile at their coming.
17:13 which I *s* you by my servants the prophets,"
17:25 so he *s* lions among them that killed some
17:26 *s* lions among them that are killing them,
18:14 *s* this message to the king of Assyria at
18:17 The king of Assyria *s* the general,
18:18 for the king, who *s* out to them Eliakim,
18:27 you that my lord *s* me to speak these words?
19: 2 He *s* Eliakim, the master of the palace,
19: 4 king of Assyria, *s* to taunt the living God,
19: 9 he *s* envoys to Hezekiah with this message:
19:16 which he *s* to taunt the living God.
19:20 son of Amoz, *s* this message to Hezekiah:
20:12 been ill, he *s* letters and gifts to him.
22: 3 year, King Josiah *s* the scribe Shaphan,
22:15 'Say to the man who *s* you to me,
22:18 of Judah who *s* you to consult the LORD,
1Chr 10: 9 these they *s* throughout the land of the
12:20 their lords took counsel and *s* him home,
14: 1 *s* envoys to David along with masons and
18:10 he *s* his son Hadoram to wish King David
18:10 He also *s* David gold,
19: 2 Therefore he *s* envoys to him to comfort
19: 4 Then he *s* them away.
19: 5 to his men, he *s* messengers to meet them,
19: 6 Hanun and the Ammonites *s* a thousand
19: 8 he *s* Joab and his whole army of warriors
19:16 the Arameans *s* messengers to bring out the
21:12 What answer am I to give him who *s* me?"
21:14 the LORD *s* pestilence upon Israel,
21:15 God also *s* an angel to destroy Jerusalem;
2Chr 1: 2 He *s* a summons to all Israel,
2: 2 Moreover, Solomon *s* this message to Huram,
2:10 wrote an answer which he *s* to Solomon:
7:10 month he *s* the people back to their tents,
8:18 *s* him ships and crewmen acquainted with
10:18 King Rehoboam then *s* out Hadoram,
16: 2 the royal palace and *s* them to Ben-hadad,
16: 4 *s* the leaders of his troops against
17: 7 year of his reign he *s* his leading men,
17: 8 With them he *s* the Levites,
23:14 Then Jehoiada the priest *s* out the
24:19 were *s* to them to convert them to the LORD,
24:23 *s* all their spoil to the king of Damascus.
25:10 come to him from Ephraim, and *s* them home.
25:15 and he *s* a prophet to him who said:
25:17 Amaziah of Judah *s* messengers to Joash,
25:18 *s* this reply to King Amaziah of Judah:
25:18 *s* a message to the cedar of the Lebanon,
28:16 At that time King Ahaz *s* an appeal for
30: 1 *s* a message to all Israel and Judah,
32: 9 he *s* his officials to Jerusalem with this
32:21 Then the LORD *s* an angel,
32:31 respect to the ambassadors [princes] *s* to him
34: 8 temple as well as the land, he *s* Shaphan,
34:23 'Tell the one who *s* you to me,
34:26 of Judah who *s* you to consult the LORD,
35:21 Neco *s* messengers to him, saying:
36:10 *s* for him and had him brought to Babylon,
Ezr 3: 7 and *s* food and drink and oil to the
4:11 is a copy of the letter that they *s* to him:
4:14 we have *s* this message to inform you,
4:17 The king *s* this answer:
4:18 *s* us has been read plainly in my presence.
5: 5 order be *s* back concerning this matter.
5: 6 of the letter *s* to King Darius by Tattenai,
5: 7 they *s* him a report in which was written
6: 5 and brought to Babylon are to be *s* back:
6:13 the instructions King Darius had *s* them.
8:16 Therefore I *s* Eliezer,
8:18 They *s* to us—for the favoring hand
8:19 They also *s* us Hashabiah,
10:44 but they *s* them away,
Neh 2: 9 also *s* with me army officers and cavalry.
6: 2 Sanballat and Geshem *s* me this message:
6: 3 I *s* messengers to them with this reply:
6: 4 Four times they *s* me this same proposal,
6: 5 Sanballat *s* me the same message by one of
6: 8 I *s* him this answer:
6:12 it was plain to me that God had not *s* him;
6:19 and Tobiah *s* letters trying to frighten me.
9:15 from a rock you *s* them in their thirst.
Tb 2:12 When she *s* back the goods to their owners,
2:12 the cloth and *s* it back to the owners.
3:17 So Raphael was *s* to heal them both:
8:13 She *s* the maid, who lit a lamp,
10:12 he said good-bye to them and *s* them away.
10:13 kissed them both and *s* them away in peace.
12:14 the dead, I was *s* to put you to the test.
12:20 I am about to ascend to him who *s* me;
Jdt 1: 7 *s* messengers to all the inhabitants of
3: 1 They therefore *s* messengers to him to sue

SENT (cont.)
4: 4 they *s* word to the whole region of Samaria,
7:18 and they *s* some of their men to the south
7:32 the women and children he *s* to their homes.
8:10 she *s* the maid who was in charge of all
11: 7 who has *s* you to set all creatures aright!
11:14 They have *s* messengers to Jerusalem to
11:16 God has *s* me to perform with you such
11:19 and I in turn have been *s* to tell you."
12: 6 she rose and *s* this message to Holofernes,
14: 5 of Israel and *s* him here to meet his death."
15: 4 Uzziah *s* messengers to Betomasthaim,
16:14 they were made, You *s* forth your spirit,
Est 1:22 He *s* letters to all the royal provinces,
3:13 *s* by couriers to all the royal provinces,
4: 4 she *s* garments for Mordecai to put on,
4:15 Esther *s* back to Mordecai the response:
8:10 he *s* by mounted couriers riding
E:17 then, to ignore the letter *s* by Haman,
9:20 these events and *s* letters to all the Jews,
9:30 when Mordecai *s* documents concerning peace
1Mc 1:29 the king *s* the Mysian commander to the
1:44 The king *s* messengers with letters to
3:39 and with them he *s* forty thousand men and
5:10 They *s* a letter to Judas and his brothers
5:38 Judas *s* men to spy on the camp,
5:48 Then Judas *s* them this peaceful message:
6: 5 the armies *s* into the land of Judah
6:61 he *s* peace terms to the Jews,
7: 9 He *s* him and the impious Alcimus,
7:10 *s* messengers who spoke deceitfully to
7:26 Then the king *s* Nicanor,
7:27 deceitfully *s* to Judas and his brothers
7:41 they who were *s* by the king blasphemed,
8:10 and *s* against the Greeks a single general
8:17 and *s* them to Rome to establish an
8:20 have *s* us to you to make a peaceful
8:22 on bronze tablets and *s* to Jerusalem,
9: 1 he again *s* Bacchides and Alcimus into the
9:35 Jonathan *s* his brother as leader of the
9:60 he *s* letters secretly to all his allies in
9:63 and *s* word to those who were in Judea.
9:70 Jonathan learned of this and *s* ambassadors
10: 3 Demetrius *s* a letter to Jonathan written
10:17 *s* Jonathan a letter written in these terms:
10:20 *s* him a purple robe and a crown of gold.
10:25 So he *s* them this message:
10:51 Alexander *s* ambassadors to Ptolemy,
10:69 *s* this message to Jonathan the high priest:
10:89 He *s* him a gold buckle,
11: 9 He *s* ambassadors to King Demetrius,
11:17 off Alexander's head and *s* it to Ptolemy.
11:41 Meanwhile Jonathan *s* the request to King
11:42 in turn, *s* this word to Jonathan:
11:44 So Jonathan *s* three thousand good fighting
11:58 *s* him gold dishes and a dinner service,
11:62 men as hostages and *s* them to Jerusalem.
12: 1 he *s* selected men to Rome to confirm and
12: 2 He also *s* letters to Sparta and other
12: 3 have *s* us to renew the earlier friendship
12: 7 was *s* to the high priest Onias from Arius,
12:16 and we have *s* them to the Romans to renew
12:19 a copy of the letter that was *s* to Onias:
12:26 The spies he had *s* into their camp came
12:47 of whom he *s* two thousand to Galilee while
12:49 Trypho *s* soldiers and cavalry to Galilee
13:11 He *s* Jonathan, son of Absalom,
13:14 him, he *s* envoys to him with this message:
13:19 So he *s* the boys and the hundred talents;
13:21 men in the citadel *s* messengers to Trypho,
13:25 *s* for the remains of his brother Jonathan,
13:34 Simon also *s* chosen men to King Demetrius
13:35 King Demetrius *s* him the following letter:
13:37 gold crown and the palm branch that you *s.*
14: 2 he *s* one of his generals to take him alive.
14:18 they *s* him inscribed tablets of bronze to
14:20 a copy of the letter that the Spartans *s:*
14:21 The envoys you *s* to our people have
14:24 Simon *s* Numenius to Rome with a great gold
15: 1 *s* a letter from the islands of the sea to
15:17 They had been *s* by Simon the high priest
15:22 *s* similar letters to Kings Demetrius,
15:24 letter was also *s* to Simon the high priest.
15:26 Simon *s* to Antiochus' support two thousand
15:28 He *s* Athenobius, one of his Friends,
16:18 *s* it to the king, asking that troops be *s*
16:19 *s* other men to Gazara to do away with John.
16:19 To the army officers he *s* letters inviting
16:20 He also *s* others to seize Jerusalem and
16:21 that Ptolemy had *s* men to kill him also.
2Mc 1:20 *s* the descendants of the priests who had
3: 7 Heliodorus and *s* him with instructions
3:37 a suitable man to be *s* to Jerusalem next,
4:19 the vile Jason *s* envoys as representatives
4:21 was *s* to Egypt for the coronation of King
4:23 Three years later Jason *s* Menelaus,
4:44 three men *s* by the senate presented to him
5: 1 *s* his second expedition into Egypt.
5:18 *s* by King Seleucus to inspect the treasury,
5:24 Jewish citizens, the king *s* Apollonius,
6: 1 Not long after this the king *s* an Athenian
8: 9 and *s* him at the head of at least twenty
8:11 immediately *s* word to the coastal cities,
11:13 He therefore *s* a message persuading them
11:32 I have also *s* Menelaus to reassure you.
11:34 The Romans also *s* them a letter as follows:
12:21 *s* on ahead of him the women and children,
12:43 which he *s* to Jerusalem to provide for an
13:20 Judas then *s* supplies to the men inside,
14:12 He *s* him off with orders to put Judas to
14:19 So he *s* Posidonius,
14:39 *s* more than five hundred soldiers to
15:22 *s* your angel in the days of King Hezekiah
15:31 the altar, and *s* for those in the citadel.
Jb 22: 9 You have *s* widows away empty-handed,
Ps(s) 18:15 *s* forth his arrows to put them to flight,
78:25 even a surfeit of provisions he *s* them.
78:45 He *s* among them flies that devoured them
104:10 You *s* forth springs into the watercourses
105:17 sustained them, He *s* a man before them,
105:20 The king *s* and released him,
105:26 He *s* Moses his servant;
105:28 He *s* the darkness; it grew dark,
106:15 asked but *s* a wasting disease against them.
107:20 He *s* forth his word to heal them and to
111: 9 He has *s* deliverance to his people;
135: 9 He *s* signs and wonders into your midst,
Prv 9: 3 She has *s* out her maidens;
17:11 merciless messenger will be *s* against him.
Wis 9:17 Wisdom and *s* your holy spirit from on high?
11:15 You *s* upon them swarms of dumb creatures
12: 8 and *s* wasps as forerunners of your army
12:25 you *s* your judgment on them as a mockery;
16: 3 *s* to plague them were so loathsome,
16:18 be burnt up that were *s* upon the wicked,
19: 2 and had anxiously *s* them on their way,
19: 3 those whom they had *s* away with entreaty,
Sir 29:18 and *s* them wandering through foreign lands.
34: 6 be a vision specially *s* by the Most High,
48: 6 You *s* kings down to destruction,
48:18 led an invasion and *s* his adjutant;
Is 9: 7 The Lord has *s* word against Jacob,
20: 1 In the year the general *s* by Sargon,
36: 2 From Lachish the king of Assyria *s* his
36:12 that my lord *s* me to speak these words?
37: 2 He *s* Eliakim,
37: 4 king of Assyria, *s* to taunt the living God,
37: 9 he *s* envoys to Hezekiah with this message:
37:17 that Sennacherib *s* to taunt the living God.
37:21 son of Amoz, *s* this message to Hezekiah:
39: 1 sickness, he *s* letters and gifts to him.
48:16 "Now the Lord GOD has *s* me,
55:11 will, achieving the end for which I *s* it.
57: 9 While you *s* your ambassadors far away,
61: 1 *s* me to bring glad tidings to the lowly,
Jer 7:25 I have *s* you untiringly all my servants
19:14 where the LORD had *s* him to prophesy,
21: 1 the LORD when King Zedekiah *s* him Pashhur,
24: 5 Judah's exiles whom I *s* away
25: 4 the LORD has *s* you without fail all his
25:17 to all the nations to which the LORD *s* me:
26:12 "It was the LORD who *s* me to prophesy
26:15 in truth it was the LORD who *s* me to you,
26:22 Thereupon King Jehoiakim *s* Elnathan,
28: 9 peace is recognized as truly *s* by the LORD
28:15 The LORD has not *s* you,
29: 1 prophet Jeremiah *s* from Jerusalem
29: 3 king of Judah, *s* to the king of Babylon,
29:20 whom I *s* away from Jerusalem to Babylon.
29:25 Because you *s* letters on your own
29:28 For he *s* us in Babylon this message:
36:14 Thereupon the princes *s* Jehudi,
36:21 happened, he *s* Jehudi to fetch the scroll.
37: 3 Yet King Zedekiah *s* Jehucal,
37: 7 of Judah who *s* you to me to consult me:
38:11 these he *s* down to Jeremiah in the cistern,
40:14 the king of the Ammonites, had *s* Ishmael,
42: 9 to whom you *s* me to offer your prayer:
43: 1 God, with which the LORD had *s* him to them,
43: 2 who *s* you to tell us not to go to Egypt to
49:14 a herald has been *s* among the nations:
Lam 1:13 on high he *s* fire down into my very frame;
Bar 1: 7 These they *s* to Jerusalem,
1:21 all the words of the prophets whom he *s* us,
4:23 With mourning and lament I *s* you forth,
6: 1 A copy of the letter which Jeremiah *s* to
6:59 in the service for which they are *s.*
6:62 *s* from on high to burn up the mountains
Ez 17: 7 vine bent its roots, *s* out its branches,
20:28 there they *s* up appeasing odors
23:16 than she *s* messengers to them in Chaldea.
23:40 they *s* for men who had to come from afar,
Dn 3:13 flew into a rage and *s* for Shadrach,
3:95 who *s* his angel to deliver the servants
5:24 By him were the wrist and hand *s,*
6:23 My God has *s* his angel and closed the
13:29 When she was *s* for,
14:37 Habakkuk, "take the lunch God has *s* you."
Hos 5:13 to Assyria, and Judah *s* to the great king.
Jl 2:25 cutter, my great army which I *s* among you.
Am 4: 7 *s* rain upon one city but not upon another;
4:10 *s* upon you a pestilence like that of Egypt,
7:10 the priest of Bethel, *s* word to Jeroboam,
Ob 1: 1 and a herald has been *s* among the nations:
Jon 2: 1 But the LORD *s* a large fish,
4: 7 dawn God *s* a worm which attacked the plant,
4: 8 the sun arose, God *s* a burning east wind;
Mi 6: 4 And I *s* before you Moses,
Hg 1:12 because the LORD, their God, had *s* him,
Zec 1:10 whom the LORD has *s* to patrol the earth."
2:12 (after he had already *s* me)
2:13 shall know that the LORD of hosts has *s* me.
2:15 that the LORD of hosts has *s* me to you.
4: 9 that the LORD of hosts has *s* me to you.
6:15 that the LORD of hosts has *s* me to you.
7: 2 Bethelsarezer *s* Regemmelech and his men to
7:12 that the LORD of hosts had *s* by his spirit
Mal 2: 4 Then you will know that I *s* you this
Mt 2: 8 Then he *s* them to Bethlehem,
10: 5 Jesus *s* these men on mission as the Twelve,
10:40 he who welcomes me welcomes him who *s* me.
11: 2 *s* a message by his disciples to ask him,
14:10 He *s* the order to have John beheaded in
14:23 When he had *s* them away,
18:32 His master *s* for him and said,
20: 2 daily wage, he *s* them out to his vineyard.
21: 1 *s* off two disciples with the instructions:
21:37 Finally he *s* his son to them,
22: 4 A second time he *s* other servants, saying:
22: 7 At this the king grew furious and *s* his
22:16 They *s* their disciples to him,
23:37 and stoner of those who were *s* to you!
26:47 They had been *s* by the chief priests and
27:19 on the bench, his wife *s* him a message:
Mk 1:12 the Spirit *s* him out toward the desert.
1:43 him a stern warning and *s* him on his way.
3:31 outside they *s* word to him to come out.
8:26 Jesus *s* him home with the admonition,
9:37 me welcomes, not me, but him who *s* me."
11: 1 he *s* off two of his disciples with the
12: 3 him, beat him, and *s* him off empty-handed.
12: 4 The second time he *s* them another servant;
12: 5 He *s* yet another and they killed him.
12: 6 He *s* him to them as a last resort,
12:13 They next *s* some Pharisees and Herodians
14:13 He *s* two of his disciples with these
14:43 people had been *s* by the chief priests,
16:20 Jesus himself *s* out from east to west
Lk 1:19 I was *s* to speak to you and bring you this
1:26 the angel Gabriel was *s* from God to a town
1:53 thing, while the rich he has *s* empty away.
4:18 has *s* me to bring glad tidings to the poor,
4:26 It was to none of these that Elijah was *s,*
4:43 reign of God, because that is why I was *s.*"
7: 3 about Jesus he *s* some Jewish elders to him,
7: 6 house, the centurion *s* friends to tell him:
7:19 two of them, John *s* them to ask the Lord,
8:39 with him, but he *s* him away with the words,
9: 2 He *s* them forth to proclaim the reign of
9:48 whoever welcomes me welcomes him who *s* me;
9:51 and *s* messengers on ahead of him.
10: 1 *s* them in pairs before him to every town
10:16 he who rejects me, rejects him who *s* me."
13:34 prophets and stone those who are *s* to you!
14: 4 the man, healed him, and *s* him on his way.
14:17 he *s* his servant to say to those invited,
15:15 *s* him to his farm to take care of the pigs.
19:14 and they immediately *s* a deputation after
19:15 Then he *s* for the servants to whom he had
19:29 he *s* two of the disciples with these
20:10 At vintage time he *s* a servant to the
20:10 they beat him and *s* him away empty-handed.
20:11 He *s* a second servant whom they also beat.
20:11 Him too they *s* away empty-handed,
20:12 He *s* still a third,
20:20 they *s* spies to him in the guise of honest
22: 8 *s* Peter and John off with the instruction,
22:35 "When I *s* you on mission without purse or
23: 7 Herod's jurisdiction, he *s* him to Herod,
23:11 robe on him and *s* him back to Pilate.
23:15 Herod, who therefore has *s* him back to us;
Jn 1: 6 There was a man named John *s* by God,
1:19 The testimony John gave when the Jews *s*
1:22 we can give some answer to those who *s* us.
1:24 had *s* proceeded to question him further:
1:33 one who *s* me to baptize with water told me,
3:28 'I am not the Messiah; I am *s* before him.'
3:34 One whom God has *s* speaks the words of God;
4:34 "Doing the will of him who *s* me and
4:38 *s* you to reap what you had not worked for.
5:23 Son refuses to honor the Father who *s* him.
5:24 in him who *s* me possesses eternal life.
5:30 my own will but the will of him who *s* me.
5:33 You have *s* to John,
5:36 on my behalf that the Father has *s* me.
5:37 the Father who *s* me has himself given
5:38 you do not believe the One he has *s.*
6:29 have faith in the One whom he *s.*"
6:38 heaven, but to do the will of him who *s* me.
6:39 It is the will of him who *s* me that I
6:44 to me unless the Father who *s* me draws him;
6:57 *s* me and I have life because of the Father,
7:16 it comes from him who *s* me.
7:18 seeks glory for him who *s* him is truthful;
7:28 I was *s* by One who has the right to send,
7:29 it is from him I come: he *s* me."
7:32 together *s* temple guards to arrest him.
7:33 you, then I am going away to him who *s* me.
8:16 at my side the One who *s* me [the Father].

8:18 behalf, the Father who *s* me is the other."
8:26 heard from him, the truthful One who *s* me."
8:29 The One who *s* me is with me.
8:42 *s* me Why do you not understand what I say?
9: 4 the deeds of him who *s* me while it is day.
9: 7 (This name means "One who has been *s*.")
10:36 Father consecrated and *s* into the world,
11: 3 The sisters *s* word to Jesus to inform him,
11:42 crowd, that they may believe that you *s* me."
12:44 not so much in me as in him who *s* me;
12:45 whoever looks on me is seeing him who *s* me.
12:49 the Father who *s* me has commanded me what
13:16 no messenger outranks the one who *s* him.
13:20 and in accepting me accepts him who *s* me."
14:24 it comes from the Father who *s* me.
15:21 for they know nothing of him who *s* me.
16: 5 Now that I go back to him who *s* me,
17: 3 the only true God, and him whom you have *s*,
17: 8 they have believed it was you who *s* me.
17:18 *s* me into the world, so as I have sent
17:21 that the world may believe that you *s* me.
17:23 So shall the world know that you *s* me,
17:25 and these men have known that you *s* me.
18:24 Annas next *s* him,
20:21 "As the Father has *s* me,
Acts 2:22 was a man whom God *s* to you with miracles,
3:26 he *s* him to you first to bless you by
5:21 They *s* word to the jail that the prisoners
7:12 *s* our fathers there on a first mission.
7:14 Then Joseph *s* for his father Jacob,
7:35 *s* to be their ruler and deliverer.
8:14 word of God, they *s* Peter and John to them.
9:17 I have been *s* by the Lord Jesus who
9:30 down to Caesarea and *s* him off to Tarsus.
9:38 *s* two men to him with the urgent request,
10:17 the men *s* by Cornelius arrived at the gate
10:20 unhesitatingly, for it is I who *s* them."
10:33 I *s* for you immediately,
10:36 the message he has *s* to the sons of Israel,
11:11 the three men who had been *s* to me from
11:22 resulting in Barnabas' being *s* to Antioch.
12:11 that the Lord has *s* his angel to rescue me
13: 3 they imposed hands on them and *s* them off.
13: 4 These two, *s* forth by the Holy Spirit,
13:15 of the synagogue *s* this message to them:
13:26 that this message of salvation was *s* forth.
15:22 *s* to Antioch along with Paul and Barnabas.
15:30 representatives *s* on their way to Antioch;
15:33 they were *s* back with greetings from the
16:36 have *s* orders that you are to be released.
17:10 brothers *s* Paul and Silas off to Beroea.
17:14 *s* Paul off directly on his way to the sea,
19:22 So he *s* two of his assistants,
19:31 Asiarchs who were friends of Paul *s* word
20:17 Paul *s* word from Miletus to Ephesus,
21:25 we *s* them a letter with our decision that
23:22 commander *s* the boy away with the order,
24:24 and *s* for Paul to hear him speak about
26:10 I *s* many of God's holy people to prison.
Rom 8: 3 Then God *s* his Son in the likeness of
10:15 And how can men preach unless they are *s*?
1Cor 4:17 This is why I have *s* you Timothy,
10:13 been *s* you that does not come to all men.
2Cor 2:17 *s* by God and of standing in his presence.
8:18 We have *s* along with him that brother whom
8:22 We have *s* along that brother whose
12:17 of you through any of the men I *s* to you?
12:18 to you, and I *s* the other brother with him.
Gal 1: 1 an apostle *s* not by men or by any man,
4: 4 come, God *s* forth his Son born of a woman,
4: 6 fact that God has *s* forth into our hearts
Eph 6:22 I have *s* him to you for the very purpose
Phil 2:25 arms, whom you *s* to take care of my needs.
4:16 Thessalonica you *s* something for my needs,
1Thes 3: 2 and so we *s* him to strengthen and
3: 5 That is why I *s* to find out about your
2Tm 1: 1 *s* to proclaim the promise of life in him,
4:12 Tychicus I have *s* to Ephesus.
Ti 1: 1 *s* as an apostle of Jesus Christ for the
Heb 1:14 *s* to serve those who are to inherit
Jas 2:25 and *s* them out by a different route?
1Pt 1:12 the power of the Holy Spirit *s* from heaven.
1Jn 4: 9 he *s* his only Son to the world that we
4:10 has *s* his Son as an offering for our sins.
4:14 has *s* the Son as savior of the world.
Rv 5: 6 of God, *s* to all parts of the world.
22: 6 has *s* his angel to show his servants what
22:16 who have *s* my angel to give you this

SENTENCE (29)

1Kgs 20:40 of Israel said to him, "That is your *s*.
2Kgs 9:36 "This is the *s* which the LORD pronounced
25: 6 king of Babylon, who pronounced *s* on him.
Ezr 9: 4 were in dread of the *s* of the God of Israel
Ps(s) 9:17 In passing *s*, the LORD is manifest;
51: 6 That you may be justified in your *s*,
149: 9 To execute on them the written *s*.
Eccl 8:11 Because the *s* against evildoers is not
Wis 17:17 unawares, he served out the inescapable *s*;
Sir 41: 2 your *s* to the weak man of failing strength,
42: 2 or of the *s* to be passed upon the sinful;
Jer 1:16 I will pronounce my *s* against them for all
4:12 And I myself now pronounce *s* upon them.
39: 5 king of Babylon pronounced *s* upon him.
52: 9 king of Babylon, who pronounced *s* on him.
Ez 16:38 you the *s* of adulteresses and murderesses;
23:45 But just men shall punish them with the *s*
Dn 4:14 by order of the holy ones, this *s*;
4:21 this is the *s* which the Most High has
13:55 the *s* from him and split you in two."
Mk 12:40 it is they who will receive the severest *s*."
14:64 verdict "guilty," with its *s* of death.
Lk 20:47 The heavier *s* will be theirs."
23:40 of God, seeing you are under the same *s*?
Rom 5:16 the *s* followed upon one offense and
9:28 will the Lord execute *s* upon the earth."
1Cor 5: 3 and have already passed *s* in the name of
2Pt 2:11 no opprobrious *s* in the Lord's presence.
Rv 16: 5 One who is and who was, in passing this *s*!

SENTENCED (1)

Jer 49:12 those not *s* to drink the cup must drink it!

SENTENCES (1)

Dn 13:53 passing unjust *s*, condemning the innocent,

SENTINEL (2)

Dn 4:10 in bed, a holy *s* came down from heaven,
4:20 As for the king's vision of a holy *s* that

SENTINELS (3)

Ps(s) 130: 6 for the LORD more than *s* wait for the dawn.
130: 6 More than *s* wait for the dawn,
Dn 4:14 By decree of the *s* is this decided,

SENTRIES (1)

Jer 51:12 Post *s*, arrange ambushes!

SEORIM (1)

1Chr 24: 8 the third to Harim, the fourth to *S*,

SEPARATE (25)

Gn 1: 6 to *s* one body of water from the other."
1:14 the dome of the sky, to *s* day from night.
1:18 and to *s* the light from the darkness.
13: 9 Please *s* from me.
32:17 in charge of his servants, in *s* droves,
Jos 18:10 for the Israelites into their *s* shares,
2Sm 19: 9 the Israelites had fled to their *s* tents,
Ezr 10:11 *s* yourselves from the peoples of the land
Wis 1: 3 For perverse counsels *s* a man from God,
Is 59: 2 it is your crimes that *s* you from your God,
Ez 20:38 I will *s* from you those who have rebelled
42:20 a wall, to *s* the sacred from the profane.
Dn 13:51 *S* these two far from one another that I
Mt 5:32 lewd conduct is a *s* case
13:49 Angels will go out and *s* the wicked from
19: 6 let no man *s* what God has joined."
19: 9 divorces his wife (lewd conduct is a *s* case)
25:32 Then he will *s* them into two groups,
Mk 10: 9 Therefore let no man *s* what God has joined."
Rom 8:35 Who will *s* us from the love of Christ?
8:39 will be able to *s* us from the love of God
1Cor 7:10 a wife must not *s* from her husband.
7:11 If she does *s*, she must either remain single
7:15 If the unbeliever wishes to *s*,
2Cor 6:17 from among them and *s* yourselves from them,'

SEPARATED (16)

Gn 1: 4 God then *s* the light from the darkness.
1: 7 and it *s* the water above the dome from the
13:11 Thus they *s* from each other;
2Sm 1:23 cherished, *s* neither in life nor in death,
2Chr 35:12 They *s* what was destined for the holocaust
Ezr 6:21 together with all those who had *s* themselves
Neh 4:13 widely *s* from one another along the wall;
9: 2 Those of Israelite descent *s* themselves
10:29 and all others who have *s* themselves from
13: 3 they *s* from Israel every foreign element.
1Mc 1:11 since we *s* from them,
Dn 13:52 After they were *s* one from the other,
Acts 15:39 which ensued was so sharp that the two *s*.
Rom 9: 3 *s* from Christ for the sake of my brothers,
Phlm 1:15 was *s* from you for a while for this reason:
Heb 7:26 holy, innocent, undefiled, *s* from sinners,

SEPARATELY (1)

Gn 43:32 It was served *s* to him,

SEPARATES (4)

Ru 1:17 besides, if aught but death *s* me from you!"
Prv 16:28 discord, and a talebearer *s* bosom friends.
17: 9 but he who gossips about it *s* friends.
Mt 25:32 groups, as a shepherd *s* sheep from goats.

SEPARATING (1)

Lv 1:17 bird down the middle without *s* the halves,

SEPARATION (1)

1Thes 2:17 we were orphaned by *s* from you for a time

SEPHAR (1)

Gn 10:30 settlements extended all the way to *S*,

SEPHARAD (1)

Ob 1:20 in *S* shall occupy the cities of the Negeb.

SEPHARVAIM (6)

2Kgs 17:24 from Babylon, Cuthah, Avva, Hamath, and *S*,
17:31 and the men of *S* immolated their children
18:34 Where are the gods of *S*, Hena, and Avva?
19:13 or the kings of the cities *S*,
Is 36:19 Where are the gods of *S*?
37:13 of Arpad, or a king of the cities of *S*,

SEPULCHER (1)

Is 22:16 Who has hewn for himself a *s* on a height

SEQUENCE (2)

Jer 33:20 day and night no longer alternate in *s*,
Lk 1: 3 the whole *s* of events from the beginning,

SERAH (3)

Gn 46:17 Ishvi, and Beriah, with their sister *S*;
Nm 26:46 The name of Asher's daughter was *S*.
1Chr 7:30 their sister was *S*.

SERAIAH (19)

2Kgs 25:18 of the guard also took *S* the high priest,
25:23 of Nethaniah, Johanan, son of Kareah, *S*,
1Chr 4:13 The sons of Kenaz were Othniel and *S*.
4:14 *S* became the father of Joab,
4:35 Joel, Jehu, son of Joshibiah, son of *S*,
5:40 Azariah became the father of *S*.
5:40 *S* became the father of Jehozadak.
Ezr 2: 2 with Zerubbabel, Jeshua, Nehemiah, *S*,
7: 1 king of Persia, Ezra, son of *S*,
Neh 10: 3 *S*, Azariah, Jeremiah, Pashhur, Amariah,
11:11 *S*, son of Hilkaiah, son of Meshullam
12: 1 *S*, Jeremiah, Ezra, Amariah, Malluch,
12:12 for *S*, Meraiah; for Jeremiah, Hananiah;
Jer 36:26 a royal prince, and *S*, son of Azriel,
40: 8 *S*, son of Tanhumeth;
51:59 errand given by the prophet Jeremiah to *S*,
51:59 *S* was chief quartermaster.
51:61 And Jeremiah said to *S*:
52:24 The captain of the guard also took *S*,

SERAPHIM (2)

Is 6: 2 *S* were stationed above;
6: 6 Then one of the *s* flew to me,

SERED (2)

Gn 46:14 *S*, Elon, and Jahleel.
Nm 26:26 through *S* the clan of the Seredites,

SEREDITES (1)

Nm 26:26 through Sered the clan of the *S*,

SERF (1)

Gn 49:15 to the burden and became a toiling *s*.

SERGIUS (1)

Acts 13: 7 court of the proconsular governor *S* Paulus,

SERIOUS (16)

Dt 15:21 is lame or blind or has any other *s* defect,
17: 1 from the flock an animal with any *s* defect;
1Sm 26:21 have been a fool and have made a *s* mistake."
2Sm 24:14 "I am in very *s* difficulty.
2Chr 16:12 Asa contracted a *s* disease in his feet.
2Mc 4: 4 the opposition was *s* and that Apollonius,
4:16 this, they found themselves in *s* trouble:
Ps(s) 19:14 shall I be blameless and innocent of *s* sin.
Sir 31: 2 more than a *s* illness it disturbs repose.
Mt 17:15 son, who is demented and in a *s* condition.
Acts 18:14 "If it were a crime or a *s* fraud,
19:23 At about that time a *s* disturbance broke
25: 7 him and leveled many *s* charges against him,
1Tm 3: 8 In the same way, deacons must be *s*,
3:11 The women, similarly, should be *s*,
Ti 2: 7 teaching must have the integrity of *s*,

SERIOUS-MINDED (1)

Ti 2: 2 older men that they must be temperate, *s*,

SERIOUSLY (2)

2Chr 35:23 "Take me away, for I am *s* wounded."
Jn 6:60 How can anyone take it *s*?"

SERON (3)

1Mc 3:13 But *S*, commander of the Syrian army,
3:23 he rushed suddenly upon *S* and his army,

SERON (cont.)

3:24 He pursued *S* down the descent of

SERPENT (28)

Gn 3: 1 Now the *s* was the most cunning of all the
3: 1 The *s* asked the woman,
3: 2 The woman answered the *s*:
3: 4 But the *s* said to the woman:
3:13 woman answered, "The *s* tricked me into it,
3:14 Then the LORD God said to the *s*:
49:17 Let Dan be a *s* by the roadside,
Ex 4: 3 it on the ground it was changed into a *s*,
7:15 your hand the staff that turned into a *s*.
Nm 21: 9 made a bronze *s* and mounted it on a pole,
21: 9 bitten by a *s* looked at the bronze serpent,
2Kgs 18: 4 smashed the bronze *s* called Nehushtan
Prv 23:32 But in the end it bites like a *s*,
30:19 in the air, the way of a *s* upon a rock,
Eccl 10: 8 breaks through a wall may be bitten by a *s*.
10:11 *s* bites because it has not been charmed,
Sir 21: 2 Flee from sin as from a *s*.
25:14 No poison worse than that of a *s*,
Is 27: 1 fleeing serpent, Leviathan the coiled *s*;
Am 9: 3 I will command the *s* there to bite them;
Mi 7:17 They shall lick the dust like the *s*,
Jn 3:14 as Moses lifted up the *s* in the desert,
2Cor 11: 3 just as the *s* seduced Eve by his cunning,
Rv 12: 9 the ancient *s* known as the devil or Satan,
12:14 in the desert, where, far from the *s*,
12:15 The *s*, however, spewed a torrent of water
20: 2 He seized the dragon, the ancient *s*,

SERPENTS (11)

Nm 21: 6 the LORD sent among the people saraph *s*,
21: 7 Pray the LORD to take the *s* from us."
Dt 8:15 desert with its saraph *s* and scorpions,
Ps(s) 58: 5 Theirs is poison like a *s*,
140: 4 make their tongues sharp as those of *s*;
Wis 11:15 worshiping dumb *s* and worthless insects,
16: 5 they were dying from the bite of crooked *s*,
Is 14:29 For out of the *s* root shall come an adder,
65:25 like the ox [but the *s* food shall be dust].
Mt 23:33 Brood of *s*!
Mk 16:18 languages, they will be able to handle *s*,

SERUG (6)

Gn 11:20 years old, he became the father of *S*.
11:21 and seven years after the birth of *S*,
11:22 When *S* was thirty years old,
11:23 *S* lived two hundred years after the birth
1Chr 1:26 Arpachshad, Shelah, Eber, Peleg, Reu, *S*,
Lk 3:35 son of Terah, son of Nahor, son of *S*,

SERVANT (447)

Gn 18: 3 favor, please do not go on past your *s*.
18: 5 that you have come this close to your *s*,
18: 7 a tender, choice steer, and gave it to a *s*,
19:19 already thought enough of your *s* to do me
24: 2 said to the senior *s* of his household,
24: 5 The *s* asked him:
24: 9 So the *s* put his hand under the thigh of
24:10 The *s* then took ten of his master's camels,
24:14 you have decided upon for your *s* Isaac.
24:17 she came up, the *s* ran toward her and said,
24:34 "I am Abraham's *s*," he began.
24:52 When Abraham's *s* heard their answer,
24:59 leave, along with Abraham's *s* and his men.
24:61 So the *s* took Rebekah and went on his way.
24:65 alighted from her camel and asked the *s*,
24:65 "That is my master," replied the *s*.
24:66 The *s* recounted to Isaac all the things he
26:24 descendants for the sake of my *s* Abraham."
32: 5 'Your *s* Jacob speaks as follows:
32:11 that you have loyally performed for your *s*:
32:18 the *s* in the lead he gave this instruction:
32:20 instructions to the second *s* and the third
32:21 to add, 'Your *s* Jacob is right behind us.'"
33: 5 whom God has graciously bestowed on your *s*."
43:28 "Your *s* our father is thriving and still
44:18 let your *s* speak earnestly to my lord,
44:18 lord, and do not become angry with your *s*,
44:24 When we returned to your *s* our father,
44:27 Then your *s* our father said to us,
44:30 with us when I go back to your *s* my father,
44:32 Besides, I, your *s*, got the boy
44:33 Let me, your *s*, therefore, remain in place
Ex 4:10 nor now that you have spoken to your *s*;
12:45 alien or hired *s* may partake of it.
14:31 and believed in him and in his *s* Moses.
Lv 22:10 or hired *s* may eat of any sacred offering.
25:40 him be like a hired *s* or like your tenant,
25:53 treat him as a *s* hired on an annual basis,
Nm 11:11 "Why do you treat your *s* so badly?"
12: 7 Not so with my *s* Moses!
12: 8 you not fear to speak against my *s* Moses?"
14:24 But because my *s* Caleb has a different
Dt 3:24 to show to your *s* your greatness and might.
24:14 not defraud a poor and needy hired *s*,
34: 5 the land of Moab, Moses, the *s* of the LORD,
Jos 1: 1 After Moses, the *s* of the LORD,
1: 2 "My *s* Moses is dead.
1: 7 law which my *s* Moses enjoined on you.
1:13 "Remember what Moses, the *s* of the LORD,
1:15 own land, which Moses, the *s* of the LORD,
5:14 to him, "What has my lord to say to his *s*?"
8:31 the Israelites of Moses, the *s* of the LORD,
8:33 instructions of Moses, the *s* of the LORD,
9:24 commanded his *s* Moses that you be given
11:12 doom on them, as Moses, the *s* of the LORD,
11:15 As the LORD had commanded his *s* Moses,
12: 6 After Moses, the *s* of the LORD,
13: 8 heritage which Moses, the *s* of the LORD,
14: 7 was forty years old when the *s* of the LORD,
18: 7 the Jordan which Moses, the *s* of the LORD,
22: 2 done all that Moses, the *s* of the LORD,
22: 4 own land, which Moses, the *s* of the LORD,
22: 5 and law which Moses, the *s* of the LORD,
24:29 events, Joshua, son of Nun, *s* of the LORD,
Jgs 2: 8 Joshua, son of Nun, the *s* of the LORD,
15:18 this great victory by the hand of your *s*.
19: 3 set out with his *s* and a pair of asses,
19: 9 was ready to go with his concubine and *s*,
19:11 the day far gone, the *s* said to his master,
19:13 Come," he said to his *s*,
19:19 for the woman and myself and for our *s*;
Ru 2:13 you have comforted me, your *s*,
2:13 would indeed that I were a *s* of yours!"
3: 9 And she replied, "I am your *s* Ruth.
1Sm 2:13 *s* would come with a three-pronged fork,
2:15 the priest's *s* would come and say to the
3: 9 'Speak, LORD, for your *s* is listening.'"
3:10 answered, "Speak, for your *s* is listening."
9: 5 Zuph, Saul said to the *s* who was with him,
9: 6 The *s* replied, "Listen!
9: 7 But Saul said to his *s*,
9: 8 Again the *s* answered Saul,
9:10 Saul then said to his *s*, "Well said!
9:22 and his *s* and brought them to the room,
9:27 to Saul, "Tell the *s* to go on ahead of us,
10:14 Saul's uncle inquired of him and his *s*,
14:41 "Why did you not answer your *s* this time?
16:18 A *s* spoke up to say:
17:34 "Your *s* used to tend his father's sheep,
17:36 Your *s* has killed both a lion and a bear,
17:58 am the son of your *s* Jesse of Bethlehem."
19: 4 not your majesty sin against his *s* David,
20: 7 If he says, 'Very well,' your *s* is safe.
20: 8 *s* because of the LORD's bond between us,
22: 8 stirred up my *s* to be an enemy against me,
22:15 *s* or anyone in my family of such a thing.
22:15 Your *s* knows nothing at all,
23:10 your *s* has heard a report that Saul plans
23:11 will Saul come down as your *s* has heard?
23:11 O LORD God of Israel, tell your *s*."
25:39 and who restrained his *s* from doing evil,
26:18 "Why does my lord pursue his *s*?
26:19 lord the king listen to the words of his *s*.
27: 5 your *s* live with you in the royal city?"
28: 2 Now you shall learn what your *s* can do."
29: 8 Or what have you against your *s* from the
2Sm 3:18 'By my *s* David I will save my people
7: 5 "Go, tell my *s* David,
7: 8 "Now then, speak thus to my *s* David,
7:19 house of your *S* for a long time to come:
7:20 You know your *s*, Lord GOD!
7:21 entire magnificent disclosure to your *s*.
7:25 have made concerning your *s* and his house,
7:26 of your *s* David stands firm before you.
7:27 Israel, who said in a revelation to your *s*,
7:27 Therefore your *s* now finds the courage to
7:28 have made this generous promise to your *s*.
7:29 your *s* that it may be before you forever;
7:29 house of your *s* shall be blessed forever."
9: 2 was a *s* of the family of Saul named Ziba.
9: 2 He replied, "Your *s*."
9: 6 "Meribbaal," and he answered, "Your *s*."
9: 8 "What is your *s* that you should pay
9:11 "Your *s* shall do just as my lord the king
11:21 'Your *s* Uriah the Hittite is also dead.'"
11:24 servants died, among them your *s* Uriah."
13:24 "Your *s* is having shearers.
13:24 come with all your retainers to your *s*."
13:34 Then the *s* on watch looked about and saw a
13:35 It is as your *s* said."
14: 6 Your *s* had two sons,
14: 7 whole clan confronted your *s* and demanded:
14:12 "Please let your *s* say still another word
14:15 And so your *s* thought:
14:16 surely consent to free his *s* from the grasp
14:19 *s* Joab who instructed me and told your *s*
14:20 Your *s* Joab did this to come at the issue
14:22 the king has granted the request of his *s*."
15: 2 *s* is of such and such a tribe of Israel,"
15: 8 in Geshur in Aram, your *s* made this vow:
15:21 your *s* shall be wherever my lord the king
15:34 and say to Absalom, 'Let me be your *s*,
15:34 I was formerly your father's *s*,
16: 1 the top when Ziba, the *s* of Meribbaal,
18:29 the king's servant Joab sent your *s* on,
19:18 Ziba, too, the *s* of the house of Saul,
19:20 take to heart the wrong that your *s* did
19:21 For your *s* knows that he has done wrong.
19:27 "My lord the king, my *s* betrayed me.
19:27 For your *s*, who is lame, said to him,
19:28 slandered your *s* before my lord the king.
19:29 your *s* among the guests at your table.
19:36 Can your *s* taste what he eats and drinks,
19:36 Why should your *s* be any further burdened
19:37 the Jordan, your *s* is doing little enough!
19:38 Please let your *s* go back to die in his
19:38 Here is your *s* Chimham.
24:10 But now, LORD, forgive the guilt of your *s*,
24:21 "Why does my lord the king come to his *s*?"
1Kgs 1:19 of the army, but not your *s* Solomon.
1:26 But me, your *s*, he did not invite;
1:26 son of Jehoiada, nor your *s* Solomon.
1:51 swear that he will not kill me, his *s*,
2:38 Your *s* will do just as the king's majesty
3: 6 "You have shown great favor to your *s*,
3: 7 O LORD, my God, you have made me, your *s*,
3: 9 Give your *s*, therefore, an understanding
8:24 you made to my father David, your *s*.
8:25 you made to my father David, your *s*,
8:26 which you made to my father David, your *s*,
8:28 on the prayer and petition of your *s*,
8:28 to the cry of supplication which I, your *s*,
8:29 may you heed the prayer which I, your *s*,
8:30 Listen to the petitions of your *s* and of
8:36 sin of your *s* and of your people Israel,
8:52 eyes be open to the petition of your *s*
8:53 as you declared through your *s* Moses
8:56 promise he made through his *s* Moses.
8:59 uphold the cause of his *s* and of his people
8:66 to his *s* David and to his people Israel.
11:11 you of the kingdom and give it to your *s*.
11:13 the sake of my *s* David and of Jerusalem,
11:26 Solomon's *s* Jeroboam, son of Nebat
11:32 remain to him for the sake of David my *s*,
11:34 as he lives for the sake of my *s* David,
11:36 that my *s* David may always have a lamp
11:38 and my commandments like my *s* David,
12: 7 be the *s* of this people and submit to them,
14: 8 Yet you have not been like my *s* David,
14:18 through his *s* the prophet Ahijah.
15:29 the LORD had pronounced through his *s*,
16: 9 His *s* Zimri, commander of half his chariots,
18:12 Your *s* has revered the LORD from his youth.
18:36 I am your *s* and have done all these things
18:43 and look out to sea," he directed his *s*,
19: 3 He left his *s* there and went a day's
20: 9 that you demanded of your *s* the first time.
20:32 "Your *s* Ben-hadad pleads for his life,"
20:39 "Your *s* went into the thick of the battle,
20:40 while your *s* was looking here and there,
2Kgs 4: 1 "My husband, your *s*, is dead.
4: 2 "This *s* of yours has nothing in the house
4:12 Then he said to his *s* Gehazi,
4:16 do not deceive your *s*."
4:19 to his mother," the father said to a *s*.
4:20 The *s* picked him up and carried him to his
4:22 husband, "Let me have a *s* and a donkey.
4:24 when the donkey was saddled, said to her *s*:
4:25 the man of God said to his *s* Gehazi:
4:38 were seated before him, he said to his *s*,
4:43 But his *s* objected,
5: 2 girl, who became the *s* of Naaman's wife.
5: 6 letter I am sending my *s* Naaman to you,
5:15 Please accept a gift from your *s*."
5:17 will not accept, please let me, your *s*,
5:18 I trust the LORD will forgive your *s* this:
5:18 May the LORD forgive your *s* this."
5:20 some distance when Gehazi, the *s* of Elisha,
5:25 answered, "Your *s* has not gone anywhere."
6:17 And the LORD opened the eyes of the *s*,
8: 4 with Gehazi, the *s* of the man of God.
8:13 exclaimed, "How can a dog like me, your *s*,
8:19 to destroy Judah, because of his *s* David.
9:36 through his *s* Elijah the Tishbite:
10:10 all that he foretold through his *s* Elijah."
14:25 of Israel, had prophesied through his *s*,
16: 7 "I am your *s* and your son.
18:12 commandments of Moses, the *s* of the LORD.
19:34 own sake, and for the sake of my *s* David.'"
20: 6 own sake, and for the sake of my *s* David.'"
21: 8 law which my *s* Moses enjoined upon them."
22:12 scribe Shaphan, and the king's *s* Asaiah:
1Chr 6:34 for Israel, as Moses, the *s* of God,
17: 4 "Go and tell my *s* David.
17: 7 Therefore, tell my *s* David,
17:18 You know your *s*.
17:23 your *s* and his house remain firm forever.
17:24 forever, while the house of David, your *s*,
17:25 to your *s* that you will build him a house,
17:25 your *s* has made bold to pray before you.
17:26 have promised this good thing to your *s*,
17:27 have deigned to bless the house of your *s*,
2Chr 1: 3 made in the desert by Moses, the LORD's *s*,
6:15 you made to my father David, your *s*.
6:16 you made to my father David, your *s*,
6:17 you made to your *s* David be confirmed.
6:19 on the prayer and petition of your *s*,
6:19 of supplication your *s* makes before you.
6:20 which I your *s* offer toward this place.
6:21 Listen to the petitions of your *s* and of
6:42 remember the devotion of David, your *s*."
13: 6 Jeroboam, son of Nebat, the *s* of Solomon,
24: 6 the tax levied by Moses, the *s* of the LORD,

24: 9 that the tax which Moses, the s of God,
32:16 the LORD God and against his s Hezekiah,
34:20 the scribe, and to Asaiah, the king's s:
Ezr 7:24 slave, or any other s of that house of God.
Neh 1: 6 open, to heed the prayer which I, your s,
1: 7 which you committed to your s Moses.
1: 8 which you gave through Moses, your s,
1:11 Grant success to your s this day,
2: 5 and if your s is deserving of your favor,
9:14 for them, by the hand of Moses your s.
10:30 was given through Moses, the s of God,
Tb 4:14 If you thus behave as God's s,
Jdt 5: 5 "My lord, hear this account from your s;
9:10 the ruler, the ruler together with his s;
11: 5 "Listen to the words of your s,
1Mc 4:30 mighty one by the hand of your s David
Jb 1: 8 said to Satan, "Have you noticed my s Job,
2: 3 said to Satan, "Have you noticed my s Job,
3:19 same, and the s is free from his master.
19:16 I call my s, but he gives no answer,
42: 7 rightly concerning me, as has my s Job.
42: 8 and seven rams, and go to my s Job,
42: 8 and let my s Job pray for you;
42: 8 rightly concerning me, as has my s Job."
Ps(s) 19:12 Though your s is careful of them,
19:14 wanton sin especially, restrain your s;
27: 9 do not in anger repel your s.
31:17 Let your face shine upon your s;
35:27 he wills the prosperity of his s!"
69:18 Hide not your face from your s;
78:70 And he chose David, his s,
86: 2 save your s who trusts in you.
86: 4 Gladden the soul of your s,
86:16 give your strength to your s,
89: 4 my chosen one, I have sworn to David my s:
89:21 I have found David, my s;
89:40 have renounced the covenant with your s,
105:26 He sent Moses his s;
105:42 remembered his holy word to his s Abraham.
109:28 be put to shame, but let your s rejoice.
116:16 O LORD, I am your s; I am your servant,
119:17 Be good to your s, that I may live
119:23 me, your s meditates on your statutes.
119:38 your s your promise to those who fear you.
119:49 to your s since you have given me hope.
119:65 You have done good to your s, O LORD,
119:84 How many are the days of your s?
119:122 Be surety for the welfare of your s;
119:124 with your s according to your kindness,
119:125 I am your s;
119:135 Let your countenance shine upon your s,
119:140 promise is very sure, and your s loves it.
119:176 seek your s, because your commands
132:10 For the sake of David your s,
136:22 The heritage of Israel his s,
143: 2 And enter not into judgment with your s,
143:12 to nought all my foes, for I am your s.
144:10 to kings, and deliver David, your s.
Prv 14:35 The king favors the intelligent s,
17: 2 s will rule over a worthless son,
29:19 By words no s can be trained;
29:21 If a man pampers his s from childhood,
30:10 Slander not a s to his master,
Eccl 7:21 lest you hear your s speaking ill of you,
10:16 Woe to you, O land, whose king was a s,
Wis 9: 5 For I am your s,
10:16 She entered the soul of the Lord's s,
18:21 the calamity, showing that he was your s.
Sir 7:20 Mistreat not a s who faithfully serves,
7:21 a wise s be dear to you as your own self;
41:21 Of trifling with a s girl you have,
42: 5 or of beating the sides of a disloyal s;
Is 20: 3 Just as my s Isaiah has gone naked and
22:20 On that day I will summon my s Eliakim,
24: 2 Layman and priest alike, s and master,
37:35 own sake, and for the sake of my s David.
41: 8 But you, Israel, my s,
41: 9 places, You whom I have called my s,
42: 1 Here is my s whom I uphold,
42:19 Who is blind but my s,
44: 1 Hear then, O Jacob, my s,
44: 2 Fear not, O Jacob, my s,
44:21 this, O Jacob, you O Israel, who are my s!
44:21 I formed you to be a s to me;
45: 4 For the sake of Jacob, my s,
48:20 say, "The LORD has redeemed his s Jacob.
49: 3 You are my s,
49: 5 who formed me as his s from the womb,
49: 6 too little, he says, for you to be my s,
52:13 See, my s shall prosper,
53:11 his suffering, my s shall justify many,
63:11 the days of old and Moses, his s;
Jer 25: 9 to Nebuchadnezzar, king of Babylon, my s);
27: 6 of Nebuchadnezzar, king of Babylon, my s;
30:10 But you, my s Jacob,
33:21 my covenant with my s David also be broken,
33:22 s David and the Levites who minister to me.
33:26 the descendants of Jacob and of my s David,
43:10 I will send for my s Nebuchadnezzar,
46:27 But you, my s Jacob,
46:28 You, my s Jacob,
Bar 1:20 which the Lord enjoined upon Moses, his s,
2:28 This was your warning through your s Moses,
3:37 and has given her to Jacob, his s,
Ez 28:25 on their land which I gave to my s Jacob;
34:23 over them to pasture them, my s David;
34:24 and my s David shall be prince among them.
37:24 My s David shall be prince over them,
37:25 on the land which I gave to my s Jacob,
37:25 with my s David their prince forever.
Dn 3:35 of Abraham, your beloved, Isaac your s,
6:21 "O Daniel, s of the living God,
9:11 recorded in the law of Moses, the s of God,
9:17 O God, the prayer and petition of your s;
10:16 How can my lord's s speak with you,
Hg 2:23 you, Zerubbabel, son of Shealtiel, my s,
Zec 3: 8 Yes, I will bring my s the Shoot.
Mal 1: 6 his father, and a s fears his master;
3:22 Remember the law of Moses my s,
Mt 12:18 "Here is my s whom I have chosen,
18:28 went out he met a fellow s who owed him
18:29 His fellow s dropped to his knees and
18:33 have dealt mercifully with your fellow s,
24:45 farsighted s whom the master has put in
24:46 Happy that s whom his master discovers at
24:48 if the s is worthless and tells himself,
25:21 You are an industrious and reliable s.
25:23 You too are an industrious and reliable s.
25:30 this worthless s into the darkness outside,
26:51 it, and slashed at the high priest's s,
Mk 9:35 the last one of all and the s of all."
12: 4 The second time he sent them another s;
14:66 the s girls of the high priest came along.
14:69 The s girl, keeping an eye on him, started
Lk 1:38 "I am the s of the Lord.
1:48 he has looked upon his s in her lowliness;
1:54 He has upheld Israel his s, ever mindful
1:69 for us in the house of David his s,
2:29 Master, you can dismiss your s in peace;
7: 2 A centurion had a s he held in high regard,
7: 3 him to come and save the life of his s.
7: 7 Just give the order and my s will be cured.
7:10 house, they found the s in perfect health.
12:43 That s is fortunate whom his master finds
12:45 But if the s says to himself, 'My master is
12:45 begins to abuse the housemen and s girls,
14:17 time he sent his s to say to those invited,
14:18 The first one said to the s, 'I have bought
14:21 The s returning reported all this to his
14:21 He said to his s, 'Go out quickly into
14:22 The s reported, after some time, 'Your
14:23 The master then said to the s, 'Go out
15:27 The s answered, 'Your brother is home,
16:13 "No s can serve two masters.
17: 7 "If one of you had a s plowing or herding
17: 9 the s who was only carrying out his orders?
20:10 At vintage time he sent a s to the tenant
20:11 He sent a second s whom they also beat.
22:26 you be as the junior, the leader as the s.
22:50 high priest's s and cut off his right ear.
22:56 A s girl saw him sitting in the light of
Jn 12:26 where I am, there will my s be.
18:17 s girl who kept the gate said to Peter,
Acts 3:13 of our fathers, has glorified his S Jesus,
3:26 When God raised up his s, he sent him to
4:25 the lips of our father David your s:
4:27 in this very city against your holy S,
4:30 worked in the name of Jesus, your holy S."
26:16 appeared to you to designate you as my s
Rom 1: 1 Greetings from Paul, a s of Christ Jesus,
13: 4 the ruler is God's s to work for your good.
13: 4 he is God's s, to inflict his avenging wrath
14: 4 are you to pass judgment on another's s?
15: 8 I affirm that Christ became the s of the
16:13 Greetings to Rufus, a chosen s of the Lord,
Col 1:23 under heaven, and I, Paul, am its s.
4:12 He is a s of Christ Jesus who is always
1Tm 1:12 has made me his s and judged me faithful.
4: 6 you will be a good s of Christ Jesus,
2Tm 2:24 and the s of the Lord must not be
Ti 1: 1 Paul, a s of God, sent as an apostle
Heb 3: 5 s charged with the task of witnessing to
Jas 1: 1 a s of God and of the Lord Jesus Christ,
2Pt 1: 1 Peter, s and apostle of Jesus Christ,
Jude 1: 1 a s of Jesus Christ and brother of James,
Rv 1: 1 known by sending his angel to his s John,
15: 3 they sang the song of Moses, the s of God,
19:10 I am merely a fellow s with you and your
22: 9 I am merely a fellow s with you and your

SERVANTS—SERVANT'S (405)

Gn 14:24 Nothing for me except what my s have used
15: 3 and so one of my s will be my heir."
19: 2 come aside into your s house for the night,
22: 3 his son Isaac, and two of his s as well,
22: 5 Then he said to his s: "Both of you stay
22:19 Abraham then returned to his s,
26:15 the wells that his father's s had dug back
26:18 the wells which his father's s had dug back
26:19 But when Isaac's s dug in the wadi and
26:20 of Gerar quarreled with Isaac's s,
26:25 there, his s began to dig a well nearby.
26:32 That same day Isaac's s came and brought
30:43 male and female s and camels and asses.
32: 6 and sheep, as well as male and female s.
32:17 He put these animals in charge of his s,
32:17 in separate droves, and he told the s,
39:11 of the household s were then in the house,
39:14 screamed for her household s and told them,
42:10 contrary, your s have come to procure food.
42:11 your s have never been spies."
42:13 "We your s," they said, "were twelve
44: 7 Far be it from your s to do such a thing!
44: 9 any of your s is found to have the goblet,
44:16 God has uncovered your s' guilt.
44:19 My lord asked your s, 'Have you a father,
44:21 Then you told your s, 'Bring him down
44:23 But you told your s, 'Unless your youngest
44:31 and your s will thus send the white head
46:34 is, you must answer, 'We your s,
47: 3 occupation was, they answered, "We your s,
47: 4 for your s' flocks in the land of Canaan,
47: 4 let your s settle in the region of Goshen."
50:17 crime that we, the s of your father's God,
Ex 5:15 "Why do you treat your s in this manner?
5:16 No straw is supplied to your s,
5:16 Look how your s are beaten!
5:21 Pharaoh and his s and have put a sword
7:10 his staff down before Pharaoh and his s,
7:20 river in full view of Pharaoh and his s,
7:28 your bed, into the houses of your s too,
7:29 all over you and your subjects and your s."
8: 5 pray for you and your s and your subjects,
8: 7 and your houses, your s and your subjects;
8:17 your s and your subjects and your houses.
8:20 house of Pharaoh and the houses of his s;
8:25 from Pharaoh and his s and his subjects.
8:27 flies from Pharaoh and his s and subjects.
9:14 upon you and your s and your subjects,
9:20 Some of Pharaoh's s feared the warning of
9:20 their s and livestock off to shelter.
9:21 left their s and livestock in the fields.
9:30 But you and your s, I know, do not yet
9:34 he with his s became obdurate,
10: 1 for I have made him and his s obdurate in
10: 6 houses of your s and of all the Egyptians;
10: 7 But Pharaoh's s said to him, "How long
11: 3 s and the people in the land of Egypt.
11: 8 s of yours shall then come down to me,
12:30 he and all his s and all the Egyptians;
14: 5 and his s changed their minds about them.
32:13 Remember your s Abraham, Isaac
Lv 25:42 out of the land of Egypt are s of mine,
25:55 Israelites belong as s; they are s of mine
Nm 22:22 on his ass, accompanied by two of his s.
31:49 "Your s have counted up the soldiers
32: 4 Now, since your s have livestock,"
32: 5 land be given to your s as their property.
32:25 Moses, "Your s will do as you command,
32:27 all your s will go across as armed troops
32:31 do what the LORD has commanded us, your s.
Dt 9:27 Remember your s, Abraham, Isaac and Jacob.
29: 1 Pharaoh and all his s and to all his land;
32:36 on his s he shall have pity.
32:43 of his s and purges his people's land.
34:11 and all his s and against all his land,
Jos 9: 8 But they answered Joshua, "We are your s."
9: 9 him, "Your s have come from a faroff land,
9:11 We are your s; we propose that you make
9:24 s were fully informed of how the LORD,
10: 6 "Do not abandon your s.
Jgs 3:24 When Ehud had left and the s came,
6:27 s and did as the LORD had commanded him.
Ru 2: 8 Stay here with my women s.
2:15 and Boaz instructed his s to let her glean
2:21 s until they complete his entire harvest."
2:22 Naomi rejoined, "to go out with his s;
2:23 So she stayed gleaning with the s of Boaz
3: 2 Now is not Boaz, with whose s you were,
1Sm 8:16 He will take your male and female s,
9: 3 "Take one of the s with you and go out
12:19 to the LORD your God for us, your s,
16:15 So the s of Saul said to him:
16:16 it, we, your s here in attendance on you,
16:17 Saul then told his s, "Find me a skillful
17: 8 I am a Philistine, and you are Saul's s.
18:22 s to speak to David privately and to say:
18:23 But when Saul's s mentioned this to David,
18:24 When his s reported to him the nature of
18:26 When the s reported this offer to David,
19: 1 with his son Jonathan and with all his s.
21: 8 One of Saul's s was there that day,
21:12 But the s of Achish said, "Is this not
21:15 Finally Achish said to his s:
22: 6 spear, while all his s were standing by.
22:14 who among all your s is as loyal as David,
22:17 But the king's s refused to lift a hand to
24: 5 David's s said to him, "This is the day
25: 8 Ask your s and they will tell you so.
25: 8 Please give your s and your son David
25:10 But Nabal answered the s of David:
25:10 are many s who run away from their masters.
25:14 was informed of this by one of the s,
25:19 She then said to her s, "Go on ahead;
25:40 When David's s came to Abigail in Carmel,
25:41 a slave to wash the feet of my lord's s."
28: 7 Then Saul said to his s, "Find me a
28: 7 His s answered him, "There is a woman

SERVANTS—SERVANT'S (cont.)

28:23 when his *s* joined the woman in urging him,
28:25 She set the meal before Saul and his *s*,
29:10 you and your lord's *s* who came with you,
2Sm 2:12 Abner, son of Ner, and the *s* of Ishbaal,
2:13 and David's *s* also set out and met them at
2:15 son of Saul, and twelve of David's *s*.
2:17 men of Israel were defeated by David's *s*.
2:30 nineteen other *s* of David were missing.
2:31 But David's *s* had fatally wounded three
3:22 Just then David's *s* and Joab were coming
3:38 The king then said to his *s*:
7:21 your *s* sake and as you have had at heart,
8:7 *s* and brought them to Jerusalem.
9:10 your sons and *s* must till the land for him.
9:10 Ziba, who had fifteen sons and twenty *s*,
10:2 So David sent his *s* with condolences to
10:2 *s* entered the country of the Ammonites,
10:4 Hanun, therefore, seized David's *s* and,
11:11 majesty's *s* are encamped in the open field.
11:13 out to sleep on his bed among his lord's *s*,
11:24 archers shot at your *s* from the wall above,
11:24 wall above, and some of the king's *s* died,
12:18 David's *s*, however, were afraid to tell him
12:19 But David noticed his *s* whispering among
12:19 He asked his *s*, "Is the child dead?"
12:21 His *s* said to him: "What is this you
13:28 But he had instructed his *s*:
13:29 *s* did to Amnon as Absalom had commanded,
13:31 *s* standing by him also rent their garments.
13:36 too, and all his *s* wept very bitterly.
14:30 He therefore instructed his *s*:
14:30 And so Absalom's *s* set the field on fire.
14:31 "Why have your *s* set my field on fire?"
15:14 all his *s* who were with him in Jerusalem:
15:15 officers answered him, "Your *s* are ready,
16:2 and summer fruits are for your *s* to eat,
16:11 the king said to Abishai and to all his *s*:
17:20 Absalom's *s* came to the woman at the house,
18:7 of Israel were defeated by David's *s*,
18:9 unexpectedly came up against David's *s*.
19:6 you have put all your *s* to shame today by
19:7 that officers and *s* mean nothing to you.
19:8 Go out and speak kindly to your *s*.
19:15 the king to return, with all his *s*.
19:18 by his fifteen sons and twenty *s*,
20:6 Take your lord's *s* and pursue him,
20:15 So David's *s* came and besieged him in Abel
21:15 down with his *s* and fought the Philistines,
21:22 they fell at the hands of David and his *s*.
24:20 noticed the king and his *s* coming toward
1Kgs 1:2 His *s* therefore said to him, "Let a young
1:47 and the king's *s* went in and paid their
2:39 two of Shimei's *s* ran away to Achish,
2:39 was informed that his *s* were in Gath.
2:40 went to Achish in Gath in search of his *s*,
3:15 and gave a banquet for all his *s*.
5:20 My *s* shall accompany yours,
5:20 you whatever you say for your *s*' salary."
5:23 My *s* shall bring them down from the
8:23 your covenant of kindness with your *s*
8:32 take action and pass judgment on your *s*.
9:27 own expert seamen with the *s* of Solomon.
10:8 Happy are your men, happy these *s* of yours,
10:13 she returned with her *s* to her own country.
11:17 Egypt with some Edomite *s* of his father.
12:7 answer, they will be your *s* forever."
20:6 this time tomorrow I will send my *s* to you,
20:6 your house and the houses of your *s*.
20:12 the assault," he commanded his *s*;
20:23 the *s* of the king of Aram said to him:
20:31 His *s* said to him: "We have heard
22:3 to the king of Israel, who said to his *s*,
22:50 my servants accompany your *s* in the ships."
2Kgs 1:13 and the lives of these fifty men, your *s*,
2:16 "Among your *s* are fifty brave men,"
5:13 But his *s* came up and reasoned with him.
5:23 the two festal garments, to two of his *s*,
5:26 sheep or cattle, male or female *s*?
6:3 "Please agree to accompany your *s*,"
6:8 with his *s* to attack a particular place.
7:12 night, the king got up; he said to his *s*:
7:13 One of his *s*, however, suggested:
9:7 I avenge the blood of my *s* the prophets,
9:7 the other *s* of the LORD shed by Jezebel,
9:11 When Jehu rejoined his master's *s*,
9:28 His *s* brought him in a chariot to
10:5 "We are your *s*, and we will do everything
17:13 and which I sent you by my *s* the prophets,"
17:23 as he had foretold through all his *s*,
18:24 repulse even one of the least *s* of my lord,
18:26 "Please speak to your *s* in Aramaic;
19:5 the *s* of King Hezekiah had come to Isaiah,
19:6 with which the *s* of the king of Assyria
19:23 Through your *s* you have insulted the Lord.
20:18 *s* in the palace of the king of Babylon."
21:10 the LORD spoke through his *s* the prophets:
22:9 "Your *s* have smelted down the metals
23:30 His *s* brought his body on a chariot from
24:2 had threatened through his *s* the prophets.
24:11 at the city while his *s* were besieging it.
1Chr 16:13 uttered, You descendants of Israel, his *s*,
17:17 *s* family reaching into the distant future,
17:19 *s* sake and in keeping with your purpose,
19:2 But when David's *s* had entered the land of
19:3 *s* rather come to you to explore the land,
19:4 Thereupon Hanun seized David's *s* and had
20:8 who died at the hands of David and his *s*.
21:8 Take away your *s* guilt,
2Chr 2:7 *s* know how to cut the wood of the Lebanon.
2:7 My *s* will labor with yours in order to
2:9 I will furnish as food for your *s*,
2:14 now, let my lord send to his *s* the wheat,
6:14 *s* who are wholeheartedly faithful to you.
6:23 take action and pass judgment on your *s*,
6:27 sin of your *s* and of your people Israel.
8:18 Huram, through his *s*, sent him ships and
8:18 who accompanied Solomon's *s* to Ophir and
9:4 the attendance of his *s* and their dress,
9:7 Happy are your men, happy these *s* of yours,
9:10 The *s* of Huram and of Solomon who brought
9:12 she returned to her own country with her *s*.
9:21 that went to Tarshish with the *s* of Huram.
10:7 their request, they will be your *s* forever."
12:8 But they shall be his *s*,
24:25 his *s* conspired against him because of the
25:3 those of his *s* who had killed the king,
33:24 His *s* conspired against him and put him to
34:16 "Your *s* are doing everything that has
35:23 shot King Josiah, who said to his *s*,
35:24 His *s* removed him from his own chariot,
36:20 where they became his and his sons' *s* until
Ezr 4:11 "To King Artaxerxes, your *s*,
5:11 'We are the *s* of the God of heaven
9:11 which you gave through your *s* the prophets:
Neh 1:6 day and night for your *s* the Israelites,
1:10 They are your *s*, your people, whom you
1:11 of all your willing *s* who revere your name.
2:20 We, his *s*, shall set about the rebuilding;
6:5 sent me the same message by one of his *s*,
9:10 all his *s* and the people of his land,
Tb 8:9 But Raguel got up and summoned his *s*.
8:18 his *s* to fill in the grave before dawn.
8:19 So the *s* began to prepare the feast.
9:2 four *s* and two camels and travel to Rages.
9:5 together with the four *s* and two camels,
Jdt 3:2 the *s* of Nebuchadnezzar the great king,
5:5 no lie shall escape your *s* lips.
6:3 but we, the *s* of Nebuchadnezzar,
6:6 the spear of my *s* will pierce your sides,
6:7 My *s* will now conduct you to the mountain
6:10 Then Holofernes ordered the *s* who were
6:11 So the *s* took him in custody and brought
6:12 Holofernes' *s* by hurling stones upon them.
7:12 Have some of your *s* keep control of the
8:7 had left her gold and silver, *s* and maids,
9:3 and the princes together with their *s*.
10:20 *s* came out and ushered her into the tent.
10:23 when Holofernes and his *s* beheld Judith,
10:23 before him, but his *s* raised her up.
11:4 well treated, as are all the *s* of my lord,
11:20 words pleased Holofernes and all his *s*;
12:5 the *s* of Holofernes led her into the tent,
12:10 Holofernes gave a banquet for his *s* alone,
13:1 When it grew late, his *s* quickly withdrew.
Est 3:2 All the king's *s* who were at the royal
3:3 The king's *s* who were at the royal gate
4:11 "All the *s* of the king and the people of
5:11 placed him above the officials and royal *s*.
6:5 The king's *s* answered him, "Haman is
1Mc 16:16 him, his two sons, and some of his *s*.
2Mc 1:2 remember his covenant with his faithful *s*,
7:6 the words, 'And he will have pity on his *s*.'"
7:33 he will again be reconciled with his *s*.
8:29 to be completely reconciled with his *s*.
Jb 4:18 Lo, he puts no trust in his *s*,
Ps(s) 34:23 But the LORD redeems the lives of his *s*;
69:37 the descendants of his *s* shall inherit it,
79:2 of your *s* as food to the birds of heaven,
79:10 you avenge the shedding of your *s*' blood.
89:51 Remember, O Lord, the insults to your *s*:
90:13 Have pity on your *s*!
90:16 by your *s* and your glory by their children;
102:15 For her stones are dear to your *s*,
102:29 The children of your *s* shall abide,
105:6 Your descendants of Abraham, his *s*,
105:25 people, and dealt deceitfully with his *s*.
113:1 Praise, you *s* of the LORD, praise
119:76 me according to your promise to your *s*.
123:2 of *s* are on the hands of their masters,
134:1 all you *s* of the LORD Who stand in the
135:9 against Pharaoh and against all his *s*.
135:14 his people, and is merciful to his *s*.
Prv 29:12 to lying words, his *s* all become wicked.
Wis 12:20 For these were enemies of your *s*,
Sir 6:11 your other self, and lords it over your *s*;
36:16 Hear the prayer of your *s*,
Is 36:9 repulse even one of the least *s* of my lord?
36:11 "Please speak to your *s* in Aramaic;
37:5 the *s* of King Hezekiah had come to Isaiah,
37:6 with which the *s* of the king of Assyria
37:24 Through your *s* you have insulted the Lord:
39:7 *s* in the palace of the king of Babylon."
43:10 my *s* whom I have chosen To know and
44:26 It is I who confirm the words of my *s*,
50:10 you fears the LORD, heeds his *s* voice,
54:17 This is the lot of the *s* of the LORD,
56:6 the name of the LORD, and becoming his *s*,
63:17 Return for the sake of your *s*, the tribes
65:8 Thus will I do with my *s*:
65:9 inherit the land, my *s* shall dwell there.
65:13 Lo, my *s* shall eat, but you shall go
65:13 My *s* shall drink, but you shall be thirsty;
65:13 My *s* shall rejoice, but you shall be put
65:14 My *s* shall shout for joy of heart,
65:15 but my *s* shall be called by another name
66:14 The LORD's power shall be known to his *s*,
Jer 7:25 sent you untiringly all my *s* the prophets.
14:3 The nobles send their *s* for water,
25:4 all his *s* the prophets with this message:
25:19 Pharaoh, king of Egypt, and his *s*,
26:5 to the words of my *s* the prophets,
29:19 I kept sending them my *s* the prophets,
34:10 to set free their male and female *s*,
35:15 I kept sending you all my *s* the prophets,
44:4 kept sending to you all my *s* the prophets,
Bar 2:20 had warned us through your *s* the prophets:
2:24 you had made through your *s* the prophets,
Ez 38:17 I spoke in ancient times through my *s*,
44:11 my sanctuary as gatekeepers and temple *s*;
46:17 part of his inheritance to one of his *s*,
Dn 1:12 Azariah, "Please test your *s* for ten days.
1:13 and treat your *s* according to what you see."
2:4 *s* the dream and we will give its meaning."
2:7 *s* the dream and we will give its meaning."
3:33 we, your *s*, who revere you, have become
3:44 be routed who inflict evils on your *s*;
3:85 *S* of the Lord, bless the Lord; praise and
3:93 *S* of the most high God, come out."
3:95 angel to deliver the *s* that trusted in him;
9:6 We have not obeyed your *s* the prophets,
9:10 you gave us through your *s* the prophets.
13:27 the old men, the *s* felt very much ashamed,
14:14 Daniel ordered his *s* to bring some ashes,
Jl 3:1 Even upon the *s* and the handmaids,
Am 3:7 without revealing his plan to his *s*,
Zec 1:6 which I entrusted to my *s* the prophets,
Mt 18:31 When his fellow *s* saw what had happened
22:3 He dispatched his *s* to summon the invited
22:4 A second time he sent other *s*, saying:
22:6 The rest laid hold of his *s*, insulted them,
22:8 Then he said to his *s*: 'The banquet is
22:10 The *s* then went out into the byroads and
24:49 coming,' and begins to beat his fellow *s*,
25:14 He called in his *s* and handed his funds
25:19 *s* came home and settled accounts with them.
Mk 13:34 He leaves home and places his *s* in charge,
Lk 12:37 It will go well with those *s* whom the
12:42 whom the master will set over his *s* to
12:46 that *s* master will come back on a day when
15:22 The father said to his *s*: 'Quick! bring
15:26 He called one of the *s* and asked him the
17:10 commanded to do, say, 'We are useless *s*.
19:13 his *s* and gave them sums of ten units each,
19:15 for the *s* to whom he had given the money,
Jn 4:51 He was on his way there when his *s* met him
18:18 and the *s* and the guards who were standing
Acts 2:18 even on my *s* and handmaids I will pour out
4:29 Grant to your *s*, even as they speak your
10:7 he called two *s* and a devout soldier from
16:17 "These men are *s* of the Most High God;
Rom 6:19 the *s* of justice for their sanctification.
14:8 the Lord, and when we die we die as his *s*.
1Cor 4:1 Men should regard us as *s* of Christ and
2Cor 4:5 and ourselves as your *s* for Jesus' sake.
Phil 1:1 Paul and Timothy, *s* of Christ Jesus,
1Pt 2:16 In a word, live as *s* of God.
Rv 1:1 show his *s* what must happen very soon.
2:20 self-styled prophetess who seduces my *s* by
6:11 of their fellow *s* and brothers to be slain,
7:3 seal on the foreheads of the *s* of our God."
10:7 which he announced to his *s* the prophets,
11:18 The time to reward your *s* the prophets and
19:2 blood of his *s* which was shed by her hand."
19:5 "Praise our God, all you his *s*,
22:3 and his *s* shall serve him faithfully.
22:6 to show his *s* what must happen very soon."

SERVE (201)

Gn 1:15 and *s* as luminaries in the dome of the sky,
6:21 may *s* as provisions for you and for them."
9:13 I set my bow in the clouds to *s* as a sign
15:14 bring judgment on the nation they must *s*,
20:16 Let that *s* you as a vindication before all
25:23 other, and the older shall *s* the younger."
27:25 Then Isaac said, *S* me your game,
27:29 "Let peoples *s* you, and nations pay you
27:40 shall live, and your brother you shall *s*;
29:15 "Should you *s* me for nothing just because
29:18 "I will *s* you seven years for your
41:36 This food will *s* as a reserve for the
43:31 of himself, gave the order, *S* the meal."
Ex 4:23 Let my son go, that he may *s* me.
14:12 Let us *s* the Egyptians'?
21:2 Hebrew slave, he is to *s* you for six years,
26:17 that shall *s* to fasten the boards in line.
Lv 24:7 which shall *s* as an oblation to the LORD,
Nm 4:37 clans who were to *s* in the meeting tent,

4:41 clans who were to s in the meeting tent,
10:10 s as a reminder of you before your God.
10:31 the desert, and you will s as eyes for us.
17: 3 they shall s as a sign to the Israelites."
35: 3 The cities shall s them to dwell in,
35: 3 s their herds and flocks and other animals.
35: 5 This shall s them as the pasture lands of
35:11 yourselves cities to s as cities of asylum,
35:12 These cities shall s you as places of
35:15 These six cities of asylum shall s not
Dt 4:28 There you shall s gods fashioned by the
6:13 him shall you s, and by his name shall
10:12 his ways exactly, to love and s the LORD,
10:20 God, shall you fear, and him shall you s;
11:16 that you s other gods and worship them.
13: 3 whom you have not known and to s them:
13: 7 entices you secretly to s other gods,
13:14 to s other gods whom you have not known,
15:12 to you, he is to s you for six years,
20:11 be found in it shall s you in forced labor.
28:14 in order to follow other gods and s them.
28:36 you will s strange gods of wood and stone,
28:47 Since you would not s the LORD,
28:48 you will s the enemies whom the LORD will
28:64 you will s strange gods of wood and stone,
29:17 our God, to go and s these pagan gods!
30:17 are led astray and adore and s other gods,
31:20 fat, if they turn to other gods and s them,
Jos 4: 7 Thus these stones are to s as a perpetual
22: 5 and s him with your whole heart and soul."
23: 7 their gods, or swear by them, or s them,
23:16 on you, s other gods and worship them,
24:14 LORD and s him completely and sincerely.
24:14 the River and in Egypt, and s the LORD.
24:15 If it does not please you to s the LORD,
24:15 the LORD, decide today whom you will s,
24:15 me and my house hold, we will s the LORD."
24:18 Therefore we also will s the LORD,
24:19 "You may not be able to s the LORD,
24:20 you forsake the LORD and s strange gods,
24:21 Joshua, "We will still s the LORD."
24:22 that you have chosen to s the LORD."
24:24 promised Joshua, "We will s the LORD,
Jgs 9:28 And why should we of Shechem s him?
9:28 Why should we s him?
9:38 'Who is Abimelech that we should s him?'
10: 6 had abandoned the LORD and would not s him,
1Sm 17: 9 him, you shall be our vassals and s us."
26:19 'Go s other gods!'
2Sm 16:19 Whom should I s, if not his son?"
1Kgs 3: 8 I s you in the midst of the people whom
12: 4 your father imposed on us, we will s you."
17: 1 LORD, the God of Israel, lives, whom I s,
18:15 "As the LORD of hosts lives, whom I s,
2Kgs 3:14 "As the LORD of hosts lives, whom I s,
4:41 pot and said, S it to the people to eat."
5:16 "As the LORD lives whom I s,
6:22 S them bread and water.
10:18 some extent, but Jehu will s him yet more.
17:35 other gods, nor worship them, nor s them,
18: 7 the king of Assyria and did not s him.
25:24 in the country and s the king of Babylon,
1Chr 16:11 seek to s him constantly.
28: 9 know the God of your father and s him with
2Chr 10: 4 your father imposed on us, we will s you."
12: 8 s me and what it is to s earthly kingdoms."
24:18 began to s the sacred poles and the idols;
30: 8 he has consecrated forever, and s the LORD,
33:16 and commanded Judah to s the LORD,
34:33 all who were in Israel to s the LORD,
35: 3 S now the LORD, your God, and his
35: 7 each to s as a Passover victim for any who
Ezr 8:20 and the princes appointed to s the Levites)
Neh 4:16 so that they might s as a guard by night
9:35 they did not s you nor did they turn away
10:37 the priests who s in the house of our God,
Tb 12:15 enter and s before the Glory of the Lord."
14: 9 S God faithfully and do what is right
Jdt 11: 1 anyone who chose to s Nebuchadnezzar,
11: 7 not only do men s him through you;
16:14 Let your every creature s you;
Est A:16 also appointed Mordecai to s at the court,
1Mc 6:23 We agreed to s your father and to follow
Jb 21:15 What is the Almighty that we should s him?
36:11 If they obey and s him, they spend their
39: 9 Will the wild ox consent to s you,
Ps(s) 2:11 S the LORD with fear, and rejoice before
22:31 my descendants shall s him.
60:10 Moab shall s as my washbowl;
72:11 pay him homage, all nations shall s him.
100: 2 s the LORD with gladness;
102:23 and the kingdoms, to s the LORD.
105: 4 seek to s him constantly.
108:10 Moab shall s as my washbowl;
119:91 all things s you.
Prv 13: 8 A man's riches s as ransom for his life,
Wis 15: 7 s for clean purposes and their opposites,
Sir 2: 1 My son, when you come to s the LORD,
3:14 be forgotten, it will s as a sin offering
4:14 Those who s her serve the Holy One;
8: 8 training to s in the presence of princes.
10:24 When free men s a prudent slave,
45:15 That he should s God in his priesthood and
Is 19:23 enter Assyria, and Egypt shall s Assyria.
44:15 and the rain made grow to s man for fuel.
47:15 Thus do your wizards s you with whom you
59: 6 Their webs cannot s as clothing,
60:12 kingdom shall perish that does not s you;
Jer 2:20 "I will not s," you said.
5:19 me to s strange gods in your own land,
5:19 you s strangers in a land not your own."
13:10 follow strange gods to s and adore them,
16:13 there you can s strange gods day and night,
25: 6 follow strange gods to s and adore them,
27: 7 shall s him and his son and his grandson,
27: 7 shall s great nations and mighty kings.
27: 8 or kingdom will not s Nebuchadnezzar,
27: 9 you, "You need not s the king of Babylon."
27:11 to the yoke of the king of Babylon to s him
27:12 s him and his people, so that you may live.
27:13 nation that will not s the king of Babylon?
27:14 say, "You need not s the king of Babylon,"
27:17 S the king of Babylon that you may live;
28:14 king of Babylon, and they shall s him;
30: 9 instead, they shall s the LORD,
34:14 six years he shall s you,
35:15 and not follow strange gods or s them,
40: 9 men not to be afraid to s the Chaldeans:
Lam 4:10 To s them as mourners' food in the
Bar 1:12 of Belshazzar, his son, and s them long,
2:22 voice so as to s the king of Babylon.
2:24 heed your voice, or s the king of Babylon,
Ez 27: 7 became your sail [to s you as a banner].
44: 8 to s me in my sanctuary in your stead.
44:11 They shall s in my sanctuary as
44:13 no longer draw near me to s as my priests,
47:12 Their fruit shall s for food,
Dn 3:12 they will not s your god or worship the
3:14 and Abednego, that you will not s my god,
3:17 If our God, whom we s, can save us from
3:18 that we will not s your god or worship the
3:95 s or worship any god except their own God.
6:17 "May your God, whom you s so constantly,
6:21 has the God whom you s so constantly been
7:14 and peoples of every language s him.
7:27 all dominions shall s and obey him."
Zep 3: 9 name of the LORD, to s him with one accord;
Mal 3:14 You have said, "It is vain to s God,
3:18 serves God, and him who does not s him.
Mt 6:24 No man can s two masters.
20:26 who aspires to greatness must s the rest,
20:27 first among you must s the needs of all.
20:28 not to be served by others, but to s,
Mk 10:43 who aspires to greatness must s the rest;
10:44 first among you must s the needs of all.
10:45 of Man has not come to be served but to s—
Lk 1:75 We should s him devoutly and through all
16:13 "No servant can s two masters.
Jn 2:10 "People usually s the choice wine first;
12:26 If anyone would s me, let him follow me;
Acts 7: 7 But I will judge that nation which they s,
27:23 of the God whose man I am and whom I s,
Rom 2:14 without the law s as a law for themselves.
7: 6 and we s in the new spirit,
7:25 So with my mind I s the law of God but
9:12 to her, "The older shall s the younger."
12:11 he whom you s is the Lord.
16:18 Such men s, not Christ our Lord, but
1Cor 10:11 that happened to them s as an example.
16:16 I urge you to s under such men and under
1Thes 1: 9 to s him who is the living and true God
1Tm 3:10 against them, they may s as deacons.
3:13 Those who s well as deacons gain a worthy
Phlm 1:13 that he might s me in your place while I
Heb 1:14 to s those who are to inherit salvation?
13:10 who s the tabernacle have no right to eat.
Rv 5:10 them a kingdom, and priests to s our God,
20: 6 they shall s God and Christ as priests,
22: 2 their leaves s as medicine for the nations.
22: 3 and his servants shall s him faithfully.

SERVED (64)

Gn 27:25 Jacob s it to him, and Isaac ate; he
29:20 So Jacob s seven years for Rachel,
29:25 Was it not for Rachel that I s you?
30:26 Let me have my wives, for whom I s you,
43:32 It was s separately to him,
Ex 38: 8 who s at the entrance of the meeting tent.
Nm 4:14 put all the utensils with which it is s:
Dt 29:25 they went and s other gods and adored them,
Jos 24: 2 dwelt beyond the River and s other gods.
24:14 fathers s beyond the River and in Egypt,
24:15 the gods your fathers s beyond the River
24:31 Israel s the LORD during the entire
Jgs 2: 7 The people s the LORD during the entire
2:13 abandoned him and s Baal and the Ashtaroth,
3: 4 These s to put Israel to the test,
3: 6 their sons in marriage, and s their gods.
3: 8 Aram Naharaim, whom they s for eight years.
3:14 The Israelites then s Eglon,
10:10 have forsaken our God and have s the Baals."
10:16 gods from their midst and s the LORD,
1Sm 19: 7 David to Saul, and David s him as before.
1Kgs 9: 9 strange gods which they worshiped and s.
22:54 He s and worshiped Baal,
2Kgs 10:18 "Ahab s Baal to some extent,
17:12 things that provoked the LORD, and s idols,
17:16 all the host of heaven, and s Baal.
17:33 venerating the LORD they s their own gods,
17:41 venerated the LORD, but also s their idols.
21: 3 worshiped and s the whole host of heaven.
21:21 and worshiping the idols his father had s.
1Chr 5:36 who s as priest in the temple Solomon
6:17 They s as singers before the Dwelling of
24: 2 only Eleazar and Ithamar s as priests.
27: 1 and other officers who s the king in all
2Chr 1:17 At these rates they s as middlemen for all
7:22 strange gods and worshiped them and s them.
Jdt 4:14 in attendance on the Lord who s his altar,
Est A: 2 a prominent man who s at the king's court,
1: 7 Liquor was s in a variety of golden cups,
1Mc 11:38 who had s under his predecessors hated him.
2Mc 5:15 to the laws and to his country, s as guide.
Ps(s) 106:36 They s their idols, which became a snare
Wis 10: 9 from tribulations those who s her.
17:17 he s out the inescapable sentence;
Sir 31:31 Rebuke not your neighbor when wine is s,
32: 5 of gold is a concert when wine is s.
47: 1 NATHAN who s in the presence of David.
Jer 8: 2 army of heaven, which they loved and s,
11:10 They also have followed and s strange gods;
15:11 me, LORD, have I not s you for their good?
16:11 strange gods, which they s and worshiped;
Bar 1:22 of our own wicked hearts, s other gods,
Ez 27: 8 of Sidon and Arvad s as your oarsmen;
36:20 they came], they s to profane my holy name,
41: 6 these s as supports,
Hos 12:13 fled to the land of Aram, he s for a wife;
Mt 20:28 of Man who has come, not to be s by others,
Mk 10:45 of Man has not come to be s but to serve
Jn 12: 2 they gave him a banquet, at which Martha s.
Acts 20:19 how I s the Lord in humility through the
20:34 s both my needs and those of my companions.
Rom 1:25 and s the creature rather than the Creator
Gal 4: 8 you s as slaves to gods who are not really
1Jn 2:19 only s to show that none of them was ours.

SERVES (17)

Prv 21:18 The wicked man s as ransom for the just,
Sir 3: 7 his father, and s his parents as rulers.
7:20 Mistreat not a servant who faithfully s,
13: 7 While it s his purpose he will beguile you,
24:21 put to shame, he who s me will never fail."
25: 8 his tongue, and he who s not his inferior.
35:16 He who s God willingly is heard;
Ez 19:14 is a lamentation and s as a lamentation.
Mal 3:17 will have compassion on his son who s him.
3:18 Between him who s God,
Mt 23:11 among you will be the one who s the rest.
Lk 22:27 who reclines at table or he who s the meal?
22:27 I am in your midst as the one who s you.
Jn 12:26 If anyone s me, him the Father will honor.
Rom 4:15 Indeed, the law s only to bring down wrath,
14:18 Whoever s Christ in this way pleases God
1Pt 4:11 The one who s is to do it with the

SERVICE (187)

Gn 29:27 for another seven years of s with me."
29:30 remained in Laban's s another seven years.
30:26 very well the s that I have rendered you."
41:46 years old when he entered the s of Pharaoh,
50: 2 physicians in his s to embalm his father.
50:10 there a very great and solemn memorial s;
Ex 14: 5 "Why, we have released Israel from our s!"
21: 3 If he comes into s alone, he shall leave
28: 3 him apart for his sacred s as my priest.
30:16 donate it to the s of the meeting tent,
31:10 the laver with its base, the s cloths,
35:19 the s cloths for use in the sanctuary;
36: 1 all the work for the s of the sanctuary,
36: 3 for establishing the s of the sanctuary.
39: 1 the s cloths for use in the sanctuary,
39:40 the s of the Dwelling of the meeting tent;
39:41 the s cloths for use in the sanctuary,
Lv 25:41 shall be released from your s and return
25:52 to his years of s shall he pay his ransom.
Nm 1: 3 years or more who are fit for military s.
1:20 who were fit for military s were polled,
1:22 who were fit for military s were polled,
1:24 who were fit for military s were polled,
1:26 who were fit for military s were polled,
1:28 who were fit for military s were polled,
1:30 who were fit for military s were polled,
1:32 who were fit for military s were polled,
1:34 who were fit for military s were polled,
1:36 who were fit for military s were polled,
1:38 who were fit for military s were polled,
1:40 who were fit for military s were polled,
1:42 who were fit for military s were polled,
1:45 years or more who were fit for military s,
3: 8 of the Israelites in the s of the Dwelling.
4: 4 "The s of the Kohathites in the meeting
4:12 Taking the utensils of the sanctuary s,
4:27 The s of the Gershonites shall be entirely
4:31 the years of their s in the meeting tent:
4:32 them all the objects connected with his s,
4:33 clans of the Merarites during all their s

SERVICE (cont.)

4:47 of *s* or transport of the meeting tent,
4:49 assignments for *s* and for transport;
7: 5 be put to use in the *s* of the meeting tent.
8:11 thus devoting them to the *s* of the LORD.
8:15 enter upon their *s* in the meeting tent.
8:22 Only then did they enter upon their *s* in
8:24 perform the required *s* in the meeting tent.
8:25 from the required *s* and work no longer.
8:26 His *s* with his fellow Levites shall
16: 9 near him for the *s* of the LORD's Dwelling
18: 6 to the LORD for the *s* of the meeting tent.
18:21 for the *s* they perform in the meeting tent.
18:23 are to perform the *s* of the meeting tent,
18:31 your recompense for *s* at the meeting tent.
26: 2 more who are fit for military *s* in Israel."
Dt 15:12 year you shall dismiss him from your *s*,
15:18 since the *s* he has given you for six years
Jos 24:16 forsake the LORD for the *s* of other gods.
Jgs 2:19 following other gods in *s* and worship,
1Sm 2:11 in the *s* of the LORD under the priest Eli.
2:21 young Samuel grew up in the *s* of the LORD.
14:52 or brave man, he took him into his *s*.
16:21 Thus David came to Saul and entered his *s*.
16:22 message, "Allow David to remain in my *s*,
17:32 at your *s* to go and fight this Philistine."
26:16 This is no creditable *s* you have performed.
2Sm 24: 9 hundred thousand men fit for military *s*;
1Kgs 4: 2 these were the officials he had in his *s*:
10: 5 and garb of his waiters, his banquet *s*,
10:26 cities and to the king's *s* in Jerusalem.
12: 4 If you now lighten the harsh *s* and the
12: 6 been in his father's *s* while he was alive,
12: 8 had grown up with him and were in his *s*.
2Kgs 25:14 pans and all the bronze vessels used for *s*.
25:19 *s* of the king who were still in the city,
1Chr 4:23 Gederah, where they lived in the king's *s*.
5:18 hundred and sixty men fit for military *s*.
7:11 two hundred men fit for military *s* . . .
7:40 twenty-six thousand men fit for military *s*.
9:13 for the work of the *s* of the house of God.
9:33 day and night they had to be ready for *s*.
12:34 From Zebulun, men fit for military *s*,
12:37 fit for military *s* and set in battle array:
23: 4 to direct the *s* of the house of the LORD,
23:24 They performed the work of the *s* of the
23:28 of Aaron in the *s* of the house of the LORD,
23:28 take part in the *s* of the house of God.
23:32 in the *s* of the house of the LORD.
24: 3 assigned the functions for the priestly *s*.
24:19 This was the appointed order of their *s*
25: 1 set apart for *s* the descendants of Asaph,
25: 1 is the list of those who performed this *s*:
26: 8 brethren, were mighty men, fit for the *s*.
26:12 watches in the *s* of the house of the LORD,
26:30 work of the LORD and in the *s* of the king.
28: 1 divisions who were in the *s* of the king,
28:13 the work of the *s* of the house of the LORD,
28:20 work for the *s* of the house of the LORD.
28:21 ready for all the *s* of the house of God;
29: 7 contributed for the *s* of the house of God
2Chr 8:14 classes of the priests for their *s*,
10: 4 If you now lighten the harsh *s* and the
10: 6 *s* of his father during Solomon's lifetime,
10: 8 had grown up with him and were in his *s*.
17:19 These were at the *s* of the king;
24:14 utensils for the *s* and the holocausts,
25:13 whom Amaziah had dismissed from battle *s*
29:35 Thus the *s* of the house of the LORD was
30:22 well skilled in the *s* of the LORD.
31: 2 to each priest and Levite his proper *s*,
31:16 their *s* in the order of their classes.
31:21 for the *s* of the house of God or for the
35: 2 them in the *s* of the Lord's house.
35:10 When the *s* had been arranged, the priests
35:16 Thus the entire *s* of the LORD was arranged
Ezr 2:69 to the treasury for the temple *s*:
6:18 divisions for the *s* of God in Jerusalem,
7:19 The utensils consigned to you for the *s* of
Neh 7:69 of the family heads contributed to the *s*.
7:70 to the treasury for the temple *s*:
10:33 year for the *s* of the house of our God,
10:34 and for every *s* of the house of our God.
10:38 take the tithe in all the cities of our *s*.
11:12 brethren who carried out the temple *s*,
11:22 appointed to the *s* of the house of God
Tb 1: 7 To the Levites who were doing *s* in
1:12 Because of this wholehearted *s* of God,
4: 6 For if you are steadfast in your *s*,
Jdt 3: 4 and their inhabitants are also at your *s*;
Est 1:14 *s* and held first rank in the realm,
4: 5 eunuchs whom he had placed at her *s*,
1Mc 11:58 also sent him gold dishes and a dinner *s*,
13:40 you are qualified for enrollment in our *s*,
2Mc 4:14 no longer cared about the *s* of the altar.
Ps(s) 101: 6 in the way of integrity shall be in my *s*.
147: 8 the mountains and herbs for the *s* of men;
Wis 8: 6 And if prudence renders *s*, who in the
15: 7 molds for our *s* each several article:
Is 14: 3 the hard *s* in which you have been enslaved,
40: 2 proclaim to her that her *s* is at an end,
43:23 did not exact from you the *s* of offerings,
45: 1 before him, and making kings run in his *s*,
Jer 34:11 had set free and again forced them into *s*.
35:19 of Jonadab, Rechab's son, standing in my *s*.
52:18 and all the bronze vessels used for *s*.
52:25 and seven men in the personal *s* of the
Bar 2:21 shoulders to the *s* of the king of Babylon,
6:59 obedient in the *s* for which they are sent.
Ez 44: 8 Instead of caring for the *s* of my temple,
44:14 But I will set them to the *s* of the temple,
44:16 to me, and they who shall carry out my *s*.
48:11 who fulfilled my *s* and did not stray along
Dn 1: 5 training they were to enter the king's *s*.
1:19 and so they entered the king's *s*.
Mt 5:41 anyone press you into *s* for one mile,
15: 8 me lip *s* but their heart is far from me.
27:32 man they pressed into *s* to carry the cross.
Mk 7: 6 me lip *s* but their heart is far from me.
12: 2 In due time he dispatched a man in his *s*
15:21 they pressed him into *s* to carry the cross.
Lk 1:23 Then, when his time of priestly *s* was over,
16: 2 Give me an account of your *s*,
Acts 17:25 man's *s* as if he were in need of it.
20:24 I can finish my race and complete the *s*
Rom 12: 7 gift of ministry; it should be used for *s*.
13: 6 themselves to his *s* with unremitting care.
16: 3 my fellow workers in the *s* of Christ Jesus
16: 9 our fellow worker in the *s* of Christ;
16:10 Apelles, who proved himself in Christ's *s*,
16:12 who has labored long in the Lord's *s*.
1Cor 16:15 and is devoted to the *s* of the saints.
2Cor 8: 4 sharing in this *s* to members of the church.
9:13 Because of your praiseworthy *s* they are
Gal 5:13 love, place yourselves at one another's *s*.
Eph 4:12 and teachers in roles of *s* for the faithful
6: 6 *s* for appearance only and to please men,
6: 7 Give your *s* willingly, doing it for the
Phil 2:17 over the sacrifical *s* of your faith,
4:22 believe, particularly those in Caesar's *s*.
2Tm 1:11 In the *s* of this gospel I have been
2:21 of the house and ready for every noble *s*.
4:11 with you, for he can be of great *s* to me.
Heb 6:10 and the love you have shown him by your *s*,
9: 6 In performing their *s* the priests used to
1Pt 4:10 put your gifts at the *s* of one another,
Rv 1: 6 of priests in the *s* of his God and Father
2:19 your love and faith and *s*—

SERVICES (17)

Ex 35:21 of the meeting tent, for all its *s*,
Lv 25:39 beside you that he sells you his *s*,
25:48 his *s* he still has the right of redemption;
1Chr 6:16 were entrusted by David with the choir *s*
6:17 their *s* in an order prescribed for them.
6:33 *s* of the Dwelling of the house of God.
28:14 in the golden vessels for the various *s*
28:14 in the silver vessels for the various *s*,
Neh 13:10 have been carrying out the *s* had deserted,
13:14 the house of my God and its *s* be forgotten!
1Mc 10:41 be handed over for the *s* of the temple.
10:42 belong to the priests who perform the *s*.
2Mc 3: 3 expenses necessary for the sacrificial *s*.
Sir 50:14 Once he had completed the *s* at the altar
50:19 As the high priest completed the *s* at the
Phil 2:30 to render me those *s* you could not render.
2Tm 1:18 And the many *s* he has performed for Christ

SERVILITY (1)

Col 2:18 by insisting on *s* in the worship of angels.

SERVING (32)

Gn 31: 6 know what effort I put into *s* your father;
Ex 28: 4 his sons are to wear in *s* as my priests,
Nm 3: 7 the meeting tent by *s* at the Dwelling.
Dt 4:19 be led astray into adoring them and *s* them.
7: 4 sons from following me to *s* other gods,
7:16 lest you be ensnared into *s* their gods.
8:19 follow other gods, *s* and worshiping them,
11:13 enjoin on you today, loving and *s* the LORD,
13: 5 heed, *s* him and holding fast to him alone.
17: 3 transgresses his covenant, by *s* other gods,
Jgs 2:11 offended the LORD by *s* the Baals.
3: 7 God, and *s* the Baals and the Asherahs,
10: 6 the LORD, *s* the Baals and Ashtaroth,
1Sm 2:18 apron, was *s* in the presence of the LORD.
2:22 women *s* at the entry of the meeting tent].
2Kgs 21:21 *s* and worshiping the idols his father had
1Chr 25: 6 harps and lyres, *s* in the house of God,
Jdt 11:17 woman, *s* the God of heaven night and day.
1Mc 16:15 While *s* them a sumptuous banquet,
Wis 16:21 and *s* the desire of him who received it,
16:24 For your creation, *s* you, its maker,
16:25 it was *s* your all-nourishing bounty
19: 6 being made over anew, *s* its natural laws,
Jer 22: 9 God, by worshiping and *s* strange gods."
28:14 of all these nations *s* Nebuchadnezzar,
44: 3 gods, *s* them and sacrificing to them,
Ez 20:32 peoples of foreign lands, *s* wood and stone."
Mt 8: 6 my *s* boy is at home in bed paralyzed,
26:69 of the *s* girls came over to him and said,
Jn 16: 2 puts you to death will claim to be *s* God!
Gal 1:10 approval, I would surely not be *s* Christ!
Phil 2:22 father's side *s* the gospel along with me.

SERVITUDE (3)

Ezr 9: 8 our eyes and given us relief in our *s*.
9: 9 but in our *s* our God has not abandoned us;
Est C:19 they are not satisfied with our bitter *s*,

SESSION (3)

2Kgs 9: 5 the commanders of the army were in *s*.
Jer 36:12 where the princes were just then in *s*:
Acts 19:38 anyone, there are courts in *s* for that.

SESSIONS (1)

Ezr 10:16 They held *s* to examine the matter,

SET (692)

Gn 1:17 God *s* them in the dome of the sky,
9:13 I *s* my bow in the clouds to serve as a
12: 5 and they *s* out for the land of Canaan.
13:11 the whole Jordan Plain and *s* out eastward.
13:17 *S* forth and walk about in the land,
15:12 As the sun was about to *s*, a trance fell
15:17 When the sun had *s* and it was dark,
18: 8 had been prepared, and *s* these before them;
18:16 The men *s* out from there and looked down
21: 2 old age, at the *s* time that God had stated.
21:28 also *s* apart seven ewe lambs of the flock,
21:29 seven ewe lambs that you have *s* apart?"
22: 3 *s* out for the place of which God had told
22:19 and they *s* out together for Beer-sheba,
24:33 But when the table was *s* for him,
28:11 a certain shrine, as the sun had already *s*,
28:18 his head, *s* it up as a memorial stone,
28:22 This stone that I have *s* up as a memorial
30:38 he then *s* upright in the watering troughs,
30:40 and he *s* these animals to face the
30:41 Jacob would *s* the rods in the troughs in
31:45 a stone and *s* it up as a memorial stone.
31:51 stone that I have *s* up between you and me.
32: 1 then he *s* out on his journey back home,
33:20 He *s* up a memorial stone there and invoked
34: 8 Shechem has his heart *s* on your daughter.
34:12 No matter how high you *s* the bridal price,
35: 5 Then, as they *s* out, a terror from God
35:14 with him, Jacob *s* up a memorial stone,
35:20 Jacob *s* up a memorial stone on her grave,
41:50 Before the famine years *s* in,
41:54 to an end, the seven years of famine *s* in,
43: 9 bring him back, to *s* him in your presence,
43:25 Then they *s* out their gifts to await
46: 1 Israel *s* out with all that was his.
Ex 1:11 taskmasters were *s* over the Israelites to
12:37 Israelites *s* out from Rameses for Succoth,
16: 1 Having *s* out from Elim,
18:21 and *s* them as officers over groups of
19: 7 When he *s* before them all that the LORD
19:12 *S* limits for the people all around the
19:23 for you yourself warned us to *s* limits
21:13 which I will *s* apart for this purpose.
23:31 I will *s* your boundaries from the Red Sea
24:13 So Moses *s* out with Joshua,
25:30 shall always keep showbread *s* before me.
25:37 seven lamps for it and so *s* up the lamps
26: 4 along the edge of the end sheet in one *s*,
26: 4 the edge of the end sheet in the other *s*.
26: 5 the edge of the end sheet in the first *s*,
26: 5 the corresponding sheet in the second *s*,
26: 9 of the sheets, edge to edge, into one *s*,
26: 9 and the other six sheets into another *s*.
26:10 along the edge of the end sheet in one *s*,
26:10 the edge of the end sheet in the second *s*.
26:18 *S* up the boards of the Dwelling as follows:
26:34 *S* the propitiatory on the ark of the
28: 3 make such vestments for Aaron as will *s*
28:12 *S* these two stones on the shoulder straps
29:23 food that you have *s* before the LORD,
29:27 "Thus shall you *s* aside the breast of
33:22 When my glory passes I will *s* you in the
36: 1 will *s* to work with Oholiab and with all
36:11 the edge of the end sheet in the first *s*,
36:11 the edge of the end sheet in the second *s*.
36:12 loops on the inner sheet in the other *s*,
36:16 sheets were sewed edge to edge into one *s*;
36:16 and the other six sheets into another *s*.
36:17 along the edge of the end sheet in one *s*,
36:17 of the corresponding sheet in the other *s*.
36:23 They were *s* up as follows:
37:16 The vessels that were *s* on the table,
39: 7 These stones were *s* on the shoulder straps
39:37 *s* up on it and with all its appurtenances,
40: 4 Bring in the table and *s* it.
40: 4 in the lampstand and *s* up the lamps on it.
40: 8 *S* up the court round about,
40:18 He placed its pedestals, *s* up its boards,
40:18 put in its bars, and *s* up its columns.
40:20 the ark and *s* the propitiatory upon it.
40:25 and he *s* up the lamps before the LORD as
40:33 he *s* up the court around the Dwelling and
40:36 Israelites would *s* out on their journey.
Lv 8: 8 He then *s* the breastpiece on him,
8:26 unleavened food that was *s* before the LORD
16:10 Azazel he shall *s* alive before the LORD,
16:16 which is *s* up among them in the midst of

17:10 I will *s* myself against that one who
18:23 nor shall a woman *s* herself in front of an
20: 5 I myself will *s* my face against that man
20:24 who has *s* you apart from the other nations.
20:25 You, too, must *s* apart, then, the clean
20:25 in the land that I have *s* apart for you.
20:26 who have *s* you apart from the other
24: 3 Aaron shall *s* up the lamps to burn before
24: 4 shall be *s* up on the pure gold lampstand,
24: 8 shall be *s* out afresh before the LORD,
26: 1 nor shall you *s* up a stone figure for
26:11 I will *s* my Dwelling among you,
27: 8 the person must be *s* before the priest,
27:11 sacrifice, it must be *s* before the priest,
27:12 and the value *s* by the priest shall stand.
27:14 and the value *s* by the priest shall stand.
Nm 1:51 it is the Levites who shall *s* it up.
2:17 shall *s* out in the middle of the line.
3: 9 they have been *s* aside from among the
8: 2 When you *s* up the seven lamps,
8:14 and thus shall you *s* aside the Levites
9:21 or even at night, they would then *s* out.
9:23 and at his bidding that they *s* out;
10: 5 encamped on the east side shall *s* out;
10: 6 encamped on the south side shall *s* out;
10: 6 encamped on the west side shall *s* out;
10: 6 encamped on the north side shall *s* out.
10:14 in companies, was the first to *s* out.
10:17 the clans of Gershon and Merari *s* out,
10:18 in companies, was the next to *s* out,
10:21 The clan of Kohath then *s* out,
10:22 The camp of the Ephraimites next *s* out,
10:25 the camps, the camp of the Danites *s* out,
10:34 And when they *s* out from camp,
10:35 Whenever the ark *s* out, Moses would say,
11:35 the people *s* out for Hazeroth.
12:16 After that the people *s* out from Hazeroth
14:25 *s* out in the desert on the Red Sea road."
14:36 had *s* the whole community grumbling
16: 3 *s* yourselves over the LORD's congregation?"
21: 4 Mount Hor they *s* out on the Red Sea road,
24:21 O smith, and your nest is *s* on a cliff;
24:25 Then Balaam *s* out on his journey home;
27:16 *s* over the community a man who shall act
31:10 while they *s* on fire all the towns where
33: 3 They *s* out from Rameses in the first month,
Dt 1:19 we *s* out from Horeb and journeyed through
1:24 They *s* out into the hill country as far as
1:27 your God, you *s* to murmuring in your tents,
4:41 Then Moses *s* apart three cities in the
4:44 law which Moses *s* before the Israelites.
7: 7 the LORD *s* his heart on you and chose you,
10: 6 *s* out from Beeroth Bene-jaakan for Moserah,
10: 7 From there they *s* out for Gudgodah,
10: 8 "At that time the LORD *s* apart the tribe
10:11 now and *s* out at the head of your people,
11:24 place where you *s* foot shall be yours:
11:25 of you through any land where you *s* foot,
11:26 "I *s* before you here, this day, a blessing
11:32 and decrees that I *s* before you today.
17:15 you shall *s* that man over you as your king
17:15 *s* over you as king must be your kinsman;
17:15 is no kin of yours, you may not *s* over you.
19: 2 you shall *s* apart three cities in the land
19: 7 is why I order you to *s* apart three cities.
23:12 then, when the sun has *s*, he may come
23:13 a place *s* aside to be used as a latrine.
26: 4 *s* it in front of the altar of the LORD,
26:10 And having *s* them before the LORD,
27: 2 *s* up some large stones and coat them with
28:36 and your king whom you have *s* over you,
28:56 to *s* the sole of her foot on the ground,
30: 1 all these things which I have *s* before you,
30:15 today *s* before you life and prosperity,
30:19 I have *s* before you life and death,
32: 8 He *s* up the boundaries of the peoples
Jos 1: 3 to you every place where you *s* foot.
2: 7 But the pursuers *s* out along the way to
4: 9 Joshua also had twelve stones *s* up in the
4:20 At Gilgal Joshua *s* up the twelve stones
8: 2 *S* an ambush behind the city."
8: 8 *s* it afire in obedience to the LORD's
8:12 and *s* them in ambush between Bethel and Ai,
8:19 the city, and immediately *s* it on fire.
10:31 where they *s* up a camp during the attack.
14: 9 'The land where you have *s* foot shall
16: 9 to each city *s* aside for the Ephraimites
18: 1 Shiloh, where they *s* up the meeting tent.
20: 7 So they *s* apart Kedesh in Galilee in the
24:26 Then he took a large stone and *s* it up
Jgs 1: 6 They *s* out in pursuit,
6:18 bring out my offering and *s* it before you."
7: 5 "You shall *s* to one side everyone who
7:22 LORD *s* the sword of one against another.
9:25 The citizens of Shechem then *s* men in
9:32 *s* an ambush tonight in the fields,
9:34 soldiers and *s* up an ambush for Shechem
9:43 and *s* up an ambush in the fields.
9:49 they *s* the crypt on fire over their heads,
9:52 very entrance of the tower to *s* it on fire.
14:18 On the seventh day, before the sun *s*,
15: 5 He then kindled the torches and *s* the
17: 8 *s* out to find another place of residence.
17:10 ten silver shekels a year, a *s* of garments,
18:11 *s* out from where they were in Zorrah and
18:30 *s* up the carved idol for themselves,
19: 3 *s* out with his servant and a pair of asses,
19:10 *s* out with a pair of saddled asses,
19:14 continued on their way till the sun *s* on
20:29 So Israel *s* men in ambush around Gibeah.
20:36 in the ambush they had *s* at Gibeah.
1Sm 2: 8 LORD's, and he has *s* the world upon them.
6: 7 So now *s* to work and make a new cart.
8:12 He will *s* them to do his plowing and his
9:24 portion that has been *s* before you.
12: 2 "I have *s* a king over you and now the
13:15 *s* out from Gilgal and went his own way;
17:20 a shepherd, David *s* out on his errand,
19:23 he *s* out from the hilltop toward the sheds,
28: 8 clothes, and *s* out with two companions.
28:22 Let me *s* something before you to eat,
28:25 *s* the meal before Saul and his servants,
30: 1 had stormed the city, and had *s* it on fire.
30:14 and we *s* Ziklag on fire."
31:12 had done to Saul, all their warriors *s* out,
2Sm 2:13 *s* out and met them at the pool of Gibeon.
2:19 in the open field, *s* out after Abner,
5: 6 Then the king and his men *s* out for
6: 2 people who were with him *s* out for Baala
6:17 The ark of the LORD was brought in and *s*
11:22 The messenger *s* out, and on his arrival
12:20 where at his request food was *s* before him,
13: 9 the pan and *s* out the cakes before him.
14:30 Go, *s* it on fire."
14:30 so Absalom's servants *s* the field on fire.
14:31 have your servants *s* my field on fire?"
15:16 Then the king *s* out, accompanied by his
18:19 *s* him free from the grasp of his enemies."
20: 5 Accordingly Amasa *s* out to summon Judah,
20: 5 delayed beyond the time *s* for him by David.
22:20 He *s* me free in the open.
22:34 as those of hinds and *s* me on the heights;
23: 5 with me, *s* forth in detail and secured.
1Kgs 6:16 space of twenty cubits was *s* off by cedar
7: 8 *s* in deeper than the tribunal and of the
7:25 the center, where the sea was *s* upon them.
7:28 panels were *s* within the framework.
8:53 because you have *s* them apart among all
9: 6 and statutes which I *s* before you,
13:24 was saddled for him, and he again *s* out.
16:34 son, Segub, when he *s* up the gates,
19:19 Elijah *s* out, and came upon Elisha,
20:34 terms," Ahab replied, "I will *s* you free."
20:34 an agreement with him and then *s* him free.
20:42 *s* free the man I doomed to destruction,
21: 9 and *s* Naboth at the head of the people.
2Kgs 3: 6 when he *s* out on a campaign from Samaria,
3: 9 So the king of Israel *s* out,
4: 4 vessels, and as each is filled, *s* it aside."
4:43 "How can I *s* this before a hundred men?"
5: 5 So Naaman *s* out, taking along ten silver
9:21 Israel, and Ahaziah, king of Judah, *s* out,
10:12 Then he *s* out for Samaria,
12:10 hole in its lid, and *s* it beside the stele,
16:14 and *s* it on the north side of his altar.
16:17 supported it, and *s* it on a stone pavement.
17: 8 [and the kings of Israel whom they *s* up].
17:10 They *s* up pillars and sacred poles for
17:29 Samarians had made, each people *s* up gods.
18: 7 he prospered in all that he *s* out to do.
21: 3 to Baal, and also *s* up a sacred pole,
21: 7 idol he had made, he *s* up in the temple,
22:13 has been *s* furiously ablaze against us,
23:29 King Josiah *s* out to confront him,
1Chr 4:41 by name *s* out during the reign of Hezekiah,
12:34 *s* in battle array with every kind of
12:36 Of the Danites, *s* in battle array:
12:37 for military service and *s* in battle array:
15:20 Benaiah, played on harps *s* to "Alamoth."
15:21 led the chant on lyres *s* to "the eighth."
16: 1 They brought in the ark of God and *s* it
18: 3 was on his way to *s* up his victory stele
18: 6 Then David *s* up garrisons in the Damascus
18:13 He *s* up garrisons in Edom,
19:10 and *s* them in array against the Arameans;
20: 3 of the city and *s* them to work with saws,
22:16 *S* to work, therefore, and the LORD be
23:13 was *s* apart to be consecrated as most holy,
25: 1 the leaders of the liturgical cult *s* apart for
28:10 Take courage and *s* to work."
2Chr 3:15 he *s* two columns thirty-five cubits high;
3:16 pomegranates which he *s* on the chains.
3:17 He *s* up the columns to correspond with the
4: 8 made ten tables and had them *s* in the nave,
14: 9 Asa went out to meet him and *s* himself in
20:23 For the Ammonites and Moabites *s* upon the
21:11 *s* up high places in the mountains of Judah;
23:11 son, *s* the crown and the insignia upon him,
25:14 of Seir, which he *s* up as his own gods;
27: 4 forest land he *s* up fortresses and towers.
28:15 and all who were weak they *s* on asses.
28:25 In every city throughout Judah he *s* up
31: 6 these they brought in and *s* out in heaps.
34:21 has been *s* furiously ablaze against us,
36:19 walls of Jerusalem, *s* all its palaces afire,
Ezr 3: 2 *s* about rebuilding the altar of the God of
4: 4 Thereupon the people of the land *s* out to
6:18 they *s* up the priests in their classes and
7:10 Ezra had *s* his heart on the study and
8:31 We *s* out for Jerusalem from the river of
Neh 2: 6 I *s* a date that was acceptable to him,
2:12 Then I *s* out by night with only a few
2:20 his servants, shall *s* about the rebuilding;
3: 1 They timbered it and *s* up its doors,
3: 3 they timbered it and *s* up its doors,
3: 6 they timbered it and *s* up its doors,
3:13 they rebuilt it and *s* up its doors,
3:14 he rebuilt it and *s* up its doors,
3:15 it, roofed it over, and *s* up its doors,
5:17 *s* my table for a hundred and fifty persons,
6: 1 I had not yet *s* up the doors in the gates),
6: 7 that you have *s* up prophets in Jerusalem
7: 1 had been rebuilt, I had the doors *s* up,
9:37 whom you *s* over us because of our sins,
12:44 over the chambers *s* aside for stores,
13: 5 had *s* aside for the latter's use a large
Tb 2: 2 The table was *s* for me, and when many
5:17 the journey, and *s* out with your kinsman.
6:18 *s* apart for you before the world existed.
6:18 with her, and his heart became *s* on her.
7:11 until you *s* aside what belongs to me."
13:12 your towers and *s* fire to your homes;
14:10 from the deadly trap Nadab had *s* for him.
Jdt 2:27 harvest, he *s* fire to all their fields,
3:10 *s* up his camp between Geba and Scythopolis,
5: 3 Who has *s* himself up as their king and the
7:23 They *s* up a great clamor and said before
8: 5 where she *s* up a tent for herself on the
8:24 let us *s* an example for our kinsmen.
11: 7 who has sent you to *s* all creatures aright!
11:19 and there I will *s* up your judgment seat.
12: 1 and bade them *s* a table for her with his
Est 3:15 *s* out in haste at the king's command;
5:14 friends said to him, "Have a gibbet *s* up,
E:20 may help them on the day *s* for their ruin,
1Mc 1:31 He plundered the city and *s* fire to it,
3:37 half of the army and *s* out from Antioch,
4: 1 and this detachment *s* out at night in
4: 3 and himself *s* out with his soldiers to
5:28 their possessions, and *s* fire to the city.
5:66 He then *s* out for the land of the
6:17 was dead, he *s* up the king's son Antiochus,
7: 1 son of Seleucus, *s* out from Rome,
7:10 They *s* out and, on arriving in the land
9: 4 Then they *s* out for Berea with twenty
9:66 these men had *s* out to go up to the siege
10:33 my kingdom I *s* at liberty without ransom;
9:67 from the city and *s* fire to the machines.
10:57 So Ptolemy with his daughter Cleopatra *s*
10:74 ten thousand men, he *s* out from Jerusalem,
11:20 and they *s* up many machines against it.
11:22 and *s* out immediately for Ptolemais.
11:48 *s* on fire and plundered on a large scale.
11:60 Jonathan *s* out and traveled through
11:61 But when he *s* out for Gaza,
12:25 He *s* out from Jerusalem and went into the
12:27 Therefore, when the sun *s*, Jonathan
12:27 He also *s* outposts all around the camp.
12:33 Simon also *s* out and went as far as
12:40 kill him, he *s* out and reached Beth-shan.
13:16 he is *s* free he will not revolt against us,
13:28 He *s* up seven pyramids facing one another
14:48 to be *s* up in a conspicuous place in the
16:10 plain of Azotus, but John *s* fire to these,
2Mc 1: 8 the lamps and *s* out the loaves of bread.
2:23 Cyrene *s* forth in detail in five volumes,
3: 8 So Heliodorus immediately *s* out on his
3:14 So on the day he had *s* he went in to take
4:11 He *s* aside the royal concessions granted
5:11 he *s* out from Egypt and took Jerusalem by
7:22 nor was it I who *s* in order the elements
8: 6 and villages, he would *s* them on fire.
8:33 they burned both those who had *s* fire to
9:14 on him, that he would *s* free the holy city,
10: 3 They also *s* out the showbread.
11: 7 Then they resolutely *s* out together.
12: 6 In a night attack he *s* the harbor on fire,
12:29 Then they *s* out from there and hastened on
14:13 and to *s* up Alcimus as high priest of the
14:16 they *s* out at once and came upon the enemy
14:21 A day was *s* on which the leaders would
14:21 came forward and thrones were *s* in place.
14:41 and calling for fire to *s* the door ablaze,
Jb 2:11 they *s* out each one from his own place:
7:12 have you *s* me up as an object of attack;
11:13 If you *s* your heart aright and stretch out
16:12 He has *s* me up for a target;
23: 4 I would *s* out my cause before him,
24: 1 Why are not times *s* by the Almighty,
28: 3 He has *s* a boundary for the darkness;
29: 7 of the city and *s* up my seat in the square
32:10 let me too *s* forth my knowledge!
34: 6 Notwithstanding my right I am *s* at nought;
34:13 or who else *s* all the land in its place?
36: 4 one perfect in knowledge I *s* before you.
38:10 When I *s* limits for it and fastened the
38:20 and *s* them on their homeward paths?
Ps(s) 2: 6 "I myself have *s* up my king on Zion,
8: 4 moon and the stars which you *s* in place

SET (cont.)

9: 8 he has *s* up his throne for judgment.
9:16 in the snare they *s*, their foot is caught;
16: 8 I *s* the LORD ever before me;
18:20 He *s* me free in the open, and rescued me,
18:34 as those of hinds and *s* me on the heights;
27: 5 of his tent, he will *s* me high upon a rock.
31: 5 will free me from the snare they *s* for me,
35: 7 without cause they *s* their snare for me,
35: 8 and let the snare they have *s* catch them;
39: 2 I will *s* a curb on my mouth."
40: 3 He *s* my feet upon a crag;
49: 5 *s* forth my riddle to the music of the harp.
54: 5 they *s* not God before their eyes.
60:10 upon Edom I will *s* my shoe;
61: 3 You will *s* me high upon a rock;
62: 4 How long will you *s* upon a man and all
62:11 wealth abound, *s* not your heart upon it.
64: 6 they conspire to *s* snares,
65: 7 You *s* the mountains in place by your power,
73: 9 They *s* their mouthings in place of heaven,
73:18 You *s* them, indeed, on a slippery road;
73:20 when you arise, *s* at nought these phantoms.
74: 4 they have *s* up their tokens of victory.
74: 7 They *s* your sanctuary on fire;
75: 4 in it quake, I have *s* firm its pillars.
78: 5 He *s* it up as a decree in Jacob,
84: 6 their hearts are *s* upon the pilgrimage:
86:14 life, nor do they *s* you before their eyes.
89:20 over the people I have *s* a youth.
89:26 I will *s* his hand upon the sea,
91:14 I will *s* him on high because he
101: 3 I will not *s* before my eyes any base thing.
104: 9 You *s* a limit they may not pass,
105:20 him, the ruler of the peoples *s* him free.
108:10 upon Edom I will *s* my shoe;
118: 5 the LORD answered me and *s* me free.
119:30 I have *s* your ordinances before me.
122: 2 And now we have *s* foot within your gates,
122: 5 In it are *s* up judgment seats,
132:11 own offspring I will *s* upon your throne;
141: 3 O LORD, *s* a watch before my mouth,
141: 9 Keep me from the trap they have *s* for me,
Prv 1:11 us, unprovoked, *s* a trap for the innocent;
1:18 blood, they *s* a trap for their own lives.
8:29 When he *s* for the sea its limit,
9: 1 her house, she has *s* up her seven columns;
22:28 ancient landmark which your fathers *s* up.
29: 8 Arrogant men *s* the city ablaze, but wise
Eccl 2: 5 and *s* out in them fruit trees of all sorts.
Sg 5:12 bathed in milk, and are *s* like jewels.
Wis 5: 1 his oppressors who *s* at nought his labors.
Sir 8:11 it will *s* him in ambush against you.
15:12 "It was he who *s* me astray";
15:16 There are *s* before you fire and water;
17: 9 He has *s* before them knowledge,
22:27 Who will *s* a guard over my mouth,
28: 6 Remember your last days, *s* enmity aside;
28:24 thorns, *s* barred doors over your mouth;
29:26 "Come here, stranger, *s* the table,
30:18 Dainties *s* before one who cannot eat are
32:20 Go not on a way that is *s* with snares,
37:15 to God to *s* your feet in the path of truth.
38:33 They *s* forth no decisions or judgments,
39:12 Once more I will *s* forth my theme to shine
49:13 defenses, and *s* up gates and bars.
Is 1:18 Come now, let us *s* things right,
10:19 be so few, Like poles *s* up for signals,
11:10 of Jesse, *s* up as a signal for the nations,
13: 2 Upon the bare mountains *s* up a signal;
14:13 the stars of God I will *s* up my throne;
16: 5 the land, A throne shall be *s* up in mercy,
17:10 plants and *s* out your foreign vine slips,
21: 5 They *s* the table, spread out the rugs;
29: 3 outposts and *s* up siege works against you.
30:33 like a stream of sulphur, will *s* it afire.
40:20 *s* up an idol that will not be unsteady?
41:19 I will *s* in the wasteland the cypress,
42: 6 you, and *s* you as a covenant of the people,
46: 7 when they *s* it in place again, it strays,
48:21 Water from the rock he *s* flowing for them;
50: 7 I have *s* my face like flint,
60:13 and glory to the place where I *s* my feet.
64: 1 As when brushwood is *s* ablaze,
66:19 I will *s* a sign among them;
Jer 1:10 day I *s* you over nations and over kingdoms.
1:15 Each king shall come and *s* up his throne
2:28 are the altars you have *s* up for Baal.
4: 7 lair, the destroyer of nations has *s* out,
5: 3 They *s* their faces harder than stone,
5:26 like fowlers they *s* traps, but it is men
9:12 abandoned my law, which I *s* before them,
12: 3 *s* them apart for the day of carnage.
17:27 I will *s* unquenchable fire to its gates,
22:17 are *s* on nothing except on your own gain,
31:21 *S* up road markers, put up guideposts;
31:29 and the children's teeth are *s* on edge,"
31:30 eats the unripe grapes shall be *s* on edge.
32:29 it shall enter this city and *s* fire to it,
32:34 me by the horrid idols they *s* up in it.
34:10 to *s* free their male and female servants,
34:11 *s* free and again forced them into service.
34:14 Every seventh year each of you shall *s*
35: 5 I *s* before these Rechabite men bowls full
37: 5 Also, Pharaoh's army had *s* out from Egypt,
37: 7 Pharaoh's army which has *s* out to help you
37:12 Jeremiah *s* out from Jerusalem for the
39: 8 The Chaldeans *s* fire to the king's palace
41:10 *s* out to make his way to the Ammonites.
41:12 all their men and *s* out to attack Ishmael,
43:10 *s* his throne upon these stones which I,
43:12 *s* fire to the temples of Egypt's gods,
44:10 which I *s* before you and your fathers.
46: 9 *S* out, warriors, Cush and Put, bearing
47: 2 the people of the land *s* up a wailing cry.
48: 9 *S* up a memorial for Moab,
49:27 I will *s* fire to the wall of Damascus,
49:31 *s* out against a nation that is at peace,
49:38 My throne I will *s* up in Elam and destroy
51:32 been seized, and the fortresses *s* on fire,
51:39 *s* a drink before them to make them drunk,
Lam 2:17 the threat He *s* forth from days of old;
3:11 He deranged my ways, *s* me astray,
3:12 and *s* me up as the target for his arrow.
Bar 1:18 the precepts which the Lord *s* before us.
2:10 precepts of the Lord which he *s* before us.
6:16 tools are their gods, *s* up in their houses;
6:33 can neither *s* up a king nor remove him.
6:52 They *s* no king over the land, not do they
Ez 2: 2 spirit entered into me and *s* me on my feet,
3:24 spirit entered into me and *s* me on my feet,
4: 2 camps, and *s* up battering rams all around.
4: 3 Then take an iron griddle and *s* it up as
5: 1 Then take a *s* of scales and divide the
12: 6 the burden and *s* out in the darkness;
12: 7 they looked on, *s* out in the darkness,
12:12 shoulder his burden and *s* out in darkness,
13:20 arms and *s* free those you have caught.
15: 7 I will *s* my face against them;
16:18 my oil and my incense you *s* before them;
16:19 you *s* before them as an appeasing odor,
16:60 will *s* up an everlasting covenant with you.
17: 4 of tradesmen, *s* it in a city of merchants.
17:16 the home of the king who *s* him up to rule,
23:16 no sooner had she *s* eyes on them than she
23:41 it, on which you had *s* my incense and oil.
24: 3 Set up the pot, *s* it up, then pour in some
24:11 Then I will *s* the pot empty on the coals
25: 4 They shall *s* up their encampments among
29: 2 Son of man, *s* your face against Pharaoh,
29:15 never more to *s* itself above the nations.
30: 8 when I *s* fire to Egypt and when all who
30:14 I will *s* fire to Zoan, and inflict
30:16 I will *s* fire to Egypt; Syene shall writhe
35: 2 Son of man, *s* your face against Mount Seir,
37: 1 LORD ans *s* me in the center of the plain,
37:28 sanctuary shall be *s* up among them forever.
40: 2 where he *s* me down on a very high mountain.
40:43 wide, were *s* on the inside all around,
42: 5 for the system of levels *s* them at a level
43: 7 is where I will *s* the soles of my feet;
43:18 when it is *s* up for the offering of holocausts
44:14 I will *s* them to the service of the temple,
45: 1 you shall *s* apart a sacred tract of land
48: 8 shall be the tract which you shall *s* apart,
48: 9 The tract that you *s* aside for the LORD
48:20 as a perfect square you shall *s* apart the
Dn 2:14 had *s* out to kill the wise men of Babylon:
2:44 of those kings the God of heaven will *s* up
3: 1 which he *s* up in the plain of Dura in the
3: 2 dedication of the statue which he had *s* up.
3: 3 statue which King Nebuchadnezzar had *s* up.
3: 5 statue which King Nebuchadnezzar has *s* up.
3: 7 statue which King Nebuchadnezzar had *s* up.
3:12 worship the golden statue which you *s* up."
3:14 or worship the golden statue that I *s* up?
3:18 worship the golden statue which you *s* up."
4:14 he will, or *s* over it the lowliest of men.'
5:24 and hand sent, and the writing *s* down.
7: 9 *s* up and the Ancient One took his throne.
11:15 he shall *s* up siegeworks and take the
11:17 He shall *s* himself to penetrate the entire
11:28 his mind *s* against the holy covenant;
11:44 he shall *s* out with great fury to slay
12:11 and the horrible abomination is *s* up,
14:11 king, *s* out the food and prepare the wine;
14:14 departed the king *s* the food before Bel,
14:36 he *s* him down in Babylon above the den.
Hos 10: 1 his land, the more sacred pillars he *s* up.
12:11 prophets, through whom I *s* forth examples.
Am 8: 9 I will make the sun *s* at midday and cover
9:14 the wine, *s* out gardens and eat the fruits.
Ob 1: 4 eagle, and your nest be *s* among the stars,
1:18 they shall *s* them ablaze and devour them;
Jon 1: 2 *S* out for the great city of Nineveh,
3: 2 *S* out for the great city of Nineveh,
Na 1:10 when a tangle of thornbushes is *s* aflame,
2: 6 the wall they rush, the mantelet is *s* up.
3: 8 than No-amon that was *s* among the streams,
Hg 1:14 so that they came and *s* to work on the
2:23 LORD, And I will *s* you as a signet ring;
Zec 6: 7 eager to *s* about patrolling the earth,
8:10 for I *s* every man against his neighbor.
Mal 3:19 the day that is coming will *s* them on fire,
3:24 the day that is coming will *s* them on fire,
Mt 2: 9 their audience with the king, they *s* out.
2:20 mother, and *s* out for the land of Israel.
4: 5 city, *s* him on the parapet of the temple,
5:14 A city *s* on a hill cannot be hidden.
5:15 They *s* it on a stand where it gives light
7:25 When the rainy season *s* in,
7:25 it had been solidly *s* on rock.
10:35 come to *s* a man at odds with his father,
11: 7 As the messengers *s* off, Jesus began to
27: 9 on his head, a price *s* by the Israelites,
Mk 8:27 Then Jesus and his disciples *s* out for the
Lk 1: 3 have decided to *s* it in writing for you,
1:39 Thereupon Mary *s* out, proceeding in haste
4: 9 *s* him on the parapet of the temple,
4:42 the town and *s* out into the open country.
7: 6 Jesus *s* out with them.
7:24 When the messengers of John had *s* off,
8:22 So they *s* out, and as they sailed he slept.
9: 6 *s* out and went from village to village,
9:33 Let us *s* up three booths, one for you,
9:56 Then they *s* off for another town.
10: 8 welcome you, eat what they *s* before you,
12:14 who has *s* me up as your judge or arbiter?"
12:42 farsighted steward whom the master will *s*
15:20 With that he *s* off for his father's house.
23:12 had previously been *s* against each other,
24:21 he was the one who would *s* Israel free.
Jn 1:43 next day he wanted to *s* out for Galilee,
4:30 that they *s* out from the town to meet him.
5:35 was the lamp, *s* aflame and burning bright,
5:45 you is Moses on whom you have *s* your hopes.
6:22 rather, they had *s* out by themselves.
6:27 on him that God the Father has *s* his seal."
8:32 the truth, and the truth will *s* you free."
Acts 2:23 up by the *s* purpose and plan of God;
2:25 'I have *s* the Lord ever before me,
8:21 Your heart is not steadfastly *s* on God.
9:39 Peter *s* out with them as they asked.
10:20 and *s* out with them unhesitatingly,
10:42 that he is the one *s* apart by God as judge
11:29 disciples determine to *s* something aside,
13: 2 *S* apart Barnabas and Saul for me to do the
13: 4 Seleucia and *s* sail from there for Cyprus.
13:20 Later on he *s* up judges to rule them until
15:16 ruins I will rebuild it and *s* it up again,
16:11 and *s* a course straight for Samothrace,
17:26 It is he who *s* limits to their epochs and
17:31 He has *s* the day on which he is going to
18:21 Then he *s* sail from Ephesus.
18:23 spending some time there he *s* out again,
20: 1 and *s* out on his journey to Macedonia.
20: 6 We ourselves *s* sail from Philippi as soon
20:13 on ahead to the ship and *s* sail for Assos,
20:18 first day I *s* foot in the province of Asia
20:33 Never did I *s* my heart on anyone's silver
22: 5 I *s* out with the intention of bringing the
25:26 may have something to *s* down in his regard.
26:32 Festus, "He could have been *s* at liberty,
27: 2 ports in the province of Asia, and *s* sail.
27:21 taken my advice and not *s* sail from Crete.
28:10 and when we eventually *s* sail they brought
28:11 Three months later we *s* sail in a ship
Rom 1: 1 called to be an apostle and *s* apart to
15:24 As soon as I can *s* out for Spain,
15:28 to them, I shall *s* out for Spain,
1Cor 4: 6 from us not to go beyond what is *s* down,
12:18 God has *s* each member of the body in the
12:28 God has *s* up in the church first apostles,
12:31 *S* your hearts on the greater gifts.
14: 1 *S* your hearts on spiritual gifts
14:12 you have *s* your hearts on spiritual gifts,
14:39 *S* your hearts on prophecy,
2Cor 7:13 his mind has been *s* at rest by all of you.
10:13 bounds the God of moderation has *s* for us
Gal 1:15 But the time came when he who had *s* me
3:15 or *s* it aside once it is legally validated.
3:17 formally ratified by God is not *s* aside
4: 2 until the time *s* by his father.
6: 1 by the spirit should gently *s* him right,
Phil 3:17 those who follow the example that we *s*.
3:19 who are *s* upon the things of this world.
Col 3: 1 *s* your heart on what pertains to higher
1Tm 5: 5 is one who has *s* her hope on God and
Ti 2: 7 you yourself fail to *s* them good example.
Heb 4: 7 because of unbelief, God once more *s* a day,
8: 2 sanctuary and of that true tabernacle *s* up,
13:23 that our brother Timothy has been *s* free.
Jas 2: 4 Have you not *s* yourselves up as judges
1Pt 1:13 *s* all your hope on the gift to be
3Jn 1: 7 for the sake of the Name that they *s* out,
Jude 1: 7 They are *s* before us to dissuade us,
Rv 17:16 will devour her flesh and *s* her on fire.

SETBACK (1)

Mt 13:21 When some *s* or persecution involving the

SETH (10)

Gn 4:25 she gave birth to a son whom she called *S.*
4:26 To *S,* in turn, a son was born,
5: 3 and he named him *S.*
5: 4 eight hundred years after the birth of *S,*
5: 6 When *S* was one hundred and five years old,
5: 7 *S* lived eight hundred and seven years

5: 8 of *S* was nine hundred and twelve years;
1Chr 1: 1 Adam, *S*, Enosh, Kenan, Mahalalel, Jared,
Sir 49:16 Glorious, too, were SHEM and *S* and ENOS;
Lk 3:38 son of Cainan, son of Enos, son of *S*,

SETS (32)

Gn 45:22 shekels of silver and five *s* of garments.
Ex 7:15 morning, when he *s* out for the water,
26: 6 with which to join the two *s* of sheets,
Lv 22: 7 his body in water, then when the sun *s*,
Dt 27:15 craftsman's hands—and *s* it up in secret!'
Jos 6:26 his youngest son when he *s* up its gates.
Jgs 14:12 linen tunics and thirty *s* of garments.
14:13 me thirty tunics and thirty *s* of garments."
1Sm 23:22 place where he *s* foot" (for he thought,
Jdt 16: 2 and *s* his encampment among his people;
Jb 5:11 He *s* up on high the lowly,
28: 9 He *s* his hand to the flinty rock,
34:24 the mighty, and *s* others in their stead,
36: 7 And with kings upon thrones he *s* them,
41:13 His breath *s* coals afire; a flame pours
Ps(s) 10: 3 covetous blasphemes, *s* the LORD at nought.
36: 5 he *s* out on a way that is not good,
146: 7 The LORD *s* captives free;
Wis 2:12 he *s* himself against our doings,
Sir 3: 2 LORD *s* a father in honor over his children;
11: 1 his head high and *s* him among princes.
11:31 with a spark he *s* many coals afire.
14:10 bread, but on his own table he *s* it stale.
43: 4 it *s* the mountains aflame with its rays;
Is 26: 1 he *s* up walls and ramparts to protect us.
51:13 But when he *s* himself to destroy,
Jer 11:16 Now he *s* fire to it, its branches burn.
15: 9 Her sun *s* in full day, she is disgraced,
Bar 6:26 move of themselves if one *s* them upright,
Heb 7:28 law *s* up as high priests men who are weak,
Jas 3: 5 the spark is that *s* a huge forest ablaze!
1Pt 3:12 but against evildoers the Lord *s* his face."

SETTING (89)

Ex 9: 5 And *s* a definite time, the LORD added,
13:20 *S* out from Succoth,
Lv 16: 7 Taking the two male goats and *s* them
Nm 8: 3 *s* up the lamps to face toward the front of
10:28 As they were *s* out, Moses said to his
10:29 "We are *s* out for the place which the
20:22 *S* out from Kadesh, the whole Israelite
21:11 *S* out from Oboth, they encamped in
21:12 *S* out from there, they encamped in the
21:13 *S* out from there, they encamped on the
33: 5 *S* out from Rameses, the Israelites camped
33: 6 *S* out from Succoth, they camped at Etham
33: 7 *S* out from Etham, they turned back to
33: 8 *S* out from Pi-hahiroth, they crossed over
33: 9 *S* out from Marah, they came to Elim,
33:10 *S* out from Elim, they camped beside the
33:11 *S* out from the Red Sea, they camped in
33:12 *S* out from the desert of Sin, they camped
33:13 *S* out from Dophkah, they camped at Alush.
33:14 *S* out from Alush, they camped at
33:15 *S* out from Rephidim, they camped in
33:16 *S* out from the desert of Sinai,
33:17 *S* out from Kibroth-hattaavah,
33:18 *S* out from Hazeroth, they camped at
33:19 *S* out from Rithmah, they camped at
33:20 *S* out from Rimmon-perez, they camped
33:21 *S* out from Libnah, they camped at Rissah.
33:22 *S* out from Rissah, they camped at
33:23 *S* out from Kehelathah, they camped at
33:24 *S* out from Mount Shepher, they camped
33:25 *S* out from Haradah, they camped at
33:26 *S* out from Makheloth, they camped at
33:27 *S* out from Tahath, they camped at Terah.
33:28 *S* out from Terah, they camped at Mithkah.
33:29 *S* out from Mithkah, they camped at
33:30 *S* out from Hashmonah,
33:31 *S* out from Moseroth, they camped at
33:32 *S* out from Bene-jaakan, they camped at
33:33 *S* out from Mount Gidgad, they camped
33:34 *S* out from Jotbathah, they camped at
33:35 *S* out from Abronah, they camped at
33:36 *S* out from Ezion-geber,
33:37 *S* out from Kadesh, they camped at
33:41] *S* out from Mount Hor,—They
33:42 *S* out from Zalmonah, they camped at
33:43 *S* out from Punon, they camped at Oboth.
33:44 *S* out from Oboth, they camped at
33:45 *S* out from Iye-abarim, they camped at
33:46 *S* out from Dibon-gad, they camped at
33:47 *S* out from Almon-diblathaim,
33:48 *S* out from the Abarim Mountains,
Dt 4: 8 whole law which I am *s* before you today?
26:12 "When you have finished *s* aside all the
27: 4 besides *s* up on Mount Ebal these stones
Jgs 4: 9 in the expedition on which you are *s* out,
1Sm 13:21 sharpening the axes and for *s* the oxgoads.
15: 5 Amalek, and after *s* an ambush in the wadi,
2Kgs 8: 2 *s* out with her family and settling in the
1Chr 9:32 charge of *s* out the showbread each sabbath.
2Chr 18:34 He died as the sun was *s*.
Neh 13: 7 in *s* aside for him a chamber in the courts
Tb 5:17 Before *s* out on his journey, Tobiah kissed
Jdt 8:12 *s* yourselves in the place of God in human
1Mc 3:40 *S* out with all their forces, they came
6:51 the sanctuary, *s* up artillery and machines,
6:52 countered by *s* up machines of their own,
9:60 Bacchides was *s* out with a large force,
13:29 the pyramids he devised a *s* of big columns,
16: 4 *S* out against Cendebeus, they spent
2Mc 1: 8 *s* fire to the gatehouse and shedding
10:21 *s* their enemies free to fight against them.
12: 9 night, *s* fire to the harbor and the fleet,
Jb 28:27 saw wisdom and appraised it, gave it its *s*,
Ps(s) 50: 1 earth, from the rising of the sun to its *s*.
83:15 forest, as a flame *s* the mountains ablaze,
104:19 the sun knows the hour of its *s*.
113: 3 From the rising to the *s* of the sun is the
Sir 32: 5 Like a seal of carnelian in a *s* of gold
Is 23:13 the impious founded, *s* up towers for her,
45: 6 rising and the *s* of the sun men may know
58: 6 *S* free the oppressed, breaking every yoke;
Jer 7:30 name by *s* up in it their abominable idols.
Dn 11:31 and *s* up the horrible abomination.
Hb 2: 9 *s* his nest on high to escape the reach of
Zec 8: 7 rising sun, and from the land of the *s* sun.
Mal 1:11 from the rising of the sun, even to its *s*,
Mk 7: 9 "You have made a fine art of *s* aside
10:17 *s* out on a journey a man came running up,
Lk 11:54 *s* traps to catch him in his speech.

SETTINGS (3)

1Chr 29: 2 made of wood, onyx stones and *s* for them,
Prv 25:11 *s* are words spoken at the proper time.
Sir 45:11 stones with seal engravings in golden *s*,

SETTLE (53)

Gn 13:18 went on to *s* near the terebinth of Mamre,
20:15 at your disposal; *s* wherever you please."
27:42 to *s* accounts with you by killing you.
34:10 you can *s* and move about freely in it,
34:16 we will *s* among you and become one kindred
34:21 *s* in the land and move about in it freely;
34:23 in to them, so that they may *s* among us."
35: 1 *S* there and build an altar there to the
45:10 You will *s* in the region of Goshen,
47: 4 your servants *s* in the region of Goshen."
47: 5 "They may *s* in the region of Goshen;
47: 6 *s* your father and brothers in the pick of
Ex 18:16 they come to me to have me *s* the matter
18:22 all the lesser cases they can *s* themselves.
Lv 24:12 from the LORD should *s* the case for them.
Nm 14:30 the land where I solemnly swore to *s* you,
33:53 take possession of the land and *s* in it,
Dt 11:31 you take possession of it and *s* there,
Jos 1:13 God, will permit you to *s* in this land.'
24: 4 the mountain region of Seir in which to *s*,
Ru 3:18 will not rest, but will *s* the matter today."
2Kgs 8: 1 with your family and *s* wherever you can,
17:27 whom I deported, to go there and *s*,
1Chr 9: 2 The first to *s* again in their cities and
2Chr 19: 8 in the name of the LORD and to *s* quarrels
1Mc 2:29 custom went out into the desert to *s* there,
3:36 He was to *s* foreigners in all their
2Mc 4:31 went off in haste to *s* the affair,
11:14 them to *s* everything on just terms,
13:13 march out and *s* the matter with God's help.
Jb 3: 5 and gloom claim it, clouds *s* upon it,
Ps(s) 139: 9 if I *s* at the farthest limits of the sea,
Sir 8:14 for he will *s* it according to his whim.
41:18 of theft from the people where you *s*,
43:18 it comes to *s* like swarms of locusts.
Is 7:19 All of them shall come and *s* in the steep
Jer 32:37 to this place and *s* them here in safety.
40:10 jars, and to *s* in the cities they occupied.
42:22 in the place where you wish to go and *s*.
43: 2 you to tell us not to go to Egypt to *s*.
44:13 the remnant of Judah that have come to *s*
44:28 to *s* in Egypt shall know whose word stands,
Ez 36:10 sown, and I will *s* crowds of men upon you,
36:11 I will *s* crowds of men and beasts upon you,
37:14 may live, and I will *s* you upon your land;
Zep 2:14 In her midst shall *s* in droves all the
Mt 5:25 *s* with your opponent while on your way to
12:45 They move in and *s* there.
18:23 decided to *s* accounts with his officials.
24:51 and *s* with him as is done with hypocrites.
Lk 12:58 try to *s* with him on the way lest he turn
18: 5 I am going to *s* in her favor or she will
1Cor 6: 5 *s* a case between one member of the church

SETTLED (70)

Gn 2:15 the man and *s* him in the garden of Eden,
3:24 man, he *s* him east of the garden of Eden;
4:16 LORD's presence and *s* in the land of Nod,
11: 2 a valley in the land of Shinar and *s* there.
11:31 But when they reached Haran, they *s* there.
13:12 while Lot *s* among the cities of the Plain,
19:30 up from Zoar and *s* in the hill country,
20: 1 Negeb, where he *s* between Kadesh and Shur.
26: 6 So Isaac *s* in Gerar.
36: 8 So Esau *s* in the highlands of Seir.
37: 1 *s* in the land where his father had stayed,
47:11 Joseph *s* his father and brothers and gave
47:27 Thus Israel *s* in the land of Egypt,
49:15 When he saw how good a *s* life was,
Ex 10: 6 first *s* on this soil up to the present day."
10:14 of Egypt and *s* down on every part of it.
16:35 for forty years, until they came to *s* land;
18:26 but all the lesser cases they *s* themselves.
24:16 The glory of the LORD *s* upon Mount Sina
40:35 because the cloud *s* down upon it and the
Nm 20: 1 first month, and the people *s* at Kadesh.
21:25 here and *s* in these towns of the Amorites,
21:31 Israel had *s* in the land of the Amorites,
31:10 where they had *s* and all their encampments.
32:40 to Machir, son of Manasseh, and he *s* there.]
Dt 3:20 until the LORD has *s* your kinsmen as well,
12:29 have replaced them and are *s* in their land,
17:14 you, and have occupied it and *s* in it,
19: 1 place and are *s* in their cities and houses,
21: 5 or violence must be *s* by their decision.
26: 1 heritage, and have occupied it and *s* in it,
Jos 1:15 them until the LORD has *s* your kinsmen,
13:21 princes of Midian, who were *s* in the land:
22: 4 has *s* your kinsmen as he promised them,
Jgs 1:16 they later left and *s* among the Amalekites.
11:11 Jephthah *s* all his affairs before the LORD.
2Sm 7: 1 King David was *s* in his palace,
1Kgs 11:24 of a band, went to Damascus, *s* there,
2Kgs 3: 8 and *s* upon the route through the desert of
17:24 and *s* them in the cities of Samaria in the
17:25 When they first *s* there,
17:26 "The nations whom you deported and *s* in
17:28 from Samaria returned and *s* in Bethel,
18:11 Israelites to Assyria and *s* them in Halah,
2Chr 8: 2 had given him, and *s* Israelites there.
Ezr 3: 1 after the Israelites had *s* in their cities,
4:10 Assurbanipal transported and *s* in the city
Neh 11:30 They were *s* from Beer-sheba to Ge-hinnom.
11:36 of the Levites from Judah *s* in Benjamin.
Tb 2:10 me, till their warm droppings *s* in my eyes,
14:12 where he *s* in Ecbatana with his
Jdt 5: 9 Here they *s*, and grew very rich in gold,
5:15 then they *s* in the land of the Amorites,
5:19 and have *s* again in the mountain region
1Mc 2: 1 of Joarib, left Jerusalem and *s* in Modein.
9:73 Jonathan *s* in Michmash;
13:48 he *s* there men who observed the law.
2Mc 14:25 so Judas married, *s* down,
Ps(s) 68:11 Your flock *s* in it; in your goodness,
78:55 and *s* the tribes of Israel in their tents.
107:36 And there he *s* the hungry,
Prv 8:25 Before the mountains were *s* into place,
Jer 24: 8 and those who have *s* in the land of Egypt.
49: 1 Gad, why have his people *s* in Gad's cities?
Lam 1:14 They have *s* about my neck,
Mt 2:23 There he *s* in a town called Nazareth.
25:19 came home and *s* accounts with them.
Acts 7: 2 in Mesopotamia and before he *s* in Haran.
7: 4 the land of the Chaldeans and *s* in Haran.
19:39 it ought to be *s* in the lawful assembly.

SETTLEMENT (2)

Jos 19:47 renamed the *s* after their ancestor Dan.
2Mc 11: 2 His plan was to make Jerusalem a Greek *s*;

SETTLEMENTS (4)

Gn 10:30 Their *s* extended all the way to Sephar,
36:43 to their *s* in their territorial holdings.
2Kgs 17: 9 They built high places in all their *s*,
Neh 12:29 had built themselves *s* about Jerusalem).

SETTLERS (1)

Gn 36:20 the Horite, the original *s* in the land:

SETTLES (4)

Sir 26:12 So she *s* down before every tent peg and
Is 14: 1 Israel and *s* them on their own soil,
Am 8: 8 Nile, and *s* back like the river of Egypt?
9: 5 Nile, and *s* back like the river of Egypt;

SETTLING (6)

Nm 22: 5 of the earth and are *s* down opposite us!
2Sm 17:12 *s* down upon him as dew alights on the
21:10 the birds of the sky from *s* on them by day,
2Kgs 8: 2 setting out with her family and *s* in the
17: 6 the Israelites to Assyria, *s* them in Halah,
Acts 18:11 ended by *s* there for a year and a half,

SEVEN (422)

Gn 5: 7 and *s* years after the birth of Enosh,
5:26 Methuselah lived *s* hundred and eighty-two
5:31 was *s* hundred and seventy-seven years;
7: 2 of every clean animal, take with you *s* pairs,
7: 3 of every clean bird of the air, *s* pairs,
7: 4 *S* days from now I will bring rain down on
7:10 As soon as the *s* days were over,
8:10 He waited *s* days more and again sent the
8:12 He waited still another *s* days and then
11:21 and *s* years after the birth of Serug,
21:28 also set apart *s* ewe lambs of the flock,
21:29 these *s* ewe lambs that you have set apart?"
21:30 "The *s* ewe lambs you shall accept from me

SEVEN (cont.)

29:18 *s* years for your younger daughter Rachel."
29:20 So Jacob served *s* years for Rachel,
29:27 for another *s* years of service with me."
29:30 in Laban's service another *s* years.
31:23 he pursued him for *s* days until he caught
33: 3 of them, bowing to the ground *s* times,
41: 2 Nile, when up out of the Nile came *s* cows,
41: 3 Behind them *s* other cows, ugly and gaunt,
41: 4 the ugly, gaunt cows ate up the *s* handsome,
41: 5 He saw *s* ears of grain, fat and healthy,
41: 6 Behind them sprouted *s* ears of grain,
41: 7 the *s* thin ears swallowed up the seven fat,
41:18 Nile, when up from the Nile came *s* cows,
41:19 Behind them came *s* other cows, scrawny,
41:20 ugly cows ate up the first *s* fat cows.
41:22 In another dream I saw *s* ears of grain,
41:23 Behind them sprouted *s* ears of grain,
41:24 *s* thin ears swallowed up the *s* healthy
41:26 The *s* healthy cows are seven years,
41:26 and the *s* healthy ears are seven years
41:27 So also, the *s* thin, ugly cows that came
41:27 cows that came up after them are *s* years,
41:27 them are seven years, as are the *s* thin,
41:27 they are *s* years of famine.
41:29 *S* years of great abundance are now coming
41:30 will be followed by *s* years of famine,
41:34 the land during the *s* years of abundance.
41:36 a reserve for the country against the *s* years
41:47 During the *s* years of plenty,
41:53 When the *s* years of abundance enjoyed by
41:54 to an end, the *s* years of famine set in,
46:25 these she bore to Jacob *s* persons in all.
50:10 observed *s* days of mourning for his father.
Ex 2:16 *s* daughters of a priest of Midian came to
7:25 *S* days passed after the LORD had struck
12:15 For *s* days you must eat unleavened bread.
12:19 For *s* days no leaven may be found in your
13: 6 For *s* days you shall eat unleavened bread,
13: 7 bread may be eaten during the *s* days;
22:29 for *s* days the firstling may stay with its
23:15 you must eat unleavened bread for *s* days
25:37 You shall then make *s* lamps for it and so
29:30 shall be clothed with them for *s* days.
29:35 *S* days you shall spend in ordaining them,
29:37 *S* days you shall spend in making atonement
34:18 For *s* days at the prescribed time in the
37:23 Its *s* lamps, as well as its trimming shears
38:24 talents and *s* hundred and thirty shekels,
38:25 *s* hundred and seventy-five shekels,
38:28 The remaining one thousand *s* hundred and
Lv 4: 6 shall sprinkle it *s* times before the LORD,
4:17 shall sprinkle it *s* times before the LORD,
8:11 some of this oil *s* times on the altar,
8:33 entrance of the meeting tent for *s* days,
8:33 for your ordination is to last for *s* days.
8:35 the meeting tent day and night for *s* days,
12: 2 to a boy, she shall be unclean for *s* days,
13: 4 quarantine the stricken man for *s* days.
13: 5 shall quarantine him for another *s* days,
13:21 the priest shall quarantine him for *s* days.
13:26 the priest shall quarantine him for *s* days.
13:31 the person with scall sore for *s* days,
13:33 shall quarantine him for another *s* days.
13:50 quarantine the infected article for *s* days.
13:54 and then quarantined for another *s* days.
14: 7 and then sprinkle *s* times the man to be
14: 8 still remain outside his tent for *s* days.
14:16 shall sprinkle it *s* times before the LORD.
14:27 sprinkle it *s* times before the LORD.
14:38 him and quarantine the house for *s* days.
14:51 water, and sprinkle the house *s* times.
15:13 he shall wait *s* days for his purification.
15:19 shall be in a state of impurity for *s* days.
15:24 impurity and shall be unclean for *s* days;
15:28 from her affliction, she shall wait *s* days,
16:14 *s* times in front of the propitiatory.
16:19 sprinkle some of the blood on it *s* times.
22:27 it shall remain with its mother for *s* days;
23: 6 For *s* days you shall eat unleavened bread.
23: 8 On each of the *s* days you shall offer an
23:15 sheaf, you shall count *s* full weeks,
23:18 holocaust of *s* unblemished yearling lambs,
23:34 of Booths, which shall continue for *s* days.
23:36 For *s* days you shall offer an oblation to
25: 8 *S* weeks of years shall you count— *s* times *s*
25: 8 the *s* cycles amount to forty-nine years.
26:24 for your sins *s* times harder than before.
Nm 1:39 sixty-two thousand *s* hundred were enrolled
2:26 the census to sixty-two thousand *s* hundred.]
3:22 they numbered *s* thousand five hundred.
4:36 numbered two thousand *s* hundred and fifty.
8: 2 When you set up the *s* lamps,
12:14 would she not hide in shame for *s* days?
12:14 be confined outside the camp for *s* days;
12:15 was confined outside the camp for *s* days,
13:22 been built *s* years before Zoan in Egypt.]
17:14 thousand *s* hundred died from the scourge,
19: 4 blood on his finger and sprinkle it *s* times
19:11 human being shall be unclean for *s* days;
19:14 already in it, shall be unclean for *s* days;
19:16 or a grave, shall be unclean for *s* days.
23: 1 *s* altars, and prepare *s* bullocks and *s*
23: 2 said to him, "I have erected the *s* altars,
23:14 where he built *s* altars and offered a
23:29 then said to him, "Here build me *s* altars;
23:29 prepare for me *s* bullocks and seven rams."
26: 7 *s* hundred and thirty men were registered.
26:34 thousand *s* hundred men were registered.
26:51 These six hundred and one thousand *s*
28:11 one ram, and *s* unblemished yearling lambs,
28:17 For *s* days unleavened bread is to be eaten.
28:19 and *s* yearling lambs that you are sure are
28:21 ram, and one tenth for each of the *s* lambs;
28:24 each day for *s* days as food offerings,
28:27 and *s* yearling lambs that you are sure are
28:29 ram, and one tenth for each of the *s* lambs.
29: 2 one ram, and *s* unblemished yearling lambs,
29: 4 ram, and one tenth for each of the *s* lambs.
29: 8 and *s* yearling lambs that you are sure are
29:10 ram, and one tenth for each of the *s* lambs.
29:12 then, for *s* days following,
29:32 the seventh day you shall offer *s* bullocks,
29:36 one ram, and *s* unblemished yearling lambs,
31:19 you shall stay outside the camp for *s* days,
31:52 thousand *s* hundred and fifty shekels.
Dt 7: 1 *s* nations more numerous and powerful than
16: 3 For *s* days you shall eat with it only
16: 4 be found in all your territory for *s* days,
16: 9 "You shall count off *s* weeks,
16:13 celebrate the feast of Booths for *s* days,
16:15 For *s* days you shall celebrate this
28: 7 direction, they will flee before you in *s*.
28:25 direction, you will flee before them in *s*,
Jos 6: 4 with *s* priests carrying ram's horns ahead
6: 4 seventh day march around the city *s* times,
6: 6 with *s* of the priests carrying ram's horns
6: 8 with the *s* priests who carried the ram's
6:13 The *s* priests bearing the ram's horns
6:15 around the city *s* times in the same manner;
6:15 did they march around the city *s* times.
18: 2 *S* tribes among the Israelites had not yet
18: 5 to me you shall divide it into *s* parts.
18: 6 the description of the land in *s* sections.
18: 9 listed its cities in writing in *s* sections
Jgs 6: 1 them into the power of Midian for *s* years,
12: 9 After having judged Israel for *s* years,
14:12 If within the *s* days of the feast you
14:17 him during the *s* days the feast lasted.
16: 7 *s* fresh bowstrings which have not dried,"
16: 8 her *s* fresh bowstrings which had not dried,
16:13 "If you weave my *s* locks of hair into the
16:14 wove his *s* locks of hair into the web,
16:19 a man who shaved off his *s* locks of hair.
20:16 *s* hundred picked men who were left-handed,
Ru 4:15 She is worth more to you than *s* sons!"
1Sm 2: 5 The barren wife bears *s* sons,
6: 1 been in the land of the Philistines *s* months
10: 8 Wait *s* days until I come to you;
11: 3 "Give us *s* days to send messengers
13: 8 He waited *s* days—the time Samuel had
16:10 way Jesse presented *s* sons before Samuel,
31:13 tree in Jabesh, and fasted for *s* days.
2Sm 2:11 David spent *s* years and six months in
5: 5 *s* years and six months in Hebron over Judah,
8: 4 David captured from him one thousand *s*
10:18 and David's men killed *s* hundred
21: 6 let *s* men from among his descendants be
21: 9 The *s* fell at the one time;
1Kgs 2:11 he reigned *s* years in Hebron and
6: 6 six cubits wide, the third *s* cubits wide,
6:38 Thus it took Solomon *s* years to build it.
8:65 before the LORD, our God, for *s* days.
11: 3 He had *s* hundred wives of princely rank
16:15 of Judah, Zimri reigned *s* days in Tirzah.
18:43 *S* times he said, "Go look again!"
19:18 Yet I will leave *s* thousand men in Israel
20:15 soldiery, who numbered *s* thousand.
20:29 encamped opposite each other for *s* days.
2Kgs 3: 9 After their roundabout journey of *s* days
3:26 the king of Moab took *s* hundred swordsmen
4:35 now sneezed *s* times and opened his eyes.
5:10 "Go and wash *s* times in the Jordan,
5:14 *s* times at the word of the man of God.
8: 2 in the land of the Philistines for *s* years.
8: 3 At the end of the *s* years, the woman
12: 1 Joash was *s* years old when he became king.
24:16 to Babylon all *s* thousand men of the army,
1Chr 3: 4 where he reigned *s* years and six months.
3:24 Akkub, Johanan, Delaiah, and Anani *s*.
5:13 Sheba, Jorai, Jacan, Zia, and Eber *s*.
5:18 forty-four thousand *s* hundred and sixty
9:13 were one thousand *s* hundred and sixty,
10:12 under the oak of Jabesh, and fasted *s* days.
12:26 *s* thousand one hundred.
12:28 with another three thousand *s* hundred,
15:26 *s* bulls and seven rams were sacrificed.
18: 4 thousand chariots, and *s* thousand horsemen.
19:18 and David slew *s* thousand of their chariot
26:30 one thousand *s* hundred police officers,
26:32 two thousand *s* hundred heads of families.
29: 4 and *s* thousand talents of refined silver,
29:27 in Hebron he reigned *s* years,
2Chr 7: 8 Egypt, celebrated the festival for *s* days.
7: 9 for seven days and the feast for *s* days.
13: 9 and *s* rams becomes a priest of no-gods.
15:11 *s* hundred oxen and seven thousand sheep
17:11 flock of *s* thousand *s* hundred rams
17:11 rams and seven thousand *s* hundred he-goats.
24: 1 Joash was *s* years old when he became king,
26:13 mighty army of three hundred *s* thousand
29:21 *S* bulls, seven rams, seven lambs
29:21 seven he-goats were brought for a sin
30:21 Bread with great rejoicing for *s* days,
30:22 they had completed the *s* days of festival,
30:23 agreed to celebrate another *s* days.
30:23 they continued the festivity *s* days longer.
30:24 bulls and *s* thousand sheep to the assembly,
35:17 feast of the Unleavened Bread for *s* days.
Ezr 2: 5 sons of Arah, *s* hundred and seventy-five;
2: 9 sons of Zaccai, *s* hundred and sixty;
2:25 and Beeroth, *s* hundred and forty-three;
2:33 Hadid, and Ono, *s* hundred and twenty-five;
2:65 *s* thousand three hundred and thirty-seven.
2:66 Their horses were *s* hundred and thirty-six,
2:67 asses six thousand *s* hundred and twenty.
6:22 the feast of Unleavened Bread for *s* days,
7:14 You are the envoy from the king and his *s*
Neh 7:14 sons of Zaccai, *s* hundred and sixty;
7:29 and Beeroth, *s* hundred and forty-three;
7:37 Hadid, and Ono, *s* hundred and twenty-one;
7:67 *s* thousand three hundred and thirty-seven.
7:67 Their horses were *s* hundred and thirty-six,
7:68 asses six thousand *s* hundred and twenty.
8:18 They kept the feast for *s* days,
Tb 3: 8 For she had been married to *s* husbands,
3: 8 You have already been married *s* times,
3:15 I have already lost *s* husbands;
6:14 woman has already been married *s* times,
7:11 I have given her in marriage to *s* men,
11:18 Tobiah's wedding feast for *s* happy days,
12:15 one of the *s* angels who enter and serve
14: 3 called his son Tobiah and Tobiah's *s* sons,
Jdt 16:24 the house of Israel mourned her for *s* days.
Est 1: 5 king gave a feast of *s* days in the garden
1:10 the *s* eunuchs who attended King Ahasuerus,
1:14 the *s* Persian and Median officials who
2: 9 out *s* maids for her from the royal palace,
1Mc 3:39 forty thousand men and *s* thousand cavalry
13:28 He set up *s* pyramids facing one another
2Mc 7: 1 It also happened that *s* brothers with
7:20 who saw her *s* sons perish in a single day,
Jb 1: 2 *S* sons and three daughters were born to him;
1: 3 and he had *s* thousand sheep,
2:13 ground with him seven days and *s* nights,
42: 8 therefore, take seven bullocks and *s* rams,
42:13 And he had *s* sons and three daughters,
Prv 6:16 hates, yes, *s* are an abomination to him;
9: 1 her house, she has set up her *s* columns;
24:16 the just man falls *s* times and rises again,
26:16 than *s* men who answer with good sense.
26:25 not, for *s* abominations are in his heart.
Eccl 11: 2 Make *s* or eight portions;
Sir 20:11 for little, but pay for it *s* times over.
20:13 for in his eyes his one gift is equal to *s*.
22:11 *S* days of mourning for the dead,
37:14 better than *s* watchmen in a lofty tower.
40: 8 with beast, but for sinners *s* times more.
Is 4: 1 *S* women will take hold of one man on that
11:15 anger And shatter it into *s* streamlets,
30:26 the light of the sun will be *s* times greater
30:26 times greater [like the light of *s* days].
Jer 15: 9 The mother of *s* swoons away,
52:25 and *s* men in the personal service of the
52:30 *s* hundred and forty-five people of Judah:
Bar 6: 2 many years, a period *s* generations long;
Ez 3:15 and for *s* days I sat among them distraught.
3:16 At the end of *s* days. . . .
39: 9 *s* years they shall make fires with them.
39:12 of Israel shall need *s* months to bury them.
39:14 For *s* months they shall keep searching.
40:22 *S* steps led up to it, and its vestibule
40:26 It was ascended by *s* steps;
41: 3 either side of it extended *s* cubits each.
43:25 Daily for *s* days you shall offer a he-goat
43:26 unblemished, shall be offered for *s* days.
44:26 he must wait an additional *s* days,
45:21 for *s* days unleavened bread is to be eaten.
45:23 On each of the *s* days of the feast he
45:23 seven bulls and *s* rams without blemish,
45:25 month, the feast day, and for *s* days,
Dn 3:19 He ordered the furnace to be heated *s*
4:13 of a beast, till *s* years pass over him.
4:20 wild beasts till *s* years pass over him'
4:22 *s* years shall pass over you,
4:29 an ox, and *s* years shall pass over you,
9:25 and a leader, there shall be *s* weeks.
14:32 In the den were *s* lions, and two carcasses
Mi 5: 4 We shall raise against it *s* shepherds,
Zec 3: 9 before Joshua, one stone with *s* facets.
4: 2 "on it are *s* lamps with their tubes,
4:10 These *s* facets are the eyes of the LORD
Mt 12:45 this time *s* spirits more evil than itself.
15:34 *S*," they replied, "and a few small fish."
15:36 He took the *s* loaves and the fish,
15:37 left over, these filled *s* hampers.
16:10 Or the *s* loaves among four thousand and
18:21 how often must I forgive him? *S* times?"
18:22 not *s* times; I say, seventy times *s* times.

22:25 Once there were *s* brothers.
22:28 she be, since all *s* of them married her?"
Mk 8: 5 *S,*" they replied.
8: 6 Taking the *s* loaves he gave thanks,
8: 8 gathered up *s* wicker baskets of leftovers.
8:20 I broke the *s* loaves for the four thousand,
8:20 did you collect?" They answered, *S.*"
12:20 There were these *s* brothers.
12:22 none of the *s* left any children behind.
12:23 All *s* married her."
16: 9 out of whom he had cast *s* demons.
Lk 2:36 having lived *s* years with her husband
8: 2 Magdalene, from whom *s* devils had gone out,
11:26 with *s* other spirits far worse than itself,
17: 4 sins against you *s* times a day, and *s* times
17: 4 and *s* times a day turns back to you saying,
20:29 Now there were *s* brothers.
20:31 *s* died without leaving her any children.
20:33 Remember, *s* married her."
24:13 Emmaus *s* miles distant from Jerusalem,
Acts 6: 3 for *s* men acknowledged to be deeply
13:19 then he destroyed *s* nations in the land of
19:14 Another time, when the *s* sons of Sceva,
21: 8 of Philip the evangelist, one of the *S,*
Rom 11: 4 "I have left for myself *s* thousand men
Heb 11:30 fell after being encircled for *s* days.
2Pt 2: 5 as a preacher of holiness, with *s* others,
Rv 1: 4 To the *s* churches in the province of Asia;
1: 4 and from the *s* spirits before his throne,
1:11 you now see and send it to the *s* churches:
1:12 When I did so I saw *s* lampstands of gold,
1:16 In his right hand he held *s* stars.
1:20 of the *s* stars you saw in my right hand,
1:20 hand, and of the *s* lampstands of gold:
1:20 the *s* stars are the presiding spirits of
1:20 the presiding spirits of the *s* churches,
1:20 the seven lampstands are the *s* churches.
2: 1 "The One who holds the *s* stars in his
2: 1 the *s* lampstands of gold has this to say:
3: 1 the seven spirits of God, the *s* stars,
4: 5 *s* flaming torches, the *s* spirits of God.
5: 1 on both sides and was sealed with *s* seals.
5: 5 to open the scroll with the *s* seals."
5: 6 He had *s* horns and *s* eyes; these eyes are the *s*
6: 1 Lamb broke open the first of the *s* seals,
8: 2 the *s* angels who minister in God's
8: 2 in God's presence were given *s* trumpets.
8: 6 The *s* angels with the seven trumpets made
10: 3 the *s* thunders raised their voices too.
10: 4 to start writing when the *s* thunders spoke,
10: 4 "Seal up what the *s* thunders have spoken
11:13 *S* thousand persons were killed during the
12: 3 flaming red, with *s* heads and ten horns;
12: 3 on his heads were *s* diadems.
13: 1 out of the sea with ten horns and *s* heads;
15: 1 *s* angels holding the seven final plagues
15: 6 the *s* angels holding the seven plagues.
15: 6 the seven angels holding the *s* plagues.
15: 7 *s* angels *s* golden bowls filled with the wrath
15: 8 *s* plagues of the *s* angels had come to an end.
16: 1 from the sanctuary say to the *s* angels,
16: 1 upon the earth the *s* bowls of God's wrath!"
17: 1 Then one of the *s* angels who were holding
17: 1 holding the *s* bowls came to me and said:
17: 3 This beast had *s* heads and ten horns.
17: 9 The *s* heads are seven hills on which the
17: 9 They are also *s* kings:
17:11 one of the *s* and is on its way to ruin.
21: 9 One of the seven angels who held the *s*
21: 9 the *s* last plagues came and said to me,

SEVEN-DAY (2)

1Chr 9:25 took turns in assisting them for *s* periods,
Acts 21:27 The *s* period was nearing completion when

SEVEN-HEADED (1)

Rv 17: 7 the *s* and ten-horned beast carrying her.

SEVEN-YEAR (3)

Dt 15: 1 "At the end of every *s* period you shall
31:10 which comes at the end of every *s* period,
2Kgs 8: 1 a *s* famine which is coming upon the land."

SEVEN-YEAR-OLD (1)

Jgs 6:25 "Take the *s* spare bullock and destroy

SEVENFOLD (10)

Gn 4:15 anyone kills Cain, Cain shall be avenged *s.*"
4:24 If Cain is avenged *s,* then Lamech
Lv 26:18 increase the chastisement for your sins *s,*
26:21 me, I will multiply my blows another *s,*
26:28 with *s* fiercer punishment for your sins,
Ps(s) 12: 7 tried silver, freed from dross, *s* refined.
79:12 And repay our neighbors *s* into their
Prv 6:31 Yet if he be caught he must pay back *s;*
Sir 7: 3 furrows of injustice, lest you harvest it *s.*
35:10 repays, and he will give back to you *s.*

SEVENTEEN (10)

Gn 37: 2 When Joseph was *s* years old, he was
47:28 lived in the land of Egypt for *s* years;
Jgs 8:26 requested weighed *s* hundred gold shekels,
1Kgs 14:21 king, and he reigned *s* years in Jerusalem,
1Chr 7:11 They numbered *s* thousand two hundred men
2Chr 12:13 king, and he reigned *s* years in Jerusalem,
Ezr 2:39 sons of Harim, one thousand and *s.*
Neh 7:42 sons of Harim, one thousand and *s.*
Tb 14:14 at the venerable age of a hundred and *s.*
Jer 32: 9 paying him the money, *s* silver shekels.

SEVENTEEN-YEAR (1)

2Kgs 13: 1 began his *s* reign over Israel in Samaria.

SEVENTEENTH (7)

Gn 7:11 second month, on the *s* day of the month:
8: 4 seventh month, on the *s* day of the month,
1Kgs 22:52 in Samaria in the *s* year of Jehoshaphat,
2Kgs 16: 1 In the *s* year of Pekah, son of Remaliah,
1Chr 24:15 the sixteenth to Immer, the *s* to Hezir,
25:24 The *s* fell to Joshbekashah, his sons,
Jdt 1:13 In the *s* year he proceeded with his army

SEVENTH (120)

Gn 2: 2 Since on the *s* day God was finished with
2: 2 *s* day from all the work he had undertaken.
2: 3 So God blessed the *s* day and made it holy,
8: 4 had so diminished that, in the *s* month,
Ex 12:15 day to the *s* shall be cut off from Israel.
12:16 a sacred assembly, and likewise on the *s.*
13: 6 *s* day shall also be a festival to the LORD.
16:26 days you can gather it, but on the *s* day,
16:27 on the *s* day some of the people went out
16:29 On the *s* day everyone is to stay home and
16:30 After that the people rested on the *s* day.
20:10 but the *s* day is the sabbath of the LORD,
20:11 but on the *s* day he rested.
21: 2 but in the *s* year he shall be given his
23:11 But the *s* year you shall let the land lie
23:12 your work, but on the *s* day you must rest,
24:16 and on the *s* day he called to Moses from
31:15 the *s* day is the sabbath of complete rest,
31:17 but on the *s* day he rested at his ease."
34:21 may work, but on the *s* day you shall rest;
35: 2 but the *s* day shall be sacred to you as
Lv 13: 5 *s* day the priest shall again examine him.
13: 6 and once more examine him on the *s* day.
13:27 the priest, when examining it on the *s* day,
13:32 and on the *s* day again examine the sore.
13:34 when examining the scall on the *s* day,
13:51 "On the *s* day the priest shall again
14: 9 On the *s* day he shall again shave off all
14:39 On the *s* day the priest shall return to
16:29 tenth day of the *s* month everyone of you,
23: 3 but the *s* day is the sabbath rest,
23: 8 Then on the *s* day you shall again hold a
23:16 and then on the day after the *s* week,
23:24 the *s* month you shall keep a sabbath rest,
23:27 of this *s* month is the Day of Atonement,
23:34 this *s* month is the LORD's feast of Booths,
23:39 the fifteenth day, then, of the *s* month,
23:41 one whole week in the *s* month of the year.
25: 4 *s* year the land shall have complete rest,
25: 9 day of the *s* month let the trumpet resound;
25:20 not say, 'What shall we eat in the *s* year,
Nm 6: 9 of his purification, that is, on the *s* day.
7:48 On the *s* day it was the turn of Elishama,
19:12 the water on the third and on the *s* day,
19:12 himself on the third and on the *s* day,
19:19 on the *s* day; thus purified on the seventh
28:25 the *s* day you shall hold a sacred assembly,
29: 1 *s* month you shall hold a sacred assembly,
29: 7 *s* month you shall hold a sacred assembly,
29:12 *s* month you shall hold a sacred assembly,
29:32 the *s* day you shall offer seven bullocks,
31:19 yourselves on the third and on the *s* day.
31:24 On the *s* day you shall wash your clothes,
Dt 5:14 but the *s* day is the sabbath of the LORD,
15: 9 the mean thought that the *s* year,
15:12 but in the *s* year you shall dismiss him
16: 8 and on the *s* there shall be a solemn
Jos 6: 4 *s* day march around the city seven times,
6:15 On the *s* day, beginning at day-break,
6:16 The *s* time around, the priests blew
19:40 The *s* lot fell to the clans of the tribe
Jgs 14:17 On the *s* day, since she importuned him,
14:18 On the *s* day, before the sun set, the men
2Sm 12:18 On the *s* day, the child died.
1Kgs 8: 2 in the month of Ethanim (the *s* month).
18:44 And the *s* time the youth reported,
20:29 On the *s* day battle was joined,
2Kgs 11: 4 But in the *s* year, Jehoiada summoned
12: 2 Joash began to reign in the *s* year of Jehu,
18: 9 Hezekiah, which was the *s* year of Hoshea,
25: 8 On the *s* day of the fifth month (this was
25:25 But in the *s* month Ishmael,
1Chr 2:15 fifth, Ozem, the sixth, and David, the *s.*
12:12 Jeremiah fifth, Attai sixth, Eliel *s,*
24:10 the sixth to Mijamin, the *s* to Hakkoz,
25:14 The *s* was Jesarelah, his sons, and his
26: 3 Jehohanan, the sixth, Eliehoenai, the *s.*
26: 5 fifth, Ammiel, the sixth, Issachar, the *s,*
27:10 *S,* for the seventh month, was Hellez,
2Chr 5: 3 king during the festival of the *s* month.
7:10 On the twenty-third day of the *s* month he
23: 1 In the *s* year, Jehoiada took courage
31: 7 and they completed them in the *s* month.
Ezr 3: 1 Now when the *s* month came,
3: 6 From the first day of the *s* month they
7: 7 Jerusalem in the *s* year of King Artaxerxes.
7: 8 the fifth month of that *s* year of the king.
Neh 8: 1 Now when the *s* month came,
8: 2 On the first day of the *s* month,
8:14 in booths during the feast of the *s* month;
10:32 We will forgo the *s* year,
Est 1:10 On the *s* day, when the king was merry
2:16 month, Tebeth, in the *s* year of his reign.
1Mc 6:53 the storerooms, because it was the *s* year,
10:21 put on the sacred vestments in the *s* month
Jb 5:19 you, and at the *s* no evil shall touch you.
Jer 28:17 That same year, in the *s* month,
34:14 Every *s* year each of you shall set free
41: 1 In the *s* month Ishmael,
52:28 in his *s* year, three thousand
Bar 1: 2 the fifth year [on the *s* day of the month,
Ez 20: 1 In the *s* year, on the tenth day
30:20 On the *s* day of the first month in the
45:20 of the *s* month for those who have sinned
45:25 On the fifteenth day of the *s* month,
Dn 14:40 *s* day the king came to mourn for Daniel.
Hg 2: 1 on the twenty-first day of the *s* month,
Zec 7: 5 and in the *s* month these seventy years,
8:19 fast days of the fourth, the fifth, the *s,*
Mt 22:26 the third, and so on, down to the *s.*
Heb 4: 4 to the *s* day Scripture somewhere says,
4: 4 rested from all his work on the *s* day";
Jude 1:14 of the *s* generation descended from Adam,
Rv 8: 1 When the Lamb broke open the *s* seal,
10: 7 comes for the *s* angel to blow his trumpet,
11:15 Then the *s* angel blew his trumpet.
16:17 the *s* angel poured out his bowl upon the
21:20 the sixth carnelian, the *s* chrysolite,

SEVENTY (72)

Gn 5:12 When Kenan was *s* years old,
11:26 When Terah was *s* years old,
46:27 come to Egypt amounted to *s* persons in all.
50: 3 and the Egyptians mourned him for *s* days.
Ex 1: 5 of the direct descendants of Jacob was *s.*
15:27 twelve springs of water and *s* palm trees,
24: 1 Abihu, and *s* of the elders of Israel.
24: 9 Nadab, Abihu, and *s* elders of Israel,
38:29 amounted to *s* talents and two thousand
Nm 7:13 and one silver basin weighing *s* shekels,
7:19 and one silver basin weighing *s* shekels,
7:25 and one silver basin weighing *s* shekels,
7:31 and one silver basin weighing *s* shekels,
7:37 and one silver basin weighing *s* shekels,
7:43 and one silver basin weighing *s* shekels,
7:49 and one silver basin weighing *s* shekels,
7:55 and one silver basin weighing *s* shekels,
7:61 and one silver basin weighing *s* shekels,
7:67 and one silver basin weighing *s* shekels,
7:73 and one silver basin weighing *s* shekels,
7:79 and one silver basin weighing *s* shekels,
7:85 thirty shekels, and each silver basin *s,*
11:16 "Assemble for me *s* of the elders of Israel,
11:24 Gathering *s* elders of the people,
11:25 on Moses, he bestowed it on the *s* elders;
33: 9 twelve springs of water and *s* palm trees,
Dt 10:22 Your ancestors went down to Egypt *s* strong,
Jgs 1: 7 At this Adonibezek said, *S* kings,
8:30 Now Gideon had *s* sons,
9: 2 that *s* men, or all Jerubbaal's sons, rule
9: 4 They also gave him *s* silver shekels from
9: 5 slew his brothers, the *s* sons of Jerubbaal,
9:18 and have killed his *s* sons upon one stone,
9:24 violence done to the *s* sons of Jerubbaal
9:56 to his father in killing his *s* brothers.
12:14 grandsons who rode on *s* saddle-asses.
1Sm 6:19 the LORD, and *s* of them were struck down.
11: 8 Israelites and *s* thousand Judahites.
2Sm 24:15 and *s* thousand of the people from Dan to
1Kgs 5:29 Solomon had *s* thousand carriers and eighty
2Kgs 10: 1 Ahab had *s* descendants in Samaria.
10: 6 [The *s* princes were in the care of
10: 7 took the princes and slew all *s* of them,
1Chr 21: 5 and in Judah four hundred and *s* thousand.
21:14 Israel, and *s* thousand men of Israel died.
2Chr 2: 1 He conscripted *s* thousand men to carry
2:17 Of these he made *s* thousand carriers and
29:32 the assembly brought forward was *s* oxen,
36:21 have rest while *s* years are fulfilled."
Ezr 8: 7 son of Athalaiah, and with him *s* males;
8:14 Uthai, son of Zakkur, and with him *s* males.
Jdt 1: 2 the wall *s* cubits high and fifty thick.
1: 4 gateway he built to a height of *s* cubits,
7: 2 Their forces numbered a hundred and *s*
1Mc 13:41 Thus in the year one hundred and *s,*
2Mc 10:20 on receiving *s* thousand drachmas,
Ps(s) 90:10 *S* is the sum of our years, or eighty, if we
Is 23:15 day, Tyre shall be forgotten for *s* years.
23:15 of another king, at the end of *s* years,
23:17 of the *s* years the LORD shall visit Tyre.

SEVENTY (cont.)

Jer 25:11 *S* years these nations shall be enslaved to
25:12 but when the *s* years have elapsed,
29:10 Only after *s* years have elapsed for
Ez 8:11 *s* of the elders of the house of Israel,
41:12 the west side was *s* cubits front to back;
Dn 9: 2 of Jerusalem *s* years must be fulfilled.
9:24 *S* weeks are decreed for your people and
14:10 There were *s* priests of Bel,
Zec 1:12 that have felt your anger these *s* years?"
7: 5 and in the seventh month these *s* years,
Mt 18:22 I say, *s* times seven times.
Acts 23:23 with two hundred infantrymen, *s* cavalrymen,

SEVENTY-FIVE (11)

Gn 12: 4 Abram was *s* years old when he left Haran.
25: 7 Abraham's life was one hundred and *s* years.
Ex 38:25 one thousand seven hundred and *s* shekels,
38:28 thousand seven hundred and *s* shekels were
Nm 31:32 to six hundred and *s* thousand sheep,
31:37 six hundred and *s* fell as tax to the LORD;
Ezr 2: 5 sons of Arah, seven hundred and *s;*
Est 9:16 They killed *s* thousand of their foes,
2Mc 12:29 on to Scythopolis, *s* miles from Jerusalem.
13: 5 There is at that place a tower *s* feet high,
Acts 7:14 and all his kinsfolk— *s* persons in all.

SEVENTY-FOUR (5)

Nm 1:27 *s* thousand six hundred were enrolled in
2: 4 in the census to *s* thousand six hundred.]
Ezr 2:40 Jeshua, Kadmiel, Binnui, and Hodaviah, *s.*
Neh 7:43 of Jeshua, Kadmiel, Binnui, Hodeviah, *s.*
1Mc 15:10 In the year one hundred and *s* Antiochus

SEVENTY-ONE (1)

1Mc 13:51 month, in the year one hundred and *s,*

SEVENTY-SEVEN (4)

Gn 5:31 of Lamech was seven hundred and *s* years;
Jgs 8:14 him the *s* princes and elders of Succoth.
Ezr 8:35 for all Israel, ninety-six rams, *s* lambs,
1Mc 16:14 to Jericho in the year one hundred and *s,*

SEVENTY-SEVENFOLD (1)

Gn 4:24 Cain is avenged sevenfold, then Lamech *s.*"

SEVENTY-SIX (2)

Nm 26:22 of whom *s* thousand five hundred men were
Acts 27:37 were two hundred and *s* of us on board.)

SEVENTY-THREE (4)

Nm 3:43 twenty-two thousand two hundred and *s.*
3:46 As ransom for the two hundred and *s*
Ezr 2:36 the house of Jeshua, nine hundred and *s;*
Neh 7:39 the house of Jeshua, nine hundred and *s;*

SEVENTY-TWO (11)

Nm 31:33 thousand sheep, *s* thousand oxen,
31:38 oxen, of which *s* fell as tax to the LORD;
Ezr 2: 3 of Parosh, two thousand one hundred and *s;*
2: 4 sons of Shephatiah, three hundred and *s;*
Neh 7: 8 of Parosh, two thousand one hundred and *s;*
7: 9 sons of Shephatiah, three hundred and *s;*
11:19 one hundred and *s* in number.
1Mc 14: 1 In the year one hundred and *s,*
14:27 of Elul, in the year one hundred and *s,*
Lk 10: 1 the Lord appointed a further *s* and sent
10:17 The *s* returned in jubilation saying,

SEVER (5)

Lv 3: 4 liver, which he shall *s* above the kidneys.
3: 9 tail, which he must *s* close to the spine,
3:10 liver, which he must *s* above the kidneys.
3:15 liver, which he must *s* above the kidneys.
4: 9 liver, which he must *s* above the kidneys.

SEVERAL (12)

Lv 15:25 for *s* days outside her menstrual period,
1Kgs 6: 5 sanctuary, an annex of *s* stories was built.
2Kgs 6:10 This happened *s* times.
Neh 1: 4 to weep and continued mourning for *s* days;
Tb 1:14 I also deposited *s* pouches containing a
Wis 15: 7 molds for our service each *s* article:
19: 6 For all creation, in its *s* kinds,
Mt 14:24 already *s* hundred yards out from shore,
Mk 2: 1 back to Capernaum after a lapse of *s* days
Acts 16:18 *s* days until finally Paul became annoyed,
24:17 "After *s* years' absence, I had come
25:14 Since they were to spend *s* days there,

SEVERE (28)

Gn 12:10 there, since the famine in the land was *s.*
12:17 *s* plagues because of Abram's wife Sarai.
35:17 When her pangs were most *s,*
41:31 so utterly *s* will that famine be.
43: 1 Now the famine in the land grew more *s.*
47: 4 of Canaan, so *s* has the famine been there.
Ex 9: 3 and flocks—with a very *s* pestilence.
Dt 28:59 your descendants with *s* and constant blows,
Jgs 11:33 so that he inflicted a *s* defeat on them,
1Sm 7:13 was *s* with them as long as Samuel lived.
23: 5 cattle and inflicted a *s* defeat on them,
1Kgs 17:17 grew more *s* until he stopped breathing.
20:21 chariots, and inflicted a *s* defeat on Aram.
2Kgs 6:25 the siege the famine in Samaria was so *s*
2Chr 13:17 his people inflicted a *s* defeat upon them;
21:15 have *s* pains from a disease in your bowels,
1Mc 8: 4 earth and had inflicted on them *s* defeat,
Jb 2: 7 smote Job with *s* boils from the soles
Prv 15:10 *S* punishment is in store for the man who
Lk 4:38 mother-in-law was in the grip of a *s* fever,
10:12 will be less *s* than that of such a town.
12:47 to fulfill them will get a *s* beating,
Acts 11:28 going to be a *s* famine all over the world.
16:26 a *s* earthquake suddenly shook the place,
2Cor 8: 2 In the midst of *s* trial their overflowing
10:10 His letters, they say, are *s* and forceful,
Rv 16: 2 *s* and festering boils broke out on the men
16:21 hailstones, because this plague was so *s.*

SEVERED (7)

Lv 7: 4 liver, which must be *s* above the kidneys.
Jgs 16: 9 a thread of tow is *s* by a whiff of flame;
Ps(s) 129: 4 just LORD has *s* the cords of the wicked.
Is 33:20 never be pulled up, nor any of its ropes *s.*
Jer 10:20 My tent is ruined, all its cords are *s.*
Jn 18:26 relative of the man whose ear Peter had *s.*
Gal 5: 4 in the law have *s* yourselves from Christ

SEVERELY (12)

1Sm 5: 6 the LORD dealt *s* with the people of Ashdod.
5: 7 for he is handling us and our god Dagon *s.*"
12:15 LORD will deal *s* with you and your king,
Neh 5: 7 I then rebuked them *s,* saying to them:
Est C:13 She afflicted her body *s;*
2Mc 6:15 to punish us more *s*
Jb 42: 8 prayer I will accept, not to punish you *s.*
Ps(s) 38: 9 I am numbed and *s* crushed;
Is 19:22 Although the LORD shall smite Egypt *s,*
64:11 Can you remain silent, and afflict us so *s?*
Mt 24:51 He will punish him *s* and settle with him
Lk 12:46 He will punish him *s* and rank him among

SEVEREST (1)

Mk 12:40 it is they who will receive the *s* sentence."

SEVERING (1)

Jn 18:10 slave of the high priest, *s* his right ear.

SEVERITY (5)

Gn 47:13 because of the extreme *s* of the famine,
Dt 25: 3 disgraced because of the *s* of the beating.
Rom 11:22 severity of God *s* toward those who fell,
2Cor 13:10 I may not have to exercise with *s* the

SEVERS (2)

Is 9:13 So the LORD *s* from Israel head and tail,
38:12 life, like a weaver who *s* the last thread.

SEW (3)

Ex 26: 9 *S* five of the sheets, edge to edge, into
Eccl 3: 7 A time to rend, and a time to *s;*
Ez 13:18 Woe to those who *s* bands for everyone's

SEWED (4)

Gn 3: 7 so they *s* fig leaves together and made
Ex 26: 3 Five of the sheets are to be *s* together,
36:10 Five of the sheets were *s* together,
36:16 sheets were *s* edge to edge into one set;

SEWS (2)

Mt 9:16 Nobody *s* a piece of unshrunken cloth on an
Mk 2:21 No one *s* a patch of unshrunken cloth on an

SEX (3)

Ex 13:15 of the male *s* that opens the womb,
Mt 19:12 renounced *s* for the sake of God's reign.
1Pt 3: 7 Treat women with respect as the weaker *s,*

SEXUAL (10)

Gn 18:12 is so old, am I still to have *s* pleasure?"
Lv 18: 6 relative to have *s* intercourse with her.
20:18 If a man lies in *s* intercourse with a
Mt 19:12 men are incapable of *s* activity from birth;
Acts 15:20 by idols, from illicit *s* union,
15:29 animals, and from illicit *s* union.
21:25 of strangled animals, and illicit *s* union."
Rom 13:13 and drunkenness, not in *s* excess and lust,
1Tm 1:10 murderers, fornicators, *s* perverts,
Jude 1: 4 our God to *s* excess and deny Jesus Christ,

SHAALABBIN (1)

Jos 19:42 territory of Zorah, Eshtaol, Irshemesh, *S,*

SHAALBIM (2)

Jgs 1:35 a firm hold in Har-heres, Aijalon and *S,*
1Kgs 4: 9 the son of Deker in Makaz, *S,*

SHAALBON (2)

2Sm 23:32 Eliahba from *S;*
1Chr 11:33 Eliahba, from *S;*

SHAALIM (1)

1Sm 9: 4 through the land of *S* without success.

SHAAPH (2)

1Chr 2:47 Regem, Jotham, Geshan, Pelet, Ephah, and *S.*
2:49 She also bore *S,*

SHAARAIM (3)

Jos 15:36 Enam, Jarmuth, Adullam, Socoh, Azekah, *S,*
1Sm 17:52 the road from *S* as far as Gath and Ekron.
1Chr 4:31 Hazar-susim, Bethbiri, and *S.*

SHAASHGAZ (1)

Est 2:14 harem under the care of the royal eunuch *S,*

SHABBETHAI (3)

Ezr 10:15 Meshullam and *S* the Levite supporting them.
Neh 8: 7 Jeshua, Bani, Sherebiah, Jamin, Akkub, *S,*
11:16 *S* and Jozabad, levitical chiefs who were

SHABBY (2)

Jos 9: 5 wore old, patched sandals and *s* garments;
Jas 2: 2 at the same time a poor man in *s* clothes.

SHACKLED (2)

2Chr 33:11 Manasseh with hooks, *s* him with chains,
Wis 17: 2 enslave the holy nation, *s* with darkness,

SHACKLES (1)

Lk 13:16 been released from her *s* on the sabbath?"

SHADE (18)

Jb 7: 2 He is a slave who longs for the *s,*
40:22 lotus trees cover him with their *s;*
Ps(s) 121: 5 the LORD is your *s;*
Sir 34:16 from the heat, a *s* from the noonday sun,
Is 4: 6 *s* from the parching heat of day,
25: 4 Shelter from the rain, *s* from the heat.
32: 2 the *s* of a great rock in a parched land.
Ez 17:23 every winged thing in the *s* of its boughs.
31: 6 its *s* dwelt numerous peoples of every race.
31:12 peoples of the land withdrew from its *s,*
31:17 in his *s* are dispersed among the nations.
Dn 4: 9 Under it the wild beasts found *s,*
4:11 let the beasts flee its *s,* and the birds its
Hos 4:13 and terebinth, because of their pleasant *s.*
14: 8 they shall dwell in his *s* and raise grain;
Jon 4: 5 himself a hut and waited under it in the *s,*
4: 6 *s* that relieved him of any discomfort,
Mk 4:32 birds of the sky to build nests in its *s.*"

SHADES (8)

Jb 26: 5 The *s* beneath writhe in terror,
Ps(s) 88:11 Will the *s* arise to give you thanks?
Prv 2:18 to death, and her footsteps lead to the *s;*
9:18 Little he knows that the *s* are there,
21:16 sense will abide in the assembly of the *s.*
Is 14: 9 It awakens the *s* to greet you,
26:14 they have no life, *s* that cannot rise;
26:19 of light, and the land of *s* gives birth.

SHADING (1)

Jer 4:30 with gold, *S* your eyes with cosmetics,

SHADOW (39)

Jgs 9:15 good faith, come and take refuge in my *s.*
9:36 him, "You see the *s* of the hills as men."
2Kgs 20: 9 Shall the *s* go forward or back ten steps?"
20:10 is easy for the *s* to advance ten steps,"
20:11 who made the *s* retreat the ten steps it
1Chr 29:15 on earth is like a *s* that does not abide.
Jb 8: 9 because our days on earth are but a *s),*
14: 2 fades, swift as a *s* that does not abide.
15:29 with no *s* to lengthen over the ground.
17: 7 and all my frame is shrunken to a *s.*
Ps(s) 17: 8 hide me in the *s* of your wings
36: 8 of men take refuge in the *s* of your wings.
57: 2 In the *s* of your wings I take refuge,
63: 8 and in the *s* of your wings I shout for joy.
80:11 The mountains were hidden in its *s;*
91: 1 High, who abide in the *s* of the Almighty,
102:12 My days are like a lengthening *s,*
109:23 Like a lengthening *s* I pass away;
144: 4 like a breath; his days, like a passing *s.*
Eccl 6:12 vain life (which God has made like a *s)?*
Sg 2: 3 I delight to rest in his *s,* and his fruit
Wis 2: 5 For our lifetime is the passing of a *s;*
5: 9 passed like a *s* and like a fleeting rumor;

Sir 29:22 Better a poor man's fare under the *s* of
Is 16: 3 at high noon let your *s* be like the night,
30: 2 protection and take refuge in Egypt's *s*;
30: 3 and refuge in Egypt's *s* your disgrace.
34:15 hatch them out and gather them in her *s*;
38: 8 I will make the *s* cast by the sun on the
49: 2 sword and concealed me in the *s* of his arm.
51:16 mouth and shielded you in the *s* of my hand,
Jer 48:45 *s* stop short the exhausted refugees;
Lam 4:20 He in whose *s* we thought we could live on
Bar 1:12 under the protective *s* of Nebuchadnezzar,
Lk 1:79 who sit in darkness and in the *s* of death,
Acts 5:15 his *s* might fall on one or another of them.
Col 2:17 All these were but a *s* of things to come;
Heb 8: 5 is only a copy and *s* of the heavenly one,
10: 1 had only a *s* of the good things to come,

SHADOWBOXING (1)

1Cor 9:26 I do not fight as if I were *s*.

SHADOWED (2)

2Kgs 9:30 had arrived in Jezreel, she *s* her eyes,
Jas 1:17 who cannot change and who is never *s* over.

SHADOWS (6)

Neh 13:19 When the *s* were falling on the gates of
Sg 2:17 the day breathes cool and the *s* lengthen,
4: 6 the day breathes cool and the *s* lengthen,
Sir 34: 2 a man who catches at *s* or chases the wind,
Jer 6: 4 the day is waning, evening *s* lengthen;
1Jn 2:11 He walks in *s*, not knowing where he is

SHADOWY (1)

Eccl 8:13 man, and he shall not prolong his *s* days,

SHADRACH (14)

Dn 1: 7 Daniel to Belteshazzar, Hananiah to *S*,
2:49 At Daniel's request the king made *S*,
3:12 *S*, Meshach, Abednego; these men,
3:13 flew into a rage and sent for *S*,
3:14 "Is it true, *S*, Meshach, and Abednego,
3:16 *S*, Meshach, and Abednego answered King
3:19 became livid with utter rage against *S*,
3:20 of the strongest men in his army bind *S*,
3:22 the flames devoured the men who threw *S*,
3:93 of the white-hot furnace and called to *S*,
3:93 Thereupon *S*, Meshach, and Abednego
3:95 exclaimed, "Blessed be the God of *S*,
3:96 that whoever blasphemes the God of *S*,
3:97 Then the king promoted *S*,

SHADY (1)

Zec 1: 8 standing among myrtle trees in a *s* place,

SHAFT (13)

Ex 25:31 its *s* and branches—with its cups
25:34 On the *s* there are to be four cups,
37:17 its *s* and branches as well as its cups and
37:20 On the *s* there were four cups,
Nm 8: 4 beaten gold in both its *s* and its branches,
1Sm 17: 7 The *s* of his javelin was like a weaver's
2Sm 5: 8 must strike at them through the water *s*.
21:19 spear with a *s* like a weaver's heddle-bar.
23: 7 arm himself with iron and the *s* of a spear,
1Chr 20: 5 spear *s* was like a weaver's heddle-bar.
Rv 9: 1 was given the key to the *s* of the abyss;
9: 2 the *s* like smoke from an enormous furnace.
9: 2 air were darkened by the smoke from the *s*.

SHAFTS (6)

Ps(s) 21:13 you shall aim your *s* against them.
58: 8 the bow, let their arrows be headless *s*.
76: 4 he shattered the flashing *s* of the bow,
Wis 5:21 Well-aimed *s* of lightnings shall go forth
Lam 3:13 He pierces my sides with *s* from his quiver.
Hb 3:14 You pierce with your *s* the heads of their

SHAGEE (1)

1Chr 11:34 Jonathan, son of *S*,

SHAHARAIM (1)

1Chr 8: 8 *S* became a father on the Moabite plateau

SHAHAZUMAH (1)

Jos 19:22 boundary reached Tabor, *S* and Beth-shemesh,

SHAKE (23)

Neh 5:13 "Thus may God *s* from his home and his
Jb 16: 5 with talk, or *s* my head with silent lips.
Ps(s) 59:12 beguile my people; *s* them by your power,
109:25 when they see me, they *s* their heads.
Sir 13: 7 will pass you by, and *s* his head over you.
Is 10:32 *s* his fist at the mount of daughter Zion,
24:18 and the foundations of the earth will *s*.
52: 2 *S* off the dust, ascend to the throne,
Jer 18:16 will be amazed, will *s* their heads.
48:27 you *s* your head whenever you speak of her?
Ez 26:10 Your walls shall *s* as he enters your gates,
Jl 2:10 them the earth trembles, the heavens *s*;
Hg 2: 6 and I will *s* the heavens and the earth,
2: 7 I will *s* all the nations, and the treasures
2:21 I will *s* the heavens and the earth;
Mt 10:14 once outside it *s* its dust from your feet.
Mk 6:11 *s* its dust from your feet in testimony
Lk 6:48 to *s* it because of its solid foundation.
9: 5 leave that town and *s* its dust from your
10:11 'We *s* the dust of this town from our feet
Jn 6:61 "Does it *s* your faith?"
Acts 18: 6 he would *s* out his garments in protest and
Heb 12:26 will once more *s* not only earth but heaven!"

SHAKEN (38)

Jgs 5: 4 The earth quaked and the heavens were *s*,
1Sm 28:20 for he was badly *s* by Samuel's message.
2Sm 19: 1 The king was *s*, and went up to the room
Neh 5:13 and may he thus be *s* out and emptied!"
Jdt 12:16 in rapture over her, and his spirit was *s*.
16:15 to their bases, and the seas, are *s*;
1Mc 1:28 land was *s* on account of its inhabitants,
6: 8 he was struck with fear and very much *s*.
Jb 38:13 till the wicked are *s* from its surface?
Ps(s) 46: 3 though the earth be *s* and mountains plunge
82: 5 all the foundations of the earth are *s*.
Wis 5: 2 this, they shall be *s* with dreadful fear,
Sir 22:16 careful deliberation *s* in a moment of fear.
27: 4 When a sieve is *s*, the husks appear;
Is 13:13 and the earth shall be *s* from its place,
24:19 burst asunder, the earth will be *s* apart,
28:16 he who puts his faith in it shall not be *s*.
32:10 a year you overconfident ones will be *s*;
54:10 leave their place and the hills be *s*,
54:10 leave you nor my covenant of peace be *s*,
Ez 21:26 he has *s* the arrows,
Na 3:12 bearing early figs That fall, when *s*,
Mt 18:31 saw what had happened they were badly *s*,
24:29 and the hosts of heaven will be *s* loose.'
26:31 them, "Tonight your faith in me will be *s*,
26:33 faith in you shaken, mine will never be *s*!"
Mk 13:25 skies, and the heavenly hosts will be *s*.
14:27 "Your faith in me shall be *s*,
14:29 to him, "Even though all are *s* in faith,
Lk 6:38 Good measure pressed down, *s* together,
21:26 The powers in the heavens will be *s*.
Jn 16: 1 all this to keep your faith from being *s*.
Acts 2:37 When they heard this, they were deeply *s*.
1Thes 3: 3 lest any one of you be *s* by these trials.
Heb 12:27 And that "once more" shows that *s*,
1Pt 2: 6 He who puts his faith in it shall not be *s*."
Rv 6:13 earth like figs *s* loose by a mighty wind.

SHAKES (7)

Jb 9: 6 He *s* the earth out of its place,
Ps(s) 29: 8 LORD shakes the desert, the LORD *s* the
Sir 22:13 trouble and be spattered when he *s* himself;
Is 23:11 stretches out over the sea, he *s* kingdoms;
Jer 8:16 neighing of his stallions *s* the whole land.
Zep 2:15 passes by her hisses, and *s* his fist!

SHAKING (3)

Is 19:16 of the LORD of hosts *s* his fist at them.
Ez 12:18 and drink your water *s* with anxiety.
38:19 shall be a great *s* upon the land of Israel.

SHALEM (1)

Is 33: 7 streets, the messengers of *S* weep bitterly.

SHALISHAH (1)

1Sm 9: 4 of Ephraim, and through the land of *S*.

SHALLECHETH (1)

1Chr 26:16 with the *S* gate at the ascending highway.

SHALLUM (29)

2Kgs 15:10 *S*, son of Jabesh, conspired against
15:13 *S*, son of Jabesh, became king
15:14 Samaria, where he attacked and killed *S*,
15:15 The rest of the acts of *S*,
22:14 She was the wife of *S*,
1Chr 2:40 Sismai became the father of *S*.
2:41 *S* became the father of Jekamiah.
3:15 the fourth, *S*.
4:25 Jachin, Zerah, and Shaul, whose son was *S*,
5:38 Zadok became the father of *S*.
5:39 *S* became the father of Hilkiah.
7:13 Naphtali were Jahziel, Guni, Jezer, and *S*.
9:17 The gatekeepers were *S*,
9:17 *S* was the chief.
9:19 *S*, son of Kore, son of Ebiasaph,
9:31 Levites, the first-born of *S* the Koreite,
2Chr 28:12 son of Meshillemoth, Jehizkiah, son of *S*,
34:22 to the prophetess Huldah, the wife of *S*,
Ezr 2:42 sons of *S*, sons of Ater, sons of Talmon,
7: 2 son of Azariah, son of Hilkiah, son of *S*,
10:24 *S*, Telem, and Uri.
10:42 Sharai, Azarel, Shelemiah, Shemariah, *S*,
Neh 3:12 the work of repair was carried out by *S*,
3:15 The Spring Gate was repaired by *S*,
7:45 sons of *S*, sons of Ater, sons of Talmon,
Jer 22:11 Thus says the LORD concerning *S*,
32: 7 Hanamel, son of your uncle *S*,
35: 4 room, above the room of Maaseiah, son of *S*,
Bar 1: 7 to Jehoiakim, son of Hilkiah, son of *S*,

SHALMAI (1)

Neh 7:48 sons of Lebana, sons of Hagaba, sons of *S*,

SHALMANESER (5)

2Kgs 17: 3 *S*, king of Assyria, advanced against him,
18: 9 of Hoshea, son of Elah, king of Israel, *S*,
Tb 1: 2 of Naphtali, who during the reign of *S*,
1:13 High granted me favor and status with *S*,
1:15 But when *S* died and his son Sennacherib

SHALMANESER'S (1)

Tb 1:16 During *S* reign I performed many charitable

SHAMA (2)

1Chr 3:18 Malchiram, Pedaiah, Shenazzar, Jekamiah, *S*,
11:44 *S* and Jeiel, sons of Hotham, from Aroer;

SHAME (169)

Gn 2:25 wife were both naked, yet they felt no *s*.
Nm 12:14 would she not hide in *s* for seven days?
1Sm 20:30 to your own *s* and to the disclosure of
20:30 and to the disclosure of your mother's *s*,
2Sm 13:12 Do not *s* me!
13:13 Where would I take my *s*?
19: 6 you have put all your servants to *s* today
2Chr 30:15 The priests and Levites, touched with *s*,
Jdt 1:14 market places, and turned its glory into *s*.
9: 3 that had felt the *s* of their own deceiving.
1Mc 1:28 all the house of Jacob was covered with *s*.
1:39 turned into mourning, Her sabbaths to *s*,
4:45 *s* to them that the Gentiles had defiled it;
10:70 am laughed at and put to *s* on your account.
2Mc 6:25 I would bring *s* and dishonor on my old age.
Jb 8:22 that hate you shall be clothed with *s*,
19: 3 reviled me, have assailed me without *s*!
20: 3 A rebuke which puts me to *s* I hear,
Ps(s) 6:11 enemies shall be put to *s* in utter terror;
6:11 they shall fall back in sudden *s*.
22: 6 they trusted, and they were not put to *s*.
25: 2 In you I trust; let me not be put to *s*,
25: 3 be put to *s*; those shall be put to shame
25:20 let me not be put to *s*, for I take refuge
31: 2 I take refuge; let me never be put to *s*.
31:18 O LORD, let me not be put to *s*,
31:18 let the wicked be put to *s*;
34: 6 joy, and your faces may not blush with *s*.
35: 4 be put to *s* and disgraced who seek my life;
35:26 Let all be put to *s* and confounded who are
35:26 with *s* and disgrace who glory over me.
37:19 They are not put to *s* in an evil time;
40:15 Let all be put to *s* and confusion who
40:16 them be dismayed in their *s* who say to me,
44: 8 foes, and those who hated us you put to *s*.
44:16 and *s* covers my face At the voice of him
53: 6 they are put to *s*, because God has
69: 7 who wait for you be put to *s* through me,
69: 8 sake I bear insult, and *s* covers my face.
69:20 know my reproach, my *s* and my ignominy;
70: 3 put to *s* and confounded who seek my life.
70: 4 Let them retire in their *s* who say to me,
71: 1 I take refuge; let me never be put to *s*.
71:13 put to *s* and consumed who attack my life;
89:46 you have covered him with *s*.
97: 7 who worship graven things are put to *s*,
109:28 may my adversaries be put to *s*,
109:29 and let them wear their *s* like a mantle.
119: 6 put to *s* when I beheld all your commands.
119:31 O LORD, let me not be put to *s*.
119:78 be put to *s* for oppressing me unjustly;
119:80 in your statutes, that I be not put to *s*.
127: 5 they shall not be put to *s* when they
129: 5 be put to *s* and fall back that hate Zion.
132:18 His enemies I will clothe with *s*,
Prv 3:35 of wise men, but fools inherit *s*.
11:16 but she who hates virtue is covered with *s*.
13: 5 but the wicked brings *s* and disgrace.
13:18 *s* befall the man who disregards correction,
18:13 his is the folly and the *s*.
19:22 From a man's greed comes his *s*;
25: 8 later on when your neighbor puts you to *s*?
Sir 3:10 shame, for his *s* is no glory to you!
3:11 disgrace for her children, a mother's *s*.
4:20 from evil, and bring upon yourself no *s*.
4:21 shame laden with guilt, and a *s* that
5:17 For *s* has been created for the thief,
6: 9 enemy, and tells of the quarrel to your *s*.
8: 5 *S* not a repentant sinner;
15: 4 he will trust in her and not be put to *s*.
20:21 One may lose his life through *s*,
20:22 A man makes a promise to a friend out of *s*,
20:25 to dishonor, his *s* remains ever with him.
22:25 in need of support no one need hide in *s*;
24:21 He who obeys me will not be put to *s*,
25:21 The man is a slave, in disgrace and *s*,

SHAME (cont.)

26: 8 great anger, for she does not hide her *s.*
31:31 served, nor put him to *s* while he is merry;
32:24 trusts in the LORD shall not be put to *s.*
41:14 My children, heed my instruction about *s;*
47:20 upon your reputation, *s* upon your marriage,
Is 20: 4 with buttocks uncovered [the *s* of Egypt].
23: 4 *S,* O Sidon, fortress on the sea, for the sea
30: 3 Pharaoh's protection shall be your *s,*
30: 5 help nor benefit, but only *s* and reproach.
33: 9 in mourning, Lebanon withers with *s;*
41:11 all shall be put to *s* and disgrace who
42:17 turned back in utter *s* who trust in idols;
44: 9 To their *s,* they neither see nor know
44:10 an idol to no purpose, will be put to *s;*
44:11 stand forth, to be reduced to fear and *s.*
45:16 Those are put to *s* and disgrace who vent
45:17 be put to *s* or disgrace in future ages."
45:24 Before him in *s* shall come all who vent
47: 3 shall be uncovered and your *s* be seen;
50: 7 knowing that I shall not be put to *s.*
54: 4 Fear not, you shall not be put to *s;*
54: 4 The *s* of your youth you shall forget,
61: 7 Since their *s* was double and disgrace and
65:13 shall rejoice, but you shall be put to *s;*
66: 5 but they shall be put to *s.*
Jer 3:25 Let us lie down in our *s,*
10:14 every artisan is put to *s* by his idol:
13:26 from you, so that your *s* will appear.
17:13 The rebels in the land shall be put to *s;*
20:11 their failure they will be put to utter *s,*
20:18 see sorrow and pain, to end my days in *s?*
23:40 eternal reproach, eternal, unforgettable *s.*
31:19 I blush with *s,* I bear the disgrace
46:12 The nations hear of your *s,*
48:39 How he turns his back in *s!*
49:23 Hamath and Arpad are covered with *s,*
50: 2 her images are put to *s,* her idols
50:12 Your mother shall be sorely put to *s,*
51:17 every artisan is put to *s* by his idol:
51:47 her whole land shall be put to *s,*
Bar 1:15 and we today are flushed with *s,*
2: 6 our fathers, are flushed with *s* even today.
6:25 men's shoulders, displaying their *s* to all;
6:38 and their worshipers will be put to *s.*
Ez 7:18 *s* shall be on all their faces and baldness
16:52 You, then, bear your *s;*
16:52 Blush for *s,* and bear the shame of having
16:54 that you may bear your *s* and be disgraced
16:63 *s* when I pardon you for all you have done,
23:18 was discovered and her *s* was revealed,
Dn 3:33 revere you, have become a *s* and a reproach.
3:40 those who trust in you cannot be put to *s.*
3:42 Do not let us be put to *s,* but deal with
Hos 2:12 bare her *s* before the eyes of her lovers,
4: 7 against me, exchanging their glory for *s.*
4:18 harlotry; in their arrogance they love *s.*
4:19 they shall have only *s* from their altars.
9:10 and consecrated themselves to the *S,*
Jl 2:26 my people shall nevermore be put to *s.*
2:27 my people shall nevermore be put to *s.*
Mi 2: 6 The *s* will not withdraw.
3: 7 Then shall the seers be put to *s,*
7:10 When my enemy sees this, *s* shall cover her:
7:16 The nations shall behold and be put to *s,*
Na 3: 5 to the nations, to the kingdoms your *s!*
3: 6 upon you, disgrace you and put you to *s;*
Hb 2:10 You have devised *s* for your household,
2:16 You are filled with *s* instead of glory;
2:16 right hand, and utter *s* on your glory.
Zep 2: 1 yourselves together, O nation without *s!*
Rom 9:33 he who believes in him will not be put to *s.*"
10:11 one who believes in him will be put to *s.*"
1Cor 1:27 the world considers absurd to *s* the wise;
1:27 out the weak of this world to *s* the strong.
4:14 I am writing you in this way not to *s* you
6: 5 I say this in an attempt to *s* you.
11: 4 his head covered brings *s* upon his head.
11: 5 her head uncovered brings *s* upon her head.
15:34 ignorant of God; I say it to your *s.*
2Cor 7:14 to him about you, I was not put to *s.*
9: 4 then I should be put to *s*—
11:21 To my *s* I must confess that we have been
Phil 1:20 I shall never be put to *s* for my hopes;
3:19 their belly and their glory is in their *s.*
Ti 2: 8 about us, and hostility will yield to *s.*
Heb 12: 2 he endured the cross, heedless of its *s.*
1Jn 2:28 and not retreat in *s* at his coming.
Jude 1:12 without *s* and only look after themselves.
Rv 3:18 the *s* of your nakedness is to be covered.

SHAME-GOD (1)

Jer 3:24 The *s* has devoured our fathers' toil from

SHAMED (14)

2Sm 13:14 he *s* her and had relations with her.
13:22 he hated him for having *s* his sister Tamar.
13:32 this ever since Amnon *s* his sister Tamar.
19: 4 that day like men *s* by flight in battle.
Ps(s) 71:24 How *s* and how disgraced are those who
83:18 Let them be *s* and put to rout forever;
Is 26:11 *s* when they see your zeal for your people:
Jer 2:26 As the thief is *s* when caught,
2:26 caught, so shall the house of Israel be *s:*
2:36 will you be *s,* as you were shamed by
Dn 3:44 Let them be *s* and powerless,
Hos 10: 6 into captivity, Israel be *s* by his schemes.
1Pt 3:16 libel your way of life in Christ may be *s.*

SHAMEFACED (3)

2Chr 32:21 that he had to return *s* to his own country.
Dn 9: 7 we are *s* even to this day:
9: 8 O LORD, we are *s,* like our kings,

SHAMEFACEDLY (1)

Lk 14: 9 have to proceed *s* to the lowest place.

SHAMEFUL (17)

Lv 18:17 this would be *s,* because they are related
20:14 be burned to death for their *s* conduct,
20:17 cut off from their people for this *s* deed;
Jos 7:15 LORD and has committed a *s* crime in Israel."
Neh 6:13 had a *s* story with which to discredit me.
2Mc 9: 2 the natives and forced to beat a *s* retreat.
11:12 Lysias himself escaped only by *s* flight.
Wis 2:20 Let us condemn him to a *s* death;
Sir 41:24 the things you should rightly avoid as *s*
Dn 11:18 a leader shall put an end to his *s* conduct,
13:63 she was found innocent of any *s* deed.
Am 8:14 Those who swear by the *s* idol of Samaria,
Rom 1:27 Men did *s* things with men,
1Cor 11: 6 If it is *s* for a woman to have her hair
2Cor 4: 2 Rather, we repudiate *s,* underhanded
Eph 5:12 It is *s* even to mention the things these
1Pt 5: 2 and not for *s* profit either, but generously.

SHAMEFULLY (5)

Jdt 9: 2 the maiden's girdle, *s* exposed her thighs,
Hos 2: 7 she that conceived them has acted *s.*
Mk 12: 4 too they beat over the head and treated *s.*
Lk 20:11 away empty-handed, after treating him *s.*
Jas 2: 6 Yet you treated this poor man *s.*

SHAMEFULNESS (1)

Lv 20:14 so that such *s* may not be found among you.

SHAMELESS (7)

Sir 22: 4 her husband, a *s* one is her father's grief.
23: 6 master me, surrender me not to *s* desires.
29:14 and only the *s* would play him false;
40:30 In the mouth of the *s* man begging is sweet,
Jer 13:27 your neighings, your *s* prostitutions:
Ez 16:30 these things, acting like a *s* prostitute,
Jude 1:13 splashing their *s* deeds abroad like foam,

SHAMELESSLY (1)

Tb 14:10 For I see that people here *s* commit all

SHAMELESSNESS (1)

Wis 14:26 lust, disorder in marriage, adultery and *s.*

SHAMES (1)

Sir 22: 5 A hussy *s* her father and her husband;

SHAMGAR (2)

Jgs 3:31 After him there was *S,*
5: 6 In the days of *S,* son of Anath,

SHAMHUTH (1)

1Chr 27: 8 for the fifth month, was the commander *S,*

SHAMIR (4)

Jos 15:48 *S,* Jattir, Socoh, Dannah, Kiriath-sannah
Jgs 10: 1 of *S* in the mountain region of Ephraim.
10: 2 years, he died and was buried in *S.*
1Chr 24:24 *S,* of the descendants of Micah;

SHAMLAI (1)

Ezr 2:46 sons of Akkub, sons of Hagab, sons of *S,*

SHAMMA (1)

1Chr 7:37 Shual, Beri, Imrah, Bezer, Hod, *S,*

SHAMMAH (8)

Gn 36:13 The sons of Reuel were Nahath, Zerah, *S,*
36:17 the clans of Nahath, Zerah, *S,* and Mizzah.
1Sm 16: 9 Next Jesse presented *S,* but Samuel said,
17:13 the second son Abinadab, and the third *S.*
2Sm 23:11 Next to him was *S,* son of Agee
23:25 *S* from En-harod;
23:33 Jonathan, son of *S* the Hararite;
1Chr 1:37 The sons of Reuel were Nahath, Zerah, *S,*

SHAMMAI (6)

1Chr 2:28 The sons of Onam were *S* and Jada.
2:28 The sons of *S* were Nadab and Abishur.
2:32 The sons of Jada, the brother of *S,*
2:44 Rekem became the father of *S.*
2:45 The son of *S:* Maon,
4:17 Jether became the father of Miriam, *S,*

SHAMMOTH (1)

1Chr 11:27 Elhanan, son of Dodo, from Bethlehem, *S,*

SHAMMUA (5)

Nm 13: 4 *S,* son of Zaccur, of the tribe of Reuben;
2Sm 5:14 *S,* Shobab,
1Chr 14: 4 *S,* Shobab,
Neh 11:17 and Abda, son of *S,*
12:18 for Bilgah, *S;*

SHAMSHERAI (1)

1Chr 8:26 *S,* Shehariah, Athaliah.

SHANKS (6)

Ex 12: 9 with its head and *s* and inner organs.
29:17 inner organs and *s* you shall first wash,
Lv 1: 9 The inner organs and the *s,*
1:13 The inner organs and the *s,*
8:21 the inner organs and the *s* with water,
9:14 Having washed the inner organs and the *s,*

SHAPE (5)

Ex 20: 4 not carve idols for yourselves in the *s*
Dt 5: 8 not carve idols for yourselves in the *s*
1Kgs 6:25 The cherubim were identical in size and *s,*
7:37 same casting, the same size, the same *s.*
Eph 2:21 and takes *s* as a holy temple in the Lord;

SHAPED (8)

Ex 25:33 to be three cups, *s* like almond blossoms,
25:33 to be three cups, *s* like almond blossoms,
25:34 to be four cups, *s* like almond blossoms,
37:19 were three cups, *s* like almond blossoms,
37:19 were three cups, *s* like almond blossoms.
37:20 were four cups, *s* like almond blossoms,
Ps(s) 94: 9 Shall he who *s* the ear not hear?
1Pt 1:14 desires that once *s* you in your ignorance.

SHAPELY (1)

Sir 26:18 bases are her *s* limbs and steady feet.

SHAPES (3)

2Mc 7:23 of the universe who *s* each man's beginning,
Is 44:12 works it over the coals, *s* it with hammers,
44:13 He *s* it with a plane and measures it off

SHAPHAM (1)

1Chr 5:12 Joel was chief, *S* was second in command,

SHAPHAN (29)

2Kgs 22: 3 year, King Josiah sent the scribe *S,*
22: 8 high priest Hilkiah informed the scribe *S,*
22: 8 Hilkiah gave the book to *S,* who read it.
22: 9 the scribe *S* went to the king and reported,
22:10 The scribe *S* also informed the king that
22:12 *S;* Achbor, son of Micaiah, the scribe *S,*
22:14 So Hilkiah the priest, Ahikam, Achbor, *S,*
25:22 governor Gedaliah, son of Ahikam, son of *S.*
25:30 governor Gedaliah, son of Ahikam, son of *S.*
2Chr 34: 8 the temple as well as the land, he sent *S,*
34:15 He reported this to *S* the scribe,
34:15 Hilkiah gave the book to *S,*
34:18 Then *S* the scribe announced to the king,
34:18 And *S* read from it before the king.
34:20 son of *S,* to Abdon, son of Michah, to *S*
Jer 26:24 But Ahikam, son of *S,* protected Jeremiah,
29: 3 Delivered in Babylon by Elasah, son of *S,*
36:10 the room of Gemariah, son of the scribe *S,*
36:11 Now Micaiah, son of Gemariah, son of *S,*
36:12 son of Achbor, Gemariah, son of *S,*
39:14 to Gedaliah, son of Ahikam, son of *S,*
40: 5 go to Gedaliah, son of Ahikam, son of *S,*
40: 9 Gedaliah, son of Ahikam, son of *S,*
40:11 them Gedaliah, son of Ahikam, son of *S,*
41: 2 swords Gedaliah, son of Ahikam, son of *S,*
43: 6 to Gedaliah, son of Ahikam, son of *S;*
Ez 8:11 among whom stood Jaazaniah, son of *S,*

SHAPHAT (7)

Nm 13: 4 *S,* son of Hori
1Kgs 19:16 and Elisha, son of *S* of Abel-meholah,
19:19 set out, and came upon Elisha, son of *S,*
2Kgs 3:11 of Israel replied, "Elisha, son of *S,*
6:31 "if the head of Elisha, son of *S,*
1Chr 3:22 Shemiah, Hattush, Igal, Bariah, Neariah, *S*—
27:29 and over the cattle in the valleys was *S,*

SHAPHIR (1)

Mi 1:11 Pass by, you who dwell in *S!*

SHAPING (1)

Sir 38:28 His eyes are fixed on the tool he is *s.*

SHARAI (1)

Ezr 10:40 Shashai, *S*, Azarel, Shelemiah, Shemariah,

SHARAR (1)

2Sm 23:33 Ahiam, son of *S* the Hararite,

SHARE (108)

Gn 14:24 the *s* that is due to the men who joined me
14:24 Eshcol and Mamre; let them take their *s*."
21:10 to *s* the inheritance with my son Isaac!"
31:54 and invited his kinsmen to *s* in the meal.
Ex 12: 4 and shall *s* in the lamb in proportion
Lv 6:11 rightful *s* in the oblations of the LORD
7:35 priestly *s* from the oblations of the LORD,
7:36 the Israelites to give them this *s*
Nm 10:32 we will *s* with you the prosperity the LORD
11:17 may *s* the burden of the people with you.
18: 8 to you and to your sons as your priestly *s*.
18: 9 to *s* in the oblations that are most sacred,
31:47 From this, the Israelites' *s*, Moses,
Dt 10: 9 has no *s* in the heritage with his brothers;
12:12 but has no *s* of his own in your heritage.
14:27 for he has no *s* in the heritage with you.
14:29 who has no *s* in the heritage with you,
18: 1 have no *s* in the heritage with Israel;
21:17 a double *s* of whatever he happens to own,
28:55 any *s* in the flesh of his children that he
32: 9 was Jacob, His hereditary *s* was Israel.
Jos 14: 4 no *s* of the land except cities to live in,
17:14 us only one lot and one *s* as our heritage?
17:17 You shall have not merely one *s*,
18: 7 For the Levites have no *s* among you,
22:19 of the LORD stands, and *s* that with us.
22:25 of Reuben and Gad have no *s* in the LORD.
22:27 our children, 'You have no *s* in the LORD.'
1Sm 26:19 day I have no *s* in the LORD's inheritance,
30:24 the *s* of the one who goes down to battle
30:24 shall be the same; they shall *s* alike."
2Sm 20: 1 in David, nor any *s* in the son of Jesse.
1Kgs 12:16 "What *s* have we in David?
2Chr 10:16 "What *s* have we in David?
Neh 2:20 *s* nor claim nor memorial in Jerusalem."
Tb 2: 2 you, so that he can *s* this meal with me.
4:17 virtuous, but do not *s* them with sinners.
1Mc 2:10 nation has not taken its *s* of her realm,
10:30 fruit of the trees that should be my *s*,
2Mc 8:28 they gave a *s* of the booty to the
Jb 31:17 alone, with no *s* in it for the fatherless,
39:17 and has given her no *s* in understanding.
Ps(s) 68:24 dogs will have their *s* of your enemies."
Prv 6:22 when you wake, she will *s* your concerns;
16:19 the meek than to *s* plunder with the proud.
17: 2 will *s* the inheritance with the brothers.
Eccl 2:10 This was my *s* for all my toil.
Wis 7:13 about her, and ungrudgingly do I *s*—
18: 9 *s* alike the same good things and dangers,
Sir 14: 8 In the miser's opinion his *s* is too small;
14:13 and give him a *s* in what you possess.
22:23 as to *s* in his inheritance when it comes.
30:10 *S* not in his frivolity lest you share in
32: 2 To *s* in their joy and win praise for your
37: 4 A false friend will *s* your joys,
41:19 of defrauding another of his appointed *s*,
Bar 6:27 but do not *s* it with the poor and the weak;
Mt 21:34 the tenants to obtain his *s* of the grapes.
25:21 Come, *s* your master's joy!'
25:23 Come, *s* your master's joy!'
Mk 10:17 what must I do to *s* in everlasting life?"
10:39 the bath I am immersed in you shall *s*.
12: 2 them his *s* of produce from the vineyard.
Lk 12:13 brother to give me my *s* of our inheritance."
15:12 the *s* of the estate that is coming to me.'
18:18 what must I do to *s* in everlasting life?"
20:10 to receive his *s* of the crop from them;
Jn 1:16 Of his fullness we have all had a *s*—
13: 8 "you will have no *s* in my heritage."
17:13 world that they may *s* my joy completely.
Acts 1:17 been given a *s* in this ministry of ours.
20:32 a *s* among all who are consecrated to him.
28:20 solely because I *s* the hope of Israel."
Rom 1:11 For I long to see you and *s* with you some
8:21 *s* in the glorious freedom of the children
8:29 he predestined to *s* the image of his Son,
11:17 come to *s* in the rich root of the olive,
1Cor 9:10 and the harvester expect a *s* in the grain.
9:13 at the altar *s* the offerings of the altar?
9:23 in the hope of having a *s* in its blessings.
10:18 eat the sacrifices do not *s* in the altar!
12:26 is honored, all the members *s* its joy.
14:26 to give, still another a revelation to *s*;
2Cor 1: 5 do we *s* abundantly in his consolation.
1: 7 you *s* in the sufferings, so you will share
Gal 6: 6 should *s* all he has with his instructor.
Eph 4:28 have something to *s* with those in need.
Phil 3:10 likewise to know how to *s* in his
4:14 kind of you to want to *s* in my hardships.
Col 1:12 worthy to *s* the lot of the saints in light.
2: 9 Yours is a *s* of this fullness,
1Thes 2: 8 that we wanted to *s* with you not only
2Tm 1: 8 *s* of the hardship which the gospel entails.
2: 6 who should have the first *s* of the crop.
Heb 2:14 flesh, Jesus likewise had a full *s* in ours,
3: 1 holy brothers who *s* a heavenly calling,
12:10 true profit, that we may *s* his holiness.
1Pt 3: 7 consideration for those who *s* your lives.
4:13 the measure that you *s* Christ's sufferings.
2Pt 2:13 *s* your feasts in a spirit of seduction.
1Jn 1: 3 turn to you so that you may *s* life with us,
3Jn 1: 8 thus to have our *s* in the work of truth.
Jude 1: 3 you, beloved, about the salvation we *s*.
Rv 1: 9 who *s* with you the distress and the kingly
20: 6 are they who *s* in the first resurrection!
22:19 God will take away his *s* in the tree of

SHARED (12)

2Sm 12: 3 She *s* the little food he had and drank
1Kgs 2:26 *s* in all the hardships my father endured."
Neh 12:43 great feast of the LORD in which they *s*.
2Mc 5:20 having *s* in the people's misfortunes,
14:25 settled down, and *s* the common life.
Prv 5:17 be yours alone, not one *s* with strangers;
Wis 19:16 those who now *s* with them the same rights.
Lk 2:10 of great joy to be *s* by the whole people.
Acts 2:44 Those who believed *s* all things in common;
Rom 15:27 *s* in the spiritual blessings of the Jews,
2Cor 1: 5 we have *s* much in the suffering of Christ,
Phil 4:15 a single congregation except yourselves *s*

SHARER (1)

1Pt 5: 1 and *s* in the glory that is to be revealed,

SHARERS (5)

1Cor 10:20 I do not want you to become *s* with demons.
Eph 3: 6 members of the same body and *s* of the
Phil 1: 7 are *s* of my gracious lot when I lie in
Heb 6: 4 gift and become *s* in the Holy Spirit,
2Pt 1: 4 lust might become *s* of the divine nature.

SHARES (8)

Nm 18: 9 *s* shall accrue to you and to your sons.
Jos 17: 5 Thus ten *s* fell to Manasseh apart from the
18:10 for the Israelites into their separate *s*,
2Sm 19:44 "We have ten *s* in the king.
Prv 14:10 bitterness, and in its joy no one else *s*.
Sir 45:22 the people nor *s* with them their heritage;
Is 34:17 his hands he marks off their *s* of her;
2Jn 1:11 whoever greets him *s* in the evil he does.

SHAREZER (2)

2Kgs 19:37 his sons Adrammelech and *S* slew him with
Is 37:38 his sons Adrammelech and *S* slew him with

SHARING (16)

Nm 8:26 Levites shall consist in *s* their responsibilities
2Chr 31:18 by *s* faithfully in the consecrated things.
2Mc 5:27 what grew wild to avoid *s* the defilement.
Wis 8:18 and fair renown in *s* her discourses,
Sir 42: 3 *s* the expenses of a business or a journey,
Is 58: 7 *S* your bread with the hungry,
1Cor 10:16 we bless a *s* in the blood of Christ?
10:16 bread we break a *s* in the body of Christ?
2Cor 7: 3 even to the *s* of death and life together.
8: 4 *s* in this service to members of the church.
9:13 generosity in *s* with them and with all.
1Tm 5:22 or you may be *s* in the misdeeds of others.
6:18 good works and generous, *s* what they have.
Phlm 1: 6 And my prayers is that your *s* of the faith
Heb 13: 3 as if you were *s* their imprisonment,
Rv 18: 4 her and *s* the plagues inflicted on her!

SHARON (6)

1Chr 27:29 that grazed in *S* was Shitrai the Sharonite,
Sg 2: 1 I am a flower of *S*.
Is 33: 9 *S* is like the steppe,
35: 2 to them, the splendor of Carmel and *S*;
65:10 *S* shall be a pasture for the flocks and
Acts 9:35 All the inhabitants of Lydda and *S*,

SHARONITE (1)

1Chr 27:29 that grazed in Sharon was Shitrai the *S*,

SHARP (23)

2Mc 9: 5 pains in his bowels and *s* internal torment,
Jb 41:22 His belly is *s* as pottery fragments;
Ps(s) 45: 6 Your arrows are *s*; peoples are subject
57: 5 and arrows, their tongue is a *s* sword.
89:44 You have turned back his *s* sword and have
120: 4 *S* arrows of a warrior with fiery coals of
140: 4 make their tongues *s* as those of serpents;
Prv 5: 4 as wormwood, as *s* as a two-edged sword.
25:18 Like a club, or a sword, or a *s* arrow,
Wis 18:16 the *s* sword of your inexorable decree.
Is 5:28 Their arrows are *s*, and all their bows
41:15 I will make of you a threshing sledge, *s*,
Ez 5: 1 a *s* sword and use it like a barber's razor,
Mk 13:34 the man at the gate to watch with a *s* eye.
Jn 18:22 nearby gave Jesus a *s* blow on the face.
Acts 15:39 ensued was so *s* that the two separated.
Rv 1:16 A *s*, two-edged sword came out of his
2:12 " 'The One with the *s*, two-edged sword
14:14 head and holding a *s* sickle in his hand.
14:17 angel, who likewise held a *s* sickle.
14:18 held the *s* sickle, "Use your sharp sickle
19:15 a *s* sword for striking down the nations.

SHARP-EDGED (1)

Is 49: 2 He made of me a *s* sword and concealed me

SHARPEN (5)

Dt 32:41 I live forever, I will *s* my flashing sword,
1Sm 13:20 to the Philistines to *s* their plowshares,
Ps(s) 7:13 they be converted, God will *s* his sword;
64: 4 Who *s* their tongues like swords,
Jer 51:11 *S* the arrows, fill the quivers; the LORD

SHARPENED (4)

Ps(s) 52: 4 your tongue is like a *s* razor,
Ez 21:14 A sword, a sword has been *s*,
21:15 To work slaughter has it been *s*,
21:16 A sword *s* and burnished to be put in the

SHARPENING (1)

1Sm 13:21 for *s* the axes and for setting the oxgoads.

SHARPENS (2)

Prv 27:17 As iron *s* iron, so man shapens

SHARPER (1)

Heb 4:12 and effective, *s* than any two-edged sword.

SHARPLY (7)

Sir 22:22 Should you speak *s* to a friend,
Mk 1:25 Jesus rebuked him *s*:
Lk 4:35 Jesus said to him *s*, "Be quiet!
Jn 7:43 fashion the crowd was *s* divided over him.
9:16 They were *s* divided over him.
10:19 words, the Jews were *s* divided once more.
Ti 1:13 Admonish them *s*, in an attempt to keep

SHARUHEN (1)

Jos 19: 6 Hazar-susah, Beth-lebaoth and *S*;

SHASHAI (1)

Ezr 10:40 *S*, Sharai, Azarel, Shelemiah, Shemariah,

SHASHAK (2)

1Chr 8:14 Their brethren were Elpaal, *S*,
8:25 Iphdeiah, and Penuel were the sons of *S*.

SHATTER (19)

Dt 12: 3 poles, and *s* the idols of their gods,
2Chr 20:37 with Ahaziah, the LORD will *s* your work."
Jdt 9: 8 *S* their strength in your might,
13: 5 to *s* the enemies who have risen against us."
Jb 40:12 tear down the wicked and *s* them.
Ps(s) 2: 9 you shall *s* them like an earthen dish."
Is 11:15 anger And *s* it into seven streamlets,
45: 2 Bronze doors I will *s*, and iron bars I
Jer 51:20 With you I *s* nations, with you I destroy
51:21 I shatter horse and rider, with you I *s*
51:22 you I *s* man and wife, with you I shatter
51:22 young, with you I *s* the youth and maiden.
51:23 *s* the shepherd and his flock, with you I *s*
51:23 team, with you I *s* satraps and prefects.
Am 6:11 the command to *s* the great house to bits,
Rv 2:27 a rod of iron and *s* them like crockery;

SHATTERED (27)

Ex 15: 6 your right hand, O LORD, has *s* the enemy.
1Sm 2:10 the LORD's foes shall be *s*.
2Kgs 11:18 They *s* its altars and images completely,
18: 4 who removed the high places, *s* the pillars,
2Chr 34: 4 molten images were *s* and beaten into dust,
Jdt 13:14 *s* our enemies by my hand this very night."
Jb 4:20 Morning or evening they may be *s*;
38:15 is withheld, and the arm of pride is *s*.
Ps(s) 76: 4 There he *s* the flashing shafts of the bow,
105:33 and *s* the trees throughout their borders.
107:16 Because he *s* the gates of brass and burst
Eccl 12: 6 broken, And the pitcher is *s* at the spring,
Sir 47: 7 and *s* their power till our own day.
48: 2 Their staff of bread he *s*,
49:13 our ruined walls, Restored our *s* defenses,
Is 10:27 shoulder, and his yoke *s* from your neck.
30:31 When the LORD speaks, Assyria will be *s*,
Jer 48:25 is broken, his might is *s* says the LORD.
48:38 I have *s* Moab like a pot that no one wants,
50: 2 is taken, Bel confounded, Merodach *s*;
50: 2 her images are put to shame, her idols *s*.
50:23 of the whole earth been broken and *s*!
Ez 21:11 with *s* strength groan bitterly while they
Dn 8: 8 height of its power the great horn was *s*,
Hb 3: 6 The eternal mountains are *s*,
Lk 9:39 then abandons him in his *s* condition.
Acts 27:41 the stern was *s* by the pounding of the sea.

SHATTERING (2)

Ps(s) 48: 8 from the east were *s* ships of Tarshish.
Jer 23:29 fire, says the LORD, like a hammer *s* rocks?

SHATTERS (1)

2Mc 12:28 who forcibly *s* the might of his enemies,

SHAUL (9)

Gn 36:37 When Samlah died, *S*,
36:38 When *S* died, Baal-hanan, son of Achbor,
46:10 Nemuel, Jamin, Ohad, Jachin, Zohar, and *S*,
Ex 6:15 Jenuel, Jamin, Ohad, Jachin, Zohar and *S*,
Nm 26:13 through *S* the clan of the Shaulites.
1Chr 1:48 *S* from Rehoboth-han-nahar succeeded him.
1:49 When *S* died, Baal-hanan, son of Achbor,
4:24 were Nemuel, Jamin, Jachin, Zerah, and *S*,
6: 9 whose son was Uzziah, whose son was *S*.

SHAULITES (1)

Nm 26:13 Soharites, through Shaul the clan of the *S*.

SHAVE (19)

Lv 13:33 below the skin, the man shall *s* himself,
14: 8 and *s* off all his hair and bathe in water;
14: 9 shall again *s* off all the hair of his head,
21: 5 of the head, nor *s* the edges of the beard,
Nm 6: 9 *s* his head on the day of his purification,
6:18 the nazirite shall *s* his dedicated head,
8: 7 then have them *s* their whole bodies and
Dt 14: 1 You shall not gash yourselves nor *s* the
21:12 she must *s* her head and pare her nails and
Is 7:20 On that day the Lord shall *s* with the
7:20 It shall also *s* off the beard.
22:12 mourn, to *s* your head and put on sackcloth.
Jer 2:16 and Tahpanhes *s* the crown of your head.
9:25 the desert dwellers who *s* their temples.
16: 6 will gash himself or *s* his head for them.
25:23 the desert dwellers who *s* their temples;
49:32 to the winds those who *s* their temples,
Ez 27:31 they *s* their heads and put on sackcloth,
44:20 They shall not *s* their heads nor let their

SHAVED (14)

Gn 41:14 After he *s* and changed his clothes,
Nm 6:19 the nazirite has *s* off his dedicated hair,
Jgs 16:17 If I am *s*, my strength will leave me,
16:19 a man who *s* off his seven locks of hair.
16:22 head began to grow as soon as it was *s* off.
2Sm 14:26 When he *s* his head—which he used to
1Chr 19: 4 seized David's servants and had them *s*
Is 15: 2 Every head is *s*, every beard sheared off.
Jer 41: 5 knew of it, eighty men with beards *s* off,
47: 5 Gaza is *s* bald, Ashkelon is reduced
48:37 head has been made bald, every beard *s*;
Acts 18:18 *s* his head because of a vow he had taken.
1Cor 11: 5 It is as if she had had her head *s*.
11: 6 to have her hair cut off or her head *s*,

SHAVEH (1)

Gn 14:17 to greet him in the Valley of *S* (that is,

SHAVEH-KIRIATHAIM (1)

Gn 14: 5 the Zuzim in Ham, the Emim in *S*,

SHAVEN (1)

Bar 6:30 with torn tunic and with *s* hair and beard,

SHAVING (2)

2Sm 10: 4 after *s* off half their beards and cutting
Acts 21:24 pay the fee for the *s* of their heads.

SHAVSHA (1)

1Chr 18:16 *S* was scribe;

SHAWL (3)

Gn 38:14 her face by covering herself with a *s*,
38:19 her *s* and put on her widow's garb again.
Jgs 5:30 an ornate *s* or two for me in the spoil."

SHAWLS (1)

Is 3:23 the mirrors, linen tunics, turbans, and *s*.

SHAWSHA (2)

2Sm 8:17 *S* was scribe.
20:25 *S* was the scribe.

SHE-ASSES (4)

Gn 32:16 twenty *s* and ten he-asses.
1Chr 27:30 over the *s* was Jehdeiah the Meronothite;
Jb 1: 3 five hundred yoke of oxen, five hundred *s*,
42:12 a thousand yoke of oxen, and a thousand *s*.

SHE-BEARS (1)

2Kgs 2:24 Then two *s* came out of the woods and tore

SHE-CAMEL (1)

Jer 2:23 A frenzied *s*, coursing near and far,

SHE-GOAT (5)

Gn 15: 9 three-year-old heifer, a three-year-old *s*,
31:38 you, no ewe or *s* of yours ever miscarried,
Lv 4:28 unblemished *s* as the offering for his sin.
5: 6 animal from the flock, a ewe lamb or a *s*.
Nm 15:27 shall bring a yearling *s* as a sin offering,

SHE-GOATS (2)

Gn 30:35 and all the speckled and spotted *s*,
32:15 two hundred *s* and twenty he-goats;

SHEAF (7)

Gn 37: 7 suddenly my *s* rose to an upright position,
37: 7 a ring around my *s* and bowed down to it."
Lv 23:10 you shall bring a *s* of the first fruits of
23:11 who shall wave the *s* before the LORD that
23:12 On this day, when your *s* is waved,
23:15 on which you bring the wave-offering *s*,
Dt 24:19 in your field and overlook a *s* there,

SHEAL (1)

Ezr 10:29 Jashub, *S*,

SHEALTIEL (13)

1Chr 3:17 *S*, Malchiram, Pedaiah, Shenazzar,
Ezr 3: 2 the priests, and Zerubbabel, son of *S*,
3: 8 in the second month, Zerubbabel, son of *S*,
5: 2 Thereupon Zerubbabel, son of *S*,
Neh 12: 1 who returned with Zerubbabel, son of *S*,
Hg 1: 1 governor of Judah, Zerubbabel, son of *S*,
1:12 Then Zerubbabel, son of *S*,
1:14 governor of Judah, Zerubbabel, son of *S*,
2: 2 governor of Judah, Zerubbabel, son of *S*,
2:23 I will take you, Zerubbabel, son of *S*,
Mt 1:12 of Shealtiel, *S* the father of Zerubbabel.
Lk 3:27 son of Rhesa, son of Zerubbabel, son of *S*,

SHEAR (3)

Gn 31:19 Now Laban had gone away to *s* his sheep,
38:13 was on his way up to Timnah to *s* his sheep,
Dt 15:19 cattle, nor *s* the firstlings of your flock.

SHEAR-JASHUB (1)

Is 7: 3 Go out to meet Ahaz, you and your son *S*,

SHEARED (2)

Is 15: 2 Every head is shaved, every beard *s* off.
Jl 1: 7 He has stripped it, *s* off its bark;

SHEARER (1)

Acts 8:32 *s* he was silent and opened not his mouth.

SHEARERS (5)

1Sm 25: 7 I have just heard that *s* are with you.
25:11 meat that I have slaughtered for my own *s*,
2Sm 13:23 Absalom had *s* in Baal-hazor near Ephraim,
13:24 "Your servant is having *s*.
Is 53: 7 to the slaughter or a sheep before the *s*,

SHEARIAH (2)

1Chr 8:38 were Azrikam, his first-born, Ishmael, *S*,
9:44 were Azrikam, his first-born, Ishmael, *S*,

SHEARING (4)

Gn 38:12 went up to Timnah for the *s* of his sheep,
Dt 18: 4 as the first fruits of the *s* of your flock;
1Sm 25: 2 present for the *s* of his flock in Carmel.
25: 4 in the desert that Nabal was *s* his flock,

SHEARINGS (1)

Tb 1: 6 of my income and the first *s* of the sheep,

SHEARS (3)

Ex 25:38 These, as well as the trimming *s* and trays,
37:23 lamps, as well as its trimming *s* and trays,
Nm 4: 9 the lampstand with its lamps, trimming *s*,

SHEATH (9)

1Sm 17:51 *s* he dispatched him and cut off his head.
2Sm 20: 8 which was slung, in its *s* near his thigh,
1Chr 21:27 to the angel to return his sword to its *s*.
Ez 21: 8 I will draw my sword from its *s* and cut
21: 9 its *s* against everyone from south to north,
21:10 the LORD, have drawn my sword from its *s*,
21:35 Return it to its *s*!
Dn 7:15 my spirit anguished within its *s* of flesh,
Jn 18:11 to Peter, "Put your sword back in its *s*.

SHEATHED (1)

Ez 21:10 its sheath, and it shall not be *s* again.

SHEAVES (15)

Gn 37: 7 There we were, binding *s* in the field,
37: 7 and your *s* formed a ring around my sheaf
Dt 33:14 the year, and the choicest *s* of the months;
Ru 2: 7 the gleanings into *s* after the harvesters;
2:15 the *s* themselves without scolding her,
3: 7 he went and lay down at the edge of the *s*,
Neh 13:15 that they were bringing in *s* of grain,
Jdt 8: 3 field supervising those who bound the *s*,
Jb 24:10 and famished are those who carry the *s*.
Ps(s) 126: 6 come back rejoicing, carrying their *s*.
129: 7 his hand, nor the gatherer of *s* his arms;
Jer 9:21 on a field, Like *s* behind the harvester,
Am 2:13 as a wagon crushes when laden with *s*.
Mi 4:12 them like *s* on the threshing floor.
Zec 12: 6 and like a burning torch among *s*,

SHEBA (30)

Gn 10: 7 descendants of Raamah: *S* and Dedan.
10:28 Diklah, Obal, Abimael, *S*,
25: 3 Jokshan became the father of *S* and Dedan.
2Sm 20: 1 individual from Benjamin named *S*,
20: 2 So all the Israelites left David for *S*,
20: 6 *S*, son of Bichri, may now do us more
20: 7 from Jerusalem to campaign in pursuit of *S*,
20:10 Joab and his brother Abishai pursued *S*,
20:13 went on after Joab in pursuit of *S*,
20:14 *S* passed through all the tribes of Israel
20:21 A man named *S*, son of Bichri, from
20:22 advice, and they cut off the head of *S*,
1Kgs 10: 1 The queen of *S*, having heard of Solomon's
10: 4 of *S* witnessed Solomon's great wisdom,
10:10 as the queen of *S* gave to King Solomon.
10:13 of *S* everything she desired and asked for,
1Chr 1: 9 The descendants of Raama were *S* and Dedan.
1:22 Hadoram, Uzal, Diklah, Ebal, Abimael, *S*,
1:32 The sons of Jokshan were *S* and Dedan.
5:13 Michael, Meshullam, *S*,
2Chr 9: 1 the queen of *S* heard of Solomon's fame,
9: 3 the queen of *S* witnessed Solomon's wisdom,
9: 9 which the queen of *S* gave to King Solomon.
9:12 *S* everything she desired and asked him for,
Jb 6:19 Tema search, the companies of *S* have hopes;
Is 60: 6 *S* shall come bearing gold and frankincense,
Jer 6:20 what use to me incense that comes from *S*,
Ez 27:22 of *S* and Raamah also traded with you,
27:23 Canneh, and Eden, the merchants of *S*,
38:13 *S* and Dedan, the merchants of Tarshish

SHEBANIAH (7)

1Chr 15:24 The priests, *S*, Joshaphat, Nethanel,
Neh 9: 4 Levites were Jeshua, Binnui, Kadmiel, *S*,
9: 5 Bani, Hashabneiah, Sherebiah, Hodiah, *S*,
10: 5 Pashhur, Amariah, Malchijah, Hattush, *S*,
10:11 and their brethren *S*, Hodiah, Kelita,
10:13 Rehob, Hashabiah, Zaccur, Sherebiah, *S*,
12:14 for *S*, Joseph; for Harim, Adna;

SHEBAT (2)

1Mc 16:14 the eleventh month (that is, the month *S*).
Zec 1: 7 on the twenty-fourth day of *S*

SHEBER (1)

1Chr 2:48 Caleb's concubine, bore *S* and Tirhanah.

SHEBNA (5)

Is 22:15 Up, go to that official, *S*, master of the
36: 3 Eliakim, son of Hilkiah, and *S* the scribe,
36:11 and *S* and Joah said to the commander,
36:22 Eliakim, son of Hilkiah, *S* the scribe,
37: 2 the master of the palace, and *S* the scribe,

SHEBNAH (4)

2Kgs 18:18 *S* the scribe; and the herald Joah,
18:26 and *S* and Joah said to the commander:
18:37 Eliakim, son of Hilkiah, *S* the scribe,
19: 2 the master of the palace, *S* the scribe,

SHECANIAH (10)

1Chr 3:21 Jeshaiah, Rephaiah, Arnan, Obadiah, and *S*.
3:22 The sons of *S* were Shemiah, Hattush,
24:11 the ninth to Jeshua, the tenth to *S*,
2Chr 31:15 Miniamin, Jeshua, Shemaiah, Amariah and *S*,
Ezr 8: 3 of the sons of David, Hattush, son of *S*;
8: 5 of the sons of Zattu, *S*, son of Jahaziel,
10: 2 Then *S*, the son of Jehiel, one of the sons
Neh 3:29 was carried out by Shemaiah, son of *S*,
6:18 him, since he was the son-in-law of *S*,
12: 3 Ezra, Amariah, Malluch, Hattush, *S*,

SHECHEM (64)

Gn 12: 6 the land as far as the sacred place at *S*,
33:18 Jacob arrived safely at the city of *S*,
33:19 the descendants of Hamor, the founder of *S*.
34: 2 When *S*, son of Hamor the Hivite,
34: 4 *S* also asked his father Hamor,
34: 5 that *S* had defiled his daughter Dinah;
34: 6 Now Hamor, the father of *S*,
34: 7 What *S* had done was an outrage in Israel;

34: 8 son S has his heart set on your daughter.
34:11 Then S, too, appealed to Dinah's father
34:13 to S and his father Hamor with guile,
34:18 seemed fair to Hamor and his son S.
34:20 So Hamor and his son S went to their town
34:24 the town agreed with Hamor and his son S,
34:26 had put Hamor and his son S to the sword,
37:12 to pasture their father's flocks at S,
37:13 you know, are tending our flocks at S.
37:14 When Joseph reached S, a man met him
48:22 you, as to the one above his brothers, S,
Nm 26:31 through S the clan of the Shechemites,
Jos 17: 2 the clans of Abiezer, Helek, Asriel, S,
17: 7 From Michmethath near S,
20: 7 S in the mountain region of Ephraim,
21:21 at S in the mountain region of Ephraim;
24: 1 together all the tribes of Israel at S,
24:25 statutes and ordinances for them at S,
24:32 were buried in S in the plot of ground
24:32 bought from the sons of Hamor, father of S,
Jgs 8:31 who lived in S also bore him a son,
9: 1 went to his mother's kinsmen in S,
9: 2 this question to all the citizens of S:
9: 3 citizens of S sympathized with Abimelech,
9: 6 Then all the citizens of S and all
9: 6 the terebinth at the memorial pillar in S.
9: 7 "Hear me, citizens of S, that God may
9:18 his handmaid, king over the citizens of S,
9:20 to devour the citizens of S and Beth-millo,
9:23 between Abimelech and the citizens of S,
9:24 killed them, and upon the citizens of S,
9:25 The citizens of S then set men in ambush
9:26 of Ebed, came over to S with his kinsmen.
9:26 The citizens of S put their trust in him,
9:28 And why should we of S serve him?
9:28 subject to the men of Hamor, father of S?
9:31 S and are stirring up the city against you.
9:34 set up an ambush for S in four companies.
9:39 citizens of S and fought against Abimelech.
9:41 Zebul drove Gaal and his kinsmen from S,
21:19 the highway that goes up from Bethel to S,
1Kgs 12: 1 Rehoboam went to S, where all Israel had
12:25 Jeroboam built up S in the hill country of
1Chr 6:52 S in the mountain region of Ephraim,
7:19 The sons of Shemida were Ahian, S,
7:28 and also S and its towns as far as Ayyah
2Chr 10: 1 to S, for all Israel had come to Shechem
Ps(s) 60: 8 "Exultantly I will apportion S,
108: 8 "Exultantly I will apportion S,
Sir 50:26 and the degenerate folk who dwell in S.
Jer 41: 5 with gashes on their bodies came from S,
Hos 6: 9 a band of priests slay on the way to S,
Jn 4: 5 brought him to a Samaritan town named S
Acts 7:16 Their remains were transferred to S and
7:16 with silver from the sons of Hamor at S.

SHECHEMITES (3)

Nm 26:31 through Shechem the clan of the S,
Jgs 9:57 all their wickedness home to the S,
Jdt 5:16 the Perizzites, the Jebusites, the S,

SHECHEM'S (1)

Gn 34:26 they took Dinah from S house and left.

SHED (46)

Gn 1:15 dome of the sky, to s light upon the earth."
1:17 dome of the sky, to s light upon the earth,
9: 6 blood of man, by man shall his blood be s;
Ex 25:37 so set up the lamps that they s their light
Nm 35:33 have no atonement for the blood s on it
35:33 except through the blood of him who s it.
Dt 19:10 innocent blood will not be s and you will
21: 7 declare, 'Our hands did not s this blood,
1Sam 25:31 for having s innocent blood or for having
1Kgs 2:31 the blood which Joab s without provocation.
2Kgs 9: 7 other servants of the LORD s by Jezebel,
24: 4 because of the innocent blood he s,
1Chr 22: 8 'You have s much blood,
22: 8 because you have s too much blood upon the
28: 3 you are a man who fought wars and s blood.'
1Mc 1:24 with great arrogance and s much blood.
1:37 they s innocent blood around the sanctuary;
7:17 blood they have s round about Jerusalem,
Ps(s) 106:38 to demons, And they s innocent blood,
119:136 My eyes s streams of tears because your
Prv 1:16 feet run to evil, they hasten to s blood.]
6:17 tongue, and hands that s innocent blood;
Sir 38:16 s tears for one who is dead with wailing
Is 1: 8 in a vineyard, Like a s in a melon patch,
59: 7 and they are quick to s innocent blood;
Jer 7: 6 no longer s innocent blood in this place,
22: 3 and do not s innocent blood in this place.
Lam 4:13 Who s in her midst the blood of the just!—
Ez 22: 4 which you s you have been made guilty,
22:12 are those in you take brides to s blood.
24: 7 For the blood she s is in her midst:
24:16 but do not mourn or weep or s any tears.
33:25 raise your eyes to your idols, you s blood
Jl 4:19 they s innocent blood in their land.
Mi 7: 2 They all lie in wait to s blood,
Hb 2: 8 Because of men's blood s, and violence
2:17 Because of men's blood s, and violence
Mt 23:35 all the blood of the just ones s on earth,
24:29 be darkened, the moon will not s her light,
Mk 13:24 be darkened, the moon will not s its light,
Lk 11:50 s since the foundation of the world.
22:20 in my blood, which will be s for you.
Acts 22:20 blood of your witness Stephen was being s,
Rom 3:15 Swiftly run their feet to s blood;
Rv 16: 6 who s the blood of saints and prophets,
19: 2 of his servants which was s by her hand."

SHEDDING (17)

Gn 37:22 Instead of s blood," he continued, 'just
Dt 19:13 from Israel the stain of s innocent blood,
21: 8 and let not the guilt of s innocent blood
1Sm 19: 5 should you become guilty of s innocent
25:26 the LORD who has kept you from s blood
25:33 this day have prevented me from s blood
2Kgs 21:16 s so much innocent blood as to fill the
Tb 7: 6 sprang up and kissed him, s tears of joy.
Est E: 5 accomplices in the s of innocent blood,
2Mc 1: 8 fire to the gatehouse and s innocent blood.
Ps(s) 79:10 you avenge the s of your servants' blood.
Jer 22:17 on your own gain, On s innocent blood,
Ez 22:27 s blood and destroying lives to get unjust
Jon 1:14 do not charge us with s innocent blood,
Mt 23:30 have joined them in s the prophets' blood.'
Heb 9:22 the s of blood there is no forgiveness.
12: 4 not yet resisted to the point of s blood.

SHEDEUR (5)

Nm 1: 6 Elizur, son of S from Simeon
2:10 [Their prince was Elizur, son of S,
7:30 day it was the turn of Elizur, son of S,
7:35 This was the offering of Elizur, son of S.
10:18 next to set out, with Elizur, son of S,

SHEDS (11)

Gn 9: 6 If anyone s the blood of man,
1Sm 19:18 Then he and Samuel went to stay in the s.
19:19 told that David was in the s near Ramah,
19:22 and was told, "At the s near Ramah."
19:23 he set out from the hilltop toward the s,
19:23 At the s near Ramah he, too, stripped
20: 1 David fled from the s near Ramah,
Jb 15:33 be like a vine that s its grapes unripened,
Ps(s) 119:130 The revelation of your words s light,
Sir 34:22 s blood who denies the laborer his wages.
Ez 22: 3 Woe to the city which s blood within

SHEEN (1)

Ez 8: 1 to be a brightness like the s of electrum.

SHEEP (210)

Gn 21:27 Then Abraham took s and cattle and gave
22: 7 wood, but where is the s for the holocaust?"
22: 8 will provide the s for the holocaust."
29: 2 with three droves of s huddled near it,
29: 9 them, Rachel arrived with her father's s;
29:10 uncle Laban, with the s of his uncle Laban,
29:10 of the well, and watered his uncle's s.
30:32 from it every dark animal among the s
30:33 a speckled or spotted goat, or a dark s,
30:35 them, as well as the fully dark-colored s;
30:40 The s, on the other hand, Jacob kept
31:19 Now Laban had gone away to shear his s,
32: 6 I own cattle, asses and s, as well as male
38:12 up to Timnah for the shearing of his s,
38:13 on his way up to Timnah to shear his s,
47:17 their flocks of s and herds of cattle,
Ex 12: 5 may take it from either the s or the goats.
13:13 of an ass you shall redeem with a s.
20:24 and peace offerings, your s and your oxen.
21:37 an ox or a s and slaughters or sells it,
21:37 the one ox, and four s for the one sheep.
22: 3 possession, be it an ox, an ass or a s,
22: 8 it be about an ox, or an ass, or a s,
22: 9 a man gives an ass, or an ox, or a s,
22:29 do the same with your oxen and your s;
Lv 1:10 is from the flock, that is, a s or a goat,
7:23 not eat the fat of any ox or s or goat.
17: 3 who slaughters an ox or a s or goat,
22:19 the ox or s or goat that he offers must be
22:23 An ox or a s that is in any way
22:28 a s on one and the same day with its young.
27:26 If it is an ox or a s, it shall be ceded to
Nm 11:22 s and cattle be slaughtered for them?
18:17 cattle, s or goats shall not be redeemed;
22:40 Here Balak slaughtered oxen and s,
27:17 may not be like s without a shepherd."
31:28 asses and s in their half of the spoil you
31:30 the different beasts, oxen, asses and s,
31:32 six hundred and seventy-five thousand s,
31:36 and thirty-seven thousand five hundred s,
31:43 and thirty-seven thousand five hundred s,
Dt 14: 4 the ox, the s, the goat, the red deer,
14: 5 the addax, the oryx, and the mountain s.
14:26 money for whatever you desire, oxen or s,
22: 1 shall not see your kinsman's ox or s driven
32:14 Butter from its cows and milk from its s,
Jos 6:21 and old, as well as oxen, s and asses.
7:24 and daughters, his ox, his ass and his s,
Jgs 6: 4 leaving no sustenance in Israel, nor s,
1Sm 14:32 So they pounced upon the spoil and took s,
14:34 of them to bring his ox or his s to me.
15: 3 women, children and infants, oxen and s,
15: 9 Agag and the best of the fat s and oxen,
15:14 this bleating of s that comes to my ears,
15:15 best s and oxen to sacrifice to the LORD,
15:21 But from the spoil the men took s and oxen,
16:11 still the youngest, who is tending the s."
17:15 Saul to tend his father's s at Bethlehem.
17:28 you left those s in the desert meanwhile?
17:34 servant used to tend his father's s,
17:34 bear came to carry off a s from the flock,
22:19 and infants, and oxen, asses and s.
25: 2 three thousand s and a thousand goats.
25:16 time we were pasturing the s near them.
25:18 loaves, two skins of wine, five dressed s,
27: 9 man or woman alive, but would carry off s,
30:20 Moreover, David took all the s and oxen,
2Sm 24:17 But these are s; what have they done?
1Kgs 1: 9 When he slaughtered s, oxen, and fatlings
1:19 oxen, fatlings, and s in great numbers;
1:25 oxen, fatlings, and s in great numbers;
5: 3 twenty pasture-fed oxen, and a hundred s,
8: 5 ark s and oxen too many to number or count.
8:63 oxen and one hundred twenty thousand s.
22:17 the mountains, like s without a shepherd,
2Kgs 3: 4 Now Mesha, king of Moab, who raised s,
5:26 olive orchards or vineyards, s or cattle,
1Chr 5:21 camels, two hundred fifty thousand s,
12:41 figs, raisins, wine oil, oxen, and s.
17: 7 from the pasture, from following the s,
21:17 But these s, what have they done?
2Chr 5: 6 before the ark were sacrificing s and oxen
7: 5 oxen, and one hundred twenty thousand s.
14:14 carried off a great number of s and camels.
15:11 thousand s of the booty they had brought.
18: 2 s and oxen for him and the people with him,
18:16 the mountains, like s without a shepherd,
29:33 were six hundred oxen and three thousand s.
30:24 bulls and seven thousand s to the assembly,
30:24 a thousand bulls and ten thousand s.
31: 6 Judah also brought in tithes of oxen, s,
32:29 he acquired s and oxen in great numbers,
Neh 3: 1 took up the task of rebuilding the S Gate.
3:32 upper chamber of the Angle and the S Gate,
12:39 as far as the S Gate [and they came to a
Tb 1: 6 income and the first shearings of the s,
10:10 male and female slaves, oxen and s,
Jdt 2:17 innumerable s, cattle, and goats for their
11:19 drive them like s that have no shepherd,
Jb 1: 3 and he had seven thousand s,
1:16 s and their shepherds and consumed them;
31:20 me when warmed with the fleece of my s;
42:12 For he had fourteen thousand s,
Ps(s) 8: 8 All s and oxen, yes, and the beasts
44:12 You marked us out as s to be slaughtered;
44:23 we are looked upon as s to be slaughtered.
49:15 s they are herded into the nether world;
74: 1 smolder against the s of your pasture?
78:52 But his people he led forth like s and
79:13 we, your people and the s of your pasture,
119:176 I have gone astray [like a lost s;
144:13 May our s be in the thousands,
Eccl 2: 7 growing herds of cattle and flocks of s,
Is 7:21 man shall keep a heifer or a couple of s,
7:25 for cattle and shall be trampled upon by s.
22:13 you slaughter oxen and butcher s,
43:23 You did not bring me s for your holocausts,
53: 6 We had all gone astray like s,
53: 7 the slaughter or a s before the shearers,
Jer 3:24 from our youth, Their s and their cattle,
5:17 your daughters, Devour your s and cattle,
12: 3 Pick them out like s for the slaughter,
13:20 to you, the s that were your glory?
23: 2 have scattered my s and driven them away.
31:12 the wine, and the oil, the s and the oxen;
49:20 be dragged away, even the smallest s,
50: 6 Lost s were my people, their shepherds
50:17 A stray s was Israel that lions pursued;
50:45 be dragged away, even the smallest s;
Bar 4:26 off by their enemies like s in a raid.
Ez 34: 2 Should not shepherds, rather, pasture s?
34: 3 fatlings, but the s you have not pastured.
34: 5 My s were scattered and wandered over all
34: 6 my s were scattered over the whole earth,
34: 8 my s have been given over to pillage,
34: 8 my s have become food for every wild beast,
34: 8 my shepherds did not look after my s,
34: 8 themselves and did not pasture my s;
34:10 I will claim my s from them and put a stop
34:10 and put a stop to their shepherding my s
34:10 I will save my s, that they may no longer
34:11 I myself will look after and tend my s.
34:12 his scattered sheep, so will I tend my s.
34:15 I myself will pasture my s;
34:17 As for you, my s, says the Lord GOD,
34:17 I will judge between one s and another,
34:19 Thus my s had to graze on what your feet
34:20 I judge between the fat and the lean s.
34:21 and butt all the weak s with your horns

SHEEP (cont.)

34:22 s so that they may no longer be despoiled,
34:22 and I will judge between one s and another.
34:31 my sheep, you are the s of my pasture,
36:37 to multiply them like s.
36:38 sacrificial sheep, the s of Jerusalem on its
45:15 One s from the flock for every two hundred
Dn 14: 3 for it six barrels of fine flour, forty s,
14:32 and two s had been given to them daily.
Hos 12:13 for a wife Israel tended s.
Jl 1:18 even the flocks of s have perished.
Am 3:12 of legs or the tip of an ear of his s,
Jon 3: 7 man nor beast, neither cattle nor s,
Mi 5: 7 like a young lion among flocks of s;
Zec 10: 2 This is why they wander like s, wretched:
11: 7 to be slaughtered for the s merchants.
11:11 The s merchants who were watching me
13: 7 the shepherd that the s may be dispersed,
Mt 9:36 from exhaustion, like s without a shepherd.
10: 6 after the lost s of the house of Israel.
10:16 is sending you out like s among wolves.
12:11 a s and it falls into a pit on the sabbath.
12:12 more precious a human being is than a s.
15:24 only to the lost s of the house of Israel,"
18:12 a hundred s and one of them wanders away;
25:32 as a shepherd separates s from goats.
25:33 The s he will place on his right hand,
26:31 and the s of the flock will be dispersed.'
Mk 6:34 for they were like s without a shepherd;
14:27 the shepherd and the s will be dispersed.'
Lk 15: 4 he has a hundred s and loses one of them,
15: 6 with me because I have found my lost s.'
17: 7 herding s and he came in from the fields,
Jn 2:14 engaged in selling oxen, s and doves,
2:15 s and oxen alike out of the temple area,
5: 2 Now in Jerusalem by the S Pool there is a
10: 2 through the gate is shepherd of the s;
10: 3 The s hear his voice as he calls his own
10: 4 and the s follow him because they
10: 8 and marauders whom the s did not heed.
10:11 good shepherd lays down his life for the s.
10:12 is no shepherd nor owner of the s—
10:12 s to be snatched and scattered by the wolf.
10:13 he has no concern for the s.
10:14 I know my sheep and my s know me in the
10:15 for these s I will give my life.
10:16 other s that do not belong to this fold.
10:26 refuse to believe because you are not my s.
10:27 My s hear my voice.
21:16 Jesus replied, "Tend my s."
21:17 Jesus said to him, "Feed my s."
Acts 8:32 "Like a s he was led to the slaughter,
Rom 8:36 we are looked upon as s to be slaughtered."
Heb 11:37 about garbed in the skins of s or goats,
13:20 the s by the blood of the eternal covenant,
1Pt 2:25 At one time you were straying like s,
Rv 18:13 cattle and s, horses and carriages; slaves

SHEEPFOLD (1)

Jn 10: 1 Whoever does not enter the s through the

SHEEPFOLDS (8)

Nm 32:16 wish only to build s here for our flocks,
32:36 and Beth-haran, and they built s.
1Sm 24: 4 When he came to the s along the way,
Jdt 2:26 burned their tents, and plundered their s.
Ps(s) 68:14 Though you rested among the s,
78:70 his servant, and took him from the s;
Sir 40:19 S and orchards bring flourishing health;
Jer 33:12 s for the shepherds to couch their flocks.

SHEEPGATE (1)

Jn 10: 7 I am the s.

SHEEP'S (1)

Mt 7:15 who come to you in s clothing but

SHEER (8)

Dt 32:25 sword in the street and by s terror at home
Prv 22:16 yield up his gains to the rich as s loss.
Wis 11: 4 and water was given them from the s rock,
Sir 40:15 for the root of the godless is on s rock;
Jer 2:12 this, O heavens, and shudder with s horror,
Mt 6: 7 hearing by the s multiplication of words.
Lk 24:41 still incredulous for s joy and wonder,
Rv 11:11 feet s terror gripped those who saw them.

SHEERAH (1)

1Chr 7:24 He had a daughter, S, who built lower

SHEET (16)

Ex 26: 4 along the edge of the end s in one set,
26: 4 the edge of the end s in the other set.
26: 5 the edge of the end s in the first set,
26: 5 of the corresponding s in the second set,
26: 9 sixth s double at the front of the tent.
26:10 along the edge of the end s in one set,
26:10 the edge of the end s in the second set.
26:12 will be an extra half s of tent covering,
36: 9 The length of each s was twenty-eight
36:11 the edge of the end s in the first set,
36:11 the edge of the end s in the second set.
36:12 Fifty loops were thus put on one inner s,
36:12 loops on the inner s in the other set,
36:15 The length of each s was thirty cubits and
36:17 along the edge of the end s in one set,
36:17 of the corresponding s in the other set.

SHEETS (20)

Ex 26: 1 s woven of fine linen twined and of violet,
26: 2 all the s shall be of the same size.
26: 3 Five of the s are to be sewed together,
26: 6 gold, with which to join the two sets of s,
26: 7 "Also make s woven of goat hair,
26: 8 Eleven such s are to be made;
26: 8 all eleven s shall be of the same size.
26: 9 Sew five of the s, edge to edge, into one
26: 9 set, and the other six s into another set.
26:13 the s of the tent will have an extra
36: 8 with its ten s woven of fine linen twined,
36: 9 all the s were of the same size.
36:10 Five of the s were sewed together,
36:13 with which the s were joined so that the
36:14 S of goat hair were also woven as a tent
36:14 Eleven such s were made.
36:15 all eleven s were the same size.
36:16 s were sewed edge to edge into one set;
36:16 and the other six s into another set.
Nm 4:25 they shall carry the s of the Dwelling,

SHEHARIAH (1)

1Chr 8:26 Shamsherai, S, Athaliah.

SHEIKHS (1)

Ez 27:21 and of all the s of Kedar belonged to you;

SHEKEL (25)

Gn 24:22 took out a gold ring weighing half a s,
Ex 30:13 sanctuary shekel, twenty gerahs to the s.
30:24 to the standard of the sanctuary s;
38:24 to the standard of the sanctuary s;
38:25 to the standard of the sanctuary s;
38:26 to the standard of the sanctuary s,
Lv 5:15 to the standard of the sanctuary s.
27:25 to the standard of the sanctuary s.
27:25 There are twenty gerahs to the s.
Nm 3:47 sanctuary shekel, twenty gerahs to the s.
18:16 sanctuary standard, twenty gerahs to the s.
1Sm 9: 8 Saul, "I have a quarter of a silver s.
13:21 and mattocks was two-thirds of a s,
13:21 and a third of a s for sharpening the axes
2Kgs 7: 1 a shekel, and two seahs of barley for a s,
7:16 a shekel and two seahs of barley for a s,
7:18 "Two seahs of barley will sell for a s,
7:18 and one seah of fine flour for a s
Neh 10:33 to give a third of a s each year for the
Ez 45:12 The s shall be twenty gerahs.
Am 8: 5 We will diminish the ephah, add to the s,

SHEKELS—SHEKEL'S (98)

Gn 20:16 given your brother a thousand s of silver.
23:15 of land worth four hundred s of silver
23:16 s of silver at the current market value.
24:22 and two gold bracelets weighing ten s,
45:22 s of silver and five sets of garments.
Ex 21:32 the owner of the slave thirty s of silver,
30:23 five hundred s of free-flowing myrrh;
30:23 amount, that is, two hundred and fifty s,
30:23 two hundred and fifty s of fragrant cane;
30:24 five hundred s of cassia
38:24 talents and seven hundred and thirty s,
38:25 thousand seven hundred and seventy-five s,
38:28 thousand seven hundred and seventy-five s
38:29 talents and two thousand four hundred s.
Lv 5:15 valued at two silver s according to the
27: 3 and sixty, the fixed sum, in sanctuary s,
27: 3 shekels, shall be fifty silver s for a man,
27: 4 for a man, and thirty s for a woman;
27: 5 fixed sum shall be twenty s for a youth,
27: 6 fixed sum shall be five silver s for a boy,
27: 7 the fixed sum shall be fifteen s for a man,
27:16 barley seed being valued at fifty silver s.
Nm 3:47 you shall take five s for each individual,
3:50 s according to the sanctuary standard.
7:13 plate weighing a hundred and thirty s
7:13 and one silver basin weighing seventy s,
7:14 cup of ten s' weight filled with incense;
7:19 plate weighing a hundred and thirty s
7:19 and one silver basin weighing seventy s,
7:20 cup of ten s' weight filled with incense,
7:25 plate weighing a hundred and thirty s
7:25 and one silver basin weighing seventy s,
7:26 cup of ten s' weight filled with incense;
7:31 plate weighing a hundred and thirty s
7:31 and one silver basin weighing seventy s,
7:32 cup of ten s' weight filled with incense;
7:37 plate weighing a hundred and thirty s
7:37 and one silver basin weighing seventy s,
7:38 cup of ten s' weight filled with incense;
7:43 plate weighing a hundred and thirty s
7:43 and one silver basin weighing seventy s,
7:44 cup of ten s weight filled with incense
7:49 plate weighing a hundred and thirty s
7:49 and one silver basin weighing seventy s,
7:50 cup of ten s' weight filled with incense;
7:55 plate weighing a hundred and thirty s
7:55 and one silver basin weighing seventy s,
7:56 cup of ten s' weight filled with incense;
7:61 plate weighing a hundred and thirty s
7:61 and one silver basin weighing seventy s,
7:62 cup of ten s' weight filled with incense;
7:67 plate weighing a hundred and thirty s
7:67 and one silver basin weighing seventy s,
7:68 cup of ten s' weight filled with incense;
7:73 plate weighing one hundred and thirty s
7:73 and one silver basin weighing seventy s,
7:74 cup of ten s' weight filled with incense;
7:79 plate weighing a hundred and thirty s
7:79 and one silver basin weighing seventy s,
7:80 cup of ten s' weight filled with incense;
7:85 plate weighed a hundred and thirty s,
7:85 amounted to two thousand four hundred s,
7:86 filled with incense weighed ten s apiece,
7:86 cups amounted to one hundred and twenty s.
18:16 s according to the sanctuary standard,
31:52 sixteen thousand seven hundred and fifty s.
Dt 22:19 besides fining him one hundred silver s,
22:29 fifty silver s and take her as his wife,
Jos 7:21 Babylonian mantle, two hundred s of silver,
7:21 and a bar of gold fifty s in weight;
Jgs 8:26 weighed seventeen hundred gold s,
9: 4 silver s from the temple of Baal of Berith,
16: 5 each give you eleven hundred s of silver."
17: 2 "The eleven hundred s of silver over
17: 3 eleven hundred s of silver to his mother,
17:10 and I will give you ten silver s a year,
1Sm 17: 5 of scale armor weighing five thousand s,
17: 7 and its iron head weighed six hundred s.
2Sm 14:26 hundred s according to the royal standard.
21:16 whose bronze spear weighed three hundred s,
24:24 floor and the oxen for fifty silver s.
1Kgs 10:16 (six hundred gold s went into each shield)
10:29 shekels, a horse one hundred and fifty s;
2Kgs 15:20 in the country, fifty silver s from each.
1Chr 21:25 Ornan six hundred s of gold for the place.
2Chr 1:17 and export them at six hundred silver s,
1:17 the horses going for a hundred and fifty s.
3: 9 The weight of the nails was fifty gold s.
9:15 s of beaten gold going into each shield,
9:16 hundred s of gold going into each buckler;
Neh 5:15 each day forty silver s for their food;
1Mc 10:40 silver s out of the royal revenues,
10:42 the dues of five thousand silver s
Jer 32: 9 paying him the money, seventeen silver s.
Ez 4:10 you eat shall be twenty s a day by weight;
45:12 Twenty s, twenty-five shekels, plus fifteen s

SHELAH (19)

Gn 10:24 of Shelah, and S became the father of Eber.
11:12 years old, he became the father of S.
11:13 and three years after the birth of S,
11:14 When S was thirty years old,
11:15 S lived four hundred and three years after
38: 5 bore still another son, whom she named S.
38:11 father's house until my son S grows up"
38:11 that S also might die like his brothers.
38:14 aware that, although S was now grown up,
38:26 I am, since I did not give her to my son S."
46:12 Er, Onan, S, Perez, and Zerah
Nm 26:20 through S the clan of the Shelahites,
1Chr 1:18 of Shelah, and S became the father of Eber.
1:24 Shem, Arpachshad, S,
2: 3 Er, Onan, and S;
4:21 The descendants of S, son of Judah, were:
Lk 3:35 Reu, son of Peleg, son of Eber, son of S,

SHELAHITES (1)

Nm 26:20 through Shelah the clan of the S,

SHELANITES (2)

1Chr 9: 5 Among the S were Asaiah,
Neh 11: 5 Joiarib, son of Zechariah, a son of the S.

SHELEMIAH (9)

Ezr 10:39 Shimei, S, Nathan, and Adaiah;
10:41 Shashai, Sharai, Azarel, S,
Neh 3:30 After him, Hananiah, son of S,
13:13 the storerooms I appointed the priest S,
Jer 36:14 sent Jehudi, son of Nethaniah, son of S,
36:26 prince, and Seraiah, son of Azriel, and S,
37: 3 Yet King Zedekiah sent Jehucal, son of S,
37:13 the guard, a man named Irijah, son of S,
38: 1 Gedaliah, son of Pashhur, Jucal, son of S,

SHELEPH (2)

Gn 10:26 Joktan became the father of Almodad, S,
1Chr 1:20 Joktan became the father of Almodad, S,

SHELESH (1)

1Chr 7:35 of his brother Hotham were Zophah, Imna, S,

SHELLING (1)
Lk 6: 1 off grain-heads, *s* them with their hands,

SHELOMI (1)
Nm 34:28 *S,* from the tribe of Naphtali:

SHELOMITH (10)
Lv 24:10 was a man born of an Israelite mother *S,*
1Chr 3:19 *S* was their sister.
23:18 *S* the chief.
24:22 *S* of the Izharites,
24:22 and Jahath of the descendatns of *S.*
26:25 whose son was Zichri, whose son was *S.*
26:26 This *S* and his brethren superintended all
26:28 was under the charge of *S* and his brethren.
2Chr 11:20 who bore him Abijah, Attai, Ziza and *S.*
Ezr 8:10 of the sons of Bani, *S,* son of Josiphiah,

SHELOMOTH (1)
1Chr 23: 9 The sons of Shimei were *S,*

SHELTER (33)
Gn 19: 8 know they have come under the *s* of my roof."
Ex 9:19 *s* shall die when the hail comes upon them."
9:20 their servants and livestock off to *s.*
Jgs 19:15 them the *s* of his home for the night.
19:18 no one has offered us the *s* of his house.
2Sm 20: 6 cities and take *s* while we look on."
22:12 He made darkness the *s* about him,
1Kgs 19: 9 There he came to a cave, where he took *s.*
Jb 24: 8 and for want of *s* they cling to the rock.
Ps(s) 27: 5 He will conceal me in the *s* of his tent,
31:21 You hide them in the *s* of your presence
32: 7 You are my *s;* from distress you will
55: 9 *s* from the violent storm and the tempest."
61: 5 take refuge in the *s* of your wings!
64: 3 *S* me against the council of malefactors,
91: 1 You who dwell in the *s* of the Most High,
Wis 5:16 For he shall *s* them with his right hand,
9:15 and the earthen *s* weighs down the mind
10:17 and became a *s* for them by day and a
Sir 2:13 trust not, who therefore will have no *s!*
6:14 A faithful friend is a sturdy *s;*
14:27 Who takes *s* with her from the heat,
34:16 and strong support, A *s* from the heat,
Is 4: 6 all, his glory will be *s* and protection:
16: 4 with you, be their *s* from the destroyer.
22: 8 the gates, and *s* over Judah is removed.
25: 4 *S* from the rain, shade from the heat.
32: 2 Each of them will be a *s* from the wind,
Lam 2: 6 has demolished his *s* like a garden booth,
Bar 6:67 by fleeing to *s* are better than they are.
Hb 3:11 to rise, the moon remains in its *s,*
Acts 27: 7 we sailed for Salmone and the *s* of Crete.
Rv 7:15 he who sits on the throne will give them *s.*

SHELTERED (6)
Jb 14:13 and keep me *s* till your wrath is past;
29: 4 in my flourishing days, when God *s* my tent;
Wis 19: 8 crossed the whole nation *s* by your hand,
Sir 28:19 Happy he who is *s* from it,
Zep 2: 3 may be *s* on the day of the LORD's anger.
Acts 27: 4 we sailed around the *s* side of Cyprus

SHELTERING (3)
1Kgs 8: 7 ark, *s* the ark and its poles from above.
2Chr 5: 8 ark, *s* the ark and its poles from above.
Is 58: 7 hungry, *s* the oppressed and the homeless;

SHELTERS (2)
Dt 33:12 who *s* him all the day while he abides
Jer 4:20 my tents are ravaged; in a flash, my *s.*

SHELUMIEL (5)
Nm 1: 6 *S,* son of Zurishaddai; from Judah:
2:12 the tribe of Simeon [Their prince was *S,*
7:36 On the fifth day it was the turn of *S,*
7:41 This was the offering of *S,*
10:19 son of Shedeur, over their host, and *S,*

SHEM (19)
Gn 5:32 years old, he became the father of *S,*
6:10 *S,* Ham, and Japheth.
7:13 precise day named, Noah and his sons *S,*
9:18 of Noah who came out of the ark were *S,*
9:23 *S* and Japheth, however, took a robe,
9:26 "Blessed be the LORD, the God of *S!*
9:27 so that he dwells among the tents of *S;*
10: 1 are the descendants of Noah's sons, *S,*
10:21 To *S* also, Japheth's oldest brother
10:22 The descendants of *S:*
10:31 These are the descendants of *S,*
11:10 This is the record of the descendants of *S.*
11:10 When *S* was one hundred years old,
11:11 *S* lived five hundred years after the birth
1Chr 1: 4 Jared, Enoch, Methuselah, Lamech, Noah, *S,*
1:17 The descendants of *S* were Elam,
1:24 *S,* Arpachshad, Shelah, Eber, Peleg, Reu,

Sir 49:16 Glorious, too, were *S* and SETH and ENOS;
Lk 3:36 son of Cainan, son of Arphaxad, son of *S,*

SHEMA (7)
Jos 15:26 Amam, *S,* Moladah.
19: 2 their heritage they received Beer-sheba, *S,*
1Chr 2:43 Hebron were Korah, Tappuah, Rekem, and *S.*
2:44 *S* became the father of Raham,
5: 8 Zechariah, and Bela, son of Azaz, son of *S,*
8:13 Lod with its nearby towns, Beriah, and *S.*
Neh 8: 4 at his right side stood Mattithiah, *S,*

SHEMAAH (1)
1Chr 12: 3 along with Joash, both sons of *S* of Gibeah;

SHEMAIAH (39)
1Kgs 12:22 However, the LORD spoke to *S,*
1Chr 4:37 son of Jedaiah, son of Shimri, son of *S*—
5: 4 His son was Joel, whose son was *S,*
9:14 Among the Levites were *S,*
9:16 Obadiah, son of *S,* son of Galal,
15: 8 of the sons of Elizaphan, *S,* their chief,
15:11 and the Levites Uriel, Asaiah, Joel, *S,*
24: 6 The scribe *S,* son of Nethanel, a Levite,
26: 4 *S,* the first-born,
26: 6 To his son *S* were born sons who ruled over
26: 7 The sons of *S* were Othni, Rephael, Obed,
2Chr 11: 2 However, the word of the LORD came to *S,*
12: 5 Then *S* the prophet came to Rehoboam and
12: 7 themselves, the word of the LORD came to *S:*
12:15 in the history of *S* the prophet and of
17: 8 With them he sent the Levites, *S,*
31:15 cities were Eden, Miniamin, Jeshua, *S,*
35: 9 Conaniah and his brothers *S,*
Ezr 8:13 whose names were Eliphelet, Jeiel, and *S,*
8:16 Therefore I sent Eliezer, Ariel, *S,*
10:21 Maaseiah, Elijah, *S,*
10:31 Eliezer, Isshijah, Malchijah, *S,*
Neh 3:29 after him the repair was carried out by *S,*
6:10 I went to the house of *S,* son of Delaiah,
10: 9 Abijah, Mijamin, Maaziah, Bilgai, *S:*
11:15 Among the Levites were *S,* son of Hasshub,
12: 6 Abijah, Mijamin, Maadiah, Bilgah, *S,*
12:18 for *S,* Jehonathan; and for Joiarib,
12:34 Ezra, Meshullam, Judah, Benjamin, *S,*
12:35 also Zechariah, son of Jonathan, son of *S,*
12:36 Zaccur, son of Asaph, and his brethren *S,*
12:42 with the trumpets, and Maaseiah, *S,*
Tb 5:14 and Nathaniah, the two sons of *S* the elder;
Jer 26:20 in the name of the LORD, Uriah, son of *S,*
29:24 Say this to *S,* the Nehelamite:
29:31 Thus says the LORD concerning *S,*
29:31 Because *S* prophesies to you without a
29:32 says the LORD, I will therefore punish *S,*
36:12 Elishama, the scribe, Delaiah, son of *S,*

SHEMARIAH (4)
1Chr 12: 6 *S;* Shephatiah the Haruphite; Elkanah,
2Chr 11:19 Jeshush, *S* and Zaham.
Ezr 10:32 Shemaiah, Shimeon, Benjamin, Malluch, *S;*
10:41 Shashai, Sharai, Azarel, Shelemiah, *S,*

SHEMEBER (1)
Gn 14: 2 Shinab king of Admah, *S* king of Zeboiim,

SHEMED (1)
1Chr 8:12 The sons of Elpaal were Eber, Misham, *S,*

SHEMEI (1)
Zec 12:13 the family of *S,* and their wives;

SHEMER (3)
1Kgs 16:24 He then bought the hill of Samaria from *S*
16:24 naming the city he built Samaria after *S,*
1Chr 6:31 son of Amzi, son of Bani, son of *S,*

SHEMIAH (2)
1Chr 3:22 The sons of Shecaniah were *S,*
2Chr 29:14 sons of Jeduthun: *S* and Uzziel.

SHEMIDA (3)
Nm 26:32 through *S* the clan of the Shemidaites,
Jos 17: 2 Helek, Asriel, Shechem, Hepher and *S,*
1Chr 7:19 The sons of *S* were Ahian,

SHEMIDAITES (1)
Nm 26:32 through Shemida the clan of the *S,*

SHEMIRAMOTH (4)
1Chr 15:18 the gatekeepers Zechariah, Uzziel, *S,*
15:20 Zechariah, Uzziel, *S,*
16: 5 second to him were Zechariah, Uzziel, *S,*
2Chr 17: 8 Shemaiah, Nethaniah, Zebadiah, Asahel, *S,*

SHEMUEL (1)
1Chr 7: 2 Rephaiah, Jeriel, Jahmai, Ibsam, and *S,*

SHENAZZAR (1)
1Chr 3:18 Shealtiel, Malchiram, Pedaiah, *S,*

SHEPHAM (2)
Nm 34:10 you shall draw a line from Hazar-enan to *S.*
34:11 *S* the boundary shall go down to Ar-Baal,

SHEPHATIAH (13)
2Sm 3: 4 the fifth, *S,* son of Abital;
1Chr 3: 3 the fifth, *S,* by Abital;
9: 8 Meshullam, son of *S,* son of Reuel, son
12: 6 *S* the Haruphite;
27:16 for the Simeonites, *S,* son of Maacah;
2Chr 21: 2 Jehiel, Zechariah, Azariah, Michael and *S;*
Ezr 2: 4 sons of *S,* three hundred and seventy-two;
2:57 sons of Darkon, sons of Giddel, sons of *S,*
8: 8 of the sons of *S,* Zebadiah, son of Michael,
Neh 7: 9 sons of *S,*
7:59 sons of Darkon, sons of Giddel, sons of *S,*
11: 4 of Zechariah, son of Amariah, son of *S,*
Jer 38: 1 *S,* son of Mattan, Gedaliah, son of Pashhur

SHEPHELAH (1)
1Mc 12:38 Simon likewise built up Adida in the *S,*

SHEPHER (2)
Nm 33:23 from Kehelathah, they camped at Mount *S.*
33:24 Setting out from Mount *S,*

SHEPHERD (67)
Gn 48:15 has been my *s* from my birth to this day,
49:24 the Mighty One of Jacob, because of the *S,*
Nm 27:17 may not be like sheep without a *s.*"
1Sm 17:20 morning, having left the flock with a *s,*
2Sm 5: 2 'You shall *s* my people Israel and shall be
24:17 it is I, the *s,* who have done wrong.
1Kgs 22:17 on the mountains, like sheep without a *s,*
1Chr 11: 2 'You shall *s* my people Israel and be ruler
2Chr 18:16 on the mountains, like sheep without a *s,*
Jdt 11:19 will drive them like sheep that have no *s,*
Ps(s) 23: 1 The LORD is my *s;* I shall not want.
49:15 death is their *s,* and the upright rule
78:71 the ewes he brought him to *s* Jacob,
80: 2 O *s* of Israel, hearken, O guide
Wis 17:17 For whether one was a farmer, or a *s,*
Sir 18:12 teaching, as a *s* guides his flock;
Is 40:11 Like a *s* he feeds his flock; in his arms
44:28 My *s,* who fulfills my every wish; He
63:11 up out of the sea the *s* of his flock?
Jer 3:15 heart, who will *s* you wisely and prudently.
22:22 The wind shall *s* all your shepherds,
23: 2 against the shepherds who *s* my people:
23: 4 shepherds for them who will *s* them
31:10 together, he guards them as a *s* his flock.
43:12 As a *s* delouses his cloak,
49:19 What *s* can stand against me?
50:44 what *s* can stand against me?
51:23 With you I shatter the *s* and his flock,
Ez 34: 5 So they were scattered for lack of a *s,*
34: 8 for every wild beast, for lack of a *s;*
34:12 As a *s* tends his flock when he finds
34:23 appoint one *s* over them to pasture them,
34:23 he shall pasture them and be their *s.*
37:24 and there shall be one *s* for them all;
Am 1: 1 The words of Amos, a *s* from Tekoa,
3:12 As the *s* snatches from the mouth of the
7:14 I was a *s* and a dresser of sycamores.
Mi 5: 3 *s* his flock by the strength of the LORD,
7:14 *S* your people with your staff, the flock
Zec 10: 2 they have no *s.*
11: 4 *S* the flock to be slaughtered.
11: 7 So I became the *s* of the flock to be
11:15 This time take the gear of a foolish *s.*
11:16 For I will raise up a *s* in the land who
11:17 Woe to my foolish *s* who forsakes the flock!
13: 7 Awake, O sword, against my *s,*
13: 7 the *s* that the sheep may be dispersed,
Mt 2: 6 come a ruler who is to *s* my people Israel.'"
9:36 from exhaustion, like sheep without a *s.*
25:32 groups, as a *s* separates sheep from goats.
26:31 'I will strike the *s* and the sheep of the
Mk 6:34 for they were like sheep without a *s;*
14:27 the *s* and the sheep will be dispersed.'
Jn 10: 2 enters through the gate is *s* of the sheep;
10:11 I am the good *s;* the good shepherd lays
10:11 good *s* lays down his life for the sheep.
10:12 who is no *s* nor owner of the sheep
10:14 "I am the good *s.*
10:16 There shall be one flock then, one *s.*
Acts 20:28 *S* the church of God,
1Cor 9: 7 What *s* does not nourish himself with the
Heb 13:20 who brought up from the dead the great *S*
1Pt 2:25 sheep, but now you have returned to the *S,*
5: 4 so that when the chief *S* appears you will
Rv 7:17 for the Lamb on the throne will *s* them.
12: 5 to *s* all the nations with an iron rod.
19:15 He will *s* them with an iron rod;

SHEPHERDING (2)

Ez 34:10 and put a stop to their *s* my sheep
34:16 the strong I will destroy], *s* them rightly.

SHEPHERDS—SHEPHERD'S (52)

Gn 26:20 the *s* of Gerar quarreled with Isaac's
29: 3 Only when all the *s* were assembled there
29: 8 "until all the *s* are here to roll the
46:32 The men are *s*, having long been keepers
46:34 since all *s* are abhorrent to the Egyptians."
47: 3 your servants, like our ancestors, are *s*.
Ex 2:17 But some *s* came and drove them away.
2:19 saved us from the interference of the *s*.
1Sm 17:40 and put them in the pocket of his *s* bag.
25: 7 Now, when your *s* were with us,
Jb 1:16 the sheep and their *s* and consumed them;
Ps(s) 95: 7 he is our God, and we are the people he *s*,
Sg 1: 8 pasture the young ones near the *s'* camps.
Is 13:20 his tent there, nor *s* couch their flocks.
31: 4 With a band of *s* assembled against it,
38:12 My dwelling, like a *s* tent, is struck down
56:11 These are the *s* who know no discretion;
Jer 2: 8 the *s* rebelled against me.
3:15 will appoint over you *s* after my own heart,
6: 3 Against her, *s* come with their flocks;
10:21 Yes, the *s* were stupid as cattle,
12:10 Many *s* have ravaged my vineyard,
22:22 The wind shall shepherd all your *s*,
23: 1 Woe to the *s* who mislead and scatter the
23: 2 against the *s* who shepherd my people:
23: 4 I will appoint *s* for them who will
25:34 Howl, you *s*, and wail!
25:35 There is no flight for the *s*, no escape for
25:36 Wailing from the *s*, howling by the leaders
33:12 sheepfolds for the *s* to couch their flocks.
50: 6 sheep were my people, their *s* mislead them,
Ez 34: 2 of man, prophesy against the *s* of Israel,
34: 2 in these words prophesy to them [to the *s*:
34: 2 Woe to the *s* of Israel who have been
34: 2 Should not *s*, rather, pasture sheep?
34: 7 Therefore, *s*, hear the word of the LORD.
34: 8 because my *s* did not look after my sheep,
34: 9 because of this, *s*, hear the word of the
34:10 I swear I am coming against these *s*.
Am 1: 2 The pastures of the *s* will languish,
Mi 5: 4 land, We shall raise against it seven *s*,
Na 3:18 how your *s* slumber, O king of Assyria,
Zep 2: 6 of the Cretans shall become fields for *s*,
Zec 10: 3 My wrath is kindled against the *s*,
11: 3 the wailing of the *s*, their glory has been
11: 5 Even their own *s* do not feel for them.
11: 8 a single month I did away with the three *s*.
Lk 2: 8 There were *s* in that region, living in
2:15 to heaven, the *s* said to one another:
2:18 at the report given them by the *s*.
2:20 The *s* returned, glorifying and praising
1Pt 5: 2 flock is in your midst; give it a *s* care.

SHEPHI (1)

1Chr 1:40 of Shobal were Alian, Manahath, Ebal, *S*,

SHEPHO (1)

Gn 36:23 descendants were Alvan, Manahath, Ebal, *S*,

SHEPHUPHAN (1)

1Chr 8: 5 Ehud were Abishua, Naaman, Ahoah, Gera, *S*,

SHERD (1)

Is 30:14 be found a *s* to scoop fire from the hearth

SHERDS (1)

Ez 23:34 it dry, and gnaw at the very *s* of the cup,

SHEREBIAH (8)

Ezr 8:18 son of Levi, son of Israel, namely *S*,
8:24 of the priestly leaders along with *S*,
Neh 8: 7 [The Levites Jeshua, Bani, *S*,
9: 4 Binnui, Kadmiel, Shebaniah, Bunni, *S*,
9: 5 Jeshua, Kadmiel, Bani, Hashabneiah, *S*,
10:13 Hanan, Mica, Rehob, Hashabiah, Zaccur, *S*,
12: 8 Levites were Jeshua, Binnui, Kadmiel, *S*,
12:24 The heads of the Levites were Hashabiah, *S*,

SHERESH (1)

1Chr 7:16 He had a brother named *S*,

SHESHACH (1)

Jer 25:26 [and after them the king of *S* shall drink].

SHESHAI (3)

Nm 13:22 reached Hebron, where Ahiman, *S* and Talmai,
Jos 15:14 *S*, Ahiman and Talmai.
Jgs 1:10 called Kiriath-arba, and defeated *S*,

SHESHAN (4)

1Chr 2:31 The sons of Ishi: *S*.
2:31 The sons of *S*: Ahlai.
2:34 *S*, who had no sons, only daughters, had
2:35 *S* gave his daughter in marriage to his

SHESHBAZZAR (4)

Ezr 1: 8 treasurer Mithredath, and counted out to *S*,
1:11 All these *S* took with him
5:14 in Babylon and consigned to a certain *S*,
5:16 Then this same *S* came and laid the

SHETHAR (1)

Est 1:14 He summoned Carshena, *S*,

SHETHAR-BOZENAI (4)

Ezr 5: 3 governor of West-of-Euphrates, and *S*,
5: 6 governor of West-of-Euphrates, and *S*,
6: 6 governor of West-of-Euphrates, and *S*,
6:13 the governor of West-of-Euphrates, and *S*,

SHEVA (1)

1Chr 2:49 bore Shaaph, the father of Madmannah, *S*,

SHIBAH (1)

Gn 26:33 He called it *S*; hence the name of the city,

SHIBBOLETH (1)

Jgs 12: 6 they would ask him to say *S*."

SHIED (1)

Ex 4: 3 into a serpent, and Moses *s* away from it.

SHIELD (62)

Gn 15: 1 I am your *s*; I will make your reward
Dt 13: 9 look with pity upon him, to spare or *s* him,
33:29 The LORD is your saving *s*, and his sword
Jgs 5: 8 Not a *s* could be seen, nor a lance, among
1Sm 17: 7 His *s* bearer went before him.
2Sm 1:21 the warriors' shields, the *s* of Saul,
22: 3 My *s*, the horn of my salvation,
22:31 he is a *s* to all who take refuge in him."
22:36 "You have given me your saving *s*,
1Kgs 10:16 hundred gold shekels went into each *s*)
2Kgs 19:32 arrow at it, nor come before it with a *s*,
19:34 will *s* and save this city for my own sake,
20: 6 I will be a *s* to this city for my own sake,
1Chr 5:18 who bore *s* and sword and who drew the bow,
12: 9 soldiers equipped with *s* and spear,
12:35 and with them, armed with *s* and lance,
2Chr 9:15 shekels of beaten gold going into each *s*,
25: 5 for war, capable of handling lance and *s*.
Jdt 5:21 otherwise their Lord and God will *s* them,
9: 7 of their infantry, trusting in *s* and spear,
1Mc 14:24 a great gold *s* weighing a thousand minas,
15:18 with them a gold *s* worth a thousand minas.
15:20 also decided to accept the *s* from them.
2Mc 15:11 not so much with the safety of *s* and spear
Jb 3:10 of the womb to *s* my eyes from trouble!
15:26 upon him with the stout bosses of his *s*,
Ps(s) 3: 4 But you, O LORD, are my *s*;
5:13 surround him with the *s* of your good will.
7:11 A *s* before me is God, who saves
18: 3 My God, my rock of refuge, my *s*,
18:31 he is a *s* to all who take refuge in him.
18:36 You have given me your saving *s*;
28: 7 the LORD is my strength and my *s*.
33:20 for the LORD, who is our help and our *s*,
35: 2 Take up the *s* and buckler,
59:12 power, and bring them down, O Lord our *s*!
76: 4 flashing shafts of the bow, *s* and sword,
84:10 O God, behold our *s*, and look upon
84:12 For a sun and a *s* is the LORD God;
89:19 For to the LORD belongs our *s*,
91: 4 his faithfulness is a buckler and a *s*.
115: 9 he is their help and their *s*.
115:10 he is their help and their *s*.
115:11 he is their help and their *s*.
119:114 You are my refuge and my *s*;
144: 2 my stronghold, my deliverer, My *s*,
Prv 2: 7 he is the *s* of those who walk honestly,
30: 5 he is a *s* to those who take refuge in him.
Wis 5:19 a *s* and whet his sudden anger for a sword,
Sir 29:13 Better than a stout *s* and a sturdy spear
34:16 he is their mighty *s* and strong support,
Is 21: 5 Rise up, O princes, oil the *s*!
31: 5 so the LORD of hosts shall *s* Jerusalem,
37:33 arrow at it, nor come before it with a *s*,
37:35 will *s* and save this city for my own sake,
38: 6 I will be a *s* to this city."
50: 6 face I did not *s* from buffets and spitting.
Jer 46: 3 Prepare *s* and buckler!
Ez 27:10 *s* and helmet they hung upon you,
Zec 9:15 The LORD of hosts shall be a *s* over them,
12: 8 LORD will *s* the inhabitants of Jerusalem,
Eph 6:16 hold faith up before you as your *s*;

SHIELD- (1)

2Chr 14: 7 thousand *s*- and lance-bearers from Judah,

SHIELD-BEARER (2)

1Sm 17:41 With his *s* marching before him,
Sir 37: 5 against your enemies he will be your *s*.

SHIELDED (2)

Dt 32:10 He *s* them and cared for them,
Is 51:16 mouth and *s* you in the shadow of my hand,

SHIELDING (1)

2Mc 10:30 Maccabeus, and *s* him with their own armor,

SHIELDS (27)

2Sm 1:21 Upon you lie begrimed the warriors' *s*,
8: 7 David also took away the golden *s* used by
1Kgs 10:16 King Solomon made two hundred *s* of beaten
14:26 well as all the gold *s* made under Solomon.
14:27 them, King Rehoboam had bronze *s* made,
14:28 the LORD, those on duty would carry the *s*,
2Kgs 11:10 the captains King David's spears and *s*,
1Chr 12:25 Judahites bearing *s* and spears:
18: 7 David took the golden *s* that were carried
2Chr 9:15 made two hundred large *s* of beaten gold,
11:12 In every city were *s* and spears,
23: 9 *s* and bucklers of king David which were in
32: 5 a great number of spears and *s* prepared.
1Mc 4:57 of the temple with gold crowns and *s*;
6:39 the sun shone on the gold and bronze *s*,
2Mc 5: 3 with brandished *s* and bristling spears,
Ps(s) 46:10 he burns the *s* with fire.
Sg 4: 4 hang upon it, all the *s* of valiant men.
Is 22: 6 mounts the horses, and Kir uncovers the *s*.
Jer 46: 9 warriors, Cush and Put, bearing your *s*,
Ez 23:24 *S*, bucklers, and helmets they shall array
26: 8 about you, and raise his *s* against you.
32:27 and whose *s* were laid over their bones,
38: 4 a great horde with bucklers and *s*,
38: 5 and Put with them [all with *s* and helmets],
39: 9 *s* and bucklers,] bows and arrows, clubs
Na 2: 4 The *s* of his warriors are crimsoned,

SHIFTED (2)

1Kgs 22:32 and *s* to fight him.
2Chr 18:31 and *s* to fight him.

SHIFTLESS (1)

Jgs 9: 4 hired *s* men and ruffians as his followers.

SHIFTS (1)

Sir 36:26 an armed band that *s* from city to city?

SHIFTY (1)

Sir 27:22 He who has *s* eyes plots mischief and no

SHIHOR-LIBNATH (1)

Jos 19:26 reached Carmel on the west, and *S*.

SHIHOR (2)

1Chr 13: 5 Israel, from *S* of Egypt to Labo of Hamath,
Is 23: 3 The grain of *S*, the harvest of the Nile,

SHIKKERON (1)

Jos 15:11 flank of Ekron, continued through *S*,

SHILHI (2)

1Kgs 22:42 mother's name was Azubah, daughter of *S*.
2Chr 20:31 His mother was named Azubah, daughter of *S*.

SHILHIM (1)

Jos 15:32 Sansannah, Lebaoth, *S* and En-rimmon;

SHILLEM (2)

Gn 46:24 Jahzeel, Guni, Jezer, and *S*.
Nm 26:49 through *S* the clan of the Shillemites.

SHILLEMITES (1)

Nm 26:49 through Shillem the clan of the *S*.

SHILOAH (1)

Is 8: 6 rejected the waters of *S* that flow gently,

SHILOH (30)

Jos 18: 1 community of the Israelites assembled at *S*,
18: 8 lots for them there before the LORD in *S*.
18: 9 and returned to Joshua in the camp at *S*.
18:10 casting lots for them before the LORD in *S*.
19:51 LORD, at the door of the meeting tent in *S*.
21: 2 the Israelites at *S* in the land of Canaan,
22: 9 Manasseh left the other Israelites at *S*
22:12 community at *S* to declare war on them.
Jgs 18:31 made as long as the house of God was in *S*.
21:12 to the camp at *S* in the land of Canaan.
21:19 of the yearly feast of the LORD at *S*,
21:21 girls of *S* come out to do their dancing,
21:21 you seize one of the girls of *S* for a wife,
1Sm 1: 3 of hosts and to sacrifice to him at *S*,

1: 9 Hannah rose after one such meal at *S*,
1:24 him at the temple of the LORD in *S*.
2:14 treated who came to the sanctuary at *S*.
4: 3 Let us fetch the ark of the LORD from *S*
4: 4 So the people sent to *S* and brought from
4:12 battlefield and reached *S* that same day,
14: 3 son of Eli, the priest of the LORD at *S*,
1Kgs 2:27 LORD had made in *S* about the house of Eli.
14: 2 Then go to *S*, where you will find
14: 4 She made the journey to *S* and entered the
Ps(s) 78:60 And he forsook the tabernacle in *S*,
Jer 7:12 You may go to *S*, which I made
7:14 you and your fathers, just as I did to *S*.
26: 6 obey them, I will treat this house like *S*,
26: 9 'This house shall be like *S*,'
41: 5 on their bodies came from Shechem, *S*,

SHILONITE (5)

1Kgs 11:29 prophet Ahijah the *S* met him on the road.
12:15 son of Nebat, through Ahijah the *S*.
15:29 through his servant, Ahijah the *S*,
2Chr 9:29 prophet, in the prophecy of Ahijah the *S*,
10:15 the son of Nebat, through Ahijah the *S*.

SHILSHAH (1)

1Chr 7:37 Shual, Beri, Imrah, Bezer, Hod, Shamma, *S*,

SHIMEA (5)

1Chr 2:13 of Abinadab, the second son, *S*,
3: 5 *S*, Shobab, Nathan, Solomon—four by
6:15 whose son was Uzzah, whose son was *S*,
6:24 Asaph was the son of Berechiah, son of *S*,
20: 7 defied Israel, and Jonathan, the son of *S*,

SHIMEAH (4)

2Sm 13: 3 named Jonadab, son of David's brother *S*,
13:32 But Jonadab, son of David's brother *S*,
1Chr 8:32 Mikloth became the father of *S*.
9:38 Mikloth became the father of *S*.

SHIMEATH (2)

2Kgs 12:22 Jozacar, son of *S*,
2Chr 24:26 Zabad, son of *S* from Ammon,

SHIMEATHITES (1)

1Chr 2:55 in Jabez were the Tirathites, the *S*,

SHIMEI (44)

Ex 6:17 as heads of clans, were Libni and *S*.
Nm 3:18 Gershon, by clans, were named Libni and *S*.
2Sm 16: 5 was approaching Bahurim, a man named *S*,
16: 7 *S* was saying as he cursed:
16:13 *S* kept abreast of them on the hillside,
19:17 *S*, son of Gera, the Benjaminite from
19:19 When *S*, son of Gera, crossed the Jordan,
19:22 *S* must be put to death for this.
19:24 Then the king said to *S*, "You shall not
21:21 Jonathan, son of David's brother *S*,
1Kgs 1: 8 the prophet, and *S* and his companions,
2: 8 "You also have with you *S*, son of Gera,
2:36 Then the king summoned *S* and said to him:
2:38 *S* answered the king:
2:38 So *S* stayed in Jerusalem for a long time.
2:39 and *S* was informed that his servants were
2:40 So *S* rose, saddled his ass, and went to
2:41 that *S* had gone from Jerusalem to Gath,
2:42 the king summoned *S* and said to him:
2:44 And the king said to *S*:
4:18 *S*, son of Ela, in Benjamin;
1Chr 3:19 The sons of Pedaiah were Zerubbabel and *S*.
4:26 whose son was Zaccur, whose son was *S*.
4:27 *S* had sixteen sons and six daughters.
5: 4 whose son was Gog, whose son was *S*,
6: 2 The sons of Gershon were named Libni and *S*.
6:14 whose son was Libni, whose son was *S*,
6:27 son of Ethan, son of Zimmah, son of *S*,
8:21 Beraiah, and Shimrath were the sons of *S*,
23: 7 To the Gershonites belonged Ladan and *S*.
23: 9 The sons of *S* were Shelomoth, Haziel,
23:10 The sons of *S* were Jahath, Zizah, Jeush,
23:10 these were the sons of *S*, four in all.
25: 3 Gedaliah, Zeri, Jeshaiah, *S*,
25:17 The tenth was *S*, his sons, and his
27:27 Over the vineyards was *S* from Ramah,
2Chr 29:14 Jehuel and *S*; of the sons of Jeduthun:
31:12 and his brother *S* was second in charge.
31:13 subject to Conaniah and his brother *S*
Ezr 10:23 Jozabad, *S*, Kelaiah (also called Kelita),
10:33 Zabad, Eliphelet, Jeremai, Manasseh, *S*;
10:38 *S*, Shelemiah, Nathan, and Adaiah;
Est A: 1 of Nisan, Mordecai, son of Jair, son of *S*,
2: 5 Jew named Mordecai, son of Jair, son of *S*,

SHIMEI'S (1)

1Kgs 2:39 two of *S* servants ran away to Achish,

SHIMEITES (1)

Nm 3:21 of the Libnites and the clan of the *S*;

SHIMEON (1)

Ezr 10:31 Eliezer, Isshijah, Malchijah, Shemaiah, *S*,

SHIMON (2)

1Chr 4:19 were *S* the Garmite and Ishi the Maacathite.
4:20 The sons of *S* were Amnon,

SHIMRATH (1)

1Chr 8:21 Beraiah, and *S* were the sons of Shimei,

SHIMRI (4)

1Chr 4:37 son of Allon, son of Jedaiah, son of *S*,
11:45 Jediael, son of *S*, and Joha, his brother,
26:10 *S*, the chief (for though he was not the
2Chr 29:13 *S* and Jeuel; of the sons of Asaph:

SHIMRITH (1)

2Chr 24:26 Ammon, and Jehozabad, son of *S* from Moab.

SHIMRON (6)

Gn 46:13 Tola, Puah, Jashub, and *S*.
Nm 26:24 through *S* the clan of the Shimronites.
Jos 11: 1 to Jobab, king of Madon, to the king of *S*,
12:20 Hepher, Aphek, Lasharon, Madon, Hazor, *S*,
19:15 Thus, with Kattah, Nahalal, *S*,
1Chr 7: 1 of Issachar were Tola, Puah, Jashub, and *S*:

SHIMRONITES (1)

Nm 26:24 through Shimron the clan of the *S*.

SHIMSHAI (4)

Ezr 4: 8 Then Rehum, the governor, and *S*,
4: 9 "Rehum, the governor, *S*, the scribe,
4:17 "To Rehum, the governor, *S*, the scribe,
4:23 been read before Rehum, the governor, *S*,

SHINAB (1)

Gn 14: 2 Birsha king of Gomorrah, *S* king of Admah,

SHINAR (7)

Gn 10:10 and Accad, all of them in the land of *S*.
11: 2 valley in the land of *S* and settled there.
14: 1 Amraphel king of *S*,
14: 9 Tidal king of Goiim, Amraphel king of *S*,
Is 11:11 and Egypt, Pathros, Ethiopia, and Elam, *S*,
Dn 1: 2 which he carried off to the land of *S*,
Zec 5:11 build a temple for it in the land of *S*;

SHINE (32)

Nm 6:25 The LORD let his face *s* upon you,
Tb 13:11 light will *s* to all parts of the earth;
2Mc 1:22 which had been clouded over, began to *s*,
Jb 3: 4 God above call for it, nor light *s* upon it!
22:28 you, and upon your ways the light shall *s*.
37:15 makes the light *s* forth from his clouds?
Ps(s) 4: 7 the light of your countenance *s* upon us!
31:17 Let your face *s* upon your servant;
67: 2 may he let his face *s* upon us.
80: 2 the cherubim, *s* forth 3 before Ephraim,
80: 4 if your face *s* upon us, then we shall be
80: 8 if your face *s* upon us, then we shall be
80:20 if your face *s* upon us, then we shall be
119:135 Let your countenance *s* upon your servant,
132:18 with shame, but upon him my crown shall *s*."
Wis 3: 7 the time of their visitation they shall *s*,
5: 6 and the light of justice did not *s* for us,
Sir 39:12 theme to *s* like the moon in its fullness!
Is 13:10 and the light of the moon does not *s*.
60:19 brightness of the moon *s* upon you at night;
Bar 3:34 the stars at their posts *s* and rejoice;
6:23 wipes away the corrosion, they do not *s*;
Dn 9:17 your face *s* upon your desolate sanctuary.
12: 3 But the wise shall *s* brightly like the
Hb 3: 4 rays *s* forth from beside him,
Mt 5:16 your light must *s* before men so that they
13:43 *s* like the sun in their Father's kingdom.
Lk 1:79 shall visit us in his mercy To *s* on those
2Cor 4: 6 who said, "Let light *s* out of darkness,"
Phil 2:15 among whom you *s* like the stars in the sky
1Jn 2: 8 is over and the real light begins to *s*.
Rv 18:23 burning lamp shall ever again *s* out in you!

SHINES (13)

Ps(s) 50: 2 From Zion, perfect in beauty, God *s* forth.
139:12 itself is not dark, and night *s* as the day.
Prv 13: 9 The light of the just *s* gaily, but the lamp
Sir 26:17 the light that *s* above the holy lampstand,
32:10 a storm is the esteem that *s* on modesty.
43: 1 of the sky *s* forth like heaven itself,
43:20 it *s* like blossoms on the thornbush.
Is 60: 1 has come, the glory of the LORD *s* upon you.
60: 2 But upon you the LORD *s*, and over you
62: 1 Until her vindication *s* forth like the
Hos 6: 3 his judgment *s* forth like the light of day!
Lk 11:36 as when a lamp *s* brightly for you."
Jn 1: 5 The light *s* on in darkness, a darkness

SHINING (18)

Neh 7: 3 still *s* they shall shut and bar the doors.
Jb 29: 3 me, While he kept his lamp *s* above my head,
41:24 Behind him he leaves a *s* path;
Ps(s) 148: 3 praise him, all you *s* stars.
Prv 4:18 But the path of the just is like *s* light,
Sir 24:30 I send my teachings forth *s* like the dawn,
43:19 Its *s* whiteness blinds the eyes, the mind
50: 6 Like a star *s* among the clouds,
50: 7 Like the sun *s* upon the temple,
Is 60: 3 your light, and kings by your *s* radiance.
Bar 3:35 *s* with joy for their Maker.
6:66 like the sun, nor *s* like the moon.
Ez 32: 8 All the *s* lights in the heavens I will
Jn 4:35 The fields are *s* for harvest!
Acts 26:13 than the sun *s* in the sky at midday.
2Cor 4: 6 the glory of God *s* on the face of Christ.
2Pt 1:19 as you would on a lamp *s* in a dark place
Rv 22:16 of David, the Morning Star *s* bright."

SHION (1)

Jos 19:19 Jezreel, Chesulloth, Shunem, Hapharaim, *S*,

SHIP (35)

Ezr 3: 7 they might *s* cedar trees from the Lebanon
1Mc 15:37 gotten aboard a *s* and escaped to Orthosia.
Prv 30:19 a rock, The way of a *s* on the high seas,
Wis 5:10 Like a *s* traversing the heaving water,
Is 23:10 Cross to your own land, O *s* of Tarshish;
33:21 boat is rowed, where no majestic *s* passes,
Ez 27: 3 Tyre, you said, "I am a *s*,
27: 9 Every *s* and sailor on the sea came to you
Jon 1: 3 down to Joppa, found a *s* going to Tarshish,
1: 4 the *s* was on the point of breaking up.
1: 5 To lighten the *s* for themselves,
1: 5 Jonah had gone down into the hold of the *s*,
Mk 4:37 the boat and it began to *s* water badly.
Lk 8:23 they began to *s* water and to be in danger.
Acts 18:24 man of eloquence, arrived by *s* at Ephesus.
20:13 on ahead to the *s* and set sail for Assos,
20:38 Then they escorted him to the *s*.
21: 2 When we found a *s* bound for Phoenicia,
21: 3 at Tyre, where the *s* had to unload cargo.
21: 6 we boarded the *s* and they returned home.
27: 2 We boarded a *s* from Adramyttium bound for
27:10 and heavy loss, not only to *s* and cargo,
27:15 Since the *s* was caught up in it and could
27:17 made use of cables to brace the *s* itself.
27:17 the ship and the *s* was carried along.
27:22 None among you will be lost—only the *s*.
27:30 Then the sailors tried to abandon *s*.
27:30 to run out anchors from the bow of the *s*,
27:31 "If these men do not stay with the *s*,
27:38 *s* further by throwing the wheat overboard.
27:39 to run the *s* aground on it if possible.
27:41 but the *s* hit a sandbar and ran aground.
27:44 on planks, or on other debris from the *s*.
28:11 Three months later we set sail in a *s*

SHIPHI (1)

1Chr 4:37 Adiel, Jesimiel, Benaiah, Ziza, son of *S*,

SHIPHMITE (1)

1Chr 27:27 for the wine cellars was Zabdi the *S*.

SHIPHRAH (1)

Ex 1:15 of whom was called *S* and the other Puah,

SHIPHTAN (1)

Nm 34:24 Kemuel, son of *S*,

SHIPMATES (1)

Lk 5: 9 they had made seized him and all his *s*,

SHIPOWNER (1)

Acts 27:11 the pilot and the *s* to listening to Paul.

SHIPOWNERS (1)

Rv 18:19 in which all *s* grew rich from their

SHIPS (33)

Gn 49:13 by the seashore [This means a shore for *s*,
Jgs 5:17 why does Dan spend his time in *s*?
1Sm 5: 6 in their *s* and overran their fields.
1Kgs 10:22 of Tarshish *s* at sea with Hiram's fleet.
10:22 Tarshish *s* would come with a cargo of gold,
22:49 made Tarshish *s* to go to Ophir for gold;
22:49 but in fact the *s* did not go,
22:50 servants accompany your servants in the *s*."
2Chr 8:18 him *s* and crewmen acquainted with the sea,
9:21 For the king had *s* that went to Tarshish
20:36 with him in building *s* to sail to Tarshish;
20:37 And the *s* were wrecked and were unable to
1Mc 8:26 give nor provide grain, arms, money, or *s*;
8:28 not be given grain, arms, money, or *s*;
11: 1 as the sands of the seashore, and many *s*;
13:29 and next to the armor he placed carved *s*,
15:14 the city, his *s* closed in along the coast,

SHIPS (cont.)

Ps(s) 48: 8 the east were shattering *s* of Tarshish.
104:26 And where *s* move about with Leviathan,
107:23 They who sailed the sea in *s*, trading on
Prv 31:14 Like merchant *s*, she secures her provisions
Is 2:16 the *s* of Tarshish and all stately vessels.
23: 1 Wail, O *s* of Tarshish, for your port is
23:14 Lament, O *s* of Tarshish, for your haven
60: 9 with the *s* of Tarshish in the lead,
Ez 27:25 *S* of Tarshish journeyed for you in your
27:29 Down from their *s* come all who ply the oar;
Dn 11:30 When *s* of the Kittim confront him,
Acts 27:16 were we able to gain control of the *s* boat.
27:19 threw even the *s* gear overboard.
27:30 they let the *s* boat down into the sea.
Jas 3: 4 It is the same with *s*:
Rv 8: 9 died, and a third of the *s* were wrecked.

SHIPWRECK (3)

Ez 27:27 the heart of the sea on the day of your *s*.
Acts 27:26 we still have to face *s* on some island."
1Tm 1:19 of conscience, have made *s* of their faith,

SHIPWRECKED (1)

2Cor 11:25 I was stoned once, *s* three times;

SHIRT (5)

Ex 28:32 a selvage, woven as at the opening of a *s*,
39:23 in its center like the opening of a *s*,
Mt 5:40 If anyone wants to go to law over your *s*,
10:10 no traveling bag, no change of *s*,
Lk 6:29 your coat, let him have your *s* as well.

SHISHA (1)

1Kgs 4: 3 Elihoreph and Ahijah, sons of *S*,

SHISHAK (8)

2Sm 8: 7 [These *S*, king of Egypt, took away when
1Kgs 11:40 for his rebellion he escaped to King *S*,
14:25 In the fifth year of King Rehoboam, *S*,
2Chr 12: 2 in the fifth year of King Rehoboam, *S*,
12: 5 who had gathered at Jerusalem because of *S*,
12: 5 I have abandoned you to the power of *S*.' "
12: 7 not be poured out upon Jerusalem through *S*.
12: 9 Therefore *S*, king of Egypt, attacked

SHITRAI (1)

1Chr 27:29 that grazed in Sharon was *S* the Sharonite,

SHITTIM (5)

Nm 25: 1 While Israel was living at *S*,
Jos 2: 1 Nun, secretly sent out two spies from *S*,
3: 1 all the Israelites from *S* to the Jordan,
Jl 4:18 of the LORD, to water the Valley of *S*.
Mi 6: 5 from *S* to Gilgal, that you may know

SHIZA (1)

1Chr 11:42 addition to the Thirty, Adina, son of *S*,

SHOA (1)

Ez 23:23 and all of Chaldea, Pekod, *S* and Koa,

SHOBAB (4)

2Sm 5:14 Shammua, *S*, Nathan, Solomon, Ibhar,
1Chr 2:18 Her sons were Jesher, *S*, and Ardon.
3: 5 Shimea, *S*, Nathan, Solomon—four by
14: 4 Shammua, *S*, Nathan, Solomon, Ibhar,

SHOBACH (2)

2Sm 10:16 They came to Helam, with *S*,
10:18 *S*, general of the army, was struck down

SHOBAI (2)

Ezr 2:42 sons of Akkub, sons of Hatita, sons of *S*,
Neh 7:45 sons of Akkub, sons of Hatita, sons of *S*,

SHOBAL (8)

Gn 36:20 Lotan, *S*, Zibeon, Anah, Dishon, Ezer,
36:29 the clans of Lotan, *S*,
1Chr 1:38 The descendants of Seir were Lotan, *S*,
1:40 The sons of *S* were Alian,
2:50 *S*, the father of Kiriath-jearim,
2:52 The sons of *S*, the father of Kiriath-jearim,
4: 1 Perez, Hezron, Carmi, Hur, and *S*.
4: 2 Reaiah, the son of *S*, became the father

SHOBAL'S (1)

Gn 36:23 *S* descendants were Alvan,

SHOBEK (1)

Neh 10:25 Hananiah, Hasshub, Hallohesh, Pilha, *S*,

SHOBI (1)

2Sm 17:27 When David came to Mahanaim, *S*,

SHOCK (1)

Jb 5:26 as a *s* of grain comes in at its season.

SHOCKED (3)

Gn 34: 7 men were *s* and seethed with indignation.
Ex 22: 5 so that *s* grain or standing grain or the
Eccl 5: 7 in the realm, do not be *s* by the fact,

SHOCKING (2)

Jer 5:30 A *s*, horrible thing has happened
23:14 prophets I saw deeds still more *s*:

SHOCKS (1)

Jgs 15: 5 burning both the *s* and the standing grain,

SHOE (2)

Ps(s) 60:10 upon Edom I will set my *s*;
108:10 upon Edom I will set my *s*;

SHOES (3)

Jer 2:25 out your *s* and parching your throat!
Dn 3:21 their coats, hats, *s* and other garments,
Lk 15:22 put a ring on his finger and *s* on his feet.

SHOHAM (1)

1Chr 24:27 *S*, Zaccur, and Ibri.

SHOMER (3)

2Kgs 12:22 son of Shimeath, and Jehozabad, son of *S*,
1Chr 7:32 Heber became the father of Japhlet, *S*,
7:34 The sons of *S* were Ahi,

SHONE (14)

Dt 33: 2 He *s* forth from Mount Paran and advanced
2Kgs 3:22 that morning, when the sun *s* on the water,
1Mc 6:39 the sun *s* on the gold and bronze shields,
Jb 31:26 Had I looked upon the sun as it *s*,
Ps(s) 68:14 the wings of the dove *s* with silver,
Wis 17:20 For the whole world *s* with brilliant light
Is 9: 1 dwelt in the land of gloom a light has *s*.
Ez 43: 2 waters, and the earth *s* with his glory.
Lk 2: 9 as the glory of the Lord *s* around them,
Acts 12: 7 Lord stood nearby and light *s* in the cell.
2Cor 3: 7 Moses' face because of the glory that *s* on it
4: 6 out of darkness," has *s* in our hearts,
Rv 1:16 his face *s* like the sun at its brightest.
10: 1 his face *s* like the sun and his legs like

SHOOK (14)

1Sm 14:15 The earth also *s* so that the panic was
2Sm 22: 8 trembled and *s* when his wrath flared up.
Neh 5:13 I also *s* out the folds of my garment,
1Mc 9:13 The earth *s* with the noise of the armies,
Ps(s) 18: 8 trembled and *s* when his wrath flared up.
Wis 17: 9 they *s* at the passing of insects and the
Sir 48:18 He *s* his fist at Zion and blasphemed God
Is 6: 4 door *s* and the house was filled with smoke.
Dn 5: 6 thoughts terrified him, his hip joints *s*,
Acts 4:31 where they were gathered *s* as they prayed.
13:51 So the two *s* the dust from their feet in
16:26 a severe earthquake suddenly *s* the place,
28: 5 But Paul *s* the snake off into the fire and
Heb 12:26 His voice then *s* the earth,

SHOOT (19)

1Sm 20:20 the third day of the month I will *s* arrows,
2Sm 11:20 know that they would *s* from the wall above?
2Kgs 13:17 Elisha said, *S*," and he shot.
19:32 not reach this city, nor *s* an arrow at it,
2Chr 26:15 walls to *s* arrows and cast large stones.
Jb 9:26 They *s* by like skiffs of reed, like an eagle
Ps(s) 11: 2 to *s* in the dark at the upright of heart.
144: 6 and put them to flight, *s* your arrows,
Is 11: 1 a *s* shall sprout from the stump of Jesse,
37:33 not reach this city, nor *s* an arrow at it,
53: 2 him, like a *s* from the parched earth;
Jer 23: 5 I will raise up a righteous *s* to David;
33:15 time, I will raise up for David a just *s*;
50:14 *S* at her, spare not your arrows, raise
Ez 17: 5 A *s* by plentiful waters, like a willow he
17:22 its topmost branches tear off a tender *s*,
Zec 3: 8 Yes, I will bring my servant the *S*.
6:12 Here is a man whose name is *S*,
9:14 and his arrow shall *s* forth as lightning;

SHOOTING (5)

1Chr 12: 2 stones and in *s* arrows with the bow.
1Mc 6:51 bows for *s* arrows and slingstones.
Ps(s) 64: 5 words, *S* from ambush at the innocent man,
64: 5 man, suddenly *s* at him without fear.
Jude 1:13 or *s* stars for whom the thick gloom of

SHOOTS (12)

Gn 30:37 Jacob, however, got some fresh *s* of poplar,
30:37 the bark down to the white core of the *s*.
Nm 17:23 had sprouted and put forth not only *s*,
Jb 8:16 and beyond his garden his *s* go forth;
14: 7 and that its tender *s* will not cease.
Ps(s) 64: 8 But God *s* his arrows at them; suddenly
80:12 to the Sea, its *s* as far as the River.
Sir 37:17 is the mind; four branches it *s* forth:
Is 18: 5 and the discarding of the lopped-off *s*.
Ez 17: 6 a vine, produced branches and put forth *s*.
19:14 came out of the branch and devoured her *s*;
Hos 14: 7 the Lebanon cedar, and put forth his *s*.

SHOP (1)

Jer 37:21 loaf of bread each day from the bakers' *s*

SHOPHACH (2)

1Chr 19:16 from the other side of the River, with *S*,
19:18 he also killed *S*, the general of the army.

SHOPKEEPER (1)

Sir 26:20 remain upright, nor a *s* free from sin:

SHORE (22)

Gn 49:13 by the seashore [This means a *s* for ships],
Jgs 5:17 Asher, who dwells along the *s*,
1Kgs 9:26 which is near Elath on the *s*
Tb 6: 4 seized the fish and hauled it up on the *s*.
Jer 5:22 I made the sandy *s* the sea's limit,
Ez 27:29 the mariners of the sea, stand on the *s*,
Dn 3:36 of heaven, or the sand on the *s* of the sea.
Jon 2:11 the fish to spew Jonah upon the *s*.
Mt 8:18 Jesus gave orders to cross to the other *s*.
13: 2 a boat while the crowd stood along the *s*.
14:24 already several hundred yards out from *s*,
14:34 crossing they reached the *s* at Gennesaret;
Mk 4: 1 while the crowd remained on the *s* nearby.
4:35 them, "Let us cross over to the farther *s*."
8:13 boat again, and went off to the other *s*.
Lk 5: 3 to pull out a short distance from the *s*;
Jn 6: 1 the Sea of Galilee [to the *s* of Tiberias;
6:21 aground on the *s* they had been approaching.
21: 4 daybreak Jesus was standing on the *s*,
Acts 28: 1 Once on *s*, we learned that the island
Rv 12:17 took up his position by the *s* of the sea.

SHORES (2)

Jer 25:22 of Sidon, and of the *s* beyond the sea;
Ez 27:28 of your mariners, the *s* begin to quake.

SHORN (3)

2Kgs 19:26 ruins, While their inhabitants, *s* of power,
Sg 4: 2 teeth are like a flock of ewes to be *s*,
Is 37:27 ruins, While their inhabitants, *s* of power,

SHORT (38)

Gn 24:55 "Let the girl stay with us a *s* while,
48: 7 we were still a *s* distance from Ephrath;
Lv 4:12 head, legs, inner organs, and offal, in *s*,
1Sm 20: 6 him go on *s* notice to his city Bethlehem,
2Sm 17:20 went by a *s* while ago toward the water."
Ezr 9: 8 "And now, but a *s* time ago, mercy came
1Mc 7:50 for a *s* time the land of Judah was quiet.
Jb 13: 2 know, I also know; I fall not *s* of you.
14: 5 There is none, however *s* his days.
20: 5 That the triumph of the wicked is *s*
Ps(s) 39: 6 A *s* span you have made my days,
89:48 Remember how *s* my life is; how frail you
102:24 he has cut *s* my days.
Wis 4:13 Having become perfect in a *s* while,
16: 6 warning, for a *s* time they were terrorized,
Sir 11:11 and drive, and fall *s* all the more.
40: 6 So *s* is his rest it seems like none,
51:16 In the *s* time I paid heed, I met with
Is 28:20 the bed shall be too *s* to stretch out in,
50: 2 Is my hand too *s* to ransom?
59: 1 the hand of the LORD is not too *s* to save,
Jer 48:45 shadow stop *s* the exhausted refugees;
Ez 16:47 in a very *s* time you became more corrupt
Mi 2: 7 of Jacob, "Is the LORD *s* of patience,
Mt 10:36 in *s*, to make a man's enemies those
Lk 5: 3 to pull out a *s* distance from the shore;
7: 6 he was only a *s* distance from the house,
Jn 16:16 Within a *s* time you will lose sight of me,
16:17 'Within a *s* time you will lose sight of me,
16:18 What does he mean by this '*s* time'?
16:19 'Within a *s* time you will lose sight of me,
Acts 27:28 after sailing on a *s* distance they again
1Cor 7:29 I tell you, brothers, the time is *s*.
Heb 12:10 prepare us for the *s* span of mortal life;
Jas 3: 2 All of us fall *s* in many respects.
Rv 12:12 no limits, for he knows his time is *s*."
17:10 he does come he will remain only a *s* while.
20: 3 the dragon is to be released for a *s* time.

SHORT-LIVED (2)

Jb 14: 1 Man born of woman is *s* and full of trouble,
Wis 9: 5 a man weak and *s* and lacking in

SHORTCOMINGS (1)

1Thes 3:10 to face and remedy any *s* in your faith?

SHORTEN (1)

Sir 30:24 Envy and anger *s* one's life, worry brings

SHORTENED (5)

Ps(s) 89:46 You have *s* the days of his youth;
Mt 24:22 Indeed, if the period had not been *s*,
24:22 of the chosen, however, the days will be *s*.
Mk 13:20 Indeed, had the Lord not *s* the period,
13:20 of those he has chosen, he has *s* the days.

SHORTLY (11)

Tb 11:15 daughter Sarah, who would arrive *s*,
2Mc 3:30 so *s* before with fear and commotion,
6:29 who *s* before had been kindly disposed,
9:10 *S* before, he had thought that he could
12:31 in Jerusalem, *s* before the feast of Weeks.
Wis 14:20 who *s* before was honored as a man.
15: 8 though he himself *s* before was made from
Hos 8:10 princes shall *s* succumb under the burden.
Mk 1:21 *S* afterward they came to Capernaum,
Lk 8:37 *S* afterward, the entire population
Acts 12:19 *S* after this, Herod left Judea to spend

SHORTNESS (1)

Eccl 5:19 he will hardly dwell on the *s* of his life,

SHORTSIGHTED (1)

2Pt 1: 9 qualities is *s* to the point of blindness.

SHOT (9)

1Sm 20:36 he *s* an arrow beyond him in the direction
20:37 had *s* the arrow Jonathan called after him,
2Sm 11:24 *s* at your servants from the wall above,
2Kgs 9:24 his bow and *s* Joram between the shoulders,
13:17 Elisha said, "Shoot," and he *s*.
2Chr 35:23 Then the archers *s* King Josiah,
2Mc 10:30 They *s* arrows and hurled thunderbolts at
Wis 5:12 Or as, when an arrow has been *s* at a mark,
Rv 9:18 and fire which *s* out of their mouths

SHOULDER (31)

Gn 24:15 Nahor) came out with a jug on her *s*.
24:45 when Rebekah came out with a jug on her *s*.
49:15 *s* to the burden and became a toiling serf.
Ex 28: 7 of *s* straps joined to its two upper ends.
28:12 Set these two stones on the *s* straps of
28:25 are attached to the *s* straps of the ephod.
28:27 fasten them to the bottom of the *s* straps
39: 4 *S* straps were made for it and joined to
39: 7 These stones were set on the *s* straps of
39:18 attached to the *s* straps of the ephod.
39:20 fastened to the bottom of the two *s* straps
Nm 6:19 priest shall take a boiled *s* of the ram,
Dt 18: 3 the flock, the priest shall receive the *s*,
Jgs 9:48 This he lifted to his *s*, then said to the men
2Mc 12:35 Dositheus and cut off his arm at the *s*.
Jb 31:22 Then may my arm fall from the *s*,
31:36 it on my *s* or put it on me like a diadem;
Ps(s) 81: 7 "I relieved his *s* of the burden;
Is 9: 3 that burdened them, the pole on their *s*,
9: 5 upon his *s* dominion rests.
10:27 day, His burden shall be taken from your *s*,
14:25 from them, and his burden from their *s*.
22:22 the key of the House of David on his *s*;
Ez 12: 6 *s* the burden and set out in the darkness;
12:12 shall *s* his burden and set out in darkness,
24: 4 thigh and *s*; Fill it with the choicest joints
25: 9 clear the *s* of Moab totally of its cities,
29: 7 splintered, throwing every *s* out of joint;
34:21 Because you push with side and *s*,
Mal 2: 3 the *s* and I will strew dung in your faces,
Lk 23:26 *s* for him to carry along behind Jesus.

SHOULDERING (1)

Ez 12: 7 on, set out in the darkness, *s* my burden.

SHOULDERS (25)

Gn 22: 6 and laid it on his son Isaac's *s*,
Ex 12:34 bowls wrapped in their cloaks on their *s*.
28:12 on his *s* as a reminder before the LORD.
Nm 7: 9 had to carry on their *s* the sacred objects
Jos 4: 5 lift to your *s* one stone apiece,
Jgs 16: 3 He hoisted them on his *s* and carried them
1Sm 9: 2 he stood head and *s* above the people.
10:23 he was head and *s* above all the crowd.
2Kgs 9:24 drew his bow and shot Joram between the *s*,
1Chr 15:15 bore the ark of God on their *s* with poles,
2Chr 35: 3 It shall no longer be a burden on your *s*.
Sir 6:26 Stoop your *s* and carry her;
Is 46: 1 They must be borne up on *s*,
46: 7 They lift it to their *s* to carry;
49:22 your daughters shall be carried on their *s*.
Jer 27: 2 and yoke bars and put them over your *s*.
Bar 2:21 *s* to the service of the king of Babylon,
6: 3 men's *s* gods of silver and gold and wood,
6:25 no feet, they are carried on men's *s*,
Ez 29:18 heads became bald and their *s* were galled;
Mt 11:29 Take my yoke upon your *s* and learn from me,
23: 4 hard to carry, to lay on other men's *s*,
Lk 15: 5 it, he puts it on his *s* in jubilation.
Jn 19: 2 around his *s* a cloak of royal purple.
Acts 15:10 to place on the *s* of these converts a yoke

SHOUT (46)

Jos 6: 5 that signal, all the people shall *s* aloud.
6:10 had been commanded by Joshua not to *s*
6:10 only then were they to *s*.
6:16 and Joshua said to the people, "Now *s*,
6:20 As the horns blew, the people began to *s*.
6:20 signal horn, they raised a tremendous *s*.
Ezr 3:11 and all the people raised a great *s* of joy,
Ps(s) 20: 6 May we *s* for joy at your victory and raise
35:27 But let those *s* for joy and be glad who
47: 2 hands, *s* to God with cries of gladness,
63: 8 in the shadow of your wings I *s* for joy.
65:14 They *s* and sing for joy.
66: 1 *S* joyfully to God, all you on earth,
71:23 shall *s* for joy as I sing your praises;
89:16 Happy the people who know the joyful *s*;
90:14 we may *s* for joy and gladness all our days.
98: 8 the mountains *s* with them for joy
118:15 *s* of victory in the tents of the just:
132: 9 let your faithful ones *s* merrily for joy.
132:16 her faithful ones shall *s* merrily for joy.
Eccl 9:17 heeded than the *s* of a ruler of fools"
Sir 50:19 All the people of the land would *s* for joy,
Is 12: 6 *S* with exultation, O city of Zion,
16:10 vineyards there is no singing, no *s* of joy;
16:10 treads grapes, the vintage *s* is stilled.
42:11 exult, and *s* from the top of the mountains.
44:23 done this; *s*, you depths of the earth.
52: 8 raise a cry, together they *s* for joy,
65:14 My servants shall *s* for joy of heart,
Jer 4:29 At the *s* of horseman and bowman each city
25:30 a *s* like that of vintagers over the grapes.
31: 7 *S* with joy for Jacob, exult at the head
48:33 treads no more, the vintage *s* is stilled.
49:29 off for themselves, and *s* from upon them,
51:14 who shall raise over you the vintage *s*!
51:48 in them shall *s* over Babylon with joy,
Lam 2: 7 Who *s* in the house of the LORD as on a
Bar 6:31 They *s* and wail before their gods as
Ez 23:42 heard the *s* of a carefree mob in the city,
Zep 3:14 *S* for joy, O daughter Zion!
Zec 9: 9 heartily, O daughter Zion, *s* for joy,
Mt 20:30 that Jesus was passing by, began to *s*,
Mk 3:11 fling themselves down at his feet, and *s*,
Acts 19:28 were overcome with fury and began to *s*,
22:22 listening to Paul, but now they began to *s*,
26:24 in this way, Festus interrupted with a *s*,

SHOUTED (39)

Gn 41:43 chariot of his vizier, and they *s* "Abrek!"
1Sm 4: 5 *s* so loudly that the earth resounded.
10:24 Then all the people *s*, "Long live
14:20 all his men *s* and rushed into the fight,
17: 8 He stood and *s* to the ranks of Israel:
26:14 He then *s*, "Will you not answer, Abner?"
30:20 and as they drove these before him, they *s*,
2Sm 18:25 The lookout *s* to inform the king,
1Kgs 1:39 They blew the horn and all the people *s*,
22:32 But Jehoshaphat *s* his battle cry,
2Kgs 2:23 "Go up, baldhead," they *s*,
9:32 Jehu looked up to the window and *s*,
2Chr 13:15 Then the men of Judah *s*;
32:18 In a loud voice they *s* in the Judean
Tb 6: 3 He *s* in alarm.
Jdt 13:11 Judith *s* to the guards from a distance:
16:11 When my lowly ones *s*, they were terrified;
Est 8:15 The city of Susa *s* with joy,
1Mc 13: 8 They *s* in reply: You are our leader
Jb 38: 7 chorus and all the sons of God *s* for joy?
Jer 43: 2 and all the insolent men *s* to Jeremiah:
Dn 5: 7 The king *s* for the enchanters, Chaldeans,
13:24 shrieked, and the old men also *s* at her,
Mt 20:31 to silence, but they only *s* the louder,
25: 6 At midnight someone *s*, 'The groom is here!
27:23 But they only *s* the louder, "Crucify
Mk 10:48 him keep quiet, but he *s* all the louder,
15:13 They *s* back, "Crucify him!"
15:14 They only *s* the louder, "Crucify him!"
Lk 18:38 He *s* out, "Jesus, Son of David, have pity
23:21 But they *s* back, "Crucify him, crucify
Jn 18:40 They *s* back, "We want Barabbas, not
19: 6 and the temple guards saw him they *s*,
19:12 was eager to release him, but the Jews *s*,
19:15 At this they *s*, "Away with him!
Acts 12:22 The assembled crowd *s* back,
14:15 they *s* frantically.
16:28 sword to kill himself; but Paul *s* to him:
21:34 in the crowd *s* out different answers.

SHOUTING (31)

Ex 32:17 Joshua heard the noise of the people *s*,
Jgs 7:21 camp fell to running and *s* and fleeing.
15:14 and the Philistines came *s* to meet him,
1Sm 4: 6 The Philistines, hearing the noise of *s*,
4: 6 loud *s* in the camp of the Hebrews mean?"
17:20 the battleground, were *s* their battle cry.
1Kgs 1:40 as to split open the earth with their *s*.
2Kgs 9:27 Jehu pursued him, *s*, "Kill him too!"
11:12 anointed him, clapping their hands and *s*,
1Chr 15:28 of the covenant of the LORD with joyful *s*,
2Chr 15:14 voice with *s* and with trumpets and horns.
Ezr 3:13 *s* from the sound of those who were weeping;
1Mc 2:27 Then Mattathias went through the city *s*,
5:31 to heaven with trumpet blasts and loud *s*,
5:33 blowing their trumpets and *s* in prayer.
Jb 39:25 battle, the roar of the chiefs and the *s*.
Is 42: 2 to the nations, Not crying out, not *s*,
Jer 4:16 *s* their war cry against the cities of
31:12 *S*, they shall mount the heights of Zion,
Ez 27:30 voice heard on your behalf, *s* bitter cries,
Mt 15:23 She keeps *s* after us."
21:15 were *s* out in the temple precincts,
Mk 9:26 *S*, and throwing the boy into convulsions,
Jn 12:13 They kept *s*: "Hosanna!
Acts 7:57 The onlookers were *s* aloud,
16:17 began to follow Paul and the rest of us *s*,
17: 6 of the brothers to the town magistrates, *s*:
19:32 various people were *s* all sorts of things,
19:34 and kept *s* for about two hours.
21:28 They seized him, *s*: "Hosanna! Blessed is
21:36 A crowd of people was following along *s*,

SHOUTS (21)

1Sm 17:52 the men of Israel and Judah, with loud *s*,
2Sm 6:15 with *s* of joy and to the sound of the horn.
Ezr 3:12 lifted up their voices in *s* of joy,
Jdt 14: 9 and their city resounded with *s* of joy.
1Mc 13:51 entered the citadel with *s* of jubilation,
2Mc 15:29 so they raised tumultuous *s* in their
Jb 39: 7 of the city, and hears no *s* of a driver.
Ps(s) 27: 6 in his tent sacrifices with *s* of gladness;
33: 3 the strings skillfully, with *s* of gladness.
47: 6 God mounts his throne amid *s* of joy;
105:43 with *s* of joy, his chosen ones.
107:22 and declare his works with *s* of joy.
Sir 20:14 often, and like a crier he *s* aloud.
Is 24: 8 timbrels, ended the *s* of the jubilant,
31: 4 by their *s* nor disturbed by their noise,
42:13 He *s* out his battle cry,
48:20 With *s* of joy proclaim this,
Ez 27:28 Hearing the *s* of your mariners, the shores
Am 2: 2 amid uproar and *s* and trumpet blasts.
Lk 23:23 crucified, and their *s* increased in violence.
Rv 19: 6 what sounded like the *s* of a great crowd,

SHOVEL (1)

Is 30:24 silage tossed to them with *s* and pitchfork.

SHOVELS (9)

Ex 27: 3 pots for removing the ashes, as well as *s*,
38: 3 the utensils of the altar, the pots, *s*,
Nm 4:14 the fire pans, forks, *s*, basins, and all
1Kgs 7:40 When Hiram made the pots, *s*,
7:45 twelve oxen supporting the sea, pots, *s*,
2Kgs 25:14 They took also the pots, the *s*,
2Chr 4:11 also made the pots, the *s* and the bowls.
4:16 likewise the pots, the *s* and the forks.
Jer 52:18 They took also the pots, the *s*,

SHOW (175)

Gn 12: 1 father's house to a land that I will *s* you.
24:49 in mind to *s* true loyalty to my master,
Ex 9:16 to *s* you my power and to make my name
13:21 of a column of cloud to *s* them the way,
25: 9 to the pattern that I will now *s* you.
31:13 the generations, to *s* that it is I,
33:19 I who *s* favors to whom I will,
Lv 13: 7 he shall once more *s* himself to the priest.
13:19 blotch, he shall *s* himself to the priest.
19:15 *S* neither partiality to the weak nor
19:32 of the aged, and *s* respect for the old;
Dt 1:33 in the fire, to *s* the way you must go.
2: 9 'Do not *s* hostility to the Moabites or
2:19 *s* hostility or come in conflict with them,
3:24 *s* to your servant your greatness and might.
7: 2 no covenant with them and *s* them no mercy.
8: 3 in order to *s* you that not by bread alone
13:18 and he may *s* you mercy and in his mercy
Jos 2:12 you in turn will *s* kindness to my family;
Jgs 1:24 and said to him, *S* us a way into the city,
4:22 him, "Come, I will *s* you the man you seek."
1Sm 1:14 long will you make a drunken *s* of yourself?
14: 8 over to those men and *s* ourselves to them.
20:14 may you *s* me the kindness of the LORD.
2Sm 9: 1 I may *s* kindness for the sake of Jonathan?"
9: 3 house to whom I may *s* God's kindness?"
15: 5 Whenever a man approached him to *s* homage,
2Kgs 20:13 all his realm that Hezekiah did not *s* them.
20:15 in my storerooms that I did not *s* them."
1Chr 19: 2 David said, "I will *s* kindness to Hanun,
19:13 Hold steadfast and let us *s* ourselves
28:21 with all those who are eager to *s* their skill
2Chr 6:14 you keep your covenant and *s* kindness to
Tb 5: 2 What can I *s* him to make him recognize me
5:10 Can you go with him to *s* him the way?
6:18 flee and never again *s* himself near her.
6:18 to *s* you mercy and grant you deliverance.
13: 6 *s* his power and majesty to a sinful nation.

SHOW (cont.)

13: 6 look with favor upon you and *s* you mercy.
Jdt 2:11 As for those who resist, *s* them no quarter,
7:30 the Lord our God, to *s* his mercy toward us;
10:13 I will *s* him the route by which he can
Est 4: 8 in Susa, to *s* and explain to Esther.
1Mc 7: 3 this, he said, "Do not *s* me their faces."
7:33 *s* him the holocaust that was being offered
11:33 Because of the good will they *s* us,
2Mc 4:17 of God, as the following period will *s*.
7:37 God to *s* mercy soon to our nation,
9:26 to *s* good will toward me and my son.
12:36 Judas called upon the Lord to *s* himself
14: 9 consideration that you *s* toward all.
14:39 Nicanor, to *s* his detestation of the Jews,
15: 2 but *s* respect for the day which the
Jb 10:16 you *s* your wondrous power against me,
13: 8 Is it for him that you *s* partiality?
13:10 you if even in secret you *s* partiality.
15:17 I will *s* you, if you listen to me; what I
32:17 I also will *s* my knowledge!
33:23 To *s* him what is right for him and bring
35:15 nor does he *s* concern that a man will die.
Ps(s) 16:11 You will *s* me the path to life,
17: 7 *S* your wondrous kindness, O savior of
27:11 *S* me, O LORD, your way, and lead me
31:20 refuge in you, you *s* in the sight of men.
32: 8 you and *s* you the way you should walk;
45: 5 may your right hand *s* you wondrous deeds.
50:23 right way I will *s* the salvation of God."
59:11 may he *s* me the fall of my foes.
68:29 *S* forth, O God, your power.
85: 8 *S* us, O LORD, your kindness, and grant
91:16 gratify him and will *s* him my salvation.
94: 1 LORD, God of vengeance, *s* yourself.
109:16 Because he remembered not to *s* kindness,
143: 8 *S* me the way in which I should walk,
Prv 24:23 To *s* partiality in judgment is not good.
28:21 To *s* partiality is never good:
29:10 but the upright *s* concern for his life.
Wis 12:13 you need *s* you have not unjustly condemned;
12:17 For you *s* your might when the perfection
Sir 4:22 *S* no favoritism to your own discredit;
7: 6 Or you will *s* favor to the ruler and mar
12:18 and hiss repeatedly, and *s* his true face.
18:20 when you have sinned, *s* repentance.
18:29 trained in her words must *s* their wisdom,
35: 8 each contribution *s* a cheerful countenance,
36: 3 you have used us to *s* them your holiness,
36: 3 so now use them to *s* us your glory.
36: 5 *s* forth the splendor of your right hand
36:11 *S* mercy to the people called by your name;
39: 8 He will *s* the wisdom of what he has
Is 30:18 Yet the LORD is waiting to *s* you favor,
39: 2 in his whole realm that he did not *s* them.
39: 4 in my storerooms that I did not *s* them."
49: 3 to me, Israel, through whom I *s* my glory.
49: 9 To those in darkness: *S* yourselves!
60:21 of my planting, my handiwork to *s* my glory.
61: 3 planted by the LORD to *s* his glory.
66: 5 *s* his glory that we may see your joy";
Jer 13:14 I will *s* no compassion, I will not spare
18:17 I will *s* them my back, not my face,
31:20 My heart stirs for him, I must *s* him mercy,
31:32 and I had to *s* myself their master,
33:26 I will change their lot and *s* them mercy.
42: 3 *s* us what way we should take and what we
Lam 2:13 What example can I *s* you for your comfort,
4:16 with favor, nor *s* kindness to the elders.
Bar 5: 3 For God will *s* all the earth your splendor:
6:66 They *s* the nations no signs in the heavens,
Ez 8:18 upon them with pity nor will I *s* mercy.
9: 5 not look on them with pity nor *s* any mercy!
9:10 look upon them with pity, nor *s* any mercy.
20:12 between me and them, to *s* that it was I,
20:20 between me and you to *s* that I am the LORD,
40: 4 strict attention to all that I will *s* you,
40: 4 brought here so that I might *s* it to you.
Dn 8:19 "I will *s* you," he said, "what is to
14: 9 But if you can *s* that Bel consumes them,
Mi 7:15 the land of Egypt, *s* us wonderful signs.
7:20 You will *s* faithfulness to Jacob,
Na 3: 5 I will *s* your nakedness to the nations,
Zec 1: 9 answered me, "I will *s* you what these are."
7: 9 and *s* kindness and compassion toward each
Mal 2: 9 ways, but *s* partiality in your decisions.
Mt 5: 7 Blest are they who *s* mercy;
8: 4 Go and *s* yourself to the priest and offer
16: 1 asked him to *s* them some sign in the sky.
16:26 What profit would a man *s* if he were to
22:19 *S* me the coin used for the tax."
23:31 Thus you *s* that you are the sons of the
Mk 8:36 What profit does a man *s* who gains the
14:15 Then he will *s* you an upstairs room,
Lk 5:14 one, but go and *s* yourself to the priest.
6:47 will *s* you with whom he is to be compared.
9:25 What profit does he *s* who gains the whole
11:48 You *s* that you stand behind the deeds of
12: 5 I will *s* you whom you ought to fear.
17:14 "Go and *s* yourselves to the priests."
20:24 their duplicity he said, *S* me a coin.
22:12 That man will *s* you an upstairs room,
Jn 2:18 *s* us authorizing you to do these things?"
5:20 will *s* him even greater works than these.
9: 3 it was to let God's works *s* forth in him.
13: 1 and would *s* his love for them to the end.
14: 8 Philip said to him, "*S* us the Father
14: 9 How can you say, *S* us the Father'?
Acts 4:16 *s* of power took place through them.
5:26 them in, but without any *s* of force,
7: 3 kinsfolk, and go to the land I will *s* you.
9:41 the widows to *s* them that she was alive.
Rom 2:15 They *s* that the demands of the law are
9:15 "I will *s* mercy to whomever I choose;
9:17 that through you I might *s* my power,
9:22 to *s* his wrath and make known his power,
11:31 since God wished to *s* you mercy
1Cor 11:22 Would you *s* contempt for the church of God,
2Cor 8: 8 love against the concern which others *s*.
8:24 *s* these men the proof of your love,
12:12 patience the signs that *s* the apostle,
Phil 4:10 course, but lacked the opportunity to *s* it.
Col 2:15 He made a public *s* of them,
2:23 *s* of wisdom in their affected piety,
Heb 6:11 each of you *s* the same zeal till the end,
13: 2 Do not neglect to *s* hospitality,
Jas 2: 9 But if you *s* favoritism, you commit sin
2:18 *S* me your faith without works,
2:18 *s* you the faith that underlies my works!
3:13 let him *s* this in practice through a
1Pt 3: 7 must *s* consideration for those who share
1Jn 2:16 for the eye, the life of empty *s*—
2:19 served to *s* that none of them was ours.
Rv 1: 1 *s* his servants what must happen very soon.
4: 1 *s* you what must take place in time to come."
17: 1 I will *s* you the judgment in store for the
21: 9 I will *s* you the woman who is the bride of
22: 6 *s* his servants what must happen very soon."

SHOWBREAD (16)

Ex 25:30 you shall always keep *s* set before me.
35:13 and all its appurtenances, and the *s*;
39:36 with all its appurtenances and the *s*,
1Sm 21: 7 no other bread was on hand except the *s*
1Kgs 7:48 the golden table on which the *s* lay;
1Chr 9:32 charge of setting out the *s* each sabbath.
23:29 They shall also have charge of the *s*,
28:16 of gold for each table to hold the *s*,
2Chr 2: 3 for the perpetual display of the *s*,
4:19 altar, the tables on which the *s* lay,
13:11 they display the *s* on the pure table,
29:18 the table for the *s* with all its utensils.
Neh 10:34 of the house of our God, for the *s*,
2Mc 10: 3 They also set out the *s*.
Sir 45:20 allotted to him, with the *s* as his portion;
Heb 9: 2 were the lampstand, the table, and the *s*;

SHOWED (57)

Gn 39:21 he *s* him kindness by making the chief
Nm 13:26 all, and *s* them the fruit of the country.
Dt 34: 1 Jericho, and the LORD *s* him all the land
Jgs 1:25 He *s* them a way into the city,
Ru 2:18 into the city and *s* to her mother-in-law.
1Sm 24:19 Great is the generosity you *s* me today,
2Sm 22:51 your king and *s* kindness to your anointed.
2Kgs 8:10 the LORD has *s* me that he will in fact die."
8:13 LORD has *s* you to me as king over Aram,"
11: 4 commitment, and then *s* them the king's son.
20:13 *s* the messengers his whole treasury,
2Chr 26:19 the moment he *s* his anger to the priests,
Neh 13:14 Let not the devotion which I *s* for the
Jdt 13:15 the head out of the pouch, *s* it to them,
Est 5: 9 gate did not rise, and *s* no fear of him,
1Mc 2:26 Thus he *s* his zeal for the law,
6:34 They *s* the elephants the juice of grapes
11:26 and *s* him great honor in the presence
2Mc 3:17 *s* those who saw him the pain that lodged
15:32 He *s* them the vile Nicanor's head and the
Ps(s) 18:51 your king and *s* kindness to your anointed,
Wis 10:10 *S* him the kingdom of God and gave him
10:14 *S* those who had defamed him false,
Sir 46: 7 and in Moses' lifetime *s* himself loyal,
Is 39: 2 therefore *s* the messengers his treasury,
40:14 or *s* him the way of understanding?
47: 6 but you *s* them no mercy,
Jer 11:18 that time you, O LORD, *s* me their doings.
24: 1 The LORD *s* me two baskets of figs placed
Dn 2:29 who reveals mysteries *s* you what is to be.
14:21 They *s* him the secret door by which they
Am 7: 1 This is what the Lord GOD *s* me:
7: 4 Then the Lord GOD *s* me this:
7: 7 Then the Lord GOD *s* me this:
8: 1 This is what the Lord GOD *s* me:
Zec 2: 3 Then the LORD *s* me four blacksmiths.
3: 1 Then he *s* me Joshua the high priest
Mt 8:10 Jesus *s* amazement on hearing this and
14:33 Those who were in the boat *s* him reverence,
Lk 4: 5 Then the devil took him up higher and *s*
7: 9 Jesus *s* amazement on hearing this,
19:17 'You *s* yourself capable in a small matter.
20:37 Moses in the passage about the bush *s* that
24:40 he said this he *s* them his hands and feet.
Jn 20:20 this, he *s* them his hands and his side.
21: 1 *s* himself to the disciples [once again].
Acts 1: 3 In the time after his suffering he *s* them
9:39 All the widows came to him in tears and *s*
15: 8 *s* his approval by granting the Holy Spirit
28: 2 The natives *s* us extraordinary kindness by
1Cor 3:10 Thanks to the favor God *s* me I laid a
2Cor 7:15 as he recalls the obedience you *s* to God
Eph 1:20 It is like the strength he *s* in raising
Heb 11:14 they *s* that they were seeking a homeland.
Rv 21:10 and *s* me the holy city Jerusalem coming
22: 1 then *s* me the river of life-giving water,
22: 8 at the feet of the angel who *s* them to me.

SHOWER (2)

Dt 32: 2 upon the grass, like a *s* upon the crops.
Dn 3:64 Every *s* and dew, bless the Lord; praise

SHOWERED (3)

Est 8:12 the more they were *s* with honors
1Mc 10:80 until evening they *s* his men with arrows.
Ps(s) 68:10 A bountiful rain you *s* down, O God,

SHOWERS (9)

Jgs 5: 4 were shaken, while the clouds sent down *s*.
Jb 36:28 with them and the *s* rain down on mankind.
Ps(s) 65:11 up its clods, Softening it with *s*,
72: 6 on the meadow, like *s* watering the earth.
Sir 1:17 and full understanding she *s* down;
18: 9 patient with men and *s* upon them his mercy.
32:13 your Creator, who *s* his favors upon you.
Jer 3: 3 Therefore the *s* were withheld,
14:22 Or can the mere heavens send *s*?

SHOWING (18)

Ex 18:20 *s* them how they are to live and what they
Nm 20:12 *s* forth my sanctity before the Israelites,
Dt 22: 1 driven astray without *s* concern about it;
22: 4 on the road without *s* concern about it;
Jos 2:12 LORD that, since I am *s* kindness to you,
2:14 we will be faithful in *s* kindness to you
Tb 2:14 Your true character is finally *s* itself!"
Eccl 3:18 *s* that they are in themselves like beasts.
Wis 14: 4 path, *S* that you can save from any danger,
18:21 the calamity, *s* that he was your servant.
Jer 2:19 the LORD, your God, And *s* no fear of me,
Acts 17: 3 *s* that the Messiah had to suffer and rise
Rom 12:10 Anticipate each other in *s* respect.
2Cor 4: 4 of the gospel *s* forth the glory of Christ,
Eph 5:33 for her part *s* respect for her husband.
1Thes 1: 3 and *s* constancy of hope in our Lord Jesus
Heb 9: 8 The Holy Spirit was *s* thereby that while
2Pt 2: 6 thereby *s* what would happen in the future

SHOWN (47)

Ex 14:31 that the LORD had *s* against the Egyptians,
18: 9 goodness that the LORD had *s* Israel
25:40 to the pattern *s* you on the mountain.
26:30 to the pattern *s* you on the mountain.
27: 8 box, just as it was *s* you on the mountain.
Lv 13: 7 after he has *s* himself to the priest to be
13:49 with leprosy and must be *s* to the priest.
Nm 8: 4 to the pattern which the LORD had *s* Moses.
2Sm 7:19 this too you have *s* to man, Lord GOD!
19: 7 For you have *s* today that officers and
1Kgs 3: 6 "You have *s* great favor to your servant,
2Chr 1: 8 have *s* great favor to my father David,
24:22 of the devotion *s* him by Jehoiada,
30:22 Levites who had *s* themselves well skilled
Tb 13: 4 he has *s* you his greatness even there.
1Mc 11: 4 *s* the temple of Dagon destroyed by fire,
14:35 loyalty and justice he had *s* his nation.
2Mc 11:10 that the Lord had *s* his mercy toward them,
12:30 good will *s* by the Scythopolitans
13: 4 When the king was *s* by Lysias that
Jb 38:12 morning and *s* the dawn its place
38:17 Have the gates of death been *s* to you,
Ps(s) 22:32 people yet to be born the justice he has *s*.
31:22 kindness he has *s* me in a fortified city.
78:11 his deeds, the wonders he had *s* them.
Wis 11: 8 once you had *s* by the thirst they then
16: 4 *s* how their enemies were being tormented.
Sir 3:22 when *s* things beyond human understanding.
Is 5:16 the holy shall be *s* holy by his justice.
60:10 yet in my good will I have *s* you mercy.
Jer 31:16 sorrow you have *s* shall have its reward,
Lam 5:12 were gibbeted by them, elders *s* no respect.
Ez 11:25 the exiles everything the LORD had *s* me.
Dn 2:23 Now you have *s* me what we asked of you,
2:28 and he has *s* King Nebuchadnezzar what is
10: 6 like chrysolite, his face *s* like lightning,
Lk 1:51 "He has *s* might with his arm;
Jn 4:52 at what time the boy had *s* improvement,
10:32 good deeds have I *s* you from the Father.
Acts 2:28 You have *s* me the paths of life;
2Cor 8: 9 the favor *s* you by our Lord Jesus Christ;
9: 3 for you in this regard may not be *s* empty.
Gal 2:17 in Christ, we are *s* to be sinners,
Col 3:25 No favoritism will be *s*.
Heb 6:10 the love you have *s* him by your service,
8: 5 to the pattern *s* you on the mountain."
Jas 2:13 judgment on the man who has not *s* mercy;

SHOWS (30)

Lv 13: 3 *s* that it has penetrated below the skin,
Dt 28:50 that *s* neither respect for the aged nor
1Sm 22: 8 None of you *s* sympathy for me or discloses
2Sm 14:13 as he has, the king *s* himself guilty,
1Mc 12: 7 are our brothers, as the attached copy *s*.
2Mc 2: 7 his people together again and *s* them mercy.
10:38 the Lord who *s* great kindness to Israel
Ps(s) 25: 8 the LORD; thus he *s* sinners the way.
25:12 LORD, he *s* him the way he should choose.
Prv 3:34 is stern, but to the humble he *s* kindness.
12:16 The fool immediately *s* his anger,
14:29 The patient man *s* much good sense,
Wis 6: 7 For the Lord of all *s* no partiality,
Sir 2:18 to his majesty is the mercy that he *s*.
17: 6 he fills them; good and evil he *s* them.
17: 7 hearts, and *s* them his glorious works,
27: 6 The fruit of a tree *s* the care it has had;
30: 3 and *s* his delight in him among his friends.
39:34 for each *s* its worth at the proper time.
Is 42:13 cry, against his enemies he *s* his might:
44:23 Jacob, and *s* his glory through Israel.
49:13 his people and *s* mercy to his afflicted.
Jer 17: 8 In the year of drought it *s* no distress,
38:21 to surrender, this is what the LORD *s* me:
Jn 5:20 and everything the Father does he *s* him.
Acts 10:34 how true it is that God *s* no partiality.
Phil 3:18 which *s* them to be enemies of the cross
Heb 12:27 And that "once more" *s* that shaken,
1Pt 5: 5 arrogant but to the humble he *s* kindness."
2Pt 3: 9 Rather, he *s* you generous patience,

SHRANK (2)

Nm 22:25 of the LORD there, she *s* against the wall;
2Mc 14:18 he *s* from deciding the issue by bloodshed.

SHREDS (1)

Mt 7: 6 at best, and perhaps even tear you to *s*.

SHREWD (12)

Prv 12:16 anger, but the *s* man passes over an insult.
12:23 A *s* man conceals his knowledge,
13:16 The *s* man does everything with prudence.
14: 8 The *s* man's wisdom gives him knowledge of
14:15 but the *s* man measures his steps.
14:18 but *s* men gain the crown of knowledge.
22: 3 The *s* man perceives evil and hides,
27:12 The *s* man perceives evil and hides;
Eccl 9:11 by the wise, nor riches by the *s*,
Sir 6:32 if you apply yourself, you will be *s*.
21:12 He can never be taught who is not *s*,
Is 10:13 have done it, and by my wisdom, for I am *s*.

SHREWDLY (2)

Ex 1:10 deal *s* with them to stop their increase;
Jdt 5:11 *s* forced them to labor at brickmaking,

SHREWDNESS (4)

Wis 17: 7 and a jeering reproof of their vaunted *s*.
Sir 19:19 There is a *s* that is detestable,
19:21 There is a *s* keen but dishonest,
21:12 but one form of *s* is thoroughly bitter.

SHRIEK (6)

Prv 23:29 Who *s?* Who have strife!
Is 10:30 Cry and *s*, O daughter of Gallim!
Jer 49: 3 Heshbon, for the ravager approaches, *s*,
Mt 8:29 With a sudden *s* they cried: "Why meddle
Mk 1:26 and with a loud *s* came out of him.
Lk 8:28 On seeing Jesus he began to *s;* then he fell

SHRIEKED (4)

1Sm 28:12 *s* at the top of her voice and said to Saul,
Dn 13:24 Then Susanna *s*, and the old men also
Mk 1:23 a man with an unclean spirit that *s:*
Lk 4:33 an unclean spirit, who *s* in a loud voice:

SHRIEKING (2)

Mk 5: 7 up and did him homage, *s* in a loud voice,
Acts 8: 7 unclean spirits, which came out *s* loudly.

SHRIEKS (1)

Nm 16:34 the Israelites near them fled at their *s*,

SHRILL (3)

Jdt 7:29 into *s* wailing and loud cries to the Lord
Is 38:14 Like a swallow I utter *s* cries;
Lam 2:19 Rise up, *s* in the night, at the beginning

SHRINE (12)

Gn 28:11 at Bethel When he came upon a certain *s*,
28:11 Taking one of the stones at the *s*,
28:17 "How awesome is this *s!*
2Kgs 10:25 into the inner *s* of the temple of Baal,
10:26 out the stele of Baal, and burned the *s*.
2Mc 12:26 marched to Karnion and the *s* of Atargatis,
14:33 I will level this *s* of God to the ground;
Ps(s) 28: 2 lifting up my hands toward your holy *s*.
74: 4 Your foes roar triumphantly in your *s;*
78:69 And he built his *s* like heaven,
Wis 13:15 a fitting *s* for it and puts it on the wall,
Is 44:13 in appearance and dignity, to occupy a *s*.

SHRINES (9)

1Kgs 13:32 against all the *s* on the high places
2Kgs 17:29 in the *s* on the high places which the
17:32 for them in the *s* on the high places.
23:19 Josiah also removed all the *s* on the high
23:20 of the high places that were at the *s*,
1Mc 1:47 to build pagan altars and temples and *s*,
Ps(s) 74: 8 burn all the *s* of God in the land."
Acts 17:23 As I walked around looking at your *s*,
19:24 who made miniature *s* of Artemis

SHRINK (4)

Tb 11: 8 the cataracts *s* and peel off from his eyes;
Jb 3:25 me, and what I *s* from comes upon me.
Jer 4:29 They *s* into the thickets, they scale
Acts 20:20 Never did I *s* from telling you what was

SHRINKS (1)

Lam 4: 8 Their skin *s* on their bones,

SHRIVEL (2)

Jb 24:24 like ears of grain they *s*.
Is 19: 5 from the sea, the river shall *s* and dry up;

SHRIVELED (7)

Gn 41:23 *s* and thin and blasted by the east wind,
Ps(s) 119:83 I am *s* like a leathern flask in the smoke,
Lam 5:10 Our skin is *s* up, as though by a furnace,
Jl 1:17 The seed lies *s* under its clods;
Mt 12:10 A man with a *s* hand happened to be there,
Mk 3: 1 where there was a man whose hand was *s* up.
3: 3 He addressed the man with the *s* hand:

SHRIVELS (1)

Is 5:24 up stubble, as dry grass *s* in the flame,

SHROUD (1)

Mk 15:46 Then, having bought a linen *s*, Joseph

SHROUDED (1)

Jude 1: 6 *s* in murky darkness against the judgment

SHRUB (4)

Gn 2: 5 while as yet there was no field *s* on earth
21:15 So she put the child down under a *s*,
Mt 13:32 It becomes so big a *s* that the birds of
Lk 13:19 It grew and became a large *s* and the birds

SHRUBS (2)

Jb 30: 4 They plucked saltwort and *s;*
Mk 4:32 springs up to become the largest of *s*,

SHRUNK (3)

Est D: 5 lovely, though her heart was *s* with fear.
Ps(s) 44:19 Our hearts have not *s* back,
Acts 20:27 for I have never *s* from announcing to you

SHRUNKEN (1)

Jb 17: 7 anguish, and all my frame is *s* to a shadow.

SHUA (3)

Gn 38: 2 met the daughter of a Canaanite named *S*,
38:12 and Judah's wife, the daughter of *S*,
1Chr 7:32 Shomer, Hotham, and their sister *S*.

SHUAH (2)

Gn 25: 2 Jokshan, Medan, Midian, Ishbak, and *S*.
1Chr 1:32 Jokshan, Medan, Midian, Ishbak, and *S*.

SHUAL (2)

1Sm 13:17 the Ophrah road toward the district of *S;*
1Chr 7:36 sons of Zophah were Suah, Harnepher, *S*,

SHUBAEL (6)

1Chr 23:16 sons of Gershon: *S* the chief.
24:20 Of the remaining Levites, there were *S*,
24:20 and Jehdeiah, of the descendants of *S;*
25: 4 Bukkiah, Mattaniah, Uzziel, *S*,
25:20 The thirteenth was *S*, his sons, and his
26:24 Izharites, Hebronites, and Uzzielites, *S*,

SHUDDER (4)

Is 32:11 *S*, you who are overconfident!
Jer 2:12 this, O heavens, and *s* with sheer horror,
Ez 32:10 and their kings shall *s* over you in horror
Jas 2:19 The demons believe that, and *s*.

SHUDDERED (1)

Ps(s) 77:17 the waters saw you and *s;*

SHUDDERING (2)

Jb 4:14 falls on men, Fear came upon me, and *s*,
Is 21: 4 My mind reels, *s* assails me;

SHUDDERS (2)

Ps(s) 119:120 My flesh *s* with dread of you,
Na 2: 7 The river gates are opened, the palace *s*,

SHUFFLES (1)

Prv 6:13 He winks his eyes, *s* his feet,

SHUH (1)

Jb 2:11 Eliphaz from Teman, Bildad from *S*,

SHUHAH (1)

1Chr 4:11 Chelub, the brother of *S*,

SHUHAM (1)

Nm 26:42 through *S* the clan of the Shuhamites.

SHUHAMITES (1)

Nm 26:42 through Shuham the clan of the *S*.

SHUHITE (4)

Jb 8: 1 Bildad the *S* spoke out and said:
18: 1 Then Bildad the *S* replied and said:
25: 1 Then Bildad the *S* answered and said:
42: 9 Eliphaz the Temanite, and Bildad the *S*,

SHULAMMITE (2)

Sg 7: 1 Turn, turn, O *S*,
7: 1 the *S* as at the dance of the two companies?

SHUMATHITES (1)

1Chr 2:53 the Ithrites, the Puthites, the *S*,

SHUN (6)

Prv 4:15 *S* it, cross it not, turn aside from it,
19: 7 how much more do his friends *s* him!
20: 3 It is honorable for a man to *s* strife,
22: 5 who would safeguard his life will *s* them.
1Cor 6:18 *S* lewd conduct.
10:14 whom I love, to *s* the worship of idols,

SHUNAMITE (5)

1Kgs 1: 3 of Israel, and found Abishag the *S*,
1:15 while Abishag the *S* was attending him
2:17 you, to give me Abishag the *S* for my wife."
2:21 "Let Abishag the *S* be given to your
2:22 why do you ask Abishag the *S* for Adonijah?"

SHUNAMMITE (3)

2Kgs 4:12 to his servant Gehazi, "Call this *S* woman."
4:25 "There is the *S!*
4:36 summoned Gehazi and said, "Call the *S*."

SHUNEM (3)

Jos 19:18 included Jezreel, Chesulloth, *S*,
1Sm 28: 4 levies advanced to *S* and encamped.
2Kgs 4: 8 One day Elisha came to *S*,

SHUNI (2)

Gn 46:16 Zephon, Haggi, *S*,
Nm 26:15 through *S* the clan of the Shunites,

SHUNITES (1)

Nm 26:15 Haggites, through Shuni the clan of the *S*,

SHUNNED (1)

Est E:24 even *s* by wild beasts and birds forever."

SHUNS (1)

Prv 14:16 The wise man is cautious and *s* evil;

SHUPHAM (3)

Gn 46:21 Becher, Ashbel, Gera, Naaman, Ahiram, *S*,
Nm 26:39 through *S* the clan of the Shuphamites,
1Chr 7:11 *S* and Hupham.

SHUPHAMITES (1)

Nm 26:39 through Shupham the clan of the *S*,

SHUR (5)

Gn 16: 7 wilderness, the spring on the road to *S*,
20: 1 where he settled between Kadesh and *S*.
Ex 15:22 and they marched out to the desert of *S*.
1Sm 15: 7 Amalek from Havilah to the approaches of *S*,
27: 8 land between Telam, on the approach to *S*,

SHUT (31)

Gn 7:16 Then the LORD *s* him in.
19: 6 When he had *s* the door behind him,
Jos 2: 5 when it was time for the gate to be *s*,

SHUT (cont.)

2: 7 and once they had left, the gate was s.
1Sm 6:10 to the cart but s up their calves indoors.
23: 7 Now he has s himself in,
Neh 7: 3 shining they shall s and bar the doors.
1Mc 5:47 But the men in the city s them out and
10:75 but the men in the city s him out because
2Mc 12: 7 When the gates of the town were s,
Jb 3:10 Because it kept not s the doors of the
24:16 By day they s themselves in;
38: 8 And who s within doors the sea,
Ps(s) 17:10 they s up their cruel hearts,
Eccl 12: 4 When the doors to the street are s,
Sir 48: 3 By God's word he s up the heavens and
Is 22:22 when he opens, no one shall s,
24:10 down is the city of chaos, s against entry,
24:22 They will be s up in a dungeon,
29:10 He has s your eyes [the prophets] and
Ez 3:24 Go s yourself up in your house.
Dn 13:17 "and s the garden doors while I bathe."
13:18 they s the garden doors and left by the
13:20 They said, "the garden doors are s,
13:36 two girls and s the doors of the garden,
14:11 then s the door and seal it with your ring.
Mal 1:10 that one among you would s the temple
Mt 23:13 You s the doors of the kingdom of God in
Lk 11: 7 is s now and my children and I are in bed.
18:16 Do not s them off.
Rv 21:25 During the day its gates shall never be s,

SHUTHELAH (3)

Nm 26:35 through S the clan of the Shuthelahites,
1Chr 7:20 S, whose son was Bered,
7:21 Ephraim's son S, and Ezer and Elead,

SHUTHELAHITES (2)

Nm 26:35 through Shuthelah the clan of the S,
26:36 The S were: through Eran the clan

SHUTHITES (1)

Nm 24:17 of Moab, and the skulls of all the S,

SHUTS (3)

Jb 37: 7 He s up all mankind indoors;
Prv 21:13 He who s his ear to the cry of the poor
Is 22:22 he opens, no one shall shut, when he s,

SHUTTING (4)

Jgs 3:23 s the doors of the upper room on him and
9:51 s themselves in and going up to the roof
Ps(s) 31: 9 Not s me up in the grip of the enemy but
Lk 3:20 added to his guilt by s John up in prison.

SHUTTLE (1)

Jb 7: 6 My days are swifter than a weaver's s;

SIA (1)

Neh 7:47 of Tabbaoth, sons of Keros, sons of S,

SIAHA (1)

Ezr 2:44 of Tabbaoth, sons of Keros, sons of S,

SIBBECAI (5)

2Sm 21:18 On that occasion S, from Husha, killed
23:27 S from Hushah; Zalmon from Ahoh;
1Chr 11:29 S, from Husha; Ilai, from Ahoh;
20: 4 At that time, S the Hushathite slew Sippai,
27:11 for the eighth month, was S the Hushathite,

SIBBOLETH (1)

Jgs 12: 6 If he said S," not being able to give the

SIBMAH (5)

Nm 32:38 and S. These towns, which they rebuilt
Jos 13:19 Jahaz, Kedemoth, Mephaath, Kiriathaim, S,
Is 16: 8 of Heshbon languish, the vines of S,
16: 9 I weep with Jazer for the vines of S;
Jer 48:32 for Jazer I weep over you, vineyard of S.

SIBRAIM (1)

Ez 47:16 Labo of Hamath, to Zedad, Berothah, and S,

SICK (55)

1Sm 19:14 to arrest David, she said, "He's s."
30:13 me because I fell s three days ago today.
2Sm 13: 2 over his sister Tamar that he became s;
13: 5 "Lie down on your bed and pretend to be s.
13: 6 So Amnon lay down and pretended to be s.
1Kgs 14: 1 that time Abijah, son of Jeroboam, took s.
14: 5 to consult you about her son, for he is s.
17:17 son of the mistress of the house fell s,
2Kgs 8: 7 a time when Ben-hadad, king of Aram, lay s.
Neh 2: 2 If you are not s, you must be sad at
1Mc 6: 8 S with grief because his designs had failed,
Prv 13:12 Hope deferred makes the heart s,
Wis 17: 8 to banish fears and terrors from the s soul
Sir 7:35 Neglect not to visit the s—
Is 1: 5 The whole head is s, the whole heart faint.
33:24 one who dwells there will say, "I am s";
38: 9 been s and had recovered from his illness:
Lam 1:22 My groans are many, and I am s at heart."
5:17 Over this our hearts are s,
Ez 34: 4 nor heal the s nor bind up the injured.
34:16 the s I will heal [but the sleek and the
Mal 1: 8 When you offer the lame or the s,
1:13 in what you seize, or the lame, or the s;
Mt 9:12 do not need a doctor; s people do.
10: 8 Cure the s, raise the dead, heal
14:14 was moved with pity, and he cured their s.
Mk 2:17 do not need a doctor; s people do.
6: 5 a few who were s by laying hands on them,
6:13 many demons, anointed the s with oil,
6:55 to bring in the s on bedrolls to the place
6:56 they laid the s in the market places and
16:18 and the s upon whom they lay their hands
16:20 and the s upon whom they lay their hands
Lk 4:40 all who had people s with a variety of
5:31 do not need a doctor; s people do.
7: 2 was at that moment s to the point of death.
10: 9 they set before you, and cure the s there.
Jn 5: 3 crowded with s people lying there blind,
5: 5 man who had been s for thirty-eight years.
5: 6 Jesus, who knew he had been s a long time,
5: 7 "Sir," the s man answered, "I do not
6: 2 saw the signs he was performing for the s.
11: 1 was a certain man named Lazarus who was s.
11: 2 (This Mary whose brother Lazarus was s was
11: 3 inform him, "Lord, the one you love is s."
11: 6 Yet, after hearing that Lazarus was s,
Acts 5:15 The people carried the s into the streets
5:16 bringing their s and those who were
19:12 touched his skin were applied to the s,
28: 8 happened that Publius' father was s in bed,
28: 9 the rest of the s on the island began to
1Cor 11:30 is why many among you are s and infirm,
Phil 2:27 He was, in fact, s to the point of death,
1Tm 6: 4 a s man in his passion for polemics and
Jas 5:14 Is there anyone s among you?

SICKBED (2)

2Chr 24:25 They killed him on his s.
Ps(s) 41: 4 The LORD will help him on his s,

SICKENED (2)

2Mc 9: 9 army was s by the stench of his corruption.
Wis 17: 8 themselves s with a ridiculous fear.

SICKLE (12)

Dt 16: 9 the s is first put to the standing grain.
23:26 do not put a s to your neighbor's grain.
Jer 50:16 and him who wields the s in harvest time!
Jl 4:13 Apply the s, for the harvest is ripe;
Mk 4:29 When the crop is ready he 'wields the s,
Rv 14:14 his head and holding a sharp s in his hand.
14:15 "Use your s and cut down the harvest,
14:16 the cloud wielded his s over all the earth
14:17 another angel, who likewise held a sharp s.
14:18 voice to the one who held the sharp s,
14:18 "Use your sharp s and gather the grapes
14:19 So the angel wielded his s over the earth

SICKLES (1)

1Sm 13:20 their plowshares, mattocks, axes, and s.

SICKLY (1)

Rv 6: 8 Now I saw a horse s green in color.

SICKNESS (20)

Ex 23:25 and I will remove all s from your midst;
Dt 7:15 The LORD will remove all s from you;
28:61 Should there be any kind of s or calamity
1Kgs 8:37 whatever plague or s there may be,
17:17 and his s grew more severe until he
2Kgs 8: 8 as to whether I shall recover from this s."
8: 9 ask you whether he will recover from his s."
13:14 from the s of which he was to die,
2Chr 6:28 there is a plague or s of any kind;
16:12 But even in his s he did not seek the LORD,
Jb 16: 3 Or what s have you that you speak on?
Eccl 5:16 sorrow, under great vexation, s and wrath.
Sir 18:18 speaking; before s prepare the cure.
31:22 do, be moderate, and no s will befall you.
37:29 choice foods, For s comes with overeating,
48: 6 and nobles, from their beds of s.
Is 39: 1 that Hezekiah had recovered from his s,
Mt 9:35 reign, and he cured every s and disease.
10: 1 and to cure s and disease of every kind.
Jn 11: 4 "This s is not to end in death;

SICYON (1)

1Mc 15:23 Sparta, Delos, Myndos, S,

SIDDIM (3)

Gn 14: 3 joined forces in the Valley of S (that is,
14: 8 of S they went into battle against them:
14:10 the Valley of S was full of bitumen pits;

SIDE (275)

Gn 6:16 Put an entrance in the s of the ark,
23: 3 Then he left the s of his dead one and
31:42 One of Isaac, had not been on my s,
Ex 17:12 hands, one on one s and one on the other,
23: 2 s with the many in perverting justice.
25:12 on one side and two on the opposite s.
25:32 of the lampstand, three branches on one s,
26:13 on either s of the Dwelling to protect it.
26:18 twenty boards on the south s,
26:20 other side of the Dwelling, the north s,
26:26 for the boards on one s of the Dwelling,
26:27 Dwelling, five for those on the other s,
26:35 the latter on the south s of the Dwelling,
26:35 table, which is to be put on the north s.
27: 7 either s of the altar when it is carried.
27: 9 On the south s the court shall have
27:11 north s there shall be similar hangings,
27:12 On the west s, across the width
27:13 court on the east s shall be fifty cubits.
27:14 On one s there shall be hangings to the
27:15 on the other s there shall be hangings to
30: 4 two on one s and two on the opposite side,
30: 4 two on one side and two on the opposite s,
34:10 deeds which I, the LORD, will do at your s.
36:23 twenty boards on the south s,
36:25 other side of the Dwelling, the north s,
36:31 for the boards on one s of the Dwelling,
36:32 Dwelling, five for those on the other s,
37: 3 for one side and two for the opposite s.
37:18 branches on one s and three on the other.
37:27 two on one side and two on the opposite s,
38: 9 south s of the court there were hangings,
38:11 On the north s there were similar hangings,
38:12 On the west s there were hangings,
38:13 the east s the court was fifty cubits long.
38:14 Toward one s there were hangings to the
38:14 toward the other s, beyond the entrance
40:22 tent, on the north s of the Dwelling,
40:24 the table, on the south s of the Dwelling,
Lv 1:11 the LORD at the north s of the altar.
1:15 out its blood against the s of the altar.
1:16 on the ash heap at the east s of the altar.
5: 9 sin offering against the s of the altar.
6: 3 altar, and lay them at the s of the altar.
Nm 2: 3 "Encamped on the east s,
2:10 s shall be the divisional camp of Reuben,
2:18 s shall be the divisional camp of Ephraim,
2:25 s shall be the divisional camp of Dan,
3:29 camped at the south s of the Dwelling.
3:35 They camped at the north s of the Dwelling.
10: 6 those encamped on the east s shall set out;
10: 6 encamped on the south s shall set out;
10: 6 those encamped on the west s shall set out;
10: 6 encamped on the north s shall set out.
21:13 they encamped on the other s of the Arnon,
22: 1 s of the Jericho stretch of the Jordan.
22:24 vineyards with a stone wall on each s.
32:19 ourselves on this eastern s of the Jordan."
32:32 property on this s of the Jordan."
34:11 ridge on the east s of Sea of Chinnereth;
34:15 s of the Jericho stretch of the Jordan,
35: 5 cubits outside the city along each s—
36:11 married relatives on their father's s
Dt 3:20 give them on the other s of the Jordan.
11:30 on the other s of the western road in the
Jos 4:11 and when all had reached the other s,
7: 2 Ai, which is near Bethel on its eastern s,
7: 7 to dwell on the other s of the Jordan.
8:11 north of Ai, on the other s of the ravine.
8:22 were hemmed in by Israelites on either s,
8:33 stood on either s of the ark facing the
12: 3 the eastern s of the Sea of Chinnereth,
12: 3 as far south as the eastern s of the Salt
15: 7 of Adummim, on the south s of the wadi;
21:44 it, the LORD gave them peace on every s,
Jgs 7: 5 "You shall set to one s everyone who laps
14:16 At Samson's s, his wife wept and said,
1Sm 12:11 from the power of your enemies on every s,
14: 1 to the Philistine outpost on the other s."
14: 4 outpost there was a rocky crag on each s,
14:40 he said to all Israel, "Stand on one s,
20:21 to him, 'Look, the arrow is this s of you;
20:25 him, while Abner sat at the king's s,
2Sm 2:13 one group on one s of the pool and the
2:13 the pool and the other on the opposite s.
2:16 and thrust his sword into his opponent's s,
7: 1 him rest from his enemies on every s,
1Kgs 1: 8 of David's army, did not s with Adonijah.
3:20 night she got up and took my son from my s,
6: 3 temple was twenty cubits from s to side,
6: 8 the annex was at the right s of the temple,
6:27 touched a s wall while the other wing,
7:33 they had wreaths on each s.
7:39 s of the temple and five on the north.
7:39 southeast from the south s of the temple.
10:19 top, and an arm on each s of the seat.
10:20 to a step, one on either s of each step.
2Kgs 2:15 in Jericho, who were on the other s,
6:16 "Our s outnumbers theirs."
9:32 the window and shouted, "Who is on my s?
10: 6 "If you are on my s and will obey me,

16:14 and set it on the north *s* of his altar.
25: 1 it, and built siege walls on every *s*.
1Chr 9:18 guard at the king's gate on the east *s*;
12:38 From the other *s* of the Jordan,
19:16 the Arameans from the other *s* of the River,
22: 9 him rest from all his enemies on every *s*.
22:18 Has he not given you rest on every *s*?
26:14 When the lot was cast for the east *s*,
26:14 counselor, and the north *s* fell to his lot.
26:15 To Obed-edom fell the south *s*,
26:16 To Hosah fell the west *s* with the
26:30 of Israel on the western *s* of the Jordan
2Chr 3:17 for the right *s* and the other for the left,
4:10 southeast from the right *s* of the temple.
9:18 and there was an arm on each *s* of the seat,
9:19 stood there, one on either *s* of each step.
14: 6 him, and he has given us rest on every *s*."
15:15 And the LORD gave them rest on every *s*.
20:30 for his God gave him rest on every *s*.
32:22 he gave them rest on every *s*.
Neh 3: 2 their *s* the men of Jericho were rebuilding,
3: 4 At their *s* Meremoth, son of Uriah,
3: 7 At their *s* were Melatiah the Gibeonite,
3: 8 guild, and at his *s* was Hananiah,
3:10 of Jerusalem, and at his *s* was Jedaiah,
3:12 At their *s* the work of repair was carried
4:12 he worked, had his sword girt at his *s*.
8: 4 at his right *s* stood Mattithiah,
1Mc 5:37 Raphon, on the other *s* of the stream.
5:41 and camps on the other *s* of the river,
8: 1 and acted amiably to all who took their *s*.
9:12 were on Judas' *s* also blew their trumpets.
9:45 us are the waters of the Jordan on one *s*,
9:48 the Jordan and swam across to the other *s*,
9:49 thousand men on Bacchides' *s* fell that day.
10:63 The king also had him seated at his *s*.
10:71 the city forces are on my *s*.
13:10 of Jerusalem, fortified it on every *s*.
15:23 Halicarnassus, Rhodes, Phaselis, Cos, *S*,
2Mc 1:11 having fought on our *s* against the king;
3:26 Standing on each *s* of him, they flogged
4:45 Menelaus, seeing himself on the losing *s*,
5: 3 and countercharges on this *s* and that,
14:21 From each *s* a chariot came forward and
Jb 18:11 On every *s* terrors affright him;
18:12 Disaster is ready at his *s*,
19:10 He breaks me down on every *s*,
Ps(s) 3: 7 of people arrayed against me on every *s*.
23: 4 for you are at my *s* With your rod and your
27: 6 is held high above my enemies on every *s*.
31:14 the crowd, that frighten me from every *s*,
55:15 at whose *s* I walked in procession in the
91: 7 at your side, ten thousand at your right *s*,
118:11 They encompassed me on every *s*;
Sg 3: 8 Each with his sword at his *s* against
Sir 9: 9 recline not at table to drink by her *s*,
25:25 If she walks not by your *s*, cut her away
47: 7 battled and subdued the enemy on every *s*.
51: 4 from flames that hemmed me in on every *s*;
Jer 6:25 of the enemy's sword; terror on every *s*!
20: 3 the LORD will name you "Terror on every *s*."
20:10 "Terror on every *s*!
46: 5 Terror on every *s*, says the LORD!
49:29 shout from upon them, "Terror on every *s*!"
50:26 Come upon her from every *s*,
52: 4 it, and built siege walls on every *s*.
Ez 1:10 but on the right *s* was the face of a lion,
1:10 lion, and on the left *s* the face of an ox,
4: 4 Then you shall lie on your left *s*,
4: 6 to lie down again, but on your right *s*,
4: 8 cords so that you cannot turn from one *s*
4: 9 it for as many days as you lie upon your *s*,
23:22 I will bring them against you from every *s*:
28:23 sword that comes against it from every *s*.
34:21 Because you push with *s* and shoulder,
40:10 of the east gate were three on either *s*,
40:10 on either *s* were also of equal size.
40:12 themselves were six cubits on either *s*,
40:13 back wall of the cell on the opposite *s*:
40:14 the court on either *s* were six cubits.
40:21 Its cells, three on either *s*, its pilasters,
40:39 gate there were two tables on either *s*,
40:40 and on the other *s* of the vestibule of the
40:41 on either *s* of the gate [eight tables],
40:48 and the side walls on either *s* of the door
40:48 and measured the pilasters on each *s*,
40:49 columns by the pilasters, one on either *s*.
41: 1 which were six cubits thick on either *s*.
41: 2 either *s* of it measured five cubits each.
41: 3 either *s* of it extended seven cubits each.
41: 5 the *s* chambers,
41: 6 There were thirty *s* chambers built one
41: 6 of the temple that enclosed the *s* chambers;
41: 7 that led upward to the *s* chambers,
41: 8 the foundations of the *s* chambers
41: 9 enclosed the *s* chambers was five cubits
41: 8 Between the *s* chambers of the temple and
41:11 *s* chambers had entrances to the open space,
41:12 west *s* was seventy cubits front to back;
41:12 it measured ninety cubits from side to *s*.
41:14 along with the free area, on the east *s*,
41:17 on every wall on every *s* in both the inner
41:19 man's face looking at a palmtree on one *s*,
41:19 on every *s* throughout the whole temple.
41:26 on both *s* walls of the vestibule,
41:26 and the *s* chambers of the temple.
42: 2 length was a hundred cubits on the north *s*,
42: 7 On the far *s* there was a wall running
42:10 To the south along the *s* of the free area
42:16 He measured the east *s*:
42:17 Then he turned and measured the north *s*:
45: 7 western *s* and eastward on the eastern side,
45: 7 side and eastward on the eastern *s*,
46:19 the entrance which is on the *s* of the gate
47: 1 down from the southern *s* of the temple,
47: 2 I saw water trickling from the southern *s*.
47:15 is the boundary of the land on the north *s*:
47:18 and Gilead on the one *s*,
47:18 and the land of Israel on the other *s*,
48:16 the north *s*, forty-five hundred cubits;
48:16 the south *s*,
48:16 and the west *s*, forty-five hundred cubits.
48:16 the east *s*, forty-five hundred cubits;
48:30 On the north *s*, measuring forty-five
48:32 On the east *s*, measuring forty-five
48:33 On the south *s*, measuring forty-five
48:34 On the west *s*, measuring forty-five
Dn 7: 5 it was raised up on one *s*,
9: 7 Justice, O Lord, is on your *s*;
13:18 the *s* gate to fetch what she had ordered,
13:26 the *s* gate to see what had happened to her.
13:56 Putting him to one *s*, he ordered
Zec 4:11 two olive trees at each *s* of the lampstand?"
Mt 14:22 the boat and precede him to the other *s*.
16: 5 when they arrived at the other *s*
Mk 5: 1 territory on the other *s* of the lake.
5:21 back to the other *s* again in the boat,
6:45 him to the other *s* toward Bethsaida,
Lk 5: 2 saw two boats moored by the *s* of the lake;
8:22 us cross over to the far *s* of the lake."
9:50 man who is not against you is on your *s*."
16:26 so, nor can anyone cross from your *s* to us.'
18:35 blind man sat at the *s* of the road begging.
19:43 you in, and press you hard from every *s*.
22:33 "at your *s* I am prepared to face
Jn 1:18 God the only Son, ever at the Father's *s*,
6:22 crowd remained on the other *s* of the lake.
6:25 they found him on the other *s* of the lake,
8:16 at my *s* the One who sent me [the Father].
17: 5 you now, Father, give me glory at your *s*,
19:18 one on either *s*, Jesus in the middle.
19:34 of the soldiers thrust a lance into his *s*,
20: 4 They were running *s* by side,
20:20 this, he showed them his hands and his *s*.
20:25 in the nailmarks and my hand into his *s*."
20:27 Put your hand into my *s*.
21: 6 "Cast your net off to the starboard *s*,"
Acts 12: 7 He tapped Peter on the *s* and woke him.
23:11 the Lord appeared at Paul's *s* and said:
27: 4 *s* of Cyprus because of strong headwinds.
27:18 some of the cargo was thrown over the *s*.
Phil 2:22 *s* serving the gospel along with me.
4: 3 struggled at my *s* in promoting the gospel,
2Tm 4:17 Lord stood by my *s* and gave me strength,
Rv 22: 2 On either *s* of the river grew the trees of

SIDEBOARD (1)

1Mc 15:32 court, the gold and silver plate on the *s*,

SIDED (2)

1Sm 14:21 the Hebrews who had previously *s*
1Kgs 2:28 news came to Joab, who had *s* with Adonijah,

SIDES (76)

Gn 26:28 be a sworn agreement between our two *s*—
Ex 25:14 put through the rings on the *s* of the ark,
25:27 on two opposite *s* of the frame as holders
25:32 are to extend from the *s* of the lampstand,
29:16 take and splash on all the *s* of the altar.
29:20 of the blood on all the *s* of the altar.
30: 3 Its grate on top, its walls on all four *s*,
32:15 tablets that were written on both *s*,
37: 5 put through the rings on the *s* of the ark,
37:18 Six branches extended from its *s*,
37:26 Its grate on top, its walls on all four *s*,
38: 7 on the *s* of the altar for carrying it.
38:16 The hangings on all *s* of the court were
Lv 1: 5 blood by splashing it on the *s* of the altar
1:11 splash its blood on the *s* of the altar.
3: 2 splash its blood on the *s* of the altar.
3: 8 splash its blood on the *s* of the altar.
3:13 splash its blood on the *s* of the altar.
7: 2 shall be splashed on the *s* of the altar.
8:19 splashed its blood on all *s* of the altar.
8:24 blood he splashed on the *s* of the altar.
9:12 he splashed it on all *s* of the altar.
9:18 Aaron splashed it on all *s* of the altar.
Nm 33:55 barbs in your eyes and thorns in your *s*,
Jos 18:20 of the Benjaminites was bounded on all *s*.
23:13 for your *s* and thorns for your eyes,
2Sm 2:16 is in Gideon, was named the Field of the *S*.
1Kgs 5:17 of the enemies surrounding him on all *s*,
5:18 LORD, my God, has given me peace on all *s*.
6:29 The walls on all *s* of both the inner and
1Chr 9:24 gatekeepers were stationed at the four *s*,
11: 8 He rebuilt the city on all *s*,
2Chr 23: 7 Levites shall surround the king on all *s*,
Jdt 6: 6 spear of my servants will pierce your *s*,
1Mc 6:45 so that they fell back from him on both *s*.
9:17 and many on both *s* fell wounded.
2Mc 2:30 and examine them thoroughly from all *s*
8: 2 people, who were being oppressed on all *s*;
10:13 on all *s* he heard himself called a traitor
13: 5 down steeply on all *s* toward the ashes.
14:41 door ablaze, Razis, now caught on all *s*,
Jb 16:13 directions, He pierces my *s* without mercy,
Ps(s) 88:18 on all *s* they close in upon me.
Wis 17: 4 crashing sounds on all *s* terrified them,
Sir 30:12 thrash his *s* while he is still small,
42: 5 or of beating the *s* of a disloyal servant;
46: 5 God when his enemies beset him on all *s*,
Jer 49:32 from all *s* I will bring ruin upon them,
50:15 raise the war cry against her on all *s*,
51: 2 her from all *s* on the day of affliction.
Lam 2:22 a feast day terrors against me from all *s*;
3:13 pierces my *s* with shafts from his quiver.
Ez 1: 9 wings] looked out on all their four *s*;
10:16 even then the wheels did not leave their *s*.
16:33 come to you from all *s* for your harlotry.
16:37 all *s* and expose you naked for them to see.
16:57 despised on all *s* by the Philistines.
36: 3 have been ridiculed and despised on all *s*
37:21 all *s* to bring them back to their land.
39:17 from all *s* gather for the slaughter I am
40:12 each of the cells on both *s* was one cubit;
40:16 Within the gateway on both *s* there were
40:16 the vestibule on both *s* there were windows.
40:25 and its vestibule had windows on both *s*,
40:29 and its vestibule had windows on both *s*;
40:33 and its vestibule had windows on both *s*;
40:36 and its vestibule had windows on both *s*;
41:15 walls on both *s* it was one hundred cubits.
41:22 corners, and its base and *s* were of wood.
45: 7 on both *s* of the combined sacred tract
47: 7 the river I saw very many trees on both *s*.
48:21 the land on both *s* of the sacred tract and
Mk 1:45 yet people kept coming to him from all *s*.
5:38 people wailing and crying loudly on all *s*.
Acts 21:30 People came running from all *s*.
Rv 5: 1 on both *s* and was sealed with seven seals.

SIDING (2)

Jer 23:14 living in lies, *s* with the wicked,
Acts 14: 4 some *s* with the Jews and others with the

SIDON (38)

Gn 10:15 Canaan became the father of *S*,
10:19 extended from *S* all the way to Gerar,
49:13 ships], and his flank shall be based on *S*.
Jos 11: 8 them and pursued them to Greater *S*,
19:28 Rehob, Hammon and Kanah, near Greater *S*.
Jgs 1:31 out the inhabitants of Acco or those of *S*,
10: 6 the gods of Aram, the gods of *S*,
18:28 since the city was far from *S* and they had
2Sm 24: 6 from there they turned toward *S*,
1Kgs 17: 9 "Move on to Zarephath of *S* and stay there.
1Chr 1:13 Canaan became the father of *S*,
Jdt 2:28 of the coastland, upon those in *S* and Tyre,
1Mc 5:15 the inhabitants of Ptolemais, Tyre, and *S*,
Is 23: 2 dwell on the coast, you merchants of *S*,
23: 4 Shame, O *S*, fortress on the sea,
23:12 who are now oppressed, virgin daughter *S*.
Jer 25:22 all the kings of Tyre, of *S*,
27: 3 Moab, of the Ammonites, of Tyre, and of *S*,
47: 4 from Tyre and *S* the last of their allies.
Ez 27: 8 of *S* and Arvad served as your oarsmen;
28:21 Son of man, look toward *S*, and prophesy
28:22 I am coming at you, *S*; I will be glorified
28:24 *S* shall no longer be a tearing thorn for
Jl 4: 4 Moreover, what are you to me, Tyre and *S*,
Zec 9: 2 also, on its border, Tyre too, and *S*,
Mt 11:21 in you had taken place in Tyre and *S*,
11:22 and *S* than for you on the day of judgment.
15:21 and withdrew to the district of Tyre and *S*.
Mk 3: 8 and the neighborhood of Tyre and *S*,
7:24 he went off to the territory of Tyre and *S*.
7:31 returned by way of *S* to the Sea of Galilee,
Lk 4:26 sent, but to a widow of Zarephath near *S*.
6:17 and Jerusalem and the coast of Tyre and *S*,
10:13 in your midst had occurred in Tyre and *S*,
10:14 of judgment for Tyre and *S* than for you.
Acts 12:20 infuriated by the people of Tyre and *S*,
27: 3 The following day we put in at *S*,
27: 4 Then, putting out from *S*, we sailed

SIDONIAN (2)

Jos 13: 6 I will drive out all the *S* inhabitants
2Kgs 23:13 built in honor of Astarte, the *S* horror,

SIDONIANS (14)

Dt 3: 9 Sirion by the *S* and Senir by the Amorites],
Jos 13: 4 Canaanites from Mearah of the *S* to Aphek,
Jgs 3: 3 and all the Canaanites, the *S*,
10:12 the Ammonites, the Philistines, the *S*,
18: 7 lived securely after the manner of the *S*,

SIDONIANS (cont.)

18: 7 the *S* and had no contact with other people.
1Kgs 5:20 is skilled in cutting timber like the *S*,
11: 1 Pharaoh (Moabites, Ammonites, Edomites, *S*,
11: 5 By adoring Astarte, the goddess of the *S*,
11:33 has worshiped Astarte, goddess of the *S*,
16:31 daughter of Ethbaal, king of the *S*,
1Chr 22: 4 The *S* and Tyrians brought great stores of
Ezr 3: 7 and sent food and drink and oil to the *S*
Ez 32:30 the princes of the north and all the *S*,

SIEGE (47)

Dt 20:12 and instead offers you battle, lay *s* to it,
20:19 at war with a city and have to lay *s* to it
20:19 that they should be included in your *s*?
28:53 of the *s* to which your enemy subjects you,
28:55 of the *s* to which your enemy will subject
28:57 in the straits of the *s* to which your
Jos 6: 1 Now Jericho was in a state of *s* because of
10: 5 Gibeon, where they took up *s* positions.
1Sm 11: 1 went up and laid *s* to Jabesh-gilead.
2Sm 12:28 join the *s* against the city and capture it,
1Kgs 16:17 by all Israel, and laid *s* to Tirzah.
2Kgs 3:27 up the *s* and returned to their own land.
6:24 his whole army and laid *s* to Samaria.
6:25 Because of the *s* the famine in Samaria was
12:18 of Aram mounted a *s* against Gath.
18: 9 of Assyria, attacked Samaria, laid *s* to it,
24:10 Jerusalem, and the city came under *s*.
25: 1 around it, and built *s* walls on every side.
25: 2 The *s* of the city continued until the
2Chr 32:10 while you remain under *s* in Jerusalem?
1Mc 6:49 food there to enable them to stand a *s*,
9:64 camp before Bethbasi, and constructing *s*,
9:66 out to go up to the *s* with their forces.
11:22 He wrote to Jonathan to discontinue the *s*
11:23 this, Jonathan ordered the *s* to continue.
13:43 He made a *s* machine,
13:44 The men who had been on the *s* machine
15:25 troops and with the *s* machines he had made.
2Mc 10:18 everything necessary to sustain a *s*,
12:15 Jericho without battering-ram or *s* machine;
Is 29: 3 outposts and set up *s* works against you.
Jer 6: 6 throw up a *s* mound against Jerusalem.
10:17 the land, O city living in a state of *s*!
19: 9 during the strict *s* by which their enemies
37:11 When the Chaldean army lifted the *s* of
52: 4 around it, and built *s* walls on every side.
52: 5 The *s* of the city continued until the
Ez 4: 2 Raise a *s* against it:
4: 3 it shall be in the state of *s*,
4: 7 Fixing your gaze on the *s* of Jerusalem,
4: 8 you have completed the days of your *s*.
5: 2 when the days of your *s* are completed;
17:17 When ramps are cast up and *s* towers are
21:27 to cast up a ramp, to build a *s* tower.
26: 8 He shall place a *s* tower against you,
Dn 1: 1 of Babylon came and laid *s* to Jerusalem.
Mi 4:14 "They have laid *s* against us!"
Na 3:14 Draw water for the *s*,

SIEGE-DEVICES (1)

1Mc 6:31 they constructed *s*,

SIEGE-WORKS (1)

2Kgs 19:32 it with a shield, nor cast up *s* against it.

SIEGEWORKS (6)

Dt 20:20 cutting them down to build *s* with which to
Eccl 9:14 it and threw up great *s* about it.
Is 37:33 it with a shield, nor cast up *s* against it.
Jer 32:24 *s* have arrived at this city to breach it;
33: 4 destroyed in the face of *s* and the sword:
Dn 11:15 up *s* and take the fortified city by storm.

SIESTA (2)

2Sm 4: 5 heat of the day, while he was taking his *s*.
11: 2 One evening David rose from his *s* and

SIEVE (2)

Sir 27: 4 When a *s* is shaken, the husks appear;
Am 9: 9 among all nations, As one sifts with a *s*,

SIFT (2)

Am 9: 9 to *s* the house of Israel among all nations,
Lk 22:31 has asked for you, to *s* you all like wheat.

SIFTING (1)

2Sm 4: 6 of the house had dozed off while *s* wheat,

SIFTS (1)

Am 9: 9 among all nations, As one *s* with a sieve,

SIGH (9)

Ps(s) 12: 6 they rob the afflicted, and the needy *s*,
42: 6 Why do you *s* within me?
42:12 Why do you *s* within me?
43: 5 Why do you *s* within me?
90: 9 we have spent our years like a *s*.
Sir 25:17 a bitter *s* escapes him unawares.
Is 16: 7 the raisin cakes of Kir-hareseth they *s*,
Lam 1: 4 deserted, her priests groan, Her virgins *s*;
Mk 8:12 a *s* from the depths of his spirit he said,

SIGHING (6)

Jb 3:24 For *s* comes more readily to me than food,
Ps(s) 5: 2 to my words, O LORD, attend to my *s*.
6: 7 I am wearied with *s*; every night I flood
31:11 is spent with grief and my years with *s*;
79:11 Let the prisoners' *s* come before you;
102: 6 insistent *s* I am reduced to skin and bone.

SIGHT (241)

Gn 4:14 on the earth, anyone may kill me at *s*."
4:15 on Cain, lest anyone should kill him at *s*.
22: 4 day Abraham got *s* of the place from afar.
31:49 and me when we are out of each other's *s*.
33:18 Canaan, and he encamped in *s* of the city.
42:35 At the *s* of their moneybags,
Ex 3: 3 must go over to look at this remarkable *s*,
4:11 who gives *s* to one and makes another blind?
10: 6 such a *s* your fathers and grandfathers
Lv 10: 3 In the *s* of all the people I will reveal
26:32 there will stand aghast at the *s* of it.
Nm 15:39 let the *s* of them remind you to keep all
19: 5 Then the heifer shall be burned in his *s*,
32:13 evil in the *s* of the LORD had died out.
35:19 the murderer, putting him to death on *s*.
35:21 of blood may execute the murderer on *s*.
Dt 4:25 this evil done in his *s* provoke the LORD,
6:18 is right and good in the *s* of the LORD,
9:18 you had committed in the *s* of the LORD
12:25 doing what is right in the *s* of the LORD.
12:28 is good and right in the *s* of the LORD,
13:19 on you today, doing what is right in his *s*.
17: 2 a woman who does evil in the *s* of the LORD,
21: 9 doing what is right in the *s* of the LORD.
28:67 feel and the *s* that your eyes must see.
31:29 because you have done evil in the LORD's *s*,
34:12 Moses exhibited in the *s* of all Israel.
Jos 3: 7 begin to exalt you in the *s* of all Israel,
4:14 LORD exalted Joshua in the *s* of all Israel,
Jgs 6:21 the angel of the LORD disappeared from *s*.
1Sm 9:17 When Samuel caught *s* of Saul,
19: 2 get out of *s* and remain in hiding.
2Sm 12: 9 spurned the LORD and done evil in his *s*?
22:25 according to my innocence in his *s*.
1Kgs 11: 6 Solomon did evil in the *s* of the LORD;
14: 4 could not see because age had dimmed his *s*.
14:22 Judah did evil in the *s* of the LORD,
15:26 He did evil in the LORD'S *s*, imitating his
15:34 He did evil in the LORD's *s*, imitating the
16: 7 the evil Baasha did in the *s* of the LORD,
16:19 doing evil in the *s* of the LORD by
16:25 LORD'S *s* beyond any of his predecessors.
16:30 did evil in the *s* of the LORD more than
21:20 yourself up to doing evil in the LORD's *s*,
21:25 of evil in the *s* of the LORD as did Ahab,
22:43 doing what was right in the LORD's *s*.
22:53 He did evil in the *s* of the LORD,
2Kgs 1:13 servants, count for something in your *s*!
3: 2 He did evil in the LORD's *s*, though not
8:18 and he did evil in the LORD's *s*.
8:27 doing evil in the LORD's *s* as they did,
13: 2 He did evil in the LORD's *s*, conducting
13:11 He did evil in the *s* of the LORD;
14:24 He did evil in the *s* of the LORD;
15: 9 the *s* of the LORD as his fathers had done,
15:18 He did evil in the *s* of the LORD,
15:24 He did evil in the *s* of the LORD,
15:28 He did evil in the *s* of the LORD,
17: 2 He did evil in the *s* of the LORD,
17:17 into evil doing in the LORD's *s*,
17:18 the LORD put them away out of his *s*.
17:23 the LORD put Israel away out of his *s*
21: 2 He did evil in the *s* of the LORD,
21: 6 in the LORD's *s* and provoked him to anger.
21:15 they have done evil in my *s* and provoked
21:16 Manasseh did evil in the *s* of the LORD,
21:20 He did evil in the *s* of the LORD,
23:27 will I put out of my *s* as I did Israel.
23:32 He did evil in the *s* of the LORD,
23:37 He did evil in the *s* of the LORD,
24: 3 put them out of his *s* for the sins Manasseh
24: 9 He did evil in the *s* of the LORD,
24:19 He also did evil in the *s* of the LORD,
1Chr 2: 3 Er, was wicked in the *s* of the LORD,
22: 8 shed too much blood upon the earth in my *s*.
2Chr 7:20 I will cast from my *s* this house which I
20:15 lose heart at the *s* of this vast multitude,
20:32 doing what was right in the LORD's *s*.
21: 6 He did evil in the *s* of the LORD,
22: 4 he did evil in the *s* of the LORD,
22:11 priest, hid the child from Athaliah's *s*,
25: 2 did what was pleasing in the *s* of the LORD,
33: 2 He did evil in the *s* of the LORD,
33: 6 with the great evil that he did in his *s*.
33:22 He did evil in the *s* of the LORD,
36: 5 He did evil in the *s* of the LORD, his God.
36: 9 He did evil in the *s* of the LORD.
36:12 He did evil in the *s* of the LORD,
Neh 3:37 not their sin be blotted out in your *s*,
9: 8 had found his heart faithful in your *s*,
9:28 they would go back to doing evil in your *s*.
Tb 4:11 *s* of the Most High for all who give them.
6: 9 on the cataracts, his *s* will be restored."
11:17 God had mercifully restored *s* to his eyes.
Jdt 5:17 did not sin in the *s* of their God,
7: 6 *s* of the Israelites who were in Bethulia.
10:10 then they lost *s* of her.
16:16 of all holocausts but little in your *s*,
Est C:17 But now we have sinned in your *s*,
1Mc 2:23 in the *s* of all to offer sacrifice on the altar
3:18 in the *s* of Heaven there is no difference
Jb 11: 4 is pure, and I am clean in your *s*"?
15:15 and if the heavens are not clean in his *s*,
18: 3 like the beasts, their equals in your *s*?
19:15 me as a stranger; I am an alien in their *s*.
21: 8 Their progeny is secure in their *s*;
25: 4 How can a man be just in God's *s*,
25: 5 and the stars are not clear in his *s*.
Ps(s) 5: 6 the arrogant may not stand in your *s*.
18:25 to the cleanness of my hands in his *s*.
23: 5 the table before me in the *s* of my foes;
31:20 refuge in you, you show in the *s* of men.
31:23 my anguish, "I am cut off from your *s*";
51: 6 I sinned, and done what is evil in your *s*—
72:14 and precious shall their blood be in his *s*.
79:10 known among the nations in our *s* that you
90: 4 thousand years in your *s* are as yesterday,
98: 2 in the *s* of the nations he has revealed
146: 8 the LORD gives *s* to the blind.
Prv 3:21 My son, let not these slip out of your *s*:
4:21 Let them not slip out of your *s*,
5:21 each man's ways are plain to the LORD's *s*;
Wis 15: 5 the *s* of which arouses yearning in the
17: 6 times when that *s* was no longer to be seen.
Sir 41: 2 and always rebuffed, with no more *s*,
Is 3: 8 a provocation in the *s* of his majesty.
5:21 Woe to those who are wise in their own *s*,
13:16 shall be dashed to pieces in their *s*;
21: 2 desert, from the fearful land, A cruel *s*,
24:23 Jerusalem, glorious in the *s* of his elders.
49: 5 I am made glorious in the *s* of the LORD,
52:10 his holy arm in the *s* of all the nations;
65:12 *s* and preferred things which displease me,
66: 4 Because they did what was evil in my *s*,
Jer 4: 1 put your detestable things out of my *s*,
18:23 crime, blot not out their sin in your *s*!
19:10 in the *s* of the men who went with you,
32:32 so that I must put it out of my *s* for all
41:13 At the *s* of Johanan, son of Kareah,
Lam 3:35 rights in the very *s* of the Most High,
3:51 at the *s* of all the daughters of my city.
Bar 1:12 serve them long, finding favor in their *s*.
1:17 sinned in the Lord's *s* and disobeyed him.
1:22 gods, and did evil in the *s* of the Lord,
2:19 do we base our plea for mercy in your *s*,
6:36 To no blind man do they restore his *s*,
6:60 lightning, when it flashes, is a goodly *s*;
Ez 4:12 loaves over human excrement in their *s*,
20: 9 the *s* of the nations among whom they were,
20:14 that it should not be profaned in the *s*
20:22 lest it be profaned in the *s* of the
20:41 my holiness in the *s* of the nations.
28:17 I made you a spectacle in the *s* of kings.
28:18 earth in the *s* of all who should see you.
28:25 through them in the *s* of the nations.
36:17 In my *s* their conduct was like the
36:23 in their *s* I prove my holiness through you.
38:16 in their *s* I prove my holiness through you,
38:23 make myself known in the *s* of many nations;
39:27 through them in the *s* of many nations.
Hos 7: 2 crimes surround them, present to my *s*.
Jon 2: 5 Then I said, "I am banished from your *s*!
Hb 1:13 and the *s* of misery you cannot endure.
3:10 at *s* of you the mountains tremble.
Hg 2:14 this people, and so is this nation in my *s*.
Mal 2:17 evildoer is good in the *s* of the LORD,
Mt 4:21 farther and caught *s* of two other brothers,
7:23 Out of my *s*, you evildoers!'
8:34 When they caught *s* of him, they begged
9: 8 At the *s*, a feeling of awe came over
9:30 and they recovered their *s*.
9:36 At the *s* of the crowds, his heart was
11: 5 the blind recover their *s*, cripples walk,
16:23 on Peter and said, "Get out of my *s*,
22:11 he caught *s* of a man not properly dressed
25:41 'Out of my *s*, you condemned, into that
28:17 At the *s* of him, those who had
Mk 1:19 little farther along, he caught *s* of James,
2:12 mat and went outside in the *s* of everyone.
3:11 Unclean spirits would catch *s* of him,
5: 6 Catching *s* of Jesus at a distance,
5:15 they caught *s* of the man who had been
8:18 Have you eyes but no *s*?
8:25 his *s* was restored and he could see
8:33 "Get out of my *s*, you satan!
9:15 Immediately on catching *s* of Jesus,
9:20 When they did so the spirit caught *s* of
10:52 *s* and started to follow him up the road.

Lk 1:75 and through all our days be holy in his *s.*
4:18 of *s* to the blind and release to prisoners,
5: 8 At the *s* of this, Simon Peter fell at
7:21 he also restored *s* to many who were blind.)
7:22 The blind recover their *s,* cripples walk,
8:35 in his full senses; this *s* terrified them.
10:33 came on him and was moved to pity at the *s.*
12:21 instead of growing rich in the *s* of God."
15:20 caught *s* of him and was deeply moved.
18:42 Jesus said to him, "Receive your *s.*
18:43 he was given his *s* and began to follow him,
19:41 Coming within *s* of the city, he wept over
24:31 whereupon he vanished from their *s.*
Jn 1:29 John caught *s* of Jesus coming toward him,
6: 5 caught *s* of a vast crowd coming toward him,
9:15 to inquire how he had recovered his *s.*
9:32 ever gave *s* to a person blind from birth.
10:12 catches *s* of the wolf coming and runs away,
16:16 Within a short time you will lose *s* of me,
16:17 'Within a short time you will lose *s* of me,
16:19 'Within a short time you will lose *s* of me,
20:14 and caught *s* of Jesus standing there.
20:20 the *s* of the Lord the disciples rejoiced.
Acts 1: 9 in a cloud which took him from their *s.*
4:19 God's *s* for us to obey you rather than God.
7:31 When Moses saw it, he marveled at the *s.*
9:12 on him so that he might recover his *s.)*
9:17 your *s* and be filled with the Holy Spirit."
9:18 fell from his eyes and he regained his *s.*
10: 4 He stared at the *s* and said in fear,
10: 4 and your generosity have risen in God's *s,*
17:16 at the *s* of idols everywhere in the city.
17:31 the *s* of all by raising him from the dead."
21: 3 We caught *s* of Cyprus but passed it by on
21:32 the crowd caught *s* of him and the soldiers,
22:13 my brother,' he said, 'recover your *s.*'
22:13 instant I regained my *s* and looked at him.
28: 4 the *s* of the snake hanging from his hand,
Rom 2:13 hear the law who are just in the *s* of God;
3:20 in God's *s* through observance of the law;
4:17 father in the *s* of God in whom he believed,
14:22 have as your rule of life in the *s* of God.
1Cor 9:26 like a man who loses *s* of the finish line.
2Cor 5: 7 We walk by faith, not by *s.*
7:12 the *s* of God the devotion you have for us.
Gal 3:11 no one is justified in God's *s* by the law,
Eph 1: 4 began, to be holy and blameless in his *s,*
1Thes 2:17 by separation from you for a time—in *s,*
Jas 4:10 Be humbled in the *s* of the Lord and he
2Pt 3:14 stain or defilement, and at peace in his *s.*
1Jn 3:22 and doing what is pleasing in his *s.*
Rv 1:17 When I caught *s* of him I fell down at his
3: 2 is less than complete in the *s* of my God.

SIGHTED (1)

Jn 6:19 miles, they *s* Jesus approaching the boat,

SIGHTLESS (1)

Jn 9:39 it, to make the *s* see and the seeing blind."

SIGHTS (1)

Prv 23:33 Your eyes behold strange *s,*

SIGN (86)

Gn 9:12 *s* that I am giving for all ages to come,
9:13 *s* of the covenant between me and the earth.
9:17 "This is the *s* of the covenant I have
47:29 as a *s* of your constant loyalty to me;
Ex 4: 8 you, nor heed the message of the first *s,*
7: 9 demands that you work a *s* or wonder,
8:19 This *s* shall take place tomorrow."
13: 9 It shall be as a *s* on your hand and as a
13:16 be as a *s* on your hand and as a pendant on
Nm 17: 3 they shall serve as a *s* to the Israelites."
Dt 6: 8 Bind them at your wrist as a *s* and let
11:18 Bind them at your wrist as a *s,*
13: 2 a dreamer who promises you a *s* or wonder,
13: 3 even though the *s* or wonder he has
28:46 as a *s* and a wonder for all time.
Jos 4: 6 the future, these are to be a *s* among you.
Jgs 6:17 give me a *s* that you are speaking with me.
1Sm 2:34 a *s* in what will happen to your two sons,
10: 1 "This will be the *s* for you that the LORD
14:10 That will be our *s.*"
1Kgs 13: 3 He gave a *s* that same day and said:
13: 3 "This is the *s* that the LORD has spoken:
13: 5 the *s* the man of God had given as the word
2Kgs 4:31 boy, but there was no sound or *s* of life.
19:29 " 'This shall be a *s* for you:
20: 8 "What is the *s* that the LORD will heal me
20: 9 "This will be the *s* for you from the LORD
2Chr 32:24 LORD, who answered him by giving him a *s.*
32:31 the *s* that had occurred in the land,
Est 4:27 that I abhor the *s* of grandeur which rests
2Mc 6:13 a *s* of great kindness to punish sinners
Wis 5:13 nought and held no *s* of virtue to display,
16: 6 though they had a *s* of salvation,
Sir 13:25 The *s* of a good heart is a cheerful
43: 6 governing the seasons, their lasting *s,*
44:17 and with a *s* to him the deluge ended;
Is 7:11 Ask for a *s* from the LORD,
7:14 the Lord himself will give you this *s:*
19:20 It shall be a *s* and a witness to the LORD
20: 3 a *s* and portent against Egypt and Ethiopia,
37:30 This shall be a *s* for you:
38: 7 "This will be the *s* for you from the LORD
38:22 "What is the *s* that I shall go up to the
55:13 renown, an everlasting imperishable *s.*
66:19 I will set a *s* among them; from them I
Jer 44:29 be fulfilled, this shall be a *s* to you,
Ez 4: 3 This shall be a *s* for the house of Israel.
12: 6 have made you a *s* for the house of Israel.
12:11 I am a *s* for you: as I have done,
20:12 my sabbaths to be a *s* between me and them,
20:20 as a *s* between me and you to show that I
24:24 Ezekiel shall be a *s* for you:
24:27 Thus you shall be a *s* to them,
Mt 12:39 evil and unfaithful age is eager for a *s!*
12:39 No *s* will be given it but that of the
16: 1 asked him to show them some *s* in the sky.
16: 4 An evil, faithless age is eager for a *s,*
16: 4 no *s* will be given it except that of Jonah."
24: 3 *s* of your coming and the end of the world?"
24:30 *s* of the Son of Man will appear in the sky,
Mk 8:11 for some heavenly *s* from him as a test.
8:12 he said, "Why does this age seek a *s?*
8:12 I assure you, no such *s* will be given it!"
13: 4 be the *s* that all this is coming to an end?"
Lk 2:12 Let this be a *s* to you: in a manger you
2:34 many in Israel, a *s* that will be opposed
11:16 him, were demanding of him a *s* from heaven.
11:29 It seeks a *s.* But no sign will be given
11:29 But no *s* will be given it except the sign
11:29 will be given it except the *s* of Jonah.
11:30 Just as Jonah was a *s* for the Ninevites,
11:30 the Son of Man be a *s* for the present age.
21: 7 will be the *s* that it is going to happen?"
Jn 2:18 "What *s* can you show us authorizing you
4:54 This was the second *s* that Jesus performed
6:14 the *s* he had performed they began to say,
6:30 *s* are you going to perform for us to see?
10:41 "John may never have performed a *s,*"
12:18 because they heard he had performed this *s.*
Rom 2:28 True circumcision is not a *s* in the flesh.
4:11 he received the *s* of circumcision as a
1Cor 11:10 to have a *s* of submission on her head,
14:22 The gift of tongues is a *s,* not for those
Rv 12: 1 A great *s* appeared in the sky, a woman
12: 3 Then another *s* appeared in the sky:
15: 1 I saw in heaven another *s,* great and

SIGNAL (18)

Jos 6: 5 on the ram's horns and you hear that *s,*
6:20 When they heard the *s* horn,
Jgs 20:38 smoke *s* they were to send up from the city.
20:40 *s* column began to rise up from the city.
1Mc 4:40 And when the *s* was given with trumpets,
2Mc 4:14 hastened, at the *s* for the discus-throwing,
Is 5:26 He will give a *s* to a far-off nation,
11:10 of Jesse, set up as a *s* for the nations,
11:12 He shall raise a *s* to the nations and
13: 2 Upon the bare mountains set up a *s;*
18: 3 When the *s* is raised on the mountain,
49:22 the nations, and raise my *s* to the peoples;
Jer 4:21 How long must I see that *s,*
6: 1 in Tekoa, raise a *s* over Beth-haccherem;
51:12 Against the walls of Babylon raise a *s,*
51:27 Raise a *s* on the earth, blow the trumpet
Mt 26:48 betrayer had arranged to give them a *s,*
Mk 14:44 The betrayer had arranged a *s* for them,

SIGNALED (3)

Lk 1:63 *s* for a writing tablet and wrote the words,
5: 7 They *s* to their mates in the other boat to
Jn 13:24 Peter *s* him to ask Jesus whom he meant.

SIGNALS (3)

Jgs 6: 2 established the fire *s* on the mountains,
1Mc 7:45 blowing the trumpets behind them as *s.*
Is 10:19 will be so few, Like poles set up for *s,*

SIGNATURE (2)

Dn 6: 9 O king, issue the prohibition over your *s,*
2Thes 3:17 I append this *s* to every letter I write.

SIGNATURES (1)

Tb 5: 3 *s* on a document written in duplicate;

SIGNED (4)

2Mc 11:17 have presented your *s* communication and
Jer 32:12 and of the witnesses who had *s* the deed,
Dn 6:10 Darius *s* the prohibition and made it law.
6:11 Daniel heard that this law had been *s,*

SIGNET (13)

Gn 41:42 his *s* ring and put it on Joseph's finger.
Est 3:10 *s* ring from his hand and gave it to Haman,
3:12 Ahasuerus and sealed with the royal *s* ring.
8: 2 The king removed his *s* ring from Haman,
8: 8 and seal the letter with the royal *s* ring."
8: 8 with the royal *s* ring cannot be revoked.
8:10 Ahasuerus and sealed with the royal *s* ring,
1Mc 6:15 him his crown, his robe, and his *s* ring,
Sir 17:17 man's goodness God cherishes like a *s* ring,
49:11 who was like a *s* ring on God's right hand,
Is 3:21 the *s* rings, and the nose rings; the court
Jer 22:24 of Judah, are a *s* ring on my right hand,
Hg 2:23 the LORD, And I will set you as a *s* ring;

SIGNIFICANT (1)

Mt 5:19 That is why whoever breaks the least *s* of

SIGNIFIED (1)

Rv 15: 2 image, and also the number that *s* its name.

SIGNIFYING (1)

Gal 2: 9 *s* that we should go to the Gentiles as

SIGNPOST (1)

Ez 21:24 Then put a *s* at the head of each road,

SIGNS (76)

Ex 4: 9 if they will not believe even these two *s,*
4:17 with it you are to perform the *s.*"
4:28 of the various *s* he had enjoined upon him.
4:30 and he performed the *s* before the people.
7: 3 despite the many *s* and wonders that I will
10: 1 I may perform these *s* of mine among them
10: 2 Egyptians and what *s* I wrought among them,
Nm 14:11 all the *s* I have performed among them?
14:22 the *s* I worked in Egypt and in the desert,
Dt 4:34 nation, by testings, by *s* and wonders,
6:22 and wrought before our eyes *s* and wonders,
7:19 your own eyes have seen, the *s* and wonders,
11: 3 *s* and deeds he wrought among the Egyptians,
26: 8 with terrifying power, with *s* and wonders;
29: 2 have seen, and those great *s* and wonders.
34:11 He had no equal in all the *s* and wonders
1Sm 10: 7 When you see these *s* fulfilled,
10: 9 That very day all these *s* came to pass. . . .
2Kgs 23: 5 to the sun, moon, and *s* of the Zodiac,
Neh 9:10 You worked *s* and wonders against Pharaoh,
Est F: 6 God worked *s* and great wonders,
Ps(s) 78:43 When he wrought his *s* in Egypt and his
105:27 They wrought his *s* among them,
135: 9 He sent *s* and wonders into your midst,
Prv 6:13 his feet, makes *s* with his fingers;
Wis 8: 8 *s* and wonders she knows in advance and the
10:16 fearsome kings with *s* and portents;
Sir 36: 5 Give new *s* and work new wonders;
Is 8:18 we are *s* and portents in Israel from the
Jer 10: 2 and have no fear of the *s* of the heavens,
32:20 you have wrought *s* and wonders in the land
32:21 Egypt amid *s* and wonders and great terror.
Bar 2:11 hand, with *s* and wonders and great might,
6:66 They show the nations no *s* in the heavens,
Dn 3:99 It has seemed good to me to publish the *s*
3:100 How great are his *s,* how mighty his
6:28 *s* and wonders in heaven and on earth,
Mi 7:15 the land of Egypt, show us wonderful *s.*
Mt 12:38 "Teacher, we want to see you work some *s.*"
16: 3 sky, can you not read the *s* of the times?]
24:24 performing *s* and wonders so great as to
Mk 13:22 appear performing *s* and wonders to mislead,
16:17 *S* like these will accompany those who have
16:20 through the *s* which accompanied them.
Lk 1:22 He kept making *s* to them,
1:62 Then, using *s,* they asked the father what
21:11 and in the sky fearful omens and great *s.*
21:25 "There will be *s* in the sun, the moon,
Jn 2:11 this first of his *s* at Cana in Galilee.
2:23 for they could see the *s* he was performing.
3: 2 for no man can perform *s* and wonders such
4:48 "Unless you people see *s* and wonders,
6: 2 saw the *s* he was performing for the sick.
6:26 looking for me because you have seen *s*
7:31 expected to perform more *s* than this man?"
9:16 a sinner, how can he perform *s* like these?"
11:47 "with this man performing all sorts of *s?*
12:37 his many *s* performed in their presence,
20:30 other signs as well *s* not recorded here
Acts 2:19 the heavens above and *s* on the earth below:
2:22 wonders, and *s* as his credentials.
2:43 and *s* were performed by the apostles.
4:30 stretching forth your hand in cures and *s*
5:12 *s* and wonders occurred among the people.
6: 8 great wonders and *s* among the people.
7:36 wonders and *s* in the land of Egypt,
8:13 *s* and the great miracles as they occurred,
14: 3 *s* and wonders to be done at their hands.
15:12 two described all the *s* and wonders God
Rom 15:19 word and deed, with mighty *s* and marvels,
1Cor 1:22 yes, Jews demand "*s*"
2Cor 12:12 great patience the *s* that show the apostle,
12:12 apostle, *s* and wonders and deeds of power.
2Thes 2: 9 accompanied by all the power and *s* and
Heb 2: 4 God then gave witness to it by *s,* miracles,

SIHON (33)

Nm 21:21 Now Israel sent men to *S,*
21:23 *S,* however, would not let Israel pass

SIHON (cont.)

21:26 Now Heshbon was the capital of S,
21:28 Heshbon and a blaze from the city of S;
21:29 be taken captive by the Amorite king S.
21:34 Do to him as you did to S,
32:33 Manasseh, son of Joseph, the kingdom of S,
Dt 1: 4 After he had defeated S, king of the
2:24 I now deliver into your hands S,
2:26 from the desert of Kedemoth to S,
2:30 But S, king of Heshbon, refused to let us
2:31 begun to hand over to you S and his land,
2:32 So S and all his people advanced against
3: 2 Do to him as you did to S,
3: 6 As we had done to S, king of Heshbon,
4:46 opposite Beth-peor, in the land of S,
29: 6 When we came to this place, S,
31: 4 with them just as he dealt with S and Og,
Jos 2:10 of Egypt, and how you dealt with S and Og,
9:10 of the Amorites beyond the Jordan, S,
12: 2 First, S, king of the Amorites, who lived
12: 5 of Gilead as far as the territory of S,
13:10 Dibon, with the rest of the cities of S,
13:21 and, generally, of the kingdom of S.
13:27 the other part of the kingdom of S,
Jgs 11:19 Then Israel sent messengers to S,
11:20 But S refused to let Israel pass through
11:21 S and all his men into the power of Israel,
1Kgs 4:19 Uri, in the land of Gilead, the land of S,
Neh 9:22 They possessed the land of S,
Ps(s) 135:11 S, king of the Amorities,
136:19 S, king of the Amorities, for his mercy
Jer 48:45 Heshbon, and a blaze from the house of S:

SIHON'S (1)

Nm 21:27 let S capital be firmly constructed.

SILAGE (1)

Is 30:24 s tossed to them with shovel and pitchfork.

SILAS (14)

Acts 15:22 Judas, known as Barsabbas, and S.
15:27 whom we are sending you are Judas and S,
15:32 Judas and S, who were themselves
15:40 chose S to accompany him on his journey,
16:19 they seized Paul and S and dragged them
16:25 while Paul and S were praying and singing
16:29 fell trembling at the feet of Paul and S.
17: 1 Paul and S took the road through
17: 4 and threw in their lot with Paul and S.
17: 5 Paul and S before the people's assembly.
17:10 the brothers sent Paul and S off to Beroea.
17:14 the sea, while S and Timothy stayed behind.
17:15 with instructions for S and Timothy to join
18: 5 S and Timothy came down from Macedonia,

SILENCE (38)

Jgs 3:19 And the king said, S!"
Est C:10 Do not s those who praise you."
Ps(s) 4: 5 and sin not; reflect, upon your beds, in s.
8: 3 foes, to s the hostile and the vengeful.
31:18 them be reduced to s in the nether world.
115:17 the LORD, nor those who go down into s;
Wis 8:12 would abide my s and attend my utterance;
Sir 20:28 a muzzle over the mouth they s reproof.
Is 23: 2 S! you who dwell on the coast,
41: 1 Keep s before me, O coastlands; you
42:14 I have looked away, and kept s,
47: 5 Go into darkness and sit in s,
Jer 7:34 of Jerusalem I will s the cry of joy,
16: 9 I will s from this place the cry of joy
47: 5 is shaved bald, Ashkelon is reduced to s;
48: 2 You, too, Madmen, shall be reduced to s;
Lam 1:16 were reduced to s when the enemy prevailed."
2:10 in s sit the old men of daughter Zion;
3:26 hope in s for the saving help of the LORD.
3:28 Let him sit alone and in s,
Ez 24:17 Groan in s, make no lament for the dead,
Am 6:10 answers, "No one," Then he shall say, S!"
8: 3 shall be the corpses, strewn everywhere— S!
Hb 1:13 do you gaze on the faithless in s while
2:20 temple; s before him, all the earth!
Zep 1: 7 S in the presence of the Lord GOD!
Zec 2:17 S, all mankind, in the presence of the
Mt 20:31 them in an effort to reduce them to s,
Lk 19:40 He replied, "If they were to keep s,
20:26 disconcerted them and reduced them to s.
Acts 9:22 to s with his proofs that this Jesus was
13:16 So Paul arose, motioned to them for s,
19:33 He motioned for s, indicating that he
21:40 on the steps and motioned the people to s.
1Cor 14:28 there should be s in the assembly,
1Tm 2:11 listen in s and be completely submissive.
1Pt 2:15 You must s the ignorant talk of foolish
Rv 8: 1 was s in heaven for about half an hour.

SILENCED (6)

Jb 29:10 The voice of the princes was s,
Ez 16:63 and that you may be utterly s for shame
Mt 22:34 heard that he had s the Sadducees,
Acts 18: 9 Go on speaking and do not be s,
Rom 3:19 This means that every mouth is s and the
Ti 1:11 These must be s. They are upsetting

SILENCES (1)

Jb 12:20 He s the trusted adviser,

SILENT (53)

Dt 27: 9 "Be s, O Israel and listen!
2Sm 19:11 s about restoring the king to his palace?"
2Kgs 7: 9 a day of good news, and we are keeping s.
18:36 remained s and did not answer him one word,
2Chr 25:16 Be s! Why should it be necessary to kill
Neh 5: 8 They remained s, for they could find no
Est 4:14 Even if you now remain s, relief and
7: 4 to be sold into slavery I would remain s,
1Mc 1: 3 the earth fell s before him, and his heart
3:45 Jacob, and the flute and the harp were s.
Jb 6:24 Teach me, and I will be s; prove to me
11: 3 Shall your babblings keep men s,
13: 5 Oh, that you would be altogether s!
13:13 Be s, let me alone!
13:19 case against me, then I shall be s and die.
16: 5 with talk, or shake my head with s lips.
29:21 they were s for my counsel.
31:34 then I should have remained s,
33:31 Be s and I will speak.
33:33 be s while I teach you wisdom.
Ps(s) 35:22 be not s; Lord, be not far from me!
39: 3 man was before me I kept dumb and s;
76: 9 and was s When God arose for judgment,
83: 2 be not s, O God, and be not still!
94:17 my help, I would soon dwell in the s grave.
109: 1 O God, whom I praise, be not s,
Prv 11:12 no sense, but the intelligent man keeps s.
17:28 Even a fool, if he keeps s, is considered
24: 7 For a fool, to be s is wisdom;
Eccl 3: 7 a time to be s, and a time to speak.
Sir 13:22 A rich man speaks and all are s,
20: 4 One man is s and is thought wise,
20: 5 One man is s because he has nothing to say;
20: 5 another is s, biding his time.
20: 6 A wise man is s till the right time comes,
Is 36:21 remained s and did not answer him one word,
53: 7 he was s and opened not his mouth.
57:11 Was I to remain s and unseeing,
62: 1 For Zion's sake I will not be s,
62: 6 Never, by day or by night, shall they be s.
64:11 Can you remain s, and afflict us so
Dn 10:15 thus to me, I fell forward and kept s.
Am 5:13 the prudent man is s at this time,
Mt 26:63 But Jesus remained s.
Mk 3: 4 At this they remained s.
9:34 At this they fell s, for on the way they
14:61 But Jesus remained s; he made no reply.
Lk 9:36 When the voice fell s, Jesus was there
14: 4 At this they kept s.
Acts 8:32 shearer he was s and opened not his mouth.
15:12 At that the whole assembly fell s.
1Cor 13: 8 Prophecies will cease, tongues will be s,
14:34 women should keep s in such gatherings.

SILENTLY (2)

Gn 24:21 s waiting to learn whether or not the LORD
1Sm 1:13 her mouth, for Hannah was praying s;

SILK (3)

Ez 16:10 you a fine linen sash and s robes to wear.
16:13 your garments were of fine linen, s,
Rv 18:12 and purple garments, s and scarlet cloth;

SILLY (4)

Sir 42: 8 Of chastisement of the s and the foolish,
Hos 7:11 Ephraim is like a dove, s and senseless;
Eph 5: 4 Nor should there be any obscene, s,
2Tm 3: 6 captives of s women burdened with sins

SILOAM (3)

Lk 13: 4 who were killed by a falling tower in S.
Jn 9: 7 he told him, "Go, wash in the pool of S."
9:11 on my eyes, telling me to go to S and wash.

SILVANUS (4)

2Cor 1:19 Jesus Christ, whom S, Timothy, and I
1Thes 1: 1 Paul, S, and Timothy, to the church
2Thes 1: 1 Paul, S, and Timothy, to the church
1Pt 5:12 I am writing briefly through S,

SILVER (372)

Gn 13: 2 Now Abram was very rich in livestock, s,
20:16 given your brother a thousand shekels of s.
23:15 of land worth four hundred shekels of s—
23:16 he weighed out to him the s that Ephron
23:16 shekels of s at the current market value.
24:35 has given him flocks and herds, s and gold,
24:53 Then he brought out objects of s and gold
37:28 to the Ishmaelites for twenty pieces of s.
44: 2 youngest one's bag put also my s goblet,
44: 4 Why did you steal the s goblet from me?
44: 8 steal s or gold from your master's house?
45:22 shekels of s and five sets of garments.
Ex 3:22 and her house guest for s and gold articles
11: 2 for s and gold articles and for clothing."
12:35 articles of s and gold and for clothing.
20:23 neither gods of s nor gods of gold shall
21:32 the owner of the slave thirty shekels of s,
25: 3 gold, s and bronze; violet, purple
26:19 forty s pedestals under the twenty boards,
26:21 north side, with their forty s pedestals,
26:25 boards, with their sixteen s pedestals,
26:32 of gold and shall rest on four s pedestals.
27:10 and bands on the columns shall be of s.
27:11 and bands on the columns shall be of s.
27:17 the court shall have bands and hooks of s,
31: 4 in making things of gold, s or bronze,
35: 5 to the LORD, gold, s and bronze;
35:24 of s or bronze offered it to the LORD;
35:32 in making things of gold, s or bronze,
36:24 forty s pedestals under the twenty boards,
36:26 north side, with their forty s pedestals,
36:30 boards, with their sixteen s pedestals,
36:36 and four s pedestals were cast for them.
38:10 hooks and bands of the columns being of s.
38:11 hooks and bands of the columns being of s.
38:12 hooks and bands of the columns being of s.
38:17 hooks and bands of the columns were of s;
38:17 columns of the court were banded with s.
38:19 bronze for it, while their hooks were of s.
38:25 The amount of the s received from the
38:27 One hundred talents of s were used for
38:28 the capitals, and for banding them with s.
Lv 5:15 valued at two s shekels according to the
27: 3 shall be fifty s shekels for a man,
27: 6 sum shall be five s shekels for a boy,
27:16 seed being valued at fifty s shekels.
Nm 3:48 Give this s to Aaron and his sons as
3:49 So Moses took the s as ransom from those
3:50 Israelites he received in s one thousand
3:51 gave this ransom s to Aaron and his sons,
7:13 His offering consisted of one s plate
7:13 and one s basin weighing seventy shekels,
7:19 He presented as his offering one s plate
7:19 and one s basin weighing seventy shekels,
7:25 His offering consisted of one s plate
7:25 and one s basin weighing seventy shekels,
7:31 His offering consisted of one s plate
7:31 and one s basin weighing seventy shekels,
7:37 His offering consisted of one s plate
7:37 and one s basin weighing seventy shekels,
7:43 His offering consisted of one s plate
7:43 and one s basin weighing seventy shekels,
7:49 His offering consisted of one s plate
7:49 and one s basin weighing seventy shekels,
7:55 His offering consisted of one s plate
7:55 and one s basin weighing seventy shekels,
7:61 His offering consisted of one s plate
7:61 and one s basin weighing seventy shekels,
7:67 His offering consisted of one s plate
7:67 and one s basin weighing seventy shekels,
7:73 His offering consisted of one s plate
7:73 and one s basin weighing seventy shekels,
7:79 His offering consisted of one s plate
7:79 and one s basin weighing seventy shekels,
7:84 twelve s plates, twelve silver basins,
7:85 Each s plate weighed a hundred and thirty
7:85 thirty shekels, and each s basin seventy,
7:85 so that all the s of these vessels
10: 2 "Make two trumpets of beaten s,
18:16 it is fixed at five s shekels according to
22:18 gave me his house full of s and gold,
24:13 Balak gave me his house full of s and gold,
31:22 Whatever can stand fire, such as gold, s,
Dt 2: 6 You shall purchase from them with s the
2:28 give me to drink, you shall be paid in s.
7:25 Do not covet the s or gold on them,
8:13 your herds and flocks, your s and gold,
17:17 he accumulate a vast amount of s and gold.
22:19 besides fining him one hundred s shekels,
22:29 fifty s shekels and take her as his wife,
29:16 idols of wood and stone, of gold and s,
Jos 6:19 All s and gold, and the articles of bronze
6:24 with all that was in it, except the s,
7:21 mantle, two hundred shekels of s,
7:21 inside my tent, with the s underneath."
7:22 them hidden there, with the s underneath.
7:24 took Achan, son of Zerah, with the s,
22: 8 with very numerous livestock, with s,
Jgs 5:19 no s booty did they take.
9: 4 They also gave him seventy s shekels from
16: 5 each give you eleven hundred shekels of s."
17: 2 "The eleven hundred shekels of s over
17: 3 eleven hundred shekels of s to his mother,
17: 3 made of them a carved idol overlaid with s.
17: 4 I have consecrated the s to the LORD as my
17: 4 by making a carved idol overlaid with s."
17:10 and I will give you ten s shekels a year,
18:14 idols, and a carved idol overlaid with s?
18:18 and the carved idol overlaid with s,
1Sm 2:36 him for a piece of s or a loaf of bread,
9: 8 Saul, "I have a quarter of a s shekel.
2Sm 8:10 also brought with him articles of s,
8:11 together with the s and gold he had taken
18:11 to give you fifty pieces of s and a belt."

18:12 a thousand pieces of *s* in my two hands,
21: 4 against Saul and his house for *s* or gold,
24:24 floor and the oxen for fifty *s* shekels.
1Kgs 7:51 of his father David, putting the *s*,
10:21 There was no *s*, for in Solomon's time it
10:22 ships would come with a cargo of gold, *s*,
10:25 *s* or gold articles, garments, weapons,
10:27 made *s* as common in Jerusalem as stones,
15:15 father's and his own votive offerings of *s*,
15:18 Asa then took all the *s* and gold remaining
15:19 I am sending you a present of *s* and gold.
16:24 for two *s* talents and built upon the hill,
20: 3 'Your *s* and gold are mine,
20: 5 sent you word to give me your *s* and gold,
20: 7 me for my wives and sons, my *s* and my gold,
20:39 with your life or pay out a talent of *s*.'
2Kgs 5: 5 Naaman set out, taking along ten *s* talents,
5:22 them a talent of *s* and two festal garments.' "
5:23 up these *s* talents in bags and gave them,
6:25 an ass's head sold for eighty pieces of *s*,
6:25 a kab of wild onion for five pieces of *s*.
7: 8 into one tent, ate and drank, and took *s*,
12:11 there was a large amount of *s* in the chest,
12:14 of the LORD were used there to make *s* cups,
12:14 basins, trumpets, or any gold or *s* article.
14:14 He took all the gold and *s* and all the
15:19 Menahem gave him a thousand talents of *s*
15:20 in the country, fifty *s* shekels from each.
16: 8 Ahaz took the *s* and gold that were in the
18:14 *s* and thirty talents of gold from Hezekiah,
20:13 the messengers his whole treasury, his *s*,
23:33 hundred talents of *s* and a talent of gold.
23:35 Jehoiakim gave the *s* and gold to Pharaoh,
23:35 the *s* and gold from the people of the land,
25:15 *s* the captain of the guard also carried off.
1Chr 18:10 gold, *s* and bronze utensils of every sort.
18:11 to the LORD along with all the *s* and gold
19: 6 Ammonites sent a thousand talents of *s*
22:14 talents of gold, a million talents of *s*,
22:16 every kind of craftsman skilled in gold, *s*,
28:14 services and the weight of *s* to be used
28:14 in the *s* vessels for the various services,
28:15 and for the *s* lampstands he specified the
28:15 of *s* for each lampstand and its lamps,
28:16 showbread, and the silver for the *s* tables;
28:17 golden bowl and the *s* for each silver bowl;
29: 2 of gold, *s* for what will be made of silver,
29: 3 my God my personal fortune in gold and *s*:
29: 4 and seven thousand talents of refined *s*,
29: 5 various utensils to be made of gold and *s*,
29: 7 darics of gold, ten thousand talents of *s*,
2Chr 1:15 The king made *s* and gold as common in
1:17 and export them at six hundred *s* shekels,
2: 6 send me men skilled at work in gold, *s*,
2:13 he knows how to work with gold, *s*,
5: 1 of his father David, putting the *s*,
9:14 the country, brought gold and *s* to Solomon.
9:20 *s* was not considered of value in Solomon's
9:21 would return with a cargo of gold and *s*,
9:24 bring his tribute *s* and gold articles,
9:27 made *s* as common in Jerusalem as stones,
15:18 *s*, gold, and various utensils.
16: 2 Asa then brought out *s* and gold from the
16: 3 See, I am sending you *s* and gold.
17:11 Jehoshaphat gifts and a tribute of *s*;
21: 3 father gave them numerous gifts of *s*,
24:14 and basins and other gold and *s* utensils.
25: 6 from Israel for a hundred talents of *s*.
25:24 He took away all the gold and *s* and all
27: 5 paid him one hundred talents of *s*,
32:27 He had treasuries made for his *s*,
36: 3 hundred talents of *s* and a talent of gold.
Ezr 1: 4 by the people of that place with *s*,
1: 6 gave them help in every way, with *s*,
1:10 *s* bowls, four hundred and ten;
1:11 Total of the gold- and *s* ware:
2:69 of gold, five thousand minas of *s*,
5:14 the gold and *s* utensils of the house of
6: 5 the gold and *s* utensils of the house of
7:15 and to bring with you the *s* and gold which
7:16 as well as all the *s* and gold which you
7:18 you with the remainder of the *s* and gold,
7:22 *s*, one hundred talents;
8:25 and I weighed out before them the *s*
8:26 *s*, six hundred and fifty talents;
8:26 *s* utensils, one hundred; gold,
8:28 the *s* and the gold are a free-will
8:30 and the Levites then took over the *s*,
8:33 On the fourth day, the *s*,
Neh 5:15 each day forty *s* shekels for their food;
7:69 for priests, and five hundred minas of *s*.
7:70 and two thousand two hundred minas of *s*.
7:71 drachmas of gold, two thousand minas of *s*,
Jdt 2:18 and much gold and *s* from the royal palace.
5: 9 settled, and grew very rich in gold, *s*,
8: 7 Manasseh, had left her gold and *s*,
10:22 to the antechamber, preceded by *s* lamps;
15:11 the tent of Holofernes, with all his *s*,
Est 1: 6 byssus from *s* rings on marble pillars.
1: 6 Gold and *s* couches were on the pavement,
3: 9 to the procurators ten thousand *s* talents
3:11 "The *s* you may keep," the king said to
4: 7 as well as the exact amount of *s* Haman

1Mc 1:23 the gold and *s* and the precious vessels;
2:18 be enriched with *s* and gold and many gifts."
3:41 fetters and a large sum of *s* and gold,
4:23 and his men collected much gold and *s*,
6: 1 famous for its wealth in *s* and gold,
6:12 the vessels of gold and *s* that were in it,
8: 3 of the *s* and gold mines in Spain,
10:40 *s* shekels out of the royal revenues,
10:42 the dues of five thousand *s* shekels that
10:60 gave them and their friends *s* and gold
11:24 He brought with him *s*,
13:16 if you send us a hundred talents of *s*,
15:26 with gold and *s* and much equipment.
15:31 pay me five hundred talents of *s* for the
15:32 the gold and *s* plate on the sideboard,
16:11 of Jericho, and he had much *s* and gold,
16:19 him so that he might present them with *s*,
2Mc 2: 2 the gold and *s* idols and their ornaments.
3:11 talents of *s* and two hundred of gold.
4: 8 king three hundred and sixty talents of *s*,
4:19 *s* drachmas for the sacrifice to Hercules.
4:24 Jason by three hundred talents of *s*.
12:43 amounting to two thousand *s* drachmas,
Jb 3:15 had gold and filled their houses with *s*.
22:25 shall be your gold and your sparkling *s*.
27:16 *s* like dust and store away mounds of clothing,
27:17 wear, and the innocent shall divide the *s*.
28: 1 There is indeed a mine for *s*,
28:15 it, nor can its price be paid with *s*.
Ps(s). 12: 7 of the LORD are sure, like tried *s*,
66:10 You have tried us as *s* is tried by fire;
68:14 the wings of the dove shone with *s*,
68:31 them prostrate themselves with bars of *s*;
105:37 he led them forth laden with *s* and gold,
115: 4 Their idols are *s* and gold, the handiwork
119:72 than thousands of gold and *s* pieces.
135:15 The idols of the nations are *s* and gold,
Prv 2: 4 If you seek her like *s*,
3:14 For her profit is better than profit in *s*,
8:10 Receive my instruction in preference to *s*,
8:19 pure gold, and my revenue than choice *s*.
10:20 Like choice *s* is the just man's tongue;
16:16 understanding is more desirable than *s*.
17: 3 The crucible for *s*, and the furnace for
22: 1 riches, and high esteem, than gold and *s*.
25: 4 Remove the dross from *s*, and it comes
25:11 Like golden apples in *s* settings are words
27:21 the crucible tests *s* and the furnace gold,
Eccl 2: 8 I amassed for myself *s* and gold,
12: 6 Before the *s* cord is snapped.
Sg 1:11 pendants of gold for you and *s* ornaments.
3:10 He made its columns of *s*, its roof of gold,
8: 9 a wall, we will build upon it a *s* parapet;
8:11 one would have to pay a thousand *s* pieces.
Wis 7: 9 and before her, *s* is to be accounted mire.
13:10 Gold and *s*, the product of art,
Sir 26:18 Golden columns on *s* bases are her shapely
28:25 As you seal up your *s* and gold,
40:25 Gold and *s* make one's way secure,
47:18 you heaped up *s* as though it were lead;
51:28 you will win *s* and gold through her.
Is 1:22 Your *s* is turned to dross, your wine is
2: 7 Their land is full of *s* and gold,
2:20 of *s* and gold which they made for worship.
7:23 vines, worth a thousand pieces of *s*,
13:17 nothing of *s* and take no delight in gold.
31: 7 shall spurn his sinful idols of *s* and gold,
39: 2 messengers his treasury, the *s* and gold,
40:19 plates with gold and fits with *s* chains?
46: 6 from a purse and weigh out *s* on the scales;
48:10 See, I have refined you like *s*,
60: 9 children from afar with their *s* and gold,
60:17 I will bring gold, instead of iron, *s*;
Jer 6:30 *S* rejected" they shall be called,
10: 4 with the adze, adorned with *s* and gold.
10: 9 *S* strips brought from Tarshish,
32: 9 paying him the money, seventeen *s* shekels.
32:10 and weighed out the *s* on the scales,
52:19 sacrificial bowls which were of gold or *s*,
Bar 1: 8 These *s* vessels Zedekiah,
3:17 up the *s* and the gold in which men trust;
6: 3 shoulders gods of *s* and gold and wood,
6: 7 they are covered with gold and *s*—
6: 9 Then sometimes the priests take the *s* and
6:10 men, these gods of *s* and gold and wood;
6:29 to these gods of *s* and gold and wood;
6:57 seize them strip off the gold and the *s*,
Ez 7:19 They shall fling their *s* into the streets,
7:19 Their *s* and gold cannot save them on the
16:13 Thus you were adorned with gold and *s*;
16:17 You took the splendid gold and *s* ornaments
22:18 dross from *s* have they become.
22:20 Just as *s*, bronze, iron, lead, and tin are
22:22 by it just as *s* is smelted in a furnace.
27:12 so great was your wealth, exchanging *s*,
28: 4 have put gold and *s* into your treasuries.
38:13 your horde, to carry off *s* and gold,
Dn 2:32 was pure gold, its chest and arms were *s*,
2:35 The iron, tile, bronze, *s*,
2:45 broke in pieces the tile, iron, bronze, *s*,
5: 2 gold and *s* vessels which Nebuchadnezzar,
5: 3 When the gold and *s* vessels taken from the
5: 4 they praised their gods of gold and *s*,

5:23 and you praised the gods of *s* and gold,
11: 8 and their precious vessels of *s* and gold,
11:38 his fathers he shall glorify with gold, *s*,
11:43 gold and *s* and all the treasures of Egypt;
Hos 2:10 wine, and the oil, And her abundance of *s*,
3: 2 of *s* and a homer and a lethech of barley.
8: 4 *s* and gold they made idols for themselves,
9: 6 Weeds shall overgrow their *s* treasures,
13: 2 images, *S* idols according to their fancy,
Jl 4: 5 You took my *s* and my gold,
Am 2: 6 Because they sell the just man for *s*,
8: 6 We will buy the lowly man for *s*,
Na 2:10 "Plunder the *s*, plunder the gold!"
Hb 2:19 See, it is overlaid with gold and *s*,
Zep 1:11 will be destroyed, all who weigh out *s*,
1:18 Neither their *s* nor their gold shall be
Hg 2: 8 *s* and mine the gold says the LORD of hosts.
Zec 6:11 *S* and gold you shall take, and make a
9: 3 a stronghold, and heaped up *s* like dust,
11:12 counted out my wages, thirty pieces of *s*.
11:13 So I took the thirty pieces of *s* and threw
13: 9 and I will refine them as *s* is refined,
14:14 shall be gathered together, gold, *s*,
Mal 3: 3 He will sit refining and purifying *s*,
3: 3 Refining them like gold or like *s* that
Mt 10: 9 gold nor *s* nor copper in your belts;
25:15 To one he disbursed five thousand *s* pieces,
25:25 your thousand *s* pieces in the ground.
26:15 They paid him thirty pieces of *s*,
27: 3 He took the thirty pieces of *s* back to the
27: 6 The chief priests picked up the *s*,
27: 9 "They took the thirty pieces of *s*,
Mk 14: 5 *s* pieces and the money given to the poor."
Lk 10:35 The next day he took out two *s* pieces and
15: 8 if she has ten *s* pieces and loses one,
15: 9 I have found the *s* piece I lost.'
Jn 12: 5 could have brought three hundred *s* pieces,
Acts 3: 6 "I have neither *s* nor gold,
7:16 with *s* from the sons of Hamor at Shechem.
17:29 like a statue of gold or *s* or stone,
19:19 it came to fifty thousand *s* pieces.
20:33 *s* or gold or envy the way he dressed.
1Cor 3:12 build on this foundation with gold, *s*,
2Tm 2:20 of gold and *s* but also of wood and clay,
Jas 5: 3 moth-eaten, your gold and *s* have corroded,
1Pt 1:18 not by any diminishable sum of *s* or gold,
Rv 9:20 demons, or of gods made from gold and *s*,
18:12 their cargoes of gold and *s*,

SILVER-PLATED (2)

Ex 38:17 the capitals were *s*, and all the columns
Is 30:22 your *s* idols and your gold-covered images;

SILVERED (6)

Bar 6:38 These gilded and *s* wooden statues are
6:50 They are wooden, gilded and *s*;
6:54 temple of these wooden or gilded or *s* gods,
6:56 these wooden and *s* and gilded gods;
6:69 are their wooden, gilded, *s* gods.
6:70 are their *s* and gilded wooden gods.

SILVERSMITH (2)

Jgs 17: 3 hundred of them and gave them to the *s*,
Acts 19:24 There was a *s* named Demetrius who made

SILVERSMITHS (1)

Wis 15: 9 and *s* and emulates molders of bronze,

SILVERWARE (2)

Ezr 1: 9 sacks of *s*, one thousand and twenty-nine;
Jdt 12: 1 her into the room where his *s* was kept,

SIMEON (43)

Gn 29:33 so she named him *S*.
34:25 in pain, Dinah's full brothers *S* and Levi,
34:30 Jacob said to *S* and Levi:
35:23 Reuben, Jacob's first-born, *S*, Levi, Judah,
42:24 he had *S* taken from them and bound before
42:36 Joseph is gone, and *S* is gone,
43:23 With that, he led *S* out to them.
46:10 The sons of *S*: Nemuel, Jamin, Ohad
48: 5 be mine as much as Reuben and *S* are mine.
49: 5 *S* and Levi, brothers indeed, weapons of
Ex 1: 2 Reuben, *S*, Levi and Judah;
6:15 The sons of *S* were Jenuel, Jamin, Ohad,
6:15 these are the clans of *S*.
Nm 1: 6 Elizur, son of Shedeur; from *S*:
1:22 Of the descendants of *S*,
1:23 hundred were enrolled in the tribe of *S*.
2:12 the tribe of *S* [Their prince was Shelumiel,
10:19 over the host of the tribe of *S*,
13: 6 son of Hori, of the tribe of *S*,
34:20 son of Jephunneh,from the tribe of *S*:
Dt 27:12 "When you cross the Jordan, *S*,
Jos 19: 1 The second lot fell to *S*.
21: 4 from the tribes of Judah, *S* and Benjamin.
Jgs 1: 3 Judah then said to his brother *S*,
1: 3 So *S* went with him.
1:17 Judah then went with his brother *S*,
1Chr 2: 1 Reuben, *S*, Levi, Judah, Issachar,

SIMEON (cont.)

4:24 The sons of S were Nemuel,
2Chr 15: 9 Manasseh and S who sojourned with them;
34: 6 in the cities of Manasseh, Ephraim, S,
Jdt 6:15 Uzziah, son of Micah of the tribe of S,
8: 1 of Salamiel, son of Sarasadai, son of S,
9: 2 "Lord, God of my forefather S!
1Mc 2: 1 days Mattathias, son of John, son of S,
2:65 is your brother S who I know is a wise man;
Ez 48:24 S: on the frontier of Benjamin,
48:25 on the frontier of S, from the eastern to
48:33 the gate of S, the gate of Issachar,
Lk 2:25 at the time a certain man named S.
2:34 S blessed them and said to Mary his mother:
3:30 son of Matthat, son of Levi, son of S,
2Pt 1: 1 S Peter, servant and apostle of Jesus
Rv 7: 7 twelve thousand from the tribe of S,

SIMEONITES (13)

Nm 7:36 son of Zurishaddai, prince of the S.
25:14 prince of an ancestral house of the S.
26:12 The S by clans were:
26:14 These were the clans of the S,
Jos 19: 1 of S lay within that of the Judahites.
19: 8 of the clans of the tribe of the S.
19: 9 S was within the confines of the Judahites;
19: 9 the S obtained their heritage within it.
21: 9 and S they designated the following cities,
1Chr 4:42 Five hundred of them (the S) went to Mount
6:50 by lot from the tribes of the Judahites, S,
12:26 Of the S, warriors fit for battle:
27:16 for the S, Shephatiah, son of Maacah;

SIMILAR (12)

Gn 32:20 He gave s instructions to the second
Ex 27:11 the north side there shall be s hangings,
38:11 On the north side there were s hangings,
1Kgs 22:12 The other prophets prophesied in a s vein,
1Mc 5:14 from Galilee to deliver a s message:
15:22 consul sent s letters to Kings Demetrius,
2Mc 2: 3 With other s words he urged them not to
Wis 16: 1 were fittingly punished by s creatures,
Zec 14:15 S to this plague shall be the plague upon
Mt 25:14 of a man who was going on a journey is s.
Acts 5:38 The present case is s.
Eph 6: 9 Masters, act in a s way toward your slaves.

SIMILARLY (17)

Lv 7: 8 S, the priest who offers a holocaust for
Jgs 1:29 S, the Ephraimites did not drive out the
2Mc 2:27 S, to win the gratitude of many we will
Bar 6:34 S, they cannot give anyone riches or
Mk 2:22 S, no man pours new wine into old wineskins.
3:26 S, if Satan has suffered mutiny in his
4:16 S, those sown on rocky ground are people
1Cor 2:11 S, no one knows what lies at the depths of
7:11 S, a husband must not divorce his wife.
11: 5 S, any woman who prays or prophesies with
14: 9 S, if you do not utter intelligible speech
1Tm 2: 9 S, the women must deport themselves
3:11 The women, s, should be serious, not
5:25 S, some good deeds stand out clearly as
2Tm 2: 5 S, if one takes part in an athletic contest,
Ti 2: 3 S, the older women must behave in ways
Jude 1: 8 S, these visionaries pollute the flesh;

SIMMAGIR (1)

Jer 39: 3 Nergal-sharezer, of S,

SIMON (147)

1Mc 2: 3 S, who was called Thassi;
5:17 Judas said to his brother S:
5:20 Three thousand men were allotted to S,
5:21 S went into Galilee and fought many
5:55 and S his brother was in Galilee opposite
9:19 Jonathan and S took their brother Judas
9:33 S and all the men with him discovered this,
9:37 was brought to Jonathan and his brother S:
9:62 Then Jonathan and S and their companions
9:65 Leaving his brother S in the city,
9:67 S and his men then sallied forth from the
10:74 and S his brother joined him to help him.
10:82 were exhausted, S attacked the phalanx,
11:59 he made Jonathan's brother S governor of
11:64 leaving his brother S in the province.
11:65 S besieged Beth-zur, attacked it
12:33 S also set out and went as far as Ashkalon
12:38 S likewise built up Adida in the Shephelah,
13: 1 When S heard that Trypho was gathering a
13:10 So S mustered all the men able to fight,
13:13 But S pitched his camp at Adida,
13:14 that S had succeeded his brother Jonathan,
13:17 Although S knew that they were speaking
13:18 say that Jonathan perished because S
13:20 but S and his army moved along opposite
13:25 S sent for the remains of his brother
13:27 Then S erected over the tomb of his father
13:33 S, on his part, built up the strongholds
13:34 S also sent chosen men to King Demetrius
13:36 sends greetings to S the high priest,
13:42 and contracts, "In the first year of S,
13:43 In those days S besieged Gazara and
13:45 loud voices, begging S to grant them peace.
13:47 So S came to terms with them and did not
13:50 They finally cried out to S for peace,
13:52 S decreed that this day should be
13:53 S made him commander of all his soldiers,
14: 4 The land was at rest all the days of S,
14:17 his brother S had been made high priest
14:20 Sparta send greetings to S the high priest,
14:23 decree has been made for S the high priest."
14:24 S sent Numenius to Rome with a great gold
14:25 said, "How can we thank S and his sons?
14:27 year under S the high priest in Asaramel,
14:29 have often been wars in our country, S,
14:32 S rose up and fought for his nation,
14:41 S shall be their permanent leader and high
14:46 "'All the people approved of granting S
14:47 and S accepted and agreed to act as high
14:49 they would be available to S and his sons.
15: 1 a letter from the islands of the sea to S,
15: 2 "King Antiochus sends greetings to S,
15:17 by S the high priest and the Jewish people,
15:21 you, hand them over to S the high priest,
15:24 letter was also sent to S the high priest.
15:26 S sent to Antiochus' support two thousand
15:27 made with S and became hostile toward him.
15:28 of his Friends, to confer with S and say:
15:33 the king's message, S said to him in reply:
16: 1 told his father S what Cendebeus was doing.
16: 2 S called his two oldest sons,
16:13 plans to do away with S and his sons.
16:14 As S was inspecting the cities of the
16:16 Then, when S and his sons had drunk freely,
16:16 in hand, rushed upon S in the banquet hall,
2Mc 3: 4 But a certain S, of the priestly course
3:11 to the calumnies of the impious S,
4: 1 The S mentioned above as the informer
4: 6 and that S would not desist from his folly.
4:23 Menelaus, brother of the aforementioned S,
8:22 army into four, placing his brothers, S,
10:19 a siege, Maccabeus left S and Joseph,
14:17 Judas' brother S had engaged Nicanor,
Sir 50: 1 the glory of his people, was S the priest,
50:11 S, Son of Jochanan When he received the
Mt 4:18 watched two brothers, S now known as Peter,
10: 2 first S, now known as Peter, and his
10: 4 S the Zealot Party member,
13:55 to be his mother and James, Joseph, S,
16:16 "You are the Messiah," S Peter answered,
16:17 replied, "Blest are you, S son of Jonah!
17:25 "What is your opinion, S?
26: 6 in Bethany at the house of S the leper,
27:32 their way out they met a Cyrenian named S.
Mk 1:16 he observed S and his brother Andrew
1:29 house of S and Andrew with James and John.
1:36 S and his companions managed to track him
3:17 S to whom he gave the name Peter;
3:18 Thaddaeus, S of the Zealot Party,
6: 3 brother of James and Joses and Judas and S?
14: 3 at table in the house of S the leper,
14:37 He said to Peter, "Asleep, S?
15:21 A man named S of Cyrene, the father
Lk 4:38 the synagogue, he entered the house of S.
5: 3 one of the boats, the one belonging to S,
5: 4 he had finished speaking he said to S,
5: 5 S answered, "Master, we have been hard
5: 8 S Peter fell at the knees of Jesus saying,
5:10 Zebedee's sons, who were partners with S.
5:10 Jesus said to S, "Do not be afraid.
6:14 S, to whom he gave the name Peter,
6:15 son of Alphaeus, and S called the Zealot,
7:40 to his thoughts, Jesus said to him, S,
7:43 S answered, "He, I presume, to whom he
7:44 Turning then to the woman, he said to S:
22:31 S, Simon! Remember that Satan has asked
22:31 "Simon, S! Remember that Satan has asked
23:26 they laid hold of one S the Cyrenean who
24:34 He has appeared to S."
Jn 1:40 hearing John was S Peter's brother Andrew.
1:41 was seek out his brother S and tell him,
1:42 who looked at him and said, "You are S,
6: 8 disciples, Andrew, S Peter's brother,
6:68 S Peter answered him, "Lord, to whom
6:71 talking about Judas, son of S the Iscariot,
13: 2 already induced Judas, son of S Iscariot,
13: 6 Thus he came to S Peter, who said to
13: 9 "Lord," S Peter said to him, "then not
13:24 S Peter signaled him to ask Jesus whom he
13:26 it and gave it to Judas, son of S Iscariot.
13:36 "Lord," S Peter said to him,
18:10 Then S Peter, who had a sword, drew it
18:15 S Peter, in company with another disciple,
18:25 S Peter had been standing there warming
20: 2 so she ran off to S Peter and the other
20: 6 S Peter came along behind him and entered
21: 2 Assembled were S Peter,
21: 3 S Peter said to them, "I am going out
21: 7 the Lord, S Peter threw on some clothes
21:11 S Peter went aboard and hauled ashore the
21:15 their meal, Jesus said to Simon Peter, S,
21:16 A second time he put his question, S,
21:17 A third time, Jesus asked him, S,
Acts 1:13 S, the Zealot party member, and Judas
8: 9 A certain man named S had been practicing
8:13 Even S believed.
8:18 S observed that it was through the laying
8:24 S responded, "I need the prayers of all
9:43 for a considerable time at the house of S,
10: 5 some men to Joppa and summon a certain S,
10: 6 He is a guest of S the leather-tanner
10:17 at the gate asking for the house of S.
10:18 inquire whether S Peter was a guest there.
10:32 to invite S known as Peter to come here.
10:32 guest in the house of S the leather-tanner,
11:13 'Send someone to Joppa and fetch S,

SIMON'S (10)

1Mc 14:35 When the Jewish people saw S loyalty and
14:40 that they had received S envoys with honor.
15:32 and on seeing the splendor of S court,
15:36 When he told him of S words,
2Mc 4: 3 When S hostility reached such a point that
4: 4 and Phoenicia, was abetting S wickedness.
10:20 But some of the men in S force who were
Mk 1:30 S mother-in-law lay ill with a fever,
Lk 4:38 S mother-in-law was in the grip of a
23:26 They put a crossbeam on S shoulder for him

SIMPLE (18)

Gn 25:27 whereas Jacob was a s man,
2Mc 2:25 aimed to please those who prefer s reading,
Ps(s) 19: 8 is trustworthy, giving wisdom to the s.
119:130 sheds light, giving understanding to the s.
Prv 1: 4 resourcefulness may be imparted to the s,
1:22 "How long, you s ones, will you love
1:32 For the self-will of the s kills them,
7: 7 And I saw among the s ones,
8: 5 You s ones, gain resource, you fools,
9: 4 "Let whoever is s turn in here;
9:16 "Let whoever is s turn in here,
19:25 beat an arrogant man, the s learn a lesson;
21:11 man is punished, the s are the wiser;
Sir 19:19 while the s man may be free from sin.
Mt 8:16 s command and cured all who were afflicted,
Mk 9:42 who leads astray one of these s believers
Rom 2:20 discipline the foolish and teach the s,
Ti 1:12 lazy gluttons," and that is the s truth!

SIMPLEMINDED (1)

Rom 16:18 the s with smooth and flattering speech.

SIMPLETON (2)

Jb 5: 2 kills the fool and indignation slays the s.
Prv 14:15 The s believes everything, but the shrewd

SIMPLETONS (3)

Prv 14:18 The adornment of s is folly,
22: 3 while s continue on and suffer the penalty.
27:12 s continue on and suffer the penalty.

SIMPLY (11)

2Chr 13: 8 s because you are a huge multitude and
Ezr 4:14 we ought not s to look on while the king
Wis 7:13 S I learned about her, and ungrudgingly
Jn 5:42 it is s that I know you,
7:17 it comes from God or is s spoken on my own.
Acts 19: 9 presence of the assembly, Paul s left them.
1Cor 3: 5 S ministers through whom you became
9:18 It is s this, that when preaching I offer
2Cor 8: 8 I am not giving an order but s testing
13: 7 but s that you may do what is good,
Jude 1: 9 He s said, "May the Lord punish you."

SIN (474)

Gn 4: 7 if not, s is a demon lurking at the door:
18:20 Gomorrah is so great, and their s so grave,
Ex 10:17 But now, do forgive me my s once more,
16: 1 community came into the desert of S,
17: 1 From the desert of S the whole Israelite
20:20 put his fear upon you, lest you should s."
23:21 him, for he will not forgive your s.
23:33 lest they make you s against me by
29:14 the camp, since this is a s offering.
29:36 a bullock each day as a s offering,
30:10 with the blood of the atoning s offering.
32:21 you should lead them into so grave a s?"
32:30 the people, "You have committed a grave s.
32:30 I may be able to make atonement for your s."
32:31 s in making a god of gold for themselves!
32:32 If you would only forgive their s!
32:34 to punish, I will punish them for their s."
34: 7 and forgiving wickedness and crime and s;
Lv 4: 2 When a person inadvertently commits a s
4: 3 as a sin offering for the s he committed.
4:14 on become known that the s was committed,
4:14 shall present a young bull as a s offering.
4:21 This is the s offering for the community.
4:22 "Should a prince commit a s inadvertently
4:23 later on he learns of the s he committed,
4:24 the goat as a s offering before the LORD,
4:25 take some of the blood of the s offering
4:26 shall make atonement for the prince's s,

4:27 a private person commits a *s* inadvertently
4:28 he later on learn of the *s* he committed,
4:28 she-goat as the offering for his *s*.
4:29 his hand on the head of the *s* offering,
4:32 for his *s* offering he presents a lamb,
4:33 he shall slaughter this *s* offering in the
4:34 take some of the blood of the *s* offering
4:35 shall make atonement for the man's *s*,
5: 1 and thus commits a *s* and has guilt to bear;
5: 5 cases shall confess the *s* he has incurred
5: 6 priest shall then make atonement for his *s*.
5: 6 the sin he has incurred and as his *s* offering
5: 6 and as his sin offering for the *s* he has
5: 7 he shall bring to the LORD as the *s* offering
5: 7 for his *s* two turtledoves or two pigeons,
5: 7 a *s* offering and the other for a holocaust.
5: 8 offer the one for the *s* offering first.
5: 9 *s* offering against the side of the altar.
5: 9 Such is the offering for *s*.
5:10 make atonement for the *s* the man committed,
5:11 he shall present as a *s* offering for his
5:11 his *s* one tenth of an ephah of fine flour.
5:11 on it, because it is a *s* offering.
5:12 and this he shall burn as a *s* offering on
5:13 the priest shall make atonement for the *s*
5:15 "If someone commits a *s* by inadvertently
5:17 commits such a *s* by doing one of the
5:21 "If someone commits a *s* of dishonesty
5:23 since he has incurred guilt by his *s*,
6:10 like the *s* offering and the guilt offering.
6:18 This is the ritual for *s* offerings.
6:18 LORD, shall the *s* offering be slaughtered.
6:19 presents the *s* offering may partake of it;
6:22 line may partake of the *s* offering,
6:23 But no one may partake of any *s* offering
7: 7 "Because the *s* offering and the guilt
7:37 holocausts, cereal offerings, *s* offerings,
8: 2 oil, the bullock for a *s* offering,
8:14 forward the bullock for a *s* offering,
9: 2 for a *s* offering and a ram for a holocaust,
9: 3 Take a he-goat for a *s* offering,
9: 7 "and offer your *s* offering and your
9: 8 the calf that was his own *s* offering.
9:10 liver that were taken from the *s* offering,
9:15 goat that was for the people's *s* offering,
9:15 it and offered it up for *s* as before.
9:22 When he came down from offering the *s*
10:16 inquired about the goat of the *s* offering,
10:17 not eat the *s* offering in the sacred place,
10:19 presented their *s* offering and holocaust
10:19 Had I then eaten of the *s* offering today,
12: 6 a pigeon or a turtledove for a *s* offering.
12: 8 a holocaust and the other for a *s* offering.
14:13 in the sacred place where the *s* offering
14:13 because, like the *s* offering,
14:19 Only after he has offered the *s* offering
14:22 a *s* offering and the other as a holocaust.
14:31 a *s* offering and the other as a holocaust,
15:15 a *s* offering and the other as a holocaust.
15:30 a *s* offering and the other as a holocaust.
16: 3 for a *s* offering and a ram for a holocaust.
16: 5 a *s* offering and one ram for a holocaust.
16: 6 his *s* offering to atone for himself and
16: 9 bring in and offer up as a *s* offering.
16:11 Aaron offer up the bullock, his *s* offering,
16:25 the fat of the *s* offering on the altar.
19:17 fellow man, do not incur *s* because of him.
19:22 before the LORD for the *s* he has committed,
23:19 goat shall be sacrificed as a *s* offering,
24:15 his God shall bear the penalty of his *s*;
Nm 6:11 a *s* offering and the other as a holocaust,
6:11 for the *s* he has committed by reason
6:14 yearling ewe lamb for a *s* offering,
6:16 the *s* offering and the holocaust for him.
7:16 one goat for a *s* offering;
7:22 one goat for a *s* offering; and two oxen,
7:28 one goat for a *s* offering; and two oxen,
7:34 one goat for a *s* offering; and two oxen,
7:40 one goat for a *s* offering; and two oxen,
7:46 one goat for a *s* offering; and two oxen,
7:52 one goat for a *s* offering; and two oxen,
7:58 one goat for a *s* offering; and two oxen,
7:64 one goat for a *s* offering; and two oxen,
7:70 one goat for a *s* offering; and two oxen,
7:76 one goat for a *s* offering; and two oxen,
7:82 one goat for a *s* offering; and two oxen,
7:87 for the *s* offerings were twelve goats.
8: 8 take another young bull for a *s* offering.
8:12 the one as a *s* offering and the other as a
8:21 themselves of *s* and washed their clothes,
9:13 man shall bear the consequences of his *s*.
12:11 the *s* that we have foolishly committed!
15:24 as well as one he-goat as a *s* offering.
15:27 bring a yearling she-goat as a *s* offering,
16:22 will one man's *s* make you angry with the
18: 9 or *s* offerings or guilt offerings;
19: 9 The heifer is a *s* offering.
19:17 the *s* offering shall be put in a vessel,
27: 3 for his own *s* without leaving any sons.
28:15 be sacrificed as a *s* offering to the LORD.
28:22 a *s* offering in atonement for yourselves.
28:30 a *s* offering in atonement for yourselves.
29: 5 a *s* offering in atonement for yourselves.
29:11 goat shall be sacrificed as a *s* offering.
29:11 in addition to the atonement *s* offering,
29:16 goat shall be sacrificed as a *s* offering.
29:19 as well as one goat for a *s* offering,
29:22 as well as one goat for a *s* offering,
29:25 as well as one goat for a *s* offering,
29:28 as well as one goat for a *s* offering,
29:31 as well as one goat for a *s* offering,
29:34 as well as one goat for a *s* offering,
29:38 as well as one goat for a *s* offering,
32:23 not do this, you will *s* against the LORD,
32:23 will not escape the consequences of your *s*.
33:11 Red Sea, they camped in the desert of *S*.
33:12 Setting out from the desert of *S*,
Dt 9:18 because of all the *s* you had committed in
9:27 people nor upon their wickedness and *s*,
20:18 gods, and you thus *s* against the LORD,
Jos 22:17 For the *s* of Peor, a plague came upon
1Sm 12:23 far be it from me to *s* against the LORD by
14:34 but you must not *s* against the LORD by
14:38 find out how this *s* was committed today.
15:23 For a *s* like divination is rebellion,
15:25 Now forgive my *s*, and return with me,
19: 4 your majesty *s* against his servant David,
2Sm 12:13 "The LORD on his part has forgiven your *s*:
1Kgs 8:33 *s* against you and are defeated by an enemy,
8:34 and forgive the *s* of your people Israel,
8:35 them, and if then they repent of their *s*,
8:36 listen in heaven and forgive the *s* of your
8:46 "When they *s* against you (for there is no
8:46 you (for there is no man who does not *s*),
12:30 This led to *s*, because the people
13:34 This was a *s* on the part of the house of
15:26 the *s* which he had caused Israel to commit.
15:34 and the *s* he had caused Israel to commit.
16: 2 and have caused my people Israel to *s*,
16:19 of Jeroboam, thus causing Israel to *s*.
16:26 Israel to *s* and to provoke to the LORD,
18: 9 Obadiah said, "What *s* have I committed,
21:22 have provoked me by leading Israel into *s*."
22:53 son of Nebat, who caused Israel to *s*.
2Kgs 3: 3 he still clung to the *s* to which Jeroboam,
13: 2 the *s* he had caused Israel to commit.
14: 6 each one shall die for his own *s*."
17:21 the LORD, causing them to commit a great *s*.
21:11 him, and has led Judah into *s* by his idols,
21:16 to the *s* which he caused Judah to commit,
21:17 the *s* he committed and all that he did,
23:15 son of Nebat, who caused Israel to *s*—
2Chr 6:25 and forgive the *s* of your people Israel,
6:26 withdraw from *s* because you afflict them,
6:27 listen in heaven and forgive the *s* of your
6:36 When they *s* against you (for there is no
6:36 you (for there is no man who does not *s*),
29:21 brought for a *s* offering for the kingdom,
29:23 Then the he-goats for the *s* offering were
29:24 the altar to atone for the *s* of all Israel;
29:24 for "The holocaust and the *s* offering,"
Neh 3:37 not their *s* be blotted out in your sight,
6:13 act on it out of fear and commit this *s*.
10:34 *s* offerings to make atonement for Israel,
13:26 the king of Israel, *s* because of them?
13:26 yet even he was made to *s* by foreign women.
Tb 4: 5 desire to *s* or to break his commandments.
4:21 a rich man if you fear God, avoid all *s*,
12: 9 saves one from death and expiates every *s*.
12:10 guilty of *s* are their own worst enemies.
14: 7 *s* shall completely disappear from the land.
Jdt 5:17 did not *s* in the sight of their God,
11:10 them, except when they *s* against their God.
12: 2 of them, lest it be an occasion of *s*;
13:16 not *s* with me to my defilement or disgrace."
2Mc 2:11 been eaten, the *s* offering was burned up."
10: 4 and that if they should *s* at any time,
12:42 soldiers to keep themselves free from *s*,
12:42 because of the *s* of those who had fallen.
12:46 dead that they might be freed from this *s*.
Jb 1:22 In all this Job did not *s*, nor did he say
10:14 If I should *s*, you would keep a watch
14:16 my steps, and not keep watch for *s* in me.
31:30 to *s* by uttering a curse against his life
34:37 For he is adding rebellion to his *s*
35: 6 If you *s*, what injury do you do to God?
Ps(s) 4: 5 Tremble, and *s* not; reflect, upon your
19:14 From wanton *s* especially, restrain your
19:14 I be blameless and innocent of serious *s*.
32: 1 fault is taken away, whose *s* is covered.
32: 5 Then I acknowledged my *s* to you,
32: 5 and you took away the guilt of my *s*.
36: 2 *S* speaks to the wicked man in his heart;
38: 4 no wholeness in my bones because of my *s*,
38:19 acknowledge my guilt; I grieve over my *s*.
39: 2 my ways, so as not to *s* with my tongue;
51: 4 me from my guilt and of my *s* cleanse me.
51: 5 my offense, and my *s* is before me always:
51: 7 I born, and in *s* my mother conceived me;
51: 9 Cleanse me of *s* with hyssop, that I may
59: 4 Not for any offense or *s* of mine,
59:13 By the *s* of their mouths and the word of
78:38 forgave their *s* and destroyed them not;
109:14 let not his mother's *s* be blotted out;
119:11 your promise, that I may not *s* against you.
Prv 5:22 meshes of his own *s* he will be held fast;
10:16 to life, the gains of the wicked, to *s*.
10:19 Where words are many, *s* is not wanting;
12:13 the *s* of his lips the evil man is ensnared,
13: 6 but the downfall of the wicked is *s*.
14:34 a nation, but *s* is a people's disgrace.
20: 9 my heart clean, I am cleansed of my *s*"?
21: 4 the tillage of the wicked is *s*.
24: 9 Beyond intrigue and folly and *s*,
28:24 father or mother and calls it no *s*,
Eccl 7:20 on earth so just as to do good and never *s*.
Wis 1: 4 nor dwells she in a body under debt of *s*.
6: 9 may learn wisdom and that you may not *s*.
10:13 when he was sold, but delivered him from *s*.
15: 2 For even if we *s* we are yours,
15: 2 but we will not *s*, knowing that we belong
Sir 3:14 forgotten, it will serve as a *s* offering
3:26 a sinner will heap *s* upon sin.
5: 5 be not overconfident, adding sin upon *s*.
7: 8 Do not plot to repeat a *s*;
7:36 your last days, and you will never *s*.
10: 7 and the *s* of oppression they both hate.
10:13 For pride is the reservoir of *s*,
13:23 Wealth is good when there is no *s*;
14: 1 grief, who is not stung by remorse for *s*.
15:20 No man does he command to *s*,
16: 9 who were uprooted because of their *s*;
16:19 If I *s*, no eye will see me; if all in secret
17:20 Return to the LORD and give up *s*,
17:21 again to the Most High and away from *s*,
18:27 *s* is rife he keeps himself from wrongdoing.
19:19 while the simple man may be free from *s*.
20:20 A man through want may be unable to *s*,
21: 2 Flee from *s* as from a serpent.
23:10 the Holy Name will not remain free from *s*.
23:11 his obligation, his *s* is doubly great.
23:12 to the devout, who do not wallow in *s*.
23:18 no one sees me; why should I fear *s*?"
26:19 And the man who passes from justice to *s*,
26:20 upright, nor a shopkeeper free from *s*:
27: 1 For the sake of profit many *s*,
27: 2 between buying and selling *s* is wedged in.
28: 6 remember death and decay, and cease from *s*!
28: 9 Commits the *s* of disrupting friendship and
31: 5 The lover of gold will not be free from *s*,
32:12 you wish, but without *s* or words of pride.
38:10 be just, cleanse your heart of every *s*;
42: 1 ashamed, lest you *s* through human respect:
47:23 the sinner who led Israel into *s*,
Is 3: 9 their *s* like Sodom they vaunt,
5:18 perversity, and at *s* as if with cart ropes!
6: 7 your wickedness is removed, your *s* purged."
27: 9 the whole fruit of the removal of his *s*:
30: 1 are not inspired by me, adding sin upon *s*.
53: 8 and smitten for the *s* of his people,
53:10 If he gives his life as an offering for *s*,
59:20 redeemer to those of Jacob who turn from *s*,
Jer 3: 9 Eager to *s*, she polluted the land,
16:10 What *s* have we committed against the LORD,
16:18 crime and their *s* of profaning my land
17: 1 *s* of Judah is written with an iron stylus,
18:23 crime, blot not out their *s* in your sight!
31:34 evildoing and remember their *s* no more.
32:35 daughters to Molech, bringing *s* upon Judah;
36: 3 I may forgive their wickedness and their *s*.
Lam 1: 8 Through the *s* of which she is guilty,
Bar 1:10 you are to procure holocausts, *s* offerings,
Ez 3:18 that wicked man shall die for his *s*,
3:19 conduct, then he shall die for his *s*,
3:20 He shall die for his *s*, and his virtuous
3:21 you have warned a virtuous man not to *s*,
7:19 for this has been the occasion of their *s*.
14: 3 keep the occasion of their *s* before them.
14: 4 keeping the occasion of his *s* before him,
14: 7 and keeps the occasion of his *s* before him,
14:10 Each shall receive punishment for his *s*,
18:24 he has broken faith and committed *s*;
33: 6 that person is taken because of his own *s*.
33:14 from his *s* and does what is right and just,
40:39 the *s* offerings and guilt offerings.
42:13 cereal offerings, *s* offerings,
43:19 young bull as a *s* offering to the priests,
43:21 Then take the bull of the *s* offering,
43:22 an unblemished he-goat as a *s* offering,
43:25 you shall offer a he-goat as a *s* offering,
44:10 shall bear the consequences of their *s*.
44:12 an occasion of *s* to the house of Israel,
44:12 shall bear the consequences of their *s*.
44:27 sanctuary, he shall present his *s* offering,
44:29 eat the cereal offering, the *s* offering,
45:17 He shall offer the *s* offerings,
45:19 take some of the blood from the *s* offering
45:22 people of the land, a bull as a *s* offering.
45:23 and as a *s* offering he shall offer one
45:25 same rites, making the same *s* offerings,
46:20 the guilt offerings and the *s* offerings,
Dn 8:12 host, while *s* replaced the daily sacrifice.
8:13 the desolating *s* which is placed there,
9:20 my *s* and the sin of my people Israel,
9:20 my sin and the *s* of my people Israel,
9:24 transgression will stop and *s* will end,
13:23 without guilt than to *s* before the Lord."
Hos 4: 7 One and all they *s* against me,
4: 8 They feed on the *s* of my people,

SIN (cont.)

8:11 When Ephraim made many altars to expiate *s*,
8:11 sin, his altars became occasions of *s*.
10: 8 Aven shall be destroyed, the *s* of Israel;
12: 9 not suffice him for the guilt of his *s*.
13: 2 Now they continue to *s*, making for
13:12 Israel is wrapped up, his *s* is stored away.
Am 4: 4 Bethel, and sin, to Gilgal, and *s* the more;
Mi 1: 5 And what is the *s* of the house of Judah?
1:13 the beginning of *s* for daughter Zion,
6: 7 the fruit of my body for the *s* of my soul?
7:18 *s* for the remnant of his inheritance;
Zec 13: 1 fountain to purify from *s* and uncleanness.
Mt 12:31 "That, I assure you, is why every *s*,
Mk 3:28 every *s* will be forgiven mankind and all
3:29 He carries the guilt of his *s* without end."
16:20 might return to the truth and *s* no more,
Jn 1:29 of God who takes away the *s* of the world!
8: 7 no *s* be the first to cast a stone at her."
8:11 But from now on, avoid this *s*
8:34 who lives in sin is the slave of *s*.
8:46 Can any one of you convict me of *s*?
9: 2 was it his *s* or that of his parents that
9: 3 "It was no *s*, either of this man or of his
9:34 "You are steeped in *s* from your birth,
9:41 you were blind there would be no *s* in that.
9:41 'But we see,' you say, and your *s* remains.
15:22 to them, they would not be guilty of *s*;
15:22 now, however, their *s* cannot be excused.
15:24 before, they would not be guilty of *s*;
16: 8 he will prove the world wrong about *s*,
16: 9 About *s*— in that they refuse to believe
19:11 me over to you is guilty of the greater *s*."
Acts 7:60 "Lord, do not hold this *s* against them."
8:23 with gall and caught in the grip of *s*."
Rom 3: 9 that they are under the domination of *s*.
5:12 man sin entered the world and with *s* death,
5:13 before the law there was *s* in the world,
5:13 *s* is not imputed when there is no law
5:16 from the *s* committed by the one man.
5:20 but despite the increase of *s*, grace has far
5:21 it, so that, as *s* reigned through death,
6: 1 us continue in *s* that grace may abound"?
6: 2 can we who died to *s* go on living in it?
6: 6 and we might be slaves to *s* no longer.
6: 7 A man who is dead has been freed from *s*.
6:10 His death was death to *s*, once for all;
6:11 to *s* but alive for God in Christ Jesus.
6:12 let *s* rule your mortal body and make you
6:13 of your body to *s* as weapons for evil.
6:14 *S* will no longer have power over you;
6:15 the law but under grace, are we free to *s*?
6:16 obey, whether yours is the slavery of *s*,
6:17 to God, though once you were slaves of *s*,
6:18 freed from your *s*, you became slaves of
6:20 When you were slaves of *s*,
6:22 freed from *s* and have become slaves of God,
6:23 The wages of *s* is death, but the gift of
7: 7 That the law is the same as *s*?
7: 7 only through the law that I came to know *s*.
7: 8 *S* seized that opportunity;
7: 8 Without law *s* is dead, and at first I lived
7: 9 with it *s* came to life, and I died,
7:11 *S* found its opportunity and used the
7:13 sin, in order to be seen clearly as *s*,
7:13 *s* might go to the limit of sinfulness.
7:14 I am weak flesh sold into the slavery of *s*.
7:17 not I who do it but *s* which resides in me.
7:20 not I who do it, but *s* which dwells in me.
7:23 the prisoner of the law of *s* in my members.
7:25 law of God but with my flesh the law of *s*.
8: 2 has freed you from the law of *s* and death.
8: 3 likeness of sinful flesh as a *s* offering,
8: 3 thereby condemning *s* in the flesh,
8:10 is in you, the body is dead because of *s*,
1Cor 6:18 other *s* a man commits is outside his body,
7:28 however, you will not be commiting *s*.
7:28 does a virgin commit *s* if she marries.
7:36 He commits no *s* if there is a marriage.
8: 9 you become an occasion of *s* to the weak.
8:12 When you *s* thus against your brothers and
8:13 brother to *s* I will never eat meat again,
8:13 that I may not be an occasion of *s* to him.
15:56 The sting of death is *s*, and sin gets its
2Cor 5:21 God made him who did not know *s* to be sin,
Gal 2:17 that mean that Christ is encouraging *s*?
3:22 all things in under the constraint of *s*.
6: 1 My brothers, if someone is detected in *s*,
Eph 2: 5 to life with Christ when we were dead in *s*.
4:26 If you are angry, let it be without *s*.
Col 2:13 dead in *s* and your flesh was uncircumcised,
1Tm 2:14 was she who was led astray and fell into *s*.
5:20 The ones who do commit *s*,
Heb 3:13 no one grows hardened by the deceit of *s*.
5: 3 by weakness and so must make *s* offerings
9:28 not to take away *s* but to bring salvation
10: 2 would have had no *s* on their conscience.
10: 6 and *s* offerings you took no delight in.
10: 8 and offerings, holocausts and *s* offerings,
10:18 there is no further offering for *s*.
10:26 we *s* willfully after receiving the truth,
10:26 remains for us no further sacrifice for *s*—
11:25 than enjoy the fleeting rewards of *s*.
12: 1 let us lay aside every encumbrance of *s*
12: 4 In your fight against *s* you have not yet
13:11 a *s* offering are burned outside the camp.
Jas 1:15 has conceived, it gives birth to *s*,
1:15 when *s* reaches maturity it begets death.
2: 9 you commit *s* and are convicted by the law
2:10 falls into *s* on one point of the law,
1Pt 2:24 to the cross, so that all of us, dead to *s*,
4: 1 suffered in the flesh has broken with *s*.
2Pt 2:14 theirs is a never-ending search for *s*.
1Jn 1: 7 of his Son Jesus cleanses us from all *s*.
1: 8 we say, "We are free of the guilt of *s*,"
2: 1 ones, I am writing this to keep you from *s*.
2: 1 But if anyone should *s*,
3: 4 sins acts lawlessly, for *s* is lawlessness.
3: 6 The man who remains in him does not *s*.
3: 9 he cannot *s* because he is begotten of God.
5:16 brother sinning, if the *s* is not deadly,
5:16 is only for those whose *s* is not deadly.
5:16 There is such a thing as a deadly *s*;
5:17 wrongdoing is sin, but not all *s* is deadly.
5:18 that no one begotten of God commits *s*;
Rv 2:22 her companions in *s* I will plunge into

SIN-OFFERING (5)

Lv 4: 8 the *s* bullock he shall remove all the fat:
4:20 just as he did with the other *s* bullock.
16:15 he shall slaughter the people's *s* goat,
16:27 The *s* bullock and goat whose blood was
Ezr 6:17 with twelve he-goats as a *s* for all Israel,

SIN-OFFERINGS (3)

2Kgs 12:17 The funds from guilt-offerings and from *s*,
Ezr 8:35 seventy-seven lambs, and twelve goats as *s*:
Ps(s) 40: 7 Holocausts or *s* you sought not;

SINAI (41)

Ex 16: 1 of Sin, which is between Elim and *S*,
19: 1 the Israelites came to the desert of *S*.
19: 2 journey from Rephidim to the desert of *S*,
19:11 Mount *S* before the eyes of all the people.
19:18 Mount *S* was all wrapped in smoke,
19:20 the LORD came down to the top of Mount *S*,
19:23 "The people cannot go up to Mount *S*,
24:16 The glory of the LORD settled upon Mount *S*.
31:18 had finished speaking to Moses on Mount *S*,
34: 2 when you are to go up Mount *S* and there
34: 4 up Mount *S* as the LORD had commanded him,
34:29 As Moses came down from Mount *S* with the
34:32 all that the LORD had told him on Mount *S*.
Lv 7:38 the LORD enjoined on Moses at Mount *S*
7:38 of *S* to bring their offerings to the LORD.
25: 1 The LORD said to Moses on Mount *S*,
26:46 LORD had Moses promulgate on Mount *S*
27:34 gave Moses on Mount *S* for the Israelites.
Nm 1: 1 in the meeting tent in the desert of *S*:
3: 1 that the LORD spoke to Moses on Mount *S*.
3: 4 fire before the LORD in the desert of *S*,
3:14 The LORD said to Moses in the desert of *S*,
9: 1 the LORD said to Moses in the desert of *S*,
9: 5 the Passover in the desert of *S* during
10:10 Departure from *S*.
10:12 moved on from the desert of *S* by stages,
26:64 of the Israelites taken in the desert of *S*.
28: 6 *S* as a sweet-smelling oblation to the LORD.
33:15 Rephidim, they camped in the desert of *S*.
33:16 Setting out from the desert of *S*,
Dt 33: 2 from *S* and dawned on his people from Seir;
Jgs 5: 5 in the presence of the LORD, the One of *S*,
Neh 9:13 On Mount *S* you came down, you spoke
Jdt 5:14 along the route to *S* and Kadesh-barnea.
Ps(s) 68: 9 of God, the God of Israel, the One of *S*.
68:18 the Lord advances from *S* to the sanctuary.
Sir 48: 7 You heard threats at *S*,
Acts 7:30 *S* in the flame of a burning thornbush.
7:38 the angel on Mount *S* and with our fathers;
Gal 4:24 One is from Mount *S*,
4:25 The mountain *S* [Hagar] is in Arabia and

SINCE (480)

Gn 2: 2 *S* on the seventh day God was finished with
4:14 *S* you have now banished me from the soil,
6: 3 remain in man forever, *s* he is but flesh.
6:12 *s* all mortals led depraved lives on earth,
8:21 *s* the desires of man's heart are evil from
9:23 *s* their faces were turned the other way,
12:10 there, *s* the famine in the land was severe.
16: 5 ever *s* she became aware of her pregnancy,
18:31 *S* I have thus dared to speak to my Lord,
19:30 *S* Lot was afraid to stay in Zoar,
21:13 of him also, *s* he too is your offspring."
22:12 *s* you did not withhold from me your own
25:21 on behalf of his wife, *s* she was sterile.
26: 7 of Rebekah, *s* she was very beautiful.
26:12 *S* the LORD blessed him, he became richer
26:24 You have no need to fear, *s* I am with you.
29:18 *S* Jacob had fallen in love with Rachel,
29:34 to me, *s* I have now borne him three sons";
30:30 *s* the LORD's blessings came upon you in my
31:43 But *s* these women are my daughters,
33:10 *s* to come into your presence is for me
33:11 *S* he so urged him, Esau accepted.
34: 3 *S* he was strongly attracted to Dinah,
34: 5 but *s* his sons were out in the fields with
34:19 *s* he was deeply in love with Jacob's
38:15 for a harlot, *s* she had covered her face.
38:26 am, *s* I did not give her to my son Shelah."
39: 2 But *s* the LORD was with him, Joseph got
39: 9 nothing but yourself, *s* you are his wife.
39:23 *s* the LORD was with him and brought
41:39 *S* God has made all this known to you,
41:56 *s* the famine had gripped the land of Egypt.
42: 5 *s* there was famine in the land of Canaan
42:23 *s* he spoke with them through an
44:20 and *s* he is the only one by that mother
44:28 by wild beasts; I have not seen him *s*.
45:11 *S* five years of famine still lie ahead,
46:34 *s* all shepherds are abhorrent to the
47:13 *S* there was no food in any country because
47:16 *S* your money is gone," replied Joseph,
47:20 *s* with the famine too much for them to
47:22 *S* the priests had a fixed allowance from
49:29 *S* I am about to be taken to my kindred,
50: 5 *S* my father, at the point of death, made
Ex 5:23 *s* I went to Pharaoh to speak in your name,
6:30 to the LORD, *S* I am a poor speaker,
7:24 *s* they could not drink from the river
9:24 seen in the land *s* Egypt became a nation.
10: 5 foliage that has *s* sprouted in your fields.
12:17 *S* it was on this very day that I brought
12:39 *S* the dough they had brought out of Egypt
18:22 be lightened, *s* they will bear it with you.
21: 8 foreigner, *s* he has broken faith with her.
21:21 punished, *s* the slave is his own property.
23: 9 *s* you were once aliens yourselves in the
28:38 *S* Aaron bears whatever guilt the
29:14 outside the camp, *s* this is a sin offering.
29:18 burned on the altar, *s* it is a holocaust,
29:22 right thigh, *s* this is the ordination ram,
29:33 layman may eat of them, *s* they are sacred.
29:34 it is not to be eaten, *s* it is sacred.
34:24 *S* I will drive out the nations before you
Lv 5:23 *s* he has incurred guilt by his sin,
6:22 of the sin offering, *s* it is most sacred.
7: 6 in a sacred place, *s* it is most sacred.
10:12 *S* it is most sacred, you must eat it in
10:17 in the sacred place, *s* it is most sacred?
11:45 *S* I, the LORD, brought you up from
13:11 him, *s* he is certainly unclean.
13:13 *s* it has all turned white,
13:28 clean, *s* it is only the scar of the burn.
13:46 himself unclean, *s* he is in fact unclean.
13:52 *s* it has malignant leprosy,
14:48 clean, *s* the infection has been healed.
16: 4 But *s* these vestments are sacred,
16:22 *S* the goat is to carry off their
16:30 *S* on this day atonement is made for you to
17:11 *S* the life of a living body is in its blood,
17:14 *S* the life of every living body is its
17:14 *S* the life of every living body is its
18: 7 Besides, *s* she is your own mother,
18:11 whom your father's wife bore to him, *s* she,
18:12 sister, *s* she is your father's relative.
18:13 sister, *s* she is your mother's relative.
18:14 by being intimate with his wife, *s* she,
20: 9 *s* he has cursed his father or mother,
20:12 *s* they have committed an abhorrent deed,
21: 6 *s* they offer up the oblations of the LORD,
22:25 *s* they are deformed or defective,
24: 9 who must eat it in a sacred place, *s*,
25:12 *S* this is the jubilee, which shall be sacred
25:15 On the basis of the number of years *s* the
25:27 to the number of years *s* the sale,
25:42 *S* those whom I brought out of the land of
Nm 5:15 it, *s* it is a cereal offering of jealousy,
6: 7 *s* his head bears his dedication to God.
14:25 *s* the Amalekites and Canaanites are living
15:26 *s* the fault of inadvertence affects all
15:31 *S* he has despised the word of the LORD and
18:31 *s* they are your recompense for service at
19:13 *S* the lustral water has not been splashed
20:21 *s* Edom refused to let them pass through
22:25 and *s* she squeezed Balaam's leg against it,
22:34 *S* it has displeased you, I will go back
30: 6 *s* her father has expressed to her his
30:13 *s* her husband has annulled them,
32: 4 Now, *s* your servants have livestock,"
35:33 *S* bloodshed desecrates the land,
Dt 2: 5 *s* I have already given Esau possession of
2: 9 *s* I have given Ar to the descendants of
2:19 *s* I have given it to the descendants of
2:33 but *s* the LORD, our God, had delivered
4:21 *S* the LORD was angered against me on your
4:31 *S* the LORD, your god, is a merciful God,
4:32 ever *s* God created man upon the earth;
5: 5 *S* you were afraid of the fire and would
9:24 Ever *s* I have known you,
12: 9 *s* you have not yet reached your resting
15: 4 *s* the LORD, your God, will bless you
15: 6 and none will rule over you, *s* the LORD,
15:16 your household, *s* he fares well with you,
15:18 *s* the service he has given you for six
16: 1 *s* it was in the month of Abib that he
16:15 *s* the LORD, your God, has blessed you

19: 6 *s* he had previously borne the slain man no
21:14 *s* she was married to you under compulsion.
21:17 *s* he is the first fruits of his manhood,
21:23 *S* God's curse rests on him who hangs on a
22:26 *s* she is not guilty of a capital offense.
23: 8 abhor the Edomite, *s* he is your brother,
23: 8 *s* you were an alien in his country.
23:15 *S* the LORD, your God, journeys along
24:15 *s* he is poor and looks forward to them.
28:47 *S* you would not serve the LORD,
32:21 *S* they have provoked me with their
32:47 *s* it is by this means that you are to
34: 9 *s* Moses had laid his hands upon him;
34:10 *S* then no prophet has arisen in Israel
Jos 2:11 is discouraged because of you, *s* the LORD,
2:12 LORD that, *s* I am showing kindness to you,
8:17 *S* they were drawn away from the city,
8:22 *S* those in the city came out to intercept
9:24 *S*, therefore, at your advance, we were in
10: 4 *s* it had concluded peace with Joshua and
10:14 before or *s* was there a day like this,
13:14 of Levi Moses assigned no heritage *s*,
13:33 to the tribe of Levi, *s* the LORD himself,
14:10 years *s* the LORD spoke thus to Moses;
15:19 *S* you have assigned to me land in the Negeb,
17: 1 *s* his eldest son, Machir, the father of
17: 6 *s* these female descendants of Manasseh
17:12 *S* the Manassehites could not conquer these
17:15 *s* the mountain regions of Ephraim are so
19: 9 for *s* the portion of the latter was too
21:10 the Levites, *s* the first lot fell to them:
22: 4 *S*, therefore, the LORD, your God, has
22:31 *S* you have not committed this act of
Jgs 1:15 *S* you have assigned land in the Negeb to me,
1:19 *S* the LORD was with Judah, he gained
3:25 *S* he did not open the doors of the upper
4:17 of Jael, wife of the Kenite Heber, *s* Jabin,
6:32 against him, *s* he destroyed his altar."
8:20 *S* Jether was still a boy, he was afraid
10: 6 *S* they had abandoned the LORD and would
13: 9 *S* her husband Manoah was not with her,
14:10 *s* it was customary for the young men to do
14:17 On the seventh day, *s* she importuned him,
17:13 me, *s* the Levite has become my priest."
18:28 *s* the city was far from Sidon and they had
19:11 *S* they were near Jebus with the day far
19:23 *S* this man is my guest, do not commit
21: 7 *s* we have sworn by the LORD not to give
21:22 *s* we did not take a woman apiece in the
Ru 1:21 *s* the LORD has pronounced against me and
2: 7 and ever *s* she came this morning she has
1Sm 1:20 Samuel, *s* she had asked the LORD for him.
2:25 *s* the LORD had decided on their death.
4:18 *s* he was an old man and heavy,
5:11 *s* the hand of God had been very heavy upon
6: 4 *s* the same plague has struck all of you
12:22 *s* the LORD himself chose to make you his
13:11 *s* you had not come by the specified time,
17:39 however, *s* he had never tried armor before.
18:16 him, *s* he led them on their expeditions.
20:18 be missed, *s* your place will be vacant.
20:34 *s* his father had railed against him.
24:12 *S* I cut off an end of your mantle and did
24:21 *s* I know that you shall surely be king and
25: 8 young men, *s* we come at a festival time.
28:15 *S* he no longer answers me through prophets
28:20 *s* he had eaten nothing all that day and
30:22 up to say, *S* they did not accompany us,
2Sm 7:11 *s* the time I first appointed judges over
10: 5 word to them, *s* the men were quite ashamed.
12:14 But *s* you have utterly spurned the LORD by
13: 2 *s* she was a virgin, Amnon thought it
13:32 this ever *s* Amnon shamed his sister Tamar.
14:22 *s* the king has granted the request of his
17: 8 *s* your father is skilled in warfare,
17:17 *s* they could not risk being seen entering
20:10 And *s* Amasa was not on his guard against
1Kgs 5:20 *s* you know that there is no one among us
5:26 Solomon, *s* they were parties to a treaty.
8:11 *s* the LORD's glory had filled the temple
8:16 *S* the day I brought my people Israel out
8:42 you *s* men will learn of your great name
11:11 *S* this is what you want,
14:13 *s* in him alone of Jeroboam's house has
20:36 *S* you did not obey the voice of the LORD,
21: 2 be my vegetable garden, *s* it is close by,
21:29 *S* he has humbled himself before me,
2Kgs 1:17 *S* he had no son, his brother Joram
3:18 *s* the LORD does not consider this enough,
4: 9 *S* he visits us often, let us arrange a little
5:13 All the more now, *s* he said to you,
7:13 *S* those who are left in the city are no
8:18 of Ahab, *s* the sister of Ahab was his wife;
8:27 did, *s* he was related to them by marriage.
10: 2 *S* your master's sons are with you,"
10:31 *s* he did not desist from the sins which
13: 4 *s* he saw the oppression to which the king
13: 7 *s* the king of Aram had destroyed them and
14: 3 *s* he did just as his father Joash had done.
14:27 *S* the LORD had not determined to blot out
17:26 *s* they do not know how to worship the God
18:29 *s* he cannot deliver you out of my hand.
25: 4 *S* the Chaldeans had the city surrounded,
1Chr 6:39 Kohathites, *s* the first lot fell to them,
7: 4 *s* they had more wives and sons than their
7:23 Beriah, *s* evil had befallen his house.
17:26 *S* you, O LORD, are truly God and have
17:27 and *s* you have deigned to bless the house
17:27 so that it will remain forever *s* it is you,
24: 4 But *s* the descendants of Eleazar were
2Chr 1:11 *S* this has been your wish and you have not
2: 5 *s* the heavens and even the highest heavens
2: 8 *s* the house I intend to build must be
5:14 *s* the LORD's glory filled the house of God.
6: 5 *S* the day I brought my people out of the
7: 7 *s* the bronze altar which Solomon had made
8:14 each gate, *s* such was the command of David,
19: 3 *s* you have removed the sacred poles from
20:26 ever *s* been called the Valley of Beracah.
22: 1 *s* all the older sons had been slain by the
22: 4 *s* they were his counselors after the
23: 8 depart on the sabbath *s* Jehoiada the priest
28:23 *S* it was the gods of the kings of Aram who
29:34 *S* the priests were too few in number to be
30:26 in Jerusalem, for *s* the days of Solomon,
31:10 *S* they began to bring the offerings to the
31:18 *s* they were to sanctify themselves by
32:15 *S* no other god of any other nation or
34:21 *s* our fathers have not kept the word of
35:18 in Israel *s* the time of the prophet Samuel,
Ezr 4: 2 sacrificed to him *s* the days of Esarhaddon,
4:14 *s* we partake of the salt of the palace,
4:15 has been fostered there *s* ancient times.
5:16 *S* that time the building has been going on,
8:22 along the way, *s* we had said to the king,
Neh 2:14 *S* there was no room here for my mount to
6: 7 *s* matters like these must reach the ear
6:18 him, *s* he was the son-in-law of Shecaniah,
Tb 5: 2 *s* he does not know me nor do I know him?
5: 3 already passed *s* I deposited that money!
6:12 *S* you are Sarah's closest relative,
6:13 *S* you have the right to marry her listen
Jdt 4: 5 *s* their fields had recently been harvested,
4: 7 passes, *s* these offered access to Judea.
5: 8 *S* they abandoned the way of their ancestors,
7:19 *s* all their enemies had them surrounded,
8:20 *S* we acknowledge no other god but the Lord,
11:12 *S* their food gave out and all their water
12:18 for at no time *s* I was born have I ever
Est 3: 4 *s* he had told them that he was a Jew.
3: 6 *S* they had told Haman of Mordecai's
7: 7 *s* he saw that the king had decided on his
1Mc 1:11 *s* we separated from them,
9:27 Israel *s* the time prophets ceased to appear
9:29 *S* your brother Judas died, there has been no
10: 5 *s* he will remember all the wrongs we have
10:42 *s* these funds belong to the priests who
11: 2 to do, *s* Ptolemy was his father-in-law.
12: 9 *s* we have for our encouragement the sacred
12:10 long time has passed *s* your mission to us.
14:22 *S* Numenius, son of Antiochus,
14:29 *S* there have often been wars in our country,
2Mc 1:11 *S* we have been saved by God from grave
3: 5 *S* he could not prevail against Onias,
3:34 *S* you have been scourged by Heaven,
7:16 *S* you have power among men,
7:23 *s* it is the Creator of the universe who
7:39 *s* he bitterly resented the boy's contempt.
9: 4 rode with him, *s* he said in his arrogance,
9:18 But *s* God's punishment had justly come
9:22 I do not despair about my health *s* I have
10:13 *S* he could not command the respect due to
11:25 *S* we desire that this people too should be
12:39 day, *s* the task had now become urgent,
14: 8 *s* our entire nation is suffering great
15:17 *s* their city and its temple with the
15:37 *S* Nicanor's doings ended in this way,
Jb 4: 7 *S* when are the upright destroyed?
9:35 *S* this is not the case with me,
15:18 contradicted *s* the days of their fathers,
20: 4 time, *s* man was placed upon the earth,
32: 4 But *s* these men were older than he,
34:33 must punish, *s* you reject what he is doing?
34:36 *s* his answers are those of the impious;
Ps(s) 22:10 have been my guide *s* I was first formed,
69: 8 of Israel, *S* for your sake I bear insult,
119:49 to your servant *s* you have given me hope.
Prv 6: 3 *s* you have fallen into your neighbor's
17:16 to buy wisdom, *s* he has no mind for it?
Eccl 2:17 *s* for me the work that is done under the
3:17 *s* there is a time for every affair and on
4:14 *s* even in his royalty he was poor at birth.
9: 6 hatred and rivalry have long *s* perished.
Wis 3:10 *s* they neglected justice and forsook the
11:14 *s* their thirst proved unlike that of the
12:27 *s* they were tortured by the very things
14:11 *s* they have become abominable amid God's
16: 3 *s* the creatures sent to plague them were
18: 1 forms, *s* now they themselves had suffered,
18:12 *s* at a single instant their nobler
19:13 *s* indeed they treated their guests with the more
19:15 *s* they received strangers unwillingly!
Sir 11:10 *s* he who is avid for wealth will not be
30: 4 *s* he leaves after him one like himself,
33:17 *S* by the LORD's blessing I have made
43:29 him the more, *s* we cannot fathom him,
44: 2 portion, his own part, *s* the days of old.
47: 5 *S* he called upon the Most High God,
51:17 *S* in this way I have profited,
Is 7:17 than any *s* Ephraim seceded from Judah.
29:13 *S* this people draws near with words only
36:14 deceive you, *s* he cannot deliver you.
40:21 *S* the earth was founded He sits enthroned
41: 4 forth the generations *s* the beginning.
46: 3 house of Israel, My burden *s* your birth,
61: 7 *S* their shame was double and disgrace and
65: 7 *S* they burned incense on the mountains,
65:12 *S* I called and you did not answer,
66: 3 *S* these have chosen their own ways and
Jer 8: 9 *S* they have rejected the word of the LORD,
25: 3 *S* the thirteenth year of Josiah,
25: 8 *S* you would not listen to my words, lo!
25:29 For *s* with this city, which is called by
30: 6 *s* when do men bear children?
32: 7 for yourself my field in Anathoth, *s* you,
34: 7 *s* these alone were left of the fortified
35:18 *S* you have obeyed the command of Jonadab,
36:22 his winter house, *s* it was the ninth month,
44:18 But *s* we stopped burning incense to the
51:62 *s* it would remain an everlasting desert."
Bar 3:38 *S* then she has appeared on earth,
Ez 3: 7 to you, *s* they will not listen to me.
16:31 a prostitute, *s* you disdained payment.
16:34 *S* you gave payment instead of receiving it,
18:18 Only the father, *s* he violated rights,
18:28 *s* he has turned away from all the sins
21:18 the Lord GOD, *s* you have spurned the rod.
32:32 *S* he spread his terror in the land of the
39:28 God, *s* I who exiled them among the nations,
44: 2 *s* the LORD, the God of Israel, has entered
Dn 2: 8 for time, *s* you know what I have decided.
6:19 *S* sleep was impossible for him,
12: 1 distress *s* nations began until that time.
13:41 *s* they were elders and judges of the
13:50 *s* God has given you the prestige of old
Hos 2:10 *S* she has not known that it was I who gave
4: 6 *S* you have rejected knowledge,
4: 6 *S* you have ignored the law of your God,
8: 1 *S* they have violated my covenant,
10: 3 *S* they do not fear the LORD,
10: 9 *S* the days of Gibeah you have sinned,
12:10 am the LORD, your God, *s* the land of Egypt;
13: 4 am the LORD, your God, *s* the land of Egypt;
Am 4:12 and *s* I will deal thus with you,
Jon 1:12 *s* I know it is because of me that this
Zec 13: 5 the soil, for I have owned land *s* my youth."
Mal 2: 9 all the people, *S* you do not keep my ways,
3: 7 *S* the days of your fathers you have turned
Mt 2: 6 *s* from you shall come a ruler who is to
2:18 no comfort for her, *s* they are no more."
13: 5 sprouted at once *s* the soil had no depth,
13:35 lain hidden *s* the creation of the world."
22:25 after marrying, and *s* he had no children,
22:28 she be, *s* all seven of them married her?"
25:21 *S* you were dependable in a small matter I
25:23 *S* you were dependable in a small matter I
27: 6 in the temple treasury *s* it is blood money."
27:17 *S* they were already assembled, Pilate said
Mk 10:20 I have kept all these *s* my childhood."
11:11 but *s* it was already late in the afternoon,
16:14 *s* they had put no faith in those who had
Lk 1:34 "How can this be *s* I do not know man?"
6:35 *s* he himself is good to the ungrateful and
7:42 *S* neither was able to repay,
7:45 has not ceased kissing my feet *s* I entered.
11:18 himself, how can his kingdom last? *s*
11:50 shed *s* the foundation of the world.
13:33 *s* no prophet can be allowed to die
18:21 "I have kept all these *s* I was a boy."
24:21 the third day *s* these things happened,
Jn 2: 9 waiters knew, *s* they had drawn the water.
7:39 as yet, *s* Jesus had not yet been glorified.)
7:51 *S* when does our law condemn any man
8:29 deserted me *s* I always do what pleases him."
9:17 *S* it was your eyes he opened,
11:10 he will stumble *s* there is no light in him."
12:50 *S* I know that his commandment means
13:29 idea that, *s* Judas held the common purse,
14:17 *s* it neither sees him nor recognizes him;
15:15 *s* I have made known to you all that I
16:19 *S* Jesus was aware that they wanted to
19:20 *s* the place where Jesus was crucified was
19:31 *S* it was the Preparation Day the Jews did
Acts 8:16 *s* they had only been baptized in the name
9:38 *S* Lydda was near Joppa,
11:24 *s* he himself was a good man filled with
13:46 but *s* you reject it and thus convict
14:12 they called Hermes, *s* he was the spokesman.
16: 2 *S* the brothers in Lystra and Iconium spoke
18:15 But *s* this is a dispute about terminology
19:36 *S* this is beyond question,
20:13 made, *s* his plan was to travel overland.
21:14 *S* he would not be dissuaded,
22:11 But *s* I could not see because of the
24:11 you, *s* you are in a position to understand.
24:11 *s* I went to Jerusalem to worship there.
25:14 *S* they were to spend several days there,
26: 3 especially *s* you are expert in all the
26: 4 "The way I have lived *s* my youth,

SINCE (cont.)
27: 7 *S* the winds would not permit us to
27:12 *S* the harbor was not fit to pass the
27:15 *S* the ship was caught up in it and could
Rom 1:20 *S* the creation of the world,
2: 1 yourself, *s* you do the very same things.
3:20 *s* no one will be justified in God's sight
8: 9 spirit, *s* the Spirit of God dwells in you.
11:31 disobedient *s* God wished to show you mercy
1Cor 1:21 *S* in God's wisdom the world did not come
11:32 but *s* it is the Lord who judges us,
14:12 *S* you have set your hearts on spiritual
14:33 the prophets' control, *s* God is a God,
2Cor 5:14 the conviction that *s* one died for all,
7: 1 *S* we have these promises, beloved, let us
9: 2 that Achaia has been ready *s* last year.
10:12 *S* people like that are their own appraisers,
11: 2 *s* I have given you in marriage to one
11:18 *S* many are bragging about their human
Gal 5:25 *S* we live by the spirit,
Phil 1: 7 in your regard *s* I hold all of you dear
3:12 *s* I have been grasped by Christ [Jesus].
Col 1: 9 Ever *s* we heard this we have been praying
3: 1 *S* you have been raised up in company with
3:15 *s* as members of the one body you have been
3:24 *s* you know full well you will receive an
1Thes 3: 6 *s* Timothy has returned to us from you
2Thes 2: 3 *S* the mass apostasy has not yet occurred
1Tm 6: 2 *s* those who will profit from their work
Phlm 1:16 *s* now you will know him both as a man and
Heb 2:14 *s* the children are men of blood and flesh,
2:18 *S* he was himself tested through what he
4: 6 Therefore, *s* it remains for some to enter,
4:14 *S*, then, we have a great high priest who
6: 6 *s* they are crucifying the Son of God for
7:25 *s* he forever lives to make intercession
9:15 *s* his death has taken place for
10: 1 *S* the law had only a shadow of the good
10:19 *s* the blood of Jesus assures our entrance
10:21 and *s* we have a great priest who is over
12: 1 *s* we for our part are surrounded by this
1Pt 1:17 *S* this is so, conduct yourselves reverently
2:21 *s* Christ suffered for you in just this way
2Pt 3: 9 *s* he wants none to perish but all to come
3:11 *S* everything is to be destroyed in this way,
1Jn 2:11 is going, *s* the dark has blinded his eyes.
4:18 And *s* fear has to do with punishment.
5:15 *s* we know that he hears us whenever we ask,
Rv 15: 4 *S* you alone are holy,

SINCERE (20)
Dt 18:13 must be altogether *s* toward the LORD,
2Sm 22:27 Toward the sincere you are *s*;
1Chr 29:17 With a *s* heart I have willingly given all
Tb 2: 2 If he is a *s* worshiper of God,
Est E: 6 slander the *s* good will of rulers.
Jb 16:17 are free from violence, and my prayer is *s*.
Ps(s) 18:27 Toward the *s* you are sincere,
78:72 And he tended them with a *s* heart,
Prv 8: 8 *S* are all the words of my mouth,
Sir 2: 2 Be *s* of heart and steadfast,
Is 57: 2 There is rest on his couch for the *s*,
Acts 2:46 *s* hearts they took their meals in common,
Rom 12: 9 Your love must be *s*.
2Cor 6: 6 patience, in the Holy Spirit, in *s* love;
11: 3 your *s* and complete devotion to Christ.
1Tm 1: 5 pure heart, a good conscience, and *s* faith.
2Tm 1: 5 I find myself thinking of your *s* faith
Jas 3:17 deeds that are its fruits, impartial and *s*.

SINCERELY (9)
Jos 24:14 the LORD and serve him completely and *s*.
1Kgs 9: 4 your father David lived, *s* and uprightly,
2Kgs 10:15 and asked, "Are you *s* disposed toward me,
Tb 14: 7 Those who *s* love God shall rejoice,
14: 9 his name *s* and with all their strength.
Jb 33: 3 my mind, my lips shall utter knowledge *s*;
Mt 22:16 are a truthful man and teach God's way *s*.
Mk 12:14 respect but teach God's way of life *s*.
Rom 6:17 you *s* obeyed that rule of teaching which

SINCERITY (10)
Ps(s) 5:10 For in their mouth there is no *s*;
41: 7 one comes to see me, he speaks without *s*;
51: 8 Behold, you are pleased with *s* of heart,
84:12 no good thing from those who walk in *s*.
Is 48: 1 the God of Israel without *s* or justice,
1Cor 5: 8 with the unleavened bread of *s* and truth.
Eph 6: 5 the awe, and the *s* you owe to Christ.
Col 3:22 in all *s* and out of reverence for the Lord.
Heb 10:22 near in utter *s* and absolute confidence,
2Pt 3: 1 as reminders urging you to *s* of outlook.

SINEW (1)
Is 48: 4 neck is an iron *s* and your forehead bronze,

SINEWS (6)
Jb 10:11 me, with bones and *s* knit me together.
40:16 loins, and his vigor in the *s* of his belly.
40:17 the *s* of his thighs are like cables.
Ez 37: 6 I will put *s* upon you, make flesh grow
37: 8 I saw the *s* and the flesh come upon them,
Col 2:19 supported and upheld by joints and *s*,

SINFUL (37)
Lv 5:22 of the *s* oaths that men make in such cases,
16:16 *s* defilements and faults of the Israelites.
16:21 he shall confess over it all the *s* faults
Dt 9:21 taking the calf, the *s* object you had made,
1Sm 15:18 *s* Amalekites under a ban of destruction.
1Kgs 16:19 by imitating the *s* conduct of Jeroboam,
16:26 closely imitated the *s* conduct of Jeroboam,
Tb 13: 6 show his power and majesty to a *s* nation.
1Mc 1:10 There sprang from these a *s* offshoot,
1:34 There they installed a *s* race,
2:62 Do not fear the words of a *s* man,
2Mc 12:42 that the *s* deed might be fully blotted out.
Jb 2:10 Through all this, Job said nothing *s*.
Wis 4:16 the just man dead condemns the *s* who live,
Sir 16: 6 Against a *s* band fire is enkindled,
23:13 to coarse talk, for in it lies *s* matter.
41: 8 Woe to you, O *s* men,
42: 2 of the sentence to be passed upon the *s*;
48:16 was right, but others were extremely *s*.
Is 1: 4 *s* nation, people laden with wickedness,
9:16 They are wholly profaned and *s*,
31: 7 shall spurn his *s* idols of silver and gold,
64: 4 Behold, you are angry, and we are *s*;
Ez 16:52 In view of your *s* deeds,
28:18 Because of your great guilt, your *s* trade,
Am 9: 8 eyes of the Lord GOD are on this *s* kingdom;
Lk 5: 8 I am a *s* man."
24: 7 must be delivered into the hands of *s* men,
Rom 3:20 law does nothing but point out what is *s*.
4: 5 yet believes in him who justifies the *s*,
6: 6 that the *s* body might be destroyed
7: 5 the *s* passions roused by the law worked in
8: 3 the likeness of *s* flesh as a sin offering,
14:23 does not accord with one's belief is *s*.
1Tm 1: 9 and unruly, the irreligious and the *s*,
Ti 3:11 recognize such a person as perverted and *s*;
1Jn 3: 5 in him there is nothing *s*.

SINFULLY (4)
Lv 5:16 what he has *s* withheld from the sanctuary,
2Chr 22: 3 because his mother counseled him to act *s*.
27: 2 the people, however, continued to act *s*.
1Jn 3: 9 acts *s* because he remains of God's stock;

SINFULNESS (4)
Ezr 9:13 have made less of our *s* than it deserved
Sir 47:24 Their *s* grew more and more,
Ez 21:29 your *s* in all your wicked deeds revealed
Rom 7:13 sin might go to the limit of *s*.

SING (122)
Ex 15: 1 I will *s* to the LORD,
15:21 *S* to the LORD, for he is gloriously
Nm 21:17 *s* to it—The well that was the princes
Dt 32: 3 For I will *s* the LORD's renown.
Jgs 5: 3 I to the LORD will *s* my song,
5:11 *S* of them to the strains of the harpers at
1Sm 21:12 During their dances do they not *s*,
29: 5 David of whom they *s* during their dances,
2Sm 22:50 nations, and I will *s* praise to your name,
1Chr 16: 7 his brethren to *s* for the first time
16: 9 Sing to him, *s* his praise,
16:23 *S* to the LORD, all the earth, announce
2Chr 20:19 rose to *s* the praises of the LORD,
20:21 he appointed some to *s* to the LORD and
29:28 and they continued to *s* the song and to
29:30 Levites to *s* the praises of the LORD
Neh 12:24 opposite them to *s* praises and thanksgiving
Tb 13: 8 majesty, and *s* his praises in Jerusalem."
13:18 of Jerusalem shall *s* hymns of gladness,
Jdt 16: 1 *S* to him a new song,
16:13 "A new hymn I will *s* to my God.
Est C:10 we shall live to *s* praise to your name,
2Mc 1:30 Then the priests began to *s* hymns.
Jb 21:12 They *s* to the timbrel and harp,
30: 9 Yet now they *s* of me in mockery;
33:27 He shall *s* before men and say,
Ps(s) 7:18 *s* praise to the name of the LORD Most High.
9: 3 I will *s* praise to your name,
9:12 *S* praise to the LORD enthroned in Zion;
13: 6 let me *s* of the LORD,
18:50 nations, and I will *s* praise to your name,
21:14 We will *s*, chant the praise of your might.
27: 6 I will *s* and chant praise to the LORD.
30: 5 *S* praise to the LORD,
30:13 soul might *s* praise to you without ceasing;
33: 3 *S* to him a new song;
42:10 I *s* to God, my rock:
45: 2 as I *s* my ode to the king,
47: 7 *S* praise to God, sing praise;
47: 7 sing praise to our king, *s* praise.
47: 8 all the earth is God; *s* hymns of praise.
57: 8 I will *s* and chant praise.
59:17 But I will *s* of your strength and revel
59:18 your praise will I *s*;
61: 9 will I *s* the praises of your name forever,
65:14 They shout and *s* for joy.
66: 2 earth, *s* praise to the glory of his name;
66: 4 sing praise to you, *s* praise to your name!"
68: 5 *S* to God, chant praise to his name,
68:33 You kingdoms of the earth, *s* to God,
71:22 I will *s* your praises with the harp,
71:23 shall shout for joy as I *s* your praises;
75:10 I will *s* praise to the God of Jacob.
81: 2 *S* joyfully to God our strength;
87: 7 And all shall *s*, in their festive dance:
89: 2 The favors of the LORD I will *s* forever;
92: 2 to the LORD, to *s* praise to your name,
95: 1 Come, let us *s* joyfully to the LORD;
95: 2 let us joyfully *s* psalms to him.
96: 1 *S* to the LORD a new song;
96: 1 *s* to the LORD, all you lands.
96: 2 *S* to the LORD; bless his name;
98: 1 *S* to the LORD a new song, for he has
98: 4 *S* joyfully to the LORD, all you lands;
98: 4 break into song; *s* praise.
98: 5 *S* praise to the LORD with the harp,
98: 6 of the horn *s* joyfully before the King,
100: 1 *S* joyfully to the LORD,
101: 1 Of kindness and judgment I will *s*;
101: 1 to you, O LORD, I will *s* praise.
104:33 I will *s* to the LORD all my life;
104:33 I will *s* praise to my God while I live.
105: 2 Sing to him, *s* his praise,
108: 2 I will *s* and chant praise.
119:172 May my tongue *s* of your promise,
135: 3 *s* praise to his name,
137: 3 *S* for us the songs of Zion!"
137: 4 we *s* a song of the LORD in a foreign land?
138: 1 of the angels I will *s* your praise;
138: 5 And they shall *s* of the ways of the LORD:
144: 9 O God, I will *s* a new song to you;
145: 7 goodness and joyfully *s* of your justice.
146: 2 I will *s* praise to my God while I live.
147: 1 *s* praise to our God, for he is gracious;
147: 7 *S* to the LORD with thanksgiving;
147: 7 *s* praise with the harp to our God,
149: 1 *S* to the LORD a new song of praise in
149: 3 them *s* praise to him with timbrel and harp.
149: 5 let them *s* for joy upon their couches;
Sir 39:10 his wisdom, and in assembly *s* his praises.
39:15 of his name, loudly *s* his praises,
39:15 *s* out with joy as you proclaim:
Is 5: 1 Let me now *s* of my friend,
12: 5 *S* praise to the LORD for his glorious
23:16 Pluck the strings skillfully, *s* many songs,
24: 9 They cannot *s* and drink wine;
26: 1 they will *s* this song in the land of Judah:
26:19 awake and *s*, you who lie in the dust.
27: 2 The pleasant vineyard, *s* about it!
30:29 *s* as on a night when a feast is observed,
35: 6 a stag, then the tongue of the dumb will *s*.
38:20 we shall *s* to stringed instruments In the
42:10 *S* to the LORD a new song,
49:13 *S* out, O heavens, and rejoice, O earth,
Jer 20:13 *S* to the LORD, praise the LORD,
Dn 3:90 Hearing them *s*, and astonished
Zep 3:14 *s* joyfully, O Israel!
3:17 love, He will *s* joyfully because of you,
Zec 2:14 *S* and rejoice, O daughter Zion!
Rom 15: 9 the Gentiles and I will *s* to your name."
15:11 the Lord, all you Gentiles and *s* his glory,
1Cor 14:15 *s* with my spirit and with my mind as well.
Eph 5:19 *S* praise to the Lord with all your hearts.
Col 3:16 *S* gratefully to God from your hearts in
Heb 2:12 I will *s* your praise in the midst of the
Jas 5:13 good spirits, he should *s* a hymn of praise.
Rv 4:10 down their crowns before the throne and *s*:

SINGED (1)
Dn 3:94 not a hair of their heads had been *s*,

SINGER (2)
Ezr 7:24 or tolls on any priest, Levite, *s*,
Ez 33:32 For them you are only a ballad *s*,

SINGERS (32)
2Sm 19:36 the voices of *s* and songstresses?
1Chr 6:17 They served as *s* before the Dwelling of
15:27 the Levites who carried the ark, the *s*,
25: 1 as *s* of inspired songs to the
2Chr 5:12 various classes), the Levites who were *s*,
5:13 When the trumpeters and *s* were heard as a
23:13 while the *s* with their musical instruments
35:15 The *s*, the sons of Asaph, were at
35:25 female *s* in their lamentations over Josiah.
Ezr 2:41 The *s*: sons of Asaph,
2:65 also had two hundred male and female *s*.
2:70 but the *s*, the gatekeepers, and the temple
7: 7 Israelites and some priests, Levites, *s*,
10:24 Of the *s*: Eliashib and Zakkur;
Neh 7: 1 and the gatekeepers [and the *s* and the
7:44 The *s*: sons of Asaph,
7:67 also had two hundred male and female *s*.
7:72 the Levites, the gatekeepers, the *s*,
10:29 people, priests, Levites, gatekeepers, *s*,

10:40 priests, the gatekeepers, and the *s*.
11:22 the *s* appointed to the service of the
11:23 the *s* assigning them their daily duties.
12:28 The levitical *s* gathered together from the
12:29 (for the *s* had built themselves settlements
12:42 The *s* were heard under the leadership of
12:45 (as did the *s* and the gatekeepers)
12:46 For the heads of the families of the *s* and
12:47 the *s* and the gatekeepers their portions,
13: 5 wine, and oil allotted to the Levites, *s*,
13:10 so that the Levites and the *s* who should
Ps(s) 68:26 The *s* lead, the minstrels follow,
Eccl 2: 8 male and female *s* and all human luxuries.

SINGING (22)

Gn 31:27 *s* to the sound of tambourines and harps.
1Sm 18: 6 of Israel to meet King Saul, *s* and dancing,
2Sm 6: 5 their strength, with *s* and with citharas,
1Chr 25: 6 in the *s* in the house of the LORD
25: 7 brethren who were trained in *s* to the LORD,
2Chr 30:22 peace offerings and *s* praises to the LORD,
Tb 12:22 They kept thanking God and *s* his praises;
Jdt 15:13 their armor, wearing garlands and *s* hymns.
1Mc 4:24 they were *s* hymns and glorifying Heaven,
13:51 lyres, and the *s* of hymns and canticles,
Sir 9: 4 With a *s* girl be not familiar,
32: 3 temper your wisdom, not to disturb the *s*.
Is 16:10 gladness, In the vineyards there is no *s*,
35:10 has ransomed will return and enter Zion *s*,
51:11 has ransomed will return and enter Zion *s*,
Jer 33:11 offerings to the house of the LORD, *s*,
Dn 3:24 the flames, *s* to God and blessing the Lord.
Mt 26:30 Then, after *s* songs of praise,
Mk 14:26 After *s* songs of praise,
Acts 16:25 Silas were praying and *s* hymns to God
Rv 14: 3 They were *s* a new hymn before the throne,
19: 1 They were *s*: "Alleluia!

SINGLE (97)

Gn 1: 9 under the sky be gathered into a *s* basin,
27:45 Must I lose both of you in a *s* day?"
31:37 a *s* object taken from your belongings?
33:13 if overdriven for a *s* day,
41: 5 fat and healthy, growing on a *s* stalk.
41:22 fat and healthy, growing on a *s* stalk.
Ex 10:19 But though not a *s* locust remained within
14:28 Not a *s* one of them escaped.
25:36 form but a *s* piece of pure beaten gold.
37:22 formed but a *s* piece of pure beaten gold.
Nm 13:23 a branch with a *s* cluster of grapes on it,
16:15 I have never taken a *s* ass from them,
35:30 The evidence of a *s* witness is not
Dt 20:16 you shall not leave a *s* soul alive.
29:20 will *s* him out from all the tribes
Jos 8:35 Every *s* word that Moses had commanded,
10:42 lands Joshua captured in a *s* campaign,
21:45 Not a *s* promise that the LORD made to the
22:20 Though he was but a *s* man,
23:14 for you, with not one *s* exception.
1Sm 3:17 to you if you hide a *s* thing he told you."
13:19 Not a *s* smith was to be found in the whole
14:45 not a *s* hair of his head shall fall to the
24:15 A dead dog, or a *s* flea!
25:22 if by morning I leave a *s* male alive among
25:34 not have had a *s* man or boy left alive."
26:20 Israel has come out to seek a *s* flea
2Sm 2:25 rallied around Abner, forming a *s* group,
19: 8 not a *s* man will remain with you overnight,
23: 8 over eight hundred slain in a *s* encounter.
1Kgs 8:56 Not a *s* word has gone unfulfilled of the
15:29 not leaving a *s* soul to Jeroboam but
16:11 sparing a *s* male relative or friend of his.
2Kgs 10:10 Know that not a *s* word which the LORD has
1Chr 11:11 hundred, whom he slew in a *s* encounter.
12:34 thousand men rallying with a *s* purpose.
23:11 as a single family, fulfilling a *s* office.
2Chr 5:13 singers were heard as a *s* voice praising
28: 6 and twenty thousand of Judah in a *s* day,
Ezr 8:15 but I could not discover a *s* Levite.
10:13 can be performed in a *s* day or even two,
Neh 3:34 they complete their restoration in a *s* day?
Tb 9: 4 If I should delay my return by a *s* day,
14: 4 *s* word of the prophecies shall prove false.
Jdt 2:13 disobey a *s* one of the orders of your lord;
7:11 thus not a *s* one of your troops will fall.
10:13 without a *s* one of his men suffering injury
12:20 he had ever drunk on one *s* day in his life.
14:18 A *s* Hebrew woman has brought disgrace on
Est 3: 7 of Mordecai's people on a *s* day,
B: 7 nether world by a violent death on a *s* day,
8:12 on a *s* day, the thirteenth of the twelfth
F: 2 not a *s* detail has been left unfulfilled
1Mc 7:46 fell by the sword; not a *s* one escaped.
8:10 Greeks a *s* general who made war on them.
9:58 he will capture all of them in a *s* night."
2Mc 2:23 we will try to condense into a *s* book.
7:20 who saw her seven sons perish in a *s* day,
Prv 17:10 A *s* reprimand does more for a man of
Eccl 9:18 and a *s* slip can ruin much that is good."
Wis 5:14 memory of the nomad camping for a *s* day.
11:20 they could have been killed at a *s* blast,
18: 5 when a *s* boy had been cast forth but saved,
18:12 all alike by a *s* death had countless dead;
18:12 since at a *s* instant their nobler
Sir 42:20 no *s* thing escapes him.
Is 10:17 his briers and his thorns in a *s* day.
21: 9 a *s* chariot, a pair of horses; He calls
47: 9 shall come to you suddenly, in a *s* day:
66: 8 one day, or a nation be born in a *s* moment?
Jer 51:60 that was to befall Babylon in a *s* book:
Ez 4: 9 in a *s* vessel and make bread out of them.
33:24 "Abraham, though but a *s* individual,
37:16 Now, son of man, take a *s* stick,
37:19 the stick of Judah, making them a *s* stick;
Dn 11:30 who forsake it he shall once more *s* out.
Am 6: 9 Should there remain ten men in a *s* house,
Jon 3: 4 and had gone but a *s* day's walk announcing,
Zec 11: 8 In a *s* month I did away with the three
Mt 5:36 (you cannot make a *s* hair white or black).
10:29 Yet not a *s* sparrow falls to the ground
18:14 Father's plan that a *s* one of these little
23:15 over sea and land to make a *s* convert,
27:14 He did not answer him on a *s* count,
Lk 4: 5 the kingdoms of the world in a *s* instant.
16:17 a *s* stroke of a letter of the law to pass.
Jn 7:21 "I have performed a *s* work and you
Rom 5:18 *s* offense brought condemnation to all men,
5:18 a *s* righteous act brought all men
1Cor 7:11 remain *s* or become reconciled to him again.
Phil 4:15 not a *s* congregation except yourselves
2Thes 3:14 *s* him out to be ostracized that he may be
Rv 18:10 In a *s* hour your doom has come!"
18:17 In a *s* hour this great wealth has been
18:19 In a *s* hour her destruction has come about!"
21:21 were twelve pearls, each made of a *s* pearl;

SINGLE-HEARTED (1)

Mt 5: 8 Blest are the *s* for they shall see God.

SINGLED (6)

Gn 18:19 I have *s* him out that he may direct his
Ex 33:16 *s* out from every other people on the earth."
Nm 16: 9 has *s* you out from the community of Israel,
Tb 1: 4 city had been *s* out of all Israel's tribes,
Jon 1: 7 So they cast lots, and thus *s* out Jonah.
1Cor 1:27 he *s* out the weak of this world to shame

SINGS (2)

Sir 24: 1 Wisdom *s* her own praises,
Zep 3:18 because of you, as one *s* at festivals.

SINGULAR (3)

Est B: 5 that this most *s* people is continually at
Ps(s) 71:16 O GOD, I will tell of your *s* justice.
Is 28:21 Gibeon, To carry out his work, his *s* work,

SINITE (1)

1Chr 1:15 the Hivite, the Arkite, the *S*,

SINITES (1)

Gn 10:17 the Hivites, the Arkites, the *S*,

SINK (11)

Dt 28:43 above you, while you *s* lower and lower.
Ps(s) 69:15 Rescue me out of the mire; may I not *s*!
139: 8 if I *s* to the nether world,
Prv 18: 8 morsels that *s* into one's inmost being.
26:22 morsels that *s* into one's inmost being.
Is 10: 4 Lest it *s* beneath the captive or fall
Jer 4:31 I *s* exhausted before the slayers!"
14: 2 Her people *s* down in mourning:
43: 9 Take with you large stones and *s* them in
51:64 Thus shall Babylon *s*.
Mt 14:30 frightened, he began to *s* and cried out,

SINKING (1)

1Mc 6:10 my eyes, for my heart is *s* with anxiety.

SINKS (1)

Prv 2:18 For her path *s* down to death,

SINLESS (2)

Jb 34: 6 my wound the arrow rankles, *s* though I am."
Ps(s) 24: 4 He whose hands are *s*,

SINNED (100)

Ex 9:27 Aaron and said to them, "I have *s* again!
9:34 and hail and thunder had ceased, *s* again:
10:16 and said, "I have *s* against the LORD,
32:33 *s* against me will I strike out of my book.
Nm 15:28 the LORD for him who *s* inadvertently;
21: 7 *s* in complaining against the LORD and you.
22:34 said to the angel of the LORD, "I have *s*.
Dt 1:41 said to me, 'We have *s* against the LORD.
9:16 I saw how you had *s* against the LORD,
Jos 7:11 Israel has *s*:
7:20 Joshua, "I have indeed *s* against the LORD,
Jgs 10:10 out to the LORD, "We have *s* against you;
10:15 Israelites said to the LORD, "We have *s*.
11:27 I have not *s* against you,
1Sm 2:17 *s* grievously in the presence of the LORD;
7: 6 confessing, "We have *s* against the LORD.
12:10 'We have *s* in forsaking the LORD and
15:24 "I have *s*, for I have disobeyed the
15:30 "I have *s*, yet honor me now before
2Sm 12:13 to Nathan, "I have *s* against the LORD."
24:10 "I have *s* grievously in what I have done.
24:17 "It is I who have *s*; it is I, the shepherd,
1Kgs 8:35 have *s* against you and you afflict them,
8:47 captors and say, 'We have *s* and done wrong;
2Kgs 17: 7 because the Israelites *s* against the LORD,
1Chr 21: 8 "I have *s* greatly in doing this thing.
21:17 I am the one who *s*, I did this wicked
2Chr 6:24 When your people Israel have *s* against you
6:26 no rain, because they have *s* against you,
6:37 and say, 'We have *s* and done wrong;
6:39 Forgive your people who have *s* against you.
Ezr 10:13 of us who have *s* in this regard are many.
Neh 9:29 they *s* against your ordinances,
Tb 3: 4 "They *s* against you, and disobeyed
Est C:17 But now we have *s* in your sight,
2Mc 7:18 account, because we have *s* against our God;
Jb 1: 5 have *s* and blasphemed God in their hearts."
7:20 Though I have *s*, what can I do to you,
8: 4 If your children have *s* against him and he
33:27 before men and say, "I *s* and did wrong,
34:32 Teach me wherein I have *s*;
35: 3 what advantage have I more than if I had *s*?"
Ps(s) 41: 5 heal me, though I have *s* against you.
51: 6 "Against you only have I *s*,
78:17 But they *s* yet more against him,
78:32 Yet for all this they *s* still more and
106: 6 We have *s*, we and our fathers;
Sir 5: 4 "I have *s*, yet what has befallen me?"
18:20 when you have *s*, show repentance.
19:15 who has not *s* with his tongue?
21: 1 My son, if you have *s*, do so no more,
31:10 He could have *s* but did not,
Is 42:24 it not the LORD, against whom we have *s*?
43:27 Your first father *s*; your spokesmen
Jer 2:35 you on that word of yours, "I have not *s*."
3: 1 But you have *s* with many lovers,
3:25 cover us, for we have *s* against the LORD,
8:14 drink, because we have *s* against the LORD.
14: 7 are many, though we have *s* against you.
14:20 that we have *s* against you.
33: 8 by which they *s* and rebelled against me,
40: 3 because you *s* against the LORD and did not
44:23 you burned incense and *s* against the LORD,
50: 7 no guilt, Because they *s* against the LORD,
50:15 for she *s* against the LORD.
Lam 3:42 We have *s* and rebelled;
5: 7 Our fathers, who *s*, are no more; but we
5:16 woe to us, for we have *s*!
Bar 1:13 for we have *s* against the Lord,
1:17 *s* in the Lord's sight and disobeyed him.
2: 5 raised up, because we *s* against the Lord,
2:12 we have *s*, been impious, and violated,
2:33 of their fathers who *s* against the Lord.
3: 2 have mercy on us, who have *s* against you:
3: 4 few, the sons of those who *s* against you;
3: 7 of our fathers who *s* against you.
Ez 3:21 man not to sin, and he has in fact not *s*,
28:16 violence was your business, and you *s*.
45:20 have *s* through inadvertence or ignorance;
Dn 3:29 *s* and transgressed by departing from you,
9: 5 We have *s*, been wicked and done evil;
9: 8 and our fathers, for having *s* against you.
9:15 for yourself even to this day, we have *s*,
Hos 7:13 Ruin to them, they have *s* against me!
8: 1 violated my covenant, and *s* against my law,
10: 9 Since the days of Gibeah you have *s*,
13: 1 but he *s* through Baal and died.
Mi 7: 9 I will endure because I have *s* against him,
Zep 1:17 because they have *s* against the LORD;
Lk 15:18 I have *s* against God and against you;
15:21 I have *s* against God and against you;
Rom 3:23 *s* and are deprived of the glory of God.
5:12 thus coming to all men inasmuch as all *s*—
5:14 not *s* by breaking a precept as did Adam,
2Cor 12:21 who *s* earlier and have not repented
13: 2 to those who *s* before and to all the rest,
Heb 3:17 Was it not those who had *s*,
4:15 in every way that we are, yet never *s*.
2Pt 2: 4 Did God spare even the angels who *s*?
1Jn 1:10 If we say, "We have never *s*,"

SINNER (35)

1Mc 2:48 of the kings and did not let the *s* triumph.
Prv 11:31 earth, how much more the wicked and the *s*!
13:22 wealth of the *s* is stored up for the just.
Eccl 2:26 but to the *s* he gives the task of
7:26 her, but the *s* will be entrapped by her.
8:12 *s* does evil a hundred times and survives.
9: 2 is for the good man, so it is for the *s*;
Sir 1:22 of the LORD is an abomination to the *s*.
2:12 hands, to the *s* who treads a double path!
3:26 a *s* will heap sin upon sin.
8: 5 Shame not a repentant *s*;
8:10 time of need, Kindle not the coals of a *s*,
10:22 wise but poor, nor proper to honor any *s*.
12: 4 Give to the good man, refuse the *s*;

SINNER (cont.)

13:16 So it is with the *s* and the just.
23: 8 Through his lips is the *s* ensnared;
25:18 may she fall to the lot of the *s!*
27:30 hateful things, yet the *s* hugs them tight.
29:19 The *s* through surety comes to grief,
32:17 The *s* turns aside reproof and distorts the
38:15 He who is a *s* toward his Maker will be
47:23 remembered, the *s* who led Israel into sin,
Lk 7:37 A woman known in the town to be a *s*
7:39 that she is a *s.*"
15: 7 more joy in heaven over one repentant *s*
15:10 the angels of God over one repentant *s.*"
18:13 and say, 'O God, be merciful to me, a *s.*'
Jn 9:16 Others objected, "If a man is a *s,*
9:24 First of all, we know this man is a *s.*"
9:25 "I do not know whether his is a *s* or not,"
Rom 3: 7 his glory, why must I be condemned as a *s?*
Jas 5:20 the person who brings a *s* back from his
1Pt 4:18 what is to become of the godless and the *s?*
1Jn 3: 8 the devil is a *s* from the beginning.
5:16 God, and thus life will be given to the *s.*

SINNERS (68)

Nm 17: 3 for these *s* have consecrated the censers
32:14 And now here you are, a brood of *s,*
Tb 4:17 the virtuous, but do not share them with *s.*
13: 6 "Turn back, you *s!*
1Mc 2:44 They gathered an army and struck down *s* in
2Mc 6:13 a sign of great kindness to punish *s*
12:23 putting the *s* to the sword and destroying
Ps(s) 1: 1 of the wicked Nor walks in the way of *s,*
1: 5 the wicked shall not stand, nor shall *s,*
25: 8 thus he shows *s* the way.
26: 9 Gather not my soul with those of *s,*
37:38 *S* shall all alike be destroyed;
51:15 your ways, and *s* shall return to you.
104:35 May *s* cease from the earth,
119:95 *S* wait to destroy me,
119:155 Far from *s* is salvation,
Prv 1:10 My son, should *s* entice you,
13:21 Misfortune pursues *s,*
23:17 Let not your heart emulate *s,*
Wis 4:10 he who lived among *s* was transported
14:31 but the retribution of *s* ever follows upon
19:13 And the punishments came upon the *s* only
Sir 9:11 Envy not a *s* fame,
11:16 were formed with *s* from their birth,
11:21 Admire not how *s* live,
12: 7 The Most High himself hates *s,*
15: 9 Unseemly is praise on a *s* lips,
19:18 nor is there prudence in the counsel of *s.*
21: 6 He who hates correction walks the *s* path,
21:10 The path of *s* is smooth stones that end in
33:14 life, so are *s* in contrast with the just;
40: 8 and with beast, but for *s* seven times more.
41: 5 A reprobate line are the children of *s,*
41: 6 Their dominion is lost to *s'* children,
Is 1:28 Rebels and *s* alike shall be crushed,
13: 9 waste the land and destroy the *s* within it!
33:14 On Zion *s* are in dread,
Dn 8:23 reign, when *s* have reached their measure,
Hos 14:10 them the just walk, but *s* stumble in them.
Am 9:10 the sword shall all *s* among my people die,
Mt 9:10 those known as *s* came to join Jesus
9:13 to call, not the self-righteous, but *s.*"
Mk 2:15 *s* joined him and his disciples at dinner.
2:17 I have come to call *s,*
16:20 sake of *s* that I was handed over to death,
Lk 5:32 self-righteous to a change of heart, but *s.*"
6:32 Even *s* love those who love them.
6:33 *S* do as much.
6:34 Even *s* lend to sinners,
7:34 drunkard, a friend of tax collectors and *s!*'
13: 2 Galileans were the greatest *s* in Galilee
15: 1 *s* were all gathering around to hear him,
15: 2 "This man welcomes *s* and eats with them."
19: 7 "He has gone to a *s* house as a guest."
Jn 9:31 We know that God does not hear *s,*
Rom 2:12 *S* who do not have the law will perish
2:12 *s* bound by the law will be judged in
5: 8 that while we were still *s,*
5:19 one man's disobedience all became *s,*
Gal 2:15 are Jews by birth, not *s* of Gentile origin.
2:17 justified in Christ, we are shown to be *s,*
1Tm 1:15 Christ Jesus came into the world to save *s.*
Heb 5: 2 is able to deal patiently with erring *s,*
7:26 innocent, undefiled, separated from *s,*
12: 3 how he endured the opposition of *s;*
Jas 4: 8 Cleanse your hands, you *s;*
Jude 1:15 and convicting those godless *s* of every

SINNING (10)

Gn 20: 6 it was I who kept you from *s* against me;
1Sm 14:33 Informed that the people were *s* against
Jdt 5:20 are at fault, and are *s* against their God,
Wis 15:13 this man more than any knows that he is *s,*
Sir 19:24 his lack of strength keeps him from *s,*
Jer 33: 8 the guilt they incurred by *s* against me;
1Cor 8:12 weak consciences, you are *s* against Christ.
15:33 Return to reason, as you ought, and stop *s.*
1Jn 5:16 Anyone who sees his brother *s,*
Rv 18: 4 for fear of *s* with her and sharing the

SINS (268)

Gn 13:13 in the *s* they committed against the LORD.
Ex 34: 9 yet pardon our wickedness and *s,*
Lv 4: 3 if it is the anointed priest who thus *s*
16:30 be cleansed of all your *s* before the LORD,
16:34 be made for all the *s* of the Israelites."
26:18 the chastisement for your *s* sevenfold,
26:21 blows another sevenfold, as your *s* deserve.
26:24 for your *s* seven times harder than before.
26:28 sevenfold fiercer punishment for your *s,*
Nm 15:27 if it is an individual who *s* inadvertently,
15:29 but one law for him who *s* inadvertently,
15:30 "But anyone who *s* defiantly,
16:26 will be swept away because of all their *s.*"
Jos 24:19 not forgive your transgressions or your *s.*
1Sm 2:25 If a man *s* against another man,
2:25 but if a man *s* against the LORD,
12:19 our other *s* the evil of asking for a king."
1Kgs 8:31 "If a man *s* against his neighbor and is
8:50 Forgive your people their *s* and all the
14:16 He will give up Israel because of the *s*
14:22 and by their *s* angered him even more than
15: 3 the *s* his father had committed before him,
15:30 because of the *s* Jeroboam committed and
16: 2 to sin, provoking me to anger by their *s,*
16:13 because of all the *s* which Baasha and his
16:19 He died because of the *s* he had committed,
16:31 for him to imitate the *s* of Jeroboam,
2Kgs 10:29 did not desist from the *s* which Jeroboam,
10:31 *s* which Jeroboam caused Israel to commit.
13: 6 they did not desist from the *s* which
13:11 desist from any of the *s* which Jeroboam,
14:24 desist from any of the *s* which Jeroboam,
15: 9 did not desist from the *s* which Jeroboam,
15:18 not desisting from the *s* which Jeroboam,
15:24 not desisting from the *s* which Jeroboam,
15:28 not desisting from the *s* which Jeroboam,
17:22 Jeroboam in all the *s* he committed,
24: 3 for the *s* Manasseh had committed in all
2Chr 6:22 "When any man *s* against his neighbor and is
7:14 and pardon their *s* and revive their land.
28:13 the LORD and increase our *s* and our guilt.
33:19 was heard, all his *s* and his infidelity,
Ezr 9:15 Here we are before you in our *s.*
Neh 1: 6 confessing the *s* which we of Israel have
9: 2 *s* and the guilty deeds of their fathers.
9:37 whom you set over us because of our *s,*
Tb 3: 3 Punish me not for my *s,*
3: 5 me as my *s* and those of my fathers deserve.
Jdt 7:28 us for our *s* and those of our forefathers,
2Mc 5:17 because of the *s* of the city's inhabitants
5:18 had not become entangled in so many *s,*
6:14 measure of their *s* before he punishes them;
6:15 when our *s* have reached their fullness.
7:32 We, indeed, are suffering because of our *s.*
13: 8 committed so many *s* against the altar
Jb 10: 6 for guilt in me and search after my *s,*
13:23 What are my faults and my *s?*
13:23 My misdeeds and my *s* make known to me!
31:33 hidden my *s* and buried my guilt in my
36: 9 have done and their *s* of boastful pride.
Ps(s) 5:11 For their many *s,* cast them out because
25: 7 The *s* of my youth and my frailties
25:18 and my suffering, and take away all my *s.*
39: 9 From all my *s* deliver me;
40:13 my *s* so overcome me that I cannot see;
51:11 Turn away your face from my *s,*
65: 4 We are overcome by our *s;*
79: 9 us and pardon our *s* for your name's sake.
85: 3 you have covered all their *s.*
90: 8 our hidden *s* in the light of your scrutiny.
103:10 according to our *s* does he deal with us,
107:17 ways and afflicted because of their *s,*
Prv 14:21 He *s* who despises the hungry;
28:13 He who conceals his *s* prospers not,
29:22 and a hotheaded man is the cause of many *s.*
Wis 4:20 they come, at the counting up of their *s,*
11:16 by the very things through which he *s.*
11:23 overlook the *s* of men that they may repent.
12: 2 remind them of the *s* they are committing,
12:11 anyone did you grant amnesty for their *s.*
12:19 you would permit repentance for their *s.*
17: 3 For they who supposed their secret *s* were
Sir 2:11 he forgives *s,* he saves in time of trouble.
3: 3 He who honors his father atones for *s;*
3:15 warmth upon frost it will melt away your *s.*
3:29 a flaming fire, and alms atone for *s.*
5: 6 my many *s* he will forgive."
12:14 of the proud man, who is involved in his *s:*
17:16 all of their *s* are before the LORD.
18:21 Delay not to forsake *s,*
19: 4 strays after them *s* against his own life.
21: 1 and for your past *s* pray to be forgiven.
23: 2 spared, nor the *s* of my heart overlooked;
23: 3 failings increase, and my *s* be multiplied;
23:16 Two types of men multiply *s,*
23:16 A man given to *s* of the flesh,
25: 8 Happy is he who *s* not with his tongue,
25:23 In woman was *s* beginning,
27:10 in wait for prey, so do *s* for evildoers.
28: 1 for he remembers their *s* in detail.
28: 2 when you pray, your own *s* will be forgiven.
28: 4 his fellows, yet seek pardon for his own *s?*
28: 5 cherishes wrath, who will forgive his *s?*
28: 8 Avoid strife and your *s* will be fewer,
34:19 many sacrifices does he forgive their *s.*
34:26 So with a man who fasts for his *s,*
39: 6 lips in prayer, to ask pardon for his *s.*
47:11 him his *s* and exalted his strength forever;
48:15 not repent, nor did they give up their *s,*
Is 1:18 Though your *s* be like scarlet,
38:17 When you cast behind your back all my *s.*
40: 2 the hand of the LORD double for all her *s.*
43:24 Instead, you burdened me with your *s,*
43:25 your *s* I remember no more.
44:22 offenses like a cloud, your *s* like a mist;
50: 1 It was for your *s* that you were sold,
53: 5 for our offenses, crushed for our *s;*
53:12 And he shall take away the *s* of many,
58: 1 and the house of Jacob their *s.*
59: 2 It is your *s* that make him hide his face
59:12 are many, our *s* bear witness against us.
Jer 5:25 your *s* have turned back these blessings
14:10 their guilt, and will punish their *s.*
17: 3 for all your *s* throughout your borders,
30:15 of your great guilt, your numerous *s,*
50:20 but it shall be no more, and Judah's *s,*
Lam 1: 5 The LORD has punished her for her many *s.*
1:14 "He has kept watch over my *s;*
1:22 As you have dealt with me for all my *s;*
3:39 complain, any mortal, in the face of his *s?*
4:13 Because of the *s* of her prophets and the
4:22 he will punish, he will lay bare your *s.*
Bar 4:12 the *s* of my children I am left desolate,
6: 1 For the *s* you committed before God,
Ez 4: 4 the *s* of the house of Israel upon you.
4: 4 as you lie thus, you shall bear their *s.*
4: 5 *s* I allot you the same number of days,
4: 5 you will bear the *s* of the house of Israel.
4: 6 the *s* of the house of Judah forty days;
4:17 terror and waste away because of his *s.*
7:13 Because of his *s,* no one shall preserve
7:16 them all to death, each one for his own *s.*
9: 9 The *s* of the house of Israel are great
14:11 may no longer be defiled by all their *s.*
14:13 when a land *s* against me by breaking faith,
16:51 Samaria did not commit half your *s!*
18: 4 only the one who *s* shall die.
18:14 who, seeing all the *s* his father commits,
18:17 one shall not die for the *s* of his father,
18:18 his people, shall in truth die for his *s.*
18:20 Only the one who *s* shall die.
18:21 man turns away from all the *s* he committed,
18:28 away from all the *s* which he committed,
23:49 and you shall pay for your *s* of idolatry.
24:23 because of your *s* and groan one to another.
33:10 say, "Our crimes and our *s* weigh us down;
33:12 will not save him on the day that he *s;*
33:12 [nor can the virtuous man, when he *s,*
33:16 *s* he committed shall be held against him;
36:31 for your *s* and your abominations.
37:23 deliver them from all their *s* of apostasy,
39:23 its *s* the house of Israel went into exile;
43:10 [that they may be ashamed of their *s,*
Dn 3:28 you have done all this because of our *s;*
3:37 in the world this day because of our *s.*
4:24 atone for your *s* by good deeds,
9:11 of God, was poured out over us for our *s.*
9:16 of our *s* and the crimes of our fathers,
13:52 Now have your past *s* come to term:
Hos 8:13 remember their guilt and punish their *s;*
9: 9 remember their iniquity and punish their *s.*
Am 5:12 many are your crimes, how grievous your *s:*
Mi 1: 5 pass, and for the *s* of the house of Israel.
3: 8 to Jacob his crimes and to Israel his *s.*
6:13 you with devastation because of your *s.*
7:19 cast into the depths of the sea all our *s;*
Mt 1:21 he will save his people from their *s.*"
3: 6 the Jordan River as they confessed their *s.*
7:11 If you, with all your *s,*
9: 2 "Have courage, son, your *s* are forgiven."
9: 5 *s* are forgiven' or 'Stand up and walk'?
9: 6 Man has authority on earth to forgive *s*—
26:28 in behalf of many for the forgiveness of *s.*
Mk 1: 4 which led to the forgiveness of *s.*
1: 5 the Jordan River as they confessed their *s.*
2: 5 man, "My son, your *s* are forgiven."
2: 7 Who can forgive *s* except God alone?"
2: 9 say to the paralytic, 'Your *s* are forgiven,'
2:10 forgive *s*" (he said to the paralyzed man),
Lk 1:77 of salvation in freedom from their *s,*
3: 3 which led to the forgiveness of *s,*
5:20 said, "My friend, your *s* are forgiven you."
5:21 Who can forgive *s* but God alone?"
5:23 to say, 'Your *s* are forgiven you,'
5:24 of Man has authority on earth to forgive *s*—
7:47 you, that is why her many *s* are forgiven
7:48 said to her then, "Your *s* are forgiven";
7:49 "Who is this that he even forgives *s?*"
11: 4 *s* for we too forgive all who do us wrong;
11:13 If you, with all your *s,*
17: 4 If he *s* against you seven times a day,
24:47 of *s* is to be preached to all the nations,

Jn 5:14 Give up your *s* so that something worse may
8:21 look for me but you will die in your *s.*
8:24 That is why I said you would die in your *s.*
8:24 *s* unless you come to believe that I AM."
20:23 If you forgive men's *s,* they are forgiven
Acts 2:38 Jesus Christ, that your *s* may be forgiven;
3:19 Turn to God, that your *s* may be wiped away!
5:31 repentance to Israel and forgiveness of *s.*
10:43 him has forgiveness of *s* through his name."
13:38 of *s* is being proclaimed to you,
22:16 wash away your *s* as you call upon his name.'
26:18 their *s* and a portion among God's people.'
Rom 3:25 sake of remitting *s* committed in the past
4: 7 are forgiven, whose *s* are covered over.
4:25 our *s* and raised up for our justification.
11:27 make with them when I take away their *s.*"
1Cor 6:18 but the fornicator *s* against his own body.
11:27 *s* against the body and blood of the Lord.
15: 3 our *s* in accordance with the Scriptures;
15:17 You are still in your *s,*
Gal 1: 4 Jesus Christ, who gave himself for our *s,*
Eph 1: 7 we have been redeemed and our *s* forgiven,
2: 1 were dead because of your *s* and offenses,
5: 6 These are *s* that bring God's wrath down on
Col 1:14 have redemption, the forgiveness of our *s.*
2:13 He pardoned all our *s.*
3: 6 These are the *s* which provoke God's wrath.
3: 7 sort, when these *s* were your very life.
1Thes 2:16 have been "filling up their quota of *s,*"
1Tm 5:24 Some men's *s* are flagrant and cry out for
5:24 while other men's *s* will appear only later.
2Tm 3: 6 with *s* and driven by desires of many kinds,
Heb 1: 3 When he had cleansed us from our *s,*
2:17 behalf, to expiate the *s* of the people.
5: 1 God, to offer gifts and sacrifices for *s.*
7:27 his own *s* and then for those of the people;
8:12 and their *s* I will remember no more."
9: 7 for himself and for the *s* of the people.
9:26 take away *s* once for all by his sacrifice.
9:28 offered up once to take away the *s* of many;
10: 3 there came only a yearly recalling of *s,*
10: 4 blood of bulls and goats to take *s* away.
10:11 sacrifices which can never take away *s.*
10:12 But Jesus offered one sacrifice for *s* and
10:17 "Their *s* and their transgressions I will
Jas 4:17 right thing to do and does not do it, he *s.*
5:15 If he has committed any *s,*
5:16 Hence, declare your *s* to one another,
5:20 from death and cancel a multitude of *s.*
1Pt 2:24 own body he brought your *s* to the cross,
3:18 reason why Christ died for *s* once for all,
4: 8 constant, for love covers a multitude of *s.*
2Pt 1: 9 forgets the cleansing of his long-past *s.*
1Jn 1: 9 But if we acknowledge our *s,*
1: 9 our *s* and cleanse us from every wrong.
2: 2 He is an offering for our *s,*
2: 2 for our sins, and not for our *s* only,
2:12 through his Name your *s* have been forgiven.
3: 4 Everyone who *s* acts lawlessly,
3: 5 he revealed himself was to take away *s;*
3: 6 man who *s* has not seen him or known him.
3: 8 The man who *s* belongs to the devil,
4:10 has sent his Son as an offering for our *s.*
Rv 1: 5 and freed us from our *s* by his own blood,
2:22 unless they repent of their *s* with her,
18: 5 For her *s* have piled up as high as heaven,

SION (1)

Dt 4:48 Wadi Arnon to Mount *S* (that is Hermon)

SIP (1)

Gn 24:17 give me a *s* of water from your jug."

SIPHMOTH (1)

1Sm 30:28 Jattir, to those in Aroer, to those in *S,*

SIPPAI (1)

1Chr 20: 4 that time, Sibbecai the Hushathite slew *S,*

SIR (37)

Gn 18: 3 *S,* if I may ask you this favor,
23: 5 "Please, *s,* listen to us!
23:11 "Please, *s,* listen to me!
23:15 *s,* listen to me!
24:18 "Take a drink, *s,*" she replied, and quickly
43:20 "If you please, *s,*" they said, "we came
Jdt 7: 9 *S,* listen to what we have to say,
7:11 Therefore, *s,* do not attack them
Dn 14:35 But Habakkuk answered, "Babylon, *s,*
Mt 8: 2 and did him homage, saying to him, *S,*
8: 6 *S,* my serving boy is at home in bed
8: 8 *S,*" the centurion said in reply,
13:27 owner's slaves came to him and said, *S,*
21:29 The son replied, 'I am on my way, *s*';
27:63 *S,*" they said, "we have recalled that
Lk 7: 6 *S,* do not trouble yourself,
13: 8 In answer, the man said, *S,*
13:25 you stand outside knocking and saying, *S,*
22:58 But Peter said, "No, *s,* not I!"
Jn 4:11 *S,*" she challenged him, "you do not have
4:15 said to him, "Give me this water, *s,*
4:19 *S,*" answered the woman, "I can see you
4:49 *S,*" the royal official pleaded with him,
5: 7 *S,*" the sick man answered,
6:34 *S,* give us this bread always,"
8:11 "No one, *s,*" she answered.
9:36 He answered, "Who is he, *s,*
12:21 *S,* we should like to see Jesus."
20:15 he was the gardener, so she said, *S,*
Acts 9: 5 "Who are you, *s?*"
10: 4 sight and said in fear, "What is it, *s?*"
10:14 *S,* it is unthinkable!
11: 8 'Not for a moment, *s!*
22: 8 I answered, 'Who are you, *s?*'
22:10 'What is it I must do, *s?*'
26:15 I said, at that, 'Who are you, *s?*'
Rv 7:14 I said to him, *S,* you should know better

SIRACH (1)

Sir 50:27 book, I, Jesus, son of Eleazar, son of *S,*

SIRAH (1)

2Sm 3:26 who brought him back from the cistern of *S.*

SIRION (3)

Dt 3: 9 Mount Hermon [which is called *S*
1Chr 5:16 all the pasture lands of *S* to the borders.
Ps(s) 29: 6 leap like a calf and *S* like a young bull.

SISERA (21)

Jgs 4: 2 The general of his army was *S,*
4: 7 I will lead *S,* the general of Jabin's army,
4: 9 will have *S* fall into the power of a woman."
4:12 It was reported to *S* that Barak,
4:13 So *S* assembled from Harosheth-ha-goiim at
4:14 the LORD has delivered *S* into your power.
4:15 And the LORD put *S* and all his chariots
4:15 *S* himself dismounted from his chariot and
4:16 entire army of *S* fell beneath the sword,
4:17 *S,* in the meantime, had fled on foot
4:18 Jael went out to meet *S* and said to him,
4:21 While *S* was sound asleep,
4:22 Then when Barak came in pursuit of *S,*
4:22 he went in with her, and there lay *S* dead,
5:20 from their courses they fought against *S.*
5:26 She hammered *S,* crushed his head;
5:28 peered down and wailed the mother of *S,*
1Sm 12: 9 them to fall into the clutches of *S,*
Ezr 2:53 sons of Harsha, sons of Barkos, sons of *S,*
Neh 7:55 sons of Harsha, sons of Barkos, sons of *S,*
Ps(s) 83:10 as with *S* and Jabin at the torrent Kishon,

SISERA'S (1)

Jgs 5:30 each man, Spoils of dyed cloth as *S* spoil,

SISMAI (2)

1Chr 2:40 Eleasah became the father of *S.*
2:40 *S* became the father of Shallum.

SISTER (105)

Gn 4:22 The *s* of Tubalcain was Naamah.
12:13 Please say, therefore, that you are my *s,*
12:19 Why did you say, 'She is my *s,*'
20: 2 he said of his wife Sarah, "She is my *s.*"
20: 5 He himself told me, 'She is my *s,*'
20:12 Besides, she is in truth my *s,*
24:30 ring and the bracelets on his *s* Rebekah
24:59 *s* Rebekah and her nurse to take leave,
24:60 *S,* may you grow into thousands of myriads;
25:20 and the *s* of Laban the Aramean.
26: 7 about his wife, he answered, "She is my *s.*"
26: 9 How could you have said, 'She is my *s'?*"
28: 9 Abraham's son Ishmael and *s* of Nebaioth.
30: 1 to Jacob, she became envious of her *s.*
30: 8 engaged in a fateful struggle with my *s,*
34:13 did because their *s* Dinah had been defiled.
34:14 "as to give our *s* to an uncircumcised man;
34:27 in reprisal for their *s* Dinah's defilement.
34:31 our *s* have been treated like a harlot?"
36: 3 daughter of Ishmael and *s* of Nebaioth.
36:22 Hori and Hemam, and Lotan's *s* was Timna.
46:17 Ishvi, and Beriah, with their *s* Serah;
Ex 2: 4 His *s* stationed herself at a distance to
2: 7 Then his *s* asked Pharaoh's daughter,
6:23 daughter, Elisheba, the *s* of Nahshon;
15:20 The prophetess Miriam, Aaron's *s,*
Lv 18: 9 shall not have intercourse with your *s,*
18:11 bore to him, since she, too, is your *s.*
18:12 not have intercourse with your father's *s,*
18:13 not have intercourse with your mother's *s,*
18:18 you shall not marry her *s* as her rival;
20:17 marriage with her *s* of his half-sister,
20:17 of having had intercourse with his own *s.*
20:19 your mother's sister or your father's *s;*
21: 3 or daughter, his brother or his maiden *s,*
21: 4 But for a *s* who has married out of his
Nm 6: 7 for his father or mother, his *s* or brother,
26:59 bore Aaron and Moses and their *s* Miriam.
Dt 27:22 relations with his *s* or his half-sister!'
Jgs 15: 2 Her younger *s* is more beautiful than she;
2Sm 13: 1 son Absalom had a beautiful *s* named Tamar,
13: 2 over his *s* Tamar that he became sick;
13: 4 in love with Tamar, my brother Absalom's *s.*"
13: 5 *s* Tamar come and encourage me to take food.
13: 6 "Please let my *s* Tamar come and prepare
13:11 Lie with me, my *s!*"
13:20 Be still now, my *s;* he is your brother.
13:22 he hated him for having shamed his *s* Tamar.
13:32 this ever since Amnon shamed his *s* Tamar.
17:25 of Jesse and *s* of Joab's mother Zeruiah.
1Kgs 11:19 him in marriage the *s* of Queen Tahpenes,
11:20 Tahpenes' *s* bore Hadad a son, Genubath.
2Kgs 8:18 of Ahab, since the *s* of Ahab was his wife;
11: 2 daughter of King Jehoram and *s* of Ahaziah,
1Chr 1:39 Timna was the *s* of Lotan.
3: 9 and Tamar was their *s.*
3:19 Shelomith was their *s.*
4: 3 their *s* was named Hazzelelponi.
4:19 sons of his Jewish wife, the *s* of Naham,
7:18 His *s* Molecheth bore Ishhod,
7:30 their *s* was Serah.
7:32 Japhlet, Shomer, Hotham, and their *s* Shua.
2Chr 22:11 daughter of King Jehoram, a *s* of Ahaziah,
Jb 17:14 and the maggot "my mother" and "my *s,*"
Prv 7: 4 Say to Wisdom, "You are my *s!*"
Sg 4: 9 You have ravished my heart, my *s,*
4:10 How beautiful is your love, my *s,*
4:12 You are an enclosed garden, my *s,*
5: 1 I have come to my garden, my *s,*
5: 2 "Open to me, my *s,*
8: 8 *s* is little and she has no breasts as yet.
8: 8 we do for our *s* when her courtship begins?
Jer 3: 7 even though her traitor *s* Judah saw that
3: 8 her traitor *s* Judah was not frightened;
3:10 the traitor *s* Judah did not return to me
22:18 *s.*" They shall not lament him,
Ez 16:45 and you are a true *s* to those who spurned
16:46 elder *s* was Samaria with her daughters,
16:46 and your younger *s,*
16:48 the Lord GOD, I swear that your *s* Sodom,
16:49 And look at the guilt of your *s* Sodom:
16:56 Was not your *s* Sodom kept in bad repute by
23: 4 elder, and the name of her *s* was Oholibah.
23:11 Though her *s* Oholibah saw all this,
23:18 her as I had become disgusted with her *s.*
23:31 Because you followed in the path of your *s,*
23:32 The cup of your *s* you shall drink,
23:33 grief, a cup of dismay, the cup of your *s.*
44:25 son, daughter, brother, or maiden *s;*
Mt 12:50 Father is brother and *s* and mother to me."
Mk 3:35 of God is brother and *s* and mother to me."
Lk 10:39 She had a *s* named Mary,
10:40 are you not concerned that my *s* has left
Jn 11: 1 the village of Mary and her *s* Martha.
11: 5 Martha and her *s* and Lazarus very much.
11:28 this she went back and called her *s* Mary.
11:39 Martha, the dead man's *s,*
19:25 there stood his mother, his mother's *s,*
Acts 23:16 The son of Paul's *s* heard about the plot,
Rom 16: 1 I commend to you our *s* Phoebe,
16:15 Philologus and Julia, to Nereus and his *s,*
Phlm 1: 2 fellow worker Philemon, to Apphia our *s,*
Jas 2:15 If a brother or *s* has nothing to wear and
2Jn 1:13 of your elect *s* send you their greetings.

SISTER-IN-LAW (3)

Dt 25: 9 'I am not willing to marry her,' his *s,*
Ru 1:15 *s* has gone back to her people and her god.
1:15 Go back after your *s!*"

SISTERS—SISTER'S (23)

Gn 29:13 Laban heard the news about his *s* son Jacob,
Jos 2:13 my father and mother, brothers and *s,*
1Chr 2:16 Their *s* were Zeruiah and Abigail.
7:15 his *s* name was Molecheth.
Jb 1: 4 their three *s* to eat and drink with them.
42:11 all his brethren and his *s* came to him,
Ez 16:51 and have even made your *s* appear just,
16:52 you are an argument in favor of your *s!*
16:52 shame of having made your *s* appear just.
16:55 Yes, your *s,* Sodom and her daughters,
16:61 conduct and be ashamed when I take your *s,*
22:11 by incest, men who coerce their *s,*
23:11 her lust was more depraved than her *s,*
Hos 2: 3 to your brothers, "Ammi," and to your *s,*
Mt 13:56 Aren't his *s* our neighbors?
19:29 who has given up home, brothers or *s,*
Mk 3:32 brothers and *s* are outside asking for you."
6: 3 Are not his *s* our neighbors here?"
10:29 one who has given up home, brothers or *s,*
10:30 times as many homes, brothers and *s,*
Lk 14:26 wife and his children, his brothers and *s,*
Jn 11: 3 The *s* sent word to Jesus to inform him,
1Tm 5: 2 women as mothers, and younger women as *s,*

SISTRUMS (2)

1Sm 18: 6 with tambourines, joyful songs, and *s.*
2Sm 6: 5 harps, tambourines, *s* and cymbals.

SIT (94)

Gn 27:19 Please *s* up and eat some of my game,

SIT (cont.)

Ex 17:12 they put a rock in place for him to *s* on.
18:14 Why do you *s* alone while all the people
Jgs 4: 5 She used to *s* under Deborah's palm tree,
Ru 4: 1 to him by name, "Come and *s* beside me!"
4: 2 of the city and asked them to *s* nearby.
1Kgs 1:13 king after me and shall *s* upon my throne?
1:17 reign after you and *s* upon your throne.
1:20 *s* on the throne after your royal majesty.
1:24 is to reign after you and *s* on your throne?
1:30 and should *s* upon my throne in my place."
1:35 and *s* upon my throne and reign in my place.
8:20 father David and *s* on the throne of Israel,
8:25 to *s* before me on the throne of Israel,
2Kgs 7: 3 "Why should we *s* here until we die?
10:30 shall *s* upon the throne of Israel."
15:12 shall *s* upon the throne of Israel,"
19:27 I am aware whether you stand or *s*;
1Chr 28: 5 *s* on the LORD'S royal throne over Israel.
2Chr 6:16 to *s* before me on the throne of Israel,
1Mc 2: 7 and to *s* idle while it is given into the
Ps(s) 50:20 You *s* speaking against your brother;
61: 8 Let him *s* enthroned before God forever;
69:13 They who *s* at the gate gossip about me,
110: 1 *S* at my right hand till I make your
132:12 too, forever shall *s* upon your throne."
139: 2 you know when I *s* and when I stand;
Prv 23: 1 When you *s* down to dine with a ruler,
Eccl 10: 6 position while the rich *s* in lowly places.
Sir 12:12 Let him not *s* at your right hand,
23:14 in mind when you *s* among the mighty,
32: 1 Take care of them first before you *s* down;
Is 16: 5 and on it shall *s* in fidelity [in David's
37:28 I am aware whether you stand or *s*;
47: 1 Come down, *s* in the dust,
47: 1 *S* on the ground, dethroned, O daughter
47: 5 Go into darkness and *s* in silence,
47:14 is no warming ember, no fire to *s* before,
Jer 15:17 *s* celebrating in the circle of merrymakers;
16: 8 to *s* with them eating and drinking.
17:25 kings who *s* upon the throne of David will
22: 2 of Judah, who *s* on the throne of David,
36:15 *S* down," they said to him, "and read it
48:18 Come down from glory, *s* on the ground,
Lam 2:10 in silence *s* the old men of daughter Zion;
3:28 Let him *s* alone and in silence,
3:63 Whether they *s* or stand,
Bar 6:42 women, girt with cords, *s* by the roads,
Ez 2: 6 reject you, and when you *s* on scorpions.
33:31 they *s* down before you and hear your words,
44: 3 Only the prince may *s* down in it to eat
47: 6 the bank of the river, where he had me *s*.
Dn 11:27 *s* at table together and exchange lies,
13:50 said, "Come, *s* with us and inform us,
Jl 4:12 For there I will *s* in judgment upon all
Mi 4: 4 Every man shall *s* under his own vine or
7: 8 though I *s* in darkness,
Zec 3: 8 who *s* before you are men of good omen.
6:13 he shall *s* as ruler upon his throne.
8: 4 shall again *s* in the streets of Jerusalem.
Mal 3: 3 He will *s* refining and purifying [silver],
Mt 14:19 ordered the crowds to *s* down on the grass.
20:21 me that these sons of mine will *s*,
22:44 Lord said to my lord, *S* at my right hand,
25:31 of heaven, he will *s* upon his royal throne,
Mk 6:39 He told them to make the people *s* down on
10:37 They replied, "See to it that we *s*,
12:36 *S* at my right hand until I make your
14:32 *S* down here while I pray,"
Lk 1:79 *s* in darkness and in the shadow of death,
9:14 them *s* down in groups of fifty or so."
14: 8 do not *s* in the place of honor in case
14:10 invited is go and *s* in the lowest place,
14:28 will he not first *s* down and calculate the
14:31 he not *s* down first and consider whether,
16: 6 said, 'Take your invoice, *s* down quickly,
17: 7 you say to him, 'Come and *s* down at table'?
20:42 *S* at my right hand while I make your
22:30 and you will *s* on thrones judging the
Jn 9: 8 this the fellow who used to *s* and beg?"
Acts 2:30 of his descendants would *s* upon his throne.
2:34 *S* at my right hand until I make your
3:10 to *s* at the Beautiful Gate of the temple.
8:31 Philip to get in and *s* down beside him.
14: 8 he used to *s* crippled,
23: 3 *s* there judging men according to the law,
Rom 14: 3 must not *s* in judgment on him who eats.
14:10 how can you *s* in judgment on your brother?
Heb 1:13 *S* at my right hand till I make your
Jas 2: 3 the well-dressed man and say, *S* right here,
2: 3 or *S* over there by my footrest."
Rv 3:21 victor the right to *s* with me on my throne,
14: 7 for his time has come to *s* in judgment.
18: 7 to herself, 'I *s* enthroned as a queen.

SITE (18)

Gn 13: 4 the *s* where he had first built the altar;
22:14 Abraham named the *s* Yahweh-yireh;
28:19 He called that *s* Bethel,
35:14 On the *s* where God had spoken with him,
35:15 Jacob named the *s* Bethel,
Nm 11:31 brought them down over the camp *s*
21:15 *s* of Ar and slant to the border of Moab."
Jos 4: 8 and carried them along to the camp *s*,
Jgs 9:45 the city, sowing the *s* with salt.
2Kgs 2:19 Elisha, "The *s* of the city is fine indeed,
Ezr 5:15 house of God be rebuilt on its former *s*.
6: 7 they are to rebuild it on its former *s*.
Is 4: 5 over the whole *s* of Mount Zion and over
Zec 12: 6 but Jerusalem shall not abide on its own *s*.
Mt 27:33 Upon arriving at a *s* called Golgotha (a
Mk 9: 5 Let us erect three booths on this *s*,
15:22 When they brought Jesus to the *s* of
Jn 4: 6 This was the *s* of Jacob's well.

SITES (4)

Gn 23: 6 your dead in the choicest of our burial *s*.
Jos 11:13 fire any of the cities built on raised *s*,
2Chr 33:19 the *s* where he built high places and
Ps(s) 16: 6 measuring lines have fallen on pleasant *s*;

SITHRI (1)

Ex 6:22 of Uzziel were Mishael, Elzaphan and *S*.

SITNAH (1)

Gn 26:21 so it was called *S*.

SITS (19)

Lv 15: 4 and any piece of furniture on which he *s*,
15: 6 Whoever *s* on a piece of furniture on which
15:20 or *s* during her impurity shall be unclean.
15:26 furniture on which she *s* becomes unclean
Ps(s) 1: 1 nor *s* in the company of the insolent,
9: 8 But the LORD *s* enthroned forever;
47: 9 the nations, God *s* upon his holy throne.
Prv 9:14 She *s* at the door of her house upon a seat
31:23 gates as he *s* with the elders of the land.
Sir 25:17 When her husband *s* among his neighbors,
40: 3 Whether he *s* on a lofty throne or grovels
Is 3:26 as the city *s* desolate on the ground.
28: 6 spirit of justice to him who *s* in judgment,
40:22 *s* enthroned above the vault of the earth,
Jer 29:16 the king who *s* on David's throne,
Rv 6:16 Hide us from the face of the One who *s* on
7:15 who *s* on the throne will give them shelter.
17: 1 harlot who *s* by the waters of the deep.
17: 9 seven hills on which the woman *s* enthroned.

SITTING (46)

Gn 19: 1 evening, as Lot was *s* at the gate of Sodom.
Lv 15: 6 on which the afflicted man was *s*,
15:22 article of furniture on which she was *s*,
Dt 22: 6 ground, and the mother bird is *s* on them,
Jgs 13: 9 to the woman as she was *s* in the field.
1Sm 1: 9 Eli the priest was *s* on a chair near the
4:13 Eli was *s* in his chair beside the gate,
19: 9 Saul as he was *s* in his house with spear
22: 6 At the time he was *s* in Gibeah under a
2Sm 18:24 Now David was *s* between the two gates,
19: 9 informed that the king was *s* at the gate,
1Kgs 13:20 But while they were *s* at table,
2Kgs 6:32 Elisha was *s* in his house in conference
18:27 Was it not rather to the men *s* on the wall,
Est 5:13 see the Jew Mordecai *s* at the royal gate."
6:10 Jew Mordecai, who is *s* at the royal gate.
Wis 6:14 for he shall find her *s* by his gate.
Sir 38:29 So with the potter *s* at his labor,
Is 36:12 Was it not rather to the men *s* on the wall,
Jer 36:22 Now the king was *s* in his winter house,
Ez 8: 1 in the sixth year, as I was *s* in my house,
8:14 and I saw *s* there the women who were
26:16 clothed in mourning and, *s* on the ground,
Dn 14:40 and looked in, there was Daniel, *s* there!
Zec 5: 7 and there was a woman *s* inside the bushel.
Mt 20:23 But *s* at my right hand or my left is not
20:30 suddenly two blind men *s* by the roadside,
26:69 Peter was *s* in the courtyard when one of
27:61 and the other Mary remained *s* there,
Mk 2: 6 the scribes were *s* there asking themselves:
4:36 him away in the boat in which he was *s*,
5:15 Legion *s* fully clothed and perfectly sane,
10:40 But as for *s* at my right or my left,
10:46 ("son of Timaeus") *s* by the roadside.
16: 5 tomb they saw a young man *s* at the right,
Lk 2:46 the temple *s* in the midst of the teachers,
5:17 *S* close by were Pharisees and teachers of
5:27 collector named Levi *s* at his customs post.
8:35 whom the devils had departed *s* at his feet
22:55 of the courtyard and were *s* beside it,
22:56 girl saw him *s* in the light of the fire.
Acts 8:28 He was *s* in his carriage reading the
20: 9 Eutychus who was *s* on the window-sill
1Cor 14:30 If another, *s* by, should happen to receive
Rv 14:16 So the one *s* on the cloud wielded his
20: 4 *s* on them were empowered to pass judgment.

SITUATED (3)

Jgs 4: 5 *s* between Ramah and Bethel in the mountain
Tb 5: 6 to Rages, for Rages is *s* at the mountains,
Ez 27: 3 that is *s* at the approaches of the sea,

SITUATION (9)

1Sm 13: 6 of the danger and of the difficult *s*,
Tb 7:10 I will explain the *s* to you very frankly.
Est 9: 1 become masters of them, the *s* was reversed:
1Mc 3:42 Judas and his brothers saw that the *s* had
Sir 37:14 A man's conscience can tell him his *s*
1Cor 1:26 Consider your *s*.
Phil 1:12 I want you to know that my *s* has worked
1:28 be intimidated by your opponents in any *s*.
4:11 for whatever the *s* I find myself in I have

SIVAN (2)

Est 8: 9 the twenty-third day of the third month, *S*,
Bar 1: 8 to the land of Judah, on the tenth of *S*.

SIX (177)

Gn 7: 6 Noah was *s* hundred years old when the
7:11 In the *s* hundredth year of Noah's life,
8:13 *s* hundred and first year of Noah's life,
30:20 now that I have borne him *s* sons";
31:41 two daughters and *s* years for your flock,
Ex 12:37 about *s* hundred thousand men on foot,
14: 7 *s* hundred first-class chariots and all
16:26 On the other *s* days you can gather it,
20: 9 *S* days you may labor and do all your work,
20:11 In *s* days the LORD made the heavens and
21: 2 slave, he is to serve you for *s* years,
23:10 "For *s* years you may sow your land and
23:12 "For *s* days you may do your work,
24:16 The cloud covered it for *s* days,
25:32 *S* branches are to extend from the sides of
25:33 *s* branches that extend from the lampstand.
26: 9 and the other *s* sheets into another set.
26:22 *s* boards for the rear of the Dwelling,
28:10 stone, and the other *s* on the other stone,
28:10 *s* of their names on one stone,
31:15 *S* days there are for doing work,
31:17 for in *s* days the LORD made the heavens
34:21 "For *s* days you may work,
35: 2 On *s* days work may be done,
36:16 and the other *s* sheets into another set.
36:27 *s* boards at the rear of the Dwelling,
37:18 *S* branches extended from its sides,
37:19 and so for the *s* branches that extended
38:26 the number of these was *s* hundred and
Lv 23: 3 "For *s* days work may be done;
24: 6 shall place in two piles, *s* in each pile,
25: 3 For *s* years you may sow your field,
25: 3 field, and for *s* years prune your vineyard,
Nm 1:25 forty-five thousand *s* hundred and fifty
1:27 seventy-four thousand *s* hundred were
1:46 houses, was *s* hundred and three thousand,
2: 4 census to seventy-four thousand *s* hundred.]
2:15 to forty-five thousand *s* hundred and fifty.
2:31 hundred and fifty-seven thousand *s* hundred.]
2:32 *s* hundred and three thousand five hundred
3:34 they numbered *s* thousand two hundred.
4:40 numbered two thousand *s* hundred and thirty.
7: 3 of *s* baggage wagons and twelve oxen,
11:21 me include *s* hundred thousand soldiers;
26:41 thousand *s* hundred men were registered.
26:51 These *s* hundred and one thousand seven
31:32 *s* hundred and seventy-five thousand sheep,
31:37 of which *s* hundred and seventy-five fell
35: 6 the *s* cities of asylum shall you must
35:13 *S* cities of asylum shall you assign:
35:15 These *s* cities of asylum shall serve not
Dt 5:13 *S* days you may labor and do all your work;
15:12 to you, he is to serve you for *s* years,
15:18 service he has given you for *s* years
16: 8 For *s* days you shall eat unleavened bread,
Jos 6: 3 Do this for *s* days,
6:14 and for *s* days in all they did the same.
15:59 *s* cities and their villages.
15:62 *s* cities and their villages.
Jgs 3:31 slew *s* hundred Philistines with an oxgoad.
12: 7 After having judged Israel for *s* years,
18:11 *s* hundred men of the clan of the Danites,
18:16 The *s* hundred men girt with weapons of war,
20:47 But *s* hundred others who turned and fled
Ru 3:15 did so, he poured out *s* measures of barley,
3:17 "He gave me these *s* measures of barley
1Sm 13: 5 thousand chariots, *s* thousand horsemen,
13:15 he had with him, who were about *s* hundred.
14: 2 with him numbered about *s* hundred men.
17: 4 he was *s* cubits and one span.
17: 7 its iron head weighed *s* hundred shekels.
23:13 and his men, about *s* hundred in number,
27: 2 his *s* hundred men and went over to Achish,
30: 9 So David went off with his *s* hundred men
2Sm 2:11 David spent seven years and *s* months in
5: 5 years and *s* months in Hebron over Judah,
6:13 the ark of the LORD had advanced *s* steps,
15:18 and the *s* hundred men of Gath who had
21:20 large stature with *s* fingers on each hand
21:20 on each hand and *s* toes on each foot
1Kgs 6: 6 cubits wide, the middle one *s* cubits wide,
10:14 *s* hundred and sixty-six gold talents,
10:16 of beaten gold *s* hundred gold shekels
10:19 The throne had *s* steps,
10:29 imported from Egypt cost *s* hundred shekels,

11:16 Joab and all Israel remained there *s*
16:23 years, the first *s* of them in Tirzah.
2Kgs 5: 5 ten silver talents, *s* thousand gold pieces,
11: 3 For *s* years he remained hidden in the
13:19 "You should have struck five or *s* times;
15: 8 was king of Israel in Samaria for *s* months.
1Chr 3: 4 *S* in all were born to him in Hebron,
3: 4 where he reigned seven years and *s* months.
3:22 Hattush, Igal, Bariah, Neariah, Shaphat *s*.
4:27 Shimei had sixteen sons and *s* daughters.
7: 2 thousand *s* hundred in the time of David.
8:38 Azel had *s* sons, whose names were
9: 6 and *s* hundred and ninety of their brethren.
9:44 Azel had *s* sons, whose names were
12:25 *s* thousand eight hundred armed troops.
12:27 thousand *s* hundred, along with Jehoiada,
12:36 twenty-eight thousand *s* hundred.
20: 6 who had *s* fingers to each hand and six
21:25 *s* hundred shekels of gold for the place.
23: 4 *s* thousand were to be officials and judges,
25: 3 *s*, under the direction of their father
26:17 On the east, *s* watched each day,
2Chr 1:17 export them at *s* hundred silver shekels,
2: 1 placed three thousand *s* hundred overseers.
2:16 one hundred fifty-three thousand *s* hundred.
2:17 and three thousand *s* hundred overseers to
3: 8 gold to the amount of *s* hundred talents.
9:13 *s* hundred and sixty-six gold talents,
9:15 *s* hundred shekels of beaten gold going
9:18 The throne had *s* steps;
22:12 For *s* years he remained hidden with them
26:12 warriors was two thousand *s* hundred,
29:33 *s* hundred oxen and three thousand sheep.
35: 8 gave to the priests two thousand *s* hundred
Ezr 2:10 sons of Bani, *s* hundred and forty-two;
2:11 sons of Bebai, *s* hundred and twenty-three;
2:13 sons of Adonikam, *s* hundred and sixty-six;
2:26 Ramah and Geba, *s* hundred and twenty-one;
2:35 three thousand *s* hundred and thirty.
2:60 sons of Nekoda, *s* hundred and fifty-two.
2:67 asses *s* thousand seven hundred and twenty.
8:26 silver, *s* hundred and fifty talents;
Neh 5:18 one beef, *s* choice muttons,
7:10 sons of Arah, *s* hundred and fifty-two;
7:15 sons of Binnui, *s* hundred and forty-eight;
7:16 sons of Bebai, *s* hundred and twenty-eight;
7:18 of Adonikam, *s* hundred and sixty-seven;
7:20 sons of Adin, *s* hundred and fifty-five;
7:30 Ramah and Geba, *s* hundred and twenty-one;
7:62 sons of Nekoda, *s* hundred and forty-two.
7:68 asses *s* thousand seven hundred and twenty.
Jdt 1: 2 three cubits in height and *s* in length.
Est 2:12 *s* months were spent with oil of myrrh,
2:12 other *s* months with perfumes and cosmetics.
1Mc 6:42 and *s* hundred men of the king's army fell.
2Mc 8: 1 to Judaism, assembled about *s* thousand men.
8:16 assembled his men, *s* thousand strong,
10:31 and *s* hundred of their horsemen were slain.
Jb 5:19 Out of *s* troubles he will deliver you,
42:12 fourteen thousand sheep, *s* thousand camels,
Prv 6:16 There are *s* things the LORD hates,
Sir 16:10 Nor the *s* hundred thousand foot soldiers
46: 8 from the *s* hundred thousand infantry,
Is 6: 2 each of them had *s* wings:
Jer 34:14 *s* years he shall serve you,
52:30 four thousand *s* hundred persons in all.
Ez 9: 2 With that I saw *s* men coming from the
40: 5 was holding a measuring rod *s* cubits long,
40:12 themselves were *s* cubits on either side,
40:14 the court on either side were *s* cubits.
41: 1 which were *s* cubits thick on either side.
41: 3 the width of the entrance was *s* cubits,
41: 5 of the temple, which was *s* cubits thick;
41: 8 a full rod of *s* cubits in extent.
46: 1 closed throughout the *s* working days,
46: 4 *s* unblemished lambs and an unblemished ram,
46: 6 also *s* lambs and a ram without blemish,
Dn 3: 1 made, sixty cubits high and *s* cubits wide,
14: 3 provided for it *s* barrels of fine flour,
14: 3 flour, forty sheep, and *s* measures of wine.
14:31 a lions' den, where he remained *s* days.
Mt 17: 1 *S* days later Jesus took Peter,
Mk 6:48 was between three and *s* in the morning.
9: 2 *S* days later, Jesus took Peter, James,
Lk 13:14 "There are *s* days for working.
Jn 2: 6 there were at hand *s* stone water jars,
12: 1 *S* days before Passover Jesus came to
Acts 11:12 These *s* brothers came along with me,
Jas 5:17 on the land for three years and *s* months.
Rv 4: 8 creatures had *s* wings and eyes all over,
13:18 The man's number is *s* hundred sixty-six.

SIXTEEN (22)

Gn 46:18 these she bore to Jacob *s* persons in all.
Ex 26:25 boards, with their *s* silver pedestals,
36:30 boards, with their *s* silver pedestals,
Nm 31:40 and *s* thousand persons,
31:46 five hundred asses, and *s* thousand persons.
31:52 *s* thousand seven hundred and fifty shekels.
Jos 15:41 *s* cities and their villages,
19:22 These *s* cities and their villages were the
2Kgs 15: 2 He was *s* years old when he began to reign,
15:33 king, and he reigned *s* years in Jerusalem.
16: 2 king, and he reigned *s* years in Jerusalem.
1Chr 4:27 Shimei had *s* sons and six daughters.
24: 4 the former were divided into *s* groups,
2Chr 13:21 fathered twenty-two sons and *s* daughters.
26: 1 Uzziah, though he was but *s* years of age,
26: 3 Uzziah was *s* years old when he became king,
27: 1 king, and he reigned *s* years in Jerusalem.
27: 8 king, and he reigned *s* years in Jerusalem.
28: 1 king, and he reigned *s* years in Jerusalem.
2Mc 11:11 foot soldiers and *s* hundred horsemen,
Ez 43:17 was sixteen cubits long and *s* cubits wide,

SIXTEEN-YEAR (1)

2Kgs 13:10 began his *s* reign over Israel in Samaria.

SIXTEEN-YEAR-OLD (1)

2Kgs 14:21 the *s* Azariah and proclaimed him king

SIXTEENTH (3)

1Chr 24:14 the fifteenth to Bilgah, the *s* to Immer,
25:23 The *s* fell to Hananiah,
2Chr 29:17 days, and on the *s* day of the first month,

SIXTH (39)

Gn 1:31 the *s* day.
30:19 conceived again and bore a *s* son to Jacob;
Ex 16: 5 On the *s* day,
16:22 the *s* day they gathered twice as much food,
16:29 the *s* day he gives you food for two days.
26: 9 *s* sheet double at the front of the tent.
Lv 25:21 bestow such blessings on you in the *s* year
Nm 7:42 On the *s* day it was the turn of Eliasaph,
29:29 the *s* day you shall offer eight bullocks,
Jos 19:32 The *s* lot fell to the Naphtalites.
2Sm 3: 5 and the *s*,
2Kgs 18:10 In the *s* year of Hezekiah,
1Chr 2:15 the fourth, Raddai, the fifth, Ozem, the *s*,
3: 3 the *s*,
12:12 fourth, Jeremiah fifth, Attai *s*,
24: 9 the fifth to Malchijah, the *s* to Mijamin,
25:13 The *s* was Bukkiah, his sons,
26: 3 fourth, Elam, the fifth, Jehohanan, the *s*,
26: 5 Nethanel, the fifth, Ammiel, the *s*,
27: 9 *S*, for the sixth month, was Ira,
Ezr 6:15 in the *s* year of the reign of King Darius.
Neh 3:30 Shelemiah, and Hanun, the *s* son of Zalaph,
2Mc 7:18 After him they brought the *s* brother.
Ez 4:11 drink shall be the *s* of a hin by measure;
8: 1 fifth day of the *s* month, in the sixth year,
45:13 one *s* of an ephah from each homer of wheat,
45:13 *s* of an ephah from each homer of barley.
46:14 as a cereal offering one *s* of an ephah,
Hg 1: 1 *s* month in the second year of King Darius,
1:15 on the twenty-fourth day of the *s* month.
Lk 1:26 In the *s* month,
1:36 to be sterile is now in her *s* month,
Rv 6:12 When I saw the Lamb break open the *s* seal,
9:13 Then the *s* angel blew his trumpet,
9:14 It said to the *s* angel,
16:12 The *s* angel poured out his bowl on the
21:20 the fifth sardonyx, the *s* carnelian,

SIXTY (44)

Gn 25:26 Isaac was *s* years old when they were born.
Lv 27: 3 persons between the ages of twenty and *s*,
27: 7 for persons of *s* or more,
Nm 7:88 all, twenty-four oxen, sixty rams, *s* goats,
7:88 rams, sixty goats, and *s* yearling lambs.
26:27 of whom *s* thousand five hundred men were
Dt 3: 4 *s* cities in all,
Jos 13:30 of Jair, which are *s* cities in Bashan.
2Sm 2:31 three hundred and *s* men of Benjamin,
1Kgs 4:13 *s* large walled cities with gates barred
5: 2 thirty kors of fine flour, *s* kors of meal,
6: 2 built for the LORD was *s* cubits long,
2Kgs 25:19 and *s* of the common people still remaining
1Chr 2:21 having married her when he was *s* years old.
2:23 is, Kenath and its towns, *s* cities in all,
5:18 hundred and *s* men fit for military service.
9:13 were one thousand seven hundred and *s*,
2Chr 3: 3 was *s* cubits according to the old measure,
11:21 had taken eighteen wives and *s* concubines,
11:21 fathered twenty-eight sons and *s* daughters.
12: 3 hundred chariots and *s* thousand horsemen,
Ezr 2: 9 sons of Zaccai, seven hundred and *s*;
2:64 to forty-two thousand three hundred and *s*,
6: 3 to be *s* cubits and its width sixty cubits.
6: 3 to be sixty cubits and its width *s* cubits.
8:10 and with him one hundred and *s* males;
8:13 Jeiel, and Shemaiah, and with them *s* males;
Neh 7:14 sons of Zaccai, seven hundred and *s*;
7:66 to forty-two thousand three hundred and *s*,
Jdt 1: 3 with a thickness of *s* cubits at the base.
1Mc 4:28 gathered together *s* thousand picked men
7:16 But he arrested *s* of them and killed them
10: 1 In the year one hundred and *s*,
10:21 one hundred and *s* at the feast of Booths,
2Mc 4: 8 king three hundred and *s* talents of silver,
Sg 3: 7 *s* valiant men surround it,
6: 8 There are *s* queens, eighty concubines,
Is 7: 9 But within *s* years and five, Ephraim shall
Jer 52:25 and *s* of the common people who were in the
Dn 3: 1 made, *s* cubits high and six cubits wide,
1Tm 5: 9 should be not less than *s* years of age.
Rv 11: 3 for those twelve hundred and *s* days,
12: 6 care of for twelve hundred and *s* days.

SIXTY- (4)

Mt 13: 8 grain a hundred- or *s*- or thirtyfold.
13:23 a yield of a hundred- or *s*- or thirtyfold."
Mk 4: 8 a rate of thirty- and *s*- and a hundredfold."
4:20 yield at thirty- and *s*- and a hundredfold."

SIXTY-EIGHT (2)

1Chr 16:38 left there Obed-edom and *s* of his brethren,
Neh 11: 6 was four hundred and *s* valiant men.

SIXTY-FIVE (5)

Gn 5:15 When Mahalalel was *s* years old,
5:21 When Enoch was *s* years old,
5:23 of Enoch was three hundred and *s* years.
Nm 3:50 one thousand three hundred and *s* shekels
1Mc 10:67 In the year one hundred and *s*,

SIXTY-FOUR (2)

Nm 26:25 of whom *s* thousand three hundred men were
26:43 of whom *s* thousand four hundred men were

SIXTY-NINE (2)

Gn 5:27 of Methuselah was nine hundred and *s* years;
2Mc 1: 7 of Demetrius, the year one hundred and *s*,

SIXTY-ONE (3)

Nm 31:34 thousand oxen, *s* thousand asses,
31:39 asses, of which *s* fell as tax to the LORD;
Ezr 2:69 *s* thousand drachmas of gold,

SIXTY-SEVEN (4)

Neh 7:18 sons of Adonikam, six hundred and *s*;
7:19 sons of Bigvai, two thousand and *s*;
7:71 of silver, and *s* garments for priests.
1Mc 11:19 became king in the year one hundred and *s*.

SIXTY-SIX (6)

Gn 46:26 numbered *s* persons in all.
Lv 12: 5 *s* days in becoming purified of her blood.
1Kgs 10:14 weighed six hundred and *s* gold talents,
2Chr 9:13 weighed six hundred and *s* gold talents,
Ezr 2:13 sons of Adonikam, six hundred and *s*;
Rv 13:18 The man's number is six hundred *s*.

SIXTY-TWO (10)

Gn 5:18 When Jared was one hundred and *s* years old,
5:20 of Jared was nine hundred and *s* years;
Nm 1:39 *s* thousand seven hundred were enrolled in
2:26 in the census to *s* thousand seven hundred.]
1Chr 26: 8 Of Obed-edom, *s*.
Tb 14: 2 was *s* years old when he lost his eyesight,
1Mc 10:57 to Ptolemais in the year one hundred and *s*.
Dn 6: 1 succeeded to the kingdom at the age of *s*.
9:25 During *s* weeks it shall be rebuilt,
9:26 After the *s* weeks an anointed shall be cut

SIZABLE (3)

Mk 10:46 place with his disciples and a *s* crowd,
12:41 Many of the wealthy put in *s* amounts;
Jn 21:11 hauled ashore the net loaded with *s* fish

SIZE (23)

Ex 26: 2 all the sheets shall be of the same *s*.
26: 8 all eleven sheets shall be of the same *s*.
36: 9 all the sheets were of the same *s*.
36:15 all eleven sheets were the same *s*.
1Kgs 6:25 The cherubim were identical in *s* and shape,
7: 9 to *s* and trimmed front and back with a saw,
7:11 Above were fine stones hewn to *s*,
7:37 made, all of the same casting, the same *s*,
1Chr 23:29 and of all measures of quantity and *s*.
1Mc 3:19 war does not depend upon the *s* of the army,
Jb 38: 5 Who determined its *s*; do you know?
Ez 13:18 *s* of head so as to entrap their owners.
31:18 in glory or *s* among the trees of Eden?
40:10 were three on either side, of equal *s*,
40:10 on either side were also of equal *s*.
40:24 they were the same *s* as the others.
40:29 vestibule were the same *s* as the others.
40:33 vestibule were the same *s* as the others;
45:11 the liquid measure shall be of the same *s*:
46:22 thirty wide, all four of them the same *s*.
Mt 17:20 if you had faith the *s* of a mustard seed,
Lk 2:40 The child grew in *s* and strength,
17: 6 "If you had faith the *s* of a mustard seed,

SIZED (1)

1Sm 17:42 When he had *s* David up,

SKIES (19)

Dt 33:13 *s* above and of the abyss crouching beneath;
33:26 his power, and rides the *s* in his majesty;
Jb 35: 5 Look up to the *s* and behold;
36:28 Till the *s* run with them and the showers
37:18 spread out with him the firmament of the *s*,
38:29 gives the hoarfrost its birth in the *s*,
Ps(s) 57:11 heavens, and your faithfulness to the *s*.
68:35 his power is in the *s*.
77:18 the *s* gave forth their voice;
78:23 *s* above and the doors of heaven he opened;
89: 7 For who in the *s* can rank with the LORD?
108: 5 heavens, and your faithfulness to the *s*.
Prv 8:28 When he made firm the *s* above,
Is 45: 8 like gentle rain let the *s* drop it down.
Mt 11:23 Capernaum, 'Are you to be exalted to the *s*?
Mk 13:25 its light, stars will fall out of the *s*,
Lk 3:21 the *s* opened and the Holy Spirit descended
10:15 Capernaum, 'Are you to be exalted to the *s*?
Acts 1:11 do you stand here looking up at the *s*?

SKIFFS (1)

Jb 9:26 They shoot by like *s* of reed,

SKILL (21)

Ex 28: 3 expert workmen whom I have endowed with *s*,
31: 3 I have filled him with divine spirit of *s*
31: 6 *s* to make all the things I have ordered
35:26 thread, All the women who possessed the *s*,
35:31 filled him with a divine spirit of *s*
35:35 them with *s* to execute all types of work:
36: 1 endowed with *s* and understanding
36: 2 experts whom the LORD had endowed with *s*,
1Kgs 7:14 He was endowed with *s*,
1Chr 28:21 their *s* in every kind of craftsmanship.
2Chr 2:12 am now sending you a craftsman of great *s*,
Ps(s) 107:27 men, and all their *s* was swallowed up.
Eccl 2:21 labored with wisdom and knowledge and *s*,
10:10 the craftsman has the advantage of his *s*.
Wis 13:13 This wood he models with listless *s*,
14: 4 so that even one without *s* may embark.
14:19 over the likeness to the best of his *s*;
Sir 38:34 their concern is for exercise of their *s*.
Jer 10:12 and stretched out the heavens by his *s*.
51:15 and stretched out the heavens by his *s*.
Eph 4:14 in human trickery and *s* in proposing error.

SKILLED (24)

1Sm 16:16 will look for a man *s* in playing the harp.
2Sm 17: 8 since your father is *s* in warfare,
1Kgs 5:20 is *s* in cutting timber like the Sidonians,
1Chr 22:16 and every kind of craftsman *s* in gold,
25: 7 in singing to the LORD, all of them *s* men,
2Chr 2: 6 Now, send me men *s* at work in gold,
30:22 well *s* in the service of the LORD.
Prv 22:29 You see a man *s* at his work?
Sg 3: 8 of them expert with the sword, *s* in battle,
Sir 9:17 *S* artisans are esteemed for their deftness;
9:17 but the ruler of his people is the *s* sage.
38:31 All these men are *s* with their hands,
44: 4 Authors *s* in composition,
47: 5 defeat the *s* warrior and raise up the might
49: 1 incense, made lasting by a *s* performer.
Is 3: 3 and the nobleman, counselor, *s* magician,
40:20 which a *s* craftsman picks out for himself,
Jer 24: 1 of Judah, the artisans and the *s* workers,
29: 2 and the *s* workmen had left Jerusalem.
50: 9 Their arrows are arrows of the *s* warrior;
Bar 1: 9 and the princes, and the *s* workers,
3:26 renowned at the first, stalwarts, *s* in war.
Ez 27: 8 *S* men of Zemer were in you to be your
Dn 8:23 arise a king, impudent and *s* in intrigue.

SKILLFUL (9)

Gn 25:27 the boys grew up, Esau became a *s* hunter,
1Sm 16:17 "Find me a *s* harpist and bring him to me."
16:18 sons of Jesse of Bethlehem is a *s* harpist.
1Chr 15:22 he directed the chanting, for he was *s*.
2Chr 34:12 All those Levites who were *s* with musical
Ps(s) 45: 2 tongue is nimble as the pen of a *s* scribe.
78:72 heart, and with *s* hands he guided them.
Prv 31:13 wool and flax and makes cloth with *s* hands.
Eccl 4: 4 Then I saw that all toil and *s* work is the

SKILLFULLY (5)

2Mc 15:38 so a *s* composed story delights the ears of
Ps(s) 33: 3 pluck the strings *s*,
Wis 13:11 tree and *s* scrape off all its bark,
Is 23:16 Pluck the strings *s*,
Mk 12:28 he realized how *s* Jesus answered them.

SKIN (71)

Gn 21:14 and a *s* of water and gave them to Hagar.
21:15 Beer-sheba, the water in the *s* was used up.
21:19 She went and filled the *s* with water,
Ex 34:29 he did not know that the *s* of his face had
34:30 how radiant the *s* of his face had become,
34:35 see that the *s* of Moses' face was radiant;
Lv 1: 6 *s* the holocaust and cut it up into pieces.
13: 2 "If someone has on his *s* a scab or
13: 3 who shall examine the sore on his *s*.
13: 3 shows that it has penetrated below the *s*,
13: 4 If, however, the blotch on the *s* is white,
13: 4 not seem to have penetrated below the *s*,
13: 5 unchanged and has not spread on the *s*,
13: 6 now dying out and has not spread on the *s*,
13: 7 clean, the eczema spreads at all on his *s*,
13: 8 the eczema has indeed spread on the *s*,
13:10 there is a white scab on the *s*
13:11 it is *s* leprosy that has long developed.
13:12 If leprosy breaks out on the *s* and,
13:12 *s* of the stricken man from head to foot,
13:18 who had a boil on his *s* which later healed,
13:20 the *s* and that the hair has turned white,
13:21 deeper than the *s* and is already dying out,
13:22 If it has then spread on the *s*,
13:24 "If a man had a burn on his *s*,
13:25 this seems to have penetrated below the *s*,
13:26 deeper than the *s* and is already dying out,
13:27 find that it has spread at all on the *s*,
13:28 on the *s* and is already dying out,
13:30 *s* and that there is fine yellow hair on it,
13:31 that it has not penetrated below the *s*,
13:32 not seem to have penetrated below the *s*,
13:34 finds that it has not spread on the *s*
13:34 that it has not penetrated below the *s*,
13:35 on his *s* after he has been declared clean,
13:36 on the *s* he need not look for yellow hair;
13:38 "When the *s* of a man or a woman is
13:39 on the *s* are white and already dying out,
13:39 only tetter that has broken out on the *s*,
13:43 *s* leprosy of the fleshy part of the body,
Nm 4: 6 these they shall put a cover of tahash *s*,
4: 8 cloth and cover all this with tahash *s*.
4:10 then enclose in a covering of tahash *s*,
4:11 this also with a covering of tahash *s*.
4:12 violet cloth and cover them with tahash *s*.
4:14 spread a covering of tahash *s* over this,
4:25 and the outer wrapping of tahash *s*,
1Sm 1:24 bull, an ephah of flour and a *s* of wine,
10: 3 loaves of bread, and the third a *s* of wine.
16:20 took five loaves of bread, a *s* of wine,
2Sm 16: 1 an ephah of summer fruits, and a *s* of wine.
2Kgs 6:30 sackcloth underneath, next to his *s*.
2Chr 29:34 to *s* all the victims for the holocausts,
2Mc 7: 7 tearing off the *s* and hair of his head,
Jb 2: 4 answered the LORD and said, *S* for skin!
7: 5 my *s* cracks and festers;
10:11 With *s* and flesh you clothed me,
16:15 I have fastened sackcloth over my *s*,
19:20 My bones cleave to my *s*,
30:30 My blackened *s* falls away from me;
Ps(s) 102: 6 sighing I am reduced to *s* and bone.
Jer 13:23 Can the Ethiopian change his *s*?
Lam 3: 4 He has worn away my flesh and my *s*,
4: 8 Their *s* shrinks on their bones,
5:10 Our *s* is shriveled up,
Ez 37: 6 flesh grow over you, cover you with *s*,
37: 8 flesh come upon them, and the *s* cover them,
Mi 3: 2 You who tear their *s* from them,
3: 3 of my people, and flay their *s* from them,
Acts 19:12 had touched his *s* were applied to the sick,

SKINK (1)

Lv 11:30 the gecko, the chameleon, the agama, the *s*,

SKINNING (1)

2Chr 35:11 blood and the Levites proceeded to the *s*.

SKINS (23)

Gn 27:16 and with the *s* of the kids she covered up
Ex 25: 5 rams' skins dyed red, and tahash *s*;
26:14 shall make a covering of rams' *s* dyed red,
26:14 and above that, a covering of tahash *s*.
35: 7 rams' skins dyed red, and tahash *s*;
35:23 hair, rams' *s* dyed red or tahash skins,
36:19 for the tent was made of rams' *s* dyed red,
36:19 and above that, a covering of tahash *s*.
39:34 the covering of rams' *s* dyed red,
39:34 skins dyed red, the covering of tahash *s*,
1Sm 25:18 together two hundred loaves, two *s* of wine,
Mt 9:17 If they do, the *s* burst, the wine spills out,
9:17 the wine spills out, and the *s* are ruined.
Mk 2:22 the *s* and both wine and skins will be lost.
2:22 No, new wine is poured into new *s*."
Lk 5:37 do so, the new wine will burst the old *s*,
5:37 will spill out, and the *s* will be lost.
5:38 New wine should be poured into fresh *s*.
Heb 11:37 about garbed in the *s* of sheep or goats,

SKIP (1)

Ps(s) 114: 6 You mountains, that you *s* like rams?

SKIPPED (1)

Ps(s) 114: 4 The mountains *s* like rams,

SKIRT (3)

Is 3:24 for the rich gown, a sackcloth *s*.
Lam 1: 9 Her filth is on her *s*;
Na 3: 5 you, and I will strip your *s* from you;

SKIRTING (3)

Jos 16: 7 to Ataroth and Naarah, and *s* Jericho,
19:14 *S* north of Hannathon,
Jdt 13:10 passed through the camp, and *s* the ravine,

SKIRTS (2)

Jer 13:22 *s* are stripped away and you are violated.
13:26 idol, I now will strip off your *s* from you,

SKULL (8)

Jgs 9:53 Abimelech's head, and it fractured his *s*.
2Kgs 9:35 her, they found nothing of her but the *s*,
1Chr 10:10 his *s* they impaled on the temple of Dagon.
Jer 48:45 the brow of Moab, the *s* of the noisemakers.
Mt 27:33 Golgotha (a name which means *S* Place),
Mk 15:22 site of Golgotha (which means *S* Place"),
Lk 23:33 When they came to *S* Place,
Jn 19:17 is called the Place of the *S* (in Hebrew,

SKULLS (1)

Nm 24:17 of Moab, and the *s* of all the Shuthites,

SKY (107)

Gn 1: 8 God called the dome "the *s*."
1: 9 the *s* be gathered into a single basin,
1: 9 under the *s* was gathered into its basin,
1:14 "Let there be lights in the dome of the *s*,
1:15 serve as luminaries in the dome of the *s*,
1:17 God set them in the dome of the *s*,
1:20 let birds fly beneath the dome of the *s*."
7:11 and the floodgates of the *s* were opened.
8: 2 and the floodgates of the *s* were closed,
8: 2 and the downpour from the *s* was held back.
11: 4 a city and a tower with its top in the *s*,
15: 5 "Look up at the *s* and count the stars,
22:17 of the *s* and the sands of the seashore;
26: 4 in the *s* and give them all these lands,
Ex 9: 8 Pharaoh let Moses scatter it toward the *s*.
9:10 Moses scattered it toward the *s*,
9:22 "Stretch out your hand toward the *s*,
9:23 stretched out his staff toward the *s*,
10:21 "Stretch out your hand toward the *s*,
10:22 Moses stretched out his hand toward the *s*,
20: 4 shape of anything in the *s* above
24:10 tilework, as clear as the *s* itself.
32:13 as numerous as the stars in the *s*;
Lv 26:19 will make the *s* above you as hard as iron,
Dt 1:10 are now as numerous as the stars in the *s*.
1:28 cities are large and fortified to the *s*;
4:11 which blazed to the very *s* with fire and
4:17 earth or of any bird that flies in the *s*,
4:32 ask from one end of the *s* to the other:
5: 8 shape of anything in the *s* above
9: 1 having large cities fortified to the *s*,
10:22 made you as numerous as the stars of the *s*.
17: 3 or the moon or any of the host of the *s*,
28:23 The *s* over your heads will be like bronze
28:24 you from the *s* until you are destroyed.
28:62 who were numerous as the stars in the *s*,
30:12 It is not up in the *s*,
30:12 the *s* to get it for us and tell us of it,
Jos 10:11 the *s* above them all the way to Azekah,
10:13 The sun halted in the middle of the *s*;
Jgs 13:20 as the flame rose to the *s* from the altar,
20:40 the *s* that the men of Israel wheeled about.
2Sm 21:10 until rain came down on them from the *s*,
21:10 of the *s* from settling on them by day,
1Kgs 8:35 "If the *s* is closed,
14:11 he will be devoured by the birds of the *s*.
16: 4 he shall be devoured by the birds of the *s*."
18:45 the *s* grew dark with clouds and wind,
21:24 field, the birds of the *s* will devour him."
2Chr 6:26 the *s* is closed so that there is no rain,
2Mc 2:10 from the *s* and consumed the sacrifices,
Ps(s) 89:38 a faithful witness in the *s*."
Sir 43: 1 of the *s* shines forth like heaven itself,
50: 7 the rainbow appearing in the cloudy *s*;
Is 7:11 deep as the nether world, or high as the *s*!
Jer 7:33 of the *s* and for the beasts of the field,
15: 3 the birds of the *s* and the beasts of the
16: 4 birds of the *s* and the beasts of the field.
19: 7 birds of the *s* and the beasts of the field.
Zep 1: 3 I will sweep away the birds of the *s*,
Mt 3:16 Suddenly the *s* opened and he saw the
6:26 "Look at the birds in the *s*.
8:20 have lairs, the birds in the *s* have nests,
13:32 birds of the *s* come and build their nests
16: 1 asked him to show them some sign in the *s*.
16: 2 ["In the evening you say, 'Red *s* at night,
16: 3 but in the morning, *S* red and gloomy,
16: 3 know how to interpret the look of the *s*,
24:29 her light, the stars will fall from the *s*,
24:30 of the Son of Man will appear in the *s*,
Mk 1:10 coming up out of the water he saw the *s* rent
4:32 birds of the *s* to build nests in its shade."
13:27 from the farthest bounds of earth and *s*.
Lk 9:58 have lairs, the birds of the *s* have nests,
10:18 Satan fall from the *s* like lightning.

12:56 can interpret the portents of earth and *s*,
17:24 flashes from one end of the *s* to the other.
21:11 and in the *s* fearful omens and great signs.
Jn 1:32 the Spirit descend like a dove from the *s*,
1:51 you shall see the *s* opened and the angels
12:28 Then a voice came from the *s*:
Acts 2: 2 in the *s* there came a noise like a strong,
7:55 to the *s* above and saw the glory of God,
7:56 he exclaimed, "I see an opening in the *s*,
9: 3 from the *s* suddenly flashed about him.
10:11 He saw the *s* open and an object come down
10:12 creatures and reptiles and birds of the *s*.
10:16 then the object was snatched up into the *s*.
11: 5 down to me from the *s* by its four corners.
11: 6 beasts and reptiles, and birds of the *s*.
11:10 in it was drawn up again into the *s*.
19:35 and of her image which fell from the *s*?
22: 6 from the *s* suddenly flashed all about me.
26:13 than the sun shining in the *s* at midday.
Phil 2:15 *s* while holding fast to the word of life.
Heb 11:12 in the *s* and the sands of the seashore.
Jas 5:18 the *s* burst forth with rain and the land
Rv 6:13 The stars in the *s* fell crashing to earth
6:14 Then the *s* disappeared as if it were a
8:10 like a torch crashed down from the *s*.
9: 1 I saw a star fall from the *s* to the earth.
11: 6 power to close up the *s* so that no rain
12: 1 A great sign appeared in the *s*,
12: 3 Then another sign appeared in the *s*:
12: 4 the *s* and hurled them down to the earth.
16:21 came crashing down on mankind from the *s*,
20:11 The earth and the *s* fled from his presence

SLACK (7)

Tb 12: 6 deeds, and do not be *s* in praising him.
Prv 10: 4 The *s* hand impoverishes,
18: 9 The man who is *s* in his work is own
Eccl 10:18 when hands are *s*,
Sir 4:29 your speech, nor lazy and *s* in your deeds.
Is 33:23 majestic ship passes, The rigging hangs *s*;
Rom 12:11 Do not grow *s* but be fervent in spirit;

SLACKEN (1)

Neh 6: 9 thinking, "Their hands will *s* in the work,

SLACKENED (1)

Neh 4: 4 *S* is the bearers' strength,

SLAIN (138)

Lv 14: 6 the bird that was *s* over the spring water,
14:51 blood of the *s* bird and the spring water,
20:15 be put to death, and the animal shall be *s*.
20:16 it, the woman and the animal shall be *s*;
Nm 17: 6 "It is you who have *s* the LORD's people."
19:16 he was *s* by the sword or died naturally,
19:18 a bone, a *s* person or other dead body,
23:24 its prey and has drunk the blood of the *s*.
25:14 *s* with the Midianite woman was Zimri,
25:15 The *s* Midianite woman was Cozbi,
31: 8 Besides those *s* in battle,
31:19 and those of you who have *s* anyone or
31:19 anyone *s* in battle shall purify yourselves
Dt 19: 6 had previously borne the *s* man no malice.
19:12 him over to be *s* by the avenger of blood.
21: 1 "If the corpse of a *s* man is found lying
32:42 With the blood of the *s* and the captured,
Jos 8:24 were *s* by the sword there in the open,
11: 6 I will stretch them *s* before Israel.
13:22 and among their *s* followers the Israelites
Jgs 5:27 where he sank down, there he fell, *s*.
9:40 *s* right up to the entrance of the gate.
15:16 jawbone of an ass I have *s* a thousand men."
16:24 our land, the one who has multiplied our *s*."
1Sm 18: 7 "Saul has *s* his thousands,
21:12 they not sing, 'Saul has *s* his thousands,
22:21 that Saul had *s* the priests of the LORD,
29: 5 their dances, 'Saul has *s* his thousands,
31: 8 the Philistines came to strip the *s*,
2Sm 1:19 glory of Israel, Saul, *s* upon your heights;
1:22 "From the blood of the *s*,
1:25 thick of the battle, *s* upon your heights!
4:11 men have *s* an innocent man in bed at home,
8:13 David became famous for having *s* eighteen
14: 7 for the life of his brother whom he has *s*;
23: 8 over eight hundred *s* in a single encounter.
23:10 after Eleazar, but only to strip the *s*.
23:18 brandished his spear over three hundred *s*.
1Kgs 11:15 of the army, while going to bury the *s*,
2Kgs 10:14 in number, then *s* at the pit of Beth-eked.
11: 2 where the princes were about to be *s*.
11:15 should not be *s* in the temple of the LORD.
11:20 been *s* with the sword at the royal palace.
23:29 was *s* at Megiddo at the first encounter.
25: 7 He had Zedekiah's sons *s* before his eyes.
1Chr 7:21 were *s* by the inhabitants of Gath because
10: 1 a number of them fell, *s* on Mount Gilboa.
10: 8 when the Philistines came to strip the *s*,
2Chr 13:17 thousand picked men of Israel fell *s*.
22: 1 older sons had been *s* by the band
22:11 the king's sons who were about to be *s*,
23: 7 Whoever tries to enter the house must be *s*.
Jdt 2: 8 *s* shall fill their ravines and wadies,
6: 6 sides, and you shall fall among their *s*.
1Mc 5:13 and they have *s* there about a thousand men."
5:51 the city, and passed through it over the *s*.
2Mc 10:31 and six hundred of their horsemen were *s*.
12:34 ensuing battle, a few of the Jews were *s*.
12:39 men went to gather up the bodies of the *s*
12:40 all that this was why these men had been *s*.
Jb 39:30 where the *s* are,
Ps(s) 44:23 for your sake we are being *s* all the day;
88: 6 the dead, like the *s* who lie in the grave,
Prv 7:26 down dead, numerous, those she has *s*.
22:13 in the streets I might be *s*."
Is 10: 4 beneath the captive or fall beneath the *s*?
14:19 corrupt, Clothed as those *s* at sword-point,
14:20 ruined your land, you have *s* your people!
22: 2 Your slain are not *s* with the sword,
26:21 upon her, and no longer conceal her *s*.
27: 7 or *s* as his slayer was slain?
34: 3 Their *s* shall be cast out,
66:16 and many shall be *s* by the LORD.
Jer 8:23 over the *s* of the daughter of my people!
9:21 corpses of the *s* lie like dung on a field,
14:18 those *s* by the sword;
18:21 young men be *s* by the sword in battle.
25:33 those whom the LORD has *s* will be strewn
26:23 who had him *s* by the sword and his corpse
39: 6 his sons were *s* at Riblah by order of the
41: 9 son of Nethaniah, filled with the *s*.
41:18 Ishmael, son of Nethaniah, had *s* Gedaliah,
51: 4 The *s* shall fall in the land of Chaldea,
51:47 and all her *s* shall lie fallen within her.
51:49 Babylon, too, must fall, O *s* of Israel,
51:49 Babylon have fallen the *s* of all the earth.
Lam 2:20 to be *s* in the sanctuary of the LORD?
2:21 You have *s* on the day of your wrath,
Ez 6: 4 cast down your *s* ones before your idols;
6: 7 [The *s* shall fall in your midst,
6:13 when their *s* shall lie amid their idols,
9: 7 to them, and fill the courts with the *s*;
11: 6 You have *s* many in this city and have
11: 6 and have filled its streets with your *s*.
11: 7 Your *s* whom you have placed within it,
28:23 Within it shall fall those *s* by the sword
30: 4 be in Ethiopia, when the *s* fall in Egypt,
30:11 Egypt, and fill the land with the *s*.
31:17 the nether world, to those *s* by the sword;
31:18 uncircumcised, with those *s* by the sword.
32:20 of those *s* by the sword shall they fall,
32:21 uncircumcised, with those *s* by the sword."
32:22 with all her company, all of them *s*,
32:23 is around Egypt's grave, all of them *s*,
32:24 throng about Egypt's grave, all of them *s*,
32:25 in the midst of the *s* they are placed.
32:26 all of them uncircumcised, *s* by the sword,
32:28 shall you lie, with those *s* by the sword.
32:29 have been placed with those *s* by the sword;
32:30 Sidonians, who have gone down with the *s*,
32:30 lie uncircumcised with those *s* by the sword
32:31 for all his hordes *s* by the sword
32:32 uncircumcised, with those *s* by the sword
33: 4 *s* by the sword that comes against him,
35: 8 With the *s* I will fill your hills,
35: 8 [in them the *s* shall fall by the sword]:
37: 9 into these *s* that they may come to life.
Dn 2:13 was issued that the wise men should be *s*,
5:30 the Chaldean king, was *s*:
7:11 until the beast was *s* and its body thrown
11:26 be overwhelmed, and many shall fall *s*.
Na 3: 3 sword, the flash of the spear, the many *s*,
Zep 2:12 shall be *s* by the sword of the LORD.
Rom 8:36 your sake we are being *s* all the day long;
Rv 5: 6 a Lamb standing, a Lamb that had been *s*.
5: 9 and break open its seals, for you were *s*.
5:12 that was *s* to receive power and riches,
6:11 their fellow servants and brothers to be *s*,
9:18 a third of mankind was *s*.
11: 5 to harm them will surely be *s* in this way.
13: 8 which belongs to the Lamb who was *s*.
13:10 If one is destined to be *s* by the sword,
13:10 by the sword, by the sword he will be *s*!
18:24 saints and of all who were *s* on the earth."
19:21 The rest were *s* by the sword which came
19:21 gorged themselves on the flesh of the *s*.

SLANDER (13)

Lv 19:16 go about spreading *s* among your kinsmen;
Est 8:12 *s* the sincere good will of rulers.
Prv 30:10 *S* not a servant to his master,
Sir 19:14 often it may be *s*;
Jer 6:28 Arch-rebels are they all, dealers in *s*,
9: 3 supplanter, every friend is guilty of *s*.
Ez 22: 9 are those in you who *s* to cause bloodshed;
Mt 5:11 every kind of *s* against you because of me.
2Cor 12:20 of anger, selfish ambitions, *s* and gossip,
Eph 4:31 all passion and anger, harsh words, *s*,
1Tm 6: 4 From these come envy, dissension, *s*,
1Pt 2:12 the pagans may *s* you as troublemakers,
Rv 2: 9 I know the *s* you endure from self-styled

SLANDERED (3)

2Sm 19:28 he *s* your servant before my lord the king.
Ps(s) 109: 4 In return for my love they *s* me,
1Cor 4:13 We are *s*, and we try conciliation.

SLANDERER (1)

Sir 21:28 A *s* besmirches himself,

SLANDERERS (2)

Rom 1:30 They are gossips and *s*,
1Cor 6:10 no *s* or robbers will inherit God's kingdom.

SLANDEROUS (4)

Sir 51: 3 mercy From the scourge of a *s* tongue,
1Tm 3:11 should be serious, not *s* gossips.
2Tm 3: 3 profane, inhuman, implacable, *s*,
Ti 2: 3 must not be *s* gossips or slaves to drink.

SLANDEROUSLY (1)

Rom 3: 8 thing that some *s* accuse us of teaching;

SLANDERS (2)

Ps(s) 15: 3 in his heart and *s* not with his tongue;
101: 5 Whoever *s* his neighbor in secret,

SLANT (1)

Nm 21:15 the site of Ar and *s* to the border of Moab."

SLAP (2)

Ez 21:17 Therefore, *s* your thigh,
2Cor 11:20 put on airs, with those who *s* your face.

SLAPPED (4)

1Kgs 22:24 came up and *s* Micaiah on the cheek saying,
2Chr 18:23 came up and *s* Micaiah on the cheek saying,
Mt 26:67 Others *s* him, saying:
Lk 22:64 They blindfolded him first, *s* him,

SLAPPING (1)

Jn 19: 3 *s* his face as they did so.

SLAPS (1)

Lk 6:29 When someone *s* you on one cheek,

SLASHED (2)

1Kgs 18:28 and *s* themselves with swords and spears,
Mt 26:51 it, and *s* at the high priest's servant,

SLAUGHTER (82)

Gn 22:10 out and took the knife to *s* his son.
34:27 sons of Jacob followed up the *s*
Ex 12:21 families, and *s* them as Passover victims.
29:11 Then *s* the bullock before the LORD,
29:16 have laid their hands on its head, *s* it.
29:20 have laid their hands on its head, *s* it.
Lv 1: 5 He shall then *s* the bull before the LORD,
1:11 This he shall *s* before the LORD at the
3: 2 *s* it at the entrance of the meeting tent;
3: 8 he shall *s* it before the meeting tent;
3:13 he shall *s* it before the meeting tent;
4: 4 hand on its head and *s* it before the LORD.
4:24 he shall *s* the goat as a sin offering
4:29 shall *s* it at the place of the holocausts.
4:33 he shall *s* this sin offering in the place
14:13 (This lamb he shall *s* in the sacred place
14:19 the priest *s* the holocaust and offer it,
16:15 he shall *s* the people's sin-offering goat,
22:28 You shall not *s* an ox or a sheep on one
Nm 25: 8 Thus the *s* of Israelites was checked;
25:18 at the time of the *s* because of Peor."
26: 1 the *s* the LORD said to Moses and Eleazar,
31:16 which began the *s* of the LORD's community.
Dt 12:15 you may *s* and eat to your heart's desire
12:21 you may *s* in the manner I have told you
Jos 10:10 The Israelites inflicted a great *s* on
10:20 the last blows in this very great *s*,
Jgs 15: 8 blows, he inflicted a great *s* on them.
1Sm 14:30 would not the *s* of the Philistines by now
14:34 *S* it here and then eat,
1Kgs 11:24 of Zobah, when David defeated them with *s*.
13: 2 who shall *s* upon you the priests of the
18: 5 we shall not have to *s* any of the beasts."
2Chr 28: 5 of Israel, who defeated him with great *s*.
Jdt 2:11 *s* and plunder in each country you occupy.
8:22 For the *s* of our kinsmen,
15: 5 struck the enemy's flanks with great *s*,
15: 7 the *s* took possession of what was left,
Est 4: 7 the royal treasury for the *s* of the Jews.
7: 4 I have been delivered to destruction, *s*,
2Mc 5:13 and children, a *s* of virgins and infants.
8: 4 to remember the criminal *s* of innocent
12:16 *s* on it that the adjacent pool,
Ps(s) 37:14 the poor, to *s* those whose path is right.
Prv 7:22 her stupidly, like an ox that is led to *s*;
Is 14:21 *s* his sons for the guilt of their fathers;
22:13 celebrate, you *s* oxen and butcher sheep,
30:25 On the day of the great *s*,
34: 2 has doomed them and given them over to *s*.
34: 6 in Bozrah, a great *s* in the land of Edom.

SLAUGHTER (cont.)

53: 7 to the *s* or a sheep before the shearers,
65:12 you shall all go down in *s*.
Jer 7:32 be called such, but rather the Valley of *S*.
11:19 Yet I, like a trusting lamb led to *s*,
12: 3 Pick them out like sheep for the *s*,
19: 6 of Ben-hinnom, but rather, the Valley of *S*.
25:34 The time for your *s* has come;
46:10 of hosts holds a *s* feast in the northland,
50:21 *S* and doom them,
50:27 all her oxen, let them go down to the *s*;
51:40 I will bring them down like lambs to the *s*,
Ez 7:23 They shall wreak *s*,
9: 1 Then *S* of the Idolaters he cried loud for
21:15 To work *s* has it been sharpened,
21:19 is doubled and tripled, this sword of *s*,
21:19 sword of *s* which threatens all around,
21:20 gates I have appointed the sword for *s*,
21:20 to flash lightning, burnished for *s*.
21:33 A sword, a sword is drawn for *s*,
39:17 for the *s* I am about to provide for you,
39:17 you, a great *s* on the mountains of Israel:
39:19 From the *s* which I will provide for you,
44:11 they shall *s* the holocausts and the
Zep 1: 7 LORD, Yes, the LORD has prepared a *s* feast,
1: 8 LORD's *s* feast I will punish the princes,
Jn 10:10 comes only to steal and *s* and destroy,
Acts 8:32 "Like a sheep he was led to the *s*,
10:13 *S*, then eat."
11: 7 *S*, then eat.'
Jas 5: 5 you fattened yourselves for the day of *s*.
Rv 6: 4 of peace by allowing men to *s* one another.

SLAUGHTERED (62)

Gn 43:16 house, and have an animal *s* and prepared,
Ex 12: 6 it shall be *s* during the evening twilight.
Lv 4:15 the bullock has been *s* before the LORD,
4:24 in the place where the holocausts are *s*.
4:33 in the place where the holocausts are *s*.
6:18 At the place where holocausts are *s*,
6:18 the LORD, shall the sin offering be *s*.
7: 2 At the place where the holocausts are *s*.
7: 2 there also shall the guilt offering be *s*.
8:15 Then Moses *s* it,
8:19 When he had *s* it,
8:23 When he had *s* it,
9: 8 *s* the calf that was his own sin offering.
9:12 Then Aaron *s* his holocaust.
9:15 *s* it and offered it up for sin as before.
9:18 Finally he *s* the ox and the ram,
14:13 the sin offering and the holocaust are *s*;
14:25 When he has *s* the guilt-offering lamb,
16:11 When he has *s* it,
Nm 11:22 Can enough sheep and cattle be *s* for them?
14:16 that is why he *s* them in the desert.'
19: 3 led outside the camp and *s* in his presence.
22:40 Here Balak *s* oxen and sheep,
Dt 28:31 Your ox will be *s* before your eyes,
1Sm 11:11 They *s* Ammonites until the heat of the day;
14:34 ox he had seized, and they *s* them there;
25:11 my meat that I have *s* for my own shearers,
28:24 calf in the house, which she now quickly *s*.
2Sm 17: 9 will say, 'Absalom's followers have been *s*.'
1Kgs 1: 9 When he *s* sheep, oxen, and fatlings
1:19 He has *s* oxen, fatlings, and sheep
1:25 He went down today and *s* oxen,
19:21 him and, taking the yoke of oxen, *s* them;
2Kgs 23:20 He *s* upon the altars all the priests of
2Chr 28: 9 have *s* them with a fury that has reached
29:22 They *s* the bulls,
29:22 *s* the rams and cast the blood on the altar;
29:22 then they *s* the lambs and cast the blood
29:24 The priests then *s* them and offered their
30:15 They *s* the Passover on the fourteenth day
35: 1 *s* on the fourteenth day of the first month.
35:11 The Passover sacrifice was *s*,
Tb 7: 9 Raguel *s* a ram from the flock and gave
8:19 and four rams which he ordered to be *s*.
Jdt 9: 3 Therefore you had their rulers *s*;
1Mc 5:28 He *s* all the male population,
5:51 He *s* every male,
2Mc 5: 6 then *s* his fellow citizens without mercy,
12:28 *s* twenty-five thousand of the people in it.
Ps(s) 44:12 will, You marked us out as sheep to be *s*;
44:23 we are looked upon as sheep to be *s*.
Jer 48:15 the flower of his youth goes down to be *s*,
Lam 2:21 on the day of your wrath, *s* without pity.
Ez 16:21 You *s* and immolated my children to them,
26: 6 on the mainland shall be *s* by the sword;
34: 3 milk, worn their wool, and *s* the fatlings,
40:39 *s* the sin offerings and guilt offerings.
40:41 tables], on which the sacrifices were *s*.
40:43 with which the holocausts were *s*.
Zec 11: 4 Shepherd the flock to be *s*.
11: 7 the flock to be *s* for the sheep merchants.
Rom 8:36 we are looked upon as sheep to be *s*."

SLAUGHTERING (4)

Gn 37:31 took Joseph's tunic, and after *s* a goat,
1Sm 14:32 *s* them on the ground and eating the flesh
2Chr 30:17 Levites were in charge of *s*
Is 66: 3 Merely *s* an ox is like slaying a man;

SLAUGHTERS (2)

Ex 21:37 steals an ox or a sheep and *s* or sells it,
Lv 17: 3 Israelite who *s* an ox or a sheep or goat,

SLAVE (126)

Gn 9:26 Let Canaan be his *s*.
9:27 and let Canaan be his *s*."
21:10 "Drive out that *s* and her son!
21:10 No son of that *s* is going to share the
21:12 about the boy or about your *s* woman.
21:13 As for the son of the *s* woman,
25:12 whom Hagar the Egyptian, Sarah's *s*,
29:24 (Laban assigned his *s* girl Zilpah to his
29:29 (Laban assigned his *s* girl Bilhah to his
39:14 brought in a Hebrew *s* to make sport of us!
39:17 *s* whom you brought here broke in on me,
39:19 story about how his *s* had treated her,
41:12 a Hebrew youth, a *s* of the chief steward;
44:10 who is found to have it shall become my *s*,
44:17 the goblet was found shall become my *s*;
44:33 in place of the boy as the *s* of my lord,
Ex 3: 7 cry of complaint against their *s* drivers,
12:44 any *s* who has been bought for money may
20:10 son or daughter, or your male or female *s*,
20:17 neighbor's wife, nor his male or female *s*,
21: 2 When you purchase a Hebrew *s*,
21: 5 If, however, the *s* declares,
21: 6 an awl, thus keeping him as his *s* forever.
21: 7 "When a man sells his daughter as a *s*,
21:20 "When a man strikes his male or female *s*
21:20 rod so hard that the *s* dies under his hand,
21:21 however, the *s* survives for a day or two,
21:21 punished, since the *s* is his own property.
21:26 "When a man strikes his male or female *s*
21:26 the *s* go free in compensation for the eye.
21:27 out a tooth of his male or female *s*,
21:27 *s* go free in compensation for the tooth.
21:32 it is a male or a female *s* that it gores,
21:32 owner of the *s* thirty shekels of silver,
Lv 19:20 carnal relations with a female *s*
22:11 But a *s* whom a priest acquires by purchase
25:39 his services, do not make him work as a *s*.
Dt 5:14 son or daughter, or your male or female *s*,
5:14 male and female *s* should rest as you do.
5:21 house or field, nor his male or female *s*,
12:18 son and daughter, your male and female *s*,
15:17 door, and he shall then be your *s* forever.
15:17 Your female *s*,
15:18 not be reluctant to let your *s* go free,
16:11 son and daughter, your male and female *s*,
16:14 son and daughter, your male and female *s*,
23:16 a *s* who has taken refuge from him with you.
Jos 9:23 every one of you shall always be a *s*
1Sm 25:41 a *s* to wash the feet of my lord's servants."
30:13 "I am an Egyptian, the *s* of an Amalekite.
2Sm 6:20 the view of the *s* girls of his followers,
6:22 the *s* girls you spoke of I will be honored."
1Kgs 14:10 line, whether *s* or freeman in Israel,
21:21 male in Ahab's line, whether *s* or freeman,
2Kgs 5: 4 *s* girl from the land of Israel had said.
9: 8 line, whether *s* or freeman in Israel.
14:26 where there was neither *s* nor freeman,
1Chr 2:34 daughters, had an Egyptian *s* named Jarha.
2:35 his daughter in marriage to his *s* Jarha,
Ezr 7:24 Levite, singer, gatekeeper, temple *s*,
Neh 2:10 Tobiah the Ammonite *s* had heard of this,
2:19 the Horonite, Tobiah the Ammonite *s*,
Jdt 9:10 lips, smite the *s* together with the ruler,
16:12 Sons of *s* girls pierced them through;
1Mc 2:11 From being free, she has become a *s*.
2Mc 8:34 the thousand *s* dealers to buy the Jews,
8:35 fled alone across country like a runaway *s*,
Jb 3:18 and hear not the voice of the *s* driver.
7: 2 He is a *s* who longs for the shade,
40:28 you that you may have him as a *s* forever?
Ps(s) 105:17 a man before them, Joseph, sold as a *s*;
Prv 11:29 and the fool will become *s* to the wise man.
19:10 much less should a *s* rule over princes.
22: 7 and the borrower is the *s* of the lender.
30:22 Under a *s* when he becomes king,
Wis 18:11 the *s* was smitten with the same retribution
Sir 10:24 When free men serve a prudent *s*,
23:10 Just as a *s* that is constantly under
25:21 The man is a *s*,
33:26 a *s* work and he will look for his rest;
33:27 Food, correction and work for a *s*;
33:27 and for a wicked *s*,
33:31 If you have but one *s*,
33:32 If you have but one *s*,
37:11 harvest, to an idle *s* about a great task:
Is 49: 7 whom the nations abhor, the *s* of rulers:
Jer 2:14 Is Israel a *s*, a bondman by birth?
Lam 1: 1 the provinces has been made a toiling *s*.
Mt 8: 9 If I tell my *s*, 'Do this,' he does it."
10:24 outranks his teacher, no *s* his master.
10:25 like his teacher, the *s* like his master.
Mk 14:47 his sword and struck the high priest's *s*,
Lk 7: 8 to my *s*,
12:47 The *s* who knew his master's wishes but did
Jn 8:34 everyone who lives in sin is the *s* of sin.
8:35 (No *s* has a permanent place in the family,
13:16 you, no *s* is greater than his master;
15:15 a *s* does not know what his master is about.
15:20 no *s* is greater than his master.
18:10 it and struck the *s* of the high priest,
Acts 16:16 met a *s* girl who had a clairvoyant spirit.
1Cor 7:21 Were you a *s* when your call came?
7:22 The *s* called in the Lord is a freedman of
7:22 who has been called is a *s* of Christ.
9:19 I made myself the *s* of all so as to win
12:13 all of us, whether Jew or Greek, *s* or free,
Gal 3:28 exist among you Jew or Greek, *s* or freeman,
4: 1 is no different from that of a *s*,
4: 7 You are no longer a *s* but a son!
4:22 Abraham had two sons, one by the *s* girl,
4:23 The son of the *s* girl had been begotten in
4:30 "Cast out *s* girl and son together;
4:30 for the *s* girl's son shall never be an
4:31 of a *s* girl but of a mother who is free.
Eph 6: 8 You know that each one, whether *s* or free,
Phil 2: 7 emptied himself and took the form of a *s*,
Col 1: 7 of Epaphras, our dear fellow *s*,
3:11 foreigner, Scythian, *s* or freeman.
4: 1 You *s* owners,
4: 7 faithful minister and fellow *s* in the Lord,
Phlm 1:16 no longer as a *s* but as more than a slave,
1:16 no longer as a slave but as more than a *s*,
2Pt 2:19 *s* of that by which he has been overcome.
Rv 6:15 wealthy and powerful, the *s* and the free
13:16 small and great, rich and poor, *s* and free,
19:18 the flesh of all men, the free and the *s*,

SLAVE-GIRL (1)

Ex 11: 5 to the first-born of the *s* at the handmill,

SLAVED (2)

Gn 31:41 I *s* fourteen years for your two daughters
Lk 15:29 'For years now I have *s* for you.

SLAVERY (41)

Gn 47:21 Pharaoh, and the people were reduced to *s*,
Ex 1:13 Israelites and reduced them to cruel *s*,
2:23 groaned and cried out because of their *s*.
6: 6 and will deliver you from their *s*.
6: 9 him because of their dejection and hard *s*.
13: 3 you came out of Egypt, that place of *s*.
13:14 brought us out of Egypt, that place of *s*.
20: 2 out of the land of Egypt, that place of *s*.
Lv 26:13 the Egyptians and freed you from their *s*,
Dt 5: 6 out of the land of Egypt, that place of *s*.
6:12 out of the land of Egypt, that place of *s*.
7: 8 with his strong hand from the place of *s*,
8:14 out of the land of Egypt, that place of *s*;
13: 6 and ransomed you from that place of *s*.
13:11 out of the land of Egypt, that place of *s*.
Jos 24:17 of the land of Egypt, out of a state of *s*.
Jgs 5: 6 of Anath, in the days of *s* caravans ceased:
6: 8 I brought you out of the place of *s*.
Neh 5: 5 had to reduce our sons and daughters to *s*,
9:17 their heads to return to their *s* in Egypt.
Est 7: 4 to be sold into *s* I would remain silent,
1Mc 8:10 and reduced them to *s* even to this day.
8:18 of the Greeks was subjecting Israel to *s*.
2Mc 5:14 and the same number being sold into *s*.
5:24 and sell the women and young men into *s*.
8:10 the Romans by selling captured Jews into *s*.
Jer 34: 9 hold a man of Judah, his brother, in *s*.
34:16 you forced them once more into *s*.
Lam 1: 3 into exile from oppression and cruel *s*;
Mi 6: 4 Egypt, from the place of *s* I released you;
Acts 7: 6 to *s* and oppressed four hundred years.
7: 9 the patriarchs sold Joseph into *s* in Egypt,
Rom 6:16 you obey, whether yours is the *s* of sin,
7:14 I am weak flesh sold into the *s* of sin.
8:15 a spirit of *s* leading you back into fear,
8:21 will be freed from its *s* to corruption
1Cor 7:21 be better off making the most of your *s*.
Gal 4:24 Sinai, and brought forth children to *s*;
4:25 which is likewise in *s* with her children.
5: 1 on yourselves the yoke of *s* a second time!
1Tm 6: 1 All under the yoke of *s* must regard their

SLAVES (124)

Gn 9:25 lowest of *s* shall he be to his brothers."
12:16 flocks and herds, male and female *s*,
17:12 including houseborn *s* and those acquired
17:13 both the houseborn *s* and those acquired
17:23 took his son Ishmael and all his *s*,
17:27 including the *s* born in his house or
20:14 male and female *s* and gave them to Abraham;
24:35 herds, silver and gold, male and female *s*,
27:37 assigned to him all his kinsmen as his *s*;
43:18 us and take our donkeys and seize us as *s*."
44: 9 rest of us, we shall become my lord's *s*."
44:16 Here we are, then, the *s* of my lord
47:19 Pharaoh's *s* and our land his property;
47:25 to my lord that we can be Pharaoh's *s*."
50:18 before him and said, "Let us be your *s*!"
Ex 1:14 the whole cruel fate of *s*.
6: 5 whom the Egyptians are treating as *s*,
14:12 Far better for us to be the *s* of the
21: 7 slave, she shall not go free as male *s* do.
Lv 25: 6 yourself and for your male and female *s*,

25:42 they shall not be sold as *s* to any man.
25:44 *S,* male and female, you may indeed
25:45 Such *s* you may own as chattels,
25:46 property, making them perpetual *s.*
Dt 5:15 remember that you too were once *s* in Egypt,
6:21 son, 'We were once *s* of Pharaoh in Egypt,
12:12 and daughters, your male and female *s,*
15:15 you too were once *s* in the land of Egypt,
16:12 Remember that you too were once *s* in Egypt,
24:18 For, remember, you were once *s* in Egypt,
24:22 For remember that you were once *s* in Egypt;
28:68 sale to your enemies as male and female *s,*
1Sm 2:27 were in Egypt as *s* to the house of Pharaoh.
4: 9 otherwise you will become *s* to the Hebrews,
4: 9 slaves to the Hebrews, as they were your *s.*
8:15 give the revenue to his eunuchs and his *s.*
8:17 and you yourselves will become his *s.*
2Sm 22:44 A people I had not known became my *s;*
2Kgs 4: 1 has come to take my two children as his *s.*"
1Chr 9: 2 the priests, the Levites, and the temple *s.*
2Chr 28:10 Judah and Jerusalem your *s* and bondwomen.
Ezr 2:43 The temple *s:* son of Ziha,
2:55 Descendants of the *s* of Solomon:
2:58 slaves and the descendants of the *s*
2:65 not counting their male and female *s,*
2:70 and the temple *s* dwelt in their cities.
7: 7 and temple *s* also came up to Jerusalem in
8:17 brethren, and to the temple *s* in Casiphia,
8:20 Of the temple *s* (those whom David and the
9: 9 For *s* we are,
Neh 3:27 [the temple *s* were dwelling on Ophel].
3:31 quarters of the temple *s* and the merchants,
7:46 The temple *s:* sons of Ziha,
7:57 Descendants of the *s* of Solomon:
7:60 slaves and the descendants of the *s*
7:67 not counting their male and female *s,*
7:72 gatekeepers, the singers, the temple *s,*
9:36 But, see, we today are *s;*
9:36 see, we have become *s* upon it!
10:29 Levites, gatekeepers, singers, temple *s,*
11: 3 Israelites, priests, Levites, temple *s,*
11: 3 and the descendants of the *s* of Solomon,
11:21 The temple *s* lived on Ophel.
11:21 and Gishpa were in charge of the temple *s.*
Tb 10:10 male and female *s,*
Jdt 4:10 *s* also girded themselves with sackcloth.
7:27 We should indeed be made *s,*
9: 3 smote the *s* together with their princes,
14:13 *s* have dared come down to give us battle,
14:18 "The *s* have duped us!
1Mc 3:41 and gold, to buy the Israelites as *s.*
2Mc 1:27 free those who are the *s* of the Gentiles,
8:11 inviting them to buy Jewish *s* and
8:11 promising to deliver ninety *s* for a talent
8:25 of those who had come to buy them as *s.*
Ps(s) 18:44 A people I had not known became my *s;*
Eccl 2: 7 female slaves, and *s* were born in my house.
10: 7 I have seen *s* on horseback,
10: 7 while princes walked on the ground like *s.*
Is 14: 2 as male and female *s* on the Lord's soil,
Jer 34: 9 Everyone was to free his Hebrew *s,*
34:10 so that they should be *s* no longer.
34:11 took back their male and female *s*
34:13 Egypt, out of the place where they were *s,*
34:16 *s* to whom you had given their freedom;
Lam 5: 8 *S* rule over us; there is no one to rescue
Ez 27:13 *s* and articles of bronze for your goods.
Zec 2:13 they become plunder for their *s.*
Mt 13:27 The owner's *s* came to him and said,
13:28 His *s* said to him,
21:34 dispatched his *s* to the tenants
21:35 The tenants responded by seizing the *s.*
21:36 time he dispatched even more *s* than before,
Jn 8:33 "Never have we been *s* to anyone.
15:15 I no longer speak of you as *s,*
18:10 (The *s* name was Malchus.)
18:26 insisted one of the high priest's *s*—
Rom 6: 6 and we might be *s* to sin no longer.
6:16 offer yourselves to someone as obedient *s,*
6:16 slaves, you are the *s* of the one you obey,
6:17 be to God, though once you were *s* of sin,
6:18 from your sin, you became *s* of justice.
6:20 When you were *s* of sin,
6:22 freed from sin and have become *s* of God,
Gal 2: 4 Christ Jesus and thereby to make *s* of us,
4: 3 *s* subordinated to the elements of the world;
4: 8 as *s* to gods who are not really divine.
Eph 6: 5 *S,* obey your human masters with the
6: 6 will with your whole heart as *s* of Christ.
6: 9 act in a similar way toward your *s.*
Col 3:22 To *s* I say,
3:24 Be *s* of Christ the Lord.
4: 1 deal justly and fairly with your *s,*
1Tm 6: 2 Those *s* whose masters are brothers in the
Ti 2: 3 not be slanderous gossips or *s* to drink.
2: 9 *S* are to be submissive to their masters.
3: 3 we were the *s* of our passions and of
Heb 2:15 had been *s* their whole life long.
1Pt 2:18 You household *s,* obey your masters
2Pt 2:19 though they themselves are *s* of corruption
Rv 18:13 *s* and human lives.

SLAY (50)

Gn 20: 4 you *s* a man even though he is innocent?
32:12 me down and *s* the mothers and children.
Ex 5:21 have put a sword in their hands to *s* us."
32:27 from gate to gate, and *s* your own kinsmen,
Lv 14: 5 The priest shall then order him to *s* one
14:50 One of the birds he shall *s* over an
Nm 14:15 If now you *s* this whole people,
31:17 *S,* therefore, every male child
Dt 9:28 brought them out to *s* them in the desert.'
13:10 hand shall be the first raised to *s* him;
2Kgs 6:22 "Do you *s* those whom you have taken
8:12 you will *s* their youth with the sword,
10:25 guards and officers, "Go in and *s* them.
2Chr 35: 6 *S* the Passover sacrifice, sanctify yourselves,
Tb 3:15 But if it please you, Lord, not to *s* me,
6:15 *s* any man who wishes to come close to her.
2Mc 5:12 to *s* those who took refuge in their houses.
Jb 13:15 *S* me though he might,
20:16 the viper's fangs shall *s* him.
Ps(s) 37:32 man spies on the just, and seeks to *s* him.
59:12 O God, *s* them,
94: 6 Widow and stranger they *s,*
Wis 11:19 their frightful appearance itself could *s*
Is 11: 4 breath of his lips he shall *s* the wicked.
14:30 with famine that shall *s* even your remnant.
27: 1 he will *s* the dragon that is in the sea.
65:15 The Lord GOD shall *s* you,
Jer 5: 6 Therefore lions from the forest *s* them,
15: 3 the sword to *s* them; dogs to drag them
18:23 you, O LORD, know all their plans to *s* me.
20: 4 to Babylon or *s* them with the sword.
29:21 Babylon, who will *s* them before your eyes.
33: 5 of those whom I *s* in my anger and wrath,
50:27 *S* all her oxen, let them go down
Ez 23:47 They shall *s* their sons and daughters,
26: 8 on the mainland he shall *s* with the sword;
26:11 Your people he shall *s* by the sword;
28: 9 a god, handed over to those who will *s* you.
Dn 11:44 out with great fury to *s* and to doom many.
Hos 2: 5 her to an arid land, and *s* her with thirst.
6: 9 a band of priests *s* on the way to Shechem,
9:11 I would *s* the darlings of their womb.
Am 2: 3 midst, and her princes I will *s* with him,
9: 1 Those who are left I will *s* with the sword;
9: 4 there will I command the sword to *s* them.
Ob 1:14 not at the crossroads to *s* his refugees;
Hb 1:17 his sword to *s* peoples without mercy?
Zec 11: 5 For they who buy them *s* them with impunity;
Lk 13:34 you *s* the prophets and stone those who are
19:27 bring them in and *s* them in my presence.'"

SLAYER (4)

Nm 35:24 between the *s* and the avenger
Is 27: 7 or slain as his *s* was slain?
Ez 21:16 burnished to be put in the hand of a *s.*
Hos 9:13 shall bring out his children to the *s.*

SLAYERS (1)

Jer 4:31 I sink exhausted before the *s!*"

SLAYING (10)

Dt 27:25 who accepts payment for *s* an innocent man!'
1Sm 17:57 when David returned from *s* the Philistine,
18: 6 (on David's return after *s* the Philistine),
22:18 *s* on that day eighty-five who wore the
1Kgs 9:16 *s* all the Canaanites living in the city,
2Chr 30:22 *s* peace offerings and singing praises to
Wis 11: 7 rebuke to the decree for the *s* of infants,
Is 66: 3 Merely slaughtering an ox is like *s* a man;
Ez 21:27 bidding him to give the order for *s,*
Acts 7:24 and avenged the victim by *s* the Egyptian.

SLAYS (12)

Lv 24:21 Whoever *s* an animal shall make restitution,
24:21 but whoever *s* a man shall be put to death.
Dt 27:24 'Cursed be he who *s* his neighbor in secret!'
Jb 5: 2 the fool and indignation *s* the simpleton.
9:23 When the scourge *s* suddenly,
Ps(s) 34:22 Vice *s* the wicked, and the enemies
Prv 21:25 The sluggard's propensity *s* him,
Wis 1:11 unpunished, and a lying mouth *s* the soul.
16:14 Man, however, *s* in his malice,
Sir 34:20 Like the man who *s* a son in his father's
34:22 He *s* his neighbor who deprives him of his
Ez 26:15 wounded, when the sword *s* in your midst,

SLEDGE (3)

Jb 41:22 spreads like a threshing *s* upon the mire.
Is 28:27 Gith is not threshed with a *s,*
41:15 I will make of you a threshing *s,*

SLEDGES (3)

2Sm 24:22 *s* and the yokes of the oxen for wood.
1Chr 21:23 holocausts, the threshing *s* for the wood,
Am 1: 3 they threshed Gilead with *s* of iron,

SLEEK (3)

Ps(s) 73: 4 their bodies are sound and *s;*
Jer 5:28 they grow powerful and rich, fat and *s.*
Ez 34:16 [but the *s* and the strong I will destroy],

SLEEP (71)

Gn 2:21 So the LORD God cast a deep *s* on the man,
28:11 his head and lay down to *s* at that spot.
28:16 When Jacob awoke from his *s,*
31:40 frost by night, while *s* fled from my eyes!
Ex 22:26 What else has he to *s* in?
Dt 24:12 not *s* in the mantle he gives as a pledge,
24:13 him at sunset that he himself may *s* in it.
Jgs 16:14 Awakening from his *s,*
16:19 She had him *s* on her lap,
16:20 and he woke from his *s,*
1Sm 2: 8 his vow, and blesses the *s* of the just.
3: 5 "Go back to *s.*"
3: 5 So he went back to *s.*
3: 6 Go back to *s.*"
3: 9 So he said to Samuel, "Go to *s,*
3: 9 When Samuel went to *s* in his place,
2Sm 11:11 to eat and to drink and to *s* with my wife?
11:13 to *s* on his bed among his lord's servants,
Tb 2: 9 went to *s* next to the wall of my courtyard.
10: 7 whole night through, getting no *s* at all.
Est 6: 1 That night the king, unable to *s,*
1Mc 6:10 *S* has departed from my eyes,
Jb 4:13 of the night, when deep *s* falls on men,
14:12 not awake, nor be roused out of their *s.*
33:15 [when deep *s* falls upon men] as they
Ps(s) 3: 6 When I lie down in *s,*
13: 4 I may not *s* in death lest my enemy say,
22:30 shall bow down all who *s* in the earth;
76: 6 they *s* their sleep;
78:65 wakes from *s* a champion overcome with wine;
90: 5 You make an end of them in their *s;*
127: 2 bread, for he gives to his beloved in *s.*
132: 3 live in, nor lie on the couch where I *s;*
132: 4 will give my eyes no *s* my eyelids no rest,
Prv 3:24 when you rest, your *s* will be sweet.
4:16 made no one stumble steals away their *s.*
6: 4 Give no *s* to your eyes, nor slumber
6: 9 when will you rise from your *s?*
6:10 A little *s,* a little slumber, a little folding
19:15 Laziness plunges a man into deep *s,*
20:13 Love not *s,* lest you be reduced to poverty;
24:33 A little *s,* a little slumber, a little folding
Eccl 4:11 So also, if two *s* together,
5:11 *S* is sweet to the laboring man,
5:11 the rich man's abundance allows him no *s.*
8:17 nor by night do his eyes find rest in *s.*
Wis 7:10 the splendor of her never yields to *s.*
17:14 world, while all sleeping the same *s,*
Sir 22: 7 like disturbing a man in the depths of *s;*
30:17 life, unending *s* to constant illness.
31:20 Distress and anguish and loss of *s,*
40: 5 to rest, his cares at night disturb his *s.*
Is 5:27 none will slumber and none will *s.*
29:10 has poured out on you a spirit of deep *s.*
56:10 Dreaming as they lie there, loving their *s.*
Jer 31:26 but my *s* was sweet to me.
51:39 that they may be overcome with perpetual *s,*
51:57 warriors, so that they sleep an eternal *s,*
Ez 34:25 in the desert and *s* in the forests.
Dn 2: 1 his spirit no rest and robbed him of his *s.*
6:19 Since *s* was impossible for him,
12: 2 who *s* in the dust of the earth shall awake;
Zec 4: 1 me, like a man awakened from his *s.*
Mt 26:45 *S* on now.
Lk 9:32 those with him had fallen into a deep *s;*
Jn 11:13 thought he meant *s* in the sense of slumber.
Rom 13:11 It is now the hour for you to wake from *s,*
1Thes 4:13 you be clear about those who *s* in death,
5: 7 *s* by night and drunkards drink by night.

SLEEPER (1)

Eph 5:14 "Awake, O *s,* arise from the dead,

SLEEPERS (1)

1Thes 5: 7 *S* sleep by night and drunkards drink by

SLEEPING (11)

1Sm 3: 3 and Samuel was *s* in the temple of the LORD
26: 5 of Ner, the general, had their *s* quarters.
26: 7 Abner and his men *s* around him.
1Kgs 3:20 from my side, as I, your handmaid, was *s.*
Jdt 14:14 tent, presuming that he was *s* with Judith.
Sg 5: 2 I was *s,* but my heart kept vigil;
Wis 17:14 nether world, while all *s* the same sleep,
Mt 8:25 Jesus was *s* soundly,
Mk 14:41 a third time and said to them, "Still *s?*
Lk 22:46 He said to them, "Why are you *s?*
Acts 12: 6 to trial, Peter was *s* between two soldiers,

SLEEPLESS (4)

2Mc 2:26 easy, is one of sweat and of *s* nights,
Ps(s) 102: 8 I am *s,* and I moan; I am like a sparrow
2Cor 6: 5 as men familiar with hard work, *s* nights,
11:27 enduring labor, hardship, many *s* nights;

SLEEPS (6)

Lv 14:47 Whoever s or eats in such a house shall
1Kgs 1: 2 If she s with your royal majesty,
1:21 when my lord the king s with his fathers,
Ps(s) 121: 4 Indeed he neither slumbers nor s,
Prv 19:23 and s without being visited by misfortune.
Hos 7: 6 All the night their anger s;

SLEPT (13)

Gn 30:16 So that night he s with her,
Jgs 16:14 So while he s, Delilah wove his seven locks
1Sm 3:15 Samuel then s until morning,
9:25 for Saul on the roof, and he s there.
2Sm 11: 9 But Uriah s at the entrance of the royal
12: 3 and drank from his cup and s in his bosom.
12:24 He went and s with her;
1Kgs 21:27 He fasted, s in the sackcloth,
Jdt 12: 5 into the tent, where she s till midnight.
Est 4: 3 they all s on sackcloth and ashes.)
Jb 3:13 had I s,
Sir 47:23 Solomon finally s with his fathers,
Lk 8:23 So they set out, and as they sailed he s.

SLEW (74)

Gn 4:25 of Abel," she said, "because Cain s him."
49: 6 For in their fury they s men,
Ex 2:12 he s the Egyptian and hid him in the sand.
12:29 s every first-born in the land of Egypt,
Nm 3:13 s all the first-born in the land of Egypt,
8:17 s all the first-born in the land of Egypt.
Jos 10:11 than the Israelites s with the sword.
11:10 Hazor and s its king with the sword;
20: 5 s his fellow man unintentionally
Jgs 1: 4 and they s ten thousand of them in Bezek.
3:29 they s about ten thousand Moabites,
3:31 s six hundred Philistines with an oxgoad.
8:17 tower of Penuel and s the men of the city.
9: 5 house in Ophrah, and s his brothers,
1Sm 4: 2 who s about four thousand men on the
14:14 s about twenty men within half a furlong.
18:27 with his men and s two hundred Philistines.
19: 5 his life in his hands and s the Philistine,
31: 2 Saul and his sons closely, and s Jonathan,
2Sm 8: 5 Zobah, David s twenty-two thousand of them.
23:12 He s the Philistines, and the LORD
23:20 It was he who s the two lions in Moab.
23:21 too, who s an Egyptian of large stature.
1Kgs 2: 5 he s the two generals of Israel's armies,
2:32 and s them with the sword without my
2Kgs 10: 7 took the princes and s all seventy of them,
10: 9 I conspired against my lord and s him,
10:11 Thereupon Jehu s all who were left of the
10:17 s all who remained there of Ahab's line,
11:18 altars and images completely, and s Mattan,
14: 5 s the officials who had murdered the king,
14: 7 s ten thousand Edomites in the Salt Valley,
19:37 Sharezer s him with the sword
21:23 against him and s the king in his palace,
21:24 s all who had conspired against king Amon,
1Chr 10:14 Therefore the LORD s him,
11:11 hundred, whom he s in a single encounter.
11:20 spear against three hundred, and s them.
11:23 He likewise s the Egyptian, a huge man
18: 5 also s twenty-two thousand of their men.
18:12 also s eighteen thousand Edomites in the
19:18 and David s seven thousand of their
20: 4 time, Sibbecai the Hushathite s Sippai,
20: 5 and Elhanan, the son of Jair, s Lahmi,
20: 7 the son of Shimea, David's brother, s him.
2Chr 22: 8 who were his attendants, and he s them.
23:17 its altars and images, and they s Mattan,
24:22 Zechariah's father, and s his son.
25: 3 he s those of his servants who had killed
28: 6 s one hundred and twenty thousand of Judah
33:25 But the people of the land s all those who
36:17 who s their young men in their own
Neh 9:26 they s your prophets who bore witness
Tb 1:18 I also buried anyone whom Sennacherib s
2Mc 4:42 thief himself they s near the treasury.
13:15 also s the lead elephant and its rider.
15:22 and he s a hundred and eighty-five
Ps(s) 78:31 God rose against them and s their best men,
78:34 While he s them they sought him and
135:10 He smote many nations and s mighty kings:
136:18 And s powerful kings,
Wis 16: 9 the bites of locusts and of flies s them,
Sir 47: 4 As a youth he s the giant and wiped out
Is 37:38 Sharezer s him with the sword
Jer 39: 6 who s also all the nobles of Judah.
41: 3 Ishmael also s all the men of Judah of
41: 7 men s them and threw them into the cistern.
52:10 the king of Babylon s his sons as well as
Lam 2: 4 as a foe, and s all on whom the eye doted;
3:43 and pursued us, you s us and took no pity;
Ez 23:10 away, and herself they s with the sword.
23:39 day they s their children for their idols,
Hos 6: 5 I s them by the words of my mouth;
Am 4:10 and with the sword I s your young men;

SLIGHT (4)

2Sm 19:44 Why do you s us?
2Mc 14:17 of the enemy suffered a s repulse.
Sir 10:10 A s illness
Lk 16:10 in a s matter is also unjust in greater.

SLIGHTED (2)

Mal 1: 7 By saying the table of the LORD may be s!
1:12 offering may be polluted, and its food s.

SLIGHTEST (2)

Ex 5:11 must not be the s reduction in your work."
1Mc 2:22 depart from our religion in the s degree."

SLIGHTLY (1)

Jn 18: 6 they retreated s and fell to the ground.

SLING (10)

Jgs 20:16 to s a stone at a hair without missing.
1Sm 17:40 With his s also ready to hand,
17:49 hurled it with the s and struck the
17:50 overcame the Philistine with s and stone;
25:29 of your enemies as from the hollow of a s.
Jdt 9: 7 trusting in shield and spear, bow and s.
Prv 26: 8 in the s is he who gives honor to a fool.
Wis 5:22 and as from his s,
Jer 10:18 I will s away the inhabitants of the land
Zec 9:15 s stones and trample them underfoot;

SLINGERS (3)

2Kgs 3:25 s had surrounded it and were attacking it.
Jdt 6:12 and all the s blocked the ascent of
1Mc 9:11 and the s and the archers came on ahead of

SLINGING (1)

1Chr 12: 2 both in s stones and in shooting arrows

SLINGSTONE (1)

Sir 47: 4 the s that crushed the pride of Goliath.

SLINGSTONES (3)

2Chr 26:14 breastplates, bows, and s
1Mc 6:51 mechanical bows for shooting arrows and s.
Jb 41:20 s used against him are but straws.

SLINK (1)

Jer 38:22 feet are stuck in the mud, they s away."

SLIP (12)

Dt 4: 9 s from your memory as long as you live,
1Sm 13: 8 Gilgal, the men began to s away from Saul.
Ps(s) 66: 9 to our souls, and has not let our feet s.
121: 3 May he not suffer your foot to s;
Prv 3:21 My son, let not these s out of your sight:
4:21 Let them not s out of your sight,
Eccl 9:18 and a single s can ruin much that is good."
Sir 12:15 but if you s,
19:15 Then, too, a man can s and not mean it;
20:17 is less sudden than a s of the tongue;
28:26 Take care not to s by your tongue and fall
Jn 5:13 great that Jesus had been able to s away.

SLIPPED (5)

2Sm 4: 6 So Rechab and his brother Baanah s past
2Kgs 6: 5 trunk, the iron axhead s into the water.
1Mc 9: 6 much afraid, and many s away from the camp,
Ps(s) 73: 2 my feet all but s,
Jn 8:59 himself and s out of the temple precincts.

SLIPPERY (3)

Ps(s) 35: 6 Let their way be dark and s,
73:18 You set them, indeed, on a s road;
Jer 23:12 their way shall become for them s ground.

SLIPPING (3)

1Sm 13:11 I saw that the men were s away from me,
Jdt 7:19 there was no way of s through their lines.
Ps(s) 94:18 When I say, "My foot is s,"

SLIPS (3)

Ps(s) 38:17 be glad on my account who, when my foot s,
Sir 13:22 If he s they cast him down.
Is 17:10 plants and set out your foreign vine s,

SLIT (1)

1Kgs 18:40 brook Kishon and there he s their throats.

SLOPE (7)

Jos 10:10 and pursued them down the Beth-horon s,
1Sm 26:13 Going across to an opposite s,
31: 7 When the Israelites on the s of the valley
2Sm 13:34 down the s from the direction of Bahurim.
Sir 46: 6 army till on the s he destroyed the foe;
Mi 1: 4 the fire, like water poured down a s.
Mk 5:11 was feeding there on the s of the mountain.

SLOPES (12)

Dt 3:17 Sea of the Arabah, under the s of Pisgah.
4:49 as the Arabah Sea under the s of Pisgah.
Jos 10:40 Negeb, the foothills, and the mountain s,
12: 3 to a point under the s of Pisgah.
12: 8 regions and foothills, the Arabah, the s,
13:20 the valley, Beth-peor, the s of Pisgah,
2Kgs 23: 4 burned outside Jerusalem on the s
Jdt 14:11 arms and went to the s of the mountain.
1Mc 9:15 and pursued them as far as the mountain s.
Jb 30: 6 To dwell on the s of the wadies,
Is 16: 8 The terraced s of Heshbon languish,
Jer 31:40 ashes, all the s toward the Kidron Valley,

SLOPING (1)

2Mc 13: 5 with a circular rim s down steeply on all

SLOTHFUL (4)

Jgs 18: 9 Do not be s about beginning your
Prv 11:16 [The s become impoverished,
12:24 will govern, but the s will be enslaved.
12:27 The s man catches not his prey,

SLOW (16)

Ex 4:10 but I am s of speech and tongue."
34: 6 s to anger and rich in kindness and
Nm 14:18 LORD is s to anger and rich in kindness,
Neh 9:17 s to anger and rich in mercy;
Ps(s) 86:15 a God merciful and gracious, s to anger,
103: 8 s to anger and abounding in kindness.
145: 8 merciful, s to anger and of great kindness.
Prv 19:11 It is good sense in a man to be s to anger,
Wis 15: 1 our God, are good and true, s to anger,
Sir 5:13 Be swift to hear, but s to answer.
Jl 2:13 gracious and merciful is he, s to anger,
Jon 4: 2 a gracious and merciful God, s to anger,
Na 1: 3 The LORD is s to anger,
Lk 24:25 How s you are to believe all that the
Jas 1:19 quick to hear, slow to speak, s to anger.

SLOWLY (1)

Gn 33:14 while I proceed more s at the pace of the

SLUGGARD (16)

Prv 6: 6 Go to the ant, O s,
6: 9 How long, O s, will you rest?
10:26 the s to those who use him as a messenger.
13: 4 The soul of the s craves in vain,
15:19 way of the s is hemmed in as with thorns,
19:15 into deep sleep, and the s must go hungry.
19:24 The s loses his hand in the dish;
20: 4 In seedtime the s plows not;
22:13 The s says, "A lion is outside;
24:30 I passed by the field of the s,
26:13 The s says, "There is a lion in the street,
26:14 The door turns on its hinges, the s,
26:15 The s loses his hand in the dish;
26:16 The s imagines himself wiser than seven
Sir 22: 1 The s is like a stone in the mud;
22: 2 The s is like a lump of dung;

SLUGGARDS (1)

Prv 21:25 The s propensity slays him,

SLUGGISH (4)

Eccl 12: 5 s and the caper berry is without effect,
Is 6:10 are to make the heart of this people s,
Mt 13:15 S indeed is this people's heart.
Acts 28:27 The mind of this people has grown s.

SLUMBER (11)

1Sm 26:12 the LORD had put them into a deep s.
Jb 33:15 falls upon men] as they s in their beds,
Ps(s) 121: 3 may he s not who guards you:
Prv 6: 4 sleep to your eyes, nor s to your eyelids;
6:10 A little sleep, a little s,
24:33 A little sleep, a little s,
Sir 31: 2 Concern for one's livelihood banishes s;
31:20 s and a clear mind next day on rising.
Is 5:27 weariness, none will s and none will sleep.
Na 3:18 how your shepherds s,
Jn 11:13 thought he meant sleep in the sense of s.

SLUMBERER (1)

Sir 22: 8 He talks with a s who talks with a fool,

SLUMBERS (2)

Ps(s) 121: 4 Indeed he neither s nor sleeps,
Prv 10: 5 a son who s during harvest,

SLUNG (2)

1Sm 17: 6 and had a bronze scimitar s from a baldric.
2Sm 20: 8 a belt over his tunic, from which was s,

SLY (1)

Sir 4:30 lion at home, nor s and suspicious at work.

SMALL (84)

Gn 19:20 It's only a *s* place.
19:20 it's a *s* place,
Ex 12: 4 If a family is too *s* for a whole lamb,
16:17 Some gathered a large and some a *s* amount.
16:18 a *s* amount did not have too little.
Nm 22:18 gold, I could not do anything, *s* or great,
26:54 heritage, to a *s* group a small heritage,
26:56 the lot falls shall each group, large or *s*,
33:54 group and a *s* heritage to a small group.
Dt 25:13 in your bag, one large and the other *s*;
25:14 in your house, one large and the other *s*.
26: 5 a *s* household and lived there as an alien.
Jos 19:47 of the Danites was too *s* for them;
1Sm 14:29 are from this *s* taste of honey I have had.
20: 2 My father does nothing, great or *s*,
22:15 servant knows nothing at all, great or *s*,
30:19 Nothing was missing, *s* or great,
1Kgs 2:20 "There is one *s* favor I would ask of you,"
8:64 the LORD was too *s* to hold these offerings.
17:10 bring me a *s* cupful of water to drink."
18:44 as *s* as a man's hand rising from the sea."
20:27 seemed like a couple of *s* flocks of goats,
2Kgs 2:23 some *s* boys came out of the city and
23: 2 prophets, and all the people, *s* and great.
25:26 Then all the people, great and *s*,
1Chr 26:13 gate, the *s* and the large families alike.
2Chr 15:13 was to be put to death, whether *s* or great,
18:30 the order, "Fight with no one, *s* or great,
31:15 to their brethren great and *s* alike,
34:30 Levites, and all the people, great and *s*;
36:18 of the house of God, the large and the *s*,
Neh 7: 4 and spacious but its population was *s*,
Jdt 13: 4 all had departed, and no one, *s* or great,
Est 1: 5 palace for all the people, great and *s*,
1Mc 3:29 the income from the province was *s*,
5:45 assembled all the Israelites, great and *s*,
9:65 Jonathan, accompanied by a *s* group of men,
Jb 3:19 *S* and great are there the same,
Ps(s) 104:25 number of living things both *s* and great,
115:13 fear the LORD, both the *s* and the great.
Eccl 9:14 Against a *s* city with few men in it
Wis 6: 7 himself made the great as well as the *s*,
Sir 6: 1 Say nothing harmful, *s* or great;
14: 8 In the miser's opinion his share is too *s*;
22:18 *S* stones lying on an open height will not
30:12 thrash his sides while he is still *s*,
Is 16:14 there shall be a remnant, very *s* and weak.
49:19 you shall be too *s* for your inhabitants,
49:20 say to you, "This place is too *s* for me,
Jer 6:13 *S* and great alike, all are greedy for gain;
8:10 *S* and great alike, all are greedy for gain,
49:15 *S* will I make you among the despised among
Bar 1: 4 and the whole people, *s* and great alike
Ez 5: 3 [But of the last take a *s* number and tie
20:37 the staff and bring back but a *s* number.
Dn 11:23 treacherously rise to power with a *s* party.
Am 6:11 to bits, and reduce the *s* house to rubble.
7: 2 He is so *s!*
7: 5 He is so *s!*
Ob 1: 2 See, I make you *s* among the nations;
Jon 3: 5 a fast and all of them, great and *s*,
Mi 5: 1 too *s* to be among the clans of Judah,
Zec 4:10 were scornful on that day of *s* beginnings
Mt 15:34 they replied, "and a few *s* fish."
22:19 When they handed him a *s* Roman coin,
25:21 Since you were dependable in a *s* matter I
25:23 Since you were dependable in a *s* matter I
Mk 7:25 whose *s* daughter had an unclean spirit,
8: 7 They also had a few *s* fish;
12:42 in two *s* copper coins worth a few cents.
Lk 7:47 Little is forgiven the one whose love is *s*."
19: 3 Jesus was like, but being *s* of stature,
19:17 'You showed yourself capable in a *s* matter.
Acts 26:22 stand here to testify to great and *s* alike.
27:16 We passed under the lee of a *s* island
27:17 they lowered the *s* anchor used for moving
Jas 3: 4 they are directed by very *s* rudders on
3: 5 It is a *s* member, yet it makes great
Rv 11:18 who revere you, the great and the *s* alike;
13:16 It forced all men, *s* and great,
19: 5 all you his servants, the *s* and the great,
19:18 free and the slave, the *s* and the great."

SMALLER (1)

Nm 35: 8 from a larger group and fewer from a *s* one,

SMALLEST (11)

Dt 7: 7 for you are really the *s* of all nations.
1Sm 9:21 of one of the *s* tribes of Israel,
Prv 30:24 Four things are among the *s* on the earth,
Is 60:22 The *s* shall become a thousand,
Jer 49:20 shall be dragged away, even the *s* sheep,
50:45 shall be dragged away, even the *s* sheep;
Mt 5:18 smallest letter of the law, not the *s* part
13:32 It is the *s* seed of all,
Mk 4:31 soil, is the *s* of all the earth's seeds,
Lk 12:26 If the *s* things are beyond your power,

SMART (1)

Tb 11:13 medicine on his eyes, and it made them *s*.

SMASH (8)

Ex 23:24 demolish them and *s* their sacred pillars.
34:13 *s* their sacred pillars,
Dt 7: 5 down their altars, *s* their sacred pillars,
12: 3 down their altars, *s* their sacred pillars,
Ps(s) 58: 7 O God, *s* their teeth in their mouths;
137: 9 and *s* your little ones against the rock!
Jer 19:11 Thus will I *s* this people and this city,
43:13 He shall *s* the obelisks of the temple of

SMASHED (17)

Jgs 5:26 she *s*, stove in his temple
2Kgs 10:27 Then they *s* the stele of Baal,
18: 4 He *s* the bronze serpent called Nehushtan
2Chr 15:16 Asa cut this down, *s* it,
23:17 They *s* its altars and images,
31: 1 cities of Judah and *s* the sacred pillars,
Ps(s) 44: 3 you *s* the peoples,
74:13 *s* the heads of the dragons in the waters.
Sir 13: 2 they knock together, the pot will be *s*:
Is 9: 3 And the rod of their taskmaster you have *s*,
21: 9 the images of her gods are *s* to the ground.' "
30:14 like a potter's jar *s* beyond rescue,
Ez 6: 6 removed, and your incense stands *s* to bits.
27:26 east wind *s* you in the heart of the sea.
Mt 21:44 falls upon that stone will be *s* to bits;
Mk 5: 4 pulled the chains apart and *s* the fetters.
Lk 20:18 falls on that stone will be *s* to pieces.

SMASHES (3)

Sir 28:17 a welt, but a blow from the tongue *s* bones;
35:21 branch, and *s* the scepter of the wicked;
Jer 19:11 *s* a clay pot so that it cannot be repaired.

SMASHING (1)

Hos 10:14 time of war, *s* mothers and their children.

SMEAR (2)

Tb 11: 8 *S* the fish gall on them.
Rv 3:18 Buy ointment to *s* on your eyes,

SMEARED (4)

Tb 11:12 Next he *s* the medicine on his eyes,
Wis 15: 4 of painters, A form *s* with varied colors,
Jn 9: 6 saliva, and *s* the man's eyes with the mud.
9:11 call Jesus made mud and *s* it on my eyes,

SMELL (4)

Dt 4:28 neither see nor hear, neither eat nor *s*.
Ps(s) 115: 6 they have noses but *s* not;
Sir 30:19 to an idol that can neither taste nor *s?*
Dn 3:94 there was not even a *s* of fire about them.

SMELLED (2)

Gn 8:21 When the LORD *s* the sweet odor,
27:27 Isaac *s* the fragrance of his clothes.

SMELLING (2)

Ex 29:18 holocaust, a sweet *s* oblation to the LORD.
1Cor 12:17 were all ear, what would happen to our *s?*

SMELLS (1)

Tb 6:18 soon as the demon *s* the odor they give off,

SMELT (4)

2Kgs 22: 4 have him *s* down the precious metals
Jer 9: 6 I will *s* them and test them;
Ez 22:20 in my furious wrath, put you in, and *s* you.
22:21 the fire of my anger and *s* you with it.

SMELTED (4)

2Kgs 22: 9 "Your servants have *s* down the metals
Ez 22:20 into a furnace and *s* in the roaring flames,
22:22 *s* by it just as silver is smelted in a furnace.

SMELTER (2)

Jer 6:29 In vain has the *s* refined,
10: 9 the craftsman and the handiwork of the *s*,

SMILE (2)

Jb 10: 3 hands, and *s* on the plan of the wicked?
Sir 26: 4 is content, and a *s* is ever on his face.

SMILED (1)

Jb 29:24 When I *s* on them they were reassured;

SMILES (2)

Sir 13: 5 and with *s* he will win your confidence;
21:20 but the prudent man at the most *s* gently.

SMILING (1)

Sir 13:11 test you, and though *s* he will probe you.

SMITE (11)

Ex 3:20 and *s* Egypt by doing all kinds of wondrous
24:11 Yet he did not *s* these chosen Israelites.
Lv 26:24 will defy you and will *s* you for your sins
Nm 24:17 Israel, That shall *s* the brows of Moab,
Dt 28:59 he will *s* you and your descendants with
Jdt 9:10 lips, *s* the slave together with the ruler,
Jb 16:10 They *s* me on the cheek insultingly;
Ps(s) 89:24 before him and those who hate him I will *s*.
Is 19:22 Although the LORD shall *s* Egypt severely,
Zec 9: 4 possessions, and *s* her power on the sea,
10:11 I will cross over to Egypt and *s* the waves

SMITER (2)

Wis 18:22 But by word he overcame the *s*,
Is 27: 7 Is he to be smitten as his *s* was smitten?

SMITES (1)

Jb 5:18 he *s*, but his hands give healing.

SMITH (6)

Nm 24:21 Your abode is enduring, O *s*,
1Sm 13:19 Not a single *s* was to be found in the
Sir 31:26 As the furnace probes the work of the *s*,
38:28 So with the *s* standing near his anvil,
Is 40:19 which the *s* plates with gold and fits with
44:12 The *s* fashions an iron image,

SMITHS (2)

2Kgs 24:14 in number, and all the craftsmen and *s*.
24:16 the army, and a thousand craftsmen and *s*,

SMITTEN (8)

Lv 10: 6 for those whom the LORD's fire has *s*;
Dt 29:21 ills with which the LORD has *s*
Wis 17:15 Were partly *s* by fearsome apparitions and
18:11 *s* with the same retribution as his master;
Is 27: 7 Is he to be smitten as his smiter was *s?*
53: 4 as stricken, as one *s* by God and afflicted.
53: 8 living, and *s* for the sin of his people,

SMOKE (46)

Gn 19:28 he saw dense *s* over the land rising like
Ex 19:18 Mount Sinai was all wrapped in *s*,
19:18 *s* rose from it as though from a furnace,
Dt 33:10 bring the *s* of sacrifice to your nostrils,
Jos 8:20 the *s* from the city was already sky-high.
8:21 taken from ambush and was going up in *s*,
Jgs 20:38 men in ambush on a *s* signal
20:40 *s* of the signal column began to rise up
2Sm 22: 9 *S* rose from his nostrils,
Tb 6: 8 if you burn them so that the *s* surrounds a
1Mc 4:20 The *s* that could be seen indicated what
2Mc 7: 5 As a cloud of *s* spread from the pan,
Ps(s) 18: 9 *S* rose from his nostrils,
37:20 like *s* they vanish.
68: 3 As *s* is driven away,
102: 4 For my days vanish like *s*,
104:32 who touches the mountains, and they *s!*
119:83 shriveled like a leathern flask in the *s*,
144: 5 touch the mountains, and they shall *s*;
Prv 10:26 As vinegar to the teeth, and *s* to the eyes,
Sg 3: 6 like a column of *s* Laden with myrrh,
Wis 2: 2 Because the breath in our nostrils is a *s*
5:14 Like *s* scattered by the wind,
11:18 forth fiery breath, Or pour out roaring *s*,
Is 6: 4 door shook and the house was filled with *s*.
9:17 thickets, which go up in columns of *s*.
14:31 For there comes a *s* from the north,
34:10 not be quenched, its *s* shall rise forever.
51: 6 Though the heavens grow thin like *s*,
Bar 6:20 faces are blackened by the *s* of the house.
Hos 13: 3 floor or like *s* out of the window.
Jl 3: 3 the earth, blood, fire, and columns of *s*;
Na 2:14 I will consume in *s* your chariots,
Acts 2:19 blood, fire, and a cloud of *s*.
Rv 8: 4 the *s* of the incense went up before God,
9: 2 he opened it and *s* poured out of the shaft
9: 2 the shaft like *s* from an enormous furnace.
9: 2 air were darkened by the *s* from the shaft.
9: 3 Out of the *s*,
9:17 their mouths came fire and sulphur and *s*.
9:18 the *s* and sulphur and fire which shot out
14:10 and the *s* of their torment shall rise
15: 8 *s* which arose from God's glory
18: 9 her when they see the *s* arise as she burns.
18:18 *s* go up as the city burned to the ground:
19: 3 *s* began to rise from her forever and ever,

SMOKES (1)

Sir 22:24 Before flames burst forth an oven *s*;

SMOKING (4)

Gn 15:17 appeared a *s* brazier and a flaming torch,
Ex 20:18 the trumpet blast and the mountain *s*,
Wis 10: 7 wickedness, there yet remain a *s* desert,
Is 4: 5 A *s* cloud by day and a light of flaming

SMOLDER (1)

Ps(s) 74: 1 anger *s* against the sheep of your pasture?

SMOLDERING (3)

Is 7: 4 before these two stumps of *s* brands
42: 3 break, and a *s* wick he shall not quench,
Mt 12:20 the *s* wick he will not quench until

SMOOTH (15)

1Sm 17:40 David selected five *s* stones from the wadi
Ps(s) 12: 3 with *s* lips they speak,
12: 4 destroy all *s* lips, every boastful tongue,
Prv 2:16 from the adulteress with her *s* words,
6:24 wife, from the *s* tongue of the adulteress.
7: 5 wife, from the adulteress with her *s* words.
7:21 with her *s* lips she leads him astray;
26:23 earthenware are *s* lips with a wicked heart.
Sir 21:10 The path of sinners is *s* stones that end
22:17 is like the polished surface of a *s* wall.
32:21 Be not too sure even of *s* roads,
Is 26: 7 The way of the just is *s*;
57: 6 the *s* stones of the wadi is your portion,
Lk 3: 5 be made straight And the rough ways *s*,
Rom 16:18 with *s* and flattering speech.

SMOOTH-SKINNED (1)

Gn 27:11 Jacob to his mother Rebekah, "and I am *s*!

SMOOTHED (1)

Bar 6: 7 Their tongues are *s* by woodworkers;

SMOOTHER (2)

Ps(s) 55:22 His words are *s* than oil,
Prv 5: 3 with honey, and her mouth is *s* than oil;

SMOOTHLY (2)

Prv 23:31 It goes down *s*;
Sg 7:10 that flows *s* for my lover,

SMOTE (15)

Ex 32:35 Thus the LORD *s* the people for having had
Jos 24: 5 and *s* Egypt with the prodigies which I
2Sm 22:39 I *s* them and they did not rise;
Jdt 9: 3 *s* the slaves together with their princes,
Jb 1:19 desert and *s* the four corners of the house.
2: 7 *s* Job with severe boils
Ps(s) 18:39 I *s* them and they could not rise;
69:27 for they kept after him whom you *s*,
78:51 He *s* every first-born in Egypt,
135: 8 He *s* the first-born in Egypt,
135:10 He *s* many nations and slew mighty kings:
136:10 Who *s* the Egyptians in their first-born,
136:17 Who *s* great kings,
Is 14:29 of you, that the rod which *s* you is broken;
Hos 6: 5 this reason I *s* them through the prophets,

SMOTHERED (1)

1Kgs 3:19 she *s* him by lying on him.

SMUGGLE (2)

Acts 16:37 Now they want to *s* us out in secret.
2Pt 2: 1 teachers who will *s* in pernicious heresies.

SMUGGLED (1)

Gal 2: 4 to the title of brother were *s* in;

SMUGNESS (1)

Prv 1:32 kills them, the *s* of fools destroys them.

SMYRNA (2)

Rv 1:11 to Ephesus, *S*,
2: 8 the presiding spirit of the church in *S*,

SNAIL (1)

Ps(s) 58: 9 Let them dissolve like a melting *s*,

SNAKE (11)

Ex 7: 9 Pharaoh, and it will be changed into a *s*."
7:10 his servants, and it was changed into a *s*.
7:12 his staff, and it was changed into a *s*.
Ps(s) 58: 5 that of a stubborn *s* that stops its ears,
Sir 12:13 Who pities a *s* charmer when he is bitten,
Am 5:19 against the wall, and a *s* should bite him.
Mt 7:10 or a poisonous *s* when he asks for a fish?
Lk 11:11 give his son a *s* if he asks for a fish,
Acts 28: 3 he had collected, when a poisonous *s*,
28: 4 the sight of the *s* hanging from his hand,
28: 5 But Paul shook the *s* off into the fire and

SNAKES (6)

Jer 8:17 Yes, I will send against you poisonous *s*,
Mt 10:16 must be clever as *s* and innocent as doves.
Lk 10:19 I have given you power to tread on *s*
Rom 1:23 mortal man, birds, beasts, and *s*.
1Cor 10: 9 of them did, only to be destroyed by *s*.
Rv 9:19 were like *s* with heads poised to strike.

SNAP (3)

Lv 1:15 the priest shall *s* its head loose and
Is 45: 2 I will shatter, and iron bars I will *s*.
Jer 30: 8 yoke from off your necks and *s* your bonds."

SNAPPED (5)

Jgs 16: 9 But he *s* the strings as a thread of tow is
16:12 But he *s* them off his arms like thread.
Eccl 12: 6 Before the silver cord is *s*.
Zec 11:10 I took my staff "Favor" and *s* it asunder,
11:14 Then I *s* asunder my other staff,

SNAPPING (1)

Lv 5: 8 *S* its head loose at the neck,

SNARE (41)

Ex 34:12 else they will become a *s* among you.
Jos 23:13 they will be a *s* and a trap for you,
Jgs 2: 3 and their gods shall become a *s* for you."
1Sm 18:21 offer her to him to become a *s* for him,
1Mc 5: 4 who had become a *s* and a stumbling block
Jb 18: 9 him by the heel, and a *s* lays hold of him.
Ps(s) 9:16 in the *s* they set,
25:15 LORD, for he will free my feet from the *s*.
31: 5 will free me from the *s* they set for me,
35: 7 For without cause they set their *s* for me,
35: 8 and let the *s* they have set catch them;
66:11 You have brought us into a *s*;
69:23 Let their own table be a *s* before them,
91: 3 will rescue you from the *s* of the fowler,
106:36 their idols, which became a *s* for them.
119:110 The wicked have laid a *s* for me,
124: 7 rescued like a bird from the fowlers' *s*;
124: 7 Broken was the *s*,
Prv 3:26 and will keep your foot from the *s*.
6: 5 Free yourself as a gazelle from the *s*,
7:23 Like a bird that rushes into a *s*,
18: 7 his lips are a *s* to his life.
22:25 learn his ways, and get yourself into a *s*.
29: 6 The wicked man steps into a *s*,
29:25 The fear of man brings a *s*,
Eccl 7:26 is a *s* and whose hands are prison bonds.
9:12 the fatal net, or birds trapped in the *s*;
Wis 14:21 And this became a *s* for mankind,
Sir 27:26 it, and he who lays a *s* is caught in it,
31: 7 who are avid for it, a *s* for every fool.
31:30 More and more wine is a *s* for the fool;
51: 3 the *s* of those who watched for my downfall,
Is 8:14 Yet he shall be a *s*,
8:14 and a *s* to those who dwell in Jerusalem;
Ez 12:13 over him, and he shall be taken in my *s*.
17:20 over him, and he shall be taken in my *s*.
Hos 5: 1 For you have become a *s* at Mizpah,
9: 8 God, yet a fowler's *s* is on all his ways,
Am 3: 5 earth by a *s* when there is no lure for it?
3: 5 Does a *s* spring up from the ground without
Rom 11: 9 "Let their table become a *s* and a trap,

SNARED (2)

Prv 6: 2 have been *s* by the utterance of your lips,
Is 8:15 them shall stumble and fall, broken, *s*,

SNARES (23)

1Sm 28: 9 Why, then, are you laying *s* for my life,
2Sm 22: 6 enmeshed me, the *s* of death overtook me.
Jb 22:10 Therefore *s* are round about you,
Ps(s) 18: 6 enmeshed me, the *s* of death overtook me.
38:13 Men lay *s* for me seeking my life;
64: 6 they conspire to set *s*,
116: 3 the *s* of the nether world seized upon me;
119:61 Though the *s* of the wicked are twined
140: 6 by the wayside they have laid *s* for me.
141: 9 set for me, and from the *s* of evildoers.
Prv 13:14 life, that a man may avoid the *s* of death.
14:27 life, that a man may avoid the *s* of death.
21: 6 tongue is chasing a bubble over deadly *s*.
22: 5 and *s* are on the path of the crooked;
Wis 14:11 *S* for the souls of men and a trap for the
Sir 9: 3 a strange woman, lest you fall into her *s*.
9:13 stepping among *s* and walking over a net.
11:29 for many are the *s* of the crafty one;
32:20 Go not on a way that is set with *s*,
Jer 18:22 to capture me, they have hid *s* for my feet;
Lam 4:20 our breath of life, was caught in their *s*,
Ez 19: 8 laid out against him *s* all about him;
Ob 1: 7 Those who eat your bread lay *s* beneath you:

SNARL (2)

Ps(s) 59: 7 *s* like dogs and prowl about the city.
59:15 *s* like dogs and prowl about the city;

SNATCH (5)

Ps(s) 40:15 and confusion who seek to *s* away my life.
107:20 heal them and to *s* them from destruction.
Jer 22:24 on my right hand, I will *s* you from it.
Hos 2:11 I will *s* away my wool and my flax,
Jn 10:28 No one shall *s* them out of my hand.

SNATCHED (13)

Ex 22: 9 if it dies, or is maimed or *s* away,
Dt 32:25 *S* away by the sword in the street and by
Jdt 16: 2 he *s* me from the hands of my presecutors.
Jb 22:16 men, Who were *s* away before their time;
Wis 4:11 *S* away,
Sir 51: 2 of the nether world you have *s* my feet;
Na 2:13 The lion *s* enough for his cubs,
Zec 3: 2 Is not this man a brand *s* from the fire?"
Jn 10:12 sheep to be *s* and scattered by the wolf.
Acts 8:39 the Spirit of the Lord *s* Philip away and
10:16 then the object was *s* up into the sky.
2Cor 12: 2 a man who was *s* up to the third heaven.
12: 4 was *s* up to Paradise to hear words which

SNATCHES (2)

Jb 21:18 and like chaff which the storm *s* away!
Am 3:12 As the shepherd *s* from the mouth of the

SNATCHING (3)

Jn 10:29 me, and there is no *s* out of his hand.
Col 2:14 *s* it up and nailing it to the cross.
Jude 1:22 you must rescue, *s* them from the fire.

SNEER (2)

Acts 2:12 one another, while a few remarked with a *s*,
1Cor 4:10 They honor you, while they *s* at us!

SNEERED (2)

Gn 19: 9 This fellow," they *s*, "came here
Acts 17:32 about the raising of the dead, some *s*,

SNEERING (1)

2Pt 3: 3 *s* men who are ruled by their passions will

SNEEZED (1)

2Kgs 4:35 who now *s* seven times and opened his eyes.

SNEEZES (1)

Jb 41:10 When he *s*, light flashes forth;

SNOBBISH (1)

1Cor 13: 4 it does not put on airs, it is not *s*.

SNORT (1)

Jer 50:11 like calves on the green, *s* like stallions!

SNORTING (2)

Jb 39:20 while his thunderous *s* spreads terror?
Jer 8:16 From Dan is heard the *s* of his steeds;

SNOUT (1)

Prv 11:22 Like a golden ring in a swine's *s* is a

SNOW (24)

Ex 4: 6 his surprise his hand was leprous, like *s*.
2Sm 23:20 lion in the cistern at the time of the *s*.
2Kgs 5:27 And Gehazi left Elisha, a leper white as *s*.
1Mc 13:22 go, there was a heavy fall of *s* that night,
Jb 6:16 with ice, and with *s* heaped upon them,
9:30 with *s* and cleanse my hands with lye,
37: 6 For he says to the *s*,
38:22 Have you entered the storehouse of the *s*,
Ps(s) 51: 9 wash me, and I shall be whiter than *s*.
68:15 the kings there, *s* fell on Zalmon."
147:16 He spreads *s* like wool;
148: 8 Fire and hail, *s* and mist,
Prv 25:13 Like the coolness of *s* in the heat of the
26: 1 Like *s* in summer, or rain in harvest,
31:21 She fears not the *s* for her household;
Wis 16:22 Yet *s* and ice withstood fire and were not
Sir 43:18 He sprinkles the *s* like fluttering birds;
Is 1:18 like scarlet, they may become white as *s*;
55:10 heavens the rain and *s* come down
Jer 18:14 the *s* of Lebanon desert the rocky heights?
Lam 4: 7 Brighter than *s* were her princes,
Dn 3:70 Ice and *s*,
7: 9 His clothing was *s* bright,
Mt 28: 3 while his garments were as dazzling as *s*.

SNOW-WHITE (2)

Nm 12:10 from the tent, there was Miriam, a *s* leper!
Rv 1:14 as *s* wool and his eyes blazed like fire.

SNOWY (1)

1Chr 11:22 of Ariel of Moab, and also, on a *s* day,

SNUFF (2)

Wis 15:15 eyes for vision, nor nostrils to *s* the air,
Ez 32: 7 When I *s* you out I will cover the heavens,

SNUFFED (1)

Is 43:17 to rise, *s* out and quenched like a wick.

SNUFFERS (5)

1Kgs 7:50 basins, *s*,
2Kgs 12:14 were used there to make silver cups, *s*,
25:14 took also the pots, the shovels, the *s*,

2Chr 4:22 gold tongs [this was the purest gold], *s*,
Jer 52:18 took also the pots, the shovels, the *s*,

SNUFFING (1)

Jer 2:24 toward the desert, *S* the wind in her ardor

SO-CALLED (6)

Mt 27:17 for you, Barabbas or Jesus the *s* Messiah?"
27:22 what am I to do with Jesus, the *s* Messiah?"
Acts 6: 9 *s* "Synagogue of Roman Freedmen" (that is,
1Cor 8: 5 are *s* gods in the heavens and on the earth
2Thes 2: 4 above every *s* god proposed for worship,
Rv 2:24 nothing of the *s* "deep secrets" of Satan;

SOAK (1)

Dt 32: 2 May my instruction *s* in like the rain,

SOAKED (3)

Is 34: 7 Their land shall be *s* with blood,
Mt 27:48 He *s* it in cheap wine,
Jn 19:29 They stuck a sponge *s* in this wine on some

SOAKING (1)

Mk 15:36 ran off, and *s* a sponge in sour wine,

SOAP (2)

Jer 2:22 Though you scour it with *s*,
Dn 13:17 "Bring me oil and *s*,"

SOAR (1)

Is 40:31 they will *s* as with eagles' wings;

SOARS (3)

Jb 39:26 Is it by your discernment that the hawk *s*,
Jer 48:40 Behold, like an eagle he *s*,
49:22 like an eagle he *s* aloft,

SOBBED (2)

Ru 1:14 Again they *s* aloud and wept;
Tb 11: 9 And she *s* aloud.

SOBBING (2)

Gn 27:34 words, Esau burst into loud, bitter *s*.
Mt 2:18 was heard at Ramah, *s* and loud lamentation:

SOBER (6)

1Sm 1:14 *S* up from your wine!"
25:37 But then, when Nabal had become *s*,
Jn 16: 7 Yet I tell you the *s* truth:
Acts 26:25 The message I proclaim is the *s* truth.
1Thes 5: 6 be asleep like the rest, but awake and *s*!
1Pt 5: 8 Stay *s* and alert.

SOBERLY (2)

Rom 12: 3 Let him estimate himself *s*,
1Pt 1:13 live *s*;

SOBS (3)

Gn 45: 2 But his *s* were so loud that the Egyptians
Ru 1: 9 them good-bye, but they wept with loud *s*,
Tb 3: 1 Then with *s* I began to pray:

SOCIETY (2)

Wis 8:18 in frequenting her *s* there is prudence,
Acts 8:10 rank of *s* were paying attention to him.

SOCKET (4)

Gn 32:26 over him, he struck Jacob's hip at its *s*,
32:26 the hip *s* was wrenched as they wrestled.
32:33 *s*, inasmuch as Jacob's hip socket

SOCKETS (1)

Zec 14:12 feet, and their eyes shall rot in their *s*,

SOCO (3)

1Chr 4:18 father of Gedor, Heber, the father of *S*,
2Chr 11: 7 up Bethlehem, Etam, Tekoa, Beth-zur, *S*,
28:18 Aijalon, Gederoth, *S* and its dependencies,

SOCOH (5)

Jos 15:35 Tappuah, Enam, Jarmuth, Adullam, *S*,
15:48 Shamir, Jattir, *S*,
1Sm 17: 1 rallied their forces for battle at *S*
17: 1 between *S* and Azekah at Ephes-dammim.
1Kgs 4:10 as in *S* and the whole region of Hepher;

SODDEN (2)

Jdt 13: 2 on his bed, for he was *s* with wine.
Jb 10:15 filled with ignominy and *s* with affliction!

SODI (1)

Nm 13:10 son of *S*, of the tribe of Zebulun;

SODOM (48)

Gn 10:19 Gerar, near Gaza, and all the way to *S*,
13:10 the LORD had destroyed *S* and Gomorrah.)
13:12 of the Plain, pitching his tents near *S*.
13:13 Now the inhabitants of *S* were very wicked
14: 2 king of Goiim made war on Bera king of *S*,
14: 8 Thereupon the king of *S*,
14:10 and as the kings of *S* and Gomorrah fled,
14:11 of *S* and Gomorrah and then went their way,
14:12 nephew Lot, who had been living in *S*,
14:17 the king of *S* went out to greet him in the
14:21 The king of *S* said to Abram,
14:22 But Abram replied to the king of *S*:
18:16 out from there and looked down toward *S*;
18:20 outcry against *S* and Gomorrah is so great,
18:22 the two men walked on farther toward *S*,
18:26 fifty innocent people in the city of *S*,
19: 1 The two angels reached *S* in the evening,
19: 1 as Lot was sitting at the gate of *S*.
19: 4 they went to bed, all the townsmen of *S*,
19:24 LORD rained down sulphurous fire upon *S*
19:28 As he looked down toward *S* and Gomorrah
Dt 29:22 of grass, destroyed like *S* and Gomorrah,
Is 1: 7 devour [a waste, like *S* overthrown]
1: 9 us a scanty remnant, We had become as *S*,
1:10 Hear the word of the LORD, princes of *S*!
3: 9 their sin like *S* they vaunt,
13:19 overthrown by God like *S* and like Gomorrah.
Jer 23:14 To me they are all like *S*,
49:18 As when *S*, Gomorrah, and their neighbors
50:40 As when God overturned *S* and Gomorrah,
Lam 4: 6 people is greater than the penalty of *S*,
Ez 16:46 the south of you, was *S* with her daughters.
16:48 the Lord GOD, I swear that your sister *S*,
16:49 And look at the guilt of your sister *S*:
16:53 the fortune of *S* and her daughters and of
16:55 Yes, your sisters, *S* and her daughters,
16:56 Was not your sister *S* kept in bad repute
Am 4:11 as when God overthrew *S* and Gomorrah:
Zep 2: 9 God of Israel, Moab shall become like *S*,
Mt 10:15 easier for the region of *S* and Gomorrah
11:23 worked in you had taken place in *S*,
11:24 for *S* than for you on the day of judgment."
Lk 10:12 on that day the fate of *S* will be less
17:29 But on the day Lot left *S*,
Rom 9:29 us a remnant, we should have become as *S*,
2Pt 2: 6 He blanketed the cities of *S* and Gomorrah
Jude 1: 7 *S*, Gomorrah, and the towns thereabout
Rv 11: 8 which has the symbolic name *S*" or "Egypt,"

SODOMITES (1)

1Cor 6: 9 or adulterers, no *s*,

SODOM'S (1)

Dt 32:32 They are a branch of *S* vinestock,

SOFT (3)

Jb 33:25 Then his flesh shall become *s* as a boy's;
Prv 25:15 and a *s* tongue will break a bone.
Wis 15: 7 potter, laboriously working the *s* earth,

SOFTENING (1)

Ps(s) 65:11 breaking up its clods, *S* it with showers,

SOFTENS (1)

Sir 38:30 he molds the clay, and with his feet *s* it.

SOFTER (1)

Ps(s) 55:22 *S* than butter is his speech,

SOHAR (1)

Nm 26:13 through *S* the clan of the Soharites,

SOHARITES (1)

Nm 26:13 through Sohar the clan of the *S*,

SOIL (59)

Gn 2: 5 earth and there was no man to till the *s*,
4: 2 of flocks, and Cain a tiller of the *s*.
4: 3 to the LORD God from the fruit of the *s*,
4:10 brother's blood cries out to me from the *s*!
4:11 Therefore you shall be banned from the *s*
4:12 If you till the *s*,
4:14 Since you have now banished me from the *s*,
9:20 Now Noah, a man of the *s*,
19:25 of the cities and the produce of the *s*.
Ex 10: 6 settled on this *s* up to the present day."
23:19 *s* you shall bring to the house of the LORD,
34:26 *s* you shall bring to the house of the LORD,
Lv 26:19 hard as iron, and your *s* as hard as bronze,
Nm 13:20 Is the *s* fertile or barren,
Dt 7:13 of your womb and the produce of your *s*,
11:17 fall, and the *s* will not yield its crops,
12: 1 to occupy, as long as you live on its *s*.
26: 2 products of the *s* which you harvest
26:10 fruits of the products of the *s* which you,
26:15 bless your people Israel and the *s*
28: 4 your *s* and the offspring of your livestock,
28:11 your livestock, and the produce of your *s*,
28:18 your *s* and the offspring of your livestock,
28:33 the fruit of your *s* and of all your labor,
28:42 all your trees and the crops of your *s*.
28:51 your livestock and the produce of your *s*,
29:18 both the watered *s* and the parched ground,
29:22 its *s* being nothing but sulphur and salt,
29:27 *s* and cast them out into a strange land,
30: 9 your livestock, and the produce of your *s*;
2Kgs 17:23 into exile from their native *s* to Assyria,
1Chr 27:26 the farm workers who tilled the *s* was Ezri,
2Chr 26:10 He was a lover of the *s*.
1Mc 11:34 of the *s* and the fruit of the trees.
Jb 8:19 the road, and out of the *s* another sprouts.
14:19 and floods wash away the *s* of the land,
Ps(s) 105:35 they devoured the fruit of their *s*.
Sg 5: 3 I have bathed my feet, am I then to *s* them?
Is 14: 1 Israel and settles them on their own *s*,
14: 2 as male and female slaves on the Lord's *s*,
30:23 the *s* produces will be rich and abundant.
32:13 the fruitful vine, And the *s* of my people,
Jer 14: 4 their heads because of the stricken *s*;
Ez 34:27 they shall dwell securely on their own *s*.
Zec 13: 5 "I am no prophet, I am a tiller of the *s*,
Mt 13: 5 on rocky ground, where it had little *s*.
13: 5 sprouted at once since the *s* had no depth,
13: 8 landed on good *s* and yielded grain a
13:23 But what was sown on good *s* is the man who
Mk 4: 5 on rocky ground where it had little *s*;
4: 5 immediately because the *s* had no depth.
4: 8 landed on good *s* and yielded grain that
4:20 good *s* are the ones who listen to the word,
4:28 The *s* produces of itself first the blade,
4:31 mustard seed which, when planted in the *s*,
Lk 8: 8 But some fell on good *s*,
14:35 fit for neither the *s* nor the manure heap;
Jas 5: 7 farmer awaits the precious yield of the *s*.
5: 7 *s* receives the winter and the spring rains.

SOILED (2)

Lam 4:14 blindly in the streets, *s* with blood,
Rv 3: 4 few persons who have not *s* their garments;

SOJOURN (7)

Gn 12:10 so Abram went down to Egypt to *s* there,
Ps(s) 15: 1 O LORD, who shall *s* in your tent?
120: 5 Woe is me that I *s* in Meshech,
Wis 19:10 mindful of what had happened in their *s*:
Is 52: 4 beginning my people went down, to *s* there;
Acts 13:17 great during their *s* in the land of Egypt,
1Pt 1:17 reverently during your *s* in a strange land.

SOJOURNED (4)

2Chr 15: 9 Manasseh and Simeon who *s* with them;
Ps(s) 105:23 to Egypt, and Jacob *s* in the land of Ham.
Ez 20:38 they *s* as aliens I will bring them out,
Heb 11: 9 By faith he *s* in the promised land as in a

SOJOURNERS (1)

2Chr 30:25 as well as the *s* from the land of Israel

SOLACE (2)

Gn 24:67 *s* after the death of his mother Sarah.
Phil 2: 1 in the name of the *s* that love can give,

SOLD (60)

Gn 25:33 So he *s* Jacob his birthright under oath.
31:15 He not only *s* us;
37:28 They *s* Joseph to the Ishmaelites for
37:36 meanwhile, *s* Joseph in Egypt to Potiphar,
45: 4 brother Joseph, whom you once *s* into Egypt.
45: 5 reproach yourselves for having *s* me here.
47:17 he *s* them food in return for their horses,
47:20 them to bear, every Egyptian *s* his field;
Ex 22: 2 he shall be *s* to pay for his theft.
Lv 25:23 "The land shall not be *s* in perpetuity;
25:25 may go and buy back what his kinsman has *s*.
25:27 the balance to the one to whom he *s* it,
25:28 what he has *s* shall remain in the
25:33 cities that had been *s* and not redeemed,
25:34 to their cities shall not be *s* at all;
25:42 they shall not be *s* as slaves to any man.
25:48 even after he has thus *s* his services he
27:27 redeemed, it shall be *s* at its fixed value.
27:28 field, shall be neither *s* nor ransomed;
Dt 32:30 Rock *s* them and the LORD delivered them up
2Kgs 6:25 ass's head *s* for eighty pieces of silver,
7:16 and then a seah of fine flour *s* for a
17:17 and *s* themselves into evil doing in the
Neh 5: 8 our fellow Jews who had been *s* to Gentiles;
Jdt 7:25 God has *s* us into their power by laying us
Est 7: 4 to be *s* into slavery I would remain silent,
1Mc 1:15 Gentiles and *s* themselves to wrongdoing.
2Mc 4:32 he had already *s* some other vessels in
5:14 and the same number being *s* into slavery.
8:14 But the others *s* everything they had left,
8:14 Nicanor had *s* before even meeting them.
10:21 accused those men of having *s* their
Ps(s) 44:13 You *s* your people for no great price;
105:17 a man before them, Joseph, *s* as a slave;

SOLD (cont.)

Wis 10:13 did not abandon the just man when he was *s*,
Is 50: 1 Or to which of my creditors have I *s* you?
50: 1 It was for your sins that you were *s*,
52: 3 You were *s* for nothing,
Jer 34:14 Hebrew brother who has *s* himself to you;
Bar 4: 6 *s* to the nations not for your destruction;
Ez 7:13 not regain what he *s* as long as he lives,
Jl 4: 3 and *s* a girl for the wine they drank.
4: 6 You *s* the people of Judah and Jerusalem to
4: 7 from the place into which you have *s* them,
Mt 10:29 Are not two sparrows *s* for next to nothing?
13:44 and *s* all he had and bought that field.
18:25 paying it, his master ordered him to be *s*,
26: 9 This could have been *s* for a good price
Mk 14: 5 It could have been *s* for over three
Lk 12: 6 Are not five sparrows *s* for a few pennies?
17:28 they ate and drank, they bought and *s*,
Jn 12: 5 "Why was not this perfume *s*?
Acts 4:34 or houses *s* them and donated the proceeds.
4:37 He *s* a farm that he owned and made a
5: 1 Sapphira likewise *s* a piece of property.
5: 4 Even when you *s* it,
7: 9 patriarchs *s* Joseph into slavery in Egypt,
Rom 7:14 I am weak flesh *s* into the slavery of sin.
1Cor 10:25 Eat whatever is *s* in the market without
Heb 12:16 like Esau, who *s* his birthright for a meal.

SOLDERING (1)

Is 41: 7 He says the *s* is good,

SOLDIER (9)

Jos 8:17 not a *s* remained in Ai [or Bethel],
1Sm 16:18 He is also a stalwart *s*,
Jn 19:23 and divided them four ways, one for each *s*.
Acts 10: 7 *s* from among those whom he could trust.
28:16 a *s* was assigned to keep guard over him.
1Cor 9: 6 What *s* in the field pays for his rations?
2Tm 2: 3 along with me like a good *s* of Christ Jesus.
2: 4 No *s* becomes entangled in the affairs of
Phlm 1: 2 our sister, to our fellow *s* Archippus,

SOLDIERS—SOLDIER'S (185)

Ex 14: 6 his chariots ready and mustered his *s*—
Nm 2: 4 and his *s* amounted in the census to
2: 6 and his *s* amounted in the census to
2: 8 and his *s* amounted in the census to
2:11 and his *s* amounted in the census to
2:13 and his *s* amounted in the census to
2:15 and his *s* amounted in the census to
2:19 and his *s* amounted in the census to forty
2:21 and his *s* amounted in the census to
2:23 and his *s* amounted in the census to
2:26 and his *s* amounted in the census to
2:28 and his *s* amounted in the census to
2:30 and his *s* amounted in the census to
11:21 around me include six hundred thousand *s*;
31:21 told the *s* who had returned from combat:
31:32 was left of the loot which the *s* had taken,
31:42 when Moses had taken it from the *s*,
31:49 have counted up the *s* under our command,
31:53 *s* had looted each one kept for himself.
Dt 2:14 generation of *s* had perished from the camp,
2:16 put an end to all the *s* among the people,
20: 2 priest shall come forward and say to the *s*:
20: 5 "Then the officials shall say to the *s*,
20: 8 In fine, the officials shall say to the *s*,
20: 9 officials have finished speaking to the *s*,
Jos 6: 3 Have all the *s* circle the city,
8: 3 Joshua and all the *s* prepared to attack Ai.
8:16 till the last of the *s* in the city had
10: 7 his picked troops and the rest of his *s*.
10:24 of the *s* who had marched with him,
Jgs 7: 1 encamped by En-harod with all his *s*.
7: 2 "You have too many *s* with you for me to
7: 3 Now proclaim to all the *s*,
7: 3 twenty-two thousand of the *s* left,
7: 4 to Gideon, "There are still too many *s*.
7: 5 When Gideon led the *s* down to the water,
7: 6 of the *s* knelt down to drink the water.
7: 7 So let all the other *s* go home."
7: 8 and such supplies as the *s* had with them,
9:34 Abimelech advanced with all his *s*
9:35 and his *s* rose from their place of ambush,
9:48 So he went up Mount Zalmon with all his *s*,
11:20 On the contrary, he gathered all his *s*,
12: 2 "My *s* and I were engaged in a critical
20: 2 hundred thousand foot *s* who were swordsmen,
20:10 procuring supplies for the *s*
20:23 But though the Israelite *s* took courage
20:31 of the Israelite *s* in the open field,
1Sm 4:10 which Israel lost thirty thousand foot *s*.
8:12 of groups of a thousand and of a hundred *s*.
13: 4 and the *s* were called up to Saul in Gilgal.
13: 5 *s* as numerous as the sands of the seashore.
13:15 people went up after Saul to meet the *s*,
13:15 Saul then numbered the *s* he had with him,
13:16 and the *s* they had with them were now
13:22 of any of the *s* with Saul or Jonathan.
14: 3 Nor did the *s* know that Jonathan had gone.
14:15 and to the countryside, and all the *s*,
14:26 *s* came to the comb the swarm had left it;
14:28 At this one of the *s* spoke up:
14:45 *s* were able to rescue Jonathan from death.
15: 4 Saul alerted the *s*,
15: 4 foot *s* and ten thousand men of Judah.
18: 5 So Saul put him in charge of his *s*,
26: 5 and all his *s* were camped around him.
26: 7 So David and Abishai went among Saul's *s*
2Sm 1: 4 He answered that the *s* had fled the battle
1:12 the *s* of the LORD of the clans of Israel,
2:27 the *s* would not have been withdrawn from
2:28 the horn, and all the *s* came to a halt,
8: 4 horsemen and twenty thousand foot *s*.
10: 6 Aramean foot *s* from Beth-rehob and Zobah,
10: 7 out Joab with the entire levy of trained *s*.
10:10 *s* under the command of his brother Abishai,
10:13 When Joab and the *s* who were with him
10:18 and forty thousand of the Aramean foot *s*.
11: 7 David questioned him about Joab, the *s*,
12:28 Therefore, assemble the rest of the *s*,
12:29 the rest of the *s* and went to Rabbah.
12:31 and all the *s* then returned to Jerusalem.
15:23 wept aloud as the last of the *s* went by,
15:23 crossed the Kidron Valley with all the *s*
15:24 until the *s* had marched out of the city.
16: 6 king's officers, even though all the *s*,
16:14 *s* with him arrived at the Jordan tired out,
17: 9 of our *s* should fall at the first attack,
18: 2 a third part of the *s* under Joab's command,
18: 2 The king then said to the *s*,
18: 4 stood by the gate as all the *s* marched out
18: 5 All the *s* heard the king instruct the
18:16 and the *s* turned back from the pursuit of
19: 4 The *s* stole into the city that day like
20:12 man noticed that all the *s* were stopping.
20:15 and all the *s* who were with Joab began
23:10 the *s* turned back after Eleazar,
23:11 When the *s* fled from the Philistines,
1Kgs 20:19 the *s* of the governors of the provinces
20:29 hundred thousand foot *s* of Aram in one day.
2Kgs 13: 7 No *s* were left to Jehoahaz,
13: 7 with ten chariots and ten thousand foot *s*,
24:16 and smiths, all of them trained *s*.
25: 4 Then the king and all the *s* left the city
25:19 he took one courtier, a commander of *s*,
1Chr 12: 9 *s* equipped with shield and spear,
12:39 All these *s*,
18: 4 took from him twenty thousand foot *s*,
19:18 and forty thousand of their foot *s*;
2Chr 8: 9 They became *s*,
17:13 works in the cities of Judah, and he had *s*,
25:22 Israel, and all the Judean *s* fled homeward.
26:11 Uzziah also had a standing army of fit *s*
28:14 Therefore the *s* left their captives and
Jdt 2: 7 cover all the land with the feet of my *s*,
7:12 Stay in your camp, and spare all your *s*.
1Mc 2:31 It was reported to the officers and *s* of
2:38 and *s* attacked them on the sabbath,
3:28 treasure chests, gave his *s* a year's pay,
4: 3 his *s* to attack the king's army at Emmaus,
4: 7 with cavalry, and made up of expert *s*.
6:37 Indian mahout, three *s* who fought from it.
6:57 king, the leaders of the army, and the *s*:
7: 2 the *s* seized Antiochus and Lysias to bring
7: 4 So the *s* killed them,
9:52 and put *s* in them and stores of provisions.
10:36 given them, as is due to all the king's *s*.
10:49 pursued him, and overpowered his *s*.
11:38 So all the *s* who had served under his
11:40 and of the hatred that his *s* had for him.
11:55 All the *s* whom Demetrius had discharged
12:43 and *s* to obey him as they would himself.
12:44 "Why have you put all your *s* to so much
12:49 Trypho sent *s* and cavalry to Galilee and
13:53 man, Simon made him commander of all his *s*,
14:33 where he stationed a garrison of Jewish *s*,
14:37 In this citadel he stationed Jewish *s*,
15:12 upon him now that his *s* had deserted him.
16: 5 was an immense army of foot *s* and horsemen,
2Mc 3:35 and returned with his *s* to the king.
5:12 He ordered his *s* to cut down without mercy
10:31 Twenty-five hundred of their foot *s* and
11: 4 confidence in his myriads of foot *s*,
11:11 foot *s* and sixteen hundred horsemen,
12:10 numbering at least five thousand foot *s*,
12:20 foot *s* and twenty-five hundred horsemen.
12:33 thousand foot *s* and four hundred horsemen.
12:42 the *s* to keep themselves free from sin,
12:43 then took up a collection among all his *s*,
13: 2 of one hundred and ten thousand foot *s*,
14:39 more than five hundred *s* to arrest him.
Sir 16:10 Nor the six hundred thousand foot *s* who
Is 13: 3 I have commanded my dedicated *s*,
Jer 34:21 to the *s* of the king of Babylon who have
38: 4 the *s* who are left in this city,
41: 3 Gedaliah and the Chaldean *s* who were there.
41:16 both the *s* and the women and children with
52: 7 Then all the *s* took to flight and left the
52:25 he took one courtier, a commander of *s*,
Ez 29:19 and pillaging it for the wages of his *s*,
39:20 riders, with warriors and *s* of every kind,
Jl 2: 7 they run, like *s* they scale the wall;
4: 9 Let all the *s* report and march!
Na 2: 4 are crimsoned, the *s* colored in scarlet;
Mt 27:27 The procurator's *s* took Jesus inside the
28:12 the *s* a large bribe with the instructions:
28:15 The *s* pocketed the money and did as they
Mk 15:16 The *s* now led Jesus away into the hall
Lk 3:14 *S* likewise asked him, "What about us?"
7: 8 of an order, having *s* under my command.
21:20 "When you see Jerusalem encircled by *s*,
23:36 The *s* also made fun of him,
Jn 18:12 Then the *s* of the cohort,
19: 2 The *s* then wove a crown of thorns and
19:23 After the *s* had crucified Jesus they took
19:24 And this was what the *s* did.
19:32 the *s* came and broke the legs of the men
19:34 One of the *s* thrust a lance into his side,
Acts 12: 4 prison, with four squads of *s* to guard him.
12: 6 trial, Peter was sleeping between two *s*,
12:18 daybreak, confusion broke out among the *s*,
21:32 Immediately the commander took his *s* and
21:32 as the crowd caught sight of him and the *s*,
21:35 the *s* because of the violence of the mob.
27:31 alerted the centurion and the *s* to this:
27:32 the *s* cut the ropes and let the boat drift.
27:42 The *s* thought at first of killing the

SOLDIERY (2)

1Kgs 20:15 them he mustered all the Israelite *s*,
2Kgs 14:12 Israel, and all the Judean *s* fled homeward.

SOLE (4)

Dt 28:56 to set the *s* of her foot on the ground,
2Sm 14:25 the *s* of his foot to the crown of his head.
Is 1: 6 From the *s* of the foot to the head there
2Cor 3: 5 Our *s* credit is from God,

SOLELY (2)

Acts 28:20 *s* because I share the hope of Israel."
1Cor 14:16 If your praise of God is *s* with the spirit,

SOLEMN (20)

Gn 28:17 In *s* wonder he cried out:
50:10 there a very great and *s* memorial service;
50:11 is a *s* funeral the Egyptians are having."
Lv 16:31 it shall be a most *s* sabbath for you,
23:36 *s* closing you shall do no sort of work.
Nm 29:35 the eighth day you shall hold a *s* meeting,
Dt 16: 8 shall be a *s* meeting in honor of the LORD,
23:24 But you must keep your *s* word and fulfill
Jgs 21: 5 For they had taken a *s* oath that anyone
2Kgs 10:20 "Proclaim a *s* assembly in honor of Baal."
Neh 8:18 days, and the *s* assembly on the eighth day,
1Mc 13:26 All Israel bewailed him with *s* lamentation,
2Mc 3:35 most *s* vows to him who had spared his life,
12:25 his *s* pledge to restore them unharmed,
Ps(s) 81: 4 new moon, at the full moon, on our *s* feast;
Mt 19:28 "I give you my *s* word,
Jn 10: 7 "My *s* word is this:
19:31 for that sabbath was a *s* feast day.
1Tm 1:18 I have a *s* charge to give you,
Jude 1:12 They join your *s* feasts without shame and

SOLEMNITIES (2)

Hos 2:13 her new moons, her sabbaths, and all her *s*.
Am 5:21 your feasts, I take no pleasure in your *s*;

SOLEMNIZED (1)

Sir 47: 9 He added beauty to the feasts and *s* the

SOLEMNLY (31)

Ex 13:19 had made the Israelites swear *s* that,
Nm 6: 2 When a man (or a woman) *s* takes the
14:30 the land where I *s* swore to settle you,
1Sm 8: 9 warn them *s* and inform them of the rights
Ez 36: 7 Therefore do I *s* swear that your
Mt 7:23 Then I will declare to them *s*,
10:23 I *s* assure you, you will not have covered
11:11 "I *s* assure you, history has not known
Mk 11:23 I *s* assure you, whoever says to this
14:25 I *s* assure you, I will never again drink
Lk 18:29 His answer was, "I *s* assure you,
Jn 1:51 He went on to tell them, "I *s* assure you,
3: 3 "I *s* assure you, no one can see the reign
3: 5 "I *s* assure you, no one can enter into
3:11 "I *s* assure you, we are talking about what
5:19 "I *s* assure you, the Son cannot do
5:24 I *s* assure you, the man who hears
5:25 I *s* assure you, an hour is coming,
6:32 "I *s* assure you, it was not Moses
6:53 "Let me *s* assure you,
8:51 I *s* assure you, if a man is true to my word
8:58 "I *s* declare it:
12:24 I *s* assure you, unless the grain of wheat
13:16 I *s* assure you, no slave is greater than
13:20 I *s* assure you, he who accepts anyone
13:21 "I tell you *s*, one of you will betray me."
14:12 I *s* assure you, the man who has faith
21:18 "I tell you *s*:
Acts 20:21 With Jews and Greeks alike I insisted *s* on
20:26 Therefore I *s* declare this day that I take
Eph 4:17 I declare and *s* attest in the Lord that

SOLES (11)

Dt 28:35 s of your feet to the crown of your head.
Jos 3:13 When the s of the feet of the priests
4:18 s of their feet regained the dry ground,
1Kgs 5:17 put these enemies under the s of his feet.
2Kgs 19:24 the s of my feet all the rivers of Egypt.
Est C: 6 s of his feet for the salvation of Israel.
Jb 2: 7 the s of his feet to the crown of his head.
Is 37:25 the s of my feet all the rivers of Egypt.
Ez 1: 7 the s of their feet were round.
43: 7 this is where I will set the s of my feet;
Mal 3:21 will become ashes under the s of your feet,

SOLICITING (1)

Mk 14:55 were busy s testimony against Jesus

SOLICITOUS (3)

2Mc 11:15 Maccabeus, s for the common good,
Col 4:13 I can certainly testify how s he is for
2Pt 1:10 s to make your call and election permanent,

SOLICITUDE (2)

Wis 6:16 in the ways, and meets them with all s.
12:20 you punished them with such s and pleading,

SOLID (13)

Lv 11:34 Any s food that was in contact with water,
Jos 3:13 down from upstream will halt in a s bank."
3:16 a s mass for a very great distance indeed,
Jb 28:15 S gold cannot purchase it,
38:38 is fused into a mass and its clods made s?
Sir 43: 4 Like a blazing furnace of s metal,
Jer 15:20 you toward this people a s wall of brass.
Lk 6:48 to shake it because of its s foundation.
1Cor 3: 2 s food because you were not ready for it.
Phil 1: 7 the s grounds on which the gospel rests.
Heb 5:12 you need milk, not s food.
5:14 S food is for the mature,
1Pt 5: 9 Resist him, s in your faith,

SOLIDLY (2)

Sir 44: 6 s established and at peace in their own
Mt 7:25 it had been s set on rock.

SOLITARY (3)

Eccl 4: 8 a s man with no companion;
4:10 Woe to the s man!
Bar 4:16 widow's cherished sons, have left me s,

SOLITUDE (1)

Lk 8:29 the demon would drive him into places of s.

SOLITUDES (2)

Wis 11: 2 desert, and in s they pitched their tents;
Hos 11: 6 with his cities and end by consuming his s.

SOLOMON (266)

2Sm 5:14 Shammua, Shobab, Nathan, S,
8: 7 in the days of Rehoboam, son of S
2Sm 12:24 and bore him a son, who was named S.
1Kgs 1:10 or the pick of the army, or his brother S.
1:12 may save your life and that of your son S.
1:13 Your son S shall be king after me and
1:17 that my son S should reign after you and
1:19 of the army, but not your servant S.
1:21 and my son S will be considered criminals."
1:26 son of Jehoiada, nor your servant S.
1:30 that your son S should reign after me and
1:33 Mount my son S upon my own mule and escort
1:34 blow the horn and cry, 'Long live King S!'
1:37 your royal majesty, so may he be with S,
1:38 down, and mounting S on King David's mule,
1:39 horn of oil from the tent and anointed S.
1:39 all the people shouted, "Long live King S!"
1:43 "Our lord, King David, has made S king.
1:46 S took his seat on the royal throne,
1:47 'May God make S more famous than you and
1:50 Adonijah, in fear of S,
1:51 S that Adonijah, in his fear of King S
1:51 S first swear that he will not kill me,
1:52 S answered,
1:53 King S sent to have him brought down from
1:53 S then said to him, "Go to your home."
2: 1 he gave these instructions to his son S:
2:12 When S was seated on the throne of his
2:13 went to Bathsheba, the mother of S.
2:17 he said, "Please ask King S,
2:19 to King S to speak to him for Adonijah,
2:22 King S answered his mother.
2:23 And King S swore by the LORD:
2:25 Then King S sent Benaiah,
2:27 So S deposed Abiathar from his office of
2:29 King S was told that Joab had fled to the
2:41 When S was informed that Shimei had gone
2:45 But King S shall be blessed,
3: 1 S allied himself by marriage with Pharaoh,
3: 3 S loved the LORD,
3: 4 its altar S offered a thousand holocausts.
3: 5 the LORD appeared to S in a dream at night.
3: 6 S answered: "You have shown great favor
3:10 Lord was pleased that S made this request.
3:15 When S awoke from his dream,
4: 1 S was king over all Israel,
4: 7 S had twelve commissaries for all Israel
4:15 to Basemath, another daughter of S,
5: 1 S ruled over all the kingdoms from the
5: 1 they paid S tribute and were his vassals
5: 5 from Dan to Beer-sheba, as long as S lived.
5: 6 S had four thousand stalls for his twelve
5: 7 provided food for King S and for all the
5: 9 God gave S wisdom and exceptional
5:10 S surpassed all the Cedemites and all the
5:12 S also uttered three thousand proverbs,
5:15 heard that S had been anointed king in
5:16 S sent back this message to Hiram:
5:21 When he had heard the words of S,
5:22 Hiram then sent word to S,
5:24 So Hiram continued to provide S with all
5:25 while S every year gave Hiram twenty
5:26 moreover, gave S wisdom as he promised him,
5:26 and there was peace between Hiram and S,
5:27 King S conscripted thirty thousand workmen
5:29 S had seventy thousand carriers and eighty
6: 2 S built for the LORD was sixty cubits long,
6:11 This word of the LORD came to S:
6:14 When S finished building the temple,
6:21 S overlaid the interior of the temple with
6:38 Thus it took S seven years to build it.
7: 1 His own palace S completed after thirteen
7: 8 Pharaoh's daughter, whom S had married.
7:13 King S had Hiram brought from Tyre.
7:14 came to King S and did all his metal work.
7:40 work for King S in the temple of the LORD:
7:45 articles which Hiram made for King S
7:47 S did not weigh all the articles because
7:48 S had all the articles made for the
7:51 S in the temple of the LORD was completed,
8: 1 At the order of S,
8: 1 Israelites, came to King S in Jerusalem,
8: 2 Israel assembled before King S
8: 5 King S and the entire community of Israel
8:12 Then S said, "The LORD intends to dwell
8:22 S stood before the altar of the LORD in
8:54 When S finished offering this entire
8:63 S offered as peace offerings to the LORD
8:65 On this occasion S and all the Israelites,
9: 1 S finished building the temple of the LORD,
9:10 years during which S built the two houses,
9:11 Tyre, supplying S with all the cedar wood,
9:11 King S gave Hiram twenty cities in the
9:12 Tyre to see the cities S had given him,
9:14 S one hundred and twenty talents of gold.
9:15 forced labor which King S levied
9:17 S then rebuilt Gezer),
9:19 S decided should be built in Jerusalem,
9:21 S conscripted as forced laborers,
9:22 But S enslaved none of the Israelites,
9:24 which he had built for her, S built Millo.
9:25 Three times a year S used to offer
9:26 King S also built a fleet at Ezion-geber,
9:27 own expert seamen with the servants of S.
9:28 and twenty talents of gold to King S.
10: 2 She came to S and questioned him on every
10: 3 S explained everything she asked about,
10:10 as the queen of Sheba gave to King S.
10:13 King S gave the queen of Sheba everything
10:14 The gold that S received every year
10:16 King S made two hundred shields of beaten
10:23 Thus King S surpassed in riches and wisdom
10:24 the whole world sought audience with S,
10:26 S collected chariots and drivers;
11: 1 King S loved many foreign women besides
11: 2 But S fell in love with them.
11: 4 When S was old his wives had turned his
11: 6 S did evil in the sight of the LORD;
11: 7 S then built a high place to Chemosh,
11: 9 The LORD, therefore, became angry with S,
11:10 strange gods, S had not obeyed him).
11:11 So the LORD said to S:
11:14 The LORD then raised up an adversary to S:
11:23 God raised up against S another adversary,
11:25 was an enemy of Israel as long as S lived;
11:27 King S was building Millo,
11:28 and when S saw that he was also an
11:34 not take any of the kingdom from S himself,
11:40 When S tried to have Jeroboam killed for
11:41 The rest of the acts of S,
11:41 in the book of the chronicles of S.
11:42 The time that S reigned in Jerusalem over
11:43 S rested with his ancestors;
12: 2 in Egypt, where he had fled from King S,
12:21 restore the kingdom to Rehoboam, son of S.
12:23 "Say to Rehoboam, son of S,
14:21 Rehoboam, son of S, reigned in Judah.
14:26 well as all the gold shields made under S.
2Kgs 21: 7 LORD had said to David and to his son S:
23:13 south of the Mount of Misconduct, which S,
24:13 and broke up all the gold utensils that S,
25:16 which S had made for the house of the LORD,
1Chr 3: 5 Shimea, Shobab, Nathan, S—
3:10 The son of S was Rehoboam, whose
5:36 priest in the temple S built in Jerusalem.
6:17 meeting tent until S built the temple
14: 4 Shammua, Shobab, Nathan, S,
18: 8 which S later used to make the bronze sea
22: 5 "My son S is young and immature:
22: 6 Then he called for his son S and commanded
22: 7 David said to S:
22: 9 For S shall be his name,
22:17 all of Israel's leaders to help his son S:
23: 1 days, he made his son S king over Israel.
28: 5 he has chosen my son S to sit on the
28: 6 S who shall build my house and my courts,
28: 9 "As for you, S,
28:11 Then David gave to his son S the pattern
28:20 Then David said to his son S:
29: 1 "My son S,
29:19 Give to my son S a wholehearted desire to
29:22 time they proclaimed David's son S king,
29:23 Thereafter S sat on the throne of the LORD
29:24 of King David, swore allegiance to King S.
29:25 S greatly in the eyes of all Israel,
29:28 glory, and his son S succeeded him as king.
2Chr 1: 1 S, son of David,
1: 5 S and the assembly consulted the LORD,
1: 6 and S offered sacrifice in the LORD's
1: 7 night God appeared to S and said to him,
1: 8 S answered God:
1:11 God then replied to S:
1:13 S returned to Jerusalem from the high
1:16 S also imported horses from Egypt and
1:18 S gave orders for the building of a house
2: 2 Moreover, S sent this message to Huram,
2:10 Tyre, wrote an answer which he sent to S:
2:16 Thereupon S took a census of all the alien
3: 1 Then S began to build the house of the
3: 3 down by S for building the house of God:
4:11 had to do for King S in the house of God:
4:16 made all these articles for King S
4:18 S made all these vessels,
4:19 S had all these articles made for the
5: 1 When all the work undertaken by S for the
5: 6 King S and the entire community of Israel
6: 1 Then S said: "The Lord intends to dwell
6:12 S then took his place before the altar of
6:13 S knelt in the presence of the whole of
7: 1 When S had ended his prayer,
7: 5 King S offered as sacrifice twenty-two
7: 7 Then S consecrated the middle part of the
7: 7 S had made could not hold the holocausts,
7: 8 On this occasion S and with him all Israel,
7:10 things the LORD had done for David, for S,
7:11 S completed the house of the LORD and the
7:12 to S during the night and said to him:
8: 1 After the twenty years during which S
8: 3 S went to Hamath of Zoba and conquered it.
8: 6 all the supply cities belonging to S,
8: 6 S decided should be built in Jerusalem,
8: 8 not destroyed S subjected to forced labor,
8: 9 But S did not enslave the Israelites for
8:11 S brought the daughter of Pharaoh up from
8:12 In those times S offered holocausts to the
8:17 In those times S went to Ezion-geber and
8:18 and fifty talents of gold to King S.
9: 1 She came to S and questioned him on every
9: 2 S explained to her everything she asked
9: 2 from S that he could not explain to her.
9: 9 which the queen of Sheba gave to King S.
9:10 The servants of Huram and of S who brought
9:12 King S gave the queen of Sheba everything
9:13 The gold that S received each year weighed
9:14 the country, brought gold and silver to S.
9:15 King S made two hundred large shields of
9:17 King S also made a large ivory throne
9:22 Thus King S surpassed all the other kings
9:23 kings of the earth sought audience with S,
9:25 S also had four thousand stalls of horses,
9:28 for S from Egypt and from all the lands.
9:29 The rest of the acts of S,
9:30 S reigned in Jerusalem over all Israel for
10: 2 in Egypt where he had fled from King S,
11: 3 "Say to Rehoboam, son of S,
11:17 of Judah and made Rehoboam, son of S,
11:17 in the way of David and S three years.
12: 9 the gold bucklers that S had made.
13: 6 Jeroboam, son of Nebat, the servant of S,
13: 7 him and overcame Rehoboam, son of S,
30:26 in Jerusalem, for since the days of S,
33: 7 which God had said to David and his son S:
35: 3 "Put the holy ark in the house built by S,
35: 4 of King David of Israel and his son S.
Ezr 2:55 Descendants of the slaves of S:
2:58 of S was three hundred and ninety-two.
Neh 7:57 Descendants of the slaves of S:
7:60 of S was three hundred and ninety-two.
11: 3 and the descendants of the slaves of S,
12:45 with the prescriptions of David and of S,
13:26 Did not S, the king of Israel, sin
2Mc 2: 8 time of Moses and when S prayed
2: 9 It is also related how S in his wisdom
2:10 so S also prayed and fire came down and

SOLOMON (cont.)

2:12 S also celebrated the feast in the same
Prv 1: 1 The Proverbs of S,
10: 1 The Proverbs of S:
25: 1 These also are proverbs of S.
Sg 1: 1 The song of songs by S.
3: 7 Ah, it is the litter of S;
3: 9 King S made himself a carriage of wood
3:11 to come forth and look upon King S
8:12 the thousand pieces are for you, O S,
Sir 47:13 S reigned during an era of peace,
47:23 S finally slept with his fathers,
Jer 52:20 King S had made for the house of the LORD.
Mt 1: 6 David was the father of S,
1: 7 S was the father of Rehoboam,
6:29 not even S in all his splendor was arrayed
12:42 of the earth to listen to the wisdom of S;
12:42 but you have a greater than S here.
Lk 11:31 of the world to listen to the wisdom of S,
11:31 but you have a greater than S here.
12:27 S in all his splendor was not arrayed like
Acts 7:47 It was S,

SOLOMON'S (30)

1Kgs 1:11 Then Nathan said to Bathsheba, S mother:
4:11 who was married to S daughter Taphath,
5: 2 S supplies for each day were thirty kors
5:14 Men came to hear S wisdom from all nations,
5:30 answerable to S prefects for the work,
5:32 S and Hiram's builders,
6: 1 in the fourth year of S reign over Israel,
9:16 given it as dowry to his daughter, S wife;
9:23 The supervisors of S works who policed the
10: 1 The queen of Sheba, having heard of S fame,
10: 4 queen of Sheba witnessed S great wisdom,
10:13 as were given her from S royal bounty.
10:21 all King S drinking vessels were of gold,
10:21 for in S time it was considered worthless.
10:28 S horses were imported from Cilicia,
11:26 S servant Jeroboam,
11:31 'I will tear away the kingdom from S grasp
11:40 in Egypt, where he remained until S death.
2Chr 5: 2 At S order the elders of Israel and all
8:10 They were also King S two hundred and
8:16 All of S work was carried out successfully
8:18 who accompanied S servants to Ophir and
9: 1 When the queen of Sheba heard of S fame,
9: 3 When the queen of Sheba witnessed S wisdom,
9:20 of King S drinking vessels were of gold,
9:20 was not considered of value in S time.
10: 6 service of his father during S lifetime,
Jn 10:23 walking in the temple area, in S Portico,
Acts 3:11 rushed over to them excitedly in S Portico.
5:12 agreement they used to meet in S Portico.

SOLUTIONS (1)

Wis 8: 8 the turns of phrases and the s of riddles;

SOLVE (3)

Jgs 14:12 of the feast you s it for me successfully,
Dn 5:12 explain enigmas, and s difficulties.
5:16 can interpret dreams and s difficulties;

SOLVED (1)

Jgs 14:18 my heifer, you would not have s my riddle."

SOMBER (1)

Wis 17: 4 and mute phantoms with s looks appeared.

SOMBERNESS (1)

Jl 2: 2 and of gloom, a day of clouds and s!

SOME (576)

Gn 3: 6 So she took s of its fruit and ate it;
3: 6 and she also gave s to her husband,
9:21 When he drank s of the wine,
15: 1 S time after these events,
18: 4 Let s water be brought,
18: 8 Then he got s curds and milk,
21:14 Early the next morning Abraham got s bread
22: 1 S time after these events,
22:20 S time afterward,
25:30 "Let me gulp down s of that red stuff;
25:34 then gave him s bread and the lentil stew;
27: 3 out into the country to hunt s game for me.
27: 5 the country to hunt s game for his father,
27: 7 'Bring me s game and with it prepare an
27:19 Please sit up and eat s of my game,
27:31 "Please, father, eat s of your son's game,
30:14 he came upon s mandrakes which he brought
30:14 let me have s of your son's mandrakes."
30:35 she-goats, all those with s white on them,
30:37 however, got s fresh shoots of poplar,
31:46 said to his kinsmen, "Gather s stones."
31:46 So they got s stones and made a mound;
32:25 Then s man wrestled with him until the
33:15 your disposal s of the men who are with me."
34: 1 out to visit s of the women of the land.
35:16 had s distance to go on the way to Ephrath,
37:28 S Midianite traders passed by,
40: 1 S time afterward, the royal cupbearer
40: 4 After they had been in custody for s time,
42: 2 Go down there and buy s for us,
42: 4 for he thought s disaster might befall him.
42:27 opened his bag to give his donkey s fodder,
42:38 If s disaster should befall him on the
43:11 Put s of the land's best products in your
43:11 s balm and honey, gum and resin,
44:25 to come back and buy s food for the family.
44:29 from me too, and s disaster befalls him,
48: 1 S time afterward, Joseph was informed,
Ex 2:17 But s shepherds came and drove them away.
4: 9 take s water from the river and pour it on
9:20 S of Pharaoh's servants feared the warning
10:10 Clearly, you have s evil in mind.
10:26 S of them we must sacrifice to the LORD
12: 7 They shall take s of its blood and apply
16:17 S gathered a large and some a small amount.
16:20 When s kept a part of it over until the
16:27 day s of the people went out to gather it,
17: 5 along with s of the elders of Israel,
18:19 listen to me, and I will give you s advice,
24: 1 You shall all worship at s distance,
29:12 Take s of its blood and with your finger
29:20 S of its blood you shall take and put on
29:21 take s of the blood that is on the altar,
29:21 together with s of the anointing oil,
29:34 s of the flesh of the ordination sacrifice or s
30:36 Grind s of it into fine dust and put this
33: 7 Moses used to pitch at s distance away,
Lv 1: 7 have put s burning embers on the altar and
1: 7 on the altar and laid s wood on them,
2:16 shall then burn s of the grits and oil,
4: 2 inadvertently commits a sin against s
4: 5 The anointed priest shall then take s of
4: 7 The priest shall also put s of the blood
4:16 bring s of its blood into the meeting tent,
4:18 He shall also put s of the blood on the
4:22 are forbidden by s commandment of the LORD,
4:25 The priest shall then take s of the blood
4:30 The priest shall then take s of its blood
4:34 The priest shall then take s of the blood
5: 3 aware of it, touches s human uncleanness,
5: 9 he shall sprinkle s of the blood of the
5:17 are forbidden by s commandment of the LORD,
6:23 partake of any sin offering of which s blood
7:21 or from s loathsome crawling creature,
8:11 s of this oil seven times on the altar,
8:12 s of the anointing oil on Aaron's head,
8:15 slaughtered it, and taking s of its blood,
8:23 Moses took s of its blood and put it on
8:24 and he put s of the blood on the tips of
8:30 Taking s of the anointing oil and some of
14: 4 live, clean birds, as well as s cedar wood,
14:14 Then the priest shall take s of the blood
14:15 s of it into the palm of his own left hand;
14:17 put s on the tip of the man's right ear,
14:25 lamb, he shall take s of its blood,
14:26 The priest shall then pour s of the oil
14:28 S of the oil in his hand the priest shall
16:14 Taking s of the bullock's blood,
16:14 propitiatory and likewise sprinkle s
16:18 s of the bullock's and the goat's blood,
16:19 sprinkle s of the blood on it seven times.
24: 7 On each pile put s pure frankincense,
25:25 poverty and has to sell s of his property,
25:49 or by s other relative or fellow clansman;
27:18 but if it is s time after this,
27:22 "If the field that s man dedicates to the
Nm 2: 2 meeting tent, but at s distance from it.
5:17 vessel he shall meanwhile put s holy water,
5:17 as well as s dust that he has taken from
9: 6 There were s,
11:17 I will also take s of the spirit that is
11:25 Taking s of the spirit that was on Moses,
13:20 best to get s of the fruit of the land."
13:23 a pole, as well as s pomegranates and figs.
17: 2 and scatter the fire s distance away,
19: 4 Eleazar the priest shall take s of its
19: 6 and the priest shall take s cedar wood,
19:18 a man who is clean shall take s hyssop,
21: 1 them in battle and took s of them captive.
22:41 and from there he saw s of the clans.
23:13 you can see only s and not all of them,
27:20 Invest him with s of your own dignity,
30:16 them s time after he first learned of them,
31:50 the LORD s gold article he has picked up,
35:22 in wait for him he throws s object at him,
Dt 1:25 taking along s of the fruit of the land,
23:26 you may pluck s of the ears with your hand,
26: 2 you shall take s first-fruits of the
27: 2 s large stones and coat them with plaster.
31:29 so that evil will befall you in s future
Jos 2: 2 king of Jericho that s Israelites
7: 5 at Ai, who killed s thirty-six of them.
11:22 However, s survived in Gaza,
15:18 induced him to ask her father for s land.
Jgs 1:14 induced him to ask her father for s land.
8: 5 you give my followers s loaves of bread?
9:48 axe in his hand, and cut down s brushwood.
11: 4 S time later,
14: 9 father and mother, he gave them s to eat,
15: 1 After s time,
17: 9 my way to find s other place of residence."
18:22 The Danites had already gone s distance,
19: 2 Judah, where she stayed for s four months.
19:13 servant, "let us make for s other place,
20:39 killing off s thirty of the men of Israel,
Ru 1: 2 S time after their arrival on the Moabite
2:14 said to her, "Come here and have s food;
2:14 he handed her s roasted grain and she ate
2:14 and she ate her fill and had s left over.
2:16 and even to let drop s handfuls and leave
1Sm 2:15 "Give me s meat to roast for the priest.
2:33 s of your family to remain at my altar,
9:11 they met s girls coming out to draw water
9:24 I explained that I was inviting s guests."
13: 6 S Israelites, aware of the danger
14:11 s Hebrews are coming out of the holes
17:18 brothers and bring home s token from them.
20: 7 you can be sure he has planned s harm.
21: 5 from women, you may eat s of that."
23:19 S of the Ziphites went up to Saul in
23:22 perhaps they are playing s trick on me).
24:11 I had s thought of killing you,
27: 1 "I shall perish s day at the hand of Saul.
2Sm 10: 1 S time later the king of the Ammonites died,
11:17 Joab, s officers of David's army fell,
11:24 above, and s of the king's servants died,
12:18 He may do s harm!"
13: 1 S time later the following incident
13: 6 and prepare s fried cakes before my eyes,
13: 7 Amnon and prepare s nourishment for him."
13:34 telling the king that he had seen s men
17: 9 in one of the caves or in s other place.
17: 9 And if s of our soldiers should fall at
18:20 On s other day you may take the good news,
1Kgs 7:10 blocks, some ten cubits and s eight cubits.
8:38 conscience and offers s prayer or petition,
11:17 with s Edomite servants of his father.
13: 7 "Come home with me for s refreshment,"
13:15 said, "Come home with me and have s bread."
13:25 S passers-by saw the body lying in the road,
14: 3 Take along ten loaves, s cakes,
17: 7 After s time,
17:17 S time later the son of the mistress of
18:12 will carry you to s place I do not know,
20:17 word that s men had marched out of Samaria.
21: 1 S time after this, as Naboth
2Kgs 2:16 him away to s mountain or some valley."
2:23 s small boys came out of the city and
4:38 s vegetable stew for the guild prophets."
4:41 "Bring s meal," Elisha said.
4:43 shall eat and there shall be s left over.'"
4:44 when they had eaten, there was s left over,
5:19 Naaman had gone s distance when Gehazi,
7:13 let s of us take five of the abandoned
9:33 and s of her blood spurted against the
10:18 "Ahab served Baal to s extent,
13:15 "Take a bow and s arrows,"
13:21 Once s people were burying a man,
17:25 among them that killed s of their number.
20:18 S of your own bodily descendants shall be
25:12 But s of the country's poor,
1Chr 9:28 S of them had charge of the liturgical
12: 2 They were s of Saul's kinsmen,
12: 9 S of the Gadites also went over to David
12:17 S Benjaminites and Judahites also came to
19:10 he chose s of the best fighters among the
2Chr 12: 7 I will give them s deliverance,
16:10 oppressed s of his people at this time.
17:11 S of the Philistines brought Jehoshaphat
18: 2 s years he went down to Ahab at Samaria;
19: 3 Yet s good things are to be found in you,
19: 8 Jehoshaphat appointed s Levites and
19: 8 s of the family heads of Israel
20: 1 and with them s Meunites came to fight
20:21 some to sing to the LORD and s to praise
21: 4 and also s of the princes of Israel.
24: 4 After s time,
28:12 At this, s of the Ephraimite leaders,
30:11 Nevertheless, s from Asher,
32:21 s of his own offspring struck him down
34:13 S of the other Levites were scribes,
35:11 priests sprinkled s of the blood
36: 7 carried away to Babylon s of the vessels
Ezr 2:68 s of the family heads made free-will
2:70 and s of the common people took up
7: 7 Some of the Israelites and s priests,
9: 2 for they have taken s of their daughters
Neh 2: 1 I took s and offered it to the king.
3: 5 s of their outstanding men would not
5: 2 S said:
5: 5 has been done to s of our daughters!
5: 7 After s deliberation,
7: 3 of Jerusalem, s at their watch posts,
7:70 S of the family heads contributed to the
11:36 S sections of the Levites from Judah
13:19 I posted s of my own men at the gates so
13:25 s of them beaten and their hair pulled out;
Tb 2: 3 out to look for s poor kinsmen of ours.
2:10 I went to see s doctors for a cure,
4: 8 have but little, distribute even s of that.
4:16 s of your bread, and to the naked some
10: 6 take care of s unexpected business there.
Jdt 7:12 Have s of your servants keep control of

7:18 and they sent *s* of their men to the south
10:15 *s* of our men will accompany you to present
1Mc 1:13 *s* from among the people promptly went to
4: 2 *S* men from the citadel were their guides.
4:38 the courts as in a forest or on *s* mountain,
5:25 There they met *s* Nabateans,
5:27 "and *s* have been imprisoned in other
5:67 At that time *s* priests fell in battle who
6:21 *S* of the besieged escaped,
6:40 the heights, while *s* were on low ground,
7:33 *S* of the priests from the sanctuary and *s*
10:14 Only in Beth-zur did *s* remain of those who
10:37 Let *s* of them be stationed in the king's
10:37 let *s* be given positions of trust
10:61 *S* pestilent Israelites,
11:21 *S* transgressors of the law,
11:23 He selected *s* elders and priests of Israel
11:25 Although *s* impious men of his own nation
16:10 *S* took refuge in the towers on the plain
16:16 him, his two sons, and *s* of his servants.
2Mc 1:19 devout priests of the time took *s* of the
1:21 ordered them to scoop *s* out and bring it.
2: 1 *s* of the aforementioned fire with them,
2: 6 *S* of those who followed him came up
3:19 some to the gates, *s* to the walls,
3:31 Soon *s* of the companions of Heliodorus
3:32 *s* foul play at the hands of the Jews,
3:38 *s* special divine power about the Place.
4:19 but should be used for *s* other purpose.
4:23 to obtain decisions on *s* important matters.
4:32 stole *s* gold vessels from the temple and
4:32 he had already sold *s* other vessels in
4:46 a colonnade, as if to get *s* fresh air,
4:49 even *s* Tyrians were indignant over the
6:21 and to pretend to be eating *s* of the meat
8:25 When they had pursued the enemy for *s* time,
8:30 them, and captured *s* very high fortresses.
9:11 arrogance, and to gain *s* understanding,
10:15 Idumeans, who held *s* important strongholds,
10:20 But *s* of the men in Simon's force who were
10:20 be bribed by *s* of the men in the towers;
12: 2 But *s* of the local governors,
12: 3 *S* people of Joppa also committed this
12:17 When they had gone on *s* ninety miles,
14: 4 as well as *s* of the customary olive
14:22 suddenly carry out *s* treacherous plan.
Ps(s) 20: 8 *S* are strong in chariots; some, in horses;
Prv 12:18 The prating of *s* men is like sword thrusts,
13:23 but *s* men perish for lack of a law court.
18:24 *S* friends bring ruin on us,
21:26 *S* are consumed with avarice all the day,
Eccl 5:13 the riches be lost through *s* misfortune,
Wis 13:14 or makes it resemble *s* worthless beast.
Sir 8: 6 Insult no man when he is old, for *s* of us,
11: 5 *s* that none would consider wear a crown.
20: 8 *S* misfortunes bring success; some things
20: 9 *S* gifts do one no good, and some
33: 9 *S* he dignifies and sanctifies,
33:12 *S* he blesses and makes great, some
36:18 yet *s* foods are more agreeable than others;
37: 7 out a way, but *s* counsel ways of their own;
44: 8 *S* of them have left behind a name and men
48:16 *S* of these did what was right,
Is 22:10 tearing *s* down to strengthen the wall;
39: 7 *S* of your own bodily descendants shall be
45:19 hiding nor from *s* dark place of the earth,
49:12 See, *s* shall come from afar,
49:12 and the west, and *s* from the land of Syene.
56:12 "Come, I will fetch *s* wine;
66:21 *S* of these I will take as priests and
Jer 19: 1 Take along *s* of the elders of the people
26:17 *s* of the elders of the land came forward
28:12 *S* time after the prophet Hananiah had
38:11 in the palace, from which he took *s* old,
39:10 But *s* of the poor who had no property were
52:16 But *s* of the country's poor,
Bar 6:32 The priests take *s* of their clothing and
6:43 aside by *s* passerby who lies with her,
Ez 5: 4 Then take *s* of these and throw them in the
6: 8 When *s* of your people have escaped to
10: 7 He took up *s* of it and put it in the hands
14:22 still *s* survivors shall be left in it who
16:16 You took *s* of your gowns and made for
17: 5 Then he took *s* seed of the land,
20: 1 *s* of the elders of Israel came to consult
24: 3 the pot, set it up, then pour in *s* water.
42: 1 bringing me to *s* chambers on the north
43:20 Take *s* of its blood and put it on the four
45:19 Then the priest shall take *s* of the blood
Dn 1: 2 and *s* of the vessels of the temple of God,
1: 3 to bring in *s* of the Israelites of royal
2:41 but yet have *s* of the hardness of iron.
3: 8 *s* of the Chaldeans came and accused the
3:20 *s* of the strongest men in his army
8:10 some of the host and *s*
8:27 I, Daniel, was weak and ill for *s* days;
11: 6 After *s* years they shall become allies:
11:13 after *s* years he shall attack with this
11:32 By his deceit he shall make *s* who were
11:35 Of the wise men, *s* shall fall,
12: 2 *s* shall live forever,
14:14 ordered his servants to bring *s* ashes,
14:27 Then Daniel took *s* pitch,

14:33 he mixed *s* bread in a bowl with the stew
Jl 4: 4 you take vengeance upon me by *s* action?
Ob 1: 5 to you, would they not leave *s* gleanings?
Mt 3: 8 Give *s* evidence that you mean to reform.
8:30 *S* distance away a large herd of swine was
9: 3 that *s* of the scribes said to themselves,
9:32 suddenly *s* people brought him a mute who
12:38 *S* of the scribes and Pharisees then spoke
12:38 "Teacher, we want to see you work *s* signs."
13:21 When *s* setback or persecution involving
14:15 the villages and buy *s* food for themselves."
16: 1 asked him to show them *s* sign in the sky.
16:14 They replied, *S* say John the Baptizer,
16:28 among those standing here there are *s*
18:15 brother should commit *s* wrong against you,
19: 3 *S* Pharisees came up to him and said,
19:12 *S* men are incapable of sexual activity
19:12 *s* have been deliberately made so;
19:12 and *s* there are who have freely renounced
21: 8 while *s* began to cut branches from the
22: 5 *S* ignored the invitation and went their way,
22:23 That same day *s* Sadducees,
23:34 *S* you will kill and crucify,
25: 8 to the sensible, 'Give us *s* of your oil.
25: 9 go to the dealers and buy yourselves *s*.'
26: 4 to arrest Jesus by *s* trick and kill him;
26:73 *s* bystanders came over to Peter and said,
27:47 *s* of the bystanders who heard it remark,
28:11 *s* of the guard went into the city and
Mk 2: 3 *s* people arrived bringing a paralyzed man
2: 6 Now *s* of the scribes were sitting there
4: 4 *S* of what he sowed landed on the footpath,
4: 5 *S* of the seed landed on rocky ground where
4: 7 Again, *s* landed among thorns,
4: 8 *S* seed,
4:17 When *s* pressure or persecution overtakes
7: 1 The Pharisees and *s* of the experts in the
7:32 *S* people brought him a deaf man who had a
8: 3 *S* of them have come a great distance."
8:11 for *s* heavenly sign from him as a test.
8:22 *s* people brought him a blind man and
8:28 They replied, *S*, John the Baptizer,
9: 1 *s* who will not taste death until they see
10: 2 Then *s* Pharisees came up and as a test
11: 5 *S* of the bystanders said to them,
11:13 Observing a fig tree *s* distance off,
12: 5 some they beat; *s* they killed.
12:13 They next sent *s* Pharisees and Herodians
12:18 Then *s* Sadducees who hold there is no
14: 1 way to arrest him by *s* trick and kill him.
14: 4 *S* were saying to themselves indignantly:
14:57 *S*, for instance, on taking the stand,
14:65 *S* of them began to spit on him.
15: 4 "Surely you have *s* answer?
Lk 3: 8 Give *s* evidence that you mean to reform.
5:18 *S* men came along carrying a paralytic on a
6: 2 *S* of the Pharisees asked,
7: 3 about Jesus he sent *s* Jewish elders to him,
8: 2 and also *s* women who had been cured of
8: 5 "A farmer went out to sow *s* seed.
8: 5 *s* fell on the footpath where it was walked
8: 6 *S* fell on rocky ground, sprouted up,
8: 7 *S* fell among briers, and the thorns
8: 8 But *s* fell on good soil,
9: 7 and was perplexed, for *s* were saying,
9:19 they replied, "and *s* say Elijah,
9:27 there are *s* standing here who will not
11:15 *S* of them said, "It is by Beelzebul,
11:49 *s* of these they will persecute and kill';
13: 1 *s* were present who told him about the
13:30 Some who are last will be first and *s*
14: 8 case *s* greater dignitary has been invited.
14:18 *s* land and must go out and inspect it.
14:22 The servant reported, after *s* time,
15:13 *S* days later this younger son collected
19:39 *S* of the Pharisees in the crowd said to him,
20:27 *S* Sadducees came forward (the ones who
20:39 *S* of the scribes responded,
21: 5 *S* were speaking of how the temple was
21:16 friends, and *s* of you will be put to death.
22: 2 began to look for *s* way to dispose of him;
23: 8 he was hoping to see him work *s* miracle.
24:22 *s* women of our group have just brought us
24:22 have just brought us *s* astonishing news.
24:24 *S* of our number went to the tomb and found
Jn 1:22 we can give *s* answer to those who sent us.
2: 8 *s* out and take it to the waiter in charge."
3:22 he spent *s* time with them there baptizing.
5:10 *s* of the Jews began telling the man who
6:23 Then *s* boats came out from Tiberias near
6:64 among you there are *s* who do not believe."
7: 1 *s* of the Jews were looking for a chance
7:12 *S* maintained, "He is a good man,"
7:25 led *s* of the people of Jerusalem to remark:
7:40 *S* in the crowd who heard these words began
7:44 *S* of them even wanted to apprehend him.
8:22 At this *s* of the Jews began to ask,
9: 9 *S* were claiming it was he;
9:16 This prompted *s* of the Pharisees to assert,
9:40 *S* of the Pharisees around him picked this
10: 1 in *s* other way is a thief and a marauder.
10:31 When *s* of the Jews again reached for rocks
11:37 But *s* said, "He opened the eyes

11:46 *S* others, however, went to the Pharisees
12:20 up to worship at the feast were *s* Greeks.
16:17 this, *s* of his disciples asked one another:
19:29 wine on *s* hyssop and raised it to his lips.
21: 7 the Lord, Simon Peter threw on *s* clothes
21: 9 there with a fish laid on it and *s* bread.
21:10 "Bring *s* of the fish you just caught,"
Acts 1:14 There were *s* women in their company,
2:41 *s* three thousand were added that day.
3:12 man walk by *s* power or holiness of our own?
5: 3 yourself *s* of the proceeds from that field?
5: 6 *S* of the young men came forward,
6:11 They persuaded *s* men to make the charge
7:26 next day while *s* of them were fighting,
8:36 moved along the road they came to *s* water,
8:37 said, "Look, there is *s* water right there.
9:23 After quite *s* time has passed,
9:25 *S* of his disciples, therefore, took him
9:30 *s* of them took him down to Caesarea and
10: 5 *s* men to Joppa and summon a certain Simon,
10:10 He became hungry and asked for *s* food,
10:23 by *s* of the brothers from Joppa.
11: 2 when Peter went up to Jerusalem *s* among
11:20 *s* men of Cyprus and Cyrene among them who
12: 1 to harass *s* of the members of the church.
12:19 left Judea to spend *s* time in Caesarea.
13:20 the end of *s* four hundred and fifty years.
13:50 But *s* of the Jews stirred up their
14: 4 *s* siding with the Jews and others with the
14:19 *s* Jews from Antioch and Iconium arrived
14:28 they spent *s* time there with the disciples.
15: 1 *S* men came down to Antioch from Judea and
15: 2 and *s* others should go up to see the
15: 5 *S* of the converted Pharisees then got up
15:24 We have heard that *s* of our number without
15:33 After passing *s* time there,
16:13 We spent *s* time in that city.
17: 4 *S* of the Jews were convinced and threw in
17: 6 *s* of the brothers to the town magistrates,
17:18 disputed with him, *s* of them asking,
17:28 being,' as *s* of your own poets have put it,
17:32 about the raising of the dead, *s* sneered,
17:32 must hear you on this topic *s* other time."
18:23 spending *s* time there he set out again,
19: 1 *s* disciples to whom he put the question,
19: 9 *s* in their obstinacy would not believe,
19:13 *S* itinerant Jewish exorcists once tried to
19:31 Even *s* of the Asiarchs who were friends of
19:33 *S* brought out of the crowd Alexander,
21:16 *S* of the disciples from Caesarea came
21:27 when *s* Jews from the province of Asia
21:38 Egyptian who caused the riot *s* time ago
23: 6 some of them were Sadducees and *s*
23: 9 *s* scribes of the Pharisee party arose and
24: 1 Ananias came down to Caesarea with *s* of
24:23 be kept in custody but allowed *s* freedom,
27: 1 Paul and *s* other prisoners were handed
27: 3 to visit *s* friends who cared for his needs.
27:18 *s* of the cargo was thrown over the side.
27:26 still have to face shipwreck on *s* island."
27:29 we should be dashed against *s* rocky coast,
27:33 Paul urged all on board to take *s* food:
27:34 Now I urge you to take *s* food,
27:35 When he had said this he took *s* bread,
28: 6 After waiting for quite *s* time,
28:14 Here we found *s* of the brothers,
28:24 *S*, indeed,
Rom 1:11 you *s* spiritual gift to strengthen you
1:13 in order to do *s* fruitful work among you,
3: 3 ask, what if *s* of them have not believed?
3: 8 that *s* slanderously accuse us of teaching;
11:14 my fellow Jews to envy and save *s* of them.
11:17 If *s* of the branches were cut off and you,
1Cor 4:18 *S* have grown full of self-importance,
6:11 And such were *s* of you;
8: 7 *s* were so recently devoted to idols,
9:22 men in order to save at least *s* of them.
10: 7 Do not become idolaters, as *s* of them did.
10: 8 not indulge in lewdness as *s* of them did,
10: 9 Let us not test the Lord as *s* of them did,
10:10 Nor are you to grumble as *s* of them did,
14: 6 if my speech does not have *s* revelation,
14:26 has a psalm, another *s* instruction to give,
15: 6 still alive, although *s* have fallen asleep.
15:12 how is it that *s* of you say there is no
15:34 *S* of you are quite ignorant of God;
15:37 but a kernel of wheat or *s* other grain.
16: 6 should like to remain with you for *s* time
16: 7 I hope to spend *s* time with you,
2Cor 2: 5 he has hurt not only me, but in *s* measure,
7: 8 Or if I did feel *s* regret (because I
8:10 *s* advice on this matter of rich and poor.
10:11 Well, let such people give this *s* thought,
Gal 1: 7 *S* who wish to alter the gospel of Christ
Phil 1:15 *s* preach Christ from motives of envy and
1:16 *S* act from unaffected love,
4: 2 come to *s* mutual understanding in the Lord.
2Thes 3:11 We hear that *s* of you are unruly,
1Tm 1: 6 *S* people have neglected these and instead
1:19 *S* men, by rejecting the guidance
4: 1 *s* will turn away from the faith
4: 8 physical training is to *s* extent valuable,
5:15 *s* have turned away to follow Satan.

SOME (cont.)

5:24 *S* men's sins are flagrant and cry out for
5:25 *s* good deeds stand out clearly as such;
6:10 *S* men in their passion for it have strayed
6:21 *s* men have missed the goal of faith.
2Tm 2:18 They are upsetting *s* people's faith.
2:20 *s* for distinguished and others for common
Heb 4: 6 since it remains for *s* to enter,
10:25 ourselves from the assembly, as *s* do,
13: 2 for by that means *s* have entertained
2Pt 3: 9 though *s* consider it "delay."
2Jn 1: 4 It has given me great joy to find *s* of
1: 5 as if I were writing you *s* new commandment;
Rv 2:10 The devil will indeed cast *s* of you into
2:14 there are *s* among you who follow the
3: 9 I mean to make *s* of Satan's assembly,
20: 4 Then I saw *s* thrones.

SOMEHOW (1)

Rom 1:10 always pleading that *s* by God's will I may

SOMEONE (119)

Gn 37:32 *s* to bring the long tunic to their father,
Ex 4:13 "If you please, Lord, send *s* else!"
Lv 3: 1 "If *s* in presenting a peace offering
5: 2 or if *s*, without being aware of it
5: 3 or if *s*, without being aware of it
5: 4 or if *s*, without being aware of it
5:15 "If *s* commits a sin by inadvertently
5:17 "If *s*,
5:21 "If *s* commits a sin of dishonesty against
7: 8 holocaust for *s* may keep for himself
7:20 *s* while in a state of uncleanness eats any
7:21 Likewise, if *s* touches anything unclean,
13: 2 "If *s* has on his skin a scab or pustule
13: 9 "When *s* is stricken with leprosy,
25:29 "When *s* sells a dwelling in a walled town,
27:14 "When *s* dedicates his house as sacred to
27:16 "If the object which *s* dedicates to the
27:20 such a field, he sells it to *s* else,
27:31 If *s* wishes to buy back any of his tithes,
Nm 6: 9 "If *s* dies very suddenly in his presence,
35:11 killed *s* unintentionally may take refuge.
35:30 "Whenever *s* kills another,
36: 8 Israelite tribes shall marry *s* belonging
Dt 19: 4 when *s* unwittingly kills his neighbor to
19:11 if *s* lies in wait for his neighbor out of
22: 8 otherwise, if *s* falls off,
Jgs 4:20 anyone comes and asks, 'Is there *s* here?'
Ru 2:22 in *s* else's field you might be insulted."
1Sm 2:13 When *s* offered a sacrifice,
10:12 And *s* from that district added,
2Sm 15: 2 *s* had a lawsuit to be decided by the king,
18:10 *S* saw this and reported to Joab that he
23:15 that *s* would give me a drink of water from
1Kgs 2: 4 *s* of your line on the throne of Israel.'
8:25 'You shall always have *s* from your line to
9: 5 *s* from your line on the throne of Israel.'
20:39 *s* turned and brought me a man and said,
22:34 *S*, however, drew his bow at random
2Kgs 4:39 *S* went out into the field to gather herbs
5: 7 should send *s* to me to be cured of leprosy?
5:21 Aware that *s* was running after him,
6:32 a murderer is sending *s* to cut off my head?
1Chr 11:17 that *s* would give me a drink from the
2Chr 6:16 'You shall always have *s* from your line to
7:18 be lacking *s* of yours as ruler in Israel.'
18:33 *S*, however, drew his bow at random
Neh 2:10 *s* had come to seek the welfare
Tb 5: 4 Tobiah went to look for *s* acquainted with
1Mc 16:21 But *s* ran ahead and brought word to John
2Mc 11:36 send *s* to us with your decisions so that
Jb 4: 2 If *s* attempts a word with you,
Prv 27: 2 *S* else
Is 21: 7 chariot, a pair of horses, *S* riding an ass,
21: 7 Someone riding an ass, *s* riding a camel,
Jer 8: 4 When *s* falls, does he not rise again?
Bar 6:23 unless *s* wipes away the corrosion,
Ez 22:30 Thus I have searched among them for *s* who
43: 6 I heard *s* speaking to me from the temple,
Dn 5:17 gifts, or give your presents to *s* else;
Mt 11: 8 you go out to see *s* luxuriously dressed?
12:47 *S* said to him,
13:31 seed which *s* took and sowed in his field.
25: 6 At midnight *s* shouted, 'The groom is here!
Mk 15:36 *S* ran off,
Lk 6:29 When *s* slaps you on one cheek,
6:29 when *s* takes your coat,
7:19 who is to come' or are we to expect *s* else?"
7:20 who is to come" or do we look for *s* else?' "
7:25 you go out to see *s* dressed luxuriously?
8:46 Jesus insisted, *S* touched me;
9:57 were making their way along, *s* said to him,
11: 5 "If one of you knows *s* who comes to him
11:22 But when *s* stronger than he comes and
12:13 *S* in the crowd said to him,
13:23 *S* asked him,
14: 8 you are invited by *s* to a wedding party,
16:12 not been trustworthy with *s* else's money,
16:30 if *s* would only go to them from the dead,
20: 5 a brief conference during which *s* said,
22:58 little while later *s* else saw him and said,
Jn 1:33 you see the Spirit descend and rest on *s*,
4:29 see *s* who told me everything I ever did!
4:33 that *s* has brought him something to eat?"
5: 7 get there, *s* else has gone in ahead of me."
5:43 But let *s* come in his own name,
9: 9 it was not but *s* who looked like him.
9:31 but that if *s* is devout and obeys his will,
18:39 I release *s* to you at Passover time.
Acts 5:25 *S* then came up to them,
5:36 to pass himself off as *s* of importance.
8: 9 himself off as *s* of great importance.
8:31 man replied, "unless *s* explains it to me?"
8:34 himself or *s* else?"
10:32 Send *s* to Joppa to invite Simon known as
11:13 'Send *s* to Joppa and fetch Simon,
13:11 groped about for *s* to lead him by the hand.
Rom 5: 7 a good man *s* may have the courage to die.
6:16 offer yourselves to *s* as obedient slaves,
10:14 can they hear unless there is *s* to preach?
14: 5 *s* else considers all days alike.
1Cor 3: 4 When *s* says, "I belong to Paul,"
3: 4 says, "I belong to Paul," and *s* else,
3:10 do, and now *s* else is building upon it.
7:18 Was *s* called after he had been circumcised?
8:10 If *s* sees you, with your "knowledge,"
10:28 But if *s* should say to you,
15:35 Perhaps *s* will say, "How are the dead
2Cor 11: 4 when *s* comes preaching another Jesus than
Gal 6: 1 My brothers, if *s* is detected in sin,
1Tm 3: 3 Nor can he be *s* who loves money.
Heb 3: 4 Every house is founded by *s*,
5:12 you need to have *s* teach you again the
6:16 Men swear by *s* greater than themselves;
Jas 5:19 among you of *s* straying from the truth,
1Pt 5: 8 a roaring lion looking for *s* to devour.
Rv 3:11 what you have lest *s* rob you of your crown.
10:11 Then *s* said to me, "You must prophesy
11: 1 *S* gave me a measuring rod and said:
22:10 Then *s* said to me:

SOMETHING (95)

Gn 30:30 now do *s* for my own household as well."
31:43 I will now do *s* for them and for the
Ex 2:20 Invite him to have *s* to eat."
17:14 down in a document as *s* to be remembered,
31:14 you must keep the sabbath as *s* sacred.
Lv 4:13 *s* that the LORD has forbidden
5: 1 as a witness of *s* he has seen or learned,
24: 9 as *s* most sacred among the various
Nm 16:30 But if the LORD does *s* entirely new,
35:20 lying in wait for him throws *s* at him,
Dt 24: 1 her because he finds in her *s* indecent,
30:14 No, it is *s* very near to you,
1Sm 3:11 "I am about to do *s* in Israel that will
28:22 Let me set *s* before you to eat,
2Sm 13: 5 she prepares *s* appetizing in my presence,
1Kgs 2:14 and added, "I have *s* to say to you."
3: 5 "Ask *s* of me and I will give it to you."
14:13 house has *s* pleasing to the LORD,
17:12 go in and prepare *s* for myself and my son;
17:13 can prepare *s* for yourself and your son.
2Kgs 1:13 your servants, count for *s* in your sight!
1:14 But now, let my life mean *s* to you!"
2:10 "You have asked *s* that is not easy,"
4:14 Elisha asked, "Can *s* be done for her?"
5:13 prophet had told you to do *s* extraordinary,
5:20 I will run after him and get *s* out of him."
Jdt 8:32 I will do *s* that will go down from
Prv 19: 6 are friends of the man who has *s* to give.
Wis 13:11 his art, produce *s* fit for daily use,
13:18 and about travel, *s* that cannot even walk.
Sir 13: 6 he needs *s* from you he will cajole you,
19:10 When a fool hears *s*,
Is 41:23 Do *s*, good or evil, that will put us
43:19 See, I am doing *s* new!
Ez 1: 4 midst of the fire] *s* gleamed like electrum.
1:13 *s* like burning coals of fire could be seen;
1:22 *s* like a firmament could be seen,
1:26 their heads *s* like a throne could be seen,
10: 1 *s* like a throne could be seen upon it.
10: 8 *S* like human hands could be seen under the
10:21 *s* like human hands were under their wings.
16: 5 thrown out on the ground as *s* loathsome,
41:21 was *s* that looked like a wooden altar,
Dn 10:16 Then *s* like a man's hand touched my lips;
Am 3: 4 out from its den unless it has seized *s*?
Mi 3: 5 Who, when their teeth have *s* to bite,
3: 5 But when one fails to put *s* in their mouth,
Mt 11: 9 A prophet indeed, and *s* more!
12: 6 there is *s* greater than the temple here.
14:16 Give them *s* to eat yourselves."
Mk 5:43 it, and told them to give her *s* to eat.
6:36 around here and buy themselves *s* to eat?"
6:37 "You give them *s* to eat," Jesus replied.
Lk 7:26 He is that, I assure you, and *s* more.
7:40 him, "Simon, I have *s* to propose to you."
8:55 he told them to give her *s* to eat.
9:13 do you not give them *s* to eat yourselves?"
Jn 4:31 disciples were urging him, "Rabbi, eat *s*."
4:33 that someone has brought him *s* to eat?"
5:14 sins so that *s* worse may not overtake you."
8: 6 so that they could have *s* to accuse him of.)
11:37 have done *s* to stop this man from dying?"
13:29 for the feast, or to give *s* to the poor.)
21: 6 he suggested, "and you will find *s*."
Acts 3: 5 them his whole attention, hoping to get *s*.
9:18 Immediately *s* like scales fell from his
11:29 the disciples determine to set *s* aside,
17:21 more than to tell about or listen to *s* new.)
17:29 *s* like a statue of gold or silver or stone,
19:33 he wanted to explain *s* to the gathering.
21:37 to the commander, "May I say *s* to you?"
23:17 he has *s* to report to him."
23:18 bring you this boy, who has *s* to tell you."
25:26 I may have *s* to set down in his regard.
27:36 new courage, and they too had *s* to eat.
Rom 9:20 Does *s* molded say to its molder,
12:20 if he is thirsty, give him *s* to drink;
14:14 *s* unclean that it becomes so for him.
14:20 God's work for the sake of *s* to eat.
1Cor 1:28 to reduce to nothing those who were *s*;
4: 7 Name *s* you have that you have not received.
7:36 come and it seems that *s* should be done,
8: 2 If a man thinks he knows *s*,
2Cor 5:12 boast about us so that you may have *s*
Gal 6: 3 If anyone thinks he amounts to *s*,
Eph 4:28 he will have *s* to share with those in need.
Phil 2: 6 deem equality with God *s* to be grasped at.
4:15 me by giving me *s* for what it had received.
4:16 at Thessalonica you sent *s* for my needs,
Heb 8: 3 necessity for this one to have *s* to offer.
Jas 3: 5 The tongue is *s* like that.
2Pt 1:19 prophetic message as *s* altogether reliable.
Rv 8: 8 *s* like a huge mountain all in flames was
9: 7 their heads they wore *s* like gold crowns;
15: 2 *s* like a sea of glass mingled with fire.

SOMETIME (1)

2Kgs 4:11 *S* later Elisha arrived and stayed in the

SOMETIMES (8)

Nm 9:20 yet *s* the cloud was over the Dwelling only
9:21 *S* the cloud remained there only from
Prv 14:12 *S* a way seems right to a man,
16:25 *S* a way seems right to a man,
Sir 18:16 *S* the word means more than the gift;
Jer 18: 7 *S* I threaten to uproot and tear down and
18: 9 *S*, again, I promise to build up and plant
Bar 6: 9 Then *s* the priests take the silver and

SOMEWHAT (1)

Mt 26:44 He left them again, withdrew *s*,

SOMEWHERE (2)

Heb 2: 6 *S* this is testified to, in the passage
4: 4 to the seventh day Scripture *s* says,

SON (2505)

Gn 4:17 a city, which he named after his *s* Enoch.
4:25 she gave birth to a *s* whom she called Seth.
4:26 To Seth, in turn, a *s* was born,
5: 3 old when he begot a *s* in his likeness,
5:28 years old, he begot a *s* and named him Noah,
9:24 what his youngest *s* had done to him,
11:31 son Abram, his grandson Lot, *s* of Haran,
11:31 Sarai, the wife of his *s* Abram,
12: 5 took his wife Sarai, his brother's *s* Lot,
16:11 "You are now pregnant and shall bear a *s*;
16:15 Abram a *s*, and Abram named the son
17:16 bless her, and I will give you a *s* by her.
17:19 your wife Sarah is to bear you a *s*,
17:23 took his *s* Ishmael and all his slaves,
17:25 and his *s* Ish-mael was thirteen years old
17:26 Abraham and his *s* Ishmael were circumcised;
18:10 next year, and Sarah will then have a *s*."
18:14 return to you, and Sarah will have a *s*."
19:37 one gave birth to a *s* whom she named Moab,
19:38 The younger one, too, gave birth to a *s*,
19:38 named him Ammon, saying, "The *s* of my kin.
21: 2 and bore Abraham a *s* in his old age,
21: 3 Isaac to this *s* of his whom Sarah bore him.
21: 4 When his *s* Isaac was eight days old,
21: 5 years old when his *s* Isaac was born to him.
21: 7 Yet I have borne him a *s* in his old age."
21: 9 Sarah noticed the *s* whom Hagar the
21: 9 borne to Abraham playing with her *s* Isaac;
21:10 "Drive out that slave and her *s*!
21:10 No *s* of that slave is going to share the
21:10 to share the inheritance with my *s* Isaac!"
21:11 especially on account of his *s* Ishmael.
21:13 As for the *s* of the slave woman,
22: 2 "Take your *s* Isaac,
22: 3 his donkey, took with him his *s* Isaac,
22: 6 and laid it on his *s* Isaac's shoulders,
22: 7 "Yes, *s*," he replied.
22: 8 *S*," Abraham answered,
22: 9 Next he tied up his *s* Isaac,
22:10 out and took the knife to slaughter his *s*.
22:12 not withhold from me your own beloved *s*."
22:13 it up as a holocaust in place of his *s*.
22:16 in not withholding from me your beloved *s*,
23: 8 Intercede for me with Ephron, *s* of Zohar,

24: 3 you will not procure a wife for my *s*
24: 4 to my kindred to get a wife for my *s* Isaac."
24: 5 *s* back to the land from which you migrated?"
24: 6 take my *s* back there for any reason,"
24: 7 and you will obtain a wife for my *s* there.
24: 8 But never take my *s* back there!"
24:15 (who was born to Bethuel, *s* of Milcah,
24:24 the daughter of Bethuel the *s* of Milcah,
24:36 Sarah bore a *s* to my master in her old age,
24:37 'You shall not procure a wife for my *s*
24:38 my own relatives, to get a wife for my *s*.'
24:40 *s* from my own kindred of my father's house.
24:44 LORD has decided upon for my master's *s*.'
24:47 'The daughter of Bethuel, *s* of Nahor,
24:48 daughter of my master's kinsman for his *s*.
24:51 she may become the wife of your master's *s*,
25: 5 everything that he owned to his *s* Isaac.
25: 6 the land of Kedem, away from his *s* Isaac.
25: 9 field of Ephron, *s* of Zohar the Hittite,
25:11 death of Abraham, God blessed his *s* Isaac,
25:12 are the descendants of Abraham's *s* Ishmael,
25:19 the family history of Isaac, *s* of Abraham;
27: 1 his older son Esau and said to him, *S!*"
27: 5 while Isaac was speaking to his *s* Esau.
27: 6 his father, Rebekah said to her *s* Jacob,
27: 8 Now, *s*,
27:13 "Let any curse against you, *s*,
27:15 her older *s* Esau that she had in the house,
27:15 gave them to her younger *s* Jacob to wear;
27:17 Then she handed her *s* Jacob the appetizing
27:20 asked, "How did you succeed so quickly, *s*?"
27:21 then said to Jacob, "Come closer, *s*,
27:21 whether you really are my *s* Esau or not."
27:24 he asked him, "Are you really my *s* Esau?"
27:25 Then Isaac said, "Serve me your game, *s*,
27:26 father Isaac said to him, "Come closer, *s*,
27:27 the fragrance of my *s* is like the
27:32 am Esau," he replied, "your first-born *s*."
27:37 What then can I do for you, *s*?"
27:42 news of what her older *s* Esau had in mind,
27:42 called her younger *s* Jacob and said to him:
27:43 Therefore, *s*, do what I tell you:
28: 5 to Laban, *s* of Bethuel the Aramean,
28: 9 *s* Ishmael and sister of Nebaioth.
29: 5 them, "Do you know Laban, *s* of Nahor?"
29:12 he was her father's relative, Rebekah's *s*,
29:13 heard the news about his sister's *s* Jacob,
29:32 Leah conceived and bore a *s*,
29:33 She conceived again and bore a *s*,
29:34 Again she conceived and bore a *s*,
29:35 Once more she conceived and bore a *s*,
30: 5 When Bilhah conceived and bore a *s*,
30: 6 he has heeded my plea and given me a *s*."
30: 7 conceived again and bore a second *s*,
30:10 Zilpah, and she conceived and bore a *s*.
30:12 Zilpah bore a second *s* to Jacob;
30:17 she conceived and bore a fifth *s* to Jacob.
30:19 again and bore a sixth *s* to Jacob;
30:23 She conceived and bore a *s*,
30:24 the LORD add another *s* to this one for me!"
34: 2 When Shechem, *s* of Hamor the Hivite,
34: 8 "My *s* Shechem has his heart set on your
34:18 seemed fair to Hamor and his *s* Shechem.
34:20 So Hamor and his *s* Shechem went to their
34:24 town agreed with Hamor and his *s* Shechem,
34:26 put Hamor and his *s* Shechem to the sword,
35:17 This time, too, you have a *s*."
36:10 *s* of Esau's wife Adah; and Reuel, son
36:12 (Esau's *s* Eliphaz had a concubine Timna,
36:17 The descendants of Esau's *s* Reuel:
36:32 Bela, *s* of Beor, became king in Edom;
36:33 When Bela died, Jobab, *s* of Zerah,
36:35 When Husham died, Hadad, *s* of Bedad,
36:38 When Shaul died, Baal-hanan, *s* of Achbor,
36:39 was the daughter of Matred, *s* of Mezahab.)
37:34 on his loins, and mourned his *s* many days.
37:35 down mourning to my *s* in the nether world."
38: 3 She conceived and bore a *s*,
38: 4 Again she conceived and bore a *s*,
38: 5 Then she bore still another *s*,
38:11 house until my *s* Shelah grows up"
38:26 since I did not give her to my *s* Shelah."
42:38 "My *s* shall not go down with you.
45: 9 'Thus says your *s* Joseph:
45:28 "My *s* Joseph is still alive!
46:10 Zohar, and Shaul, *s* of a Canaanite woman.
47:29 he called his *s* Joseph and said to him:
48: 2 was told, "Your *s* Joseph has come to you,"
48:19 "I know it, *s*," he said, "I know.
49: 9 whelp, you have grown up on prey, my *s*.
50:23 *s* Machir were also born on Joseph's knees.
Ex 2: 2 a Levite woman, who conceived and bore a *s*.
2:10 adopted him as her *s* and called him Moses;
2:22 She bore him a *s*,
4:22 Israel is my *s*, my first-born.
4:23 Let my *s* go, that he may serve me.
4:23 let him go, I warn you, I will kill your *s*,
6:15 Shaul, who was the *s* of a Canaanite woman;
6:25 Aaron's *s*,
10: 2 you may recount to your *s* and grandson
13: 8 On this day you shall explain to your *s*,
13:12 to the LORD every *s* that opens the womb;
13:13 Every first-born *s* you must redeem.
13:14 If your *s* should ask you later on,
20:10 then either by you, or your *s* or daughter,
21: 9 If he destines her for his *s*,
23:12 and that the *s* of your maidservant and the
31: 2 "See, I have chosen Bezalel, *s* of Uri,
31: 2 have chosen Bezalel, son of Uri, *s* of Hur,
31: 6 I have appointed Oholiab, *s* of Ahisamach,
33:11 but his young assistant, Joshua, *s* of Nun,
35:30 has chosen Bezalel, son of Uri, *s* of Hur,
35:34 given both him and Oholiab, *s* of Ahisamach,
38:21 of Ithamar, *s* of Aaron the priest.
38:22 it was Bezalel, son of Uri, *s* of Hur,
38:23 he was assisted by Oholiab, *s* of Ahisamach,
Lv 12: 6 for a *s* or for a daughter are fulfilled,
21: 2 his mother or father, his *s* or daughter,
Nm 1: 5 Elizur, *s* of Shedeur; from Simeon:
1: 6 Shelumiel, *s* of Zurishaddai; from Judah:
1: 7 Nahshon, *s* of Amminadab; from Issachar:
1: 8 Nethanel, *s* of Zuar; from Zebulun:
1: 9 Eliab, *s* of Helon; from Ephraim:
1:10 Elishama, *s* of Ammihud, and from Manasseh:
1:10 Gamaliel, *s* of Pedahzur,
1:11 Abidan, *s* of Gideoni; from Dan:
1:12 Ahiezer, *s* of Ammishaddai; from Asher:
1:13 Pagiel, *s* of Ochran; from Gad:
1:14 Eliasaph, *s* of Reuel; from Naphtali:
1:15 Ahira, *s* of Enan."
2: 3 the Judahites was Nahshon, *s* of Amminadab,
2: 5 [Their prince was Nethanel, *s* of Zuar,
2: 7 [Their prince was Eliab, *s* of Helon,
2:10 [Their prince was Elizur, *s* of Shedeur,
2:12 prince was Shelumiel, *s* of Zurishaddai,
2:14 [Their prince was Eliasaph, *s* of Reuel,
2:18 [Their prince was Elishama, *s* of Ammihud,
2:20 [Their prince was Gamaliel, *s* of Pedahzur,
2:22 [Their prince was Abidan, *s* of Gideoni,
2:25 prince was Ahiezer, *s* of Ammishaddai,
2:27 [Their prince was Pagiel, *s* of Ochran,
2:29 [Their prince was Ahira, *s* of Enan,
3:24 ancestral house was Eliasaph, *s* of Lael.
3:30 ancestral house was Elizaphan, *s* of Uzziel.
3:32 was Eleazar, *s* of Aaron the priest;
3:35 clans of Merari was Zuriel, *s* of Abihail.
4:16 "Eleazar, *s* of Aaron the priest,
4:28 of Ithamar, *s* of Aaron the priest.
4:33 of Ithamar, *s* of Aaron the priest."
7: 8 of Ithamar, *s* of Aaron the priest.
7:12 the first day was Nahshon, *s* of Amminadab,
7:17 the offering of Nahshon, *s* of Amminadab.
7:18 On the second day Nethanel, *s* of Zuar,
7:23 was the offering of Nethanel, *s* of Zuar.
7:24 day it was the turn of Eliab, *s* of Helon,
7:29 This was the offering of Eliab, *s* of Helon.
7:30 it was the turn of Elizur, *s* of Shedeur,
7:35 was the offering of Elizur, *s* of Shedeur.
7:36 the turn of Shelumiel, *s* of Zurishaddai,
7:41 offering of Shelumiel, *s* of Zurishaddai.
7:42 it was the turn of Eliasaph, *s* of Reuel,
7:47 was the offering of Eliasaph, *s* of Reuel.
7:48 it was the turn of Elishama, *s* of Ammihud,
7:53 was the offering of Elishama, *s* of Ammihud.
7:54 it was the turn of Gamaliel, *s* of Pedahzur,
7:59 the offering of Gamaliel, *s* of Pedahzur.
7:60 it was the turn of Abidon, *s* of Gideoni,
7:65 was the offering of Abidan, *s* of Gideoni.
7:66 was the turn of Ahiezer, *s* of Ammishaddai,
7:71 the offering of Ahiezer, *s* of Ammishaddai.
7:72 day it was the turn of Pagiel, *s* of Ochran,
7:77 was the offering of Pagiel, *s* of Ochran.
7:78 day it was the turn of Ahira, *s* of Enan,
7:83 This was the offering of Ahira, *s* of Enan.
10:14 Nahshon, *s* of Amminadab,
10:15 over their host, and Nethanel, *s* of Zuar,
10:16 tribe of Issachar, and Eliab, *s* of Helon,
10:18 next to set out, with Elizur, *s* of Shedeur,
10:19 host, and Shelumiel, *s* of Zurishaddai,
10:20 tribe of Simeon, and Eliasaph, *s* of Reuel,
10:22 in companies, with Elishama, *s* of Ammihud,
10:23 their host, and Gamaliel, *s* of Pedahzur,
10:24 of Manasseh, and Abidan, *s* of Gideoni,
10:25 companies, with Ahiezer, *s* of Ammishaddai,
10:26 over their host, and Pagiel, *s* of Ochran,
10:27 the tribe of Asher, and Ahira, *s* of Enan,
10:29 Hobab, *s* of Reuel the Midianite,
11:28 in the camp," Joshua, *s* of Nun,
13: 4 Shammua, *s* of Zaccur,
13: 5 Saphat, *s* of Hori,
13: 6 Caleb, *s* of Jephunneh,
13: 7 *s* of Joseph],
13: 8 *s* of Nun,
13: 9 *s* of Raphu,
13:10 *s* of Sodi,
13:11 *s* of Susi, of the tribe of Manasseh,
13:12 the Josephites, withAmmiel, *s* of Gemalli,
13:13 *s* of Michael,
13:14 *s* of Vophsi, of the tribe of Naphtali;
13:15 Geuel, *s* of Machi,
13:16 But Hoshea, *s* of Nun, Moses called Joshua.
14: 6 son of Nun, and Caleb, *s* of Jephunneh,
14:30 son of Jephunneh, and Joshua, *s* of Nun.
14:38 son of Nun, and Caleb, *s* of Jephunneh,
16: 1 *s* of Izhar, son of Kohath, son of Levi,
16: 1 sons of Eliab, *s* of Pallu, son of Reuben
17: 2 "Tell Eleazar, *s* of Aaron the priest,
20:25 *s* Eleazar and bring them up on Mount Hor.
20:26 his garments and put them on his *s* Eleazar;
20:28 his garments and put them on his *s* Eleazar.
22: 2 Now Balak, *s* of Zippor,
22: 4 *s* who was king of Moab at that time,
22: 5 time, sent messengers to Balaam, *s* of Beor,
22:10 Balaam answered God, "Balak, *s* of Zippor,
22:16 him, "This is what Balak, *s* of Zippor,
23:18 give ear to my testimony, O *s* of Zippor!
24: 3 The utterance of Balaam, *s* of Beor,
24:15 The utterance of Balaam, *s* of Beor,
25: 7 Phinehas, *s* of Eleazar, son of Aaron
25:11 son of Eleazar, *s* of Aaron the priest,
25:14 the Midianite woman was Zimri, *s* of Salu,
26: 1 Moses and Eleazar, *s* of Aaron the priest,
26:33 Zelophehad, *s* of Hepher,
26:65 son of Jephunneh, and Joshua, *s* of Nun.
27: 1 *s* of Hepher, son of Gilead, son of Machir,
27: 1 *s* of Manasseh, son of Joseph,
27: 4 from his clan merely because he had no *s*?
27: 8 If a man dies without leaving a *s*,
27:18 replied to Moses, "Take Joshua, *s* of Nun,
31: 6 each tribe, with Phinehas, *s* of Eleazar,
31: 8 and they also executed Balaam, *s* of Beor,
32:12 son of Jephunneh, and Joshua, *s* of Nun,
32:28 to the priest Eleazar, to Joshua, *s* of Nun,
32:33 as half the tribe of Manasseh, *s* of Joseph,
32:39 The descendants of Machir, *s* of Manasseh,
32:40 gave Gilead to Machir, *s* of Manasseh,
34:17 Eleazar the priest, and Joshua, *s* of Nun,
34:19 Caleb, *s* of Jephunneh,from
34:20 Samuel, *s* of Ammihud;from
34:21 Elidad, *s* of Chislon;from
34:22 Bukki, *s* of Jogli;from
34:23 Hanniel, *s* of Ephod;
34:24 Kemuel, *s* of Shiphtan,
34:25 Elizaphan, *s* of Parnach;from
34:26 Paltiel, *s* of Azzan;from
34:27 Ahihud, *s* of Shelomi;
34:28 Pedahel, *s* of Ammihud."
36: 1 of Gilead, son of Machir, *s* of Manasseh
36:12 the descendants of Manasseh, *s* of Joseph;
Dt 1:36 your fathers, except Caleb, *s* of Jephunneh;
1:38 there, but your aide Joshua, *s* of Nun,
5:14 whether by you, or your *s* or daughter,
6: 2 your *s* and your grandson may fear the LORD,
6:20 when your *s* asks you what these ordinances,
6:21 enjoined on you, you shall say to your *s*,
8: 5 you even as a man disciplines his *s*.
10: 6 his *s* Eleazar succeeding him in the
12:18 he chooses, along with your *s* and daughter,
13: 7 own full brother, or your *s* or daughter,
16:11 presence together with your *s* and daughter,
16:14 feast, together with your *s* and daughter,
18:10 immolates his *s* or daughter in the fire,
21:16 his first-born the *s* of the wife he loves,
21:16 the *s* of the wife whom he dislikes.
21:17 first-born the *s* of her whom he dislikes,
21:18 "If a man has a stubborn and unruly *s* who
21:20 'This *s* of ours is a stubborn and unruly
23: 5 and because Moab hired Balaam, *s* of Beor,
25: 5 together and one of them dies without a *s*,
25: 6 The first-born *s* she bears shall continue
28:56 begrudge her beloved husband and her *s*
31:23 the LORD commissioned Joshua, *s* of Nun,
32:44 So Moses, together with Joshua, *s* of Nun,
34: 9 Now Joshua, *s* of Nun,
Jos 1: 1 LORD said to Moses' aide Joshua, *s* of Nun:
2: 1 Then Joshua, *s* of Nun, secretly sent out
2:23 crossed the Jordan to Joshua, *s* of Nun,
6: 6 Summoning the priests, Joshua, *s* of Nun,
6:26 his youngest *s* when he sets up its gates.
7: 1 son of Carmi, son of Zerah, *s* of Zara
7:18 son of Carmi, *s* of Zabdi, son of Zerah
7:19 Joshua said to Achan, "My *s*,
7:24 and all Israel took Achan, *s* of Zerah,
13:22 also the soothsayer Balaam, *s* of Beor.
13:31 the descendants of Machir, *s* of Manasseh,
14: 1 Eleazar the priest, Joshua, *s* of Nun,
14: 6 the Kenizzite Caleb, *s* of Jephunneh,
14:13 Joshua blessed Caleb, *s* of Jephunneh,
14:14 of the Kenizzite Caleb, *s* of Jephunneh,
15:13 Joshua gave Caleb, *s* of Jephunneh,
15:17 Othniel, *s* of Caleb's brother Kenaz,
17: 1 since his eldest *s*, Machir, the father
17: 2 male children of Manasseh, *s* of Joseph.
17: 3 son of Hepher, *s* of Gilead, son of Machir,
17: 3 *s* of Manasseh, had had no sons
17: 4 to Eleazar the priest, to Joshua, *s* of Nun,
19:49 in their midst to Joshua, *s* of Nun.
19:51 which Eleazar the priest, Joshua, *s* of Nun,
21: 1 to Eleazar the priest, to Joshua, *s* of Nun,
21:12 had been given to Caleb, *s* of Jephunneh,
22:13 of Phinehas, *s* of Eleazar the priest,
22:20 When Achan, *s* of Zerah,
22:31 Phinehas, *s* of Eleazar the priest,
22:32 Phinehas, *s* of Eleazar the priest,
24: 9 Then Balak, *s* of Zippor,
24: 9 He summoned Balaam, *s* of Beor,
24:29 After these events, Joshua, *s* of Nun,
24:33 When Eleazar, *s* of Aaron,
24:33 given to his *s* Phinehas in the mountain

SON (cont.)
Jgs 1:13 *s* of Caleb's younger brother Kenaz,
2: 8 LORD had done for Israel, Joshua, *s* of Nun,
3: 9 *s* of Caleb's younger brother Kenaz,
3:11 for forty years, until Othniel, *s* of Kenaz,
3:15 a savior, the Benjaminite Ehud, *s* of Gera,
3:31 After him there was Shamgar, *s* of Anath,
4: 6 She sent and summoned Barak, *s* of Abinoam,
4:12 to Sisera that Barak, *s* of Abinoam,
5: 1 that day Deborah [and Barak, *s* of Abinoam,]
5: 6 In the days of Shamgar, *s* of Anath,
5:12 make despoilers your spoil, *s* of Abinoam.
6:11 While his *s* Gideon was beating out wheat
6:29 to the conclusion that Gideon, *s* of Joash,
6:30 Joash, "Bring out your *s* that he may die,
7:14 sword of the Israelite Gideon, *s* of Joash,"
8:13 Then Gideon, *s* of Joash,
8:22 you, your son, and your son's *s*—
8:23 over you, nor shall my *s* rule over you.
8:29 Then Jerubbaal, *s* of Joash,
8:31 who lived in Shechem also bore him a *s*,
8:32 At a good old age Gideon, *s* of Joash,
9: 1 Abimelech, *s* of Jerubbaal,
9: 5 Only the youngest *s* of Jerubbaal,
9:18 have made Abimelech, the *s* of his handmaid,
9:26 Now Gaal, *s* of Ebed, came over
9:28 Gaal, *s* of Ebed, said, "Who is Abimelech?
9:28 Were not the *s* of Jerubbaal and his
9:30 At the news of what Gaal, *s* of Ebed,
9:31 "Gaal, *s* of Ebed, and his kinsmen
9:35 Gaal, *s* of Ebed, went out and stood
9:57 for the curse of Jotham, *s* of Jerubbaal,
10: 1 Issacharite Tola, son of Puah, *s* of Dodo,
11: 2 family, for you are the *s* of another woman."
11:25 are you any better than Balak, *s* of Zippor,
11:34 he had neither *s* nor daughter besides her.
12:13 him the Pirathonite Abdon, *s* of Hillel,
12:15 the Pirathonite Abdon, *s* of Hillel,
13: 3 yet you will conceive and bear a *s*.
13: 5 As for the *s* you will conceive and bear,
13: 7 'You will be with child and will bear a *s*.
13:24 The woman bore a *s* and named him Samson.
17: 4 his mother said, "May the LORD bless my *s*!
17: 4 to the LORD as my gift in favor of my *s*,
18:29 Dan after their ancestor Dan, *s* of Israel.
18:30 and Jonathan, son of Gershom, *s* of Moses,
20:28 and Phinehas, son of Eleazar, *s* of Aaron,
Ru 4:13 enabled her to conceive and she bore a *s*.
1Sm 1: 1 son of Jeroham, son of Elihu, *s* of Tohu,
1: 1 *s* of Zuph, an Ephraimite.
1:20 her term bore a *s* whom she called Samuel,
1:23 and nursed her *s* until she had weaned him.
3: 6 he answered, "I did not call you, my *s*.
3:16 but Eli called to him, "Samuel, my *s*!"
4:16 He asked, "What happened, my *s*?"
4:20 You have given birth to a *s*."
7: 1 appointing his *s* Eleazar as guardian of
8: 2 first-born was named Joel, his second *s*,
9: 1 Kish, who was the son of Abiel, *s* of Zeror,
9: 1 son of Zeror, son of Becorath, *s* of Aphiah,
9: 2 He had a *s* named Saul,
9: 3 Kish said to his *s* Saul,
10: 2 you and says, What shall I do about my *s*?'
10:11 "What has happened to the *s* of Kish?
10:21 was chosen, and finally Saul, *s* of Kish,
13:16 Saul, his *s* Jonathan,
13:22 Only Saul and his *s* Jonathan had them.
14: 1 One day Jonathan, *s* of Saul,
14: 3 Ahijah, *s* of Ahitub,
14: 3 who was the son of Phinehas, *s* of Eli,
14:39 even if my *s* Jonathan has committed it,
14:40 and my *s* Jonathan will stand on the other."
14:41 for this resides in me or my *s* Jonathan,
14:42 "Cast lots between me and my *s* Jonathan."
14:50 his general was Abner, *s* of Saul's uncle.
16:19 to ask Jesse to send him his *s* David,
16:20 kid, and sent them to Saul by his *s* David.
17:12 was the *s* of an Ephrathite named Jesse,
17:13 first-born Eliab, the second *s* Abinadab,
17:17 [Now Jesse said to his *s* David:
17:55 Abner, "Abner, whose *s* is that youth?"
17:56 king said, "Find out whose *s* the lad is."
17:58 Saul then asked him, "Whose *s* are you,
17:58 the *s* of your servant Jesse of Bethlehem."
19: 1 his *s* Jonathan and with all his servants.
19: 1 But Saul's *s* Jonathan,
20:27 *s* Jonathan, "Why has the son of Jesse
20:30 *S* of a rebellious woman,
20:30 shame, you are the companion of Jesse's *s*?
20:31 as the *s* of Jesse lives upon the earth,
22: 7 Will the *s* of Jesse give all of you fields
22: 8 *s* has made an agreement with the son
22: 8 my *s* has stirred up my servant
22: 9 *s* of Jesse come to Ahimelech, son
22:11 to Ahimelech the priest, *s* of Ahitub,
22:12 Then Saul said, "Listen, *s* of Ahitub!"
22:13 conspire against me with the *s* of Jesse
22:20 One son of Ahimelech, *s* of Ahitub,
23: 6 Abiathar, *s* of Ahimelech,
23:16 Horesh in the barrens near Ziph, Saul's *s*,
24:17 answered, "Is that your voice, my *s* David?"
25: 8 and your *s* David whatever you can manage.'"
25:10 Who is the *s* of Jesse?
25:43 Saul's own daughter, to Palti, *s* of Laish,
26: 5 the spot where Saul and Abner, *s* of Ner,
26: 6 Abishai, *s* of Zeruiah and brother of Joab,
26:13 at a great distance from Abner, *s* of Ner,
26:17 asked, "Is that your voice, my *s* David?"
26:21 Come back, my *s* David,
26:25 "Blessed are you, my *s* David!
27: 2 men and went over to Achish, *s* of Maoch,
30: 7 to Abiathar, the priest, *s* of Ahimelech,
2Sm 1: 4 dead, among them Saul and his *s* Jonathan.
1: 5 know that Saul and his *s* Jonathan are dead?"
1:12 until evening for Saul and his *s* Jonathan,
1:13 "I am the *s* of an Amalekite immigrant."
1:17 this elegy for Saul and his *s* Jonathan,
2: 8 *s* of Ner, Saul's general, took Ishbaal, son
2:10 Ishbaal, *s* of Saul,
2:12 Ner, and the servants of Ishbaal, Saul's *s*,
2:13 Joab, *s* of Zeruiah, and David's servants
2:15 of the Benjaminites of Ishbaal, *s* of Saul,
3: 3 *s* of Maacah the daughter of Talmai,
3: 4 *s* of Haggith; the fifth, Shephatiah, son
3: 7 And Ishbaal, *s* of Saul,
3:14 sent messengers to Ishbaal, *s* of Saul,
3:15 away from her husband Paltiel, *s* of Laish,
3:23 he was informed, "Abner, *s* of Ner,
3:29 for the death of Abner, *s* of Ner,
3:37 no part in the killing of Abner, *s* of Ner.
4: 1 When Ishbaal, *s* of Saul, heard that
4: 2 Ishbaal, *s* of Saul,
4: 4 *s* of Saul, had a son named Meribbaal
4: 8 the head of Ishbaal, *s* of your enemy Saul,
7:14 a father to him, and he shall be a *s* to me.
8: 3 David defeated Hadadezer, *s* of Rehob,
8: 7 in the days of Rehoboam, *s* of Solomon.]
8:10 he sent his *s* Hadoram to King David to
8:12 from the plunder of Hadadezer, *s* of Rehob,
8:16 Joab, *s* of Zeruiah,
8:16 Jehoshaphat, *s* of Ahilud, was chancellor.
8:17 *s* of Ahitub, and Ahimelech, son
8:18 Benaiah, *s* of Jehoiada,
9: 3 the king, "There is still Jonathan's *s*,
9: 4 is in the house of Machir, *s* of Ammiel,
9: 5 from the house of Machir, *s* of Ammiel,
9: 6 When Meribbaal, son of Jonathan, *s* of Saul,
9: 9 "I am giving your lord's *s* all that
9:10 But Meribbaal, your lord's *s*,
9:12 had a young *s* whose name was Mica;
10: 1 and his *s* Hanun succeeded him as king.
10: 2 "I will be kind to Hanun, *s* of Nahash,
11:21 Who killed Abimelech, *s* of Jerubbaal?
11:27 She became his wife and bore him a *s*.
12:24 and she conceived and bore him a *s*,
13: 1 David's *s* Absalom had a beautiful sister
13: 1 named Tamar, and David's *s* Amnon loved her.
13: 3 Jonadab, *s* of David's brother Shimeah,
13:21 spark the resentment of his *s* Amnon,
13:25 But the King said to Absalom, "No, my *s*,
13:32 But Jonadab, *s* of David's brother Shimeah,
13:37 taken flight, went to Talmai, *s* of Ammihud,
13:39 during all that time to mourn over his *s*;
14: 1 When Joab, *s* of Zeruiah,
14:11 and that my *s* may not be done away with."
14:11 a hair of your *s* shall fall to the ground."
14:13 for not bringing back his own banished *s*.
14:16 and my *s* as well from God's inheritance.'"
15:27 own son Ahimaaz, and Abiathar's *s* Jonathan.
15:36 son Ahimaaz and Abiathar's *s* Jonathan.
16: 3 king said, "And where is your lord's *s*?"
16: 5 the *s* of Gera of the same clan as Saul's
16: 8 given over the kingdom to your *s* Absalom.
16: 9 Abishai, *s* of Zeruiah, said to the king:
16:11 "If my own *s*, who came forth from
16:19 Whom should I serve, if not his *s*?"
17:25 was the *s* of an Ishamelite named Ithra,
17:27 *s* of Nahash from Rabbah of the Ammonites,
17:27 Machir, *s* of Ammiel from Lodebar,
18: 2 Abishai, *s* of Zeruiah and brother of Joab,
18:12 two hands, I would not harm the king's *s*,
18:18 said, "I have no *s* to perpetuate my name."
18:19 Then Ahimaaz, *s* of Zadok,
18:20 news, for in fact the king's *s* is dead."
18:22 But Ahimaaz, *s* of Zadok,
18:22 "Why do you want to run, my *s*?
18:27 first one runs like Ahimaaz, *s* of Zadok."
19: 1 "My *s* Absalom! my *s*, my *s*
19: 1 died instead of you, Absalom, my son, my *s*!"
19: 3 heard that the king was grieving for his *s*.
19: 5 cried out in a loud voice, "My *s* Absalom!
19: 5 My son, my *s*!"
19:17 Shimei, *s* of Gera,
19:19 When Shimei, *s* of Gera,
19:22 But Abishai, *s* of Zeruiah, countered:
19:25 Meribbaal, *s* of Saul,
20: 1 from Benjamin named Sheba, the *s* of Bichri,
20: 1 in David, nor any share in the *s* of Jesse.
20: 2 left David for Sheba, *s* of Bichri.
20: 6 "Sheba, *s* of Bichri,
20: 7 campaign in pursuit of Sheba, *s* of Bichri.
20:10 brother Abishai pursued Sheba, *s* of Bichri.
20:13 Joab in pursuit of Sheba, *s* of Bichri.
20:21 A man named Sheba, *s* of Bichri,
20:22 cut off the head of Sheba, *s* of Bichri,
20:23 Benaiah, *s* of Jehoiada, was in command
20:24 Jehoshaphat, *s* of Ahilud,
21: 7 Meribbaal, son of Jonathan, *s* of Saul,
21: 7 a bond between David and Saul's *s* Jonathan.
21: 8 to Adriel, *s* of Barzillai the Meholathite,
21:12 bones of Saul and of his *s* Jonathan
21:13 the bones of Saul and of his *s* Jonathan,
21:14 Then the bones of Saul and of his *s*
21:17 to kill David, but Abishai, *s* of Zeruiah,
21:19 in which Elhanan, *s* of Jair from Bethlehem,
21:21 Jonathan, *s* of David's brother Shimei,
23: 1 "The utterance of David, *s* of Jesse;
23: 8 Ishbaal, *s* of Hachamoni, was the first
23: 9 was Eleazar, *s* of Dodo the Ahohite.
23:11 to him was Shammah, *s* of Agee the Hararite.
23:18 Abishai, brother of Joab, *s* of Zeruiah,
23:20 Benaiah, *s* of Jehoiada, a stalwart from
23:22 deeds performed by Benaiah, *s* of Jehoiada.
23:24 Elhanan, *s* of Dodo,
23:26 Ira, *s* of Ikkesh,
23:29 son of Baanah, from Netophah; Ittai, *s*
23:33 *s* of Shammah the Hararite; Ahiam, son
23:34 *s* of Ahasbai, from Beth-maacah; Eliam, *s*
23:36 Igal, *s* of Nathan,
23:37 armor-bearer of Joab, *s* of Zeruiah;
1Kgs 1: 5 relations with herAdonijah, *s* of Haggith,
1: 7 He conferred with Joab, *s* of Zeruiah,
1: 8 Zadok the priest, Benaiah, *s* of Jehoiada,
1:11 you not heard that Adonijah, *s* of Haggith,
1:12 save your life and that of your *s* Solomon.
1:13 Your *s* Solomon shall be king after me and
1:17 that my *s* Solomon should reign after you
1:21 my *s* Solomon will be considered criminals."
1:26 the priest, nor Benaiah, *s* of Jehoiada,
1:30 that your *s* Solomon should reign after me
1:32 the prophet, and Benaiah, *s* of Jehoiada.
1:33 Mount my *s* Solomon upon my own mule and
1:36 answer to the king, Benaiah, *s* of Jehoiada,
1:38 Nathan the prophet, Benaiah, *s* of Jehoiada,
1:42 Jonathan, *s* of Abiathar the priest,
1:44 Nathan the prophet, Benaiah, *s* of Jehoiada,
2: 1 gave these instructions to his *s* Solomon:
2: 5 You yourself know what Joab, *s* of Zeruiah,
2: 5 Abner, son of Ner, and Amasa, *s* of Jether.
2: 8 "You also have with you Shimei, *s* of Gera,
2:13 firmly established, Adonijah, *s* of Haggith,
2:22 Abiathar the priest and Joab, *s* of Zeruiah."
2:25 King Solomon sent Benaiah, *s* of Jehoiada,
2:29 He sent Benaiah, *s* of Jehoiada,
2:32 Abner, *s* of Ner,
2:32 of Israel's army, and Amasa, *s* of Jether.
2:34 Benaiah, *s* of Jehoiada,
2:35 The king appointed Benaiah, *s* of Jehoiada,
2:39 servants ran away to Achish, *s* of Maacah,
2:46 gave the order to Benaiah, *s* of Jehoiada,
3: 6 today, seating a *s* of his on his throne.
3:19 This woman's *s* died during the night;
3:20 she got up and took my *s* from my side,
3:21 I saw it was not the *s* whom I had borne."
3:22 The living one is my *s*,
3:26 The woman whose *s* it was,
4: 2 Azariah, *s* of Zadok,
4: 3 Jehoshaphat, *s* of Ahilud, chancellor,
4: 4 [Benaiah, *s* of Johoiada,
4: 5 Abiathar, priests;] Azariah, *s* of Nathan,
4: 5 Zabud, *s* of Nathan, companion to the king
4: 6 and Adoniram, *s* of Abda,
4: 8 *s* of Hur in the hill country of Ephraim;
4: 9 the *s* of Deker in Makaz, Shaalbim,
4:10 the *s* of Hesed in Arubboth as well as in
4:11 the *s* of Abinadab, who was married
4:12 Baana, *s* of Ahilud, in Taanach
4:13 the *s* of Geber in Ramoth-gilead,
4:13 of the villages of Jair, *s* of Manasseh,
4:14 Ahinadab, *s* of Iddo, in Mahanaim;
4:16 Naphtali; Baana, *s* of Hushai, in Asher
4:17 Jehoshaphat, *s* of Paruah, in Issachar;
4:18 Shimei, *s* of Ela, in Benjamin; Geber,
4:19 Geber, *s* of Uri, in the land of Gilead,
5:19 'It is your *s* whom I will put upon your
5:21 a wise *s* to rule this numerous people."
7:14 *s* of a widow from the tribe of Naphtali;
8:19 but the *s* who will spring from you,
9:21 Zechariah, *s* of Meshelemiah
11:12 it is your *s* whom I will deprive.
11:13 I will leave your *s* one tribe for the sake
11:20 Tahpenes' sister bore Hadad a *s*, Genubath.
11:23 adversary, in Rezon, the *s* of Eliada,
11:26 Solomon's servant Jeroboam, *s* of Nebat,
11:36 I will give his *s* one tribe,
11:43 and his *s* Rehoboam succeeded him as king.
12: 2 Jeroboam, *s* of Nebat,
12:15 he had uttered to Jeroboam, *s* of Nebat,
12:16 We have no heritage in the *s* of Jesse.
12:21 the kingdom to Rehoboam, *s* of Solomon.
12:23 "Say to Rehoboam, *s* of Solomon,
14: 1 At that time Abijah, *s* of Jeroboam,
14: 5 wife is coming to consult you about her *s*,
14:20 and his *s* Nadab succeeded him as king.
14:21 Rehoboam, *s* of Solomon, reigned in Judah.
14:31 His *s* Abijam succeeded him as king.
15: 1 year of King Jeroboam, *s* of Nebat,
15: 4 raising up his *s* after him and permitting
15: 8 David, and his *s* Asa succeeded him as king.

15:18 Ben-hadad, son of Tabrimmon, *s* of Hezion,
15:24 his *s* Jehoshaphat succeeded him as king.
15:25 Asa, king of Judah, Nadab, *s* of Jeroboam,
15:27 Baasha, *s* of Ahijah,
15:33 of Asa, king of Judah, Baasha, *s* of Ahijah,
16: 1 spoke against Baasha to Jehu, *s* of Hanani,
16: 3 house like that of Jeroboam, *s* of Nebat.
16: 6 and his *s* Elah succeeded him as king.
16: 7 [Through the prophet Jehu, *s* of Hanani,
16: 8 of Asa, king of Judah, Elah, *s* of Baasha,
16:13 Baasha and his *s* Elah committed
16:21 divided, half following Tibni, *s* of Ginath,
16:22 prevailed over those of Tibni, *s* of Ginath.
16:26 the sinful conduct of Jeroboam, *s* of Nebat,
16:28 and his *s* Ahab succeeded him as king.
16:29 year of Asa, king of Judah, Ahab *s* of Omri,
16:30 Ahab, *s* of Omri, did evil in the sight
16:31 imitate the sins of Jeroboam, *s* of Nebat.
16:34 He lost his first-born *s*, Abiram,
16:34 laid the foundation, and his youngest *s*,
16:34 LORD had foretold through Joshua, *s* of Nun.
17:12 and prepare something for myself and my *s*;
17:13 prepare something for yourself and your *s*.
17:15 eat for a year, and he and her *s* as well;
17:17 *s* of the mistress of the house fell sick,
17:18 attention to my guilt and to kill my *s*?"
17:19 "Give me your *s*," Elijah said to her.
17:20 with whom I am staying by killing her *s*?"
17:23 Elijah said to her, "your *s* is alive."
19:16 anoint Jehu, son of Jehu, *s* of Nimshi,
19:16 and Elisha, *s* of Shaphat of Abel-meholah,
19:19 out, and came upon Elisha, *s* of Shaphat,
21:22 son of Nebat, and like that of Baasha, *s*
21:29 upon his house during the reign of his *s*."
22: 8 consult the LORD, Micaiah, *s* of Imlah;
22: 9 and said to him, "Get Micaiah, *s* of Imlah,
22:11 Zedekiah, *s* of Chenaanah,
22:24 Thereupon Zedekiah, *s* of Chenaanah,
22:26 of the city, and to Joash, the king's *s*,
22:40 and his *s* Ahaziah succeeded him as king.
22:41 Jehoshaphat, *s* of Asa,
22:50 Then Ahaziah, *s* of Ahab,
22:51 His *s* Jehoram succeeded him as king.
22:52 Ahaziah, *s* of Ahab,
22:53 his mother, and Jeroboam, *s* of Nebat,
2Kgs 1:17 Since he had no *s*,
1:17 second year of Jehoram, *s* of Jehoshaphat,
3: 1 Joram, *s* of Ahab,
3: 3 to the sin to which Jeroboam, *s* of Nebat,
3:11 of Israel replied, "Elisha, *s* of Shaphat,
4: 6 the vessels were filled, she said to her *s*,
4:14 "She has no *s*, and her husband
4:16 next year you will be fondling a baby *s*."
4:17 following year she had given birth to a *s*,
4:28 "Did I ask my lord for a *s*?"
4:36 and Elisha said to her, "Take your *s*."
4:37 then she took her *s* and left the room.
6:28 'Give up your *s* that we may eat him today;
6:28 then tomorrow we will eat my *s*.'
6:29 So we boiled my *s* and ate him.
6:29 'Now give up your *s* that we may eat him.'
6:29 But she hid her *s*."
6:31 "if the head of Elisha, *s* of Shaphat,
6:32 "Do you know that this *s* of a murderer is
8: 1 the woman whose *s* he had restored to life:
8: 5 the very woman whose *s* Elisha had restored
8: 5 *s* of hers whom Elisha restored to life."
8: 9 the prophet and said, "Your *s* Ben-hadad,
8:16 *s* of Ahab, king of Israel, Jehoram, son
8:24 His *s* Ahaziah succeeded him as king.
8:25 Ahaziah, *s* of Jehoram, king of Judah,
8:25 in the twelfth year of Joram, *s* of Ahab,
8:28 He joined Joram, *s* of Ahab,
8:29 Then Ahaziah, *s* of Jehoram,
9: 2 for Jehu, son of Jehoshaphat, *s* of Nimshi.
9: 9 with the house of Jeroboam, *s* of Nebat,
9: 9 and with the house of Baasha, *s* of Ahijah.
9:14 Jehu, son of Jehoshaphat, *s* of Nimshi,
9:20 driving is like that of Jehu, *s* of Nimshi,
9:29 in the eleventh year of Joram, *s* of Ahab.
10:15 there, Jehu met Jehonadab, *s* of Rechab,
10:23 them, Jehu, with Jehonadab, *s* of Rechab,
10:29 from the sins which Jeroboam, *s* of Nebat,
10:35 His *s* Jehoahaz succeeded him as king.
11: 1 mother of Ahaziah, saw that her *s* was dead,
11: 2 and sister of Ahaziah, took Joash, his *s*,
11: 4 and then showed them the king's *s*.
11:12 Then Jehoiada led out the king's *s* and put
12:22 *s* of Shimeath, and Jehozabad, son
12:22 and his *s* Amaziah succeeded him as king.
13: 1 *s* of Ahaziah, king of Judah, Jehoahaz, son
13: 2 himself like Jeroboam, *s* of Nebat,
13: 3 of Aram, and of Ben-hadad, *s* of Hazael.
13: 9 His *s* Joash succeeded him as king.
13:10 king of Judah, Jehoash, *s* of Jehoahaz,
13:11 any of the sins which Jeroboam, *s* of Nebat,
13:24 and his *s* Ben-hadad succeeded him as king,
13:25 *s* of Jehoahaz, took back from Ben-hadad, *s*
14: 1 *s* of Jehoahaz, king of Israel, Amaziah, son
14: 8 to Jehoash, son of Jehoahaz, *s* of Jehu,
14: 9 'Give your daughter to my *s* in marriage,'
14:13 Amaziah, son of Jehoash, *s* of Ahaziah,
14:16 His *s* Jeroboam succeeded him as king.
14:17 Amaziah, *s* of Joash,
14:17 of Judah, survived Jehoash, *s* of Jehoahaz,
14:23 son of Joash, king of Judah, Jeroboam, *s*
14:24 any of the sins which Jeroboam, *s* of Nebat,
14:25 servant, the prophet Jonah, *s* of Amittai,
14:27 he saved them through Jeroboam, *s* of Joash.
14:29 and his *s* Zechariah succeeded him as king.
15: 1 Azariah, *s* of Amaziah,
15: 5 a house apart, while Jotham, the king's *s*,
15: 7 His *s* Jotham succeeded him as king.
15: 8 king of Judah, Zechariah, *s* of Jeroboam,
15: 9 from the sins which Jeroboam, *s* of Nebat,
15:10 Shallum, *s* of Jabesh, conspired against
15:13 Shallum, *s* of Jabesh, became king
15:14 Menahem, *s* of Gadi, came up from Tirzah
15:14 attacked and killed Shallum, *s* of Jabesh,
15:17 Azariah, king of Judah, Menahem, *s* of Gadi,
15:18 from the sins which Jeroboam, *s* of Nebat,
15:22 and his *s* Pekahiah succeeded him as king.
15:23 king of Judah, Pekahiah, *s* of Menahem,
15:24 from the sins which Jeroboam, *s* of Nebat,
15:25 His adjutant Pekah, *s* of Remaliah,
15:27 king of Judah, Pekah, *s* of Remaliah,
15:28 from the sins which Jeroboam, *s* of Nebat,
15:30 *s* of Elah, conspired against Pekah, son
15:30 *s* of Uzziah] The rest of the acts of
15:32 *s* of Remaliah, king of Israel, Jotham, son
15:37 king of Aram, and Pekah, *s* of Remaliah,
15:38 His *s* Ahaz succeeded him as king.
16: 1 Pekah, son of Remaliah, Ahaz, *s* of Jotham,
16: 3 Israel, and even immolated his *s* by fire,
16: 5 king of Aram, and Pekah, *s* of Remaliah,
16: 7 "I am your servant and your *s*.
16:20 His *s* Hezekiah succeeded him as king.
17: 1 of Ahaz, king of Judah, Hoshea, *s* of Elah,
17:21 of David, they made Jeroboam, *s* of Nebat,
18: 1 son of Elah, king of Israel, Hezekiah, *s*
18: 9 was the seventh year of Hoshea, *s* of Elah,
18:18 who sent out to them Eliakim, *s* of Hilkiah,
18:18 and the herald Joah, *s* of Asaph.
18:26 Then Eliakim, *s* of Hilkiah,
18:37 of the palace, Eliakim, *s* of Hilkiah,
18:37 scribe, and the herald Joah, *s* of Asaph,
19: 2 to tell the prophet Isaiah, *s* of Amoz,
19:20 Then Isaiah, *s* of Amoz,
19:37 His *s* Esarhaddon reigned in his stead.
20: 1 ill, the phophet Isaiah, *s* of Amoz,
20:12 time, when Merodach-baladan, *s* of Baladan,
20:21 and his *s* Manasseh succeeded him as king.
21: 6 He immolated his *s* by fire.
21: 7 had said to David and to his *s* Solomon:
21:18 His *s* Amon succeeded him as king.
21:24 proclaimed his *s* Josiah king in his stead.
21:26 and his *s* Josiah succeeded him as king.
22: 3 Shaphan, son of Azaliah, *s* of Meshullam,
22:12 son of Shaphan, Achbor, *s* of Micaiah,
22:14 of Shallum, son of Tikvah, *s* of Harhas,
23:15 high place built by Jeroboam, *s* of Nebat,
23:30 of the land took Jehoahaz, *s* of Josiah,
23:34 Neco then appointed Eliakim, *s* of Josiah,
24: 6 and his *s* Jehoiachin succeeded him as king.
25:22 Gedaliah, son of Ahikam, *s* of Shaphan.
25:23 son of Nethaniah, Johanan, *s* of Kareah,
25:23 Seraiah, *s* of Tanhumeth the Netophathite,
25:25 Ishmael, son of Nethaniah, *s* of Elishama,
25:30 Gedaliah, son of Ahikam, *s* of Shaphan.
1Chr 1:43 Bela, *s* of Beor, the name of whose city
1:44 When Bela died, Jobab, *s* of Zerah,
1:46 Husham died and Hadad, *s* of Bedad,
1:49 When Shaul died, Baal-hanan, *s* of Achbor,
2:13 his first-born, of Abinadab, the second *s*,
2:18 By his wife Azubah, Caleb, *s* of Hezron,
2:45 The *s* of Shammai:
3: 2 the third, Absalom, *s* of Maacah,
3: 2 Geshur, the fourth, Adonijah, *s* of Haggith;
3:10 The *s* of Solomon was Rehoboam,
3:10 son was Abijah, whose *s* was Asa, whose *s*
3:11 whose son was Joram, whose *s* was Ahaziah,
3:11 whose son was Ahaziah, whose *s* was Joash,
3:12 whose son was Amaziah, whose *s* was Azariah,
3:12 whose son was Azariah, whose *s* was Jotham,
3:13 whose son was Ahaz, whose *s* was Hezekiah,
3:13 whose *s* was Manasseh,
3:14 whose son was Amon, whose *s* was Josiah.
3:16 Jeconiah, his son; Zedekiah, his *s*.
4: 2 Reaiah, the *s* of Shobal,
4: 8 as of the clans of Aharhel, *s* of Harum.
4:15 The sons of Caleb, *s* of Jephunneh,
4:20 *s* of Ishi was Zoheth and the son of Zoheth.
4:21 The descendants of Shelah, *s* of Judah,
4:25 *s* was Shallum, whose son was Mibsam,
4:25 Mibsam, whose *s* was Mishma.
4:26 descendants of Mishma were his *s* Hammuel,
4:26 whose son was Zaccur, whose *s* was Shimei.
4:34 Meshobab, Jamlech, Joshah, *s* of Amaziah,
4:35 *s* of Joshibiah, son of Seraiah, son of Asiel,
4:37 *s* of Shiphi, son of Allon, son of Jedaiah,
4:37 Jedaiah, *s* of Shimri, son of Shemaiah—
5: 1 given to the sons of Joseph, *s* of Israel,
5: 4 *s* was Joel, whose son was Shemaiah,
5: 4 *s* was Gog, whose son was Shimei,
5: 5 *s* was Micah, whose son was Reaiah,
5: 5 Reaiah, whose *s* was Baal,
5: 6 *s* was Beerah, whom Tiglath-pileser,
5: 8 Bela, *s* of Azaz, son of Shema, son of Joel.
5:14 *s* of Michael, son of Jeshishai,
5:14 *s* of Huri, son of Jaroah, son of Gilead,
5:14 *s* of Jahdo, son of Buz.
5:15 Ahi, *s* of Abdiel, son of Guni,
6: 5 *s* Libni, whose son was Jahath, whose son
6: 6 whose son was Zerah, whose *s* was Jetherai.
6: 6 whose *s* was Joah, whose son was Iddo,
6: 7 his *s* Amminadab, whose son was Korah,
6: 7 Korah, whose *s* was Assir,
6: 8 whose *s* was Elkanah whose son was Ebiasaph,
6: 8 Ebiasaph, whose *s* was Assir,
6: 9 whose *s* was Tahath, whose son was Uriel,
6: 9 whose son was Uzziah, whose *s* was Shaul.
6:11 whose son was Elkanah, whose *s* was Zophai,
6:11 Zophai, whose *s* was Nahath,
6:12 whose son was Eliab, whose *s* was Jeroham,
6:12 whose son was Elkanah, whose *s* was Samuel.
6:14 whose son was Libni, whose *s* was Shimei,
6:14 Shimei, whose *s* was Uzzah,
6:15 whose son was Shimea, whose *s* was Haggiah,
6:15 Haggiah, whose *s* was Asaiah.
6:18 the chanter, son of Joel, *s* of Samuel,
6:19 *s* of Elkanah, son of Jeroham, son of Eliel,
6:19 Eliel, *s* of Toah,
6:20 son of Zuth, son of Elkanah, *s* of Mahath,
6:20 Mahath, *s* of Amasi,
6:21 son of Elkanah, son of Joel, *s* of Azariah,
6:21 Azariah, *s* of Zaphaniah,
6:22 son of Tahath, son of Assir, *s* of Ebiasaph,
6:22 Ebiasaph, *s* of Korah,
6:23 son of Izhar, son of Kohath, *s* of Levi,
6:23 Levi, *s* of Israel.
6:24 was the son of Berechiah, *s* of Shimea,
6:25 Shimea, *s* of Michael,
6:25 Michael, son of Baaseiah, *s* of Malchijah,
6:26 son of Ethni, son of Zerah, *s* of Adaiah,
6:27 son of Ethan, son of Zimmah, *s* of Shimei,
6:28 son of Jahath, son of Gershon, *s* of Levi.
6:29 son of Kishi, son of Abdi, *s* of Malluch,
6:30 son of Hashabiah, *s* of Amaziah,
6:30 son of Amaziah, *s* of Hilkiah,
6:31 son of Amzi, son of Bani, *s* of Shemer,
6:32 son of Mahli, son of Mushi, *s* of Merari,
6:32 Merari, *s* of Levi.
6:35 his son Eleazar, whose *s* was Phinehas,
6:35 Phinehas, whose *s* was Abishua,
6:36 whose son was Bukki, whose *s* was Uzzi,
6:36 Uzzi, whose *s* was Zerahiah,
6:37 son was Meraioth, whose *s* was Amariah,
6:37 Amariah, whose *s* was Ahitub,
6:38 whose son was Zadok, whose *s* was Ahimaaz.
6:41 been given to Caleb, the *s* of Jephunneh.
7:15 Manasseh's second *s* was named Zelophehad,
7:16 wife, bore a *s* whom she named Peresh.
7:17 the son of Machir, the *s* of Manasseh.
7:20 whose son was Bered, whose *s* was Tahath,
7:20 whose son was Eleadah, whose *s* was Tahath,
7:21 whose *s* was Zabad.
7:21 Ephraim's *s* Shuthelah,
7:23 and bore a *s* whom he named Beriah,
7:25 son was Rephah, whose *s* was Resheph,
7:25 whose son was Telah, whose *s* was Tahan,
7:26 whose son was Ladan, whose *s* was Ammihud,
7:26 Ammihud, whose *s* was Elishama,
7:27 whose son was Nun, whose *s* was Joshua.
7:29 the descendants of Joseph, the *s* of Israel.
8: 1 his first-born, Ashbel, the second *s*,
8:30 also his first-born *s*,
8:34 The *s* of Jonathan was Meribbaal,
8:37 the father of Binea, whose *s* was Raphah,
8:37 whose son was Eleasah, whose *s* was Azel.
8:39 Ulam, his first-born, Jeush, the second *s*,
9: 4 son of Ammihud, son of Omri, *s* of Imri, *s*
9: 4 of the descendants of Perez, *s* of Judah.
9: 7 son of Meshullam, son of Hodaviah, *s*
9: 8 Ibneiah, *s* of Jeroham;
9: 8 Elah, son of Uzzi, *s* of Michri;
9: 8 Meshullam, son of Shephatiah, *s* of Reuel,
9:11 *s* of Hilkiah, *s* of Meshullam, *s* of Zadok, *s*
9:11 son of Zadok, son of Meraioth, *s* of Ahitub,
9:12 son of Jeroham, *s* of Pashhur, son
9:12 *s* of Adiel, son of Jahzerah, *s* of Meshullam,
9:12 Meshullam, son of Meshillemith, *s* of Immer.
9:14 son of Hasshub, son of Azrikam, *s*
9:15 Mattaniah, son of Mica, *s* of Zichri,
9:16 Obadiah, son of Shemaiah, *s* of Galal,
9:16 and Berechiah, son of Asa, *s* of Elkanah,
9:19 Shallum, son of Kore, *s* of Ebiasaph,
9:20 Phinehas, *s* of Eleazar, had been their chief
9:36 His first-born *s* was Abdon;
9:40 The *s* of Jonathan was Meribbaal,
9:43 whose son was Eleasah, whose *s* was Azel.
9:43 son was Rephaiah, whose *s* was Eleasah,
10:14 his kingdom to David, the *s* of Jesse.
11: 6 Joab, the *s* of Zeruiah, was the first to go
11:11 Ishbaal, the *s* of Hachamoni,
11:12 to him Eleazar, the *s* of Dodo the Ahohite,
11:22 Benaiah, *s* of Jehoiada, a valiant man
11:24 as these of Benaiah, the *s* of Jehoiada,
11:26 Elhanan, *s* of Dodo,
11:28 Ira, *s* of Ikkesh,

SON (cont.)

11:30 Heled, *s* of Baanah,
11:31 Ithai, *s* of Ribai,
11:34 Jonathan, *s* of Shagee, from En-harod;
11:35 from En-harod; Ahiam, *s* of Sachar,
11:35 Elipheleth, *s* of Abasabi,
11:37 Naarai, the *s* of Ezbai;
11:39 the armor-bearer of Joab, *s* of Zeruiah;
11:41 Uriah the Hittite; Zabad, *s* of Ahlai,
11:42 addition to the Thirty, Adina, *s* of Shiza,
11:45 Jediael, *s* of Shimri, and Joha, his brother
12: 1 under banishment from Saul, *s* of Kish;
12:19 O David, we are with you, O *s* of Jesse.
15:17 the Levites appointed Heman, *s* of Joel,
15:17 among his brethren, Asaph, *s* of Berechiah;
15:17 their brethren, Ethan, *s* of Kushaiah;
16:38 including Obed-edom, *s* of Jeduthun,
17:13 a father to him, and he shall be a *s* to me,
18:10 he sent his *s* Hadoram to wish King David
18:12 Abishai, the *s* of Zeruiah,
18:15 Joab, *s* of Zeruiah,
18:15 Jehoshaphat, *s* of Ahilud,
18:16 *s* of Ahitub, and Ahimelech, son
18:17 Benaiah, *s* of Jehoiada,
19: 1 died and his *s* succeeded him as king.
19: 2 show kindness to Hanun, the *s* of Nahash,
20: 5 Philistines, and Elhanan, the *s* of Jair,
20: 7 Israel, and Jonathan, the *s* of Shimea,
22: 5 "My *s* Solomon is young and immature:
22: 6 Then he called for his *s* Solomon and
22: 7 "My *s*, it was my purpose to build a house
22: 9 However, a *s* is to be born to you.
22:10 he shall be a *s* to me,
22:11 Now, my *s*, the LORD be with you,
22:17 of Israel's leaders to help his *s* Solomon:
23: 1 he made his *s* Solomon king over Israel.
24: 6 The scribe Shemaiah, *s* of Nethanel,
24: 6 priest, and of Ahimelech, *s* of Abiathar,
24:26 Mushi, and the descendants of his *s* Uzziah.
24:27 descendants of Merari through his *s* Uzziah:
26: 1 Korahites was Meshelemiah, the *s* of Kore,
26: 2 the first-born, Jediael, the second *s*,
26: 4 the first-born, Jehozabad, a second *s*,
26: 6 To his *s* Shemaiah were born sons who ruled
26:11 made him chief), Hilkiah, the second *s*,
26:14 Then they cast lots for his *s* Zechariah,
26:24 Shubael, son of Gershon, *s* of Moses,
26:25 son was Rehabiah, whose *s* was Jeshaiah,
26:25 *s* was Joram, whose son was Zichri, whose *s*
26:28 son of Kish, Abner, *s* of Ner, Joab, son
27: 2 the first month was Ishbaal, *s* of Zabdiel,
27: 4 of the second month was Eleazar, *s* of Dodo,
27: 5 was Benaiah, *s* of Jehoiada the priest,
27: 6 His *s* Ammizabad was over his division.
27: 7 of Joab, and after him his *s* Zebadiah,
27: 9 for the sixth month, was Ira, *s* of Ikkesh,
27:16 the leader was Eliezer, *s* of Zichri;
27:16 the Simeonites, Shephatiah, *s* of Maacah;
27:17 for Levi, Hashabiah, *s* of Kemuel;
27:18 for Issachar, Omri, *s* of Michael;
27:19 *s* of Obadiah; for Naphtali, Jeremoth, *s*
27:20 the sons of Ephraim, Hoshea, *s* of Azaziah;
27:20 half-tribe of Manasseh, Joel, *s* of Pedaiah;
27:21 *s* of Zechariah; for Benjamin, Jaasiel, *s*
27:22 for Dan, Azarel, *s* of Jeroham.
27:24 Joab, *s* of Zeruiah, began to take the census
27:25 of the king was Azmaveth, the *s* of Adiel.
27:25 and the towers was Jonathan, *s* of Uzziah.
27:26 who tilled the soil was Ezri, *s* of Chelub.
27:29 in the valleys was Shaphat, the *s* of Adlai;
27:32 he and Jehiel, the *s* of Hachmoni,
27:34 Ahithophel came Jehoiada, the *s* of Benaiah,
28: 5 he has chosen my *s* Solomon to sit on the
28: 6 'It is your *s* Solomon who shall build my
28: 6 my courts, for I have chosen him for my *s*,
28: 9 "As for you, Solomon, my *s*,
28:11 Then David gave to his *s* Solomon the
28:20 Then David said to his *s* Solomon:
29: 1 "My *s* Solomon, whom alone God
29:19 Give to my *s* Solomon a wholehearted desire
29:22 they proclaimed David's *s* Solomon king,
29:26 Thus David, the *s* of Jesse,
29:28 and his *s* Solomon succeeded him as king.
2Chr 1: 1 Solomon, *s* of David,
1: 5 The bronze altar made by Bezalel, *s* of Uri,
1: 5 made by Bezalel, son of Uri, *s* of Hur,
2:11 a wise *s* of intelligence and understanding,
2:13 *s* of a Danite woman and of a father from
6: 9 your *s* whom you will beget shall build the
9:29 seer which concern Jeroboam, *s* of Nebat.
9:31 and his *s* Rehoboam succeeded him as king.
10: 2 When Jeroboam, *s* of Nebat,
10:15 had uttered to Jeroboam, the *s* of Nebat,
10:16 We have no heritage in the *s* of Jesse.
11: 3 "Say to Rehoboam, *s* of Solomon,
11:17 of Judah and made Rehoboam, *s* of Solomon,
11:18 of Jerimoth, *s* of David and of Abihail,
11:18 of Abihail, daughter of Eliab, *s* of Jesse.
11:22 Rehoboam constituted Abijah, *s* of Maacah,
12:16 His *s* Abijah succeeded him as king.
13: 6 *s* of Nebat, the servant of Solomon, son
13: 7 him and overcame Rehoboam, *s* of Solomon,
13:23 His *s* Asa succeeded him as king.
15: 1 Upon Azariah, *s* of Oded,
17: 1 His *s* Jehoshaphat succeeded him as king
17:16 Next to him, Amasiah, *s* of Zichri,
18: 7 That is Micaiah, *s* of Imlah."
18: 8 to whom he said, "Get Micaiah, *s* of Imlah,
18:10 Zedekiah, *s* of Chenaanah,
18:23 Thereupon Zedekiah, *s* of Chenaanah,
18:25 of the city, and to Joash the king's *s*,
19: 2 Jehu the seer, *s* of Hanani,
19:11 to the LORD, and Zebadiah, *s* of Ishmael,
20:14 *s* of Zechariah, *s* of Benaiah, *s* of Jeiel, *s*
20:34 in the chronicle of Jehu, *s* of Hanani,
20:37 But Eliezer, *s* of Dodavahu from Mareshah,
21: 1 Jehoram, his *s*, succeeded him as king.
21:17 there was left to him only one *s*,
22: 1 of Jerusalem made Ahaziah, his youngest *s*,
22: 1 Thus Ahaziah, *s* of Jehoram,
22: 5 when he accompanied Jehoram, *s* of Ahab,
22: 6 of this illness, Ahaziah, *s* of Jehoram,
22: 6 went down to visit Jehoram, *s* of Ahab,
22: 7 rode out with Jehoram to Jehu, *s* of Nimshi,
22:10 of Ahaziah, learned that her *s* was dead,
22:11 secretly took Ahaziah's *s* Joash from among
23: 1 *s* of Jehoram; Ishmael, son of Jehohanan;
23: 1 *s* of Obed; Masseiah, son of Adaiah;
23: 1 and Elishaphat, *s* of Zichri.
23: 3 "Here is the king's *s* who must reign,
23:11 Then they brought out the king's *s*,
24:20 Zechariah, *s* of Jehoiada the priest.
24:22 Zechariah's father, and slew his *s*.
24:25 the murder of the *s* of Jehoiada the priest.
24:26 Zabad, *s* of Shimeath from Ammon,
24:26 and Jehozabad, *s* of Shimrith from Moab.
24:27 His *s* Amaziah succeeded him as king.
25:17 to Joash, son of Jehoahaz, *s* of Jehu,
25:18 'Give your daughter to my *s* for his wife.'
25:23 king of Judah, son of Joash, *s* of Jehoahaz,
25:25 *s* of Joash, king of Judah, survived Joash, *s*
26:21 Therefore his *s* Jotham was regent of the
26:22 The prophet Isaiah, *s* of Amos,
26:23 His *s* Jotham succeeded him as king.
27: 9 and his *s* Ahaz succeeded him as king.
28: 6 For Pekah, *s* of Remaliah,
28: 7 warrior, killed Maaseiah, the king's *s*,
28:12 *s* of Johanan, Berechiah, *s* of Meshillemoth,
28:12 son of Shallum, and Amasa, *s* of Hadlai,
28:27 His *s* Hezekiah succeeded him as king.
29:12 son of Amasai, and Joel, *s* of Azariah,
29:12 son of Abdi, and Azariah, *s* of Jehallel;
29:12 Joah, son of Zimmah, and Eden, *s* of Joah;
30:26 for since the days of Solomon, *s* of David,
31:14 Kore, the *s* of Imnah,
32:20 Hezekiah and the prophet Isaiah, *s* of Amos,
32:32 Vision of the Prophet Isaiah, *s* of Amos,
32:33 His *s* Manasseh succeeded him as king.
33: 7 God had said to David and his *s* Solomon:
33:20 His *s* Amon succeeded him as king.
33:25 land, made his *s* Josiah king in his stead.
34: 8 as the land, he sent Shaphan, *s* of Azaliah,
34: 8 ruler of the city, and Joah, *s* of Joahaz,
34:20 son of Shaphan, to Abdon, *s* of Michah,
34:22 of Shallum, son of Tokhath, *s* of Hasrah,
35: 3 in the house built by Solomon, *s* of David,
35: 4 of King David of Israel and his *s* Solomon.
36: 1 *s* of Josiah and made him king in Jerusalem
36: 8 His *s* Jehoiachin succeeded him as king.
Ezr 3: 2 Then Jeshua, *s* of Jozadak,
3: 2 priests, and Zerubbabel, *s* of Shealtiel,
3: 8 son of Shealtiel, and Jeshua, *s* of Jozadak,
3: 9 with Kadmiel and Binnui, *s* of Henadad,
5: 1 prophets Haggai and Zechariah, *s* of Iddo,
5: 2 son of Shealtiel, and Jeshua, *s* of Jozadak,
6:14 prophets, Haggai and Zechariah, *s* of Iddo.
7: 1 *s* of Seraiah, son of Azariah, *s* of Hilkiah,
7: 2 son of Shallum, son of Zadok, *s* of Ahitub,
7: 3 *s* of Amariah, son of Azariah, *s* of Meraioth,
7: 4 son of Zerahiah, son of Uzzi, *s* of Bukki,
7: 5 of Bukki, son of Abishua, *s* of Phinehas,
7: 5 son of Eleazar, *s* of the high priest Aaron
8: 3 the sons of David, Hattush, *s* of Shecaniah;
8: 4 of Pahathmoab, Eliehoenai, *s* of Zerahiah,
8: 5 sons of Zattu, Shecaniah, *s* of Jahaziel,
8: 6 of the sons of Adin, Ebed, *s* of Jonathan,
8: 7 the sons of Elam, Jeshaiah, *s* of Athaliah,
8: 8 sons of Shephatiah, Zebadiah, *s* of Michael,
8: 9 of the sons of Joab, Obadiah, *s* of Jehiel,
8:10 sons of Bani, Shelomith, *s* of Josiphiah,
8:11 the sons of Bebai, Zechariah, *s* of Bebai,
8:12 the sons of Azgad, Johanan, *s* of Hakkatan,
8:14 of the sons of Bigvai, Uthai, *s* of Zakkur,
8:18 sons of Mahli, son of Levi, *s* of Israel,
8:33 *s* of Uriah, who was assisted by Eleazar, *s*
8:33 by the Levites Jozabad, *s* of Jeshua,
8:33 son of Jeshua, and Noadiah, *s* of Binnui.
10: 2 Then Shecaniah, the *s* of Jehiel,
10: 6 the chamber of Johanan, *s* of Eliashib,
10:15 son of Asahel, and Jahzeiah, *s* of Tikvah,
10:18 Of the sons of Jeshua, *s* of Jozadak,
Neh 1: 1 The words of Nehemiah, the *s* of Hacaliah.
3: 2 and next to them was Zaccur, *s* of Imri.
3: 4 side Meremoth, son of Uriah, *s* of Hakkoz,
3: 4 son of Berechiah, *s* of Meshezabel;
3: 4 and next to him was Zadok, *s* of Baana.
3: 6 *s* of Paseah; and Meshullam, *s* of Besodeiah;
3: 8 was carried out by Uzziel, *s* of Harhaiah,
3: 9 was carried out by Rephaiah, *s* of Hur,
3:10 and at his side was Jedaiah, *s* of Harumaph,
3:10 Next to him Hattush, *s* of Hashabneiah,
3:11 was repaired by Malchijah, *s* of Harim,
3:12 was carried out by Shallum, *s* of Hallohesh,
3:14 was repaired by Malchijah, *s* of Rechab,
3:15 was repaired by Shallum, *s* of Colhozeh,
3:16 was carried out by Nehemiah, *s* of Azbuk,
3:17 Rehum, *s* of Bani.
3:18 Binnui, *s* of Henadad,
3:19 next to him Ezer, *s* of Jeshua,
3:20 After him, Baruch, *s* of Zabbai,
3:21 him, Meremoth, son of Uriah, *s* of Hakkoz,
3:23 Azariah, son of Maaseiah, *s* of Ananiah,
3:24 After him, Binnui, *s* of Henadad,
3:25 Palal, *s* of Uzai, carried out the work
3:25 After him, Pedaiah, *s* of Parosh,
3:29 Zadok, *s* of Immer, carried out the repair
3:29 carried out by Shemaiah, *s* of Shecaniah,
3:30 *s* of Shelemiah, and Hanun, the sixth *s*
3:30 after them, Meshullam, *s* of Berechiah,
6:10 Shemaiah, son of Delaiah, *s* of Mehetabel,
6:18 *s* of Arah, and his son Jehohanan
6:18 the daughter of Meshullam, *s* of Berechiah.
8:17 sort from the days of Jeshua, *s* of Nun,
10: 2 His Excellency Nehemiah, *s* of Hacaliah,
10:10 Jeshua, *s* of Azaniah; Binnui, of the sons
11: 4 *s* of Uzziah, son of Zechariah, son
11: 4 son of Shephatiah, *s* of Mehallalel,
11: 5 Maaseiah, son of Baruch, *s* of Colhozeh,
11: 5 *s* of Hazaiah, son of Adaiah,
11: 5 *s* of Adaiah, son of Joiarib,
11: 5 of Hazaiah, son of Adaiah, *s* of Joiarib,
11: 5 son of Zechariah, a *s* of the Shelanites.
11: 7 Sallu, son of Meshullam, *s* of Joed,
11: 7 *s* of Pedaiah, son of Kolaiah,
11: 7 of Kolaiah, son of Maaseiah,
11: 7 of Maaseiah, son of Ithiel, *s* of Jeshaiah,
11: 9 Joel *s* of Zichri,
11: 9 their commander, and Judah, *s* of Hassenuah,
11:11 Seraiah, son of Hilkaiah, *s* of Meshullam,
11:11 son of Zadok, son of Meraioth, *s* of Ahitub,
11:12 Adaiah, son of Jeroham, *s* of Pelaliah,
11:12 *s* of Amzi, son of Zechariah, son of
11:12 Pashhur, *s* of Malchijah,
11:13 Meshillemoth, *s* of Immer,
11:13 of Azarel, son of Ahzai, *s* of Meshillemoth,
11:14 Their commander was Zabdiel, *s* of Haggadol.
11:15 Zarikam, son of Hashabiah, *s* of Bunni:
11:15 Shemaiah, son of Hasshub, *s* of Azrikam,
11:17 Mattaniah, *s* of Micah; son of Zabdi,
11:17 Zabdi, *s* of Asaph, director of the psalms,
11:17 and Abda, son of Shammua, *s* of Galal,
11:17 Galal, *s* of Jeduthun.
11:22 Uzzi, *s* of Bani, son of Hashabiah,
11:22 of Hashabiah, son of Mattaniah, *s* of Micah;
11:24 Pethahiah, *s* of Meshezabel,
11:24 a descendant of Zerah, *s* of Judah,
12: 1 returned with Zerubbabel, *s* of Shealtiel,
12:23 the time of Johanan, the *s* of Eliashib.
12:26 Joiakim, *s* of Jeshua, son of Jozadak
12:35 Zechariah, son of Jonathan, *s* of Shemaiah,
12:35 Shemaiah, son of Mattaniah, *s* of Micaiah,
12:35 Micaiah, son of Zaccur, *s* of Asaph,
12:45 of David and of Solomon, his *s*.
13:13 with Hanan, son of Zaccur, *s* of Mattaniah,
13:28 of Joiada, *s* of Eliashib the high priest,
Tb 1: 1 *s* Tobiel, son of Hananiel son of Aduel, son
1: 9 By her I had a *s* whom I named Tobiah.
1:14 money with my kinsman Gabael, *s* of Gabri,
1:15 his *s* Sennacherib succeeded him as king,
1:20 except for my wife Anna and my *s* Tobiah.
1:21 His *s* Esarhaddon, who succeeded him
1:21 king, placed Ahiqar, my brother Anael's *s*,
2: 1 Anna and my *s* Tobiah were restored to me.
2: 2 placed before me I said to my *s* Tobiah:
2: 2 "My *s*, go out and try to find a poor man
2: 2 Indeed, *s*,
2: 3 I said to him, "What is it, *s*?"
3: 9 May we never see a *s* or daughter of yours!"
3:17 daughter Sarah to Tobit's *s* Tobiah,
4: 2 why should I not call my *s* Tobiah and let
4: 3 So he called his *s* Tobiah;
4: 3 "My *s*, when I die, give me a decent burial.
4: 4 Remember, my *s*,
4: 5 "Through all your days, my *s*,
4: 8 *S*, give alms in proportion to what you own.
4:12 "Be on your guard, *s*, against every form
4:13 Therefore, my *s*, love your kinsmen.
4:14 Keep a close watch on yourself, my *s*,
4:19 my *s*, keep in mind my commandments,
4:20 "And now, *s*, I wish to inform you
4:20 with Gabri's *s* Gabael at Rages in Media.
5: 3 Tobit answered his *s* Tobiah:
5: 3 So now, my *s*, find yourself a trustworthy
5: 9 trustworthy enough to travel with you, *s*."
5:10 "My *s* Tobiah wants to go to Media."
5:12 for a hired man to travel with your *s*?"
5:12 wish to know truthfully whose *s* you are,
5:13 "I am Azariah, *s* of Hananiah the elder,
5:15 wages, plus expenses for you and for my *s*.

5:15 If you go with my s,
5:17 Then he called his s and said to him:
5:17 "My s, prepare whatever you need
5:17 his angel accompany you for safety, my s."
5:19 Rather let it be a ransom for our s!
5:21 Our s will leave in good health and come
6:15 And they have no other s to bury them!"
7:7 You are the s of a noble and good father.
7:11 But now, s, eat and drink.
7:11 And tonight, s,
8:21 Be of good cheer, my s!
8:21 So be happy, s!"
9:5 bond and told him about Tobit's s Tobiah,
9:6 and good child, s of a noble and good,
10:1 days was reached and his s did not appear,
10:4 "My s has perished and is no longer among
10:4 began to weep aloud and to wail over her s:
10:7 watch all day at the road her s had taken,
10:11 "Goodbye, my s.
11:5 the road by which her s was to come.
11:6 to his father, "Tobit, your s is coming,
11:9 Then Anna ran up to her s,
11:9 him, "Now that I have seen you again, s,
11:13 When Tobit saw his s,
11:14 He exclaimed, "I can see you, s,
11:15 Behold, I now see my s Tobiah!"
11:17 reached Sarah, the wife of his s Tobiah,
11:17 Blessed is my s Tobiah,
12:1 s Tobiah and said to him, "Son,
12:4 Tobit answered, "It is only fair, s,
14:3 his s Tobiah and Tobiah's seven sons,
14:3 S, take your children and flee into Media
14:8 "Now, as for you, my s,
14:10 Think, my s,
Jdt 6:15 Uzziah, s of Micah of the tribe of Simeon,
6:15 son of Gothoniel, and Charmis, s
8:1 son of Joseph, son of Oziel, s of Elkiah,
8:1 son of Ananias, s of Gideon, son of
8:1 son of Ahitob, son of Elijah, s of Hilkiah,
8:1 son of Eliab, s of Nathanael, son of Salamiel,
8:1 son of Sarasadai, s of Simeon, son of Israel,
Est A:1 Nisan, Mordecai, son of Jair, s of Shimei,
A:1 son of Jair, son of Shimei, s of Kish,
A:17 however, s of Hammedatha the Agagite,
2:5 son of Jair, son of Shimei, s of Kish,
3:1 raised Haman, s of Hammedatha the Agagite,
3:10 it to Haman, s of Hammedatha the Agagite,
8:5 schemer Haman, s of Hammedatha the Agagite,
E:10 "For instance, Haman, s of Hammedatha,
E:17 the letter sent by Haman, s of Hammedatha,
9:10 the ten sons of Haman, s of Hammedatha,
9:24 Haman, s of Hammedatha the Agagite,
1Mc 1:1 Alexander the Macedonian, Philip's s,
1:10 Antiochus Epiphanes, s of King Antiochus,
2:1 days Mattathias, son of John, s of Simeon,
2:26 just as Phinehas did with Zimri, s of Salu.
3:1 Then his s Judas, who was called
3:33 of his s Antiochus until his own return.
3:38 Lysias chose Ptolemy, s of Dorymenes,
4:30 into the hand of Jonathan, the s of Saul,
5:18 In Judea he left Joseph, s of Zechariah,
5:56 opposite Ptolemais, Joseph, s of Zechariah,
6:2 left there by Alexander, s of Philip,
6:15 s Antiochus and bring him up to be king.
6:17 was dead, he set up the king's s Antiochus,
6:55 to train his s Antiochus to be king,
7:1 and fifty-one, Demetrius, s of Seleucus,
8:17 s of John, son of Accos, and Jason, son
10:1 who was called Epiphanes, s of Antiochus,
10:67 and sixty-five, Demetrius, s of Demetrius,
11:39 bringing up Alexander's young s Antiochus.
11:70 son of Absalom, and Judas, s of Chalphi.
12:16 s of Antiochus, and Antipater, s of Jason,
13:11 He sent Jonathan, s of Absalom,
13:53 Seeing that his s John was now a grown man,
14:22 s of Antiochus, and Antipater, s of Jason,
14:29 country, Simon, s of the priest Mattathias,
15:1 Antiochus, s of King Demetrius,
16:11 Ptolemy, s of Abubus, had been appointed
16:15 The s of Abubus gave them a deceitful
2Mc 2:20 Antiochus Epiphanes and his s Eupator,
3:11 was the property of Hyrcanus, s of Tobias,
4:4 and that Apollonius, s of Menestheus,
4:21 When Apollonius, s of Menestheus,
4:45 side, promised Ptolemy, s of Dorymenes,
7:26 through the motions of persuading her s.
7:27 to her s and said in their native language:
7:27 S, have pity on me,
8:9 promptly selected Nicanor, s of Patroclus,
9:25 therefore appointed as king my s Antiochus,
9:26 to show good will toward me and my s.
9:29 but fearing Antiochus' s,
10:10 the s of that godless man and shall give a
12:2 Timothy and Apollonius, s of Gennaeus,
14:1 men learned that Demetrius, s of Seleucus,
Jb 18:19 neither s nor grandson among his people,
25:6 man, who is but a maggot, the s of man,
32:2 anger of Elihu, s of Barachel the Buzite,
32:6 So Elihu, s of Barachel the Buzite,
Ps(s) 2:7 The LORD said to me, "You are my s;
8:5 the s of man that you should care for him?
50:20 against your mother's s you spread rumors.
72:1 king, and with your justice, the king's s;
72:20 prayers of David the s of Jesse are ended.
80:16 s of man whom you yourself made strong].
80:18 the s of man whom you yourself made strong.
86:16 servant, and save the s of your handmaid.
116:16 I am your servant, the s of your handmaid;
144:3 s of man, that you take thought of him?
Prv 1:1 The Proverbs of Solomon, the s of David,
1:8 Hear, my s, your father's instruction,
1:10 My s, should sinners entice you,
1:15 My s, walk not in the way with them,
2:1 My s, if you receive my words
3:1 My s, forget not my teaching,
3:11 The discipline of the LORD, my s,
3:12 reproves, and he chastises the s he favors.
3:21 My s, let not these slip out of your sight:
4:10 Hear, my s, and receive my words.
4:20 My s, to my words be attentive,
5:1 My s, to my wisdom be attentive,
5:20 Why then, my s, should you go astray
6:1 My s, if you have become surety
6:3 So do this, my s, to free yourself,
6:20 Observe, my s, your father's bidding,
7:1 My s, keep my words, and treasure my
10:1 s makes his father glad, but a foolish son
10:5 A s who fills the granaries in summer is a
10:5 a s who slumbers during harvest,
13:1 A wise s loves correction,
13:24 He who spares his rod hates his s,
15:20 A wise s makes his father glad,
17:2 servant will rule over a worthless s,
17:25 A foolish s is vexation to his father,
19:13 The foolish s is ruin to his father,
19:18 Chastise your s, for in this there is hope;
19:26 mother, is a worthless and disgraceful s.
19:27 If a s ceases to hear instruction,
23:15 My s, if your heart be wise,
23:19 Hear, my s, and be wise,
23:24 who begets a wise s will have joy in him.
23:26 My s, give me your heart,
24:13 If you eat honey, my s,
24:21 My s, fear the LORD and the king;
27:11 If you are wise, my s,
28:7 He who keeps the law is a wise s,
29:17 Correct your s, and he will bring you
30:1 The words of Agur, s of Jakeh the Massaite:
31:2 What, my s, my first-born!
31:2 O son of my womb; what, O s of my vows!
Eccl 1:1 The words of David's s,
4:8 with neither s nor brother.
5:13 he may have a s when he is without means.
12:12 As to more than these, my s, beware.
Wis 2:18 For if the just one be the s of God,
9:5 I am your servant, the s of your handmaid,
18:13 acknowledged that the people was God's s.
Sir 2:1 My s, when you come to serve
3:12 My s, take care of your father
3:17 My s, conduct your affairs with humility,
4:1 My s, rob not the poor man
4:10 Thus will you be like a s to the Most High,
6:18 My s, from your youth embrace discipline;
6:24 Listen, my s, and heed my advice;
6:32 My s, if you wish, you can be taught;
10:27 My s, with humility have self-esteem;
11:10 My s, why increase your cares,
11:20 My s, hold fast to your duty,
14:11 My s, use freely whatever you have
16:22 Hearken to me, my s, take my advice,
17:25 in men, for not immortal is any s of man.
18:14 My s, to your charity add no reproach,
21:1 My s, if you have sinned, do so no more,
23:22 and offers as heir her s by a stranger.
30:1 He who loves his s chastises him often,
30:2 disciplines his s will benefit from him,
30:3 who educates his s makes his enemy jealous,
30:7 spoils his s will have wounds to bandage,
30:8 a s left to himself grows up unruly.
30:13 Discipline your s, make heavy his yoke,
31:22 Listen to me, my s, and scorn me not;
33:20 Let neither s nor wife, neither brother
34:20 Like the man who slays a s in his father's
37:26 My s, while you are well,
38:9 My s, when you are ill,
38:16 My s, shed tears for one who is dead
40:28 My s, live not the life of a beggar,
45:23 PHINEHAS too, the s of Eleazar,
45:25 the s of Jesse of the tribe of Judah,
45:25 an individual heritage through one s alone;
46:1 Valiant leader was JOSHUA, s of Nun,
46:7 loyal, He and CALEB, s of Jephunneh,
47:12 merits he had as his successor a wise s,
49:12 God's right hand, And Jeshua, Jozadak's s?
50:1 was SIMON the priest, s of Jochanan,
50:11 S of Jochanan When he received the
50:27 in this book, I, Jesus, s of Eleazar,
50:27 I, Jesus, son of Eleazar, s of Sirach,
Is 1:1 The vision which Isaiah, s of Amoz,
2:1 This is what Isaiah, s of Amoz,
7:1 king of Judah, son of Jotham, s of Uzziah,
7:1 and Pekah, king of Israel, s of Remaliah,
7:3 to meet Ahaz, you and your s Shear-jashub,
7:4 the Arameans, and of the s of Remaliah],
7:5 and the s of Remaliah] plots against you,
7:6 and appoint the s of Tabeel king there."
7:8 and Remaliah's s the head of Samaria.
7:14 virgin shall be with child, and bear a s,
8:2 priest, and Zechariah, s of Jeberechiah.
8:3 prophetess and she conceived and bore a s.
8:6 the loftiness of Rezin and Remaliah's s,
9:5 For a child is born to us, a s is given us;
13:1 a vision of Isaiah, s of Amoz.
14:12 the heavens, O morning star, s of the dawn!
20:2 a warning through Isaiah, the s of Amoz:
22:20 summon my servant Eliakim, s of Hilkiah;
36:3 of the palace, Eliakim, s of Hilkiah,
36:3 scribe, and the herald Joah, s of Asaph.
36:22 of the palace, Eliakim, s of Hilkiah,
36:22 scribe, and the herald Joah, s of Asaph,
37:2 to tell the prophet Isaiah, s of Amoz:
37:21 Then Isaiah, s of Amoz,
37:38 His s Esarhaddon reigned in his stead.
38:1 ill, the prophet Isaiah, s of Amoz,
39:1 time when Merodach-baladan, s of Baladan,
56:2 does this, the s of man who holds to it;
66:13 As a mother comforts her s,
Jer 1:1 The words of Jeremiah, s of Hilkiah,
1:2 to him in the days of Josiah, s of Amon,
1:3 the reign of Jehoiakim, s of Josiah,
1:3 the eleventh year of Zedekiah, s of Josiah,
15:4 because of what Manasseh, s of Hezekiah,
20:1 things by the priest Pashhur, s of Immer,
20:15 news to my father, saying, "A child, a s,
21:1 s of Malchiah, and the priest Zephaniah, s
22:11 the LORD concerning Shallum, s of Josiah,
22:18 the LORD concerning Jehoiakim, s of Josiah,
22:24 the LORD, if you, Coniah, s of Jehoiakim,
24:1 from Jerusalem Jeconiah, s of Jehoiakim,
25:1 the fourth year of Jehoiakim, s of Josiah,
25:3 the thirteenth year of Josiah, s of Amon,
26:1 of the reign of Jehoiakim, s of Josiah,
26:20 the name of the LORD, Uriah, s of Shemaiah,
26:22 King Jehoiakim sent Elnathan, s of Achbor,
26:24 Ahikam, s of Shaphan, protected Jeremiah,
27:1 of the reign of Jehoiakim, s of Josiah,
27:7 shall serve him and his s and his grandson,
27:20 when he exiled Jeconiah, s of Jehoiakim,
28:1 year, the prophet Hananiah, s of Azzur,
28:4 to this place Jeconiah, s of Jehoiakim,
29:3 s of Shaphan, and by Gemariah, son
29:21 Ahab, s of Kolaiah, and Zedekiah, son
29:25 to Zephaniah, the priest, s of Maaseiah,
31:20 Is Ephraim not my favored s,
32:7 Hanamel, s of your uncle Shallum,
32:8 the LORD foretold, Hanamel, my uncle's s,
32:12 to Baruch, son of Neriah, s of Mahseiah,
32:16 deed of purchase to Baruch, s of Neriah,
33:21 not have a s to be king upon his throne,
35:1 LORD in the days of Jehoiakim, s of Josiah,
35:3 son of Jeremiah, s of Habazziniah,
35:4 room of the sons of Hanan, s of Igdaliah,
35:4 above the room of Maaseiah, s of Shallum,
35:6 "Jonadab, Rechab's s, our father, forbade
35:8 Now we have heeded Jonadab, Rechab's s,
35:14 The advice of Jonadab, Rechab's s,
35:16 Yes, the children of Jonadab, Rechab's s,
35:19 to be a descendant of Jonadab, Rechab's s,
36:1 the fourth year of Jehoiakim, s of Josiah,
36:4 So Jeremiah called Baruch, s of Neriah,
36:8 Baruch, s of Neriah, did everything
36:9 the fifth year of Jehoiakim, s of Josiah,
36:10 room of Gemariah, s of the scribe Shaphan,
36:11 Now Micaiah, son of Gemariah, s of Shaphan,
36:12 son of Shemaiah, Elnathan, s of Achbor,
36:12 son of Shaphan, Zedekiah, s of Hananiah,
36:14 Jehudi, son of Nethaniah, s of Shelemiah,
36:14 Shelemiah, s of Cushi, to Baruch
36:14 Scroll in hand, Baruch, s of Neriah,
36:26 son of Azriel, and Shelemiah, s of Abdeel,
36:32 it to his secretary, Baruch, s of Neriah;
37:1 Coniah, s of Jehoiakim,
37:1 succeeded by King Zedekiah, s of Josiah;
37:3 s of Shelemiah, and Zephaniah, son
37:13 Irijah, son of Shelemiah, s of Hananiah;
38:1 son of Mattan, Gedaliah, s of Pashhur,
38:1 s of Shelemiah, and Pashhur, son
39:14 to Gedaliah, son of Ahikam, s of Shaphan,
40:5 to Gedaliah, son of Ahikam, s of Shaphan,
40:6 Jeremiah went to Gedaliah, s of Ahikam,
40:7 of Babylon had given Gedaliah, s of Ahikam,
40:8 s of Nethaniah; Johanan, son of Kareah;
40:8 Seraiah, s of Tanhumeth;
40:9 Gedaliah, son of Ahikam, s of Shaphan,
40:11 them Gedaliah, son of Ahikam, s of Shaphan,
40:13 Now Johanan, s of Kareah,
40:14 had sent Ishmael, s of Nethaniah,
40:15 But Gedaliah, s of Ahikam,
40:15 Then Johanan, s of Kareah,
40:15 me go and kill Ishmael, s of Nethaniah;
40:16 s of Ahikam, answered Johanan, son
41:1 Ishmael, son of Nethaniah, s of Elishama,
41:1 came with ten men to Gedaliah, s of Ahikam,
41:2 table in Mizpah, Ishmael, s of Nethaniah,
41:2 Gedaliah, son of Ahikam, s of Shaphan,
41:6 Ishmael s of Nethaniah,
41:7 "Come to Gedaliah, s of Ahikam,"
41:7 inside the city, Ishmael, s of Nethaniah,
41:9 this cistern Ishmael, s of Nethaniah,

SON (cont.)
41:10 Ishmael, *s* of Nethaniah, led away
41:10 had confided to Gedaliah, *s* of Ahikam.
41:10 these captives, Ishmael, *s* of Nethaniah,
41:11 But when Johanan, *s* of Kareah,
41:11 of the crimes Ishmael, *s* of Nethaniah,
41:12 set out to attack Ishmael, *s* of Nethaniah.
41:13 At the sight of Johanan, *s* of Kareah,
41:14 Mizpah went over to Johanan, *s* of Kareah.
41:15 But Ishmael, *s* of Nethaniah, escaped
41:16 Then Johanan, *s* of Kareah,
41:16 guardians, whom Ishmael, *s* of Nethaniah,
41:16 after he killed Gedaliah, *s* of Ahikam.
41:18 son of Nethaniah, had slain Gedaliah, *s*
42: 1 son of Kareah, Azariah, *s* of Hoshaiah,
42: 8 Then he called Johanan, *s* of Kareah,
43: 2 son of Hoshaiah, Johanan, *s* of Kareah,
43: 3 It is Baruch, *s* of Neriah, who stirs you
43: 4 *s* of Kareah, and the rest of the leaders
43: 5 In-stead, Johanan, *s* of Kareah,
43: 6 to Gedaliah, son of Ahikam, *s* of Shaphan;
43: 6 the prophet, and Baruch, *s* of Neriah.
45: 1 Jeremiah gave to Baruch, *s* of Neriah,
45: 1 the fourth year of Jehoiakim, *s* of Josiah,
46: 2 the fourth year of Jehoiakim, *s* of Josiah,
51:59 to Seraiah, son of Neriah, *s* of Mahseiah,
Bar 1: 1 of the scroll which Baruch, *s* of Neriah,
1: 1 of Neriah, son of Mahseiah, *s* of Zedekiah,
1: 1 of Zedekiah, son of Hasadiah, *s* of Hilkiah,
1: 3 this scroll for Jeconiah, *s* of Jehoiakim,
1: 7 to Jehoiakim, son of Hilkiah, *s* of Shallum,
1: 8 These silver vessels Zedekiah, *s* of Josiah,
1:11 of Babylon, and that of Belshazzar, his *s*,
1:12 of Babylon, and that of Belshazzar, his *s*,
2: 3 eat the flesh of his *s* or of his daughter.
3:37 his servant, to Israel, his beloved *s*.
Ez 1: 3 came to the priest Ezekiel, the *s* of Buzi,
2: 1 *S* of man, stand up!
2: 3 *S* of man, I am sending you
2: 6 But as for you, *s* of man,
2: 8 As for you, *s* of man,
3: 1 *S* of man, eat what is before you;
3: 3 *S* of man, he then said to me, feed
3: 4 *S* of man, go now to the house of Israel,
3:10 *S* of man, he said to me, take
3:17 *S* of man, I have appointed you
3:25 [As for you, *s* of man,
4: 1 As for you, *s* of man,
4:16 *S* of man, I am breaking the staff
5: 1 As for you, *s* of man,
6: 2 *S* of man, turn toward the mountains
7: 2 *S* of man, now say:
8: 5 *S* of man, look toward the north!
8: 6 *S* of man, he asked me, do you see
8: 8 *S* of man, he ordered, dig through
8:11 among whom stood Jaazaniah, *s* of Shaphan,
8:12 Do you see, *s* of man,
8:15 Do you see this, *s* of man?
8:17 Do you see, *s* of man?
11: 1 son of Azzur, and Pelatiah, *s* of Benaiah,
11: 2 *S* of man, these are the men
11: 4 Therefore prophesy against them, *s* of man,
11:13 prophesying, Pelatiah, the *s* of Benaiah,
11:15 *S* of man, it is about your kinsmen,
12: 2 *S* of man, you live in the midst
12: 3 Now, *s* of man,
12: 9 *S* of man, did not the house of Israel,
12:18 *S* of man, eat your bread trembling,
12:22 *S* of man, what is this proverb
12:27 *S* of man, listen to the house of Israel
13: 2 *S* of man, prophesy against the prophets
13:17 Now, *s* of man,
14: 3 *S* of man, these men have the memory
14:13 *S* of man, when a land sins against me
14:20 they could save neither *s* nor daughter;
15: 2 *S* of man, what makes the wood
16: 2 *S* of man, make known to Jerusalem
17: 2 *S* of man, propose a riddle,
17:12 *S* of man, say now to the rebellious
18: 1 *S* of man, what is the meaning
18: 4 of the father is like the life of the *s*,
18:10 But if he begets a *s* who is a thief,
18:11 of them), a *s* who eats on the mountains,
18:13 this *s* certainly shall not live.
18:14 On the other hand, if a man begets a *s* who,
18:15 a *s* who does not eat on the mountains,
18:19 the *s* charged with the guilt of his father?"
18:19 the *s* has done what is right and just,
18:20 The *s* shall not be charged with the guilt
18:20 father be charged with the guilt of his *s*.
19: 1 As for you, *s* of man,
20: 3 *S* of man, speak with the elders
20: 4 Will you judge, *s* of man?
20:27 speak to the house of Israel, *s* of man,
21: 2 *S* of man, look southward,
21: 7 *S* of man, look toward Jerusalem,
21:11 As for you, *s* of man, groan!
21:14 *S* of man, prophesy!
21:17 Cry out and wail, *s* of man,
21:19 As for you, *s* of man,
21:24 *S* of man, make for yourself two roads
21:33 As for you, *s* of man, prophesy:
22: 2 You, *s* of man,
22:18 *S* of man, the house of Israel
22:24 *S* of man,
23: 2 *S* of man, there were two women,
23:36 *S* of man, would you judge Oholah
24: 2 *S* of man, write down this date today,
24:15 *S* of man, by a sudden blow I am taking
24:25 As for you, *s* of man,
25: 2 *S* of man, turn toward the Ammonites
26: 2 *S* of man, because of what Tyre said
27: 2 As for you, *s* of man,
28: 2 *S* of man, say to the prince of Tyre:
28:12 *S* of man, utter a lament
28:21 *S* of man, look toward Sidon,
29: 2 *S* of man, set your face against Pharaoh,
29:18 *S* of man, Nebuchadnezzar, the king
30: 2 *S* of man, speak this prophecy:
30:21 *S* of man, I have broken the arm
31: 2 *S* of man, say to Pharaoh,
32: 2 *S* of man, utter a lament over Pharaoh,
32:18 *S* of man, lament over the throngs
33: 2 *S* of man, speak thus to your countrymen:
33: 7 You, *s* of man,
33:10 As for you, *s* of man,
33:12 As for you, *s* of man, tell your countrymen:
33:24 *S* of man, they who live in the ruins
33:30 As for you, *s* of man,
34: 2 *S* of man, prophesy against the shepherds
35: 2 *S* of man, set your face against
36: 1 As for you, *s* of man,
36:17 *S* of man, when the house of Israel lived
37: 3 *S* of man, can these bones come to life?
37: 9 Prophesy to the spirit, prophesy, *s* of man,
37:11 *S* of man, these bones are the whole
37:16 Now, *s* of man,
38: 2 *S* of man, turn toward Gog
38:14 Therefore prophesy, *s* of man,
39: 1 Now, *s* of man,
39:17 As for you, *s* of man,
40: 4 The man said to me, *S* of man,
43: 7 *S* of man, this is where my throne
43:10 As for you, *s* of man,
43:18 *S* of man, thus says the Lord GOD:
44: 5 *S* of man, pay strict attention,
44:25 unless it be their father, mother, *s*,
47: 6 asked me, "Have you seen this, *s* of man?"
Dn 3:92 fire, and the fourth looks like a *s* of God."
5:22 You, his *s*, Belshazzar, have not humbled
7:13 I saw One like a *s* of man coming,
8:17 But he said to me, "Understand, *s* of man,
9: 1 the first year that Darius, *s* of Ahasuerus,
11: 6 who brought her, her *s* and her husband.
Hos 1: 1 Lord that came to Hosea, the *s* of Beeri,
1: 1 and in the days of Jeroboam, *s* of Joash,
1: 3 and she conceived and bore him a *s*.
1: 8 Lo-ruhama, she conceived and bore a *s*.
11: 1 I loved him, out of Egypt I called my *s*.
Jl 1: 1 LORD which came to Joel, the *s* of Pethuel.
Am 1: 1 and in the days of Jeroboam, *s* of Joash,
2: 7 *S* and father go to the same prostitute,
8:10 I will make them mourn as for an only *s*,
Jon 1: 1 the LORD that came to Jonah, *s* of Amittai:
Mi 6: 5 planned, and how Balaam, the *s* of Beor,
7: 6 For the *s* dishonors his father,
Zep 1: 1 the son of Cushi, the *s* of Gedaliah,
1: 1 the son of Amariah, the *s* of Hezekiah,
1: 1 in the days of Josiah, the *s* of Amon,
Hg 1: 1 of Judah, Zerubbabel, *s* of Shealtiel,
1: 1 to the high priest Joshua, *s* of Jehozadak:
1:12 Then Zerubbabel, *s* of Shealtiel,
1:12 and the high priest Joshua, *s* of Jehozadak,
1:14 of Judah, Zerubbabel, *s* of Shealtiel,
1:14 of the high priest Joshua, *s* of Jehozadak,
2: 2 of Judah, Zerubbabel, *s* of Shealtiel,
2: 2 to the high priest Joshua, *s* of Jehozadak,
2: 4 Joshua, high priest, *s* of Jehozadak,
2:23 will take you, Zerubbabel, *s* of Shealtiel,
Zec 1: 1 Zechariah, son of Berechiah, *s* of Iddo:
1: 7 Zechariah, son of Berechiah, *s* of Iddo,
6:10 *s* of Zephaniah (these had come from
6:11 it on the head of [Joshua, *s* of Jehozadak,
6:14 Tobijah, Jedaiah, and the *s* of Zephaniah.
12:10 mourn for him as one mourns for an only *s*,
Mal 1: 6 A *s* honors his father,
3:17 compassion on his *s* who serves him.
Mt 1: 1 Jesus Christ, son of David, *s* of Abraham.
1:20 "Joseph, *s* of David, have no fear
1:21 She is to have a *s* and you are to name him
1:23 shall be with child and give birth to a *s*,
1:25 with her at any time before she bore a *s*,
2:15 "Out of Egypt I have called my *s*."
3:17 the heavens said, "This is my beloved *S*.
4: 3 and said to him, "If you are the *S* of God,
4: 6 and said, "If you are the *S* of God,
4:21 of two other brothers, James, Zebedee's *s*,
7: 9 hand his *s* a stone when he asks for a loaf,
8:20 the *S* of Man has nowhere to lay his head."
8:29 "Why meddle with us, *S* of God?
9: 2 said to the paralytic, "Have courage, *s*,
9: 6 To help you realize that the *S* of Man has
9:27 men came after him crying out, *S* of David,
10: 2 James, Zebedee's *s*,
10: 3 James, *s* of Alphaeus,
10:23 towns of Israel before the *S* of Man comes.
10:37 loves father or mother, *s* or daughter,
11:19 The *S* of Man appeared eating and drinking,
11:27 No one knows the *S* but the Father,
11:27 and no one knows the Father but the *S*—
12: 8 The *S* of Man is indeed Lord of the sabbath."
12:23 "Might this not be David's *s*?"
12:32 against the *S* of Man will be forgiven,
12:40 so will the *S* of Man spend three days and
13:37 farmer sowing good seed is the *S* of Man;
13:41 The *S* of Man will dispatch his angels to
13:55 Isn't this the carpenter's *s*?
14:33 "Beyond doubt you are the *S* of God!"
15:22 crying out to him, "Lord, *S* of David,
16:13 "Who do people say that the *S* of Man is?"
16:16 Peter answered, "the *S* of the living God!"
16:17 replied, "Blest are you, Simon *s* of Jonah!
16:27 The *S* of Man will come with his Father's
16:28 they see the *S* of Man come in his kingship."
17: 5 is my beloved *S* on whom my favor rests.
17: 9 until the *S* of Man rises from the dead."
17:12 The *S* of Man will suffer at their hands in
17:15 "Lord," he said, "take pity on my *s*,
17:22 "The *S* of Man is going to be delivered
19:28 in the new age when the *S* of Man takes his
20:18 There the *S* of Man will be handed over to
20:28 is the case with the *S* of Man who has come,
20:30 by, began to shout, "Lord, *S* of David,
20:31 shouted the louder, "Lord, *S* of David,
21: 9 "Hosanna to the *S* of David!
21:15 precincts, "Hosanna to the *S* of David!"
21:28 He approached the elder and said, *S*,
21:29 The *s* replied, 'I am on my way, sir';
21:30 to his second *s* and said the same thing.
21:30 This *s* said in reply, 'No, I will not';
21:37 Finally he sent his *s* to them,
21:37 to them, thinking, 'They will respect my *s*.'
21:38 When they saw the *s*, the tenants said
22: 2 king who gave a wedding banquet for his *s*.
22:42 Whose *s* is he?"
22:45 calls him 'lord,' how can he be his *s*?"
23:35 to the blood of Zechariah *s* of Barachiah,
24:27 so will the coming of the *S* of Man be.
24:30 of the *S* of Man will appear in the sky,
24:30 *S* of Man coming on the clouds
24:36 it, neither the angels in heaven nor the *S*,
24:37 The coming of the *S* of Man will repeat
24:39 will it be at the coming of the *S* of Man.
24:44 The *S* of Man is coming at the time you
25:31 "When the *S* of Man comes in his glory,
26: 2 and that the *S* of Man is to be handed over
26:24 The *S* of Man is departing,
26:24 that man by whom the *S* of Man is betrayed.
26:45 The hour is on us when the *S* of Man is to
26:63 whether you are the Messiah, the *S* of God."
26:64 Soon you will see the *S* of Man seated at
27:40 down off that cross if you are God's *S*!"
27:43 After all, he claimed, 'I am God's *S*.'"
27:54 and said, "Clearly this was the *S* of God!"
28:19 in the name of the Father, and of the *S*,
Mk 1: 1 the gospel of Jesus Christ, the *S* of God.
1:11 "You are my beloved *S*.
1:19 he caught sight of James, Zebedee's *s*,
2: 5 he said to the paralyzed man, "My *s*,
2:10 That you may know that the *S* of Man has
2:14 *s* of Alphaeus at his tax collector's post,
2:28 the *S* of Man is lord even of the sabbath."
3:11 feet, and shout, "You are the *S* of God!"
3:17 James, *s* of Zebedee;
3:18 Matthew, Thomas, James *s* of Alphaeus;
5: 7 meddle with me, Jesus, *S* of God Most High?
6: 3 Is this not the carpenter, the *s* of Mary,
8:31 them that the *S* of Man had to suffer much,
8:38 the *S* of Man will be ashamed of him when
9: 7 "This is my *S*, my beloved.
9: 9 the *S* of Man had risen from the dead.
9:12 Yet why does Scripture say of the *S* of Man
9:17 "I have brought my *s* to you because he is
9:31 "The *S* of Man is going to be delivered
10:33 where the *S* of Man will be handed over to
10:45 The *S* of Man has not come to be served but
10:46 a blind beggar Bartimaeus("*s* of Timaeus")
10:47 he began to call out, "Jesus, *S* of David,
10:48 but he shouted all the louder, *S* of David,
12: 6 the *s* whom he loved.
12: 6 thinking, 'They will have to respect my *s*.'
12:35 scribes claim, 'The Messiah is David's *s*'?
12:37 as 'Lord,' in what sense can he be his *s*?"
13:26 Then men will see the *S* of Man coming in
13:32 the angels in heaven nor even the *S*,
14:21 The *S* of Man is going the way the
14:21 that man by whom the *S* of Man is betrayed.
14:41 You will see that the *S* of Man is to be
14:61 you the Messiah, the *S* of the Blessed One?"
14:62 and you will see the *S* of Man seated at
15:39 "Clearly this man was the *S* of God!"
Lk 1:13 shall bear a *s* whom you shall name John.
1:31 and bear a *s* and give him the name Jesus.
1:32 and he will be called *S* of the Most High.
1:35 to be born will be called *S* of God.
1:36 kinswoman has conceived a *s* in her old age;
1:57 delivery arrived, she gave birth to a *s*.
2: 7 She gave birth to her first-born *s* and
2:48 *S*, why have you done this to us?

3: 2 to John s of Zechariah in the desert.
3:22 "You are my beloved S.
3:23 the son of Joseph, s of Heli,
3:24 son of Matthat, son of Levi, s of Melchi,
3:24 Melchi, son of Jannai, s of Joseph,
3:25 Joseph, s of Mattathias, son of Amos
3:25 son of Nahum, s of Esli, son of Naggai,
3:26 Esli, son of Naggai, s of Maath,
3:26 of Maath, son of Mattathias, s of Semein,
3:26 Semein, s of Josech, son of Joda, son
3:27 Joda, s of Joanan, son of Rhesa,
3:27 Rhesa, son of Zerubbabel, s of Shealtiel,
3:27 Shealtiel, s of Neri, son of Melchi,
3:28 Melchi, s of Addi, son of Cosam,
3:28 son of Cosam, son of Elmadam, s of Er,
3:29 son of Joshua, son of Eliezer, s of Jorim,
3:29 Jorim, son of Matthat, s of Levi,
3:30 son of Simeon, son of Judah, s of Joseph,
3:30 Joseph, son of Jonam, s of Eliakim,
3:31 son of Melea, son of Menna, s of Mattatha,
3:31 Mattatha, son of Nathan, s of David,
3:32 son of Jesse, son of Obed, s of Boaz,
3:32 Boaz, son of Sala, s of Nashon,
3:33 son of Amminadab, son of Admin, s of Arni,
3:33 son of Hezron, s of Perez, son of Judah,
3:34 son of Jacob, son of Isaac, s of Abraham,
3:34 Abraham, son of Terah, s of Nahor,
3:35 son of Serug, s of Reu, s of Peleg,
3:35 Peleg, son of Eber, s of Shelah,
3:36 son of Cainan, son of Arphaxad, s of Shem,
3:36 Shem, son of Noah, s of Lamech,
3:37 son of Methuselah, s of Enoch,
3:37 Methuselah, son of Enoch, s of Jared,
3:37 Jared, son of Mahalaleel, s of Cainan,
3:38 son of Enos, son of Seth, s of Adam,
3:38 Adam, s of God.
4: 3 said to him, "If you are the S of God,
4: 9 and said to him, "If you are the S of God,
4:22 They also asked, "Is not this Joseph's s?"
4:41 out as they did so, "You are the S of God!"
5:24 to make it clear to you that the S of Man
6: 5 "The S of Man is Lord even of the sabbath."
6:15 Matthew and Thomas, James s of Alphaeus,
6:16 Simon called the Zealot, Judas s of James,
6:22 your name as evil because of the S of Man.
7:12 out, the only s of a widowed mother.
7:34 S of Man came and he both ate and drank,
8:28 of his voice, "Jesus, S of God Most High,
9:22 "The S of Man," he said, "must first
9:26 the S of Man will be ashamed of him when
9:35 came a voice which said, "This is my S,
9:38 "Teacher, I beg you to look at my s;
9:41 Bring your s here to me."
9:44 the S of Man must be delivered into the
9:58 the S of Man has nowhere to lay his head."
10:22 No one knows the S except the Father and
10:22 Son—and anyone to whom the S
11:11 give his s a snake if he asks for a fish,
11:30 the S of Man be a sign for the present age.
12: 8 the S of Man will acknowledge him before
12:10 against the S of Man will be forgiven,
12:40 The S of Man will come when you least
12:53 be split against son and s against father,
14: 5 has a s or an ox and he falls into a pit,
15:13 Some days later this younger s collected
15:18 I no longer deserve to be called your s.
15:21 The s said to him, 'Father, I have sinned
15:21 I no longer deserve to be called your s.'
15:24 Let us eat and celebrate because this s
15:25 the elder s was out on the land.
15:28 s grew angry at this and would not go in;
15:30 when this s of yours returns after having
15:31 "'My s,' replied the father, 'you are
17:22 day of the S of Man but will not see it.
17:24 The S of Man in his day will be like the
17:26 so will it be in the days of the S of Man.
17:30 that on the day the S of Man is revealed.
18: 8 But when the S of Man comes,
18:31 the S of Man may be accomplished.
18:38 He shouted out, "Jesus, S of David,
18:39 but he cried out all the more, S of David,
19: 9 this is what it means to be a s of Abraham.
19:10 The S of Man has come to search out and
20:13 Perhaps if I send the s I love,
20:14 "But when the tenant farmers saw the s,
20:41 say that the Messiah is the s of David?
20:44 him the title 'lord,' how can he be his s?"
21:27 men will see the S of Man coming on a
21:36 and to stand secure before the S of Man."
22:22 The S of Man is following out his
22:48 would you betray the S of Man with a kiss?"
22:69 the S of Man will have his seat at the
22:70 "So you are the S of God?"
24: 7 that the S of Man must be delivered into
Jn 1:14 glory of an only S coming from the Father,
1:18 It is God the only S,
1:42 him and said, "You are Simon, s of John;
1:45 Jesus, s of Joseph,
1:49 said Nathanael, "you are the S of God;
1:51 ascending and descending on the S of Man."
3:13 the S of Man [who is in heaven].
3:14 desert, so must the S of Man be lifted up,
3:16 loved the world that he gave his only S,
3:17 the S into the world to condemn the world,
3:18 not believing in the name of God's only S.
3:35 the S and has given everything over to him.
3:36 Whoever believes in the S has life eternal.
3:36 Whoever disobeys the S will not see life,
4: 5 land which Jacob had given to his s Joseph.
4:46 to be a royal official whose s was ill.
4:47 to come down and restore health to his s,
4:50 Your s will live."
4:53 had told him, "Your s is going to live."
5:19 you, the S cannot do anything by himself
5:19 the Father does, the S does likewise.
5:20 For the Father loves the S and everything
5:21 S grants life to those to whom he wishes.
5:22 but has assigned all judgment to the S,
5:23 honor the S just as they honor the Father.
5:23 S refuses to honor the Father who sent him.
5:25 dead shall hear the voice of the S of God,
5:26 it to the S to have life in himself.
5:27 to pass judgment because he is S of Man;
6:27 food which the S of Man will give you;
6:40 everyone who looks upon the S
6:42 "Is this not Jesus, the s of Joseph?
6:53 flesh of the S of Man and drink his blood,
6:62 S of Man ascend to where he was before . . .
6:71 about Judas, s of Simon the Iscariot,
8:28 "When you lift up the S of Man,
8:35 but the s has a place there forever.)
8:36 That is why, if the s frees you,
9:19 "Is this your s?"
9:20 "We know this is our s,
9:35 him, "Do you believe in the S of Man?"
10:36 into the world, I said, 'I am God's S'?
11: 4 through it the S of God may be glorified."
11:27 that you are the Messiah, the S of God:
12:23 has come for the S of Man to be glorified.
12:34 claim that the S of Man must be lifted up?
12:34 Just who is this S of Man'?"
13: 2 already induced Judas, s of Simon Iscariot,
13:26 and gave it to Judas, s of Simon Iscariot.
13:31 "Now is the S of Man glorified and God is
14:13 do, so as to glorify the Father in the S.
17: 1 your Son that your S may give glory to you,
19: 7 must die because he made himself God's S."
19:26 to his mother, "Woman, there is your s."
20:31 that Jesus is the Messiah, the S of God,
21:15 said to Simon Peter, "Simon, s of John,
21:16 he put his question, "Simon, s of John,
21:17 time, Jesus asked him, "Simon, s of John,
Acts 1:13 James s of Alpheus;
1:13 Zealot party member, and Judas s of James.
4:36 Barnabas (meaning "s of encouragement")
7:21 him and brought him up as her own s.
7:56 the S of Man standing at God's right hand."
9:20 the synagogues that Jesus was the S of God.
13:10 s of Satan and enemy of all that is right!
13:21 for a king, God gave them Saul s of Kish,
13:22 'I have found David s of Jesse to be a man
13:33 written in the second psalm, 'You are my s;
20: 4 him were Sopater, s of Pyrrhus,
23:16 s of Paul's sister heard about the plot,
Rom 1: 3 the gospel concerning his S,
1: 4 but was made S of God in power
1: 9 preaching the gospel of his S
5:10 reconciled to him by the death of his S,
8: 3 Then God sent his S in the likeness of
8:29 to share the image of his S, that the Son
8:32 he who did not spare his own S
9: 9 at this time, and Sarah shall have a s."
1Cor 1: 9 he who called you to fellowship with his S,
4:17 my beloved and faithful s in the Lord.
15:28 finally, all has been subjected to the S,
2Cor 1:19 Timothy, and I preached to you as S of God,
Gal 1:16 by his favor chose to reveal his S to me,
2:20 but it is a life of faith in the S of God,
3:26 Each one of you is a s of God because of
4: 4 come, God sent forth his S born of a woman,
4: 6 the spirit of his S which cries out "Abba!"
4: 7 You are no longer a slave but a s!
4: 7 fact that you are a s makes you an heir,
4:23 The s of the slave girl had been begotten
4:23 but the s of the free woman was the fruit
4:29 But just as in those days the s born in
4:30 s together; for the slave girl's son
4:30 terms with the s" of the one born free.
Eph 4:13 in faith and in the knowledge of God's S,
Phil 2:22 how he was like a s at his father's side
Col 1:13 us into the kingdom of his beloved S.
1Thes 1:10 from heaven the S he raised from the dead
2Thes 2: 3 that s of perdition and adversary who
2Tm 2: 1 So you, my s, must be strong in the grace
Heb 1: 2 age, he has spoken to us through his S,
1: 3 S is the reflection of the Father's glory,
1: 5 angels did God ever say, "You are my s;
1: 5 will be his father, and he shall be my s"?
1: 8 but of the S, "Your throne, O God,
2: 6 the s of man that you should care for him?
3: 6 faithful as the S placed over God's house.
4:14 through the heavens, Jesus, the S of God,
5: 5 the One who said to him, "You are my s;
5: 8 S though he was, he learned obedience
6: 6 since they are crucifying the S of God for
7: 3 the S of God he remains a priest forever.
7:28 after the law appoints as priest the S,
10:29 is due the man who disdains the S of God,
11:17 was ready to sacrifice his only s,
11:24 be known as the s of Pharaoh's daughter;
12: 6 he scourges every s he receives."
12: 7 For what s is there whom his father does
Jas 2:21 when he offered his s Isaac on the altar?
1Pt 5:13 you, sends you greeting, as does Mark my s.
2Pt 1:17 "This is my beloved S,
2:15 off on the path taken by Balaam, s of Beor.
1Jn 1: 3 of ours is with the Father and with his S,
1: 7 of his S Jesus cleanses us from all sin.
2:22 antichrist, denying the Father and the S.
2:23 denies the S has no claim on the Father,
2:23 the S can claim the Father as well.
2:24 will remain in the S and in the Father,
3: 1 us is that it never recognized the S.
3: 7 is holy indeed, even as the S is holy.
3: 8 works that the S of God revealed himself.
3:23 we are to believe in the name of his S,
4: 9 he sent his only S to the world that we
4:10 has sent his S as an offering for our sins.
4:14 has sent the S as savior of the world.
4:15 acknowledges that Jesus is the S of God,
5: 5 who believes that Jesus is the S of God.
5:10 Whoever believes in the S of God possesses
5:11 us eternal life, and this life is in his S.
5:12 Whoever possesses the S possesses life;
5:12 possess the S of God does not possess life.
5:13 who believe in the name of the S of God.
5:20 that the S of God has come and has given
5:20 is true, for we are in his S Jesus Christ.
2Jn 1: 3 and from Jesus Christ, the Father's S.
1: 9 possesses both the Father and the S.
Rv 1:13 a S of Man wearing an ankle-length robe,
2:18 " 'The S of God, whose eyes blaze like fire
12: 5 She gave birth to a s—
14:14 on the cloud sat One like a S of Man
21: 7 I will be his God and he shall be my s.

SON-IN-LAW (13)

Jgs 15: 6 were told, "Samson, the s of the Timnite,
19: 5 But the girl's father said to his s,
1Sm 18:18 Israel that I should become the king's s?"
18:21 to David, "You shall become my s today."]
18:22 You should become the king's s."
18:23 you think it easy to become the king's s?
18:26 with the prospect of becoming the king's s.
18:27 that he might thus become the king's s.
22:14 is as loyal as David, the king's s,
Neh 6:18 with him, since he was the s of Shecaniah,
13:28 was the s of Sanballat the Horonite!
1Mc 10:54 as your s, I will give to you and to her
16:12 and gold, being the s of the high priest.

SONG (65)

Ex 15: 1 and the Israelites sang this s to the LORD:
Nm 21:17 Then it was that Israel sang this s:
Dt 31:19 Write out this s, then, for yourselves.
31:19 so that this s may be a witness for me
31:21 evils and troubles befall them, this s,
31:22 So Moses wrote this s that same day,
31:30 the words of this s from beginning to end,
32:44 the words of this s for the people to hear.
Jgs 5: 1 [and Barak, son of Abinoam,] sang this s:
5: 3 I to the LORD will sing my s,
5:12 awake, awake, strike up a s.
1Sm 18: 8 Saul was very angry and resentful of the s,
2Sm 22: 1 David sang the words of this s to the LORD
2Chr 23:18 in the law of Moses, with rejoicing and s,
29:27 began, they also began the s of the LORD,
29:28 and they continued to sing the s and to
Tb 12: 6 by blessing and extolling his name in s.
12:18 thank him every day; praise him with s.
Jdt 15:14 led all Israel in this s of thanksgiving,
16: 1 instruments, a s to my God with timbrels,
16: 1 Sing to him a new s,
Jb 36:24 his work, which men have praised in s.
Ps(s) 28: 7 exults, and with my s I give him thanks.
33: 3 Sing to him a new s;
40: 4 And he put a new s into my mouth,
42: 9 his grace, and at night I have his s,
69:31 I will praise the name of God in s,
96: 1 Sing to the LORD a new s;
98: 1 Sing to the LORD a new s,
98: 4 break into s;
98: 5 the harp, with the harp and melodious s.
100: 2 come before him with joyful s.
104:12 among the branches they send forth their s.
119:54 the theme of my s in the place of my exile.
137: 4 we sing a s of the LORD in a foreign land?
144: 9 O God, I will sing a new s to you;
149: 1 Sing to the LORD a new s of praise in
Eccl 7: 5 rebuke than to hearken to the s of fools;
12: 4 but all the daughters of s are suppressed;
Sg 1: 1 The s of songs by Solomon.
2:12 and the s of the dove is heard in our land.
Wis 17:18 s of birds in the spreading branches,
Sir 22: 6 s in time of mourning is inopportune talk,
47:17 With s and story and riddle,
Is 5: 1 my friend's s concerning his vineyard.
14: 7 earth rests peacefully, s breaks forth;

SONG (cont.)

23:15 be for Tyre as in the *s* about the harlot:
26: 1 they will sing this *s* in the land of Judah:
35: 2 flowers, and rejoice with joyful *s*.
38: 9 The *s* of Hezekiah,
42:10 Sing to the LORD a new *s*,
44:23 Break forth, you mountains, into *s*,
49:13 and rejoice, O earth, break forth into *s*,
51: 3 in her thanksgiving and the sound of *s*.
52: 9 Break out together in *s*,
54: 1 did not bear, break forth in jubilant *s*,
55:12 and hills shall break out in *s* before you,
Jer 25:10 end the song of joy and the *s* of gladness,
Lam 3:63 they sit or stand, see, I am their taunt *s*.
Gal 4:27 break into *s*,
Rv 15: 3 God, and they sang the *s* of Moses,
15: 3 the servant of God, and the *s* of the Lamb:
19: 1 the loud *s* of a great assembly in heaven.

SONGS (27)

1Sm 18: 6 and dancing, with tambourines, joyful *s*,
1Kgs 5:12 and his *s* numbered a thousand and five.
1Chr 13: 8 enthusiasm, amid *s* and music on lyres,
25: 1 as singers of inspired *s* to the
25: 2 inspired *s* under the guidance of the king.
25: 3 inspired *s* to the accompaniment of a lyre,
Ezr 3:11 *s* of praise and thanksgiving to the LORD,
Tb 2: 6 mourning, And all your *s* into lamentation."
1Mc 4:54 that very day it was reconsecrated with *s*,
13:47 the city with hymns and *s* of praise.
2Mc 12:37 cry in his ancestral language, and with *s*,
15:25 to the sound of trumpets and battle *s*.
Ps(s) 69:13 and drunkards make me the butt of their *s*.
137: 3 captors asked of us the lyrics of our *s*,
137: 3 "Sing for us the *s* of Zion!"
Sg 1: 1 The song of *s* by Solomon.
Is 23:16 Pluck the strings skillfully, sing many *s*,
24:16 From the end of the earth we hear *s*:
Jer 30:19 From them will resound *s* of praise,
Ez 26:13 I will put an end to the noise of your *s*,
Am 5:23 Away with your noisy *s*!
8: 3 temple *s* shall become wailings on that day,
8:10 mourning and all your *s* into lamentations.
Mt 26:30 Then, after singing *s* of praise,
Mk 14:26 After singing *s* of praise,
Eph 5:19 another in psalms and hymns and inspired *s*.
Col 3:16 hearts in psalms, hymns, and inspired *s*.

SONGSTRESSES (1)

2Sm 19:36 appreciate the voices of singers and *s*?

SONS—SON'S (1161)

Gn 5: 4 of Seth, and he had other *s* and daughters.
5: 7 of Enosh, and he had other *s* and daughters.
5:10 of Kenan, and he had other *s* and daughters.
5:13 and he had other *s* and daughters.
5:16 of Jared, and he had other *s* and daughters.
5:19 of Enoch, and he had other *s* and daughters.
5:22 and he had other *s* and daughters.
5:26 Lamech, and he had other *s* and daughters.
5:30 of Noah, and he had other *s* and daughters.
6: 2 the *s* of heaven saw how beautiful the
6: 4 after the *s* of heaven had intercourse with
6: 4 with the daughters of man, who bore them *s*.
6:10 age, for he walked with God, begot three *s*:
6:18 and your sons, your wife and your *s*' wives,
7: 7 with his sons, his wife, and his *s*' wives,
7:13 the precise day named, Noah and his *s* Shem,
7:13 wives of Noah's *s* had entered the ark,
8:16 your wife and your *s* and your sons' wives.
8:18 his wife and his sons and his *s*' wives;
9: 1 blessed Noah and his *s* and said to them:
9: 8 God said to Noah and to his *s* with him:
9:18 The *s* of Noah who came out of the ark were
9:19 These three were the *s* of Noah,
10: 1 sons, Shem, Ham, and Japheth, to whom *s*
10:21 of all the children of Eber, *s* were born.
10:25 To Eber two *s* were born:
10:32 These are the groupings of Noah's *s*,
11:11 and he had other *s* and daughters.
11:13 Shelah, and he had other *s* and daughters.
11:15 of Eber, and he had other *s* and daughters.
11:17 of Peleg, and he had other *s* and daughters.
11:19 of Reu, and he had other *s* and daughters.
11:21 of Serug, and he had other *s* and daughters.
11:23 of Nahor, and he had other *s* and daughters.
11:25 of Terah, and he had other *s* and daughters.
16: 2 perhaps I shall have *s* through her."
18:19 singled him out that he may direct his *s*
19:12 Your *s* [sons-in-law] and your daughters
22:20 "Milcah too has borne *s*,
25: 6 To his *s* by concubinage,
25: 9 His *s* Isaac and Ishmael buried him in the
25:13 These are the names of Ishmael's *s*,
25:16 These are the *s* of Ishmael,
27:18 "Which of my *s* are you?"
27:29 and may your mother's *s* bow down to you.
27:31 "Please, father, eat some of your *s* game,
29:34 me, since I have now borne him three *s*";
30:14 let me have some of your *s* mandrakes."
30:15 that you must now take my *s* mandrakes too?"
30:15 "In exchange for your *s* mandrakes,
30:16 I have paid for you with my *s* mandrakes."
30:20 now that I have borne him six *s*";
30:35 in charge of his *s*.
31: 1 Jacob learned that Laban's *s* were saying,
34: 5 but since his *s* were out in the fields
34: 7 Jacob's *s* were coming in from the fields.
34:13 Jacob's *s* replied to Shechem and his
34:25 Simeon and Levi, two of Jacob's *s*,
34:27 Then the other *s* of Jacob followed up the
35: 5 so that no one pursued the *s* of Jacob.
35:22 The *s* of Jacob were now twelve.
35:23 The *s* of Leah:
35:24 the *s* of Rachel:
35:25 the *s* of Rachel's maid Bilhah:
35:26 the *s* of Leah's maid Zilpah:
35:26 These are the *s* of Jacob who were born to
35:29 His *s* Esau and Jacob buried him.
36: 5 These are the *s* of Esau who were born to
36: 6 Esau took his wives, his *s*,
36:10 These are the names of Esau's *s*;
36:11 The *s* of Eliphaz were Teman,
36:13 The *s* of Reuel were Nahath,
37: 2 *s* of his father's wives Bilhah and Zilpah,
37: 3 Israel loved Joseph best of all his *s*,
37: 4 their father loved him best of all his *s*,
37:32 See whether it is your *s* tunic or not."
37:33 "My *s* tunic!
37:35 his *s* and daughters tried to console him,
41:50 set in, Joseph became the father of two *s*,
42: 1 were available in Egypt, he said to his *s*:
42: 5 the *s* of Israel were among those who came
42:11 All of us are *s* of the same man.
42:13 brothers, *s* of a certain man in Canaan;
42:32 of us brothers, *s* of the same father;
42:37 my own two *s* if I do not return him to you."
44:27 to us, 'As you know, my wife bore me two *s*.
45:21 The *s* of Israel acted accordingly.
46: 5 and the *s* of Israel put their father and
46: 7 His *s* and his grandsons,
46: 9 Jacob's first-born, and the *s* of Reuben:
46:10 The *s* of Simeon:
46:11 The *s* of Levi:
46:12 The *s* of Judah:
46:12 and the *s* of Perez were Hezron and Hamul.
46:13 The *s* of Issachar:
46:14 The *s* of Zebulun:
46:15 *s* whom Leah bore to Jacob in Paddan-aram,
46:16 The *s* of Gad:
46:17 The *s* of Asher:
46:17 and the *s* of Beriah:
46:19 The *s* of Jacob's wife Rachel:
46:21 The *s* of Benjamin:
46:22 These were the *s* whom Rachel bore to Jacob
46:23 The *s* of Dan:
46:24 The *s* of Naphtali:
46:25 These were the *s* of Bilhah,
46:26 not counting the wives of Jacob's *s*—
46:27 Joseph's *s* who were born to him in Egypt
47: 5 Jacob and his *s* came to Joseph in Egypt,
48: 1 So he took along with him his two *s*,
48: 5 Your two *s*, therefore, who were born
48: 8 When Israel saw Joseph's *s*,
48: 9 "They are my *s*," Joseph answered
48:10 When Joseph brought his *s* close to him,
49: 1 Jacob called his *s* and said:
49: 2 "Assemble and listen, *s* of Jacob,
49: 8 the *s* of your father shall bow down to you.
49:33 giving these instructions to his *s*,
50:12 *s* did for him as he had instructed them.
50:25 Then, putting the *s* of Israel under oath,
Ex 1: 1 These are the names of the *s* of Israel who,
3:22 clothing to put on your *s* and daughters.
4:20 So Moses took his wife and his *s*,
4:25 of flint and cut off her *s* foreskin and,
6:14 The *s* of Reuben, the first-born of Israel,
6:15 The *s* of Simeon were Jenuel,
6:16 The names of the *s* of Levi,
6:17 The *s* of Gershon, as heads of clans,
6:18 The *s* of Kohath were Amram,
6:19 The *s* of Merari were Mahli and Mushi.
6:21 The *s* of Izhar were Korah,
6:22 The *s* of Uzziel were Mishael,
6:24 The *s* of Korah were Assir,
10: 9 "our *s* and daughters as well as our
13:15 and why I redeem every first-born of my *s*.'
18: 3 Moses had sent back to him, and her two *s*.
18: 5 Together with Moses' wife and *s*,
18: 6 to you, along with your wife and her two *s*."
21: 4 a wife and she bears him *s* or daughters,
22:28 You shall give me the first-born of your *s*.
27:21 From evening to morning Aaron and his *s*
28: 1 brother Aaron, together with his *s* Nadab,
28: 4 his *s* are to wear in serving as my priests,
28: 9 on them the names of the *s* of Israel;
28:11 engraved with the names of the *s* of Israel
28:12 as memorial stones of the *s* of Israel.
28:21 them to match the names of the *s* of Israel,
28:29 bear the names of the *s* of Israel
28:40 glorious adornment of Aaron's *s*
28:41 shall clothe your brother Aaron and his *s*.
28:43 Aaron and his *s* shall wear them whenever
29: 4 Aaron and his *s* you shall also bring to
29: 8 his *s* also and clothe them with the tunics,
29: 9 and thus shall you ordain Aaron and his *s*.
29:10 his *s* shall lay their hands on its head.
29:15 his *s* have laid their hands on its head,
29:19 his *s* have laid their hands on its head,
29:20 tips of his *s*' right ears
29:21 *s* and their vestments, that his sons
29:24 put into the hands of Aaron and his *s*,
29:27 else belonging to Aaron or to his *s*.
29:28 Such things are due to Aaron and his *s*
29:32 Aaron and his *s* shall eat the flesh
29:35 and his *s* just as I have given them to you.
29:44 Aaron and his *s* to be my priests.
30:19 Aaron and his *s* shall use it in washing
30:30 Aaron and his *s* you shall also anoint and
31:10 the vestments for his *s* in their ministry,
32: 2 "Have your wives and *s* and daughters take
32:29 you were against your own *s* and kinsmen,
34:16 take their daughters as wives for your *s*;
34:16 gods, they will make your *s* do the same.
34:20 first-born among your *s* you shall redeem.
35:19 vestments worn by his *s* in their ministry."
39: 6 with the names of the *s* of Israel.
39: 7 as memorial stones of the *s* of Israel,
39:14 to match the names of the *s* of Israel,
39:27 For Aaron and his *s* there were also woven
39:41 to be worn by his *s* in their ministry.
40:12 his *s* to the entrance of the meeting tent,
40:14 Bring forward his *s* also,
40:31 *s* used to wash their hands and feet there,
Lv 1: 5 the bull before the LORD, but Aaron's *s*,
1: 7 After Aaron's *s*, the priests, have put
1:11 Then Aaron's *s*, the priests, shall splash
2: 2 When he has brought it to Aaron's *s*,
2: 3 cereal offering belongs to Aaron and his *s*.
2:10 cereal offering belongs to Aaron and his *s*.
3: 2 but Aaron's *s*,
3: 5 All this Aaron's *s* shall then burn on the
3: 8 but Aaron's *s* shall splash its blood on
3:13 but Aaron's *s* shall splash its blood on
6: 2 Aaron and his *s* the following command:
6: 7 *s* shall first present it before the LORD,
6: 9 The rest of it Aaron and his *s* may eat;
6:13 offering that Aaron and his *s* shall present
6:18 LORD said to Moses, "Tell Aaron and his *s*:
7:10 to all of Aaron's *s* without distinction.
7:31 but the breast belongs to Aaron and his *s*.
7:34 and to his *s* by a perpetual ordinance as a
7:35 allotted to Aaron and his *s* on the day he
8: 2 said to Moses, "Take Aaron and his *s*,
8: 6 Bringing forward Aaron and his *s*,
8:13 Moses likewise brought forward Aaron's *s*,
8:14 and his *s* laid their hands on its head.
8:18 and his *s* laid their hands on its head.
8:22 and his *s* laid their hands on its head.
8:24 Moses had the *s* of Aaron also come forward,
8:27 things into the hands of Aaron and his *s*,
8:30 as well as his *s* and their vestments,
8:30 vestments and his *s* and their vestments.
8:31 Finally, Moses said to Aaron and his *s*,
8:31 'Aaron and his *s* shall eat of it.'
8:36 So Aaron and his *s* did all that the LORD
9: 1 eighth day Moses summoned Aaron and his *s*,
9: 9 When his *s* presented the blood to him,
9:12 When his *s* brought him the blood,
9:18 When his *s* brought him the blood,
10: 1 *s* Nadab and Abihu took their censers and,
10: 4 Elzaphan, the *s* of Aaron's uncle Uzziel,
10: 6 to Aaron and his *s* Eleazar and Ithamar,
10: 9 your *s* are forbidden under pain of death,
10:12 Moses said to Aaron and his surviving *s*,
10:13 oblations of the LORD, and that of your *s*;
10:14 With your *s* and daughters you shall also
10:16 he was angry with the surviving *s* of Aaron,
16: 1 After the death of Aaron's two *s*,
17: 2 to Moses, "Speak to Aaron and his *s*,
18:10 not have intercourse with your *s* daughter
18:15 she is your *s* wife,
18:17 her *s* daughter or her daughter's daughter;
21: 1 LORD said to Moses, "Speak to Aaron's *s*,
21:24 Aaron and his *s* and to all the Israelites.
22: 2 "Tell Aaron and his *s* to respect the
22:18 Aaron and his *s* and to all the Israelites,
24: 9 It shall belong to Aaron and his *s*,
25:46 to your *s* as their hereditary property,
26:29 eat the flesh of your own *s* and daughters.
Nm 3: 2 The *s* of Aaron were Nadab his first-born,
3: 3 These are the names of the *s* of Aaron,
3: 4 in the presence of the LORD, and left no *s*.
3: 9 shall give the Levites to Aaron and his *s*;
3:17 The *s* of Levi were named Gershon,
3:38 camped Moses and Aaron and the latter's *s*.
3:48 and his *s* as ransom for the extra number."
3:51 gave this ransom silver to Aaron and his *s*,
4: 5 Aaron and his *s* shall go in and take down
4:15 "Only after Aaron and his *s* have finished
4:19 Aaron and his *s* shall go in and assign to
4:27 under the direction of Aaron and his *s*,
6:23 "Speak to Aaron and his *s* and tell them:
8:13 the Levites stand before Aaron and his *s*
8:19 his *s* to discharge the duties
8:22 under the supervision of Aaron and his *s*.
10: 8 "It is the *s* of Aaron, the priests,

16: 1 Levi, [and Dathan and Abiram, *s* of Eliab,
16:12 summoned Dathan and Abiram, *s* of Eliab,
16:27 with their wives and *s* and little ones,
18: 1 "You and your *s* as well as the other
18: 1 shall rest on you and your *s* alone.
18: 2 while you and your *s* are in front of the
18: 7 But only you and your *s* are to have charge
18: 8 you and to your *s* as your priestly share.
18: 9 shares shall accrue to you and to your *s*.
18:11 it to you and to your *s* and daughters.
18:19 your *s* and daughters all the contributions
21:29 He let his *s* become fugitives and his
21:35 him down with his *s* and all his people,
26:19 The *s* of Judah who died in the land of
26:28 The *s* of Joseph were Manasseh and Ephraim.
26:33 Zelophehad, son of Hepher, had no *s*,
27: 3 died for his own sin without leaving any *s*.
Dt 1:36 to his *s* I will give the land he trod upon,
2:33 defeated him and his *s* and all his people.
7: 3 *s* nor taking their daughters for your sons.
7: 3 sons nor taking their daughters for your *s*.
7: 4 *s* from following me to serving other gods,
11: 6 Reubenites Dathan and Abiram, *s* of Eliab,
12:12 LORD, your God, with your *s* and daughters,
12:31 their *s* and daughters to their gods.
18: 5 has chosen him and his *s* out of all your
21:15 and if both bear him *s*,
21:16 bequeath his property to his *s*
28:32 Your *s* and daughters will be given to a
28:41 Though you beget *s* and daughters,
28:53 of your own *s* and daughters whom the LORD,
32: 8 peoples after the number of the *s* of God;
32:19 and anger toward his *s* and daughters.
32:20 race they are, *s* with no loyalty in them!
33:24 "More blessed than the other *s* be Asher!
Jos 7:24 bar of gold, and with his *s* and daughters,
16: 4 of Manasseh and Ephraim, *s* of Joseph,
17: 3 of Machir, son of Manasseh, had had no *s*,
17: 6 received each a portion among his *s*.
24:32 Jacob had bought from the *s* of Hamor,
Jgs 1:20 who then drove from it the three *s* of Anak.
3: 6 their own daughters to their *s* in marriage,
8:19 "They were my brothers, my mother's *s*,"
8:22 you, your son, and your *s* son
8:30 Now Gideon had seventy *s*,
9: 2 that seventy men, or all Jerubbaal's *s*,
9: 5 his brothers, the seventy *s* of Jerubbaal,
9:18 have killed his seventy *s* upon one stone,
9:24 repay the violence done to the seventy *s*
10: 4 He had thirty *s* who rode on thirty
11: 2 Gilead's wife had also borne him *s*,
11: 2 the *s* of the wife had driven Jephthah away,
12: 9 He had thirty *s*.
12: 9 brought in as wives for his *s*
12:14 He had forty *s* and thirty grandsons who
17: 5 idols, and consecrated one of his *s*,
17:11 man, to whom he became as one of his own *s*.
Ru 1: 1 and two *s* to reside on the plateau of Moab.
1: 2 wife Naomi, and his *s* Mahlon and Chilion;
1: 3 died, and she was left with her two *s*,
1: 5 with neither her two *s* nor her husband.
1:11 *s* in my womb who may become your husbands
1:12 if tonight I had a husband
1:13 of husbands until those *s* grew up?
4:15 She is worth more to you than seven *s*!"
1Sm 1: 3 to him at Shiloh, where the two *s* of Eli,
1: 4 Peninnah and to all her *s* and daughters,
1: 8 Am I not more to you than ten *s*?"
2: 5 The barren wife bears seven *s*,
2:12 Now the *s* of Eli were wicked;
2:21 birth to three more *s* and two daughters,
2:22 he heard repeatedly how his *s* were
2:24 No, my *s*, you must not do these things!
2:29 do you honor your *s* in preference to me,
2:34 a sign in what will happen to your two *s*,
3:13 though he knew his *s* were blaspheming God,
4: 4 The two *s* of Eli, Hophni and Phinehas,
4:11 ark of God was captured, and Eli's two *s*,
4:17 Your two *s*, Hophni and Phinehas,
8: 1 Samuel appointed his *s* judges over Israel.
8: 3 His *s* did not follow his example but
8: 5 old, and your *s* do not follow your example,
8:11 He will take your *s* and assign them to his
12: 2 I am old and gray, and have *s* among you.
12: 8 When Jacob and his *s* went to Egypt and the
14:49 The *s* of Saul were Jonathan,
14:51 and Ner, Abner's father, were *s* of Abiel.
16: 1 for I have chosen my king from among his *s*."
16: 5 He also had Jesse and his *s* cleanse
16:10 way Jesse presented seven *s* before Samuel,
16:11 Jesse, "Are these all the *s* you have?"
16:18 "I have observed that one of the *s* of
17:12 He had eight *s*, and in the days
17:13 oldest *s* of Jesse had followed Saul to war;
17:13 three *s* who had gone off to war were named,
28:19 By tomorrow you and your *s* will be with me,
30: 3 their wives, *s* and daughters taken captive.
30: 6 over the fate of their *s* and daughters.
30:19 small or great, booty or *s* or daughters,
31: 2 Philistines pursued Saul and his *s* closely,
31: 2 Abinadab, and Malchishua, *s* of Saul.
31: 6 Thus Saul, his three *s*,
31: 7 had fled and that Saul and his *s* were dead,
31: 8 Saul and his three *s* lying on Mount Gilboa.
31:12 Saul and his *s* from the wall of Beth-shan,
2Sm 2:18 The three *s* of Zeruiah were there
3: 2 *S* were born to David in Hebron:
3:39 this day, and these men, the *s* of Zeruiah,
4: 3 and Rechab, *s* of Rimmon the Beerothite
4: 5 The *s* of Rimmon the Beerothite,
4: 9 brother Baanah, *s* of Rimmon the Beerothite:
5:13 and more *s* and daughters were born to him
6: 3 Uzzah and Ahio, *s* of Abinadab,
8:18 And David's *s* were priests.
9:10 *s* and servants must till the land for him.
9:10 who had fifteen *s* and twenty servants,
9:11 at David's table like one of the king's *s*.
14: 6 Your servant had two *s*,
14:27 Absalom had three *s* born to him,
15:27 city in peace, and both your *s* with you,
16:10 is it of mine or of yours, *s* of Zeruiah,
19: 6 your life and your *s*' and daughters' lives,
19:18 by his fifteen *s* and twenty servants,
19:23 has come between you and me, *s* of Zeruiah,
21: 8 the two *s* that Aiah's daughter Rizpah had
21: 8 and the five *s* of Saul's daughter Merob
1Kgs 1: 9 invited all his brothers, the king's *s*,
1:19 he has invited all the king's *s*,
1:25 he invited all the king's *s*,
1:48 this day seated one of my *s* upon my throne,
2: 4 'If your *s* so conduct themselves that they
2: 7 kind to the *s* of Barzillai the Gileadite,
4: 3 Elihoreph and Ahijah, *s* of Shisha,
11:20 where he then lived with Pharaoh's own *s*.
11:35 kingdom from his *s* and will give it to you
13:11 whose *s* came and told him all that the man
13:12 And his *s* pointed out to him the road
13:13 Then he said to his *s*,
13:27 Then he said to his *s*,
13:31 After he had buried him, he said to his *s*,
18:31 for the number of tribes of the *s* of Jacob,
20: 3 your wives and your promising *s* are mine.'"
20: 5 silver and gold, your wives and your *s*.
20: 7 When he sent to me for my wives and *s*
2Kgs 9:26 blood of Naboth and the blood of his *s*,'
10: 2 "Since your master's *s* are with you,"
10: 6 count the heads of your master's *s* and
10:30 your *s* to the fourth generation shall sit
17:17 immolated their *s* and daughters by fire,
17:41 And their *s* and grandsons,
19:37 his *s* Adrammelech and Sharezer slew him
23:10 *s* or daughters by fire in honor of Molech.
25: 7 He had Zedekiah's *s* slain before his eyes.
1Chr 1:19 Two *s* were born to Eber;
1:23 all these were the *s* of Joktan.
1:28 The *s* of Abraham were Isaac and Ishmael.
1:32 The *s* of Jokshan were Sheba and Dedan.
1:34 The *s* of Isaac were Esau and Israel.
1:35 The *s* of Esau were Eliphaz,
1:36 The *s* of Eliphaz were Teman,
1:37 The *s* of Reuel were Nahath,
1:39 The *s* of Lotan were Hori and Homam;
1:40 The *s* of Shobal were Alian,
1:40 The *s* of Zibeon were Aiah and Anah.
1:41 The *s* of Anah:
1:41 The *s* of Dishon were Hemdan,
1:42 The *s* of Ezer were Bilhan,
1:42 The *s* of Dishan were Uz and Aran.
2: 1 These were the *s* of Israel:
2: 3 The *s* of Judah were:
2: 4 and Zerah, so that he had five *s* in all.
2: 5 The *s* of Perez were Hezron and Hamul.
2: 6 The *s* of Zerah were Zimri,
2: 7 The *s* of Zimri: Carmi.
2: 7 The *s* of Carmi: Achar, who brought
2: 8 The *s* of Ethan:
2: 9 The *s* born to Hezron were Jerahmeel,
2:16 Zeruiah had three *s*:
2:18 Her *s* were Jesher, Shobab, and Ardon.
2:23 all, which had belonged to the *s* of Machir,
2:25 The *s* of Jerahmeel,
2:27 The *s* of Ram,
2:28 The *s* of Onam were Shammai and Jada.
2:28 The *s* of Shammai were Nadab and Abishur.
2:30 The *s* of Nadab were Seled and Appaim.
2:30 Seled died without *s*.
2:31 The *s* of Appaim:
2:31 The *s* of Ishi:
2:31 The *s* of Sheshan:
2:32 The *s* of Jada,
2:32 Jether died without *s*.
2:33 The *s* of Jonathan were Peleth and Zaza.
2:34 Sheshan, who had no *s*,
2:42 Then the *s* of Mareshah,
2:43 The *s* of Hebron were Korah,
2:47 The *s* of Jahdai were Regem,
2:50 These were descendants of Caleb, *s* of Hur,
2:52 The *s* of Shobal,
3: 1 *s* of David who were born to him in Hebron:
3: 9 All these were *s* of David,
3: 9 in addition to other *s* by concubines;
3:15 The *s* of Josiah were:
3:16 The *s* of Jehoiakim were:
3:17 The *s* of Jeconiah the captive were:
3:19 *s* of Pedaiah were Zerubbabel and Shimei.
3:19 The *s* of Zerubbabel were Meshullam and
3:20 The *s* of Meshullam were Hashubah,
3:21 The *s* of Hananiah were Pelatiah,
3:22 The *s* of Shecaniah were Shemiah,
3:23 The *s* of Neariah were Elioenai,
3:24 The *s* of Elioenai were Hodaviah,
4: 7 The *s* of Helah were Zereth,
4:13 The *s* of Kenaz were Othniel and Seraiah.
4:13 *s* of Othniel were Hathath and Meonothai;
4:15 The *s* of Caleb, son of Jephunneh,
4:15 The *s* of Elah were . . .
4:16 The *s* of Jehallelel were Ziph,
4:17 The *s* of Ezrah were Jether,
4:18 These were the *s* of Bithiah,
4:19 The *s* of his Jewish wife,
4:20 The *s* of Shimon were Amnon,
4:24 The *s* of Simeon were Nemuel,
4:27 Shimei had sixteen *s* and six daughters.
4:27 brothers, however, did not have many *s*,
4:42 Neariah, Rephaiah, and Uzziel, *s* of Ishi.
5: 1 The *s* of Reuben, the first-born of Israel.
5: 1 birthright was given to the *s* of Joseph,
5: 3 The *s* of Reuben, the first-born of Israel,
5:14 These were the *s* of Abihail,
5:27 The *s* of Levi were Gershon,
5:28 The *s* of Kohath were Amram,
5:29 The *s* of Aaron were Nadab,
6: 1 The *s* of Levi were Gershon,
6: 2 *s* of Gershon were named Libni and Shimei.
6: 3 The *s* of Kohath were Amram,
6: 4 The *s* of Merari were Mahli and Mushi.
6:10 The *s* of Elkanah were Amasai and Ahimoth,
6:13 The *s* of Samuel were Joel,
7: 1 The *s* of Issachar were Tola,
7: 2 The *s* of Tola were Uzzi,
7: 3 The *s* of Uzzi:
7: 3 The *s* of Izarahiah were Michael,
7: 4 wives and *s* than their fellow tribesmen.
7: 6 The *s* of Benjamin were Bela,
7: 7 The *s* of Bela were Ezbon,
7: 8 The *s* of Becher were Zemirah,
7: 8 all these were *s* of Becher.
7:10 The *s* of Jediael:
7:10 The *s* of Bilhan were Jeush,
7:12 The *s* of Dan:
7:13 The *s* of Naphtali were Jahziel,
7:16 named Sheresh, whose *s* were Ulam and Rakem
7:17 The *s* of Ulam:
7:19 The *s* of Shemida were Ahian,
7:20 The *s* of Ephraim:
7:30 The *s* of Asher were Imnah,
7:31 Beriah's *s* were Heber and Malchiel,
7:33 The *s* of Japhlet were Pasach,
7:33 these were the *s* of Japhlet.
7:34 The *s* of Shomer were Ahi,
7:35 The *s* of his brother Hotham were Zophah,
7:36 The *s* of Zophah were Suah,
7:38 The *s* of Jether were Jephunneh,
7:39 The *s* of Ulla were Arah,
8: 3 The *s* of Bela were Addar and Gera,
8: 4 The *s* of Ehud were Abishua,
8: 6 These were the *s* of Ehud,
8:10 These were his *s*, family heads.
8:12 The *s* of Elpaal were Eber,
8:16 Ishpah, and Joha were the *s* of Beriah.
8:18 Izliah, and Jobab were the *s* of Elpaal.
8:21 and Shimrath were the *s* of Shimei,
8:25 Iphdeiah, and Penuel were the *s* of Shashak.
8:27 Elijah, and Zichri were the *s* of Jeroham.
8:35 The *s* of Micah were Pithon,
8:38 Azel had six *s*, whose names were
8:38 all these were the *s* of Azel.
8:39 The *s* of Eshek, his brother, were Ulam,
8:40 The *s* of Ulam were combat archers,
8:40 and many were their *s* and grandsons:
9: 5 were Asaiah, the first-born, and his *s*.
9:23 Thus they and their *s* kept guard over the
9:30 It was the *s* of priests,
9:41 The *s* of Micah were Pithon,
9:44 Azel had six *s*, whose names were
9:44 these were the *s* of Azel.
10: 2 pressed hard after Saul and his *s*.
10: 2 Abinadab, and Malchishua, *s* of Saul,
10: 6 Thus, with Saul and his three *s*,
10: 7 that Saul and his *s* had died in the rout,
10: 8 *s* where they had fallen on Mount Gilboa.
10:12 recovered the bodies of Saul and his *s*
11:22 He killed the two *s* of Ariel of Moab,
11:44 Shama and Jeiel, *s* of Hotham,
11:46 Jeribai and Joshaviah, *s* of Elnaam;
12: 3 with Joash, both *s* of Shemaah of Gibeah;
12: 3 also Jeziel and Pelet, *s* of Azmaveth;
12: 8 finally, and Zebadiah, *s* of Jeroham,
14: 3 became the father of more *s* and daughters.
15: 4 together the *s* of Aaron and the Levites:
15: 5 of the *s* of Kohath, Uriel, their chief,
15: 6 of the *s* of Merari, Asaiah, their chief,
15: 7 of the *s* of Gershon, Joel, their chief,
15: 8 of the *s* of Elizaphan, Shemaiah,
15: 9 of his brethren, of the *s* of Hebron,
15:10 of the *s* of Uzziel,
15:17 and among the *s* of Merari,
16:13 of Israel, his servants, *s* of Jacob,
16:42 The *s* of Jeduthun kept the gate.

SONS—SON'S (cont.)
17:11 after you who will be one of your own *s*,
18:17 *s* were the chief assistants to the king.
21:20 the king, and his four *s* who were with him,
23: 6 into classes according to the *s* of Levi:
23: 8 The *s* of Ladan:
23: 9 The *s* of Shimei were Shelomoth,
23:10 The *s* of Shimei were Jahath,
23:10 these were the *s* of Shimei,
23:11 but Jeush and Beriah had not many *s*,
23:12 The *s* of Kohath:
23:13 The *s* of Amram were Aaron and Moses.
23:13 as most holy, he and his *s* forever,
23:14 his *s* were counted as part of the tribe of
23:15 The *s* of Moses were Gershom and Eliezer.
23:16 The *s* of Gershom:
23:17 The *s* of Eliezer were Rehabiah the chief
23:17 Eliezer had no other *s*, but the sons
23:18 The *s* of Izhar:
23:19 The *s* of Hebron:
23:20 The *s* of Uzziel:
23:21 The *s* of Merari:
23:21 The *s* of Mahli:
23:22 no sons, only daughters; the *s* of Kish,
23:23 The *s* of Mushi:
23:24 These were the *s* of Levi according to
23:28 duty shall be to assist the *s* of Aaron
23:32 tent, the sanctuary, and the *s* of Aaron,
24: 1 The *s* of Aaron were Nadab,
24: 2 died before their father, leaving no *s*;
24:28 of Mahli were Eleazar, who had no *s*,
25: 2 Of the *s* of Aspah:
25: 2 Nethaniah, and Asharelah, *s* of Aspah,
25: 3 Of Jeduthun, these *s* of Jeduthun:
25: 4 Of Heman, these *s* of Heman:
25: 5 All these were the *s* of Heman,
25: 5 gave Heman fourteen *s* and three daughters.
25: 9 he and his *s* and his brethren were twelve.
25: 9 he and his brethren and his *s* were twelve.
25:10 The third was Zaccur, his *s*,
25:11 The fourth fell to Izri, his *s*,
25:12 The fifth was Nethaniah, his *s*,
25:13 The sixth was Bukkiah, his *s*,
25:14 The seventh was Jesarelah, his *s*,
25:15 The eighth was Jeshaiah, his *s*,
25:16 The ninth was Mattaniah, his *s*,
25:17 The tenth was Shimei, his *s*,
25:18 The eleventh was Uzziel, his *s*,
25:19 The twelfth fell to Hashabiah, his *s*,
25:20 The thirteenth was Shubael, his *s*,
25:21 The fourteenth was Mattithiah, his *s*,
25:22 The fifteenth fell to Jeremoth, his *s*,
25:23 The sixteenth fell to Hananiah, his *s*,
25:24 seventeenth fell to Joshbekashah, his *s*,
25:25 The eighteenth fell to Hanani, his *s*,
25:26 The nineteenth fell to Mallothi, his *s*,
25:27 The twentieth fell to Eliathah, his *s*,
25:28 The twenty-first fell to Hothir, his *s*,
25:29 The twenty-second fell to Giddalti, his *s*,
25:30 The twenty-third fell to Mahazioth, his *s*,
25:31 twenty-fourth fell to Romamti-ezer, his *s*,
26: 1 the son of Kore, one of the *s* of Abiasaph.
26: 2 Meshelemiah's *s*:
26: 4 Obed-edom's *s*:
26: 6 were born *s* who ruled over their family,
26: 7 The *s* of Shemaiah were Othni,
26: 8 *s* of Obed-edom, who together with their *s*
26: 9 Of Meshelemiah, eighteen *s* and brethren,
26:10 Hosah, a descendant of Merari, had these *s*:
26:11 the *s* and brethren of Hosah were thirteen.
26:15 south side, and to his *s* the storehouse.
26:29 Chenaniah and his *s* were in charge of
27:10 from Beth-phelet, of the *s* of Ephraim,
27:20 for the *s* of Ephraim,
27:32 of Hachmoni, were tutors of the king's *s*.
28: 1 king's estates and possessions, and his *s*,
28: 4 and finally, among all the *s* of my father,
28: 5 *s*— for the LORD has given me many sons
29:24 and also all the other *s* of King David,
2Chr 5:12 Heman, Jeduthun, and their *s* and brothers,
11:14 *s* repudiated them as priests of the LORD.
11:19 She bore him *s*:
11:21 twenty-eight *s* and sixty daughters.
11:23 distributing various of his *s* throughout
13: 5 to David forever, to him and to his *s*,
13: 8 of the LORD commanded by the *s* of David,
13: 9 the priests of the LORD, the *s* of Aaron,
13:10 ministering to the LORD are *s* of Aaron,
13:21 twenty-two *s* and sixteen daughters.
20:13 ones, their wives, and their young *s*.
21: 2 His brothers, *s* of Jehoshaphat,
21: 2 these were *s* of King Jehoshaphat of Judah.
21: 7 to give him and his *s* a lamp for all time.
21:17 palace, along with his *s* and his wives;
22: 1 since all the older *s* had been slain by
22:11 the king's *s* who were about to be slain,
23: 3 LORD promised concerning the *s* of David.
23:11 Jehoiada and his *s* anointed him,
24: 3 he became the father of *s* and daughters.
24: 7 For the wicked Athaliah and her *s* had
24:27 Of his *s*, and the great tribute imposed
26:18 LORD, but for the priests, the *s* of Aaron,
28: 3 and immolated his *s* by fire according to
28: 8 of their brethren's wives, *s* and daughters;
29: 9 as you know, fell by the sword, and our *s*,
29:11 My *s*, be not negligent any longer,
29:12 of the *s* of Merari:
29:13 of the *s* of Elizaphan:
29:13 Shimri and Jeuel; of the *s* of Asaph:
29:14 of the *s* of Heman:
29:14 Jehuel and Shimei; of the *s* of Jeduthun:
29:21 for Judah, and he ordered the *s* of Aaron,
31:18 their little ones, wives, *s* and daughters
31:19 The *s* of Aaron,
33: 6 his *s* by fire in the Valley of Ben-hinnom.
35:14 Indeed the priests, the *s* of Aaron,
35:14 and for the priests, the *s* of Aaron.
35:15 The singers, the *s* of Asaph,
36:20 where they became his and his *s*' servants
Ezr 2: 3 *s* of Parosh,
2: 4 *s* of Shephatiah,
2: 5 *s* of Arah,
2: 6 *s* of Pahath-moab, who were sons
2: 7 *s* of Elam,
2: 8 *s* of Zattu,
2: 9 *s* of Zaccai, seven hundred and sixty;
2:10 *s* of Bani, six hundred and forty-two;
2:11 *s* of Bebai, six hundred and twenty-three;
2:12 six hundred and twenty-three; *s* of Azgad,
2:13 *s* of Adonikam, six hundred and sixty-six;
2:14 *s* of Bigvai, two thousand and fifty-six;
2:15 *s* of Adin, four hundred and fifty-four;
2:16 sons of Ater, who were *s* of Hezekiah,
2:17 *s* of Bezai,
2:18 *s* of Jorah, one hundred and twelve;
2:19 one hundred and twelve; *s* of Hashum,
2:20 *s* of Gibeon, ninety-five;
2:21 ninety-five *s* of Bethlehem,
2:29 *s* of Nebo, fifty-two;
2:30 *s* of Magbish, one hundred and fifty-six;
2:31 *s* of the other Elam, one thousand two
2:32 *s* of Harim, three hundred and twenty;
2:33 *s* of Lod, Hadid, and Ono,
2:34 *s* of Jericho, three hundred
2:35 *s* of Senaah, three thousand six hundred
2:36 *s* of Jedaiah, who were of the house
2:37 *s* of Immer, one thousand and fifty-two;
2:38 *s* of Pashhur, one thousand two hundred
2:39 *s* of Harim, one thousand and seventeen.
2:40 *s* of Jeshua, Kadmiel, Binnui,
2:41 *s* of Asaph, one hundred and twenty-eight.
2:42 *s* of Shallum, sons of Ater, sons of Talmon,
2:42 sons of Akkub, sons of Hatita, *s* of Shobai,
2:43 *s* of Ziha, sons of Hasupha, sons
2:44 sons of Keros, *s* of Siaha, sons of Padon,
2:45 of Lebanah, sons of Hagabah, *s* of Akkub,
2:46 sons of Hagab, sons of Shamlai, *s* of Hanan,
2:47 sons of Giddel, sons of Gahar, *s* of Reaiah,
2:48 sons of Rezin, sons of Nekoda, *s* of Gazzam,
2:49 sons of Uzza, sons of Paseah, *s* of Besai,
2:50 of Besai, sons of Asnah, *s* of the Meunites,
2:50 Meunites, *s* of the Nephusites,
2:51 *s* of Bakbuk, sons of Hakupha,
2:51 Hakupha, *s* of Harhur,
2:52 *s* of Bazluth, sons of Mehida,
2:52 Mehida, *s* of Harsha,
2:53 sons of Barkos, sons of Sisera, *s* of Temah,
2:54 sons of Neziah, *s* of Hatipha.
2:55 sons of Sotai, *s* of Hassophereth,
2:56 Hassophereth, sons of Peruda, *s* of Jaalah,
2:56 of Jaalah, sons of Darkon, *s* of Giddel,
2:57 sons of Shephatiah, *s* of Hattil,
2:57 sons of Pochereth-hazzebaim, *s* of Ami.
2:60 *s* of Delaiah, sons of Tobiah,
2:60 *s* of Nekoda, six hundred and fifty-two.
2:61 sons of Habaiah, *s* of Hakkoz, sons
3: 9 Jeshua and his *s* and brethren,
3: 9 of Henadad, and their *s* and their brethren,
3:10 the trumpets and the Levites, *s* of Asaph,
6:10 pray for the life of the king and his *s*.
7:23 come upon the realm of the king and his *s*.
8: 2 *s* of Phinehas, Gershon; of the sons
8: 2 of the *s* of David,
8: 3 of the *s* of Parosh,
8: 4 of the *s* of Pahathmoab,
8: 5 of the *s* of Zattu,
8: 6 of the *s* of Adin, Ebed, son of Jonathan,
8: 7 of the *s* of Elam, Jeshaiah,
8: 8 of the *s* of Shephatiah,
8: 9 of the *s* of Joab, Obadiah, son of Jehiel,
8:10 *s* of Bani, Shelomith, son of Josiphiah,
8:11 *s* of Bebai, Zechariah, son of Bebai,
8:12 *s* of Azgad, Johanan, son of Hakkatan,
8:13 of the sons of Adonikam, younger *s*,
8:14 of the *s* of Bigvai, Uthai, son of Zakkur,
8:18 well-instructed man, one of the *s* of Mahli,
8:18 namely Sherebiah, with his *s* and brethren,
8:19 and with him Jeshaiah, *s* of Merari,
8:19 of Merari, and their brethren and their *s*,
9: 2 as wives for themselves and their *s*,
9:12 give your daughters to their *s* in marriage,
9:12 and do not take their daughters for your *s*.
10: 2 the son of Jehiel, one of the *s* of Elam,
10:18 Of the *s* of Jeshua, son of Jozadak,
10:20 Of the *s* of Immer:
10:21 Hanani and Zebadiah; of the *s* of Harim:
10:22 of the *s* of Pashhur:
10:25 Of the *s* of Parosh:
10:26 of the *s* of Elam:
10:27 of the *s* of Zattu:
10:28 of the *s* of Bebai:
10:29 of the *s* of Bani:
10:30 and Jeremoth; of the *s* of Pahathmoab:
10:31 and Manasseh; of the *s* of Harim:
10:33 Shemariah; of the *s* of Hashum:
10:34 Manasseh, Shimei; of the *s* of Bengui:
10:38 and Jaasu; of the *s* of Binnui:
10:40 Adaiah; of the *s* of Zachai:
10:43 Shallum, Amariah, Joseph, of the *s* of Nebo:
Neh 3: 3 Gate was rebuilt by the *s* of Hassenaah;
4: 8 for your brethren, your *s* and daughters,
5: 2 "We are forced to pawn our *s* and
5: 5 to reduce our *s* and daughters to slavery,
7: 8 *s* of Parosh, two thousand one hundred
7: 9 *s* of Shephatiah, three hundred and
7:10 *s* of Arah, six hundred and fifty-two;
7:11 *s* of Pahath-moab who were sons of Jeshua
7:12 *s* of Elam, one thousand two hundred
7:13 *s* of Zattu, eight hundred and forty-five;
7:14 *s* of Zaccai, seven hundred and sixty;
7:15 *s* of Binnui, six hundred and forty-eight;
7:16 *s* of Bebai, six hundred and twenty-eight;
7:16 *s* of Azgad, two thousand three hundred
7:18 *s* of Adonikam, six hundred
7:19 *s* of Bigvai, two thousand and sixty-seven;
7:20 *s* of Adin, six hundred and fifty-five;
7:21 sons of Ater who were *s* of Hezekiah,
7:22 *s* of Hashum, three hundred
7:23 *s* of Bezai, three hundred and twenty-four;
7:24 *s* of Hariph, one hundred and twelve;
7:25 *s* of Gibeon, ninety-five;
7:34 *s* of another Elam,
7:35 *s* of Harim, three hundred and twenty;
7:36 *s* of Jericho, three hundred and forty-five;
7:37 *s* of Lod, Hadid, and Ono,
7:38 *s* of Senaah, three thousand nine hundred
7:39 *s* of Jedaiah who were of the house of
7:40 *s* of Immer, one thousand and fifty-two
7:40 *s* of Pashhur, one thousand two hundred
7:42 *s* of Harim, one thousand and seventeen.
7:43 *s* of Jeshua, Kadmiel, Binnui,
7:44 *s* of Asaph, one hundred and forty-eight.
7:45 sons of Shallum, sons of Ater, *s* of Talmon,
7:45 sons of Akkub, sons of Hatita, *s* of Shobai,
7:46 *s* of Ziha, sons of Hasupha, sons
7:47 sons of Keros, sons of Sia, *s* of Padon,
7:48 *s* of Lebana, sons of Hagaba, *s* of Shalmai,
7:49 sons of Hanan, sons of Giddel, *s* of Gahar,
7:50 sons of Reaiah, sons of Rezin, *s* of Nekoda,
7:51 sons of Gazzam, sons of Uzza, *s* of Paseah,
7:52 *s* of Besai, sons of the Meunites,
7:52 Meunites, *s* of the Nephusites,
7:53 *s* of Bakbuk, sons of Hakupha, *s* of Harhur,
7:54 *s* of Bazlith, sons of Mehida, *s* of Harsha,
7:55 sons of Barkos, sons of Sisera, *s* of Temah,
7:56 sons of Neziah, *s* of Hatipha.
7:57 *s* of Sotai, sons of Sophereth, *s* of Perida,
7:58 sons of Jaala, sons of Darkon, *s* of Giddel,
7:59 sons of Shephatiah, *s* of Hattil,
7:59 sons of Pochereth-hazzebaim, *s* of Amon.
7:62 *s* of Delaiah, sons of Tobiah, *s* of Nekoda,
7:63 *s* of Hobaiah, sons of Hakkoz, sons
9:24 *s* went in to take possession of the land,
10:10 Binnui, of the *s* of Henadad;
10:29 the law of God, with their wives, their *s*,
10:31 we will not take their daughters for our *s*.
11: 4 son of Mehallalel, of the *s* of Perez;
11: 6 The total of the *s* of Perez who dwelt in
11:22 he was one of the *s* of Asaph,
12:23 The *s* of Levi:
12:47 the Levites made theirs to the *s* of Aaron.
13:25 shall not marry your daughters to their *s*
13:25 daughters for your *s* or for yourselves!
13:28 One of the *s* of Joiada,
Tb 1: 7 and present them to the priests, Aaron's *s*,
1:21 the king was assassinated by two of his *s*,
4:12 tribe, because we are *s* of the prophets.
4:13 kinsmen the *s* and daughters of your people,
5:14 Nathaniah, the two *s* of Shemaiah the elder;
14: 3 called his son Tobiah and Tobiah's seven *s*,
Jdt 9: 4 spoils you divided among your favored *s*,
16:12 *S* of slave girls pierced them through;
16:12 supposed *s* of rebel mothers cut them down;
Est 5:11 of his riches, the large number of his *s*,
9:10 Aridai, and Vaizatha, the ten *s* of Haman,
9:12 hundred men, as well as the ten *s* of Haman.
9:13 the ten *s* of Haman be hanged on gibbets."
9:14 So the ten *s* of Haman were hanged,
9:25 he and his *s* should be hanged on gibbets.
1Mc 1: 9 so did their *s* after them for many years,
1:48 animals, to leave their *s* uncircumcised,
2: 2 He had five *s*:
2:14 Mattathias and his *s* tore their garments,
2:16 and his *s* gathered in a group apart.
2:17 in this city, supported by *s* and kinsmen.
2:18 Then you and your *s* shall be numbered
2:20 yet I and my *s* and my kinsmen will keep to
2:28 he fled to the mountains with his *s*,
2:30 desert to settle there, they and their *s*,

2:49 for Mattathias to die, he said to his *s*:
2:50 Therefore, my *s*, be zealous for the law
5: 3 the *s* of Esau at Akrabattene in Idumea,
5: 4 remembered the malice of the *s* of Baean,
5:65 *s* of Esau in the country toward the south;
6:24 *s* of our people have become our enemies;
9:36 But the *s* of Jambri from Medaba made a
9:37 "The *s* of Jambri are celebrating a great
9:53 He took as hostages the *s* of the leaders
9:66 and the *s* of Phasiron in their encampment;
11:62 He took the *s* of their chief men as
13:16 and two of his *s* as hostages to guarantee
14:25 said, "How can we thank Simon and his *s*?
14:49 they would be available to Simon and his *s*.
16: 2 Simon called his two oldest *s*,
16:13 plans to do away with Simon and his *s*.
16:14 he and his *s* Mattathias and Judas went
16:16 when Simon and his *s* had drunk freely,
16:16 banquet hall, and killed him, his two *s*,
2Mc 7:20 who saw her seven *s* perish in a single day,
7:41 The mother was last to die after her *s*.
Jb 1: 2 *s* and three daughters were born to him;
1: 4 His *s* used to take turns giving feasts,
1: 5 "It may be that my *s* have sinned and
1: 6 when the *s* of God came to present
1:13 while his *s* and his daughters were eating
1:18 "Your *s* and daughters were eating and
2: 1 Once again the *s* of God came to present
14:21 If his *s* are honored,
38: 7 and all the *s* of God shouted for joy?
42:13 And he had seven *s* and three daughters,
Ps(s) 17:14 Their *s* are enriched and bequeath their
29: 1 Give to the LORD, you *s* of God,
45: 3 Fairer in beauty are you than the *s* of men;
45:17 place of your fathers your *s* shall have;
69: 9 my brothers, a stranger to my mother's *s*,
77:16 your people, the *s* of Jacob and Joseph.
78: 4 to us, We will not hide from their *s*;
78: 5 fathers they should make known to their *s*;
78: 6 to come might know, their *s* yet to be born,
78: 6 they too may rise and declare to their *s*
78: 9 The *s* of Ephraim,
82: 6 are gods, all of you *s* of the Most High;
83: 9 they are the forces of the *s* of Lot.
89: 7 Who is like the LORD among the *s* of God?
89:31 "If his *s* forsake my law and walk not
105: 6 of Abraham, his servants, *s* of Jacob,
106:37 their *s* and their daughters to demons,
106:38 the blood of their *s* and their daughters,
127: 3 Behold, *s* are a gift from the LORD;
127: 4 hand of a warrior are the *s* of one's youth.
132:12 If your *s* keep my covenant and the decrees
132:12 decrees which I shall teach them, Their *s*,
144:12 May our *s* be like plants well-nurtured
Prv 8:31 and I found delight in the *s* of men.
30: 4 What is his name, what is his *s* name,
Wis 5: 5 See how he is accounted among the *s* of God;
9: 6 though one be perfect among the *s* of men,
9: 7 and magistrate for your *s* and daughters.
12:19 And you gave your *s* good ground for hope
12:21 With what exactitude you judged your *s*,
16:10 of poisonous reptiles overcame your *s*,
16:26 That your *s* whom you loved might learn,
18: 4 who had kept your *s* confined through whom
18: 5 you carried off their multitude of *s*
Sir 3: 2 mother's authority he confirms over her *s*.
7:23 If you have *s*,
40: 1 and a heavy yoke, to the *s* of men;
45:13 be worn by any Except his *s* and them alone,
47:23 father, and left behind him one of his *s*,
48:10 the hearts of fathers toward their *s*,
50:13 All the *s* of Aaron in their dignity
50:16 God, The *s* of Aaron would sound a blast,
Is 1: 2 *S* have I raised and reared,
14:21 his *s* for the guilt of their fathers;
27:12 shall be gleaned one by one, O *s* of Israel.
37:38 his *s* Adrammelech and Sharezer slew him
38:19 Fathers declare to their *s*,
43: 6 Bring back my *s* from afar,
49:22 They shall bring your *s* in their arms,
49:25 you I will oppose, and your *s* I will save.
51:18 no one to guide her of all the *s* she bore;
51:18 her by the hand, of all the *s* she reared!—
51:20 Your *s* lie helpless at every street corner
54:13 All your *s* shall be taught by the LORD,
56: 5 and a name Better than *s* and daughters;
57: 3 But you, draw near, you *s* of a sorceress,
60: 4 Your *s* come from afar,
Jer 3:19 How I should like to treat you as *s*,
3:24 their cattle, their *s* and their daughters.
5: 7 Your *s* have forsaken me,
5:17 bread, devour your *s* and your daughters,
6: 1 Flee, *s* of Benjamin, out of Jerusalem!
6:21 Fathers and *s* alike,
7:31 in fire their *s* and their daughters,
10:20 My *s* have left me, they are no more:
11:22 their *s* and daughters shall die by famine.
13:14 against each other, fathers and *s* together,
14:16 one shall bury them, their wives, their *s*,
16: 2 not have *s* or daughters in this place,
16: 3 concerning the *s* and daughters
17: 2 when their *s* remember their altars and
19: 5 their *s* in fire as holocausts to Baal:

19: 9 eat the flesh of their *s* and daughters;
29: 6 *s* and daughters; find wives for your sons
29: 6 so that they may bear *s* and daughters
30:20 His *s* shall be as of old,
31:17 Your *s* shall return to their own borders.
32:18 into the lap of their *s* who follow them.
32:35 immolated their *s* and daughters to Molech,
35: 3 Habazziniah, his brothers and all his *s*,
35: 4 of the LORD, to the room of the *s* of Hanan,
35: 8 wine, neither we, nor our wives, nor our *s*,
38:23 and *s* shall be led forth to the Chaldeans,
39: 6 his *s* were slain at Riblah by order of the
40: 8 the *s* of Ephai of Netopha;
48:46 Your *s* are taken into exile,
49: 1 Has Israel no *s*?
49:10 *s*, and brothers, and neighbors,
52:10 the king of Babylon slew his *s* as well as
Lam 1:16 My *s* were reduced to silence when the
3:33 joy in afflicting or grieving the *s* of men.
4: 2 Zion's precious *s*,
Bar 1: 4 the nobles, the kings' *s*, the elders,
3: 4 few, the *s* of those who sinned against you;
3:23 The *s* of Hagar who seek knowledge on earth,
4:10 God has brought upon my *s* and daughters.
4:14 of the captivity of my *s* and daughters,
4:16 have led away this widow's cherished *s*,
4:32 fearful the city that took your *s*.
4:37 Here come your *s* whom you once let go,
Ez 5:10 shall eat sons, and *s* shall eat fathers.
14:16 they could save neither *s* nor daughters;
14:18 be unable to save either *s* or daughters;
14:22 in it who will bring out *s* and daughters;
16:20 The *s* and daughters you had borne me you
23: 4 They became mine and bore *s* and daughters.
23:10 her *s* and daughters they took away,
23:25 They shall take away your *s* and daughters,
23:47 They shall slay their *s* and daughters,
24:21 The *s* and daughters you left behind shall
24:25 of their hearts, their *s* and daughters,
46:16 any of his sons, it shall belong to his *s*;
46:17 inheritance given to his *s* is permanent.
46:18 for his *s* from his own property,
Dn 3:82 You *s* of men,
11:10 "But his *s* shall prepare and assemble a
Hos 4: 6 law of your God, I will also ignore your *s*.
11:10 his *s* shall come frightened from the west,
Jl 3: 1 Your *s* and daughters shall prophesy,
4: 8 I will sell your *s* and your daughters to
Am 2:11 I who raised up prophets among your *s*,
7:17 *s* and daughters shall fall by the sword;
Mi 5: 6 for no man, nor tarry for the *s* of men.
Zep 1: 8 will punish the princes, and the king's *s*,
Zec 9:13 I will arouse your *s*,
9:13 arouse your sons, O Zion, [against your *s*,
Mal 3: 3 [silver], and he will purify the *s* of Levi,
3: 6 change, nor do you cease to be *s* of Jacob.
Mt 5: 9 they shall be called *s* of God.
5:45 that you are *s* of your heavenly Father,
15:26 *s* and daughters and throw it to the dogs."
17:25 of the world take tax or toll from their *s*,
17:26 "Then their *s* are exempt.
20:20 sons came up to him accompanied by her *s*,
20:21 "Promise me that these *s* of mine will sit,
21:28 There was a man who had two *s*.
23:31 you are the *s* of the prophets' murderers.
26:37 He took along Peter and Zebedee's two *s*,
27:56 and Jo-seph, and the mother of Zebedee's *s*.
Mk 3:17 Boanerges, or "*s* of thunder"
7:27 "Let the *s* of the household satisfy
10:24 "My *s*, how hard it is to enter
10:35 Zebedee's *s*, James and John,
Lk 1:16 Many of the *s* of Israel will he bring back
5:10 as well as James and John, Zebedee's *s*,
6:35 will rightly be called *s* of the Most High,
15:11 "A man had two *s*.
20:36 *S* of the resurrection, they are sons of God.
Jn 4:12 drank from it with his *s* and his flocks?"
12:36 thus you will become *s* of light."
21: 2 (from Cana in Galilee), Zebedee's *s*,
Acts 2:17 Your *s* and daughters shall prophesy,
7:16 with silver from the *s* of Hamor at Shechem.
7:29 where he became the father of two *s*.
10:36 the message he has sent to the *s* of Israel,
19:14 Another time, when the seven *s* of Sceva,
Rom 8:14 are led by the Spirit of God are *s* of God.
8:19 awaits the revelation of the *s* of God.
9:26 they shall be called *s* of the living God."
2Cor 6:18 to you and you will be my *s* and daughters,'
Gal 3: 7 that those who believe are *s* of Abraham.
4: 5 we might receive our status as adopted *s*.
4: 6 The proof that you are *s* is the fact that
4:22 it is written that Abraham had two *s*,
Eph 1: 5 through Christ Jesus to be his adopted *s*—
Heb 2:10 that when bringing many *s* to glory God,
11:21 dying, blessed each of the *s* of Joseph,
12: 5 encouraging words addressed to you as *s*:
12: 5 "My *s*, do not disdain the discipline
12: 7 discipline of God, who deals with you as *s*.
12: 8 the discipline of sons, you are not *s*
1Pt 1:14 As obedient *s*,
1Jn 5: 9 God has given on his own *S* behalf.
5:10 testimony he has given on his own *S* behalf.

SONS-IN-LAW (3)

Gn 19:12 Your sons *s* and your daughters and all who
19:14 So Lot went out and spoke to his *s*,
19:14 But his *s* thought he was joking.

SOON (119)

Gn 7:10 As *s* as the seven days were over,
18:33 *s* as he had finished speaking with Abraham,
19:17 As *s* as they had been brought outside,
24:30 As *s* as he saw the ring and the bracelets
29:10 As *s* as Jacob saw Rachel,
39:19 As *s* as the master heard his wife's story
41:32 by God and that God will *s* bring it about.
42: 7 he recognized them as *s* as he saw them.
44:30 as *s* as he sees that the boy is missing;
46:29 As *s* as he saw him, he flung himself
Ex 2:18 "How is it you have returned so *s* today?"
8:25 "As *s* as I leave your presence I will
9:29 "As *s* as I leave the city I will extend
32: 8 They have *s* turned aside from the way I
Lv 13:14 But as *s* as raw flesh appears on him,
Nm 22: 4 *S* this horde will devour all the country
Dt 11:17 and you will *s* perish from the good land
31:16 *S* you will be at rest with your fathers,
Jos 8:19 toward the city, and as *s* as he did so,
Jgs 16:22 began to grow as *s* as it was shaved off.
1Sm 25:23 As *s* as Abigail saw David,
29:10 morning start, as *s* as it grows light,
2Sm 6:13 As *s* as the bearers of the ark of the LORD
17:21 As *s* as they left, Ahimaaz and Jonathan
22:45 as *s* as they heard me,
1Kgs 9:24 As *s* as Pharaoh's daughter went up from
12: 2 from Egypt as *s* as he learned this.
2Kgs 10:25 As *s* as he finished offering the holocaust,
2Chr 31: 5 As *s* as the order was promulgated,
Ezr 4:23 As *s* as a copy of King Artaxerxes' letter
Neh 3:38 which was *s* filled in and completed up to
9:28 "As *s* as they had relief,
Tb 5: 4 As *s* as he went out, he found the angel
6:18 As *s* as the demon smells the odor they
10: 6 He will be here *s*."
Jdt 7: 4 *S* they will devour the whole country.
10: 1 As *s* as Judith had thus concluded,
11:16 "As *s* as I, your handmaid, learned
13: 9 *S* afterward, she came out
1Mc 2:40 they will *s* destroy us from the earth."
11:22 a conference at Ptolemais as *s* as possible.
12:48 as *s* as Jonathan had entered Ptolemais,
2Mc 1:15 As *s* as he entered the temple,
1:32 As *s* as this was done, a flame blazed up,
2:18 that he will *s* have mercy on us and gather
3:31 *S* some of the companions of Heliodorus
5:18 presumptuous action as *s* as he approached.
7:37 God to show mercy *s* to our nation,
8: 7 *S* the fame of his valor spread everywhere.
9: 4 of the Jews as *s* as I arrive there."
10:28 As *s* as dawn broke,
11: 1 Very *s* afterward, Lysias, guardian
11:36 As *s* as you have considered them,
12: 5 As *s* as Judas heard of the barbarous deed
Jb 7:21 For *s* I shall lie down in the dust;
32:22 if I did, my Maker would *s* take me away.
Ps(s) 4: 9 As *s* as I lie down,
18:45 as *s* as they heard me they obeyed.
94:17 help, I would *s* dwell in the silent grave.
106:13 But *s* they forgot his works;
Wis 14:20 *s* thought he should be worshiped who
Sir 6:20 little, and *s* you will eat of her fruits.
Is 5:11 drink as *s* as they rise in the morning,
30:19 out, as *s* as he hears he will answer you.
51:14 The oppressed shall *s* be released;
Jer 27:16 will be brought back from Babylon *s* now,"
Bar 4:24 they *s* see God's salvation come to you,
4:25 and you will *s* see their destruction and
Ez 7: 8 *S* now I will pour out my fury upon you and
11: 3 we not," they say, "be building houses *s*?
23:17 As *s* as she was defiled by them,
36: 8 my people Israel, for they shall *s* return.
Dn 3: 7 *s* as they heard the sound of the trumpet,
10:20 *S* I must fight the prince of Persia again.
11:20 kingdom, but he shall *s* be destroyed,
13:19 As *s* as the maids had left,
14:18 As *s* as he had opened the door,
Mt 13:21 involving the message occurs, he *s* falters.
26:64 *S* you will see the Son of Man seated at
Mk 4:15 ones to whom, as *s* as they hear the word,
7:25 *S* a woman, whose small daughter
11: 2 and as *s* as you enter it you will find
15: 1 As *s* as it was daybreak the chief priests,
15:44 surprised that Jesus should have died so *s*.
Lk 7:11 *S* afterward he went to a town called Naim,
Jn 11:29 As *s* as Mary heard this,
13:32 him in himself, and will glorify him *s*.
16:16 but *s* after that you shall see me again."
16:17 of me, but *s* after that you will see me'?
16:19 of me, but *s* after that you will see me.'
19: 6 As *s* as the chief priests and the temple
Acts 9:20 and *s* began to proclaim in the synagogues
17:10 As *s* as it was night,
17:15 and Timothy to join him as *s* as possible.
19:27 may *s* be stripped of her magnificence."
20: 6 We ourselves set sail from Philippi as *s*

SOON (cont.)

21:32 As *s* as the crowd caught sight of him and
25: 4 that he himself would be returning there *s.*
Rom 15:24 As *s* as I can set out for Spain,
1Cor 4:19 But I shall come to you *s,*
Gal 1: 6 I am amazed that you are so *s* deserting
2:14 As *s* as I observed that they were not
Phil 2:19 Lord Jesus, to send Timothy to you very *s,*
2:23 him as *s* as I see how things go with me.
2:24 in the Lord that I myself will be coming *s.*
1Tm 3:14 Although I hope to visit you *s,*
2Tm 4: 9 Do your best to join me *s,*
Heb 6: 8 it is *s* cursed,
13:19 that I may be restored to you very *s.*
13:23 If he is able to join me *s,*
3Jn 1:14 Rather, I hope to see you *s,*
Rv 1: 1 show his servants what must happen very *s.*
2:16 I will come to you *s* and fight against
3:11 I am coming *s.*
11:14 The third is coming very *s.*
22: 6 show his servants what must happen very *s.*"
22: 7 "Remember, I am coming *s!*
22:12 "Remember, I am coming *s!*
22:20 this testimony says, "Yes, I am coming *s!*"

SOONER (10)

Nm 16:31 No *s* had he finished saying all this
Jos 3:15 No *s* had these priestly bearers of the ark
2Sm 13:36 No *s* had he finished speaking than the
Ez 23:16 no *s* had she set eyes on them than she
Dn 11: 4 No *s* shall he appear than his kingdom
Mt 26:52 the sword are *s* or later destroyed by it.
Jn 13:30 No *s* had Judas eaten the morsel than he
20:14 She had no *s* said this than she turned
Acts 1: 9 No *s* had he said this than he was lifted
22:25 No *s* had they bound Paul than he said to

SOOT (3)

Ex 9: 8 a double handful of *s* from a furnace,
9:10 So they took *s* from a furnace and stood in
Lam 4: 8 Now their appearance is blacker than *s,*

SOOTHING (1)

Prv 15: 4 A *s* tongue is a tree of life,

SOOTHSAYER (2)

Dt 18:10 in the fire, nor a fortune-teller, *s,*
Jos 13:22 put to the sword also the *s* Balaam,

SOOTHSAYERS (5)

Dt 18:14 listen to their *s* and fortune-tellers,
Is 2: 6 they are filled with fortune-tellers and *s,*
Jer 27: 9 and dreamers, to your *s* and sorcerers,
50:36 A sword upon the *s,*
Mi 5:11 and there shall no longer be *s* among you.

SOOTHSAYING (2)

Lv 19:26 Do not practice divination or *s.*
2Kgs 21: 6 He practiced *s* and divination,

SOPATER (1)

Acts 20: 4 Accompanying him were *S,*

SOPHERETH (1)

Neh 7:57 sons of Sotai, sons of *S,*

SOPHERIM (1)

1Chr 2:55 *S* dwelling in Jabez were the Tirathites,

SOPHISTRIES (1)

2Cor 10: 4 We demolish *s* and every proud pretension

SORCERERS (6)

Ex 7:11 Pharaoh, in turn, summoned wise men and *s,*
Jer 27: 9 and dreamers, to your soothsayers and *s,*
Dn 2: 2 ordered that the magicians, enchanters, *s,*
Mal 3: 5 be swift to bear witness Against the *s,*
Rv 21: 8 and murderers, the fornicators and *s,*
22:15 Outside are the dogs and *s,*

SORCERESS (2)

Ex 22:17 "You shall not let a *s* live.
Is 57: 3 But you, draw near, you sons of a *s,*

SORCERIES (3)

Wis 18:13 disbelieved at every turn on account of *s,*
Is 47: 9 *s* and the great number of your spells;
47:12 Keep up, now, your spells and your many *s.*

SORCERY (4)

Nm 23:23 No, there is no *s* against Jacob,
Gal 5:20 impurity, licentiousness, idolatry, *s,*
Rv 9:21 they repent of their murders or their *s,*
18:23 you led all nations astray by your *s.*

SORDID (2)

Ti 1:11 and all for *s* gain!
Rv 17: 4 the abominable and *s* deeds of her lewdness.

SORE (24)

Lv 13: 2 which appears to be the *s* of leprosy,
13: 3 who shall examine the *s* on his skin.
13: 3 sore has turned white and the *s* itself
13: 3 the skin, it is indeed the *s* of leprosy;
13: 5 If he judges that the *s* has remained
13: 6 If the *s* is now dying out and has not
13:17 find that the *s* has indeed turned white,
13:20 it is the *s* of leprosy that has broken out
13:29 or a woman has a *s* on the head or cheek,
13:30 find that the *s* has penetrated below the
13:31 if the priest, on examining the scall *s*
13:31 the person with scall *s* for seven days,
13:32 and on the seventh day again examine the *s.*
13:42 pink *s* on his bald crown or bald forehead,
13:43 and if the scab on the *s* of the bald spot
13:44 him unclean by reason of the *s* on his head.
13:45 "The one who bears the *s* of leprosy shall
13:46 As long as the *s* is on him he shall
14: 3 the *s* of leprosy has healed in the leper,
22:22 that has a running *s* or mange or ringworm,
Jer 30:13 your cause, no remedy for your running *s,*
Hos 5:13 saw his infirmity, and Judah his *s,*
5:13 he cannot heal you nor take away your *s.*

SOREK (1)

Jgs 16: 4 woman in the Wadi *S* whose name was Delilah.

SORELY (5)

Jgs 4: 3 he *s* oppressed the Israelites
1Mc 10:46 in Israel, and how *s* he had afflicted them.
Prv 31: 6 is perishing, and wine to the *s* depressed;
Jer 50:12 Your mother shall be *s* put to shame,
2Thes 1: 7 will provide relief to you who are *s* tried,

SORES (3)

Ps(s) 38: 6 and festering are my *s* because of my folly,
Lk 16:20 named Lazarus who was covered with *s.*
16:21 The dogs even came and licked his *s.*

SORREL (1)

Zec 1: 8 a shady place, and behind him were red, *s,*

SORROW (49)

Gn 48: 7 Paddan, your mother Rachel died, to my *s,*
49: 4 father's bed and defiled my couch to my *s.*
1Sm 1:16 has been prompted by my deep *s* and misery."
Ezr 3:12 cried out in *s* as they watched the
Tb 2: 5 I washed myself and ate my food in *s.*
3:10 go down to the nether world laden with *s.*
6:15 mother down to their grave in *s* over me.
Est C:10 your inheritance and turn our *s* into joy:
9:22 which was turned for them from *s* into joy,
1Mc 6: 9 he remained many days, overwhelmed with *s,*
6:11 I come, and in what floods of *s* am I now.
Ps(s) 6: 8 My eyes are dimmed with *s;*
10:14 You do see, for you behold misery and *s,*
13: 3 How long shall I harbor *s* in my soul,
31:10 with *s* my eye is consumed;
77:11 And I say, "This is my *s,*
107:39 low through oppression, affliction and *s.*
116: 3 I fell into distress and *s,*
119:28 My soul weeps for *s;*
Prv 14:13 may be sad, and the end of joy may be *s.*
17:25 father, and bitter *s* to her who bore him.
25:20 maggot in wood, *s* gnaws at the human heart.
Eccl 1:18 For in much wisdom there is much *s,*
2:23 his days *s* and grief are his occupation;
5:16 of his life are passed in gloom and *s,*
7: 3 *S* is better than laughter,
Sir 3:26 A stubborn man will be burdened with *s;*
6:10 who will not be with you when *s* comes.
30:10 in his frivolity lest you share in his *s,*
37: 2 Is it not a *s* unto death when your bosom
38:17 mourning fully, pay your tribute of *s,*
Is 14: 3 On the day the LORD relieves you of *s* and
35:10 joy and gladness, *s* and mourning will flee.
51:11 joy and gladness, *s* and mourning will flee.
Jer 20:18 forth from the womb, to see *s* and pain,
31:16 The *s* you have shown shall have its reward,
Mt 26:37 and began to experience *s* and distress.
26:38 them, "My heart is nearly broken with *s.*
Mk 14:34 is filled with *s* to the point of death.
Lk 2:48 and I have been searching for you in *s.*"
2Cor 2: 4 is why I wrote you in great *s* and anguish,
2: 7 not be crushed by too great a weight of *s.*
7: 9 were filled with a *s* that came from God;
7:10 *s* for God's sake produces a repentance
7:10 salvation, whereas worldly *s* brings death.
7:11 the fruit of this *s* which stems from God.
Phil 2:27 too, so as to spare me one *s* after another.
Heb 13:17 fulfill their task with joy, not with *s,*
Jas 4: 9 turned into mourning and your joy into *s.*

SORROWFUL (1)

2Cor 6:10 *s,*

SORROWFULLY (2)

Dn 6:21 As he drew near, he cried out to Daniel *s,*
Mk 14:19 They began to say to him *s,*

SORROWING (2)

Tb 8:20 shall bring joy to my daughter's *s* spirit.
Mt 5: 4 Blest too are the *s;*

SORROWS (5)

Ps(s) 16: 4 They multiply their *s* who court other gods.
32:10 Many are the *s* of the wicked,
Is 13: 8 pangs and *s* take hold of them,
Jer 31:13 console and gladden them after their *s.*
Acts 20:19 served the Lord in humility through the *s*

SORRY (4)

Gn 6: 7 of the air, for I am *s* that I made them."
Ex 5:19 foremen knew they were in a *s* plight,
Jer 42:12 *s* for you and let you return to your land.
Lk 17: 4 a day turns back to you saying, 'I am *s,*'

SORT (50)

Ex 12:16 these days you shall not do any *s* of work,
18:14 "What *s* of thing is this that you are
Lv 11:37 Any *s* of cultivated grain remains clean
23: 7 hold a sacred assembly and do no *s* of work.
23: 8 hold a sacred assembly and do no *s* of work."
23:21 assembly, and no *s* of work may be done.
23:25 you shall then do no *s* of work,
23:35 assembly, and you shall do no *s* of work.
23:36 solemn closing you shall do no *s* of work.
Nm 28:18 a sacred assembly, and do no *s* of work.
28:25 a sacred assembly, and do no *s* of work.
28:26 a sacred assembly, and do no *s* of work.
29: 1 a sacred assembly, and do no *s* of work;
29: 7 mortify yourselves, and do no *s* of work.
29:12 a sacred assembly, and do no *s* of work;
29:35 hold a solemn meeting, and do no *s* of work.
Dt 16: 8 on that day you shall not do any *s* of work.
1Chr 18:10 silver and bronze utensils of every *s.*
Neh 8:17 nothing of this *s* from the days of Jeshua,
Jdt 5: 3 what *s* of people is this that dwells in
2Mc 5: 3 ornaments, together with armor of every *s.*
Jb 16: 2 I have heard this *s* of thing many times.
Sir 6: 8 *s* of friend is a friend when it suits him,
Jer 18: 4 another object of whatever *s* he pleased.
Ez 20:29 *s* of high place do you betake yourselves?—and
47: 9 every *s* of living creature that can
Mt 8:27 "What *s* of man is this,"
Mk 5:26 *s* and exhausted her savings in the process,
13:24 trials of every *s* the sun will be darkened,
Lk 3:18 Using exhortations of this *s,*
7:39 what *s* of woman this is that touches him
8:25 "What *s* of man can this be who commands
16:16 people of every *s* are forcing their way in.
Jn 6:60 "This *s* of talk is hard to endure!
12:33 indicated the *s* of death he had to die.)
18:32 indicating the *s* of death he had to die.)
21:19 (What he said indicated the *s* of death by
Eph 4:19 the indulgence of every *s* of lewd conduct.
5: 3 or promiscuousness or lust of any *s,*
5:27 stain or wrinkle or anything of that *s.*
6:18 using prayers and petitions of every *s.*
Col 1:10 every *s* and grow in the knowledge of God.
3: 7 Your own conduct was once of this *s,*
1Thes 2: 3 or impure motives or any *s* of trickery;
Jas 1: 2 when you are involved in every *s* of trial.
1: 8 A man of this *s,* devious and erratic
2Pt 3:11 in this way, what *s* of men must you not be!
Rv 2: 2 apostles who are nothing of the *s,*
21: 8 idol-worshipers and deceivers of every *s*
21:19 was ornate with precious stones of every *s:*

SORTIE (3)

Jos 8: 5 a *s* against us as they did the last time,
2Sm 11:17 the men of the city made a *s* against Joab,
1Mc 6:31 *s* and burned these and they fought bravely.

SORTS (11)

Dt 6:11 of goods of all *s* that you did not garner,
Tb 14:10 commit all *s* of wickedness and treachery.
Eccl 2: 5 and set out in them fruit trees of all *s.*
Wis 16:25 very time, transformed in all *s* of ways,
Mt 13:47 the lake, which collected all *s* of things.
Mk 4:19 cravings of other *s* come to choke it off;
Jn 11:47 "with this man performing all *s* of signs?
Acts 19:32 people were shouting all *s* of things,
1Cor 9:12 we put up with all *s* of hardships so as
9:25 Athletes deny themselves all *s* of things.
Rv 18:12 all *s* of ivory pieces and expensive wooden

SOSIPATER (3)

2Mc 12:19 But Dositheus and *S,*
12:24 hands of the men under Dositheus and *S;*
Rom 16:21 too, do my kinsmen Lucius, Jason, and *S.*

SOSTHENES (2)

Acts 18:17 Then they all pounced on S,
1Cor 1: 1 apostle of Christ Jesus, and S our brother,

SOSTRATUS (2)

2Mc 4:28 to the king, in spite of the demand of S,
4:29 the high priesthood, while S left Crates,

SOTAI (2)

Ezr 2:55 sons of S, sons of Hassophereth,
Neh 7:57 sons of S, sons of Sophereth,

SOUGHT (79)

Ex 2:15 of the affair and s to put him to death.
4:19 for all the men who s your life are dead."
Dt 13:11 he s to lead you astray from the LORD,
Jos 2:22 who had s them all along the road without
1Sm 8: 3 but s illicit gain and accepted bribes,
13:12 and I have not yet s the LORD'S blessing.'
13:14 The LORD has s out a man after his own
23:14 Though Saul s him continually,
2Sm 4: 8 son of your enemy Saul, who s your life.
16:23 was as though one had s divine revelation.
1Kgs 1: 2 "Let a young virgin be s to attend you,
1: 3 So they s for a beautiful girl throughout
10:24 the whole world s audience with Solomon,
1Chr 10:13 because he had s counsel of a necromancer,
2Chr 9:23 kings of the earth s audience with Solomon,
11:23 and s an abundance of wives for them.
14: 6 land is still ours, for we have s the LORD,
14: 6 we s him,
15: 4 to the LORD, the God of Israel, and s him,
15:15 whole heart and s him with complete desire,
17: 4 he s the God of his father and observed
22: 9 who s the LORD with his whole heart."
26: 5 and as long as he s the LORD,
35:22 he had s a pretext for fighting with him.
Neh 12:27 the Levites were s out wherever they lived
Est A:17 s to harm Mordecai and his people because
2: 2 beautiful young virgins be s for the king.
3: 6 nationality, he s to destroy all the Jews,
9: 2 to attack those who s to do them harm,
1Mc 2:29 Many who s to live according to
9:26 These s out and hunted down the friends of
9:32 Bacchides learned of it, he s to kill him.
11: 1 and he s by deceit to take Alexander's
11:10 him my daughter, for he has s to kill me."
12:53 the nations round about s to destroy them.
14: 4 of Simon, who s the good of his nation.
14:31 When the enemies of the Jews s to invade
14:35 In every way he s to exalt his people.
16:13 and s to get control of the country.
Ps(s) 34: 5 I s the LORD, and he answered me
37:36 I s him,
40: 7 Holocausts or sin-offerings you s not;
71:24 how disgraced are those who s to harm me!
78:34 they s him and inquired after God again,
119:94 save me, for I have s your precepts.
Eccl 7:25 I s and pursued wisdom and reason,
12:10 Qoheleth s to find pleasing sayings,
Sg 3: 1 bed at night I s him whom my heart loves
3: 1 I s him but I did not find him.
3: 2 I s him but I did not find him.
5: 6 I s him but I did not find him;
Wis 8: 2 Her I loved and s after from my youth;
8: 2 I s to take her for my bride and was
19:17 each s the entrance of his own gate.
Sir 21:17 of a prudent man are s in an assembly,
24: 7 Among all these I s a resting place;
46:15 As a trustworthy prophet he was s out and
46:20 when he lay buried, his guidance was s;
51: 3 and from the power of those who s my life;
51:13 When I was young and innocent, I s wisdom.
Is 65: 1 me not, to be found by those who s me not.
65:10 for the cattle of my people who have s me.
Jer 10:21 were stupid as cattle, the LORD they s not;
13: 7 s out and took the loincloth from the
26:21 of his words, the king s to kill him.
Lam 1:19 Where they s food for themselves,
Ez 16:34 No one s you out for prostitution.
26:21 you shall be s,
Dn 2:13 Daniel and his companions were also s out.
4:33 My nobles and lords s me out;
8:15 s the meaning of the vision I had seen,
Mal 2: 7 and instruction is to be s from his mouth,
Mt 21:46 Although they s to arrest him,
Jn 1:45 Philip s out Nathanael and told him,
9:35 his expulsion, he s him out and asked him,
Acts 13: 8 s to turn the governor away from the faith.
28:23 He s to convince them about Jesus by
2Tm 1:17 Rome, he s me out earnestly and found me.
Heb 12:17 even though he s the blessing with tears.

SOUL (162)

Gn 49: 6 Let not my s enter their council,
Dt 4:29 him with your whole heart and your whole s.
6: 5 with all your heart, and with all your s,
10:12 God, with all your heart and all your s,
11:13 God, with all your heart and all your s,
11:18 these words of mine into your heart and s.
13: 4 with all your heart and with all your s.
20:16 you shall not leave a single s alive.
26:16 with all your heart and with all your s.
30: 2 voice with all your heart and all your s,
30: 6 God, with all your heart and all your s,
30:10 God, with all your heart and all your s.
Jos 22: 5 and serve him with your whole heart and s."
23:14 acknowledge with your whole heart and s
1Kgs 2: 4 their whole heart and with their whole s,
8:48 if with their whole heart and s they turn
15:29 s to Jeroboam but destroying him utterly,
2Kgs 23:25 he did, with his whole heart, his whole s,
1Chr 28: 9 him with a perfect heart and a willing s,
2Chr 6:38 with their whole s they turn back
15:12 their fathers, with all their heart and s;
34:31 and statutes with his whole heart and s,
2Mc 3:16 his face manifested the anguish of his s.
6:30 joy in my s because of my devotion to him."
15:30 who was ever in body and s the chief
Jb 7:11 I will complain in the bitterness of my s.
10: 1 I will speak from the bitterness of my s.
12:10 In his hand is the s of every living thing,
14:22 flesh pains him, and his s grieves for him.
19: 2 How long will you vex my s,
21:25 Another dies in bitterness of s,
27: 2 the Almighty, who has made bitter my s,
30:16 My s ebbs away from me;
30:25 was not my s grieved for the destitute?
33:18 He withholds his s from the pit and his
33:22 His s draws near to the pit,
33:28 He delivered my s from passing to the pit,
33:30 back his s from the pit to the light,
Ps(s) 6: 4 My s,
7:10 the just, O searcher of heart and s,
13: 3 How long shall I harbor sorrow in my s,
16: 9 my heart is glad and my s rejoices,
16:10 will not abandon my s to the nether world,
19: 8 of the LORD is perfect, refreshing the s;
22:21 Rescue my s from the sword,
22:30 And to him my s shall live;
23: 3 he refreshes my s.
25: 1 To you I lift up my s, O LORD, my God.
26: 2 test my s and my heart.
26: 9 Gather not my s with those of sinners,
30:13 s might sing praise to you without ceasing;
31:10 my s also,
33:20 Our s waits for the LORD,
34: 3 Let my s glory in the LORD;
35: 3 Say to my s,
35:12 for good, bringing bereavement to my s.
42: 2 the running waters, so my s longs for you,
42: 3 thirst is my s for God, the living god.
42: 5 now that I pour out my s within me,
42: 6 Why are you so downcast, O my s?
42: 7 Within me my s is downcast;
42:12 Why are you so downcast, O my s?
43: 5 Why are you so downcast, O my s?
57: 9 Awake, O my s; awake, lyre and harp!
62: 2 Only in God is my s at rest;
62: 6 Only in God be at rest, my s,
63: 2 pines and my s thirsts like the earth,
63: 6 of a banquet shall my s be satisfied,
63: 9 My s clings fast to you;
71:23 My s also,
73:21 heart was embittered and my s was pierced,
77: 3 my s refuses comfort.
84: 3 My s yearns and pines for the courts of
86: 4 Gladden the s of your servant,
86: 4 for to you, O Lord, I lift up my s;
88: 4 For my s is surfeited with troubles and my
94:19 within me, your comfort gladdens my s.
103: 1 Bless the LORD, O my s;
103: 2 Bless the LORD, O my s,
103:22 Bless the LORD, O my s!
104: 1 Bless the LORD, O my s!
104:35 Bless the LORD, O my s!
107: 9 Because he satisfied the longing s and
107: 9 and filled the hungry s with good things.
108: 3 Awake, O my s;
116: 7 Return, O my s,
116: 8 For he has freed my s from death,
119:20 My s is consumed with longing for your
119:28 My s weeps for sorrow;
119:81 My s pines for your salvation;
119:175 Let my s live to praise you,
130: 5 my s trusts in his word.
130: 6 My s waits for the LORD more than
131: 2 and quieted my s like a weaned child.
131: 2 on its mother's lap, [so is my s within me.]
139:14 My s also you knew full well;
143: 6 my s thirsts for you like parched land.
143: 8 I should walk, for to you I lift up my s.
146: 1 Praise the LORD, O my s;
Prv 2:10 your heart, knowledge will please your s,
3:22 So will they be life to your s,
13: 4 The s of the sluggard craves in vain,
13: 4 but the diligent s is amply satisfied.
13:19 Lust indulged starves the s,
15:32 who rejects admonition despises his own s,
21:10 The s of the wicked man desires evil;
24:14 Such, you must know, is wisdom to your s.
25:13 [He refreshes the s of his master.]
27: 9 heart, but by grief the s is torn asunder.
29:17 you comfort, and give delight to your s.
Eccl 7:28 which my s still seeks and has not found:
Wis 1: 4 into a s that plots evil wisdom enters not,
1:11 unpunished, and a lying mouth slays the s.
4:11 pervert his mind or deceit beguile his s;
4:14 for his s was pleasing to the Lord,
9:15 For the corruptible body burdens the s and
10: 7 ripens, and the tomb of a disbelieving s,
10:16 She entered the s of the Lord's servant,
13:17 not ashamed to address the thing without a s.
15:11 him, and breathed into him a quickening s,
16:14 he bring back the s once it is confined.
17: 8 s themselves sickened with a ridiculous fear.
Sir 4: 6 if in the bitterness of his s he curse you,
6:27 With all your s draw close to her;
7:29 With all your s, fear God,
34:15 Happy the s that fears the LORD!
38:23 rally your courage, once the s has left.
40:20 Wine and music delight the s,
51: 6 my s was nearing the depths of the nether
Is 10:18 will be consumed, s and body;
15: 4 of Moab tremble, his s quivers within him;
26: 9 My s yearns for you in the night,
38:15 my years despite the bitterness of my s.
61:10 in the LORD, in my God is the joy of my s;
Jer 4:10 for the sword touches our very s."
12: 7 my s I deliver into the hand of her foes.
31:25 For I will refresh the weary s;
31:25 every s that languishes I will replenish.
32:41 in this land, with all my heart and s.
Lam 3:17 My s is deprived of peace,
3:20 and over leaves my s downcast within me.
3:24 My portion is the LORD, says my s;
3:25 who waits for him, to the s that seeks him;
3:51 My eyes torment my s at the sight of all
Bar 2:18 He whose s is deeply grieved,
2:18 feeble, with failing eyes and famished s,
Ez 24:21 delight of your eyes, the desire of your s.
24:25 of their eyes, the desire of their s,
Jon 2: 8 When my s fainted within me,
Mi 6: 7 the fruit of my body for the sin of my s?
Mt 10:28 the body of life but cannot destroy the s.
10:28 who can destroy both body and s in Gehenna.
22:37 with your whole heart, with your whole s,
Mk 12:30 God with all your heart, with all your s,
Lk 10:27 god with all your heart, with all your s,
Jn 12:27 My s is troubled now,
Acts 2:27 will not abandon my s to the nether world,
1Cor 15:45 Adam, the first man, became a living s;
1Thes 5:23 preserve you whole and entire, spirit, s,
Heb 4:12 It penetrates and divides s and spirit,
Jas 5:20 sinner back from his way will save his s
1Pt 2:11 By their nature they wage war on the s.

SOULLESS (1)

Wis 14:29 For as their trust is in s idols,

SOULS (24)

2Kgs 23: 3 and decrees with their whole hearts and s,
1Chr 22:19 hearts and s to seeking the LORD your God.
Jdt 7:27 wives and children breathing out their s.
Jb 24:12 and the s of the wounded cry out [yet God
Ps(s) 44:26 For our s are bowed down to the dust,
66: 9 He has given life to our s,
123: 4 Our s are more than sated with the mockery
Wis 2:22 nor discern the innocent s' reward.
3: 1 the s of the just are in the hand of God,
3:13 shall bear fruit at the visitation of s.
7:27 And passing into holy s from age to age,
11:26 they are yours, O Lord and lover of s.
14:11 Snares for the s of men and a trap for the
14:26 neglect of gratitude, besmirching of s,
17: 1 therefore the unruly s were wrong.
17:15 and partly stricken by their s surrender;
Sir 21: 2 are lion's teeth, destroying the s of men.
Is 26: 8 and your title are the desire of our s.
57:16 faint before me, the s that I have made.
Jer 6:16 thus you will find rest for your s.
Bar 3: 1 s and dismayed spirits call to you.
Dn 3:86 Spirits and s of the just,
Mt 11:29 Your s will find rest,
1Pt 2:25 to the Shepherd, the Guardian of your s.

SOUND (146)

Gn 3: 8 When they heard the s of the LORD God
31:27 singing to the s of tambourines and harps.
44:17 you may go back safe and s to your father."
Ex 32:18 "It does not s like cries of victory,
32:18 nor does it s like cries of defeat;
Nm 10: 5 When you s the first alarm,
10: 6 when you s the second alarm,
10: 6 when you s the third alarm,
10: 6 when you s the fourth alarm,
10: 9 you, you shall s the alarm on the trumpets,
29: 1 shall be a day on which you s the trumpet.
Dt 4:12 You heard the s of the words,
Jos 10:21 no man uttering a s against the Israelites.
Jgs 4:21 While Sisera was s asleep,
18:25 him, "Let us hear no further s from you,
1Sm 20:12 s out my father about this time tomorrow.
2Sm 5:24 When you hear a s of marching in the tops

SOUND (cont.)

6:15 shouts of joy and to the *s* of the horn.
15:10 to say, "When you hear the *s* of the horn,
1Kgs 1:41 When Joab heard the *s* of the horn,
14: 6 *s* of her footsteps as she entered the door,
18:26 But there was no *s*, and no one answering.
18:29 But there was not a *s*;
18:41 drink, for there is the *s* of a heavy rain."
19:12 the fire there was a tiny whispering *s*.
2Kgs 4:31 boy, but there was no *s* or sign of life.
7: 6 to hear the *s* of chariots and horses,
1Chr 14:15 When you hear the *s* of marching in the
15:16 and cymbals, to make a loud *s* of rejoicing.
15:28 with joyful shouting, to the *s* of horns,
16: 5 lyres, while Asaph was to *s* the cymbals,
2Chr 5:13 and when they raised the *s* of the trumpets,
13:12 with trumpets to *s* the attack against you.
29:28 *s* the trumpets until the holocaust
Ezr 3:13 and no one could distinguish the *s* of the
3:13 from the *s* of those who were weeping;
Neh 4:14 wherever you hear the trumpet *s*,
Tb 5:17 way and bring you back to me safe and *s*;
5:21 the day when he returns to you safe and *s*.
8:13 went in, and found them *s* asleep together.
12: 3 He led me back safe and *s*;
Jdt 3: 7 garlands and dancing to the *s* of timbrels.
16:11 at the *s* of their war cry,
1Mc 9:41 and the *s* of music into lamentation.
2Mc 15:25 to the *s* of trumpets and battle songs.
Jb 15:21 The *s* of terrors is in his ears;
21:12 harp, and make merry to the *s* of the flute.
33: 8 as I listened to the *s* of your words:
37: 4 the majestic *s* of his thunder.
39:24 he holds not back at the *s* of the trumpet,
Ps(s) 6: 9 for the LORD has heard the *s* of my weeping;
27: 7 Hear, O LORD, the *s* of my call;
28: 2 Hear the *s* of my pleading,
28: 6 for he has heard the *s* of my pleading;
31:23 *s* of my pleading when I cried out to you.
66: 8 our God, you peoples, loudly *s* his praise;
66:19 he has hearkened to the *s* of my prayer.
73: 4 their bodies are *s* and sleek;
81: 3 Take up a melody, and *s* the timbrel,
86: 6 prayer and attend to the *s* of my pleading.
98: 6 With trumpets and the *s* of the horn sing
104: 7 the *s* of your thunder they took to flight;
115: 7 they utter no *s* from their throat.
Prv 1: 5 an intelligent man will gain *s* guidance,
Eccl 12: 4 are shut, and the *s* of the mill is low;
Wis 1: 9 the *s* of his words shall reach the Lord,
7: 3 I uttered that first *s* common to all.
7:17 he gave me *s* knowledge of existing things,
17:18 branches, Or the steady *s* of rushing water,
Sir 18:29 *s* proverbs like life-giving waters.
31:20 Moderate eating ensures *s* slumber and a
32:16 His judgment is *s* who fears the LORD;
40:25 secure, but better than either, *s* judgment.
45: 9 through whose pleasing *s* at each step He
50:16 God, The sons of Aaron would *s* a blast,
Is 1: 6 of the foot to the head there is no *s* spot:
6: 4 At the *s* of that cry,
24:18 at the *s* of terror will fall into the pit;
30:21 from behind, a voice shall *s* in your ears:
33: 3 At the roaring *s*,
51: 3 found in her thanksgiving and the *s* of song.
65:19 shall the *s* of weeping be heard there,
65:19 weeping be heard there, or the *s* of crying;
66: 6 A *s* of roaring from the city,
66: 6 roaring from the city, a *s* from the temple,
66: 6 The *s* of the LORD repaying his enemies
Jer 4:19 For I have heard the *s* of the trumpet,
4:21 I see that signal, hear that trumpet *s*!
6:17 "Hearken to the *s* of the trumpet!"
6:23 They *s* like the roaring sea as they ride
25:10 the *s* of the millstone and the light of
31:15 In Ramah is heard the *s* of moaning,
33:11 the *s* of those who bring thank offerings
49: 2 of the Ammonites I will *s* the battle alarm;
50:42 They *s* like the roaring sea,
Ez 1:24 Then I heard the *s* of their wings,
1:24 the *s* of the tumult was like the din of an
7:14 *s* the trumpet and make everything ready,
26:13 the *s* of your lyres shall be heard no more.
43: 2 heard a *s* like the roaring of many waters,
Dn 3: 4 when you hear the *s* of the trumpet,
3: 7 as soon as they heard the *s* of the trumpet,
3:10 everyone who heard the *s* of the trumpet,
3:15 whenever you hear the *s* of the trumpet,
10: 9 When I heard the *s* of his voice,
Hos 5: 8 *S* the alarm in Beth-aven:
Jl 2: 1 in Zion, *s* the alarm on my holy mountain!
Na 3: 2 of the whip, the rumbling *s* of wheels;
Hb 3:16 at the *s*,
Zec 9:14 The Lord GOD shall *s* the trumpet,
Mt 7:17 Any *s* tree bears good fruit,
7:18 A *s* tree cannot bear bad fruit any more
12:13 it became as *s* as the other.
15:31 the mute speaking, the deformed made *s*,
Mk 4:38 through it all, *s* asleep on a cushion.
Lk 11:34 When your eyesight is *s*,
15:25 home, he heard the *s* of music and dancing.
Jn 3: 8 You hear the *s* it makes but you do not
Acts 2: 6 These heard the *s*,
4:10 this man stands before you perfectly *s*.
5: 5 At the *s* of these words,
20: 9 He finally went *s* asleep,
22:14 Just One, and to hear the *s* of his voice;
Rom 2:18 to make *s* judgments on disputed points.
14: 2 A man of *s* faith knows he can eat anything,
1Cor 14: 7 case of lifeless things which produce a *s*,
14: 8 If the bugle's *s* is uncertain,
14:10 in the world and all are marked by *s*;
15:52 of an eye, at the *s* of the last trumpet.
15:52 The trumpet will *s* and the dead will be
1Thes 4:16 at the *s* of the archangel's voice and
1Tm 1:10 flout the *s* teaching
4: 6 *s* doctrine you have faithfully followed.
6: 3 not holding to the *s* doctrines of our Lord
2Tm 1:13 of *s* teaching what you have heard me say,
4: 3 when people will not tolerate *s* doctrine,
Ti 1: 9 encourage men to follow *s* doctrine
1:13 an attempt to keep them close to *s* faith,
2: 1 speech be consistent with your *s* doctrine.
2: 2 likewise *s* in the faith,
2: 8 *s* words to which no one can take exception.
Rv 1:10 a piercing voice like the *s* of a trumpet,
9: 9 Their wings made a *s* like the roar of many
14: 2 I heard a *s* from heaven which resembled
14: 2 the *s* I heard was like the melody of
18:22 No *s* of the millstone shall ever again be

SOUNDED (19)

Ex 14:25 the Egyptians *s* the retreat before Israel,
Nm 10: 6 shall the alarm be *s* for them to depart.
Jgs 3:27 On his arrival he *s* the horn in the
1Sm 13: 3 Then Saul *s* the horn throughout the land,
2Sm 2:28 Joab then *s* the horn,
18:16 Joab then *s* the horn,
20: 1 He *s* the horn and cried out,
20:22 He then *s* the horn,
1Chr 15:19 Heman, Asaph, and Ethan, *s* brass cymbals.
15:24 *s* the trumpets before the ark of God.
2Chr 13:14 to the LORD and the priests *s* the trumpets.
1Mc 6:33 prepared for battle, while the trumpets *s*.
Jer 31:37 or the foundations below the earth be *s*,
Dn 10: 6 his voice *s* like the roar of a multitude.
Lk 1:44 The moment your greeting *s* in my ears,
Rom 10:18 "their voice has *s* over the whole earth,
Rv 1:15 voice *s* like the roar of rushing waters.
19: 1 After this I heard what *s* like the loud
19: 6 what *s* like the shouts of a great crowd,

SOUNDING (5)

Nm 10: 7 an ordinary blast, without *s* the alarm.
31: 6 vessels and the trumpets for *s* the alarm.
Ps(s) 150: 5 Praise him with *s* cymbals,
Acts 27:28 a *s* and found a depth of twenty fathoms;
27:28 again took a *s* and found it to be fifteen.

SOUNDLY (1)

Mt 8:25 Jesus was sleeping *s*.

SOUNDS (11)

Ex 32:17 to Moses, "That *s* like a battle in camp."
32:18 the *s* that I hear are cries of revelry."
Jb 30:31 mourning, and my reed pipe to *s* of weeping.
Ps(s) 51:10 Let me hear the *s* of joy and gladness;
Wis 17: 4 for crashing *s* on all sides terrified them,
17:19 from the hollow of the hills, these *s*,
Jer 46:22 She *s* like a retreating reptile!
Bar 2:23 The *s* of joy and the sounds of gladness,
Am 3: 6 If a trumpet *s* in a city,
Acts 17:18 "He *s* like a promoter of foreign gods,"

SOUR (4)

Mk 15:36 ran off, and soaking a sponge in *s* wine,
Lk 23:36 to offer him their *s* wine and saying,
Rv 10: 9 It will be *s* in your stomach,
10:10 when I swallowed it my stomach turned *s*.

SOURCE (27)

Gn 26:35 a *s* of embitterment to Isaac and Rebekah.
Jdt 7:12 servants keep control of the *s* of water
Est 4:14 will come to the Jews from another *s*;
2Mc 4: 8 as eighty talents from another *s* of income.
Jb 4: 6 Is not your piety a *s* of confidence,
28: 6 Its stones are the *s* of sapphires,
Ps(s) 52: 9 man who made not God the *s* of his strength,
Prv 18: 4 but the *s* of wisdom is a flowing brook.
Wis 12:16 For your might is the *s* of justice;
13: 3 the original *s* of beauty fashioned them.
14:12 *s* of wantonness is the devising of idols;
14:27 the reason and *s* and extremity of all evil.
Sir 10:13 of sin, a *s* which runs over with vice;
37:16 A word is the *s* of every deed;
Jer 2:13 have forsaken me, the *s* of living waters;
17:13 forsaken the *s* of living waters [the LORD].
Jon 2: 9 vain idols forsake their *s* of mercy.
Acts 16:19 saw that their *s* of profit was gone,
Rom 2:29 its *s* is the spirit,
15: 5 the *s* of all patience and encouragement,
15:13 So may God, the *s* of hope,
Phil 4:13 In him who is the *s* of my strength I have
Col 2:19 a growth from this *s* which comes from God.
2Tm 3:15 the *s* of the wisdom which through faith in
Heb 5: 9 he became the *s* of eternal salvation for
Jas 3:12 no more can a brackish *s* yield fresh water.
Rv 3:14 Witness and true, the *S* of God's creation,

SOURCES (6)

1Kgs 18: 5 to all *s* of water and to all the streams.
Jdt 7: 7 to their city and located their *s* of water;
Jb 38:16 Have you entered into the *s* of the sea,
Prv 4:23 your heart, for in it are the *s* of life.
5:16 How may your water *s* be dispersed abroad,
Acts 9:13 I have heard from many *s* about this man

SOUTH (105)

Gn 13:14 where you are, gaze to the north and *s*,
28:14 spread out east and west, north and *s*.
Ex 26:18 twenty boards on the *s* side,
26:35 the latter on the *s* side of the Dwelling,
27: 9 On the *s* side the court shall have
36:23 twenty boards on the *s* side,
38: 9 *s* side of the court there were hangings,
40:24 the table, on the *s* side of the Dwelling,
Nm 2:10 "On the *s* side shall be the divisional
3:29 camped at the *s* side of the Dwelling.
10: 6 those encamped on the *s* side shall set out;
34: 4 Sea, and turning *s* of the Akrabbim Pass,
34: 4 extend *s* of Kadesh-barnea to Hazar-addar;
35: 5 east, *s*,
Dt 3:27 the west, and to the north, and to the *s*,
33:23 The lake and *s* of it are his possession!"
Jos 12: 3 as far *s* as the eastern side of the Salt
13: 3 also where the Avvim are in the *s*;
15: 1 the extreme *s* toward the boundary of Edom,
15: 3 Zin, up to a point *s* of Kadesh-barnea,
15: 7 pass of Adummim, on the *s* side of the wadi;
17: 9 Manasseh were those to the *s* of that wadi;
17:10 The land on the *s* belonged to Ephraim and
18: 5 Judah is to retain its territory in the *s*,
18:13 on the mountaintop *s* of Lower Beth-horon.
18:14 the boundary line swung *s* from the
19:34 it touched Zebulun on the *s*,
Jgs 21:19 from Bethel to Shechem, and *s* of Lebonah.
1Sm 14: 5 north, toward Michmash, the other to the *s*,
23:19 the hill of Hachilah, *s* of the wasteland.
23:24 Maon, in the Arabah *s* of the wasteland.
2Sm 24: 5 near Aroer, *s* of the city in the wadi,
1Kgs 7:25 north, three facing west, three facing *s*,
7:39 *s* side of the temple and five on the north.
7:39 southeast from the *s* side of the temple.
2Kgs 23:13 of Jerusalem, *s* of the Mount of Misconduct,
1Chr 9:24 the east, the west, the north, and the *s*.
26:15 To Obed-edom fell the *s* side,
26:17 on the north, four each day, on the *s*,
2Chr 4: 4 three facing north, three west, three *s*,
Tb 1: 2 is *s* of Kedesh Naphtali in upper Galilee,
Jdt 2:23 of the desert toward the *s* of Chaldea.
7:18 to the *s* and to the east opposite Egrebel,
1Mc 3:57 off, and they camped to the *s* of Emmaus.
5:65 sons of Esau in the country toward the *s*;
Jb 9: 9 Pleiades and the constellations of the *s*;
23: 9 by the *s* he is veiled,
37:17 when a calm from the *s* comes over the land,
39:26 that he spreads his wings toward the *s*?
Ps(s) 78:26 and by his power brought on the *s* wind.
89:13 North and *s* you created;
107: 3 and the west, from the north and the *s*.
Prv 27:16 he cannot tell north from *s*.
Eccl 1: 6 Blowing now toward the *s*,
11: 3 a tree falls to the *s* or to the north,
Sg 4:16 Come, *s* wind!
Sir 43:17 A word from him drives on the *s* wind,
Is 43: 6 and to the *s*:
Ez 16:46 younger sister, living to the *s* of you,
21: 2 man, look southward, preach toward the *s*,
21: 3 but from *s* to north every face shall be
21: 9 sheath against everyone from *s* to north,
40:24 Then he led me *s*,
40:28 south gate, where he measured the *s* gate.
40:44 south, and the other beside the *s* gate,
40:45 "This chamber which faces *s* is for the
41:11 entrance on the north and another on the *s*.
42:10 To the *s* along the side of the free area
42:12 Below the chambers to the *s* there was an
42:13 "The north and *s* chambers which border on
42:18 to the *s* and measured five hundred
46: 9 north gate they shall leave by the *s* gate,
46: 9 *s* gate they shall leave by the north gate;
47: 1 side of the temple, *s* of the altar.
48: 8 thousand cubits from north to *s*,
48: 9 across by twenty thousand north and *s*.
48:10 east, and twenty-five thousand on the *s*;
48:13 across and twenty thousand north and *s*.
48:16 the *s* side,
48:17 cubits, *s* two hundred and fifty cubits,
48:33 On the *s* side,
Dn 8: 4 ram butting toward the west, north, and *s*.
8: 9 horn which kept growing toward the *s*,
11: 5 "The king of the *s* shall grow strong,
11: 6 the daughter of the king of the *s* shall
11: 9 shall invade the land of the king of the *s*,
11:11 around the stronghold, the king of the *s*,

11:14 times many shall resist the king of the *s*,
11:15 The power of the *s* shall not withstand him,
11:25 *s* with a great army; the king of the south
11:29 appointed he shall come again to the *s*,
11:40 king of the *s* shall come to grips with him,
Zec 6: 6 spotted ones went toward the land of the *s*.
9:14 trumpet, and come in a storm from the *s*.
14: 4 very deep valley, and half of it to the *s*.
Mt 12:42 the queen of the *S* will rise with the
Lk 11:31 The queen of the *S* will rise at the
12:55 When the wind blows from the *s*,
13:29 and the west, from the north and the *s*,
Acts 8:26 "Head *s* toward the road which goes from
27:13 When a gentle *s* wind began to blow,
28:13 A day later a *s* wind began to blow which
Rv 21:13 gates facing east, three north, three *s*,

SOUTHEAST (2)

1Kgs 7:39 to the *s* from the south side of the temple.
2Chr 4:10 to the *s* from the right side of the temple.

SOUTHEASTERN (1)

Jos 13:27 to the *s* tip of the Sea of Chinnereth.

SOUTHERN (23)

Nm 34: 3 "Your *s* boundary shall be at the desert
Jos 15: 2 bay that forms the *s* end of the Salt Sea,
15: 4 [This is your *s* boundary.]
15: 8 on the *s* flank of the Jebusites [that is,
15:21 in the extreme *s* district toward Edom were:
18:13 over to the *s* flank of Luz (that is,
18:15 The *s* boundary began at the limits of
18:16 Hinnom along the *s* flank of the Jebusites,
18:19 the Salt Sea, at the *s* end of the Jordan.
18:19 This was the *s* boundary.
2Kgs 11:11 *s* to the northern limit of the enclosure,
2Chr 23:10 from the *s* to the northern extremity of
Jdt 2:25 he proceeded to the *s* borders of Japheth,
Ps(s) 126: 4 O LORD, like the torrents in the *s* desert.
Ez 21: 2 prophesy against the forest of the *s* land.
21: 3 you shall say to the *s* forest.
40:24 led me south, to where there was a *s* gate,
40:27 The inner court also had a *s* gate;
47: 1 flowed down from the *s* side of the temple,
47: 2 I saw water trickling from the *s* side.
47:19 The *s* boundary:
47:19 This is the *s* boundary.
48:28 frontier of Gad shall be the *s* boundary,

SOUTHWARD (3)

Jos 15: 3 Salt Sea, *s* below the pass of Akrabbim,
17: 7 ran *s* to include the natives of En-Tappuah,
Ez 21: 2 Son of man, look *s*,

SOUTHWEST (1)

Acts 27:12 port exposed on the *s* and the northwest.

SOVEREIGN (14)

2Mc 3:28 clearly experienced the *s* power of God.
5:20 glory, once the great *S* became reconciled.
12:15 the aid of the great *S* of the world,
12:28 invoking the *S* who forcibly shatters the
15:23 *S* of the heavens, send a good angel
15:29 native tongue in praise of the divine *S*.
Ps(s) 150: 2 mighty deeds, praise him for his *s* majesty.
Eccl 8: 4 he pleases, because his word is *s*,
Is 47: 5 shall you be called *s* mistress of kingdoms.
47: 7 shall remain always a *s* mistress forever!"
Acts 4:24 *S* Lord, who made heaven and earth
25:26 definite to write about him to our *s*.
1Pt 2:13 whether to the emperor as *s* or to the
2Pt 1:17 for we were eyewitnesses of his *s* majesty.

SOVEREIGNTY (14)

1Sm 24:21 shall surely be king and that *s* over
1Kgs 2:12 David, with his *s* firmly established,
9: 5 your throne of *s* over Israel forever,
2Kgs 8:20 the *s* of Judah and chose a king of its own.
1Chr 29:11 yours, O LORD, is the *s*;
2Chr 21: 8 time Edom revolted against the *s* of Judah;
21:10 the *s* of Judah down to the present time.
21:10 *s* because he had forsaken the LORD,
Wis 6: 3 you by the Lord and *s* by the Most High,
Sir 10: 4 *S* over the earth is in the hand of God,
10: 5 *S* over every man is in the hand of God,
1Cor 15:24 end, when, after having destroyed every *s*,
Rv 17:17 making them agree to bestow their *s*
17:18 which has *s* over the kings of the earth."

SOW (39)

Ex 23:10 may *s* your land and gather in its produce.
Lv 19:19 do not *s* a field of yours with two
25: 3 For six years you may *s* your field,
25: 4 *s* your field nor prune your vineyard.
25:11 your year of jubilee, you shall not *s*,
25:20 year, if we do not then *s* or reap our crop?'
25:22 When you *s* in the eighth year,
26:16 You will *s* your seed in vain,
27:16 to the amount of seed required to *s* it,
Dt 11:10 *s* your seed and then water it by hand,
22: 9 "You shall not *s* your vineyard with two
2Kgs 19:29 But in the third year, *s* and reap,
Jb 4: 8 those who plow for mischief and *s* trouble,
31: 8 stain clings to my hands, Then may I *s*,
Ps(s) 126: 5 Those that *s* in tears shall reap rejoicing.
Eccl 11: 4 One who pays heed to the wind will not *s*,
11: 6 In the morning *s* your seed,
Sir 7: 3 *S* not in the furrows of injustice,
Is 28:25 does he not scatter gith and *s* cumin,
30:23 rain for the seed that you *s* in the ground,
32:20 Happy are you who *s* beside every stream,
37:30 But in the third year, *s* and reap,
Jer 4: 3 your untilled ground, *s* not among thorns.
35: 7 Build no house and *s* no seed;
Hos 2:25 I will *s* him for myself in the land,
8: 7 When they *s* the wind,
10:12 *S* for yourselves justice,
Mi 6:15 You shall *s*,
Mt 6:26 They do not *s* or reap,
13:27 did you not *s* good seed in your field?
25:24 not *s* and gather where you did not scatter,
25:26 not *s* and gather where I did not scatter.
Lk 8: 5 "A farmer went out to *s* some seed.
12:24 they do not *s*,
1Cor 15:36 you *s* does not germinate unless it dies.
15:37 you sow, you do not *s* the full-blown plant,
2Cor 9:10 you *s* and increase your generous yield.
2Pt 2:22 and, "A *s* bathes by wallowing in the mire."

SOWED (11)

Gn 26:12 Isaac *s* a crop in that region and reaped a
Ps(s) 107:37 They *s* fields and planted vineyards,
Zec 10: 9 I *s* them among the nations,
Mt 13: 4 Part of what he *s* landed on a footpath,
13:24 to a man who *s* good seed in his field.
13:25 enemy came and *s* weeds through his wheat,
13:31 seed which someone took and *s* in his field.
13:39 one and the enemy who *s* them is the devil.
Mk 4: 4 Some of what he *s* landed on the footpath,
Lk 19:21 You reap what you never *s*.'
19:22 I never deposited, reaping what I never *s*!

SOWER (5)

Jer 50:16 Cut off from Babylon the *s* and him who
Mt 13:18 "Mark well, then, the parable of the *s*.
Mk 4:14 What the *s* is sowing is the word.
Jn 4:36 that *s* and reaper may rejoice together.
2Cor 9:10 He who supplies seed for the *s* and bread

SOWING (10)

Gn 47:23 Pharaoh, here is your seed for *s* the land.
Lv 26: 5 and your vintage till the time for *s*,
Jgs 6: 3 when the Israelites had completed their *s*,
9:45 demolished the city, *s* the site with salt.
Sir 6:19 As though plowing and *s*,
Mt 13: 4 "One day a farmer went out *s*.
13:37 "The farmer *s* good seed is the Son of Man;
Mk 4: 3 A farmer went out *s*.
4:14 What the sower is *s* is the word.
Lk 8: 5 In the *s*,

SOWN (25)

Ex 23:16 of the crop that you have *s* in the field;
Lv 27:16 the acreage *s* with a homer of barley seed
Dt 14:22 that grows in the field you have *s*;
21: 4 at a place that has not been plowed or *s*,
22: 9 you have *s* and the yield of the vineyard.
1Chr 11:14 He made a stand on the *s* ground,
Ps(s) 126: 6 forth weeping, carrying the seed to be *s*,
Is 19: 7 All the *s* land along the Nile shall dry up
40:24 Scarcely are they planted or *s*,
Jer 12:13 They have *s* wheat and reaped thorns,
Ez 36: 9 you will be tilled and *s*,
Hg 1: 6 You have *s* much,
Mt 13:19 him to steal away what was *s* in his mind.
13:22 What was *s* among briers is the man who
13:23 But what was *s* on good soil is the man who
Mk 4:15 comes to carry off what was *s* in them.
4:16 those *s* on rocky ground are people who on
4:18 Those *s* among thorns are another class.
4:20 But those *s* on good soil are the ones who
4:32 all the earth's seeds, yet once it is *s*,
1Cor 9:11 If we have *s* for you in the spirit,
15:42 What is *s* in the earth is subject to decay,
15:43 What is *s* is ignoble,
15:43 Weakness is *s*, strength rises up.
Jas 3:18 *s* in peace for those who cultivate peace.

SOWS (14)

Prv 6:14 heart, is always plotting evil, *s* discord.
6:19 lies, and he who *s* discord among brothers.
11:18 but he who *s* virture has a sure reward.
13:10 The stupid man *s* discord by his insolence,
16:28 An intriguer *s* discord,
22: 8 He who *s* iniquity reaps calamity,
Sir 28: 9 and *s* discord among those at peace.
Is 55:10 to him who *s* and bread to him who eats,
Am 9:13 and the vintager, him who *s* the seed;
Jn 4:37 'One man *s*; another reaps.'
2Cor 9: 6 He who *s* sparingly will reap sparingly,
9: 6 he who *s* bountifully will reap bountifully.
Gal 6: 7 A man will reap only what he *s*.
6: 8 If he *s* in the field of the flesh,

SPACE (24)

Gn 32:17 keep a *s* between one drove and the next."
Ex 25:37 light on the *s* in front of the lampstand.
Nm 16:24 from the *s* around the Dwelling" [of Korah,
16:35 from the *s* around the Dwelling [of Korah,
Jos 3: 4 But let there be a *s* of two thousand
1Kgs 6:16 At the rear of the temple a *s* of twenty
6:24 cherub measured five cubits so that the *s*
7:36 the panels, wherever there was a clear *s*,
2Kgs 16:14 from the *s* between the new altar and the
2Chr 29: 4 gathered them in the open *s* to the east,
32: 6 open *s* at the gate of the city
Neh 8: 1 man in the open *s* before the Water Gate,
2Mc 5:14 In the *s* of three days,
14:44 he fell into the middle of the empty *s*
Jb 26: 7 He stretches out the North over empty *s*,
41: 8 so close to the next that no *s* intervenes;
Wis 12:10 bit by bit, you gave them *s* for repentance.
Is 54: 2 Enlarge the *s* for your tent,
Jer 7:32 For lack of *s*,
Ez 41: 4 He measured the *s* beyond the nave,
41:10 chambers of the court was an open *s*
41:11 side chambers had entrances to the open *s*,
41:11 surrounding the open *s* was five cubits.
45: 2 surrounded by a free *s* of fifty cubits,

SPACES (2)

Neh 8:16 and in the open *s* of the Water Gate and
Lam 2:11 faint away in the open *s* of the town.

SPACIOUS (8)

Ex 3: 8 out of that land into a good and *s* land,
1Chr 4:40 and good pastures, and the land was *s*,
Neh 7: 4 wide and *s* but its population was small,
Is 30:23 day your cattle will graze in *s* meadows;
Jer 22:14 Who says, "I will build myself a *s* house,
51:58 of *s* Babylon shall be leveled utterly;
Mk 14:15 Then he will show you an upstairs room, *s*,
Lk 22:12 show you an upstairs room, *s* and furnished.

SPADED (1)

Is 5: 2 He *s* it,

SPAIN (3)

1Mc 8: 3 of the silver and gold mines in *S*,
Rom 15:24 As soon as I can set out for *S*,
15:28 to them, I shall set out for *S*,

SPAN (17)

Gn 23: 1 The *s* of Sarah's life was one hundred and
25: 7 The whole *s* of Abraham's life was one
25:17 The *s* of Ishmael's life was one
47:28 the *s* of his life came to a hundred and
Ex 23:26 and I will give you a full *s* of life.
28:16 folded double, a *s* high and a span wide.
39: 9 *s* high and a span wide in its folded form.
1Sm 17: 4 he was six cubits and one *s*.
Ps(s) 39: 6 A short *s* you have made my days,
Wis 15: 9 is to die nor that his *s* of life is brief;
15:12 and our *s* of life a holiday for gain;
Is 40:12 sea, and marked off the heavens with a *s*?
Ez 43:13 deep, with a rim around its edges of one *s*.
Heb 12:10 prepare us for the short *s* of mortal life;

SPANNED (1)

2Chr 3:11 The wings of the cherubim *s* twenty cubits:

SPANS (2)

Sir 39:20 His gaze *s* all the ages;
43:12 It *s* the heavens with its glory,

SPARE (46)

Gn 18:24 rather than *s* it for the sake of the fifty
18:26 I will *s* the whole place for their sake."
Nm 31:18 But you may *s* and keep for yourselves all
Dt 13: 9 with pity upon him, to *s* or shield him,
Jos 2:13 that you are to *s* my father and mother,
9:15 and entered into an agreement to *s* them,
9:20 Let us therefore *s* their lives and so deal
Jgs 1:24 us a way into the city, and we will *s* you."
6:25 "Take the seven-year-old *s* bullock and
6:26 Then take the *s* bullock and offer it as a
6:28 and the *s* bullock offered on the altar
11:37 *S* me for two months,
1Sm 15: 3 Do not *s* him,
1Kgs 20:31 Perhaps he will *s* your life."
2Kgs 7: 4 If they *s* us,
Jdt 7:12 Stay in your camp, and *s* all your soldiers.
Est C: 8 God, King, God of Abraham, *s* your people,
7: 3 I beg that you *s* the lives of my people.
2Mc 12:24 he asked them to *s* his life and let him go,
Jb 2: 6 "He is in your power; only *s* his life."
Eccl 9: 8 white, and *s* not the perfume for your head.
Wis 2:10 let us neither *s* the widow nor revere the

SPARE (cont.)

11:26 But you *s* all things,
13:13 he takes and carves to occupy his *s* time.
Sir 16: 9 Nor did he *s* the doomed people who were
Is 9:16 the Lord does not *s* their young men,
13:18 The fruit of the womb they shall not *s*,
27:11 therefore their maker shall not *s* them,
31: 5 To protect and deliver, to *s* and rescue it.
Jer 13:14 show no compassion, I will not *s* or pity,
14:10 to wander that they do not *s* their feet.
50:14 Shoot at her, *s* not your arrows,
51: 3 *S* not her young men,
Dn 1: 8 chief chamberlain to *s* him this defilement.
Jl 2:17 ministers of the LORD weep, And say, *S*,
Zec 11: 6 I *s* the inhabitants of the earth any more,
Acts 20:29 come among you who will not *s* the flock.
Rom 8:32 Is it possible that he who did not *s* his
11:21 If God did not *s* the natural branches,
11:21 branches, he will certainly not *s* you.
1Cor 7:28 life, and these I should like to *s* you.
2Cor 13: 2 that if I come again I shall not *s* you.
Phil 2:27 so as to *s* me one sorrow after another.
2Pt 2: 4 Did God *s* even the angels who sinned?
2: 5 Nor did he *s* the ancient world
Rv 6: 6 But *s* the olive oil and the wine!"

SPARED (44)

Gn 12:13 account and my life may be *s* for your sake."
32:31 face," he said, "yet my life has been *s*."
Ex 9:16 But this is why I have *s* you:
10:15 the fruit of whatever trees the hail had *s*.
12:27 struck down the Egyptians, he *s* our houses.'"
Nm 22:33 her I would have *s*."
31:15 "So you have *s* all the women!"
Jos 6:17 are in the house with her are to be *s*,
6:25 *s* her with her family and all her kin,
Jgs 8:19 the LORD lives, if you had *s* their lives,
21:14 women of Jabesh-gilead whom they had *s*;
1Sm 15: 9 He and his troops *s* Agag and the best of
15:15 The men *s* the best sheep and oxen to
2Sm 8: 2 for execution, and a full length to be *s*.
21: 7 The king, however, *s* Meribbaal,
2Kgs 10:14 Not one of them was *s*.
2Chr 30:20 The LORD heard Hezekiah and *s* the people.
Ezr 9:15 yet we have been *s*,
Jdt 10:19 to be *s* they could beguile the whole world."
11: 3 Your life is *s* tonight and for the future.
11: 9 When the men of Bethulia *s* him,
Est 7: 3 your majesty, I ask that my life be *s*,
1Mc 2:33 king's command, and your lives will be *s*."
7:21 *s* no pains to maintain his high priesthood,
2Mc 3:31 the man who was about to expire might be *s*.
3:33 for his sake that the Lord has *s* your life.
3:35 most solemn vows to him who had *s* his life,
Jb 21:30 the evil man is *s* calamity when it comes;
Ps(s) 7: 5 who *s* those who without cause were my foes
78:50 of his anger he *s* them not from death,
Wis 12: 8 But even these, as they were men, you *s*,
Sir 16: 8 He *s* not the neighbors of Lot
23: 2 discipline, That my failings may not be *s*,
46: 8 *s* from the six hundred thousand infantry,
Is 26:10 The wicked man, *s*,
Jer 11:23 None shall be *s* among them,
25:29 to inflict evil, how can you possibly be *s*?
25:29 You shall not be *s*!
38: 2 his life shall be *s* him as booty,
38:20 go well with you, and your life will be *s*.
39:18 Your life shall be *s* as booty,
41: 8 And so he *s* them and did not kill them,
Dn 13:62 Thus was innocent blood *s* that day.
Mt 16:22 "May you be *s*, Master!
Lk 8:50 is needed is trust and her life will be *s*."

SPARES (3)

Prv 13:24 He who *s* his rod hates his son,
17:27 He who *s* his words is truly wise,
Is 9:18 No man *s* his brother,

SPARING (6)

1Kgs 16:11 *s* a single male relative or friend of his.
2Chr 36:17 building, *s* neither young man nor maiden,
Est 4:11 to him the golden scepter, thus *s* his life.
Prv 11:24 another is too *s*,
Sir 35: 7 to the LORD, be not *s* of freewill gifts.
Jer 15: 6 hand to destroy you, I was weary of *s* you.

SPARINGLY (2)

2Cor 9: 6 He who sows *s* will reap sparingly,
9: 6 He who sows sparingly will reap *s*,

SPARK (7)

2Sm 13:21 however, *s* the resentment of his son Amnon,
Wis 2: 2 reason is a *s* at the beating of our hearts,
Sir 11:31 with a *s* he sets many coals afire.
28:12 If you blow upon a *s*,
42:23 even to the *s* and the fleeting vision!
Is 1:31 to tow, and his work shall become a *s*;
Jas 3: 5 the *s* is that sets a huge forest ablaze!

SPARKLE (3)

2Sm 23: 4 making the greensward *s* after rain.'
Sir 34:17 up the spirits, brings a *s* to the eyes,
Rv 4: 3 had a gemlike *s* as of jasper and carnelian.

SPARKLED (2)

Ez 1: 7 They *s* with a gleam like burnished bronze.
Rv 21:11 of a precious jewel that *s* like a diamond.

SPARKLES (2)

Prv 23:31 when it is red, when it *s* in the glass.
Sir 24:25 It *s* like the Nile with knowledge,

SPARKLING (3)

Jb 22:25 shall be your gold and your *s* silver.
Sir 43: 9 that adorn with their *s* the heights of God,
Ez 1:16 wheels had the *s* appearance of chrysolite,

SPARKS (4)

Jb 5: 7 himself begets mischief, as *s* fly upward.
41:11 *s* of fire leap forth.
Wis 3: 7 and shall dart about as *s* through stubble;
11:18 or flash terrible *s* from their eyes.

SPARROW (4)

Ps(s) 84: 4 Even the *s* finds a home,
102: 8 I am like a *s* alone on the housetop.
Prv 26: 2 Like the *s* in its flitting,
Mt 10:29 Yet not a single *s* falls to the ground

SPARROWS (5)

Hos 11:11 Egypt they shall come trembling, like *s*,
Mt 10:29 Are not two *s* sold for next to nothing?
10:31 are worth more than an entire flock of *s*.
Lk 12: 6 Are not five *s* sold for a few pennies?
12: 7 You are worth more than a flock of *s*.

SPARTA (5)

1Mc 12: 2 to *S* and other places for the same purpose.
14:16 Rome and even in *S* that Jonathan had died,
14:20 *S* send greetings to Simon the high priest,
14:23 the people of *S* may have a record of them.
15:23 Sampsames, *S*,

SPARTANS (6)

1Mc 12: 5 of the letter that Jonathan wrote to the *S*:
12: 6 send greetings to their brothers the *S*.
12:20 "Arius, king of the *S*,
12:21 that the *S* and the Jews are brothers;
14:20 is a copy of the letter that the *S* sent:
2Mc 5: 9 into Egypt, he crossed the sea to the *S*,

SPAT (4)

2Mc 6:19 to a life of defilement, he *s* out the meat,
Mt 27:30 They also *s* at him.
Lk 18:32 He will be mocked and outraged and *s* upon.
Jn 9: 6 With that Jesus *s* on the ground,

SPATE (1)

Sir 40:13 out of wickedness is like a wadi in *s*:

SPATTERED (1)

Sir 22:13 trouble and be *s* when he shakes himself;

SPATTERING (1)

2Sm 22:12 him, with *s* rain and thickening clouds,

SPEAK (345)

Gn 17: 3 himself, God continued to *s* to him:
18:27 "See how I am presuming to *s* to my Lord,
18:31 "Since I have thus dared to *s* to my Lord,
18:32 Lord grow angry if I *s* up this last time.
19:21 I will not overthrow the town you *s* of.
42:24 When he was able to *s* to them again,
44:18 let your servant *s* earnestly to my lord,
Ex 4:15 You are to *s* to him,
4:16 He shall *s* to the people for you:
5:23 since I went to Pharaoh to *s* in your name,
20:19 away and said to Moses, "You *s* to us,
20:19 but let not God *s* to us,
20:22 "Thus shall you *s* to the Israelites:
29:42 tent, where I will meet you and *s* to you.
33:11 The LORD used to *s* to Moses face to face,
Lv 1: 2 *S* to the Israelites and tell them:
11: 2 Aaron, *S* to the Israelites and tell them:
15: 2 Aaron, *S* to the Israelites and tell them:
17: 2 said to Moses, *S* to Aaron and his sons,
18: 2 Moses, *S* to the Israelites and tell them:
19: 2 *S* to the whole Israelite community and
19:11 shall not lie or *s* falsely to one another.
21: 1 The LORD said to Moses, *S* to Aaron's sons,
21:17 said to Moses, *S* to Aaron and tell him:
22:18 *S* to Aaron and his sons and to all the
23: 2 Moses, *S* to the Israelites and tell them:
23:10 Moses, *S* to the Israelites and tell them:
25: 2 Sinai, *S* to the Israelites and tell them:
27: 2 Moses, *S* to the Israelites and tell them:
Nm 5:12 Moses, *S* to the Israelites and tell them:
6: 2 *S* to the Israelites and tell them:
6:23 *S* to Aaron and his sons and tell them:
7:89 entered the meeting tent to *s* with him,
9:10 *S* to the Israelites and say:
11:17 you, I will come down and *s* with you there.
12: 2 Does he not *s* through us also?"
12: 6 myself to him, in dreams will I *s* to him;
12: 8 face to face I *s* to him,
12: 8 you not fear to *s* against my servant Moses?"
15:18 Moses, *S* to the Israelites and tell them:
15:38 *S* to the Israelites and tell them that
16:24 Moses, *S* to the community and tell them:
17:17 *S* to the Israelites and get one staff from
22:38 I can *s* only what God puts in my mouth."
23: 5 him, "Go back to Balak, and *s* accordingly."
23:16 him, "Go back to Balak, and *s* accordingly."
23:19 God is not man that he should *s* falsely,
23:19 Is he one to *s* and not act,
Dt 3:26 *S* to me no more of this.
6: 7 *S* of them at home and abroad,
18:20 But if a prophet presumes to *s* in my name
18:20 oracle that I have not commanded him to *s*,
18:22 it is an oracle which the LORD did not *s*.
31:28 that I may *s* these words for them to hear,
32: 1 Give ear, O heavens, while I *s*;
Jos 2: 4 said, "True, the men you *s* of came to me,
22:28 should *s* thus to us or to our descendants,
Jgs 6:39 "Do not be angry with me if I *s* once more.
14: 7 However, on the journey to *s* for the woman,
1Sm 2: 3 *S* boastfully no longer,
3: 9 sleep, and if you are called, reply, *S*,
3:10 Samuel answered, *S*,
15:16 *S*!" he replied.
18:22 to *s* to David privately and to say:
19: 3 where you are, and will *s* to him about you.
25:24 Please let your handmaid *s* to you,
2Sm 3:27 gate as though to *s* with him privately.
7: 8 "Now then, *s* thus to my servant David,
13:13 So please, *s* to the king;
14: 3 go to the king and *s* to him in this manner."
14:12 He replied, *S*."
14:15 to *s* of this matter to your majesty,
14:15 'Let me *s* to the king.
14:18 The woman said, "Let my lord the king *s*."
17: 6 If not, *s* up."
19: 8 Go out and *s* kindly to your servants.
19:44 we not first to *s* of restoring the king?"
20:16 Joab to come here, that I may *s* with him."
1Kgs 2:16 And she said, *S* on."
2:18 Bathsheba, "I will *s* to the king for you."
2:19 to King Solomon to *s* to him for Adonijah,
22: 8 not your majesty *s* of evil against you."
22:24 of the LORD, then left me to *s* with you?"
2Kgs 6:12 the very words you *s* in your bedroom."
18:26 "Please *s* to your servants in Aramaic;
18:26 Do not *s* to us in Judean within earshot of
18:27 you that my lord sent me to *s* these words?
2Chr 18: 7 not your Majesty *s* of evil against you."
18:23 of the LORD go when he left me to *s* to you?"
Neh 13:24 and none of them knew how to *s* Jewish;
Tb 6:13 tonight we must *s* for the girl,
13: 8 Let all men *s* of his majesty,
13:12 are all who *s* a harsh word against you;
Jdt 8:30 that they forced us to *s* to them as we did,
10:16 give him the report you *s* of,
11: 5 and let your handmaid *s* in your presence!
Est B: 9 Invoke the Lord and *s* to the king for us:
D:12 *S* to me."
Jb 2:10 even you going to *s* as senseless women do?
6: 3 Because of this I *s* without restraint.
7:11 I will *s* in the anguish of my spirit;
9:35 I might *s* without being afraid of him.
10: 1 I will *s* from the bitterness of my soul.
11: 5 But oh, that God would *s*,
13: 3 But I would *s* with the Almighty;
13: 7 Is it for God that you *s* falsehood?
13:13 that I may *s* and give vent to my feelings.
13:22 or let me *s* first,
15: 5 mouth, and you choose to *s* like the crafty.
16: 3 Or what sickness have you that you *s* on?
16: 6 If I *s*,
19:18 when I appear, they *s* against me.
21: 3 Bear with me while I *s*;
27: 4 my nostrils, My lips shall not *s* falsehood,
32: 7 Days should *s*,
32:16 Now that they *s* no more,
32:17 ceased to make reply, I too will *s* my part;
32:20 Let me *s* and obtain relief;
33:14 For God does *s*,
33:31 Be silent and I will *s*.
33:32 *S* out!
34:16 Hearken to the words I *s*!
34:33 *s*, therefore, what you know.
37:20 Will he be told about it when I *s*,
Ps(s) 5: 7 you destroy all who *s* falsehood;
12: 3 with smooth lips they *s*,
17:10 their cruel hearts, their mouths *s* proudly.
28: 3 Who *s* civilly to their neighbors though
31:19 strike their lying lips that *s* insolence
32: 3 As long as I would not *s*,
35:20 For civil words they *s* not,

38:13 they look to my misfortune, they *s* of ruin,
49: 4 My mouth shall *s* wisdom;
50: 7 "Hear, my people, and I will *s*;
63:12 of those who *s* falsely shall be stopped.
71:10 me not, For my enemies *s* against me,
73: 8 They scoff and *s* evil;
73:15 Had I thought, "I will *s* as they do,"
75: 6 *s* not haughtily against the Rock.
77: 5 I am troubled and cannot *s*.
109:20 and upon those who *s* evil against me.
109:30 I will *s* my thanks earnestly to the
115: 5 They have mouths but *s* not;
119:46 I will *s* of your decrees before kings
120: 7 When I *s* of peace, they are ready for war.
135:16 They have mouths but *s* not;
145: 5 They *s* of the splendor of your glorious
145:11 glory of your kingdom and *s* of your might,
145:21 May my mouth *s* the praise of the LORD,
Prv 8: 6 for noble things I *s*;
15:26 but the pure *s* what is pleasing to him.
23: 9 *S* not for the fool's hearing;
23:16 will exult, when your lips *s* what is right.
24: 2 violence, and their lips *s* of foul play.
Eccl 3: 7 a time to be silent, and a time to *s*.
Wis 7:15 Now God grant I *s* suitably and value these
Sir 8: 4 man, lest he *s* ill of your forebears.
13: 5 have anything he will *s* fair words to you,
22:12 *S* but seldom with the stupid man,
22:22 Should you *s* sharply to a friend,
32: 7 Young man, *s* only when necessary,
34: 4 can the liar ever *s* the truth?
37:11 *S* not to a woman about her rival,
39:10 Peoples will *s* of his wisdom,
39:17 had but to *s* and the reservoirs were made.
51:25 I open my mouth and *s* of her:
Is 14:10 All of them *s* out and say to you,
28:11 he will *s* to this people to whom he said:
29: 4 Prostrate you shall *s* from the earth,
30:10 *s* flatteries to us,
32: 4 the stutterers will *s* fluently and clearly.
32: 6 to *s* perversely against the LORD,
36:11 "Please *s* to your servants in Aramaic;
36:11 Do not *s* to us in Judean within earshot of
36:12 that my lord sent me to *s* these words?
40: 2 *S* tenderly to Jerusalem,
41: 1 Let them draw near and *s*;
43:26 *S* up, prove your innocence!
44: 7 Let him stand up and *s*,
48:16 from the beginning did I *s* it in secret;
50: 4 *s* to the weary a word that will rouse them.
59: 3 Your lips *s* falsehood,
Jer 1: 6 I said, "I know not how to *s*;
1: 7 whatever I command you, you shall *s*.
5: 5 will go to the great ones and *s* with them;
6:10 To whom shall I *s*?
7:27 When you *s* all these words to them,
8: 6 they *s* what is not true;
10: 5 a cucumber field are they, they cannot *s*;
11: 2 *S* to the men of Judah and to the citizens
13:12 Now *s* to them this word:
14:14 I gave them no command nor did I *s* to them.
14:17 *S* to them this word:
18:20 I stood before you to *s* in their behalf,
19: 2 proclaim the words which I will *s* to you:
20: 8 Whenever I *s*, I must cry out,
20: 9 mention him, I will *s* in his name no more.
23:16 Visions of their own fancy they *s*,
23:21 I did not *s* to them,
23:28 him who has my word *s* my word truthfully!
26: 2 *s* to the people of all the cities of Judah
26: 7 *s* these words in the house of the LORD.
26: 8 that the LORD bade him *s* to all the people,
26:15 you, to *s* all these things for you to hear."
32: 4 They shall meet and *s* face to face,
34: 3 king of Babylon and *s* to him face to face.
35: 2 Approach the Rechabites and *s* to them;
48:27 you shake your head whenever you *s* of her?
Bar 6: 7 but they are a fraud, and cannot *s*.
Ez 2: 1 I wish to *s* with you.
2: 7 [But *s* my words to them,
2: 8 you, son of man, obey me when I *s* to you:
3: 1 scroll, then go, *s* to the house of Israel.
3: 4 house of Israel, and *s* my words to them.
3:10 your heart all my words that I *s* to you;
3:18 and you do not warn him or *s* out to
3:22 into the plain, where I will *s* with you.
3:27 Only when I *s* with you and open your mouth,
12:24 because it is I, the LORD, who will *s*.
12:25 Whatever I *s* is final,
12:25 house, whatever I *s* I will bring about,
12:28 whatever I *s* is final,
14: 4 Therefore *s* with them,
17: 2 and *s* this proverb to the house of Israel:
20: 3 *s* with the elders of Israel and say to
20:27 Therefore *s* to the house of Israel,
29:21 I will cause you to *s* out in their midst;
30: 2 Son of man, *s* this prophecy:
32:20 the mighty warriors shall *s* to Egypt:
33: 2 ,Son of man, *s* thus to your countrymen:
33: 8 and you do not *s* out to dissuade the
33:10 you, son of man, *s* to the house of Israel:
36: 5 with burning jealousy I *s* against the rest
36: 6 With jealous fury I *s*,
Dn 7:25 He shall *s* against the Most High and
10:16 How can my lord's servant *s* with you,
10:20 spoke to me, I grew strong and said, *S*,
Hos 2:16 her into the desert and *s* to her heart.
Ob 1:12 *S* not haughtily on the day of distress!
Mi 6:12 whose inhabitants *s* falsehood with
Zep 3:13 They shall do no wrong and *s* no lies;
Zec 8:16 *S* the truth to one another;
10: 2 For the teraphim *s* nonsense,
Mt 9:33 the demon was expelled the mute began to *s*,
10:27 I tell you in darkness, *s* in the light.
11: 7 Jesus began to *s* to the crowds about John:
12:22 cured the man so that he could *s* and see.
12:36 for every unguarded word they *s*.
12:46 brothers appeared outside to *s* with him.
12:47 out there and they wish to *s* to you."
13:10 him, "Why do you *s* to them in parables?"
13:13 *s* to them because they look but do not see,
17:25 house asked, without giving him time to *s*:
Mk 1:34 But he would not permit the demons to *s*,
3:23 then began to *s* to them by way of examples:
6:20 he heard him *s* he was very much disturbed;
7:35 the impediment, and he began to *s* plainly.
7:37 He makes the deaf hear and the mute *s*!"
9:39 my name can at the same time *s* ill of me.
16:17 demons, they will *s* entirely new languages,
Lk 1:19 to *s* to you and bring you this good news.
1:20 unable to *s*—
1:22 came out he was unable to *s* to them,
1:64 loosed, and he began to *s* in praise of God.
4:41 rebuked them and did not allow them to *s*
6:26 "Woe to you when all *s* well of you.
7:15 The dead man sat up and began to *s*.
7:24 Jesus began to *s* about him to the crowds.
7:40 "Teacher," he said, "*S*."
11:29 him he began to *s* to them in these words:
11:53 to make him *s* on a multitude of questions,
12: 1 He began to *s* first to his disciples:
21:31 see all the things happening of which I *s*,
21:35 The day I *s* of will come upon all who
Jn 4:26 Jesus replied, "I who *s* to you am he."
9:21 He is old enough to *s* for himself."
12:49 has commanded me what to say and how to *s*.
14:10 The words I *s* are not spoken of myself;
15:15 I no longer *s* of you as slaves,
16:13 He will not *s* on his own, but will *s* only
19:10 "Do you refuse to *s* to me?"
Acts 1: 4 promise, of which you have heard me *s*.
2:29 I can *s* confidently to you about our
4:18 to *s* the name of Jesus or teach about him.
4:29 your servants, even as they *s* your words,
4:31 continued to *s* God's word with confidence.
5:40 not to *s* again about the name of Jesus,
8:33 justice, Who will ever *s* of his posterity,
13:15 to address to the people, please *s* up."
13:42 the people invited them to *s* on this
17:18 to *s* of "Jesus" and "the resurrection,"
18:14 Paul was about to *s* in self-defense when
19: 6 to *s* in tongues and to utter prophecies.
19: 9 but chose to *s* ill of the new way in the
20:25 I know as I *s* these words that none of you
21:40 on them as he began to *s* to them in Hebrew.
24:24 to hear him *s* about faith in Christ Jesus.
25:24 The governor began to *s*:
26:26 Before him I can *s* freely.
28:20 why I have asked to see you and *s* with you.
Rom 3: 5 (I *s* in a merely human way.)
9: 1 I *s* the truth in Christ:
9: 5 the Messiah (I *s* of his human origins).
15:18 I will not dare to *s* of anything except
1Cor 2: 2 I would *s* of nothing but Jesus Christ
2:13 We *s* of these, not in words of human
9: 8 does not the law itself *s* of these things?
12:28 administrators, and those who *s* in tongues.
12:30 Do all *s* in tongues,
13: 1 I *s* with human tongues and angelic as well,
14:18 God, I *s* in tongues more than any of you,
14:21 in alien speech I will *s* to this people,
14:29 Let no more than two or three prophets *s*,
14:31 You can all *s* your prophecies,
14:34 They may not *s*.
14:39 and do not forbid those who *s* in tongues,
2Cor 2:17 We *s* in Christ's name,
3: 1 Am I beginning to *s* well of myself again?
3:12 hope being such, we *s* with full confidence.
4:13 We believe and so we *s*,
6:13 then (I *s* as a father to his children),
7: 4 I *s* to you with utter frankness and boast
7:11 not to *s* of readiness to defend yourselves!
11:17 I *s* not as the Lord desires but after the
11:21 I *s* with absolute foolishness now
12: 1 *s* of visions and revelations of the Lord.
12: 4 be uttered, words which no man may *s*.
Gal 4:20 be with you now and can *s* to you differently!
Eph 3:12 faith in him we can *s* freely to God,
4:25 let everyone *s* the truth to his neighbor,
Phil 1:14 emboldened to *s* the word of God fearlessly.
Col 4: 4 Pray that I may *s* it clearly, as I must.
1Thes 2: 4 we *s* like those who strive to please God,
1Tm 2: 7 me, I am not lying but *s* the truth),
5:14 our enemies no occasion to *s* ill of us.
Ti 3: 2 not to *s* evil of anyone or be quarrelsome.
Heb 2: 5 that world of which we *s*—
6: 9 Beloved, even though we *s* in this way,
7: 9 Levi, who receives tithes, was, so to *s*,
9: 5 We cannot *s* now of each of these in detail.
Jas 1:19 Let every man be quick to hear, slow to *s*,
2:12 Always *s* and act as men destined for
4:11 Do not, my brothers, *s* ill of one another.
1Pt 3:16 to reply, but *s* gently and respectfully.
3Jn 1:10 if I come I will *s* publicly of what he is

SPEAKER (7)

Ex 4:14 I know that he is an eloquent *s*.
6:12 will listen to me, poor *s* that I am!"
6:30 to the LORD, "Since I am a poor *s*,
1Sm 16:18 stalwart soldier, besides being an able *s*,
Sir 21: 7 *s* but the wise man knows his own faults.
1Cor 14: 5 unless the *s* can also interpret for the
14:11 to the *s* and he a foreigner to me.

SPEAKERS (2)

Mt 10:20 You yourselves will not be the *s*;
Acts 4:13 the *s* were uneducated men of no standing,

SPEAKING (126)

Gn 11: 6 are one people, all *s* the same language,
17:22 When he had finished *s* with him,
18:33 as soon as he had finished *s* with Abraham,
27: 5 while Isaac was *s* to his son Esau.
34:13 *s* as they did because their sister Dinah
45:12 that it is I, Joseph, who am *s* to you.
46: 2 God, *s* to Israel in a vision by night,
50:21 By thus *s* kindly to them,
Ex 4:12 *s* and will teach you what you are to say."
4:15 I will assist both you and him in *s* and
19: 9 so that when the people hear me *s* with you,
19:19 was *s* and God answering him with thunder.
31:18 had finished *s* to Moses on Mount Sinai,
34:33 When he finished *s* with them,
Dt 4:33 the voice of God *s* from the midst of fire,
4:36 fire, and you heard him *s* out of the fire.
5:26 of the living God *s* from the midst of fire,
5:28 words as you were *s* to me and said to me,
11:19 children, *s* of them at home and abroad,
20: 9 officials have finished *s* to the soldiers,
31: 1 had finished *s* these words to all Israel,
32:45 finished *s* all these words to all Israel,
Jgs 6:17 you, give me a sign that you are *s* with me.
15:17 finished *s* he threw the jawbone from him;
1Sm 14:19 While Saul was *s* to the priest,
17:28 oldest brother, heard him *s* with the men,
18: 1 [By the time David finished *s* with Saul,
2Sm 13:36 he finished *s* than the princes came in,
1Kgs 1:14 while you are still there *s* to the king,
1:22 While she was still *s* to the king,
1:42 As he was *s*,
2Kgs 6:33 While Elisha was still *s*,
2Chr 10:14 *s* to them according to the advice of the
25:16 While he was still *s*,
32:17 the God of Israel, *s* of him in these terms:
Jdt 14: 8 she left till the time she began *s* to them.
Est 6:14 While they were *s* with him,
1Mc 3:23 When he finished *s*, he rushed suddenly
13:17 knew that they were *s* deceitfully to him,
2Mc 7: 2 One of the brothers, *s* for the others,
7:30 scarcely finished *s* when the youth said:
Jb 1:16 While he was yet *s*, another came and said,
1:17 While he was yet *s*, another came and said,
1:18 While he was yet *s*, another came and said,
4: 2 For how can anyone refrain from *s*?
16: 8 rises up my traducer, *s* openly against me;
29: 9 The chief men refrained from *s* and covered
Ps(s) 34:14 from evil and your lips from *s* guile;
50:20 You sit *s* against your brother;
Eccl 7:21 lest you hear your servant *s* ill of you,
Sir 4:23 Refrain not from *s* at the proper time,
18:18 Be informed before *s*;
Is 19:18 Egypt *s* the language of Canaan
58:13 your own interests, or *s* with malice
65:24 while they are yet *s*,
Jer 7:22 In *s* to your fathers on the day I brought
23:35 Thus you shall ask, when *s* to one another,
26: 8 When Jeremiah finished *s* all that the LORD
38: 1 Jeremiah *s* these words to all the people:
38: 4 all the people, by *s* such things to them;
43: 1 When Jeremiah finished *s* to the people all
Ez 2: 2 and I heard the one who was *s* say to me:
14: 9 prophet, if he is beguiled into *s* a word,
43: 6 I heard someone *s* to me from the temple,
Dn 8:13 I heard a holy one *s*,
10:11 "understand the words which I am *s* to you;
10:15 While he was *s* thus to me,
Hos 1: 2 In the beginning of the Lord's *s* to Hosea,
Zec 8:23 of every nationality, *s* different tongues,
Mt 9:18 Before Jesus had finished *s* to them,
10:20 the Spirit of your Father will be *s* in you.
13: 3 at length in parables, *s* in this fashion:
15:31 in the crowds as they beheld the mute *s*,
16:11 Why is it you do not see that I was not *s*
17: 5 He was still *s* when suddenly a bright
17:13 had been *s* to them about John the Baptizer.
21:45 they realized he was *s* about them.
26:47 While he was still *s*,

SPEAKING (cont.)

Mk 5:35 He had not finished *s* when people from the
13:11 not be yourselves *s* but the Holy Spirit.
14:43 Even while he was still *s*,
16:19 Then, after *s* to them,
Lk 5: 4 When he had finished *s* he said to Simon,
6:39 He also used images in *s* to them:
8:49 He was still *s* when a man came from the
9:34 While he was *s*, a cloud came
11:37 As he was *s*, a Pharisee invited him
11:45 "Teacher, in *s* this way you insult us too."
21: 5 Some were *s* of how the temple was adorned
22:47 While he was still *s* a crowd came,
24:36 While they were still *s* about all this,
24:53 temple constantly, *s* the praises of God.
Jn 4:27 surprised that Jesus was *s* with a woman.
5:18 still, was *s* of God as his own Father,
7:26 Here he is *s* in public and they don't say
8:27 grasp that he was *s* to them of the Father.
9:37 "He is *s* to you now."
11:13 Jesus had been *s* about his death,
12:29 Others maintained, "An angel was *s* to him."
14:30 I shall not go on *s* to you longer;
16:29 "At last you are *s* plainly,"
18:38 *S* for myself, I find no case
21:19 When Jesus had finished *s* he said to him,
Acts 1: 3 days and *s* to them about the reign of God.
2: 6 one heard these men *s* his own language.
2: 7 not all of these men who are *s* Galileans?
2:11 Yet each of us hears them *s* in his own
4:20 help *s* of what we have heard and seen."
6:11 him *s* blasphemies against Moses and God,
9:27 and how Saul had been *s* out fearlessly in
10:28 there, and he began *s* to them thus:
10:46 could hear *s* in tongues and glorifying God.
18: 9 Go on *s* and do not be silenced,
20: 7 the next day, he kept on *s* until midnight.
22: 9 light but did not hear the voice *s* to me.
22:18 I fell into a trance and saw Jesus *s* to me.
Rom 7: 1 (I am *s* to men who know what law is),
9:24 I am *s* about us whom he called,
1Cor 5:10 I was not *s* of association with immoral
14: 6 that I should come to you *s* in tongues.
14: 9 speech because you are *s* in a tongue,
14:23 is assembled and everyone is *s* in tongues,
14:28 each one *s* only to himself and to God.
Eph 3: 4 about in *s* of the mystery of Christ,
Heb 12:19 nor a voice *s* words such that those who
Jas 4:11 or judges his brother is *s* against the law.

SPEAKS (69)

Gn 32: 5 'Your servant Jacob *s* as follows:
Ex 33:11 face to face, as one man *s* to another.
Nm 12: 2 it through Moses alone that the LORD *s*?
Dt 18:19 listen to my words which he *s* in my name,
18:20 to speak, or *s* in the name of other gods,
18:22 though a prophet *s* in the name of the LORD,
Jdt 11:21 other looks so beautiful and *s* so wisely!"
Jb 34:35 "Job *s* without intelligence,
36:33 His thunder *s* for him and incites the fury
Ps(s) 2: 5 Then in anger he *s* to them;
12: 3 Everyone *s* falsehood to his neighbor;
27: 8 Of you my heart *s*;
36: 2 Sin *s* to the wicked man in his heart;
41: 7 comes to see me, he *s* without sincerity;
101: 7 *s* falsehood shall not stand before my eyes.
Prv 12:17 sure of, but a lying witness *s* deceitfully.
16:13 and the man who *s* what is right he loves.
26:25 When he *s* graciously,
Sg 2:10 My lover *s*;
Sir 12:16 With his lips an enemy *s* sweetly,
13:21 the supporters for a rich man when he *s*;
13:21 When a poor man *s* they make sport of him;
13:21 he *s* wisely and no attention is paid him.
13:22 A rich man *s* and all are silent,
13:22 A poor man *s* and they say:
25: 9 a friend and he who *s* to attentive ears.
27: 4 so do a man's faults when he *s*.
27: 7 Praise no man before he *s*,
29: 5 *s* with respect of his creditor's wealth;
34: 9 a man of experience *s* sense.
Is 1: 2 and listen, O earth, for the LORD *s*:
30:31 When the LORD *s*,
32: 6 For the fool *s* foolishly,
33:15 He who practices virtue and *s* honestly,
Jer 9: 4 one deceives the other, no one *s* the truth.
9: 7 He *s* cordially with his friends,
10: 1 Hear the word which the LORD *s* to you,
13:15 Give ear, listen humbly, for the LORD *s*.
26:16 name of the LORD, our God, that he *s* to us."
Ez 10: 5 the voice of God the Almighty when he *s*.
16:59 For thus *s* the Lord GOD:
17: 3 Thus *s* the Lord GOD:
20: 5 Thus *s* the Lord GOD:
37:21 Thus *s* the Lord GOD:
Am 3: 8 The Lord GOD *s*— who will not prophesy!
5:10 at the gate and abhor him who *s* the truth.
Mi 7: 3 for a price, The great man *s* as he pleases,
Mt 12:34 The mouth *s* whatever fills the mind.
Lk 6:45 Each man *s* from his heart's abundance.
12:10 *s* against the Son of Man will be forgiven,
Jn 3:31 is earthly, and he *s* on an earthly plane.
3:34 One whom God has sent *s* the words of God;
7:18 *s* on his own is bent on self-glorification.
8:47 Whoever is of God hears every word God *s*.
1Cor 12: 3 who *s* in the Spirit of God ever says,
14: 2 A man who *s* in a tongue is talking not to
14: 3 other hand, *s* to men for their upbuilding,
14: 4 He who *s* in a tongue builds up himself,
14: 5 is greater than one who *s* in tongues,
14:13 This means that the man who *s* in a tongue
14:26 one *s* in a tongue,
14:35 a disgrace when a woman *s* in the assembly.
2Cor 13: 3 for a proof of the Christ who *s* in me.
Heb 11: 4 although Abel is dead, he still *s*.
12:24 which *s* more eloquently than that of Abel.
12:25 Do not refuse to hear him who *s*.
12:25 if we turn away from him who *s* from heaven!
Jas 4:11 The one who *s* ill of his brother or judges
1Pt 4:11 The one who *s* is to deliver God's message.

SPEAR (43)

1Sm 13:22 neither sword nor *s* could be found
17:45 against me with sword and *s* and scimitar,
17:47 is not by sword or *s* that the LORD saves.
18:10 other times, while Saul was holding his *s*.
18:11 Saul poised the *s*,
19: 9 sitting in his house with *s* in hand
19:10 *s*, but David eluded Saul, so that the spear
19:10 Saul, so that the *s* struck only the wall,
20:33 this Saul brandished his *s* to strike him,
21: 9 "Do you have a *s* or a sword on hand?
22: 6 tree on the high place, holding his *s*,
26: 7 with his *s* thrust into the ground at his
26: 8 him to the ground with one thrust of the *s*;
26:11 *s* which is at his head and the water jug,
26:12 So David took the *s* and the water jug from
26:16 *s* and the water jug that was at his head?"
26:22 "Here is the king's *s*.
2Sm 1: 6 Gilboa and saw Saul leaning on his *s*,
21:16 bronze *s* weighed three hundred shekels,
21:19 *s* with a shaft like a weaver's heddle-bar.
23: 7 arm himself with iron and the shaft of a *s*,
23:18 brandished his *s* over three hundred slain.
23:21 Although the Egyptian was armed with a *s*,
23:21 and wrested the *s* from the Egyptian's hand,
23:21 hand, then killed him with his own *s*.
1Chr 11:11 He brandished his *s* against three hundred,
11:20 he brandished his *s* against three hundred,
11:23 a *s* that was like a weaver's heddle-bar,
11:23 wrested the *s* from the Egyptian's hand,
11:23 hand, and killed him with his own *s*.
12: 9 soldiers equipped with shield and *s*,
20: 5 *s* shaft was like a weaver's heddle-bar.
2Chr 23:10 all the people, each with his *s* in hand,
Jdt 6: 6 *s* of my servants will pierce your sides,
9: 7 their infantry, trusting in shield and *s*,
11: 2 Nor would I have raised my *s* against your
2Mc 15:11 *s* as with the encouragement of noble words,
Jb 39:23 quiver, flashes the *s* and the javelin.
41:18 nor will the *s*,
41:21 he laughs at the crash of the *s*.
Sir 29:13 *s* it will fight for you against the foe.
Na 3: 3 flame of the sword, the flash of the *s*,
Hb 3:11 arrows, at the gleam of your flashing *s*.

SPEARMEN (1)

Acts 23:23 seventy cavalrymen, and two hundred *s*.

SPEARS (20)

1Sm 13:19 the Hebrews will make swords or *s*."
1Kgs 18:28 and slashed themselves with swords and *s*,
2Kgs 11:10 the captains King David's *s* and shields,
1Chr 12:25 Judahites bearing shields and *s*:
2Chr 11:12 In every city were shields and *s*,
23: 9 the priest gave the captains the *s*,
32: 5 a great number of *s* and shields prepared.
Neh 4: 7 family groups with their swords, their *s*,
4:10 work, while the other half, armed with *s*,
4:15 work, half of the men with *s* at the ready,
Jdt 1:15 mountains of Ragae, ran him through with *s*,
7:10 These Israelites do not rely on their *s*,
2Mc 5: 3 with brandished shields and bristling *s*,
Jb 40:31 hide with barbs, or his head with fish *s*?
Ps(s) 46:10 he splinters the *s*;
57: 5 Their teeth are *s* and arrows,
Is 2: 4 plowshares and their *s* into pruning hooks;
Jer 46: 4 polish your *s*,
Jl 4:10 swords, and your pruning hooks into *s*;
Mi 4: 3 plowshares, and their *s* into pruning hooks;

SPECIAL (15)

Gn 27: 4 I may give you my *s* blessing before I die."
27:19 so that you may give me your *s* blessing."
27:31 that you may then give me your *s* blessing."
30:40 Thus he produced *s* flocks of his own,
Ex 19: 5 my covenant, you shall be my *s* possession,
Lv 7:29 a part of it as his *s* offering to him,
21:10 has been ordained to wear the *s* vestments,
Dt 12:11 *s* offering you have vowed to the LORD.
2Chr 7: 9 On the eighth day they held a *s* meeting,
2Mc 3:38 some *s* divine power about the Place.
Wis 18:21 bearing the weapon of his *s* office,
Mal 3:17 the LORD of hosts, my own *s* possession,
1Cor 3: 7 nor he who waters is of any *s* account,
Phil 1:29 is your *s* privilege to take Christ's part
Rv 12: 6 a *s* place had been prepared for her by God;

SPECIALLY (1)

Sir 34: 6 it be a vision *s* sent by the Most High,

SPECIES (11)

Gn 7:16 male and female, and of all *s* they came,
Lv 11:14 osprey, the kite, the various *s* of falcons,
11:15 species of falcons, the various *s* of crows,
11:16 nightjar, the gull, the various *s* of hawks,
11:19 the stork, the various *s* of herons,
19:19 animals with others of a different *s*;
Dt 14:14 and falcons, all the various *s* of crows,
14:15 nightjar, the gull, the various *s* of hawks,
14:18 the stork, the various *s* of herons,
Prv 30:25 Ants—a *s* not strong,
30:26 a *s* not mighty,

SPECIFIC (1)

1Thes 5: 1 As regards *s* times and moments,

SPECIFICATIONS (2)

1Chr 28:19 to writing the exact *s* of the pattern,
2Chr 3: 3 These were the *s* laid down by Solomon for

SPECIFIED (7)

1Sm 13:11 me, since you had not come by the *s* time,
1Chr 28:14 He *s* the weight of gold to be used in the
28:15 he *s* the weight of gold for each lampstand
28:15 and for the silver lampstands he *s* the
28:16 He *s* the weight of gold for each table to
Jdt 8:33 and within the days you have *s* before you
Dn 1:18 time the king had *s* for their preparation,

SPECIMENS (1)

Gn 41:19 ugly *s* as these in all the land of Egypt!

SPECIOUS (3)

Lam 2:14 prophets had for you false and *s* visions;
Phil 1:18 whether from *s* motives or genuine ones,
Col 2: 4 no one may delude you with *s* arguments.

SPECK (6)

Mt 7: 3 Why look at the *s* in your brother's eye
7: 4 'Let me take that *s* out of your eye,'
7: 5 to take the *s* from your brother's eye.
Lk 6:41 "Why look at the *s* in your brother's eye
6:42 let me remove the *s* from your eye,'
6:42 to remove the *s* from your brother's eye.

SPECKLED (8)

Gn 30:32 and every spotted or *s* one among the goats.
30:33 possession that is not a *s* or spotted goat,
30:35 and all the *s* and spotted she-goats,
30:39 brought forth streaked, *s* and spotted kids.
31: 8 said, 'The *s* animals shall be your wages,'
31: 8 the entire flock would bear *s* young;
31:10 he-goats that were streaked, *s* and mottled.
31:12 as they mate, are streaked, *s* and mottled,

SPECTACLE (4)

Ez 28:17 I made you a *s* in the sight of kings.
Lk 23:48 assembled for this *s* saw what had happened,
1Cor 4: 9 We have become a *s* to the universe,
Heb 12:21 so fearful was the *s* that Moses said,

SPECTATORS (1)

Mk 5:16 The *s* explained what had happened to the

SPECULATE (1)

Wis 13: 9 that they could *s* about the world,

SPECULATING (1)

Rom 1:21 themselves through *s* to no purpose,

SPECULATIONS (1)

1Tm 1: 4 which promote idle *s* rather than that

SPED (6)

2Sm 17:18 They *s* on their way and reached the house
18:21 The Cushite bowed to Joab and *s* away.
18:23 Ahimaaz *s* off by way of the Jordan plain
Est 8:14 *s* forth in haste at the king's order,
Ps(s) 77:18 your arrows also *s* abroad.
Wis 4:14 he *s* him out of the midst of wickedness.

SPEECH (69)

Gn 11: 9 the LORD confused the *s* of all the world.
Ex 4:10 but I am slow of *s* and tongue."
4:11 one man *s* and makes another deaf and dumb?
Jdt 9:13 Let my guileful *s* bring wound and wale on
11: 9 "As for Achior's *s* in your council,
Est E: 5 the fair *s* of friends entrusted with the

1Mc 4:19 As Judas was finishing this *s*,
2Mc 15:12 gentle in manners, distinguished in *s*,
Jb 13:17 Pay careful heed to my *s*,
15: 3 Should he argue in *s* which does not avail,
15:11 for you, and *s* that deals gently with you?
19:16 answer, though in my *s* I plead with him.
Ps(s) 35:20 in the land they fashion treacherous *s*.
39: 3 I refrained from rash *s*.
52: 5 than good, falsehood rather than honest *s*.
55:22 Softer than butter is his *s*,
Prv 2:12 way of evil men, from men of perverse *s*,
4:24 talk, deceitful *s* put far from you.
12: 6 ambush, but the *s* of the upright saves them.
16:21 pleasing *s* increases his persuasiveness.
17:27 who is chary of *s* is a man of intelligence.
22:11 of winning *s* has the king for his friend.
Eccl 1: 8 All *s* is labored;
7: 8 Better is the end of *s* than its beginning;
Wis 10:21 of the dumb, and gave ready *s* to infants.
Sir 4:24 it is through *s* that wisdom becomes known,
4:29 Be not surly in your *s*,
8: 3 Dispute not with a man of railing *s*,
9:18 Feared in the city is the man of railing *s*,
11: 8 interrupt no one in the middle of his *s*.
26:14 A gift from the LORD is her governed *s*,
27: 6 a man's *s* disclose the bent of his mind.
36:23 And if, besides, her *s* is kindly,
Is 3: 8 *s* and their deeds are before the LORD,
33:19 look no more, the people of obscure *s*,
58: 9 false accusation and malicious *s*;
Jer 5:15 know not, whose *s* you cannot understand.
7:27 the word itself is banished from their *s*.
Bar 4:15 afar, a nation ruthless and of alien *s*,
6:40 when they see a deaf mute, incapable of *s*,
Ez 3: 5 *s* and barbarous language am I sending you,
3: 6 difficult *s* and barbarous language]
Mt 21:16 'From the *s* of infants and children you
22:15 to plot how they might trap Jesus in *s*.
Mk 7:32 deaf man who had a *s* impediment
12:13 Herodians after him to catch him in his *s*.
Lk 4:36 "What is there about his *s*?
11:54 setting traps to catch him in his *s*.
20:20 the guise of honest men to trap him in *s*,
20:26 They were unable to trap him publicly in *s*.
Jn 8:44 Lying *s* is his native tongue;
16:25 shall tell you about the Father in plain *s*.
Acts 4: 4 many of those who had heard the *s* believed;
5:39 This *s* persuaded them.
14:18 Yet even with a *s* such as this,
19:28 When they heard this *s*,
22:22 his *s* the crowd had been listening to Paul,
Rom 8:26 groanings that cannot be expressed in *s*.
16:18 with smooth and flattering *s*.
1Cor 1: 5 endowed with every gift of *s* and knowledge.
14: 6 you if my *s* does not have some revelation,
14: 9 *s* because you are speaking in a tongue,
14:21 and in alien *s* I will speak to this people,
2Cor 11: 6 I may be unskilled in *s* but I know that I
Col 3:17 Whatever you do, whether in *s* or in action,
4: 6 *s* be always gracious and in good taste,
Ti 2: 1 *s* be consistent with your sound doctrine.
Jas 3: 2 in *s* he is a man in the fullest sense,
Rv 13:15 so that the image had the power of *s*

SPEECHES (2)

Ps(s) 94: 4 the wicked glory, Mouthing insolent *s*,
Jer 23:31 LORD, who borrow *s* to pronounce oracles.

SPEECHLESS (6)

2Mc 3:29 he lay *s* and deprived of all hope of aid,
Ps(s) 39:10 I was *s* and opened not my mouth,
Wis 4:19 For he shall strike them down *s* and
Is 52:15 because of him kings shall stand *s*;
Lk 1:22 making signs to them, for he remained *s*.
Acts 9: 7 who were traveling with him stood there *s*.

SPEED (3)

Is 5:19 say, "Let him make haste and *s* his work,
Dn 14:36 with the *s* of the wind,
Ti 3:13 *S* Zenas the lawyer and Apollos on their

SPEEDILY (5)

Dt 28:20 until you are *s* destroyed and perish for
Ps(s) 102: 3 in the day when I call, answer me *s*.
Is 5:26 *s* and promptly will they come.
51: 5 I will make my justice come *s*;
Jl 4: 4 you do take action against me, swiftly, *s*,

SPEEDING (1)

Wis 5:11 and cleft by the rushing force Of *s* wings,

SPEEDS (1)

Sir 43:13 *s* the arrows of his judgment to their goal.

SPELL (3)

Mk 11:18 crowd was under the *s* of his teaching.
Acts 8:11 the *s* of his magic over a long period;
Gal 3: 1 Who has cast a *s* over you

SPELLBOUND (5)

Mt 7:28 and left the crowds *s* at his teaching.
22:33 crowds who listened were *s* by his teaching.
Mk 1:22 The people were *s* by his teaching because
Lk 4:32 They were *s* by his teaching,
Acts 8: 9 in the town and holding the Samaritans *s*.

SPELLS (4)

Dt 18:11 charmer, diviner, or caster of *s*,
Ps(s) 58: 6 the voice of enchanters casting cunning *s*.
Is 47: 9 sorceries and the great number of your *s*;
47:12 up, now, your *s* and your many sorceries.

SPELT (3)

Ex 9:32 But the wheat and the *s* were not ruined,
Is 28:25 in wheat and barley, with *s* as its border?
Ez 4: 9 and beans and lentils, and millet and *s*;

SPEND (44)

Gn 24:23 your father's house for us to *s* the night?"
24:25 she added, "and room to *s* the night."
Ex 29:35 "Seven days you shall *s* in ordaining them,
29:37 Seven days you shall *s* in making atonement
Lv 12: 4 and then she shall *s* thirty-three days
12: 5 after which she shall *s* sixty-six days in
Dt 28:38 "Though you *s* much seed on your field,
32:23 I will *s* on them woe upon woe and exhaust
Jgs 5:17 why does Dan *s* his time in ships?
19: 6 to *s* the night here and enjoy yourself?"
19: 9 *S* the night here and enjoy yourself.
19:11 of the Jebusites and *s* the night in it."
19:13 either Gibeah or Ramah, to *s* the night."
19:20 do not *s* the night in the public square."
2Sm 17: 8 he will not *s* the night with the people.
17:16 *s* the night at the fords near the desert,
Neh 4:16 people to *s* the nights inside Jerusalem,
13:21 do you *s* the night alongside the wall?
Jb 27:12 why then do you *s* yourselves in idle words!
36:11 serve him, they *s* their days in prosperity,
Sg 7:12 fields and *s* the night among the villages.
Sir 27:12 Limit the time you *s* among fools,
29:10 *S* your money for your brother and friend,
42:12 men, or *s* her time with married women;
Is 10:29 "We will *s* the night at Geba."
21:13 thicket in the nomad country *s* the night,
55: 2 Why *s* your money for what is not bread;
Bar 6: 9 from their gods and *s* it on themselves,
Ez 5:13 Thus shall my anger *s* itself,
5:13 in my jealousy when I *s* my fury upon them.
6:12 so will I *s* my fury upon them.
7: 8 my fury upon you and *s* my anger upon you;
Jl 1:13 Come, *s* the night in sackcloth,
Mt 12:40 so will the Son of Man *s* three days and
Mk 6:37 "Are we to go and *s* two hundred days'
Lk 21:37 city to *s* the night on the Mount of Olives.
Acts 12:19 left Judea to *s* some time in Caesarea.
25:14 Since they were to *s* several days there,
1Cor 16: 6 even to *s* the winter with you
16: 7 I hope to *s* some time with you,
2Cor 12:15 *s* myself and be spent for your sakes.
Ti 3:12 I have decided to *s* the winter there.
Jas 4:13 go to such and such a town, *s* a year there,
1Pt 4: 2 You are not to *s* what remains of your

SPENDING (8)

1Mc 14:32 *s* large sums of his own money to equip the
Is 65: 4 the graves and *s* the night in caverns,
Ez 20: 8 *s* my anger on them there in the land
20:21 them, of *s* my anger on them in the desert;
Lk 6:12 to pray, *s* the night in communion with God.
Acts 18:23 After *s* some time there he set out again,
25: 6 After *s* eight or ten days in Jerusalem,
27:12 of making Phoenix and *s* the winter there.

SPENDS (1)

Jb 39:28 On the cliff he dwells and *s* the night,

SPENT (45)

Gn 24:54 eaten and drunk, they *s* the night there.
31:41 years that I have now *s* in your household,
47:15 all the money in Egypt and Canaan was *s*,
47:18 *s* and our livestock made over to my lord,
50: 3 embalmed Israel, they *s* forty days at it,
Ex 4:24 journey, at a place where they *s* the night,
Lv 26:20 so that your strength will be *s* in vain;
Nm 14:34 Forty days you *s* in scouting the land;
Dt 10:10 "After I had *s* these other forty days and
Jos 8: 9 Joshua, however, *s* that night in the plain.
Jgs 19: 4 and so he *s* three days with this
19: 7 him he went back and *s* the night there.
2Sm 1: 1 of the Amalekites and *s* two days in Ziklag.
2:11 David *s* seven years and six months in
1Kgs 5:28 so that they *s* one month in the Lebanon
Ezr 10: 6 where he *s* the night neither eating food
Neh 13:20 *s* the night once or twice outside
Est 2:12 six months were *s* with oil of myrrh,
2:21 time that Mordecai *s* at the king's gate,
1Mc 11: 6 greeted each other and *s* the night there.
16: 4 Cendebeus, they *s* the night at Modein,
2Mc 4:19 the money should not be *s* on a sacrifice,
10: 6 they had *s* the feast of Booths living like
Ps(s) 31:11 is *s* with grief and my years with sighing;
90: 9 we have *s* our years like a sigh.
Wis 18:14 the night in its swift course was half *s*,
Is 49: 4 and for nothing, uselessly, *s* my strength,
Lam 3:22 are not exhausted, his mercies are not *s*;
4:11 The LORD has *s* his anger,
Ez 13:15 *s* my fury on the wall and its whitewashers,
Mt 12:40 Just as Jonah *s* three days and three
13:54 Jesus next went to his native place and *s*
21:17 the city to Bethany, where he *s* the night.
Mk 6: 6 villages instead, and *s* his time teaching.
Lk 15:14 After he had *s* everything,
Jn 3:22 he *s* some time with them there baptizing.
Acts 13:36 *s* a lifetime in carrying out God's will,
14: 3 Paul and Barnabas *s* considerable time
14:28 they *s* some time there with the disciples.
16:13 We *s* some time in that city.
20: 6 we joined them in Troas, where we *s* a week.
21: 7 the brothers and *s* the day with them.
28:12 put in at Syracuse and *s* three days there.
Rom 13:12 The night is far *s*; the day draws near.
2Cor 12:15 spend myself and be *s* for your sakes.

SPEW (2)

Jon 2:11 the fish to *s* Jonah upon the shore.
Rv 3:16 hot nor cold, I will *s* you out of my mouth!

SPEWED (2)

Rv 12:15 *s* a torrent of water out of his mouth to
12:16 flood which the dragon *s* out of his mouth.

SPICE (3)

2Chr 9: 9 There was no other *s* like that which the
Sg 5:13 beds of *s* with ripening aromatic herbs.
6: 2 down to his garden, to the beds of *s*,

SPICED (3)

1Chr 9:30 however, who mixed the *s* ointments.
Ps(s) 75: 9 LORD's hand, full of *s* and foaming wine,
Sg 8: 2 you *s* wine to drink and pomegranate juice.

SPICES (26)

Ex 25: 6 *s* for the anointing oil and for the
30:23 LORD said to Moses, "Take the finest *s*:
35: 8 *s* for the anointing oil and for the
35:28 as well as *s*,
1Kgs 10: 2 retinue, and with camels bearing *s*,
10:10 gold talents, a very large quantity of *s*,
10:10 did anyone bring such an abundance of *s*
10:25 or gold articles, garments, weapons, *s*,
2Kgs 20:13 treasury, his silver, gold, *s* and fine oil,
1Chr 9:29 wine, the oil, the frankincense, and the *s*.
2Chr 9: 1 numerous retinue and by camels bearing *s*,
9: 9 talents and a very large quantity of *s*,
9:24 and gold articles, garments, weapons, *s*,
16:14 couch which was filled with *s*
32:27 for his silver, gold, precious stones, *s*,
Sg 4:10 the fragrance of your ointments than all *s*!
4:14 Myrrh and aloes, with all the finest *s*.
5: 1 I gather my myrrh and my *s*,
8:14 or a young stag on the mountains of *s*!
Sir 24:15 Like galbanum and onycha and sweet *s*,
Is 39: 2 the silver and gold, the *s* and fine oil,
Jer 34: 5 and burn *s* for your burial as they did for
Ez 27:22 for your wares the very choicest *s*,
Lk 23:56 they went home to prepare *s* and perfumes.
24: 1 the tomb bringing the *s* they had prepared.
Rv 5: 8 vessels of gold filled with aromatic *s*,

SPIDERS (2)

Jb 8:14 a gossamer thread and his trust is a *s* web.
Is 59: 5 They hatch adders' eggs, and weave *s*' webs:

SPIED (7)

Gn 22:13 *s* a ram caught by its horns in the thicket.
Jos 6:22 the two men who had *s* out the land,
1Sm 6:13 When they looked up and *s* the ark,
2Sm 18:26 nearer, the lookout *s* another runner.
2Kgs 4:25 When he *s* her at a distance,
13:21 when suddenly they *s* such a raiding band.
Mt 12: 2 When the Pharisees *s* this, they protested:

SPIES (15)

Gn 42: 9 "You are *s*.
42:11 your servants have never been *s*."
42:14 Joseph persisted; "you are *s*.
42:16 are untrue, as Pharaoh lives, you are *s*!"
42:31 we have never been *s*.
42:34 I know that you are honest men and not *s*,
Nm 21:32 of the Amorites, Moses sent *s* to Jazer;
Jos 2: 1 Nun, secretly sent out two *s* from Shittim,
2: 8 Before the *s* fell asleep,
6:23 The *s* entered and brought out Rahab,
2Sm 15:10 *s* throughout the tribes of Israel to say,
1Mc 12:26 The *s* he had sent into their camp came
Ps(s) 37:32 The wicked man *s* on the just,
Lk 20:20 they sent *s* to him in the guise of honest

SPIES (cont.)

Heb 11:31 for she had peacefully received the *s.*

SPIKES (2)

Eccl 12:11 *s* are the topics given by one collector.
Sir 44: 4 and forgers of epigrams with their *s;*

SPILL (1)

Lk 5:37 burst the old skins, the wine will *s* out,

SPILLED (1)

Lv 6:20 If any of its blood is *s* on a garment,

SPILLING (2)

Jn 2:15 the money-changers' tables, *s* their coins.
Acts 1:18 burst wide open, all his entrails *s* out.

SPILLS (1)

Mt 9:17 they do, the skins burst, the wine *s* out,

SPIN (2)

Mt 6:28 They do not work, they do not *s.*
Lk 12:27 they do not *s,*

SPINDLE (1)

Prv 31:19 to the distaff, and her fingers ply the *s.*

SPINE (1)

Lv 3: 9 tail, which he must sever close to the *s,*

SPINNERS (2)

Ex 35:25 who were expert *s* brought hand-spun violet,
Is 19:10 The *s* shall be crushed,

SPINNING (1)

Ez 21: 5 not this the one who is forever *s* parables?' "

SPIRIT (579)

Gn 6: 3 "My *s* shall not remain in man forever,
41: 8 Next morning his *s* was agitated.
41:38 "a man so endowed with the *s* of God?"
45:27 the *s* of their father Jacob revived.
49: 6 or my *s* be joined with their company;
Ex 31: 3 I have filled him with divine *s* of skill
35:21 as his heart suggested and his *s* prompted,
35:31 and has filled him with a divine *s* of
Nm 11:17 I will also take some of the *s* that is on
11:25 Taking some of the *s* that was on Moses,
11:25 and as the *s* came to rest on them,
11:26 yet the *s* came to rest on them also,
11:29 the LORD might bestow his *s* on them all!"
14:24 a different *s* and follows me unreservedly,
24: 2 tribe by tribe, the *s* of God came upon him,
27:18 "Take Joshua, son of Nun, a man of *s,*
Dt 28:65 heart and wasted eyes and a dismayed *s.*
34: 9 of Nun, was filled with the *s* of wisdom,
Jgs 3:10 The *s* of the LORD came upon him,
6:34 The *s* of the LORD enveloped Gideon;
11:29 The *s* of the LORD came upon Jephthah.
13:25 the *s* of the LORD first stirred him in
14: 6 But the *s* of the LORD came upon Samson,
14:19 The *s* of the LORD came upon him,
15:14 meet him, the *s* of the LORD came upon him:
15:19 drank till his *s* returned and he revived.
1Sm 10: 6 The *s* of the LORD will rush upon you,
10:10 met him, and the *s* of God rushed upon him,
11: 6 the *s* of God rushed upon him and he became
16:13 on, the *s* of the LORD rushed upon David.
16:14 The *s* of the LORD had departed from Saul,
16:14 tormented by an evil *s* sent by the LORD.
16:15 An evil *s* from God is tormenting you.
16:16 When the evil *s* from God comes over you,
16:23 Whenever the *s* from God seized Saul,
16:23 better, for the evil *s* would leave him.
18:10 next day an evil *s* from God came over Saul,
19: 9 Then an evil *s* from the LORD came upon
19:23 the sheds, the *s* of God came upon him also,
2Sm 23: 2 The *s* of the LORD spoke through me;
1Kgs 18:12 the *s* of the LORD will carry you to some
22:22 lying *s* in the mouths of all his prophets.'
22:23 the LORD has put a lying *s* in the mouths
22:24 the cheek saying, "Has the *s* of the LORD,
2Kgs 2: 9 "May I receive a double portion of your *s.*"
2:15 said, "The *s* of Elijah rests on Elisha."
2:16 Perhaps the *s* of the LORD has carried him
5:26 "Was I not present in *s* when the man
19: 7 I am about to put in him such a *s* that,
1Chr 12:19 Then *s* enveloped Amasai,
2Chr 15: 1 Azariah, son of Oded, came the *s* of God.
18:20 until a *s* came forward and presented
18:21 lying *s* in the mouths of all his prophets.'
18:22 *s* in the mouths of these your prophets,
18:23 "Which way did the *s* of the LORD go when
20:14 And the *s* of the LORD came upon Jahaziel,
24:20 Then the *s* of God possessed Zechariah,
Neh 9:20 "Your good *s* you bestowed on them,
9:30 witness against them through your *s,*
Tb 3: 1 Grief-stricken in *s,* I groaned
3:10 That day she was deeply grieved in *s.*
4: 3 her, and do not grieve her *s* in any way.
6: 8 who is afflicted by a demon or evil *s,*
8:20 bring joy to my daughter's sorrowing *s.*
13: 7 and my *s* rejoices in the King of heaven.
13:15 My *s* blesses the Lord,
14:11 But now my *s* is about to leave me."
Jdt 12:16 in rapture over her, and his *s* was shaken.
16:14 and they were made, You sent forth your *s,*
1Mc 13: 7 heard these words, their *s* was rekindled.
2Mc 5:17 Puffed up in *s,* Antiochus did not
7:21 Filled with a noble *s* that stirred her
9:11 At last, broken in *s,* he began to give up
14:46 and of *s* to give these back to him again.
Jb 3:20 the toilers, and life to the bitter in *s?*
4:15 Then a *s* passed before me,
6: 4 pierce me, and my *s* drinks in their poison;
7:11 I will speak in the anguish of my *s;*
10:12 and your providence has preserved my *s.*
17: 1 My *s* is broken,
20: 2 from my understanding a *s* gives me a reply.
32: 8 But it is a *s* in man,
32:18 the *s* within me compels me.
33: 4 For the *s* of God has made me,
34:14 If he were to take back his *s* to himself,
Ps(s) 31: 6 Into your hands I commend my *s;*
32: 2 not guilt, in whose *s* there is no guile.
34:19 and those who are crushed in *s* he saves.
51:12 O God, and a steadfast *s* renew within me.
51:13 presence, and your holy *s* take not from me.
51:14 salvation, and a willing *s* sustain in me.
51:19 My sacrifice, O God, is a contrite *s;*
77: 4 when I ponder, my *s* grows faint.
77: 7 I ponder, and my *s* broods:
78: 8 steadfast nor its *s* faithful toward God.
104:30 When you send forth your *s,*
106:33 their account, For they embittered his *s,*
139: 7 Where can I go from your *s?*
142: 4 When my *s* is faint within me,
143: 4 And my *s* is faint within me,
143: 7 to answer me, O LORD, for my *s* fails me.
143:10 May your good *s* guide me on level ground.
146: 4 When his *s* departs he returns to his earth;
Prv 1:23 I will pour out to you my *s,*
15: 4 of life, but a perverse one crushes the *s.*
15:13 but by mental anguish the *s* is broken.
16: 2 eyes, but it is the LORD who proves the *s.*
16:18 disaster, and a haughty *s* before a fall.
17:22 body, but a depressed *s* dries up the bones.
18:14 A man's *s* sustains him in infirmity
18:14 but a broken *s* who can bear?
29:23 but he who is humble of *s* obtains honor.
Eccl 7: 8 is the patient *s* than the lofty spirit.
7: 9 Do not in *s* become quickly discontented,
Wis 1: 5 For the holy *s* of discipline flees deceit
1: 6 For wisdom is a kindly *s,*
1: 7 For the *s* of the Lord fills the world,
2: 3 our *s* will be poured abroad
5: 3 rueful and groaning through anguish of *s:*
7: 7 I pleaded and the *s* of Wisdom came to me.
7:22 For in her is a *s* intelligent,
9:17 Wisdom and sent your holy *s* from on high?
11:20 and winnowed out by your mighty *s;*
12: 1 for your imperishable *s* is in all things!
15:11 a quickening soul, and infused a vital *s.*
15:16 whose *s* has been lent him fashioned them.
16:14 his malice, but when the *s* has come away,
Sir 30:15 well-being, contentment of *s* than coral.
35: 7 In generous *s* pay homage to the LORD,
35: 8 and pay your tithes in a *s* of joy.
39: 6 will be filled with the *s* of understanding;
40:29 *s* to one who understands inward feelings:
48:12 filled with a twofold portion of his *s,*
48:24 By his powerful *s* he looked into the
Is 11: 2 The *s* of the LORD shall rest upon him:
11: 2 a *s* of wisdom and of understanding,
11: 2 A *s* of counsel and of knowledge
11: 2 a *s* of fear of the Lord
19:14 has prepared among them a *s* of dizziness,
26: 9 yes, my *s* within me keeps vigil for you;
28: 6 A *s* of justice to him who sits in judgment,
29:10 has poured out on you a *s* of deep sleep.
29:24 who err in *s* shall acquire understanding,
31: 3 not God, their horses are flesh, not *s;*
32:15 the *s* from on high is poured out on us.
33:11 my *s* shall consume you like fire.
34:16 it, and his *s* shall gather them there.
37: 7 I am about to put in him such a *s* that,
38:16 the life of my *s.*
40:13 Who has directed the *s* of the LORD,
42: 1 I am pleased, Upon whom I have put my *s;*
42: 5 its people and *s* to those who walk on it:
44: 3 I will pour out my *s* upon your offspring,
48:16 "Now the Lord GOD has sent me, and his *s.*"
54: 6 like a wife forsaken and grieved in *s,*
57:15 and with the crushed and dejected in *s,*
59:21 My *s* which is upon you and my words that I
61: 1 The *s* of the LORD GOD is upon me,
61: 3 a glorious mantle instead of a listless *s.*
63:10 But they rebelled, and grieved his holy *s;*
63:11 is he who put his holy *s* in their midst;
63:14 the plain, the *s* of the LORD guiding them?
65:14 grief of heart and howl for anguish of *s.*
Jer 51:11 LORD has stirred up the *s* of Media's kings;
Bar 6:24 at any price, and there is no *s* in them.
Ez 1:12 wherever the *s* wished to go,
1:20 Wherever the *s* wished to go,
1:20 for the *s* of the living creatures was in
2: 2 *s* entered into me and set me on my feet,
3:12 Then *s* lifted me up, and I heard behind
3:14 The *s* which had lifted me up seized me,
3:24 *s* entered into me and set me on my feet,
8: 3 *S* lifted me up in the air and brought me
10:17 for the living creatures' *s* was in them.
11: 1 *S* lifted me up and brought me to the east
11: 5 Then the *s* of the LORD fell upon me,
11:19 a new heart and put a new *s* within them;
11:24 *S* lifted me up and brought me
11:24 exiles in Chaldea [in a vision, by God's *s.*
13: 3 follow their own *s* and have seen no vision.
18:31 for yourselves a new heart and a new *s.*
21:12 fall helpless, every *s* shall be daunted,
36:26 a new heart and place a new *s* within you,
36:27 I will put my *s* within you and make you
37: 1 and he led me out in the *s* of the LORD
37: 5 I will bring *s* into you,
37: 6 and put *s* in you so that you may come to
37: 8 cover them, but there was no *s* in them.
37: 9 Prophesy to the *s,*
37: 9 prophesy, son of man, and say to the *s:*
37: 9 From the four winds come, O *s,*
37:10 as he told me, and the *s* came into them;
37:14 I will put my *s* in you that you may live,
39:29 poured out my *s* upon the house of Israel,
43: 5 but *s* lifted me up and brought me to the
Dn 2: 1 his *s* no rest and robbed him of his sleep.
2: 3 my *s* no rest until I know what it means."
3:39 heart and humble *s* let us be received;
4: 5 god, and in whom is the *s* of the holy God.
4: 6 I know that the *s* of the holy God is in
4:15 because the *s* of the holy God is in you."
5:11 kingdom in whom is the *s* of the holy God;
5:14 I have heard that the *s* of God is in you,
5:20 proud and his *s* hardened by insolence,
6: 4 because an extraordinary *s* was in him,
7:15 my *s* anguished within its sheath of flesh,
13:45 up the holy *s* of a young boy named Daniel,
Hos 4:12 For the *s* of harlotry has led them astray;
5: 4 For the *s* of harlotry is in them,
9: 7 prophet is a fool, the man of the *s* is mad!"
Jl 3: 1 I will pour out my *s* upon all mankind.
3: 1 in those days, I will pour out my *s.*
Mi 3: 8 filled with power, with the *s* of the LORD,
Hg 1:14 stirred up the *s* of the governor of Judah,
1:14 and the *s* of the high priest Joshua,
1:14 and the *s* of all the remnant of the people,
2: 5 of Egypt, And my *s* continues in your midst;
Zec 4: 6 Not by an army, nor by might, but by my *s,*
6: 8 make my *s* rest in the land of the north."
7:12 sent by his *s* through the former prophets.
12: 1 earth, and forms the *s* of man within him:
12:10 of Jerusalem a *s* of grace and petition;
13: 2 and the *s* of uncleanness from the land.
Mal 2:15 he not make one being, with flesh and *s:*
Mt 1:18 with child through the power of the Holy *S.*
1:20 Holy *S* that she has conceived this child.
3:11 will baptize you in the Holy *S* and fire.
3:16 Suddenly the sky opened and he saw the *S*
4: 1 desert by the *S* to be tempted by the devil.
5: 3 "How blest are the poor in *s:*
10:20 *S* of your Father will be speaking in you.
12:18 I will endow him with my *s* and he will
12:28 it is by the *S* of God that I expel demons,
12:31 against the *S* will not be forgiven.
12:32 against the Holy *S* will not be forgiven,
12:43 "When the unclean *s* departs from a man,
26:41 The *s* is willing but nature is weak."
27:50 in a loud voice, and then gave up his *s.*
28:19 Father, and of the Son, and of the Holy *S.*
Mk 1: 8 he will baptize you in the Holy *S.*"
1:10 and the *S* descending on him like a dove.
1:12 point the *S* sent him out toward the desert.
1:23 a man with an unclean *s* that shrieked:
1:26 At that the unclean *s* convulsed the man
1:27 new teaching in a *s* of authority!
3:29 against the Holy *S* will never be forgiven.
3:30 said, "He is possessed by an unclean *s.*"
5: 2 a man from the tombs who had an unclean *s.*
5: 8 (Jesus had been saying to him, "Unclean *s,*
7:22 envy, blasphemy, arrogance, an obtuse *s.*
7:25 whose small daughter had an unclean *s,*
8:12 a sigh from the depths of his *s* he said,
9:17 to you because he is possessed by a mute *s.*
9:20 When they did so the *s* caught sight of
9:25 unclean *s* by saying to him, "Mute and deaf *s,*
12:36 David himself, inspired by the Holy *S,*
13:11 not be yourselves speaking but the Holy *S.*
14:38 The *s* is willing but nature is weak."
Lk 1:15 with the Holy *S* from his mother's womb.
1:17 before him, in the *s* and power of Elijah,
1:35 "The Holy *S* will come upon you and the
1:41 the Holy *S* and cried out in a loud voice:
1:47 the Lord, my *s* finds joy in God my savior,
1:67 his father, filled with the Holy *S,*
1:80 The child grew up and matured in *s.*
2:25 of Israel, and the Holy *S* was upon him.

2:26 It was revealed to him by the Holy S that
2:27 came to the temple now, inspired by the S;
3:16 will baptize you in the Holy S and in fire.
3:22 the skies opened and the Holy S descended
4: 1 Jesus, full of the Holy S,
4: 1 by the S into the desert for forty days,
4:14 returned in the power of the S to Galilee,
4:18 "The s of the Lord is upon me;
4:33 there was a man with an unclean s,
8:15 those who hear the word in a s of openness,
8:29 the unclean s to come out of the man.
8:29 This s had taken hold of him many a time.
9:39 A s takes possession of him and with a
9:40 to cast out the s but they could not."
9:42 s threw him into convulsions on the ground.
9:42 Jesus then rebuked the unclean s,
10:21 Jesus rejoiced in the Holy S and said:
11:13 give the Holy S to those who ask him."
11:24 "When an unclean s has gone out of a man,
12:10 the Holy S will never be forgiven.
12:12 The Holy S will teach you at that moment
13:11 by a s which drained her strength.
23:46 "Father, into your hands I recommend my s."
Jn 1:32 saw the S descend like a dove from the sky,
1:33 you see the S descend and rest on someone,
1:33 it is he who is to baptize with the Holy S.'
3: 5 without being begotten of water and S.
3: 6 Flesh begets flesh, S begets spirit.
3: 8 So it is with everyone begotten of the S."
3:34 he does not ration his gift of the S.
4:23 will worship the Father in S and truth.
4:24 God is S,
4:24 worship him must worship in S and truth."
6:63 It is the s that gives life;
6:63 The words I spoke to you are s and life.
7:39 (Here he was referring to the S,
7:39 There was, of course, no S as yet,
11:33 her also weeping, he was troubled in s,
11:38 Once again troubled in s,
14:17 the S of truth,
14:26 S whom the Father will send in my name,
15:26 the S of truth who comes from the Father
16:13 S of truth he will guide you to all truth.
19:30 bowed his head, and delivered over his s.
20:22 "Receive the Holy S.
Acts 1: 2 apostles he had chosen through the Holy S.
1: 5 days you will be baptized with the Holy S."
1: 8 power when the Holy S comes down on you;
1:16 Scripture uttered long ago by the Holy S
2: 4 All were filled with the Holy S.
2: 4 bold proclamations as the S prompted them.
2:17 pour out a portion of my s on all mankind:
2:18 pour out a portion of my s in those days,
2:33 the promised Holy S from the Father,
2:33 the Father, then poured this S out on us.
2:38 you will receive the gift of the Holy S.
4: 8 Then Peter, filled with the Holy S,
4:25 you have said by the Holy S through the
4:31 They were filled with the Holy S and
5: 3 make you lie to the Holy S
5: 9 scheme to put the S of the Lord to test?
5:32 So too does the Holy S,
6: 5 a man filled with faith and the Holy S;
6:10 for the wisdom and s with which he spoke.
7:51 Holy S just as your fathers did before you.
7:55 Stephen meanwhile, filled with the Holy S,
7:59 heard praying, "Lord Jesus, receive my s."
8:15 prayed that they might receive the Holy S.
8:17 hands on them and they received the Holy S.
8:18 hands that the apostles conferred the S,
8:19 hands on anyone he will receive the Holy S."
8:29 The S said to Philip,
8:39 the S of the Lord snatched Philip away and
9:17 your sight and be filled with the Holy S."
9:31 the increased consolation of the Holy S.
10:19 the vision when the S said to him:
10:38 God anointed him with the Holy S and power.
10:44 when the Holy S descended upon all
10:45 gift of the Holy S should have been poured
10:47 these people who have received the Holy S,
11:12 The S instructed me to accompany them
11:15 to address them the Holy S came upon them,
11:16 but you will be baptized with the Holy S.'
11:24 good man filled with the Holy S and faith.
13: 2 and were fasting, the Holy S spoke to them:
13: 4 These two, sent forth by the Holy S,
13: 9 known as Paul) was filled with the Holy S;
13:52 not but be filled with joy and the Holy S.
15: 8 the Holy S to them just as he did to us.
15:28 'It is the decision of the Holy S,
16: 6 prevented by the Holy S from preaching
16: 7 again the S of Jesus would not allow them.
16:16 met a slave girl who had a clairvoyant s.
16:18 annoyed, turned around, and said to the s,
16:18 Then and there the s left her.
19: 2 the Holy S when you became believers?"
19: 2 so much as heard that there is a Holy S."
19: 6 the Holy S came down on them and they
19:15 were doing this, the evil s answered,
19:16 s sprang at them and overpowered them all.
20:22 compelled by the S and not knowing what
20:23 except that the Holy S has been warning me
20:28 flock the Holy S has given you to guard.
21:11 Then he said, "Thus says the Holy S:
23: 9 If a s or an angel has spoken to him.
28:25 "The Holy S stated it well when he said
Rom 1: 4 in power according to the s of holiness,
1: 9 The God I worship in the s by preaching
1:18 the irreligious and perverse s of men who,
2:29 its source is the s,
5: 5 the Holy S who has been given to us.
7: 6 and we serve in the new s,
8: 2 law of the s the s of life in Christ Jesus,
8: 4 to the flesh, but according to the s.
8: 5 according to the spirit, on those of the s.
8: 6 but that of the s toward life and peace.
8: 9 you are in the spirit, since the S of God
8: 9 If anyone does not have the S of Christ,
8:10 sin, while the s lives because of justice.
8:11 If the S of him who raised Jesus from the
8:11 life also, through his S dwelling in you.
8:13 but if by the s you put to death the evil
8:14 are led by the S of God are sons of God.
8:15 a s of slavery leading you back into fear,
8:15 a s of adoption through which we cry out,
8:16 S himself gives witness with our spirit
8:16 with our s that we are children of God.
8:23 although we have the S as first fruits,
8:26 The S too helps us in our weakness,
8:26 but the S himself makes intercession for
8:27 Spirit means, for the S intercedes
9: 1 bears me witness in the Holy S
11: 8 "God gave them a s of stupor;
12:11 Do not grow slack but be fervent in s;
14:17 and the joy that is given by the Holy S.
15: 2 so as to do him good by building up his s.
15: 5 another according to the s of Christ Jesus,
15:13 the Holy S you may have hope in abundance.
15:16 sacrifice, consecrated by the Holy S.
15:19 and marvels, by the power of God's S.
15:30 Lord Jesus Christ and the love of the S,
15:32 joy and be refreshed in s by your company.
1Cor 2: 4 but the convincing power of the S.
2:10 revealed this wisdom to us through the S.
2:10 The S scrutinizes all matters,
2:11 self but the man's own s within him?
2:11 lies at the depths of God but the S of God.
2:12 The S we have received is not the world's
2:12 is not the world's spirit but God's S,
2:13 human wisdom but in words taught by the S,
2:14 not accept what is taught by the S of God.
3:16 God, and that the S of God dwells in you?
4:21 with a rod, or with love and a gentle s?
5: 3 though absent in body I am present in s,
5: 4 s with you and empowered by our Lord Jesus,
5: 5 his s may be saved on the day of the Lord.
6:11 Lord Jesus Christ and in the S of our God.
6:17 joined to the Lord becomes one s with him.
6:19 Holy Spirit, who is within—the S
7:34 Lord, in pursuit of holiness in body and s.
7:40 that in this I have the S of God.
9:11 If we have sown for you in the s,
12: 3 who speaks in the S of God ever says,
12: 3 "Jesus is Lord," except in the Holy S.
12: 4 There are different gifts but the same S;
12: 7 of the S is given for the common good.
12: 8 To one the S gives wisdom in discourse,
12: 9 S one receives faith; by the same Spirit
12:10 power to distinguish one s from another.
12:11 the same S who produces all these gifts,
12:13 It was in one S that all of us,
12:13 us have been given to drink of the one S.
14: 2 him, because he utters mysteries in the S.
14:14 If I pray in a tongue my s is at prayer
14:15 I want to pray with my s,
14:15 to sing with my s and with my mind as well.
14:16 your praise of God is solely with the s,
14:37 thinks he is a prophet or a man of the S,
15:45 the last Adam has become a life-giving s.
16:18 They have refreshed my s as they did yours.
2Cor 1:22 depositing the first payment, the S,
3: 3 with ink but by the S of the living God,
3: 6 a covenant not of a written law but of s.
3: 6 written law kills, but the S gives life.
3: 8 will be the glory of the ministry of the S?
3:17 the Spirit, and where the S of the Lord is,
3:18 his very image by the Lord who is the S.
4:13 s of faith of which the Scripture says,
5: 5 and has given us the S as a pledge of it.
6: 6 knowledge, and patience, in the Holy S,
7: 1 from every defilement of flesh and s,
7: 6 who gives heart to those who are low in s,
11: 4 different s than the one you have received,
12:18 Did we not act in the one s,
13:13 fellowship of the Holy S be with you all!
Gal 3: 2 how did you receive the S?
3: 3 After beginning in the s,
3: 5 S on you and works wonders in your midst?
3:14 us to receive the promised S through faith.
4: 6 the s of his Son which cries out "Abba!"
4:15 What has happened to your open-hearted s?
4:17 not courting your favor in any generous s.
4:29 the one whose birth was in the realm of s,
5: 5 It is in the s that we eagerly await the
5:16 should live in accord with the s
5:17 the spirit and the s against the flesh;
5:18 If you are guided by the s,
5:22 In contrast, the fruit of the s is love,
5:25 Since we live by the s,
6: 1 live by the s should gently set him right,
6: 8 but if his seed-ground is the s,
6:18 of our Lord Jesus Christ be with your s.
Eph 1:13 with the Holy S who had been promised.
1:17 grant you a s of wisdom and insight to
2: 2 that s who is even now at work among the
2:18 we both have access in one S to the Father.
2:22 become a dwelling place for God in the S.
3: 5 by the S to the holy apostles and prophets.
3:16 you inwardly through the working of his S.
4: 3 preserve the unity which has the S
4: 4 There is but one body and one S,
4:30 Do nothing to sadden the Holy S with whom
5:18 Be filled with the S,
6:17 helmet of salvation and the sword of the s,
6:18 At every opportunity pray in the S,
Phil 1:19 I receive from the S of Jesus Christ.
1:27 you are standing firm in unity of s
2: 1 that love can give, of fellowship in s,
2: 2 the one love, united in s and ideals.
3: 3 who worship in the s of God and glory in
4:23 of the Lord Jesus Christ be with your s.
Col 1: 8 it was who told us of your love in the S.
2: 5 be absent in body but I am with you in s,
2: 6 Lord, in the s in which you received him.
4: 2 to prayer, and pray in a s of thanksgiving.
1Thes 1: 5 the Holy S and out of complete conviction.
1: 6 with the joy that comes from the Holy S.
4: 8 man, but God who sends his Holy S upon you.
5:19 Do not stifle the S.
5:23 May he preserve you whole and entire, s,
2Thes 2:11 God is sending upon them a perverse s
2:13 in holiness of s and fidelity to truth.
1Tm 3:16 in the flesh, vindicated in the S;
4: 1 The S distinctly says that in later times
6:11 faith, love, steadfastness, and a gentle s.
2Tm 1: 7 Spirit God has given us is no cowardly s,
1:14 help of the Holy S who dwells within us.
4:22 The Lord be with your s.
Ti 3: 5 of new birth and renewal by the Holy S.
3: 6 This S he lavished on us through Jesus
Phlm 1:25 of our Lord Jesus Christ be with your s.
Heb 2: 4 of the gifts of the Holy S as he willed.
3: 7 Wherefore, as the Holy S says:
3:12 s and fall away from the living God.
4:12 It penetrates and divides soul and s,
6: 4 gift and become sharers in the Holy S,
9: 8 The Holy S was showing thereby that while
9:14 s offered himself up unblemished to God,
10:15 The Holy S attests this to us,
10:29 be ordinary, and insults the S of grace?
Jas 4: 5 "The s he has implanted in us tends
1Pt 1: 2 consecrated by the S to a life of
1:11 S of Christ within them was pointing to,
1:12 the power of the Holy S sent from heaven.
2: 2 of the s to make you grow into salvation,
2: 5 living stones, built as an edifice of s,
3:18 but was given life in the realm of the s.
3:19 It was in the s also that he went to
4: 6 might live in the s in the eyes of God.
4:14 S in its glory has come to rest on you.
2Pt 1:21 Holy S have spoken under God's influence.
2: 3 you with fabricated tales, in a s of greed.
2:13 they share your feasts in a s of seduction.
3:15 you this in the s of wisdom that is his,
1Jn 3:24 from the S that he gave us.
4: 1 Beloved, do not trust every s,
4: 2 This is how you can recognize God's S:
4: 2 every s that acknowledges Jesus Christ
4: 3 while every s that fails to acknowledge
4: 3 Such is the s of the antichrist which,
4: 6 s of truth from the spirit of deception.
4:13 he in us is that he has given us of his S.
5: 6 S who testifies to this, and the Spirit
5: 8 testify, the S and the water and the blood
3Jn 1: 2 in all other ways as you do in the s.
Jude 1:19 These sensualists, devoid of the S,
1:20 holy faith through prayer in the Holy S.
Rv 2: 1 the presiding s of the church in Ephesus,
2: 8 the presiding s of the church in Smyrna,
2:12 the presiding s of the church in Pergamum,
2:18 the presiding s of the church in Thyatira,
3: 1 the presiding s of the church in Sardis,
3: 7 presiding s of the church in Philadelphia,
3:14 the presiding s of the church in Laodicea,
14:13 The S added,
17: 3 The angel then carried me away in s to a
18: 2 She is a cage for every unclean s,
19:10 s proves itself by witnessing to Jesus."
21:10 He carried me away in s to the top of a
22:17 The S and the Bride say, "Come!"

SPIRITED (1)

2Kgs 11: 2 took Joash, his son, and s him away,

SPIRITS (69)

Nm 16:22 out, "O God, God of the s of all mankind,
27:16 the LORD, the God of the s of all mankind,
Dt 18:11 and s or seeks oracles from the dead.

SPIRITS (cont.)

Jgs 16:25 When their s were high,
1Kgs 22:21 until one of the s came forth and
2Kgs 21: 6 the consulting of ghosts and s.
23:24 with the consultation of ghosts and s,
2Chr 33: 6 appointed necromancers and diviners of s,
Est 5: 9 That day Haman left happy and in good s.
2Mc 3:24 the Lord of s who holds all power
Wis 7:23 all-seeing, And pervading all s,
Sir 16:15 what am I in the world of s?
34:17 He buoys up the s,
51:29 Let your s rejoice in the mercy of God,
Is 19: 3 consult idols and charmers, ghosts and s.
57:15 in spirit, To revive the s of the dejected,
57:16 For their s would faint before me,
Bar 2:17 whose s have been taken from within them,
3: 1 souls and dismayed s call to you.
Dn 3:86 S and souls of the just,
Mt 8:16 He expelled the s by a simple command and
10: 1 gave them authority to expel unclean s
12:45 it this time seven s more evil than itself.
22:43 under the S influence calls him 'lord,'
Mk 1:27 He gives orders to unclean s and they obey!"
3:11 Unclean s would catch sight of him,
5:13 unclean s came out and entered the swine.
6: 7 two, giving them authority over unclean s.
16:20 by s to grasp the true power of God.
Lk 4:36 the unclean s with authority and power,
6:18 were troubled with unclean s were cured;
7:21 their diseases, afflictions, and evil s;
8: 2 who had been cured of evil s and maladies;
11:26 with seven other s far worse than itself,
21:34 "Be on guard lest your s become bloated
Acts 5:16 and those who were troubled by unclean s,
8: 7 There were many who had unclean s,
14:17 your s he fills with food and delight."
19:12 were cured and evil s departed from them.
19:13 over those who were possessed by evil s,
21: 4 Under the S prompting,
23: 8 and that there are neither angels nor s,
1Cor 14:32 The s of the prophets are under the
Gal 5:25 by the spirit, let us follow the s lead.
Eph 6:12 of darkness, the evil s in regions above.
1Tm 4: 1 will heed deceitful s and things taught
Heb 1:14 Are they not all ministering s,
12: 9 not all the more submit to the Father of s,
12:23 of all, to the s of just men made perfect,
Jas 5:13 If a person is in good s,
1Pt 3:19 that he went to preach to the s in prison.
1Jn 4: 1 s to a test to see if they belong to God,
Rv 1: 4 and from the seven s before his throne,
1:20 are the presiding s of the seven churches,
2: 7 has ears heed the S word to the churches!
2:11 has ears heed the S word to the churches!
2:17 has ears heed the S word to the churches!
2:29 has ears heed the S word to the churches!'
3: 1 " 'The One who holds the seven s of God,
3: 6 has ears heed the S word to the churches!'
3:13 has ears heed the S word to the churches!
3:22 has ears heed the S word to the churches.' "
4: 5 seven flaming torches, the seven s of God,
5: 6 these eyes are the seven s of God,
6: 9 I saw under the altar the s of those who
16:13 I saw three unclean s like frogs come from
16:14 these s were devils who worked prodigies.
20: 4 I also saw the s of those who had been
22: 6 the Lord, the God of prophetic s,

SPIRITUAL (27)

Mk 16:20 and inherit the s and immortal glory of
Acts 6: 3 acknowledged to be deeply s and prudent,
18:25 Apollos was a man full of s fervor.
Rom 1:11 with you some s gift to strengthen you
7:14 We know that the law is s,
12: 1 holy and acceptable to God, your s worship.
15:27 have shared in the s blessings of the Jews,
1Cor 1: 7 lack no s gift as you wait for the revelation
2:13 interpreting s things in spiritual terms.
2:14 because it must be appraised in a s way.
2:15 The s man, on the other hand,
3: 1 to you as s men but only as men of flesh,
10: 3 All ate the same s food.
10: 4 s drink (they drank from the spiritual rock
12: 1 to leave you in ignorance about s gifts.
14: 1 Set your hearts on s gifts
14:12 Since you have set your hearts on s gifts,
15:44 body is put down and a s body comes up.
15:44 body, be sure there is also a s body.
15:46 Take note, the s was not first;
15:46 came the natural and after that the s.
Eph 1: 3 in Christ every s blessing in the heavens!
4:23 and acquire a fresh, s way of thinking.
Col 1: 9 will through perfect wisdom and s insight.
1Pt 2: 5 offering s sacrifices acceptable to God

SPIRITUALLY (3)

Ez 3:14 me up seized me, and I went off s stirred,
1Cor 2: 6 wisdom which we express among the s mature.
Phil 3:15 who are s mature must have this attitude.

SPIT (7)

Nm 12:14 "Suppose her father had s in her face,
Dt 25: 9 his sandal from his foot and s in his face,
Jb 30:10 me, they do not hesitate to s in my face!
Sir 28:12 it quickens into flame, if you s on it,
Mt 26:67 they began to s in his face and hit him.
Mk 10:34 Gentiles, who will mock him and s at him,
14:65 Some of them began to s on him.

SPITE (10)

1Mc 9: 8 But in s of his discouragement,
2Mc 4:28 the king, in s of the demand of Sostratus,
4:34 persuaded him, in s of his suspicions,
Jb 18: 6 in s of him,
Ps(s) 33:19 death and preserve them in s of famine.
Jer 31:36 these natural laws give way in s of me,
Mi 7:16 put to shame, in s of all their strength;
Jn 21:11 In s of the great number, the net was not
Acts 5:40 In s of it, however, the Sanhedrin called
Rom 2: 5 In s of this, your hard and impenitent

SPITS (1)

Lv 15: 8 If the afflicted man s on a clean man,

SPITTING (3)

Is 50: 6 face I did not shield from buffets and s.
Mk 7:33 his fingers into the man's ears and, s,
15:19 Jesus on the head with a reed and s at him,

SPITTLE (3)

Jb 7:19 let me alone long enough to swallow my s?
Is 61: 7 and disgrace and s were their portion,
Mk 8:23 Putting s on his eyes he laid his hands on

SPLASH (8)

Ex 29:16 take and s on all the sides of the altar.
29:20 S the rest of the blood on all the sides
Lv 1:11 s its blood on the sides of the altar.
3: 2 s its blood on the sides of the altar.
3: 8 s its blood on the sides of the altar.
3:13 s its blood on the sides of the altar.
17: 6 The priest shall s the blood on the altar
Nm 18:17 Their blood you must s on the altar

SPLASHED (8)

Ex 24: 6 the other half he s on the altar.
Lv 7: 2 blood shall be s on the sides of the altar.
8:19 s its blood on all sides of the altar.
8:24 the blood he s on the sides of the altar.
9:12 blood, he s it on all sides of the altar.
9:18 Aaron s it on all sides of the altar.
Nm 19:13 the lustral water has not been s over him,
19:20 the lustral water has not been s over him,

SPLASHES (1)

Lv 7:14 who s the blood of the peace offering.

SPLASHING (2)

Lv 1: 5 shall offer up its blood by s it on the
Jude 1:13 s their shameless deeds abroad like foam,

SPLAYED (4)

1Kgs 6: 4 S windows with trellises were made for the
Ez 40:16 on both sides there were s windows
41:16 There were s windows with trellises about
41:26 There were s windows [and palmtrees] on

SPLENDID (18)

1Sm 16:12 to behold and making a s appearance.
Jdt 15: 9 You are the s boast of our people.
Est C:12 Taking off her s garments,
1Mc 14:15 the temple s and enriched its equipment.
2Mc 12:45 But if he did this with a view to the s
14:33 and erect here a s temple to Dionysus."
Wis 5:16 Therefore shall they receive the s crown,
Sir 6:31 robe of glory, bear her as your s crown.
27: 8 attain it, and put it on like a s robe.
40: 4 Whether he bears a s crown or is wrapped
45: 8 He clothed him with s apparel,
50: 5 How s he was as he appeared from the tent,
Is 10:18 His s forests and orchards.
Ez 16:17 You took the s gold and silver ornaments
16:39 garments and take away your s ornaments,
23:26 your clothes and seize your s ornaments.
23:42 women's arms and s diadems on their heads.
28: 7 they shall run them through your s apparel.

SPLENDIDLY (2)

2Mc 3:26 strikingly beautiful, and s attired,
Lk 16:19 purple and linen and feasted s every day.

SPLENDOR (67)

1Chr 16:27 S and majesty go before him;
29:11 LORD, are grandeur and power, majesty, s,
Tb 14: 5 and they shall rebuild Jerusalem with s.
Est 8:16 and there was s and merriment for the Jews,
1Mc 10:58 great s according to the custom of kings.
15:32 and on seeing the s of Simon's court,
15:36 he told him of Simon's words, of his s,
Jb 31:26 or the moon in the s of its progress,
37:22 From the North the s comes,
39:19 his strength, and endow his neck with s?
40:10 and array yourself with glory and s.
Ps(s) 21: 6 majesty and s you conferred upon him.
45: 4 In your s and your majesty ride on
49:13 Thus man, for all his s,
49:21 Man, for all his s,
89:18 For you are the s of their strength,
93: 1 The LORD is king, in s robed;
96: 6 S and majesty go before him;
110: 3 power in the day of your birth, in holy s;
145: 5 They speak of the s of your glorious
145:12 might and the glorious s of your kingdom.
Wis 7:10 because the s of her never yields to sleep.
8: 3 nobility the s of companionship with God;
Sir 1: 9 Fear of the LORD is glory and s,
36: 5 forth the s of your right hand and arm;
42:25 can one ever see enough of their s?
43:11 its Maker, for majestic indeed is its s;
45:12 Majestic, glorious, renowned for s,
49:16 that of any living being was the s of ADAM.
50:11 robes, and wearing his garments of s,
Is 2:10 of the LORD and the s of his majesty!
2:19 of the LORD and the s of his majesty,
2:21 of the LORD and the s of his majesty,
4: 2 be honor and s for the survivors of Israel.
10:34 with the axe, and Lebanon in its s falls.
24:16 S to the Just One!"
33:17 Your eyes will see a king in his s,
35: 2 given to them, the s of Carmel and Sharon;
35: 2 the glory of the LORD, the s of our God.
60: 1 Rise up in s!
60: 7 and I will enhance the s of my house.
Bar 4: 2 walk by her light toward s.
4:24 great glory and the s of the Eternal God.
5: 1 put on the s of glory from God forever:
5: 3 For God will show all the earth your s:
Ez 1:27 he was surrounded with s.
1:28 a rainy day was the s that surrounded him.
16:14 of my s which I had bestowed on you,
27:10 they hung upon you, increasing your s.
28:17 for the sake of s you debased your wisdom.
Dn 4:27 as a royal residence for my s and majesty?"
4:33 my majesty and my s returned to me.
12: 3 shine brightly like the s of the firmament,
Hos 14: 7 His s shall be like the olive tree and his
Hb 3: 4 His s spreads like the light;
Mt 6:29 in all his s was arrayed like one of these.
6:30 clothe in such s the grass of the field,
Lk 7:25 eat in s are to be found in royal palaces.
12:27 his s was not arrayed like any one of them.
12:28 clothes in such s the grass of the field,
1Cor 15:40 The s of the heavenly bodies is one thing,
15:41 The sun has a s of its own,
2Cor 4: 4 they do not see the s of the gospel showing
1Pt 1: 7 than the passing s of fire-tried gold,
2Pt 1:17 came to him out of the majestic s:
Rv 18:14 All your luxury and s are gone;
21:11 It gleamed with the s of God.

SPLINTERED (3)

Ex 9:25 thing and s every tree in the fields.
Jb 24:20 accursed, and wickedness is s like wood.
Ez 29: 7 When they held you in hand, you s,

SPLINTERS (2)

Jb 41:21 Clubs he esteems as s;
Ps(s) 46:10 he s the spears;

SPLIT (16)

Gn 15:10 He brought him all these, s them in two,
Ex 14:16 over the sea, s the sea in two,
Lv 1:17 having s the bird down the middle without
Nm 16:31 this than the ground beneath them s open,
Jgs 15:19 Then God s the cavity in Lehi,
1Sm 6:14 the wood of the cart was s up and the cows
1Kgs 1:40 as to s open the earth with their shouting.
Ps(s) 60: 4 You have rocked the country and s it open;
136:13 Who s the Red Sea in twain,
Dn 13:55 the sentence from him and s you in two."
Mi 1: 4 melt under him and the valleys s open,
Hb 3: 9 Into streams you s the earth;
Mt 12:25 s into factions cannot last for long.
27:52 The earth quaked, boulders s,
Lk 12:53 be s against son and son against father,
Rv 16:19 The great city was s into three parts,

SPLITS (1)

Jb 28:10 He s channels in the rocks;

SPOIL (32)

Nm 31: 9 their herds and flocks and wealth as s,
31:29 sheep in their half of the s
Jos 8: 2 you may take its s and livestock as booty.
8:27 booty the livestock and the s of that city,
11:14 The Israelites took all the s and
Jgs 5:12 arise, Barak, make despoilers your s,

5:30 "They must be dividing the s they took:
5:30 man, Spoils of dyed cloth as Sisera's s,
5:30 an ornate shawl or two for me in the s."
1Sm 2:5 for bread, while the hungry batten on s.
14:32 So they pounced upon the s and took sheep,
15:19 You have pounced on the s,
15:21 But from the s the men took sheep and oxen,
30:20 him, they shouted, "This is David's s!"
30:26 sent part of the s to the elders of Judah,
30:26 from the s of the enemies of the LORD":
2Chr 20:25 they were three days taking the s,
24:23 sent all their s to the king of Damascus.
Jdt 16:4 children a prey, and seize my virgins as s.
Est 3:13 and that their goods should be seized as s.
8:11 and to seize their goods as s throughout
1Mc 11:51 they returned to Jerusalem with much s.
Ps(s) 119:162 your promise, as one who has found rich s.
Eccl 9:18 that dies can s the perfumer's ointment,
Sir 18:14 no reproach, nor s any gift by harsh words.
Is 8:4 the wealth of Damascus and the s of
33:4 gather s as caterpillars are gathered up;
42:22 as booty, with no one to rescue them, as s,
Jer 17:3 and all your treasures I will give as s.
49:32 be your booty, their many herds your s;
Dn 11:24 he shall distribute s,
Hb 2:7 You shall become their s!

SPOILED (1)

Ez 7:21 s and defiled by the wicked of the earth.

SPOILER (2)

Jb 15:21 all is prosperous, the s comes upon him.
Jer 15:8 the mother of youths the s at midday;

SPOILERS (1)

Jer 8:10 wives to strangers, their fields to s.

SPOILS (29)

Gn 49:27 prey, and evenings he distributes the s."
Ex 15:9 will divide the s and have my fill of them:
Nm 31:11 captives, together with the s and booty,
Dt 13:17 up all its s in the middle of its square,
13:17 s as a whole burnt offering to the LORD,
Jos 7:21 Among the s,
22:8 divide these s of your enemies with your
Jgs 5:30 man, S of dyed cloth as Sisera's spoil,
2Kgs 3:23 To the s, Moabites!"
2Chr 14:12 his army, which carried away enormous s.
Jdt 2:7 soldiers, to whom I will deliver them as s.
9:4 the s you divided among your favored sons,
1Mc 2:9 ornaments have been carried off as s,
5:22 the Gentiles fell, and he gathered their s.
7:47 the Jews collected the s and the booty;
9:40 the mountain, all their s were taken.
2Mc 8:27 stripped them of their s
8:31 rest of the s they carried to Jerusalem.
Ps(s) 68:13 and the household shall divide the s.
Sir 30:7 who s his son will have wounds to bandage,
37:6 neglect him not when you distribute your s.
Is 9:2 harvest, as men make merry when dividing s.
21:2 the traitor betrays, the despoiler s.
33:23 s and the lame will carry off the loot.
53:12 and he shall divide the s with the mighty,
Mi 2:8 in confidence, as though it were s of war.
4:13 You shall devote their s to the LORD,
Zec 14:1 when the s shall be divided in your midst.
Lk 11:22 on which he was relying and divides the s.

SPOKE (236)

Gn 11:1 The whole world s the same language,
16:13 To the LORD who s to her she gave a name,
18:27 Abraham s up again:
19:14 So Lot went out and s to his sons-in-law,
22:7 on together, Isaac s to his father Abraham.
27:39 Finally Isaac s again and said to him:
41:9 chief cupbearer s up and said to Pharaoh:
42:7 identity from them and s sternly to them.
42:23 he s with them through an interpreter.
43:27 how is your aged father, of whom you s?
50:4 was over, Joseph s to Pharaoh's courtiers.
50:17 When they s these words to him,
Ex 3:15 God s further to Moses,
6:13 s to Moses and Aaron and gave them his
6:27 These are the ones who s to Pharaoh,
6:28 day the LORD s to Moses in Egypt he said,
7:7 Aaron eighty-three when they s to Pharaoh.
13:1 The LORD s to Moses and said,
16:11 The LORD s to Moses and said,
33:9 its entrance while the LORD s with Moses.
34:31 Moses then s to them.
Lv 16:1 the LORD s to Moses and said to him,
Nm 3:1 that the LORD s to Moses on Mount Sinai.
7:89 and it s to him. . . .
8:1 The LORD s to Moses,
11:25 then came down in the cloud and s to him.
12:1 Miriam and Aaron s against Moses on the
14:40 to go up to the place that the LORD s of:
17:21 So Moses s to the Israelites,
33:50 The LORD s to Moses on the plains of Moab
Dt 1:1 These are the words which Moses s to all
1:3 Moses s to the Israelites all the commands
4:12 LORD s to you from the midst of the fire.
4:15 saw no form at all on the day the LORD s
5:4 The LORD s with you face to face on the
5:22 the LORD s with a loud voice to your
9:10 copy of all the words that the LORD s
10:4 the ten commandments which he s to you on
Jos 14:10 years since the LORD s thus to Moses;
20:2 cities of which I s to them through Moses,
24:27 heard all the words which the LORD s to us.
Jgs 13:11 to him, "Are you the one who s to my wife?"
13:13 from all the things of which I s to her.
1Sm 4:1 and Samuel s to all Israel.
14:28 At this one of the soldiers s up:
15:10 Then the LORD s to Samuel:
16:18 A servant s up to say:
17:23 of the Philistines and s as before,
17:32 Then David s to Saul:
19:4 then s well of David to his father Saul,
22:9 standing with the officers of Saul, s up:
30:6 difficulty, for the men s of stoning him,
30:22 who had accompanied David s up to say,
2Sm 3:19 Abner also s personally to Benjamin,
6:22 the slave girls you s of I will be honored."
7:4 that night the LORD s to Nathan and said:
12:18 "When the child was alive, we s to him,
13:32 son of David's brother Shimeah, s up:
19:44 s even more fiercely than the Israelites.
21:2 king called the Gibeonites and s to them.
23:2 The spirit of the LORD s through me;
23:3 The God of Israel s;
1Kgs 5:13 out of the wall, and he s about beasts,
8:24 You who s that promise,
12:22 However, the LORD s to Shemaiah,
13:20 s to the prophet who had brought him back,
16:1 The LORD s against Baasha to Jehu,
18:1 in the third year, the LORD s to Elijah,
21:6 s to Naboth the Jezreelite and said to him,
2Kgs 21:10 LORD s through his servants the prophets:
25:28 He s kindly to him and gave him a throne
1Chr 12:19 Amasai, the chief of the Thirty, who s:
21:9 Then the LORD s to Gad,
2Chr 6:15 With your own mouth you s it,
29:31 Hezekiah now s out this command:
30:22 Hezekiah s encouragingly to all the
32:19 They s of the God of Israel as though he
33:10 The LORD s to Manasseh and his people,
33:18 seers who s to him in the name of the LORD,
34:22 They s to her as they had been instructed,
36:12 Jeremiah, who s the word of the LORD.
Neh 9:13 came down, you s with them from heaven;
13:24 Of their children, half s Ashdodite,
Jdt 16:14 for you s, and they were made,
1Mc 1:30 He s to them deceitfully in peaceful terms,
7:10 sent messengers who s deceitfully to Judas
7:15 s with them peacefully and swore to them,
7:34 them, defiled them, and s disdainfully.
7:42 Nicanor s wickedly against your sanctuary;
8:19 envoys entered the senate and s as follows:
2Mc 6:28 He s thus,
7:11 out his hands, as he s these noble words:
Jb 2:13 nights, but none of them s a word to him;
3:2 Job s out and said:
4:1 Then s Eliphaz the Temanite, who said:
8:1 Bildad the Shuhite s out and said:
11:1 And Zophar the Naamathite s out and said:
15:1 Then Eliphaz the Temanite s and said:
20:1 Then Zophar the Naamathite s and said:
26:1 Then Job s again and said:
29:22 Once I s, they said no more,
32:6 son of Barachel the Buzite, s out and said:
Ps(s) 33:9 For he s,
39:4 I s out with my tongue:
78:19 Yes, they s against God,
89:20 Once you s in a vision,
99:7 From the pillar of cloud he s to them;
105:31 He s, and there came swarms of flies;
105:34 He s, and there came locusts
106:23 Then he s of exterminating them,
Sg 5:4 within me, and I grew faint when he s.
Wis 8:12 and as I s on further,
Is 7:10 Again the LORD s to Ahaz:
8:5 Again the Lord s to me:
16:13 of the LORD s against Moab in times past.
41:26 Not one of you foretold it, not one s;
65:12 did not answer, I s and you did not listen,
66:4 when I called, no one answered, when I s,
Jer 7:13 not listen, though I s to you untiringly;
19:5 a thing as I neither commanded nor s of,
22:21 I s to you when you were secure,
25:2 This word the prophet Jeremiah s to all
25:3 has come to me and I s to you untiringly,
27:12 king of Judah, I s the same words:
27:16 and to all the people I s as follows:
30:4 which the LORD s to Israel and to Judah:
35:14 I s to you untiringly and insistently.
35:17 because when I s they did not obey,
36:2 the nations, from the day I first s to you,
38:25 If the princes hear I s to you,
39:16 fulfilling the words I s against this city,
50:1 The word which the LORD s against Babylon,
52:32 He s kindly to him and gave him a throne
Ez 2:2 As he s to me, spirit entered me
3:24 me and set me on my feet, and he s with me.
24:19 I therefore s to the people that morning,
38:17 I s in ancient times through my servants,
Dn 4:28 on the king's lips, a voice s from heaven,
7:8 like a man, and a mouth that s arrogantly.
7:11 of the arrogant words which the horn s,
7:20 the eyes and the mouth that s arrogantly,
8:13 said to whichever one it was that s,
8:18 As he s to me, I fell forward in a faint;
9:2 which the LORD s to the prophet Jeremiah:
9:6 prophets, who s in your name to our kings,
9:12 You carried out the threats you s against
10:20 When he s to me,
Hos 7:13 to redeem them, they s lies against me.
12:5 Bethel he met God and there he s with him;
12:11 granted many visions and s to the prophets,
Zec 1:9 and the angel who s with me answered me,
1:10 among the myrtle trees s up and said,
1:12 Then the angel of the LORD s out and said,
1:13 To the angel who s with me,
1:14 And the angel who s with me said to me,
2:2 the angel who s with me what these were.
2:7 Then the angel who s with me advanced,
3:4 He s and said to those who were standing
4:1 who s with me returned and awakened me,
4:4 Then I said to the angel who s with me,
4:5 And the angel who s with me replied,
5:5 who s with me came forward and said to me,
5:10 the air, I said to the angel who s with me,
6:4 I asked the angel who s with me,
7:7 the LORD s through the former prophets,
Mal 3:16 they who fear the LORD s with one another,
Mt 11:13 well as the law s prophetically until John.
11:25 On one occasion Jesus s thus:
12:38 of the scribes and Pharisees then s up,
13:34 He s to them in parables only,
14:28 Peter s up and said,
15:15 Then Peter s up to say,
26:25 Then Judas, his betrayer, s:
28:5 Then the angel s, addressing the women:
Mk 3:30 He s thus because they had said,
4:34 To them he s only by way of parable,
9:5 Then Peter s to Jesus:
14:56 Many s against him falsely under oath but
Lk 4:22 All who were present s favorably of him;
8:4 He s to them in a parable:
8:54 He took her by the hand and s these words:
9:11 them and s to them of the reign of God,
9:31 appeared in glory and s of his passage,
11:14 when the devil was cast out the dumb man s.
13:6 Jesus s this parable:
17:16 at the feet of Jesus and s his praises.
18:9 He then s this parable addressed to those
22:59 hour after that another s more insistently:
24:44 words I s to you when I was still with you:
Jn 1:45 have found the one Moses s of in the law
4:50 put his trust in the word Jesus s to him,
6:63 The words I s to you are spirit and life.
7:46 "No man ever s like that before,"
7:50 (the man who had come to him), s up to say,
8:12 Jesus s to them once again.
8:20 He s these words while teaching at the
8:30 Because he s this way,
9:29 We know that God s to Moses,
12:41 seen Jesus' glory, and it was of him he s.
18:16 came out and s to the woman at the gate,
18:21 Question those who heard me when I s.
18:23 evidence, but if I s the truth why hit me?"
Acts 2:16 No, it is what Joel the prophet s of:
3:21 s of long ago through his holy prophets.
4:8 Peter, filled with the Holy Spirit, s up:
6:1 the ones who s Greek complained that their
6:1 with the widows of those who s Hebrew.
6:10 for the wisdom and spirit with which he s.
7:44 as God prescribed it when he s to Moses,
10:7 who s these words had disappeared,
11:9 time the voice from the heavens s out:
13:2 were fasting, the Holy Spirit s to them:
13:43 who s to them and urged them to hold fast
13:46 Paul and Barnabas s out fearlessly,
14:1 s in such a way as to convince a good number
14:3 time there and s out fearlessly,
15:13 concluded their presentation, James s up:
16:2 in Lystra and Iconium s highly of him,
16:13 and s to the women who were gathered there.
18:25 He s and taught accurately about Jesus,
23:6 Consequently he s out before the Sanhedrin:
26:1 Agrippa now s to Paul:
1Cor 14:5 should like it if all of you s in tongues,
2Cor 4:13 says, "Because I believed, I s out."
Heb 1:1 God s in fragmentary and varied ways to
4:7 s through David the words we have quoted:
11:22 life, s of the Exodus of the Israelites,
12:25 to listen as God s to them on earth,
13:7 your leaders who s the word of God to you;
Jas 5:10 the prophets who s in the name of the Lord.
2Pt 2:16 A mute beast s with a human voice to
Rv 1:12 to see whose voice it was that s to me.
10:4 start writing when the seven thunders s,
10:8 I heard from heaven s to me again and said,
13:11 horns like a ram and it s like a dragon.
21:15 The one who s to me held a rod of gold for

SPOKEN (141)

Gn 32:29 "You shall no longer be s of as Jacob,
35:14 On the site where God had s with him,
35:15 Bethel, because God had s with him there.
41:24 I have s to the magicians,
Ex 4:10 nor now that you have s to your servant;
20:22 that I have s to you from heaven.
Dt 5:24 can still live after God has s with him.
5:28 heard the words these people have s to you,
18:21 recognize an oracle which the LORD has s?,
18:22 The prophet has s it presumptuously,
25:10 And his lineage shall be s of in Israel as
Ru 4: 1 relative of whom he had s come along,
1Sm 17:31 had s were overheard and reported to Saul,
2Sm 2:27 replied, "As God lives, if you had not s,
7:19 you have also s of the house of your
24:11 morning, the LORD had s to the prophet Gad,
1Kgs 13: 3 "This is the sign that the LORD has s:
13:11 father the words he had s to the king,
14:11 For the LORD has s!"
22:28 in safety, the LORD has not s through me."
2Kgs 1:17 of the prophecy of the LORD s by Elijah.
10:10 not a single word which the LORD has s
10:17 prophecy which the LORD had s to Elijah.
19:21 is the word the LORD has s concerning him:
20:19 of the LORD which you have s is favorable."
22:14 When they had s to her,
2Chr 18:27 in safety, the LORD has not s through me."
34:27 s against this place and its inhabitants;
36:21 fulfill the word of the LORD s by Jeremiah:
36:22 fulfill the word of the LORD s by Jeremiah,
Ezr 1: 1 fulfill the word of the LORD s by Jeremiah,
Tb 14: 4 word which was s by Nahum against Nineveh.
14: 4 whatever God has s will be accomplished.
Jdt 2:12 I have s I will accomplish by my power.
6: 4 for he has s,
6: 9 I have s and my words shall not prove
8: 9 lack of water, had s against their ruler,
8:28 that you have said was s with good sense,
11:23 fair to behold, and your words are well s.
Est 7: 8 s when the face of Haman was covered over.
1Mc 1:24 s with great arrogance and shed much blood.
2Mc 7: 4 tongue of the one who had s for the others,
Jb 21: 3 and after I have s,
40: 5 Though I have s once,
42: 7 after the LORD had s these words to Job,
42: 7 for you have not s rightly concerning me,
42: 8 For you have not s rightly concerning me,
Ps(s) 40:11 and your salvation I have s of;
50: 1 God the LORD has s and summoned the earth,
103:20 who do his bidding, obeying his s word.
109: 2 They have s to me with lying tongues,
Prv 25:11 settings are words s at the proper time.
Eccl 7:21 Do not give heed to every word that is s
7:22 that you have many times s ill of others.
Sg 1: 3 Your name s is a spreading perfume
Sir 15: 8 impious is she, not to be s of by liars.
20:19 A proverb when s by a fool is unwelcome,
36:14 fulfill the prophecies s in your name,
Is 1:20 for the mouth of the LORD has s!
16:14 But now the LORD has s:
21:17 for the LORD, the God of Israel, has s.
22:25 for the LORD has s.
23: 4 fortress on the sea, for the sea has s:
25: 8 for the LORD has s.
37:22 is the word the LORD has s concerning him:
39: 8 of the LORD which you have s is favorable."
40: 5 for the mouth of the LORD has s.
45:19 I have not s from hiding nor from some
46:11 Yes, I have s, I will accomplish it;
48:15 I myself have s, I have called him,
49: 5 For now the LORD has s who formed me as
53: 9 he had done no wrong nor s any falsehood.
58:14 father, for the mouth of the LORD has s.
Jer 4:28 I have s, I will not repent,
9:11 the mouth of the LORD has s make it known:
11:19 living, so that his name will be s no more."
25:13 I will fulfill all the words I have s
30: 2 all the words I have s to you in a book:
36: 2 the words I have s to you against Israel,
36: 4 all the words which the LORD had s to him.
37: 2 of the LORD s by Jeremiah the prophet.
42:19 It is the LORD who has s to you,
Ez 5:13 have s in my jealousy when I spend my fury
5:15 I, the LORD, have s!
5:17 I, the LORD, have s!
13: 8 s falsehood and have seen lying visions,
17:21 you shall know that I, the LORD, have s.
17:24 As I, the LORD, have s, so will I do.
21:22 I, the LORD, have s.
21:37 not be remembered, for I, the LORD, have s.
22:14 I, the LORD, have s, and I will act.
22:28 Lord GOD," although the LORD has not s.
23:34 for I have s, says the Lord GOD,
24:14 I, the LORD, have s:
26: 5 I have s, says the Lord GOD:
26:14 Never shall you be rebuilt, for I have s,
28:10 at the hands of foreigners, for I have s,
30:12 I, the LORD, have s.
34:24 I, the LORD, have s.
35:13 and wild words you have s against me.
Dn 1:19 When the king had s with all of them,
8:26 evenings and the mornings is true, as s;
Jl 4: 8 Indeed, the LORD has s.
Ob 1:18 of the house of Esau, for the LORD has s.
Mi 4: 4 for the mouth of the LORD of hosts has s.
Zec 8: 9 hear these words s by the prophets
13: 3 you have s a lie in the name of the LORD."
Mal 3:13 yet you ask, "What have we s against you?"
Mt 3: 3 that the prophet Isaiah had s when he said:
26:13 what she did will be s of as her memorial."
Mk 4: 9 Having s this parable, he added:
Lk 3: 2 s to John son of Zechariah in the desert.
19:28 Having s thus he went ahead with his
22:61 the word that the Lord had s to him,
Jn 2:22 the Scripture and the word he had s.
4:41 his own s word many more came to faith.
7:17 it comes from God or is simply s on my own.
12:48 has his judge, namely, the word I have s—
12:49 For I have not s on my own;
12:50 I say is s just as he instructed me."
14:10 The words I speak are not s of myself;
15: 3 thanks to the word I have s to you.
15:22 If I had not come to them and s to them,
16:25 s these things to you in veiled language.
17: 1 After he had s these words,
18:20 have s publicly to any who would listen.
Acts 3:24 "Moreover, all the prophets who have s,
6: 8 s of was a man filled with grace and power,
22:12 well s of by all the Jews who lived there,
23: 9 If a spirit or an angel has s to him.
2Cor 6: 8 honored or dishonored, s of well or ill.
6:11 Men of Corinth, we have s to you frankly,
Gal 3:16 s to Abraham and to his "descendant."
Heb 1: 2 final age, he has s to us through his Son,
2: 2 the word s through angels stood unchanged,
3: 5 the task of witnessing to what would be s;
4: 8 would not have s afterward of another day.
Jas 1:18 bring us to birth with a word s in truth
2Pt 1:21 Holy Spirit have s under God's influence.
Rv 4: 1 trumpetlike voice which had s to me before.
10: 4 thunders have s and do not write it down!"

SPOKES (1)

1Kgs 7:33 their axles, fellies, s,

SPOKESMAN (4)

Gn 20: 7 as a s he will intercede for you
Ex 4:16 he shall be your s, and you shall be as God
Jb 16:19 witness is in heaven, and my s is on high.
Acts 14:12 they called Hermes, since he was the s.

SPOKESMEN (2)

Jdt 3: 5 After the s had reached Holofernes and
Is 43:27 your s rebelled against me Till I

SPONGE (3)

Mt 27:48 one of them ran off and got a s.
Mk 15:36 ran off, and soaking a s in sour wine,
Jn 19:29 They stuck a s soaked in this wine on some

SPORT (18)

Gn 27:12 He will think I am making s of him,
39:14 brought in a Hebrew slave to make s of us!
39:17 here broke in on me, to make s of me.
1Sm 31: 4 these uncircumcised come and make s of me."
2Mc 7: 7 they brought the second to be made s of.
7:10 After him the third suffered their cruel s.
Jb 12: 4 I have become the s of my neighbors:
39:18 of foot she makes s of the horse and rider.
40:20 to him, and of all wild animals he makes s.
Ps(s) 104:26 which you formed to make s of it.
Sir 6: 4 owner and makes him the s of his enemies.
13:21 When a poor man speaks they make s of him;
18:31 they will make you the s of your enemies.
42:11 lest she make you the s of your enemies,
47: 3 made s of lions as though they were kids,
Is 57: 4 Of whom do you make s,
Bar 3:17 and made s of the birds of the heavens:
Mt 20:19 to be made s of and flogged and crucified.

SPOT (30)

Gn 28:11 his head and lay down to sleep at that s.
28:16 exclaimed, "Truly, the LORD is in this s,
Lv 13:33 shave himself, but not on the diseased s.
13:43 if the scab on the sore of the bald s
Jos 4: 3 take up twelve stones from this s in the bed
4: 9 set up in the bed of the Jordan on the s
1Sm 19:23 prophetic condition until he reached the s.
20:19 Go to the s where you hid on the other
20:37 When the boy made for the s where Jonathan
26: 5 and examined the s where Saul and Abner,
2Sm 2:23 He fell there and died on the s.
6: 7 God struck him on that s,
18:11 you not strike him to the ground on the s?
2Kgs 5:11 God, and would move his hand over the s,
6: 6 When he pointed out to the s,
2Chr 3: 1 David, on the s which David had selected,
Sir 24: 8 he who formed me chose the s for my tent,
Is 1: 6 the foot to the head there is no sound s:
22:23 I will fix him like a peg in a sure s,
22:25 the peg fixed in a sure s shall give way,
46: 7 it strays, and does not move from the s.
Jer 38: 9 He will die of famine on the s,
Hos 9:13 planted in a beauteous s;
13: 8 I will devour them on the s like a lion,
Mt 15:33 in this deserted s to satisfy such a crowd?"
Mk 1:20 He summoned them on the s.
2: 4 up the roof over the s where Jesus was.
8: 4 people sufficient bread in this deserted s?"
Lk 19: 5 Jesus came to the s he looked up and said,
Jn 11:30 still at the s where Martha had met him.)

SPOTLESS (2)

Wis 7:26 light, the s mirror of the power of God,
1Pt 1:19 blood of a s, unblemished lamb

SPOTS (2)

Sir 11:30 yet like a spy he will pick out the weak s.
Jer 13:23 the leopard his s?

SPOTTED (8)

Gn 30:32 every s or speckled one among the goats.
30:33 that is not a speckled or s goat,
30:35 Laban removed the streaked and s he-goats
30:35 and all the speckled and s she-goats,
30:39 forth streaked, speckled and s kids.
Lv 13:38 a man or a woman is s with white blotches,
Zec 6: 3 horses, and the fourth chariot s horses
6: 6 s ones went toward the land of the south.

SPOUSE (4)

Ex 4:25 she said, "You are a s of blood to me."
4:26 At that time she said, "A s of blood,"
Is 62: 4 delights in you, and makes your land his s.
Jl 1: 8 girt with sackcloth for the s of her youth.

SPOUTING (1)

Ez 32: 2 a monster in the sea, s in your streams,

SPRANG (18)

Gn 10: 5 and from them s the maritime nations,
10:14 the Caphtorim from whom the Philistines s.
Ex 37:22 The knobs and branches s so directly from
37:25 high, having horns that s directly from it.
38: 2 were made that s directly from the altar.
1Sm 20:34 Jonathan s up from the table in great
1Chr 1:12 and Caphtorim, from whom the Philistines s.
Tb 2: 4 I s to my feet,
7: 6 Raguel s up and kissed him,
9: 6 He s up and greeted Gabael,
Est D: 8 In great anxiety he s from his throne,
1Mc 1:10 There s from these a sinful offshoot,
2:24 he s forward and killed him upon the altar.
16:16 had drunk freely, Ptolemy and his men s up,
Dn 7: 8 a little horn, s out of their midst,
7:20 on its head, and the other one that s up,
Mk 4: 8 yielded grain that s up to produce
Acts 19:16 spirit s at them and overpowered them all.

SPRAWLED (2)

1Kgs 13:24 His corpse lay s on the road,
Prv 23:34 of the sea, now s at the top of the mast.

SPREAD (152)

Gn 10:18 the clans of the Canaanites s out,
28:14 through them you shall s out east and west,
41:56 When the famine had s throughout the land,
Ex 1:12 oppressed, the more they multiplied and s.
22: 4 s so that it burns in another's field,
25:20 shall have their wings s out above,
29: 2 with oil, and unleavened wafers s with oil,
37: 9 The cherubim had their wings s out above,
40:19 He s the tent over the Dwelling and put
Lv 2: 4 oil, or of unleavened wafers s with oil.
7:12 with oil, unleavened wafers s with oil,
13: 5 unchanged and has not s on the skin,
13: 6 is now dying out and has not s on the skin,
13: 8 that the eczema has indeed s on the skin,
13:22 If it has then s on the skin,
13:27 day, find that it has s at all on the skin,
13:32 If the scall has not s and has no yellow
13:34 finds that it has not s on the skin and
13:36 If the scall has indeed s on the skin he
13:51 If it has s on the garment,
13:53 finds that it has not s on the garment,
13:55 appearance, even though it may not have s,
14:39 that the infection has s on the walls,
14:44 that the infection has s in the house,
14:48 has in fact not s after the plastering,
Nm 4: 6 and on top of this s an all-violet cloth.
4: 7 On the table of the Presence they shall s
4: 8 Over these they shall s a scarlet cloth
4:11 golden altar they shall s a violet cloth,
4:13 ashes, they shall s a purple cloth over it.
4:14 then s a covering of tahash skin over this,
6:15 oil and of unleavened wafers s with oil.
11:32 Then they s them out all around the camp.
13:32 So they s discouraging reports among the
Dt 11:25 will s the fear and dread of you through
22:17 And they shall s out the cloth before the

32:11 So he *s* his wings to receive them and bore
33:27 He *s* out the primeval tent;
Jos 2: 6 them among her stalks of flax *s* out there.
6:27 so that his fame *s* throughout the land.
7:23 Israelites, and *s* them out before the LORD.
Jgs 8:25 and *s* out a cloak into which everyone
Ru 3: 9 *S* the corner of your cloak over me,
1Sm 9:25 a mattress was *s* for Saul on the roof,
14:15 panic *s* to the army and to the countryside,
19:13 hair at its head and covering it with a *s*.
2Sm 17:19 took the cover and *s* it over the cistern,
18: 8 The battle *s* out over that entire region,
21:10 took sackcloth and *s* it out for herself on
1Kgs 1: 1 *s* covers over him he could not keep warm.
5:11 fame *s* throughout the neighboring nations.
6:27 of the temple, with their wings *s* wide,
8: 7 wings *s* out over the place of the ark,
2Kgs 6:23 The king *s* a great feast for them.
8:15 dipped it in water, and *s* it over
9:13 *s* it under Jehu on the bare steps,
1Chr 4:38 and their ancestral houses *s* out to such
14:17 fame was *s* abroad through every land,
28:18 the cherubim that *s* their wings and
2Chr 5: 8 wings *s* out over the place of the ark,
26: 8 to Uzziah and his fame *s* as far as Egypt,
26:15 His fame *s* far and wide,
Neh 9:35 land that you had *s* out before them,
Tb 3:11 At that time, then, she *s* out her hands,
Jdt 7: 3 and *s* out in breadth toward Dothan as far
7:18 was *s* out in profusion everywhere.
10:18 the news of her arrival *s* among the tents,
12:15 Meanwhile her maid went ahead and *s* out on
1Mc 3: 3 He *s* abroad the glory of his people,
11:47 around him and *s* out through the city.
2Mc 4:39 When word was *s* that a large number of
7: 5 As a cloud of smoke *s* from the pan,
8: 7 Soon the fame of his valor *s* everywhere.
10:36 *s* the fire and burned the blasphemers
15:23 angel now to *s* fear and dread before us.
Jb 1:10 and his livestock are *s* over the land.
17:13 dwelling, if I *s* my couch in the darkness,
29:19 My root is *s* out to the waters;
37:18 *s* out with him the firmament of the skies,
Ps(s) 23: 5 You *s* the table before me in the sight
50:20 against your mother's son you *s* rumors.
78:19 saying, "Can God *s* a table in the desert?
104: 2 have *s* out the heavens like a tent-cloth;
105:39 He *s* a cloud to cover them and fire
136: 6 Who *s* out the earth upon the waters,
140: 6 They have *s* cords for a net;
Prv 1:17 a net is *s* before the eyes of any bird
7:16 With coverlets I have *s* my couch,
9: 2 mixed her wine, yes, she has *s* her table.
Sg 4:16 my garden that its perfumes may *s* abroad.
Wis 17:21 Over them alone was *s* oppressive night,
Sir 24:16 I *s* out my branches like a terebinth,
Is 1:15 When you *s* out your hands,
8: 8 *s* its wings the full width of your land,
16: 8 branches *s* forth and extended over the sea.
17:14 In the evening, they *s* terror,
19: 8 *s* their nets in the water shall pine away.
21: 5 They set the table, *s* out the rugs;
33:23 the mast in place, nor keep the sail *s* out.
44:24 when I *s* out the earth,
48:13 my right hand *s* out the heavens.
54: 2 tent, *s* out your tent cloths unsparingly;
54: 3 *s* abroad to the right and to the left;
57: 8 Deserting me, you *s* out your high,
65:11 You who *s* a table for Fortune and fill
66:12 I will *s* prosperity over her like a river,
Jer 8: 2 *s* out before the sun and the moon
49:16 The terror you *s* beguiled you,
51:46 for fear of rumors *s* in the land;
Lam 1:13 He *s* a net for my feet,
Ez 1:11 Each had two wings *s* out above so that
12:13 But I will *s* my net over him,
13:12 Where is the whitewash you *s* on?
16: 8 So I *s* the corner of my cloak over you to
17:20 I will *s* my net over him,
19: 8 They *s* their net to take him,
23:41 for them, with a table *s* before it,
26:17 *s* terror into all that dwelt by the sea.
31: 7 beautiful and stately in its *s* of foliage,
32: 3 I will *s* my net over you [with a host of
32: 8 And I will *s* darkness over your land,
32:23 who *s* terror in the land of the living.
32:24 *s* their terror in the land of the living,
32:26 *s* their terror in the land of the living.
32:32 he *s* his terror in the land of the living,
Dn 3:48 cubits above the furnace, and *s* out,
Hos 5: 1 a snare at Mizpah, and a net *s* over Tabor.
7:12 as they go I will *s* my net around them,
Na 3:17 grasshoppers will *s* their wings and fly,
Mt 9:31 and *s* word of him through the whole area.
10:34 that my mission on earth is to *s* peace.
10:34 My mission is to *s*,
14:35 him they *s* the word throughout the region.
21: 8 The huge crowd *s* their cloaks on the road,
Mk 1:28 From that point on his reputation *s*
11: 8 Many people *s* their cloaks on the road,
11: 8 *s* reeds which they had cut in the fields.
Lk 4:14 and his reputation *s* throughout the region.
4:25 years and a great famine *s* over the land.
5:15 His reputation *s* more and more,
7:17 This was the report that *s* about him
19:36 They *s* their cloaks on the roadway as he
Jn 21:23 This is how the report *s* among the
Acts 6: 7 The word of God continued to *s*,
12:24 of the Lord continued to *s* and increase.
16:34 up into his house, *s* a table before them,
19:20 continue to *s* with influence and power.
19:29 long, confusion *s* throughout the city.
Rom 1: 5 that we may *s* his name and bring to
Gal 1:16 that I might *s* among the Gentiles the good
2Tm 2:17 of their talk will *s* like the plague.

SPREADING (25)

Lv 13:23 the blotch remains in its place without *s*,
13:28 *s* on the skin and is already dying out,
19:16 not go about *s* slander among your kinsmen;
Nm 14:36 by *s* discouraging reports about the land;
Jgs 20:42 had been in the city were *s* destruction.
1Sm 2:24 I hear the people of the LORD *s* about you.
2Kgs 19:14 of the LORD, and *s* it out before him,
Est 9: 4 and the report was *s* through all the
Jb 5: 3 I have seen a fool *s* his roots,
26: 9 of the full moon by *s* his clouds before it.
Prv 29: 5 his neighbor is *s* a net under his feet.
Sg 1: 3 Your name spoken is a *s* perfume
7:10 my lover, *s* over the lips and the teeth.
Wis 17:18 melodious song of birds in the *s* branches,
Is 37:14 of the LORD, and *s* it out before him,
47:14 cannot save themselves from the *s* flames.
Jer 11:16 A *s* olive tree, goodly to behold,
Ez 16:25 obscenely, *s* your legs for every passer-by,
47:10 En-gedi to Eneglaim, *s* their nets there.
Jl 2: 2 Like dawn *s* over the mountains,
Lk 4:37 kept *s* through the surrounding country.
9: 6 *s* the good news everywhere and curing
Acts 4:17 To stop this from *s* further among the
21:28 This is the man who is *s* his teaching
3Jn 1:10 he is doing in *s* evil nonsense about us.

SPREADS (18)

Ex 22: 5 If the fire *s* further,
Lv 13: 7 clean, the eczema *s* at all on his skin,
13:35 But if the scall *s* at all on his skin
Jb 12:23 he *s* peoples abroad and he abandons them.
36:29 he *s* the clouds in layers as the carpeting
38:24 whence the east wind *s* over the earth?
39:20 while his thunderous snorting *s* terror?
39:26 that he *s* his wings toward the south?
41:22 he *s* like a threshing sledge upon the mire.
Ps(s) 147:16 He *s* snow like wool;
Prv 10:18 but he who *s* accusations is a fool.
Is 40:22 a veil, *s* them out like a tent to dwell in.
42: 5 out, who *s* out the earth with its crops,
Jer 25:31 the earth to its very ends the uproar *s*;
48:40 an eagle he soars, *s* his wings over Moab.
49:22 soars aloft, and *s* his wings over Bozrah;
Hb 3: 4 His splendor *s* like the light;
Zec 12: 1 Thus says the LORD, who *s* out the heavens,

SPRING (63)

Gn 16: 7 found her by a *s* in the wilderness,
16: 7 the wilderness, the *s* on the road to Shur,
24:13 While I stand here at the *s* and the
24:16 She went down to the *s* and filled her jug.
24:30 Laban rushed outside to the man at the *s*.
24:30 was still standing by the camels at the *s*.
24:42 "When I came to the *s* today, I prayed:
24:43 While I stand here at the *s*,
24:45 she went down to the *s* and drew water,
26:19 the wadi and reached *s* water in their well,
49:22 is a wild colt, a wild colt by a *s*,
Ex 25:36 Their knobs and branches shall so *s* from
27: 2 made that they *s* directly from the altar.
30: 2 high, with horns that *s* directly from it.
Lv 11:36 a *s* or a cistern for collecting water
14: 5 over an earthen vessel with *s* water in it.
14: 6 the bird that was slain over the *s* water,
14:50 over an earthen vessel with *s* water in it.
14:51 blood of the slain bird and the *s* water,
14:52 with the bird's blood and the *s* water,
Nm 19:17 and *s* water shall be poured on them.
21:17 *S* up, O well!—so
Jos 18:15 and projected to the *s* at Nephtoah.
Jgs 15:19 *s* in Lehi is called En-hakkore to this day.
1Sm 29: 1 encamped at the *s* of Harod near Jezreel.
1Kgs 8:19 but the son who will *s* from you,
2Kgs 2:21 went out to the *s* and threw salt into it,
2:21 again shall death or miscarriage *s* from it.' "
Neh 2:13 the Valley Gate, passed by the Dragon *S*,
2:14 over to the *S* Gate and to the King's Pool.
3:15 The *S* Gate was repaired by Shallum,
12:37 At the *S* Gate they went straight up by the
Jdt 7: 3 at the *s* in the valley near Bethulia,
12: 7 she washed herself at the *s* of the camp.
Est A: 9 river, a flood of water from a little *s*.
F: 3 the tiny *s* that grew into a river,
Jb 5: 6 nor does trouble *s* out of the ground;
29:23 they drank in my words like the *s* rains.
Ps(s) 84: 7 of the mastic trees they make a *s* of it;
85:12 Truth shall *s* out of the earth,
Prv 16:15 and his favor is like a rain cloud in *s*.
25:26 Like a troubled fountain or a polluted *s*
Eccl 12: 6 And the pitcher is shattered at the *s*,
Wis 11: 6 Instead of a *s*, when the perennial river
Sir 21:13 a flood, and his counsel, like a living *s*;
45: 1 was to *s* the man who won the favor of all:
Is 42: 9 Before they *s* into being,
44: 4 They shall *s* up amid the verdure like
45: 8 let justice also *s* up!
58:11 garden, like a *s* whose water never fails.
61:11 plants, and a garden makes its growth *s* up,
61:11 and praise *s* up before all the nations.
Jer 3: 3 showers were withheld, the *s* rain failed.
8:23 Oh, that my head were a *s* of water,
Hos 6: 3 rain, like *s* rain that waters the earth."
13:15 from the desert, That shall dry up his *s*,
Am 3: 5 Does a snare *s* up from the ground without
Zec 10: 1 Ask of the LORD rain in the *s* season!
Jn 8:44 The father you *s* from is the devil,
1Thes 2: 3 The exhortation we deliver does not *s* from
Jas 3:11 Does a *s* gush forth fresh water and foul
5: 7 soil receives the winter and the *s* rains.
Rv 21: 6 cost from the *s* of life-giving water.

SPRINGING (4)

Ex 25:31 and knobs and petals *s* directly from it.
37: 8 *s* directly from the propitiatory at its
37:17 and knobs and petals *s* directly from it.
Sg 2: 8 here he comes *s* across the mountains,

SPRINGS (33)

Ex 15:27 twelve *s* of water and seventy palm trees,
25:19 so that one cherub *s* direct from each end.
Nm 23:24 Here is a people that *s* up like a lioness,
33: 9 twelve *s* of water and seventy palm trees,
Dt 8: 7 with *s* and fountains welling up in the
33:22 a lion's whelp, that *s* forth from Bashan!"
2Kgs 3:19 fell every fruit tree, stop up all the *s*,
3:25 all the *s* they stopped up and every useful
2Chr 32: 3 stop the waters of the *s* outside the city.
32: 4 was gathered which stopped all the *s*
Jdt 6:11 till they reached the *s* below Bethulia.
7:17 water supply and the *s* of the Israelites.
Jb 14: 2 trouble, Like a flower that *s* up and fades,
Ps(s) 74:15 You released the *s* and torrents;
90: 6 changing grass, Which at dawn *s* up anew,
104:10 You sent forth *s* into the watercourses
107:33 into desert, water *s* into thirsty ground,
107:35 of water, waterless land into water *s*.
114: 8 pools of water, the flint into flowing *s*.
Prv 8:24 when there were no fountains or *s* of water;
Is 35: 7 pools, and the thirsty ground, *s* of water;
41:18 and the dry ground into *s* of water,
43:19 Now it *s* forth, do you not perceive it?
49:10 them and guides them beside *s* of water.
Dn 3:77 You *s*, bless the Lord;
Mk 4:32 sown, *s* up to become the largest of shrubs,
1Tm 1: 5 is the love that *s* from a pure heart,
Heb 12:15 *s* up through which many may become defiled;
2Pt 2:17 These men are waterless *s*,
Rv 7:17 will lead them to *s* of life-giving water.
8:10 fell on a third of the rivers and the *s*.
14: 7 earth, the Creator of the sea and the *s*."
16: 4 poured out his bowl on the rivers and *s*.

SPRINGTIME (2)

Wis 2: 7 perfumes, and let no *s* blossom pass us by;
Sir 50: 8 Like the blossoms on the branches in *s*,

SPRINKLE (19)

Ex 12:22 *s* the lintel and the two doorposts with
29:21 oil, and *s* this on Aaron and his vestments,
Lv 4: 6 he shall *s* it seven times before the LORD,
4:17 he shall *s* it seven times before the LORD,
5: 9 he shall *s* some of the blood of the sin
14: 7 and then *s* seven times the man to be
14:16 he shall *s* it seven times before the LORD.
14:27 *s* it seven times before the LORD.
14:51 spring water, and *s* the house seven times.
16:14 he shall *s* it with his finger on the fore
16:14 likewise *s* some of the blood with his finger
16:19 *s* some of the blood on it seven times.
Nm 8: 7 *S* them with the water of remission;
19: 4 *s* it seven times toward the front
19:18 dip it in this water and *s* it on the tent
19:19 The clean man shall *s* the unclean on the
2Kgs 16:15 You must also *s* on it all the blood of
2Mc 1:21 ordered the priests to *s* with the water
Ez 36:25 I will *s* clean water upon you to cleanse

SPRINKLED (14)

Ex 24: 8 he took the blood and *s* it on the people,
Lv 8:11 Then he *s* some of this oil seven times on
8:30 Moses *s* with it Aaron and his vestments,
2Chr 30:16 *s* the blood given them by the Levites;
35:11 whereupon the priests *s* some of the blood
1Mc 3:47 they *s* ashes on their heads and tore their
4:39 they *s* their heads with ashes and fell
2Mc 14:15 they *s* themselves with earth and prayed to
Prv 7:17 I have *s* my bed with myrrh,

SPRINKLED (cont.)

Heb 9:19 hyssop, and *s* the book and all the people,
9:21 He also *s* the tabernacle and all the
10:22 our hearts *s* clean from the evil which lay
11:28 kept the Passover and *s* the lamb's blood,
12:24 and to the *s* blood which speaks more

SPRINKLES (2)

Nm 19:21 "One who *s* the lustral water shall wash
Sir 43:18 He *s* the snow like fluttering birds;

SPRINKLING (7)

Lv 16:15 *s* it on the propitiatory and before it.
2Kgs 16:13 and *s* the blood of his peace-offerings on
2Mc 10:25 *s* earth upon their heads and girding their
Ez 43:18 upon it and for the *s* of blood against it.
Hos 7: 9 Of gray hairs, too, there is a *s*,
Mk 7: 4 from the market without first *s* it.
Heb 9:13 *s* of a heifer's ashes can sanctify those

SPROUT (10)

Nm 17:20 the staff of the man of my choice shall *s*.
Jb 14: 7 that it will *s* again and that its tender
Ps(s) 132:17 will I make a horn to *s* forth for David;
147: 8 Who makes grass to *s* on the mountains and
Is 11: 1 a shoot shall *s* from the stump of Jesse,
27: 6 take root, Israel shall *s* and blossom,
Ez 17: 6 he placed it, To *s* and grow up a vine,
29:21 will make a horn *s* for the house of Israel,
Zec 6:12 name is Shoot, and where he is he shall *s*,
Mk 13:28 runs high and it begins to *s* leaves,

SPROUTED (9)

Gn 2: 5 on earth and no grass of the field had *s*,
41: 6 Behind them *s* seven ears of grain,
41:23 Behind them *s* seven ears of grain,
Ex 10: 5 foliage that has since *s* in your fields.
Nm 17:23 Levi, had *s* and put forth not only shoots,
Hg 2:19 Indeed, the seed has not *s*,
Mt 13: 5 It *s* at once since the soil had no depth,
Mk 4: 5 it *s* immediately because the soil had no
Lk 8: 6 Some fell on rocky ground, *s* up,

SPROUTS (5)

Jb 8:19 the road, and out of the soil another *s*.
Sir 14:18 one falls off and another *s*—
Is 17:11 make your *s* blossom on the next morning,
Mt 24:32 When its branch grows tender and *s* leaves,
Mk 4:27 Through it all the seed *s* and grows

SPRUNG (3)

Dt 13:14 it said that certain scoundrels have *s* up
2Sm 7:12 up your heir after you, *s* from your loins,
Is 48: 1 name of Israel, *s* from the stock of Judah,

SPUN (2)

Ex 35:26 women who possessed the skill, *s* goat hair.
Ps(s) 45:14 her raiment is threaded with *s* gold.

SPUR (1)

Jb 39:28 on the *s* of the cliff or the fortress.

SPURIOUS (2)

Wis 4: 3 their *s* offshoots shall not strike deep
Jer 2:21 you turn out obnoxious to me, a *s* vine?

SPURN (16)

Lv 26:15 if you reject my precepts and *s* my decrees,
26:44 enemies' land, I will not reject or *s* them,
Nm 14:11 to Moses, "How long will this people *s* me?
1Sm 2:30 me, but those who *s* me shall be accursed.
Est C: 9 Do not *s* your portion,
Jb 10: 3 to oppress, to *s* the work of your hands,
Ps(s) 51:19 and humbled, O God, you will not *s*.
Prv 3:11 *s* not his reproof;
5:12 I hate instruction, and my heart *s* reproof!
Sir 8: 8 *S* not the discourse of the wise,
Is 31: 7 *s* his sinful idols of silver and gold,
Jer 4:30 Your lovers *s* you, they seek your life.
14:21 For your name's sake *s* us not,
33:24 They *s* my people as if it were no longer a
Am 5:21 I hate, I *s* your feasts,
Jude 1: 8 they *s* God's dominion and revile the

SPURNED (25)

Lv 26:43 *s* my precepts and abhorred my statutes.
Nm 11:20 you have *s* the LORD who is in your midst,
14:23 None of these who have *s* me shall see it.
14:31 and they shall appreciate the land you *s*.
Dt 32:15 They *s* the God who made them and scorned
2Sm 12: 9 you *s* the LORD and done evil in his sight?
12:14 you have utterly *s* the LORD by this deed,
Ps(s) 22:25 For he has not *s* nor disdained the
89:39 and *s* and been enraged at your anointed.
Prv 1:30 ignored my counsel, they *s* all my reproof;
Is 1: 4 the LORD, *s* the Holy One of Israel,
5:24 they have *s* the law of the LORD of hosts,
33: 8 Covenants are broken, their terms are *s*;
53: 3 He was *s* and avoided by men,
53: 3 of those from whom men hide their faces, *s*,
Ez 5: 6 she has *s* my ordinances and has not lived
16:45 the mother who *s* her husband and children,
16:45 to those who *s* their husbands and children
17:16 who set him up to rule, whose oath he *s*,
17:18 He *s* his oath, breaking his covenant.
17:19 As I live, my oath which he *s*,
21:15 You have *s* the rod and every judgment!
21:18 the Lord GOD, since you have *s* the rod.
22: 8 What is holy to me you have *s*,
Am 2: 4 Because they *s* the law of the LORD,

SPURNS (4)

Ps(s) 69:34 and his own who are in bonds he *s* not.
Prv 14: 2 but he who is devious in his ways *s* him.
15: 5 The fool *s* his father's admonition,
Is 33:15 who *s* what is gained by oppression,

SPURTED (2)

2Kgs 9:33 *s* against the wall and against the horses.
Is 63: 3 Their blood *s* on my garments;

SPURTS (1)

Prv 15: 2 but the mouth of fools *s* forth folly.

SPY (7)

Jos 2: 2 come there that night to *s* out the land.
2: 3 they have come to *s* out the entire land."
2Sm 10: 3 not rather to explore the city, to *s* on it,
1Mc 5:38 Judas sent men to *s* on the camp,
Ps(s) 10: 8 his eyes *s* upon the unfortunate.
Sir 11:30 like a *s* he will pick out the weak spots.
Gal 2: 4 they wormed their way into the group to *s*

SPYING (2)

Gn 42:30 us in custody as if we were *s* on the land.
1Chr 19: 3 the land, *s* it out for its overthrow?"

SQUADRONS (3)

1Mc 9:11 The cavalry were divided into two *s*,
9:12 Flanked by the two *s*,
2Mc 5: 3 *s* of cavalry in battle array,

SQUADS (1)

Acts 12: 4 with four *s* of soldiers to guard him.

SQUALL (1)

Mk 4:37 It happened that a bad *s* blew up.

SQUANDERED (1)

Lk 15:13 where he *s* his money on dissolute living.

SQUANDERING (1)

Jas 4: 3 to *s* what you receive on your pleasures.

SQUANDERS (1)

Prv 29: 3 he who consorts with harlots *s* his wealth.

SQUARE (32)

Gn 19: 2 we shall pass the night in the town *s*."
Ex 27: 1 make an altar of acacia wood, on a *s*,
28:16 It is to be *s* when folded double,
30: 2 an altar of acacia wood, with a *s* surface,
37:25 incense was made of acacia wood, on a *s*,
38: 1 was made of acacia wood, on a *s*,
39: 9 It was *s* and folded double a span high and
Dt 13:17 up all its spoils in the middle of its *s*,
Jgs 19:15 in the public *s* of the city he had entered,
19:17 the traveler in the public *s* of the city,
19:20 and do not spend the night in the public *s*."
2Sm 21:12 secretly from the public *s* of Beth-shan,
Neh 3: 8 as far as the wall of the public *s*.
Est 4: 6 in the public *s* in front of the royal gate,
6: 9 on the horse in the public *s* of the city,
6:11 had him ride in the public *s* of the city,
1Mc 10:11 Zion with *s* stones for its fortification,
Jb 29: 7 of the city and set up my seat in the *s*—
Prv 26:13 the street, a lion in the middle of the *s*!"
Is 59:14 For truth stumbles in the public *s*,
Ez 40:47 and a hundred cubits wide, a perfect *s*.
41:21 The way into the nave was a *s* doorframe.
43:16 The hearth was a *s*:
43:17 The upper ledge was also a *s*:
43:17 The lower ledge, likewise a *s*,
45: 2 Of this land a *s* plot,
48:20 as a perfect *s* you shall set apart the
Am 5:16 In every *s* there shall be lamentation,
Acts 16:19 the main *s* before the local authorities.
17: 5 who engaged loafers from the public *s*
17:17 in the public *s* with ordinary passers-by.
Rv 21:16 The city is perfectly *s*,

SQUARES (10)

1Mc 14: 9 Old men sat in the *s*,
Prv 1:20 street, in the open *s* she raises her voice;
7:12 she is in the streets, now in the open *s*,
Sir 9: 7 of the city and wander not through its *s*;
Is 15: 3 the rooftops and in the *s* everyone wails.
Jer 9:20 in the street, young people in the *s*.
48:38 of Moab and in all his *s* there is mourning;
Na 2: 5 through the streets And wheel in the *s*,
Mt 11:16 are like children squatting in the town *s*,
Lk 7:32 the city *s* and calling to their playmates,

SQUAT (1)

Bar 6:30 and in their temples the priests *s* with

SQUATTING (2)

Mt 11:16 are like children *s* in the town squares,
Lk 7:32 They are like children *s* in the city

SQUEEZE (1)

Lv 1:15 snap its head loose and *s* out its blood

SQUEEZED (2)

Lv 5: 9 be *s* out against the base of the altar.
Nm 22:25 and since she *s* Balaam's leg against it,

SQUEEZING (1)

Jgs 6:38 the fleece, *s* out of it a bowlful of water.

STABBED (3)

2Sm 3:27 There he *s* him in the abdomen,
20:10 hand, Joab *s* him in the abdomen with it,
1Mc 6:46 under the elephant and *s* it in the belly,

STABILITY (4)

Est B: 5 so that *s* of government cannot be obtained,
Prv 29: 4 By justice a king gives *s* to the land;
Wis 6:24 and a prudent king, the *s* of his people;
Sir 10: 1 A wise magistrate lends *s* to his people,

STABLE (1)

Est B: 7 affairs *s* and undisturbed for the future."

STACHYS (1)

Rom 16: 9 and to my beloved *S*.

STACKED (1)

1Mc 11: 4 in the war and *s* up along his route.

STADIUM (1)

1Cor 9:24 the runners in the *s* take part in the race,

STAFF (76)

Gn 32:11 the Jordan here with nothing but my *s*,
38:18 "Your seal and cord, and the *s* you carry."
38:25 seal and cord and whose *s* these are."
40:20 when he gave a banquet to all his *s*,
Ex 4: 2 "A *s*," he answered.
4: 4 hold of it, and it became a *s* in his hand.
4:17 Take this *s* in your hand;
4:20 The *s* of God he carried with him.
7: 9 your *s* and throw it down before Pharaoh,
7:10 *s* down before Pharaoh and his servants,
7:12 Each one threw down his *s*,
7:12 But Aaron's *s* swallowed their staffs.
7:15 your hand the *s* that turned into a serpent.
7:17 the water of the river with the *s* I hold,
7:19 Take your *s* and stretch out your hand over
7:20 Aaron raised his *s* and struck the waters
8: 1 *s* over the streams and canals and pools,
8:12 out his *s* and strike the dust of the earth,
8:13 and with his *s* he struck the dust of the
9:23 Moses stretched out his *s* toward the sky,
10:13 stretched out his *s* over the land of Egypt,
12:11 sandals on your feet and your *s* in hand,
14:16 And you, lift up your *s* and,
17: 5 go, the *s* with which you struck the river.
17: 9 of the hill with the *s* of God in my hand."
21:19 up and walk around with the help of his *s*.
Nm 17:17 one *s* from them for each ancestral house,
17:17 Mark each man's name on his *s*;
17:18 and mark Aaron's name on Levi's *s*,
17:18 Levi's ancestral house shall also have a *s*.
17:20 the *s* of the man of my choice shall sprout.
17:21 and Aaron's *s* was with them.
17:23 when Moses entered the tent, Aaron's *s*,
17:24 prince identified his own *s* and took it,
17:25 Aaron's *s* in front of the commandments,
20: 8 "Take the *s* and assemble the community,
20: 9 took the *s* from its place before the LORD,
20:11 Moses struck the rock twice with his *s*,
24:17 from Jacob, and a *s* shall rise from Israel,
Jgs 5:14 from Zebulun wielders of the marshal's *s*.
6:21 stretched out the tip of the *s* he held,
1Sm 14:27 thrust out the end of the *s* he was holding
14:43 honey from the end of the *s* I was holding.
17:40 *s* in hand, David selected five smooth stones
17:43 I a dog that you come against me with a *s*?"
2Kgs 4:29 to Gehazi, "take my *s* with you and be off;
4:29 Lay my *s* upon the boy."
4:31 on ahead and had laid the *s* upon the boy,

18:21 This Egypt, the *s* on which you rely,
1Chr 11:23 but he came against him with a *s*,
Tb 5:18 Is he not the *s* to which we cling,
Est 5: 2 toward her the golden *s* which he held.
5: 2 and touched the top of the *s*
Ps(s) 23: 4 your rod and your *s* that give me courage.
Sir 48: 2 Their *s* of bread he shattered,
Is 10: 5 My rod in anger, my *s* in wrath.
10:15 who lifts it, or a *s* him who is not wood!
10:24 with a rod, and raises his *s* against you.
10:26 his *s* over the sea as he did against Egypt.
14: 5 rod of the wicked, the *s* of the tyrants
28:27 But gith is beaten out with a *s*,
36: 6 This Egypt, the *s* on which you rely,
Jer 48:17 How the strong *s* is broken,
Ez 4:16 I am breaking the *s* of bread in Jerusalem.
5:16 of hunger, I will break your *s* of bread;
14:13 hand against it and break its *s* of bread,
20:37 the *s* and bring back but a small number.
29: 6 have been a reed *s* for the house of Israel:
Mi 7:14 Shepherd your people with your *s*,
Zec 8: 4 each with *s* in hand because of old age,
11:10 took my *s* "Favor" and snapped it asunder,
11:14 Then I snapped asunder my other *s*,
Mt 10:10 change of shirt, no sandals, no walking *s*.
Lk 9: 3 neither walking *s* nor traveling bag;
10: 4 Do not carry a walking *s* or traveling bag;
Heb 11:21 God, leaning on the head of his *s*.

STAFFS (7)

Ex 7:12 But Aaron's staff swallowed their *s*.
Nm 17:17 for each ancestral house, twelve *s* in all,
17:21 Israelites, and their princes gave him *s*,
17:22 Then Moses laid the *s* down before the LORD
17:24 Moses thereupon brought out all the *s* from
21:18 dug, with their scepters and their *s*."
Zec 11: 7 I took two *s*,

STAG (5)

Prv 7:22 Like a *s* that minces toward the net,
Sg 2: 9 My lover is like a gazelle or a young *s*.
2:17 or a young *s* upon the mountains of Bether.
8:14 or a young *s* on the mountains of spices!
Is 35: 6 Then will the lame leap like a *s*,

STAGE (1)

Phil 3:16 course, no matter what *s* we have reached.

STAGES (9)

Gn 12: 9 Then Abram journeyed on by *s* to the Negeb.
13: 3 the Negeb he traveled by *s* toward Bethel,
Ex 17: 1 whole Israelite community journeyed by *s*,
40:38 of Israel in all the *s* of their journey.
Nm 10:12 moved on from the desert of Sinai by *s*,
33: 1 The following are the *s* by which the
33: 2 the starting places of the various *s*.
33: 2 starting places of the successive *s* were:
Mt 24: 8 These are the early *s* of the birth pangs.

STAGGER (8)

Jb 12:25 he makes them *s* like drunken men.
Is 19:14 have made Egypt *s* in whatever she does,
28: 7 *s* from wine and stumble from strong drink:
28: 7 Priest and prophet *s* from strong drink,
29: 9 Be drunk, but not from wine, *s*,
40:30 and grow weary, and youths *s* and fall,
Lam 5:13 boys *s* under their loads of wood;
Hb 2:16 drink, you too, and *s*!

STAGGERED (6)

2Sm 22:46 they *s* forth from their fortresses."
Est D: 7 the height of majestic anger, the queen *s*,
Ps(s) 18:46 they *s* forth from their fortresses.
107:27 They reeled and *s* like drunken men,
Lam 4:14 They *s* blindly in the streets,
Am 4: 8 Though two or three cities *s* to one city

STAGGERING (3)

Is 28: 7 astray by strong drink, *s* in their visions,
51:17 Who drained to the dregs the bowl of *s*!
51:22 I am taking from your hand the cup of *s*;

STAGGERS (1)

Is 19:14 she does, as a drunkard *s* in his vomit.

STAIN (12)

Dt 19:13 Israel the *s* of shedding innocent blood,
1Mc 9:10 kinsmen and not leave a *s* upon our glory!"
Jb 31: 7 my eyes, or any *s* clings to my hands,
Wis 13:14 red and crimsoned its surface with red *s*,
Sir 11:33 only evil, lest you incur a lasting *s*.
44:19 of many peoples, kept his glory without *s*:
Jer 2:22 The *s* of your guilt is still before me,
Eph 5:27 *s* or wrinkle or anything of that sort.
Jas 1:27 without *s* before our God and Father.
1Pt 3:21 This baptism is no removal of physical *s*,
2Pt 2:13 they are *s* and defilement as they share
3:14 effort to be found without *s* or defilement,

STAINED (3)

Lv 6:20 *s* part must be washed in a sacred place.
Is 59: 3 For your hands are *s* with blood,
63: 3 all my apparel I *s*.

STAIRCASE (1)

2Kgs 20:11 descended on the *s* to the terrace of Ahaz.

STAIRS (2)

1Kgs 6: 8 and *s* with intermediate landings led up to
2Chr 9:11 With the cabinet wood the king made *s* for

STAIRWAY (5)

Gn 28:12 a *s* rested on the ground,
Is 38: 8 make the shadow cast by the sun on the *s*
Ez 40:31 pilasters, and it had a *s* of eight steps.
40:34 and there, and it had a *s* of eight steps.
40:37 and there, and it had a *s* of eight steps.

STAKE (5)

Gn 40:19 up your head and have you impaled on a *s*,
Lv 19:16 by idly when your neighbor's life is at *s*.
Ezr 9: 8 remnant and gave us a *s* in his holy place;
Prv 7:23 a snare, unaware that its life is at *s*.
Acts 16:24 going so far as to chain their feet to a *s*.

STAKES (1)

Is 54: 2 lengthen your ropes and make firm your *s*.

STALE (1)

Sir 14:10 bread, but on his own table he sets it *s*.

STALK (6)

Gn 41: 5 fat and healthy, growing on a single *s*.
41:22 fat and healthy, growing on a single *s*.
Jb 15:32 His *s* shall wither before its time,
Ps(s) 68:22 crowns of those who *s* about in their guilt.
Ez 5:17 and bloodshed shall *s* through you,
Hos 8: 7 The *s* of grain that forms no ear can yield

STALKS (6)

Nm 23:24 up like a lioness, and *s* forth like a lion;
Jos 2: 6 them among her *s* of flax spread out there.
Is 17: 5 of *s* when he gathers the standing grain;
Jer 25:32 calamity *s* from nation to nation;
48: 2 behind you *s* the sword.
Lam 1:20 the sword bereaves, at home death *s*.

STALL (3)

Am 6: 4 from the flock, and calves from the *s*!
Mal 3:20 out of the *s* and tread down the wicked;
Lk 13:15 out of the *s* on the sabbath to water it?

STALL-FED (2)

1Sm 28:24 The woman had a *s* calf in the house,
Am 5:22 nor consider your *s* peace offerings.

STALLION (1)

Sir 33: 6 A fickle friend is like the *s* that neighs,

STALLIONS (4)

Jer 5: 8 Lustful *s* they are,
8:16 neighing of his *s* shakes the whole land.
50:11 like calves on the green, snort like *s*!
Ez 23:20 an ass, and whose heat is like that of *s*.

STALLS (7)

1Kgs 5: 6 *s* for his twelve thousand chariot horses.
2Chr 9:25 Solomon also had four thousand *s* of horses,
Sir 38:26 he keeps a watch on the beasts in the *s*.
Hos 14: 3 as offerings the bullocks from our *s*.
Hb 3:17 the fold and there be no herd in the *s*,
Mt 21:12 tables and the *s* of the dove-sellers,
Mk 11:15 tables and the *s* of the men selling doves;

STALWART (7)

1Sm 9: 1 was a *s* man from Benjamin named Kish,
16:18 He is also a *s* soldier,
2Sm 23:20 Benaiah, son of Jehoiada, a *s* from Kabzeel,
Jdt 9:11 nor does your power depend upon *s* men;
Ps(s) 37:35 wicked man, fierce, and *s* as a flourishing,
Sir 44: 6 *S* men, solidly established and at peace
Is 21:17 Few of Kedar's *s* archers shall remain,

STALWARTS (1)

Bar 3:26 born the giants, renowned at the first, *s*,

STAMMERING (2)

Is 28:11 with *s* lips and in a strange language he
33:19 speech, *s* in a language not understood.

STAMP (2)

Dt 12: 3 that you may *s* out the remembrance of them
Ez 6:11 Clap your hands, *s* your feet,

STAMPED (3)

Ez 25: 6 you clapped your hands and *s* your feet,
28:12 You were *s* with the seal of perfection,
Rv 13:16 to accept a *s* image on their right hand or

STAMPING (1)

Jer 47: 3 They hear the *s* hooves of his steeds,

STAND (265)

Gn 19: 9 They replied, *S* back!
24:13 While I *s* here at the spring and the
24:43 While I *s* here at the spring,
39: 9 a wrong and thus *s* condemned before God
43: 9 I myself will *s* surety for him.
Ex 3: 5 for the place where you *s* is holy ground.
8:17 *s* shall be filled with swarms of flies.
9:11 magicians could not *s* in Moses' presence,
12: 2 month shall *s* at the head of your calendar;
14:13 *S* your ground, and you will see the victory
18:14 to *s* about you from morning till evening?"
18:23 orders you will be able to *s* the strain,
33: 8 and *s* at the entrance of their own tents,
33: 9 cloud would come down and *s* at its entrance
33:10 of cloud *s* at the entrance of the tent,
Lv 19:16 nor shall you *s* by idly when your
19:32 *S* up in the presence of the aged,
25:17 but *s* in fear of your God.
25:43 them harshly, but *s* in fear of your God.
26:32 there will *s* aghast at the sight of it.
26:37 will you be to take a *s* against your foes!
27:12 and the value set by the priest shall *s*.
27:14 and the value set by the priest shall *s*.
Nm 5:16 woman come forward and *s* before the LORD.
5:30 wife, he shall have her *s* before the LORD,
8:13 the Levites *s* before Aaron and his sons,
11:24 the people, he had them *s* around the tent.
16: 9 *s* before the community to minister for them?
16:18 they took their *s* by the entrance of the
16:21 to Moses and Aaron, *S* apart from this band,
22:24 Then the angel of the LORD took his *s* in a
23: 3 *S* here by your holocaust while I go over
23:15 said to Balak, *S* here by your holocaust,
27:19 Have him *s* in the presence of the priest
27:22 Taking Joshua and having him *s* in the
31:22 Whatever can *s* fire,
31:23 cannot *s* fire you shall put into the water.
Dt 7:24 No man will be able to *s* up against you,
9: 2 of them, 'Who can *s* up against the Anakim?'
11:25 None shall *s* up against you;
19:15 "One witness alone shall not take the *s*
19:16 "If an unjust witness takes the *s* against
27:12 Joseph and Benjamin shall *s* on Mount
27:13 shall *s* on Mount Ebal to pronounce curses.
28:10 of the LORD, they will *s* in awe of you.
28:65 no repose, not a foot of ground to *s* upon,
28:66 suspense and *s* in dread both day and night,
Jos 7:10 *S* up.
7:12 Israelites cannot *s* up to their enemies,
7:13 You cannot *s* up to your enemies until you
10:12 *S* still, O sun, at Gibeon,
Jgs 4:20 *S* at the entrance of the tent,"
1Sm 6:20 can *s* in the presence of this Holy One?
10:19 take your *s* before the LORD according to
12: 3 Here I *s*!
12: 7 Now, therefore, take your *s*,
12:16 *s* ready to witness the great marvel the
14:40 So he said to all Israel, *S* on one side,
14:40 I and my son Jonathan will *s* on the other."
17:16 his *s* morning and evening for forty days.
19: 3 will go out and *s* beside my father in the
2Sm 1: 9 Then he said to me, *S* up to me,
2:25 single group, and made a *s* on the hilltop.
7:16 your throne shall *s* firm forever.'"
15: 2 *s* alongside the road leading to the gate.
18:13 of the king, and you would *s* aloof."
23:12 he took his *s* in the middle of the plot
1Kgs 7:30 *s* had four bronze wheels and bronze axles.
7:32 of the wheels and the *s* were of one piece.
7:33 The four legs of each *s* had cast braces,
7:34 each stand, were of one piece with the *s*.
7:35 On the top of the *s* there was a raised
7:35 were of one piece with the top of the *s*.
10: 8 who *s* before you always and listen to your
19:11 and *s* on the mountain before the LORD;
2Kgs 5:11 out and *s* there to invoke the LORD his God,
19:27 I am aware whether you *s* or sit;
1Chr 11:14 He made a *s* on the sown ground,
29:15 For we *s* before you as aliens:
2Chr 9: 7 who *s* before you always and listen to your
20: 9 we will *s* before this house and before you,
20:17 Take your places, *s* firm,
24:20 his *s* above the people and said to them:
26:15 devices contrived to *s* on the towers and
29:11 whom the LORD has chosen to *s* before him,
35: 5 *S* in the sanctuary according to the
Ezr 9:15 this, we can no longer *s* in your presence."
10: 4 We will *s* by you,
Neh 2:17 "You see the evil plight in which we *s*:
Jdt 8:33 *S* at the gate tonight to let me pass
10:16 When you *s* before him,
13: 3 her maid to *s* outside the bedroom and wait,

STAND (cont.)

1Mc 4:18 But now *s* firm against our enemies and
6:49 no food there to enable them to *s* a siege,
10:72 Men say that you cannot make a *s* against
2Mc 13:12 encouraged them and told them to *s* ready.
Jb 11:15 you may *s* firm and unafraid.
19:25 that he will at last *s* forth upon the dust;
30:10 They abhor me, they *s* aloof from me,
30:20 you *s* off and look at me,
33: 5 draw up your arguments and *s* forth.
37:14 *S* and consider the wondrous works of God!
41: 2 who then dares *s* before him?
Ps(s) 1: 5 in judgment the wicked shall not *s*,
5: 6 the arrogant may not *s* in your sight.
10: 1 Why, O LORD, do you *s* aloof?
20: 9 bow down and fall, yet we *s* erect and firm.
24: 3 or who may *s* in his holy place?
38:12 companions *s* back because of my affliction;
38:12 my neighbors *s* afar off.
41:13 me and let me *s* before you forever.
78:13 and he made the waters *s* as in a mound.
94:16 Who will *s* by me against the evildoers?
101: 7 falsehood shall not *s* before my eyes.
109: 6 and let the accuser *s* at his right hand.
119:91 to your ordinances they still *s* firm:
130: 3 O LORD, mark iniquities, Lord, who can *s*?
134: 1 all you servants of the LORD Who *s* in the
135: 2 Who *s* in the house of the LORD,
139: 2 you know when I sit and when I *s*;
144:12 such as *s* at the corners of the temple.
Prv 8: 2 road, at the crossroads she takes her *s*;
22:29 He will *s* in the presence of kings;
22:29 will not *s* in the presence of obscure men.
27: 4 but before jealousy who can *s*?
Sir 1:20 A patient man need *s* firm but for a time,
12:12 Let him not *s* near you,
12:15 While you *s* firm,
22:26 friend all will *s* aloof who hear of it.
27:14 oath-filled talk makes the hair *s* on end,
37: 9 be, and then *s* by to watch your misfortune.
39:32 So from the first I took my *s*,
41:12 for it will *s* by you better than precious
42:17 the strength to *s* firm before his glory.
50:12 a garland, like a *s* of cedars on Lebanon;
Is 7: 7 This shall not *s*, it shall not be!
8:12 fear not, nor *s* in awe of what they fear.
14:24 As I have proposed, so shall it *s*:
19:17 they shall *s* in dread because of the plan
21: 8 O my Lord, I *s* constantly by day;
27: 9 no sacred poles or incense altars shall *s*.
28:18 pact with the nether world shall not *s*.
37:28 I am aware whether you *s* or sit;
44: 7 Let him *s* up and speak,
44:11 they will all assemble and *s* forth,
46:10 I say that my plan shall *s*,
47:13 Let the astrologers *s* forth to save you,
48:13 When I call them, they *s* forth at once.
49: 7 When kings see you, they shall *s* up,
52:15 because of him kings shall *s* speechless;
60:11 Your gates shall *s* open constantly;
61: 5 shall *s* ready to pasture your flocks,
Jer 1:17 *s* up and tell them all that I command you.
6:16 *S* beside the earliest roads,
7: 2 *S* at the gate of the house of the LORD,
7:10 and yet come to *s* before me in this house
14: 6 The wild asses *s* on the bare heights,
15:19 I restore you, in my presence you shall *s*;
17:19 Go, *s* at the Gate of Benjamin,
26: 2 *S* in the court of the house of the LORD
30:20 old, his assembly before me shall *s* firm;
46: 5 They flee headlong without making a *s*.
46:14 Take your *s*,
46:15 has Apis fled, your mighty one failed to *s*?
46:21 turn and flee together, *s* not their ground,
48:19 *S* by the wayside, watch closely,
49:19 What shepherd can *s* against me?
50:44 what shepherd can *s* against me?
51:50 have escaped the sword, go on, *s* not still;
Lam 2: 4 in his right hand He took his *s* as a foe,
3:63 Whether they sit or *s*,
Bar 5: 5 *s* upon the heights; look to the east
6: 4 their alien example and *s* in fear of them,
Ez 2: 1 Son of man, *s* up!
11:23 LORD rose from the city and took a *s*
13: 5 about the house of Israel that would *s* firm
22:30 who could build a wall or *s* in the breach
27:29 the mariners of the sea, *s* on the shore,
28:19 peoples, all who knew you *s* aghast at you;
31:14 by water may *s* by itself in its loftiness.
44:11 *s* before the people to minister for them.
44:15 *s* before me to offer me fat and blood,
44:24 In capital cases they shall *s* as judges,
Dn 2:44 put an end to them, and it shall *s* forever.
7: 4 the ground to *s* on two feet like a man,
7:17 "These four great beasts *s* for four
8:18 he touched me and made me *s* up.
10:11 *s* up, for my mission now is to you."
11:11 whose great host shall make a *s* but shall
Hos 10: 9 There they took their *s*;
Am 2:15 his life, nor the bowman *s* his ground;
7: 2 How can Jacob *s*?
7: 5 How can Jacob *s*?
Ob 1:14 *S* not at the crossroads to slay his
Mi 5: 3 He shall *s* firm and shepherd his flock by
Na 1: 6 Before his wrath, who can *s* firm,
Hb 2: 1 I will *s* at my guard post,
Zec 4:14 who *s* by the LORD of the whole earth."
14:12 shall rot while they *s* upon their feet,
Mal 3: 2 And who can *s* when he appears?
Mt 5:15 *s* where it gives light to all in the house.
6: 5 like the hypocrites who love to *s* and pray
9: 5 'Your sins are forgiven' or *S* up and walk'?
9: 6 then said to the paralyzed man— *S* up!
18:16 *s* on the word of two or three witnesses.
26:60 the many false witnesses who took the *s*.
Mk 2: 9 'Your sins are forgiven,' or to say, *S* up,
2:11 *S* up!
3: 3 *S* up here in front!"
4:21 Is it not meant to be put on a *s*?
11:25 When you *s* to pray,
14:57 Some, for instance, on taking the *s*,
Lk 1:19 am Gabriel, who *s* in attendance before God.
6: 8 was withered, "Get up and *s* here in front."
11:48 you *s* behind the deeds of your fathers:
13:25 door and you *s* outside knocking and saying,
17:19 He said to the man, *S* up and go your way;
21:28 happen, *s* erect and hold your heads high,
21:36 and to *s* secure before the Son of Man."
Jn 5: 8 Jesus said to him, *S* up!
8: 3 They made her *s* there in front of everyone.
8: 9 woman, who continued to *s* there before him.
Acts 1:11 do you *s* here looking up at the skies?
5: 9 They *s* ready to carry you out too."
5:27 in and made them *s* before the Sanhedrin,
7:33 for the place where you *s* is holy ground.
9:40 to the dead body, he said, "Tabitha, *s* up."
10:33 All of us *s* before God at this moment to
11:28 Agabus was inspired to *s* up and proclaim
14:10 He called out to him in a loud voice, *S* up!
22:30 Paul down and made him *s* before them.
25: 9 *s* trial before me there on these charges?"
25:10 "I *s* before the imperial bench;
25:20 and *s* trial there on these charges.
26: 6 But today I *s* trial because of my hope in
26: 7 Your Majesty, that I *s* accused by the Jews.
26:16 Get up now and *s* on your feet.
26:22 *s* here to testify to great and small alike.
Rom 5: 2 by faith to the grace in which we now *s*,
9:11 in order that God's decree might *s* fast
14: 4 *s* he will, for the Lord is able to make him
14: 4 will, for the Lord is able to make him *s*.
1Cor 11:19 for the tried and true to *s* out clearly.
15: 1 which you received and in which you *s* firm.
16:13 Be on your guard, *s* firm in the faith,
Gal 4:24 the two women *s* for two covenants.
5: 1 So *s* firm, and do not take on yourselves
Eph 6:11 to *s* firm against the tactics of the devil.
6:14 *S* fast, with the truth as the belt
Phil 4: 1 my dear ones, to *s* firm in the Lord.
4: 7 will *s* guard over your hearts and minds,
Col 1:11 endowed with the strength needed to *s* fast,
2:18 a one takes his *s* on his own experience;
4:12 earnestly in prayer that you *s* firm,
1Thes 3: 5 when I could *s* the suspense no longer,
3: 8 to flourish only if you *s* firm in the Lord!
2Thes 2:15 Therefore, brothers, *s* firm.
1Tm 5:25 some good deeds *s* out clearly as such;
Jas 2: 3 were to say to the poor man, "You can *s*!"
1Pt 3:14 do not *s* in awe of what this people fears."
Jude 1:24 make you *s* unblemished and exultant
Rv 3:10 Because you have kept my plea to *s* fast,
3:20 "'Here I *s*, knocking at the door.
11: 4 *s* in the presence of the Lord of the earth.

STANDARD (35)

Ex 30:13 according to the *s* of the sanctuary shekel,
30:24 according to the *s* of the sanctuary shekel;
38:24 according to the *s* of the sanctuary shekel;
38:25 according to the *s* of the sanctuary shekel;
38:26 according to the *s* of the sanctuary shekel,
Lv 5:15 according to the *s* of the sanctuary shekel.
27:25 according to the *s* of the sanctuary shekel.
Nm 3:47 according to the *s* of the sanctuary shekel,
3:50 shekels according to the sanctuary *s*.
7:13 shekels according to the sanctuary *s*
7:19 shekels according to the sanctuary *s*
7:25 shekels according to the sanctuary *s*
7:31 shekels according to the sanctuary *s*
7:37 shekels according to the sanctuary *s*
7:43 shekels according to the sanctuary *s*
7:49 shekels according to the sanctuary *s*
7:55 shekels according to the sanctuary *s*
7:61 shekels according to the sanctuary *s*
7:67 shekels according to the sanctuary *s*
7:73 shekels according to the sanctuary *s*
7:79 shekels according to the sanctuary *s*
7:85 shekels, according to the sanctuary *s*.
7:86 apiece, according to the sanctuary *s*,
10:14 under its own *s* and arranged in companies,
10:18 under its own *s* and arranged in companies,
10:22 under its own *s* and arranged in companies,
10:25 under its own *s* and arranged in companies,
18:16 shekels according to the sanctuary *s*,
2Sm 14:26 hundred shekels according to the royal *s*.
Is 31: 9 princes shall flee in terror from his *s*,
62:10 of stones, raise up a *s* over the nations.
Jer 4: 6 Bear the *s* to Zion,
2Cor 5:16 Christ, we no longer know him by this *s*.
Heb 13: 9 to those who take them as a *s* for living.
Rv 19:11 *s* in passing judgment and in waging war.

STANDARDS (4)

Ps(s) 20: 6 and raise the *s* in the name of our God.
Sir 13:23 but poverty is evil by the *s* of the proud.
Mt 16:23 are not judging by God's *s* but by man's."
Mk 8:33 are not judging by God's *s* but by man's."

STANDING (146)

Gn 18: 2 Looking up, he saw three men *s* nearby.
18:22 Sodom, the LORD remained *s* before Abraham.
24:30 he was still *s* by the camels at the spring.
28:13 there was the LORD *s* beside him and saying:
41: 1 He saw himself *s* by the Nile,
41: 3 and *s* on the bank of the Nile beside the
41:17 my dream, I was *s* on the bank of the Nile,
Ex 17: 6 I will be *s* there in front of you on the
17: 9 I will be *s* on top of the hill with the
22: 5 *s* grain or the field itself is burned up,
Nm 12: 5 cloud, and *s* at the entrance of the tent,
16:27 had come out and were *s* at the entrances
17:13 *s* there between the living and the dead,
22:23 of the LORD *s* on the road with sword drawn,
22:31 of the LORD *s* on the road with sword drawn;
23: 6 who was still *s* by his holocaust together
23:17 who was still *s* by his holocaust together
27: 2 forward, and *s* in the presence of Moses,
Dt 16: 9 the sickle is first put to the *s* grain.
29: 9 "You are all now *s* before the LORD,
Jos 4: 3 where the priests have been *s* motionless.
5:15 for the place on which you are *s* is holy."
20: 4 and *s* at the entrance of the city gate,
Jgs 6:31 Joash replied to all who were *s* around him,
7:21 all remained *s* in place around the camp,
9: 7 to the top of Mount Gerizim, and *s* there,
15: 5 loose in the *s* grain of the Philistines,
15: 5 burning both the shocks and the *s* grain,
1Sm 4:14 Hearing the outcry of the men *s* near him,
4:20 when the women *s* around her said to her,
17:26 David now said to the men *s* by:
22: 6 spear, while all his servants were *s* by.
22: 9 who was *s* with the officers of Saul,
22:17 The king then commanded his henchmen *s* by:
2Sm 13:31 servants *s* by him also rent their garments.
24:16 The angel of the LORD was then *s* at the
1Kgs 13: 1 was *s* at the altar to offer sacrifice.
13:24 on the road, and the ass remained *s* by it,
13:25 in the road, with the lion *s* beside it,
13:28 road with the ass and the lion *s* beside it.
22:19 heaven *s* by to his right and to his left.
2Kgs 9:17 The watchman *s* on the tower in Jezreel saw
11:14 When she saw the king *s* by the pillar,
13: 6 The sacred pole also remained *s* in Samaria.
23: 3 *S* by the column,
23:16 was *s* by the altar on the feast day.
1Chr 21:15 The angel of the LORD was then *s* by the
21:16 of the LORD *s* between earth and heaven,
2Chr 7: 6 The priests were *s* at their stations,
9:18 the seat, with two lions *s* beside the arms.
18:18 heaven *s* by to his right and to his left.
20:13 All Judah was *s* before the LORD,
23:13 king *s* beside his pillar at the entrance,
26:11 Uzziah also had a *s* army of fit soldiers
34:31 *S* at his post, the king made a covenant
Ezr 10: 9 *s* in the open place before the house of
Neh 8: 3 *S* at one end of the open place that was
8: 5 he was *s* higher up than any of the people);
9: 4 *S* on the platform of the Levites were
Tb 5: 4 he found the angel Raphael *s* before him,
Jdt 5:22 the people *s* round about the tent murmured;
6:10 who were *s* by in his tent to seize Achior,
10: 6 of the city, Chabri and Charmis, *s* there.
Est B: 7 whose present ill will is of long *s*,
5: 2 He saw Queen Esther *s* in the courtyard,
8: 4 So she rose and, *s* in his presence, said:
10: 3 King Ahasuerus, in high *s* among the Jews,
2Mc 3:26 *S* on each side of him,
14:46 Then, *s* on a steep rock,
Wis 10: 7 of a disbelieving soul, a *s* pillar of salt.
Sir 38:28 So with the smith *s* near his anvil,
50:10 fruit, like a cypress *s* against the clouds;
Is 3:13 LORD rises to accuse, *s* to try his people.
17: 5 of stalks when he gathers the *s* grain;
Jer 35:19 of Jonadab, Rechab's son, *s* in my service.
Ez 40: 3 he was *s* in the gate,
46: 2 and remain *s* at the doorpost of the gate;
47:10 be *s* along it from En-gedi to Eneglaim,
Dn 8: 3 *s* by the river a ram with two great horns,
8: 6 two-horned ram I had seen *s* by the river,
8:17 When he came near where I was *s*,
11: 1 *s* as a reinforcement and a bulwark for me.
12: 5 others, one *s* on either bank of the river.
Am 7: 7 he was *s* by a wall, plummet in hand.
9: 1 I saw the Lord *s* beside the altar,
Zec 1: 8 *s* among myrtle trees in a shady place,
1:10 *s* among the myrtle trees spoke up and said,
1:11 who was *s* among the myrtle trees and said,
3: 1 high priest *s* before the angel of the LORD,

3: 3 Now Joshua was *s* before the angel,
3: 4 and said to those who were *s* before him,
3: 5 Then the angel of the LORD, *s*,
3: 7 I will give you access among these *s* here.
Mt 11:23 taken place in Sodom, it would be *s* today.
12: 1 a sabbath Jesus walked through the *s* grain.
12:47 *s* out there and they wish to speak to you."
16:28 among those *s* here there are some who will
20: 3 men *s* around the marketplace without work,
20: 6 afternoon he found still others *s* around.
20: 6 'Why have you been *s* here idle all day?'
24:15 prophet Daniel foretold *s* on holy ground
24:33 will know that he is near, *s* at your door.
Mk 2:23 was walking through *s* grain on the sabbath,
9: 1 among those *s* here there are some who will
9:14 disciples, they saw a large crowd *s* around,
13:14 presence *s* where it should not be
Lk 1:11 *s* at the right of the altar of incense.
6: 1 Jesus was walking through the *s* grain.
6: 8 The man rose and remained *s*.
8:20 are *s* outside and they wish to see you."
9:27 there are some *s* here who will not taste
9:32 saw the two men who were *s* with him.
13:11 quite incapable of *s* erect.
19:24 He said to those *s* around,
23:49 were *s* at a distance watching everything.
Jn 18:16 while Peter was left *s* at the gate.
18:18 servants and the guards who were *s* around
18:22 one of the guards who was *s* nearby gave
18:25 Peter had been *s* there warming himself.
20:14 around and caught sight of Jesus *s* there.
21: 4 after daybreak Jesus was *s* on the shore,
Acts 4:13 the speakers were uneducated men of no *s*,
4:14 man who had been cured *s* there with them,
5:25 put in jail are *s* over there in the temple,
7:55 of God, and Jesus *s* at God's right hand.
7:56 and the Son of Man *s* at God's right hand."
11:13 *s* in his house and that the angel had said:
22:25 than he said to the centurion who was *s* by,
1Cor 6: 4 judges those who have no *s* in the church?
10:12 he is *s* upright watch out lest he fall!
2Cor 1:24 As regards faith, you are *s* firm.
2:17 been sent by God and of *s* in his presence.
5:11 *S* in awe of the Lord we try to persuade men,
Phil 1:27 it will be clear that you are *s* firm in
Heb 9: 8 while the first tabernacle was still *s*,
2Pt 3: 5 out of the waters and *s* between the waters,
Rv 4: 2 A throne was *s* there in heaven,
5: 6 creatures and the elders, I saw a Lamb *s*,
7: 1 angels *s* at the four corners of the earth;
7:11 All the angels who were *s* around the
10: 5 Then the angel whom I saw *s* on the sea and
10: 8 of the angel *s* on the sea and on the land."
14: 1 He was *s* on Mount Zion,
15: 2 On the sea of glass were *s* those who had
19:17 Next I saw an angel *s* on the sun.
20:12 great and the lowly, *s* before the throne.

STANDS (63)

Lv 26:30 high places, overthrow your incense *s*,
Nm 5:18 Then, as the woman *s* before the LORD,
14:14 Your cloud *s* over them,
Jos 22:19 where the Dwelling of the LORD *s*,
22:29 LORD, our God, which *s* before his Dwelling."
2Sm 7:26 of your servant David *s* firm before you.
1Kgs 7:27 Ten *s* were also made of bronze,
7:28 When these *s* were constructed,
7:37 This was how the ten *s* were made,
7:38 one basin for the top of each of the ten *s*.
7:39 *s* were placed, five on the south side
7:43 columns, ten stands, ten basins on the *s*,
2Chr 4:14 made the stands, and the basins on the *s*;
14: 4 and incense *s* from all the cities of Judah,
34: 4 *s* erected above them were torn down;
34: 7 incense *s* throughout the land of Israel.
Est 7: 9 of Haman *s* a gibbet fifty cubits high.
1Mc 2:27 and who *s* by the covenant follow after me!
Ps(s) 21: 8 kindness of the Most High he *s* unshaken.
26:12 My foot *s* on level ground;
33:11 But the plan of the LORD *s* forever;
45: 7 Your throne, O God, *s* forever and ever;
89:29 him, and my covenant with him *s* firm.
93: 2 Your throne *s* firm from of old;
119:90 have established the earth, and it *s* firm.
119:161 cause but my heart *s* in awe of your word.
125: 1 which forever *s*.
Prv 12: 7 no more, but the house of the just *s* firm.
29:14 of the poor, his throne *s* firm forever.
Sg 2: 9 Here he *s* behind our wall,
5:10 he *s* out among thousands.
Sir 37: 4 joys, but in time of trouble he *s* afar off.
Is 17: 8 the sacred poles or the incense *s*.
32: 8 noble things, and by noble things he *s*.
40: 8 wilts, the word of our God *s* forever."
59:14 Right is repelled, and justice *s* far off;
65: 6 Lo, before me it *s* written;
66:17 groves, as followers of one who *s* within,
Jer 17: 6 no change of season, But *s* in a lava waste,
27:19 the pillars, the bronze sea, the *s*,
44:28 to settle in Egypt shall know whose word *s*,
Lam 5:19 your throne *s* from age to age.
Ez 6: 4 laid waste, your incense *s* shall be broken,
6: 6 and your incense *s* smashed to bits.
21:26 the two roads divide *s* the king of Babylon,
Hos 7: 1 heal Israel, The guilt of Ephraim *s* out,
Acts 4:10 name this man *s* before you perfectly sound.
10: 6 leather-tanner whose house *s* by the sea."
Rom 3:19 and the whole world *s* convicted before God,
14: 4 alone can judge whether he *s* or falls.
1Cor 3:14 has raised on this foundation still *s*,
7:37 man, however, who *s* firm in his resolve,
2Tm 1:18 When he *s* before the Lord on the great Day,
2:19 But the foundation God has laid *s* firm.
Ti 3:11 he *s* self-condemned.
Heb 1: 8 "Your throne, O God, *s* forever and ever;
10:11 other priest *s* ministering day by day,
Jas 5: 9 The judge *s* at the gate.
1Pt 1: 5 *s* ready to be revealed in the last days.
4: 5 *s* ready to judge the living and the dead.
Rv 13:18 it is a number that *s* for a certain man.

STANDSTILL (1)

Mt 2: 9 to a *s* over the place where the child was.

STAR (15)

Nm 24:17 A *s* shall advance from Jacob,
Dt 4:19 the moon or any *s* among the heavenly hosts,
Sir 50: 6 Like a *s* shining among the clouds,
Is 14:12 you fallen from the heavens, O morning *s*,
Am 5:26 Sakkuth, your king, and Kaiwan, your *s* god,
Mt 2: 2 We observed his *s* at its rising and have
2: 9 The *s* which they had observed at its
2:10 They were overjoyed at seeing the *s*,
Acts 7:43 tent of Moloch and the *s* of the god Rephan,
2Pt 1:19 and the morning *s* rises in your hearts.
Rv 2:28 and I will give him the morning *s*.
8:10 a huge *s* burning like a torch crashed down
9: 1 I saw a *s* fall from the sky to the earth.
9: 1 The *s* was given the key to the shaft of
22:16 of David, the Morning *S* shining bright."

STARBOARD (1)

Jn 21: 6 "Cast your net off to the *s* side,"

STARE (5)

Sg 1: 6 Do not *s* at me because I am swarthy,
Sir 26: 9 *s* an unchaste wife can be recognized.
Is 14:16 When they see you they will *s*,
Acts 3:12 Why do you *s* at us as if we had made this
Rv 11: 9 *s* at their corpses for three and a half

STARED (5)

2Kgs 8:11 *s* him down until Hazael became ill at ease.
Acts 6:15 Sanhedrin who sat there *s* at him intently.
10: 4 He *s* at the sight and said in fear,
11: 6 As I *s* at it I could make out four-legged
13: 9 he *s* at him and exclaimed:

STARGAZERS (1)

Is 47:13 the *s* who forecast at each new moon what

STARING (1)

Est C:11 strength, for death was *s* them in the face.

STARK (4)

Ez 16: 7 hair had grown, but you were still *s* naked.
16:22 girl, *s* naked and weltering in your blood.
16:39 splendid ornaments, leaving you *s* naked.
23:29 have worked for and leaving you *s* naked,

STARRY (1)

Wis 10:17 for them by day and a *s* flame by night.

STARS (64)

Gn 1:16 and he made the *s*.
15: 5 "Look up at the sky and count the *s*,
22:17 *s* of the sky and the sands of the seashore;
26: 4 *s* in the sky and give them all these lands,
37: 9 moon and eleven *s* were bowing down to me."
Ex 32:13 as numerous as the *s* in the sky;
Dt 1:10 are now as numerous as the *s* in the sky.
10:22 made you as numerous as the *s* of the sky.
28:62 you who were numerous as the *s* in the sky,
Jgs 5:20 From the heavens the *s*, too, fought;
1Chr 27:23 multiply Israel like the *s* of the heavens.
Neh 4:15 ready, from daybreak till the *s* came out.
9:23 as numerous as the *s* of the heavens,
2Mc 9:10 that he could reach the *s* of heaven,
Jb 3: 9 May the *s* of its twilight be darkened;
9: 7 he seals up the *s*.
22:12 the heights of the heavens, behold the *s*,
25: 5 and the *s* are not clear in his sight.
38: 7 While the morning *s* sang in chorus and all
Ps(s) 8: 4 the moon and the *s* which you set in place
136: 9 The moon and the *s* to rule over the night,
147: 4 He tells the number of the *s*;
148: 3 praise him, all you shining *s*.
Eccl 12: 2 and the light, and the moon, and the *s*,
Wis 7:19 Cycles of years, positions of the *s*,
7:29 and surpasses every constellation of the *s*.
13: 2 the swift air, or the circuit of the *s*,
17: 5 *s* succeed in lighting up that gloomy night.
Sir 43: 9 of the heavens are the *s* that adorn with
44:21 dust, and exalt his posterity like the *s*;
Is 13:10 The *s* and constellations of the heavens
14:13 Above the *s* of God I will set up my throne;
Jer 31:35 the day, moon and *s* to light the night;
Bar 3:34 the *s* at their posts shine and rejoice;
6:59 The sun and moon and *s* are bright,
Ez 32: 7 the heavens, and all their *s* I will darken;
Dn 3:36 their offspring like the *s* of heaven,
3:63 *S* of heaven, bless the Lord;
8:10 and some of the *s* and trampled on them.
12: 3 man to justice shall be like the *s* forever.
Jl 2:10 and the *s* withhold their brightness.
4:15 and the *s* withhold their brightness.
Ob 1: 4 eagle, and your nest be set among the *s*,
Na 3:16 your couriers more numerous than the *s*,
Mt 2: 7 them the exact time of the *s* appearance.
24:29 her light, the *s* will fall from the sky,
Mk 13:25 its light, *s* will fall out of the skies,
Lk 21:25 be signs in the sun, the moon, and the *s*.
Acts 27:20 neither the sun nor the *s* were to be seen,
1Cor 15:41 so has the moon, and the *s* have theirs.
15:41 Even among the *s*,
Phil 2:15 whom you shine like the *s* in the sky
Heb 11:12 descendants as numerous as the *s* in the
Jude 1:13 or shooting *s* for whom the thick gloom of
Rv 1:16 In his right hand he held seven *s*.
1:20 of the seven *s* you saw in my right hand,
1:20 the seven *s* are the presiding spirits of
2: 1 "The One who holds the seven *s* in his
3: 1 the seven spirits of God, the seven *s*,
6:13 The *s* in the sky fell crashing to earth
8:11 The *s* name was "Wormwood" because a
8:12 and a third of the *s* were hit hard enough
12: 1 feet, and on her head a crown of twelve *s*.
12: 4 His tail swept a third of the *s* from the

START (21)

Gn 8:21 of man's heart are evil from the *s*;
Nm 12:15 not *s* out again until she was brought back.
Jgs 19: 9 Early tomorrow you can *s* your journey home."
19:27 of the house to *s* out again on his journey,
Ru 3: 8 the man gave a *s* and turned around to find
1Sm 6: 8 *S* it on its way, and let it go.
9:26 "Get up, and I will *s* you on your journey."
29:10 But make an early morning *s*,
1Kgs 18:23 and place it on the wood, but *s* no fire.
18:23 place it on the wood, but shall *s* no fire.
18:25 Call upon your gods, but do not *s* the fire."
21:18 *S* down to meet Ahab,
Tb 9: 6 *s* and traveled to the wedding celebration.
Prv 17:14 *s* of strife is like the opening of a dam;
Sir 5:11 wind, and *s* not off in every direction.
Jn 6:64 (Jesus knew from the *s*,
Acts 17: 5 to form a mob and *s* a riot in the town.
Phil 4:15 that at the *s* of my evangelizing,
1Jn 2: 7 but an old one which you had from the *s*.
2Jn 1: 5 is a commandment we have had from the *s*):
Rv 10: 4 to *s* writing when the seven thunders spoke,

STARTED (27)

Gn 11: 6 the same language, they have *s* to do this,
24:61 Then Rebekah and her maids *s* out;
Ex 4:20 his sons, and *s* back to the land of Egypt,
22: 5 who *s* the fire must make full restitution.
Nm 14:40 next morning they *s* up into the foothills,
Jgs 19:28 her on an ass and *s* out again for home.
1Kgs 14:17 So Jeroboam's wife *s* back;
21:16 Ahab *s* off on his way down to the vineyard
2Kgs 4:30 So he *s* to go back with her.
Tb 8: 5 and they *s* to pray and beg that
Dn 10:12 Because of it I *s* out,
Mt 16:21 From then on Jesus [the Messiah] *s* to
Mk 10:52 his sight and *s* to follow him up the road.
14:69 eye on him, *s* again to tell the bystanders,
Lk 23: 2 They *s* his prosecution by saying,
Jn 4: 3 he left Judea and *s* back for Galilee again.
4:50 word Jesus spoke to him, and *s* for home.
6:41 *s* to murmur in protest because he claimed,
8: 2 and when the people *s* coming to him,
8: 6 *s* tracing on the ground with his finger.
11:29 she got up and *s* out in his direction.
20: 3 *s* out on their way toward the tomb.
Acts 12: 1 King Herod *s* to harass some of the members
13:50 a persecution *s* against Paul and Barnabas.
16:36 Get *s*, now.
19:34 he was a Jew, they *s* to chant in unison,
21:15 we got ready and *s* up toward Jerusalem.

STARTING (5)

Gn 44:12 *s* with the oldest and ending with the
Nm 33: 2 the *s* places of the various stages.
33: 2 The *s* places of the successive stages were:
Mt 20:17 As Jesus was *s* to go up to Jerusalem,
Acts 8:35 with this Scripture passage as his *s* point,

STARTLE (1)

Is 52:15 So shall he *s* many nations,

STARTLED (1)

Is 16: 2 Like flushed birds, like *s* nestlings,

STARTS (1)

Prv 20: 3 shun strife, while every fool *s* a quarrel.

STARVATION (1)

1Mc 13:49 from hunger, and many of them died of *s*.

STARVES (1)

Prv 13:19 Lust indulged *s* the soul,

STARVING (5)

Gn 25:30 I'm *s*" (That is why he was called Edom.)
42:19 take home provisions for your *s* families.
42:33 go home with rations for your *s* families.
43: 8 our children are to keep from *s* to death.
Lk 15:17 more than enough to eat, while here I am *s*!

STATE (39)

Gn 30:28 "*S* what wages you want from me
Lv 7:20 someone while in a *s* of uncleanness eats
14:57 a state of uncleanness and when a *s*
15:19 shall be in a *s* of impurity for seven days.
22: 3 dares, while he is in a *s* of uncleanness,
Jos 6: 1 Now Jericho was in a *s* of siege because of
24:17 the land of Egypt, out of a *s* of slavery.
Jgs 19:30 note of it, and *s* what you propose to do."
20: 7 O Israelites, *s* what you propose to do."
1Sm 10: 5 meet a band of prophets, in a prophetic *s*,
10: 6 *s* and will be changed into another man.
10:10 that he joined them in their prophetic *s*.
10:11 him in a prophetic *s* among the prophets,
10:13 When he came out of the prophetic *s*,
19:20 frenzy, they too fell into the prophetic *s*.
19:21 who also fell into the prophetic *s*.
19:21 but they too fell into the prophetic *s*.
19:24 the prophetic *s* in the presence of Samuel;
1Kgs 18:29 *s* until the time for offering sacrifice.
22:10 clothed in their robes of *s* on a threshing
2Chr 18: 9 clothed in their robes of *s* on a threshing
Est D: 2 In making her *s* appearance,
D: 6 royal throne, clothed in full robes of *s*,
1Mc 15: 3 it, that I may restore it to its former *s*.
2Mc 14:10 it is impossible for the *s* to enjoy peace."
14:26 that Nicanor was plotting against the *s*,
Jb 5: 8 to God, and to God I would *s* my plea.
8: 7 Your former *s* will be of little moment,
33: 3 I will *s* directly what is in my mind,
Jer 10:17 the land, O city living in a *s* of siege!
Ez 4: 3 it shall be in the *s* of siege,
16:55 shall return to their former *s* [you and
16:55 daughters shall return to your former *s*.
Mt 12:45 *s* of that man becomes worse than the first.
Lk 11:26 last *s* of the man is worse than the first."
Acts 26: 1 "You have permission to *s* your case."
1Cor 4:13 that is the present *s* of affairs.
8:10 his conscience in its weak *s* be influenced

STATED (9)

Gn 20: 5 'She is my sister,' and she herself also *s*,
21: 2 old age, at the set time that God had *s*.
2Kgs 1:16 and went down with him and *s* to the king:
24: 3 This befell Judah because the LORD had *s*
Neh 10:35 of our family houses at *s* times each year,
13:31 wood at *s* times and for the first fruits.
Jer 44:25 You and your wives have *s* your intentions,
Mt 26:61 Finally two came forward who *s*:
Acts 28:25 "The Holy Spirit *s* it well when he said

STATELY (7)

Prv 30:29 Three things are *s* in their stride,
30:29 stride, yes, four are *s* in their carriage:
Is 2:16 the ships of Tarshish and all *s* vessels.
53: 2 in him no *s* bearing to make us look at him,
Ez 19:11 *S* was her height amid the dense foliage;
31: 7 beautiful and *s* in its spread of foliage,
Zec 10: 3 of Judah, and make them his *s* war horse.

STATEMENT (3)

Jb 13:17 heed to my speech, and give my *s* a hearing.
Jn 1:20 was the direct *s*, "I am not the Messiah."
12:33 (This *s* indicated the sort of death he had

STATEMENTS (2)

Jb 32:12 Job, not one of you who could refute his *s*.
Acts 6:13 *s* against the holy place and the law."

STATES (2)

Prv 12:17 tells the truth who *s* what he is sure of,
1Cor 14:34 Rather, as the law *s*, submissiveness

STATING (4)

Tb 7:13 contract *s* that he gave Sarah to Tobiah
1Mc 12: 7 over you, *s* that you are our brothers,
12:21 A document has been found *s* that the
2Mc 14:27 *s* that he was displeased with the treaty,

STATION (6)

Ex 33:21 me where you shall *s* yourself on the rock.
2Chr 1:14 drivers he could *s* in the chariot cities
Is 21: 6 Go, *s* a watchman,
22:19 your office and pull you down from your *s*.
Dn 11:39 he shall *s* a people of a foreign god.
Hb 2: 1 guard post, and *s* myself upon the rampart,

STATIONED (33)

Gn 3:24 and he *s* the cherubim and the fiery
Ex 2: 4 His sister *s* herself at a distance to find
19:17 *s* themselves at the foot of the mountain.
Nm 22:22 and the angel of the LORD *s* himself on the
Jgs 16:24 Then they *s* him between the columns.
1Sm 17: 3 The Philistines were *s* on one hill and the
1Kgs 12:32 and he *s* in Bethel priests of the high
2Kgs 3:21 arms was called up and *s* at the border.
10:24 had *s* eighty men outside with this warning,
1Chr 9:24 The gatekeepers were *s* at the four sides,
2Chr 23:10 He *s* all the people,
23:19 he *s* guards at the gates of the LORD's
29:25 He *s* the Levites in the LORD's house with
29:26 were *s* with the instruments of David,
33:14 He *s* army officers in all the fortified
Ezr 3:10 were *s* there with the cymbals to praise
Neh 4: 7 about to attack us, I *s* guards down below,
Jdt 3: 6 and *s* garrisons in the fortified cities;
15: 3 Those also who were *s* in the mountain
1Mc 5:42 he *s* the officers of the people beside the
6:38 The remaining cavalry were *s* on one or the
6:50 Beth-zur and *s* a garrison there to hold it.
10:37 Let some of them be *s* in the king's
11: 3 cities, he *s* garrison troops in each one.
14:33 where he *s* a garrison of Jewish soldiers,
14:37 In this citadel he *s* Jewish soldiers,
15:41 Kedron and *s* horsemen and infantry there,
2Mc 15:20 and their cavalry *s* on the flanks.
15:31 countrymen, *s* the priests before the altar,
Is 6: 2 Seraphim were *s* above;
62: 6 your walls, O Jerusalem, I have *s* watchmen;
Ez 8: 4 *s* to the right of the temple
Rv 21:12 twelve gates at which twelve angels were *s*.

STATIONING (1)

Jdt 7: 7 he seized, *s* armed detachments around them,

STATIONS (4)

Jos 8:13 Thus the people took up their *s*,
2Chr 7: 6 The priests were standing at their *s*,
35:15 was no need for them to leave their *s*,
Neh 13:11 together and had them resume their *s*.

STATISTICS (1)

2Mc 2:24 In view of the flood of *s*,

STATUE (18)

Is 48: 5 might not say, "My idol did them, my *s*,
Ez 8: 3 the *s* of jealousy which stirs up jealousy.
8: 5 of the gate the altar of the *s* of jealousy.
Dn 2:31 "In your vision, O king, you saw a *s*,
2:32 The head of the *s* was pure gold,
2:34 While you looked at the *s*,
2:35 But the stone that struck the *s* became a
3: 1 King Nebuchadnezzar had a golden *s* made,
3: 2 dedication of the *s* which he had set up.
3: 3 the *s* which King Nebuchadnezzar had set up.
3: 5 *s* which King Nebuchadnezzar has set up.
3: 7 *s* which King Nebuchadnezzar had set up.
3:10 should fall down and worship the golden *s*;
3:12 or worship the golden *s* which you set up."
3:14 god, or worship the golden *s* that I set up?
3:15 to fall down and worship the *s* I had made,
3:18 or worship the golden *s* which you set up."
Acts 17:29 like a *s* of gold or silver or stone,

STATUES (3)

1Mc 5:68 altars and burned the *s* of their gods;
Bar 6:38 *s* are like stones from the mountains
Mi 1: 7 in the fire, and all her *s* I will destroy.

STATURE (12)

1Sm 2:26 young Samuel was growing in *s* and in worth
16: 7 from his appearance or from his lofty *s*,
2Sm 21:20 man of large *s* with six fingers on each hand
23:21 he, too, who slew an Egyptian of large *s*.
Sg 5:15 His *s* is like the trees on Lebanon,
Is 10:33 The tall of *s* are felled,
45:14 of Ethiopia, and the Sabeans, tall of *s*,
Ez 31: 3 Lebanon, beautiful of branch, lofty of *s*,
31:10 Because it became lofty in *s*,
31:14 in *s* or raise its crest among the clouds;
Lk 19: 3 what Jesus was like, but being small of *s*,
Eph 4:13 perfect man who is Christ come to full *s*.

STATUS (2)

Tb 1:13 granted me favor and *s* with Shalmaneser,
Gal 4: 5 we might receive our *s* as adopted sons.

STATUTE (9)

Lv 23:14 This shall be a perpetual *s* for you and
23:21 a perpetual *s* for you wherever you dwell.
23:31 This is a perpetual *s* for you and your
23:41 By perpetual *s* for you and your
24: 3 a perpetual *s* for you and your descendants,
Nm 10: 8 perpetual *s* for you and your descendants.
1Chr 16:17 Which he established for Jacob by *s*,
Ps(s) 81: 5 For it is a *s* in Israel,
105:10 Which he established for Jacob by *s*,

STATUTES (127)

Lv 18: 4 and my *s* you shall take care to follow.
18: 5 Keep, then, my *s* and decrees,
18:26 must keep my *s* and decrees forbidding all
19:19 "Keep my *s*:
19:37 then, to observe all my *s* and decrees.
20:22 to observe all my *s* and all my decrees;
26:43 spurned my precepts and abhorred my *s*.
Nm 30:17 These are the *s* which the LORD prescribed
Dt 4: 1 hear the *s* and decrees which I am teaching
4: 5 I teach you the *s* and decrees as the LORD,
4: 6 who will hear of all these *s* and say,
4: 8 Or what great nation has *s* and decrees
4:14 at that time to teach you the *s* and decrees
4:40 You must keep his *s* and commandments
4:45 *s* and decrees which he proclaimed to them
5: 1 the *s* and decrees which I proclaim in your
5:31 the *s* and decrees you must teach them,
6: 1 the *s* and decrees which the LORD,
6: 2 *s* and commandments which I enjoin on you,
6:17 ordinances and *s* he has enjoined on you.
6:20 *s* and decrees mean which the LORD,
6:24 to observe all these *s* in fear of the LORD,
7:11 the *s* and the decrees which I enjoin on
8:11 decrees and *s* which I enjoin on you today:
10:13 keep the commandments and *s* of the LORD
11: 1 his *s*, decrees and commandments.
11:32 *s* and decrees that I set before you today.
12: 1 "These are the *s* and decrees which you
16:12 in Egypt, and carry out these *s* carefully.
17:19 all the words of this law and these *s*.
26:16 you to observe these *s* and decrees.
26:17 are to walk in his ways and observe his *s*,
27:10 and *s* which I enjoin on you today."
28:45 keep the commandments and *s* he gave you.
30:10 and keep his commandments and *s* that are
30:16 keeping his commandments, *s* and decrees,
Jos 24:25 made *s* and ordinances for them at Shechem,
2Sm 22:23 present to me, and his *s* I put not from me;
1Kgs 2: 3 following his ways and observing his *s*,
3: 3 LORD, and obeyed the *s* of his father David;
3:14 me by keeping my *s* and commandments,
6:12 you observe my *s*, carry out my ordinances,
8:58 in everything and keep the commands, *s*,
8:61 his *s* and keeping his commandments,
9: 4 commanded you, keeping my *s* and decrees,
9: 6 commandments and *s* which I set before you,
11:11 covenant and my *s* which I enjoined on you,
11:33 to me according to my *s* and my decrees,
11:34 I chose, who kept my commandments and *s*.
11:38 and please me by keeping my *s* and my
2Kgs 17:13 evil ways and keep my commandments and *s*,
17:15 They rejected his *s*,
17:34 the LORD nor observe the *s* and regulations,
17:37 to observe forever the *s* and regulations,
23: 3 *s* and decrees with their whole hearts and
1Chr 29:19 keep your commandments, precepts, and *s*,
2Chr 7:17 you and keeping my *s* and ordinances,
7:19 *s* and commands which I placed before you,
19:10 or questions of law, command, *s*,
33: 8 the *s* and the ordinances given by Moses."
34:31 and *s* with his whole heart and soul,
Ezr 7:10 and on teaching *s* and ordinances in Israel.
7:11 the LORD's commandments and *s* for Israel:
Neh 1: 7 you, not keeping the commandments, the *s*,
9:13 them just ordinances, firm laws, good *s*,
9:14 you made known to them, commandments, *s*,
10:30 LORD, our LORD, his ordinances and his *s*.
Ps(s) 18:23 his *s* I put not from me
50:16 "Why do you recite my *s*,
89:32 they violate my *s* and keep not my commands,
105:45 they might keep his *s* and observe his laws.
119: 5 be firm in the ways of keeping your *s*!
119: 8 I will keep your *s*;
119:12 Blessed are you, O LORD; teach me your *s*.
119:16 In your *s* I will delight;
119:23 me, your servant meditates on your *s*.
119:26 teach me your *s*.
119:33 me, O LORD, in the way of your *s*,
119:48 to your commands and meditate on your *s*.
119:54 Your *s* are the theme of my song in the
119:64 teach me your *s*.
119:68 teach me your *s*.
119:71 been afflicted, that I may learn your *s*.
119:80 Let my heart be perfect in your *s*,
119:83 in the smoke, I have not forgotten your *s*.
119:112 in my heart to fulfill your *s* always,
119:117 I may be safe and ever delight in your *s*.
119:118 You despise all who stray from your *s*,
119:124 to your kindness, and teach me your *s*.
119:135 upon your servant, and teach me your *s*.

119:145 I will observe your *s.*
119:155 is salvation, because they seek not your *s.*
119:171 your praise, because you teach me your *s.*
147:19 Jacob, his *s* and his ordinances to Israel.
Is 10: 1 unjust *s* and who write oppressive decrees,
24: 5 who have transgressed laws, violated *s,*
Jer 44:10 *s* which I set before you and your fathers.
44:23 of the LORD, not living by his law, his *s,*
Bar 2:12 and violated, O Lord, our God, all your *s.*
4:13 of God, and did not acknowledge his *s;*
Ez 5: 6 and against my *s* more than the foreign
5: 6 my ordinances and has not lived by my *s.*
5: 7 by my *s* nor fulfilling my ordinances,
11:12 am the LORD, by whose *s* you have not lived,
11:20 so that they will live according to my *s,*
18: 9 *s* and is careful to observe my ordinances,
18:17 but keeps my ordinances and lives by my *s*—
18:19 and has been careful to observe all my *s,*
18:21 all my *s* and does what is right and just,
20:11 *s* and made known to them my ordinances,
20:13 They did not observe my *s,*
20:16 to their idols, they had not lived by *s,*
20:18 *s* of your parents or keep their ordinances;
20:19 my *s* and be careful to keep my ordinances;
20:21 they did not observe my *s* or keep my
20:24 despised my *s* and desecrated my sabbaths,
20:25 Therefore I gave them *s* that were not good,
33:15 goods, living by the *s* that bring life,
36:27 within you and make you live by my *s,*
37:24 by my *s* and carefully observe my decrees.
43:11 exits and entrances, all its *s* and laws;
43:11 may carefully observe all its laws and *s.*
43:18 These are the *s* for the altar when it is
44: 5 about the *s* and laws of the LORD's temple;
44:24 observe my laws and *s* on all my festivals,
Am 2: 4 law of the LORD, and did not keep his *s;*
Mal 3: 7 fathers you have turned aside from my *s,*
3:22 Horeb, The *s* and ordinances for all Israel.

STAUNCH (2)

Acts 21:20 all of them *s* defenders of the law.
22: 3 I was a *s* defender of God,

STAVES (1)

Sir 44: 4 of the folk, and governors with their *s;*

STAY (116)

Gn 6:20 come into the ark with you, to *s* alive.
19:30 Since Lot was afraid to *s* in Zoar,
21:23 in which you *s* as I have acted toward you."
22: 5 "Both of you *s* here with the donkey,
24:55 "Let the girl *s* with us a short while,
26: 3 *S* in this land,
27:44 and *s* with him a while until your
29:19 *S* with me."
38:11 *S* as a widow in your father's house until
39:10 to lie beside her, or even *s* near her.
42: 2 we may *s* alive rather than die of hunger."
42:16 while the rest of you *s* here under arrest.
46:34 that you may *s* in the region of Goshen,
47: 4 continued, "in order to *s* in this country,
Ex 9:28 you need *s* no longer."
16:29 is to *s* home and no one is to go out."
22:29 days the firstling may *s* with its mother,
28:28 so that the breastpiece will *s* right above
Nm 22: 8 he said to them in reply, *S* here overnight,
22:19 But, you too shall *s* here overnight,
31:19 shall *s* outside the camp for seven days,
32:15 make them *s* still longer in the desert,
35:25 and he shall *s* there until the death of
35:28 the homicide was bound to *s* in his city of
Dt 1:46 you had to *s* as long as you did at Kadesh.
Jos 4: 3 and place them where you are to *s* tonight."
Jgs 5:16 Why do you *s* beside your hearths listening
8:29 son of Joash, went back home to *s.*
13:15 of the LORD, "Can we persuade you to *s,*
17:10 *S* with me," Micah said to him.
17:11 the young Levite decided to *s* with the man,
19: 9 *S* for the night.
19:10 man, however, refused to *s* another night;
Ru 2: 8 *S* here with my women servants.
2:21 "that I should *s* with his servants until
3:13 *S* as you are for tonight,
1Sm 9:27 of us, but *s* here yourself for the moment,
14: 9 to us, *S* there until we can come to you,'
19:18 Then he and Samuel went to *s* in the sheds.
22: 3 "Let my father and mother *s* with you,
22:23 *S* with me.
25:15 them during our *s* in the open country.
2Sm 10: 5 *S* in Jericho until your beards grow,"
11:12 David said to Uriah, *S* here today also,
15:19 Go back and *s* with the king,
16:18 Israel have chosen, and with him I will *s.*
19:33 the king during his *s* in Mahanaim.
24:16 *S* your hand."
1Kgs 17: 9 on to Zarephath of Sidon and *s* there.
2Kgs 2: 2 *S* here, please," Elijah said to Elisha.
2: 4 Then Elijah said to him, *S* here,
2: 6 Elijah said to Elisha, "Please *s* here;
4:10 so that when he comes to us he can *s* there."
11: 8 *s* with the king,
14:10 Enjoy your glory, but *s* at home!
1Chr 21:15 *S* your hand!"
2Chr 23: 7 *S* with the king wherever he goes."
Tb 5: 6 I used to *s* with our kinsman Gabael,
6:11 "Tonight we must *s* with Raguel,
10: 8 *S,* my child, stay with me.
14:10 do not even *s* overnight within the
Jdt 7:12 *S* in your camp,
1Mc 11:40 During his *s* there of many days,
12:45 Pick out a few men to *s* with you,
Jb 30:13 me, they attack with none to *s* them;
Ps(s) 26: 4 I *s* not with worthless men,
26: 5 and with the wicked I will not *s.*
Sir 6:34 whoever is wise, *s* close to him.
38:32 could be lived in, and wherever they *s,*
Is 21: 8 And I *s* at my post through all the watches
29: 9 blind yourselves and *s* blind!
Jer 17: 8 the heat when it comes, its leaves *s* green;
40: 5 *s* with him among the people,
40: 9 to *s* in the land and submit to the king of
42:15 go to Egypt, when you arrive there to *s,*
42:17 men who determine to go to Egypt to *s,*
43: 4 LORD's command to *s* in the land of Judah.
Dn 2:43 intermarriage, but they shall not *s* united,
4:32 is no one who can *s* his hand or say to him,
Mt 2:13 *S* there until I tell you otherwise.
10:11 you come to and *s* with him until you leave.
24:42 *S* awake, therefore!
26:36 *S* here while I go over there and pray."
26:38 Remain here and *s* awake with me."
26:40 could not *s* awake with me for even an hour?
Mk 6:10 in, *s* there until you leave the locality.
13:33 *S* awake!
14:34 Remain here and *s* awake."
14:37 You could not *s* awake for even an hour?
Lk 9: 4 *S* at whatever house you enter and proceed
10: 7 *S* in the one house eating and drinking
19: 5 I mean to *s* at your house today."
24:29 *S* with us.
24:29 So he went in to *s* with them.
Jn 1:38 (which means Teacher), where do you *s*?"
4:40 him, they begged him to *s* with them awhile.
15: 7 you live in me, and my words *s* part of you,
21:22 "Suppose I want him to *s* until I come,"
21:23 *s* until I come [how does that concern you]?"
Acts 10:48 asked him to *s* with them for a few days.
16:15 in the Lord, come and *s* at my house."
18:20 asked him to *s* on longer but he declined.
21:10 During our few days' *s,*
21:15 At the conclusion of our *s,*
21:16 an early disciple, with whom we were to *s.*
27:31 "If these men do not *s* with the ship,
28:14 who urged us to *s* on with them for a week.
1Cor 16: 8 I intend to *s* in Ephesus until Pentecost.
2Cor 10:13 we will not go over the mark but will *s*
Phil 1:25 me with confidence that I will *s* with you,
1Tm 1: 3 *s* on in Ephesus in order to warn certain
6:20 *S* clear of worldly, idle talk
2Tm 3: 5 *S* clear of them.
4: 2 to *s* with this task whether convenient or
1Pt 5: 8 *S* sober and alert.

STAYED (68)

Gn 13: 6 could not support them if they *s* together;
13:12 Abram *s* in the land of Canaan,
15:11 on the carcasses, but Abram *s* with them.
20: 1 While he *s* in Gerar, he said of his wife
32:22 of him, while he *s* that night in the camp.
35:27 is, Hebron], where Abraham and Isaac had *s.*
37: 1 in the land where his father had *s,*
Ex 2:15 fled from him and *s* in the land of Midian.
12:40 The time the Israelites had *s* in Egypt was
24:18 there he *s* for forty days and forty nights.
34:28 So Moses *s* there with the LORD for forty
39:21 so that the breastpiece *s* right above the
Nm 9:18 As long as the cloud *s* over the Dwelling,
9:20 bidding of the LORD that they *s* in camp,
20:15 went down to Egypt, where we *s* a long time,
Dt 1: 6 'You have *s* long enough at this mountain.
9: 9 Meanwhile I *s* on the mountain forty days
Jos 2:22 they *s* three days until their pursuers,
10:13 And the sun stood still, and the moon *s,*
Jgs 19: 2 of Judah, where she *s* for some four months.
19: 6 *s* and the two men ate and drank together.
Ru 1:14 mother-in-law good-bye, but Ruth *s* with her.
2:23 So she *s* gleaning with the servants of
1Sm 22: 4 and they *s* with him as long as David
24: 1 there and *s* in the refuges behind Engedi.
2Sm 13:38 of Geshur, and *s* in Geshur for three years.
1Kgs 2:38 So Shimei *s* in Jerusalem for a long time.
15:21 left off fortifying Ramah, and *s* in Tirzah.
2Kgs 2:22 And the water has *s* pure even to this day,
4:11 arrived and *s* in the room overnight.
4:20 he *s* with her until noon,
1Chr 9:33 They *s* in the chambers when free of duty,
21:22 that the plague may be *s* from the people."
Tb 9: 5 in Media, where they *s* at Gabael's house.
Jdt 3:10 and *s* there a whole month to refurbish all
5:10 *s* there as long as they found sustenance,
12: 7 Thus she *s* in the camp three days.
Est 7: 7 Haman *s* to beg Queen Esther for his life,
1Mc 11:70 *s* except the army commanders Mattathias,
2Mc 14:23 Nicanor *s* on in Jerusalem,
Eccl 2: 9 my wisdom, too, *s* with me.
Jer 38:28 Thus Jeremiah *s* in the quarters of the
40: 6 and *s* with him among the people left in
Ez 20:22 I *s* my hand, acting for my name's sake,
Mt 2:15 He *s* there until the death of Herod,
Mk 1:13 He *s* in the wasteland forty days,
1:45 He *s* in desert places;
5:21 around him and he *s* close to the lake.
Jn 1:39 he was lodged, and *s* with him that day.
2:12 but they *s* there only a few days.
4:40 So he *s* there two days,
7: 9 Having said this, he *s* on in Galilee.
10:40 while he *s* there many people came to him.
11: 6 he *s* on where he was for two days more.
11:54 the desert, where he *s* with his disciples.
18:15 *s* with Jesus as far as the high priests'
Acts 9:28 Saul *s* on with them,
9:43 Thus it happened that Peter *s* on in Joppa
17:14 the sea, while Silas and Timothy *s* behind.
18:18 Paul *s* on in Corinth for quite a while;
19:22 while he himself *s* on for a time in Asia.
20: 3 in Greece, where he *s* for three months.
21: 4 disciples there and *s* with them for a week.
21: 8 one of the Seven, with whom we *s.*
28:30 years Paul *s* on in his rented lodgings,
Gal 1:18 to know Cephas, with whom I *s* fifteen days.
2Tm 4:20 Erastus has *s* in Corinth,
1Jn 2:19 belonged to us, they would have *s* with us.

STAYING (15)

Gn 17: 8 after you the land in which you are now *s,*
24:31 Why are you *s* outside when I have made the
28: 4 possession of the land where you are *s,*
32: 5 I have been *s* with Laban and have been
36: 7 land in which they were *s* could not support
Ex 24:14 Aaron and Hur are *s* with you.
2Sm 16: 3 answered the king, "He is *s* in Jerusalem,
17:17 Jonathan and Ahimaaz were *s* at En-rogel,
1Kgs 17:19 him to the upper room where he was *s,*
17:20 widow with whom I am *s* by killing her son?"
2Kgs 2:18 to Elisha in Jericho, where he was *s,*
Acts 1:13 to the upstairs room where they were *s:*
2: 5 *S* in Jerusalem at the time were devout
2:14 are Jews, indeed all of you *s* in Jerusalem!
11:11 Caesarea came to the house where we were *s.*

STAYS (8)

2Kgs 6:31 of Elisha, son of Shaphat, *s* on him today!"
Eccl 1: 4 and another comes, but the world forever *s.*
Is 46: 7 when they set it in place again, it *s*
Jer 49:33 Where no man lives, no human being *s.*
Mk 2:19 So long as the groom *s* with them,
1Cor 7:40 though, in my opinion, if she *s* unmarried.
2Pt 3: 4 but everything *s* just as it was when the
Rv 16:15 Happy the man who *s* wide awake and fully

STEAD (19)

Dt 20: 6 and another enjoy its fruits in his *s.*
Jos 5: 7 up in their *s* whom Joshua circumcised,
Jgs 6:31 him, "Do you intend to act in Baal's *s,*
Ru 4: 6 Put in a claim yourself in my *s,*
2Sm 16: 8 family of Saul, in whose *s* you became king,
1Kgs 15:28 Asa, king of Judah, and reigned in his *s.*
2Kgs 8:15 And Hazael reigned in his *s.*
19:37 His son Esarhaddon reigned in his *s.*
21:24 proclaimed his son Josiah king in his *s.*
2Chr 22: 1 Ahaziah, his youngest son, king in his *s,*
33:25 land, made his son Josiah king in his *s.*
36: 1 him king in Jerusalem in his father's *s.*
Jb 34:24 the mighty, and sets others in their *s,*
Prv 11: 8 and the wicked man falls into it in his *s.*
Sir 10:14 and establishes the lowly in their *s.*
Is 37:38 His son Esarhaddon reigned in his *s.*
Bar 3:19 world, and others have risen up in their *s.*
Ez 44: 8 to serve me in my sanctuary in your *s.*
Dn 11:20 In his *s* one shall arise who will send a

STEADFAST (31)

Dt 31: 6 Be brave and *s;* have no fear or dread
31: 7 all Israel said to him, "Be brave and *s,*
31:23 of Nun, and said to him, "Be brave and *s,*
Jos 1: 6 Be firm and *s,* so that you may give
1: 7 Above all, be firm and *s,*
1: 9 be firm and *s!*
1:18 But be firm and *s.*"
10:25 not be afraid or dismayed, be firm and *s.*
1Chr 19:13 Hold *s* and let us show ourselves
22:13 Be brave and *s;* do not fear or lose heart.
28:20 "Be firm and *s;* go to work without fear
2Chr 32: 7 "Be brave and *s;* do not be afraid
Tb 4: 6 For if you are *s* in your service,
Est B: 3 for constant devotion and *s* loyalty,
Ps(s) 17: 5 My steps have been *s* in your paths,
51:12 me, O God, and a *s* spirit renew within me.
57: 8 My heart is *s,* O God;
57: 8 my heart is *s;* I will sing and chant praise.
78: 8 heart *s* nor its spirit faithful toward God.
78:37 Though their hearts were not *s* toward him,
108: 2 My heart is *s,* O God; my heart is steadfast;
108: 2 my heart is *s;*

STEADFAST (cont.)
112: 8 His heart is s; he shall not fear
117: 2 For s is his kindness toward us,
119:86 All your commands are s;
Sir 2: 2 Be sincere of heart and s,
5:12 s be your words.
1Cor 15:58 Be s and persevering,
Col 1:23 to faith, be firmly grounded and s in it,
Ti 2: 2 likewise sound in the faith, loving, and s.
1Pt 5:12 Be s in it.

STEADFASTLY (1)
Acts 8:21 Your heart is not s set on God.

STEADFASTNESS (2)
1Tm 6:11 after integrity, piety, faith, love, s,
Jas 5:11 You have heard of the s of Job,

STEADIED (1)
2Sm 6: 6 out his hand to the ark of God and s it,

STEADILY (8)
2Sm 5:10 David grew s more powerful,
2Chr 17:12 Jehoshaphat grew s greater.
Jdt 5:18 for them, they were ground down s,
1Mc 6:40 they marched forward s and in good order.
Wis 19:18 melody, while the flow of music s persists.
Na 3:19 For who has not been overwhelmed, s,
Lk 2:52 progressed s in wisdom and age and grace
Acts 9:22 Saul for his part grew s more powerful,

STEADY (12)
Ex 17:12 so that his hands remained s till sunset.
1Chr 13: 9 Uzzah stretched out his hand to s the ark,
Wis 14: 3 sea a road, and through the waves a s path,
17:18 branches, Or the s sound of rushing water,
Sir 26:18 bases are her shapely limbs and s feet.
43:19 eyes, the mind is baffled by its s fall.
Is 33:16 fastness, his food and drink in s supply.
41: 7 good, and he fastens it with nails to s it.
Acts 9:31 making s progress in the fear of the Lord;
2Tm 4: 5 As for you, be s and self-possessed;
Ti 1: 8 s, just, holy, and self-controlled.
Jas 5: 8 S your hearts,

STEADYING (1)
Sir 36:24 richest treasure, a helpmate, a s column.

STEAL (24)
Gn 31:30 your father's house, why did you s my gods?"
44: 4 Why did you s the silver goblet from me?
44: 8 s silver or gold from your master's house?
Ex 20:15 "You shall not s.
Lv 19:11 "You shall not s.
Dt 5:19 'You shall not s.
2Sm 19:42 "Why did our brothers the Judahites s you
Jb 24: 2 they s away herds and pasture them.
Ps(s) 69: 5 Must I restore what I did not s?
Prv 30: 9 " Or, being in want, I s,
Jer 7: 9 Are you to s and murder,
23:30 the LORD, who s my words from each other.
Ob 1: 5 they not s merely till they had enough?
Mt 6:19 thieves break in and s.
6:20 rust corrode nor thieves break in and s.
13:19 him to s away what was sown in his mind.
19:18 'You shall not s';
27:64 may go and s him and tell the people,
Mk 10:19 You shall not s;
Lk 18:20 You shall not s.
Jn 10:10 comes only to s and slaughter and destroy,
Rom 2:21 You who preach against stealing, do you s?
13: 9 you shall not s; you shall not covet,"
Eph 4:28 man who has been stealing must s no longer;

STEALING (7)
Gn 31:27 Why did you dupe me by s away secretly?
2Sm 15: 6 s away the loyalties of the men of Israel.
Hos 4: 2 swearing, lying, murder, s and adultery!
Mt 15:19 murder, adulterous conduct, fornication, s,
Rom 2:21 You who preach against s, do you steal?
Eph 4:28 man who has been s must steal no longer;
Ti 2:10 not contradicting them nor s from them,

STEALS (3)
Ex 21:37 "When a man s an ox or a sheep and
Prv 4:16 made no one stumble s away their sleep.
6:30 Men despise not the thief if he s to

STEALTH (4)
Tb 1:18 to take their bodies by s and bury them;
Dn 8:25 be proud of heart and destroy many by s.
11:21 By s and fraud he shall seize the kingdom.
11:24 By s he shall enter prosperous provinces

STEALTHILY (4)
Jos 7:11 They have s taken goods subject to the ban,
Jgs 4:21 she s approached him and drove the peg
1Sm 24: 5 up and s cut off an end of Saul's mantle.
Jb 4:12 For a word was s brought to me,

STEALTHY (1)
Wis 1:11 For a s utterance does not go unpunished,

STEAM (1)
Jb 41:12 From his nostrils issues s,

STEED (4)
1Kgs 20:20 king of Aram, escaped on a chariot s.
Jb 39:20 Do you make the s to quiver while his
Ps(s) 147:10 In the strength of the s he delights not,
Jer 8: 6 his course, like a s dashing into battle.

STEEDS (18)
Jgs 5:22 with the dashing, dashing of his s.
Est 8:10 couriers riding thoroughbred royal s.
8:14 s sped forth in haste at the king's order,
Ps(s) 76: 7 O God of Jacob, chariots and s lay stilled.
Sg 1: 9 s of Pharaoh's chariots would I liken you,
Sir 43: 5 made it, at whose orders it urges on its s.
Is 30:16 "Upon swift s we will ride."
Jer 4:13 Swifter than eagles are his s:
6:23 the roaring sea as they ride forth on s,
8:16 From Dan is heard the snorting of his s;
47: 3 They hear the stamping hooves of his s,
50:42 the roaring sea, as they ride forth on s,
Ez 26:10 cover you with dust, amid the noise of s,
27:14 From Beth-togarmah horses, s,
Jl 2: 4 like s they run.
Mi 1:13 Harness s to the chariots,
Hb 3: 8 you drive the s of your victorious chariot?
3:15 s amid the churning of the deep waters.

STEEL (1)
Na 2: 4 Fiery s are the chariots on the day of his

STEEP (3)
2Mc 14:46 Then, standing on a s rock,
Sir 39:24 are level, to the haughty they are s;
Is 7:19 in the s ravines and in the rocky clefts,

STEEPE (1)
Is 42:11 Let the s and its cities cry out,

STEEPED (1)
Jn 9:34 "You are s in sin from your birth,

STEEPLY (1)
2Mc 13: 5 down s on all sides toward the ashes.

STEER (2)
Gn 18: 7 the herd, picked out a tender, choice s,
18: 8 as well as the s that had been prepared,

STEERMANS (1)
Jas 3: 4 whatever course the s impulse may select.

STEERS (1)
Tb 8:19 went out to the herd and picked out two s

STELE (4)
2Kgs 10:26 the temple of Baal, took out the s of Baal,
10:27 Then they smashed the s of Baal,
12:10 hole in its lid, and set it beside the s,
1Chr 18: 3 up his victory s at the river Euphrates.

STEM (6)
Gn 17: 6 kings shall s from you.
35:11 an assembly of nations, shall s from you,
49:11 vine, his purebred ass to the choicest s.
Sir 10:16 down their s to the level of the ground,
Is 40:24 scarcely is their s rooted in the earth,
Mt 15:19 From the mind s evil designs

STEMS (1)
2Cor 7:11 the fruit of this sorrow which s from God.

STENCH (9)
Ex 8:10 gathered up and there was a s in the land.
2Mc 9: 9 was sickened by the s of his corruption.
9:10 the man because of this intolerable s.
9:12 When he could no longer bear his own s,
Is 3:24 Instead of perfume there will be s,
34: 3 cast out, their corpses shall send up a s;
Jl 2:20 shall go up, and his s shall go up.
Am 4:10 nostrils I brought the s of your camps;
Jn 11:39 surely there will be a s!"

STEP (20)
1Sm 5: 5 they always s over it.
20: 3 there is but a s between me and death."
2Sm 18:30 S aside and remain in attendance here."
1Kgs 10:20 other lions stood on the steps, two to a s,
10:20 to a step, one on either side of each s.
14:12 As you s inside the city,
2Chr 9:19 stood there, one on either side of each s.
Jb 18:11 they harry him at each s.
Prv 4:12 When you walk, your s will not be impeded,
Eccl 4:17 your s when you go to the house of God.
Wis 6:17 For the first s toward discipline is a
Sir 23:19 s a man takes and peer into hidden corners.
45: 9 s He would be heard within the sanctuary,
Is 3:16 go, their anklets tinkling with every s,
Jer 6:25 into the field, s not into the street,
10:23 choice, nor is it for him to direct his s.
Ez 13: 5 You did not s into the breach,
26:16 of the sea shall s down from their thrones,
Acts 11: 4 to them s by step from the beginning:
11: 4 to them step by s from the beginning:

STEPHANAS (3)
1Cor 1:16 Oh, and I baptized the household of S.
16:15 You know that the household of S is the
16:17 I was very happy at the arrival of S,

STEPHEN (9)
Acts 6: 5 Following this they selected S,
6: 8 The S already spoken of was a man filled
6: 9 would undertake to engage S in debate,
7: 2 To this S replied: "My brothers!
7:55 S meanwhile, filled with the Holy Spirit,
7:59 As S was being stoned he could be heard
8: 2 Devout men buried S, bewailing him loudly
11:19 because of S went as far as Phoenicia,
22:20 the blood of your witness S was being shed,

STEPHEN'S (1)
Acts 6:15 S face seemed like that of an angel.

STEPMOTHER (1)
Lv 20:11 the man and his s shall be put to death;

STEPPE (5)
Jb 24: 5 s provides food for the young among them;
Is 33: 9 Sharon is like the s,
35: 1 the s will rejoice and bloom.
35: 6 forth in the desert, and rivers in the s.
42:11 Let the s and its cities cry out,

STEPPED (13)
Gn 44:18 Judah then s up to him and said:
Jgs 8:21 s forward and killed Zebah and Zalmunna.
14: 8 he s aside to look at the remains of the
1Sm 24: 9 David also s out of the cave,
2Sm 18:30 So he s aside and remained there.
19: 9 So the king s out and sat at the gate.
2Kgs 18:28 Then the commander s forward and cried out
Is 36:13 Then the commander s forward and cried out
Mt 25:22 received the two thousand then s forward.
25:24 who had received the thousand s forward.
26:50 they s forward to lay hands on Jesus,
Lk 7:14 Then he s forward and touched the litter;
Jn 18: 4 happen to him, s forward and said to them,

STEPPING (2)
Sir 9:13 are s among snares and walking over a net.
Mt 3: 7 and Sadducees were s forward for this bath,

STEPS (57)
Ex 20:26 You shall not go up by s to my altar,
Jos 18: 3 s to possess the land which the LORD,
1Sm 25:12 So David's young men retraced their s and
2Sm 6:13 of the ark of the LORD had advanced six s,
22:37 You made room for my s;
1Kgs 10:19 throne had six s, a back with a round top,
10:20 and twelve other lions stood on the s,
2Kgs 9:13 spread it under Jehu on the bare s,
20: 9 Shall the shadow go forward or back ten s?"
20:10 is easy for the shadow to advance ten s,"
20:10 "Rather, let it go back ten s."
20:11 who made the shadow retreat the ten s
2Chr 9:18 The throne had six s;
Neh 3:15 s that lead down from the City of David.
12:37 went straight up by the s of the City of David
Jb 14:16 Surely then you would count my s,
18: 7 His vigorous s are hemmed in,
23:11 My foot has always walked in his s;
31: 4 he not see my ways, and number all my s?
31: 7 If my s have turned out of the way,
31:37 Of all my s I should give him an account;
34:21 the ways of man, and he beholds all his s.
Ps(s) 17: 5 My s have been steadfast in your paths,
17:11 Their s even now surround me;
18:37 You made room for my s;
37:23 By the LORD are the s of a man made firm,
37:31 is in his heart, and his s do not falter.
40: 3 he made firm my s.
44:19 nor our s turned aside from your path,
56: 7 gather together in hiding, they watch my s.
74: 3 Turn your s toward the utter ruins;
85:14 him, and salvation, along the way of his s.
Prv 5: 5 to death, to the nether world her s attain;
14: 7 To avoid the foolish man, take s!

14:15 but the shrewd man measures his *s*.
16: 9 his course, but the LORD directs his *s*.
20:24 Man's *s* are from the LORD;
29: 6 The wicked man *s* into a snare,
Sir 21:22 The fool *s* boldly into a house,
Is 38: 8 of Ahaz go back the ten *s* it has advanced."
38: 8 sun came back the ten *s* it had advanced.
Lam 4:18 *s* so that we could not walk in our streets;
Ez 40: 6 gate which faced the east, climbed its *s*,
40:22 Seven *s* led up to it,
40:26 It was ascended by seven *s*;
40:31 and it had a stairway of eight *s*.
40:34 there, and it had a stairway of eight *s*.
40:37 there, and it had a stairway of eight *s*.
40:49 ten *s* led up to it,
43:17 The *s* of the altar face the east.
Hb 3: 5 and the plague follows in his *s*.
Mk 8:34 take up his cross, and follow in my *s*.
16:13 These men retraced their *s* and announced
Lk 9:23 up his cross each day, and follow in my *s*.
Acts 14:21 their *s* to Lystra and Iconium first,
21:35 When Paul reached the *s*,
21:40 the *s* and motioned the people to silence.

STERILE (6)

Gn 25:21 on behalf of his wife, since she was *s*.
Jb 15:34 For the breed of the impious shall be *s*,
Sir 42:10 home, or be *s* in that of her husband.
Lk 1: 7 They were childless, for Elizabeth was *s*;
1:36 thought to be *s* is now in her sixth month,
23:29 when they will say, 'Happy are the *s*,

STERN (12)

Dt 28:50 do not understand, a nation of *s* visage,
Prv 3:34 he is dealing with the arrogant, he is *s*,
Sg 8: 6 For *s* as death is love,
Wis 6: 5 you, because judgment is *s* for the exalted
10:12 she gave him the prize for his *s* struggle
11:10 as a *s* king you probed and condemned.
Mk 1:43 him a *s* warning and sent him on his way.
4:38 Jesus was in the *s* through it all,
Acts 4:17 we must give them a *s* warning never
27:29 anchors from the *s* and prayed for daylight.
27:41 *s* was shattered by the pounding of the sea.
1Pt 5: 5 because God "is *s* with the arrogant but

STERNER (1)

Sir 28:10 greater a man's strength, the *s* his anger,

STERNLY (7)

Gn 42: 7 own identity from them and spoke *s* to them.
42:30 "spoke to us *s* and put us in custody as
Jb 15:26 One shall rush *s* upon him with the stout
Mt 9:30 Then Jesus warned them *s*,
12:16 though he *s* ordered them not to make
Mk 3:12 ordering them *s* not to reveal who he was.
Lk 18:39 in the lead *s* ordered him to be quiet,

STEW (6)

Gn 25:29 Once, when Jacob was cooking a *s*,
25:34 then gave him some bread and the lentil *s*;
2Kgs 4:38 some vegetable *s* for the guild prophets."
4:39 vegetable *s* without anybody's knowing it.
4:40 The *s* was poured out for the men to eat,
Dn 14:33 bread in a bowl with the *s* he had boiled,

STEWARD (21)

Gn 15: 2 and have as my heir the *s* of my house,
37:36 a courtier of Pharaoh and his chief *s*.
39: 1 courtier of Pharaoh and his chief *s*)
40: 3 in custody in the house of the chief *s*
40: 4 The chief *s* assigned Joseph to them,
41:10 in custody in the house of the chief *s*.
41:12 a Hebrew youth, a slave of the chief *s*;
43:16 Benjamin with them, he told his head *s*,
43:17 the *s* conducted the men to Joseph's house.
43:19 So they went up to Joseph's head *s* and
43:24 The *s* then brought the men inside Joseph's
44: 1 Joseph gave his head *s* these instructions:
44: 2 The *s* carried out Joseph's instructions.
44: 4 the city when Joseph said to his head *s*:
44: 6 When the *s* overtook them and repeated
Sir 15:10 its rightful *s* will proclaim it.
Dn 1:11 Then Daniel said to the *s* whom the chief
1:16 So the *s* continued to take away the food
Lk 8: 3 out, Joanna, the wife of Herod's *s* Chuza,
12:42 farsighted *s* whom the master will set over
Ti 1: 7 The bishop as God's *s* must be blameless.

STEWARDS (1)

Est 1: 8 he had instructed all the *s* of his household

STICK (13)

Nm 22:27 in anger, he again beat the ass with his *s*.
2Kgs 6: 6 out to the spot, Elisha cut off a *s*,
Prv 26: 9 Like a thorn *s* brandished by the hand of a
Ez 3:26 I will make your tongue *s* to your palate
29: 4 the fish of your Niles *s* to your scales,
37:16 Now, son of man, take a single *s*,
37:16 Then take another *s* and write on it:
37:16 Joseph [the *s* of Ephraim] and all the
37:17 so that they form one *s* in your hand.
37:19 [I will take the *s* of Joseph,
37:19 the stick of Judah, making them a single *s*;
37:19 him, and I will join to it the *s* of Judah,
Mk 6: 8 nothing on their journey but a walking *s*—

STICKING (2)

Ez 29: 4 the fish of your Niles *s* to your scales.
Mt 27:48 it in cheap wine, and *s* it on a reed,

STICKS (4)

1Kgs 17:10 of the city, a widow was gathering *s* there;
17:12 Just now I was collecting a couple of *s*,
Ez 37:17 Then join the two *s* together,
37:20 The *s* on which you write you shall hold up

STIFF (2)

Gn 49:24 But each one's bow remained *s*,
Neh 9:16 *s* and would not obey your commandments.

STIFF-NECKED (12)

Ex 33: 3 your company, because you are a *s* people;
33: 5 You are a *s* people.
34: 9 This is indeed a *s* people;
Dt 9: 6 land to possess, for you are a *s* people.
9:13 idol, I have seen now how *s* this people is,'
10:16 your hearts, therefore, and be no longer *s*.
31:27 know how rebellious and *s* you will be.
2Kgs 17:14 not listen, but were as *s* as their fathers,
Prv 29: 1 The man who remains *s* and hates rebuke
Bar 2:30 not heed me, because they are a *s* people.
2:33 shall turn back from their *s* stubbornness,
Acts 7:51 "You *s* people, uncircumcised in heart

STIFFENED (5)

Neh 9:17 They *s* their necks and turned their heads
9:29 They turned stubborn backs, *s* their necks,
Jer 7:26 they have *s* their necks and done worse
17:23 but *s* their necks so as not to hear or
19:15 *s* their necks and have not obeyed my words.

STIFFNECKED (3)

Ex 32: 9 I see how *s* this people is,"
2Chr 36:13 He became *s* and hardened his heart rather
Sir 16:11 And had there been but one *s* man,

STIFLE (1)

1Thes 5:19 Do not *s* the Spirit.

STIFLED (2)

Lk 8: 7 and the thorns growing up with it *s* it.
8:14 but their progress is *s* by the cares and

STILL (330)

Gn 8:12 He waited *s* another seven days and then
9: 4 its lifeblood *s* in it you shall not eat.
18:12 is so old, am I *s* to have sexual pleasure?"
18:31 *S* he went on, "Since I have thus dared
18:32 But he *s* persisted:
24:30 was *s* standing by the camels at the spring.
25: 6 he made grants while he was *s* living,
25:23 peoples are quarreling while *s* within you;
26:22 moved on from there, he dug *s* another well;
29: 7 "There is *s* much daylight left;
29: 9 While he was *s* talking with them,
31:14 *s* an heir's portion in our father's house?
32: 9 "the remaining camp may *s* survive."
34:25 the third day, while they were *s* in pain,
35:16 but while they *s* had some distance to go
38: 5 Then she bore *s* another son,
40:14 So if you will *s* remember,
43: 7 'Is your father *s* living?
43:27 Is he *s* in good health?"
43:28 father is thriving and *s* in good health,"
44:14 reentered Joseph's house, he was *s* there;
45: 3 "Is my father *s* in good health?"
45:11 Since five years of famine *s* lie ahead,
45:26 When they told him, "Joseph is *s* alive
45:28 "My son Joseph is *s* alive!
46:30 seen for myself that Joseph is *s* alive."
47:26 for the land in Egypt, which is *s* in force,
48: 7 we were *s* a short distance from Ephrath;
Ex 2:23 *S* the Israelites groaned and cried out
4:18 in Egypt, to see whether they are *s* living."
5:16 servants, and *s* we are told to make bricks.
5:18 you must *s* deliver your quota of bricks."
6:13 *S*, the LORD, to bring the Israelites out
9: 7 he *s* remained obdurate and would not let
9:17 Will you *s* block the way for my people by
14:14 you have only to keep *s*."
16:27 *S*, on the seventh day some of the people
20:21 *S* the people remained at a distance,
21:16 sells his victim or *s* has him when caught,
21:19 *S*, he must compensate him for his enforced
22:16 he must *s* pay him the customary marriage
24:11 gazing on God, they could *s* eat and drink.
33:20 cannot see, for no man sees me and *s* lives.
36: 3 *S*, morning after morning the people
Lv 13:57 it is *s* virulent and the thing infected
14: 8 *s* remain outside his tent for seven days.
18:18 While your wife is *s* living you shall not
19:26 "Do not eat meat with the blood *s* in it.
25:22 in, you will *s* have the old to eat from.
25:48 services he *s* has the right of redemption;
26:23 you *s* refuse to be chastened by me and
26:26 not enough food to *s* your hunger.
26:27 you *s* persist in disobeying and defying me,
Nm 5:28 has not defiled herself, but is *s* pure,
5:28 immune and will *s* be able to bear children.
9:10 journey, he may *s* keep the LORD's Passover.
11:33 while the meat was *s* between their teeth,
19:13 his uncleanness *s* clings to him.
20:20 Edom *s* said, "No, you shall not pass
23: 6 who was *s* standing by his holocaust
23:17 who was *s* standing by his holocaust
30: 4 while *s* a maiden in her father's house,
30:17 she is *s* a maiden in her father's house.
31:35 thousand girls who were *s* virgins.
32:14 rising up in your fathers' place to add *s* more
32:15 will make them stay *s* longer in the desert,
Dt 3:11 is *s* preserved in Rabbah of the Ammonites.]
5:24 can *s* live after God has spoken with him.
29:28 [Both what is *s* hidden and what has
31:15 which stood *s* at the entrance of the tent.
Jos 9:12 This bread of ours was *s* warm when we
9:27 the same time he made them, as they *s* are,
10:12 Stand *s*, O sun, at Gibeon,
10:13 And the sun stood *s*,
13: 1 part of the land *s* remains to be conquered.
14:11 I am *s* as strong today as I was the day
22:18 We are *s* not free of that;
24:21 Joshua, "We will *s* serve the LORD."
Jgs 1:26 city and called it Luz, as it is *s* called.
5:27 At her feet he sank down, fell, lay *s*;
6:24 day it is *s* in Ophrah of the Abiezrites.
7: 4 to Gideon, "There are *s* too many soldiers.
8:20 Since Jether was *s* a boy,
10:13 you *s* forsook me and worshiped other gods.
18:19 They said to him, "Be *s*:
19: 7 The man *s* made a move to go,
21:11 and every woman who was not *s* a virgin.
21:15 The people were *s* disconsolate over
Ru 3:12 to you, you have another relative *s* closer.
1Sm 2:13 fork, while the meat was *s* boiling,
6:18 ark of the LORD was placed is *s* in the field
12:20 *s*, you must not turn from the LORD,
16:11 Jesse replied, "There is *s* the youngest,
17:57 David was *s* holding the Philistine's head.
20:14 if I am *s* alive, may you show me
30:25 and a custom in Israel, as it *s* is today.
2Sm 2:23 *S* he refused to stop.
3:35 console David with food while it was *s* day.
9: 3 the king, "There is *s* Jonathan's son,
12: 8 enough, I could count up for you *s* more.
13:20 Be *s* now, my sister; he is your brother.
13:30 While they were *s* on the road,
14:12 say *s* another word to my lord the king."
14:32 I would be better off if I were *s* there!'
18:14 of Absalom, *s* hanging from the tree alive.
19:29 *s* have to make further appeal to the king?"
19:36 or *s* appreciate the voices of singers and
1Kgs 1:14 while you are *s* there speaking to the king,
1:22 While she was *s* speaking to the king,
12: 2 Jeroboam, son of Nebat, who was *s* in Egypt,
20:32 "Is he *s* alive?"
2Kgs 2: 3 "Keep *s*."
2: 5 "Keep *s*."
2:10 *S*, if you see me taken up from you,
3: 3 he *s* clung to the sin to which Jeroboam,
5:16 and despite Naaman's urging, he *s* refused.
6:33 While Elisha was *s* speaking,
12: 4 *S*, the high places did not disappear;
25:19 service of the king who were *s* in the city,
25:19 the common people *s* remaining in the city.
1Chr 4:41 against them the ban that is *s* in force
11: 2 Even formerly, when Saul was *s* the king,
12: 1 while he was *s* under banishment from Saul,
20: 6 In *s* another battle,
29: 1 God has chosen, is *s* young and immature;
2Chr 14: 6 The land is *s* ours,
18: 7 "There is *s* another through whom we may
25:16 While he was *s* speaking,
32:16 His officials said *s* more against the LORD
34: 3 year of his reign, while he was *s* a youth,
Neh 5: 4 *S* others said: To pay the king's tax
7: 3 and while the sun is *s* shining they shall
9:30 *s* they would not listen.
Tb 11: 3 the rest of the party are *s* on the way."
Jdt 6: 9 If you *s* cherish the hope that they will
8:31 cisterns, lest we be weakened *s* further."
15: 1 those *s* in their tents were amazed,
1Mc 1: 6 kingdom among them while he was *s* alive.
2:13 Why are we *s* alive?"
4: 4 forces were *s* scattered away from the camp.
12:36 for making the walls of Jerusalem *s* higher,
2Mc 7: 5 he was completely maimed but *s* breathing,
7:24 As the youngest brother was *s* alive,
9: 9 while he was *s* alive in hideous torments,
10:36 *S* others broke down the gates and let in
11: 8 Suddenly, while they were *s* near Jerusalem,

STILL (cont.)

14:45 S breathing, and inflamed with anger,
Jb 2: 3 He s holds fast to his innocence although
2: 9 him, "Are you s holding to your innocence?
4:16 was before my eyes, and I heard a s voice:
6:10 Then I should s have consolation and could
6:29 Think it over; I s am right.
8: 5 left them in the grip of their guilt, S,
20:13 let it go but keeps it s within his mouth.
27: 3 So long as I s have life in me and the
36: 2 are s words to be said on God's behalf.
Ps(s) 65: 8 You s the roaring of the seas,
78:30 and their food was s in their mouths,
78:32 s more and believed not in his wonders.
83: 2 be not silent, O God, and be not s!
89:10 you s the swelling of its waves.
119:91 to your ordinances they s stand firm:
139:18 the end of them, I should s be with you.
141: 5 but I will s pray under these afflictions.
Prv 9: 9 a wise man, and he becomes s wiser;
11:24 One man is lavish yet grows s richer;
31:15 She rises while it is s night,
Eccl 3:16 And s under the sun in the judgment place
4: 2 in death than are the living to be s alive.
5: 7 him and above these are others higher s—
6: 3 s if he has not the full benefit of his
7:28 which my soul s seeks and has not found:
Wis 18:16 he s reached to heaven,
19: 3 For while they were s engaged in funeral
19:10 For they were s mindful of what had
Sir 12:11 you will find that there is s corrosion.
18: 5 and when he stops he is s bewildered.
23:20 exist s knows them all after they are made.
24:20 He who eats of me will hunger s,
30:12 thrash his sides while he is s small,
33:21 While breath of life is s in you,
35:19 will not be s Till he breaks the back of
39:17 his word the waters become s as in a flask;
41: 1 who s can enjoy life's pleasures.
43:31 though he is s beyond your power to praise;
Is 5:25 back, and his hand is s outstretched.
6:13 If there be s a tenth part in it,
9:11 back, and his hand is s outstretched!
9:16 turned back, his hand is s outstretched!
9:20 turned back, his hand is s outstretched!
10: 4 turned back, his hand is s outstretched!
15: 9 blood, but I will bring s more upon Dimon:
65: 8 them, for there is s good in them";
Jer 2:22 The stain of your guilt is s before me,
2:29 How dare you s plead with me?
4:19 My heart beats wildly, I cannot be s;
11:15 Will you s be jubilant when you hear the
17: 8 it shows no distress, but s bears fruit.
23:14 prophets I saw deeds s more shocking:
31:20 threaten him, I s remember him with favor;
33: 1 s imprisoned in the quarters of the guard:
37: 4 he s came and went freely among the people.
39:15 s imprisoned in the quarters of the guard,
40: 7 When the army leaders who were s in the
47: 6 Return into your scabbard; stop, be s!
51:50 escaped the sword, go on, stand not s;
Ez 1:24 [And when they stood s,
8: 6 But you shall see s greater abominations!
8:13 You shall see s greater abominations that
10:17 When they stood s,
10:17 When they stood still, the wheels stood s;
14:22 s some survivors shall be left in it who
15: 4 is scorched, is it s good for anything?
16: 7 hair had grown, but you were s stark naked.
16:28 harlot with them, you were s not satisfied.
16:29 but despite this, you were s not satisfied.
17:15 Can he break a covenant and s go free?
18:24 wicked man does, can he do this and s live?
33:20 s you say, "The way of the LORD
Dn 4:28 these words were s on the king's lips,
9:20 I was s occupied with my prayer,
9:21 I was s occupied with this prayer,
11: 5 s and govern a domain greater than his.
11:35 the end time which is s appointed to come.
Hos 8:13 He shall s remember their guilt and punish
12: 1 Judah is s rebellious against God,
Am 4: 7 when the harvest was s three months away;
Jon 1:13 S the men rowed hard to regain the land,
4: 2 I said while I was s in my own country?
Na 1:12 s they shall be mown down and disappear.
Hb 2: 3 For the vision s has its time,
Zec 13: 3 If a man s prophesies,
Mt 12:46 He was s addressing the crowds when his
13:31 He proposed s another parable:
13:33 He offered them s another image:
15:16 you, too, s incapable of understanding?"
16: 9 Do you s not understand?
16:14 s others Jeremiah or one of the prophets."
17: 5 He was s speaking when suddenly a bright
20: 6 he found s others standing around.
26:39 S, let it be as you would have it,
26:47 While he was s speaking,
27:19 While he was s presiding on the bench,
27:63 while he was s alive made the claim,
Mk 2:19 fast as long as the groom is s among them?
4:39 Be s!"
6:15 s others, "He is a prophet equal to any
8: 5 S he asked them, "How many loaves
8:17 Do you s not see or comprehend?
8:21 to them again, "Do you s not understand?"
8:28 the Baptizer, others, Elijah, s others,
12: 6 He s had one to send
14:21 S, accursed be that man by whom the Son of
14:41 a third time and said to them, S sleeping?
14:41 S taking your ease?
14:43 Even while he was s speaking,
Lk 5:34 groom fast while the groom is s with them?
8:49 He was s speaking when a man came from the
9: 8 s others, "One of the prophets of old
14:22 carried out, my lord, and there is s room.'
14:32 while the enemy is s at a distance,
15:20 While he was s a long way off,
20:12 He sent s a third,
22:47 While he was s speaking a crowd came,
24: 4 s at a loss over what to think of this,
24: 6 he said to you while he was s in Galilee
24:36 While they were s speaking about all this,
24:41 s incredulous for sheer joy and wonder,
24:44 words I spoke to you when I was s with you:
Jn 3:10 and s you do not understand these matters?
5:18 was breaking the sabbath but, worse s,
6:17 was dark, and Jesus had s not joined them;
6:36 you have seen me, you s do not believe.
7:27 S, we know where this man is from.
8:20 S, he went unapprehended because his hour
11:30 was s at the spot where Martha had met him.)
12:35 s have it or darkness will come over you.
14: 9 you all this time, you s do not know me?
14:25 have I told you while I was s with you;
17:13 I say all this while I am s in the world
19:37 is s another Scripture passage which says:
20: 1 first day of the week, while it was s dark,
21:25 are s many other things that Jesus did,
Acts 1:10 They were s gazing up into the heavens
2:39 s far off whom the Lord our God calls."
4: 1 Peter and John were s addressing the crowd,
5: 4 you sold it, was not the money s yours?
7: 2 Abraham when he was s in Mesopotamia
9: 1 s breathing murderous threats against the
9:39 Dorcas had made when she was s with them.
10:19 Peter was s pondering the vision when the
13:35 That is why he said in s another place,
16:28 We are all s here."
22: 2 them in Hebrew, they grew quieter s.
27:26 we s have to face shipwreck on some island."
27:27 were s being driven across the Ionian Sea,
Rom 4:11 through faith while he was s uncircumcised.
4:12 which Abraham walked while s uncircumcised.
5: 6 appointed time, when we were s powerless,
5: 8 while we were s sinners, Christ died for us.
7: 3 if, while her husband is s alive,
1Cor 1:12 "I belong to Apollos," s another,
3: 3 being s very much in a natural condition.
3: 4 clear that you are s at the human level?
3:14 has raised on this foundation s stands,
5: 2 S you continue to be self-satisfied,
7: 7 S, each one has his own gift from God,
12:10 healing, and s another miraculous powers.
14:26 to give, s another a revelation to share;
15: 6 brothers at once, most of whom are s alive,
15:17 You are s in your sins,
2Cor 7: 7 for me, so that my joy is greater s.
Gal 2:20 I s live my human life,
5:11 brothers, if I am s preaching circumcision,
Col 2:21 were s living a life bounded by this world?
1Thes 1: 5 proved to be like when, while s among you,
3: 4 When we were s with you,
4: 1 you must learn to make s greater progress.
2Thes 2: 5 about these things when I was s with you?
2Tm 2:13 are unfaithful he will s remain faithful,
Heb 3:13 one another daily while it is s "today,"
4: 1 promise of entrance into his rest s holds,
4: 9 rest s remains for the people of God.
7:10 for he was s in his father's loins when
7:15 The matter is clearer s if another priest
9: 8 while the first tabernacle was s standing,
11: 4 although Abel is dead, he s speaks.
11:20 Jacob and Esau blessings that were s to be.
11:36 S others endured mockery,
Rv 9:14 sixth angel, who was s holding his trumpet,

STILLBORN (1)

Nm 12:12 Let her not thus be like the s babe that

STILLED (11)

Jb 30:17 my inward parts seethe and will not be s.
38:11 and here shall your proud waves be s!
Ps(s) 76: 7 O God of Jacob, chariots and steeds lay s.
107:29 breeze, and the billows of the sea were s;
131: 2 s and quieted my soul like a weaned child.
Is 14: 4 how the turmoil is s!
16:10 one treads grapes, the vintage shout is s.
24: 8 S are the cheerful timbrels,
24: 8 of the jubilant, s is the cheerful harp.
Jer 48:33 treads no more, the vintage shout is s.
49:26 streets, and all her warriors shall be s.

STILLNESS (1)

Wis 18:14 For when peaceful s compassed everything

STILLS (1)

Jer 51:55 LORD lays Babylon waste, s her loud cry,

STIMULUS (1)

Wis 14:18 the artisan's ambition provided a s.

STING (5)

Hos 13:14 where is your s, O nether world!
1Cor 15:55 O death, where is your s?"
15:56 The s of death is sin,
Rv 9: 3 as powerful as scorpions in their s.
9: 5 inflicted was like that of a scorpion's s.

STINGERS (1)

Rv 9:10 They had tails with s like scorpions;

STINGINESS (1)

Sir 31:24 and this testimony to his s is lasting.

STINGY (4)

1Sm 30:22 But all the s and worthless men among
Sir 14: 5 To whom will he be generous who is s with
14: 6 more s than he who is stingy with himself;

STINT (1)

Dt 8: 9 without s and where you will lack nothing,

STIPULATED (1)

Gn 23:16 had s in the hearing of the Hittites,

STIPULATION (1)

Gal 2:10 The only s was that we should be mindful

STIPULATIONS (3)

2Kgs 22:13 the s of this book that has been found,
22:13 fathers did not obey the s of this book,
23:24 he might carry out the s of the law

STIR (14)

Tb 8:20 fourteen days you shall not s from here,.
2Mc 14: 6 who s up sedition and keep the kingdom
15:17 valor and s young hearts to courage,
Ps(s) 140: 3 in their hearts, and s up wars every day.
Prv 6: 3 Go, hurry, s up your neighbor!
Sg 2: 7 do not s up love before its own time.
3: 5 do not s up love before its own time.
8: 4 the field, Do not arouse, do not s up love,
Ez 23:22 I will now s up your lovers against you,
32:13 The foot of man shall s them no longer,
Acts 17:13 to cause a commotion and s up the crowds.
21:27 and began to s up the whole crowd there.
Rom 11:11 come to the Gentiles to s Israel to envy.
2Tm 1: 6 I remind you to s into flame the gift of

STIRRED (28)

Gn 7:21 All creatures that s on earth perished:
Jgs 13:25 of the LORD first s him in Mahaneh-dan,
1Sm 22: 8 s up my servant to be an enemy against me,
2Chr 21:16 Then the LORD s up against Jehoram the
2Mc 7:21 s her womanly heart with manly courage,
14:27 S up by the villain's calumnies,
15:10 Having s up their courage,
Ps(s) 39: 3 But my grief was s up;
74:13 on earth, You s up the sea by your might;
78:26 He s up the east wind in the heavens,
Sir 51:21 whole being was s as I learned about her;
Is 41: 2 s up from the East the champion of justice,
41:25 I have s up one from the north,
45:13 I who s up one for the triumph of justice;
Jer 51:11 LORD has s up the spirit of Media's kings;
Ez 3:14 seized me, and I went off spiritually s,
Dn 7: 2 four winds of heaven s up the great sea,
13:45 God s up the holy spirit of a young boy
Hos 11: 8 My heart is overwhelmed, my pity is s.
Jl 2:18 Then the LORD was s to concern for his
Hg 1:14 s up the spirit of the governor of Judah,
Zec 8: 2 for Zion, s to jealous wrath for her.
Mt 21:10 the whole city was s to its depths,
Jn 5: 7 into the pool once the water has been s up.
Acts 13:50 But some of the Jews s up their
14: 2 But the Jews who remained unconvinced s up
17: 8 In this way they s up the crowd.
2Cor 9: 2 Your zeal has s up most of them.

STIRRING (7)

Jgs 9:31 Shechem and are s up the city against you.
Prv 30:33 For the s of milk brings forth curds,
30:33 and the s of anger brings forth blood.
Is 13:17 I am s up against them the Medes,
Jer 50: 9 I am s against Babylon a band of great
Ez 32: 2 S the water with your feet and churning
Hos 7: 4 Whose fire the baker desists from s once

STIRS (17)

Jb 26:12 By his power he s up the sea,
Ps(s) 50:11 of the air, and whatever s in the plains,

Prv 10:12 Hatred *s* up disputes,
15: 1 calms wrath, but a harsh word *s* up anger.
15:18 An ill-tempered man *s* up strife,
28:25 The greedy man *s* up disputes,
29:22 An ill-tempered man *s* up disputes,
Is 9:10 them and *s* up their enemies to action:
42:13 a hero, like a warrior he *s* up his ardor;
51:15 who *s* up the sea so that its waves roar;
Jer 31:20 My heart *s* for him,
31:35 Who *s* up the sea till its waves roar,
43: 3 son of Neriah, who *s* you up against us,
Ez 8: 3 the statue of jealousy which *s* up jealousy.
Zec 2:17 for he *s* forth from his holy dwelling.
Lk 23: 5 "He *s* up the people by his teaching
Acts 24: 5 man is a troublemaker who *s* up sedition

STOCK (10)

Jdt 5:21 become the laughing *s* of the whole world."
Jb 5:24 taking *s* of your household,
Is 48: 1 name of Israel, sprung from the *s* of Judah,
48:19 and those born of your *s* like its grains,
Jer 2:21 you, a choice vine of fully tested *s*;
Jn 8:37 I realize you are one of Abraham's *s*.
Acts 17:26 From one *s* he made every nation of mankind
Eph 2:11 You men of Gentile *s*—
Phil 3: 5 the *s* of Israel and the tribe of Benjamin,
1Jn 3: 9 sinfully because he remains of God's *s*;

STOCKS (9)

2Chr 16:10 with the seer and imprisoned him in the *s*,
Jb 13:27 You put my feet in the *s*;
33:11 He puts my feet in the *s*;
Prv 31:24 sells them, and *s* the merchants with belts.
Wis 14:21 the incommunicable Name on *s* and stones.
Sir 33:27 for a wicked slave, punishment in the *s*.
Jer 20: 2 prophet scourged and placed in the *s*
20: 3 Pashhur had released Jeremiah from the *s*,
29:26 by putting them into the *s* or the pillory.

STOIC (1)

Acts 17:18 and *S* philosophers disputed with him,

STOKE (1)

Dn 3:46 continued to *s* the furnace with brimstone,

STOLE (5)

Ex 22: 3 what he *s* is found alive in his possession,
Ru 3: 7 down at the edge of the sheaves, she *s* up,
2Sm 19: 4 The soldiers *s* into the city that day like
2Mc 4:32 *s* some gold vessels from the temple and
Mt 28:13 the night and *s* him while we were asleep.'

STOLEN (13)

Gn 31:32 had no idea that Rachel had *s* the idols.
31:39 responsible for anything *s* by day or night.
Ex 22: 3 shall restore two animals for each one *s*.
22: 6 and it is *s* from the latter's house,
Lv 5:21 a deposit or a pledge or a *s* article,
5:23 restore the thing that was *s* or unjustly
Dt 28:31 Your ass will be *s* in your presence,
Tb 2:13 Perhaps it was *s*!
2:13 its owners, we have no right to eat *s* food!"
2Mc 4:39 a large number of gold vessels had been *s*,
Jb 20:19 and *s* a patrimony he had not built up,
Prv 9:17 for to him I say, *S* water is sweet,
Ez 33:15 giving back pledges, restoring *s* goods,

STOMACH (12)

Dt 18: 3 receive the shoulder, the jowls and the *s*.
Jb 20:14 Yet in his *s* the food shall turn;
Sir 31:21 too much, once you have emptied your *s*,
Is 29: 8 he is eating and awakens with an empty *s*,
Ez 3: 3 your *s* with this scroll I am giving you.
Mt 15:17 the *s* and is discharged into the latrine,
Mk 7:19 his *s* only and passes into the latrine."
1Cor 6:13 is for the *s* and the stomach for food,
1Tm 5:23 Take a little wine for the good of your *s*,
Rv 10: 9 It will be sour in your *s*,
10:10 but when I swallowed it my *s* turned sour.

STONE (204)

Gn 11: 3 They used bricks for *s*,
28:18 took the *s* that he had put under his head,
28:18 under his head, set it up as a memorial *s*,
28:22 This *s* that I have set up as a memorial
28:22 up as a memorial *s* shall be God's abode.
29: 2 A large *s* covered the mouth of the well.
29: 3 roll the *s* away from the mouth of the well
29: 3 *s* back again over the mouth of the well.
29: 8 roll the *s* away from the mouth of the well;
29:10 the *s* away from the mouth of the well,
31:13 anointed a memorial *s* and made a vow to me.
31:45 took a stone and set it up as a memorial *s*.
31:51 *s* that I have set up between you and me.
31:52 and this memorial *s* shall be witness,
33:20 set up a memorial *s* there and invoked "El,
35:14 with him, Jacob set up a memorial *s*,
35:20 Jacob set up a memorial *s* on her grave,
Ex 7:19 blood, even in the wooden pails and *s* jars."
8:22 to them, will not the Egyptians *s* us?
15: 5 they sank into the depths like a *s*.
15:16 might of your arm they were frozen like *s*,
17: 4 A little more and they will *s* me!"
20:25 If you make an altar of *s* for me,
20:25 of stone for me, do not build it of cut *s*,
21:18 the other with a *s* or with his fist,
24:12 I will give you the *s* tablets on which I
28:10 stone, and the other six on the other *s*,
28:21 each *s* engraved like a seal with the name
31:18 *s* tablets inscribed by God's own finger.
34: 1 Moses, "Cut two *s* tablets like the former,
34: 4 then cut two *s* tablets like the former,
34: 4 him, taking along the two *s* tablets.
39:14 and each *s* was engraved like a seal with
Lv 20: 2 Let his fellow citizens *s* him.
24:14 on his head, let the whole community *s* him.
24:16 The whole community shall *s* him;
26: 1 set up a *s* figure for worship in your land;
Nm 14:10 the whole community threatened to *s* them.
15:35 the whole community *s* him outside the camp."
22:24 vineyards with a *s* wall on each side.
33:52 all their *s* figures and molten images,
35:17 *s* in his hand and causes his death,
35:23 *s* which strikes him and causes his death,
Dt 4:13 which he wrote on two tablets of *s*.
4:28 by the hands of man out of wood and *s*,
5:22 upon two tablets of *s* and gave them to me.
9: 9 up the mountain to receive the *s* tablets
9:10 gave me the two tablets of *s* inscribed,
9:11 given me the two *s* tablets of the covenant,
10: 1 me, 'Cut two tablets of *s* like the former;
10: 3 and cut two tablets of *s* like the former,
13:11 You shall *s* him to death,
17: 5 out to your city gates and *s* him to death.
21:21 his fellow citizens shall *s* him to death.
22:21 there her townsmen shall *s* her to death,
22:24 gate of the city and there *s* them to death:
24: 6 or even its upper *s* as a pledge for debt,
28:36 you will serve strange gods of wood and *s*,
28:64 you will serve strange gods of wood and *s*,
29:16 you saw the loathsome idols of wood and *s*,
Jos 4: 5 lift to your shoulders one *s* apiece,
24:26 Then he took a large *s* and set it up there
24:27 the people, "This *s* shall be our witness,
Jgs 9: 5 the seventy sons of Jerubbaal, on one *s*.
9:18 have killed his seventy sons upon one *s*,
20:16 to sling a *s* at a hair without missing.
1Sm 6:14 At a large *s* in the field,
6:15 were, and had placed them on the great *s*.
6:18 The large *s* on which the ark of the LORD
7:12 Samuel then took a *s* and placed it between
14:33 Roll a large *s* here for me."
17:49 his hand into the bag and took out a *s*,
17:49 The *s* embedded itself in his brow,
17:50 overcame the Philistine with sling and *s*;
25:37 died within him, and he became like a *s*.
2Sm 20: 8 the great *s* in Gibeon when Amasa met them.
1Kgs 1: 9 oxen, and fatlings at the *s* Zoheleth,
5:31 to give the temple a foundation of hewn *s*.
6: 7 was built of *s* dressed at the quarry,
6:18 all was of cedar, and no *s* was to be seen.
8: 9 nothing in the ark but the two *s* tablets
21:10 Then take him out and *s* him to death."
2Kgs 3:25 Kirhareseth was left behind its *s* walls,
12:13 LORD, and to the lumbermen and *s* cutters,
12:13 and hewn *s* used in repairing the breaches,
16:17 supported it, and set it on a *s* pavement.
19:18 but the work of human hands, wood and *s*.
22: 6 of wood and hewn *s* for the temple repairs.
1Chr 22: 2 out *s* blocks for building the house of God.
29: 2 stones, every other kind of precious *s*,
2Chr 2: 1 seventy thousand men to carry *s*
2: 1 thousand to cut the *s* in the mountains,
2:13 silver, bronze and iron, with *s* and wood,
16: 6 all of Judah to carry away the *s* and wood
34:11 carpenters and the masons to buy hewn *s*
Ezr 5: 8 it is being rebuilt of cut *s* and the walls
6: 4 courses of cut *s* for each one of timber.
Neh 9:11 depths, like a *s* into the mighty waters.
Jdt 1: 2 this city he built a wall of blocks of *s*,
1Mc 10:73 is not a *s* or a pebble or a place to flee."
Jb 28: 2 the earth, and copper is melted out of *s*.
30: 6 of the wadies, in caves of sand and *s*;
38:30 waters lie covered as though with *s*
41:15 His heart is hard as *s*;
Ps(s) 91:12 up, lest you dash your foot against a *s*.
118:22 The *s* which the builders rejected has
Prv 17: 8 has a bribe to offer rates it a magic *s*;
24:31 with nettles, and its *s* wall broken down.
26: 8 Like one who entangles the *s* in the sling
26:27 and a *s* comes back upon him who rolls it.
27: 3 *S* is heavy, and sand a burden,
Wis 11: 4 for their thirst from the hard *s*.
13:10 and likenesses of beasts, or useless *s*,
Sir 6:22 will be like a burdensome *s* to test him,
22: 1 The sluggard is like a *s* in the mud;
27:25 As a *s* falls back on him who throws it up,
29:10 and hide it not under a *s* to perish;
Is 8:14 a stumbling *s* to both the houses of Israel,
9: 9 have fallen, but we will build with cut *s*;
28:16 See, I am laying a *s* in Zion,
28:16 a stone in Zion, a *s* that has been tested,
37:19 but the work of human hands, wood and *s*.
Jer 2:27 of wood, "You are my father," and to a *s*,
3: 9 land, committing adultery with *s* and wood.
5: 3 They set their faces harder than *s*,
51:26 from you a cornerstone, or a foundation *s*;
51:63 a *s* to it and throw it in the Euphrates.
Lam 3:53 in the pit, and sealed me in with a *s*.
Ez 10: 1 cherubim what appeared to be a sapphire *s*;
10: 9 to have the luster of chrysolite *s*.
16:40 to *s* you and hack you with their swords.
20:32 of foreign lands, serving wood and *s*."
23:47 The assembly shall *s* them and hack them to
28:13 precious *s* was your covering [carnelian,
40:42 four tables for holocausts, made of cut *s*,
Dn 2:34 a *s* which was hewn from a mountain without
2:35 But the *s* that struck the statue became a
2:45 That is the meaning of the *s* you saw hewn
5: 4 silver, bronze and iron, wood and *s*.
5:23 and gold, bronze and iron, wood and *s*,
6:18 *s* that had been brought to block
Am 5:11 Though you have built houses of hewn *s*,
Mi 1: 6 I will make Samaria a *s* heap in the field,
Hb 2:11 For the *s* in the wall shall cry out,
2:19 to dumb *s*, "Arise!"
Hg 2:15 Before there was a *s* laid upon a stone in
Zec 3: 9 at the *s* that I have placed before Joshua,
3: 9 before Joshua, one *s* with seven facets.
4:10 the select *s* in the hands of Zerubbabel.
12: 3 make Jerusalem a weighty *s* for all peoples.
Mt 4: 6 you that you may never stumble on a *s*.'"
7: 9 hand his son a *s* when he asks for a loaf,
21:42 'The *s* which the builders rejected has
21:44 falls upon that *s* will be smashed to bits;
24: 2 you, not one *s* will be left on another
27:60 Then he rolled a huge *s* across the
27:66 of the guard, after fixing a seal to the *s*.
28: 2 He came to the *s*,
Mk 12:10 'The *s* rejected by the builders has become
13: 1 blocks of *s* and the enormous buildings!"
13: 2 Not one *s* will be left upon another
15:46 rolled a *s* across the entrance of the tomb.
16: 3 the *s* for us from the entrance to the tomb?"
16: 4 they found that the *s* had been rolled back.
Lk 4: 3 of God, command this *s* to turn into bread."
4:11 you, that you may never stumble on a *s*.'"
13:34 prophets and *s* those who are sent to you!
19:44 and leave not a *s* on a stone within you,
19:44 and leave not a stone on a *s* within you,
20: 6 we say, 'From men,' the people will *s* us,
20:17 'The *s* which the builders rejected has
20:18 falls on that *s* will be smashed to pieces.
21: 6 when not one *s* will be left on another,
24: 2 found the *s* rolled back from the tomb;
Jn 2: 6 there were at hand six *s* water jars,
8: 7 has no sin be the first to cast a *s* at her."
10:31 the Jews again reached for rocks to *s* him,
10:32 For which of these do you *s* me?"
11: 8 the Jews only recently trying to *s* you,
11:38 It was a cave with a *s* laid across it.
11:39 "Take away the *s*," Jesus directed.
11:41 the *s* and Jesus looked upward and said:
19:13 bench at the place called the *S* Pavement
20: 1 She saw that the *s* had been moved away,
Acts 4:11 This Jesus is 'the *s* rejected by you the
7:58 him out of the city, and began to *s* him.
14: 5 with their leaders, to abuse and *s* them.
17:29 like a statue of gold or silver or *s*,
Rom 9:32 They stumbled over the stumbling *s*,
9:33 I am placing in Zion a *s* to make men
11: 9 a trap, a stumbling *s* and a retribution;
2Cor 3: 3 of *s* but on tablets of flesh in the heart.
3: 7 ministry of death, carved in writing on *s*,
1Pt 2: 4 Come to him, a living *s*,
2: 6 a cornerstone in Zion, an approved *s*,
2: 7 The *s* is of value for you who have faith.
2: 7 "A *s* which the builders rejected that
2: 8 likewise "an obstacle and a stumbling *s*."
Rv 2:17 white *s* upon which is inscribed a new name,
9:20 and silver, from bronze and *s* and wood,
18:21 A powerful angel picked up a *s* like a

STONECUTTERS (4)

1Kgs 5:29 and eighty thousand *s* in the mountain.
1Chr 22: 2 and he appointed them *s* to hew out stone
22:15 an unlimited supply of workmen, *s*,
Ezr 3: 7 They then hired *s* and carpenters,

STONED (21)

Ex 19:13 must be *s* to death or killed with arrows.
21:28 man or a woman to death, the ox must be *s*;
21:29 or a woman, not only must the ox be *s*,
21:32 shekels of silver, and the ox must be *s*.
Lv 24:23 the blasphemer outside the camp and *s* him;
Nm 15:36 him outside the camp and *s* him to death,
Jos 7:25 And all Israel *s* him to death and piled a
1Kgs 12:18 labor, but all Israel *s* him to death.
21:13 led him out of the city and *s* him to death.
21:14 to Jezebel that Naboth had been *s* to death.
21:15 learned that Naboth had been *s* to death,
2Chr 10:18 labor, but the Israelites *s* him to death.
24:21 and at the king's order they *s* him to
Mt 21:35 beat one, killed another, and *s* a third.

STONED (cont.)

Jn 8: 5 the law, Moses ordered such women to be *s.*
Acts 5:26 of force, for fear of being *s* by the crowd.
7:59 was being *s* he could be heard praying,
14:19 *s* Paul and dragged him out of the town,
2Cor 11:25 I was *s* once, shipwrecked three times;
Heb 11:37 They were *s,* sawed in two, put to death
12:20 the mountain, it must be *s* to death."

STONER (1)

Mt 23:37 and *s* of those who were sent to you!

STONES (150)

Gn 28:11 Taking one of the *s* at the shrine,
31:46 Jacob said to his kinsmen, "Gather some *s.*"
31:46 So they got some *s* and made a mound;
Ex 25: 7 onyx *s* and other gems for mounting on the
28: 9 "Get two onyx *s* and engrave on them the
28:11 so shall you have the two *s* engraved with
28:12 Set these two *s* on the shoulder straps of
28:12 ephod as memorial *s* of the sons of Israel.
28:17 it you shall mount four rows of precious *s:*
28:20 *s* are to be mounted in gold filigree work,
31: 5 bronze, in cutting and mounting precious *s,*
35: 9 onyx *s* and other gems for mounting on the
35:27 The princes brought onyx *s* and other gems
35:33 in cutting and mounting precious *s,*
39: 6 The onyx *s* were prepared and mounted in
39: 7 These *s* were set on the shoulder straps of
39: 7 ephod as memorial *s* of the sons of Israel,
39:10 Four rows of precious *s* were mounted on it:
39:14 These *s* were twelve,
Lv 14:40 he shall order the infected *s* to be pulled
14:42 Then new *s* shall be brought and put in the
14:42 brought and put in the place of the old *s,*
14:43 once more after the *s* have been pulled
14:45 It shall be pulled down, and all its *s,*
Dt 8: 9 a land whose *s* contain iron and in whose
27: 2 some large *s* and coat them with plaster.
27: 4 *s* concerning which I command you today,
27: 5 made of *s* that no iron tool has touched.
27: 6 of the LORD, your God, with undressed *s,*
27: 8 On the *s* you shall inscribe all the words
Jos 4: 3 them to take up twelve *s* from this spot
4: 6 children ask you what these *s* mean to you,
4: 7 Thus these *s* are to serve as a perpetual
4: 8 they took up as many *s* from the bed of the
4: 9 Joshua also had twelve *s* set up in the bed
4:20 *s* which had been taken from the Jordan,
4:21 you ask their fathers what these *s* mean,
7:26 death and piled a great heap of *s* over him,
8:29 a great heap of *s* was piled up over it,
8:31 *s* on which no iron tool had been used,
8:32 the *s* a copy of the law written by Moses.
10:11 the LORD hurled great *s* from the sky above
10:18 "Roll large *s* to the mouth of the cave
10:27 the mouth of the cave large *s* were placed,
1Sm 17:40 David selected five smooth *s* from the wadi
2Sm 12:30 weighed a talent, of gold and precious *s;*
16: 6 *s* at David and at all the king's officers,
16:13 cursing and throwing *s* and dirt as he went.
18:17 very large mound of *s* was erected over him.
1Kgs 5:32 the wood and *s* for building the temple.
6:36 of hewn *s* and one course of cedar beams.
7: 9 All these buildings were of fine *s,*
7:11 Above were fine *s* hewn to size,
7:12 hewn *s* and a bonding course of cedar beams.
10: 2 a large amount of gold, and precious *s.*
10:10 large quantity of spices, and precious *s.*
10:11 quantity of cabinet wood and precious *s.*
10:27 made silver as common in Jerusalem as *s,*
15:22 and they carried away the *s* and beams with
18:31 He took twelve *s,* for the number of tribes
18:32 an altar in honor of the LORD with the *s,*
18:38 down and consumed the holocaust, wood, *s,*
2Kgs 3:19 and ruin every fertile field with *s.*"
3:25 each of them cast *s* onto every fertile
23:15 up the *s* and grinding them to powder,
1Chr 12: 2 *s* and in shooting arrows with the bow.
20: 2 and it contained precious *s,*
22:14 I have also stored up wood and *s,*
29: 2 made of wood, onyx *s* and settings for them,
29: 2 settings for them, carnelian and mosaic *s,*
29: 8 Those who had precious *s* gave them into
2Chr 1:15 and gold as common in Jerusalem as *s,*
3: 6 decorated the building with precious *s.*
9: 1 bearing spices, much gold, and precious *s.*
9: 9 quantity of spices, as well as precious *s.*
9:10 also brought cabinet wood and precious *s.*
9:27 made silver as common in Jerusalem as *s,*
26:15 the walls to shoot arrows and cast large *s.*
32:27 made for his silver, gold, precious *s,*
Neh 3:34 Will they recover these *s,*
3:35 attacked it would breach their wall of *s!*"
Tb 13:16 and all your walls with precious *s,*
13:17 shall be paved with rubies and *s* of Ophir;
Jdt 6:12 servants by hurling *s* upon them.
10:21 and gold, emeralds and other precious *s.*
Est 1: 6 marble, mother-of-pearl, and colored *s.*
D: 6 and covered with gold and precious *s,*
1Mc 2:36 they neither threw *s,*
4:43 *s* of the Abomination to an unclean place.
4:46 *s* in a suitable place on the temple hill,
4:47 Then they took uncut *s,*
5:47 them out and blocked up the gates with *s.*
10:11 Zion with square *s* for its fortification,
13:27 father and his brothers a monument of *s,*
2Mc 1:16 hurled *s* at the leader and his companions
1:31 of the liquid to be poured upon large *s.*
4:41 the people picked up *s* or pieces of wood
Jb 5:23 shall be in league with the *s* of the field,
6:12 Have I the strength of *s,*
8:17 About a heap of *s* are his roots entwined;
14:19 As waters wear away the *s* and floods wash
28: 6 Its *s* are the source of sapphires,
Ps(s) 102:15 For her *s* are dear to your servants,
Eccl 3: 5 A time to scatter *s,*
10: 9 He who moves *s* may be hurt by them,
Wis 14:21 the incommunicable Name on stocks and *s.*
18:24 were carved in four rows upon the *s,*
Sir 21: 8 is collecting *s* for his funeral mound.
21:10 The path of sinners is smooth *s* that end
22:18 Small *s* lying on an open height will not
22:20 He who throws *s* at birds drives them away,
27: 2 Like a peg driven between fitted *s,*
40:14 Which, in its rising, rolls along the *s,*
45:11 *s* with seal engravings in golden settings,
50: 9 of beaten gold, studded with precious *s;*
Is 5: 2 He spaded it, cleared it of *s,*
27: 9 the *s* of the altars like pieces of chalk;
54:12 and all your walls of precious *s.*
57: 6 the smooth *s* of the wadi is your portion,
60:17 In place of wood, bronze, instead of *s,*
62:10 up, build up the highway, clear it of *s,*
Jer 43: 9 Take with you large *s* and sink them in
43:10 will set his throne upon these *s* which I,
Lam 3: 9 He has blocked my ways with fitted *s,*
4: 1 sacred *s* lie strewn at every street corner!
Bar 6:38 statues are like *s* from the mountains;
Ez 26:12 Your *s,* your timber, and your clay
27:22 choicest spices, all kinds of precious *s,*
28:14 mountain of God, walking among the fiery *s.*
28:16 Cherub drove you from among the fiery *s.*
46:23 A wall of *s* surrounded each of the four,
46:23 built beneath the *s* all the way around.
Dn 11:38 glorify with gold, silver, precious *s,*
Hos 12:12 heaps of *s* in the furrows of the field.
Mi 1: 6 I will throw down into the valley her *s,*
Zec 5: 4 his house, consuming it, timber and *s.*"
9:15 sling *s* and trample them underfoot;
Mt 3: 9 up children to Abraham from these very *s.*
4: 3 of God, command these *s* to turn into bread."
Mk 5: 5 he screamed and gashed himself with *s.*
Lk 3: 8 raise up children to Abraham from these *s.*
19:40 I tell you the very *s* would cry out."
21: 5 with precious *s* and votive offerings.
22:41 He withdrew from them about a *s* throw,
1Cor 3:12 foundation with gold, silver, precious *s,*
1Pt 2: 5 You too are living *s,*
Rv 18:12 of gold and silver, precious *s* and pearls;
21:14 had twelve courses of *s* as its foundation,
21:19 was ornate with precious *s* of every sort:
21:19 the first course of *s* was jasper,

STONING (3)

Lv 20:27 fortune-teller shall be put to death by *s;*
1Sm 30: 6 difficulty, for the men spoke of *s* him,
Jn 10:33 not for any 'good deed' that we are *s* you,"

STONY (3)

Dt 32:13 and olive oil from its hard, *s* ground;
Ez 11:19 will remove the *s* heart from their bodies,
36:26 *s* hearts and giving you natural hearts.

STOOD (184)

Gn 13: 3 and Ai where his tent had formerly *s,*
19:27 where he had *s* in the LORD's presence.
Ex 9:10 a furnace and *s* in the presence of Pharaoh.
15: 8 up, the flowing waters *s* like a mound,
32:26 he *s* at the gate of the camp and cried,
34: 5 *s* with him there and proclaimed his name,
Lv 9: 5 had come forward and *s* before the LORD,
Nm 16: 2 They *s* before Moses,
22:34 that you *s* against me to oppose my journey.
Dt 4:10 was the day on which you *s* before the LORD,
4:11 near and *s* at the foot of the mountain,
5: 5 I *s* between the LORD and you at that time,
31:15 which *s* still at the entrance of the tent.
32:17 of whom their fathers had never *s* in awe.
Jos 4: 9 priests *s* who were carrying the ark
5:13 his eyes and saw one who *s* facing him,
8:33 *s* on either side of the ark facing the
10:13 And the sun *s* still,
20: 6 he has *s* judgment before the community,
24: 1 When they *s* in ranks before God,
Jgs 9:35 out and *s* at the entrance of the city gate.
9:44 in and *s* by the entrance of the city gate,
18:16 Danites, *s* by the entrance of the gate,
18:16 of the gate, and the priest *s* there also.
1Sm 1:26 lord, I am the woman who *s* near you here,
5: 7 seeing how matters *s,* the men of Ashdod
9: 2 he *s* head and shoulders above the people.
10:23 and when he *s* among the people,
17: 8 He *s* and shouted to the ranks of Israel:
17:51 Then David ran and *s* over him;
26:13 David *s* on a remote hilltop at a great
28:25 Then they *s* up and left the same night.
2Sm 1:10 So I *s* up to him and dispatched him,
12:17 The elders of his house *s* beside him
13:31 king *s* up, rent his garments,
18: 4 and he *s* by the gate as all the soldiers
20:11 of Joab's attendants *s* by Amasa and said,
20:16 the city *s* on the outworks and called out,
23:10 but he *s* his ground and fought the
1Kgs 1:28 the king's presence and *s* before him,
2:19 king *s* up to meet her and paid her homage.
3:15 *s* before the ark of the covenant of the
3:16 harlots came to the king and *s* before him.
8:14 the whole community of Israel as they *s.*
8:22 Solomon *s* before the altar of the LORD in
8:55 He *s* and blessed the whole community of
10:19 Next to each arm *s* a lion;
10:20 and twelve other lions *s* on the steps,
19:13 and went and *s* at the entrance of the cave.
2Kgs 2: 7 at the Jordan, *s* facing them at a distance.
2:13 went back and *s* at the bank of the Jordan.
4:12 He did so, and when she *s* before Elisha,
4:15 she had been called, and *s* at the door.
5:15 On his arrival he *s* before him and said,
5:25 He went in and *s* before Elisha his master,
8: 9 arrival, he *s* before the prophet and said,
16:14 The bronze altar that *s* before the LORD he
23: 3 people *s* as participants in the covenant.
1Chr 6:24 His brother Asaph *s* at his right hand.
6:29 brothers, the Merarites, *s* at the left:
9:18 Previously they had *s* guard at the king's
2Chr 3:13 They *s* upon their own feet,
5:12 harps and lyres, *s* east of the altar,
6: 3 the whole community of Israel as they *s.*
7: 6 priests blew the trumpets and all Israel *s.*
8:14 the various classes *s* guard at each gate,
9:19 Twelve other lions also *s* there,
13: 4 Abijah *s* on Mount Zemariam,
13: 6 has *s* up and rebelled against his lord!
20: 5 Jehoshaphat *s* up in the assembly of Judah
28:12 themselves *s* up in opposition to those who
30:16 They *s* in the places prescribed for them
Ezr 3: 9 *s* as one man to supervise those who were
10:10 Ezra, the priest, *s* up and said to them:
Neh 4:10 *s* guard behind the whole house of Judah as
4:13 Also, a trumpeter *s* beside me,
8: 4 Ezra the scribe *s* on a wooden platform
8: 4 at his right side *s* Mattithiah,
9: 2 then *s* forward and confessed their sins
12:24 Their brethren who *s* opposite them to sing
Jdt 10:18 They came and *s* around her as she waited
13: 4 Judith *s* by Holofernes' bed and said
Est D: 6 till she *s* face to face with the king,
5: 1 garments and *s* in the inner courtyard,
1Mc 7:36 and *s* before the altar and the sanctuary.
14:26 have *s* firm and repulsed Israel's enemies.
2Mc 3:33 again appeared and *s* before Heliodorus.
Jb 4:15 before me, and the hair of my flesh *s* up.
22:20 these have been destroyed where they *s,*
29: 8 withdrew, while the elders rose up and *s;*
Ps(s) 33: 9 he commanded, and it *s* forth.
104: 6 above the mountains the waters *s.*
106:30 Then Phinehas *s* forth in judgment and the
109:31 For he *s* at the right hand of the poor man,
Wis 10:11 *S* by him against the greed of his
18:16 to heaven, while he *s* upon the earth.
18:23 he *s* in the midst and checked the anger,
19:22 *s* by them in every time and circumstance.
Sir 50:12 while he *s* before the sacrificial wood,
Jer 15: 1 Even if Moses and Samuel *s* before me,
18:20 I *s* before you to speak in their behalf,
19:14 he *s* in the court of the house of God and
23:18 Now, who has *s* in the council of the LORD,
23:22 Had they *s* in my council,
Ez 1:24 [And when they *s* still,
8: 3 where *s* the statue of jealousy which stirs
8:11 Before these *s* seventy of the elders of
8:11 house of Israel, among whom *s* Jaazaniah,
9: 2 They entered and *s* beside the bronze altar.
10: 6 the man entered and *s* by one of the wheels.
10:17 When they stood still, the wheels *s* still;
10:19 They *s* at the entrance of the eastern gate
37:10 they came alive and *s* upright,
40:47 The altar *s* in front of the temple.
43: 6 from the temple, while the man *s* beside me.
Dn 2:31 in appearance as it *s* before you.
3: 3 came together for the dedication and *s*
3:25 In the fire Azariah *s* up and prayed aloud:
8:15 I had seen, a manlike figure *s* before me,
10:11 When he said this to me, I *s* up trembling.
10:13 of Persia *s* in my way for twenty-one days,
13:48 He *s* in their midst and continued,
Ob 1:11 On the day when you *s* by,
Zec 3: 1 Satan *s* at his right hand to accuse him.
Mal 2: 5 and he feared me, and *s* in awe of my name.
Mt 8:26 Then he *s* up and took the winds and the
9: 7 The man *s* up and went toward his home.
9:19 Jesus *s* up and followed him,
13: 2 a boat while the crowd *s* along the shore.
18: 2 over and *s* him in their midst and said:
28: 9 warning, Jesus *s* before them and said,

Mk 2:12 The man *s* and picked up his mat and went
3:31 and as they *s* outside they sent word to
5:42 *s* up immediately and began to walk around.
9:36 took a little child, *s* him in their midst,
15:39 The centurion who *s* guard over him,
Lk 4:16 habit of doing, he *s* up to do the reading.
4:39 He *s* over her and addressed himself to the
5: 1 As he *s* by the Lake of Gennesaret,
5:25 At once the man *s* erect before them.
5:28 behind, Levi *s* up and became his follower.
7:38 perfumed oil and *s* behind him at his feet,
10:25 a lawyer *s* up to pose him this problem:
13:13 she *s* up straight and began thanking God.
19: 8 *s* his ground and said to the Lord:
22:28 who have *s* loyally by me in my temptations.
23:35 The people *s* there watching,
24: 4 two men in dazzling garments *s* beside them.
24:36 himself *s* in their midst [and said to them,
Jn 7:37 of the festival, Jesus *s* up and cried out:
18:18 joined them and *s* there warming himself.
19:25 Near the cross of Jesus there *s* his mother,
20:11 Meanwhile, Mary *s* weeping beside the tomb.
20:19 of the Jews, Jesus came and *s* before them.
20:26 locked doors, Jesus came and *s* before them.
Acts 1:10 two men dressed in white *s* beside them.
1:15 Peter *s* up in the center of the brothers;
2:14 Peter *s* up with the Eleven,
3: 8 he jumped up, *s* for a moment,
3:11 the man *s* there clinging to Peter and John,
5:34 Then a member of the Sanhedrin *s* up,
9: 7 were traveling with him *s* there speechless.
10:30 when a man in dazzling robes *s* before me.
12: 7 Lord *s* nearby and light shone in the cell.
14:13 temple of Zeus, which *s* outside the town,
16: 9 of Macedonia *s* before him and invited him,
17:22 Then Paul *s* up in the Areopagus and
21:40 With his permission Paul then *s* on the
22:13 the Jews who lived there, came and *s* by me.
22:20 was being shed, I *s* by and approved it.
24:20 me guilty of when I *s* before the Sanhedrin,
24:21 what I called out as I *s* in their presence:
27:21 time when Paul *s* up among them and said:
27:23 whose man I am and whom I serve, *s* by me.
Col 2:14 bond that *s* against us with all its claims,
2Tm 4:17 the Lord *s* by my side and gave me strength,
Heb 2: 2 the word spoken through angels *s* unchanged,
Rv 4: 6 *s* four living creatures covered with eyes
7: 9 They *s* before the throne and the Lamb,
11:11 When they *s* on their feet sheer terror
12: 4 *s* before the woman about to give birth,
13:17 or with the number that *s* for its name.
18:17 then *s* at a distance and cried out when

STOOP (3)

Sir 6:26 *S* your shoulders and carry her;
Is 46: 2 They *s* and bow down together;
Mk 1: 7 not fit to *s* and untie his sandal straps.

STOOPED (7)

Ps(s) 18:36 me, and you have *s* to make me great.
38: 7 I am *s* and bowed down profoundly;
40: 2 LORD, and he *s* toward me and heard my cry.
Hos 11: 4 Yet, though I *s* to feed my child,
Lk 13:11 She was badly *s*—
24:12 He *s* down but could see nothing but the
Jn 20:11 Even as she wept, she *s* to peer inside,

STOOPS (2)

Ps(s) 10:10 He *s* and lies prone till by his violence
Is 46: 1 Bel bows down, Nebo *s*,

STOP (57)

Gn 11: 6 nothing will later *s* them from doing
19:17 Don't look back or *s* anywhere on the Plain.
Ex 1:10 shrewdly with them to *s* their increase;
Nm 11:28 aide, said, "Moses, my lord, *s* them."
Jgs 15: 7 not *s* until I have taken revenge on you."
1Sm 14: 9 can come to you,' we shall *s* where we are;
15:16 *S!*
2Sm 2:22 *S* pursuing me!
2:23 Still he refused to *s*.
2:26 people to *s* the pursuit of their brothers?"
2Kgs 3:19 every fruit tree, *s* up all the springs,
4: 8 he passed by, he used to *s* there to dine.
4:24 Do not *s* my donkey unless I tell you to."
2Chr 32: 3 warriors to *s* the waters of the springs
Ezr 4:21 that will *s* the work of these men.
Neh 6: 3 why should the work *s*,
Tb 10: 7 But she retorted, *S* it,
1Mc 6:27 these, and you will not be able to *s* them."
11:50 let the Jews *s* attacking us and our city."
Wis 18:21 the wrath and put a *s* to the calamity,
Sir 27:14 on end, their brawls make one *s* one's ears.
31:17 Be the first to *s*, as befits good manners:
46: 4 Did he not by his power *s* the sun,
Jer 2:25 *S* wearing out your shoes and parching your
15: 5 Who will *s* to ask about your welfare?
47: 6 Return into your scabbard; *s*, be still!
48:45 shadow *s* short the exhausted refugees;
Ez 34:10 put a *s* to their shepherding my sheep
45: 9 *S* evicting my people!
Dn 9:24 Then transgression will *s* and sin will end,
11:16 He shall *s* in the glorious land,
Na 2: 9 like a pool whose waters escape; *S!*
2: 9 *S!*"
Mt 6:31 *S* worrying,
7: 1 want to avoid judgment, *s* passing judgment.
Mk 9:38 to *s* him because he is not of our company."
9:39 "Do not try to *s* him.
Lk 8:52 *S* crying for she is not dead but asleep."
9:49 to *s* him because he is not of our company."
9:50 Jesus told him in reply, "Do not *s* him,
12:29 *S* worrying.
Jn 2:16 *S* turning my Father's house into a
6:43 *S* your murmuring," Jesus told them.
7:24 *S* judging by appearances and make an
11:37 done something to *s* this man from dying?"
Acts 4:17 To *s* this from spreading further among the
10:47 "What can *s* these people who have
12:14 that she did not *s* to open the door,
13:10 Will you never *s* trying to make crooked
14:18 they could scarcely *s* the crowds from
1Cor 4: 5 so *s* passing judgment before the time of
15:33 to reason, as you ought, and *s* sinning.
Eph 6: 9 *S* threatening them.
Col 3: 9 *S* lying to one another.
1Tm 5:23 *S* drinking water only.
2Tm 2:14 before God to *s* disputing about mere words.
4: 4 They will *s* listening to the truth and

STOPPED (43)

Gn 11: 8 the earth, and they *s* building the city.
18:11 and Sarah had *s* having her womanly periods.
26:15 (The Philistines had *s* up and filled with
26:18 Philistines had *s* up after Abraham's death;
28:11 had already set, he *s* there for the night.
29:35 Then she *s* bearing children.
41:49 so vast that at last he *s* measuring it,
Ex 36: 6 So the people *s* bringing their offerings;
Nm 22:26 and *s* next in a passage so narrow that
1Sm 6:14 of Joshua the Beth-shemite and *s* there.
2Sm 16:14 Jordan tired out, and *s* there for a rest.
1Kgs 17:17 grew more severe until he *s* breathing.
2Kgs 2: 7 followed, and when the two *s* at the Jordan,
3:25 *s* up and every useful tree they felled.
4: 6 And then the oil *s*.
5: 9 and *s* at the door of Elisha's house.
10: 9 morning, he *s* and said to all the people:
13:18 He struck the ground three times and *s*.
18:17 *s* at the conduit of the upper pool on the
2Chr 16: 5 he *s* his work.
32: 4 crowd was gathered which *s* all the springs
32:30 This same Hezekiah *s* the upper outflow of
Ezr 4:23 and *s* their work by force of arms.
Tb 6: 1 Then she *s* weeping.
Ps(s) 46:10 He has *s* wars to the end of the earth:
63:12 of those who speak falsely shall be *s*.
Is 36: 2 When he *s* at the conduit of the upper pool,
Jer 14: 8 like a traveler who has *s* but for a night?
41:17 of Chimham near Bethlehem, where they *s*,
44:18 But since we *s* burning incense to the
Ez 31:15 I *s* its streams so that the deep waters
Zec 7:11 backs and *s* their ears so as not to hear.
Mt 20:32 Jesus then *s* and called out to them,
Mk 10:49 Then Jesus *s* and said, "Call him over."
Lk 6:17 he *s* at a level stretch where were many of
8:44 Immediately her bleeding *s*.
11:52 yet you have *s* those who wished to enter!"
Acts 5:42 they never *s* teaching and proclaiming the
8:38 He ordered the carriage *s*,
11:18 When they heard this they *s* objecting,
21:32 and the soldiers, they *s* assaulting Paul.
Eph 1:16 I have never *s* thanking God for you and
Heb 10: 2 the priests would have *s* offering them,

STOPPING (4)

2Sm 20:12 man noticed that all the soldiers were *s*.
20:12 him, because all who came up to him were *s*.
2Mc 9: 4 without *s* until he finished the journey.
Is 33:15 *s* his ears lest he hear of bloodshed,

STOPS (7)

1Kgs 18:44 leave the mountain before the rain *s* you.'"
Ps(s) 58: 5 that of a stubborn snake that *s* its ears,
Sir 18: 5 and when he *s* he is still bewildered.
23:16 who never *s* until the fire breaks forth;
Lam 3: 8 when I cry out for help, he *s* my prayer;
Na 3: 1 full of plunder, whose looting never *s!*
Acts 6:13 "This man never *s* making statements

STORAX (1)

Ex 30:34 *s* and onycha and galbanum,

STORE (30)

Gn 6:21 food that is to be eaten, and *s* it away,
Dt 28:39 you will not drink or *s* up the wine,
1Sm 25:17 *s* for our master and for his whole family.
2Chr 16: 4 and all the *s* cities of Naphtali.
17:12 built strongholds and *s* cities in Judah.
Tb 5:10 God has healing in *s* for you;
12: 8 is better to give alms than to *s* up gold;
Jdt 7:18 Their enormous *s* of tents and equipment
Jb 15:20 and limited years are in *s* for the tyrant;
20:26 Complete darkness is in *s* for him;
21:19 not *s* up the man's misery for his children;
27:16 like dust and *s* away mounds of clothing,
Ps(s) 31:20 which you have in *s* for those who fear you,
37:16 Better is the scanty *s* of the just than
144:13 be full, affording every kind of *s*;
Prv 2: 7 He has counsel in *s* for the upright,
10:14 Wise men *s* up knowledge,
15:10 is in *s* for the man who goes astray;
30:25 yet they *s* up their food in the summer;
Sg 7:14 fruits, my lover, I have kept in *s* for you.
Sir 29:12 *S* up almsgiving in your treasure house,
Jer 40:10 the fruit and the oil, to *s* them in jars,
Mt 6:20 practice instead to *s* up heavenly treasure,
12:35 man produces good from his *s* of goodness;
12:35 an evil man produces evil from his evil *s*.
Lk 6:45 man produces evil out of his *s* of evil.
12:17 'I have no place to *s* my harvest.
20:15 owner of the vineyard has in *s* for them?
Col 1: 4 by the hope held in *s* for you in heaven.
Rv 17: 1 I will show you the judgment in *s* for the

STORED (27)

Gn 41:35 authority, to be *s* in the towns for food.
41:48 Egypt was enjoying and *s* it in the towns,
Lv 26:10 So much of the old crops will you have *s*
2Kgs 20:17 that your fathers have *s* up until this day,
1Chr 22:14 I have also *s* up wood and stones,
29: 2 reason I have *s* up for the house of my God,
29: 3 to all that I *s* up for the holy house,
Ezr 6: 1 which the Babylonian records were *s* away;
Neh 13: 5 had previously been *s* the cereal offerings,
Jdt 4: 5 *s* up provisions in preparation for war.
1Mc 4:46 They *s* the stones in a suitable place on
13:33 and he *s* up provisions in the fortresses.
14:33 previously the enemy's arms had been *s*.
2Mc 8:31 and carefully *s* them in suitable places;
Jb 27:17 What he has *s* the just man shall wear,
Ps(s) 56: 9 my tears are *s* in your flask;
Prv 13:22 wealth of the sinner is *s* up for the just.
Eccl 1:16 I have become great and *s* up wisdom beyond
2: 9 I *s* up more than all others before me in
Sir 43:10 weapon against the flood waters *s* on high,
Is 10:28 Migron, at Michmash his supplies are *s*.
15: 7 So now whatever they have acquired or *s*
23:18 It shall not be *s* up or laid away,
39: 6 that your fathers have *s* up until this day,
Hos 13:12 of Israel is wrapped up, his sin is *s* away.
Lk 1:66 heard *s* these things up in their hearts,
Jas 5: 3 *s* up for yourselves against the last days.

STOREHOUSE (7)

Dt 32:34 in my treasury, sealed up in my *s*,
1Chr 26:15 fell the south side, and to his sons the *s*.
26:17 day, and at the *s* they were two and two;
Jb 38:22 Have you entered the *s* of the snow,
Ps(s) 135: 7 he brings forth the winds from his *s*.
Sir 43:14 At it, the *s* is opened,
Mal 3:10 Bring the whole tithe into the *s*,

STOREHOUSES (1)

2Chr 32:28 also *s* for the harvest of grain,

STOREROOM (1)

Mt 13:52 bring from his *s* both the new and the old."

STOREROOMS (9)

2Kgs 20:13 his armory, and all that was in his *s*;
20:15 nothing in my *s* that I did not show them."
1Chr 28:11 and of the building itself, with its *s*,
Neh 12:25 They kept watch over the *s* at the gates.
13:12 tithes of grain, wine, and oil to the *s*;
13:13 of the *s* I appointed the priest Shelemiah,
1Mc 6:53 But there were no provisions in the *s*,
Is 39: 2 armory, and everything that was in his *s*;
39: 4 nothing in my *s* that I did not show them."

STORES (22)

Dt 14:28 that year and deposit them in community *s*,
1Chr 22: 3 He also laid up large *s* of iron to make
22: 4 brought great *s* of cedar logs to David,
26:20 Their brother Levites superintended the *s*
26:20 house of God and the *s* of votive offerings.
26:26 his brethren superintended all the *s*
27:25 Over the *s* in the country,
27:28 Gederite, and over the *s* of oil was Joash.
28:12 compartments for the *s* for the house
28:12 of God and the *s* of the votive offerings,
Neh 12:44 over the chambers set aside for *s*,
1Mc 9:52 put soldiers in them and *s* of provisions.
Ps(s) 39: 7 he heaps up *s*,
41: 7 his heart *s* up malice;
Prv 6: 8 summer, *s* up her provisions in the harvest.
27:16 He who keeps her *s* up a stormwind;
Eccl 1:18 and he who *s* up knowledge stores up grief.
1:18 and he who stores up knowledge *s* up grief.
Sir 3: 4 he *s* up riches who reveres his mother.
Jer 41: 8 we have *s* buried in the field:

STORES (cont.)
Jl 1:17 the *s* are destroyed,
Hb 2:6 Woe to him who *s* up what is not his:

STORIES (4)
1Kgs 6:5 sanctuary, an annex of several *s* was built.
2Chr 9:6 you have surpassed the *s* I heard.
Est E:7 ancient *s* that have been handed down to us,
Ez 41:6 built one above the other in three *s*,

STORING (4)
Tb 4:9 you will be *s* up a goodly treasure for
1Mc 1:35 inside it, *s* up weapons and provisions,
Am 3:10 *S* up in their castles what they have
Rom 2:5 your hard and impenitent heart is *s* up

STORK (5)
Lv 11:19 owl, the desert owl, the buzzard, the *s*,
Dt 14:18 owl, the buzzard, the cormorant, the *s*,
Ps(s) 104:17 fir trees are the home of the *s*.
Jer 8:7 Even the *s* in the air knows its seasons;
Zec 5:9 for they had wings like the wings of a *s*.

STORM (46)
1Kgs 20:12 and they made ready to *s* the city.
2Chr 32:1 cities, and proposed to take them by *s*.
2Mc 5:11 set out from Egypt and took Jerusalem by *s*.
Jb 21:18 and like chaff which the *s* snatches away!
27:21 The *s* wind seizes him and he disappears;
36:33 for him and incites the fury of the *s*.
38:1 LORD addressed Job out of the *s* and said:
38:34 or veil yourself in the waters of the *s*?
40:6 LORD addressed Job out of the *s* and said:
Ps(s) 50:3 around him is a raging *s*.
55:9 shelter from the violent *s* and the tempest."
83:16 your tempest and rout them with your *s*.
107:25 up a *s* wind which tossed its waves on high.
107:29 He hushed the *s* to a gentle breeze,
135:7 raises *s* clouds from the end of the earth;
148:8 and mist, *s* winds that fulfill his word;
Prv 1:27 When terror comes upon you like a *s*,
23:7 For in his greed he is like a *s*.
Sir 32:10 a *s* is the esteem that shines on modesty.
33:2 and is tossed about like a boat in a *s*.
39:28 There are *s* winds created to punish,
43:15 *s* its power and breaks off the hailstones.
43:17 angry north wind, the hurricane and the *s*.
Is 4:6 of day, refuge and cover from *s* and rain.
17:13 on the mountains, like tumbleweed in a *s*.
27:8 them off with my cruel wind in time of *s*.
28:2 like a downpour of hail, a destructive *s*,
29:6 earthquake, and great noise, whirlwind, *s*,
30:30 of consuming fire, in driving *s* and hail.
41:16 them off and the *s* shall scatter them.
Jer 4:13 like *s* clouds he advances,
23:19 See, the *s* of the LORD!
23:19 *s* that bursts upon the heads of the wicked.
25:32 *s* is unleashed from the ends of the earth.
30:23 See, the *s* of the LORD!
30:23 *s* that bursts upon the heads of the wicked.
Ez 38:9 You shall come up like a sudden *s*,
Dn 11:15 and take the fortified city by *s*.
Jon 1:12 me that this violent *s* has come upon you."
Zec 9:14 trumpet, and come in a *s* from the south.
10:1 It is the LORD who makes *s* clouds.
Mt 8:24 warning a violent *s* came up on the lake,
Acts 27:18 We were being pounded by the *s* so
27:20 to be seen, so savagely did the *s* rage.
27:27 It was the fourteenth night of the *s*,
Heb 12:18 gloomy darkness and *s* and trumpet blast,

STORM-BATTERED (1)
Is 54:11 O afflicted one, *s* and unconsoled,

STORM-DRIVEN (1)
Hos 13:3 Like chaff *s* from the threshing floor or

STORMED (5)
Jos 6:20 *s* the city in a frontal attack and took it.
1Sm 30:1 the Negeb and Ziklag, had *s* the city,
1Mc 6:20 and fifty they assembled and *s* the citadel,
2Mc 10:35 bravely *s* the wall and with savage fury
12:15 then they furiously *s* the ramparts.

STORMS (2)
Prv 21:22 The wise man *s* a city of the mighty,
Sir 51:10 of trouble, in the midst of *s* and dangers.

STORMWIND (6)
Prv 27:16 He who keeps her stores up a *s*;
Is 40:24 and the *s* carries them away like straw.
Ez 1:4 As I looked, a *s* came from the North,
13:11 shall fall, and a *s* shall break out.
Am 1:14 day of battle and *s* in a time of tempest.
Hb 1:9 of a *s* that heaps up captives like sand.

STORMWINDS (3)
Jer 10:13 rain, and releases *s* from their chambers.
51:16 rain, and releases *s* from their chambers.
Ez 13:13 In my fury I will let loose *s*;

STORMY (1)
Mt 16:3 'Sky red and gloomy, the day will be *s*.'

STORY (30)
Gn 2:4 Such is the *s* of the heavens and the earth
39:17 Then she told him the same *s*:
39:19 *s* about how his slave had treated her,
1Kgs 6:6 Its lowest *s* was five cubits wide,
6:8 story and from the middle *s* to the third.
6:10 annex, with its lowest *s* five cubits high,
2Kgs 8:6 the woman, and she told him her *s*.
Neh 6:13 a shameful *s* with which to discredit me.
Tb 1:1 This book tells the *s* of Tobit,
2Mc 2:19 the *s* of Judas Maccabeus and his brothers,
2:32 a *s* and then abbreviate the story itself.
6:17 further ado we must go on with our *s*.
15:37 I will bring my own *s* to an end here too.
15:38 so a skillfully composed *s* delights the
Sir 19:14 every *s* you must not believe.
43:25 who go down to the sea tell part of its *s*,
47:17 With song and *s* and riddle,
Ez 41:7 the lowest to the middle and the highest *s*.
Mt 8:33 the *s* about the two possessed men.
28:15 This is the *s* that circulates among the
Mk 1:45 whole matter freely, making the *s* public.
Lk 24:11 but the *s* seemed like nonsense and they
Jn 4:42 longer does our faith depend on your *s*.
Acts 4:24 voices in prayer to God on hearing the *s*:
15:3 *s* caused great joy among the brothers.
17:8 the town's magistrates heard the whole *s*,
20:9 and fell from the third *s* to the ground.
Gal 1:13 the *s* of my former way of life in Judaism.

STOUT (2)
Jb 15:26 upon him with the *s* bosses of his shield,
Sir 29:13 Better than a *s* shield and a sturdy spear

STOUTHEARTED (5)
1Mc 9:14 Judas, with all the most *s* rallying to him,
Ps(s) 27:14 be *s*, and wait for the LORD.
31:25 who act proudly Take courage and be *s*,
76:6 Despoiled are the *s*;
Am 2:16 *s* of warriors shall flee naked on that day,

STOVE (1)
Jgs 5:26 she smashed, *s* in his temple.

STRADDLE (1)
1Kgs 18:21 and said, "How long will you *s* the issue?

STRAGGLER (1)
Is 14:31 from the north, without a *s* in the ranks.

STRAGGLERS (1)
1Mc 5:53 *s* and encouraging the people the whole way,

STRAGGLING (1)
Jer 50:6 shepherds mislead them, *s* on the mountains;

STRAIGHT (51)
Gn 24:27 me *s* to the house of my master's brother."
Nm 20:17 but we will go *s* along the royal road
21:22 but we will go *s* along the royal road
1Sm 6:12 The cows went *s* for the route to
9:12 The girls answered, "Yes, there *s* ahead.
Neh 12:37 At the Spring Gate they went *s* up by the
Tb 4:19 and ask him to make all your paths *s* and
7:1 Azariah, lead me *s* to our kinsman Raguel."
Ps(s) 5:9 make *s* your way before me.
Prv 2:13 the *s* paths to walk in the way of darkness,
3:6 of him, and he will make *s* your paths.
4:25 Let your eyes look *s* ahead and your glance
9:15 to passers-by as they go on their *s* way:
11:5 The honest man's virtue makes his way *s*,
15:21 the man of understanding goes the *s* way.
Eccl 1:15 What is crooked cannot be made *s*,
7:13 Who can make *s* what he has made crooked?
7:29 God made mankind *s*,
Wis 9:18 were the paths of those on earth made *s*,
Sir 2:6 make *s* your ways and hope in him.
8:15 For he will go his own way *s*,
Is 40:3 *s* in the wasteland a highway for our God!
42:16 light before them, and make crooked ways *s*.
Jer 31:39 *s* to the hill Gareb and then turn to Goah.
Ez 1:7 and four wings, and their legs went *s* down;
1:9 went *s* forward [Each went straight forward;
1:12 went straight forward [Each went *s* forward;
1:22 crystal, stretched *s* out above their heads.
10:11 *s* towards it without veering as they moved.
10:22 each one went *s* forward.
Hos 14:10 *S* are the paths of the LORD,
Mt 3:3 the way of the Lord, make *s* his paths.'"
21:2 "Go into the village *s* ahead of you and
Mk 1:3 the way of the Lord, clear him a *s* path.'"
11:2 "Go to the village *s* ahead of you,
Lk 1:76 before the Lord to prepare *s* paths for him,
3:4 the way of the Lord, Clear him a *s* path.
3:5 shall be made *s* And the rough ways smooth,
4:30 went *s* through their midst and walked away.
13:13 she stood up *s* and began thanking God.
19:30 "Go into the village *s* ahead of you.
Jn 1:23 Make *s* the way of the Lord!'"
Acts 9:11 Lord said to him, "Go at once to *S* Street,
13:10 to make crooked the *s* paths of the Lord?
16:11 Troas and set a course *s* for Samothrace,
21:1 we put out to sea and sailed *s* to Cos.
1Thes 3:11 Lord Jesus make our path to you a *s* one!
2Thes 3:6 any brother who wanders from the *s* path
2Tm 2:15 a *s* course in preaching the truth.
Heb 12:13 Make *s* the paths you walk on,
2Pt 2:15 They have abandoned the *s* road and wander

STRAIGHTEN (1)
Mt 28:14 we will *s* it out with him and keep you out

STRAIGHTENED (2)
Jn 8:7 questioning, he *s* up and said to them,
8:10 Jesus finally *s* up and said to her,

STRAIGHTFORWARD (5)
Prv 4:11 wisdom I direct you, I lead you on *s* paths.
Is 57:2 rest on his couch for the sincere, *s* man.
Gal 2:14 not being *s* about the truth of the gospel,
Phil 2:15 prove yourselves innocent and *s*,
1Tm 3:8 the same way, deacons must be serious, *s*,

STRAIGHTWAY (1)
Wis 5:12 the parted air *s* flows together again so

STRAIN (4)
Ex 18:23 orders you will be able to stand the *s*,
Ps(s) 119:82 My eyes *s* after your promise;
119:123 My eyes *s* after your salvation and your
Mt 23:24 You *s* out the gnat and swallow the camel!

STRAINS (2)
Jgs 5:11 them to the *s* of the harpers at the wells,
Sir 50:18 over the throng sweet *s* of praise resound.

STRAITS (13)
Dt 28:55 nothing else is left him in the *s* of the siege
28:57 in the *s* of the siege to which your enemy
1Sm 28:15 "I am in great *s*,
2Sm 13:2 He was in such *s* over his sister Tamar
1Chr 21:13 "I am in dire *s*.
Jb 20:22 to overflowing, he shall be brought into *s*,
Ps(s) 107:6 from their *s* he rescued them.
107:13 from their *s* he rescued them.
107:19 from their *s* he rescued them.
107:28 from their *s* he rescued them.
118:5 In my *s* I called upon the LORD;
Sir 48:2 in his zeal he reduced them to *s*;
Is 38:14 O Lord, I am in *s*; be my surety!

STRAND (1)
Sg 4:3 Your lips are like a scarlet *s*;

STRANGE (47)
Dt 28:36 you will serve *s* gods of wood and stone,
28:64 you will serve *s* gods of wood and stone,
29:27 their soil and cast them out into a *s* land,
31:16 rendering wanton worship to the *s* gods
32:12 was their leader, no *s* god was with him.
32:16 They provoked him with *s* gods and angered
Jos 24:20 you, you forsake the LORD and serve *s* gods,
24:23 put away the *s* gods that are among you and
1Sm 8:8 day, deserting me and worshiping *s* gods,
1Kgs 9:6 and proceed to venerate and worship *s* gods,
9:9 *s* gods which they worshiped and served.
11:4 his wives had turned his heart to *s* gods,
11:10 him this very act of following *s* gods,
14:9 *s* gods and molten images to provoke me;
2Chr 7:19 you proceed to venerate and worship *s* gods,
7:22 *s* gods and worshiped them and served them.
Ps(s) 44:21 God and stretched out our hands to a *s* god,
81:10 There shall be no *s* god among you nor
Prv 23:33 Your eyes behold *s* sights,
Wis 14:18 observance among those to whom it was *s*,
Sir 9:3 Be not intimate with a *s* woman,
11:4 For *s* are the works of the LORD,
Is 28:11 with stammering lips and in a *s* language
28:21 work, to perform his deed, his *s* deed.
43:12 I made it known, not any *s* god among you;
Jer 1:16 to *s* gods and adoring their own handiwork.
5:19 me to serve *s* gods in your own land,
7:6 place, or follow *s* gods to your own harm,
7:9 to Baal, go after *s* gods that you know not,
7:18 poured out to *s* gods in order to hurt me.
11:10 They also have followed and served *s* gods;
13:10 and follow *s* gods to serve and adore them,
16:11 me, says the LORD, and followed *s* gods,
16:13 there you can serve *s* gods day and night,
19:4 by burning in it incense to *s* gods
19:13 heaven and poured out libations to *s* gods.

22: 9 God, by worshiping and serving *s* gods."
25: 6 not follow *s* gods to serve and adore them,
32:29 out to *s* gods as a provocation to me.
35:15 and not follow *s* gods or serve them,
44: 3 they did to provoke me, going after *s* gods,
44: 5 from the evil of sacrificing to *s* gods.
44: 8 by sacrificing to *s* gods here in the land
44:15 their wives were burning incense to *s* gods,
1Cor 14:21 "In *s* tongues and in alien speech I will
Heb 13: 9 be carried away by all kinds of *s* teaching.
1Pt 1:17 reverently during your sojourn in a *s* land.

STRANGER (26)

Ex 2:22 for he said, "I am a *s* in a foreign land."
18: 3 for he said, "I am a *s* in a foreign land."
Jos 8:33 And all Israel, *s* and native alike,
20: 9 cities to which any Israelite or *s* living
Tb 4:12 a *s* who is not of your father's tribe,
1Mc 1:38 She became a *s* to her own offspring,
Jb 19:15 Even my handmaids treat me as a *s*;
29:16 the rights of the *s* I studied,
31:32 Because no *s* lodged in the street,
Ps(s) 69: 9 to my brothers, a *s* to my mother's sons,
94: 6 Widow and *s* they slay,
Prv 27:13 for another, and for the sake of a *s*,
Eccl 6: 2 to partake of them, but a *s* devours them.
Sir 4:17 She walks with him as a *s*,
8:18 a *s* do nothing that should be kept secret,
11:34 Lodge a *s* with you,
11:34 and make a *s* of you to your own household.
14: 4 and in his possessions a *s* will revel.
23:22 husband and offers as heir her son by a *s*.
29:26 "Come here, *s*, set the table,
29:27 Away, *s*, for one more worthy;
Jer 14: 8 Why should you be a *s* in this land,
Mal 3: 5 those who turn aside the *s*,
Mt 25:35 I was a *s* and you welcomed me,
Jn 10: 5 They will not follow a *s*;
Gal 4:27 song, you *s* to the pains of childbirth!

STRANGERS (39)

Jos 8:35 and the *s* who had accompanied Israel.
2Sm 1:20 rejoice, lest the daughters of the *s* exult!
1Chr 16:19 were few in number, a handful, and *s* there,
1Mc 1:38 fled away, and she became the abode of *s*.
2: 7 and the sanctuary into the hands of *s*?
12:10 so as not to become *s* to you altogether;
Ps(s) 105:12 were few in number, a handful, and *s* there,
109:11 and *s* plunder the fruit of his labors.
146: 9 The LORD protects *s*;
Prv 5:10 Lest *s* have their fill of your wealth,
5:17 be yours alone, not one shared with *s*;
20:16 surety for another, and for *s* yield it up!
Wis 19:15 theirs since they received *s* unwillingly!
Sir 29:22 roof than sumptuous banquets among *s*.
Is 1: 7 land before your eyes *s* devour [a waste,
2: 6 they covenant with *s*.
61: 5 *S* shall stand ready to pasture your flocks,
Jer 2:25 I love these *s*, and after them I must go."
3:13 How you ran hither and yon to *s* [under
5:19 shall you serve *s* in a land not your own."
6:12 Their houses will fall to *s*,
8:10 Therefore, I will give their wives to *s*,
30: 8 *S* shall no longer enslave them;
51:51 *s* have entered the holy places of the
Lam 5: 2 inherited lands have been turned over to *s*,
Hos 7: 9 *S* have sapped his strength,
8: 7 Even if it could, *s* would swallow it.
8:12 ordinances, they are considered as a *s*.
Jl 4:17 holy, and *s* shall pass through her no more.
Ob 1:11 *s* entered his gates and cast lots over
Jn 10: 5 because they do not recognize a *s* voice."
Acts 7: 6 posterity will be *s* in a foreign land,
Eph 2:12 You were *s* to the covenant and its promise;
2:19 means that you are *s* and aliens no longer.
1Tm 5:10 Has she been hospitable to *s*?
Heb 11:13 to be *s* and foreigners on the earth,
1Pt 1: 1 who live as *s* scattered throughout Pontus,
2:11 Beloved, you are *s* and in exile;
3Jn 1: 5 for the brothers even though they are *s*;

STRANGLED (5)

Tb 2: 3 in the market place where he was just *s*!"
Na 2:13 for his cubs, and *s* for his lionesses;
Acts 15:20 sexual union, from the meat of *s* animals,
15:29 from blood, from the meat of *s* animals,
21:25 to idols, blood, the flesh of *s* animals,

STRANGLES (1)

Tb 3: 8 "You are the one who *s* your husbands!

STRAP (4)

Gn 14:23 or a sandal *s* from anything that is yours,
1Kgs 6:34 each door was banded by a metal *s*,
Lk 3:16 I am not fit to loosen his sandal *s*.
Jn 1:27 the *s* of whose sandal I am not worthy to

STRAPS (9)

Ex 28: 7 of shoulder *s* joined to its two upper ends.
28:12 Set these two stones on the shoulder *s* of
28:25 attached to the shoulder *s* of the ephod.
28:27 bottom of the shoulder *s* next to where
39: 4 Shoulder *s* were made for it and joined to
39: 7 These stones were set on the shoulder *s* of
39:18 attached to the shoulder *s* of the ephod.
39:20 two shoulder *s* next to where they joined
Mk 1: 7 not fit to stoop and untie his sandal *s*.

STRATAGEM (3)

2Mc 1:13 a deceitful *s* employed by Nanea's priests.
13:18 tried to take their positions by a *s*.
14:29 opportunity to carry out this order by a *s*.

STRATEGIC (2)

2Mc 8: 6 He captured *s* positions,
15:20 their elephants placed in *s* positions,

STRATEGY (4)

2Kgs 18:20 words substitute for *s* and might in war?
Jdt 11: 8 and distinguished in military *s*.
Is 36: 5 words substitute for *s* and might in war?
Mt 28:12 with the elders and worked out their *s*,

STRAW (20)

Gn 24:25 is plenty of *s* and fodder at our place,"
24:32 unloaded and provided with *s* and fodder,
Ex 5: 7 Let them go and gather *s* themselves!
5: 7 shall no longer supply the people with *s*
5:10 I will not provide you with *s*.
5:11 Go and gather the *s* yourselves,
5:12 the land of Egypt to gather stubble for *s*,
5:13 daily amount as when your *s* was supplied."
5:16 No *s* is supplied to your servants,
5:18 *S* shall not be provided for you,
Jgs 19:19 We have *s* and fodder for our asses,
1Kgs 5: 8 of barley and *s* to the required place.
Jb 13:25 a wind-driven leaf, or pursue a withered *s*?
21:18 Let them be like *s* before the wind,
41:19 He regards iron as *s*,
Is 25:10 down as a *s* is trodden down in the mire.
40:24 and the stormwind carries them away like *s*.
41: 2 them to dust, with his bow, to driven *s*.
Jer 23:28 What has *s* to do with the wheat?
1Cor 3:12 silver, precious stones, wood, hay or *s*,

STRAWS (1)

Jb 41:20 slingstones used against him are but *s*.

STRAY (14)

Lv 19: 9 nor shall you glean the *s* ears of grain.
23:22 shall you glean the *s* ears of your grain.
Jgs 2:17 to *s* from the way their fathers had taken,
Tb 5:14 No, they did not *s* from the right path;
Ps(s) 40: 5 idolatry or to those who *s* after falsehood.
119:10 let me not *s* from your commands.
119:118 You despise all who *s* from your statutes,
Jer 4: 1 things out of my sight, and do not *s*,
31:22 How long will you continue to *s*,
50:17 A *s* sheep was Israel that lions pursued;
Bar 4:28 hearts have been disposed to *s* from God,
Ez 14:11 house of Israel may no longer *s* from me
48:11 who fulfilled my service and did not *s*
Mt 18:12 out on the hills and go in search of the *s*?

STRAYED (8)

Ps(s) 119:110 me, but from your precepts I have not *s*.
Wis 5: 6 We, then, have *s* from the way of truth,
Ez 34: 4 did not bring back the *s* nor seek the lost,
34:16 I will seek out, the *s* I will bring back,
44:10 Israel *s* from me to pursue their idols,
44:15 my sanctuary when the Israelites *s* from me,
Hos 7:13 Woe to them, they have *s* from me!
1Tm 6:10 their passion for it have *s* from the faith,

STRAYING (3)

Jos 23: 6 the law of Moses, not *s* from it in anyway,
Jas 5:19 among you of someone *s* from the truth,
1Pt 2:25 At one time you were *s* like sheep,

STRAYS (3)

Prv 21:16 The man who *s* from the way of good sense
Sir 19: 4 who *s* after them sins against his own life.
Zec 11:16 note of those that perish, nor seek the *s*,

STREAKED (7)

Gn 30:35 That same day Laban removed the *s* and
30:39 by the rods, and so they brought forth *s*,
30:40 *s* or fully dark-colored animals of Laban.
31: 8 said, 'The *s* animals shall be your wages,'
31: 8 the entire flock would bear *s* young.
31:10 in which I saw mating he-goats that were *s*,
31:12 in the flock, as they mate, are *s*,

STREAKS (1)

2Pt 1:19 dark place until the first *s* of dawn appear

STREAM (35)

Gn 2: 6 but a *s* was welling up out of the earth
32:24 *s* and had brought over all his possessions,
Nm 24: 6 They are like gardens beside a *s*,
Dt 21: 4 down to a wadi with an everflowing *s*
Jos 13: 3 (from the *s* adjoining Egypt to the boundary
1Kgs 17: 4 You shall drink of the *s*,
17: 6 in the evening, and he drank from the *s*.
2Chr 32: 4 also the running *s* in the valley nearby.
1Mc 5:37 Raphon, on the other side of the *s*.
5:39 to help them, and have camped beyond the *s*,
5:40 his army were approaching the running *s*,
5:42 But when Judas reached the running *s*,
5:42 beside the *s* and gave them this order:
16: 5 and between the two armies was a *s*.
16: 6 that his men were afraid to cross the *s*,
Jb 14:11 a lake fail, or a *s* grows dry and parches,
Ps(s) 36: 9 your delightful *s* you give them to drink.
46: 5 a *s* whose runlets gladden the city of God,
105:41 it flowed through the dry lands like a *s*,
Prv 21: 1 Like a *s* is the king's heart in the hand
Sir 4:25 and struggle not against the rushing *s*.
24:28 Now I, like a rivulet from her *s*,
24:29 mine became a river, then this *s* of mine,
35:15 Do not the tears that *s* down her cheek cry
40:13 like a mighty *s* with lightning and thunder,
50: 8 like a lily on the banks of a *s*;
Is 2: 2 All nations shall *s* toward it;
30:33 breath of the LORD, like a *s* of sulphur,
32:20 Happy are you who sow beside every *s*,
Jer 14:17 Let my eyes *s* with tears day and night,
17: 8 that stretches out its roots to the *s*:
51:44 peoples shall *s* to him no more.
Dn 7:10 surging *s* of fire flowed out from
Am 5:24 water, and goodness like an unfailing *s*.
Mi 4: 1 above the hills, And peoples shall *s* to it:

STREAMING (3)

Sg 4: 1 of goats *s* down the mountains of Gilead.
6: 5 like a flock of goats *s* down from Gilead.
Jer 31:12 they shall come *s* to the LORD's blessings:

STREAMLETS (1)

Is 11:15 fierce anger And shatter it into seven *s*,

STREAMS (37)

Ex 7:19 their *s* and canals and pools,
8: 1 your staff over the *s* and canals and pools,
Dt 8: 7 a good country, a land with *s* of water,
1Kgs 18: 5 to all sources of water and to all the *s*.
Jb 12:21 He breaks down the barriers of the *s* and
20:17 He shall see no *s* of oil,
28:11 He probes the wellsprings of the *s*,
29: 6 milk, and the rock flowed with *s* of oil;
37:17 whom the *s* of water fail when a calm from
Ps(s) 78:16 He made *s* flow from the crag and brought
78:20 waters gushed forth, and the *s* overflowed;
78:44 of Zoan, And changed into blood their *s*—
119:136 My eyes shed *s* of tears because your law
137: 1 By the *s* of Babylon we sat and wept when
Prv 5:16 abroad, *s* of water in the streets?
Wis 5:22 them and the *s* shall abruptly overflow;
Is 7:18 the fly that is in the farthest *s* of Egypt,
19: 6 Its *s* shall become foul,
30:25 hill there will be *s* of running water.
32: 2 will be like *s* of water in a dry country,
33:21 and wide *s* on which no boat is rowed,
34: 9 Edom's *s* shall be changed into pitch and
35: 6 *S* will burst forth in the desert,
44: 3 thirsty ground, and *s* upon the dry land;
47: 2 train, bare your legs, pass through the *s*.
Lam 3:48 My eyes run with *s* of water over the
Ez 31: 4 its *s* to all the trees of the field.
31:15 *s* so that the deep waters were held back.
32: 2 a monster in the sea, spouting in your *s*,
32: 2 water with your feet and churning its *s*.
32:14 waters clear, and their *s* flow like oil,
Jl 1:20 For the *s* of water are dried up,
Mi 6: 7 thousands of rams, with myriad *s* of oil?
Na 3: 8 than No-amon that was set among the *s*,
Hb 3: 8 Is your anger against the *s*, O LORD?
3: 8 Is your wrath against the *s*,
3: 9 Into *s* you split the earth;

STREET (24)

Dt 32:25 "Snatched away by the sword in the *s* and
Tb 2: 4 from the *s* and put him in one of the rooms,
Jb 31:32 Because no stranger lodged in the *s*,
Prv 1:20 Wisdom cries aloud in the *s*,
7: 8 sense, Going along the *s* near the corner,
26:13 sluggard says, "There is a lion in the *s*,
Eccl 10: 3 When the fool walks through the *s*,
12: 4 When the doors to the *s* are shut,
12: 5 one fears heights, and perils in the *s*;
Is 42: 2 not making his voice heard in the *s*.
51:20 at every *s* corner like antelopes in a net.
51:23 the ground, like the *s* for them to walk on.
Jer 6:11 I will pour it out upon the child in the *s*,
6:25 forth into the field, step not into the *s*,
9:20 It cuts down the children in the *s*,

STREET (cont.)

Lam 2:19 faint from hunger at the corner of every *s.*
4: 1 sacred stones lie strewn at every *s* corner!
Ez 16:25 At every *s* corner you built a dais for
16:31 building your platform at every *s* corner
Am 5:16 lamentation, and in every *s* they shall cry,
Na 3:10 dashed to pieces at the corner of every *s;*
Mt 6: 5 or on *s* corners in order to be noticed.
Mk 11: 4 a colt tethered out on the *s* near a gate,
Acts 9:11 said to him, "Go at once to Straight *S,*

STREETS (68)

2Sm 1:20 Gath, herald it not in the *s* of Ashkelon,
22:43 like the mud in the *s* I trampled them down.
Tb 13:17 The *s* of Jerusalem shall be paved with
Jdt 7:14 will be laid low in the *s* of their city.
7:22 in the *s* and gateways of the city,
1Mc 1:55 at the doors of houses and in the *s.*
2: 9 Her infants have been murdered in her *s,*
11:46 control of the main *s* and began to fight.
2Mc 3:19 below their breasts, filled the *s;*
Ps(s) 18:43 like the mud in the *s* I trampled them down.
55:12 and fraud never depart from its *s.*
144:14 in the walls, no exile, no outcry in our *s.*
Prv 5:16 abroad, streams of water in the *s?*
7:12 Now she is in the *s,*
22:13 in the *s* I might be slain."
Eccl 12: 5 lasting home, and mourners go about the *s;*
Sg 3: 2 in the *s* and crossings I will seek Him
Sir 23:21 man will be punished in the *s* of the city;
49: 6 the holy city and left its *s* desolate,
Is 5:25 corpses shall be like refuse in the *s.*
10: 6 and tread them down like the mud of the *s.*
15: 3 In the *s* they wear sackcloth,
24:11 In the *s* they cry out for lack of wine;
33: 7 See, the men of Ariel cry out in the *s,*
Jer 2:28 And as many as the *s* of Jerusalem are the
5: 1 Roam the *s* of Jerusalem,
7:17 the cities of Judah, in the *s* of Jerusalem?
7:34 In the cities of Judah and in the *s* of
11: 6 cities of Judah and in the *s* of Jerusalem:
11:13 And as many as the *s* of Jerusalem are the
14:16 the *s* of Jerusalem by famine and the sword.
33:10 the *s* of Jerusalem that are now deserted,
44: 6 the cities of Judah and the *s* of Jerusalem,
44: 9 the land of Judah and the *s* of Jerusalem?
44:17 the cities of Judah and the *s* of Jerusalem.
44:21 the cities of Judah and the *s* of Jerusalem:
49:26 But now her young men shall fall in her *s,*
50:30 her young men shall fall in her *s,*
51: 4 land of Chaldea, the transfixed, in her *s;*
Lam 1:20 In the *s* the sword bereaves,
2:12 away like the wounded in the *s* of the city,
2:21 in the dust of the *s* lie young and old;
4: 5 accustomed to dainty food perish in the *s;*
4: 8 than soot, they are unrecognized on the *s;*
4:14 They staggered blindly in the *s,*
4:18 steps so that we could not walk in our *s;*
Bar 2:23 from the *s* of Jerusalem The sounds of joy
Ez 7:19 They shall fling their silver into the *s,*
11: 6 city and have filled its *s* with your slain.
26:11 of his horses he shall trample all your *s;*
28:23 pestilence, and blood shall flow in its *s.*
Dn 9:25 it shall be rebuilt, With *s* and trenches,
Mi 7:10 trampled underfoot, like the mire in the *s.*
Na 2: 5 through the *s* And wheel in the squares,
Zep 3: 6 I have made their *s* deserted,
Zec 8: 4 age, shall again sit in the *s* of Jerusalem.
8: 5 with boys and girls playing in her *s.*
9: 3 like dust, and gold like the mire of the *s.*
10: 5 trampling the mire of the *s* in battle;
Mt 6: 2 and *s* like hypocrites looking for applause.
12:19 out, nor will his voice be heard in the *s.*
Lk 10:10 do not welcome you, go into its *s* and say,
13:26 You taught in our *s.'*
14:21 'Go out quickly into the *s* and alleys of
Acts 5:15 the *s* and laid them on cots and mattresses,
Rv 11: 8 will lie in the *s* of the great city,
21:21 and the *s* of the city were of pure gold,
22: 2 Lamb and flowed down the middle of the *s.*

STRENGTH (239)

Gn 48: 2 you," he rallied his *s* and sat up in bed.
49: 3 my *s* and the first fruit of my manhood,
Ex 15: 2 My *s* and my courage is the LORD,
15:13 *s* you guided them to your holy dwelling.
Lv 26:20 so that your *s* will be spent in vain;
Dt 6: 5 with all your soul, and with all your *s.*
8:17 'It is my own power and the *s* of my own
32:36 When he sees their *s* failing,
33:25 may your *s* endure through all your days!"
Jos 17:18 if, despite their *s* and iron chariots,
Jgs 5:12 *S!* arise, Barak,
6:14 "Go with the *s* you have and save Israel
8:21 us yourself, for a man's *s* is like the man."
16: 5 and find out the secret of his great *s,*
16: 6 "Tell me the secret of your great *s*
16: 9 and the secret of his *s* remained unknown.
16:15 and not told me the secret of your great *s!"*
16:17 If I am shaved, my *s* will leave me,
16:19 to mistreat him, for his *s* had left him.
1Sm 2: 4 are broken, while the tottering gird on *s.*
2: 9 For not by *s* does man prevail;
2:10 the earth, Now may he give *s* to his king,
2:31 *s* and the strength of your father's family,
28:20 Moreover, he had no bodily *s* left,
28:22 you may have *s* when you go on your way."
2Sm 6: 5 merry before the LORD with all their *s,*
15:12 So the conspiracy gained *s,*
22:33 girded me with *s* and kept my way unerring;
22:40 "You girded me with *s* for war;
2Kgs 19: 3 but there is no *s* to bring them forth.
23:25 heart, his whole soul, and his whole *s,*
1Chr 16:11 Look to the LORD in his *s;*
29:12 it is yours to give grandeur and *s* to all.
2Chr 30:21 of the LORD day after day with all their *s.*
Neh 4: 4 "Slackened is the bearers' *s,*
8:10 for rejoicing in the LORD must be your *s!"*
Tb 14: 9 his name sincerely and with all their *s.*
Jdt 2:12 For as I live, and by the *s* of my kingdom,
4:15 they cried to the Lord with all their *s*
5: 3 In what does their power and *s* consist?
7:22 of the city, with no *s* left in them.
9: 8 "Shatter their *s* in your might,
9:11 "Your *s* is not in numbers,
11: 7 the birds of the air, because of your *s,*
13:11 Once more he has made manifest his *s* in
Est C:11 Israel, too, cried out with all their *s,*
1Mc 2:61 that none who hope in him shall fail in *s.*
3:19 the army, but on *s* that comes from Heaven.
4:32 with fear, weaken the boldness of their *s,*
6:47 When the Jews saw the *s* of the royal army
7:25 Judas and his followers were gaining *s*
10:71 and let us test each other's *s* there;
2Mc 10:34 inside, relying on the *s* of the place,
12:14 Relying on the *s* of their walls and their
12:35 cloak and dragged him along by main *s,*
Jb 6:11 What *s* have I that I should endure?
6:12 Have I the *s* of stones,
9: 4 God is wise in heart and mighty in *s;*
9:19 If it be a question of *s,* he is mighty;
12:16 With him are *s* and prudence;
17: 9 and he who has clean hands increase in *s.*
24:23 He sustains the mighty by his *s,*
26: 2 to the powerless, what *s* to the feeble arm!
30: 2 Such *s* as they had, to me meant nought;
39:11 *s* and leave to him the fruits of your toil?
39:19 Do you give the horse his *s,*
40:16 Behold the *s* in his loins,
41: 4 I need hardly mention his limbs, his *s,*
41:14 *S* abides in his neck,
Ps(s) 10:15 the *s* of the wicked and of the evildoer;
18: 2 I love you, O LORD, my *s,*
18:33 girded me with *s* and kept my way unerring;
18:40 And you girded me with *s* for war;
20: 7 with the *s* of his victorious right hand.
21: 2 I O Lord, in your *s* the king is glad;
21:14 Be extolled, O LORD, in your *s!*
28: 7 the LORD is my *s* and my shield.
28: 8 The LORD is the *s* of his people,
29:11 May the LORD give *s* to his people;
30: 8 will you had endowed me with majesty and *s:*
31:11 My *s* has failed through affliction,
32: 4 my *s* was dried up as by the heat of summer.
33:16 nor is a warrior delivered by great *s.*
33:17 great though its *s,*
38: 5 they are like a heavy burden, beyond my *s.*
38:11 my *s* forsakes me;
43: 2 For you, O God, are my *s.*
46: 2 God is our refuge and our *s,*
52: 9 man who made not God the source of his *s,*
52: 9 great wealth, and his *s* in harmful plots."
59:10 O my *s!*
59:17 your *s* and revel at dawn in your kindness;
59:18 O my *s!*
61: 4 my refuge, a tower of *s* against the enemy.
62: 8 and my glory, he is the rock of my *s;*
66: 3 your great *s* your enemies fawn upon you.
68:36 he gives power and *s* to his people.
69: 5 *s* are they who wrongfully are my enemies.
71: 6 from my mother's womb you are my *s;*
71: 9 as my *s* fails, forsake me not,
71:18 your *s* to every generation that is to come.
78: 4 and his *s* and the wonders that he wrought.
78:61 And he surrendered his *s* into captivity,
81: 2 Sing joyfully to God our *s;*
84: 6 Happy the men whose *s* you are!
84: 8 They go from strength to *s;*
86:16 give your *s* to your servant,
88: 5 I am a man without *s.*
89:18 For you are the splendor of their *s,*
93: 1 robed is the LORD and girt about with *s,*
102:24 He has broken down my *s* in the way;
103:20 LORD, all you his angels, you mighty in *s,*
105: 4 Look to the LORD in his *s;*
118:14 My *s* and my courage is the LORD,
138: 3 you built up *s* within me.
140: 8 O GOD, my Lord, my *s* and my salvation;
147:10 In the *s* of the steed he delights not,
150: 1 praise him in the firmament of his *s.*
Prv 8:14 Mine is *s;* I am understanding.
11: 7 what is expected from *s* comes to nought.
14: 4 large crops come through the *s* of the bull.
20:29 The glory of young men is their *s,*
24:10 of adversity, your *s* will depart from you.
31: 3 women, nor your *s* to those who ruin kings.
31:17 She is girt about with *s,*
31:25 She is clothed with *s* and dignity,
Wis 2:11 But let our *s* be our norm of justice;
11:21 For with you great *s* abides always;
14:16 practice gained *s* and was observed as law,
16:19 fire blazed beyond its *s* so as to consume
16:23 be nourished, forgot even its proper *s;*
18:22 overcame the bitterness not by bodily *s,*
19:20 Fire in water maintained its own *s,*
Sir 3:13 revile him not in the fullness of your *s.*
3:20 not, into things beyond your *s* search not.
5: 2 *s* in following the desires of your heart.
6: 2 lest, like fire, it consume your *s;*
6:27 with all your *s* keep her ways.
7: 6 judge if you have not *s* to root out crime,
7:30 With all your *s,* love your Creator,
11:12 a failure, with little *s* and great misery
15:20 to sin, to none does he give *s* for lies.
17: 3 He endows man with a *s* of his own,
19:24 his lack of *s* keeps him from sinning,
28:10 The greater a man's *s,*
31:25 not wine-drinking be the proof of your *s,*
31:30 it lessens his *s* and multiplies his wounds.
41: 2 sentence to the weak man of failing *s,*
42:17 the *s* to stand firm before his glory.
43:32 Extol him with renewed *s,*
46: 9 And the *s* he gave to Caleb remained with
47: 5 who gave *s* to his right arm To defeat the
47:11 him his sins and exalted his *s* forever;
49:10 Gave new *s* to Jacob and saved him by their
Is 11: 2 spirit of counsel and of *s*
12: 2 My *s* and my courage is the LORD,
17:10 and remembered not the Rock, your *s.*
28: 6 And *s* to those who turn back the battle at
30: 2 They find their *s* in Pharaoh's protection
30:15 saved, in quiet and in trust your *s* lies.
33: 2 Be our *s* every morning,
37: 3 but there is no *s* to bring them forth.
40:26 *s* of his power not one of them is missing!
40:29 He gives *s* to the fainting;
40:31 that hope in the LORD will renew their *s,*
49: 4 and for nothing, uselessly, spent my *s,*
49: 5 sight of the LORD, and my God is now my *s!*
50: 2 Have I not the *s* to deliver?
51: 9 Awake, awake, put on *s,* O arm of the LORD!
52: 1 Put on your *s,* O Zion:
57:10 New *s* you found,
58:11 He will renew your *s,*
63: 1 marching in the greatness of his *s?*
Jer 9:22 wisdom, nor the strong man glory in his *s,*
16:19 O LORD, my *s,* my fortress, my refuge
16:21 them in no doubt Of my *s* and my power:
17: 5 in human beings, who seeks his *s* in flesh,
47: 5 Ashdod, the remnant of their *s,*
48:25 Moab's *s* is broken,
49: 4 Why do you glory in your *s,*
49: 4 you glory in your strength, your ebbing *s,*
51:30 Dried up is their *s,*
Lam 1: 6 gone off without *s* before their captors.
1:14 my neck, he has brought my *s* to its knees;
2: 3 wrath, the horn that was Israel's whole *s;*
Bar 1:12 and that the Lord may give us *s,*
3:14 Learn where prudence is, where *s,*
Ez 7:24 I will put an end to their proud *s,*
21:11 *s* groan bitterly while they look on.
30: 6 fall, and down shall come her proud *s:*
33:28 so that its proud *s* will come to an end,
Dn 2:37 God of heaven has given dominion and *s,*
3:44 shamed and powerless, and their *s* broken;
4:27 Was it not I, with my great *s,*
7: 7 horrible, and of extraordinary *s;*
8:22 issue from his nation, but without his *s.*
10: 8 No *s* remained in me;
10:16 For now no *s* or even breath is left in me."
11:15 picked troops shall have the *s* to resist.
11:17 to penetrate the *s* of his kingdom.
11:25 He shall call on his *s* and cleverness to
Hos 7: 9 Strangers have sapped his *s,*
Am 2:14 and the strong man shall not retain his *s;*
3:11 the land, and strip you of your *s,*
6:13 and say, "Have we not, by our own *s,*
Mi 5: 3 shepherd his flock by the *s* of the LORD,
7:16 be put to shame, in spite of all their *s;*
Na 2: 2 road, gird your loins, marshall all your *s!*
3: 9 Ethiopia was her *s,*
Hb 1:11 this culprit who makes his own *s* his god!
3:19 God, my Lord, is my *s;*
Zec 12: 5 have their *s* in the LORD of hosts,
Mk 12:30 with all your mind, and with all your *s.'*
12:33 with all our thoughts and with all our *s,*
Lk 1:69 *s* for us in the house of David his servant,
2:40 The child grew in size and *s,*
10:27 with all your soul, with all your *s,*
13:11 possessed by a spirit which drained her *s.*
21:36 the *s* to escape whatever is in prospect,
Jn 4:39 on the *s* of the woman's word of testimony:
Acts 9:19 *s* returned to him after he had taken food.
27:34 food, which will give you *s* to survive.
1Cor 10:13 will not let you be tested beyond your *s.*
15:43 Weakness is sown, *s* rises up.
2Cor 1: 8 we were crushed beyond our *s,*
7: 6 gave me *s* with the arrival of Titus.

Eph 1:19 It is like the *s* he showed in raising
6:10 your *s* from the Lord and his mighty power.
Phil 4:13 of my *s* I have strength for everything.
Col 1:11 be endowed with the *s* needed to stand fast,
2Tm 1: 8 but with the *s* which comes from God bear
4:17 the Lord stood by my side and gave me *s*,
1Pt 4:11 is to do it with the *s* provided by God.
2Pt 2:11 though greater than men in *s* and power,
Rv 3: 8 I know that your *s* is limited;
5:12 to receive power and riches, wisdom and *s*,
14:10 poured full *s* into the cup of his anger.

STRENGTHEN (31)

Dt 3:28 Commission Joshua, and encourage and *s* him,
Jgs 16:28 *S* me, O God, this last time
2Sm 11:25 *S* your attack on the city and destroy it.'
Jdt 13: 7 hair of his head, and said, *S* me this day,
1Mc 6:18 trying to harm them and to *s* the Gentiles.
15:39 and to fortify Kedron and *s* its gates,
Jb 16: 5 I could *s* you with talk,
Ps(s) 119:28 *s* me according to your words.
Sg 2: 5 *S* me with raisin cakes,
Is 22:10 Jerusalem, tearing some down to *s* the wall;
35: 3 *S* the hands that are feeble,
41:10 I will *s* you, and help you,
Ez 30:24 I will *s* the arms of the king of Babylon,
34: 4 You did not *s* the weak nor heal the sick
Na 3:14 water for the siege, *s* your fortresses;
Zec 10: 6 I will *s* the house of Judah,
10:12 I will *s* them in the LORD,
Lk 22:32 You in turn must *s* your brothers."
22:43 then appeared to him from heaven to *s* him.
Rom 1:11 with you some spiritual gift to *s* you
14:19 aim to work for peace and to *s* one another.
16:25 Now to him who is able to *s* you in the
1Cor 1: 8 He will *s* you to the end,
Eph 3:16 May he *s* you inwardly through the working
1Thes 3: 2 and so we sent him to *s* and encourage you
3:13 May he *s* your hearts,
2Thes 2:17 and *s* them for every good work and word.
3: 3 *s* you and guard you against the evil one.
Heb 12:12 *s* your drooping hands and your weak knees.
1Pt 5:10 Christ, will himself restore, confirm, *s*,
Rv 3: 2 Wake up, and *s* what remains before it dies.

STRENGTHENED (29)

Jgs 3:12 LORD, who because of this offense *s* Eglon,
1Sm 23:16 to David and *s* his resolve in the LORD.
1Kgs 19: 8 then *s* by that food, he walked forty days
2Chr 1: 1 son of David, *s* his hold on the kingdom,
11:11 Then he *s* the fortifications and put
11:17 *s* the kingdom of Judah and made Rehoboam,
17: 1 him as king and *s* his hold against Israel.
25: 3 After he had *s* his hold on the kingdom,
32: 5 He *s* the Millo of the City of David and
1Mc 9:62 they rebuilt and *s* its fortifications that
12:38 and *s* its fortifications by providing them
13:52 he also *s* the fortifications of the temple
14:14 He *s* all the lowly among his people and
14:37 and he *s* its fortifications for the
Jb 4: 4 you have *s* his faltering knees.
Ps(s) 147:13 For has *s* the bars of your gates;
Sir 45: 2 and the Lord *s* him with fearful powers;
50: 4 brigands and *s* his city against the enemy.
Dn 10:18 like a man touched me again and *s* me,
10:20 said, "Speak, my lord, for you have *s* me."
11: 2 *S* by his riches,
Hos 7:15 Though I trained and *s* their arms,
Acts 3:16 that has *s* the limbs of this man whom you
15:32 *s* the community and gave them reassurance
18:27 he greatly *s* those who through God's favor
Rom 4:20 he was *s* in faith and gave glory to God,
Col 2: 2 I wish their hearts to be *s* and themselves
1Tm 1:12 thank Christ Jesus our Lord, who has *s* me,
Heb 13: 9 It is good to have our hearts *s* by the

STRENGTHENING (4)

2Kgs 15:19 assistance in *s* his hold on the kingdom.
1Mc 10:23 friendship of the Jews and thus *s* himself?
13:33 *s* their fortifications with high towers,
Ps(s) 10:17 *s* their hearts, you pay heed

STRESS (7)

Jb 38:23 hail Which I have reserved for times of *s*,
Ps(s) 32: 6 faithful man pray to you in time of *s*.
Prv 17:17 and a brother is born for the time of *s*.
Sir 40:24 A brother, a helper, for times of *s*;
Mt 24:29 "Immediately after the *s* of that period,
1Cor 7:26 In the present time of *s* it seems good to
2Cor 7: 5 I was under all kinds of *s*—

STRETCH (44)

Ex 3:20 I will *s* out my hand,
7: 5 as I *s* out my hand against Egypt and lead
7:19 *s* out your hand over the waters of Egypt
8: 1 *S* out your hand and your staff over the
8:12 "Tell Aaron to *s* out his staff and strike
9:22 to Moses, *S* out your hand toward the sky,
10:12 *S* out your hand over the land of Egypt,
10:21 to Moses, *S* out your hand toward the sky,
14:26 told Moses, *S* out your hand over the sea,
Nm 22: 1 other side of the Jericho *s* of the Jordan.
26: 3 of Moab along the Jericho *s* of the Jordan,
26:63 of Moab along the Jericho *s* of the Jordan.
31:12 of Moab, along the Jericho *s* of the Jordan.
33:48 of Moab along the Jericho *s* of the Jordan.
33:50 Jericho *s* of the Jordan and said to him:
34:15 side of the Jericho *s* of the Jordan,
35: 1 of Moab beside the Jericho *s* of the Jordan:
36:13 of Moab beside the Jericho *s* of the Jordan.
Jos 8:18 *S* out the javelin in your hand toward Ai,
11: 6 tomorrow I will *s* them slain before Israel.
Jb 11:13 aright and *s* out your hands toward him,
Ps(s) 88:10 to you I *s* out my hands.
110: 2 your power the LORD will *s* forth from Zion:
143: 6 I *s* out my hands to you;
Sir 15:16 to whichever you choose, *s* forth your hand.
Is 25:11 He will *s* forth his hands in Moab as a
28:20 For the bed shall be too short to *s* out in,
Jer 6:12 For I will *s* forth my hand against those
43:10 have sunk, and *s* his canopy over them.
51:25 I will *s* forth my hand against you,
Ez 6:14 I will *s* out my hand against them,
13: 9 But I will *s* out my hand against the
14: 9 I will *s* out my hand against him and root
14:13 I *s* out my hand against it and break its
25: 7 therefore I will *s* out my hand against you.
25:13 I will *s* out my hand against Edom and cut
35: 3 I will *s* out my hand against you and make
Zep 1: 4 I will *s* out my hand against Judah,
2:13 He will *s* out his hand against the north,
Mt 12:13 To the man he said, *S* out your hand."
Mk 3: 5 Then he said to the man, *S* out your hand."
Lk 6:10 all and said to the man, *S* out your hand."
6:17 *s* where there were many of his disciples;
Jn 21:18 you are older you will *s* out your hands,

STRETCHED (59)

Ex 8: 2 *s* out his hand over the waters of Egypt,
8:13 Aaron *s* out his hand,
9:15 For by now I would have *s* out my hand and
9:23 When Moses *s* out his staff toward the sky,
10:13 *s* out his staff over the land of Egypt,
10:22 So Moses *s* out his hand toward the sky,
14:21 Then Moses *s* out his hand over the sea,
14:27 So Moses *s* out his hand over the sea,
15:12 of wonders, when you *s* out your right hand,
Jos 8:18 Joshua *s* out the javelin in his hand
8:26 Joshua kept the javelin in his hand *s* out
Jgs 6:21 LORD *s* out the tip of the staff he held,
2Sm 24:16 But when the angel *s* forth his hand toward
1Kgs 13: 4 *s* forth his hand from the altar and said,
13: 4 the hand he *s* forth against him withered,
17:21 Then he *s* himself out upon the child three
2Kgs 4:34 As Elisha *s* himself over the child,
1Chr 13: 9 Uzzah *s* out his hand to steady the ark,
21:16 sword in his hand *s* out against Jerusalem.
2Chr 6:12 community of Israel and *s* forth his hands.
6:13 Israel and *s* forth his hands toward heaven.
Est 8: 4 king *s* forth the golden scepter to Esther.
2Mc 14:34 priests *s* out their hands toward heaven,
15:21 *s* out his hands toward heaven and called
15:32 arm that had been boastfully *s* out
Jb 15:25 Because he has *s* out his hand against God
38: 5 Who *s* out the measuring line for it?
Ps(s) 44:21 God and *s* out our hands to a strange god,
77: 3 night my hands are *s* out without flagging;
Sir 50:15 High, And had *s* forth his hand for the cup,
Is 14:27 His hand is *s* out; who can turn it back?
42: 5 who created the heavens and *s* them out,
44:24 all things, who alone *s* out the heavens;
45:12 It was my hands that *s* out the heavens;
51:13 who *s* out the heavens and laid the
51:16 of my hand, I, who *s* out the heavens,
65: 2 I have *s* out my hands all the day to a
Jer 10:12 wisdom, and *s* out the heavens by his skill.
15: 6 And so I *s* out my hand to destroy you,
31:39 The measuring line shall be *s* from there
48:32 down to the sea, as far as Jazer they *s*.
51:15 wisdom, and *s* out the heavens by his skill.
Lam 1:10 foe *s* out his hand to all her treasures;
1:17 Zion *s* out her hands,
2: 8 He *s* out the measuring line;
Ez 1:22 crystal, *s* straight out above their heads.
1:23 the firmament their wings were *s* out,
2: 9 It was then I saw a hand *s* out to me,
8: 2 He *s* out what appeared to be a hand and
10: 7 Thereupon its cherub *s* out his hand toward
16:27 Therefore I *s* out my hand against you,
Am 6: 4 of ivory, *s* comfortably on their couches,
Zec 1:16 a measuring line shall be *s* over Jerusalem.
Mt 8: 3 *s* out his hand and touched him and said,
14:31 at once *s* out his hand and caught him.
Mk 1:41 Moved with pity, Jesus *s* out his hand,
Lk 5:13 Jesus *s* out his hand to touch him and said,
Acts 26: 1 Paul *s* out his hand and began his defense.
Rom 10:21 "All day long I *s* out my hands to an

STRETCHER (1)

2Mc 3:27 Men picked him up and laid him on a *s*.

STRETCHES (11)

Dt 25:11 if she *s* out her hand and seizes the
2Chr 6:29 pain, *s* out his hands toward this temple,
Jb 9: 8 He alone *s* out the heavens and treads upon
26: 7 He *s* out the North over empty space,
Is 23:11 His hand he *s* out over the sea,
31: 3 When the LORD *s* forth his hand,
40:22 He *s* out the heavens like a veil,
44:13 The carpenter *s* a line and marks with a
Jer 4:31 Zion gasping, as she *s* forth her hands:
17: 8 waters that *s* out its roots to the stream:
Lk 11:51 Their guilt *s* from the blood of Abel to

STRETCHING (8)

1Kgs 8:22 and *s* forth his hands toward heaven.
8:38 *s* out his hands toward this temple,
Ezr 9: 5 knees, *s* out my hands to the LORD my God.
2Mc 15:15 *S* out his right hand,
Sir 41:18 and of *s* out your elbow when you dine;
Jer 46: 9 your shields, Men of Lud, *s* your bows!"
Ez 25:16 I am *s* out my hand against the Philistines;
Acts 4:30 complete assurance by *s* forth your hand in

STREW (8)

Lam 2:10 They *s* dust on their heads and gird
Ez 5: 2 the final third *s* in the wind,
29:12 the nations and *s* them over foreign lands.
30:23 the nations and *s* them over foreign lands.
30:26 the nations and *s* them over foreign lands.]
43:24 the priests shall *s* salt on them and offer
Mal 2: 3 shoulder and I will *s* dung in your faces,
Rom 3:16 ruin and misery *s* their course.

STREWING (3)

Lv 10: 1 *s* incense on the fire they had put in
2Sm 17:19 *s* ground grain on the cover so that
Ez 27:30 bitter cries, *S* dust on their heads,

STREWN (11)

1Kgs 13: 3 up and the ashes on it shall be *s* about."
13: 5 up and the ashes from it were *s* about
2Kgs 7:15 and the whole route was *s* with garments
2Chr 34: 4 which was *s* over the tombs of those who
Jdt 4:11 building, with ashes *s* on their heads,
9: 1 down prostrate, with ashes *s* upon her head,
1Mc 7:17 "The flesh of your saints they have *s*,
Ps(s) 141: 7 are *s* by the edge of the nether world.
Jer 25:33 *s* from one end of the earth to the other.
Lam 4: 1 sacred stones lie *s* at every street corner!
Am 8: 3 Many shall be the corpses, *s* everywhere

STREWS (1)

Ps(s) 147:16 frost he *s* like ashes.

STRICKEN (16)

Lv 13: 4 shall quarantine the *s* man for seven days.
13: 9 "When someone is *s* with leprosy,
13:12 the skin of the *s* man from head to foot,
13:13 body, he shall declare the *s* man clean;
13:17 white, he shall declare the *s* man clean,
13:22 shall declare him unclean; the man is *s*.
13:25 declare him unclean and *s* with leprosy.
13:27 declare the man unclean and *s* with leprosy.
22: 4 descendant of Aaron who is *s* with leprosy,
Tb 12:16 *S* with fear, the two men fell
Ps(s) 107:17 *S* because of their wicked ways and
Wis 17:15 and partly *s* by their soul's surrender;
Is 16: 7 of Kir-hareseth they sigh *s* with grief
53: 4 he endured, While we thought of him as *s*,
Jer 14: 4 cover their heads because of the *s* soil;
Hos 9:16 Ephraim is *s*, their root is dried up;

STRICT (12)

Dt 23:22 your God, is *s* in requiring it of you.
1Sm 14:28 father put the people under a *s* oath,
1Kgs 7: 4 at either end, with windows in *s* alignment.
Ezr 7:26 king, let *s* judgment be executed upon him,
Sir 26:10 Keep a *s* watch over an unruly wife,
Is 8:21 there shall be *s* darkness without any dawn;
Jer 19: 9 eat one another's flesh during the *s* siege
Ez 40: 4 *s* attention to all that I will show you,
44: 5 Son of man, pay *s* attention,
Mk 8:30 them *s* orders not to tell anyone about him.
Acts 5:28 you *s* orders not to teach about that name,
2Thes 1: 6 even if *s* justice would require that God

STRICTER (1)

Jas 3: 1 who do so will be called to the *s* account.

STRICTEST (1)

Acts 26: 5 as a Pharisee, the *s* sect of our religion.

STRICTLY (11)

Gn 43: 3 "The man *s* warned us.
Nm 8:16 the Israelites, are *s* dedicated to me;
Dt 4:15 Be *s* on your guard,
2Mc 3: 1 laws were *s* observed because of the piety
Mt 16:20 Then he *s* ordered his disciples not to

STRICTLY (cont.)

Mk 5:43 them *s* not to let anyone know about it,
7:36 Then he enjoined them *s* not to tell anyone;
9: 9 he *s* enjoined them not to tell anyone what
Lk 9:21 He *s* forbade them to tell this to anyone.
Acts 15:28 burden beyond that which is *s* necessary,
22: 3 was educated *s* in the law of our fathers.

STRIDE (4)

Dt 33:29 fawn upon you, as you *s* upon their heights."
2Sm 22:37 unwavering was my *s*.
Ps(s) 18:37 unwavering was my *s*.
Prv 30:29 Three things are stately in their *s*,

STRIDES (1)

Am 4:13 and *s* upon the heights of the earth:

STRIFE (25)

Gn 13: 8 "Let there be no *s* between you and me,
2Sm 22:44 "You rescued me from the *s* of my people;
Ps(s) 18:44 You rescued me from the *s* of the people;
31:21 within your abode from the *s* of tongues.
55:10 for in the city I see violence and *s*;
78:49 his fierce anger, wrath and fury and *s*,
Prv 15:18 An ill-tempered man stirs up *s*,
17: 1 peace than a house full of feasting with *s*.
17:14 start of *s* is like the opening of a dam;
17:19 He who loves *s* loves guilt;
18: 6 The fool's lips lead him into *s*,
20: 3 It is honorable for a man to shun *s*,
22:10 *s* and insult cease.
23:29 Who have *s*?
26:20 when there is no talebearer, *s* subsides.
26:21 such is a contentious man in enkindling *s*.
Sir 11: 9 in the *s* of the arrogant take no part.
28: 8 Avoid *s* and your sins will be fewer,
31:29 disgrace is wine drunk amid anger and *s*.
40: 5 and dread, terror of death, fury and *s*.
Jer 15:10 a man of *s* and contention to all the land!
Hb 1: 3 there is *s*, and clamorous discord.
Mt 12:25 torn by *s* is headed for its downfall.
Mk 3:24 If a kingdom is torn by civil *s*,
Jas 3:16 Where there are jealousy and *s*,

STRIKE (95)

Gn 3:15 He will *s* at your head,
3:15 at your head, while you *s* at his heel."
8:21 will I ever again *s* down all living beings,
32:12 I fear that when he comes he will *s* me
Ex 7:17 I will *s* the water of the river with the
8:12 out his staff and *s* the dust of the earth,
12:13 thus, when I *s* the land of Egypt,
12:23 come into your houses to *s* you down.
17: 6 *S* the rock, and the water will flow
32:32 *s* me out of the book that you have written."
32:33 sinned against me will I *s* out of my book.
Nm 1:53 God's wrath will *s* the Israelite community.
8:19 so that no plague may *s* among the
14:12 *s* them with pestilence and wipe them out.
34:11 shall *s* the ridge on the east side of Sea
Dt 19: 6 homicide and overtake him and *s* him dead,
28:22 The LORD will *s* you with wasting and fever,
28:27 *s* you with Egyptian boils and with tumors,
28:28 And the LORD will *s* you with madness,
28:35 The LORD will *s* you with malignant boils
Jgs 5:12 awake, awake, *s* up a song.
1Sm 17:35 me, I would seize it by the jaw, *s* it,
17:46 I will *s* you down and cut off your head.
18:17 let the Philistines *s* him."
18:21 for him, so that the Philistines may *s* him."
20:33 At this Saul brandished his spear to *s* him,
22:17 lift a hand to *s* the priests of the LORD.
26:10 must be the LORD himself who will *s* him,
2Sm 1:15 and said to him, "Come, *s* him down";
2:22 Why must I *s* you to the ground?
5: 8 must *s* at them through the water shaft.
17: 2 him flee, I shall *s* down the king alone.
18:11 you not *s* him to the ground on the spot?
1Kgs 2:29 Jehoiada, with the order, "Go, *s* him down."
2:31 as he has said, *S* him down and bury him,
14:15 The LORD will *s* Israel like a reed tossed
20:35 by the LORD to say to his companion, *S* me."
20:35 But he refused to *s* him.
20:37 The prophet met another man and said, *S* me."
2Kgs 6:18 prayed to the LORD, *S* this people blind,
13:18 Elisha said to him, *S* the ground!"
19:30 shall again *s* root below and bear fruit
1Chr 14:15 you to *s* the army of the Philistines."
21:17 LORD, my God, *s* me and my father's family,
2Chr 21:14 than you, the LORD will *s* your people,
Jdt 6: 3 will *s* them down as one man,
14: 4 them and *s* them down in their tracks.
16: 1 *S* up the instruments, a song to my God
1Mc 4:32 *S* them with fear, weaken the boldness
4:33 *S* them down by the sword of those who love
9:47 Jonathan raised his arm to *s* Bacchides,
2Mc 14:43 of the struggle he failed to *s* exactly.
Jb 16:13 his arrows *s* me from all directions,
36:32 and he commands it to *s* the mark.
Ps(s) 3: 8 For you *s* all my enemies on the cheek;
9:21 *S* them with terror, O LORD;
31:19 Let dumbness *s* their lying lips that speak
141: 5 Let the just man *s* me;
Wis 4: 3 shall not *s* deep root nor take firm hold.
4:19 For he shall *s* them down speechless and
Is 5:25 his people, he raises his hand to *s* them;
11: 4 *s* the ruthless with the rod of his mouth,
25:12 raze, and *s* it down level with the earth,
37:31 again *s* root below and bear fruit above.
47:12 make them avail, perhaps you can *s* terror!
49:10 shall the scorching wind or the sun *s* them;
Jer 21: 6 I will *s* the inhabitants of this city,
21: 7 He shall *s* them with the edge of the sword,
30:14 I struck you as an enemy would *s*,
31:19 I have come to myself, I *s* my breast;
43:11 He shall come and *s* the land of Egypt:
Ez 5: 2 around the city and *s* it with the sword;
7: 9 you know that it is I, the LORD, who *s*.
9: 5 Pass through the city after him and *s*!
9: 7 then go out and *s* in the city.
9: 8 As they began to *s*, I was left alone.
32:15 when I *s* all who live there,
39: 3 Then I will *s* the bow from your left hand,
Hos 14: 6 He shall *s* root like the Lebanon cedar,
Am 3:15 I *s* the winter house and the summer house;
9: 1 *S* the bases, so that the doorjambs
Mi 4:14 they *s* on the cheek the ruler of Israel.
6:13 Rather I will begin to *s* you with
Zec 12: 4 the LORD, I will *s* every horse with fright,
12: 4 will *s* blind all the horses of the peoples,
13: 7 *S* the shepherd that the sheep may be
14:12 plague with which the LORD shall *s* all
Mal 3:24 Lest I come and *s* the land with doom.
Mt 24:30 and 'all the clans of earth will *s* their
26:31 'I will *s* the shepherd and the sheep of
Mk 14:27 'I will *s* the shepherd and the sheep will
Lk 22:50 One of them went so far as to *s* the high
Acts 23: 2 his attendants to *s* Paul on the mouth.
23: 3 "You are the one God will *s*,
Rv 9:19 were like snakes with heads poised to *s*.

STRIKES (20)

Ex 21:12 *s* a man a mortal blow must be put to death.
21:15 Whoever *s* his father or mother shall be
21:18 *s* the other with a stone or with his fist,
21:20 "When a man *s* his male or female slave
21:26 "When a man *s* his male or female slave in
Nm 35:16 "If a man *s* another with an iron
35:17 If a man *s* another with a death-dealing
35:18 If a man *s* another with a death-dealing
35:21 or if he *s* another out of enmity and
35:23 stone which *s* him and causes his death,
Dt 19:11 and rising up against him, *s* him mortally,
1Chr 11: 6 "Whoever *s* the Jebusites first shall be
Jdt 7:14 and even before the sword *s* them they will
2Mc 3:39 and he *s* down and destroys those who come
Ps(s) 29: 7 The voice of the LORD *s* fiery flames;
Is 10:24 the Assyrian, though he *s* you with a rod,
30:31 will be shattered, as he *s* with the rod;
41: 7 with the hammer, him who *s* on the anvil;
Jer 11:12 them no help whatever when misfortune *s*.
Mt 5:39 When a person *s* you on the right cheek,

STRIKING (13)

Ex 2:11 labor, he saw an Egyptian *s* a Hebrew,
2:13 "Why are you *s* your fellow Hebrew?"
12:12 Egypt, *s* down every first-born of the land,
12:23 the LORD will go by, *s* down the Egyptians.
2Sm 24:17 David saw the angel who was *s* the people,
2Kgs 3:24 the countryside *s* down the Moabites,
2Mc 3:24 all power manifested himself in so *s* a way
Ps(s) 35:15 they gathered together *s* me unawares.
Is 58: 4 and fighting, *s* with wicked claw.
Ez 3:13 of the living creatures *s* one another,
Mt 27:30 of the reed and kept *s* him on the head.
Mk 15:19 Continually *s* Jesus on the head with a
Rv 19:15 came a sharp sword for *s* down the nations.

STRIKINGLY (2)

Gn 39: 6 was *s* handsome in countenance and body.
2Mc 3:26 young men, remarkably strong, *s* beautiful,

STRING (4)

Ps(s) 11: 2 they place the arrow on the *s* to shoot
45: 9 from ivory palaces *s* music brings you joy.
Sir 32: 6 seal is *s* music with delicious wine.
47: 9 of each year With *s* music before the altar,

STRINGED (3)

Sir 39:15 music on the harp and all *s* instruments;
Is 38:20 we shall sing to *s* instruments In the
Hb 3:19 For the leader; with *s* instruments.

STRINGS (5)

Jgs 16: 9 But he snapped the *s* as a thread of tow is
Ps(s) 33: 3 pluck the *s* skillfully,
150: 4 and dance, praise him with *s* and pipe.
Wis 19:18 among themselves, like *s* of the harp,
Is 23:16 Pluck the *s* skillfully,

STRIP (30)

Lv 16:23 he shall *s* off and leave in the sanctuary
Nm 20:26 Then *s* Aaron of his garments and put them
24: 8 like grass, their bones he shall *s* bare.
Dt 25: 9 shall go up to him and *s* his sandal from
1Sm 31: 8 the Philistines came to *s* the slain,
2Sm 2:21 young men and take what you can *s* from him
23:10 after Eleazar, but only to *s* the slain.
1Chr 10: 8 when the Philistines came to *s* the slain,
Jb 41: 5 Who can *s* off his outer garment,
Ps(s) 141: 8 *s* me not of life.
Is 32:11 *S* yourselves bare, with only a loincloth
47: 2 *S* off your train,
Jer 13:26 I now will *s* off your skirts from you,
49:10 So I myself will *s* Esau;
Bar 6:57 seize them *s* off the gold and the silver,
Ez 16:39 they shall *s* you of your garments and take
17: 9 it out by the roots and *s* off its fruit,
23:26 They shall *s* off your clothes and seize
26:16 and *s* off their embroidered garments.
45: 3 Also from this sector measure off a *s*,
45: 5 Also there shall be a *s* twenty-five
45: 6 you shall designate a *s* five thousand cubits
Dn 4:11 *s* off its leaves and scatter its fruit;
Hos 2: 5 between her breasts, Or I will *s* her naked,
Am 3:11 the land, and *s* you of your strength,
Na 3: 5 you, and I will *s* your skirt from you;
Zec 9: 4 Lo, the LORD will *s* her of her possessions,
Jas 1:21 *S* away all that is filthy,
1Pt 2: 1 So *s* away everything vicious,
Rv 17:16 will *s* off her finery and leave her naked;

STRIPE (3)

Ex 21:25 for burn, wound for wound, *s* for stripe.
Acts 4: 7 in whose name have men of your *s* done this?"

STRIPES (8)

Gn 30:37 and he made white *s* in them by peeling off
Dt 25: 2 guilty party, if the latter deserves *s*,
25: 2 receive the number of *s* his guilt deserves.
25: 3 Forty *s* may be given him,
25: 3 if he were beaten with more *s* than these,
Ps(s) 89:33 crime with a rod and their guilt with *s*.
Is 53: 5 makes us whole, by his *s* we were healed.
Lk 12:48 to be flogged will get off with fewer *s*.

STRIPLINGS (1)

Is 3: 4 I will make *s* their princes;

STRIPPED (26)

Gn 37:23 they *s* him of the long tunic he had on;
Nm 20:28 Moses *s* Aaron of his garments and put them
Dt 25:10 as 'the family of the man *s* of his sandal.'
1Sm 19:24 he, too, *s* himself of his garments and he,
31: 9 cut off Saul's head and *s* him of his armor,
1Chr 10: 9 They *s* him, cut off his head,
1Mc 1:22 He *s* off everything,
2Mc 4:38 *s* Andronicus of his purple robe,
8:27 They collected the enemy's arms and *s* them
11:12 got away were wounded and *s* of their arms,
Jb 19: 9 He has *s* me of my glory,
22: 6 pawn, left them *s* naked of their clothing.
Sir 19: 1 wastes the little he has will be *s* bare.
Is 24: 3 The earth is utterly laid waste, utterly *s*,
33: 9 the steppe, Bashan and Carmel are *s* bare.
Jer 13:22 skirts are *s* away and you are violated.
Jl 1: 7 He has *s* it, sheared off its bark;
Mi 2: 8 you have *s* off the mantle covering the
Mt 27:28 They *s* off his clothes and wrapped him in
27:31 a fool of him, they *s* him of the cloak,
Mk 15:20 mocking him, they *s* him of the purple,
Lk 10:30 They *s* him, beat him, and then went off
Jn 21: 7 he was *s*— and jumped into the water.
Acts 16:22 *s* them and ordered them to be flogged.
19:27 revere may soon be *s* of her magnificence."
2Cor 5: 4 down because we do not wish to be *s* naked

STRIPS (4)

Ps(s) 29: 9 the LORD twists the oaks and *s* the forests,
Jer 10: 9 Silver *s* brought from Tarshish,
Jn 11:44 came out bound head and foot with linen *s*,
Col 2:11 which *s* off the carnal body completely.

STRIVE (14)

Jos 23: 6 Therefore *s* hard to observe and carry out
Jb 9:29 guilty, why then should I *s* in vain?
Sir 27: 8 If you *s* after justice you will attain it,
Is 27: 8 and expelling, I should *s* against them,
41:12 shall not find, those who *s* against you;
Hos 6: 3 Let us know, let us *s* to know the LORD;
Acts 24:16 In this regard I too always *s* to keep my
Rom 2: 7 eternal life to those who *s* for glory,
2Cor 6: 4 *s* to present ourselves as ministers of God,
7: 1 *s* to fulfill our consecration perfectly.
Col 4: 6 and *s* to respond properly to all who
1Thes 2: 4 we speak like those who *s* to please God,
Heb 4:11 Let us *s* to enter into that rest,
12:14 *S* for peace with all men,

STRIVES (1)

Jb 27:22 dragon as from his hand it *s* to flee.

STROKE (2)

1Mc 9:55 Just at that time he had a *s*,
Lk 16:17 a single *s* of a letter of the law to pass.

STROLLED (1)

2Sm 11: 2 and *s* about on the roof of the palace.

STRONG (193)

Ex 1: 7 and *s* that the land was filled with them.
1:20 The people too, increased and grew *s*.
10:19 changed the wind to a very *s* west wind,
13: 3 a *s* hand that the LORD brought you away.
13: 9 a *s* hand the LORD brought you out of Egypt.
13:14 a *s* hand the LORD brought us out of Egypt,
13:16 a *s* hand the LORD brought us out of Egypt."
14:21 and the LORD swept the sea with a *s* east
32:11 with such great power and with so *s* a hand?
Lv 10: 9 generations, to drink any wine or *s* drink.
Nm 6: 3 he shall abstain from wine and *s* drink;
13:18 Are the people living there *s* or weak,
13:28 and the towns are fortified and very *s*.
13:31 they are too *s* for us."
Dt 2:10 *s* and numerous and tall like the Anakim;
2:21 *s* and numerous and tall like the Anakim.
4:34 war, with his *s* hand and outstretched arm,
5:15 there with his *s* hand and outstretched arm.
6:21 brought us out of Egypt with his *s* hand,
7: 8 with his *s* hand from the place of slavery,
7:19 his *s* hand and outstretched arm with which
9:26 and brought out of Egypt with your *s* hand.
10:22 ancestors went down to Egypt seventy *s*,
11: 2 majesty, his *s* hand and outstretched arm;
11: 8 that you may be *s* enough to enter in and
14:26 you desire, oxen or sheep, wine or *s* drink,
26: 5 he became a nation great, *s* and numerous.
26: 8 Egypt with his *s* hand and outstretched arm,
Jos 14:11 I am still as *s* today as I was the day
17:17 "You are a numerous people and very *s*.
23: 9 LORD has driven out large and *s* nations,
Jgs 3:29 Moabites, all of them *s* and valiant men.
9:51 was a *s* tower in the middle of the city,
13: 4 wine or *s* drink and to eat nothing unclean.
13: 7 So take neither wine nor *s* drink,
13:14 from the vine, nor take wine or *s* drink,
14:14 and out of the *s* came forth sweetness."
1Sm 14:52 When Saul saw any *s* or brave man,
2Sm 11:16 a place where he knew the defenders were *s*.
23:15 Now David had a *s* craving and said,
1Kgs 19:11 A *s* and heavy wind was rending the
2Kgs 6:14 there a *s* force with horses and chariots.
1Chr 19:12 "If the Arameans prove too *s* for me,
19:12 and if the Ammonites prove too *s* for you,
2Chr 11:12 and spears, and he made them very *s*.
14:10 you to help the powerless against the *s*.
15: 7 But as for you, be *s* and do not relax,
26:16 But after he had become *s*,
27: 6 Thus Jotham continued to grow *s* because he
Ezr 9:12 thus you will grow *s*, enjoy the produce
Neh 1:10 freed by your great might and your *s* hand.
Jdt 5:23 powerless people, incapable of a *s* defense.
9: 9 me, a widow, the *s* hand to execute my plan.
1Mc 1: 4 a very *s* army and conquered provinces,
1:17 He invaded Egypt with a *s* force,
1:20 to Israel and to Jerusalem with a *s* force.
1:29 and he came to Jerusalem with a *s* force.
1:33 with a high, massive wall and *s* towers,
2:49 "Arrogance and scorn have now grown *s*;
2:64 be courageous and *s* in keeping the law,
3:27 the forces of his kingdom, a very *s* army.
4: 7 army of the Gentiles, *s* and breastplated,
4:30 Seeing that the army was *s*,
4:60 high walls and *s* towers around Mount Zion,
5: 6 where he found a *s* army and a large body
6: 6 Lysias had gone at first with a *s* army
6: 6 they had grown *s* by reason of the arms,
6:37 A *s* wooden tower covering each elephant,
6:41 for the army was very great and *s*.
6:57 scanty, the place we are besieging is *s*,
11:15 him with a *s* force and put him to flight.
11:45 one hundred and twenty thousand *s*,
11:63 come with a *s* force to Kadesh in Galilee,
2Mc 1:24 God, creator of all things, awesome and *s*,
3:26 Then two other young men, remarkably *s*,
8:16 assembled his men, six thousand *s*,
10:18 thousand took refuge in two very *s* towers,
11: 5 Jerusalem, launched a *s* attack against it.
12:18 behind in one place a very *s* garrison.
13:19 against Beth-zur, a *s* fortress of the Jews;
Jb 30:21 mercy and with your *s* hand you buffet me.
Ps(s) 20: 8 Some are *s* in chariots;
20: 8 but we are *s* in the name of the LORD,
22:13 the *s* bulls of Bashan encircle me.
24: 8 The LORD, *s* and mighty,
35:10 the afflicted man from those too *s* for him,
38:20 But my undeserved enemies are *s*;
50:13 Do I eat the flesh of *s* bulls,
68:31 the herd of *s* bulls and the bullocks,
71: 7 am I to many, but you are my *s* refuge!
77:16 With your *s* arm you redeemed your people,
80:16 [the son of man whom you yourself made *s*.
80:18 the son of man whom you yourself made *s*.
89:11 your *s* arm you have scattered your enemies.
89:14 *s* is your hand, exalted your right hand.
89:22 with him, and that my arm may make him *s*.
90:10 sum of our years, or eighty, if we are *s*,
142: 7 my persecutors, for they are too *s* for me.
Prv 10:15 The rich man's wealth is his *s* city;
14:26 In the fear of the LORD is a *s* defense;
18:10 The name of the LORD is a *s* tower;
18:11 The rich man's wealth is his *s* city;
18:19 brother is a better defense than a *s* city,
20: 1 Wine is arrogant, *s* drink is riotous;
23:11 For their redeemer is *s*;
24: 5 A wise man is more powerful than a *s* man,
30:25 species not *s*, yet they store up their food
31: 4 *s* drink is not for princes!
31: 6 Give *s* drink to one who is perishing,
Eccl 12: 3 the house tremble, and the *s* men are bent,
Sir 30:14 Better a poor man *s* and robust,
34:16 he is their mighty shield and *s* support,
Is 1:31 The *s* man shall turn to tow,
5:11 Woe to those who demand *s* drink as soon as
5:22 wine, the valiant at mixing *s* drink!
17: 9 On that day his *s* cities shall be like
18: 2 near and far, a nation *s* and conquering,
18: 7 near and far, a nation *s* and conquering,
24: 9 *s* drink is bitter to those who partake of
25: 3 Therefore a *s* people will honor you,
26: 1 "A *s* city have we; he sets up walls
27: 1 his sword that is cruel, great, and *s*,
28: 2 Behold, the LORD has a *s* one and a mighty,
28: 7 stagger from wine and stumble from *s* drink:
28: 7 Priest and prophet stagger from *s* drink,
28: 7 Led astray by *s* drink,
29: 9 from wine, stagger, but not from *s* drink!
35: 4 Be *s*, fear not!
40:10 power the Lord GOD, who rules by his *s* arm;
44:12 with hammers, and forges it with his *s* arm.
56:12 let us carouse with *s* drink,
Jer 9:22 nor the *s* man glory in his strength,
20: 7 you were too *s* for me,
32:21 With *s* hand and outstretched arm you
48:17 How the *s* staff is broken,
50:34 *S* is their avenger, whose name is LORD
51:12 Babylon raise a signal, make *s* the watch;
51:53 and make her *s* heights inaccessible,
Bar 6:35 death, nor deliver the weak from the *s*.
Ez 19:11 *s* branch she put out as a royal scepter.
19:12 Then her *s* branch withered up,
19:14 She is now without a *s* branch,
22:14 heart remain firm, will your hands be *s*,
30:21 that it may be *s* enough to hold the sword.
30:22 I will break his *s* arm,
30:25 make the arms of the king of Babylon *s*,
34:16 [but the sleek and the *s* I will destroy],
Dn 2:40 There shall be a fourth kingdom, *s* as iron;
2:42 shall be partly *s* and partly fragile.
4: 8 It was large and *s*,
4:17 The large, *s* tree that you saw,
4:19 you are that tree, O king, large and *s*!
8:24 He shall be *s* and powerful,
9:15 out of the land of Egypt with a *s* hand,
10:19 take courage and be *s*."
10:20 When he spoke to me, I grew *s* and said,
11: 5 "The king of the south shall grow *s*,
11:25 for battle with a very large and *s* army,
11:32 loyal to their God shall take *s* action.
Am 2: 9 as the cedars, and as *s* as the oak trees.
2:14 the *s* man shall not retain his strength;
5: 9 Who flashes destruction upon the *s*,
Mi 2:11 pour you wine and *s* drink as my prophecy,"
4: 3 and impose terms on *s* and distant nations;
4: 7 and of those driven far off a *s* nation;
Zec 6: 3 all of them *s* horses.
6: 7 As these *s* horses emerged,
8: 9 Let your hands be *s*,
8:13 do not fear, but let your hands be *s*.
8:22 Many people and *s* nations shall come to
Mt 12:29 "How can anyone enter a *s* man's house and
14:24 about in the waves raised by *s* head winds.
14:30 But when he perceived how *s* the wind was,
Mk 3:27 No one can enter a *s* man's house and
5: 4 No one had proved *s* enough to tame him.
Lk 1:15 He will never drink wine or *s* drink,
11:21 a *s* man fully armed guards his courtyard,
Jn 6:18 moreover, with a *s* wind blowing,
Acts 2: 2 up in the sky there came a noise like a *s*,
3: 7 the beggar's feet and ankles became *s*;
27: 4 side of Cyprus because of *s* headwinds.
Rom 15: 1 We who are *s* in faith should be patient
1Cor 1:27 out the weak of this world to shame the *s*.
4:10 We are the weak ones, you the *s*!
16:13 In a word, be *s*.
2Cor 12:10 I am powerless, it is then that I am *s*.
13: 9 rejoice when we are weak and you are *s*.
2Tm 1: 7 spirit, but rather one that makes us *s*,
2: 1 must be *s* in the grace which is ours in
Heb 11:34 were made powerful, became *s* in battle,
1Jn 2:14 I address you, young men, for you are *s*,
Jude 1:20 grow *s* in your holy faith through prayer
Rv 18: 2 He cried out in a *s* voice:

STRONGER (23)

Nm 22: 6 they are *s* than we are.
Dt 1:28 reporting that the people are *s* and taller
9: 1 nations greater and *s* than yourselves,
Jos 17:13 When the Israelites grew *s* they impressed
Jgs 1:28 When the Israelites grew *s*,
14:18 than honey, and what is *s* than a lion?"
18:26 and Micah, seeing that they were *s* than he,
2Sm 1:23 death, swifter than eagles, *s* than lions!
3: 1 and that of David, in which David grew *s*,
10:11 Joab said, "If the Arameans are *s* than I,
10:11 But if the Ammonites are *s* than you,
2Chr 13:21 he died, while Abijah continued to grow *s*.
26: 8 far as Egypt, for he grew stronger and *s*.
1Mc 12:24 to attack him with a *s* army than before.
Ps(s) 105:24 his people and made them *s* than their foes,
Eccl 6:10 in judgment with one who is *s* than he.
Dn 11: 5 one of his princes shall grow *s* still
13:39 could not hold, because he was *s* than we;
Lk 11:22 someone *s* than he comes and overpowers him,
Acts 16: 5 *s* in faith and daily increased in numbers.
1Cor 10:22 Surely we are not *s* than he!
Col 2: 7 built up in him, growing ever *s* in faith,

STRONGEST (1)

Dn 3:20 of the *s* men in his army bind Shadrach,

STRONGHOLD (59)

Jgs 6:26 to the LORD, your God, on top of this *s*.
2Sm 5: 7 But David did take the *s* of Zion,
5: 9 David then dwelt in the *s*,
22: 3 My shield, the horn of my salvation, my *s*,
2Kgs 15:25 killed him within the palace *s* in Samaria,
1Chr 11:16 David was then in the *s*,
12: 9 when he was at the *s* in the wilderness.
12:17 and Judahites also came to David at the *s*.
Ezr 6: 2 Ecbatana, the *s* in the province of Media,
Est 1: 2 the royal throne in the *s* of Susa,
1: 5 great and small, who were in the *s* of Susa.
2: 3 virgins to the harem in the *s* of Susa.
2: 5 the *s* of Susa a certain Jew named Mordecai,
2: 8 to the *s* of Susa under the care of Hegai,
3:15 decree was promulgated in the *s* of Susa.
8:14 decree was promulgated in the *s* of Susa.
9: 6 In the *s* of Susa, the Jews killed
9:11 in the *s* of Susa was reported to the king,
9:12 "In the *s* of Susa the Jews have killed
1Mc 4:61 the people might have a *s* facing Idumea.
5: 9 these then fled to the *s* of Dathema.
5:11 and seize this *s* to which we have fled.
5:29 and they marched toward the *s* of Dathema.
5:30 ladders and devices for capturing the *s*,
12:34 over this *s* to the supporters of Demetrius.
15: 7 all the *s* you have built
16: 8 wounded, and the rest fled toward the *s*.
16:15 the little *s* called Dok which he had built.
2Mc 10:32 fled to a well-fortified *s* called Gazara,
12:19 men that Timothy had left in the *s*.
Ps(s) 9:10 The LORD is a *s* for the oppressed,
9:10 the oppressed, a *s* in times of distress.
18: 3 my shield, the horn of my salvation, my *s*!
31: 3 my rock of refuge, a *s* to give me safety.
46: 4 our *s* is the God of Jacob.
46: 8 our *s* is the God of Jacob.
46:12 our *s* is the God of Jacob.
48: 4 renowned is he as a *s*.
59:10 for you, O God, are my *s*,
59:17 You have been my *s*,
59:18 for you, O God, are my *s*,
62: 3 only is my rock and my salvation, my *s*;
62: 7 only is my rock and my salvation, my *s*;
71: 3 my rock of refuge, a *s* to give me safety,
91: 9 you have made the Most High your *s*.
94:22 innocent blood, Yet the LORD is my *s*,
144: 2 My refuge and my fortress, my *s*,
Prv 10:29 The LORD is a *s* to him who walks honestly,
12:12 The *s* of evil men will be demolished,
21:22 and overthrows the *s* in which it trusts.
Is 33:16 heights, his *s* shall be the rocky fastness,
Jer 48: 1 Disgraced and overthrown is the *s*:
Ez 24:21 my sanctuary, the *s* of your pride,
30:15 pour out my wrath on Pelusium, Egypt's *s*,
Dn 11: 7 and enter the *s* of the king of the north,
11:10 When it returns and surges around the *s*,
11:31 at his command and defile the sanctuary *s*,
Jl 4:16 to his people, a *s* to the men of Israel.
Zec 9: 3 Tyre built herself a *s*, and heaped up silver

STRONGHOLDS (32)

Jgs 6: 2 mountains, the caves for refuge, and the *s*.
2Chr 17:12 He built *s* and store cities in Judah.
1Mc 5:27 their enemies plan to attack the *s*
5:65 its *s* and burned the towers around it.
8:10 tore down their *s* and reduced them to
9:50 to Jerusalem, Bacchides built *s* in Judea:
10:12 in the *s* that Bacchides had built,
10:37 be stationed in the king's principal *s*
11:18 were killed by the inhabitants of the *s*.
11:41 citadel of Jerusalem and from the other *s*,
12:33 as far as Ashkalon and its neighboring *s*.
12:35 them he made plans for building *s* in Judea,

STRONGHOLDS (cont.)

12:45 together with other *s* and their garrisons,
13:33 on his part, built up the *s* of Judea,
13:38 *s* that you have built shall remain yours.
14:42 concerning the country, its weapons and *s*,
15: 7 all the *s* you have built
2Mc 10:15 the Idumeans, who held some important *s*,
10:16 quickly against the *s* of the Idumeans.
10:23 more than twenty thousand men in the two *s*.
11: 6 learned that Lysias was besieging the *s*,
Ps(s) 89:41 you have laid his *s* in ruins.
Is 23:11 has ordered the destruction of Canaan's *s*.
Jer 48:18 come up against you, he has ruined your *s*.
48:41 Cities are taken, *s* seized:
51:30 ceased to fight, they remain in their *s*;
Ez 19: 7 He ravaged their *s*,
Dn 11:19 He shall turn to the *s* of his own land,
11:24 them and devise plots against their *s*;
11:38 he shall give glory to the god of *s*;
11:39 To defend the *s* he shall station a people
2Cor 10: 4 God's power for the destruction of *s*.

STRONGLY (9)

Gn 19: 3 He urged them so *s*,
34: 3 Since he was *s* attracted to Dinah,
2Chr 25: 8 on your own, *s* prepared for the conflict;
1Mc 5:46 a large and *s* fortified city along the way,
1Cor 16:12 urged him *s* to go to you with the brothers,
Phil 1:23 I am *s* attracted by both:
2Thes 3:12 we urge them *s* in the Lord Jesus Christ,
2Tm 4:15 guard, for he has *s* resisted our preaching.
Heb 6:18 might be *s* encouraged to seize the hope

STROVE (2)

Est E:12 he *s* to deprive us of kingdom and of life;
Sir 51:18 the good I persistently *s* for.

STRUCK (135)

Gn 12:17 But the LORD *s* Pharaoh and his household
19:11 *s* the men at the entrance of the house,
32:26 over him, he *s* Jacob's hip at its socket,
32:33 hip socket was *s* at the sciatic muscle.
Ex 7:20 Aaron raised his staff and *s* the waters of
7:25 days passed after the LORD had *s* the river.
8:13 and with his staff he *s* the dust of the
9:15 would have stretched out my hand and *s* you
9:25 It *s* down every man and beast that was in
12:27 when he *s* down the Egyptians,
17: 5 go, the staff with which you *s* the river.
19:21 otherwise many of them will be *s* down.
21:19 the one who *s* the blow shall be acquitted,
Nm 11:33 and he *s* them with a very great plague.
14:37 the land were *s* down by the LORD and died.
20:11 Moses *s* the rock twice with his staff,
21:35 So they *s* him down with his sons and all
33: 4 first-born all of whom the LORD had *s* down;
Jos 3:14 people *s* their tents to cross the Jordan,
8:21 up in smoke, they *s* back at the men of Ai.
10:26 Thereupon Joshua *s* and killed them,
11: 8 They *s* them all down,
Jgs 7:13 It came to our tent and *s* it,
11:35 *s* me down and brought calamity upon me.
1Sm 4: 8 These are the gods that *s* the Egyptians
6: 4 plague has *s* all of you and your lords.
6: 9 not, we will know it was not he who *s* us,
6:19 the LORD, and seventy of them were *s* down.
17:49 sling and *s* the Philistine on the forehead.
17:50 he *s* the Philistine mortally,
19:10 Saul, so that the spear *s* only the wall,
25:38 ten days later the LORD *s* him and he died.
2Sm 1:15 and the youth *s* him a mortal blow.
2:23 So Abner *s* him in the abdomen with the
4: 7 They *s* and killed him,
6: 7 God *s* him on that spot,
10:18 the army, was *s* down and died on the field.
11:15 pull back and leave him to be *s* down dead."
12:15 The LORD *s* the child that the wife of
14: 6 one of them *s* his brother and killed him.
21:17 assistance and *s* and killed the Philistine.
1Kgs 2:25 Benaiah, son of Jehoiada, who *s* him dead.
2:32 because he *s* down two men better and more
2:34 went back, *s* him down and killed him;
2:46 son of Jehoiada, who *s* him dead as he left.
15:27 *s* him down at Gibbethon of the Philistines,
16:10 he *s* and killed him in the twenty-seventh
20:20 each of them *s* down his man.
20:29 and the Israelites *s* down one hundred
20:37 The man *s* him a blow and wounded him.
2Kgs 2: 8 his mantle, rolled it up and *s* the water,
2:14 he *s* the water in his turn and said,
2:14 *s* the water it divided and he crossed over.
6:18 the prophet's prayer the LORD *s* them blind.
13:18 He *s* the ground three times and stopped.
13:19 "You should have *s* five or six times;
19:35 angel of the LORD went forth and *s* down
25:21 had them *s* down and put to death in Riblah,
1Chr 13:10 LORD became angry with Uzzah and *s* him;
2Chr 13:20 the LORD *s* him down and he died,
32:21 offspring *s* him down there with the sword.
Jdt 5:12 and he *s* the land of Egypt with plagues
13: 8 Then with all her might she *s* him twice in
13:15 The Lord *s* him down by the hand of a woman.
14: 7 all who hear of you will be *s* with terror.
15: 5 *s* the enemy's flanks with great slaughter,
16: 6 Not by youths was their mighty one *s* down,
Est 9: 5 *s* down all their enemies with the sword,
1Mc 2:44 They gathered an army and *s* down sinners
5: 7 with them, routed them, and *s* them down.
6: 8 he was *s* with fear and very much shaken.
9:66 He *s* down Odomera and his kinsmen and the
10: 8 The men in the citadel were *s* with fear
2Mc 1:16 leader and his companions and *s* them down.
9: 5 *s* him down with an unseen but incurable
10: 3 Then, with fire *s* from flint,
15:24 By the might of your arm may those be *s*
Jb 1:16 has fallen from heaven and *s* the sheep
18:20 they who went before are *s* with horror.
19:21 my friends, for the hand of God has *s* me!
Ps(s) 44: 6 Our foes through you we *s* down;
64: 8 suddenly they are *s*.
78:20 For when he *s* the rock,
105:33 He *s* down their vines and their fig trees
105:36 *s* every first-born throughout their land,
118:15 right hand of the LORD has *s* with power:
118:16 right hand of the LORD has *s* with power."
Prv 7:26 For many are those she has *s* down dead,
23:35 "They *s* me, but it pained me not;
Sg 5: 7 They *s* me, and wounded me,
Wis 13: 4 if they were *s* by their might and energy,
16:18 know they were *s* by the judgment of God;
18:20 and in the desert a plague *s* the multitude;
19:17 And they were *s* with blindness,
Sir 24:12 I have *s* root among the glorious people,
27:25 blow *s* in treachery injures more than one.
48:21 God *s* the camp of the Assyrians and routed
Is 1: 5 Where would you yet be *s*,
9:12 The people do not turn to him who *s* them,
10:20 will no more lean upon him who *s* them;
10:26 such as *s* Midian at the rock of Oreb;
14: 6 *s* the peoples in wrath relentless blows;
33:20 as a quiet abode, a tent not to be *s*,
34: 7 Wild oxen shall be *s* down with fatlings,
37:36 The angel of the LORD went forth and *s*
38:12 tent, is *s* down and borne away from me;
57:17 wicked avarice I was angry, and *s* them,
60:10 Though I *s* you in my wrath,
Jer 2:30 In vain I *s* your children;
5: 3 You *s* them, but they did not cringe;
14:19 have you *s* us a blow that cannot be healed?
15: 8 Suddenly I *s* her with anguish and terror.
30:14 I *s* you as an enemy would strike,
52:27 had them *s* down and put to death in Riblah,
Lam 3:30 Let him offer his cheek to be *s*,
3:53 They *s* me down alive in the pit,
Dn 2:34 being put to it, *s* its iron and tile feet,
2:35 But the stone that *s* the statue became a
Hos 6: 1 he has *s* us, but he will bind
Am 4: 9 I *s* you with blight and searing wind;
Jon 1:16 *S* with great fear of the LORD,
Mi 1: 9 is no remedy for the blow she has been *s*;
Hg 2:17 I *s* you in all the works of your hands
Mt 26:68 Who *s* you?"
Mk 5:38 Jesus was *s* by the noise of people wailing
14:47 his sword and *s* the high priest's slave,
Lk 4:36 All were *s* with astonishment,
22:64 "Play the prophet; which one *s* you?"
Jn 18:10 drew it and *s* the slave of the high priest,
Acts 3:10 They were *s* with astonishment
12:23 The angel of the Lord *s* Herod down at once
23: 3 the law yourself by ordering me to be *s!*"
27:14 It was not long before a hurricane *s*,
1Cor 10: 5 them, for "they were *s* down in the desert."
2Cor 4: 9 we are *s* down but never destroyed.

STRUCTURE (7)

Ezr 5: 4 names of the men who are building this *s?*"
2Mc 2:29 must give his attention to the whole *s*,
Ez 40: 5 the width and the height of the *s*,
Mt 21:42 rejected has become the keystone of the *s*.
Mk 12:10 builders has become the keystone of the *s*.
Lk 20:17 rejected has become the keystone of the *s'?*
Eph 2:21 Through him the whole *s* is fitted together

STRUCTURES (1)

1Mc 10:44 restoring the *s* of the sanctuary shall be

STRUGGLE (15)

Gn 30: 8 "I engaged in a fateful *s* with my sister,
1Sm 4: 2 *s* Israel was defeated by the Philistines,
1Mc 5:31 When Judas perceived that the *s* had begun
2Mc 14:43 of the *s* he failed to strike exactly.
Eccl 8: 8 There is no exemption from the *s*,
Wis 10:12 she gave him the prize for his stern *s*
Sir 4:25 and *s* not against the rushing stream.
11:11 One may toil and *s* and drive,
27: 1 sin, and the *s* for wealth blinds the eyes.
Is 16: 4 When the *s* is ended,
Rom 15:30 the *s* by your prayers to God on my behalf.
Phil 1:30 Yours is the same *s* as mine,
Col 1:29 For this I work and *s*,
1Tm 4:10 This explains why we work and *s* as we do;
Heb 12: 3 do not grow despondent or abandon the *s*.

STRUGGLED (1)

Phil 4: 3 have *s* at my side in promoting the gospel,

STRUGGLES (2)

Wis 3:15 For the fruit of noble *s* is a glorious one;
Sir 40: 6 till in his dreams he *s* as he did by day,

STRUGGLING (2)

1Sm 15:32 Agag came to him *s* and saying,
Col 2: 1 I want you to know how hard I am *s* for you

STRUT (1)

Ps(s) 12: 9 *s* and in high place are the basest of men.

STRUTTING (1)

Prv 30:31 The *s* cock, and the he-goat,

STUBBLE (10)

Ex 5:12 the land of Egypt to gather *s* for straw,
15: 7 loosed your wrath to consume them like *s*
Wis 3: 7 and shall dart about as sparks through *s*;
Is 5:24 as the tongue of fire licks up *s*,
33:11 You conceive dry grass, bring forth *s*;
47:14 Lo, they are like *s*,
Jl 2: 5 crackling of a fiery flame devouring *s*;
Ob 1:18 The house of Esau shall be *s*,
Na 1:10 of thornbushes is set aflame, like dry *s*,
Mal 3:19 all the proud and all evildoers will be *s*,

STUBBORN (19)

Dt 2:30 made him *s* in mind and obstinate in heart
21:18 "If a man has a *s* and unruly son who will
21:20 'This son of ours is a *s* and unruly fellow
Jgs 2:19 none of their evil practices or *s* conduct.
1Sm 6: 6 Why should you become *s*,
6: 6 as the Egyptians and Pharaoh were *s?*
Neh 9:29 They turned *s* backs,
Ps(s) 58: 5 like that of a *s* snake that stops its ears,
Prv 29:21 from childhood, he will turn out to be *s*.
Sir 3:25 A *s* man will fare badly in the end,
3:26 A *s* man will be burdened with sorrow;
10:18 to a man, nor *s* anger to one born of woman.
30: 8 A colt untamed turns out *s*;
30:12 he is still small, Lest he become *s*,
Is 48: 4 Because I know that you are *s* and that
Jer 5:23 this people's heart is *s* and rebellious;
Ez 3: 7 Israel is *s* of brow and obstinate in heart.
3: 8 as theirs, and your brow as *s* as theirs,
Hos 4:16 For Israel is as *s* as a heifer;

STUBBORNLY (2)

Ex 13:15 When Pharaoh *s* refused to let us go,
Zec 7:11 they *s* turned their backs and stopped

STUBBORNNESS (8)

Dt 9:27 Look not upon the *s* of this people nor
29:18 he can safely persist in his *s* of heart,
Sir 10:12 beginning of pride is man's *s*
Jer 13:10 words, who walk in the *s* of their hearts,
18:12 according to the *s* of his evil heart!"
Bar 2:33 shall turn back from their stiff-necked *s*,
Mt 19: 8 of your *s* Moses let you divorce your wives,"
Mk 10: 5 that commandment for you because of your *s*.
16:14 to task for their disbelief and their *s*,

STUCK (6)

Jb 29:10 tongues *s* to the roofs of their mouths.
Jer 38:22 Now that your feet are *s* in the mud,
Mt 27:29 his head, and *s* a reed in his right hand.
Mk 15:36 *s* it on a reed to try to make him drink.
Jn 19:29 They *s* a sponge soaked in this wine on
Acts 27:41 The bow *s* fast and could not be budged,

STUDDED (1)

Sir 50: 9 of beaten gold, *s* with precious stones;

STUDENT (2)

Lk 6:40 A *s* is not above his teacher;
6:40 but every *s* when he has finished his

STUDIED (2)

Jb 29:16 the rights of the stranger I *s*,
Acts 17:11 Each day they *s* the Scriptures to see

STUDIES (3)

Sir 32:15 He who *s* the law masters it,
39: 3 He *s* obscure parables,
Lk 6:40 his *s* will be on a par with his teacher.

STUDIOUS (1)

2Mc 2:25 the *s* who wish to commit things to memory,

STUDY (6)

Dt 17: 9 They shall *s* the case and then hand down
Ezr 7:10 Ezra had set his heart on the *s* and
Prv 6: 6 O sluggard, *s* her ways and learn wisdom;

Eccl 12:12 in much *s* there is weariness for the flesh.
Sir 2:10 *S* the generations long past and understand;
39: 1 to the *s* of the law of the Most High!

STUDYING (1)

Wis 13: 1 *s* the works did not discern the artisan:

STUFF (2)

Gn 25:30 "Let me gulp down some of that red *s*;
Wis 15:13 when out of earthen *s* he creates fragile

STULTIFIED (1)

Rom 1:21 they *s* themselves through speculating to

STUMBLE (30)

Ps(s) 27: 2 my enemies themselves *s* and fall
Prv 3:23 your foot will never *s*;
4:12 and should you run, you will not *s*.
4:16 have made no one *s* steals away their sleep.
4:19 they know not on what they *s*.
24:16 and rises again, but the wicked *s* to ruin.
Sir 25:20 *S* not through a woman's beauty,
41: 9 When you *s*, there is lasting joy;
Is 5:27 None of them will *s* with weariness,
8:15 And many among them shall *s* and fall,
28: 7 stagger from wine and *s* from strong drink:
28:13 So that when they walk, they *s* backward,
31: 3 forth his hand, the helper shall *s*,
59:10 We *s* at midday as at dusk,
Jer 13:16 Before your feet *s* on darkening mountains;
18:15 They *s* out of their ways,
20:11 my persecutors will *s*,
31: 9 on a level road, so that none shall *s*.
46: 6 on the Euphrates' bank, they *s* and fall.
Dn 11:19 of his own land, but shall *s* and fall,
Hos 4: 5 You shall *s* in the day,
4: 5 and the prophets shall *s* with you at night;
14:10 them the just walk, but sinners *s* in them.
Na 3: 3 corpses, the endless bodies to *s* upon!
Mt 4: 6 you that you may never *s* on a stone.'"
Lk 4:11 you, that you may never *s* on a stone.'"
Jn 11: 9 man goes walking by day he does not *s*
11:10 he will *s* since there is no light in him."
Rom 9:33 to make men *s* and a rock to make them fall;
1Pt 2: 8 Those who *s* and fall are the disbelievers

STUMBLED (5)

Tb 11:10 up and *s* out through the courtyard gate.
Ps(s) 35:15 I *s* they were glad and gathered together;
107:12 when they *s*, there was no one to help
Jer 46:16 he *s* repeatedly,
Rom 9:32 They *s* over the stumbling stone,

STUMBLER (1)

Jb 4: 4 Your words have upheld the *s*;

STUMBLES (6)

Prv 24:17 not when your enemy falls, and when he *s*,
Sir 13:20 a rich man *s* he is supported by a friend;
Is 59:14 For truth *s* in the public square,
Jer 50:32 Insolence *s* and falls;
Hos 5: 5 Ephraim *s* in his guilt,
5: 5 in his guilt, and Judah *s* with them.

STUMBLING (23)

Lv 19:14 or put a *s* block in front of the blind,
26:37 *s* over one another as if to escape a
1Mc 5: 4 become a snare and a *s* block
Ps(s) 56:14 me from death, my feet, too, from *s*;
116: 8 death, my eyes from tears, my feet from *s*.
119:165 peace, and for them there is no *s* block.
Sir 31: 7 is a *s* block to those who are avid for it,
34:16 from the noonday sun, a guard against *s*,
Is 8:14 and a *s* stone to both the houses of Israel,
57:14 remove the *s* blocks from my people's path.
63:13 Who led them without *s* through the depths
Ez 3:20 wrong when I place a *s* block before him,
Mt 11: 6 is the man who finds no *s* block in me."
Lk 7:23 is that man who finds no *s* block in me."
Rom 9:32 They stumbled over the *s* stone,
11: 9 and a trap, a *s* stone and a retribution;
11:11 their *s* mean that they are forever fallen?
14:13 *s* block or hindrance in your brother's way.
14:21 your brother an occasion for *s* or scandal,
1Cor 1:23 preach Christ crucified—a *s* block to Jews,
Gal 5:11 were, the cross would be a *s* block no more.
1Pt 2: 8 It is likewise "an obstacle and a *s* stone."
Rv 2:14 who instructed Balak to throw a *s* block in

STUMP (5)

Jb 14: 8 in the earth, and its *s* die in the dust,
Is 11: 1 a shoot shall sprout from the *s* of Jesse,
Dn 4:12 But leave in the earth its *s* and roots,
4:20 it, but leave in the earth its *s* and roots,
4:23 The command that the *s* and roots of the

STUMPS (1)

Is 7: 4 fail before these two *s* of smoldering brands

STUNG (4)

Wis 16:11 reminder of your injunctions, they were *s*,
Sir 14: 1 no grief, who is not *s* by remorse for sin.
Acts 5:33 were *s* to fury and wanted to kill them.
7:54 listened to his words were *s* to the heart;

STUNNED (4)

Jb 16: 7 But now that I am exhausted and *s*,
26:11 tremble and are *s* at his thunderous rebuke;
Ps(s) 48: 6 They also see, and at once are *s*,
Jer 4: 9 priests will be amazed, and the prophets *s*.

STUNTED (1)

Lv 22:23 that is in any way ill-proportioned or *s*

STUPEFIED (4)

Ezr 9: 3 from my head and beard, and sat there *s*.
Is 28: 1 on the head of him who is *s* with wine.
29: 9 Be irresolute, *s*; blind yourselves
Acts 3:10 utterly *s* at what had happened to him.

STUPEFY (1)

Zec 12: 2 a bowl to *s* all peoples round about.

STUPEFYING (1)

Ps(s) 60: 5 you have given us *s* wine.

STUPENDOUS (2)

Wis 19: 8 by your hand, after they beheld *s* wonders.
Sir 43:26 In it are his creatures, *s*,

STUPID (17)

Dt 32: 6 thus repaid by you, O *s* and foolish people?
2Mc 11:13 But Lysias was not a *s* man.
Ps(s) 49:11 likewise the senseless and the *s* pass away,
73:22 was pierced, I was *s* and understood not;
74:18 and how a *s* people has reviled your name.
Prv 12: 1 knowledge, but he who hates reproof is *s*.
13:10 The *s* man sows discord by his insolence,
30: 2 Why, I am the most *s* of men,
Sir 21:18 *s* man knows it only as inscrutable words.
22:12 Speak but seldom with the *s* man,
22:15 iron mass are easier to bear than a *s* man.
Is 19:11 of Pharaoh's advisers give *s* counsel.
Jer 10:14 Every man is *s*,
10:21 Yes, the shepherds were *s* as cattle,
51:17 Every man is *s*,
Gal 3: 3 How could you be so *s*?
Ti 3: 9 abstain from *s* arguments and genealogies,

STUPIDITY (1)

2Tm 3: 9 *s* of these will be plain for all to see.

STUPIDLY (1)

Prv 7:22 He follows her *s*,

STUPOR (1)

Rom 11: 8 "God gave them a spirit of *s*;

STURDY (5)

Gn 30:42 would go to Laban, but the *s* ones to Jacob.
Ps(s) 92:15 vigorous and *s* shall they be,
Prv 31:17 about with strength, and *s* are her arms.
Sir 6:14 A faithful friend is a *s* shelter;
29:13 Better than a stout shield and a *s* spear

STUTTERERS (1)

Is 32: 4 and the *s* will speak fluently and clearly.

STYGIAN (1)

Is 59:10 at midday as at dusk, in *S* darkness,

STYLES (2)

Wis 2:13 of God and *s* himself a child of the Lord.
1Tm 2: 9 and not be decked out in fancy hair *s*,

STYLUS (2)

Is 44:13 and marks with a *s* the outline of an idol.
Jer 17: 1 sin of Judah is written with an iron *s*,

SUAH (1)

1Chr 7:36 The sons of Zophah were *S*,

SUBDIVISIONS (1)

Gn 36:40 according to their *s* and localities:

SUBDUE (6)

Gn 1:28 fill the earth and *s* it.
9: 7 abound on earth and *s* it."
Dt 9: 3 them to nothing and *s* them before you,
1Chr 17:10 And I will *s* all your enemies.
1Mc 4:28 men and five thousand cavalry, to *s* them.
Dn 2:40 break in pieces and *s* all these others,

SUBDUED (14)

Gn 14: 7 and they *s* the whole country both of the
Nm 32:22 of his way and the land is *s* before him,
32:29 when the land has been *s* before you.
Jos 18: 1 After they had *s* the land,
1Sm 7:13 Thus were the Philistines *s*,
2Sm 22:40 you *s* my adversaries beneath me.
1Kgs 21:27 slept in the sackcloth, and went about *s*.
1Chr 18: 1 David defeated the Philistines and *s* them;
20: 4 of the Raphaim, and the Philistines were *s*.
22:18 land is *s* before the LORD and his people.
2Chr 13:18 The Israelites were *s* on that occasion and
1Mc 5:44 So Carnaim was *s*,
Ps(s) 18:40 you *s* my adversaries beneath me.
Sir 47: 7 he battled and *s* the enemy on every side.

SUBDUERS (1)

Sir 44: 2 *S* of the land in kingly fashion,

SUBDUES (2)

Ps(s) 144: 2 in whom I trust, who *s* peoples under me.
Is 41: 2 he delivers the nations and *s* the kings;

SUBDUING (1)

Is 45: 1 right hand I grasp, *S* nations before him,

SUBJECT (45)

Gn 14: 4 years they had been *s* to Chedorlaomer,
Dt 28:55 enemy will *s* you in all your communities.
28:57 your enemy will *s* you in your communities.
Jos 7:11 have stealthily taken goods *s* to the ban,
Jgs 3:10 into his power, so that he made him *s*.
6: 2 seven years, so that Midian held Israel *s*.
9:28 Zebul once *s* to the men of Hamor,
2Sm 22:48 who made peoples *s* to me and helped me
1Kgs 10: 2 him on every *s* in which she was interested.
2Chr 9: 1 him on every *s* in which she was interested.
31:13 Benaiah were supervisors *s* to Conaniah
2Mc 9:12 he said, "It is right to be *s* to God,
Ps(s) 18:48 *s* to me and preserved me from my enemies,
45: 6 peoples are *s* to you;
Sir 15:14 man, he made him *s* to his own free choice.
Jer 34: 1 armies and the earth's kingdoms *s* to him,
Bar 2: 4 us *s* to all the kingdoms round about us,
Mt 6:13 *S* us not to the trial but deliver us from
Lk 3:19 was censured by John on the *s* of Herodias,
10:17 even the demons are *s* to us in your name."
10:20 devils are *s* to you as that your names
11: 4 and *s* us not to the trial."
Acts 7: 6 and they will be *s* to slavery and
13:42 on this *s* again on the following sabbath.
Rom 8: 7 it is not *s* to God's law.
8:20 Creation was made *s* to futility,
10: 3 did not *s* themselves to the justice of God.
1Cor 9:16 the gospel is not the *s* of a boast;
9:21 To those not *s* to the law I became like
9:21 I became like one not *s* to it
9:21 of God, for I am *s* to the law of Christ),
9:21 that I might win those not *s* to the law.
15:27 it says that everything has been made *s*,
15:27 made everything *s* to Christ is excluded.
15:28 he will then *s* himself to the One who made
15:28 to the One who made all things *s* to him,
15:42 What is sown in the earth is *s* to decay,
Gal 4:21 You who want to be *s* to the law, tell me:
Phil 3:21 by his power to *s* everything to himself.
Ti 3: 1 *s* to the government and its officials,
Heb 2: 5 that world of which we speak *s* to angels.
2: 8 present we do not see all things thus *s*,
7: 8 And whereas men *s* to death receive tithes,
1Pt 3: 6 was *s* to Abraham and called him her master.
2Pt 2: 2 the true way will be made *s* to contempt.

SUBJECTED (9)

2Kgs 13: 4 to which the king of Aram had *s* Israel.
2Chr 8: 8 Solomon *s* to forced labor,
Tb 8:10 die, we would be *s* to ridicule and insult."
2Mc 13:11 to be *s* again to blasphemous Gentiles.
Lk 22:46 pray that you may not be *s* to the trial."
Rom 8:20 of its own accord but by him who once *s* it;
1Cor 15:28 When, finally, all has been *s* to the Son,
Gal 4: 5 from the law those who were *s* to it,
1Pt 3:22 with angelic rulers and powers *s* to him.

SUBJECTING (2)

1Mc 8:18 of the Greeks was *s* Israel to slavery.
Heb 2: 8 In *s* all things to him,

SUBJECTION (2)

Jgs 8:28 Midian brought into *s* by the Israelites;
11:33 Ammonites brought into *s* by the Israelites.

SUBJECTS (35)

Ex 1: 9 He said to his *s*,
1:22 Pharaoh then commanded all his *s*,
7:28 houses of your servants too, and your *s*,
7:29 all over you and your *s* and your servants."
8: 4 LORD to remove the frogs from me and my *s*,
8: 5 pray for you and your servants and your *s*,

SUBJECTS (cont.)

8: 7 and your houses, your servants and your *s*;
8:17 your servants and your *s* and your houses.
8:25 from Pharaoh and his servants and his *s*.
8:27 flies from Pharaoh and his servants and *s*.
9:14 upon you and your servants and your *s*,
9:15 struck you and your *s* with such pestilence
9:27 it is I and my *s* who are at fault.
Dt 28:53 of the siege to which your enemy *s* you,
1Sm 11: 1 a treaty with us, and we will be your *s*."
26:15 when one of his *s* went to kill the king,
2Sm 8: 6 of Damascus, and the Arameans became *s*,
8:14 Thus all the Edomites became David's *s*,
10:19 with the Israelites and became their *s*.
2Kgs 21:23 *S* of Amon conspired against him and slew
1Chr 18: 2 Moab, and the Moabites became his *s*,
18: 6 of Aram, and the Arameans became his *s*,
18:13 and all the Edomites became David's *s*.
19:19 made peace with David and became his *s*.
21: 3 LORD king, are not all of them my lord's *s*?
Est B: 2 for my *s* a life of complete tranquillity;
E: 3 Not only do they seek to do harm to our *s*;
1Mc 11:51 in the eyes of the king and all his *s*,
2Mc 11:23 we wish the *s* of our kingdom to be
Prv 14:28 In many *s* lies the glory of the king;
Wis 8:14 govern peoples, and nations would be my *s*—
14:15 down to his *s* mysteries and sacrifices.
Is 11:14 possessions, and the Ammonites their *s*.
Jn 18:36 my *s* would be fighting to save me from
Acts 17:20 You are introducing *s* unfamiliar to us and

SUBJUGATED (2)

2Kgs 18: 8 He also *s* the watchtowers and walled
1Mc 8: 5 them in battle had been overwhelmed and *s*.

SUBLIME (4)

Jb 36:22 Behold, God is *s* in his power.
Ps(s) 131: 1 great things, nor with things too *s* for me.
Eccl 9:13 wise deed under the sun, which I thought *s*.
Sir 3:20 What is too *s* for you,

SUBMERGED (3)

Gn 7:19 the highest mountains everywhere were *s*,
7:20 fifteen cubits higher than the *s* mountains.
Ex 15: 4 of his officers were *s* in the Red Sea.

SUBMISSION (2)

1Sm 15:22 than sacrifice, and *s* than the fat of rams.
1Cor 11:10 ought to have a sign of *s* on her head,

SUBMISSIVE (5)

Eph 5:22 Wives should be *s* to their husbands as if
Col 3:18 You who are wives, be *s* to your husbands.
1Tm 2:11 must listen in silence and be completely *s*.
Ti 2: 5 busy at home, kindly, *s* to their husbands.
2: 9 Slaves are to be *s* to their masters.

SUBMISSIVENESS (1)

1Cor 14:34 as the law states, *s* is indicated for them.

SUBMIT (12)

Gn 16: 9 mistress and *s* to her abusive treatment.
Ex 10: 3 How long will you refuse to *s* to me?
1Kgs 12: 7 the servant of this people and *s* to them,
Neh 3: 5 not *s* to the labor asked by their lords.
Sir 51:26 *S* your neck to her yoke,
Jer 27:12 *S* your necks to the yoke of the king of
40: 9 in the land and *s* to the king of Babylon,
Gal 2: 5 us, but we did not *s* to them for a moment.
Eph 5:24 should *s* to their husbands in every thing.
Heb 12: 9 all the more *s* to the Father of spirits,
13:17 Obey your leaders and *s* to them,
Jas 4: 7 Therefore *s* to God,

SUBMITS (2)

Jer 27:11 The people that *s* its neck to the yoke of
Eph 5:24 As the church *s* to Christ,

SUBMITTED (7)

Nm 25: 3 Israel thus *s* to the rites of Baal of Peor,
25: 5 who have *s* to the rites of Baal of Peor."
2Mc 11:36 he passed judgment should be *s* to the king.
13:23 parleyed with the Jews, *s* to their terms,
Ps(s) 106:28 they *s* to the rites of Baal of Peor
Is 53: 7 treated, he *s* and opened not his mouth;
Lam 5: 6 To Egypt we *s*, and to Assyria,

SUBORDINATE (1)

Est B: 1 to Ethiopia, and the governors *s* to them,

SUBORDINATED (1)

Gal 4: 3 like slaves *s* to the elements of the world;

SUBORNED (1)

Ezr 4: 5 They also *s* counselors to work against

SUBSEQUENTLY (1)

Acts 23:29 I *s* discovered that he was accused in

SUBSIDE (1)

Gn 8: 1 over the earth, and the waters began to *s*.

SUBSIDED (3)

Jgs 8: 3 he said this, their anger against him *s*.
Jdt 6: 1 the crowd surrounding the council had *s*,
Lk 8:24 The waves *s* and it grew calm.

SUBSIDES (3)

Gn 27:44 him a while until your brother's fury *s*
27:45 you *s* and he forgets what you did to him.
Prv 26:20 and when there is no talebearer, strife *s*.

SUBSISTENCE (1)

Sir 31: 4 The poor man toils for a meager *s*,

SUBSTANCE (4)

2Kgs 15:20 it from all the men of *s* in the country,
Jb 5: 5 and the thirsty shall swallow their *s*,
Ps(s) 109:24 fasting, and my flesh is wasted of its *s*.
Wis 16:21 For this *s* of yours revealed your sweetness

SUBSTANCES (1)

Ex 30:34 LORD told Moses, "Take these aromatic *s*:

SUBSTANTIAL (2)

2Mc 4:45 a *s* sum of money if he would win the king
Acts 16:16 *s* profit to her masters by fortune-telling.

SUBSTANTIATE (1)

Acts 24:13 *s* the charges they are making against me.

SUBSTITUTE (8)

Lv 27:10 The offerer shall not present a *s* for it
27:10 and its *s* shall be treated as sacred.
27:33 and its *s* shall be treated as sacred,
2Kgs 18:20 mere words *s* for strategy and might in war?
2Mc 4:29 as his *s* in the high priesthood,
4:29 commander of the Cypriots, as his *s*.
Prv 10:22 brings wealth, and no effort can *s* for it.
Is 36: 5 mere words *s* for strategy and might in war?

SUBTLE (4)

1Kgs 10: 1 fame, came to test him with *s* questions.
2Chr 9: 1 to Jerusalem to test him with *s* questions,
Wis 7:22 intelligent, holy, unique, Manifold, *s*,
7:23 they be intelligent, pure and very *s*.

SUBTLETIES (1)

Sir 1: 5 Who knows her *s*?

SUBTRACT (1)

Dt 4: 2 add to what I command you nor *s* from it.

SUBTRACTING (1)

Dt 13: 1 neither adding to it nor *s* from it.

SUBURBS (4)

1Mc 11: 4 by fire, Azotus and its *s* demolished,
11:61 besieged it and burned and plundered its *s*.
Jer 32:44 land of Benjamin, in the *s* of Jerusalem,
33:13 land of Benjamin and the *s* of Jerusalem,

SUBVERSION (1)

2Mc 8:17 as the *s* of their ancestral way of life.

SUBVERT (2)

Jb 30:12 To *s* my paths they rise up;
Sir 11:34 with you, and he will *s* your course,

SUBVERTED (1)

Dn 13:56 seduced you, lust has *s* your conscience.

SUBVERTING (1)

Lk 23: 2 saying, "We found this man *s* our nation,

SUBVERTS (2)

Sir 28:14 A meddlesome tongue *s* many,
Lk 23:14 this man before me as one who *s* the people.

SUCATHITES (1)

1Chr 2:55 Tirathites, the Shimeathites, and the *S*.

SUCCEED (43)

Gn 27:20 Isaac asked, "How did you *s* so quickly,
Nm 14:41 This cannot *s*.
Dt 29: 8 them, that you may *s* in whatever you do.
Jos 1: 7 the left, that you may *s* wherever you go.
Jgs 18: 5 the undertaking we are engaged in will *s*."
1Sm 26:25 certainly *s* in whatever you undertake."
1Kgs 1:27 was to *s* to your majesty's kingly throne?"
2: 3 Moses, that you may *s* in whatever you do,
3: 7 your servant, king to *s* my father David;
19:16 of Abel-meholah, as prophet to *s* you.
22:12 "Go up to Ramoth-gilead; you shall *s*.
22:15 "Go up," he answered, "you shall *s*!
22:22 replied, 'You shall *s* in deceiving him.
2Kgs 14:21 him king to *s* his father Amaziah.
23:30 and proclaimed him king to *s* his father.
1Chr 22:11 and may you *s* in building the house of the
22:13 Only then shall you *s*,
2Chr 1: 8 and you have allowed me to *s* him as king.
13:12 fathers, O Israelites, for you will not *s*!"
18:11 You shall *s*; the LORD will deliver it
18:14 "Go up," he answered, "and *s*;
18:21 'You shall *s* in deceiving him.
20:20 Trust in his prophets and you will *s*."
26: 1 him king to *s* his father Amaziah.
2Mc 15: 5 did not *s* in carrying out his cruel plan.
Jb 22:28 you make a decision, it shall *s* for you,
Ps(s) 21:12 you, devising plots, they cannot *s*,
Prv 15:22 but they *s* when counselors are many.
16: 3 works to the LORD, and your plans will *s*.
20:18 Plans made after advice *s*;
Eccl 4:15 the heir apparent who will *s* to his place.
Wis 13: 1 seen did not *s* in knowing him who is,
17: 5 stars *s* in lighting up that gloomy night.
Sir 24:26 nor will the last *s* in fathoming her.
Jer 13:13 land, the kings who *s* to David's throne,
22: 4 kings who *s* to the throne of David will
36:30 of his shall *s* to David's throne;
Dn 8:24 fearful ruin, and *s* in his undertaking.
8:25 holy ones, his treacherous conduct shall *s*.
11: 7 descendant of her line shall *s* to his rank,
11:17 kingdom, but this shall not *s* in his favor.
11:25 *s* because of the plots devised against him.
Mi 7: 3 Their hands *s* at evil;

SUCCEEDED (74)

Gn 36:33 son of Zerah, from Bozrah, *s* him as king.
36:34 the land of the Temanites, *s* him as king.
36:35 died, Hadad, son of Bedad, *s* him as king.
36:36 died, Samlah, from Masrekah, *s* him as king.
36:37 from Rehoboth-on-the-River, *s* him as king.
36:38 Baal-hanan, son of Achbor, *s* him as king.
36:39 When Baal-hanan died, Hadar *s* him as king;
2Sm 10: 1 died, and his son Hanun *s* him as king.
1Kgs 8:20 I have *s* my father David and sit on the
11:43 David, and his son Rehoboam *s* him as king.
14:20 ancestors, and his son Nadab *s* him as king.
14:31 His son Abijam *s* him as king.
15: 8 of David, and his son Asa *s* him as king.
15:24 and his son Jehoshaphat *s* him as king.
16: 6 in Tirzah, and his son Elah *s* him as king.
16:28 im Samaria, and his son Ahab *s* him as king.
22:40 and his son Ahaziah *s* him as king.
22:51 His son Jehoram *s* him as king.
2Kgs 1:17 no son, his brother Joram *s* him as king,
8:24 His son Ahaziah *s* him as king.
10:35 His son Jehoahaz *s* him as king.
12:22 David, and his son Amaziah *s* him as king.
13: 9 His son Joash *s* him as king.
13:24 died and his son Ben-hadad *s* him as king,
14:16 His son Jeroboam *s* him as king.
14:29 and his son Zechariah *s* him as king.
15: 7 His son Jotham *s* him as king.
15:22 and his son Pekahiah *s* him as king.
15:38 His son Ahaz *s* him as king.
16:20 His son Hezekiah *s* him as king.
20:21 and his son Manasseh *s* him as king.
21:18 His son Amon *s* him as king.
21:26 of Uzza, and his son Josiah *s* him as king.
24: 6 and his son Jehoiachin *s* him as king.
1Chr 1:44 Jobab, son of Zerah, from Bozrah, *s* him.
1:45 from the land of the Temanites, *s* him.
1:46 Husham died and Hadad, son of Bedad, *s* him.
1:47 Hadad died and Samlah of Masrekah *s* him.
1:48 and Shaul from Rehoboth-han-nahar *s* him.
1:49 died, Baal-hanan, son of Achbor, *s* him.
1:50 Baal-hanan died and Hadad *s* him.
19: 1 Ammonites, died and his son *s* him as king.
29:28 glory, and his son Solomon *s* him as king.
2Chr 6:10 I have *s* my father David and have taken my
9:31 David, and his son Rehoboam *s* him as king.
12:16 His son Abijah *s* him as king.
13:23 His son Asa *s* him as king.
17: 1 Jehoshaphat *s* him as king and strengthened
21: 1 Jehoram, his son, *s* him as king.
24:27 His son Amaziah *s* him as king.
26:23 His son Jotham *s* him as king.
27: 9 of David, and his son Ahaz *s* him as king.
28:27 His son Hezekiah *s* him as king.
32:33 His son Manasseh *s* him as king.
33:20 His son Amon *s* him as king.
36: 8 His son Jehoiachin *s* him as king.
Tb 1:15 died and his son Sennacherib *s* him as king,
1:21 His son Esarhaddon, who *s* him as king,
1Mc 8: 7 the kings who *s* him to pay a heavy tribute,
13:14 that Simon had *s* his brother Jonathan,
14:36 they *s* in driving the Gentiles out
16: 2 and many times we *s* in saving Israel.
16:24 time that he *s* his father as high priest.

2Mc 4: 7 surnamed Epiphanes *s* him on the throne,
10:11 When Eupator *s* to the kingdom,
Wis 13: 9 For if they so far *s* in knowledge that
Is 18: 5 and the blooms are *s* by ripening grapes,
Jer 22:11 king of Judah, who *s* his father as king.
37: 1 son of Jehoiakim, was *s* by King Zedekiah,
Dn 6: 1 *s* to the kingdom at the age of sixty-two.
14: 1 Cyrus the Persian *s* to his kingdom.
Mt 2:22 had *s* his father Herod as king of Judea,
23: 2 and the Pharisees have *s* Moses as teachers;
Acts 24:27 which Felix was *s* by Porcius Festus.

SUCCEEDING (3)

Dt 10: 6 son Eleazar *s* him in the priestly office.
Sir 44:16 *s* generations might learn by his example.]
Dn 8:12 the ground, and was *s* in its undertaking.

SUCCEEDS (6)

Ex 29:30 The descendant who *s* him as priest and who
Lv 6:15 Aaron's descendant who *s* him as the
Wis 15:16 no man *s* in fashioning a god like himself;
Sir 43:27 For him each messenger *s*,
Is 48:15 him, I have brought him, and his way *s*!
Mt 18:13 If he *s* in finding it,

SUCCESS (24)

Gn 39: 3 him and brought him *s* in whatever he did,
39:23 was with him and brought *s* to all he did.
1Sm 9: 4 through the land of Shaalim without *s*.
25:30 promise of *s* he has made concerning you,
Neh 1:11 Grant *s* to your servant this day,
2:20 is the God of heaven who will grant us *s*.
Tb 4: 6 service, your good works will bring *s*,
4:19 to grant *s* to all your endeavors and plans.
11:15 his father that his journey had been a *s*;
Jdt 10: 8 to favor, and make your undertaking a *s*,
11: 6 handmaid, God will give you complete *s*,
1Mc 4:55 and praised Heaven, who had given them *s*.
2Mc 10:28 the one having as pledge of *s* and victory
Jb 5:12 cunning, so that their hands achieve no *s*;
Prv 17: 8 at every turn it brings him *s*.
31:18 She enjoys the *s* of her dealings;
Wis 13:19 And for profit in business and *s* with his
Sir 9:12 Rejoice not at a proud man's *s*;
11:17 his favor brings continued *s*.
20: 8 Some misfortunes bring *s*;
Jer 2:37 you trust, with them you will have no *s*.
10:21 Therefore they had no *s*,
50:34 He will defend their cause with *s*,
Dn 11:27 exchange lies, but they shall have no *s*,

SUCCESSFUL (20)

Gn 24:21 or not the LORD had made his errand *s*.
24:40 messenger with you and make your errand *s*,
24:42 will to make *s* the errand I am engaged on!
24:56 now that the LORD has made my errand *s*;
1Sm 14:47 he turned, he was *s* and fought bravely.
18:15 Seeing how *s* he was,
18:30 David was more *s* against them than any
Tb 5:22 will go with him, his journey will be *s*,
10:14 King of all, for making his journey so *s*.
2Mc 8: 8 his *s* advances were becoming more frequent,
8:35 was eminently *s* in destroying his own army.
10:23 he was *s* at arms in all his undertakings,
Ps(s) 37: 7 *s* path of the man who does malicious deeds.
Prv 16:20 He who plans a thing will be *s*;
19: 8 he who keeps understanding will be *s*.
Eccl 11: 6 you know not which of the two will be *s*,
Sir 12: 9 a man is *s* even his enemy is friendly;
41: 1 For the man unruffled and always *s*,
2Cor 8: 6 among you, to bring it to *s* completion:
8:11 Carry it through now to a *s* completion,

SUCCESSFULLY (6)

Jos 1: 8 then you will *s* attain your goal.
Jgs 14:12 days of the feast you solve it for me *s*,
1Sm 18: 5 out *s* every mission on which Saul sent him.
1Chr 28:19 He had *s* committed to writing the exact
2Chr 7:11 he *s* accomplished everything he had
8:16 All of Solomon's work was carried out *s*

SUCCESSION (1)

Lv 16:32 to the priesthood in *s* to his father.

SUCCESSIVE (3)

Nm 33: 2 The starting places of the *s* stages were:
2Sm 21: 1 reign there was a famine for three *s* years.
1Chr 24: 6 listing two *s* family groups from Eleazar

SUCCESSOR (5)

2Mc 9:23 in the hinterland, would name his *s*,
14:26 against the kingdom, to be his *s*.
Sir 47:12 of his merits he had as his *s* a wise son,
48: 8 inflict vengeance, and a prophet as your *s*.
Jer 33:17 a *s* on the throne of the house of Israel,

SUCCESSORS (1)

Bar 6:47 have left frauds and opprobrium to their *s*.

SUCCOR (2)

Dt 23: 5 because they would not *s* you with food and
Neh 13: 2 not *s* the Israelites with food and water,

SUCCOTH (18)

Gn 33:17 journey back to Seir, Jacob journeyed to *S*.
33:17 That is why the place was called *S*.
Ex 12:37 The Israelites set out from Rameses for *S*,
13:20 Setting out from *S*, they camped at Etham
Nm 33: 5 from Rameses, the Israelites camped at *S*.
33: 6 Setting out from *S*, they camped at Etham
Jos 13:27 Beth-haram, Bethnimrah, *S*,
Jgs 8: 5 So he said to the men of *S*,
8: 6 But the princes of *S* replied,
8: 8 of Penuel answered him as had the men of *S*.
8:14 He captured a young man of *S*,
8:14 the seventy-seven princes and elders of *S*.
8:15 So he went to the men of *S* and said,
8:16 and ground these men of *S* into them.
1Kgs 7:46 the clayey ground between *S* and Zarethan.
2Chr 4:17 in the clayey ground between *S* and Zeredah.
Ps(s) 60: 8 Shechem, and measure off the valley of *S*.
108: 8 Shechem, and measure off the valley of *S*;

SUCCUMB (2)

Sir 23: 3 Lest I *s* to my foes, and my enemy rejoice
Hos 8:10 princes shall shortly *s* under the burden.

SUCCUMBED (1)

Lam 2: 8 grief on wall and rampart till both *s*.

SUCH (409)

Gn 2: 4 *S* is the story of the heavens and the
3:13 the woman, "Why did you do *s* a thing?"
17:14 *s* a one shall be cut off from his people;
18:25 Far be it from you to do *s* a thing,
19:11 with *s* a blinding light that they were
20: 9 *s* monstrous guilt on me and my kingdom?
20:10 him, "that you should have done *s* a thing?"
26:14 He acquired *s* flocks and herds,
27: 4 an appetizing dish for me, *s* as I like,
27: 9 dish for your father, *s* as he likes.
27:14 an appetizing dish, *s* as his father liked.
30:32 Only *s* animals shall be my wages.
34: 7 *s* a thing could not be tolerated.
34:14 "We could not do *s* a thing,"
36:19 *S* are the descendants of Esau [that is,
39:11 One *s* day, when Joseph came
41:19 Never have I seen *s* ugly specimens as
42:36 Why must *s* things always happen to me?"
44: 7 "How can my lord say *s* things?
44: 7 be it from your servants to do *s* a thing!
44:15 "How could you do *s* a thing?"
44:15 "You should have known that *s* a man as I
Ex 5:22 And why did you send me on *s* a mission?
9:15 with *s* pestilence as would wipe you from
9:18 at this hour I will rain down *s* fierce hail
9:24 *s* fierce hail as had never been seen in
10: 6 *s* a sight your fathers and grandfathers
10:14 had there been *s* a fierce swarm of locusts,
10:21 be *s* intense darkness that one can feel it."
11: 6 the land of Egypt, *s* as has never been,
19:13 *S* a one, man or beast,
26: 8 Eleven *s* sheets are to be made;
28: 3 instructions to make *s* vestments for Aaron
28:37 ribbon in *s* a way that it rests on the front
29:28 *S* things are due to Aaron and his sons
32:11 *s* great power and with so strong a hand?
34:10 eyes of all your people I will work *s* marvels
35:29 *s* voluntary offerings as they thought best,
36:14 Eleven *s* sheets were made.
Lv 1: 2 *s* an offering must be from the herd or
2: 6 *S* a cereal offering must be broken into
2:12 *S* you may indeed present to the LORD in
5: 4 *s* as men are accustomed to utter rashly,
5: 4 recognizes that he is guilty of *s* an oath;
5: 9 *S* is the offering for sin.
5:17 commits *s* a sin by doing one of the things
5:19 *S* is the offering for guilt;
5:22 the sinful oaths that men make in *s* cases,
6:23 *s* an offering must be burned up in the
7:25 *s* a one shall be cut off from his people.
10: 1 profane fire, *s* as he had not authorized.
10:13 *s* is the command I have received.
11:24 *S* is the uncleanness that you contract,
11:28 *S* is their uncleanness for you.
11:32 Any *s* article that men use,
11:34 men drink, in any *s* vessel become unclean.
12: 7 *S* is the law for the woman who gives birth
14:30 or pigeons, *s* as the man can afford,
14:47 in *s* a house shall also wash his garments.
15: 3 *S* is his uncleanness from this flow that
15:10 up any *s* thing shall wash his garments,
15:26 she lies during *s* a flow becomes unclean,
17: 4 *s* a man shall be cut off from among his
17: 5 *s* sacrifices as they used to offer up in
18:22 *s* a thing is an abomination.
18:23 *s* things are abhorrent.
18:26 decrees forbidding all *s* abominations
19: 8 *S* a one shall be cut off from his people.
20: 3 I myself will turn against *s* a man and cut
20: 4 Even if his fellow citizens connive at *s* a
20: 6 *s* a one and cut him off from his people.
20:14 *s* shamefulness may not be found among you.
21:21 who has any *s* defect may draw near
22: 3 *s* a one shall be cut off from my presence.
22: 6 the one who touches *s* as these shall be
22:14 If *s* a one eats of a sacred offering
22:20 *s* a one would not be acceptable for you.
22:22 do not put *s* an animal on the altar as an
22:25 receive from a foreigner any *s* animals
25:21 I will bestow *s* blessings on you in the
25:30 But if *s* a house in a walled town has not
25:45 *S* slaves you may own as chattels,
25:47 your countrymen is reduced to *s* poverty
25:51 The more *s* years there are,
27: 9 that may be sacrificed, every *s* animal,
27:20 If, instead of redeeming *s* a field,
27:26 which as *s* already belongs to the LORD,
Nm 4:37 *S* was the census of all the men of the
4:41 *S* was the census of all the men of the
4:45 *S* was the census of the men of the
5:30 or when *s* a feeling of jealousy comes over
5:31 woman shall bear *s* guilt as she may have."
14:15 who have heard *s* reports of you will say,
18:15 beast, *s* as are to be offered to the LORD,
30:10 pledge to which *s* a woman binds herself,
31:22 Whatever can stand fire, *s* as gold,
31:50 article he has picked up, *s* as an anklet,
Dt 5:29 that they might always be of *s* a mind,
6:14 *s* as those of the surrounding nations,
7:10 he does not dally with *s* a one,
12: 3 out the remembrance of them in any *s* place.
13:12 again do *s* evil as this in your midst.
16:22 you erect a sacred pillar, *s* as the LORD,
18:12 *s* things is an abomination to the LORD,
18:12 and because of *s* abominations the LORD,
19: 4 take refuge in *s* a place to save his life:
19:21 Do not look on *s* a man with pity.
20:18 lest they teach you to make any *s*
22: 5 *s* things is an abomination to the LORD,
22:25 that a man comes upon *s* a betrothed maiden,
24: 4 bring *s* guilt upon the land which the LORD,
28:64 *s* as you and your fathers have not known.
29:17 bear *s* poison and wormwood among you.
29:18 If any *s* person, upon hearing the words
Jgs 7: 8 *s* supplies as the soldiers had with them,
1Sm 1: 9 Hannah rose after one *s* meal at Shiloh,
2:23 "Why are you doing *s* things?
7:10 and threw them into *s* confusion that they
9:21 Why say *s* things to me?"
22:15 or anyone in my family of *s* a thing.
24: 7 that I should do *s* a thing to my master,
2Sm 11:11 and as you live, I will do no *s* thing."
13: 2 He was in *s* straits over his sister Tamar
15: 2 servant is of *s* and such a tribe of Israel,"
16:23 *S* was all his counsel both to David and to
23:12 *S* were the deeds of the Three warriors.
23:22 *S* were the deeds performed by Benaiah,
1Kgs 3:13 *s* riches and glory that among kings there
5:17 until *s* a time as the LORD should put
10:10 Never again did anyone bring *s* an
10:12 No more *s* wood was brought or seen to the
10:13 besides *s* presents as were given her from
2Kgs 13:21 when suddenly they spied *s* a raiding band.
19: 7 I am about to put in him *s* a spirit that,
21:12 bring *s* evil on Jerusalem and Judah that,
23:22 No Passover *s* as this had been observed
1Chr 4:38 ancestral houses spread out to *s* an extent
11:19 *S* deeds as these the Three warriors
11:19 "God forbid that I should do *s* a thing!
11:24 *S* deeds as these of Benaiah,
17: 6 whom I commanded to guide my people, *s* as,
22:14 and bronze and iron in *s* great quantities
23:31 feast days, in *s* numbers as are prescribed,
29:18 keep *s* thoughts in the hearts and minds of
29:25 giving him a glorious reign *s* as had not
2Chr 1:12 and glory, *s* as kings before you never had,
2: 3 *s* is Israel's perpetual obligation.
8:14 gate, since *s* was the command of David,
32: 1 he had proved his fidelity by *s* deeds,
32:15 you further and deceive you in any *s* way.
35:18 No *s* Passover had been observed in Israel
Tb 3: 6 command me to be delivered from *s* anguish;
3:10 I need no longer live to hear *s* insults."
3:13 the earth, never again to hear *s* insults.
4:13 For in *s* arrogance there is ruin and great
5:21 "Have no *s* thought.
5:22 no *s* thought; do not worry about them,
7: 7 But what a terrible misfortune that *s* a
Jdt 5:10 and grew into *s* a great multitude that the
8:15 to protect us at *s* time as he pleases,
8:19 It was for *s* conduct that our forefathers
10:19 this people that has *s* women among them?
11:16 God has sent me to perform with you *s*
12:12 It would be a disgrace for us to have *s* a
Est E: 3 incapable of bearing *s* greatness,
E:14 For by *s* measures he hoped to catch us
11: 6 *s* as have not occurred among the nations.
1Mc 1:51 *S* were the orders he published throughout
3:17 as we are, fight *s* a mighty host as this?
4: 6 who lacked *s* armor and swords as they
9:10 me to do *s* a thing as to flee from them!

SUCH (cont.)

9:27 There had not been *s* great distress in
10:32 in it *s* men as he shall choose to guard it.
10:73 cavalry and *s* a force as this in the plain,
10:77 *s* a large number of horsemen to rely on.
10:89 *s* as is usually given to King's Kinsmen;
15:15 left Rome with letters *s* as this addressed
2Mc 4: 3 When Simon's hostility reached *s* a point
4:13 and foreign customs reached *s* a pitch,
4:24 he flattered him with *s* an air of
6:21 providing, *s* as he could legitimately eat,
6:24 would be unbecoming to make *s* a pretense;
7: 5 to die bravely, saying *s* words as these:
7:18 *s* astonishing things have happened to us.
8: 7 as being especially helpful for *s* attacks.
8:21 With *s* words he encouraged them and made
9:28 sufferings *s* as he had inflicted on others,
10: 4 might never again fall into *s* misfortunes,
10: 9 *S* was the end of Antiochus surnamed
10:35 of Maccabeus, angered over *s* blasphemies,
11: 9 their hearts were filled with *s* courage
12:16 they inflicted *s* indescribable slaughter
12:22 they rushed away in *s* headlong flight that
13: 7 In *s* a manner was Menelaus,
14:40 *s* a man he would deal the Jews a hard blow.
14:46 *S* was the manner of his death.
15: 4 that there was indeed *s* a ruler in heaven,
Jb 8: 2 How long will you utter *s* things?
12: 3 for who does not know *s* things as these?
12: 5 a disgrace *s* as awaits unsteady feet;
14: 3 Upon *s* a one will you cast your eyes so as
15:13 God and let *s* words escape your mouth!
17:12 *S* men change the night into day;
18:21 *s* is the place of him who knows not God!
22:20 where they stood, and *s* as were left,
23:14 and many *s* things may yet be in his mind.
30: 2 *S* strength as they had,
Ps(s) 14: 1 *S* are corrupt; they do abominable deeds
24: 6 *S* is the race that seeks for him,
27:12 against me, and *s* as breathe out violence.
48:15 tell a future generation that *s* is God,
53: 2 *S* are corrupt; they do abominable deeds;
73:10 to *s* a pass that they have not even water!"
73:12 *S*, then, are the wicked;
125: 5 But *s* as turn aside to crooked ways may
139: 6 *S* knowledge is too wonderful for me;
144:12 *s* as stand at the corners of the temple.
Prv 24:14 *S*, you must know, is wisdom to your soul.
26:21 *s* is a contentious man in enkindling
29: 7 the wicked man has no *s* concern.
30:20 *S* is the way of an adulterous woman:
Eccl 2:11 to the toil at which I had taken *s* pains,
5: 5 lest God be angered by *s* words and destroy
6: 5 dead child is at rest rather than *s* a man.
Sg 5:16 Such is my lover, and *s* my friend,
Wis 7:21 *S* things as are hidden I learned and such
12:20 them with *s* solicitude and pleading,
14:22 war of ignorance, they call *s* evils peace.
15: 6 and worthy of *s* hopes are they who make
16: 9 they deserved to be punished by *s* means;
Sir 6:16 remedy, *s* as he who fears God finds;
16: 5 Many *s* things has my eye seen,
16:21 *S* are the thoughts of senseless men,
19:25 a wise man is known as *s* when first met.
20:14 hateful indeed is *s* a man.
23:12 For all *s* words are foreign to the devout,
23:21 *S* a man will be punished in the streets of
23:24 *S* a woman will be dragged before the
51:20 *s* that I will never forsake her.
51:24 how long will you endure *s* bitter thirst?
Is 10:26 *s* as struck Midian at the rock of Oreb;
17:14 *S* is the portion of those who despoil us,
23: 8 Who has planned *s* a thing against Tyre,
37: 7 I am about to put in him *s* a spirit that,
64: 3 *s* as they had not heard of from of old.
64: 3 doing *s* deeds for those who wait for him.
66: 8 Who ever heard of *s* a thing,
Jer 5: 9 *s* as this shall I not take vengeance?
5:29 *s* as this shall I not take vengeance?
7:31 *s* a thing as I never commanded or had in
7:32 of Ben-hinnom will no longer be called *s*,
9: 8 *s* as this shall I not take vengeance?
9:23 For with *s* am I pleased,
17:12 from the beginning, *s* is our holy place.
19: 3 I am going to bring *s* evil upon this place
19: 5 *s* a thing as I neither commanded nor spoke
32:35 that they should practice *s* abominations.
38: 4 the people, by speaking *s* things to them;
Lam 5:21 give us anew *s* days as we had of old.
Bar 1: 6 collected *s* funds as each could furnish.
3:36 *S* is our God; no other is to be compared
Ez 1:28 *S* was the vision of the likeness of the
8:17 Is it *s* a trivial matter for the house of
10:15 *S* were the living creatures I had seen by
17:15 Can he who does *s* things escape?
31:18 *S* are Pharaoh and all his hordes,
44: 8 you have appointed *s* as these to serve me
48:29 *S* is the land which you shall apportion as
Dn 1: 4 *s* as could take their place in the king's
2:10 mighty, asked *s* a thing of any magician,
13:27 had any *s* thing been said about Susanna.
13:48 midst and continued, "Are you *s* fools,
Hos 8: 6 *s* is the calf of Samaria!
9: 4 *S* food as they have shall be for
Am 4:11 I brought upon you *s* upheaval as when God
Jon 1:10 "How could you do *s* a thing!"—They
Mi 2: 7 LORD short of patience, or are *s* his deeds?"
Hb 2:19 Can *s* a thing give oracles?
Zep 2:10 *S* shall be the requital of their pride,
Mt 1:20 *S* was his intention when suddenly the
6:30 in *s* splendor the grass of the field,
9: 8 praised God for giving *s* authority to men.
13: 2 *S* great crowds gathered around him that he
13:22 *S* a one produces no yield.
13:54 man get *s* wisdom and miraculous powers?
14: 2 *s* miraculous powers are at work in him!"
15:33 in this deserted spot to satisfy *s* a crowd?"
16:22 forbid that any *s* thing ever happen to you!"
18: 5 one *s* child for my sake welcomes me.
19:14 The kingdom of God belongs to *s* as these."
20:28 *S* is the case with the Son of Man who has
24: 6 *S* things are bound to happen,
26: 8 "What is the point of *s* extravagance?
Mk 2:16 "Why does he eat with *s* as these?"
4: 1 *S* a huge crowd gathered around him that he
4:33 By means of many *s* parables he taught them
6: 2 How is it that *s* miraculous deeds are
6:14 why *s* miraculous powers are at work in him."
7:13 you have many other *s* practices besides."
7:29 Then he said to her, "For *s* a reply,
8:12 I assure you, no *s* sign will be given it!"
9:37 a child *s* as this for my sake welcomes me.
10:14 *s* as these that the kingdom of God belongs.
13: 7 *S* things are bound to happen,
Lk 5: 6 Upon doing this they caught *s* a great
10:12 will be less severe than that of *s* a town.
11:19 In *s* case, let them act as your judges.
11:22 *s* a one carries off the arms on which he
12:28 in *s* splendor the grass of the field,
12:30 Your Father knows that you need *s* things.
18:16 The reign of God belongs to *s* as these.
22:23 as to which of them would do *s* a deed.
24:38 Why do *s* ideas cross your mind?
Jn 3: 2 *s* as you perform unless God is with him."
3: 9 "How can *s* a thing happen?"
4:23 it is just *s* worshipers the Father seeks.
4:27 however, *s* as "What do you want of him?"
5:16 It was because Jesus did things *s* as this
5:34 that I myself accept *s* human testimony
8: 5 law, Moses ordered *s* women to be stoned.
8:13 *S* testimony cannot be valid."
9:33 God, he could never have done *s* a thing."
10: 5 *s* a one they will flee,
13:34 *S* as my love has been for you,
15:24 Had I not performed *s* works among them as
Acts 3:16 *S* faith has given him perfect health,
5: 4 How could you ever concoct *s* a scheme?
5: 8 piece of property for *s* and such an amount?"
5: 8 piece of property for such and *s* an amount?"
9:21 "Isn't this the man who worked *s* havoc in
9:21 come here purposely to apprehend *s* people
10:41 but only by *s* witnesses as had been chosen
14: 1 spoke in *s* a way as to convince a good
14:15 just *s* follies as these to the living God,
14:18 Yet even with a speech *s* as this,
15: 5 demanded that *s* Gentiles be circumcised
18:15 I refuse to judge *s* matters."
20:35 by *s* hard work that you must help the weak.
22:24 out why they made *s* an outcry against him.
26:12 "On one *s* occasion I was traveling toward
Rom 1:32 that all who do *s* things deserve death;
2: 2 judgment on men who do *s* things is just."
2:29 *S* a one receives his praise,
16:18 *S* men serve, not Christ our Lord,
1Cor 2:14 He cannot come to know *s* teaching because
5:11 clear that you must not eat with *s* a man.
6: 4 If you have *s* matters to decide,
6:11 And *s* were some of you;
7:15 husband or wife is not bound in *s* cases.
7:28 But *s* people will have trials in this life,
8: 5 to be sure, many *s* "gods" and "lords"
10: 6 to keep us from wicked desires *s* as theirs.
14: 7 produce a sound, *s* as a flute or a harp,
14:34 women should keep silent in *s* gatherings.
16:16 I urge you to serve under *s* men and under
16:18 You should recognize the worth of *s* men.
2Cor 2: 6 by the majority on *s* a one is enough;
2:16 For *s* a mission as this,
3: 7 was inaugurated with *s* glory that the
3:12 Our hope being *s*, we speak with full
4: 3 it is *s* only for those who are headed
10:11 Well, let *s* people give this some thought,
11:13 *S* men are false apostles.
11:21 that we have been too weak to do *s* things.
Gal 3: 4 *s* remarkable experiences all to no purpose
3:19 is the relevance of the law, in *s* case?
3:21 was given was *s* that it could impart life,
5: 8 *S* enticement does not come from him who
5:21 those who do *s* things will not inherit the
5:23 Against *s* there is no law!
Eph 1: 5 adopted sons *s* was his will and pleasure
5:13 but when *s* deeds are condemned they are
Phil 1: 7 right that I should entertain *s* expectations
3:19 *S* as these will end in disaster!
Col 2:18 *S* a one takes his stand on his own
2:22 *S* prescriptions deal with things that
1Thes 3: 3 enough that *s* trials are our common lot.
4: 6 for the Lord is an avenger of all *s* things,
5:18 *s* is God's will for you in Christ Jesus.
2Thes 1: 9 *S* as these will suffer the penalty of
3:12 We enjoin all *s*, and we urge them strongly
1Tm 1: 7 the matters they discuss with *s* assurance.
4:11 *S* are the things you must urge and teach.
5:25 some good deeds stand out clearly as *s*;
6: 5 *S* men value religion only as a means of
6:21 In laying claim to *s* knowledge,
2Tm 3: 6 It is *s* as these who worm their way into
Ti 3:11 *s* a person as perverted and sinful;
Heb 7:26 that we should have *s* a high priest:
8: 1 we have *s* a high priest,
12:19 nor a voice speaking words *s* that those
Jas 2:14 *S* faith has no power to save one, has it?
2:18 To *s* a person one might say,
3: 6 The tongue is *s* a flame.
4:13 tomorrow we shall go to *s* and such a town,
4:16 All *s* boasting is reprehensible.
1Pt 2:15 *S* obedience is the will of God.
1Jn 2: 4 in *s* a one there is no truth.
2:18 so now many *s* antichrists have appeared.
4: 3 *S* is the spirit of the antichrist which,
5:16 There is *s* a thing as a deadly sin;
2Jn 1: 7 *S* is the deceitful one!
3Jn 1: 8 we owe it to *s* men to support them and
Rv 13:10 *S* is the faithful endurance that
16:18 *S* was its violence that there has never

SUCK (5)

Dt 32:13 Giving them honey to *s* from its rocks and
33:19 Because you *s* up the abundance of the seas
Jb 3:12 or why did I *s* at the breasts?
Is 60:16 You shall *s* the milk of nations,
66:11 you may *s* fully of the milk of her comfort,

SUCKLE (1)

Lam 4: 3 bare their breasts and *s* their young;

SUCKLING (2)

Sir 46:16 called upon God, and offered him a *s* lamb;
Lam 4: 4 The tongue of the *s* cleaves to the roof of

SUCKLINGS (2)

Gn 33:13 the flocks and herds, which now have *s*;
Ps(s) 8: 3 Out of the mouths of babes and *s* you have

SUD (1)

Bar 1: 4 all who lived in Babylon by the river *S*.

SUDDEN (17)

Jgs 20:37 men in ambush made a *s* dash into Gibeah,
2Mc 14:17 but because of the *s* appearance of the
Jb 22:10 you, and a *s* terror causes you dismay,
Ps(s) 6:11 they shall fall back in *s* shame.
78:33 days and their years with *s* destruction.
Prv 3:25 Be not afraid of *s* terror,
Wis 5:20 a shield and whet his *s* anger for a sword,
14:14 and therefore a *s* end is devised for them.
17:15 for fear came upon them, *s* and unexpected.
Sir 20:17 ground is less *s* than a slip of the tongue;
Is 65:23 vain, nor beget children for *s* destruction;
Jer 6:26 wailing, For *s* upon us comes the destroyer.
Ez 24:16 by a *s* blow I am taking away from you the
38: 9 You shall come up like a *s* storm,
Zep 1:18 For he shall make an end, yes, a *s* end,
Mt 8:29 With a *s* shriek they cried:
Lk 9:39 with a *s* cry throws him into a convulsion

SUDDENLY (72)

Gn 37: 7 *s* my sheaf rose to an upright position,
Nm 6: 9 "If someone dies very *s* in his presence,
1Kgs 20:39 and *s* someone turned and brought me a man
2Kgs 13:21 man, when *s* they spied such a raiding band.
2Chr 29:36 people, and at how *s* this had been done.
Tb 6: 3 a large fish *s* leaped out of the water
1Mc 1:30 Then he attacked the city *s*,
3:23 he rushed *s* upon Seron and his army,
5:14 reading this letter, *s* other messengers,
5:28 Judas *s* changed direction with his army,
9:39 and *s* saw a noisy crowd with baggage;
2Mc 3:27 *S* he fell to the ground,
5: 5 a thousand men and *s* attacked the city.
11: 8 *S*, while they were still near Jerusalem,
14:22 might *s* carry out some treacherous plan.
Jb 1:19 when *s* a great wind came across the desert
5: 3 his roots, but his household *s* decayed.
9:23 When the scourge slays *s*,
Ps(s) 2:12 from the way, when his anger blazes *s*.
64: 5 man, *s* shooting at him without fear.
64: 8 *s* they are struck.
73:19 How *s* they are made desolate!
Prv 6:15 Therefore *s* ruin comes upon him;
24:22 For *s* arises the destruction they send,
29: 1 hates rebuke will be crushed *s* beyond cure.
Eccl 9:12 when the evil time falls *s* upon them.
Sir 5: 9 For *s* his wrath flames forth;
11:21 For it is easy with the LORD *s*,
24:29 And *s* this rivulet of mine became a river,

27: 3 the LORD, *s* your house will be thrown down.
40:14 its rising, rolls along the stones, but *s*,
Is 29: 5 Then *s*, in an instant,
30:13 out in a high wall whose crash comes *s*,
30:28 in a ravine that reaches *s* to the neck,
47: 9 Both these things shall come to you *s*,
47:11 *S* there shall come upon you ruin which
48: 3 then *s* I took action and they came to be.
Jer 15: 8 *S* I struck her with anguish and terror.
18:22 when *s* you send plunderers against them.
51: 8 Babylon *s* falls and is crushed:
Dn 5: 5 *S*, opposite the lampstand,
7: 2 *s* the four winds of heaven stirred up the
7: 8 the ten horns it had, when *s* another,
8: 5 horn on its forehead *s* came from the west
Hb 2: 7 Shall not your creditors rise *s*?
Mal 3: 1 And *s* there will come to the temple the
Mt 1:20 Such was his intention when *s* the angel of
2:13 the angel of the Lord *s* appeared in a
3:16 *S* the sky opened and he saw the Spirit of
8: 2 *S* a leper came forward and did him homage,
9:32 *s* some people brought him a mute who was
17: 3 *S* Moses and Elijah appeared to them
17: 5 when *s* a bright cloud overshadowed them.
20:30 *s* two blind men sitting by the roadside,
26:51 *S* one of those who accompanied Jesus put
27:51 *S* the curtain of the sanctuary was torn in
28: 2 *S* there was a mighty earthquake as the
28: 9 *S*, without warning, Jesus stood before them
Mk 9: 8 *S* looking around they no longer saw anyone
13:36 Do not let him come *s* and catch you asleep.
Lk 2:13 *S*, there was with the angel a multitude of
9:30 *S* two men were talking with him
9:38 *S* a man from the crowd exclaimed:
21:34 day will *s* close in on you like a trap.
Jn 6:21 but *s* it came aground on the shore they
Acts 2: 2 *S* from up in the sky there came a noise
9: 3 a light from the sky *s* flashed about him.
12: 7 *S* an angel of the Lord stood nearby and
12:10 a narrow alley, when *s* the angel left him.
16:26 a severe earthquake *s* shook the place,
22: 6 light from the sky *s* flashed all about me.
28: 6 to see him swell up or *s* fall dead.

SUDDENNESS (1)

1Thes 5: 3 the *s* of pains overtaking a woman in labor,

SUE (1)

Jdt 3: 1 to him to *s* for peace in these words:

SUED (1)

1Mc 11:66 When they *s* for peace,

SUET (3)

Lv 1: 8 of meat, together with the head and the *s*,
1:12 lay these, together with the head and *s*,
8:20 the head, the cut-up pieces and the *s*,

SUFFER (61)

Gn 35:16 to be in labor and to *s* great distress.
43:14 I am to suffer bereavement, I shall *s* it."
45:11 and all that are yours may not *s* want.
Nm 14:34 forty years shall you *s* for your crimes:
2Sm 16: 8 now you *s* ruin because you are a murderer."
Ezr 10: 8 *s* the confiscation of all his possessions,
Jdt 16:17 flesh, and they shall burn and *s* forever."
2Mc 7:18 We *s* these things on our own account,
9: 4 he planned to make the Jews *s* for the
12:24 of many of them, and could make these *s*.
14:42 and *s* outrages unworthy of his noble birth.
Jb 9:18 He need not *s* me to draw breath,
24:11 They tread the wine presses, yet *s* thirst,
Ps(s) 16:10 *s* your faithful one to undergo corruption.
39: 9 a fool's taunt let me not *s*.
73:14 For I *s* affliction day after day and
107:38 nor did he *s* their cattle to decrease.
121: 3 May he not *s* your foot to slip;
Prv 21:17 He who loves pleasure will *s* want;
22: 3 simpletons continue on and *s* the penalty.
27:12 simpletons continue on and *s* the penalty.
Sir 20:24 inveterate liar, yet both will *s* disgrace;
23:11 just, and all his house will *s* affliction.
28: 1 The vengeful will *s* the LORD's vengeance,
41: 7 father, for they *s* disgrace through him.
Is 47: 8 be a widow, or *s* the loss of my children"
48:11 why should I *s* profanation?
Jer 4:19 how I *s*!
Mt 16:21 *s* greatly there at the hands of the elders,
17:12 Man will *s* at their hands in the same way."
Mk 8:31 them that the Son of Man had to *s* much,
9:12 of Man that he must *s* much and be despised?
Lk 17:25 *s* much and be rejected by the present age.
22:15 to eat this Passover with you before I *s*.
24:46 *s* and rise from the dead on the third day.
Jn 16:33 You will *s* in the world.
Acts 2:27 *s* your faithful one to undergo corruption.
3:18 that his Messiah would *s*.
9:16 him how much he will have to *s* for my name."
13:35 *s* your faithful one to undergo corruption.'
17: 3 Messiah had to *s* and rise from the dead:
26:23 namely, that the Messiah must *s*,
Rom 8:17 *s* with him so as to be glorified with him.
1Cor 3:15 if a man's building burns, he will *s* loss.
8: 8 We *s* no loss through failing to eat,
12:26 member suffers, all the members *s* with it;
2Cor 7: 9 thus you did not *s* any loss from us.
Phil 1:29 to believe in him but also to *s* for him.
2Thes 1: 5 it is for his kingdom you *s*—
1: 9 Such as these will *s* the penalty of
1Tm 6: 1 of God and the church's teaching *s* abuse.
2Tm 2: 9 in preaching it I *s* as a criminal,
Heb 9:26 he would have had to *s* death over and over
13: 3 yourselves, for you may yet *s* as they do.
1Pt 1: 6 time have to *s* the distress of many trials:
2:19 When a man can *s* injustice and endure
2:23 When he was made to *s*,
3:14 if you should have to *s* for justice' sake,
3:17 If it should be God's will that you *s*,
4:19 let those who *s* as God's will requires

SUFFERED (33)

1Sm 4:17 in fact, the troops *s* heavy losses.
Jdt 8: 3 who bound the sheaves, he *s* sunstroke;
1Mc 13:49 they *s* greatly from hunger,
2Mc 3:32 *s* some foul play at the hands of the Jews,
4:48 vessels, quickly *s* unjust punishment.
7: 8 in turn *s* the same tortures as the first.
7:10 After him the third *s* their cruel sport.
11:13 He reflected on the defeat he had *s*,
13: 9 than those they *s* in his father's time.
14:17 appearance of the enemy *s* a slight repulse.
15:19 who remained in the city *s* a like agony,
Jb 31:30 Even though I had not *s* my mouth to sin by
Wis 12:27 the things through which they *s* distress,
18: 1 forms, since now they themselves had *s*,
18:11 even the plebeian *s* the same as the king.
18:19 lest they perish unaware of why they *s* ill.
19:13 For they justly *s* for their own misdeeds,
Jer 44:17 we *s* no misfortune.
Mt 9:20 a woman who had *s* from hemorrhages for
11:12 now the kingdom of God has *s* violence,
Mk 3:26 if Satan has *s* mutiny in his ranks and is
Lk 13: 2 in Galilee just because they *s* this?
14: 2 front of him was a man who *s* from dropsy.
Acts 28: 5 fire and *s* no ill effects from the bite.
1Thes 2: 2 from the humiliation we had *s* at Philippi
2:14 You *s* the same treatment from your fellow
Heb 2: 9 with glory and honor because he *s* death:
2:18 he was himself tested through what he *s*,
5: 8 was, he learned obedience from what he *s*;
1Pt 2:21 since Christ *s* for you in just this way
4: 1 Christ *s* in the flesh;
4: 1 who has *s* in the flesh has broken with sin.
5:10 establish those who have *s* a little while.

SUFFERING (32)

Ex 3: 7 drivers, so I know well what they are *s*.
Nm 5: 2 leper, and everyone *s* from a discharge,
14:33 for forty years, *s* for your faithlessness,
16:29 merely *s* the fate common to all mankind,
2Sm 1: 9 and finish me off, for I am in great *s*,
3:29 never be without one *s* from a discharge,
2Kgs 13:14 *s* from the sickness of which he was to die,
2Chr 24:25 from him, leaving him in grievous *s*,
Jdt 10:13 one of his men *s* injury or loss of life."
2Mc 6:30 but also *s* it with joy in my soul because
7:32 We, indeed, are *s* because of our sins.
14: 8 since our entire nation is *s* great
Jb 2:13 for they saw how great was his *s*.
33:19 by pain and unceasing *s* within his frame,
Ps(s) 25:18 Put an end to my affliction and my *s*,
Is 53: 3 spurned and avoided by men, a man of *s*,
53:11 Through his *s*, my servant shall justify
Lam 1:12 Whether there is any suffering like my *s*,
1:18 Listen, all you peoples, and behold my *s*:
Mt 8: 6 is at home in bed paralyzed, *s* painfully."
Acts 1: 3 In the time after his *s* he showed them in
2Cor 1: 5 As we have shared much in the *s* of Christ,
Col 1:24 I find my joy in the *s* I endure for you.
Heb 2:10 in the work of salvation perfect through *s*.
10:32 you endured a great contest of *s*.
Jas 5:10 your models in *s* hardship and in patience,
5:13 If anyone among you is *s* hardship,
1Pt 2:20 you put up with *s* for doing what is right,
2Pt 2:12 *s* the reward of their wickedness.
Rv 2:22 I will plunge into intense *s* unless they repent
16:11 heaven because of their *s* and their boils.

SUFFERINGS (21)

Gn 41:51 *s* I endured at the hands of my family";
2Mc 7:12 because he regarded his *s* as nothing.
9:18 come upon him, his *s* were not lessened,
9:28 *s* such as he had inflicted on others,
Sir 25:13 Worst of all *s* is that from one's foes,
Is 53: 4 that he bore, our *s* that he endured,
Mt 8:17 our infirmities he bore, our *s* he endured."
Lk 9:22 he said, "must first endure many *s*,
Rom 8:18 I consider the *s* of the present to be as
2Cor 1: 6 may endure patiently the same *s* we endure.
1: 7 we know that just as you share in the *s*,
11:28 Leaving other *s* unmentioned,
Phil 3:10 likewise to know how to share in his *s*
Col 1:24 the *s* of Christ for the sake of his body,
2Tm 3:11 through persecutions and *s* in Antioch,
Heb 10:34 You even joined in the *s* of those who were
1Pt 1:11 for he predicted the *s* destined for Christ
4:13 in the measure that you share Christ's *s*.
5: 1 a witness of Christ's *s* and sharer in the
5: 9 undergoing the same *s* throughout the world.
Rv 2:10 Have no fear of the *s* to come.

SUFFERS (10)

Ex 21:22 woman, so that she *s* a miscarriage,
Lv 15:25 *s* this unclean flow she shall be unclean,
22: 4 with leprosy, or who *s* from a flow,
Est 4:11 summoned, *s* the automatic penalty of death,
Prv 13:25 but the belly of the wicked *s* want.
14:14 scoundrel *s* the consequences of his ways,
28:27 He who gives to the poor *s* no want,
1Cor 12:26 If one member *s*, all the members suffer
1Pt 4:15 it that none of you *s* for being a murderer,
4:16 If anyone *s* for being a Christian,

SUFFICE (5)

2Mc 6:17 Let these words *s* for recalling this truth.
Sir 31:19 Does not a little *s* for a well-bred man?
Is 40:16 Lebanon would not *s* for fuel,
Hos 12: 9 shall not *s* him for the guilt of his sin.
Zec 10:10 into Lebanon, but these shall not *s* them;

SUFFICIENCY (1)

1Tm 6: 6 provided one is content with a *s*.

SUFFICIENT (8)

Lv 25:26 *s* means to buy it back in his own name,
25:28 not acquire *s* means to buy back his land,
Nm 5:13 her husband has not *s* evidence of the fact,
35:30 is not *s* for putting a person to death.
2Chr 30: 3 had not sanctified themselves in *s* numbers,
2Mc 10:19 and his men, in *s* numbers to besiege them,
Wis 18:12 the living were not even *s* for the burial,
Mk 8: 4 these people *s* bread in this deserted spot?"

SUGGEST (3)

1Chr 28:18 gold for what would *s* a chariot throne:
Est 6: 4 to *s* to the king that Mordecai should be
Acts 23:15 you must *s* to the commander that he have

SUGGESTED (7)

Ex 18:24 father-in-law and did all that he had *s*.
35:21 as his heart *s* and his spirit prompted,
Jos 2:16 up into the hill country," she *s* to them,
2Kgs 7:13 One of his servants, however, *s*:
Est 2: 2 Then the king's personal attendants *s*:
2:15 eunuch Hegai, custodian of the women, *s*.
Jn 21: 6 your net off to the starboard side," he *s*,

SUGGESTION (5)

Est 2: 4 This *s* pleased the king,
5:14 This *s* pleased Haman,
2Mc 6: 8 At the *s* of the citizens of Ptolemais,
Mt 14:15 on, his disciples came to him with the *s*:
Mk 6:35 and his disciples came to him with a *s*:

SUGGESTIVE (1)

Eph 5: 4 there be any obscene, silly, or *s* talk;

SUIT (4)

2Sm 15: 3 say to him, "Your *s* is good and just,
Ps(s) 17: 1 Hear, O LORD, a just *s*; attend to my outcry;
Sir 32:17 and distorts the law to *s* his purpose.
Is 59: 4 No one brings *s* justly,

SUITABLE (9)

Gn 2:18 I will make a *s* partner for him."
2:20 proved to be the *s* partner for the man.
2Sm 19: 7 of us dead, you would think that more *s*.
1Mc 4:46 the stones in a *s* place on the temple hill,
2Mc 3:37 be a *s* man to be sent to Jerusalem next,
8:31 and carefully stored them in *s* places;
14:22 posted armed men in readiness at *s* points
Wis 13:11 A carpenter may saw out a *s* tree and
Sir 36:21 yet one girl will be more *s* than another:

SUITABLY (2)

Jgs 20:10 deal fully and *s* with Gibeah of Benjamin
Wis 7:15 Now God grant I speak *s* and value these

SUITED (2)

Wis 19: 4 a compulsion *s* to this ending drew them on,
Sir 37:27 nor is everything *s* to every taste.

SUITS (2)

1Mc 13:29 carved *s* of armor as a perpetual memorial,
Sir 6: 8 sort of friend is a friend when it *s* him,

SUKKITES (1)

2Chr 12: 3 Libyans, *S* and Ethiopians.

SULLEN (1)

Sir 25:16 looks, and makes her *s* as a female bear.

SULLIED (2)

Wis 7:25 therefore nought that is *s* enters into her.
Ez 24:13 Because you have *s* yourself with lewdness

SULPHUR (9)

Dt 29:22 all its soil being nothing but *s* and salt,
Is 30:33 the breath of the LORD, like a stream of *s*,
34: 9 changed into pitch and her earth into *s*,
Rv 9:17 of their mouths came fire and *s* and smoke.
9:18 *s* and fire which shot out of their mouths
14:10 He will be tormented in burning *s* before
19:20 alive into the fiery pool of burning *s*.
20:10 was hurled into the pool of burning *s*,
21: 8 their lot is the fiery pool of burning *s*,

SULPHUROUS (1)

Gn 19:24 LORD rained down *s* fire upon Sodom

SUM (26)

Lv 27: 2 are to be ransomed at a fixed *s* of money,
27: 3 the ages of twenty and sixty, the fixed *s*,
27: 5 *s* shall be twenty shekels for a youth,
27: 6 *s* shall be five silver shekels for a boy,
27: 7 *s* shall be fifteen shekels for a man,
27: 8 the vow is too poor to meet the fixed *s*,
27: 8 who shall determine the *s* for his ransom
2Chr 24:11 they had collected a large *s* of money.
Tb 1:14 a great *s* of money with my kinsman Gabael,
4:20 you that I have deposited a great *s* of money
1Mc 3:31 provinces, and so raise a large *s* of money.
3:41 fetters and a large *s* of silver and gold,
2Mc 3: 6 total *s* of money was incalculable
4:45 *s* of money if he would win the king over.
Ps(s) 90:10 Seventy is the *s* of our years,
139:17 how vast the *s* of them!
Sir 6:15 beyond price, no *s* can balance his worth.
18: 7 The *s* of a man's days is great if it
Lk 7:43 presume, to whom he remitted the larger *s*."
19:16 *s* you gave me has earned you another ten.'
Acts 5: 8 She answered, "Yes, that was the *s*."
22:28 cost me quite a *s* to get my citizenship."
Rom 5:18 To *s* up, then: just as a single offense
1Cor 7:38 To *s* up: the man who marries his virgin
1Pt 1:18 by any diminishable *s* of silver or gold,
Rv 3: 2 I find that the *s* of your deeds is less

SUMMARY (3)

2Mc 2:28 our efforts to giving only a *s* outline.
10:10 a *s* of the chief evils caused by the wars.
1Pt 3: 8 In *s*, then, all of you should be like-minded,

SUMMED (1)

Rom 13: 9 there may be are all *s* up in this,

SUMMER (20)

Gn 8:22 heat, seedtime and harvest, *S* and winter,
2Sm 16: 1 of pressed raisins, an ephah of *s* fruits,
16: 2 and *s* fruits are for your servants to eat,
Ps(s) 32: 4 strength was dried up as by the heat of *s*.
74:17 *s* and winter you made.
Prv 6: 8 or ruler, She procures her food in the *s*,
10: 5 who fills the granaries in *s* is a credit;
26: 1 Like snow in *s*, or rain in harvest,
30:25 yet they store up their food in the *s*;
Sir 50: 8 Like the trees of Lebanon in *s*,
Is 16: 9 For on your *s* fruits and harvests the
18: 6 The birds of prey shall *s* on them and on
28: 4 valley Will be like an early fig before *s*:
Jer 8:20 harvest has passed, the *s* is at an end,
Dn 2:35 as the chaff on the threshing floor in *s*,
Am 3:15 I strike the winter house and the *s* house;
Zec 14: 8 sea, and it shall be so in *s* and in winter.
Mt 24:32 sprouts leaves, you realize that *s* is near.
Mk 13:28 to sprout leaves, you know that *s* is near.
Lk 21:30 and know for yourselves that *s* is near.

SUMMIT (4)

2Chr 25:12 to the *s* of the Rock and then cast down,
Jdt 7:10 not easy to reach the *s* of their mountains.
Am 1: 2 will languish, and the *s* of Carmel wither.
9: 3 Though they hide on the *s* of Carmel,

SUMMITS (5)

Dt 32:13 He had them ride triumphant over the *s* of
Jdt 4: 5 guards on all the *s* of the high mountains,
5: 1 fortified the *s* of all the higher peaks,
7:13 go up to the *s* of the nearby mountains,
Sir 46: 9 Till he won his way onto the *s* of the land;

SUMMON (28)

Nm 3: 6 *S* the tribe of Levi and present them to
22:20 to him, "If these men have come to *s* you,
Dt 25: 8 of his city shall *s* him and admonish him.
31:14 *S* Joshua, and present yourselves
2Sm 20: 4 *S* the Judahites for me within three days.
20: 5 Accordingly Amasa set out to *s* Judah,
1Kgs 18:19 Now *s* all Israel to me on Mount Carmel,
2Kgs 10:19 Now *s* for me all Baal's prophets,
1Chr 13: 2 let us *s* the rest of our brethren from all
Tb 5: 9 Tobiah went out to *s* the man,
Jdt 7:26 *s* them and deliver the whole city as booty
14: 5 doing this, *s* for me Achior the Ammonite,
Is 22:20 On that day I will *s* my servant Eliakim,
41:25 from the east I *s* him by name;
55: 5 So shall you *s* a nation you knew not,
Jer 4: 5 trumpet through the land, *s* the recruits!
9:16 wailing women to come, *s* the best of them;
30:21 When I *s* him, he shall approach me;
51:27 against her, *s* against her the kingdoms,
Ez 23:46 *S* an assembly against them,
38:21 Against him I will *s* every terror,
Dn 5:12 *s* Daniel to tell you what this means."
Am 5:16 They shall *s* the farmers to wail and
9: 6 I *s* the waters of the sea and pour them
Mt 18:16 If he does not listen, *s* another,
22: 3 to *s* the invited guests to the wedding,
Acts 10: 5 some men to Joppa and *s* a certain Simon,
10:22 by a holy messenger to *s* you to his house.

SUMMONED (107)

Gn 12:18 Then Pharaoh *s* Abram and said to him:
20: 9 Then Abimelech *s* Abraham and said to him:
41: 8 So he *s* all the magicians and sages of
41:14 Pharaoh therefore had Joseph *s*,
Ex 1:18 So the king *s* the midwives and asked them,
7:11 Pharaoh, in turn, *s* wise men and sorcerers,
8: 4 Then Pharaoh *s* Moses and Aaron and said,
8:21 *s* Moses and Aaron and said to them,
9:27 Pharaoh *s* Moses and Aaron and said to them,
10:16 Hastily Pharaoh *s* Moses and Aaron and said,
10:24 Pharaoh then *s* Moses and Aaron and said,
12:31 night Pharaoh *s* Moses and Aaron and said,
19: 7 Moses went and *s* the elders of the people.
19:20 he *s* Moses to the top of the mountain,
Lv 9: 1 the eighth day Moses *s* Aaron and his sons,
10: 4 Then Moses *s* Mishael and Elzaphan,
Nm 16:12 Moses *s* Dathan and Abiram, sons of Eliab,
24:10 was to curse my foes that I *s* you here;
Dt 5: 1 Moses *s* all Israel and said to them,
29: 1 Moses *s* all Israel and said to them,
31: 7 Then Moses *s* Joshua and in the presence of
Jos 9:22 Joshua *s* the Gibeonites and said to them,
10:24 Joshua *s* all the men of Israel and said to
22: 1 At that time Joshua *s* the Reubenites,
23: 2 he *s* all Israel (including their elders,
24: 9 He *s* Balaam, son of Beor, to curse you;
Jgs 4: 6 She sent and *s* Barak,
4:10 Barak *s* Zebulun and Naphtali to Kedesh,
6:34 blew the horn that *s* Abiezer to follow him.
12: 2 I *s* you, but you did not rescue me
16:18 she *s* the lords of the Philistines,
1Sm 5: 8 So they *s* all the Philistine lords and
6: 2 they *s* priests and fortune-tellers to ask,
19: 7 So Jonathan *s* David and repeated the whole
29: 6 So Achish *s* David and said to him:
2Sm 9: 2 He was *s* to David,
11:13 On the day following, David *s* him,
14:29 Then he *s* Joab to send him to the king,
14:29 Although he *s* him a second time,
19:15 one man, and so they *s* the king to return,
1Kgs 1:32 Then King David *s* Zadok the priest,
2:36 Then the king *s* Shimei and said to him:
2:42 the king *s* Shimei and said to him:
12:20 they *s* him to an assembly and made him
15:22 King Asa *s* all Judah without exception,
18: 4 Samaria was bitter, and Ahab had *s* Obadiah,
20: 7 then *s* all the elders of the land and said:
2Kgs 4:36 Elisha *s* Gehazi and said,
7:10 They came and *s* the city gatekeepers.
11: 4 Jehoiada *s* the captains of the Carians and
12: 8 King Joash *s* the priest Jehoiada and the
23: 1 and of Jerusalem *s* together before him.
1Chr 15:11 David *s* the priests Zadok and Abiathar,
2Chr 10: 3 Jeroboam was *s* to the assembly,
24: 6 Then the king *s* Jehoiada,
29: 4 He *s* the priests and Levites,
Tb 8: 9 But Raguel got up and *s* his servants.
8:20 *s* Tobiah and made an oath in his presence,
Jdt 2: 2 He *s* all his ministers and nobles,
2: 4 king of the Assyrians, *s* Holofernes,
2:14 of his lord, and *s* all the princes,
5: 2 anger he *s* all the rulers of the Moabites,
13:12 to their city gate and *s* the city elders.
Est 1:14 He *s* Carshena,
2:14 was pleased with her and had her *s* by name.
3:12 So the royal scribes were *s*;
4: 5 Esther then *s* Hathach,
4:11 king in the inner court without being *s*,
4:11 not been *s* to the king for thirty days."
5:10 where he *s* his friends and his wife Zeresh.
8: 9 month, Sivan, the royal scribes were *s*.
1Mc 1: 6 He therefore *s* his officers,
6:14 Then he *s* Philip, one of his Friends,
2Mc 4:28 this reason, both were *s* before the king.
8: 1 the village secretly, *s* their kinsmen,
12: 5 against his countrymen, he *s* his men;
Ps(s) 50: 1 God the LORD has spoken and *s* the earth,
Wis 18: 8 in this you glorified us whom you had *s*.
Is 13: 3 dedicated soldiers, I have *s* my warriors,
41: 2 of justice, and *s* him to be his attendant?
41: 9 of the earth and *s* from its far-off places,
Jer 38:14 Once King Zedekiah *s* the prophet Jeremiah
Lam 1:15 *s* an army against me to crush my young men;
2:22 "You *s* as for a feast day terrors against
Ez 38:13 it for pillage that you have *s* your horde,
Dn 2: 2 be *s* to interpret the dream for him.
3: 2 officials of the provinces to be *s*
Mt 10: 1 Then he *s* his twelve disciples and gave
15:10 He *s* the crowd and said to them:
28:16 to the mountain to which Jesus had *s* them.
Mk 1:20 He *s* them on the spot.
3:13 and *s* the men he himself had decided on,
6: 7 Jesus *s* the Twelve and began to send them
7:14 He *s* the crowd again and said to them:
8:34 He *s* the crowd with his disciples and
15:44 He *s* the centurion and inquired whether
Lk 16: 2 He *s* him and said, 'What is this I hear
19:13 He *s* ten of his servants and gave them
Jn 9:18 until they *s* the parents of this man who
9:24 A second time they *s* the man who had been
18:33 went back into the praetorium and *s* Jesus.
Acts 10:29 of course, like to know why you *s* me."
13: 7 a man of intelligence who had *s* Barnabas
16:10 had *s* us to proclaim the good news there.
22:30 He *s* the chief priests and the whole
23:23 *s* two of his centurions and said to them,
Phil 1: 7 am *s* to defend the solid grounds

SUMMONING (11)

Nm 22: 5 of the Amawites, *s* him with these words,
Jos 4: 4 *S* the twelve men whom he had selected from
6: 6 *S* the priests, Joshua, son of Nun,
24: 1 of Israel at Shechem, *s* their elders,
2Sm 14:32 "I was *s* you to come here,
Jer 1:15 Lo, I am *s* all the kingdoms of the north,
Mt 2: 4 *S* all of the chief priests and scribes of
Mk 3:23 *S* them, he then began to speak to them
Lk 7:18 *S* two of them, John sent them to ask
21:12 you, *s* you to synagogues and prisons,
Acts 20:17 Ephesus, *s* the presbyters of that church.

SUMMONS (11)

Gn 46:33 *s* you and asks what your occupation is,
Nm 22:37 to Balaam, "I sent an urgent *s* to you!
Jgs 6:35 Manasseh, which also obeyed his *s*;
1Sm 5:11 *s* to all the Philistine lords and pleaded:
22:11 the king sent a *s* to Ahimelech the priest,
2Chr 1: 2 He sent a *s* to all Israel,
Jdt 1:11 land disregarded the *s* of Nebuchadnezzar,
Ps(s) 50: 4 He *s* the heavens from above,
Am 5: 8 Who *s* the waters of the sea,
Acts 10:29 to your *s* without raising any objection.
24: 2 Following Paul's *s* to the bar,

SUMPTUOUS (3)

1Mc 16:15 While serving them a *s* banquet,
Sir 29:22 roof than *s* banquets among strangers.
Hb 1:16 his portion is generous, and his repast *s*.

SUMPTUOUSLY (1)

2Mc 4:49 the crime and provided *s* for their burial.

SUMS (4)

1Mc 14:32 spending large *s* of his own money to equip
Ps(s) 10: 4 "There is no God," *s* up his thoughts.
Mt 7:12 this *s* up the law and the prophets.
Lk 19:13 servants and gave them *s* of ten units each,

SUN (161)

Gn 15:12 As the *s* was about to set,
15:17 When the *s* had set and it was dark,
19:23 The *s* was just rising over the earth as
28:11 a certain shrine, as the *s* had already set,
37: 9 the *s* and the moon and eleven stars were
Ex 16:21 but when the *s* grew hot,
Lv 22: 7 his body in water, then when the *s* sets,
Dt 4:19 look up to the heavens and behold the *s*
17: 3 or by worshiping the *s* or the moon or any
23:12 then, when the *s* has set,
Jos 10:12 Stand still, O *s*,
10:13 And the *s* stood still,
10:13 The *s* halted in the middle of the sky;
Jgs 5:31 friends be as the *s* rising in its might!
14:18 On the seventh day, before the *s* set,
19:14 So they continued on their way till the *s*
1Sm 11: 9 that tomorrow, while the *s* is hot,
2Sm 2:24 The *s* had gone down when they came to the
12:12 of all Israel, and with the *s* looking down.'"
2Kgs 3:22 morning, when the *s* shone on the water,
23: 5 who burned incense to Baal, to the *s*,
23:11 the kings of Judah had dedicated to the *s*;
23:11 The chariots of the *s* he destroyed by fire.
2Chr 18:34 He died as the *s* was setting.
Neh 7: 3 the *s* is hot, and while the sun
Jdt 14: 2 At daybreak, when the *s* rises on the earth,
Est A:10 The light of the *s* broke forth;
F: 3 that grew into a river, the light of the *s*,

1Mc 6:39 the *s* shone on the gold and bronze shields,
12:27 Therefore, when the *s* set,
2Mc 1:22 When this was done and in time the *s*,
Jb 9: 7 He commands the *s*,
30:28 I go about in gloom, without the *s*;
31:26 Had I looked upon the *s* as it shone,
Ps(s) 19: 5 He has pitched a tent there for the *s*,
50: 1 from the rising of the *s* to its setting.
58: 9 an untimely birth that never sees the *s*.
72: 5 May he endure as long as the *s*,
72:17 as long as the *s* his name shall remain.
74:16 you fashioned the moon and the *s*.
84:12 For a *s* and a shield is the LORD God;
89:37 his throne shall be like the *s* before me;
104:19 the *s* knows the hour of its setting.
104:22 When the *s* rises,
113: 3 *s* is the name of the LORD to be praised.
121: 6 The *s* shall not harm you by day,
136: 8 The *s* to rule over the day,
148: 3 Praise him, *s* and moon;
Eccl 1: 3 the labor which he toils at under the *s*?
1: 5 sun rises and the *s* goes down
1: 9 Nothing is new under the *s*.
1:13 all things that are done under the *s*.
1:14 seen all things that are done under the *s*,
2:11 wind, with nothing gained under the *s*.
2:17 the work that is done under the *s* is evil;
2:18 all the fruits of my labor under the *s*,
2:19 the fruits of my wise labor under the *s*.
2:20 of all the fruits of my labor under the *s*.
2:22 with which he has labored under the *s*?
3:16 *s* in the judgment place I saw wickedness,
4: 1 oppressions that take place under the *s*:
4: 3 the wicked work that is done under the *s*.
4: 7 Again I found this vanity under the *s*:
4:15 live and move about under the *s* with the heir
5:12 evil which I have seen under the *s*:
5:17 all the fruits of his labor under the *s*
6: 1 another evil which I have seen under the *s*,
6: 5 though it has not seen or known the *s*,
6:12 a man what will come after him under the *s*?
7:11 and an advantage to those that see the *s*.
8: 9 to every work that is done under the *s*,
8:15 the *s* except eating and drinking and mirth:
8:15 the life which God gives him under the *s*.
8:17 all God's work that is done under the *s*,
9: 3 all the things that happen under the *s*,
9: 6 part in anything that is done under the *s*.
9: 9 life that is granted you under the *s*.
9: 9 for the toil of your labors under the *s*.
9:11 *s* that the race is not won by the swift,
9:13 hand I saw this wise deed under the *s*,
10: 5 I have seen under the *s* another evil,
11: 7 it is pleasant for the eyes to see the *s*.
12: 2 Before the *s* is darkened.
Sg 1: 6 I am swarthy, because the *s* has burned me.
6:10 as the moon, as resplendent as the *s*,
Wis 5: 6 for us, and the *s* did not rise for us.
7:29 For she is fairer than the *s* and surpasses
18: 3 and the mild *s* for an honorable migration.
Sir 17:15 their actions are clear as the *s* to him,
17:26 Is anything brighter than the *s*?
23:19 ten thousand times brighter than the *s*,
26:16 Like the *s* rising in the LORD's heavens,
33: 7 when it is the *s* that lights up every day?
34:16 from the heat, a shade from the noonday *s*,
42:16 As the rising *s* is clear to all,
43: 2 The orb of the *s*,
46: 4 Did he not by his power stop the *s*,
48:23 the *s* and prolonged the life of the king.
50: 7 Like the *s* shining upon the temple,
Is 13:10 The *s* is dark when it rises,
19:18 one shall be called "City of the *S*."
24:23 the moon will blush and the *s* grow pale,
30:26 of the moon will be like that of the *s*
30:26 light of the *s* will be seven times greater
38: 8 I will make the shadow cast by the *s* on
38: 8 *s* came back the ten steps it had advanced.
45: 6 rising and the setting of the *s* men may know
49:10 the scorching wind or the *s* strike them;
60:19 No longer shall the *s* be your light by day,
60:20 No longer shall your *s* go down,
Jer 8: 2 spread out before the *s* and the moon
15: 9 Her *s* sets in full day,
31:35 LORD, He who gives the *s* to light the day,
43:13 smash the obelisks of the temple of the *s*
Bar 6:59 The *s* and moon and stars are bright,
6:66 heavens, nor are they brilliant like the *s*,
Ez 8:16 they were bowing down to the *s*.
32: 7 The *s* I will cover with clouds,
Dn 3:62 *S* and moon, bless the Lord;
Jl 2:10 The *s* and the moon are darkened,
3: 4 The *s* will be turned to darkness,
4:15 *S* and moon are darkened,
Am 8: 9 I will make the *s* set at midday and cover
Jon 4: 8 And when the *s* arose,
4: 8 and the *s* beat upon Jonah's head
Mi 3: 6 The *s* shall go down upon the prophets,
Na 3:17 Yet when the *s* warms them,
Hb 3:10 The *s* forgets to rise,
Zec 8: 7 sun, and from the land of the setting *s*.
Mal 1:11 your hands, For from the rising of the *s*,
3:20 the *s* of justice with its healing rays;
Mt 5:45 for his *s* rises on the bad and the good,
13: 6 depth, but when the *s* rose and scorched it,
13:43 shine like the *s* in their Father's kingdom.
17: 2 His face became as dazzling as the *s*,
24:29 of that period, 'the *s* will be darkened,
Mk 4: 6 Then, when the *s* rose and scorched it,
13:24 of every sort the *s* will be darkened,
Lk 21:25 "There will be signs in the *s*,
23:44 midafternoon with an eclipse of the *s*.
Acts 2:20 The *s* shall be turned to darkness and the
13:11 be blind, unable so much as to see the *s*."
26:13 than the *s* shining in the sky at midday.
27:20 the *s* nor the stars were to be seen,
1Cor 15:41 The *s* has a splendor of its own,
Eph 4:26 The *s* must not go down on your wrath;
Jas 1:11 When the *s* comes up with its scorching
Rv 1:16 his face shone like the *s* at its brightest.
6:12 the *s* turned black as a goat's-hair
7:16 shall the *s* or its heat beat down on them,
8:12 angel blew his trumpet, a third of the *s*,
9: 2 The *s* and the air were darkened by the
10: 1 the *s* and his legs like pillars of fire.
12: 1 in the sky, a woman clothed with the *s*,
16: 8 fourth angel poured out his bowl on the *s*.
19:17 Next I saw an angel standing on the *s*.
21:23 The city had no need of *s* or moon,
22: 5 will need no light from lamps or the *s*,

SUNBEAM (1)

Wis 16:27 fire, when merely warmed by a momentary *s*,

SUNBURSTS (1)

Is 3:18 do away with the finery of the anklets, *s*,

SUNDERED (1)

Sir 50:12 When he received the *s* victims

SUNDOWN (2)

Dt 24:15 day's wages before *s* on the day itself,
1Sm 30:17 From dawn to *s* David attacked them,

SUNG (4)

Wis 18: 9 previously *s* the praises of the fathers.
Sir 47: 8 his Maker and daily had his praises *s*;
Ez 32:16 This is a dirge, and it shall be *s*:
Mi 2: 4 On that day a satire shall be *s* over you,

SUNK (9)

Jb 38: 6 Into what were its pedestals *s*,
Ps(s) 9:16 nations are *s* in the pit they have made;
38: 3 For your arrows have *s* deep in me,
69: 3 I am *s* in the abysmal swamp where there is
Wis 10: 5 the nations were *s* in universal wickedness,
Jer 43:10 these stones which I, Jeremiah, have *s*,
Lam 2: 9 *S* into the ground are her gates;
Hos 5: 2 perversity they have *s* into wickedness,
9: 9 They have *s* to the depths of corruption,

SUNLIGHT (2)

Tb 3:17 eyes, so that he might again see God's *s*;
5:10 I am, a blind man who cannot see God's *s*,

SUNRISE (11)

Gn 32:32 At *s*, as he left Penuel, Jacob limped
Ex 22: 2 But if after *s* he is thus beaten,
Nm 2: 3 "Encamped on the east side, toward the *s*,
3:38 front of the meeting tent, toward the *s*,
34:15 stretch of the Jordan, toward the *s*."
Jgs 9:33 Promptly at *s* tomorrow morning,
2Sm 23: 4 morning light at *s* on a cloudless morning,
Jb 8:16 He is full of sap before *s*,
Wis 16:28 that one must give you thanks before the *s*,
Mk 16: 2 Very early, just after *s*,
Lk 12:38 or before *s* and find them prepared,

SUNS (2)

Wis 2: 4 by the *s* rays and overpowered by its heat.
7:18 *s* course and the variations of the seasons.

SUNSET (16)

Ex 17:12 so that his hands remained steady till *s*.
22:25 you shall return it to him before *s*;
Dt 16: 6 of his name, and in the evening at *s*,
24:13 him at *s* that he himself may sleep in it.
Jos 8:29 then at *s* Joshua ordered the body removed
10:27 At *s* they were removed from the trees at
2Sm 3:35 if I eat bread or anything else before *s*."
1Kgs 22:36 At *s* a cry went through the army,
Tb 2: 4 rooms, so that I might bury him after *s*.
2: 7 Then at *s* I went out,
10: 7 At *s* she would go back home to wait and
1Mc 10:50 He pressed the battle hard until *s*,
Dn 6:15 he worked till *s* to rescue him.
Mk 1:32 After *s*, as evening drew on,
Lk 4:40 At *s*, all who had people sick
9:12 As *s* approached the Twelve came and said

SUNSHINE (1)

Is 18: 4 where I dwell, Like the glowing heat of *s*,

SUNSTROKE (1)

Jdt 8: 3 who bound the sheaves, he suffered *s*;

SUPER-APOSTLES (2)

2Cor 11: 5 inferior to the "*s*" in nothing.
12:11 in no way inferior to the "*s*."

SUPERFICIALLY (1)

2Cor 10: 7 You view things *s*.

SUPERHUMAN (1)

2Mc 9: 8 he who previously, in his *s* presumption,

SUPERINTENDED (3)

1Chr 26:20 Their brother Levites *s* the stores for the
26:22 *s* the treasures of the house of the LORD.
26:26 This Shelomith and his brethren *s* all the

SUPERINTENDENT (6)

1Kgs 4: 6 son of Abda, *s* of the forced labor.
12:18 sent out Adoram, *s* of the forced labor,
16: 9 house of Arza, *s* of his palace in Tirzah,
1Chr 26:24 of Moses, was chief *s* over the treasures.
2Chr 10:18 out Hadoram, who was *s* of the forced labor,
2Mc 3: 4 who had been appointed *s* of the temple,

SUPERIOR (3)

Phil 2: 3 think humbly of others as *s* to themselves.
Heb 1: 4 as far *s* to the angels as the name he has
1: 4 the name he has inherited is *s* to theirs.

SUPERIORITY (1)

Rom 3: 9 do we find ourselves in a position of *s*?

SUPERIORS (1)

1Mc 10:37 Let their *s* and their rulers be taken from

SUPERVENED (1)

Heb 7:19 But a better hope has *s*,

SUPERVISE (3)

Ezr 3: 8 to *s* the work on the house of the LORD.
3: 9 stood as one man to *s* those who were
7:14 king and his seven counselors to *s* Judah

SUPERVISED (1)

Nm 7: 2 princes of the tribes who *s* the census.

SUPERVISING (1)

Jdt 8: 3 in the field *s* those who bound the sheaves,

SUPERVISION (6)

Nm 4:28 and they shall be under the *s* of Ithamar,
4:33 in the meeting tent under the *s* of Ithamar,
7: 8 to their duties, under the *s* of Ithamar,
8:22 tent under the *s* of Aaron and his sons.
2Mc 3: 4 high priest about the *s* of the city market.
Gal 4: 2 for he is under the *s* of guardians and

SUPERVISOR (1)

Nm 3:32 he was *s* over those who had charge of the

SUPERVISORS (7)

1Kgs 9:23 The *s* of Solomon's works who policed the
2Chr 31:13 Mahath and Benaiah were *s* subject to
Dn 6: 3 these were accountable to three *s*,
6: 4 Daniel outshone all the *s* and satraps
6: 5 Therefore the *s* and satraps tried to find
6: 7 So these *s* and satraps went thronging to
6: 8 All the *s* of the kingdom,

SUPH (1)

Dt 1: 1 [in the desert, in the Arabah, opposite *S*,

SUPHAH (1)

Nm 21:14 "Waheb in *S* and the waidies,

SUPPER (14)

Mt 26:17 wish us to prepare the Passover *s* for you?"
26:19 had ordered, and prepared the Passover *s*.
Mk 14:12 us to go to prepare the Passover *s* for you?"
14:16 them, and they prepared the Passover *s*.
Lk 17: 8 Would you not rather say, 'Prepare my *s*.
22: 8 "Go and prepare our Passover *s* for us."
22:13 accordingly they prepared the Passover *s*.
Jn 13: 2 so, during the *s*, Jesus—fully aware
18:28 if they were to eat the Passover *s*.
21:20 against Jesus' chest during the *s* and said,
1Cor 11:20 assemble it is not to eat the Lord's *S*,
11:21 for everyone is in haste to eat his own *s*.
11:25 In the same way, after the *s*,

SUPPER (cont.)
Rv 3:20 I will enter his house and have *s* with him,

SUPPLANT (1)
Dt 31: 3 nations before you, that you may *s* them.

SUPPLANTED (2)
Gn 27:36 He has now *s* me twice!
Hos 12: 4 In the womb he *s* his brother,

SUPPLANTER (1)
Jer 9: 3 Every brother apes Jacob, the *s*,

SUPPLANTS (1)
Wis 7:30 for that, indeed, night *s*,

SUPPLIANTS (1)
Tb 3:16 the prayer of these two *s* was heard in the

SUPPLICATION (21)
1Kgs 8:28 my God, and listen to the cry of *s* which I,
2Chr 6:19 the cry of *s* your servant makes before you.
33:19 His prayer and how his *s* was heard,
Est 9:31 upon their race the duty of fasting and *s*.
1Mc 11:49 courage and cried out to the king in *s*,
2Mc 3:18 their houses in crowds to make public *s*,
3:20 with hands raised toward heaven, making *s*.
8:29 When this was done, they made *s* in common,
9:18 letter to the Jews in the form of a *s*.
10:25 Maccabeus and his men made *s* to God,
12:42 Turning to *s*, they prayed
15:26 his men met the army with *s* and prayers.
Jb 8: 5 recourse to God and make *s* to the Almighty,
Ps(s) 116: 1 LORD because he has heard my voice in *s*,
119:170 Let my *s* reach you;
130: 2 your ears be attentive to my voice in *s*:
140: 7 hearken, O LORD, to my voice in *s*.
Jer 14:12 If they fast, I will not listen to their *s*.
36: 7 Perhaps they will lay their *s* before the
Bar 2:14 Hear, O Lord, our prayer of *s*,
4:20 have put on sackcloth for my prayer of *s*,

SUPPLICATIONS (2)
1Tm 5: 5 continues night and day in *s* and prayers.
Heb 5: 7 and *s* with loud cries and tears to God,

SUPPLIED (16)
Gn 45:21 he *s* them with provisions for the journey.
Ex 5:13 same daily amount as when your straw was *s*."
5:16 No straw is *s* to your servants,
Nm 4: 9 containers of oil from which it is *s*.
1Kgs 4: 7 who *s* food for the king and his household,
18: 4 two caves, and *s* them with food and drink.
18:13 two caves, and *s* them with food and drink?
20:27 were called to arms and *s* with provisions;
Jdt 12: 2 amply *s* from the things I brought with me."
1Mc 14:10 He *s* the cities with food and equipped
Eccl 1:15 straight, and what is missing cannot be *s*.
Sir 39:16 in its own time every need is *s*.
Jn 18: 3 *s* by the chief priests and the Pharisees,
Acts 12:20 was *s* with food from the king's territory.
2Cor 11: 9 who came from Macedonia *s* my needs.
Phil 4:18 I am well *s* because of what I received

SUPPLIES (15)
Gn 14:11 seized all the possessions and food *s*
Ex 7:19 canals and pools, all their *s* of water
Jgs 7: 8 and such *s* as the soldiers had with them,
20:10 and procuring *s* for the soldiers who will
1Sm 22:10 consulted the LORD for him and gave him *s*,
1Kgs 5: 2 Solomon's *s* for each day were thirty kors
9:19 the desert of Judah, all his cities for *s*,
2Chr 11:11 and put commanders in them, with *s* of food,
Jdt 12: 4 your handmaid will not use up her *s* till
2Mc 12:27 were large *s* of machines and missiles.
13:20 Judas then sent *s* to the men inside,
Is 3: 1 and prop [all *s* of bread and water]:
10:28 Migron, at Michmash his *s* are stored.
2Cor 9:10 He who *s* seed for the sower and bread for
9:12 benefit not only *s* the needs of the members

SUPPLY (21)
Gn 42: 3 to buy an emergency *s* of grain from Egypt.
Ex 1:11 Pharaoh the *s* cities of Pithom and Raamses.
5: 7 "You shall no longer *s* the people with
Lv 26:26 And as I cut off your *s* of bread,
Dt 2:28 For the food I eat which you will *s*,
Jos 22: 8 iron, and with a very large *s* of clothing,
1Chr 22:15 have available an unlimited *s* of workmen,
2Chr 8: 4 in the desert region and all the *s* cities,
8: 6 all the *s* cities belonging to Solomon,
31:10 This great *s* is what was left over."
Ezr 7:20 *s* for the needs of the house of your God,
Jdt 2:17 sheep, cattle, and goats for their food *s*;
7:17 water *s* and the springs of the Israelites.
2Mc 12:11 promised to *s* the Jews with cattle
12:14 of their walls and their *s* of provisions,
Prv 27:27 milk to supply you, [to *s* your household,]
Is 33:16 fastness, his food and drink in steady *s*.
2Cor 8:14 Your plenty at the present time should *s*
8:14 that their surplus may one day *s* your need,
Phil 4:19 My God in turn will *s* your needs fully,

SUPPLYING (1)
1Kgs 9:11 of Tyre, *s* Solomon with all the cedar wood,

SUPPORT (43)
Gn 13: 6 could not *s* them if they stayed together;
36: 7 not *s* them because of their livestock.
Jgs 16:26 *s* the temple and may rest against them."
Ru 4:15 be your comfort and the *s* of your old age,
2Sm 22:19 day of calamity, but the LORD came to my *s*.
2Chr 31: 4 provide the *s* of the priests and Levites,
32: 3 When they had pledged him their *s*,
Ezr 5: 2 with the prophets of God giving them *s*.
8:36 *s* to the people and to the house of God.
Tb 8: 6 him his wife Eve to be his help and *s*;
Jdt 7: 1 the allied troops that had come to his *s*,
7: 4 valleys and hills can *s* the mass of them."
Est D: 3 on the one she leaned gently for *s*,
1Mc 12:15 with the help of Heaven for our *s*,
15:26 to Antiochus' *s* two thousand elite troops,
Jb 24:23 of his life he gives safety and *s*.
Ps(s) 18:19 of my calamity, but the LORD came to my *s*.
55:23 your care upon the LORD, and he will *s* you;
Prv 28:17 to flee to the grave, none should *s* him.
Sir 3:30 when he falls, he finds a *s*.
22:25 in need of *s* no one need hide in shame;
34:15 In whom does he trust, and who is his *s*?
34:16 he is their mighty shield and strong *s*,
40:26 he who has it need seek no other *s*:
Is 3: 1 from Jerusalem and from Judah *s* and prop
59:16 victory, and his justice lent him its *s*.
63: 5 appalled that there was no one to lend *s*;
63: 5 the victory and my own wrath lent me its *s*.
Lam 2: 3 He withheld the *s* of his right hand when
Ez 7:11 violence has risen to *s* wickedness.
30: 6 Those who *s* Egypt shall fall,
Mt 4: 6 with their hands they will *s* you that you
15: 5 Any *s* you might have had from me is
Mk 7:11 Any *s* you might have had from me is
Lk 4:11 again, 'With their hands they will *s* you,
Acts 2:40 In *s* of his testimony he used many other
Rom 11:18 boast, remember that you do not *s* the root;
2Cor 2: 7 you should now relent and *s* him so that he
11: 8 *s* from them in order to minister to you.
Phil 1:19 thanks to your prayers and the *s* I receive
1Thes 5:14 *s* the weak; be patient toward all.
1Tm 5: 4 fittingly *s* their parents and grandparents;
3Jn 1: 8 we owe it to such men to *s* them and thus

SUPPORTED (16)
Ex 17:12 Meanwhile Aaron and Hur *s* his hands,
1Kgs 1: 7 with Abiathar the priest, and they *s* him.
7: 2 it was *s* by four rows of cedar columns,
2Kgs 16:17 bronze sea from the bronze oxen that *s* it,
1Chr 11:10 *s* him in his reign in order to make him
Ezr 6:14 building, *s* by the message of the prophets,
Est 9: 3 *s* the Jews from fear of Mordecai;
1Mc 2:17 man in this city, *s* by sons and kinsmen.
2:43 from the disaster joined them and *s* them.
3: 2 and all who had joined his father *s* him,
2Mc 7:27 up, educated and *s* you to your present age.
Sir 13:20 a rich man stumbles he is *s* by a friend;
Acts 24: 9 The Jews *s* this indictment and maintained
1Cor 9:13 who work in the temple are *s* by the temple,
Col 2:19 mutually *s* and upheld by joints and sinews,
1Tm 5:19 unless it is *s* by two or three witnesses.

SUPPORTER (1)
Jdt 9:11 helper of the oppressed, the *s* of the weak,

SUPPORTERS (7)
2Kgs 10:11 in Jezreel, as well as all his powerful *s*,
1Mc 7: 7 and let him punish them and all their *s*."
12:34 over this stronghold to the *s* of Demetrius.
Jb 31:21 because I saw that I had *s* at the gate
Sir 13:21 are the *s* for a rich man when he speaks;
Acts 5:17 high priest and all his *s* (that is,
5:21 his *s* arrived they convoked the Sanhedrin,

SUPPORTING (3)
1Kgs 7:44 the stands, one sea, twelve oxen *s* the sea,
Ezr 10:15 and Shabbethai the Levite *s* them.
Eph 4:16 joined firmly together by each *s* ligament,

SUPPORTS (13)
Ex 25:12 and fasten them on the four *s* of the ark,
37: 3 rings were cast and put on its four *s*,
1Kgs 7:35 with *s* and panels which were of one piece
7:36 On the surfaces of the *s* and on the panels,
10:12 With the wood the king made *s* for the
Jdt 13: 9 off the bed and took the canopy from its *s*.
Ps(s) 37:17 shall be broken, but the LORD *s* the just.
Prv 12: 9 Better a lowly man who *s* himself than one
Sir 25:21 and shame, when a wife *s* her husband.
Ez 41: 6 these served as *s*,
41: 6 there were no *s* in the temple wall proper.
Dn 10:21 No one *s* me against all these
Rom 11:18 the root *s* you.

SUPPOSE (29)
Gn 18:24 *S* there were fifty innocent people in the
27:12 *S* my father feels me?
50:15 *S* Joseph has been nursing a grudge against
Ex 4: 1 "*s* they will not believe me,
Nm 12:14 Moses, *S* her father had spit in her face,
2Sm 16:10 *S* the LORD has told him to curse David;
Tb 6:18 And I *s* that you will have children by her,
Est E: 4 they *s* they will escape the vindictive
Mt 10:34 "Do not *s* that my mission on earth is to
12:11 *S* one of you has a sheep and it falls into
16: 8 do you *s* it is because you have no bread?
21:40 What do you *s* the owner of the vineyard
26:53 Do you not *s* I can call on my Father to
Mk 8:17 *s* that it is because you have no bread?
12: 9 do you *s* the owner of the vineyard will do?
Lk 18: 7 Will he delay long over them, do you *s*?
20:15 What fate do you *s* the owner of the
Jn 4:33 "Do you *s* that someone has brought him
21:22 *S* I want him to stay until I come,"
21:23 *S* I want him to stay until I come [how
Acts 13:25 would say, 'What you *s* me to be I am not.
Rom 2: 3 Do you *s*, then, that you will escape
2:17 Let us *s* you bear the name of "Jew" and
1Cor 14: 6 Just *s*, brothers, that I should come to you
2Cor 1:17 Do you *s* that in making those plans I was
Heb 10:29 Do you not *s* that a much worse punishment
Jas 2: 2 *S* there should come into your assembly a
2: 3 *S* further that you were to take notice of
4: 5 *s* it is to no purpose that Scripture says,

SUPPOSED (7)
Jdt 16:12 the *s* sons of rebel mothers cut them down;
Wis 17: 3 For they who *s* their secret sins were hid
Mt 20:10 group appeared they *s* they would get more;
Lk 3:23 so it was *s*— the son of Joseph,
Jn 7:27 comes, no one is *s* to know his origins."
20:15 She *s* he was the gardener,
1Tm 1: 8 one uses it in the way law is *s* to be used

SUPPOSING (2)
1Cor 7:21 Even *s* you could go free,
Eph 4:21 I am *s*, of course, that he has been preached

SUPPRESS (2)
Nm 17:20 Thus will I *s* from my presence the
Tb 4: 5 and *s* every desire to sin or to break his

SUPPRESSED (4)
1Mc 14:14 he *s* all the lawless and the wicked.
Eccl 12: 4 bird, but all the daughters of song are *s*;
Sir 46: 7 from the people and *s* the wicked complaint
Dn 13: 9 They *s* their consciences;

SUPREME (4)
1Mc 14:47 and to exercise *s* authority over all.'"
Jb 34:17 or will you condemn the *s* Just One,
Ps(s) 47:10 he is *s*.
Sir 45:12 splendor, a delight to the eyes, beauty *s*.

SUR (2)
2Kgs 11: 6 another third shall be at the gate *S*;
Jdt 2:28 Tyre, and those who dwelt in *S* and Ocina,

SURCEASE (1)
Dt 28:33 and crushed at all times without *s*,

SURE (63)
Gn 20: 7 you can be *s* that you and all who are
32:21 be *s* to add, 'Your servant Jacob
Nm 28:19 lambs that you are *s* are unblemished,
28:27 lambs that you are *s* are unblemished,
29: 8 lambs that you are *s* are unblemished,
32:23 and you can be *s* that you will not escape
Dt 12:23 *s* that you do not partake of the blood;
28:66 day and night, never *s* of your existence.
31:29 For I know that after my death you are *s*
1Sm 9: 6 all that he says is *s* to come true.
20: 7 you can be *s* he has planned some harm.
23:22 Go now and make *s* once more!
23:23 Then come back to me with *s* information,
1Kgs 20:23 level ground, we shall be *s* to defeat them.
2Kgs 10:23 "Search and be *s* that there is no
Tb 7:11 I am *s* the Lord will look after you both."
1Mc 11:37 Be *s*, therefore, to have a copy
11:52 King Demetrius was *s* of his royal throne,
2Mc 1:19 making *s* that the place would be unknown
Ps(s) 12: 7 The promises of the LORD are *s*,
111: 7 *s* are all his precepts,
119:140 Your promise is very *s*,
Prv 4:26 for your feet, and let all your ways be *s*.
11:18 but he who sows virture has a *s* reward.
12:17 tells the truth who states what he is *s* of,
14:16 the fool is reckless and *s* of himself.
21: 5 The plans of the diligent are *s* of profit,
28: 1 just man, like a lion, feels *s* of himself.

Wis 1: 6 *s* observer of his heart and the listener
5:18 and shall wear *s* judgment for a helmet;
18: 6 with *s* knowledge of the oaths in which
Sir 32:21 Be not too *s* even of smooth roads,
37:12 man, who you are *s* keeps the commandments;
Is 22:23 I will fix him like a peg in a *s* spot,
22:25 the peg fixed in a *s* spot shall give way,
28:16 A precious cornerstone as a *s* foundation;
Dn 2: 9 that I may be *s* that you can also give its
2:45 what you dreamed, and its meaning is *s*."
Hos 5: 9 of Israel I announce what is *s* to be.
Mt 6: 2 You can be *s* of this much,
24:43 "Be *s* of this:
Lk 16: 3 My employer is *s* to dismiss me.
16: 4 Here is a way to make *s* that people will
Jn 8:52 "Now we are *s* you are possessed,"
11:22 I am *s* that God will give you whatever you
Acts 21:22 your coming, of which they are *s* to hear?
26:27 I am *s* you do."
Rom 2:25 Circumcision, to be *s*,
1Cor 2: 6 There is, to be *s*,
8: 5 there are, to be *s*,
9:10 You can be *s* it was written for us,
14:40 but make *s* that everything is done
15:44 body, be *s* there is also a spiritual body.
16:10 come, be *s* to put him at ease among you.
Gal 2: 2 to make *s* the course I was pursuing,
Eph 3: 2 I am *s* you have heard of the ministry
Phil 1: 6 I am *s* of this much:
Heb 6:19 Like a *s* and firm anchor,
1Jn 2: 3 The way we can be *s* of our knowledge of
2: 5 The way we can be *s* we are in union with
2:29 you can be *s* that everyone who acts in
3:21 we can be *s* that God is with us and that
5: 2 We can be *s* that we love God's children

SURELY (103)

Gn 2:17 you eat from it you are *s* doomed to die."
18:10 *s* return to you about this time next year,
20:11 would *s* be no fear of God in this place,
40: 8 Joseph said to them, *S*,
45:12 *S*, you can see for yourselves,
50:24 God will *s* take care of you and lead you
Ex 18:18 "You will *s* wear yourself out,
22:22 cry out to me, I will *s* hear their cry.
Lv 13:36 the man is *s* unclean.
Nm 20:19 *S* there is no harm in merely letting us
26:65 them that they would *s* die in the desert,
Dt 5:25 *S* this great fire will consume us.
32:36 *S*, the LORD shall do justice for his people:
32:40 As *s* as I live forever,
Jgs 20:39 them as *s* as in the earlier fighting,
1Sm 14:39 Jonathan has committed it, he shall *s* die!"
16: 6 *S* the LORD'S anointed is here before him."
22:21 was there, that he would *s* tell Saul.
24:21 since I know that you shall *s* be king and
28: 9 "You are *s* aware of what Saul has done,
30: 8 shall *s* overtake them and effect a rescue."
2Sm 5:19 *s* deliver the Philistines into your grip."
9: 7 "I will *s* be kind to you for the sake of
12:14 deed, the child born to you must *s* die."
14:16 For the king must *s* consent to free his
1Kgs 20:25 level ground, and we shall *s* defeat them."
2Kgs 5:11 "I thought that he would *s* come out and
8:10 Elisha answered, "that he will *s* recover.
8:14 "He told me that you would *s* recover,"
9:26 'As *s* as I saw yesterday the blood of
18:30 the LORD, saying, The LORD will *s* save us;
1Chr 11: 1 *S*, we are of the same bone and flesh as you.
Jdt 12: 4 Judith answered him, "As *s* as you,
Est 6:13 against him, but will *s* be defeated by him."
Jb 1:11 and *s* he will blaspheme you to your face."
2: 5 and *s* he will blaspheme you to your face."
6:28 *s* I will not lie to your face.
8: 6 *s* now he will awake for you and restore
11:15 *S* then you may lift up your face in
13:11 *S* will his majesty affright you and the
14:16 *S* then you would count my steps,
31:36 *S*, I should wear it on my shoulder or put
34:12 *S*, God cannot act wickedly,
Ps(s) 68:22 *S* God crushes the heads of his enemies,
139:11 If I say, *S* the darkness shall hide me,
140:14 *S* the just shall give thanks to your name:
Prv 23:18 For you will *s* have a future,
Is 8:20 That kind of thing they will *s* say.
36:15 LORD, saying, "The LORD will *s* save us;
56: 3 LORD will *s* exclude me from his people";
Jer 16:14 However, days will *s* come,
19:15 I will *s* bring upon this city all the evil
22:22 *S* then you shall be ashamed and confounded
36:29 Babylon's king shall *s* come and lay waste
44:29 That you may know how *s* my threats of
49:12 you shall *s* drink it.
51:36 *S* I will defend your cause,
51:56 is a God who requites, he will *s* repay.
Bar 2:29 *s* this great and numerous throng will
Ez 3:18 I say to the wicked man, You shall *s* die;
3:21 he shall *s* live because of the warning,
18: 9 he shall *s* live,
18:13 all these abominations, he shall *s* die;
18:17 the sins of his father, but shall *s* live.
18:19 observe all my statutes, he shall *s* live.
18:21 what is right and just, he shall *s* live,
18:28 sins which he committed, he shall *s* live,
30: 9 on the day of Egypt, which is *s* coming.
33: 8 I tell the wicked man that he shall *s* die,
33:13 to the virtuous man that he shall *s* live,
33:14 say to the wicked man that he shall *s* die,
33:15 life, and doing no wrong, he shall *s* live,
33:16 what is right and just, he shall *s* live.
33:33 But when it comes—and it is *s* coming!—they
Am 7:11 and Israel shall *s* be exiled from its land."
Hb 2: 3 If it delays, wait for it, it will *s* come,
Zep 3: 7 I said, *S* now you will fear me,
Mal 3: 6 not fear me, says the LORD of hosts, *S* I,
Mt 26:22 to him one after another, *S* it is not I,
26:25 *S* it is not I, Rabbi?"
27:13 *S* you hear how many charges they bring
Mk 14:19 to him sorrowfully, one by one, *S* not I!"
15: 4 *S* you have some answer?
Lk 5:35 midst, they will *s* fast in those days."
23:47 God by saying, *S* this was an innocent man."
Jn 4:12 *S* you do not pretend to be greater than
7:35 *S* he is not going off to the Diaspora
7:41 *S* the Messiah is not to come from Galilee?
8:24 You will *s* die in your sins unless you
8:53 *S* you do not pretend to be greater than
10:21 *S* a devil cannot open the eyes of the blind!"
11:39 *s* there will be a stench!"
Acts 4:20 *S* we cannot help speaking of what we have
Rom 14:11 It is written, "As *s* as I live,
1Cor 1:26 and *s* not many are well-born.
6: 3 *S*, then, we are up to deciding everyday
10:22 *S* we are not stronger than he!
Gal 1:10 approval, I would *s* not be serving Christ!
Heb 2:16 *S* he did not come to help angels,
Jas 1:13 *S* God, who is beyond the grasp of evil,
2Pt 1:10 *s* those who do so will never be lost.
2:19 for *s* anyone is the slave of that by which
Rv 11: 5 to harm them will *s* be slain in this way.

SURETY (17)

Gn 43: 9 I myself will stand *s* for him.
44:32 the boy from his father by going *s* for him,
Jdt 8:16 make the Lord our God give *s* for his plans.
Jb 17: 3 who is there that will give *s* for me?
Ps(s) 119:122 Be *s* for the welfare of your servant;
Prv 6: 1 son, if you have become *s* to your neighbor,
11:15 is in a bad way who becomes *s* for another,
17:18 in pledge, who becomes *s* for his neighbor.
20:16 Take his garment who becomes *s* for another,
22:26 in pledge, of those who become *s* for debts;
27:13 Take his garment who becomes *s* for another,
Sir 8:13 Go not *s* beyond your means;
29:14 A good man goes *s* for his neighbor,
29:17 Going *s* has ruined many prosperous men and
29:19 The sinner through *s* comes to grief,
29:20 Go *s* for your neighbor according to your
Is 38:14 O Lord, I am in straits; be my *s!*

SURF (1)

Jas 1: 6 like the *s* tossed and driven by the wind.

SURFACE (27)

Gn 2: 6 and was watering all the *s* of the ground
7: 4 and so I will wipe out from the *s* of the
7:18 but the ark floated on the *s* of the waters.
8:13 saw that the *s* of the ground was drying up.
Ex 10:15 They covered the *s* of the whole land,
16:14 there on the *s* of the desert were fine
30: 2 an altar of acacia wood, with a square *s*,
Lv 14:37 seem to go deeper than the *s* of the wall,
1Sm 20:15 enemies of David from the *s* of the earth.
2Kgs 6: 6 the water, and brought the iron to the *s*.
Jb 26:10 He has marked out a circle on the *s* of the
37:12 in their task upon the *s* of the earth,
38:13 till the wicked are shaken from its *s?*
38:30 stone that holds captive the *s* of the deep?
Prv 8:31 the while, playing on the *s* of his earth;
20: 5 human heart is like water far below the *s*,
24:31 its *s* was covered with nettles,
Wis 13:14 red and crimsoned its *s* with red stain,
Sir 16:28 Its *s* he covered with all manner of life
22:17 is like the polished *s* of a smooth wall.
38: 8 in its efficacy on the *s* of the earth.
39:22 Euphrates it enriches the *s* of the earth.
43: 3 At noon it seethes the *s* of the earth,
Is 28:25 When he has leveled the *s*,
Ez 37: 2 how many they were on the *s* of the plain.
Am 5: 8 and pours them out upon the *s* of the earth;
9: 6 sea and pour them upon the *s* of the earth,

SURFACES (1)

1Kgs 7:36 On the *s* of the supports and on the panels,

SURFEIT (1)

Ps(s) 78:25 even a *s* of provisions he sent them.

SURFEITED (2)

Ps(s) 78:29 So they ate and were wholly *s*;
88: 4 For my soul is *s* with troubles and my life

SURGE (6)

Wis 14: 5 have been safe crossing the *s* on a raft.
Is 17:12 that *s* like the surging of mighty waves!
63:15 your might, your *s* of pity and your mercy?
Jer 46: 8 "I will *s* forward," he says, "and cover
Ez 26:10 *s* of his horses shall cover you with dust,
Am 5:24 holocausts, then let justice *s* like water,

SURGED (2)

2Sm 22: 5 "The breakers of death *s* round about me.
Ps(s) 18: 5 The breakers of death *s* round about me,

SURGES (4)

Jb 40:23 though the torrent *s* about his mouth.
Jer 46: 7 Who is this that *s* forward like the Nile,
46: 8 Egypt *s* like the Nile,
Dn 11:10 it returns and *s* around the stronghold,

SURGING (5)

Ps(s) 46: 4 and foam and the mountains quake at its *s*.
89:10 You rule over the *s* of the sea;
Is 17:12 The *s* of nations that surge like the
17:12 that surge like the *s* of mighty waves!
Dn 7:10 A *s* stream of fire flowed out from where

SURIVE (1)

Jb 21: 7 Why do the wicked *s*, grow old,

SURLY (1)

Sir 4:29 Be not *s* in your speech, nor lazy

SURMOUNTED (3)

1Kgs 7:31 This was *s* by a crown one cubit high
2Kgs 25:17 capital five cubits high *s* each pillar,
Jer 52:22 capital five cubits high *s* the one pillar,

SURNAME (1)

Is 44: 5 "The LORD's," and Israel shall be his *s*.

SURNAMED (3)

2Mc 4: 7 *s* Epiphanes succeeded him on the throne,
10: 9 Such was the end of Antiochus *s* Epiphanes.
10:12 Ptolemy, *s* Macron,

SURPASS (3)

Gn 25:23 But one shall *s* the other,
48:19 his younger brother shall *s* him,
1Kgs 10: 7 wisdom and prosperity *s* the report I heard.

SURPASSED (6)

2Sm 13:15 which far *s* the love he had had for her.
1Kgs 5:10 Solomon *s* all the Cedemites and all the
10:23 Thus King Solomon *s* in riches and wisdom
2Chr 9: 6 you have *s* the stories I heard.
9:22 Thus King Solomon *s* all the other kings of
Rom 5:20 the increase of sin, grace has far *s* it,

SURPASSES (7)

Jb 28:18 it *s* pearls and Arabian topaz.
Prv 12:26 The just man *s* his neighbor,
Wis 7:29 sun and *s* every constellation of the stars.
Sir 25:11 Fear of the LORD *s* all else.
36:22 up, for it *s* all else that charms the eye;
Mt 5:20 unless your holiness *s* that of the scribes
Eph 3:19 experience this love which *s* all knowledge,

SURPASSING (7)

Jdt 15: 9 glory of Jerusalem, the *s* joy of Israel;
Ps(s) 103:11 so *s* is his kindness toward those who fear
Sir 26:14 speech, and her firm virtue is of *s* worth.
2Cor 3:10 that limited glory with this *s* glory,
4: 7 its *s* power comes from God and not from us.
9:14 because of the *s* grace God has given you.
Phil 3: 8 of the *s* knowledge of my Lord Jesus Christ.

SURPLUS (4)

Mk 12:44 They gave from their *s* wealth,
Lk 21: 4 They make contributions out of their *s*,
2Cor 8:14 that their *s* may one day supply your need,
9: 8 of everything and even a *s* for good works,

SURPRISE (13)

Ex 4: 6 withdrew it, to his *s* his hand was leprous,
4: 7 *s* it was again like the rest of his body.
Jos 10: 9 And when Joshua made his *s* attack upon
11: 7 them at the waters of Merom in a *s* attack.
1Mc 4: 2 the camp of the Jews and take them by *s*.
Ps(s) 55:16 Let death *s* them;
Prv 14: 7 But knowing lips one meets with by *s*.
Mt 9:33 to speak, to the great *s* of the crowds.
27:14 a single count, much to the procurator's *s*.
Mk 15: 5 But greatly to Pilate's *s*,
Acts 3:12 "Fellow Israelites, why does this *s* you?
2Cor 11:15 It comes as no *s* that his ministers
Rv 6: 2 To my *s*, I saw a white horse;

SURPRISED (14)

Gn 26: 8 s to see Isaac fondling his wife Rebekah.
42:27 s to see his money in the mouth of his bag.
Ex 3: 2 looked on, he was s to see that the bush,
Sir 26:11 are bold, and be not s if she betrays you;
Dn 13:58 me under what tree you s them together."
Mk 15:44 was s that Jesus should have died so soon.
Lk 11:38 the Pharisee was s that he had not first
Jn 3: 7 Do not be s that I tell you you must all
4:27 s that Jesus was speaking with a woman.
5:28 no need for you to be s at this,
Acts 10:45 Peter were s that the gift of the Holy Spirit
1Pt 4: 4 blasphemers are s when you do not plunge
4:12 Do not be s, beloved, that a trial by fire
1Jn 3:13 brothers, to be s if the world hates you.

SURPRISING (1)

Is 29:14 with this people in s and wondrous fashion:

SURRENDER (18)

Lv 26:25 you, till you are forced to s to the enemy.
1Sm 11: 3 If no one rescues us, we will s to you."
11:10 to Nahash, "Tomorrow we will s to you,
2Sm 20:21 S him alone, and I will withdraw
2Kgs 18:31 Make peace with me and s!
Jdt 2:10 If they s to you,
7:13 carry them off, and they will s their city.
8:33 before you will s the city to our enemies,
2Mc 14:31 sacrifices, and ordered them to s Judas.
Wis 17:12 the s of the helps that come from reason;
17:15 and partly stricken by their soul's s;
Sir 9: 6 to harlots, lest you s your inheritance.
23: 6 master me, s me not to shameless desires.
Is 36:16 'Make peace with me and s!
Jer 38:17 If you s to the princes of Babylon's king,
38:18 do not s to the princes of Babylon's king,
38:21 But if you refuse to s,
Heb 10:35 Do not, then, s your confidence;

SURRENDERED (5)

2Sm 21: 9 Meholathite, and s them to the Gibeonites.
2Kgs 24:12 functionaries, s to the king of Babylon,
2Chr 24:24 LORD s a very large force into their power,
Ps(s) 78:61 And he s his strength into captivity,
Is 53:12 Because he s himself to death and was

SURRENDERS (2)

Jer 21: 9 But whoever leaves and s to the besieging
50:15 war cry against her on all sides, She s,

SURROUND (18)

Ex 25:25 S it with a frame,
Nm 34:12 be yours, with the boundaries that s it."
2Kgs 11: 8 You shall s the king,
2Chr 14: 6 build these cities and s them with walls,
23: 7 The Levites shall s the king on all sides,
Ps(s) 5:13 s him with the shield of your good will.
7: 8 Let the assembly of the peoples s you;
17:11 Their steps even now s me;
22:13 Many bullocks s me;
22:17 Indeed, many dogs s me,
140:10 Those who s me lift up their heads;
Sg 3: 7 sixty valiant men s it,
Jer 4:17 Like watchmen of the fields they s her,
Ez 5:14 a reproach among the nations that s you,
5:15 terrible warning to the nations that s you.
Hos 7: 2 Even now their crimes s them,
Am 3:11 An enemy shall s the land,
2Tm 4: 3 will s themselves with teachers who tickle

SURROUNDED (38)

Nm 32:33 its towns and the districts that s them.
Jgs 16: 2 the men of Gaza s him with an ambush at
19:22 corrupt, s the house and beat on the door.
20: 5 me by night and s the house in which I was.
20:43 The men of Benjamin had been s,
2Kgs 3:25 slingers had s it and were attacking it.
6:14 They arrived by night and s the city.
8:21 s him and the commanders of his chariots.
25: 4 Since the Chaldeans had the city s,
25:10 guard tore down the walls that s Jerusalem.
2Chr 21: 9 s him and the commanders of his chariots.
Jdt 2:26 He s all the Midianites,
7:19 since all their enemies had them s,
7:20 kept them thus s for thirty-four days.
1Mc 6: 7 had s with high walls both the sanctuary,
10:80 was an ambush behind him, his army was s.
13:43 Simon besieged Gazara and s it with troops.
2Mc 10:30 They s Maccabeus, and shielding him
Jb 1:10 Have you not s him and his family and all
Eccl 9:14 who s it and threw up great siegeworks
Wis 19:17 When, s by yawning darkness,
Jer 12: 9 is a prey for hyenas, is s by vultures;
52:14 tore down all the walls that s Jerusalem.
Ez 1:27 he was s with splendor.
1:28 on a rainy day was the splendor that s him.
5: 5 I placed her, s by foreign countries.
40: 5 an outer wall that completely s the temple.
42:20 It was s by a wall,
45: 2 cubits, s by a free space of fifty cubits,
46:23 A wall of stones s each of the four,
Hos 12: 1 Ephraim has s me with lies,
Na 3: 8 was set among the streams, S by waters,
Acts 25: 7 Jerusalem s him and leveled many serious
25:18 His accusers s him but they did not charge
26:13 s me and those who were traveling with me.
Heb 12: 1 our part are s by this cloud of witnesses,
Rv 5:11 voices of many angels who s the throne
20: 9 They invaded the whole country and s the

SURROUNDING (37)

Lv 25:31 considered as belonging to the s farm land;
Nm 3:37 of the s court with their pedestals,
4:32 of the s court with their pedestals,
Dt 1: 7 of the Amorites and to all the s regions,
6:14 other gods, such as those of the s nations,
17:14 a king over you like all the s nations,
1Sm 14:47 Saul waged war on all their s enemies
1Kgs 5:17 because of the enemies s him on all sides,
2Kgs 6:15 with its horses and chariots s the city.
11:11 s the altar and the temple on the king's
17:15 they followed the s nations whom the LORD
1Chr 28:12 with the s compartments for the stores for
29:30 Israel and all the kingdoms of the s lands.
2Chr 17:10 all the kingdoms of the countries s Judah,
20:29 God came upon all the kingdoms of the s lands
34: 6 of the s country as far as Naphtali;
Neh 3:22 out by the priests, men of the s country.
Jdt 6: 1 of the crowd s the council had subsided,
1Mc 1:31 it, demolished its houses and its s walls,
1:54 s cities of Judah they built pagan altars.
7:46 From all the s villages of Judea people
Jb 37:22 splendor comes, s God's awesome majesty!
Jer 52: 7 With the Chaldeans s the city,
Ez 5: 6 more than the foreign countries s her;
5: 7 to the ordinances of the s nations;
5: 7 more rebellious than the nations s you,
41:11 the wall s the open space was five cubits.
43:12 its whole s area on the mountain top shall
43:17 cubits wide, with a half-cubit rim s it.
Zec 7: 7 the s cities were inhabited and at peace,
12: 6 devour right and left all the s peoples;
14:14 the s nations shall be gathered together,
Mk 1:28 spread throughout the s region of Galilee.
Lk 4:37 kept spreading through the s country.
7:17 him throughout Judea and the s country.
Acts 14: 6 of Lystra and Derbe and to the s country,
Rv 4: 4 S this throne were twenty-four other

SURROUNDINGS (2)

Dt 29:15 "You know in what s we lived in the land
Jer 21:14 in its forest that shall devour all its s.

SURROUNDS (4)

Tb 6: 8 burn them so that the smoke s a man
Ps(s) 32:10 but kindness s him who trusts in the LORD.
89: 9 you, O LORD, and your faithfulness s you.
Sir 23:18 Darkness s me, walls hide me;

SURVEILLANCE (2)

Mt 27:64 the tomb kept under s until the third day.
27:66 they went and kept it under s of the guard,

SURVEY (4)

Jos 18: 4 commission them to begin a s of the land,
18: 8 Joshua instructed them to s the land,
Prv 4:26 S the path for your feet,
Hb 3: 6 He pauses to s the earth;

SURVEYS (1)

Prv 5:21 all their paths he s;

SURVIOR (1)

Jb 18:19 his people, nor any s where once he dwelt.

SURVIVAL (2)

Gn 50:20 his present end, the s of many people.
Acts 27:20 Toward the end, we abandoned any hope of s.

SURVIVE (30)

Gn 32: 9 reasoned, "the remaining camp may still s."
47:19 give us seed, that we may s and not perish,
Lv 26:36 "Those of you who s in the lands of their
26:39 Those of you who s in the lands of their
Nm 24:23 Alas, who shall s of Ishmael,
Jos 13:13 s in the midst of Israel to this day.
23: 4 as their heritage the nations that s
23: 7 with these nations while they s among you.
23:12 of these nations while they s among you,
Jgs 21:17 "Those of Benjamin who s must have heirs,
2Sm 1:10 for I knew that he could not s his wound.
17:12 None shall s—
Ezr 9:13 deserved and have allowed us to s as we do
Tb 13:16 remnant of my offspring s to see your glory
Jdt 6: 4 Not a trace of them shall s our attack:
Ps(s) 10:15 let them not s.
Jer 21: 7 the people in this city who s pestilence,
29:32 None of them shall s among this people to
42:17 not one shall s or escape the evil that I
44:13 in the land of Egypt shall escape or s.
48: 6 to s like the wild ass in the desert!"
Ez 33:10 How can we s?"
Ob 1:18 Then none shall s of the house of Esau,
Mk 3:25 to loyalties, that household will not s.
Acts 7:19 to exposure so that the people would not s.
27:31 with the ship, you have no chance to s."
27:34 food, which will give you strength to s.
Gal 2: 5 the gospel might s intact for your benefit.
1Thes 4:15 that we who live, who s until his coming,
1Jn 3:17 how can God's love s in a man who has

SURVIVED (9)

Nm 14:38 son of Nun, and Caleb, son of Jephunneh, s.
Dt 5:26 God speaking from the midst of fire, and s?
Jos 11:22 However, some s in Gaza,
2Sm 13:30 the princes and that not one of them had s.
2Kgs 14:17 son of Joash, king of Judah, s Jehoash,
2Chr 25:25 son of Joash, king of Judah, s Joash,
Ezr 1: 4 Let everyone who has s,
Ez 38: 8 against a nation which has s the sword,
Rv 7:14 ones who have s the great period of trial;

SURVIVES (4)

Ex 21:21 If, however, the slave s for a day or two,
2Mc 3:38 back well-flogged, if indeed he s at all;
Eccl 8:12 the sinner does evil a hundred times and s.
Zec 11:16 nor heal the injured, nor feed what s—

SURVIVING (7)

Lv 10:12 Moses said to Aaron and his s sons,
10:16 So he was angry with the s sons of Aaron,
Dt 28:54 and his beloved wife and his s children,
Jgs 4:16 fell beneath the sword, not even one man s.
1Kgs 18:22 "I am the only s prophet of the LORD,
1Chr 4:43 attacked the s Amalekites who had escaped,
Eccl 7:15 and a wicked one s in his wickedness.

SURVIVOR (12)

Nm 21:35 his people, until not a s was left to him,
Dt 2:34 we left no s.
3: 3 him so completely that we left him no s.
3:11 was the last remaining s of the Rephaim.
Jos 12: 4 Og, king of Bashan, a s of the Rephaim,
13:12 in Bashan of Og, a s of the Rephaim,
2Sm 9: 1 "Is there any s of Saul's house to whom I
9: 3 "Is there any s of Saul's house to whom I
2Kgs 10:11 intimates, and priests, leaving him no s.
Ezr 9:14 us as to destroy us without remnant or s?
Lam 2:22 day of your wrath, either fugitive or s;
Am 9: 1 not one shall flee, no s shall escape.

SURVIVORS (37)

Dt 7:20 s who have hidden from you are destroyed.
Jos 8:22 without any fugitives or s except the king,
10:20 and the s had escaped from them into the
10:28 and on every person in it, leaving no s.
10:30 with every person there, leaving no s.
10:33 him and his people, leaving him no s.
10:37 and every person there, leaving no s,
10:39 doom on every person there, leaving no s.
10:40 He left no s, but fulfilled the doom
11: 8 They struck them all down, leaving no s.
Jgs 21: 7 What can we do about wives for the s,
21:16 "What shall we do for wives for the s?
1Sm 11:11 by then the s were so scattered that no
2Sm 21: 2 were not Israelites, but s of the Amorites;
1Kgs 20:30 s, twenty-seven thousand of them,
2Kgs 19:30 remaining s of the house of Judah
19:31 come a remnant, and from Mount Zion, s.
21:14 I will cast off the s of my inheritance
2Chr 14:12 the Ethiopians fell until there were no s,
20:24 corpses fallen on the ground, with no s.
Neh 1: 3 "The s of the captivity there in the
1Mc 2:44 and the s fled to the Gentiles for safety.
9:40 and after the s fled toward the mountain,
Jb 27:15 s, when they die, shall have no burial,
Ps(s) 76:11 the s of Hamath shall keep your festivals.
Sir 44:17 Because of his worth there were s,
Is 4: 2 be honor and splendor for the s of Israel.
10:20 of Israel, the s of the house of Jacob,
37:31 The remaining s of the house of Judah
37:32 come a remnant, and from Mount Zion, s.
49: 6 of Jacob, and restore the s of Israel;
Jer 8: 3 by all the s of this wicked race who remain
15: 9 Their s I will give to the sword before
Ez 14:22 still some s shall be left in it who will
17:21 s shall be scattered in every direction.
Jl 3: 5 in Jerusalem s whom the LORD shall call.
Zep 2: 9 them, the s of my nation dispossess them.
1Thes 4:17 Then we, the living, the s,

SUSA (23)

Neh 1: 1 I was in the citadel of S when Hanani,
Est A: 2 He was a Jew residing in the city of S,
1: 2 the royal throne in the stronghold of S,
1: 5 and small, who were in the stronghold of S.
2: 3 to the harem in the stronghold of S.
2: 5 of S a certain Jew named Mordecai,

2: 8 stronghold of *S* under the care of Hegai,
3:15 was promulgated in the stronghold of *S.*
3:15 the city of *S* was thrown into confusion.
4: 8 which had been promulgated in *S,*
4:16 and assemble all the Jews who are in *S;*
E:18 entire household, before the gates of *S.*
8:14 was promulgated in the stronghold of *S.*
8:15 The city of *S* shouted with joy,
9: 6 In the stronghold of *S,* the Jews killed
9:11 stronghold of *S* was reported to the king,
9:12 "In the stronghold of *S* the Jews have
9:13 let the Jews in *S* be permitted again
9:14 effect, and the decree was published in *S.*
9:15 and the Jews in *S* mustered again on the
9:15 of Adar and killed three hundred men in *S.*
9:18 (The Jews in *S,* however, mustered
Dn 8: 2 the fortress of *S* in the province of Elam;

SUSANNA (11)

Dn 13: 2 a very beautiful and God-fearing woman, *S,*
13: 7 *S* used to enter her husband's garden for a
13:22 "I am completely trapped," *S* groaned.
13:24 *S* shrieked, and the old men also shouted
13:27 never had any such thing been said about *S.*
13:28 came, fully determined to put *S* to death.
13:29 "Send for *S,* the daughter of Hilkiah,
13:31 *S,* very delicate and beautiful, was veiled
13:42 *S* cried aloud: O Eternal God
13:63 his wife praised God for their daughter *S,*
Lk 8: 3 the wife of Herod's steward Chuza, *S,*

SUSI (1)

Nm 13:11 Gaddi, son of *S,* of the tribe of Manasseh

SUSIAN (1)

Ezr 4: 9 Urukian, Babylonian, *S* (that is Elamite),

SUSPECT (2)

Nm 5:14 of jealousy that makes him *s* his wife,
Acts 27:27 the sailors began to *s* that land was near.

SUSPECTING (2)

2Mc 7:24 Antiochus, *s* insult in her words,
12: 4 not *s* treachery and wishing to live on

SUSPENDS (1)

Jb 26: 7 space, and *s* the earth over nothing at all;

SUSPENSE (5)

Dt 28:66 *s* and stand in dread both day and night,
Hos 11: 7 His people are in *s* about returning to him;
Jn 10:24 "How long are you going to keep us in *s?*
Acts 27:33 fourteen days you have been in constant *s;*
1Thes 3: 5 faith when I could stand the *s* no longer,

SUSPICIONS (2)

2Mc 4:34 joined, persuaded him, in spite of his *s,*
1Tm 6: 4 come envy, dissension, slander, evil *s*—

SUSPICIOUS (3)

Nm 5:30 over a man that he becomes *s* of his wife,
Jgs 3:25 They waited until they finally grew *s.*
Sir 4:30 not a lion at home, nor sly and *s* at work.

SUSTAIN (6)

2Mc 10:18 everything necessary to *s* a siege,
Ps(s) 7:10 the wicked come to an end, but *s* the just,
20: 3 from the sanctuary, from Zion may he *s* you.
41:13 *s* me and let me stand before you forever.
51:14 salvation, and a willing spirit *s* in me.
Sir 51: 7 one to help me, I looked for one to *s* me,

SUSTAINED (5)

Gn 47:12 And Joseph *s* his father and brothers and
Neh 9:21 Forty years in the desert you *s* them:
Ps(s) 89:44 sharp sword and have not *s* him in battle.
105:16 the land and ruined the crop that *s* them,
Sir 45: 3 his words and *s* him in the king's presence.

SUSTAINS (11)

Jb 24:23 He *s* the mighty by his strength,
Ps(s) 3: 6 in sleep, I wake again, for the LORD *s* me.
37:24 prostrate, for the hand of the LORD *s* him.
54: 6 God is my helper; the Lord *s* my life.
94:18 is slipping," your kindness, O LORD, *s* me;
146: 9 the fatherless and the widow he *s,*
147: 6 The LORD *s* the lowly;
Prv 18:14 A man's spirit *s* him in infirmity
Is 9: 6 he confirms and *s* By judgment and justice,
Heb 1: 3 and he *s* all things by his powerful word.
Rv 14:12 This is what *s* the holy ones,

SUSTENANCE (7)

Dt 24: 6 would be taking the debtor's *s* as a pledge.
Jgs 6: 4 outskirts of Gaza, leaving no *s* in Israel,
Jdt 5:10 They stayed there as long as they found *s,*
Prv 22: 9 for he gives of his *s* to the poor.
Sir 38: 2 wisdom, and the king provides for his *s.*
Lam 5: 9 the peril of our lives we bring in our *s,*
Acts 7:11 and Canaan, our fathers could find no *s.*

SWADDLING (5)

Jb 38: 9 its garment and thick darkness its *s* bands?
Wis 7: 4 In *s* clothes and with constant care I was
Ez 16: 4 rubbed with salt, nor swathed in *s* clothes.
Lk 2: 7 him in *s* clothes and laid him in a manger,
2:12 will find an infant wrapped in *s* clothes."

SWALLOW (15)

Nm 16:34 saying, "The earth might *s* us too!"
Tb 6: 3 out of the water and tried to *s* his foot.
Jdt 5:24 army, Lord Holofernes, will *s* them up."
Jb 5: 5 and the thirsty shall *s* their substance,
7:19 let me alone long enough to *s* my spittle?
Ps(s) 69:16 overwhelm me, nor the abyss *s* me up,
84: 4 the *s* a nest in which she puts her young
Prv 1:12 Let us *s* them up,
26: 2 in its flitting, like the *s* in its flight,
Sir 36:18 The throat can *s* any food,
Is 38:14 Like a *s* I utter shrill cries;
Jer 8: 7 *s* and thrush observe their time of return,
Hos 8: 7 Even if it could, strangers would *s* it.
Ob 1:16 Yes, they shall drink and *s,*
Mt 23:24 You strain out the gnat and *s* the camel!

SWALLOWED (22)

Gn 41: 7 and the seven thin ears *s* up the seven fat,
41:24 thin ears *s* up the seven healthy ears.
Ex 7:12 But Aaron's staff *s* their staffs.
15:12 out your right hand, the earth *s* them!
Lv 26:38 Gentiles, *s* up in your enemies' country.
Nm 16:32 earth opened its mouth and *s* them
21:28 Moab and *s* up the high places of the Arnon.
26:10 The earth opened its mouth and *s* them as a
Dt 11: 6 and *s* them up out of the midst of Israel,
1Sm 2: 1 I have *s* up my enemies;
Jb 20:15 The riches he *s* he shall disgorge;
Ps(s) 35:25 Let them not say, "We have *s* him up!"
106:17 The earth opened and *s* up Dathan,
107:27 drunken men, and all their skill was *s* up.
124: 3 us, then would they have *s* us alive.
Is 49:19 while those who *s* you up will be far away.
Jer 51:34 He has *s* me like a dragon:
51:44 Babylon, and make him disgorge what he *s;*
Hos 8: 8 Israel is *s* up;
Jon 2: 1 the LORD sent a large fish, that *s* Jonah;
1Cor 15:54 "Death is *s* up in victory."
Rv 10:10 but when I *s* it my stomach turned sour.

SWALLOWING (1)

Rv 12:16 *s* the flood which the dragon spewed out

SWALLOWS (3)

Nm 16:30 *s* them alive down into the nether world,
Is 28: 4 a man sees it, he picks and *s* it at once.
Bar 6:21 Bats and *s* alight on their bodies and on

SWAM (2)

1Mc 9:48 the Jordan and *s* across to the other side,
Wis 19:19 and those that *s* went over on to the land.

SWAMP (4)

Jb 40:21 trees he lies, in coverts of the reedy *s.*
Ps(s) 40: 3 of destruction, out of the mud of the *s;*
69: 3 the abysmal *s* where there is no foothold;
1Pt 4: 4 into the same *s* of profligacy as they.

SWAMPED (1)

Mt 8:24 and the boat began to be *s* by the waves.

SWAMPS (1)

Ez 47:11 its marshes and *s* shall not be made fresh;

SWARM (13)

Ex 7:29 The frogs will *s* all over you and your
10:12 that locusts may *s* over it and eat up all
10:14 had there been such a fierce *s* of locusts,
Lv 11:29 "Of the creatures that *s* on the ground,
11:41 "All the creatures that *s* on the ground
11:46 move about in the water or *s* on the ground,
Jgs 14: 8 *s* of bees and honey in the lion's carcass.
1Sm 14:26 came to the comb the *s* had left it;
1Kgs 8:37 if blight comes, or mildew, or a locust *s,*
Wis 16: 1 and were tormented by a *s* of insects.
Jl 1: 4 the cutter left, the locust *s* has eaten;
1: 4 What the locust *s* left,
Am 7: 1 He was forming a locust *s* when the late

SWARMED (6)

Gn 7:21 wild animals, and all that *s* on the earth,
Ex 10:14 They *s* over the whole land of Egypt and
1Sm 5: 6 *s* in their ships and overran their fields.
2Mc 9: 9 The body of this impious man *s* with worms,
Ps(s) 105:30 Their land *s* with frogs,
Wis 19:10 of fishes the river *s* with countless frogs.

SWARMING (7)

Lv 5: 2 animal, or that of an unclean *s* creature,
11:31 Among the various *s* creatures,
11:42 has many legs, you shall eat no *s* creature:
11:43 loathsome or unclean with any *s* creature
11:44 any *s* creature that crawls on the ground.
20:25 beast or bird or of any *s* creature in the land
22: 5 *s* creature or any man whose uncleanness,

SWARMS (7)

Ex 8:17 I will loose *s* of flies upon you and your
8:17 they stand shall be filled with *s* of flies.
8:20 Thick *s* of flies entered the house of
Ps(s) 105:31 He spoke, and there came *s* of flies;
Wis 11:15 them *s* of dumb creatures for vengeance;
Sir 43:18 it comes to settle like *s* of locusts.
Na 3:17 scribes as locust *s* gathered on the rubble

SWARTHY (1)

Sg 1: 6 Do not stare at me because I am *s,*

SWATHED (1)

Ez 16: 4 with salt, nor *s* in swaddling clothes.

SWAY (4)

Est B: 2 and to hold *s* over the whole world,
Sir 24: 6 over every people and nation I held *s.*
Is 10:15 As if a rod could *s* him who lifts it,
24:20 like a drunkard, and it will *s* like a hut;

SWAYED (3)

2Sm 22: 8 "The earth *s* and quaked:
Ps(s) 18: 8 The earth *s* and quaked;
Lk 7:24 a reed *s* by the wind?

SWAYING (1)

Mt 11: 7 a reed *s* in the wind?

SWEAR (73)

Gn 21:23 *s* to me by God at this place that you will
21:24 To this Abraham replied, "I so *s.*"
22:16 "I *s* by myself, declares the LORD,
24: 3 thigh, and I will make you *s* by the LORD,
25:33 But Jacob insisted, *S* to me first!"
42:15 I *s* by the life of Pharaoh that you shall
47:31 But his father demanded, *S* it to me!"
Ex 13:19 had made the Israelites *s* solomnly that,
22: 7 to *s* that he himself did not lay hands on
22:10 the custodian shall *s* by the LORD that he
Lv 19:12 You shall not *s* falsely by my name,
Dt 6:13 you serve, and by his name shall you *s.*
10:20 hold fast to him and *s* by his name.
32:40 "To the heavens I raise my hand and *s:*
Jos 2:12 Now then, *s* to me by the LORD that,
23: 7 must not invoke their gods, or *s* by them,
Jgs 15:12 *S* to me that you will not kill me
1Sm 3:14 I *s* to the family of Eli that no sacrifice
24:22 *s* to me by the LORD that you will not
30:15 *S* to me by God that you will not kill me
2Sm 19: 8 I *s* by the LORD that if you do not go out,
1Kgs 1:13 you not, lord king, *s* to your handmaid:
1:51 Solomon first *s* that he will not kill me,
2:42 "Did I not have you *s* by the LORD to your
18:10 and nation *s* they could not find you.
2Chr 36:13 Nebuchadnezzar, who had made him *s* by
Jdt 13:16 I *s* that it was my face that seduced
Ps(s) 119:106 resolve and *s* to keep your just ordinances.
139:20 your foes *s* faithless oaths.
144: 8 Whose mouths *s* false promises while their
144:11 Whose mouths *s* false promises while
Is 45:23 By myself I *s,* uttering my just decree
45:23 by me every tongue shall *s,*
48: 1 You who *s* by the name of the LORD and
65:16 in the land shall *s* by the God of truth;
Jer 4: 2 sight, and do not stray, Then you can *s,*
5: 2 say, "As the LORD lives," they *s* falsely.
5: 7 forsaken me, they *s* by gods that are not.
12:16 taught my people to *s* by Baal shall be built
22: 5 do not obey these commands, I *s* by myself,
44:26 I *s* by my own great name,
Ez 5:11 abominations, I *s* to cut you down.
14:16 I *s* they could save neither sons nor
14:20 I *s* that they could save neither son nor
16:48 the Lord GOD, I *s* that your sister Sodom,
17:16 broke, there in Babylon I *s* he shall die!
17:19 he broke, I *s* to bring down upon his head.
18: 3 I *s* that there shall no longer be anyone
20: 3 I *s* I will not allow myself to be
20:31 I *s* I will not let myself be consulted by
20:33 wrath, I *s* I will be king over you!
33:11 I *s* I take no pleasure in the death of the
33:27 in the ruins I *s* shall fall by the sword;
34:10 I *s* I am coming against these shepherds.
35: 6 have been guilty of blood, and blood, I *s,*
36: 7 Therefore do I solemnly *s* that your
38:19 and in my jealousy, in my fiery wrath, I *s:*
Dn 12: 7 and I heard him *s* by him who lives forever
Hos 4:15 not to Gilgal, nor up to Beth-aven, to *s,*
10: 4 Nothing but make promises, *s* false oaths,

SWEAR (cont.)
8:14 who *s* by the shameful idol of Samaria,
Zep 1: 5 those who adore the LORD but *s* by Milcom;
Mt 5:34 do not *s* at all.
5:34 Do not *s* by heaven (it is God's throne),
5:36 do not *s* by your head (you cannot make a
Mk 6:23 He went so far as to *s* to her:
14:71 He began to curse, and to *s*,
1Cor 15:31 I *s* to you, brothers, by the very pride you
2Cor 11:10 I *s* by the Christ who is in me that this
Heb 3:18 *s* that they would not enter into his rest?
6:13 by himself, having no one greater to *s* by.
6:16 Men *s* by someone greater than themselves;
Jas 5:12 else, my brothers, you must not *s* an oath,

SWEARING (8)
Jdt 8: 9 *s* that he would hand over the city to the
Sir 23: 9 Let not your mouth form the habit of *s*,
Is 19:18 of Canaan and *s* by the LORD of hosts;
Jer 12:16 learn my people's custom of *s* by my name,
Hos 4: 2 False *s*, lying, murder, stealing and adultery
Mt 23:20 altar is *s* by it and by everything on it.
23:21 is *s* by it and by him who dwells there.
23:22 The man who swears by heaven is *s* by God's

SWEARS (15)
Lv 5:22 he denies the fact and *s* falsely about it
Ps(s) 24: 4 is vain, nor *s* deceitfully to his neighbor.
63:12 everyone who *s* by him shall glory,
Eccl 9: 2 as it is for him who *s* rashly,
Sir 23:10 So one who *s* continually by the Holy Name
23:11 A man who often *s* heaps up obligations;
23:11 If he *s* in error, he incurs guilt;
23:11 *s* without reason he cannot be found just,
Mt 23:16 'If a man *s* by the temple it means nothing,
23:16 but if he *s* by the gold of the temple he
23:18 'If a man *s* by the altar it means nothing,
23:18 but if he *s* by the gift on the altar he
23:20 The man who *s* by the altar is swearing by
23:21 The man who *s* by the temple is swearing by
23:22 The man who *s* by heaven is swearing by

SWEAT (4)
Gn 3:19 *s* of your face shall you get bread to eat,
2Mc 2:26 easy, is one of *s* and of sleepless nights,
Ez 44:18 themselves with anything that causes *s*.
Lk 22:44 and his *s* became like drops of blood

SWEEP (17)
Gn 8: 1 So God made a wind *s* over the earth,
18:23 you *s* away the innocent with the guilty?
Lv 26:25 the avenger of my covenant, *s* over you.
Dt 29:18 as though to *s* away both the watered soil
Jb 20:28 The flood shall *s* away his house with the
Prv 21: 7 oppression of the wicked will *s* them away,
Sg 8: 7 cannot quench love, nor floods *s* it away.
Is 14:23 I will *s* it with the broom of destruction,
25:11 low their pride as his hands *s* over them.
28:17 Hail shall *s* away the refuge of lies,
30:32 While at every *s* of the rod which the LORD
Zep 1: 2 I will completely *s* away all things from
1: 3 I will *s* away man and beast,
1: 3 beast, I will *s* away the birds of the sky,
Lk 15: 8 does not light a lamp and *s* the house in a
Jn 11:48 in and *s* away our sanctuary and our nation."
Rv 12:15 to search out the woman and *s* her away.

SWEEPING (3)
Lv 26: 6 the sword of war from *s* across your land.
Is 21: 1 whirlwinds *s* in waves through the Negeb,
Jer 25:38 their land is made desolate By the *s* sword,

SWEEPS (4)
Jb 27:21 it *s* him out of his place.
37:21 the wind comes by and *s* the clouds away.
Ps(s) 103:16 The wind *s* over him and he is gone,
Sir 10:17 The traces of the proud God *s* away and

SWEET (36)
Gn 8:21 When the LORD smelled the *s* odor,
Ex 29:18 a *s* smelling oblation to the LORD.
Neh 8:10 "Go eat rich foods and drink *s* drinks,
Jdt 16:16 the *s* odor of every sacrifice is a trifle,
Jb 20:12 Though wickedness is *s* in his mouth,
21:33 *S* to him are the clods of the valley,
Ps(s) 119:103 How *s* to my palate are your promises,
Prv 3:24 when you rest, your sleep will be *s*.
9:17 for to him I say, Stolen water is *s*,
16:24 *s* to the taste and healthful to the body.
20:17 The bread of deceit is *s* to a man,
24:13 good, if virgin honey is *s* to your taste;
27: 7 man who is hungry, any bitter thing is *s*.
Eccl 5:11 Sleep is *s* to the laboring man,
11: 7 Light is *s*!
Sg 2: 3 shadow, and his fruit is *s* to my mouth.
2:14 me hear your voice, For your voice is *s*,
Sir 23:17 is *s* and who is never through till he dies;
24:15 Like galbanum and onycha and *s* spices,
35: 5 and rises as a *s* odor before the Most High.
39:14 Send up the *s* odor of incense,
39:14 Send up the *s* odor of your hymn of praise;
40:17 Wealth or wages can make life *s*,
40:21 The flute and the harp offer *s* melody,
40:30 mouth of the shameless man begging is *s*,
45:16 burn sacrifices of *s* odor for a memorial,
47: 9 providing *s* melody for the psalms So that
50:18 the throng *s* strains of praise resound.
Is 5:20 bitter into sweet, and *s* into bitter!
43:24 You did not buy me *s* cane for money,
Jer 6:20 from Sheba, or *s* cane from far-off lands?
31:26 but my sleep was *s* to me.
Ez 3: 3 it, and it was as *s* as honey in my mouth.
Rv 10: 9 in your mouth it will taste as *s* as honey."
10:10 In my mouth it tasted as *s* as honey,

SWEET-SMELLING (36)
Ex 29:25 on the altar as a *s* oblation to the LORD.
29:41 offer this as a *s* oblation to the LORD.
Lv 1: 9 as a holocaust, a *s* oblation to the LORD.
1:13 as a holocaust, a *s* oblation to the LORD.
1:17 as a holocaust, a *s* oblation to the LORD.
2: 2 a token offering, a *s* oblation to the LORD.
2: 9 on the altar as a *s* oblation to the LORD.
3: 5 over the fire, as a *s* oblation to the LORD.
3:16 on the altar as the food of the *s* oblation.
6: 8 token offering, a *s* oblation to the LORD.
6:14 present it as a *s* oblation to the LORD.
8:21 as a holocaust, a *s* oblation to the LORD,
8:28 offering, a *s* oblation to the LORD.
23:13 with oil, as a *s* oblation to the LORD;
23:18 and libations, as a *s* oblation to the LORD.
26:31 refusing to accept your *s* offerings.
Nm 15: 3 *s* oblation from the herd or from the flock,
15: 7 wine, thus making a *s* offering to the LORD.
15:10 a hin of wine, as a *s* oblation to the LORD.
15:13 they present a *s* oblation to the LORD.
15:14 who presents a *s* oblation to the LORD,
15:24 bull as a *s* oblation pleasing to the LORD,
18:17 you must burn as a *s* oblation to the LORD,
28: 2 that are offered to me as *s* oblations.
28: 6 at Mount Sinai as a *s* oblation to the LORD.
28: 8 the morning, as a *s* oblation to the LORD.
28:13 holocaust may be a *s* oblation to the LORD.
28:24 its libation, for a *s* oblation to the LORD.
28:27 as a *s* holocaust to the LORD two bullocks,
29: 2 as a *s* holocaust to the LORD one bullock,
29: 6 for them, as a *s* oblation to the LORD.
29: 8 as a *s* holocaust to the LORD one bullock,
29:13 *s* holocaust to the LORD thirteen bullocks,
29:36 as a *s* oblation to the LORD one bullock,
Sir 38:11 Offer your *s* oblation and petition,
50:15 the altar, a *s* odor to the Most High God,

SWEETENED (1)
Sir 38: 5 *s* by a twig that men might learn his power?

SWEETER (4)
Jgs 14:18 city said to him, "What is *s* than honey,
Ps(s) 19:11 *S* also than syrup or honey from the comb.
119:103 your promises, *s* than honey to my mouth!
Sir 24:19 You will remember me as *s* than honey,

SWEETLY (1)
Sir 12:16 With his lips an enemy speaks *s*,

SWEETMEATS (2)
Sg 4:11 bride, *s* and milk are under your tongue;
5: 1 and my spices, I eat my honey and my *s*,

SWEETNESS (4)
Jgs 9:11 'Must I give up my *s* and my good fruit,
14:14 food, and out of the strong came forth *s*."
Sg 5:16 His mouth is *s* itself; he is all delight.
Wis 16:21 yours revealed your *s* toward your children,

SWELL (5)
Nm 5:21 thighs to waste away and your belly to *s*!
5:22 your belly *s* and your thighs waste away!'
5:27 will *s* and her thighs will waste away,
Dt 8: 4 nor did your feet *s* these forty years.
Acts 28: 6 to see him *s* up or suddenly fall dead.

SWELLED (1)
Jdt 15:14 and the people *s* this hymn of praise:

SWELLING (3)
Gn 7:18 The *s* waters increased greatly,
Jdt 2: 8 *s* torrent shall be choked with their dead;
Ps(s) 89:10 you still the *s* of its waves.

SWEPT (19)
Gn 1: 2 while a mighty wind *s* over the waters.
19:15 be *s* away in the punishment of the city."
19:17 the hills at once, or you will be *s* away."
Ex 14:21 and the LORD *s* the sea with a strong east
Nm 16:26 will be *s* away because of all their sins."
Jgs 5:21 The Wadi Kishon *s* them away;
Jdt 15: 6 *s* down on the camp of the Assyrians,
Jb 22:16 whose foundations a flood *s* away?
Ps(s) 88:17 Your furies have *s* over me;
109:23 I am *s* away like the locust.
124: 4 The torrent would have *s* over us;
124: 5 us then would have *s* the raging waters.
136:15 *s* Pharaoh and his army into the Red Sea,
Is 57: 1 Devout men are *s* away,
Zec 5: 3 with it shall every thief be *s* away,
Mt 12:44 unoccupied, though *s* and tidied now.
Lk 11:25 returns, to find the house *s* and tidied.
Gal 2:13 even Barnabas was *s* away by their pretense.
Rv 12: 4 His tail *s* a third of the stars from the

SWERVE (2)
Jos 1: 7 Do not *s* from it either to the right or to
Prv 22: 6 even when he is old, he will not *s* from it.

SWERVED (1)
Ti 1:14 invented by men who have *s* from the truth.

SWERVING (1)
Jl 2: 7 his own lane, without *s* from their paths.

SWIFT (23)
Jos 10:13 for a whole day did it resume its *s* course.
2Sm 22:34 Who made my feet *s* as those of hinds and
1Chr 12: 9 were as *s* as the gazelles on the mountains.
2Mc 9: 2 the people had *s* recourse to arms,
Jb 14: 2 fades, *s* as a shadow that does not abide.
Ps(s) 18:34 Who made my feet *s* as those of hinds and
Eccl 9:11 the sun that the race is not won by the *s*,
Sg 8:14 Be *s*, my lover, like a gazelle
Wis 13: 2 But either fire, or wind, or the *s* air,
18:14 the night in its *s* course was half spent,
Sir 5:13 Be *s* to hear, but slow to answer.
45: 3 God wrought *s* miracles at his words and
Is 18: 2 Go, *s* messengers,
19: 1 is riding on a *s* cloud on his way to Egypt;
30:16 "Upon *s* steeds we will ride."
30:16 —Not so *s* as your pursuers.
Jer 46: 6 The *s* cannot flee, nor the hero escape:
Am 2:14 Flight shall perish from the *s*,
2:15 The *s* of foot shall not escape,
Hb 3:19 he makes my feet *s* as those of hinds and
Mal 3: 5 be *s* to bear witness Against the sorcerers,
Lk 18: 8 I tell you, he will give them *s* justice.
2Pt 2: 1 thereby bringing on themselves *s* disaster.

SWIFTER (6)
2Sm 1:23 in life nor in death, *s* than eagles,
Jb 7: 6 My days are *s* than a weaver's shuttle;
9:25 My days are *s* than a runner,
Jer 4:13 *S* than eagles are his steeds:
Lam 4:19 Our pursuers were *s* than eagles in the air,
Hb 1: 8 *S* than leopards are his horses,

SWIFTLY (11)
Est E:18 Thus *s* has God, who governs all,
Ps(s) 147:15 *s* runs his word!
Prv 6:18 wicked schemes, feet that run *s* to evil,
Wis 4:16 and youth *s* completed condemns the many
6: 5 Terribly and *s* shall he come against you,
16:11 they were stung, and *s* they were saved,
Is 60:22 will *s* accomplish these things when their
Bar 4:22 will *s* reach you from your eternal savior.
Jl 4: 4 But if you do take action against me, *s*,
Zep 1:14 day of the LORD, near and very *s* coming,
Rom 3:15 *S* run their feet to shed blood;

SWIFTNESS (1)
Jb 39:18 Yet in her *s* of foot she makes sport of

SWIM (4)
Lv 11:10 creatures that crawl or *s* in the water,
Is 25:11 Moab as a swimmer extends his hands to *s*;
Acts 27:42 so that none might *s* away and escape;
27:43 he ordered those who could *s* to jump

SWIMMER (1)
Is 25:11 in Moab as a *s* extends his hands to swim;

SWIMMING (3)
Gn 1:21 of *s* creatures with which the water teems,
Ez 47: 5 that could not be crossed except by *s*.
Jas 3: 7 four-footed or winged, crawling or *s*,

SWIMS (1)
Ps(s) 8: 9 sea, and whatever *s* the paths of the seas.

SWINE (12)
1Mc 1:47 to sacrifice *s* and unclean animals,
Mt 7: 6 holy to dogs or toss your pearls before *s*.
8:30 away a large herd of *s* was feeding.
8:31 you expel us, send us into the herd of *s*."
8:32 At that they came forth and entered the *s*.
Mk 5:11 It happened that a large herd of *s* was
5:12 "Send us into the *s*," they begged him.

5:13 unclean spirits came out and entered the s.
5:16 possessed man, and told them about the s.
Lk 8:32 of s was feeding nearby on the hillside,
8:32 asked him to permit them to enter the s.
8:33 came out of the man and entered the s,

SWINEHERDS (3)

Mt 8:33 The s took to their heels,
Mk 5:14 The s ran off and brought the news to
Lk 8:34 When the s saw what had happened,

SWINES (4)

Prv 11:22 Like a golden ring in a s snout is a
Is 65: 4 the night in caverns, Eating s flesh,
66: 3 a cereal offering, like offering s blood;
66:17 who stands within, they who eat s flesh,

SWING (2)

Ex 28:28 belt of the ephod and not s loose from it.
39:21 of the ephod and did not s loose from it.

SWINGS (1)

Dt 19: 5 wood, and as he s his ax to fell a tree,

SWIRLED (1)

Jon 2: 6 waters s about me, threatening my life

SWOLLEN (1)

Neh 9:21 worn, and their feet did not become s.

SWOONS (1)

Jer 15: 9 The mother of seven s away,

SWOOP (1)

Is 11:14 But they shall s down on the foothills of

SWOOPED (1)

Gn 15:11 Birds of prey s down on the carcasses,

SWOOPING (1)

Jb 9:26 of reed, like an eagle s upon its prey.

SWOOPS (1)

Dt 28:49 of the earth, that s down like an eagle,

SWORD (435)

Gn 3:24 the cherubim and the fiery revolving s,
27:40 "By your s you shall live,
34:26 put Hamor and his son Shechem to the s,
48:22 from the Amorites with my s and bow."
Ex 5: 3 he will punish us with pestilence or the s."
5:21 and have put a s in their hands to slay us."
15: 9 I will draw my s;
17:13 and his people with the edge of the s.
18: 4 he has rescued me from Pharaoh's s."
22:23 flare up, and I will kill you with the s;
32:27 Put your s on your hip, every one of you!
Lv 26: 6 s of war from sweeping across your land.
26: 7 your enemies and lay them low with your s.
26: 8 of them, till they are cut down by your s.
26:25 I will make the s,
26:33 the nations at the point of my drawn s,
26:36 they will flee headlong, as if from the s,
Nm 14: 3 this land only to have us fall by the s?
14:43 face you, and you will fall by the s.
19:16 he was slain by the s or died naturally,
20:18 do, I will advance against you with the s."
21:24 Israel defeated him at the point of the s,
22:23 the LORD standing on the road with s drawn,
22:29 the ass, "that if I but had a s at hand,
22:31 the LORD standing on the road with s drawn;
31: 8 executed Balaam, son of Beor, with the s.
Dt 13:16 put the inhabitants of that city to the s,
13:16 that is in it, even its cattle, to the s.
20:13 your hand, put every male in it to the s;
32:25 "Snatched away by the s in the street and
32:41 forever, I will sharpen my flashing s,
32:42 and my s shall gorge itself with flesh
33:29 saving shield, and his s is your glory.
Jos 5:13 one who stood facing him, drawn s in hand.
6:21 to the s all living creatures in the city:
8:24 were slain by the s there in the open,
8:24 and put to the s those inside the city.
10:11 than the Israelites slew with the s.
10:28 captured and put to the s at that time.
10:30 He put it to the s with every person there,
10:32 put it to the s with every person in it,
10:35 it the same day, putting it to the s.
10:37 They put it to the s with its king,
10:39 They put them to the s and fulfilled the
11:10 Hazor and slew its king with the s;
11:11 by putting every person there to the s,
11:12 with their cities and put them to the s,
11:14 but the people they put to the s,
13:22 put to the s also the soothsayer Balaam,
19:47 which they captured and put to the s.
24:12 it was not your s or your bow.
Jgs 1: 8 and captured it, putting it to the s;
1:25 the city, which they then put to the s;
4:16 entire army of Sisera fell beneath the s,
7:14 can only be the s of the Israelite Gideon,
7:20 cried out, "A s for the LORD and Gideon!"
7:22 the LORD set the s of one against another.
8:20 boy, he was afraid and did not draw his s.
9:54 said to him, "Draw your s and dispatch me,
18:27 to the s and destroyed their city by fire.
20:37 it, and put the whole city to the s.
20:48 to the s the inhabitants of the cities,
21:10 and put those who lived there to the s,
1Sm 2:33 the men of your family shall die by the s.
13:22 And so on the day of battle neither s nor
15: 8 effect the ban of destruction by the s.
15:33 "As your s has made women childless,
17:39 himself with Saul's s over the tunic.
17:45 against me with s and spear and scimitar,
17:47 is not by s or spear that the LORD saves.
17:50 and did it without a s
17:51 with the Philistine's own s [which he drew
18: 4 along with his military dress, and his s,
21: 9 "Do you have a spear or a s on hand?
21: 9 brought along neither my s nor my weapons,
21:10 "The s of Goliath the Philistine,
21:10 there is no s here except that one."
22:10 the s of Goliath the Philistine as well."
22:13 food and a s and by consulting God for him,
22:19 put the priestly city of Nob to the s.
25:13 to his men, "Let everyone gird on his s."
25:13 everyone, David included, girded on his s.
31: 4 "Draw your s and run me through,
31: 4 So Saul took his own s and fell upon it.
31: 5 he too fell upon his s and died with him.
2Sm 1:12 Israel, because they had fallen by the s.
1:22 back, or the s of Saul return unstained.
2:16 and thrust his s into his opponent's side,
2:26 "Must the s destroy to the utmost?
3:29 or one unmanly, one falling by the s,
11:25 for the s devours now here and now there.
12: 9 cut down Uriah the Hittite with the s;
12: 9 him you killed with the s of the Ammonites.
12:10 the s shall never depart from your house,
15:14 disaster upon us and put the city to the s."
18: 8 more combatants that day than did the s.
20: 8 a s that could be drawn with a downward
20:10 guard against the s in Joab's other hand,
21:16 with a new s and planned to kill David,
23:10 and became cramped, holding fast to the s.
1Kgs 1:51 will not kill me, his servant, with the s."
2: 8 the LORD that I would not put him to the s.
2:32 the s without my father David's knowl-edge:
3:24 The king continued, "Get me a s."
3:24 When they brought the s before him,
19: 1 that he had put all the prophets to the s.
19:10 altars, and put your prophets to the s.
19:14 altars, and put your prophets to the s.
19:17 If anyone escapes the s of Hazael,
19:17 If he escapes the s if Jehu,
2Kgs 6:22 you have taken captive with your s or bow?
8:12 you will slay their youth with the s,
10:25 put them to the s and cast them out.
11:15 her," he added, "Let him die by the s,"
11:20 been slain with the s at the royal palace.
19: 7 there I will cause him to fall by the s.'"
19:37 the s and fled into the land of Ararat.
1Chr 5:18 who bore shield and s and who drew the bow,
10: 4 your s and thrust me through with it,
10: 4 So Saul took his own s and fell on it.
10: 5 armor-bearer also fell on his s and died.
21: 5 of men capable of wielding a s,
21:12 with the s of your foes ever at your back;
21:12 or three days of the LORD's own s,
21:16 with a naked s in his hand stretched out
21:27 to the angel to return his s to its sheath.
21:30 fearful of the s of the angel of the LORD.
2Chr 20: 9 evil comes upon us, the s of judgment,
21: 4 he put to the s all his brothers and also
23:14 tries to follow her, let him die by the s.
23:21 Athaliah had been put to death by the s.
29: 9 our fathers, as you know, fell by the s,
32:21 offspring struck him down there with the s.
36:20 the s he carried captive to Babylon,
Ezr 9: 7 of the kings of foreign lands, to the s,
Neh 4:12 he worked, had his s girt at his side.
Jdt 1:12 with his s all the inhabitants of Moab,
2:27 plains, and put all their youths to the s.
6: 6 the s of my army or the spear of my
7:14 and even before the s strikes them they
8:19 were handed over to the s and to pillage,
9: 2 You put a s into his hand to take revenge
11:10 nor does the s prevail against them,
13: 6 of Holofernes, and taking his s from it,
16: 4 to burn my land, put my youths to the s,
16: 9 The s cut through his neck.
Est E:24 be ruthlessly destroyed with fire and s,
9: 5 struck down all their enemies with the s,
1Mc 2: 9 her young men by the s of the enemy.
3: 3 battles and protected the camp with his s.
3:12 and the s of Apollonius was taken by Judas,
4:15 Their whole rearguard fell by the s,
4:33 them down by the s of those who love you,
7:38 and his army, and let them fall by the s.
7:46 them in, and all the enemies fell by the s;
8:23 may s and enemy be far from them.
9:73 Then the s ceased in Israel.
10:85 Those who fell by the s,
12:48 entered with him, they killed with the s.
2Mc 12: 6 to the s those who had taken refuge there.
12:23 putting the sinners to the s and
14:41 on all sides, turned his s against himself,
15:15 hand, Jeremiah presented a gold s to Judas.
15:16 "Accept this holy s as a gift from God;
Jb 1:15 They put the herdsmen to the s,
1:17 off, and put those tending them to the s,
5:15 of the s and from the hand of the mighty,
5:20 and in war from the threat of the s;
15:22 the darkness, and looks ever for the s;
19:29 Be afraid of the s for yourselves,
19:29 for these crimes deserve the s;
27:14 children be many, the s is their destiny.
39:22 he turns not back from the s.
41:18 Should the s reach him,
Ps(s) 7:13 they be converted, God will sharpen his s;
17:13 rescue me by your s from the wicked,
22:21 Rescue my soul from the s,
37:14 A s the wicked draw;
44: 4 with their own s did they conquer the land,
44: 7 my bow did I trust, nor did my s save me;
45: 4 Gird your s upon your thigh, O mighty one!
57: 5 and arrows, their tongue is a sharp s.
63:11 They shall be delivered over to the s,
76: 4 flashing shafts of the bow, shield and s,
78:62 s and was enraged against his inheritance.
78:64 Their priests fell by the s,
89:44 s and have not sustained him in battle.
144:11 From the evil s deliver me;
Prv 5: 4 as wormwood, as sharp as a two-edged s.
12:18 The prating of some men is like s thrusts,
25:18 Like a club, or a s,
Sg 3: 8 All of them expert with the s,
3: 8 Each with his s at his side against
Wis 5:20 shield and whet his sudden anger for a s,
18:16 the sharp s of your inexorable decree.
Sir 21: 3 Every offense is a two-edged s;
22:21 Should you draw a s against a friend,
26:19 sin, for whom the LORD makes ready the s.
28:18 Many have fallen by the edge of the s,
39:30 the avenging s to exterminate the wicked;
40: 9 Plague and bloodshed, wrath and the s,
Is 1:20 refuse and resist, the s shall consume you:
2: 4 shall not raise the s against another,
3:25 Your men will fall by the s,
13:15 to a man, they shall fall by the s,
21:15 flee from the sword, from the whetted s;
22: 2 townYour slain are not slain with the s,
27: 1 LORD will punish with his s that is cruel,
31: 8 shall fall by a s not wielded by man,
31: 8 by man, no mortal s shall devour him;
31: 8 He shall flee before the s,
34: 5 my s has drunk its fill in the heavens,
34: 6 The LORD has a s filled with blood,
37: 7 there I will cause him to fall by the s.'"
37:38 the s and fled into the land of Ararat.
41: 2 With his s he reduces them to dust,
49: 2 He made of me a sharp-edged s and
51:19 Desolation and destruction, famine and s!
65:12 for Destiny, You I will destine for the s;
66:16 LORD shall judge all mankind by fire and s.
Jer 2:30 Your s devoured your prophets like a
4:10 for the s touches our very soul."
5:12 us, neither s nor famine shall we see.
5:17 s the fortified city in which you trust.
6:25 into the street, Beware of the enemy's s;
9:15 I will send the s to pursue them until I
11:22 The young men shall die by the s;
12:12 The LORD has a s which consumes the land,
14:12 Rather, I will destroy them with the s,
14:13 who say to them, "You shall not see the s;
14:15 S and famine shall not befall this land":
14:15 by the s and famine shall these prophets
14:16 streets of Jerusalem by famine and the s.
14:18 those slain by the s;
15: 2 whoever is marked for the s,
15: 2 whoever is marked for the sword, to the s;
15: 3 the s to slay them;
15: 9 I will give to the s before their enemies,
16: 4 S and famine will make an end of them,
18:21 to famine, do away with them by the s.
18:21 young men be slain by the s in battle.
19: 7 them fall by the s before their enemies,
20: 4 see them fall by the s of their enemies.
20: 4 captive to Babylon or slay them with the s.
21: 7 in this city who survive pestilence, s,
21: 7 shall strike them with the edge of the s,
21: 9 shall die by the s or famine or pestilence.
24:10 I will send upon them the s,
25:16 because of the s I will send among them.
25:27 before the s that I will send among you!
25:29 down the s upon all who inhabit the earth,
25:31 The godless shall be given to the s,
25:38 land is made desolate By the sweeping s,
26:23 who had him slain by the s and his corpse
27: 8 Babylon, I will punish that nation with s,
27:13 should you and your people die by the s,
29:17 I am sending against them s,

SWORD (cont.)

29:18 I will pursue them with *s*,
31: 2 the *s* have found favor in the desert.
32:24 the Chaldeans who are attacking it, amid *s*,
32:36 handed over to the king of Babylon amid *s*,
33: 4 in the face of siegeworks and the *s*:
34: 4 LORD to you, you shall not die by the *s*.
34:17 you free, says the LORD, for the *s*,
38: 2 who remains in this city shall die by *s*,
39:18 that you escape and do not fall by the *s*.
42:16 the *s* you fear shall reach you in the land
42:17 go to Egypt to stay, shall die by the *s*,
42:22 no doubt of this, you shall die by the *s*,
43:11 the sword, all who are intended for the *s*.
44:12 High and low, they shall die by the *s*,
44:12 fall by the *s* or be consumed by hunger.
44:13 Egypt, just as I punished Jerusalem with *s*,
44:18 are being destroyed by the *s* and by hunger.
44:27 Judah in Egypt shall perish by the *s*
44:28 Those who escape the *s* to return from the
46:10 *s* devours, is sated, drunk with their blood
46:14 the *s* has already devoured your neighbors.
46:16 our birth, away from the destroying *s*."
47: 6 Alas, *s* of the LORD!
48: 2 behind you stalks the *s*.
48:10 cursed he who holds back his *s* from blood.]
49:37 I will send the *s* to pursue them until I
50:16 Before the destroying *s*,
50:35 A *s* upon the Chaldeans, says the LORD
50:36 A *s* upon the soothsayers,
50:36 A *s* upon her warriors,
50:37 A *s* upon her motley throng,
50:37 A *s* upon her treasures,
50:38 A *s* upon her waters,
51:50 You who have escaped the *s*,
Lam 1:20 In the streets the *s* bereaves,
2:21 and young men have fallen by the *s*;
4: 9 by the *s* than for those who die of hunger,
Bar 2:25 anguish, by hunger and the *s* and plague.
Ez 5: 1 a sharp *s* and use it like a barber's razor,
5: 2 around the city and strike it with the *s*;
5: 2 in the wind, and pursue it with the *s*.
5:12 third shall fall by the *s* all around you;
5:12 and I will pursue them with the *s*.
5:17 you, and I will bring the *s* upon you.
6: 3 See, I am bringing a *s* against you,
6: 8 have escaped to other nations from the *s*,
6:11 Israel, for which they shall fall by the *s*,
6:12 he that is near shall fall by the *s*,
7:15 The *s* is outside;
7:15 that is in the country shall die by the *s*;
11: 8 the sword, but the *s* I will bring upon you,
11:10 By the *s* you shall fall;
12:14 direction, and pursue them with the *s*.
12:16 will leave a few of them to escape the *s*,
14:17 Or if I brought the *s* upon this country,
14:17 commanding the *s* to pass through the land
14:21 my four cruel punishments, the *s*,
17:21 among his forces shall fall by the *s*,
21: 8 I will draw my *s* from its sheath and cut
21: 9 Thus my *s* shall leave its sheath against
21:10 the LORD, have drawn my *s* from its sheath,
21:14 a sword has been burnished:
21:14 A sword, a sword has been sharpened, a *s*,
21:16 A *s* sharpened and burnished to be put in
21:17 of Israel, victims of the *s* with my people.
21:18 slap your thigh, for the *s* has been tested;
21:19 While the *s* is doubled and tripled,
21:19 doubled and tripled, this *s* of slaughter,
21:19 *s* of slaughter which threatens all around,
21:20 gates I have appointed the *s* for slaughter,
21:24 the *s* of the king of Babylon can come.
21:25 so that the *s* can come to Rabbah of the
21:33 A sword, a *s* is drawn for slaughter,
23:10 away, and herself they slew with the *s*.
23:25 what is left of you shall fall by the *s*.
24:21 you left behind shall fall by the *s*.
25:13 they shall fall by the *s*.
26: 6 mainland shall be slaughtered by the *s*;
26: 8 on the mainland he shall slay with the *s*;
26:11 Your people he shall slay by the *s*;
26:15 wounded, when the *s* slays in your midst,
28:23 *s* that comes against it from every side.
29: 8 I will bring the *s* against you,
30: 4 Then a *s* shall come upon Egypt,
30: 5 territory shall fall by the *s* with them.
30: 6 to Syene they shall fall there by the *s*,
30:17 of On and of Pibeseth shall fall by the *s*,
30:21 that it may be strong enough to hold the *s*.
30:22 arm, so that the *s* drops from his hand.
30:24 king of Babylon, and put my *s* in his hand,
30:25 when I put my *s* in the hand of the king of
31:17 the nether world, to those slain by the *s*;
31:18 uncircumcised, with those slain by the *s*.
32:10 in horror when they see me brandish my *s*,
32:11 The *s* of the king of Babylon shall come
32:12 of those slain by the *s* shall they fall,
32:21 uncircumcised, with those slain by the *s*."
32:23 grave, all of them slain, fallen by the *s*,
32:24 grave, all of them slain, fallen by the *s*:
32:26 all of them uncircumcised, slain by the *s*,
32:28 shall you lie, with those slain by the *s*.
32:29 been placed with those slain by the *s*;
32:30 uncircumcised with those slain by the *s*
32:31 for all his hordes slain by the *s*—
32:32 uncircumcised, with those slain by the *s*—
33: 2 When I bring the *s* against a country,
33: 3 seeing the *s* coming against the country,
33: 4 slain by the *s* that comes against him,
33: 6 But if the watchman sees the *s* coming and
33: 6 so that the *s* comes and takes anyone,
33:26 You rely on your *s*,
33:27 in the ruins I swear shall fall by the *s*;
35: 5 of the *s* at the time of their trouble,
35: 8 [in them the slain shall fall by the *s*:
38: 8 against a nation which has survived the *s*,
38:21 GOD, every man's *s* against his brother.
39:23 foes, so that all of them fell by the *s*.
Dn 11:33 a time they will become victims of the *s*,
13:59 "for the angel of God waits with a *s*
14:26 will kill this dragon without *s* or club."
Hos 1: 7 I will not save them by war, by *s* or bow,
2:20 and *s* and war I will destroy from the land,
7:16 Their princes shall fall by the *s* because
11: 6 The *s* shall begin with his cities and end
14: 1 They shall fall by the *s*,
Am 1:11 Because he pursued his brother with the *s*,
4:10 and with the *s* I slew your young men;
7: 9 attack the house of Jeroboam with the *s*.
7:11 Jeroboam shall die by the *s*,
7:17 sons and daughters shall fall by the *s*;
9: 1 Those who are left I will slay with the *s*;
9: 4 there will I command the *s* to slay them.
9:10 *s* shall all sinners among my people die,
Mi 4: 3 shall not raise the *s* against another,
5: 5 shall tend the land of Assyria with the *s*,
5: 5 and the land of Nimrod with the drawn *s*;
6:14 you do save, I will deliver up to the *s*.
Na 2:14 and the *s* shall devour your young lions;
3: 3 Cavalry charging, The flame of the *s*,
3:15 consume you, the *s* shall cut you down.
Hb 1:17 his *s* to slay peoples without mercy?
Zep 2:12 shall be slain by the *s* of the LORD.
Hg 2:22 horses shall go down by one another's *s*.
Zec 9:13 and I will use you as a warrior's *s*.
11:17 *s* fall upon his arm and upon his right eye;
13: 7 Awake, O *s*, against my shepherd
Mt 26:51 accompanied Jesus put his hand to his *s*,
26:52 "Put back your *s* where it belongs.
26:52 the *s* are sooner or later destroyed by it.
Mk 14:47 his *s* and struck the high priest's slave,
Lk 2:35 you yourself shall be pierced with a *s*—
21:24 The people will fall before the *s*:
22:36 without a *s* must sell his coat and buy one.
22:49 they said, "Lord, shall we use the *s*?"
Jn 18:10 Then Simon Peter, who had a *s*,
18:11 to Peter, "Put your *s* back in its sheath.
Acts 16:27 had escaped, he drew his *s* to kill himself;
Rom 8:35 hunger, or nakedness, or danger, or the *s*?
13: 4 purpose that the ruler carries the *s*;
Eph 6:17 of salvation and the *s* of the spirit,
Heb 4:12 effective, sharper than any two-edged *s*.
11:34 out raging fires, escaped the devouring *s*;
Rv 1:16 A sharp, two-edged *s* came out of his mouth,
2:12 the sharp, two-edged *s* has this to say:
2:16 fight against them with the *s* of my mouth.
6: 4 For this he was given a huge *s*.
6: 8 to kill with *s* and famine and plague and
13:10 by the sword, by the *s* he will be slain!
13:14 had been wounded by the *s* and yet lived.
19:15 a sharp *s* for striking down the nations.
19:21 The rest were slain by the *s* which came

SWORD-POINT (1)

Is 14:19 and corrupt, Clothed as those slain at *s*,

SWORDS (31)

Gn 34:25 Levi, two of Jacob's sons, took their *s*,
1Sm 13:19 the Hebrews will make *s* or spears."
14:20 confused, were thrusting *s* at one another.
1Kgs 18:28 and slashed themselves with *s* and spears,
Neh 4: 7 them by family groups with their *s*,
Est B: 6 destroyed by the *s* of their enemies,
1Mc 4: 6 such armor and *s* as they would have wished.
2Mc 5: 3 fully armed with lances and drawn *s*;
12:22 another, pierced by the *s* of their own men.
Ps(s) 37:15 But their *s* shall pierce their own hearts,
55:22 smoother than oil, but they are drawn *s*.
64: 4 Who sharpen their tongues like *s*,
149: 6 let two-edged *s* be in their hands:
Prv 30:14 There is a group whose incisors are *s*,
Is 2: 4 They shall beat their *s* into plowshares
Jer 41: 2 him, rose up and attacked with *s* Gedaliah,
Ez 16:40 you to stone you and hack you with their *s*.
23:47 them and hack them to pieces with their *s*.
28: 7 draw their *s* against your beauteous wisdom,
30:11 They shall draw their *s* against Egypt,
32:27 whose *s* were placed under their heads and
38: 4 and shields, all of them carrying *s*:
Jl 4:10 Beat your plowshares into *s*,
Mi 4: 3 They shall beat their *s* into plowshares,
Mt 26:47 by a great crowd with *s* and clubs.
26:55 come armed with *s* and clubs to arrest me?
Mk 14:43 accompanied by a crowd with *s* and clubs;
14:48 with *s* and clubs as if against a brigand.
Lk 22:38 They said, "Lord, here are two *s*!"
22:52 come out after me armed with *s* and clubs?
Heb 11:37 sawed in two, put to death at *s* point;

SWORDSMEN (8)

Jgs 8:10 and twenty thousand *s* having fallen.
20: 2 hundred thousand foot soldiers who were *s*,
20:15 The number of the Benjaminite *s* from the
20:17 four hundred thousand *s* ready for battle,
20:25 thousand Israelites, all of them *s*.
20:35 one hundred men of Benjamin, all of them *s*.
20:46 day were in all twenty-five thousand *s*,
2Kgs 3:26 *s* to break through to the king of Aram,

SWORE (78)

Gn 24: 9 Abraham and *s* to him in this undertaking.
26: 3 the oath that I *s* to your father Abraham.
47:31 So Joseph *s* to him.
Ex 6: 8 into the land which I *s* to give to Abraham,
13: 5 he *s* to your fathers he would give you,
13:11 which he *s* to you and your fathers he
32:13 and how you *s* to them by your own self,
33: 1 from here to the land which I *s* to Abraham,
Lv 5:24 found or whatever else he *s* falsely about;
Nm 14:16 people into the land he *s* to give them;
14:30 the land where I solemnly *s* to settle you,
32:10 the wrath of the LORD flared up, and he *s*,
Dt 1: 8 and occupy the land I *s* to your fathers,
1:35 he *s*, 'Not one man of this evil generation
1:35 the good land I *s* to give to your fathers,
4:21 *s* that I should not cross the Jordan
6:10 into the land which he *s* to your fathers,
7:13 he *s* to your fathers he would give you.
8:18 the covenant which he *s* to your fathers.
10:11 I *s* to their fathers I would give them.'
11: 9 land which the LORD *s* to your fathers
11:21 LORD *s* to your fathers he would give them.
19: 8 your territory, as he *s* to your fathers,
26: 3 which he *s* to our fathers he would give us.'
28: 9 a people sacred to himself, as he *s* to you;
28:11 he *s* to your fathers he would give you.
29:12 you and as he *s* to your fathers Abraham,
30:20 *s* he would give to your fathers Abraham,
31: 7 LORD *s* to their fathers he would give them;
34: 4 "This is the land which I *s* to Abraham,
Jos 1: 6 I *s* to their fathers I would give them.
5: 6 For the LORD *s* that he would not let them
6:22 all her kin, as you *s* to her you would do."
14: 9 On that occasion Moses *s* this oath,
1Sm 14:24 And Saul *s* a very rash oath that day,
19: 6 Saul heeded Jonathan's plea and *s*,
28:10 But Saul *s* to her by the LORD,
2Sm 3: 9 carry out for David what the LORD *s* to him
3:35 David *s*, "May God do thus and so to me
21:17 Then David's men *s* to him,
1Kgs 1:17 you *s* to me your handmaid by the LORD,
1:29 presence and stood before him, the king *s*,
1:30 fulfill the oath I *s* to you by the LORD,
2: 8 I *s* to him by the LORD that I would not
2:23 And King Solomon *s* by the LORD:
1Chr 29:24 King David, *s* allegiance to King Solomon.
2Chr 15:14 They *s* to the LORD with a loud voice with
Ezr 10: 5 and they *s* it.
Jdt 1:12 and *s* by his throne and his kingdom that
1Mc 6:61 the king and the leaders *s* an oath to them,
7:15 spoke with them peacefully and *s* to them,
7:18 the agreement and the oath that they *s*."
7:35 In a rage he *s*:
9:71 He *s* an oath to him that he would never
2Mc 13:23 their terms, and *s* to observe their rights.
14:33 hand toward the temple and *s* this oath:
Ps(s) 95:11 Therefore I *s* in my anger:
106:26 Then with raised hand he *s* against them to
132: 2 How he *s* to the LORD,
132:11 The LORD *s* to David a firm promise from
Wis 14:30 deliberately *s* false oaths despising piety.
Is 54: 9 when I *s* that the waters of Noah should
Jer 11: 5 fulfill the oath which I *s* to your fathers,
38:16 But King Zedekiah *s* to Jeremiah secretly:
Ez 16: 8 I *s* an oath to you and entered into a
20: 5 *s* to the descendants of the house of Jacob;
20: 5 of Egypt I revealed myself to them and *s*:
20: 6 That day I *s* to bring them out of the land
20:15 Nevertheless I *s* to them in the desert not
20:23 Nevertheless I *s* to them in the desert
20:42 the land which I *s* to give to your fathers.
47:14 land which I *s* to give to your fathers,
Mt 14: 7 delighted Herod so much that he *s* he would
26:74 At that he began cursing, and *s*,
Lk 1:73 *s* to Abraham our father he would grant us:
Heb 3:11 "Thus I *s* in my anger,
4: 3 "Thus I *s* in my anger.
6:13 his promise to Abraham, he *s* by himself,

SWORN (45)

Gn 14:22 "I have *s* to the LORD,
26:28 be a *s* agreement between our two sides
Nm 14:35 have *s* to do this to all this wicked
Dt 2:14 the camp, as the LORD had *s* they should.
7: 8 to the oath he had *s* to your fathers,
Jos 9:18 of the community had *s* to them by the LORD,

9:19 people, "We have *s* to them by the LORD,
9:20 be punished for the oath we have *s* to them."
21:43 had *s* to their fathers he would give them.
Jgs 2:15 as in his warning he had *s* he would do,
21: 1 Now the men of Israel had *s* at Mizpah that
21: 7 since we have *s* by the LORD not to give
21:18 marriage, because the Israelites have *s*,
1Sm 20:42 what we two have *s* by the name of the LORD:
2Kgs 11: 4 the LORD, exacted from them a *s* commitment,
2Chr 15:15 for they had *s* with their whole heart and
Neh 9:15 you had *s* with upraised hand to give them.
Tb 9: 3 You witnessed the oath that Raguel has *s*;
10: 7 Raguel had *s* to hold for his daughter,
1Mc 6:62 he broke the oath he had *s* and gave orders
2Mc 4:34 through *s* pledges with right hands joined,
Ps(s) 89: 4 chosen one, I have *s* to David my servant:
89:36 Once, by my holiness, have I *s*;
110: 4 LORD has *s*, and he will not repent:
Wis 12:21 gave the *s* covenants of goodly promises!
14:29 expect no harm when they have *s* falsely.
14:31 For not the might of those that are *s* by
18:22 the *s* covenants with their fathers.
Is 5: 9 In my hearing the LORD of hosts has *s*:
14:24 The LORD of hosts has *s*:
54: 9 So I have *s* not to be angry with you,
62: 8 *s* by his right hand and by his mighty arm:
Jer 49:13 By my own self I have *s*, says the LORD:
51:14 The LORD of hosts has *s* by himself:
51:15 He has *s* who made the earth by his power,
Ez 20:28 them to the land I had *s* to give them,
21:28 they are bound by the oaths they have *s*,
44:12 therefore I have *s* an oath against them,
Dn 9:11 not heeding your voice, the *s* malediction,
Am 4: 2 The Lord GOD has *s* by his holiness:
6: 8 The Lord GOD has *s* by his very self,
8: 7 The LORD has *s* by the pride of Jacob:
Mi 7:20 you have *s* to our fathers from days of old.
Acts 2:30 He was a prophet and knew that God had *s*
Heb 7:21 "The Lord has *s*, and he will not repent:

SWUNG (2)
Jos 18:14 the boundary line *s* south from the
2Mc 10:36 up the same way *s* around on the defenders,

SYCAMORE (2)
Lk 17: 6 a mustard seed, you could say to this *s*,
19: 4 a *s* tree which was along Jesus' route,

SYCAMORES (7)
1Kgs 10:27 as numerous as the *s* of the foothills.
1Chr 27:28 Over the olive trees and *s* of the
2Chr 1:15 as numerous as the *s* of the foothills.
9:27 as numerous as the *s* of the foothills.
Ps(s) 78:47 vines with hail and their *s* with frost.
Is 9: 9 *S* are felled, but we will replace them
Am 7:14 I was a shepherd and a dresser of *s*.

SYENE (4)
Is 49:12 and the west, and some from the land of *S*.
Ez 29:10 a waste and a desolation from Migdol to *S*,
30: 6 to *S* they shall fall there by the sword,
30:16 *S* shall writhe in anguish;

SYMBOL (4)
Is 57: 8 the doorpost you placed your indecent *s*.
57: 8 you carved the *s* and gazed upon it
Heb 9: 9 This is a *s* of the present time,
11:19 so he received Isaac back as a *s*.

SYMBOLIC (2)
Rv 11: 8 which has the *s* name "Sodom" or "Egypt,"
17: 5 On her forehead was written a *s* name,

SYMBOLISM (1)
Rv 17: 7 I will explain to you the *s* of the woman

SYMEON (2)
Acts 13: 1 Barnabas, *S* known as Niger,
15:14 *S* has told you how God first concerned

SYMPATHETIC (3)
Acts 17: 4 did a great number of Greeks *s* to Judaism,
17:17 with the Jews and those *s* to Judaism,
1Pt 3: 8 then, all of you should be like-minded, *s*,

SYMPATHIZE (1)
Heb 4:15 who is unable to *s* with our weakness,

SYMPATHIZED (1)
Jgs 9: 3 the citizens of Shechem *s* with Abimelech,

SYMPATHIZERS (2)
Mt 22:16 to him, accompanied by Herodian *s*,
Acts 13:50 women *s* and the leading men of the town,

SYMPATHY (7)
1Sm 22: 8 None of you shows *s* for me or discloses to
23:21 "The LORD bless you for your *s* toward me.
Jb 2:11 together to give him *s* and comfort.
Ps(s) 69:21 my heart, and I am weak, I looked for *s*,
Jer 16: 5 go not there to lament or offer *s*.
Dn 1: 9 the favor and *s* of the chief chamberlain,
Jas 3:17 *s* and the kindly deeds that are its fruits,

SYNAGOGUE (42)
Mt 9:18 speaking to them, a *s* leader came up,
9:23 When Jesus arrived at the *s* leader's house
12: 9 He left that place and went into their *s*.
13:54 spent his time teaching them in their *s*.
Mk 1:21 he entered the *s* and began to teach.
1:23 There appeared in their *s* a man with an
1:29 Immediately upon leaving the *s*,
3: 1 He returned to the *s* where there was a man
5:22 One of the officials of the *s*,
5:38 they approached the house of the *s* leader,
6: 2 he began to teach in the *s* in a way
Lk 4:16 and entering the *s* on the sabbath as he
4:20 All in the *s* had their eyes fixed on him.
4:28 in the *s* was filled with indignation.
4:33 *s* there was a man with an unclean spirit,
4:38 Leaving the *s*, he entered the house
6: 6 another sabbath he came to teach in a *s*
7: 5 our people, and even built our *s* for us."
8:41 man named Jairus, who was chief of the *s*,
13:14 chief of the *s*, indignant that Jesus
Jn 6:59 said this in a *s* instruction at Capernaum.
9:22 as the Messiah would be put out of the *s*.
12:42 for fear they might be ejected from the *s*.
18:20 I always taught in a *s* or in the temple
Acts 6: 9 so-called *S* of Roman Freedmen" (that is,
13:14 day they entered the *s* and sat down.
13:15 men of the *s* sent this message to them:
14: 1 they entered the Jewish *s* and spoke in
17: 1 Thessalonica, where there was a Jewish *s*.
17:10 their arrival, they went to the Jewish *s*.
17:17 In the *s* he used to hold discussions with
18: 4 Every sabbath, in the *s*, Paul led discussions
18: 7 his house was next door to the *s*.
18: 8 A leading man of the *s*,
18:17 on Sosthenes, a leading man of the *s*,
18:19 the *s* to hold discussions with the Jews.
18:26 to express himself fearlessly in the *s*.
19: 8 Paul entered the *s*,
22:19 in you and flogged them in every *s*.
24:12 Neither in the temple area, nor in the *s*,
26:11 Many a time, in *s* after synagogue,

SYNAGOGUES (22)
Mt 4:23 He taught in their *s*,
6: 2 do not blow a horn before you in *s*
6: 5 who love to stand and pray in *s*
9:35 He taught in their *s*,
10:17 into court, they will flog you in their *s*.
23: 6 at banquets and the front seats in *s*,
23:34 in your *s* and hunt down from city to city;
Mk 1:39 So he went into their *s* preaching the good
12:39 of respect in public, front seats in the *s*,
13: 9 You will be beaten in *s*.
Lk 4:15 He was teaching in their *s*,
4:44 he continued to preach in the *s* of Judea.
11:43 seats in *s* and marks of respect in public.
12:11 When they bring you before *s*,
13:10 day he was teaching in one of the *s*.
20:46 of respect in public, front seats in *s*,
21:12 you, summoning you to *s* and prisons,
Jn 16: 2 Not only will they expel you from *s*;
Acts 9: 2 asked him for letters to the *s* in Damascus
9:20 in the *s* that Jesus was the Son of God.
13: 5 the word of God in the Jewish *s*,
15:21 been read aloud in the *s* on every sabbath."

SYNTYCHE (1)
Phil 4: 2 I plead with Evodia just as I do with *S*:

SYRACUSE (1)
Acts 28:12 We put in at *S* and spent three days there.

SYRIA (11)
Jdt 1:12 territories of Cilicia and Damascus and *S*,
1Mc 11: 2 He entered *S* with peaceful words,
11:60 forces of *S* espoused his cause as allies.
Mt 4:24 his reputation traveled the length of *S*.
Lk 2: 2 place while Quirinius was governor of *S*.
Acts 15:23 brothers of Gentile origin in Antioch, *S*,
15:41 He traveled throughout *S* and Cilicia,
18:18 leave of the brothers and sailed for *S*,
20: 3 As he was on the point of embarking for *S*,
21: 3 by on our left as we continued on toward *S*.
Gal 1:21 I entered the regions of *S* and Cilicia.

SYRIAN (4)
Jdt 8:26 all that happened to Jacob in *S* Mesopotamia
1Mc 3:13 But Seron, commander of the *S* army,
7:39 at Beth-horon, where the *S* army joined him.
Lk 4:27 yet not one was cured except Naaman the *S*."

SYRO-PHOENICIAN (1)
Mk 7:26 *S* by birth—began to beg him

SYRTIS (1)
Acts 27:17 they would be driven on the reef of *S*,

SYRUP (2)
2Kgs 18:32 and orchards, of olives, oil and fruit *s*.
Ps(s) 19:11 Sweeter also than *s* or honey from the comb.

SYSTEM (1)
Ez 42: 5 for the *s* of levels set them at a level

SYSTEMATICALLY (1)
Acts 18:23 traveling *s* through the Galatian country

T

TAANACH (8)
Jos 12:21 Madon, Hazor, Shimron, Achshaph, *T*,
17:11 and natives, *T* and its towns and natives,
21:25 two cities of *T* with its pasture lands
Jgs 1:27 with its towns or of *T* with its towns.
5:19 of Canaan, At *T* by the waters of Megiddo;
1Kgs 4:12 Baana, son of Ahilud, in *T* and Megiddo,
1Chr 6:55 *T* with its pasture lands and Ibleam with
7:29 Bethshean and its towns, *T* and its towns,

TAANATH-SHILOH (1)
Jos 16: 6 their boundary curved eastward around *T*,

TABBAOTH (2)
Ezr 2:43 sons of Ziha, sons of Hasupha, sons of *T*,
Neh 7:46 sons of Ziha, sons of Hasupha, sons of *T*,

TABBATH (1)
Jgs 7:22 near the border of Abelmeholah at *T*.

TABBUR-HAARES (1)
Jgs 9:37 are coming down from the region of *T*,

TABEEL (2)
Ezr 4: 7 Mithredath wrote in concert with *T*
Is 7: 6 force, and appoint the son of *T* king there."

TABERAH (2)
Nm 11: 3 Hence that place was called *T*,
Dt 9:22 "At *T*, at Massah,

TABERNACLE (11)
Ps(s) 78:60 And he forsook the *t* in Shiloh,
Wis 9: 8 *t* which you had established from of old.
Heb 8: 2 of the sanctuary and of that true *t* set up,
8: 5 one, for Moses, when about to erect the *t*,
9: 2 For a *t* was constructed,
9: 3 veil was the *t* called the holy of holies,
9: 6 used to go into the outer *t* constantly,
9: 8 that while the first *t* was still standing,
9:11 and more perfect *t* not made by hands,
9:21 He also sprinkled the *t* and all the
13:10 those who serve the *t* have no right to eat.

TABITHA (2)
Acts 9:36 woman convert named *T* (in Greek Dorcas,
9:40 Turning to the dead body, he said, *T*,

TABLE (116)
Gn 24:33 But when the *t* was set for him,
43:34 were brought to them from Joseph's *t*,
Ex 25:23 "You shall also make a *t* of acacia wood,
25:27 as holders for the poles to carry the *t*.
25:28 These poles for carrying the *t* you shall
25:30 On the *t* you shall always keep showbread
26:35 you shall place the *t* and the lampstand,
26:35 south side of the Dwelling, opposite the *t*,
30:27 the *t* and all its appurtenances,
31: 8 of the tent, the *t* with its appurtenances,
35:13 *t*, with its poles
37:10 The *t* was made of acacia wood,
37:14 as holders for the poles to carry the *t*.
37:16 The vessels that were set on the *t*,
39:36 the *t* with all its appurtenances and the
40: 4 Bring in the *t* and set it.
40:22 He put the *t* in the meeting tent,
40:24 in the meeting tent, opposite the *t*,
Lv 24: 6 pile, on the pure gold *t* before the LORD.
Nm 3:31 of whatever pertained to the ark, the *t*,
4: 7 On the *t* of the Presence they shall spread
4: 7 bread offering shall remain on the *t*.
Jgs 1: 7 cut off, used to pick up scraps under my *t*.
1Sm 20:24 new moon, when the king sat at *t* to dine,
20:27 of Jesse not come to *t* yesterday or today?"
20:29 is why he has not come to the king's *t*."
20:34 Jonathan sprang up from the *t* in great

TABLE (cont.)

2Sm 9: 7 Saul, and you shall always eat at my t."
9:10 your lord's son, shall always eat at my t."
9:11 at David's t like one of the king's sons.
9:13 because he always ate at the king's t.
11: 8 was sent out after him from the king's t.
19:29 your servant among the guests at your t.
19:43 have portions from his t been given to us?"
1Kgs 2: 7 the Gileadite, and have them eat at your t.
5: 7 and for all the guests at the royal t.
7:48 the golden t on which the showbread lay;
10: 5 palace he had built, the food at his t,
13:20 But while they were sitting at t,
18:19 prophets of Asherah who eat at Jezebel's t."
2Kgs 4:10 roof and furnish it for him with a bed, t,
25:29 ate at the king's t as long as he lived.
1Chr 28:16 of gold for each t to hold the showbread,
2Chr 9: 4 palace he had built, the food at his t,
13:11 they display the showbread on the pure t,
29:18 t for the showbread with all its utensils.
Neh 5:17 I set my t for a hundred and fifty persons,
Tb 2: 2 The t was set for me,
2:12 and also gave her a young goat for the t.
9: 6 house, they found Tobiah reclining at t.
Jdt 12: 1 and bade them set a t for her with his own
Est C:28 have never eaten at the t of Haman,
1Mc 1:22 with all its fixtures, the offering t,
4:49 of incense, and the t into the temple.
4:51 on the t and hung up curtains
Ps(s) 23: 5 the t before me in the sight of my foes;
69:23 Let their own t be a snare before them,
78:19 saying, "Can God spread a t in the desert?
128: 3 children like olive plants around your t.
Prv 9: 2 mixed her wine, yes, she has spread her t.
Sir 9: 9 not, recline not at t to drink by her side,
9:16 Have just men for your t companions;
14:10 bread, but on his own t he sets it stale.
29:26 "Come here, stranger, set the t,
30:25 and gay while at t benefits from his food.
31:12 man, bring not a greedy gullet to his t,
31:16 Behave at t like a favored guest,
31:18 If there are many with you at t,
40:29 When one has to look to another's t,
Is 21: 5 They set the t,
65:11 You who spread a t for Fortune and fill
Jer 41: 1 while they were together at t in Mizpah,
52:33 ate at the king's t as long as he lived.
Ez 23:41 for them, with a t spread before it,
39:20 be filled at my t with horses and riders,
41:22 "This is the t which is before the LORD.
44:16 who shall approach my t to minister to me,
Dn 1: 5 portion of food and wine from the royal t.
1:13 other young men who eat from the royal t,
1:15 of the young men who ate from the royal t.
11:26 his t companions shall seek to destroy him,
11:27 sit at t together and exchange lies,
14:13 because under the t they had made a secret
14:18 the king looked at the t and cried aloud,
14:21 used to enter to consume what was on the t.
Mal 1: 7 saying the t of the LORD may be slighted!
1:12 LORD's t and its offering may be polluted,
Mt 9:10 while Jesus was at t in Matthew's home,
26: 7 him at t and began to pour it on his head.
26:20 grew dark he reclined at t with the Twelve.
Mk 7:27 household satisfy themselves at t first.
7:28 under the t eat the family's leavings."
14: 3 at t in the house of Simon the leper,
14:18 They reclined at t,
16:14 Finally, as they were at t,
Lk 11:37 He entered and reclined at t.
12:37 he will put on an apron, seat them at t,
14: 7 trying to get the places of honor at the t:
16:21 the scraps that fell from the rich man's t.
17: 7 you say to him, 'Come and sit down at t'?
22:14 the hour arrived, he took his place at t,
22:21 hand of my betrayer is with me at this t.
22:27 reclines at t or he who serves the meal?
22:27 Is it not the one who reclines at t?
22:30 my kingdom you will eat and drink at my t,
Jn 2: 5 His mother instructed those waiting on t,
12: 2 Lazarus was one of those at t with him.
13:12 cloak back on and reclined at t once more.
13:28 at t understood why Jesus said this to him.
Acts 16:34 up into his house, spread a t before them,
Rom 11: 9 "Let their t become a snare and a trap,
1Cor 8:10 reclining at t in the temple of an idol,
10:21 t of the Lord and likewise the t of demons.
10:27 invites you to his t and you want to go,
Heb 9: 2 one, in which were the lampstand, the t,

TABLELAND (5)

Jos 13: 9 itself, through the t of Medeba and Dibon,
13:16 wadi itself, through the t about Medeba,
13:17 and all its towns which are on the t,
13:21 and the other cities of the t and,
20: 8 Bezer on the open t in the tribe of Reuben,

TABLES (17)

1Chr 28:16 and the silver for the silver t;
2Chr 4: 8 He made ten t and had them set in the nave,
4:19 altar, the t on which the showbread lay,
Sir 36:20 an experienced man can turn the t on him.
Is 28: 8 all the t are covered with filthy vomit,
Ez 40:39 the gate there were two t on either side,
40:40 entrance of the north gate, were two t,
40:40 vestibule of the gate there were two t.
40:41 four t on either side of the gate [eight t
40:42 There were four t for holocausts,
40:43 On the t themselves the flesh was laid.
Mt 15:27 leavings that fall from their masters' t."
21:12 t and the stalls of the dove-sellers,
Mk 11:15 t and the stalls of the men selling doves;
Jn 2:15 and knocked over the money-changers' t,
Acts 6: 2 the word of God in order to wait on t.

TABLET (4)

Prv 7: 3 fingers, write them on the t of your heart.
Is 30: 8 Now come, write it on a t they can keep,
Ez 4: 1 As for you, son of man, take a clay t;
Lk 1:63 for a writing t and wrote the words,

TABLETS (38)

Ex 24:12 I will give you the stone t on which I
31:18 two t of the commandments, the stone t
32:15 the two t of the commandments in his hands,
32:15 hands, t that were written on both sides,
32:16 t that were made by God,
32:19 so that he threw the t down and broke them
34: 1 Moses, "Cut two stone t like the former,
34: 1 which were on the former t that you broke.
34: 4 Moses then cut two stone t like the former,
34: 4 him, taking along the two stone t.
34:28 wrote on the t the words of the covenant,
34:29 the two t of the commandments in his hands,
Dt 4:13 which he wrote on two t of stone.
5:22 upon two t of stone and gave them to me.
9: 9 up the mountain to receive the stone t
9:10 LORD gave me the two t of stone inscribed,
9:11 given me the two stone t of the covenant,
9:15 the two t of the covenant in both my hands,
9:17 Raising the two t with both hands I threw
10: 1 to me, 'Cut two t of stone like the former;
10: 2 I will write upon the t the commandments
10: 2 that were on the former t that you broke,
10: 3 and cut two t of stone like the former,
10: 3 went up the mountain carrying the two t.
10: 5 and placed the t in the ark I had made.
1Kgs 8: 9 stone t which Moses had put there at Horeb,
2Chr 5:10 two t which Moses put there on Horeb, the t
1Mc 8:22 on bronze t and sent to Jerusalem,
14:18 they sent him inscribed t of bronze to
14:26 So they made an inscription on bronze t,
14:48 should be engraved on bronze t,
Jer 17: 1 upon the t of their hearts.
Hb 2: 2 Write down the vision Clearly upon the t,
2Cor 3: 3 not on t of stone but on tablets of flesh
Heb 9: 4 had blossomed, and the t of the covenant.

TABOR (10)

Jos 19:22 The boundary reached T,
Jgs 4: 6 "go, march on Mount T,
4:12 son of Abinoam, had gone up to Mount T.
4:14 So Barak went down Mount T,
8:18 "Where now are the men you killed at T?"
1Sm 10: 3 on, when you arrive at the terebinth of T,
1Chr 6:62 lands, and T with its pasture lands.
Ps(s) 89:13 T and Hermon rejoice at your name.
Jer 46:18 Like T among the mountains he shall come,
Hos 5: 1 a snare at Mizpah, and a net spread over T.

TABRIMMON (1)

1Kgs 15:18 King Asa sent them to Ben-hadad, son of T,

TACITURN (1)

Sir 32: 8 those few words, be like the wise man, t.

TACTICS (1)

Eph 6:11 to stand firm against the t of the devil.

TADMOR (1)

2Chr 8: 4 He built T in the desert region and all

TAHAN (2)

Nm 26:35 through T the clan of the Tahanites.
1Chr 7:25 whose son was Telah, whose son was T,

TAHANITES (1)

Nm 26:35 Bechrites, through Tahan the clan of the T.

TAHASH (14)

Gn 22:24 Tebah, Gaham, T, and Maacah.
Ex 25: 5 rams' skins dyed red, and t skins;
26:14 red, and above that, a covering of t skins.
35: 7 rams' skins dyed red, and t skins;
35:23 goat hair, rams' skins dyed red or t skins,
36:19 red, and above that, a covering of t skins.
39:34 skins dyed red, the covering of t skins,
Nm 4: 6 these they shall put a cover of t skin,
4: 8 cloth and cover all this with t skin.
4:10 shall then enclose in a covering of t skin,
4:11 cover this also with a covering of t skin.
4:12 in violet cloth and cover them with t skin.
4:14 then spread a covering of t skin over this,
4:25 covering and the outer wrapping of t skin,

TAHATH (6)

Nm 33:26 out from Makheloth, they camped at T.
33:27 Setting out from T, they camped at Terah.
1Chr 6: 9 whose son was Assir, whose son was T,
6:22 of Azariah, son of Zaphaniah, son of T,
7:20 whose son was Bered, whose son was T,
7:20 whose son was Eleadah, whose son was T,

TAHPANHES (7)

Jdt 1: 9 to T, Raamses, all the land of Goshen,
Jer 2:16 Memphis and T shave the crown of your head.
43: 7 they went to Egypt, and arrived at T. . . .
43: 8 word of the LORD came to Jeremiah in T:
43: 9 the entrance to the royal building in T,
44: 1 who were living in Egypt, at Migdol, T,
46:14 it in Migdol, proclaim it in Memphis and T!

TAHPENES (2)

1Kgs 11:19 gave him in marriage the sister of Queen T,
11:20 T' sister bore Hadad a son, Genubath.

TAHREA (1)

1Chr 9:41 The sons of Micah were Pithon, Melech, T,

TAIL (15)

Ex 4: 4 LORD said to him, "and take hold of its t."
29:22 fatty t, the fat that covers its inner organs,
Lv 3: 9 whole fatty t, which he must sever close
7: 3 fatty t, the fatty membrane over the inner
8:25 t and all the fat over the inner organs,
9:19 from the ox and from the ram, the fatty t,
Dt 28:13 LORD will make you the head, not the t,
28:44 He will become the head, you the t.
Jgs 15: 4 Turning them tail to t,
Jb 40:17 He carries his t like a cedar;
Is 9:13 So the LORD severs from Israel head and t,
9:14 the prophet who teaches falsehood is the t
19:15 shall have no work to do for head or t,
Rv 12: 4 His t swept a third of the stars from the

TAILS (5)

Jgs 15: 4 of t one of the torches he had at hand.
Rv 9:10 had t with stingers like scorpions; in their t
9:19 but in their t; for their t were like snakes

TAINTED (2)

Sir 34:18 T his gifts who offers in sacrifice
Ti 1:15 Their very minds and consciences are t.

TAKE (883)

Gn 3:22 hand to t fruit from the tree of life also,
7: 2 every clean animal, t with you seven pairs,
12:19 T her and be gone!"
14:23 that I would not t so much as a thread or
14:24 let them t their share."
19:12 to you in the city t them away from it!
19:15 T with you your wife and your two
22: 2 T your son Isaac,
22:17 your descendants shall t possession of the
24: 5 Should I then t your son back to the land
24: 6 "Never t my son back there for any reason,"
24: 8 But never t my son back there!"
24:14 I may drink,' and she answers, T a drink,
24:18 T a drink, sir," she replied,
24:46 jug she was carrying and said, T a drink,
24:51 t her with you,
24:59 sister Rebekah and her nurse to t leave,
27: 3 T your gear,
30: 2 Jacob retorted, "Can I t the place of God,
30:15 it not enough for you to t away my husband,
30:15 that you must now t my son's mandrakes too
31:24 T care not to threaten Jacob with any
31:29 T care not to threaten Jacob with any harm!'
31:31 t your daughters away from me by force.
31:32 anything here as belonging to you, t it."
31:50 or t other wives besides my daughters,
34: 9 to us, and t our daughters for yourselves.
34:16 you our daughters and t yours in marriage;
34:17 we will t our daughter and go away."
37:21 "We must not t his life.
41:34 should also t action to appoint overseers,
42:19 while the rest of you may go and t home
42:36 is gone, and now you would t away Benjamin!
43:11 and t them down to the man as gifts:
43:12 Also t extra money along,
43:13 T your brother,
43:16 head steward, T these men into the house,
43:18 and t our donkeys and seize us as slaves."
44:29 If you now t this one away from me too,
45:19 T wagons from the land of Egypt for your
47:19 T us and our land in exchange for food,
47:22 the priests' lands Joseph did not t over.
50:19 Can I t the place of God?
50:24 God will surely t care of you and lead you

Ex 2: 9 to her, *T* this child and nurse it for me,
4: 4 LORD said to him, "and *t* hold of its tail."
4: 5 will *t* place so that they may believe,"
4: 9 *t* some water from the river and pour it on
4: 9 The water you *t* from the river will become
4:17 *T* this staff in your hand;
6: 7 I will *t* you as my own people,
7: 9 *T* your staff and throw it down before
7:19 *T* your staff and stretch out your hand
8:19 This sign shall *t* place tomorrow."
9: 8 *T* a double handful of soot from a furnace,
9:21 did not *t* the warning of the LORD to heart
10:17 to *t* at least this deadly pest from me."
12: 5 *t* it from either the sheep or the goats.
12: 7 They shall *t* some of its blood and apply
12:22 Then *t* a bunch of hyssop,
12:32 *T* your flocks,
12:46 not *t* any of its flesh outside the house.
16:29 *T* note!
16:33 *T* an urn and put an omer of manna in it.
19:12 *T* care not to go up the mountain,
20: 7 "You shall not *t* the name of the LORD,
21:14 you must *t* him even from my altar and put
22:25 If you *t* your neighbor's cloak as a pledge,
23: 8 Never *t* a bribe,
23:30 enough to *t* possession of the land.
25: 2 the Israelites to *t* up a collection for me.
29: 3 *T* the basket of them along with the
29: 5 *T* the vestments and clothe Aaron with the
29: 7 *t* the anointing oil and anoint him with it,
29:12 *T* some of its blood and with your finger
29:13 on them, you shall *t* and burn on the altar.
29:15 "Then *t* one of the rams,
29:16 *t* and splash on all the sides of the altar.
29:19 "After this *t* the other ram,
29:20 Some of its blood you shall *t* and put on
29:21 *t* some of the blood that is on the altar,
29:22 "Now from this ram you shall *t* its fat:
29:23 you shall *t* one of the loaves of bread,
29:26 *t* the breast of Aaron's ordination ram and
29:31 "You shall *t* the flesh of the ordination
30:12 "When you *t* a census of the Israelites
30:23 LORD said to Moses, *T* the finest spices:
30:34 told Moses, *T* these aromatic substances:
31:13 *T* care to keep my sabbaths,
32: 2 *t* off the golden earrings they are wearing,
32:24 'Let anyone who has gold jewelry *t* it off.'
33: 5 *T* off your ornaments,
34:12 *T* care, therefore, not to make a covenant
34:16 *t* their daughters as wives for your sons;
35: 5 *T* up among you a collection for the LORD.
36: 2 moved them to come and *t* part in the work.
40: 9 *T* the anointing oil and anoint the
Lv 2: 2 *t* a handful of this fine flour and oil,
2: 8 to the priest, who shall *t* it to the altar.
4: 5 The anointed priest shall then *t* some of
4:19 he shall *t* from it and burn on the altar,
4:25 The priest shall then *t* some of the blood
4:30 The priest shall then *t* some of its blood
4:34 The priest shall then *t* some of the blood
5:12 the latter shall *t* a handful of this flour
6: 3 shall *t* away the ashes to which the fire
6: 8 Then he shall *t* from it a handful of its
8: 2 LORD said to Moses, *T* Aaron and his sons,
9: 2 *T* a calf for a sin offering and a ram for
9: 3 *T* a he-goat for a sin offering,
10:12 *T* the cereal offering left over from the
12: 8 she may *t* two turtledoves or two pigeons,
14:10 day he shall *t* two unblemished male lambs,
14:14 Then the priest shall *t* some of the blood
14:15 The priest shall also *t* a log of oil and
14:21 shall *t* one male lamb for a guilt offering,
14:25 lamb, he shall *t* some of its blood,
14:49 To purify the house, he shall *t* two birds,
15:14 he shall *t* two turtledoves or two pigeons,
15:29 On the eighth day she shall *t* two
16:12 he shall *t* a censer full of glowing embers
18: 4 and my statutes you shall *t* care to follow.
19:18 *T* no revenge and cherish no grudge against
24: 5 *t* fine flour and bake it into twelve cakes,
24:14 Moses, *T* the blasphemer outside the camp,
26:17 will *t* to flight though no one pursues you.
26:37 will you be to *t* a stand against your foes!
Nm 1: 2 *T* a census of the whole community of the
1:51 is to move on, the Levites shall *t* it down;
3:15 *T* a census of the Levites by ancestral
3:40 *T* a census of all the first-born males of
3:45 *T* the Levites in place of all the
3:47 shall *t* five shekels for each individual,
4: 2 the Levites *t* a total of the Kohathites,
4: 5 shall go in and *t* down the screening curtain
4:22 *T* a total among the Gershonites also,
5:15 shall *t* along as an offering for her
5:25 But first he shall *t* the cereal offering
5:26 where he shall *t* a handful of the cereal
6:19 shall *t* a boiled shoulder of the ram,
8: 6 *T* the Levites from among the Israelites
8: 8 They shall *t* a young bull,
8: 8 *t* another young bull for a sin offering.
11:17 I will also *t* some of the spirit that is
16: 6 *t* your censers [Korah and all his band]
16:17 and fifty followers shall *t* his own censer,
17:11 Then Moses said to Aaron, *T* your censer,
19: 4 Eleazar the priest shall *t* some of its
19: 6 and the priest shall *t* some cedar wood,
19:18 a man who is clean shall *t* some hyssop,
20: 8 *T* the staff and assemble the community,
20:25 *T* Aaron and his son Eleazar and bring them
21: 7 Pray the LORD to *t* the serpents from us."
26: 2 son of Aaron the priest, *T* a census,
27:11 clan, who shall then *t* possession of it."
27:18 And the LORD replied to Moses, *T* Joshua,
31:30 you shall *t* one out of every fifty persons,
33:53 *t* possession of the land and settle in it,
35: 6 as places where a homicide can *t* refuge,
35: 8 *t* more from a larger group and fewer from
35:11 someone unintentionally may *t* refuge.
35:15 another unintentionally may *t* refuge there.
Dt 1:22 we must follow and the cities we must *t*.'
4: 1 *t* possession of the land which the LORD,
4: 9 *t* care and be earnestly on your guard not
4:22 over and *t* possession of that good land.
4:23 *T* heed, therefore, lest, forgetting
4:34 Or did any god venture to go and *t* a
4:42 that a homicide might *t* refuge there if he
5: 1 may learn them and *t* care to observe them.
5:11 'You shall not *t* the name of the LORD,
5:12 *T* care to keep holy the sabbath day as the
6: 6 *T* to heart these words which I enjoin on
6:12 your fill, *t* care not to forget the LORD,
7:25 or gold on them, nor *t* it for yourselves,
9: 5 are going in to *t* possession of their land;
9:23 *t* possession of the land he was giving you,
11: 8 to enter in and *t* possession of the land
11:18 *t* these words of mine into your heart and
11:31 you *t* possession of it and settle there,
12:13 *T* care not to offer up your holocausts in
12:19 *T* care, also, that you do not neglect
13: 6 the LORD, your God, has directed you to *t*,
15:17 you shall *t* an awl and thrust it through
16:19 You shall not *t* a bribe;
19: 4 *t* refuge in such a place to save his life:
19: 5 he may *t* refuge in one of these cities to
19:15 "One witness alone shall not *t* the stand
20: 7 he die in battle and another *t* her to wife.'
20:14 worth plundering you may *t* as your booty,
21: 3 the elders of that city shall *t* a heifer
21:10 into your hand, so that you *t* captives,
21:12 as wife, you may *t* her home to your house.
22: 2 *t* it to your own place and keep it with
22: 6 you shall not *t* away the mother bird along
22: 7 her go, although you may *t* her brood away.
22:15 girl shall *t* the evidence of her virginity
22:18 elders shall *t* the man and chastise him,
22:29 fifty silver shekels and *t* her as his wife,
24: 4 may not again *t* her as his wife after she
24: 6 "No one shall *t* a hand mill or even its
24: 8 *T* care to act in accordance with the
24:17 nor *t* the clothing of a widow as a pledge.
26: 2 you shall *t* some first-fruits of the
28:63 *t* delight in ruining and destroying you,
30: 9 will again *t* delight in your prosperity,
31:16 and then this people will *t* to rendering
31:26 *T* this scroll of the law and put it beside
32:46 *T* to heart all the warning which I have
Jos 1:11 *t* possession of the land which the LORD,
2:17 how we will fulfill the oath you made us *t*:
2:20 be quit of the oath you have made us *t*."
3: 4 follow it, that you may know the way to *t*,
3: 6 And he directed the priests to *t* up the
4: 3 and instruct them to *t* up twelve stones
6: 6 then ordered them to *t* up the ark of the
6:12 had the priests *t* up the ark of the LORD.
6:18 But be careful not to *t*,
8: 1 *T* all the army with you and prepare to
8: 2 you may *t* its spoil and livestock as booty.
8: 7 from ambush and *t* possession of the city,
9:11 *T* along provisions for the journey and go
23: 5 *t* possession of their land as the LORD,
23:11 *T* great care, however, to love the LORD,
Jgs 1:27 Manasseh did not *t* possession of
1:31 those of Sidon, or *t* possession of Mahaleb,
2: 6 to *t* possession of his own hereditary land.
4: 6 and *t* with you ten thousand Naphtalites
5:19 no silver booty did they *t*.
6:20 *T* the meat and unleavened cakes and lay
6:25 *T* the seven-year-old spare bullock and
6:26 Then *t* the spare bullock and offer it as a
6:32 the words, "Let Baal *t* action against him,
9:15 good faith, come and *t* refuge in my shadow.
11:15 Israel did not *t* the land of Moab or the
13: 4 be careful to *t* no wine or strong drink
13: 7 So *t* neither wine nor strong drink,
13:14 from the vine, nor *t* wine or strong drink,
14: 3 that you must go and *t* a wife from the
15:10 they answered, "To *t* Samson prisoner;
15:12 to him, "We have come to *t* you prisoner,
19: 3 after her to forgive her and *t* her back.
19:30 *T* note of it,
21:22 we did not *t* a woman apiece in the war.
Ru 3: 4 down, *t* note of the place where he does so.
3:15 to her, *T* off your cloak and hold it out."
4: 5 Naomi, you must *t* also Ruth the Moabite,
4: 7 *t* off his sandal and give it to the other.
4:10 I also *t* Ruth the Moabite,
1Sm 1:22 I will *t* him to appear before the LORD and
2:16 as is the custom, then *t* whatever you wish,"
2:16 it to me now, or else I will *t* it by force."
4: 9 *T* courage and be manly,
6: 7 Then *t* two milch cows that have not borne
6: 8 You shall next *t* the ark of the LORD and
8:11 He will *t* your sons and assign them to his
8:14 He will *t* the best of your fields,
8:16 He will *t* your male and female servants,
9: 3 *T* one of the servants with you and go out
10: 4 of bread, which you will *t* from them.
10:19 *t* your stand before the LORD according to
12: 7 Now, therefore, *t* your stand,
16: 2 *T* a heifer along and say,
16:23 Saul, David would *t* the harp and play,
17:17 *T* this ephah of roasted grain and these
17:18 *t* these ten cheeses for the field officer.
18:25 he may thus *t* vengeance on his enemies."
20:40 and said to him, "Go, *t* them to the city."
21:10 If you wish to *t* that, take it;
23:22 *T* note of the place where he sets foot"
24:12 you are hunting me down to *t* my life.
24:14 So I will *t* no action against you.
24:16 May he see this, and *t* my part,
25:11 Must I *t* my bread,
25:40 us to you that he may *t* you as his wife."
26:11 Now *t* the spear which is at his head and
29:10 Do not decide to *t* umbrage at this;
30:22 Let them *t* those along and be on their way."
2Sm 2: 7 *T* courage, therefore, and prove yourselves
2:21 men and *t* what you can strip from him."
3:10 *t* away the kingdom from the house of Saul
3:18 Now *t* action, for the LORD has said
5: 7 But David did *t* the stronghold of Zion,
12: 4 but he would not *t* from his own flocks and
12:11 will *t* your wives while you live to see it,
12:17 would not, nor would he *t* food with them.
12:21 the child is dead, you rise and *t* food."
13: 5 Tamar come and encourage me to *t* food.
13: 6 that I may *t* nourishment from her hand."
13:13 Where would I *t* my shame?
13:20 Do not *t* this affair to heart."
14:14 he does *t* thought how not to banish anyone
15:14 Let us *t* flight,
15:16 he left behind to *t* care of the palace.
15:20 Return and *t* your brothers with you and,
15:25 *T* the ark of God back to the city.
16:21 he left behind to *t* care of the palace.
16:21 father, all your partisans will *t* courage."
18:19 "Let me run to *t* the good news to the
18:20 On some other day you may *t* the good news,
19:20 and may he not remember and *t* to heart the
20: 3 he had left behind to *t* care of the palace
20: 6 *T* your lord's servants and pursue him,
20: 6 cities and *t* shelter while we look on."
21:16 shekels, was about to *t* him captive.
22:31 he is a shield to all who *t* refuge in him."
24:22 king *t* and offer up whatever he may wish.
1Kgs 1:33 *T* with you the royal attendants.
2: 2 *T* courage and be a man.
5:23 up the rafts, and you shall *t* the lumber.
8:31 to *t* an oath sanctioned by a curse,
8:32 *t* action and pass judgment on your
11:13 Nor will I *t* away the whole kingdom.
11:31 *T* ten pieces for yourself;
11:34 *t* any of the kingdom from Solomon himself,
11:35 But I will *t* the kingdom from his sons and
11:37 I will *t* you; you shall reign over all
14: 3 *T* along ten loaves,
19: 4 *T* my life, for I am no better than
19:10 alone am left, and they seek to *t* my life."
19:14 alone am left, and they seek to *t* my life."
19:15 *t* the road back to the desert near
20: 6 and *t* away whatever they consider valuable.'
20:18 peace or for war, in any case *t* them alive."
20:24 *T* the kings from their posts and put
21:10 Then *t* him out and stone him to death."
21:15 *t* possession of the vineyard of Naboth the
21:16 the Jezreelite, to *t* possession of it.
21:18 of which he has come to *t* possession.
21:19 After murdering, do you also *t* possession?
22: 3 nothing to *t* it from the king of Aram?"
22:26 "Seize Micaiah and *t* him back to Amon,
22:34 "Rein about and *t* me out of the ranks,
2Kgs 2: 1 to *t* Elijah up to heaven in a whirlwind,
2: 3 will *t* your master from over you today?"
2: 5 will *t* your master from over you today?"
4: 1 come to *t* my two children as his slaves."
4:29 to Gehazi, *t* my staff with you and be off;
4:36 call, and Elisha said to her, *T* your son."
5: 7 *T* note!
5:16 LORD lives whom I serve, I will not *t* it,"
5:23 "Please *t* two talents,"
5:26 this a time to *t* money or to take garments,
5:26 this a time to take money or to *t* garments,
6:13 he said, "so that I may *t* him captive."
6:19 I will *t* you to the man you want."
7:12 hoping to *t* us alive and enter our city
7:13 let some of us *t* five of the abandoned
8: 8 *T* a gift with you and go call on the man
9: 1 your loins, *t* this flask of oil with you,
9: 2 Enter and *t* him away from his companions
9:25 *T* him and throw him into the field of
9:26 So now *t* him into this plot of ground,

TAKE (cont.)
10:14 *T* them alive," Jehu ordered.
12: 6 the priests may *t* for themselves,
12: 8 must no longer *t* funds from your clients,
12: 9 they would neither *t* funds from the people
13:15 *T* a bow and some arrows,"
13:18 said to the king of Israel, *T* the arrows,"
18:32 I come to *t* you to a land like your own,
1Chr 7:21 had gone down to *t* away their livestock.
9:29 Others were appointed to *t* care of the
13:13 Therefore he did not *t* the ark back with
21: 8 *T* away your servant's guilt,
21:23 *T* it as your own,
21:24 I will not *t* what is yours for the LORD,
23:28 *t* part in the service of the house of God.
27:24 son of Zeruiah, began to *t* the census,
28:10 *T* courage and set to work."
29: 3 of the delight I *t* in the house of my God,
29:17 and that you *t* pleasure in uprightness.
2Chr 2:15 whence you may *t* them up to Jerusalem."
6:22 to *t* an oath of execration against himself,
6:23 *t* action and pass judgment on your servants,
18:25 "Seize Micaiah and *t* him back to Amon,
18:33 "Rein about and *t* me out of the ranks,
19: 6 *T* care what you do,
20:17 *T* your places, stand firm,
20:25 and his people came to *t* plunder,
23:14 *T* her outside through the ranks,
25:16 let you *t* counsel to your own destruction,
30:14 *t* down the altars that were in Jerusalem;
32: 1 cities, and proposed to *t* them by storm.
35:23 who said to his servants, *T* me away,
36: 6 bound him with chains to *t* him to Babylon.
Ezr 4:22 *T* care that you do not neglect this matter,
5:15 *T* these utensils and deposit them in the
7:17 You must *t* care, therefore, to use
9:11 the land which you are entering to *t* as
9:12 and do not *t* their daughters for your sons.
10: 4 stand by you, so have courage and *t* action!"
Neh 2: 6 my journey would *t* and when I would return.
3:36 *T* note, O our God, how we were mocked!
6:11 "A man like me *t* flight?
9:24 sons went in to *t* possession of the land,
9:32 *t* into account all the disasters that have
10:30 *t* this oath to follow the law of God
10:31 we will not *t* their daughters for our sons.
10:38 shall *t* the tithe in all the cities of our
10:39 be with the Levites when they *t* the tithe,
11: 2 agreed to *t* up residence in Jerusalem.
13:25 nor *t* any of their daughters for your sons
Tb 1:18 to *t* their bodies by stealth and bury them;
4:13 to *t* a wife for yourself from among them.
5: 2 roads to *t* for the journey into Media!"
5:10 Raphael said, *T* courage!
5:10 so *t* courage!"
6: 4 *T* hold of the fish and don't let it get
6: 5 "Cut the fish open and *t* out its gall,
6:13 we will *t* her and bring her back with us
6:17 chamber, *t* the fish's liver and heart,
6:18 who will *t* the place of brothers for you.
7:11 *T* your kinswoman;
7:12 *T* her according to the law.
7:12 *T* her and bring her safely to your father.
8: 7 I *t* this wife of mine not because of lust,
8:21 *T*, to begin with, half of whatever I own
9: 2 *t* along with you four servants and two
10: 6 *t* care of some unexpected business there.
12: 5 *T* as your wages half of all that you have
14: 3 *t* your children and flee into Media for I
14: 4 shall *t* place in the time appointed for it.
Jdt 2: 5 presence, *t* with you men of proven valor,
2:10 "You go before me and *t* possession of all
8:35 before you to *t* vengeance upon our enemies!"
9: 2 You put a sword into his hand to *t* revenge
10:13 *t* possession of the whole mountain district
11: 1 *T* courage, lady; have no fear in your heart!
11: 3 *T* courage!
14: 1 *T* this head and hang it on the parapet of
Est 2:13 she was allowed to *t* with her from the
4: 4 on, so that he might *t* off his sackcloth;
D: 9 *T* courage!
6:10 *T* the robe and horse as you have proposed,
1Mc 3:15 to help him *t* revenge on the Israelites.
3:33 and commissioned him to *t* care of his son
3:50 with these men, and where shall we *t* them?
4: 2 camp of the Jews and *t* them by surprise.
4:18 Afterward you can freely *t* the plunder."
5: 5 He forced them to *t* refuge in towers,
5:19 *T* charge of these people,"
6:56 he was seeking to *t* over the government.
6:57 to *t* care of the affairs of the kingdom.
7: 9 with orders to *t* revenge on the Israelites.
7:38 *T* revenge on this man and his army,
8:30 hereafter decide to add or *t* away anything,
8:30 they shall add or *t* away shall be valid.
11: 1 and he sought by deceit to *t* Alexander's
14: 2 he sent one of his generals to *t* him alive.
15: 4 *t* revenge on those who have ruined it
15:21 from their country *t* refuge with you,
16: 3 *T* my place and my brother's,
2Mc 2: 1 *t* some of the aforementioned fire with them,
3:14 he went in to *t* an inventory of the funds.
4:14 to *t* part in the unlawful exercises on the

11: 4 did not *t* God's power into account at all,
11: 7 himself was the first to *t* up arms,
13:13 invade Judea and *t* possession of the city,
13:18 tried to *t* their positions by a stratagem.
15: 5 and my orders are that you *t* up arms and
Jb 1: 4 His sons used to *t* turns giving feasts,
5: 5 [or God shall *t* it away by blight;]
7:21 not pardon my offense, or *t* away my guilt?
8:20 neither will he *t* the hand of the wicked.
11:19 you shall *t* your rest with none to disturb.
13:14 between my teeth, and *t* my life in my hand.
23:15 when I *t* thought, I fear him.
24: 3 they *t* the widow's ox for a pledge.
32:22 if I did, my Maker would soon *t* me away.
33:24 to justice, He will *t* pity on him and say,
34:14 If he were to *t* back his spirit to himself,
35:13 or that the Almighty does not *t* notice.
36:21 *T* heed, turn not to evil;
37: 8 the wild beasts *t* to cover and remain
38:20 That you may *t* them to their boundaries
42: 8 therefore, *t* seven bullocks and seven rams,
Ps(s) 2:10 *t* warning, you rulers of the earth.
2:12 Happy are all who *t* refuge in him!
5:12 *t* refuge in you be glad and exult forever.
7: 2 O LORD, my God, in you I *t* refuge;
11: 1 In the LORD I *t* refuge;
16: 1 Keep me, O God, for in you I *t* refuge;
16: 4 nor will I *t* their names upon my lips.
18:31 he is a shield to all who *t* refuge in him.
25:18 and my suffering, and *t* away all my sins.
25:20 not be put to shame, for I *t* refuge in you.
31: 2 In you, O LORD, I *t* refuge;
31:14 together against me, plotting to *t* my life.
31:20 which, toward those who *t* refuge in you,
31:25 act proudly *T* courage and be stouthearted,
35: 2 *T* up the shield and buckler,
36: 8 men *t* refuge in the shadow of your wings.
37: 4 *T* delight in the LORD,
37:40 saves them, because they *t* refuge in him.
39:11 *T* away your scourge from me;
41: 4 will *t* away all his ailment when he is ill.
49:18 For when he dies, he shall *t* none of it;
50: 9 I *t* from your house no bullock,
51:13 and your holy spirit *t* not from me.
57: 2 have pity on me, for in you I *t* refuge.
57: 2 In the shadow of your wings I *t* refuge,
59: 5 no guilt of mine they hurry to *t* up arms.
61: 5 *t* refuge in the shelter of your wings!
62:11 in plunder *t* no empty pride;
71: 1 In you, O LORD, I *t* refuge;
71:10 watch against my life *t* counsel together.
80:15 *T* care of this vine,
81: 3 *T* up a melody, and sound the timbrel,
83:13 "Let us *t* for ourselves the dwelling
89:34 Yet my kindness I will not *t* from him,
91: 4 and under his wings you shall *t* refuge;
102:25 *T* me not hence in the midst of my days;
104:29 if you *t* away their breath,
109: 8 may another *t* his office.
116:13 The cup of salvation I will *t* up,
118: 8 *t* refuge in the LORD than to trust in man.
118: 9 It is better to *t* refuge in the LORD than
119:22 *T* away from me reproach and contempt,
119:43 *T* not the word of truth from my mouth,
119:109 Though constantly I *t* my life in my hands,
139: 9 If I *t* the wings of the dawn,
141: 8 in you I *t* refuge; strip me not of life.
144: 3 the son of man, that you *t* thought of him?
Prv 6:27 Can a man *t* fire to his bosom,
13:10 but with those who *t* counsel is wisdom.
14: 7 To avoid the foolish man, *t* steps!
20:16 *T* his garment who becomes surety for
23: 6 Do not *t* food with a grudging man,
27:13 *T* his garment who becomes surety for
27:23 *T* good care of your flocks,
30: 5 is a shield to those who *t* refuge in him.
Eccl 4: 1 the oppressions that *t* place under the sun:
7: 2 man, and the living should *t* it to heart.
Sg 7: 9 palm tree, I will *t* hold of its branches.
Wis 2:20 to his own words, God will *t* care of him."
4: 3 shall not strike deep root nor *t* firm hold.
4:14 nor did they *t* this into account.
5:17 He shall *t* his zeal for armor and he shall
5:19 He shall *t* invincible rectitude as a
6:25 so *t* instruction from my words,
8: 2 I sought to *t* her for my bride and was
8: 9 So I determined to *t* her to live with me,
8:16 dwelling, I should *t* my repose beside her;
8:18 I went about seeking to *t* her for my own.
Sir 3:12 son, *t* care of your father when he is old;
3:14 it will *t* lasting root.
8:17 *T* no counsel with a fool,
9:13 offend him not, lest he *t* away your life;
9:14 As best you can, *t* your neighbors' measure,
11: 9 in the strife of the arrogant *t* no part.
12:11 *t* care to be on your guard against him.
12:12 you, lest he oust you and *t* your place.
13:13 *t* care never to accompany men of violence.
14:16 Give, *t*, and treat yourself well,
16:18 Of me, therefore, he will *t* no thought;
16:22 Hearken to me, my son, *t* my advice,
19:23 not observed, he will *t* advantage of you:
23:25 Her children will not *t* root;

28:22 It will not *t* hold among the just nor
28:26 *T* care not to slip by your tongue and fall
29:20 means, but *t* care lest you fall thereby.
32: 1 *T* care of them first before you sit down;
32: 2 fulfilled your duty, then *t* your place,
32:11 There *t* your ease,
36:12 *T* pity on your holy city,
51: 8 For he saves those who *t* refuge in him,
51:23 *t* up lodging in the house of instruction;
Is 1:24 I will *t* vengeance on my foes and fully
3: 1 shall *t* away from Jerusalem and from Judah
3: 6 Be our ruler, and *t* in hand this ruin!"—
4: 1 women will *t* hold of one man on that day,
5: 5 *T* away its hedge, give it to grazing,
7: 4 *T* care you remain tranquil and do not fear;
8: 1 *T* a large cylinder-seal, and inscribe on it
11:11 The Lord shall again *t* it in hand to
13: 8 pangs and sorrows *t* hold of them,
13:17 nothing of silver and *t* no delight in gold.
14: 2 *t* them and bring them along to its place,
14: 4 you will *t* up this taunt-song against the
14:13 I will *t* my seat on the Mount of Assembly,
16: 3 Offer counsel, *t* their part:
20: 2 Go and *t* off the sackcloth from your waist,
23:16 *T* a harp, go about the city,
27: 6 In days to come Jacob shall *t* root,
28:19 Whenever it passes, it shall *t* you;
30: 2 protection and *t* refuge in Egypt's shadow;
36:17 I come to *t* you to a land like your own,
47: 2 *T* the millstone and grind flour,
47: 3 I will *t* vengeance,
53:12 And he shall *t* away the sins of many,
54: 7 with great tenderness I will *t* you back.
54: 8 But with enduring love I *t* pity on you,
58: 3 afflict ourselves, and you *t* no note of it?"
62: 6 who are to remind the LORD, *t* no rest
66:21 of these I will *t* as priests and Levites,
Jer 2:30 the correction they did not *t*.
2:31 generation, *t* note of the word of the Lord:
3:14 I will *t* you, one from a city,
5: 9 such as this shall I not *t* vengeance?
5:29 such as this shall I not *t* vengeance?
7:27 of the LORD, its God, or *t* correction.
9: 8 such as this shall I not *t* vengeance?
11:20 Let me witness the vengeance you *t* on them,
13: 4 *T* the loincloth which you bought and are
14: 7 crimes bear witness against us, *t* action,
17:21 *t* care not to carry burdens on the sabbath
17:23 necks so as not to hear or *t* correction.
18:11 *T* care!
18:20 that they should dig a pit to *t* my life?
19: 1 *T* along some of the elders of the people
20: 4 who shall *t* them captive to Babylon or
20:10 we can prevail, and *t* our vengeance on him."
20:12 Let me witness the vengeance you *t* on them,
23: 2 I will *t* care to punish your evil deeds.
25:15 *T* this cup of foaming wine from my hand,
25:28 to *t* the cup from your hand and drink,
27:20 Babylon, did not *t* when he exiled Jeconiah,
29: 6 *T* wives and beget sons and daughters;
29:26 to *t* action against all madmen and those
30:21 one *t* the deadly risk of approaching me?
32:14 *T* these deeds, both the sealed
32:28 for Nebuchadnezzar, king of Babylon, to *t*.
32:41 I will *t* delight in doing good to them:
33:26 so as not to *t* from his descendants rulers
35:13 you not *t* correction and obey my words?
36: 2 *T* a scroll and write on it all the words I
36:28 *T* another scroll, and write on it
37:12 to *t* part with his family in the division
38:10 the Cushite to *t* three men along with him,
39:12 *T* him and look after him;
42: 3 what way we should *t* and what we should do
43: 9 *T* with you large stones and sink them in
44:12 I will *t* away the remnant of Judah who
46:11 Go up to Gilead, and *t* balm,
46:14 *T* your stand, prepare yourselves,
49:24 Distress and pangs *t* hold of her,
50:14 *T* your posts encircling Babylon,
50:15 *T* revenge on her, as she has done,
51:26 They will not *t* from you a cornerstone,
Bar 2:16 your holy dwelling and *t* thought of us;
4:14 to *t* note of the captivity of my sons and
4:34 I will *t* from her the joyous throngs,
5: 1 *t* off your robe of mourning and misery;
6: 4 *T* care that you yourselves do not imitate
6: 9 Then sometimes the priests *t* the silver
6:32 The priests *t* some of their clothing and
Ez 3:10 *t* into your heart all my words that I
4: 1 As for you, son of man, *t* a clay tablet;
4: 3 Then *t* an iron griddle and set it up as an
4: 9 Again, *t* wheat and barley,
5: 1 *t* a sharp sword and use it like a barber's
5: 1 Then *t* a set of scales and divide the hair
5: 3 [But of the last *t* a small number and tie
5: 4 Then *t* some of these and throw them in the
7:24 who shall *t* possession of their houses.
10: 6 linen to *t* fire from within the wheelwork,
11: 7 but you I will *t* out of it.
16:39 and *t* away your splendid ornaments,
16:61 and be ashamed when I *t* your sisters,
17:22 I, too, will *t* from the crest of the cedar,
19: 8 They spread their net to *t* him,

22:12 are those in you *t* brides to shed blood.
23:25 They shall *t* away your sons and daughters,
24: 6 *T* out its pieces, one by one,
24:25 the day I *t* away from them their bulwark,
26:20 to *t* your place in the land of the living.
33: 5 the trumpet blast yet refused to *t* warning;
33:11 I swear I *t* no pleasure in the death of
36:12 they shall *t* possession of you,
36:24 I will *t* you away from among the nations,
37:16 Now, son of man, *t* a single stick,
37:16 Then *t* another stick and write on it:
37:19 [I will *t* the stick of Joseph,
37:21] I will *t* the Israelites from among the
38:13 and gold, to *t* away cattle and goods,
43:20 *T* some of its blood and put it on the four
43:21 Then *t* the bull of the sin offering,
44:19 they shall *t* off the garments in which
44:22 They shall not *t* for their wives either
45:19 Then the priest shall *t* some of the blood
46:20 so that they do not have to *t* them into
Dn 1: 4 could *t* their place in the king's palace;
1:16 So the steward continued to *t* away the
2:39 Another kingdom shall *t* your place,
3:35 Do not *t* away your mercy from us,
4:24 Therefore, O king, *t* my advice;
10:19 *t* courage and be strong."
11:15 and *t* the fortified city by storm.
11:18 He shall turn to the coastland and *t* many,
11:32 loyal to their God shall *t* strong action.
11:36 ready, for what is determined must *t* place.
12:13 Go, *t* your rest,
14:34 *T* the lunch you have to Daniel in the
14:37 Habakkuk, *t* the lunch God has sent you."
Hos 1: 2 Go, *t* a harlot wife and harlot's children,
2:11 I will *t* back my grain in its time,
2:20 I will let them *t* their rest in security.
5:13 he cannot heal you nor *t* away your sore.
13:11 in my anger, and I *t* him away in my wrath.
14: 3 *T* with you words, and return
Jl 4: 4 you *t* vengeance upon me by some action?
4: 4 But if you do *t* action against me,
Am 5:21 I *t* no pleasure in your solemnities;
9: 3 there too I will hunt them and *t* them away;
Ob 1:17 And the house of Jacob shall *t* possession
Jon 4: 3 And now, LORD, please *t* my life from me;
Mi 2: 2 houses, and they *t* them;
2: 9 you *t* away forever the honor I gave them.
Na 3:14 tread the clay, *t* hold of the brick mold!
Hb 1: 6 of the land to *t* dwellings not his own.
2: 6 not all these *t* up a taunt against him,
Zep 3:12 Who shall *t* refuge in the name of the LORD;
Hg 1: 8 may *t* pleasure in it and receive my glory,
2: 4 But now *t* courage, Zerubbabel,
2: 4 Zerubbabel, says the LORD, and *t* courage,
2: 4 priest, son of Jehozadak, And *t* courage,
2:23 day, says the LORD of hosts, I will *t* you,
Zec 3: 4 before him, *T* off his filthy garments,
3: 9 *t* away the guilt of the land in one day.
6:10 *T* from the returned captives Heldai,
6:11 Silver and gold you shall *t*,
8:23 shall *t* hold, yes, *t* hold of every Jew
9: 7 and *t* from his mouth his bloody meat,
11:15 This time *t* the gear of a foolish shepherd.
11:16 who will *t* no note of those that perish,
13: 2 I will also *t* away the prophets and the
14:21 to sacrifice shall *t* them and cook in them.
Mal 3:17 special possession, on the day I *t* action.
3:21 soles of your feet, on the day I *t* action,
Mt 2:13 "Get up, *t* the child and his mother,
2:20 "Get up, *t* the child and his mother,
4: 6 'He will bid his angels *t* care of you;
5:33 your forefathers, 'Do not *t* a false oath;
6:34 Let tomorrow *t* care of itself.
7: 4 'Let me *t* that speck out of your eye,'
7: 5 to *t* the speck from your brother's eye.
10:38 He who will not *t* up his cross and come
11:12 violence, and the violent *t* it by force.
11:29 *T* my yoke upon your shoulders and learn
12:11 Will he not *t* hold of it and pull it out?
13:29 and you might *t* the wheat along with them.
15:26 "It is not right to *t* the food of sons
16:24 he must deny his very self, *t* up his cross,
17:15 "Lord," he said, *t* pity on my son,
17:25 of the world *t* tax or toll from their sons,
17:27 a line, and *t* out the first fish you catch.
17:27 *T* it and give it to them for you and me."
19:28 shall likewise *t* your places on twelve thrones
20:14 *T* your pay and go home.
22:24 his brother must *t* the wife and produce
24:15 on holy ground (let the reader *t* note!),
25:28 *T* the thousand away from him and give it
26:26 *T* this and eat it,"
26:48 shall embrace is the one; *t* hold of him."
Mk 3:21 heard of this they came to *t* charge of him,
4:20 ones who listen to the word, *t* it to heart,
6: 8 He instructed them to *t* nothing on their
7: 5 *t* food without purifying their hands?"
7:27 It is not right to *t* the food of the
8: 6 the crowd to *t* their places on the ground.
8:34 he must deny his very self, *t* up his cross,
10:15 like a little child shall not *t* part in it."
11: 6 told them to, and the men let them *t* it.
12:19 his brother must *t* the wife and produce
13:11 When men *t* you off into custody,
13:14 let the reader *t* note!—those
13:30 pass away until all these things *t* place.
14:22 *T* this," he said, "this is my body."
14:36 *T* this cup away from me.
15:23 drugged with myrrh, but he would not *t* it.
15:24 dice for them to see what each should *t*.
15:36 see whether Elijah comes to *t* him down."
Lk 1:20 until the day these things *t* place,
5:24 *T* your mat with you,
8:18 *T* heed, therefore, how you hear:
9: 3 *T* nothing for the journey,
9:23 his very self, *t* up his cross each day,
9:61 first let me *t* leave of my people at home."
11: 8 *t* care of the man because of friendship,
11:35 *T* care, then, that your light is not
12:27 "Or *t* the lilies:
13: 4 Or *t* those eighteen who were killed by a
13:29 and will *t* their place at the feast in the
14:27 Anyone who does not *t* up his cross and
15:15 sent him to his farm to *t* care of the pigs.
15:23 *T* the fatted calf and kill it.
16: 4 *t* me into their homes when I am let go.'
16: 6 The manager said, *T* your invoice,
16: 7 said, *T* your invoice and make it eighty.'
16: 8 Because the worldly *t* more initiative than
19:17 For that you can *t* over ten villages.'
19:19 His word to him was, *T* over five villages.'
19:24 standing around, *T* from him what he has,
21: 8 He said, *T* care not to be misled.
21:15 can *t* exception to or contradict.
22:17 *T* this and divide it among you;
22:42 if it is your will, *t* this cup from me;
Jn 2: 8 some out and *t* it to the waiter in charge."
6:21 They wanted to *t* him into the boat,
6:60 How can anyone *t* it seriously?"
10:17 that I lay down my life to *t* it up again.
10:18 it down, and I have power to *t* it up again.
11:39 *T* away the stone," Jesus directed.
14: 3 then I shall come back to *t* you with me,
16:22 rejoice with a joy no one can *t* from you.
16:33 But *t* courage!
17:15 do not ask you to *t* them out of the world,
18:31 "Why do you not *t* him and pass judgment
19: 1 move was to *t* Jesus and have him scourged.
19: 6 said, *T* him and crucify him yourselves;
20:15 you have laid him and I will *t* him away."
20:27 *T* your finger and examine my hands.
Acts 1:20 And again, 'May another *t* his office.'
5:20 "Go out now and *t* your place in the
9: 8 They had to *t* him by the hand and lead him
10:37 I *t* it you know what has been reported all
15:37 Barnabas wanted to *t* along John,
20:12 they were able to *t* the boy away alive.
20:26 that I *t* the blame for no man's conscience,
21:24 *T* them along with you and join with them
23:10 their midst and *t* him back to headquarters.
23:17 he said, *T* this young man to the commander;
23:30 his accusers to *t* the matter up with you."
26:26 all, it did not *t* place in a dark corner!
27:33 Paul urged all on board to *t* some food:
27:34 Now I urge you to *t* some food,
28:16 Paul was allowed to *t* a lodging of his own,
Rom 11:27 make with them when I *t* away their sins."
13:11 *T* care to do all these things,
15:15 I *t* this liberty because God has given me
15:17 This means I can *t* glory in Christ Jesus
1Cor 6:15 Would you have me *t* Christ's members and
8: 9 *T* care, however, lest in exercising your
9:24 runners in the stadium *t* part in the race,
10: 7 and drink, and arose to *t* their pleasure."
15:31 brothers, by the very pride you *t* in me,
15:46 *T* note, the spiritual was not first;
16: 3 have chosen to *t* your gift to Jerusalem.
2Cor 3: 5 of ourselves to *t* credit for anything.
5:12 those who *t* pride in external appearances,
12:17 Did I ever *t* advantage of you through any
12:18 Did Titus *t* advantage of you in any way?
Gal 5: 1 and do not *t* on yourselves the yoke of
5:15 and tearing one another to pieces, *t* care!
Eph 5:11 *T* no part in vain deeds done in darkness;
6:17 *T* the helmet of salvation and the sword of
Phil 1:29 your special privilege to *t* Christ's part
2:25 arms, whom you sent to *t* care of my needs.
3:17 *T* as your guide those who follow the
Col 4:17 *T* care to discharge the ministry you have
1Tm 3: 5 how can he *t* care of the church of God?
5:23 *T* a little wine for the good of your
6: 2 not *t* liberties with them on that account.
6: 7 nor have we the power to *t* anything out.
6:12 *T* firm hold on the everlasting life to
2Tm 1:13 *T* as a model of sound teaching what you
Ti 2: 8 words to which no one can *t* exception.
3: 1 to be ready to *t* on any honest employment.
3:14 work in order to *t* care of their needs,
Heb 3:12 *T* care, my brothers, lest any of you have
5: 4 not *t* this honor on his own initiative,
9:26 *t* away sins once for all by his sacrifice.
9:28 offered up once to *t* away the sins of many;
9:28 not to *t* away sin but to bring salvation
10: 4 blood of bulls and goats to *t* sins away.
10:11 sacrifices which can never *t* away sins.
10:38 if he draws back I *t* no pleasure in him.
13: 9 those who *t* them as a standard for living.
Jas 1: 9 Let the brother in humble circumstances *t*
2: 3 *t* notice of the well-dressed man and say,
4: 7 God, resist the devil and he will *t* flight.
5:10 *t* the prophets who spoke in the name of
1Pt 5:12 whom I *t* to be a faithful brother to you.
2Pt 3: 5 they do not *t* into account that of old
1Jn 3: 5 he revealed himself was to *t* away sins;
Rv 3:18 *T* my advice.
4: 1 show you what must *t* place in time to come."
10: 8 *t* the open scroll from the hand of the
10: 9 He said to me, "Here, *t* it and eat it!
11: 1 "Come and *t* the measurements of God's
22:19 God will *t* away his share in the tree of

TAKEN (329)

Gn 2:22 a woman the rib that he had *t* from the man.
2:23 for out of 'her man' this one has been *t*."
3:19 to the ground, from which you were *t*;
3:23 till the ground from which he had been *t*.
12:15 So she was *t* into Pharaoh's palace.
20: 3 to die because of the woman you have *t*,
25: 8 and he was *t* to his kinsmen.
25:17 his last and died, he was *t* to his kinsmen.
26:10 "It would have *t* very little for one of
27:36 and now he has *t* away my blessing."
31: 1 *t* everything that belonged to our father,
31:34 Now Rachel had *t* the idols,
31:37 a single object *t* from your belongings?
32:24 After he had *t* them across the stream and
35:29 as an old man and was *t* to his kinsmen.
37:25 gum, balm and resin to be *t* down to Egypt.
39: 1 When Joseph was *t* down to Egypt,
42:24 *t* from them and bound before their eyes.
43:18 bags the first time, that we are *t* inside;
47:30 have me *t* out of Egypt and buried in their
49:29 "Since I am about to be *t* to my kindred,
49:33 his last, and was *t* to his kindred.
Ex 8: 5 that the frogs may be *t* away from you and
Lv 6: 4 having *t* off these garments and put on
7: 3 its fat shall be *t* from it and offered up:
7:34 I have *t* the breast that is waved
9:10 liver that were *t* from the sin offering,
16:27 atonement, shall be *t* outside the camp,
21:14 but a virgin, *t* from his own people,
25:12 except as *t* directly from the field.
Nm 1:44 in the census *t* by Moses and Aaron and the
2:32 of the Israelites *t* by ancestral houses.
5:17 he has *t* from the floor of the Dwelling.
6:21 in keeping with the vow he has *t*."
8:16 I have *t* them for myself in place of
8:18 first-born Israelites I have *t* the Levites;
14: 3 wives and little ones will be *t* as booty.
14:31 however, who you said would be *t* as booty,
16:15 I have never *t* a single ass from them,
18: 6 it is I who have *t* your kinsmen,
20:24 "Aaron is about to be *t* to his people,
20:26 for there Aaron shall be *t* in death."
21:29 be *t* captive by the Amorite king Sihon.
26:63 the census of the Israelites *t* on the plains
26:64 of the Israelites *t* in the desert of Sinai.
27:13 it, you too shall be *t* to your people,
31: 2 and then you shall be *t* to your people."
31:26 captives and the beasts that have been *t*;
31:32 left of the loot which the soldiers had *t*,
31:42 when Moses had *t* it from the soldiers,
32:18 has *t* possession of his heritage,
35:26 the city of asylum where he has *t* refuge,
Dt 2:22 have *t* their place down to the present.
4:20 he has *t* and led out of that iron foundry,
19: 1 and you have *t* their place and are settled
19:12 send for him and have him *t* from there,
20: 7 a woman and not yet *t* her as his wife?
23:16 a slave who has *t* refuge from him with you.
32:50 climbed, and shall be *t* to your people,
32:50 on Mount Hor and there was *t* to his people;
Jos 2: 4 woman had *t* the two men and hidden them,
4:20 stones which had been *t* from the Jordan,
7:11 have stealthily *t* goods subject to the ban,
8: 8 When you have *t* the city,
8:21 *t* from ambush and was going up in smoke,
11:19 all were *t* in battle.
19:47 Once they had *t* possession of Leshem,
Jgs 2:17 to stray from the way their fathers had *t*,
7: 8 as the soldiers had with them, were *t* up,
11: 3 and had *t* up residence in the land of Tob.
15: 6 his wife was *t* and given to his best man."
15: 7 not stop until I have *t* revenge on you."
16:18 had *t* her completely into his confidence,
17: 2 in my hearing when they were *t* from you,
18:18 When they had gone in and *t* the ephod,
18:23 do you want, that you have *t* up arms?"
18:24 "You have *t* my god,
18:27 Having *t* what Micah had made,
19: 1 who had *t* for himself a concubine
20: 3 asked to be told how the crime had *t* place,
21: 5 For they had *t* a solemn oath that anyone
1Sm 6:15 had *t* down the ark of God and the box
7:14 had *t* from Israel were restored to them.
12: 3 Whose ox have I *t*?
12: 3 Whose ass have I *t*?
21: 7 replaced by fresh bread when it was *t* away.

TAKEN (cont.)

30: 2 They had *t* captive the women and all who
30: 3 their wives, sons and daughters *t* captive.
30:12 he had not *t* food nor drunk water for
30:16 all the rich booty they had *t* from the land
30:18 recovered everything the Amalekites had *t*,
30:19 of all that the Amalekites had *t*.
2Sm 6: 3 *t* away from the house of Abinadab
8:11 had *t* from every nation he had conquered;
12:10 have *t* the wife of Uriah to be your wife.'
12:27 against Rabbah and have *t* the watercity.
13:34 Meanwhile, Absalom had *t* flight.
13:37 But Absalom, who had *t* flight,
18:17 Absalom was *t* up and cast into a deep pit
18:18 During his lifetime Absalom had *t* a pillar
18:31 that this day the LORD has *t* your part,
23: 6 they cannot be *t* up by hand.
1Kgs 9:16 king of Egypt, had come up and *t* Gezer and,
13:12 the road *t* by the man of God
2Kgs 2: 9 I may do for you before I am *t* from you."
2:10 "Still, if you see me *t* up from you,
6:22 you have *t* captive with your sword or bow?
10:14 They were *t* alive,
12:18 When he had *t* it, Hazael decided
13:25 had *t* in battle from his father Jehoahaz.
18:10 of Hosea, king of Israel, Samaria was *t*.
20:18 descendants shall be *t* and made servants
23:16 *t* from the graves and burned on the altar,
24: 7 for the king of Babylon had *t* all that
1Chr 9:28 tallying it as it was brought in and *t* out.
13: 1 After David had *t* counsel with his
17: 1 David had *t* up residence in his house,
18:11 and gold that he had *t* from the nations:
23:25 and has *t* up his dwelling in Jerusalem.
26:27 from the booty they had *t* in the wars,
2Chr 2:16 the census David his father had *t* of them),
6:10 and have *t* my seat on the throne of Israel,
11:21 had *t* eighteen wives and sixty concubines,
15: 8 he had *t* in the highlands of Ephraim,
17: 2 of Ephraim which his father Asa had *t*.
25:17 Having *t* counsel, King Amaziah
29: 9 wives have been *t* captive because of this.
34:28 and you shall be *t* to your grave in peace.
Ezr 1: 7 Nebuchadnezzar had *t* away from Jerusalem
2:64 The entire assembly *t* together came to
5:14 Nebuchadnezzar had *t* from the temple
6:11 edict, a beam is to be *t* from his house,
9: 2 for they have *t* some of their daughters as
9: 2 have *t* a leading part in this apostasy!"
10:14 in our cities who have *t* foreign women
10:17 the men who had *t* foreign women for wives.
10:18 found to have *t* foreign women for wives:
10:44 All these had *t* foreign wives;
Neh 6: 8 "Nothing of what you report has *t* place;
6:15 it had *t* fifty-two days.
6:16 the nations round about had *t* note of it,
7:66 The entire assembly *t* together came to
9: 3 When they had *t* their places,
Tb 1: 2 king of Assyria, was *t* captive from Thisbe,
1:20 All that I had was *t* to the king's palace,
3: 6 and command my life breath to be *t* from me,
10: 7 watch all day at the road her son had *t*,
Jdt 4:12 to be seized, their wives to be *t* captive,
5:18 finally *t* as captives into foreign lands.
6: 5 until I have *t* revenge on this race of
6: 9 cherish the hope that they will not be *t*,
8:21 If we are *t*, all Judea will fall,
16:19 that she herself had *t* from his bedroom.
Est 0: 3 had *t* from Jerusalem with Jeconiah,
2: 6 with the captives *t* with Jeconiah,
2: 7 Mordecai had *t* her as his own daughter.
1Mc 2:10 nation has not *t* its share of her realm,
2:11 All her adornment has been *t* away.
2:58 zeal for the law, was *t* up to heaven.
3:12 and the sword of Apollonius was *t* by Judas,
6: 6 *t* from the armies they had destroyed;
8: 7 They had *t* him alive and obliged him and
9:40 the mountain, all their spoils were *t*.
9:42 Having *t* their revenge for the blood of
9:72 he had previously *t* from the land of Judah.
10:37 and their rulers be *t* from among them,
10:42 shekels that used to be *t* from the revenue
10:52 *t* my seat on the throne of my fathers,
10:84 Dagon and the men who had *t* refuge in it.
15:29 *t* possession of many districts in my realm.
15:30 of Judea of which you have *t* possession;
2Mc 2:26 For us who have *t* upon ourselves the labor
5: 5 back and the city was finally being *t*,
8:33 who had *t* refuge in a little house;
10:12 had *t* the lead in treating the Jews fairly
11:23 our father has *t* his place among the gods,
12: 6 to the sword those who had *t* refuge there.
13: 4 he ordered him to be *t* to Beroea and
15:30 right arm to be cut off and *t* to Jerusalem.
Jb 1:21 The LORD gave and the LORD has *t* away;
10:19 have been *t* from the womb to the grave.
19: 9 of my glory, and *t* the diadem from my brow.
28: 2 Iron is *t* from the earth,
33: 6 have been *t* from the same clay by God.
34: 5 am innocent, but God has *t* what is my due.
Ps(s) 32: 1 Happy is he whose fault is *t* away,
68:19 You have ascended on high, *t* captives,
88: 9 You have *t* my friends away from me;
88:19 and neighbor you have *t* away from me;
Prv 22:27 to pay, your bed will be *t* from under you.
27:25 is *t* away and the aftergrowth appears,
Eccl 2:11 to the toil at which I had *t* such pains,
9:12 his own time than fish *t* in the fatal net,
Sg 5: 3 I have *t* off my robe,
Wis 14:15 image of the child so quickly *t* from him,
15: 8 after a little, is to go whence he was *t*,
17:17 at tasks in the wasteland, *T* unawares,
Sir 1: 7 her, has seen her and *t* note of her.
31:27 is very life to man if *t* in moderation.
42:22 same, With nothing added, nothing *t* away;
44:16 [ENOCH walked with the LORD and was *t* up,
46:19 bribe or secret gift have I *t* from any man!"
48: 9 You were *t* aloft in a whirlwind,
49:14 the equal of ENOCH, for he was *t* up bodily.
Is 6: 6 which he had *t* with tongs from the altar.
8:23 Anguish has *t* wing, dispelled is darkness:
10:27 His burden shall be *t* from your shoulder,
16:10 the orchards are *t* away joy and gladness,
23: 7 feet have *t* her to dwell in distant lands?
28: 9 weaned from milk, those *t* from the breast?
29:16 as though the potter were *t* to be the clay:
38:21 of figs to be *t* and applied to the boil,
39: 7 descendants shall be *t* and made servants
41: 9 You whom I have *t* from the ends of the
42:22 They are *t* as booty,
49:24 Can booty be *t* from a warrior?
49:25 Yes, captives can be *t* from a warrior,
52: 5 My people have been *t* away without redress;
53: 8 Oppressed and condemned, he was *t* away,
57: 1 he is *t* away from the presence of evil,
66: 3 and *t* pleasure in their own abominations,
Jer 6:11 Yes, all will be *t*, husband and wife,
10:18 I will hem them in, that they may be *t*.
12: 2 they have *t* root, they keep on growing
27:18 and in Jerusalem might not be *t* to Babylon.
32: 5 face, and Zedekiah shall be *t* to Babylon.
34: 3 Then you shall be *t* to Babylon.
38:28 of the guard till the day Jerusalem was *t*.
39:14 *t* out of the quarters of the guard,
48:41 Cities are *t*, strongholds seized:
48:46 Your sons are *t* into exile,
49:20 which he has *t* against Edom;
49:29 Their tents and herds shall be *t* away,
49:30 For counsel has been *t* against you,
50: 2 Babylon is *t*, Bel confounded,
50: 9 there they advance, and she shall be *t*.
50:45 of the LORD which he has *t* against Babylon;
51:31 the king of Babylon that all his city is *t*.
Bar 2:17 whose spirits have been *t* from within them,
3:29 Who has gone up to the heavens and *t* her,
4:20 I have *t* off the garment of peace,
4:24 Zion's neighbors lately saw you *t* captive,
6:53 nor do they recover what is unjustly *t*,
Ez 12:13 over him, and he shall be *t* in my snare.
17:20 over him, and he shall be *t* in my snare.
21:28 and the arrow *t* in hand marks their guilt.
21:29 been drawn to you), you shall be *t* in hand.
24: 5 joints *t* from the pick of the flock.
25:12 Because Edom has *t* vengeance on the house
25:15 and have *t* vengeance with destructive
29: 5 field, you shall not be *t* up or buried;
33: 5 for had he *t* warning he would have escaped
33: 6 that person is *t* because of his own sin.
33:21 from Jerusalem and said, "The city is *t*!"
40: 1 fourteen years after the city was *t*,
48:19 shall be *t* from all the tribes of Israel.
Dn 4:28 that your kingdom is *t* from you!
5: 2 father, had *t* from the temple in Jerusalem,
5: 3 When the gold and silver vessels *t* from
7:14 dominion that shall not be *t* away,
7:26 *t* away by final and absolute destruction,
14: 7 it has never *t* any food or drink."
Hos 10: 6 Ephraim shall be *t* into captivity,
Am 2: 8 *t* in pledge they recline beside my altar;
6: 4 couches, They eat lambs *t* from the flock,
Mi 7:11 on that day the boundary shall be *t* away.
Zec 3: 5 said, "See, I have *t* away your guilt."
10:11 cast down, and the scepter of Egypt *t* away.
14: 2 the city shall be *t*, houses plundered,
Mt 9:15 the day comes that the groom is *t* away,
11:21 in you had *t* place in Tyre and Sidon,
11:23 worked in you had *t* place in Sodom,
21:43 the kingdom of God will be *t* away from you
22:22 *T* aback by this reply,
24:40 one will be *t* and one will be left.
24:41 one will be *t* and one will be left.
Mk 2:20 when the groom will be *t* away from them;
4:25 not, what little they have will be *t* away."
5: 3 The man had *t* refuge among the tombs;
6:46 When he had *t* leave of them,
6:51 They were *t* aback by these happenings,
16:19 the Lord Jesus was *t* up into heaven and
Lk 5:36 the piece *t* from it will not match the old.
6:44 Figs are not *t* from thornbushes,
8:29 This spirit had *t* hold of him many a time.
9:51 when he was to be *t* from this world,
11:52 You have *t* away the key of knowledge.
17:34 one will be *t* and the other left.
17:35 one will be *t* and the other left."
24:51 he left them, and was *t* up to heaven.
Jn 7:47 "Do not tell us you too have been *t* in!"
19:31 legs be broken and the bodies be *t* away.
20: 2 them, "The Lord has been *t* from the tomb!
20:13 them, "Because the Lord has been *t* away,
Acts 1: 2 taught until the day he was *t* up to heaven,
1:11 Jesus who has been *t* from you will return,
1:22 of John until the day he was *t* up from us,
9:19 returned to him after he had *t* food.
9:21 Any who heard it were greatly *t* aback.
15:38 mission, he was not fit to be *t* along now.
17: 7 Now they come here and Jason has *t* them in.
17:15 Paul was *t* as far as Athens by his escort,
18:18 shaved his head because of a vow he had *t*.
21: 1 When we had finally *t* leave of them,
22:11 I had to be *t* by the hand and led into
27:21 *t* my advice and not set sail from Crete.
Rom 3:12 All have *t* the wrong course,
1Cor 14:24 he will be *t* to task by all and called to
16: 2 will not have to be *t* up after I arrive.
2Cor 3:14 it is only in Christ that it is *t* away.
2Thes 2: 7 that restrainer shall be *t* from the scene.
1Tm 2:15 her chastity being *t* for granted.
3:16 in throughout the world, *t* up into glory."
2Tm 2:18 that the resurrection has already *t* place.
2:26 Thus, *t* captive by God to do his will,
Heb 5: 1 Every high priest is *t* from among men and
6:18 we who have *t* refuge in him might be
8: 1 who has *t* his seat at the right hand of
9:15 since his death has *t* place for
11: 5 By faith Enoch was *t* away without dying,
11: 5 testifies that, before he was *t* up,
12: 2 He has *t* his seat at the right of the
Jas 1:21 welcome the word that has *t* root in you,
2Pt 2:15 and wander off on the path *t* by Balaam,
Jude 1:11 They have *t* the road Cain took.
Rv 5: 8 When he had *t* the scroll,
12: 6 there she was *t* care of for twelve hundred
12:14 she could be *t* care of for a year and for
17: 7 "Why are you so *t* aback?

TAKES (84)

Gn 50:25 continued, "When God thus *t* care of you,
Ex 17:16 he said, "The LORD *t* in hand his banner;
20: 7 unpunished him who *t* his name in vain.
21:10 If he *t* another wife,
Lv 24:17 "Whoever *t* the life of any human being
24:18 whoever *t* the life of an animal shall make
Nm 6: 2 When a man (or a woman) solemnly *t* the
11:23 or not what I have promised you *t* place."
Dt 5:11 unpunished him who *t* his name in vain.
19:11 and then *t* refuge in one of these cities,
19:16 "If an unjust witness *t* the stand against
22:28 *t* her and has relations with her,
1Sm 8:18 When this *t* place, you will complain
14:24 be the man who *t* food before evening,
14:28 'Cursed be the man who *t* food this day!'
1Kgs 8:31 when he comes and *t* the oath before your
1Mc 10:43 Whoever *t* refuge in the temple of
Jb 8:17 among the rocks he *t* hold.
12:20 adviser, and *t* discretion from the aged.
12:24 He *t* understanding from the leaders of the
20: 8 a dream he *t* flight and is not found again;
21: 6 am dismayed, and horror *t* hold on my flesh.
30:17 My frame *t* no rest by night;
34:20 He brings on nobles, and *t* them away,
Ps(s) 15: 3 nor *t* up a reproach against his neighbor;
34: 9 happy the man who *t* refuge in him.
34:13 life, and *t* delight in prosperous days?
34:23 no one incurs guilt who *t* refuge in him.
45:10 the queen *t* her place at your right hand
64:11 is glad in the LORD and *t* refuge in him;
Prv 1:19 *t* away the life of him who acquires it.
8: 2 road, at the crossroads she *t* her stand;
11:30 a tree of life, but violence *t* lives away.
12:10 The just man *t* care of his beast,
13:24 he who loves him *t* care to chastise him.
16:13 The king *t* delight in honest lips,
16:32 who rules his temper, than he who *t* a city.
18: 2 The fool *t* no delight in understanding,
Eccl 4:16 people, to all over whom he *t* precedence;
Wis 7:29 Compared to light, she *t* precedence;
13:13 he *t* and carves to occupy his spare time.
15: 9 and *t* pride in modeling counterfeits.
Sir 12: 7 and upon the wicked he *t* vengeance.
14:27 Who *t* shelter with her from the heat,
23:19 step a man *t* and peer into hidden corners.
50:28 things, wise the man who *t* them to heart!
Is 10:14 As one *t* eggs left alone,
22: 6 Elam *t* up the quivers,
44:14 He cuts down cedars, *t* a holm or an oak,
57: 1 man perishes, but no one *t* it to heart;
57:13 who *t* refuge in me shall inherit the land,
65:16 He who *t* an oath in the land shall swear
Jer 4:29 horseman and bowman each city *t* to flight;
6:24 fall our hands, Anguish *t* hold of us,
12:11 all the land, because no one *t* it to heart.
Lam 3:32 Though he punishes, he *t* pity,
Bar 6:44 that *t* place around these gods is a fraud:
Ez 33: 6 so that the sword comes and *t* anyone,
Hos 7: 9 his strength, but he *t* no notice of it;
7: 9 is a sprinkling, but he *t* no notice of it.
Mi 7: 9 sinned against him, Until he *t* up my cause,
Na 1: 7 *t* care of those who have recourse to him,

Mt 13:23 the man who hears the message and *t* it in.
19:28 Son of Man *t* his seat upon a throne
24:34 will not pass away until all this *t* place.
Lk 6:29 when someone *t* your coat,
6:30 When a man *t* what is yours,
8:12 but the devil comes and *t* the word out of
9:39 A spirit *t* possession of him and with a
21:32 will not pass away until all this *t* place.
Jn 1:29 of God who *t* away the sin of the world!
10:18 No one *t* it from me; I lay it down freely.
13:19 before it *t* place, so that when it *t* place
14:29 before it *t* place, so that when it *t* place
1Cor 15:54 When the corruptible frame *t* on
Eph 2:21 and *t* shape as a holy temple in the Lord;
3:15 family in heaven and on earth *t* its name;
5:29 he nourishes it and *t* care of it as Christ
Col 2:18 a one *t* his stand on his own experience;
2Tm 2: 5 if one *t* part in an athletic contest,
Heb 10: 9 he *t* away the first covenant to establish
Rv 22:19 *t* from the words of this prophetic book,

TAKING (115)

Gn 14:12 their way, *t* with them Abram's nephew Lot,
28:11 *T* one of the stones at the shrine,
31:23 *T* his kinsmen with him,
38:28 and the midwife, *t* a crimson thread,
Ex 5: 4 by *t* the people away from their work?
24: 7 *T* the book of the covenant,
32:20 *T* the calf they had made, he fused it
34: 4 him, *t* along the two stone tablets.
Lv 8:10 *T* the anointing oil, Moses anointed
8:15 slaughtered it, and *t* some of its blood,
8:16 *T* all the fat that was over the inner
8:30 *T* some of the anointing oil and some of
9:15 *T* the goat that was for the people's sin
9:17 *t* a handful of it, he burned it
14: 6 *T* the living bird with the cedar wood,
14:12 *T* one of the male lambs,
14:24 *T* the guilt-offering lamb,
14:51 Then, *t* the cedarwood,
16: 7 *T* the two male goats and setting them
16:14 *T* some of the bullock's blood,
16:18 *T* some of the bullock's and the goat's
Nm 4:12 *T* the utensils of the sanctuary service,
11:25 *T* some of the spirit that was on Moses,
25: 7 left the assembly, and *t* a lance in hand,
27:22 *T* Joshua and having him stand in the
Dt 1:25 *t* along some of the fruit of the land,
2:12 them out of the way and *t* their place,
7: 3 sons nor *t* their daughters for your sons.
9:21 Then, *t* the calf, the sinful object
24: 6 be *t* the debtor's sustenance as a pledge.
30: 3 and *t* pity on you, he will again gather
Jos 1: 7 *t* care to observe the entire law which my
8: 9 *t* up their position to the west of Ai,
18: 3 *t* steps to possess the land which the LORD,
Jgs 3:13 Israel, *t* possession of the city of palms.
9:42 next day, when the people were *t* the field,
20:10 *t* from all the tribes of Israel ten men
1Sm 6:10 *T* two milch cows, they hitched them
11: 7 *T* a yoke of oxen, he cut them into pieces
14:47 After *t* over the kingship of Israel,
20:25 dine, *t* his usual place against the wall,
23: 6 with David to Keilah, *t* the ephod with him.
28:24 Then *t* flour, she kneaded it and baked
2Sm 4: 5 heat of the day, while he was *t* his siesta.
4: 7 Then, *t* the head, they traveled on
13: 8 *T* dough and kneading it,
18:14 And *t* three pikes in hand,
19:32 for his crossing, *t* leave of him there.
1Kgs 12:28 After *t* counsel, the king made two
17:19 *T* him from her lap,
17:23 *T* the child, Elijah brought him down
18:26 *T* the young bull that was turned over to
19:21 Elisha left him and, *t* the yoke of oxen,
20:11 armor to boast as though he were *t* it off.' "
2Kgs 5: 5 Naaman set out, *t* along ten silver talents,
1Chr 12:22 helped David by *t* charge of his troops,
21: 1 he enticed David into *t* a census of Israel.
2Chr 20:25 they were three days *t* the spoil,
Ezr 10: 2 *t* foreign women of the peoples of the land.
10:10 "Your unfaithfulness in *t* foreign women
Neh 5:15 *t* from them each day forty silver shekels
Jdt 2: 1 about *t* revenge on the whole world,
8:22 kinsmen, for the *t* of exiles from the land,
13: 6 of Holofernes, and *t* his sword from it,
Est C:13 *T* off her splendid garments,
C:15 but you, for I am *t* my life in my hand.
E: 9 *t* advantage of changing conditions and
1Mc 1:24 *T* all this, he went back to his own
9:16 Judas and his men, *t* them in the rear.
11:12 After *t* his daughter away and giving her
2Mc 4:30 While these things were *t* place,
10:13 high office, he ended his life by *t* poison.
10:28 other *t* fury as their leader in the fight.
10:36 the defenders, *t* the besieged in the rear;
Jb 5:24 *t* stock of your household,
38:13 place For *t* hold of the ends of the earth,
Ps(s) 10:14 misery and sorrow, *t* them in your hands.
Eccl 2: 3 concerned with wisdom, and of *t* up folly,
3:14 there is no adding to it, or *t* from it.
Wis 6:15 For *t* thought of her is the perfection of
12:24 *t* for gods the worthless and disgusting
Is 8:11 *t* hold of me and warning me not to walk in
42:20 You see many things without *t* note;
51:22 am *t* from your hand the cup of staggering;
Jer 34:16 profaned my name by *t* back your male
Ez 24:16 *t* away from you the delight of your eyes,
25:12 grievously guilty by *t* vengeance on them,
36:26 *t* from your bodies your stony hearts and
Jon 1:14 let us not perish for *t* this man's life;
Zec 5:10 with me, "Where are they *t* the bushel?"
6:13 of the LORD, and *t* up the royal insignia,
Mt 1:20 have no fear about *t* Mary as your wife.
25: 3 The foolish ones, in *t* their torches,
27:59 *T* the body, Joseph wrapped it in fresh
Mk 5:41 *T* her hand, he said to her,
6:41 Then, *t* the five loaves and the two fish,
8: 6 *T* the seven loaves he gave thanks,
10:32 *T* the Twelve aside once more,
12:41 *T* a seat opposite the treasury,
14:41 Still *t* your ease?
14:44 him and lead him away, *t* every precaution."
14:57 Some, for instance, on *t* the stand,
Lk 9:10 *T* them with him, he retired to a town
9:16 Then, *t* the five loaves and the two fish,
12:45 'My master is *t* his time about coming,'
18:31 *T* the Twelve aside, he said to them:
22:17 Then *t* a cup he offered a blessing in
22:19 Then, *t* bread and giving thanks,
Acts 12: 9 this was *t* place through the angel's help.
12:25 the relief mission, *t* with them John Mark.
15:14 *t* from among the Gentiles a people to bear
21:11 He came up to us, and *t* Paul's belt,
Gal 2: 1 with Barnabas, this time *t* Titus with me.
2:12 He had been *t* his meals with the Gentiles
Phil 1:14 in Christ, *t* courage from my chains,

TALE (4)

Gn 24:33 "I will not eat until I have told my *t*."
Sir 18: 3 power, or exhaust the *t* of his mercies?
20:18 Insipid food is the untimely *t*;
Lk 24:23 but returned with the *t* that they had seen

TALEBEARER (5)

Prv 16:28 discord, and a *t* separates bosom friends.
18: 8 The words of a *t* are like dainty morsels
26:20 and when there is no *t*,
26:22 The words of a *t* are like dainty morsels
Sir 11:31 The *t* turns good into evil;

TALENT (10)

Ex 25:39 Use a *t* of pure gold for the lampstand and
37:24 A *t* of pure gold was used for the
38:27 of the veil, one *t* for each pedestal,
2Sm 12:30 It weighed a *t*,
1Kgs 20:39 with your life or pay out a *t* of silver.'
2Kgs 5:22 them a *t* of silver and two festal garments.' "
23:33 hundred talents of silver and a *t* of gold.
1Chr 20: 2 It was found to weigh a *t* of gold;
2Chr 36: 3 hundred talents of silver and a *t* of gold.
2Mc 8:11 to deliver ninety slaves for a *t*—

TALENTS (50)

Ex 38:24 *t* and seven hundred and thirty shekels,
38:25 one hundred *t* and one thousand seven
38:27 One hundred *t* of silver were used for
38:27 hundred *t* for the one hundred pedestals.
38:29 *t* and two thousand four hundred shekels.
1Kgs 9:14 Solomon one hundred and twenty *t* of gold.
9:28 and twenty *t* of gold to King Solomon.
10:10 the king one hundred and twenty gold *t*,
10:14 weighed six hundred and sixty-six gold *t*,
16:24 for two silver *t* and built upon the hill,
2Kgs 5: 5 Naaman set out, taking along ten silver *t*,
5:23 "Please take two *t*,"
5:23 up these silver *t* in bags and gave them,
15:19 and Menahem gave him a thousand *t* of
18:14 king of Assyria exacted three hundred *t*
18:14 silver and thirty *t* of gold from Hezekiah,
23:33 a hundred *t* of silver and a talent of gold.
1Chr 19: 6 the Ammonites sent a thousand *t* of silver
22:14 talents of gold, a million *t* of silver,
29: 4 three thousand *t* of Ophir gold,
29: 4 and seven thousand *t* of refined silver,
29: 7 thousand *t* and ten thousand darics of gold,
29: 7 ten thousand *t* of silver, eighteen thousand *t*
29: 7 bronze, and one hundred thousand *t* of iron.
2Chr 3: 8 fine gold to the amount of six hundred *t*.
8:18 and fifty *t* of gold to King Solomon.
9: 9 gold *t* and a very large quantity of spices,
9:13 weighed six hundred and sixty-six gold *t*,
25: 6 from Israel for a hundred *t* of silver.
25: 9 *t* that I paid for the troops of Israel?"
27: 5 Ammonites paid him one hundred *t* of silver,
36: 3 hundred *t* of silver and a talent of gold.
Ezr 7:22 silver, one hundred *t*;
8:26 silver, six hundred and fifty *t*;
8:26 gold, one hundred *t*;
Est 3: 9 silver *t* for deposit in the royal treasury."
1Mc 11:28 promising him in return three hundred *t*.
13:16 if you send us a hundred *t* of silver,
13:19 So he sent the boys and the hundred *t*;
15:31 pay me five hundred *t* of silver for the
15:31 five hundred *t* more for the tribute money
15:35 to pay you a hundred *t* for these cities."
2Mc 3:11 *t* of silver and two hundred of gold.
4: 8 king three hundred and sixty *t* of silver,
4: 8 as eighty *t* from another source of income.
4:24 Jason by three hundred *t* of silver.
5:21 off eighteen hundred *t* from the temple,
8:10 two thousand *t* of tribute owed by the king

TALES (2)

1Tm 4: 7 to do with profane myths or old wives' *t*.
2Pt 2: 3 They will deceive you with fabricated *t*,

TALITHA (1)

Mk 5:41 Taking her hand, he said to her, *T*,

TALK (42)

Gn 37: 8 the more because of his *t* about his dreams.
45:15 then were his brothers able to *t* with him.
1Sm 25:17 He is so mean that no one can *t* to him."
2Sm 19:11 When the *t* of all Israel reached the king,
2Kgs 9:11 You know that kind of man and his *t*,
Jb 16: 4 I also could *t* as you do,
16: 5 I could strengthen you with *t*,
17:12 is darkness they *t* of approaching light.
Ps(s) 38:13 of ruin, treachery they *t* of all the day.
119:23 Though princes meet and *t* against me,
Prv 4:24 Put away from you dishonest *t*,
6:12 a villain, is he who deals in crooked *t*.
14:23 is profit, but mere *t* tends only to penury.
Eccl 10:13 and the end of his *t* is utter madness;
Sir 13:11 For by prolonged *t* he will test you,
21:25 the impious *t* of what is not their concern,
22: 6 song in time of mourning is inopportune *t*,
23:13 Let not your mouth become used to coarse *t*,
27:14 oath-filled *t* makes the hair stand on end,
27:23 In your presence he uses honeyed *t*,
32: 3 Being older, you may *t*;
Ez 11: 5 This is the way you *t*,
Mk 2: 7 "Why does the man *t* in that way?
Jn 6:60 "This sort of *t* is hard to endure!
7:13 No one dared *t* openly about him,
19: 8 When Pilate heard this kind of *t*,
Acts 11:20 to Antioch began to *t* even to the Greeks,
1Cor 3: 1 I could not *t* to you as spiritual men
4:20 of God does not consist in *t* but in power.
13:11 I was a child I used to *t* like a child,
14:27 If any are going to *t* in tongues let it be
Eph 4:29 Never let evil *t* pass your lips;
5: 4 be any obscene, silly, or suggestive *t*;
1Tm 1: 6 and instead have turned to meaningless *t*,
6:20 idle *t* and the contradictions of what is
2Tm 2:16 Avoid worldly, idle *t*,
2:17 of their *t* will spread like the plague.
1Pt 2:15 *t* of foolish men by your good behavior.
2Pt 2:18 They *t* empty bombast while baiting their
1Jn 3:18 and in truth and not merely *t* about it.
2Jn 1:12 to visit you and *t* with you face to face,
3Jn 1:14 see you soon, when we can *t* face to face.

TALKATIVE (1)

Sir 20: 4 thought wise, another is *t* and is disliked.

TALKED (8)

Gn 43:19 and *t* to him at the entrance of the house.
1Mc 3:26 the Gentiles *t* about the battles of Judas.
Lk 2:38 she gave thanks to God and *t* about the
24:32 hearts burning inside us as he *t* to us
Acts 20: 8 Paul *t* on and on,
20:11 Then he *t* for a long while
24:25 As Paul *t* on about uprightness,
26:31 they *t* matters over among themselves and

TALKERS (1)

Ti 1:10 men who are empty *t* and deceivers.

TALKING (26)

Gn 29: 9 While he was still *t* with them,
1Sm 17:23 While he was *t* with them,
17:29 I was only *t*."
2Sm 19:30 "Why do you go on *t*?
2Kgs 8: 4 The king was *t* with Gehazi,
1Mc 14: 9 in the squares, all *t* about the good times,
Sir 5:15 Honor and dishonor through *t*!
Ez 33:30 your countrymen are *t* about you along the
Mt 26:70 "I do not know what you are *t* about!"
Mk 14:68 "I do not know what you are *t* about!
14:71 do not even know the man you are *t* about!"
Lk 9:30 Suddenly two men were *t* with him
22:60 friend, I do not know what you are *t* about."
Jn 2:21 he was *t* about the temple of his body.
3:11 assure you, we are *t* about what we know,
4:27 or "Why are you *t* with her?"
6:71 (He was *t* about Judas,
16:18 We do not know what he is *t* about."
16:29 exclaimed, "without *t* in veiled language!
Acts 10:27 then went in, *t* with him all the while.
1Cor 14: 2 in a tongue is *t* not to men but to God.
14: 9 You will be *t* to the air.

TALKING (cont.)

2Cor 11:23 Now I am really *t* like a fool—I am more:
Eph 3: 4 realize that I know what I am *t* about
Phil 3:19 I am *t* about those who are set upon the
1Tm 5:13 as well, *t* about things they ought not.

TALKS (4)

Sir 9:18 speech, and he who *t* rashly is hated.
20: 7 He who *t* too much is detested;
22: 8 talks with a slumberer who *t* with a fool,

TALL (10)

Dt 2:10 strong and numerous and *t* like the Anakim;
2:21 strong and numerous and *t* like the Anakim.
9: 2 the sky, the Anakim, a people great and *t*.
1Chr 11:23 the Egyptian, a huge man five cubits *t*.
Is 10:33 The *t* of stature are felled,
18: 2 messengers, to a nation *t* and bronzed,
18: 7 LORD of hosts from a people *t* and bronzed,
45:14 of Ethiopia, and the Sabeans, *t* of stature,
Ez 19:11 Notably *t* was she with her many clusters.
Am 2: 9 before them, who were as *t* as the cedars,

TALLER (2)

Dt 1:28 the people are stronger and *t* than we
Ez 31: 5 grew *t* than every other tree of the field,

TALLYING (1)

1Chr 9:28 *t* it as it was brought in and taken out.

TALMAI (6)

Nm 13:22 Hebron, where Ahiman, Sheshai and *T*.
Jos 15:14 Sheshai, Ahiman and *T*.
Jgs 1:10 and defeated Sheshai, Ahiman and *T*.
2Sm 3: 3 Absalom, son of Maacah the daughter of *T*,
13:37 Absalom, who had taken flight, went to *T*,
1Chr 3: 2 son of Maacah, who was the daughter of *T*,

TALMON (5)

1Chr 9:17 The gatekeepers were Shallum, Akkub, *T*,
Ezr 2:42 sons of Shallum, sons of Ater, sons of *T*,
Neh 7:45 sons of Shallum, sons of Ater, sons of *T*,
11:19 The gatekeepers were Akkub, *T*,
12:25 Meshullam, *T*, and Akkub were gatekeepers.

TAMAR (27)

Gn 38: 6 got a wife named *T* for his first-born,
38:11 Judah said to his daughter-in-law *T*,
38:11 So *T* went to live in her father's house.
38:13 When *T* was told that her father-in-law was
38:24 his daughter-in-law *T* had played the harlot
Ru 4:12 the house of Perez, whom *T* bore to Judah."
2Sm 13: 1 son Absalom had a beautiful sister named *T*,
13: 2 over his sister *T* that he became sick;
13: 4 Amnon said to him, "I am in love with *T*,
13: 5 *T* come and encourage me to take food.
13: 6 "Please let my sister *T* come and prepare
13: 7 David then sent home a message to *T*,
13: 8 *T* went to the house of her brother Amnon,
13:10 they had all left him, Amnon said to *T*,
13:10 So *T* picked up the cakes she had prepared
13:19 *T* put ashes on her head and tore the long
13:20 But *T* remained grief-stricken and forlorn
13:22 hated him for having shamed his sister *T*.
13:32 this ever since Amnon shamed his sister *T*.
14:27 born to him, besides a daughter named *T*,
1Kgs 9:18 Baalath, *T* in the desert of Judah,
1Chr 2: 4 daughter-in-law *T* bore him Perez and Zerah,
3: 9 and *T* was their sister.
Ez 47:18 down to the eastern sea as far as *T*.
47:19 from *T* to the waters of Meribath-kadesh,
48:28 from *T* to the waters of Meribath-kadesh,
Mt 1: 3 of Perez and Zerah, whose mother was *T*.

TAMARISK (3)

Gn 21:33 Abraham planted a *t* at Beer-sheba,
1Sm 22: 6 in Gibeah under a *t* tree on the high place,
31:13 and buried them under the *t* tree in Jabesh,

TAMBOURINE (1)

Ex 15:20 Aaron's sister, took a *t* in her hand,

TAMBOURINES (9)

Gn 31:27 merry singing to the sound of *t* and harps.
Ex 15:20 women went out after her with *t* dancing,
Jgs 11:34 who came forth, playing the *t* and dancing.
1Sm 10: 5 from the high place preceded by lyres, *t*,
18: 6 King Saul, singing and dancing, with *t*,
2Sm 6: 5 with singing and with citharas, harps, *t*,
1Chr 13: 8 amid songs and music on lyres, harps, *t*,
1Mc 9:39 with *t* and musicians and much equipment.
Jer 31: 4 Carrying your festive *t*,

TAME (7)

Gn 8: 1 Noah and all the animals, wild and *t*,
8:19 and all the animals, wild and *t*,
9:10 and the various *t* and wild animals that
Ps(s) 148:10 You wild beasts and all *t* animals,
Dn 3:81 All you beasts, wild and *t*,
Mk 5: 4 No one had proved strong enough to *t* him.
Jas 3: 8 the tongue no man can *t*.

TAMED (2)

Jas 3: 7 swimming, can be tamed, and has been *t*,

TAMMUZ (1)

Ez 8:14 there the women who were weeping for *T*.

TAMPERING (1)

Dn 6:18 To forestall any *t*, the king sealed

TANGLE (1)

Na 1:10 As when a *t* of thornbushes is set aflame,

TANHUMETH (2)

2Kgs 25:23 Kareah, Seraiah, son of *T* the Netophathite,
Jer 40: 8 Seraiah, son of *T*;

TANIS (1)

Jdt 1:10 Raamses, all the land of Goshen, *T*,

TANNER (1)

Acts 9:43 time at the house of Simon, a *t* of leather.

TAPHATH (1)

1Kgs 4:11 who was married to Solomon's daughter *T*,

TAPPED (1)

Acts 12: 7 He *t* Peter on the side and woke him.

TAPPUAH (7)

Jos 12:17 Libnah, Adullam, Makkedah, Bethel, *T*,
15:34 Zorah, Ashnah, Zanoah, Engannim, *T*,
16: 8 From *T* the boundary ran westward to the
17: 8 *T* belonged to Manasseh, although *T* itself
2Kgs 15:16 At that time, Menahem punished *T*,
1Chr 2:43 The sons of Hebron were Korah, *T*,

TARALAH (1)

Jos 18:27 Chephirah, Mozah, Rekem, Irpeel, *T*,

TAREA (1)

1Chr 8:35 The sons of Micah were Pithon, Melech, *T*,

TARGET (4)

1Sm 20:20 will shoot arrows, as though aiming at a *t*.
Jb 7:12 or why should I be a *t* for you?
16:12 He has set me up for a *t*;
Lam 3:12 bow, and set me up as the *t* for his arrow.

TARNISH (1)

Sir 33:23 let no one *t* your glory.

TARNISHED (1)

Lam 4: 1 How *t* is the gold,

TARRIED (2)

Nm 9:19 Even when the cloud *t* many days over the
9:22 Whether the cloud *t* over the Dwelling for

TARRY (6)

Jgs 19: 8 yourself and *t* until the afternoon."
Sir 14:12 Remember that death does not *t*,
32:11 When it is time to leave, *t* not;
Is 46:13 is not far off, my salvation shall not *t*;
Jer 50:40 dwell there, no human being shall *t* there.
Mi 5: 6 wait for no man, nor *t* for the sons of men.

TARSHISH (29)

Gn 10: 4 Elishah, *T*, the Kittim, and the Rodanim.
1Kgs 10:15 in addition to what came from the *T* fleet,
10:22 fleet of *T* ships at sea with Hiram's fleet.
10:22 of *T* ships would come with a cargo of gold,
22:49 made *T* ships to go to Ophir for gold;
1Chr 1: 7 The descendants of Javan were Elishah, *T*,
7:10 Benjamin, Ehud, Chenaanah, Zethan, *T*,
2Chr 9:21 that went to *T* with the servants of Huram.
9:21 Once every three years the fleet of *T*
20:36 with him in building ships to sail to *T*;
20:37 were wrecked and were unable to sail to *T*.
Est 1:14 He summoned Carshena, Shethar, Admatha, *T*,
Ps(s) 48: 8 from the east were shattering ships of *T*.
72:10 kings of *T* and the Isles shall offer gifts;
Is 2:16 all the ships of *T* and all stately vessels.
23: 1 Wail, O ships of *T*, for your port
23: 6 Pass over to *T*,
23:10 Cross to your own land, O ship of *T*;
23:14 Lament, O ships of *T*,
60: 9 assembled, with the ships of *T* in the lead,
66:19 to *T*, Put and Lud, Mosoch,
Jer 10: 9 Silver strips brought from *T*,
Ez 27:12 *T* traded with you,
27:25 *T* journeyed for you in your merchandising.
38:13 of *T* and all her young lions shall ask you:
Jon 1: 3 made ready to flee to *T* away from the LORD.
1: 3 down to Joppa, found a ship going to *T*,
1: 3 and went aboard to journey with them to *T*,
4: 2 This is why I fled at first to *T*.

TARSUS (7)

2Mc 3: 5 against Onias, he went to Apollonius of *T*,
4:30 the people of *T* and Mallus rose in revolt,
Acts 9:11 house of Judas ask for a certain Saul of *T*.
9:30 him down to Caesarea and sent him off to *T*.
11:25 Barnabas went off to *T* to look for Saul;
21:39 "I am a Jew, a citizen of *T* in Cilicia
22: 3 "I am a Jew, born in *T* in Cilicia,

TARTAK (1)

2Kgs 17:31 the men of Avva made Nibhaz and *T*;

TARTARUS (1)

2Pt 2: 4 He held them captive in *T*—

TASK (46)

Ex 18:18 The *t* is too heavy for you;
Nm 4:19 each of them his *t* and what he must carry;
4:24 is the *t* of the clans of the Gershonites,
4:26 be done with these things shall be their *t*.
4:28 *t* of the Gershonites in the meeting tent;
4:33 is the *t* of the clans of the Merarites
34:18 tribes whom you shall designate for this *t*.
1Sm 23:20 our *t* to deliver him into the king's grasp."
1Chr 9:19 assigned *t* the guarding of the threshold
2Chr 24:13 and the *t* of restoration progressed under
29:34 assisted them until the *t* was completed
34:12 The men worked faithfully at their *t*;
Ezr 10:13 this is not a *t* that can be performed in a
Neh 3: 1 took up the *t* of rebuilding the Sheep Gate.
4: 9 went back, each to his own *t* at the wall.
13:11 I took the magistrates to *t*,
13:17 I took the nobles of Judah to *t*,
13:25 I took them to *t* and cursed them;
13:30 Levites, so that each had his appointed *t*.
2Mc 2:26 the labor of making this digest, the *t*,
2:30 is the *t* of the professional historian;
12:39 day, since the *t* had now become urgent,
Jb 24: 5 these go forth to their *t* of seeking food;
37:12 in their *t* upon the surface of the earth,
Eccl 1:13 A thankless *t* God has appointed for men to
2:26 but to the sinner he gives the *t* of
3:10 I have considered the *t* which God has
4: 8 This also is vanity and a worthless *t*.
Sir 7:20 nor a laborer who devotes himself to his *t*.
7:25 your daughter in marriage ends a great *t*;
11:20 with it, grow old while doing your *t*.
37:11 harvest, to an idle slave about a great *t*:
38:31 hands, each one an expert at his own *t*;
Mt 8:26 up and took the winds and the sea to *t*.
Mk 13:34 servants in charge, each with his own *t*;
16:14 He took them to *t* for their disbelief and
Acts 6: 3 and we shall appoint them to this *t*.
14:26 of God for the *t* they had now completed.
Rom 15:28 When I have finished my *t* and have safely
1Cor 14:24 to *t* by all and called to account by all,
1Thes 5:12 respect those among you whose *t* it is to
1Tm 3: 1 wants to be a bishop aspires to a noble *t*.
2Tm 4: 2 to stay with this *t* whether convenient or
4:17 the preaching *t* might be completed
Heb 3: 5 *t* of witnessing to what would be spoken;
13:17 act that they may fulfill their *t* with joy,

TASKMASTER (2)

Jb 40:19 ways, and was made the *t* of his fellows;
Is 9: 3 And the rod of their *t* you have smashed,

TASKMASTERS (5)

Ex 1:11 *t* were set over the Israelites to oppress
5: 6 the *t* and foremen of the people this order:
5:10 So the *t* and foremen of the people went
5:13 straw, while the *t* kept driving them on,
5:14 whom the *t* of Pharaoh had placed over them,

TASKS (17)

Nm 4: 3 undertake obligatory *t* in the meeting tent.
4:23 undertake obligatory *t* in the meeting tent.
4:30 undertake obligatory *t* in the meeting tent.
4:35 undertake obligatory *t* in the meeting tent,
4:39 undertake obligatory *t* in the meeting tent,
4:43 undertake obligatory *t* in the meeting tent,
4:47 to undertake *t* of service or transport
Jos 14:11 vigor whether for war or for ordinary *t*.
Prv 24:27 Complete your outdoor *t*,
Wis 17:17 or a worker at *t* in the wasteland,
Sir 7:15 Hate not laborious *t*,
16:24 and, as he made them, assigned their *t*,
16:25 grow weary, nor ever cease from their *t*.
51:30 Work at your *t* in due season,
Lk 10:40 left me to do the household *t* all alone?
1Tm 4:16 Persevere at both *t*.
6: 2 must perform their *t* even more faithfully,

TASSEL (5)

Nm 15:38 fastening each corner *t* with a violet cord.
Mt 9:20 behind him and touched the *t* on his cloak.
14:36 do no more than touch the *t* of his cloak.
Mk 6:56 to let them touch just the *t* of his cloak.
Lk 8:44 behind him and touched the *t* on his cloak.

TASSELS (3)

Nm 15:38 put *t* on the corners of their garments,
15:39 When you use these *t*,
Mt 23: 5 widen their phylacteries and wear huge *t*.

TASTE (22)

1Sm 14:29 are from this small *t* of honey I have had.
2Sm 19:36 Can your servant *t* what he eats and drinks,
2Mc 6:20 it is unlawful to *t* even for love of life.
13:18 king, having had a *t* of the Jews' daring,
Jb 6:30 tongue, or cannot my *t* discern falsehood?
34: 3 the ear tests words, as the *t* does food.
Ps(s) 34: 9 *T* and see how good the LORD is;
Prv 16:24 sweet to the *t* and healthful to the body.
24:13 good, if virgin honey is sweet to your *t*;
Wis 16:20 all delights and conforming to every *t*.
Sir 30:19 to an idol that can neither *t* nor smell?
37:27 nor is everything suited to every *t*.
49: 1 is his memory, like honey to the *t*,
Jer 48:11 Thus he kept his *t*,
Jon 3: 7 neither cattle nor sheep, shall *t* anything;
Mk 9: 1 there are some who will not *t* death
Lk 9:27 *t* death until they see the reign of God."
14:24 invited shall *t* a morsel of my dinner.' "
Col 2:21 Do not *t*!
4: 6 speech be always gracious and in good *t*,
Heb 2: 9 he might *t* death for the sake of all men.
Rv 10: 9 in your mouth it will *t* as sweet as honey."

TASTED (11)

Ex 16:31 and it *t* like wafers made with honey.
Nm 11: 8 loaves, which *t* like cakes made with oil.
1Sm 14:24 So none of the people *t* food.
14:43 "I only *t* a little honey from the end of
Jb 21:25 of soul, having never *t* happiness.
Mt 27:34 with gall, which he *t* but refused to drink.
Jn 2: 9 The waiter in charge *t* the water made wine,
Heb 6: 4 enlightened and have *t* the heavenly gift
6: 5 when they have *t* the good word of God and
1Pt 2: 3 now that you have *t* that the Lord is good.
Rv 10:10 In my mouth it *t* as sweet as honey,

TASTELESS (1)

Mk 9:50 but if salt becomes *t*,

TASTES (1)

Jb 12:11 the ear judge words as the mouth *t* food?

TATAM (1)

Jos 15:59 is, Bethlehem), Peor, Etam, Kulom, *T*,

TATTENAI (4)

Ezr 5: 3 At that time there came to them *T*,
5: 6 of the letter sent to King Darius by *T*,
6: 6 "Now, therefore, *T*,
6:13 Then *T*, the governor of West-of-Euphrates,

TATTERED (2)

Jer 38:11 from which he took some old, *t* rags;
38:12 *t* rags between your armpits and the ropes."

TATTERS (2)

Dt 8: 4 The clothing did not fall from you in *t*,
29: 4 you in *t* nor your sandals from your feet;

TATTOO (1)

Lv 19:28 for the dead, and do not *t* yourselves.

TAUGHT (47)

Dt 6: 1 has ordered that you be *t* to observe in
31:22 same day, and he *t* it to the Israelites.
2Sm 1:18 Book of Jashar to be *t* to the Judahites.
2Kgs 17:28 and *t* them how to venerate the LORD.
2Chr 17: 9 They *t* in Judah,
17: 9 the cities of Judah and *t* among the people.
26: 5 as Zechariah lived, who *t* him to fear God;
Jb 35:11 *T* us rather than the beasts of the earth,
Ps(s) 71:17 O God, you have *t* me from my youth,
Prv 4: 4 yet the darling of my mother, He *t* me,
Eccl 12: 9 wise, Qoheleth *t* the people knowledge,
Wis 7:22 for Wisdom, the artificer of all, *t* me.
12:19 And you *t* your people,
Sir 6:32 My son, if you wish, you can be *t*;
21:12 He can never be *t* who is not shrewd,
Is 40:14 Who *t* him the path of judgment,
54:13 All your sons shall be *t* by the LORD,
Jer 9:13 and the Baals, as their fathers had *t* them;
12:16 they who formerly *t* my people to swear by
13:21 you those whom you *t* to be your lovers?
Dn 1: 4 they were to be *t* the language and
Hos 11: 3 Yet it was I who *t* Ephraim to walk,
Mt 4:23 He *t* in their synagogues,
7:29 The reason was that he *t* with authority
9:35 He *t* in their synagogues,
13:34 Jesus *t* the crowds in the form of parables.
Mk 1:22 his teaching because he *t* with authority,
2:13 kept coming to him in crowds and he *t* them.
4:33 By means of many such parables he *t* them
6:30 all that they had done and what they had *t*.
Lk 11: 1 teach us to pray, as John *t* his disciples."
13:26 You *t* in our streets.'
23:16 to release him, once I have *t* him a lesson."
Jn 6:45 'They shall all be *t* by God,'
8:28 I say only what the Father has *t* me.
18:20 I always *t* in a synagogue or in the temple
Acts 1: 1 *t* until the day he was taken up to heaven,
18:25 He spoke and *t* accurately about Jesus,
28:31 of God and *t* about the Lord Jesus Christ.
1Cor 2:13 human wisdom but in words *t* by the Spirit,
2:14 not accept what is *t* by the Spirit of God.
Eph 4:21 that he has been preached and *t* to you in
Col 2: 7 ever stronger in faith, as you were *t*,
1Thes 4: 9 God himself has *t* you to love one another,
1Tm 4: 1 things *t* by demons through plausible liars
2Pt 1:16 myths that we *t* you about the coming
1Jn 2:27 remain in him as that anointing *t* you.

TAUNT (11)

2Kgs 19: 4 king of Assyria, sent to *t* the living God,
19:16 which he sent to *t* the living God.
Ps(s) 39: 9 a fool's *t* let me not suffer.
Sg 8: 1 I would kiss you and none would *t* me.
Is 37: 4 king of Assyria, sent to *t* the living God,
37:17 that Sennacherib sent to *t* the living God.
Jer 24: 9 a reproach and a byword, a *t* and a curse,
38:22 Babylon's king, and they shall *t* you thus:
Lam 3:14 for all nations, their *t* all the day long;
3:63 they sit or stand, see, I am their *t* song.
Hb 2: 6 not all these take up a *t* against him,

TAUNT-SONG (1)

Is 14: 4 take up this *t* against the king of Babylon:

TAUNTED (4)

Jgs 8:15 Zebah and Zalmunna, with whom you *t* me,
1Kgs 18:27 When it was noon, Elijah *t* them:
Lk 22:64 him first, slapped him, and then *t* him:
Jn 7:52 us you are a Galilean too," they *t* him.

TAUNTING (2)

Mt 27:44 with him kept *t* him in the same way.
Mk 15:32 crucified with him likewise kept *t* him.

TAUNTS (1)

Jer 51:51 We are ashamed because we have heard *t*,

TAUT (2)

Is 21:15 From the *t* bow, from the fury of battle.
Lam 2: 4 Like an enemy he made *t* his bow;

TAVERNS (1)

Acts 28:15 Forum of Appius and the Three *T* to meet us.

TAX (46)

Nm 31:28 You shall levy a *t* for the LORD on the
31:37 and seventy-five fell as *t* to the LORD;
31:38 of which seventy-two fell as *t* to the LORD;
31:39 of which sixty-one fell as *t* to the LORD;
31:40 of whom thirty-two fell as *t* to the LORD,
2Kgs 12: 5 the census *t*, personal redemption money,
2Chr 24: 6 Judah and Jerusalem the *t* levied by Moses,
24: 9 Judah and Jerusalem that the *t* which Moses,
Neh 5: 4 "To pay the king's *t* we have borrowed
1Mc 10:29 all the Jews, from the tribute, the salt *t*,
10:31 and her tolls, be sacred and free from *t*.
11:35 the *t* on the salt pans and the crown tax.
13:39 now, as well as the crown *t* that you owe.
13:39 Any other *t* that may have been collected
15: 5 I confirm to you all the *t* exemptions that
Dn 11:20 a *t* collector through the glorious kingdom,
Mt 5:46 Do not *t* collectors do as much?
9:10 many *t* collectors and those known as
9:11 Teacher have for eating with *t* collectors
10: 3 Thomas and Matthew the *t* collector;
11:19 of *t* collectors and those outside the law!'
17:24 of the temple *t* approached Peter and said,
17:24 "Does your master not pay the temple *t*?"
17:25 the world take *t* or toll from their sons,
17:27 there a coin worth twice the temple *t*.
18:17 as you would a Gentile or a *t* collector.
21:31 "I assure you that *t* collectors and
21:32 but the *t* collectors and the prostitutes
22:17 lawful to pay *t* to the emperor or not?"
22:19 Show me the coin used for the *t*."
Mk 2:14 son of Alphaeus at his *t* collector's post,
2:15 many *t* collectors and those known as
2:16 *t* collectors and offenders against the law,
12:14 lawful to pay the *t* to the emperor or not?
Lk 3:12 *T* collectors also came to be baptized,
5:27 Afterward he went out and saw a *t*
5:29 crowd of *t* collectors and others at dinner.
5:30 *t* collectors and non-observers of the law?"
7:29 had heard Jesus, even the *t* collectors,
7:34 a friend of *t* collectors and sinners!'
15: 1 The *t* collectors and sinners were all
18:10 was a Pharisee, the other a *t* collector.
18:11 or even like this *t* collector.
19: 2 the chief *t* collector and a wealthy man.
20:22 May we pay *t* to the emperor or not?"

TAXATION (1)

1Mc 13:34 that he grant the land a release from *t*,

TAXED (1)

2Kgs 23:35 but *t* the land to raise the amount Pharaoh

TAXES (14)

Nm 31:41 to the LORD, The *t* contributed to the LORD,
Ezr 4:13 up again, they will no longer pay *t*,
4:20 ruled over all West-of-Euphrates, and *t*,
6: 8 royal revenue, the *t* of West-of-Euphrates,
7:24 you that it is not permitted to impose *t*,
1Mc 10:33 let all their *t*, even those on their cattle,
11:34 the royal *t* that formerly the king received
2Mc 4:28 whose duty it was to collect the *t*.
Prv 29: 4 but he who imposes heavy *t* ruins it.
Mt 9: 9 Matthew at his post where *t* were collected.
Lk 23: 2 opposing the payment of *t* to Caesar,
Rom 13: 5 You pay *t* for the same reason,
13: 7 taxes to whom *t* are due;

TEACH (100)

Ex 4:12 and will *t* you what you are to say."
4:15 will *t* the two of you what you are to do.
35:34 the tribe of Dan, the ability to *t* others.
Lv 10:11 you must *t* the Israelites all the laws
Dt 4: 5 *t* you the statutes and decrees as the LORD,
4: 9 but *t* them to your children and to your
4:10 in the land and may so *t* their children.'
4:14 The LORD charged me at that time to *t* you
5:31 the statutes and decrees you must *t* them,
11:19 *T* them to your children,
20:18 lest they *t* you to make any such
31:19 *T* it to the Israelites and have them
Jgs 13: 8 return to us to *t* us what to do for the
1Sm 12:23 you and to *t* you the good and right way.
14:12 they said, "and we will *t* you a lesson."
2Kgs 17:27 to *t* them how to worship the God of the
2Chr 6:27 But *t* them the right way to live,
17: 7 and Micaiah, to *t* in the cities of Judah.
Jb 6:24 *T* me, and I will be silent; prove to me
8:10 Will they not *t* you and tell you and utter
12: 7 But now ask the beasts to *t* you,
21:22 Can anyone *t* God knowledge,
27:11 I will *t* you the manner of God's dealings,
32: 7 speak, I thought, and many years *t* wisdom!
33:33 be silent while I *t* you wisdom.
34:32 *T* me wherein I have sinned;
37:19 *T* us then what we shall say to him;
Ps(s) 25: 4 *t* me your paths,
25: 5 paths, Guide me in your truth and *t* me,
34:12 I will *t* you the fear of the LORD.
51: 8 and in my inmost being you *t* me wisdom.
51:15 I will *t* transgressors your ways,
86:11 *T* me, O LORD, your way
90:12 *T* us to number our days aright,
94:12 instruct, O LORD, whom by your law you *t*,
105:22 to be like him and *t* his elders wisdom.
119:12 O LORD; *t* me your statutes.
119:26 *t* me your statutes.
119:64 the earth is full; *t* me your statutes.
119:66 *T* me wisdom and knowledge,
119:68 good and bountiful; *t* me your statutes.
119:108 homage of my mouth, and *t* me your decrees.
119:124 to your kindness, and *t* me your statutes.
119:135 upon your servant, and *t* me your statutes.
119:171 praise, because you *t* me your statutes.
132:12 and the decrees which I shall *t* them,
143:10 *T* me to do your will,
Prv 9: 9 *t* a just man, and he advances
22:21 To *t* you truly how to give a dependable
Sg 8: 2 There you would *t* me to give you spiced
Sir 9: 1 lest you *t* her to do evil against you.
45: 5 That he might *t* his precepts to Jacob,
45:17 To *t* the precepts to his people,
Is 48:17 your God, *t* you what is for your good,
Jer 5:31 falsely, and the priests *t* as they wish;
9:19 *T* your daughters this dirge,
10: 8 these idols they *t* about are wooden:
31:34 No longer will they have need to *t* their
Ez 22:26 nor *t* the difference between the unclean
44:23 They shall *t* my people to distinguish
Mt 5: 2 around him, and he began to *t* them:
11: 1 locality to *t* and preach in their towns.
22:16 a truthful man and *t* God's way sincerely.
28:20 *T* them to carry out everything I have
Mk 1:21 he entered the synagogue and began to *t*.
4: 1 occasion he began to *t* beside the lake.
6: 2 When the sabbath came he began to *t* in the
6:34 and he began to *t* them at great length.

TEACH (cont.)

7: 7 they *t* as dogmas mere human precepts.'
8:31 He began to *t* them that the Son of Man had
10: 1 him, and as usual he began to *t* them.
11:17 Then he began to *t* them:
12:14 respect but *t* God's way of life sincerely.
Lk 5: 3 he continued to *t* the crowds from the boat.
6: 6 On another sabbath he came to *t* in a
6:46 and not put into practice what I *t* you?
11: 1 disciples asked him, "Lord, *t* us to pray,
12:12 The Holy Spirit will *t* you at that moment
20:21 of persons but *t* the way of God in truth.
21:37 He would *t* in the temple by day,
Jn 7:14 went into the temple area and began to *t*.
7:35 the Diaspora among the Greeks, to *t* them?
8: 2 to him, he sat down and began to *t* them.
Acts 4:18 to speak the name of Jesus or *t* about him.
5:28 you strict orders not to *t* about that name,
15: 1 from Judea and began to *t* the brothers:
21:21 Yet they have been informed that you *t* the
Rom 2:20 discipline the foolish and *t* the simple,
2:21 of others, are you failing to *t* yourself?
1Cor 4:17 just as I *t* them in all the churches.
11:14 Does not nature itself *t* you that it is
Col 1:28 and *t* them in the full measure of wisdom,
1Tm 4:11 Such are the things you must urge and *t*.
6: 2 These are the things you must *t* and preach.
2Tm 2: 2 men who will be able to *t* others.
Ti 1:11 by teaching things they have no right to *t*—
2: 3 By their good example they must *t* the
Heb 5:12 you need to have someone *t* you again the
8:11 *t* their fellow citizens or their brothers,
1Jn 2:27 means you have no need for anyone to *t* you.

TEACHER (63)

Jb 36:22 What *t* is there like him?
Sir 33:28 idle, for idleness is an apt *t* of mischief.
51:17 I will give my *t* grateful praise.
Is 30:20 No longer will your *T* hide himself,
30:20 with your own eyes you shall see your *T*,
Jl 2:23 He has given you the *t* of justice:
Mt 8:19 A scribe approached him and said, *T*,
9:11 "What reason can the *T* have for eating
10:24 "No pupil outranks his *t*,
10:25 pupil should be glad to become like his *t*,
12:38 and Pharisees then spoke up, saying, *T*,
19:16 time a man came up to him and said, *T*,
22:16 *T*, we know you are a truthful man and
22:24 *T*, Moses declared,
22:36 an attempt to trip him up, asked him, *T*,
23: 8 One among you is your *t*,
23:10 Only one is your *t*, the Messiah.
26:18 man in the city and tell him, 'The *T* says,
Mk 4:38 They finally woke him and said to him, *T*,
5:35 Why bother the *T* further?"
9:17 *T*," a man in the crowd replied,
9:38 John said to him, *T*,
10:17 knelt down before him and asked, "Good *T*,
10:20 He replied, *T*, I have kept all these
10:35 *T*," they said, "We want you to grant
12:14 *T*, we know you are a truthful man,
12:19 *T*, we were left this in writing by Moses:
12:32 "Excellent, *T*!
13: 1 area, one of his disciples said to him, *T*,
14:14 he enters, say to the owner, 'The *T* asks,
Lk 3:12 to be baptized, and they said to him, *T*,
6:40 A student is not above his *t*;
6:40 his studies will be on a par with his *t*.
7:18 their *t* word of all these happenings.
7:40 *T*," he said, "speak."
8:49 do not bother the *T* further."
9:38 *T*, I beg you to look at my son;
10:25 *T*, what must I do to inherit everlasting
11:45 reply one of the lawyers said to him, *T*,
12:13 Someone in the crowd said to him, *T*,
18:18 the ruling class asked him then, "Good *t*,
19:39 the Pharisees in the crowd said to him, *T*,
20:21 *T*, we know that your words and your
20:39 of the scribes responded, "Well said, *T*."
21: 7 They asked him, "When will this be, *T*—
22:11 and say to the owner, 'The *T* asks you:
Jn 1:38 They said to him, "Rabbi (which means *T*),
3: 2 said, "we know you are a *t* come from God,
3:10 "You hold the office of *t* of Israel and
7:15 man get his education when he had no *t*?"
8: 4 *T*," they said to him,
11:28 "The *T* is here, asking for you,"
13:13 You address me as *T*' and 'Lord,'
13:14 I who am *T* and Lord
20:16 "Rabbouni!" (meaning "*T*").
Acts 5:34 a *t* of the law highly regarded by all the
Rom 2:21 Now then, *t* of others,
12: 7 is a *t* should use his gift for teaching;
1Tm 2: 7 the *t* of the nations in the true faith.
2:12 I do not permit a woman to act as *t*,
3: 2 He should be a good *t*.
2Tm 1:11 been appointed preacher and apostle and *t*,
2:24 He must be an apt *t*,

TEACHERS (16)

Ps(s) 119:99 my *t* when your decrees are my meditation.
Prv 5:13 Why did I not listen to the voice of my *t*,
Mt 23: 2 the Pharisees have succeeded Moses as *t*;
23:10 Avoid being called *t*.
Lk 2:46 the temple sitting in the midst of the *t*,
5:17 Sitting close by were Pharisees and *t* of
Acts 13: 1 church at Antioch certain prophets and *t*:
1Cor 12:28 first apostles, second prophets, third *t*,
12:29 Are all *t*?
Eph 4:11 pastors and *t* in roles of service for the
1Tm 1: 7 wanting to be *t* of the law but actually
2Tm 3:14 believed, because you know who your *t* were.
4: 3 themselves with *t* who tickle their ears.
Ti 1:10 There are many irresponsible *t*,
Jas 3: 1 Not many of you should become *t*,
2Pt 2: 1 *t* who will smuggle in pernicious heresies.

TEACHES (8)

Ps(s) 25: 9 humble to justice, he *t* the humble his way.
94:10 not chastise, he who *t* men knowledge?
Wis 8: 7 For she *t* moderation and prudence,
Is 9:14 the prophet who *t* falsehood is the tail.]
Mt 5:19 these commands and *t* others to do so
5:19 Whoever fulfills and *t* these commands
1Tm 6: 3 Whoever *t* in any other way,
1Jn 2:27 *t* you about all things and is true

TEACHING (91)

Dt 4: 1 and decrees which I am *t* you to observe,
1Kgs 8:36 *t* them the right way to live and sending
Ezr 7:10 and on *t* statutes and ordinances in Israel.
Jb 11: 4 "My *t* is pure,
Ps(s) 78: 1 Hearken, my people, to my *t*;
Prv 1: 8 and reject not your mother's *t*;
3: 1 My son, forget not my *t*,
4: 2 my *t* do not forsake.
6:20 bidding, and reject not your mother's *t*;
6:23 the bidding is a lamp, and the *t* a light,
7: 2 and live, my *t* as the apple of your eye;
13:14 The *t* of the wise is a fountain of life,
Sir 18:12 all flesh, Reproving, admonishing, *t*,
22: 7 *T* a fool is like gluing a broken pot,
51:26 her yoke, that your mind may accept her *t*.
Is 42: 4 the coastlands will wait for his *t*.
51: 7 justice, you people who have my *t* at heart:
Jer 32:33 though I kept *t* them, they would not
Zec 7:12 as not to hear the *t* and the message
Mt 7:28 and left the crowds spellbound at his *t*.
13:54 spent his time *t* them in their synagogue.
16:12 against the Pharisees' and Sadducees' *t*.
19:11 said, "Not everyone can accept this *t*,
19:12 Let him accept this *t* who can."
21:23 the temple precincts, and while he was *t*,
22:33 who listened were spellbound by his *t*.
26:55 day to day I sat *t* in the temple precincts,
Mk 1:22 by his *t* because he taught with authority,
1:27 completely new *t* in a spirit of authority!
4: 2 parables, and in the course of his *t* said:
6: 6 villages instead, and spent his time *t*.
9:31 He was *t* his disciples in this vein:
9:32 *T* They returned to Capernaum and Jesus,
11:18 whole crowd was under the spell of his *t*.
12:35 As Jesus was *t* in the temple precincts he
12:38 In the course of his *t* he said:
14:49 reach daily, *t* in the temple precincts,
Lk 4:15 He was *t* in their synagogues,
4:32 They were spellbound by his *t*,
5:17 One day Jesus was *t*,
13:10 day he was *t* in one of the synagogues.
13:22 He went through cities and towns *t*—
19:47 was *t* in the temple area from day to day.
20: 1 One day when he was *t* the people in the
23: 5 by his *t* throughout the whole of Judea,
Jn 7:28 this, Jesus, who was *t* in the temple area,
8:20 these words while *t* at the temple treasury.
8:31 "If you live according to my *t*,
18:19 about his disciples, then about his *t*.
Acts 4: 2 angry because they were *t* the people and
5:21 the temple at dawn and resumed their *t*.
5:25 over there in the temple, *t* the people."
5:28 you have filled Jerusalem with your *t*
5:42 they never stopped *t* and proclaiming the
13:12 impressed was he by the *t* about the Lord.
15:35 *t* and preaching the word of the Lord.
17:19 know what this new *t* is that you propose.
18:11 a year and a half, *t* them the word of God.
20:20 or from *t* you in public or in private.
21:28 his *t* everywhere against our people,
Rom 3: 8 that some slanderously accuse us of *t*;
6:17 that rule of *t* which was imparted to you;
12: 7 is a teacher should use his gift for *t*;
16:17 contrary to the *t* you have received.
1Cor 2:14 He cannot come to know such *t* because it
1Tm 1: 3 certain people there against *t* false doctrines
1:10 those who in other ways flout the sound *t*
4:13 reading of Scripture, to preaching and *t*.
4:16 Watch yourself and watch your *t*.
5:17 those whose work is preaching and *t*.
6: 1 of God and the church's *t* suffer abuse.
6: 3 Christ and the *t* proper to true religion,
2Tm 1:13 of sound *t* what you have heard me say,
3:10 have followed closely my *t* and my conduct.
3:16 is inspired of God and is useful for *t*—
4: 2 constantly *t* and never losing patience.
Ti 1: 9 In his *t* he must hold fast to the
1:11 by *t* things they have no right to teach
2: 7 Your *t* must have the integrity of serious,
Heb 5:12 by this time you should be *t* others,
6: 1 *t* about Christ and advance to maturity,
13: 9 be carried away by all kinds of strange *t*.
2Pt 3: 2 *t* delivered long ago by the holy prophets,
2Jn 1: 9 in the *t* of Christ does not possess God,
1: 9 *t* possesses both the Father and the Son.
1:10 comes to you who does not bring this *t*,
Rv 2:14 some among you who follow the *t* of Balaam,
2:15 you who hold to the *t* of the Nicolaitans.
2:20 seduces my servants by *t* them to practice
2:24 do not uphold this *t* and know nothing

TEACHINGS (1)

Sir 24:30 do I send my *t* forth shining like the dawn,

TEAM (1)

Jer 51:23 with you I shatter the farmer and his *t*,

TEAMS (1)

2Kgs 9:25 we were driving *t* behind his father Ahab,

TEAR (44)

Ex 34:13 *T* down their altars;
Lv 10: 6 not bare your heads or *t* your garments,
13:56 *t* the infected part out of the garment,
Dt 7: 5 *T* down their altars,
12: 3 *T* down their altars,
1Kgs 11:31 'I will *t* away the kingdom from Solomon's
1Mc 4:45 happy thought came to them to *t* it down,
9:54 But he only began to *t* it down.
2Mc 14:33 I will *t* down the altar,
Jb 1:20 began to *t* his cloak and cut off his hair.
18: 4 You who *t* yourself in your anger,
40:12 *t* down the wicked and shatter them.
Ps(s) 28: 5 may he *t* them down and not build them up.
Eccl 3: 3 a time to *t* down, and a time to build.
Sir 28:23 like a panther, it will *t* them to pieces.
Is 7: 6 saying, "Let us go up and *t* Judah asunder,
Jer 1:10 To root up and to *t* down,
5:10 *T* away her tendrils,
18: 7 *t* down and destroy a nation or a kingdom.
24: 6 to build them up, not to *t* them down;
42:10 I will build you up, and not *t* you down;
Ez 13:14 I will *t* down the wall that you have
13:20 I will *t* them from their arms and set free
13:21 I will *t* off your veils and rescue my
16:39 I will hand you over to them to *t* down
17: 9 Will he not rather *t* it out by the roots
17:22 its topmost branches *t* off a tender shoot,
22:25 princes are like roaring lions that *t* prey;
22:27 within her are like wolves that *t* prey,
23:34 the cup, and you shall *t* out your breasts;
Hos 13: 8 and *t* their hearts from their breasts;
Mi 3: 2 You who *t* their skin from them,
5:10 your land and *t* down all your fortresses.
5:13 *t* out the sacred poles from your midst,
Zec 11:16 of the fat ones and *t* off their hoofs!
Mal 1: 4 They indeed may build, but I will *t* down,
Mt 7: 6 at best, and perhaps even *t* you to shreds.
Mk 2:21 and the *t* would get worse.
9:47 If your eye is your downfall, *t* it out!
Lk 5:36 If he does, he will only *t* the new coat,
Jn 19:24 said to each other, "We should not *t* it.
Acts 23:10 feared they would *t* Paul to pieces.
Rv 7:17 and God will wipe every *t* from their eyes."
21: 4 He shall wipe every *t* from their eyes,

TEARFULLY (1)

Est 8: 3 Esther fell at his feet and *t* implored him

TEARING (6)

2Mc 7: 7 After *t* off the skin and hair of his head,
Is 22:10 *t* some down to strengthen the wall;
Jer 45: 4 What I have built, I am *t* down;
Ez 17: 4 *t* off its topmost branch,
28:24 be a *t* thorn for the house of Israel,
Gal 5:15 go on biting and *t* one another to pieces,

TEARS (55)

Gn 29:11 Then Jacob kissed Rachel and burst into *t*.
43:30 his brother that he was on the verge of *t*.
50:17 these words to him, Joseph broke into *t*.
Jgs 14: 6 he tore the lion in pieces as one *t* a kid.
2Kgs 20: 5 I have heard your prayer and seen your *t*.
Tb 3:10 She went in *t* to an upstairs room in her
7: 6 up and kissed him, shedding *t* of joy.
7:16 over her, she wiped away the *t* and said:
2Mc 11: 6 and *t* to send a good angel to save Israel.
Jb 8:18 Yet if one *t* him from his place,
16:20 before God my eyes drop *t*,
Ps(s) 6: 7 I drench my couch with my *t*.
42: 4 My *t* are my food day and night,
56: 9 my *t* are stored in your flask;
80: 6 You have fed them with the bread of *t* and
80: 6 and given them *t* to drink in ample measure.
102:10 like bread and mingle my drink with *t*,
116: 8 freed my soul from death, my eyes from *t*,

119:136 of *t* because your law has not been kept.
126: 5 Those that sow in *t* shall reap rejoicing.
Prv 14: 1 but Folly *t* hers down with her own hands.
Eccl 4: 1 *t* of the victims with none to comfort them!
Sir 12:16 Though your enemy has *t* in his eyes,
22:19 One who jabs the eye brings *t*:
34:23 If one man builds up and another *t* down,
35:15 Do not the *t* that stream down her cheek
38:16 shed *t* for one who is dead with wailing
Is 16: 9 I water you with *t*,
25: 8 GOD will wipe away the *t* from all faces;
38: 5 I have heard your prayer and seen your *t*.
Jer 8:23 of water, my eyes a fountain of *t*,
9:17 be wet with weeping, our cheeks run with *t*.
13:17 in secret many *t*; My eyes will run with *t*
14:17 Let my eyes stream with *t* day and night,
31: 9 They departed in *t*,
31:16 of mourning, wipe the *t* from your eyes.
Lam 1: 2 she weeps at night, *t* upon her cheeks,
1:16 "At this I weep, my eyes run with *t*:
2:18 your *t* flow like a torrent day and night;
Ez 24:16 but do not mourn or weep or shed any *t*.
Dn 13:35 Through her *t* she looked up to heaven,
Hos 12: 5 angel and triumphed, entreating him with *t*.
Mi 5: 7 When it passes through, it tramples and *t*,
Mal 2:13 the altar of the LORD you cover with *t*,
Lk 5:36 "No one *t* a piece from a new coat to
7:38 weeping so that her *t* fell upon his feet.
7:44 with her *t* and wiped them with her hair.
Acts 9:39 All the widows came to him in *t* and showed
20:31 you individually even to the point of *t*.
2Cor 2: 4 great sorrow and anguish, with copious *t*—
Phil 3:18 this time I say it with *t*.
2Tm 1: 4 Recalling your *t* when we parted,
Heb 5: 7 supplications with loud cries and *t* to God,
12:17 even though he sought the blessing with *t*.

TEBAH (2)

Gn 22:24 *T*, Gaham, Tahash, and Maacah.
2Sm 8: 8 From *T* and Berothai,

TEBALIAH (1)

1Chr 26:11 him chief), Hilkiah, the second son, *T*,

TEBETH (1)

Est 2:16 in his palace in the tenth month, *T*,

TEEM (2)

Gn 1:20 *t* with an abundance of living creatures,
Ex 7:28 The river will *t* with frogs.

TEEMING (1)

Gn 48:16 may become *t* multitudes upon the earth!"

TEEMS (2)

Gn 1:21 swimming creatures with which the water *t*,
Ps(s) 5:10 their heart *t* with treacheries.

TEETH (49)

Gn 49:12 than wine, and his *t* are whiter than milk.
Nm 11:33 while the meat was still between their *t*,
Dt 32:24 *t* of wild beasts I will send among them,
Jb 4:10 yet the *t* of the young lions are broken;
13:14 I will carry my flesh between my *t*,
16: 9 wrath assails, he gnashes his *t* against me.
19:20 I have escaped with my flesh between my *t*.
29:17 from his *t* I forced the prey.
41: 6 of his mouth, close to his terrible *t*?
Ps(s) 3: 8 the *t* of the wicked you break.
35:16 they mocked me, gnashing their *t* at me.
37:12 against the just and gnashes his *t* at them;
57: 5 Their *t* are spears and arrows,
58: 7 O God, smash their *t* in their mouths;
112:10 he shall gnash his *t* and pine away;
124: 6 who did not leave us a prey to their *t*.
Prv 10:26 As vinegar to the *t*,
30:14 incisors are swords, whose *t* are knives,
Sg 4: 2 *t* are like a flock of ewes to be shorn,
5:12 waters, His *t* would seem bathed in milk,
6: 6 Your *t* are like a flock of ewes which
7:10 lover, spreading over the lips and the *t*.
Sir 21: 2 Its teeth are lion's *t*,
30:10 finally your *t* are clenched in remorse.
Jer 31:29 and the children's *t* are set on edge,"
31:30 the *t* of him who eats the unripe grapes
Lam 2:16 They hiss and gnash their *t*.
3:16 He has broken my *t* with gravel,
Ez 18: 2 thus their children's *t* are on edge"?
Dn 7: 5 among the *t* in its mouth were three tusks.
7: 7 iron *t* with which it devoured and crushed,
7:19 crushing with its iron *t* and bronze claws,
Jl 1: 6 His *t* are the teeth of a lion,
Am 4: 6 your *t* clean of food in all your cities,
Mi 3: 5 Who, when their *t* have something to bite,
Zec 9: 7 and his abominations from between his *t*:
Mt 8:12 will be heard there, and the grinding of *t*."
13:42 where they will wail and grind their *t*.
13:50 where they will wail and grind their *t*.
22:13 out into the night to wail and grind his *t*.'
24:51 will be wailing then and grinding of *t*.
25:30 outside, where he can wail and grind his *t*.'
Mk 9:18 mouth and grinds his *t* and becomes rigid.
Lk 13:28 and grinding of *t* when you see Abraham,
Acts 7:54 they ground their *t* in anger at him.
Rv 9: 8 Their teeth were like the *t* of lions,

TEHAPHNEHES (1)

Ez 30:18 In *T* the day shall be darkened when I

TEHINNAH (1)

1Chr 4:12 the father of Bethrapha, Paseah, and *T*,

TEKEL (2)

Dn 5:25 MENE, *T*, and PERES.
5:27 *T*, you have been weighed on the scales

TEKOA (14)

Jos 15:59 *T*, Ephrathah (that is,
2Sm 14: 2 to *T* and brought from there a gifted woman,
14: 4 So the woman of *T* went to the king and
14: 9 The woman of *T* answered him,
23:26 Ira, son of Ikkesh, from *T*;
1Chr 2:24 and she bore him Ashhur, the father of *T*.
4: 5 Ashhur, the father of *T*,
11:28 Ira, son of Ikkesh, from *T*;
27: 9 month, was Ira, son of Ikkesh, from *T*,
2Chr 11: 6 He built up Bethlehem, Etam, *T*,
20:20 they hastened out to the wilderness of *T*.
1Mc 9:33 and they fled to the desert of *T* and
Jer 6: 1 Blow the trumpet in *T*,
Am 1: 1 The words of Amos, a shepherd from *T*,

TEKOITES (2)

Neh 3: 5 him the *T* carried out the work of repair;
3:27 the *T* repaired the adjoining sector

TEL-ABIB (1)

Ez 3:15 exiles who lived at *T* by the river Chebar,

TEL-HARSHA (2)

Ezr 2:59 following who returned from Tel-melah, *T*,
Neh 7:61 following who returned from Tel-melah, *T*,

TEL-MELAH (2)

Ezr 2:59 The following who returned from *T*,
Neh 7:61 The following who returned from *T*

TELAH (1)

1Chr 7:25 whose son was Resheph, whose son was *T*,

TELAIM (1)

1Sm 15: 4 and at *T* reviewed two hundred thousand

TELAM (2)

1Sm 27: 8 living in the land between *T*,
2Sm 3:12 Then Abner sent messengers to David in *T*,

TELASSAR (2)

2Kgs 19:12 Gozan, Haran, Rezeph, or the Edenites in *T*?
Is 37:12 Haran, Rezeph, and the Edenites in *T*?

TELEM (2)

Jos 15:24 Ziph, *T*, Bealoth, Hazor-hadattah,
Ezr 10:24 Shallum, *T*, and Uri.

TELL (449)

Gn 3: 1 "Did God really *t* you not to eat from any
12:18 Why didn't you *t* me she was your wife?
24:23 *T* me, please, And is there room in your
26: 2 to camp wherever in this land I *t* you.
27: 6 overheard your father *t* your brother Esau,
27: 8 Now, son, listen carefully to what I *t* you.
27:43 Therefore, son, do what I *t* you:
29:12 son, and she ran to *t* her father.
29:15 *T* me what your wages should be."
32:30 Jacob then asked him, "Do *t* me your name,
37:16 *t* me where they are tending the flocks?"
40: 8 Please *t* the dreams to me."
41:21 them, no one could *t* that they had done so,
42:22 "Didn't I *t* you," broke in Reuben,
45: 9 "Hurry back, then, to my father and *t* him:
45:13 *T* my father all about my high position in
49: 1 that I may *t* you what is to happen to you
Ex 3:13 what am I to *t* them?"
3:14 "This is what you shall *t* the Israelites:
3:16 the elders of the Israelites, and *t* them:
4:23 Hence I *t* you:
6:11 the LORD said to Moses, "Go and *t* Pharaoh,
6:29 Pharaoh, king of Egypt, all that I *t* you."
7: 2 You shall *t* him all that I command you.
7: 2 your brother Aaron shall *t* Pharaoh to let
7:26 said to Moses, "Go to Pharaoh and *t* him:
8:12 *T* Aaron to stretch out his staff and
9: 1 said to Moses, "Go to Pharaoh and *t* him:
12: 3 *T* the whole community of Israel:
13:14 you shall *t* him, 'With a strong hand
14: 2 *T* the Israelites to turn about and camp
14:12 Did we not *t* you this in Egypt,
14:15 *T* the Israelites to go forward.
16: 9 to Aaron, *T* the whole Israelite community:
16:12 *T* them:
19: 4 *t* the Israelites;
19: 6 That is what you must *t* the Israelites."
19: 7 that the LORD had ordered him to *t* them,
19:12 people all around the mountain, and *t* them:
23:22 heed his voice and carry out all I *t* you,
25: 2 *T* the Israelites to take up a collection
25:22 I will *t* you all the commands that I wish
31:13 to Moses, "You must also *t* the Israelites:
33: 5 The LORD said to Moses, *T* the Israelites:
34:34 he would *t* the Israelites all that had
Lv 1: 2 "Speak to the Israelites and *t* them:
4: 2 The LORD said to Moses, *T* the Israelites:
6:18 LORD said to Moses, *T* Aaron and his sons:
7:23 The LORD said to Moses, *T* the Israelites:
7:29 The LORD said to Moses, *T* the Israelites:
9: 3 *T* the elders of Israel, too:
11: 2 "Speak to the Israelites and *t* them:
12: 2 The LORD said to Moses, *T* the Israelites:
15: 2 "Speak to the Israelites and *t* them:
16: 2 *T* your brother Aaron that he is not to
17: 2 well as to all the Israelites, and *t* them:
17: 8 *T* them, therefore:
18: 2 "Speak to the Israelites and *t* them:
19: 2 the whole Israelite community and *t* them:
20: 2 The LORD said to Moses, *T* the Israelites:
21: 1 to Aaron's sons, the priests, and *t* them:
21:17 said to Moses, "Speak to Aaron and *t* him:
22: 2 *T* Aaron and his sons to respect the sacred
22: 3 *T* them:
22:18 sons and to all the Israelites, and *t* them:
23: 2 "Speak to the Israelites and *t* them:
23:10 "Speak to the Israelites and *t* them:
23:24 The LORD said to Moses, *T* the Israelites:
23:34 The LORD said to Moses, *T* the Israelites:
24:15 *T* the Israelites:
25: 2 "Speak to the Israelites and *t* them:
27: 2 "Speak to the Israelites and *t* them:
Nm 5: 6 The LORD said to Moses, *T* the Israelites:
5:12 "Speak to the Israelites and *t* them:
6: 2 "Speak to the Israelites and *t* them:
6:23 "Speak to Aaron and his sons and *t* them:
9: 2 *T* the Israelites to celebrate the Passover
11:12 that you *t* me to carry them at my bosom,
14:14 to *t* of it to the inhabitants of this land?
14:28 *T* them:
15:18 "Speak to the Israelites and *t* them:
15:38 "Speak to the Israelites and *t* them that
16:24 Moses, "Speak to the community and *t* them:
17: 2 The LORD said to Moses, *T* Eleazar,
18:30 *T* them also:
19: 2 *T* the Israelites to procure for you a red
22:19 till I learn what else the LORD may *t* me."
22:20 condition that you do exactly as I *t* you."
22:35 but you may say only what I *t* you."
23: 3 then I will *t* you whatever he lets me see."
27: 8 Therefore, *t* the Israelites:
28: 3 "You shall *t* them therefore:
33:51 *T* the Israelites:
35: 2 *T* the Israelites that out of their
35:10 The LORD said to Moses, *T* the Israelites:
Dt 5:27 God, will say, and then *t* us what the LORD,
5:30 Go, *t* them to return to their tents.
18:18 he shall *t* them all that I command him.
30:12 in the sky to get it for us and *t* us of it,
30:13 the sea to get it for us and *t* us of it,
30:18 I *t* you now that you will certainly perish;
32: 7 you, ask your elders and they will *t* you:
Jos 4:10 LORD had commanded Joshua to *t* the people.
7:13 *T* them to sanctify themselves before
20: 2 *T* the Israelites to designate the cities
Jgs 2: 3 For now I *t* you, I will not clear them
7: 4 *t* you that a certain man is to go with you,
7: 4 But no one is to go if I *t* you he must not."
13: 6 he came from, nor did he *t* me his name.
14:16 my father or my mother, must I *t* it to you?"
16: 6 *T* me the secret of your great strength and
16:10 Now *t* me how you may be bound."
16:13 *T* me how you may be bound."
Ru 3: 4 He will *t* you what to do."
4: 4 if you do not wish to claim it, *t* me so,
1Sm 3:15 He feared to *t* Eli the vision,
6: 2 *T* us what we should send back with it."
9: 6 he can *t* us how to accomplish our errand."
9: 8 to the man of God, he will *t* us our way."
9:18 said, "Please *t* me where the seer lives."
9:19 you, I will *t* you whatever you wish.
9:27 Saul, *T* the servant to go on ahead of us,
10: 8 I shall then *t* you what you must do."
10:15 Then Saul's uncle said, *T* me,
11: 9 *T* the inhabitants of Jabesh-gilead that
14:34 "Mingle with the people and *t* each of
14:43 said to Jonathan, *T* me what you have done."
15:16 *t* you what the LORD said to me last night."
16: 3 and I myself will *t* you what to do;
20:10 "Who will *t* me if your father gives you a
22:21 was there, that he would surely *t* Saul.
23:11 O LORD God of Israel, *t* your servant."
25: 8 Ask your servants and they will *t* you so.
25:19 But she did not *t* her husband Nabal.

TELL (cont.)
28: 8 said to her, *T* my fortune through a ghost;
28:15 I have called you to *t* me what I should do."
2Sm 1: 4 *T* me what happened," David bade him.
1:20 *T* it not in Gath,
7: 5 "Go, *t* my servant David,
12:18 afraid to *t* him that the child was dead,
12:18 How can we *t* him the child is dead?
13: 4 Why not *t* me?"
18:21 *t* the king what you have seen" The
20:16 *T* Joab to come here,
1Kgs 14: 3 will *t* you what will happen to the child."
14: 5 This is what you must *t* her.
14: 7 Go, *t* Jeroboam,
18: 8 "Go *t* your master, 'Elijah is here!' "
18:11 And now you say, 'Go *t* your master:
18:14 And now you say, 'Go *t* your master:
20:11 The king of Israel replied, *T* him,
21:19 This is what you shall *t* him.
22:16 I adjure you to *t* me nothing but the truth
22:18 "Did I not *t* you he prophesies not good
2Kgs 1: 6 back to the king who sent you and *t* him:
2:18 said to them, "Did I not *t* you not to go?"
4: 2 *T* me what you have in the house."
4:24 Do not stop my donkey unless I *t* you to."
6:11 "Will you not *t* me,"
6:12 "The Israelite prophet Elisha can *t* the
7:12 me *t* you what the Arameans have done to us.
8: 4 *T* me," he said, "all the great things
8:10 "Go and *t* him," Elisha answered,
8:14 "What did Elisha *t* you?"
9:12 Come, *t* us."
10: 5 and we will do everything you *t* us.
18:19 The commander said to them, *T* Hezekiah,
19: 2 in sackcloth, to *t* the prophet Isaiah,
19: 6 he said to them, *T* this to your master:
20: 5 "Go back and *t* Hezekiah,
1Chr 16:24 after day *T* his glory among the nations;
17: 4 "Go and *t* my servant David.
17: 7 Therefore, *t* my servant David,
21:10 "Go, *t* David:
21:18 LORD commanded Gad to *t* David to go up
2Chr 9: 6 did not *t* me the half of your great wisdom;
18:15 times must I adjure you to *t* me nothing
18:17 *t* you that he prophesies no good about me,
34:23 *T* the one who sent you to me,
Tb 5: 7 young man, till I go back and *t* my father;
5: 9 to *t* his father Tobit what had happened.
5:11 Tobit asked, "Brother, *t* me,
12:11 "I will now *t* you the whole truth;
12:12 I can now *t* you that when you,
14: 9 you must *t* your children to do what is
Jdt 2: 7 *T* them to have earth and water ready,
5: 3 "Now *t* me, you Canaanites,
5: 5 I will *t* you the truth about this people
6: 2 and to *t* us not to fight against the
8:34 *t* you until my plan has been accomplished."
11: 3 *t* me why you fled from them and came to us.
11: 5 I will *t* no lie to my lord this night,
11:17 He will *t* me when the Israelites have
11:19 and I in turn have been sent to *t* you."
13:19 by those who *t* of the might of God.
14: 8 *t* me all that you did during these days."
1Mc 13: 9 and we will do everything that you *t* us."
2Mc 8:19 He went on to *t* them of the times when
Jb 1:15 sword, and I alone have escaped to *t* you."
1:16 and I alone have escaped to *t* you."
1:17 sword, and I alone have escaped to *t* you."
1:19 and I alone have escaped to *t* you."
8:10 Will they not teach you and *t* you and
11: 6 And *t* you that the secrets of wisdom are
12: 7 you, and the birds of the air to *t* you;
15:17 what I have seen I will *t*—
33:12 In this you are not just, let me *t* you;
38: 3 question you, and you *t* me the answers!
38: 4 *T* me, if you have understanding.
38:18 *T* me, if you know all:
40: 7 will question you, and you *t* me the answers!
Ps(s) 40: 6 Should I wish to declare or to *t* them,
48:14 *t* a future generation that such is God,
50:12 If I were hungry, I should not *t* you,
71:16 O GOD, I will *t* of your singular justice.
87: 4 I *t* of Egypt and Babylon
96: 3 *T* his glory among the nations;
106: 2 Who can *t* the mighty deeds of the LORD,
145: 5 majesty and *t* of your wondrous works.
Prv 27:16 he cannot *t* north from south.
Eccl 6:12 who is there to *t* a man what will come
9: 1 Love from hatred man cannot *t*;
10:14 who can *t* him what is to come after him?
10:20 a winged creature may *t* what you say.
Sg 5: 8 What shall you *t* him?—
Sir 19: 7 *T* nothing to friend or foe;
19:25 One can *t* a man by his appearance;
37: 9 He may *t* you how good your way will be,
37:14 A man's conscience can *t* him his situation
43:25 who go down to the sea *t* part of its story,
Is 19:12 Let them *t* you and make known What the
21: 6 station a watchman, let him *t* what he sees.
36: 4 commander said to them, *T* King Hezekiah:
37: 2 in sackcloth, to *t* the prophet Isaiah,
37: 6 *T* this to your master:
38: 5 "Go, *t* Hezekiah:
38:15 What am I to say or *t* him?
41:22 *T* us, that we may reflect on them
58: 1 *T* my people their wickedness,
59: 4 They trust in emptiness and *t* lies;
Jer 1:17 stand up and *t* them all that I command you.
8: 4 *T* them:
9:16 *t* the wailing women to come,
15: 2 they ask you where they should go, *t* them,
15:11 *T* me, LORD, have I not served you
18:11 *t* this to the men of Judah and the
25:27 *T* them:
26: 2 whatever I command you, *t* them,
27: 4 *T* your masters:
28:13 Go *t* Hananiah this:
32:25 and yet you *t* me, O Lord God:
33: 3 I will *t* you things great beyond reach of
34: 2 Go to Zedekiah, king of Judah, and *t* him:
36:16 must certainly *t* the king all these things."
36:17 *T* us, please, how you came to write down
38:15 If I *t* you anything, you will have me
38:20 the voice of the LORD and do as I *t* you;
38:25 ask you, *T* us what you said to the king;
39:16 Go, *t* this to Ebed-melech the Cushite:
42: 4 the LORD answers you, I will *t* you;
43: 2 you to *t* us not to go to Egypt to settle.
51:10 come, let us *t* in Zion what the LORD,
Lam 3:18 I *t* myself my future is lost,
Ez 12:10 *T* them:
12:16 so that they may *t* of all their
13:15 I *t* you there shall be no wall,
20:27 house of Israel, son of man, and *t* them:
24:19 "Will you not *t* us what all these things
33: 8 *t* the wicked man that he shall surely die,
33:12 As for you, son of man, *t* your countrymen:
33:27 *T* them this:
37:18 you not *t* us what you mean by all this?",
37:21 *T* them:
40: 4 *T* the house of Israel all that you see."
44: 5 I will *t* you about the statutes
Dn 2: 4 *T* your servants the dream and we will give
2: 5 unless you *t* me the dream and its meaning,
2: 6 But if you *t* me the dream and its meaning,
2: 6 Now *t* me the dream and its meaning."
2: 7 "Let the king *t* his servants the dream
2: 9 If you do not *t* me the dream,
2: 9 *T* me the dream, therefore,
2:11 there is no one who can *t* it to the king
2:24 will *t* him the interpretation of the dream."
2:26 "Can you *t* me the dream that I had,
4: 4 but none of them could *t* me its meaning.
4: 6 *t* me the meaning of the visions that I saw
4:15 Now, Belteshazzar, *t* me its meaning.
4:15 men in my kingdom can *t* me the meaning,
5: 8 the writing or *t* the king what it meant.
5:12 summon Daniel to *t* you what this means."
5:15 to read this writing and *t* me its meaning,
5:16 to read the writing and *t* me what it means,
5:17 for you, O king, and *t* you what it means.
10:21 *t* you what is written in the truthful book.
11: 2 Now I shall *t* you the truth.
13:10 they did not *t* each other their trouble,
13:41 the young man was, but she refused to *t* us.
13:54 *t* me under what tree you saw them together."
13:58 *t* me under what tree you surprised them
14: 8 "Unless you *t* me who it is that consumes
Jl 1: 3 *T* it to your children,
Jon 1: 8 *T* us," they said, "what is your business?
3: 2 to it the message that I will *t* you."
Hg 2: 2 *T* this to the governor of Judah,
2:21 *T* this to Zerubbabel,
Zec 2: 8 to him, "Run, *t* this to that young man:
10: 2 Deceitful dreams they *t*,
Mt 2:13 Stay there until I *t* you otherwise.
3: 9 I *t* you, God can raise up children
5:20 I *t* you, unless your holiness surpasses
5:34 What I *t* you is:
7:20 You can *t* a tree by its fruit.
8: 4 "See to it that you *t* no one.
8: 9 If I *t* my slave, 'Do this,' he does it."
10:27 What I *t* you in darkness,
11: 8 *T* me, what did you go out to see
12:33 other, for you can *t* a tree by its fruit.
14:28 you, *t* me to come to you across the water."
16:20 not to *t* anyone that he was the Messiah.
17: 9 "Do not *t* anyone of the vision until the
18:19 "Again I *t* you,
21: 5 *T* the daughter of Zion,
21:24 then I will *t* you on what authority I do
21:27 "Then neither will I *t* you on what
21:43 For this reason, I *t* you,
22: 4 *T* those who were invited,
23: 3 and observe everything they *t* you.
23:39 I *t* you, you will not see me
24: 3 *T* us, when will all this occur?
24:26 so if they *t* you, 'Look, he is in the desert,'
25:12 But he answered, 'I *t* you,
26:18 "Go to this man in the city and *t* him,
26:29 I *t* you, I will not drink this fruit
26:63 "I order you to *t* us under oath before
26:64 But I *t* you this:
27:64 may go and steal him and *t* the people,
28: 7 Then go quickly and *t* the disciples:
Mk 1:30 thing they did was to *t* him about her.
7:36 he enjoined them strictly not to *t* anyone;
8:30 strict orders not to *t* anyone about him.
9: 9 them not to *t* anyone what they had seen,
10:32 to *t* them what was going to happen to him.
11:29 I will *t* you on what authority I do the
11:30 *T* me, was John's baptism of divine origin
11:33 "Then neither will I *t* you on what
13: 4 *T* us, when will this occur?
14:69 on him, started again to *t* the bystanders,
16: 7 Go now and *t* his disciples and Peter,
Lk 3: 8 I *t* you, God can raise up children
5:14 *T* no one, but go and show yourself
7: 6 house, the centurion sent friends to *t* him:
7: 9 which was following him to say, "I *t* you,
7:47 I *t* you, that is why her many sins
8:56 them not to *t* anyone what had happened.
9:21 strictly forbade them to *t* this to anyone.
9:44 "Pay close attention to what I *t* you:
10:24 I *t* you, many prophets and kings
10:40 *T* her to help me."
11: 8 I *t* you, even though he does not get up
11:51 Yes, I *t* you, this generation
12: 5 Yes, I *t* you, fear him.
12: 8 "I *t* you, whoever acknowledges me
12:13 *t* my brother to give me my share of our
12:27 but I *t* you, Solomon in all his splendor
12:37 I *t* you, he will put on an apron,
12:57 *T* me, why do you not judge
13: 3 But I *t* you, you will all come
13: 5 But I *t* you, you will all come to the same
13:24 Many, I *t* you, will try to enter
13:27 But he will answer, 'I *t* you,
13:32 "Go *t* that fox, 'Today and tomorrow
14:24 but I *t* you that not one of those invited
15: 7 I *t* you, there will likewise be more joy
15:10 I *t* you, there will be the same kind of joy
17:20 "You cannot *t* by careful watching when
17:23 They will *t* you he is to be found in this
17:34 I *t* you, on that night there will be two
18: 8 I *t* you, he will give them swift justice.
18:17 Trust me when I *t* you that whoever does
19:11 to these things he went on to *t* a parable,
19:40 I *t* you the very stones would cry out."
20: 2 approached him with the question, *T* us,
20: 8 will I *t* you by whose authority I act."
20: 9 to *t* the people the following parable:
20:16 I will *t* you.
21:32 Let me *t* you this:
22:16 I *t* you, I will not eat again
22:18 I *t* you, from now on I will not drink
22:34 Jesus replied, "I *t* you,
22:37 among the wicked,' and this, I *t* you,
22:66 him before their council, they said, *T* us,
22:67 He replied, "If I *t* you,
Jn 1:22 *T* us who you are,
1:41 was seek out his brother Simon and *t* him,
1:51 He went on to *t* them,
3: 7 *t* you you must all be begotten from above.
3:12 believe when I *t* you about earthly things,
3:12 believe when I *t* you about those of heaven?
4:25 "When he comes, he will *t* us everything."
7:47 "Do not *t* us you too have been taken in!"
7:52 "Do not *t* us you are a Galilean too,"
8:26 *t* the world what I have heard from him,
8:38 I *t* you what I have seen in the Father's
9:27 *t* me you want to become his disciples too?"
10: 6 did not grasp what he was trying to *t* them.
10:24 are the Messiah, *t* us so in plain words."
10:25 "I did *t* you, but you do not believe.
12:22 Philip went to *t* Andrew;
13:19 I *t* you this now, before it takes place,
13:21 "I *t* you solemnly, one of you will betray
13:38 "I *t* you truly, the cock will not crow
14:29 I *t* you this now, before it takes place,
15:11 All this I *t* you that my joy may be yours
16: 7 Yet I *t* you the sober truth:
16:12 I have much more to *t* you,
16:20 "I *t* you truly:
16:25 *t* you about the Father in plain speech.
16:33 I *t* you all this that in me you may find
19:21 priests of the Jews tried to *t* Pilate,
20:15 *t* me where you have laid him and I will
20:17 Rather, go to my brothers and *t* them,
21:18 "I *t* you solemnly:
Acts 5: 8 Peter said to her, *T* me,
8:34 The eunuch said to Philip, *T* me,
11:14 In the light of what he will *t* you,
17:21 than to *t* about or listen to something new.)
19: 4 He used to *t* the people about the one who
21: 4 they tried to *t* Paul that he should not go
21:23 Please do as we *t* you.
23:18 you this boy, who has something to *t* you."
23:22 *t* anyone that you gave me this information."
1Cor 7:29 I *t* you, brothers, the time is short.
12: 3 That is why I *t* you that nobody who speaks
15:12 *T* me, if Christ is preached as raised from
15:51 Now I am going to *t* you a mystery.
2Cor 6:16 *T* me what agreement there is between the
12:19 Before God I *t* you,
Gal 4:16 your enemy just because I *t* you the truth?
4:21 who want to be subject to the law, *t* me:
5: 2 when I *t* you that if you have yourselves
Col 2: 4 I *t* you all this so that no one may delude

4: 9 They will *t* you all that has happened here.
2Thes 2: 5 do you not remember how I used to *t* you
1Tm 6:17 *T* those who are rich in this world's goods
Ti 2: 2 *T* the older men that they must be temperate,
2: 6 *T* the young men to keep themselves
3: 2 *T* them not to speak evil of anyone or be
Heb 11:32 I have no time to *t* of Gideon,

TELLING (33)

Gn 31:20 by not *t* him of his intended flight.
43: 6 by *t* the man that you had another brother?"
46:31 "I will go and inform Pharaoh, *t* him:
Ex 33:12 indeed, are *t* me to lead this people on;
Jos 7:19 glory and honor by *t* me what you have done;
Jgs 7:13 one man was *t* another about a dream.
14: 9 without *t* them that he had scooped the
2Sm 13:34 *t* the king that he had seen some men
1Kgs 10: 7 that they were not *t* me the half.
Tb 10: 6 But Tobit kept *t* her:
1Mc 9:60 *t* them to seize Jonathan and his
Sir 7:13 Delight not in *t* lie after lie,
Jer 35:15 servants the prophets, *t* you to turn back,
51:31 *T* the king of Babylon that all his city is
Mk 10:49 the blind man over, *t* him as they did so,
Lk 9:36 *t* nothing of what they had seen at that
Jn 5:10 Jews began *t* the man who had been cured,
8:25 I have been *t* you from the beginning.
8:46 If I am *t* the truth,
9:11 on my eyes, *t* me to go to Siloam and wash.
13:29 *t* him to buy what was needed for the feast,
16: 4 comes you may remember my *t* you of them.
18:34 own, or have others been *t* you about me?"
20:25 The other disciples kept *t* him:
Acts 8:35 point, *t* him the good news of Jesus.
15: 3 *t* everyone about the conversion of the
17: 3 Jesus I am *t* you about is the Messiah!"
20:20 from *t* you what was for your own good,
1Cor 10:14 I am *t* you, whom I love,
2Cor 12: 6 in me because I would only be *t* the truth.
1Thes 3: 6 and *t* us that you constantly remember us
Jude 1:18 how they kept *t* you, "In the last days
Rv 13:14 *t* them to make an idol in honor of the

TELLS (21)

Nm 23:26 you that I must do all that the LORD *t* me?"
Dt 5:27 then tell us what the LORD, our God, *t* you;
15:16 *t* you that he does not wish to leave you,
1Sm 22: 8 no one *t* me that my son has made
1Kgs 22:14 "I shall say whatever the LORD *t* me."
2Chr 18:13 answered, "I will say what my God *t* me."
Tb 1: 1 This book *t* the story of Tobit,
2Mc 2: 4 The same document also *t* how the prophet,
Ps(s) 37:30 The mouth of the just man *t* of wisdom and
147: 4 He *t* the number of the stars;
Prv 12:17 *t* the truth who states what he is sure of,
Sir 6: 9 enemy, and *t* of the quarrel to your shame.
16:20 Who *t* him of just deeds and what could I
Dn 5: 7 reads this writing and *t* me what it means,"
Mt 24:23 If anyone *t* you at that time,
24:48 if the servant is worthless and *t* himself,
Mk 13:21 If anyone *t* you at that time,
14:21 is going the way the Scripture *t* of him.
Jn 2: 5 waiting on table, "Do whatever he *t* you."
19:35 He *t* what he knows is true,
Acts 19:26 He *t* them that man-made gods are no gods

TEMA (5)

Gn 25:15 Mibsam, Mishma, Dumah, Massa, Hadad, *T*,
1Chr 1:30 Mibsam, Mishma, Dumah, Massa, Hadad, *T*,
Jb 6:19 The caravans of *T* search,
Is 21:14 you who dwell in the land of *T*,
Jer 25:23 Dedan and *T* and Buz,

TEMAH (2)

Ezr 2:53 sons of Barkos, sons of Sisera, sons of *T*,
Neh 7:55 sons of Barkos, sons of Sisera, sons of *T*,

TEMAN (14)

Gn 36:11 The sons of Eliphaz were *T*,
36:15 the clans of *T*,
36:42 Jetheth, Oholibamah, Elah, Pinon, Kenaz, *T*,
1Chr 1:36 The sons of Eliphaz were *T*,
1:53 Oholibamah, Elah, Pinon, Kenaz, *T*,
Jb 2:11 Eliphaz from *T*,
Jer 49: 7 Is there no more wisdom in *T*,
49:20 he has made against those that live in *T*:
Bar 3:22 not been heard of in Canaan, nor seen in *T*.
3:23 on earth, the merchants of Midian and *T*,
Ez 25:13 I will make it a waste from *T* to Dedan;
Am 1:12 wrath to the end, I will send fire upon *T*,
Ob 1: 9 Your warriors, O *T*,
Hb 3: 3 God comes from *T*,

TEMANITE (5)

Jb 4: 1 Then spoke Eliphaz the *T*, who said:
15: 1 Then Eliphaz the *T* spoke and said:
22: 1 Then Eliphaz the *T* answered and said:
42: 7 Job, that the LORD said to Eliphaz the *T*,
42: 9 Then Eliphaz the *T*,

TEMANITES (2)

Gn 36:34 Jobab died, Husham, from the land of the *T*,
1Chr 1:45 Jobab died, Husham, from the land of the *T*,

TEMENITES (1)

1Chr 4: 6 Hepher, the *T* and the Ahashtarites.

TEMERITY (1)

Wis 12:17 and in those who know you, you rebuke *t*.

TEMPER (8)

2Mc 4:25 he had the *t* of a cruel tyrant and the
Ps(s) 32: 9 with bit and bridle their *t* must be curbed,
Prv 16:32 than a warrior, and he who rules his *t*,
19:19 The man of violent *t* pays the penalty;
Sir 20: 2 better to admonish than to lose one's *t*,
32: 3 that is only your right, but *t* your wisdom,
Col 3: 8 all the anger and quick *t*,
1Tm 3: 2 married only once, of even *t*,

TEMPERATE (2)

1Tm 3:11 They should be *t* and entirely trustworthy.
Ti 2: 2 Tell the older men that they must be *t*,

TEMPERATELY (1)

Ti 2:12 ways and worldly desires, and live *t*,

TEMPERED (2)

Ps(s) 45: 7 a *t* rod is your royal scepter.
Wis 16:18 For now the flame was *t* so that the beasts

TEMPERS (1)

Wis 7:20 stars, natures of animals, *t* of beasts,

TEMPEST (11)

Jb 9:17 With a *t* he might overwhelm me,
27:20 at night the *t* carries him off.
30:22 I am tossed about by the *t*.
37: 9 Out of its chamber comes forth the *t*;
Ps(s) 55: 9 shelter from the violent storm and the *t*."
83:16 with your *t* and rout them with your storm.
Prv 10:25 When the *t* passes, the wicked man is no
Wis 5:23 confront them and a *t* winnow them out;
Am 1:14 day of battle and stormwind in a time of *t*.
Jon 1: 4 and in the furious *t* that arose the ship
Na 1: 3 In hurricane and *t* is his path,

TEMPEST-DRIVEN (1)

Wis 5:14 borne on the wind, and like fine, *t* foam;

TEMPLE (565)

Gn 38:21 of the place, "Where is the *t* prostitute,
38:21 "There has never been a *t* prostitute here."
38:22 place said there was no *t* prostitute there."
Dt 23:18 be no *t* harlot among the Israelite women,
23:18 nor a *t* prostitute among the Israelite men.
Jgs 4:21 the peg through his *t* down into the ground,
4:22 dead, with the tent peg through his *t*.
5:26 she smashed, stove in his *t*.
9: 4 shekels from the *t* of Baal of Berith,
9:27 a festival and went to the *t* of their god,
9:46 went into the crypt of the *t* of El-berith.
16:26 support the *t* and may rest against them."
16:27 The *t* was full of men and women:
16:29 *t* rested and braced himself against them,
16:30 and the *t* fell upon the lords and all the
1Sm 1: 9 a chair near the doorpost of the LORD's *t*.
1:24 him at the *t* of the LORD in Shiloh.
3: 3 the *t* of the LORD where the ark of God was.
3:15 and opened the doors of the *t* of the LORD.
5: 2 of God and brought it into the *t* of Dagon,
5: 5 enter the *t* of Dagon tread on the threshold
31:10 They put his armor in the *t* of Astarte,
2Sm 22: 7 From his *t* he heard my voice,
1Kgs 3: 1 building his palace, and the *t* of the LORD,
3: 2 *t* had been built to the name of the LORD.
5:17 could not build a *t* in honor of the LORD,
5:19 purpose to build a *t* in honor of the LORD,
5:19 place who shall build the *t* in my honor.'
5:31 to give the *t* a foundation of hewn stone.
5:32 the wood and stones for building the *t*.
6: 1 of the *t* of the LORD was begun.
6: 2 The *t* which King Solomon built for the
6: 3 the *t* was twenty cubits from side to side,
6: 3 and ten cubits deep in front of the *t*.
6: 4 with trellises were made for the *t*,
6: 5 temple, and adjoining the wall of the *t*,
6: 6 were offsets along the outside of the *t*
6: 6 not be fastened into the walls of the *t*.
6: 7 *t* was built of stone dressed at the quarry,
6: 7 be heard in the *t* during its construction.)
6: 8 the annex was at the right side of the *t*,
6: 9 When the *t* was built to its full height,
6:10 was built all along the outside of the *t*,
6:12 "As to this *t* you are building
6:14 When Solomon finished building the *t*,
6:16 At the rear of the *t* a space of twenty
6:17 or part of the *t* in front of the sanctuary,
6:18 The cedar in the interior of the *t* was
6:19 In the innermost part of the *t* was located
6:21 the interior of the *t* with pure gold.
6:22 The entire *t* was overlaid with gold so
6:27 were placed in the inmost part of the *t*,
6:37 The foundations of the LORD's *t* were laid
7:12 of the *t* of the LORD and the temple porch.
7:21 erected adjacent to the porch of the *t*,
7:39 south side of the *t* and five on the north.
7:39 the southeast from the south side of the *t*.
7:40 work for King Solomon in the *t* of the LORD:
7:45 the *t* of the LORD were of burnished bronze.
7:48 made for the interior of the *t* of the LORD:
7:51 Solomon in the *t* of the LORD was completed,
7:51 in the treasuries of the *t* of the LORD.
8: 6 the sanctuary, the holy of holies of the *t*.
8:10 the cloud filled the *t* of the LORD so that
8:11 LORD's glory had filled the *t* of the LORD.
8:16 Israel for the building of a *t* to my honor;
8:17 to build a *t* to the honor of the LORD,
8:18 him, 'In wishing to build a *t* to my honor,
8:19 not be you, however, who will build the *t*;
8:19 from you, he shall build the *t* to my honor.'
8:20 and I have built this *t* to honor the LORD,
8:27 how much less this *t* which I have built!
8:29 your eyes watch night and day over this *t*,
8:31 the oath before your altar in this *t*,
8:33 pray to you, and entreat you in this *t*,
8:38 stretching out his hands toward this *t*,
8:42 when he comes and prays toward this *t*,
8:43 and may acknowledge that this *t* which I
8:44 and the *t* I have built in your honor,
8:48 and the *t* I have built in your honor,
8:63 the Israelites dedicated the *t* of the LORD.
8:64 of the court facing the *t* of the LORD;
9: 1 finished building the *t* of the LORD,
9: 3 consecrated this *t* which you have built;
9: 7 the *t* I have consecrated to my honor.
9: 8 and this *t* shall become a heap of ruins.
9: 8 LORD done this to the land and to this *t*?'
9:10 the *t* of the LORD and the palace of the
9:15 levied in order to build the *t* of the LORD,
9:25 and he kept the *t* in repair.
10: 5 holocausts he offered in the *t* of the LORD,
10:12 king made supports for the *t* of the LORD
12:27 in the *t* of the LORD in Jerusalem,
14:26 including the treasures of the *t* of the LORD
14:28 the king visited the *t* of the LORD,
15:12 banishing the *t* prostitutes from the land
15:15 He brought into the *t* of the LORD his
15:18 the *t* of the LORD and of the royal palace.
16:32 in the *t* of Baal which he built in Samaria,
2Kgs 5:18 enters the *t* of Rimmon to worship there,
5:18 adjutant, must bow down in the *t* of Rimmon.
10:21 without exception came into the *t* of Baal,
10:23 entered the *t* of Baal and said to the
10:25 into the inner shrine of the *t* of Baal,
11: 3 he remained hidden in the *t* of the LORD,
11: 4 had them come to him in the *t* of the LORD,
11: 7 guard over the *t* of the LORD for the king.
11:10 shields, which were in the *t* of the LORD.
11:11 the altar and the *t* on the king's behalf.
11:13 appeared before them in the *t* of the LORD.
11:15 should not be slain in the *t* of the LORD.
11:18 went to the *t* of Baal and demolished it.
11:18 a detachment for the *t* of the LORD,
11:19 led the king down from the *t* of the LORD
12: 5 that are brought to the *t* of the LORD
12: 5 are freely brought to the *t* of the LORD
12: 6 repairs on the *t* may prove necessary."
12: 7 had not made needed repairs on the *t*.
12: 8 "Why do you not repair the *t*?"
12: 9 the people nor make the repairs on the *t*.
12:10 the right as one entered the *t* of the LORD.
12:10 that were brought to the *t* of the LORD.
12:11 the funds that were in the *t* of the LORD,
12:12 to the master workmen in the *t* of the LORD.
12:12 and builders working in the *t* of the LORD,
12:13 that were necessary to repair the *t*.
12:14 None of the funds brought to the *t* of the
12:15 with them they repaired the *t* of the LORD.
12:17 were not brought to the *t* of the LORD;
12:19 in the treasuries of the *t* and the palace,
14:14 utensils there were in the *t* of the LORD
15:35 built the Upper Gate of the *t* of the LORD.
16: 8 and gold that were in the *t* of the LORD
16:14 LORD he brought from the front of the *t*—
16:14 the new altar and the *t* of the LORD
16:18 the king of Assyria he removed from the *t*
16:18 which had been built in the *t* for a throne,
18:15 *t* of the LORD and in the palace treasuries.
18:16 the uprights of the *t* of the LORD
19: 1 sackcloth, and went into the *t* of the LORD.
19:14 then he went up to the *t* of the LORD,
19:37 was worshiping in the *t* of his god Nisroch,
20: 5 three days you shall go up to the LORD's *t*;
20: 8 up to the *t* of the LORD on the third day?"
21: 4 He built altars in the *t* of the LORD,
21: 5 host of heaven, in the two courts of the *t*.
21: 7 idol he had made, he set up in the *t*,

TEMPLE (cont.)
21: 7 “In this *t* and in Jerusalem,
22: 3 to the *t* of the LORD with orders to go to
22: 4 that had been donated to the *t* of the LORD,
22: 5 to the master workmen in the *t* of the LORD,
22: 5 and lumbermen making repairs on the *t*,
22: 6 of wood and hewn stone for the *t* repairs.
22: 8 the book of the law in the *t* of the LORD.”
22: 9 metals available in the *t* and have consigned
22: 9 to the master workmen in the *t* of the LORD.”
23: 2 The king went up to the *t* of the LORD with
23: 2 that had been found in the *t* of the LORD,
23: 4 remove from the *t* of the LORD all the
23: 6 From the *t* of the LORD he also removed the
23: 7 which were in the *t* of the LORD,
23:11 were at the entrance of the *t* of the LORD,
23:12 in the two courts of the *t* of the LORD.
23:24 Helkiah had found in the *t* of the LORD.
23:27 which I chose, and the *t* of which I said,
24:13 the *t* of the LORD and those of the palace,
24:13 Israel, had provided in the *t* of the LORD,
1Chr 5:36 priest in the *t* Solomon built in Jerusalem.
6:17 built the *t* of the LORD in Jerusalem,
9: 2 the priests, the Levites, and the *t* slaves.
10:10 his skull they impaled on the *t* of Dagon.
2Chr 4:10 the southeast from the right side of the *t*.
5: 1 for the *t* of the LORD had been completed,
5: 7 the sanctuary, the holy of holies of the *t*.
5:13 of the LORD's *t* was filled with a cloud.
6: 5 Israel for the building of a *t* to my honor,
6: 7 to build a *t* to the honor of the LORD,
6: 8 ‘In wishing to build a *t* to my honor,
6: 9 However, you shall not build the *t*;
6: 9 you will beget shall build the *t* to my
6:10 have built the *t* to the honor of the LORD,
6:18 how much less this *t* which I have built!
6:20 your eyes watch day and night over this *t*,
6:22 for the oath before your altar in this *t*,
6:24 pray to you and entreat you in this *t*,
6:29 stretches out his hands toward this *t*,
6:32 arm, when they come in prayer to this *t*,
7:21 This *t* which is so exalted
9:11 *t* of the LORD and the palace of the king;
12: 9 *t* of the LORD and of the king's palace.
12:11 the king visited the *t* of the LORD,
16: 2 gold from the treasuries of the *t* of the LORD
23: 5 will be in the courts of the LORD's *t*.
23:10 the altar and the *t* on the king's behalf.
23:12 went to the people in the *t* of the LORD.
23:14 must not put her to death in the LORD's *t*.”
23:17 went to the *t* of Baal and tore it down.
23:18 *t* into the hands of the levitical priests,
23:18 *t* for offering the holocausts of the LORD,
23:19 guards at the gates of the LORD's *t*
24: 4 Joash decided to restore the LORD's *t*.
24: 7 the dedicated resources of the LORD's *t*.
24: 8 they put outside the gate of the LORD's *t*.
24:12 in charge of the labor on the LORD's *t*,
24:12 masons and carpenters to restore the *t*,
24:14 it made into utensils for the LORD's *t*,
24:14 They offered holocausts in the LORD's *t*
24:16 particular with respect to God and his *t*.
24:18 They forsook the *t* of the LORD,
24:21 him to death in the court of the LORD's *t*.
26:16 He entered the *t* of the LORD to make an
26:20 was leprous, they expelled him from the *t*.
27: 2 though he did not enter the *t* of the LORD;
29:16 they found in the LORD's *t* that was unclean
32:21 And when he entered the *t* of his god,
33: 4 He even built altars in the *t* of the LORD,
34: 8 order to cleanse the *t* as well as the land,
34:10 who were restoring and repairing the *t*.
35:20 Josiah had done all this to restore the *t*,
36:10 precious vessels from the *t* of the LORD.
36:14 *t* which he had consecrated in Jerusalem.
Ezr 2:43 The *t* slaves: sons of Ziha,
2:58 The total of the *t* slaves and the
2:69 to the treasury for the *t* service:
2:70 and the *t* slaves dwelt in their cities.
3: 6 of the *t* of the LORD had not yet been laid.
3:10 had laid the foundation of the LORD's *t*,
4: 1 the exiles were building a *t* for the LORD,
5:14 Nebuchadnezzar had taken from the *t*
5:14 and carried off to the *t* in Babylon,
5:14 Cyrus ordered to be removed from the *t*
5:15 and deposit them in the *t* of Jerusalem,
6: 5 Nebuchadnezzar took from the *t* of Jerusalem
6: 5 to be returned to their place in the *t* of
7: 7 and *t* slaves also came up to Jerusalem in
7:24 Levite, singer, gatekeeper, *t* slave,
8:17 brethren, and to the *t* slaves in Casiphia,
8:20 Of the *t* slaves (those whom David and the
Neh 3:27 [the *t* slaves were dwelling on Ophel].
3:31 quarters of the *t* slaves and the merchants,
6:10 in the house of God, inside the *t* building;
6:10 let us lock the doors of the *t*.
6:11 a man like me enter the *t* to save his life?
7:46 The *t* slaves:
7:60 The total of the *t* slaves and the
7:70 to the treasury for the *t* service:
7:72 the gatekeepers, the singers, the *t* slaves,
10:29 Levites, gatekeepers, singers, *t* slaves,
11: 3 lay Israelites, priests, Levites, *t* slaves,
11:12 brethren who carried out the *t* service,
11:21 The *t* slaves lived on Ophel.
11:21 and Gishpa were in charge of the *t* slaves.
Tb 1: 4 offer sacrifice in the place where the *t*,
14: 4 God's *t* there shall be burnt to the ground
14: 5 They shall rebuild the *t*,
14: 5 In her the *t* of God shall also be rebuilt;
Jdt 4: 2 for Jerusalem and the *t* of the Lord,
4: 3 and the *t* been purified from profanation.
4:11 themselves in front of the *t* building,
5:18 The *t* of their God was razed to the ground,
8:24 and the defense of the sanctuary, the *t*,
9: 1 in the *t* of God in Jerusalem that evening,
9:13 things against your covenant, your holy *t*,
Est 4:20 the glory of your *t* and your altar;
1Mc 1:22 the golden ornament on the façade of the *t*.
2: 8 “Her *t* has become like a man disgraced,
4:46 stones in a suitable place on the *t* hill,
4:48 interior of the *t* and purified the courts.
4:49 altar of incense, and the table into the *t*.
4:50 the lampstand, and these illuminated the *t*.
4:57 of the *t* with gold crowns and shields;
5:43 and fled to the *t* enclosure at Carnaim.
6: 2 and gold, and that its *t* was very rich,
7:35 return victorious I will burn this *t* down.”
10:41 be handed over for the services of the *t*.
10:43 *t* of Jerusalem or in any of its precincts,
10:83 entered Beth-dagon, the *t* of their idol,
10:84 and destroyed by fire both the *t* of Dagon
11: 4 was shown the *t* of Dagon destroyed by fire,
13:52 of the *t* hill alongside the citadel,
14:15 the *t* splendid and enriched its equipment.
14:31 their country and to lay hands on their *t*,
14:36 *t* and inflict grave injury on its purity.
14:42 over them, and shall have charge of the *t*,
14:48 place in the precincts of the *t*,
15: 7 Jerusalem and its *t* shall be free.
15: 9 honor you and your nation and the *t*,
16:20 to seize Jerusalem and the mount of the *t*.
2Mc 1:13 they were cut to pieces in the *t* of the
1:15 a few attendants came to the *t* precincts.
1:15 As soon as he entered the *t*,
1:18 be celebrating the purification of the *t*
1:18 the rebuilder of the *t* and the altar,
2: 9 the dedication and the completion of the *t*.
2:16 the feast of the purification of the *t*,
2:19 of the purification of the great *t*,
2:22 regained possession of the world-famous *t*,
3: 2 the *t* with the most magnificent gifts.
3: 4 been appointed superintendent of the *t*,
3:12 of a *t* venerated all over the world.
3:30 and the *t*, charged so shortly before
4:14 the *t* and neglecting the sacrifices,
4:32 the *t* and presented them to Andronicus;
5:15 dared to enter the holiest *t* in the world;
5:21 off eighteen hundred talents from the *t*,
6: 2 also to profane the *t* in Jerusalem and
6: 4 filled the *t* with debauchery and revelry;
6: 4 into the *t* things that were forbidden,
8: 2 to have pity on the *t*,
9: 2 to rob the *t* and gain control of the city.
9:16 holy *t* which he had previously despoiled;
10: 1 had recovered the *t* and the city,
10: 3 After purifying the *t*,
10: 5 the *t* had been profaned by the Gentiles,
10: 5 the purification of the *t* took place.
11: 3 to levy tribute on the *t*,
11:25 our decision is that their *t* be restored
13:11 law, their country, and their holy *t*;
13:14 fight nobly to death for the laws, the *t*,
13:23 and honored the *t* with a generous donation.
14: 4 of the customary olive branches from the *t*.
14:13 up Alcimus as high priest of the great *t*.
14:31 the man, he went to the great and holy *t*,
14:33 hand toward the *t* and swore this oath:
14:33 and erect here a splendid *t* to Dionysus.”
14:35 of a *t* for your dwelling place among us.
15:17 *t* with the sacred vessels were in danger.
15:33 other wages of his folly opposite the *t*.
Ps(s) 5: 8 worship at your holy *t* in fear of you,
11: 4 The LORD is in his holy *t*;
18: 7 From his *t* he heard my voice,
27: 4 of the LORD and contemplate his *t*.
29: 9 strips the forests, and in his *t* all say,
48:10 God, we ponder your kindness within your *t*.
65: 5 of your house, the holy things of your *t*!
68:30 For your *t* in Jerusalem let the kings
79: 1 they have defiled your holy *t*,
138: 2 your holy *t* and give thanks to your name,
144:12 such as stand at the corners of the *t*.
Wis 3:14 a more gratifying heritage in the Lord's *t*.
9: 8 You have bid me build a *t* on your holy
Sir 36:13 with your majesty, your *t* with your glory.
49:12 They erected the holy *t*,
50: 1 in whose days the *t* was reinforced.
50: 2 with powerful turrets for the *t* precincts;
50: 7 Like the sun shining upon the *t*,
Is 6: 1 the train of his garment filling the *t*.
37: 1 sackcloth, and went into the *t* of the LORD.
37:14 then he went up to the *t* of the LORD,
37:38 was worshiping in the *t* of his god Nisroch,
38: 5 three days you shall go up to the LORD's *t*;
38:22 that I shall go up to the *t* of the LORD?”
44:28 “Let her be rebuilt,” and of the *t*,
64:10 Our holy and glorious *t* in which our
66: 6 roaring from the city, a sound from the *t*,
Jer 7: 4 “This is the *t* of the LORD!
7: 4 The *t* of the LORD!
7: 4 The *t* of the LORD!”
24: 1 of figs placed before the *t* of the LORD.
26:18 of ruins, and the *t* mount a forest ridge.
28: 3 of the *t* of the LORD which Nebuchadnezzar,
43:13 He shall smash the obelisks of the *t* of
51:11 vengeance of the LORD, vengeance for his *t*.
Bar 1: 8 the Lord that had been removed from the *t*,
6:54 For when fire breaks out in the *t* of these
Ez 8: 4 stationed to the right of the *t*
8:14 the entrance of the north gate of the *t*,
8:16 and there at the door of the LORD's *t*,
8:16 LORD's *t* and their faces toward the east;
9: 6 [the elders] who were in front of the *t*.
9: 7 Defile the *t*, he said to them,
10: 2 it had been, to the threshold of the *t*.
10: 4 threshold of the *t*; the *t* was filled
10:18 of the *t* and rested upon the cherubim.
11: 1 and brought me to the east gate of the *t*.
40: 5 wall that completely surrounded the *t*.
40:45 for the priests who have charge of the *t*,
40:47 The altar stood in front of the *t*.
40:48 *t* and measured the pilasters on each side,
41: 5 Then he measured the wall of the *t*,
41: 5 which extended all the way around the *t*,
41: 6 of the *t* that enclosed the side chambers;
41: 6 were no supports in the *t* wall proper.
41: 7 for the *t* was enclosed all the way around
41: 7 therefore the *t* had a broad way running
41: 8 About the *t* was a raised pavement
41: 8 Between the side chambers of the *t* and the
41:10 twenty cubits wide going all around the *t*.
41:13 He measured the *t*,
41:14 The façade of the *t*,
41:17 interior part of the *t* as well as outside,
41:19 on every side throughout the whole *t*.
41:26 vestibule, and the side chambers of the *t*.
42:15 he had finished measuring the inner *t* area,
43: 4 *t* by way of the gate which faces the east,
43: 5 *t* was filled with the glory of the LORD.
43: 6 I heard someone speaking to me from the *t*,
43:10 describe the *t* to the house of Israel
43:11 to them the form and design of the *t*,
43:12 This is the law of the *t*:
43:21 to be burnt in a designated part of the *t*,
44: 4 of the north gate to the façade of the *t*,
44: 4 the glory of the LORD filling the LORD's *t*,
44: 5 the statutes and laws of the LORD's *t*;
44: 5 those who are to be admitted to the *t*
44: 8 Instead of caring for the service of my *t*,
44:11 my sanctuary as gatekeepers and *t* servants;
44:14 I will set them to the service of the *t*,
44:17 gates of the inner court or within the *t*.
45: 5 for the Levites, the ministers of the *t*,
45:19 and put it on the doorposts of the *t*,
45:20 thus you shall make atonement for the *t*.
46:24 “These are the kitchens where the *t*
47: 1 brought me back to the entrance of the *t*,
47: 1 the threshold of the *t* toward the east,
47: 1 the façade of the *t* was toward the east;
47: 1 down from the southern side of the *t*,
48:21 sanctuary of the *t* shall be in the middle.
Dn 1: 2 and some of the vessels of the *t* of God,
1: 2 and placed in the *t* treasury of his god.
3:53 are you in the *t* of your holy glory,
5: 2 father, had taken from the *t* in Jerusalem,
5:23 the vessels of his *t* brought before you,
9:27 On the *t* wing shall be the horrible
14:10 king went with Daniel into the *t* of Bel,
14:14 which they scattered through the whole *t*;
14:22 over to Daniel, who destroyed it and its *t*.
Am 7:13 it is the king's sanctuary and a royal *t*.”
8: 3 *t* songs shall become wailings on that day,
Jon 2: 5 yet would I again look upon your holy *t*.”
2: 8 My prayer reached you in your holy *t*.
Mi 1: 2 against you, the Lord from his holy *t*.
3:12 And the mount of the *t* to a forest ridge.
Na 1:14 From your *t* I will abolish the carved and
Hb 2:20 But the LORD is in his holy *t*;
Hg 2:15 laid upon a stone in the *t* of the LORD,
2:18 day on which the *t* of the LORD was founded,
Zec 5:11 build a *t* for it in the land of Shinar;
5:11 when the *t* is ready, they will deposit
6:12 and he shall build the *t* of the LORD.
6:13 Yes, he shall build the *t* of the LORD,
6:14 in the *t* of the LORD in favor of Heldai,
6:15 shall come and build the *t* of the LORD,
8: 9 hosts was laid for the building of the *t*.
Mal 1:10 that one among you would shut the *t* gates
2:11 has profaned the *t* which the LORD loves,
3: 1 will come to the *t* the LORD whom you seek,
Mt 4: 5 city, set him on the parapet of the *t*,
12: 5 priests on *t* duty can break the sabbath rest
12: 6 there is something greater than the *t* here.
17:24 of the *t* tax approached Peter and said,
17:24 said, “Does your master not pay the *t* tax?”
17:27 there a coin worth twice the *t* tax.
21:12 Jesus entered the *t* precincts and drove
21:14 to him inside the *t* area and he cured them.

21:15 were shouting out in the *t* precincts,
21:23 After Jesus had entered the *t* precincts,
23:16 'If a man swears by the *t* it means nothing,
23:16 by the gold of the *t* he is obligated.'
23:17 the gold or the *t* which makes it sacred?
23:21 The man who swears by the *t* is swearing by
23:35 between the *t* building and the altar.
23:38 'You will find your *t* deserted.'
24: 1 Jesus left the *t* precincts then,
24: 1 out to him the buildings of the *t* area.
26:55 to day I sat teaching in the *t* precincts,
27: 5 Judas flung the money into the *t* and left.
27: 6 in the *t* treasury since it is blood money."
27:40 destroy the *t* and rebuild it in three days!
Mk 11:11 Jerusalem and went into the *t* precincts.
11:15 he entered the *t* precincts and began to drive
11:16 anyone to carry things through the *t* area.
11:27 in the *t* precincts the chief priests,
12:35 in the *t* precincts he went on to say:
13: 1 As he was making his way out of the *t* area,
13: 3 on the Mount of Olives facing the *t*,
14:49 reach daily, teaching in the *t* precincts,
14:54 he found a seat with the *t* guard
14:58 'I will destroy this *t* made by human hands,'
15:29 destroy the *t* and rebuild it in three days!
Lk 1:21 Zechariah, wondering at his delay in the *t*.
2:27 He came to the *t* now,
2:37 She was constantly in the *t*,
2:46 the *t* sitting in the midst of the teachers,
4: 9 set him on the parapet of the *t*,
13:35 Your *t* will be abandoned.
18:10 "Two men went up to the *t* to pray;
18:14 from the *t* justified but the other did not.
19:45 *t* and began ejecting the traders saying:
19:47 was teaching in the *t* area from day to day.
20: 1 in the *t* and proclaiming the good news,
21: 5 Some were speaking of how the *t* was
21:37 He would teach in the *t* by day,
21:38 all the people came to hear him in the *t*.
22:52 chief priests, the chiefs of the *t* guard,
22:53 the *t* you never raised a hand against me.
24:53 they were to be found in the *t* constantly,
Jn 2:14 In the *t* precincts he came upon people
2:15 sheep and oxen alike out of the *t* area,
2:19 "Destroy this *t*," was Jesus' answer,
2:20 "This *t* took forty-six years to build,
2:21 he was talking about the *t* of his body.
5:14 him in the *t* precincts and said to him:
7:14 went into the *t* area and began to teach.
7:28 Jesus, who was teaching in the *t* area,
7:32 together sent *t* guards to arrest him.
7:45 When the *t* guards came back,
8: 2 At daybreak he reappeared in the *t* area;
8:20 words while teaching at the *t* treasury.
8:59 himself and slipped out of the *t* precincts.
10:23 Jesus was walking in the *t* area,
11:56 in the *t* vicinity saying to each other,
18:20 *t* area where all the Jews come together.
19: 6 and the *t* guards saw him they shouted,
Acts 2:46 They went to the *t* area together every day,
3: 1 the *t* for prayer at the three o'clock hour,
3: 2 put him at the *t* gate called "the Beautiful"
3: 8 He went into the *t* with them
3:10 used to sit at the Beautiful Gate of the *t*.
4: 1 the priests, the captain of the *t* guard,
5:20 take your place in the *t* precincts
5:21 the *t* at dawn and resumed their teaching.
5:22 But when the *t* guard got to the jail they
5:24 the captain of the *t* guard and the high
5:25 in jail are standing over there in the *t*,
5:42 Day after day, both in the *t* and at home,
14:13 Even the priest of the *t* of Zeus,
19:27 but even that the *t* of the great goddess
19:35 custodian of the *t* of the great Artemis,
21:26 Then he entered the *t* precincts to give
21:27 recognized Paul in the *t* precincts
21:28 *t* area and thus profaned this sacred place."
21:29 that Paul had brought him into the *t*.
21:30 seized Paul, dragged him outside the *t*,
22:17 I was praying in the court of the *t*,
24: 6 He even tried to desecrate our *t*,
24:12 Neither in the *t* area,
24:18 found me in the *t* court completing the rites
25: 8 or against the *t* or against the emperor."
26:21 me in the *t* court and tried to murder me.
1Cor 3:16 you not aware that you are the *t* of God,
3:17 If anyone destroys God's *t*,
3:17 temple of God is holy, and you are that *t*.
6:19 that your body is a *t* of the Holy Spirit,
8:10 reclining at table in the *t* of an idol,
9:13 work in the *t* are supported by the temple,
2Cor 6:16 there is between the *t* of God and idols.
6:16 You are the *t* of the living God,
Eph 2:21 and takes shape as a holy *t* in the Lord;
2:22 in him you are being built into this *t*,
2Thes 2: 4 *t* and even declares himself to be God
Rv 3:12 *t* of my God and he shall never leave it.
7:15 and night they minister to him in his *t*;
11: 1 take the measurements of God's *t* and altar,
11: 2 Exclude the outer court of the *t*,
11:19 God's *t* in heaven opened and in the *t*
14:15 Another angel came out of the *t* and in a
14:17 out of the *t* in heaven came another angel,
21:22 I saw no *t* in the city.
21:22 The Lord, God the Almighty, is its *t*—

TEMPLE-CITADEL (1)

Neh 2: 8 wood for timbering the gates of the *t*

TEMPLE-GATE (1)

Jer 36:10 house, at the entrance of the New *T*,

TEMPLE-ROBBERS (1)

Acts 19:37 men whom you have brought here are not *t*.

TEMPLES (12)

Lv 19:27 Do not clip your hair at the *t*,
1Kgs 12:31 He also built *t* on the high places and
Jdt 4: 1 despoiled all their *t* and destroyed them,
1Mc 1:47 to build pagan altars and *t* and shrines,
Jer 9:25 and the desert dwellers who shave their *t*.
25:23 all the desert dwellers who shave their *t*;
43:12 He shall set fire to the *t* of Egypt's gods,
43:13 with fire the *t* of the Egyptian gods.
49:32 to the winds those who shave their *t*,
Bar 6:30 and in their *t* the priests squat with torn
Jl 4: 5 brought my precious treasures into your *t*!
Rom 2:22 You who abhor idols, do you rob *t*?

TEMPORAL (1)

Rom 15:27 to contribute to their *t* needs in return.

TEMPORARY (1)

Lv 25:47 has a permanent or a *t* residence among you,

TEMPT (4)

Is 7:12 I will not *t* the LORD!"
Mal 3:15 prosper, and even *t* God with impunity."
1Cor 7: 5 *t* you through your lack of self-control.
Jas 1:14 and lure of his own passion *t* every man.

TEMPTATION (3)

Lk 8:13 for a while, but fall away in time of *t*.
Gal 6: 1 you trying to avoid falling into *t* himself.
1Tm 6: 9 to be rich are falling into *t* and a trap.

TEMPTATIONS (1)

Lk 22:28 ones who have stood loyally by me in my *t*.

TEMPTED (11)

Ps(s) 78:18 And they *t* God in their hearts by
78:41 *t* God and provoked the Holy One of Israel.
78:56 *t* and rebelled against God the Most High,
95: 9 in the desert, Where your fathers *t* me;
106:14 in the desert and *t* God in the wilderness.
Mt 4: 1 desert by the Spirit to be *t* by the devil.
Lk 4: 2 forty days, where he was *t* by the devil.
Heb 2:18 he is able to help those who are *t*.
4:15 but one who was *t* in every way that we are,
Jas 1:13 is *t* is free to say, "I am being tempted

TEMPTER (2)

Mt 4: 3 The *t* approached and said to him,
1Thes 3: 5 fearing that the *t* had put you to the test

TEMPTING (2)

Lk 4:13 devil had finished all the *t* he left him,
Rv 2:14 by *t* them to eat food sacrificed to idols

TEMPTS (1)

Jas 1:13 who is beyond the grasp of evil, *t* no one.

TEN (213)

Gn 5:14 of Kenan was nine hundred and *t* years;
16: 3 had lived *t* years in the land of Canaan,
18:32 What if there are at least *t* there?"
18:32 "For the sake of those *t*,"
24:10 servant then took *t* of his master's camels,
24:22 and two gold bracelets weighing *t* shekels,
24:55 stay with us a short while, say *t* days;
32:16 *t* bulls; twenty she-asses and *t* he-asses.
42: 3 So *t* of Joseph's brothers went down to buy
45:23 *t* jackasses loaded with the finest products
45:23 *t* jennies loaded with grain and bread
50:22 He lived a hundred and *t* years.
50:26 Joseph died at the age of a hundred and *t*.
Ex 26:16 The length of each board is to be *t* cubits,
27:12 long, with ten columns and *t* pedestals.
34:28 words of the covenant, the *t* commandments.
36: 8 its *t* sheets woven of fine linen twined,
36:21 The length of each board was *t* cubits,
38:12 long, with ten columns and *t* pedestals,
Lv 26: 8 of you will chase *t* thousand of them,
26:26 *t* women will need but one oven for baking
27: 5 shekels for a youth, and *t* for a maiden;
27: 7 shekels for a man, and *t* for a woman.
Nm 7:14 of *t* shekels' weight filled with incense;
7:20 of *t* shekels' weight filled with incense,
7:26 of *t* shekels' weight filled with incense;
7:32 of *t* shekels' weight filled with incense;
7:38 of *t* shekels' weight filled with incense;
7:44 of *t* shekels' weight filled with incense;
7:50 of *t* shekels' weight filled with incense;
7:56 of *t* shekels' weight filled with incense;
7:62 of *t* shekels' weight filled with incense;
7:68 of *t* shekels' weight filled with incense;
7:74 of *t* shekels' weight filled with incense;
7:80 of *t* shekels' weight filled with incense;
7:86 with incense weighed *t* shekels apiece,
11:19 for one day, or two days, or five, or *t*,
11:32 got the least gathered *t* homers of them.
14:22 have put me to the test *t* times already
29:23 the fourth day you shall offer *t* bullocks,
Dt 4:13 the *t* commandments, which he wrote
10: 4 the *t* commandments which he spoke to you
32:30 or two men put *t* thousand to flight,
Jos 15:57 *t* cities and their villages.
17: 5 Thus *t* shares fell to Manasseh apart from
21: 5 The rest of the Kohathites obtained *t*
21:26 rest of the Kohathite clans were *t* in all.
22:14 son of Eleazar the priest, and *t* princes,
24:29 LORD, died at the age of a hundred and *t*.
Jgs 1: 4 and they slew *t* thousand of them in Bezek.
2: 8 was a hundred and *t* years old when he died;
3:29 they slew about *t* thousand Moabites,
4: 6 you *t* thousand Naphtalites and Zebulunites.
4:10 to Kedesh, and *t* thousand men followed him.
4:14 Tabor, followed by his *t* thousand men.
6:27 So Gideon took *t* of his servants and did
7: 3 the soldiers left, but *t* thousand remained.
12:11 When he had judged Israel for *t* years,
17:10 I will give you *t* silver shekels a year,
20:10 tribes of Israel *t* men for every hundred,
20:10 thousand, a thousand for every *t* thousand,
20:34 *t* thousand picked men from all Israel,
Ru 1: 4 When they had lived there about *t* years,
4: 2 Then Boaz picked out *t* of the elders of
1Sm 1: 8 Am I not more to you than *t* sons?"
14:24 whole people, about *t* thousand combatants,
15: 4 foot soldiers and *t* thousand men of Judah.
17:17 grain and these *t* loaves for your brothers,
17:18 take these *t* cheeses for the field officer.
18: 7 his thousands, and David his *t* thousands."
18: 8 "They give David *t* thousands,
21:12 his thousands, but David his *t* thousands'?"
25: 5 shearing his flock, he sent *t* young men,
25:38 About *t* days later the LORD struck him and
29: 5 his thousands, but David his *t* thousands'?"
2Sm 15:16 except for *t* concubines whom he left
18: 3 You are equal to *t* thousand of us.
18:15 *t* of Joab's young armor-bearers closed in
19:44 "We have *t* shares in the king.
20: 3 he took the *t* concubines whom he had left
1Kgs 5: 3 flour, sixty kors of meal, *t* fatted oxen,
5:28 each month in relays of *t* thousand
6: 3 and *t* cubits deep in front of the temple.
6:23 were two cherubim, each *t* cubits high,
6:24 wing tip to wing tip of each was *t* cubits.
6:26 shape, and each was exactly *t* cubits high.
7:10 some *t* cubits and some eight cubits.
7:23 rim, and measured *t* cubits across,
7:24 it, *t* to the cubit all the way around;
7:27 *T* stands were also made of bronze,
7:37 This was how the *t* stands were made,
7:38 *T* bronze basins were then made,
7:38 basin for the top of each of the *t* stands.
7:43 ten stands, *t* basins on the stands,
11:31 "Take *t* pieces for yourself;
11:31 grasp and will give you *t* of the tribes.
11:33 The *t* I will give you because he has
11:35 that is, the *t* tribes.
14: 3 Take along *t* loaves,
2Kgs 5: 5 set out, taking along *t* silver talents,
5: 5 gold pieces, and *t* festal garments.
13: 7 *t* chariots and ten thousand foot soldiers,
14: 7 *t* thousand Edomites in the Salt Valley,
15:17 began his *t* year reign over Samaria
20: 9 the shadow go forward or back *t* steps?"
20:10 is easy for the shadow to advance *t* steps,"
20:10 "Rather, let it go back *t* steps."
20:11 who made the shadow retreat the *t* steps it
24:14 and men of the army, *t* thousand in number,
25:25 of royal descent, came with *t* men,
1Chr 6:46 The other Kohathites obtained *t* cities by
29: 7 *t* thousand darics of gold, *t* thousand talents
2Chr 4: 1 long, twenty cubits wide and *t* cubits high.
4: 2 was perfectly round, *t* cubits in diameter,
4: 3 of oxen encircled the sea, *t* to the cubit,
4: 6 Then he made *t* basins for washing,
4: 7 of gold, *t* of them as was prescribed,
4: 8 made *t* tables and had them set in the nave,
13:23 time, *t* years of peace began in the land.
25:11 there they killed *t* thousand men of Seir.
25:12 also brought back another *t* thousand alive,
27: 5 together with *t* thousand kors of wheat and
27: 5 kors of wheat and *t* thousand of barley.
30:24 a thousand bulls and *t* thousand sheep.
36: 9 three months [and *t* days] in Jerusalem.
Ezr 1:10 silver bowls, four hundred and *t*;
8:12 and with him one hundred and *t* males;
8:24 Hashabiah, and *t* of their brethren,
Neh 4: 6 and had told us *t* times over that they
5:18 kinds of wine in abundance every *t* days,

TEN (cont.)

11: 1 bring one man in *t* to reside in Jerusalem,
Est 3: 9 to the procurators *t* thousand silver talents
9:10 Aridai, and Vaizatha, the *t* sons of Haman,
9:12 men, as well as the *t* sons of Haman.
9:13 the *t* sons of Haman be hanged on gibbets."
9:14 So the *t* sons of Haman were hanged,
1Mc 4:29 and Judas met them with *t* thousand men.
10:74 Choosing *t* thousand men,
2Mc 12:19 destroyed the force of more than *t* thousand
13: 2 one hundred and *t* thousand foot soldiers,
Jb 19: 3 These *t* times you have reviled me,
Ps(s) 91: 7 your side, *t* thousand at your right side,
Eccl 7:19 man than would be *t* princes in the city,
Wis 7: 2 I was molded into flesh in a *t*'
Sir 23:19 *t* thousand times brighter than the sun,
41: 4 lived a thousand years, a hundred, or *t*,
Is 5:10 *T* acres of vineyard shall yield but one
38: 8 Ahaz go back the *t* steps it has advanced."
38: 8 sun came back the *t* steps it had advanced.
Jer 41: 1 king's nobles, came with *t* men to Gedaliah,
41: 2 of Nethaniah, and the *t* who were with him,
41: 8 were *t* among them who pleaded with Ishmael:
42: 7 *T* days passed before the word of the LORD
Bar 4:28 God, turn now *t* times the more to seek him;
Ez 40:11 gate's entrance, which was *t* cubits wide,
40:49 *t* steps led up to it,
41: 2 The width of the entrance was *t* cubits,
42: 4 *t* cubits broad and a wall of one cubit;
45: 3 thousand cubits long and *t* thousand wide,
45: 5 thousand cubits long and *t* thousand wide
45:14 the kor of *t* liquid measures [or a homer,
45:14 homer, for *t* liquid measures make a homer].
48:10 *t* thousand on the west, *t* thousand on the east,
48:13 twenty-five thousand cubits by *t* thousand.
48:18 *t* thousand cubits to the east and ten
Dn 1:12 "Please test your servants for *t* days.
1:14 this request, and tested them for *t* days;
1:15 after *t* days they looked healthier and
1:20 he found them *t* times better than all the
7: 8 I was considering the *t* horns it had,
7:20 about the *t* horns on its head,
7:24 The *t* horns shall be ten kings rising out
Am 5: 3 out with a hundred shall be left with *t*,
6: 9 there remain *t* men in a single house,
Hg 2:16 for twenty measures, it would yield but *t*;
Zec 5: 2 it is twenty cubits long and *t* cubits wide."
8:23 In those days *t* men of every nationality,
Mt 4:25 him came from Galilee, the *T* Cities,
20:24 The other *t*, on hearing this,
25: 1 "The reign of God can be likened to *t*
25:28 and give it to the man with the *t* thousand.
Mk 5:20 the *T* Cities what Jesus had done for him.
7:31 Galilee, into the district of the *T* Cities.
10:41 The other *t*, on hearing this, became
Lk 14:31 and consider whether, with *t* thousand men,
15: 8 if she has *t* silver pieces and loses one,
17:12 was entering a village, *t* lepers met him.
17:17 to say, "Were not all *t* made whole?
19:13 He summoned *t* of his servants and gave
19:13 and gave them sums of *t* units each,
19:16 sum you gave me has earned you another *t*.'
19:17 For that you can take over *t* villages.'
19:24 he has, and give it to the man with the *t*.'
19:25 'Yes, but he already has *t*,' they said.
Acts 25: 6 spending eight or *t* days in Jerusalem,
1Cor 4:15 you have *t* thousand guardians in Christ,
14:19 others than *t* thousand words in a tongue.
Rv 2:10 you will be tried over a period of *t* days.
12: 3 flaming red, with seven heads and *t* horns;
13: 1 of the sea with *t* horns and seven heads;
13: 1 on its horns were *t* diadems and on its
17: 3 This beast had seven heads and *t* horns.
17:12 The *t* horns you saw represent ten kings
17:16 The *t* horns you saw on the beast will turn

TEN-HORNED (1)

Rv 17: 7 the seven-headed and *t* beast carrying her.

TEN-STRINGED (3)

Ps(s) 33: 2 with the *t* lyre chant his praises.
92: 4 the night, With *t* instrument and lyre,
144: 9 with a *t* lyre I will chant your praise,

TENANT (10)

Lv 22:10 "Neither a lay person nor a priest's *t* or
25:35 to him the privileges of an alien or a *t*,
25:40 be like a hired servant or like your *t*,
Sir 10:21 Be it *t* or wayfarer, alien or pauper,
Mt 21:33 it out to *t* farmers and went on a journey.
Mk 12: 1 it to *t* farmers and went on a journey.
Lk 20: 9 planted a vineyard, leased it to *t* farmers,
20:10 he sent a servant to the *t* farmers
20:14 "But when the *t* farmers saw the son,
20:16 *t* farmers and give the vineyard to others."

TENANTS (11)

Lv 25: 6 hired help and the *t* who live with you,
25:23 you are but aliens who have become my *t*.
2Sm 9:12 *t* of Ziba's family worked for Meribbaal.
Jb 31:39 payment and grieved the hearts of its *t*;
Mt 21:34 to the *t* to obtain his share of the grapes.
21:35 The *t* responded by seizing the slaves.
21:38 saw the son, the *t* said to one another,
21:40 vineyard will do to those *t* when he comes?"
Mk 12: 2 dispatched a man in his service to the *t*
12: 7 But those *t* said to one another,
12: 9 *t* and turn his vineyard over to others.

TEND (9)

Gn 30:31 I will again pasture and *t* your flock,
1Sm 17:15 Saul to *t* his father's sheep at Bethlehem.
17:34 servant used to *t* his father's sheep,
2Sm 7: 7 whom I charged to *t* my people Israel,
Ez 34:11 I myself will look after and *t* my sheep.
34:12 his scattered sheep, so will I *t* my sheep.
Mi 5: 5 shall *t* the land of Assyria with the sword,
Jn 21:16 Jesus replied, *T* my sheep."
Rom 6:22 as you *t* toward eternal life.

TENDED (3)

Gn 29: 9 she was the one who *t* them.
Ps(s) 78:72 And he *t* them with a sincere heart,
Hos 12:13 for a wife Israel *t* sheep.

TENDENCY (2)

Rom 8: 6 The *t* of the flesh is toward death but
8: 7 The flesh in its *t* is at enmity with God;

TENDER (7)

Gn 18: 7 He ran to the herd, picked out a *t*,
1Mc 15: 6 your own money, as legal *t* in your country.
Jb 14: 7 and that its *t* shoots will not cease.
40:27 after time, or address you with *t* words?
Sir 4:10 and he will be more *t* to you than a mother.
Ez 17:22 its topmost branches tear off a *t* shoot,
Mt 24:32 When its branch grows *t* and sprouts leaves,

TENDERLY (1)

Is 40: 2 Speak *t* to Jerusalem,

TENDERNESS (3)

Is 49:15 be without *t* for the child of her womb?
54: 7 you, but with great *t* I will take you back.
Bar 4:15 reverence for age nor *t* for childhood;

TENDING (8)

Gn 37: 2 old, he was *t* the flocks with his brothers;
37:13 you know, are *t* our flocks at Shechem.
37:16 please tell me where they are *t* the flocks?"
Ex 3: 1 *t* the flock of his father-in-law Jethro,
1Sm 16:11 is still the youngest, who is *t* the sheep."
Jdt 8:26 while he was *t* the flocks of Laban,
Jb 1:17 off, and put those *t* them to the sword,
Rom 6:21 now ashamed of, all of them *t* toward death.

TENDRILS (4)

Jer 5:10 Tear away her *t*,
6: 9 like a vintager, repeatedly over the *t*.
48:32 Your *t* trailed down to the sea,
Na 2: 3 have ravaged them and ruined the *t*.

TENDS (5)

Ps(s) 100: 3 his people, the flock he *t*.
Prv 14:23 is profit, but mere talk *t* only to penury.
27:18 He who *t* a fig tree eats its fruit,
Ez 34:12 As a shepherd *t* his flock when he finds
Jas 4: 5 he has implanted in us *t* toward jealousy"?

TENS (7)

Ex 18:21 of hundreds, of fifties, and of *t*.
18:25 of hundreds, of fifties, and of *t*.
Dt 1:15 over hundreds, over fifties and over *t*,
1Mc 3:55 over hundreds, over fifties, and over *t*.
Sir 47: 6 praises and ascribed to him *t* of thousands.
Dn 11:12 his heart, he shall lay low *t* of thousands,
Rv 5:11 and *t* of thousands and they all cried out:

TENSE (1)

Wis 16:24 grows *t* for punishment against the wicked,

TENSION (1)

2Cor 11:28 there is that daily *t* pressing on me,

TENT (316)

Gn 9:21 he became drunk and lay naked inside his *t*.
12: 8 pitching his *t* with Bethel to the west and
13: 3 and Ai where his *t* had formerly stood,
18: 1 Mamre, as he sat in the entrance of his *t*,
18: 2 from the entrance of the *t* to greet them;
18: 6 Abraham hastened into the *t* and told Sarah,
18: 9 "There in the *t*," he replied.
18:10 was listening at the entrance of the *t*,
24:67 Then Isaac took Rebekah into his *t*;
26:25 After he had pitched his *t* there,
31:33 in and searched Jacob's *t* and Leah's tent,
31:33 Leaving Leah's *t*, he went into Rachel's.
31:34 the rest of her *t* without finding them,
33:19 ground on which he had pitched his *t*
35:21 on and pitched his *t* beyond Migdal-eder.
38: 1 *t* near a certain Adullamite named Hirah.
Ex 16:16 each man providing for those of his own *t*."
18: 7 greeted each other, they went into the *t*.
26: 7 be used as a *t* covering over the Dwelling.
26: 9 sixth sheet double at the front of the *t*.
26:11 the loops, to join the *t* into one whole.
26:12 will be an extra half sheet of *t* covering,
26:13 the sheets of the *t* will have an extra
26:14 Over the *t* itself you shall make a
26:36 the *t* make a variegated curtain of violet,
27:19 tent pegs and all the *t* pegs of the court,
27:21 them before the LORD in the meeting *t*,
28:43 whenever they go into the meeting *t*
29: 4 bring to the entrance of the meeting *t*,
29:10 the bullock in front of the meeting *t*.
29:11 the LORD, at the entrance of the meeting *t*.
29:30 who is to enter the meeting *t* to minister
29:32 At the entrance of the meeting *t* Aaron and
29:42 the LORD at the entrance of the meeting *t*,
29:44 consecrate the meeting *t* and the altar,
30:16 donate it to the service of the meeting *t*,
30:18 it between the meeting *t* and the altar,
30:20 they are about to enter the meeting *t*,
30:26 meeting *t* and the ark of the commandments,
30:36 in the meeting *t* where I will meet you.
31: 7 the meeting *t*, the ark
31: 7 top of it, all the furnishings of the *t*,
33: 7 The tent, which was called the meeting *t*,
33: 7 go to this meeting *t* outside the camp.
33: 8 Whenever Moses went out to the *t*,
33: 8 watching Moses until he entered the *t*.
33: 9 As Moses entered the *t*,
33:10 of cloud stand at the entrance of the *t*,
33:11 son of Nun, would not move out of the *t*.
35:11 the Dwelling, with its *t*,
35:18 *t* pegs for the Dwelling and for the court,
35:21 for the construction of the meeting *t*,
36:14 were also woven as a *t* over the Dwelling.
36:18 *t* was joined so that it formed one whole.
36:19 for the *t* was made of rams' skins dyed red,
36:37 the entrance of the *t* was made of violet,
38: 8 served at the entrance of the meeting *t*.
38:20 All the *t* pegs for the Dwelling and for
38:30 at the entrance of the meeting *t*,
38:31 and all the *t* pegs for the Dwelling and
39:32 Dwelling of the meeting *t* was completed.
39:33 Dwelling, the *t* with all its appurtenances,
39:38 the curtain for the entrance of the *t*,
39:40 of the court with its ropes and *t* pegs,
39:40 service of the Dwelling of the meeting *t*;
40: 2 shall erect the Dwelling of the meeting *t*.
40: 6 entrance of the Dwelling of the meeting *t*.
40: 7 laver between the meeting *t* and the altar,
40:12 his sons to the entrance of the meeting *t*,
40:19 He spread the *t* over the Dwelling and put
40:19 and put the covering on top of the *t*,
40:22 He put the table in the meeting *t*,
40:24 He placed the lampstand in the meeting *t*,
40:26 placed the golden altar in the meeting *t*,
40:29 entrance of the Dwelling of the meeting *t*,
40:30 the laver between the meeting *t* and altar,
40:32 into the meeting *t* or approached the altar,
40:34 Then the cloud covered the meeting *t*,
40:35 Moses could not enter the meeting *t*,
Lv 1: 1 from the meeting *t* gave him this message:
1: 3 bring it to the entrance of the meeting *t*
1: 5 which is at the entrance of the meeting *t*.
3: 2 it at the entrance of the meeting *t*;
3: 8 shall slaughter it before the meeting *t*;
3:13 shall slaughter it before the meeting *t*;
4: 4 bullock to the entrance of the meeting *t*,
4: 5 blood and bring it into the meeting *t*,
4: 7 which is before the LORD in the meeting *t*.
4: 7 which is at the entrance of the meeting *t*.
4:14 They shall bring it before the meeting *t*,
4:16 some of its blood into the meeting *t*,
4:18 which is before the LORD in the meeting *t*.
4:18 which is at the entrance of the meeting *t*.
6: 9 court of the meeting *t* they shall eat it.
6:19 place, in the court of the meeting *t*.
6:23 *t* to make atonement in the sanctuary;
8: 3 community at the entrance of the meeting *t*."
8: 4 at the entrance of the meeting *t*,
8:31 flesh at the entrance of the meeting *t*,
8:33 entrance of the meeting *t* for seven days,
8:35 the meeting *t* day and night for seven days,
9:23 Moses and Aaron went into the meeting *t*.
10: 7 you go beyond the entry of the meeting *t*,
10: 9 "When you are to go to the meeting *t*,
12: 6 at the entrance of the meeting *t*
14: 8 still remain outside his *t* for seven days.
14:11 the LORD at the entrance of the meeting *t*.
14:23 entrance of the meeting *t* before the LORD.
15:14 LORD, to the entrance of the meeting *t*,
15:29 priest at the entrance of the meeting *t*.

16: 7 the LORD at the entrance of the meeting t,
16:16 He shall do the same for the meeting t,
16:17 No one else may be in the meeting t from
16:20 the sanctuary, the meeting t and the altar,
16:23 Aaron has again gone into the meeting t,
16:33 sanctuary, the meeting t and the altar,
17: 4 to the entrance of the meeting t to present it
17: 5 entrance of the meeting t and sacrificing
17: 6 entrance of the meeting t and there burn
17: 9 of the meeting t to offer it to the LORD,
19:21 t a ram as his guilt offering to the LORD.
24: 3 In the meeting t, outside the veil
Nm 1: 1 in the meeting t in the desert of Sinai:
2: 2 They shall camp around the meeting t,
2:17 "Then the meeting t and the camp of the
3: 7 the meeting t by serving at the Dwelling.
3: 8 all the furnishings of the meeting t
3:25 At the meeting t they had charge of
3:25 to the Dwelling, the t and its covering,
3:25 curtain at the entrance of the meeting t,
3:38 that is, in front of the meeting t,
4: 3 obligatory tasks in the meeting t.
4: 4 meeting t concerns the most sacred objects.
4:15 meeting t that the Kohathites shall carry.
4:23 obligatory tasks in the meeting t.
4:25 the meeting t with its covering and the
4:25 curtain at the entrance of the meeting t,
4:28 task of the Gershonites in the meeting t;
4:30 obligatory tasks in the meeting t.
4:31 years of their service in the meeting t:
4:33 meeting t under the supervision of Ithamar,
4:35 obligatory tasks in the meeting t,
4:37 clans who were to serve in the meeting t,
4:39 obligatory tasks in the meeting t,
4:41 clans who were to serve in the meeting t,
4:43 obligatory tasks in the meeting t,
4:47 of service or transport of the meeting t,
6:10 priest at the entrance of the meeting t.
6:13 shall go to the entrance of the meeting t,
6:18 Then at the entrance of the meeting t the
7: 5 put to use in the service of the meeting t.
7:89 entered the meeting t to speak with him,
8: 9 come forward in front of the meeting t,
8:15 enter upon their service in the meeting t.
8:19 meeting t and to make atonement for them,
8:22 enter upon their service in the meeting t
8:24 the required service in the meeting t.
8:26 their responsibilities in the meeting t,
9:15 the Dwelling, the t of the commandments;
9:17 Whenever the cloud rose from the t,
10: 3 you at the entrance of the meeting t;
11:16 people, and bring them to the meeting t.
11:24 the people, he had them stand around the t.
11:26 the list, but had not gone out to the t;
12: 4 "Come out, you three, to the meeting t."
12: 5 and standing at the entrance of the t,
12:10 and the cloud withdrew from the t,
14:10 at the meeting t to all the Israelites.
16:18 the meeting t along with Moses and Aaron.
16:19 them at the entrance of the meeting t,
17: 7 and Aaron turned toward the meeting t,
17: 8 Aaron came to the front of the meeting t,
17:15 to Moses at the entrance of the meeting t.
17:19 Then lay them down in the meeting t,
17:22 the LORD in the t of the commandments.
17:23 The next day, when Moses entered the t,
18: 2 are in front of the t of the commandments.
18: 3 look after your persons and the whole t;
18: 4 all the work connected with the meeting t.
18: 6 the LORD for the service of the meeting t.
18:21 the service they perform in the meeting t.
18:22 may no longer approach the meeting t;
18:23 to perform the service of the meeting t,
18:31 recompense for service at the meeting t.
19: 4 times toward the front of the meeting t.
19:14 dies in a tent, everyone who enters the t,
19:18 sprinkle it on the t and on all the vessels
20: 6 assembly to the entrance of the meeting t,
25: 6 weeping at the entrance of the meeting t.
27: 2 community at the entrance of the meeting t,
31:54 and put it in the meeting t as a memorial
32:41 clan, campaigned against the t villages,
Dt 31:14 t that I may give him his commission."
31:14 and presented themselves at the meeting t.
31:15 appeared at the t in a column of cloud,
31:15 which stood still at the entrance of the t.
33:27 He spread out the primeval t;
Jos 7:21 are now hidden in the ground inside my t,
7:22 to the t and found them hidden there,
7:23 They took them from the t,
7:24 his ox, his ass and his sheep, his t,
18: 1 at Shiloh, where they set up the meeting t.
19:51 at the door of the meeting t in Shiloh.
Jgs 4:11 his t by the terebinth of Zaanannim,
4:17 had fled on foot to the t of Jael,
4:18 So he went into her t,
4:20 "Stand at the entrance of the t,"
4:21 got a t peg and took a mallet in her hand.
4:22 dead, with the t peg through his temple.
7:13 It came to our t and struck it,
7:13 and as it fell it turned the t upside down."
20: 8 to leave for his t or return to his home.
1Sm 2:22 serving at the entry of the meeting t.
4:10 every man fled to his own t.
17:54 but he kept Goliath's armor in his own t.
2Sm 6:17 within the t David had pitched for it.
7: 2 cedar, while the ark of God dwells in a t!"
7: 6 I have been going about in a t under cloth.
16:22 So a t was pitched on the roof for Absalom,
20: 1 Every man to his t, O Israel!"
1Kgs 1:39 of oil from the t and anointed Solomon.
2:28 he fled to the t of the LORD and seized
2:29 to the t of the LORD and was at the altar.
2:30 went to the t of the LORD and said to him,
8: 4 the meeting t with all the sacred vessels
8: 4 all the sacred vessels that were in the t.
2Kgs 7: 8 of the camp, they went first into one t,
7: 8 Back they came into another t,
1Chr 6:17 the Dwelling of the meeting t until Solomon
9:19 the guarding of the threshold of the t,
9:21 guarded the gate of the meeting t.
9:23 of the LORD, the house which was then a t.
15: 1 the ark of God, pitching a t for it there.
16: 1 the t which David had pitched for it.
17: 5 but I have been lodging in t or pavilion
23:32 for them concerning the meeting t,
2Chr 1: 3 at Gibeon, because the meeting t of God,
1: 4 provided a place and pitched a t for it.)
1: 6 on the bronze altar at the meeting t;
1:13 high place at Gibeon, from the meeting t,
5: 5 carried the ark and the meeting t
5: 5 all the sacred vessels that were in the t;
24: 6 of Israel, for the t of the testimony?"
Tb 13:10 that his t may be rebuilt in you with joy.
Jdt 5:22 people standing round about the t murmured;
6:10 were standing by in his t to seize Achior,
8: 5 a t for herself on the roof of her house.
8:36 from the t and returned to their posts.
9: 8 the t where your glorious name resides,
10:15 Now go to his t; some of our men
10:17 conducted them to the t of Holofernes.
10:18 as she waited outside the t of Holofernes,
10:20 came out and ushered her into the t.
12: 5 servants of Holofernes led her into the t,
12: 9 Then she returned purified to the t,
13: 1 Bagoas closed the t from the outside and
13: 2 was left alone in the t with Holofernes,
14: 3 to the t of Holofernes and do not find him,
14: 7 "Blessed are you in every t of Judah;
14:13 They came to the t of Holofernes and said
14:14 in, and knocked at the entry of the t,
14:17 the t where Judith had her quarters;
15:11 camp, giving Judith the t of Holofernes,
1Mc 5:42 "Do not allow any man to pitch a t;
2Mc 2: 4 ordered that the t and the ark should
2: 5 a room in a cave in which he put the t,
Jb 4:21 The pegs of their t are plucked up;
5:24 And you shall know that your t is secure;
8:22 and the t of the wicked shall be no more.
11:14 and let not injustice dwell in your t,
18: 6 The light is darkened in his t;
18:14 Fiery destruction lodges in his t,
18:14 He is plucked from the security of his t;
19:12 to attack me, and they encamp around my t.
22:23 if you put iniquity far from your t,
29: 4 flourishing days, when God sheltered my t;
31:31 Had not the men of my t exclaimed,
36:29 clouds in layers as the carpeting of his t.
Ps(s) 15: 1 O LORD, who shall sojourn in your t?
19: 5 He has pitched a t there for the sun,
27: 5 He will conceal me in the shelter of his t,
27: 6 his t sacrifices with shouts of gladness;
52: 7 He shall pluck you from your t,
61: 5 Oh, that I might lodge in your t forever,
78:60 in Shiloh, the t where he dwelt among men.
78:67 And he rejected the t of Joseph,
91:10 nor shall affliction come near your t,
Prv 14:11 but the t of the upright will flourish.
Sir 14:24 and fastens his t pegs next to her walls;
14:25 Who pitches his t beside her,
24: 8 he who formed me chose the spot for my t,
24:10 In the holy t I ministered before him,
26:12 t peg and opens her quiver for every arrow.
50: 5 splendid he was as he appeared from the t,
Is 13:20 The Arab shall not pitch his t there,
16: 5 it shall sit in fidelity [in David's t
33:20 as a quiet abode, a t not to be struck,
38:12 My dwelling, like a shepherd's t,
40:22 spreads them out like a t to dwell in.
54: 2 tent, spread out your t cloths unsparingly;
Jer 10:20 My t is ruined, all its cords are severed.
10:20 no one to pitch my t,
37:10 only the wounded remained, each in his t,
49:29 away, their t curtains and all their goods;
Lam 2: 4 Over the t of daughter Zion he poured out
Acts 7:43 t of Moloch and the star of the god Rephan,
7:44 had the meeting t as God prescribed it
2Cor 5: 1 we know that when the earthly t in which
5: 4 While we live in our present t we groan;
2Pt 1:14 how close is the day when I must fold my t.
Rv 15: 5 which is the t of witness opened up,

TENT-CLOTH (1)

Ps(s) 104: 2 You have spread out the heavens like a t;

TENT-DWELLING (1)

Jgs 5:24 among women by Jael, blessed among t women.

TENTCLOTH (2)

1Chr 17: 1 of the covenant of the LORD dwells under t."
Rv 6:12 t and the moon grew red as blood.

TENTH (61)

Gn 8: 5 continued to diminish until the t month,
8: 5 t month the tops of the mountains appeared.
14:20 Then Abram gave him a t of everything.
28:22 I will faithfully return a t part to you."
Ex 12: 3 On the t of this month every one of your
16:36 [An omer is one t of an ephah.]
29:40 With the first lamb there shall be a t of
Lv 5:11 his sin one t of an ephah of fine flour.
6:13 one t of an ephah of fine flour for the
14:21 one t of an ephah of fine flour mixed with
16:29 t day of the seventh month everyone of you,
23:27 "The t of this seventh month is the Day
25: 9 on the t day of the seventh month let the
27:32 ceding to the LORD as sacred every t animal
Nm 5:15 for her a t of an ephah of barley meal.
7:66 On the t day it was the turn of Ahiezer,
15: 4 cereal offering consisting of a t of an ephah
28: 5 offering of one t of an ephah of fine flour
28:13 and one t of an ephah of fine flour mixed
28:21 ram, and one t for each of the seven lambs;
28:29 ram, and one t for each of the seven lambs.
29: 4 ram, and one t for each of the seven lambs.
29: 7 "On the t day of this seventh month you
29:10 ram, and one t for each of the seven lambs.
29:15 and one t for each of the fourteen lambs.
Dt 23: 3 descendant of his even to the t generation.
23: 4 of theirs even to the t generation,
Jos 4:19 the Jordan on the t day of the first month,
2Kgs 25: 1 In the t month of the ninth year of
25: 1 reign, on the t day of the month,
1Chr 12:14 Johanan eighth, Elzabad ninth, Jeremiah t,
24:11 the ninth to Jeshua, the t to Shecaniah,
25:17 The t was Shimei,
27:13 T, for the tenth month, was Maharai
Ezr 10:16 with the first day of the t month.
Tb 1: 6 together with a t of my income and the
Est 2:16 Ahasuerus in his palace in the t month,
Sir 25: 7 as blessed, a t whom my tongue proclaims:
Is 6:13 If there be still a t part in it,
Jer 32: 1 from the LORD in the t year of Zedekiah,
39: 1 the t month of the ninth year of Zedekiah,
52: 4 the t month of the ninth year of his reign,
52: 4 of his reign, on the t day of the month,
52:12 On the t day of the fifth month (this was
Bar 1: 8 to the land of Judah, on the t of Sivan.
Ez 20: 1 year, on the t day of the fifth month,
24: 1 On the tenth day of the t month,
29: 1 day of the tenth month in the t year,
33:21 On the fifth day of the t month,
40: 1 On the t day of the month beginning the
45:11 the liquid measure equal to a t of a homer;
45:11 the ephah equal to a t of a homer
45:14 for every measure of oil, a t of a measure,
Zec 8:19 and the t months shall become occasions of
Heb 7: 2 apportioned to him one t of all his booty.
7: 4 the patriarch gave one t of his booty!
Rv 11:13 and a t of the city fell in ruins.
21:20 beryl, the ninth topaz, the t chrysoprase,

TENTHS (19)

Lv 14:10 three t of an ephah of fine flour mixed
23:13 t of an ephah of fine flour mixed with oil,
23:17 loaves of bread made of two t of an ephah
24: 5 two t of an ephah of flour for each cake.
Nm 15: 6 present a cereal offering of two t of a ephah
15: 9 offering of three t of an ephah of fine flour
28: 9 t of an ephah of fine flour mixed with oil,
28:12 with three t of an ephah of fine flour
28:12 two t of an ephah of fine flour mixed with
28:20 three t of an ephah for each bullock,
28:20 ephah for each bullock, two t for the ram,
28:28 three t of an ephah for each bullock,
28:28 ephah for each bullock, two t for the ram,
29: 3 three t of an ephah for the bullock,
29: 3 ephah for the bullock, two t for the ram,
29: 9 three t of an ephah for the bullock,
29: 9 ephah for the bullock, two t for the ram,
29:14 offering three t of an ephah for each of
29:14 bullocks, two t for each of the two rams,

TENTING-PLACE (1)

Ps(s) 26: 8 in which you dwell, the t of your glory.

TENTMAKERS (1)

Acts 18: 3 with them and they worked together as t.

TENTS (75)

Gn 4:20 of all who dwell in t and keep cattle.
9:27 so that he dwells among the t of Shem;
13: 5 Abram, also had flocks and herds and t,
13:12 of the Plain, pitching his t near Sodom.

TENTS (cont.)

13:18 Abram moved his *t* and went on to settle
25:27 Jacob was a simple man, who kept to his *t*.
31:25 Jacob's *t* were pitched in the highlands;
31:25 Laban also pitched his *t* there,
31:33 as well as the *t* of the two maidservants;
Ex 33: 8 and stand at the entrance of their own *t*,
33:10 and worship at the entrance of their own *t*.
Nm 11:10 family, crying at the entrance of their *t*,
16:26 "Keep away from the *t* of these wicked men
16:27 standing at the entrances of their *t*
24: 5 How goodly are your *t*,
Dt 1:27 your God, you set to murmuring in your *t*,
5:30 Go, tell them to return to their *t*.
11: 6 with their families and *t* and every living
16: 7 in the morning you may return to your *t*.
33:18 pursuits, and you, Issachar, in your *t*!
Jos 3:14 people struck their *t* to cross the Jordan,
22: 4 may now return to your *t* beyond the Jordan;
22: 6 them and sent them away to their own *t*.
22: 7 them off to their *t* with his blessing was,
22: 8 returning to your own *t* with great wealth,
Jgs 6: 5 *t* would become as numerous as locusts;
7: 8 the rest of the Israelites to their *t*,
1Sm 13: 2 the rest of the people back to their *t*.
2Sm 11:11 ark and Israel and Judah are lodged in *t*,
18:17 And all the Israelites fled to their own *t*.
19: 9 Israelites had fled to their separate *t*,
20:22 scattered from the city to their own *t*,
1Kgs 12:16 To your *t*, O Israel!
12:16 So Israel went off to their *t*,
2Kgs 7: 7 twilight they fled, abandoning their *t*,
7:10 tethered, and the *t* just as they were left."
1Chr 4:41 and attacked the *t* of Ham (for Hamites
5:10 *t* throughout the region east of Gilead.
2Chr 7:10 month he sent the people back to their *t*,
10:16 Everyone to your *t*, O Israel!
10:16 So all Israel went off to their *t*.
14:14 They attacked also the *t* of the
Jdt 2:26 all the Midianites, burned their *t*,
7:18 Their enormous store of *t* and equipment
10:18 the news of her arrival spread among the *t*,
15: 1 happened, those still in their *t* were amazed,
2Mc 12:12 exchanged, the Arabs withdrew to their *t*.
Jb 12: 6 Yet the *t* of robbers are prosperous,
15:34 fire shall consume the *t* of extortioners.
Ps(s) 69:26 in their *t* let there be no one to dwell.
78:28 midst of their camp round about their *t*.
78:51 first fruits of manhood in the *t* of Ham;
78:55 settled the tribes of Israel in their *t*.
83: 7 The *t* of Edom and the Ishmaelites,
84:11 my God than dwell in the *t* of the wicked.
106:25 They murmured in their *t*,
118:15 shout of victory in the *t* of the just:
120: 5 Meshech, that I dwell amid the *t* of Kedar!
Prv 14: 9 Guilt lodges in the *t* of the arrogant,
Sg 1: 5 As the *t* of Kedar,
Wis 11: 2 and in solitudes they pitched their *t*;
Jer 4:20 In an instant my *t* are ravaged;
6: 3 all around, they pitch their *t*,
30:18 I will restore the *t* of Jacob,
35: 7 You shall dwell in *t* all your life,
35:10 or fields or crops, and we live in *t*;
49:29 Their *t* and herds shall be taken away,
Ez 25: 4 encampments among you and pitch their *t*;
Dn 11:45 He shall pitch the *t* of his royal pavilion
Hos 9: 6 treasures, and thorns invade their *t*.
12:10 I will again have you live in *t*,
Hb 3: 7 I see the *t* of Cushan collapse;
Zec 12: 7 The LORD shall save the *t* of Judah first,
Mal 2:12 witness and advocate out of the *t* of Jacob,
Heb 11: 9 dwelling in *t* with Isaac and Jacob,

TEPHON (1)

1Mc 9:50 Bethel, Timnath, Pharathon, and *T*,

TERAH (14)

Gn 11:24 years old, he became the father of *T*.
11:25 and nineteen years after the birth of *T*,
11:26 When *T* was seventy years old,
11:27 This is the record of the descendants of *T*.
11:27 *T* became the father of Abram,
11:28 Haran died before his father *T*,
11:31 *T* took his son Abram,
11:32 The lifetime of *T* was two hundred and five
11:32 then *T* died in Haran.
Nm 33:27 Setting out from Tahath, they camped at *T*.
33:28 Setting out from *T*,
Jos 24: 2 In times past your fathers, down to *T*,
1Chr 1:26 Shelah, Eber, Peleg, Reu, Serug, Nahor, *T*,
Lk 3:34 son of Isaac, son of Abraham, son of *T*,

TERAPHIM (2)

Ez 21:26 has shaken the arrows, inquired of the *t*,
Zec 10: 2 For the *t* speak nonsense,

TEREBINTH (19)

Gn 12: 6 sacred place at Shechem, by the *t* of Moreh.
13:18 and went on to settle near the *t* of Mamre,
14:13 was camping at the *t* of Mamre the Amorite,
18: 1 appeared to Abraham by the *t* of Mamre,
Dt 11:30 opposite the Gilgal beside the *t* of Moreh?]
Jgs 4:11 had pitched his tent by the *t* of Zaanannim,
6:11 LORD came and sat under the *t* in Ophrah
6:19 out to him under the *t* and presented them.
9: 6 by the *t* at the memorial pillar in Shechem.
1Sm 10: 3 on, when you arrive at the *t* of Tabor,
17: 2 gathered and camped in the Vale of the *T*,
17:19 the Philistines in the Vale of the *T*."
21:10 whom you killed in the Vale of the *T*,
2Sm 18: 9 passed under the branches of a large *t*,
18:10 that he had seen Absalom hanging from a *t*.
1Kgs 13:14 man of God, whom he found seated under a *t*.
Sir 24:16 I spread out my branches like a *t*,
Is 6:13 As with a *t* or an oak whose trunk remains
Hos 4:13 burn incense, Beneath oak and poplar and *t*,

TEREBINTHS (2)

Is 1:29 shall be ashamed of the *t* which you prized,
57: 5 You who are in heat among the *t*,

TERESH (1)

Est 6: 2 in which Mordecai reported Bagathan and *T*,

TERM (8)

Gn 29:21 with her, for my *t* is now completed."
Ru 4:22 and prophecy to fulfillment, history to *t*,
1Sm 1:20 of her *t* bore a son whom she called Samuel,
Jer 51:13 come, the *t* at which you shall be cut off!
Dn 13:52 Now have your past sins come to *t*:
Lk 23: 3 He answered, "That is your *t*."
Jn 1:41 (This *t* means the Anointed.)
4:25 (This *t* means Anointed.)

TERMED (2)

Wis 13:10 who *t* gods things made by human hands:
14: 8 because though corruptible, it was *t* a god.

TERMINATE (3)

Nm 34: 5 to the Wadi of Egypt, shall *t* at the Sea.
34: 9 shall reach to Ziphron and *t* at Hazar-enan.
34:12 along the Jordan and *t* with the Salt Sea.

TERMINOLOGY (1)

Acts 18:15 about *t* and titles and your own law,

TERMS (40)

Gn 23:16 Abraham accepted Ephron's *t*;
34:17 comply with our *t* regarding circumcision,
Dt 20:10 attack a city, first offer it *t* of peace.
20:11 your *t* of peace and opens its gates to you,
29: 8 Keep the *t* of this covenant,
1Kgs 20:34 "On these *t*," Ahab replied,
2Kgs 23: 3 thus reviving the *t* of the covenant which
2Chr 32:17 God of Israel, speaking of him in these *t*:
34:31 the *t* of the covenant written in this book.
1Mc 1:30 He spoke to them deceitfully in peaceful *t*,
6:58 Therefore let us now come to *t* with these
6:60 he sent peace *t* to the Jews,
6:61 these *t* they evacuated the fortification.
7:10 to Judas and his brothers in peaceful *t*.
8:29 On these *t* the Romans have made an
10: 3 a letter to Jonathan written in peaceful *t*,
10:17 sent Jonathan a letter written in these *t*:
11:50 "Give us your *t* and let the Jews stop
13:37 We are willing to be on most peaceful *t*
13:47 to *t* with them and did not destroy them.
2Mc 11:14 them to settle everything on just *t*,
11:16 These are the *t* of the letter which Lysias
12: 4 and wishing to live on friendly *t*,
13:23 with the Jews, submitted to their *t*,
14:20 After a long discussion of the *t*,
Jb 22:21 Come to *t* with him to be at peace.
Wis 4: 8 time, nor can it be measured in *t* of years.
Is 2: 4 the nations, and impose *t* on many peoples.
33: 8 Covenants are broken, their *t* are spurned;
Jer 11: 3 does not observe the *t* of this covenant,
34:18 did not observe the *t* of the agreement
Hos 12: 2 he comes to *t* with Assyria,
Mi 4: 3 and impose *t* on strong and distant nations;
Lk 14:32 still at a distance, asking for *t* of peace.
1Cor 2:13 spiritual things in spiritual *t*.
2Cor 5:16 look on anyone in *t* of mere human judgment.
11:12 ministry they work on the same *t* as we do.
Gal 3:12 Its *t* are:
4:30 *t* with the son" of the one born free.
Col 2:16 to pass judgment on you in *t* of what you

TERRACE (9)

2Kgs 1: 2 his roof *t* at Samaria and had been injured.
20:11 on the staircase to the *t* of Ahaz.
23:12 of Judah on the roof (the roof *t* of Ahaz),
Is 38: 8 the sun on the stairway to the *t* of Ahaz
Bar 6:10 or give part of it to the harlots on the *t*.
Ez 42: 6 therefore they were on a lower *t* of the
Mt 24:17 If a man is on the roof *t*,
Mk 13:15 If a man is on the roof *t*,
Acts 10: 9 city, Peter went up to the roof *t* to pray.

TERRACED (1)

Is 16: 8 The *t* slopes of Heshbon languish,

TERRACES (3)

Jer 5:10 Climb to her *t*, and ravage them,
22:13 his house on wrong, his *t* on injustice;
Hb 3:17 fail and the *t* produce no nourishment,

TERRAIN (1)

2Mc 12:21 because of the difficult *t* of that region.

TERRIBLE (29)

Ex 15:11 O *t* in renown, worker of wonders,
Lv 26:16 I will punish you with *t* woes
Dt 8:15 guided you through the vast and *t* desert
10:21 and *t* things which your own eyes have seen.
Jgs 13: 6 appearance of an angel of God, *t* indeed.
Tb 7: 7 But what a *t* misfortune that such a
1Mc 1:63 *T* affliction was upon Israel.
2Mc 6:30 *t* pain in my body from this scourging,
Jb 41: 6 doors of his mouth, close to his *t* teeth?
Ps(s) 76: 8 You are *t*; and who can withstand you
76:12 the *t* Lord Who checks the pride of princes,
76:13 who is *t* to the kings of the earth.
89: 8 God is *t* in the council of the holy ones;
106:22 the land of Ham, *t* things at the Red Sea.
145: 6 of your *t* deeds and declare your greatness.
Wis 8:15 *t* princes, hearing of me, would be afraid;
11:18 smoke, or flash *t* sparks from their eyes.
12: 9 once by *t* beasts or by one decisive word;
Is 10:33 hosts, lops off the boughs with *t* violence;
Ez 5:15 *t* warning to the nations that surround you.
Dn 7:19 so very *t* and different from the others,
Jl 2:11 is the day of the LORD, and exceedingly *t*;
3: 4 Day of the Lord, the great and *t* day.
Hb 1: 7 *T* and dreadful is he,
Mal 3:23 day of the LORD comes, the great and *t* day.
3:24 day of the LORD comes, the great and *t* day.
Mt 18: 7 What *t* things will come on the world
Mk 16:20 fulfilled, but other *t* things are imminent.
2Tm 3: 1 there will be *t* times in the last days.

TERRIBLY (2)

Wis 6: 5 *T* and swiftly shall he come against you,
Mt 15:22 My daughter is *t* troubled by a demon."

TERRIFIED (27)

Dt 7:21 Therefore, do not be *t* by them,
Jdt 16:11 When my lowly ones shouted, they were *t*;
1Mc 4:21 When they realized this, they were *t*;
Jb 4:14 me, and shuddering, that *t* me to the bones.
31:34 multitude and the scorn of the tribes *t* me
Ps(s) 6: 4 My soul, too, is utterly *t*;
30: 8 but when you hid your face I was *t*.
48: 6 They also see, and at once are stunned, *t*,
Wis 17: 3 in fearful trembling, *t* by apparitions.
17: 4 for crashing sounds on all sides *t* them,
Sir 40: 6 did by day, *T* by what his mind's eye sees,
Ez 26:18 The isles in the sea are *t* at your passing.
27:35 are aghast over you, Their kings are *t*,
Dn 4:16 appalled for a while, *t* by his thoughts.
5: 6 his thoughts *t* him,
5: 9 Then King Belshazzar was greatly *t*;
7: 1 bed, and was *t* by the visions of his mind.
7:15 and I was *t* by the visions of my mind.
7:28 I, Daniel, was greatly *t* by my thoughts,
Mt 14:26 saw him walking on the water, they were *t*.
Mk 4:40 Then he said to them, "Why are you so *t*?
6:50 They had all seen him and were *t*.
Lk 8:35 this sight *t* them.
24: 5 *T*, the women bowed to the ground.
2Thes 2: 2 not to be so easily agitated or *t*,
Heb 12:21 that Moses said, "I am *t* and trembling."
Rv 11:13 so *t* that they worshiped the God of heaven.

TERRIFIES (3)

Jb 33:16 of men and as a warning to them, *t* them;
Ps(s) 2: 5 he *t* them in his wrath:
Dn 11:44 news from the east and the north *t* him,

TERRIFY (8)

2Chr 32:18 to frighten and *t* them so that they might
Jb 7:14 me with dreams and with visions *t* me,
Ps(s) 10:18 that man, who is of earth, may *t* no more.
Sir 13: 7 then twice or three times he will *t* you;
Ez 30: 9 at my command to *t* unsuspecting Ethiopia;
Dn 4:16 "let not the dream or its meaning *t* you."
Hb 2:17 the destruction of the beasts shall *t* you;
Zec 2: 4 but these have come to *t* them:

TERRIFYING (8)

Gn 15:12 and a deep, *t* darkness enveloped him.
Dt 26: 8 hand and outstretched arm, with *t* power,
28:25 *t* example to all the kingdoms of the earth.
34:12 and for the might and the *t* power that
Jb 6:21 you see a *t* thing and are afraid.
Dn 2:31 *t* in appearance as it stood before you.
4: 2 I had a *t* dream as I lay in bed,
7: 7 beast, different from all the others, *t*,

TERRITORIAL (1)

Gn 36:43 to their settlements in their *t* holdings.

TERRITORIES (4)

Jos 13:12 Moses conquered and occupied these *t*,
Jdt 1:12 the *t* of Cilicia and Damascus and Syria,
2:10 and take possession of all their *t* for me.
1Mc 15:29 You have laid waste their *t*,

TERRITORY (109)

Gn 31:52 may I pass beyond this mound into your *t*,
47:21 from one end of Egypt's *t* to the other.
Ex 7:27 send a plague of frogs over all your *t*.
13: 7 leavened may be found in all your *t*.
34:24 nations before you to give you a large *t*,
Nm 20:16 at the town of Kadesh at the edge of your *t*.
20:17 left, until we have passed through your *t*."
20:21 refused to let them pass through their *t*,
21:13 that extends from the *t* of the Amorites;
21:22 road until we have passed through your *t*."
21:23 would not let Israel pass through his *t*,
22:36 on the Arnon at the end of the Moabite *t*.
34: 2 this is the *t* that shall fall to you as
Dt 2: 4 to pass through the *t* of your kinsmen,
2:18 about to leave Ar and the *t* of Moab behind.
3: 8 the *t* from the Wadi Arnon to Mount
3:12 I gave Reuben and Gad the *t* from Aroer,
3:16 Gad the *t* from Gilead to the Wadi Arnon
11:24 River to the Western Sea, shall be your *t*.
12:20 the LORD, your God, has enlarged your *t*,
16: 4 may be found in all your *t* for seven days,
19: 8 if the LORD, your God, enlarges your *t*,
Jos 12: 5 half of Gilead as far as the *t* of Sihon,
13: 3 in the north is reckoned Canaanite *t*,
13: 5 and the Gebalite *t*; and all the Lebanon
13:11 the *t* of the Geshurites and Maacathites,
13:16 Their *t* reached from Aroer,
13:25 Their *t* included Jazer,
13:30 Their *t* included Mahanaim,
16: 9 within the *t* of the Manassehites.
17: 9 thus the *t* of Manasseh ran north of the
18: 5 Judah is to retain its *t* in the south,
18: 5 the house of Joseph its *t* in the north.
18:11 The *t* allotted them lay between the
19:17 The *t* of the clans of the Issacharites
19:25 Their *t* included Helkath,
19:41 Their heritage was the *t* of Zorah,
19:47 *t* of the Danites was too small for them;
21:41 within the *t* of the Israelites which,
Jgs 1: 3 up with me into the *t* allotted to me,
1: 3 accompany you into the *t* allotted to you."
1:18 however, did not occupy Gaza with its *t*,
1:18 with its territory, or Ekron with its *t*.
1:36 The *t* of the Amorites extended from the
11:18 Thus they did not go through the *t* of Moab,
11:20 refused to let Israel pass through his *t*.
11:22 the whole *t* from the Arnon to the Jabbok,
12: 4 in *t* belonging to Ephraim and Manasseh."
19:29 and sent them throughout the *t* of Israel.
20: 6 her through every part of the *t* of Israel,
20:48 withdrew through the *t* of the Benjaminites,
21:23 the dancers, and went back to their own *t*,
1Sm 6: 9 Beth-shemesh along the route to his own *t*,
7:13 never again to enter the *t* of Israel,
7:14 Israel also freed the *t* of these cities
10: 2 tomb at Zelzah in the *t* of Benjamin,
11: 3 messengers throughout the *t* of Israel.
11: 7 *t* of Israel by couriers with the message,
14:46 Philistines, who returned to their own *t*.
30:14 Negeb of the Cherethites, the *t* of Judah,
2Sm 17:26 and Absalom encamped in the *t* of Gilead.
21: 5 might have no place in all the *t* of Israel,
21:14 father Kish at Zela in the *t* of Benjamin.
1Kgs 1: 3 beautiful girl throughout the *t* of Israel,
2Kgs 10:32 throughout their *t* east of the Jordan
15:29 Kedesh, Hazor, all the *t* of Naphtali,
18: 8 Philistines, all the way to Gaza and its *t*.
2Chr 34:33 from all the *t* belonging to the Israelites,
Jdt 2:25 He seized the *t* of Cilicia,
3: 8 whole *t* and cut down their sacred groves,
14: 4 inhabitants of the whole *t* of Israel will
15: 5 slaughter, even beyond Damascus and its *t*.
1Mc 1: 8 took over his kingdom, each in his own *t*,
2:46 boys whom they found in the *t* of Israel.
3:36 their *t* and distribute their land by lot.
3:42 that armies were encamped within their *t*;
4:22 to attack, they all fled to Philistine *t*.
5: 9 the Israelites who were in their *t*;
5:48 to cross your *t* in order to reach our own;
6:25 against us, but throughout their whole *t*.
9:72 country and never came into their *t* again.
10:31 Let Jerusalem and her *t*,
10:89 him Ekron and all its *t* as a possession.
11:34 possession, not only of the *t* of Judea,
14: 2 heard that Demetrius had invaded his *t*,
15:30 the districts outside the *t* of Judea
2Mc 13:24 and civil governor of the *t* from Ptolemais
15: 1 his companions were in the *t* of Samaria,
Ps(s) 125: 3 shall not remain upon the *t* of the just,
Ez 30: 5 allied *t* shall fall by the sword with them.
48:12 domain, next to the *t* of the Levites.
48:13 a *t* corresponding to that of the priests,
48:21 a *t* parallel with the tribal portions for
48:22 the *t* between the portions of Judah and of
Am 1:13 in Gilead, while extending their *t*,
6: 2 kingdoms, or is your *t* wider than theirs?
Zep 2: 8 my people and made boasts against their *t*.
Mt 4:13 the sea near the *t* of Zebulun and Naphtali,
10: 5 pagan *t* and do not enter a Samaritan town.
Mk 5: 1 Gerasene *t* on the other side of the lake.
7:24 he went off to the *t* of Tyre and Sidon.
7:31 He then left Tyrian *t* and returned by way
Lk 8:37 *t* asked Jesus to leave their neighborhood,
Jn 3:22 and his disciples came into Judean *t*,
Acts 12:20 was supplied with food from the king's *t*.
13:50 Jews finally expelled them from their *t*.
16: 6 traveled through Phrygia and Galatian *t*
2Cor 10:16 already done by another in his alloted *t*.

TERROR (72)

Gn 35: 5 *t* from God fell upon the towns round about,
Ex 15:16 *t* and dread fell upon them.
Dt 32:25 sword in the street and by sheer *t* at home
1Kgs 1:49 All the guests of Adonijah left in *t*,
2Chr 29: 8 he has made them an object of *t*,
Jdt 14: 7 all who hear of you will be struck with *t*.
1Mc 13: 2 saw that the people were in dread and *t*,
2Mc 3:17 The *t* and bodily trembling that had come
3:24 at God's power and fainted away in *t*.
12:22 *t* at the manifestation of the All-seeing.
13:16 filled the camp with *t* and confusion.
Jb 13:21 me, and let not the *t* of you frighten me.
22:10 you, and a sudden *t* causes you dismay,
26: 5 The shades beneath writhe in *t*,
30:15 over me rolls the *t*.
39:20 while his thunderous snorting spreads *t*?
41:14 abides in his neck, and *t* leaps before him.
Ps(s) 6: 3 heal me, O LORD, for my body is in *t*;
6:11 enemies shall be put to shame in utter *t*;
9:21 Strike them with *t*,
55: 5 the *t* of death has fallen upon me.
91: 5 You shall not fear the *t* of the night nor
Prv 1:26 I will mock when *t* overtakes you;
1:27 When *t* comes upon you like a storm,
3:25 Be not afraid of sudden *t*,
21:15 is a joy for the just, but *t* for evildoers.
Wis 17: 6 And in their *t* they thought beholding
17:19 of the hills, these sounds, inspiring *t*,
Sir 30: 9 your child and he will be a *t* for you,
40: 5 and envy, trouble and dread, *t* of death,
Is 2:10 From the *t* of the LORD and the splendor of
2:19 From the *t* of the LORD and the splendor of
2:21 From the *t* of the LORD and the splendor of
10:29 Ramah is in *t*, Gibeah of Saul has fled.
13: 8 Every man's heart melts in *t*;
17:14 In the evening, they spread *t*,
19:17 of Judah shall be a *t* to the Egyptians.
24:17 *T*, pit, and trap are upon you,
24:18 at the sound of *t* will fall into the pit;
28:19 *t* alone shall convey the message.
31: 9 princes shall flee in *t* from his standard,
33:18 Your mind will dwell on the *t*:
47:12 make them avail, perhaps you can strike *t*!
Jer 6:25 *t* on every side!
8:15 for a time of healing, but *t* comes instead.
14:19 for a time of healing, but *t* comes instead.
15: 8 Suddenly I struck her with anguish and *t*.
20: 3 the LORD will name you *T* on every side."
20: 4 Indeed, I will deliver you to *t*,
20:10 *T* on every side!
32:21 Egypt amid signs and wonders and great *t*.
46: 5 *T* on every side, says the LORD!
48:39 one wants, says the LORD How *t* seizes Moab,
48:43 *T*, pit, and trap be upon you, people
48:44 He who flees from the *t* falls into the pit;
49: 5 I am bringing *t* upon you,
49:16 The *t* you spread beguiled you,
49:29 and shout from upon them, *T* on every side!"
Lam 3:47 *T* and the pit have been our lot.
Ez 4:17 with *t* and waste away because of his sins.
7:27 while the prince shall be enveloped in *t*,
23:46 and deliver them over to *t* and plunder.
26:17 spread *t* into all that dwelt by the sea.
32:23 who spread *t* in the land of the living.
32:24 spread their *t* in the land of the living,
32:26 spread their *t* in the land of the living.
32:27 men caused *t* in the land of the living.
32:30 because of the *t* their might inspired;
32:32 he spread his *t* in the land of the living,
38:21 Against him I will summon every *t*,
Dn 8:17 I was standing, I fell prostrate in *t*.
Rv 11:11 feet sheer *t* gripped those who saw them.

TERROR-STRICKEN (4)

1Sm 14:15 outpost and the raiding parties, were *t*.
17:11 of the Philistine, were dismayed and *t*.
28:21 to Saul, and seeing that he was quite *t*,
Mt 27:54 keeping watch over Jesus were *t* at seeing

TERRORIZED (1)

Wis 16: 6 a warning, for a short time they were *t*,

TERRORS (12)

Dt 4:34 hand and outstretched arm, and by great *t*,
2Chr 15: 5 many *t* upon the inhabitants of the lands.
Jb 6: 4 the *t* of God are arrayed against me.
9:34 Would that his *t* did not frighten me;
15:21 The sound of *t* is in his ears;
18:11 On every side *t* affright him;
18:14 tent, and marches him off to the king of *t*.
20:25 *t* shall fall upon him.
27:20 *T* rush upon him by day;
Ps(s) 88:17 your *t* have cut me off.
Wis 17: 8 they who undertook to banish fears and *t*
Lam 2:22 a feast day *t* against me from all sides;

TERTIUS (1)

Rom 16:22 I, *T*, who have written this letter,

TERTULLUS (2)

Acts 24: 1 some of the elders and an attorney named *T*.
24: 2 *T* began his prosecution by addressing

TEST (70)

Gn 22: 1 these events, God put Abraham to the *t*.
Ex 15:25 regulations for them, put them to the *t*.
16: 4 thus will I *t* them,
17: 2 Why do you put the LORD to a *t*?"
20:20 only to *t* you and put his fear upon you,
Nm 14:22 have put me to the *t* ten times already
Dt 6:16 shall not put the LORD, your God, to the *t*,
8: 2 so as to *t* you by affliction and find out
8:16 that he might afflict you and *t* you,
33: 8 For you put him to the *t* at Massah and you
Jgs 3: 4 These served to put Israel to the *t*,
6:39 me make just one more *t* with the fleece.
7: 3 Gideon put them to this *t* on the mountain,
7: 4 the water and I will *t* them for you there.
1Kgs 10: 1 fame, came to *t* him with subtle questions.
1Chr 29:17 that you put hearts to the *t* and that you
2Chr 9: 1 Jerusalem to *t* him with subtle questions,
32:31 in the land, God forsook him to *t* him,
Tb 12:14 the dead, I was sent to put you to the *t*.
Jdt 8:12 you should have put God to the *t* this day,
8:25 the Lord our God, for putting us to the *t*,
1Mc 10:71 and let us *t* each other's strength there;
Ps(s) 17: 3 Though you *t* my heart,
26: 2 *t* my soul and my heart.
35:16 they put me to the *t*;
Prv 18:17 his opponent comes and puts him to the *t*.
Wis 1: 2 Because he is found by those who *t* him not,
2:19 put him to the *t* that we may have proof
6: 6 the mighty shall be mightily put to the *t*.
Sir 4:17 and at first she puts him to the *t*;
6: 7 When you gain a friend, first *t* him,
6:22 will be like a burdensome stone to *t* him,
13:11 For by prolonged talk he will *t* you,
27: 5 As the *t* of what the potter molds is in
27: 5 so in his conversation is the *t* of a man.
Jer 6:27 appointed you, to search and *t* their way.
9: 6 I will smelt them and *t* them;
17:10 LORD, alone probe the mind and *t* the heart,
20:12 O LORD of hosts, you who *t* the just,
Dn 1:12 "Please *t* your servants for ten days.
Zec 13: 9 and I will *t* them as gold is tested.
Mt 4: 7 shall not put the Lord your God to the *t*.'"
16: 1 and as a *t* asked him to show them some
19: 3 came up to him and said, to *t* him,
26:41 and pray that you may not undergo the *t*.
Mk 1:13 forty days, put to the *t* there by Satan.
8:11 for some heavenly sign from him as a *t*.
10: 2 Then some Pharisees came up and as a *t*
14:38 and pray that you may not be put to the *t*.
Lk 4:12 shall not put the Lord your God to the *t*.'"
11:16 Others, to *t* him, were demanding of him
14:19 yoke of oxen and I am going out to *t* them.
22:40 "Pray that you may not be put to the *t*."
Jn 6: 6 but he asked this to *t* Philip's response.)
Acts 5: 9 scheme to put the Spirit of the Lord to *t*?
15:10 do you put God to the *t* by trying to place
1Cor 3:13 fire will *t* the quality of each man's work.
10: 9 Let us not *t* the Lord as some of them did,
10:13 No *t* has been sent you that does not come
10:13 Along with the *t* he will give you a way
2Cor 2: 9 The reason I wrote you was to *t* you and
13: 5 *T* yourselves to see whether you are living
1Thes 2: 4 having met the *t* imposed on us by God,
3: 5 that the tempter had put you to the *t*
5:21 *T* everything; retain what is good.
Heb 11:17 By faith Abraham, when put to the *t*,
1Pt 4:12 It is a *t* for you,
1Jn 4: 1 to a *t* to see if they belong to God,
Rv 2:10 of you into prison to put you to the *t*;
3:10 on the whole world, to *t* all men on earth.

TESTAMENT (2)

Heb 9:16 When there is a *t*,
9:17 For a *t* comes into force only in the case

TESTATOR (2)

Heb 9:16 that the death of the *t* be confirmed.
9:17 it has no force while the *t* is alive.

TESTED (29)

Gn 42:15 This is how you shall be *t*:
42:16 Thus shall your words be *t* for their truth;
Ex 17: 7 Israelites quarreled there and *t* the LORD,
Ps(s) 66:10 For you have *t* us, O God!
81: 8 I *t* you at the waters of Meribah.
95: 9 they *t* me though they had seen my works.
Prv 27:21 so a man is *t* by the praise he receives.
30: 5 Every word of God is *t*;
Wis 11:10 the latter you *t*, admonishing them
Sir 2: 5 For in fire gold is *t*,
27: 7 he speaks, for it is then that men are *t*.
31:10 he has been *t* by gold and come off safe,
42: 4 and balances, or of *t* measures and weights;
44:20 ordinance, and when *t* he was found loyal.
Is 28:16 a stone in Zion, a stone that has been *t*,
48:10 silver, *t* you in the furnace of affliction.
Jer 2:21 you, a choice vine of fully *t* stock;
Ez 21:18 slap your thigh, for the sword has been *t*;
Dn 1:14 to this request, and *t* them for ten days;
11:35 shall fall, so that the rest may be *t*,
12:10 Many shall be refined, purified, and *t*,
Zec 13: 9 refined, and I will test them as gold is *t*.
Rom 5: 4 for tested virtue, and *t* virtue for hope.
1Cor 10:13 will not let you be *t* beyond your strength.
Heb 2:18 he was himself *t* through what he suffered,
3: 9 desert, When your fathers *t* and tried me,
Jas 1: 3 your faith is *t* this makes for endurance.
Rv 2: 2 you have *t* those self-styled apostles who

TESTER (3)

Prv 17: 3 for gold, but the *t* of hearts is the LORD.
Jer 6:27 A *t* among my people I have appointed you,
1Thes 2: 4 to please God, "the *t* of our hearts,"

TESTICLES (2)

Lv 22:24 One that has its *t* bruised or crushed or
Dt 23: 2 "No one whose *t* have been crushed or

TESTIFIED (16)

Jgs 20: 4 the husband of the murdered woman, *t*:
2Sm 1:16 for you *t* against yourself when you said,
2Mc 8:36 Jerusalem *t* that the Jews had a champion,
12:30 But when the Jews who lived there *t* to the
Sir 46:19 *t* before the LORD and his anointed prince,
Dn 13:43 know that they have *t* falsely against me.
13:49 court, for they have *t* falsely against her."
Mk 14:57 on taking the stand, *t* falsely by alleging,
Jn 1:15 John *t* to him by proclaiming:
1:34 Now I have seen for myself and have *t*,
4:44 (Jesus himself had *t* that no one esteems a
5:33 have sent to John, who has *t* to the truth.
Acts 13:22 on his behalf God *t*,
Ti 1:12 Crete, one of their own prophets, has *t*,
Heb 2: 6 Somewhere this is *t* to,
3Jn 1: 6 they have *t* to your love before the church.

TESTIFIES (6)

Wis 17:11 nature cowardly, *t* in its own condemnation,
Jn 3:32 above all] *t* to what he has seen and heard,
Heb 7: 8 tithes, Scripture *t* that this man lives on.
7:17 Scripture *t*:
11: 5 Scripture *t* that, before he was taken up,
1Jn 5: 6 It is the Spirit who *t* to this,

TESTIFY (22)

Gn 30:33 wages of mine, let my honesty *t* against me:
Ps(s) 50: 7 Israel, I will *t* against you;
Dn 13:21 we will *t* against you that you dismissed
13:41 We *t* to this."
Mk 13: 9 and have to *t* to your faith before them.
14:60 no answer to what these men *t* against you?"
Jn 1: 7 who came as a witness to *t* to the light,
1: 8 but only to *t* to the light,
5:36 *t* on my behalf that the Father has sent me.
5:39 they also *t* on my behalf.
18:37 came into the world, is to *t* to the truth.
Acts 5:32 We *t* to this.
10:43 To him all the prophets *t*,
26: 5 with me for a long time and can *t*,
26:22 I stand here to *t* to great and small alike.
Rom 10: 2 I can *t* that they are zealous for God
2Cor 8: 3 indeed I can *t* even beyond their means
Gal 4:15 I can *t* on your behalf that if it were
Phil 1: 8 God himself can *t* how much I long for each
Col 4:13 I can certainly *t* how solicitous he is for
1Jn 4:14 We have seen for ourselves, and can *t*,
5: 7 Thus there are three that *t*,

TESTIFYING (6)

Ex 23: 2 wrong, nor shall you, when *t* in a lawsuit,
Jn 3:11 we know, we are *t* to what we have seen,
3:26 the one about whom you have been *t*—
5:32 but there is another who is *t* on my behalf,
8:18 I am one of those *t* in my behalf,
12:17 and raised him from the dead kept *t* to it.

TESTIMONIAL (2)

3Jn 1:12 is one who gets a good *t* from all,
1:12 We give our *t* as well,

TESTIMONY (59)

Nm 23:18 give ear to my *t*,
Dt 17: 6 The *t* of two or three witnesses is
17: 6 put to death on the *t* of only one witness.
19:15 only on the *t* of two or three witnesses.
2Chr 24: 6 assembly of Israel, for the tent of the *t*?"
Wis 10: 7 Where as a *t* to its wickedness,
Sir 26: 5 and lying *t* are harder to bear than death,
31:23 and this *t* to his goodness is lasting;
31:24 and this *t* to his stinginess is lasting.
Mt 26:59 busy trying to obtain false *t* against Jesus
26:62 you no answer to the *t* leveled against you?"
Mk 6:11 your feet in *t* against them as you leave."
14:55 were busy soliciting *t* against Jesus
14:56 under oath but their *t* did not agree.
14:59 Even so, their *t* did not agree.
Lk 9: 5 dust from your feet as a *t* against them."
10:11 this town from our feet as *t* against you.
Jn 1:19 The *t* John gave when the Jews sent priests
1:32 John gave this *t* also:
2:25 no one to give him *t* about human nature.
3:11 we have seen, but you do not accept our *t*.
3:32 seen and heard, but no one accepts his *t*.
3:33 this *t* certifies that God is truthful.
4:39 on the strength of the woman's word of *t*:
5:31 on my own behalf, you cannot verify my *t*;
5:32 the *t* he renders me I know can be verified.
5:34 (Not that I myself accept such human *t*—
5:36 Yet I have *t* greater than John's,
5:37 sent me has himself given *t* on my behalf.
8:13 Such *t* cannot be valid."
8:14 My *t* is valid nonetheless,
13:21 He went on to give this *t*:
19:35 (This *t* has been given by an eyewitness,
19:35 given by an eyewitness, and his *t* is true.
21:24 it is he who wrote them down and his *t*,
Acts 2:40 of his *t* he used many other arguments,
8:25 *t* and proclaiming the word of the Lord,
22:18 they will not accept your *t* about me.'
23:11 you have given *t* to me here in Jerusalem,
1Cor 2: 1 I did not come proclaiming God's *t*
2Cor 1:12 Conscience gives *t* to the boast that in
13: 1 only on the *t* of two or three witnesses."
1Thes 4: 6 as we once indicated to you by our *t*.
2Tm 1: 8 never be ashamed of your *t* to our Lord,
Heb 10:28 mercy on the *t* of two or three witnesses.
Jas 5: 3 their corrosion shall be a *t* against you;
1Pt 5:12 my *t* that this is the true grace of God.
1Jn 5: 9 Do we not accept human *t*?
5: 9 The *t* of God is much greater:
5: 9 *t* God has given on his own Son's behalf.
5:10 of God possesses that *t* within his heart.
5:10 the *t* he has given on his own Son's behalf.
5:11 The *t* is this:
3Jn 1:12 as well, and you know that our *t* is true.
Rv 1: 2 the word of God and the *t* of Jesus Christ.
11: 7 When they have finished giving their *t*,
12:11 of the Lamb and by the word of their *t*;
22:16 to give you this *t* about the churches.
22:20 The One who gives this *t* says,

TESTING (4)

Dt 13: 4 is *t* you to learn whether you really love
Eccl 3:18 it is God's way of *t* them and of showing
2Cor 8: 8 I am not giving an order but simply *t* your
Heb 3: 8 the revolt in the day of *t* in the desert,

TESTINGS (3)

Dt 4:34 from the midst of another nation, by *t*,
7:19 the great *t* which your own eyes have seen,
29: 2 the great *t* your own eyes have seen,

TESTS (4)

Jb 34: 3 For the ear *t* words,
Prv 24:12 does not he who *t* hearts perceive it?
27:21 the crucible *t* silver and the furnace gold,
Sir 36:19 As the palate *t* meat by its savor,

TETHERED (4)

2Kgs 7:10 human voice, only the horses and asses *t*,
Mt 21: 2 find an ass *t* and her colt with her.
Mk 11: 2 *t* there a colt on which no one has ridden.
11: 4 a colt *t* out on the street near a gate,

TETHERS (1)

Gn 49:11 He *t* his donkey to the vine,

TETRARCH (7)

Mt 14: 1 On one occasion Herod the *t*,
Lk 3: 1 procurator of Judea, Herod *t* of Galilee,
3: 1 Philip his brother *t* of the region of
3: 1 and Trachonitis, and Lysanias *t* of Abilene,
3:19 Herod the *t* was censured by John on the
9: 7 Herod the *t* heard of all that was
Acts 13: 1 (who had been brought up with Herod the *t*),

TETTER (1)

Lv 13:39 is only *t* that has broken out on the skin,

TEXT (8)

2Chr 34:30 the entire *t* of the book of the covenant
Ezr 6: 2 was found containing the following *t*:
7:11 the scribe of the *t* of the LORD's
Neh 6: 6 bore an unsealed letter containing this *t*:
1Mc 7:16 one day, according to the *t* of Scripture:
Jer 36:27 with the *t* Jeremiah had dictated to Baruch:
Mt 12: 7 If you understood the meaning of the *t*,
Jn 15:25 this only fulfills the *t* in their law:

THADDAEUS (2)

Mt 10: 3 James, son of Alphaeus, and *T*;
Mk 3:18 *T*, Simon of the Zealot Party,

THANK (25)

1Chr 16: 4 the ark of the LORD, to celebrate, *t*,
2Chr 29:31 and *t* offerings for the house of the LORD.
29:31 brought forward the sacrifices and *t* offerings
33:16 on it peace offerings and *t* offerings,
Tb 12: 6 *T* God!
12:17 *T* God now and forever.
12:18 So continue to *t* him every day;
1Mc 14:25 said, "How can we *t* Simon and his sons?
2Mc 9:20 are going as you wish, I *t* God very much,
Ps(s) 52:11 I will *t* you always for what you have done,
56:13 your *t* offerings I will fulfill.
107:22 Let them make *t* offerings and declare his
Sir 51:12 For this reason I *t* him and I praise him;
Jer 17:26 and *t* offerings to the house of the LORD.
33:11 bring *t* offerings to the house of the LORD,
Jn 11:41 "Father, I *t* you for having heard me.
1Cor 1: 4 I continually *t* my God for you because of
1:14 *T* God, I baptized none of you except
14:18 *T* God, I speak in tongues more than
1Thes 2:13 That is why we *t* God constantly that in
2Thes 1: 3 right that we *t* God unceasingly for you,
2:13 We are bound to *t* God for you always,
1Tm 1:12 I *t* Christ Jesus our Lord,
2Tm 1: 3 I *t* God, the God of my forefathers
Phlm 1: 4 I *t* God always,

THANKED (5)

2Mc 11: 9 all of them together *t* God for his mercy,
12:31 Judas and his men *t* them and exhorted them
Wis 18: 2 wronged did not harm them, they *t* them,
Acts 28:15 saw them, he *t* God and took fresh courage.
2Cor 1:11 on our behalf God may be *t* for the gift

THANKFULLY (1)

1Cor 10:30 And why is it, if I partake *t*,

THANKFULNESS (1)

Col 3:15 Dedicate yourselves to *t*.

THANKING (7)

Tb 12:22 They kept *t* God and singing his praises;
Ps(s) 42: 6 For I shall again be *t* him,
42:12 For I shall again be *t* him,
43: 5 For I shall again be *t* him,
Lk 13:13 she stood up straight and began *t* God.
Eph 1:16 I have never stopped *t* God for you and
1Thes 1: 2 We keep *t* God for all of you and we

THANKLESS (1)

Eccl 1:13 A *t* task God has appointed for men to be

THANKS (116)

1Chr 16: 8 Give *t* to the LORD, invoke his name;
16:34 Give *t* to the LORD, for he is good,
16:35 That we may give *t* to your holy name and
16:41 designated by name to give *t* to the LORD,
23:30 morning to offer *t* and to praise the LORD,
25: 3 a lyre, to give *t* and praise to the LORD.
29:13 *t* and we praise the majesty of your name."
2Chr 5:13 voice praising and giving *t* to the LORD,
5:13 instruments to "give *t* to the LORD,
20:21 "Give *t* to the LORD, for his mercy
2Mc 1:11 we give him great *t* for having fought on
4:50 *t* to the covetousness of the men in power,
8:27 with fervent praise and *t* to the Lord
Ps(s) 6: 6 in the nether world who gives you *t*?
7:18 I will give *t* to the LORD for his justice,
9: 2 I will give *t* to you, O LORD,
26: 7 your altar, O LORD, Giving voice to my *t*,
28: 7 exults, and with my song I give him *t*.
30: 5 faithful ones, and give *t* to his holy name.
30:10 give you *t* or proclaim your faithfulness?
30:13 O LORD, my God, forever will I give you *t*.
33: 2 Give *t* to the LORD on the harp;
35:18 I will give you *t* in the vast assembly,
43: 4 Then will I give you *t* upon the harp,
57:10 I will give *t* to you among the peoples,
71:22 will I give you *t* with music on the lyre,
75: 2 We give you *t*, O God, we give thanks.
79:13 your pasture, will give *t* to you forever;

86:12 I will give *t* to you,
88:11 Will the shades arise to give you *t?*
92: 2 It is good to give *t* to the LORD,
97:12 you just, and give *t* to his holy name.
100: 4 Give *t* to him; bless his name,
105: 1 Give *t* to the LORD,
106:47 That we may give *t* to your holy name and
107: 1 "Give *t* to the LORD,
107: 8 Let them give *t* to the LORD for his
107:15 Let them give *t* to the LORD for his
107:21 Let them give *t* to the LORD for his
107:31 Let them give *t* to the LORD for his
108: 4 I will give *t* to you among the peoples,
109:30 I will speak my *t* earnestly to the
111: 1 I will give *t* to the LORD with all my
118:19 I will enter them and give *t* to the LORD.
118:21 I will give *t* to you,
118:28 You are my God, and I give *t* to you;
118:29 Give *t* to the LORD,
119: 7 I will give you *t* with an upright heart,
119:62 give you *t* because of your just ordinances.
122: 4 Israel, to give *t* to the name of the LORD.
136: 1 Give *t* to the LORD,
136: 2 Give *t* to the God of gods,
136: 3 Give *t* to the Lord of lords,
136:26 Give *t* to the God of heaven,
138: 1 I will give *t* to you, O LORD,
138: 2 your holy temple and give *t* to your name,
138: 4 the kings of the earth shall give *t* to you,
139:14 I give you *t* that I am fearfully,
140:14 Surely the just shall give *t* to your name:
142: 8 prison, that I may give *t* to your name.
145:10 Let all your works give you *t,*
Prv 28:23 He who rebukes a man gets more *t* in the
Wis 16:28 one must give you *t* before the sunrise,
Sir 20:15 has no friends, nor *t* for his generosity;
29:25 The visitor has no *t* for filling the cups;
39: 6 of wisdom and in prayer give *t* to the LORD,
47: 8 every deed he offered *t* to God Most High,
51: 1 I give you *t,* O God of my father;
Is 12: 1 I give you *t,* O LORD;
12: 4 Give *t* to the LORD, acclaim his name;
38:18 is not the nether world that gives you *t,*
38:19 The living, the living give you *t,*
Jer 33:11 singing, "Give *t* to the LORD of hosts,
Dn 2:23 O God of my fathers, I give *t* and praise,
3:89 Give *t* to the Lord,
3:90 praise him and give him *t,*
6:11 kneel in prayer and give *t* to his God
Hb 1:16 For *t* to them his portion is generous,
Mt 15:36 and after giving *t* he broke them and gave
26:27 Then he took a cup, gave *t,*
Mk 8: 6 Taking the seven loaves he gave *t,*
14:23 took a cup, gave *t* and passed it to them,
Lk 2:38 she gave *t* to God and talked about the
17:18 and give *t* to God except this foreigner?"
18:11 'I give you *t,* O God, that I am not like
22:17 a cup he offered a blessing in *t* and said:
22:19 Then, taking bread and giving *t,*
Jn 6:11 then took the loaves of bread, gave *t,*
6:23 eaten the bread after the Lord had given *t.*
15: 3 *t* to the word I have spoken to you.
Acts 27:35 bread, gave *t* to God before all of them,
Rom 1: 8 I give *t* to God through Jesus Christ for
1:21 did not glorify him as God or give him *t;*
6:17 *T* be to God, though once you were slaves
14: 6 to honor the Lord, and he gives *t* to God.
14: 6 honor the Lord, and he too gives *t* to God.
1Cor 3:10 *T* to the favor God showed me I laid a
7:25 who is trustworthy, *t* to the Lord's mercy.
10:30 be blamed for the food over which I gave *t?*
11:24 took bread, and after he had given *t,*
15:57 But *t* be to God who has given us the
2Cor 2:14 *T* be to God, who unfailingly leads us
4:15 to God because they who give *t* are many.
8:16 *T* be to God, who has put an equal zeal
9:11 through us it results in *t* offered to God.
9:15 *T* be to God for his indescribable gift!
Eph 5: 5 Instead, give *t.*
5:20 Give *t* to God the Father always and for
Phil 1: 3 give *t* to my God every time I think of you
1:19 *t* to your prayers and the support I
Col 1: 3 We always give *t* to God,
1:12 giving *t* to the Father for having made you
3:17 Give *t* to God the Father through him.
1Thes 3: 9 What *t* can we give to God for all the joy
5:18 never cease praying, render constant *t;*

THANKSGIVING (27)

Lv 7:12 When anyone makes a peace offering in *t,*
7:12 together with his *t* sacrifice he shall
7:13 the victim of his peace offering for *t.*
7:15 "The flesh of the *t* sacrifice shall be
19:24 be sacred to the LORD as a *t* feast to him.
22:29 you offer a *t* sacrifice to the LORD,
2Chr 31: 2 holocausts or peace offerings, *t* or praise,
Ezr 3:11 in songs of praise and *t* to the LORD,
Neh 11:17 of the psalms, who led the *t* at prayer;
12:24 *t* in fulfillment of the command of David,
12:27 with *t* hymns and the music of cymbals,
12:46 the hymns of praise and *t* to God came
Jdt 15:14 Judith led all Israel in this song of *t,*
Ps(s) 42: 5 of God, Amid loud cries of joy and *t,*
69:31 in song, and I will glorify him with *t;*
95: 2 Let us greet him with *t;*
100: 4 Enter his gates with *t,*
116:17 To you will I offer sacrifice of *t,*
147: 7 Sing to the LORD with *t;* sing praise
Is 51: 3 be found in her *t* and the sound of song.
Am 4: 5 Burn leavened food as a *t* sacrifice,
1Cor 14:16 be able to say "Amen" to your *t?*
Col 4: 2 to prayer, and pray in a spirit of *t.*
1Tm 2: 1 and *t* be offered for all men,
4: 3 with *t* by believers who know the truth.
4: 4 to be rejected when it is received with *t,*
Rv 7:12 Praise and glory, wisdom and *t* and honor,

THARES (2)

Est A:12 lodged at the court with Bagathan and *T,*
2:21 spent at the king's gate, Bagathan and *T,*

THASSI (1)

1Mc 2: 3 Simon, who was called *T;*

THATS (1)

Acts 24:25 *T* enough for now!

THEATER (2)

Acts 19:29 *t* and dragged in Gaius and Aristarchus,
19:31 him advising him not to venture into the *t.*

THEBES (3)

Jer 46:25 I will punish Amon of *T,*
Ez 30:14 fire to Zoan, and inflict punishments on *T.*
30:16 *T* shall be breached and its walls shall be

THEBEZ (2)

Jgs 9:50 Abimelech proceeded to *T,*
2Sm 11:21 from the wall above, so that he died in *T?*

THEFT (6)

Gn 30:33 goat, or a dark sheep, got there by *t!*"
Ex 22: 2 nothing, he shall be sold to pay for his *t.*
22:11 if the custodian is really guilty of *t,*
Wis 14:25 blood and murder, *t* and guile,
Sir 41:18 of *t* from the people where you settle,
Mk 7:21 acts of fornication, *t,*

THEFTS (2)

2Mc 4:39 Many sacrilegious *t* had been committed by
Rv 9:21 sorcery, their fornication or their *t.*

THEIRS (41)

Ex 29: 9 shall the priesthood be *t* by perpetual law,
Nm 16:26 men and do not touch anything that is *t:*
23:10 just, may my descendants be as many as *t!*
Dt 23: 4 of *t* even to the tenth generation,
1Kgs 22:13 Let your word be the same as any of *t;*
2Kgs 6:16 "Our side outnumbers *t.*"
2Chr 18:12 the king, let your word, like each of *t,*
24:18 and because of this crime of *t,*
Neh 5: 5 kinsmen and our children are as good as *t,*
12:47 the Levites made *t* to the sons of Aaron.
Tb 8: 5 pray and beg that deliverance might be *t.*
Jdt 5:20 God, and if we verify this offense of *t,*
2Mc 13:22 giving them his pledge and receiving *t,*
Ps(s) 58: 5 *T* is poison like a serpent's,
Wis 19:15 but what punishment was to be *t* since they
Is 61: 7 in their land, everlasting joy shall be *t.*
Jer 23:10 *T* is an evil course, theirs is unjust power.
44:28 shall know whose word stands, mine or *t.*
Ez 3: 8 But I will make your face as hard as *t,*
3: 8 as theirs, and your brow as stubborn as *t,*
16:52 sinful deeds, more abominable than *t,*
44:29 is under the ban in Israel shall be *t.*
46:16 that property is *t* by inheritance.
Hos 9: 4 *T* will be like mourners' bread,
Am 6: 2 or is your territory wider than *t?*
Zec 9:17 For what wealth is *t,* and what beauty!
Mt 5: 3 the reign of God is *t.*
5: 7 mercy shall be *t.*
5:10 for holiness' sake; the reign of God is *t.*
Lk 20:47 The heavier sentence will be *t.*"
Rom 1:18 spirit of men who, in this perversity of *t,*
9: 4 *T* were the adoption,
9: 5 *t* were the patriarchs,
1Cor 10: 6 to keep us from wicked desires such as *t.*
15:39 Birds are of their kind, fish are of *t.*
15:41 own, so has the moon, and the stars have *t.*
Phil 4:21 My brothers here send you *t,*
Heb 1: 4 the name he has inherited is superior to *t.*
2Pt 2:14 woman, *t* is a never-ending search for sin.
1Jn 4: 5 that is why *t* is the language of the world

THEME (10)

Jb 29: 1 Job took up his *t* anew and said;
36: 4 For indeed, my *t* cannot fail me:
Ps(s) 45: 2 My heart overflows with a goodly *t;*
104:34 Pleasing to him be my *t;*
119:54 the *t* of my song in the place of my exile.
Sir 39:12 *t* to shine like the moon in its fullness!
39:32 I took my stand, and wrote down as my *t:*
Mt 3: 1 in the desert of Judea, this was his *t:*
4:17 time on Jesus began to proclaim this *t:*
Mk 1: 7 The *t* of his preaching was:

THEMES (1)

Sir 44: 5 psalms, or discoursers on lyric *t;*

THEMSELVES (307)

Gn 3: 7 leaves together and made loincloths for *t.*
3: 8 the man and his wife hid *t* from the LORD
34:22 male among us be circumcised as they *t* are.
43:15 way down to Egypt to present *t* to Joseph.
44:14 so they flung *t* on the ground before him.
50:18 to fling *t* down before him and said,
Ex 5: 7 Let them go and gather straw *t!*
18:22 but all the lesser cases they can settle *t.*
18:26 but all the lesser cases they settled *t.*
19:10 have them sanctify *t* today and tomorrow.
19:14 them sanctify *t* and wash their garments.
19:17 stationed *t* at the foot of the mountain.
19:22 who approach the LORD must sanctify *t;*
29:33 They *t* are to eat of these things by which
32: 8 for *t* a molten calf and worshiping it,
32:31 a grave sin in making a god of gold for *t!*
40:32 for they washed *t* whenever they went into
Lv 18:24 am driving out of your way have defiled *t.*
20:27 have no one but *t* to blame for their death."
Nm 8: 7 and wash their clothes, and so purify *t.*
8:21 cleansed *t* of sin and washed their clothes,
25: 1 the people degraded *t* by having illicit
Dt 9:12 to them and have made for *t* a molten idol,
31:14 went and presented *t* at the meeting tent.
Jos 7:13 Tell them to sanctify *t* before tomorrow,
8:27 the Israelites took for *t* as booty the
14: 4 The Levites *t* received no share of the
17: 4 These presented *t* to Eleazar the priest,
Jgs 2:17 abandoned *t* to the worship of other gods.
8:33 Israelites again abandoned *t* to the Baals,
9: 8 the trees went to anoint a king over *t.*
9:51 *t* in and going up to the roof of the tower.
18:30 The Danites set up the carved idol for *t,*
19:22 While they were enjoying *t,*
20: 2 *t* in the assembly of the people of God.
Ru 2:15 among the sheaves *t* without scolding her,
1Sm 2: 5 The well-fed hire *t* out for bread,
13: 6 of the difficult situation, hid *t* in caves,
16: 5 *t* and invited them to the sacrifice.
2Sm 12:19 *t* and realized that the child was dead.
17:18 They let *t* down into this,
19:10 Israel all the people were arguing among *t,*
1Kgs 2: 4 'If your sons so conduct *t* that they
14:15 poles for *t* and thus provoked the LORD.
14:23 They, too, built for *t* high places,
18:28 and slashed *t* with swords and spears,
2Kgs 3:23 have fought among *t* and killed one another.
7: 6 large army, and they had reasoned among *t,*
12: 6 the priests may take for *t,*
17:10 set up pillars and sacred poles for *t*
17:15 The vanity they pursued, they *t* became:
17:16 God, and made for *t* two molten calves;
17:17 sold *t* into evil doing in the LORD's sight,
22:14 *t* to the Second Quarter in Jerusalem,
1Chr 12: 9 shield and spear, who bore *t* like lions,
15:14 *t* to bring up the ark of the LORD,
19: 6 that they had put *t* in bad odor with David,
19:16 Seeing *t* vanquished by Israel,
19:19 of Hadadezer saw *t* vanquished by Israel,
21:16 sackcloth, prostrated *t* face to the ground,
29:20 *t* before the LORD and before the king.
2Chr 5:11 priests who were present had purified *t*
7:14 has been pronounced, humble *t* and pray,
11:13 *t* to him from all parts of their land,
12: 6 of Israel and the king humbled *t* saying,
12: 7 When the LORD saw that they had humbled *t,*
12: 7 "Because they have humbled *t,*
28:12 *t* stood up in opposition to those who had
29:15 their brethren together and sanctified *t;*
29:29 who were with him knelt and prostrated *t.*
29:30 was full, then fell down and prostrated *t.*
29:34 and the priests had sanctified *t;*
29:34 willing than the priests to sanctify *t.*
30: 3 had not sanctified *t* in sufficient numbers,
30:11 Zebulun humbled *t* and came to Jerusalem.
30:15 sanctified *t* and brought holocausts into
30:17 many in the assembly had not sanctified *t,*
30:18 Issachar and Zebulun, had not cleansed *t.*
30:22 *t* well skilled in the service of the LORD.
30:24 The priests sanctified *t* in great numbers,
31: 4 devote *t* entirely to the law of the LORD.
31:18 since they were to sanctify *t* by sharing
34:32 conformed *t* to the covenant of God,
35:14 the Passover for *t* and for the priests.
35:14 Levites prepared for *t* and for the priests,
Ezr 6:20 for their brethren the priests, and for *t.*
6:21 who had separated *t* from the uncleanness
9: 1 Levites have kept *t* aloof from the peoples
9: 2 daughters as wives for *t* and their sons,
10:19 They pledged *t* to dismiss their wives,
Neh 8: 6 down and prostrated *t* before the LORD,
8:16 with which they made booths for *t,*

THEMSELVES (cont.)
9: 2 t from all who were of foreign extraction,
9: 3 and prostrated t before the LORD their God.
9:18 they made for t a molten calf,
9:25 and feast t on your immense good gifts.
10:29 who have separated t from the peoples
12:29 had built t settlements about Jerusalem).
12:30 The priests and Levites first purified t,
13:22 to purify t and to go and watch the gates,
Jdt 4:10 and slaves also girded t with sackcloth.
4:11 t in front of the temple building,
9: 7 a vast force, priding t on horse and rider,
11: 2 not despised me and brought this upon t.
15: 8 came to see for t the good things that the
15:13 crowned t with garlands of olive leaves.
Est 8:12 to defend t against those who attack them.
8:13 on that day to avenge t on their enemies.
9:16 provinces, also mustered and defended t,
9:23 The Jews took upon t for the future this
9:27 the Jews established and took upon t,
9:31 enjoined upon t and upon their race
1Mc 1:15 they allied t with the Gentiles and sold t
1:34 perverse men, who fortified t inside it,
1:48 and to let t be defiled with every kind of
4:55 prostrated t and adored and praised Heaven,
5:67 to fight in their desire to distinguish t.
8:15 They had made for t a senate house,
9:38 up and hid t under cover of the mountain.
10:83 the temple of their idol, to save t.
14:29 and his brothers have put t in danger and
14:36 who had built for t a citadel from which
2Mc 3: 2 the kings t honored the Place and
3:15 t in their priestly robes before the altar,
4:16 of this, they found t in serious trouble:
4:19 But the bearers t decided that the money
6: 4 they amused t with prostitutes and had
6:11 day, they had scruples about defending t.
8:15 and because they t bore his holy,
8:28 they divided among t and their children.
8:30 half to t and the rest to the persecuted,
10: 4 they prostrated t and begged the Lord that
10:20 were money lovers let t be bribed by some
11:11 Hurling t upon the enemy like lions,
12:38 they purified t according to custom and
12:42 the soldiers to keep t free from sin,
14:14 of the Jews would mean prosperity for t.
14:15 they sprinkled t with earth and prayed to
14:21 set on which the leaders would meet by t.
Jb 1: 6 of God came to present t before the LORD,
2: 1 of God came to present t before the LORD,
24:16 By day they shut t in;
36:13 The impious in heart lay up anger for t;
Ps(s) 27: 2 My foes and my enemies t tumble and fall.
66: 7 rebels may not exalt t.
68:31 Let them prostrate t with bars of silver;
Eccl 3:18 of showing that they are in t like beasts.
Wis 2: 1 they who said among t,
5: 3 They shall say among t,
14:28 or live lawlessly or lightly forswear t.
14:30 thought ill of God and devoted t to idols,
17: 8 soul t sickened with a ridiculous fear.
17:21 to t more burdensome than the darkness.
18: 1 their forms, since now they t had suffered,
19: 2 That though they t had agreed to the
19:18 the elements, in variable harmony among t,
Sir 2:17 their hearts and humble t before him.
32: 1 up, but with the guests be as one of t;
47:25 and more, and they lent t to every evil.
Is 3: 9 they deal out evil to t.
23:18 their fill and clothe t in choice attire.
43: 9 them produce witnesses to prove t right,
44: 9 are of no avail, as they t give witness.
47:14 cannot save t from the spreading flames.
49: 7 t Because of the LORD who is faithful,
56: 6 And the foreigners who join t to the LORD,
59: 6 nor can they cover t with their works.
66:17 sanctify and purify t to go to the groves,
Jer 2: 5 Went after empty idols, and became empty t?
2:13 They have dug t cisterns,
2:24 No beasts need tire t seeking her;
5:13 May their threats be carried out against t!"
7:19 is it not rather t, to their own confusion?
12:13 they have tired t out to no purpose;
31:12 They t shall be like watered gardens,
49:29 Their camels they shall carry off for t,
51:58 for the flames the peoples weary t.
51:64 [To "weary t" are the words of Jeremiah.]
Lam 1:19 Where they sought food for t,
2:10 on their heads and gird t with sackcloth;
Bar 6: 9 gold from their gods and spend it on t,
6:18 They light more lamps for them than for t,
6:26 neither move of t if one sets them upright,
6:40 the Chaldeans t have no respect for them;
6:41 t unable to reflect and abandon these gods,
6:48 among t where they can hide with them.
6:49 save t either from war or from disaster?
6:54 they t are burnt up in the fire like beams.
6:57 that was on them, and they cannot help t.
6:67 The beasts which can help t by fleeing to
6:71 they t will in the end be comsumed,
Ez 6: 9 shall loathe t because of their evil deeds,
14:14 they could save only t by their virtue,
14:20 they would save only t by their virtue.
30:17 and the cities t shall go into captivity.
34: 2 of Israel who have been pasturing t!
34: 8 pastured t and did not pasture my sheep,
34:10 sheep so that they may no longer pasture t.
37:23 shall they defile t with their idols,
40:12 the cells t were six cubits on either side,
40:43 On the tables t the flesh was laid.
44:18 not gird t with anything that causes sweat.
44:25 t unclean by coming near any dead person,
44:25 for these they may make t unclean.
Dn 2: 2 When they came and presented t to the king,
6: 6 Then these men said to t,
10: 7 they fled and hid t,
13:16 who had hidden t and were watching her.
13:32 her face so as to sate t with her beauty.
Hos 2: 2 t one head and come up from other lands,
4:18 carousing is over, they give t to harlotry;
7: 2 t that I remember all their wickedness.
7:14 For wheat and wine they lacerated t,
8: 4 silver and gold they made idols for t,
9: 4 Such food as they have shall be for t;
9:10 Baal-peor and consecrated t to the Shame,
13: 2 to sin, making for t molten images,
Jl 4:12 t and come up to the Valley of Jehoshaphat;
Am 6: 6 from bowls and anoint t with the best oils;
Jon 1: 5 To lighten the ship for t,
Zec 2:15 shall join t to the LORD on that day,
12: 3 attempt to lift it shall injure t badly,
12: 5 and the princes of Judah shall say to t,
Mt 2:11 They prostrated t and did him homage.
9: 3 At that some of the scribes said to t,
14:12 t to carry his body away and bury it.
14:15 go to the villages and buy some food for t."
15:35 directed the crowd to seat t on the ground.
17: 1 and led them up on a high mountain by t.
21:25 They thought to t, "If we say 'divine,'
23: 4 t will not lift a finger to budge them.
Mk 2: 6 of the scribes were sitting there asking t:
2: 8 their reasoning, though they kept it to t,
3:11 sight of him, fling t down at his feet,
6:32 off in the boat by t to a deserted place.
6:36 around here and buy t something to eat?"
7:27 of the household satisfy t at table first.
8:16 t that it was because they had no bread.
9: 2 t with him and led them up a high mountain.
9:10 They kept this word of his to t,
11:31 They thought to t, "If we say 'divine,'
14: 4 Some were saying to t indignantly:
Lk 7:49 his fellow guests began to ask among t,
8:35 went out to see for t what had happened.
9:12 neighborhood and find t lodging and food,
14:18 But they began to excuse t, one and all.
22:23 t as to which of them would do such a deed.
22:63 men guarding Jesus amused t at his expense.
Jn 4:45 They t had been at the feast and had seen
6:22 rather, they had set out by t.
6:52 At this the Jews quarreled among t,
7:35 This caused the Jews to exclaim among t:
9:22 who had already agreed among t that anyone
18:18 had made a charcoal fire to warm t by.
18:28 They did not enter the praetorium t,
Acts 1:14 Together they devoted t to constant prayer.
2: 4 They began to express t in foreign tongues
2:42 They devoted t to the apostles'
15:26 t to the cause of our Lord Jesus Christ.
15:32 Judas and Silas, who were t prophets,
20:30 men will present t distorting the truth
23:12 they bound t by oath not to eat or drink
23:20 "The Jews have agreed among t to ask you
23:21 they have bound t by oath not to eat or
26:31 talked matters over among t and admitted,
28:25 Without reaching any agreement among t,
Rom 1:21 t through speculating to no purpose,
2:14 without the law serve as a law for t.
10: 3 did not subject t to the justice of God.
13: 2 thus shall draw condemnation down upon t.
13: 6 t to his service with unremitting care.
1Cor 7:30 conduct t as though they owned nothing,
9:25 Athletes deny t all sorts of things.
15:29 who have t baptized on behalf of the dead?
2Cor 5:15 those who live might live no longer for t,
8: 5 t to God and then to us by the will of God.
10:12 with certain people who recommend t.
10:12 appraisers, comparing t with one another,
11:15 t as ministers of the justice of God.
Gal 5:12 you might go the whole way, and castrate t!
6:13 circumcision do not follow the law t.
Eph 2:11 on their flesh, call t "circumcised"
4:19 they have abandoned t to lust
Phil 2: 3 think humbly of others as superior to t.
Col 2: 2 and t to be closely united in love,
1Tm 1: 4 t with interminable myths and genealogies,
2: 9 the women must deport t properly.
3:13 deacons gain a worthy place for t
6: 9 They are letting t be captured by foolish
2Tm 3:13 bad to worse, deceiving others, t deceived.
4: 3 t with teachers who tickle their ears.
Ti 2: 6 men to keep t completely under control
3: 8 have committed t to God may be careful
3:14 Let our people devote t to honest work in
Heb 6: 6 God for t and holding him up to contempt.
6:16 Men swear by someone greater than t;
9:23 realities t called for better sacrifices.
11:13 By acknowledging t to be strangers and
1Pt 1:12 they were providing, not for t but for you,
3: 5 of past ages used to adorn t in this way,
2Pt 2: 1 own, thereby bringing on t swift disaster.
2:19 though they t are slaves of corruption
Jude 1:11 have abandoned t to Balaam's error for pay,
1:12 feasts without shame and only look after t.
Rv 6:15 all hid t in caves and mountain crags.
19:21 birds gorged t on the flesh of the slain.

THENCE (14)

Nm 34: 4 t it shall cross to Azmon,
34: 9 T the boundary shall reach to Ziphron and
34:12 t the boundary shall continue along the
Jos 15: 7 T it climbed to Debir,
15:10 t it descended to Beth-shemesh,
15:11 to Mount Baalah, t to include Jabneel,
16: 3 and to Gezer, ending t at the sea.
16: 6 to Upper Beth-horon and t to the sea.
18:17 extended to En-shemesh, and t to Geliloth,
19:29 t it cut back to Hosah and ended at the
2Kgs 2:25 Mount Carmel, and t he returned to Samaria.
Jb 39:29 From t he watches for his prey;
Jer 43: 5 t to dwell again in the land of Judah:
Ez 47:19 of Meribath-kadesh, t to the Wadi of Egypt,

THENCEFORTH (3)

Jos 4:14 and t during his whole life they respected
1Chr 11: 7 which t was called the City of David.
1Thes 4:17 T we shall be with the Lord unceasingly.

THEODOTUS (1)

2Mc 14:19 T and Mattathias to arrange an agreement.

THEOPHILUS (2)

Lk 1: 3 decided to set it in writing for you, T,
Acts 1: 1 In my first account, T,

THEREABOUT (1)

Jude 1: 7 Gomorrah, and the towns t indulged in lust,

THEREAFTER (9)

Lv 6:21 which it has been cooked shall t be broken;
Nm 3: 4 T only Eleazar and Ithamar performed the
1Chr 29:23 T Solomon sat on the throne of the LORD as
2Chr 20:30 T Jehoshaphat's kingdom enjoyed peace,
32:23 who t was exalted in the eyes of all the
Ezr 3: 5 T they offered the established holocaust,
1Mc 10:10 T Jonathan dwelt in Jerusalem,
Acts 13:31 and for many days t Jesus appeared to
Gal 1:21 T I entered the regions of Syria and

THEREBY (25)

Lv 4: 3 and t makes the people also become guilty,
15: 2 flow from his private parts is t unclean.
15:32 an emission of seed, and t becomes unclean;
17:11 atonement may t be made for your own lives,
21: 9 and t dishonors her father also,
Nm 30: 9 he t annuls the vow she had made or the
30:15 he t allows as valid any vow or any pledge
Dt 19: 3 You shall t divide into three regions the
2Kgs 23:19 Israel had erected, t provoking the LORD;
2Chr 34:32 He t committed all who were of Jerusalem
Sir 23: 8 the railer and the arrogant man fall t.
29:20 your means, but take care lest you fall t.
Mt 8:17 t fulfilling what had been said through
Jn 5:18 own Father, t making himself God's equal.
Acts 11:24 T large numbers were added to the Lord.
13:36 his fathers, t undergoing corruption.
Rom 8: 3 offering, t condemning sin in the flesh,
2Cor 1:22 sealed us, t depositing the first payment,
Gal 2: 4 in Christ Jesus and t to make slaves of us,
3:14 t making it possible for us to receive the
Heb 9: 8 The Holy Spirit was showing t that while
11: 7 He t condemned the world and inherited the
11:23 his birth, t disregarding the king's edict,
2Pt 2: 1 t bringing on themselves swift disaster.
2: 6 t showing what would happen in the future

THESSALONIANS (2)

1Thes 1: 1 to the church of the T who belong to God
2Thes 1: 1 to the church of the T who belong to God

THESSALONICA (7)

Acts 17: 1 Amphipolis and Apollonia and came to T,
17:11 were better disposed than those in T,
17:13 But when the Jews of T learned that the
20: 4 Aristarchus and Secundus from T;
27: 2 With us was a Macedonian, Aristarchus of T.
Phil 4:16 I was at T you sent something for my needs,
2Tm 4:10 present world, has left me and gone to T.

THEUDAS (1)

Acts 5:36 Not long ago a certain T came on the scene

THICK (20)

Ex 8:20 T swarms of flies entered the house of
2Sm 1:25 in the t of the battle,

1Kgs 7:26 It was a handbreadth *t*,
20:39 servant went into the *t* of the battle,
2Chr 4:5 It was a handbreadth *t*,
Jdt 1:2 the wall seventy cubits high and fifty *t*.
1Mc 13:33 fortifications with high towers, *t* walls,
Jb 22:13 Can he judge from the *t* darkness?
23:17 that *t* gloom were before me to conceal me.
38:9 garment and *t* darkness its swaddling bands?
Sir 50:10 Like a luxuriant olive tree *t* with fruit,
Is 60:2 the earth, and *t* clouds cover the peoples;
Jer 52:21 each was four fingers *t*,
Bar 6:12 of the house dust which is *t* upon them.
Ez 17:3 wings, with long pinions, with *t* plumage,
41:1 which were six cubits *t* on either side.
41:5 of the temple, which was six cubits *t*;
41:12 the building was five cubits *t* all around,
Zep 1:15 and gloom, A day of *t* black clouds,
Jude 1:13 or shooting stars for whom the *t* gloom of

THICKEN (2)

Jb 10:10 pour me out as milk, and *t* me like cheese?
Zep 1:12 I will punish the men who *t* on their lees,

THICKENING (1)

2Sm 22:12 him, with spattering rain and *t* clouds,

THICKER (2)

1Kgs 12:10 little finger is *t* than my father's body.
2Chr 10:10 little finger is *t* than my father's body.

THICKET (5)

Gn 22:13 spied a ram caught by its horns in the *t*.
Jb 38:40 in their dens, or lie in wait in the *t*?
Is 21:13 the *t* in the nomad country spend the night,
Jer 49:19 As when a lion comes up from the *t* of
50:44 *t* to the permanent feeding grounds,

THICKETS (7)

1Sm 13:6 situation, hid themselves in caves, in *t*,
2Sm 18:8 and the *t* consumed more combatants that
1Mc 9:45 on one side, marsh and *t* on the other,
Is 9:17 It kindles the forest *t*,
10:34 The forest *t* are felled with the axe,
Jer 4:29 They shrink into the *t*,
12:5 what will you do in the *t* of the Jordan?

THICKNESS (2)

1Kgs 7:15 their metal was of four fingers' *t*.
Jdt 1:3 with a *t* of sixty cubits at the base.

THIEF (28)

Ex 22:1 "[If a *t* is caught in the act of
22:6 is stolen from the latter's house, the *t*,
22:7 If the *t* is not caught,
2Mc 4:42 *t* himself they slew near the treasury.
Jb 24:15 In the night the *t* roams about,
30:5 men, with an outcry like that against a *t*—
Ps(s) 50:18 When you see a *t*, you keep pace with him
Prv 6:30 Men despise not the *t* if he steals to
29:24 The accomplice of a *t* is his own enemy:
Sir 5:17 For shame has been created for the *t*,
20:24 Better a *t* than an inveterate liar,
Jer 2:26 As the *t* is shamed when caught,
Ez 18:10 But if he begets a son who is a *t*,
Zec 5:3 with it shall every *t* be swept away,
5:4 and it shall come into the house of the *t*,
Mt 24:43 if the owner of the house knew when the *t*
Lk 12:33 no *t* comes near nor any moth destroys.
12:39 head of the house knew when the *t* was
Jn 10:1 in some other way is a *t* and a marauder.
10:10 The *t* comes only to steal and slaughter
12:6 for the poor, but because he was a *t*.
1Cor 5:11 an abusive person, a drunkard, or a *t*.
1Thes 5:2 the Lord is coming like a *t* in the night.
5:4 day should catch you off guard, like a *t*.
1Pt 4:15 of you suffers for being a murderer, a *t*,
2Pt 3:10 The day of the Lord will come like a *t*,
Rv 3:3 yourselves I will come upon you like a *t*,
16:15 I come like a *t*.

THIEVES (16)

Is 1:23 Your princes are rebels and comrades of *t*;
Jer 7:11 my name become in your eyes a den of *t*?
48:27 Was she caught among *t*,
49:9 If *t* by night, they would destroy
Bar 6:56 They are safe from neither *t* nor bandits,
Hos 7:1 They practice falsehood, *t* break in,
Jl 2:9 In at the windows they come like *t*.
Ob 1:5 If *t* came to you, robbers by night,
Mt 6:19 *t* break in and steal.
6:20 nor rust corrode nor *t* break in and steal.
21:13 but you are turning it into a den of *t*."
Mk 11:17 but you have turned it into a den of *t*."
Lk 19:46 prayer' but you have made it 'a den of *t*.'"
Jn 10:8 All who came before me were *t* and
1Cor 5:10 world, or the covetous or *t* or idolaters.
6:10 no homosexual perverts, sodomites, *t*,

THIGH (13)

Gn 24:2 "Put your hand under my *t*,
24:9 So the servant put his hand under the *t* of
47:29 *t* as a sign of your constant loyalty to me;
Ex 29:22 the fat that is on them, and its right *t*,
29:27 *t* of whatever raised offering is raised up,
Jgs 3:16 wore it under his clothes over his right *t*.
3:21 left hand drew the dagger from his right *t*,
2Sm 20:8 which was slung, in its sheath near his *t*,
Ps(s) 45:4 Gird your sword upon your *t*, O mighty one!
Sir 19:11 man's *t* is gossip in the breast of a fool.
Ez 21:17 Therefore, slap your *t*,
24:4 *t* and shoulder; Fill it with the choicest
Rv 19:16 the part of the cloak that covered his *t*:

THIGHS (8)

Ex 28:42 naked flesh from their loins to their *t*.
Nm 5:21 *t* to waste away and your belly to swell!
5:22 your belly swell and your *t* waste away!'
5:27 belly will swell and her *t* will waste away,
Jdt 9:2 maiden's girdle, shamefully exposed her *t*,
Jb 40:17 the sinews of his *t* are like cables.
Sg 7:2 Your rounded *t* are like jewels,
Dn 2:32 arms were silver, its belly and *t* bronze,

THIN (10)

Gn 41:6 of grain, *t* and blasted by the east wind;
41:7 seven *t* ears swallowed up the seven fat,
41:23 and *t* and blasted by the east wind,
41:24 *t* ears swallowed up the seven healthy ears.
41:27 So also, the seven *t*,
41:27 them are seven years, as are the seven *t*,
Sg 4:2 big with twins, none of them *t* and barren.
6:6 big with twins, none of them *t* and barren.
Is 17:4 shall fade, and his full body grow *t*,
51:6 Though the heavens grow *t* like smoke,

THING (147)

Gn 3:13 the woman, "Why did you do such a *t*?"
7:14 every kind of creeping *t* of the earth,
7:23 The LORD wiped out every living *t* on earth:
8:17 with you every living *t* that is with you
18:25 Far be it from you to do such a *t*,
19:7 you my brothers, not to do this wicked *t*.
20:10 him, "that you should have done such a *t*?"
22:12 "Do not do the least *t* to him.
24:50 "This *t* comes from the LORD;
30:31 your flock, if you do this one *t* for me:
31:28 What you have now done is a senseless *t*.
34:7 such a *t* could not be tolerated.
34:14 "We could not do such a *t*,"
44:7 be it from your servants to do such a *t*!
44:15 "How could you do such a *t*?"
Ex 9:22 and every growing *t* in the land of Egypt."
9:25 *t* and splintered every tree in the fields.
18:14 "What sort of *t* is this that you are
22:8 where another claims that the *t* is his,
Lv 5:2 being aware of it, touches any unclean *t*,
5:23 restore the *t* that was stolen or unjustly
5:24 make full restitution of the *t* itself,
13:49 the *t* is indeed infected with leprosy and
13:57 the *t* infected shall be destroyed by fire.
13:58 the *t* shall be washed a second time,
15:10 up any such *t* shall wash his garments,
18:22 such a *t* is an abomination.
Nm 18:15 Every living *t* that opens the womb,
Dt 7:26 not bring any abominable *t* into your house,
7:26 and abhor it utterly as a *t* that is doomed.
11:6 and every living *t* that belonged to them.
14:3 "You shall not eat any abominable *t*.
19:20 and never again do a *t* so evil among you.
1Sm 3:17 to you if you hide a single *t* he told you."
22:15 servant or anyone in my family of such a *t*.
24:7 that I should do such a *t* to my master,
29:10 So the first *t* tomorrow,
2Sm 3:13 But one *t* I require of you.
11:11 lives and as you live, I will do no such *t*."
14:13 same kind of *t* against the people of God?
24:3 my lord the king to order a *t* of this kind?"
1Chr 11:19 "God forbid that I should do such a *t*!
17:19 your purpose, you have done this great *t*.
17:26 have promised this good *t* to your servant,
21:3 why does my lord seek to do this *t*?
21:8 "I have sinned greatly in doing this *t*.
21:17 am the one who sinned, I did this wicked *t*.
2Chr 25:16 this *t* and have refused to hear my counsel."
34:33 Josiah removed every abominable *t* from all
Ezr 9:3 When I had heard this *t*,
Neh 13:7 evil *t* that Eliashib had done for Tobiah,
13:17 "What is this evil *t* that you are doing,
Tb 2:8 down for execution because of this very *t*;
12:12 the same *t* when you used to bury the dead.
Est C:3 and every wonderful *t* under the heavens.
1Mc 9:10 me to do such a *t* as to flee from them!
2Mc 4:16 whom they desired to imitate in every *t*,
Jb 6:6 Can a *t* insipid be eaten without salt?
6:21 you see a terrifying *t* and are afraid.
12:10 In his hand is the soul of every living *t*,
12:14 If he breaks a *t* down,
16:2 I have heard this sort of *t* many times.
Ps(s) 27:4 One *t* I ask of the LORD; this I seek:
34:11 those who seek the LORD want for no good *t*.
62:12 One *t* God said; these two things which
84:12 no good *t* from those who walk in sincerity.
101:3 I will not set before my eyes any base *t*.
145:16 and satisfy the desire of every living *t*.
Prv 16:20 He who plans a *t* will be successful;
27:7 man who is hungry, any bitter *t* is sweet.
Eccl 1:10 Even the *t* of which we say,
7:27 adding one *t* to another that I might
Wis 11:25 And how could a *t* remain,
13:17 not ashamed to address the *t* without a soul.
13:19 of a *t* with hands completely inert.
14:10 and the *t* made shall be punished with its
15:17 he makes a dead *t* with his lawless hands.
17:9 even though no monstrous *t* frightened them,
Sir 1:8 every living *t* according to his bounty;
13:14 every living *t* loves
32:20 and let not the same *t* trip you twice.
39:19 not a *t* escapes his eye.
41:11 Man's body is a fleeting *t*,
41:14 nor is it always the proper *t* to blush:
42:20 no single *t* escapes him.
Is 8:20 That kind of *t* they will surely say.
23:8 Who has planned such a *t* against Tyre,
24:3 stripped, for the LORD has decreed this *t*.
44:20 a *t* that cannot save itself when the flame
44:20 "Is not this *t* in my right hand a fraud?"
66:8 Who ever heard of such a *t*,
Jer 5:30 horrible *t* has happened in the land:
7:31 a *t* as I never commanded or had in mind.
18:15 burn incense to a *t* that does not exist.
19:5 a *t* as I neither commanded nor spoke of,
31:22 LORD has created a new *t* upon the earth:
44:22 a *t* accursed and without inhabitants,
Lam 1:17 has become in their midst a *t* unclean.
3:38 Most High, whether the *t* be good or bad!
Ez 17:23 every winged *t* in the shade of its boughs.
Dn 2:10 and mighty, asked such a *t* of any magician,
13:27 had any such *t* been said about Susanna.
Hos 6:10 house of Israel I have seen a horrible *t*:
8:8 is now among the nations a *t* of no value.
9:10 became as abhorrent as the *t* they loved.
13:15 It shall loot his land of every precious *t*.
Am 8:7 Never will I forget a *t* they have done!
Jon 1:10 "How could you do such a *t*— They
Hb 2:19 Can such a *t* give oracles?
Mal 2:11 an abominable *t* has been done in Israel
Mt 9:16 *t* he has used to cover the hole will pull,
12:4 a *t* forbidden to him and his men or anyone
16:22 forbid that any such *t* ever happen to you!"
21:30 came to his second son and said the same *t*.
22:26 The same *t* happened to the second,
24:15 you see the abominable and destructive *t*
Mk 1:30 first *t* they did was to tell him about her.
2:21 the very *t* he has used to cover the hole
2:24 they do a *t* not permitted on the sabbath?"
10:21 him, "There is one *t* more you must do.
12:21 The same *t* happened to the third;
Lk 1:53 The hungry he has given every good *t*,
10:42 one *t* only is required.
18:22 "There is one *t* further you must do.
22:35 "Not a *t*," they replied.
Jn 1:41 The first *t* he did was seek out his
3:9 "How can such a *t* happen?"
9:33 God, he could never have done such a *t*."
21:5 "Not a *t*," they answered.
Acts 9:41 The next *t* he did was to call in those who
12:9 The whole *t* seemed to him a mirage.
22:14 The next *t* he said was,
Rom 3:8 This is the very *t* that some slanderously
7:13 Did this good *t* then become death for me?
1Cor 5:6 This boasting of yours is an ugly *t*.
15:40 splendor of the heavenly bodies is one *t*,
2Cor 5:5 God has fashioned us for this very *t* and
8:20 There is one *t* I wish to avoid,
Gal 2:10 one *t* that I was making every effort to do.
3:2 I want to learn only one *t* from you:
Eph 5:24 should submit to their husbands in every *t*.
Phil 1:23 with Christ, for that is the far better *t*;
1Tm 6:17 not to rely on so uncertain a *t* as wealth.
Heb 10:31 *t* to fall into the hands of the living God.
11:29 attempted the same *t* they were drowned.
Jas 4:17 knows the right *t* to do and does not do it,
1Jn 5:16 There is such a *t* as a deadly sin;
3Jn 1:6 And you will do a good *t* if,

THINGS (533)

Gn 1:24 cattle, creeping *t*, and wild animals
1:25 and all kinds of creeping *t* of the earth.
1:28 all the living *t* that move on the earth."
6:7 the creeping *t* and the birds of the air,
6:20 of beasts, and of all kinds of creeping *t*,
7:23 the creeping *t* and the birds of the air;
8:17 or animals or creeping *t* of the earth
24:66 recounted to Isaac all the *t* he had done.
27:20 your God, let *t* turn out well with me."
31:12 all the *t* that Laban has been doing to you.
31:37 Now that you have ransacked all my *t*,
38:23 "Let her keep the *t*,"
38:25 whom these *t* belong that I am with child.
42:36 Why must such *t* always happen to me?"
44:7 "How can my lord say such *t*?

THINGS (cont.)

Ex 21:11 If he does not grant her these three t,
29:24 All these t you shall put into the hands
29:28 Such t are due to Aaron and his sons from
29:33 They themselves are to eat of these t by
31: 4 of embroidery, in making t of gold,
31: 6 make all the t I have ordered you to make:
31:11 All these t they shall make just as I have
35:32 of embroidery, in making t of gold,
Lv 4: 2 the LORD by doing one of the forbidden t,
4:22 doing one of the t which are forbidden
4:27 sin inadvertently by doing one of the t
5:17 the t which are forbidden by some
8:27 t into the hands of Aaron and his sons,
18:23 such t are abhorrent.
18:24 not defile yourselves by any of these t
19:10 These t you shall leave for the poor and
20:23 because all these t that they have done
21:23 not profane these t that are sacred to me,
23:22 These t you shall leave for the poor and
Nm 4:26 be done with these t shall be their task.
7: 5 that these t may be put to use in the
27:17 who shall act as their leader in all t,
Dt 4: 9 forget the t which your own eyes have seen,
4:30 when all these t shall have come upon you,
10:21 terrible t which your own eyes have seen.
18: 3 a right to the following t from the people:
18:12 does such t is an abomination to the LORD,
22: 5 does such t is an abomination to the LORD,
23:19 these t are an abomination to the LORD,
26:11 merry over all these good t which the LORD,
30: 1 all these t which I have set before you,
Jgs 13:13 from all the t of which I spoke to her.
1Sm 2:23 "Why are you doing such t?
2:24 No, my sons, you must not do these t!
9:21 Why say such t to me?"
12:24 in mind the great t he has done among you.
13:14 but as t are, your kingdom shall not
24:17 When David finished saying these t to Saul,
2Sm 7:23 and by doing awe-inspiring t as you
14:19 your servant all these t she was to say.
14:20 of God, so that he knows all t on earth."
1Kgs 18:36 and have done all these t by your command.
2Kgs 1: 7 who came up to you and said these t to you?"
7: 8 came into another tent, took t from it,
8: 4 "all the great t that Elisha has done."
9:18 "What does it matter to you how t are?"
9:19 "What does it matter to you how t are?"
17:11 They did evil t that provoked the LORD,
23:17 t you have done to the altar of Bethel."
1Chr 16:26 the gods of the nations are t of nought,
29:17 I have willingly given all these t
2Chr 6:41 may your faithful ones rejoice in good t.
7:10 at the good t the LORD had done for David,
19: 3 Yet some good t are to be found in you,
31: 6 t that had been consecrated to the LORD,
31:12 t were deposited there in safekeeping.
31:12 of these t was Conaniah the Levite,
31:14 and the most holy of the consecrated t.
31:18 by sharing faithfully in the consecrated t.
32:27 jewels, and other precious t of all kinds;
36: 8 of Jehoiakim, the abominable t that he did,
Neh 6:14 O my God, because of these t they did;
9:25 of houses filled with all good t,
9:35 in the midst of the many good t that you
9:36 that they might eat its fruits and good t—
Tb 4:19 but the Lord himself gives all good t.
12: 6 the many good t he has done for you,
12:20 down all these t that have happened to you."
Jdt 6: 5 for saying these t in a moment of
8:10 was in charge of all her t to ask Uzziah,
8:14 you fathom God, who has made all these t,
9: 6 the t you decide on come forward and say,
9:13 have planned dire t against your covenant,
11:12 consume all the t which God in his laws
11:13 t which no layman should even touch with
11:14 inhabitants there have also done these t.
12: 2 supplied from the t I brought with me."
12:19 She then took the t her maid had prepared,
14:13 said to the one in charge of all his t,
15: 8 good t that the Lord had done for Israel,
15:11 wagons to them, and loaded these t on them.
16:19 all the t of Holofernes that the people
Est A:15 Then the king had these t recorded;
C: 2 almighty King, all t are in your power,
C: 5 You know all t.
C:25 "You know all t.
F: 2 recall the dream I had about these very t,
1Mc 3:48 to learn about the t for which the
4:27 because t in Israel had not turned out as
6:27 them, they will do even worse t than these,
6:59 that they became angry and did all these t."
10:22 When Demetrius heard of these t,
11:35 other t that would henceforth be due to us,
12: 9 Though we have no need of these t,
14:25 When the people heard of these t,
16:24 and his other achievements these t are
2Mc 1:24 "Lord, Lord God, creator of all t,
2: 8 Then the Lord will disclose these t,
2:13 Besides these t, it is also told in the records
2:25 studious who wish to commit t to memory,
3: 9 and he asked if these t were really true.
4:30 While these t were taking place,

6: 4 into the temple t that were forbidden,
7:18 We suffer these t on our own account,
7:18 why such astonishing t have happened to us.
7:28 God did not make them out of existing t;
11:18 the t that were acceptable he has granted.
12:41 who brings to light the t that are hidden.
13: 9 inflicting on the Jews worse t than those
Jb 2:10 We accept good t from God;
8: 2 How long will you utter such t?
9:10 does great t past finding out, marvelous t
10:13 Yet these t you have hidden in your heart;
12: 3 for who does not know such t as these?
13:20 These t only do not use against me,
22:18 he had filled their houses with good t!
23:14 and many such t may yet be in his mind.
28:11 the streams, and brings hidden t to light.
33:29 Lo, all these t God does,
37: 5 He does great t beyond our knowing;
42: 2 I know that you can do all t,
42: 3 great t that I do not understand; t too
Ps(s) 8: 7 your hands, putting all t under his feet:
15: 5 who does these t shall never be disturbed.
35:11 t I knew not of, they lay to my charge.
46: 9 the astounding t he has wrought on earth:
50:21 When you do these t,
62:12 these two t which I heard:
65: 5 with the good t of your house, the holy t
71:19 You have done great t;
78:12 Before their fathers he did wondrous t,
87: 3 Glorious t are said of you, O city of God!
96: 5 the gods of the nations are t of nought,
97: 7 All who worship graven t are put to shame,
97: 7 put to shame, who glory in the t of nought;
104:25 number of living t both small and great,
104:28 your hand, they are filled with good t.
106:22 the land of Ham, terrible t at the Red Sea.
107: 9 and filled the hungry soul with good t.
107:43 t and to understand the favors of the LORD?
119:91 all t serve you.
126: 2 "The LORD has done great t for them."
126: 3 The LORD has done great t for us;
131: 1 things, nor with t too sublime for me.
138: 2 above all t your name and your promise.
144:15 Happy the people for whom t are thus;
148:10 you creeping t and you winged fowl.
Prv 6:16 There are six t the LORD hates,
8: 6 for noble t I speak;
12:14 of his words a man has his fill of good t,
13: 2 the fruit of his words a man eats good t,
30: 7 Two t I ask of you, deny them not
30:15 Three t are never satisfied,
30:18 Three t are too wonderful for me,
30:21 Under three t the earth trembles,
30:24 Four t are among the smallest on the earth,
30:29 Three t are stately in their stride,
Eccl 1: 2 All t are vanity!
1:13 wisdom all t that are done under the sun.
1:14 seen all t that are done under the sun,
2: 1 with pleasure and the enjoyment of good t."
2:24 provide himself with good t by his labors.
4: 8 do I toil and deprive myself of good t?"
6: 2 that he lacks none of all the t he craves;
7:14 On a good day enjoy good t,
7:15 have seen all manner of t in my vain days:
7:22 All these t I probed in wisdom.
8: 1 man, and who knows the explanation of t?
8: 9 All these t I considered and I applied my
9: 3 Among all the t that happen under the sun,
9: 3 worst, that t turn out the same for all.
12: 8 vanities, says Qoheleth, all t are vanity!
Wis 1: 8 one who utters wicked t can go unnoticed,
1:14 fashioned all t that they might have being;
2: 6 let us enjoy the good t that are real,
2:16 aloof from our paths as from t impure.
4:12 For the witchery of paltry t obscures what
7:11 good t together came to me in her company,
7:17 he gave me sound knowledge of existing t,
7:21 Such t as are hidden I learned and such
7:24 and pervades all t by reason of her purity.
7:27 And she, who is one, can do all t,
8: 1 to end mightily and governs all t well.
8: 5 more rich than Wisdom, who produces all t?
8: 8 copious learning, she knows the t of old,
9: 1 you who have made all t by your word
9:11 For she knows and understands all t,
9:16 And scarce do we guess the t on earth,
9:16 but when t are in heaven,
10: 2 fall, and gave him power to rule all t.
10:10 of God and gave him knowledge of holy t;
11: 5 For by the t through which their foes were
11:16 by the very t through which he sins.
11:20 all t by measure and number and weight.
11:23 mercy on all, because you can do all t;
11:24 For you love all t that are and loathe
11:26 But you spare all t, because they are yours,
12: 1 for your imperishable spirit is in all t!
12:15 as you are just, you govern all t justly;
12:16 over all t makes you lenient to all.
12:27 the t through which they suffered distress,
12:27 tortured by the very t they deemed gods,
13: 1 and who from the good t seen did not
13: 4 let them from these t realize how much
13: 5 beauty of created t their original author,

13: 7 what they see, because the t seen are fair.
13:10 are they, and in dead t are their hopes,
13:10 who termed gods t made by human hands:
14:16 t were worshiped by princely decrees.
15: 6 Lovers of evil t, and worthy of such hopes
15:17 For he is better than the t he worships;
18: 9 share alike the same good t and dangers,
Sir 1: 4 Before all t else wisdom was created;
2: 9 You who fear the LORD, hope for good t,
3:20 into t beyond your strength search not.
3:22 when shown t beyond human understanding.
6:11 When t go well, he is your other self,
7:35 for these t you will be loved.
11: 3 Least is the bee among winged t,
14:14 Deprive not yourself of present good t,
16: 5 Many such t has my eye seen,
17: 3 and with power over all t else on earth.
18: 1 is the judge of all t without exception;
18:26 before the LORD all t are fleeting.
18:27 A wise man is circumspect in all t;
20: 8 some t gained are a man's loss.
23:20 He who knows all t before they exist still
25: 1 With three t I am delighted,
26: 5 There are three t at which my heart quakes,
27:30 Wrath and anger are hateful t,
29:28 Painful t to a sensitive man are abuse at
30:20 who groans at the good t his eyes behold!
39:25 Good t for the good he provided from the
39:25 but for the wicked good t and bad.
41:24 These are the t you should rightly avoid
42: 1 But of these t be not ashamed,
42:18 sees from of old the t that are to come:
43:34 Beyond these, many t lie hid;
43:35 It is the LORD who has made all t,
44: 3 prudence, or seers of all t in prophecy;
48:25 end of time, hidden t yet to be fulfilled.
50:22 of all, who has done wondrous t on earth;
50:28 Happy the man who meditates upon these t,
Is 1:12 in to visit me, who asks these t of you?
1:18 Come now, let us set t right,
1:19 obey, you shall eat the good t of the land;
32: 8 noble man plans noble t, and by noble things
41: 5 these t are near, they come to pass.
41:22 What are the t of long ago?
41:22 or declare to us the t to come!
41:23 Foretell the t that shall come afterward,
42: 9 See, the earlier t have come to pass,
42:16 These t I do for them,
42:20 You see many t without taking note;
43: 9 this, or foretold to us the earlier t?
43:18 the past, the t of long ago consider not;
44: 7 Let them foretell to us the t to come.
44:24 I am the LORD, who made all t,
45: 7 I, the LORD, do all these t.
46: 8 remember the former t,
46:10 in advance, t not yet done.
47: 7 But you did not lay these t to heart,
47: 9 Both these t shall come to you suddenly,
48: 3 T of the past I foretold long ago,
48: 6 From now on I announce new t to you,
48:14 Who among you foretold these t?
57: 6 Should I decide not to punish these t?
60:22 accomplish these t when their time comes.
65: 5 These t enkindle my wrath,
65:12 sight and preferred t which displease me,
65:17 The t of the past shall not be remembered
66: 2 all these t when all of them came to be,
66:17 eat swine's flesh, loathsome t and mice,
Jer 2:11 have changed their glory for useless t.
4: 1 you put your detestable t out of my sight,
5: 7 Why should I pardon you these t?
5: 9 Shall I not punish them for these t?
5:19 "Why has the LORD done all these t to us?"
5:25 Your crimes have prevented these t,
5:29 Shall I not punish these t?
6:15 they have done abominable t,
8:12 they have done abominable t,
9: 8 For these t, says the LORD,
10:16 he is the creator of all t;
13:22 ask in your heart why these t befall you:
14:22 You alone have done all these t.
18:13 Truly horrible t has virgin Israel done!
20: 1 prophesying these t by the priest Pashhur,
25:30 against them all these t and say to them:
26:10 princes of Judah were informed of these t,
26:15 you, to speak all these t for you to hear."
26:20 he prophesied the same t against this city
28: 6 May he fulfill the t you have prophesied
29:23 alleging in my name t I did not command.
33: 3 you t great beyond reach of your knowledge.
34: 6 Jeremiah told all these t to Zedekiah,
36:16 must certainly tell the king all these t."
38: 4 all the people, by speaking such t to them;
44:22 deeds, the horrible t which you were doing;
45: 5 And do you seek great t for yourself?
48:44 For I will bring these t upon Moab in the
50:38 they shall be made frantic by fearful t.
51:19 of Jacob, he is the creator of all t;
Bar 3:32 Yet he who knows all t knows her;
Ez 8:10 all kinds of creeping t and loathsome beasts
8:17 to do the abominable t they have done here
16: 5 or compassion to do any of these t for you.
16:30 the Lord GOD, that you did all these t,

16:43 a girl, but enraged me with all these *t*,
16:51 You have done more abominable *t* than they,
17:15 Can he who does such *t* escape?
17:18 his hand in pledge, he did all these *t*.
18:10 *t* (though the father does none of them),
18:12 his eyes to idols, does abominable *t*,
18:24 of abominable *t* that the wicked man does,
20: 7 the detestable *t* that have held your eyes;
20: 8 the detestable *t* that had held their eyes,
20:43 because of all the evil *t* you did.
22: 9 in your midst are those who do lewd *t*.
22:11 *t* with the wives of their neighbors,
22:25 seizing their wealth and precious *t*,
23:30 and harlotry have brought these *t* upon you,
24:19 all these *t* that you are doing mean for us?"
33:26 rely on your sword, you do abominable *t*,
33:29 of all abominable the *t* they have done.
35:12 I have heard all the contemptuous *t* you
44:13 of my sacred things, or the most sacred *t*.
Dn 2:22 hidden *t* and knows what is in the darkness,
7:16 he made known to me the meaning of the *t*:
12: 6 it be to the end of these appalling *t*?"
12: 7 brought to an end, all these *t* should end.
13:42 are aware of all *t* before they come to be:
13:43 though I have done none of the *t* with
Hos 2:20 and with the *t* that crawl on the ground.
14:10 Let him who is wise understand these *t*;
Jl 2:21 for the LORD has done great *t*.
Mi 2: 6 preach, "let them not preach of these *t*!"
Na 2:10 their wealth in precious *t* of every kind!
Hb 1:14 the sea, like creeping *t* without a ruler.
Zep 1: 2 away all *t* from the face of the earth,
Zec 4: 4 who spoke with me, "What are these *t*,
4: 5 "Do you not know what these *t* are?"
8:12 all these *t* I will have the remnant of the
8:16 These then are the *t* you should do:
8:17 For all these *t* I hate, says the LORD.
Mt 6:32 are always running after these *t*.
6:33 and all these *t* will be given you besides.
7:11 Father give good *t* to anyone who asks him!
13:47 the lake, which collected all sorts of *t*.
15:18 It is *t* like these that make a man impure.
15:20 These are the *t* that make a man impure.
18: 7 *t* will come on the world through scandal!
19:26 but for God all *t* are possible."
21:23 "On what authority are you doing these *t*?
21:24 tell you on what authority I do the *t* I do.
21:27 tell you on what authority I do the *t* I do."
24: 6 Such *t* are bound to happen,
24:33 when you see all these *t* happening,
Mk 4:22 *T* are hidden only to be revealed at a
4:34 explaining *t* privately to his disciples.
8:32 He said these *t* quite openly.
10:27 With God all *t* are possible."
11:16 anyone to carry *t* through the temple area.
11:28 "On what authority are you doing these *t*?
11:29 tell you on what authority I do the *t* I do.
11:33 tell you on what authority I do the *t* I do."
13: 7 Such *t* are bound to happen,
13:29 same way, when you see these *t* happening,
13:30 not pass away until all these *t* take place.
14:36 (O Father), you have the power to do all *t*.
16:20 but other terrible *t* are imminent.
Lk 1:20 until the day these *t* take place,
1:49 God who is mighty has done great *t* for me,
1:66 heard stored these *t* up in their hearts,
2:19 these *t* and reflected on them in her heart.
2:51 meanwhile kept all these *t* in memory.
4:23 *t* we have heard you have done in Capernaum.'
5:26 saying, "We have seen incredible *t* today!"
10:41 you are anxious and upset about many *t*;
11:13 know how to give your children good *t*,
11:42 These are the *t* you should practice,
12:26 If the smallest *t* are beyond your power,
12:30 world are always running after these *t*.
12:30 Your Father knows that you need such *t*.
16:10 If you can trust a man in little *t*,
18:27 *T* that are impossible for men are possible
19:11 to these *t* he went on to tell a parable,
19:32 errand and found *t* just as he had said.
20: 2 us, by what authority do you do these *t*?
21: 6 He said, "These *t* you are contemplating
21: 9 These *t* are bound to happen first,
21:28 When these *t* begin to happen,
21:31 see all the *t* happening of which I speak,
23:31 If they do these *t* in the green wood,
24: 9 all these *t* to the Eleven and the others.
24:18 *t* that went on there these past few days?"
24:19 He said to them, "What *t*?"
24:21 the third day since these *t* happened,
Jn 1: 3 Through him all *t* came into being,
1:50 You will see much greater *t* than that."
2:18 you show us authorizing you to do these *t*?"
3:12 believe when I tell you about earthly *t*,
5:16 It was because Jesus did *t* such as this on
5:34 I refer to these *t* only for your salvation.)
7: 4 If you are going to do *t* like these,
13:17 Once you know all these *t*,
16: 4 But I have told you these *t* that when
16:13 and will announce to you the *t* to come.
16:25 spoken these *t* to you in veiled language.
21:24 disciple who is the witness to these *t*;
21:25 are still many other *t* that Jesus did,
Acts 2:44 Those who believed shared all *t* in common;
4:28 They have brought about the very *t* which
7:50 Did not my hand make all these *t*?
15:18 these *t* known to him from of old.'
15:29 You will be well advised to avoid these *t*.
17: 3 He explained many *t*,
17:11 Scriptures to see whether these *t* were so.
19:32 people were shouting all sorts of *t*,
23: 8 while the Pharisees believe in all these *t*.)
Rom 1:20 recognized through the *t* he has made.
1:27 Men did shameful *t* with men,
1:32 that all who do such *t* deserve death;
2: 1 yourself, since you do the very same *t*.
2: 2 judgment on men who do such *t* is just."
2: 3 these *t* in others yet do them yourself?
4:17 into being those *t* which had not been.
6:21 *T* you are now ashamed of,
8: 5 the flesh are intent on the *t* of the flesh,
8:28 We know that God makes all *t* work
8:32 of us all will not grant us all *t* besides?
11:36 him and through him and for him all *t* are.
13:11 Take care to do all these *t*,
1Cor 2:10 all matters, even the deep *t* of God.
2:13 spiritual *t* in spiritual terms.
3:21 All *t* are yours, whether it be Paul,
7:34 is concerned with *t* of the Lord,
8: 6 from whom all *t* come and for whom we live;
9: 8 does not the law itself speak of these *t*?
9:22 I have made myself all *t* to all men in
9:25 Athletes deny themselves all sorts of *t*.
10: 6 These *t* happened as an example to keep us
10:11 The *t* that happened to them serve as an
10:23 "All *t* are lawful" but not all are
10:23 "All *t* are lawful"—which does not mean
13:13 There are in the end three *t* that last:
14: 7 case of lifeless *t* which produce a sound,
15:27 that God "has placed all *t* under his feet."
15:28 to the One who made all *t* subject to him,
2Cor 10: 7 You view *t* superficially.
11:21 that we have been too weak to do such *t*.
Gal 2:18 to build up the very *t* I had demolished,
3:12 "Whoever does these *t* shall live by them."
3:22 all *t* in under the constraint of sin.
5:21 such *t* will not inherit the kingdom of God!
Eph 1:10 to bring all *t* in the heavens and on earth
1:22 all *t* under Christ's feet and has made him,
4:29 say only the good *t* men need to hear,
4:29 need to hear, *t* that will really help them.
5:12 mention the *t* these people do in secret;
Phil 1:10 learn to value the *t* that really matter,
2:19 courage from learning how *t* go with you.
2:23 send him as soon as I see how *t* go with me.
3: 1 I find writing you these *t* no burden,
3: 7 But those *t* I used to consider gain I have
3:19 those who are set upon the *t* of this world.
Col 1:16 earth was created, *t* visible and invisible,
2:17 All these were but a shadow of *t* to come;
2:22 deal with *t* that perish in their use.
3: 2 on things above rather than on *t* of earth.
1Thes 4: 6 for the Lord is an avenger of all such *t*,
2Thes 2: 5 about these *t* when I was still with you?
1Tm 4: 1 *t* taught by demons through plausible liars
4:11 Such are the *t* you must urge and teach.
5:13 as well, talking about *t* they ought not.
6: 2 These are the *t* you must teach and preach.
6:17 provides us richly with all *t* for our use.
2Tm 2: 2 The *t* which you have heard from me through
2:14 Keep reminding people of these *t* and
2:21 of evil *t* he may be a distinguished vessel,
Ti 1:11 by teaching *t* they have no right to teach
1:15 To the clean all *t* are clean,
2:15 These are the *t* you are to say.
3: 8 great weight on the *t* I have been saying,
Heb 1: 2 whom he has made heir of all *t* and
1: 3 and he sustains all *t* by his powerful word.
2: 8 and honor, and put all *t* under his feet."
2: 8 In subjecting all *t* to him,
2: 8 present we do not see all *t* thus subject,
2:10 God, for whom and through whom all *t* exist,
6: 9 are persuaded of better *t* in your regard,
6: 9 your regard, *t* pointing to your salvation.
6:18 so that, by two *t* that are unchangeable,
7:13 these *t* are said was of a different tribe,
9:11 priest of the good *t* which have come to be,
10: 1 had only a shadow of the good *t* to come,
11: 1 for, and conviction about *t* we do not see.
11: 7 By faith Noah, warned about *t* not yet seen,
12:27 that shaken, created *t* will pass away,
2Pt 1: 4 on us the great and precious *t* he promised,
1:12 intend to recall these *t* to you constantly,
1:15 these *t* frequently after my departure.
2:12 pour abuse on *t* of which they are ignorant.
1Jn 2:15 world, nor the *t* that the world affords.
2:26 these *t* about those who try to deceive you.
2:27 teaches you about all *t* and is true
Jude 1: 5 I wish to remind you of certain *t*,
1:10 through the very *t* they know by instinct,
Rv 4:11 For you have created all *t*;
21: 5 throne said to me, "See, I make all *t* new!"
22: 8 is I, John, who heard and saw all these *t*,

THINK (85)

Gn 27:12 He will *t* I am making sport of him,
Nm 22:37 Did you *t* I could not reward you?"
Dt 10:14 *T*! The heavens,
32: 7 *T* back on the days of old,
Jos 8: 6 for they will *t* we are fleeing from them
9:25 power, do with us what you *t* fit and right."
1Sm 1:16 Do not *t* your handmaid a ne'er-do-well;
1:18 She replied, *T* kindly of your maidservant,"
1:23 "Do what you *t* is best;
14:36 They replied, "Do what you *t* best."
14:40 The people responded, "Do what you *t* best."
18:23 *t* it easy to become the king's son-in-law?
20:29 Now, therefore, if you *t* well of me,
2Sm 10: 3 "Do you *t* that David is honoring your
13:32 "Let not my lord *t* that all the young
14:13 do you *t* of this same kind of thing
18: 4 to them, "I will do what you *t* best";
19: 7 of us dead, you would *t* that more suitable.
2Kgs 10: 5 do whatever you *t* best."
18:20 Do you *t* mere words substitute for
1Chr 19: 3 to Hanun, "Do you *t* David is doing this
2Chr 13: 8 do you *t* you are a match for the kingdom
Tb 4:18 *t* lightly of any advice that can be useful.
5: 3 *T* of it, twenty years have already passed
10: 6 "Hush, do not *t* about it,
14:10 *T*, my son, of all that Nadab did
2Mc 2:29 for ornamentation, so I *t* it is with us.
3:32 Fearing that the king might *t* that
6:24 many young men would *t* the ninety-year-old
7:16 not *t* that our nation is forsaken by God.
7:19 Do not *t* then, that you will go
9:12 God, and not to *t* one's mortal self divine."
Jb 6:29 *T* it over; let there be no injustice.
6:29 *T* it over; I still am right.
21: 6 When I *t* of it, I am dismayed,
35: 2 Do you *t* it right to say,
41:24 would *t* the deep had the hoary head of age.
Ps(s) 50:21 Or do you *t* that I am like yourself?
Prv 31: 7 misery, and *t* no more of their burdens.
Wis 1: 1 *t* of the Lord in goodness,
12:22 *t* earnestly of your goodness when we judge.
Sir 8:13 *t* any pledge a debt you must pay.
16:21 men, which only the foolish knave will *t*.
18:24 *T* of wrath and the day of death,
28: 7 *T* of the commandments,
38:20 *t* rather of the end.
Is 13:17 who *t* nothing of silver and take no
36: 5 Do you *t* mere words substitute for
Jer 3:16 They will no longer *t* of it,
23:27 they *t* to make my people forget my name
26:14 do with me what you *t* good and right.
27: 5 and I can give them to whomever I *t* fit.
40: 4 go wherever you *t* good and proper";
Lam 1: 8 *t* her vile now that they see her nakedness;
Ez 8:12 They *t*:
9: 9 They *t* that the LORD has forsaken the land,
13:18 Do you *t* to entrap the lives of my people,
28: 2 god, however you may *t* yourself like a god.
Dn 14: 6 "You do not *t* Bel is a living god?
Mt 5:17 "Do not *t* that I have come to abolish the
6: 7 They *t* they will win a hearing by the
12:12 *t* how much more precious a human being is
16: 7 and Sadducees," they could *t* only,
21:28 "What do you *t* of this case?
Mk 9:22 You would *t* it would kill him.
Lk 12:51 Do you *t* I have come to establish peace on
13: 2 "Do you *t* that these Galileans were the
13: 4 Do you *t* they were more guilty than anyone
24: 4 still at a loss over what to *t* of this,
Jn 5:39 in which you *t* you have eternal life
11:56 saying to each other, "What do you *t*?
Acts 2:15 these men are not drunk, as you seem to *t*.
4:14 with them, they could *t* of nothing to say,
5:35 *t* twice about what you are going to do
17:29 we ought not to *t* of divinity as something
Rom 12: 3 to *t* more highly of himself than he ought.
1Cor 9: 8 You may *t* the reasons I am giving you are
13:11 used to talk like a child, *t* like a child,
2Cor 11:16 let no one *t* me foolish.
12: 7 lest anyone *t* more of me than what he sees
12:19 Do you *t* throughout this recital that I am
Phil 1: 3 thanks to my God every time I *t* of you
2: 3 let all parties *t* humbly of others as
3:13 I do not *t* of myself as having reached the

THINKING (34)

Ex 2:14 *t* of killing me as you killed the Egyptian?"
Dt 29:18 should beguile himself into *t* that he can
Jgs 9: 3 of Shechem sympathized with Abimelech, *t*,
1Sm 1:13 Eli, *t* her drunk,
18:11 the spear, *t* to nail David to the wall,
27:12 And Achish trusted David, *t*,
2Sm 4:10 *t* himself the bearer of good news for
12:22 child was living, I fasted and wept, *t*,
2Chr 25:19 You are *t*, 'See, I have beaten Edom!',
Neh 6: 9 They were all trying to frighten us, *t*,
1Mc 5:61 brothers, *t* that they would do brave deeds.
2Mc 4:32 Then Menelaus, *t* this a good opportunity,
14:14 *t* that the misfortunes and calamities of
Wis 2: 1 who said among themselves, *t* not aright:
8:17 *T* thus within myself, and reflecting

THINKING (cont.)

Sir 37: 8 For he may be *t* of himself alone;
Ez 20:32 What you are *t* of shall never happen:
Dn 7:25 *t* to change the feast days and the law.
Mal 1:12 But you behave profanely toward me by *t*
Mt 9: 4 was aware of what they were *t* and said:
21:37 Finally he sent his son to them, *t*,
Mk 12: 6 He sent him to them as a last resort, *t*,
Lk 2:44 *T* he was in the party,
Jn 11:31 *t* she was going to the tomb to weep there.
Acts 7:28 'Are you *t* of killing me as you killed the
8:20 money rot *t* that God's gift can be bought!
8:22 Lord may pardon you for *t* the way you have.
16:27 *T* that the prisoners had escaped,
1Cor 4:18 *t* that I will not come to you.
Eph 4:23 and acquire a fresh, spiritual way of *t*.
Phil 1:17 *t* that it will make my imprisonment even
2Tm 1: 5 I find myself *t* of your sincere faith
Heb 11:15 If they had been *t* back to the place from
2Pt 2:13 *T* daytime revelry a delight,

THINKS (14)

Ps(s) 15: 2 who *t* the truth in his heart and slanders
40:18 afflicted and poor, yet the Lord *t* of me.
Prv 18: 2 but rather in displaying what he *t*.
Lk 8:18 not, will lose even the little he *t* he has."
16:15 What man *t* important,
Rom 14:14 it is only when a man *t* something unclean
1Cor 3:18 one of you *t* he is wise in a worldly way,
7:36 If anyone *t* he is behaving dishonorably
8: 2 If a man *t* he knows something,
10:12 let anyone who *t* he is standing upright
14:37 *t* he is a prophet or a man of the Spirit,
Gal 6: 3 If anyone *t* he amounts to something,
Phil 3: 4 If anyone *t* he has a right to put his
Heb 10:29 *t* the covenant-blood by which he was

THIRD (193)

Gn 1:13 morning followed—the *t* day.
2:14 The name of the *t* river is the Tigris;
6:16 shall make with bottom, second and *t* decks.
22: 4 On the *t* day Abraham got sight of the
31:22 On the *t* day, word came to Laban
32:20 to the second servant and the *t*
34:25 On the *t* day, while they were still in pain,
40:20 And in fact, on the *t* day,
42:18 On the *t* day Joseph said to them:
50:23 saw Ephraim's children to the *t* generation,
Ex 19: 1 In the *t* month after their departure from
19:11 be ready for the *t* day; for on the *t* day
19:15 He warned them, "Be ready for the *t* day.
19:16 On the morning of the *t* day there were
20: 5 me, down to the *t* and fourth generation;
28:19 in the *t* row, a jacinth,
34: 7 grandchildren to the *t* and fourth generation
39:12 in the *t* row a jacinth,
Lv 7:17 the sacrifice be left over on the *t* day,
7:18 the peace offering is eaten on the *t* day,
19: 6 the *t* day shall be burned up in the fire.
19: 7 If any of it is eaten on the *t* day,
Nm 2:24 These shall be *t* on the march.
7:24 On the *t* day it was the turn of Eliab,
10: 6 when you sound the *t* alarm,
14:18 children to the *t* and fourth generation
15: 6 fine flour mixed with a *t* of a hin of oil,
15: 7 and a libation of a *t* of a hin of wine,
19:12 the water on the *t* and on the seventh day,
19:12 himself on the *t* and on the seventh day,
19:19 unclean on the *t* and on the seventh day;
28:14 for each bullock, a *t* of a hin for the ram,
29:20 the *t* day you shall offer eleven bullocks,
31:19 yourselves on the *t* and on the seventh day.
Dt 5: 9 down to the *t* and fourth generation but
14:28 "At the end of every *t* year you shall
23: 9 Children born to them may in the *t*
26:12 the tithes of your produce in the *t* year,
Jos 9:17 The *t* day on the road,
17:11 towns and natives [the *t* is Naphathdor].
19:10 *t* lot fell to the clans of the Zebulunites.
Jgs 20:30 up against the Benjaminites for the *t* time
1Sm 3: 8 LORD called Samuel again, for the *t* time.
10: 3 loaves of bread, and the *t* a skin of wine.
13:18 and the *t* took the road for Geba that
13:21 and a *t* of a shekel for sharpening the
17:13 the second son Abinadab, and the *t* Shammah.
19:21 For the *t* time Saul sent messengers,
20:20 the *t* day of the month I will shoot arrows,
30: 1 and his men reached Ziklag on the *t* day,
2Sm 1: 2 On the *t* day a man came from Saul's camp,
3: 3 the *t*, Absalom, son of Maacah
18: 2 David then put a *t* part of the soldiers
18: 2 command, a *t* under command of Abishai,
18: 2 and a *t* under command of Ittai the Gittite.
1Kgs 3:18 On the *t* day after I gave birth this woman
6: 6 six cubits wide, the *t* seven cubits wide,
6: 8 story and from the middle story to the *t*.
12:12 On the *t* day all Israel came back to King
15:28 Baasha killed him in the *t* year of Asa,
15:33 In the *t* year of Asa, king of Judah,
18: 1 Long afterward, in the *t* year,
18:34 a *t* time," he said, and they did it a third
22: 2 In the *t* year, however,
2Kgs 1:13 Again, for the *t* time,
1:13 When the *t* captain arrived,
11: 5 the *t* of you who come on duty on the
11: 6 another *t* shall be at the gate Sur;
11: 6 *t* shall be at the gate behind the guards.
18: 1 In the *t* year of Hoshea,
19:29 But in the *t* year, sow and reap,
20: 8 up to the temple of the LORD on the *t* day?"
1Chr 2:13 Abinadab, the second son, Shimea, the *t*,
3: 2 the *t*, Absalom, son of Maacah,
3:15 the *t*, Zedekiah;
8: 1 Ashbel, the second son, Aharah, the *t*,
8:39 the second son, and Eliphelet, the *t*.
12:10 their chief, Obadiah was second, Eliab *t*,
23:19 Amariah, the second, Jahaziel, the *t*,
24: 8 the second to Jedaiah, the *t* to Harim,
24:23 Amariah, the second, Jahaziel, the *t*,
25:10 The *t* was Zaccur,
26: 2 Jediael, the second son, Zebadiah, the *t*,
26: 4 Jehozabad, a second son, Joah, the *t*,
26:11 Hilkiah, the second son, Tebaliah, the *t*,
27: 5 *t* army commander, chief for the *t* month,
2Chr 10:12 On the *t* day, Jeroboam and all the people
15:10 They gathered at Jerusalem in the *t* month
17: 7 In the *t* year of his reign he sent his
23: 4 a *t* of your number, both priests and
23: 5 another *t* must be at the king's palace and
23: 5 and the final *t* at the Foundation Gate,
27: 5 to him also in the second and in the *t* year.
31: 7 It was in the *t* month that they began to
Ezr 6:15 this house on the *t* day of the month Adar,
Neh 10:33 to give a *t* of a shekel each year for the
Tb 1: 8 The *t* tithe I gave to orphans and widows,
1: 8 *t* year I would bring them this offering,
Est 1: 3 of Susa, in the *t* year of his reign,
D: 1 On the *t* day, putting an end to her
5: 1 [Now on the *t* day,
8: 9 on the twenty-third day of the *t* month,
1Mc 10:30 Instead of collecting the *t* of the grain
14:27 the *t* year under Simon the high priest in
2Mc 7:10 After him the *t* suffered their cruel sport.
Jb 42:14 the second Keziah, and the *t* Keren-happuch.
Sir 23:16 of men multiply sins, a *t* draws down wrath;
26:19 to my heart, and the *t* arouses my horror:
45:23 was the courageous *t* of his line When,
50:25 two nations, the *t* is not even a people:
Is 19:24 shall be a *t* party with Egypt and Assyria,
37:30 But in the *t* year,
Jer 38:14 at the *t* entrance to the house of the LORD.
Ez 5: 2 Burn a *t* in the fire, within the city
5: 2 place another *t* around the city and strike
5: 2 the final *t* strew in the wind,
5:12 A *t* of your people shall die of pestilence
5:12 *t* shall fall by the sword all around you;
5:12 and a *t* I will scatter in every direction,
10:14 second that of a man, the *t* that of a lion,
31: 1 day of the *t* month in the eleventh year,
46:14 with a *t* of a hin of oil to moisten the
Dn 1: 1 In the *t* year of the reign of Jehoiakim,
2:39 place, inferior to yours, then a *t* kingdom,
5: 7 and be *t* in the government of the kingdom."
5:16 and be *t* in the government of the kingdom."
5:29 him *t* in the government of the kingdom.
8: 1 the *t* year of the reign of King Belshazzar.
10: 1 In the *t* year of Cyrus, king of Persia,
Hos 6: 2 on the *t* day he will raise us up,
Am 4: 4 morning bring your sacrifices, every *t* day,
Zec 6: 3 black horses, the *t* chariot white horses,
13: 8 cut off and perish and one *t* shall be left.
13: 9 I will bring the one *t* through fire,
Mt 16:21 put to death, and raised up on the *t* day.
17:23 and he will be raised up on the *t* day."
20:19 But on the *t* day he will be raised up."
21:35 beat one, killed another, and stoned a *t*.
22:26 same thing happened to the second, the *t*,
25:15 second two thousand, and to a *t* a thousand.
26:44 somewhat, and began to pray a *t* time,
27:64 kept under surveillance until the *t* day.
Mk 12:21 The same thing happened to the *t*;
14:41 He returned a *t* time and said to them,
Lk 2:46 On the *t* day they came upon him in the
9:22 death, and then be raised up on the *t* day."
13:32 on the *t* day my purpose is accomplished.
14:20 A *t* said, 'I am newly married
18:33 death, and on the *t* day he will rise again."
19:20 The *t* came in and said:
20:12 He sent still a *t*,
20:31 brother married the widow, then the *t*,
23:22 He said to them for the *t* time,
24: 7 be crucified, and on the *t* day rise again."
24:21 the *t* day since these things happened,
24:46 suffer and rise from the dead on the *t* day.
Jn 2: 1 On the *t* day there was a wedding at Cana
21:14 This marked the *t* time that Jesus appeared
21:17 A *t* time, Jesus asked him,
21:17 was hurt because he had asked a *t* time,
Acts 10:40 up on the *t* day and grant that he be seen,
20: 9 and fell from the *t* story to the ground.
27:19 On the *t* day they deliberately threw even
1Cor 12:28 apostles, second prophets, *t* teachers,
15: 4 with the Scriptures, rose on the *t* day;
2Cor 12: 2 a man who was snatched up to the *t* heaven.
12:14 is the *t* time that I am about to visit you,
13: 1 is the *t* time I shall be coming to you.
Rv 4: 7 the *t* had the face of a man,
6: 5 Lamb broke open the *t* seal, I heard the *t*
8: 7 *t* of the land was scorched, along with a *t*
8: 8 A *t* of the sea turned to blood,
8: 9 *t* of the creatures living in the sea died,
8: 9 died, and a *t* of the ships were wrecked.
8:10 When the *t* angel blew his trumpet,
8:10 fell on a *t* of the rivers and the springs.
8:11 *t* part of all the water turned to wormwood.
8:12 third of the sun, a *t* of the moon, and a third
8:12 The day lost a *t* of its light,
9:15 had been prepared, to kill a *t* of mankind.
9:18 a *t* of mankind was slain.
11:14 The *t* is coming very soon.
12: 4 His tail swept a *t* of the stars from the
14: 9 A *t* angel followed the others and said in
16: 4 The *t* angel poured out his bowl on the
21:19 the second sapphire, the *t* chalcedony,

THIRDLY (1)

Sir 23:23 *T*, in her wanton adultery she has borne

THIRDS (1)

Zec 13: 8 two *t* of them shall be cut off and perish

THIRST (35)

Ex 17: 3 Here, then, in their *t* for water,
17: 3 of *t* with our children and our livestock?"
Dt 28:48 of every kind, therefore in hunger and *t*,
Jgs 15:18 Must I now die of *t* or fall into the hands
2Chr 32:11 you over to a death of famine and *t*,
Neh 9:15 water from a rock you sent them in their *t*.
9:20 mouths, and you gave them water in their *t*.
Jdt 7:13 Then *t* will begin to carry them off,
7:22 women and youths were consumed with *t*
7:25 before them in *t* and utter exhaustion.
8:30 were so tortured with *t* that they forced
Jb 24:11 They tread the wine presses, yet suffer *t*,
Ps(s) 69:22 and in my *t* they gave me vinegar to drink.
104:11 field, till the wild asses quench their *t*.
Prv 25:25 from *t* is good news from a far country.
Wis 11: 4 for their *t* from the hard stone.
11: 8 once you had shown by the *t* they then had
11:14 their *t* proved unlike that of the just.
Sir 24:20 still, he who drinks of me will *t* for more;
51:24 how long will you endure such bitter *t?*
Is 5:13 and their masses are parched with *t*.
30:20 you need and the water for which you *t*.
41:17 in vain, their tongues are parched with *t*.
48:21 not *t* when he led them through dry lands;
49:10 They shall not hunger or *t*,
50: 2 fish rot for lack of water, and die of *t*.
Lam 4: 4 cleaves to the roof of its mouth in *t*;
Hos 2: 5 her to an arid land, and slay her with *t*.
Am 4: 8 for water that did not quench their *t*;
8:11 Not a famine of bread, or *t* for water,
8:13 virgins and young men shall faint from *t*;
Mt 5: 6 are they who hunger and *t* for holiness;
Jn 6:35 no one who believes in me shall ever *t*.
2Cor 11:27 in hunger and *t* and frequent fastings;
Rv 7:16 Never again shall they know hunger or *t*,

THIRSTED (1)

Wis 11: 4 When they *t*, they called upon you,

THIRSTS (4)

Ps(s) 63: 2 flesh pines and my soul *t* like the earth,
143: 6 my soul *t* for you like parched land.
Jn 7:37 "If anyone *t*, let him come to me;
Rv 21: 6 To anyone who *t* I will give to drink

THIRSTY (28)

Jgs 4:19 I am *t*."
15:18 Being very *t*, he cried to the LORD
Ru 2: 9 When you are *t*, you may go and drink
2Sm 17:29 been hungry and tired and *t* in the desert."
Jb 5: 5 and the *t* shall swallow their substance,
22: 7 To the *t* you have given no water to drink,
Ps(s) 107: 5 Hungry and *t*, their life was wasting away
107:33 into desert, water springs into *t* ground,
Prv 25:21 hungry, give him food to eat, if he be *t*,
Sir 26:12 As a *t* traveler with eager mouth drinks
Is 21:14 Meet the *t*, bring them water;
29: 8 Or when a *t* man dreams he is drinking and
32: 6 hungry go empty and the *t* be without drink.
35: 7 sands will become pools, and the *t* ground,
44: 3 I will pour out water upon the *t* ground,
55: 1 All you who are *t*, come to the water!
65:13 servants shall drink, but you shall be *t*;
Mt 25:35 me food, I was *t* and you gave me drink.
25:37 feed you or see you *t* and give you drink?
25:42 no food, I was *t* and you gave me no drink.
25:44 when did we see you hungry or *t* or away
Jn 4:13 who drinks this water will be *t* again.
4:14 the water I give him will never be *t*;
4:15 so that I shall not grow *t* and have to
19:28 said to fulfill the Scripture, "I am *t*."
Rom 12:20 if he is *t*, give him something to drink;
1Cor 4:11 Up to this very hour we go hungry and *t*,

Rv 22:17 Let him who is t come forward;

THIRTEEN (13)

Gn 17:25 and his son Ishmael was t years old when
Nm 29:13 holocaust to the LORD t bullocks,
29:14 of an ephah for each of the t bullocks,
Jos 19: 6 t cities and their villages.
21: 4 t cities by lot from the tribes of Judah,
21: 6 The Gershonites obtained t cities by lot
21:19 descendants of Aaron, were t in all.
21:33 to the Gershonite clans were t in all.
1Kgs 7: 1 completed after t years of construction.
1Chr 6:45 they had t cities with their pasture lands.
6:47 t cities from the tribes of Issachar,
26:11 All the sons and brethren of Hosah were t.
Ez 40:11 of the gate's passage itself was t cubits.

THIRTEENTH (16)

Gn 14: 4 but in the t year they rebelled.
1Chr 24:13 the twelfth to Jakim, the t to Huppah,
25:20 The t was Shubael,
Est 3: 7 lot fell on the t day of the twelfth month,
3:12 on the t day of the first month they wrote,
3:13 in one day, the t day of the twelfth month,
8:12 a single day, the t of the twelfth month,
E:20 their ruin, the t day of the twelfth month,
9: 1 out, the t day of the twelfth month,
9:17 plunder, on the t day of the month of Adar.
9:18 on the t and fourteenth of the month.
1Mc 7:43 in battle on the t day of the month Adar.
7:49 be observed every year on the t of Adar.
2Mc 15:36 it on the t day of the twelfth month,
Jer 1: 2 king of Judah, in the t year of his reign,
25: 3 Since the t year of Josiah,

THIRTIETH (2)

2Mc 11:30 those who return by the t of Xanthicus
Ez 1: 1 In the t year, on the fifth day

THIRTY (118)

Gn 5: 3 Adam was one hundred and t years old when
5: 5 of Adam was nine hundred and t years;
5:16 and t years after the birth of Jared,
6:15 fifty cubits, and its height t cubits.
11:14 When Shelah was t years old,
11:17 and t years after the birth of Peleg,
11:18 When Peleg was t years old,
11:22 When Serug was t years old,
18:30 What if only t are found there?"
18:30 doing it if I can find but t there."
32:16 t milch camels and their young;
41:46 Joseph was t years cld when he entered the
47: 9 as a wayfarer amount to a hundred and t.
Ex 12:40 in Egypt was four hundred and t years.
12:41 At the end of four hundred and t years,
21:32 the owner of the slave t shekels of silver,
26: 8 the length of each shall be t cubits,
36:15 was t cubits and the width four cubits;
38:24 talents and seven hundred and t shekels,
Lv 27: 4 for a man, and t shekels for a woman;
Nm 4: 3 between t and fifty years of age;
4:23 the men between t and fifty years of age;
4:30 their men between t and fifty years of age;
4:35 the men between t and fifty years of age.
4:39 the men between t and fifty years of age.
4:40 numbered two thousand six hundred and t.
4:43 the men from t up to fifty years of age.
4:47 of all the men between t and fifty years
7:13 weighing a hundred and t shekels
7:19 silver plate weighing a hundred and t shekels
7:25 a hundred and t shekels according
7:31 plate weighing a hundred and t shekels
7:37 a hundred and t shekels according to the
7:43 one silver plate weighing a hundred and t
7:49 and t shekels according to the sanctuary
7:55 plate weighing a hundred and t shekels
7:61 plate weighing a hundred and t shekels
7:67 plate weighing a hundred and t shekels
7:73 silver plate weighing one hundred and t shekels
7:79 silver plate weighing a hundred and t shekels
7:85 plate weighed a hundred and t shekels,
20:29 and for t days the whole house of Israel
26: 7 seven hundred and t men were registered.
26:51 t were the Israelites who were registered.
31:39 t thousand five hundred asses,
31:45 oxen, t thousand five hundred asses,
Dt 34: 8 For t days the Israelites wept for Moses
Jos 8: 3 Picking out t thousand warriors,
Jgs 10: 4 He had thirty sons who rode on t
10: 4 possessed t cities in the land of Gilead;
12: 9 He had t sons.
12: 9 had t daughters married outside the family,
12: 9 sons t young women from outside the family.
12:14 He had forty sons and t grandsons who rode
14:11 they brought t men to be his companions.
14:12 thirty linen tunics and t sets of garments.
14:13 me t tunics and thirty sets of garments."
14:19 killed t of their men and despoiled them;
20:31 they killed off about t of the Israelite soldiers
20:39 by killing off some t of the men of Israel,
1Sm 4:10 which Israel lost t thousand foot soldiers.
9:22 of the guests, of whom there were about t.
2Sm 5: 4 David was t years old when he became king,
6: 1 picked men of Israel, t thousand in number.
23:13 During the harvest three of the T went
23:18 son of Zeruiah, was at the head of the T.
23:18 He was listed among the T and commanded
23:19 and commanded greater respect than the T,
23:22 He was listed among the T warriors and
23:23 and commanded greater respect than the T.
23:24 Among the T were:
1Kgs 5: 2 for each day were t kors of fine flour,
5:27 t thousand workmen from all Israel.
7: 2 cubits long, fifty wide, and t high;
7: 6 hall he made fifty cubits long and t wide.
7:23 five in height, and t in circumference.
2Kgs 18:14 silver and t talents of gold from Hezekiah,
1Chr 11:15 of the T chiefs went down to the rock,
11:20 He was the chief of the T;
11:21 as any of the T and became their commander,
11:25 He was more famous than any of the T,
11:42 son of Ahlai, and, in addition to the T,
12: 4 a warrior on the level of the T,
12:19 enveloped Amasai, the chief of the T,
15: 7 and one hundred and t of his brethren;
23: 3 Levites t years old and above were counted,
27: 6 a warrior among the Thirty and over the T.
2Chr 4: 2 five in depth, and t in circumference;
24:15 was a hundred and t years old when he died.
31:16 houses of males t years of age and over,
35: 7 of lambs and kids, t thousand in number,
Ezr 1: 9 sacks of goldware, t; sacks of of silverware
1:10 golden bowls, t;
2:35 Senaah, three thousand six hundred and t.
Neh 7:38 Senaah, three thousand nine hundred and t.
7:69 gold, fifty basins, t garments for priests,
Jdt 15:11 For t days the whole populace plundered
Est 4:11 not been summoned to the king for t days."
1Mc 10:36 "Let t thousand Jews be enrolled in the
2Mc 12: 9 visible as far as Jerusalem, t miles away.
12:23 and destroying as many as t thousand men.
Prv 22:20 Have I not written for you the T,"
Ez 40:17 were on the pavement, were t in number.
41: 6 There were t side chambers built one above
46:22 minor courts, forty cubits long and t wide,
Dn 6: 8 any petition to god or man for t days,
6:13 a petition to god or man for t days,
Zec 11:12 counted out my wages, t pieces of silver.
11:13 So I took the t pieces of silver and threw
Mt 26:15 They paid him t pieces of silver,
27: 3 He took the t pieces of silver back to the
27: 9 "They took the t pieces of silver,
Lk 3:23 began his work he was about t years of age,
Gal 3:17 into being four hundred and t years later,

THIRTY- (2)

Mk 4: 8 a rate of t- and sixty- and a hundredfold."
4:20 yield at t- and sixty- and a hundredfold."

THIRTY-EIGHT (4)

Dt 2:14 T years had elapsed between our departure
1Chr 23: 3 number was found to be t thousand men.
Neh 7:45 Hatita, sons of Shobai, one hundred and t.
Jn 5: 5 was one man who had been sick for t years.

THIRTY-EIGHTH (2)

1Kgs 16:29 In the t year of Asa,
2Kgs 15: 8 In the t year of Azariah,

THIRTY-FIFTH (1)

2Chr 15:19 was no war until the t year of Asa's reign.

THIRTY-FIRST (1)

1Kgs 16:23 In the t year of Asa,

THIRTY-FIVE (10)

Gn 11:12 When Arpachshad was t years old,
Nm 1:37 t thousand four hundred were enrolled in
2:23 in the census to t thousand four hundred.
1Kgs 22:42 was t years old when he began to reign,
2Chr 3:15 building he set two columns t cubits high;
20:31 He was t years old when he became king,
Ezr 2:67 their camels four hundred and t,
Neh 7:68 their camels four hundred and t,
2Mc 15:27 hearts, they laid low at least t thousand,
Dn 12:12 the one thousand three hundred and t days.

THIRTY-FOUR (3)

Gn 11:16 When Eber was t years old,
1Chr 7: 7 records listed twenty-two thousand and t.
Jdt 7:20 kept them thus surrounded for t days.

THIRTY-NINE (1)

Ezr 2:42 sons of Shobai, one hundred and t in all.

THIRTY-NINTH (3)

2Kgs 15:13 became king in the t year of Uzziah,
15:17 In the t year of Azariah,
2Chr 16:12 In the t year of his reign,

THIRTY-ONE (3)

Jos 12:24 t kings in all.
2Kgs 22: 1 reign, and he reigned t years in Jerusalem.
2Chr 34: 1 king, and he reigned t years in Jerusalem.

THIRTY-SECOND (2)

Neh 5:14 of Judah, from his twentieth to his t year
13: 6 Jerusalem, for in the t year of Artaxerxes,

THIRTY-SEVEN (9)

Gn 25:17 Ishmael's life was one hundred and t years.
Ex 6:16 Levi lived one hundred and t years.
6:20 Amram lived one hundred and t years.
Nm 31:36 hundred and t thousand five hundred sheep,
31:43 hundred and t thousand five hundred sheep,
1Chr 12:35 with shield and lance, t thousand men.
Ezr 2:65 were seven thousand three hundred and t.
Neh 7:67 were seven thousand three hundred and t.
1Mc 1:10 hundred and t of the kingdom of the Greeks.

THIRTY-SEVENTH (3)

2Kgs 13:10 In the t year of Joash,
25:27 In the t year of the exile of Jehoiachin,
Jer 52:31 In the t year of the exile of Jehoiachin,

THIRTY-SIX (6)

Nm 31:38 t thousand oxen, of which seventy-two fell
31:44 five hundred sheep, t thousand oxen,
Jos 6: 5 by those at Ai, who killed some t of them.
1Chr 7: 4 numbered t thousand men in organized
Ezr 2:66 Their horses were seven hundred and t,
Neh 7:67 Their horses were seven hundred and t,

THIRTY-SIXTH (1)

2Chr 16: 1 In the t year of Asa's reign,

THIRTY-THREE (6)

Ex 6:18 Kohath lived one hundred and t years.
Lv 12: 4 and then she shall spend t days more in
2Sm 5: 5 and t years in Jerusalem over all Israel
1Kgs 2:11 years in Hebron and t years in Jerusalem.
1Chr 3: 4 Then he reigned t years in Jerusalem,
29:27 he reigned seven years, and in Jerusalem t.

THIRTY-TWO (16)

Gn 11:20 When Reu was t years old,
Nm 1:35 t thousand two hundred were enrolled in
2:21 in the census to t thousand two hundred.]
26:37 of whom t thousand five hundred men were
31:35 t thousand girls who were still virgins.
31:40 persons, of whom t fell as tax to the LORD,
1Kgs 20: 1 by t kings with horses and chariotry,
20:15 of the provinces, two hundred t of them.
20:16 with the t kings who were his allies.
22:31 given his t chariot commanders the order,
2Kgs 8:17 He was t years old when he began to reign,
1Chr 19: 7 They hired t thousand chariots along with
2Chr 21: 5 was t years old when he became king,
21:20 He was t years old when he became king,
1Mc 6:30 cavalry, and t elephants trained for war.
Jer 52:29 eight hundred and t persons from Jerusalem;

THIRTYFOLD (2)

Mt 13: 8 yielded grain a hundred- or sixty- or t.
13:23 bears a yield of a hundred- or sixty- or t."

THISBE (1)

Tb 1: 2 king of Assyria, was taken captive from T,

THISTLE (4)

2Kgs 14: 9 "The t of Lebanon sent word to the cedar
14: 9 passed by and trampled the t underfoot.
2Chr 25:18 "The t of the Lebanon sent a message to
25:18 Lebanon passed by and trampled the t down.

THISTLEDOWN (1)

Wis 5:14 of the wicked is like t borne on the wind,

THISTLES (7)

Gn 3:18 Thorns and t shall it bring forth to you,
Jb 31:40 Then let the t grow instead of wheat and
Ps(s) 58:10 like a thorn-bush, or like t,
Prv 24:31 it was all overgrown with t;
Is 34:13 thorns, her fortresses with t and briers.
Hos 10: 8 thorns and t shall overgrow their altars.
Heb 6: 8 But if it bears thorns and t,

THOMAS (11)

Mt 10: 3 T and Matthew the tax collector;
Mk 3:18 Andrew, Philip, Bartholomew, Matthew, T,
Lk 6:15 Philip and Bartholomew, Matthew and T,
Jn 11:16 Then T (the name means "Twin") said to
14: 5 "Lord," said T, "we do now know where
20:24 of the Twelve, T (the name means "Twin"),
20:26 in the room, and this time T was with them.
20:27 "Peace be with you," he said; then, to T:

THOMAS (cont.)

20:28 T said in response, "My Lord
21: 2 were Simon Peter, T (the "Twin"),
Acts 1:13 Philip and T, Bartholomew

THONG (1)

Is 5:27 belt loose, nor the t of his sandal broken.

THONGS (1)

Is 58: 6 bound unjustly, untying the t of the yoke;

THORN (6)

Ex 22: 5 further, and catches on to t bushes,
Prv 26: 9 Like a t stick brandished by the hand of a
Is 9:17 burns like fire, devouring brier and t;
Ez 28:24 be a tearing t for the house of Israel,
Mi 7: 4 a brier, the most upright like a t hedge.
2Cor 12: 7 conceited I was given a t in the flesh,

THORN-BUSH (1)

Ps(s) 58:10 Unexpectedly, like a t,

THORNBUSH (5)

Sir 43:20 it shines like blossoms on the t.
Is 55:13 In place of the t,
Bar 6:70 Just like a t in a garden on which perches
Acts 7:30 Mount Sinai in the flame of a burning t.
7:35 the angel appearing to him in the t,

THORNBUSHES (4)

Is 7:19 rocky clefts, on all t and in all pastures.
Na 1:10 As when a tangle of t is set aflame,
Mt 7:16 Do you ever pick grapes from t,
Lk 6:44 Figs are not taken from t,

THORNS (34)

Gn 3:18 T and thistles shall it bring forth to you,
Nm 33:55 as barbs in your eyes and t in your sides,
Jos 23:13 scourge for your sides and t for your eyes,
Jgs 8: 7 in with the t and briers of the desert."
8:16 the city, and t and briers of the desert,
2Sm 23: 6 the wicked are all like t to be cast away;
Ps(s) 118:12 bees, they flared up like fire among t;
Prv 15:19 of the sluggard is hemmed in as with t,
22: 5 T and snares are on the path of the crooked;
Eccl 7: 6 For as the crackling of t under a pot,
Sg 2: 2 As a lily among t, so is my beloved
Sir 28:24 As you hedge round your vineyard with t,
Is 5: 6 or hoed, but overgrown with t and briers;
7:23 of silver, shall be turned to briers and t.
7:24 for all the country shall be briers and t.
7:25 For fear of briers and t you shall not go
10:17 his briers and his t in a single day.
27: 4 angry, but if I were to find briers and t,
32:13 of my people, overgrown with t and briers;
34:13 Her castles shall be overgrown with t,
Jer 4: 3 Till your untilled ground, sow not among t.
12:13 They have sown wheat and reaped t,
Hos 2: 8 way with t and erect a wall against her,
9: 6 silver treasures, and t invade their tents.
10: 8 t and thistles shall overgrow their altars.
Mt 13: 7 Again, part of the seed fell among t,
27:29 a crown out of t they fixed it on his head,
Mk 4: 7 Again, some landed among t,
4:18 Those sown among t are another class.
15:17 then wove a crown of t and put it on him,
Lk 8: 7 and the t growing up with it stifled it.
Jn 19: 2 wove a crown of t and fixed it on his head,
19: 5 the crown of t and the purple cloak,
Heb 6: 8 But if it bears t and thistles,

THOROUGH (3)

Lv 19: 9 t that you reap the field to its very edge,
23:22 t that you reap the field to its very edge,
Dt 19:18 and if after a t investigation the judges

THOROUGHBRED (1)

Est 8:10 by mounted couriers riding t royal steeds.

THOROUGHGOING (1)

Acts 13:10 "You are an impostor and a t fraud,

THOROUGHLY (9)

Dt 13:15 into the matter and investigate it t.
2Mc 2:30 questions and examine them t from all sides
4:40 As the crowds, now t enraged,
Ps(s) 51: 4 T wash me from my guilt and of my sin
Sir 21:12 but one form of shrewdness is t bitter.
Jer 7: 5 if you t reform your ways and your deeds;
Mk 16: 6 This frightened them t,
Ti 1:16 and t incapable of any decent action.
Jas 2:17 It is t lifeless.

THOUGH (508)

Gn 18:27 to my Lord, t I am but dust and ashes!
20: 4 would you slay a man even t he is innocent?
31:50 remember that even t no one else is about,
37:35 T his sons and daughters tried to console
38:23 kid, even t you were unable to find her."
44:10 "Even t it ought to be as you propose,
50:20 Even t you meant harm to me,
Ex 3: 2 surprised to see that the bush, t on fire,
8:14 T the magicians tried to bring forth gnats
9: 7 But t Pharaoh's messengers informed him
10:19 But t not a single locust remained within
13:17 Philistines' land, t this was the nearest;
15:19 t the Israelites had marched on dry land
19: 5 all other people, t all the earth is mine.
19:18 The smoke rose from it as t from a furnace,
21:29 of goring people and its owner, t warned,
Lv 10:19 "Even t they presented their sin offering
11:37 t one of their dead bodies falls on it;
13:31 skin, t the hair on it may not be black,
13:55 appearance, even t it may not have spread,
19:17 T you may have to reprove your fellow man,
25:50 as t he had been hired as a day laborer.
26:17 will take to flight t no one pursues you.
26:25 T you then huddle together in your walled
26:36 if from the sword, t no one pursues them;
Nm 5:13 t her husband has not sufficient evidence
14:44 even t neither the ark of the covenant of
23:25 "Even t you cannot curse them,"
24:17 I see him, t not now; I behold him, t not
Dt 2: 4 T they are afraid of you, be very careful
13: 3 even t the sign or wonder he has foretold
18:14 T these nations whom you are to dispossess
18:22 t a prophet speaks in the name of the LORD,
19: 6 even t he does not merit death since he
21:18 not obey them even t they chastise him,
22:24 not cry out for help t she was in the city,
22:27 and t the betrothed maiden may have cried
23: 6 t the LORD, your God, would not listen
28: 7 t they come out against you from but one
28:25 t you advance against them from one
28:30 T you betroth a wife, another man will
28:30 T you build a house, you will not live
28:30 T you plant a vineyard, you will not enjoy
28:38 T you spend much seed on your field,
28:39 T you plant and cultivate vineyards,
28:40 T you have olive trees throughout your
28:41 T you beget sons and daughters,
29:18 as t to sweep away both the watered soil
30: 4 T you may have been driven to the farthest
Jos 5: 5 T all the men who came out were circumcised,
13: 1 T now you are old and advanced in years,
13: 3 t held by the five lords of the
13:12 T Moses conquered and occupied these
14: 3 and t the Levites were given no heritage
16:10 t they have been impressed as laborers.
20: 5 T the avenger of blood pursues him,
22:20 T he was but a single man,
Jgs 13: 3 T you are barren and have had no children,
19:16 t he lived among the Benjaminite
20:23 But t the Israelite soldiers took courage
20:36 it had looked as t the enemy were defeated,
20:39 And t the men of Benjamin had begun by
Ru 3:12 Now, t indeed I am closely related to you,
1Sm 1: 5 loved her, t the LORD had made her barren.
1:13 t her lips were moving,
3:13 t he knew his sons were blaspheming God,
12:12 us,' even t the LORD your God is your king.
14:45 t it was he who brought Israel this great
15:17 T little in your own esteem,
20:20 will shoot arrows, as t aiming at a target.
23:14 T Saul sought him continually,
24:12 t you are hunting me down to take my life.
26:23 t the LORD delivered you into my grasp,
2Sm 2: 7 valiant men, for t your lord Saul is dead,
3:27 city gate as t to speak with him privately.
13:25 And t Absalom urged him,
14:14 Yet, t God does not bring back life,
16: 6 king's officers, even t all the soldiers,
16:23 was as t one had sought divine revelation.
19: 6 T they saved your life and your sons' and
19:29 For t my father's entire house deserved
22:28 people, t on the lofty your eyes look down.
1Kgs 1: 1 t they spread covers over him he could not
2:26 T you deserve to die, I will not put you
2:28 sided with Adonijah, t not with Absalom,
10: 7 T I did not believe the report until I
11:10 (for t the LORD had forbidden him
14:10 completely, as t dung were being burned.
20:11 armor to boast as t he were taking it off.' "
2Kgs 3: 2 t not as much as his father and mother.
3:17 says, T you will see neither wind nor rain,
7:12 T it was night, the king got up;
17:13 And t the LORD warned Israel and Judah by
1Chr 5: 2 him, t the birthright had been Joseph's.)
12:18 my enemies t my hands have done no wrong,
26:10 the chief (for t he was not the first-born
2Chr 24:24 T the Aramean force came with few men,
25: 2 sight of the LORD, t not wholeheartedly.
26: 1 Uzziah, t he was but sixteen years of age,
27: 2 t he did not enter the temple of the LORD;
28:21 T Ahaz plundered the LORD's house and the
30:19 t he be not clean as holiness requires."
32:19 They spoke of the God of Israel as t he
33:17 T the people continued to sacrifice on the
Ezr 3: 6 t the foundation of the temple of the LORD
9:13 our evil deeds and our great guilt t you,
Neh 1: 9 even t your outcasts have been driven to
2: 2 T I was seized with great fear,
5: 5 And t these are our own kinsmen and our
5:16 t I had acquired no land of my own,
5:17 T I set my table for a hundred and fifty
5:18 and t the daily preparations were made at
6: 1 was no breach left in it t up to that time
9:18 T they made themselves a molten calf,
13: 2 t our God turned the curse into a blessing."
13:26 T among the many nations there was no king
13:26 and t he was beloved of his God and God
Tb 5: 4 t he did not know that this was an angel
5:10 T alive, I am among the dead.
12:19 Even t you watched me eat and drink.
13: 3 for t he has scattered you among them,
Jdt 9: 2 This they did, t you forbade it.
16:16 T the sweet odor of every sacrifice
Est D: 5 lovely, t her heart was shrunk with fear.
D:14 my lord, t your glance is full of kindness."
1Mc 10:77 as t he were going on through the country,
12: 9 T we have no need of these things,
2Mc 7:16 you have power among men, mortal t you are,
7:33 T our living Lord treats us harshly for a
14:35 of all, t you are in need of nothing,
Jb 4:10 T the lion roars, though the king of beasts
5:14 at noonday they grope as t it were night,
6:14 t he have forsaken the fear of the
6:16 T they may be black with ice,
6:20 are disappointed, t they were confident;
7:20 T I have sinned, what can I do to you,
9:15 Even t I were right,
9:20 T I were right, my own mouth
9:21 T I am innocent, I myself cannot know it;
10: 7 Even t you know that I am not wicked,
10:19 I should be as t I had never lived;
13:15 Slay me t he might, I will wait for him;
13:28 T he wears out like a leather bottle,
14: 8 Even t its root grow old in the earth,
19:16 answer, t in my speech I plead with him.
19:22 Why do you hound me as t you were divine,
20: 6 T his pride mount up to the heavens and
20:11 T his frame is full of youthful vigor,
20:12 T wickedness is sweet in his mouth,
20:13 T he retains it and will not let it go but
20:18 t his wealth increases, he shall not rejoice.
20:20 T he has known no quiet in his greed,
22: 2 T to himself a wise man be profitable!
22:12 heavens, behold the stars, high t they are?
23: 2 T I know my complaint is bitter,
26: 3 How you counsel, as t he had no wisdom;
27:14 T his children be many,
27:16 T he heap up silver like dust and store
28: 5 The earth, t out of it comes forth bread,
31:18 T like a father God has reared me from my
31:30 Even t I had not suffered my mouth to sin
33:14 once, or even twice, t one perceive it not.
34: 6 my wound the arrow rankles, sinless t I am."
35:12 T thus they cry out,
35:14 Even t you say that you see him not,
37:24 men revere him, t none can see him,
38:14 the seal, and dyed as t it were a garment;
38:30 When the waters lie covered as t with
40: 5 T I have spoken once,
40: 5 t twice, I will do so no more.
40:23 t the torrent surges about his mouth.
Ps(s) 13: 6 my downfall t I trusted in your kindness.
15: 4 Who, t it be to his loss,
17: 3 T you test my heart,
17: 3 it in the night, t you try me with fire,
19:12 T your servant is careful of them,
20: 9 T they bow down and fall,
21:10 Make them burn as t in a fiery furnace,
21:12 T they intend evil against you,
23: 4 t I walk in the dark valley I fear no evil;
27: 3 T an army encamp against me,
27: 3 T war be waged upon me,
27:10 T my father and mother forsake me,
28: 3 their neighbors t evil is in their hearts.
32: 6 T deep waters overflow,
33:17 great t its strength
35:14 As t it were a friend of mine,
37:10 t you mark his place he will not be there.
37:24 T he fall, he does not lie prostrate,
40:18 T I am afflicted and poor,
41: 5 heal me, t I have sinned against you.
44:18 come upon us, t we have not forgotten you,
44:20 T you thrust us down into a place of
46: 3 t the earth be shaken and mountains plunge
46: 4 T its waters rage and foam and the
46: 7 T nations are in turmoil,
48: 8 As t a wind from the east were shattering
49:12 t they have called lands by their names.
49:19 T in his lifetime he counted himself
50:17 T you hate discipline and cast my words
59: 8 T they bay with their mouths,
62: 4 beat him down as t he were a sagging fence,
62:11 t wealth abound, set not your heart
68:14 T you rested among the sheepfolds,
71:15 your salvation, t I know not their extent.
71:20 T you have made me feel many bitter
73: 3 when I saw them prosper t they were wicked.
73:16 T I tried to understand this it seemed to
73:20 As t they were the dream of one who had
73:26 T my flesh and my heart waste away,

75: 4 *T* the earth and all who dwell in it quake,
77:20 waters, *t* your footsteps were not seen.
78:37 *T* their hearts were not steadfast toward
91: 7 *T* a thousand fall at your side,
92: 8 *T* the wicked flourish like grass and all
94:21 *T* they attack the life of the just and
95: 9 they tested me *t* they had seen my works.
99: 8 were to them, *t* requiting their misdeeds.
102:27 *t* all of them grow old like a garment.
118:18 *T* the LORD has indeed chastised me,
119:23 *T* princes meet and talk against me,
119:51 *T* the proud scoff bitterly at me,
119:61 *T* the snares of the wicked are twined
119:69 *T* the proud forge lies against me,
119:83 *T* I am shriveled like a leathern flask in
137: 3 *T* there our captors asked of us the lyrics
138: 7 *T* I walk amid distress,
Prv 6: 7 For *t* she has no chief,
23: 7 says to you, *t* his heart is not with you;
27:22 *T* you should pound the fool to bits with
28:17 *T* a man burdened with human blood were to
Eccl 1:16 *T* I said to myself,
2: 3 wine, *t* my mind was concerned with wisdom,
6: 4 *T* it came in vain and goes into darkness
6: 5 *t* it has not seen or known the sun,
6:11 For *t* there are many sayings that multiply
8:12 *T* indeed I know that it shall be well with
8:14 there are just men treated as *t* they had
8:14 men treated as *t* they had done justly.
8:17 even *t* neither by day nor by night do his
9:15 But in the city lived a man who, *t* poor,
9:16 *T* I had said, "Wisdom is better
10:10 dull, *t* at first he made easy progress,
11:10 presence, *t* the dawn of youth is fleeting.
Wis 2: 2 hereafter we shall be as *t* we had not been;
4: 4 even *t* their branches flourish for a time,
4: 7 But the just man, *t* he die early,
6: 4 *t* you were ministers of his kingdom,
7:12 *t* I had not known that she is the mother
7:23 all spirits, *t* they be intelligent,
8:10 esteem from the elders *t* I be but a youth.
9: 6 *t* one be perfect among the sons of men,
11: 9 had been tried, *t* only mildly chastised,
12:18 But *t* you are master of might,
12:25 Therefore as *t* upon unreasoning children,
13: 6 *t* they seek God and wish to find him.
14: 8 produced it, and it, because *t* corruptible,
14:17 to flatter him when absent, as *t* present.
14:22 *t* they live in a great war of ignorance,
15: 8 *t* he himself shortly before was made from
16: 6 terrorized, *t* they had a sign of salvation,
17: 9 even *t* no monstrous thing frightened them,
17:14 during that night, powerless *t* it was,
18:13 For *t* they disbelieved at every turn on
19: 2 That *t* they themselves had agreed to the
Sir 6:19 As *t* plowing and sowing,
11:30 *T* he seem like a bird confined in a cage,
12:11 *t* he acts humbly and peaceably toward you,
12:16 *T* your enemy has tears in his eyes,
13:11 test you, and *t* smiling he will probe you.
13:21 *t* what he says is odious,
16: 2 Many *t* they be, exult not in them
16:11 *t* on the wicked alights his wrath.
19:24 Even *t* his lack of strength keeps him from
26: 5 *T* false charges in public,
31: 6 gold, *t* destruction lay before their eyes;
35:13 *T* not unduly partial toward the weak,
36:21 *T* any man may be accepted as a husband,
37:20 *T* a man may be wise,
42:17 wonders of the LORD, *T* God has given these,
43:22 and the flowering plains as *t* by flames,
43:31 *t* he is still beyond your power to praise;
43:32 and weary not, *t* you cannot reach the end;
44: 9 And they are as *t* they had not lived,
47: 3 He made sport of lions as *t* they were kids,
47:18 you heaped up silver as *t* it were lead;
49: 3 his whole heart, and, *t* times were evil,
Is 1:15 *T* you pray the more, I will not listen.
1:18 *T* your sins be like scarlet,
1:18 *T* they be crimson red,
9:19 *T* they hack on the right,
9:19 *t* they eat on the left,
10:22 For *t* your people,
10:24 the Assyrian, *t* he strikes you with a rod,
12: 1 *t* you have been angry with me,
17:10 *t* you plant your pagan plants and set out
17:11 *T* you make them grow the day you plant
29:13 lips alone, *t* their hearts are far from me,
29:16 as *t* the potter were taken to be the clay:
29:16 As *t* what is made should say of its maker,
40: 8 *T* the grass withers and the flower wilts,
40:30 *T* young men faint and grow weary,
42:21 *T* it pleased the LORD in his justice to
43: 8 are blind *t* they have eyes, who are deaf *t*
45: 4 giving you a title, *t* you knew me not.
45: 5 It is I who arm you, *t* you know me not,
46: 5 or match me against, as *t* we were alike?
48: 2 *T* you are named after the holy city and
49: 4 *T* I thought I had toiled in vain,
49:19 *T* you were waste and desolate,
51: 6 *T* the heavens grow thin like smoke,
53: 7 *T* he was harshly treated,
53: 9 *T* he had done no wrong nor spoken any
54:10 *T* the mountains leave their place and the
57: 1 *T* he is taken away from the presence of
57:10 *T* worn out by your many misdeeds,
60:10 *T* I struck you in my wrath,
Jer 1:17 as *t* I would leave you crushed before them;
2:22 *T* you scour it with soap,
3: 7 even *t* her traitor sister Judah saw that
5: 2 *T* they say, "As the LORD lives,"
5:22 *t* it may, it is to no avail; though its billows
6:14 They would repair, as *t* it were nought,
6:14 they say, *t* there is no peace.
7:13 not listen, *t* I spoke to you untiringly;
7:13 because you did not answer, *t* I called you,
8:11 They would repair, as *t* it were nought,
8:11 they say, *t* there is no peace.
10: 2 of the heavens, *t* the nations fear them.
11:12 *T* they cry out to me,
14: 7 Even *t* our crimes bear witness against us,
14: 7 *t* our rebellions are many, *t* we have sinned
14:15 prophesy in my name, *t* I did not send them;
15:20 *T* they fight against you,
17:23 fathers, *t* they did not listen or give ear,
22: 6 *T* you be to me like Gilead,
23:38 of the LORD," *t* I forbade you to use it,
25: 4 *T* you refused to listen or pay heed,
26: 5 send you constantly *t* you do not obey them,
29:19 *t* I kept sending them my servants the
30: 7 for Jacob, *t* he shall be saved from it.
32:33 *t* I kept teaching them,
34:10 But *t* they agreed and freed them,
36:25 And *t* Elnathan, Delaiah,
44: 4 *T* I kept sending to you all my servants
44:14 *t* they yearn to return and live there.
46:23 says the LORD, impenetrable *t* it be;
49:16 *T* you build your nest high as the eagle,
51:53 *T* Babylon scale the heavens,
51:55 *T* her waves were roaring like mighty
Lam 3:32 *T* he punishes, he takes pity,
4: 9 Who waste away, as *t* pierced through,
4:21 *T* you rejoice and are glad,
5:10 skin is shriveled up, as *t* by a furnace,
Bar 6:11 but *t* they are wrapped in purple clothing,
6:19 *T* the insects out of the ground consume
6:40 make noise, as *t* the man could understand;
6:54 gods, *t* the priests flee and are safe,
Ez 1:16 as *t* one wheel were within another.
10:10 as *t* they were a wheel within a wheel.
11:16 *T* I have removed them far among the
12: 3 on, prepare your baggage as *t* for exile,
12: 7 my baggage as *t* it were that of an exile,
13: 6 *t* the LORD did not send them;
14:21 Even *t* I send Jerusalem my four cruel
16:61 *t* I am not bound by my covenant with you.
17:18 *T* he gave his hand in pledge,
18:11 things *t* the father does none of them),
23:11 *T* her sister Oholibah saw all this,
32:27 *t* the mighty men caused terror in the land
33: 6 even *t* that person is taken because of his
33:13 *T* I say to the virtuous man that he shall
33:14 And *t* I say to the wicked man that he
33:24 "Abraham, *t* but a single individual,
Dn 1: 9 *T* God had given Daniel the favor and
3:40 *t* it were holocausts of rams and bullocks,
3:50 as *t* a dew-laden breeze were blowing
5: 8 But *t* all the king's wise men came in,
5:22 humbled your heart, *t* you knew all this;
11:20 destroyed, *t* not in conflict or in battle.
11:33 *t* for a time they will become victims of
13:10 *T* both were enamored of her,
13:43 *t* I have done none of the things with
Hos 3: 1 *t* they turn to other gods and are fond of
4:15 *T* you play the harlot,
4:16 them broad pastures as *t* they were lambs?
7:13 *T* I wished to redeem them,
7:15 *T* I trained and strengthened their arms,
8:10 Even *t* they bargain with the nations,
8:12 *T* I write for him my many ordinances,
8:13 *T* they offer sacrifice,
9:12 Even *t* they bring up their children,
11: 4 Yet, *t* I stooped to feed my child,
11: 7 and God, *t* in unison they cry out to him,
12: 9 *T* Ephraim says, "How rich I have
13: 8 lion, as *t* a wild beast were to rend them.
13:15 *T* he be fruitful among his fellows,
Jl 2: 8 *T* they fall into the ditches,
Am 4: 6 *T* I have made your teeth clean of food in
4: 7 *T* I also withheld the rain from you when
4: 8 *T* two or three cities staggered to one
5:11 *T* you have built houses of hewn stone,
5:11 *T* you have planted choice vineyards,
9: 2 *T* they break through to the nether world,
9: 2 *T* they climb to the heavens,
9: 3 *T* they hide on the summit of Carmel,
9: 3 *T* they hide from my gaze in the bottom of
9: 4 *T* they are led into captivity by their
Ob 1: 4 *T* you go as high as the eagle,
1:16 and shall become as *t* they had not been.
Mi 2: 8 in confidence, as *t* it were spoils of war.
7: 8 *t* I have fallen, I will arise; though I sit
Na 1:12 *T* I have humbled you,
2: 3 *T* ravagers have ravaged them and ruined
Hb 3:17 For *t* the fig tree blossom not nor fruit
3:17 *T* the yield of the olive fail and the
3:17 *T* the flocks disappear from the fold and
Zec 2: 8 live in Jerusalem as *t* in open country,
10: 6 shall be as *t* I had never cast them off,
Mal 2:14 have broken faith *t* she is your companion,
Mt 12:16 *t* he sternly ordered them not to make
12:44 unoccupied, *t* swept and tidied now.
17:12 I assure you, *t*, that Elijah has already
26:33 *T* all may have their faith in you shaken,
26:35 replied, "Even *t* I have to die with you,
Mk 2: 8 reasoning, *t* they kept it to themselves,
9:10 *t* they continued to discuss what "to rise
9:32 *T* they failed to understand his words,
14:29 to him, "Even *t* all are shaken in faith,
Lk 6: 4 even *t* only priests are allowed to eat it?"
11: 8 even *t* he does not get up and take care of
Jn 1:31 *t* the very reason I came baptizing with
6:10 *t* the men numbered about five thousand,
6:36 *t* you have seen me,
6:71 the Iscariot, who, *t* one of the Twelve,
7:22 Moses gave you circumcision *t* it did not
8:55 for your God, even *t* you do not know him.
10: 6 Even *t* Jesus used this figure with them,
10:38 them, even *t* you put no faith in me,
11:26 whoever believes in me, *t* he should die,
13:10 just as you are; *t* not all."
20:19 even *t* the disciples had locked the doors
21: 4 *t* none of the disciples knew it was Jesus.
Acts 9: 8 unable to see, even *t* his eyes were open.
13:28 Even *t* they found no charge against him
17:27 *t* he is not really far from any one of us.
27:26 *t* we still have to face shipwreck on some
28:19 *t* I had no cause to make accusations
Rom 1:13 often planned to visit you *t* up to now
3: 4 true even *t* every man be proved a liar,
3:21 even *t* both law and prophets bear witness
5: 7 *t* it is barely possible that for a good
5:13 *t* sin is not imputed when there is no law
6:17 be to God, *t* once you were slaves of sin,
7:21 that even *t* I want to do what is right,
9:27 *T* the number of the Israelites should be
10: 2 for God *t* their zeal is unenlightened.
12: 5 have the same function, so too we, *t* many,
1Cor 2:15 *t* he himself can be appraised by no one.
5: 3 *t* absent in body I am present in spirit,
7:10 I give this command *t* it is not mine;
7:29 with wives should live as *t* they had none;
7:30 should live as *t* they were not weeping,
7:30 who rejoice as *t* they were not rejoicing;
7:30 conduct themselves as *t* they owned nothing,
7:31 of the world as *t* they were not using it,
7:40 She will be happier, *t*, in my opinion,
8: 5 Even *t* there are so-called gods in the
10:17 loaf of bread is one, we, many *t* we are,
12:12 but all the members, many *t* they are,
2Cor 3: 7 shone on it (even *t* it was a fading glory),
4:16 even *t* our body is being destroyed
6:10 sorrowful, *t* we are always rejoicing;
7:14 For *t* I had boasted to him about you,
8: 9 sake he made himself poor *t* he was rich,
12:11 Even *t* I am nothing,
13: 7 is good, even *t* we may seem to have failed.
Gal 4: 1 even *t* in name he is master of all his
Phil 2: 6 *T* he was in the form of God,
3: 4 the flesh *t* I can be confident even there.
Col 2:21 as *t* you were still living a life bounded
1Thes 2: 7 even *t* we could have insisted on our own
Heb 5: 8 Son *t* he was, he learned obedience
6: 9 Beloved, even *t* we speak in this way,
7: 5 *t* all of them are descendants of Abraham;
11:11 power to conceive *t* she was past the age,
11:34 *t* weak they were made powerful,
12:17 even *t* he sought the blessing with tears.
Jas 2:10 law, even *t* he keeps the entire remainder,
3: 9 *t* they are made in the likeness of God.
1Pt 2:12 *T* the pagans may slander you as
2Pt 1:12 even *t* you already understand and are
2: 5 even *t* he preserved Noah as a preacher of
2:11 *t* greater than men in strength and power,
2:19 *t* they themselves are slaves of corruption
3: 9 his promise *t* some consider it "delay."
3Jn 1: 5 for the brothers even *t* they are strangers;
Jude 1: 5 even *t* you may already be very well aware
Rv 1:17 of him I fell down at his feet as *t* dead.
2: 4 I hold this against you, *t*:
2: 9 and your poverty, even *t* you are rich.
17:11 no longer, even *t* it is an eighth king,

THOUGHTFUL (4)

Sir 22: 4 A *t* daughter becomes a treasure to her
27:12 fools, but frequent the company of *t* men.
32:18 The *t* man will not neglect direction;
Eph 5:15 Do not act like fools, but like *t* men.

THOUGHTFULNESS (1)

Sir 26:13 her husband, her *t* puts flesh on his bones;

THOUGHTS (74)

1Chr 28: 9 hearts and understands all the mind's *t*.
29:18 keep such *t* in the hearts and minds of
2Mc 2: 2 of the Lord or be led astray in their *t*,
Jb 4:13 In my *t* during visions of the night,
20: 2 So now my *t* provide me with an answer,

THOUGHTS (cont.)

21:27 Behold, I know your t,
31: 1 and entertained any t against a maiden;
Ps(s) 10: 4 "There is no God," sums up his t.
39: 4 in my t, a fire blazed forth
64: 7 deep are the t of each heart.
92: 6 How very deep are your t!
94:11 The LORD knows the t of men,
139: 2 you understand my t from afar.
139:23 try me, and know my t;
Prv 23:33 and your heart utters disordered t;
Eccl 7:25 I turned my t toward knowledge;
10:20 in your t do not make light of the king,
Wis 2:14 To us he is the censure of our t;
2:21 These were their t, but they erred;
3:10 receive a punishment to match their t,
3:14 who held no wicked t against the Lord
7:20 beasts, Powers of the winds and t of men,
11:15 in return for their senseless, wicked t,
Sir 5:12 Be consistent in your t;
9: 5 Entertain no t against a virgin,
16:21 Such are the t of senseless men,
17:26 How obscure then the t of flesh and blood!
21:26 Fools' t are in their mouths,
23: 2 Who will apply the lash to my t,
24:27 For deeper than the sea are her t;
33: 5 his t revolve in circles.
35:22 and repays men according to their t;
38:20 Turn not your t to him again;
40: 2 to the mother of all the living, His t,
41:21 and of entertaining t about another's wife;
Is 55: 7 forsake his way, and the wicked man his t;
55: 8 For my t are not your thoughts,
55: 9 your ways and my thoughts above your t.
59: 7 Their t are destructive thoughts,
65: 2 walk in evil paths and follow their own t,
66:17 all perish with their deeds and their t,
Jer 4:14 must your pernicious t lodge within you?
12: 2 their lips, but far from their inmost t.
Ez 13:17 of your people who prophesy their own t;
38:10 At that time t shall arise in your mind,
Dn 2:29 t about what should happen in the future,
2:30 you may understand the t in your own mind.
4:16 appalled for a while, terrified by his t.
5: 6 his t terrified him,
7:28 I, Daniel, was greatly terrified by my t,
Am 4:13 the wind, and declares to man his t;
Mi 4:12 But they know not the t of the LORD,
Mt 5:28 committed adultery with her in his t.
9: 4 "Why do you harbor evil t?
12:25 Knowing their t, he said to them:
16: 8 Jesus knew their t and said,
Mk 2: 8 "Why do you harbor these t?
12:33 with all our t and with all our strength,
Lk 1:51 has confused the proud in their inmost t.
2:35 that the t of many hearts may be laid bare."
5:22 "Why do you harbor these t?
6: 8 He knew their t, however, and said
7:40 In answer to his t, Jesus said to him,
9:47 Jesus, who knew their t, took a little child
11:17 Because he knew their t, he said to them:
Rom 2:15 and their t will accuse or defend them on
12:16 t and associate with those who are lowly.
1Cor 3:20 Lord knows how empty are the t of the wise."
2Cor 11: 3 your t may be corrupted and you may fall
Phil 4: 8 your t should be wholly directed to all
Heb 4:12 judges the reflections and t of the heart.

THOUSAND (585)

Gn 20:16 given your brother a t shekels of silver.
Ex 12:37 Succoth, about six hundred t men on foot,
32:28 day there fell about three t of the people.
34: 7 his kindness for a t generations,
38:25 t seven hundred and seventy-five shekels,
38:26 and three t five hundred and fifty men.
38:28 The remaining one t seven hundred and
38:29 talents and two t four hundred shekels.
Lv 26: 8 a hundred of you will chase ten t of them,
Nm 1:21 forty-six t five hundred were enrolled in
1:23 fifty-nine t three hundred were enrolled
1:25 forty-five t six hundred and fifty were
1:27 seventy-four t six hundred were enrolled
1:29 fifty-four t four hundred were enrolled in
1:31 fifty-seven t four hundred were enrolled
1:33 forty t five hundred were enrolled in the
1:35 thirty-two t two hundred were enrolled in
1:37 thirty-five t four hundred were enrolled
1:39 sixty-two t seven hundred were enrolled in
1:41 forty-one t five hundred were enrolled in
1:43 fifty-three t four hundred were enrolled
1:46 houses, was six hundred and three t,
2: 4 the census to seventy-four t six hundred.]
2: 6 in the census to fifty-four t four hundred.]
2: 8 the census to fifty-seven t four hundred.]
2: 9 one hundred and eighty-six t four hundred.]
2:11 in the census to forty-six t five hundred.]
2:13 the census to fifty-nine t three hundred.]
2:15 to forty-five t six hundred and fifty.
2:16 and fifty-one t four hundred and fifty.]
2:19 in the census to forty t five hundred.]
2:21 in the census to thirty-two t two hundred.]
2:23 the census to thirty-five t four hundred.
2:24 was one hundred and eight t one hundred.]
2:26 in the census to sixty-two t seven hundred.]
2:28 in the census to forty-one t five hundred.]
2:30 the census to fifty-three t four hundred.
2:31 one hundred and fifty-seven t six hundred.]
2:32 hundred and three t five hundred and fifty.
3:22 they numbered seven t five hundred.
3:28 they numbered eight t three hundred.
3:34 they numbered six t two hundred.
3:39 with the LORD's command, was twenty-two t.
3:43 twenty-two t two hundred and seventy-three.
3:50 one t three hundred and sixty-five shekels
4:36 numbered two t seven hundred and fifty.
4:40 they numbered two t six hundred and thirty.
4:44 clans, they numbered three t two hundred.
4:48 was eight t five hundred and eighty,
7:85 amounted to two t four hundred shekels,
11:21 around me include six hundred t soldiers;
17:14 t seven hundred died from the scourge,
25: 9 but only after twenty-four t had died.
26: 7 of whom forty-three t seven hundred and
26:14 t two hundred men were registered.
26:18 forty t five hundred men were registered.
26:22 t five hundred men were registered.
26:25 t three hundred men were registered.
26:27 sixty t five hundred men were registered.
26:34 t seven hundred men were registered.
26:37 t five hundred men were registered.
26:41 t six hundred men were registered.
26:43 t four hundred men were registered.
26:47 t four hundred men were registered.
26:50 t four hundred men were registered.
26:51 These six hundred and one t seven hundred
26:62 who were registered, was twenty-three t.
31: 4 you shall send a band of one t men to war."
31: 5 a t men of each tribe were levied,
31: 5 that there were twelve t men armed for war.
31: 6 out on the campaign, a t from each tribe,
31:32 to six hundred and seventy-five t sheep,
31:33 thousand sheep, seventy-two t oxen,
31:34 thousand oxen, sixty-one t asses,
31:35 thirty-two t girls who were still virgins.
31:36 and thirty-seven t five hundred sheep,
31:38 as tax to the LORD; thirty-six t oxen,
31:39 thirty t five hundred asses,
31:40 and sixteen t persons,
31:43 and thirty-seven t five hundred sheep,
31:44 five hundred sheep, thirty-six t oxen,
31:45 thousand oxen, thirty t five hundred asses,
31:46 five hundred asses, and sixteen t persons.
31:52 sixteen t seven hundred and fifty shekels.
35: 4 assigned the Levites shall extend a t cubits
35: 5 t cubits outside the city along each side
Dt 1:11 your fathers, increase you a t times over,
32:30 thousand, or two men put ten t to flight,
Jos 3: 4 of two t cubits between you and the ark.
4:13 About forty t troops equipped for battle
7: 3 if only about two or three t go up,
7: 4 three t of the people made the attack,
8: 3 Picking out thirty t warriors,
8:12 [He took about five t men and set them in
8:25 that day a total of twelve t men and women,
23:10 One of you puts to flight a t,
Jgs 1: 4 and they slew ten t of them in Bezek.
3:29 occasion they slew about ten t Moabites,
4: 6 with you ten t Naphtalites and Zebulunites.
4:10 to Kedesh, and ten t men followed him.
4:14 Mount Tabor, followed by his ten t men.
5: 8 seen, nor a lance, among forty t in Israel!
7: 3 twenty-two t of the soldiers left, but ten t
8:10 with their force of about fifteen t men;
8:10 and twenty t swordsmen having fallen.
9:49 of Migdal-shechem, about a t men and women,
12: 6 forty-two t Ephraimites fell at that time.
15:11 Three t men of Judah went down to the
15:15 grasped it, and with it killed a t men.
15:16 the jawbone of an ass I have slain a t men."
16:27 and from the roof about three t men and
20: 2 hundred t foot soldiers who were swordsmen,
20:10 hundred for every t, a t for every ten t,
20:15 cities on that occasion was twenty-six t,
20:17 four hundred t swordsmen ready for battle,
20:21 city and felled twenty-two t men of Israel.
20:25 against them felled eighteen t Israelites,
20:34 Gibeah, ten t picked men from all Israel,
20:35 twenty-five t one hundred men of Benjamin,
20:44 of Gibeah, while eighteen t of them fell,
20:45 picked off five t men among them,
20:45 Gidom, killed another two t of them there.
20:46 day were in all twenty-five t swordsmen,
21:10 sent twelve t warriors with orders to go
1Sm 4: 2 slew about four t men on the battlefield.
4:10 which Israel lost thirty t foot soldiers.
8:12 of groups of a t and of a hundred soldiers.
11: 8 three hundred t Israelites and seventy t
13: 2 Saul chose three t men of Israel,
13: 2 of whom two t remained with him in
13: 2 and one t were with Jonathan in Gibeah of
13: 5 three thousand chariots, six t horsemen,
14:24 the whole people, about ten t combatants,
15: 4 thousand foot soldiers and ten t men of Judah.
17: 5 of scale armor weighing five t shekels,
22: 7 you an officer over a t or a hundred men,
24: 3 So Saul took three t picked men from all
25: 2 owning three t sheep and a thousand goats.
26: 2 of Ziph with three t picked men of Israel,
29: 2 their groups of a hundred and a t,
2Sm 6: 1 picked men of Israel, thirty t in number.
8: 4 one t seven hundred horsemen and twenty t
8: 5 of Zobah, David slew twenty-two t of them.
8:13 eighteen t Edomites in the Salt Valley;
10: 6 hired twenty t Aramean foot soldiers
10: 6 thousand men, and twelve t men from Tob.
10:18 and forty t of the Aramean foot soldiers.
17: 1 "Please let me choose twelve t men,
18: 1 of groups of a t and groups of a hundred.
18: 3 You are equal to ten t of us.
18: 4 out in units of a hundred and of a t.
18: 7 that day were heavy—twenty t men.
18:12 held a t pieces of silver in my two hands,
19:18 accompanied by a t men from Benjamin.
24: 9 hundred t men fit for military service;
24: 9 in Judah, five hundred t.
24:15 and seventy t of the people from Dan to
1Kgs 3: 4 its altar Solomon offered a t holocausts.
5: 6 four t stalls for his twelve t chariot horses.
5:12 Solomon also uttered three t proverbs,
5:12 and his songs numbered a t and five.
5:25 gave Hiram twenty t kors of wheat
5:25 and twenty t measures of pure oil.
5:27 thirty t workmen from all Israel.
5:28 the Lebanon each month in relays of ten t,
5:29 seventy t carriers and eighty t stonecutters
5:30 to three t three hundred overseers,
7:26 Its capacity was two t measures.
8:63 offerings to the LORD twenty-two t oxen
8:63 oxen and one hundred twenty t sheep.
10:26 he had one t four hundred chariots and
10:26 four hundred chariots and twelve t drivers;
12:21 one hundred and eighty t seasoned warriors
19:18 Yet I will leave seven t men in Israel
20:15 Israelite soldiery, who numbered seven t.
20:29 hundred t foot soldiers of Aram in one day.
20:30 The survivors, twenty-seven t of them,
2Kgs 3: 4 as tribute a hundred t lambs and the wool
3: 4 lambs and the wool of a hundred t rams.
5: 5 ten silver talents, six t gold pieces,
13: 7 with ten chariots and ten t foot soldiers,
14: 7 slew ten t Edomites in the Salt Valley,
15:19 and Menahem gave him a t talents of silver
18:23 two t horses if you can put riders on them.
19:35 and eighty-five t men in Assyrian camp.
24:14 and men of the army, ten t in number,
24:16 to Babylon all seven t men of the army,
24:16 of the army, and a t craftsmen and smiths,
1Chr 5:18 forty-four t seven hundred and sixty men
5:21 t men they also captured their livestock:
5:21 fifty t camels, two hundred fifty t sheep,
5:21 fifty thousand sheep, and two t asses.
7: 2 t six hundred in the time of David.
7: 4 t men in organized military troops,
7: 5 t warriors in their family records.
7: 7 listed twenty-two t and thirty-four.
7: 9 Their family records listed twenty t two
7:11 They numbered seventeen t two hundred men
7:40 twenty-six t men fit for military service.
9:13 houses, were one t seven hundred and sixty,
12:25 six t eight hundred armed troops.
12:26 seven t one hundred.
12:27 four t six hundred, along with Jehoiada,
12:28 Aaron, with another three t seven hundred,
12:30 three t— until this time,
12:31 twenty t eight hundred warriors,
12:32 eighteen t, designated by name
12:34 fifty t men rallying with a single purpose.
12:35 one t captains, and with them, armed
12:35 with shield and lance, thirty-seven t men.
12:36 twenty-eight t six hundred.
12:37 set in battle array: forty t.
12:38 one hundred and twenty t.
16:15 which he made binding for a t generations
18: 4 David took from him twenty t foot soldiers,
18: 4 twenty t foot soldiers, one t chariots,
18: 5 David also slew twenty-two t of their men.
18:12 eighteen t Edomites in the Valley of Salt.
19: 6 Hanun and the Ammonites sent a t talents
19: 7 They hired thirty-two t chariots along
19:18 and David slew seven t of their chariot
19:18 and forty t of their foot soldiers;
21: 5 in all Israel one million one hundred t,
21: 5 and in Judah four hundred and seventy t.
21:14 Israel, and seventy t men of Israel died.
22:14 of the LORD a hundred t talents of gold,
23: 3 number was found to be thirty-eight t men.
23: 4 twenty-four t were to direct the service
23: 4 six t were to be officials and judges,
23: 5 and judges, four t were to be gatekeepers,
23: 5 and four t were to praise the LORD with
26:30 one t seven hundred police officers,
26:32 two t seven hundred heads of families.
27: 1 the divisions, of twenty-four t men each,
27: 2 and in his division were twenty-four t men;
27: 4 and in his division were twenty-four t men.
27: 5 and in his division were twenty-four t men.
27: 7 and in his division were twenty-four t men.
27: 8 and in his division were twenty-four t men.

27: 9 and in his division were twenty-four *t* men.
27:10 in his division were twenty-four *t* men.
27:11 and in his division were twenty-four *t* men.
27:12 and in his division were twenty-four *t* men.
27:13 and in his division were twenty-four *t* men.
27:14 and in his division were twenty-four *t* men.
27:15 and in his division were twenty-four *t* men.
29: 4 three *t* talents of Ophir gold, and seven *t*
29: 7 five *t* talents and ten *t* darics of gold,
29: 7 *t* talents of silver, eighteen *t* talents of bronze,
29: 7 bronze, and one hundred *t* talents of iron.
29:21 a *t* bulls, a thousand rams, and a thousand
2Chr 1: 6 he offered a *t* holocausts upon it.
1:14 so that he had one *t* four hundred chariots
1:14 four hundred chariots and twelve *t* drivers
2: 1 He conscripted seventy *t* men to carry
2: 1 eighty *t* to cut the stone in the mountains,
2: 1 he placed three *t* six hundred overseers.
2: 9 twenty *t* kors of wheat, twenty thousand
2: 9 thousand kors of barley, twenty *t* measures
2:16 one hundred fifty-three *t* six hundred.
2:17 seventy *t* carriers and eighty thousand
2:17 and three *t* six hundred overseers to keep
4: 5 It had a capacity of three *t* measures.
7: 5 offered as sacrifice twenty-two *t* oxen,
7: 5 oxen, and one hundred twenty *t* sheep.
9:25 Solomon also had four *t* stalls of horses,
9:25 of horses, chariots, and twelve *t* horsemen,
11: 1 a hundred and eighty *t* seasoned warriors,
12: 3 hundred chariots and sixty *t* horsemen,
13: 3 a force of four hundred *t* picked warriors,
13: 3 hundred *t* picked and valiant warriors.
13:17 hundred *t* picked men of Israel fell slain.
14: 7 *t* shield- and lance-bearers from Judah,
14: 7 and two hundred and eighty *t* from Benjamin
15:11 *t* sheep of the booty they had brought.
17:11 him a flock of seven *t* seven hundred rams
17:11 rams and seven *t* seven hundred he-goats.
17:14 with him three hundred *t* valiant warriors.
17:15 and with him two hundred eighty *t*.
17:16 with him two hundred *t* valiant warriors.
17:17 two hundred *t* armed with bow and buckler.
17:18 one hundred and eighty *t* equipped for war.
25: 5 be three hundred *t* picked men fit for war,
25: 6 He also hired a hundred *t* valiant warriors
25:11 and there they killed ten *t* men of Seir.
25:12 also brought back another ten *t* alive,
25:13 They killed three *t* of the inhabitants and
26:12 valiant warriors was two *t* six hundred,
26:13 army of three hundred seven *t* five hundred
27: 5 thousand kors of wheat and ten *t* of barley.
28: 6 and twenty *t* of Judah in a single day,
28: 8 two hundred *t* of their brethren's wives,
29:33 were six hundred oxen and three *t* sheep.
30:24 thousand bulls and seven *t* sheep to the
30:24 assembly a *t* bulls and ten thousand sheep.
35: 7 of lambs and kids, thirty *t* in number,
35: 7 who were present, and also three *t* oxen;
35: 8 gave to the priests two *t* six hundred
35: 9 to the Levites five *t* Passover victims,
Ezr 1: 9 sacks of silverware, one *t* and twenty-nine;
1:10 other ware, one *t* pieces.
1:11 five *t* four hundred pieces.
2: 3 Parosh, two *t* one hundred and seventy-two;
2: 6 and Joab, two *t* eight hundred and twelve;
2: 7 of Elam, one *t* two hundred and fifty-four;
2:12 of Azgad, one *t* two hundred and twenty-two;
2:14 sons of Bigvai, two *t* and fifty-six;
2:31 Elam, one *t* two hundred and fifty-four;
2:35 of Senaah, three *t* six hundred and thirty.
2:37 sons of Immer, one *t* and fifty-two;
2:38 Pashhur, one *t* two hundred and forty-seven;
2:39 sons of Harim, one *t* and seventeen.
2:64 to forty-two *t* three hundred and sixty,
2:65 seven *t* three hundred and thirty-seven.
2:67 their asses six *t* seven hundred and twenty.
2:69 sixty-one *t* drachmas of gold, five *t* minas
8:27 twenty golden bowls valued at a *t* darics;
Neh 3:13 a *t* cubits of the wall up to the Dung Gate.
7: 8 Parosh, two *t* one hundred and seventy-two;
7:11 and Joab, two *t* eight hundred and eighteen;
7:12 of Elam, one *t* two hundred and fifty-four;
7:17 Azgad, two *t* three hundred and twenty-two;
7:19 sons of Bigvai, two *t* and sixty-seven;
7:34 Elam, one *t* two hundred and fifty-four;
7:38 of Senaah, three *t* nine hundred and thirty.
7:40 sons of Immer, one *t* and fifty-two
7:40 Pashhur, one *t* two hundred and forty-seven;
7:42 sons of Harim, one *t* and seventeen.
7:66 to forty-two *t* three hundred and sixty,
7:67 seven *t* three hundred and thirty-seven.
7:68 their asses six *t* seven hundred and twenty.
7:69 into the treasury one *t* drachmas of gold,
7:70 thousand drachmas of gold and two *t* two
7:71 thousand drachmas of gold, two *t* minas
Jdt 2: 5 *t* infantry and twelve thousand cavalry,
2:15 a hundred and twenty *t* picked troops,
2:15 commanded, and twelve *t* mounted archers,
7: 2 *t* infantry and twelve thousand horsemen,
7:17 moved camp, together with five *t* Assyrians.
Est 3: 9 deliver to the procurators ten *t* silver talents
9:16 They killed seventy-five *t* of their foes,
1Mc 2:38 their cattle, to the number of a *t* persons.
3:39 forty thousand men and seven *t* cavalry
4: 1 thousand infantry and a *t* picked cavalry,
4: 6 appeared in the plain with three *t* men,
4:15 About three *t* of their men fell.
4:28 *t* picked men and five thousand cavalry,
4:29 and Judas met them with ten *t* men.
4:34 and about five *t* of Lysias' men fell in
5:13 and they have slain there about a *t* men."
5:20 Three *t* men were allotted to Simon,
5:20 go into Galilee, and eight *t* men to Judas,
5:22 About three *t* men of the Gentiles fell,
5:34 About eight *t* of their men fell that day.
5:60 and about two *t* Israelites fell that day.
6:30 thousand foot-soldiers, twenty *t* cavalry,
6:35 assigned to it a *t* men in coats of mail,
7:40 But Judas camped in Adasa with three *t* men.
7:41 killed a hundred and eighty-five *t* of them.
9: 4 with twenty *t* men and two thousand cavalry.
9: 5 Judas, with three *t* picked men,
9:49 A *t* men on Bacchides' side fell that day.
10:36 "Let thirty *t* Jews be enrolled in the
10:40 personal grant of fifteen *t* silver shekels
10:42 the dues of five *t* silver shekels that
10:74 Choosing ten *t* men, he set out from
10:77 *t* horsemen and an innumerable infantry.
10:79 had left a *t* cavalry in hiding behind them.
10:85 burned alive, came to about eight *t* men.
11:44 *t* good fighting men to him at Antioch.
11:45 populace, one hundred and twenty *t* strong,
11:47 killed about a hundred *t* men in the city,
11:74 *t* of the foreign troops fell on that day.
12:41 with forty *t* picked fighting men and came
12:47 thousand men, of whom he sent two *t* to
14:24 a great gold shield weighing a *t* minas,
15:13 thousand infantry and eight *t* horsemen.
15:18 with them a gold shield worth a *t* minas.
15:26 to Antiochus' support two *t* elite troops,
16: 4 in the land twenty *t* warriors and horsemen.
16:10 and about two *t* of the enemy perished.
2Mc 4:40 three *t* armed men under the leadership
5: 5 a *t* men and suddenly attacked the city.
5:14 space of three days, eighty *t* were lost,
5:14 were lost, forty *t* meeting a violent death,
5:24 at the head of an army of twenty-two *t*
8: 1 to Judaism, assembled about six *t* men.
8: 9 the head of at least twenty *t* armed men
8:10 Nicanor planned to raise the two *t* talents
8:16 Maccabeus assembled his men, six *t* strong,
8:19 eighty-five *t* of his men were destroyed,
8:20 only eight *t* Jews fought along with four *t*
8:20 eight *t* routed one hundred and twenty *t*
8:24 they killed more than nine *t* of the enemy,
8:30 killed more than twenty *t* of them,
8:34 the *t* slave dealers to buy the Jews,
10:17 them, killing as many as twenty *t* men.
10:18 *t* took refuge in two very strong towers,
10:20 on receiving seventy *t* drachmas,
10:23 than twenty *t* men in the two strongholds.
11: 2 mustered about eighty *t* infantry and all
11:11 they laid low eleven *t* foot soldiers and
12:10 numbering at least five *t* foot soldiers,
12:19 destroyed the force of more than ten *t* men
12:20 a hundred and twenty *t* foot soldiers
12:23 and destroying as many as thirty *t* men.
12:26 where he killed twenty-five *t* people.
12:28 twenty-five *t* of the people in it.
12:33 *t* foot soldiers and four hundred horsemen.
12:43 amounting to two *t* silver drachmas,
13: 2 of one hundred and ten *t* foot soldiers,
13:15 men and killed about two *t* in the camp.
15:22 eighty-five *t* men of Sennacherib's army.
15:27 they laid low at least thirty-five *t*,
Jb 1: 3 had seven thousand sheep, three *t* camels,
9: 3 he could not answer him once in a *t* times.
33:23 there be for him an angel, one out of a *t*,
42:12 had fourteen thousand sheep, six *t* camels,
42:12 a thousand yoke of oxen, and a *t* she-asses.
Ps(s) 50:10 forests, beasts by the *t* on my mountains.
84:11 one day in your courts than a *t* elsewhere;
90: 4 a *t* years in your sight are as yesterday,
91: 7 Though a *t* fall at your side, ten *t* at your
105: 8 which he made binding for a *t* generations
Eccl 6: 6 twice a *t* years and not enjoy his goods,
7:28 One man out of a *t* have I come upon,
Sg 4: 4 A *t* bucklers hang upon it,
8:11 one would have to pay a *t* silver pieces.
8:12 the *t* pieces are for you,
Wis 12:22 and our enemies with a *t* blows you punish,
Sir 6: 6 be many, but one in a *t* your confidant.
16: 3 For one can be better than a *t*;
16:10 Nor the six hundred *t* foot soldiers who
23:19 LORD, ten *t* times brighter than the sun,
39:11 While he lives he is one out of a *t*,
41: 4 Whether one has lived a *t* years,
46: 8 two spared from the six hundred *t* infantry,
Is 7:23 thousand vines, worth a *t* pieces of silver,
30:17 A *t* shall tremble at the threat of one;
36: 8 'I will give you two *t* horses,
37:36 and eighty-five *t* in the Assyrian camp.
60:22 The smallest shall become a *t*,
Jer 32:18 your kindness through a *t* generations;
52:28 three *t* and twenty-three people of Judah;
52:30 four *t* six hundred persons in all.
Ez 45: 1 *t* cubits long and twenty thousand wide;
45: 3 thousand cubits long and ten *t* wide,
45: 5 thousand cubits long and ten *t* wide
45: 6 five *t* cubits wide and twenty-five thousand
47: 3 *t* cubits and had me wade through the water,
47: 4 Again he measured off a *t* and had me wade;
47: 5 Once more he measured off a *t*,
48: 8 twenty-five *t* cubits from north to south,
48: 9 thousand cubits across by twenty *t* north
48:10 have twenty-five *t* cubits on the north,
48:10 ten *t* on the west, ten *t* on the east,
48:13 twenty-five *t* cubits by ten thousand.
48:13 thousand cubits across and twenty *t* north
48:15 The remaining five *t* cubits along the
48:18 ten *t* cubits to the east and ten thousand
48:20 thousand by twenty-five *t* cubits;
48:35 perimeter of the City is eighteen *t* cubits.
Dn 5: 1 gave a great banquet for a *t* of his lords,
8:14 two *t* three hundred evenings and mornings;
12:11 shall be one *t* two hundred and ninety days.
12:12 one *t* three hundred and thirty-five days.
Am 5: 3 with a *t* shall be left without a hundred,
Jon 4:11 hundred and twenty *t* persons who cannot
Mt 14:21 Those who ate were about five *t*,
15:38 The people who were fed numbered four *t*,
16: 9 *t* and how many baskets-full you picked up?
16:10 *t* and how many hampers-full you retrieved?
25:15 To one he disbursed five *t* silver pieces,
25:15 a second two thousand, and to a third a *t*.
25:16 *t* went to invest it and made another five.
25:17 who received the two *t* doubled his figure.
25:18 The man who received the *t* went off
25:20 The man who had received the five *t* came
25:20 lord,' he said, 'you let me have five *t*.
25:20 See, I have made five *t* more.'
25:22 received the two *t* then stepped forward.
25:22 two thousand and I have made two *t* more.'
25:24 man who had received the *t* stepped forward.
25:25 buried your *t* silver pieces in the ground.
25:28 Take the *t* away from him and give it to
25:28 him and give it to the man with the ten *t*.
Mk 5:13 The herd of about two *t* went rushing down
6:44 had eaten the loaves numbered five *t* men.
8: 9 Those who had eaten numbered about four *t*.
8:19 I broke the five loaves for the five *t*,
8:20 I broke the seven loaves for the four *t*,
Lk 9:14 (There were about five *t* men.)
14:31 first and consider whether, with ten *t* men,
14:31 an enemy coming against him with twenty *t*?
Jn 6:10 Even though the men numbered about five *t*,
Acts 2:41 some three *t* were added that day.
4: 4 the number of the men came to about five *t*.
19:19 assessed, it came to fifty *t* silver pieces.
21:38 of four *t* cutthroats out into the desert?"
Rom 11: 4 *t* men who have not bowed the knee to Baal."
1Cor 4:15 Granted you have ten *t* guardians in Christ,
10: 8 so that in one day twenty-three *t* perished.
14:19 others than ten *t* words in a tongue.
2Pt 3: 8 *t* years and a thousand years are as a day.
Rv 7: 4 forty-four *t* from every tribe of Israel;
7: 5 twelve *t* from the tribe of Judah,
7: 5 Judah, twelve *t* from the tribe of Reuben,
7: 5 of Reuben, twelve *t* from the tribe of Gad,
7: 6 of Gad, twelve *t* from the tribe of Asher,
7: 6 Asher, twelve *t* from the tribe of Naphtali,
7: 6 twelve *t* from the tribe of Manasseh,
7: 7 twelve *t* from the tribe of Simeon,
7: 7 of Simeon, twelve *t* from the tribe of Levi,
7: 7 Levi, twelve *t* from the tribe of Issachar,
7: 8 twelve *t* from the tribe of Zebulun,
7: 8 Zebulun, twelve *t* from the tribe of Joseph,
7: 8 and twelve *t* from the tribe of Benjamin.
11:13 Seven *t* persons were killed during the
14: 1 hundred and forty-four *t* who had his name
14: 3 *t* who had been ransomed from the world.
20: 2 or Satan, and chained him up for a *t* years.
20: 3 nations astray until the *t* years are over.
20: 4 and reigned with Christ for a *t* years.
20: 5 come to life till the *t* years were over.
20: 6 and shall reign with him for a *t* years.
20: 7 When the *t* years are over,
21:16 and found it twelve *t* furlongs in length,

THOUSANDS (42)

Gn 24:60 "Sister, may you grow into *t* of myriads;
Ex 18:21 and set them as officers over groups of *t*,
18:25 of the people as officers over groups of *t*,
Dt 1:15 them your leaders as officials over *t*,
33:17 of Ephraim, and these the *t* of Manasseh.]
1Sm 18: 7 slain his thousands, and David his ten *t*."
18: 8 "They give David ten *t*, but only thousands
21:12 slain his thousands, but David his ten *t*'?"
29: 5 slain his *t*, but David his ten thousands'?"
29: 5 slain his thousands, but David his ten *t*'?"
1Chr 12:15 over hundreds and the greater over *t*.
12:21 and Zillethai, chiefs of *t* of Manasseh.
13: 1 with his commanders of *t* and of hundreds,
15:25 and the commanders of *t* went to bring up
26:26 the commanders of *t* and of hundreds,
27: 1 heads, commanders of *t* and of hundreds,
28: 1 king, the commanders of *t* and of hundreds,
29: 6 the commanders of *t* and of hundreds,

THOUSANDS (cont.)

2Chr 1: 2 to the commanders of *t* and of hundreds,
17:14 Of Judah, the commanders of *t*:
25: 5 houses, under leaders of *t* and of hundreds.
1Mc 3:55 officers among the people, over *t*,
2Mc 11: 4 of foot soldiers, his *t* of horsemen,
Ps(s) 68:18 chariots of God are myriad, *t* on thousands;
119:72 precious than *t* of gold and silver pieces.
144:13 May our sheep be in the *t*,
Sg 5:10 he stands out among *t*.
Sir 41:12 better than precious treasures in the *t*;
47: 6 his praises and ascribed to him tens of *t*.
Dn 3:40 of rams and bullocks, or *t* of fat lambs,
7:10 *T* upon thousands were ministering to him,
11:12 of his heart, he shall lay low tens of *t*,
Mi 6: 7 Will the LORD be pleased with *t* of rams,
Lk 12: 1 Meanwhile a crowd of *t* had gathered,
Acts 21:20 how many *t* of Jews have come to believe,
Rv 5:11 *t* and tens of thousands and they all cried

THOUSANDTH (3)

Ex 20: 6 bestowing mercy down to the *t* generation,
Dt 5:10 bestowing mercy, down to the *t* generation,
7: 9 merciful covenant down to the *t* generation

THRACIAN (1)

2Mc 12:35 when a *T* horseman attacked Dositheus and

THRASH (1)

Sir 30:12 young, *t* his sides while he is still small,

THREAD (16)

Gn 14:23 not take so much as a *t* or a sandal strap
38:28 and the midwife, taking a crimson *t*,
Ex 28: 6 they shall make of gold *t* and of violet,
28: 8 from it and, like it, be made of gold *t*,
28:15 like the ephod with gold *t* and violet,
35:25 purple and scarlet yarn and fine linen *t*,
35:35 purple and scarlet yarn and fine linen *t*,
39: 2 ephod was woven of gold *t* and of violet,
39: 5 from it, and like it, was made of gold *t*,
39: 8 like the ephod, with gold *t* and violet,
Lv 19:19 woven with two different kinds of *t*.
Dt 22:11 not wear cloth of two different kinds of *t*,
Jgs 16: 9 a *t* of tow is severed by a whiff of flame;
16:12 But he snapped them off his arms like *t*.
Jb 8:14 gossamer *t* and his trust is a spider's web.
Is 38:12 life, like a weaver who severs the last *t*.

THREADED (1)

Ps(s) 45:14 her raiment is *t* with spun gold.

THREADS (1)

Ex 39: 3 into gold leaf and then cut up into *t*,

THREAT (8)

Jos 23:15 for you, so will he fulfill every *t*,
1Kgs 5:18 There is no enemy or *t* of danger.
1Mc 1:35 And they became a great *t*.
Jb 5:20 death, and in war from the *t* of the sword;
Is 30:17 A thousand shall tremble at the *t* of one;
Jer 37:11 Jerusalem at the *t* of the army of Pharaoh,
51:12 his *t* against the inhabitants of Babylon.
Lam 2:17 the *t* He set forth from days of old;

THREATEN (8)

Gn 31:24 "Take care not to *t* Jacob with any harm!"
31:29 'Take care not to *t* Jacob with any harm!'
Ps(s) 69: 2 Save me, O God, for the waters *t* my life;
73: 8 outrage from on high they *t*.
140:10 the mischief which they *t* overwhelm them.
Is 30:17 if five *t* you, you shall flee,
Jer 18: 7 Sometimes I *t* to uproot and tear down and
31:20 Often as I *t* him, I still remember him

THREATENED (25)

Ex 32:14 he had *t* to inflict on his people.
Nm 14:10 the whole community *t* to stone them.
Dt 9:25 the LORD, because he had *t* to destroy you.
1Sm 3:12 Eli everything I *t* against his family.
19:17 "He *t* me, 'Let me go or I will kill
1Kgs 16: 7 the LORD had *t* Baasha and his house
2Kgs 22:16 all the evil that is *t* in the book
24: 2 had *t* through his servants the prophets.
Jdt 2: 1 revenge on the whole world, as he had *t*.
16: 4 He *t* to burn my land,
2Mc 4: 1 it was Onias who *t* Heliodorus
Is 31: 2 he will not turn from what he has *t* to do.
Jer 18: 8 nation which I have *t* turns from its evil,
18: 8 I also repent of the evil which I *t* to do.
19:15 this city all the evil with which I *t* it,
26:19 of the evil with which he had *t* them?
27:13 with which the LORD has *t* the nation that
32:24 What you *t* has happened,
35:17 citizens of Jerusalem every evil that I *t*;
36: 7 with which the LORD has *t* this people.
40: 3 he has brought about in deed what he *t*;
51:62 LORD, you yourself *t* to destroy this place,
Ez 6:10 LORD, *t* to inflict this calamity upon them.
Dn 14:30 When he saw himself *t* with violence,
Jon 3:10 of the evil that he had *t* to do to them;

THREATENING (3)

Is 59:13 back from following our God, *T* outrage,
Jon 2: 6 The waters swirled about me, *t* my life;
Eph 6: 9 Stop *t* them.

THREATENS (3)

Jer 6: 1 For evil *t* from the north,
26:13 repent of the evil with which he *t* you.
Ez 21:19 sword of slaughter which *t* all around,

THREATS (17)

Jgs 2: 4 had made these *t* to all the Israelites,
2Kgs 22:18 As for the *t* you have heard,
22:19 when you heard my *t* that this place
2Chr 34:26 of Israel, concerning the *t* you have heard:
Jdt 6:17 and of all the boasting *t* of Holofernes
8:16 is not man that he should be moved by *t*,
Sir 48: 7 You heard *t* at Sinai,
Jer 5:13 their *t* be carried out against themselves!"
11: 8 till I brought upon them all the *t* of this
36:31 all the *t* of evil which went unheeded.
44:29 *t* of punishment for you shall be fulfilled,
Bar 2:24 and you fulfilled the *t* you had made
Dn 9:12 You carried out the *t* you spoke against us
Mk 13: 7 When you hear about wars and *t* of war,
Acts 4:29 look at the *t* they are leveling against us.
9: 1 murderous *t* against the Lord's disciples,
1Pt 2:23 made to suffer, he did not counter with *t*.

THREE (491)

Gn 5:22 Enoch lived *t* hundred years after the
5:23 Enoch was *t* hundred and sixty-five years.
6:10 age, for he walked with God, begot *t* sons:
6:15 of the ark shall be *t* hundred cubits,
7:13 *t* wives of Noah's sons had entered the ark,
9:19 These *t* were the sons of Noah,
9:28 *t* hundred and fifty years after the flood.
11:13 and *t* years after the birth of Shelah,
11:15 and *t* years after the birth of Eber,
14:14 *t* hundred and eighteen of his retainers,
18: 2 Looking up, he saw *t* men standing nearby.
18: 6 told Sarah, "Quick, *t* seahs of fine flour!
29: 2 with *t* droves of sheep huddled near it,
29:34 to me, since I have now borne him *t* sons";
30:36 *t* days' journey between himself and Jacob,
38:24 About *t* months later, Judah was told
40:10 of me, and on the vine were *t* branches.
40:12 The three branches are *t* days;
40:13 within *t* days Pharaoh will lift up your
40:16 In it I had *t* wicker baskets on my head;
40:18 The three baskets are *t* days;
40:19 within *t* days Pharaoh will lift up your
42:17 them up in the guardhouse for *t* days.
45:22 but to Benjamin he gave *t* hundred shekels
Ex 2: 2 a goodly child, she hid him for *t* months.
3:18 to go a *t* days' journey in the desert,
5: 3 Let us go a *t* days' journey in the desert,
8:23 We must go a *t* days' journey in the desert
10:22 throughout the land of Egypt for *t* days.
10:23 they move from where they were, for *t* days.
15:22 After traveling for *t* days through the
21:11 If he does not grant her these *t* things,
23:14 *T* times a year you shall celebrate a
25:32 *t* branches on one side, and three
25:33 On one branch there are to be *t* cups,
25:33 the opposite branch there are to be *t* cups,
25:35 knob below each of the *t* pairs of branches
27: 1 it shall be *t* cubits high.
27:14 cubits, with *t* columns and three pedestals;
27:15 cubits, with *t* columns and three pedestals.
32:28 there fell about *t* thousand of the people.
34:23 *T* times a year all your men shall appear
34:24 *t* times a year to appear before the LORD,
37:18 *t* branches on one side and three on the
37:19 On one branch there were *t* cups,
37:19 on the opposite branch there were *t* cups,
37:21 each of the *t* pairs of branches that
38: 1 its height was *t* cubits.
38:14 cubits, with three columns and *t* pedestals;
38:15 cubits, with three columns and *t* pedestals.
38:26 and *t* thousand five hundred and fifty men.
Lv 14:10 *t* tenths of an ephah of fine flour mixed
19:23 For *t* years, while its fruit remains
25:21 there will then be crop enough for *t* years.
27: 6 silver shekels for a boy, and *t* for a girl;
Nm 1:23 fifty-nine thousand *t* hundred were
1:46 houses, was six hundred and *t* thousand,
2:13 census to fifty-nine thousand *t* hundred.]
2:32 and *t* thousand five hundred and fifty.
3:28 they numbered eight thousand *t* hundred.
3:50 one thousand *t* hundred and sixty-five shekels
4:44 they numbered *t* thousand two hundred.
10:33 mountain of the LORD, a *t* days' journey,
10:33 place went the *t* days' journey with them.
12: 4 and Aaron and Miriam, "Come out, you *t*,
12: 4 And the *t* of them went.
15: 9 a cereal offering of *t* tenths of an ephah
22:28 you that you should beat me these *t* times?"
22:32 have you beaten your ass these *t* times?
22:33 me, she turned away from me these *t* times.
24:10 yet *t* times now you have even blessed them
26:25 thousand *t* hundred men were registered.
28:12 with *t* tenths of an ephah of fine flour
28:20 *t* tenths of an ephah for each bullock,
28:28 *t* tenths of an ephah for each bullock,
29: 3 *t* tenths of an ephah for the bullock,
29: 9 *t* tenths of an ephah for the bullock,
29:14 offering *t* tenths of an ephah for each of
31:36 *t* hundred and thirty-seven thousand five
31:43 *t* hundred and thirty-seven thousand five
33: 8 a *t* days' journey in the desert of Etham,
35:14 *t* beyond the Jordan, and three in the land
Dt 4:41 *t* cities in the region east of the Jordan,
16:16 *T* times a year, then, every male among
17: 6 The testimony of two or *t* witnesses is
19: 2 apart *t* cities in the land which the LORD,
19: 3 into *t* regions the land which the LORD,
19: 7 is why I order you to set apart *t* cities.
19: 9 then add three cities to these *t*.
19:15 on the testimony of two or *t* witnesses.
Jos 1:11 for *t* days from now you shall cross the
2:16 Hide there for *t* days,
2:22 they stayed *t* days until their pursuers,
3: 2 *T* days later the officers went through the
7: 3 if only about two or *t* thousand go up,
7: 4 *t* thousand of the people made the attack,
9:16 *T* days after the agreement was entered into,
15:14 Caleb drove out from there the *t* Anakim,
18: 4 Choose *t* men from each of your tribes;
21:32 and from the tribe of Naphtali, *t* cities:
Jgs 1:20 who then drove from it the *t* sons of Anak.
7: 6 to their mouths by hand numbered *t* hundred,
7: 7 "By means of the *t* hundred who lapped up
7: 8 to their tents, but kept the *t* hundred men.
7:16 the *t* hundred men into three companies,
7:20 All *t* companies blew horns and broke their
7:22 the *t* hundred men kept blowing the horns,
8: 4 and crossed it with his *t* hundred men,
9:22 Abimelech had ruled Israel for *t* years,
9:43 divided the men he had into *t* companies,
11:26 *T* hundred years have passed;
14:15 After *t* days' failure to answer the riddle,
15: 4 So Samson left and caught *t* hundred foxes.
15:11 *T* thousand men of Judah went down to the
16:15 *T* times already you have mocked me,
16:27 and from the roof about *t* thousand men and
19: 4 *t* days with this father-in-law of his,
1Sm 2:21 birth to *t* more sons and two daughters,
9:20 As for the asses you lost *t* days ago,
10: 3 be met by *t* men going up to God at Bethel;
10: 3 one will be bringing *t* kids, another *t* loaves
11: 8 there were *t* hundred thousand Israelites
11:11 Saul arranged his troops in *t* companies
13: 2 Saul chose *t* thousand men of Israel,
13: 5 for battle, with *t* thousand chariots,
13:17 the camp of the Philistines in *t* bands.
17:13 The *t* oldest sons of Jesse had followed
17:13 *t* sons who had gone off to war were named,
17:14 While the *t* oldest had joined Saul.
20:41 ground *t* times before Jonathan in homage.
24: 3 So Saul took *t* thousand picked men from
25: 2 *t* thousand sheep and a thousand goats.
26: 2 Ziph with *t* thousand picked men of Israel,
30:12 drunk water for three days and *t* nights.
30:13 me because I fell sick *t* days ago today.
31: 6 Thus Saul, his *t* sons,
31: 8 Saul and his *t* sons lying on Mount Gilboa.
2Sm 2:18 The *t* sons of Zeruiah were there
2:31 *t* hundred and sixty men of Benjamin,
6:11 of Obed-edom the Gittite for *t* months,
13:38 Geshur, and stayed in Geshur for *t* years.
14:27 Absalom had *t* sons born to him,
18:14 And taking *t* pikes in hand,
20: 4 the Judahites for me within *t* days.
21: 1 there was a famine for *t* successive years.
21:16 bronze spear weighed *t* hundred shekels,
23: 8 son of Hachamoni, was the first of the *T*.
23: 9 Next to him, among the *T* warriors,
23:12 Such were the deeds of the *T* warriors.
23:13 During the harvest *t* of the Thirty went
23:16 So the *T* warriors broke through the
23:18 brandished his spear over *t* hundred slain.
23:19 However, he did not attain to the *T*.
23:23 However, he did not attain to the *T*.
24:12 I offer you *t* alternatives;
24:13 a *t* years' famine to come upon your land,
24:13 your enemy *t* months while he pursues you,
24:13 to have a *t* days' pestilence in your land?
1Kgs 2:39 But *t* years later, two of Shimei's servants
5:12 Solomon also uttered *t* thousand proverbs,
5:30 to three thousand *t* hundred overseers,
6:36 by means of *t* courses of hewn stones
7: 4 There were *t* window frames at either end,
7: 5 doorways faced each other, *t* at either end.
7:12 The great court was enclosed by *t* courses
7:25 *t* . . . north, *t* . . . west, *t* . . . south, and *t*
7:27 four cubits long, four wide, and *t* high.
9:25 *T* times a year Solomon used to offer
10:17 *t* hundred bucklers of beaten gold (three
10:22 Once every *t* years the fleet of Tarshish
11: 3 of princely rank and *t* hundred concubines,

12: 5 "Come back to me in *t* days,"
15: 2 He reigned *t* years in Jerusalem.
17:21 child *t* times and called out to the LORD:
22: 1 *T* years passed without war between Aram
2Kgs 2:17 searched for *t* days without finding him.
3:10 *t* kings to put them in the grasp of Moab."
3:13 "The LORD has called these *t* kings
9:32 two or *t* eunuchs looked down toward him.
13:18 He struck the ground *t* times and stopped.
13:19 Now, you will defeat Aram only *t* times."
13:25 Joash defeated Ben-hadad *t* times,
17: 5 Samaria, which he besieged for *t* years.
18:10 siege to it, and after *t* years captured it.
18:14 The king of Assyria exacted *t* hundred
20: 5 In *t* days you shall go up to the LORD's
23:31 and he reigned *t* months in Jerusalem.
24: 1 Jehoiakim became his vassal for *t* years.
24: 8 and he reigned *t* months in Jerusalem.
25:18 priest, and the *t* keepers of the entry.
1Chr 2: 3 these *t* were born to him of Bathshua,
2:16 Zeruiah had *t* sons:
3:23 were Elioenai, Hizkiah, and Azrikam *t*.
7: 6 Benjamin were Bela, Becher, and Jediael *t*.
10: 6 Thus, with Saul and his *t* sons,
11:11 the son of Hachamoni, chief of the *T*.
11:11 He brandished his spear against *t* hundred,
11:12 of Dodo the Ahohite, one of the *T* warriors.
11:15 *T* of the Thirty chiefs went down to the
11:18 Thereupon the *T* broke through the
11:19 deeds as these the *T* warriors performed.
11:20 he brandished his spear against *t* hundred,
11:20 he had a reputation like that of the *T*.
11:21 commander, but he did not attain to the *T*.
11:24 gave him a reputation like that of the *T*.
11:25 the Thirty, but he did not attain to the *T*.
12:28 with another *t* thousand seven hundred,
12:30 *t* thousand—until this time,
12:40 They remained with David for *t* days,
13:14 of Obed-edom with his family for *t* months,
21:10 I offer you *t* alternatives;
21:12 *t* years of famine; or *t* months of fleeing
21:12 or *t* days of the LORD's own sword,
23: 8 then Zetham and Joel; *t* in all.
23: 9 Shelomoth, Haziel, and Haran; *t*.
23:23 Mahli, Eder, and Jeremoth; *t* in all.
25: 5 gave Heman fourteen sons and *t* daughters.
29: 4 *t* thousand talents of Ophir gold,
2Chr 2: 1 he placed *t* thousand six hundred overseers.
2:17 and *t* thousand six hundred overseers to
4: 4 *t* facing north, *t* west, *t* south, and *t* east,
4: 5 It had a capacity of *t* thousand measures.
6:13 long, five cubits wide, and *t* cubits high,
8:13 and on the fixed festivals *t* times a year:
9:16 *t* hundred bucklers of beaten gold, three
9:21 Once every *t* years the fleet of Tarshish
10: 5 "In *t* days," he answered them,
11:17 son of Solomon, prevail for *t* years;
11:17 in the way of David and Solomon *t* years.
13: 2 he reigned *t* years in Jerusalem.
14: 7 Asa had an army of *t* hundred thousand
14: 8 of one million men and *t* hundred chariots,
17:14 him *t* hundred thousand valiant warriors.
20:25 they were *t* days taking the spoil,
25: 5 *t* hundred thousand picked men fit for war,
25:13 They killed *t* thousand of the inhabitants
26:13 mighty army of *t* hundred seven thousand
29:33 were six hundred oxen and *t* thousand sheep.
35: 7 who were present, and also *t* thousand oxen;
35: 8 victims together with *t* hundred oxen.
36: 2 king, and he reigned *t* months in Jerusalem.
36: 9 *t* months [and ten days] in Jerusalem.
Ezr 2: 4 of Shephatiah, *t* hundred and seventy-two;
2:17 sons of Bezai, *t* hundred and twenty-three;
2:32 sons of Harim, *t* hundred and twenty;
2:34 sons of Jericho, *t* hundred and forty-five;
2:35 Senaah, *t* thousand six hundred and thirty.
2:58 of Solomon was *t* hundred and ninety-two.
2:64 to forty-two thousand *t* hundred and sixty,
2:65 seven thousand *t* hundred and thirty-seven.
6: 4 It shall have *t* courses of cut stone for
8: 5 of Jahaziel, and with him *t* hundred males;
8:15 Ahava, where we made camp for *t* days.
8:32 where we first rested for *t* days.
10: 8 failed to appear within *t* days would,
Neh 2:11 Jerusalem, I first rested there for *t* days.
7: 9 of Shephatiah, *t* hundred and seventy-two;
7:17 two thousand *t* hundred and twenty-two;
7:22 sons of Hashum, *t* hundred and twenty-eight;
7:23 sons of Bezai, *t* hundred and twenty-four;
7:35 sons of Harim, *t* hundred and twenty;
7:36 sons of Jericho, *t* hundred and forty-five;
7:38 Senaah, *t* thousand nine hundred and thirty.
7:60 of Solomon was *t* hundred and ninety-two.
7:66 to forty-two thousand *t* hundred and sixty,
7:67 seven thousand *t* hundred and thirty-seven.
Jdt 1: 2 each *t* cubits in height and six in length.
8: 4 remained *t* years and four months at home,
12: 7 Thus she stayed in the camp *t* days.
16:20 For *t* months the people continued their
Est 4:16 or drinking, night or day, for *t* days.
9:15 of Adar and killed *t* hundred men in Susa.
1Mc 4: 6 appeared in the plain with *t* thousand men,
4:15 About *t* thousand of their men fell.
5:20 *T* thousand men were allotted to Simon,
5:22 About *t* thousand men of the Gentiles fell,
5:24 and marched for *t* days through the desert.
5:33 He came up behind them with *t* columns
6:37 mahout, *t* soldiers who fought from it.
7:40 Judas camped in Adasa with *t* thousand men.
8:15 day *t* hundred and twenty men took counsel,
9: 5 Judas, with *t* thousand picked men,
10:30 from the *t* districts annexed from Samaria.
10:34 and the *t* days that precede each feast day,
10:34 each feast day, and the *t* days that follow,
10:38 "Let the *t* districts that have been added
10:77 he drew up *t* thousand horsemen and an
11:18 But *t* days later King Ptolemy himself died,
11:28 the *t* districts of Samaria from tribute,
11:28 promising him in return *t* hundred talents.
11:34 but also of the *t* districts of Aphairema,
11:44 So Jonathan sent *t* thousand good fighting
11:74 *T* thousand of the foreign troops fell on
12:47 But he kept with him *t* thousand men,
2Mc 4: 8 king *t* hundred and sixty talents of silver,
4:19 to bring there *t* hundred silver drachmas
4:23 *T* years later Jason sent Menelaus,
4:24 Jason by *t* hundred talents of silver.
4:40 *t* thousand armed men under the leadership
4:44 *t* men sent by the senate presented to him
5:14 In the space of *t* days,
7:27 for nine months, nursed you for *t* years,
12:33 who opposed them with *t* thousand foot
13: 2 and *t* hundred chariots armed with scythes.
13:12 and fasting and prostrations for *t* days,
14: 1 *T* years later, Judas and his men learned
Jb 1: 2 sons and *t* daughters were born to him;
1: 3 seven thousand sheep, *t* thousand camels,
1: 4 their *t* sisters to eat and drink with them.
1:17 and said, "The Chaldeans formed *t* columns,
2:11 Now when *t* of Job's friends heard of all
32: 1 Then the *t* men ceased to answer Job,
32: 3 He was angry also with the *t* friends
32: 5 was no reply in the mouths of the *t* men,
35: 4 reply to you and your *t* companions as well.
42:13 And he had seven sons and *t* daughters,
Prv 30:15 *T* things are never satisfied,
30:18 *T* things are too wonderful for me,
30:21 Under *t* things the earth trembles,
30:29 *T* things are stately in their stride,
Sir 13: 7 then twice or *t* times he will terrify you;
25: 1 With *t* things I am delighted,
25: 2 *T* kinds of men I hate;
26: 5 are *t* things at which my heart quakes,
26: 6 and a scourging tongue like the other *t*.
48: 3 the heavens and *t* times brought down fire.
Is 16:14 In *t* years, like those of a hireling,
17: 6 Two or *t* olives remain at the very top,
20: 3 gone naked and barefoot for *t* years as a sign
38: 5 in *t* days you shall go up to the LORD's
Jer 25: 3 to this day—these *t* and twenty years
36:23 Each time Jehudi finished reading *t* or
38:10 the Cushite to take *t* men along with him,
52:24 priest, and the *t* keepers of the entry.
52:28 *t* thousand and twenty-three people of
Ez 4: 5 same number of days, *t* hundred and ninety,
4: 9 lie upon your side, *t* hundred and ninety.
14:14 and even if these *t* men were in it,
14:16 wild beasts, and these *t* men were in it,
14:18 man and beast, and these *t* men were in it,
40:10 of the east gate were *t* on either side,
40:21 Its cells, *t* on either side,
40:48 either side of the door measured *t* cubits.
41: 6 built one above the other in *t* stories,
41:22 like a wooden altar, *t* cubits in height,
42: 3 there were *t* parallel rows of them on
42: 6 for they were in *t* rows and had no
48:31 hundred cubits, there shall be *t* gates:
48:32 hundred cubits, there shall be *t* gates:
48:33 hundred cubits, there shall be *t* gates:
48:34 hundred cubits, there shall be *t* gates:
Dn 1: 5 after *t* years' training they were to enter
3:23 But these *t* fell, bound, into the midst
3:51 these *t* in the furnace with one voice sang,
3:91 we not cast *t* men bound into the fire?"
6: 3 these were accountable to *t* supervisors,
6:11 his God in the upper chamber *t* times a day,
6:14 *t* times a day he offers his prayer."
7: 5 among the teeth in its mouth were *t* tusks.
7: 8 and *t* of the previous horns were torn away
7:20 that sprang up, before which *t* horns fell;
7:24 before him, who shall lay low *t* kings.
8:14 thousand *t* hundred evenings and mornings;
10: 2 days, I, Daniel, mourned *t* full weeks.
10: 3 myself at all until the end of the *t* weeks.
11: 2 *T* kings of Persia are yet to come;
12:12 thousand *t* hundred and thirty-five days.
Am 1: 3 For *t* crimes of Damascus,
1: 6 For *t* crimes of Gaza,
1: 9 For *t* crimes of Tyre
1:11 For *t* crimes of Edom,
1:13 For *t* crimes of the Ammonites,
2: 1 For *t* crimes of Moab,
2: 4 For *t* crimes of Judah,
2: 6 For *t* crimes of Israel,
4: 7 when the harvest was still *t* months away;
4: 8 Though two or *t* cities staggered to one
Jon 2: 1 belly of the fish three days and *t* nights.
3: 3 it took *t* days to go through it.
Zec 11: 8 month I did away with the *t* shepherds.
Mt 12:40 Just as Jonah spent *t* days and *t* nights
12:40 Son of Man spend *t* days and *t* nights
13:33 took and kneaded into *t* measures of flour.
14:25 At about *t* in the morning,
15:32 By now they have been with me *t* days,
17: 4 your permission I will erect *t* booths here,
18:16 stand on the word of two or *t* witnesses.
18:20 Where two or *t* are gathered in my name,
26:34 crows tonight you will deny me *t* times."
26:61 God's sanctuary and rebuild it in *t* days.'"
26:75 the cock crows, you will deny me *t* times."
27:40 the temple and rebuild it in *t* days!
27:63 made the claim, 'After *t* days I will rise.'
Mk 6:48 time was between *t* and six in the morning.
8: 2 with me *t* days and have nothing to eat.
8:31 be put to death, and rise *t* days later.
9: 5 Let us erect *t* booths on this site,
9:31 *t* days after his death he will rise."
10:34 But *t* days later he will rise."
14: 5 It could have been sold for over *t* hundred
14:30 cock crows twice, you will deny me *t* times."
14:58 and 'In *t* days I will construct another
14:72 cock crows twice you will deny me *t* times."
15:29 the temple and rebuild it in *t* days!
Lk 1:56 about *t* months and then returned home.
4:25 heavens remained closed for *t* and a half
9:33 Let us set up *t* booths,
10:36 "Which of these *t*,
11: 5 and says to him, 'Friend, lend me *t* loaves,
12:52 three against two and two against *t*;
13: 7 For *t* years now I have come in search of
13:21 took to knead into *t* measures of flour
22:34 you have *t* times denied that you know me."
22:61 cock crows today you will deny me *t* times."
Jn 2:19 answer, "and in *t* days I will raise it up."
2:20 you are going to 'raise it up in *t* days'!"
6:19 when they had rowed *t* or four miles,
12: 5 could have brought *t* hundred silver pieces,
13:38 crow before you have *t* times disowned me!
Acts 2:41 some *t* thousand were added that day.
3: 1 temple for prayer at the *t* o'clock hour,
5: 7 *T* hours later Ananias' wife came in,
7:20 For the first *t* months he was reared in
9: 9 For *t* days he continued blind,
10: 3 One afternoon at about *t* he had a vision
10:16 This happened *t* times; then the object
10:30 "Just *t* days ago at this very hour,
10:30 ago at this very hour, namely *t* o'clock,
11:10 This happened *t* times; then the canvas
11:11 the *t* men who had been sent to me from
17: 2 them about the Scriptures for *t* sabbaths.
19: 8 synagogue, and over a period of *t* months,
20: 3 in Greece, where he stayed for *t* months.
20:31 Do not forget that for *t* years,
25: 1 *T* days after Festus had arrived in the
28: 7 in and gave us kind hospitality for *t* days.
28:11 *T* months later we set sail in a ship which
28:12 put in at Syracuse and spent *t* days there.
28:15 of Appius and the *T* Taverns to meet us.
28:17 *T* days later Paul invited the prominent
1Cor 13:13 There are in the end *t* things that last:
14:27 in tongues let it be at most two or *t*,
14:29 Let no more than two or *t* prophets speak,
2Cor 11:25 *t* times I was beaten with rods;
11:25 I was stoned once, shipwrecked *t* times;
12: 8 *T* times I begged the Lord that this might
13: 1 on the testimony of two or *t* witnesses."
Gal 1:18 *T* years after that I went up to Jerusalem
1Tm 5:19 it is supported by two or *t* witnesses.
Heb 10:28 on the testimony of two or *t* witnesses.
11:23 hid him for *t* months after his birth,
Jas 5:17 on the land for *t* years and six months.
1Jn 5: 7 Thus there are *t* that testify,
5: 8 and these *t* are of one accord.
Rv 6: 6 of wheat and the same for *t* of barley!
8:13 the other *t* angels are about to blow!"
9:18 By these *t* plagues
11: 9 *t* and a half days but refuse to bury them.
11:11 But after the *t* and a half days,
16:13 I saw *t* unclean spirits like frogs come
16:19 The great city was split into *t* parts,
21:13 three gates facing east, three north, *t* south,
21:13 three north, three south, and *t* west.

THREE-DAY (2)

Ezr 10: 9 together in Jerusalem within the *t* period:
Jdt 2:21 After a *t* march from Nineveh,

THREE-PLY (1)

Eccl 4:12 A *t* cord is not easily broken.

THREE-PRONGED (1)

1Sm 2:13 priest's servant would come with a *t* fork,

THREE-YEAR-OLD (4)

Gn 15: 9 He answered him, "Bring me a *t* heifer,
15: 9 a *t* she-goat, a three-year-old ram,
1Sm 1:24 him up with her, along with a *t* bull,

THRESH (5)

Jb 39:12 Can you rely on him to *t* out your grain
Is 28:28 No, he does not *t* it unendingly,
41:15 To *t* the mountains and crush them,
Hos 10:11 was a trained heifer, willing to *t*;
Mi 4:13 Arise and *t*, O daughter Zion;

THRESHED (3)

Is 21:10 O my people who have been *t*,
28:27 Gith is not *t* with a sledge,
Am 1: 3 Because they *t* Gilead with sledges of iron,

THRESHES (1)

Prv 20:26 the wicked, and *t* them under the cartwheel.

THRESHING (46)

Lv 26: 5 your *t* will last till vintage time,
Nm 15:20 you offer a contribution from the *t* floor.
18:27 the *t* floor or new wine from the press.
18:30 of the *t* floor or of the wine press.
Dt 15:14 from your flock and *t* floor and wine press,
16:13 produce from your *t* floor and wine press.
Jgs 6:37 putting this woolen fleece on the *t* floor.
Ru 3: 2 he will be winnowing barley at the *t* floor.
3: 3 best attire and go down to the *t* floor.
3: 6 So she went down to the *t* floor and did
3:14 known that this woman came to the *t* floor."
1Sm 14: 2 near the *t* floor on the outskirts of Geba;
19:22 cistern of the *t* floor on the bare hilltop,
23: 1 Keilah and plundering the *t* floors.
2Sm 6: 6 When they came to the *t* floor of Nodan,
24:16 at the *t* floor of Araunah the Jebusite.
24:18 on the *t* floor of Araunhah the Jebusite."
24:20 coming toward him while he was *t* wheat.
24:21 "To buy the *t* floor from you to build an
24:22 and *t* sledges and the yokes of the oxen
24:24 So David bought the *t* floor and the oxen
1Kgs 22:10 clothed in their robes of state on a *t* floor
2Kgs 6:27 from the *t* floor or the winepress?"
1Chr 13: 9 As they reached the *t* floor of Chidon,
21:15 by the *t* floor of Ornan the Jebusite.
21:18 LORD on the *t* floor of Ornan the Jebusite.
21:20 While Ornan was *t* wheat,
21:21 the *t* floor and bowed down before David,
21:22 "Sell me the ground of this *t* floor,
21:23 the holocausts, the *t* sledges for the wood,
21:28 him on the *t* floor of Ornan the Jebusite,
2Chr 3: 1 had selected the *t* of Ornan
18: 9 robes of state on a *t* floor at the entrance
Jb 39:12 and gather in the yield of your *t* floor?
41:22 he spreads like a *t* sledge upon the mire.
Is 21:10 have been threshed, beaten on my *t* floor!
41:15 I will make of you a *t* sledge,
Jer 51:33 like a *t* floor at the time it is trodden;
Dn 2:35 fine as the chaff on the *t* floor in summer,
Hos 9: 1 loving a harlot's hire upon every *t* floor.
9: 2 *T* floor and wine press shall not nourish
13: 3 *t* floor or like smoke out of the window.
Jl 2:24 The *t* floors shall be full of grain and
Mi 4:12 gathered them like sheaves on the *t* floor.
Mt 3:12 *t* floor and gather his grain into the barn,
Lk 3:17 *t* floor and gather the wheat into his barn;
1Tm 5:18 a muzzle on an ox when he is *t* the grain,"

THRESHOLD (19)

Jgs 19:27 of the house with her hands on the *t*.
1Sm 5: 4 and hands broken off and lying on the *t*,
5: 5 the *t* of Dagon in Ashdod to this very day;
1Kgs 14:17 Tirzah and crossed the *t* of her house,
1Chr 9:19 task the guarding of the *t* of the tent,
9:22 at the *t* were two hundred and twelve.
2Chr 34: 9 which the Levites, the guardians of the *t*,
Ps(s) 84:11 I had rather lie at the *t* of the house of
Ez 10: 2 which it had been, to the *t* of the temple.
10: 4 over the cherubim to the *t* of the temple;
10:18 Then the glory of the LORD left the *t* of
40: 6 its steps, and measured the gate's *t*,
40: 7 The *t* of the gate adjoining the vestibule
41:16 with trellises about them [facing the *t*.
43: 8 When they placed their *t* against my
43: 8 my *t* and their doorpost next to mine,
46: 2 at the *t* of the gate and then leave;
47: 1 the *t* of the temple toward the east,
Zep 1: 9 on that day, all who leap over the *t*,

THRESHOLDS (2)

2Chr 3: 7 The house, its beams and *t*,
23: 4 come in on the sabbath must guard the *t*,

THREW (70)

Gn 37:24 they took him and *t* him into the cistern,
39:20 He seized Joseph and *t* him into the jail
50: 1 Joseph *t* himself on his father's face and
Ex 4: 3 When he *t* it on the ground it was changed
7:10 Aaron *t* his staff down before Pharaoh and
7:12 Each one *t* down his staff,
14:24 force a glance that *t* it into a panic;
15:25 When he *t* this into the water,
32:19 so that he *t* the tablets down and broke
32:24 gave it to me, and I *t* it into the fire,
Dt 9:17 with both hands I *t* them from me
9:21 which I *t* into the wadi that went down the
Jos 7: 6 and they *t* dust on their heads.
10:10 the LORD *t* them into disorder before him.
Jgs 8:25 which everyone *t* a ring from his booty.
15:17 speaking he *t* the jawbone from him;
1Sm 5: 9 the LORD *t* the city into utter turmoil:
7:10 and *t* them into such confusion that they
2Sm 11:21 Was it not a woman who *t* a millstone down
16: 6 He *t* stones at David and at all the king's
20:15 They *t* up a mound against the city,
20:22 Sheba, son of Bichri, and *t* it out to Joab.
1Kgs 19:19 went over to him and *t* his cloak over him.
2Kgs 2:21 went out to the spring and *t* salt into it,
4:41 He *t* it into the pot and said,
6: 6 cut off a stick, *t* it into the water,
9:33 They *t* her down,
23:12 them and *t* the dust into the Kidron Valley.
Tb 11: 9 ran up to her son, *t* her arms around him,
11:13 his son, he *t* his arms around him and wept.
Jdt 9: 1 Judith *t* herself down prostrate,
10:23 She *t* herself down prostrate before him,
14: 7 *t* himself at the feet of Judith in homage,
1Mc 2:36 they neither *t* stones,
5:43 they *t* away their arms and fled to the
7:44 was dead, they *t* down their arms and fled.
11:50 So they *t* down their arms and made peace.
11:71 tore his clothes, *t* earth on his head,
2Mc 4:41 handfuls of the ashes lying there and *t* them
14:43 courage *t* himself down into the crowd.
Jb 2:12 their cloaks and *t* dust upon their heads.
Eccl 9:14 it and *t* up great siegeworks about it.
Jer 38: 6 *t* him into the cistern of Prince Malchiah,
41: 7 men slew them and *t* them into the cistern.
41: 9 The cistern into which Ishmael *t* all the
Ez 20: 8 none of them *t* away the detestable things
Dn 3:22 the flames devoured the men who *t* Shadrach,
8: 7 It *t* the ram, which had not the force
14:31 They *t* Daniel into a lions' den,
14:42 had tried to destroy him he *t* into the den,
Jon 1: 5 themselves, they *t* its cargo into the sea.
1:15 they took Jonah and *t* him into the sea,
Zec 11:13 I took the thirty pieces of silver and *t* them
Mt 13:48 What was useless they *t* away.
Mk 9:20 and immediately *t* the boy into convulsions.
10:50 He *t* aside his cloak,
11: 7 Jesus and *t* their cloaks across its back,
Lk 4:35 the demon *t* him to the ground before
9:42 *t* him into convulsions on the ground.
15:20 to meet him, *t* his arms around his neck,
17:16 He *t* himself on his face at the feet of
Jn 9:34 With that they *t* him out bodily.
21: 7 the Lord, Simon Peter *t* on some clothes
Acts 5:18 apostles and *t* them into the public jail.
8: 3 men and women out, and *t* them into jail.
16:37 even a trial, then they *t* us into jail,
17: 4 and *t* in their lot with Paul and Silas.
20:10 down immediately and *t* himself on him,
27:19 *t* even the ship's gear overboard.
Rv 14:19 He *t* them into the huge winepress of God's

THRICE (2)

Ex 23:17 *T* a year shall all your men appear before
Jb 33:29 all these things God does, twice, or *t*,

THRICE-SINFUL (1)

2Mc 15: 3 At this the *t* wretch asked if there was a

THRILLS (1)

Sir 38:25 who *t* in wielding the goad like a lance,

THRIVE (4)

Jb 39: 4 When their offspring *t* and grow,
Ps(s) 92: 8 flourish like grass and all evildoers *t*,
Jer 22:30 who will never *t* in his lifetime!
3Jn 1: 2 may you *t* in all other ways as you do in

THRIVING (1)

Gn 43:28 our father is *t* and still in good health,"

THROAT (11)

Dt 21: 4 shall cut the heifer's *t* there in the wadi.
21: 6 the heifer whose *t* was cut in the wadi,
Ps(s) 5:10 Their *t* is an open grave;
22:16 My *t* is dried up like baked clay,
69: 4 I am wearied with calling, my *t* is parched;
115: 7 they utter no sound from their *t*.
Prv 23: 2 to your *t* if you have a ravenous appetite.
Sir 36:18 The *t* can swallow any food,
Is 5:14 its *t* and opens its maw without limit;
Jer 2:25 wearing out your shoes and parching your *t*!
Hb 2: 5 who opens wide his *t* like the nether world,

THROATS (3)

1Kgs 18:40 the brook Kishon and there he slit their *t*.
Ps(s) 149: 6 let the high praises of God be in their *t*.
Rom 3:13 Their *t* are open tombs;

THROB (1)

Is 60: 5 you see, your heart shall *t* and overflow,

THROBS (1)

Ps(s) 38:11 My heart *t*; my strength forsakes me;

THROES (2)

Jer 6:24 of us, *t* like a mother's in childbirth.
50:43 him, *t* like a mother's in childbirth.

THRONE (201)

Gn 41:40 in respect to the *t* shall I outrank you.
Ex 11: 5 from the first-born of Pharaoh on the *t*
12:29 Pharaoh on the *t* to the first-born
1Sm 2: 8 and make a glorious *t* their heritage.
2Sm 3:10 establish the *t* of David over Israel
7:13 And I will make his royal *t* firm forever.
7:16 your *t* shall stand firm forever.'"
14: 9 you and your *t* are innocent."
1Kgs 1:13 be king after me and shall sit upon my *t*?
1:17 should reign after you and sit upon your *t*.
1:20 to sit on the *t* after your royal majesty.
1:24 is to reign after you and sit on your *t*?
1:27 was to succeed to your majesty's kingly *t*?"
1:30 me and should sit upon my *t* in my place."
1:35 in and sit upon my *t* and reign in my place.
1:37 exalt his *t* even more than that of my lord,
1:46 Solomon took his seat on the royal *t*,
1:47 you and exalt his *t* more than your own!'
1:48 this day seated one of my sons upon my *t*,
2: 4 someone of your line on the *t* of Israel.'
2:12 was seated on the *t* of his father David,
2:19 upon his throne, and a *t* was provided
2:24 who has seated me firmly on the *t* of my
2:33 his descendants, and his house, and his *t*."
2:45 *t* shall endure before the LORD forever."
3: 6 even today, seating a son of his on his *t*.
5:19 I will put upon your *t* in your place
7: 7 vestibule of the *t* where he gave judgment
8:20 my father David and sit on the *t* of Israel,
8:25 line to sit before me on the *t* of Israel,
9: 5 your *t* of sovereignty over Israel forever,
9: 5 someone from your line on the *t* of Israel.'
10: 9 pleased to place you on the *t* of Israel.
10:18 The king also had a large ivory *t* made,
10:19 The *t* had six steps,
16:11 Once he was seated on the royal *t*,
22:10 of Judah were seated, each on his *t*,
22:19 I saw the LORD seated on his *t*,
2Kgs 10: 3 offspring, place him on his father's *t*,
10:30 generation shall sit upon the *t* of Israel."
11:19 where Joash took his seat on the royal *t*.
13:13 his ancestors, and Jeroboam occupied the *t*.
15:12 generation shall sit upon the *t* of Israel,"
16:18 which had been built in the temple for a *t*,
25:28 He spoke kindly to him and gave him a *t*
1Chr 17:12 house, and I will establish his *t* forever.
17:14 his *t* shall be firmly established forever."
22:10 the *t* of his kingship over Israel forever.'
28: 5 to sit on the LORD's royal *t* over Israel.
28:18 gold for what would suggest a chariot *t*:
29:23 Thereafter Solomon sat on the *t* of the
2Chr 6:10 and have taken my seat on the *t* of Israel,
6:16 line to sit before me on the *t* of Israel,
7:18 I will establish your royal *t* as I
9: 8 to place you on his *t* as king for the LORD,
9:17 ivory *t* which he overlaid with fine gold.
9:18 The *t* had six steps; a footstool of gold
18: 9 of Judah were seated each on his *t*,
18:18 I saw the LORD seated on his *t*,
23:20 they seated the king upon the royal *t*.
Ezr 4:13 thus it can only result in harm to the *t*.
4:22 the evil grow to the detriment of the *t*."
Jdt 1:12 and swore by his *t* and his kingdom that he
Est 1: 2 the royal *t* in the stronghold of Susa,
D: 6 the king, who was seated on his royal *t*,
D: 8 In great anxiety he sprang from his *t*,
5: 1 on his royal *t* in the audience chamber,
E:11 he attained the rank second to the royal *t*.
1Mc 2:57 as a heritage a *t* of everlasting royalty.
7: 4 them, and Demetrius sat on the royal *t*.
10:52 taken my seat on the *t* of my fathers,
10:53 and his army, and recovered the royal *t*—
10:55 and took your seat on their royal *t*!
11:52 King Demetrius was sure of his royal *t*,
2Mc 4: 7 surnamed Epiphanes succeeded him on the *t*,
Ps(s) 9: 5 my right and my cause, seated on your *t*,
9: 8 he has set up his *t* for judgment.
11: 4 the LORD's *t* is in heaven.
33:14 *t* he beholds all who dwell on the earth,
45: 7 Your *t*, O God, stands forever
47: 6 God mounts his *t* amid shouts of joy;
47: 9 over the nations, God sits upon his holy *t*.
55:20 and will humble them from his eternal *t*;
68:17 at the mountain God has chosen for his *t*,
80: 2 From your *t* upon the cherubim,
89: 5 and establish your *t* for all generations."
89:15 and judgment are the foundation of your *t*;
89:30 forever and his *t* as the days of heaven.
89:37 and his *t* shall be like the sun before me;
89:45 his luster and hurled his *t* to the ground.

93: 2 Your *t* stands firm from of old;
97: 2 and judgment are the foundation of his *t*.
103:19 The LORD has established his *t* in heaven,
132:11 own offspring I will set upon your *t*;
132:12 sons, too, forever shall sit upon your *t*."
Prv 16:12 for by righteousness the *t* endures.
20: 8 A king seated on the *t* of judgment dispels
20:28 the king, and he upholds his *t* by justice.
25: 5 his *t* is made firm through righteousness.
29:14 of the poor, his *t* stands firm forever.
Wis 6:21 then, you find pleasure in *t* and scepter,
7: 8 I preferred her to scepter and *t*,
9: 4 Give me Wisdom, the attendant at your *t*,
9:10 from your glorious *t* dispatch her That she
9:12 justly and be worthy of my father's *t*.
18:15 word from heaven's royal *t* bounded,
Sir 1: 6 and truly awe-inspiring, seated upon his *t*:
6:30 Her fetters will be your *t* of majesty;
11: 5 The oppressed often rise to a *t*,
24: 4 did I dwell, my *t* on a pillar of cloud.
40: 3 on a lofty *t* or grovels in dust and ashes,
47:11 of royalty and established his *t* in Israel.
Is 6: 1 saw the Lord seated on a high and lofty *t*,
9: 6 vast and forever peaceful, From David's *t*,
14:13 Above the stars of God I will set up my *t*;
16: 5 the land, A *t* shall be set up in mercy,
52: 2 Shake off the dust, ascend to the *t*,
66: 1 The heavens are my *t*,
Jer 1:15 set up his *t* at the gateways of Jerusalem, Call
3:17 they will call Jerusalem the LORD's *t*;
13:13 land, the kings who succeed to David's *t*,
13:18 come down from your *t*;
14:21 us not, disgrace not the *t* of your glory;
17:12 A *t* of glory, exalted from the beginning,
17:25 upon the *t* of David will continue to enter,
22: 2 king of Judah, who sit on the *t* of David,
22: 4 kings who succeed to the *t* of David will
22:30 the *t* of David as ruler again over Judah.
29:16 concerning the king who sits on David's *t*,
33:17 successor on the *t* of the house of Israel,
33:21 will not have a son to be king upon his *t*,
36:30 of his shall succeed to David's *t*;
43:10 will set his *t* upon these stones which I,
49:38 My *t* I will set up in Elam and destroy
52:32 He spoke kindly to him and gave him a *t*
Lam 5:19 your *t* stands from age to age.
Ez 1:26 heads something like a *t* could be seen,
10: 1 something like a *t* could be seen upon it.
28: 2 occupy a godly *t* in the heart of the sea!—"
43: 7 Son of man, this is where my *t* shall be,
Dn 3:54 Blessed are you on the *t* of your kingdom,
3:55 the depths from your *t* upon the cherubim,
5:20 from his royal *t* and deprived of his glory;
7: 9 were set up and the Ancient One took his *t*.
7: 9 His *t* was flames of fire,
Jon 3: 6 the king of Nineveh, he rose from his *t*,
Zec 6:13 insignia, he shall sit as ruler upon his *t*.
Mt 5:34 Do not swear by heaven (it is God's *t*),
19:28 his seat upon a *t* befitting his glory,
23:22 throne and by him who is seated on that *t*.
25:31 of heaven, he will sit upon his royal *t*,
Lk 1:32 will give him the *t* of David his father.
Acts 2:30 of his descendants would sit upon his *t*.
7:49 'The heavens are my *t*,
Heb 1: 8 "Your *t*, O God, stands forever and ever;
4:16 So let us confidently approach the *t* of
8: 1 hand of the *t* of the Majesty in heaven,
12: 2 his seat at the right of the *t* of God.
Rv 1: 4 and from the seven spirits before his *t*,
2:13 the very place where Satan's *t* is erected;
3:21 victor the right to sit with me on my *t*,
3:21 and took my seat beside my Father on his *t*.
4: 2 *t* was standing there in heaven, and on the *t*
4: 3 *t* was a rainbow as brilliant as emerald.
4: 4 Surrounding this *t* were twenty-four other
4: 5 From the *t* came flashes of lightning and
4: 6 The floor around the *t* was like a sea of
4: 6 At the very center, around the *t* itself,
4: 9 and praise to the One seated on the *t*,
4:10 fall down before the One seated on the *t*,
4:10 down their crowns before the *t* and sing:
5: 1 of the One who sat on the *t* I saw a scroll.
5: 6 between the *t* with the four living
5: 7 the right hand of the One who sat on the *t*.
5:11 *t* and the living creatures and the elders.
5:13 "To the One seated on the *t*,
6:16 on the *t* and from the wrath of the Lamb!
7: 9 They stood before the *t* and the Lamb,
7:10 is from our God, who is seated on the *t*,
7:11 the angels who were standing around the *t*
7:11 fell down before the *t* to worship God.
7:15 was this that brought them before God's *t*:
7:15 who sits on the *t* will give them shelter.
7:17 for the Lamb on the *t* will shepherd them.
8: 3 on the altar of gold in front of the *t*,
12: 5 child was caught up to God and to his *t*.
13: 2 The dragon gave it his own power and *t*,
14: 3 They were singing a new hymn before the *t*,
16:10 poured out his bowl on the *t* of the beast.
16:17 From the *t* in the sanctuary came a loud
19: 4 and worshiped God seated on the *t* and sang,
19: 5 A voice coming from the *t* cried out:
20:11 a large white *t* and the One who sat on it.
20:12 great and the lowly, standing before the *t*.
21: 3 I heard a loud voice from the *t* cry out:
21: 5 The One who sat on the *t* said to me,
22: 1 which issued from the *t* of God and of the
22: 3 *t* of God and of the Lamb shall be there,

THRONED (2)

Ps(s) 2: 4 He who is *t* in heaven laughs;
99: 1 he is *t* upon the cherubim;

THRONES (15)

2Mc 14:21 came forward and *t* were set in place.
Jb 36: 7 And with kings upon *t* he sets them,
Wis 5:23 and evildoing overturn the *t* of potentates.
Sir 10:14 The *t* of the arrogant God overturns and
Is 14: 9 the kings of all nations rise from their *t*.
Bar 5: 6 to you borne aloft in glory as on royal *t*.
Ez 26:16 of the sea shall step down from their *t*,
Dn 7: 9 *T* were set up and the Ancient One took his
Hg 2:22 I will overthrow the *t* of kingdoms,
Mt 19:28 *t* to judge the twelve tribes of Israel.
Lk 1:52 *t* and raised the lowly to high places.
22:30 on *t* judging the twelve tribes of Israel.
Col 1:16 and invisible, whether *t* or dominations,
Rv 4: 4 twenty-four other *t* upon which were seated
20: 4 Then I saw some *t*.

THRONG (20)

2Kgs 7:13 off than all the *t* that has perished,
2Chr 20:24 of the desert and looked toward the *t*,
32: 7 and all the *t* that is coming with him,
Jdt 6: 1 of the whole *t* of coastland peoples,
6:16 They placed Achior in the center of the *t*,
Ps(s) 35:18 in the mighty *t* I will praise you.
42: 5 When I went with the *t* and led them in
109:30 in the midst of the *t* I will praise him,
Sir 50:18 over the *t* sweet strains of praise resound.
Is 13: 4 that of an immense *t*!
Jer 5: 7 to the harlot's house they *t*.
31: 8 they shall return as an immense *t*.
50:37 A sword upon her motley *t*,
Bar 2:29 surely this great and numerous *t* will
Ez 7:12 mourn, for wrath shall be upon all the *t*.
7:13 lives, for wrath shall be upon all the *t*.
7:14 go to war, for my wrath is upon all the *t*.
32:24 is Elam with all her *t* about Egypt's grave,
32:26 and Tubal and all their *t* about her grave,
Mt 14:14 When he disembarked and saw the vast *t*,

THRONGING (2)

Jer 3:23 indeed are the hills, the *t* mountains;
Dn 6: 7 satraps went *t* to the king and said to him,

THRONGS (6)

2Mc 14:23 He got rid of the *t* of ordinary people who
Wis 6: 2 multitude and lord it over *t* of peoples!
Is 5:14 their masses, their *t* and their revelry.
Bar 4:34 I will take from her the joyous *t*,
Ez 30:10 *t* of Egypt by the hand of Nebuchadnezzar,
32:18 Son of man, lament over the *t* of Egypt,

THROTTLED (1)

Mt 18:28 He seized him and *t* him.

THROUGHOUT (155)

Gn 17: 7 you *t* the ages as an everlasting pact,
17: 9 after you must keep my covenant *t* the ages.
17:12 *T* the ages, every male among you
41:29 are now coming *t* the land of Egypt;
41:46 presence, he traveled *t* the land of Egypt.
41:54 food was available *t* the land of Egypt.
41:55 When hunger came to be felt *t* the land of
41:56 When the famine had spread *t* the land,
49: 7 them in Jacob, disperse them *t* Israel.
Ex 5:12 scattered *t* the land of Egypt to gather
7:19 *T* the land of Egypt there shall be blood,
7:21 There was blood *t* the land of Egypt.
8:12 be turned into gnats *t* the land of Egypt."
8:13 was turned into gnats *t* the land of Egypt.
8:20 *t* Egypt the land was infested with flies.
9: 9 boils on man and beast *t* the land."
9:16 and to make my name resound *t* the earth!
9:25 that was in the open *t* the land of Egypt;
10:15 on any tree or plant *t* the land of Egypt.
10:22 *t* the land of Egypt for three days.
11: 6 shall be loud wailing *t* the land of Egypt,
12:17 you must celebrate this day *t* your
12:30 and there was a loud wailing *t* Egypt,
12:42 a vigil for the LORD *t* their generations.
14:21 *t* the night and so turned it into dry land.
27:21 for the Israelites *t* their generations.
29:42 *T* your generations this established
30: 8 *T* your generations this shall be the
30:10 *T* your generations this atonement is to be
30:21 and his descendants *t* their generations."
30:31 this shall belong to me *t* your generations.
31:13 token between you and me *t* the generations,
31:16 keeping it *t* their generations as a
36: 6 a proclamation to be made *t* the camp:
40:15 priesthood *t* all future generations."
Lv 6:11 of the LORD perpetually *t* your generations.
7:36 a perpetual ordinance *t* their generations.
10: 9 a perpetual ordinance *t* your generations,
25: 9 trumpet blast shall re-echo *t* your land.
Nm 12: 7 *T* my house he bears my trust:
15:21 *T* your generations you shall give a
26: 2 *t* the community of the Israelites of all
Dt 6: 2 God, and keep, *t* the days of your lives,
16:18 appoint judges and officials *t* your tribes
28:40 Though you have olive trees *t* your country,
28:52 *t* the land which the LORD your God,
Jos 6:27 Joshua so that his fame spread *t* the land.
Jgs 6:35 He sent messengers, too, *t* Manasseh,
7:22 and *t* the camp the LORD set the sword of
7:24 *t* the mountain region of Ephraim to say,
19:29 and sent them *t* the territory of Israel.
20:12 sent men *t* the tribe of Benjamin to say,
1Sm 11: 3 messengers *t* the territory of Israel.
11: 7 which he sent *t* the territory of Israel by
13: 3 Then Saul sounded the horn *t* the land,
27: 1 search for me *t* the land of Israel,
31: 9 and then sent the good news *t* the land of
31:12 set out, and after marching *t* the night,
2Sm 15:10 sent spies *t* the tribes of Israel to say,
19:10 but *t* the tribes of Israel all the people
1Kgs 1: 3 a beautiful girl *t* the territory of Israel,
5:11 his fame spread *t* the neighboring nations.
2Kgs 10:21 Jehu sent word of it *t* the land of Israel.
10:32 Hazael defeated the Israelites *t* their
1Chr 5:10 their tents *t* the region east of Gilead.
10: 9 these they sent *t* the land of the
16:14 *t* the earth his judgments prevail He
27: 1 came and went month by month *t* the year.
2Chr 11:13 Now the priests and Levites *t* Israel
11:23 *t* all the districts of Judah and Benjamin,
17:19 placed in the fortified cities *t* all Judah.
24: 9 They had it proclaimed *t* Judah and
24:14 continually *t* the lifetime of Jehoiada.
28:25 In every city *t* Judah he set up high
30: 5 *t* all Israel from Beer-sheba to Dan,
31: 1 down the high places and altars *t* Judah,
34: 7 the incense stands *t* the land of Israel.
36:22 to issue this proclamation *t* his kingdom,
Ezr 1: 1 to issue this proclamation *t* his kingdom,
7:16 you may receive *t* the province of Babylon,
10: 7 A proclamation was made *t* Judah and
Neh 8:15 made *t* their cities and in Jerusalem:
Tb 11:14 his holy name be praised *t* all the ages,
Jdt 4:13 a fast of many days' duration *t* Judea,
7: 5 their bastions, and kept watch *t* the night.
7:32 *T* the city they were in great misery.
11: 8 that *t* the kingdom you alone
11:16 that people *t* the world will be astonished
11:23 and shall be renowned *t* the earth."
16:21 of her life she was renowned *t* the land.
Est 1:16 populace *t* the provinces of King Ahasuerus.
1:20 king will issue is published *t* his realm,
3: 6 people, *t* the realm of King Ahasuerus.
3: 8 nations *t* the provinces of your kingdom,
B: 4 mixed in with all the races *t* the world,
8:12 as spoil *t* the provinces of King Ahasuerus;
9: 2 The Jews mustered in their cities *t* the
F:10 *t* all future generations of his people Israel."
1Mc 1:51 were the orders he published *t* his kingdom.
6:25 against us, but *t* their whole territory.
11:51 and they became renowned *t* his kingdom.
12:27 armed, ready for combat, *t* the night.
14: 4 his power and his magnificence *t* his reign.
2Mc 3:14 There was great distress *t* the city.
9:24 the people *t* the realm would know to whom
Ps(s) 92: 3 at dawn and your faithfulness *t* the night,
105: 7 *t* the earth his judgments prevail.
105:31 gnats, *t* all their borders.
105:32 hail, with flashing fires *t* their land.
105:33 and shattered the trees *t* their borders.
105:35 And they devoured every plant *t* the land;
105:36 he struck every first-born *t* their land,
Sir 45:26 forgotten, or your authority, *t* all time.
Is 8: 8 shall pass into Judah, and flood it all *t*:
12: 5 let this be known *t* all the earth.
Jer 17: 3 for all your sins *t* your borders,
Ez 21:37 the fire, your blood shall flow *t* the land.
41:19 figured on every side *t* the whole temple.
46: 1 shall remain closed *t* the six working days,
Dn 6:27 I decree that *t* my royal domain the God of
Jon 3: 7 Then he had this proclaimed *t* Nineveh,
Mt 9:26 News of this circulated *t* the district.
14:35 him they spread the word *t* the region.
24:14 be proclaimed *t* the world as a witness
26:13 the good news is proclaimed *t* the world,
Mk 1:28 spread *t* the surrounding region of Galilee.
1:39 expelling demons *t* the whole of Galilee.
5:20 man went off and began to proclaim *t*
14: 9 the good news is proclaimed *t* the world,
16:20 The Lord continued to work with them *t* and
Lk 1:65 *t* the hill country of Judea these
4:14 and his reputation spread *t* the region.
7:17 him *t* Judea and the surrounding country.
23: 5 by his teaching *t* the whole of Judea,
Acts 1: 8 in Jerusalem, *t* Judea and Samaria,
6:15 *T*, Stephen's face seemed like that of an
8: 1 *t* the countryside of Judea and Samaria.
9:31 Meanwhile *t* all Judea,

THROUGHOUT (cont.)

13:49 word of the Lord was carried *t* that area.
15:41 He traveled *t* Syria and Cilicia,
19:26 Ephesus but *t* most of the province of Asia,
19:29 Before long, confusion spread *t* the city.
20: 2 He traveled *t* its regions,
Rom 1: 8 because your faith is heralded *t* the world.
9:17 name might be proclaimed *t* all the earth."
2Cor 12:19 Do you think *t* this recital that I am
Phil 1:13 become well known *t* the praetorium here,
1Thes 1: 8 *t* every region your faith in God is
3: 7 by your faith *t* our distress and trial
4:10 respect to all the brothers *t* Macedonia.
1Tm 3:16 the Gentiles, Believed in *t* the world,
1Pt 1: 1 who live as strangers scattered *t* Pontus,
4:11 to him be glory and dominion *t* the ages.
5: 9 undergoing the same sufferings *t* the world.
5:11 Dominion be his *t* the ages!

THROW (44)

Gn 27:40 you shall *t* off his yoke from your neck."
37:20 and *t* him into one of the cisterns here;
37:22 "just *t* him into that cistern there in
Ex 1:22 *T* into the river every boy that is born to
4: 3 The LORD then said, *T* it on the ground."
7: 9 your staff and *t* it down before Pharaoh,
22:30 *t* it to the dogs.
23:27 I will *t* into panic every nation you reach.
Nm 8: 2 have them *t* their light toward the front
19: 6 hyssop and scarlet yarn and *t* them into
2Sm 20:15 Joab began battering the wall to *t* it down.
2Kgs 9:25 "Take him and *t* him into the field of
9:33 *T* her down," he ordered.
Neh 4: 2 Jerusalem and thus to *t* us into confusion.
Tb 6: 5 but *t* away the entrails.
Ps(s) 50:18 him, and with adulterers you *t* in your lot.
Is 2:20 On that day men will *t* to the moles and
30:22 You shall *t* them away like filthy rags to
Jer 6: 6 *t* up a siege mound against Jerusalem.
7:29 Cut off your dedicated hair and *t* it away!
51:63 a stone to it and *t* it in the Euphrates.
Ez 5: 4 Then take some of these and *t* them in the
15: 4 If you *t* it on the fire as fuel and the
20: 7 *T* away, each of you, the detestable
Jon 1:12 them, "Pick me up and *t* me into the sea,
Mi 1: 6 I will *t* down into the valley her stones,
Zec 11:13 the LORD said to me, *T* it in the treasury,
Mt 4: 6 you are the Son of God, *t* yourself down.
5:25 to the guard, who will *t* you into prison.
5:29 your trouble, gouge it out and *t* it away!
5:30 is your trouble, cut it off and *t* it away!
15:26 sons and daughters and *t* it to the dogs."
17:27 them go to the lake, *t* in a line,
18: 8 your undoing, cut it off and *t* it from you!
22:13 'Bind him hand and foot and *t* him out into
25:30 *T* this worthless servant into the darkness
Mk 7:27 food of the children and *t* it to the dogs."
Lk 4: 9 the Son of God, *t* yourself down from here,
12:58 jailer, and the jailer *t* you into prison.
22:41 He withdrew from them about a stone's *t*,
Jn 8:59 At that they picked up rocks to *t* at Jesus,
19:24 Let us *t* dice to see who gets it."
Rv 2:14 who instructed Balak to *t* a stumbling
4:10 They *t* down their crowns before the throne

THROWING (8)

Jgs 8:12 captive, *t* the entire army into panic.
2Sm 16:13 cursing and *t* stones and dirt as he went.
1Mc 7:19 deserted to him, *t* them into the great pit.
Ez 29: 7 splintered, *t* every shoulder out of joint;
Mk 9:26 Shouting, and *t* the boy into convulsions,
Jn 19: 2 *t* around his shoulders a cloak of royal
Acts 20:37 *t* their arms around him and kissing him,
27:38 the ship further by *t* the wheat overboard.

THROWN (48)

Lv 1:16 feathers shall be removed and *t* on the ash
Jgs 20:41 the men of Benjamin were *t* into confusion,
2Sm 20:21 head shall be *t* to you across the wall."
2Kgs 7:15 the Arameans had *t* away in their haste.
2Chr 29:19 reign had *t* away because of his apostasy,
Neh 13: 8 household goods *t* outside the chamber.
Tb 1:17 and been *t* outside the walls of Nineveh,
Est 3:15 but the city of Susa was *t* into confusion.
7: 8 Haman had *t* himself on the couch on which
2Mc 6:10 then *t* down from the top of the city wall.
9: 8 was now *t* to the ground and had to be
9:15 but fit only to be *t* out with their
10:30 and blinded, *t* into confusion and routed.
Jb 30:11 and have *t* off restraint in my presence.
Sir 27: 3 LORD, suddenly your house will be *t* down.
Jer 22:28 cast out, why *t* into a land they know not?
31:40 shall the city be rooted up or *t* down.
37:15 and had Jeremiah beaten and *t* into prison
Ez 16: 5 *t* out on the ground as something loathsome,
Dn 3:46 Now the king's men who had *t* them in
5: 9 ashen, and his lords were *t* into confusion.
7:11 its body *t* into the fire to be burnt up.
Hos 8: 3 The men of Israel have *t* away what is good;
Mi 2:12 they shall not be *t* into panic by men.
Mt 3:10 will be cut down and *t* into the fire.
5:13 but to be *t* out and trampled underfoot.
6:30 blooms today and is *t* on the fire tomorrow,
7:19 good fruit is cut down and *t* into the fire.
13:47 God is also like a dragnet *t* into the lake,
18: 8 crippled than be *t* with two hands
18: 9 eye than be *t* with both into fiery Gehenna.
21:21 mountain, 'Be lifted up and *t* into the sea,'
Mk 9:45 than to be *t* into Gehenna with both feet.
9:47 than to be *t* with both eyes into Gehenna,
11:23 mountain, 'Be lifted up and *t* into the sea,'
Lk 3: 9 will be cut down and *t* into the fire."
12:28 grows today and is *t* on the fire tomorrow,
14:35 it has to be *t* away.
17: 2 He would be better off *t* into the sea with
23:19 This Barabbas had been *t* in prison for
23:25 *t* in prison for insurrection and murder,
Jn 3:24 of course, had not yet been *t* into prison.)
15: 6 picked up to be *t* in the fire and burnt.
Acts 12: 4 he had him arrested and *t* into prison,
16:23 many lashes they were *t* into prison,
27:18 day some of the cargo was *t* over the side.
2Tm 2: 9 even to the point of being *t* into chains
Rv 20:10 and the false prophet had also been *t*.

THROWS (8)

Nm 35:20 lying in wait for him *t* something at him,
35:22 in wait for him he *t* some object at him,
35:23 or without seeing him *t* a death-dealing
Sir 22:20 He who *t* stones at birds drives them away,
27:25 As a stone falls back on him who *t* it up,
Mk 9:18 Whenever it seizes him it *t* him down;
9:22 "Often it *t* him into fire and into water.
Lk 9:39 with a sudden cry *t* him into a convulsion

THRUSH (1)

Jer 8: 7 and *t* observe their time of return,

THRUST (28)

Dt 9: 4 LORD, your God, has *t* them out of your way,
15:17 awl and *t* it through his ear into the door,
Jgs 3:21 right thigh, and *t* it into Eglon's belly.
19:25 his concubine and *t* her outside to them.
1Sm 2:14 boiling, and would *t* it into the basin,
14:27 *t* out the end of the staff he was holding
26: 7 with his spear *t* into the ground at his
26: 8 him to the ground with one *t* of the spear;
26: 8 I will not need a second *t*!"
2Sm 2:16 and *t* his sword into his opponent's side,
18:14 in hand, he *t* for the heart of Absalom,
20:10 and he died without receiving a second *t*.
1Chr 10: 4 "Draw your sword and *t* me through with it,
Jb 16:14 He pierces me with *t* upon thrust;
Ps(s) 36:13 they are *t* down and cannot rise.
44:20 Though you *t* us down into a place of
Sir 7:14 *T* not yourself into the deliberations of
Is 22:19 I will *t* you from your office and pull you
Jer 46:15 The LORD *t* him down;
Ez 26:20 then I will *t* you down with those who
28: 8 They shall *t* you down to the pit,
32:18 *t* them down to the bottom of the earth,
Zec 5: 8 and he *t* her inside the bushel,
12:10 shall look on him whom they have *t* through,
13: 3 father and mother, shall *t* him through.
Jn 19:34 of the soldiers *t* a lance into his side,
Acts 7:39 *t* him aside and longed to return to Egypt.

THRUSTING (2)

Dt 6:19 *t* all your enemies out of your way.
1Sm 14:20 confused, were *t* swords at one another.

THRUSTS (1)

Prv 12:18 The prating of some men is like sword *t*,

THUMB (5)

Lv 8:23 right ear, on the *t* of his right hand,
14:14 man's right ear, the *t* of his right hand,
14:17 man's right ear, the *t* of his right hand,
14:25 being purified, on the *t* of his right hand,
14:28 man's right ear, the *t* of his right hand,

THUMBS (4)

Ex 29:20 right ears and on the *t* of their right hands
Lv 8:24 right ears, on the *t* of their right hands,
Jgs 1: 6 caught him, cut off his *t* and his big toes.
1: 7 kings, with their *t* and big toes cut off,

THUMMIM (6)

Ex 28:30 of decision you shall put the Urim and *T*,
Lv 8: 8 on him, with the Urim and *T* in it,
Dt 33: 8 "To Levi belong your *T*,
1Sm 14:41 is in your people Israel, respond with *T*."
Ezr 2:63 should be a priest bearing the Urim and *T*.
Neh 7:65 should be a priest bearing the Urim and *T*.

THUNDER (29)

Ex 9:23 the LORD sent forth hail and peals of *t*.
9:28 for we have had enough of God's *t* and hail.
9:29 the *t* will cease,
9:33 Then the *t* and the hail ceased,
9:34 that the rain and hail and *t* had ceased,
19:16 day there were peals of *t* and lightning,
19:19 was speaking and God answering him with *t*.
20:18 the people witnessed the *t* and lightning,
1Sm 12:17 to the LORD, and he will send *t* and rain.
12:18 and the LORD sent *t* and rain that day.
Est A: 4 was noise and tumult, *t* and earthquake
Jb 36:33 His *t* speaks for him and incites the fury
37: 4 the majestic sound of his *t*.
40: 9 of God, or can you *t* with a voice like his?
Ps(s) 77:19 Your *t* resounded in the whirlwind;
81: 8 Unseen, I answered you in *t*;
104: 7 at the sound of your *t* they took to flight;
Sir 40:13 like a mighty stream with lightning and *t*,
43:16 The *t* of his voice makes the earth writhe;
Is 29: 6 be visited by the LORD of hosts, With *t*,
Mk 3:17 two the name Boanerges, or "sons of *t*");
Jn 12:29 heard the voice, they said it was *t*.
Rv 4: 5 came flashes of lightning and peals of *t*;
6: 1 living creatures cry out in a voice like *t*,
8: 5 of *t* and flashes of lightning followed,
11:19 were flashes of lightning and peals of *t*,
14: 2 roaring of the deep, or loud peals of *t*;
16:18 followed lightning flashes and peals of *t*,
19: 6 roaring of the deep, or mighty peals of *t*,

THUNDERBOLTS (3)

2Mc 10:30 They shot arrows and hurled *t* at the enemy,
Jb 28:26 rules for the rain and a path for the *t*,
Wis 19:13 forewarnings from the violence of the *t*.

THUNDERED (4)

1Sm 7:10 the LORD *t* loudly against the Philistines,
2Sm 22:14 "The LORD *t* from heaven;
Ps(s) 18:14 And the LORD *t* from heaven,
Sir 46:17 Then the LORD *t* forth from heaven,

THUNDEROUS (2)

Jb 26:11 tremble and are stunned at his *t* rebuke;
39:20 quiver while his *t* snorting spreads terror?

THUNDERS (7)

1Sm 2:10 The Most High in heaven *t*;
Ps(s) 29: 3 is over the waters, the God of glory *t*,
Jer 10:13 When he *t*, the waters in the heavens
51:16 When he *t*, the waters in the heavens roar,
Rv 10: 3 out, the seven *t* raised their voices too.
10: 4 to start writing when the seven *t* spoke,
10: 4 *t* have spoken and do not write it down!"

THUNDERSTORM (1)

Jb 38:25 *t* a path To bring rain to no man's land,

THUNDERSTRUCK (1)

Sir 43:25 its story, and when we hear them we are *t*;

THWART (3)

Ezr 4: 5 work against them and *t* their plans
Is 14:27 who can *t* him?
1Cor 1:19 wise, and *t* the cleverness of the clever."

THWARTED (2)

Jdt 16: 5 "But the Lord Almighty *t* them,
Is 8:10 Form a plan, and it shall be *t*;

THWARTS (2)

Ps(s) 146: 9 sustains, but the way of the wicked he *t*.
Prv 10: 3 hunger, but the craving of the wicked he *t*.

THYATIRA (4)

Acts 16:14 dealer in purple goods from the town of *T*.
Rv 1:11 to Ephesus, Smyrna, Pergamum, *T*,
2:18 the presiding spirit of the church in *T*,
2:24 I address myself to you others in *T*

TIBERIAS (3)

Jn 6: 1 the Sea of Galilee [to the shore] of *T*;
6:23 Then some boats came out from *T* near the
21: 1 Later, at the Sea of *T*,

TIBERIUS (1)

Lk 3: 1 the fifteenth year of the rule of *T* Caesar,

TIBHATH (1)

1Chr 18: 8 He likewise took away from *T* and Cun,

TIBNI (3)

1Kgs 16:21 of Israel were divided, half following *T*,
16:22 of Omri prevailed over those of *T*,
16:22 *T* died and Omri became king.

TICKLE (1)

2Tm 4: 3 themselves with teachers who *t* their ears.

TIDAL (2)

Gn 14: 1 and *T* king of Goiim made war on Bera king

14: 9 king of Elam, *T* king of Goiim,

TIDE-OVER (1)

1Mc 6:53 and the *t* provisions had been eaten up by

TIDIED (2)

Mt 12:44 unoccupied, though swept and *t* now.
Lk 11:25 returns, to find the house swept and *t*.

TIDINGS (13)

Ps(s) 68:12 women bear the glad *t*,
Is 40: 9 a high mountain, Zion, herald of glad *t*;
41:27 I will pick out a bearer of the glad *t*."
52: 7 are the feet of him who brings glad *t*,
61: 1 has sent me to bring glad *t* to the lowly,
Lk 2:10 I come to proclaim good news to you *t* of
4:18 He has sent me to bring glad *t* to the poor,
Gal 1:16 the Gentiles the good *t* concerning him.
Eph 1:13 when you heard the glad *t* of salvation,
1Thes 2: 2 *t* to you in the face of great opposition.
2: 4 by God, as men entrusted with the good *t*,
2: 8 you not only God's *t* but our very lives,
2: 9 we preached God's good *t* to you in order

TIE (6)

Ex 29: 9 with the sashes, and *t* the turbans on them.
Jos 2:18 *t* this scarlet cord in the window through
2Chr 34:11 buy hewn stone and timber for the *t* beams
Jer 51:63 *t* a stone to it and throw it in the
Ez 5: 3 and *t* them in the hem of your garment.
Jn 21:18 and another will *t* you fast and carry you

TIED (13)

Gn 22: 9 Next he *t* up his son Isaac,
38:28 taking a crimson thread, *t* it on his hand,
Ex 28:37 This plate is to be *t* over the miter with
39:31 was *t* over the miter with a violet ribbon,
Jos 2:21 gone, she *t* the scarlet cord in the window.
Jgs 15: 4 he *t* between each pair of tails one of the
2Kgs 5:23 He *t* up these silver talents in bags and
Mk 6:53 came ashore at Gennesaret, and *t* up there.
Lk 8:29 man used to be *t* with chains and fetters,
19:30 an ass *t* there which no one has yet ridden.
Jn 13: 4 picked up a towel and *t* it around himself.
Acts 21:11 belt, *t* his own hands and feet with it.
Rv 9:14 the four angels who are *t* up on the banks

TIES (2)

Mt 12:29 property unless he first *t* him securely?
Acts 7:13 his family *t* became known to the Pharaoh.

TIGHT (2)

Jgs 16:11 "If they bind me *t* with new ropes,
Sir 27:30 hateful things, yet the sinner hugs them *t*.

TIGHTENED (1)

Is 28:22 be arrogant no more lest your bonds be *t*,

TIGHTLY (2)

Gn 20:18 for God had *t* closed every womb in
Jb 41: 7 scales are on his back, *t* sealed together;

TIGLATH-PILESER (5)

2Kgs 15:29 the reign of Pekah, king of Israel, *T*,
16: 7 Meanwhile, Ahaz sent messengers to *T*,
16:10 King Ahaz went to Damascus to meet *T*,
1Chr 5: 6 was Baal, whose son was Beerah, whom *T*,
5:26 anger of Pul, king of Assyria, and of *T*,

TIGRIS (5)

Gn 2:14 The name of the third river is the *T*;
Tb 6: 2 and made camp beside the *T* River.
Jdt 1: 6 all who dwelt along the Euphrates, the *T*,
Sir 24:23 like the *T* in the days of the new fruits.
Dn 10: 4 was on the bank of the great river, the *T*.

TIKVAH (2)

2Kgs 22:14 She was the wife of Shallum, son of *T*,
Ezr 10:15 son of Asahel, and Jahzeiah, son of *T*,

TILE (8)

Dn 2:33 iron, its feet partly iron and partly *t*.
2:34 put to it, struck its iron and *t* feet,
2:35 The iron, *t*, bronze, silver, and gold
2:41 partly of potter's *t* and partly of iron,
2:41 As you saw the iron mixed with clay *t*,
2:42 and the toes partly iron and partly *t*,
2:43 The iron mixed with clay *t* means that they
2:45 put to it, which broke in pieces the *t*,

TILES (1)

Lk 5:19 let him down with his mat through the *t*

TILEWORK (1)

Ex 24:10 his feet there appeared to be sapphire *t*,

TILGATH-PILNESER (1)

2Chr 28:20 *T*, king of Assyria,

TILL (180)

Gn 2: 5 earth and there was no man to *t* the soil,
3:23 *t* the ground from which he had been taken.
4:12 If you *t* the soil,
Ex 10:15 the whole land, *t* it was black with them.
16:21 they gathered it, *t* each had enough to eat;
17:12 so that his hands remained steady *t* sunset.
18:14 to stand about you from morning *t* evening?"
23:18 my feast be kept overnight *t* the next day.
Lv 7:15 none of it may be kept *t* the next day.
12: 4 the sanctuary *t* the days of her purification
24: 3 the LORD regularly, from evening *t* morning.
24:12 who kept him in custody *t* a decision from
26: 5 your threshing will last *t* vintage time,
26: 5 and your vintage *t* the time for sowing,
26: 8 of them, *t* they are cut down by your sword.
26:17 *t* you are beaten down before your enemies
26:22 *t* your population dwindles away and your
26:25 *t* you are forced to surrender to the enemy.
26:29 *t* you begin to eat the flesh of your own
Nm 9:12 and not leaving any of it over *t* morning,
14:33 *t* the last of you lies dead in the desert.
22:19 *t* I learn what else the LORD may tell me."
23:24 It rests not *t* it has devoured its prey
24:18 all the Shuthites, *T* Edom is dispossessed,
Dt 2:15 *t* he wiped them out of the camp completely.
7:24 against you, *t* you have put an end to them.
9:10 *t* the LORD gave me the two tablets of
34: 8 *t* they had completed the period of grief
Jos 7: 5 front of the city gate *t* they broke ranks,
8:16 *t* the last of the soldiers in the city
11:11 there to the sword, *t* none was left alive.
18:12 *t* it reached the desert of Beth-aven.
18:14 *t* it reached Kiriath-baal (that is,
20: 6 live on in that city *t* the death of the high
Jgs 2:15 he would do, *t* they were in great distress.
4:24 *t* at length they destroyed the Canaanite
9:43 watched *t* he saw the people leave the city,
15:19 drank *t* his spirit returned and he revived.
16:16 complaints *t* he was deathly weary of them.
19:10 and traveled *t* they came opposite Jebus,
19:14 So they continued on their way *t* the sun
Ru 1:19 went on together *t* they reached Bethlehem.
2Sm 9:10 sons and servants must *t* the land for him.
22:35 war *t* my arms could bend a bow of brass.
22:38 nor did I turn again *t* I made an end
2Kgs 3:25 fertile field *t* they had loaded it down;
4:25 She kept going *t* she reached the man of
17:18 in the LORD's sight, provoking him *t*,
24:20 Judah *t* he cast them out from his presence.
2Chr 29:30 They sang praises *t* their joy was full,
Ezr 8:29 Keep good watch over them *t* you weigh them
10:14 *t* we have turned away from us our God's
Neh 2: 7 afford me safe-conduct *t* I arrive in Judah;
2:15 *t* I once more reached the Valley Gate,
4:15 ready, from daybreak *t* the stars came out.
8: 3 out of the book from daybreak *t* midday,
13:19 them to be reopened *t* after the sabbath.
Tb 2:10 *t* their warm droppings settled in my eyes,
3: 4 and death, *t* we were an object lesson,
4:15 Do not drink wine *t* you become drunk,
5: 7 young man, *t* I go back and tell my father;
6: 2 The travelers walked *t* nightfall,
6: 7 on together *t* they were near Media.
Jdt 2:10 them for me *t* the day of their punishment.
6: 8 die *t* you are destroyed together with them.
6:11 *t* they reached the springs below Bethulia.
11:19 you through Judea, *t* you come to Jerusalem,
12: 4 use up her supplies *t* the Lord accomplishes
12: 5 into the tent, where she slept *t* midnight.
12:14 will be a joy for me *t* the day of my death."
14: 8 left *t* the time she began speaking to them.
15: 7 *t* the towns and villages in the mountains
Est 4: 2 *t* he came before the royal gate,
4:29 From the day I was brought here *t* now,
D: 6 *t* she stood face to face with the king,
1Mc 14:10 *t* his glorious name reached the ends of
Jb 12:25 *t* they grope in the darkness without light;
14:12 *T* the heavens are no more,
14:13 and keep me sheltered *t* your wrath is past;
27: 5 *t* I die I will not renounce my innocence.
31:12 to the abyss *t* it consumed all my possessions
31:38 against me *t* its very furrows complained;
36:28 *T* the skies run with them and the showers
37:21 *t* the wind comes by and sweeps the clouds
38:13 *t* the wicked are shaken from its surface?
38:27 ground *t* the desert blooms with verdure?
Ps(s) 10:10 *t* by his violence fall the unfortunate.
18:38 did I turn again *t* I made an end of them.
57: 2 your wings I take refuge, *t* harm pass by.
59:14 consume, *t* they are no more;
71:17 and *t* the present I proclaim your wondrous
71:18 forsake me not *T* I proclaim your strength
72: 7 and profound peace, *t* the moon be no more.
73:17 *T* I entered the sanctuary of God and
94:13 evil days, *t* the pit be dug for the wicked.
104:11 *t* the wild asses quench their thirst.
104:23 his work and to his tillage *t* the evening.
105:19 *T* his prediction came to pass and the word
109:15 *t* he banish the memory of these parents
110: 1 hand *t* I make your enemies your footstool."
112: 8 not fear *t* he looks down upon his foes.
123: 2 on the LORD, our God, *t* he have pity on us.
132: 5 no rest, *T* I find a place for the LORD,
133: 2 *t* it runs down upon the collar of his robe.
Prv 4:18 that grows in brilliance *t* perfect day.
7:20 not *t* the full moon will he return home."
7:23 the net, *t* an arrow pierces its liver;
Sg 3: 4 would not let him go *t* I should bring him
Wis 15: 5 *t* he longs for the inanimate form of a
Sir 11:19 be *t* he dies and leaves them to others.
18:21 sins, neglect it not *t* you are in distress.
20: 6 wise man is silent *t* the right time comes,
23:16 not to be quenched *t* it burns itself out:
23:17 sweet and who is never through *t* he dies;
33:17 *t* like a vintager I have filled my winepress,
35:17 it does not rest *t* it reaches its goal,
35:18 will it withdraw *t* the Most High responds,
35:20 will not be still *T* he breaks the backs of
35:21 *T* he destroys the haughty root and branch,
35:22 *T* he requites mankind according to its
35:23 *T* he defends the cause of his people,
38:27 he keeps watch *t* he finishes his design.
38:28 he keeps watch *t* he perfects it in detail.
40: 2 his troubled forebodings *t* the day he dies
40: 6 *t* in his dreams he struggles as he did by
46: 6 army *t* on the slope he destroyed the foe;
46: 9 *T* he won his way onto the summits
47: 7 and shattered their power *t* our own day.
48: 1 *T* like a fire there appeared the prophet
48:25 foretold what should be *t* the end of time,
Is 5: 8 field with field, *T* no room remains,
22:14 not be pardoned this wickedness *t* you die,
30:24 The oxen and the asses that *t* the ground
43:17 army, *T* they lie prostrate together,
43:28 against me *T* I repudiated the holy gates,
55:10 return there *t* they have watered the earth,
Jer 4: 3 *T* your untilled ground,
4: 4 like fire, and burn *t* none can quench it,
4: 7 *t* your cities lie waste and empty.
11: 8 *t* I brought upon them all the threats of
27:11 says the LORD, to *t* it and dwell in it.
31:35 Who stirs up the sea *t* its waves roar,
38:28 of the guard *t* the day Jerusalem was taken.
47: 6 how long *t* you find rest?
49:36 *t* there is no nation to which the outcasts
50:19 Ephraim and Gilead, *t* she has her fill.
Lam 2: 8 grief on wall and rampart *t* both succumbed.
3:50 *T* the LORD from heaven looks down and sees.
Bar 2:11 made for yourself a name *t* the present day:
Ez 4:14 been made unclean, and from my youth *t* now,
5:13 wreak my fury upon them *t* I am appeased;
24:10 *T* the meat has been cooked, *t* the broth
24:11 *t* its metal glows red hot, *t* the impurities
Dn 2: 9 to present me with *t* the crisis is past.
4:13 of a beast, *t* seven years pass over him.
4:20 wild beasts *t* seven years pass over him'
6:15 he worked *t* sunset to rescue him.
11:36 shall prosper only *t* divine wrath is ready,
Hos 9:12 make them childless, *t* not one is left.
10:12 *t* he come and rain down justice upon you."
Am 9: 1 so that the doorjambs totter *t* you break
Ob 1: 5 they not steal merely *t* they had enough?
1: 9 crushed, *t* all on Mount Esau are destroyed.
Jon 4: 9 upon Jonah's head *t* he became
Na 3: 7 *T* everyone who sees you runs from you,
3:11 too, shall drink of this *t* you faint away;
Hb 2:15 make them drunk, *t* their nakedness is seen!
Zep 1:17 will hem men in *t* they walk like the blind,
Zec 9:15 *t* they are filled with it like libation
Mt 10:22 holds out *t* the end will escape death.
Mk 13:13 the man who holds out *t* the end is the one
Lk 12:50 What anguish I feel *t* it is over!
Gal 2:13 *t* even Barnabas was swept away by their
Eph 4:13 *t* we become one in faith and in the
Heb 1:13 *t* I make your enemies your footstool"?
6:11 each of you show the same zeal *t* the end,
Rv 2:26 victory, who keeps to my ways *t* the end,
20: 5 to life *t* the thousand years were over.

TILLAGE (4)

Gn 45: 6 five more years *t* will yield no harvest.
Ps(s) 104:23 to his work and to his *t* till the evening.
Prv 13:23 A lawsuit devours the *t* of the poor,
21: 4 the *t* of the wicked is sin.

TILLED (4)

Jos 24:13 not *t* and cities which you had not built,
1Chr 27:26 the farm workers who *t* the soil was Ezri,
Ez 36: 9 you will be *t* and sown,
36:34 the desolate land shall be *t*,

TILLER (2)

Gn 4: 2 keeper of flocks, and Cain a *t* of the soil.
Zec 13: 5 "I am no prophet, I am a *t* of the soil,

TILLS (1)

Prv 12:11 He who *t* his own land has food in plenty,

TILON (1)

1Chr 4:20 Amnon, Rinnah, Benhanan, and T.

TILTS (1)

Jb 38:37 Or who t the water jars of heaven So that

TIMAEUS (1)

Mk 10:46 ("son of T") sitting by the roadside.

TIMBER (8)

1Kgs 5:20 is skilled in cutting t like the Sidonians,
2Chr 34:11 buy hewn stone and t for the tie beams
Ezr 5: 8 and the walls are being reinforced with t;
6: 4 courses of cut stone for each one of t.
Is 40:20 for himself, Choosing t that will not rot,
Ez 26:12 Your stones, your t, and your clay
Hg 1: 8 bring t, and build the house
Zec 5: 4 his house, consuming it, t and stones."

TIMBERED (3)

Neh 3: 1 They t it and set up its doors,
3: 3 they t it and set up its doors,
3: 6 they t it and set up its doors,

TIMBERING (1)

Neh 2: 8 that he may give me wood for t the gates

TIMBREL (5)

Jb 21:12 They sing to the t and harp,
Ps(s) 81: 3 Take up a melody, and sound the t,
149: 3 them sing praise to him with t and harp.
150: 4 lyre and harp, Praise him with t and dance,
Is 5:12 With harp and lyre, t and flute,

TIMBRELS (5)

Jdt 3: 7 garlands and dancing to the sound of t.
16: 1 the instruments, a song to my God with t,
Ps(s) 68:26 in their midst the maidens play on t.
Is 24: 8 Stilled are the cheerful t,
30:29 of Israel, accompanied by the t and lyres.

TIME (916)

Gn 2: 4 At the t when the LORD God made the earth
3: 8 in the garden at the breezy t of the day,
4: 3 In the course of t Cain brought an
4:26 t men began to invoke the LORD by name.
6: 4 At that t the Nephilim appeared on earth
8:12 and this t it did not come back.
10:25 Peleg, for in his t the world was divided;
13: 7 (At this t the Canaanites and the
15: 1 Some t after these events,
17:21 shall bear to you by this t next year."
18:10 return to you about this t next year,
18:14 At the appointed t, about this time next
18:32 Lord grow angry if I speak up this last t.
19:11 at the same t they struck the men at the
19:24 at the same t the LORD rained down
21: 2 old age, at the set t that God had stated.
21:22 About that t Abimelech,
22: 1 Some t after these events,
22:20 Some t afterward, the news came
24:11 at the t when women go out to draw water,
24:21 The man watched her the whole t,
25:24 When the t of her delivery came,
26: 8 But when he had been there for a long t,
26:13 him, he became richer and richer all the t,
27: 2 I am so old that I may now die at any t.
27:41 the t of mourning for my father comes,
29: 7 is hardly the t to bring the animals home.
29:35 "This t I will give grateful praise to
30:20 This t my husband will offer me presents,
31: 7 me and changed my wages t after time.
31:41 while you changed my wages t after time.
34:19 man lost no t in acting in the matter,
35:17 This t, too, you have a son."
37: 9 "this t, the sun and the moon
38: 1 About that t Judah parted from his
38:27 When the t of her delivery came,
39: 7 After a t, his master's wife
40: 1 Some t afterward, the royal cupbearer
40: 4 After they had been in custody for some t,
43:18 money put back in our bags the first t,
46:29 on his neck and wept a long t in his arms.
47:29 When the t approached for Israel to die,
48: 1 Some t afterward, Joseph was informed,
Ex 1:10 in t of war they too may join our enemies
2:23 A long t passed, during which the king
4:26 At that t she said, "A spouse of blood,"
8: 5 "Do me the favor of appointing the t
9: 5 And setting a definite t,
9:14 or this t I will hurl all my blows upon
12:40 The t the Israelites had stayed in Egypt
13:10 rite at its appointed t from year to year.
23:15 at the prescribed t in the month of Abib,
32:34 When it is t for me to punish,
34:18 For seven days at the prescribed t in the
Lv 7:38 at the t when he commanded the Israelites
10: 1 During this t Aaron's sons Nadab and Abihu
13:58 the thing shall be washed a second t,
14: 2 of leprosy at the t of his purification.
16:17 from the t he enters the sanctuary
23: 4 at their proper t with a sacred assembly.
25:29 the t of one full year from its sale.
25:31 they may be redeemed at any t,
26: 5 last till vintage t, and your vintage till the t
26:34 sabbaths during all the t it lies waste,
26:35 during all the t that it lies desolate,
27:18 but if it is some t after this,
Nm 3: 1 at the t that the LORD spoke to Moses
9: 2 celebrate the Passover at the prescribed t.
9: 3 prescribed t when you shall celebrate it,
9: 7 proper t along with the other Israelites?"
9:13 the LORD's offering at the prescribed t.
10:13 The first t that they broke camp at the
15:14 residing with you permanently or for a t,
15:23 from the t the LORD first issues the
17:28 Every t anyone approaches the Dwelling of
20:15 down to Egypt, where we stayed a long t,
22: 4 son who was king of Moab at that t,
25:18 at the t of the slaughter because of Peor."
30:16 them some t after he first learned of them,
32:10 At that t the wrath of the LORD flared up,
Dt 1: 9 "At that t I said to you,
1:16 I charged your judges at that t,
2: 1 around the highlands of Seir for a long t.
2:34 At that t we seized all his cities and
3: 4 At that t we captured all his cities,
3: 8 "And so at that t we took from the two
3:12 "When we occupied the land at that t,
3:18 "At that t I charged them as follows:
4:14 The LORD charged me at that t to teach you
4:26 of t but shall be promptly wiped out.
4:32 now of the days of old, before your t,
5: 5 stood between the LORD and you at that t,
9:20 had I not prayed for him also at that t.
10: 1 "At that t the LORD said to me,
10: 8 "At that t the LORD set apart the tribe
17: 9 or to the judge who is in office at that t.
19:17 the priests or judges in office at that t;
20:19 to it for a long t before you capture it,
24:20 shall not go over the branches a second t;
24:21 shall not go over the vineyard a second t;
26: 3 priest in office at that t and say to him,
27: 3 Also write on them, at the t you cross,
28:46 as a sign and a wonder for all t.
31:10 at the prescribed t in the year of
31:14 "The t is now approaching for you to die.
31:17 that t my anger will flare up against them;
31:17 At that t they will indeed say,
31:18 at that t only because of all the evil
31:21 are inclined to do even at the present t,
32:35 against the t they lose their footing?"
Jos 2: 5 when it was t for the gate to be shut,
5: 2 the Israelite nation for the second t."
6:16 The seventh t around,
8: 5 a sortie against us as they did the last t,
8: 6 are fleeing from them as we did the last t.
8:20 By the t the men of Ai looked back,
9:27 the Israelites, at the same t he made them,
10:28 captured and put to the sword at that t.
10:33 At that t Horam, king of Gezer,
11: 6 for by this t tomorrow I will stretch them
11:10 At that t Joshua, turning back,
11:18 war against all these kings for a long t.
11:21 At that t Joshua penetrated the mountain
20: 6 the high priest who is in office at the t.
22: 1 At that t Joshua summoned the Reubenites,
24: 7 to Egypt, and dwelt a long t in the desert,
Jgs 3:30 under the power of Israel at that t;
4: 4 At this t the prophetess Deborah,
5:17 why does Dan spend his t in ships?
11: 4 Some t later, the Ammonites warred
11:26 why did you not recover them during that t?
12: 6 thousand Ephraimites fell at that t.
14: 4 at that t they had dominion over Israel.
15: 1 After some t, in the season of wheat
15: 3 "This t the Philistines cannot blame me
16:18 the Philistines, saying, "Come up this t,
16:20 good his escape as he had done t and again,
16:28 this last t that for my two eyes I may
18: 1 At that t there was no king in Israel.
18: 1 for up to that t they had received no
18:30 until the t of the captivity of the land.
19: 1 At that t, when there was no king
20:24 met the Benjaminites for the second t,
20:30 for the third t and formed their line
21:14 When Benjamin returned at that t,
21:24 Also at that t the Israelites dispersed;
Ru 1: 1 Once in the t of the judges there was a
1: 2 Some t after their arrival on the Moabite
1Sm 1: 7 each t they made their pilgrimage to the
1: 9 at the t, Eli the priest was sitting
1:21 The next t her husband Elkanah was going
2:19 which she would bring him each t she went
2:31 the t is coming when I will break your
3: 1 During the t young Samuel was minister to
3: 7 t Samuel was not familiar with the LORD,
3: 8 LORD called Samuel again, for the third t.
4: 1 At that t, the Philistines gathered
6:18 Joshua the Beth-shemite at the present t.
7: 2 came to rest in Kiriath-jearim a long t—
8: 9 but at the same t, warn them solemnly
9:16 "At this t tomorrow I will send you a man
12:10 Each t they appealed to the LORD and said,
12:17 Are we not in the harvest t for wheat?
13: 8 the t Samuel had determined.
13:11 since you had not come by the specified t,
14:18 ephod in front of the Israelites at that t.)
14:35 the first t he built an altar to the LORD.
14:41 did you not answer your servant this t?
18: 1 the t David finished speaking with Saul,
18:19 when it was t for Saul's daughter Merob to
18:21 [Thus for the second t Saul said to David,
18:30 forays, but each t they took the field,
19:21 For the third t Saul sent messengers,
20:12 sound out my father about this t tomorrow.
22: 6 At the t he was sitting in Gibeah under a
22:15 the first t I have consulted God for him?
23:24 At this t David and his men were in the
25: 2 At this t he was present for the shearing
25: 8 young men, since we come at a festival t.
25:16 t we were pasturing the sheep near them.
26:10 him, whether the t comes for him to die,
27: 6 to the kings of Judah up to the present t.
27:10 who asked, "Whom did you raid this t?"
2Sm 3:14 same t David sent messengers to Ishbaal,
3:17 t you have been seeking David as your king.
7:11 since the t I first appointed judges over
7:12 t comes and you rest with your ancestors,
7:19 house of your Servant for a long t to come:
7:25 confirm for all t the prophecy you have
10: 1 t later the king of the Ammonites died,
11: 4 at a t when she was just purified after
13: 1 t later the following incident occurred.
13:39 during all that t to mourn over his son;
14:29 Although he summoned him a second t,
16:23 that t was as though one had sought divine
17: 7 t Ahithophel has not given good counsel."
18:14 "I will not waste t with you in this way."
20: 5 delayed beyond the t set for him by David.
21: 9 The seven fell at the one t;
21:12 them at the t they killed Saul on Gilboa.
23:14 At that t David was in the refuge,
23:20 lion in the cistern at the t of the snow.
24:15 Now it was the t of the wheat harvest when
24:15 Israel from morning until the t appointed,
1Kgs 2: 1 When the t of David's death drew near,
2: 5 for the blood of war in a t of peace,
2:26 die, I will not put you to death this t,
2:38 So Shimei stayed in Jerusalem for a long t.
3: 2 for up to that t no temple had been built
5:17 until such a t as the LORD should put
9: 2 the LORD appeared to him a second t,
10:21 in Solomon's t it was considered worthless.
11:29 At that t Jeroboam left Jerusalem,
11:42 The t that Solomon reigned in Jerusalem
14: 1 At that t Abijah, son of Jeroboam,
16:21 that t the people of Israel were divided,
17: 7 After some t, however, the brook ran dry,
17:17 Some t later the son of the mistress of
18:29 until the t for offering sacrifice.
18:34 time," he said, and they did it a third t.
18:36 At the t for offering sacrifice,
18:44 And the seventh t the youth reported,
19: 2 if by this t tomorrow I have not done
19: 7 angel of the LORD came back a second t,
20: 6 t tomorrow I will send my servants to you,
20: 9 you demanded of your servant the first t.
21: 1 Some t after this,
21:29 me, I will not bring the evil in his t.
2Kgs 1:13 Again, for the third t,
3:20 In the morning, at the t of the sacrifice,
4:16 "This t next year you will be fondling a
4:17 and by the same t the following year she
5:26 this a t to take money or to take garments,
7: 1 'At this t tomorrow a seah of fine flour
7:18 at this t tomorrow at the gate of Samaria."
8: 7 came to Damascus at a t when Ben-hadad,
8:19 a lamp in the LORD's presence for all t.
8:22 Libnah also revolted at that t.
10: 6 come to me in Jezreel at this t tomorrow."
10:32 that t the LORD began to dismember Israel.
13: 3 a long t left them in the power of Hazael,
13:20 At the t, bands of Moabites used to raid
15:16 At that t, Menahem punished Tappuah,
15:37 at that t that the LORD first loosed Rezin,
16: 6 At the same t the king of Edom recovered
16:11 completed by the t the king returned home.
18: 4 because up to that t the Israelites were
20:12 At that t, when Merodach-baladan,
20:17 t is coming when all that is in your house,
23:29 In his t Pharaoh Neco,
24:10 At that t the officials of Nebuchadnezzar,
1Chr 1:19 Peleg (for in his t the world was divided),
5:17 in the family records in the t of Jotham,
5:22 dwelling place until the t of the exile.
6:16 from the t when the ark had obtained
7: 2 thousand six hundred in the t of David.
7:22 Their father Ephraim mourned a long t,
10: 6 three sons, his whole house died at one t.
12:30 until this t, most of them had held their
15: 2 At that t he said, "No one may carry
15:13 Because you were not with us the first t,
16: 7 for the first t these praises of the LORD:
17: 5 house, from the t when I led Israel onward,

17:10 and during all the *t* when I appointed
20: 1 following year, the *t* when kings go to war,
20: 4 At that *t*, Sibbecai the Hushathite slew
21:29 were at that *t* on the high place at Gibeon.
22: 9 and in his *t* I will bestow peace and
23:27 from the *t* they were twenty years old.
29:22 *t* they proclaimed David's son Solomon king,
29:27 The *t* that he reigned over Israel was
2Chr 9:20 was not considered of value in Solomon's *t*.
13:20 not regain power during the *t* of Abijah;
13:23 During his *t*, ten years of peace began
15: 3 For a long *t* Israel had no true God,
15: 5 In that former *t* there was no peace for
15:11 at that *t* seven hundred oxen and seven
16: 7 At that *t* Hanani the seer came to Asa,
16:10 oppressed some of his people at this *t*.
21: 7 to give him and his sons a lamp for all *t*.
21: 8 During his *t* Edom revolted against the
21:10 sovereignty of Judah down to the present *t*.
21:10 Libnah also revolted at that *t* against
21:19 As *t* went on until a period of two years
24: 4 After some *t*, Joash decided to restore
25:27 *t* that Amaziah ceased to follow the LORD,
28:16 At that *t* King Ahaz sent an appeal for
30: 3 celebrate it at the *t* of the restoration:
32:26 his anger on them during the *t* of Hezekiah.
34:16 *t* that he was making his report to him.
35:18 Israel since the *t* of the prophet Samuel,
36:21 during all the *t* it lies waste it shall
Ezr 4: 7 Again, in the *t* of Artaxerxes,
5: 3 At that *t* there came to them Tattenai,
5:16 that *t* the building has been going on,
8:34 At that same *t*, those who had returned
9: 5 Then, at the *t* of the evening sacrifice,
9: 7 From the *t* of our fathers even to this day
9: 8 "And now, but a short *t* ago,
Neh 4:10 From that *t* on, however,
4:16 At the same *t* I told the people to spend
5:14 Moreover, from the *t* that
6: 1 up to that *t* I had not yet set up the doors
6: 4 proposal, and each *t* I gave the same reply.
6: 5 Then, the fifth *t*, Sanballat sent me
6:17 At that same *t*, however, many letters
9:27 But in the *t* of their oppression they
9:32 *t* of the kings of Assyria until this day!
12:22 In the *t* of Eliashib, Joiada, Johanan
12:23 of Chronicles, up until the *t* of Johanan,
12:26 All these lived in the *t* of Joiakim,
12:26 son of Jozadak [and in the *t* of Nehemiah
12:44 At that *t* men were appointed over the
13: 1 At that *t*, when there was reading from
13: 6 all this *t* I had not been in Jerusalem,
13: 6 After due *t*, however, I asked leave
13:21 From that *t* on, they did not return
Tb 2:11 At that *t* my wife Anna worked for hire at
3:11 At that *t*, then, she spread out her hands,
3:15 relative whom I might bide my *t* to marry.
3:16 At that very *t*, the prayer of these two
10: 1 *t* Tobiah would need to go and to return.
10:13 cause her grief at any *t* in your life.
12:14 At the same *t*, however, God
14: 4 shall take place in the *t* appointed for it.
Jdt 1: 1 At that *t* Arphaxad ruled over the Medes in
2:27 of Damascus at the *t* of the wheat harvest,
5: 8 to Mesopotamia and dwelt there a long *t*.
5:16 and they lived in these mountains a long *t*.
8: 2 had died at the *t* of the barley harvest.
8:11 within that *t* the Lord comes to our aid,
8:15 to protect us at such *t* as he pleases,
12:16 *t* to seduce her from the day he saw her.
12:18 for at no *t* since I was born have I ever
13: 5 now is the *t* for aiding your heritage and
14: 8 left till the *t* she began speaking to them.
16:22 *t* of the death and burial of her husband,
16:25 of Judith and for a long *t* after her death,
Est 1: 5 At the end of this *t* the king gave a feast
2:19 *t* the virgins had been brought together,
2:19 was passing his *t* at the king's gate,
2:21 *t* that Mordecai spent at the king's gate,
4:14 Who knows but that it was for a *t* like
4:23 the *t* of our distress and give me courage.
8: 9 At that *t*, on the twenty-third day
9:24 for the *t* of their defeat and destruction.
9:27 by this letter, and at the *t* appointed.
9:31 were established, for their appointed *t*,
11: 8 lots were fulfilled in the hour, the *t*,
1Mc 2:25 At the same *t*, he also killed the messenger
2:49 When the *t* came for Mattathias to die,
2:49 it is a *t* of disaster and violent anger.
3:49 who had completed the *t* of their vows.
4:60 At that *t* they built high walls and strong
5:55 During the *t* that Judas and Jonathan were
5:67 At that *t* some priests fell in battle who
6:52 their own, and kept up the fight a long *t*.
7:50 for a short *t* the land of Judah was quiet.
9: 7 he had no *t* to gather them together.
9:10 If our *t* has come, let us die bravely
9:27 since the *t* prophets ceased to appear
9:55 Just at that *t* he had a stroke,
10:77 at the same *t* he advanced into the plain,
11:14 King Alexander was in Cilicia at that *t*,
11:20 At that *t* Jonathan gathered together the
11:48 men in the city, which, at the same *t*,

12:10 long *t* has passed since your mission to us.
12:25 giving them no *t* to enter his province.
13: 5 to save my own life in any *t* of distress,
14:36 " 'In his *t* and under his guidance they
15: 8 be canceled for you, now and for all *t*.
15:33 a *t* had been unjustly held by our enemies.
16:24 from the *t* that he succeeded his father as
2Mc 1: 5 and never forsake you in *t* of adversity.
1:19 devout priests of the *t* took some of the
1:22 When this was done and in *t* the sun,
2: 8 just as it appeared in the *t* of Moses and
3: 5 who at that *t* was governor of Coelesyria
5: 1 About this *t* Antiochus sent his second
6:26 Even if, for the *t* being,
7:26 After he had urged her for a long *t*,
7:29 so that in the *t* of mercy I may receive
8:14 and at the same *t* besought the Lord to
8:19 both the *t* of Sennacherib,
8:20 and the *t* of the battle in Babylonia
8:25 they had pursued the enemy for some *t*,
9: 1 About that *t* Antiochus retreated in
10: 3 sacrifice for the first *t* in two years,
10: 4 and that if they should sin at any *t*,
10:15 At the same *t* the Idumeans,
12:32 they lost no *t* in marching against Gorgias,
12:36 been fighting for a long *t* and were weary,
13: 9 than those they suffered in his father's *t*.
14: 3 incurred defilement at the *t* of the revolt,
14:31 at a *t* when the priests were offering the
15:10 at the same *t* the perfidy of the Gentiles
15:37 possession of the Hebrews from that *t* on,
Jb 8: 7 for in *t* to come you will flourish indeed.
14:13 would fix a *t* for me,
15:32 His stalk shall wither before its *t*,
20: 4 Do you not know this from olden *t*,
22:16 men, Who were snatched away before their *t*;
27:19 He lies down a rich man, one last *t*;
32: 4 Elihu bided his *t* before addressing Job.
34:23 of his *t* to come before God in judgment.
39: 2 and fix the *t* of their bringing forth?
40:27 Will he then plead with you, *t* after time,
Ps(s) 20: 2 The LORD answer you in *t* of distress;
32: 6 faithful man pray to you in *t* of stress.
37:19 They are not put to shame in an evil *t*;
37:39 he is their refuge in *t* of distress.
50:15 Then call upon me in *t* of distress;
69:14 to you, O LORD, for the *t* of your favor,
75: 3 "When I seize the appointed *t*,
102:14 mercy on Zion, for it is *t* to pity her,
102:14 to pity her, for the appointed *t* has come.
104:27 all look to you to give them food in due *t*.
119:126 It is *t* for the LORD to act:
Prv 7: 9 dusk of day, at the *t* of the dark of night.
17:17 and a brother is born for the *t* of stress.
24:10 you remain indifferent in *t* of adversity,
25:11 settings are words spoken at the proper *t*.
25:19 on] a faithless man in *t* of trouble.
29:11 but by biding his *t*, the wise man calms it.
Eccl 3: 1 *t* for everything, and a time for every
3: 2 A time to be born, and a *t* to die;
3: 2 time to plant, and a *t* to uproot the plant.
3: 3 A time to kill, and a *t* to heal;
3: 3 a time to tear down, and a *t* to build.
3: 4 A time to weep, and a *t* to laugh;
3: 4 a time to mourn, and a *t* to dance.
3: 5 time to scatter stones, and a *t* to gather
3: 5 time to embrace, and a *t* to be far from
3: 6 A time to seek, and a *t* to lose;
3: 6 a time to keep, and a *t* to cast away.
3: 7 A time to rend, and a *t* to sew;
3: 7 a time to be silent, and a *t* to speak.
3: 8 A time to love, and a *t* to hate;
3: 8 a time of war, and a *t* of peace.
3:11 has made everything appropriate to its *t*,
3:17 since there is a *t* for every affair and on
7:17 Why should you die before your *t*?"
8: 6 there is a *t* and a judgment for everything."
9:11 for a *t* of calamity comes to all alike.
9:12 his own *t* than fish taken in the fatal net,
9:12 when the evil *t* falls suddenly upon them.
10:17 *t* (for vigor and not in drinking bouts).
11: 1 after a long *t* you may find it again.
Sg 2: 7 do not stir up love before its own *t*.
2:12 the *t* of pruning the vines has come,
3: 5 do not stir up love before its own *t*.
8: 4 do not stir up love, before its own *t*.
Wis 2: 4 Even our name will be forgotten in *t*,
2:10 old man for his hair grown white with *t*.
3: 7 the *t* of their visitation they shall shine,
4: 4 though their branches flourish for a *t*,
4: 8 honorable comes not with the passing of *t*,
12:20 *t* and opportunity to abandon wickedness,
13:13 he takes and carves to occupy his spare *t*.
14:16 Then, in *t*, the impious practice gained
16: 6 for a short *t* they were terrorized,
16:25 Therefore at that very *t*, transformed in
18:20 of death touched at one *t* even the just,
19:22 stood by them in every *t* and circumstance.
Sir 1:20 patient man need stand firm but for a *t*,
2: 2 steadfast, undisturbed in *t* of adversity.
2:11 he forgives sins, he saves in *t* of trouble.
3:15 In *t* of tribulation it will be recalled to
4:20 Use your *t* well; guard yourself from evil,

4:23 Refrain not from speaking at the proper *t*,
4:31 receive and clenched when it is *t* to give.
5: 4 for the LORD bides his *t*.
5: 9 at the *t* of vengeance,
6: 8 he will not be with you in *t* of distress.
8: 9 the knowledge how to answer in *t* of need,
10:25 affairs, and boast not in your *t* of need.
11:22 man, and in due *t* his hopes bear fruit.
14:12 have you been told the grave's appointed *t*.
16:25 He ordered for all *t* what they were to do
18:19 the *t* of visitation you will have a ransom.
18:24 *t* of vengeance when he will hide his face.
18:25 the *t* of hunger in the time of plenty,
19: 8 it against you, and in *t* become your enemy.
20: 5 another is silent, biding his *t*.
20: 6 wise man is silent till the right *t* comes,
20: 6 but a boasting fool ignores the proper *t*.
20:19 for he does not utter it at the proper *t*.
22: 6 song in *t* of mourning is inopportune talk,
22:23 In *t* of trouble remain true to him,
24:24 like the Jordan at harvest *t*.
24:25 knowledge, like the Gihon at vintage *t*.
27:12 Limit the *t* you spend among fools,
31:28 are wine drunk freely at the proper *t*.
32: 4 and flaunt not your wisdom at the wrong *t*.
32:11 When it is *t* to leave,
33:24 the *t* of death distribute your inheritance.
35:24 *t* of distress as rain clouds in *t* of drought.
36: 7 Hasten the day, bring on the *t*;
37: 4 but in *t* of trouble he stands afar off.
39:16 in its own *t* every need is supplied.
39:29 his treasury also, kept for the proper *t*,
39:34 for each shows its worth at the proper *t*.
42:12 men, or spend her *t* with married women;
44: 1 men, our ancestors, each in his own *t*:
44: 7 All these were glorious in their *t*,
44:13 And for all *t* their progeny will endure,
44:17 renewed the race in the *t* of devastation.
45:13 generation after generation, for all *t*.
45:26 or your authority, throughout all *t*.
48:10 in *t* to come to put an end to wrath before
48:25 foretold what should be till the end of *t*,
49:12 In their *t* they built the house of God;
50: 1 In whose *t* the house of God was renovated,
50: 2 In his *t* also the wall was built with
50: 3 In his *t* the reservoir was dug,
51:10 Do not abandon me in *t* of trouble,
51:12 kind and preserved me in *t* of trouble.
51:16 In the short *t* I paid heed,
51:30 in his own *t* God will give you your reward.
Is 7:15 by the *t* he learns to reject the bad
13:22 Her *t* is near at hand and her days shall
18: 4 sunshine, like a cloud of dew at harvest *t*.
19:17 Every *t* they remember Judah,
27: 8 them off with my cruel wind in *t* of storm.
33: 2 morning, our salvation in *t* of trouble!
39: 1 At that *t* when Merodach-baladan,
42:23 listens and pays heed for the *t* to come?
48:16 At the *t* it comes to pass,
49: 8 In a *t* of favor I answer you,
60:22 accomplish these things when their *t* comes.
Jer 1:13 A second *t* the word of the LORD came to me
2:27 yet, in their *t* of trouble they cry out,
2:28 Will they save you in your *t* of trouble?
3:17 At that *t* they will call Jerusalem the
4:11 At that *t* it will be said of this people
5:24 gives us rain early and late, in its *t*;
6:15 their *t* of punishment they shall go down,
8: 1 At that *t*, says the LORD,
8: 7 and thrush observe their *t* of return,
8:12 their *t* of punishment they shall go down,
8:15 for a *t* of healing, but terror comes
10:15 they will perish in their *t* of punishment.
10:18 this *t* I will sing away the inhabitants of
11:14 call to me at the *t* of their misfortune.
11:18 at that *t* you, O LORD, showed me
13: 3 *t* the word of the LORD came to me thus:
14: 8 of Israel, O LORD, our savior in *t* of need!
14:19 for a *t* of healing, but terror comes
15:11 you in the *t* of misfortune and anguish?
16:21 this *t* I will leave them in no doubt Of my
18:23 against them in the *t* of your anger.
23:20 When the *t* comes,
25:34 The *t* for your slaughter has come;
27: 7 and his grandson, until the *t* of his land,
28:12 Some *t* after the prophet Hananiah had
29:28 It will be a long *t*;
30: 7 A *t* of distress for Jacob,
30:24 When the *t* comes, you will fully
31: 1 At that *t*, says the LORD,
32: 2 At that *t* the army of the king of Babylon
32:14 so that they can be kept there a long *t*.
33: 1 LORD came to Jeremiah a second *t*
33:15 In those days, in that *t*,
36:23 Each *t* Jehudi finished reading three or
37: 4 At this *t* Jeremiah had not yet been put
37:16 dungeon, where he remained a long *t*.
39:10 given at the same *t* vineyards and farms.
46:17 the name "The noise that let its *t* go by."
46:21 comes upon them, the *t* of their punishment.
50: 4 In those days, at that *t*,
50:16 and him who wields the sickle in harvest *t*!
50:20 In those days, at that *t*, says the LORD:

TIME (cont.)

50:27 day has come, the *t* of their punishment.
50:31 day has come, the *t* for me to punish you.
51: 6 This is a *t* of vengeance for the LORD,
51:18 that will perish in their *t* of punishment.
51:33 a threshing floor at the *t* it is trodden;
51:33 while, and the harvest *t* will come for her.
Lam 4:18 our *t* had expired.
5:20 you forget us, abandon us so long a *t*?
Bar 1: 2 at the *t* when the Chaldeans took Jerusalem
1:19 From the *t* the Lord led our fathers out of
1:20 at the *t* he led our fathers forth from the
3: 5 at this *t* not the misdeeds of our fathers,
3:32 He who established the earth for all *t*,
4:35 her from the Eternal God, for a long *t*,
4:35 demons shall dwell in her from that *t* on.
Ez 7: 7 The *t* has come, near is the day:
7: 7 a *t* of consternation, not of rejoicing.
7:12 The *t* has come, the day dawns.
16:47 in a very short *t* you became more corrupt
22: 3 within herself so that her *t* has come,
22:24 is, not rained on] at the *t* of my fury.
35: 5 of the sword at the *t* of their trouble,
38:10 that *t* thoughts shall arise in your mind,
Dn 1:18 At the end of the *t* the king had specified
2: 8 for certain that you are bargaining for *t*,
2:16 Daniel went and asked for *t* from the king,
4:33 At the same *t* my reason returned to me,
7:12 prolongation of life for a *t* and a season.
7:22 and the *t* came when the holy ones
8:17 man, that the vision refers to the end *t*."
8:19 for at the appointed *t*, there will be an end.
9:21 flight at the *t* of the evening sacrifice.
9:25 streets and trenches, in *t* of affliction.
11:24 but only for a *t*.
11:29 At the *t* appointed he shall come again to
11:29 but this *t* it shall not be as before.
11:33 a *t* they will become victims of the sword,
11:35 the end *t* which is still appointed to come.
11:40 "At the appointed *t* the king of the south
12: 1 "At that *t* there shall arise Michael,
12: 1 It shall be a *t* unsurpassed in distress
12: 1 distress since nations began until that *t*.
12: 1 At that *t* your people shall escape,
12: 4 message and seal the book until the end *t*;
12: 9 be kept secret and sealed until the end *t*.
12:11 From the *t* that the daily sacrifice is
13:13 us be off for home, it is *t* for lunch."
Hos 2:11 I will take back my grain in its *t*,
10:12 a new field, for it is *t* to seek the LORD,
10:14 As Salman ravaged Beth-arbel in *t* of war,
12:10 you live in tents, as in that appointed *t*.
13:13 For when it is *t* he shall not present
Jl 4: 1 Yes, in those days, and at that *t*,
Am 1:14 of battle and stormwind in a *t* of tempest.
5:13 silent at this time, for it is an evil *t*.
8: 2 The *t* is ripe to have done with my people
Jon 3: 1 word of the LORD came to Jonah a second *t*:
Mi 2: 3 with head high, for it will be a *t* of evil.
3: 4 shall he hide his face from them at that *t*,
5: 2 *t* when she who is to give birth has borne,
7: 4 now is the *t* of your confusion.
Na 1: 9 The enemy shall not rise a second *t*;
Hb 2: 3 For the vision still has its *t*,
Zep 1:12 that *t* I will explore Jerusalem with lamps;
3:19 *t* I will deal with all who oppress you;
3:20 *t* I will bring you home, and at that time
Hg 1: 2 *t* come to rebuild the house of the LORD.
1: 4 Is it *t* for you to dwell in your own
2:20 The message of the LORD came a second *t* to
Zec 11:15 This *t* take the gear of a foolish shepherd.
14: 7 for in the evening *t* there shall be light.
Mt 1:11 brothers at the *t* of the Babylonian exile.
1:25 with her at any *t* before she bore a son,
2: 7 them the exact *t* of the star's appearance.
3: 5 At that *t* Jerusalem, all Judea,
4:17 *t* on Jesus began to proclaim this theme:
5:25 Lose no *t*; settle with your opponent
7: 4 all the *t* the plank remains in your own?
8:29 come to torture us before the appointed *t*?"
11:12 From John the Baptizer's *t* until now the
11:19 Yet *t* will prove where wisdom lies."
12:45 this *t* seven spirits more evil than itself.
13:21 he has no roots, so he lasts only for a *t*.
13:30 at harvest *t* I will order the harvesters,
13:54 his *t* teaching them in their synagogue.
17:25 house asked, without giving him *t* to speak:
18:29 give me *t* and I will pay you back in full.'
19:16 Another *t* a man came up to him and said,
21:34 When vintage *t* arrived he dispatched his
21:36 A second *t* he dispatched even more slaves
21:41 see to it that he has grapes at vintage *t*."
22: 4 A second *t* he sent other servants, saying:
23:30 'Had we lived in our forefathers' *t* we
23:39 see me from this *t* on until you declare,
24:23 If anyone tells you at that *t*,
24:37 Man will repeat what happened in Noah's *t*.
24:44 of Man is coming at the *t* you least expect.
24:48 himself, 'My master is a long *t* in coming,'
26: 2 that in two days' *t* it will be Passover,
26: 3 At that *t* the chief priests and elders of
26:16 and from that *t* on he kept looking for an
26:18 Teacher says, My appointed *t* draws near.
26:42 Withdrawing a second *t*, he began to pray:
26:44 somewhat, and began to pray a third *t*,
26:55 At that very *t* Jesus said to the crowd:
27:16 the *t* a notorious prisoner named Barabbas.
Mk 1: 9 During that *t*, Jesus came from Nazareth
1:15 "This is the *t* of fulfillment.
2:13 Another *t*, while he went walking
4:22 hidden only to be revealed at a later *t*;
4:24 He said to them another *t*:
4:29 the sickle, for the *t* is ripe for harvest.'"
6: 6 villages instead, and spent his *t* teaching.
6:48 *t* was between three and six in the morning.
8: 1 about that *t* another large crowd assembled,
8:25 a second *t* Jesus laid hands on his eyes,
9:39 my name can at the same *t* speak ill of me.
11:13 it was not the *t* for figs.
11:18 They were at the same *t* afraid of him
12: 2 In due *t* he dispatched a man in his
12: 4 The second *t* he sent them another servant;
13:19 of creation and now, and for all *t* to come.
13:21 If anyone tells you at that *t*,
13:33 do not know when the appointed *t* will come.
14: 1 Bread were to be observed in two days' *t*,
14:33 at the same *t* he took along with him Peter,
14:41 He returned a third *t* and said to them,
15:16 the same *t* they assembled the whole cohort.
15:34 At that *t* Jesus cried in a loud voice,
Lk 1:23 when his *t* of priestly service was over,
1:57 When Elizabeth's *t* for delivery arrived,
2:25 at the *t* a certain man named Simeon.
4: 2 During that *t* he ate nothing,
4:27 in Israel in the *t* of Elisha the prophet;
7:21 *t* he was curing many of their diseases,
8:13 a while, but fall away in *t* of temptation.
8:27 For a long *t* he had not worn any clothes;
8:29 This spirit had taken hold of him many a *t*.
9:36 of what they had seen at that *t* to anyone.
9:51 As the *t* approached when he was to be
12:45 'My master is taking his *t* about coming,'
12:46 not expect him, at a *t* he does not know.
12:56 why can you not interpret the present *t*?
13: 1 At that *t*, some were present who told him
13:35 not see me until the *t* comes when you say,
14:17 At dinner *t* he sent his servant to say to
14:22 The servant reported, after some *t*,
16: 1 Another *t* he said to his disciples:
16:16 From his *t* on, the good news of God's
17:22 "A *t* will come when you will long to see
18: 4 For a *t* he refused, but finally he thought,
19:44 to recognize the *t* of your visitation."
20: 9 tenant farmers, and went away for a long *t*.
20:10 At vintage *t* he sent a servant to the
21: 8 saying, 'I am he' and 'The *t* is at hand.'
21:21 Judea at the *t* must flee to the mountains;
23: 7 also happened to be in Jerusalem at the *t*.
23: 8 him he had wanted for a long *t* to see him,
23:22 He said to them for the third *t*,
Jn 3:22 he spent some *t* with them there baptizing.
4:52 at what *t* the boy had shown improvement,
5: 6 who knew he had been sick a long *t*,
5: 7 By the *t* I get there,
6:17 By this *t* it was dark,
6:66 From this *t* on, many of his disciples
7: 6 not yet the right *t* for me, whereas the *t*
7: 8 because the *t* is not yet ripe for me."
7:14 The feast was half over by the *t* Jesus
8: 8 *t* he bent down and wrote on the ground.
9:24 A second *t* they summoned the man who had
10:22 and the *t* came for the feast of the
14: 9 "after I have been with you all this *t*,
16: 2 a *t* will come when anyone who puts you to
16:16 Within a short *t* you will lose sight of me,
16:17 a short *t* you will lose sight of me,
16:18 "What does he mean by this 'short *t*'?
16:19 a short *t* you will lose sight of me,
16:20 you will grieve for a *t*,
16:21 is in labor she is sad that her *t* has come.
16:22 In the same way, you are sad for a *t*,
16:25 A *t* will come when I shall no longer do so,
18:39 I release someone to you at Passover *t*.
19: 4 went out a second *t* and said to the crowd:
20:26 the room, and this *t* Thomas was with them.
21:14 This marked the third *t* that Jesus
21:16 A second *t* he put his question,
21:17 A third *t*, Jesus asked him, "Simon, son
21:17 was hurt because he had asked a third *t*,
Acts 1: 3 In the *t* after his suffering he showed
1: 7 "The exact *t* it is not yours to know.
2: 5 Staying in Jerusalem at the *t* were devout
3:21 Jesus must remain in heaven until the *t* of
5:37 Judas the Galilean at the *t* of the census.
6: 7 while at the same *t* a number of the
7:13 The second *t*, Joseph made himself known
7:17 "When the *t* drew near for the fulfillment
7:20 "It was at this *t* that Moses was born.
7:45 So it was until the *t* of David,
9: 4 and at the same *t* heard a voice saying,
9: 9 during which *t* he neither ate nor drank.
9:23 After quite some *t* has passed,
9:31 at the same *t* it enjoyed the increased
9:37 At about that *t* she fell ill and died.
9:43 for a considerable *t* at the house of Simon,
10:15 The voice was heard a second *t*:
11: 9 *t* the voice from the heavens spoke out:
11:26 were called Christians for the first *t*.
11:27 At about that *t*, certain prophets came
12:11 Peter had recovered his senses by this *t*,
12:19 left Judea to spend some *t* in Caesarea.
13:11 For a *t* you shall be blind,
13:20 them until the *t* of the prophet Samuel.
14: 3 *t* there and spoke out fearlessly,
14:28 they spent some *t* there with the disciples.
15:33 After passing some *t* there,
15:36 After a certain *t* Paul said to Barnabas,
16:13 We spent some *t* in that city.
17:32 must hear you on this topic some other *t*."
18:23 spending some *t* there he set out again,
19:14 Another *t*, when the seven sons of Sceva,
19:22 while he himself stayed on for a *t* in Asia.
19:23 At about that *t* a serious disturbance
20:16 past Ephesus so as not to lose *t* in Asia,
21: 5 Then, when our *t* was up,
21:26 at which *t* the offering was to be made for
21:38 Egyptian who caused the riot some *t* ago
24: 4 But now, lest I impose on your *t* unduly,
24: 6 our temple, but we apprehended him in *t*.
24:14 At the same *t*, I believe all that is written
24:25 I'll send for you again when I find the *t*."
24:26 At the same *t*, he hoped he would be
26: 5 with me for a long *t* and can testify,
26:11 Many a *t*, in synagogue after synagogue,
27: 9 Much *t* had now gone by.
27:21 *t* when Paul stood up among them and said:
27:40 *t* they untied the guy-ropes of the rudders,
28: 6 After waiting for quite some *t*,
Rom 5: 6 At the appointed *t*, when we were still
9: 9 "I will return at this *t*, and Sarah shall
11: 5 in the present *t* there is a remnant chosen
13:11 for you know the *t* in which we are living.
15: 4 our *t* was written for our instruction,
1Cor 4: 5 judgment before the *t* of his return.
4: 5 At that *t*, everyone will receive his praise
7: 5 unless perhaps by mutual consent for a *t*,
7:26 In the present *t* of stress it seems good
7:29 I tell you, brothers, the *t* is short.
11:26 Every *t*, then, you eat this bread
16: 6 should like to remain with you for some *t*—
16: 7 I hope to spend some *t* with you,
16: 9 but at the same *t* there are many opposed.
16:12 but he did not wish to go at this *t*.
2Cor 1:13 you will in *t* come to know us well,
4:16 our body is being destroyed at the same *t*.
5:16 If at one *t* we so regarded Christ,
6: 2 "In an acceptable *t* I have heard you;
6: 2 Now is the acceptable *t*!
7: 8 that the letter caused you grief for a *t*),
8:14 Your plenty at the present *t* should supply
10: 9 At the same *t*, I do not wish to intimidate
12:14 the third *t* that I am about to visit you,
13: 1 is the third *t* I shall be coming to you.
13: 2 said before when I was there the second *t*—
Gal 1:15 But the *t* came when he who had set me
2: 1 with Barnabas, this *t* taking Titus with me.
4: 2 until the *t* set by his father.
4: 4 but when the designated *t* had come,
4:25 and corresponds to the Jerusalem of our *t*,
5: 1 yourselves the yoke of slavery a second *t*!
6: 9 in due *t* we shall reap our harvest.
Eph 1:10 to be carried out in the fullness of *t*:
1:15 from the *t* I first heard of your faith in
5: 8 There was a *t* when you were darkness,
Phil 1: 3 thanks to my God every *t* I think of you
3:18 this *t* I say it with tears.
1Thes 2: 9 how we worked day and night all the *t* we
2:16 All this *t* they have been "filling up
2:17 orphaned by separation from you for a *t*—
2Thes 2: 6 until he shall be revealed in his own *t*.
1Tm 2: 6 This truth was attested at the fitting *t*.
6:15 God will bring to pass at his chosen *t*.
2Tm 4: 3 For the *t* will come when people will not
4: 6 The *t* of my dissolution is near.
Ti 1: 3 manifested in his own good *t* as his word,
3:10 Warn a heretic once and then a second *t*;
Heb 4:16 and favor and to find help in *t* of need.
5:12 by this *t* you should be teaching others,
9: 9 This is a symbol of the present *t*,
9:10 imposed until the *t* of the new order.
9:28 he will appear a second *t* not to take away
11:32 I have no *t* to tell of Gideon,
12:11 At the *t* it is administered, all discipline
Jas 2: 2 at the same *t* a poor man in shabby clothes.
1Pt 1: 6 You may for a *t* have to suffer the
2:25 At one *t* you were straying like sheep,
3:20 At that *t*, a few persons, eight in all,
4: 3 devoted enough *t* to what the pagans enjoy,
5: 6 so that in due *t* he may lift you high.
2Pt 2: 3 condemnation has not lain idle all this *t*,
Rv 1: 3 written in it, for the appointed *t* is near!
1:19 what you see now and will see in *t* to come.
2:13 have in me, not even at the *t* when Antipas,
3: 3 you like a thief, at a *t* you cannot know.
3:10 I will keep you safe in the *t* of trial
4: 1 show you what must take place in *t* to come."
6: 5 This *t* I saw a black horse,
9: 6 During that *t* these men will seek death
10: 7 When the *t* comes for the seventh angel to

11: 6 will fall during the *t* of their mission.
11:18 The *t* to reward your servants the prophets
11:18 The *t* to destroy those who lay the earth
12:12 no limits, for he knows his *t* is short."
14: 7 for his *t* has come to sit in judgment.
14:15 down the harvest, for now is the *t* to reap;
16:18 in all the *t* men have lived on the earth.
20: 3 the dragon is to be released for a short *t*.
22:10 of this book, for the appointed *t* is near!

TIME-SPAN (1)

Gn 15:16 fourth *t* the others shall come back here;

TIME-WASTERS (1)

1Tm 5:13 only *t* but gossips and busybodies as well,

TIMELESS (2)

Dt 33:15 mountains and the best from the *t* hills;
Eccl 3:11 time, and has put the *t* into their hearts,

TIMELY (1)

Sir 40:23 A friend, a neighbor, are *t* guides,

TIMES (163)

Gn 1:14 Let them mark the fixed *t*,
33: 3 of them, bowing to the ground seven *t*,
43:34 was five *t* as large as anyone else's.
Ex 23:14 "Three *t* a year you shall celebrate a
34:23 Three *t* a year all your men shall appear
34:24 three *t* a year to appear before the LORD,
Lv 4: 6 shall sprinkle it seven *t* before the LORD,
4:17 shall sprinkle it seven *t* before the LORD,
8:11 some of this oil seven *t* on the altar,
14: 7 *t* the man to be purified from his leprosy.
14:16 shall sprinkle it seven *t* before the LORD.
14:27 sprinkle it seven *t* before the LORD.
14:51 water, and sprinkle the house seven *t*.
16:14 seven *t* in front of the propitiatory.
16:19 sprinkle some of the blood on it seven *t*.
25: 8 seven *t* seven years
26:24 for your sins seven *t* harder than before.
Nm 14:22 *t* already and have failed to heed my voice,
19: 4 *t* toward the front of the meeting tent.
22:28 you that you should beat me these three *t*?"
22:32 have you beaten your ass these three *t*?
22:33 me, she turned away from me these three *t*.
24:10 *t* now you have even blessed them instead!
28: 2 At the *t* I have appointed,
Dt 1:11 fathers, increase you a thousand *t* over,
16:16 "Three *t* a year, then, every male among
28:33 and crushed at all *t* without surcease,
Jos 6: 4 seventh day march around the city seven *t*,
6:15 around the city seven *t* in the same manner;
6:15 did they march around the city seven *t*.
24: 2 In *t* past your fathers, down to Terah,
Jgs 16:15 Three *t* already you have mocked me,
1Sm 9: 9 (In former *t* in Israel,
18:10 attendance, playing the harp as at other *t*,
20:41 ground three *t* before Jonathan in homage.
1Kgs 9:25 Three *t* a year Solomon used to offer
17:21 child three *t* and called out to the LORD:
18:43 Seven *t* he said, "Go look again!"
22:16 "How many *t* must I adjure you to tell me
2Kgs 4:35 now sneezed seven *t* and opened his eyes.
5:10 "Go and wash seven *t* in the Jordan,
5:14 seven *t* at the word of the man of God.
6:10 This happened several *t*.
13:18 He struck the ground three *t* and stopped.
13:19 "You should have struck five or six *t*;
13:19 Now, you will defeat Aram only three *t*."
13:25 Joash defeated Ben-hadad three *t*,
1Chr 9:20 of Eleazar, had been their chief in *t* past
12:33 the *t* and who knew what Israel had to do:
2Chr 8:12 In those *t* Solomon offered holocausts to
8:13 and on the fixed festivals three *t* a year:
8:17 In those *t* Solomon went to Ezion-geber and
18:15 "How many *t* must I adjure you to tell me
Ezr 4:15 has been fostered there since ancient *t*.
4:19 it was verified that from ancient *t* this
10:14 women for wives appear at appointed *t*,
Neh 4: 6 *t* over that they were about to attack us,
6: 4 Four *t* they sent me this same proposal,
9:28 them according to your mercy, many *t* over.
10:35 of our family houses at stated *t* each year,
12:46 the days of David and Asaph in *t* of old.
13:31 wood at stated *t* and for the first fruits.
Tb 3: 8 You have already been married seven *t*,
4:19 At all *t* bless the Lord God,
5: 6 "Yes, I have been there many *t*.
6:14 woman has already been married seven *t*,
14: 5 when the appointed *t* shall be completed.
14: 9 to be mindful of God and at all *t* to bless
1Mc 1:36 and a wicked adversary to Israel at all *t*.
2:51 the deeds that our fathers did in their *t*,
12: 1 When Jonathan saw that the *t* favored him,
14: 9 the squares, all talking about the good *t*,
16: 2 and many *t* we succeeded in saving Israel.
2Mc 8:19 *t* when help had been given their ancestors;
9:16 restore all the sacred vessels many *t* over;
12:30 kind treatment even in *t* of adversity,
Jb 9: 3 could not answer him once in a thousand *t*.
16: 2 I have heard this sort of thing many *t*.
19: 3 These ten *t* you have reviled me,
24: 1 Why are not *t* set by the Almighty,
38:23 hail Which I have reserved for *t* of stress,
Ps(s) 4: 7 Many say, "Oh, that we might see better *t*!"
9:10 oppressed, a stronghold in *t* of distress.
10: 1 Why hide in *t* of distress?
10: 5 His ways are secure at all *t*;
34: 2 I will bless the LORD at all *t*; his praise
42: 5 Those *t* I recall, now that I pour out my
62: 9 Trust in him at all *t*, O my people!
106:43 Many *t* did he rescue them,
119:20 with longing for your ordinances at all *t*.
119:164 Seven *t* a day I praise you for your just
Prv 24:16 the just man falls seven *t* and rises again,
Eccl 7:10 is it that former *t* were better than these?
7:22 that you have many *t* spoken ill of others.
8: 5 the wise man's heart knows *t* and judgments;
8:12 sinner does evil a hundred *t* and survives.
9: 8 At all *t* let your garments be white,
Wis 7:18 and the end and the midpoint of *t*,
8: 8 in advance and the outcome of *t* and ages.
17: 6 *t* when that sight was no longer to be seen.
Sir 13: 7 then twice or three *t* he will terrify you;
20:11 for little, but pay for it seven *t* over.
20:16 How many *t* they laugh him to scorn!
22: 6 lashes and discipline are at all *t* wisdom.
23:19 LORD, ten thousand *t* brighter than the sun,
38:13 There are *t* that give him an advantage,
40: 8 with beast, but for sinners seven *t* more.
40:24 A brother, a helper, for *t* of stress;
43: 6 The moon, too, that marks the changing *t*,
48: 3 the heavens and three *t* brought down fire.
49: 3 his whole heart, and, though *t* were evil,
Is 16:13 of the LORD spoke against Moab in *t* past.
30:26 *t* greater [like the light of seven days].
Jer 46:26 shall be inhabited again, as in *t* past,
Bar 4:28 God, turn now ten *t* the more to seek him;
Ez 16:25 passer-by, playing the harlot countless *t*.
16:26 so many *t* that I was provoked to anger.
38:17 I spoke in ancient *t* through my servants,
39:26 and all the *t* they broke faith with me,
Dn 1:20 he found them ten *t* better than all the
2:21 He causes the changes of the *t* and seasons,
3:19 furnace to be heated seven *t* more
6:11 his God in the upper chamber three *t* a day,
6:14 three *t* a day he offers his prayer."
11:14 *t* many shall resist the king of the south,
Mi 5: 1 origin is from of old, from ancient *t*.
Mt 16: 3 can you not read the signs of the *t*
18:21 how often must I forgive him? Seven *t*?"
18:22 "No," Jesus replied, "not seven *t*;
18:22 I say, seventy *t* seven times.
19:29 *t* as much and inherit everlasting life.
26:34 crows tonight you will deny me three *t*."
26:75 the cock crows, you will deny me three *t*."
Mk 10:30 this present age a hundred *t* as many homes,
13:19 Those *t* will be more distressful than any
14:30 cock crows twice, you will deny me three *t*."
14:72 cock crows twice you will deny me three *t*."
Lk 1:70 his holy ones, the prophets of ancient *t*:
17: 4 seven times a day, and seven *t* a day
21:24 until the *t* of the Gentiles are fulfilled.
22:34 you have three *t* denied that you know me."
22:61 cock crows today you will deny me three *t*."
Jn 13:38 crow before you have three *t* disowned me!
Acts 10:16 This happened three *t*; then the object
11:10 This happened three *t*; then the canvas
2Cor 11:24 Five *t* at the hands of the Jews I received
11:25 three *t* I was beaten with rods;
11:25 I was stoned once, shipwrecked three *t*;
12: 8 Three *t* I begged the Lord that this might
Gal 4:18 be courted for the right reasons at all *t*,
Eph 2:12 remember that, in former *t*, you had no
1Thes 5: 1 As regards specific *t* and moments,
1Tm 4: 1 Spirit distinctly says that in later *t* some
2Tm 3: 1 there will be terrible *t* in the last days.
Heb 1: 1 In *t* past, God spoke in fragmentary
10:33 At *t* you were publicly exposed to insult
10:33 at other *t* you associated yourselves with
1Pt 1:11 They investigated the *t* and the
2Pt 2: 1 In *t* past there were false prophets among
Rv 2:19 efforts of recent *t* are greater than ever.
22: 2 life which produce fruit twelve *t* a year,

TIMID (2)

Wis 9:14 For the deliberations of mortals are *t*,
Sir 22:18 Neither can a *t* resolve based on foolish

TIMNA (6)

Gn 36:12 (Esau's son Eliphaz had a concubine *T*,
36:22 Hori and Hemam, and Lotan's sister was *T*.
36:40 the clans of *T*, Alvah, Jetheth,
1Chr 1:36 Omar, Zephi, Gatam, Kenaz, *T* and Amalek.
1:39 *T* was the sister of Lotan.
1:51 the chiefs of *T*, Aliah, Jetheth

TIMNAH (11)

Gn 38:12 went up to *T* for the shearing of his sheep,
38:13 was on his way up to *T* to shear his sheep,
38:14 to Enaim, which is on the way to *T*;
Jos 15:10 to Beth-shemesh, and ran across to *T*.
15:57 Jokdeam, Zanoah, Kain, Gibbeah and *T*;
19:43 Shaalabbin, Aijalon, Ithlah, Elon, *T*,
Jgs 14: 1 Samson went down to *T* and saw there one of
14: 2 "There is a Philistine woman I saw in *T*
14: 5 went down to *T* with his father and mother.
14: 5 When they had come to the vineyards of *T*,
2Chr 28:18 its dependencies, *T* and its dependencies,

TIMNAH-SERAH (1)

Jos 19:50 *T* in the mountain region of Ephraim.

TIMNATH (1)

1Mc 9:50 as well as Emmaus, Beth-horon, Bethel, *T*,

TIMNATH-HERES (1)

Jgs 2: 9 within the borders of his heritage at *T*

TIMNATH-SERAH (1)

Jos 24:30 within the limits of his heritage at *T*

TIMNITE (1)

Jgs 15: 6 told, "Samson, the son-in-law of the *T*,

TIMON (1)

Acts 6: 5 Philip, Prochorus, Nicanor, *T*,

TIMOTHY (40)

1Mc 5: 6 body of people with *T* as their leader.
5:11 *T* is the leader of their army.
5:34 army of *T* realized that it was Maccabeus,
5:37 After these events *T* assembled another
5:40 stream, *T* said to the officers of his army:
2Mc 8:30 challenged the forces of *T* and Bacchides,
10:24 *T*, who had previously been defeated by the
10:32 *T*, however fled to a well-fortified
10:37 *T* had hidden in a cistern,
12: 2 of the local governors, *T* and Apollonius,
12:10 mile from there in the campaign against *T*,
12:18 But they did not find *T* in that region,
12:19 men that *T* had left in the stronghold.
12:20 each cohort, and went in pursuit of *T*;
12:21 When *T* learned of the approach of Judas,
12:24 *T* himself fell into the hands of the men
Acts 16: 1 where there was a disciple named *T*,
17:14 the sea, while Silas and *T* stayed behind.
17:15 and *T* to join him as soon as possible.
18: 5 Silas and *T* came down from Macedonia,
19:22 sent two of his assistants, *T* and Erastus,
20: 4 *T*; Tychicus and Trophimus from Asia.
Rom 16:21 *T*, my fellow worker, sends you his
1Cor 4:17 This is why I have sent you *T*,
16:10 If *T* should come, be sure to put him
2Cor 1: 1 apostle of Jesus Christ, and *T* his brother,
1:19 Jesus Christ, whom Silvanus, *T*,
Phil 1: 1 Paul and *T*, servants of Christ Jesus
2:19 the Lord Jesus, to send *T* to you very soon,
Col 1: 1 by the will of God, and *T* our brother,
1Thes 1: 1 Paul, Silvanus, and *T*, to the church of
3: 2 to remain alone at Athens and send you *T*.
3: 6 since *T* has returned to us from you
2Thes 1: 1 Paul, Silvanus, and *T*,
1Tm 1: 2 our savior and Christ Jesus our hope, to *T*,
1:18 I have a solemn charge to give you, *T*,
6:20 O *T*, guard what has been committed to you.
2Tm 1: 2 proclaim the promise of life in him, to *T*,
Phlm 1: 1 of Christ Jesus, and *T* our brother,
Heb 13:23 know that our brother *T* has been set free.

TIMOTHY'S (3)

2Mc 8:32 They also killed the commander of *T* forces,
9: 3 had happened to Nicanor and to *T* forces.
Phil 2:22 know from experience what *T* qualities are,

TIN (4)

Nm 31:22 as gold, silver, bronze, iron, *t* and lead,
Ez 22:18 All of them are bronze and *t*,
22:20 and *t* are gathered into a furnace and
27:12 your wealth, exchanging silver, iron, *t*,

TINGLE (1)

Jer 19: 3 all who hear of it will feel their ears *t*.

TINKLING (2)

Ex 28:35 that its *t* may be heard as he enters and
Is 3:16 they go, their anklets *t* with every step,

TINY (5)

1Kgs 19:12 the fire there was a *t* whispering sound.
Est F: 3 the *t* spring that grew into a river,
Sir 48:15 But Judah remained, a *t* people,
Jer 30:19 they will not be *t*, for I will glorify them.
Jas 3: 5 See how *t* the spark is that sets a huge

TIP (15)

Ex 29:20 and put on the *t* of Aaron's right ear

TIP (cont.)

Lv 8:23 and put it on the *t* of Aaron's right ear,
14:14 and put it on the *t* of the man's right ear,
14:17 put some on the *t* of the man's right ear,
14:25 and put it on the *t* of the right ear of
14:28 also put on the *t* of the man's right ear,
Jos 13:27 southeastern *t* of the Sea of Chinnereth.
18:19 extended to the northern *t* of the Salt Sea,
Jgs 6:21 stretched out the *t* of the staff he held,
2Sm 6: 6 steadied it, for the oxen were making it *t*.
1Kgs 6:24 wing *t* to wing tip of each was ten cubits.
Ps(s) 66:17 words, praise was on the *t* of my tongue.
Am 3:12 of legs or the *t* of an ear of his sheep,
Lk 16:24 Send Lazarus to dip the *t* of his finger in

TIPHSAH (1)

1Kgs 5: 4 land west of the Euphrates, from *T* to Gaza,

TIPS (2)

Ex 29:20 and on the *t* of his sons' right ears
Lv 8:24 of the blood on the *t* of their right ears,

TIRAS (2)

Gn 10: 2 Magog, Madai, Javan, Tubal, Meshech, and *T*.
1Chr 1: 5 Magog, Madai, Javan, Tubal, Meshech, and *T*.

TIRATHITES (1)

1Chr 2:55 the Sopherim dwelling in Jabez were the *T*,

TIRE (2)

Is 1:14 they weigh me down, I *t* of the load.
Jer 2:24 No beasts need *t* themselves seeking her;

TIRED (9)

Ex 17:12 Moses' hands, however, grew *t*;
2Sm 16:14 with him arrived at the Jordan *t* out,
17:29 hungry and *t* and thirsty in the desert."
21:15 fought the Philistines, but David grew *t*.
23:10 until his hand grew *t* and became cramped,
Jdt 13: 1 they were all *t* from the prolonged banquet.
1Mc 10:81 whereas the enemy's horses became *t* out.
Jer 12:13 they have *t* themselves out to no purpose;
Jn 4: 6 Jesus, *t* from his journey,

TIRHAKAH (2)

2Kgs 19: 9 The king of Assyria heard a report that *T*,
Is 37: 9 The king of Assyria heard a report that *T*,

TIRHANAH (1)

1Chr 2:48 Caleb's concubine, bore Sheber and *T*.

TIRIA (1)

1Chr 4:16 sons of Jehallelel were Ziph, Ziphah, *T*,

TIRZAH (18)

Nm 26:33 were Mahlah, Noah, Hoglah, Milcah and *T*.
27: 1 named Mahlah, Noah, Hoglah, Milcah, and *T*.
36:11 Mahlah, *T*,
Jos 12:24 foreign king of Gilgal, and the king of *T*:
17: 3 were Mahlah, Noah, Hoglah, Milcah, and *T*.
1Kgs 14:17 *T* and crossed the threshold of her house,
15:21 left off fortifying Ramah, and stayed in *T*.
15:33 twenty-four-year reign over Israel in *T*.
16: 6 he was buried in *T*, and his son Elah
16: 8 began his two-year reign over Israel in *T*.
16: 9 As he was in *T*, drinking to excess
16: 9 Arza, superintendent of his palace in *T*,
16:15 of Judah, Zimri reigned seven days in *T*.
16:17 by all Israel, and laid siege to *T*.
16:23 twelve years, the first six of them in *T*.
2Kgs 15:14 son of Gadi, came up from *T* to Samaria,
15:16 on his way from *T* they did not let him in.
Sg 6: 4 You are as beautiful as *T*, my beloved,

TISHBE (1)

1Kgs 17: 1 Elijah the Tishbite, from *T* in Gilead,

TISHBITE (6)

1Kgs 17: 1 Elijah the *T*, from Tishbe in Gilead,
21:17 But the LORD said to Elijah the *T*:
21:28 Then the LORD said to Elijah the *T*,
2Kgs 1: 3 the angel of the LORD said to Elijah the *T*:
1: 8 "It is Elijah the *T*!"
9:36 through his servant Elijah the *T*:

TITANS (1)

Jdt 16: 6 one struck down, nor did *t* bring him low,

TITHE (18)

Nm 18:26 from them to the LORD, a *t* of the tithes;
Dt 12:17 partake of your *t* of grain or wine or oil,
14:22 "Each year you shall *t* all the produce
14:23 eat in his presence your *t* of the grain,
14:24 you and you are not able to bring your *t*,
14:25 you, you may exchange the *t* for money and,
26:14 I have not eaten any of the *t* as a mourner;
1Sm 8:15 He will *t* your crops and your vineyards,
8:17 He will *t* your flocks and you yourselves
2Chr 31: 5 they gave a generous *t* of everything.
Neh 10:38 The *t* of our fields we will bring to the
10:38 the *t* in all the cities of our service.
10:39 the *t*, and the Levites shall bring the tithe
Tb 1: 7 in Jeusalem I would give the *t* of grain,
1: 7 years, I used to give a second *t* in money,
1: 8 The third *t* I gave to orphans and widows,
Mal 3:10 Bring the whole *t* into the storehouse,

TITHED (1)

Heb 7: 9 so to speak, *t* in the person of his father,

TITHES (34)

Lv 27:30 "All *t* of the land, whether in grain from
27:31 someone wishes to buy back any of his *t*,
27:32 The *t* of the herd and the flock shall be
Nm 18:21 I hereby assign all *t* in Israel as their
18:24 heritage the *t* which the Israelites give
18:26 the Israelites the *t* I have assigned you
18:26 from them to the LORD, a tithe of the *t*;
18:28 all the *t* you receive from the Israelites,
18:30 the rest of the *t* will be credited to you
Dt 12: 6 your *t* and personal contributions,
12:11 your *t* and personal contributions,
14:28 all the *t* of your produce for that year
26:12 the *t* of your produce in the third year,
26:12 in the third year, the year of the *t*,
2Chr 31: 6 cities of Judah also brought in *t* of oxen,
31:12 *t* and consecrated things were deposited
Neh 10:39 the tithe of the *t* to the house of our God,
12:44 stores, offerings, first fruits, and *t*;
13: 5 incense and utensils, the *t* in grain,
13:12 Judah once more brought in the *t* of grain,
Jdt 11:13 *t* of wine and oil which they had sanctified
1Mc 3:49 vestments, the first fruits, and the *t*;
10:31 and her territory, her *t* and her tolls,
11:35 of *t* and tribute and of the tax on the
Sir 35: 8 and pay your *t* in a spirit of joy.
Am 4: 4 your sacrifices, every third day, your *t*;
Mal 3: 8 In *t* and in offerings!
Mt 23:23 You pay *t* on mint and herbs and seeds
Lk 11:42 You pay *t* on mint and rue and all the
18:12 I pay *t* on all I possess.'
Heb 7: 5 of Levi should receive *t* from the people,
7: 6 received *t* of Abraham and blessed him who
7: 8 whereas men subject to death receive *t*,
7: 9 Levi, who receives *t*,

TITLE (11)

Ex 3:15 this is my *t* for all generations.
1Mc 6:17 and he gave him the *t* Eupator.
Ps(s) 135:13 LORD is your *t* through all generations,
Is 26: 8 and your *t* are the desire of our souls.
45: 4 called you by your name, giving you a *t*,
Jer 32:11 sealed copy, containing *t* and conditions,
Mt 23: 8 As to you, avoid the *t* 'Rabbi.'
Lk 20:44 Now if David accords him the *t* 'lord,'
1Cor 5:11 bears the *t* "brother" if he is immoral,
Gal 2: 4 to the *t* of brother were smuggled in;
Jas 2:23 for this he received the *t* "God's friend."

TITLES (2)

Jb 32:21 to anyone, nor give flattering *t* to any.
Acts 18:15 about terminology and *t* and your own law,

TITUS (16)

2Mc 11:34 "Quintus Memmius and *T* Manius,
Acts 18: 7 to the house of a Gentile named *T* Justus,
2Cor 2:13 because I did not find my brother *T* there.
7: 6 gave me strength with the arrival of *T*.
7: 7 *T* had already received from you,
7:13 *T* because his mind has been set at rest
7:14 boasting to *T* has been proved equally true.
8: 6 That is why I have exhorted *T*,
8:16 an equal zeal for you in the heart of *T*!
8:23 As for *T*, he is my companion and fellow
12:18 I urged *T* to go to you,
12:18 Did *T* take advantage of you in any way?
Gal 2: 1 with Barnabas, this time taking *T* with me.
2: 3 Not even *T*, who was with me, was
2Tm 4:10 has gone to Galatia and *T* to Dalmatia.
Ti 1: 4 Paul to *T*, my own true child in our

TIZITE (1)

1Chr 11:45 of Shimri, and Joha, his brother, the *T*;

TOAH (1)

1Chr 6:19 son of Jeroham, son of Eliel, son of *T*,

TOB (4)

Jgs 11: 3 had taken up residence in the land of *T*.
11: 5 went to bring Jephthah from the land of *T*.
2Sm 10: 6 men, and twelve thousand men from *T*.
10: 8 Rehob and the men of *T* and Maacah

TOBIADS (1)

1Mc 5:13 who were among the *T* have been killed;

TOBIAH (74)

Ezr 2:60 sons of Delaiah, sons of *T*,
Neh 2:10 and *T* the Ammonite slave had heard of this,
2:19 the Horonite, *T* the Ammonite slave,
3:35 *T* the Ammonite was beside him,
4: 1 When Sanballat, *T*, the Arabs,
6: 1 When it had been reported to Sanballat, *T*,
6:12 because *T* and Sanballat had bribed him,
6:14 Keep in mind *T* and Sanballat,
6:17 were going to *T* from the nobles of Judah,
6:19 and *T* sent letters trying to frighten me.
7:62 sons of Delaiah, sons of *T*,
13: 4 of our God and who was an associate of *T*,
13: 7 evil thing that Eliashib had done for *T*,
Tb 1: 9 By her I had a son whom I named *T*.
1:20 except for my wife Anna and my son *T*.
2: 1 wife Anna and my son *T* were restored to me.
2: 2 were placed before me I said to my son *T*:
2: 3 *T* went out to look for some poor kinsmen
3:17 Raguel's daughter Sarah to Tobit's son *T*,
3:17 For *T* had the right to claim her before
4: 2 why should I not call my son *T* and let him
4: 3 So he called his son *T*;
5: 1 Then *T* replied to his father Tobit:
5: 3 Tobit answered his son *T*:
5: 4 *T* went to look for someone acquainted with
5: 5 *T* said to him, "Who are you, young
5: 5 *T* said, "Do you know the way to Media?"
5: 7 *T* said to him, "Wait for me, young man,
5: 9 *T* went back to tell his father Tobit what
5: 9 *T* went out to summon the man,
5:10 "My son *T* wants to go to Media.
5:17 journey, *T* kissed his father and mother.
6: 2 *T* out of the house and went with them.
6:11 Raphael said to the boy, "Brother *T*!"
6:14 *T* objected, however: "Brother Azariah,
6:18 When *T* heard Raphael say that she was his
7: 1 When they entered Ecbatana, *T* said,
7: 5 Then *T* exclaimed, "He is my father!"
7: 7 He said to *T*: "My child, God bless you!
7: 7 to weep in the arms of his kinsman *T*.
7: 9 and reclined to eat, *T* said to Raphael,
7:11 *T* answered, "I will eat or drink nothing
7:12 the hand and gave her to *T* with the words:
7:13 stating that he gave Sarah to *T* as his wife
8: 2 At this point *T*, mindful of Raphael's
8: 4 *T* arose from bed and said to his wife,
8:10 "I must do this, because if *T* should die,
8:12 maids in to see whether *T* is alive or dead,
8:14 told the girl's parents that *T* was alive,
8:20 *T* and made an oath in his presence,
9: 1 Then *T* called Raphael and said to him:
9: 5 his bond and told him about Tobit's son *T*,
9: 6 they found *T* reclining at table
10: 1 the time *T* would need to go and to return.
10: 7 for his daughter, *T* went to him and said:
10: 8 Raguel said to *T*: "Stay, my child,
10: 9 But *T* insisted, "No, I beg you to let me
10:10 promptly handed over to *T* Sarah his wife,
10:11 He embraced *T* and said to him:
10:13 Then Edna said to *T*: "My child
10:14 When *T* left Raguel, he was full of
11: 4 both went on ahead and Raphael said to *T*,
11: 7 said to *T* before he reached his father:
11:10 *T* went up to him with the fish gall in his
11:13 *T* used both hands to peel off the
11:15 Behold, I now see my son *T*!"
11:15 *T* told his father that his journey had
11:17 Tobit reached Sarah, the wife of his son *T*,
11:17 Blessed is my son *T*,
12: 1 Tobit called his son *T* and said to him,
12: 2 *T* said: "Father, how much shall I pay
12: 5 So *T* called Raphael and said, "Take as
14: 3 called his son *T* and Tobiah's seven sons,
14:15 *T* praised God for all that he had done

TOBIAH'S (5)

Neh 6:17 of Judah, and *T* letters were reaching them,
13: 8 and I had all of *T* household goods thrown
Tb 11:18 *T* wedding feast for seven happy days,
14: 3 he called his son Tobiah and *T* seven sons,
14:12 When *T* mother died,

TOBIAS (1)

2Mc 3:11 was the property of Hyrcanus, son of *T*,

TOBIEL (2)

Tb 1: 1 book tells the story of Tobit, son of *T*,
1: 8 of Deborah, the mother of my father *T*;

TOBIJAH (3)

2Chr 17: 8 Shemiramoth, Jehonathan, Adonijah and *T*,
Zec 6:10 Take from the returned captives Heldai, *T*,
6:14 temple of the LORD in favor of Heldai, *T*,

TOBIT (43)

Tb 1: 1 This book tells the story of *T*,
1: 3 I, *T*, have walked all the days of my life
3:17 *T* returned from the courtyard to his house,
4: 1 That same day *T* remembered the money he

5: 1 Then Tobiah replied to his father T:
5: 3 T answered his son Tobiah:
5: 9 to tell his father T what had happened.
5: 9 T said, "Call the man, so that I may find
5:10 entered the house, T greeted him first.
5:10 T replied: "What joy is left for me
5:10 T then said: "My son Tobiah wants
5:11 T asked, "Brother, tell me, please, what
5:12 T replied, "I wish to know truthfully
5:14 T exclaimed: "Welcome! God save you
5:17 T said, "God bless you, brother."
5:17 T said to him, "Have a safe journey."
5:18 She said to T: "Why have you decided
5:21 T reassured her: "Have no such thought
7: 2 young man looks just like my kinsman T!"
7: 4 She said, "Do you know our kinsman T?"
7: 7 when he heard that T had lost his eyesight,
7: 8 His wife Edna also wept for T;
9: 6 I have seen the very image of my cousin T!"
10: 1 T was keeping track of the time Tobiah
10: 6 But T kept telling her:
10: 8 I am sending messengers to your father T,
11: 6 coming, she exclaimed to his father, T,
11:10 T got up and stumbled out through the
11:13 When T saw his son, he threw his arms
11:15 Then T went back in, rejoicing and
11:16 T went out to the gate of Nineveh to meet
11:17 Before them all T proclaimed how God had
11:17 When T reached Sarah,
11:18 nephew Nadab also came to rejoice with T.
12: 1 T called his son Tobiah and said to him,
12: 4 T answered, "It is only fair, son, that he
12:12 I can now tell you that when you, T,
13: 1 Then T composed this joyful prayer:
14: 1 T died peacefully at the age of a hundred
14:13 estate as well as that of his father T.

TOBIT'S (5)

Tb 3:17 to remove the cataracts from T eyes,
3:17 Raguel's daughter Sarah to T son Tobiah,
9: 5 his bond and told him about T son Tobiah,
11:13 Then, beginning at the corners of T eyes,
13:18 The end of T hymn of praise.

TOCHEN (1)

1Chr 4:32 Etam, also, and Ain, Rimmon, T,

TODAY (211)

Gn 19:37 He is the ancestor of the Moabites of t.
19:38 He is the ancestor of the Ammonites of t.
24:12 let it turn out favorably for me t and thus
24:42 "When I came to the spring t, I prayed:
30:32 go through your whole flock t and remove
40: 7 master's house, "Why do you look so sad t?"
Ex 2:18 "How is it you have returned so soon t?"
5:14 amount of bricks yesterday and t,
14:13 the victory the LORD will win for you t.
14:13 whom you see t you will never see again.
16:25 it today, for t is the sabbath of the LORD.
19:10 them sanctify themselves t and tomorrow.
32:29 T you have been dedicated to the LORD,
34:11 keep the commandments I am giving you t.
Lv 8:34 done t be done to make atonement for you.
9: 4 for t the LORD will reveal himself to you."
10:19 offering and holocaust before the LORD t,
10:19 Had I then eaten of the sin offering t,
Dt 3:14 Bashan Havvothjair, the name it bears t
4: 4 to the LORD, your God, are all alive t.
4: 8 whole law which I am setting before you t?
4:20 might be his very own people, as you are t.
4:38 make their land your heritage, as it is t.
4:40 and commandments which I enjoin on you t,
5:24 have found out t that man can still live
6: 6 heart these words which I enjoin on you t.
6:24 prosperous and happy a life as we have t;
7:11 and the decrees which I enjoin on you t.
8: 1 all the commandments I enjoin on you t,
8:11 and statutes which I enjoin on you t:
9: 3 Understand, then, t that it is the LORD,
10:13 which I enjoin on you t for your own good?
11: 8 then, which I enjoin on you t,
11:13 my commandments which I enjoin on you t,
11:27 LORD, your God, which I enjoin on you t;
11:28 aside from the way I ordain for you t,
11:32 and decrees that I set before you t.
13:19 his commandments which I enjoin on you t,
15: 5 commandments which I enjoin on you t,
15:15 That is why I am giving you this command t.
19: 9 commandments which I enjoin on you t,
20: 3 T you are going into battle against your
26: 3 say to him, T I acknowledge to the LORD,
26:17 T you are making this agreement with the
26:18 And t the LORD is making this agreement
27: 1 these commandments which I enjoin on you t.
27: 4 stones concerning which I command you t,
27:10 and statutes which I enjoin on you t."
28: 1 his commandments which I enjoin on you t,
28:13 which I order you t to observe carefully,
28:15 his commandments which I enjoin on you t,
29:11 with you t under this sanction of a curse,
29:14 with those who are not here among us t
29:27 out into a strange land, where they are t.'
30:11 t is not too mysterious and remote for you.
30:15 have t set before you life and prosperity,
30:16 LORD, your God, which I enjoin on you t,
30:19 heaven and earth t to witness against you:
Jos 3: 7 T I will begin to exalt you in the sight
5: 9 T I have removed the reproach of Egypt
7:25 "The LORD bring upon you t the misery
8:28 mound of ruins, as it remains t.
14:11 t as I was the day Moses sent me forth,
22:18 You are rebelling against the LORD t and
23:14 T, as you see, I am going the way of all
24:15 the LORD, decide t whom you will serve,
Jgs 21: 3 t one tribe of Israel should be lacking?"
21: 6 T one of the tribes of Israel has been cut
Ru 2:19 said to her, "Where did you glean t?
2:19 at whose place I worked t is named Boaz,"
3:18 not rest, but will settle the matter t."
4: 9 "You are witnesses t that I have acquired
4:10 Do you witness this t?"
4:14 not failed to provide you t with an heir!
1Sm 4: 3 us to be defeated t by the Philistines?
4:16 I fled from there t."
9:12 just t he came to the city,
9:12 have a sacrifice t on the high place.
9:19 of me to the high place and eat with me t.
10: 2 When you leave me t, you will meet two
10:19 But t you have rejected your God,
11:13 this day, for t the LORD has saved Israel."
14:30 if the people had eaten freely t of their
14:38 and find out how this sin was committed t.
14:45 for God was with him in what he did t!"
16: 5 yourselves and join me t for the banquet."
17:10 "I defy the ranks of Israel t.
17:46 T the LORD shall deliver you into my hand;
18:21 "You shall become my son-in-law t
20:27 of Jesse not come to table yesterday or t?"
21: 6 All the more so t,
22: 8 be an enemy against me, as is the case t."
22:13 me and become my enemy, as is the case t?"
24:11 You see for yourself t that the LORD just
24:19 Great is the generosity you showed me t,
25:32 God of Israel, who sent you to meet me t.
26:21 because you have held my life precious t.
26:23 T, though the LORD delivered you into my
26:24 As I valued your life highly t,
28:18 Amalek, the LORD has done this to you t.
30:13 me because I fell sick three days ago t.
30:25 and a custom in Israel, as it still is t.
2Sm 3:38 a great general has fallen t in Israel.
6:20 the king of Israel has honored himself t,
11:12 David said to Uriah, "Stay here t also,
15:20 shall I have you wander about with us t,
18:20 "You are not the man to bring the news t.
18:20 but t you would not be bringing good news,
19: 6 put all your servants to shame t by loving
19: 7 For you have shown t that officers and
19: 7 if Absalom were alive t and all of us dead,
19:21 to come down t to meet my lord the king."
19:23 Should anyone die t in Israel?
19:23 Am I not aware that t I am king of Israel?"
1Kgs 1:25 He went down t and slaughtered oxen,
3: 6 this great favor toward him, even t,
12: 7 "If t you will be the servant of this
14:14 T, at this very moment, the LORD will
18:15 I serve, I will present myself to him t."
20:13 When I deliver it up to you t,
2Kgs 2: 3 LORD will take your master from over you t?"
2: 5 LORD will take your master from over you t?"
4:23 "Why are you going to him t?"
6:28 'Give up your son that we may eat him t;
6:31 of Elisha, son of Shaphat, stays on him t!"
10:27 turned it into a latrine, as it remains t.
21:15 fathers came forth from Egypt until t.'"
Ezr 9: 7 pillage, and to disgrace, as is the case t.
9:15 we have been spared, the remnant we are t.
Neh 8: 9 T is holy to the LORD your God.
8:10 for t is holy to our Lord.
8:11 the people saying, "Hush, for t is holy,
9:36 But, see, we t are slaves;
Tb 7:11 She is yours t and ever after.
Jdt 6: 2 to prophesy among us as you have done t,
6: 5 you shall not see my face after t,
8:11 you said to the people t is not proper.
8:18 generations, nor does there exist t,
8:29 Not t only is your wisdom made evident,
12:18 have I ever enjoyed life as much as I do t."
13:17 who t have brought to nought the enemies
Est 5: 4 "come t with Haman to a banquet I have
1Mc 2:63 T he is exalted, and tomorrow he is not
3:17 Besides, we are weak t from fasting."
4:10 fathers, and destroy this army before us t.
5:32 men of his army, "Fight for our kinsmen t."
7:42 the same way, crush this army before us t,
9:30 t to be our ruler and leader in his place,
9:44 t is not like yesterday and the day before.
10:20 you t to be high priest of your nation;
16: 2 battles of Israel from our youth until t,
Jb 23: 3 Oh, that t I might find him,
Ps(s) 95: 7 Oh, that t you would hear his voice:
Prv 7:14 offerings, and t I have fulfilled my vows;
Sir 10:10 the doctor jests, a king t—
20:14 He lends t, he asks it back tomorrow;
38:22 for him it was yesterday, for you t.
Is 10:32 Even t he will halt at Nob,
38:19 the living give you thanks, as I do t.
56:12 strong drink, And tomorrow will be like t,
58: 4 Would that t you might fast so as to make
Jer 11: 5 the one you have t.
25:18 and cursing, as they are t Pharaoh,
34:15 T you indeed repented and did what is
36: 2 to you, in the days of Josiah, until t.
40: 4 t from the fetters that bind your hands;
42:21 T I proclaim his message,
44: 2 T they are ruins and uninhabited,
44: 6 they became the ruinous waste they are t.
44:22 and without inhabitants, as it is t.
Bar 1:15 and we t are flushed with shame,
1:20 with milk and honey, cling to us even t.
2: 6 our fathers, are flushed with shame even t.
2:26 which bears your name to what it is t,
3: 8 Behold us t in our captivity,
Ez 24: 2 Son of man, write down this date t,
Dn 3:40 presence t as we follow you unreservedly;
Mt 6:11 Give us t our daily bread,
6:30 t and is thrown on the fire tomorrow,
6:34 T has troubles enough of its own.
11:23 place in Sodom, it would be standing t.
21:28 'Son, go out and work in the vineyard t.'
27: 8 That is why that field, even t,
27:19 about him t which has greatly upset me."
Lk 4:21 T this Scripture passage is fulfilled in
5:26 saying, "We have seen incredible things t!"
7:31 comparison can I use for the men of t?
12:28 grows t and is thrown on the fire tomorrow,
13:32 T and tomorrow I cast out devils and
13:33 For all that, I must proceed on course t,
19: 5 I mean to stay at your house t."
19: 9 T salvation has come to this house,
22:34 the cock will not crow t until you have
22:61 cock crows t you will deny me three times."
24:21 Besides all this, t, the third day since
Acts 4: 9 If we must answer t for a good deed done
22: 3 defender of God, just as all of you are t.
24:21 t because of the resurrection of the dead.'"
26: 2 able to make my defense t in your presence,
26: 6 But t I stand trial because of my hope in
26:29 who listen to me t might become what I am
Heb 1: 5 t I have begotten you"?
3: 7 T, if you should hear his voice,
3:13 one another daily while it is still t,"
3:15 When Scripture says, T, if you should
4: 7 of unbelief, God once more set a day, t,"
4: 7 T, if you should hear his voice,
5: 5 t I have begotten you";
13: 8 Jesus Christ is the same yesterday, t,
Jas 4:13 T or tomorrow we shall go to such and such

TODAY'S (2)

Est 9:13 tomorrow to act according to t decree,
Acts 19:40 accused of rioting because of t conduct.

TOE (6)

Lv 8:23 hand, and on the big t of his right foot.
14:14 hand, and the big t of his right foot.
14:17 hand, and the big t of his right foot,
14:25 hand, and on the big t of his right foot.
14:28 hand, and the big t of his right foot,
Acts 28:13 sailed around the t and arrived at Rhegium.

TOES (8)

Ex 29:20 hands and the great t of their right feet.
Lv 8:24 and on the big t of their right feet.
Jgs 1: 6 him, cut off his thumbs and his big t.
1: 7 kings, with their thumbs and big t cut off,
2Sm 21:20 on each hand and six t on each foot
1Chr 20: 6 to each hand and six t to each foot;
Dn 2:41 The feet and t you saw,
2:42 and the t partly iron and partly tile,

TOGARMAH (2)

Gn 10: 3 Ashkenaz, Riphath, and T.
1Chr 1: 6 of Gomer were Ashkenaz, Riphath, and T.

TOGETHER (335)

Gn 3: 7 t and made loincloths for themselves.
7: 7 T with his sons, his wife, and his sons'
7:14 the ark, t with every kind of wild beast,
8:16 t with your wife and your sons and your
8:18 t with his wife and his sons and his sons'
13: 6 could not support them if they stayed t;
13: 6 were so great that they could not dwell t.
19:25 t with the inhabitants of the cities and
22: 7 As the two walked on t, Isaac spoke to
22:19 and they set out t for Beer-sheba,
23:17 t with its cave and all the trees anywhere
36: 7 had become too great for them to dwell t,
44: 2 goblet, t with the money for his rations."
46:27 T with Joseph's sons who were born to him
50:14 t with his brothers and all who had gone
50:22 in Egypt, t with his father's family.
Ex 14:20 camps coming any closer t all night long.
18: 5 T with Moses' wife and sons,

TOGETHER (cont.)
19: 8 to tell them, the people all answered t,
26: 3 Five of the sheets are to be sewed t,
28: 1 your brother Aaron, t with his sons Nadab,
29:13 kidneys, t with the fat that is on them,
29:21 altar, t with some of the anointing oil,
30:24 t with a hin of olive oil;
36:10 Five of the sheets were sewed t,
39:16 t with two gold filigree rosettes and two
Lv 1: 8 of meat, t with the head and the suet,
1:12 shall lay these, t with the head and suet,
2: 2 flour and oil, t with all the frankincense,
2:16 grits and oil, t with all the frankincense,
6: 8 t with all the frankincense that is on it,
7:12 t with his thanksgiving sacrifice he shall
7:30 fat is to be brought in, t with the breast,
8: 2 Aaron and his sons, t with the vestments,
9: 1 and his sons, t with the elders of Israel,
14:20 and offer it, t with the cereal offering,
14:51 the scarlet yarn, t with the living bird,
25:41 jubilee year, when he, t with his children,
25:54 be released, t with his children,
26:25 you then huddle t in your walled cities,
Nm 4:26 t with their ropes and all other objects
4:37 tent, which Moses took, t with Aaron,
4:41 tent, which Moses took, t with Aaron,
4:45 clans which Moses took, t with Aaron,
21:16 LORD said to Moses, "Bring the people t,
23: 6 holocaust t with all the princes of Moab.
23:17 his holocaust t with the princes of Moab.
24:10 Balak beat his palms t in a blaze of anger
27: 3 t against the LORD [in Korah's band],
28:31 these offerings, t with their libations,
29: 6 t with the libations prescribed for them,
31:11 the captives, t with the spoils and booty,
Dt 16:11 his presence t with your son and daughter,
16:14 your feast, t with your son and daughter,
22:10 not plow with an ox and an ass harnessed t.
22:11 kinds of thread, wool and linen, woven t.
25: 5 live t and one of them dies without a son,
26:11 t with the Levite and the aliens who live
29:10 t with your wives and children and the
32:44 So Moses, t with Joshua,
33: 5 assembled and the tribes of Israel came t
Jos 7: 6 Joshua, t with the elders of Israel,
11: 5 they encamped t to fight against Israel.
24: 1 t all the tribes of Israel at Shechem,
Jgs 4: 7 Kishon, t with his chariots and troops,
9: 6 and all Beth-millo came t and proceeded
9:47 citizens of Migdal-shechem were gathered t.
12: 1 gathered t and crossed over to Zaphon.
12: 4 Then Jephthah called t all the men of
19: 6 stayed and the two men ate and drank t.
20:11 exception were leagued t against the city,
Ru 1:19 they went on t till they reached Bethlehem.
4:13 When they came t as man and wife,
1Sm 9:26 and he and Samuel went outside the city t.
10:17 Samuel called the people t to the LORD at
11:11 were so scattered that no two were left t.
17:10 Give me a man and let us fight t."
20:11 When they were out in the open country t,
20:41 They kissed each other and wept aloud t.
25:18 Abigail quickly got t two hundred loaves,
31: 6 his armor-bearer died t on that same day.
2Sm 2:16 his opponent's side, and all fell down t.
8:11 t with the silver and gold he had taken
1Kgs 12:21 Rehoboam gathered t all the house of Judah
22: 6 The king of Israel gathered t the prophets,
2Kgs 2: 6 And so the two went on t.
3:10 "The LORD has called t these three kings
3:13 kings t to put them in the grasp of Moab."
6:11 the king of Aram called t his officers.
10:18 gathered all the people t and said to them:
23: 1 and of Jerusalem summoned t before him.
23:18 So they left his bones undisturbed t with
24:12 king of Judah, t with his mother,
1Chr 4:33 t with all their outlying villages as far
6:18 the following, t with their descendants.
11:10 chief warriors who, t with all Israel,
12:33 t with all their brethren under their
15: 4 called t the sons of Aaron and the Levites:
15:18 and, t with these, their brethren of
19:17 to David, he gathered all Israel t,
22: 2 lived in the land of Israel be brought t,
22: 3 t with so much bronze that it could not be
23: 2 t all the leaders of Israel, together with
25: 7 t with that of their brethren who were
26: 8 who, t with their sons and their brethren,
28: 1 and his sons, t with the courtiers,
29:16 we have brought t to build you a house
29:21 t with their libations and many other
29:30 t with the particulars of his reign and
2Chr 1:14 He gathered t chariots and drivers,
11: 1 gathered t the house of Judah and Benjamin,
15: 9 and Benjamin, t with those of Ephraim,
17: 8 t with the priests Elishama and Jehoram.
21: 3 objects, t with fortified cities in Judah,
24: 5 t the priests and Levites and said to them:
25:24 t with the treasures of the palace,
27: 5 t with ten thousand kors of wheat and ten
29:15 their brethren t and sanctified themselves;
30:25 t with the priests and Levites and the
32: 6 He gathered them t in his presence in the
35: 8 Passover victims t with three hundred oxen.
35: 9 Passover victims, t with five hundred oxen.
Ezr 1: 4 t with freewill offerings for the house
2:64 The entire assembly taken t came to
3: 2 Jozadak, t with his brethren the priests,
3: 2 son of Shealtiel, t with his brethren,
3: 8 Jozadak, t with the rest of their brethren,
6:17 t with twelve he-goats as a sin-offering
6:21 from the exile partook of it t with all those
7:16 t with the freewill offerings which the
7:28 I gathered t Israelite family heads to
10: 7 the exiles should gather t in Jerusalem,
10: 9 t in Jerusalem within the three-day period:
Neh 4: 2 Thereupon they all plotted t to come and
5:11 houses, t with the interest on the money,
6: 2 council t at Caphirim in the plain of Ono."
6: 7 of the king, come, let us hold council t."
7: 5 put it into my mind to gather t the nobles,
7:66 The entire assembly taken t came to
9: 1 gathered t fasting and in sackcloth,
12: 8 the last-mentioned, t with his brethren,
12:28 gathered t from the region about Jerusalem,
13:11 t and had them resume their stations.
13:13 Pedaiah, one of the Levites, t with Hanan,
13:15 loading them on their asses, t with wine,
Tb 1: 6 t with a tenth of my income and the first
5:14 to Jerusalem, where we would worship t.
6: 7 traveled on t till they were near Media.
8: 7 and allow us to live t to a happy old age."
8: 8 They said t, "Amen, amen."
8:13 went in, and found them sound asleep t.
9: 5 t with the four servants and two camels,
10:10 his wife, t with half of all his property:
13:13 t and shall bless the Lord of the ages.
14: 7 shall be gathered t and go to Jerusalem;
Jdt 1: 6 came t to resist the people of Cheleoud.
4: 3 all the people of Judea been gathered t,
6: 8 not die till you are destroyed t with them.
7: 8 t with the generals of the seacoast,
7:17 moved camp, t with five thousand Assyrians.
9: 3 t with their princes, and the princes t
9:10 together with the ruler, the ruler t with
13:10 t as they were accustomed to do for prayer.
Est 2: 3 realm to bring t all beautiful young virgins
2: 8 many maidens brought t to the stronghold
2:19 the time the virgins had been brought t,
B: 6 us, shall, t with their wives and children,
8:11 city to group t and defend their lives,
E:13 royal consort, t with their whole race.
E:18 been hanged, t with his entire household,
F:10 t with joy and happiness before God,
1Mc 3: 9 he gathered t those who were perishing.
3:10 Gentiles, t with a large army from Samaria,
3:44 The assembly gathered t to prepare for
3:52 are gathered t against us to destroy us.
4:28 So the following year he gathered t sixty
6:19 called all the people t to besiege them.
6:28 was angry, and he called t all his Friends,
9: 7 because he had no time to gether them t.
9:28 of Judas came t and said to Jonathan:
9:63 he gathered t his whole force and sent
10:43 t with all the goods he possesses in my
10:48 King Alexander gathered t a large army and
10:85 sword, t with those who were burned alive,
11:20 At that time Jonathan gathered t the men
11:34 districts, t with all their dependencies,
12:37 therefore worked t on building up the city,
12:45 I will hand it over to you t with other
15:26 t with gold and silver and much equipment.
2Mc 1:27 Gather t our scattered people,
2: 7 his people t again and shows them mercy.
2:18 mercy on us and gather us t from
3:19 maidens secluded indoors ran t,
4:36 t with the Greeks who detested the crime,
5: 3 gold ornaments, t with armor of every sort.
11: 7 Then they resolutely set out t.
11: 9 all of them t thanked God for his mercy,
12: 3 them, t with their wives and children,
14:30 So he gathered t a large number of his men,
Jb 2:11 t to give him sympathy and comfort.
3:18 There the captives are at ease t,
9:32 him, that we should come t in judgment.
10:11 me, with bones and sinews knit me t.
17:16 Shall we go down t into the dust?
30: 7 under the nettles they huddled t.
34:15 his breath, All flesh would perish t,
40:13 bury them in the dust t;
41: 7 scales are on his back, tightly sealed t;
Ps(s) 2: 2 and the princes conspire t against the
31:14 every side, as they consult t against me,
34: 4 the LORD with me, let us t extol his name.
35:15 gathered t; they gathered together striking
41: 8 All my foes whisper t against me;
47:10 t with the people of the God of Abraham.
48: 5 the kings assemble, they come on t;
56: 7 They gather t in hiding,
59: 4 mighty men come t against me.
62: 4 set upon a man and all t beat him down
62:10 In a balance they prove lighter, all t,
71:10 keep watch against my life take counsel t.
83: 6 Yes, they consult t with one mind,
102:23 in Jerusalem, When the peoples gather t,
Eccl 4:11 So also, if two sleep t,
4:12 lone man may be overcome, two t can resist.
Wis 5:12 the parted air straightway flows t again
7:11 good things t came to me in her company,
Sir 13: 2 When they knock t, the pot will be
Is 1:31 Both shall burn t, and there shall be none
9:20 t they turn on Judah.
11: 6 The calf and the young lion shall browse t,
11: 7 be neighbors, t their young shall rest;
11:14 west, t they shall plunder the Kedemites;
22: 3 All your leaders fled away t,
22: 3 All who were in you were captured t,
24:22 be gathered t like prisoners into a pit;
31: 3 fall, and both of them shall perish t.
40: 5 revealed, and all mankind shall see it t;
41: 1 let us come t for judgment.
41:19 t with the plane tree and the pine,
43: 9 Let all the nations gather t,
43:17 powerful army, Till they lie prostrate t,
45:20 Come and assemble, gather t,
45:21 Come here and declare in counsel t:
46: 2 They stoop and bow down t;
50: 8 wishes to oppose me, let us appear t.
52: 8 watchmen raise a cry, t they shout for joy,
52: 9 Break out t in song, O ruins of Jerusalem!
Jer 3:17 all nations will be gathered t to honor
3:18 t they will come from the land of the
6:11 the street, upon the young men gathered t.
12: 9 Come, gather t, all you beasts of the field,
13:14 against each other, fathers and sons t,
29:14 I will gather you t from all the nations
31:10 who scattered Israel, now gathers them t,
31:24 who lead the flock, shall dwell there t.
32:37 t from all the lands to which in anger,
41: 1 And while they were t at table in Mizpah,
46:12 Warrior trips over warrior, both fall t.
46:21 They too turn and flee t, stand not their
49:14 Gather t, move against her, rise up
Ez 1:20 were raised t with the living creatures;
16:37 t all your lovers whom you tried to please,
22:19 I must gather you t within Jerusalem.
22:20 so I will gather you t in my furious wrath,
37: 7 it was a rattling as the bones came t,
37:17 Then join the two sticks t,
39:17 Come t, from all sides gather for
41:13 area, t with the building and its walls,
41:15 and t with its walls on both sides it was
46: 5 t with a cereal offering of one ephah for
48:20 the sacred tract t with the City property.
Dn 3: 3 all these came t for the dedication and
3:94 governors, and nobles of the king came t,
11: 6 be given up, t with those who brought her,
11:27 shall sit at table t and exchange lies,
13:39 We saw them lying t, but the man we
13:54 tell me under what tree you saw them t."
13:58 me under what tree you surprised them t."
14:27 these he boiled t and made into cakes.
Hos 2:22 Judah and of Israel shall be gathered t;
5: 7 new moon devour them t with their fields.
Am 3: 3 Do two walk t unless they have agreed?
Zep 2: 1 Gather, gather yourselves t,
3: 8 it is my decision to gather t the nations,
Zec 10: 8 I will whistle for them to come t,
14:14 surrounding nations shall be gathered t,
Mt 1:18 to Joseph, but before they lived t,
13:30 Let them grow t until harvest;
20:25 Jesus then called them t and said:
Mk 5:24 two went off t and a large crowd followed,
10:42 Jesus called them t and said to them:
14:53 priests, the elders and the scribes came t.
Lk 5: 7 and t they filled the two boats until they
6:38 Good measure pressed down, shaken t,
9: 1 Jesus now called the Twelve t and gave
13:34 gather your children t as a mother bird
17:35 Two women will be grinding grain t;
23:13 Pilate then called t the chief priests,
Jn 4:36 life, that sower and reaper may rejoice t.
7:32 t sent temple guards to arrest him.
18:20 the temple area where all the Jews come t.
Acts 1:14 T they devoted themselves to constant
1:15 have been a hundred and twenty gathered t.
2:46 They went to the temple area t every day,
4:26 the princes gathered t against the Lord
6:12 All t they confronted him,
14: 5 by Gentiles and Jews, t with their leaders,
14:27 they called the congregation t and related
15:30 the assembly t to deliver the letter.
18: 3 with them and they worked t as tentmakers.
19:29 People rushed t to the theater and dragged
19:32 not even knowing why they had come t.
20: 1 brought his disciples t to encourage them.
21:26 Paul gathered the men t and went through
23:13 than forty of them who took the oath t.)
23:15 Now, t with the Sanhedrin,
Rom 2:15 conscience bears witness t with that law,
8:28 We know that God makes all things work t
1Cor 16:19 t with the assembly that meets in their
2Cor 1:20 address our Amen to God when we worship t.
7: 3 even to the sharing of death and life t.
Gal 4:30 "Cast out slave girl and son t;
Eph 2:21 whole structure is fitted t and takes shape
4:16 firmly t by each supporting ligament,
Col 3:14 binds the rest t and makes them perfect.
1Thes 5:10 awake or asleep, t might live with him.

Heb 9:19 *t* with water and crimson wool and hyssop,
1Pt 5:13 that is in Babylon, chosen *t* with you,
Rv 8: 3 *t* with the prayers of all God's holy ones.
13: 2 power and throne, *t* with great authority.
19:17 Gather *t* for the great feast God has

TOHU (1)

1Sm 1: 1 the son of Jeroham, son of Elihu, son of *T*,

TOI (2)

2Sm 8: 9 When *T*, king of Hamath,
8:10 *T* had been in many battles with Hadadezer.

TOIL (35)

Gn 3:17 In *t* shall you eat its yield all the days
5:29 from our work and the *t* of our hands."
31:42 God saw my plight and the fruits of my *t*,
Dt 26: 7 our affliction, our *t* and our oppression.
Jb 39:11 and leave to him the fruits of your *t*?
Ps(s) 78:46 the fruits of their *t* to the locust.
90:10 strong, And most of them are fruitless *t*,
Prv 23: 4 *T* not to gain wealth,
Eccl 2:10 my heart rejoiced in the fruit of all my *t*.
2:10 This was my share for all my *t*.
2:11 to the *t* at which I had taken such pains,
2:22 man from all the *t* and anxiety of heart
3: 9 What advantage has the worker from his *t*?
4: 4 Then I saw that all *t* and skillful work is
4: 6 than two with *t* and a chase after wind!
4: 8 Yet there is no end to all his *t*,
4: 8 do I *t* and deprive myself of good things?"
5:15 What then does it profit him to *t* for wind?
5:18 lot and finds joy in the fruits of his *t*,
6: 7 All man's *t* is for his mouth,
8:15 for this is the accompaniment of his *t*
9: 9 for the *t* of your labors under the sun.
Wis 15: 8 And with misspent *t* he molds a meaningless
Sir 11:11 One may *t* and struggle and drive,
28:15 and rob them of the fruit of their *t*;
38:24 is free from *t* can become a wise man.
Is 65:23 They shall not *t* in vain,
Jer 3:24 has devoured our fathers' *t* from our youth,
51:58 The *t* of the nations is for nothing;
Ez 29:20 his *t* I have given him the land of Egypt,
Hb 2:13 peoples *t* for the flames,
1Cor 3: 8 receive his wages in proportion to his *t*.
15:58 You know that your *t* is not in vain when
Phil 1:22 the flesh, that means productive *t* for me
1Thes 2: 9 recall, brothers, our efforts and our *t*:

TOILED (7)

Ps(s) 105:44 and they took what the peoples had *t* for,
Sir 33:18 you that not for myself only have I *t*,
Is 47:13 at which you *t* from your youth;
47:15 you with whom you have *t* from your youth;
49: 4 Though I thought I had *t* in vain,
62: 8 drink your wine, for which you *t*.
Jer 20: 5 this city, all it has *t* for and holds dear,

TOILERS (1)

Jb 3:20 Why is light given to the *t*,

TOILING (2)

Gn 49:15 shoulder to the burden and became a *t* serf.
Lam 1: 1 the provinces has been made a *t* slave.

TOILS (7)

Jb 18:10 the ground, and the *t* for him on the way.
Eccl 1: 3 all the labor which he *t* at under the sun?
8:17 However much man *t* in searching,
Wis 19:16 oppressed with awful *t* those who now
Sir 31: 4 The poor man *t* for a meager subsistence,
38:28 flesh, yet he *t* away in the furnace heat.
1Cor 16:16 everyone who cooperates and *t* with them.

TOKEN (11)

Ex 31:13 for that is to be the *t* between you and me
31:17 Israelites it is to be an everlasting *t*;
Lv 2: 2 he shall burn on the altar as a *t* offering,
2: 9 Its *t* offering the priest shall then lift
2:16 For its *t* offering the priest shall then
5:12 a handful of this flour as a *t* offering,
6: 8 shall burn on the altar as its *t* offering,
24: 7 to the LORD, a *t* offering for the bread.
Nm 5:26 as its *t* offering and burn it on the altar.
Jos 2:12 and give me an unmistakable *t* that you are
1Sm 17:18 brothers and bring home some *t* from them.

TOKENS (2)

Ps(s) 74: 4 they have set up their *t* of victory.
Wis 2: 9 everywhere let us leave *t* of our rejoicing,

TOKHATH (1)

2Chr 34:22 Huldah, the wife of Shallum, son of *T*,

TOLA (6)

Gn 46:13 *T*, Puah, Jashub, and Shimron.
Nm 26:23 through *T* the clan of the Tolaites,
Jgs 10: 1 rose to save Israel the Issacharite *T*,
1Chr 7: 1 The sons of Issachar were *T*,
7: 2 The sons of *T* were Uzzi,
7: 2 warrior heads of the ancestral houses of *T*.

TOLAD (1)

1Chr 4:29 Moladah, Hazar-shual, Bilhah, Ezem, *T*,

TOLAITES (1)

Nm 26:23 through Tola the clan of the *T*,

TOLD (376)

Gn 3:11 he asked, "Who *t* you that you were naked?
9:17 God *t* Noah: "This is the sign
9:22 and he *t* his two brothers outside about it.
16: 6 Abram *t* Sarai: your maid is in
16: 9 But the LORD'S messenger *t* her:
17:23 on that same day, as God had *t* him to do.
18: 6 Abraham hastened into the tent and *t* Sarah,
19:14 "Get up and leave this place," he *t* them;
19:17 as they had been brought outside, he was *t*:
20: 5 He himself *t* me, 'She is my sister,'
21: 7 Who would have *t* Abraham,"
21:26 "In fact, you never *t* me about it,
22: 3 out for the place of which God had *t* him.
22: 9 came to the place of which God had *t* him,
24: 6 back there for any reason," Abraham *t* him.
24:28 off and *t* her mother's household about it.
24:33 "I will not eat until I have *t* my tale."
26:32 they *t* him, "We have reached water!"
27:19 I did as you *t* me.
29:12 He *t* her that he was her father's relative,
30:16 are now to come in with me," she *t* him,
31:16 Therefore, do just as God has *t* you."
31:27 You should have *t* me, and I would have
32:10 You *t* me, O LORD 'Go back to the land
32:17 in separate droves, and he *t* the servants,
35: 2 So Jacob *t* his family and all the others
37: 5 had a dream, which he *t* to his brothers:
37: 9 and this one, too, he *t* to his brothers.
37:10 When he also *t* it to his father,
37:17 The man *t* him, "They have moved on
38:13 When Tamar was *t* that her father-in-law
38:22 He went back to Judah and *t* him,
38:24 Judah was *t* that his daughter-in-law Tamar
39: 8 "As long as I am here," he *t* her,
39:14 for her household servants and *t* them,
39:17 Then she *t* him the same story:
40: 9 the chief cupbearer *t* Joseph his dream.
40:22 as Joseph had *t* them in his interpretation.
41:12 and when we *t* him our dreams,
41:13 And it turned out just as he had *t* us:
41:15 you are *t* a dream you can interpret it."
41:28 It is just as I *t* Pharaoh:
41:41 Herewith," Pharaoh *t* Joseph,
41:44 "I, Pharaoh, proclaim," he *t* Joseph,
41:55 to go to Joseph and do whatever he *t* them.
42:29 they *t* him all that had happened to them.
42:37 Then Reuben *t* his father:
43: 5 we will not go down, because the man *t* us,
43:11 Their father Israel then *t* them:
43:16 Benjamin with them, he *t* his head steward,
43:29 your youngest brother, of whom you *t* me?"
44:21 Then you *t* your servants, 'Bring him
44:23 But you *t* your servants, 'Unless your
44:25 our father *t* us to come back and buy some
45: 4 "Come closer to me," he *t* his brothers.
45:17 So Pharaoh *t* Joseph:
45:24 sent his brothers on their way, he *t* them,
45:26 When they *t* him, "Joseph is still alive
45:27 to him all that Joseph had *t* them,
47: 1 Joseph went and *t* Pharaoh, "My father
47:23 Joseph *t* the people: "Now that I
48: 2 When Jacob was *t*, "Your son Joseph
Ex 1:15 The king of Egypt *t* the Hebrew midwives,
4:30 Aaron *t* them everything the LORD had said
5:10 foremen of the people went out and *t* them,
5:16 and still we are *t* to make bricks.
5:19 *t* not to reduce the daily amount of bricks.
6: 9 But when Moses *t* this to the Israelites,
7: 8 The LORD *t* Moses and Aaron,
8: 1 The LORD then *t* Moses, "Say to Aaron:
8:16 LORD *t* Moses, "Early tomorrow morning
9:13 Then the LORD *t* Moses, "Early tomorrow
10: 3 Moses and Aaron went to Pharaoh and *t* him,
11: 1 LORD *t* Moses, "One more plague will
14:26 LORD *t* Moses, "Stretch out your hand
15:26 voice of the LORD, your God," he *t* them,
16: 6 So Moses and Aaron *t* all the Israelites,
16:15 But Moses *t* them, "This is the bread
16:19 Moses also *t* them, "Let no one keep
16:23 came and reported this to Moses, he *t* them,
16:33 Moses then *t* Aaron, "Take an urn
17:10 So Joshua did as Moses *t* him:
18: 8 Moses then *t* his father-in-law of all that
19: 9 The LORD also *t* him, "I am coming
19:21 Then the LORD *t* Moses, "Go down
19:25 went down to the people and *t* them this.
20:22 The LORD *t* Moses, "Thus shall you
23:13 Give heed to all that I have *t* you.
24: 1 Moses himself was *t*, "Come up to the
24: 3 will do everything that the LORD has *t* us."
24:14 The elders, however, had been *t* by him,
30:34 The LORD *t* Moses, "Take these aromatic
32:24 So I *t* them, 'Let anyone who has gold
32:27 Levites then rallied to him, and he *t* them,
32:34 and lead the people whither I have *t* you.
33: 1 The LORD *t* Moses, "You and the
34:32 all that the LORD had *t* him on Mount Sinai.
35: 4 Moses *t* the whole Israelite community,
36: 5 left the work they were doing, and *t* Moses,
Lv 8: 5 Moses *t* them what the LORD had ordered to
9: 7 Come up to the altar," Moses then *t* Aaron,
10: 7 So they did as Moses *t* them.
17:12 That is why I have *t* the Israelites:
17:14 body is its blood, I have *t* the Israelites:
21:24 *t* this to Aaron and his sons and to all
24:23 When Moses *t* this to the Israelites,
Nm 1:48 For the LORD had *t* Moses.
9: 4 *t* the Israelites to celebrate the Passover.
11:24 and *t* the people what the LORD had said.
11:27 So, when a young man quickly *t* Moses,
13:27 They *t* Moses: "We went into the land
22:13 Balaam arose and *t* the princes of Balak,
22:16 On coming to Balaam they *t* him,
25: 5 So Moses *t* the Israelite judges,
26:65 For the LORD had *t* them that they would
31: 3 So Moses *t* the people, "Select men
31:21 Eleazar the priest *t* the soldiers who had
Dt 10: 9 heritage, as the LORD, your God, has *t* him.
12:21 manner I have *t* you any of your herd
18: 2 himself is his heritage, as he has *t* him.
28:68 I *t* you that you were never to see again;
31: 2 *t* me that I shall not cross this Jordan.
Jos 10:17 When Joshua was *t* that the five kings had
Jgs 6:13 wondrous deeds of which our fathers *t* us
7:17 "Watch me and follow my lead," he *t* them.
13: 6 The woman went and *t* her husband,
13:10 the woman ran in haste and *t* her husband.
14: 2 On his return he *t* his father and mother,
14:16 countrymen, but have not *t* me the answer."
14:16 not *t* it even to my father or my mother,
14:17 she importuned him, he *t* her the answer,
15: 6 asked who had done this, they were *t*,
16:10 Samson, "You have mocked me and *t* me lies.
16:13 to now you have mocked me and *t* me lies.
16:15 not *t* me the secret of your great strength!"
16:17 completely into his confidence and *t* her,
20: 3 to be *t* how the crime had taken place,
21:11 They were *t* to include under the ban all
Ru 1:10 and *t* her they would return with her to
2:19 Then she *t* her mother-in-law with whom she
2:21 "He even *t* me," added Ruth the Moabite,
3:16 So she *t* her all the man had done for her,
1Sm 3:17 to you if you hide a single thing he *t* you."
3:18 So Samuel *t* him everything,
8:11 He *t* them: "The rights of the king
9:17 him, "This is the man of whom I *t* you;
9:23 portion I gave you and *t* you to put aside."
16:17 Saul then *t* his servants, "Find me
17:34 Then David *t* Saul: "Your servant
19: 2 who was very fond of David, *t* him:
19:19 *t* that David was in the sheds near Ramah,
19:22 and was *t*, "At the sheds near Ramah."
21: 3 "The king gave me a commission and *t* me
22:21 When Abiathar *t* David that Saul had slain
23: 7 Saul was *t* that David had entered Keilah,
24: 2 *t* that David was in the desert near Engedi.
25:36 So she *t* him nothing at all before
25:37 sober, his wife *t* him what had happened.
26:19 share in the LORD's inheritance, but am *t*:
27: 4 Saul was *t* that David had fled to Gath,
2Sm 5: 6 David was *t*, "You cannot enter here:
7:22 no God but you, as we have heard it *t*.
8: 2 He *t* off two lengths of line for execution,
10: 5 When he was *t* of it, King David sent
11: 3 inquiries made about the woman and was *t*,
11:10 David was *t* that Uriah had not gone home.
11:23 He *t* David: "The men had us
14:19 Joab who instructed me and *t* your servant
16:10 Suppose the LORD has *t* him to curse David;
16:11 let him curse, for the LORD has *t* him to.
19: 2 Joab was *t* that the king was weeping and
1Kgs 1:27 without my being *t* who was to succeed
2:29 King Solomon was *t* that Joab had fled to
10: 6 and your wisdom is true," she *t* the king.
13:11 whose sons came and *t* him all that the man
13:17 "for I was *t* by the word of the LORD
13:18 and an angel *t* me in the word of the LORD
13:22 in the place where he *t* you to do neither,
18:13 Have you not been *t*.
19: 1 Ahab *t* Jezebel all that Elijah had done
2Kgs 4: 7 She went and *t* the man of God,
4:13 when she stood before Elisha, he *t* Gehazi,
5: 4 Naaman went and *t* his lord just what the
5:13 had *t* you to do something extraordinary,
7:15 The messengers returned and *t* the king.
8: 6 the woman, and she *t* him her story.
8: 7 was *t* that the man of God had come there,
8:14 "He *t* me that you would surely recover,"
9:12 *t* them what the young man had said to him,
9:36 They returned to Jehu, and when they *t* him,
10: 8 princes," a messenger came in and *t* him.
17:12 served idols, although the LORD had *t* them,

TOLD (cont.)

1Chr 19: 5 "Remain at Jericho," the king *t* them,
2Chr 9: 5 and your wisdom is true," she *t* the king.
35:21 kingdom, and God has *t* me to hasten.
Neh 2:12 I had not *t* anyone what my God had
4: 6 and had *t* us ten times over that they were
4:16 At the same time I *t* the people to spend
Tb 2:14 and *t* her to give it back to its owners.
6: 5 The angel then *t* him:
7:13 her mother and *t* her to bring a scroll,
7:16 and made the bed in the room, as she was *t*,
8:14 *t* the girl's parents that Tobiah was alive,
8:18 Then he *t* his servants to fill in the
9: 5 bond and *t* him about Tobit's son Tobiah,
10: 7 I have already *t* you how I left him."
11:15 Tobiah *t* his father that his journey had
Jdt 11: 9 him, he *t* them all he had said to you.
11:19 This was *t* me, and announced to me
14: 8 So Judith *t* him, in the presence
Est 2:20 because Mordecai had *t* her not to;
2:22 known to Mordecai, he *t* Queen Esther,
3: 4 since he had *t* them that he was a Jew.
3: 6 they had *t* Haman of Mordecai's nationality,
4: 4 Esther's maids and eunuchs came and *t* her.
4: 7 and Mordecai *t* him all that had happened,
4: 9 to Esther and *t* her what Mordecai had said.
6:13 When he *t* his wife Zeresh and all his
1Mc 4:26 went and *t* Lysias all that had occurred.
5:25 who received them peacefully and *t* them
8: 2 He was also *t* of their battles and the
10:15 he was also *t* of the battles and valiant
11: 5 he was *t* what the latter had done;
11:40 he *t* him of all that Demetrius had done
12:23 given orders that you should be *t* of this."
15:36 When he *t* him of Simon's words,
16: 1 John then went up from Gazara and *t* his
2Mc 1:33 and the king of the Persians was *t* that,
2:13 it is also *t* in the records and in
3: 9 he *t* him about the information that had
3:33 to the high priest Onias," they *t* him.
6:23 He *t* them to send him at once to the abode
7:10 put out his tongue at once when *t* to do so,
10:21 When Maccabeus was *t* what had happened he
11:29 Menelaus has *t* us of your wish to return
13:12 encouraged them and *t* them to stand ready.
Jb 7: 3 and troubled nights have been *t* off for me.
37:20 Will he be *t* about it when I speak,
Ps(s) 22:31 Let the coming generation be *t* of the LORD
52: 2 when Doeg the Edomite went and *t* Saul,
59:13 for the lies they have *t* under oath.
Prv 25: 7 For it is better that you be *t*,
Sir 14:12 have you been *t* the grave's appointed time.
Is 52:15 For those who have not been *t* shall see,
Jer 13: 6 the loincloth which I *t* you to hide there.
22: 1 The LORD *t* me this:
26:18 of Judah, and he *t* all the people of Judah:
34: 6 Jeremiah *t* all these things to Zedekiah,
36:20 they *t* him everything that had happened,
Ez 11: 5 the LORD fell upon me, and he *t* me to say:
11:25 I *t* the exiles everything the LORD
12: 7 I did as I was *t*.
37: 7 I prophesied as I had been *t*,
37:10 I prophesied as he *t* me,
Dn 1: 3 The king *t* Ashpenaz,
2:15 When Arioch *t* him, Daniel went
14:34 the field, when an angel of the Lord *t* him,
Jon 1:10 from the LORD, because he had *t* them.—
Mi 6: 8 You have been *t*, O man, what is good,
Hb 1: 5 you would not have believed, were it *t*.
Zep 2:15 That *t* herself, "There is no other
Mt 3: 7 Who *t* you to flee from the wrath to come?
8:22 But Jesus *t* him, "Follow me, and let
9:28 "Yes, Lord," they *t* him.
12:48 He said to the one who had *t* him,
14: 4 That was because John had *t* him,
17:20 you have so little trust," he *t* them.
19:21 Jesus *t* him, "If you seek perfection, go,
20: 7 'No one has hired us,' they *t* him.
20:23 He *t* them: "From the cup I drink of,
20:33 "Lord," they *t* him, "open our eyes!"
23: 1 Then Jesus *t* the crowds and his disciples:
24:25 I have *t* you all about it beforehand;
27:65 Pilate *t* them, "You have a guard.
Mk 1:37 down, and when they found him, they *t* him,
3: 9 he *t* his disciples to have a fishing boat
3:32 The crowd seated around him *t* him,
4:11 He *t* them: "To you the mystery
5:16 possessed man, and *t* them about the swine.
5:19 not grant his request, but *t* him instead:
5:33 in front of him and *t* him the whole truth.
5:43 and *t* them to give her something to eat.
6:18 That was because John had *t* Herod,
6:22 The king *t* the girl, "Ask for anything
6:39 He *t* them to make the people sit down on
7:27 He *t* her: "Let the sons
8: 7 fish, he *t* them to distribute these also.
9:12 He *t* them: "Elijah will indeed come
9:29 He *t* them,
10: 5 But Jesus *t* them: "He wrote that
10:11 He *t* them, "Whoever divorces his wife
10:21 Jesus looked at him with love and *t* him,
10:38 Jesus *t* them, "You do not know what
10:39 "We can," they *t* him.
11: 6 They answered as Jesus had *t* them to,
11:22 In reply Jesus *t* them:
12:16 "Caesar's," they *t* him.
12:26 about the burning bush, how God *t* him,
12:34 the insight of this answer and *t* him,
12:43 He called his disciples over and *t* them:
13:23 I have *t* you about it beforehand.
14: 9 what she has done will be *t* in her memory."
14:16 city they found it just as he had *t* them,
16: 7 where you will see him just as he *t* you.'"
16:15 Then he *t* them: "Go into the whole
Lk 2:17 what had been *t* them concerning this child.
2:20 seen, in accord with what had been *t* them.
3: 7 Who *t* you to flee from the wrath to come?
3:14 He *t* them, "Don't bully anyone.
8:20 He was *t*, "Your mother and your
8:21 He *t* them in reply, "My mother
8:36 They were *t* by witnesses how the possessed
8:55 he *t* them to give her something to eat.
9:50 Jesus *t* him in reply, "Do not stop him,
12:16 He *t* them a parable in these words:
13: 1 some were present who *t* him about the
18: 1 He *t* them a parable on the necessity of
20:19 he had *t* the parable with them in mind.
21:29 Then he *t* them a parable:
24: 9 they *t* all these things to the Eleven and
24:10 other women with them also *t* the apostles,
Jn 1:33 one who sent me to baptize with water *t* me,
1:45 Philip sought out Nathanael and *t* him,
1:50 I *t* you I saw you under the fig tree?
2: 3 the wine ran out, and Jesus' mother *t* him,
2:16 He *t* those who were selling doves:
4:21 Jesus *t* her: "Believe me, woman,
4:29 see someone who *t* me everything I ever did!
4:32 But he *t* them: "I have food to eat
4:39 "He *t* me everything I ever did."
4:42 As they *t* the woman:
4:50 Jesus *t* him, "Return home.
4:52 the boy had shown improvement, they *t* him,
4:53 the father realized, that Jesus had *t* him,
5:11 "It was the man who cured me who *t* me,
5:12 person who *t* you to pick it up and walk,"
6:12 they had had enough, he *t* his disciples,
6:20 They were frightened, but he *t* them,
6:36 But as I *t* you—though you have seen
6:43 "Stop your murmuring," Jesus *t* them.
6:65 "This is why I have *t* you that no one can
8:39 Jesus *t* them: "If you were Abraham's
8:40 a man who has *t* you the truth which I have
9: 7 Then he *t* him, "Go, wash in the pool
9:15 He *t* them, "He put mud on my eyes.
9:27 "I have *t* you once, but you would not
11:25 Jesus *t* her: "I am the resurrection
11:44 "Untie him," Jesus *t* them,
13:10 Jesus *t* him, "The man who has bathed
14: 2 how could I have *t* you that I was going to
14: 6 Jesus *t* him: "I am the way,
14:25 have I *t* you while I was still with you;
14:26 and remind you of all that I *t* you.
15:20 Remember what I *t* you:
16: 1 "I have *t* you all this to keep your faith
16: 4 But I have *t* you these things that when
18: 8 "I have *t* you, I am he," Jesus said.
20: 2 disciple (the one Jesus loved) and *t* them,
21:10 the fish you just caught," Jesus *t* them.
21:12 "Come and eat your meal," Jesus *t* them.
21:23 Jesus never *t* him, as a matter of fact,
Acts 1: 4 them, he *t* them not to leave Jerusalem:
4:23 two went back to their own people and *t*
9: 6 the city, where you will be *t* what to do."
12: 8 Then the angel *t* him, "Now put on your
13:41 would have believed even if you had been *t*.'"
15: 5 circumcised and *t* to keep the Mosaic law.
15:14 Symeon has *t* you how God first concerned
21:24 nothing in what they have been *t* about you,
22:10 *t* about everything you are destined to do.'
23:16 him to enter, and he *t* Paul about it.
27:25 will all work out just as I have been *t*,
Rom 4:18 many nations, just as it was once *t* him,
Col 1: 8 it was who *t* us of your love in the Spirit.
Rv 6:11 and they were *t* to be patient a little
7:14 He then *t* me, "These are the ones

TOLERATE (5)

Est 3: 8 so it is not proper for the king to *t* them.
Dn 13:57 of Judah did not *t* your wickedness.
2Tm 4: 3 come when people will not *t* sound doctrine,
Rv 2: 2 I know you cannot *t* wicked men;
2:20 you *t* a Jezebel

TOLERATED (1)

Gn 34: 7 such a thing could not be *t*.

TOLL (3)

Mt 17:25 of the world take tax or *t* from their sons,
Rom 13: 7 *t* to whom toll is due;
13: 7 toll to whom *t* is due;

TOLLS (4)

Ezr 4:13 will no longer pay taxes, tributes, or *t*;
4:20 taxes, tributes, and *t* were paid to them.
7:24 impose taxes, tributes, or *t* on any priest,
1Mc 10:31 and her territory, her tithes and her *t*,

TOMB (58)

Gn 50: 5 bury him in the *t* that he had prepared
Jgs 8:32 died and was buried in the *t* of his father
1Sm 10: 2 *t* at Zelzah in the territory of Benjamin,
2Sm 2:32 buried him in his father's *t* in Bethlehem.
17:23 he died and was buried in his father's *t*.
19:38 own city by the *t* of his father and mother.
21:14 were buried in the *t* of his father Kish
2Kgs 9:28 *t* of his ancestors in the City of David.
2Chr 16:14 They buried him in the *t* he had hewn for
Jdt 16:23 they buried her in the *t* of her husband,
1Mc 9:19 him in the *t* of their fathers at Modein.
13:27 Then Simon erected over the *t* of his
13:30 This *t* which he built at Modein is there
2Mc 5:10 or any place in the *t* of his ancestors.
Wis 10: 7 ripens, and the *t* of a disbelieving soul,
Sir 30:18 are like the offerings placed before a *t*.
Is 14:18 nations lie in glory, each in his own *t*;
22:16 on a height and carved his *t* in the rock:
22:16 that here you have hewn for yourself a *t*?"
Ez 39:11 Gog for his *t* a well-known place in Israel,
Mt 27:60 fresh linen and laid it in his own new *t*
27:60 across the entrance of the *t* and went away.
27:61 Mary remained sitting there, facing the *t*.
27:64 You should issue an order having the *t*
27:65 Go and secure the *t* as best you can."
28: 1 came with the other Mary to inspect the *t*.
28: 8 hurried away from the *t* half-overjoyed,
Mk 6:29 carried his body away and laid it in a *t*.
15:46 him in a *t* which had been cut out of rock.
15:46 a stone across the entrance of the *t*.
16: 2 first day of the week they came to the *t*.
16: 3 stone for us from the entrance to the *t*?"
16: 5 On entering the *t* they saw a young man
16: 8 fled from the *t* bewildered and trembling;
Lk 23:53 and laid it in a *t* hewn out of the rock,
23:55 They saw the *t* and how his body was buried.
24: 1 *t* bringing the spices they had prepared.
24: 2 found the stone rolled back from the *t*;
24: 3 but when they entered the *t*,
24: 9 On their return from the *t*,
24:12 Peter, however, got up and ran to the *t*.
24:22 *t* before dawn and failed to find his body,
24:24 Some of our number went to the *t* and found
Jn 11:17 had already been in the *t* four days.
11:31 she was going to the *t* to weep there.
11:38 troubled in spirit, Jesus approached the *t*.
12:17 when he called Lazarus out of the *t*
19:41 new *t* in which no one had ever been buried.
19:42 Jesus there, for the *t* was close at hand.
20: 1 still dark, Mary Magdalene came to the *t*.
20: 2 them, "The Lord has been taken from the *t*!
20: 3 started out on their way toward the *t*.
20: 4 outran Peter and reached the *t* first.
20: 6 came along behind him and entered the *t*.
20: 8 who had arrived first at the *t* went in.
20:11 Meanwhile, Mary stood weeping beside the *t*.
Acts 7:16 placed in the *t* which Abraham had bought
13:29 him down from the tree and laid him in a *t*.

TOMBS (23)

2Chr 21:20 of David, but not in the *t* of the kings.
24:25 of David, but not in the *t* of the kings.
28:27 bring him to the *t* of the kings of Israel.
32:33 to the *t* of the descendants of David.
34: 4 the *t* of those who had sacrificed to them;
35:24 He was buried in the *t* of his ancestors,
Neh 3:16 to a place opposite the *t* of David,
1Mc 2:70 buried in the *t* of his fathers in Modein.
2Mc 12:39 with their kinsmen in their ancestral *t*.
Ps(s) 49:12 *T* are their homes forever,
Mt 8:28 he encountered two men coming out of the *t*.
23:27 You are like whitewashed *t*,
23:29 You erect *t* for the prophets and decorate
27:52 The earth quaked, boulders split, *t* opened.
27:53 they came forth from their *t* and entered
Mk 5: 2 a man from the *t* who had an unclean spirit.
5: 3 The man had taken refuge among the *t*;
5: 5 and day, amid the *t* and on the hillsides,
Lk 11:44 like hidden *t* over which men walk unawares."
11:47 You build the *t* of the prophets,
11:48 committed the murders and you erect the *t*.
Jn 5:28 *t* shall hear his voice and come forth.
Rom 3:13 Their throats are open *t*;

TOMBSTONE (1)

2Kgs 23:17 words, he asked, "What is that *t* I see?"

TOMBSTONES (1)

Lk 8:27 did not live in a house, but among the *t*.

TOMORROW (70)

Ex 7:15 *T* morning, when he sets out for
8: 6 *T*," said Pharaoh.
8:16 "Early *t* morning present yourself to
8:19 This sign shall take place *t*."
8:25 that the flies may depart *t* from Pharaoh

9: 5 T the LORD shall do this in the land."
9:13 "Early t morning present yourself to
9:18 t at this hour I will rain down such
10: 4 t I will bring locusts into your country.
16:19 no one keep any of it over until t morning."
16:23 T is a day of complete rest,
17: 9 and t go out and engage Amalek in battle.
19:10 have them sanctify themselves today and t.
32: 5 and proclaimed, T is a feast of the LORD."
34: 2 Get ready for t morning,
Nm 11:18 Sanctify yourselves for t,
14:25 turn away t and set out in the desert on
16: 5 "May the LORD make known t morning who
16: 7 place incense in them before the LORD t.
16:16 your band shall appear before the LORD t—
Jos 3: 5 for t the LORD will perform wonders among
7:13 Tell them to sanctify themselves before t,
11: 6 t I will stretch them slain before Israel.
22:18 the LORD today and by t he will be angry
Jgs 9:33 Promptly at sunrise t morning,
16: 2 waited, saying, T morning we will kill him."
19: 9 Early t you can start your journey home."
20:28 for t I will deliver him into your power."
Ru 3:13 Stay as you are for tonight, and t,
1Sm 9:16 "At this time t I will send you a man
11: 9 the inhabitants of Jabesh-gilead that t,
11:10 said to Nahash, T we will surrender to you,
19: 2 please be on your guard t morning;
19:10 yourself tonight, t you will be killed."
20: 5 T is the new moon,
20:12 will sound out my father about this time t.
20:18 T is the new moon;
28:19 By t you and your sons will be with me,
29:10 So the first thing t, you and your lord's
2Sm 11:12 here today also, I shall dismiss you t."
1Kgs 19: 2 if by this time t I have not done with
20: 6 this time t I will send my servants to you,
2Kgs 6:28 then t we will eat my son.'
7: 1 'At this time t a seah of fine flour will
7:18 at this time t at the gate of Samaria."
10: 6 and come to me in Jezreel at this time t."
2Chr 20:16 Go down against them t.
20:17 T go out to meet them,
Est 5: 8 come with Haman t to a banquet which I
5:12 again t I am to be her guest,
9:13 again t to act according to today's decree,
1Mc 2:63 he is exalted, and t he is not to be found,
5:27 T their enemies plan to attack the
Prv 3:28 "Go, and come again, t I will give,"
27: 1 Boast not of t, for you know not what any
Sir 10:10 doctor jests, a king today t he is dead.
20:14 He lends today, he asks it back t;
Is 22:13 "Eat and drink, for t we die!"
56:12 strong drink, And t will be like today,
Mt 6:30 blooms today and is thrown on the fire t,
6:34 Enough, then, of worrying about t.
6:34 Let t take care of itself.
Lk 12:28 grows today and is thrown on the fire t,
13:32 and t I cast out devils and perform cures,
13:33 that, I must proceed on course today, t,
Acts 23:20 to ask you t to have Paul brought down
25:22 T you shall hear him," replied Festus.
1Cor 15:32 "Let us eat and drink, for t we die!"
Jas 4:13 or t we shall go to such and such a town,
4:14 no idea what kind of life will be yours t.

TONE (2)

Sir 27:23 his t and twists your words to your ruin.
Mt 27:46 midafternoon Jesus cried out in a loud t,

TONGS (3)

1Kgs 7:49 with their flowers, lamps, and t of gold;
2Chr 4:21 and gold t [this was the purest gold],
Is 6: 6 which he had taken with t from the altar.

TONGUE (118)

Ex 4:10 but I am slow of speech and t."
Dt 28:49 a nation whose t you do not understand,
Jgs 7: 5 up the water as a dog does with its t;
2Sm 23: 2 his word was on my t.
2Mc 7: 4 t of the one who had spoken for the others,
7:10 put out his t at once when told to do so,
15:29 native t in praise of the divine Sovereign.
15:33 He cut out the t of the godless Nicanor,
Jb 5:21 the scourge of the t you shall be hidden,
6:30 Is there insincerity on my t,
20:12 in his mouth, and he hides it under his t,
27: 4 not speak falsehood, nor my t utter deceit!
33: 2 my t and my voice form words.
40:25 with a hook, or curb his t with a bit?
Ps(s) 5:10 they flatter with their t.
10: 7 under his t are mischief and iniquity.
12: 4 LORD destroy all smooth every boastful t,
15: 3 in his heart and slanders not with his t;
22:16 like baked clay, my t cleaves to my jaws;
34:14 Keep your t from evil and your lips from
35:28 Then my t shall recount your justice,
37:30 of wisdom and his t utters what is right.
39: 2 watch my ways, so as not to sin with my t;
39: 4 I spoke out with my t:
45: 2 my t is nimble as the pen of a skillful
50:19 for evil, you harness your t to deceit.
51:16 then my t shall revel in your justice.
52: 4 your t is like a sharpened razor,
52: 6 that means ruin, you of the deceitful t!
57: 5 and arrows, their t is a sharp sword.
66:17 in words, praise was on the tip of my t.
71:24 and my t day by day shall discourse on
114: 1 house of Jacob from a people of alien t,
119:172 May my t sing of your promise,
120: 2 me from lying lip, from treacherous t.
120: 3 on you, with more besides, O treacherous t?
126: 2 with laughter, and our t with rejoicing.
137: 6 may my t cleave to my palate if I remember
139: 4 Even before a word is on my t,
140:12 of wicked t shall not abide in the land;
Prv 6:17 Haughty eyes, a lying t,
6:24 wife, from the smooth t of the adulteress.
10:20 Like choice silver is the just man's t;
10:31 wisdom, but the perverse t will be cut off.
12:18 thrusts, but the t of the wise is healing.
12:19 Truthful lips endure forever, the lying t,
15: 2 The t of the wise pours out knowledge,
15: 4 A soothing t is a tree of life,
16: 1 but what the t utters is from the LORD.
17: 4 listens to falsehood from a mischievous t.
18:21 Death and life are in the power of the t;
21: 6 t is chasing a bubble over deadly snares.
21:23 mouth and his t keeps himself from trouble.
25:15 persuaded, and a soft t will break a bone.
25:23 and a backbiting t an angry countenance.
26:28 The lying t is its owner's enemy,
28:23 in the end than one with a flattering t.
31:26 in wisdom, and on her t is kindly counsel.
Sg 4:11 sweetmeats and milk are under your t;
Wis 1: 6 of his heart and the listener to his t.
Sir 5:15 A man's t can be his downfall.
5:16 use not your t for calumny;
6: 1 "That for the evil man with double t!"
15:10 But praise is offered by the wise man's t;
19:15 who has not sinned with his t?
20:16 Those who eat his bread have an evil t.
20:17 is less sudden than a slip of the t;
22:27 through them, that my t may not destroy me?
25: 7 as blessed, a tenth whom my t proclaims:
25: 8 Happy is he who sins not with his t,
26: 6 and a scourging t like the other three.
28:14 A meddlesome t subverts many,
28:15 A meddlesome t can drive virtuous women
28:17 welt, but a blow from the t smashes bones;
28:18 of the sword, but not as many as by the t.
28:26 Take care not to slip by your t and fall
37:18 and life, their absolute mistress is the t.
51: 3 mercy From the scourge of a slanderous t,
51:22 reward, and my t will declare his praises.
Is 5:24 as the t of fire licks up stubble,
11:15 shall dry up the t of the Sea of Egypt,
30:27 with fury, his t is like a consuming fire;
33:19 people of alien t you will look no more,
35: 6 a stag, then the t of the dumb will sing.
45:23 by me every t shall swear,
50: 4 Lord GOD has given me a well-trained t,
54:17 every t you shall prove false that
57: 4 open wide your mouth, and put out your t?
59: 3 speak falsehood, and your t utters deceit.
Jer 9: 7 A murderous arrow is his t,
18:18 And so, let us destroy him by his own t;
Lam 4: 4 The t of the suckling cleaves to the roof
Ez 3:26 I will make your t stick to your palate so
Zep 3:13 be found in their mouths a deceitful t;
Mk 7:33 man's ears and, spitting, touched his t;
Lk 1:64 his mouth was opened and his t loosed,
16:24 tip of his finger in water to refresh my t,
Jn 8:44 Lying speech is his native t;
Acts 2: 8 that each of us hears them in his native t?
2:11 t about the marvels God has accomplished."
2:26 heart has been glad and my t has rejoiced,
Rom 14:11 me and every t shall give praise to God."
1Cor 14: 2 in a t is talking not to men but to God.
14: 4 He who speaks in a t builds up himself,
14: 9 speech because you are speaking in a t,
14:13 This means that the man who speaks in a t
14:14 If I pray in a t my spirit is at prayer
14:19 others than ten thousand words in a t.
14:26 one speaks in a t, another interprets
Phil 2:11 t proclaim to the glory of God the Father:
Jas 1:26 control his t imagines that he is devout,
3: 5 The t is something like that.
3: 6 The t is such a flame.
3: 6 The t defiles the entire body.
3: 8 the t no man can tame.
1Pt 3:10 must keep his t from evil and his lips from
Rv 5: 9 purchased for God men of every race and t,
7: 9 from every nation and race, people and t.

TONGUES (44)

Jb 29:10 their t stuck to the roofs of their mouths.
Ps(s) 12: 5 Those who say, "We are heroes with our t;
31:21 within your abode from the strife of t.
64: 4 Who sharpen their t like swords,
64: 9 He brings them down by their own t;
68:24 the t of your dogs will have their share
78:36 their mouths and lied to him with their t,
109: 2 They have spoken to me with lying t,
140: 4 make their t sharp as those of serpents;
Wis 1:11 and from calumny withhold your t;
Sir 4:24 and knowledge through the t rejoinder.
17: 5 He forms men's t and eyes and ears,
51: 6 of lies, from the arrows of dishonest t.
Is 41:17 in vain, their t are parched with thirst.
Jer 9: 2 They ready their t like a drawn bow;
9: 4 They have accustomed their t to lying,
Bar 6: 7 Their t are smoothed by woodworkers;
Hos 7:16 sword because of the insolence of their t;
Mi 6:12 falsehood with deceitful t in their heads!
Zec 8:23 every nationality, speaking different t,
14:12 and their t shall rot in their mouths.
Acts 2: 3 T as of fire appeared,
2: 4 began to express themselves in foreign t
10:46 hear speaking in t and glorifying God.
19: 6 to speak in t and to utter prophecies.
Rom 3:13 they use their t to deceive;
1Cor 12:10 gift of t, another that of interpreting the t.
12:28 administrators, and those who speak in t.
12:30 in t, all have the gift of interpretation of t?
13: 1 I speak with human t and angelic as well,
13: 8 Prophecies will cease, t will be silent,
14: 5 I should like it if all of you spoke in t,
14: 5 is greater than one who speaks in t,
14: 6 that I should come to you speaking in t.
14:18 God, I speak in t more than any of you,
14:21 "In strange t and in alien speech I will
14:22 The gift of t is a sign,
14:23 assembled and everyone is speaking in t,
14:27 talk in t let it be at most two or three,
14:39 and do not forbid those who speak in t,
Rv 16:10 men bit their t in pain and blasphemed the
17:15 large numbers of peoples and nations and t.

TONIGHT (20)

Gn 19: 5 are the men who came to your house t?
19:34 Let us ply him with wine again t,
30:15 son's mandrakes, Jacob may lie with you t."
Jos 4: 3 and place them where you are to stay t."
Jgs 9:32 set an ambush t in the fields,
Ru 1:12 or if t I had a husband or had borne sons,
3:13 Stay as you are for t, and tomorrow,
1Sm 19:10 informed him, "Unless you save yourself t,
2Sm 17: 1 men, and be off in pursuit of David t.
Tb 6:11 T we must stay with Raguel,
6:13 T I will ask the girl's father to let us
6:13 t we must speak for the girl,
6:16 that t you shall have her for your wife!
7:10 "Eat and drink and be merry t,
7:11 And t, son, may the Lord of heaven
Jdt 8:33 gate t to let me pass through with my maid;
11: 3 Your life is spared t and for the future.
Mt 26:31 to them, T your faith in me will be shaken,
26:34 cock crows t you will deny me three times."
Acts 23:23 to leave for Caesarea by nine o'clock t,

TOOK (661)

Gn 2:15 The LORD God then t the man and settled
2:21 he t out one of his ribs and closed up its
3: 6 So she t some of its fruit and ate it;
4:19 Lamech t two wives;
5:24 and he was no longer here, for God t him.
6: 2 and so they t for their wives as many
9:23 Shem and Japheth, however, t a robe,
11:29 Abram and Nahor t wives;
11:31 Terah t his son Abram, his grandson Lot,
12: 5 Abram t his wife Sarai, his brother's
12:19 is my sister,' so that I t her for my wife?
15: 5 He t him outside and said:
16: 3 land of Canaan, his wife Sarai t her maid,
17:23 t his son Ishmael and all his slaves,
20: 2 Abimelech, king of Gerar, sent and t Sarah.
20:14 Then Abimelech t flocks and herds and male
21: 1 t note of Sarah as he had said he would;
21:27 Then Abraham t sheep and cattle and gave
21:31 the two t an oath there.
22: 3 his donkey, t with him his son Isaac,
22: 6 Thereupon Abraham t the wood for the
22:10 out and t the knife to slaughter his son.
22:13 So he went and t the ram and offered it up
24: 7 who t me from my father's house and the
24:10 servant then t ten of his master's camels,
24:22 t out a gold ring weighing half a shekel,
24:61 the servant t Rebekah and went on his way.
24:67 Then Isaac t Rebekah into his tent;
27:15 Rebekah then t the best clothes of her
27:36 First he t away my birthright,
28:18 t the stone that he had put under his head,
29:23 At nightfall he t his daughter Leah and
31:45 Then Jacob t a stone and set it up as a
31:53 t the oath by the Awesome One of Isaac.
32:23 however, Jacob arose, t his two wives,
34:25 Levi, two of Jacob's sons, t their swords,
34:26 they t Dinah from Shechem's house and left.
34:29 and t for loot whatever was in the houses.
36: 2 t his wives from among the Canaanite women:
36: 6 Esau t his wives, his sons, his daughters,
37:24 they t him and threw him into the cistern,
37:28 up out of the cistern and t him to Egypt.
37:31 They t Joseph's tunic,

TOOK (cont.)

38: 7 so the LORD *t* his life.
38:10 the LORD, and the LORD *t* his life too.
38:14 his sheep, she *t* off her widow's garb,
38:19 she *t* off her shawl and put on her
39: 4 he *t* a liking to Joseph and made him his
40:11 so I *t* the grapes, pressed them out into
41:42 Pharaoh *t* off his signet ring and put it
43:15 *t* double the amount of money with them,
46: 6 They *t* with them their livestock and the
46: 7 he *t* with him to Egypt.
48: 1 So he *t* along with him his two sons,
48:13 Then Joseph *t* the two,
48:17 so he *t* hold of his father's hand,
Ex 2: 3 hide him no longer, she *t* a papyrus basket,
2: 9 woman therefore *t* the child and nursed it.
4:20 So Moses *t* his wife and his sons,
4:25 But Zipporah *t* a piece of flint and cut
9:10 So they *t* soot from a furnace and stood in
10:19 which *t* up the locusts and hurled them
12:34 *t* their dough before it was leavened,
13:19 Moses also *t* Joseph's bones along,
14:19 the front, *t* up its place behind them,
15:20 Aaron's sister, *t* a tambourine in her hand,
18: 2 his father-in-law Jethro *t* along Zipporah,
18:11 for he *t* occasion of their being dealt
20:18 So they *t* up a position much farther away
24: 6 Moses *t* half of the blood and put it in
24: 8 *t* the blood and sprinkled it on the people,
32: 3 So all the people *t* off their earrings and
40:20 *t* the commandments and put them in the ark;
Lv 8:23 Moses *t* some of its blood and put it on
8:25 He then *t* the fat:
8:26 before the LORD he *t* one unleavened cake,
8:29 He then *t* the breast and waved it as a
10: 1 sons Nadab and Abihu *t* their censers and,
10: 5 So they went in and *t* them,
24:23 they *t* the blasphemer outside the camp and
27: 8 if the one who *t* the vow is too poor to
Nm 1:17 Aaron *t* these men who had been designated,
3:16 *t* their census in accordance with the
3:42 So Moses *t* a census of all the first-born
3:49 So Moses *t* the silver as ransom from those
4:37 serve in the meeting tent, which Moses *t*,
4:41 serve in the meeting tent, which Moses *t*,
4:45 men of the Merarite clans which Moses *t*,
9:15 until morning it *t* on the appearance of fire
16: 1 son of Reuben] *t* two hundred and fifty
16:18 So they all *t* their censers,
16:18 they *t* their stand by the entrance of the
17:12 Aaron *t* his censer and ran in among the
17:24 prince identified his own staff and *t* it,
20: 9 *t* the staff from its place before the LORD,
21: 1 them in battle and *t* some of them captive.
21:24 and *t* possession of his land from the
21:35 to him, and they *t* possession of his land.
22:24 Then the angel of the LORD *t* his stand in
22:41 morning Balak *t* Balaam up on Bamoth-baal,
23:28 So he *t* Balaam to the top of Peor,
31:11 Then they *t* all the booty,
31:27 giving half to those who *t* active part in
31:47 LORD had ordered, *t* one out of every fifty,
35:25 to the city of asylum where he *t* refuge;
Dt 1:15 So I *t* outstanding men of your tribes,
1:30 *t* your part before your very eyes in Egypt,
2:21 who ousted them and *t* their place.
2:23 villages as far as Gaza, and *t* their place.]
3: 7 of each city we *t* as booty for ourselves.
3: 8 "And so at that time we *t* from the two
3:14 *t* all the region of Argob as far as the
28:63 *t* delight in making you grow and prosper,
29: 7 but we defeated them and *t* over their land,
30: 9 even as he *t* delight in your fathers',
Jos 4: 8 they *t* up as many stones from the bed of
6:20 the city in a frontal attack and *t* it.
7: 1 of Judah, *t* goods that were under the ban,
7:21 shekels in weight; in my greed I *t* them.
7:23 They *t* them from the tent,
7:24 Then Joshua and all Israel *t* Achan,
8:12 [He *t* about five thousand men and set them
8:13 Thus the people *t* up their stations,
8:23 whom they *t* alive and brought to Joshua.
8:27 the Israelites *t* for themselves as booty
9: 5 all the bread they *t* was dry and crumbly.
10: 5 Gibeon, where they *t* up siege positions.
10:13 while the nation *t* vengeance on its foes.
11:14 The Israelites *t* all the spoil and
24: 8 You *t* possession of their land,
24:26 Then he *t* a large stone and set it up
Jgs 2:18 it was thus the LORD *t* pity on their
3: 6 fact, they *t* their daughters in marriage,
3:25 upper room, they *t* the key and opened them.
3:26 and, passing the idols, *t* refuge in Seirah.
4:21 got a tent peg and *t* a mallet in her hand.
5: 2 Of chiefs who *t* the lead in Israel,
5:30 "They must be dividing the spoil they *t*:
6:27 So Gideon *t* ten of his servants and did as
6:38 That is what *t* place.
8:12 pursued them and *t* the two kings of Midian,
8:16 He *t* the elders of the city,
8:21 he also *t* the crescents that were on the
9:48 all his soldiers, *t* his axe in his hand,
11:13 "Israel *t* away my land from the Arnon to
12: 3 I *t* my life in my own hand and went on to
12: 5 *t* the fords of the Jordan toward Ephraim.
13:19 Then Manoah *t* the kid with a cereal
16:12 *t* new ropes and bound him with them.
16:17 So he *t* her completely into his confidence
17: 2 It was I who *t* them;
17: 3 she *t* two hundred of them and gave them to
18:20 The priest, agreeing, *t* the ephod,
18:22 that of Micah *t* up arms and overtook them.
19:29 he *t* a knife to the body of his concubine,
20: 6 So I *t* my concubine and cut her up and
20:23 But though the Israelite soldiers *t*
Ru 2:18 which she *t* into the city and showed to
2:19 May he who *t* notice of you be blessed!"
4: 1 Boaz went and *t* a seat at the gate;
4:13 Boaz *t* Ruth.
4:16 Naomi *t* the child, placed him on her lap,
1Sm 5: 2 They then *t* the ark of God and brought it
7: 9 Samuel therefore *t* an unweaned lamb and
7:12 Samuel then *t* a stone and placed it
9:22 Samuel then *t* Saul and his servant and
9:24 cook *t* up the leg and what went with it,
13:17 One band *t* the Ophrah road toward the
13:18 and the third *t* the road for Geba that
14:32 So they pounced upon the spoil and *t* sheep,
14:52 or brave man, he *t* him into his service.
15: 8 He *t* Agag, king of Amalek, alive,
15:21 from the spoil the men *t* sheep and oxen,
16:13 When Samuel *t* his leave, he went to Ramah.
16:20 Then Jesse *t* five loaves of bread,
17:16 the Philistine came forward and *t* his stand
17:39 So he *t* them off.
17:49 his hand into the bag and *t* out a stone,
17:51 hero was dead, the Philistines *t* to flight.
17:54 David *t* the head of the Philistine and
17:57 Abner *t* him and presented him to Saul.
18:30 forays, but each time they *t* the field,
19: 5 When he *t* his life in his hands and slew
19:13 Michal *t* the household idol and laid it in
20:34 and *t* no food that second day of the month,
21:11 That same day David *t* to flight from Saul,
21:13 David *t* note of these remarks and became
23:26 gorge, David and his men *t* to the other.
24: 3 So Saul *t* three thousand picked men from
24:11 killing you, but I *t* pity on you instead.
25:35 David then *t* from her what she had brought
26:12 So David *t* the spear and the water jug
28:21 I *t* my life in my hands and fulfilled the
30:20 Moreover, David *t* all the sheep and oxen,
31: 4 So Saul *t* his own sword and fell upon it.
31:13 Then they *t* their bones and buried them
2Sm 2: 8 son of Ner, Saul's general, *t* Ishbaal,
2:32 They *t* up Asahel and buried him in his
3:15 and *t* her away from her husband Paltiel,
3:27 Joab *t* him aside within the city gate as
4: 4 Jezreel, and his nurse *t* him up and fled.
4:12 But he *t* the head of Ishbaal and buried it
5:13 David *t* more concubines and wives in
5:17 they all *t* the field in search of him.
7: 8 It was I who *t* you from the pasture and
8: 7 David also *t* away the golden shields used
8: 7 *t* away when he came to Jerusalem in the
11: 4 Then David sent messengers and *t* her.
12: 4 Instead he *t* the poor man's ewe lamb and
12: 9 you *t* his wife as your own,
12:30 it, he *t* the crown from Milcom's head.
13: 9 *t* the pan and set out the cakes before him.
15:29 So Zadok and Abiathar *t* the ark of God
17:19 *t* the cover and spread it over the cistern,
18: 6 army then *t* the field against Israel,
20: 3 he *t* the ten concubines whom he had left
21: 8 But the king *t* Armoni and Meribbaal,
21:10 *t* sackcloth and spread it out for herself
23:12 he *t* his stand in the middle of the plot
1Kgs 1:39 Then Zadok the priest *t* the horn of oil
1:46 Solomon *t* his seat on the royal throne,
2: 5 He *t* revenge for the blood of war in a
3:20 night she got up and *t* my son from my side,
6:38 Thus it *t* Solomon seven years to build it.
8: 3 had arrived, the priests *t* up the ark;
8:48 the land of the enemies who *t* them captive,
11:30 Ahijah *t* off his new cloak,
14: 1 that time Abijah, son of Jeroboam, *t* sick.
14:26 He *t* everything, including the treasures
15:18 Asa then *t* all the silver and gold
18: 4 of the LORD, Obadiah *t* a hundred prophets,
18:31 He *t* twelve stones, for the number of
19: 9 he came to a cave, where he *t* shelter.
20:21 Israel went out, *t* the horses and chariots,
20:25 He *t* their advice and did this.
20:30 too, fled, and *t* refuge within the city,
20:33 the men quickly *t* him at his word and said,
20:34 cities which my father *t* from your father,
2Kgs 2: 8 Elijah *t* his mantle,
3:26 the king of Moab *t* seven hundred swordsmen
3:27 So he *t* his first-born, his heir apparent,
4:21 The mother *t* him upstairs and laid him on
4:37 then she *t* her son and left the room.
5:24 reached the hill, Gehazi *t* what they had,
7: 8 into one tent, ate and drank, and *t* silver,
7: 8 came into another tent, *t* things from it,
7:14 They *t* two chariots, and horses,
8:15 The next day, however, Hazael *t* a cloth,
9:13 At once each *t* his garment,
10: 7 *t* the princes and slew all seventy of them,
10:16 And he *t* him along in his own chariot.
10:26 temple of Baal, *t* out the stele of Baal,
11: 2 Jehoram and sister of Ahaziah, *t* Joash,
11:19 where Joash *t* his seat on the royal throne.
12:10 The priest Jehoiada then *t* a chest,
12:19 But King Jehoash of Judah *t* all the
13:25 son of Jehoahaz, *t* back from Ben-hadad,
14: 7 in the Salt Valley, and *t* Sela in battle.
14:14 He *t* all the gold and silver and all the
14:21 Thereupon all the people of Judah *t* the
15:29 king of Assyria, came and *t* Ijon,
16: 8 Ahaz *t* the silver and gold that were in
16:17 he also *t* down the bronze sea from the
17: 6 of Hoshea, the king of Assyria *t* Samaria,
17:24 They *t* possession of Samaria and dwelt in
19:14 Hezekiah *t* the letter from the hand of the
23:30 Then the people of the land *t* Jehoahaz,
23:33 Pharaoh Neco *t* him prisoner at Riblah in
23:34 Jehoahaz he *t* away with him to Egypt,
24:12 eighth year of his reign, *t* him captive.
25:14 They *t* also the pots,
25:18 the guard also *t* Seraiah the high priest,
25:19 And from the city he *t* one courtier,
25:29 Jehoiachin *t* off his prison garb and ate
1Chr 2:23 and Aram *t* from them the villages of Jair,
5: 6 the king of Assyria, *t* into exile;
5:22 and they *t* over their dwelling place until
7:15 Machir *t* a wife whose name was Maacah;
9:25 who had lived in their own villages *t* turns
10: 4 So Saul *t* his own sword and fell on it;
10: 9 him, cut off his head, and *t* his armor;
11: 7 David *t* up his residence in the fortress,
12:20 their lords *t* counsel and sent him home,
13:13 but he *t* it instead to the house of
14: 3 David *t* other wives in Jerusalem and
17: 7 I *t* you from the pasture,
18: 1 and he *t* Gath and its towns away from the
18: 4 *t* from him twenty thousand foot soldiers,
18: 7 David *t* the golden shields that were carried
18: 8 He likewise *t* away from Tibhath and Cun,
19:15 *t* to flight before his brother Abishai,
20: 2 *t* the crown of Milcom from the idol's head.
2Chr 2:16 Thereupon Solomon *t* a census of all the
5: 4 had arrived, the Levites *t* up the ark,
6:12 Solomon then *t* his place before the altar
9: 4 house of the LORD, it *t* her breath away.
11: 5 Rehoboam *t* up residence in Jerusalem and
11:18 Rehoboam *t* to himself as wife Mahalath,
12: 9 He *t* everything, including the gold
13:19 pursued Jeroboam and *t* cities from him:
13:21 He *t* to himself fourteen wives and
20:25 They *t* so much that they were unable to
22:11 secretly *t* Ahaziah's son Joash from among
23: 1 Jehoiada *t* courage and entered a
23:20 Then he *t* the captains,
24:11 *t* it back and returned it to its place.
24:20 He *t* his stand above the people and said
25:13 of the inhabitants and *t* away much booty.
25:24 He *t* away all the gold and silver and all
28: 8 The Israelites *t* away as captives two
28: 8 they also *t* from them much plunder,
29:16 where the Levites *t* it from them and
32: 8 And the people *t* confidence from the words
33:11 they *t* Manasseh with hooks,
35:10 been arranged, the priests *t* their places,
36: 1 The people of the land *t* Jehoahaz,
36: 4 Neco *t* his brother Jehoahaz away and
Ezr 1:11 All these Sheshbazzar *t* with him when the
2:70 common people *t* up residence in Jerusalem;
6: 5 which Nebuchadnezzar *t* from the temple
7:28 I therefore *t* courage, and, with the hand
8:30 and the Levites then *t* over the silver,
Neh 2: 1 I *t* some and offered it to the king.
3: 1 *t* up the task of rebuilding the Sheep Gate.
4:10 only half my able men *t* a hand in the work,
4:17 that accompanied me *t* off his clothes;
7:72 all Israel *t* up residence in their cities.
9:25 they *t* possession of houses filled with
11: 1 of the people *t* up residence in Jerusalem,
11: 3 province who *t* up residence in Jerusalem.
12:40 choirs *t* up a position in the house of God;
13:11 I *t* the magistrates to task,
13:17 I *t* the nobles of Judah to task,
13:25 I *t* them to task and cursed them;
Tb 1:19 then in my fear I *t* to flight.
1:21 *t* control over the entire administration.
2:10 however, *t* care of me for two years,
4:12 all of them *t* wives from among their own
7:12 He *t* her by the hand and gave her to
8: 2 *t* the fish's liver and heart from the bag
14:13 He *t* respectful care of his aging
Jdt 1:14 chariots, and *t* possession of his cities.
1:14 He pressed on to Ecbatana and *t* its towers,
2:17 He *t* along a very large number of camels,
2:22 From there Holofernes *t* his whole force,
5:15 *t* possession of the whole mountain region.
6:11 So the servants *t* him in custody and
6:13 So they *t* cover below the mountain,
8:11 God and yourselves this oath which you *t*.
10: 3 She *t* off the sackcloth she had on,
10:12 The men *t* her in custody and asked her,

12:19 then *t* the things her maid had prepared,
13: 9 the bed and *t* the canopy from its supports.
13:15 Then she *t* the head out of the pouch,
14:11 Then all the Israelite men *t* up their arms
15: 3 district around Bethulia *t* to flight.
15: 5 rest of the mountain region *t* part in this,
15: 7 slaughter *t* possession of what was left,
15:12 She *t* branches in her hands and
16: 7 She *t* off her widow's garb to raise up the
16:11 sound of their war cry, they *t* to flight.
Est 3:10 The king *t* the signet ring from his hand
D: 1 she *t* off her penitential garments and
D: 2 God and savior, she *t* with her two maids;
6:11 So Haman *t* the robe and horse,
9:23 The Jews *t* upon themselves for the future
9:27 the Jews established and *t* upon themselves,
1Mc 1: 5 But after all this he *t* to his bed,
1: 8 So his officers *t* over his kingdom,
1:21 the sanctuary and *t* away the golden altar,
1:23 and *t* away the gold and silver and the
1:23 *t* all the hidden treasures he could find.
1:27 Every bridegroom *t* up lamentation,
1:32 walls, *t* captive the women and children,
3: 1 who was called Maccabeus, *t* his place.
3:37 The king *t* the remaining half of the army
4: 1 Now Gorgias *t* five thousand infantry and a
4:47 Then they *t* uncut stones,
5:23 He *t* with him the Jews who were in Galilee
5:28 male population, *t* all their possessions,
5:36 From there he moved on and *t* Chaspho,
5:50 the men of the army *t* up their positions,
5:65 he *t* Hebron and its villages,
6: 8 his designs had failed, he *t* to his bed.
6:50 The king *t* Beth-zur and stationed a
6:63 fought against him and *t* the city by force.
7:22 They *t* possession of the land of Judah and
7:24 and *t* revenge on the men who had deserted,
8: 1 and acted amiably to all who *t* their side.
8: 8 The Romans *t* these from him and gave them
8:10 Romans *t* their wives and children captive.
8:10 plundered them, *t* possession of their land,
8:15 day three hundred and twenty men *t* counsel,
9: 2 They *t* the road to Galilee,
9:11 out of camp and *t* its position for combat.
9:19 Jonathan and Simon *t* their brother Judas
9:31 and *t* the place of Judas his brother.
9:53 He *t* as hostages the sons of the leaders
9:59 So they went and *t* counsel with him.
10: 1 son of Antiochus, came up and *t* Ptolemais.
10:12 that Bacchides had built, *t* flight,
10:55 and *t* your seat on their royal throne!
10:76 and so Jonathan *t* possession of Joppa.
11: 8 King Ptolemy *t* possession of the cities
11:46 But he *t* refuge in the palace,
11:62 He *t* the sons of their chief men as
11:66 them from the city, *t* possession of it,
11:72 the enemy that they *t* to flight.
14: 7 He *t* many enemies prisoners of war and
15:33 what we *t* is not the property of others,
15:40 he *t* people captive or massacred them.
16: 6 his men *t* their position against the enemy.
16:10 Some *t* refuge in the towers on the plain
2Mc 1:19 devout priests of the time *t* some of the
4:21 so he *t* measures for his own security.
5: 5 taken, Menelaus *t* refuge in the citadel.
5: 7 *t* refuge in the country of the Ammonites.
5:11 out from Egypt and *t* Jerusalem by storm.
5:12 to slay those who *t* refuge in their houses.
6:21 ritual meal *t* the man aside privately,
8:20 thousand and *t* a great quantity of booty,
8:23 he himself *t* charge of the first division
10: 5 the purification of the temple *t* place.
10:18 *t* refuge in two very strong towers,
10:27 they *t* up their arms and advanced a
10:36 the troops, who *t* possession of the city.
12: 4 the people of Joppa *t* them out to sea and
12:27 *t* up their posts in defense of the walls,
12:43 *t* up a collection among all his soldiers,
13:26 But Lysias *t* the platform,
14:26 other, he *t* the treaty that had been made,
Jb 2: 8 And he *t* a potsherd to scrape himself,
29: 1 Job *t* up his theme anew and said;
29:25 *t* comfort from my cheerful glance.
29:25 I *t* a king's place in the armed forces.
Ps(s) 30:12 you *t* off my sackcloth and clothed me with
32: 5 LORD," and you *t* away the guilt of my sin.
68:29 power, O God, with which you *t* our part;
74: 2 where you *t* up your abode
78:70 his servant, and *t* him from the sheepfolds;
80:10 for it, and it *t* root and filled the land.
104: 7 the sound of your thunder they *t* to flight;
105:44 and they *t* what the peoples had toiled for,
109:17 he *t* no delight in blessing;
Prv 1:24 I extended my hand and no one *t* notice;
7:20 A bag of money he *t* with him,
Sg 3: 4 I *t* hold of him and would not let him go
5: 7 and wounded me, and *t* my mantle from me,
Wis 3: 6 sacrificial offerings he *t* them to himself.
10:18 She *t* them across the Red Sea and brought
11: 3 enemies and *t* vengeance on their foes.
11:12 For a twofold grief *t* hold of them and a
12: 6 *t* with their own hands defenseless lives,
12:26 But they who *t* no heed of punishment
14: 6 of the universe, who *t* refuge on a raft,
19:18 exactly from a review of what *t* place.
Sir 39:32 So from the first I *t* my stand,
Is 8: 2 And I *t* reliable witnesses,
10:14 eggs left alone, so I *t* in all the earth;
37:14 Hezekiah *t* the letter from the hand of the
42:25 it burned them, but they *t* it not to heart.
48: 3 suddenly I *t* action and they came to be.
48: 5 before they *t* place I let you hear of them,
Jer 13: 7 sought out and *t* the loincloth from the
25:17 I *t* the cup from the hand of the LORD and
28: 3 Babylon, *t* away from this place to Babylon.
28:10 Thereupon the prophet Hananiah *t* the yoke
31:32 I made with their fathers the day I *t* them
32:23 They entered and *t* possession of it,
34:11 afterward they *t* back their male and
36:32 Jeremiah *t* another scroll,
38: 6 And so they *t* Jeremiah and threw him into
38:11 Ebed-melech *t* the men along with him,
38:11 in the palace, from which he *t* some old,
40: 2 of the bodyguard *t* charge of Jeremiah,
41:12 they *t* all their men and set out to attack
41:16 *t* charge of the remnant of the people,
43: 5 and all the army leaders *t* along the whole
52: 7 Then all the soldiers *t* to flight and left
52:18 They *t* also the pots,
52:24 The captain of the guard also *t* Seraiah,
52:25 And from the city he *t* one courtier,
52:31 of his reign, *t* up the case of Jehoiachin,
52:33 Jehoiachin *t* off his prison garb and ate
Lam 2: 4 in his right hand He *t* his stand as a foe,
3:43 and pursued us, you slew us and *t* no pity;
Bar 1: 2 *t* Jerusalem and burnt it with fire].
4:32 fearful the city that *t* your sons.
Ez 10: 7 He *t* up some of it and put it in the hands
10: 7 dressed in linen, who *t* it and came out.
11:23 the LORD rose from the city and *t* a stand
16:16 You *t* some of your gowns and made for
16:17 You *t* the splendid gold and silver
16:18 You *t* your embroidered gowns to cover them;
16:20 borne me you *t* and offered as sacrifices
17: 3 He *t* the crest of the cedar.
17: 5 Then he *t* some seed of the land,
17:12 and *t* away its king and princes with him
19: 4 *t* him away with hooks to the land of Egypt.
19: 5 She *t* another of her whelps,
19: 9 cage and *t* him away to the king of Babylon,
23:10 her sons and daughters they *t* away,
27: 5 from Lebanon they *t* to make you a mast;
Dn 2:14 Daniel prudently *t* counsel with Arioch,
7: 9 set up and the Ancient One *t* his throne.
8:27 I arose and *t* care of the king's affairs.
10: 3 I ate no savory food, I *t* no meat or wine,
14:27 Then Daniel *t* some pitch,
14:42 Daniel he *t* out, but those who had tried
Hos 1: 3 So he went and *t* Gomer,
10: 9 There they *t* their stand; war was not
11: 3 Ephraim to walk, who *t* them in my arms;
Jl 2:18 for his land and *t* pity on his people.
4: 5 You *t* my silver and my gold,
Am 1: 6 Because they *t* captive whole groups to
7:15 The LORD *t* me from following the flock,
Jon 1:15 they *t* Jonah and threw him into the sea,
3: 3 it *t* three days to go through it.
Zec 11: 7 I *t* two staffs, one of which I called
11:10 Then I *t* my staff "Favor" and snapped it
11:13 So I *t* the thirty pieces of silver and
Mt 2:14 Joseph got up and *t* the child and his
2:21 He got up, *t* the child and his mother,
4: 5 Next the devil *t* him to the holy city,
4: 8 The devil then *t* him up a very high
8:15 *t* her by the hand and the fever left her.
8:26 up and *t* the winds and the sea to task.
8:33 The swineherds *t* to their heels,
9:25 put out he entered and *t* her by the hand,
13: 2 that he went and *t* his seat in a boat
13:31 which someone *t* and sowed in his field.
13:33 *t* and kneaded into three measures of flour.
14:11 given to the girl, who *t* it to her mother.
14:19 He *t* the five loaves and two fish,
15:36 He *t* the seven loaves and the fish,
16:22 Peter *t* him aside and began to remonstrate
17: 1 Six days later Jesus *t* Peter,
20:17 he *t* the Twelve aside on the road and said
25: 1 ten bridesmaids who *t* their torches
25: 4 *t* flasks of oil as well as their torches.
26:26 During the meal Jesus *t* bread,
26:27 Then he *t* a cup, gave thanks, and gave
26:37 He *t* along Peter and Zebedee's two sons,
26:60 the many false witnesses who *t* the stand.
27: 1 of the people *t* formal action against Jesus
27: 3 He *t* the thirty pieces of silver back to
27: 9 "They *t* the thirty pieces of silver,
27:27 The procurator's soldiers *t* Jesus inside
27:30 Afterward they *t* hold of the reed and kept
Mk 4:36 they *t* him away in the boat in which he
5:40 Jesus *t* the child's father and mother and
6:40 *t* their places in hundreds and fifties,
7:33 *t* him off by himself away from the crowd.
8:23 Jesus *t* the blind man's hand and led him
8:32 Peter then *t* him aside and began to
9: 2 Six days later, Jesus *t* Peter,
9:27 But Jesus *t* him by the hand and helped him
9:36 Then he *t* a little child,
12:20 The eldest *t* a wife and died,
12:21 The second *t* the woman,
14:22 During the meal he *t* bread,
14:23 He likewise *t* a cup, gave thanks
14:33 at the same time he *t* along with him Peter,
15:46 bought a linen shroud, Joseph *t* him down,
16:14 He *t* them to task for their disbelief and
16:19 heaven and *t* his seat at God's right hand.
Lk 2: 2 This first census *t* place while Quirinius
2:28 he *t* him in his arms and blessed God in
4: 5 Then the devil *t* him up higher and showed
4:40 with a variety of diseases *t* them to him,
6: 4 how he entered God's house and *t* and ate
8:34 they *t* to their heels and brought the news
8:54 He *t* her by the hand and spoke these words:
9:28 eight days after saying this he *t* Peter,
9:47 *t* a little child and placed it beside him,
10:35 The next day he *t* out two silver pieces
13:19 which a man *t* and planted in his garden.
13:21 It is like yeast which a woman *t* to knead
14: 4 He *t* the man, healed him, and sent him
17:17 Jesus *t* the occasion to say, "Were not all
17:27 ate and drank, they *t* husbands and wives,
22: 3 Then Satan *t* possession of Judas,
22:14 the hour arrived, he *t* his place at table,
23:53 He *t* it down, wrapped it in fine linen,
24:30 himself with them to eat, he *t* bread,
24:43 fish, which he *t* and ate in their presence.
Jn 2:20 "This temple *t* forty-six years to build,
6:11 Jesus then *t* the loaves of bread,
9:13 they *t* the man who had been born blind to
11:41 They then *t* away the stone and Jesus
13: 4 rose from the meal and *t* off his cloak.
13:26 the morsel, then *t* it and gave it to Judas,
18: 3 Judas *t* the cohort as well as guards
19:13 then brought Jesus outside and *t* a seat on
19:23 *t* his garments and divided them four ways,
19:27 onward, the disciple *t* her into his care.
19:30 When Jesus *t* the wine,
19:36 *t* place for the fulfillment of Scripture:
19:38 it, so they came and *t* the body away.
19:40 They *t* Jesus' body, and in accordance
21: 1 This is how the appearance *t* place.
21: 6 and *t* so many fish they could not haul the
21:13 came over, *t* the bread and gave it to them,
Acts 1: 9 in a cloud which *t* him from their sight.
2:46 hearts they *t* their meals in common,
3: 7 *t* him by the right hand and pulled him up.
4:16 show of power *t* place through them.
5: 2 he *t* and laid at the feet of the apostles.
7:29 He *t* up his residence as an alien in the
7:43 You *t* along the tent of Moloch and the
9:25 *t* him along the wall one night and lowered
9:27 Then Barnabas *t* him in charge and
9:30 some of them *t* him down to Caesarea and
9:39 arrival they *t* him upstairs to the room.
11: 2 among the circumcised *t* issue with him,
12: 3 of the Jews, he *t* Peter into custody too.
12:21 *t* his seat on the rostrum and publicly
13:29 they *t* him down from the tree and laid him
15: 7 Peter *t* the floor and said to them:
15:39 Barnabas *t* Mark along with him and sailed
16:33 night he *t* them in and bathed their wounds;
17: 1 Paul and Silas *t* the road through
18: 3 He *t* up lodgings with them and they worked
18:18 but eventually he *t* leave of the brothers
18:26 they *t* him home and explained to him God's
19: 9 He *t* his disciples with him,
20:14 we *t* him aboard and sailed to Mitylene.
20:15 From there we *t* off the next day,
21:32 Immediately the commander *t* his soldiers
23:13 than forty of them who *t* the oath together.)
23:18 The centurion *t* him in charge and led him
23:19 The commander *t* him by the hand and drew
23:31 the infantry *t* Paul and escorted him that
25: 6 On the following day he *t* his seat on the
25:17 The very next day I *t* my seat on the bench
27:28 They *t* a sounding and found a depth of
27:28 *t* a sounding and found it to be fifteen.
27:35 When he had said this he *t* some bread,
28: 7 He *t* us in and gave us kind hospitality
28:15 them, he thanked God and *t* fresh courage.
1Cor 11:23 the night in which he was betrayed *t* bread,
11:25 same way, after the supper, he *t* the cup,
Gal 4:14 you *t* me to yourselves as an angel of God,
Eph 4: 8 *t* a host of captives and gave gifts to men."
Phil 2: 7 emptied himself and *t* the form of a slave,
2:27 the point of death, but God *t* pity on him;
1Thes 2:13 in receiving his message from us you *t* it,
2Tm 4:16 of my case in court, no one *t* my part.
Heb 1: 3 he *t* his seat at the right hand of the
8: 9 I made with their fathers the day I *t* them
9:19 people, he *t* the blood of goats and calves,
10: 6 and sin offerings you *t* no delight in.
10:12 one sacrifice for sins and *t* his seat forever
11: 5 "he was seen no more because God *t* him."
1Jn 2:19 was from our ranks that they *t* their leave
Jude 1:11 They have taken the road Cain *t*.
Rv 3:21 *t* my seat beside my Father on his throne.
8: 3 He *t* his place at the altar of incense and
8: 5 Then the angel *t* the censer,
10: 6 *t* an oath by the One who lives forever

TOOK (cont.)
10:10 I *t* the little scroll from the angel's
12:17 *t* up his position by the shore of the sea.

TOOL (7)
Ex 20:25 for by putting a *t* to it you desecrate it.
32: 4 and fashioning this gold with a graving *t*,
Dt 27: 5 made of stones that no iron *t* has touched.
Jos 8:31 stones on which no iron *t* had been used,
1Kgs 6: 7 or iron *t* was to be heard in the temple
Sir 38:28 His eyes are fixed on the *t* he is shaping.
Bar 6:58 his valor, or a handy *t* in a house,

TOOLS (2)
Sir 48:17 With iron *t* he cut through the rock and he
Bar 6:15 useless as one's broken *t* are their gods,

TOOTH (11)
Ex 21:24 life for life, eye for eye, tooth for *t*,
21:27 knocks out a *t* of his male or female slave,
21:27 slave go free in compensation for the *t*.
Lv 24:20 Limb for limb, eye for eye, tooth for *t*!
Dt 19:21 Life for life, eye for eye, tooth for *t*,
Prv 25:19 Like an infected *t* or an unsteady foot is
Mt 5:38 'An eye for an eye, a tooth for a *t*.'

TOP (73)
Gn 11: 4 a city and a tower with its *t* in the sky,
22: 9 and put him on *t* of the wood on the altar.
28:12 ground, with its *t* reaching to the heavens;
28:18 memorial stone, and poured oil on *t* of it.
40:17 in the *t* one were all kinds of bakery
Ex 17: 9 I will be standing on *t* of the hill with
17:10 to the *t* of the hill with Aaron and Hur.
19:20 the LORD came down to the *t* of Mount Sinai,
19:20 he summoned Moses to the *t* of the mountain,
25:11 put a molding of gold around the *t* of it.
25:21 you shall then place on *t* of the ark.
26:24 the bottom, and likewise double at the *t*,
29:25 you shall burn them on *t* of the holocaust
30: 3 Its grate on *t*, its walls on all four sides,
31: 7 with the propitiatory on *t* of it,
34: 2 yourself to me on the *t* of the mountain.
36:29 the bottom, and likewise double at the *t*,
37:26 Its grate on *t*, its walls on all four sides,
40:19 and put the covering on *t* of the tent,
Lv 1: 8 on *t* of the wood and embers on the altar.
1:12 on *t* of the wood and the fire on the altar.
8:26 *t* of the portions of fat and the right leg.
9:20 he placed on *t* of the breasts and burned
Nm 4: 6 on *t* of this spread an all-violet cloth.
20:28 Then Aaron died there on *t* of the mountain.
23: 9 For from the *t* of the crags I see him,
23:14 to the lookout field on the *t* of Pisgah,
23:28 So he took Balaam to the *t* of Peor,
Dt 3:27 the *t* of Pisgah and look out to the west,
Jos 15: 8 the boundary rose to the *t* of the mountain
15: 9 From the *t* of the mountain it ran to the
Jgs 6:26 LORD, your God, on *t* of this stronghold.
9: 7 him, Jotham went to the *t* of Mount Gerizim,
16: 3 them to the *t* of the ridge opposite Hebron.
1Sm 28:12 at the *t* of her voice and said to Saul,
2Sm 15:32 When David reached the *t*,
16: 1 had gone a little beyond the *t* when Ziba,
1Kgs 7:16 in bronze, to place on *t* of the columns,
7:17 of the) capitals on *t* of the columns,
7:19 The capitals on *t* of the columns were
7:35 On the *t* of the stand there was a raised
7:35 were of one piece with the *t* of the stand.
7:38 basin for the *t* of each of the ten stands.
7:41 nodes for the capitals on *t* of the columns,
7:41 nodes for the capitals on *t* of the columns,
10:19 had six steps, a back with a round *t*,
18:42 while Elijah climbed to the *t* of Carmel,
Neh 12:31 to the right, along the *t* of the wall,
12:37 continued along the *t* of the wall
12:38 along the *t* of the wall past the Oven
Est 5: 2 up to him, and touched the *t* of the staff.]
1Mc 6:46 The beast fell to the ground on *t* of him,
2Mc 6:10 thrown down from the *t* of the city wall.
14:43 he gallantly ran up to the *t* of the wall
Prv 8: 2 On the *t* of the heights along the road,
23:34 the sea, now sprawled at the *t* of the mast.
Sg 4: 8 the *t* of Amana, from the top of Senir
Is 17: 6 Two or three olives remain at the very *t*,
40: 9 Cry out at the *t* of your voice,
42:11 and shout from the *t* of the mountains.
Ez 43:12 on the mountain *t* shall be most sacred.
43:15 and extending from the *t* of the hearth
Dn 4: 8 strong, with its *t* touching the heavens,
4:17 you saw, with its *t* touching the heavens,
Zec 4: 2 all of gold, with a bowl at the *t*,"
Mt 27:51 sanctuary was torn in two from *t* to bottom.
Mk 15:38 sanctuary was torn in two from *t* to bottom.
Lk 8:28 feet and exclaimed at the *t* of his voice,
Jn 19:23 one piece from *t* to bottom and had no seam.
Rv 6:10 They cried out at the *t* of their voices:
7: 2 He cried out at the *t* of his voice to the
21:10 He carried me away in spirit to the *t* of a

TOPAZ (5)
Ex 28:17 first row, a carnelian, a *t* and an emerald;
39:10 first row a carnelian, a *t* and an emerald;
Jb 28:19 it surpasses pearls and Arabian *t*.
Ez 28:13 stone was your covering [carnelian, *t*,
Rv 21:20 chrysolite, the eighth beryl, the ninth *t*,

TOPHEL (1)
Dt 1: 1 opposite Suph, between Paran and *T*,

TOPHETH (9)
2Kgs 23:10 also defiled *T* in the Valley of Ben-hinnom,
Jer 7:31 they have built the high place of *T*
7:32 when *T* and the Valley of Ben-hinnom will
7:32 lack of space, *T* will be a burial place.
19: 6 this place will no longer be called *T*,
19:11 And *T* shall be a burial place,
19:12 I will make this city like *T*.
19:13 shall be defiled like the place of *T*,
19:14 When Jeremiah returned from *T*,

TOPIC (1)
Acts 17:32 must hear you on this *t* some other time."

TOPICS (1)
Eccl 12:11 spikes are the *t* given by one collector.

TOPMOST (2)
Ez 17: 4 tearing off its *t* branch,
17:22 its *t* branches tear off a tender shoot,

TOPPING (4)
2Chr 3:15 the capital *t* each was of five cubits.
4:12 nodes for the capitals *t* these two columns,
4:12 the nodes of the capitals *t* the columns;
4:13 two nodes of the capitals *t* the columns.

TOPS (6)
Gn 8: 5 month the *t* of the mountains appeared.
2Sm 5:24 of marching in the *t* of the mastic trees,
1Chr 14:15 of marching in the *t* of the mastic trees,
Ps(s) 72:16 on the *t* of the mountains the crops shall
95: 4 earth, and the *t* of the mountains are his.
Is 14:14 I will ascend above the *t* of the clouds;

TORCH (5)
Gn 15:17 appeared a smoking brazier and a flaming *t*,
2Mc 10:36 they put the towers to the *t*,
Is 62: 1 the dawn and her victory like a burning *t*.
Zec 12: 6 and like a burning *t* among sheaves,
Rv 8:10 burning like a *t* crashed down from the sky.

TORCHES (14)
Jgs 7:16 and with empty jars and *t* inside the jars.
7:20 They held the *t* in their left hands,
15: 4 pair of tails one of the *t* he had at hand.
15: 5 He then kindled the *t* and set the foxes
1Mc 6:39 their brightness and blazed like flaming *t*.
Ez 1:13 they seemed like *t*, moving to and fro
Dn 10: 6 lightning, his eyes were like fiery *t*,
Mt 25: 1 their *t* and went out to welcome the groom.
25: 3 The foolish ones, in taking their *t*,
25: 4 ones took flasks of oil as well as their *t*.
25: 7 the virgins woke up and got their *t* ready.
25: 8 Our *t* are going out.'
Jn 18: 3 came there with lanterns, *t* and weapons.
Rv 4: 5 before it burned seven flaming *t*,

TORCHLIGHTS (1)
2Mc 4:22 who escorted him with *t* and acclamations;

TORE (53)
Gn 37:29 Joseph was not in it, he *t* his clothes,
44:13 At this, they *t* their clothes.
Nm 14: 6 *t* their garments and said to the whole
Jgs 14: 6 he *t* the lion in pieces as one tears a kid.
16: 3 and the two gateposts, and *t* them loose,
1Sm 15:27 a loose end of his mantle, and it *t* off.
2Sm 13:19 *t* the long tunic in which she was clothed.
1Kgs 11:30 off his new cloak, *t* it into twelve pieces,
21:27 he *t* his garments and put on sackcloth
2Kgs 2:12 gripped his own garment and *t* it in two.
2:24 and *t* forty-two of the children to pieces.
5: 7 of Israel *t* his garments and exclaimed:
6:30 heard the woman's words, he *t* his garments.
10:27 the stele of Baal, *t* down the building,
11:14 trumpets, she *t* her garments and cried out,
14:13 He went on to Jerusalem where he *t* down
17:21 he *t* Israel away from the house of David,
19: 1 Hezekiah heard this, he *t* his garments,
22:11 he *t* his garments and issued this command
22:19 you *t* your garments and wept before me;
23: 7 He *t* down the apartments of the cult
23: 8 also *t* down the high place of the satyrs,
23:15 this same altar and high place he *t* down,
25:10 *t* down the walls that surrounded Jerusalem.
2Chr 23:13 Athaliah *t* her garments and cried out,
23:17 went to the temple of Baal and *t* it down.
25:23 Then he *t* down the wall of Jerusalem from
31: 1 and *t* down the high places and altars
34: 7 and *t* down the incense stands throughout
34:19 he *t* his garments and issued this command
36:19 of God, *t* down the walls of Jerusalem,
Ezr 9: 3 this thing, I *t* my cloak and my mantle,
Est 4: 1 all that was happening, he *t* his garments,
1Mc 1:56 law which they found they *t* up and burnt.
2:14 Mattathias and his sons *t* their garments,
2:25 to sacrifice, and he *t* down the altar.
2:45 went about and *t* down the pagan altars;
3:47 ashes on their heads and *t* their clothes.
4:39 *t* their clothes and made great lamentation;
4:45 so they *t* down the altar.
8:10 *t* down their strongholds and reduced them
11:71 Jonathan *t* his clothes,
2Mc 4:38 his purple robe, *t* off his other garments,
14:46 he *t* out his entrails and flung them with
Jb 2:12 they *t* their cloaks and threw dust upon
Ps(s) 35:15 They *t* at me without ceasing;
Is 37: 1 Hezekiah heard this, he *t* his garments,
49:17 as those who *t* you down and laid you waste
Jer 2:20 you broke your yoke, you *t* off your bonds.
52:14 *t* down all the walls that surrounded
Mt 26:65 At this the high priest *t* his robes:
Mk 14:63 that the high priest *t* his robes and said:
Acts 14:14 they *t* their garments and rushed out into

TORMENT (17)
2Mc 7:17 power will *t* you and your descendants."
9: 5 pains in his bowels and sharp internal *t*,
Jb 15:20 The wicked man is in *t* all his days,
Sg 6: 5 Turn your eyes from me, for they *t* me.
Wis 3: 1 the hand of God, and no *t* shall touch them.
17:13 of not knowing the cause that brings on *t*.
Sir 30:21 to sadness, *t* not yourself with brooding;
Is 38:12 Day and night you give me over to *t*;
38:13 [day and night you give me over to *t*.
Lam 3:51 My eyes *t* my soul at the sight of all the
Jl 2: 6 Before them peoples are in *t*,
Lk 8:28 Do not *t* me, I beg you."
16:23 the abode of the dead where he was in *t*,
16:25 consolation here, but you have found *t*.
16:28 that they may not end in this place of *t*.'
Rv 14:10 of their *t* shall rise forever and ever.
18: 7 and sensuality, repay her in *t* and grief!

TORMENTED (8)
1Sm 16:14 was *t* by an evil spirit sent by the LORD.
Wis 11: 9 wicked, condemned in anger, were being *t*.
12:23 you *t* through their own abominations.
16: 1 and were *t* by a swarm of insects.
16: 4 be shown how their enemies were being *t*.
Heb 11:37 of sheep or goats, needy, afflicted, *t*.
2Pt 2: 8 felt himself *t* by seeing and hearing about
Rv 14:10 He will be *t* in burning sulphur before the

TORMENTING (1)
1Sm 16:15 An evil spirit from God is *t* you.

TORMENTORS (1)
Is 51:23 I will put it into the hands of your *t*,

TORMENTS (4)
2Mc 9: 6 the bowels of others with many barbarous *t*.
9: 9 and while he was still alive in hideous *t*,
Wis 11:13 their own *t* was a benefit to these others,
19: 4 might fill out the *t* of their punishment,

TORN (53)
Gn 31:39 brought you an animal *t* by wild beasts;
37:33 Joseph has been *t* to pieces!"
44:28 must have been *t* to pieces by wild beasts;
Ex 22:30 *t* to pieces in the field you shall not eat;
28:32 of a shirt, to keep it from being *t*.
39:23 around the opening to keep it from being *t*.
Lv 22:24 has its testicles bruised or crushed or *t* out
Jos 9: 4 asses, and old wineskins, *t* and mended.
9:13 when we filled them, but now they are *t*.
1Sm 4:12 clothes *t* and his head covered with dirt.
15:28 *t* the kingdom of Israel from you this day,
28:17 he has *t* the kingdom from your grasp and
2Sm 1: 2 with his clothes *t* and dirt on his head.
14:30 Joab's farmhands came to him with *t*
1Kgs 19:10 forsaken your covenant, *t* down your altars,
19:14 forsaken your covenant, *t* down your altars,
2Kgs 5: 8 that the king of Israel had *t* his garments,
5: 8 "Why have you *t* your garments?
18:37 came to Hezekiah with their garments *t*,
2Chr 33: 3 which his father Hezekiah had *t* down,
34: 4 stands erected above them were *t* down;
34:27 yourself before me, have *t* your garments,
Ezr 9: 5 with cloak and mantle *t* I fell on my knees,
1Mc 5:14 suddenly other messengers, in *t* clothes,
9:54 inner court of the sanctuary to be *t* down,
Ps(s) 7: 3 like the lion's prey, to be *t* to pieces,
Prv 27: 9 heart, but by grief the soul is *t* asunder.
Is 36:22 came to Hezekiah with their garments *t*,
Jer 5: 5 had broken the yoke, *t* off the harness.

5: 6 all who come out are *t* to pieces For their
50:15 her bastions fall, her walls are *t* down:
51:35 My *t* flesh be upon Babylon,
Lam 2: 2 He has *t* down in his anger the fortresses
Bar 6:30 *t* tunic and with shaven hair and beard,
Ez 4:14 carrion flesh or that *t* by wild beasts;
19:12 was *t* up in fury and flung to the ground;
19:12 wind withered her up, her fruit was *t* off;
26:12 Your walls shall be *t* down,
Dn 7: 8 horns were *t* away to make room for it.
11: 4 *t* to pieces and belong to others than they.
Mt 12:25 *t* by strife is headed for its downfall.
12:26 Satan, he must be *t* by dissension.
24: 2 left on another—it will all be *t* down."
27:51 sanctuary was *t* in two from top to bottom.
Mk 3:24 If a kingdom is *t* by civil strife,
3:26 mutiny in his ranks and is *t* by dissension,
13: 2 left upon another—all will be *t* down."
15:38 sanctuary was *t* in two from top to bottom.
Lk 11:17 Any house *t* by dissension falls.
21: 6 left on another, but it will all be *t* down."
23:45 The curtain in the sanctuary was *t* in two.
Jn 21:11 of the great number, the net was not *t*.
Rom 11: 3 prophets, they have *t* down your altars;

TORPOR (1)

Prv 23:21 to poverty, and *t* clothes a man in rags.

TORQUE (1)

Prv 1: 9 a *t* for your neck.

TORRENT (12)

Jdt 2: 8 swelling *t* shall be choked with their dead;
Jb 40:23 though the *t* surges about his mouth.
Ps(s) 83:10 as with Sisera and Jabin at the *t* Kishon,
124: 4 The *t* would have swept over us;
Is 66:12 of the nations like an overflowing *t*.
Jer 47: 2 are rising from the north, a *t* in flood;
Lam 2:18 Let your tears flow like a *t* day and night;
Dn 9:26 Then the end shall come like a *t*;
Hb 3:10 A *t* of rain descends;
Lk 6:48 floods came the *t* rushed in on that house,
6:49 When the *t* rushed upon it,
Rv 12:15 spewed a *t* of water out of his mouth to

TORRENTS (6)

Jdt 16: 3 Their numbers blocked the *t*,
Jb 20:17 no streams of oil, no *t* of honey or milk.
Ps(s) 74:15 You released the springs and *t*;
126: 4 O LORD, like the *t* in the southern desert.
Mt 7:25 the *t* came and the winds blew and buffeted
7:27 The rains fell, the *t* came,

TORRID (1)

Hos 13: 5 I fed you in the desert, in the *t* land.

TORTUOUS (1)

Jer 17: 9 More *t* than all else is the human heart,

TORTURE (7)

2Mc 6:19 of his own accord to the instrument of *t*,
6:28 went immediately to the instrument of *t*.
Wis 2:19 With revilement and *t* let us put him to
Mt 8:29 you come to *t* us before the appointed time?"
24: 9 They will hand you over to *t* and kill you.
Mk 5: 7 I implore you in God's name, do not *t* me!"
Rv 9: 5 them but only to *t* them for five months;

TORTURED (9)

Jdt 8:30 were so *t* with thirst that they forced us
2Mc 7: 1 and *t* with whips and scourges by the king,
7: 7 rather than have your body *t* limb by limb?"
7:13 they *t* and maltreated the fourth brother
9: 6 punishment for him who had *t* the bowels
Wis 12:27 were *t* by the very things they deemed gods,
Lk 16:24 my tongue, for I am *t* in these flames.'
Heb 11:35 were *t* and would not receive deliverance,
Rv 20:10 There they will be *t* day and night,

TORTURERS (1)

Mt 18:34 the *t* until he paid back all that he owed.

TORTURES (1)

2Mc 7: 8 in turn suffered the same *t* as the first.

TOSS (4)

Is 22:18 And roll you up and *t* you like a ball
Jer 5:22 *T* though it may, it is to no avail;
49:23 they *t* like the sea which cannot rest.
Mt 7: 6 holy to dogs or *t* your pearls before swine.

TOSSED (11)

1Kgs 14:15 The LORD will strike Israel like a reed *t*
2Mc 1:16 heads and *t* them to the people outside.
Jb 30:22 I am *t* about by the tempest.
Ps(s) 107:25 up a storm wind which *t* its waves on high.
Sir 29:17 men and *t* them about like waves of the sea,
33: 2 and is *t* about like a boat in a storm.
Is 30:24 silage *t* to them with shovel and pitchfork.
Mt 14:24 was being *t* about in the waves raised by
Mk 6:48 seeing them *t* about as they tried to row
Eph 4:14 be children no longer, *t* here and there,
Jas 1: 6 is like the surf *t* and driven by the wind.

TOSSES (1)

Am 8: 8 While it rises up and *t* like the Nile,

TOSSING (4)

Sir 31:20 of sleep, and restless *t* for the glutton!
Is 57:20 are like the *t* sea which cannot be calmed,
Mt 27:39 insulting him, *t* their heads and saying:
Mk 15:29 insulting him, *t* their heads and saying,

TOTAL (34)

Ex 1: 5 The *t* number of the direct descendants of
Nm 1:45 The *t* number of the Israelites of twenty
2: 9 The *t* number of those registered by
2:16 The *t* number of those registered by
2:24 The *t* number of those registered by
2:31 The *t* number of those registered by
2:32 The *t* number of those registered by
3:39 The *t* number of male Levites a month old
3:40 old or more, and compute their *t* number.
4: 2 the Levites take a *t* of the Kohathites,
4:22 "Take a *t* among the Gershonites also,
4:48 the *t* number registered was eight thousand
26:62 The *t* number of male Levites one month or
35: 7 a *t* of forty-eight cities with their
Jos 8:25 day a *t* of twelve thousand men and women,
15:32 a *t* of twenty-nine cities with their
21:38 from the tribe of Gad a *t* of four cities:
21:41 Thus the *t* number of cities within the
Jgs 20:16 Included in this *t* were seven hundred
1Chr 7: 5 was a *t* of eighty-seven thousand warriors
23: 3 and their *t* number was found to be
Ezr 1:11 *T* of the gold- and silver ware:
2:58 The *t* of the temple slaves and the
8:34 weight, and the *t* weight was registered.
Neh 7:60 The *t* of the temple slaves and the
11: 6 The *t* of the sons of Perez who dwelt in
11:18 The *t* of the Levites in the holy city was
Jdt 2: 2 urged the *t* destruction of those countries.
2Mc 3: 6 that the *t* sum of money was incalculable
3:11 the *t* amounted to four hundred talents of
Jer 50:13 she shall be empty, and become a *t* desert;
Mt 1:17 Thus the *t* number of generations is:
Lk 7:41 one owed a *t* of five hundred coins,
2Cor 8: 7 and discourse, in knowledge, in *t* concern,

TOTALLY (2)

Ez 25: 9 clear the shoulder of Moab *t* of its cities,
Mt 24:39 They were *t* unconcerned until the flood

TOTTER (4)

Ps(s) 46: 7 Though nations are in turmoil, kingdoms *t*,
109:24 My knees *t* from my fasting,
Jer 10: 4 they are fastened, that they may not *t*.
Am 9: 1 so that the doorjambs *t* till you break

TOTTERING (5)

1Sm 2: 4 are broken, while the *t* gird on strength.
Ps(s) 60: 4 repair the cracks in it, for it is *t*.
Prv 24:11 and from those *t* to execution withdraw not.
Sir 41: 2 of failing strength, *T* and always rebuffed,
Is 28: 7 in their visions, *t* when giving judgment.

TOU (2)

1Chr 18: 9 When *T*, king of Hamath,
18:10 for Hadadezer had been at war with *T*.

TOUBIANI (1)

2Mc 12:17 where there were certain Jews known as *T*.

TOUCH (54)

Gn 3: 3 said, 'You shall not eat it or even *t* it,
20: 6 that is why I did not let you *t* her.
Ex 19:12 go up the mountain, or even to *t* its base.
19:13 No hand shall *t* him; he must be stoned
Lv 7:19 Should the flesh *t* anything unclean,
11: 8 eat, and their dead bodies you shall not *t*;
12: 4 she shall not *t* anything sacred nor enter
Nm 4:15 But they shall not *t* the sacred objects;
6: 5 nazirite vow, no razor shall *t* his hair.
16:26 men and do not *t* anything that is theirs:
Dt 14: 8 eat, and their dead bodies you shall not *t*.
Jos 3:13 the whole earth, *t* the water of the Jordan,
Jgs 13: 5 and bear, no razor shall *t* his head,
16:26 "Put me where I may *t* the columns that
1Sm 1:11 drink, and no razor shall ever *t* his head."
18:17 Saul had in mind, "I shall not *t* him;
24:13 I shall not *t* you.
26:11 But the LORD forbid that I *t* his anointed!
2Sm 14:10 to me, and he shall not *t* you again."
23: 7 He who wishes to *t* them must arm himself
1Chr 16:22 *T* not my anointed, and to my prophets
Jdt 11:13 no layman should even *t* with his hands.
Jb 1:11 forth your hand and *t* anything that he has,
2: 5 your hand and *t* his bone and his flesh,
5:19 and at the seventh no evil shall *t* you.
6: 7 I refuse to *t* them; they are loathsome
Ps(s) 105:15 *T* not my anointed, and to my prophets
144: 5 *t* the mountains, and they shall smoke;
Wis 3: 1 hand of God, and no torment shall *t* them.
Is 52:11 come forth from there, *t* nothing unclean!
65: 5 Crying out, "Hold back, do not *t* me;
Lam 4:14 people could not *t* even their garments:
Ez 9: 6 But do not *t* any marked with the X;
33:32 with a pleasant voice and a clever *t*.
44:13 nor shall they *t* any of my sacred things,
Dn 4:19 has become so great as to *t* the heavens,
Am 9: 5 GOD of hosts, I melt the earth with my *t*,
Mt 9:21 "If only I can *t* his cloak,"
14:36 do no more than *t* the tassel of his cloak.
Mk 3:10 kept pushing toward him to *t* him.
5:28 "If I just *t* his clothing,"
6:56 to let them *t* just the tassel of his cloak.
8:22 him a blind man and begged him to *t* him.
10:13 little children to him to have him *t* them,
Lk 5:13 stretched out his hand to *t* him and said,
6:19 the whole crowd was trying to *t* him
24:39 *T* me, and see that a ghost does not have
24:53 *T* me, and see that a ghost does not have
Acts 23:14 by oath to *t* no food until we kill Paul.
2Cor 6:17 says the Lord; 'and *t* nothing unclean.
Col 2:19 when he should be in close *t* with the head.
2:21 Do not *t*!"
Heb 11:28 angel might not *t* the first-born of Israel.
1Jn 5:18 by him, and so the evil one cannot *t* him.

TOUCHED (48)

Lv 15:12 *t* by the afflicted man shall be broken;
Nm 19:18 that were in it, or on him who *t* a bone,
31:19 slain anyone or *t* anyone slain in battle
Dt 27: 5 made of stones that no iron tool has *t*.
Jos 19:34 it *t* Zebulun on the south,
Jgs 6:21 held, and *t* the meat and unleavened cakes.
16:17 and told her, "No razor has *t* my head,
1Sm 10:26 by warriors whose hearts the LORD had *t*.
1Kgs 6:27 cherub *t* a side wall while the other wing,
6:27 *t* the corresponding wing of the second
19: 5 *t* him and ordered him to get up and eat.
19: 7 of the LORD came back a second time, *t* him,
2Chr 3:12 *t* the corresponding wing of the second
30:15 The priests and Levites, *t* with shame,
Est D:12 the golden scepter, he *t* her neck with it,
5: 2 came up to him, and *t* the top of the staff.]
Wis 18:20 trial of death *t* at one time even the just,
Is 6: 7 He *t* my mouth with it.
6: 7 he said, "now that this has *t* your lips,
Jer 1: 9 the LORD extended his hand and *t* my mouth,
Ez 1: 8 and the wings of one *t* those of another.
1:11 out above so that they *t* one another's,
17:10 not rather wither, when *t* by the east wind,
Dn 3:50 no way *t* them or caused them pain or harm.
8:18 he *t* me and made me stand up.
10:10 But then a hand *t* me,
10:16 Then something like a man's hand *t* my lips;
10:18 like a man *t* me again and strengthened me,
Mt 8: 3 stretched out his hand and *t* him and said,
9:20 behind him and *t* the tassel on his cloak.
9:29 At that he *t* their eyes and said,
14:36 many as *t* it were fully restored to health.
20:34 Moved with compassion, Jesus *t* their eyes,
Mk 1:41 pity, Jesus stretched out his hand, *t* him,
5:30 he began to ask, "Who *t* my clothing?"
5:31 hems you in, yet you ask, 'Who *t* me?'"
6:56 All who *t* him got well.
7:33 the man's ears and, spitting, *t* his tongue;
Lk 7:14 Then he stepped forward and *t* the litter;
8:44 behind him and *t* the tassel on his cloak.
8:45 Jesus asked, "Who *t* me?"
8:46 Jesus insisted, "Someone *t* me;
8:47 *t* him and how she had been instantly cured.
18:15 They even brought babies to be *t* by him.
22:51 Then he *t* the ear and healed the man.
Acts 19:12 had *t* his skin were applied to the sick,
1Pt 1: 8 and rejoice with inexpressible joy *t* with
Rv 1:17 He *t* me with his right hand and said:

TOUCHES (45)

Ex 19:12 If anyone *t* the mountain,
29:37 and whatever *t* it will become sacred.
30:29 whatever *t* them shall be sacred.
Lv 5: 2 being aware of it, *t* any unclean thing,
5: 3 aware of it, *t* some human uncleanness,
6:11 Whatever *t* the oblations becomes sacred."
6:20 Whatever *t* its flesh shall become sacred.
7:21 Likewise, if someone *t* anything unclean,
11:24 that everyone who *t* their dead bodies
11:26 everyone who *t* them becomes unclean.
11:27 everyone who *t* their dead bodies shall be
11:31 Everyone who *t* them when they are dead
11:36 whoever *t* the dead body becomes unclean.
11:39 anyone who *t* its dead body shall be
15: 5 who *t* his bed shall wash his garments,
15: 7 Whoever *t* the body of the afflicted man
15:10 Whoever *t* anything that was under him
15:11 Anyone whom the afflicted man *t* with

TOUCHES (cont.)

15:19 who *t* her shall be unclean until evening.
15:21 who *t* her bed shall wash his garments,
15:22 Whoever *t* any article of furniture on
15:23 is on the bed or on the seat when he *t* it,
15:27 Anyone who *t* them becomes unclean;
22: 4 if anyone *t* a person who has become
22: 5 or if anyone *t* any swarming creature or
22: 6 the one who *t* such as these shall be
Nm 19:11 "Whoever *t* the dead body of any human
19:16 who in the open country *t* a dead person,
19:16 or who *t* a human bone or a grave,
19:22 unclean person *t* becomes unclean itself,
19:22 who *t* it becomes unclean until evening."
Jb 4: 5 when it *t* yourself, you are dismayed.
Ps(s) 104:32 who *t* the mountains, and they smoke!
Prv 6:29 none who *t* her shall go unpunished.
Sir 13: 1 He who *t* pitch blackens his hand;
22: 2 whoever *t* him wipes his hands.
34:25 a man again *t* a corpse after he has bathed,
Jer 4:10 for the sword *t* our very soul."
51: 9 judgment reaches heaven, it *t* the clouds.
Hg 2:12 fold of his garment and the fold *t* bread,
2:13 from contact with a corpse *t* any of these,
Zec 2:12 Whoever touches you *t* the apple of my eye.
Lk 7:39 and what sort of woman this is that *t* him
Heb 12:20 "If even an animal *t* the mountain,

TOUCHING (5)

Ex 4:25 off her son's foreskin and, *t* his person,
Nm 19:13 after *t* the body of any deceased person,
Dn 4: 8 and strong, with its top *t* the heavens,
4:17 that you saw, with its top *t* the heavens,
8: 5 the whole earth without *t* the ground.

TOUR (2)

2Sm 24: 2 *T* all the tribes in Israel from Dan to
Mt 9:35 his *t* of all the towns and villages.

TOURED (2)

2Sm 24: 8 Thus they *t* the whole country,
Mt 4:23 Jesus *t* all of Galilee.

TOW (4)

Jgs 16: 9 thread of *t* is severed by a whiff of flame;
Sir 21: 9 A band of criminals is like a bundle of *t*;
Is 1:31 The strong man shall turn to *t*,
Dn 3:46 stoke the furnace with brimstone, pitch, *t*,

TOWARD (351)

Gn 4: 7 his urge is *t* you, yet you can be his
13: 3 the Negeb he traveled by stages *t* Bethel,
18:16 set out from there and looked down *t* Sodom;
18:22 the two men walked on farther *t* Sodom,
19:28 As he looked down *t* Sodom and Gomorrah
21:23 but will act as loyally *t* me and the land
21:23 in which you stay as I have acted *t* you."
24:17 came up, the servant ran *t* her and said,
24:27 let his constant kindness *t* my master fail.
24:63 One day *t* evening he went out . . .
24:65 out there, walking through the fields *t* us?"
26:29 you shall not act unkindly *t* us,
26:29 *t* you and have let you depart in peace.
28:10 from Beer-sheba and proceeded *t* Haran.
31: 2 *t* him was not what it had previously been.
31: 5 attitude *t* me is not as it was in the past;
33:11 God has been generous *t* me,
34:21 "These men are friendly *t* us.
39:21 the chief jailer well-disposed *t* him.
43:14 dispose the man to be merciful *t* you,
Ex 3:21 so well-disposed *t* this people that,
9: 8 of Pharaoh let Moses scatter it *t* the sky.
9:10 Moses scattered it *t* the sky,
9:22 Moses, "Stretch out your hand *t* the sky,
9:23 Moses stretched out his staff *t* the sky,
9:23 Lightning flashed *t* the earth,
10:21 Moses, "Stretch out your hand *t* the sky,
10:22 So Moses stretched out his hand *t* the sky,
11: 3 the Egyptians well-disposed *t* the people;
12:36 Egyptians so well-disposed *t* the people
13:18 *t* the Red Sea by way of the desert road.
14:27 Egyptians were fleeing head on *t* the sea,
16:10 community, they turned *t* the desert,
19:21 through *t* the LORD in order to see him;
22:24 *t* him by demanding interest from him.
25:20 *t* each other, but with their faces looking *t*
26:27 and five for those at the rear, *t* the west.
34: 3 are not to go grazing *t* this mountain."
37: 9 They were turned *t* each other,
37: 9 their faces looking *t* the propitiatory.
38:14 *T* one side there were hangings to the
38:14 *t* the other side, beyond the entrance
Lv 4: 6 the LORD, *t* the veil of the sanctuary.
4:17 it seven times before the LORD, *t* the veil.
Nm 2: 3 "Encamped on the east side, *t* the sunrise,
3:38 front of the meeting tent, *t* the sunrise,
8: 2 their light *t* the front of the lampstand."
8: 3 lamps to face *t* the front of the lampstand,
10:29 with us, and we will be generous *t* you,
13:30 however, to quiet the people *t* Moses,
17: 7 Moses and Aaron turned *t* the meeting tent,
19: 4 times *t* the front of the meeting tent.
21:15 gorges That reach back *t* the site of Ar
24: 1 omens, but turned his gaze *t* the desert.
31:16 Israelites *t* the LORD in the Peor affair,
34:15 stretch of the Jordan, *t* the sunrise."
Dt 2: 8 and we went on *t* the desert of Moab.
3: 1 "Then we turned and proceeded *t* Bashan.
7: 9 down to the thousandth generation *t* those
9: 7 place, you have been rebellious *t* the LORD.
18:13 must be altogether sincere *t* the LORD,
23:12 the camp, and not return until, *t* evening,
25: 7 does not intend to perform his duty *t* me
32:19 and anger *t* his sons and daughters.
Jos 3:16 those flowing downstream *t* the Salt Sea
8: 9 their position to the west of Ai, *t* Bethel,
8:14 in battle at the descent *t* the Arabah,
8:15 fled in seeming defeat *t* the desert,
8:18 out the javelin in your hand *t* Ai,
8:18 out the javelin in his hand *t* the city,
8:20 *t* the desert now turned on their pursuers;
11:17 from Mount Halak that rises *t* Seir as far
12: 7 valley to Mount Halak which rises *t* Seir,
13:25 as far as Aroer, *t* Rabbah (that is,
15: 1 the extreme south *t* the boundary of Edom,
15:21 the extreme southern district *t* Edom were:
Jgs 2:20 In his anger *t* Israel the LORD said,
9:19 honor *t* Jerubbaal and his family this day,
12: 5 took the fords of the Jordan *t* Ephraim.
1Sm 2:13 nor for the priests' duties *t* the people.
9:14 coming *t* them on his way to the high place.
13:17 the Ophrah road *t* the district of Shual;
13:18 the Valley of the Hyenas *t* the desert.
14: 5 *t* Michmash, the other to the south, *t*
17:48 while David ran quickly *t* the battle line
19:23 As he set out from the hilltop *t* the sheds,
20:12 Whether he is well disposed *t* David or not,
23:21 LORD bless you for your sympathy *t* me.
2Sm 2:24 east of the valley *t* the desert near Geba.
13: 2 impossible to carry out his designs *t* her.
14: 1 observed how the king felt *t* Absalom,
15: 6 By behaving in this way *t* all the
15:23 way of the Mount of Olives, *t* the desert.
17:20 went by a short while ago *t* the water."
22:24 But I was wholehearted *t* him,
22:26 *T* the faithful you are faithful; toward
22:27 Toward the sincere you are sincere; but *t*
24: 5 and went in the direction of Gad *t* Jazer.
24: 6 from there they turned *t* Sidon,
24:16 forth his hand *t* Jerusalem to destroy it,
24:20 coming *t* him while he was threshing wheat.
1Kgs 3: 6 David, because he behaved faithfully *t* you,
3: 6 you have continued this great favor *t* him,
6:12 I will fulfill *t* you the promise I made to
6:27 wing, pointing *t* the middle of the room,
7:25 east, with their haunches all *t* the center,
8:22 and stretching forth his hands *t* heaven.
8:38 stretching out his hands *t* this temple,
8:42 when he comes and prays *t* this temple,
8:44 *t* the city you have chosen and the temple
8:48 to you *t* the land you gave their fathers,
8:54 with his hands outstretched *t* heaven.
11:17 fled *t* Egypt with some Edomite servants of
2Kgs 9:27 Ahaziah, king of Judah, fled *t* Beth-haggan.
9:32 two or three eunuchs looked down *t* him.
10:15 disposed toward me, as I am *t* you?"
13:17 and said, "Open the window *t* the east."
17: 9 They adopted unlawful practices *t* the LORD,
23:29 went up *t* the river Euphrates to the king
1Chr 5: 9 *t* the east they dwelt as far as the desert
18: 3 defeated Hadadezer, king of Zobah *t* Hamath,
21:21 But as David came on *t* him,
29:18 forever, and direct their hearts *t* you.
2Chr 3:13 upon their own feet, facing *t* the nave.
4: 4 east, with their haunches all *t* the center;
6:13 and stretched forth his hands *t* heaven.
6:20 which I your servant offer *t* this place.
6:21 Israel which they direct *t* this place.
6:26 pray *t* this place and praise your name,
6:29 stretches out his hands *t* this temple,
20:12 to do, hence our eyes are turned *t* you."
20:24 of the desert and looked *t* the throng,
20:27 turned back *t* Jerusalem celebrating the
Ezr 8:15 assemble by the river that flows *t* Ahava,
9: 9 the good will of the kings of Persia *t* us.
Neh 1: 5 covenant of mercy *t* those who love you
9:10 Because you knew of their insolence *t* them;
Tb 4:13 Do not be so proudhearted *t* your kinsmen
8:17 for you were merciful *t* two only children.
Jdt 2:23 of the desert *t* the south of Chaldea.
2:25 the southern borders of Japheth, *t* Arabia.
7: 3 out in breadth *t* Dothan as far as Balbaim,
7:30 the Lord our God, to show his mercy *t* us;
12: 9 her food was brought to her *t* evening.
Est 5: 1 courtyard, looking *t* the royal palace,
5: 2 *t* her the golden staff which he held.
5: 9 of him, he was filled with anger *t* him.
E:11 the good will which we have *t* all peoples
1Mc 4:12 looked up and saw them marching *t* them,
4:14 were defeated and fled *t* the plain.
5:29 they marched *t* the stronghold of Dathema.
5:35 *t* Alema and attacked and captured it;
5:58 who were with them, and marched *t* Jamnia.
5:65 sons of Esau in the country *t* the south;
5:68 *t* Azotus in the land of the Philistines.
9:40 after the survivors fled *t* the mountain,
15:27 made with Simon and became hostile *t* him.
16: 8 and the rest fled *t* the stronghold.
2Mc 3:20 all of them with hands raised *t* heaven,
6:29 now became hostile *t* him because what he
9:14 *t* which he had been hurrying with the
9:26 continue to show good will *t* me and my son.
11:10 that the Lord had shown his mercy *t* them,
12: 3 There was no hint of enmity *t* them;
13: 5 down steeply on all sides *t* the ashes.
14: 9 gracious consideration that you show *t* all.
14:33 hand *t* the temple and swore this oath:
14:34 priests stretched out their hands *t* heaven,
15:21 stretched out his hands *t* heaven and
15:34 everyone looked *t* heaven and praised the
Jb 11:13 aright and stretch out your hands *t* him,
15: 4 with piety, and you lessen devotion *t* God,
21: 4 Is my complaint *t* man?
22:26 and you shall lift up your face *t* God.
31: 9 If my heart has been enticed *t* a woman,
39:26 that he spreads his wings *t* the south?
Ps(s) 18:24 not from me, But I was wholehearted *t* him,
18:26 Toward the faithful you are faithful, *t*
18:27 *T* the sincere you are sincere, but toward
25:10 constancy *t* those who keep his covenant
25:15 My eyes are ever *t* the LORD,
25:16 Look *t* me, and have pity on me,
28: 2 lifting up my hands *t* your holy shrine.
31:20 And which, *t* those who take refuge in you,
36:11 Keep up your kindness *t* your friends,
40: 2 LORD, and he stooped *t* me and heard my cry.
63: 3 Thus have I gazed *t* you in the sanctuary
69:17 in your great mercy turn *t* me.
71:21 Renew your benefits *t* me,
74: 3 toward the utter ruins; *t* all the damage
78: 8 steadfast nor its spirit faithful *t* God.
78:37 their hearts were not steadfast *t* him,
86:13 Great has been your kindness *t* me;
86:16 Turn *t* me, and have pity on me;
89:29 Forever I will maintain my kindness *t* him,
90:11 indignation *t* those who should fear you?
98: 3 and his faithfulness *t* the house of Israel.
103:11 is his kindness *t* those who fear him.
103:17 *t* those who fear him, And his justice *t*
117: 2 For steadfast is his kindness *t* us,
121: 1 I lift up my eyes *t* the mountains;
134: 2 Lift up your hands *t* the sanctuary,
141: 8 For *t* you, O GOD, my Lord, my eyes
145: 9 to all and compassionate *t* all his works.
Prv 7:22 Like a stag that minces *t* the net,
11:19 Virtue directs *t* life, but he who pursues
23: 5 wings, like the eagle that flies *t* heaven.
Eccl 1: 6 now toward the south, then *t* the north,
7:25 I turned my thoughts *t* knowledge;
8:12 who fear God, for their reverence *t* him:
8:13 days, for his lack of reverence *t* God.
Sg 7: 5 the tower on Lebanon that looks *t* Damascus.
Wis 6:17 For the first step *t* discipline is a very
16: 7 For he who turned *t* it was saved,
16:21 revealed your sweetness *t* your children,
Sir 12:11 though he acts humbly and peaceably *t* you,
31:14 *T* what he eyes, do not put out a hand;
35:13 Though not unduly partial *t* the weak,
38:15 toward his Maker will be defiant *t*
48:10 back the hearts of fathers *t* their sons,
50:24 May his goodness *t* us endure in Israel as
Is 2: 2 All nations shall stream *t* it;
3: 5 be bold *t* the elder, and the base toward
17: 7 his eyes turned *t* the Holy One of Israel.
30:29 Toward the mountain of the LORD, *t*
45: 6 so that *t* the rising and the setting of
Jer 2:24 near and far, breaking away *t* the desert,
3:12 Go, proclaim these words *t* the north,
4:11 a wind comes *t* the daughter of my people."
15: 1 me, my heart would not turn *t* this people.
15:20 you *t* this people a solid wall of brass.
19: 2 and go out *t* the Valley of Ben-hinnom,
31: 3 so I have kept my mercy *t* you.
31:40 ashes, all the slopes *t* the Kidron Valley,
Lam 3:41 us reach out our hearts *t* God in heaven!
Bar 4: 2 walk by her light *t* splendor.
Ez 1:23 wings were stretched out, one *t* the other.
6: 2 Son of man, turn *t* the mountains of Israel,
8: 5 Son of man, look *t* the north!
8: 5 I looked *t* the north and saw northward of
8:16 LORD's temple and their faces *t* the east;
10: 7 *t* the fire that was among the cherubim.
13:17 turn *t* the daughters of your people who
17: 6 and low-lying, Its branches turned *t* him,
21: 2 of man, look southward, preach *t* the south,
21: 7 Son of man, look *t* Jerusalem,
23:27 you shall no longer look *t* it,
25: 2 *t* the Ammonites and prophesy against them.
28:21 Son of man, look *t* Sidon,
31: 7 for its roots were turned *t* abundant water.
38: 2 Son of man, turn *t* Gog [the land of Magog],
40: 7 of the gate *t* the inside measured one rod.
40: 9 The vestibule of the gate was *t* the inside.
40:22 to it, and its vestibule was *t* the inside.
40:26 its vestibule was *t* the inside;
40:31 But its vestibule was *t* the outer court;

40:34 But its vestibule was *t* the outer court;
40:37 Its vestibule was *t* the outer court;
46: 1 The gate *t* the east of the inner court
47: 1 the threshold of the temple *t* the east,
47: 1 the façade of the temple was *t* the east;
47:18 between the Hauran *t* Damascus
Dn 6:11 a day, with the windows open *t* Jerusalem.
8: 4 I saw the ram butting *t* the west,
8: 6 river, and rushed *t* it with savage force.
8: 9 little horn which kept growing *t* the south,
9: 4 merciful covenant *t* those who love you
9: 7 them because of their treachery *t* you.
11:28 turn back *t* his land with great riches,
13:38 the garden, saw this crime, we ran *t* them.
Jl 2:20 and waste, With his van *t* the eastern sea,
2:20 sea, and his rear *t* the western sea;
Zec 6: 6 horses was turning *t* the land of the north,
6: 6 spotted ones went *t* the land of the south.
7: 9 show kindness and compassion *t* each other.
11: 8 of them, and they behaved badly *t* me.
Mal 1:12 But you behave profanely *t* me by thinking
Mt 5:22 who uses abusive language *t* his brother
8:25 so they made their way *t* him and woke him:
9: 7 The man stood up and went *t* his home.
12:49 Then, extending his hand *t* his disciples,
14:25 he came walking *t* them on the lake.
14:29 began to walk on the water, moving *t* Jesus.
17: 7 came *t* them and laying his hand on them,
26:12 has contributed *t* my burial preparation.
27:46 Then *t* midafternoon Jesus cried out in a
Mk 1:12 point the Spirit sent him out *t* the desert.
3: 7 withdrew *t* the lake with his disciples.
3:10 kept pushing *t* him to touch him.
6:45 precede him to the other side *t* Bethsaida,
6:48 them, he came walking *t* them on the water;
Lk 9:51 he firmly resolved to proceed *t* Jerusalem,
9:55 He turned *t* them only to reprimand them.
13:22 all the while making his way *t* Jerusalem.
Jn 1:29 John caught sight of Jesus coming *t* him,
1:47 When Jesus saw Nathanael coming *t* him,
6: 5 caught sight of a vast crowd coming *t* him,
6:17 intending to cross the lake *t* Capernaum.
20: 3 started out on their way *t* the tomb.
Acts 8:26 "Head south *t* the road which goes from
10: 3 messenger of God coming *t* him and calling,
21: 3 by on our left as we continued on *t* Syria.
21:15 we got ready and started up *t* Jerusalem.
26:12 "On one such occasion I was traveling *t*
27:20 *T* the end, we abandoned any hope of
27:27 when *t* midnight the sailors began to
Rom 1:30 wrongdoing and rebellious *t* their parents.
6:21 ashamed of, all of them tending *t* death.
6:22 sanctification as you tend *t* eternal life.
8: 6 The tendency of the flesh is *t* death but
8: 6 but that of the spirit *t* life and peace.
9:23 known the riches of his glory *t* the vessels
10:12 rich in mercy *t* all who call upon him.
11:22 severity *t* those who fell,
11:22 toward those who fell, kindness *t* you,
12:16 Have the same attitude *t* all.
1Cor 7: 3 his conjugal obligations *t* his wife,
7: 3 his wife, the wife hers *t* her husband.
7:36 he is behaving dishonorably *t* his virgin
2Cor 1:12 in our behavior *t* all and especially toward
1:24 I prefer to work with you *t* your happiness.
4: 3 for those who are headed *t* destruction.
10: 1 am lowly, but when absent am bold *t* you.
Gal 5:26 or challenging, or jealous *t* one another.
Eph 6: 9 act in a similar way *t* your slaves.
Phil 2:13 It is God who, in his good will *t* you,
3:14 as I run *t* the prize to which God calls me
Col 1: 4 and the love you bear *t* all the saints
3:19 Avoid any bitterness *t* them.
1Thes 2:10 our conduct was *t* you who are believers.
5:14 support the weak; be patient *t* all.
2Tm 2:24 be quarrelsome but must be kindly *t* all.
Ti 3: 2 and display a perfect courtesy *t* all men.
Phlm 1: 5 *t* the Lord Jesus and all God's people.
Jas 4: 5 he has implanted in us tends *t* jealousy"?
1Pt 3: 8 sympathetic, loving *t* one another,
2Pt 3:15 Lord's patience is directed *t* salvation.

TOWARDS (1)

Ez 10:11 *t* it without veering as they moved.

TOWEL (2)

Jn 13: 4 picked up a *t* and tied it around himself.
13: 5 and dry them with the *t* he had around him.

TOWER (37)

Gn 11: 4 a city and a *t* with its top in the sky,
11: 5 the city and the *t* that the men had built.
Jgs 8: 9 return in triumph, I will demolish this *t*."
8:17 *t* of Penuel and slew the men of the city.
9:51 was a strong *t* in the middle of the city,
9:51 in and going up to the roof of the *t*.
9:52 came up to the *t* and fought against it,
9:52 very entrance of the *t* to set it on fire.
2Kgs 9:17 The watchman standing on the *t* in Jezreel
Neh 3: 1 the rebuilding to the *T* of Hananel.
3:11 adjoining sector, as far as the Oven *T*,
3:25 the *t* projecting from the Upper Palace
3:26 Gate on the east, and the projecting *t*.
3:27 sector opposite the great projecting *t*,
12:38 past the Oven *T* as far as the Broad Wall,
12:39 the Tower of Hananel, and the Hundred *T*,
1Mc 6:37 A strong wooden *t* covering each elephant,
2Mc 13: 5 at that place a *t* seventy-five feet high,
14:41 troops, on the point of capturing the *t*,
Ps(s) 61: 4 refuge, a *t* of strength against the enemy.
Prv 18:10 The name of the LORD is a strong *t*;
Sg 4: 4 is like David's *t* girt with battlements;
7: 5 Your neck is like a *t* of ivory.
7: 5 *t* on Lebanon that looks toward Damascus.
Sir 37:14 better than seven watchmen in a lofty *t*.
Is 2:15 every lofty *t* and every fortified wall,
32:19 Hill and *t* will become wasteland forever
Jer 31:38 from the *T* of Hananel to the Corner Gate.
Ez 4: 2 build a *t*, lay out a ramp, pitch camps,
21:27 to cast up a ramp, to build a siege *t*.
26: 8 He shall place a siege *t* against you,
Zec 14:10 *T* of Hananel to the king's wine presses,
Mt 21:33 around it, dug out a vat, and erected a *t*.
Mk 12: 1 around it, dug out a vat, and erected a *t*.
Lk 13: 4 who were killed by a falling *t* in Siloam.
14:28 If one of you decides to build a *t*,

TOWERING (2)

Nm 23:22 him out of Egypt, a wild bull of *t* might.
24: 8 him out of Egypt, a wild bull of *t* might.

TOWERS (36)

1Chr 27:25 the villages, and the *t* was Jonathan,
2Chr 14: 6 cities and surround them with walls, *t*,
26: 9 built *t* in Jerusalem at the Corner Gate,
26:10 *t* in the desert and dug numerous cisterns,
26:15 devices contrived to stand on the *t*
27: 4 the forest land he set up fortresses and *t*.
32: 5 where it was broken down, raised *t* upon it,
Tb 13:12 your *t* and set fire to your homes;
13:16 *t* of Jerusalem shall be built with gold,
Jdt 1: 3 the gates he raised *t* of a hundred cubits,
1:14 He pressed on to Ecbatana and took its *t*,
7:32 returned to the walls and *t* of the city;
1Mc 1:33 with a high, massive wall and strong *t*,
4:60 high walls and strong *t* around Mount Zion,
5: 5 He forced them to take refuge in *t*,
5: 5 the *t* along with all the persons in them.
5:65 its strongholds and burned the *t* around it.
13:33 their fortifications with high *t*,
13:43 and attacked and captured one of the *t*.
16:10 refuge in the *t* on the plain of Azotus,
2Mc 10:18 thousand took refuge in two very strong *t*,
10:20 be bribed by some of the men in the *t*;
10:22 and without delay captured the two *t*.
10:36 they put the *t* to the torch,
Ps(s) 48:13 Zion, make the round; count her *t*.
57:11 For your kindness *t* to the heavens,
108: 5 For your kindness *t* to the heavens,
Sg 8:10 I am a wall, and my breasts are like *t*.
Is 23:13 the impious founded, setting up *t* for her,
30:25 of the great slaughter, when the *t* fall,
33:18 Where is he who counted the *t*?"
Lam 2: 7 of her *t* he has handed over to the enemy,
Ez 17:17 When ramps are cast up and siege *t* are
26: 4 destroy the walls of Tyre and raze her *t*.
26: 9 and break down your *t* with his weapons.
27:11 walls, and the Gamadites were in your *t*;

TOWING (1)

Jn 21: 8 came in the boat, *t* the net full of fish.

TOWN (93)

Gn 19: 2 we shall pass the night in the *t* square."
19:20 this *t* ahead is near enough to escape to.
19:21 I will not overthrow the *t* you speak of.
19:22 That is why the *t* is called Zoar.
23:10 of the Hittites who sat on his *t* council:
23:18 the Hittites who sat on Ephron's *t* council.
28:19 the former name of the *t* had been Luz.
34:20 his son Shechem went to their *t* council
34:24 *t* agreed with Hamor and his son Shechem,
41:48 each *t* the crops of the fields around it.
Lv 25:29 someone sells a dwelling in a walled *t*,
25:30 But if such a house in a walled *t* has not
25:32 the *t* houses that are their property.
25:33 Any *t* house of the Levites in their cities
25:33 for the *t* houses of the Levites are their
Nm 20:16 *t* of Kadesh at the edge of our territory.
1Sm 9:11 and inquired of them, "Is the seer in *t*?"
9:27 As they were approaching the edge of *t*,
14:24 in every *t* in the hill country of Ephraim.
2Sm 12: 1 In a certain *t* there were two men,
15:12 an invitation to come from his *t*,
2Kgs 15:16 of the *t* and of its whole district,
Jdt 8:18 exist today, any tribe, or clan, or *t*,
2Mc 12: 7 When the gates of the *t* were shut,
Is 22: 2 O wanton *t*, your slain are not slain
Jer 49:25 of glory be forsaken, the *t* of delight!
Lam 2:11 faint away in the open spaces of the *t*.
Hb 2:12 and establishes a *t* by wickedness!
Mt 2:23 There he settled in a *t* called Nazareth.
8:33 the *t* related everything that had happened,
8:34 that the entire *t* came out to meet Jesus.
9: 1 the crossing, and came back to his own *t*.
10: 5 territory and do not enter a Samaritan *t*.
10:11 "Look for a worthy person in every *t* or
10:14 you have to say, leave that house or *t*,
10:15 day of judgment than it will for that *t*.
10:23 When they persecute you in one *t*,
11:16 like children squatting in the *t* squares,
12:25 A *t* or household split into factions
Mk 1:33 the whole *t* was gathered outside the door.
1:45 possible for Jesus to enter a *t* openly.
Lk 1:26 from God to a *t* of Galilee named Nazareth,
1:39 into the hill country to a *t* of Judah,
2: 3 went to register, each to his own *t*.
2: 4 from the *t* of Nazareth in Galilee to Judea,
2: 4 to Judea, to David's *t* of Bethlehem
2:39 to Galilee and their own *t* of Nazareth.
4:29 They rose up and expelled him from the *t*,
4:31 went down to Capernaum, a *t* of Galilee,
4:42 the *t* and set out into the open country.
5:12 On one occasion in a certain *t*,
7:11 Soon afterward he went to a *t* called Naim,
7:12 of the *t* a dead man was being carried out,
7:37 A woman known in the *t* to be a sinner
8: 4 resorting to him from one *t* after another.
8:27 from the *t* who was possessed by demons.
8:34 the news to the *t* and country roundabout.
8:39 The man went all through the *t* making
9: 5 leave that *t* and shake its dust from your
9:10 him, he retired to a *t* called Bethsaida,
9:52 *t* to prepare for his passing through,
9:56 Then they set off for another *t*.
10: 1 to every *t* and place he intended to visit.
10:10 of any *t* you enter do not welcome you,
10:11 *t* from our feet as testimony against you.
10:12 will be less severe than that of such a *t*.
14:21 *t* and bring in the poor and the crippled,
23:51 He was from Arimathea, a Jewish *t*,
Jn 1:44 Bethsaida, the same *t* as Andrew and Peter.
4: 5 him to a Samaritan *t* named Shechem
4: 8 had gone off to the *t* to buy provisions.)
4:28 left her water jar and went off into the *t*.
4:30 that they set out from the *t* to meet him.
4:39 Many Samaritans from that *t* believed in
11:54 He withdrew instead to a *t* called Ephraim
Acts 8: 5 went down to the *t* of Samaria and there
8: 8 rejoicing in that *t* rose to fever pitch.
8: 9 *t* and holding the Samaritans spellbound.
13:50 sympathizers and the leading men of the *t*,
14:13 temple of Zeus, which stood outside the *t*,
14:19 stoned Paul and dragged him out of the *t*,
14:20 long he got up and went back into the *t*.
14:21 news in that *t* and made numerous disciples,
15:21 Moses has been proclaimed in every *t*
16: 4 As they made their way from town to *t*,
16:14 in purple goods from the *t* of Thyatira.
17: 5 to form a mob and start a riot in the *t*.
17: 6 some of the brothers to the *t* magistrates,
19:35 Finally the *t* clerk quieted the mob.
27: 8 called Fair Havens, near the *t* of Lasea.
Ti 1: 5 the appointment of presbyters in every *t*.
Jas 4:13 tomorrow we shall go to such and such a *t*,

TOWNS (70)

Gn 35: 5 from God fell upon the *t* round about,
41:35 authority, to be stored in the *t* for food.
41:48 Egypt was enjoying and stored it in the *t*,
Nm 13:19 *t* in which they dwell open or fortified?
13:28 and the *t* are fortified and very strong.
21:25 the towns here and settled in these *t* of
31:10 while they set on fire all the *t* where
32:16 for our flocks, and *t* for our families;
32:17 can remain here in the fortified *t*,
32:24 Build the *t*, then, for your families,
32:26 other livestock remain in the *t* of Gilead,
32:33 *t* and the districts that surrounded them.
32:34 Gadites rebuilt the fortified *t* of Dibon,
32:38 These *t*, which they rebuilt,
Dt 3: 5 nothing of the great number of unwalled *t*.
3:19 remain behind in the *t* I have given you,
Jos 10:37 it to the sword with its king, all its *t*,
10:39 capturing it with its king and all its *t*.
13:17 and all its *t* which are on the tableland,
15:45 Ekron and its *t* and villages,
15:46 sea, all the *t* that lie alongside Ashdod,
15:47 towns and villages; Gaza and its *t* and
17:11 *t*, Ibleam and its towns, Dor and its towns
17:11 its *t* and natives, Taanach and its towns
17:11 *t* and natives [the third is Naphathdor].
17:16 particular those in Beth-shean and its *t*,
Jgs 1:27 with its *t* or of Taanach with its towns.
1:27 and its towns, those of Ibleam and its *t*,
1:27 its towns, or those of Megiddo and its *t*.
1Sm 27: 5 a place to live in one of the country *t*.
2Sm 8: 8 From Tebah and Berothai, *t* of Hadadezer,
1Chr 2:23 of Jair, that is, Kenath and its *t*,
5:16 They dwelt in Gilead, in Bashan and its *t*,
7:28 their dwellings were in Bethel and its *t*.
7:28 *t* to the west, and also Shechem and its *t*
7:28 and its towns as far as Ayyah and its *t*.
7:29 and its *t*, Taanach and its towns,

TOWNS (cont.)
7:29 Megiddo and its *t*, and Dor and its *t*.
8:12 who built Ono and Lod with its nearby *t*,
18: 1 *t* away from the control of the Philistines.
Jdt 6: 7 leave you at one of the *t* along the ascent.
15: 7 till the *t* and villages in the mountains
1Mc 10:84 plundered Azotus with its neighboring *t*,
2Mc 8: 6 Coming unexpectedly upon *t* and villages,
Mt 9:35 his tour of all the *t* and villages.
10:23 *t* of Israel before the Son of Man comes.
11: 1 locality to teach and preach in their *t*.
11:20 He began to reproach the *t* where most
14:13 of it and followed him on foot from the *t*.
Mk 6:33 all the *t* hastened on foot to the place,
6:56 put in an appearance, in villages, in *t*,
Lk 4:43 "To other *t* I must announce the good news
8: 1 After this he journeyed through *t* and
13:22 He went through cities and *t* teaching
Acts 5:16 from the *t* around Jerusalem would gather,
8:40 in all the *t* until he reached Caesarea.
14: 6 they fled to the Lycaonian *t* of Lystra and
15:36 of the *t* where we proclaimed the word
17: 8 the *t* magistrates heard the whole story,
Jude 1: 7 and the *t* thereabout indulged in lust,

TOWNSFOLK (1)
Lk 7:12 A considerable crowd of *t* were with her.

TOWNSMEN (4)
Gn 19: 4 they went to bed, all the *t* of Sodom,
24:13 of the *t* are coming out to draw water,
34:20 presented the matter to their fellow *t*:
Dt 22:21 and there her *t* shall stone her to death,

TOWNSPEOPLE (6)
Jgs 6:27 through fear of his family and of the *t*,
6:28 Early the next morning the *t* found that
6:30 So the *t* said to Joash,
19:16 he lived among the Benjaminite *t* of Gibeah.
Ru 3:11 all my *t* know you for a worthy woman.
Acts 14: 4 Most of the *t* were divided over them,

TRACE (6)
Gn 41:31 no *t* of the abundance will be found in the
Jdt 6: 4 Not a *t* of them shall survive our attack:
Jb 13:27 all my paths and *t* out all my footsteps.
Wis 5:10 when it has passed, no *t* can be found,
Bar 3:18 for money, but there is no *t* of their work:
Dn 2:35 wind blew them away without leaving a *t*.

TRACED (2)
Bar 3:37 He has *t* out all the way of understanding,
Lk 1: 3 I too have carefully *t* the whole sequence

TRACES (2)
Wis 2: 4 life will pass away like the *t* of a cloud,
Sir 10:17 The *t* of the proud God sweeps away and

TRACHONITIS (1)
Lk 3: 1 tetrarch of the region of Ituraea and *T*,

TRACING (1)
Jn 8: 6 started *t* on the ground with his finger.

TRACK (4)
Tb 10: 1 Tobit was keeping *t* of the time Tobiah
Jer 18:15 To travel on bypaths, not the beaten *t*.
Jl 2: 8 another, each advances in his own *t*;
Mk 1:36 and his companions managed to *t* him down,

TRACKED (1)
Hos 6: 8 is a city of evildoers, *t* with blood.

TRACKLESS (1)
Ps(s) 107:40 and sends them astray through a *t* waste,

TRACKS (2)
Jdt 14: 4 them and strike them down in their *t*.
Sg 1: 8 Follow the *t* of the flock and pasture the

TRACT (14)
Ez 45: 1 set apart a sacred *t* of land for the LORD,
45: 6 thousand long, parallel to the sacred *t*;
45: 7 of the combined sacred *t* and City property,
48: 8 shall be the *t* which you shall set apart,
48: 8 the center of the *t* shall be the sanctuary.
48: 9 The *t* that you set aside for the LORD
48:10 In this sacred *t* the priests shall have
48:12 *t* of land their own most sacred domain,
48:13 The whole *t* shall be twenty-five thousand
48:18 shall remain an area along the sacred *t*,
48:20 The entire *t* shall be twenty-five thousand
48:20 sacred *t* together with the City property.
48:21 of the sacred *t* and the City property,
48:21 The sacred *t* and the sanctuary of the

TRADE (11)
Ez 27: 3 the *t* of the peoples to many a coastland:
27: 9 sailor on the sea came to you to carry *t*.
27:21 The *t* of Arabia and of all the sheikhs of
28:16 in you, the result of your far-flung *t*;
28:18 of your great guilt, your sinful *t*,
Acts 18: 3 pair, whose *t* he had in common with them.
19:27 not only that our *t* will be discredited,
2Cor 2:17 not like so many who *t* on the word of God.
Jas 4:13 and such a town, spend a year there, *t*,
Rv 18:19 grew rich from their profitable *t* with her!
18:22 in any *t* shall ever again be found in you!

TRADED (8)
Ez 27:12 Tarshish *t* with you,
27:15 many coastlands *t* with you;
27:16 Edom *t* with you,
27:18 Damascus *t* with you,
27:20 Dedan *t* with you for riding gear.
27:22 of Sheba and Raamah also *t* with you,
27:24 of Sheba, Asshur, and Chilmad *t* with you,
27:27 of your seams, those who *t* for your goods,

TRADERS (7)
Gn 37:28 Some Midianite *t* passed by,
Jb 40:30 Will the *t* bargain for him?
Is 23: 8 whose *t* are the earth's honored men?
Ez 16:29 now going to Chaldea, the land of the *t*;
27:13 Tubal, and Meshech were also *t* with you,
27:36 The *t* among the peoples now hiss at you;
Lk 19:45 the temple and began ejecting the *t* saying:

TRADESMEN (1)
Ez 17: 4 branch, And brought it to a land of *t*,

TRADING (2)
Ps(s) 107:23 the sea in ships, *t* on the deep waters,
Ez 28: 5 to your *t* you have heaped up your riches;

TRADITION (7)
Sir 8: 9 Reject not the *t* of old men which they
Mt 15: 2 act contrary to the *t* of our ancestors?
15: 3 of God for the sake of your *t*?
15: 6 of your *t* you have nullified God's word.
Mk 7: 5 not follow the *t* of our ancestors,
7: 8 commandment and cling to what is human *t*."
2Thes 3: 6 does not follow the *t* you received from us.

TRADITIONAL (1)
2Mc 6: 6 keep the sabbath or celebrate the *t* feasts,

TRADITIONS (8)
1Mc 2:40 the Gentiles for our lives and our *t*,
Mk 7: 4 There are many other *t* they observe
7: 9 in the interests of keeping your *t*!
7:13 word in favor of the *t* you have handed on.
1Cor 11: 2 to the *t* just as I handed them on to you.
Gal 1:14 zeal to live out all the *t* of my ancestors.
Col 2: 8 philosophy that follows mere human *t*,
2Thes 2:15 Hold fast to the *t* you received from us,

TRADUCER (1)
Jb 16: 8 As a witness there rises up my *t*,

TRAFFIC (1)
1Kgs 10:15 Tarshish fleet, from the *t* of merchants,

TRAFFICKED (2)
Ez 27:15 The Rhodanites *t* with you;
27:17 Judah and the land of Israel *t* with you,

TRAILED (1)
Jer 48:32 Your tendrils *t* down to the sea,

TRAIN (16)
1Kgs 1:35 When you come back in his *t*,
Jdt 7: 2 *t* or the men who accompanied it on foot
Est D: 3 the other followed her, bearing her *t*.
1Mc 6:55 to *t* his son Antiochus to be king,
Jb 38:32 their season, or guide the Bear with its *t*?
Ps(s) 45:15 the virgins of her *t* are brought to you.
105:22 That he might *t* his princes to be like him
Prv 22: 6 *T* a boy in the way he should go;
Is 2: 4 another, nor shall they *t* for war again.
6: 1 the *t* of his garment filling the temple.
47: 2 Strip off your *t*,
Dn 11:43 Libya and Ethiopia shall be in his *t*.
Mi 4: 3 another, nor shall they *t* for war again.
2Cor 2:14 leads us on in Christ's triumphal *t*,
1Tm 4: 7 *T* yourself for the life of piety,
Rv 6: 8 Death, and the nether world was in his *t*.

TRAINED (16)
2Sm 10: 7 Joab with the entire levy of *t* soldiers.
22:35 Who *t* my hands for war till my arms could
2Kgs 24:16 and smiths, all of them *t* soldiers.
1Chr 5:18 sword and who drew the bow, *t* in warfare
25: 7 brethren who were *t* in singing to the LORD,
1Mc 6:30 and thirty-two elephants *t* for war.
2Mc 15:12 and *t* from childhood in every virtuous
Ps(s) 18:35 Who *t* my hands for war and my arms to
Prv 29:19 By words no servant can be *t*;
Sir 18:29 *t* in her words must show their wisdom,
Dn 13: 3 her pious parents had *t* their daughter
Hos 7:15 Though I *t* and strengthened their arms,
10:11 Ephraim was a *t* heifer,
Heb 5:14 for those whose faculties are *t* by
12:11 justice to those who are *t* in its school.
2Pt 2:14 Their hearts are *t* in greed.

TRAINING (13)
Jgs 3: 1 [just to instruct, by *t* them in battle,
Prv 1: 3 May receive *t* in wise conduct,
15:33 The fear of the LORD is *t* for wisdom,
Wis 2:12 and charges us with violations of our *t*.
Sir 8: 8 the *t* to serve in the presence of princes.
33: 4 draw upon your *t*,
34: 9 A man with *t* gains wide knowledge;
42: 5 Of constant *t* of children,
Dn 1: 5 *t* they were to enter the king's service.
Eph 6: 4 the *t* and instruction befitting the Lord.
1Tm 1: 4 than that *t* in faith which God requires.
4: 8 physical *t* is to some extent valuable,
2Tm 3:16 and *t* in holiness so that the man of God

TRAINS (2)
Ps(s) 144: 1 LORD, my rock, who *t* my hands for battle,
Ti 2:12 It *t* us to reject godless ways and worldly

TRAIT (1)
Ps(s) 119:160 Permanence is your word's chief *t*;

TRAITOR (8)
2Mc 5:15 that *t* both to the laws and to his country,
10:13 called a *t* for having abandoned Cyprus,
Is 21: 2 the *t* betrays, the despoiler spoils.
33: 1 never destroyed, O *t* never betrayed!
Jer 3: 7 even though her *t* sister Judah saw that
3: 8 her *t* sister Judah was not frightened;
3:10 the *t* sister Judah did not return to me
Lk 6:16 of James, and Judas Iscariot, who turned *t*.

TRAITOROUS (1)
Jer 3:11 Israel is inwardly more just than *t* Judah.

TRAITORS (5)
2Mc 10:22 So he put them to death as *t*,
Ps(s) 59: 6 have no pity on any worthless *t*.
Is 24:16 The *t* betray:
24:16 with treachery have the *t* betrayed!
Rv 21: 8 As for the cowards and *t* to the faith,

TRAMP (1)
1Mc 6:41 of their numbers, the *t* of their marching,

TRAMPLE (20)
Jb 39:15 them, that the wild beasts may *t* them,
Ps(s) 7: 6 let him *t* my life to the ground,
56: 2 Have pity on me, O God, for men *t* upon me;
56: 3 My adversaries *t* upon me all the day;
57: 4 may he make those a reproach who *t* upon me;
91:13 you shall *t* down the lion and the dragon.
94: 5 Your people, O LORD, they *t* down,
Sir 9: 2 power over you to *t* upon your dignity.
Is 1:13 *T* my courts no more!
14:25 in my land and *t* him on my mountains;
28: 3 With feet that will *t* the majestic garland
41:25 He shall *t* the rulers down like red earth,
Bar 4:25 their destruction and *t* upon their necks.
Ez 26:11 of his horses he shall *t* all your streets;
34:18 *t* the rest of your pastures with your feet?
Am 2: 7 They *t* the heads of the weak into the dust
8: 4 you who *t* upon the needy and destroy the
Hb 3:12 the earth, in fury you *t* the nations.
Zec 9:15 overcome sling stones and *t* them underfoot;
Mt 7: 6 They will *t* them under foot,

TRAMPLED (28)
2Sm 22:43 like the mud in the streets I *t* them down.
2Kgs 7:17 but the people *t* him to death at the gate,
7:20 for the people *t* him to death at the gate.
13: 7 had destroyed them and *t* them like dust.
14: 9 passed by and *t* the thistle underfoot.
2Chr 25:18 Lebanon passed by and *t* the thistle down.
1Mc 3:45 The sanctuary was *t* on,
3:51 your sanctuary has been *t* on and profaned,
Ps(s) 18:43 like the mud in the streets I *t* them down.
44: 6 your name we *t* down our adversaries.
Is 5: 5 break through its wall, let it be *t*!
7:25 for cattle and shall be *t* upon by sheep.
9: 4 For every boot that *t* in battle,
14:19 as those slain at sword-point, a *t* corpse.
26: 6 It is *t* underfoot by the needy,
28:18 scourge passes, you shall be *t* down by it.
63: 3 in my anger, and *t* them down in my wrath;

63: 6 I t down the peoples in my anger,
63:18 why have our enemies t your sanctuary?
Ez 34:19 had t and drink what your feet had fouled.
Dn 7: 7 and what was left it t with its feet.
8: 7 withstand it, to the ground, and t upon it;
8:10 host and some of the stars and t on them.
8:13 there, the sanctuary, and the t host?"
Am 5:11 because you have t upon the weak and
Mi 7:10 now shall she be t underfoot,
Mt 5:13 but to be thrown out and t underfoot.
Lk 21:24 Jerusalem will be t by the Gentiles,

TRAMPLES (3)

Prv 27: 7 One who is full, t on virgin honey;
Lam 3:34 t underfoot all the prisoners in the land.
Mi 5: 7 When it passes through, it t and tears,

TRAMPLING (4)

1Mc 4:60 and t over it as they had done before.
Is 16: 4 and they have done with t the land,
Dn 7:19 claws, and t with its feet what was left;
Zec 10: 5 t the mire of the streets in battle;

TRANCE (4)

Gn 15:12 sun was about to set, a t fell upon Abram,
Acts 10:10 it was being prepared he fell into a t.
11: 5 prayer in the city of Joppa when, in a t,
22:17 fell into a t and saw Jesus speaking to me.

TRANQUIL (12)

Jb 3:13 then I should have lain down and been t;
34:29 If he remains t, who then can condemn?
40:23 he is t though the torrent surges about
Prv 14:30 A t mind gives life to the body,
Wis 7:23 beneficent, kindly, Firm, secure, t,
Sir 47:13 of peace, for God made t all his borders.
Is 7: 4 Take care you remain t and do not fear;
Jer 30:10 find rest, shall be t and undisturbed,
46:27 find rest, shall be t and undisturbed.
48:11 Moab has been t from his youth,
Zec 1:11 see, the whole earth is t and at rest!"
1Tm 2: 2 and t lives in perfect piety and dignity.

TRANQUILITY (5)

1Chr 22: 9 time I will bestow peace and t on Israel.
Est B: 2 for my subjects a life of complete t;
Ps(s) 116: 7 Return, O my soul, to your t,
Eccl 4: 6 Better is one handful with t than two
Sir 20:20 to sin, yet in this t he cannot rest.

TRANQUILLY (1)

Jb 21:13 and t go down to the nether world.

TRANSACTION (1)

Gn 23:19 After this t, Abraham buried his wife

TRANSFER (3)

1Chr 12:24 David at Hebron to t to him Saul's kingdom,
Est E:14 defenseless and to t the rule of the Persians
1Mc 10:32 Jerusalem, and I t it to the high priest,

TRANSFERRED (9)

Gn 23:20 Thus the field with its cave was t from
1Sm 5: 1 ark of God, t it from Ebenezer to Ashdod.
2Sm 15:13 Israelites have t their loyalty to Absalom."
1Chr 10:14 LORD slew him, and t his kingdom to David,
Est 2: 9 he t both her and her maids to the best
8: 2 and t it into the keeping of Mordecai;
1Mc 11:34 were t from Samaria to Judea in favor of
Sir 10: 8 Dominion is t from one people to another
Acts 7:16 Their remains were t to Shechem and placed

TRANSFIGURED (2)

Mt 17: 2 He was t before their eyes.
Mk 9: 2 He was t before their eyes and his clothes

TRANSFIXED (1)

Jer 51: 4 shall fall in the land of Chaldea, the t,

TRANSFORMED (5)

Jdt 10: 7 Judith t in looks and differently dressed,
Wis 16:25 at that very time, t in all sorts of ways,
Is 38:17 thus is my bitterness t into peace.
Rom 12: 2 age but be t by the renewal of your mind,
2Cor 3:18 are being t from glory to glory into his

TRANSFORMS (1)

Wis 4:12 the whirl of desire t the innocent mind.

TRANSGRESS (4)

Jos 23:16 If you t the covenant of the LORD,
2Mc 7: 2 rather than t the laws of our ancestors."
Prv 8:29 that the waters should not t his command;
Sir 10:19 Those who t the commandments.

TRANSGRESSED (7)

Jb 6:10 I have not t the commands of the Holy One.
Ps(s) 17: 4 My mouth has not t after the manner of man;
Is 24: 5 of its inhabitants, who have t laws,
Ez 20:38 those who have rebelled and t against me;
39:23 for they t against me,
Dn 3:29 we have sinned and t by departing from you,
9:11 all Israel t your law and went astray,

TRANSGRESSES (1)

Dt 17: 2 of the LORD, your God, and t his covenant,

TRANSGRESSING (2)

2Chr 24:20 says, 'why are you t the LORD's commands,
Is 59:13 T, and denying the LORD,

TRANSGRESSION (9)

1Sm 25:28 Please forgive the t of your handmaid,
Jb 33: 9 "I am clean and without t;
Wis 3:13 undefiled, knew not t of the marriage bed;
14:31 ever follows upon the t of the wicked.
Dn 9:24 Then t will stop and sin will end,
Rom 4:15 for where there is no law there is no t.
11:11 by their t salvation has come to the
11:12 But if their t and their diminishing have
Heb 2: 2 and all t and disobedience received its

TRANSGRESSIONS (11)

Lv 16:21 the sinful faults and t of the Israelites,
Jos 24:19 who will not forgive your t or your sins.
Ps(s) 103:12 the west, so far has he put our t from us.
Wis 1: 9 the Lord, for the chastisement of his t;
2:12 Reproaches us for t of the law and charges
Ez 37:23 idols, their abominations, and all their t.
39:24 uncleanness and their t I dealt with them,
2Cor 5:19 himself, not counting men's t against them,
Gal 3:19 in view of t and promulgated by angels,
Heb 9:15 from t committed under the first covenant,
10:17 sins and their t I will remember no more."

TRANSGRESSOR (4)

2Mc 5: 8 by all men, hated as a t of the laws,
13: 7 a manner was Menelaus, the t of the law,
Gal 2:18 demolished, I should then indeed be a t.
Jas 2:11 murder, you have become a t of the law.

TRANSGRESSORS (6)

1Mc 9:23 the t of the law raised their heads in
9:58 the t of the law held a council and said:
10:61 Some pestilent Israelites, t of the law,
11:21 Some t of the law, enemies of their own
Ps(s) 51:15 I will teach t your ways, and sinners
Jas 2: 9 sin and are convicted by the law as t.

TRANSIENT (2)

Ex 12:45 t alien or hired servant may partake of it.
Nm 35:15 all the resident or t aliens among them,

TRANSITORY (1)

2Cor 4:18 What is seen is t; what is unseen lasts

TRANSJORDAN (1)

Mk 3: 8 to him from Judea, Jerusalem, Idumea, T,

TRANSLATION (1)

Ezr 4: 7 in Aramaic and was accompanied by a t.

TRANSMIT (1)

Ez 44:19 thus they will not t holiness to the

TRANSMITTED (4)

Prv 25: 1 The men of Hezekiah, king of Judah, t them.
Lk 1: 2 precisely as those events were t to us by
Acts 16: 4 they t to the people for observance the
28:28 of God has been t to the Gentiles

TRANSMITTING (1)

Ez 46:20 at the risk of t holiness to the people."

TRANSPARENT (1)

Rv 21:21 of the city were of pure gold, t as glass.

TRANSPLANTED (2)

Ps(s) 80: 9 A vine from Egypt you t; you drove away
Lk 17: 6 sycamore, 'Be uprooted and t into the sea,'

TRANSPORT (6)

Gn 45:19 and to t your father on your way back here.
45:27 the wagons that Joseph had sent for his t,
46: 5 the wagons that Pharaoh had sent for his t.
Nm 4:47 tasks of service or of the meeting tent,
4:49 assignments for service and for t;
2Mc 9:10 no one could endure to t the man because

TRANSPORTED (4)

1Chr 13: 7 They t the ark of God on a new cart from
2Chr 33:11 him with chains, and t him to Babylon.
Ezr 4:10 Assurbanipal t and settled in the city
Wis 4:10 he who lived among sinners was t—

TRAP (31)

Jos 23:13 they will be a snare and a t for you,
Tb 14:10 from the deadly t Nadab had set for him.
14:10 But Nadab himself fell into the deadly t,
Jb 18: 9 A t seizes him by the heel,
40:24 by his eyes, or pierce his nose with a t?
Ps(s) 140: 6 the proud who have hidden a t for me;
141: 9 Keep me from the t they have set for me,
142: 4 which I walk they have hid a t for me.
Prv 1:11 us, unprovoked, set a t for the innocent;
1:18 blood, they set a t for their own lives.
6:26 married, she is a t for your precious life.
20:25 to pledge a sacred gift is a t for a man,
Eccl 7:26 I find the woman who is a hunter's t,
Wis 14:11 men and a t for the feet of the senseless.
Sir 27:20 he has fled like a gazelle from the t.
27:29 The t seizes those who rejoice in pitfalls,
32:15 it, but the hypocrite finds it a t.
Is 8:14 A t and a snare to those who dwell in
24:17 Terror, pit, and t are upon you,
24:18 out of the pit will be caught in the t.
Jer 48:43 Terror, pit, and t be upon you,
48:44 climbs from the pit is caught in the t;
Mt 22:15 to plot how they might t Jesus in speech.
Lk 20:20 the guise of honest men to t him in speech,
20:26 were unable to t him publicly in speech.
21:34 day will suddenly close in on you like a t.
Jn 8: 6 (They were posing this question to t him,
Rom 11: 9 "Let their table become a snare and a t,
1Tm 3: 7 not fall into disgrace and the devil's t.
6: 9 rich are falling into temptation and a t.
2Tm 2:26 his will, they shall escape the devil's t.

TRAPDOOR (1)

2Mc 1:16 Then they opened a hidden t in the ceiling,

TRAPPED (5)

Ps(s) 9:17 are t by the work of their own hands.
Eccl 9:12 in the fatal net, or birds t in the snare;
Is 42:22 and plundered, all of them t in holes,
Jer 20:10 "Perhaps he will be t;
Dn 13:22 "I am completely t," Susanna groaned.

TRAPPINGS (1)

Jgs 8:26 t that were on the necks of their camels.

TRAPS (2)

Jer 5:26 like fowlers they set t, but it is men
Lk 11:54 setting t to catch him in his speech.

TRAVAIL (7)

Jer 4:31 I hear the moaning, as of a woman in t,
22:23 upon you, like the pangs of a woman in t!
48:41 heroes are like the heart of a woman in t.
49:22 shall be like the heart of a woman in t.
49:24 hold of her, like those of a woman in t.
Mi 4: 9 are seized with pains like a woman in t?
4:10 faint, O daughter Zion, like a woman in t;

TRAVEL (21)

Gn 33:12 I will t alongside you."
Ex 13:21 Thus they could t both day and night.
Neh 9:12 the way in which they must t.
9:19 for them the way by which they were to t.
Tb 5: 4 the roads who would t with him to Media.
5: 6 a good two days' t from Ecbatana to Rages,
5: 9 he is trustworthy enough to t with you,
5:12 looking for a hired man to t with your son?"
9: 2 servants and two camels and t to Rages.
Ps(s) 104: 3 you t on the wings of the wind.
Wis 13:18 the wholly incompetent, and about t,
Sir 8:15 T not with a ruthless man,
34:10 with t a man adds to his resourcefulness.
Jer 18:15 ways, the paths of old, To t on bypaths,
Mt 7:13 the road is clear, and many choose to t it.
8:28 savage that no one could t along that road.
23:15 You t over sea and land to make a single
Jn 7: 1 He had decided not to t in Judea because
Acts 13:14 They continued to t on from Perga and came
19:21 to t through Macedonia and Achaia again,
20:13 made, since his plan was to t overland.

TRAVELED (22)

Gn 13: 3 the Negeb he t by stages toward Bethel,
41:46 he t throughout the land of Egypt.
Jgs 5: 6 who t the roads went by roundabout paths.
18: 2 they t as far as the house of Micah in the
19:10 asses, and t till they came opposite Jebus,
2Sm 4: 7 they t on the Arabah road all night long.
2Chr 17: 9 they t through all the cities of Judah and
Tb 5: 6 I have often t to Media; I used to stay
5:10 I have often t to Media and crossed all
6: 7 t on together till they were near Media.

TRAVELED (cont.)
9: 5 and two camels, *t* to Rages in Media,
9: 6 start and *t* to the wedding celebration.
11: 6 son is coming, and the man who *t* with him!"
1Mc 11:60 *t* through West-of-Euphrates and its cities,
11:62 *t* on through the province as far as Damascus.
Mt 4:24 this, his reputation *t* the length of Syria.
Acts 9: 3 he *t* along and was approaching Damascus,
13: 6 *t* over the whole island as far as Paphos,
15:41 He *t* throughout Syria and Cilicia,
16: 6 They next *t* through Phrygia and Galatian
20: 2 He *t* throughout its regions,
2Cor 11:26 I *t* continually, endangered by floods,

TRAVELER (4)
Jgs 19:17 the *t* in the public square of the city,
Sir 26:12 As a thirsty *t* with eager mouth drinks
Jer 14: 8 like a *t* who has stopped but for a night?
Ez 35: 7 desolate waste, and cut off from it any *t*.

TRAVELERS (6)
2Chr 9:14 from *t* and what the merchants brought.
Tb 6: 2 The *t* walked till nightfall,
Is 33: 8 are desolate, *t* have quit the paths,
Jer 9: 1 Would that I had in the desert a *t*' lodge!
Ez 39:11 Abarim east of the sea [it is blocked to *t*.
Lk 2: 7 room for them in the place where *t* lodged.

TRAVELING (19)
Ex 15:22 After *t* for three days through the desert
Jgs 19:18 "We are *t* from Bethlehem of Judah far up
Tb 10: 6 The man who is *t* with him is trustworthy,
Zec 7:14 after them with no one *t* to and fro;
Mt 10:10 no *t* bag, no change of shirt, no sandals
Mk 6: 8 no food, no *t* bag,
13:34 It is like a man *t* abroad.
Lk 9: 3 journey, neither walking staff nor *t* bag;
10: 4 Do not carry a walking staff or *t* bag;
22:35 mission without purse or *t* bag or sandals,
22:36 the same with the *t* bag.
Acts 9: 7 who were *t* with him stood there speechless.
10: 9 men were *t* along and approaching the city,
18:23 *t* systematically through the Galatian
19:29 Paul's *t* companions from Macedonia.
22: 6 As I was *t* along, approaching Damascus
26:12 "On one such occasion I was *t* toward
26:13 surrounded me and those who were *t* with me.
2Cor 8:19 appointed our *t* companion by the churches,

TRAVELS (2)
Sir 34:11 I have seen much in my *t*,
39: 5 He *t* among the peoples of foreign lands to

TRAVERSE (1)
Wis 14: 1 and about to *t* the wild waves cries out

TRAVERSED (6)
Dt 29:15 and what we passed by in the nations we *t*,
1Chr 21: 4 Joab, who departed and *t* all of Israel,
2Chr 30: 6 and his princes, *t* all Israel and Judah,
1Mc 12:32 on to Damascus and *t* that whole region.
Wis 5:11 the rushing force Of speeding wings, is *t*:
Ez 14:15 *t* by none because of the wild beasts,

TRAVERSING (2)
1Mc 6: 1 King Antiochus was *t* the inland provinces,
Wis 5:10 Like a ship *t* the heaving water,

TRAYS (3)
Ex 25:38 as well as the trimming shears and *t*,
37:23 as well as its trimming shears and *t*,
Nm 4: 9 with its lamps, trimming shears, and *t*,

TREACHERIES (1)
Ps(s) 5:10 their heart teems with *t*.

TREACHEROUS (17)
1Mc 16:13 *t* plans to do away with Simon and his sons.
2Mc 14:22 enemy might suddenly carry out some *t* plan.
Ps(s) 35:20 in the land they fashion *t* speech.
78:57 they recoiled like a *t* bow.
109: 2 have opened wicked and *t* mouths against me.
120: 2 deliver me from lying lip, from *t* tongue.
120: 3 on you, with more besides, O *t* tongue?
Prv 13: 2 good things, but the *t* one craves violence.
Sir 22:22 or a *t* attack will drive away any friend.
Is 48: 8 Yes, I know you are utterly *t*,
Jer 12: 1 propser, why live all the *t* in contentment?
15:18 You have indeed become for me a *t* brook,
Dn 8:25 the holy ones, his *t* conduct shall succeed.
Hos 7:16 have again become useless, like a *t* bow.
Hb 2: 4 Wealth, too, is *t*:
Zep 3: 4 Her prophets are insolent, *t* men;
2Tm 3: 4 They will be *t*, reckless, pompous,

TREACHEROUSLY (3)
1Mc 13:31 dealt *t* with the young King Antiochus.
2Mc 4:34 and by *t* reassuring him through sworn
Dn 11:23 shall *t* rise to power with a small party.

TREACHERY (14)
Jos 22:16 What act of *t* is this you have committed
22:22 out of rebellion or *t* against the LORD,
22:31 committed this act of *t* against the LORD,
Tb 14:10 commit all sorts of wickedness and *t*.
1Mc 7:30 Nicanor had come to him with *t* in mind,
2Mc 5: 7 the end received only disgrace for his *t*,
12: 4 *t* and wishing to live on friendly terms,
Ps(s) 38:13 speak of ruin, *t* they talk of all the day.
55:12 *t* is in its midst;]
Sir 27:25 a blow struck in *t* injures more than one.
Is 24:16 with *t* have the traitors betrayed!
Jer 5:27 as full of *t* as a bird-cage is of birds;
Dn 9: 7 them because of their *t* toward you.
11:34 them, but many shall join them out of *t*.

TREAD (16)
1Sm 5: 5 *t* on the threshold of Dagon in Ashdod
Tb 4: 5 life, and do not *t* the paths of wrongdoing.
Jb 24:11 They *t* the wine presses,
Ps(s) 60:14 it is he who will *t* down our foes.
91:13 You shall *t* upon the asp and the viper;
108:14 it is he who will *t* down our foes.
Is 10: 6 *t* them down like the mud of the streets.
41: 3 loss, by a path his feet do not even *t*.
Bar 4:13 *t* the disciplined paths of his justice.
Jl 4:13 Come and *t*, for the wine press is full;
Mi 6:15 shall sow, yet not reap, *t* out the olive,
Na 3:14 Go down into the mud and *t* the clay,
Hb 3:15 You *t* the sea with your steeds amid the
Mal 3:21 out of the stall and *t* down the wicked;
Lk 10:19 I have given you power to *t* on snakes and
Rv 19:15 it is he who will *t* out in the winepress

TREADER (1)
Jer 48:33 from the wine vats, the *t* treads no more,

TREADING (4)
Dt 25: 4 not muzzle an ox when it is *t* out grain.
Neh 13:15 were *t* the winepresses on the sabbath;
Mi 7:19 compassion on us, *t* underfoot our guilt?
Lk 12: 1 so dense that they were *t* on one another.

TREADS (10)
Jb 9: 8 heavens and *t* upon the crests of the sea.
Sir 2:12 hands, to the sinner who *t* a double path!
Is 16:10 In the wine presses no one *t* grapes,
41:25 like red earth, as the potter *t* the clay.
59: 8 crooked, whoever *t* them knows no peace.
Jer 48:33 from the wine vats, the treader *t* no more,
Mi 1: 3 and *t* upon the heights of the earth.
5: 4 invades our country and *t* upon our land,
5: 5 it invades our land and *t* upon our borders.
1Cor 9: 8 not muzzle an ox while it *t* out grain."

TREASON (6)
2Kgs 9:23 about and fled, crying to Ahaziah, *T*,
11:14 her garments and cried out, "Treason, *t*!"
2Chr 23:13 tore her garments and cried out, *T*! *T*!"
1Mc 16:17 vicious act of *t* he repaid good with evil.

TREASURE (34)
Dt 28:12 up for you his rich *t* house of the heavens,
Tb 4: 9 you will be storing up a goodly *t* for
1Mc 3:28 He opened his *t* chests, gave his soldiers
4:23 violet and crimson cloth, and great *t*.
Ps(s) 119:11 Within my heart I *t* your promise,
Prv 2: 1 if you receive my words and *t* my commands,
7: 1 My son, keep my words, and *t* my commands.
21:20 *t* remains in the house of the wise,
Wis 7:14 unfailing *t*; those who gain this treasure
Sir 6:14 he who finds one finds a *t*.
20:29 Hidden wisdom and unseen *t*—
22: 4 daughter becomes a *t* to her husband,
29:11 of your *t* as the Most High commands,
29:12 Store up almsgiving in your *t* house,
30:16 No *t* greater than a healthy body;
36:24 A wife is her husband's richest *t*,
40:17 but better than either is finding a *t*.
42: 9 is a *t* that keeps her father wakeful,
Is 33: 6 the fear of the LORD is her *t*.
Jer 51:13 You who dwell by mighty waters, rich in *t*,
Ez 7:22 face from them, and my *t* shall be profaned:
Na 2:10 There is no end to the *t*,
Mt 6:19 not lay up for yourselves an earthly *t*.
6:20 practice instead to store up heavenly *t*,
6:21 Remember, where your *t* is,
13:44 a buried *t* which a man found in a field.
19:21 You will then have *t* in heaven.
Mk 10:21 you will then have *t* in heaven.
Lk 12:33 a never-failing *t* with the Lord which no
12:34 Wherever your *t* lies, there your heart
18:22 You will have *t* in heaven.
2Cor 4: 7 This *t* we possess in earthen vessels,
Col 2: 3 every *t* of wisdom and knowledge is hidden.

TREASURED (2)
Jb 23:12 words of his mouth I have *t* in my heart.
Lk 2:19 Mary *t* all these things and reflected on

TREASURER (3)
Ezr 1: 8 had them brought forth by the *t* Mithredath,
Tb 1:22 keeper of the seal, administrator, and *t*;
Rom 16:24 Erastus, the city *t*,

TREASURERS (3)
Ezr 7:21 decree to all the *t* of West-of-Euphrates:
Dn 3: 2 and governors, the counselors, *t*,
3: 3 and governors, the counselors, *t*,

TREASURES (43)
Gn 43:23 must have put *t* in your bags for you.
Dt 33:19 of the seas and the hidden *t* of the sand."
1Kgs 14:26 including the *t* of the temple of the LORD
2Kgs 24:13 He carried off all the *t* of the temple of
1Chr 9:26 of the chambers and *t* of the house of God.
26:22 the *t* of the house of the LORD.
26:24 Moses, was chief superintendent over the *t*.
27:25 Over the *t* of the king was Azmaveth,
2Chr 1:11 you have not asked for riches, *t* and glory,
1:12 I will also give you riches, *t* and glory,
12: 9 carried off the *t* of the temple of the LORD
25:24 together with the *t* of the palace,
36:18 and the *t* of the LORD's house and of the
1Mc 1:23 also took all the hidden *t* he could find.
2Mc 1:14 place to get its great *t* by way of dowry.
1:15 of the Nanaeon had displayed the *t*,
Jb 3:21 search for it rather than for hidden *t*,
20:20 in his greed, his *t* shall not save him.
Ps(s) 17:14 where with your *t* you fill their bellies.
Prv 2: 4 silver, and like hidden *t* search her out:
10: 2 Ill-gotten *t* profit nothing,
Sir 1:22 wisdom's *t* is the paragon of prudence;
39: 2 He *t* the discourses of famous men,
41:12 better than precious *t* in the thousands;
Is 2: 7 and gold, and there is no end to their *t*;
10:13 of peoples, their *t* I have pillaged,
30: 6 and their *t* on the humps of camels
45: 3 I will give you *t* out of the darkness,
Jer 17: 3 wealth and all your *t* I will give as spoil.
20: 5 dear, all the *t* of the kings of Judah,
48: 7 you trusted in your works and your *t*,
49: 4 You who trust in your *t*,
50:37 A sword upon her *t*, that they may be
Lam 1:10 foe stretched out his hand to all her *t*;
1:11 They give their *t* for food,
Dn 11:38 gold, silver, precious stones, and other *t*.
11:43 of gold and silver and all the *t* of Egypt;
Hos 9: 6 Weeds shall overgrow their silver *t*,
Jl 4: 5 brought my precious *t* into your temples!
Hg 2: 7 and the *t* of all the nations will come in,
Heb 11:26 greater riches than the *t* of Egypt,
Rv 21:24 the kings of the earth shall bring their *t*.
21:26 The *t* and wealth of the nations shall be

TREASURIES (13)
1Kgs 7:51 in the *t* of the temple of the LORD.
15:18 gold remaining in the *t* of the temple
2Kgs 12:19 was in the *t* of the temple and the palace,
14:14 temple of the LORD and the *t* of the palace,
16: 8 temple of the LORD and in the palace *t*
18:15 the temple of the LORD and in the palace *t*.
2Chr 5: 1 articles in the *t* of the house of God.
8:15 to the priests and Levites or the *t*.
16: 2 from the *t* of the temple of the LORD
32:27 He had *t* made for his silver,
Prv 8:21 to those who love me, and filling their *t*.
Bar 3:15 of wisdom, who has entered into her *t*?
Ez 28: 4 You have put gold and silver into your *t*.

TREASURY (35)
Dt 32:34 "Is not this preserved in my *t*,
Jos 6:19 They shall be put in the *t* of the LORD."
6:24 placed in the *t* of the house of the LORD.
2Kgs 20:13 showed the messengers his whole *t*,
1Chr 29: 8 for the *t* of the house of the LORD.
Ezr 2:69 to the *t* for the temple service:
7:20 of your God, you may draw from the royal *t*.
Neh 7:69 into the *t* one thousand drachmas of gold,
7:70 to the *t* for the temple service:
10:39 house of our God, to the chambers of the *t*.
Est 3: 9 silver talents for deposit in the royal *t*."
4: 7 the royal *t* for the slaughter of the Jews.
1Mc 3:29 that this exhausted the money in his *t*;
13:15 that he owed the royal *t* in connection
14:49 copies of it should be deposited in the *t*,
15: 8 to the royal *t* shall be canceled for you,
2Mc 3: 6 and reported to him that the *t* in
3:13 money must be confiscated for the royal *t*.
3:24 was approaching the *t* with his bodyguards,
3:28 had entered that *t* with a great retinue
3:40 and the preservation of the *t* turned out.
4:42 thief himself they slew near the *t*.
5:18 sent by King Seleucus to inspect the *t*,
Jb 38:22 and seen the *t* of the hail Which I have
Sir 39:29 In his *t* also, kept for the proper time,

Is 39: 2 and therefore showed the messengers his t,
Dn 1: 2 and placed in the temple t of his god.
Zec 11:13 the LORD said to me, "Throw it in the t,
11:13 them into the t in the house of the LORD.
Mt 27: 6 in the temple t since it is blood money."
Mk 12:41 Taking a seat opposite the t,
12:43 than all the others who donated to the t.
Lk 21: 1 rich putting their offerings into the t.
Jn 8:20 these words while teaching at the temple t.
Acts 8:27 official in charge of the entire t of Candace

TREAT (46)

Gn 19: 9 We'll t you worse than them!"
Ex 5:15 do you t your servants in this manner?
5:22 "Lord, why do you t this people so badly?
21: 9 his son, he shall t her like a daughter.
30:37 you must t it as sacred to the LORD.
Lv 11:11 for you, and you shall t them as loathsome.
19:34 You shall t the alien who resides with
21: 8 t him as sacred, because I, the LORD,
25:53 The alien shall t him as a servant hired
Nm 11:11 "Why do you t your servant so badly?"
18:10 them you shall t them as most sacred;
25:17 T the Midianites as enemies and crush them,
33:56 will t you as I had intended to treat them."
33:56 will treat you as I had intended to t them."
Dt 15:17 slave, also, you shall t in the same way.
1Sm 8: 8 strange gods, so do they t you too.
1Kgs 8:39 so t them that they may fear you as long
Jdt 10:16 you speak of, and he will t you well."
1Mc 13:46 "Do not t us according to our evil deeds,"
2Mc 9:27 he will t you with mildness and kindness
Jb 19:15 Even my handmaids t me as a stranger;
22:24 from your tent, And t raw gold like dust,
24:12 out [yet God does not t it as unseemly].
Ps(s) 71:16 I will t of the mighty works of the Lord;
Sir 14:16 Give, take, and t yourself well,
33:31 have but one slave, t him like yourself,
Jer 3:19 How I should like to t you as sons,
12: 8 has roared against me, I t her as an enemy.
24: 8 even so will I t Zedekiah,
26: 6 obey them, I will t this house like Shiloh,
33: 6 I will t and assuage the city's wounds;
39:12 him, but t him as he himself requests."
Ez 35:15 of the house of Israel, so will I t you.
Dn 1:13 t your servants according to what you see."
Hos 11: 8 How could I t you as Admah,
Mt 7:12 T others the way you would have them treat
18:17 then t him as you would a Gentile or a tax
18:35 My heavenly Father will t you in exactly
Lk 15:19 T me like one of your hired hands.'
1Cor 16:11 as I do, so let no one t him disdainfully.
Gal 2:21 not t God's gracious gift as pointless.
2Thes 3:15 But do not t him like an enemy;
1Tm 5: 1 You should t younger men as brothers,
1Pt 3: 7 T women with respect as the weaker sex,
2Pt 2:10 how to t those who live for the flesh in

TREATED (45)

Gn 18:25 innocent and the guilty would be t alike!
20: 9 You have t me in an intolerable way.
34:31 our sister have been t like a harlot?"
39:19 wife's story about how his slave had t her,
50:17 of your brothers, who t you so cruelly.'
Ex 3:16 and about the way you are being t in Egypt;
19: 4 seen for yourselves how I t the Egyptians
30:32 is sacred, and shall be t as sacred by you.
30:36 incense shall be t as most sacred by you.
Lv 11:35 unclean and shall be t as unclean by you.
27:10 and its substitute shall be t as sacred.
27:33 and its substitute shall be t as sacred,
Dt 25: 9 'This is how one should be t who will not
32: 5 has he been t by his degenerate children,
Jgs 9:16 and if you have t him as he deserved for
1Sm 2:14 were t who came to the sanctuary at Shiloh.
2:17 t the offerings to the LORD with disdain.
8: 8 As they have t me constantly from the day
24:18 you have t me generously,
2Kgs 10:30 and have t the house of Ahab as I desire,
1Chr 19: 2 Nahash, for his father t me with kindness."
Jdt 11: 4 Rather, you will be well t,
1Mc 11:26 the king t him just as his predecessors
2Mc 6:22 and be t kindly because of their old
7:39 and t him even worse than the others,
12:14 besieged t Judas and his men with contempt,
Eccl 8:14 there are just men t as though they had
8:14 men t as though they had done justly.
Wis 19:13 since indeed they t their guests with the
Sir 49: 7 for they had t him badly who even in the
Is 10:11 Samaria, Just as I t Samaria and her idols,
53: 7 Though he was harshly t, he submitted
Lam 2:20 whom have you ever t thus?
Bar 6:33 Whether they are t well or ill by anyone,
Zec 1: 6 has t us according to our ways and deeds,
Mt 21:36 than before, but they t them the same way.
Mk 12: 4 they beat over the head and t shamefully.
Lk 6:23 it was that their fathers t the prophets.
6:26 t the false prophets in just this way.
10:37 came, "The one who t him with compassion."
23:11 guards then t him with contempt and insult,
Acts 10:23 Peter invited them in and t them as guests.
1Cor 4:11 hungry and thirsty, poorly clad, roughly t,
1Tm 1:13 in my unbelief, I have been t mercifully,
Jas 2: 6 Yet you t this poor man shamefully.

TREATING (5)

Ex 6: 5 whom the Egyptians are t as slaves,
Nm 22:30 been in the habit of t you this way before?"
1Sm 2:22 repeatedly how his sons were t all Israel
2Mc 10:12 had taken the lead in t the Jews fairly
Lk 20:11 away empty-handed, after t him shamefully.

TREATMENT (10)

Gn 16: 9 your mistress and submit to her abusive t.
Est 2:12 Of this period of beautifying t,
E: 9 t matters coming to our attention.
2Mc 2:31 and to omit detailed t of the matter.
12: 8 like t to the Jews who lived among them,
12:30 to their kind t even in times of adversity,
Sir 38:14 be correct and his t bring about a cure.
Is 66: 4 I in turn will choose ruthless t for them
Mk 5:26 She had received t at the hands of doctors
1Thes 2:14 You suffered the same t from your fellow

TREATS (2)

Jgs 18: 4 "This is how Micah t me,"
2Mc 7:33 Though our living Lord t us harshly for a

TREATY (14)

1Sm 11: 1 Jabesh begged Nahash, "Make a t with us,
11: 2 "This is my condition for a t with you:
1Kgs 5:26 Solomon, since they were parties to a t.
15:19 "There is a t between you and me,
15:19 Go, break your t with Baasha,
2Chr 16: 3 "There is a t between you and me,
16: 3 Go, break your t with Baasha,
1Mc 10:26 We have heard how you have kept the t with
2Mc 4:11 to establish a t of friendship with them);
13:25 of that city were angered by the peace t;
13:26 defended the t as well as he could and won
14:20 was expressed, they assented to the t.
14:26 other, he took the t that had been made,
14:27 stating that he was displeased with the t,

TREE (164)

Gn 1:11 every kind of fruit t on earth that bears
1:12 every kind of fruit t on earth that bears
1:29 every t that has seed-bearing fruit on it
2: 9 with the t of life in the middle of the
2: 9 and the t of the knowledge of good and bad.
2:17 except the t of knowledge of good and bad.
2:17 From that t you shall not eat;
3: 3 fruit of the t in the middle of the garden
3: 6 The woman saw that the t was good for food,
3:11 the t of which I had forbidden you to eat!"
3:12 she gave me fruit from the t,
3:17 the t of which I had forbidden you to eat,
3:22 hand to take fruit from the t of life also,
3:24 sword, to guard the way to the t of life.
18: 4 feet, and then rest yourselves under the t.
18: 8 waited on them under the t while they ate.
Ex 9:25 thing and splintered every t in the fields.
10:15 t or plant throughout the land of Egypt.
Lv 19:23 into the land and plant any fruit t there,
Dt 12: 2 and under every leafy t where the nations
19: 5 wood, and as he swings his ax to fell a t,
21:22 put to death and his corpse hung on a t,
21:23 on a tree, it shall not remain on the t
22: 6 or eggs in it, in any t or on the ground,
Jos 8:29 the king of Ai hanged on a t until evening;
8:29 ordered the body removed from the t
Jgs 4: 5 She used to sit under Deborah's palm t,
9: 8 So they said to the olive t, 'Reign over
9: 9 But the olive t answered them, 'Must I
9:10 Then the trees said to the fig t,
9:11 But the fig t answered them, 'Must I give
1Sm 14: 2 command post was under the pomegranate t
22: 6 under a tamarisk t on the high place,
31:13 buried them under the tamarisk t in Jabesh,
2Sm 18: 9 terebinth, his hair caught fast in the t.
18:14 of Absalom, still hanging from the t alive.
1Kgs 5: 5 or under his fig t from Dan to Beer-sheba,
14:23 every high hill and under every green t.
19: 4 he came to a broom t and sat beneath it.
19: 5 down and fell asleep under the broom t,
2Kgs 3:19 every fortified city, fell every fruit t,
3:25 stopped up and every useful t they felled.
6: 5 While one of them was felling a t trunk,
16: 4 places, on hills, and under every leafy t.
17:10 on every high hill and under every leafy t.
18:31 eat of his own vine and of his own fig t
2Chr 28: 4 on hills, and under every leafy t.
Neh 10:38 and our offerings of the fruit of every t,
1Mc 14:12 Every man sat under his vine and his fig t,
Jb 14: 7 For a t there is hope, if it be cut down,
15:33 and like an olive t casting off its bloom.
19:10 my hope he has uprooted like a t.
Ps(s) 1: 3 He is like a t planted near running water,
37:35 and stalwart as a flourishing, age-old t.
52:10 like a green olive t in the house of God,
92:13 just man shall flourish like the palm t,
Prv 3:18 She is a t of life to those who grasp her,
11:30 The fruit of virtue is a t of life,
13:12 sick, but a wish fulfilled is a t of life.
15: 4 A soothing tongue is a t of life,
27:18 He who tends a fig t eats its fruit,
Eccl 11: 3 a t falls to the south or to the north,
12: 5 When the almond t blooms,
Sg 2: 3 an apple t among the trees of the woods,
2:13 The fig t puts forth its figs,
7: 8 Your very figure is like a palm t.
7: 9 I will climb the palm t,
8: 5 Under the apple t I awakened you;
Wis 13:11 t and skillfully scrape off all its bark,
Sir 6: 3 destroy, and you will be left a dry t,
14:18 with the leaves that grow on a vigorous t:
24:14 on Mount Hermon, Like a palm t in Engedi,
24:14 fair olive tree in the field, like a plane t
27: 6 The fruit of a t shows the care it has had;
50:10 Like a luxuriant olive t thick with fruit,
Is 1:30 shall become like a t with falling leaves,
17: 6 As when an olive t has been beaten,
24:13 As with an olive t after it is beaten,
34: 4 the vine, or as the fig withers on the t.
36:16 eat of his own vine and of his own fig t,
41:19 together with the plane t and the pine,
56: 3 let the eunuch say, "See, I am a dry t."
57: 5 among the terebinths, under every green t;
65:22 As the years of a t, so the years of my
Jer 2:20 On every high hill, under every green t,
3: 6 every green t she has played the harlot.
3:13 green t and would not listen to my voice,
11:16 A spreading olive t, goodly to behold,
11:19 "Let us destroy the t in its vigor;
17: 8 He is like a t planted beside the waters
Bar 5: 8 The forests and every fragrant kind of t
Ez 6:13 beneath every green t and leafy oak,
17:24 low the high t, lift high the lowly tree,
17:24 green tree, and make the withered t bloom.
31: 5 taller than every other t of the field,
31: 8 t in the garden of God matched its beauty.
31:14 Thus no t may grow lofty in stature or
31:14 no t fed by water may stand by itself in
Dn 4: 7 I saw a t of great height at the center of
4:11 down the t and lop off its branches,
4:17 The large, strong t that you saw,
4:19 you are that t, O king, large and strong!
4:20 'Cut down the t and destroy it,
4:23 roots of the t are to be left means that
13:54 tell me under what t you saw them together."
13:55 "Under a mastic t," he answered.
13:58 under what t you surprised them together."
Hos 9:10 the first fruits of the fig t in its prime,
14: 7 t and his fragrance like the Lebanon cedar.
14: 9 "I am like a verdant cypress t—
Jl 1: 7 laid waste my vine, and blighted my fig t;
1:12 vine has dried up, the fig t is withered;
2:22 The t bears its fruit,
2:22 the fig t and the vine give their yield.
Mi 4: 4 under his own vine or under his own fig t,
Hb 3:17 t blossom not nor fruit be on the vines,
Hg 2:19 the pomegranate and the olive t yet borne.
Mt 3:10 now the ax is laid to the root of the t.
3:10 Every t that is not fruitful will be cut
7:17 t bears good fruit, while a decayed tree
7:18 A sound t cannot bear bad fruit any more
7:18 more than a decayed t can bear good fruit.
7:19 Every t that does not bear good fruit is
7:20 You can tell a t by its fruit.
12:33 t good and its fruit good or declare a tree
12:33 other, for you can tell a t by its fruit.
21:19 a fig t by the roadside he went over to it,
21:20 "Why did the fig t wither up so quickly?"
21:21 only will you do what I did to the fig t,
24:32 From the fig t learn a lesson.
Mk 11:13 Observing a fig t some distance off,
11:20 they saw the fig t withered to its roots.
11:21 The fig t you cursed has withered up."
13:28 Learn a lesson from the fig t.
Lk 3: 9 now the ax is laid to the root of the t.
3: 9 Every t that is not fruitful will be cut
6:43 "A good t does not produce decayed fruit
6:43 more than a decayed t produces good fruit.
6:44 Each t is known by its yield.
13: 6 man had a fig t growing in his vineyard,
13: 7 of fruit on this fig t and found none.
19: 4 a sycamore t which was along Jesus' route,
21:29 "Notice the fig tree, or any other t.
Jn 1:48 answered, "I saw you under the fig t."
1:50 I told you I saw you under the fig t?
Acts 5:30 whom you put to death, hanging him on a t.
10:40 killed him, finally, hanging him on a t,
13:29 him down from the t and laid him in a tomb.
Rom 11:17 off and you, a branch of the wild olive t,
11:24 nature be grafted into their own olive t.
Gal 3:13 "Accursed is anyone who is hanged on a t."
Jas 3:12 A fig t, brothers, cannot produce olives,
Rv 2: 7 that the victor eats from the t of life
7: 1 wind blew on land or sea or through any t.
9: 4 to any plant or t but only to those men
22:14 access to the t of life and enter the city
22:19 t of life and the holy city described here!

TREES (121)

Gn 2: 9 the LORD God made various t grow

TREES (cont.)

2:16 "You are free to eat from any of the *t* of
3: 1 not to eat from any of the *t* in the garden?"
3: 2 eat of the fruit of the *t* in the garden;
3: 8 the LORD God among the *t* of the garden.
23:17 and all the *t* anywhere within its limits,
30:37 shoots of poplar, almond and plane *t*,
Ex 10:15 fruit of whatever *t* the hail had spared.
15:27 twelve springs of water and seventy palm *t*,
Lv 23:40 you shall gather foliage from majestic *t*,
26: 4 will bear its crops, and the *t* their fruit;
26:20 will bear no crops, and its *t* no fruit.
27:30 from the fields or in fruit from the *t*,
Nm 33: 9 twelve springs of water and seventy palm *t*,
Dt 8: 8 and fig *t* and pomegranates, of olive trees
20:19 not destroy its *t* by putting an ax to them.
20:19 fruit, but you must not cut down the *t*.
20:19 After all, are the *t* of the field men,
20:20 those *t* which you know are not fruit trees
24:20 you knock down the fruit of your olive *t*,
28:40 you have olive *t* throughout your country,
28:42 all your *t* and the crops of your soil.
33:24 the oil of his olive *t* runs over his feet!
Jos 10:26 killed them, and hanged them on five *t*,
10:27 At sunset they were removed from the *t* at
Jgs 9: 8 *t* went to anoint a king over themselves.
9: 9 are honored, and go to wave over the *t*?'
9:10 Then the *t* said to the fig tree,
9:11 my good fruit, and go to wave over the *t*?'
9:12 Then the *t* said to the vine,
9:13 gods and men, and go to wave over the *t*?'
9:14 Then all the *t* said to the buckthorn,
9:15 But the buckthorn replied to the *t*,
2Sm 5:23 rear and meet them before the mastic *t*.
5:24 of marching in the tops of the mastic *t*,
1Kgs 5:22 provide all the cedars and fir *t* you wish.
5:24 with all the cedars and fir *t* he wished;
6:29 had carved figures of cherubim, palm *t*,
6:32 with carved figures of cherubim, palm *t*,
6:32 also molded to the cherubim and the palm *t*.
6:35 and back, and had carved cherubim, palm *t*,
7:36 cherubim, lions, and palm *t* were carved,
2Kgs 6: 4 arrived at the Jordan they began to fell *t*.
1Chr 14:14 them from the direction of the mastic *t*.
14:15 of marching in the tops of the mastic *t*,
16:33 the *t* of the forest exult before the LORD,
22: 4 not be weighed, and cedar *t* without number.
27:28 Over the olive *t* and sycamores of the
2Chr 2:15 For our part, we will cut *t* on Lebanon,
Ezr 3: 7 *t* from the Lebanon to the port of Joppa,
Neh 8:15 country and bring in branches of olive *t*,
8:15 myrtle, palm and other leafy *t*,
9:25 olive groves, and fruit *t* in abundance.
10:36 fruits of our fields and of our fruit *t*,
1Mc 10:30 the fruit of the *t* that should be my share,
11:34 produce of the soil and the fruit of the *t*.
14: 8 produce and the *t* of the field their fruit.
Jb 40:21 Under the lotus *t* he lies,
40:22 The lotus *t* cover him with their shade;
Ps(s) 74: 6 men coming up with axes to a clump of *t*
84: 7 of the mastic *t* they make a spring of it;
96:12 the *t* of the forest exult before the LORD,
104:16 Well watered are the *t* of the LORD,
104:17 fir *t* are the home of the stork.
105:33 fig *t* and shattered the *t* throughout
148: 9 you hills, you fruit *t* and all you cedars;
Eccl 2: 5 and set out in them fruit *t* of all sorts.
Sg 2: 3 As an apple tree among the *t* of the woods,
5:15 His stature is like the *t* on Lebanon,
Sir 50: 8 Like the *t* of Lebanon in summer,
Is 7: 2 as the *t* of the forest tremble in the wind.
10:19 of the *t* in his forest will be so few,
32:19 it comes, as *t* come down in the forest!
44:14 and lays hold of other *t* of the forest,
44:23 into song, you forest, with all your *t*.
55:12 and all the *t* of the countryside shall
Jer 5:17 and cattle, devour your vines and fig *t*;
6: 6 Hew down her *t*, throw up a siege mound
7:20 *t* of the field and the fruits of the earth;
8:13 grapes on the vine, No figs on the fig *t*,
17: 2 their sacred poles, beside the green *t*,
Ez 15: 2 That branch among the *t* of the forest!
15: 6 wood of the vine among the *t* of the forest,
17:24 all the *t* of the field shall know that I,
20:28 they saw all its high hills and leafy *t*,
21: 3 a fire in you that shall devour all *t*,
31: 4 its streams to all the *t* of the field.
31: 8 nor could the fir *t* match its boughs,
31: 8 were the plane *t* like it for branches;
31: 9 envy of all Eden's *t* in the garden of God.
31:15 the *t* in the land dropped on his account.
31:16 the land below, all Eden's *t* were consoled,
31:18 equal in glory or size among the *t* of Eden?
31:18 down with the *t* of Eden to the land below.
34:27 The *t* of the field shall bear their fruits,
36:30 on your *t* and the crops in your fields;
47: 7 the river I saw very many *t* on both sides.
47:12 river, fruit *t* of every kind shall grow;
Hos 2:14 I will lay waste her vines and fig *t*,
Jl 1:12 apple, all the *t* of the field are dried up;
1:19 flame has enkindled all the *t* of the field.
Am 2: 9 as the cedars, and as strong as the oak *t*.
4: 9 fig trees and olive *t* the locust devoured;
Na 3:12 All your fortresses are but fig *t*,
Zec 1: 8 standing among myrtle *t* in a shady place,
1:10 among the myrtle *t* spoke up and said,
1:11 was standing among the myrtle *t* and said,
3:10 one another under your vines and fig *t*."
4: 3 tubes, and beside it are two olive *t*,
4:11 two olive *t* at each side of the lampstand?"
11: 2 Wail, you cypress *t*,
Mt 21: 8 from the *t* and lay them along his path.
Mk 8:24 see people but they look like walking *t*!"
Jude 1:12 *t* at the year's end they bear no fruit,
Rv 7: 3 no harm to the land or the sea or the *t*
8: 7 a third of the *t* and every green plant.
11: 4 These are the two olive *t* and the two
22: 2 On either side of the river grew the *t* of

TRELLISES (2)

1Kgs 6: 4 windows with *t* were made for the temple,
Ez 41:16 with *t* about them [facing the threshold].

TREMBLE (38)

Dt 2:25 your name they will quake and *t* before you.'
1Chr 16:30 *T* before him, all the earth; he has made
1Mc 4:32 and let them *t* at their own destruction.
Jb 9: 6 of its place, and the pillars beneath it *t*.
26:11 *t* and are stunned at his thunderous rebuke;
Ps(s) 4: 5 *T*, and sin not; reflect, upon your beds,
96: 9 *T* before him, all the earth; say among
99: 1 The LORD is king; the peoples *t*;
114: 7 Before the face of the Lord, *t*,
Eccl 12: 3 When the guardians of the house *t*,
Sir 16:16 earth and the abyss *t* at his visitation;
Is 7: 2 as the trees of the forest *t* in the wind.
13:13 For this I will make the heavens *t* and the
14:16 "Is this the man who made the earth *t*,
15: 4 At this the loins of Moab *t*,
19: 1 The idols of Egypt *t* before him,
30:17 A thousand shall *t* at the threat of one;
32:11 *T*, you who are complacent!
41: 5 the ends of the earth *t*:
64: 1 enemies and the nations would *t* before you,
66: 5 word of the LORD, you who *t* at his word:
Jer 5:22 says the LORD, should you not *t* before me?
23: 2 heart within me is broken, my bones all *t*;
23: 4 so that they need no longer fear and *t*;
50:36 sword upon her warriors, that they may *t*;
Ez 7:27 and the hands of the common people shall *t*.
21:20 all around, That every heart may *t*;
26:16 *t* at every moment and be horrified at you.
32:10 them shall continuously *t* for his own life.
38:20 Before me shall *t* the fish of the sea and
Jl 2: 1 Let all who dwell in the land *t*,
Am 8: 8 Shall not the land *t* because of this,
Hb 2: 7 Shall not they who make you *t* awake?
3: 6 his look makes the nations *t*.
3:10 at sight of you the mountains *t*.
3:16 invades my bones, my legs *t* beneath me.
Mk 5:33 to *t* now as she realized what had happened,
Acts 7:32 Moses began to *t* and dared look no more.

TREMBLED (11)

Ex 19:16 so that all the people in the camp *t*.
19:18 and the whole mountain *t* violently.
20:18 mountain smoking, they all feared and *t*.
Jgs 5: 5 Mountains *t* in the presence of the LORD,
2Sm 22: 8 *t* and shook when his wrath flared up.
Jdt 16:11 when my weaklings cried out, they *t*;
1Mc 6:41 marching, and the clashing of the arms, *t*;
Ps(s) 18: 8 *t* and shook when his wrath flared up.
Sg 5: 4 my heart *t* within me,
Is 7: 2 of the king and heart of the people *t*,
Rv 8: 5 of lightning followed, and the earth *t*.

TREMBLES (7)

Jb 37: 1 this my heart *t* and leaps out of its place.
Ps(s) 97: 4 the earth sees and *t*.
104:32 He who looks upon the earth, and it *t*;
Prv 30:21 Under three things the earth *t*,
Is 66: 2 lowly and afflicted man who *t* at my word.
Jl 2:10 Before them the earth *t*,
Hb 3:16 I hear, and my body *t*;

TREMBLING (31)

Gn 27:33 was seized with a fit of uncontrollable *t*.
42:28 *T*, they asked one another,
Ex 15:15 *t* seized the chieftains of Moab;
1Sm 16: 4 the city came *t* to meet him and inquired,
21: 2 of Nob, who came *t* to meet him and asked,
Ezr 10: 9 were *t* both over the matter at hand and
Jdt 15: 2 were amazed, and overcome with fear and *t*.
2Mc 3:17 The terror and bodily *t* that had come over
Jb 35:14 with *t* should you wait upon him.
39:24 Frenzied and *t* he devours the ground;
Ps(s) 2:11 with *t* pay homage to him,
55: 6 Fear and *t* come upon me.
Wis 17: 3 of oblivion Were scattered in fearful *t*,
17:10 the hissing of reptiles, And perished *t*,
Is 19:16 Egyptians shall be like women, *t* with fear,
33:14 sinners are in dread, *t* grips the impious:
Jer 4:24 I looked at the mountains, and they were *t*,
33: 9 They shall be in fear and *t* over all the
Bar 3:33 it departs, calls it, and it obeys him *t*;
Ez 12:18 Son of man, eat your bread *t*,
Dn 10:11 When he said this to me, I stood up *t*.
Hos 3: 5 shall come *t* to the LORD and to his bounty,
11:11 the west, Out of Egypt they shall come *t*,
Mi 7:17 fastnesses, *t* in fear of you [the LORD,
Na 2:11 melting hearts and *t* knees,
Hb 3: 7 *t* are the pavilions of the land of Midian.
Mk 16: 8 and fled from the tomb bewildered and *t*;
Lk 8:47 had not gone unnoticed, she came forward *t*.
Acts 16:29 and fell *t* at the feet of Paul and Silas.
2Cor 7:15 to God when you received him in fear and *t*.
Heb 12:21 that Moses said, "I am terrified and *t*."

TREMENDOUS (7)

Dt 29:27 in his furious wrath and *t* anger the LORD
Jos 6:20 the signal horn, they raised a *t* shout.
2Mc 10:24 gathered a *t* force of foreign troops and
Ps(s) 66: 3 Say to God, "How *t* are your deeds!
66: 5 the works of God, his *t* deeds among men.
Sir 46: 5 answer to him in hailstones of *t* power,
46:17 and the *t* roar of his voice was heard.

TRENCH (3)

1Kgs 18:32 and made a *t* around the altar large enough
18:35 altar, and the *t* was filled with the water.
18:38 dust, and it lapped up the water in the *t*.

TRENCHES (1)

Dn 9:25 it shall be rebuilt, With streets and *t*,

TREPIDATION (1)

1Cor 2: 3 in weakness and in fear, and with much *t*.

TRESSES (2)

Jdt 16: 8 with a fillet she fastened her *t*,
Sg 7: 6 a king is held captive in its *t*.

TRIAL (38)

1Mc 2:52 Was not Abraham found faithful in *t*,
Jb 34:24 Without a *t* he breaks the mighty,
Ps(s) 37:33 nor let him be condemned when he is on *t*.
50: 4 and the earth, to the *t* of his people:
Wis 18:20 But the *t* of death touched at one time
18:25 for the mere *t* of anger was enough.
Sir 26: 5 charges in public, *t* before all the people,
Is 43:26 you have me remember, have us come to *t*?
Mi 6: 2 people, and he enters into *t* with Israel.
Mt 6:13 to the *t* but deliver us from the evil one.'
10:18 be brought to *t* before rulers and kings,
Lk 11: 4 and subject us not to the *t*."
21:12 you to *t* before kings and governors,
22:46 that you may not be subjected to the *t*."
Acts 7:11 and great *t* came upon Egypt and Canaan,
12: 6 night before Herod was to bring him to *t*,
16:37 flogged us in public without even a *t*,
22:25 legal to flog a Roman citizen without a *t*?"
23: 6 I find myself on *t* now because of my hope
24:21 'I am on *t* before you today because of the
24:22 he heard these words he adjourned the *t*,
25: 9 stand *t* before me there on these charges?"
25:20 and stand *t* there on these charges.
26: 6 But today I stand *t* because of my hope in
Rom 8:35 *T*, or distress, or persecution, or hunger,
12:12 Rejoice in hope, be patient under *t*,
2Cor 4:17 present burden of our *t* is light enough,
8: 2 In the midst of severe *t* their overflowing
1Thes 3: 4 used to warn you that we would undergo *t*;
3: 7 your faith throughout our distress and *t*—
2Thes 1: 4 and your faith in persecution and *t*.
Heb 10:33 you were publicly exposed to insult and *t*;
Jas 1: 2 when you are involved in every sort of *t*.
1:12 the man who holds out to the end through *t*!
1Pt 4:12 a *t* by fire is occurring in your midst.
2Pt 2: 9 knows how to rescue devout men from *t*,
Rv 3:10 of *t* which is coming on the whole world,
7:14 who have survived the great period of *t*;

TRIALS (15)

Tb 4: 4 *t* for your sake while you were in her womb.
Prv 23:30 those who engage in *t* of blended wine.
Sir 2: 1 to serve the LORD, prepare yourself for *t*.
33: 1 through *t*, again and again he is safe.
Mk 13:24 *t* of every sort the sun will be darkened,
Acts 14:22 *t* if we are to enter into the reign of God."
20:19 in humility through the sorrows and *t*
1Cor 7:28 But such people will have *t* in this life,
2Cor 6: 4 God, acting with patient endurance amid *t*,
Eph 3:13 be disheartened by the *t* I endure for you;
1Thes 1: 6 Lord, receiving the word despite great *t*,
3: 3 lest any one of you be shaken by these *t*.
3: 3 well enough that such *t* are our common lot.
Heb 12: 7 Endure your *t* as the discipline of God,
1Pt 1: 6 time have to suffer the distress of many *t*:

TRIBAL (9)

Gn 25:16 twelve chieftains of as many *t* groups.
Nm 17:17 in all, one from each of their *t* princes.

17:21 twelve in all, one from each *t* prince;
Dt 1:15 and over tens, and other *t* officers.
5:23 the person of all your *t* heads and elders,
31:28 your *t* elders and your officials before me,
Ez 45: 7 in length to one of the *t* portions
48: 8 and as wide as one of the *t* portions from
48:21 with the *t* portions for the prince.

TRIBE (209)

Gn 48:19 That one too shall become a *t*,
49:16 for his kindred like any other *t* of Israel.
Ex 31: 2 son of Uri, son of Hur, of the *t* of Judah,
31: 6 Oholiab, son of Ahisamach, of the *t* of Dan.
35:30 son of Uri, son of Hur, of the *t* of Judah,
35:34 Oholiab, son of Ahisamach, of the *t* of Dan,
38:22 son of Uri, son of Hur, of the *t* of Judah,
38:23 Oholiab, son of Ahisamach, of the *t* of Dan,
Lv 24:10 of the *t* of Dan) and an Egyptian father.
Nm 1: 4 you there shall be a man from each *t*,
1:21 hundred were enrolled in the *t* of Reuben.
1:23 hundred were enrolled in the *t* of Simeon.
1:25 and fifty were enrolled in the *t* of Gad.
1:27 hundred were enrolled in the *t* of Judah.
1:29 hundred were enrolled in the *t* of Issachar.
1:31 hundred were enrolled in the *t* of Zebulun.
1:33 hundred were enrolled in the *t* of Ephraim.
1:35 hundred were enrolled in the *t* of Manasseh.
1:37 hundred were enrolled in the *t* of Benjamin.
1:39 hundred were enrolled in the *t* of Dan.
1:41 hundred were enrolled in the *t* of Asher.
1:43 hundred were enrolled in the *t* of Naphtali.
1:47 registered by ancestral *t* with the others.
1:49 "The *t* of Levi alone you shall not enroll
2: 5 *t* of Issachar [Their prince was Nethanel,
2: 7 and the *t* of Zebulun.
2:12 *t* of Simeon [Their prince was Shelumiel,
2:14 and next the *t* of Gad.
2:20 *t* of Manasseh [Their prince was Gamaliel,
2:22 and the *t* of Benjamin.
2:27 the *t* of Asher [Their prince was Pagiel,
2:29 and next the *t* of Naphtali.
3: 6 "Summon the *t* of Levi and present them to
7:12 son of Amminadab, prince of the *t* of Judah.
10:15 Zuar, over the host of the *t* of Issachar.
10:16 Helon, over the host of the *t* of Zebulun.
10:19 over the host of the *t* of Simeon,
10:20 of Reuel, over the host of the *t* of Gad.
10:23 over the host of the *t* of Manasseh,
10:24 over the host of the *t* of Benjamin.
10:26 of Ochran, over the host of the *t* of Asher,
10:27 Enan, over the host of the *t* of Naphtali.
13: 2 shall send one man from each ancestral *t*,
13: 4 son of Zaccur, of the *t* of Reuben;
13: 5 son of Hori, of the *t* of Simeon;
13: 6 son of Jephunneh, of the *t* of Judah;
13: 7 [son of Joseph], of the *t* of Issachar;
13: 8 son of Nun, of the *t* of Ephraim; 9Palti,
13: 9 son of Raphu, of the *t* of Benjamin;Gaddiel,
13:10 son of Sodi, of the *t* of Zebulun;Gaddi,
13:11 son of Susi, of the *t* of Manasseh,
13:12 son of Gemalli, of the *t* of Dan;Sethur,
13:13 son of Michael, of the *t* of Asher; Nahbi,
13:14 son of Vophsi, of the *t* of Naphtali;
13:15 son of Machi, of the *t* of Gad.
18: 2 also your other kinsmen of the *t* of Levi,
18: 2 of the tribe of Levi, your ancestral *t*,
24: 2 eyes and saw Israel encamped, tribe by *t*,
26:59 the tribe of Levi, born to the *t* in Egypt.
31: 5 a thousand men of each *t* were levied,
31: 6 on the campaign, a thousand from each *t*,
32:33 as well as half the *t* of Manasseh,
33:54 be within the heritage of his ancestral *t*.
34:14 the ancestral houses of the *t* of Reuben,
34:14 and the ancestral houses of the *t* of Gad,
34:14 Gad, as well as half of the *t* of Manasseh,
34:19 from the *t* of Judah:
34:20 son of Jephunneh, from the *t* of Simeon:
34:21 from the *t* of Benjamin:
34:22 Elidad, son of Chislon; from the *t* of Dan:
34:23 from the *t* of Manasseh:
34:24 from the *t* of Ephraim:
34:25 from the *t* of Zebulun:
34:26 from the *t* of Issachar:
34:27 from the *t* of Asher:
34:28 Shelomi; from the *t* of Naphtali:
36: 3 to that of the *t* into which they marry;
36: 4 to that of the *t* into which they marry
36: 4 be withdrawn from that of our ancestral *t*."
36: 5 "The *t* of the Josephites are right in
36: 6 marry into a clan of their ancestral *t*,
36: 7 Israelites will pass from one *t* to another,
36: 8 to a clan of her own ancestral *t*,
36: 9 no heritage can pass from one *t* to another,
36:12 remained in the *t* of their father's clan.
36:13 be withdrawn from that of our ancestral *t*."
Dt 1:23 men from your number, one from each *t*.
10: 8 "At that time the LORD set apart the *t* of
18: 1 "The whole priestly *t* of Levi shall have
29: 7 Gadites, and half the *t* of Manasseh.
29:17 no man or woman, no clan or *t* among you,
Jos 4: 2 men from the people, one from each *t*,
4: 4 from among the Israelites, one from each *t*,
7: 1 of Zerah, son of Zara of the *t* of Judah,
7:14 The *t* which the LORD designates shall come
7:16 tribes, and the *t* of Judah was designated.
7:18 of Zabdi, son of Zerah of the *t* of Judah,
13: 8 Now the other half of the *t* of Manasseh as
13:14 *t* of Levi Moses assigned no heritage since,
13:33 Moses gave no heritage to the *t* of Levi,
15: 1 The lot for the clans of the Judahite *t*
15:20 of the clans of the *t* of Judahites:
15:21 The cities of the *t* of the Judahites in
17: 1 *t* of Manasseh as the first-born of Joseph:
18:11 fell to the clans of the *t* of Benjaminites.
18:21 clans of the *t* of the Benjaminites were:
19: 1 The heritage of the clans of the *t* of
19: 8 of the clans of the *t* of the Simeonites.
19:24 to the clans of the *t* of the Asherites.
19:31 of the clans of the *t* of the Asherites.
19:39 of the clans of the *t* of the Naphtalites.
19:40 lot fell to the clans of the *t* of Danites.
19:48 of the clans of the *t* of the Danites.
20: 8 on the open tableland in the *t* of Reuben,
20: 8 Reuben, Ramoth in Gilead in the *t* of Gad,
20: 8 and Golan in Bashan in the *t* of Manasseh.
21: 5 of the tribe of Ephraim, from the *t* of Dan,
21: 6 the tribe of Issachar, from the *t* of Asher,
21: 6 the tribe of Asher, from the *t* of Naphtali,
21:17 From the *t* of Benjamin they obtained the
21:20 obtained by lot, from the *t* of Ephraim,
21:23 From the *t* of Dan they obtained the four
21:28 From the *t* of Issachar they obtained the
21:29 from the *t* of Asher,
21:32 and from the *t* of Naphtali,
21:34 received from the *t* of Zebulun the four
21:36 across the Jordan, from the *t* of Reuben,
21:38 from the *t* of Gad a total of four cities:
22: 7 to half the *t* of Manasseh Moses had
22:14 ten princes, one from every *t* of Israel,
Jgs 17: 7 the *t* of Judah at Bethlehem of Judah.
18: 1 Moreover the *t* of Danites were in search
18:19 to be priest for a *t* and a clan in Israel?"
18:30 were priests for the *t* of the Danites
20:12 men throughout the *t* of Benjamin to say,
21: 3 today one *t* of Israel should be lacking?"
21:24 for his own heritage in his own clan and *t*.
1Sm 9:21 among the clans of the *t* of Benjamin?
10:20 forward, and the *t* of Benjamin was chosen.
10:21 the *t* of Benjamin come forward in clans,
2Sm 4: 2 the Beer-othite, of the *t* of Benjamin.
15: 2 servant is of such and such a *t* of Israel,"
1Kgs 7:14 the son of a widow from the *t* of Naphtali;
8:16 *t* of Israel for the building of a temple
11:13 I will leave your son one *t* for the sake
11:32 One *t* shall remain to him for the sake of
11:36 I will give his son one *t*,
12:20 David's house except the *t* of Judah alone.
12:21 the house of Judah and the *t* of Benjamin
2Kgs 17:18 Only the *t* of Judah was left.
1Chr 6:45 Also from the *t* of Benjamin:
6:46 lot for their clans from the *t* of Ephraim,
6:46 the tribe of Ephraim, from the *t* of Dan,
6:51 cities by lot from the *t* of Ephraim.
6:54 From the *t* of Dan:
6:57 From the *t* of Issachar:
6:59 From the *t* of Asher:
6:61 From the *t* of Naphtali:
6:62 Merarites received from the *t* of Zebulun:
6:63 Jordan] they received from the *t* of Reuben:
6:65 From the *t* of Gad:
11:42 the Reubenite, chief of the *t* of Reuben;
23:14 sons were counted as part of the *t* of Levi.
Tb 1: 1 the family of Asiel, of the *t* of Naphtali,
1: 4 the entire *t* of my forefather Naphtali had
1: 5 rest of the *t* of my forefather Naphtali,
4:12 a stranger who is not of your father's *t*,
5: 9 find out what family and *t* he comes from,
5:11 me, please, what family and *t* are you from?"
5:12 Do you need a *t* and a family?
Jdt 3: 8 and every people and *t* invoke him as a god.
6:15 Uzziah, son of Micah of the *t* of Simeon,
8: 2 husband, Manasseh, of her own *t* and clan,
8:18 nor does there exist today, any *t*,
Est A: 1 Shimei, son of Kish, of the *t* of Benjamin,
Ps(s) 74: 2 the *t* you redeemed as your inheritance,
78:67 Joseph, and the *t* of Ephraim he chose not;
78:68 But he chose the *t* of Judah,
Sir 45: 6 his brother AARON, of the *t* of Levi.
45:25 David, the son of Jesse of the *t* of Judah,
Jer 10:16 Israel is his very own *t*,
51:19 Israel is his very own *t*,
Ez 47:23 In whatever *t* the alien may be resident,
Mi 6: 9 Hear, O *t* and city council,
Lk 2:36 daughter of Phanuel of the *t* of Asher.
Acts 13:21 Saul son of Kish, of the *t* of Benjamin,
Rom 11: 1 from Abraham, of the *t* of Benjamin.
Phil 3: 5 the stock of Israel and the *t* of Benjamin,
Heb 7: 5 that the priests of the *t* of Levi
7:13 things are said was of a different *t*,
7:14 that our Lord rose from the *t* of Judah,
Rv 5: 5 The Lion of the *t* of Judah,
7: 4 forty-four thousand from every *t* of Israel;
7: 5 twelve thousand from the *t* of Judah,
7: 5 twelve thousand from the *t* of Reuben,
7: 5 Reuben, twelve thousand from the *t* of Gad,
7: 6 Gad, twelve thousand from the *t* of Asher,
7: 6 twelve thousand from the *t* of Naphtali,
7: 6 twelve thousand from the *t* of Manasseh,
7: 7 twelve thousand from the *t* of Simeon,
7: 7 Simeon, twelve thousand from the *t* of Levi,
7: 7 twelve thousand from the *t* of Issachar,
7: 8 twelve thousand from the *t* of Zebulun,
7: 8 twelve thousand from the *t* of Joseph,
7: 8 and twelve thousand from the *t* of Benjamin.

TRIBES (125)

Gn 48: 4 and raise you into an assembly of *t*,
49:28 All these are the twelve *t* of Israel,
Ex 24: 4 twelve pillars for the twelve *t* of Israel.
28:21 seal with the name of one of the twelve *t*.
39:14 seal with the name of one of the twelve *t*.
Nm 1:16 community, princes of their ancestral *t*,
7: 2 princes of the *t* who supervised the census.
26:55 as the heritage of the various ancestral *t*.
30: 2 said to the heads of the Israelite *t*,
31: 4 From each of the *t* of Israel you shall
32:28 heads of the ancestral *t* of the Israelites:
34:13 to be given to the nine and one half *t*.
34:15 these two and one half *t* have received
34:18 *t* whom you shall designate for this task.
36: 3 marry into one of the other Israelite *t*,
36: 8 of the Israelite *t* shall marry someone
36: 9 but all the Israelite *t* will retain their
Dt 1:13 and experienced men from each of your *t*,
1:15 So I took outstanding men of your *t*,
12: 5 chooses out of all your *t* and designates
12:14 which the LORD chooses from among your *t*;
16:18 officials throughout your *t* to administer
18: 5 chosen him and his sons out of all your *t*
29:20 him out from all the *t* of Israel for doom,
33: 5 and the *t* of Israel came together
33:19 You who invite the *t* to the mountains
Jos 3:12 men, one from each of the *t* of Israel.]
4: 5 equal in number the *t* of the Israelites.
4: 8 Jordan as there were *t* of the Israelites,
7:14 morning you must present yourselves by *t*.
7:16 Joshua had Israel come forward by *t*,
11:23 heritage, apportioning it among the *t*.
12: 7 Joshua apportioned to the *t* of Israel.
13: 7 apportion among the nine *t* and the
14: 1 and the heads of families in the *t* of the
14: 2 concerning the remaining nine and a half *t*.
14: 3 For to two and a half *t* Moses had already
14: 3 were given no heritage among the *t*,
14: 4 the descendants of Joseph formed two *t*,
18: 2 Seven *t* among the Israelites had not yet
18: 4 Choose three men from each of your *t*;
19:51 and the heads of families in the *t* of the
21: 1 of families of the other *t* of the Israelites
21: 4 thirteen cities by lot from the *t* of Judah,
21: 7 twelve cities from the *t* of Reuben,
21: 9 From the *t* of the Judahites and Simeonites
21:16 nine cities from the two *t* mentioned.
23: 4 I have apportioned among your *t*
24: 1 together all the *t* of Israel at Shechem,
Jgs 6:35 and these *t* advanced to meet the others.
18: 1 received no heritage among the *t* of Israel.
20:10 the *t* of Israel ten men for every hundred,
20:12 the *t* of Israel sent men throughout the
21: 5 "Are there any among all the *t* of Israel
21: 6 one of the *t* of Israel has been cut off.
21: 8 *t* of Israel had not come up to the LORD
21:15 had made a breach among the *t* of Israel.
21:17 one of the Israelite *t* will be wiped out.
1Sm 2:28 of all the *t* of Israel to be my priests,
9:21 of one of the smallest *t* of Israel,
10:19 the LORD according to *t* and families."
10:20 had all the *t* of Israel come forward,
15:17 are you not leader of the *t* of Israel?
2Sm 5: 1 All the *t* of Israel came to David in
15:10 spies throughout the *t* of Israel to say,
19:10 but throughout the *t* of Israel all the
20:14 all the *t* of Israel to Abel Beth-maacah.
24: 2 "Tour all the *t* in Israel from Dan to
1Kgs 8: 1 of Israel and all the leaders of the *t*,
11:31 grasp and will give you ten of the *t*.
11:32 I have chosen out of all the *t* of Israel.
11:35 that is, the ten *t*.
14:21 city in which, out of all the *t* of Israel,
18:31 for the number of *t* of the sons of Jacob,
2Kgs 21: 7 I have chosen out of all the *t* of Israel,
1Chr 6:47 thirteen cities from the *t* of Issachar,
6:48 twelve cities by lot from the *t* of Reuben,
6:50 them by lot from the *t* of the Judahites,
27:16 Over the *t* of Israel,
27:22 were the commanders of the *t* of Israel.
28: 1 the leaders of Israel, the heads of the *t*,
29: 6 families, the leaders of the *t* of Israel,
2Chr 5: 2 of Israel and all the leaders of the *t*,
6: 5 any city from among all the *t* of Israel
11:16 *t* who firmly desired to seek the LORD,
12:13 city in which, out of all the *t* of Israel,
33: 7 *t* of Israel I shall place my name forever.
Ezr 6:17 keeping with the number of the *t* of Israel.
Tb 1: 4 had been singled out of all Israel's *t*,
Jdt 9:14 Let your whole nation and all the *t* know
Jb 31:34 and the scorn of the *t* terrified me

TRIBES (cont.)

Ps(s) 72:17 shall all the *t* of the earth be blessed;
78:55 and settled the *t* of Israel in their tents.
105:37 gold, with not a weakling among their *t*.
122: 4 To it the *t* go up, the tribes of the LORD,
Sir 36:10 Gather all the *t* of Jacob,
44:23 He fixed the boundaries for his *t*,
45:11 in incised letters each of the *t* of Israel;
48:10 sons, and to reestablish the *t* of Jacob.
Is 19:13 The chiefs of her *t* have led Egypt astray,
49: 6 be my servant, to raise up the *t* of Jacob,
63:17 of your servants, the *t* of your heritage.
Jer 10:25 not, on the *t* that call not upon your name;
25: 9 send for and fetch all the *t* of the north,
31: 1 I will be the God of all the *t* of Israel,
33:24 rejected the two *t* which he had chosen"?
Ez 37:19 and of the *t* of Israel associated with him,
45: 8 the house of Israel according to their *t*.
47:13 *t* of Israel [Joseph having two portions].
47:21 yourselves according to the *t* of Israel.
47:22 receive inheritances among the *t* of Israel.
48: 1 This is the list of the *t*.
48:19 shall be taken from all the *t* of Israel.
48:23 These are the remaining *t*.
48:29 as inheritances among the *t* of Israel,
48:30 of which are named after the *t* of Israel.
Hos 5: 9 *t* of Israel I announce what is sure to be.
10:14 Turmoil shall break out among your *t*
Zec 9: 1 are the LORD's, as are all the *t* of Israel,
Mt 19:28 thrones to judge the twelve *t* of Israel.
Lk 22:30 on thrones judging the twelve *t* of Israel.
Acts 26: 7 The twelve *t* of our people fervently
Jas 1: 1 To the twelve *t* in the dispersion,
Rv 21:12 gates, the names of the twelve *t* of Israel.

TRIBESMEN (3)

Jgs 20: 2 of all the people and all the *t* of Israel,
1Chr 7: 5 more wives and sons than their fellow *t*.
8:32 in Jerusalem, opposite their fellow *t*.

TRIBULATION (4)

Est A: 7 *T* and distress,
1Mc 6:11 'Into what *t* have I come,
Sir 3:15 of *t* it will be recalled to your advantage,
Rv 2: 9 I know of your *t* and your poverty,

TRIBULATIONS (2)

Wis 10: 9 delivered from *t* those who served her.
Acts 7:10 with him and rescued him from all his *t*.

TRIBUNAL (5)

1Kgs 7: 7 that is, the *t*;
7: 8 than the *t* and of the same construction.
7: 8 this *t* was built for Pharaoh's daughter,
Ps(s) 94:20 the *t* of wickedness be leagued with you,
2Cor 5:10 to be revealed before the *t* of Christ

TRIBUNE (1)

Jn 18:12 Then the soldiers of the cohort, their *t*,

TRIBUTARIES (1)

1Mc 1: 4 nations, and rulers, and they became his *t*.

TRIBUTARY (2)

2Sm 8: 2 Thus the Moabites became *t* to David.
8: 6 the Arameans became subjects, *t* to David.

TRIBUTE (33)

Gn 49:10 his legs, While *t* is brought to him,
Jgs 3:15 that the Israelites sent their *t* to Eglon,
3:17 He presented the *t* to Eglon,
3:18 presentation went off with the *t* bearers.
1Sm 6: 5 and give them as a *t* to the God of Israel.
1Kgs 5: 1 *t* and were his vassals as long as he lived.
10:25 Each one brought his yearly *t*:
2Kgs 3: 4 of Israel as *t* a hundred thousand lambs
17: 3 Hoshea became his vassal and paid him *t*.
17: 4 pay the annual *t* to his Assyrian overlord.
18:14 and I will pay whatever *t* you impose on me."
1Chr 18: 2 the Moabites became his subjects, paying *t*.
18: 6 the Arameans became his subjects, paying *t*.
2Chr 9:24 and year out, each one would bring his *t*—
17:11 Jehoshaphat gifts and a *t* of silver;
24:27 his sons, and the great *t* imposed on him,
26: 8 The Ammonites paid *t* to Uzziah and his
Est 10: 1 King Ahasuerus laid *t* on the land and on
1Mc 3:31 go to Persia and levy *t* on those provinces,
8: 2 conquering them and forcing them to pay *t*.
8: 4 and the rest paid *t* to them every year.
8: 7 kings who succeeded him to pay a heavy *t*,
10:29 as I also exempt all the Jews, from the *t*,
11:28 and the three districts of Samaria from *t*,
11:35 of tithes and *t* and of the tax on the salt
13:37 our official to grant you release from *t*.
15:30 and the *t* money of the districts outside
15:31 more for the *t* money of the cities.
2Mc 8:10 two thousand talents of *t* owed by the king
8:36 So he who had promised to provide *t* for
11: 3 to levy *t* on the temple,

Ps(s) 72:10 the kings of Arabia and Seba shall bring *t*.
Sir 38:17 mourning fully, pay your *t* of sorrow,

TRIBUTES (4)

Ezr 4:13 again, they will no longer pay taxes, *t*,
4:20 over all West-of-Euphrates, and taxes, *t*,
7:24 it is not permitted to impose taxes, *t*,
Ez 20:40 *t* and the first fruits of your offerings,

TRICE (1)

1Kgs 18:45 In a *t*, the sky grew dark with clouds

TRICK (5)

1Sm 19:17 "Why did you play this *t* on me?
23:22 perhaps they are playing some *t* on me).
Bar 6:10 They *t* them out in garments like men,
Mt 26: 4 to arrest Jesus by some *t* and kill him;
Mk 14: 1 a way to arrest him by some *t* and kill him.

TRICKED (1)

Gn 3:13 woman answered, "The serpent *t* me into it,

TRICKERY (6)

Prv 16:30 He who winks his eye is plotting *t*;
Is 32: 7 And the trickster uses wicked *t*,
Dn 14:18 there is no *t* in you."
2Cor 4: 2 not resort to *t* or falsify the word of God.
Eph 4:14 in human *t* and skill in proposing error.
1Thes 2: 3 deceit or impure motives or any sort of *t*;

TRICKLING (1)

Ez 47: 2 where I saw water *t* from the southern side.

TRICKSTER (2)

Is 32: 5 noble, nor the *t* be considered honorable.
32: 7 And the *t* uses wicked trickery,

TRIED (63)

Gn 37:21 this, he *t* to save him from their hands,
37:35 his sons and daughters *t* to console him,
39:10 Although she *t* to entice him day after day,
Ex 8:14 *t* to bring forth gnats by their magic arts,
Nm 35:12 unless he is first *t* before the community.
1Sm 17:39 however, since he had never *t* armor before.
17:39 these, because I have never *t* them before."
19:10 *t* to nail David to the wall with the spear,
1Kgs 11:40 When Solomon *t* to have Jeroboam killed for
Tb 6: 3 out of the water and *t* to swallow his foot.
14:10 darkness, for he had *t* to kill Ahiqar.
Jdt 8:26 he dealt with Abraham, and how he *t* Isaac,
Est A:11 He kept it in mind, and *t* in every way,
D:16 and all his attendants *t* to revive her.
1Mc 6: 3 and *t* to capture and pillage the city.
9: 9 They *t* to dissuade him, saying:
2Mc 13:18 *t* to take their positions by a stratagem.
Jb 34:36 Let Job be *t* to the limit,
Ps(s) 12: 7 of the LORD are sure, like *t* silver,
66:10 You have tried us as silver is *t* by fire;
73:16 Though I *t* to understand this it seemed to
Wis 3: 5 *t* them and found them worthy of himself.
11: 9 For when they had been *t*,
Jer 18: 4 turned out badly in his hand, he *t* again,
51: 9 "We have *t* to heal Babylon,
Ez 16:37 all your lovers whom you *t* to please,
Dn 6: 5 Therefore the supervisors and satraps *t* to
9: 2 *t* to understand in the Scriptures the
14:42 had *t* to destroy him he threw into the den,
Mt 3:14 John *t* to refuse him with the protest,
27:48 sticking it on a reed, *t* to make him drink.
Mk 6:48 they *t* to row with the wind against them,
9:38 to expel demons and we *t* to stop him
15:23 they *t* to give him wine drugged with myrrh,
Lk 4:42 him they *t* to keep him from leaving them.
9:49 and we *t* to stop him because he is not of
20:19 high priests *t* to get their hands on him,
Jn 7:30 At this they *t* to seize him,
10:39 At these words they again *t* to arrest him,
19:21 chief priests of the Jews *t* to tell Pilate,
Acts 5:36 Theudas came on the scene and *t* to pass
7:26 and *t* to reconcile them by saying:
9:26 Jerusalem he *t* to join the disciples there;
12:19 he had the guards *t* and executed.
16: 7 to Mysia they *t* to go on into Bithynia,
16:39 They came along and *t* to quiet them;
19:13 Some itinerant Jewish exorcists once *t* to
21: 4 they *t* to tell Paul that he should not go
21:33 He *t* to find out who he was and what he
24: 6 He even *t* to desecrate our temple,
25:10 that is where I must be *t*.
26:21 me in the temple court and *t* to murder me.
27:30 Then the sailors *t* to abandon ship.
28:18 The Romans *t* my case and wanted to release
1Cor 11:19 for the *t* and true to stand out clearly.
Gal 1:13 the church of God and *t* to destroy it;
1:23 is now preaching the faith he *t* to destroy,"
1Thes 2:18 So we *t* to come to you
2:18 I, Paul, *t* more than once
2Thes 1: 7 relief to you who are sorely *t*
Heb 3: 9 desert, When your fathers tested and *t* me,
Rv 2:10 you will be *t* over a period of ten days.

TRIES (8)

2Kgs 11: 8 and if anyone *t* to approach the cordon,
2Chr 23: 7 Whoever *t* to enter the house must be slain.
23:14 the ranks, and if anyone *t* to follow her,
Sir 4:17 upon him and *t* him with her discipline;
18:23 be not one who *t* the LORD.
Jer 48:19 man who flees, the woman who *t* to escape:
Lk 17:33 *t* to preserve his life will lose it;
Rv 11: 5 If anyone *t* to harm them,

TRIFLE (2)

Jdt 16:16 the sweet odor of every sacrifice is a *t*,
Mi 2:10 For any *t* you exact a crippling pledge.

TRIFLING (1)

Sir 41:21 Of *t* with a servant girl you have,

TRIM (1)

Lv 19:27 the temples, nor *t* the edges of your beard.

TRIMMED (3)

2Sm 19:25 He had not washed his feet nor *t* his
1Kgs 7: 9 to size and *t* front and back with a saw,
Ez 44:20 but they shall keep their hair carefully *t*.

TRIMMING (3)

Ex 25:38 These, as well as the *t* shears and trays,
37:23 lamps, as well as its *t* shears and trays,
Nm 4: 9 the lampstand with its lamps, *t* shears,

TRIMS (1)

Jn 15: 2 ones he *t* clean to increase their yield.

TRIP (7)

Ps(s) 140: 5 from violent men Who plan to *t* up my feet
Sir 12:17 feigning to help, he will *t* you up,
32:20 and let not the same thing *t* you twice.
Mt 16:23 You are trying to make me *t* and fall.
22:18 to them, "Why are you trying to *t* me up,
22:35 them, a lawyer, in an attempt to *t* him up,
Mk 12:15 to them, "Why are you trying to *t* me up?

TRIPLED (1)

Ez 21:19 While the sword is doubled and *t*,

TRIPOLIS (1)

2Mc 14: 1 port of *T* with a powerful army and a fleet,

TRIPS (2)

Sir 13:20 a poor man *t* he is pushed down by a friend.
Jer 46:12 Warrior *t* over warrior,

TRIREMES (1)

2Mc 4:20 who brought it, to the construction of *t*.

TRIUMPH (21)

Ex 14: 8 even while they were marching away in *t*.
Nm 23:21 with him is the *t* of his King.
33: 3 morrow the Israelites went forth in *t*,
Jgs 8: 9 Penuel, too, he said, "When I return in *t*,
11:31 when I return in *t* from the Ammonites
Jdt 12: 8 to direct her way for the *t* of his people.
Est 8:16 merriment for the Jews, exultation and *t*.
1Mc 2:48 of the kings and did not let the sinner *t*.
11:16 King Ptolemy's *t* was complete when the
2Mc 5: 6 not realizing that *t* over one's own
13:16 Finally they withdrew in *t*,
Jb 20: 5 That the *t* of the wicked is short and the
Ps(s) 13: 3 How long will my enemy *t* over me?
41:12 by this, that my enemy does not *t* over me,
60:10 I will *t* over Philistia."
108:10 I will *t* over Philistia."
Wis 4: 2 And forever it marches crowned in *t*,
Is 45:13 I who stirred up one for the *t* of justice;
Jer 20:11 persecutors will stumble, they will not *t*.
Dn 11:12 low tens of thousands, but he shall not *t*.
Lk 22:53 But this is your hour—the *t* of darkness!"

TRIUMPHAL (1)

2Cor 2:14 leads us on in Christ's *t* train,

TRIUMPHANT (5)

Ex 15: 1 sing to the LORD, for he is gloriously *t*;
15:21 Sing to the LORD, for he is gloriously *t*;
Dt 32:13 He had them ride *t* over the summits of the
Ps(s) 45: 4 your splendor and your majesty ride on *t*
Prv 28:12 When the just are *t*,

TRIUMPHANTLY (1)

Ps(s) 74: 4 Your foes roar *t* in your shrine;

TRIUMPHED (4)

Jer 20: 7 you were too strong for me, and you *t*.
Lam 1: 9 LORD, upon her misery, for the enemy has *t*!
Hos 12: 5 He contended with the angel and *t*,

Col 2:15 off captive, *t* in the person of Christ.

TRIUMPHS (1)

Jas 2:13 but mercy *t* over judgment.

TRIVIAL (2)

Dt 32:47 For this is no *t* matter for you;
Ez 8:17 Is it such a *t* matter for the house of

TROAS (6)

Acts 16: 8 through Mysia instead, they came down to *T.*
16:11 We put out to sea from *T* and set a course
20: 5 went on ahead and waited for us in *T.*
20: 6 Five days later we joined them in *T,*
2Cor 2:12 I came to *T* to preach the gospel of Christ,
2Tm 4:13 bring the cloak I left in *T* with Carpus,

TROD (4)

Dt 1:36 to his sons I will give the land he *t* upon,
Jgs 9:27 harvested their grapes and *t* them out.
2Kgs 21:21 exactly the path his father had *t,*
Is 63: 3 I *t* them in my anger,

TRODDEN (11)

Tb 3: 5 have we *t* the paths of truth before you.
Jb 22:15 keep to the ancient way *t* by worthless men,
28: 8 The proud beasts have not *t* it,
Is 25:10 Moab will be *t* down as a straw is *t*
63: 3 "The wine press I have *t* alone,
Jer 12:10 my vineyard, have *t* my heritage underfoot;
51:33 a threshing floor at the time it is *t;*
Lam 1:15 *t* in the wine press virgin daughter Judah.
Bar 4:26 My pampered children have *t* rough roads,
Rv 14:20 The winepress was *t* outside the city,

TROOP (1)

2Kgs 9:17 saw the *t* of Jehu coming and reported,

TROOPS (98)

Nm 1:16 tribes, chiefs of the *t* of Israel.
10: 4 the princes, the chiefs of the *t* of Israel,
10:36 ride upon the clouds, to the *t* of Israel.
32:17 march as *t* in the van of the Israelites,
32:20 "If you keep your word to march as *t* in
32:27 as armed *t* to battle before the LORD,
32:29 with you as combat *t* before the LORD,
32:30 with you as combat *t* before the LORD,
32:32 the land of Canaan as *t* before the LORD,
Dt 3:18 But all you *t* equipped for battle must
Jos 4:13 About forty thousand *t* equipped for battle
6: 7 *t* marching ahead of the ark of the LORD.
6: 9 with the horns marched the picked *t;*
6:13 Ahead of these marched the picked *t,*
8:11 When all the *t* he led were drawn up in
8:13 and Joshua waited overnight among his *t.*
10: 7 his picked *t* and the rest of his soldiers.
11: 4 They came out with all their *t,*
Jgs 4: 7 Kishon, together with his chariots and *t,*
5:14 behind you was Benjamin, among your *t.*
1Sm 4: 3 When the *t* retired to the camp,
4:17 in fact, the *t* suffered heavy losses.
11:11 Saul arranged his *t* in three companies and
14:17 *t* and find out if any of us are missing."
15: 9 He and his *t* spared Agag and the best of
26:13 distance from Abner, son of Ner, and the *t.*
2Sm 10: 9 a selection from all the picked *t* of Israel
10:15 by Israel with a full mustering of *t;*
18: 1 After mustering the *t* he had with him,
1Kgs 15:20 of his *t* against the cities of Israel.
2Kgs 25:10 Then the Chaldean *t* who were with the
1Chr 7: 4 thousand men in organized military *t,*
12:19 and placed them among the leaders of his *t.*
12:22 helped David by taking charge of his *t,*
12:24 of armed *t* that came to David
12:25 six thousand eight hundred armed *t.*
2Chr 12:11 of the LORD, the *t* would come bearing them,
16: 4 of his *t* against the cities of Israel.
25: 9 talents that I paid for the *t* of Israel?"
25:10 the *t* that had come to him from Ephraim,
Ezr 8:22 have been ashamed to ask the king for *t*
Neh 3:34 of his brethren and the *t* of Samaria:
Jdt 2:15 a hundred and twenty thousand picked *t,*
3: 6 them he impressed picked *t* as auxiliaries.
7: 1 the allied *t* that had come to his support,
7: 7 them, while he himself returned to his *t.*
7: 9 that there may be no losses among your *t.*
7:11 thus not a single one of your *t* will fall.
7:26 the *t* of Holofernes and to all his forces;
14:17 her, he rushed out to the *t* and cried:
1Mc 4:31 them ashamed of their *t* and their cavalry.
7:20 over to Alcimus, leaving *t* to help him,
9: 6 his men saw the great number of the *t,*
11: 3 he stationed garrison *t* in each one.
11:38 except the foreign *t* which he had hired
11:39 that all the *t* were grumbling at Demetrius,
11:41 to King Demetrius to withdraw his *t*
11:43 for me, because all my *t* have revolted."
11:74 thousand of the foreign *t* fell on that day.
12:46 He dismissed his *t,*
13:20 His *t* went around by the road that leads
13:43 besieged Gazara and surrounded it with *t.*
15: 3 recruited a large number of mercenary *t*
15:10 ancestors, and all the *t* rallied to him,
15:25 *t* and with the siege machines he had made.
15:26 Antiochus' support two thousand elite *t,*
15:39 He ordered him to move his *t* against Judea
16:18 asking that *t* be sent to help him and that
2Mc 10:14 he employed foreign *t* and used every
10:24 gathered a tremendous force of foreign *t*
10:36 the gates and let in the rest of the *t,*
14:20 each leader communicated them to his *t;*
14:41 But when these *t,* on the point of capturing
14:43 So while the *t* rushed in through the doors,
15:20 near with their *t* drawn up in battle line,
Jb 10:17 in waves your *t* come against me.
19:12 His *t* advance as one man;
25: 3 Is there any numbering of his *t?*
Sg 6: 4 as awe-inspiring as bannered *t,*
6:10 the sun, as awe-inspiring as bannered *t?*
Jer 52:14 And the Chaldean *t* who were with the
Ez 12:14 his *t* I will scatter in every direction,
17:17 Pharaoh with a great army and numerous *t.*
17:21 *t* among his forces shall fall by the sword,
38: 6 and helmets], Gomer with all its *t,*
38: 6 the recesses of the north with all its *t,*
38: 9 all your *t* and the many peoples with you.
38:22 I will rain upon him, upon his *t,*
39: 4 your *t* and the peoples who are with you.
Dn 11:15 picked *t* shall have the strength to resist.
Hos 10:10 I gathered *t* against them when I chastised
Na 2: 6 His picked *t* are called,
3:13 See, the *t* are women in your midst;
Mt 8: 9 myself and I have *t* assigned to me.
Acts 23:10 He therefore ordered his *t* to go down and
23:27 I intervened with my *t* and rescued him.
Rv 9:16 Their cavalry *t,*
20: 8 and muster for war the *t* of Gog and Magog,

TROPHIMUS (3)

Acts 20: 4 Tychicus and *T* from Asia.
21:29 They had seen *T,*
2Tm 4:20 while *T* I had to leave ill at Miletus.

TROPHY (1)

1Sm 15:12 where he erected a *t* in his own honor,

TROUBLE (50)

Gn 34:25 advanced against the city without any *t,*
34:30 "You have brought *t* upon me by making me
43: 6 "Why did you bring this *t* on me by
1Sm 14:29 "My father brings *t* to the land.
2Kgs 6:28 Then the king asked her, "What is your *t?*"
1Chr 2: 7 brought *t* upon Israel by violating the ban.
1Mc 11:53 received from him, he caused him much *t.*
12:44 to so much *t* when we are not at war?
2Mc 1: 7 we Jews wrote to you during the *t*
4:16 this, they found themselves in serious *t:*
4:47 Menelaus, who was the cause of all the *t,*
13: 4 that Menelaus was to blame for all the *t,*
Jb 3:10 doors of the womb to shield my eyes from *t!*
3:26 I have no rest, for *t* comes!
4: 8 it, those who plow for mischief and sow *t,*
5: 6 earth, nor does *t* spring out of the ground;
14: 1 of woman is short-lived and full of *t,*
Ps(s) 27: 5 will hide me in his abode in the day of *t;*
107:12 And he humbled their hearts with *t;*
Prv 10:10 He who winks at a fault causes *t,*
11: 8 The just man escapes *t,*
12:13 is ensnared, but the just comes free of *t.*
17:20 and a double-tongued man falls into *t.*
21:23 mouth and his tongue keeps himself from *t.*
25:19 on] a faithless man in time of *t.*
Eccl 11:10 heart and put away *t* from your presence,
Sir 2:11 he forgives sins, he saves in time of *t.*
22:13 *t* and be spattered when he shakes himself;
22:23 In time of *t* remain true to him,
34:23 tears down, what do they gain but *t?*
37: 4 joys, but in time of *t* he stands afar off.
40: 5 Are of wrath and envy, *t* and dread,
51:10 Do not abandon me in time of *t,*
51:12 every kind and preserved me in time of *t.*
Is 33: 2 every morning, our salvation in time of *t!*
Jer 2:27 yet, in their time of *t* they cry out,
2:28 Will they save you in your time of *t?*
Ez 35: 5 power of the sword at the time of their *t,*
Dn 13:10 her, they did not tell each other their *t,*
Mt 5:29 If your right eye is your *t,*
5:30 Again, if your right hand is your *t,*
9: 5 Which is less *t* to say, 'Your sins are
28:14 it out with him and keep you out of *t.*"
Lk 7: 6 "Sir, do not *t* yourself,
Acts 25:26 The *t* is, I have nothing definite to write
1Cor 3: 1 the *t* was that I could not talk to you as
2Cor 1: 4 enables us to comfort those who are in *t,*
1: 8 you in the dark about the *t* we had in Asia;
Gal 2:12 to avoid *t* with those who were circumcised.
6:17 Henceforth, let no man *t* me,

TROUBLED (25)

1Sm 4:13 for he was *t* at heart about the ark of God.
Est D:13 my heart was *t* with fear of your majesty.
D:16 The king became *t* and all his attendants
1Mc 3: 5 who *t* his people he destroyed by fire.
10:68 Alexander heard of it he was greatly *t,*
Jb 7: 3 and *t* nights have been told off for me.
Ps(s) 55: 3 I rock with grief, and am *t*
77: 5 I am *t* and cannot speak.
77:17 the very depths were *t.*
Prv 25:26 Like a *t* fountain or a polluted spring is
Wis 11: 6 when the perennial river was *t* with impure
Sir 40: 2 and his *t* forebodings till the day he dies
Is 30: 6 and *t* land of the lioness and roaring lion,
44: 8 Fear not, be not *t:*
Dn 5:10 Be not *t* in mind, nor look so pale!
Mt 15:22 My daughter is terribly *t* by a demon."
Lk 1:29 She was deeply *t* by his words,
6:18 who were *t* with unclean spirits were cured;
Jn 11:33 her also weeping, he was *t* in spirit,
11:38 Once again *t* in spirit, Jesus approached
12:27 My soul is *t* now,
13:21 After saying this, Jesus grew deeply *t.*
14: 1 "Do not let your hearts be *t.*
Acts 5:16 and those who were *t* by unclean spirits,
2Cor 2:13 Yet I was inwardly *t* because I did not

TROUBLEMAKER (2)

Jn 7:11 looking for him, asking, "Where is that *t?*"
Acts 24: 5 We have found that this man is a *t* who

TROUBLEMAKERS (2)

1Mc 15:21 *t* from their country take refuge with you,
1Pt 2:12 Though the pagans may slander you as *t,*

TROUBLES (10)

Dt 31:17 and many evils and *t* will befall them.
31:21 then, when many evils and *t* befall them,
1Sm 1:15 I was only pouring out my *t* to the LORD.
1Mc 10:15 brothers and the *t* that they had endured.
15:12 realizing what a mass of *t* had come upon
Jb 5:19 Out of six *t* he will deliver you,
Ps(s) 25:17 and afflicted Relieve the *t* of my heart,
34:20 Many are the *t* of the just man,
88: 4 For my soul is surfeited with *t* and my
Mt 6:34 Today has *t* enough of its own.

TROUBLESOME (3)

1Mc 10:63 on any grounds or be *t* to him in any way."
12:14 We did not wish to be *t* to you and to the
2Mc 9:21 of Persia, I fell victim to a *t* illness;

TROUBLING (4)

Jos 15:18 the ass, Caleb asked her, "What is *t* you?"
Jgs 1:14 the ass, Caleb asked her, "What is *t* you?"
Jb 3:17 There the wicked cease from *t,*
Gal 5:12 those who are *t* you might go the whole way,

TROUBLOUS (1)

Wis 2: 1 "Brief and *t* is our lifetime;

TROUGH (1)

Gn 24:20 emptied her jug into the drinking *t*

TROUGHS (4)

Gn 30:38 he then set upright in the watering *t,*
30:38 front of the animals that drank from the *t.*
30:41 in the *t* in full view of these animals,
Ex 2:16 fill the *t* to water their father's flock.

TROWEL (1)

Dt 23:14 keep a *t* in your equipment and with it,

TRUE (125)

Gn 24:49 in mind to show *t* loyalty to my master,
Lv 19:36 You shall have a true scale and *t* weights,
Nm 11:16 *t* elders and authorities among the people,
24: 3 the utterance of the man whose eye is *t,*
24:15 the utterance of the man whose eye is *t,*
Dt 1:16 and administer *t* justice to both parties
13:15 If you find that it is *t* and an
16:18 to administer *t* justice for the people
17: 4 that it is *t* and an established fact
21:16 loves, in preference to his *t* first-born,
22:20 "But if this charge is *t,*
25:15 use a *t* and just weight, and a true
Jos 2: 4 two men and hidden them, so she said, *T,*
14:12 *T,* the Anakim are there,
Jgs 13:12 "Now, when that which you say comes *t,*
13:17 we may honor you when your words come *t?*"
1Sm 9: 6 all that he says is sure to come *t.*
12:20 "It is *t* you have committed all this evil;
1Kgs 10: 6 about your deeds and your wisdom is *t,*"
1Chr 11:10 in his reign in order to make him *t* king,
2Chr 9: 5 about your deeds and your wisdom is *t,*"
15: 3 For a long time Israel had no *t* God,
Tb 2:14 Your *t* character is finally showing itself!"
3: 5 your judgments are many and *t* in dealing
14: 6 be converted and shall offer God *t* worship;
Jdt 11:10 his word, but bear it in mind, for it is *t.*
1Mc 14:41 and high priest until a *t* prophet arises.

TRUE (cont.)

2Mc 1: 1 the Jews in Egypt, and wish them *t* peace!
3: 9 and he asked if these things were really *t.*
Ps(s) 19:10 The ordinances of the LORD are *t,*
105:19 pass and the word of the LORD proved him *t.*
Prv 18:24 a *t* friend is more loyal than a brother.
Eccl 12:10 and to write down *t* sayings with precision.
Wis 2:17 Let us see whether his words be *t;*
12:27 *t* God whom before they had refused to know;
15: 1 But you, our God, are good and *t,*
Sir 12:18 and hiss repeatedly, and show his *t* face.
22:23 In time of trouble remain *t* to him,
24:22 *t* of the book of the Most High's covenant,
36:15 in you, and let your prophets be proved *t.*
37: 5 A *t* friend will fight with you against the
40:21 but better than either, a voice that is *t.*
46:15 out and his words proved him *t* as a seer.
Is 25: 1 wonderful plans of old, faithful and *t.*
41:26 beforehand, that we might say it is *t?*
43: 9 that one may hear and say, "It is *t!*"
Jer 8: 6 they speak what is not *t;*
10:10 The LORD is *t* God,
22:16 Is this not *t* knowledge of me?
Ez 16:45 you are the *t* daughter of the mother who
16:45 and you are a *t* sister to those who
17:10 *T,* it is planted, but will it prosper?
Dn 3:14 "Is it *t,* Shadrach, Meshach,
8:26 of the evenings and the mornings is *t,*
Zec 7: 9 Render *t* judgment, and show kindness
Mal 2: 6 *T* doctrine was in his mouth,
Mt 5:18 be done away with until it all comes *t.*
11:26 Father, it is *t.*
Mk 11:32 who all regarded John as a *t* prophet.)
16:20 by spirits to grasp the *t* power of God.
Lk 1:20 They will all come *t* in due season."
12:51 I assure you, the contrary is *t;*
24:34 It is *t!*
Jn 1:47 "This man is a *t* Israelite.
4:18 What you said is *t.*"
8:51 is *t* to my word he shall never see death."
10:41 whatever John said about this man was *t.*"
14:23 "Anyone who loves me will be *t* to my word,
15: 1 the *t* vine and my Father is the vinegrower.
17: 3 to know you, the only *t* God,
19:35 by an eyewitness, and his testimony is *t.*
19:35 He tells what he knows is *t,*
21:24 them down and his testimony, we know, is *t.*
Acts 7: 1 priest asked whether the charges were *t.*
10: 1 The same was *t* of his whole household.
10:34 how *t* it is that God shows no partiality.
12:15 said to her, but she insisted it was *t.*
22:27 rushed in and asked Paul, "Is it *t?*
Rom 2:28 *T* circumcision is not a sign in the flesh.
2:29 and *t* circumcision is of the heart;
3: 4 *t* even though every man be proved a liar,
4:16 holds *t* for all Abraham's descendants,
9: 6 For not all Israelites are *t* Israelites
14:20 *T,* all foods are clean;
1Cor 11:19 for the tried and *t* to stand out clearly.
2Cor 7:14 as everything I ever said to you was *t,*
7:14 to Titus has been proved equally *t.*
13: 4 It is *t* he was crucified out of weakness,
Gal 1:20 God that what I have just written is *t.*
Phil 1:15 It is *t,* some preach Christ from motives
4: 8 be wholly directed to all that is *t,*
1Thes 1: 8 This is *t* not only in Macedonia and Achaia;
1: 9 to serve him who is the living and *t* God
1Tm 1: 2 hope, to Timothy, my own *t* child in faith.
2: 7 the teacher of the nations in the *t* faith.
6: 3 and the teaching proper to *t* religion,
Ti 1: 4 Titus, my own *t* child in our common faith:
3: 3 foolish, disobedient, and far from *t* faith;
3: 8 You can depend on this to be *t.*
Heb 8: 2 sanctuary and of that *t* tabernacle set up,
9:24 made by hands, a mere copy of the *t* one;
12:10 but God does so for our *t* profit,
1Pt 5:12 testimony that this is the *t* grace of God.
5:14 one another with the embrace of *t* love.
2Pt 1: 8 in *t* knowledge of our Lord Jesus Christ.
2: 2 the *t* way will be made subject to contempt.
1Jn 2:27 teaches you about all things and is *t*—
5:17 *T,* all wrongdoing is sin,
5:20 discernment to recognize the One who is *t.*
5:20 And we are in the One who is *t,*
5:20 He is the *t* God and eternal life.
3Jn 1:12 well, and you know that our testimony is *t.*
Rv 3: 7 " 'The holy One, the *t,*
3:14 " 'The Amen, the faithful Witness and *t,*
6:10 long will it be, O Master, holy and *t,*
15: 3 Righteous and *t* are your ways,
16: 7 Almighty, your judgments are *t* and just!"
19: 2 God, for his judgments are *t* and just!
19: 9 The angel continued, "These words are *t;*
19:11 its rider was called "The Faithful and *T.*"
21: 5 down, for the words are trustworthy and *t!*"
22: 6 "These words are trustworthy and *t;*

TRULY (54)

Gn 7: 1 in this age have I found to be *t* just.
28:16 awoke from his sleep, he exclaimed, *T,*
Ex 3: 9 and I have *t* noted that the Egyptians are
Dt 4: 6 nation is *t* a wise and intelligent people.'
11:13 you *t* heed my commandments which I enjoin
1Sm 17:55 replied, "As *t* as your majesty is alive,
1Kgs 8:13 I have *t* built you a princely house,
17:24 word of the LORD comes *t* from your mouth."
2Kgs 9:15 "If you are *t* with me,"
19:17 *T,* O LORD, the kings of Assyria
1Chr 4:10 may *t* bless me and extend my boundaries!
14: 2 had *t* confirmed him as king over Israel,
17:26 are *t* God and have promised this good
2Chr 6: 2 *t* built you a princely house and dwelling,
12:14 for he had not *t* resolved to seek the LORD.
Tb 14: 7 in those days will *t* be mindful of God,
2Mc 7: 6 looking on, and he *t* has compassion on us,
Jb 18: 5 *T,* the light of the wicked is extinguished;
22:20 *T* these have been destroyed where they
Ps(s) 18:49 *T* above my adversaries you exalt me and
58:12 say, *T* there is a reward for the just;
58:12 *t* there is a God who is judge on earth!"
62: 5 *T* from my place on high they plan to
90: 7 *T* we are consumed by your anger,
139:13 *T* you have formed my inmost being;
Prv 11:21 *T* the evil man shall not go unpunished,
17:27 He who spares his words is *t* wise,
22:21 To teach you *t* how to give a dependable
Wis 12: 3 For *t,* the ancient inhabitants of your
13:16 for, *t,* it is an image and needs help.
15: 7 For *t* the potter,
Sir 1: 6 There is but one, wise and *t* awe-inspiring,
42: 8 Thus you will be *t* cautious and recognized
Is 37:18 *T,* O LORD, the kings of Assyria have
45:15 *T* with you God is hidden,
Jer 18:13 *T* horrible things has virgin Israel done!
28: 9 peace is recognized as *t* sent by the LORD
42: 5 we will *t* and faithfully follow all the
Ez 24:25 As for you, son of man, *t,*
36: 5 *T,* with burning jealousy I speak against
Dn 2:47 *T* your God is the God of gods and Lord of
Am 4: 2 *T* the days are coming upon you When they
5:14 Then *t* will the LORD,
Jn 8:31 to my teaching, you are *t* my disciples;
10: 1 *T* I assure you:
13:38 "I tell you *t,* the cock will not crow
14:28 If you *t* loved me you would rejoice to
16:20 "I tell you *t:*
1Cor 14:25 God, crying out, "God is *t* among you."
Eph 2:10 We are *t* his handiwork,
1Thes 2:13 it, not as the word of men, but as it *t* is,
1Jn 2: 5 *t* has the love of God been made perfect in
3Jn 1: 3 to how *t* you walk in the path of truth.
Rv 3:18 refined by fire if you would be *t* rich.

TRUMPET (58)

Ex 19:16 over the mountain, and a very loud *t* blast,
19:19 The *t* blast grew louder and louder,
20:18 the *t* blast and the mountain smoking,
Lv 23:24 and with the *t* blasts as a reminder;
25: 9 day of the seventh month let the *t* resound;
25: 9 *t* blast shall re-echo throughout your land.
Nm 29: 1 it shall be a day on which you sound the *t.*
2Kgs 9:13 under Jehu on the bare steps, blew the *t,*
Neh 4:14 wherever you hear the *t* sound,
1Mc 4:13 battle, and the men with Judas blew the *t.*
5:31 to heaven with *t* blasts and loud shouting,
Jb 39:24 he holds not back at the sound of the *t,*
Ps(s) 47: 6 the LORD, amid *t* blasts.
81: 4 Blow the *t* at the new moon,
150: 3 Praise him with the blast of the *t,*
Is 18: 3 When the *t* blows, listen!
27:13 On that day, A great *t* shall blow,
58: 1 lift up your voice like a *t* blast;
Jer 4: 5 Blow the *t* through the land,
4:19 For I have heard the sound of the *t,*
4:21 must I see that signal, hear that *t* sound!
6: 1 Blow the *t* in Tekoa,
6:17 "Hearken to the sound of the *t!*"
42:14 no more of war, hear the *t* alarm no longer,
51:27 on the earth, blow the *t* among the nations;
Ez 7:14 sound the *t* and make everything ready,
33: 3 country, blows the *t* to warn the people,
33: 4 but not heeding the warning of the *t*
33: 5 the *t* blast yet refused to take warning;
33: 6 coming and fails to blow the warning *t,*
Dn 3: 4 when you hear the sound of the *t,*
3: 7 as soon as they heard the sound of the *t,*
3:10 everyone who heard the sound of the *t,*
3:15 whenever you hear the sound of the *t,*
Hos 5: 8 Blow the horn in Gibeah, the *t* in Ramah!
8: 1 A *t* to your lips,
Jl 2: 1 Blow the *t* in Zion, sound the alarm
2:15 Blow the *t* in Zion!
Am 2: 2 and uproar amid shouts and *t* blasts.
3: 6 If a *t* sounds in a city,
Zep 1:16 a day of *t* blasts and battle alarm
Zec 9:14 The Lord GOD shall sound the *t,*
Mt 24:31 dispatch his angels 'with a mighty *t* blast,
1Cor 15:52 of an eye, at the sound of the last *t.*
15:52 The *t* will sound and the dead will be
1Thes 4:16 of the archangel's voice and God's *t;*
Heb 12:19 nor gloomy darkness and storm and *t* blast,
Rv 1:10 me a piercing voice like the sound of a *t,*
8: 7 When the first angel blew his *t,*
8: 8 When the second angel blew his *t,*
8:10 When the third angel blew his *t,*
8:12 When the fourth angel blew his *t,*
8:13 from the *t* blasts the other three angels
9: 1 Then the fifth angel blew his *t,*
9:13 Then the sixth angel blew his *t,*
9:14 sixth angel, who was still holding his *t,*
10: 7 comes for the seventh angel to blow his *t,*
11:15 Then the seventh angel blew his *t.*

TRUMPETER (1)

Neh 4:13 Also, a *t* stood beside me,

TRUMPETERS (5)

2Kgs 11:14 custom, and the captains and *t* near him,
1Chr 16: 6 *t* before the ark of the covenant of God.
2Chr 5:13 When the *t* and singers were heard as a
23:13 the officers and the *t* around him,
Rv 18:22 harpists and minstrels, of flutists and *t,*

TRUMPETLIKE (1)

Rv 4: 1 the *t* voice which had spoken to me before.

TRUMPETS (38)

Nm 10: 2 "Make two *t* of beaten silver,
10: 8 Aaron, the priests, who shall blow the *t;*
10: 9 you, you shall sound the alarm on the *t,*
10:10 you shall blow the *t* over your holocausts
31: 6 vessels and the *t* for sounding the alarm.
2Kgs 11:14 of the land rejoicing and blowing *t,*
12:14 to make silver cups, snuffers, basins, *t,*
1Chr 13: 8 lyres, harps, tambourines, cymbals, and *t.*
15:24 sounded the *t* before the ark of God.
15:28 joyful shouting, to the sound of horns, *t,*
16:42 with *t* and cymbals for accompaniment,
2Chr 5:12 a hundred and twenty priests blowing *t.*
5:13 and when they raised the sound of the *t,*
7: 6 priests blew the *t* and all Israel stood.
13:12 with *t* to sound the attack against you.
13:14 to the LORD and the priests sounded the *t.*
15:14 voice with shouting and with *t* and horns.
20:28 house of the LORD, with harps, lyres and *t.*
23:13 of the land rejoicing and blowing *t,*
29:26 of David, and the priests with the *t.*
29:27 of the *t* and the instruments of David,
29:28 *t* until the holocaust had been completed.
Ezr 3:10 vested priests with the *t* and the Levites,
Neh 12:35 and Jeremiah, priests with the *t,*
12:41 Elioenai, Zechariah, Hananiah, with the *t,*
1Mc 3:54 Then they blew the *t* and cried out loudly.
4:40 And when the signal was given with *t,*
5:33 blowing their *t* and shouting in prayer.
6:33 prepared for battle, while the *t* sounded.
7:45 blowing the *t* behind them as signals.
9:12 the phalanx attacked as they blew their *t.*
9:12 who were on Judas' side also blew their *t.*
16: 8 They blew the *t,* and Cendebeus and his
2Mc 15:25 to the sound of *t* and battle songs.
Ps(s) 98: 6 With *t* and the sound of the horn sing
Sir 50:16 the priests, on their *t* of beaten metal;
Rv 8: 2 in God's presence were given seven *t.*
8: 6 with the seven *t* made ready to blow them.

TRUNK (5)

1Sm 5: 4 lying on the threshold, his *t* alone intact.
2Kgs 6: 5 While one of them was felling a tree *t,*
Is 6:13 *t* remains when its leaves have fallen.
6:13 [Holy offspring is the *t*
Ez 31:13 fallen *t* rested all the birds of the air,

TRUST (144)

Nm 12: 7 Throughout my house he bears my *t:*
Dt 1:32 Despite this, you would not *t* the LORD,
9:23 your God, and would not *t* or obey him.
28:52 *t* in come tumbling down all over your land.
Jgs 9:26 The citizens of Shechem put their *t* in him,
1Sm 30: 6 But with renewed *t* in the LORD his God,
2Kgs 5:18 *t* the LORD will forgive your servant this:
6:33 Why should I *t* in the LORD any longer?"
12:16 workmen, because they held positions of *t.*
18: 5 He put his *t* in the LORD,
22: 7 to them, because they held positions of *t.*
1Chr 5:20 them because they had put their *t* in him.
9:22 established them in their position of *t.*
2Chr 20:20 *T* in the LORD,
20:20 *T* in his prophets and you will succeed."
Tb 5: 2 to make him recognize me and *t* me,
1Mc 1:30 in peaceful terms, and won their *t.*
7: 7 send a man whom you *t* to go and see all
10:37 of *t* in the affairs of the kingdom.
2Mc 2:18 We *t* in God,
3:12 who had placed their *t* in the sanctity
3:22 secure for those who had placed them in *t,*
7:40 undefiled, putting all his *t* in the Lord.
8:18 "They *t* in weapons and acts of daring,"
8:18 he said, "but we *t* in almighty God,
Jb 4:18 Lo, he puts no *t* in his servants,
8:14 thread and his *t* is a spider's web.
31:24 *t* in gold or called fine gold my security;
39:11 Will you *t* him for his great strength and
Ps(s) 4: 6 Offer just sacrifices, and *t* in the LORD.

9:11 They *t* in you who cherish your name,
25: 2 In you I *t;* let me not be put to shame,
26: 1 and in the LORD I *t* without wavering,
27: 3 war be waged upon me, even then will I *t.*
31: 7 vain idols, but my *t* is in the LORD.
31:15 But my *t* is in you, O LORD; I say,
33:21 in his holy name we *t.*
37: 3 *T* in the LORD and do good,
37: 5 Commit to the LORD your way; *t* in him,
40: 4 shall look on in awe and *t* in the LORD.
40: 5 Happy the man who makes the LORD his *t;*
41:10 who had my *t* and partook of my bread,
44: 7 For not in my bow did I *t,*
49: 7 They *t* in their wealth;
49:14 This is the way of those whose *t* is folly,
52: 9 But put his *t* in his great wealth,
52:10 *T* in the kindness of God forever and ever.
55:24 But I *t* in you, O LORD.
56: 4 when I begin to fear, in you will I *t.*
56: 5 promise I glory, in God I *t* without fear;
56:12 promise I glory, in God I *t* without fear;
62: 9 *T* in him at all times, O my people!
62:11 *T* not in extortion;
71: 5 my *t,* O GOD, from my youth.
84:13 LORD of hosts, happy the men who *t* in you!
91: 2 and my fortress, my God, in whom I *t.*"
93: 5 Your decrees are worthy of *t* indeed:
115:11 Those who fear the LORD *t* in the LORD;
118: 8 take refuge in the LORD than to *t* in man.
118: 9 refuge in the LORD than to *t* in princes.
119:42 who reproach me, for I *t* in your words.
119:66 and knowledge, for in your commands I *t.*
125: 1 They who *t* in the LORD are like Mount Zion,
130: 5 I *t* in the LORD; my soul trusts
143: 8 me hear of your kindness, for in you I *t.*
144: 2 my deliverer, My shield, in whom I *t,*
146: 3 Put not your *t* in princes,
Prv 3: 5 *T* in the LORD with all your heart,
20: 6 but who can find one worthy of *t?*
20:22 *T* in the LORD and he will help you.
22:19 That your *t* may be in the LORD,
26:25 When he speaks graciously, *t* him not,
Wis 3: 9 Those who *t* in him shall understand truth,
14: 5 men *t* their lives even to frailest wood.
14:29 For as their *t* is in soulless idols,
16:24 relaxed in benefit for those who *t* in you.
Sir 2: 6 *T* God and he will help you;
2: 8 You who fear the LORD, *t* him,
2:13 Woe to the faint of heart who *t* not,
6: 7 be not too ready to *t* him
7:26 but where there is ill-feeling, *t* her not.
11:21 but *t* in the LORD and wait for his light;
12:10 Never *t* your enemy,
13:11 discussion with him, *t* not his many words;
15: 4 he will *t* in her and not be put to shame.
34:15 In whom does he *t,* and who is his support?
35:11 *T* not in sacrifice of the fruits of
36:26 Who will *t* an armed band that shifts from
Is 8:17 For I will *t* in the LORD,
26: 3 in peace, for its *t* in you."
26: 4 *T* in the LORD forever!
30:12 put your *t* in what is crooked and devious,
30:15 in quiet and in *t* your strength lies.
31: 1 *t* in chariots because of their number,
42:17 turned back in utter shame who *t* in idols;
59: 4 They *t* in emptiness and tell lies;
Jer 2:37 the LORD has rejected those in whom you *t,*
5:17 sword the fortified city in which you *t.*
7: 4 Put not your *t* in the deceitful words:
7: 8 your *t* in deceitful words to your own loss!
7:14 this house named after me, in which you *t,*
9: 3 put no *t* in any brother.
46:25 her kings, Pharaoh, and those who *t* in him.
49: 4 You who *t* in your treasures,
49:11 your widows, let them *t* in me.
Bar 3:17 up the silver and the gold in which men *t;*
Ez 29:16 they be for the house of Israel to *t* in,
Dn 3:40 those who *t* in you cannot be put to shame.
Mi 7: 5 Put no *t* in a friend,
7: 7 the LORD, I will put my *t* in God my savior;
Hb 2:18 oracle, that its very maker should *t* in it,
Mal 3:16 those who fear the LORD and *t* in his name.
Mt 17:20 "Because you have so little *t,*"
21:21 "Believe me, if you *t* and do not falter,
Mk 5:36 What is needed is *t.*"
9:24 Help my lack of *t!*"
11:22 "Put your *t* in God.
Lk 8:50 is needed is *t* and her life will be spared."
12:46 and rank him among those undeserving of *t.*
16:10 If you can *t* a man in little things,
16:10 things, you can also *t* him in greater;
16:11 wealth, who will *t* you with lasting?
18:17 *T* me when I tell you that whoever does not
Jn 2:24 *t* himself to them because he knew them all.
4:50 put his *t* in the word Jesus spoke to him,
Acts 3:16 It is his name, and *t* in this name,
10: 7 soldier from among those whom he could *t.*
27:25 I *t* in God that it will all work out just
Rom 15:24 I *t* that you will send me on my journey
1Cor 13: 7 no limit to love's forbearance, to its *t,*
2Cor 1: 9 condemned to death so that we might *t,*
7:16 I rejoice because I *t* you utterly.
8:22 this work because of his great *t* in you.
9: 4 for having had this *t.*
Gal 5:10 I *t* that, in the Lord, you will not adopt
Phil 1:20 I firmly *t* and anticipate that I shall
3: 3 rather than putting our *t* in the flesh
3: 4 a right to put his *t* in external evidence,
1Tm 6:17 Let them *t* in the God who provides us
Heb 2:13 and "I will put my *t* in him";
10:23 he who made the promise deserves our *t*
11:11 who had made the promise was worthy of *t.*
1Jn 4: 1 Beloved, do not *t* every spirit,

TRUSTED (24)

1Sm 27:12 And Achish *t* David,
1Mc 7:16 So they *t* him.
Jb 12:20 He silences the *t* adviser,
Ps(s) 13: 6 my downfall though I *t* in your kindness.
22: 5 In you our fathers *t;*
22: 5 they *t,* and you delivered them.
22: 6 in you they *t,* and they were not put
78:22 they believed not God nor *t* in his help.
Sir 27:16 He who betrays a secret cannot be *t,*
Jer 13:25 have forgotten me, and *t* in the lying idol,
39:18 be spared as booty, because you *t* in me,
48: 7 you *t* in your works and your treasures,
48:13 was disappointed by Bethel in which they *t.*
Bar 4:22 have *t* in the Eternal God for your welfare,
Dn 3:95 to deliver the servants that *t* in him;
6:24 the den, unhurt because he *t* in his God.
13:35 for she *t* in the Lord wholeheartedly.
Hos 10:13 Because you have *t* in your chariots,
Zep 3: 2 In the LORD she has not *t,*
Mt 8:13 It shall be done because you *t.*"
Lk 1:20 place, because you have not *t* my words.
1:45 Blest is she who *t* that the Lord's words
16:11 If you cannot be *t* with elusive wealth,
1Jn 1: 9 he who is just can be *t* to forgive our

TRUSTING (8)

Jgs 18: 7 the manner of the Sidonians, quiet and *t,*
18:10 Those against whom you go are a *t* people,
18:27 they attacked Laish, a quiet and *t* people;
20:36 *t* in the ambush they had set at Gibeah.
Jdt 9: 7 of their infantry, *t* in shield and spear,
Ps(s) 112: 7 his heart is firm, *t* in the LORD.
Is 50:10 *T* in the name of the LORD and relying on
Jer 11:19 Yet I, like a *t* lamb led to slaughter,

TRUSTS (22)

Ps(s) 21: 8 For the king *t* in the LORD,
28: 7 In him my heart *t,* and I find help;
32:10 who *t* in the LORD.
86: 2 save your servant who *t* in you.
115: 8 be like them, everyone that *t* in them.
115: 9 The house of Israel *t* in the LORD;
115:10 The house of Aaron *t* in the LORD;
130: 5 my soul *t* in his word.
135:18 be like them, everyone that *t* in them.
Prv 11:28 He who *t* in his riches will fall,
16:20 happy is he who *t* in the LORD!
21:22 overthrows the stronghold in which it *t.*
28:25 but he who *t* in the LORD will prosper.
28:26 He who *t* in himself is a fool,
29:25 a snare, but he who *t* in the LORD is safe.
Sir 4:16 If one *t* her, he will possess her;
19: 4 He who lightly *t* in them has no sense,
32:24 *t* in the LORD shall not be put to shame.
33: 3 The prudent man *t* in the word of the LORD,
Jer 17: 5 Cursed is the man who *t* in human beings,
17: 7 Blessed is the man who *t* in the LORD,
Mk 9:23 Everything is possible to a man who *t.*"

TRUSTWORTHINESS (1)

Sir 45: 4 For his *t* and meekness God selected him

TRUSTWORTHY (22)

Ex 18:21 men, *t* men who hate dishonest gain,
Neh 7: 2 was a more *t* and God-fearing man than most.
13:13 for these men were held to be *t.*
Tb 5: 3 a *t* man who will make the journey with you.
5: 9 whether he is *t* enough to travel with you,
10: 6 The man who is traveling with him is *t,*
Jdt 10:13 of your forces, to give him a *t* report;
Ps(s) 19: 8 The decree of the LORD is *t,*
33: 4 word of the LORD, and all his works are *t.*
Prv 11:13 secrets, but a *t* man keeps a confidence.
13:17 but a *t* envoy is a healing remedy.
28:20 The *t* man will be richly blessed;
Sir 46:15 As a *t* prophet he was sought out and his
Dn 6: 5 because he was *t,* no fault of neglect
Lk 16:12 have not been *t* with someone else's money,
1Cor 4: 2 of an administrator is that he prove *t.*
7:25 but I give my opinion as one who is *t,*
1Thes 5:24 He who calls us is *t,*
1Tm 3:11 They should be temperate and entirely *t.*
2Tm 2: 2 to *t* men who will be able to teach others.
Rv 21: 5 matters down, for the words are *t* and true!"
22: 6 "These words are *t* and true;

TRUTH (157)

Gn 20:12 Besides, she is in *t* my sister,
40:15 The *t* is that I was kidnaped from the land
42:16 shall your words be tested for their *t;*
2Sm 7:28 GOD, you are God and your words are *t;*
1Kgs 22:16 nothing but the *t* in the name of the LORD?
2Chr 18:15 nothing but the *t* in the name of the LORD?"
Tb 1: 3 life on the paths of *t* and righteousness.
3: 2 All your ways are mercy and *t;*
3: 5 have we trodden the paths of *t* before you.
5:14 wanting to learn the *t* about your family.
12:11 "I will now tell you the whole *t;*
Jdt 5: 5 I will tell you the *t* about this people
1Mc 7:18 "There is no *t* or justice among them;
8:13 In *t* those whom they desired to help to a
2Mc 6:17 these words suffice for recalling this *t.*
Ps(s) 15: 2 who thinks the *t* in his heart and
25: 5 paths, Guide me in your *t* and teach me,
26: 3 is before my eyes, and I walk in your *t.*
40:11 kindness and your *t* in the vast assembly.
40:12 your kindness and your *t* ever preserve me.
45: 5 the cause of *t* and for the sake of justice;
85:11 Kindness and *t* shall meet;
85:12 *T* shall spring out of the earth,
86:11 LORD, your way that I may walk in your *t;*
89:15 kindness and *t* go before you.
111: 8 forever and ever, wrought in *t* and equity.
115: 1 of your kindness, because of your *t.*
119:30 The way of *t* I have chosen;
119:43 Take not the word of *t* from my mouth,
119:90 Through all generations your *t* endures;
138: 2 name, Because of your kindness and your *t;*
145:18 upon him, to all who call upon him in *t.*
Prv 8: 7 Yes, the *t* my mouth recounts,
12:17 tells the *t* who states what he is sure of,
23:23 Get the *t,* and sell it not— wisdom,
Wis 3: 9 Those who trust in him shall understand *t,*
5: 6 We, then, have strayed from the way of *t,*
6:22 of her, nor shall I diverge from the *t.*
Sir 4:25 Never gainsay the *t,*
4:28 Even to the death fight for *t,*
34: 4 can the liar ever speak the *t?*
37:15 to God to set your feet in the path of *t.*
48:22 prophet Isaiah, who saw the *t* in visions.
Is 10:20 the LORD, the Holy One of Israel, in *t.*
59:14 For *t* stumbles in the public square,
65:16 in the land shall swear by the God of *t;*
Jer 4: 2 can swear, "As the LORD lives," in *t,*
9: 2 with lying, and not with *t,*
9: 4 deceives the other, no one speaks the *t.*
26:15 in *t* it was the LORD who sent me to you,
Ez 18:18 his people, shall in *t* die for his sins.
Dn 7:16 and asked him what all this meant in *t;*
8:12 It cast *t* to the ground,
11: 2 Now I shall tell you the *t.*
Am 5:10 the gate and abhor him who speaks the *t.*
Zec 8:16 Speak the *t* to one another;
Mk 5:33 in front of him and told him the whole *t.*
16:20 they might return to the *t* and sin no more,
Lk 12: 7 In very *t,* even the hairs of your head
20:21 of persons but teach the way of God in *t.*
Jn 3:21 But he who acts in *t* comes into the light,
4:23 will worship the Father in Spirit and *t.*
4:24 worship him must worship in Spirit and *t.*"
5:33 sent to John, who has testified to the *t.*
7:28 The *t* is, I have not come of myself.
8:32 the truth, and the *t* will set you free."
8:40 told you the *t* which I have heard from God.
8:44 and has never based himself on *t;*
8:44 the *t* is not in him.
8:45 But because I deal in the *t,*
8:46 If I am telling the *t,* why do you not
14: 6 "I am the way, and the *t,*
14:17 the Spirit of *t,* whom the world cannot
15:26 the Spirit of *t* who comes from the Father
16: 7 Yet I tell you the sober *t:*
16:13 Spirit of truth he will guide you to all *t.*
17: 8 They have known that in *t* I came from you,
17:17 Consecrate them by means of *t*—
17:17 'Your word is *t.*'
17:19 now, that they may be consecrated in *t.*
18:23 evidence, but if I spoke the *t* why hit me?"
18:37 into the world, is to testify to the *t.*
18:37 Anyone committed to the *t* hears my voice."
18:38 *T!*" said Pilate. "What does that mean?"
Acts 20:30 *t* and leading astray any who follow them.
21:34 not get at the *t* because of the uproar,
26:25 The message I proclaim is the sober *t.*
Rom 1:18 in this perversity of theirs, hinder the *t.*
1:25 these men who exchanged the *t* of God for a
2: 8 disobey the *t* and obey wickedness.
2:20 at hand a clear pattern of knowledge and *t.*
3: 7 light God's *t* and thus promotes his glory,
9: 1 I speak the *t* in Christ:
1Cor 5: 8 the unleavened bread of sincerity and *t.*
13: 6 in what is wrong but rejoices with the *t.*
2Cor 4: 2 We proclaim the *t* openly and commend
6: 7 with the message of *t* and the power of God;
12: 6 me because I would only be telling the *t.*
13: 8 We cannot do anything against the *t,*
13: 8 the truth, but only for the sake of the *t.*
Gal 2: 5 We resisted so that the *t* of the gospel
2:14 straightforward about the *t* of the gospel,
4:16 your enemy just because I tell you the *t?*
5: 7 who diverted you from the path of *t?*
Eph 1:13 glad tidings of salvation, the word of *t,*

TRUTH (cont.)

4:15 let us profess the t in love and and the
4:21 you in accord with the t that is in Jesus:
4:24 whose justice and holiness are born of t.
4:25 let everyone speak the t to his neighbor,
5: 9 every kind of goodness and justice and t.
6:14 with the t as the belt around your waist,
Col 1: 5 of this hope through the message of t,
2Thes 2:10 their hearts to the t in order to be saved.
2:12 so that all who have not believed the t
2:13 in holiness of spirit and fidelity to t.
1Tm 2: 4 men to be saved and come to know the t.
2: 5 And the t is this: "God is one.
2: 6 This t was attested at the fitting time.
2: 7 me, I am not lying but speak the t),
3:15 living God, the pillar and bulwark of t.
4: 3 thanksgiving by believers who know the t.
6: 5 twisted minds who have lost all sense of t.
2Tm 2:15 a straight course in preaching the t.
2:18 who have gone far wide of the t in saying
2:25 will enable them to repent and know the t.
3: 7 never able to reach a knowledge of the t.
3: 8 Moses, so these men also oppose the t;
4: 4 to the t and will wander off to fables.
Ti 1: 1 of the t as our religion embodies it.
1:12 lazy gluttons," and that is the simple t!
1:14 by men who have swerved from the t.
Phlm 1:11 He has become in t Onesimus [Useful],
Heb 10:26 If we sin willfully after receiving the t,
Jas 1:18 bring us to birth with a word spoken in t
3:14 arrogant and false claims against the t.
5:19 among you of someone straying from the t,
1Pt 1:22 By obedience to the t you have purified
2Pt 1:12 and are firmly rooted in the t you possess.
1Jn 1: 6 darkness, we are liars and do not act in t.
1: 8 the t is not to be found in us.
2: 4 in such a one there is no t.
2:21 that you do not know the t but that you do,
2:21 no lie has anything in common with the t.
3:18 deed and in t and not merely talk about it.
3:19 are committed to the t and are at peace
4: 6 spirit of t from the spirit of deception.
5: 6 who testifies to this, and the Spirit is t.
2Jn 1: 1 In t I love each of you
1: 1 also all those who have come to know the t.
1: 2 This love is based on the t that abides in
1: 3 In t and love, then, we shall have grace,
1: 4 your children walking in the path of t,
3Jn 1: 3 to how truly you walk in the path of t.
1: 8 thus to have our share in the work of t.
1:12 testimonial from all, even from t itself.

TRUTHFUL (12)

Prv 12:19 T lips endure forever,
12:22 LORD, but those who are t are his delight.
14: 5 A t witness does not lie,
14:25 The t witness saves lives,
Dn 10:21 tell you what is written in the t book.
Mt 22:16 are a t man and teach God's way sincerely.
Mk 12:14 "Teacher, we know you are a t man,
Jn 3:33 this testimony certifies that God is t.
7:18 who seeks glory for him who sent him is t;
8:26 have heard from him, the t One who sent me."
2Cor 6: 8 We are called imposters, yet we are t;
1Tm 3: 8 must be serious, straightforward, and t.

TRUTHFULLY (3)

Tb 5:12 "I wish to know t whose son you are,
Is 59: 4 one brings suit justly, no one pleads t;
Jer 23:28 let him who has my word speak my word t!

TRY (34)

Gn 44:16 we plead or how t to prove our innocence?
Jgs 3: 1 so that through them he might t all those
1Chr 14:14 "Do not t to pursue them,
Tb 2: 2 go out and t to find a poor man from among
Jdt 8:27 put them in the crucible to t their hearts,
1Mc 7:15 will not t to injure you or your friends."
9:71 t to injure him for the rest of his life;
2Mc 2:23 we will t to condense into a single book.
Jb 7:18 each new day and t him at every moment!
Ps(s) 17: 3 it in the night, though you t me with fire,
26: 2 wavering, Search me, O LORD, and t me;
139:23 t me, and know my thoughts;
Eccl 2: 1 let me t you with pleasure and the
Wis 2:19 proof of his gentleness and t his patience.
Is 3:13 rises to accuse, standing to t his people.
22: 4 Do not t to comfort me for the ruin of the
Mal 3:10 may be food in my house, and t me in this,
Mt 15:10 "Give ear and t to understand.
Mk 7:14 "Hear me, all of you, and t to understand.
9:39 "Do not t to stop him.
15:36 stuck it on a reed to t to make him drink.
Lk 12:58 t to settle with him on the way lest he
13:24 T to come in through the narrow door.
13:24 I tell you, will t to enter and be unable.
1Cor 4:13 We are slandered, and we t conciliation.
7:18 He should not t to hide his circumcision.
10:33 just as I t to please all in any way I can
14:12 t to be rich in those that build up the
2Cor 5:11 in awe of the Lord we t to persuade men,
Eph 5:17 but t to discern the will of the Lord.
1Thes 2:16 they t to keep us from preaching salvation
2Tm 2:15 T hard to make yourself worthy of God's
Ti 2: 9 They should t to please them in every way,
1Jn 2:26 things about those who t to deceive you.

TRYING (34)

1Sm 19: 2 "My father Saul is t to kill you.
24:10 to those who say, 'David is t to harm you'?
Neh 3:34 "What are these miserable Jews t to do?
6: 9 They were all t to frighten us,
6:14 other prophets who were t to frighten me.
6:19 and Tobiah sent letters t to frighten me.
1Mc 6:18 continually t to harm them and to
Ez 33: 9 the wicked man, t to turn him from his way,
Mt 16:23 You are t to make me trip and fall.
22:18 to them, "Why are you t to trip me up,
23:13 nor admitting those who are t to enter.
26:59 were busy t to obtain false testimony
Mk 12:15 to them, "Why are you t to trip me up?
Lk 5:18 t to bring him in and lay him before Jesus;
6:19 the whole crowd was t to touch him because
13:31 Herod is t to kill you."
14: 7 t to get the places of honor at the table:
19: 3 He was t to see what Jesus was like,
Jn 8:37 you are t to kill me because my word finds
8:40 The fact is, you are t to kill me,
10: 6 did not grasp what he was t to tell them.
11: 8 the Jews only recently t to stone you,
Acts 7:26 Why are you t to hurt each other?'
9:29 for their part responded by t to kill him.
10:17 While Peter was t to make out the meaning
13:10 Will you never stop t to make crooked the
15:10 do you put God to the test by t to place
17:18 "What is this magpie t to say to us?"
Rom 11:14 t to rouse my fellow Jews to envy and save
Gal 1:10 you say I am t to please at this point
1:10 If I were t to win man's approval,
6: 1 t to avoid falling into temptation himself.
6:12 Those who are t to force you to be
2Pt 3:12 of the day of God and t to hasten it!

TRYPHAENA (1)

Rom 16:12 Greetings, too, to T and Tryphosa,

TRYPHO (23)

1Mc 11:39 When a certain T,
11:40 T kept urging Imalkue to hand over the boy
11:54 After this T returned and brought with him
11:56 T captured the elephants and occupied
12:39 T was determined to become king of Asia,
12:42 But when T saw that Jonathan had arrived
12:49 T sent soldiers and cavalry to Galilee and
13: 1 When Simon heard that T was gathering a
13:12 Then T moved from Ptolemais with a large
13:14 When T learned that Simon had succeeded
13:18 would not send T the money and the boys.
13:19 but T broke his promise and would not let
13:21 men in the citadel sent messengers to T,
13:22 Although T got all his cavalry ready to go,
13:24 Then T returned to his own country.
13:31 T dealt treacherously with the young King
13:34 for all that T did was to plunder the land.
14: 1 to obtain help so that he could fight T.
15:10 to him, so that few were left with T.
15:11 Pursued by Antiochus, T fled to Dor,
15:25 He blockaded T by preventing anyone from
15:37 T had gotten aboard a ship and escaped to
15:39 Meanwhile the king went in pursuit of T.

TRYPHOSA (1)

Rom 16:12 Greetings, too, to Tryphaena and T,

TUANTS (1)

Prv 27:11 and I will be able to rebut him who t me.

TUBAL (8)

Gn 10: 2 Gomer, Magog, Madai, Javan, T,
1Chr 1: 5 were Gomer, Magog, Madai, Javan, T,
Is 66:19 Tarshish, Put and Lud, Mosoch, T and Javan,
Ez 27:13 Javan, T, and Meshech were also traders
32:26 and T and all their throng about her grave,
38: 2 Magog], the chief prince of Meshech and T,
38: 3 at you, Gog, chief prince of Meshech and T.
39: 1 at you, Gog, chief prince of Meshech and T.

TUBALCAIN (2)

Gn 4:22 Zillah, on her part, gave birth to T,
4:22 The sister of T was Naamah.

TUBES (2)

Jb 40:18 His bones are like t of bronze;
Zec 4: 2 "on it are seven lamps with their t,

TUFTS (1)

Zec 4:12 "What are the two olive t which freely

TUG (2)

Is 5:18 who t at guilt with cords of perversity,
Jas 1:14 the t and lure of his own passion tempt

TUMBLE (1)

Ez 38:20 shall be overturned, and cliffs shall t,

TUMBLES (2)

Gn 49:17 horse's heel, so that the rider t backward.
Is 26: 5 He t it to the ground,

TUMBLEWEED (1)

Is 17:13 chaff on the mountains, like t in a storm.

TUMBLING (1)

Dt 28:52 trust in come t down all over your land.

TUMORS (1)

Dt 28:27 strike you with Egyptian boils and with t,

TUMULT (9)

1Sm 14:19 t in the Philistine camp kept increasing.
Est A: 4 There was noise and t,
1Mc 13:44 into the city and caused a great t there.
Ps(s) 64: 3 malefactors, against the t of evildoers,
65: 8 of their waves and the t of the peoples.
83: 3 For behold, your enemies raise a t,
93: 3 the floods lift up their t.
Ez 1:24 sound of the t was like the din of an army.
Zec 14:13 be among them a great t from the LORD:

TUMULTUOUS (2)

2Mc 15:29 so they raised t shouts in their native
Lk 8:24 awoke and rebuked the wind and the t waves.

TUNE (3)

Hb 3: 1 To a plaintive t.
Mt 11:17 'We piped you a t but you did not dance!
Lk 7:32 'We piped you a t but you did not dance,

TUNES (1)

Rv 18:22 No t of harpists and minstrels,

TUNIC (25)

Gn 37: 3 and he made him a long t.
37:23 they stripped him of the long t he had on;
37:31 They took Joseph's t,
37:31 a goat, dipped the t in its blood.
37:32 to bring the long t to their father,
37:32 See whether it is your son's t or not."
37:33 "My son's t!
Ex 28: 4 an ephod, a robe, a brocaded t,
28:39 "The t of fine linen shall be brocaded.
29: 5 the vestments and clothe Aaron with the t,
Lv 8: 7 Then he put the t on Aaron,
16: 4 He shall wear the sacred linen t,
1Sm 17:38 Then Saul clothed David in his own t,
17:39 himself with Saul's sword over the t.
2Sm 13:18 Now she had on a long t,
13:19 tore the long t in which she was clothed.
20: 8 Now Joab had a belt over his t,
2Mc 12:40 But under the t of each of the dead they
Jb 30:18 by the collar of my t he seizes me:
Sir 45: 8 Breeches and t and robe with pomegranates
Bar 6:30 with torn t and with shaven hair and beard,
Mi 2: 8 t Of those who go their way in confidence,
Mk 6: 9 "Do not bring a second t,"
Jn 19:23 There was also his t,
19:23 but this t was woven in one piece from top

TUNICS (10)

Ex 28:40 shall have t and sashes and turbans made.
29: 8 his sons also and clothe them with the t,
39:27 sons there were also woven t of fine linen;
40:14 his sons also, and clothe them with the t.
Lv 8:13 forward Aaron's sons, clothed them with t,
10: 5 So they went in and took them, in their t,
Jgs 14:12 thirty linen t and thirty sets of garments.
14:13 me thirty t and thirty sets of garments."
Jdt 14:19 their t and were seized with consternation.
Is 3:23 the mirrors, linen t,

TURBAN (4)

Jb 29:14 justice was my robe and my t.
Sir 45:12 On his t the diadem of gold,
Ez 21:31 Off with the t and away with the crown!
24:17 no lament for the dead, bind on your t,

TURBANS (9)

Ex 28:40 shall have tunics and sashes and t made.
29: 9 with the sashes, and tie the t on them.
39:28 the ornate t of fine linen;
Lv 8:13 girded them with sashes, and put t on them,
Jdt 4:15 With ashes upon their t,
Is 3:23 the mirrors, linen tunics, t,
Ez 23:15 their waists, flowing t on their heads,

24:23 Your t shall remain on your heads,
44:18 They shall have linen t on their heads and

TURBULENT (2)

Jon 1:11 For the sea was growing more and more t.
1:13 could not, for the sea grew ever more t.

TURMOIL (7)

1Sm 5: 9 the LORD threw the city into utter t:
Ps(s) 46: 7 Though nations are in t,
Prv 15: 6 but the earnings of the wicked are in t.
Wis 14:25 and guile, corruption, faithlessness, t,
Is 14: 4 how the t is stilled!
Hos 10:14 T shall break out among your tribes and
Acts 21:30 Before long the whole city was in t.

TURN (336)

Gn 4:26 To Seth, in t, a son was born,
24:12 let it t out favorably for me today and
27:20 your God, let things t out well with me."
37:30 And I—where can I t?"
47:19 and that our land may not t into a waste."
Ex 7: 2 In t, your brother Aaron shall tell
7:11 Pharaoh, in t, summoned wise men
9: 9 It will then t into fine dust over the
14: 2 to t about and camp before Pi-hahiroth,
23:27 make all your enemies t from you in flight,
Lv 19: 4 "Do not t aside to idols,
20: 3 I myself will t against such a man and cut
20: 6 Should anyone t to mediums and
20: 6 I will t against such a one and cut him
26:16 and breaking my covenant, then I, in t,
26:17 I will t against you,
Nm 7:24 On the third day it was the t of Eliab,
7:30 On the fourth day it was the t of Elizur,
7:36 On the fifth day it was the t of Shelumiel,
7:42 On the sixth day it was the t of Eliasaph,
7:48 the seventh day it was the t of Elishama,
7:54 On the eighth day it was the t of Gamaliel,
7:60 On the ninth day it was the t of Abidon,
7:66 On the tenth day it was the t of Ahiezer,
7:72 On the eleventh day it was the t of Pagiel,
7:78 On the twelfth day it was the t of Ahira,
8:12 The Levites in t shall lay their hands on
14:25 t away tomorrow and set out in the desert
21:22 not t aside into any field or vineyard,
31:29 of the spoil you shall t over to the priest
32:15 If you t away from following him,
Dt 1:40 t about and proceed into the desert on the
2: 1 "When we did t and proceed into the
2: 3 t and go north.
7: 4 For they would t your sons from following
11:28 but t aside from the way I ordain for you
17:20 nor t aside to the right or to the left
29:17 now t away their hearts from the LORD,
30:17 you t away your hearts and will not listen,
31:20 if they t to other gods and serve them,
31:29 sure to become corrupt and to t aside
Jos 2:12 you in t will show kindness to my family;
7:12 enemies, but must t their back to them,
24:19 Joshua in t said to the people,
24:23 among you and t your hearts to the LORD,
Jgs 9:19 Abimelech and may he in t rejoice in you.
19:11 let us t off to this city of the Jebusites
19:12 will not t off to a city of foreigners,
1Sm 1:28 Now I, in t, give him to the LORD;
9: 5 who was with him, "Come, let us t back,
12:20 still, you must not t from the LORD,
12:21 Do not t to meaningless idols which can
28:22 Now you, in t, please listen to your
2Sm 1:22 The bow of Jonathan did not t back,
2:21 Abner said to him, T right or left;
11: 1 At the t of the year, when kings go out
11:21 Then you in t shall say, 'Your servant
15:31 LORD, t the counsel of Ahithophel to folly!"
17:17 in t were to go and report to King David.
19:44 Then the Judahites in t spoke even more
22:38 nor did I t again till I made an end of
1Kgs 2: 3 in whatever you do, wherever you t,
8:48 whole heart and soul they t back to you
11: 2 "they will t your hearts to their gods."
2Kgs 2:14 he struck the water in his t and said,
12: 8 but you shall t them over for the repairs."
12:12 They in t would give it to the carpenters
22:17 by everything to which they t their hands,
22:19 I in t have listened, says the LORD.
2Chr 6:38 with their whole soul they t back to you
7:14 my presence and t from their evil ways,
7:19 But if you t away and forsake my statutes
10:15 for this t of events was divinely ordained
24:23 At the t of the year a force of Arameans
30: 8 he may t away his burning anger from you.
30: 9 and he will not t away his face from you
34:10 and these in t used it to pay the workmen
34:27 have wept before me, I in t have listened
36:10 At the t of the year, King
Neh 3:36 T back their derision upon their own heads
9:35 nor did they t away from their evil deeds.
Tb 3:12 Lord, to you I t my face and raise my eyes.
4: 7 not t your face away from any of the poor,
13: 6 When you t back to him with all your heart,
13: 6 before him, Then he will t back to you,
13: 6 T back, you sinners!
Jdt 11:19 and I in t have been sent to tell you."
14:12 these, in t, went to the generals
Est 2:12 Each girl went in t to visit King
2:15 Mordecai, when her t came to visit the king,
2:22 who in t informed the king for Mordecai.
C:10 your inheritance and t our sorrow into joy:
C:22 but t their own counsel against them and
C:24 and t his heart to hatred for our enemy,
8: 8 you in t may write in the king's name what
1Mc 1:51 Judah to offer sacrifices, each city in t.
11:42 Demetrius, in t,
2Mc 7: 8 t suffered the same tortures as the first.
Jb 6:18 Caravans t aside from their routes;
10: 8 will you then t and destroy me?
15:13 So that you t your anger against God and
17:10 But t now, and come on again; for I
20:14 Yet in his stomach the food shall t;
30:21 Then you t upon me without mercy and with
30:23 Indeed I know you will t me back in death
36:10 and exhorts them to t back from evil.
36:21 Take heed, t not to evil;
Ps(s) 9:18 the nether world the wicked shall t back,
18:38 did I t again till I made an end of them.
22:25 Nor did he t his face away from him,
22:28 the earth shall remember and t to the LORD;
34:15 T from evil, and do good; seek peace,
37:27 T from evil and do good,
39:14 T your gaze from me,
45:11 t your ear, forget your people and your
51:11 T away your face from my sins,
54: 7 T back the evil upon my foes;
55: 2 t not away from my pleading;
56:10 Then do my enemies t back,
69:17 in your great mercy t toward me.
74: 3 T your steps toward the utter ruins;
81:15 against their foes I would t my hand.
86:16 T toward me, and have pity on me;
90: 3 You t man back to dust,
106:23 the breach to t back his destructive wrath.
114: 5 O Jordan, that you t back?
119:21 proud, who t away from your commands.
119:37 T away my eyes from seeing what is vain;
119:39 T away from me the reproach which I dread,
119:51 bitterly at me, I t not away from your law.
119:79 Let those t to me who fear you and
119:102 From your ordinances I t not away,
119:132 pity as you t to those who love your name.
119:157 are many, I t not away from your decrees.
125: 5 But such as t aside to crooked ways may
Prv 1:23 how long will you t away at my reproof?
1:26 I, in my t, will laugh at your doom;
3: 7 fear the LORD and t away from evil;
4: 5 forget or t aside from the words I utter.
4:15 Shun it, cross it not, t aside from it,
4:27 T neither to right nor to left,
6:22 wherever you t, she will guide you.
7:25 Let not your heart t to her ways,
9: 4 "Let whoever is simple t in here;
9:16 "Let whoever is simple t in here,
13:19 the soul, but fools hate to t from evil.
17: 8 at every t it brings him success.
29:21 childhood, he will t out to be stubborn.
Eccl 9: 3 worst, that things t out the same for all.
9:10 Anything you can t your hand to,
11: 6 or whether both alike will t out well.
Sg 6: 5 as bannered troops, T your eyes from me,
7: 1 Turn, turn, O Shulammite, turn, t,
Wis 16:28 the sunrise, and t to you at daybreak.
18:13 at every t on account of sorceries,
Sir 2: 7 for his mercy, t not away lest you fall.
4: 1 force not the eyes of the needy to t away.
4: 5 From the needy t not your eyes,
7: 2 wickedness, and it will t aside from you.
17:21 T again to the Most High and away from sin,
22:13 T away from him and you will find rest and
29:16 t a pledge on their behalf into misfortune,
36:20 an experienced man can t the tables on him.
38:20 T not your thoughts to him again;
39:27 good, but for the wicked they t out evil.
42:25 them has he made in vain, For each in t,
43:21 he sends that t the ponds to lumps of ice.
48:10 To t back the hearts of fathers toward
Is 1:25 I will t my hand against you,
1:31 The strong man shall t to tow,
6:10 understand, and they will t and be healed.
6:13 in it, then this in t shall be laid waste;
9:12 The people do not t to him who struck them,
9:20 together they t on Judah.
13:14 t to his kindred and flee to his own land.
14:27 who can t it back?
19: 9 the combers and weavers shall t pale;
19:22 they shall t to the LORD and he shall be
22: 4 T away from me, let me weep bitterly;
24: 6 Therefore they who dwell on earth t pale,
28: 6 to those who t back the battle at the gate.
30:21 you would t to the right or to the left.
31: 2 not t from what he has threatened to do.
41:18 I will t the desert into a marshland,
42:15 I will t the rivers into marshes,
42:16 I will t darkness into light before them,
44:25 I t wise men back and make their knowledge
45:22 T to me and be safe,
50: 2 I dry up the sea, I t rivers into a desert;
55: 7 Let him t to the LORD for mercy;
59:20 redeemer to those of Jacob who t from sin,
66: 4 I in t will choose ruthless treatment for
Jer 2:21 How could you t out obnoxious to me,
2:27 They t to me their backs,
4: 7 his place, To t your land into desolation,
4:28 repent, I have resolved, I will not t back.
5:23 they t and go away,
6: 8 Lest I t you into a desert,
8: 4 if he goes astray, does he not t back?
8: 5 cling to deceptive idols, refuse to t back?
9:10 I will t Jerusalem into a heap of ruins,
10:22 To t the cities of Judah into a desert
11:15 meat t away your misfortune from you?
15: 1 my heart would not t toward this people.
15:19 turn to you, and you shall not t to them;
18:20 behalf, to t away your wrath from them.
21: 4 I will t back in your hands the weapons
22: 6 peak of Lebanon, I will t you into a waste,
25: 5 T back, each of you, from your evil way
25:12 land I will t into everlasting desert.
26: 3 Perhaps they will listen and t back,
27: 7 Then it in t shall serve great nations and
31:13 I will t their mourning into joy,
31:19 I t in repentance;
31:21 T your attention to the highway,
31:21 T back, O virgin Israel, turn back
31:39 to the hill Gareb and then t to Goah.
34:22 I will t into a desert where no man dwells.
35:15 the prophets, telling you to t back,
36: 3 they will t back each from his evil way,
36: 7 and will all t back from their evil way;
44: 5 accept the warning to t away from the evil
46:21 They too t and flee together,
47: 3 Fathers t not to save their children;
48:12 when I will send him coopers to t him over;
48:34 even the waters of Nimrim t into a desert.
50: 3 against her to t her land into a desert,
Bar 2: 8 we did not plead before the Lord, or t,
2:16 t, O Lord, your ear to hear us.
2:33 Then they shall t back from their
4: 2 T, O Jacob, and receive her:
4:28 God, t now ten times the more to seek him;
Ez 1: 9 they did not t when they moved,
1:12 they did not t when they moved.]
4: 8 cords so that you cannot t from one side
6: 2 of man, t toward the mountains of Israel,
7:22 I will t away my face from them,
8:18 Therefore I in t will act furiously:
13:17 t toward the daughters of your people who
13:22 t from his evil conduct and save his life;
14: 6 t yourselves away from all your
14: 8 I will t against that man,
15: 7 am the LORD, when I t my face against them.
18:30 T and be converted from all your crimes,
25: 2 t toward the Ammonites and prophesy
30:12 I will t the Niles into dry land and sell
32:15 When I t Egypt into a waste,
33: 9 wicked man, trying to t him from his way,
33: 9 his way, and he refuses to t from his way,
33:11 T, turn from your evil ways!
35: 4 Your cities I will t into ruins,
36: 9 See, I come to you, it is to you that I t;
38: 2 of man, t toward Gog [the land of Magog],
39: 2 I will t you about,
Dn 11:18 He shall t to the coastland and take many,
11:19 shall t to the strongholds of his own land,
11:28 t back toward his land with great riches,
Hos 2:14 I will t them into rank growth and wild
3: 1 though they t to other gods and are fond
3: 3 I in t will wait for you."
3: 5 of Israel shall t back and seek the LORD,
9:12 Woe to them when I t away from them!
Am 1: 8 I will t my hand against Ekron,
5: 7 Woe to those who t judgment to wormwood
8:10 I will t your feasts into mourning and all
Jon 3: 8 every man shall t from his evil way and
Zec 1: 4 T from your evil ways and from your wicked
1:16 I will t to Jerusalem in mercy;
13: 7 I will t my hand against the little ones.
14:10 Negeb, all the land shall t into a plain;
Mal 3: 5 those who t aside the stranger,
3:24 To t the hearts of the fathers to their
Mt 4: 3 God, command these stones to t into bread."
5:39 the right cheek, t and offer him the other.
5:42 Do not t your back on the borrower.
10:21 children will t against parents and have
13:15 with their hearts, and t back to me,
14:19 who in t gave them to the people.
15:36 who in t gave them to the crowds.
19:27 Then it was Peter's t to say to him:
20:19 They will t him over to the Gentiles,
21:27 He said in t, "Then neither will I tell
22:41 In t Jesus put a question to the assembled
23:32 Now it is your t:
24:18 he must not t back to pick up his cloak.
25:44 Then they in t will ask:
28:12 They, in t, convened with the elders
Mk 11:25 Father may in t forgive you your faults."
11:33 In t, Jesus said to them, "Then neither
12: 9 tenants and t his vineyard over to others.

TURN (cont.)

13:12 children will *t* against their parents and
13:16 he must not *t* back to pick up his cloak.
Lk 1: 8 when it was the *t* of Zechariah's class and
1:17 to *t* the hearts of fathers to their
4: 3 of God, command this stone to *t* into bread."
6:29 you on one cheek, *t* and give him the other;
12:31 over you, and the rest will follow in *t*.
12:58 on the way lest he *t* you over to the judge,
22:32 You in *t* must strengthen your brothers."
Jn 9:15 The Pharisees, in *t*, began to inquire how
12:22 and Andrew in *t* came to inform Jesus.
13:32 God will, in *t*, glorify him in himself,
19:27 In *t* he said to the disciple,
Acts 3:19 *T* to God, that your sins may be wiped
7:52 *t* have become his betrayers and murderers.
13: 8 to *t* the governor away from the faith.
13:46 everlasting life, we now *t* to the Gentiles.
18: 6 From now on, I will *t* to the Gentiles."
26:18 to *t* them from darkness to light and from
Rom 8:30 and those he justified he in *t* glorified.
1Cor 11: 7 Woman, in *t*, is the reflection of man's
14:27 let it be at most two or three, each in *t*,
14:38 ignores it, he in *t* should be ignored.
2Cor 4: 6 that we in *t* might make known the glory of
11:12 depriving at every *t* those who look for a
Phil 1:19 that this will *t* out to my salvation,
4:19 My God in *t* will supply your needs fully,
1Thes 1: 6 You, in *t*, became imitators of us
1Tm 4: 1 later times some will *t* away from the faith
2Tm 2:22 *t* from youthful passions and pursue
Heb 12:25 we *t* away from him who speaks from heaven!
Jas 5:14 They in *t* are to pray over him,
1Pt 3:11 He must *t* from evil and do good,
2Pt 1: 6 with virtue, and your self-control, in *t*,
1Jn 1: 3 we have seen and heard we proclaim in *t*
2:24 then you in *t* will remain in the Son and
Rv 2:21 but she refuses to *t* from her lewdness.
11: 6 They also have power to *t* water into blood
16:11 did not *t* away from their wicked deeds.
17:16 will *t* against the harlot with hatred;

TURNED (253)

Gn 9:23 since their faces were *t* the other way,
14: 7 They *t* back and came to Enmishpat (that is,
19: 3 *t* aside to his place and entered his house.
19:26 back, and she was *t* into a pillar of salt.
41:13 And it *t* out just as he had told us:
44:12 the goblet *t* up in Benjamin's bag.
Ex 7:15 your hand the staff that *t* into a serpent.
7:23 He *t* away and went into his house,
8:12 *t* into gnats throughout the land of Egypt."
8:13 *t* into gnats throughout the land of Egypt.
10: 6 With that he *t* and left Pharaoh.
14:21 the night and so *t* it into dry land.
16:10 community, they *t* toward the desert,
25:20 they shall be *t* toward each other,
32: 8 *t* aside from the way I pointed out to them,
32:15 Moses then *t* and came down the mountain
37: 9 They were *t* toward each other,
Lv 13: 3 If the hair on the sore has *t* white and
13: 4 below the skin, nor has the hair *t* white,
13:10 on the skin which has *t* the hair white
13:13 since it has all *t* white,
13:17 him, find that the sore has indeed *t* white,
13:20 the skin and that the hair has *t* white,
13:25 If the hair has *t* white on the blotch and
Nm 12:10 When Aaron *t* and saw her a leper,
14:43 You have *t* back from following the LORD;
17: 7 Moses and Aaron *t* toward the meeting tent,
21:33 *t* and went up along the road to Bashan.
22:23 she *t* off the road and went into the field,
22:33 me, she *t* away from me these three times.
22:33 If she had not *t* away from me,
24: 1 omens, but *t* his gaze toward the desert.
25: 4 blazing wrath may be *t* away from Israel."
25:11 has *t* my anger from the Israelites by his
33: 7 out from Etham, they *t* back to Pi-hahiroth,
Dt 3: 1 "Then we *t* and proceeded toward Bashan.
9:12 they have already *t* aside from the way I
9:16 you had already *t* aside from the way which
10: 5 to me, I *t* and came down the mountain,
23: 6 and *t* his curse into a blessing for you,
Jos 7: 8 that Israel has *t* its back to its enemies?
8:20 toward the desert now *t* on their pursuers;
10:38 all Israel *t* back to Debir and attacked it,
19:13 extended to Rimmon, and *t* to Neah.
19:29 Then the boundary *t* back to Ramah and to
Jgs 2:15 the LORD *t* into disaster for them,
6:14 The LORD *t* to him and said,
7:13 and as it fell it *t* the tent upside down."
18: 3 the young Levite and *t* in that direction.
18:21 As they *t* to depart, they placed their
18:23 the Danites, who *t* about and said to Micah,
19:15 they *t* off to enter Gibeah for the night.
20:45 The rest *t* and fled through the desert to
20:47 But six hundred others who *t* and fled
Ru 3: 8 *t* around to find a woman lying at his feet.
1Sm 1: 6 *t* it into a constant reproach to her that
7: 2 whole Israelite population *t* to the LORD.
10: 9 As Saul *t* to leave Samuel,
11: 7 of the LORD, the people *t* out to a man.
13:18 another *t* in the direction of Beth-horon;
14:13 as the Philistines *t* to flee him,
14:21 *t* to join the Israelites under Saul and
14:47 Wherever he *t*, he was successful
15:11 has *t* from me and has not kept my command
15:27 As Samuel *t* to go,
17:30 Yet he *t* from him to another and asked the
2Sm 1: 7 He *t* around and, seeing me, called me
2:20 Abner *t* around and said,
3:16 And he *t* back.
18:16 and the soldiers *t* back from the pursuit
19: 3 and that day's victory was *t* into mourning
23:10 the soldiers *t* back after Eleazar,
24: 6 from there they *t* toward Sidon,
1Kgs 8:14 The king *t* and greeted the whole community
11: 3 concubines, and his wives *t* his heart.
11: 4 his wives had *t* his heart to strange gods,
11: 9 because his heart was *t* away from the LORD,
18:26 the young bull that was *t* over to them,
20:39 someone *t* and brought me a man and said,
21: 4 bed, he *t* away from food and would not eat.
2Kgs 2:24 The prophet *t* and saw them,
5:12 With this, he *t* about in anger and left.
10:27 down the building, and *t* it into a latrine,
12:12 The amount thus realized they *t* over to
14:28 Damascus and *t* back Hamath from Israel,
18: 6 the LORD, Hezekiah never *t* away from him,
20: 2 He *t* his face to the wall and prayed to
23:16 When Josiah *t* and saw the graves there on
23:25 been no king who *t* to the LORD as he did,
24: 1 Then Jehoiakim *t* and rebelled against him.
1Chr 21:20 wheat, he *t* around and saw the king,
2Chr 12:12 the anger of the LORD *t* from him so that
13:14 When Judah *t* and saw that they had to
15: 4 when in their distress they *t* to the LORD,
20:12 to do, hence our eyes are *t* toward you."
20:27 *t* back toward Jerusalem celebrating the
24: 7 had even *t* over to the Baals
29: 6 *t* away their faces from the LORD's
29: 6 LORD's dwelling, and *t* their backs on him.
34: 9 came to Hilkiah the high priest and *t* over
34:10 They *t* it over to the master workmen in
34:17 have *t* into bullion the metals deposited
Ezr 9: 9 he has *t* the good will of the kings of
10:14 till we have *t* away from us our God's
Neh 9:17 They stiffened their necks and *t* their
9:29 They *t* stubborn backs,
13: 2 though our God *t* the curse into a blessing."
Tb 2: 6 "Your festivals shall be *t* into mourning,
4: 7 and God's face will not be *t* away from you.
Jdt 1:11 them, and *t* away his envoys empty-handed,
1:14 market places, and *t* its glory into shame.
8:21 enslavement will not be *t* to our benefit,
Est E:21 has *t* that day for them from one of
9:22 which was *t* for them from sorrow into joy,
9:25 Jews should instead be *t* against Haman
1Mc 1:39 her feasts were *t* into mourning,
1:40 and her exaltation was *t* into mourning.
3: 8 He *t* away wrath from Israel
4:27 because things in Israel had not *t* out
5:35 Then he *t* toward Alema and attacked and
5:68 Judas then *t* toward Azotus in the land of
9:16 they *t* and followed Judas and his men,
9:41 Thus the wedding was *t* into mourning,
12:31 So Jonathan *t* aside against the Arabs who
12:33 He then *t* to Joppa and occupied it,
12:51 to fight for their lives, they *t* back.
16:18 him and that the country be *t* over to him.
2Mc 3:40 and the preservation of the treasury *t* out.
5:18 would have been flogged and *t* back from
14:41 on all sides, *t* his sword against himself,
Jb 19:19 those whom I loved have *t* against me!
23:11 his way I have kept and have not *t* aside.
30:31 My harp is *t* to mourning,
31: 7 If my steps have *t* out of the way,
34:27 Because they *t* away from him and heeded
Ps(s) 9: 4 Most High, Because my enemies are *t* back,
35: 4 Let those be *t* back and confounded who
40:15 be *t* back in disgrace who desire my ruin.
44:19 back, nor our steps *t* aside from your path,
70: 3 be *t* back in disgrace who desire my ruin.
78:38 Often he *t* back his anger and let none of
78:57 They *t* back and were faithless like their
89:44 You have *t* back his sharp sword and have
105:29 He *t* their waters into blood and killed
114: 3 The sea beheld and fled; Jordan *t* back.
114: 8 Jacob, Who *t* the rock into pools of water,
119:59 my ways and *t* my feet to your decrees.
141: 8 toward you, O GOD, my Lord, my eyes are *t*;
Eccl 2:11 But when I *t* to all the works that my
2:20 So my feelings *t* to despair of all the
7:25 I *t* my thoughts toward knowledge;
Wis 16: 3 be *t* from even the craving of necessities,
16: 7 For he who *t* toward it was saved,
Sir 48:23 In his lifetime he *t* back the sun and
49: 3 He *t* to God with his whole heart,
51: 7 I *t* every way, but there was no one
Is 1:21 How has she *t* adulteress,
1:22 Your silver is *t* to dross,
5:25 For all this, his wrath is not *t* back,
7:23 of silver, shall be *t* to briers and thorns.
9:11 For all this, his wrath is not *t* back,
9:16 For all this, his wrath is not *t* back,
9:20 For all this, his wrath is not *t* back,
10: 4 For all this, his wrath is not *t* back,
17: 7 his eyes *t* toward the Holy One of Israel.
21: 4 My yearning for twilight has *t* into dread.
23:13 destroyed, and has been *t* into a ruin.
38: 2 Then Hezekiah *t* his face to the wall and
42:17 *t* back in utter shame who trust in idols;
50: 5 And I have not rebelled, have not *t* back.
63:10 So he *t* on them like an enemy,
Jer 2:35 at least, his anger is *t* away from me."
4: 8 wrath of the LORD is not *t* away from us."
5:25 sins have *t* back these blessings from you.
7:24 of their evil hearts and *t* their backs,
7:34 for the land will be *t* to rubble.
12: 8 has *t* on me like a lion in the jungle;
12:10 me they have *t* into a desert waste,
15: 6 me, says the LORD, *t* your back upon me;
18: 4 he was making *t* out badly in his hand,
18:16 Their land shall be *t* into a desert,
21:10 For I have *t* against this city,
30: 6 Why have all their faces *t* deathly pale?
32:33 They *t* their backs to me,
48: 9 are *t* into ruins where no one dwells.
Lam 3: 9 with fitted stones, and *t* my paths aside.
5: 2 lands have been *t* over to strangers,
5:15 has ceased, our dance has *t* into mourning;
5:22 in full measure *t* your wrath against us.
Bar 4:12 because they *t* from the law of God,
4:34 and her exultation shall be *t* to mourning:
Ez 3:19 yet he has not *t* away from his evil nor
6: 9 their adulterous hearts that *t* away from me
17: 6 and low-lying, Its branches *t* toward him,
18:28 since he has *t* away from all the sins
21:21 wherever your edge is *t*.
29:16 guilt for having *t* to follow after them.
31: 7 for its roots were *t* toward abundant water.
41:17 He *t* to the south
42:16 Then he *t* and measured the north side:
42:19 Then he *t* to the west and measured five
Dn 9: 3 I *t* to the Lord God,
9:16 wrath be *t* away from your city Jerusalem,
10: 8 I *t* the color of death and was powerless.
13:14 but both *t* back, and when they met
13:47 All the people *t* and asked him,
14:28 they were angry and *t* against the king.
Hos 14: 5 for my wrath is *t* away from them.
Jl 3: 4 The sun will be *t* to darkness,
Am 6:12 Yet you have *t* judgment into gall,
Jon 3:10 actions how they *t* from their evil way,
Zep 3:15 against you, he has *t* away your enemies;
Zec 7:11 they stubbornly *t* their backs and stopped
Mal 2: 6 in uprightness, and *t* many away from evil.
2: 8 But you have *t* aside from the way,
3: 7 fathers you have *t* aside from my statutes,
Mt 9:22 Jesus *t* around and saw her and said,
16:23 Jesus *t* on Peter and said,
Mk 8:33 At this he *t* around and,
11:17 but you have *t* it into a den of thieves."
Lk 6:16 James, and Judas Iscariot, who *t* traitor.
7: 9 and *t* to the crowd which was following him
9:55 He *t* toward them only to reprimand them.
14:25 crowd was with him, he *t* to them and said,
22:61 The Lord *t* around and looked at Peter,
23:28 Jesus *t* to them and said:
Jn 1:38 *t* around and noticed them following him,
16:20 a time, but your grief will be *t* into joy.
20:14 She had no sooner said this than she *t*
20:16 She *t* to him and said [in Hebrew],
21:20 Peter *t* around at that,
Acts 2:20 The sun shall be *t* to darkness and the
7:42 But God *t* away from them and abandoned
9:26 it *t* out that they were all afraid of him.
16:18 finally Paul became annoyed, *t* around,
16:20 They *t* them over to the magistrates with
Rom 1:22 to be wise, but *t* into fools instead:
1Cor 1:20 God *t* the wisdom of this world into folly?
1Thes 1: 9 from you, and how you *t* to God from idols,
1Tm 1: 6 and instead have *t* to meaningless talk,
1:20 these I have *t* over to Satan so that they
5:15 Already, some have *t* away to follow Satan.
2Tm 1:15 and Hermogenes, have *t* their backs on me.
Heb 11:34 in battle, and *t* back foreign invaders.
Jas 4: 9 *t* into mourning and your joy into sorrow.
2Pt 2:21 than to have *t* their backs on the holy law
Rv 1:12 I *t* around to see whose voice it was that
2: 4 you have *t* aside from your early love.
6:12 the sun *t* black as a goat's-hair tentcloth
8: 8 A third of the sea *t* to blood,
8:11 third part of all the water *t* to wormwood.
10:10 but when I swallowed it my stomach *t* sour.
16: 3 The sea *t* to blood like that of a corpse,
16: 4 These also *t* to blood.

TURNING (37)

Gn 42:24 But *t* away from them, he wept.
Nm 20:17 road without *t* to the right or the left,
34: 4 Salt Sea, and *t* south of the Akrabbim Pass,
34: 5 and *t* from Azmon to the Wadi of Egypt,
Dt 2:27 without *t* aside to the right or the left.
5:32 not *t* aside to the right or to the left,
17:11 without *t* aside to the right or to the
28:14 not *t* aside to the right or to the left

31:18 the evil they have done in *t* to other gods.
Jos 11:10 At that time Joshua, *t* back,
Jgs 15: 4 *T* them tail to tail,
18:15 So *t* in that direction, they went
1Sm 6:12 as they went, without *t* right or left.
2Sm 2:19 *t* neither right nor left in his pursuit.
2Chr 6: 3 *T* about, the king greeted the whole
2Mc 12:42 *T* to supplication, they prayed that
Jb 33:17 By *t* man from evil and keeping pride away
Prv 2: 2 my commands, *T* your ear to wisdom,
Sir 51:19 I burned with desire for her, never *t* back.
Is 58: 7 see them, and not *t* your back on your own.
59:13 the LORD, *t* back from following our God,
Jer 51:29 *T* the land of Babylon into a desert where
Lam 4: 6 in an instant without the *t* of a hand.
Ez 18:27 *t* from the wickedness he has committed,
31: 4 *t* its streams to all the trees of the
38:12 *t* my hand against the ruins that were
Dn 9:13 by *t* back from our wickedness and
Hos 1: 2 itself to harlotry, *t* away from the Lord.
Zec 6: 6 horses was *t* toward the land of the north,
Mt 21:13 but you are *t* it into a den of thieves."
Lk 7:44 *T* then to the woman, he said to Simon:
10:23 *T* to his disciples he said to them
14:26 *t* his back on his father and mother,
Jn 2:16 *t* my Father's house into a marketplace!"
Acts 3:26 to bless you by *t* you from your evil ways."
9:40 *T* to the dead body, he said, "Tabitha,

TURNS (47)

Lv 13:16 If, however, the raw flesh again *t* white,
1Sm 20: 6 If it *t* out that your father misses me,
1Chr 9:25 *t* in assisting them for seven-day periods,
2Chr 23:18 to whom David had assigned *t* in the temple
Neh 12: 9 brethren ministered opposite them by *t*.
Tb 5:14 So it *t* out that you are a kinsman,
Jb 1: 4 His sons used to take *t* giving feasts,
34:25 he *t* at night and crushes them.
39:22 he *t* not back from the sword.
Ps(s) 40: 5 who *t* not to idolatry or to those who
Prv 26:14 The door *t* on its hinges,
28: 9 one *t* away his ear from hearing the law,
Eccl 1: 6 the north, the wind *t* again and again,
10: 2 man's understanding *t* him to his right;
10: 2 the fool's understanding *t* him to his left.
Wis 8: 8 *t* of phrases and the solutions of riddles;
Sir 6:12 he *t* against you and avoids meeting you.
11:31 The talebearer *t* good into evil;
30: 8 A colt untamed *t* out stubborn;
31: 8 without fault, who *t* not aside after gain!
32:17 The sinner *t* aside reproof and distorts
38:29 his products, and *t* them out in quantity.
39:23 and *t* fertile land into a salt marsh.
Is 24: 2 he *t* it upside down,
59:15 and the man who *t* from evil is despoiled.
Jer 13:16 the light you look for *t* to darkness,
17: 5 in flesh, whose heart *t* away from the LORD.
18: 8 which I have threatened *t* from its evil,
23:14 the wicked, so that no one *t* from evil;
48:39 How he *t* his back in shame!
49:24 Damascus is weakened, she *t* to flee,
50:16 sword, each of them *t* to his own people,
Lam 1: 8 She herself groans and *t* away.
Ez 3:20 If a virtuous man *t* away from virtue and
18:21 man *t* away from all the sins he committed,
18:23 he *t* from his evil way that he may live?
18:24 *t* from the path of the virtue to do evil,
18:26 man *t* away from virtue to commit iniquity,
33:12 on the day that he *t* from his wickedness
33:14 if he *t* away from his sin and does what is
33:18 *t* away from what is right and does wrong,
33:19 But when a wicked man *t* away from
Am 5: 8 and Orion, who *t* darkness into dawn,
Na 2: 9 but none *t* back.
Lk 2: 8 keeping night watch by *t* over their flocks.
17: 4 and seven times a day *t* back to you saying,
2Cor 3:16 "But whenever he *t* to the Lord,

TURRETS (1)

Sir 50: 2 with powerful *t* for the temple precincts;

TURTLEDOVE (4)

Gn 15: 9 she-goat, a three-year-old ram, a *t*,
Lv 1:14 choose a *t* or a pigeon as his offering.
12: 6 and a pigeon or a *t* for a sin offering.
Jer 8: 7 *T*, swallow and thrush observe their time

TURTLEDOVES (9)

Lv 5: 7 offering for his sin two *t* or two pigeons,
5:11 unable to afford even two *t* or two pigeons,
12: 8 a lamb, she may take two *t* or two pigeons,
14:22 a log of oil, and two *t* or pigeons,
14:30 Then, of the *t* or pigeons,
15:14 day he shall take two *t* or two pigeons,
15:29 On the eighth day she shall take two *t* or
Nm 6:10 On the eighth day he shall bring two *t* or
Lk 2:24 "a pair of *t* or two young pigeons,"

TUSKS (2)

Ez 27:15 *t* and ebony wood they gave you for payment.
Dn 7: 5 among the teeth in its mouth were three *t*.

TUTORS (1)

1Chr 27:32 son of Hachmoni, were *t* of the king's sons.

TWAIN (1)

Ps(s) 136:13 Who split the Red Sea in *t*,

TWELFTH (27)

Nm 7:78 On the *t* day it was the turn of Ahira,
1Kgs 19:19 he was following the *t*.
2Kgs 8:25 Judah, became king in the *t* year of Joram,
17: 1 In the *t* year of Ahaz,
25:27 on the twenty-seventh day of the *t* month,
1Chr 24:12 the eleventh to Eliashib, the *t* to Jakim,
25:19 The *t* fell to Hashabiah,
27:15 *T*, for the twelfth month,
2Chr 34: 3 and in his *t* year he began to purge Judah
Ezr 8:31 of Ahava on the *t* day of the first month.
Jdt 1: 1 the *t* year of the reign of Nebuchadnezzar,
Est 3: 7 Nisan, in the *t* year of King Ahasuerus,
3: 7 fell on the thirteenth day of the *t* month,
B: 6 one day, the thirteenth day of the *t* month,
3:13 on the fourteenth day of the *t* month,
8:12 single day, the thirteenth of the *t* month,
E:20 ruin, the thirteenth day of the *t* month,
9: 1 out, the thirteenth day of the *t* month,
2Mc 15:36 it on the thirteenth day of the *t* month,
Jer 52:31 on the twenty-fifth day of the *t* month,
Ez 29: 1 *t* day of the tenth month in the tenth year,
32: 1 day of the *t* month in the twelfth year,
32: 1 day of the twelfth month in the *t* year,
32:17 day of the first month in the *t* year,
33:21 tenth month, in the *t* year of our exile,
Rv 21:20 the eleventh hyacinth, and the *t* amethyst.

TWELVE (198)

Gn 5: 8 of Seth was nine hundred and *t* years;
14: 4 For *t* years they had been subject to
17:20 He shall become the father of *t* chieftains,
25:16 *t* chieftains of as many tribal groups.
35:22 The sons of Jacob were now *t*.
42:13 servants," they said, "were *t* brothers,
42:32 There were *t* of us brothers,
49:28 All these are the *t* tribes of Israel,
Ex 15:27 *t* springs of water and seventy palm trees,
24: 4 twelve pillars for the *t* tribes of Israel.
28:21 *t* of them to match the names of the sons
28:21 seal with the name of one of the *t* tribes.
39:14 These stones were *t*,
39:14 seal with the name of one of the *t* tribes.
Lv 24: 5 take fine flour and bake it into *t* cakes,
Nm 1:44 and Aaron and the *t* princes of Israel.
7: 3 consisted of six baggage wagons and *t* oxen,
7:84 *t* silver plates,
7:84 twelve silver basins, and *t* gold cups.
7:86 The *t* gold cups that were filled with
7:87 were, in all, twelve young bulls, *t* rams,
7:87 those for the sin offerings were *t* goats.
17:17 for each ancestral house, *t* staffs in all,
17:21 their princes gave him staffs, *t* in all,
29:17 the second day you shall offer *t* bullocks,
31: 5 there were *t* thousand men armed for war.
33: 9 *t* springs of water and seventy palm trees,
Dt 1:23 proposal, I chose *t* men from your number,
Jos 3:12 [Now choose *t* men,
4: 2 to Joshua, "Choose *t* men from the people,
4: 3 and instruct them to take up *t* stones from
4: 4 Summoning the *t* men whom he had selected
4: 8 *t* Israelites did as Joshua had commanded:
4: 9 Joshua also had *t* stones set up in the bed
4:20 At Gilgal Joshua set up the *t* stones which
8:25 day a total of *t* thousand men and women,
18:24 *t* cities and their villages.
19:15 there were *t* cities and their villages to
21: 7 *t* cities from the tribes of Reuben,
21:40 of the Levites, were therefore *t* in all.
Jgs 19:29 of his concubine, cut her into *t* pieces,
21:10 sent *t* thousand warriors with orders to go
2Sm 2:15 *t* of the Benjaminites of Ishbaal,
2:15 son of Saul, and *t* of David's servants.
10: 6 thousand men, and *t* thousand men from Tob.
17: 1 "Please let me choose *t* thousand men,
1Kgs 4: 7 Solomon had *t* commissaries for all Israel
5: 6 stalls for his *t* thousand chariot horses.
7:15 cubits high and *t* cubits in circumference;
7:25 This rested on *t* oxen,
7:44 stands, one sea, *t* oxen supporting the sea,
10:20 and *t* other lions stood on the steps,
10:26 hundred chariots and *t* thousand drivers;
11:30 off his new cloak, tore it into *t* pieces,
16:23 he reigned over Israel *t* years,
18:31 He took *t* stones,
19:19 as he was plowing with *t* yoke of oxen;
2Kgs 3: 1 king of Judah, and he reigned for *t* years].
21: 1 was *t* years old when he began to reign,
1Chr 6:48 *t* cities by lot from the tribes of Reuben,
9:22 at the threshold were two hundred and *t*.
15:10 and one hundred and *t* of his brethren.
25: 9 he and his sons and his brethren were *t*.
25: 9 he and his brethren and his sons were *t*.
25:10 Zaccur, his sons, and his brethren: *t*.
25:11 Izri, his sons, and his brethren: *t*.
25:12 Nethaniah, his sons, and his brethren: *t*.
25:13 Bukkiah, his sons, and his brethren: *t*.
25:14 Jesarelah, his sons, and his brethren: *t*.
25:15 Jeshaiah, his sons, and his brethren: *t*.
25:16 Mattaniah, his sons, and his brethren: *t*.
25:17 Shimei, his sons, and his brethren: *t*.
25:18 Uzziel, his sons, and his brethren: *t*.
25:19 Hashabiah, his sons, and his brethren: *t*.
25:20 Shubael, his sons, and his brethren: *t*.
25:21 Mattithiah, his sons, and his brethren: *t*.
25:22 Jeremoth, his sons, and his brethren: *t*.
25:23 Hananiah, his sons, and his brethren: *t*.
25:24 Joshbekashah, his sons, and his brethren: *t*.
25:25 Hanani, his sons, and his brethren: *t*.
25:26 Mallothi, his sons, and his brethren: *t*.
25:27 Eliathah, his sons, and his brethren: *t*.
25:28 Hothir, his sons, and his brethren: *t*.
25:29 Giddalti, his sons, and his brethren: *t*.
25:30 Mahazioth, his sons, and his brethren: *t*.
25:31 his sons, and his brethren: *t*.
2Chr 1:14 and *t* thousand drivers he could station
4: 4 It rested on *t* oxen,
4:15 one sea, and the *t* oxen under it;
9:19 *T* other lions also stood there,
9:25 horses, chariots, and *t* thousand horsemen,
12: 3 He came up with *t* hundred chariots and
33: 1 was *t* years old when he became king,
Ezr 2: 6 Joab, two thousand eight hundred and *t*;
2:18 sons of Jorah, one hundred and *t*;
6:17 together with *t* he-goats as a sin-offering
8:24 Next I selected *t* of the priestly leaders
8:35 the God of Israel *t* bulls for all Israel,
8:35 lambs, and *t* goats as sin-offerings:
Neh 5:14 during these *t* years neither I nor my
7:24 sons of Hariph, one hundred and *t*;
Tb 14: 1 peacefully at the age of a hundred and *t*,
Jdt 2: 5 thousand infantry and *t* thousand cavalry,
2:15 commanded, and *t* thousand mounted archers,
7: 2 thousand infantry and *t* thousand horsemen,
Est 2:12 after the *t* months' preparation decreed
1Mc 1: 7 Alexander had reigned *t* years when he died.
Sir 44:23 for his tribes, and their division into *t*.
49:10 Then, too, the *T* PROPHETS
Jer 52:20 and the *t* oxen of bronze under the sea,
52:21 cubits high and *t* cubits in diameter;
Ez 40:49 was twenty cubits wide and *t* cubits deep;
43:16 twelve cubits long and *t* cubits wide.
47:13 the land among the *t* tribes of Israel
Dn 4:26 *T* months later, as he was walking
Mt 9:20 had suffered from hemorrhages for *t* years
10: 1 Then he summoned his *t* disciples and gave
10: 2 The names of the *t* apostles are these:
10: 5 Jesus sent these men on mission as the *T*,
11: 1 had finished instructing his *t* disciples,
14:20 when gathered up, filled *t* baskets.
19:28 on *t* thrones to judge the twelve tribes
19:28 thrones to judge the *t* tribes of Israel.
20:17 the *T* aside on the road and said to them:
26:14 Then one of the *T* whose name was Judas
26:20 grew dark he reclined at table with the *T*.
26:47 was still speaking, Judas, one of the *T*,
26:53 notice more than *t* legions of angels?
Mk 3:14 He named *t* as his companions whom he
3:16 He appointed the *T* as follows:
4:10 the *T* questioned him about the parables.
5:42 The girl, a child of *t*, stood up
6: 7 *T* and began to send them out two by two,
6:43 up enough leftovers to fill *t* baskets,
8:19 They answered, *T*."
9:35 down and called the *T* around him and said,
10:32 Taking the *T* aside once more,
11:11 went out to Bethany accompanied by the *T*.
14:10 Then Judas Iscariot, one of the *T*,
14:17 As it grew dark he arrived with the *T*.
14:20 He said, "It is one of the *T*—
14:43 was still speaking, Judas, one of the *T*,
Lk 2:42 and when he was *t* they went up for the
6:13 and selected *t* of them to be his apostles:
8: 1 The *T* accompanied him,
8:42 his only daughter, a girl of about *t*,
8:43 with a hemorrhage of *t* years' duration,
9: 1 Jesus now called the *T* together and gave
9:12 approached the *T* came and said to him,
9:17 had left, over and above, filled *t* baskets.
18:31 Taking the *T* aside, he said to them:
22: 3 the one called Iscariot, a member of the *T*.
22:30 on thrones judging the *t* tribes of Israel.
22:47 led by the man named Judas, one of the *T*.
Jn 6:13 they gathered *t* baskets full of pieces
6:67 Jesus then said to the *T*,
6:70 "Did I not choose the *T* of you myself?
6:71 the Iscariot, who, though one of the *T*,
11: 9 "Are there not *t* hours of daylight?
20:24 It happened that one of the *T*, Thomas
Acts 6: 2 The *T* assembled the community of the
7: 8 for Jacob, and Jacob for the *t* patriarchs.
19: 7 were in the company about *t* men in all.
24:11 Not more than *t* days have passed since I
26: 7 The *t* tribes of our people fervently
1Cor 15: 5 that he was seen by Cephas, then by the *T*.
Jas 1: 1 To the *t* tribes in the dispersion,

TWELVE (cont.)

Rv 7: 5 Judah, *t* thousand from the tribe of Reuben,
7: 5 Reuben, *t* thousand from the tribe of Gad,
7: 6 *t* thousand from the tribe of Asher,
7: 6 *t* thousand from the tribe of Naphtali,
7: 6 *t* thousand from the tribe of Manasseh,
7: 7 *t* thousand from the tribe of Simeon,
7: 7 *t* thousand from the tribe of Levi,
7: 7 *t* thousand from the tribe of Issachar,
7: 8 *t* thousand from the tribe of Zebulun,
7: 8 *t* thousand from the tribe of Joseph,
7: 8 and *t* thousand from the tribe of Benjamin.
11: 3 for those *t* hundred and sixty days,
12: 1 feet, and on her head a crown of *t* stars.
12: 6 taken care of for *t* hundred and sixty days.
21:12 had *t* gates at which twelve angels were
21:12 *T* names were written on the gates,
21:12 the names of the *t* tribes of Israel.
21:14 had *t* courses of stones as its foundation,
21:14 the names of the *t* apostles of the Lamb.
21:16 and found it *t* thousand furlongs in length,
21:21 The twelve gates were *t* pearls,
22: 2 of life which produce fruit *t* times a year,

TWENTIETH (9)

Nm 10:11 year, on the *t* day of the second month,
1Kgs 15: 9 In the *t* year of Jeroboam,
2Kgs 15:30 in his place [in the *t* year of Jotham,
1Chr 24:16 to Pethahiah, the *t* to Jehezkel,
25:27 The *t* fell to Eliathah,
Ezr 10: 9 the ninth month, on the *t* day of the month.
Neh 1: 1 In the month Chislev of the *t* year,
2: 1 Nisan of the *t* year of King Artaxerxes,
5:14 from his *t* to his thirty-second year

TWENTY (169)

Gn 6: 3 shall comprise one hundred and *t* years."
18:31 my Lord, what if there are no more than *t*?"
18:31 it," he answered, "for the sake of the *t*."
31:38 "In the *t* years that I was under you,
31:41 Of the *t* years that I have now spent in
32:15 two hundred she-goats and *t* he-goats;
32:15 two hundred ewes and *t* rams;
32:16 *t* she-asses and ten he-asses.
37:28 to the Ishmaelites for *t* pieces of silver.
Ex 26:18 *t* boards on the south side,
26:19 forty silver pedestals under the *t* boards,
26:20 *t* boards on the other side of the Dwelling,
27:10 *t* columns and twenty pedestals of bronze;
27:11 *t* columns and twenty pedestals of bronze;
27:16 be a variegated curtain, *t* cubits long,
30:13 sanctuary shekel, *t* gerahs to the shekel.
30:14 Everyone of *t* years or more who enters the
36:23 *t* boards on the south side,
36:24 forty silver pedestals under the *t* boards,
36:25 *t* boards on the other side of the Dwelling,
38:10 *t* columns and twenty pedestals of bronze,
38:11 *t* columns and twenty pedestals of bronze,
38:18 twined, *t* cubits long and five cubits wide,
38:26 was received from every man of *t* years or
Lv 27: 3 persons between the ages of *t* and sixty,
27: 5 fixed sum shall be *t* shekels for a youth
27: 5 persons between the ages of five and *t*,
27:25 There are *t* gerahs to the shekel.
Nm 1: 3 all the men in Israel of *t* years or more
1:18 Every man of *t* years or more then declared
1:20 when all the males of *t* years or more who
1:22 when all the males of *t* years or more who
1:24 when all the males of *t* years or more who
1:26 when all the males of *t* years or more who
1:28 when all the males of *t* years or more who
1:30 when all the males of *t* years or more who
1:32 when all the males of *t* years or more who
1:34 when all the males of *t* years or more who
1:36 when all the males of *t* years or more who
1:38 when all the males of *t* years or more who
1:40 when all the males of *t* years or more who
1:42 when all the males of *t* years or more who
1:45 The total number of the Israelites of *t*
3:47 sanctuary shekel, *t* gerahs to the shekel.
7:86 cups amounted to one hundred and *t* shekels.
11:19 or two days, or five, or ten, or *t* days,
14:29 Of all your men of *t* years or more,
18:16 sanctuary standard, *t* gerahs to the shekel.
26: 2 Israelites of all those of *t* years or more
26: 4 registered those of *t* years or more,
32:11 none of these men of *t* years or more who
Dt 31: 2 "I am now one hundred and *t* years old and
34: 7 one hundred and *t* years old when he died,
Jgs 4: 3 oppressed the Israelites for *t* years.
8:10 and *t* thousand swordsmen having fallen.
11:33 Aroer to the approach of Minnith *t* cities
15:20 *t* years in the days of the Philistines.
16:31 He had judged Israel for *t* years.
1Sm 7: 2 rest in Kiriath-jearim a long time *t* years
14:14 slew about *t* men within half a furlong.
2Sm 3:20 When Abner, accompanied by *t* men,
8: 4 horsemen and *t* thousand foot soldiers.
9:10 Ziba, who had fifteen sons and *t* servants,
10: 6 the Ammonites sent for and hired *t*
18: 7 there that day were heavy *t* thousand men.
19:18 by his fifteen sons and *t* servants,
24: 8 again after nine months and *t* days.
1Kgs 5: 3 meal, ten fatted oxen, *t* pasture-fed oxen,
5:25 year gave Hiram *t* thousand kors of wheat
5:25 and *t* thousand measures of pure oil.
6: 2 for the LORD was sixty cubits long, *t* wide,
6: 3 the temple was *t* cubits from side to side,
6:16 At the rear of the temple a space of *t*
6:20 *t* cubits long, twenty wide, and twenty high.
8:63 oxen and one hundred *t* thousand sheep.
9:10 After the *t* years during which Solomon
9:11 gave Hiram *t* cities in the land of Galilee.
9:14 Solomon one hundred and *t* talents of gold.
9:28 and *t* talents of gold to King Solomon.
10:10 the king one hundred and *t* gold talents,
2Kgs 4:42 *t* barely loaves made from the first fruits,
16: 2 Ahaz was *t* years old when he became king,
1Chr 7: 9 Their family records listed *t* thousand two
12:31 *t* thousand eight hundred warriors,
12:38 one hundred and *t* thousand.
15: 5 and one hundred and *t* of his brethren;
15: 6 and two hundred and *t* of his brethren;
18: 4 took from him *t* thousand foot soldiers,
23:24 of the LORD from *t* years of age upward,
23:27 from the time they were *t* years old.
27:23 those who were *t* years of age or younger,
2Chr 2: 9 who cut the wood, *t* thousand kors of wheat,
2: 9 kors of wheat, *t* thousand kors of barley,
2: 9 of barley, *t* thousand measures of wine,
2: 9 of wine, and *t* thousand measures of oil."
3: 3 old measure, and the width was *t* cubits;
3: 4 twenty cubits, and it was *t* cubits high.
3: 8 twenty cubits, and its width was also *t*
3:11 The wings of the cherubim spanned *t* cubits:
3:13 of the two cherubim was thus *t* cubits.
4: 1 altar twenty cubits long, *t* cubits wide
5:12 a hundred and *t* priests blowing trumpets.
7: 5 oxen, and one hundred *t* thousand sheep.
8: 1 After the *t* years during which Solomon
9: 9 Then she gave the king one hundred and *t*
25: 5 he had counted those of *t* years and over,
28: 1 Ahaz was *t* years old when he became king,
28: 6 and *t* thousand of Judah in a single day,
31:17 and the Levites of *t* years and over
Ezr 2:32 sons of Harim, three hundred and *t*;
2:67 asses six thousand seven hundred and *t*.
3: 8 by appointing the Levites *t* years of age
8:19 and their brethren and their sons, *t* men.
8:20 the Levites) there were two hundred and *t*.
8:27 *t* golden bowls valued at a thousand
Neh 7:35 sons of Harim, three hundred and *t*;
7:68 asses six thousand seven hundred and *t*.
7:70 *t* thousand drachmas of gold and two
7:71 amounted to *t* thousand drachmas of gold,
Tb 5: 3 *t* years have already passed since I
Jdt 1:16 and feasted for a hundred and *t* days.
2: 5 a hundred and *t* thousand infantry and
2:15 a hundred and *t* thousand picked troops,
1Mc 6:30 thousand foot-soldiers, *t* thousand cavalry,
8: 6 with a hundred and *t* elephants
8:15 day three hundred and *t* men took counsel,
9: 4 *t* thousand men and two thousand cavalry.
11:45 one hundred and *t* thousand strong,
15:13 with a hundred and *t* thousand infantry
16: 4 the land *t* thousand warriors and horsemen.
2Mc 8: 9 head of at least *t* thousand armed men
8:20 routed one hundred and *t* thousand
8:30 killed more than *t* thousand of them,
10:17 them, killing as many as *t* thousand men.
10:23 than *t* thousand men in the two strongholds.
10:35 *t* young men in the army of Maccabeus,
11: 5 place about *t* miles from Jerusalem,
12:20 a hundred and *t* thousand foot soldiers
Jer 25: 3 these three and *t* years
Ez 4:10 you eat shall be *t* shekels a day by weight;
40:49 was *t* cubits wide and twelve cubits deep;
41: 2 to be forty cubits, while its width was *t*.
41: 4 nave, *t* cubits long and twenty cubits wide,
41:10 *t* cubits wide going all around the temple.
42: 3 Across the *t* cubits of the inner court and
45: 1 thousand cubits long and *t* thousand wide;
45:12 The shekel shall be *t* gerahs.
45:12 *T* shekels,
48: 9 across by *t* thousand north and south.
48:13 across and *t* thousand north and south.
Dn 6: 2 entire kingdom one hundred and *t* satraps,
Jon 4:11 a hundred and *t* thousand persons
Hg 2:16 one went to a heap of grain for *t* measures,
2:16 draw fifty measures, there would be but *t*.
Zec 5: 2 it is *t* cubits long and ten cubits wide."
Lk 14:31 enemy coming against him with *t* thousand?
Acts 1:15 been a hundred and *t* gathered together.
27:28 a sounding and found a depth of *t* fathoms;
Rv 19: 4 the four and *t* elders and the four living

TWENTY-EIGHT (13)

Ex 26: 2 The length of each shall be *t* cubits,
36: 9 was *t* cubits and the width four cubits;
2Kgs 10:36 reign over Israel in Samaria was *t* years.
1Chr 12:36 *t* thousand six hundred.
2Chr 11:21 and he fathered *t* sons and sixty daughters.
Ezr 2:23 men of Anathoth, one hundred and *t*;
2:41 sons of Asaph, one hundred and *t*.
8:11 son of Bebai, and with him *t* males;
Neh 7:16 sons of Bebai, six hundred and *t*;
7:22 sons of Hashum, three hundred and *t*;
7:27 men of Anathoth, one hundred and *t*;
11: 8 warriors, nine hundred and *t* in number.
11:14 his brethren, warriors, one hundred and *t*.

TWENTY-FIFTH (9)

Nm 8:24 Each from his *t* year onward shall perform
Neh 6:15 The wall was finished on the *t* day of Elul;
1Mc 1:59 On the *t* day of each month they sacrificed
4:52 morning on the *t* day of the ninth month,
4:59 days, from the *t* day of the month Chislev.
2Mc 1:18 temple on the *t* day of the month Chislev,
10: 5 that is, the *t* of the same month Chislev,
Jer 52:31 Judah, on the *t* day of the twelfth month,
Ez 40: 1 month beginning the *t* year of our exile,

TWENTY-FIRST (4)

Ex 12:18 the evening of the *t* day of this month
1Chr 24:17 the twentieth to Jehezkel, the *t* to Jachin,
25:28 The *t* fell to Hothir,
Hg 2: 1 on the *t* day of the seventh month,

TWENTY-FIVE (41)

Jgs 20:35 *t* thousand one hundred men of Benjamin,
20:46 that day were in all *t* thousand swordsmen,
1Kgs 6: 2 sixty cubits long, twenty wide, and *t* high.
22:42 reign, and he reigned *t* years in Jerusalem.
2Kgs 14: 2 He was *t* years old when he became king,
15:33 He was *t* years old when he became king,
18: 2 He was *t* years old when he became king,
23:36 was *t* years old when he began to reign,
2Chr 20:31 king, and he reigned *t* years in Jerusalem.
25: 1 was *t* years old when he became king,
27: 1 Jotham was *t* years old when he became king,
27: 8 He was *t* years old when he became king,
29: 1 was *t* years old when he became king,
36: 5 was *t* years old when he became king,
Ezr 2:33 Lod, Hadid, and Ono, seven hundred and *t*;
2Mc 10:31 *T* hundred of their foot soldiers and six
12:20 foot soldiers and *t* hundred horsemen.
12:26 where he killed *t* thousand people.
12:28 slaughtered *t* thousand of the people in it.
Ez 8:16 were about *t* men with their backs to the
11: 1 At the entrance of the gate I saw *t* men,
40:13 the width was *t* cubits.
40:14 measured the vestibule, which was *t* cubits.
40:21 it was fifty cubits long and *t* cubits wide.
40:25 It was fifty cubits long and *t* cubits wide.
40:29 it was fifty cubits long and *t* cubits wide.
40:33 it was fifty cubits long and *t* cubits wide.
40:36 it was fifty cubits long and *t* cubits wide.
45: 1 *t* thousand cubits long and twenty thousand
45: 3 *t* thousand cubits long and ten thousand
45: 5 Also there shall be a strip *t* thousand
45: 6 thousand cubits wide and *t* thousand long,
45:12 Twenty shekels, *t* shekels,
48: 8 *t* thousand cubits from north to south,
48: 9 set aside for the LORD shall be *t* thousand
48:10 shall have *t* thousand cubits on the north,
48:10 on the east, and *t* thousand on the south;
48:13 priests, *t* thousand cubits by ten thousand.
48:13 The whole tract shall be *t* thousand cubits
48:20 twenty-five thousand by *t* thousand cubits;
Jn 2: 6 jars, each holding fifteen to *t* gallons.

TWENTY-FOUR (23)

Nm 7:88 the peace offerings were, in all, *t* oxen,
25: 9 but only after *t* thousand had died.
1Chr 20: 6 hand and six toes to each foot; *t* in all.
23: 4 *t* thousand were to direct the service of
27: 1 to the divisions, of *t* thousand men each,
27: 2 and in his division were *t* thousand men;
27: 4 and in his division were *t* thousand men.
27: 5 and in his division were *t* thousand men.
27: 7 and in his division were *t* thousand men.
27: 8 and in his division were *t* thousand men.
27: 9 and in his division were *t* thousand men.
27:10 and in his division were *t* thousand men.
27:11 and in his division were *t* thousand men.
27:12 and in his division were *t* thousand men.
27:13 and in his division were *t* thousand men.
27:14 and in his division were *t* thousand men.
27:15 and in his division were *t* thousand men.
Neh 7:23 sons of Bezai, three hundred and *t*;
Rv 4: 4 Surrounding this throne were *t* other
4: 4 thrones upon which were seated *t* elders;
4:10 the *t* elders fall down before the One
5: 8 and the *t* elders fell down before the Lamb.
11:16 The *t* elders who were enthroned in God's

TWENTY-FOUR-YEAR (1)

1Kgs 15:33 began his *t* reign over Israel in Tirzah.

TWENTY-FOURTH (10)

1Chr 24:18 twenty-third to Delaiah, the *t* to Maaziah.
25:31 The *t* fell to Romamti-ezer,
Neh 9: 1 On the *t* day of this month,
2Mc 11:21 and forty-eight, the *t* of Dioscorinthius.

Dn 10: 4 On the *t* day of the first month I was on
Hg 1:15 their God, on the *t* day of the sixth month.
2:10 On the *t* day of the ninth month,
2:18 from the *t* day of the ninth month.
2:20 time to Haggai on the *t* day of the month:
Zec 1: 7 year of Darius, on the *t* day of Shabat,

TWENTY-NINE (8)

Gn 11:24 When Nahor was *t* years old,
Ex 38:24 amounted to *t* talents and seven hundred
Jos 15:32 a total of *t* cities with their villages.
2Kgs 14: 2 king, and he reigned *t* years in Jerusalem.
18: 2 king, and he reigned *t* years in Jerusalem.
2Chr 25: 1 king, and he reigned *t* years in Jerusalem.
29: 1 king, and he reigned *t* years in Jerusalem.
Ezr 1: 9 sacks of silverware, one thousand and *t*;

TWENTY-ONE (7)

2Kgs 24:18 was *t* years old when he became king,
2Chr 36:11 was *t* years old when he became king,
Ezr 2:26 men of Ramah and Geba, six hundred and *t*;
Neh 7:30 men of Ramah and Geba, six hundred and *t*;
7:37 Lod, Hadid, and Ono, seven hundred and *t*;
Jer 52: 1 was *t* years old when he became king,
Dn 10:13 of Persia stood in my way for *t* days,

TWENTY-SECOND (3)

1Chr 24:17 the twenty-first to Jachin, the *t* to Gamul,
25:29 The *t* fell to Giddalti,
Jdt 2: 1 year, on the *t* day of the first month,

TWENTY-SEVEN (7)

Gn 23: 1 Sarah's life was one hundred and *t* years.
1Kgs 20:30 The survivors, *t* thousand of them,
Est 1: 1 and *t* provinces from India to Ethiopia
3:13 and *t* provinces from India to Ethiopia,
8: 9 and *t* provinces from India to Ethiopia:
8:12 and *t* satrapies from India to Ethiopia,
9:30 and *t* provinces of Ahasuerus' kingdom.

TWENTY-SEVENTH (6)

Gn 8:14 second month, on the *t* day of the month,
1Kgs 16:10 struck and killed him in the *t* year of Asa,
16:15 In the *t* year of Asa,
2Kgs 15: 1 became king in the *t* year of Jeroboam,
25:27 Judah, on the *t* day of the twelfth month,
Ez 29:17 first day of the first month in the *t* year,

TWENTY-SIX (2)

Jgs 20:15 cities on that occasion was *t* thousand,
1Chr 7:40 *t* thousand men fit for military service.

TWENTY-SIXTH (1)

1Kgs 16: 8 In the *t* year of Asa,

TWENTY-THIRD (8)

2Kgs 12: 7 as the *t* year of the reign of King Joash,
13: 1 In the *t* year of Joash,
1Chr 24:18 twenty-second to Gamul, the *t* to Delaiah,
25:30 The *t* fell to Mahazioth,
2Chr 7:10 On the *t* day of the seventh month he sent
Est 8: 9 that time, on the *t* day of the third month,
1Mc 13:51 On the *t* day of the second month,
Jer 52:30 in the *t* year of Nebuchadnezzar,

TWENTY-THREE (13)

Nm 26:62 age, who were registered, was *t* thousand.
33:39 and *t* years old when he died on Mount Hor.
Jgs 10: 2 When he had judged Israel *t* years,
2Kgs 23:31 was *t* years old when he began to reign,
1Chr 2:22 possessed *t* cities in the land of Gilead.
2Chr 36: 2 was *t* years old when he became king
Ezr 2:11 sons of Bebai, six hundred and *t*;
2:17 sons of Bezai, three hundred and *t*;
2:19 sons of Hashum, two hundred and *t*;
2:21 sons of Bethlehem, one hundred and *t*;
2:28 men of Bethel and Ai, two hundred and *t*;
Neh 7:32 men of Bethel and Ai, one hundred and *t*;
Jer 52:28 year, three thousand and *t* people of Judah;
1Cor 10: 8 so that in one day *t* thousand perished.

TWENTY-TWO (27)

Nm 3:39 with the LORD's command, was *t* thousand.
3:43 *t* thousand two hundred and seventy-three.
26:14 *t* thousand two hundred men were registered.
Jos 19:30 there were *t* cities and their villages to
Jgs 7: 3 mountain, *t* thousand of the soldiers left,
10: 3 came after him and judged Israel *t* years.
20:21 city and felled *t* thousand men of Israel.
2Sm 8: 5 of Zobah, David slew *t* thousand of them.
1Kgs 8:63 offerings to the LORD *t* thousand oxen
14:20 The length of Jeroboam's reign was *t* years.
16:29 reigned over Israel in Samaria for *t* years.
2Kgs 8:26 He was *t* years old when he began his reign,
21:19 was *t* years old when he began to reign,
1Chr 7: 2 Their kindred numbered *t* thousand six
7: 7 records listed *t* thousand and thirty-four.
12:29 with *t* princes of his father's house.
18: 5 David also slew *t* thousand of their men.
2Chr 7: 5 offered as sacrifice *t* thousand oxen,
13:21 and fathered *t* sons and sixteen daughters.
22: 2 He was *t* years old when he became king,
33:21 Amon was *t* years old when he became king,
Ezr 2:12 of Azgad, one thousand two hundred and *t*;
2:27 men of Michmas, one hundred and *t*;
Neh 7:17 Azgad, two thousand three hundred and *t*;
7:31 men of Michmas, one hundred and *t*;
11:12 the temple service, eight hundred and *t*;
2Mc 5:24 an army of *t* thousand
13: 2 fifty-three hundred horsemen, *t* elephants,

TWENTY-YEAR (1)

2Kgs 15:27 began his *t* reign over Israel in Samaria.

TWICE (30)

Gn 27:36 He has now supplanted me *t*!
41:32 That Pharaoh had the same dream *t* means
43:10 we could have been there and back *t* by now!"
Ex 16: 5 let it be *t* as much as they gather on the
16:22 the sixth day they gathered *t* as much food,
Nm 20:11 Moses struck the rock *t* with his staff,
Dt 15:18 six years was worth *t* a hired man's salary;
1Sm 18:11 David to the wall, but *t* David escaped him.]
1Kgs 11: 9 who had appeared to him *t* (for though the
1Chr 11:21 He was *t* as famous as any of the Thirty
Neh 13:20 the night once or *t* outside Jerusalem,
Jdt 13: 8 him *t* in the neck and cut off his head.
1Mc 10:72 were *t* put to flight in their own land.
Jb 11: 6 the secrets of wisdom are *t* as effective:
33:14 God does speak, perhaps once, or even *t*,
33:29 Lo, all these things God does, *t*,
40: 5 though *t*, I will do so no more.
42:10 gave to Job *t* as much as he had before.
Eccl 6: 6 *t* a thousand years and not enjoy his goods,
Sir 13: 7 then *t* or three times he will terrify you;
32:20 and let not the same thing trip you *t*.
45:14 with the established sacrifice *t* each day;
Mt 17:27 there a coin worth *t* the temple tax.
23:15 a devil of him *t* as wicked as yourselves.
Mk 14:30 this very night before the cock crows *t*,
14:72 cock crows *t* you will deny me three times."
Lk 18:12 I fast *t* a week.
Acts 5:35 think *t* about what you are going to do
Phil 4:16 something for my needs, not once but *t*.
Rv 18: 6 into her cup *t* the amount she concocted!

TWICE-LENGTHENED (1)

Sir 26: 1 the husband of a good wife, *t* are his days;

TWIG (1)

Sir 38: 5 by a *t* that men might learn his power?

TWIGS (1)

Wis 4: 5 Their *t* shall be broken off untimely,

TWILIGHT (17)

Ex 12: 6 shall be slaughtered during the evening *t*.
16:12 In the evening *t* you shall eat flesh,
29:39 and the other lamb at the evening *t*.
29:41 lamb you shall offer at the evening *t*,
30: 8 the lamps, and again in the evening *t*,
Lv 23: 5 day of the first month, at the evening *t*.
Nm 9: 3 The evening *t* of the fourteenth day of
9: 5 *t* of the fourteenth day of the first month,
9:11 *t* of the fourteenth day of that month,
28: 4 and the other during the evening *t*,
28: 8 lamb, to be offered during the evening *t*,
2Kgs 7: 5 At *t* they left for the Arameans;
7: 7 Then in the *t* they fled,
Jb 3: 9 May the stars of its *t* be darkened;
24:15 The eye of the adulterer watches for the *t*;
Prv 7: 9 In the *t*, at dusk of day, at the time
Is 21: 4 My yearning for *t* has turned into dread.

TWIN (6)

Sg 4: 5 Your breast are like *t* fawns,
7: 4 Your breasts are like *t* fawns,
Jn 11:16 means *T*") said to his fellow disciples,
20:24 of the Twelve, Thomas (the name means *T*"),
21: 2 were Simon Peter, Thomas (the *T*"),
Rom 9:10 had conceived *t* children by one man,

TWINED (23)

Ex 26: 1 sheets woven of fine linen *t* and of violet,
26:31 and scarlet yarn, and of fine linen *t*,
26:36 and scarlet yarn and of fine linen *t*.
27: 9 cubits long, woven of fine linen *t*,
27:16 and scarlet yarn and of fine linen *t*.
27:18 Fine linen *t* must be used,
28: 6 yarn, embroidered on cloth of fine linen *t*.
28: 8 and scarlet yarn, and of fine linen *t*.
28:15 and scarlet yarn on cloth of fine linen *t*.
28:33 purple and scarlet yarn and fine linen *t*,
36: 8 with its ten sheets woven of fine linen *t*,
36:35 and scarlet yarn, and of fine linen *t*,
36:37 and scarlet yarn, and of fine linen *t*,
38: 9 were hangings, woven of fine linen *t*,
38:16 of the court were woven of fine linen *t*.
38:18 and scarlet yarn and of fine linen *t*,
39: 2 and scarlet yarn and of fine linen *t*.
39: 5 and scarlet yarn, and of fine linen *t*,
39: 8 and scarlet yarn on cloth of fine linen *t*.
39:24 and scarlet yarn and of fine linen *t*;
39:28 drawers of linen [of fine linen *t*;
39:29 work made of fine linen *t* and of violet,
Ps(s) 119:61 *t* about me your law I have not forgotten.

TWINKLING (1)

1Cor 15:52 in an instant, in the *t* of an eye,

TWINS (5)

Gn 25:24 delivery came, there were *t* in her womb.
38:27 came, she was found to have *t* in her womb.
Sg 4: 2 from the washing, All of them big with *t*,
6: 6 from the washing, All of them big with *t*,
Acts 28:11 with the "Heavenly *T*" as its figurehead.

TWISTED (10)

Ex 28:14 as two chains of pure gold, *t* like cords,
28:22 the chains of pure gold, *t* like cords,
39:15 Chains of pure gold, *t* like cords,
Dt 22:12 "You shall put *t* cords on the four
2Sm 13: 8 she *t* it into cakes before his eyes and
Ez 21:32 *T*, twisted, twisted will I leave it;
Phil 2:15 the midst of a *t* and depraved generation
1Tm 6: 5 *t* minds who have lost all sense of truth.

TWISTS (4)

Ex 23: 8 and *t* the words even of the just.
Dt 16:19 the wise and *t* the words even of the just.
Ps(s) 29: 9 the LORD *t* the oaks and strips the forests,
Sir 27:23 his tone and *t* your words to your ruin.

TWO (804)

Gn 1:16 God made the *t* great lights,
2:24 wife, and the *t* of them become one body.
4:19 Lamech took *t* wives;
6:19 creatures you shall bring *t* into the ark,
6:20 *t* of each shall come into the ark with you,
7: 9 *t* by two] male and female entered the ark
7: 9 [two by *t* male and female entered the ark
9:22 he told his *t* brothers outside about it.
10:25 To Eber *t* sons were born:
11:10 of Arpachshad, *t* years after the flood.
11:19 Peleg lived *t* hundred and nine years after
11:21 Reu lived *t* hundred and seven years after
11:23 *t* hundred years after the birth of Nahor,
11:32 of Terah was *t* hundred and five years;
15:10 He brought him all these, split them in *t*,
18:22 the *t* men walked on farther toward Sodom,
19: 1 The *t* angels reached Sodom in the evening,
19: 8 I have *t* daughters who have never had
19:15 wife and your *t* daughters who are here,
19:16 the hands of his wife and his *t* daughters
19:30 he and his *t* daughters went up from Zoar
19:30 he lived with his *t* daughters in a cave.
21:27 them to Abimelech and the *t* made a pact.
21:31 the *t* took an oath there.
22: 3 son Isaac, and *t* of his servants as well,
22: 7 As the *t* walked on together, Isaac
22: 8 Then the *t* continued going forward.
24:22 and *t* gold bracelets weighing ten shekels,
25:23 *T* nations are in your womb,
25:23 *t* peoples are quarreling while still
26:28 be a sworn agreement between our *t* sides
27: 9 Go to the flock and get me *t* choice kids.
29:16 Now Laban had *t* daughters;
31:33 as well as the tents of the *t* maidservants;
31:37 and mine, and let them decide between us *t*.
31:41 *t* daughters and six years for your flock,
32: 8 his flocks, herds and camels, into *t* camps.
32:11 staff, I have now grown into *t* companies.
32:15 *t* hundred she-goats and twenty he-goats;
32:15 *t* hundred ewes and twenty rams;
32:23 however, Jacob arose, took his *t* wives,
32:23 the *t* maidservants and his eleven children,
33: 1 among Leah, Rachel and the *t* maidservants,
34:25 Simeon and Levi, *t* of Jacob's sons,
40: 2 Pharaoh was angry with his *t* courtiers,
41: 1 After a lapse of *t* years, Pharaoh
41:50 set in, Joseph became the father of *t* sons,
42:37 own *t* sons if I do not return him to you."
44:27 us, 'As you know, my wife bore me *t* sons.
45: 6 For *t* years now the famine has been in the
46:27 who were born to him in Egypt *t* persons
48: 1 So he took along with him his *t* sons,
48: 5 Your *t* sons, therefore, who were born
48: 6 recorded in the names of their *t* brothers.
48:13 Then Joseph took the *t*,
Ex 2:13 out again, and now *t* Hebrews were fighting!
4: 9 they will not believe even these *t* signs,
4:15 will teach the *t* of you what you are to do.
12: 7 blood and apply it to the *t* doorposts
12:22 lintel and the *t* doorposts with this blood.
12:23 blood on the lintel and the *t* doorposts,
14:16 over the sea, split the sea in *t*,
16:22 as much food, *t* omers for each person.

TWO (cont.)
16:29 the sixth day he gives you food for *t* days.
18: 3 Moses had sent back to him, and her *t* sons.
18: 6 you, along with your wife and her *t* sons."
21:21 the slave survives for a day or *t*,
22: 3 restore *t* animals for each one stolen.
25:10 of acacia wood, *t* and a half cubits long,
25:12 *t* rings on one side and two on the
25:17 of pure gold, *t* cubits and a half long,
25:18 Make *t* cherubim of beaten gold for the two
25:22 *t* cherubim on the ark of the commandments.
25:23 make a table of acacia wood, *t* cubits long,
25:27 on *t* opposite sides of the frame as
26: 6 with which to join the *t* sets of sheets,
26:17 Each board shall have *t* arms that shall
26:19 there are *t* pedestals under each board,
26:20 pedestals under each board, at its *t* arms;
26:21 forty silver pedestals, *t* under each board;
26:23 and *t* boards for the corners at the rear
26:24 These *t* shall be double at the bottom,
26:25 pedestals, *t* pedestals under each board.
28: 7 shoulder straps joined to its *t* upper ends.
28: 9 "Get *t* onyx stones and engrave on them
28:11 so shall you have the *t* stones engraved
28:12 Set these *t* stones on the shoulder straps
28:14 of gold, as well as *t* chains of pure gold,
28:23 you shall then make *t* rings of gold for it
28:23 to the *t* upper ends of the breastpiece.
28:24 cords are then to be fastened to the *t* rings
28:25 the other *t* ends of the cords being
28:25 cords being fastened in front to the *t* filigree
28:26 Make *t* other rings of gold and put them on
28:26 on the *t* lower ends of the breastpiece,
28:27 Then make *t* more rings of gold and fasten
29: 1 a young bull and *t* unblemished rams.
29: 3 them along with the bullock and the *t* rams.
29:13 as the lobe of its liver and its *t* kidneys,
29:22 its *t* kidneys with the fat that is on them,
29:38 *t* yearling lambs as the sacrifice
30: 2 long, a cubit wide, and *t* cubits high,
30: 4 *t* on one side and two on the opposite side,
30:23 that is, *t* hundred and fifty shekels,
30:23 *t* hundred and fifty shekels of fragrant
31:18 gave him the *t* tablets of the commandments,
32:15 *t* tablets of the commandments in his hands,
34: 1 "Cut *t* stone tablets like the former,
34: 4 then cut *t* stone tablets like the former,
34: 4 him, taking along the *t* stone tablets.
34:29 *t* tablets of the commandments in his hands,
36:22 Each board had *t* arms,
36:24 there were *t* pedestals under each board,
36:24 pedestals under each board, at its *t* arms;
36:26 forty silver pedestals, *t* under each board;
36:28 and *t* boards at the corners in the rear of
36:30 pedestals, *t* pedestals under each board.
37: 1 of acacia wood, *t* and a half cubits long,
37: 3 *t* rings for one side and two for the
37: 6 *t* and a half cubits long and one and a
37: 7 *T* cherubim of beaten gold were made for
37: 7 made for the *t* ends of the propitiatory,
37: 8 from the propitiatory at its *t* ends.
37:10 was made of acacia wood, *t* cubits long,
37:25 long, a cubit wide, and *t* cubits high,
37:27 two on one side and *t* on the opposite side,
38:29 and *t* thousand four hundred shekels.
39: 4 made for it and joined to its *t* upper ends.
39:16 together with *t* gold filigree rosettes and
39:16 gold filigree rosettes and *t* gold rings.
39:16 The *t* rings were fastened to the two upper
39:17 The *t* gold chains were then fastened to
39:17 the *t* rings at the ends of the breastpiece.
39:18 The other two ends of the *t* chains were
39:18 in front to the *t* filigree rosettes,
39:19 *T* other gold rings were made and put on
39:19 put on the *t* lower ends of the breastpiece,
39:20 *T* more gold rings were made and fastened
39:20 to the bottom of the *t* shoulder straps
Lv 3: 4 adheres to them, as well as the *t* kidneys,
3:10 adheres to them, as well as the *t* kidneys,
3:15 adheres to them, as well as the *t* kidneys,
4: 9 adheres to them, as well as the *t* kidneys,
5: 7 for his sin two turtledoves or *t* pigeons,
5:11 afford even two turtledoves or *t* pigeons,
5:15 valued at *t* silver shekels according to
7: 4 as well as the *t* kidneys with the fat on
8: 2 the bullock for a sin offering, the *t* rams,
8:16 the liver and the *t* kidneys with their fat,
8:25 the liver and the *t* kidneys with their fat,
9:19 over the inner organs, the *t* kidneys,
12: 8 she may take *t* turtledoves or two pigeons,
14: 4 man who is to be purified, to get *t* live,
14:10 day he shall take *t* unblemished male lambs,
14:22 a log of oil, and *t* turtledoves or pigeons,
14:49 To purify the house, he shall take *t* birds,
15:14 he shall take two turtledoves or *t* pigeons,
15:29 On the eighth day she shall take *t*
15:29 she shall take two turtledoves or *t* pigeons
16: 1 After the death of Aaron's *t* sons,
16: 5 receive *t* male goats for a sin offering
16: 7 Taking the *t* male goats and setting them
19:19 of yours with *t* different kinds of seed;
19:19 woven with *t* different kinds of thread.
20:14 the man and the *t* women as well shall be
23:13 Its cereal offering shall be *t* tenths of
23:17 from wherever you live *t* loaves of bread
23:17 of *t* tenths of an ephah of fine flour
23:18 yearling lambs, one young bull, and *t* rams,
23:19 and *t* yearling lambs as a peace offering.
23:20 *t* lambs as a wave offering before the LORD;
24: 5 using *t* tenths of an ephah of flour for
24: 6 These you shall place in *t* piles,
Nm 1:35 thirty-two thousand *t* hundred were
2:21 census to thirty-two thousand *t* hundred.]
3:34 they numbered six thousand *t* hundred.
3:43 thousand *t* hundred and seventy-three.
3:46 As ransom for the *t* hundred and
4:36 *t* thousand seven hundred and fifty.
4:40 numbered *t* thousand six hundred and thirty.
4:44 they numbered three thousand *t* hundred.
6:10 On the eighth day he shall bring *t*
6:10 he shall bring two turtledoves or *t* pigeons
7: 3 oxen, that is, a wagon for every *t* princes,
7: 7 He gave *t* wagons and four oxen to the
7:17 one goat for a sin offering; and *t* oxen,
7:23 one goat for a sin offering; and *t* oxen,
7:29 one goat for a sin offering; and *t* oxen,
7:35 one goat for a sin offering; and *t* oxen,
7:41 one goat for a sin offering; and *t* oxen,
7:47 one goat for a sin offering; and *t* oxen,
7:53 one goat for a sin offering; and *t* oxen,
7:59 one goat for a sin offering; and *t* oxen,
7:65 one goat for a sin offering; and *t* oxen,
7:71 one goat for a sin offering; and *t* oxen,
7:77 one goat for a sin offering; and *t* oxen,
7:83 one goat for a sin offering; and *t* oxen,
7:85 to *t* thousand four hundred shekels,
7:89 commandments, from between the *t* cherubim;
9:22 for *t* days or for a month or longer,
10: 2 "Make *t* trumpets of beaten silver,
11:19 will eat it, not for one day, or *t* days,
11:26 Now *t* men, one named Eldad
11:31 over the camp site at a height of *t* cubits
13:23 on it, which *t* of them carried on a pole,
15: 6 offering of *t* tenths of a ephah of fine flour
16: 2 son of Reuben] took *t* hundred and fifty
16:17 Then each of your *t* hundred and fifty
16:35 consumed the *t* hundred and fifty men
22:22 his ass, accompanied by *t* of his servants.
26:10 the fire consumed *t* hundred and fifty men.
26:14 thousand *t* hundred men were registered.
28: 3 *t* unblemished yearling lambs each day as
28: 9 shall offer *t* unblemished yearling lambs,
28: 9 *t* tenths of an ephah of fine flour mixed
28:11 as a holocaust to the LORD *t* bullocks,
28:12 *t* tenths of an ephah of fine flour mixed
28:19 LORD, which shall consist of *t* bullocks,
28:20 for each bullock, *t* tenths for the ram,
28:27 holocaust to the LORD *t* bullocks,
28:28 for each bullock, *t* tenths for the ram,
29: 3 for the bullock, *t* tenths for the ram,
29: 9 for the bullock, *t* tenths for the ram,
29:13 to the LORD thirteen bullocks, *t* rams,
29:14 *t* tenths for each of the two rams,
29:17 you shall offer twelve bullocks, *t* rams,
29:20 you shall offer eleven bullocks, *t* rams,
29:23 day you shall offer ten bullocks, *t* rams,
29:26 day you shall offer nine bullocks, *t* rams,
29:29 day you shall offer eight bullocks, *t* rams,
29:32 day you shall offer seven bullocks, *t* rams,
34:15 these *t* and one half tribes have received
35: 5 Thus you shall measure out *t* thousand
Dt 3: 8 "And so at that time we took from the *t*
4:13 which he wrote on *t* tablets of stone.
4:47 the land of these *t* kings of the Amorites
5:22 *t* tablets of stone and gave them to me.
9:10 gave me the *t* tablets of stone inscribed,
9:11 me the *t* stone tablets of the covenant,
9:15 *t* tablets of the covenant in both my hands,
9:17 Raising the *t* tablets with both hands I
10: 1 'Cut *t* tablets of stone like the former;
10: 3 and cut *t* tablets of stone like the former,
10: 3 up the mountain carrying the *t* tablets.
17: 6 The testimony of *t* or three witnesses is
19:15 on the testimony of *t* or three witnesses.
19:17 the *t* parties in the dispute shall appear
21:15 *t* wives loves one and dislikes the other;
22: 9 vineyard with *t* different kinds of seed;
22:11 wear cloth of *t* different kinds of thread,
25:11 "When *t* men are fighting and the wife of
25:13 not keep *t* differing weights in your bag,
25:14 keep *t* different measures in your house,
32:30 or *t* men put ten thousand to flight,
Jos 2: 1 secretly sent out *t* spies from Shittim,
2: 1 When the *t* reached Jericho,
2: 4 woman had taken the *t* men and hidden them,
2:10 *t* kings of the Amorites beyond the Jordan,
2:23 Then the *t* came back down from the hills,
3: 4 *t* thousand cubits between you and the ark.
6:22 the *t* men who had spied out the land,
7: 3 if only about *t* or three thousand go up,
7:21 mantle, *t* hundred shekels of silver,
9:10 *t* kings of the Amorites beyond the Jordan,
14: 3 For to *t* and a half tribes Moses had
14: 4 the descendants of Joseph formed *t* tribes,
15:60 and Rabbah; *t* cities and their villages.
21:16 nine cities from the *t* tribes mentioned.
21:25 *t* cities of Taanach with its pasture lands
21:27 from the half-tribe of Manasseh *t* cities:
24: 8 them [the *t* kings of the Amorites] before
Jgs 5:30 there must be a damsel or *t* for each man,
5:30 an ornate shawl or *t* for me in the spoil."
7:25 They captured the *t* princes of Midian,
8:12 them and took the *t* kings of Midian,
9:44 while the other *t* companies rushed upon
11:37 Spare me for *t* months,
11:38 he replied, and sent her away for *t* months.
11:39 of the *t* months she returned to her father,
15:13 So they bound him with *t* new ropes and
16: 3 doors of the city gate and the *t* gateposts,
16:28 this last time that for my *t* eyes I may
16:29 Samson grasped the *t* middle columns on
17: 3 she took *t* hundred of them and gave them
19: 6 and the *t* men ate and drank together.
20:45 killed another *t* thousand of them there.
Ru 1: 1 *t* sons to reside on the plateau of Moab.
1: 3 died, and she was left with her *t* sons,
1: 5 with neither her *t* sons nor her husband.
1: 7 She and her *t* daughters-in-law left the
1: 8 Naomi said to her *t* daughters-in-law,
1Sm 1: 2 He had *t* wives, one named Hannah,
1: 3 to him at Shiloh, where the *t* sons of Eli,
2:21 birth to three more sons and *t* daughters,
2:34 a sign in what will happen to your *t* sons,
4: 4 The *t* sons of Eli,
4:11 ark of God was captured, and Eli's *t* sons,
4:17 Your *t* sons, Hophni and Phinehas,
6: 7 *t* milch cows that have not borne the yoke;
6:10 Taking *t* milch cows,
10: 2 you will meet *t* men near Rachel's tomb at
10: 4 and offer you *t* wave offerings of bread,
11:11 so scattered that no *t* were left together.
13: 1 *t*) years over Israel.]
13: 2 of whom *t* thousand remained with him in
14:11 the *t* of them appeared before the outpost
14:49 his *t* daughters were named,
15: 4 and at Telaim reviewed *t* hundred thousand
18:27 his men and slew *t* hundred Philistines.
20:42 we *t* have sworn by the name of the LORD:
25:13 while *t* hundred remained with the baggage.
25:18 quickly got together *t* hundred loaves,
25:18 two hundred loaves, *t* skins of wine,
25:18 and *t* hundred cakes of pressed figs,
27: 3 had his family, and David had his *t* wives,
28: 8 clothes, and set out with *t* companions.
29: 3 He has been with me now for a year or *t*,
30: 5 David's *t* wives,
30:10 but *t* hundred were too exhausted to cross
30:12 a cake of pressed figs and *t* cakes of
30:18 had taken, and rescued his *t* wives.
30:21 When David came to the *t* hundred men who
2Sm 1: 1 the Amalekites and spent *t* days in Ziklag.
2: 2 went up there accompanied by his *t* wives,
2:10 over Israel, and he reigned for *t* years.
4: 2 *t* company leaders named Baanah and Rechab,
8: 2 told off *t* lengths of line for execution,
12: 1 In a certain town there were *t* men,
13:23 After a period of *t* years, Absalom had
14: 6 Your servant had *t* sons,
14:26 the hair weighed *t* hundred shekels
14:28 *t* years without appearing before the king.
15:11 *T* hundred men had accompanied Absalom
16: 1 asses laden with *t* hundred loaves of bread,
18:12 a thousand pieces of silver in my *t* hands,
18:24 Now David was sitting between the *t* gates,
21: 8 the *t* sons that Aiah's daughter Rizpah had
23:20 It was he who slew the *t* lions in Moab.
1Kgs 2: 5 he slew the *t* generals of Israel's armies,
2:32 *t* men better and more just than himself,
2:39 *t* of Shimei's servants ran away to Achish,
3:16 *t* harlots came to the king and stood
3:18 there was no one there but us *t*.
3:25 him, he said, "Cut the living child in *t*,
5:28 month in the Lebanon and *t* months at home.
6:23 In the sanctuary were *t* cherubim,
6:32 The *t* doors were of olive wood,
6:34 The *t* doors were of fir wood;
7:15 *T* hollow bronze columns were cast,
7:16 There were also *t* capitals cast in bronze,
7:17 *T* pieces of network with a chainlike mesh
7:18 *t* hundred of them in a double row
7:18 piece of network on each of the *t* capitals.
7:24 the gourds were in *t* rows and were cast in
7:26 Its capacity was *t* thousand measures.
7:41 two columns, *t* nodes for the capitals
7:41 *t* pieces of network covering the nodes for
7:42 that covered the *t* nodes of the capitals
8: 9 There was nothing in the ark but the *t*
9:10 during which Solomon built the *t* houses,
10:16 King Solomon made *t* hundred shields of
10:20 lions stood on the steps, *t* to a step,
11:29 The *t* were alone in the area,
12:28 *t* calves of gold and said to the people:
15:25 he reigned over Israel *t* years.
16:24 *t* silver talents and built upon the hill,
18: 4 hid them away fifty each in *t* caves,
18:13 of the LORD, fifty each in *t* caves,
18:23 Give us *t* young bulls.
18:32 altar large enough for *t* seahs of grain.
20:15 provinces, *t* hundred thirty-two of them.

21:10 get *t* scoundrels to face him and accuse
21:13 *T* scoundrels came in and confronted him
22:52 he reigned *t* years over Israel.
2Kgs 1:14 consuming *t* captains with their companies
2: 6 And so the *t* went on together.
2: 7 and when the *t* stopped at the Jordan,
2:12 gripped his own garment and tore it in *t*.
2:24 Then *t* she-bears came out of the woods and
4: 1 come to take my *t* children as his slaves."
5:17 your servant, have *t* mule-loads of earth,
5:22 to say, *T* young men have just come to me,
5:22 a talent of silver and *t* festal garments.'"
5:23 "Please take *t* talents," Naaman said,
5:23 two festal garments, to *t* of his servants,
7: 1 shekel, and *t* seahs of barley for a shekel,
7:14 They took *t* chariots,
7:16 shekel and *t* seahs of barley for a shekel,
7:18 *T* seahs of barley will sell for a shekel,
9:32 *t* or three eunuchs looked down toward him.
10: 4 said, "If *t* kings could not withstand him,
10: 8 "Pile them in *t* heaps at the entrance of
11: 7 The *t* of your divisions who are going off
17:16 and made for themselves *t* molten calves;
18:23 I will give you *t* thousand horses if you
21: 5 of heaven, in the *t* courts of the temple.
21:19 reign, and he reigned *t* years in Jerusalem.
23:12 in the *t* courts of the temple of the LORD.
25: 4 *t* walls which was near the king's garden.
25:16 The weight in bronze of the *t* pillars,
1Chr 1:19 *T* sons were born to Eber;
4: 5 Ashbur, the father of Tekoa, had *t* wives,
5:21 camels, *t* hundred fifty thousand sheep,
5:21 fifty thousand sheep, and *t* thousand asses.
7: 9 twenty thousand *t* hundred of their kindred
7:11 *t* hundred men fit for military service . . .
9:22 at the threshold were *t* hundred and twelve.
11:22 He killed the *t* sons of Ariel of Moab,
12:33 *t* hundred chiefs, together with all their
15: 6 and *t* hundred and twenty of his brethren;
15: 8 their chief, and *t* hundred of his brethren,
24: 6 listing *t* successive family groups from
25: 7 men, was *t* hundred and eighty-eight.
26:17 and at the storehouse they were two and *t*;
26:18 at the highway and *t* at the large building.
26:32 *t* thousand seven hundred heads of families.
2Chr 3:10 he made *t* cherubim of carved workmanship,
3:13 of the *t* cherubim was thus twenty cubits.
3:15 he set *t* columns thirty-five cubits high;
4: 3 there were *t* rows of these cast in the
4:12 *t* columns, two nodes for the capitals
4:12 topping these *t* columns, and two networks
4:13 hundred pomegranates for the *t* networks,
4:13 *t* rows of pomegranates to each network,
4:13 to cover the *t* nodes of the capitals
5:10 *t* tablets which Moses put there on Horeb,
8:10 They were also King Solomon's *t* hundred
9:15 *t* hundred large shields of beaten gold,
9:18 with *t* lions standing beside the arms.
14: 7 and *t* hundred and eight thousand from
17:15 and with him *t* hundred eighty thousand.
17:16 him *t* hundred thousand valiant warriors.
17:17 and with him *t* hundred thousand armed with
21:19 on until a period of *t* years had elapsed,
24: 3 Jehoiada provided him with *t* wives,
26:12 warriors was *t* thousand six hundred,
28: 8 The Israelites took away as captives *t*
29:32 one hundred rams, and *t* hundred lambs:
33: 5 heaven in the *t* courts of the LORD's house.
33:21 king, and he reigned *t* years in Jerusalem.
35: 8 gave to the priests *t* thousand six hundred
Ezr 2: 3 *t* thousand one hundred and seventy-two;
2: 6 Joab, *t* thousand eight hundred and twelve;
2: 7 one thousand *t* hundred and fifty-four;
2:12 one thousand *t* hundred and twenty-two;
2:14 sons of Bigvai, *t* thousand and fifty-six;
2:19 sons of Hashum, *t* hundred and twenty-three;
2:28 Bethel and Ai, *t* hundred and twenty-three;
2:31 one thousand *t* hundred and fifty-four;
2:38 one thousand *t* hundred and forty-seven;
2:65 also had *t* hundred male and female singers.
2:66 their mules *t* hundred and forty-five,
6:17 offered one hundred bulls, *t* hundred rams,
8: 4 of Zerahiah, and with him *t* hundred males;
8: 9 and with him *t* hundred and eighteen males;
8:20 Levites) there were *t* hundred and twenty.
8:27 *t* vases of excellent polished bronze,
10:13 be performed in a single day or even *t*,
Neh 7: 8 *t* thousand one hundred and seventy-two;
7:11 *t* thousand eight hundred and eighteen;
7:12 one thousand *t* hundred and fifty-four;
7:17 *t* thousand three hundred and twenty-two;
7:19 sons of Bigvai, *t* thousand and sixty-seven;
7:34 one thousand *t* hundred and fifty-four;
7:40 one thousand *t* hundred and forty-seven;
7:67 also had *t* hundred male and female singers.
7:67 their mules *t* hundred and forty-five,
7:70 and two thousand *t* hundred minas of silver.
7:71 of gold, *t* thousand minas of silver,
11:13 family heads, *t* hundred and forty-two;
11:18 holy city was *t* hundred and eighty-four.
12:31 the wall, and I arranged *t* great choirs.
12:40 The *t* choirs took up a position in the
Tb 1:21 the king was assassinated by *t* of his sons,
2:10 however, took care of me for *t* years,
3:16 the prayer of these *t* suppliants was heard
5: 3 I divided it into *t* parts,
5: 6 good *t* days' travel from Ecbatana to Rages,
5:14 the *t* sons of Shemaiah the elder;
8: 6 and from these *t* the human race descended.
8:17 you were merciful toward *t* only children.
8:19 and picked out *t* steers and four rams
9: 2 servants and *t* camels and travel to Rages.
9: 5 with the four servants and *t* camels,
12: 6 the *t* men aside privately and said to them:
12:16 with fear, the *t* men fell to the ground.
Jdt 1:12 Egypt as far as the borders of the *t* seas.
4: 7 defile was only wide enough for *t* abreast.
13:10 and the *t* went off together as they were
13:13 opened the gate and welcomed the *t* women.
13:13 and when they gathered around the *t*,
Est A: 5 *T* great dragons came on,
A:12 *t* eunuchs of the king who were court
A:14 the king had the *t* eunuchs questioned and,
A:17 because of the *t* eunuchs of the king.
2:21 *t* of the royal eunuchs who guarded the
D: 2 God and savior, she took with her *t* maids;
6: 2 *t* of the royal eunuchs who guarded the
9:27 obligation of celebrating these *t* days
F: 4 The *t* dragons are myself and Haman.
F: 7 For this purpose he arranged *t* lots:
F: 8 These *t* lots were fulfilled in the hour,
1Mc 1:29 *T* years later, the king sent the Mysian
5:60 about *t* thousand Israelites fell that day.
6:38 or the other of the *t* flanks of the army,
9: 4 twenty thousand men and *t* thousand cavalry.
9:11 The cavalry were divided into *t* squadrons,
9:12 Flanked by the *t* squadrons,
9:57 the land of Judah was quiet for *t* years.
10:49 The *t* kings joined battle,
10:60 where he met the *t* kings and gave them and
11:13 he thus wore *t* crowns on his head,
12:47 of whom he sent *t* thousand to Galilee
13:16 and *t* of his sons as hostages to guarantee
15:26 Antiochus' support *t* thousand elite troops,
16: 2 Simon called his *t* oldest sons,
16: 5 and between the *t* armies was a stream.
16: 7 *t* corps and put his cavalry between them,
16:10 and about *t* thousand of the enemy perished.
16:16 banquet hall, and killed him, his *t* sons,
2Mc 3:11 talents of silver and *t* hundred of gold.
3:26 Then *t* other young men,
6:10 *t* women who were arrested for having
8:10 Nicanor planned to raise the *t* thousand
10: 3 sacrifice for the first time in *t* years,
10:18 took refuge in *t* very strong towers,
10:22 and without delay captured the *t* towers.
10:23 twenty thousand men in the *t* strongholds.
12: 4 sea and drowned at least *t* hundred of them.
12:19 and Sosipater, *t* of Maccabeus' captains,
12:43 amounting to *t* thousand silver drachmas,
13:15 and killed about *t* thousand in the camp.
Jb 42: 7 am angry with you and with your *t* friends;
Ps(s) 62:12 God said; these *t* things which I heard:
Prv 30:15 The *t* daughters of the leech are,
Eccl 4: 6 than *t* with toil and a chase after wind!
4: 9 *T* are better than one:
4:11 So also, if *t* sleep together,
4:12 man may be overcome, *t* together can resist.
11: 6 know not which of the *t* will be successful,
Sg 7: 1 as at the dance of the *t* companies?
8:12 *t* hundred for the caretakers of its fruit.
Sir 23:16 *T* types of men multiply sins,
26:19 These *t* bring grief to my heart,
38:18 of sorrow, as he deserves, One or *t* days,
46: 4 stop the sun, so that one day became *t*?
46: 8 they were the only *t* spared from the six
47:21 Thus *t* governments came into being,
50:25 My whole being loathes *t* nations,
Is 6: 2 with *t* they veiled their faces,
6: 2 their faces, with *t* they veiled their feet,
6: 2 their feet, and with *t* they hovered aloft.
7: 4 before these *t* stumps of smoldering brands
7:16 *t* kings whom you dread shall be deserted.
17: 6 *T* or three olives remain at the very top,
22:11 the *t* walls for the water of the old pool.
36: 8 'I will give you *t* thousand horses,
Jer 2:13 *T* evils have my people done:
3:14 take you, one from a city, *t* from a clan,
24: 1 The LORD showed me *t* baskets of figs
28: 3 Within *t* years I will restore to this
28:11 within *t* years I will break the yoke of
33:24 the *t* tribes which he had chosen"?
34:18 make like the calf which they cut in *t*,
34:18 in two, between those *t* parts they passed.
39: 4 Road through the gate between the *t* walls.
52: 7 *t* walls which was near the king's garden.
52:20 carried off, as well as the *t* pillars,
Ez 1:11 Each had *t* wings spread out above so that
1:11 the other *t* wings of each covered his body.
1:23 [Each of them had *t* covering his body.]
21:24 make for yourself *t* roads over which the
21:26 *t* roads divide stands the king of Babylon,
23: 2 Son of man, there were *t* women,
35:10 The *t* nations and the two lands have
35:10 nations and the *t* lands have become mine;
37:17 Then join the *t* sticks together,
37:22 Never again shall they be *t* nations,
37:22 shall they be divided into *t* kingdoms.
40: 9 and its pilasters, which were *t* cubits.
40:39 gate there were *t* tables on either side,
40:40 entrance of the north gate, were *t* tables,
40:40 vestibule of the gate there were *t* tables.
40:44 inner court where there were *t* chambers,
41: 3 that entrance, which were *t* cubits;
41:18 a palmtree between every *t* cherubim.
41:18 Each cherub had *t* faces:
41:22 height, two cubits long, and *t* cubits wide.
41:24 Each door had *t* movable leaves;
41:24 *t* leaves were on one doorjamb and two on
43:14 up to the lower edge it was *t* cubits high,
45:15 *t* hundred from the pasturage of Israel,
47:13 of Israel [Joseph having *t* portions].
48:17 extend north *t* hundred and fifty cubits,
48:17 cubits, south *t* hundred and fifty cubits,
48:17 cubits, east *t* hundred and fifty cubits,
48:17 and west *t* hundred and fifty cubits.
Dn 7: 4 the ground to stand on *t* feet like a man,
7:25 be handed over to him for a year, *t* years,
8: 3 by the river a ram with *t* great horns,
8:14 "For *t* thousand three hundred evenings
11:27 The *t* kings, resolved on evil, shall sit
12: 5 I, Daniel, looked and saw *t* others,
12: 7 that it should be for a year, *t* years,
12:11 be one thousand *t* hundred and ninety days.
13: 5 *t* elders of the people were appointed
13:15 the garden as usual, with *t* maids only.
13:16 Nobody else was there except the *t* elders,
13:19 the *t* old men got up and hurried to her.
13:28 next day, the *t* wicked elders also came,
13:34 In the midst of the people the *t* elders
13:36 *t* girls and shut the doors of the garden,
13:51 "Separate these *t* far from one another
13:55 the sentence from him and split you in *t*."
13:59 you in *t* so as to make an end of you both."
13:61 They rose up against the *t* elders,
14:32 and *t* carcasses and two sheep had been
14:32 and *t* sheep had been given to them daily.
Hos 6: 2 He will revive us after *t* days;
10:10 when I chastised them for their *t* crimes.
Am 1: 1 of Israel, *t* years before the earthquake:
3: 3 Do *t* walk together unless they have agreed?
4: 8 Though *t* or three cities staggered to one
Zec 4: 3 tubes, and beside it are *t* olive trees,
4:11 "What are these *t* olive trees at each
4:12 "What are the *t* olive tufts which freely
4:12 fresh oil through the *t* golden channels?"
4:14 "These are the *t* anointed who stand by
5: 9 Then I raised my eyes and saw *t* women
6: 1 coming out from between *t* mountains;
6:13 and between the *t* of them there shall be
11: 7 I took *t* staffs,
13: 8 *t* thirds of them shall be cut off and
14: 4 *t* from east to west by a very deep valley,
14: 5 of those *t* mountains reaches its edge;
Mt 2:16 He ordered the massacre of all the boys *t*
4:18 the Sea of Galilee he watched *t* brothers,
4:21 and caught sight of *t* other brothers,
5:41 service for one mile, go with him *t* miles.
6:24 No man can serve *t* masters.
8:28 encountered *t* men coming out of the tombs.
8:33 the story about the *t* possessed men.
9:27 *t* blind men came after him crying out,
10:29 not *t* sparrows sold for next to nothing?
14:19 He took the five loaves and *t* fish,
18: 8 with *t* hands or two feet into endless fire.
18: 8 with two hands or *t* feet into endless fire.
18:15 fault, but keep it between the *t* of you.
18:16 stand on the word of *t* or three witnesses.
18:19 if *t* of you join your voices on earth to
18:20 Where *t* or three are gathered in my name,
19: 5 his wife, and the *t* shall become as one'?
19: 6 Thus they are no longer *t* but one flesh.
20:24 this, became indignant at the *t* brothers.
20:30 *t* blind men sitting by the roadside,
21: 1 sent off *t* disciples with the instructions:
21:28 There was a man who had *t* sons.
21:31 Which of the *t* did what the father wanted?"
22:40 *t* commandments the whole law is based,
24:40 *T* men will be out in the field;
24:41 *T* women will be grinding meal;
25:15 silver pieces, to a second *t* thousand,
25:17 received the *t* thousand doubled his figure.
25:22 the *t* thousand then stepped forward.
25:22 'you entrusted me with *t* thousand and I
25:22 thousand and I have made *t* thousand more.'
25:32 Then he will separate them into *t* groups,
26: 2 that in *t* days' time it will be Passover,
26:37 He took along Peter and Zebedee's *t* sons,
26:60 Finally *t* came forward who stated:
27:38 *T* insurgents were crucified along with him,
27:51 sanctuary was torn in *t* from top to bottom.
Mk 1:10 he saw the sky rent in *t* and the Spirit
3:17 James (he gave these *t* the name Boanerges,
5:13 The herd of about *t* thousand went rushing
5:24 The *t* went off together and a large crowd
6: 7 Twelve and began to send them out *t* by two,
6: 7 and began to send them out two by *t*,
6:37 "Are we to go and spend *t* hundred days'
6:38 number they answered, "Five, and *t* fish."

TWO (cont.)

6:41 taking the five loaves and the *t* fish,
6:41 He divided the *t* fish among all of them
9: 4 the *t* were in conversation with Jesus.
10: 8 and mother and the *t* shall become as one.
10: 8 They are no longer *t* but one flesh.
11: 1 *t* of his disciples with the instruction:
12:14 The *t* groups came and said to him:
12:42 in *t* small copper coins worth a few cents.
14: 1 Bread were to be observed in *t* days' time,
14:13 *t* of his disciples with these instructions:
15:27 With him they crucified *t* insurgents,
15:38 sanctuary was torn in *t* from top to bottom.
16:12 as *t* of them were walking along on their
Lk 2:24 "a pair of turtledoves or *t* young pigeons,"
3:11 man with *t* coats give to him who has none.
5: 2 saw *t* boats moored by the side of the lake;
5: 7 filled the *t* boats until they nearly sank.
7:18 Summoning *t* of them, John sent them
7:41 *T* men owed money to a certain money-lender;
9: 3 No one is to have *t* coats.
9:13 have nothing but five loaves and *t* fish.
9:16 taking the five loaves and the *t* fish,
9:30 Suddenly *t* men were talking with him
9:32 saw the *t* men who were standing with him.
10:35 The next day he took out *t* silver pieces
12:52 three against *t* and two against three;
12:52 three against two and *t* against three;
15:11 "A man had *t* sons.
16:13 "No servant can serve *t* masters.
17:34 that night there will be *t* men in one bed;
17:35 *T* women will be grinding grain together;
18:10 *T* men went up to the temple to pray;
19:29 *t* of the disciples with these instructions:
21: 2 a poor widow putting in *t* copper coins.
22:38 They said, "Lord, here are *t* swords!"
23:32 *T* others who were criminals were led along
23:45 The curtain in the sanctuary was torn in *t*.
24: 4 *t* men in dazzling garments stood beside
24:13 *T* of them that same day were making their
Jn 1:35 was there again with *t* of his disciples.
1:37 The *t* disciples heard what he said,
1:40 One of the *t* who had followed him after
4:40 So he stayed there *t* days,
4:43 When the *t* days were over,
6: 7 "Not even with *t* hundred days' wages
8:17 that evidence given by *t* persons is valid.
11: 6 he stayed on where he was for *t* days more.
11:18 just under *t* miles
19:18 they crucified him, and *t* others with him;
20:12 there she saw *t* angels in dazzling robes.
21: 2 Zebedee's sons, and *t* other disciples.
Acts 1:10 *t* men dressed in white stood beside them.
1:23 At that they nominated *t*, Joseph
1:24 *t* you choose for this apostolic ministry,
1:26 Then they drew lots between the *t* men.
4:23 the *t* went back to their own people and
5: 9 "How could you *t* scheme to put the Spirit
7:29 where he became the father of *t* sons.
8:15 The *t* went down to these people and prayed
9:38 sent *t* men to him with the urgent request,
10: 7 he called *t* servants and a devout soldier
10:19 "There are *t* men in search of you.
12: 6 Peter was sleeping between *t* soldiers,
13: 4 These *t*, sent forth by the Holy Spirit,
13:51 So the *t* shook the dust from their feet
15:12 Barnabas and Paul as the *t* described all
15:39 ensued was so sharp that the *t* separated.
16:40 *t* first made their way to Lydia's house,
19:10 This continued for *t* years,
19:22 So he sent *t* of his assistants, Timothy
19:34 and kept shouting for about *t* hours.
23:23 *t* of his centurions and said to them,
23:23 tonight, with *t* hundred infantrymen,
23:23 seventy cavalrymen, and *t* hundred spearmen.
24:27 *T* years passed, following which Felix
27:37 *t* hundred and seventy-six of us on board.)
28:13 enabled us to reach Puteoli in *t* days.
28:30 For *t* full years Paul stayed on in his
1Cor 6:16 says, "The *t* shall become one flesh."
14:27 in tongues let it be at most *t* or three,
14:29 Let no more than *t* or three prophets speak,
2Cor 13: 1 on the testimony of *t* or three witnesses."
Gal 4:22 it is written that Abraham had *t* sons,
4:24 the two women stand for *t* covenants.
5:17 the *t* are directly opposed.
Eph 2:14 and who made the *t* of us one by breaking
2:15 from us who had been *t* and to make peace,
5:31 his wife, and the *t* shall be made into one."
1Tm 5:19 it is supported by *t* or three witnesses.
2Tm 3: 9 as with those *t* men,
Heb 6:18 so that, by *t* things that are unchangeable,
10:28 on the testimony of *t* or three witnesses.
11:37 They were stoned, sawed in *t*,
Rv 9:12 There are *t* more to come.
9:16 I heard, were *t* hundred million in number
11: 3 I will commission my *t* witnesses to
11: 4 These are the two olive trees and the *t*
11:10 *t* prophets harassed everyone on earth.
11:12 The *t* prophets heard a loud voice from
12:14 for a year and for *t* and a half years more.
13:11 it had *t* horns like a ram and it spoke
14:20 winepress that for *t* hundred miles around,

TWO-EDGED (7)

Jgs 3:16 Ehud made himself a *t* dagger a foot long,
Ps(s) 149: 6 And let *t* swords be in their hands:
Prv 5: 4 bitter as wormwood, as sharp as a *t* sword.
Sir 21: 3 Every offense is a *t* sword;
Heb 4:12 and effective, sharper than any *t* sword.
Rv 1:16 A sharp, *t* sword came out of his mouth,
2:12 with the sharp, *t* sword has this to say:

TWO-HORNED (2)

Dn 8: 6 the *t* ram I had seen standing by the river,
8:20 "The *t* ram you saw represents the kings

TWO-THIRDS (1)

1Sm 13:21 plowshares and mattocks was *t* of a shekel,

TWO-YEAR (2)

1Kgs 16: 8 began his *t* reign over Israel in Tirzah.
2Kgs 15:23 began his *t* reign over Israel in Samaria.

TWOFOLD (5)

Ex 22: 6 thief, if caught, must make *t* restitution.
22: 8 must make *t* restitution to the other.
Wis 11:12 For a *t* grief took hold of them and a
Sir 12: 6 With *t* evil you will meet for every good
48:12 filled with a *t* portion of his spirit,

TYCHICUS (5)

Acts 20: 4 *T* and Trophimus from Asia.
Col 4: 6 *T* and Onesimus.
4: 7 *T*, our dear brother,
2Tm 4:12 *T* I have sent to Ephesus.
Ti 3:12 I send Artemas to you, or perhaps *T*,

TYPE (3)

2Chr 2:13 to devise every *t* of artistic work
Wis 5: 3 as a laughingstock and as a *t* for mockery,
Rom 5:14 as did Adam, that *t* of the man to come.

TYPES (4)

Ex 35:35 them with skill to execute all *t* of work:
Sir 23:16 Two *t* of men multiply sins,
2Pt 2:14 They lure the weaker *t*.
Jude 1: 4 their way into your midst, godless *t*,

TYRANNICAL (1)

Zep 3: 1 rebellious and polluted, to the *t* city!

TYRANNIZE (1)

2Mc 1:28 who *t* over us and arrogantly mistreat us.

TYRANNIZES (1)

Eccl 8: 9 while one man *t* over another to his hurt.

TYRANNUS (1)

Acts 19: 9 from day to day in the lecture hall of *T*.

TYRANNY (1)

Wis 14:21 that men enslaved to either grief or *t*

TYRANT (9)

2Mc 4:25 of a cruel *t* and the rage of a wild beast.
7:27 In derision of the cruel *t*,
Jb 15:20 and limited years are in store for the *t*;
Is 3:12 a babe in arms will be their *t*,
29:20 For the *t* will be no more and the arrogant
49:24 or captives be rescued from a *t*?
49:25 a warrior, and booty be rescued from a *t*;
Jer 51:46 violence in the land, tyrant against *t*.

TYRANTS (4)

Is 13:11 arrogant, the insolence of *t* I will humble.
14: 5 the rod of the wicked, the staff of the *t*
14:21 and fill the breadth of the world with *t*.
29: 5 dust, the horde of the *t* like flying chaff.

TYRE (61)

Jos 19:29 to Ramah and to the fortress city of *T*;
2Sm 5:11 Hiram, king of *T*,
24: 7 going to the fortress of *T* and to all the
1Kgs 5:15 When Hiram, king of *T*,
7:13 King Solomon had Hiram brought from *T*.
7:14 his father had been from *T*.
9:11 Hiram, king of *T*,
9:12 *T* to see the cities Solomon had given him,
1Chr 14: 1 Hiram, king of *T*,
2Chr 2: 2 sent this message to Huram, king of *T*:
2:10 Huram, king of *T*,
2:13 of a Danite woman and of a father from *T*;
Jdt 2:28 the coastland, upon those in Sidon and *T*,
1Mc 5:15 that the inhabitants of Ptolemais, *T*,
11:59 the Ladder of *T* to the frontier of Egypt.
2Mc 4:18 were held at *T* in the presence of the king,
4:32 vessels in *T* and in the neighboring cities.
4:44 When the king came to *T*,
Ps(s) 45:13 And the city of *T* is here with gifts;
83: 8 Philistia with the inhabitants of *T*;
87: 4 Of Philistia, *T*,
Is 23: 1 Oracle on *T*:
23: 5 they shall be in anguish at the news of *T*.
23: 8 Who has planned such a thing against *T*,
23:15 *T* shall be forgotten for seventy years.
23:15 be for *T* as in the song about the harlot:
23:17 the seventy years the LORD shall visit *T*.
Jer 25:22 all the kings of *T*,
27: 3 of Edom, of Moab, of the Ammonites, of *T*,
47: 4 from *T* and Sidon the last of their allies.
Ez 26: 2 man, because of what *T* said of Jerusalem:
26: 3 I am coming at you, *T*;
26: 4 destroy the walls of *T* and raze her towers.
26: 7 I am now bringing up against *T* from the
26:15 Thus says the Lord GOD to *T*:
27: 2 you, son of man, utter a lament over *T*,
27: 3 and say to *T* that is situated at the
27: 3 *T*, you said, "I am a ship, perfect
27:32 destroyed like *T* in the midst of the sea?
28: 2 Son of man, say to the prince of *T*:
28:12 of man, utter a lament over the king of *T*,
29:18 army in an exhausting campaign against *T*.
29:18 from *T* for the campaign he led against it.
Hos 9:13 Ephraim, as I saw, was like *T*,
Jl 4: 4 Moreover, what are you to me, *T* and Sidon,
Am 1: 9 For three crimes of *T*,
1:10 I will send fire upon the wall of *T*,
Mi 7:12 and from Egypt, From *T* even to the River,
Zec 9: 2 Israel, Hamath also, on its border, *T* too,
9: 3 *T* built herself a stronghold,
Mt 11:21 in you had taken place in *T* and Sidon,
11:22 it will go easier for *T* and Sidon than for
15:21 withdrew to the district of *T* and Sidon.
Mk 3: 8 and the neighborhood of *T* and Sidon,
7:24 went off to the territory of *T* and Sidon.
Lk 6:17 and Jerusalem and the coast of *T* and Sidon,
10:13 in your midst had occurred in *T* and Sidon,
10:14 of judgment for *T* and Sidon than for you.
Acts 12:20 infuriated by the people of *T* and Sidon,
21: 3 Finally we put in at *T*,
21: 7 our voyage from *T* we put in at Ptolemais,

TYRIAN (1)

Mk 7:31 He then left *T* territory and returned by

TYRIANS (4)

1Chr 22: 4 The Sidonians and *T* brought great stores
Ezr 3: 7 and drink and oil to the Sidonians and *T*
Neh 13:16 In Jerusalem itself the *T* who were
2Mc 4:49 even some *T* were indignant over the crime

U

UEL (1)

Ezr 10:34 Maadai, Amram, *U*,

UGLY (7)

Gn 41: 3 Behind them seven other cows, *u* and gaunt,
41: 4 bank of the Nile beside the others, the *u*,
41:19 Never have I seen such *u* specimens as
41:20 *u* cows ate up the first seven fat cows.
41:21 so, because they looked as *u* as before.
41:27 *u* cows that came up after them are seven
1Cor 5: 6 This boasting of yours is an *u* thing.

ULAI (2)

Dn 8: 2 I was beside the river *U*.
8:16 the *U* I heard a human voice that cired out,

ULAM (4)

1Chr 7:16 Sheresh, whose sons were *U* and Rakem.
7:17 The sons of *U*:
8:39 The sons of Eshek, his brother, were *U*,
8:40 The sons of *U* were combat archers,

ULLA (1)

1Chr 7:39 The sons of *U* were Arah,

ULTIMATUM (1)

Jdt 8:16 nor human, that he may be given an *u*.

UMBLEMISHED (1)

Heb 9:14 eternal spirit offered himself up *u* to God,

UMBRAGE (1)

1Sm 29:10 Do not decide to take *u* at this;

UMMAH (1)

Jos 19:30 Thus, with Mahalab, Achzib, *U*,

UNABATED (1)

Dt 34: 7 yet his eyes were undimmed and his vigor *u*.

UNABLE (40)

Gn 19:11 they were utterly *u* to reach the doorway.
38:23 kid, even though you were *u* to find her."
Ex 7:18 the Egyptians will be *u* to drink its water."
Lv 5:11 "If he is *u* to afford even two
25:35 to poverty and is *u* to hold out beside you,
Dt 1: 9 I said to you, 'Alone, I am *u* to carry you.
28:29 blind man in the dark, *u* to find your way.
1Kgs 9:21 the Israelites had been *u* to accomplish,
2Kgs 16: 5 besieged Ahaz, they were *u* to conquer him.
2Chr 20:25 so much that they were *u* to carry it all;
20:37 wrecked and were *u* to sail to Tarshish.
Ezr 2:59 and Immer were *u* to prove that their
Neh 6: 3 a great enterprise and am *u* to come down;
6:10 son of Mehetabel, who was *u* to go about,
7:61 and Immer were *u* to prove that their
Jdt 6: 3 be *u* to withstand the force of our cavalry.
Est 6: 1 That night the king, *u* to sleep,
7: 4 the enemy will be *u* to compensate for the
1Mc 10:73 Now you too will be *u* to withstand our
Eccl 8:17 I recognized that man is *u* to find out all
8:17 says that he knows, he is *u* to find it out.
Sir 20:20 A man through want may be *u* to sin,
Is 46: 2 *u* to save those who bear them,
Lam 1:14 me into their grip, I am *u* to rise.
Bar 6:41 *u* to reflect and abandon these gods,
6:53 what is unjustly taken, for they are *u;*
Ez 3:26 you will be dumb and *u* to rebuke them
14:18 be *u* to save either sons or daughters;
Hos 8: 5 they be *u* to attain innocence in Israel?
Mk 2: 4 The four who carried him were *u* to bring
6:19 and wanted to kill him but was *u* to do so.
9:18 to expel him, but they were *u* to do so."
Lk 1:20 But now you will be mute *u* to speak
1:22 finally came out he was *u* to speak to them,
13:24 I tell you, will try to enter and be *u.*
19: 3 was *u* to do so because of the crowd.
20:26 They were *u* to trap him publicly in speech.
Acts 9: 8 Saul got up from the ground *u* to see,
13:11 be blind, *u* so much as to see the sun."
Heb 4:15 who is *u* to sympathize with our weakness,

UNACCEPTABLE (1)

Lv 19: 7 day, the sacrifice will be *u* as refuse,

UNACCUSTOMED (1)

2Mc 14:30 and acting with *u* rudeness when they met;

UNAFFECTED (2)

Phil 1:16 Some act from *u* love,
Ti 1:14 and *u* by Jewish myths or rules invented by

UNAFRAID (3)

Jb 11:15 you may stand firm and *u.*
Ps(s) 78:53 He led them on secure and *u,*
Is 12: 2 I am confident and *u.*

UNALTERABLE (1)

Is 45:23 uttering my just decree and my *u* word:

UNANIMITY (1)

Phil 2: 2 by your *u,* possessing the one love

UNANIMOUSLY (5)

1Kgs 22:13 are *u* predicting good for the king.
2Chr 18:12 the prophets *u* predict good for the king,
2Mc 15:36 By public vote it was *u* decreed never to
Acts 6: 5 proposal was *u* accepted by the community.
15:25 Therefore we have *u* resolved to choose

UNAPPREHENDED (1)

Jn 8:20 went *u* because his hour had not yet come.

UNAPPROACHABLE (1)

1Tm 6:16 has immortality and who dwells in *u* light,

UNASSISTED (1)

Jb 29:12 out for help, the orphans, and the *u;*

UNAWARE (7)

Prv 7:23 into a snare, *u* that its life is at stake.
Wis 12:10 You were not *u* that their race was wicked
18:19 they perish *u* of why they suffered ill.
Is 56:10 My watchmen are blind, all of them *u;*
Dn 13:18 *u* that the elders were hidden inside.
Acts 5: 7 wife came in, *u* of what had happened.
Rom 10: 3 *U* of God's justice and seeking to

UNAWARES (5)

Ps(s) 35: 8 Let ruin come upon them *u,*
35:15 they gathered together striking me *u.*
Wis 17:17 worker at tasks in the wasteland, Taken *u,*
Sir 25:17 his neighbors, a bitter sigh escapes him *u.*
Lk 11:44 like hidden tombs over which men walk *u.*"

UNBALANCED (1)

Sir 3:23 many, and false reasoning *u* their judgment.

UNBARRED (2)

Wis 17:16 into that *u* prison and was kept confined.
Is 45: 1 doors before him and leaving the gates *u:*

UNBECOMING (1)

2Mc 6:24 age it would be *u* to make such a pretense;

UNBELIEF (8)

Jn 20:27 Do not persist in your *u,* but believe!"
Rom 3: 3 their *u* put an end to God's faithfulness?
11:20 of *u* and you are there because of faith.
11:23 in their *u* they will be grafted back on,
1Tm 1:13 I did not know what I was doing in my *u,*
Heb 3:19 was their *u* that kept them from entering.
4: 6 was first announced did not because of *u,*
4:11 in imitation of the example of Israel's *u.*

UNBELIEVABLE (1)

Jdt 13:13 assembled, for her return seemed *u.*

UNBELIEVER (7)

1Cor 7:12 is an *u* but is willing to live with him,
7:13 is an *u* but is willing to live with her,
7:15 If the *u* wishes to separate,
10:27 If an *u* invites you to his table and you
14:24 But if an *u* or an uninitiate enters while
2Cor 6:15 what common lot between believer and *u?*
1Tm 5: 8 he is worse than an *u.*

UNBELIEVERS (8)

Mt 6:32 *u* are always running after these things.
Lk 12:30 The *u* of this world are always running
Rom 15:31 I may be kept safe from the *u* in Judea,
1Cor 6: 6 brother into court, and before *u* at that?
14:23 If the uninitiated or *u* should come in
2Cor 6:14 not yoke yourselves in a mismatch with *u.*
Ti 1:15 but to those defiled *u* nothing is clean.
Heb 11:31 escaped from being destroyed with the *u,*

UNBELIEVING (8)

Mt 17:17 "What an *u* and perverse lot you are!
Mk 9:19 to the crowd, "What an *u* lot you are!
Lk 9:41 "What an *u* and perverse lot you are!
Rom 10:21 my hands to an *u* and contentious people."
1Cor 7:14 The *u* husband is consecrated by his
7:14 the *u* wife is consecrated by her believing
2Cor 4: 4 Their *u* minds have been blinded by the god
Phil 3: 2 Beware of *u* dogs.

UNBLEMISHED (44)

Ex 29: 1 Procure a young bull and two *u* rams.
Lv 4: 3 *u* bull as a sin offering for the sin he
4:23 shall bring as his offering an *u* male goat.
4:28 an *u* she-goat as the offering for his sin.
4:32 a lamb, he shall bring an *u* female.
5:15 his guilt offering an *u* ram from the flock,
5:18 as a guilt offering to the priest an *u* ram
5:25 he shall bring to the LORD an *u* ram
9: 3 a calf and a lamb, both *u* yearlings,
14:10 eighth day he shall take two *u* male lambs,
14:10 male lambs, one *u* yearling ewe lamb,
22:19 or goat that he offers must be an *u* male.
22:21 if it is to find acceptance, it must be *u;*
23:12 LORD for a holocaust an *u* yearling lamb.
23:18 LORD a holocaust of seven *u* yearling lambs,
Nm 6:14 LORD one *u* yearling lamb for a holocaust,
6:14 one *u* yearling ewe lamb for a sin offering,
6:14 offering, one *u* ram as a peace offering,
28: 3 two *u* yearling lambs each day as the
28: 9 day you shall offer two *u* yearling lambs,
28:11 one ram, and seven *u* yearling lambs,
28:19 yearling lambs that you are sure are *u,*
28:27 yearling lambs that you are sure are *u,*
29: 2 one ram, and seven *u* yearling lambs,
29: 8 yearling lambs that you are sure are *u,*
29:13 and fourteen yearling lambs that are *u,*
29:17 two rams, and fourteen *u* yearling lambs,
29:20 two rams, and fourteen *u* yearling lambs,
29:23 two rams, and fourteen *u* yearling lambs,
29:26 two rams, and fourteen *u* yearling lambs,
29:29 two rams, and fourteen *u* yearling lambs,
29:32 two rams, and fourteen *u* yearling lambs,
29:36 one ram, and seven *u* yearling lambs,
Ez 43:22 day present an *u* he-goat as a sin offering,
43:23 bring an *u* young bull and an unblemished
43:25 young bull and a ram from the flock, all *u,*
45:18 shall use an *u* young bull as a sacrifice
46: 4 of six *u* lambs and an unblemished ram,
46: 6 new moon he shall provide an *u* young bull,
46:13 holocaust to the LORD an *u* yearling lamb;
1Pt 1:19 *u* lamb chosen before the world's
Jude 1:24 make you stand *u* and exultant

UNBORN (2)

Eccl 4: 3 And better off than both is the yet *u,*
Rom 9:11 yet *u* and had done neither good nor evil,

UNBOWED (1)

Lk 18:11 with head *u* prayed in this fashion:

UNBROKEN (2)

Dn 14:17 "Are the seals *u,* Daniel?"
14:17 And Daniel answered, "They are *u,*

UNBURIED (4)

2Mc 5:10 he who had cast out so many to lie *u*
Jer 16: 4 *u* they will lie like dung on the ground.
16: 6 this land, and shall go *u* and unlamented.
Ez 39:14 through the land burying those who lie *u,*

UNCALLED-FOR (1)

Prv 26: 2 in its flight, a curse *u* arrives nowhere.

UNCEASING (3)

Jb 33:19 by pain and *u* suffering within his frame,
Ps(s) 74:23 who rebel against you is *u.*
Wis 4:19 corpses and an *u* mockery among the dead.

UNCEASINGLY (6)

1Sm 7: 8 "Implore the LORD our God *u* for us,
2Mc 3:26 they flogged him *u* until they had given
9:11 of God, for he was racked with pain *u.*
Col 1: 9 we have been praying for you *u*
1Thes 4:17 Thenceforth we shall be with the Lord *u.*
2Thes 1: 3 than right that we thank God *u* for you,

UNCERTAIN (3)

Wis 17:13 the more one's expectation is of itself *u,*
1Cor 14: 8 If the bugle's sound is *u,*
1Tm 6:17 and not to rely on so *u* a thing as wealth.

UNCHANGEABLE (1)

Heb 6:18 oath, so that, by two things that are *u,*

UNCHANGED (2)

Lv 13: 5 remained *u* and has not spread on the skin,
Heb 2: 2 if the word spoken through angels stood *u,*

UNCHASTE (1)

Sir 26: 9 haughty stare an *u* wife can be recognized.

UNCHASTENESS (1)

Dt 22:21 Israel by her *u* in her father's house.

UNCHECKED (2)

Jgs 5:15 too, was in the valley, his course *u.*
Is 14: 6 the nations in anger, with oppression *u.*

UNCIRCUMCISED (44)

Gn 17:14 If a male is *u,*
34:14 said, "as to give our sister to an *u* man;
Ex 12:48 But no man who is *u* may partake of it.
Lv 19:23 first look upon its fruit as if it were *u.*
19:23 For three years, while its fruit remains *u,*
26:41 when their *u* hearts are humbled and they
Jgs 14: 3 go and take a wife from the *u* Philistines?"
15:18 of thirst or fall into the hands of the *u?*"
1Sm 14: 6 let us go over to that outpost of the *u.*
17:26 Who is this *u* Philistine
17:36 this *u* Philistine will be as one of them,
31: 4 lest these *u* come and make sport of me."
1Chr 10: 4 that these *u* may not come and maltreat me."
Est C:26 abhor the bed of the *u* or of any foreigner.
1Mc 1:48 unclean animals, to leave their sons *u,*
2:46 also enforced circumcision for any *u* boys
Is 52: 1 shall the *u* or the unclean enter you.
Jer 6:10 their ears are *u,* they cannot give heed;
9:25 the whole house of Israel, are *u* in heart.
Ez 28:10 death of the *u* at the hands of foreigners,
31:18 You shall lie with the *u,*
32:21 down, you and your allies, lie with the *u,*
32:24 gone down *u* to the bottom of the earth,
32:26 throng about her grave, all of them *u,*
32:28 But in the midst of the *u* shall you lie,
32:29 with the *u* they lie,
32:30 they lie *u* with those slain by the sword
32:32 therefore is he laid to rest among the *u,*
44: 7 foreigners, *u* both in heart and flesh,
44: 9 No foreigners, *u* in heart and in flesh,
Acts 7:51 stiff-necked people, *u* in heart and ears,
11: 3 the house of *u* men and ate with them."
Rom 2:25 but if you break it you might as well be *u!*
2:26 an *u* person keeps the precepts of the law,
2:27 If a man who is *u* keeps the law,
3:30 and the *u* on the basis of faith.
4: 9 to the circumcised, or to the *u* as well?
4:11 through faith while he was still *u.*
4:11 to be the father of all the *u* who believe,
4:12 faith which Abraham walked while still *u.*
Gal 2: 7 been entrusted with the gospel for the *u,*
Eph 2:11 called *u*" by those who,
Col 2:13 you were dead in sin and your flesh was *u,*
3:11 is no Greek or Jew here, circumcised or *u,*

UNCLE (13)

Gn 28: 2 from among the daughters of your *u* Laban.
29:10 uncle Laban, with the sheep of his *u* Laban,
Lv 10: 4 and Elzaphan, the sons of Aaron's *u* Uzziel,
20:20 If a man disgraces his *u* by having
25:49 of his own brothers, or by his *u* or cousin,
1Sm 10:14 Saul's *u* inquired of him and his servant,
10:15 Then Saul's *u* said, "Tell me, then,
10:16 Saul said to his *u*, "He assured us
14:50 of his general was Abner, son of Saul's *u*.
2Kgs 24:17 of Babylon appointed his *u* Mattaniah king,
1Chr 27:32 David's *u* and a man of intelligence,
Jer 32: 7 Hanamel, son of your *u* Shallum,

UNCLEAN (223)

Gn 7: 2 and of the *u* animals,
7: 3 male and a female, and of all the *u* birds,
7: 8 Of the clean animals and the *u*,
Lv 5: 2 being aware of it, touches any *u* thing,
5: 2 thing, as the carcass of an *u* wild animal,
5: 2 animal, or that of an *u* domestic animal,
5: 2 animal, or that of an *u* swarming creature,
5: 2 creature, and thus becomes *u* and guilty;
7:19 Should the flesh touch anything *u*,
7:21 Likewise, if someone touches anything *u*,
10:10 between what is clean and what is *u*;
11: 4 not have hoofs and is therefore *u* for you;
11: 5 not have hoofs and is therefore *u* for you;
11: 6 not have hoofs and is therefore *u* for you;
11: 7 chew the cud and is therefore *u* for you.
11: 8 they are *u* for you.
11:24 their dead bodies shall be *u* until evening,
11:25 wash his garments and be *u* until evening.
11:26 or do not chew the cud are *u* for you;
11:26 everyone who touches them becomes *u*.
11:27 all those that walk on paws are *u* for you;
11:27 their dead bodies shall be *u* until evening,
11:28 wash his garments and be *u* until evening.
11:29 on the ground, the following are *u* for you:
11:31 swarming creatures, these are *u* for you.
11:31 they are dead shall be *u* until evening.
11:32 one of them falls when dead becomes *u*.
11:32 be put in water and remain *u* until evening,
11:33 a clay vessel, everything in it becomes *u*,
11:34 men drink, in any such vessel become *u*.
11:35 one of their dead bodies falls, becomes *u*;
11:35 *u* and shall be treated as unclean by you.
11:36 whoever touches the dead body becomes *u*.
11:38 it becomes *u* when one of these falls on it.
11:39 its dead body shall be *u* until evening.
11:40 wash his garments and be *u* until evening;
11:40 wash his garments and be *u* until evening.
11:43 Do not make yourselves loathsome or *u* with
11:44 You shall not make yourselves *u*,
11:47 distinguish between the clean and the *u*,
12: 2 to a boy, she shall be *u* for seven days,
12: 5 she shall be as *u* as at her menstruation.
13: 3 on seeing this, shall declare the man *u*.
13: 8 on the skin, he shall declare the man *u*;
13:11 the man *u* without first quarantining him,
13:11 quarantining him, since he is certainly *u*.
13:14 soon as raw flesh appears on him, he is *u*;
13:15 raw flesh, the priest shall declare him *u*,
13:15 him unclean, because raw flesh is *u*;
13:20 turned white, he shall declare the man *u*;
13:22 the skin, the priest shall declare him *u*;
13:25 declare him *u* and stricken with leprosy.
13:27 the man *u* and stricken with leprosy.
13:30 it, the priest shall declare the person *u*,
13:36 the man is surely *u*.
13:40 is not *u* merely because of his bald crown.
13:41 not *u* merely because of his bald forehead.
13:44 of the body, the man is leprous and *u*,
13:44 him *u* by reason of the sore on his head.
13:45 he shall cry out, 'Unclean, *u*!'
13:46 himself unclean, since he is in fact *u*.
13:51 is malignant leprosy, and the article is *u*.
13:55 is *u* and shall be destroyed by fire.
13:59 to determine whether it is clean or *u*."
14:36 lest everything in the house become *u*.
14:40 and cast in an *u* place outside the city.
14:41 be dumped in an *u* place outside the city.
14:44 is corrosive leprosy, and the house is *u*.
14:45 hauled away to an *u* place outside the city.
14:46 it is quarantined shall be *u* until evening.
15: 2 flow from his private parts is thereby *u*.
15: 4 man afflicted with the flow lies, is *u*,
15: 4 piece of furniture on which he sits, is *u*.
15: 5 bathe in water, and be *u* until evening.
15: 6 bathe in water, and be *u* until evening.
15: 7 bathe in water, and be *u* until evening.
15: 8 bathe in water, and be *u* until evening.
15: 9 on which the afflicted man rides, is *u*.
15:10 was under him shall be *u* until evening;
15:10 bathe in water, and be *u* until evening.
15:11 bathe in water, and be *u* until evening.
15:16 whole body in water and be *u* until evening.
15:17 washed with water and be *u* until evening.
15:18 both bathe in water and be *u* until evening.
15:19 who touches her shall be *u* until evening.
15:20 or sits during her impurity shall be *u*.
15:21 bathe in water, and be *u* until evening.
15:22 bathe in water, and be *u* until evening.
15:23 he touches it, he shall be *u* until evening.
15:24 her impurity and shall be *u* for seven days;
15:24 bed on which he then lies also becomes *u*.
15:25 suffers this *u* flow she shall be unclean,
15:26 she lies during such a flow becomes *u*,
15:26 becomes *u* just as during her menstruation.
15:27 Anyone who touches them becomes *u*;
15:27 bathe in water, and be *u* until evening.
15:30 atonement before the LORD for her *u* flow.
15:32 emission of seed, and thereby becomes *u*;
15:33 also for the man who lies with an *u* woman."
17:15 bathe in water, and be *u* until evening,
18:19 with her while she is *u* from menstruation.
20:25 apart, then, the clean animals from the *u*,
20:25 unclean, and the clean birds from the *u*,
21: 1 *u* for any dead person among his people,
21: 3 for these he may make himself *u*.
21: 4 of his family he shall not make himself *u*;
21:11 he thus become *u* or leave the sanctuary;
22: 4 who has become *u* by contact with a corpse,
22: 6 such as these shall be *u* until evening
22: 8 He shall not make himself *u* by eating of
27:11 is *u* and therefore unfit for sacrifice,
27:27 but if it is an *u* animal,
Nm 5: 2 who has become *u* by contact with a corpse.
6: 7 brother, should they die, may he become *u*,
6: 9 so that his dedicated head becomes *u*,
6:12 valid, because his dedicated head became *u*.
9: 6 who were *u* because of a human corpse and
9: 7 "Although we are *u* because of a corpse,
9:10 your descendants is *u* because of a corpse,
18:15 first-born of man, as well as of *u* animals,
19: 7 He remains *u* until the evening,
19: 8 his body in water, and be *u* until evening.
19:10 wash his garments and be *u* until evening.
19:11 any human being shall be *u* for seven days;
19:13 not been splashed over him, he remains *u*:
19:14 already in it, shall be *u* for seven days;
19:15 or with its lid unfastened, shall be *u*.
19:16 bone or a grave, shall be *u* for seven days.
19:17 For anyone who is thus *u*,
19:19 the *u* on the third and on the seventh day;
19:20 Any *u* man who fails to have himself
19:20 not been splashed over him, he remains *u*.
19:21 with this water shall be *u* until evening.
19:22 *u* person touches becomes unclean itself,
19:22 who touches it becomes *u* until evening."
Dt 12:15 and the *u* as well as the clean may eat it,
12:22 the *u* and the clean eating it alike.
14: 7 not have hoofs and are therefore *u* for you;
14: 8 chew the cud and is therefore *u* for you.
14:10 they are *u* for you.
14:19 too, are *u* for you and shall not be eaten.
15:22 it, the *u* and the clean eating it alike,
23:11 becomes *u* because of a nocturnal emission,
26:14 I have not brought any of it out as one *u*;
Jos 22:19 you consider the land you now possess *u*,
Jgs 13: 4 wine or strong drink and to eat nothing *u*.
13: 7 wine nor strong drink, and eat nothing *u*.
13:14 wine or strong drink, nor eat anything *u*.
1Sm 20:26 "He must have become *u* by accident,
2Chr 23:19 that no one *u* in any respect might enter.
29:16 found in the LORD's temple that was *u*
30:17 Passover victims for all who were *u*
Ezr 9:11 land *u* with the filth of the peoples
1Mc 1:47 shrines, to sacrifice swine and *u* animals,
1:62 in their hearts not to eat anything *u*;
1:63 *u* food or to profane the holy covenant;
4:43 stones of the Abomination to an *u* place.
Eccl 9: 2 good and the bad, for the clean and the *u*,
Sir 34: 4 Can the *u* produce the clean?
Is 6: 5 For I am a man of *u* lips,
6: 5 lips, living among a people of *u* lips;
30:22 And you shall consider *u* your
35: 8 No one *u* may pass over it,
52: 1 shall the uncircumcised or the *u* enter you.
52:11 come forth from there, touch nothing *u*!
64: 5 all of us have become like *u* men,
Jer 2:33 in your wickedness, have gone by ways *u*!
Lam 1:17 has become in their midst a thing *u*.
4:15 "Away you *u*!"
Ez 4:13 *u* among the nations where I scatter them.
4:14 "Never have I been made *u*,
4:14 never has any *u* meat entered my mouth."
22:26 the difference between the *u* and the clean;
44:23 the difference between the clean and the *u*.
44:25 *u* by coming near any dead person,
44:25 for these they may make themselves *u*.
Hos 9: 3 and in Assyria they shall eat *u* food.
9: 4 bread, that makes *u* all who eat of it;
Am 7:17 and you yourself shall die in an *u* land;
Hg 2:13 If a person *u* from contact with a corpse
2:13 touches any of these, do they become *u*?
2:13 The priests answered, "They become *u*."
2:14 and what they offer there is *u*.
Mt 10: 1 gave them authority to expel *u* spirits
12:43 "When the *u* spirit departs from a man,
Mk 1:23 a man with an *u* spirit that shrieked:
1:26 At that the *u* spirit convulsed the man
1:27 He gives orders to *u* spirits and they obey!"
3:11 *U* spirits would catch sight of him,
3:30 had said, "He is possessed by an *u* spirit."
5: 2 a man from the tombs who had an *u* spirit.
5: 8 (Jesus had been saying to him, *U* spirit,
5:13 *u* spirits came out and entered the swine.
6: 7 two, giving them authority over *u* spirits.
7:25 whose small daughter had an *u* spirit,
9:25 reprimanded the *u* spirit by saying to him,
16:20 who does not allow what is *u* and dominated
Lk 4:33 synagogue there was a man with an *u* spirit,
4:36 the *u* spirits with authority and power,
6:18 were troubled with *u* spirits were cured;
8:29 the *u* spirit to come out of the man.
9:42 Jesus then rebuked the *u* spirit,
11:24 "When an *u* spirit has gone out of a man,
Acts 5:16 and those who were troubled by *u* spirits,
8: 7 There were many who had *u* spirits,
10:14 eaten anything *u* or impure in my life."
10:15 God has purified you are not to call *u*."
10:28 no one should call any man *u* or impure.
11: 8 *u* or impure has ever entered my mouth!'
11: 9 God has purified you are not to call *u*.'
Rom 1:24 them up in their lusts to *u* practices;
14:14 the Lord Jesus that nothing is *u* in itself;
14:14 something *u* that it becomes so for him.
1Cor 7:14 were otherwise, your children should be *u*;
2Cor 6:17 'and touch nothing *u*.
Eph 5: 5 no fornicator, no *u* or lustful person
Rv 16:13 I saw three *u* spirits like frogs come from
18: 2 She is a cage for every *u* spirit,

UNCLEANNESS (27)

Lv 5: 3 being aware of it, touches some human *u*,
5: 3 whatever kind of *u* this may be,
7:20 someone while in a state of *u* eats any of
7:21 whether the *u* be of human or of animal
11:24 "Such is the *u* that you contract,
11:28 Such is their *u* for you.
12: 2 with the same *u* as at her menstrual period.
14:19 for the man's *u* shall the priest slaughter
14:57 a state of *u* and when a state of cleanness.
15: 3 Such is his *u* from this flow that it makes
15: 3 his *u* remains.
15:31 shall warn the Israelites of their *u*,
15:31 midst, their *u* be the cause of their death.
16:16 set up among them in the midst of their *u*.
20:25 you may not be contaminated with the *u*
22: 3 dares, while he is in a state of *u*,
22: 5 any swarming creature or any man whose *u*,
Nm 19:13 his *u* still clings to him.
Ezr 6:21 from the *u* of the peoples of the land
9:11 it from one end to the other in their *u*.
Ez 22:15 foreign lands, so that I may purge your *u*.
24:13 and you refused to be purified of your *u*,
39:24 According to their *u* and their
Zec 13: 1 a fountain to purify from sin and *u*.
13: 2 prophets and the spirit of *u* from the land.
2Cor 12:21 earlier and have not repented of the *u*,
Col 3: 5 fornication, *u*,

UNCLES (3)

Gn 29:10 mouth of the well, and watered his *u* sheep.
Lv 20:20 by having intercourse with his *u* wife,
Jer 32: 8 as the LORD foretold, Hanamel, my *u* son,

UNCOMMON (1)

1Sm 3: 1 of the LORD was *u* and vision infrequent.

UNCONCERNED (4)

Dt 22: 3 you may not be *u* about them.
Lam 3:36 crooked claim, the Lord does not look on *u*.
Mt 24:39 *u* until the flood came and destroyed them.
Mk 12:14 a truthful man, *u* about anyone's opinion.

UNCONSOLED (1)

Is 54:11 O afflicted one, storm-battered and *u*,

UNCONTROLLABLE (1)

Gn 27:33 Isaac was seized with a fit of *u* trembling.

UNCONVINCED (1)

Acts 14: 2 But the Jews who remained *u* stirred up the

UNCONVINCING (1)

Jb 6:25 yet how *u* is your argument!

UNCOVER (5)

Nm 5:18 the priest shall *u* her head and place in
Ru 3: 4 Then go, *u* a place at his feet,
Jer 49:10 will *u* his retreats so that he cannot hide.
Ez 22:10 those who *u* the nakedness of their fathers,
Dn 13:32 wicked men ordered her to *u* her face

UNCOVERED (8)

Gn 44:16 God has *u* your servants' guilt.
Ex 20:26 on which you must not be indecently *u*.
Ru 3: 7 she stole up, *u* a place at his feet,
Tb 2: 9 Because of the heat I left my face *u*.
Is 20: 4 with buttocks *u* [the shame of Egypt].
47: 3 shall be *u* and your shame be seen;

Bar 6:30 hair and beard, and with their heads *u.*
1Cor 11: 5 with her head *u* brings shame upon her head.

UNCOVERS (2)

Ex 21:33 "When a man *u* or digs a cistern and does
Is 22: 6 mounts the horses, and Kir *u* the shields.

UNCUT (2)

1Mc 4:47 Then they took *u* stones,
Jb 8:12 While it is yet green and *u,*

UNDEFILED (6)

2Mc 7:40 Thus he too died *u,*
14:36 holiness, preserve forever *u* this house,
15:34 be he who has kept his own Place *u!"*
Wis 3:13 Yes, blessed is she who, childless and *u,*
Heb 7:26 holy, innocent, *u,* separated from sinners,
13: 4 every way and the marriage bed be kept *u,*

UNDEPENDABLE (1)

Jb 6:15 My brethren are *u* as a brook,

UNDERFOOT (8)

2Kgs 14: 9 passed by and trampled the thistle *u.*
Is 26: 6 It is trampled *u* by the needy,
Jer 12:10 my vineyard, have trodden my heritage *u;*
Lam 3:34 tramples *u* all the prisoners in the land.
Mi 7:10 now shall she be trampled *u,*
7:19 compassion on us, treading *u* our guilt?
Zec 9:15 overcome sling stones and trample them *u;*
Mt 5:13 but to be thrown out and trampled *u.*

UNDERGIRD (1)

2Pt 1: 5 every effort to *u* your virtue with faith,

UNDERGO (12)

Ps(s) 16:10 suffer your faithful one to *u* corruption.
Mt 26:41 and pray that you may not *u* the test.
Lk 24:26 *u* all this so as to enter into his glory?"
Acts 2:27 suffer your faithful one to *u* corruption.
2:31 world, nor did his body *u* corruption,
13:35 suffer your faithful one to *u* corruption.'
13:37 God has raised up did not *u* corruption.
14:22 "We must *u* many trials if we are to enter
Gal 2: 3 was with me, was ordered to *u* circumcision,
1Thes 3: 4 we used to warn you that we would *u* trial;
2Tm 1:12 and for its sake I *u* present hardships.
Jude 1: 7 us, as they *u* a punishment of eternal fire.

UNDERGOING (2)

Acts 13:36 joined his fathers, thereby *u* corruption.
1Pt 5: 9 *u* the same sufferings throughout the world.

UNDERGROUND (1)

2Chr 32:30 and led it *u* westward to the City of David.

UNDERHANDED (1)

2Cor 4: 2 Rather, we repudiate shameful, *u* practices.

UNDERLIES (1)

Jas 2:18 I will show you the faith that *u* my works!

UNDERLYING (1)

Sir 28:10 wood, the greater the fire, the more *u* it,

UNDERNEATH (7)

Ex 30: 4 *U* the molding you shall put gold rings,
37:27 *U* the molding gold rings were placed,
Jos 7:21 ground inside my tent, with the silver *u."*
7:22 found them hidden there, with the silver *u.*
2Kgs 6:30 people saw that he was wearing sackcloth *u,*
Jb 28: 5 comes forth bread, is in fiery upheaval *u.*
Mt 7:15 clothing but *u* are wolves on the prowl.

UNDERSTAND (114)

Gn 11: 7 so that one will not *u* what another says."
Dt 7: 9 *U,* then, that the LORD, your God,
9: 3 *U,* then, today that it is the LORD,
9: 6 *U* this, therefore:
11: 2 who must now *u* the discipline of the LORD,
28:49 eagle, a nation whose tongue you do not *u,*
29: 3 day has the LORD yet given you a mind to *u,*
1Sm 12:17 Thus you will see and *u* how greatly the
1Kgs 20: 7 *U* clearly that this man wants to ruin us.
2Kgs 18:26 to your servants in Aramaic; we *u* it.
Neh 8: 2 women, and those children old enough to *u.*
8: 3 women, and those children old enough to *u;*
8: 8 it so that all could *u* what was read.
Jdt 8:13 will you never *u* anything?
8:14 things, discern his mind, and *u* his plan?
Est A:11 every way, until night, to *u* its meaning.
2Mc 11:24 We *u* that the Jews do not agree with our
Jb 17: 4 therefore they do not *u.*
23: 5 answer, and *u* what he would reply to me.
32: 9 who are wise, nor the aged who *u* the right.
42: 3 dealt with great things that I do not *u;*
Ps(s) 36: 4 he has ceased to *u* how to do good.
73:16 to *u* this it seemed to me too difficult,
82: 5 "They know not, neither do they *u;*
92: 7 man knows not, nor does a fool *u* this.
94: 8 *U,* you senseless ones among the people;
107:43 things and to *u* the favors of the LORD?
119:27 Make me *u* the way of your precepts,
139: 2 you *u* my thoughts from afar.
Prv 1: 2 discipline, may *u* words of intelligence;
2: 5 Then will you *u* the fear of the LORD;
2: 9 Then you will *u* rectitude and justice,
20:24 how, then, can a man *u* his way?
28: 5 Evil men *u* nothing of justice,
28: 5 justice, but those who seek the LORD *u* all.
30:18 too wonderful for me, yes, four I cannot *u:*
Eccl 2: 3 until I should *u* what is best for men to
11: 9 Yet *u* that as regards all this God will
Wis 3: 9 Those who trust in him shall *u* truth,
4:14 But the people saw and did not *u,*
4:17 do not *u* what the Lord intended for him,
6: 1 Hear, therefore, kings, and *u;*
Sir 2:10 Study the generations long past and *u;*
23:19 He does not *u* that the eyes of the LORD,
23:27 and all who inhabit the world shall *u*
Is 5:13 go into exile, because they do not *u;*
6: 9 Listen carefully, but you shall not *u!*
6:10 will see, their ears hear, their heart *u,*
29:16 should say of the potter, "He does not *u."*
36:11 to your servants in Aramaic; we *u* it.
41:20 That all may see and know, observe and *u,*
43:10 know and believe in me and *u* that it is I.
44:18 and their hearts so that they cannot *u.*
Jer 5:15 you know not, whose speech you cannot *u.*
9:11 Who is so wise that he can *u* this?
17: 9 heart, beyond remedy; who can *u* it?
23:20 When the time comes, you shall fully *u.*
24: 7 a heart with which to *u* that I am the LORD.
30:24 When the time comes, you will fully *u.*
Bar 6:40 to make noise, as though the man could *u;*
Ez 3: 6 language] whose words you cannot *u.*
17:12 Do you not *u* what this means?
Dn 2:21 to the wise and knowledge to those who *u.*
2:30 you may *u* the thoughts in your own mind.
8:17 But he said to me, *U,* son of man,
8:27 at the vision, which I could not *u.*
9: 2 tried to *u* in the Scriptures the counting
9:23 mark the answer and *u* the vision.
9:25 Know and *u* this:
10:11 me, *u* the words which I am speaking to you;
10:14 and came to make you *u* what shall happen
12: 8 I heard, but I did not *u;*
Hos 14:10 Let him who is wise *u* these things;
Mi 4:12 thoughts of the LORD, nor *u* his counsel,
Mt 13:13 not see, they listen but do not hear or *u.*
13:14 'Listen as you will, you shall not *u,*
13:15 with their ears, and *u* with their hearts,
15:10 "Give ear and try to *u.*
16: 9 Do you still not *u?*
22:29 to *u* the Scriptures and the power of God.
Mk 4:12 and not see, listen carefully and not *u,*
4:13 "You do not *u* this parable?
4:13 are you going to *u* other figures like it?
4:33 them the message in a way they could *u.*
7:14 "Hear me, all of you, and try to *u.*
8:21 said to them again, "Do you still not *u?"*
9:32 Though they failed to *u* his words,
12:24 to *u* the Scriptures or the power of God.
Lk 8:10 not perceive, and hearing they may not *u.'*
9:45 They failed, however, to *u* this warning;
Jn 3:10 and still you do not *u* these matters?
4:22 You people worship what you do not *u,*
4:22 not understand, while we *u* what we worship;
8:43 he who sent me Why do you not *u* what I say?
12:16 first, the disciples did not *u* all this,
13: 7 now what I am doing, but later you will *u!"*
13:12 "Do you *u* what I just did for you?
20: 9 as yet they did not *u* the Scripture that
Acts 7:25 He assumed that his kinsmen would *u* that
24:11 you, since you are in a position to *u.*
28:26 may listen carefully yet you will never *u;*
28:27 hear with their ears, *u* with their minds,
Rom 7:15 I cannot even *u* my own actions.
10:19 question again, did Israel really not *u?*
15:21 him, and they who have never heard will *u."*
2Cor 1:13 write anything that you cannot read and *u.*
7: 8 Or if I did feel some regret (because I *u*
13: 6 I hope you will *u* that we have not failed.
Gal 4:12 *U,* you have not done me any wrong.)
Eph 1: 9 given us the wisdom to *u* fully the mystery,
2Pt 1:12 even though you already *u* and are firmly
1:20 First you must *u* this:
3:16 are certain passages in them hard to *u.*
1Jn 3:16 The way we came to *u* love was that he

UNDERSTANDING (112)

Ex 31: 3 skill and *u* and knowledge in every craft:
35:31 skill and *u* and knowledge in every craft:
36: 1 the LORD has endowed with skill and *u*
Dt 32:28 are a people devoid of reason, having no *u.*
1Kgs 2:42 LORD to your clear *u* of my warning that,
3: 9 an *u* heart to judge your people and to
3:11 for *u* so that you may know what is right
3:12 I give you a heart so wise and *u* that
5: 9 wisdom and exceptional *u* and knowledge,
7:14 He was endowed with skill, *u,*
1Chr 12:33 who were endowed with an *u* of the times
2Chr 2:11 David a wise son of intelligence and *u,*
Neh 9:20 you bestowed on them, to give them *u;*
2Mc 9:11 excessive arrogance, and to gain some *u,*
Jb 8:10 and tell you and utter their words of *u?*
11:12 Will empty man then gain *u,*
12:12 age is wisdom, and with length of days *u.*
12:13 his are counsel and *u.*
12:24 He takes *u* from the leaders of the land,
20: 2 and from my *u* a spirit gives me a reply.
28:12 be obtained, and where is the place of *u?*
28:20 comes wisdom, and where is the place of *u?*
28:28 LORD is wisdom; and avoiding evil is *u.*
32: 8 breath of the Almighty, that gives him *u.*
34:10 Therefore, men of *u,* hearken to me:
34:34 Men of *u* will say to me,
38: 4 Tell me, if you have *u.*
38:36 in the heart, and gives the cock its *u?*
39:17 from her and has given her no share in *u.*
Ps(s) 119:99 I have more *u* than all my teachers when
119:130 words sheds light, giving *u* to the simple.
Prv 2: 2 ear to wisdom, inclining your heart to *u;*
2: 3 to intelligence, and to *u* raise your voice;
2: 6 from his mouth come knowledge and *u;*
2:11 will watch over you, *u* will guard you;
3:13 man who finds wisdom, the man who gains *u!*
3:19 the earth, established the heavens by *u;*
4: 1 be attentive, that you may gain *u!*
4: 5 "Get wisdom, get *u!*
4: 7 at the cost of all you have, get *u.*
5: 2 may watch over you, and *u* may guard you.
7: 4 call *U,* "Friend!"
8: 1 not Wisdom call, and *U* raise her voice?
8:14 Mine is strength; I am *u.*
9: 4 to him who lacks *u,*
9: 6 advance in the way of *u.*
9:10 LORD, and knowledge of the Holy One is *u.*
9:16 is simple turn in here, or who lacks *u;*
15:21 but the man of *u* goes the straight way.
15:32 own soul, but he who heeds reproof gains *u.*
16:16 To acquire *u* is more desirable than silver.
18: 2 The fool takes no delight in *u,*
19: 8 he who keeps *u* will be successful.
21:30 There is no wisdom, no *u,*
23:23 wisdom, instruction and *u.*
24: 3 is a house built, by *u* is it made firm;
Eccl 10: 2 The wise man's *u* turns him to his right;
10: 2 the fool's *u* turns him to his left.
10: 3 his lack of *u* he calls everything foolish.
Wis 3:15 and unfailing is the root of *u.*
4: 9 Rather, *u* is the hoary crown for men,
8: 4 For she is instructress in the *u* of God,
Sir 1: 4 else wisdom was created; and prudent *u,*
1:17 Knowledge and full *u* she showers down;
3:22 not, when shown things beyond human *u.*
11:15 Wisdom and *u* and knowledge of affairs,
15: 3 Nourish him with the bread of *u,*
17: 5 and ears, and imparts to them an *u* heart.
19:20 There are those with little *u* who fear God,
22:17 A resolve that is backed by prudent *u* is
24:24 It runs over, like the Euphrates, with *u,*
25: 5 is wisdom, *u* and prudence to the venerable!
39: 6 he will be filled with the spirit of *u;*
39: 9 Many will praise his *u;*
42:20 No *u* does he lack; no single thing
45: 5 the commandments, the law of life and *u,*
47:15 Your *u* covered the whole earth,
50:27 as they gushed forth from my heart's *u.*
51:20 *u* such that I will never forsake her.
Is 11: 2 a spirit of wisdom and of *u,*
27:11 This is not an *u* people;
29:14 perish and the *u* of its prudent men be hid.
29:24 Those who err in spirit shall acquire *u,*
40:14 of judgment, or showed him the way of *u?*
Jer 4:22 Senseless children they are, having no *u;*
Bar 3:14 prudence is, where strength, where *u;*
3:20 land, But the way to *u* they have not known,
3:27 choose, nor did he give them the way of *u;*
3:37 He has traced out all the way of *u,*
Dn 1:17 to Daniel the *u* of all visions and dreams.
9:22 "Daniel, I have now come to give you *u.*
10:12 acquire *u* and humble yourself before God,
12:10 none of them shall have *u,* but the wise
Hos 4:11 Old wine and new deprive my people of *u.*
4:14 So must a people without *u* come to ruin.
Ob 1: 7 There is no *u* in him!
1: 8 from Edom, and *u* from the mount of Esau?
Zec 6:13 the two of them there shall be friendly *u.*
Mt 13:19 the message about God's reign without *u* it.
15:16 "Are you, too, still incapable of *u?"*
Mk 7:18 "Are you, too, incapable of *u?"*
Lk 24:45 their minds to the *u* of the Scriptures.
Jn 11:49 "You have no *u* whatever!
2Cor 3:15 when Moses is read a veil covers their *u.*
Eph 4:18 their minds empty, their *u* darkened.
Phil 1: 9 abound, both in *u* and wealth of experience.
4: 2 come to some mutual *u* in the Lord.

UNDERSTANDING (cont.)

4: 7 God's own peace, which is beyond all *u*,
1Tm 1: 7 actually not *u* the words they are using,
1: 9 that is, with the *u* that it is aimed,
Jas 3:13 If one of you is wise and *u*,
1Pt 1:13 So gird the loins of your *u*;

UNDERSTANDS (12)

1Chr 28: 9 all hearts and *u* all the mind's thoughts.
Prv 29:19 for he *u* what is said, but obeys not.
Wis 8: 8 She *u* the turns of phrases and the
9: 9 Who *u* what is pleasing in your eyes and
9:11 For she knows and *u* all things,
Sir 14:21 her ways in his heart, and *u* her paths;
15:19 he *u* man's every deed.
18:10 He sees and *u* that their death is grievous,
40:29 of spirit to one who *u* inward feelings:
42:18 their innermost being he *u*.
Rom 3:11 there is no one who *u*, no one in search
1Cor 14: 2 No one *u* him, because he utters

UNDERSTOOD (21)

Gn 42:23 of course, that Joseph *u* what they said,
Nm 20:29 the community *u* that Aaron had passed away;
1Sm 3: 8 Eli *u* that the LORD was calling the youth.
1Chr 14: 2 David now *u* that the LORD had truly
17:20 no God but you, just as we have always *u*.
2Chr 33:13 Manasseh *u* that the LORD is indeed God.
Neh 8:12 for they *u* the words that had been
Ps(s) 73:22 soul was pierced, I was stupid and *u* not;
Is 1: 3 Israel does not know, my people has not *u*.
33:19 speech, stammering in a language not *u*.
40:21 Have you not *u*?
Bar 3:31 the way to her, nor has any *u* her paths.
Dn 5:12 He knew and *u* how to interpret dreams,
10: 1 a great war; he *u* it from the vision.
Zec 11:11 me *u* that this was the word of the LORD.
Mt 12: 7 If you *u* the meaning of the text,
13:51 "Have you *u* all this?"
Mk 6:52 for they had not *u* about the loaves.
Lk 2:17 they *u* what had been told them concerning
18:34 They *u* nothing of this.
Jn 13:28 at table *u* why Jesus said this to him.

UNDERTAKE (13)

Nm 4: 3 to *u* obligatory tasks in the meeting tent.
4:23 to *u* obligatory tasks in the meeting tent.
4:30 to *u* obligatory tasks in the meeting tent.
4:35 to *u* obligatory tasks in the meeting tent,
4:39 to *u* obligatory tasks in the meeting tent,
4:43 to *u* obligatory tasks in the meeting tent,
4:47 who were to *u* tasks of service or transport
Dt 14:29 your God, may bless you in all that you *u*.
28:20 and frustration in every enterprise you *u*,
1Sm 26:25 shall certainly succeed in whatever you *u*."
Ezr 6:12 overthrow every king or people who may *u*
Is 3: 7 "I will not *u* to cure this,
Acts 6: 9 Asia) would *u* to engage Stephen in debate,

UNDERTAKEN (7)

Gn 2: 2 the seventh day from all the work he had *u*.
1Kgs 7:51 When all the work *u* by King Solomon in the
2Chr 5: 1 When all the work *u* by Solomon for the
29:31 "You have *u* a work for the LORD.
Est C:19 but have *u* to do away with the decree you
1Mc 4:51 Thus they finished all the work they had *u*.
Lk 1: 1 Many have *u* to compile a narrative of the

UNDERTAKES (2)

2Mc 2:29 while the man who *u* the decoration and the
Sir 29:19 and he who *u* too much falls into lawsuits.

UNDERTAKING (7)

Gn 24: 9 master Abraham and swore to him in this *u*.
Jgs 18: 5 the *u* we are engaged in will succeed."
18: 6 is favorable to the *u* you are engaged in."
Jdt 10: 8 you to favor, and make your *u* a success,
13: 4 on my *u* for the exaltation of Jerusalem;
Dn 8:12 to the ground, and was succeeding in its *u*.
8:24 about fearful ruin, and succeed in his *u*.

UNDERTAKINGS (14)

Dt 2: 7 your God, has blessed you in all your *u*;
12: 7 shall eat and make merry over all your *u*,
12:18 LORD, you shall make merry over all your *u*.
15:10 bless you for this in all your works and *u*.
16:15 you in all your crops and in all your *u*,
23:21 *u* on the land you are to enter and occupy.
24:19 your God, may bless you in all your *u*.
28: 8 upon you, on your barns and on all your *u*,
28:12 rain in due season, blessing all your *u*,
2Sm 8: 6 LORD brought David victory in all his *u*.
8:14 LORD brought David victory in all his *u*.
2Chr 32:30 Hezekiah prospered in all his *u*.
Jdt 11: 6 and my lord will not fail in any of his *u*.
2Mc 10:23 As he was successful at arms in all his *u*,

UNDERTOOK (5)

Jgs 2:15 Whatever they *u*, the LORD turned into
2Chr 31:21 Everything that he *u*, for the service
Neh 2:18 And they *u* the good work with vigor.
Eccl 2: 4 I *u* great works; I built myself houses
Wis 17: 8 For they who *u* to banish fears and terrors

UNDESERVED (2)

Ps(s) 35:19 let not my *u* foes wink knowingly.
38:20 But my *u* enemies are strong;

UNDESERVEDLY (1)

Rom 3:24 men are now *u* justified by the gift of God,

UNDESERVING (2)

Est E: 7 influence of those *u* of authority.
Lk 12:46 and rank him among those *u* of trust.

UNDIMMED (2)

Dt 34: 7 yet his eyes were *u* and his vigor unabated.
Prv 31:18 at night her lamp is *u*.

UNDISCLOSED (1)

Dn 8:26 Do you, however, keep this vision *u*,

UNDISTURBED (15)

Dt 33:28 has been *u* In a land of grain and wine,
2Kgs 23:18 So they left his bones *u* together with the
1Chr 17: 9 them in it to dwell there henceforth *u*;
Est B: 7 our affairs stable and *u* for the future."
E: 8 the kingdom *u* and peaceful for all men,
2Mc 11:23 to be *u* in conducting their own affairs.
11:25 desire that this people too should be *u*,
Jb 12: 5 The *u* esteem my downfall a disgrace such
Sir 2: 2 and steadfast, *u* in time of adversity.
Is 17: 2 given over to flocks to lie in *u*.
Jer 30:10 again find rest, shall be tranquil and *u*,
46:27 again find rest, shall be tranquil and *u*.
Mi 4: 4 his own vine or under his own fig tree, *u*;
Lk 11:21 guards his courtyard, his possessions go *u*.
1Tm 2: 2 that we may be able to lead *u* and tranquil

UNDIVIDED (1)

2Chr 15:17 yet Asa's heart was *u* as long as he lived.

UNDO (2)

2Sm 15:34 will *u* for me the counsel of Ahithophel.
17:14 had decided to *u* Ahithophel's good counsel,

UNDOING (3)

Jer 26:19 of committing this great evil to our own *u*."
Mt 18: 8 If your hand or foot is your *u*,
Mk 9:45 If your foot is your *u*, cut it off!

UNDONE (4)

Jos 11:15 He left nothing *u* that the LORD had
Sir 22:21 against a friend, despair not, it can be *u*.
Jer 10:19 I am *u*, my wound is incurable;
Ti 1: 5 you might accomplish what had been left *u*,

UNDOUBTEDLY (1)

Jn 6:14 "This is *u* the Prophet who is to come

UNDRESSED (1)

Dt 27: 6 altar of the LORD, your God, with *u* stones,

UNDULY (2)

Sir 35:13 Though not *u* partial toward the weak,
Acts 24: 4 But now, lest I impose on your time *u*,

UNDYING (2)

Wis 1:15 nether world on earth, For justice is *u*.
Ez 25:15 malice in their hearts, with an *u* enmity,

UNEDUCATED (1)

Acts 4:13 the speakers were *u* men of no standing,

UNENDING (2)

Sir 30:17 bitter life, *u* sleep to constant illness.
Phil 4:20 All glory to our God and Father for *u* ages!

UNENDINGLY (1)

Is 28:28 No, he does not thresh it *u*,

UNENLIGHTENED (1)

Rom 10: 2 are zealous for God though their zeal is *u*.

UNEQUAL (1)

Est E:12 But, *u* to this dignity,

UNERRING (4)

2Sm 22:31 God's way is *u*;
22:33 girded me with strength and kept my way *u*;
Ps(s) 18:31 God's way is *u*,
18:33 me with strength and kept my way *u*;

UNEXPECTED (5)

Tb 10: 6 have to take care of some *u* business there.
2Mc 9:24 *u* happened or any unwelcome news came,
Wis 17:15 for fear came upon them, sudden and *u*.
18:17 perturbed them and *u* fears assailed them;
Sir 39:20 to him there is nothing *u*.

UNEXPECTEDLY (3)

2Sm 18: 9 Absalom *u* came up against David's servants.
2Mc 8: 6 Coming *u* upon towns and villages,
Ps(s) 58:10 *U*, like a thorn-bush,

UNFADING (4)

Wis 6:12 Resplendent and *u* is Wisdom,
Sir 39: 9 *U* will be his memory,
1Pt 3: 4 *u* beauty of a calm and gentle disposition.
5: 4 win for yourselves the *u* crown of glory.

UNFAILING (8)

2Mc 14:34 *u* defender of our nation in these words:
Prv 31:11 his heart to her, has an *u* prize.
Wis 3:15 and *u* is the root of understanding.
7:14 For to men she is an *u* treasure;
8:18 and *u* riches in the works of her hands,
19:22 *u*, you stood by them in every time
Am 5:24 like water, and goodness like an *u* stream.
Eph 6:24 who love our Lord Jesus Christ with *u* love.

UNFAILINGLY (2)

Zep 3: 5 after morning he renders judgment *u*,
2Cor 2:14 *u* leads us on in Christ's triumphal train,

UNFAIR (2)

Ez 18:25 Is it my way that is *u*,
18:25 is unfair, or rather, are not your ways *u*?

UNFAIRLY (3)

Lv 25:14 or buy any from him, do not deal *u*.
25:17 Do not deal *u*,
Jb 19: 6 Know then that God has dealt *u* with me,

UNFAITHFUL (13)

Nm 5:12 If a man's wife goes astray and becomes *u*
5:27 she has been impure and *u* to her husband,
Jgs 19: 2 His concubine was *u* to him and left him
2Chr 12: 2 Jerusalem, for they had been *u* to the LORD.
28:22 King Ahaz became even more *u* to the LORD.
Ps(s) 73:27 you destroy everyone who is *u* to you.
Sir 23:22 So also with the woman who is *u* to her
42:10 seduced, or, as a wife, lest she prove *u*;
Hos 9: 1 For you have been *u* to your God,
Mt 12:39 "An evil and *u* age is eager for a sign!
2Tm 2:13 If we are *u* he will still remain faithful,
Heb 3:12 *u* spirit and fall away from the living God.
Jas 4: 4 O you *u* ones, are you not aware

UNFAITHFULNESS (2)

Nm 31:16 advice prompted the *u* of the Israelites
Ezr 10:10 "Your *u* in taking foreign women as wives

UNFAMILIAR (2)

Wis 19:14 those others did not receive *u* visitors,
Acts 17:20 You are introducing subjects *u* to us and

UNFASTEN (2)

Jn 1:27 strap of whose sandal I am not worthy to *u*."
Acts 13:25 am not worthy to *u* the sandals on his feet.'

UNFASTENED (1)

Nm 19:15 vessel that is open, or with its lid *u*,

UNFATHOMABLE (2)

Prv 25: 3 earth in depth, the heart of kings is *u*.
Eph 3: 8 grace to preach to the Gentiles the *u* riches

UNFETTERED (1)

Dn 3:92 he replied, "I see four men *u* and unhurt,

UNFIT (3)

Lv 27:11 is unclean and therefore *u* for sacrifice,
Mt 22: 8 but those who were invited were *u* to come.
Lk 9:62 looking back is *u* for the reign of God."

UNFORGETTABLE (3)

2Mc 6:31 of courage and an *u* example of virtue
Jer 20:11 to utter shame, to lasting, *u* confusion.
23:40 you eternal reproach, eternal, *u* shame.

UNFORTUNATE (6)

1Mc 5:16 what they should do for their *u* kinsmen
Jb 5:16 Thus the *u* have hope,
36:15 he saves the *u* through their affliction,
Ps(s) 10: 8 his eyes spy upon the *u*.
10:10 lies prone till by his violence fall the *u*.
10:14 On you the *u* man depends;

UNFORTUNATELY (1)

Phil 3:18 *U,* many go about in a way which shows them

UNFOUNDED (1)

2Mc 7:34 insolence, concern yourself with *u* hopes,

UNFRUITFUL (3)

Dt 29:22 and salt, a burnt-out waste, unsown and *u,*
2Kgs 2:19 see, but the water is bad and the land *u.*"
Hos 9:14 Give them an *u* womb, and dry breasts!

UNFULFILLED (7)

Jos 23:14 your God, made to you has remained *u.*
1Kgs 8:56 Not a single word has gone *u* of the entire
2Kgs 10:10 against the house of Ahab shall go *u.*
Tb 14: 4 Not one of all the oracles shall remain *u,*
Jdt 6: 4 spoken, and his words shall not remain *u.*
Est F: 2 and not a single detail has been left *u*—
Sir 16:13 a just man's hope God does not leave *u.*

UNGENEROUS (1)

1Sm 25: 3 Calebite, was harsh and *u* in his behavior.

UNGODLINESS (1)

Jer 23:15 *u* has gone forth into the whole land.

UNGODLY (2)

2Mc 4:13 of the *u* pseudo-high-priest Jason,
8:14 those whom the *u* Nicanor had sold

UNGRATEFUL (2)

Lk 6:35 he himself is good to the *u* and the wicked.
2Tm 3: 2 abusive, disobedient to their parents, *u,*

UNGRUDGINGLY (2)

Wis 7:13 I learned about her, and *u* do I share
Jas 1: 5 the God who gives generously and *u* to all,

UNGUARDED (1)

Mt 12:36 accountable for every *u* word they speak.

UNHAMPERED (1)

Wis 7:22 Not baneful, loving the good, keen, *u,*

UNHAPPY (1)

1Sm 1:15 "I am an *u* woman.

UNHARMED (4)

1Sm 24:20 meets his enemy, does he send him away *u?*
Tb 5:22 will be successful, and he will return *u.*"
2Mc 12:25 his solemn pledge to restore them *u,*
Wis 19: 6 that your children might be preserved *u.*

UNHARVESTED (1)

Ex 23:11 you shall let the land lie untilled and *u,*

UNHEARD (2)

Jer 9: 9 crosses them, *u* is the bleat of the flock;
Jn 9:32 It is *u* of that anyone ever gave sight to

UNHEARD-OF (2)

Wis 14:23 or frenzied carousals in *u* rites,
Sir 10:13 *u* afflictions and brings men to utter ruin.

UNHEEDED (3)

Eccl 9:16 poor man is despised and his words go *u.*
Jer 29:19 the prophets, only to have them go *u,*
36:31 all the threats of evil which went *u.*

UNHESITATINGLY (1)

Acts 10:20 Go downstairs and set out with them *u,*

UNHEWN (1)

Jos 8:31 of *u* stones on which no iron tool had been

UNHOLY (2)

1Cor 6: 9 *u* will not fall heir to the kingdom of God?
1Jn 3:10 No one whose actions are *u* belongs to God,

UNHOPED-FOR (1)

Wis 11: 7 You gave them abundant water in an *u* way,

UNHURT (3)

Ex 10: 5 up the remnant you saved *u* from the hail,
Dn 3:92 "I see four men unfettered and *u,*
6:24 the den, *u* because he trusted in his God.

UNIMPEDED (1)

Wis 19: 7 Out of the Red Sea an *u* road,

UNIMPRESSIVE (1)

2Cor 10:10 he is *u* and his word makes no great impact.

UNINHABITED (5)

1Mc 3:45 Jerusalem was *u,*
Wis 11: 2 They journeyed through the *u* desert,
Jer 22: 6 I will turn you into a waste, a city *u.*
44: 2 Today they are ruins and *u,*
Ez 29:11 it, and it will be *u* for forty years.

UNINITIATE (1)

1Cor 14:24 *u* enters while all are uttering prophecy,

UNINITIATED (1)

1Cor 14:23 If the *u* or unbelievers should come in

UNINTELLIGENT (1)

Rom 1:14 and non-Greeks, to learned and *u* alike.

UNINTENDED (1)

Jos 20: 3 one guilty of accidental and *u* homicide

UNINTENTIONALLY (3)

Nm 35:11 who has killed someone *u* may take refuge.
35:15 has killed another *u* may take refuge there.
Jos 20: 5 man *u* and not out of previous hatred.

UNINTERRUPTEDLY (1)

Mk 5: 5 *U* night and day, amid the tombs

UNION (5)

Dt 23: 3 No child of an incestuous *u* may be
Acts 15:20 by idols, from illicit sexual *u,*
15:29 animals, and from illicit sexual *u.*
21:25 of strangled animals, and illicit sexual *u.*"
1Jn 2: 5 The way we can be sure we are in *u* with

UNIONS (1)

Wis 4: 6 For children born of lawless *u* give

UNIQUE (2)

Wis 7:22 in her is a spirit intelligent, holy, *u,*
2Pt 1:17 when that *u* declaration came to him

UNISON (4)

1Chr 14: 8 Israel, they went up in *u* to seek him out.
Wis 10:20 name and praised in *u* your conquering hand
Hos 11: 7 and God, though in *u* they cry out to him,
Acts 19:34 he was a Jew, they started to chant in *u,*

UNIT (1)

Rv 21:17 by the *u* of measurement the angel used.

UNITE (3)

Gn 19:31 to *u* with us as was the custom everywhere.
34:30 if these people *u* against me and attack me,
38: 8 said to Onan, *U* with your brother's widow,

UNITED (11)

Jos 10: 5 *u* all their forces and marched against
Jdt 14:10 and he has been *u* with the house of Israel
1Mc 2:69 them, and he was *u* with his fathers.
10:61 of the law, *u* against him to accuse him,
13: 6 nations out of hatred have *u* to destroy us."
Dn 2:43 intermarriage, but they shall not stay *u,*
Rom 6: 5 *u* with him through likeness to his death,
1Cor 1:10 rather, be *u* in mind and judgment.
5: 4 *U* in spirit with you and empowered by our
Phil 2: 2 the one love, *u* in spirit and ideals.
Col 2: 2 and themselves to be closely *u* in love,

UNITS (2)

2Sm 18: 4 out in *u* of a hundred and of a thousand.
Lk 19:13 servants and gave them sums of ten *u* each,

UNITY (5)

Est B: 4 so that the *u* of empire blamelessly
Ps(s) 122: 3 Jerusalem, built as a city with compact *u.*
Jn 17:23 that their *u* may be complete.
Eph 4: 3 Make every effort to preserve the *u* which
Phil 1:27 that you are standing firm in *u* of spirit

UNIVERSAL (15)

Wis 10: 5 when the nations were sunk in *u* wickedness,
Jer 13:19 All Judah is banished in *u* exile.
Acts 3:21 time of *u* restoration which God spoke

UNIVERSE (15)

2Mc 7:23 of the *u* who shapes each man's beginning,
Eccl 11: 5 of God which he is accomplishing in the *u.*
Wis 5:20 *u* shall war with him against the foolhardy.
7:17 of the *u* and the force of its elements,
11:17 had fashioned the *u* from formless matter,
11:22 the whole *u* is as a grain from a balance.
14: 6 were being destroyed, the hope of the *u,*
16:17 For the *u* fights on behalf of the just.
Sir 36: 1 Come to our aid, O God of the *u,*
42:24 The *u* lives and abides forever;
1Cor 4: 9 We have become a spectacle to the *u,*
Eph 1:23 of him who fills the *u* in all its parts.
Heb 1: 2 through whom he first created the *u.*
Jas 3: 6 among our members as a whole *u* of malice.
Rv 5:13 everything in the *u* cried aloud:

UNJUST (25)

Ex 23: 1 in putting your hand, as an *u* witness,
Dt 19:16 "If an *u* witness takes the stand against
2Mc 4:35 and angry over the *u* murder of the man.
4:48 vessels, quickly suffered *u* punishment.
Jb 27: 7 be as the wicked and my adversary as the *u!*
Ps(s) 35:11 *U* witnesses have risen up;
Wis 10: 3 the *u* man withdrew from her in his anger,
12:12 into your presence as vindicator of *u* men?
12:23 Hence those *u* also, who lived a life
Sir 1:19 One cannot justify *u* anger;
33:30 it over any human being, and do nothing *u.*
Is 10: 1 Woe to those who enact *u* statutes and who
Jer 23:10 is an evil course, theirs is *u* power.
Ez 22:13 because of the *u* profits you have made
22:27 blood and destroying lives to get *u* gain.
Dn 3:32 to an *u* king, the worst in all the world.
13:53 passing *u* sentences,
Mt 5:45 the good, he rains on the just and the *u.*
Lk 16:10 while anyone *u* in a slight matter is also
16:10 in a slight matter is also *u* in greater.
Acts 1:18 bought a piece of land with his *u* gains,
Rom 3: 5 "Is not God *u* when he inflicts punishment?"
9:14 That God is *u?*
Heb 6:10 God is not *u;* he will not forget
1Pt 3:18 all, the just man for the sake of the *u,*

UNJUSTIFIED (1)

2Mc 4:40 Lysimachus launched an *u* attack against

UNJUSTLY (13)

Lv 5:21 retaining his neighbor's goods *u,*
5:23 that was stolen or *u* retained by him
1Mc 2:37 are our witnesses that you destroy us *u.*"
15:33 for a time had been *u* held by our enemies.
2Mc 8:16 number of the Gentiles attacking them *u,*
Jb 22: 6 have *u* kept your kinsmen's goods in pawn,
Ps(s) 82: 2 judge *u* and favor the cause of the wicked?
119:78 proud be put to shame for oppressing me *u;*
Wis 12:13 you need show you have not *u* condemned;
Is 58: 6 releasing those bound *u,*
Jer 17:11 her own is the man who acquires wealth *u:*
Bar 6:53 nor do they recover what is *u* taken,
Col 3:25 *u* will be repaid for the wrong he has done.

UNKINDLY (1)

Gn 26:29 you shall not act *u* toward us,

UNKNOWN (16)

Dt 8: 3 manna, a food *u* to you and your fathers,
8:16 with manna, a food *u* to your fathers,
Jgs 16: 9 and the secret of his strength remained *u.*
2Mc 1:19 sure that the place would be *u* to anyone.
2: 7 "The place is to remain *u* until God
Ps(s) 19:13 Cleanse me from my *u* faults!
139:15 frame *u* to you When I was made in secret,
Prv 14:33 abides, but in the bosom of fools it is *u.*
Wis 11:18 *u* beasts to breathe forth fiery breath,
18: 3 pillar which was a guide on the *u* way,
Is 42:16 by paths *u* I will guide them.
Dn 11:38 a god *u* to his fathers he shall glorify
Lk 2:43 Jesus remained behind *u* to his parents.
Acts 17:23 discovered an altar inscribed, 'To a God *U.*'
Rom 3:17 The path of peace is *u* to them;
Eph 3: 5 *u* to men in former ages but now revealed

UNLAMENTED (2)

Jer 16: 4 *U* and unburied they will lie like dung on
16: 6 in this land, and shall go unburied and *u.*

UNLAWFUL (6)

2Kgs 17: 9 They adopted *u* practices toward the LORD,
2Mc 4:14 in the *u* exercises on the athletic field.
6:20 it is *u* to taste even for love of life.
6:21 *u* ritual meal took the man aside privately,
Prv 1:19 *u* gain takes away the life of him who
Wis 3:16 and the progeny of an *u* bed will disappear

UNLEASH (2)

Lv 26:22 I will *u* the wild beasts against you,
Ez 7: 3 I will *u* my anger against you and judge

UNLEASHED (1)

Jer 25:32 storm is *u* from the ends of the earth.

UNLEAVENED (61)

Ex 12: 8 flesh with *u* bread and bitter herbs.
12:15 For seven days you must eat *u* bread.
12:17 "Keep, then, this custom of the *u* bread.
12:18 day of this month you shall eat *u* bread.
12:20 you dwell you may eat only *u* bread."
12:39 not leavened, they baked it into *u* loaves.

UNLEAVENED (cont.)

13: 6 For seven days you shall eat *u* bread,
13: 7 *u* bread may be eaten during the seven days;
23:15 You shall keep the feast of *U* Bread.
23:15 you must eat *u* bread for seven days at the
29: 2 wheat flour make *u* cakes mixed with oil,
29: 2 with oil, and *u* wafers spread with oil,
29:23 *u* food that you have set before the LORD,
34:18 "You shall keep the feast of *U* Bread.
34:18 the month of Abib you are to eat *u* bread,
Lv 2: 4 *u* cakes made of fine flour mixed with oil,
2: 4 with oil, or of *u* wafers spread with oil.
2: 5 must be of fine flour mixed with oil and *u*.
2:11 that you present to the LORD shall be *u*,
6: 9 the form of *u* cakes and in a sacred place:
7:12 he shall offer *u* cakes mixed with oil,
7:12 mixed with oil, *u* wafers spread with oil,
8: 2 the two rams, and the basket of *u* food.
8:26 from the basket of *u* food that was set
8:26 was set before the LORD he took one *u* cake,
10:12 it beside the altar in the form of *u* cakes.
23: 6 this month is the LORD's feast of *U* Bread.
23: 6 For seven days you shall eat *u* bread.
Nm 6:15 and a basket of *u* cakes of fine flour
6:15 with oil and of *u* wafers spread with oil.
6:17 and libation, and the basket of *u* cakes.
6:19 as one *u* cake and one unleavened wafer
9:11 eating it with *u* bread and bitter herbs,
28:17 For seven days *u* bread is to be eaten.
Dt 16: 3 days you shall eat with it only *u* bread,
16: 8 For six days you shall eat *u* bread,
16:16 at the feast of *U* Bread,
Jos 5:11 in the form of *u* cakes and parched grain.
Jgs 6:19 an ephah of flour in the form of *u* cakes.
6:20 meat and *u* cakes and lay them on this rock;
6:21 he held, and touched the meat and *u* cakes.
6:21 rock which consumed the meat and *u* cakes,
1Sm 28:24 flour, she kneaded it and baked *u* bread.
2Kgs 23: 9 with their relatives, ate the *u* bread.
1Chr 23:29 cereal offering, of the wafers of *u* bread,
2Chr 8:13 on the feast of the *U* Bread,
30:13 the feast of *U* Bread in the second month;
30:21 Jerusalem celebrated the feast of *U* Bread
35:17 the feast of the *U* Bread for seven days.
Ezr 6:22 kept the feast of *U* Bread for seven days,
Ez 45:21 for seven days *u* bread is to be eaten.
Mt 26:17 On the first day of the feast of *U* Bread,
Mk 14: 1 The feasts of Passover and *U* Bread were to
14:12 On the first day of *U* Bread,
Lk 22: 1 The feast of *U* Bread known as the Passover
22: 7 The day of *U* Bread arrived on which it was
Acts 12: 3 During the feast of *U* Bread he had him
20: 6 soon as the festival of *U* Bread was over.
1Cor 5: 7 make of yourselves fresh dough, *u* loaves,
5: 8 with the *u* bread of sincerity and truth.

UNLESS (68)

Gn 42:15 *u* your youngest brother comes here,
43: 3 in my presence *u* your brother is with you.'
43: 5 in my presence *u* your brother is with you.' "
44:23 *U* your youngest brother comes back with
Ex 3:19 will not allow you to go *u* he is forced.
Lv 22: 4 sacred offerings, *u* he again becomes clean.
Nm 35:12 *u* he is first tried before the community.
Dt 32:30 *U* it was because their Rock sold them and
Jos 7:12 I will not remain with you *u* you remove
1Sm 19:10 informed him, *U* you save yourself tonight,
2Sm 3:13 appear before me *u* you bring back Michal,
2Kgs 4:24 Do not stop my donkey *u* I tell you to."
2Chr 2: 5 *u* it be to offer incense in his presence?
Jdt 8:11 *u* within that time the Lord comes
Est 2:14 She could not return to the king *u* he was
4:11 *u* the king extends to him the golden
1Mc 3:53 we be able to resist them *u* you help us?"
6:27 *U* you quickly forestall them,
2Mc 4: 6 He saw that *u* the king intervened,
Ps(s) 7:13 *U* they be converted,
127: 1 *U* the LORD build the house, they labor
127: 1 *U* the LORD guard the city,
Prv 4:16 For they cannot rest *u* they have done evil;
Wis 11:25 how could a thing remain, *u* you willed it;
Sir 27: 3 *U* you earnestly hold fast to the fear of
34: 6 *U* it be a vision specially sent by the
Is 1: 9 *U* the LORD of hosts had left us a scanty
7: 9 *U* your faith is firm you shall not be firm!
Bar 6:23 *u* someone wipes away the corrosion,
Ez 44:25 near any dead person, *u* it be their father,
Dn 2: 5 *u* you tell me the dream and its meaning,
6: 6 this Daniel *u* by way of the law of his God."
14: 8 *U* you tell me who it is that consumes
Am 3: 3 Do two walk together *u* they have agreed?
3: 4 out from its den *u* it has seized something?
Mt 5:20 *u* your holiness surpasses that of the
12:29 his property *u* he first ties him securely?
18: 3 *u* you change and become like little
18:35 the same way *u* each of you forgives
Mk 3:27 *u* he has first put him under restraint.
Lk 13: 3 will all come to the same end *u* you reform.
13: 5 will all come to the same end *u* you reform."
Jn 3: 2 such as you perform *u* God is with him."
3: 3 reign of God *u* he is begotten from above."
3:27 on anything *u* it is given him from on high.
4:48 *U* you people see signs and wonders,
6:44 to me *u* the Father who sent me draws him;
6:65 to me *u* it is granted him by the Father."
8:24 your sins *u* you come to believe that I AM."
12:24 *u* the grain of wheat falls to the earth
19:11 me whatever *u* it were given you from above.
Acts 8:31 man replied, *u* someone explains it to me?"
15: 1 *U* you are circumcised according to Mosaic
24:21 *u* it was what I called out as I stood in
Rom 7: 7 what evil desire was *u* the law had said,
9:29 *U* the Lord of hosts had left us a remnant,
10:14 can they believe *u* they have heard of him?
10:14 can they hear *u* there is someone to preach?
10:15 And how can men preach *u* they are sent?
1Cor 7: 5 *u* perhaps by mutual consent for a time,
14: 5 *u* the speaker can also interpret for the
15:36 seed you sow does not germinate *u* it dies.
2Cor 12: 5 about myself *u* it be about my weaknesses.
13: 5 not realize that Christ Jesus is in you *u*,
1Tm 5:19 *u* it is supported by two or three witnesses.
2Tm 2: 5 the winner's crown *u* he has kept the rules.
Rv 2:22 *u* they repent of their sins with her,
13:17 or sell anything *u* he was first marked

UNLIFTED (1)

2Cor 3:14 old covenant is read the veil remains *u*;

UNLIKE (6)

Wis 11:14 their thirst proved *u* that of the just.
Sir 33:11 his great knowledge the LORD makes men *u*;
Ez 16:31 Yet you were *u* a prostitute,
Jn 6:58 *U* your ancestors who ate and died
Heb 7:21 without an oath, *u* Jesus to whom God said:
7:27 *U* the other high priests,

UNLIMITED (1)

1Chr 22:15 you have available an *u* supply of workmen,

UNLOAD (1)

Acts 21: 3 in at Tyre, where the ship had to *u* cargo.

UNLOADED (1)

Gn 24:32 being *u* and provided with straw and fodder,

UNLOOKED-FOR (1)

Wis 5: 2 fear, and amazed at the *u* salvation.

UNLOVED (3)

Gn 29:31 When the LORD saw that Leah was *u*,
29:33 "It means, 'The LORD heard that I was *u*,'
2Chr 21:20 *u* and was buried in the City of David,

UNMAKES (1)

Dn 2:21 times and seasons, makes kings and *u* them.

UNMANLY (1)

2Sm 3:29 from a discharge, or a leper, or one *u*,

UNMARRIED (7)

Lv 21: 3 is of his own family while she remains *u*;
Sir 42: 9 Lest she pass her prime *u*,
42:10 While *u*, lest she be seduced,
Acts 21: 9 had four *u* daughters gifted with prophecy.
1Cor 7:32 The *u* man is busy with the Lord's affairs,
7:34 The virgin—indeed, any *u* woman
7:40 though, in my opinion, if she stays *u*.

UNMENTIONED (1)

2Cor 11:28 Leaving other sufferings *u*,

UNMINDFUL (7)

Dt 8:14 become haughty of heart and *u* of the LORD,
32:18 You were *u* of the Rock that begot you,
2Chr 24:22 *u* of the devotion shown him by Jehoiada,
Jb 39:15 in the sand, *U* that a foot may crush them,
Ps(s) 74:19 *u* of the lives of your afflicted ones.
74:23 Be not *u* of the voice of your foes;
Lam 2: 1 *U* of his footstool on the day of his wrath.

UNMISTAKABLE (1)

Jos 2:12 and give me an *u* token that you are to

UNMOURNED (1)

2Mc 5:10 many to lie unburied went *u* himself

UNMOVED (1)

Ps(s) 83: 2 O God, do not remain *u*;

UNNATURAL (3)

Wis 14:26 of gratitude, besmirching of souls, *u* lust,
Rom 1:26 women exchanged natural intercourse for *u*,
Jude 1: 7 they practiced *u* vice.

UNNI (2)

1Chr 15:18 Zechariah, Uzziel, Shemiramoth, Jehiel, *U*,
15:20 Zechariah, Uzziel, Shemiramoth, Jehiel, *U*,

UNNO (1)

Neh 12: 9 while Bakbukiah and *U* and their brethren

UNNOTICED (2)

Wis 1: 8 no one who utters wicked things can go *u*,
Lk 8:47 the woman saw that her act had not gone *u*,

UNOBSERVED (1)

2Mc 15:36 decreed never to let this day pass *u*,

UNOCCUPIED (2)

Jdt 5:19 again in the mountain region which was *u*.
Mt 12:44 from,' and returns to find the dwelling *u*,

UNPEOPLED (1)

Jb 38:26 rain to no man's land, the *u* wilderness;

UNPRINCIPLED (2)

Prv 19:28 An *u* witness perverts justice,
2Pt 2: 7 by the conduct of men *u* in their lusts.

UNPROTECTED (2)

Dt 32:36 their protected and *u* alike disappearing,
Jos 8:17 [or Bethel], and the city was open and *u*.

UNPROVED (1)

Nm 5:13 so that her impurity remains *u* for lack of

UNPROVIDED (1)

1Kgs 5: 7 They left nothing *u*.

UNPROVOKED (2)

Ps(s) 35:19 Let not my *u* enemies rejoice over me;
Prv 1:11 lie in wait for the honest man, let us, *u*,

UNPUNISHED (23)

Ex 20: 7 not leave *u* him who takes his name in vain.
21:28 The owner of the ox, however, shall go *u*.
Dt 5:11 not leave *u* him who takes his name in vain.
1Sm 26: 9 hands on the LORD's anointed and remain *u*?
1Kgs 2: 9 But you must not let him go *u*.
2Mc 7:19 go *u* for having dared to fight against God."
Prv 6:29 none who touches her shall go *u*.
11:21 Truly the evil man shall not go *u*,
16: 5 I assure you that he will not go *u*.
17: 5 he who is glad at calamity will not go *u*.
19: 5 The false witness will not go *u*,
19: 9 The false witness will not go *u*,
28:20 who is in haste to grow rich will not go *u*.
Wis 1:11 For a stealthy utterance does not go *u*,
Sir 7: 8 not even for one will you go *u*.
9:12 remember he will not reach death *u*.
16:11 man, it were a wonder had he gone *u*.
Jer 30:11 as you deserve, I will not let you go *u*.
46:28 as you deserve, I will not let you go *u*.
49:12 Shall you then go *u*?
49:12 You shall not go *u*;
Jl 4:21 avenge their blood, and not leave it *u*.
Na 1: 3 and the LORD never leaves the guilty *u*.

UNQUENCHABLE (4)

Jer 17:27 sabbath, I will set *u* fire to its gates,
Mt 3:12 barn, but the chaff he will burn in *u* fire."
Mk 9:43 hands and enter Gehenna with its *u* fire.
Lk 3:17 but the chaff he will burn in *u* fire."

UNQUENCHABLY (1)

Sir 28:23 victims to it, as it burns among them *u*!

UNRAINED (1)

Ez 22:24 You are a land *u* on [that is,

UNREADY (1)

2Cor 9: 4 Macedonians come with me and find you *u*;

UNREAL (1)

Sir 34: 5 Divination, omens and dreams all are *u*;

UNREASONABLE (1)

2Mc 14: 8 the *u* conduct of the people just mentioned.

UNREASONING (1)

Wis 12:25 Therefore as though upon *u* children,

UNRECOGNIZED (1)

Lam 4: 8 than soot, they are *u* on the streets;

UNREMEMBERED (1)

Ps(s) 31:13 I am forgotten like the *u* dead;

UNREMITTING (5)

1Sm 14:52 An *u* war was waged against the Philistines

Jb 6:10 consolation and could exult through *u* pain,
Wis 16:16 rains and hailstorms and *u* downpours,
Sir 51: 4 From the midst of *u* fire,
Rom 13: 6 themselves to his service with *u* care.

UNRESERVEDLY (6)

Nm 14:24 has a different spirit and follows me *u*,
32:11 'Because they have not followed me *u*,
32:12 son of Nun, who have followed the LORD *u*.'
Dt 1:36 upon, because he has followed the LORD *u*.'
1Kgs 11: 6 follow him *u* as his father David had done.
Dn 3:40 in your presence today as we follow you *u*;

UNRESISTING (1)

Wis 2: 3 spirit will be poured abroad like *u* air.

UNRESPONSIVE (1)

Wis 16:11 and become *u* to your beneficence.

UNREST (2)

Is 14: 3 relieves you of sorrow and *u* and the hard
Jer 50:34 earth, but *u* to those who live in Babylon.

UNRIGHTEOUS (1)

Jb 31: 3 Is it not calamity for the *u*,

UNRIGHTEOUSNESS (1)

Ti 2:14 to redeem us from all *u* and to cleanse for

UNRINSED (1)

Lv 15:11 with *u* hands shall wash his garments,

UNRIPE (5)

Nm 6: 4 not even *u* grapes or grapeskins.
Dt 28:40 ointment, for your olives will drop off *u*.
Wis 4: 5 and their fruit be useless, *u* for eating,
Jer 31:29 no longer say, "The fathers ate *u* grapes,
31:30 who eats the *u* grapes shall be set on edge.

UNRIPENED (1)

Jb 15:33 be like a vine that sheds its grapes *u*,

UNROLLED (3)

1Mc 3:48 They *u* the scroll of the law,
Ez 2:10 was a written scroll which he *u* before me.
Lk 4:17 he *u* the scroll and found the passage

UNRUFFLED (1)

Sir 41: 1 For the man *u* and always successful,

UNRULY (17)

Gn 49: 4 *U* as water, you shall no longer excel,
Dt 21:18 "If a man has a stubborn and *u* son who
21:20 and *u* fellow who will not listen to us;
Prv 7:11 She is fickle and *u*,
Wis 17: 1 therefore the *u* souls were wrong.
Sir 6:21 How irksome she is to the *u*!
8: 4 Be not too familiar with an *u* man,
20:18 the *u* are always ready to offer it.
20:23 yet it is constantly on the lips of the *u*.
22: 3 An *u* child is a disgrace to its father;
26:10 Keep a strict watch over an *u* wife,
30: 8 a son left to himself grows up *u*.
33:29 if he becomes *u*,
Hb 1: 6 up Chaldea, that bitter and *u* people,
1Thes 5:14 We exhort you to admonish the *u*;
2Thes 3:11 We hear that some of you are *u*,
1Tm 1: 9 not at good men but at the lawless and *u*,

UNSAFE (1)

Tb 1:15 him as king, the roads to Media became *u*,

UNSCALABLE (1)

Dt 28:52 *u* walls you trust in come tumbling down

UNSCATHED (1)

Jb 9: 4 who has withstood him and remained *u*?

UNSEALED (1)

Neh 6: 5 who bore an *u* letter containing this text:

UNSEARCHABLE (2)

Ps(s) 145: 3 his greatness is *u*.
Rom 11:33 inscrutable his judgments, how *u* his ways!

UNSEEING (1)

Is 57:11 Was I to remain silent and *u*,

UNSEEMLY (4)

Jb 24:12 cry out [yet God does not treat it as *u*.
Sir 15: 9 *U* is praise on a sinner's lips,
Jer 23:13 Among Samaria's prophets I saw *u* deeds:
Rom 1:28 their own depraved sense to do what is *u*.

UNSEEN (6)

2Mc 9: 5 him down with an *u* but incurable blow;
Ps(s) 81: 8 *U*,
Wis 17:19 rocks, Or the *u* gallop of bounding animals,
Sir 20:29 Hidden wisdom and *u* treasure
2Cor 4:18 our gaze on what is seen but on what is *u*.
4:18 what is *u* lasts forever.

UNSELFISH (1)

Phil 4: 5 Everyone should see how *u* you are.

UNSETTLING (1)

Gal 5:10 fall on whoever it is that is *u* you!

UNSHAKABLE (1)

Heb 12:28 *u* kingdom should hold fast to God's grace,

UNSHAKEN (3)

Ps(s) 21: 8 the kindness of the Most High he stands *u*.
Col 1:23 *u* in the hope promised you by the gospel
Heb 12:27 away, so that only what is *u* may remain.

UNSHRUNKEN (2)

Mt 9:16 sews a piece of *u* cloth on an old cloak;
Mk 2:21 sews a patch of *u* cloth on an old cloak.

UNSKILLED (1)

2Cor 11: 6 I may be *u* in speech but I know that I am

UNSOLD (1)

Acts 5: 4 Was it not yours so long as it remained *u*?

UNSOUND (1)

Wis 14: 1 wood more *u* than the boat that bears him.

UNSOWN (2)

Dt 29:22 salt, a burnt-out waste, *u* and unfruitful,
Jer 2: 2 Following me in the desert, in a land *u*.

UNSPARINGLY (3)

Prv 21:26 all the day, but the just man gives *u*.
Is 54: 2 your tent, spread out your tent cloths *u*;
58: 1 Cry out full-throated and *u*,

UNSPOTTED (1)

Jas 1:27 distress and keeping oneself *u* by the world

UNSTABLE (2)

Hb 2: 4 the proud, *u* man
2Pt 3:16 The ignorant and the *u* distort them (just

UNSTAINED (2)

2Sm 1:22 turn back, or the sword of Saul return *u*.
Wis 7:22 unique, Manifold, subtle, agile, clear, *u*,

UNSTEADY (5)

Gn 49:24 bow remained stiff, as their arms were *u*,
Jb 12: 5 downfall a disgrace such as awaits *u* feet;
Prv 25:19 Like an infected tooth or an *u* foot is
Wis 4: 4 are *u* and shall be rocked by the wind and,
Is 40:20 to set up an idol that will not be *u*?

UNSTINTED (1)

Est 1: 8 ordinance of the king the drinking was *u*,

UNSUBJECTED (1)

Heb 2: 8 all things to him, God left nothing *u*.

UNSUCCESSFUL (1)

Acts 12:19 When it proved *u*,

UNSULLIED (3)

Wis 4: 2 in triumph, victorious in *u* deeds of valor.
4: 9 is the hoary crown for men, and an *u* life,
8:20 rather, being noble, I attained an *u* body.

UNSURE (1)

Wis 9:14 of mortals are timid, and *u* are our plans.

UNSURPASSABLE (1)

Jdt 16:13 and glorious, wonderful in power and *u*.

UNSURPASSED (1)

Dn 12: 1 It shall be a time *u* in distress since

UNSUSPECTING (1)

Ez 30: 9 forth at my command to terrify *u* Ethiopia;

UNSWERVINGLY (4)

1Kgs 22:43 followed all the ways of his father Asa *u*,
2Kgs 22: 2 *u* just as his ancestor David had done.
2Chr 20:32 He followed the path of his father Asa *u*,
Heb 10:23 *u* to our profession which gives us hope,

UNTAMED (2)

Sir 30: 8 A colt *u* turns out stubborn;
Jer 31:18 I was an *u* calf.

UNTHINKABLE (5)

2Mc 3:12 He added that it was utterly *u* to defraud
Bar 6:63 so that it is *u*,
Acts 10:14 "Sir, it is *u*!
Gal 2:17 Christ is encouraging sin? *U*!
3:21 Again, *u*! If the law that was given

UNTHINKING (1)

2Chr 13: 7 of Solomon, when Rehoboam was young and *u*,

UNTIE (5)

Mt 21: 2 *U* them and lead them back to me.
Mk 1: 7 not fit to stoop and *u* his sandal straps.
11: 2 *U* it and bring it back.
Lk 19:30 *U* it and lead it back.
Jn 11:44 *U* him," Jesus told them, "and let him go

UNTIED (3)

Mk 11: 4 out on the street near a gate, they *u* it.
Lk 19:33 As they *u* the ass,
Acts 27:40 time they *u* the guy-ropes of the rudders,

UNTIL (472)

Gn 3:19 bread to eat, *U* you return to the ground,
7:19 *u* all the highest mountains everywhere
8: 5 continued to diminish *u* the tenth month,
8: 7 *u* the waters dried off from the earth.
15:16 not have reached its full measure *u* then."
19:22 I cannot do anything *u* you arrive there."
21:26 about it, nor did I ever hear of it *u* now."
24:19 camels, too, *u* they have drunk their fill."
24:20 *u* she had drawn enough for all the camels.
24:33 "I will not eat *u* I have told my tale."
26:13 all the time, *u* he was very wealthy indeed.
27:44 and stay with him a while *u* your brother's
27:45 fury subsides *u* your brother's anger against
28:15 you *u* I have done what I promised you."
29: 8 *u* all the shepherds are here to roll the
31:23 he pursued him for seven days *u* he caught
32: 5 Laban and have been detained there *u* now.
32:25 man wrestled with him *u* the break of dawn.
32:27 "I will not let you go *u* you bless me."
33: 3 seven times, *u* he reached his brother.
33:14 of my children, *u* I join my lord in Seir."
34: 5 he held his peace *u* they came home.
38:11 father's house *u* my son Shelah grows up"
38:17 you leave a pledge *u* you send it."
39:16 the cloak with her *u* his master came home.
46:34 of livestock from the beginning *u* now,'
Ex 10:26 to him *u* we arrive at the place itself."
12: 6 keep it *u* the fourteenth day of this month,
12:18 *u* the evening of the twenty-first day
12:22 none of you shall go outdoors *u* morning.
16:19 one keep any of it over *u* tomorrow morning."
16:20 a part of it over *u* the following morning,
16:35 forty years, *u* they came to settled land;
16:35 manna *u* they reached the borders of Canaan.
18:13 waited about him from morning *u* evening.
23:30 *u* you have grown numerous enough to take
24:14 him, "Wait here for us *u* we return to you.
33: 8 watching Moses *u* he entered the tent.
33:22 cover you with my hand *u* I have passed by.
34:34 he removed the veil *u* he came out again.
34:35 *u* he went in to converse with the LORD.
Lv 6: 2 of the altar all night *u* the next morning,
8:33 *u* the days of your ordination are
11:24 dead bodies shall be unclean *u* evening,
11:25 wash his garments and be unclean *u* evening.
11:27 dead bodies shall be unclean *u* evening,
11:28 wash his garments and be unclean *u* evening.
11:31 they are dead shall be unclean *u* evening.
11:32 put in water and remain unclean *u* evening,
11:39 its dead body shall be unclean *u* evening.
11:40 wash his garments and be unclean *u* evening;
11:40 wash his garments and be unclean *u* evening.
14:46 is quarantined shall be unclean *u* evening.
15: 5 bathe in water, and be unclean *u* evening.
15: 6 bathe in water, and be unclean *u* evening.
15: 7 bathe in water, and be unclean *u* evening.
15: 8 bathe in water, and be unclean *u* evening.
15:10 was under him shall be unclean *u* evening;
15:10 bathe in water, and be unclean *u* evening.
15:11 bathe in water, and be unclean *u* evening.
15:16 body in water and be unclean *u* evening.
15:17 washed with water and be unclean *u* evening.
15:18 bathe in water and be unclean *u* evening.
15:19 who touches her shall be unclean *u* evening.
15:21 bathe in water, and be unclean *u* evening.
15:22 bathe in water, and be unclean *u* evening.
15:23 touches it, he shall be unclean *u* evening.
15:27 bathe in water, and be unclean *u* evening.
16: 4 on *u* he has first bathed his body in water.
16:17 sanctuary to make atonement *u* he departs.
17:15 bathe in water, and be unclean *u* evening,

UNTIL (cont.)

19: 6 Whatever is left over *u* the third day
19:25 Not *u* the fifth year may you eat its fruit.
22: 6 such as these shall be unclean *u* evening
22: 6 *u* he has first bathed his body in water,
22:30 of it shall be left over *u* the next day.
23:14 *U* this day, when you bring your God
25:28 possession of the purchaser *u* the jubilee,
25:40 working with you *u* the jubilee year,
27:18 of years left *u* the next jubilee year,
27:23 to the number of years *u* the next jubilee,
Nm 6: 5 *U* the period of his dedication to the LORD
9: 8 "Wait *u* I learn what the LORD will
9:15 but from evening *u* morning it took on the
9:21 remained there only from evening *u* morning;
10:12 *u* the cloud came to rest in the desert of
11:20 but for a whole month *u* it comes out of
12:15 not start out again *u* she was brought back.
14:19 as you have forgiven them from Egypt *u* now."
19: 7 He remains unclean *u* the evening,
19: 8 body in water, and be unclean *u* evening.
19:10 wash his garments and be unclean *u* evening.
19:21 with this water shall be unclean *u* evening.
19:22 who touches it becomes unclean *u* evening."
20:17 *u* we have passed through your territory."
21:22 *u* we have passed through your territory."
21:35 people, *u* not a survivor was left to him,
22:30 have you not always ridden upon me *u* now?
32:13 *u* the whole generation that had done evil
32:17 *u* we have led them to their destination.
32:18 We will not return to our homes *u* every
32:21 *u* he has driven his enemies out of his way
35:25 and he shall stay there *u* the death of the
35:28 of asylum *u* the death of the high priest.
Dt 1:31 your journey *u* you arrived at this place.'
2:29 *u* I cross the Jordan into the land which
3:20 *u* the LORD has settled your kinsmen as
7:20 *u* the survivors who have hidden from you
7:23 rout them utterly *u* they are annihilated.
9: 7 land of Egypt *u* you arrived in this place,
11: 5 in the desert *u* you arrived in this place;
22: 2 place and keep it with you *u* he claims it;
23:11 go outside the camp, and not return *u*,
24:11 but shall wait outside *u* the man to whom
28:20 *u* you are speedily destroyed and perish
28:21 that will persist *u* he has exterminated you
28:22 wind, that will plague you *u* you perish.
28:24 upon you from the sky *u* you are destroyed.
28:27 eczema and the itch, *u* you cannot be cured.
28:34 *u* you are driven mad by what your eyes
28:45 and overwhelming you, *u* you are destroyed,
28:48 iron yoke on your neck, *u* he destroys you.
28:51 produce of your soil, *u* you are destroyed;
28:51 *u* they have brought about your ruin.
28:52 in each of your communities, *u* the great,
28:61 will bring upon you *u* you are destroyed.
Jos 1:15 them *u* the LORD has settled your kinsmen,
2:16 Hide there for three days, *u* they return;
2:22 they stayed three days *u* their pursuers,
3:17 bed of the Jordan *u* the whole nation had
4:10 *u* everything had been done that the LORD
4:23 Jordan in front of you *u* you crossed over,
4:23 dried up in front of us *u* we crossed over;
5: 1 before the Israelites *u* they crossed over,
5: 6 *u* all the warriors among the people that
5: 8 in camp where they were, *u* they recovered.
6:10 any noise or outcry *u* he gave the word:
7: 6 before the ark of the LORD *u* evening;
7:13 You cannot stand up to your enemies *u* you
8: 6 us *u* we have drawn them away from the city,
8:26 stretched out *u* he had fulfilled the doom
8:29 the king of Ai hanged on a tree *u* evening;
10:26 where they remained hanging *u* evening.
10:27 were placed, which remain *u* this very day.
11:14 *u* they had exterminated the last of them,
20: 9 *u* he could appear before the community.
23:13 *u* you perish from this good land which the
Jgs 3:11 was at rest for forty years, *u* Othniel,
3:25 They waited *u* they finally grew suspicious.
6:18 *u* I come back to you and bring out my
13: 7 God from the womb, *u* the day of his death.'"
15: 7 not stop *u* I have taken revenge on you."
16: 3 Samson rested there *u* midnight.
18:30 *u* the time of the captivity of the land.
19: 8 yourself and tarry *u* the afternoon."
19:25 abused her all night *u* the following dawn,
19:26 was a guest, where she lay *u* the morning.
20:22 went up and wept before the LORD *u* evening.
20:26 before the LORD *u* evening of that day,
21: 2 and remained there before God *u* evening,
Ru 1:13 of husbands *u* those sons grew up?
2: 7 this morning she has remained here *u* now,
2:17 She gleaned in the field *u* evening,
2:21 *u* they complete his entire harvest."
2:23 *u* the end of the barley and wheat harvests.
3:13 Lie there *u* morning."
3:14 So she lay at his feet *u* morning,
3:18 my daughter, *u* you learn what happens,
1Sm 1:23 wait *u* you have weaned him.
1:23 and nursed her son *u* she had weaned him.
3:15 Samuel then slept *u* morning,
9:13 The people will not eat *u* he arrives;
9:24 for it was kept for you *u* your arrival;
10: 8 Wait seven days *u* I come to you;
11:11 Ammonites *u* the heat of the day;
14: 9 to us, 'Stay there *u* we can come to you,'
14:36 them *u* daybreak and to kill them all off."
15:18 against them *u* you have exterminated them.'
16:11 the sacrificial banquet *u* he arrives here."
19:23 prophetic condition *u* he reached the spot.
20: 5 go and hide in the open country *u* evening.
22: 3 you, *u* I learn what God will do for me."
29: 3 the day he came over to me *u* the present."
30: 4 him wept aloud *u* they could weep no more.
2Sm 1:12 *u* evening for Saul and his son Jonathan,
2:27 the pursuit of their brothers *u* morning."
10: 5 "Stay in Jericho *u* your beards grow,"
15:24 *u* the soldiers had marched out of the city.
15:28 desert *u* I receive information from you."
19: 8 has afflicted you from your youth *u* now."
19:25 the day the king left *u* he returned safely.
21:10 *u* rain came down on them from the sky,
23:10 *u* his hand grew tired and became cramped,
24:15 Israel from morning *u* the time appointed,
1Kgs 3: 1 *u* he should finish building his palace,
5:17 *u* such a time as the LORD should put these
10: 7 report *u* I came and saw with my own eyes,
11:16 *u* they had killed off every male in Edom.
11:40 Egypt, where he remained *u* Solomon's death.
17:14 *u* the day when the LORD sends rain upon
17:17 grew more severe *u* he stopped breathing.
18:28 was their custom, *u* blood gushed over them.
18:29 state *u* the time for offering sacrifice.
19: 4 *u* he came to a broom tree and sat beneath
22:11 shall gore Aram *u* you have destroyed them.'"
22:21 *u* one of the spirits came forth and
22:27 of bread and water *u* I return in safety.'"
2Kgs 2:17 urging him, *u* he was embarrassed and said,
4:20 he stayed with her *u* noon,
7: 3 "Why should we sit here *u* we die?
7: 9 If we wait *u* morning breaks,
8: 6 from the day she left the land *u* now."
8:11 him down *u* Hazael became ill at ease.
10: 8 at the entrance of the city *u* morning,"
16: 6 which they have occupied *u* the present.
18:32 *u* I come to take you to a land like your
20:17 your fathers have stored up *u* this day,
21:15 fathers came forth from Egypt *u* today.'"
23:23 *u* the eighteenth year of king Josiah,
25: 2 continued *u* the eleventh year of Zedekiah.
1Chr 4:31 *U* David came to reign,
5:22 dwelling place *u* the time of the exile.
6:17 *u* Solomon built the temple of the LORD in
12:23 David's help *u* there was a vast encampment,
12:30 three thousand *u* this time,
19: 5 told them, *u* your beards have grown again;
2Chr 8:16 *u* the house of the LORD had been completed
9: 6 report *u* I came and saw with my own eyes.
14:12 Ethiopians fell *u* there were no survivors,
15:19 war *u* the thirty-fifth year of Asa's reign.
18:10 shall gore Aram *u* you have destroyed them.'"
18:20 *u* a spirit came forward and presented
18:26 of bread and water *u* I return in safety!'"
18:34 his chariot facing the Arameans *u* evening.
21:19 on *u* a period of two years had elapsed,
24:10 and cast it into the chest *u* it was filled.
24:11 *u* they had collected a large sum of money.
29:28 *u* the holocaust had been completed.
29:34 assisted them *u* the task was completed
31: 1 Ephraim and Manasseh, *u* all were destroyed.
35:14 holocausts and the fatty portions *u* night;
36:16 *u* the anger of the LORD against his people
36:20 servants *u* the kingdom of the Persians came
36:21 *U* the land has retrieved its lost sabbaths,
Ezr 2:63 *u* there should be a priest bearing the Urim
4: 5 king of Persia, and *u* the reign of Darius,
4:21 *u* a further decree has been issued by me.
4:24 *u* the second year of the reign of Darius,
5: 5 *u* a report could go to Darius and then a
9: 4 motionless *u* the evening sacrifice.
Neh 7: 3 are not to be opened *u* the sun is hot,
7:65 *u* there should be a priest bearing the Urim
8:17 of Jeshua, son of Nun, *u* this occasion;
9:32 time of the kings of Assyria *u* this day!
12:22 up *u* the reign of Darius the Persian.
12:23 of Chronicles, up *u* the time of Johanan,
12:37 *u* they came to the Water Gate on the east.
Tb 1:14 Every now and then *u* his death I would go
2:10 cataracts became, *u* I could see no more.
2:10 of me for two years, *u* he left for Elymais.
7:11 nothing *u* you set aside what belongs to me."
14: 5 *u* the era when the appointed times shall
Jdt 2:24 along the Wadi Abron, *u* he reached the sea.
6: 5 *u* I have taken revenge on this race of
8:34 tell you *u* my plan has been accomplished."
12: 9 and remained there *u* her food was brought
Est A:11 in mind, and tried in every way, *u* night,
D: 8 held her in his arms *u* she recovered,
1Mc 3:33 care of his son Antiochus *u* his own return.
4:46 *u* a prophet should come and decide what to
5:19 not fight against the Gentiles *u* we return."
5:53 whole way, *u* he reached the land of Judah.
9: 6 camp, *u* only eight hundred men remained.
9:13 the battle raged from morning *u* evening.
10:50 He pressed the battle hard *u* sunset,
10:80 From morning *u* evening they showered his
12:29 did not know what had happened *u* morning.
14:41 and high priest *u* a true prophet arises.
16: 2 battles of Israel from our youth *u* today,
16: 9 pursued them *u* Cendebeus reached Kedron,
2Mc 2: 7 "The place is to remain unknown *u* God
3:26 *u* they had given him innumerable blows.
5:25 and waited *u* the holy day of the sabbath;
6:14 the Lord patiently waits *u* they reach the
8:35 like a runaway slave, *u* he reached Antioch.
9: 4 without stopping *u* he finished the journey.
Jb 7: 4 I am filled with restlessness *u* the dawn.
14:14 I would wait, *u* my relief should come.
Prv 7:18 let us drink our fill of love, *u* morning,
Eccl 2: 3 *u* I should understand what is best for men
Sg 2:17 *U* the day breathes cool and the shadows
4: 6 *U* the day breathes cool and the shadows
Wis 10:14 *U* she brought him the scepter of royalty
19: 1 wicked, merciless wrath assailed *u* the end.
Sir 4:17 the proof, *u* his heart is fully with her.
23:16 who never stops *u* the fire breaks forth;
47:23 *U* one arose who should not be remembered,
48:15 *U* they were rooted out of their land and
51:14 beauty, and *u* the end I will cultivate her.
Is 6:11 *U* the cities are desolate,
6:12 *U* the LORD removes men far away,
24:20 rebellion will weigh it down, *u* it falls,
26:20 for a brief moment, *u* the wrath is past.
30:17 *U* you are left like a flagstaff on the
32:15 *U* the spirit from on high is poured out on
36:17 *u* I come to take you to a land like your
38:13 I cry out *u* the dawn.
39: 6 your fathers have stored up *u* this day,
42: 4 *U* he establishes justice on the earth;
44:16 he eats what he has roasted *u* he is full,
62: 1 *U* her vindication shines forth like the
62: 7 *u* he reestablishes Jerusalem And makes of
65: 6 I will not be quiet *u* I have paid in full
Jer 1: 3 and *u* the downfall and exile of Jerusalem
9:15 them *u* I have completely destroyed them.
23:20 The anger of the LORD shall not abate *u* he
24:10 *u* they have disappeared from the land
27: 7 and his grandson, *u* the time of his land,
27: 8 says the LORD *u* I give them into his hand.
27:22 shall remain, *u* the day I look for them,
30:24 The anger of the LORD will not abate *u* he
32: 5 There he shall remain, *u* I attend to him,
32:20 other men, *u* now you have gained renown.
36: 2 to you, in the days of Josiah, *u* today.
36:23 *u* the entire roll was consumed in the fire.
37:21 *u* all the bread in the city was eaten up.
44:27 or famine *u* they are utterly destroyed.
49:37 *u* I have completely made an end of them;
52: 5 *u* the eleventh year of King Zedekiah.
52:11 and kept in prison *u* the day of his death.
52:34 days of his life *u* the day of his death.
Bar 1:19 out of the land of Egypt *u* the present day,
Ez 4: 8 cannot turn from one side to the other *u*
21:32 it shall not be the same *u* he comes who
24:13 not be purified *u* I wreak my fury on you.
28:15 you were created, *U* evil was found in you,
34:21 with your horns *u* you have driven them out,
39:15 *u* others have buried it in the Valley of
39:19 you shall eat fat *u* you are filled and
39:19 are filled and drink blood *u* you are drunk.
42:14 *u* they have left here the clothing in which
46: 2 the gate shall not be closed *u* evening.
46:17 to the latter only *u* the year of release,
Dn 1:21 there *u* the first year of King Cyrus.
2: 3 my spirit no rest *u* I know what it means."
4:22 *u* you know that the Most High rules over
4:29 *u* you learn that the Most High rules over
4:30 *u* his hair grew like the feathers of an
5:21 *u* he learned that the Most High God rules
7:11 *u* the beast was slain and its body thrown
7:22 was victorious *u* the Ancient One arrived;
9:25 rebuilt *U* one who is anointed and a leader,
9:26 *u* the end there shall be war,
9:27 *u* the ruin that is decreed is poured out
10: 3 myself at all *u* the end of the three weeks.
10:13 way for twenty-one days, *u* finally Michael,
11:35 *u* the end time which is still appointed to
12: 1 distress since nations began *u* that time.
12: 4 message and seal the book *u* the end time;
12: 9 be kept secret and sealed *u* the end time.
12:12 the man who has patience and perseveres *u*
Hos 5:15 I will go back to my place *u* they pay for
7: 4 once the dough is kneaded *u* it has risen.
Mi 5: 2 *u* the time when she who is to give birth
7: 9 sinned against him, *U* he takes up my cause,
Mt 2: 9 *u* it came to a standstill over the place
2:13 Stay there *u* I tell you otherwise.
5:18 *u* heaven and earth pass away,
5:18 be done away with *u* it all comes true.
5:26 be released *u* you have paid the last penny.
10:11 you come to and stay with him *u* you leave.
11:12 From John the Baptizer's time *u* now the
11:13 well as the law spoke prophetically *u* John.
12:20 not quench *u* judgment is made victorious.
13:12 has, more will be given *u* he grows rich;
13:30 Let them grow together *u* harvest;
15:37 All ate *u* they were full.
17: 9 *u* the Son of Man rises from the dead."
18:30 put in jail *u* he paid back what he owed.

18:34 torturers *u* he paid back all that he owed.
22:44 *u* I humble your enemies beneath your feet'?
23:35 *u* retribution overtakes you for all the
23:39 not see me from this time on *u* you declare,
24:21 of the world *u* now or in all ages to come.
24:34 will not pass away *u* all this takes place.
24:39 *u* the flood came and destroyed them.
25:29 who have will get more *u* they grow rich,
26:29 *u* the day when I drink it new with you
27:45 over the whole land *u* midafternoon.
27:64 kept under surveillance *u* the third day.
28:20 am with you always, *u* the end of the world!"
Mk 6:10 in, stay there *u* you leave the locality.
6:42 them and they ate *u* they had their fill.
8: 8 in the crowd ate *u* they had their fill;
9: 1 not taste death *u* they see the reign of God
12:36 hand *u* I make your enemies your footstool.'
13:30 pass away *u* all these things take place.
14:25 drink of the fruit of the vine *u* the day when
15:33 countryside and lasted *u* midafternoon.
Lk 1:20 to speak *u* the day these things take place,
1:80 He lived in the desert *u* the day when he
2:26 *u* he had seen the Anointed of the Lord.
2:37 and then as a widow *u* she was eighty-four.
5: 7 filled the two boats *u* they nearly sank.
9:17 They all ate *u* they had enough.
9:27 taste death *u* they see the reign of God."
12:59 from there *u* you have paid the last penny."
13:21 *u* the whole mass of dough began to rise."
13:35 not see me *u* the time comes when you say,
15: 4 and follow the lost one *u* he finds it?
15: 8 search *u* she has retrieved what she lost?
16:16 law and the prophets were in force *u* John.
19:13 saying to them, 'Invest this *u* I get back.'
21:24 *u* the times of the Gentiles are fulfilled.
21:32 will not pass away *u* all this takes place.
22:16 *u* it is fulfilled in the kingdom of God."
22:18 the vine *u* the coming of the reign of God."
22:34 the cock will not crow today *u* you have
23:44 *u* midafternoon with an eclipse of the sun.
24:49 *u* you are clothed with power from on high."
Jn 2:10 have done is keep the choice wine *u* now."
5:17 "My Father is at work *u* now,
9:18 *u* they summoned the parents of this man
16:24 *U* now you have not asked for anything in
21:22 "Suppose I want him to stay *u* I come,"
21:23 stay *u* I come [how does that concern you]?"
Acts 1: 2 taught *u* the day he was taken up to heaven,
1:22 of John *u* the day he was taken up from us,
2:35 hand *u* I make your enemies your footstool.'
3:21 Jesus must remain in heaven *u* the time of
7:18 *u* a new king came to power in Egypt,
7:45 So it was *u* the time of David,
8:40 in all the towns *u* he reached Caesarea.
13:20 rule them *u* the time of the prophet Samuel.
16:18 several days *u* finally Paul became annoyed,
20: 7 next day, he kept on speaking *u* midnight.
20:11 for a long while *u* his departure at dawn.
23:12 not to eat or drink *u* they had killed Paul.
23:14 by oath to touch no food *u* we kill Paul.
23:21 oath not to eat or drink *u* they kill him.
25:21 Paul appealed to be kept here *u* there
25:21 custody *u* I could send him to the emperor."
Rom 8:22 creation groans and is in agony even *u* now.
11:25 *u* the full number of Gentiles enter in,
1Cor 11:26 proclaim the death of the Lord *u* he comes!
15:25 *u* God has put all enemies under his feet,
16: 8 I intend to stay in Ephesus *u* Pentecost.
Gal 3:19 it was to be valid only *u* that descendant
3:23 locked in *u* the faith that was coming
3:24 the law was our monitor *u* Christ came to
4: 2 *u* the time set by his father.
4:19 in labor pains *u* Christ is formed in you.
1Thes 4:15 that we who live, who survive *u* his coming,
2Thes 2: 6 him *u* he shall be revealed in his own time.
2: 7 holds him back *u* that restrainer shall be
1Tm 4:13 *U* I arrive, devote yourself to the reading
6:14 *u* our Lord Jesus Christ shall appear.
2Tm 1:12 what has been entrusted to me *u* that Day.
Heb 9:10 flesh, imposed *u* the time of the new order.
10:13 *u* his enemies are placed beneath his feet.
Jas 5: 7 my brothers, *u* the coming of the Lord.
1Pt 3:20 God patiently waited *u* the ark was built.
2Pt 1:19 dark place *u* the first streaks of dawn appear
2: 4 pits of darkness, to be guarded *u* judgment.
Rv 2:10 Remain faithful *u* death and I will give
2:25 case, hold fast to what you have *u* I come.
6:11 a little while longer *u* the quota was filled
7: 3 *u* we imprint this seal on the foreheads
15: 8 *u* the seven plagues of the seven angels had
17:17 on the beast *u* his will is accomplished.
20: 3 astray *u* the thousand years are over.
20:11 presence *u* they could no longer be seen.

UNTILLED (4)

Ex 23:11 shall let the land lie *u* and unharvested,
Jb 24: 6 they harvest at night in the *u* land.
Ps(s) 65:13 The *u* meadows overflow with it,
Jer 4: 3 Till your *u* ground, sow not among thorns.

UNTIMELY (5)

Jb 3:16 why was I not buried away like an *u* birth,
Ps(s) 58: 9 like an *u* birth that never sees the sun.
Wis 4: 5 Their twigs shall be broken off *u*,
14:15 For a father, afflicted with *u* mourning,
Sir 20:18 Insipid food is the *u* tale;

UNTIRINGLY (4)

Jer 7:13 did not listen, though I spoke to you *u*;
7:25 sent you *u* all my servants the prophets.
25: 3 LORD has come to me and I spoke to you *u*,
35:14 although I spoke to you *u* and insistently.

UNTOILED-FOR (1)

Wis 16:20 them bread from heaven, ready to hand, *u*,

UNTOLD (1)

2Mc 3: 6 full of *u* riches that the total sum of money

UNTOUCHABLE (1)

Heb 12:18 near to an *u* mountain and a blazing fire,

UNTOUCHED (2)

Gn 24:16 was very beautiful, a virgin, *u* by man.
Tb 2: 4 I sprang to my feet, leaving the dinner *u*;

UNTRAVERSED (1)

Jer 9:11 land ravaged, scorched like a wasteland *u*?

UNTRIMMED (2)

Lv 25: 5 nor shall you pick the grapes of your *u* vines
25:11 or pick the grapes from the *u* vines.

UNTRODDEN (1)

Est E:24 that it will be left not merely *u* by men,

UNTRUE (3)

Gn 42:16 if they are *u*,
Hos 5: 7 They have been *u* to the LORD,
6: 7 there they were *u* to me.

UNTURNED (1)

Hos 7: 8 the nations, Ephraim is a hearth cake *u*.

UNTUTORED (1)

Sir 51:23 Come aside to me, you *u*,

UNTYING (3)

Is 58: 6 bound unjustly, *u* the thongs of the yoke;
Mk 11: 5 to them, "What do you mean by *u* that colt?"
Lk 19:31 should ask you, 'Why are you *u* the beast?'

UNUSUAL (1)

Acts 28: 6 and seeing nothing *u* happen to him,

UNVEILED (4)

Nm 24: 4 Almighty sees, enraptured, and with eyes *u*:
24:16 Almighty sees, enraptured and with eyes *u*.
1Cor 11:13 Is it proper for a woman to pray to God *u*?
2Cor 3:18 gazing on the Lord's glory with *u* faces,

UNVISITED (1)

Is 60:15 Once you were forsaken, hated and *u*,

UNWALLED (1)

Dt 3: 5 say nothing of the great number of *u* towns.

UNWASHED (1)

Mt 15:20 As for eating with *u* hands

UNWAVERING (2)

2Sm 22:37 *u* was my stride.
Ps(s) 18:37 *u* was my stride.

UNWEANED (1)

1Sm 7: 9 Samuel therefore took an *u* lamb and

UNWELCOME (2)

2Mc 9:24 unexpected happened or any *u* news came,
Sir 20:19 A proverb when spoken by a fool is *u*,

UNWILLING (7)

Gn 24: 5 the woman is *u* to follow me to this land?
24: 8 If the woman is *u* to follow you,
Jgs 11:17 sent to the king of Moab, but he too was *u*.
2Kgs 8:19 Even so, the LORD was *u* to destroy Judah,
13:23 He was *u* to destroy them or to cast them
Mt 1:19 an upright man *u* to expose her to the law,
Jn 5:40 are *u* to come to me to possess that life.

UNWILLINGLY (2)

Wis 19:15 be theirs since they received strangers *u*!
1Cor 9:17 if *u*,

UNWILLINGNESS (1)

Lv 26:21 you become defiant in your *u* to obey me,

UNWISE (1)

Hos 13:13 come for him, but he shall be an *u* child;

UNWITTINGLY (4)

Lv 5:18 for the fault which was *u* committed,
Nm 15:24 if the community itself *u* becomes guilty
Dt 4:42 take refuge there if he *u* killed his neighbor
19: 4 when someone *u* kills his neighbor to whom

UNWONTED (1)

Wis 16:16 Pursued by *u* rains and hailstorms and

UNWORTHILY (1)

1Cor 11:27 *u* sins against the body and blood of the

UNWORTHY (5)

Gn 32:11 I am *u* of all the acts of kindness that
2Mc 14:42 and suffer outrages *u* of his noble birth.
Wis 12:15 you regard it as *u* of your power to punish
Acts 13:46 yourselves as *u* of everlasting life,
1Cor 6: 2 be thought *u* of judging in minor matters?

UPBRAIDED (1)

Gn 31:36 Jacob, now enraged, *u* Laban.

UPBRAIDS (1)

Sir 18:17 Only a fool *u* before giving;

UPBRINGING (1)

Sir 23:14 you commit a blunder and disgrace your *u*,

UPBUILD (1)

1Thes 5:11 Therefore, comfort and *u* one another,

UPBUILDING (3)

1Cor 14: 3 the other hand, speaks to men for their *u*,
14: 5 can also interpret for the *u* of the church.
2Cor 10: 8 us for your *u* and not for your destruction,

UPBUILDS (1)

1Cor 8: 1 But whereas "knowledge" inflates, love *u*.

UPHEAVAL (3)

Gn 19:29 of Abram by sending Lot away from the *u*
Jb 28: 5 forth bread, is in fiery *u* underneath.
Am 4:11 *u* as when God overthrew Sodom and

UPHELD (5)

Jb 4: 4 Your words have *u* the stumbler;
Ps(s) 9: 5 For you *u* my right and my cause,
18:36 your right hand has *u* me,
Lk 1:54 He has *u* Israel his servant,
Col 2:19 supported and *u* by joints and sinews,

UPHOLD (6)

Dt 33: 9 keep your words, and your covenant they *u*.
1Kgs 8:59 that he may *u* the cause of his servant and
2Chr 6:39 prayer and petitions, and *u* their cause.
Is 41:10 and *u* you with my right hand of justice.
42: 1 Here is my servant whom I *u*,
Rv 2:24 in Thyatira who do not *u* this teaching

UPHOLDING (1)

Is 16: 5 A judge *u* right and prompt to do justice.

UPHOLDS (3)

Ps(s) 63: 9 your right hand *u* me.
Prv 20:28 the king, and he *u* his throne by justice.
Is 50: 8 He is near who *u* my right;

UPLIFTED (1)

Is 26:11 O LORD, your hand is *u*,

UPPER (44)

Ex 28: 7 shoulder straps joined to its two *u* ends.
28:23 them to the two *u* ends of the breastpiece.
28:24 two rings at the *u* ends of the breastpiece,
39: 4 made for it and joined to its two *u* ends.
39:16 to the two *u* ends of the breastpiece.
Dt 24: 6 or even its *u* stone as a pledge for debt,
Jos 15:19 So he gave her the *u* and the lower pools.
16: 5 to *U* Beth-horon and thence to the sea.
Jgs 1:15 So Caleb gave her the *u* and the lower pool.
1:35 as the house of Joseph gained the *u* hand,
3:20 him where he sat alone in his cool *u* room,
3:23 of the *u* room on him and locking them.
3:24 that the doors of the *u* room were locked,
3:25 he did not open the doors of the *u* room,
9:53 But a certain woman cast the *u* part of a
1Kgs 17:19 him to the *u* room where he was staying,
17:23 from the *u* room and gave him to his mother.

UPPER (cont.)

2Kgs 15:35 built the *U* Gate of the temple of the LORD.
18:17 stopped at the conduit of the *u* pool
1Chr 7:24 lower and *u* Beth-horon and Uzzensheerah.
28:11 storerooms, its *u* rooms and inner chambers,
2Chr 3: 9 *u* chambers he likewise covered with gold.
8: 5 He built *U* Beth-horon and Lower Beth-horon,
23:20 come within the *u* gate of the king's house,
27: 3 He built the *u* gate of the LORD's house
32:30 This same Hezekiah stopped the *u* outflow
Neh 3:25 the *U* Palace at the quarters of the guard.
3:31 and as far as the *u* chamber of the Angle.
3:32 *u* chamber of the Angle and the Sheep Gate,
Tb 1: 2 is south of Kedesh Naphtali in *u* Galilee,
8: 3 by the odor of the fish, fled into *U* Egypt;
Jdt 1: 8 the peoples of Carmel, Gilead, *U* Galilee,
2:21 the mountains to the north of *U* Cilicia.
Is 7: 3 at the end of the conduit of the *u* pool,
36: 2 he stopped at the conduit of the *u* pool,
Jer 20: 2 in the stocks at the *u* Gate of Benjamin
36:10 in the *u* court of the LORD's house,
44: 1 Tahpanhes, and Memphis, and in *U* Egypt:
44:15 the people who lived in Lower and *U* Egypt,
Ez 9: 2 of the *u* gate which faces the north,
43:14 to the *u* ledge it was four cubits high,
43:17 The *u* ledge was also a square:
Dn 6:11 his God in the *u* chamber three times a day,
Am 9: 6 I have built heaven, my *u* chamber,

UPPERMOST (1)

Lam 1: 5 Her foes are *u*,

UPRAISED (3)

Neh 9:15 you had sworn with *u* hand to give them.
Bar 2:11 and great might, and with your *u* arm,
Lk 24:50 them out near Bethany, and with hands *u*,

UPRIGHT (63)

Gn 30:38 he then set *u* in the watering troughs,
37: 7 suddenly my sheaf rose to an *u* position,
Dt 32: 4 God, without deceit, how just and *u* he is!
1Kgs 3: 6 toward you, with justice and an *u* heart;
2Chr 31:20 was good, *u* and faithful before the LORD,
Tb 9: 6 of a noble and good, *u* and charitable man,
14: 9 children to do what is *u* and to give alms,
Jb 1: 1 there was a blameless and *u* man named Job,
1: 8 no one on earth like him, blameless and *u*,
2: 3 no one on earth like him, faultless and *u*,
4: 7 Since when are the *u* destroyed?
8: 6 Almighty, Should you be blameless and *u*,
8:20 Behold, God will not cast away the *u*;
17: 8 *U* men are astonished at this,
23: 7 There the *u* man might reason with him,
Ps(s) 7:11 before me is God, who saves the *u* of heart;
11: 2 to shoot in the dark at the *u* of heart.
11: 7 the *u* shall see his face.
25: 8 Good and *u* is the LORD;
32:11 exult, all you *u* of heart.
33: 1 in the LORD, praise from the *u* is fitting.
33: 4 For *u* is the word of the LORD,
36:11 your just defense of the *u* of heart.
37:37 the whole hearted man, and mark the *u*;
49:15 their shepherd, and the *u* rule over them.
64:11 in him glory all the *u* of heart.
73: 1 How good God is to the *u*;
94:15 and all the *u* of heart shall follow it.
97:11 and gladness, for the *u* of heart.
107:42 The *u* see this and rejoice,
112: 2 the *u* generation shall be blessed.
112: 4 through the darkness, a light for the *u*;
119: 7 I will give you thanks with an *u* heart,
125: 4 O LORD, to the good and to the *u* of heart.
140:14 the *u* shall dwell in your presence.
Prv 2: 7 He has counsel in store for the *u*,
2:21 For the *u* will dwell in the land,
3:32 but with the *u* is his friendship.
11: 3 The honesty of the *u* guides them;
11: 6 The virtue of the *u* saves them,
12: 6 ambush, but the speech of the *u* saves them.
14:11 but the tent of the *u* will flourish.
15: 8 but the prayer of the *u* is his delight.
16:17 The path of the *u* avoids misfortune;
21:29 but the *u* man pays heed to his ways.
28:10 He who seduces the *u* into an evil way will
29:10 man, but the *u* show concern for his life.
Sir 26:20 A merchant can hardly remain *u*,
Is 1:21 turned adulteress, the faithful city, so *u*!
26:10 in an *u* land he acts perversely,
Bar 6:26 move of themselves if one sets them *u*,
6:26 sets them upright, nor come *u* if they fall;
Ez 13:22 Because you have disheartened the *u* man
37:10 they came alive and stood *u*,
Mi 7: 2 the earth, among men the *u* are no more!
7: 4 a brier, the most *u* like a thorn hedge.
Mt 1:19 *u* man unwilling to expose her to the law,
Mk 6:20 John, knowing him to be an *u* and holy man,
Lk 23:50 an *u* and holy member of the Sanhedrin,
Acts 10:22 Cornelius, who is an *u* and Godfearing man,
1Cor 10:12 he is standing *u* watch out lest he fall!
1Thes 2:10 witnesses, as is God himself, of how *u*,
1Pt 2:14 of criminals and the recognition of the *u*.

UPRIGHTLY (10)

1Kgs 9: 4 your father David lived, sincerely and *u*,
Tb 4: 6 to you, but also to all those who live *u*.
Jdt 13:20 our disaster, walking *u* before our God."
Prv 14: 2 He who walks *u* fears the LORD,
28:18 He who walks *u* is safe,
29:27 walks *u* is an abomination to the wicked.
Jer 5: 1 one Who lives *u* and seeks to be faithful,
Mi 2: 7 my words promise good to him who walks *u*?
Acts 10:35 fears God and acts *u* is acceptable to him.
Rom 3:12 not one of them acts *u*,

UPRIGHTNESS (7)

1Chr 29:17 the test and that you take pleasure in *u*.
1Mc 2:52 in trial, and it was reputed to him as *u*?
Ps(s) 25:21 Let integrity and *u* preserve me,
Is 59:14 in the public square, *u* cannot enter.
Jer 9:23 about kindness justice and *u* on the earth;
Mal 2: 6 He walked with me in integrity and in *u*,
Acts 24:25 As Paul talked on about *u*,

UPRIGHTS (1)

2Kgs 18:16 He broke up the door panels and the *u* of

UPRISING (2)

Mk 15: 7 rebels who had committed murder in the *u*.
Lk 23:19 in prison for causing an *u* in the city,

UPROAR (12)

1Sm 4:13 his news, which put the whole city in an *u*.
1Kgs 1:41 asked, "What does this *u* in the city mean?"
1:45 rejoicing, so that the city is in an *u*.
Jb 30:14 Amid the *u* they come on in waves;
39: 7 He scoffs at the *u* of the city,
Ps(s) 74:23 the *u* of those who rebel against you is
Is 25: 5 even so you quell the *u* of the wanton.
Jer 10:22 closer, a great *u* from the northern land:
25:31 the earth to its very ends the *u* spreads;
Am 2: 2 death amid *u* and shouts and trumpet blasts.
Acts 21:34 not get at the truth because of the *u*,
23: 9 A loud *u* ensued.

UPROOT (10)

2Chr 7:20 *u* the people from the land I gave them;
Ps(s) 52: 7 and *u* you from the land of the living.
101: 8 *u* from the city of the LORD all evildoers.
Eccl 3: 2 a time to plant, and a time to *u* the plant.
Sir 47:22 does not *u* the posterity of his chosen one,
Jer 12:17 I will *u* and destroy that nation entirely,
18: 7 Sometimes I threaten to *u* and tear down
31:28 once watched over them to *u* and pull down,
42:10 I will plant you, not *u* you;
44:11 and I will *u* all Judah.

UPROOTED (10)

Dt 29:27 anger the LORD *u* them from their soil
Jb 19:10 my hope he has *u* like a tree.
Ps(s) 9: 7 of the cities you *u* has perished.
Wis 4: 4 wind and, by the violence of the winds, *u*;
Sir 16: 9 people who were *u* because of their sin;
Zep 2: 4 drive out at midday, and Ekron shall be *u*.
Mt 15:13 put down by my heavenly Father will be *u*."
Lk 17: 6 'Be *u* and transplanted into the sea,'
Jude 1:12 end they bear no fruit, being dead and *u*.
Rv 6:14 mountain and island was *u* from its base.

UPROOTING (1)

Jer 45: 4 what I have planted, I am *u*:

UPROOTS (1)

Sir 3: 9 but a mother's curse *u* the growing plant.

UPSET (5)

1Sm 1: 6 Her rival, to *u* her,
Neh 4: 9 been warned and that God had *u* their plan,
Mt 27:19 about him today which has greatly *u* me."
Lk 10:41 you are anxious and *u* about many things;
Acts 15:24 without any instructions from us have *u* you

UPSETS (2)

Prv 11:29 He who *u* his household has empty air for a
19: 3 A man's own folly *u* his way,

UPSETTING (3)

1Chr 13: 9 to steady the ark, for the oxen were *u* it.
2Tm 2:18 They are *u* some people's faith.
Ti 1:11 They are *u* whole families by teaching

UPSHOT (1)

Mt 8:34 The *u* was that the entire town came out to

UPSIDE (2)

Jgs 7:13 and as it fell it turned the tent *u* down."
Is 24: 2 he turns it *u* down,

UPSTAIRS (9)

2Kgs 4:21 The mother took him *u* and laid him on the
Tb 3:10 She went in tears to an *u* room in her
Mk 14:15 Then he will show you an *u* room,
Lk 22:12 That man will show you an *u* room,
Acts 1:13 went to the *u* room where they were staying:
9:37 her body and laid it out in an *u* room.
9:39 his arrival they took him *u* to the room.
20: 8 in the *u* room where we were assembled.
20:11 Afterward Paul went *u* again,

UPSTREAM (4)

Jos 3:13 down from *u* will halt in a solid bank."
3:16 than the waters flowing from *u* halted,
Dn 12: 6 to the man clothed in linen, who was *u*,
12: 7 The man clothed in linen, who was *u*,

UPSURGINGS (1)

2Sm 1:21 dew nor rain upon you, nor *u* of the deeps!

UPWARD (12)

1Chr 23:24 of the LORD from twenty years of age *u*,
Jb 5: 7 himself begets mischief, as sparks fly *u*.
Prv 15:24 The path of life leads the prudent man *u*,
Eccl 3:21 life-breath of the children of men goes *u*
Is 8:21 He shall look *u*,
Ez 1:27 *U* from what resembled his waist I saw what
8: 2 from his waist *u* there seemed to be a
8:11 fragrance of the incense was rising *u*.
41: 7 passageway that led *u* to the side chambers,
41: 7 all the way around and all the way *u*;
41: 7 the temple had a broad way running *u*
Jn 11:41 away the stone and Jesus looked *u* and said:

UR (4)

Gn 11:28 in his native land, in *U* of the Chaldeans.
11:31 and brought them out of *U* of the Chaldeans,
15: 7 who brought you from *U* of the Chaldeans
Neh 9: 7 who brought him out from *U* of the Chaldees,

URBANUS (1)

Rom 16: 9 to *U*,

URGE (14)

Gn 3:16 Yet your *u* shall be for your husband,
4: 7 his *u* is toward you,
Ru 1:18 Naomi then ceased to *u* her,
Wis 14: 2 For the *u* for profits devised this latter,
Sir 13: 9 then he will *u* you all the more.
Jer 7:16 Do not *u* me, for I will not listen to you.
Ez 39: 2 I will turn you about, I will *u* you on,
Acts 27:22 I *u* you now to keep up your courage.
27:34 Now I *u* you to take some food,
1Cor 16:16 I *u* you to serve under such men and under
2Thes 3:12 *u* them strongly in the Lord Jesus Christ,
1Tm 2: 1 First of all, I *u* that petitions,
4:11 Such are the things you must *u* and teach.
1Pt 2:11 I *u* you not to indulge your carnal desires.

URGED (27)

Gn 19: 3 He *u* them so strongly,
19:15 As dawn was breaking the angels *u* Lot on,
27:38 But Esau *u* his father,
33:11 Since he so *u* him, Esau accepted.
43: 8 Then Judah *u* his father Israel:
Ex 12:33 The Egyptians likewise *u* the people on,
1Sm 20: 6 'David *u* me to let him go on short notice
2Sm 13:25 And though Absalom *u* him,
1Kgs 21:25 LORD as did Ahab, *u* on by his wife Jezebel.
2Kgs 4: 8 of influence, who *u* him to dine with her.
Jdt 2: 2 *u* the total destruction of those countries.
13:14 the two, Judith *u* them with a loud voice:
2Mc 2: 3 With other similar words he *u* them not to
6:21 *u* him to bring meat of his own providing,
7:26 After he had *u* her for a long time,
13:10 he *u* the people to call upon the LORD
14:25 He *u* him to marry and have children;
15: 8 He *u* his men not to fear the enemy,
Ps(s) 137: 3 And our despoilers *u* us to be joyous:
Jer 36:25 Gemariah *u* the king not to burn the scroll,
Acts 13:43 *u* them to hold fast to the grace of God.
21:12 *u* Paul not to proceed to Jerusalem.
26:20 I *u* them to act in conformity with their
27:33 dawn Paul *u* all on board to take some food:
28:14 who *u* us to stay on with them for a week.
1Cor 16:12 I *u* him strongly to go to you with the
2Cor 12:18 I *u* Titus to go to you,

URGENT (6)

Nm 22:37 to Balaam, "I sent an *u* summons to you!
1Sm 21: 9 weapons, because the king's business was *u*."
2Mc 12:39 day, since the task had now become *u*,
Dn 3:22 other garments, for the king's order was *u*.
Acts 9:38 sent two men to him with the *u* request,
Phil 1:24 more *u* that I remain alive for your sakes.

URGENTLY (4)

1Sm 20:28 *u* asked me to let him go to his city,

2Mc 10:19 off to places where he was more *u* needed.
Jer 11: 7 *U* and constantly I warned your fathers to
Mk 15:43 Pilate and *u* requested the body of Jesus.

URGES (3)

Prv 16:26 labors for him, for his mouth *u* him on.
Sir 38:25 Who guides the ox and *u* on the bullock,
43: 5 it, at whose orders it *u* on its steeds.

URGING (16)

Dt 13: 3 sign or wonder, *u* you to follow other gods,
1Sm 28:23 his servants joined the woman in *u* him,
2Sm 12:17 beside him *u* him to rise from the ground:
13:27 At Absalom's *u*,
2Kgs 2:17 However, they kept *u* him,
5:16 and despite Naaman's *u*,
1Mc 11:40 kept *u* Imalkue to hand over the boy to him,
13:21 *u* him to come to them by way of the desert,
2Mc 7:25 *u* her to advise her boy to save his life.
13: 3 with great duplicity kept *u* Antiochus on,
Prv 7:21 She wins him over by her repeated *u*,
Jn 4:31 Meanwhile the disciples were *u* him,
Acts 2:40 he used many other arguments, and kept *u*,
25: 3 and *u* Festus to send him to Jerusalem.
Phil 2:12 beloved, obedient as always to my *u*,
2Pt 3: 1 as reminders *u* you to sincerity of outlook.

URI (8)

Ex 31: 2 "See, I have chosen Bezalel, son of *U*,
35:30 the LORD has chosen Bezalel, son of *U*,
38:22 However, it was Bezalel, son of *U*,
1Kgs 4:19 Geber, son of *U*,
1Chr 2:20 Hur became the father of *U*,
2:20 of Uri, and *U* became the father of Bezalel.
2Chr 1: 5 bronze altar made by Bezalel, son of *U*,
Ezr 10:24 Shallum, Telem, and *U*.

URIAH (38)

2Sm 11: 3 of [Joab's armor-bearer] *U* the Hittite."
11: 6 a message to Joab, "Send me *U* the Hittite."
11: 6 So Joab sent *U* to David.
11: 7 going, and *U* answered that all was well.
11: 8 David then said to *U*,
11: 8 *U* left the palace,
11: 9 But *U* slept at the entrance of the royal
11:10 David was told that *U* had not gone home.
11:10 So he said to *U*,
11:11 *U* answered David,
11:12 Then David said to *U*,
11:12 So *U* remained in Jerusalem that day.
11:14 wrote a letter to Joab which he sent by *U*.
11:15 "Place *U* up front,
11:16 he assigned *U* to a place where he knew the
11:17 fell, and among them *U* the Hittite died.
11:21 'Your servant *U* the Hittite is also dead.' "
11:24 servants died, among them your servant *U*."
11:26 wife of *U* heard that her husband had died,
12: 9 have cut down *U* the Hittite with the sword;
12:10 have taken the wife of *U* to be your wife.'
12:15 that the wife of *U* had borne to David,
23:39 *U* the Hittite
1Kgs 15: 5 lived, except in the case of *U* the Hittite.
2Kgs 16:10 King Ahaz sent to *U* the priest a model of
16:11 *U* the priest built an altar according to
16:15 altar," King Ahaz commanded *U* the priest,
16:16 *U* the priest did just as King Ahaz had
1Chr 11:41 *U* the Hittite;
Ezr 8:33 to the priest Meremoth, son of *U*,
Neh 3: 4 At their side Meremoth, son of *U*,
3:21 After him, Meremoth, son of *U*,
8: 4 side stood Mattithiah, Shema, Anaiah, *U*,
Is 8: 2 I took reliable witnesses, *U* the priest,
Jer 26:20 who prophesied in the name of the LORD, *U*,
26:21 *U* heard of it and fled in fear to Egypt.
26:23 him into Egypt to bring *U* back to the king,
Mt 1: 6 whose mother had been the wife of *U*.

URIEL (4)

1Chr 6: 9 whose son was Tahath, whose son was *U*,
15: 5 of the sons of Kohath, *U*,
15:11 Zadok and Abiathar, and the Levites *U*,
2Chr 13: 2 named Michaiah, daughter of *U* of Gibeah.

URIM (8)

Ex 28:30 decision you shall put the *U* and Thummim,
Lv 8: 8 on him, with the *U* and Thummim in it,
Nm 27:21 decisions of the *U* in the LORD'S presence;
Dt 33: 8 Thummim, to the man of your favor your *U*;
1Sm 14:41 LORD, God of Israel, respond with *U*;
28: 6 in dreams or by the *U* or through prophets.
Ezr 2:63 be a priest bearing the *U* and Thummim.
Neh 7:65 be a priest bearing the *U* and Thummim.

URINE (2)

2Kgs 18:27 eat their own excrement and drink their *u*?"
Is 36:12 their own excrement and drink their own *u*?"

URN (1)

Ex 16:33 "Take an *u* and put an omer of manna in it.

URUKIAN (1)

Ezr 4: 9 and agents from among the Persian, *U*,

USAGE (2)

Lk 1: 9 priestly *u* to enter the sanctuary of the Lord
1Cor 11:16 the churches of God recognize any other *u*.

USE (104)

Gn 43:18 they want to *u* it as a pretext to attack
Ex 21:26 in the eye and destroys the *u* of the eye,
25:39 *U* a talent of pure gold for the lampstand
26: 9 *U* the sixth sheet double at the front of
27:19 of the Dwelling, whatever be their *u*,
28: 5 serving as my priests, they shall *u* gold,
30:19 shall *u* it in washing their hands and feet.
35:19 the service cloths for *u* in the sanctuary;
39: 1 the service cloths for *u* in the sanctuary,
39:41 the service cloths for *u* in the sanctuary,
Lv 7:24 by wild beasts may be put to any other *u*,
11:32 Any such article that men *u*,
13:51 or on the leather, whatever be its *u*,
Nm 4: 9 They shall *u* a violet cloth to cover the
4:26 and all other objects necessary in their *u*.
7: 5 to *u* in the service of the meeting tent.
10: 2 which you shall *u* in assembling the
10: 8 and the *u* of them is prescribed by
15:39 When you *u* these tassels,
Dt 20:14 and you may *u* this plunder of your enemies
25:15 But *u* a true and just weight,
Jos 9: 4 making *u* of old sacks for their asses,
1Sm 8:13 will *u* your daughters as ointment-makers,
8:16 and your asses, and *u* them to do his work.
1Kgs 13: 6 king recovered the normal *u* of his hand.
1Chr 12: 2 could *u* either the right or the left hand,
28:15 *u* to which each lampstand was to be put.
Ezr 7:17 therefore, to *u* this money to buy bulls,
Neh 13: 5 had set aside for the latter's *u* a large
Jdt 3: 3 make *u* of them as you please.
11:13 They decreed that they would *u* up the
12: 4 your handmaid will not *u* up her supplies
12:15 for her daily *u* in reclining at her dinner.
Est 2:23 was written in the annals for the king's *u*
Jb 13:20 These things only do not *u* against me,
Ps(s) 7:14 them, and *u* fiery darts for arrows.
17: 9 from the wicked who *u* violence against me.
39: 7 up stores, and knows not who will *u* them.
104:14 the cattle, and vegetation for men's *u*,
Prv 10:26 sluggard to those who *u* him as a messenger.
17:16 Of what *u* in the fool's hand are the means
Eccl 5:10 Of what *u* are they to the owner except to
Wis 2: 6 and *u* the freshness of creation avidly.
13:11 art, produce something fit for daily *u*,
13:12 and *u* up the refuse from his handiwork in
15: 7 As to what shall be the *u* of each vessel
15:15 which have no *u* of the eyes for vision,
Sir 4:20 *U* your time well;
5:16 *u* not your tongue for calumny;
12: 5 give him, lest he *u* them against yourself;
13: 4 rich man can *u* you he will enslave you,
14: 3 and to the miser, of what *u* is gold?
14:11 *u* freely whatever you have and enjoy it as
26:10 finding an opportunity, she make *u* of it;
31:31 *U* no harsh words with him and distress
36: 3 so now *u* them to show us your glory.
37:19 benefit many, yet be of no *u* to himself.
Is 22: 3 together, captured without the *u* of a bow.
Jer 2:22 you scour it with soap, and *u* much lye,
2:25 But you say, "No *u*!
4: 2 shall the nations *u* his name in blessing,
6:20 what *u* to me incense that comes from Sheba,
16:19 of our fathers, empty idols of no *u*."
18:12 But they will say, "No *u*!
23:38 Because you *u* this phrase,
23:38 the LORD," though I forbade you to *u* it,
27: 6 of the field I have given him for his *u*.
46:11 No *u* to multiply remedies;
Ez 5: 1 sharp sword and *u* it like a barber's razor,
15: 3 you *u* its wood to make anything worthwhile?
16:25 for yourself to *u* your beauty obscenely,
28:22 upon it and *u* it to manifest my holiness.
45:18 you shall *u* an unblemished young bull
Mi 5:11 the means of divination from your *u*,
Zec 9:13 and I will *u* you as a warrior's sword.
Mt 6:25 you are to eat or drink or *u* for clothing.
11:16 comparison can I *u* to describe this breed?
13:13 "I *u* parables when I speak to them
26:52 Those who *u* the sword are sooner or later
Mk 4: 2 them at great length, by the *u* of parables,
4:30 comparison shall we *u* for the reign of God?
16:17 they will *u* my name to expel demons,
Lk 7:31 comparison can I *u* for the men of today?
16: 9 through your *u* of this world's goods,
22:49 they said, "Lord, shall we *u* the sword?"
Acts 2:23 made *u* of pagans to crucify and kill him.
27:17 made *u* of cables to brace the ship itself.
Rom 3:13 they *u* their tongues to deceive;
6:19 (I *u* the following example from human
12: 6 its *u* should be in proportion to his faith.
12: 7 a teacher should *u* his gift for teaching;
14:22 *U* the faith you have as your rule of life
1Cor 7:31 and those who make *u* of the world as
9:18 *u* of the authority the gospel gives me.
2Cor 10: 2 assurance I might dare to *u* courageously
Gal 5: 2 circumcised, Christ will be of no *u* to you!
Col 2:22 deal with things that perish in their *u*.
1Tm 6:17 us richly with all things for our *u*.
2Tm 2:20 for distinguished and others for common *u*.
Jas 3: 9 We *u* it to say,
3: 9 then we *u* it to curse men,
1Pt 2:16 do not *u* your freedom as a cloak for vice.
Rv 14:15 *U* your sickle and cut down the harvest,
14:18 *U* your sharp sickle and gather the grapes

USED (132)

Gn 11: 3 They *u* bricks for stone,
14:24 for me except what my servants have *u* up
21:15 Beer-sheba, the water in the skin was *u* up.
31:15 has even *u* up the money that he got for us!
40:13 *u* to do when you were his cupbearer.
43: 2 So when they had *u* up all the rations they
Ex 26: 7 be *u* as a tent covering over the Dwelling.
27:18 Fine linen twined must be *u*,
27:20 of crushed olives, to be *u* for the light,
30: 4 as holders for the poles *u* in carrying it.
30:32 be *u* in any ordinary anointing of the body,
33: 7 Moses *u* to pitch at some distance away,
33:11 The LORD *u* to speak to Moses face to face,
37:24 A talent of pure gold was *u* for the
38:21 of the various amounts *u* on the Dwelling,
38:24 All the gold *u* in the entire construction
38:27 One hundred talents of silver were *u* for
38:28 were *u* for making the hooks on the columns,
40:31 sons *u* to wash their hands and feet there,
Lv 14:21 to be *u* as a wave offering in atonement
17: 5 such sacrifices as they *u* to offer up in
17: 7 whom they *u* to render their wanton worship.
Nm 11: 5 the fish we *u* to eat without cost in Egypt,
Dt 23:13 a place set aside to be *u* as a latrine.
Jos 8:31 stones on which no iron tool had been *u*,
Jgs 1: 7 off, *u* to pick up scraps under my table.
4: 5 She *u* to sit under Deborah's palm tree,
6: 3 And it *u* to be that when the Israelites
Ru 4: 7 Now it *u* to be the custom in Israel that,
1Sm 1: 4 he *u* to give a portion each to his wife
1: 8 Her husband Elkanah *u* to ask her:
2:19 mother *u* to make a little garment for him,
7:17 Then he *u* to return to Ramah,
9: 9 anyone who went to consult God *u* to say,
17:34 servant *u* to tend his father's sheep,
2Sm 8: 7 David also took away the golden shields *u*
14:26 which he *u* to do at the end of every year,
15: 2 Absalom *u* to rise early and stand
15:32 the top, where men *u* to worship God,
1Kgs 9:25 Three times a year Solomon *u* to offer
10:11 fleet, which *u* to bring gold from Ophir,
19:21 he *u* the plowing equipment for fuel to
2Kgs 3: 4 *u* to pay the king of Israel as tribute a
4: 8 he passed by, he *u* to stop there to dine.
12:13 and hewn stone *u* in repairing the breaches,
12:14 the LORD were *u* there to make silver cups,
13:20 of Moabites *u* to raid the land each year.
21:13 with the plummet I *u* for the house of Ahab.
25:14 and all the bronze vessels *u* for service.
1Chr 14:11 "God has *u* me to break through my enemies
18: 8 which Solomon later *u* to make the bronze
28:14 He specified the weight of gold to be *u* in
28:14 weight of silver to be *u* in the silver vessels
28:16 gold to be *u* for the forks and pitchers,
28:18 weight, to be *u* for the altar of incense;
2Chr 7: 6 when David *u* them to accompany the hymns.
34:10 and these in turn *u* it to pay the workmen
Tb 1: 5 *u* to offer sacrifice on all the mountains
1: 7 years, I *u* to give a second tithe in money,
1:18 But I *u* to take their bodies by stealth
5: 6 I *u* to stay with our kinsman Gabael,
5:14 they *u* to make the pilgrimage to Jerusalem,
11:13 *u* both hands to peel off the cataracts.
12:12 the same thing when you *u* to bury the dead.
Jdt 10: 2 she *u* only on sabbaths and feast days.
1Mc 1:58 So they *u* their power against Israel,
10:14 for they *u* it as a place of refuge.
10:42 shekels that *u* to be taken from the revenue
14:36 they *u* to sally forth to defile the environs
2Mc 4:19 but should be *u* for some other purpose.
10:14 and *u* every opportunity to attack the Jews.
Jb 1: 4 His sons *u* to take turns giving feasts,
41:20 slingstones *u* against him are but straws.
Prv 16:11 the weights *u* with them are his concern.
Sir 23:13 Let not your mouth become *u* to coarse talk,
36: 3 you have *u* us to show them your holiness,
Is 1:21 Justice *u* to lodge within her,
7:23 place where there *u* to be a thousand vines,
7:25 which *u* to be hoed with the mattock:
65:15 Shall be *u* by my chosen ones for cursing;
Jer 26:18 *u* to prophesy in the days of Hezekiah,
32:44 shall be *u* in the land of Benjamin,
52:18 and all the bronze vessels *u* for service.
Ez 15: 5 and scorched it, can it be *u* for anything!
16:15 *u* your renown to make yourself a harlot,
44:12 *u* to minister for them before their idols,
Dn 13: 7 *u* to enter her husband's garden for a walk.
14:21 secret door by which they *u* to enter
Hos 2:10 silver, and of gold, which they *u* for Baal,

USED (cont.)

Mt 7: 2 which you measure will be *u* to measure you.
9:16 thing he has *u* to cover the hole will pull,
16:12 issuing a warning against yeast *u* for bread
22:19 Show me the coin *u* for the tax."
27: 7 they *u* it to buy the potter's field as a
Mk 2:21 he has *u* to cover the hole would pull away
Lk 2:41 His parents *u* to go every year to
6:39 He also *u* images in speaking to them:
8:29 man *u* to be tied with chains and fetters,
Jn 9: 8 this the fellow who *u* to sit and beg?"
10: 6 Even though Jesus *u* this figure with them,
12: 6 and *u* to help himself to what was
Acts 2:40 of his testimony he *u* many other arguments,
3:10 beggar who *u* to sit at the Beautiful Gate
4:35 They *u* to lay them at the feet of the
5:12 they *u* to meet in Solomon's Portico.
7: 6 These are the words God *u*:
14: 8 he *u* to sit crippled,
16:16 She *u* to bring substantial profit to her
17:17 In the synagogue he *u* to hold discussions
19: 4 He *u* to tell the people about the one who
24:26 so he *u* to send for him frequently to
27:17 they lowered the small anchor *u* for moving
28:27 They have scarcely *u* their ears to listen;
Rom 7: 8 it *u* the commandment to rouse in me every
7:11 its opportunity and *u* the commandment:
7:13 *u* what was good to bring about my death.
12: 7 it should be *u* for service.
1Cor 9:12 But we have not *u* this right.
9:15 for me, I have not *u* any of these rights,
13:11 I was a child I *u* to talk like a child,
2Cor 3:13 who *u* to hide his face with a veil so that
Phil 3: 7 But those things I *u* to consider gain I
1Thes 3: 4 *u* to warn you that we would undergo trial;
2Thes 2: 5 do you not remember how I *u* to tell you
3:10 when we were with you we *u* to lay down the
1Tm 1: 8 it in the way law is supposed to be *u*—
Heb 9: 6 In performing their service the priests *u*
1Pt 3: 5 ages *u* to adorn themselves in this way,
Rv 13:12 It *u* the authority of the first beast to
15: 2 were holding the harps *u* in worshiping God,
21:17 by the unit of measurement the angel *u*.

USEFUL (11)

2Kgs 3:25 stopped up and every *u* tree they felled.
Tb 4:18 think lightly of any advice that can be *u*.
6: 5 gall, heart, and liver make *u* medicines."
2Mc 12:12 they could indeed be *u* in many respects,
Wis 8: 7 in life is more *u* for men than these.
2Tm 2:21 dedicated and *u* to the master of the house
3:16 is inspired of God and is *u* for teaching
Phlm 1:11 He has become in truth Onesimus *U*,
1:11 you is now *u* indeed both to you and to me.
1:20 I want to make you *u*" to me in the Lord.
Heb 6: 7 *u* to those for whom it is cultivated,

USELESS (22)

2Mc 12:44 *u* and foolish to pray for them in death.
Ps(s) 33:17 *U* is the horse for safety;
Prv 11: 4 Wealth is *u* on the day of wrath,
Wis 2:11 for weakness proves itself *u*.
4: 5 broken off untimely, and their fruit be *u*,
13:10 art, and likenesses of beasts, or *u* stone,
15:15 even their feet are *u* to walk with.
16:29 a wintry frost and runs off like *u* water.
Jer 2: 8 prophesied by Baal, and went after *u* idols.
2:11 have changed their glory for *u* things.
Bar 6:15 As *u* as one's broken tools are their gods,
Hos 7:16 They have again become *u*,
Mt 13:48 What was *u* they threw away.
Mk 5:36 "Fear is *u*.
Lk 8:50 "Fear is *u*;
17:10 commanded to do, say, 'We are *u* servants.
Jn 6:63 the flesh is *u*.
2Cor 12: 1 I must go on boasting, however *u* it may be,
Gal 2: 2 I was pursuing, or had pursued, was not *u*.
Ti 3: 9 They are *u* and have no point.
Phlm 1:11 for he who was formerly *u* to you is now
Heb 13: 9 foods which are *u* to those who take them

USELESSLY (1)

Is 49: 4 I had toiled in vain, and for nothing, *u*,

USELESSNESS (1)

Heb 7:18 annulled because of its weakness and *u*,

USES (7)

Gn 44: 5 drinks and which he *u* for divination.
Dt 28:57 *u* them for food for want of anything else,
Wis 7:20 of men, *u* of plants and virtues of roots
Sir 27:23 In your presence he *u* honeyed talk,
Is 32: 7 And the trickster *u* wicked trickery,
Mt 5:22 any man who *u* abusive language toward his
1Tm 1: 8 provided one *u* it in the way law is

USHERED (2)

Jdt 10:20 servants came out and *u* her into the tent.
Est 1:17 that Queen Vashti be *u* into his presence,

USING (18)

Gn 11: 1 spoke the same language, *u* the same words.
31: 1 wealth of his by *u* our father's property."
Lv 19:35 *u* measures of length or weight or capacity.
24: 5 *u* two tenths of an ephah of flour for each
Dt 28:55 his children that he himself is *u* for food
Sir 41:22 Of *u* harsh words with friends,
Jer 37:15 the scribe, which they were *u* as a jail.
Mt 22: 1 to address them, once more *u* parables.
Mk 9:38 we saw a man *u* your name to expel demons
9:39 No man who performs a miracle *u* my name
Lk 1:62 Then, *u* signs,
3:18 *U* exhortations of this sort,
9:49 we saw a man *u* your name to expel demons,
Acts 7:25 God was *u* him to bring them deliverance;
9:25 him to the ground, *u* ropes and a hamper.
1Cor 7:31 of the world as though they were not *u* it,
Eph 6:18 *u* prayers and petitions of every sort.
1Tm 1: 7 not understanding the words they are *u*,

USUAL (11)

Lv 5:10 be offered as a holocaust in the *u* way.
9:16 holocaust, and offered it in the *u* manner.
1Sm 3: 2 One day Eli was asleep in his *u* place.
20:25 dine, taking his *u* place against the wall,
Dn 3:19 to be heated seven times more than *u*
13:15 right moment, she entered the garden as *u*,
14:15 The priests entered that night as *u*,
Mt 20: 2 agreement with them for the *u* daily wage,
20:13 You agreed on the *u* wage, did you not?
Mk 10: 1 him, and as *u* he began to teach them.
Acts 17: 2 Following his *u* custom,

USUALLY (3)

Dt 23:20 else on which interest is *u* demanded.
1Mc 10:89 such as is *u* given to King's Kinsmen;
Jn 2:10 "People *u* serve the choice wine first;

USURER (1)

Ps(s) 109:11 May the *u* ensnare all his belongings,

USURPED (1)

Sir 47:21 into being, when in Ephraim kingship was *u*.

USURY (6)

Neh 5:10 Let us put an end to this *u*!
Ps(s) 15: 5 who lends not his money at *u* and
Ez 18: 8 he does not lend at interest nor exact *u*;
18:13 things, lends at interest and exacts *u*—
18:17 from evildoing, accepts no interest or *u*,
22:12 You exact interest and *u*;

UTENSILS (37)

Ex 38: 3 All the *u* of the altar,
Nm 3:31 the *u* with which the ministry of the
4:10 The lampstand with all its *u* they shall
4:12 Taking the *u* of the sanctuary service,
4:14 put all the *u* with which it is served:
4:14 basins, and all the *u* of the altar.
4:15 objects and all their *u* on breaking camp,
4:16 the sacred objects and *u* that are in it."
1Kgs 10:21 and all the *u* in the hall of the Forest of
15:15 offerings of silver, gold, and various *u*.
2Kgs 14:14 all the gold and silver and all the *u*
24:13 and broke up all the gold *u* that Solomon,
1Chr 9:29 care of the *u* and all the sacred vessels,
18:10 gold, silver and bronze *u* of every sort.
29: 5 various *u* to be made of gold and silver,
2Chr 9:20 and all the *u* in the hall of the Forest of
15:18 silver, gold, and various *u*.
24:14 had it made into *u* for the LORD's temple,
24:14 *u* for the service and the holocausts,
24:14 and basins and other gold and silver *u*.
28:24 *u* of God's house and broke them in pieces.
29:18 the altar of holocausts with all its *u*,
29:18 the table for the showbread with all its *u*.
36:18 All the *u* of the house of God,
Ezr 1: 7 had the *u* of the house of the LORD brought
5:14 the gold and silver *u* of the house of God
5:15 Take these *u* and deposit them in the
6: 5 the gold and silver *u* of the house of God
7:19 The *u* consigned to you for the service of
8:25 and the *u* offered for the house of our God
8:26 silver *u*,
8:28 the LORD, and the *u* are also consecrated;
8:30 gold, and the *u* that had been weighed out,
8:33 and the *u* were weighed out in the house of
Neh 10:40 also are housed the *u* of the sanctuary,
13: 5 the cereal offerings, incense and *u*,
13: 9 replace there the *u* of the house of God,

UTHAI (2)

1Chr 9: 4 Among the Judahites was *U*,
Ezr 8:14 of the sons of Bigvai, *U*,

UTMOST (2)

2Sm 2:26 "Must the sword destroy to the *u*?
2Mc 15:17 by hand-to-hand combat with the *u* courage,

UTTER (62)

Ex 16: 8 he heeds the grumbling you *u* against him,
Lv 5: 4 such as men are accustomed to *u* rashly,
Dt 28:48 and thirst, in nakedness and *u* poverty,
1Sm 5: 9 the LORD threw the city into *u* turmoil:
2Sm 7: 7 did I ever *u* word to any one of the
1Kgs 8:28 I, your servant, *u* before you this day.
Jdt 7:25 before them in thirst and *u* exhaustion.
14:13 to give us battle, to their *u* destruction."
1Mc 9:55 so that he could no longer *u* a word to
2Mc 6:29 what he had said seemed to them *u* madness.
15: 6 In his *u* boastfulness and arrogance
Jb 8: 2 How long will you *u* such things?
8:10 you and *u* their words of understanding?
13: 6 *u* and listen to the reproof from my lips.
13: 7 Is it for him that you *u* deceit?
27: 4 speak falsehood, nor my tongue *u* deceit!
32:18 For I am full of matters to *u*;
33: 3 mind, my lips shall *u* knowledge sincerely;
Ps(s) 2: 1 the nations rage and the peoples *u* folly?
6:11 enemies shall be put to shame in *u* terror;
22:26 gift will I *u* praise in the vast assembly;
74: 3 Turn your steps toward the *u* ruins;
78: 2 a parable, I will *u* mysteries from of old.
115: 7 they *u* no sound from their throat.
Prv 4: 5 forget or turn aside from the words I *u*.
5:14 I have all but come to *u* ruin,
Eccl 10:13 and in the end of his talk is *u* madness;
Wis 3: 3 their going forth from us, *u* destruction.
Sir 10:13 afflictions and brings men to *u* ruin.
11: 6 The exalted often fall into *u* disgrace;
20:19 for he does not *u* it at the proper time.
Is 15: 5 the way to Horonaim they *u* rending cries.
19:11 *U* fools are the princes of Zoan!
38:14 Like a swallow I *u* shrill cries;
42:12 LORD, and *u* his praise in the coastlands.
42:17 turned back in *u* shame who trust in idols;
Jer 11:14 of this people, nor *u* a plea for them.
14:14 Lies these prophets *u* in my name,
20:11 their failure they will be put to *u* shame,
48: 9 for Moab, for it is an *u* wasteland;
Ez 26:17 Then they shall *u* a lament over you:
27: 2 for you, son of man, *u* a lament over Tyre,
27:32 In their mourning they *u* a lament over you;
28:12 of man, *u* a lament over the king of Tyre,
32: 2 Son of man, *u* a lament over Pharaoh,
36: 5 who with wholehearted joy and *u* contempt
Dn 3:19 became livid with *u* rage against Shadrach,
11:36 he shall *u* dreadful blasphemies against
Hos 10:15 you, Bethel, Because of your *u* wickedness:
Am 5: 1 Hear this word which I *u* over you,
Mi 1: 8 I *u* lamentation like the jackals,
Hb 2:16 right hand, and *u* shame on your glory.
Mt 5:11 persecute you and *u* every kind of slander
12:34 How can you *u* anything good,
Mk 3:28 mankind and all the blasphemies men *u*,
Acts 2: 7 They asked in *u* amazement,
19: 6 to speak in tongues and to *u* prophecies.
1Cor 2: 7 No, what we *u* is God's wisdom:
14: 9 if you do not *u* intelligible speech
2Cor 7: 4 with *u* frankness and boast much about you.
Phil 1: 4 is constantly, in every prayer I *u*—
Heb 10:22 in *u* sincerity and absolute confidence,

UTTERANCE (27)

Gn 4:23 wives of Lamech, listen to my *u*:
Nm 23: 5 When he had put an *u* in Balaam's mouth,
23:16 Balaam, and having put an *u* in his mouth,
24: 3 The *u* of Balaam,
24: 3 Beor, the *u* of the man whose eye is true,
24: 4 true, The *u* of one who hears what God says,
24:15 The *u* of Balaam,
24:15 Beor, the *u* of the man whose eye is true,
24:16 true, The *u* of one who hears what God says,
2Sm 23: 1 "The *u* of David,
23: 1 the *u* of the man God raised up,
Jb 7:11 My own *u* I will not restrain;
Ps(s) 49: 4 prudence shall be the *u* of my heart.
106:33 his spirit, and the rash *u* passed his lips.
Prv 6: 2 You have been snared by the *u* of your lips,
15:23 There is joy for a man in his *u*;
15:28 The just man weighs well his *u*,
Eccl 5: 1 Be not hasty in your *u* and let not your
5: 2 many cares, and a fool's *u* with many words.
Wis 1:11 For a stealthy *u* does not go unpunished,
8:12 would abide my silence and attend my *u*;
Is 10:12 the *u* of the king of Assyria's proud heart,
Dn 9:25 From the *u* of the word that Jerusalem was
Mt 4: 4 every *u* that comes from the mouth of God.' "
Lk 18:34 His *u* remained obscure to them,
Jn 12:36 After this *u*, Jesus left them and went
2Thes 2: 2 or terrified, whether by an oracular *u*,

UTTERANCES (1)

Eccl 5: 5 Let not your *u* make you guilty,

UTTERED (29)

Nm 30: 3 must fulfill exactly the promise he has *u*.
Jgs 9:38 to him, "Where now is the boast you *u*,
1Kgs 5:12 Solomon also *u* three thousand proverbs,
12:15 fulfill the prophecy he had *u* to Jeroboam,

1Chr 16:12 his portents, and the judgments he has *u*,
17:23 may the promise that you have *u* concerning
2Chr 10:15 the prophecy the LORD had *u* to Jeroboam,
Tb 1:18 King because of the blasphemies he had *u*.
Est A: 5 They *u* a mighty cry,
1Mc 7:40 Here Judas *u* this prayer:
2Mc 8: 4 and the blasphemies *u* against his name;
9: 5 for scarcely had he *u* those words when he
Jb 26: 4 With whose help have you *u* those words,
Ps(s) 66:14 *u* and my words promised in my distress.
105: 5 his portents, and the judgments he has *u*,
Wis 7: 3 I *u* that first sound common to all.
Sir 48:20 they *u* and saved them through ISAIAH.
Bar 2: 1 fulfilled the warning he had *u* against us:
Ez 35:12 you have *u* against the mountains of Israel:
Zep 2: 8 I have heard the revilings *u* by Moab,
Lk 1:67 with the Holy Spirit, *u* this prophecy:
23:46 Jesus *u* a loud cry and said,
Jn 12:41 Isaiah *u* these words because he had seen
Acts 1:16 "the saying in Scripture *u* long ago by
27: 9 It was then that Paul *u* this warning:
Rom 15: 3 reproaches they *u* against you fell on me."
2Cor 12: 4 Paradise to hear words which cannot be *u*,
Jas 5:15 *u* in faith will reclaim the one who is ill,
Jude 1:15 every harsh word they have *u* against him."

UTTERING (14)

Jos 10:21 no man *u* a sound against the Israelites.
2Sm 16:12 benefits for the curses he is *u* this day."
2Mc 10:34 blasphemies and *u* abominable words.
12:14 them and even *u* blasphemies and profanity.
Jb 31:30 mouth to sin by *u* a curse against his life
Is 45:23 *u* my just decree and my unalterable word:
59:13 *u* words of falsehood the heart has
Mk 15:37 Then Jesus, *u* a loud cry,
Jn 11:11 After *u* these words,
1Cor 14:17 You will be *u* praise very well indeed,
14:24 uninitiate enters while all are *u* prophecy,
1Pt 3:10 from evil and his lips from *u* deceit.
Jude 1:16 They live by their passions, *u* bombast.
Rv 13: 5 a mouth for *u* proud boasts and blasphemies,

UTTERLY (41)

Gn 19:11 they were *u* unable to reach the doorway.
41:31 so *u* severe will that famine be.
Dt 7:23 rout them *u* until they are annihilated.
7:26 and abhor it *u* as a thing that is doomed.
8:19 you this day that you will perish *u*.
2Sm 12:14 you have *u* spurned the LORD by this deed,
1Kgs 15:29 soul to Jeroboam but destroying him *u*,
2Chr 28:19 own way and proved *u* faithless to the LORD.
Jdt 1:15 through with spears, and *u* destroyed him.
6: 4 they shall *u* perish,
7:30 he will not *u* forsake us.
Est B: 6 *u* destroyed by the swords of their enemies,
1Mc 3:42 given to destroy and *u* wipe out the people.
16:22 On hearing this, John was *u* astounded.
2Mc 3:12 He added that it was *u* unthinkable to
6: 3 in an intolerable and *u* disgusting way.
Jb 30: 2 they were *u* destitute.
Ps(s) 6: 4 My soul, too, is *u* terrified;
13: 2 Will you *u* forget me?
77: 9 Will his kindness *u* cease,
78:59 and was enraged and *u* rejected Israel.
119: 8 do not *u* forsake me.
Wis 4:19 They shall be *u* laid waste and shall be in
Is 24: 3 The earth is *u* laid waste,
24: 3 earth is utterly laid waste, *u* stripped,
31: 6 of Israel, to him whom you have *u* deserted.
32:19 The city will be *u* laid low.
48: 8 Yes, I know you are *u* treacherous,
60:12 those nations shall be *u* destroyed.
Jer 10:25 For they have devoured Jacob *u*,
44:27 sword or famine until they are *u* destroyed.
51:58 of spacious Babylon shall be leveled *u*;
Lam 2:22 I bore and reared my enemy has *u* destroyed."
Ez 11:13 will you *u* wipe out what remains of Israel?"
16:63 and that you may be *u* silenced for shame
Hos 1: 6 rather, I abhor them *u*.
10:15 At dawn the king of Israel shall perish *u*.
Na 1:10 like dry stubble, they shall be *u* consumed.
Hb 1: 5 over the nations and see, and be *u* amazed!
Acts 3:10 *u* stupefied at what had happened to him.
2Cor 7:16 I rejoice because I trust you *u*.

UTTERS (15)

Lv 5: 4 of it, rashly *u* an oath to do good or evil,
Ps(s) 37:30 of wisdom and his tongue *u* what is right.
Prv 1:21 out, at the city gates she *u* her words:
6:19 to evil, The false witness who *u* lies,
14: 5 but a false witness *u* lies
14:25 lives, but he who *u* lies is a betrayer.
16: 1 but what the tongue *u* is from the LORD.
19: 5 and he who *u* lies will not escape.
19: 9 unpunished, and he who *u* lies will perish.
23:33 and your heart *u* disordered thoughts;
Wis 1: 8 one who *u* wicked things can go unnoticed,
Is 59: 3 speak falsehood, and your tongue *u* deceit.
Jer 9: 7 arrow is his tongue, his mouth *u* deceit;
Lk 5:21 "Who is this man who *u* blasphemies?
1Cor 14: 2 him, because he *u* mysteries in the Spirit.

UZ (8)

Gn 10:23 *U*, Hul, Gether, and Mash.
22:21 *U*, his first-born,
36:28 The descendants of Dishan were *U* and Aran.
1Chr 1:17 The descendants of Aram were *U*,
1:42 The sons of Dishan were *U* and Aran.
Jb 1: 1 In the land of *U* there was a blameless and
Jer 25:20 all the kings of the land of *U*;
Lam 4:21 Edom, you who dwell in the land of *U*,

UZAI (1)

Neh 3:25 After him Palal, son of *U*,

UZAL (3)

Gn 10:27 Sheleph, Hazarmaveth, Jerah, Hadoram, *U*,
1Chr 1:21 Sheleph, Hazarmaveth, Jerah, Hadoram, *U*,
Ez 27:19 and aromatic cane from *U* for your wares.

UZZA (5)

2Kgs 21:18 in his palace garden, the garden of *U*.
21:26 in his own grave in the garden of *U*,
1Chr 8: 7 exile, became the father of *U* and Ahihud.
Ezr 2:49 sons of Nekoda, sons of Gazzam, sons of *U*,
Neh 7:51 sons of Nekoda, sons of Gazzam, sons of *U*,

UZZAH (9)

2Sm 6: 3 *U* and Ahio, sons of Abinadab,
6: 6 *U* reached out his hand to the ark of God
6: 7 But the LORD was angry with *U*;
6: 8 because the LORD had vented his anger on *U*.
1Chr 6:14 whose son was Shimei, whose son was *U*,
13: 7 *U* and Ahio were guiding the cart,
13: 9 *U* stretched out his hand to steady the ark,
13:10 LORD became angry with *U* and struck him;
13:11 the LORD's anger had broken out against *U*.

UZZEN-SHEERAH (1)

1Chr 7:24 who built lower and upper Beth-horon and *U*.

UZZI (11)

1Chr 5:31 Bukki became the father of *U*.
5:32 *U* became the father of Zerahiah.
6:36 whose son was Bukki, whose son was *U*,
7: 2 The sons of Tola were *U*,
7: 3 The sons of *U*:
7: 7 The sons of Bela were Ezbon, *U*,
9: 8 Elah, son of *U*,
Ezr 7: 4 of Meraioth, son of Zerahiah, son of *U*,
Neh 11:22 prefect of the Levites in Jerusalem was *U*,
12:19 for Jedaiah, *U*;
12:42 and Maaseiah, Shemaiah, Eleazar, *U*,

UZZIA (1)

1Chr 11:44 *U*,

UZZIAH (44)

2Kgs 15:13 became king in the thirty-ninth year of *U*,
15:30 son of *U* The rest of the acts of Pekah,
15:32 Remaliah, king of Israel, Jotham, son of *U*,
15:34 the LORD, just as his father *U* had done.
1Chr 6: 9 whose son was Uriel, whose son was *U*,
24:26 Mushi, and the descendants of his son *U*.
24:27 descendants of Merari through his son *U*:
27:25 and the towers was Jonathan, son of *U*.
2Chr 26: 1 All the people of Judah chose *U*,
26: 3 *U* was sixteen years old when he became king,
26: 8 to *U* and his fame spread as far as Egypt,
26: 9 *U* built towers in Jerusalem at the Corner
26:11 *U* also had a standing army of fit soldiers
26:14 *U* provided for them
26:18 They opposed King *U*, saying to him:
26:18 "It is not for you, *U*,
26:19 *U*, who was holding a censer for burning
26:21 *U* remained a leper to the day of his death.
26:22 of Amos, wrote the rest of the acts of *U*,
26:23 *U* rested with his ancestors;
27: 2 the LORD just as his father *U* had done,
Ezr 10:21 Maaseiah, Elijah, Shemaiah, Jehiel, and *U*;
Neh 11: 4 Athaiah, son of *U*,
Jdt 6:15 of the city, who in those days were *U*,
6:16 *U* questioned him about what had happened.
6:21 *U* brought him from the assembly to his home,
7:23 in a crowd to *U* and the rulers of the city.
7:30 *U* said to them, "Courage, my brothers!
8: 9 of all that *U* had said to them in reply,
8:10 was in charge of all her things to ask *U*,
8:28 Then *U* said to her: "All that you have
8:35 *U* and the rulers said to her,
10: 6 and found *U* and the elders of the city,
13:18 *U* said to her: "Blessed are you
14: 6 So they called Achior from the house of *U*.
15: 4 *U* sent messengers to Betomasthaim,
Is 1: 1 Judah and Jerusalem in the days of *U*,
6: 1 In the year King *U* died,
7: 1 king of Judah, son of Jotham, son of *U*,
Hos 1: 1 Hosea, the son of Beeri, in the days of *U*,
Am 1: 1 concerning Israel, in the days of *U*,
Zec 14: 5 earthquake in the days of King *U* of Judah.
Mt 1: 8 the father of Joram, Joram the father of *U*.
1: 9 *U* was the father of Jotham,

UZZIEL (20)

Ex 6:18 of Kohath were Amram, Izhar, Hebron and *U*.
6:22 The sons of *U* were Mishael,
Lv 10: 4 and Elzaphan, the sons of Aaron's uncle *U*,
Nm 3:19 by clans, were Amram, Izhar, Hebron and *U*.
3:30 ancestral house was Elizaphan, son of *U*.
1Chr 4:42 of Pelatiah, Neariah, Rephaiah, and *U*,
5:28 of Kohath were Amram, Izhar, Hebron, and *U*.
6: 3 of Kohath were Amram, Izhar, Hebron, and *U*.
7: 7 The sons of Bela were Ezbon, Uzzi, *U*,
15:10 of the sons of *U*,
15:18 the gatekeepers Zechariah, *U*,
15:20 Zechariah, *U*,
16: 5 and second to him were Zechariah, *U*,
23:12 Amram, Izhar, Hebron, and *U*:
23:20 The sons of *U*:
24:24 The descendants of *U* were Micah;
25: 4 Bukkiah, Mattaniah, *U*,
25:18 The eleventh was *U*,
2Chr 29:14 Shemiah and *U*.
Neh 3: 8 the work of repair was carried out by *U*,

UZZIELITES (2)

Nm 3:27 the Izharites, the Hebronites, and the *U*;
1Chr 26:23 Amramites, Izharites, Hebronites, and *U*,

V

VACANT (3)

1Sm 20:18 will be missed, since your place will be *v*.
20:25 the king's side, and David's place was *v*.
20:27 day of the month, David's place was *v*.

VAGRANTS (1)

Ps(s) 109:10 May his children be roaming *v* and beggars;

VAIN (54)

Ex 20: 7 take the name of the LORD, your God, in *v*.
20: 7 unpunished him who takes his name in *v*.
Lv 26:16 You will sow your seed in *v*,
26:20 so that your strength will be spent in *v*;
Dt 5:11 take the name of the LORD, your God, in *v*.
5:11 unpunished him who takes his name in *v*.
32:21 'no-god' and angered me with their *v* idols,
1Sm 10:21 But they looked for him in *v*.
25:21 it was in *v* that I guarded all this man's
2Mc 7:18 "Have no *v* illusions.
Jb 9:29 guilty, why then should I strive in *v*?
13: 4 over falsehoods and offering *v* remedies,
15:31 for *v* shall be his bartering.
21:34 How then can you offer me *v* comfort,
Ps(s) 4: 3 love what is *v* and seek after falsehood?
24: 4 who desires not what is *v*,
31: 7 You hate those who worship *v* idols,
73:13 Is it but in *v* I have kept my heart
94:11 the thoughts of men, and that they are *v*.
109: 7 forth condemned, and may his plea be in *v*.
119:37 Turn away my eyes from seeing what is *v*;
119:118 statutes, for their deceitfulness is in *v*.
127: 1 the house, they labor in *v* who build it.
127: 1 the city, in *v* does the guard keep vigil.
127: 2 It is *v* for you to rise early,
Prv 1:17 It is in *v* that a net is spread before the
13: 4 The soul of the sluggard craves in *v*,
14: 6 The senseless man seeks in *v* for wisdom,
Eccl 6: 4 Though it came in *v* and goes into darkness
6:12 *v* life (which God has made like a shadow)?
7:15 seen all manner of things in my *v* days:
9: 1 both appear equally *v*,
Wis 3:11 *V* is their hope,
Sir 20:12 fools pour forth their blandishments in *v*.
42:25 yet none of them has he made in *v*,
Is 30: 7 to Egypt whose help is futile and *v*,
41:17 afflicted and the needy seek water in *v*,
49: 4 Though I thought I had toiled in *v*,
65:23 They shall not toil in *v*,
Jer 2:30 In *v* I struck your children;
4:30 with cosmetics, beautifying yourself in *v*?
6:29 In *v* has the smelter refined,
Lam 2:12 *v*, As they faint away like the wounded in
4:17 ever wasted away, looking in *v* for aid;
Ez 6:10 shall know that it was not in *v* that I,
19: 5 Then she saw that in *v* she had waited,
Jon 2: 9 *v* idols forsake their source of mercy.
Mal 1:10 you from kindling fire on my altar in *v*!
3:14 You have said, "It is *v* to serve God,
1Cor 15: 2 Otherwise you have believed in *v*.
15:58 is not in *v* when it is done in the Lord.
2Cor 6: 1 you not to receive the grace of God in *v*.
Eph 5:11 Take no part in *v* deeds done in darkness;
Phil 2:16 run the race in *v* or work to no purpose.

VAINLY (1)

Jb 41: 1 Whoever might *v* hope to do so need only

VAIZATHA (1)

Est 9: 9 Parmashta, Arisai, Aridai, and *V*,

VALE (5)

Jos 15: 7 climbed to Debir, north of the *v* of Achor,
1Sm 17: 2 and camped in the *V* of the Terebinth,
17:19 the Philistines in the *V* of the Terebinth."
21:10 whom you killed in the *V* of the Terebinth,
2Sm 23:13 clan was encamped in the *V* of Rephaim.

VALIANT (32)

Jgs 3:29 Moabites, all of them strong and *v* men.
18: 2 detail of five *v* men of Zorah and Eshtaol,
2Sm 1:22 of the slain, from the bodies of the *v*,
2: 7 therefore, and prove yourselves *v* men,
2Kgs 5: 1 But *v* as he was, the man was a leper.
1Chr 9:13 *v* for the work of the service of the house
11:22 son of Jehoiada, a *v* man of mighty deeds,
12: 9 They were *v* warriors,
2Chr 13: 3 hundred thousand picked and *v* warriors.
14: 7 and were archers, all of them *v* warriors.
17:13 of Judah, and he had soldiers, *v* warriors,
17:14 with him three hundred thousand *v* warriors.
17:16 with him two hundred thousand *v* warriors.
17:17 Eliada, a *v* warrior,
25: 6 He also hired a hundred thousand *v*
26:12 *v* warriors was two thousand six hundred,
28: 6 Judah in a single day, all of them *v* men,
32:21 an angel, who destroyed every *v* warrior,
Neh 11: 6 was four hundred and sixty-eight *v* men.
1Mc 2:42 by a group of Hasideans, *v* Israelites,
5:63 The *v* Judas and his brothers were greatly
8: 1 They were *v* fighters and acted amiably to
9:11 and all the *v* men were in the front line.
10:15 told of the battles and *v* deeds of Jonathan
Eccl 9:11 won by the swift, nor the battle by the *v*,
Sg 3: 7 sixty *v* men surround it,
3: 7 men surround it, of the *v* men of Israel:
4: 4 hang upon it, all the shields of *v* men.
Sir 46: 1 *V* leader was JOSHUA,
Is 5:22 wine, the *v* at mixing strong drink!
Jer 48:14 you say, "We are heroes, men *v* in war"?
Zec 10: 7 Then Ephraim shall be *v* men,

VALIANTLY (4)

Nm 24:18 Israel shall do *v*,
2Mc 12:27 of the walls, from which they fought *v*;
Ps(s) 60:14 Under God we shall do *v*;
108:14 Under God we shall do *v*;

VALID (15)

Nm 6:12 The previous period is not *v*,
30: 5 vow or any pledge she has made remains *v*.
30: 8 the vow or pledge she had made remains *v*.
30:10 to which such a woman binds herself, is *v*.
30:12 vow or any pledge she has made remains *v*.
30:14 allow to remain *v* or render null and void.
30:15 as *v* any vow or any pledge she has made;
30:15 he has allowed them to remain *v*,
1Mc 8:30 they shall add or take away shall be *v*.
Jn 8:13 Such testimony cannot be *v*."
8:14 My testimony is *v* nonetheless,
8:16 of mine is *v* because I am not alone:
8:17 that evidence given by two persons is *v*.
Acts 19:40 no *v* excuse for this wild demonstration."
Gal 3:19 it was to be *v* only until that descendant

VALIDATED (1)

Gal 3:15 will or set it aside once it is legally *v*.

VALLEY (124)

Gn 11: 2 *v* in the land of Shinar and settled there.
14: 3 joined forces in the *V* of Siddim (that is,
14: 8 and in the *V* of Siddim they went into
14:10 the *V* of Siddim was full of bitumen pits;
14:17 Valley of Shaveh (that is, the King's *V*).
37:14 So he sent him off from the *v* of Hebron.
Lv 23:40 and boughs of myrtles and of *v* poplars,
Jos 7:24 and led them off to the *V* of Achor.
7:26 place is called the *V* of Achor to this day.
10:12 at Gibeon, O moon, in the *v* of Aijalon!
11: 8 and eastward to the *v* of Mizpeh.
11:17 the Lebanon *v* at the foot of Mount Hermon.
12: 7 *v* to Mount Halak which rises toward Seir,
13:19 Zereth-shahar on the knoll within the *v*,
13:27 and in the Jordan *v*:
15: 8 Climbing again to the *V* of Ben-hinnom on
15: 8 at the northern end of the *V* of Rephaim,
15: 8 which bounds the *V* of Hinnom on the west.
17:16 in the *v* region all have iron chariots,
17:16 its towns, and those in the *v* of Jezreel."
18:16 mountain on the north of the *V* of Rephaim,
18:16 where it faces the *V* of Ben-hinnom;
18:16 and continuing down the *V* of Hinnom along
19:14 the boundary ended at the *v* of Iphtahel.
19:27 reached Zebulun and the *v* of Iphtahel;
Jgs 5:14 From Ephraim, princes were in the *v*;
5:15 Barak, too, was in the *v*,
6:33 and crossed over into the *v* of Jezreel,
7: 1 was in the *v* north of Gibeath-hammoreh.
7: 8 camp of Midian was beneath him in the *v*.
7:12 and all the Kedemites lay in the *v*,
18:28 was in the *v* that belongs to Beth-rehob,
1Sm 6:13 were harvesting the wheat in the *v*.
13:18 the *V* of the Hyenas toward the desert.
17: 3 on an opposite hill, with a *v* between them.
31: 7 When the Israelites on the slope of the *v*
2Sm 2:24 east of the *v* toward the desert near Geba.
5:18 came and overran the *v* of Rephaim.
5:22 came up again and overran the *v* of Rephaim.
8:13 eighteen thousand Edomites in the Salt *V*;
15:23 and the king crossed the Kidron *V* with all
18:18 erected it for himself in the King's *V*,
1Kgs 2:37 For if you leave, and cross the Kidron *V*,
15:13 this object and burned it in the Kidron *V*.
2Kgs 2:16 him away to some mountain or some *v*."
14: 7 slew ten thousand Edomites in the Salt *V*,
23: 6 removed the sacred pole, to the Kidron *V*,
23:10 defiled Topheth in the *V* of Ben-hinnom,
23:12 them and threw the dust into the Kidron *V*.
1Chr 4:39 to the approaches of Gedor, east of the *v*,
10: 7 Israelites who were in the *v* saw that Saul
11:15 were encamped in the *v* of Rephaim.
11:32 Hurai, from the *v* of Gaash;
14: 9 had come and raided the *v* of Rephaim.
14:13 Once again the Philistines raided the *v*;
18:12 thousand Edomites in the *V* of Salt.
2Chr 14: 9 in battle array in the *v* of Zephathah,
15:16 smashed it, and burnt it in the Kidron *V*.
20:26 they held an assembly in the *V* of Beracah
20:26 ever since been called the *V* of Beracah.
25:11 They proceeded to the *V* of Salt,
26: 9 at the Corner Gate, at the *V* Gate,
28: 3 offered sacrifice in the *V* of Ben-hinnom,
29:16 them and carried it out to the Kidron *V*.
30:14 of incense and cast them into the Kidron *V*.
32: 4 also the running stream in the *v* nearby.
33: 6 his sons by fire in the *V* of Ben-hinnom.
33:14 of David to the west of Gihon in the *v*,
Neh 2:13 I rode out at night by the *V* Gate,
2:15 while till I once more reached the *V* Gate,
3:13 The *V* Gate was repaired by Hanun and the
11:35 Lod, Ono, and the *V* of the Artisans.
Jdt 4: 4 to Choba and Aesora, and to the *v* of Salem.
7: 3 at the spring in the *v* near Bethulia,
7:17 They encamped in the *v*,
10:10 went down the mountain and crossed the *v*;
10:11 and her maid walked directly across the *v*,
15: 2 both through the *v* and in the mountains.
Jb 21:33 Sweet to him are the clods of the *v*,
Ps(s) 23: 4 though I walk in the dark *v* I fear no evil;
60: 8 Shechem, and measure off the *v* of Succoth.
84: 7 When they pass through the *v* of the mastic
108: 8 Shechem, and measure off the *v* of Succoth;
Prv 30:17 be plucked out by the ravens in the *v*;
Sg 2: 1 a lily of the *v*.
6:11 to look at the fresh growth of the *v*,
Is 17: 5 one gleans the ears in the *V* of Rephaim.
22: 1 Oracle of the *V* of Vision:
22: 5 Lord, the GOD of hosts, in the *V* of Vision.
28: 4 *V* Will be like an early fig before summer:
28:21 bestir himself as in the *V* of Gibeon,
40: 4 Every *v* shall be filled in,
40: 4 made a plain, the rough country, a broad *v*.
65:10 *v* of Achor a resting place for the cattle
Jer 2:23 Consider your conduct in the *V*,
7:31 In the *V* of Ben-hinnom they have built the
7:32 when Topheth and the *V* of Ben-hinnom will
7:32 called such, but rather the *V* of Slaughter.
19: 2 and go out toward the *V* of Ben-hinnom,
19: 6 be called Topheth, or the *V* of Ben-hinnom,
19: 6 Ben-hinnom, but rather, the *V* of Slaughter.
31:40 The whole *v* of corpses and ashes,
31:40 ashes, all the slopes toward the Kidron *V*,
32:35 high places to Baal in the *V* of Ben-hinnom,
48: 8 Ruined is the *v*,
Ez 39:11 the *V* of Abarim east of the sea [it is
39:11 and it shall be named *V* of Hamon-gog."
39:15 have buried it in the *V* of Hamon-gog.
Hos 1: 5 the bow of Israel in the *v* of Jezreel.
2:17 had, and the *v* of Achor as a door of hope.
Jl 4: 2 bring them down to the *V* of Jehoshaphat,
4:12 and come up to the *V* of Jehoshaphat;
4:14 Crowd upon crowd in the *v* of decision;
4:14 the day of the LORD in the *v* of decision.
4:18 of the LORD, to water the *V* of Shittim.
Am 1: 5 root out those who live in the *V* of Aven,
Mi 1: 6 I will throw down into the *v* her stones,
Zec 14: 4 in two from east to west by a very deep *v*,
14: 5 And the *v* of the LORD's mountain shall be
14: 5 *v* of those two mountains reaches its edge;
Lk 3: 5 Every *v* shall be filled And every mountain
Jn 18: 1 out with his disciples across the Kidron *V*.

VALLEY-SITE (1)

Jer 21:13 I am against you, *V*,

VALLEYS (19)

Nm 14:25 and Canaanites are living in the *v*,
Dt 8: 7 fountains welling up in the hills and *v*,
11:11 and *v* that drinks in rain from the heavens,
1Chr 12:16 were in the *v* to the east and to the west.
27:29 and over the cattle in the *v* was Shaphat,
Jdt 7: 4 *v* and hills can support the mass of them."
Jb 39:10 furrow, and will he harrow the *v* after you?
Ps(s) 65:14 flocks and the *v* blanketed with grain.
104: 8 the *v* to the place you had fixed for them.
Is 22: 7 Your choice *v* are filled with chariots,
41:18 heights, and fountains in the broad *v*;
Ez 6: 3 the mountains and hills, the ravines and *v*:
7:16 to the mountains like the doves of the *v*—
31:12 Its foliage was brought low in all the *v*,
32: 5 and fill the *v* with your carcass.
35: 8 the slain I will fill your hills, your *v*,
36: 4 mountains and hills, the ravines and *v*,
36: 6 the mountains and hills, the ravines and *v*:
Mi 1: 4 melt under him and the *v* split open,

VALOR (20)

2Sm 10:12 let us prove our *v* for the sake of our
1Kgs 15:23 of Asa, with all his *v* and accomplishments,
16: 5 Baasha, with all his *v* and accomplishments,
16:27 Omri, with all his *v* and accomplishments,
2Kgs 10:34 of Jehu, his *v* and all his accomplishments,
13: 8 with all his *v* and accomplishments,
13:12 the *v* with which he fought against Amaziah,
14:15 The rest of the acts of Jehoash, his *v*,
14:28 his *v* and all his accomplishments,
20:20 rest of the acts of Hezekiah, all his *v*,
1Chr 29:30 with the particulars of his reign and *v*,
2Chr 26:13 *v* to help the king against his enemies.
Jdt 2: 5 presence, take with you men of proven *v*,
Est 10: 2 All the acts of his power and *v*,
2Mc 8: 7 Soon the fame of his *v* spread everywhere.
10:28 *v* but also their reliance on the Lord,
14:18 heard of the *v* of Judas and his men,
15:17 instill *v* and stir young hearts to courage,
Wis 4: 2 victorious in unsullied deeds of *v*.
Bar 6:58 much better to be a king displaying his *v*,

VALUABLE (4)

1Kgs 20: 6 and take away whatever they consider *v*.'"
Mt 6:25 Is not the body more *v* than clothes?
13:46 When he found one really *v* pearl,
1Tm 4: 8 physical training is to some extent *v*,

VALUATION (5)

Lv 27:13 he shall pay one fifth more than this *v*.
27:16 its *v* shall be made according to the
27:17 of a jubilee period, the full *v* shall hold;
27:18 year, with a corresponding rebate on the *v*.
27:25 "Every *v* shall be made according to the

VALUE (33)

Gn 23:16 shekels of silver at the current market *v*.
Ex 21:34 restoring the *v* of the animal to its owner;
Lv 5:16 sanctuary, adding to it a fifth of its *v*.
5:18 ram of the flock of the established *v*.
5:24 give the owner one fifth of its *v*.
5:25 ram of the flock of the established *v*.
27:12 who shall determine its *v* in keeping with
27:12 and the *v* set by the priest shall stand.
27:14 *v* in keeping with its good or bad points,
27:14 and the *v* set by the priest shall stand.
27:18 the priest shall estimate its money *v*
27:23 the priest shall compute its *v* in
27:27 by paying one fifth more than its fixed *v*.
27:27 redeemed, it shall be sold at its fixed *v*.
27:31 he shall pay one fifth more than their *v*.
Nm 5: 7 fifth of their *v* to the one he has wronged.
1Sm 26:24 so may the LORD *v* my life highly and
1Kgs 21: 2 you prefer, I will give you its *v* in money."
2Chr 9:20 was not considered of *v* in Solomon's time.
Tb 6: 7 medicinal *v* is there in the fish's heart,
Prv 31:10 a worthy wife, her *v* is far beyond pearls.
Wis 7:15 and *v* these endowments at their worth:
Sir 20:29 of what *v* is either?
37:11 about business, to a buyer about *v*,
Hos 8: 8 is now among the nations a thing of no *v*.
Mt 27: 9 the *v* of a man with a price on his head,
Acts 19:19 When the *v* of these was assessed,
20:24 I put no *v* on my life if only I can finish
Rom 2:25 to be sure, has *v* if you observe the law,
3: 1 a Jew, and what *v* is there in circumcision?
Phil 1:10 learn to *v* the things that really matter,
1Tm 6: 5 Such men *v* religion only as a means of
1Pt 2: 7 The stone is of *v* for you who have faith.

VALUED (5)

Lv 5:15 *v* at two silver shekels according to the
27:16 seed being *v* at fifty silver shekels.
1Sm 26:24 As I *v* your life highly today,
Ezr 8:27 twenty golden bowls *v* at a thousand darics;
Zec 11:13 the handsome price at which they *v* me."

VAN (2)

Nm 32:17 march as troops in the *v* of the Israelites,
Jl 2:20 waste, With his *v* toward the eastern sea,

VANGUARD (4)

Nm 32:20 word to march as troops in the LORD's *v*

Dt 3:18 over in the *v* of your brother Israelites.
Jos 4:12 armed, marched in the *v* of the Israelites,
Is 60:11 of nations, and their kings, in the *v*.

VANIAH (1)

Ezr 10:36 Amram, Uel, Benaiah, Bedeiah, Cheluhi, *V*,

VANISH (6)

Ps(s) 37:20 meadows, vanish; like smoke they *v*.
58: 8 Let them *v* like water flowing off;
102: 4 For my days *v* like smoke,
Na 3:17 will spread their wings and fly, and *v*,
2Pt 3:10 on that day the heavens will *v* with a roar;

VANISHED (5)

Jb 23:17 Yes, would that I had *v* in darkness,
Ps(s) 12: 2 faithfulness has *v* from among men.
Sir 41: 2 rebuffed, with no more sight, with *v* hope.
Bar 3:19 They have *v* down into the nether world,
Lk 24:31 whereupon he *v* from their sight.

VANISHES (4)

Jb 7: 9 As a cloud dissolves and *v*,
30:15 on the wind, and my welfare *v* like a cloud.
Ps(s) 1: 6 of the just, but the way of the wicked *v*.
Jas 4:14 You are a vapor that appears briefly and *v*.

VANITIES (3)

Eccl 1: 2 *v* of vanities, says Qoheleth, vanity of *v*!
12: 8 Vanity of *v*, says Qoheleth,

VANITY (30)

2Kgs 17:15 The *v* they pursued,
Eccl 1: 2 *V* of vanities, says Qoheleth, vanity of vanities!
1: 2 All things are *v*!
1:14 behold, all is *v* and a chase after wind.
2: 1 But behold, this too was *v*.
2:11 all was *v* and a chase after wind,
2:15 I concluded in my heart that this too is *v*.
2:17 for all is *v* and a chase after wind.
2:19 This also is *v*.
2:21 This also is *v* and a great misfortune.
2:23 This also is *v*.
2:26 This also is *v* and a chase after wind.
3:19 but all is *v*.
4: 4 This also is *v* and a chase after wind.
4: 7 Again I found this *v* under the sun:
4: 8 This also is *v* and a worthless task.
4:16 This also is *v* and a chase after wind.
5: 9 so this too is *v*.
6: 2 This is *v* and a dire plague.
6: 9 This also is *v* and a chase after wind.
6:11 there are many sayings that multiply *v*,
7: 6 This also is *v*,
8:10 This also is *v*.
8:14 This is a *v* which occurs on earth:
8:14 This, too, I say is *v*.
11: 8 All that is to come is *v*.
12: 8 *V* of vanities, says Qoheleth, all things are *v*!
Wis 14:14 by the *v* of men they came into the world,

VANQUISH (1)

Jb 32:13 God may *v* him out not man!"

VANQUISHED (4)

1Chr 19:16 Seeing themselves *v* by Israel,
19:19 of Hadadezer saw themselves *v* by Israel,
2Chr 20:22 coming against Judah, so that they were *v*.
Wis 12: 9 to have the wicked *v* in battle by the just,

VAPOR (2)

Ps(s) 39: 7 like *v* only are his restless pursuits;
Jas 4:14 are a *v* that appears briefly and vanishes.

VARIABLE (1)

Wis 19:18 elements, in *v* harmony among themselves,

VARIANCE (1)

Est B: 5 people is continually at *v* with all men,

VARIATIONS (1)

Wis 7:18 the sun's course and the *v* of the seasons.

VARICOLORED (1)

Ez 27:24 mantles, embroidered cloth, *v* carpets,

VARIED (3)

Wis 15: 4 of painters, A form smeared with *v* colors,
Heb 1: 1 *v* ways to our fathers through the prophets;
2: 4 to it by signs, miracles, *v* acts of power,

VARIEGATED (8)

Ex 26:36 of the tent make a *v* curtain of violet,
27:16 of the court there shall be a *v* curtain,
28:39 The sash shall be of *v* work.
35:35 the making of *v* cloth of violet,
36:37 of fine linen twined, woven in a *v* manner.
38:18 of the court there was a *v* curtain,
38:23 and a weaver of *v* cloth of violet,
39:29 and sashes of *v* work made of fine linen

VARIETY (2)

Est 1: 7 Liquor was served in a *v* of golden cups,
Lk 4:40 sick with a *v* of diseases took them to him,

VARIOUS (83)

Gn 2: 9 Out of the ground the LORD God made *v*
2:19 *v* wild animals and *v* birds of the air,
6:14 of gopherwood, put *v* compartments in it,
9:10 and the *v* tame and wild animals that were
25:18 camp in opposition to his *v* kinsmen.
36: 6 well as his livestock comprising *v* animals
Ex 4:28 of the *v* signs he had enjoined upon him.
11:10 these *v* wonders in Pharaoh's presence,
28: 3 to the *v* expert workmen whom I have
35:22 rings, necklaces and *v* other gold articles.
35:29 for the *v* kinds of work which the LORD had
36: 4 the *v* kinds of work for the sanctuary,
36: 8 The *v* experts who were executing the work,
37:24 for the lampstand and its *v* appurtenances.
38:21 of the *v* amounts used on the Dwelling,
Lv 11: 9 the *v* creatures that live in the water,
11:10 But of the *v* creatures that crawl or swim
11:14 osprey, the kite, the *v* species of falcons,
11:15 species of falcons, the *v* species of crows,
11:16 nightjar, the gull, the *v* species of hawks,
11:19 the stork, the *v* species of herons,
11:20 "The *v* winged insects that walk on all
11:21 But of the *v* winged insects that walk on
11:22 the *v* kinds of locusts,
11:22 of locusts, the *v* kinds of grasshoppers,
11:22 of grasshoppers, the *v* kinds of katydids,
11:22 of katydids, and the *v* kinds of crickets.
11:27 Of the *v* quadrupeds,
11:29 the rat, the mouse, the *v* kinds of lizards,
11:31 Among the *v* swarming creatures,
23:38 your *v* votive offerings and the freewill
24: 9 sacred among the *v* oblations to the LORD,
Nm 4: 9 as well as the *v* containers of oil from
18: 8 the *v* sacred offerings of the Israelites;
26:55 as the heritage of the *v* ancestral tribes.
33: 2 the starting places of the *v* stages.
Dt 14: 9 the *v* creatures that live in the water,
14:13 the osprey, the *v* kites and falcons,
14:14 and falcons, all the *v* species of crows,
14:15 nightjar, the gull, the *v* species of hawks,
14:18 the stork, the *v* species of herons,
26: 2 some first fruits of the *v* products of the soil
Jgs 2:12 other gods of the *v* nations around them,
1Sm 4: 8 with *v* plagues and with pestilence.
23:23 all the *v* hiding places he is holding out.
2Sm 18: 5 the *v* leaders with regard to Absalom.
1Kgs 15:15 offerings of silver, gold, and *v* utensils.
2Kgs 17:29 in the *v* cities in which they were living;
1Chr 9: 9 *v* families were nine hundred and fifty-six.
28:14 used in the golden vessels for the *v* services
28:14 in the silver vessels for the *v* services,
29: 5 *v* utensils to be made of gold and silver,
2Chr 5:11 to the rotation of their *v* classes),
8:14 *v* classes of the priests for their service,
8:14 of the *v* classes stood guard at each gate,
11:23 distributing *v* of his sons throughout all
15:18 silver, gold, and *v* utensils.
16:14 filled with spices and *v* kinds of aromatics
31: 1 the Israelites returned to their *v* cities,
31:17 according to their *v* offices and classes.
32:28 the *v* kinds of cattle and for the flocks.
35:12 gave it to *v* groups of the ancestral houses
Neh 12:44 were to collect from the fields of the *v* cities
13:20 The merchants and sellers of *v* kinds of
13:24 to the languages of the *v* other peoples.
13:30 *v* functions for the priests and Levites,
Tb 2:10 more they anointed my eyes with *v* salves,
1Mc 12: 4 to the authorities in the *v* places,
15:15 as this addressed to *v* kings and countries:
15:19 decided to write to *v* kings and countries,
2Mc 8: 9 twenty thousand armed men of *v* nations
Wis 16:26 not the *v* kinds of fruits that nourish man,
Mt 4:24 with *v* diseases and racked with pain:
Mk 13: 8 in *v* places and there will be famine.
Lk 21:11 plagues and famines in *v* places
Jn 11:56 *v* people in the temple vicinity saying to
Acts 9:39 showed him the *v* garments Dorcas had made
19:32 *v* people were shouting all sorts of things,
26: 3 in all the *v* Jewish customs and disputes.
Ti 3: 3 our passions and of pleasures of *v* kinds.
Heb 9:10 of food and drink and *v* ritual washings:

VARIOUSLY (2)

2Mc 3:21 It was pitiful to see the populace *v*
Mk 1:34 Those whom he cured, who were *v* afflicted,

VARY (1)

Sir 38:27 and whose concern is to *v* the pattern.

VARYING (3)

Prv 20:10 Varying weights, *v* measures,
20:23 *V* weights are an abomination to the LORD,

VASE (1)

Lk 7:37 She brought in a *v* of perfumed oil and

VASES (1)

Ezr 8:27 two *v* of excellent polished bronze,

VASHTI (10)

Est 1: 9 Queen *V* also gave a feast for the women
1:11 to bring Queen *V* into his presence wearing
1:12 But Queen *V* refused to come at the royal
1:15 "What is to be done by law with Queen *V*
1:16 "Queen *V* has not wronged the king alone,
1:17 that Queen *V* be ushered into his presence,
1:19 forbidding *V* to come into the presence of
2: 1 he thought over what *V* had done and what
2: 4 pleases the king shall reign in place of *V*."
2:17 her head and made her queen in place of *V*.

VASSAL (4)

1Sm 27:12 I shall have him as my *v* forever."
2Sm 10:19 All of Hadadezer's *v* kings,
2Kgs 17: 3 Hoshea became his *v* and paid him tribute.
24: 1 and Jehoiakim became his *v* for three years.

VASSALS (5)

Jos 13:21 in Heshbon, Moses had killed, with his *v*,
1Sm 17: 9 in combat and kills me, we will be your *v*;
17: 9 kill him, you shall be our *v* and serve us."
1Kgs 5: 1 tribute and were his *v* as long as he lived.
1Chr 19:19 When the *v* of Hadadezer saw themselves

VAST (33)

Gn 41:49 so *v* that at last he stopped measuring it,
Dt 1:19 desert, *v* and fearful as you have seen,
2: 7 about your journey through this *v* desert.
8:15 who guided you through the *v* and terrible
17:17 accumulate a *v* amount of silver and gold.
33:20 "Blessed be he who has made Gad so *v*!
1Kgs 3: 8 so *v* that it cannot be numbered or counted.
3: 9 is able to govern this *v* people of yours?"
5: 9 as *v* as the sand on the seashore.
1Chr 12:23 help until there was a *v* encampment,
2Chr 16: 8 not the Ethiopians and Libyans a *v* army,
20:12 this *v* multitude that comes against us.
20:15 heart at the sight of this *v* multitude,
Jdt 1: 5 war against King Arphaxad in the *v* plain,
1: 8 Galilee, and the *v* plain of Esdraelon,
9: 7 "Here are the Assyrians, a *v* force,
Est 1:20 published throughout his realm, *v* as it is,
Ps(s) 22:26 gift will I utter praise in the *v* assembly;
29: 3 of glory thunders, the LORD, over *v* waters.
35:18 I will give you thanks in the *v* assembly,
40:10 I announced your justice in the *v* assembly;
40:11 kindness and your truth in the *v* assembly.
68:12 women bear the glad tidings, a *v* army:
139:17 how *v* the sum of them!
Is 9: 6 His dominion is *v* and forever peaceful,
33:17 his splendor, they will look upon a *v* land.
Bar 3:24 O Israel, how *v* is the house of God,
3:25 *V* and endless, high and immeasurable!
Ez 37:10 came alive and stood upright, a *v* army.
Mt 14:14 When he disembarked and saw the *v* throng,
Mk 6:34 Upon disembarking Jesus saw a *v* crowd.
Jn 6: 2 a *v* crowd kept following him because they
6: 5 sight of a *v* crowd coming toward him,

VASTNESS (1)

Sir 50: 3 was dug, the pool with a *v* like the sea's.

VAT (3)

Hg 2:16 went to the *v* to draw fifty measures,
Mt 21:33 put a hedge around it, dug out a *v*,
Mk 12: 1 put a hedge around it, dug out a *v*,

VATS (4)

Prv 3:10 grain, with new wine your *v* will overflow.
Jer 48:33 I drain the wine from the wine *v*,
Jl 2:24 and the *v* shall overflow with wine and oil.
4:13 The *v* overflow,

VAULT (6)

Jb 22:14 he walks upon the *v* of the heavens!"
Prv 8:27 marked out the *v* over the face of the deep;
Sir 24: 5 The *v* of heaven I compassed alone,
43: 1 The clear *v* of the sky shines forth like
Is 40:22 He sits enthroned above the *v* of the earth,
Am 9: 6 and established my *v* over the earth;

VAULTED (1)

Jer 37:16 And so Jeremiah entered the *v* dungeon,

VAUNT (3)

Jgs 7: 2 lest Israel *v* itself against me and say,

VAUNT (cont.)

Jb 19: 5 if you would *v* yourselves against me and
Is 3: 9 their sin like Sodom they *v*,

VAUNTED (2)

Ps(s) 55:13 he who hates me had *v* himself against me,
Wis 17: 7 a jeering reproof of their *v* shrewdness.

VEERING (3)

Ez 1:17 they faced, without *v* as they moved.
10:11 four directions without *v* as they moved;
10:11 towards it without *v* as they moved.

VEERS (1)

Hb 1:11 Then he *v* like the wind and is gone

VEGETABLE (4)

Dt 11:10 then water it by hand, as in a *v* garden.
1Kgs 21: 2 "Give me your vineyard to be my *v* garden,
2Kgs 4:38 make some *v* stew for the guild prophets."
4:39 pot of *v* stew without anybody's knowing it.

VEGETABLES (3)

Dn 1:12 Give us *v* to eat and water to drink.
1:16 wine they were to receive, and gave them *v*.
Rom 14: 2 while one who is weak in faith eats only *v*.

VEGETATION (6)

Gn 1:11 God said, "Let the earth bring forth *v*:
Ex 10:12 all the *v* and whatever the hail has left."
10:15 They ate up all the *v* in the land and the
Ps(s) 104:14 grass for the cattle, and *v* for men's use,
Jer 14: 6 grow dim, because there is no *v* to be seen.
Heb 6: 7 and brings forth *v* useful to those for

VEHEMENTLY (2)

Mk 14:31 But Peter kept reasserting *v*,
Lk 23:10 and scribes were at hand to accuse him *v*.

VEIL (48)

Gn 24:65 Then she covered herself with her *v*.
Ex 26:31 "You shall have a *v* woven of violet,
26:33 Hang the *v* from clasps.
26:33 behind this *v* which divides the holy place
26:35 "Outside the *v* you shall place the table
27:21 *v* which hangs in front of the commandments.
30: 6 in front of the *v* that hangs before the ark
34:33 with them, he put a *v* over his face.
34:34 he removed the *v* until he came out again.
34:35 so he would again put the *v* over his face
35:12 the propitiatory, and the curtain *v*;
36:35 The *v* was woven of violet,
38:27 the sanctuary and the pedestals of the *v*,
39:34 covering of tahash skins, the curtain *v*;
40: 3 in it, and screen off the ark with the *v*.
40:21 into the Dwelling and hung the curtain *v*,
40:22 north side of the Dwelling, outside the *v*,
40:26 in the meeting tent, in front of the *v*,
Lv 4: 6 the LORD, toward the *v* of the sanctuary.
4:17 seven times before the LORD, toward the *v*.
16: 2 pleases into the sanctuary, inside the *v*,
16:12 incense, and bringing them inside the *v*.
16:15 goat, and bringing its blood inside the *v*,
21:23 he may not approach the *v* nor go up to the
24: 3 *v* that hangs in front of the commandments,
Nm 3:31 of the sanctuary was exercised, and the *v*.
18: 7 the altar and the room within the *v*.
22:31 Then the LORD removed the *v* from Balaam's
2Chr 3:14 He made the *v* of violet,
Jb 38:34 or *v* yourself in the waters of the storm?
Sg 4: 1 Your eyes are doves behind your *v*.
4: 3 is like a half-pomegranate behind your *v*.
6: 7 is like a half-pomegranate behind your *v*.
Wis 17: 3 secret sins were hid under the dark *v*
Sir 50: 5 the tent, as he came from within the *v*!
Is 25: 7 will destroy the *v* that veils all peoples,
40:22 He stretches out the heavens like a *v*,
47: 2 millstone and grind flour, remove your *v*;
1Cor 11: 6 Indeed, if a woman will not wear a *v*,
11: 6 it is clear that she ought to wear a *v*.
2Cor 3:13 who used to hide his face with a *v* so that
3:14 covenant is read the *v* remains unlifted;
3:15 is read a *v* covers their understanding.
3:16 turns to the Lord, the *v* will be removed."
Heb 6:19 extends beyond the *v* through which Jesus,
9: 3 Behind the second *v* was the tabernacle
10:20 the *v* (the "veil" meaning his flesh),
10:20 the veil (the *v*" meaning his flesh),

VEILED (10)

Gn 38:14 *v* her face by covering herself with a
Jb 19: 8 he has *v* my path in darkness;
23: 9 by the south he is *v*,
Is 6: 2 with two they *v* their faces,
6: 2 their faces, with two they *v* their feet,
Lam 3:43 You *v* yourself in wrath and pursued us,
Dn 13:32 very delicate and beautiful, was *v*;
Jn 16:25 spoken these things to you in *v* language.
16:29 exclaimed, "without talking in *v* language!
2Cor 4: 3 our gospel can be called *v*" in any sense,

VEILS (4)

Is 3:19 the pendants, bracelets, and *v*;
25: 7 will destroy the veil that *v* all peoples,
Ez 13:18 make *v* for every size of head so as to entrap
13:21 *v* and rescue my people from your power,

VEIN (3)

1Kgs 22:12 other prophets prophesied in a similar *v*,
2Chr 18:11 other prophets prophesied in the same *v*,
Mk 9:31 He was teaching his disciples in this *v*:

VENERABLE (2)

Tb 14:14 at the *v* age of a hundred and seventeen.
Sir 25: 5 understanding and prudence to the *v*!

VENERATE (12)

Jgs 6:10 you shall not *v* the gods of the Amorites
1Kgs 9: 6 and proceed to *v* and worship strange gods,
2Kgs 17:25 settled there, they did not *v* the LORD,
17:28 Bethel, and taught them how to *v* the LORD.
17:34 [They did not *v* the LORD nor observe the
17:35 "You must not *v* other gods,
17:36 him shall you *v*,
17:37 for you, and you must not *v* other gods.
17:38 you must not *v* other gods.
17:39 But the LORD, your God, you must *v*;
2Chr 7:19 you proceed to *v* and worship strange gods,
1Pt 3:15 *V* the Lord, that is, Christ, in your hearts.

VENERATED (4)

2Kgs 17: 7 of Egypt, and because they *v* other gods.
17:32 They also *v* the LORD,
17:41 Thus these nations *v* the LORD,
2Mc 3:12 of a temple *v* all over the world.

VENERATING (1)

2Kgs 17:33 *v* the LORD they served their own gods,

VENERATION (1)

1Kgs 16:31 and went over to the *v* and worship of Baal.

VENGEANCE (57)

Nm 31: 3 and execute the LORD'S *v* on them.
Dt 32:35 Against the day of *v* and requital,
32:41 "With *v* I will repay my foes and requite
Jos 10:13 while the nation took *v* on its foes.
Jgs 11:36 *v* for you on your enemies the Ammonites."
1Sm 18:25 that he may thus take *v* on his enemies."
2Sm 22:48 of my salvation, O God, who granted me *v*,
Jdt 8:27 Not for *v* did the Lord put them in the
8:35 go before you to take *v* upon our enemies!"
Ps(s) 18:48 O God, who granted me *v*,
58:11 The just man shall be glad when he sees *v*;
94: 1 God of vengeance, LORD, God of *v*,
149: 7 to execute *v* on the nations,
Prv 6:34 he will have no pity on the day of *v*;
Wis 11: 3 withstood enemies and took *v* on their foes.
11:15 upon them swarms of dumb creatures for *v*;
Sir 5: 9 at the time of *v*,
12: 7 sinners, and upon the wicked he takes *v*.
18:24 the time of *v* when he will hide his face.
25:13 worst of all *v* is that of one's enemies:
27:28 and *v* lies in wait for them like a lion.
28: 1 The vengeful will suffer the LORD'S *v*,
35:20 the merciless and wreaks *v* upon the proud;
48: 8 You anointed kings who should inflict *v*,
Is 1:24 *v* on my foes and fully repay my enemies!
34: 8 For the LORD has a day of *v*,
47: 3 I will take *v*,
59:17 He clothed himself with garments of *v*,
63: 4 For the day of *v* was in my heart,
Jer 5: 9 a nation such as this shall I not take *v*?
5:29 a nations such as this shall I not take *v*?
9: 8 a nation such as this shall I not take *v*?
11:20 Let me witness the *v* you take on them,
20:10 then we can prevail, and take our *v* on him."
20:12 Let me witness the *v* you take on them,
46:10 hosts, a day of vengeance, *v* on his foes!
50:15 *V* of the LORD is this!
50:28 They announce in Zion the *v* of the LORD,
51: 6 This is a time of *v* for the LORD,
51:11 vengeance of the LORD, *v* for his temple.
Ez 24: 8 To work up my wrath, to excite my *v*,
25:12 Because Edom has taken *v* on the house of
25:12 grievously guilty by taking *v* on them,
25:14 My *v* upon Edom I will entrust to my people
25:14 thus they shall know my *v*,
25:15 *v* with destructive malice in their hearts,
25:17 I will execute great acts of *v* on them,
25:17 I am the LORD, when I wreak my *v* on them.
Jl 4: 4 Would you take *v* upon me by some action?
Mi 5:14 I will wreak *v* in anger and wrath upon the
Na 1: 2 The LORD brings *v* on his adversaries,
Rom 12:19 *V* is mine; I will repay,' says the Lord."
Heb 10:30 We know who said, *V* is mine;
Rv 6:17 The great day of *v* has come.

VENGEFUL (2)

Ps(s) 8: 3 foes, to silence the hostile and the *v*.
Sir 28: 1 The *v* will suffer the LORD's vengeance,

VENOM (8)

Dt 32:24 with the *v* of reptiles gliding in the dust.
32:33 Their wine is the *v* of dragons and the
Jb 20:14 it shall be *v* of asps inside him.
Ps(s) 140: 4 the *v* of asps is under their lips.
Wis 16: 5 For when the dire *v* of beasts came upon
Sir 25:14 serpent, no *v* greater than that of a woman.
Rom 3:13 The *v* of asps lies behind their lips,
Rv 9:10 was enough *v* to harm men for five months.

VENT (10)

Ex 19:22 else he will *v* his anger upon them."
19:24 else he will *v* his anger upon them."
2Chr 32:26 and therefore the LORD did not *v* his anger
Jb 13:13 that I may speak and give *v* to my feelings.
Prv 29:11 The fool gives *v* to all his anger;
Is 9:16 sinful, and every mouth gives *v* to folly.
41:11 and disgrace who *v* their anger against you;
45:16 and disgrace who *v* their anger against him;
45:24 come all who *v* their anger against him.
Hos 11: 9 I will not give *v* to my blazing anger,

VENTED (1)

2Sm 6: 8 because the LORD had *v* his anger on Uzzah.

VENTURE (4)

Dt 4:34 Or did any god *v* to go and take a nation
28:56 she would not *v* to set the sole of her foot
Acts 19:31 him advising him not to *v* into the theater.
Jude 1: 9 did not *v* to charge him with blasphemy.

VENTURED (1)

1Mc 12:10 we have *v* to send word to you for the

VERDANT (3)

Ps(s) 23: 2 In *v* pastures he gives me repose;
Sg 1:16 Our couch, too, is *v*;
Hos 14: 9 "I am like a *v* cypress tree"

VERDICT (6)

Dt 17:11 give you and the *v* they pronounce for you,
Mt 7: 2 Your *v* on others will be the verdict
7: 2 on others will be the *v* passed on you.
26:66 What is your *v*?"
Mk 14:64 What is your *v*?"
14:64 They all concurred in the *v* "guilty,"

VERDURE (3)

Jb 38:27 ground till the desert blooms with *v*?
Ps(s) 72:16 shall flourish like the *v* of the fields.
Is 44: 4 *v* like poplars beside the flowing waters.

VERGE (1)

Gn 43:30 his brother that he was on the *v* of tears.

VERIFIED (7)

Gn 42:20 Your words will thus be *v*,
Dt 18:22 LORD, if his oracle is not fulfilled or *v*,
Ezr 4:19 it was *v* that from ancient times this city
Est 2:23 The matter was investigated and *v*,
E: 7 This can be *v* in the ancient stories that
Jn 4:37 Here we have the saying *v*:
5:32 testimony he renders me I know can be *v*.

VERIFY (4)

Gn 38:25 Please *v*,"
Ezr 4:15 discover and *v* that this city is a rebellious
Jdt 5:20 God, and if we *v* this offense of theirs,
Jn 5:31 my own behalf, you cannot *v* my testimony;

VERIFYING (1)

2Mc 1:34 the sacrifices, the king, after *v* the fact,

VERITABLE (1)

Nm 13:33 *v* giants [the Anakim were a race of

VERMILLION (2)

Jer 22:14 panels it with cedar, and paints it with *v*.
Ez 23:14 the images of Chaldeans drawn with *v*,

VERSED (1)

Est 1:13 conferred with the wise men *v* in the law,

VESSEL (23)

Lv 6:21 A clay *v* in which it has been cooked shall
6:21 if it is cooked in a bronze *v*,
11:33 any of these creatures fall into a clay *v*,
11:33 unclean, and the *v* itself you must break.
11:34 men drink, in any such *v* become unclean.
14: 5 over an earthen *v* with spring water in it.
14:50 over an earthen *v* with spring water in it.

Nm 5:17 v he shall meanwhile put some holy water,
19:15 likewise, every v that is open,
19:17 from the sin offering shall be put in a v,
2Kgs 4: 6 she said to her son, "Bring me another v."
Wis 15: 7 shall be the use of each v of either class
Sir 50: 9 Like a v of beaten gold,
Is 29:16 Or the v should say of the potter,
Jer 22:28 Is this man Coniah a v despised,
51:34 of Babylon,] he has left me as an empty v;
Ez 4: 9 in a single v and make bread out of them.
15: 3 a peg from it, to hang on it any kind of v?
Mt 23:32 up the v measured out by your forefathers.
Acts 27: 6 an Alexandrian v bound for Italy,
28:11 It was an Alexandrian v with the
Rom 9:21 to make from the same lump of clay one v
2Tm 2:21 evil things he may be a distinguished v,

VESSELS (65)

Ex 37:16 The v that were set on the table,
Nm 7:85 so that all the silver of these v amounted to
18: 3 not come near the sacred v or the altar,
19:18 on all the v and persons that were in it,
31: 6 v and the trumpets for sounding the alarm.
Ru 2: 9 drink from the v the young men have filled."
1Kgs 8: 4 all the sacred v that were in the tent.
10:21 all King Solomon's drinking v were of gold,
2Kgs 4: 3 said, "borrow v from all your neighbors
4: 3 as many empty v as you can.
4: 4 pour the oil into all the v,
4: 5 As they handed her the v,
4: 6 When all the v were filled,
25:14 pans and all the bronze v used for service.
1Chr 9:29 care of the utensils and all the sacred v,
18: 8 sea and the pillars and the v of bronze.
22:19 God's sacred v may be brought into
28:13 the liturgical v of the house of the LORD.
28:14 weight of gold to be used in the golden v
28:14 in the silver v for the various services,
2Chr 4:18 Solomon made all these v,
5: 5 all the sacred v that were in the tent;
9:20 of King Solomon's drinking v were of gold,
20:25 personal property, garments and precious v.
25:24 all the v he found in the house of God
36: 7 carried away to Babylon some of the v
36:10 precious v from the temple of the LORD.
Jdt 4: 3 Judea been gathered together, and the v,
1Mc 1:23 the gold and silver and the precious v;
4:49 new sacred v and brought the lampstand,
6:12 the v of gold and silver that were in it,
2Mc 4:32 stole some gold v from the temple and
4:32 v in Tyre and in the neighboring cities.
4:39 a large number of gold v had been stolen,
4:48 city, for the people, and for the sacred v,
5:16 He laid his impure hands on the sacred v
9:16 restore all the sacred v many times over;
15:17 temple with the sacred v were in danger.
Jb 28:17 equal it, nor can golden v reach its worth.
Wis 15: 7 Both the v that serve for clean purposes
15:13 stuff he creates fragile v and idols alike.
Is 2:16 the ships of Tarshish and all stately v.
52:11 you who carry the v of the LORD.
60: 9 All the v of the sea are assembled,
66:20 to the house of the LORD in clean v.
Jer 27:16 "The v of the house of the LORD will be
27:18 that the v which remain in the house of
27:19 the rest of the v that remain in this city,
27:21 the v that remain in the house of the LORD,
28: 3 restore to this place all the v of the temple
28: 6 you have prophesied by bringing the v of
52:18 and all the bronze v used for service.
Bar 1: 8 [This was when he received the v of the
1: 8 These silver v Zedekiah,
Dn 1: 2 and some of the v of the temple of God,
5: 2 the gold and silver v which Nebuchadnezzar,
5: 3 When the gold and silver v taken from the
5:23 had the v of his temple brought before you,
11: 8 and their precious v of silver and gold,
Rom 9:22 endured with much patience v fit for wrath,
9:23 of his glory toward the v for mercy,
2Cor 4: 7 This treasure we possess in earthen v,
2Tm 2:20 In every large household there are v not
Heb 9:21 and all the v of worship with blood.
Rv 5: 8 v of gold filled with aromatic spices,

VESTED (2)

Ezr 3:10 the v priests with the trumpets and the
Sir 50:11 V in his magnificent robes,

VESTIBULE (38)

1Kgs 7: 7 the v of the throne where he gave judgment
2Chr 15: 8 LORD which was before the v of the LORD.
29: 7 They also closed the doors of the v,
29:17 month they arrived at the v of the LORD;
Ez 8:16 LORD's temple, between the v and the altar,
40: 7 The threshold of the gate adjoining the v
40: 8 He measured the v of the gate,
40: 9 The v of the gate was toward the inside.
40:14 He measured the v,
40:15 of the v on the inside was fifty cubits.
40:16 the v on both sides there were windows.
40:21 and its v had the same measurements as
40:22 Its windows, the windows of its v,
40:22 up to it, and its v was toward the inside.
40:24 whose cells, pilasters, and v he measured;
40:25 gate and its v had windows on both sides,
40:26 its v was toward the inside.
40:29 and its v were the same size as the others.
40:29 gate and its v had windows on both sides;
40:31 But its v was toward the outer court;
40:33 and its v were the same size as the others;
40:33 gate and its v had windows on both sides;
40:34 But its v was toward the outer court;
40:36 of its cells, its pilasters, and its v,
40:36 gate and its v had windows on both sides;
40:37 Its v was toward the outer court;
40:38 a chamber opening off the v of the gate,
40:39 In the v of the gate there were two tables
40:40 Along the wall of the v,
40:40 the v of the gate there were two tables.
40:48 Then he brought me into the v of the
40:49 The v was twenty cubits wide and twelve
41:15 The inner nave and the outer v were
41:25 Before the v outside was a wooden lattice.
41:26 palmtrees] on both side walls of the v,
44: 3 He must enter by way of the v of the gate,
46: 2 from outside by way of the v of the gate
46: 8 enter and depart by the v of the gate.

VESTIGE (1)

Zep 1: 4 destroy from this place the last v of Baal,

VESTMENTS (32)

Ex 28: 2 brother Aaron you shall have sacred v made.
28: 3 shall give instructions to make such v
28: 4 These are the v they shall make:
28: 4 In making these sacred v which your
29: 5 Take the v and clothe Aaron with the tunic,
29:21 oil, and sprinkle this on Aaron and his v,
29:21 as well as on his sons and their v,
29:21 that his sons and their v may be sacred.
29:29 "The sacred v of Aaron shall be passed
31:10 cloths, the sacred v for Aaron the priest,
31:10 the v for his sons in their ministry,
35:19 the sacred v for Aaron,
35:19 the v worn by his sons in their ministry."
35:21 for all its services, and for the sacred v.
39: 1 as well as the sacred v for Aaron,
39:41 the sacred v for Aaron the priest,
39:41 v to be worn by his sons in their ministry.
40:13 Aaron with the sacred v and anoint him,
Lv 8: 2 Aaron and his sons, together with the v,
8:30 Moses sprinkled with it Aaron and his v,
8:30 as well as his sons and their v,
8:30 and his vestments and his sons and their v.
16: 4 But since these v are sacred,
16:23 v he had put on when he entered there.
16:24 in a sacred place, he shall put on his v,
16:32 wear the linen garments, the sacred v,
21:10 has been ordained to wear the special v,
1Mc 3:49 They brought with them the priestly v,
10:21 Jonathan put on the sacred v in the
Sir 45: 8 and adorned him with the glorious v:
45:10 The sacred v of gold,

VESTURE (2)

Ps(s) 22:19 among them, and for my v they cast lots.
Is 50: 3 in mourning, and make sackcloth their v.

VEX (1)

Jb 19: 2 How long will you v my soul,

VEXATION (2)

Prv 17:25 A foolish son is v to his father,
Eccl 5:16 passed in gloom and sorrow, under great v,

VEXATIOUS (1)

Prv 21:19 than with a quarrelsome and v wife.

VEXED (6)

Jgs 16:16 She importuned him continually and v him
Ps(s) 37: 1 Be not v over evildoers,
37: 7 Be not v at the successful path of the man
37: 8 be not v,
112:10 The wicked man shall see it and be v;
Ez 16:42 I will be quiet and no longer v.

VICAR (1)

2Kgs 23: 4 commanded the high priest Hilkiah, his v,

VICE (4)

Ps(s) 34:22 V slays the wicked,
Sir 10:13 of sin, a source which runs over with v;
1Pt 2:16 do not use your freedom as a cloak for v.
Jude 1: 7 they practiced unnatural v.

VICINITY (4)

1Sm 5: 6 the city and its v with hemorrhoids;
2Kgs 23: 5 cities of Judah and in the v of Jerusalem,
Jn 11:56 in the temple v saying to each other,
Acts 28: 7 v of that place was the estate of Publius,

VICIOUS (3)

1Mc 16:17 v act of treason he repaid good with evil.
Jas 1:21 away all that is filthy, every v excess.
1Pt 2: 1 So strip away everything v,

VICTIM (9)

Ex 21:16 sells his v or still has him when caught,
Lv 7:13 v of his peace offering for thanksgiving.
14: 2 "This is the law for the v of leprosy at
Dt 18: 3 the v is from the herd or from the flock,
2Chr 35: 7 as a Passover v for any who were present,
2Mc 9:21 Persia, I fell v to a troublesome illness;
Sir 28:26 and fall v to your foe waiting in ambush.
Jer 22: 3 the v from the hand of his oppressor.
Acts 7:24 and avenged the v by slaying the Egyptian.

VICTIMS (12)

Ex 12:21 families, and slaughter them as Passover v.
2Chr 4: 6 were cleansed the v for the holocausts;
29:34 able to skin all the v for the holocausts,
30:17 in charge of slaughtering the Passover v
35: 8 v together with three hundred oxen.
35: 9 to the Levites five thousand Passover v,
Eccl 4: 1 tears of the v with none to comfort them!
Sir 28:23 who forsake the LORD will fall v to it,
50:12 When he received the sundered v from
Jer 33:18 burn cereal offerings, and to sacrifice v.
Ez 21:17 of Israel, v of the sword with my people.
Dn 11:33 for a time they will become v of the sword,

VICTOR (6)

Rv 2: 7 I will see to it that the v eats from the
2:11 The v shall never be harmed by the second
2:17 To the v I will give the hidden manna;
3: 5 " 'The v shall go clothed in white.
3:12 " 'I will make the v a pillar in the
3:21 v the right to sit with me on my throne,

VICTORIES (3)

2Sm 22:51 You who gave great v to your king and
Ps(s) 18:51 You who gave great v to your king and
44: 5 king and my God, who bestowed v on Jacob.

VICTORIOUS (17)

Dt 33:29 Where else is a nation v in the LORD?
1Chr 18: 6 the LORD made David v in all his campaigns.
18:10 on having waged a v war against Hadadezer;
18:13 the LORD made David v in all his campaigns.
2Chr 13:18 were v because they relied on the LORD,
Jdt 1:13 King Arphaxad, and was v in his campaign.
1Mc 7:35 I return v I will burn this temple down."
2Mc 12:11 his companions, with God's help, were v.
Ps(s) 20: 7 with the strength of his v right hand.
44: 4 land, nor did their own arm make them v,
Wis 4: 2 in triumph, v in unsullied deeds of valor.
Jer 43:12 delouse the land of Egypt and depart v.
Dn 7:21 and was v until the Ancient One arrived;
Hb 3: 8 you drive the steeds of your v chariot?
Mt 12:20 will not quench until judgment is made v.
Rv 6: 2 He rode forth v, to conquer yet again.
17:14 v,

VICTORS (1)

Gn 14:11 The v seized all the possessions and food

VICTORY (61)

Gn 14:17 When Abram returned from his v over
Ex 14:13 see the v the LORD will win for you today.
32:18 "It does not sound like cries of v,
Dt 20: 4 you against your enemies and give you v.'
32:27 mistakenly boast, 'Our own hand won the v;
Jgs 7: 2 me and say, 'My own power brought me the v.'
15:18 this great v by the hand of your servant.
1Sm 2: 1 I rejoice in my v.
14: 6 to grant v through a few than through many."
14:39 the LORD lives who has given v to Israel,
14:45 it was he who brought Israel this great v?
19: 5 about a great v for all Israel through him,
2Sm 8: 6 brought David v in all his undertakings.
8:10 him for his v over Had-adezer in battle,
8:14 brought David v in all his undertakings.
19: 3 and that day's v was turned into mourning
23:10 LORD brought about a great v on that day;
23:12 and the LORD brought about a great v.
2Kgs 5: 1 through him the LORD had brought v to Aram.
13:17 prophet exclaimed, "The LORD's arrow of v!
13:17 The arrow of v over Aram!
1Chr 5:22 had fallen in battle, for v is from God;
11:14 Thus the LORD brought about a great v.
18: 3 set up his v stele at the river Euphrates.
2Chr 20:27 celebrating the joyful v the LORD had given
Jdt 11:22 of your people, to bring v to our arms,
Est E:23 for loyal Persians, a celebration of v,
1Mc 3:19 for v in war does not depend upon the size
2Mc 5: 6 that he was winning a v over his enemies,
8:33 celebrating the v in their ancestral city,
10:28 the one having as pledge of success and v

VICTORY (cont.)

10:38 great kindness to Israel and grants them *v*.
13:15 Giving his men the battle cry "God's *V*,"
15: 6 monument of *v* over Judas and his men.
15: 8 too, *v* would be given them by the Almighty.
15:21 that *v* is won by those who deserve it.
Ps(s) 20: 6 May we shout for joy at your *v* and raise
20: 7 that the LORD has given *v* to his anointed,
20:10 O LORD, grant *v* to the king,
21: 2 in your *v* how greatly he rejoices!
21: 6 Great is his glory in your *v*;
74: 4 they have set up their tokens of *v*.
98: 1 His right hand has won *v* for him,
118:15 joyful shout of *v* in the tents of the just:
144:10 chant your praise, You who give *v* to kings,
149: 4 his people, and he adorns the lowly with *v*.
Prv 21:31 for the day of battle, but *v* is the LORD's.
24: 6 and the *v* is due to a wealth of counselors.
Is 42: 6 LORD, have called you for the *v* of justice,
46:12 you who seem far from the *v* of justice:
59:16 So his own arm brought about the *v*,
62: 1 the dawn and her *v* like a burning torch.
63: 5 the *v* and my own wrath lent me its support.
1Cor 15:54 "Death is swallowed up in *v*."
15:55 "O death, where is your *v*?
15:57 us the *v* through our Lord Jesus Christ.
Rv 2:26 " 'To the one who wins the *v*,
3:21 as I myself won the *v* and took my seat
5: 5 has won the right by his *v* to open the
15: 2 had won the *v* over the beast and its image,
21: 7 who wins the *v* shall inherit these gifts;

VICTUALS (1)

Neh 13:15 I warned them to sell none of these *v*.

VIE (1)

Jb 11: 7 you *v* with the perfection of the Almighty?

VIES (1)

Wis 15: 9 he *v* with goldsmiths and silversmiths and

VIEW (40)

Gn 30:41 in the troughs in full *v* of these animals,
Ex 7:20 in full *v* of Pharaoh and his servants,
Nm 20:27 Mount Hor in *v* of the whole community,
25: 6 in the *v* of Moses and of the whole Israelite
27:12 and *v* the land that I am giving to
33: 3 went forth in triumph, in *v* of all Egypt.
Dt 32:49 and *v* the land of Canaan,
32:52 You may indeed *v* the land at a distance,
2Sm 6:20 the *v* of the slave girls of his followers,
10: 6 *v* of the offense they had given to David,
10:19 kings, in *v* of their defeat by Israel,
16:22 his father's concubines in *v* of all Israel.
Neh 10: 1 In *v* of all this,
Jdt 10:10 The men of the city kept her in *v* as she
2Mc 2:24 In *v* of the flood of statistics,
12:43 he had the resurrection of the dead in *v*;
12:45 But if he did this with a *v* to the
Ps(s) 56: 8 of their wickedness keep them in *v*:
68:25 They *v* your progress,
Prv 3:21 keep advice and counsel in *v*;
Eccl 8: 2 of the king, and in *v* of your oath to God,
Wis 3: 2 They seemed, in the *v* of the foolish,
7: 9 Because all gold, in *v* of her,
Jer 16:17 from me, nor does their guilt escape my *v*.
Ez 16:52 In *v* of your sinful deeds,
Mt 23:28 Thus you present to *v* a holy exterior
Mk 3: 9 In *v* of their numbers,
Lk 19:42 but you have completely lost it from *v*!
Acts 18:17 and beat him in full *v* of the bench;
Rom 4: 2 grounds for boasting, but not in God's *v*;
4:13 in *v* of the justice that comes from faith.
4:23 were not written with him alone in *v*;
1Cor 9:22 a weak person with a *v* to winning the weak.
2Cor 10: 7 You *v* things superficially.
11: 7 humbling myself with a *v* to exalting you?
Gal 3: 1 Christ was displayed to *v* upon his cross?
3:19 It was given in *v* of transgressions and
5:10 the Lord, you will not adopt a different *v*.
Heb 2: 1 In *v* of this, we must attend all the more
Jas 4: 3 with a *v* to squandering what you receive

VIEWED (1)

Nm 27:13 When you have *v* it,

VIEWS (3)

Jb 34:34 say to me, every wise man who hears my *v*:
Sir 21:17 The *v* of a prudent man are sought in an
Acts 28:22 we are anxious to hear you present your *v*.

VIGIL (8)

Ex 12:42 This was a night of *v* for the LORD,
12:42 all the Israelites must keep a *v* for the LORD
2Sm 12:21 living, you fasted and wept and kept *v*;
Ps(s) 127: 1 the city, in vain does the guard keep *v*.
Sg 5: 2 I was sleeping, but my heart kept *v*;
Wis 6:15 keeps *v* shall quickly be free from care;
Sir 33:16 Now I am the last to keep *v*,
Is 26: 9 yes, my spirit within me keeps *v* for you;

VIGILANT (1)

Ps(s) 35:23 Awake, and be *v* in my defense;

VIGILS (1)

Sir 43:10 their place and never relax in their *v*.

VIGOR (15)

Dt 34: 7 his eyes were undimmed and his *v* unabated.
Jos 14:11 *v* whether for war or for ordinary tasks.
Neh 2:18 And they undertook the good work with *v*.
Jb 5:26 You shall approach the grave in full *v*,
14:10 But when a man dies, all *v* leaves him;
20:11 Though his frame is full of youthful *v*,
21:23 One dies in his full *v*,
40:16 and his *v* in the sinews of his belly.
Prv 3: 8 health for your flesh and *v* for your bones.
31: 3 Give not your *v* to women,
Eccl 10:17 time (for *v* and not in drinking bouts).
Wis 13:17 And for *v* he invokes the powerless;
Sir 40:26 Wealth and *v* build up confidence,
Is 40:29 for the weak he makes *v* abound.
Jer 11:19 "Let us destroy the tree in its *v*;

VIGOROUS (5)

Jb 18: 7 His *v* steps are hemmed in,
Ps(s) 92:15 *v* and sturdy shall they be,
Sir 14:18 As with the leaves that grow on a *v* tree:
Na 1:12 the LORD, be they ever so many and so *v*,
Acts 18:28 He was *v* in his public refutation of the

VIGOROUSLY (2)

2Mc 10:17 Attacking *v*,
12:23 Judas pressed the pursuit *v*,

VILE (9)

2Mc 4:19 the *v* Jason sent envoys as representatives
9:13 Then this *v* man vowed to the Lord,
12:35 intending to capture the *v* wretch alive,
14:42 rather than fall into the hands of *v* men
15:32 He showed them the *v* Nicanor's head and
Sir 11:12 he raises him free of the *v* dust,
Jer 15:19 you bring forth the precious without the *v*,
Lam 1: 8 her *v* now that they see her nakedness;
Jas 3:16 inconstancy and all kinds of *v* behavior.

VILEST (1)

2Mc 7:34 But you, wretch, *v* of all men!

VILLAGE (21)

2Mc 8: 1 and his companions entered the *v* secretly,
14:16 and came upon the enemy at the *v* of Adasa.
Mt 10:11 for a worthy person in every town or *v*
21: 2 "Go into the *v* straight ahead of you and
Mk 5:14 off and brought the news to field and *v*,
8:23 blind man's hand and led him outside the *v*.
8:26 admonition, "Do not even go into the *v*."
11: 2 "Go to the *v* straight ahead of you,
Lk 5:17 *v* of Galilee and from Judea and Jerusalem.
9: 6 So they set out and went from *v* to village,
9: 6 they set out and went from village to *v*,
10:38 On their journey Jesus entered a *v* where a
17:12 As he was entering a *v*,
19:30 "Go into the *v* straight ahead of you.
24:13 making their way to a *v* named Emmaus
24:28 were near the *v* to which they were going,
Jn 7:42 from Bethlehem, the *v* where David lived?"
11: 1 the *v* of Mary and her sister Martha.
11:18 The *v* was not far from Jerusalem
11:30 Jesus had not yet come into the *v*
12: 1 the *v* of Lazarus whom Jesus had raised

VILLAGES (75)

Gn 25:16 their names by their *v* and encampments;
Lv 25:31 houses in *v* that are not encircled by
Nm 32:41 clan, campaigned against the tent *v*,
Dt 2:23 Avvim, who once dwelt in *v* as far as Gaza,
Jos 13:23 These cities and their *v* were the heritage
13:28 These cities and their *v* were the heritage
13:30 Og, king of Bashan, and all the *v* of Jair,
15:32 a total of twenty-nine cities with their *v*.
15:36 fourteen cities and their *v*.
15:41 sixteen cities and their *v*,
15:44 nine cities and their *v*.
15:45 Ekron and its towns and *v*,
15:46 that lie alongside Ashdod, and their *v*;
15:47 Ashdod and its towns and *v*;
15:47 Gaza and its towns and *v*,
15:51 eleven cities and their *v*.
15:54 nine cities and their *v*.
15:57 ten cities and their *v*.
15:59 six cities and their *v*.
15:59 eleven cities and their *v*.
15:60 two cities and their *v*.
15:62 six cities and their *v*.
16: 9 including the *v* that belonged to each city
18:24 twelve cities and their *v*.
18:28 fourteen cities and their *v*.
19: 6 thirteen cities and their *v*.
19: 7 four cities and their *v*,
19: 8 besides all the *v* around these cities as
19:15 were twelve cities and their *v* to comprise
19:22 These sixteen cities and their *v* were the
19:30 twenty-two cities and their *v* to comprise
19:38 nineteen cities and their *v*,
19:48 These cities and their *v* were the heritage
21:12 although the open country and *v* belonging
Jgs 11:26 when Israel occupied Heshbon and its *v*,
11:26 Heshbon and its villages, Aroer and its *v*,
1Sm 6:18 including fortified cities and open *v*.
1Kgs 4:13 having charge of the *v* of Jair,
1Chr 2:23 and Aram took from them the *v* of Jair,
4:32 reign, these were their cities and their *v*.
4:33 with all their outlying *v* as far as Baal.
6:41 open country and the *v* belonging to the city
9:16 lived in the *v* of the Netophathites.
9:22 inscribed in the family records of their *v*.
9:25 kinsmen who had lived in their own *v*
27:25 stores in the country, the cities, the *v*,
2Chr 34: 6 and in the ruined *v* of the surrounding
Neh 11:25 As concerns their *v* in the country:
11:25 its dependencies, in Jekabzeel and its *v*,
11:30 Jarmuth, Zanoah, Adullam, and their *v*,
12:28 Jerusalem, from the *v* of the Netophathites,
Jdt 4: 5 of the high mountains, fortified their *v*,
15: 7 till the towns and *v* in the mountains and
Est 9:19 is why the rural Jews, who dwell in *v*,
1Mc 5: 8 After seizing Jazer and its *v*,
5:65 he took Hebron and its *v*,
7:46 From all the surrounding *v* of Judea people
2Mc 8: 6 Coming unexpectedly upon towns and *v*,
Ps(s) 10: 8 He lurks in ambush near the *v*;
Sg 7:12 fields and spend the night among the *v*.
Is 42:11 cities cry out, the *v* where Kedar dwells;
Ez 25: 5 and the *v* of the Ammonites a resting place
38:11 "I will go up against a land of open *v*
Mt 9:35 continued his tour of all the towns and *v*.
14:15 to the *v* and buy some food for themselves."
Mk 1:38 "Let us move on to the neighboring *v* so
6: 6 the rounds of the neighboring *v* instead,
6:36 that they can go to the crossroads and *v*
6:56 Wherever he put in an appearance, in *v*,
8:27 set out for the *v* around Caesarea Philippi.
Lk 8: 1 he journeyed through towns and *v* preaching
9:12 so that they can go into the *v* and farms
19:17 For that you can take over ten *v*.'
19:19 His word to him was, 'Take over five *v*.'
Acts 8:25 good news to many *v* of Samaria on the way.

VILLAIN (1)

Prv 6:12 A scoundrel, a *v*,

VILLAINS (2)

1Mc 15: 3 Whereas certain *v* have gained control of
2Mc 14:27 Stirred up by the *v* calumnies,

VINDICATE (2)

Prv 25:22 heap on his head, and the LORD will *v* you.
Bar 6:53 They neither *v* their own rights,

VINDICATED (5)

Gn 30: 6 bore a son, Rachel said, "God has *v* me;
Ps(s) 51: 6 in your sentence, *v* when you condemn.
Lk 7:35 God's wisdom is *v* by all who accept it."
Rom 3: 4 says, "You shall be *v* in what you say,
1Tm 3:16 manifested in the flesh, *v* in the Spirit;

VINDICATION (13)

Gn 20:16 you as a *v* before all who are with you;
Jb 36: 6 rights, but grants *v* to the oppressed,
Ps(s) 37: 6 bright as the noonday shall be your *v*.
Is 35: 4 Here is your God, he comes with *v*;
45:25 In the LORD shall be the *v* and the glory
48:18 and your *v* like the waves of the sea;
54:17 the servants of the LORD, their *v* from me,
58: 8 Your *v* shall go before you,
61: 2 from the LORD and a day of *v* by our God,
62: 1 Until her *v* shines forth like the dawn and
62: 2 Nations shall behold your *v*,
63: 1 "It is I, I who announce *v*,
Bar 2:17 who will give glory and *v* to the Lord.

VINDICATOR (2)

Jb 19:25 But as for me, I know that my *V* lives,
Wis 12:12 come into your presence as *v* of unjust men?

VINDICTIVE (2)

Est E: 4 the *v* judgment of the all-seeing God.
Prv 6:34 For *v* is the husband's wrath,

VINDICTIVENESS (1)

Lam 3:60 You see all their *v*,

VINE (49)

Gn 40: 9 he said, "I saw a *v* in front of me,
40:10 of me, and on the *v* were three branches.
49:11 He tethers his donkey to the *v*,
Nm 6: 4 not eat anything of the produce of the *v*;
Jgs 9:12 Then the trees said to the *v*,

9:13 But the *v* answered them,
13:14 not eat anything that comes from the *v*,
1Kgs 5: 5 every man under his *v* or under his fig
2Kgs 4:39 field to gather herbs and found a wild *v*,
18:31 eat of his own *v* and of his own fig-tree,
1Mc 14:12 Every man sat under his *v* and his fig tree,
Jb 15:33 like a *v* that sheds its grapes unripened,
Ps(s) 80: 9 A *v* from Egypt you transplanted;
80:15 Take care of this *v*,
128: 3 a fruitful *v* in the recesses of your home;
Sg 7: 9 your breasts be like clusters of the *v*
Sir 24:17 I bud forth delights like the *v*,
Is 17:10 plants and set out your foreign *v* slips,
24: 7 The wine mourns, the *v* languishes,
32:12 for the pleasant fields, the fruitful *v*,
34: 4 wither away, As the leaf wilts on the *v*,
36:16 eat of his own *v* and of his own fig tree,
Jer 2:21 you, a choice *v* of fully tested stock;
2:21 you turn out obnoxious to me, a spurious *v*?
6: 9 glean like a *v* the remnant of Israel;
8:13 no grapes on the *v*,
Ez 15: 2 wood of the *v* better than any other wood?
15: 6 of the *v* among the trees of the forest,
17: 6 he placed it, To sprout and grow up a *v*,
17: 6 Thus it became a *v*,
17: 7 To him this *v* bent its roots,
17: 8 bear fruit, and become a majestic *v*.
19:10 mother was like a *v* planted by the water;
Hos 10: 1 luxuriant *v* whose fruit matches its growth.
14: 8 They shall blossom like the *v*,
Jl 1: 7 He has laid waste my *v*,
1:12 The *v* has dried up,
2:22 the fig tree and the *v* give their yield.
Mi 4: 4 under his own *v* or under his own fig tree,
Na 2: 3 The LORD will restore the *v* of Jacob,
Hg 2:19 the seed has not sprouted, nor have the *v*,
Zec 8:12 the *v* shall yield its fruit,
Mal 3:11 And the *v* in the field will not be barren,
Mt 26:29 I will not drink this fruit of the *v* from
Mk 14:25 never again drink of the fruit of the *v* until
Lk 22:18 the *v* until the coming of the reign of God."
Jn 15: 1 the true *v* and my Father is the vinegrower.
15: 4 can bear fruit of itself apart from the *v*,
15: 5 I am the *v*, you are the branches.

VINE-KEEPER (1)

Jb 27:18 cobwebs, or like a booth put up by the *v*.

VINEDRESSER (1)

Lk 13: 7 He said to the *v*, 'Look here!

VINEDRESSERS (5)

2Kgs 25:12 of the guard, left behind as *v* and farmers.
2Chr 26:10 and *v* in the highlands and the garden land.
Is 61: 5 foreigners shall be your farmers and *v*.
Jer 52:16 of the guard, left behind as *v* and farmers.
Jl 1:11 wail, you *v*!

VINEGAR (4)

Nm 6: 3 he may neither drink wine *v*,
6: 3 may neither drink wine vinegar, other *v*,
Ps(s) 69:22 and in my thirst they gave me *v* to drink.
Prv 10:26 As *v* to the teeth,

VINEGROWER (1)

Jn 15: 1 am the true vine and my Father is the *v*.

VINES (21)

Lv 25: 5 you pick the grapes of your untrimmed *v*
25:11 or pick the grapes from the untrimmed *v*.
Nm 20: 5 grain nor figs nor *v* nor pomegranates?
Dt 8: 8 of *v* and fig trees and pomegranates,
28:39 wine, for the grubs will eat the *v* clean.
Ps(s) 78:47 *v* with hail and their sycamores with frost.
105:33 He struck down their *v* and their fig trees
Sg 2:12 earth, the time of pruning the *v* has come,
2:13 fig tree puts forth its figs, and the *v*,
6:11 the valley, To see if the *v* were in bloom.
7:13 vineyards, and see if the *v* are in bloom,
Is 5: 2 it of stones, and planted the choicest *v*;
7:23 place where there used to be a thousand *v*,
16: 8 of Heshbon languish, the *v* of Sibmah,
16: 9 I weep with Jazer for the *v* of Sibmah;
Jer 5:17 and cattle, devour your *v* and fig trees;
Hos 2:14 I will lay waste her *v* and fig trees,
Mi 7: 1 gathered, as when the *v* have been gleaned;
Hb 3:17 tree blossom not nor fruit be on the *v*,
Zec 3:10 one another under your *v* and fig trees."
Rv 14:18 gather the grapes from the *v* of the earth,

VINESTOCK (1)

Dt 32:32 They are a branch of Sodom's *v*,

VINEYARD (69)

Gn 9:20 of the soil, was the first to plant a *v*.
Ex 22: 4 a man is burning over a field or a *v*,
22: 4 the best produce of his own field or *v*.
23:11 in regard to your *v* and your olive grove.
Lv 19:10 Likewise, you shall not pick your *v* bare,
25: 3 your field, and for six years prune your *v*,
25: 4 neither sow your field nor prune your *v*.
Nm 21:22 will not turn aside into any field or *v*,
Dt 20: 6 a *v* and never yet enjoyed its fruits?
22: 9 your *v* with two different kinds of seed;
22: 9 crop you have sown and the yield of the *v*.
23:25 "When you go through your neighbor's *v*,
24:21 you shall not go over the *v* a second time;
28:30 Though you plant a *v*,
1Kgs 21: 1 a *v* in Jezreel next to the palace of Ahab,
21: 2 "Give me your *v* to be my vegetable garden,
21: 2 I will give you a better *v* in exchange,
21: 6 and said to him, 'Sell me your *v*,
21: 6 prefer, I will give you a *v* in exchange.'
21: 6 But he refused to let me have his *v*."
21: 7 the *v* of Naboth the Jezreelite for you."
21:15 take possession of the *v* of Naboth the
21:16 way down to the *v* of Naboth the Jezreelite,
21:18 He will be in the *v* of Naboth,
Jb 24:11 they glean in the the *v* of the wicked.
Prv 24:30 by the *v* of the man without sense;
31:16 out of her earnings she plants a *v*.
Sg 1: 6 my own *v* I have not cared for.
8:11 Solomon had a *v* at Baal-hamon;
8:11 he gave over the *v* to caretakers.
8:12 My *v* is at my own disposal;
Sir 28:24 As you hedge round your *v* with thorns,
36:25 A *v* with no hedge will be overrun;
Is 1: 8 daughter Zion is left like a hut in a *v*,
3:14 It is you who have devoured the *v*;
5: 1 friend, my friend's song concerning his *v*.
5: 1 My friend had a *v* on a fertile hillside;
5: 3 men of Judah, judge between me and my *v*:
5: 4 there to do for my *v* that I had not done?
5: 5 let you know what I mean to do to my *v*:
5: 7 The *v* of the LORD of hosts is the house of
5:10 of *v* shall yield but one liquid measure,
27: 2 The pleasant *v*,
Jer 12:10 Many shepherds have ravaged my *v*,
35: 7 neither plant nor own a *v*,
48:32 for Jazer I weep over you, *v* of Sibmah.
Am 5:17 And in every *v* there shall be lamentation
Mt 20: 1 went out at dawn to hire workmen for his *v*.
20: 2 daily wage, he sent them out to his *v*.
20: 4 my *v* and I will pay you whatever is fair.'
20: 7 He said, 'You go to the *v* too.'
20: 8 the owner of the *v* said to his foreman,
21:28 said, 'Son, go out and work in the *v* today.'
21:33 was a property owner who planted a *v*,
21:39 they seized him, dragged him outside the *v*,
21:40 *v* will do to those tenants when he comes?"
21:41 lease his *v* out to others who will see to it
Mk 12: 1 "A man planted a *v*,
12: 2 from them his share of produce from the *v*.
12: 8 killed him and dragged him outside the *v*.
12: 9 do you suppose the owner of the *v* will do?
12: 9 tenants and turn his *v* over to others.
Lk 13: 6 "A man had a fig tree growing in his *v*,
20: 9 "A man planted a *v*,
20:13 The owner of the *v* asked himself,
20:15 dragged him outside the *v* and killed him.
20:15 the owner of the *v* has in store for them?
20:16 tenant farmers and give the *v* to others."
1Cor 9: 7 plants a *v* and does not eat of its yield?

VINEYARDS (45)

Nm 16:14 giving us fields and *v* for our inheritance,
20:17 We will not cross any fields or *v*,
22:24 between *v* with a stone wall on each side.
Dt 6:11 *v* and olive groves that you did not plant;
28:39 Though you plant and cultivate *v*,
32:32 Sodom's vinestock, from the *v* of Gomorrah.
Jos 24:13 *v* and olive groves which you did not plant.
Jgs 14: 5 When they had come to the *v* of Timnah,
15: 5 and the *v* and olive orchards as well.
21:20 "Go and lie in wait in the *v*.
21:21 leave the *v* and each of you seize one of
1Sm 8:14 He will take the best of your fields, *v*,
8:15 He will tithe your crops and your *v*,
22: 7 son of Jesse give all of you fields and *v*?
2Kgs 5:26 or to take garments, olive orchards or *v*,
19:29 sow and reap, plant *v* and eat their fruit!
1Chr 27:27 Over the *v* was Shimei from Ramah,
Neh 5: 3 'We are forced to pawn our fields, our *v*,
5: 4 borrowed money on our fields and our *v*.
5: 5 for our fields and our *v* belong to others."
5:11 them this very day their fields, their *v*,
9:25 all good things, cisterns already dug, *v*,
1Mc 3:56 or were just married, or were planting *v*,
Ps(s) 107:37 They sowed fields and planted *v*,
Eccl 2: 4 I built myself houses and planted *v*;
Sg 1: 6 they charged me with the care of the *v*:
1:14 a cluster of henna from the *v* of Engedi.
2:15 foxes, the little foxes that damage the *v*;
2:15 for our *v* are in bloom!
7:13 Let us go early to the *v*,
Is 16:10 and gladness, In the *v* there is no singing,
36:17 a land of grain and wine, of bread and *v*.
37:30 sow and reap, plant *v* and eat their fruit!
65:21 and eat the fruit of the *v* they plant;
Jer 31: 5 shall plant *v* on the mountains of Samaria;
32:15 and *v* shall again be bought in this land.
35: 9 we own no *v* or fields or crops,
39:10 were given at the same time *v* and farms.
Ez 28:26 security, building houses and planting *v*.
Hos 2:17 From there I will give her the *v* she had,
Am 4: 9 your many gardens and *v*,
5:11 Though you have planted choice *v*,
9:14 ruined cities, Plant *v* and drink the wine,
Mi 1: 6 heap in the field, a place to plant for *v*;
Zep 1:13 but shall not dwell in them, plant *v*,

VINTAGE (16)

Lv 26: 5 your threshing will last till *v* time,
26: 5 time, and your *v* till the time for sowing,
Jgs 8: 2 of Ephraim better than the *v* of Abiezer?
Sir 24:25 with knowledge, like the Gihon at *v* time.
33:16 to keep vigil, like a gleaner after the *v*;
Is 16:10 one treads grapes, the *v* shout is stilled.
18: 5 Before the *v*,
24:13 as with a gleaning when the *v* is done.
32:10 The *v* will fail,
Jer 48:32 Upon your harvest, upon your *v*,
48:33 treads no more, the *v* shout is stilled.
51:14 who shall raise over you the *v* shout!
Mt 21:34 When *v* time arrived he dispatched his
21:41 see to it that he has grapes at *v* time."
Lk 20:10 At *v* time he sent a servant to the tenant
Jn 2:10 have been drinking awhile, a lesser *v*.

VINTAGER (3)

Sir 33:17 till like a *v* I have filled my winepress,
Jer 6: 9 Pass your hand, like a *v*,
Am 9:13 shall overtake the reaper, and the *v*,

VINTAGERS (3)

Jer 25:30 a shout like that of *v* over the grapes.
49: 9 If *v* came upon you,
Ob 1: 5 If *v* came to you,

VIOLATE (12)

Nm 30: 3 of abstinence, he shall not *v* his word,
Dt 24:17 *v* the rights of the alien or of the orphan,
Ezr 9:14 shall we again *v* your commandments by
Tb 9: 3 I cannot *v* his oath."
Est 7: 8 "Will he also *v* the queen while she is
Jb 34:12 wickedly, the Almighty cannot *v* justice.
Ps(s) 89:32 *v* my statutes and keep not my commands,
89:35 "I will not *v* my covenant;
Prv 31: 5 and *v* the rights of all who are in need.
Sir 19:20 those of great intelligence who *v* the law.
Ez 22:26 *v* my law and profane what is holy to me;
Acts 23: 3 yet you *v* the law yourself by ordering me

VIOLATED (17)

Dt 22:24 the man because he *v* his neighbor's wife.
Jos 7: 1 But the Israelites *v* the ban;
7:11 *v* the covenant which I enjoined on them.
7:15 because he has *v* the covenant of the LORD
22:20 When Achan, son of Zerah, *v* the ban,
Jgs 2:20 "Inasmuch as this nation has *v* my
2Kgs 18:12 of the LORD, their God, but *v* his covenant,
Jdt 9: 2 her thighs, and disgracefully *v* her body.
1Mc 7:18 they *v* the agreement and the oath that
Is 24: 5 who have transgressed laws, *v* statutes,
Jer 13:22 skirts are stripped away and you are *v*.
34:18 The men who *v* my covenant and did not
Bar 2:12 we have sinned, been impious, and *v*,
Ez 18:18 Only the father, since he *v* rights,
Hos 5:11 Is Ephraim maltreated, his rights *v*?
6: 7 But they, in their land, *v* the covenant;
8: 1 Since they have *v* my covenant,

VIOLATES (4)

Dt 27:19 be he who *v* the rights of the alien,
Ezr 6:11 If any man *v* this edict,
1Mc 14:45 Whoever acts otherwise or *v* any of these
Ps(s) 55:21 hands on his associates, and *v* his pact.

VIOLATING (3)

1Chr 2: 7 brought trouble upon Israel by *v* the ban.
Sir 41:21 servant girl you have, and of *v* her couch;
Mal 2:10 each other, *v* the covenant of our fathers?

VIOLATION (4)

2Mc 7: 1 force them to eat pork in *v* of God's law.
15:10 of the Gentiles and their *v* of oaths.
Eccl 5: 7 and *v* of rights and justice in the realm,
Jn 7:23 the sabbath to prevent a *v* of Mosaic law,

VIOLATIONS (1)

Wis 2:12 law and charges us with *v* of our training.

VIOLENCE (66)

Gn 49: 5 indeed, weapons of *v* are their knives.
Dt 21: 5 or *v* must be settled by their decision.
Jgs 9:24 This was to repay the *v* done to the
2Sm 22: 3 refuge, my savior, from *v* you keep me safe.
Neh 5: 5 *v* has been done to some of our daughters!
1Mc 12:42 a large army he was afraid to offer him *v*.

VIOLENCE (cont.)

2Mc 1: 7 wrote to you during the trouble and *v* that
Jb 16:17 my eyes, Although my hands are free from *v*,
Ps(s) 7:17 the crown of his head his *v* shall rebound.
10:10 prone till by his *v* fall the unfortunate.
11: 5 the lover of *v* he hates.
17: 9 from the wicked who use *v* against me.
27:12 up against me, and such as breathe out *v*.
55:10 for in the city I see *v* and strife;
72:14 From fraud and *v* he shall redeem them,
73: 6 as a robe *v* enwraps them.
74:20 in the land and the plains are full of *v*.
Prv 4:17 of wickedness and drink the wine of *v*.
10:11 but the mouth of the wicked conceals *v*.
10:13 [but the mouth of the wicked conceals *v*.
11:30 is a tree of life, but *v* takes lives away.
13: 2 things, but the treacherous one craves *v*.
24: 2 For their hearts plot *v*,
26: 6 He cuts off his feet, he drinks down *v*,
Eccl 4: 1 From the hand of their oppressors comes *v*,
Wis 4: 4 by the wind and, by the *v* of the winds,
19:13 from the *v* of the thunderbolts.
Sir 10: 6 matter the wrong, do no *v* to your neighbor,
10: 8 another because of the *v* of the arrogant.
13:13 and take care never to accompany men of *v*.
21: 4 *V* and arrogance wipe out wealth;
40:15 The offshoot of *v* will not flourish,
Is 10:33 lops off the boughs with terrible *v*;
28: 2 overflowing, levels to the ground with *v*;
59: 6 and deeds of *v* come from their hands.
60:18 No longer shall *v* be heard of in your land,
Jer 6: 7 *V* and destruction resound in her;
9: 5 Violence upon *v*, deceit upon deceit:
20: 8 must cry out, *v* and outrage is my message;
51:46 year the rumor comes, then *v* in the land,
Ez 7:11 *v* has risen to support wickedness.
7:23 with bloodshed and the city full of *v*.
8:17 they have filled the land with *v*,
12:19 *v* of all its inhabitants that now fills it.
28:16 *v* was your business,
45: 9 Put away *v* and oppression,
Dn 14:30 When he saw himself threatened with *v*,
Jl 4:19 Because of *v* done to the people of Judah,
Am 6: 3 evil day, yet you hasten the reign of *v*!
Ob 1:10 Because of *v* to your brother Jacob,
Jon 3: 8 his evil way and from the *v* he has in hand.
Mi 6:12 council, You whose rich men are full of *v*,
Hb 1: 2 I cry out to you, *V*!"
1: 3 Destruction and *v* are before me;
2: 8 men's blood shed, and *v* done to the land,
2:17 For the *v* done to Lebanon shall cover you,
2:17 men's blood shed, and *v* done to the land,
Zep 1: 9 house of their master with *v* and deceit.
3: 4 profane what is holy, and do *v* to the law.
Mt 11:12 now the kingdom of God has suffered *v*,
Lk 18: 5 in her favor or she will end by doing me *v*.' "
23:23 crucified, and their shouts increased in *v*.
Acts 21:35 the soldiers because of the *v* of the mob.
Rv 16:18 Such was its *v* that there has never been
18:21 city shall be cast down like this, with *v*,

VIOLENT (27)

2Sm 22:49 exalt me and from the *v* man you rescue me.
Jdt 1:12 fell into a *v* rage against all that land,
Est B: 7 nether world by a *v* death on a single day,
1Mc 2:49 it is a time of disaster and *v* anger.
15:36 he had seen, the king fell into a *v* rage.
2Mc 5:14 lost, forty thousand meeting a *v* death,
9: 7 part of his body was racked by the *v* fall.
Jb 40:23 If the river grows *v*,
Ps(s) 18:49 me and from the *v* man you have rescued me.
55: 9 shelter from the *v* storm and the tempest."
71: 4 from the grasp of the criminal and the *v*.
140: 2 preserve me from *v* men,
140: 5 me from *v* men Who plan to trip up my feet
140:12 evil shall abruptly entrap the *v* man.
Prv 19:19 The man of *v* temper pays the penalty;
21:14 anger, and a concealed present, *v* wrath.
Jer 15:21 and rescue you from the grasp of the *v*.
Jon 1: 4 however, hurled a *v* wind upon the sea,
1:12 of me that this *v* storm has come upon you."
Mt 8:24 warning a *v* storm came up on the lake,
11:12 violence, and the *v* take it by force.
Acts 13:45 countered with *v* abuse whatever Paul said.
Ti 1: 7 or arrogant, a drunkard, a *v* or greedy man.
Rv 6:12 the sixth seal, there was a *v* earthquake;
11:13 At that moment there was a *v* earthquake
11:19 thunder, an earthquake, and a *v* hailstorm.
16:18 and peals of thunder, then a *v* earthquake.

VIOLENTLY (7)

Ex 19:18 furnace, and the whole mountain trembled *v*.
Ps(s) 25:19 my enemies are many, and they hate me *v*.
Ez 22:12 you despoil your neighbors *v*;
Dn 2:12 At this the king became *v* angry and
Mk 1:26 *v* and with a loud shriek came out of him.
Acts 19:16 He dealt with them so *v* that they fled
27:18 We were being pounded by the storm so *v*

VIOLET (48)

Ex 25: 4 *v*, purple and scarlet yarn;
26: 1 woven of fine linen twined and of *v*,
26: 4 Make loops of *v* yarn along the edge of the
26:31 "You shall have a veil woven of *v*,
26:36 the tent make a variegated curtain of *v*,
27:16 curtain, twenty cubits long, woven of *v*,
28: 5 as my priests, they shall use gold, *v*,
28: 6 they shall make of gold thread and of *v*,
28: 8 like it, be made of gold thread, of *v*,
28:15 like the ephod with gold thread and *v*,
28:28 *V* ribbons shall bind the rings of the
28:31 you shall make entirely of *v* material.
28:33 you shall make pomegranates, woven of *v*,
28:37 is to be tied over the miter with a *v* ribbon
35: 6 *v*, purple and scarlet yarn;
35:23 Everyone who happened to have *v*,
35:25 were expert spinners brought hand-spun *v*,
35:35 the making of variegated cloth of *v*,
36: 8 having cherubim embroidered on them with *v*,
36:11 Loops of *v* yarn were made along the edge
36:35 The veil was woven of *v*,
36:37 the entrance of the tent was made of *v*,
38:18 was a variegated curtain, woven of *v*,
38:23 and a weaver of variegated cloth of *v*,
39: 1 With *v*,
39: 2 ephod was woven of gold thread and of *v*,
39: 3 into threads, which were woven with the *v*,
39: 5 like it, was made of gold thread, of *v*,
39: 8 like the ephod, with gold thread and *v*,
39:21 *V* ribbons bound the rings of the
39:22 of the ephod was woven entirely of *v* yarn,
39:24 of the robe pomegranates were made of *v*,
39:29 work made of fine linen twined and of *v*,
39:31 It was tied over the miter with a *v* ribbon,
Nm 4: 7 *v* cloth and put on it the plates and cups,
4: 9 They shall use a *v* cloth to cover the
4:11 golden altar they shall spread a *v* cloth,
4:12 in *v* cloth and cover them with tahash skin.
15:38 fastening each corner tassel with a *v* cord.
2Chr 2: 6 iron, in purple, crimson, and *v* fabrics,
2:13 iron, with stone and wood, with purple, *v*,
3:14 He made the veil of *v*,
Est 1: 6 were white cotton draperies and *v* hangings,
8:15 in a royal robe of *v* and of white cotton,
1Mc 4:23 much gold and silver, *v* and crimson cloth,
Sir 45:10 The sacred vestments of gold, of *v*,
Jer 10: 9 of the smelter, Clothed with *v* and purple
Ez 27:24 with you rich garments, *v* mantles,

VIPER (4)

Gn 49:17 by the roadside, a horned *v* by the path,
Ps(s) 91:13 You shall tread upon the asp and the *v*;
Is 30: 6 roaring lion, of the *v* and flying saraph,
59: 5 of them is pressed, it will hatch as a *v*;

VIPERS (6)

Jb 20:16 the *v* fangs shall slay him.
Sir 39:30 disease, Ravenous beasts, scorpions, *v*,
Mt 3: 7 "You brood of *v*!
12:34 you utter anything good, you brood of *v*,
23:33 *V'* nest!
Lk 3: 7 "You brood of *v*!

VIRGIN (37)

Gn 24:16 The girl was very beautiful, a *v*,
Ex 22:15 a man seduces a *v* who is not betrothed,
Lv 21:13 "The priest shall marry a *v*.
21:14 lost her honor as a prostitute, but a *v*,
Dt 22:14 relations with her I did not find her a *v*,'
22:17 I did not find your daughter a *v*.
22:19 because the man defamed a *v* in Israel.
Jgs 21:11 and every woman who was not still a *v*.
2Sm 13: 2 since she was a *v*,
1Kgs 1: 2 "Let a young *v* be sought to attend you,
2Kgs 19:21 laughs you to scorn, the *v* daughter Zion!
Prv 24:13 is good, if *v* honey is sweet to your taste;
27: 7 One who is full, tramples on *v* honey;
Sir 9: 5 Entertain no thoughts against a *v*,
Is 7:14 the *v* shall be with child,
23:12 who are now oppressed, *v* daughter Sidon.
37:22 laughs you to scorn, the *v* daughter Zion;
47: 1 sit in the dust, O *v* daughter Babylon;
62: 5 As a young man marries a *v*,
Jer 2:32 Does a *v* forget her jewelry,
14:17 overwhelms the *v* daughter of my people,
18:13 Truly horrible things has *v* Israel done!
31: 4 you, and you shall be rebuilt, O *v* Israel;
31:21 Turn back, O *v* Israel,
46:11 Gilead, and take balm, O *v* daughter Egypt!
Lam 1:15 trodden in the wine press *v* daughter Judah.
2:13 show you for your comfort, *v* daughter Zion?
Jl 1: 8 Lament like a *v* girt with sackcloth for
Am 5: 2 is fallen, to rise no more, the *v* Israel;
Mt 1:23 "The *v* shall be with child and give birth
Lk 1:27 to a *v* betrothed to a man named Joseph,
1Cor 7:28 Neither does a *v* commit sin if she marries.
7:34 The *v*— indeed, any unmarried woman
7:36 he is behaving dishonorably toward his *v*
7:37 his will makes up his mind to keep his *v*,
7:38 the man who marries his *v*,
2Cor 11: 2 presenting you as a chaste *v* to Christ.

VIRGINAL (2)

Ez 23: 3 their bosoms and fondled their *v* breasts.
23: 8 fondling her *v* breasts and pouring out

VIRGINITY (5)

Dt 22:15 the girl shall take the evidence of her *v*
22:17 here is the evidence of my daughter's *v*!'
22:20 and evidence of the girl's *v* is not found,
Jgs 11:37 mountains to mourn my *v* with my
11:38 and mourned her *v* on the mountains.

VIRGINS (19)

Ex 22:16 pay him the customary marriage price for *v*.
Nm 31:35 thirty-two thousand girls who were still *v*.
Jgs 21:12 of Jabesh-gilead four hundred young *v*,
Jdt 16: 4 children a prey, and seize my *v* as spoil.
Est 2: 2 beautiful young *v* be sought for the king.
2: 3 *v* to the harem in the stronghold of Susa.
2:17 the *v* she won his favor and benevolence.
2:19 the time the *v* had been brought together,
1Mc 1:26 *V* and young men languished,
2Mc 5:13 and children, a slaughter of *v* and infants.
Ps(s) 45:15 her the *v* of her train are brought to you.
Is 23: 4 birth, nor raised young men, nor reared *v*."
Jer 31:13 Then the *v* shall make merry and dance,
Lam 1: 4 deserted, her priests groan, Her *v* sigh;
Ez 44:22 women, but only *v* of the race of Israel;
Am 8:13 *v* and young men shall faint from thirst;
Mt 25: 7 the *v* woke up and got their torches ready.
Lk 1:27 The *v* name was Mary.
1Cor 7:25 With respect to *v*,

VIRTUE (43)

2Chr 6:23 and rewarding him according to his *v*.
2Mc 6:31 courage and an unforgettable example of *v*
Prv 10: 2 profit nothing, but *v* saves from death.
11: 4 the day of wrath, but *v* saves from death.
11: 5 The honest man's *v* makes his way straight,
11: 6 The *v* of the upright saves them,
11:16 but she who hates *v* is covered with shame.
11:19 *V* directs toward life,
11:30 The fruit of *v* is a tree of life,
13: 6 *V* guards one who walks honestly,
14:34 *V* exalts a nation,
15: 9 LORD, but he loves the man who pursues *v*.
16: 8 Better a little with *v*,
20: 6 Many are declared to be men of *v*:
Sg 8:14 er *v* and boasts of having found welcome
Wis 4: 1 Better is childlessness with *v*;
5:13 to nought and held no sign of *v* to display,
Sir 17:17 cherishes like a signet ring, a man's *v*,
26:14 and her firm *v* is of surpassing worth.
49: 3 though times were evil, he practiced *v*.
Is 33:15 He who practices *v* and speaks honestly,
Ez 3:20 If a virtuous man turns away from *v* and
14:14 they could save only themselves by their *v*,
14:20 they would save only themselves by their *v*.
18:20 The virtuous man's *v* shall be his own,
18:22 live because of the *v* he has practiced.
18:24 turns from the path of *v* to do evil,
18:26 man turns away from *v* to commit iniquity,
33:12 The *v* which a man has practiced will not
33:13 he then presumes on his *v* and does wrong,
Rom 5: 4 for endurance, and endurance for tested *v*,
5: 4 for tested virtue, and tested *v* for hope.
12: 3 Thus, in *v* of the favor given to me,
Gal 3:18 is no longer conferred in *v* of the promise.
Eph 1:21 high above every principality, power, *v*,
2:11 *v* of a hand-executed rite on their flesh,
Heb 7:16 not in *v* of a law expressed in a
7:16 but in *v* of the power of a life which
1Pt 4:16 rather glorify God in *v* of that name.
2Pt 1: 4 By *v* of them he has bestowed on us the
1: 5 effort to undergird your *v* with faith,
1: 5 with faith, your discernment with *v*,
Rv 22:11 *v* and the holy ones in their holiness!

VIRTUES (4)

Wis 7:20 of men, uses of plants and *v* of roots
8: 7 justice, the fruits of her works are *v*;
Sir 44:10 godly men whose *v* have not been forgotten;
Col 3:14 Over all these *v* put on love,

VIRTUOUS (27)

Tb 2:14 Where are your *v* acts?
4:17 your bread and wine at the burial of the *v*,
2Mc 15:12 the former high priest, a good and *v* man,
15:12 trained from childhood in every *v* practice,
Prv 16:31 it is gained by *v* living.
Sir 11:15 love and *v* paths are from the LORD.
26:16 of a *v* wife is the radiance of her home.
28:15 A meddlesome tongue can drive *v* women from
39:24 For the *v* his paths are level,
41:11 but a *v* name will never be annihilated.
Ez 3:20 If a *v* man turns away from virtue and does
3:20 and his *v* deeds shall not be remembered;
3:21 hand, you have warned a *v* man not to sin,
18: 5 If a man is *v*—
18: 9 to observe my ordinances, that man is *v*—
18:20 The *v* man's virtue shall be his own,

18:24 And if the v man turns from the path of
18:24 None of his v deeds shall be remembered,
18:26 When a v man turns away from virtue to
21: 8 and cut off from you the v and the wicked.
33:12 from his wickedness [nor can the v man,
33:13 say to the v man that he shall surely live,
33:13 none of his v deeds shall be remembered;
33:18 When a v man turns away from what is right
Phil 4: 8 that is honest, pure, admirable, decent, v,
Rv 19: 8 linen dress is the v deeds of God's saints.)
22:11 The v must live on in their virtue and the

VIRTURE (1)

Prv 11:18 but he who sows v has a sure reward.

VIRULENT (1)

Lv 13:57 it is still v and the thing infected shall

VISAGE (1)

Dt 28:50 do not understand, a nation of stern v,

VISIBLE (8)

Ex 10: 5 so that the ground itself will not be v.
2Mc 12: 9 of the flames was v as far as Jerusalem,
Lk 3:22 descended on him in v form like a dove.
Rom 1:20 eternal power and divinity, have become v,
Col 1:16 earth was created, things v and invisible,
Heb 11: 3 is v came into being through the invisible.
1Jn 1: 1 (This life became v;
1: 1 present to the Father and became v to us.)

VISION (93)

Gn 15: 1 this word of the LORD came to Abram in a v:
16:13 a name, saying, "You are the God of V";
16:13 seen God and remained alive after my v?"
46: 2 God, speaking to Israel in a v by night,
1Sm 3: 1 of the LORD was uncommon and v infrequent.
3:15 He feared to tell Eli the v,
2Sm 7:17 all these words and this entire v to David.
1Chr 17:15 whole v Nathan related exactly to David.
2Chr 32:32 written in the V of the Prophet Isaiah,
Tb 12:19 what you were seeing was a v.
2Mc 5: 4 prayed that this v might be a good omen.
15:11 them all by relating a dream, a kind of v,
Jb 20: 8 he fades away like a v of the night.
33:15 In a dream, in a v of the night,
Ps(s) 89:20 Once you spoke in a v,
Eccl 11: 9 the ways of your heart, the v of your eyes;
Wis 15:15 gods, which have no use of the eyes for v,
Sir 34: 6 it be a v specially sent by the Most High,
42:23 even to the spark and the fleeting v!
43: 1 forth like heaven itself, a v of glory.
49: 8 EZEKIEL beheld the v and described the
Is 1: 1 The v which Isaiah,
13: 1 a v of Isaiah,
22: 1 Oracle of the Valley of V:
22: 5 Lord, the GOD of hosts, in the Valley of V.
29: 7 Then like a dream, a v in the night,
Lam 2: 9 have not received any v from the LORD.
2:14 for you in v false and misleading portents.
Ez 1:28 v of the likeness of the glory of the LORD.
7:26 Prophetic v shall fade;
8: 4 Israel, like the v I had seen in the plain.
11:24 me back to the exiles in Chaldea [in a v,
11:24 Then the v I had seen left me, :
12:22 drag on, and no v ever comes to anything"?
12:23 hand, and also the fulfillment of every v.
12:27 saying, "The v he sees is a long way off;
13: 3 follow their own spirit and have seen no v.
13: 7 Was not the v you saw false,
43: 3 The v was like that which I had seen when
Dn 2:19 the mystery was revealed to Daniel in a v,
2:31 "In your v, O king, you saw a statue,
4:10 In the v I saw while in bed,
4:20 As for the king's v of a holy sentinel
7: 2 In the v I saw during the night,
8: 1 After this first v, I, Daniel, had another
8: 2 In my v I saw myself in the fortress of
8:13 this v last concerning the daily sacrifice,
8:15 sought the meaning of the v I had seen,
8:16 out, "Gabriel, explain the v to this man."
8:17 of man, that the v refers to the end time."
8:26 The v of the evenings and the mornings is
8:26 Do you, however, keep this v undisclosed,
8:27 But I was appalled at the v,
9:21 the one whom I had seen before in v,
9:23 mark the answer and understand the v.
9:24 be introduced, v and prophecy ratified,
10: 1 a great war; he understood it from the v.
10: 7 I alone, Daniel, saw the v;
10: 7 although they did not see the v.
10: 8 So I was left alone, seeing this great v.
10:14 for there is yet a v concerning those days."
10:16 with pangs at the v and I was powerless.
11:14 people shall rise up in fulfillment of v,
Am 1: 1 which he received in v concerning Israel,
Ob 1: 1 The v of Obadiah.
Mi 1: 1 the v he received concerning Samaria and
3: 6 you shall have night, not v darkness,
Na 1: 1 The book of the v of Nahum of Elkosh.
Hb 1: 1 which Habakkuk the prophet received in v.
2: 2 Write down the v Clearly upon the tablets,
2: 3 For the v still has its time,
Zec 1: 8 I had a v during the night.
13: 4 shall be ashamed to prophesy his v,
Mt 17: 9 v until the Son of Man rises from the dead."
Lk 1:22 they realized that he had seen a v inside.
24:23 a v of angels who declared he was alive.
Acts 9:10 to whom the Lord had appeared in a v.
9:12 (Saul saw in a v a man named Ananias
10: 3 One afternoon at about three he had a v in
10:17 make out the meaning of the v he had had,
10:19 the v when the Spirit said to him:
11: 5 city of Joppa when, in a trance, I saw a v.
16: 9 There one night Paul had a v.
16:10 After this v,
18: 9 One night in a v the Lord said to Paul:
26:19 I could not disobey that heavenly v.
Eph 1:18 May he enlighten your innermost v that you
Rv 4: 1 After this I had another v:
5:11 As my v continued, I heard the voices
8:13 As my v continued, I heard an eagle
9:17 Now, in my v,
14: 1 Then the Lamb appeared in my v.
15: 5 After this I had another v.

VISIONARIES (1)

Jude 1: 8 Similarly, these v pollute the flesh;

VISIONARY (1)

Am 7:12 "Off with you, v,

VISIONS (37)

Nm 12: 6 you, in v will I reveal myself to him,
2Chr 9:29 v of Iddo the seer which concern Jeroboam,
Jb 4:13 In my thoughts during v of the night,
7:14 me with dreams and with v terrify me,
35:10 my Maker, who has given v in the night,
Wis 18:17 v in horrible dreams perturbed them and
Sir 48:22 prophet Isaiah, who saw the truth in v.
Is 28: 7 by strong drink, staggering in their v,
30:10 They say to the seers, "Have no v";
Jer 14:14 Lying v,
23:16 V of their own fancy they speak,
Lam 2:14 had for you false and specious v;
Ez 1: 1 the heavens opened, and I saw divine v.
8: 3 and brought me in divine v to Jerusalem,
12:24 There shall no longer be any false v or
13: 6 v are false and their divination lying.
13: 8 spoken falsehood and have seen lying v,
13: 9 who have false v and who foretell lies.
13:16 for it v of peace when there was no peace,
13:23 longer see false v and practice divination,
21:34 because you planned with false v and lying
22:28 pretending to v that are false and
40: 2 me in divine v to the land of Israel,
Dn 1:17 the understanding of all v and dreams.
4: 2 images and the v of my mind frightened me.
4: 6 meaning of the v that I saw in my dream.
4: 7 "These were the v I saw while in bed:
7: 1 and was terrified by the v of his mind.
7: 7 the v of the night I saw the fourth beast,
7:13 As the v during the night continued,
7:15 and I was terrified by the v of my mind.
Hos 12:11 I granted many v and spoke to the prophets,
Jl 3: 1 dream dreams, your young men shall see v;
Zec 10: 2 speak nonsense, the diviners have false v:
Acts 2:17 see v and your old men shall dream dreams.
2Cor 12: 1 and speak of v and revelations of the Lord.
Rv 1:19 down, therefore, whatever you see in v—

VISIT (59)

Gn 24:41 If you v my kindred and they refuse you,
34: 1 out to v some of the women of the land.
Dt 18: 6 in which he ordinarily resides, to v,
1Sm 16: 4 him and inquired, "Is your v peaceful,
20:29 well of me, give me leave to v my brothers.'
25: 5 Pay Nabal a v and greet him in my name.
2Sm 13: 5 When your father comes to v you,
13: 6 When the king came to v him,
15:14 then v disaster upon us and put the city
1Kgs 1:13 Go, v King David,
2Kgs 8: 9 Hazael went to v him,
8:29 to Jezreel to v him there in his illness.
9:16 Ahaziah, king of Judah, had come to v him.
10:13 "We are going down to v the princes and
13:14 King Joash of Israel went down to v him.
1Chr 13: 3 for in the days of Saul we did not v it."
2Chr 22: 6 king of Judah, went down to v Jehoram,
Jdt 8:10 Charmis, the elders of the city, to v her.
Est 2:12 Each girl went in turn to v King Ahasuerus
2:13 Then, when the girl was to v the king,
2:15 Mordecai, when her turn came to v the king,
2Mc 3: 8 v the cities of Coelesyria and Phoenicia,
9:17 he would become a Jew himself and v every
Ps(s) 106: 4 v me with your saving help,
Sir 7:35 Neglect not to v the sick
29:27 for my brother's v I need the room!"
Is 1:12 When you come in to v me,
23:17 of the seventy years the LORD shall v Tyre.
Jer 15:15 Remember me, LORD, v me,
29:10 will I v you and fulfill for you my promise
49:18 no one shall v there.
Am 3:14 crimes, I will v also the altars of Bethel:
Zep 2: 7 For the LORD their God shall v them,
Zec 10: 3 For the LORD of hosts will v his flock,
Mt 10: 5 "Do not v pagan territory and do not
25:36 me, in prison and you came to v me.'
25:39 we v you when you were ill or in prison?'
Lk 1:78 shall v us in his mercy To shine on those
10: 1 to every town and place he intended to v.
Jn 11:45 many of the Jews who had come to v Mary,
Acts 7:23 he was forty, he decided to v his kinsmen,
18: 2 Paul went to v the pair,
19:21 been there," he said, "I must v Rome too."
21:18 Paul and the rest of us paid a v to James
27: 3 to v some friends who cared for his needs.
28:17 men of the Jewish community to v him.
Rom 1:10 I may at last find my way clear to v you.
1:13 to know that I have often planned to v you
15:23 to v you which I have had for many years.
15:29 I am certain that when I do v you,
2Cor 1:15 I wanted to v you first so that a double
1:16 I planned to v you,
2: 1 to v you again in painful circumstances.
12:14 is the third time that I am about to v you,
2Thes 1: 6 v hardships on those who visit them on you.
1Tm 3:14 Although I hope to v you soon,
2Jn 1:12 to v you and talk with you face to face,
Rv 22:18 God will v him with all the plagues

VISITATION (8)

Wis 3: 7 In the time of their v they shall shine,
3:13 she shall bear fruit at the v of souls.
14:11 the idols of the nations shall a v come,
Sir 2:14 what will you do at the v of the LORD?
16:16 the earth and the abyss tremble at his v;
18:19 at the time of v you will have a ransom.
Lk 19:44 you failed to recognize the time of your v."
1Pt 2:12 they may give glory to God on the day of v.

VISITED (19)

Ex 2:11 when he v his kinsmen and witnessed their
Jgs 15: 1 of the wheat harvest, Samson v his wife,
16: 1 to Gaza, where he saw a harlot and v her.
Ru 1: 6 LORD had v his people and given them food.
2Sm 16:22 and he v his father's concubines in view
1Kgs 1:15 So Bathsheba v the king in his room,
14:28 Whenever the king v the temple of the LORD,
2Kgs 7:17 of God had predicted when the king v him.
1Chr 7:23 had come and comforted him, he v his wife,
2Chr 12:11 Whenever the king v the temple of the LORD,
Ezr 5: 8 king that we have v the province of Judah
Jdt 15: 9 When they had v her,
Ps(s) 65:10 You have v the land and watered it;
Prv 19:23 and sleeps without being v by misfortune.
Sir 46:14 nation, when he v the encampments of Jacob.
Is 29: 6 you shall be v by the LORD of hosts,
Zep 3: 7 not fail to see all I have v upon her.
Lk 1:68 because he has v and ransomed his people.
7:16 and, "God has v his people."

VISITING (2)

Nm 22: 9 Balaam and said, "Who are these men v you?"
Rom 15:22 I have so often been hindered from v you.

VISITOR (3)

2Sm 12: 4 Now, the rich man received a v,
12: 4 ewe lamb and made a meal of it for his v."
Sir 29:25 The v has no thanks for filling the cups;

VISITORS (4)

Jos 2: 3 out the v who have entered your house,
Wis 19:14 those others did not receive unfamiliar v,
Acts 2:10 There are even v from Rome
1Tm 5:10 Has she washed the feet of Christian v?

VISITS (2)

2Kgs 4: 9 Since he v us often,
2Mc 9:25 I made hurried v to the outlying provinces.

VITAL (1)

Wis 15:11 a quickening soul, and infused a v spirit.

VIVID (1)

Sir 38:27 His care is to produce a v impression,

VIZIER (4)

Gn 41:43 then had him ride in the chariot of his v,
1Kgs 18: 4 and Ahab had summoned Obadiah, his v,
2Kgs 10: 5 So the v and the ruler of the city,
15: 5 v and regent for the people of the land.

VOICE (301)

Gn 4:23 "Adah and Zillah, hear my v;
27:22 him, he said, "Although the v is Jacob's,
Ex 15:26 you really listen to the v of the LORD,
19: 5 you hearken to my v and keep my covenant,
23:21 Be attentive to him and heed his v.

VOICE (cont.)
23:22 heed his *v* and carry out all I tell you,
24: 3 of the LORD, they all answered with one *v*,
Nm 7:89 he heard the *v* addressing him from above
14:22 already and have failed to heed my *v*,
23: 7 Then Balaam gave *v* to his oracle:
23:18 Balaam gave *v* to his oracle:
24: 3 came upon him, and he gave *v* to his oracle:
24:15 Then Balaam gave *v* to his oracle:
24:20 seeing Amalek, Balaam gave *v* to his oracle:
24:21 the Kenites, he gave *v* to his oracle:
24:23 he gave *v* to his oracle:
Dt 4:12 there was only a *v*.
4:30 to the LORD, your God, and heed his *v*.
4:33 *v* of God speaking from the midst of fire,
4:36 he let you hear his *v* to discipline you;
5:22 the LORD spoke with a loud *v* to your
5:23 heard the *v* from the midst of the darkness,
5:24 We have heard his *v* from the midst of the
5:25 If we hear the *v* of the LORD,
5:26 the *v* of the living God speaking from the
8:20 perish for not heeding the *v* of the LORD,
13: 5 you observe, and his *v* shall you heed,
13:19 because you have heeded the *v* of the LORD,
15: 5 If you but heed the *v* of the LORD,
18:16 'Let us not again hear the *v* of the LORD,
26:14 I have thus hearkened to the *v* of the LORD,
26:17 and decrees, and to hearken to his *v*.
27:10 therefore hearken to the *v* of the LORD,
28: 1 if you continue to heed the *v* of the LORD,
28: 2 When you hearken to the *v* of the LORD,
28:15 if you do not hearken to the *v* of the LORD,
28:45 you would not hearken to the *v* of the LORD,
28:62 you would not hearken to the *v* of the LORD,
30: 2 *v* with all your heart and all your soul,
30: 8 must again heed the LORD's *v* and carry out
30:10 if only you heed the *v* of the LORD,
30:20 loving the LORD, your God, heeding his *v*,
Jos 10:14 this, when the LORD obeyed the *v* of a man;
24:24 serve the LORD, our God, and obey his *v*."
Jgs 9: 7 there, cried out to them in a loud *v*:
18: 3 they recognized the *v* of the young Levite
1Sm 1:13 lips were moving, her *v* could not be heard.
24:17 to Saul, Saul answered, "Is that your *v*,
26:17 Saul recognized David's *v* and asked,
26:17 David's voice and asked, "Is that your *v*,
28:12 at the top of her *v* and said to Saul,
2Sm 19: 5 covered his face and cried out in a loud *v*,
22: 7 From his temple he heard my *v*,
22:14 the Most High gave forth his *v*.
1Kgs 8:55 community of Israel, saying in a loud *v*:
19:13 A *v* said to him,
20:36 "Since you did not obey the *v* of the LORD,
2Kgs 7:10 not a human *v*,
18:28 and cried out in a loud *v* in Judean,
19:22 your *v* And lifted up your eyes on high?
2Chr 5:13 *v* praising and giving thanks to the LORD,
15:14 They swore to the LORD with a loud *v* with
30:27 their *v* was heard and their prayer reached
32:18 In a loud *v* they shouted in the Judean
Ezr 10:12 the whole assembly cried out with a loud *v*:
Neh 9: 4 out to the LORD their God, with a loud *v*.
Tb 5:10 I can hear a man's *v*,
11:15 in, rejoicing and praising God with full *v*.
13: 6 done for you, and praise him with full *v*.
Jdt 9: 1 Judith prayed to the Lord with a loud *v*:
13:12 When the citizens heard her *v*,
13:14 the two, Judith urged them with a loud *v*:
Est C:30 than all, hear the *v* of those in despair.
1Mc 2:19 But Mattathias answered in a loud *v*:
Jb 3:18 and hear not the *v* of the slave driver.
4:16 was before my eyes, and I heard a still *v*:
29:10 The *v* of the princes was silenced,
30:28 I rise up in public to *v* my grief.
33: 2 my tongue and my *v* form words.
37: 2 angry *v* as it rumbles forth from his mouth!
37: 4 Again his *v* roars
38:34 Can you raise your *v* among the clouds,
40: 9 God, or can you thunder with a *v* like his?
Ps(s) 5: 4 at dawn you hear my *v*;
18: 7 From his temple he heard my *v*,
18:14 heaven, the Most High gave forth his *v*;
19: 4 word nor a discourse whose *v* is not heard;
19: 5 Through all the earth their *v* resounds,
26: 7 your altar, O LORD, Giving *v* to my thanks,
29: 3 The *v* of the LORD is over the waters,
29: 4 The *v* of the LORD is mighty;
29: 4 the *v* of the LORD is majestic.
29: 5 The *v* of the LORD breaks the cedars,
29: 7 The *v* of the LORD strikes fiery flames;
29: 8 the *v* of the LORD shakes the desert,
29: 9 The *v* of the LORD twists the oaks and
41: 7 when he leaves he gives *v* to it outside.
44:17 At the *v* of him who mocks and blasphemes,
46: 7 turmoil, kingdoms totter, his *v* resounds,
55: 4 and am troubled at the *v* of the enemy and
55:18 grieve and moan, and he will hear my *v*.
58: 6 *v* of enchanters casting cunning spells.
64: 2 Hear, O God, my *v* in my lament;
68:34 Behold, his voice resounds, the *v* of power:
74:23 Be not unmindful of the *v* of your foes;
77:18 the skies gave forth their *v*;
81:12 "But my people heard not my *v*,
93: 3 up, O LORD, the floods lift up their *v*;
95: 7 Oh, that today you would hear his *v*:
106:25 tents, and obeyed not the *v* of the LORD.
116: 1 because he has heard my *v* in supplication,
119:149 Hear my *v* according to your kindness,
130: 1 Lord, hear my *v*!
130: 2 ears be attentive to my *v* in supplication:
140: 7 hearken, O LORD, to my *v* in supplication.
141: 1 hearken to my *v* when I call upon you.
142: 2 With a loud *v* I cry out to the LORD;
142: 2 with a loud *v* I beseech the LORD.
Prv 1:20 in the open squares she raises her *v*;
2: 3 and to understanding raise your *v*;
5:13 did I not listen to the *v* of my teachers,
8: 1 Wisdom call, and Understanding raise her *v*?
27:14 greets his neighbor with a loud *v* in the early
Eccl 10:20 the birds of the air may carry your *v*,
Sg 2:14 Let me see you, let me hear your *v*,
2:14 me hear your voice, For your *v* is sweet,
8:13 my friends are listening for your *v*,
Sir 17:11 beheld, his glorious *v* their ears heard.
21:20 A fool raises his *v* in laughter,
34:24 another curses, whose *v* will the Lord hear?
40:21 but better than either, a *v* that is true.
43:16 thunder of his *v* makes the earth writhe;
45: 5 He permitted him to hear his *v*,
46:17 and the tremendous roar of his *v* was heard.
46:20 the grave he raised his *v* as a prophet,
51: 9 So I raised my *v* from the very earth,
51:11 Thereupon the LORD heard my *v*,
Is 6: 8 Then I heard the *v* of the Lord saying,
24:14 These lift up their *v* in acclaim;
28:23 Give ear and hear my *v*,
29: 4 *v* shall be like a ghost's from the earth,
30:21 from behind, a *v* shall sound in your ears:
30:30 The LORD will make his glorious *v* heard,
32: 9 complacent ladies, rise up and hear my *v*,
36:13 and cried out in a loud *v* in Judean,
37:23 your *v* And lifted up your eyes on high?
40: 3 A *v* cries out: In the desert prepare
40: 6 A *v* says, "Cry out!"
40: 9 Cry out at the top of your *v*,
42: 2 not making his *v* heard in the street.
50:10 you fears the LORD, heeds his servant's *v*,
58: 1 lift up your *v* like a trumpet blast;
58: 4 fast so as to make your *v* heard on high!
Jer 3:13 green tree] and would not listen to my *v*,
3:25 we listened not to the *v* of the LORD,
7:23 Listen to my *v*;
7:27 which does not listen to the *v* of the LORD,
7:34 the *v* of the bridegroom and the voice of
7:34 of the bridegroom and the *v* of the bride;
9:12 have not followed it or listened to my *v*,
11: 4 to my *v* and do all that I command you.
11: 7 I warned your fathers to obey my *v*,
16: 9 the *v* of the bridegroom and the voice of
16: 9 of the bridegroom and the *v* of the bride.
18:10 is evil in my eyes, refusing to obey my *v*,
22:20 and cry out, in Bashan lift up your *v*;
22:21 way from your youth, not to listen to my *v*.
25:10 the *v* of the bridegroom and the voice of
25:30 from his holy dwelling he raises his *v*;
26:13 listen to the *v* of the LORD your God,
32:23 of it, but they did not listen to your *v*;
33:11 cry of gladness, the *v* of the bridegroom,
33:11 of the bridegroom, the *v* of the bride,
38:20 the *v* of the LORD and do as I tell you;
40: 3 against the LORD and did not obey his *v*,
42:13 But if you disobey the *v* of the LORD,
42:21 message, but you obey the *v* of the LORD,
44:23 the LORD, not obeying the *v* of the LORD,
Bar 1:18 We have neither heeded the *v* of the Lord,
1:19 God, and only too ready to disregard his *v*.
1:21 For we did not heed the *v* of the Lord,
2: 5 the Lord, our God, not heeding his *v*.
2:10 us to do, but we did not heed his *v*,
2:22 *v* so as to serve the king of Babylon.
2:23 the *v* of the bridegroom and the voice of
2:23 of the bridegroom and the *v* of the bride;
2:24 But we did not heed your *v*,
2:29 If you do not heed my *v*,
3: 4 they did not heed the *v* of the Lord,
Ez 1:24 mighty waters, like the *v* of the Almighty.
10: 5 the *v* of God the Almighty when he speaks.
11:13 I fell prone and cried out in a loud *v*;
19: 9 So that his *v* would not be heard on the
21:27 slaying, to raise his *v* in the battle cry,
27:30 shore, Making their *v* heard on your behalf,
33:32 with a pleasant *v* and a clever touch.
43: 7 The *v* said to me: Son of man, this is
Dn 3:51 these three in the furnace with one *v* sang,
4:28 on the king's lips, a *v* spoke from heaven,
8:16 the Ulai I heard a human *v* that cried out,
9:11 law and went astray, not heeding your *v*,
9:14 have done, for we did not listen to your *v*.
10: 6 his *v* sounded like the roar of a multitude.
10: 9 When I heard the sound of his *v*,
Jl 2:11 LORD raises his *v* at the head of his army;
4:16 Zion, and from Jerusalem raises his *v*;
Am 1: 2 from Zion, and from Jerusalem raise his *v*:
Jon 2: 3 world I cried for help, and you heard my *v*.
Mi 6: 1 mountains, and let the hills hear your *v*!
Zep 3: 2 She hears no *v*, accepts no correction;
Hg 1:12 the people listened to the *v* of the LORD,
Zec 6:15 heed carefully the *v* of the LORD your God.
Mt 3: 3 "A herald's *v* in the desert;
3:17 With that, a *v* from the heavens said,
12:19 nor will his *v* be heard in the streets.
17: 5 Out of the cloud came a *v* which said,
27:50 Once again Jesus cried out in a loud *v*,
Mk 1: 3 a herald's *v* in the desert,
1:11 Then a *v* came from the heavens:
5: 7 and did him homage, shrieking in a loud *v*,
9: 7 them, and out of the cloud a *v*:
15:34 At that time Jesus cried in a loud *v*,
Lk 1:42 the Holy Spirit and cried out in a loud *v*:
3: 4 "A herald's *v* in the desert,
3:22 A *v* from heaven was heard to say:
4:33 unclean spirit, who shrieked in a loud *v*:
8:28 feet and exclaimed at the top of his *v*,
9:35 Then from the cloud came a *v* which said,
9:36 When the *v* fell silent,
17:15 cured, came back praising God in a loud *v*.
Jn 1:23 prophet Isaiah, "I am 'a *v* in the desert,
3:29 for him and is overjoyed to hear his *v*.
5:25 dead shall hear the *v* of the Son of God,
5:28 tombs shall hear his *v* and come forth.
5:37 His *v* you have never heard,
10: 3 The sheep hear his *v* as he calls his own
10: 4 follow him because they recognize his *v*.
10: 5 they do not recognize a stranger's *v*."
10:16 lead them, too, and they shall hear my *v*.
10:27 My sheep hear my *v*.
12:28 Then a *v* came from the sky:
12:29 When the crowd of bystanders heard the *v*,
12:30 "That *v* did not come for my sake,
18:37 Anyone committed to the truth hears my *v*."
Acts 2:14 stood up with the Eleven, raised his *v*,
7:31 it carefully, the *v* of the Lord was heard:
7:60 to his knees and cried out in a loud *v*,
9: 4 and at the same time heard a *v* saying,
9: 5 The *v* answered, "I am Jesus,
9: 7 They had heard the *v* but could see no one.
10:13 A *v* said to him: "Get up, Peter!
10:15 The *v* was heard a second time:
11: 7 I listened as a *v* said to me,
11: 9 time the *v* from the heavens spoke out:
12:14 On recognizing his *v* she was so overjoyed
12:22 shouted back, "This is the *v* of a god,
14:10 He called out to him in a loud *v*,
22: 7 fell to the ground and heard a *v* say to me,
22: 9 but did not hear the *v* speaking to me.
22:14 Just One, and to hear the sound of his *v*;
26:14 and I heard a *v* saying to me in Hebrew,
Rom 10:18 "their *v* has sounded over the whole earth,
15: 6 with one heart and *v* you may glorify God,
1Thes 4:16 of the archangel's *v* and God's trumpet;
Heb 3: 7 "Today, if you should hear his *v*,
3:15 says, "Today, if you should hear his *v*,
3:16 those that revolted when they heard that *v*?
4: 7 "Today, if you should hear his *v*,
12:19 nor a *v* speaking words such that those who
12:26 His *v* then shook the earth,
2Pt 2:16 human *v* to restrain the prophet's madness.
Rv 1:10 a piercing *v* like the sound of a trumpet,
1:12 to see whose *v* it was that spoke to me.
1:15 *v* sounded like the roar of rushing waters.
4: 1 *v* which had spoken to me before.
5: 2 a mighty angel who proclaimed in a loud *v*:
6: 1 creatures cry out in a *v* like thunder,
6: 6 I heard what seemed to be a *v* coming from
6: 7 *v* of the fourth living creature cry out,
7: 2 He cried out at the top of his *v* to the
7:10 They cried out in a loud *v*,
8:13 flying in midheaven cry out in a loud *v*,
9:13 and I heard a *v* coming from between the
10: 4 spoke, but I heard a *v* from heaven say,
10: 8 Then the *v* which I heard from heaven spoke
11:12 heard a loud *v* from heaven say to them,
12:10 Then I heard a loud *v* in heaven say:
14: 7 He said in a loud *v*:
14: 9 followed the others and said in a loud *v*:
14:13 I heard a *v* from heaven say to me:
14:15 *v* cried out to him who sat on the cloud,
14:18 *v* to the one who held the sharp sickle,
16: 1 I heard a mighty *v* from the sanctuary say
16:17 in the sanctuary came a loud *v* which said,
18: 2 He cried out in a strong *v*:
18: 4 Then I heard another *v* from heaven say:
19: 5 A *v* coming from the throne cried out:
19:17 *v* to all the birds flying in midheaven.
21: 3 I heard a loud *v* from the throne cry out:

VOICED (1)

Neh 6:12 he *v* this prophecy concerning me that I

VOICES (15)

Jgs 21: 2 evening, raising their *v* in bitter lament.
2Sm 19:36 the *v* of singers and songstresses?
Ezr 3:12 lifted up their *v* in shouts of joy,
1Mc 13:45 garments rent, and cried out in loud *v*,
Wis 18: 1 heard their *v* but did not see their forms,
Sir 43:31 Lift up your *v* to glorify the LORD,
Mt 18:19 *v* on earth to pray for anything whatever,
Lk 17:13 distance, they raised their *v* and said,

Acts 4:24 v in prayer to God on hearing the story:
Rv 5:11 I heard the v of many angels who
5:13 Then I heard the v of every creature in
6:10 They cried out at the top of their v:
10: 3 the seven thunders raised their v too.
11:15 Loud v in heaven cried out,
18:23 No v of bride and groom shall ever again

VOID (13)

Lv 26:44 them out, I make v my covenant with them;
Nm 30: 6 pledge she has made becomes null and v;
30:13 vow or in her pledge becomes null and v;
30:14 allow to remain valid or render null and v.
Sir 41:10 nought, so too the godless from v to void.
Is 40:17 nought, as nothing and v he accounts them.
55:11 It shall not return to me v,
Jer 4:23 at the earth, and it was waste and v;
Dn 3:34 us up forever, or make v your covenant.
Mal 2: 8 You have made v the covenant of Levi,
1Cor 1:17 of Christ be rendered v of its meaning!
15:14 v of content and your faith is empty too.

VOLUMES (1)

2Mc 2:23 of Cyrene set forth in detail in five v,

VOLUNTARILY (1)

2Cor 8: 3 and v,

VOLUNTARY (2)

Ex 35:29 LORD such v offerings as they thought best,
36: 3 to bring their v offerings to Moses.

VOLUNTEERS (1)

Is 13: 2 Wave for them to enter the gates of the v.

VOLUPTUOUS (1)

Is 47: 8 Now hear this v one,

VOMIT (10)

Lv 18:25 by making it v out its inhabitants.
18:28 will v you out also for having defiled it,
20:22 I am bringing you to dwell will v you out.
Prv 23: 8 The little you have eaten you will v up,
25:16 you become glutted with it and v it up.
26:11 As the dog returns to his v,
Is 19:14 she does, as a drunkard staggers in his v.
28: 8 all the tables are covered with filthy v,
Jer 25:27 become drunk and v;
2Pt 2:22 "The dog returns to its v,"

VOMITED (1)

Lv 18:28 just as it v out the nations before you.

VOMITS (1)

Jer 48:26 make Moab drunk so that he retches and v,

VOPHSI (1)

Nm 13:14 son of V, of the tribe of Naphtali;

VOTE (3)

2Mc 12: 4 this was done by public v of the city.
15:36 By public v it was unanimously decreed
Acts 26:10 be put to death I cast my v against them.

VOTED (1)

1Mc 14:23 have v to receive the men with honor,

VOTIVE (18)

Lv 7:16 sacrifice is a v or a freewill offering,
22:18 brings a holocaust as a v offering or as a
22:23 it will not be acceptable as a v offering.
23:38 your various v offerings and the freewill
Nm 29:39 present as your v or freewill offerings."
Dt 12: 6 your v and freewill offerings,
12:26 gifts or v offerings that you may have,
23:19 of v offering in the house of the LORD,
23:24 your solemn word and fulfill the v offering
1Kgs 15:15 father's and his own v offerings of silver,
1Chr 26:20 house of God and the stores of v offerings.
26:26 of the v offerings dedicated by King David,
28:12 of God and the stores of the v offerings,
2Chr 15:18 God his father's v offerings and his own:
Jdt 4:14 the daily holocaust, the v offerings,
16:19 Judith dedicated, as a v offering to God,
2Mc 5:16 v offerings made by other kings for
Lk 21: 5 with precious stones and v offerings.

VOW (45)

Gn 28:20 Jacob then made this v:
31:13 a memorial stone and made a v to me.
Lv 22:21 herd or the flock in fulfillment of a v,
27: 2 When anyone fulfills a v of offering one
27: 8 the v is too poor to meet the fixed sum,
27: 8 with the means of the one who made the v.
27:26 the LORD, may not be dedicated by v to him.
Nm 6: 2 nazirite v to dedicate himself to the LORD,
6: 5 While he is under the nazirite v,
6:21 which is included in his v of dedication
6:21 in keeping with the v he has taken."
15: 3 in holocaust, in fulfillment of a v,
15: 8 as a holocaust, or in fulfillment of a v,
21: 2 Israel then made this v to the LORD:
30: 3 When a man makes a v to the LORD or binds
30: 4 her father's house, makes a v to the LORD,
30: 5 if her father learns of her v or the
30: 5 v or any pledge she has made remains valid.
30: 6 then any v or any pledge she has made
30: 7 "If she marries while under a v or under
30: 8 the v or pledge she had made remains valid.
30: 9 he thereby annuls the v she had made or
30:10 The v of a widow or of a divorced woman,
30:11 v or binds herself under oath to a pledge,
30:12 v or any pledge she has made remains valid.
30:13 v or in her pledge becomes null and void;
30:14 "Any v or any pledge that she makes under
30:15 as valid any v or any pledge she has made;
Dt 23:22 "When you make a v to the LORD,
23:23 Should you refrain from making a v,
Jgs 11:30 Jephthah made a v to the LORD.
11:35 made a v to the LORD and I cannot retract."
11:36 replied, "you have made a v to the LORD.
1Sm 1:11 LORD, weeping copiously, and she made a v,
2: 8 He gives to the vower his v,
2Sm 15: 7 Hebron and fulfill a v I made to the LORD.
15: 8 Geshur in Aram, your servant made this v:
Prv 20:25 trap for a man, or to regret a v once made.
Eccl 5: 3 When you make a v to God,
5: 4 make a v than make it and not fulfill it.
Sir 18:23 making a v have the means to fulfill it;
Bar 6:34 if one fails to fulfill a v to them,
Mal 1:14 his v sacrifices to the LORD a gelding;
Acts 18:18 his head because of a v he had taken.
21:23 are four men among us who have made a v.

VOWED (12)

Lv 27: 9 "If the offering v to the LORD is an
27: 9 every such animal, when v to the LORD,
27:11 If the animal v to the LORD is unclean and
Dt 12:11 special offering you have v to the LORD.
12:17 herd or flock, of any offering you have v,
Jgs 11:36 Do with me as you have v,
11:39 to her father, who did to her as he had v.
1Mc 5: 5 he v their annihilation and burned down
2Mc 9:13 Then this vile man v to the Lord,
Ps(s) 132: 2 to the LORD, v to the Mighty One of Jacob:
Eccl 5: 3 fulfill what you have v.
Jon 2:10 What I have v I will pay:

VOWER (1)

1Sm 2: 8 He gives to the v his vow,

VOWS (24)

Lv 27:28 which a man v as doomed to the LORD,
1Sm 1:21 to the LORD and to fulfill his v,
1Mc 3:49 who had completed the time of their v.
2Mc 3:35 solemn v to him who had spared his life,
Jb 22:27 hear you, and your v you shall fulfill.
Ps(s) 22:26 fulfill my v before those who fear him.
50:14 and fulfill your v to the Most High;
56:13 I am bound, O God, by v to you;
61: 6 You indeed, O God, have accepted my v;
61: 9 name forever, fulfilling my v day by day.
65: 2 To you must v be fulfilled,
66:13 to you I will fulfill the v Which my
76:12 Make v to the LORD,
116:14 My v to the LORD I will pay in the
116:18 My v to the LORD I will pay in the
Prv 7:14 and today I have fulfilled my v;
31: 2 what, O son of my v!
Sir 18:22 prevent the prompt payment of your v;
Is 19:21 and fulfill the v they make to the LORD.
Jer 11:15 Can v and sacred meat turn away your
44:25 "We will continue to fulfill the v we
44:25 keep your v, carry out your resolutions!
Jon 1:16 men offered sacrifice and made v to him.
Na 2: 1 your feasts, O Judah, fulfill your v!

VOYAGE (3)

Wis 14: 1 one preparing for a v and about to
Acts 21: 7 our v from Tyre we put in at Ptolemais,
27:10 I can see that this v is bound to meet

VULTURE (3)

Lv 11:13 the eagle, the v,
Dt 14:12 the eagle, the v,
Ps(s) 74:19 Give not to the v the life of your dove;

VULTURES (6)

2Mc 9:15 children to be eaten by v and wild animals;
Jb 15:23 A wanderer, food for the v,
Sir 43:14 opened, and like v the clouds hurry forth.
Jer 12: 9 is a prey for hyenas, is surrounded by v;
Mt 24:28 Where the carcass lies, there the v gather.
Lk 17:37 the carcass is, there will the v gather."

W

WADE (4)

Ez 47: 3 cubits and had me w through the water,
47: 4 and once more had me w through the water,
47: 4 he measured off a thousand and had me w;
47: 5 now a river through which I could not w;

WADED (1)

Jos 3:15 w into the waters at the edge of the Jordan,

WADI (68)

Gn 15:18 from the W of Egypt to the Great River
26:17 and made the W Gerar his regular campsite.
26:19 w and reached spring water in their well,
Nm 13:23 They also reached the W Eshcol,
13:24 there that they called the place W Eshcol.
21:12 from there, they encamped in the W Zered.
21:15 Arnon and the w gorges That reach back
32: 9 the W Eshcol and reconnoitered the land,
34: 5 and turning from Azmon to the W of Egypt,
Dt 1:24 the hill country as far as the W Eshcol,
2:13 Get ready, then, to cross the W Zered.'
2:24 "'Advance now across the W Arnon.
2:36 From Aroer on the edge of the W Arnon and
2:36 Arnon and from the city in the w itself,
2:37 the region bordering on the W Jabbok,
3: 8 from the W Arnon to Mount Hermon
3:12 from Aroer, on the edge of the W Arnon,
3:16 Gilead to the W Arnon—including the w
3:16 and to the W Jabbok,
4:48 from Aroer on the edge of the W Arnon to
9:21 into the w that went down the mountainside.
21: 4 and bringing it down to a w with an
21: 4 cut the heifer's throat there in the w.
21: 6 the heifer whose throat was cut in the w,
Jos 12: 2 of the Wadi Arnon, to include the w itself,
12: 2 through half of Gilead to the W Jabbok,
13: 9 W Arnon and the city in the wadi itself,
13: 9 Wadi Arnon and the city in the w itself,
13:16 Wadi Arnon, and the city in the w itself,
15: 4 W of Egypt before coming out at the sea.
15: 7 of Adummim, on the south side of the w;
15:47 W of Egypt and the coast of the Great Sea.
16: 8 to the W Kanah and ended at the sea.
17: 9 boundary continued down to the W Kanah.
17: 9 were those to the south of that w;
17: 9 ran north of the w and ended at the sea.
19:11 Dabbesheth and the w that is near Jokneam.
Jgs 4: 7 Jabin's army, out to you at the W Kishon,
4:13 from Harosheth-ha-goiim at the W Kishon
5:21 The W Kishon swept them away; a wadi
16: 4 in the W Sorek whose name was Delilah.
1Sm 15: 5 and after setting an ambush in the w,
17:40 selected five smooth stones from the w
30: 9 hundred men and came as far as the W Besor,
30:10 to cross the W Besor and remained behind.
30:21 and whom he had left behind at the W Besor,
2Sm 24: 5 near Aroer, south of the city in the w,
1Kgs 8:65 from Labo of Hamath to the W of Egypt,
17: 3 here, go east and hide in the W Cherith,
17: 5 He went and remained by the W Cherith,
2Kgs 3:16 LORD, 'Provide many catch basins in this w.'
3:17 this w will be filled with water for you,
24: 7 from the W of Egypt to the Euphrates River.
2Chr 7: 8 from Labo of Hamath to the W of Egypt,
20:16 w which opens on the wilderness of Jeruel.
Neh 2:15 I continued on foot up the w by night,
Jdt 2:24 every fortified city along the W Abron,
7:18 Egrebel, near Chusi, which is on W Mochmur.
Sir 40:13 out of wickedness is like a w in spate:
Is 27:12 between the Euphrates and the W of Egypt,
57: 6 the smooth stones of the w is your portion,
Ez 47:19 Meribath-kadesh, thence to the W of Egypt,
48:28 and from there to the W of Egypt,
Am 6:14 from Labo of Hamath even to the W Arabah.

WADIES (5)

Dt 10: 7 a region where there is water in the w
Jdt 2: 8 slain shall fill their ravines and w,
Jb 6:15 as watercourses that run dry in the w;
30: 6 To dwell on the slopes of the w,
Is 57: 5 You who immolate children in the w,

WAFER (2)

Lv 8:26 loaf of bread made with oil, and one w;
Nm 6:19 cake and one unleavened w from the basket,

WAFERS (7)

Ex 16:31 and it tasted like w made with honey.
29: 2 with oil, and unleavened w spread with oil,
29:23 the cakes made with oil, and one of the w.
Lv 2: 4 oil, or of unleavened w spread with oil.
7:12 with oil, unleavened w spread with oil,
Nm 6:15 oil and of unleavened w spread with oil.
1Chr 23:29 offering, of the w of unleavened bread,

WAFT (1)

Jb 31:27 enticed to w them a kiss with my hand;

WAG (3)
Jb 16: 4 declaim over you, or w my head at you;
Ps(s) 22: 8 me with parted lips, they w their heads:
Lam 2:15 and w their heads over daughter Jerusalem:

WAGE (16)
Jos 11:20 to encourage them to w war against Israel,
1Mc 8:26 and to those who w war they shall not give
15:19 or w war against them or their cities or
Prv 20:18 so with wise guidance w your war.
24: 6 it is by wise guidance that you w your war,
Eccl 4: 9 they get a good w for their labor.
Is 31: 4 w war upon the mountain and hill of Zion.
Zec 10: 5 shall w war because the LORD is with them,
Mt 20: 2 agreement with them for the usual daily w,
20:11 yet they received the same daily w.
20:13 You agreed on the usual w, did you not?
Lk 10: 7 they have, for the laborer is worth his w.
2Cor 10: 3 but we do not w war with human resources.
1Pt 2:11 By their nature they w war on the soul.
Rv 11: 7 w war against them and conquer and kill
13: 7 The beast was allowed to w war against

WAGED (12)
Ex 17: 8 Amalek came and w war against Israel.
Nm 31: 7 They w war against the Midianites,
Jos 11:18 Joshua w war against all these kings for a
1Sm 14:47 w war on all their surrounding enemies
14:52 An unremitting war was w against the
1Chr 5:10 reign of Saul they w war with the Hagrites,
5:19 When they w war against the Hagrites and
18:10 w a victorious war against Hadadezer;
22: 8 shed much blood, and you have w great wars.
2Chr 14: 5 war was w against him during these years,
Jdt 1: 5 Then King Nebuchadnezzar w war against
Ps(s) 27: 3 Though war be w upon me,

WAGER (2)
2Kgs 18:23 "Now, make a w with my lord,
Is 36: 8 make a w with my lord the king of Assyria:

WAGES (39)
Gn 29:15 Tell me what your w should be."
30:28 continued, "state what w you want from me,
30:32 Only such animals shall be my w.
30:33 whenever you check on these w of mine,
31: 7 me and changed my w time after time.
31: 8 'The speckled animals shall be your w,'
31: 8 'The streaked animals shall be your w,'
31:41 while you changed my w time after time.
Lv 19:13 overnight the w of your day laborer.
Dt 24:15 day's w before sundown on the day itself,
Tb 2:14 given to me as a bonus over and above my w."
4:14 the w of any man who works for you,
5:15 you are away I will give you the normal w,
5:16 my son, I will even add a bonus to your w!"
12: 5 w half of all that you have brought back,
2Mc 15:33 other w of his folly opposite the temple.
Jb 7: 2 the shade, a hireling who waits for his w.
Sir 34:22 sheds blood who denies the laborer his w.
40:17 Wealth or w can make life sweet,
Is 55: 2 your w for what fails to satisfy?
Jer 22:13 neighbor without pay, and gives him no w.
Ez 29:18 neither he nor his army received any w
29:19 and pillaging it for the w of his soldiers,
Mi 1: 7 all her w shall be burned in the fire,
1: 7 As the w of a harlot they were gathered,
1: 7 and to the w of a harlot shall they return.
Hg 1: 6 w earned them for a bag with holes in it.
Zec 8:10 before those days there were no w for men,
11:12 "If it seems good to you, give me my w;
11:12 And they counted out my w,
Mal 3: 5 those who defraud the hired man of his w,
Mk 6:37 two hundred days' w for bread to feed them?"
Jn 4:36 his w and gathers a yield for eternal life,
6: 7 "Not even with two hundred days' w
Rom 4: 4 his w are not regarded as a favor but as
6:23 The w of sin is death,
1Cor 3: 8 receive his w in proportion to his toil.
1Tm 5:18 and also, "The worker deserves his w."
Jas 5: 4 are the w you withheld from the farmhands

WAGING (3)
1Sm 28:15 w war against me and God has abandoned me.
2Kgs 6: 8 When the king of Aram was w war on Israel,
Rv 19:11 standard in passing judgment and in w war.

WAGON (2)
Nm 7: 3 oxen, that is, a w for every two princes,
Am 2:13 as a w crushes when laden with sheaves.

WAGONS (10)
Gn 45:19 Take w from the land of Egypt for your
45:21 Joseph gave them the w,
45:27 w that Joseph had sent for his transport,
46: 5 w that Pharaoh had sent for his transport.
Nm 7: 3 consisted of six baggage w and twelve oxen,
7: 6 So Moses accepted the w and oxen,
7: 7 He gave two w and four oxen to the
7: 8 and four w and eight oxen to the Merarites
Jdt 15:11 harnessed her mules, hitched her w to them,
Ez 23:24 north with chariots and w and many peoples.

WAGS (2)
2Kgs 19:21 Behind you she w her head,
Is 37:22 Behind you she w her head,

WAHEB (1)
Nm 21:14 W in Suphah and the waidies,

WAIDIES (1)
Nm 21:14 "Waheb in Suphah and the w,

WAIL (32)
Tb 10: 4 began to weep aloud and to w over her son:
10: 7 go back home to w and cry
Wis 18:10 and the piteous w of mourning for children
Sir 35:14 He is not deaf to the w of the orphan,
Is 15: 8 the wailing, and to Beer-elim, the w.
16: 7 Moab wails for Moab, everywhere they w;
23: 1 W, O ships of Tarshish,
Jer 4: 8 yourselves with sackcloth, mourn and w:
25:34 Howl, you shepherds, and w!
48:31 And so I w over Moab,
48:36 the w of flutes for Moab is in my heart;
48:36 Kir-heres the w of flutes is in my heart;
Bar 6:31 They shout and w before their gods as
Ez 21:17 Cry out and w,
27:32 thus they w over you:
Hos 10: 5 mourn for it and its priests w over it,
Jl 1: 5 w,
1:11 w, you vinedressers!
1:13 w, O ministers of the altar!
Am 5:16 to w and professional mourners to lament,
Mi 1: 8 Judgment For this reason I lament and w,
Zep 1:10 the Fish Gate, a w from the New Quarter,
1:11 W, O inhabitants of the Mortar!
Zec 11: 2 W, you cypress trees,
11: 2 W, you oaks of Bashan,
Mt 11:17 We sang you a dirge but you did not w!'
13:42 where they will w and grind their teeth.
13:50 where they will w and grind their teeth.
22:13 into the night to w and grind his teeth.'
25:30 where he can w and grind his teeth.'
Lk 7:32 We sang you a dirge but you did not w.'
Jas 5: 1 weep and w over your impending miseries.

WAILED (5)
Nm 11:20 your midst, and in his presence you have w,
14: 1 cries, and even in the night the people w.
Jgs 5:28 peered down and w the mother of Sisera,
Hos 7:14 their hearts when they w upon their beds;
Rv 12: 2 she w aloud in pain as she labored to give

WAILING (19)
Ex 11: 6 be loud w throughout the land of Egypt,
12:30 and there was a loud w throughout Egypt,
Jdt 7:29 w and loud cries to the Lord their God.
Wis 7: 3 w,
Sir 38:16 one who is dead with w and bitter lament;
Is 15: 8 As far as Eglaim the w,
23: 6 Pass over to Tarshish, w,
Jer 6:26 Mourn as for an only child with bitter w,
9:16 tell the w women to come,
25:36 W from the shepherds,
47: 2 All the people of the land set up a w cry.
48:39 the LORD How terror seizes Moab, and w!
Ez 2:10 Lamentation and w and woe!
Zec 11: 3 the w of the shepherds,
Mt 8:12 W will be heard there,
24:51 There will be w then and grinding of teeth.
Mk 5:38 of people w and crying loudly on all sides.
5:39 "Why do you make this din with your w?
Lk 13:28 "There will be w and grinding of teeth

WAILINGS (1)
Am 8: 3 temple songs shall become w on that day,

WAILS (3)
Is 15: 2 Over Nebo and over Medeba Moab w.
15: 3 the rooftops and in the squares everyone w.
16: 7 Therefore Moab w for Moab,

WAIST (17)
1Kgs 2: 5 belt about my w and the sandal on my foot.
20:32 they dressed in sackcloth girded at the w,
Is 5:27 None will have his w belt loose,
11: 5 Justice shall be the band around his w,
20: 2 Go and take off the sackcloth from your w,
Ez 1:27 his w I saw what gleamed like electrum;
1:27 his w I saw what looked like fire;
8: 2 seemed to be his w, there was fire; from his w
9: 2 in linen, with a writer's case at his w.
9: 3 in linen with the writer's case at his w,
9:11 the writing case at his w make his report:
47: 4 the water was up to my w.
Dn 10: 5 with a belt of fine gold around his w.
Mt 3: 4 hair, and wore a leather belt around his w.
Mk 1: 6 hair, and wore a leather belt around his w.
Eph 6:14 with the truth as the belt around your w,

WAISTCLOTH (1)
Jb 12:18 but a w to bind the king's own loins.

WAISTS (2)
Ez 23:15 with sashes girded about their w,
Lk 12:35 your w and your lamps be burning ready.

WAIT (92)
Ex 24:14 him, W here for us until we return to you.
Lv 15:13 he shall w seven days for his purification.
15:28 her affliction, she shall w seven days,
Nm 9: 8 W until I learn what the LORD will command
35:20 lying in w for him throws something at him,
35:22 in w for him he throws some object at him,
Dt 5:31 Then you w here near me and I will give
19:11 w for his neighbor out of hatred for him,
24:11 but shall w outside until the man to whom
Jgs 16: 9 in w in the chamber and so she said to him,
16:12 there were men lying in w in the chamber.
21:20 "Go and lie in w in the vineyards.
Ru 1:13 would you then w and deprive yourselves of
3:18 Naomi then said, W here,
1Sm 1:23 w until you have weaned him.
10: 8 W seven days until I come to you;
20:19 other occasion and w near the mound there.
2Sm 3:30 his brother Abishai had lain in w for Abner
2Kgs 5:21 alighted from his chariot to w for him.
5:26 man alighted from his chariot to w for you?
7: 9 If we w until morning breaks,
Tb 2: 2 son, I shall w for you to come back."
5: 7 Tobiah said to him, W for me,
5: 8 replied, "Very well, I will w for you;
Jdt 7:30 us w five days more for the Lord our God,
8:17 we w for the salvation that comes from him,
13: 3 maid to stand outside the bedroom and w,
2Mc 7:17 Only w and you will see how his great
Jb 3:21 They w for death and it comes not;
11:20 cut off from them, they shall w to expire.
13:15 Slay me though he might, I will w for him;
14:14 all the days of my drudgery I would w,
31: 9 and I have lain in w at my neighbor's door;
32:16 Must I w?
35:14 with trembling should you w upon him.
36: 2 W yet a little and I will instruct you,
38:40 in their dens, or lie in w in the thicket?
Ps(s) 10: 9 he lies in w to catch the afflicted;
25: 5 God my savior, and for you I w all the day.
25:21 preserve me, because I w for you,
27:14 of the living W for the LORD with courage;
27:14 be stouthearted, and w for the LORD.
37: 7 Leave it to the LORD, and w for him;
37: 9 who w for the LORD shall possess the land.
37:34 W for the LORD,
38:16 Because for you, O LORD, I w;
39: 8 And now, for what do I w, O LORD?
59: 4 For behold, they lie in w for my life;
69: 7 who w for you be put to shame through me,
88:14 with my morning prayer I w upon you.
119:95 Sinners w to destroy me,
119:166 I w for your salvation,
130: 6 LORD more than sentinels w for the dawn.
130: 6 More than sentinels w for the dawn,
130: 7 for the dawn, let Israel w for the LORD,
Prv 1:11 Let us lie in w for the honest man,
1:18 These men lie in w for their own blood,
23:28 Yes, she lies in w like a robber,
24:15 not in w against the home of the just man,
Sir 2: 7 You who fear the LORD, w for his mercy,
11:21 but trust in the LORD and w for his light;
11:32 The evil man lies in w for blood,
14:22 a scout, and lies in w at her entry way;
18:22 w not to fulfill them when you are dying.
27:10 As a lion crouches in w for prey,
27:28 vengeance lies in w for them like a lion.
Is 8:17 yes, I will w for him.
30:18 blessed are all who w for him!
33: 2 O LORD, have pity on us, for you we w.
41: 1 you peoples, w for my words!
42: 4 the coastlands will w for his teaching.
64: 3 doing such deeds for those who w for him.
Jer 8:15 We w for peace to no avail;
14:19 We w for peace,
Ez 13: 6 then they w for him to fulfill their word!
44:26 he must w an additional seven days,
Hos 3: 3 "Many days you shall w for me;
3: 3 I in turn will w for you."
Mi 5: 6 raindrops on the grass, Which w for no man,
7: 2 They all lie in w to shed blood,
Hb 2: 3 If it delays, w for it,
Zep 3: 8 Therefore, w for me,
Mt 8:15 She got up at once and began to w on him.
Mk 1:31 She immediately began to w on them.
Lk 12:37 them at table, and proceed to w on them.
17: 8 apron and w on me while I eat and drink.
Acts 1: 4 W, rather, for the fulfillment of my
6: 2 the word of God in order to w on tables.
23:21 More than forty of them are lying in w;
1Cor 1: 7 no spiritual gift as you w for the revelation

11:33 assemble for the meal, w for one another.

WAITED (28)

Gn 8:10 He w seven days more and again sent the
8:12 He w still another seven days and then
18: 8 he w on them under the tree while they ate.
Ex 18:13 who w about him from morning until evening.
Jos 8:13 and Joshua w overnight among his troops.
Jgs 3:25 They w until they finally grew suspicious.
16: 2 And all the night they w,
19:15 The man w in the public square of the city
1Sm 13: 8 He w seven days
25: 9 fully to Nabal in David's name, and then w.
1Kgs 20:38 went on and w for the king on the road,
Jdt 10:18 as she w outside the tent of Holofernes,
2Mc 5:25 and w until the holy day of the sabbath;
Jb 29:21 For me they listened and w;
29:23 They w for me as for the rain;
32:11 Behold, I have w for your discourses,
Ps(s) 40: 2 I have waited, w for the LORD,
56: 7 As they have w for my life,
106:13 they w not for his counsel.
Jer 3: 2 you w for them like an Arab in the desert.
Ez 19: 5 Then she saw that in vain she had w,
Jon 4: 5 himself a hut and w under it in the shade,
Mt 4:11 left him, and angels came and w on him.
Mk 1:13 with the wild beasts, and angels w on him.
Lk 4:39 She got up immediately and w on them.
Acts 20: 5 went on ahead and w for us in Troas.
1Pt 3:20 God patiently w until the ark was built.

WAITER (3)

Jn 2: 8 some out and take it to the w in charge."
2: 9 The w in charge tasted the water made wine,
2: 9 Then the w in charge called the groom over

WAITERS (2)

1Kgs 10: 5 the attendance and garb of his w,
Jn 2: 9 only the w knew,

WAITING (24)

Gn 24:21 silently w to learn whether or not the
Ex 5:20 Moses and Aaron, who were w to meet them,
2Sm 15:28 I shall be w at the fords near the desert
1Kgs 1:20 all Israel is w for you to make known to
Est 6: 5 answered him, "Haman is w in the court."
2Mc 7:30 "What are you w for?
9:25 and w to see what will happen.
Prv 8:34 daily at my gates, w at my doorposts;
Sir 28:26 and fall victim to your foe w in ambush.
29: 8 keep him not w for your alms;
Is 30:15 By w and by calm you shall be saved,
30:18 Yet the LORD is w to show you favor,
Dn 13:15 while they were w for the right moment,
Zec 9:12 return to the fortress of the w prisoners,
Lk 1:21 Meanwhile, the people were w for Zechariah,
8:40 indeed, they were all w for him.
20:20 W their chance,
Jn 2: 5 His mother instructed those w on table,
5: 4 disabled w for the movement of the water].
Acts 17:16 While Paul was w for them in Athens,
23:21 are all ready now, w only for your consent."
28: 6 After w for quite some time,
Heb 6:15 And so, after patient w,
2Pt 3:14 So, beloved, while w for this,

WAITS (11)

2Mc 6:14 the Lord patiently w until they reach the
Jb 7: 2 the shade, a hireling who w for his wages.
Ps(s) 10: 9 He w in secret like a lion in his lair;
25: 3 No one who w for you shall be put
33:20 Our soul w for the LORD,
130: 6 My soul w for the LORD more than sentinels
Eccl 12: 4 When one w for the chirp of a bird,
Lam 3:25 Good is the LORD to one who w for him,
Dn 13:59 "for the angel of God w with a sword to
Jn 3:29 The groom's best man w there listening for
Heb 10:13 now he w until his enemies are placed

WAKE (10)

Ps(s) 3: 6 When I lie down in sleep, I w again,
7: 7 w to the judgment you have decreed.
57: 9 I will w the dawn.
108: 3 I will w the dawn.
Prv 6:22 she will watch over you, and when you w,
Jl 1: 5 W up, you drunkards, and weep;
Lk 22:46 W up, and pray that you may not
Jn 11:11 asleep, but I am going there to w him."
Rom 13:11 It is now the hour for you to w from sleep,
Rv 3: 2 W up, and strengthen what remains before

WAKEFUL (1)

Sir 42: 9 is a treasure that keeps her father w,

WAKEN (1)

Jdt 14:13 in charge of all his things, W our master,

WAKES (2)

Ps(s) 78:65 w from sleep a champion overcome with wine;
Sir 40: 7 he w up astonished that there was nothing

WAKING (1)

Ps(s) 17:15 on w,

WALE (1)

Jdt 9:13 Let my guileful speech bring wound and w

WALK (127)

Gn 13:17 Set forth and w about in the land,
17: 1 W in my presence and be blameless.
Ex 21:19 up and w around with the help of his staff.
Lv 11:20 that w on all fours are loathsome for you.
11:21 But of the various winged insects that w
11:27 those that w on paws are unclean for you;
26:13 had laid upon you and letting you w erect.
Dt 26:17 to w in his ways and observe his statutes,
28: 9 of the LORD, your God, and w in his ways,
2Chr 6:31 So may they fear you and w in your ways as
Neh 5: 9 Should you not w in the fear of our God,
Est 2:11 w about in front of the court of the harem,
Ps(s) 23: 4 I w in the dark valley I fear no evil;
26: 3 is before my eyes, and I w in your truth.
26:11 But I w in integrity;
32: 8 you and show you the way you should w;
56:14 w before God in the light of the living.
78:10 according to his law they would not w;
81:14 would hear me, and Israel w in my ways,
84:12 good thing from those who w in sincerity.
85:14 Justice shall w before him,
86:11 LORD, your way that I may w in your truth;
89:16 light of your countenance, O LORD, they w.
89:31 law and w not according to my ordinances,
101: 2 I will w in the integrity of my heart,
115: 7 they have feet but w not;
116: 9 I shall w before the LORD in the lands of
119: 1 is blameless, who w in the law of the LORD.
119: 3 heart, And do no wrong, but w in his ways.
119:45 And I will w at liberty,
128: 1 you who fear the LORD, who w in his ways!
138: 7 Though I w amid distress,
142: 4 which I w they have hid a trap for me.
143: 8 Show me the way in which I should w,
Prv 1:15 My son, w not in the way with them,
2: 7 he is the shield of those who w honestly,
2:13 straight paths to w in the way of darkness,
2:20 Thus you may w in the way of good men,
4:12 When you w,
4:14 enter not, w not on the way of evil men;
6:28 Or can a man w on live coals,
8:20 On the way of duty I w,
11:20 those who w blamelessly are his delight.
13:20 W with wise men and you will become wise,
Wis 6: 4 law, nor w according to the will of God,
13:18 about travel, something that cannot even w.
15:15 even their feet are useless to w with.
Sir 10: 6 and do not w the path of arrogance.
33:11 in different paths he has them w.
Is 2: 3 us in his ways, and we may w in his paths."
2: 5 come, let us w in the light of the LORD!
3:16 and w with necks outstretched Ogling and
8:11 me not to w in the way of this people:
28:13 So that when they w,
30:21 w in it,"
35: 9 to make, and on it the redeemed will w.
40:31 and not grow weary, w and not grow faint.
42: 5 its people and spirit to those who w on it:
42:24 In his ways they refused to w,
43: 2 When you w through fire,
50:11 W by the light of your own fire and by the
51:23 to bow down, that they might w over you,
51:23 ground, like the street for them to w on.
59: 9 for brightness, but we w in gloom!
60: 3 Nations shall w by your light,
65: 2 Who w in evil paths and follow their own
Jer 3:17 and they will w no longer in their
6:16 of old Which is the way to good, and w it;
6:16 But they said, "We will not w it."
7:23 W in all the ways that I command you,
10: 5 must be carried about, for they cannot w.
13:10 who w in the stubbornness of their hearts,
14:18 If I w out into the field, look!
Lam 3: 2 he has led and forced to w in darkness,
4:18 so that we could not w in our streets;
Bar 4: 2 w by her light toward splendor.
4:13 ways of God's commandments they did not w,
Ez 16:47 Yet not only in their ways did you w,
36:12 are the ones whom I will have w upon you;
37: 2 He made me w among them in every direction
42: 4 w ten cubits broad and a wall of one cubit;
Dn 4:34 those who w in pride he is able to humble.
13: 7 used to enter her husband's garden for a w.
13: 8 old men saw her enter every day for her w,
Hos 11: 3 Yet it was I who taught Ephraim to w,
14:10 the paths of the LORD, in them the just w,
Am 3: 3 Do two w together unless they have agreed?
Jon 3: 4 had gone but a single day's w announcing,
Mi 2: 3 Nor shall you w with head high,
4: 2 us in his ways, that we may w in his paths."
4: 5 w each in the name of its god, But we will w
6: 8 goodness, and to w humbly with your God.
Zep 1:17 will hem men in till they w like the blind,
Zec 3: 7 If you w in my ways and heed my charge,
10:12 in the LORD, and they shall w in his name,
Mt 9: 5 sins are forgiven' or 'Stand up and w'?
11: 5 the blind recover their sight, cripples w,
14:29 of the boat and began to w on the water,
Mk 2: 9 'Stand up, pick up your mat, and w again'?
5:42 stood up immediately and began to w around.
Lk 5:23 forgiven you,' or to say, 'Get up and w'?
7:22 The blind recover their sight, cripples w,
11:44 hidden tombs over which men w unawares."
24:15 approached and began to w along with them.
Jn 1:36 As he watched Jesus w by he said, "Look!
5: 8 Pick up your mat and w!"
5: 9 he picked up his mat and began to w.
5:11 me who told me, 'Pick up your mat and w.'"
5:12 person who told you to pick it up and w,"
8:12 follower of mine shall ever w in darkness;
12:35 W while you still have it or darkness will
Acts 3: 6 the name of Jesus Christ, the Nazorean, w!"
3: 8 stood for a moment, then began to w around.
3:12 man w by some power or holiness of our own?
14:10 The man jumped up and began to w around.
2Cor 5: 7 We w by faith, not by sight.
6:16 "I will dwell with them and w among them.
12:18 in the one spirit, w in the same footsteps?
Heb 12:13 Make straight the paths you w on,
1Jn 1: 6 him," while continuing to w in darkness,
1: 7 But if we w in light,
2Jn 1: 6 is the way in which you should w.
3Jn 1: 3 to how truly you w in the path of truth.
Rv 3: 4 w with me in white because they are worthy.
9:20 and wood, which cannot see or hear or w.
21:24 The nations shall w by its light;

WALKED (44)

Gn 5:24 Then Enoch w with God,
6:10 blameless in that age, for he w with God,
9:23 they w backward and covered their father's
18:22 the two men w on farther toward Sodom,
22: 7 As the two w on together,
24:40 LORD, in whose presence I have always w,
48:15 whose ways my fathers Abraham and Isaac w,
Ex 2: 5 while her maids w along the river bank.
1Sm 17:39 He w with difficulty,
1Kgs 19: 8 he w forty days and forty nights to the
2Kgs 2:11 As they w on conversing,
2Chr 11:17 for they w in the way of David and Solomon
17: 3 for he w in the ways his father had
21:13 but instead have w in the way of the kings
Tb 1: 3 have w all the days of my life on the
6: 2 The travelers w till nightfall,
Jdt 10:11 and her maid w directly across the valley,
Est 4: 1 and w through the city crying out loudly
Jb 23:11 My foot has always w in his steps;
29: 3 and by his light I w through darkness;
31: 5 If I have w in falsehood and my foot has
38:16 sea, or w about in the depths of the abyss?
Ps(s) 26: 1 for I have w in integrity,
55:15 side I w in procession in the house of God!
81:13 they w according to their own counsels.
Eccl 10: 7 while princes w on the ground like slaves.
Sir 44:16 [ENOCH w with the LORD and was taken up,
Is 9: 1 who w in darkness have seen a great light;
Jer 7:24 They w in the hardness of their evil
Bar 3:13 Had you w in the way of God,
Ez 47: 3 Then when he had w off to the east with a
Dn 3:24 They w about in the flames,
Mi 6:16 of Ahab, and you have w in their counsels;
Mal 2: 6 w with me in integrity and in uprightness,
Mt 4:21 He w along farther and caught sight of two
12: 1 sabbath Jesus w through the standing grain.
26:30 praise, they w out to the Mount of olives.
Mk 14:26 praise, they w out to the Mount of Olives.
Lk 4:30 straight through their midst and w away.
8: 5 w on and the birds of the air ate it up.
Jn 9: 1 As he w along,
Acts 14: 8 sit crippled, never having w in his life.
17:23 As I w around looking at your shrines,
Rom 4:12 which Abraham w while still uncircumcised.

WALKING (46)

Gn 18:16 Abraham was w with them,
24:65 out there, w through the fields toward us?"
Dt 8: 6 your God, by w in his ways and fearing him.
19: 9 the LORD, your God, and ever w in his ways:
22: 6 "If, while w along,
30:16 you today, loving him, and w in his ways,
2Sm 6: 4 guided the cart, with Ahio w before it,
15:30 head was covered, and he was w barefoot.
2Kgs 6:26 the king of Israel was w on the city wall,
6:30 And as he was w on the wall,
Tb 11:16 people of Nineveh saw him w along briskly,
Jdt 13:20 our disaster, w uprightly before our God."
Prv 7: 8 then w in the direction of her house
Sir 9:13 are stepping among snares and w over a net.
Is 20: 2 This he did, w naked and barefoot.
Jer 16:12 w in the hardness of his evil heart
Ez 28:14 mountain of God, w among the fiery stones.
Dn 3:92 men unfettered and unhurt, w in the fire,
4:26 as he was w on the roof of the royal

WALKING (cont.)

13:36 "As we were *w* in the garden alone,
Mt 4:18 As he was *w* along the Sea of Galilee he
10:10 no change of shirt, no sandals, no *w* staff.
14:25 morning, he came *w* toward them on the lake.
14:26 When the disciples saw him *w* on the water,
15:31 the deformed made sound, cripples *w* about,
Mk 2:13 time, while he went *w* along the lakeshore,
2:23 *w* through standing grain on the sabbath,
6: 8 nothing on their journey but a *w* stick
6:48 them, he came *w* toward them on the water;
6:49 When they saw him *w* on the lake,
8:24 can see people but they look like *w* trees!"
10:32 up to Jerusalem, with Jesus *w* in the lead.
11:20 Early next morning, as they were *w* along,
11:27 As he was *w* in the temple precincts the
16:12 were *w* along on their way to the country,
Lk 6: 1 Jesus was *w* through the standing grain.
9: 3 journey, neither *w* staff nor traveling bag;
10: 4 Do not carry a *w* staff or traveling bag;
Jn 6:19 Jesus approaching the boat, *w* on the water.
10:23 Jesus was *w* in the temple area,
11: 9 If a man goes *w* by day he does not stumble
11:10 But if he goes *w* at night he will stumble
Acts 3: 8 He went into the temple with them *w*,
2Jn 1: 4 of your children *w* in the path of truth,
1: 6 our *w* according to the commandments,
3Jn 1: 4 hear that my children are *w* in this path.

WALKS (28)

Jb 22:14 he *w* upon the vault of the heavens!"
Ps(s) 1: 1 of the wicked Nor *w* in the way of sinners,
15: 2 He who *w* blamelessly and does justice;
101: 6 He who *w* in the way of integrity shall be
Prv 10: 9 He who walks honestly *w* securely,
10:29 LORD is a stronghold to him who *w* honestly,
13: 6 Virtue guards one who *w* honestly,
14: 2 He who *w* uprightly fears the LORD,
19: 1 Better a poor man who *w* in his integrity
20: 7 When a man *w* in integrity and justice,
28: 6 Better a poor man who *w* in his integrity
28:18 He who *w* uprightly is safe,
28:26 is a fool, but he who *w* in wisdom is safe.
29:27 and he who *w* uprightly is an abomination
Eccl 2:14 in his head, but the fool *w* in darkness.
10: 3 When the fool *w* through the street,
Sir 4:17 She *w* with him as a stranger,
21: 6 who hates correction *w* the sinner's path,
25:25 If she *w* not by your side,
Is 50:10 voice, And *w* in darkness without any light,
Jer 23:17 And to everyone who *w* in hardness of heart,
Bar 2:18 is deeply grieved, who *w* bowed and feeble,
Mi 2: 7 words promise good to him who *w* uprightly?
Jn 10: 4 those that are his, he *w* in front of them,
12:35 The man who *w* in the dark does not know
1Jn 2:11 He *w* in shadows,
Rv 2: 1 *w* among the seven lampstands of gold

WALL (171)

Ex 14:22 like a *w* to their right and to their left.
14:29 like a *w* to their right and to their left.
Lv 14:37 to go deeper than the surface of the *w*,
Nm 22:24 vineyards with a stone *w* on each side.
22:25 the LORD there, she shrank against the *w*;
Jos 2:15 she lived in a house built into the city *w*.
6: 5 The *w* of the city will collapse,
6:20 The *w* collapsed,
1Sm 18:11 the spear, thinking to nail David to the *w*,
19:10 to nail David to the *w* with the spear,
19:10 Saul, so that the spear struck only the *w*,
20:25 taking his usual place against the *w*,
31:10 impaled his body on the *w* of Beth-shan.
31:12 Saul and his sons from the *w* of Beth-shan,
2Sm 11:20 that they would shoot from the *w* above?
11:21 a millstone down on him from the *w* above,
11:21 Why did you go near the *w*?'
11:24 shot at your servants from the *w* above,
18:24 to the roof of the gate above the city *w*,
20:15 began battering the *w* to throw it down.
20:21 head shall be thrown to you across the *w*."
22:30 and by the help of my God I leap over a *w*.
1Kgs 3: 1 of the LORD, and the *w* around Jerusalem.
5:13 to the hyssop growing out of the *w*,
6: 5 temple, and adjoining the *w* of the temple,
6:27 touched a side *w* while the other wing,
9:15 his palace, Millo, the *w* of Jerusalem,
20:30 city of Aphek, and there the *w* collapsed.
2Kgs 3:27 and offered him as a holocaust upon the *w*.
6:26 king of Israel was walking on the city *w*,
6:30 And as he was walking on the *w*,
9:33 against the *w* and against the horses.
14:13 down four hundred cubits of the city *w*,
18:26 earshot of the people who are on the *w*."
18:27 it not rather to the men sitting on the *w*,
20: 2 his face to the *w* and prayed to the LORD:
2Chr 3:12 in length, extended to a *w* of the building,
25:23 Then he tore down the *w* of Jerusalem from
27: 3 much construction done on the *w* of Ophel.
32: 5 he rebuilt the *w* where it was broken down,
32: 5 upon it, and built another *w* outside.
32:18 the people of Jerusalem who were on the *w*,
33:14 Afterward he built an outer *w* for the
Neh 1: 3 Also, the *w* of Jerusalem lies breached,
2: 8 city *w* and the house that I shall occupy."
2:15 inspecting the *w* all the while till I once
2:17 Come, let us rebuild the *w* of Jerusalem,
3: 8 as far as the *w* of the public square.
3:13 cubits of the *w* up to the Dung Gate.
3:15 He also repaired the *w* of the Aqueduct
3:27 to the *w* of Ophel [the temple slaves were
3:33 heard that we were rebuilding the *w*,
3:35 attacked it would breach their *w* of stones!"
3:38 We, however, continued to build the *w*,
4: 4 Never shall we be able the *w* to rebuild."
4: 7 stationed guards down below, behind the *w*,
4: 9 went back, each to his own task at the *w*.
4:11 whole house of Judah as they rebuilt the *w*.
4:13 separated from one another along the *w*;
5:16 own, I did my part in this work on the *w*,
6: 1 rebuilt the *w* and that there was no breach
6: 6 for this reason you are rebuilding the *w*;
6:15 The *w* was finished on the twenty-fifth day
7: 1 When the *w* had been rebuilt,
12:27 At the dedication of the *w* of Jerusalem,
12:30 purified the people, the gates, and the *w*.
12:31 I had the princes of Judah mount the *w*,
12:31 to the right, along the top of the *w*,
12:37 continued along the top of the *w* above
12:38 along the top of the *w* past the Oven Tower
12:38 past the Oven Tower as far as the Broad *W*,
13:21 do you spend the night alongside the *w*?
Tb 2: 9 to sleep next to the *w* of my courtyard.
2:10 there were birds perched on the *w* above me,
Jdt 1: 2 this city he built a *w* of blocks of stone,
1: 2 the *w* seventy cubits high and fifty thick.
14: 1 head and hang it on the parapet of your *w*.
14:11 they hung the head of Holofernes on the *w*.
1Mc 1:33 with a high, massive *w* and strong towers,
6:62 for the encircling *w* to be destroyed.
9:54 Alcimus ordered the *w* of the inner court
12:37 the east *w* above the ravine had collapsed.
13:45 wives and children, went up on the *w*,
14:37 the *w* of Jerusalem to a greater height.
2Mc 6:10 thrown down from the top of the city *w*.
10:35 bravely stormed the *w* and with savage fury
14:43 he gallantly ran up to the top of the *w*
15:35 up Nicanor's head on the *w* of the citadel,
Ps(s) 18:30 and by the help of my God I leap over a *w*.
62: 4 he were a sagging fence, a battered *w*?
Prv 18:11 he fancies it a high *w*.
24:31 with nettles, and its stone *w* broken down.
Eccl 10: 8 through a *w* may be bitten by a serpent.
Sg 2: 9 Here he stands behind our *w*,
8: 9 If she is a *w*,
8:10 I am a *w*, and my breasts are like towers.
Wis 13:15 fitting shrine for it and puts it on the *w*,
Sir 22:17 is like the polished surface of a smooth *w*.
50: 2 In his time also the *w* was built with
Is 2:15 every lofty tower and every fortified *w*,
5: 5 give it to grazing, break through its *w*,
22:10 tearing some down to strengthen the *w*;
30:13 out in a high *w* whose crash comes suddenly,
36:11 earshot of the people who are on the *w*."
36:12 it not rather to the men sitting on the *w*,
38: 2 his face to the *w* and prayed to the LORD:
59:10 Like blind men we grope along the *w*,
Jer 1:18 city, A pillar of iron, a *w* of brass,
15:20 you toward this people a solid *w* of brass.
49:27 I will set fire to the *w* of Damascus,
51:44 The *w* of Babylon falls!
Lam 2: 8 for destruction the *w* of daughter Zion:
2: 8 grief on *w* and rampart till both succumbed.
Ez 4: 3 up as an iron *w* between you and the city.
8: 7 where I saw there was a hole in the *w*.
8: 8 Son of man, he ordered, dig through the *w*.
8: 8 I dug through the *w* and saw a door.
8:10 all around upon the *w* were pictured
12: 5 dig a hole in the *w* and pass through it;
12: 7 dug a hole through the *w* with my hand and,
12:12 through a hole that he has dug in the *w*.
13: 5 nor did you build a *w* about the house of
13:10 was no peace, and that, as one built a *w*,
13:12 And when the *w* has fallen,
13:14 I will tear down the *w* that you have
13:15 my fury on the *w* and its whitewashers,
13:15 I tell you there shall be no *w*,
22:30 who could build a *w* or stand in the breach
23:14 When she saw men drawn on the *w*,
38:20 and every *w* shall fall to the ground.
40: 5 *w* that completely surrounded the temple.
40:13 from the back *w* of one cell to the back *w*
40:40 Along the *w* of the vestibule,
41: 5 Then he measured the *w* of the temple,
41: 6 offsets in the outside *w* of the temple
41: 6 were no supports in the temple *w* proper.
41: 9 The width of the outside *w* which
41:11 The width of the *w* surrounding the open
41:12 the *w* of the building was five cubits
41:17 on every *w* on every side in both the inner
42: 4 walk ten cubits broad and a *w* of one cubit;
42: 7 On the far side there was a *w* running
42: 8 length the *w* measured one hundred cubits.
42:10 court where the *w* of the court began.
42:12 of the way which led to the back *w*,
42:20 It was surrounded by a *w*,
43: 8 to mine, so that only a *w* was between us,
46:23 A *w* of stones surrounded each of the four,
Dn 5: 5 the plaster of the *w* in the king's palace.
Hos 2: 8 way with thorns and erect a *w* against her,
Jl 2: 7 they run, like soldiers they scale the *w*;
2: 9 assault the city, they run upon the *w*,
Am 1: 7 Edom, I will send fire upon the *w* of Gaza,
1:10 I will send fire upon the *w* of Tyre,
1:14 I will kindle a fire upon the *w* of Rabbah,
5:19 he were to rest his hand against the *w*,
7: 7 he was standing by a *w*, plummet in hand.
9:11 I will *w* up its breaches,
Na 2: 6 To the *w* they rush,
3: 8 the flood for her rampart and water her *w*?
Hb 2:11 For the stone in the *w* shall cry out,
Zec 2: 9 I will be for her an encircling *w* of fire,
Acts 9:25 *w* one night and lowered him to the ground,
23: 3 the one God will strike, you whitewashed *w*!
2Cor 11:33 a window in the *w* and escaped his hands.
Rv 21:12 Its *w*, massive and high, had twelve gates
21:14 The *w* of the city had twelve courses of
21:15 measuring the city, its gates, and its *w*.
21:17 Its *w* measured a hundred and forty-four
21:18 The *w* was constructed of jasper;
21:19 The foundation of the city *w* was ornate

WALLED (10)

Lv 25:29 someone sells a dwelling in a *w* town,
25:30 But if such a house in a *w* town has not
26:25 you then huddle together in your *w* cities,
1Kgs 4:13 *w* cities with gates barred with bronze;
6:36 The inner court was *w* off by means of
2Kgs 17: 9 the watchtowers as well as the *w* cities.
18: 8 and *w* cities of the Philistines,
Sir 28:14 It destroys *w* cities,
Jer 8:14 Let us form ranks and enter the *w* cities,
Bar 6:17 Their courtyards are *w* in like those of a

WALLEYED (1)

Lv 21:20 hand, or who is humpbacked or weakly or *w*,

WALLOW (1)

Sir 23:12 foreign to the devout, who do not *w* in sin.

WALLOWED (1)

Rv 18: 9 fornication with her and *w* in her sensuality

WALLOWING (1)

2Pt 2:22 and, "A sow bathes by *w* in the mire."

WALLS (107)

Ex 26:15 of acacia wood as *w* for the Dwelling.
30: 3 Its grate on top, its *w* on all four sides,
36:20 wood were made as *w* for the Dwelling.
37:26 Its grate on top, its *w* on all four sides,
Lv 14:37 finds that the infection on the *w* of the
14:39 that the infection has spread on the *w*,
25:31 villages that are not encircled by *w*
Nm 35: 4 cubits from the city *w* in each direction.
Dt 3: 5 fortified with high *w* and gates and bars.
28:52 unscalable *w* you trust in come tumbling
Jgs 5: 7 Gone was freedom beyond the *w*,
1Kgs 6: 6 not be fastened into the *w* of the temple.
6:15 its *w* were lined from floor to ceiling
6:29 The *w* on all sides of both the inner and
2Kgs 3:25 Kirhareseth was left behind its stone *w*,
25: 1 around it, and built siege *w* on every side.
25: 4 no more bread, the city *w* were breached.
25: 4 the two *w* which was near the king's garden.
25:10 tore down the *w* that surrounded Jerusalem.
1Chr 29: 4 silver, for overlaying the *w* of the rooms,
2Chr 3: 7 thresholds, as well as its *w* and its doors,
3: 7 gold, and he engraved cherubim upon the *w*.
8: 5 Lower Beth-horon, fortified cities with *w*,
14: 6 these cities and surround them with *w*,
26: 6 the Philistines and razed the *w* of Gath,
26:15 *w* to shoot arrows and cast large stones.
36:19 house of God, tore down the *w* of Jerusalem,
Ezr 4:12 They are raising up its *w*,
4:13 is rebuilt and its *w* are raised up again,
4:16 is rebuilt and its *w* are raised up again,
5: 8 and the *w* are being reinforced with timber;
Neh 2:13 observing how the *w* of Jerusalem lay in
4: 1 of the *w* of Jerusalem was progressing
Tb 1:17 and been thrown outside the *w* of Nineveh,
13:12 all who destroy you and pull down your *w*,
13:16 and all your *w* with precious stones,
Jdt 7:32 returned to the *w* and towers of the city;
1Mc 1:31 its houses and its surrounding *w*,
4:60 high *w* and strong towers around Mount Zion,
6: 7 surrounded with high *w* both the sanctuary,
9:50 and Tephon, with high *w* and gates and bars.
10:11 He ordered the workmen to build the *w* and
10:45 Likewise the cost of building the *w* of
10:45 it all around, and of building *w* in Judea,
12:36 for making the *w* of Jerusalem still higher,
13:10 and quickly completing the *w* of Jerusalem,
13:33 fortifications with high towers, thick *w*,
16:23 he performed, his rebuilding of the *w*,
2Mc 3:19 some to the gates, some to the *w*,

5: 5 As the defenders on the *w* were forced back
10:17 places, drove back all who manned the *w*,
11: 9 most savage beasts, yes, even *w* of iron.
12:14 of their *w* and their supply of provisions,
12:27 took up their posts in defense of the *w*,
Ps(s) 51:20 kindness by rebuilding the *w* of Jerusalem;
55:11 day and night they prowl about upon its *w*.
80:13 Why have you broken down its *w*,
89:41 You have broken down all his *w*;
122: 7 May peace be within your *w*,
144:14 May there be no breach in the *w*,
Sg 5: 7 my mantle from me, the guardians of the *w*.
Sir 14:24 and fastens his tent pegs next to her *w*;
23:18 Darkness surrounds me, *w* hide me;
49:13 He rebuilt our ruined *w*,
Is 22: 5 *W* crash; they cry for help to
22:11 the two *w* for the water of the old pool.
26: 1 he sets up *w* and ramparts to protect us.
49:16 your *w* are ever before me.
54:12 and all your *w* of precious stones.
56: 5 I will give, in my house and within my *w*,
60:10 Foreigners shall rebuild your *w*,
60:18 *w* "Salvation" and your gates "Praise."
62: 6 your *w*, O Jerusalem, I have stationed
Jer 1:15 Opposite her *w* all around and opposite all
4:19 The *w* of my heart!
21: 4 Chaldeans who besiege you outside the *w*.
39: 4 Road through the gate between the two *w*.
39: 8 people, and demolished the *w* of Jerusalem.
50:15 her bastions fall, her *w* are torn down:
51:12 Against the *w* of Babylon raise a signal,
51:58 The *w* of spacious Babylon shall be leveled
52: 4 around it, and built siege *w* on every side.
52: 7 no more bread, the city *w* were breached.
52: 7 the two *w* which was near the king's garden.
52:14 down all the *w* that surrounded Jerusalem.
Lam 2: 7 The *w* of her towers he has handed over to
Ez 26: 4 destroy the *w* of Tyre and raze her towers.
26: 9 He shall pound your *w* with battering-rams
26:10 Your *w* shall shake as he enters your gates,
26:12 Your *w* shall be torn down,
27:11 The men of Arvad were all about your *w*,
27:11 hung their bucklers all around on your *w*,
30:16 be breached and its *w* shall be demolished.
33:30 along the *w* and in the doorways of houses.
38:11 in security, all of them living without *w*,
40:48 and the side *w* on either side of the door
41: 2 and the *w* at either side of it measured
41: 3 and the *w* at either side of it extended
41:13 area, together with the building and its *w*,
41:15 *w* on both sides it was one hundred cubits.
41:20 and palmtrees were carved on the *w*.
41:25 and palmtrees, like those carved on the *w*.
41:26 palmtrees] on both side *w* of the vestibule,
Am 4: 3 the breached *w* each by the most direct way,
Mi 7:11 It is the day for building your *w*;
Lk 19:44 out, you and your children within your *w*,
Heb 11:30 the *w* of Jericho fell after being

WAND (1)

Hos 4:12 and their *w* makes pronouncements for them,

WANDER (13)

Nm 14:33 where your children must *w* for forty years,
32:13 LORD made them *w* in the desert forty years,
2Sm 15:20 and shall I have you *w* about with us today,
Ps(s) 59:16 They *w* about as scavengers;
Eccl 6: 9 is better than what the desires *w* after."
Sir 9: 7 of the city and *w* not through its squares;
Is 63:17 Why do you let us *w*,
Jer 14:10 to *w* that they do not spare their feet.
Am 8:12 Then shall they *w* from sea to sea and rove
Zec 10: 2 This is why they *w* like sheep, wretched:
Mt 18:13 about the ninety-nine that did not *w* away.
2Tm 4: 4 to the truth and will *w* off to fables.
2Pt 2:15 road and *w* off on the path taken by Balaam,

WANDERED (10)

Dt 2: 3 have *w* round these highlands long enough;
Jos 5: 6 Israelites had *w* forty years in the desert,
1Sm 9: 3 asses of Saul's father, Kish, had *w* off.
23:13 left Keilah and *w* from place to place.
1Chr 17: 6 long as I have *w* about with all of Israel.
Sir 24: 5 alone, through the deep abyss I *w*.
Jer 50: 6 From mountain to hill they *w*,
Lam 4:15 If they left and *w* among the nations,
Ez 34: 6 *w* over all the mountains and high hills;
Heb 11:38 They *w* about in deserts and on mountains,

WANDERER (5)

Gn 4:12 You shall become a restless *w* on the earth."
4:14 and become a restless *w* on the earth,
Jb 15:23 A *w*,
31:19 If I have seen a *w* without clothing,
Sir 36:25 a man with no wife becomes a homeless *w*.

WANDERERS (1)

Hos 9:17 they shall be *w* among the nations.

WANDERING (9)

Gn 20:13 When God sent me *w* from my father's house,
37:15 met him as he was *w* about in the fields.
Ex 14: 3 are *w* about aimlessly in the land.
Dt 26: 5 'My father was a *w* Aramean who went down
1Chr 16:20 strangers there, *W* from nation to nation,
Ps(s) 105:13 *W* from nation to nation and from one
Sg 1: 7 *w* after the flocks of your companions.
Sir 29:18 and sent them *w* through foreign lands.
1Cor 4:11 clad, roughly treated, *w* about homeless.

WANDERINGS (2)

2Sm 7: 7 all my *w* everywhere among the Israelites,
Ps(s) 56: 9 My *w* you have counted;

WANDERS (6)

Jb 18: 8 into a net, and he *w* into a pitfall.
Prv 19:27 instruction, he *w* from words of knowledge.
Is 47:15 Each *w* his own way,
Mt 18:12 a hundred sheep and one of them *w* away;
Lk 11:24 it *w* through arid wastes searching for a
2Thes 3: 6 to avoid any brother who *w* from the

WANES (1)

Sir 43: 7 this light-giver which *w* in its course:

WANING (1)

Jer 6: 4 the day is *w*,

WANT (121)

Gn 30:28 "state what wages you *w* from me,
32:30 "Why should you *w* to know my name?"
43:18 they *w* to use it as a pretext to attack us
45:11 and all that are yours may not suffer *w*.
Ex 10:11 After all, that is what you *w*."
Nm 20:19 "We *w* only to go up along the highway.
Dt 2: 7 with you, and you have never been in *w*.'
28:57 uses them for food for *w* of anything else,
Jgs 18:23 about and said to Micah, "What do you *w*,
18:24 How, then, can you ask me what I *w*?"
19:24 them, or do whatever you *w* with them;
1Sm 12:13 "Now you have the king you *w*,
28:11 him, "Whom do you *w* me to conjure up?"
2Sm 14: 5 The king said to her, "What do you *w*?"
18:22 "Why do you *w* to run, my son?
18:23 he insisted, "Come what may, I *w* to run."
24:13 "Do you *w* a three years' famine to come
1Kgs 11:11 "Since this is what you *w*,
2Kgs 3:13 "What do you *w* with me?"
6:19 I will take you to the man you *w*."
Neh 9:21 did not *w*; their garments did not become
Jb 5:22 At destruction and *w* you shall laugh;
24: 8 for *w* of shelter they cling to the rock.
30: 3 In *w* and hunger was their lot,
Ps(s) 23: 1 The LORD is my shepherd; I shall not *w*.
34:11 who seek the LORD *w* for no good thing.
107:10 and gloom, bondsmen in *w* and in chains,
Prv 6:11 a highway man, and *w* like an armed man.
10:21 nourish many, but fools die for *w* of sense.
13:25 but the belly of the wicked suffers *w*.
21:17 He who loves pleasure will suffer *w*;
24:34 like a highwayman, and *w* like an armed man.
28:22 and he knows not when *w* will come upon him.
28:27 He who gives to the poor suffers no *w*,
30: 9 being in *w*, I steal, and profane the name
Wis 16: 4 those oppressors, inexorable *w* had to come;
Sir 18:25 plenty, poverty and *w* in the day of wealth.
20:20 A man through *w* may be unable to sin,
26:19 A wealthy man reduced to *w*;
29: 9 precept, help the needy, and in their *w*,
31: 4 if ever he rests, he finds himself in *w*.
Is 51:14 into the pit, nor shall they *w* for bread.
Hos 4: 6 My people perish for *w* of knowledge!
Mt 7: 1 "If you *w* to avoid judgment,
10:42 he is a disciple will not *w* for his reward."
12:38 "Teacher, we *w* to see you work some signs."
13:28 'Do you *w* us to go out and pull them up?'
20:21 "What is it you *w*?"
20:32 to them, "What do you *w* me to do for you?"
Mk 1:24 "What do you *w* of us, Jesus of Nazareth?
6:22 anything you *w* and I will give it to you."
6:25 "I *w* you to give me,
6:26 of the guests, he did not *w* to refuse her.
9:30 but he did not *w* anyone to know about it.
10:35 they said, "we *w* you to grant our request."
10:51 him, "What do you *w* me to do for you?"
10:51 the blind man said, "I *w* to see."
12:43 "I *w* you to observe that this poor widow
12:44 surplus wealth, but she gave from her *w*,
15: 9 "Do you *w* me to release the king of the
Lk 4:34 What do you *w* of us, Jesus of Nazareth?
14:23 I *w* my house to be full,
18:41 him, "What do you *w* me to do for you?"
18:41 "Lord," he answered, "I *w* to see."
19:27 enemies of mine who do not *w* me to be king,
21: 4 her *w* has given what she could not afford
22: 9 him, "Where do you *w* us to get it ready?"
Jn 4:27 however, such as "What do you *w* of him?"
5: 6 him lying there, "Do you *w* to be healed?"
6:67 to the Twelve, "Do you *w* to leave me too?"
7:25 "Is this not the one they *w* to kill?
9:27 "Why do you *w* to hear it all over again?
9:27 tell me you *w* to become his disciples too?"
18: 4 and said to them, "Who is it you *w*?"
18: 7 question to them again, "Who is it you *w*?"
18: 8 "If I am the one you *w*,
18:39 Do you *w* me to release to you the king of
18:40 They shouted back, "We *w* Barabbas,
19:31 Jews did not *w* to have the bodies left
21:22 "Suppose I *w* him to stay until I come,"
21:23 "Suppose I *w* him to stay until I come
Acts 16:37 Now they *w* to smuggle us out in secret.
19:38 *w* to bring charges against anyone,
19:39 is any further matter you *w* to investigate,
23:20 that they *w* to question him more carefully.
Rom 1:13 I *w* you to know that I have often planned
7:15 do not do what I *w* to do but what I hate.
7:21 that even though I *w* to do what is right,
11:25 I do not *w* you to be ignorant of this
15:20 for I did not *w* to build on a foundation
16:19 I *w* you to be wise in regard to what is
1Cor 7:35 on you, but I do *w* to promote what is good,
10: 1 Brothers, I *w* you to remember this:
10:20 do not *w* you to become sharers with demons.
10:27 invites you to his table and you *w* to go,
11: 3 I *w* you to know that theConcerning Idol
12: 1 I do not *w* to leave you in ignorance about
14:15 I *w* to pray with my spirit,
14:15 I *w* to sing with my spirit and with my
14:35 If they *w* to learn anything,
15: 1 I *w* to remind you of the gospel I preached
16: 7 I do not *w* to see you just in passing.
2Cor 11: 9 and in *w* I was a burden to none of you,
12:14 I do not want what you have, I only *w* you.
Gal 3: 2 I *w* to learn only one thing from you:
4:17 What they really *w* is to exclude you so
4:21 You who *w* to be subject to the law,
6:13 They *w* you to be circumcised only that
Phil 1:12 I *w* you to know that my situation has
4:11 I do not say this because I am in *w*,
4:14 kind of you to *w* to share in my hardships.
Col 2: 1 I *w* you to know how hard I am struggling
1Thes 4:12 example to outsiders and *w* for nothing.
1Tm 5:11 them from Christ they will *w* to marry.
6: 9 Those who *w* to be rich are falling into
Ti 3: 8 I *w* you to lay great weight on the things
Phlm 1:14 not *w* to do anything without your consent,
1:20 *w* to make you "useful" to me in the Lord.
Jas 2:20 Do you *w* proof,
Rv 3:17 am so rich and secure that I *w* for nothing."

WANTED (32)

Tb 1:19 knew all about me and *w* to put me to death,
8: 1 drinking, the girl's parents *w* to retire.
1Mc 3:34 concerning everything he *w* done.
2Mc 13:25 that they *w* to annul its provisions.
14:32 that they did not know where the *w* man was,
15:38 and to the point, that is what I *w*;
Ps(s) 35:25 This is what we *w*!"
Mt 14: 5 Herod *w* to kill John but was afraid of
21:31 Which of the two did what the father *w*?"
Mk 6:19 and *w* to kill him but was unable to do so.
7:24 house and *w* no one to recognize him;
12:12 They *w* to arrest him at this,
Lk 13:34 How often have I *w* to gather your children
23: 8 him he had *w* for a long time to see him,
23:20 for he *w* Jesus to be the one he released.
Jn 1:43 The next day he *w* to set out for Galilee,
6:11 with the dried fish, as much as they *w*,
6:21 They *w* to take him into the boat,
7:44 Some of them even *w* to apprehend him.
16:19 was aware that they *w* to question him,
Acts 5:33 they were stung to fury and *w* to kill them.
15:37 Barnabas *w* to take along John,
18:27 He *w* to go on to Achaia,
19:30 Paul *w* to go before this gathering but his
19:33 he *w* to explain something to the gathering.
24:27 *w* to ingratiate himself with the Jews,
28:18 The Romans tried my case and *w* to release
1Cor 12:18 of the body in the place he *w* it to be.
2Cor 1:15 I *w* to visit you first so that a double
1Thes 2: 8 that we *w* to share with you not only God's
Phlm 1:13 I had *w* to keep him with me,
Heb 12:17 he *w* to inherit his father's blessing,

WANTING (7)

Tb 5:14 for *w* to learn the truth about your family.
Prv 10:19 Where words are many, sin is not *w*;
Sir 40:26 Fear of the LORD leaves nothing *w*;
Lam 2: 9 priestly instruction is *w*,
Ez 20:17 on them with pity, not *w* to destroy them,
Dn 5:27 been weighed on the scales and found *w*;
1Tm 1: 7 *w* to be teachers of the law but actually

WANTON (24)

Ex 34:15 when they render their *w* worship to their
34:16 render their *w* worship to their gods,
Lv 17: 7 whom they used to render their *w* worship.
20: 5 who join him in his *w* worship of Molech.
20: 6 and fortune-tellers and follow their *w* ways,
Dt 31:16 people will take to rendering *w* worship

WANTON (cont.)

Jgs 19:24 the man you must not commit this *w* crime."
Ps(s) 19:14 From *w* sin especially,
106:39 by their works, and *w* in their crimes.
Sir 10: 3 A *w* king destroys his people,
21:15 the *w* hears them with scorn and casts them
23:23 in her *w* adultery she has borne children
27:13 is offensive, their laughter is *w* guilt.
31: 3 wealth, and his only rest is *w* pleasure;
42: 8 aged and infirm answering for *w* conduct.
Is 22: 2 O *w* town Your slain are not slain with the
23: 7 Is this your *w* city,
25: 5 even so you quell the uproar of the *w*.
32:13 For all the joyful houses, the *w* city.
57: 3 sons of a sorceress, adulterous, *w* race!
Hos 10:10 the *w* people I came and I chastised them;
Am 6: 7 their *w* revelry shall be done away with.
Jas 5: 5 You lived in *w* luxury on the earth;
1Pt 4: 3 orgies, carousing, and *w* idolatry.

WANTONLY (1)

Nm 15:39 without going *w* astray after the desires

WANTONNESS (3)

Wis 2: 9 Let no meadow be free from our *w*;
14:12 the source of *w* is the devising of idols
Rv 18: 3 merchants grew rich from her wealth and *w*."

WANTS (19)

1Kgs 20: 7 clearly that this man *w* to ruin us.
Tb 5:10 "My son Tobiah *w* to go to Media.
Sir 37: 8 advice, find out first of all what he *w*.
Jer 22:28 be broken up, an instrument that no one *w*?
48:38 shattered Moab like a pot that no one *w*,
Mt 5:40 If anyone *w* to go to law over your shirt,
20:27 and whoever *w* to rank first among you must
27:43 let God rescue him now if he *w* to.
Mk 10:44 whoever *w* to rank first among you must
Lk 5:39 No one, after drinking old wine, *w* new.
Jn 7:20 "Who *w* to kill you?"
Acts 24:23 prevent his friends from seeing to his *w*.
1Cor 11:16 If anyone *w* to argue about this,
1Tm 2: 4 for he *w* all men to be saved and come to
3: 1 *w* to be a bishop aspires to a noble task.
5: 4 this is the way God *w* it to be.
2Tm 3:12 Anyone who *w* to live a godly life in
1Pt 3:10 "He who cares for life and *w* to see
2Pt 3: 9 since he *w* none to perish but all to come

WAR (173)

Gn 14: 2 king of Goiim made *w* on Bera king of Sodom,
31:26 carrying off my daughters like *w* captives?
Ex 1:10 in time of *w* they too may join our enemies
17: 8 Amalek came and waged *w* against Israel.
17:16 *w* against Amalek through the centuries."
Lv 26: 6 sword of *w* from sweeping across your land.
Nm 10: 9 *w* against an enemy that is attacking you,
31: 3 men from your midst and arm them for *w*,
31: 4 shall send a band of one thousand men to *w*."
31: 5 there were twelve thousand men armed for *w*.
31: 7 They waged *w* against the Midianites,
31:27 part in the *w* by going out to combat,
32: 6 "Are your kinsmen, then, to engage in *w*,
Dt 4:34 by testings, by signs and wonders, by *w*,
20: 1 "When you go out to *w* against your
20:19 "When you are at *w* with a city and have
21:10 out to *w* against your enemies and the LORD,
Jos 11:18 *w* against all these kings for a long time.
11:20 to encourage them to wage *w* against Israel,
14:11 vigor whether for *w* or for ordinary tasks.
22:12 community at Shiloh to declare *w* on them.
22:33 against declaring *w* on the Reubenites
24: 9 king of Moab, prepared to *w* against Israel.
Jgs 3:10 When he went out to *w*,
5: 8 then the *w* was at their gates.
10:17 had gathered for *w* and encamped in Gilead,
10:18 "The one who begins the *w* against the
11:25 or did he *w* against them when Israel
18:11 Danites, fully armed with weapons of *w*,
18:16 six hundred men girt with weapons of *w*,
21:22 we did not take a woman apiece in the *w*.
1Sm 8:12 of *w* and the equipment of his chariots.
12: 9 the king of Moab, who made *w* against them.
14:47 waged *w* on all their surrounding enemies
14:52 An unremitting *w* was waged against the
17:13 sons of Jesse had followed Saul to *w*;
17:13 sons who had gone off to *w* were named,
19: 8 When *w* broke out again,
23: 8 Saul then called all the people to *w*,
28:15 *w* against me and God has abandoned me.
2Sm 1:27 fallen, the weapons of *w* have perished!"
3: 1 There followed a long *w* between the house
3: 6 During the *w* between the house of Saul and
11: 7 the soldiers, and how the *w* was going,
22:35 *w* till my arms could bend a bow of brass.
22:40 "You girded me with strength for *w*;
1Kgs 2: 5 for the blood of *w* in a time of peace,
8:44 people forth to *w* against their enemies,
15: 6 There was *w* between Abijam and Jeroboam.
15:16 There was *w* between Asa and Baasha,
15:32 [There was *w* between Asa and Baasha,
20:18 they have come out for peace or for *w*,
22: 1 passed without *w* between Aram and Israel.
2Kgs 6: 8 the king of Aram was waging *w* on Israel,
18:20 substitute for strategy and might in *w*?
1Chr 5:10 of Saul they waged *w* with the Hagrites,
5:19 *w* against the Hagrites and against Jetur,
10: 1 Now the Philistines were at *w* with Israel;
12:34 array with every kind of weapon for *w*:
12:38 equipped with every kind of weapon of *w*:
18:10 waged a victorious *w* against Hadadezer;
18:10 for Hadadezer had been at *w* with Tou.
19: 7 from their cities and came out for *w*.
20: 1 year, the time when kings go to *w*,
20: 5 again there was *w* with the Philistines,
2Chr 6:34 people go forth to *w* against their enemies,
12:15 There was *w* continually between Rehoboam
13: 2 There was *w* between Abijah and Jeroboam.
14: 5 for the land had peace and no *w* was waged
15:19 There was no *w* until the thirty-fifth year
17:10 so that they did not *w* against Jehoshaphat.
17:18 hundred and eighty thousand equipped for *w*.
25: 5 hundred thousand picked men fit for *w*,
28:12 to those who had returned from the *w*.
35:21 this day, for my *w* is with another kingdom,
Jdt 1: 5 *w* against King Arphaxad in the vast plain,
1:11 and would not go with him to the *w*.
4: 5 stored up provisions in preparation for *w*.
16:11 at the sound of their *w* cry,
Est A: 6 at their cry every nation prepared for *w*,
1Mc 1:18 with a large fleet, to make *w* on Ptolemy,
2:66 army and direct the *w* against the nations.
3: 2 and they carried on Israel's *w* joyfully.
3: 3 He armed himself with weapons of *w*;
3:13 an assembly of faithful men ready for *w*,
3:19 for victory in *w* does not depend upon the
6:30 and thirty-two elephants trained for *w*.
8:10 Greeks a single general who made *w* on them.
8:24 But if *w* is first made on Rome,
8:26 *w* they shall not give nor provide grain,
8:27 if *w* is made first on the Jewish nation,
8:32 justice and make *w* on you by land and sea.'"
11: 4 in the *w* and stacked up along his route.
12:44 to so much trouble when we are not at *w*?
12:53 let us make *w* on them and wipe out their
14: 7 of *w* and made himself master of Gazara,
14: 9 young men wore the glorious apparel of *w*.
15:19 or wage *w* against them or their cities or
15:31 do this, we will come and make *w* on you."
2Mc 2:14 that had been scattered because of the *w*,
8: 9 commander, well-versed in the art of *w*.
10:15 Jerusalem and endeavored to continue the *w*.
Jb 5:20 and in *w* from the threat of the sword;
20:23 and rain down his missiles of *w* upon him.
38:23 of stress, for the days of *w* and of battle?
Ps(s) 18:35 for *w* and my arms to bend a bow of brass.
18:40 And you girded me with strength for *w*;
27: 3 Though *w* be waged upon me,
35: 1 *w* against those who make war upon me.
55:19 and peace from those who *w* against me,
55:22 is his speech, but *w* is in his heart;
68:31 scatter the peoples who delight in *w*.
76: 4 bow, shield and sword, and weapons of *w*.
120: 7 I speak of peace, they are ready for *w*.
144: 1 my hands for battle, my fingers for *w*;
Prv 20:18 so with wise guidance wage your *w*.
24: 6 is by wise guidance that you wage your *w*,
28: 4 but those who keep the law *w* against him.
Eccl 3: 8 a time of *w*,
Wis 5:20 shall *w* with him against the foolhardy.
8:15 I should appear noble, and in *w* courageous.
14:22 though they live in a great *w* of ignorance,
Sir 37:11 about her rival, nor to a coward about *w*,
Is 2: 4 another, nor shall they train for *w* again.
3:25 by the sword, and your champions, in *w*;
19: 2 brother will *w* against brother,
29: 7 horde of all the nations who *w* against Ariel
29: 8 the nations be, who make *w* against Zion.
31: 4 wage *w* upon the mountain and hill of Zion.
36: 5 substitute for strategy and might in *w*?
Jer 4:16 their *w* cry against the cities of Judah."
4:19 the sound of the trumpet, the alarm of *w*.
6: 4 "Prepare for *w* against her, Up!
20:16 Let him hear *w* cries in the morning,
28: 8 who were before you and me prophesied *w*,
42:14 to Egypt, where we will see no more of *w*,
48:14 say, "We are heroes, men valiant in *w*"?
50:15 raise the *w* cry against her on all sides,
51:20 You are my hammer, my weapon for *w*;
51:27 Dedicate peoples to *w* against her,
51:28 Dedicate peoples to *w* against her:
Bar 3:26 at the first, stalwarts, skilled in *w*.
6:14 it cannot save itself from *w* or pillage.
6:48 For when *w* or disaster comes upon them,
6:49 themselves either from *w* or from disaster?
Ez 7:14 everything ready, yet no one shall go to *w*,
32:27 the nether world with their weapons of *w*,
Dn 7:21 that horn made *w* against the holy ones and
9:26 until the end there shall be *w*,
10: 1 a great *w*; he understood it from
Hos 1: 7 But I will not save them by *w*,
2:20 sword and *w* I will destroy from the land,
10: 9 *w* was not to reach them in Gibeah.
10:14 As Salman ravaged Beth-arbel in time of *w*,
Jl 4: 9 proclaim a *w*, rouse the warriors to arms!
Ob 1: 1 let us go to *w* against him!"
Mi 2: 8 confidence, as though it were spoils of *w*.
3: 5 in their mouth, proclaim *w* against him.
4: 3 another, nor shall they train for *w* again.
Zec 10: 3 Judah, and make them his stately *w* horse.
10: 5 shall wage *w* because the LORD is with them,
Mk 13: 7 When you hear about wars and threats of *w*,
Rom 7:23 another law at *w* with the law of my mind;
2Cor 10: 3 but we do not wage *w* with human resources.
Jas 4: 1 cravings that make *w* within your members?
1Pt 2:11 By their nature they wage *w* on the soul.
Rv 11: 7 *w* against them and conquer and kill them.
12: 7 Then *w* broke out in heaven;
12:17 off to make *w* on the rest of her offspring,
13: 7 *w* against God's people and conquer them.
19:11 in passing judgment and in waging *w*.
20: 8 muster for *w* the troops of Gog and Magog,

WARD (4)

Jdt 4: 7 be easy to *w* off the attacking forces,
Eccl 11:10 *W* off grief from your heart and put away
Sir 23: 5 *w* off passion from my heart,
27:22 plots mischief and no one can *w* him off;

WARDROBE (4)

2Kgs 10:22 Then Jehu said to the custodian of the *w*,
22:14 of Tikvah, son of Harhas, keeper of the *w*.
2Chr 34:22 son of Hasrah, the guardian of the *w*;
Jas 5: 2 rotted, your fine *w* has grown moth-eaten,

WARE (2)

Ezr 1:10 other *w*,
1:11 Total of the gold- and silver *w*:

WARES (7)

Ez 27:12 silver, iron, tin, and lead for your *w*.
27:14 and mules were exchanged for your *w*.
27:16 fine linen, coral, and rubies for your *w*.
27:19 and aromatic cane from Uzal for your *w*.
27:22 for your *w* the very choicest spices,
27:27 Your wealth, your goods, your *w*,
27:34 Your *w* and all your crew have gone down

WARFARE (8)

1Sm 8:20 and to lead us in *w* and fight our battles."
2Sm 17: 8 since your father is skilled in *w*,
1Kgs 14:19 acts of Jeroboam, with his *w* and his reign,
14:30 constant *w* between Rehoboam and Jeroboam.
1Chr 5:18 sword and who drew the bow, trained in *w*—
Jdt 9: 8 not know that "'You, the Lord, crush *w*;
16: 2 he crushes *w*,
2Cor 10: 4 The weapons of our *w* are not merely human.

WARM (13)

Jos 9:12 This bread of ours was still *w* when we
1Kgs 1: 1 spread covers over him he could not keep *w*.
1: 2 your royal majesty, you will be kept *w*."
2Kgs 4:34 himself over the child, the body became *w*.
Tb 2:10 till their *w* droppings settled in my eyes,
Eccl 4:11 two sleep together, they keep each other *w*.
4:11 How can one alone keep *w*?
Is 44:16 I am *w*, I feel the fire."
Dn 13:15 decided to bathe, for the weather was *w*.
Mk 14:54 guard and began to *w* himself at the fire.
Jn 18:18 made a charcoal fire to *w* themselves by.
Acts 21:17 the brothers there gave us a *w* welcome.
Jas 2:16 Keep *w* and well fed,"

WARMED (3)

Jb 31:20 me when *w* with the fleece of my sheep;
Wis 16:27 fire, when merely *w* by a momentary sunbeam,
Hg 1: 6 have clothed yourselves, but not been *w*;

WARMING (4)

Is 47:14 This is no *w* ember, no fire to sit before,
Mk 14:67 When she noticed Peter *w* himself,
Jn 18:18 joined them and stood there *w* himself.
18:25 Peter had been standing there *w* himself.

WARMONGERS (1)

2Mc 14: 6 Hasideans, led by Judas Maccabeus, are *w*,

WARMS (4)

Sir 1:10 Fear of the LORD *w* the heart,
Is 44:15 With a part of their wood he *w* himself,
44:16 he is full, and then *w* himself and says,
Na 3:17 Yet when the sun *w* them,

WARMTH (1)

Sir 3:15 *w* upon frost it will melt away your sins.

WARN (32)

Ex 4:23 If you refuse to let him go, I *w* you,
7:27 me, If you refuse to let them go, I *w* you,
8:17 If you will not let my people go, I *w* you,
9: 3 go and persist in holding them, I *w* you,

9:18 I *w* you, then, tomorrow at this hour
10: 4 If you refuse to let my people go, I *w* you,
19:21 "Go down and *w* the people not to break
Lv 15:31 *w* the Israelites of their uncleanness,
Nm 23:26 "Did I not *w* you that I must do all that
24:12 *w* the very messengers whom you sent to me.
24:14 let me first *w* you what this people will
Dt 1:42 But the LORD said to me, *W* them:
1Sm 8: 9 *w* them solemnly and inform them of the
2Chr 19:10 *w* them lest they become guilty before the
Wis 12: 2 rebuke offenders little by little, *w* them,
Jer 6:10 whom shall I *w*, and be heard?
42:19 never say that I did not *w* you this day.
Ez 3:17 from my mouth, you shall *w* them for me.
3:18 and you do not *w* him or speak out to
3:20 for his death if you did not *w* him.
33: 3 country, blows the trumpet to *w* the people,
33: 7 me say anything, you shall *w* them for me.
33: 9 But if you *w* the wicked man,
Mt 5:26 I *w* you, you will not be released until
6:25 I *w* you, then: do not worry about your
Lk 12:22 "That is why I *w* you,
12:59 I *w* you, you will not be released from
Rom 12: 3 I *w* each of you not to think more highly
Gal 5:21 I *w* you, as I have warned you before:
1Thes 3: 4 used to *w* you that we would undergo trial;
1Tm 1: 3 stay on in Ephesus in order to *w* certain
Ti 3:10 *W* a heretic once and then a second time;

WARNED (26)

Gn 31:24 to Laban the Aramean in a dream and *w* him,
43: 3 "The man strictly *w* us.
Ex 19:15 He *w* them, "Be ready for the third day.
19:23 for you yourself *w* us to set limits around
21:29 of goring people and its owner, though *w*,
Nm 16:26 Then he *w* the community,
1Sm 15: 6 an ambush in the wadi, *w* the Kenites:
2Kgs 17:13 And though the LORD *w* Israel and Judah by
Neh 4: 9 been *w* and that God had upset their plan,
13:15 I *w* them to sell none of these victuals.
13:21 twice outside Jerusalem, but then I *w* them,
2Mc 12:42 The noble Judas *w* the soldiers to keep
Sir 12:12 when you groan with regret, as I *w* you.
Jer 6: 8 Be *w*, O Jerusalem, lest I be estranged
11: 7 I *w* your fathers to obey my voice,
Bar 2: 7 which the Lord has *w* us have come upon us:
2:20 *w* us through your servants the prophets:
Ez 3:19 the other hand, you have *w* the wicked man,
3:21 hand, you have *w* a virtuous man not to sin,
6: 8 I have *w* you.]
23:48 will be *w* not to imitate your lewdness.
Zec 1: 4 your fathers whom the former prophets *w*:
Mt 9:30 Then Jesus *w* them sternly,
Gal 5:21 I warn you, as I have *w* you before:
Heb 8: 5 when about to erect the tabernacle, was *w*,
11: 7 By faith Noah, *w* about things not yet seen,

WARNING (44)

Gn 26:11 therefore gave this *w* to all his men:
Ex 9:20 Some of Pharaoh's servants feared the *w* of
9:21 did not take the *w* of the LORD to heart
Nm 17:25 to be kept there as a *w* to the rebellious,
26:10 its mouth and swallowed them as a *w*
Dt 1:43 I gave you this *w* but you would not listen.
17:16 against the LORD's *w* that you must never
32:46 "Take to heart all the *w* which I have
Jgs 2:15 them, as in his *w* he had sworn he would do,
1Sm 2:25 But they disregarded their father's *w*,
8:19 refused to listen to Samuel's *w* and said,
2Sm 17:16 So send a *w* to David immediately,
1Kgs 2:42 to your clear understanding of my *w* that,
15:29 according to the *w* which the LORD had
2Kgs 10:24 stationed eighty men outside with this *w*,
18:12 they had not heeded the *w* of the LORD,
Jb 33:16 opens the ears of men and as a *w* to them,
Ps(s) 2:10 take *w*,
Wis 16: 6 But as a *w*, for a short time they were
Is 8:11 *w* me not to walk in the way of this people:
20: 2 it, the LORD gave a *w* through Isaiah,
Jer 44: 5 they would not listen or accept the *w*
Bar 2: 1 fulfilled the *w* he had uttered against us:
2:28 This was your *w* through your servant Moses,
Ez 3:21 he shall surely live because of the *w*,
5:15 *w* to the nations that surround you.
33: 4 hearing but not heeding the *w* of the trumpet
33: 5 the trumpet blast yet refused to take *w*;
33: 5 *w* he would have escaped with his life.
33: 6 coming and fails to blow the *w* trumpet,
Mt 2:22 because of a *w* received in a dream,
8:24 *w* a violent storm came up on the lake,
16:11 *w* you against the yeast of the Pharisees?"
16:12 realized he was not issuing a *w* against yeast
28: 9 without *w*, Jesus stood before them
Mk 1:43 gave him a stern *w* and sent him on his way.
Lk 9:45 failed, however, to understand this *w*;
16:28 Let him be a *w* to them so that they may
Acts 4:17 must give them a stern *w* never to mention
20:23 Holy Spirit has been *w* me from city to city
20:31 I never ceased *w* you individually even to
27: 9 It was then that Paul uttered this *w*:
1Cor 10:11 They have been written as a *w* to us,
1Tm 1: 5 What we are aiming at in this *w* is the

WARNINGS (4)

2Kgs 17:15 fathers, and the *w* which he had given them.
2Chr 24:19 the people would not listen to their *w*.
36:16 the messengers of God, despised his *w*,
Acts 4:21 point they were dismissed with further *w*.

WARPED (1)

Prv 12: 8 praised, but one with a *w* mind is despised.

WARRED (1)

Jgs 11: 4 Some time later, the Ammonites *w* on Israel.

WARRING (1)

Jgs 11:27 you, but you wrong me by *w* against me,

WARRIOR (30)

Ex 15: 3 The LORD is a *w*, LORD is his name!
Jos 17: 1 Machir, the father of Gilead, was a *w*,
1Sm 17:33 while he has been a *w* from his youth."
2Sm 17:10 all Israel knows that your father is a *w*
1Chr 7: 2 *w* heads of the ancestral houses of Tola.
12: 4 Gibeonite, a *w* on the level of the Thirty,
12:29 seven hundred, and Zadok, a young *w*,
27: 6 a *w* among the Thirty and over the Thirty.
2Chr 17:17 Eliada, a valiant *w*,
28: 7 Zichri, an Ephraimite *w*,
32:21 an angel, who destroyed every valiant *w*,
1Mc 2:66 And Judas Maccabeus, a *w* from his youth,
10:19 are a mighty *w* and worthy to be our friend.
Jb 16:14 he attacks me like a *w*.
Ps(s) 33:16 nor is a *w* delivered by great strength.
120: 4 of a *w* with fiery coals of brushwood.
127: 4 hand of a *w* are the sons of one's youth.
Prv 16:32 A patient man is better than a *w*,
Wis 18:15 heaven's royal throne bounded, a fierce *w*,
Sir 35:19 God indeed will not delay, and like a *w*,
47: 5 *w* and raise up the might of his people,
Is 3: 2 Hero and *w*,
42:13 a hero, like a *w* he stirs up his ardor;
49:24 Can booty be taken from a *w*?
49:25 Yes, captives can be taken from a *w*,
Jer 46:12 *W* trips over warrior, both fall together.
50: 9 Their arrows are arrows of the skilled *w*;
Jl 4:10 let the weak man say, "I am a *w*!"
Am 2:14 The *w* shall not save his life,

WARRIORS—WARRIOR'S (95)

Ex 14: 7 chariots of Egypt, with *w* on them all.
Nm 31:28 the LORD on the *w* who went out to combat:
Jos 1:14 But all the *w* among you must cross over
5: 6 until all the *w* among the people that came
8: 3 Picking out thirty thousand *w*,
Jgs 5:13 people of the LORD came down for me as *w*.
5:23 to my help, as *w* to the help of the LORD."
20:44 eighteen thousand of them fell, *w* to a man.
20:46 twenty-five thousand swordsmen, *w* to a man.
21:10 sent twelve thousand *w* with orders to go
1Sm 10:26 by *w* whose hearts the LORD had touched.
31:12 had done to Saul, all their *w* set out,
2Sm 1:19 how can the *w* have fallen!
1:21 Upon you lie begrimed the *w*' shields,
1:25 "How can the *w* have fallen
1:27 "How can the *w* have fallen,
17: 8 know that your father and his men are *w*,
20: 7 all the *w* marched out behind Abishai
23: 8 These are the names of David's *w*.
23: 9 Next to him, among the Three *w*,
23:12 Such were the deeds of the Three *w*.
23:16 So the Three *w* broke through the
23:22 He was listed among the Thirty *w* and
1Kgs 12:21 hundred and eighty thousand seasoned *w*—
1Chr 5:18 and half-tribe of Manasseh were *w*,
5:24 men who were *w*,
7: 5 thousand *w* in their family records.
7: 7 were heads of their ancestral houses and *w*.
7: 9 were heads of their ancestral houses and *w*.
7:11 Jediael, heads of ancestral houses and *w*.
7:40 of ancestral houses, distinguished men, *w*,
10:12 had done to Saul, its *w* rose to a man,
11:10 These were David's chief *w* who,
11:11 Here is the list of David's *w*:
11:12 of Dodo the Ahohite, one of the Three *w*.
11:19 Such deeds as these the Three *w* performed.
11:26 Also these *w*: Asahel, the brother
12: 1 among the *w* who helped him in his battles.
12: 9 They were valiant *w*,
12:22 all *w* and became commanders of his army.
12:26 Of the Simeonites, *w* fit for battle:
12:31 twenty thousand eight hundred *w*,
19: 8 Joab and his whole army of *w* against them.
26: 6 ruled over their family, for they were *w*.
28: 1 courtiers, the *w* and every important man.
29:24 All the leaders and *w*,
2Chr 8: 9 They became soldiers, commanders of his *w*,
11: 1 a hundred and eighty thousand seasoned *w*,
13: 3 a force of four hundred thousand picked *w*,
13: 3 hundred thousand picked and valiant *w*.
14: 7 and were archers, all of them valiant *w*,
17:13 of Judah, and he had soldiers, valiant *w*,
17:14 with him three hundred thousand valiant *w*.
17:16 with him two hundred thousand valiant *w*.
25: 6 also hired a hundred thousand valiant *w*
26:12 valiant *w* was two thousand six hundred,
32: 3 decided in counsel with his princes and *w*
Neh 11: 8 son of Jeshaiah, and his brethren, *w*,
11:14 son of Immer, and his brethren, *w*,
Jdt 1:16 with all his numerous, motley horde of *w*;
15: 3 Then all the Israelite *w* overwhelmed them.
1Mc 16: 4 in the land twenty thousand *w* and horsemen.
Is 13: 3 dedicated soldiers, I have summoned my *w*,
Jer 5:16 all of them are *w*.
39: 4 saw them, he and all his *w* fled by night,
46: 9 Set out, *w*,
49:26 streets, and all her *w* shall be stilled.
50:30 all her *w* shall perish on that day,
50:36 A sword upon her *w*,
51:30 Babylon's *w* have ceased to fight,
51:32 set on fire, while *w* are in panic.
51:57 her governors, her prefects, and her *w*,
Ez 23: 5 lovers, the Assyrians, *w* dressed in purple,
23:12 and officers, *w* impeccably clothed,
23:15 their heads, all looking like chariot *w*
23:23 governors and officers, charioteers and *w*,
27:10 and Lud and Put were in your army as *w*;
27:27 for your goods, all your *w* who were in you,
32:12 cut down your horde with the blades of *w*,
32:20 world, the mighty *w* shall speak to Egypt:
39:18 You shall eat the flesh of *w* and drink the
39:20 riders, with *w* and soldiers of every kind,
Hos 10:13 in your chariots, and in your many *w*,
Jl 2: 7 Like *w* they run, like soldiers they scale
4: 9 proclaim a war, rouse the *w* to arms!
4:11 [Bring down, O Lord, your *w*
Am 2:16 of *w* shall flee naked on that day,
Ob 1: 9 Your *w*,
Na 2: 4 The shields of his *w* are crimsoned,
Zep 1:14 bitter, then, the *w* cry.
Zec 9:10 The *w* bow shall be banished,
9:13 O Yavan,] and I will use you as a *w* sword.
10: 4 chief, from him *w* bow and every officer.
10: 5 They shall all be *w*,
Rv 19:18 the flesh of kings, of commanders and *w*,

WARS (18)

Nm 21:14 said in the "Book of the *W* of the LORD":
1Chr 22: 8 much blood, and you have waged great *w*.
26:27 from the booty they had taken in the *w*,
28: 3 you are a man who fought *w* and shed blood.'
2Chr 16: 9 matter, for from now on you will have *w*."
27: 7 acts of Jotham, his *w* and his activities,
Jdt 5:18 steadily, more and more, by frequent *w*,
1Mc 12:13 But many hardships and *w* have beset us,
12:14 rest of our allies and friends in these *w*;
14:29 there have often been *w* in our country,
16:23 his *w* and the brave deeds he performed,
2Mc 10:10 summary of the chief evils caused by the *w*.
Ps(s) 46:10 He has stopped *w* to the end of the earth:
140: 3 in their hearts, and stir up *w* every day.
Mt 24: 6 You will hear of *w* and rumors of wars.
Mk 13: 7 When you hear about *w* and threats of war,
Lk 21: 9 when you hear of *w* and insurrections.

WARSHIPS (1)

1Mc 15: 3 equipped *w* to make a landing in my country

WASH (67)

Ex 19:10 Make them *w* their garments and be ready
19:14 sanctify themselves and *w* their garments.
29: 4 meeting tent, and there *w* them with water.
29:17 inner organs and shanks you shall first *w*,
30:20 the meeting tent, they must *w* with water,
30:21 the LORD they must *w* their hands and feet,
40:12 meeting tent, and there *w* them with water.
40:31 sons used to *w* their hands and feet there,
Lv 1: 9 the offerer shall first *w* with water.
1:13 the offerer shall first *w* with water.
11:25 shall *w* his garments and be unclean until
11:28 shall *w* his garments and be unclean until
11:40 anyone who eats of its dead body shall *w*
11:40 removes its dead body shall *w* his garments
13: 6 shall *w* his garments and so become clean.
13:34 the latter shall *w* his garments,
14: 8 The man being purified shall then *w* his
14: 9 *w* his garments and bathe his body in water;
14:47 in such a house shall also *w* his garments.
15: 5 who touches his bed shall *w* his garments,
15: 6 man was sitting, shall *w* his garments,
15: 7 of the afflicted man shall *w* his garments,
15: 8 clean man, the latter shall *w* his garments,
15:10 up any such thing shall *w* his garments,
15:11 with unrinsed hands shall *w* his garments,
15:13 Then he shall *w* his garments and bathe
15:21 who touches her bed shall *w* his garments,
15:22 she was sitting, shall *w* his garments,
15:27 he shall *w* his garments,
16:26 *w* his garments and bathe his body in water;
16:28 *w* his garments and bathe his body in water;
17:15 by a wild beast, shall *w* his garments,
17:16 he does not *w* or does not bathe his body,
Nm 5:23 then *w* them off into the bitter water,
8: 7 their whole bodies and *w* their clothes,

WASH (cont.)

19: 7 w his garments and bathe his body in water.
19: 8 who burned the heifer shall w his garments,
19:10 ashes of the heifer shall also w his garments
19:19 w his garments and bathe his body in water,
19:21 the lustral water shall w his garments,
31:24 the seventh day you shall w your clothes,
Dt 21: 6 city nearest the corpse shall w their hands
1Sm 25:41 slave to w the feet of my lord's servants."
2Kgs 5:10 "Go and w seven times in the Jordan,
5:12 Could I not w in them and be cleansed?"
5:13 now, since he said to you, W and be clean,'
2Chr 4: 6 but the sea was for the priests to w in.
Tb 6: 3 boy went down to w his feet in the river,
Jb 9:30 If I should w myself with snow and
14:19 and floods w away the soil of the land,
Ps(s) 26: 6 I w my hands in innocence,
51: 4 Thoroughly w me from my guilt and of my
51: 9 w me,
Is 1:16 W yourselves clean!
Mt 6:17 that you groom your hair and w your face.
15: 2 They do not w their hands,
Jn 9: 7 he told him, "Go, w in the pool of Siloam."
9:11 my eyes, telling me to go to Siloam and w.
9:11 When I did go and w, I was able to see."
13: 5 began to w his disciples' feet and dry them
13: 6 to him, "Lord, are you going to w my feet?"
13: 8 Peter replied, "You shall never w my feet!"
13: 8 "If I do not w you,"
13:10 has no need to w [except for his feet];
13:14 then you must w each other's feet.
Acts 22:16 w away your sins as you call upon his name.'
Rv 22:14 Happy are they who w their robes so as to

WASHBOWL (2)

Ps(s) 60:10 Moab shall serve as my w;
108:10 Moab shall serve as my w;

WASHED (36)

Ex 40:32 for they w themselves whenever they went
Lv 6:20 stained part must be w in a sacred place.
8: 6 and his sons, he first w them with water.
8:21 then having w the inner organs and the
9:14 Having w the inner organs and the shanks,
13:54 orders to have the infected article w
13:55 the infected article after it has been w.
13:58 the thing shall be w a second time,
15:17 w with water and be unclean until evening.
Nm 8:21 themselves of sin and w their clothes,
Jgs 19:21 Then they w their feet, and ate and drank.
2Sm 12:20 the ground, David w and anointed himself,
19:25 He had not w his feet nor trimmed his
19:25 nor w his clothes from the day the king left
1Kgs 22:38 the chariot was w at the pool of Samaria,
Tb 2: 5 I w myself and ate my food in sorrow.
Jdt 10: 3 of her widowhood, w her body with water,
12: 7 she w herself at the spring of the camp.
Ps(s) 73:13 clean and w my hands as an innocent man?
Is 18: 2 and conquering, whose land is w by rivers.
18: 7 and conquering, whose land is w by rivers
Ez 16: 4 you were neither w with water nor anointed,
16: 9 I bathed you with water, w away your blood,
Mt 27:24 and w his hands in front of the crowd,
Mk 7: 2 that is to say, w—
Lk 7:44 She has w my feet with her tears and wiped
Jn 9: 7 So the man went off and w,
9:15 I w it off, and now I can see."
13:11 (The reason he said, "Not all are w clean,"
13:12 After he had w their feet,
13:14 But if I w your feet
Acts 9:37 They w her body and laid it out in an
1Cor 6:11 but you have been w,
1Tm 5:10 Has she w the feet of Christian visitors?
Heb 10:22 conscience and our bodies w in pure water.
Rv 7:14 they have w their robes and made them

WASHES (2)

Gn 49:11 In wine he w his garments,
Is 4: 4 w away the filth of the daughters of Zion,

WASHING (11)

Gn 43:31 After w his face,
Ex 30:19 shall use it in w their hands and feet.
40:30 tent and altar, and put water in it for w.
Lv 13:56 finds that it is dying out after the w,
13:58 if, after the w, the infection has left
2Chr 4: 6 Then he made ten basins for w,
Sg 4: 2 to be shorn, which come up from the w,
6: 6 a flock of ewes which come up from the w,
Mk 7: 3 eat without scrupulously w their hands.
7: 4 the w of cups and jugs and kettles.
Lk 5: 2 had disembarked and were w their nets.

WASHINGS (2)

Jn 2: 6 As prescribed for Jewish ceremonial w,
Heb 9:10 of food and drink and various ritual w:

WASPS (1)

Wis 12: 8 and sent w as forerunners of your army

WASTE (112)

Gn 47:19 and that our land may not turn into a w."
Lv 26:31 I will lay w your cities and devastate
26:34 sabbaths during all the time it lies w,
26:39 in the lands of their enemies will w away
Nm 5:21 thighs to w away and your belly to swell!
5:22 your belly swell and your thighs w away!'
5:27 will swell and her thighs will w away,
21:30 Ar is laid w;
Dt 29:22 but sulphur and salt, a burnt-out w,
Jgs 6: 5 when they came into the land to lay it w.
2Sm 18:14 "I will not w time with you in this way."
2Kgs 19:17 have laid w the nations and their lands,
1Chr 20: 1 force, laid w the land of the Ammonites,
2Chr 36:21 during all the time it lies w it shall
1Mc 2:12 and our beauty and our glory laid w,
15: 4 it and laid w many cities in my realm.
15:29 You have laid w their territories,
15:35 to our people and laying w our country;
Jb 7:16 I w away:
38:27 To enrich the w and desolate ground till
Ps(s) 73:26 Though my flesh and my heart w away,
79: 7 devoured Jacob and laid w his dwelling.
80:14 fruit, The boar from the forest lays it w,
107:40 sends them astray through a trackless w,
Wis 4:19 They shall be utterly laid w and shall be
5:23 lawlessness shall lay the whole earth w
Is 1: 7 Your country is w,
1: 7 before your eyes strangers devour [a w,
6:11 a man, and the earth is a desolate w.
6:13 in it, then this in turn shall be laid w;
13: 9 To lay w the land and destroy the sinners
15: 1 Laid w in a night,
15: 6 The waters of Nimrim have become a w;
17: 9 they shall be laid w.
24: 2 the LORD empties the land and lays it w;
24: 3 The earth is utterly laid w,
34:10 generation to generation she shall lie w,
34:11 to be an empty w for satyrs to dwell in.
37:18 laid w all the nations and their lands,
42:15 I will lay w mountains and hills,
45:18 Not creating it to be a w,
45:19 of Jacob, "Look for me in an empty w."
49:17 you down and laid you w go forth from you;
49:19 Though you were w and desolate,
64: 9 a desert, Zion is a desert, Jerusalem a w.
64:10 all that was dear to us is laid w.
Jer 2:15 They have made his land a w;
4: 7 till your cities lie w and empty.
4:20 the whole earth is laid w.
4:23 looked at the earth, and it was w and void;
4:27 W shall the whole land be;
9:10 The cities of Judah I will make into a w,
10:25 Jacob utterly, and laid w his dwelling.
12:10 me they have turned into a desert w,
12:11 waste, They have made it a mournful w,
17: 6 change of season, But stands in a lava w,
22: 6 peak of Lebanon, I will turn you into a w,
25:36 For the LORD lays w their grazing place,
36:29 w this land and empty it of man and beast?"
44: 6 they became the ruinous w they are today.
44:22 and so your land became a w,
48: 1 Woe to Nebo, it is laid w;
50:12 last of the nations, a desert, dry and w.
51: 2 winnowers to winnow her and lay w her land;
51:55 For the LORD lays Babylon w,
Lam 4: 9 for those who die of hunger, Who w away,
Ez 4:17 with terror and w away because of his sins.
5:14 I will make you a w and a reproach among
6: 4 Your altars shall be laid w,
6: 6 be made desolate and high places laid w,
6: 6 altars will be made desolate and laid w,
6:14 live I will make the land a desolate w,
12:20 be in ruins, and the land shall be a w;
14:15 depopulating it so that it became a w,
14:16 would be saved, and the land would be a w.
15: 8 I will make the land a w,
25:13 I will make it a w from Teman to Dedan;
29: 9 land of Egypt shall become a desolate w;
29:10 a w and a desolation from Migdol to Syene,
32:12 They shall lay w the glory of Egypt,
32:15 When I turn Egypt into a w,
33:28 I will make the land a desolate w,
33:29 when I make the land a desolate w because
35: 3 hand against you and make you a desolate w.
35: 4 turn into ruins, and you shall be a w;
35: 7 I will make Mount Seir a desolate w,
35:15 A w shall you be,
36:35 "The cities that were in ruins, laid w,
Hos 2:14 I will lay w her vines and fig trees,
5: 9 become a w on the day of chastisement:
Jl 1: 7 He has laid w my vine,
2: 3 before them, and after them a desert w;
2:20 and drive him out into a land arid and w,
4:19 shall be a waste, and Edom a desert w,
Am 7: 9 The high places of Isaac shall be laid w,
Mi 7:13 land shall be a w because of its citizens,
Na 1: 5 The earth is laid w before him,
2:11 Emptiness, desolation, w;
Zep 2: 4 be forsaken, and Ashkelon shall be a w,
2: 9 of nettles and a salt pit and a w forever.
2:11 he makes all the gods of earth to w away;
2:13 He will make Nineveh a w,
2:15 How has she become a w,
3: 6 nations, their battlements are laid w;
Zec 11: 3 lions, the jungle of the Jordan is laid w.
Mal 1: 3 I made his mountains a w,
Mk 14: 4 the point of this extravagant w of perfume?
Lk 11:17 kingdom divided against itself is laid w.
Jn 6:12 are left over so that nothing will go to w."
Rv 11:18 time to destroy those who lay the earth w."

WASTED (15)

Gn 38: 9 widow, he w his seed on the ground,
Dt 28:65 heart and w eyes and a dismayed spirit.
Jb 33:21 His flesh is w so that it cannot be seen,
Ps(s) 32: 3 bones w away with my groaning all the day,
39:11 at the blow of your hand I w away.
73:19 They are completely w away amid horrors.
109:24 and my flesh is w of its substance.
Prv 23: 8 and you will have w your agreeable words.
Sir 30:14 and robust, than a rich man with w frame.
Is 24:16 But I said, "I am wasted, w away.
Jer 48: 8 Ruined is the valley, w the plain,
Lam 4:17 Our eyes ever w away,
Ez 19: 7 their strongholds, their cities he w.
Gal 4:11 all my efforts with you may have been w.

WASTELAND (20)

Gn 1: 2 and the earth, the earth was a formless w,
Dt 32:10 in a wilderness, a w of howling desert.
1Sm 23:19 or on the hill of Hachilah, south of the w.
23:24 below Maon, in the Arabah south of the w.
26: 1 the hill of Hachilah at the edge of the w.
26: 3 the hill of Hachilah, at the edge of the w.
Ps(s) 78:17 rebelling against the Most High in the w,
Wis 17:17 a shepherd, or a worker at tasks in the w,
Is 32:19 w forever for wild asses to frolic in,
40: 3 straight in the w a highway for our God!
41:19 I will set in the w the cypress,
43:19 In the desert I make a way, in the w,
43:20 in the w for my chosen people to drink,
51: 3 Eden, her w like the garden of the LORD;
Jer 9:11 ravaged, scorched like a w untraversed?
48: 9 a memorial for Moab, for it is an utter w;
Ez 36:34 a w exposed to the gaze of every passer-by.
Mt 11: 7 "What did you go out to the w to see
Mk 1:13 He stayed in the w forty days,
Lk 15: 4 not leave the ninety-nine in the w and follow

WASTELANDS (2)

Jb 30: 3 their lot, they who fled to the parched w:
Is 21: 1 Oracle on the w by the sea:

WASTES (6)

Sir 19: 1 w the little he has will be stripped bare.
31: 1 Keeping watch over riches w the flesh,
Is 61: 4 the former w they shall raise up And
Jer 2: 6 desert, through a land of w and gullies,
Mt 12:43 it roams through arid w searching for a
Lk 11:24 arid w searching for a resting place;

WASTING (4)

Lv 26:16 with w and fever to dim the eyes and sap
Dt 28:22 The LORD will strike you with w and fever,
Ps(s) 106:15 asked but sent a w disease against them.
107: 5 thirsty, their life was w away within them.

WATCH (88)

Gn 21:16 to herself, "Let me not w the child die."
31:49 "May the LORD keep w between you and me
Ex 14:24 In the night w just before dawn the LORD
Nm 24:22 even as I w—
Jos 8: 4 then all of you be on the w.
Jgs 7:17 W me and follow my lead," he told them.
7:19 the camp at the beginning of the middle w,
Ru 2: 9 W to see which field is to be harvested,
1Sm 6: 9 Then w! If it goes to Beth-shemesh
11:11 and invaded the camp during the dawn w.
2Sm 13:28 "Now w! When Amnon is merry with wine
13:34 Then the servant on w looked about and saw
1Kgs 8:29 your eyes w night and day over this temple,
2Chr 6:20 your eyes w day and night over this temple,
Ezr 8:29 Keep good w over them till you weigh them
Neh 4: 3 We prayed to our God and posted a w
7: 3 of Jerusalem, some at their w posts,
11:19 their brethren, who kept w over the gates;
12:25 kept w over the storerooms at the gates.
13:22 themselves and to go and w the gates,
Tb 4:14 Keep a close w on yourself,
10: 7 w all day at the road her son had taken,
Jdt 7: 5 bastions, and kept w throughout the night.
12: 5 In the night w just before dawn,
2Mc 5:26 All those who came out to w,
9:25 are on the w for opportunities and waiting
Jb 7:12 of the deep, that you place a w over me?
10:14 should sin, you would keep a w against me,
13:27 you w all my paths and trace out all my
14:16 my steps, and not keep w for sin in me.
21:33 and over him the funeral mound keeps w,
39: 1 goats, w for the birth pangs of the hinds,
Ps(s) 39: 2 I said, "I will w my ways,

56: 7 gather together in hiding, they *w* my steps.
59:10 for you I *w*;
66: 7 his eyes *w* the nations;
71:10 *w* against my life take counsel together.
90: 4 that it is past, or as a *w* of the night.
141: 3 O LORD, set a *w* before my mouth,
Prv 2:11 your soul, Discretion will *w* over you,
5: 2 your ear, That discretion may *w* over you,
6:22 When you lie down she will *w* over you,
15: 3 place, keeping *w* on the evil and the good.
Sir 1:26 over your lips keep *w*.
26:10 Keep a strict *w* over an unruly wife,
31: 1 Keeping *w* over riches wastes the flesh,
37: 9 be, and then stand by to *w* your misfortune.
38:26 he keeps a *w* on the beasts in the stalls.
38:27 and he keeps *w* till he finishes his design.
38:28 he keeps *w* till he perfects it in detail.
38:30 and he keeps *w* on the fire of his kiln.
42:11 Keep a close *w* on your daughter,
Jer 5: 6 them, Leopards keep *w* round their cities:
20:10 are on the *w* for any misstep of mine.
31:28 I will *w* over them to build and to plant,
48:19 Stand by the wayside, *w* closely,
51:12 Babylon raise a signal, make strong the *w*;
Lam 1:14 "He has kept *w* over my sins;
2:19 in the night, at the beginning of every *w*;
Bar 2: 9 And the Lord kept *w* over the evils,
Dn 9:14 *w* over the calamity and brought it upon us.
Hos 8: 1 lips, You who *w* over the house of the LORD!
13: 7 like a panther by the road I will keep *w*.
Na 2: 2 guard the rampart, Keep *w* on the road,
Hb 2: 1 And keep *w* to see what he will say to me,
Mt 27:36 they sat down there and kept *w* over him.
27:54 men who were keeping *w* over Jesus
Mk 13:33 Be constantly on the *w*!
13:34 the man at the gate to *w* with a sharp eye.
Lk 2: 8 keeping night *w* by turns over their flocks.
4:10 it, 'He will bid his angels *w* over you';
6: 7 The scribes and Pharisees were on the *w* to
21:36 So be on the *w*.
Jn 17:12 I kept careful *w*,
Acts 9:24 They went so far as to keep close *w* on the
12: 6 chains, while guards kept *w* at the door.
20:28 "Keep *w* over yourselves,
Rom 16:17 I beg you to be on the *w* against those who
1Cor 10:12 he is standing upright *w* out lest he fall!
2Cor 11:32 close *w* on the city in order to arrest me,
Eph 5:15 Keep careful *w* over your conduct.
Phil 3: 2 *W* out for workers of evil.
1Tm 4:16 Watch yourself and *w* your teaching.
Heb 13:17 for they keep *w* over you as men who must
1Pt 5: 2 *W* over it willingly as God would have you

WATCHED (27)

Gn 24:21 The man *w* her the whole time,
Jgs 9:43 He *w* till he saw the people leave the city,
1Sm 1:12 at prayer before the LORD, Eli *w* her mouth,
21:14 as they *w*, he feigned insanity and acted
1Chr 26:17 On the east, six *w* each day,
Ezr 3:12 cried out in sorrow as they *w* the
5: 5 But their God *w* over the elders of the
Tb 12:19 Even though you *w* me eat and drink.
1Mc 9:39 They *w*, and suddenly saw a noisy crowd
2Mc 14:29 so he *w* for an opportunity to carry out
Jb 29: 2 as in the days when God *w* over me,
Ps(s) 31: 8 my affliction and *w* over me in my distress,
Sir 51: 3 the snare of those who *w* for my downfall,
Jer 31:28 I once *w* over them to uproot and pull down,
Lam 4:17 we *w* for a nation that could not save us.
Dn 7: 4 While I *w*, the wings were plucked;
7: 9 As I *w*, Thrones were set up and
7:11 I *w*, then, from the first of the arrogant
7:21 For, as I *w*, that horn made war against
13:12 Day by day they *w* eagerly for her.
Mt 4:18 along the Sea of Galilee he *w* two brothers,
Lk 10:18 *w* Satan fall from the sky like lightning.
Jn 1:36 As he *w* Jesus walk by he said, "Look!
Acts 8:13 He *w* the signs and the great miracles as
Rv 6: 1 Then I *w* while the Lamb broke open the
8: 2 as I *w*, the seven angels who minister
14:14 Then, as I *w*, a white cloud appeared,

WATCHER (1)

Jb 7:20 sinned, what can I do to you, O *w* of men?

WATCHES (17)

1Chr 26:12 *w* in the service of the house of the LORD,
26:16 For each family, *w* were established.
2Mc 3:39 heaven *w* over that Place and protects it,
Jb 24:15 eye of the adulterer *w* for the twilight;
33:11 he *w* all my ways!"
39:29 From thence he *w* for his prey;
Ps(s) 1: 6 For the LORD *w* over the way of the just,
34:21 He *w* over all his bones;
37:18 LORD *w* over the lives of the wholehearted;
119:148 the night *w* in meditation on your promise.
Prv 31:27 She *w* the conduct of her household,
Eccl 11: 4 and one who *w* the clouds will never reap.
Sg 3: 8 side against danger in the *w* of the night.
Wis 6:14 he who *w* for her at dawn shall not be
Sir 17:27 God *w* over the hosts of highest heaven,
Is 21: 8 at my post through all the *w* of the night.
Jer 5:24 Who *w* for us over the appointed weeks of

WATCHFUL (2)

Ps(s) 77: 5 You keep my eyes *w*;
Mt 24:43 the thief was coming he would keep a *w* eye

WATCHING (14)

Ex 33: 8 tents, *w* Moses until he entered the tent.
1Sm 4:13 in his chair beside the gate, *w* the road,
Tb 11: 5 *w* the road by which her son was to come.
1Mc 12:29 and his men were *w* the lights burning,
Prv 8:34 my ways, Happy the man *w* daily at my gates,
Eccl 5: 7 official has another higher than he *w* him
Sir 46: 6 the LORD was *w* over his people's battles.
Jer 1:12 you seen, for I am *w* to fulfill my word.
44:27 I am *w* over them to do evil, not good.
Dn 13:16 who had hidden themselves and were *w* her.
Zec 11:11 The sheep merchants who were *w* me
Lk 17:20 careful *w* when the reign of God will come.
23:35 The people stood there *w*.
23:49 were standing at a distance *w* everything.

WATCHING-TREE (1)

Jer 1:11 "I see a branch of the *w*," I replied.

WATCHMAN (15)

2Kgs 9:17 The *w* standing on the tower in Jezreel saw
9:18 The *w* reported to the king,
9:20 *w* reported, "The messenger has reached
Is 21: 6 Go, station a *w*,
21: 8 Then the *w* cried,
21:11 They call to me from Seir, *W*,
21:11 *W*, how much longer the night?"
21:12 The *w* replies, "Morning has come,
Ez 3:17 appointed you a *w* for the house of Israel.
33: 2 select one of their number to be their *w*,
33: 3 number to be their watchman, and the *w*,
33: 6 But if the *w* sees the sword coming and
33: 6 the *w* responsible for that person's death,
33: 7 I have appointed *w* for the house of Israel;
Hos 9: 8 A prophet is Ephraim's *w* with God,

WATCHMEN (11)

Neh 7: 3 Appoint as *w* the inhabitants of Jerusalem,
Sg 3: 3 The *w* came upon me as they made their
5: 7 The *w* came upon me as they made their
Sir 37:14 better than seven *w* in a lofty tower.
Is 52: 8 Your *w* raise a cry,
56:10 My *w* are blind,
62: 6 walls, O Jerusalem, I have stationed *w*;
Jer 4:17 Like *w* of the fields they surround her,
6:17 When I raised up *w* for them:
31: 6 when the *w* will call out on Mount Ephraim:
Mi 7: 4 The day announced by your *w*!

WATCHTOWER (4)

2Chr 20:24 When Judah came to the *w* of the desert and
Is 5: 2 Within it he built a *w*,
21: 8 Then the watchman cried, "On the *w*,
Lam 4:17 From our *w* we watched for a nation that

WATCHTOWERS (2)

2Kgs 17: 9 the *w* as well as the walled cities.
18: 8 the *w* and walled cities of the Philistines,

WATCHWORD (1)

2Mc 8:23 from the holy book and giving them the *w*,

WATER (491)

Gn 1: 6 to separate one body of *w* from the other."
1: 7 *w* above the dome from the water below it.
1: 9 "Let the *w* under the sky be gathered into
1: 9 the *w* under the sky was gathered into its
1:10 and the basin of the *w* he called "the sea."
1:20 "Let the *w* teem with an abundance of
1:21 swimming creatures with which the *w* teems,
1:22 multiply, and fill the *w* of the seas;
2:10 A river rises in Eden to *w* the garden;
8: 9 ark, for there was *w* all over the earth.
8:13 month, the *w* began to dry up on the earth.
18: 4 Let some *w* be brought,
21:14 and a skin of *w* and gave them to Hagar.
21:15 Beer-sheba, the *w* in the skin was used up.
21:19 opened her eyes, and she saw a well of *w*.
21:19 She went and filled the skin with *w*,
24:11 at the time when women go out to draw *w*,
24:13 of the townsmen are coming out to draw *w*,
24:14 a drink, and let me give *w* to your camels,
24:17 "Please give me a sip of *w* from your jug."
24:19 she said, "I will draw *w* for your camels,
24:20 and ran back to the well to draw more *w*,
24:32 *w* was brought to bathe his feet and the
24:43 comes out to draw *w*, Please give me a little *w*
24:44 a drink, but I will give *w* to your camels,
24:45 she went down to the spring and drew *w*,
24:46 drink, and let me bring *w* for your camels,
26:19 wadi and reached spring *w* in their well,
26:20 servants, saying, "The *w* belongs to us!"
26:32 they told him, "We have reached *w*!"
29: 3 the mouth of the well and *w* the flocks.
29: 7 Why don't you *w* the flocks now,
29: 8 only then can we *w* the flocks."
36:24 (He is the Anah who found *w* in the desert
43:24 He gave them *w* to bathe their feet,
49: 4 Unruly as *w*, you shall no longer excel,
Ex 2:10 for she said, "I drew him out of the *w*."
2:16 came to draw *w* and fill the troughs to water
2:19 even drew *w* for us and watered the flock!"
4: 9 take some *w* from the river and pour it on
4: 9 The *w* you take from the river will become
7:15 morning, when he sets out for the *w*,
7:17 the *w* of the river with the staff I hold,
7:18 Egyptians will be unable to drink its *w*."
7:19 canals and pools, all their supplies of *w*—
7:20 the *w* of the river was changed into blood.
7:21 that the Egyptians could not drink its *w*.
7:24 neighborhood of the river for drinking *w*,
7:24 they could not drink from the river *w*.
8:16 to Pharaoh when he goes forth to the *w*,
14:21 When the *w* was thus divided,
14:22 with the *w* like a wall to their right and
14:26 the *w* may flow back upon the Egyptians,
14:28 As the *w* flowed back,
14:29 with the *w* like a wall to their right and
15:22 days through the desert without finding *w*,
15:23 at Marah, where they could not drink the *w*,
15:25 he threw this into the *w*, the *w* became fresh.
15:27 twelve springs of *w* and seventy palm trees,
15:27 trees, and they camped there near the *w*.
17: 1 there was no *w* for the people to drink.
17: 2 with Moses and said, "Give us *w* to drink."
17: 3 Here, then, in their thirst for *w*,
17: 6 and the *w* will flow from it for the people
29: 4 meeting tent, and there wash them with *w*.
30:18 tent and the altar, and put *w* in it.
30:20 the meeting tent, they must wash with *w*,
32:20 on the *w* and made the Israelites drink.
34:28 without eating any food or drinking any *w*,
40: 7 tent and the altar, and put *w* in it.
40:12 meeting tent, and there wash them with *w*.
40:30 and altar, and put *w* in it for washing.
Lv 1: 9 the offerer shall first wash with *w*.
1:13 the offerer shall first wash with *w*.
6:21 be scoured afterward and rinsed with *w*.
8: 6 and his sons, he first washed them with *w*.
8:21 the inner organs and the shanks with *w*.
11: 9 the various creatures that live in the *w*,
11:10 creatures that crawl or swim in the *w*,
11:12 Every *w* creature that lacks fins or scales
11:32 put in *w* and remain unclean until evening,
11:34 Any solid food that was in contact with *w*,
11:36 a cistern for collecting *w* remains clean;
11:46 move about in the *w* or swarm on the ground,
14: 5 over an earthen vessel with spring *w* in it.
14: 6 the bird that was slain over the spring *w*,
14: 8 and shave off all his hair and bathe in *w*;
14: 9 wash his garments and bathe his body in *w*;
14:50 over an earthen vessel with spring *w* in it.
14:51 blood of the slain bird and the spring *w*,
14:52 with the bird's blood and the spring *w*,
15: 5 bed shall wash his garments, bathe in *w*,
15: 6 shall wash his garments, bathe in *w*,
15: 7 man shall wash his garments, bathe in *w*,
15: 8 latter shall wash his garments, bathe in *w*,
15:10 thing shall wash his garments, bathe in *w*,
15:11 hands shall wash his garments, bathe in *w*,
15:12 wooden article shall be rinsed with *w*.
15:13 garments and bathe his body in fresh *w*,
15:16 body in *w* and be unclean until evening.
15:17 washed with *w* and be unclean until evening.
15:18 bathe in *w* and be unclean until evening.
15:21 bed shall wash his garments, bathe in *w*,
15:22 shall wash his garments, bathe in *w*,
15:27 he shall wash his garments, bathe in *w*,
16: 4 on until he has first bathed his body in *w*.
16:24 bathing his body with *w* in a sacred place,
16:26 wash his garments and bathe his body in *w*;
16:28 wash his garments and bathe his body in *w*;
17:15 shall wash his garments, bathe in *w*,
22: 6 until he has first bathed his body in *w*.
Nm 5:17 vessel he shall meanwhile put some holy *w*,
5:18 hold the bitter *w* that brings a curse.
5:19 to the curse brought by this bitter *w*.
5:22 May this *w*,
5:23 then wash them off into the bitter *w*,
5:26 then shall he have the woman drink the *w*.
5:27 *w* that brings a curse will go into her,
8: 7 Sprinkle them with the *w* of remission;
19: 7 wash his garments and bathe his body in *w*.
19: 8 wash his garments, bathe his body in *w*,
19: 9 lustral *w* for the Israelite community.
19:12 the *w* on the third and on the seventh day,
19:13 lustral *w* has not been splashed over him,
19:17 and spring *w* shall be poured on them.
19:18 dip it in this *w* and sprinkle it on the
19:19 wash his garments and bathe his body in *w*,
19:20 lustral *w* has not been splashed over him,
19:21 the lustral *w* shall wash his garments,
19:21 with this *w* shall be unclean until evening.
20: 2 As the community had no *w*,
20: 5 Here there is not even *w* to drink!"

WATER (cont.)

20: 8 From the rock you shall bring forth *w* for
20:10 Are we to bring *w* for you out of this rock?"
20:11 and *w* gushed out in abundance for the
20:17 or vineyards, nor drink of any well *w*,
20:19 If we or our livestock drink any of your *w*,
21: 5 this desert, where there is no food or *w*?
21:16 people together, and I will give them *w*."
21:22 or vineyard, nor will we drink any well *w*,
27:14 my sanctity to them by means of the *w*."
27:14 [This is the *w* of Meribah of Kadesh in the
31:23 it must also be purified with lustral *w*.
31:23 cannot stand fire you shall put into the *w*.
33: 9 twelve springs of *w* and seventy palm trees,
33:14 there was no *w* for the people to drink.
Dt 2: 6 the food you eat and the well *w* you drink.
2:28 supply, and for the *w* you give me to drink,
8: 7 a good country, a land with streams of *w*,
8:15 who brought forth *w* for you from the
10: 7 a region where there is *w* in the wadies.]
11: 4 the *w* of the Red Sea as they pursued you,
11:10 would sow your seed and then *w* it by hand,
12:16 but must pour it out on the ground like *w*.
12:24 but pour it out on the ground like *w*.
14: 9 the various creatures that live in the *w*,
15:23 must be poured out on the ground like *w*.
23: 5 and *w* on your journey after you left Egypt,
23:12 until, toward evening, he has bathed in *w*;
29:10 those who hew wood and draw *w* for you
Jos 3:13 the whole earth, touch the *w* of the Jordan,
3:13 for the *w* flowing down from upstream will
7: 5 of the people melted away like *w*.
9:21 and drawers of *w* for the entire community;
9:23 and drawers of *w* for the house of my God."
9:27 hewers of wood and drawers of *w* for the
15:19 land in the Negeb, give me also pools of *w*."
Jgs 1:15 the Negeb to me, give me also pools of *w*."
4:19 her, "Please give me a little *w* to drink.
5:25 He asked for *w*, she gave him milk;
6:38 fleece, squeezing out of it a bowlful of *w*.
7: 4 the *w* and I will test them for you there.
7: 5 Gideon led the soldiers down to the *w*,
7: 5 up the *w* as a dog does with its tongue;
7: 6 Those who lapped up the *w* raised to their
7: 6 of the soldiers knelt down to drink the *w*.
7: 7 who lapped up the *w* I will save you
7:24 and seize the *w* courses against them as
7:24 seized the *w* courses as far as Beth-barah,
15:19 the cavity in Lehi, and *w* issued from it,
1Sm 7: 6 they drew *w* and poured it out on the
9:11 coming out to draw *w* and inquired of them,
26:11 spear which is at his head and the *w* jug,
26:12 the *w* jug from their place at Saul's head,
26:16 spear and the *w* jug that was at his head?"
30:11 food, which he ate, and given *w* to drink;
30:12 drunk *w* for three days and three nights.
2Sm 5: 8 must strike at them through the *w* shaft.
14:14 we are then like *w* that is poured out on
17:20 went by a short while ago toward the *w*."
17:21 Cross the *w* at once,
23:15 that someone would give me a drink of *w*
23:16 drew *w* from the cistern that is by the gate
1Kgs 13: 8 nor eat bread or drink *w* in this place.
13: 9 *w* and not to return by the way I came."
13:16 bread or drink *w* with you in this place,"
13:17 LORD neither to eat bread nor drink *w* here,
13:18 and to have you eat bread and drink *w*."
13:19 and ate bread and drank *w* in his house.
13:22 returned and ate bread and drank *w*
13:23 After he had eaten bread and drunk *w*,
14:15 Israel like a reed tossed about in the *w*
17:10 bring me a small cupful of *w* to drink."
18: 5 to all sources of *w* and to all the streams.
18:34 "Fill four jars with *w*," he said, "and pour
18:35 The *w* flowed around the altar,
18:35 and the trench was filled with the *w*.
18:38 dust, and it lapped up the *w* in the trench.
19: 6 his head was a hearth cake and a jug of *w*.
22:27 of bread and *w* until I return in safety.'"
2Kgs 2: 8 his mantle, rolled it up and struck the *w*,
2:14 he struck the *w* in his turn and said,
2:14 the *w* it divided and he crossed over.
2:19 but the *w* is bad and the land unfruitful."
2:21 says the LORD, 'I have purified this *w*.
2:22 And the *w* has stayed pure even to this day,
3: 9 seven days the *w* gave out for the army
3:11 who poured *w* on the hands of Elijah,
3:17 this wadi will be filled with *w* for you,
3:20 *w* came from the direction of Edom and
3:22 shone on the *w*, the Moabites saw the *w*
6: 5 trunk, the iron axhead slipped into the *w*.
6: 6 cut off a stick, threw it into the *w*,
6:22 Serve them bread and *w*.
8:15 took a cloth, dipped it in *w*, and spread
18:31 and drink the *w* of his own cistern,
19:24 I dug wells and drank *w* in foreign lands;
20:20 by which *w* was brought into the city,
1Chr 11:18 drew *w* from the cistern by the gate at
14:11 my enemies just as *w* breaks through a dam."
2Chr 18:26 of bread and *w* until I return in safety!'"
32: 4 of Assyria come and find an abundance of *w*?"
32:30 Hezekiah stopped the upper outflow of *w*
Ezr 10: 6 night neither eating food nor drinking *w*,
Neh 3:26 to a point opposite the *W* Gate on the east,
8: 1 man in the open space before the *W* Gate,
8: 3 the open place that was before the *W* Gate,
8:16 of the *W* Gate and the Gate of Ephraim.
9:15 *w* from a rock you sent them in their
9:20 and you gave them *w* in their thirst.
12:37 until they came to the *W* Gate on the east.
13: 2 not succor the Israelites with food and *w*,
Tb 6: 3 out of the *w* and tried to swallow his foot.
Jdt 2: 7 Tell them to have earth and *w* ready,
7: 7 their city and located their sources of *w*;
7:12 servants keep control of the source of *w*
7:13 the inhabitants of Bethulia get their *w*.
7:17 *w* supply and the springs of the Israelites.
7:20 of *w* failed the inhabitants of Bethulia,
7:21 drink, but their drinking *w* was rationed.
8: 9 people, discouraged by their lack of *w*,
10: 3 of her widowhood, washed her body with *w*,
11:12 food gave out and all their *w* ran low,
Est A: 9 river, a flood of *w* from a little spring.
2Mc 1:21 could not find any fire, but only muddy *w*,
1:21 with the *w* the wood and what lay on it.
15:38 is harmful to drink wine alone or *w* alone,
15:38 whereas mixing wine with *w* makes a more
Jb 3:24 than food, and my groans well forth like *w*.
5:10 upon the earth and sends *w* upon the fields;
8:11 Can the reed grass flourish without *w*?
14: 9 Yet at the first whiff of *w* it may
15:16 man, who drinks in iniquity like *w*!
22: 7 the thirsty you have given no *w* to drink,
34: 7 He drinks in blasphemies like *w*,
37:17 whom the streams of *w* fail when a calm
38:37 Or who tilts the *w* jars of heaven So that
Ps(s) 1: 3 He is like a tree planted near running *w*,
22:15 I am like *w* poured out;
58: 8 Let them vanish like *w* flowing off;
63: 2 the earth, parched, lifeless and without *w*.
66:12 we went through fire and *w*,
73:10 to such a pass that they have not even *w*!"
77:18 The clouds poured down *w*;
78:15 desert and gave them *w* in copious floods.
78:44 their running *w*,
79: 3 their blood like *w* round about Jerusalem,
88:18 They encompass me like *w* all the day;
104:13 You *w* the mountains from your palace;
105:41 He cleft the rock, and the *w* gushed forth;
107:33 into desert, *w* springs into thirsty ground,
107:35 desert into pools of *w*, waterless land into *w*
109:18 like *w* and like oil into his bones;
114: 8 Jacob, Who turned the rock into pools of *w*,
Prv 5:15 Drink *w* from your own cistern, running *w*
5:16 *w* sources be dispersed abroad, streams of *w*
8:24 there were no fountains or springs of *w*;
9:17 for to him I say, Stolen *w* is sweet,
20: 5 heart is like *w* far below the surface,
25:25 Like cool *w* to one faint from thirst is
30:16 the earth, that is never saturated with *w*,
Eccl 2: 6 reservoirs to *w* a flourishing woodland.
Sg 4:15 a well of *w* flowing fresh from Lebanon.
Wis 5:10 Like a ship traversing the heaving *w*,
5:22 The *w* of the sea shall be enraged against
11: 4 and *w* was given them from the sheer rock,
11: 7 gave them abundant *w* in an unhoped-for way,
13: 2 the circuit of the stars, or the mighty *w*,
16:17 expectation, in *w* which quenches anything,
16:19 And again, even in the *w*,
16:29 a wintry frost and runs off like useless *w*.
17:18 Or the steady sound of rushing *w*,
18: 5 them perish all at once in the mighty *w*.
19: 7 and out of what had before been *w*,
19:19 creatures were changed into *w* creatures,
19:20 *w* maintained its own strength, and *w* forgot
Sir 3:29 *W* quenches a flaming fire,
15: 3 and give him the *w* of learning to drink.
15:16 There are set before you fire and *w*;
18: 8 Like a drop of sea *w*,
24:14 like a plane tree growing beside the *w*.
24:29 Said to myself, "I will *w* my plants,
25:24 Allow *w* no outlet,
26:12 mouth drinks from any *w* that he finds,
29:21 Life's prime needs are *w*,
38: 5 Was not the *w* sweetened by a twig that men
39:26 of all needs for human life are *w* and fire,
43:21 He freezes over every body of *w*,
48:17 his city and had *w* brought into it;
48:17 the rock and he built reservoirs for *w*.
Is 1:22 turned to dross, your wine is mixed with *w*.
1:30 leaves, like a garden that has no *w*.
3: 1 and prop [all supplies of bread and *w*:
11: 9 knowledge of the LORD, as *w* covers the sea.
12: 3 will draw *w* at the fountain of salvation,
16: 9 I *w* you with tears,
19: 8 spread their nets in the *w* shall pine away.
21:14 Meet the thirsty, bring them *w*;
22: 9 you collected the *w* of the lower pool.
22:11 the two walls for the *w* of the old pool.
27: 3 LORD, am its keeper, I *w* it every moment;
28: 2 a destructive storm, Like a flood of *w*,
30:14 from the hearth or dip *w* from the cistern.
30:20 you need and the *w* for which you thirst.
30:25 hill there will be streams of running *w*.
32: 2 will be like streams of *w* in a dry country,
35: 7 and the thirsty ground, springs of *w*;
36:16 tree, and drink the *w* of his own cistern,
37:25 I dug wells and drank *w* in foreign lands;
41:17 The afflicted and the needy seek *w* in vain,
41:18 and the dry ground into springs of *w*,
43: 2 When you pass through the *w*,
43:20 For I put *w* in the desert and rivers in
44: 3 I will pour out *w* upon the thirsty ground,
44:12 weak, drinks no *w* and becomes exhausted.
48:21 *W* from the rock he set flowing for them;
49:10 them and guides them beside springs of *w*.
50: 2 Their fish rot for lack of *w*,
55: 1 All you who are thirsty, come to the *w*!
58:11 garden, like a spring whose *w* never fails.
64: 1 is set ablaze, or fire makes the *w* boil!
Jer 2:13 cisterns, broken cisterns, that hold no *w*.
8:23 Oh, that my head were a spring of *w*,
13: 1 it on your loins, but do not put it in *w*.
14: 3 The nobles send their servants for *w*,
14: 3 They find no *w* and return with empty jars.
31: 9 I will lead them to brooks of *w*,
38: 6 There was no *w* in the cistern,
Lam 2:19 heart like *w* in the presence of the Lord;
3:48 My eyes run with streams of *w* over
5: 4 The *w* we drink we must buy,
Ez 4:11 And the *w* you drink shall be the sixth of
4:16 *w* which they have measured out fearfully,
4:17 owing to the scarcity of bread and *w*,
7:17 limp, and all their knees shall run with *w*.
12:18 and drink your *w* shaking with anxiety.
12:19 in anxiety and drink their *w* in horror,
16: 4 were neither washed with *w* nor anointed,
16: 9 Then I bathed you with *w*,
17: 7 That he might *w* it more freely than the
19:10 mother was like a vine planted by the *w*;
19:10 branchy was she because of the abundant *w*.
21:12 daunted, and every knee shall run with *w*.
24: 3 up the pot, set it up, then pour in some *w*.
31: 5 longer of branch because of the abundant *w*.
31: 7 its roots were turned toward abundant *w*.
31:14 by *w* may stand by itself in its loftiness.
31:16 choice and best, all that were fed by *w*.
32: 2 *w* with your feet and churning its streams.
32: 6 I will *w* the land with what flows from you,
34:18 enough for you to drink the clearest *w*,
36:25 I will sprinkle clean *w* upon you to
47: 1 and I saw *w* flowing out from beneath the
47: 1 the *w* flowed down from the southern side
47: 2 I saw *w* trickling from the southern side.
47: 3 cubits and had me wade through the *w*,
47: 4 and once more had me wade through the *w*,
47: 4 the *w* was up to my waist.
47: 5 for the *w* had risen so high it had become
47: 8 "This *w* flows into the eastern district
47: 9 this *w* comes the sea shall be made fresh.
Dn 1:12 Give us vegetables to eat and *w* to drink.
3:79 You dolphins and all *w* creatures,
Hos 2: 7 she said, "who give me my bread and my *w*,
5:10 Upon them I will pour out my wrath like *w*.
Jl 1:20 For the streams of *w* are dried up,
4:18 the channels of Judah shall flow with *w*:
4:18 of the LORD, to *w* the Valley of Shittim.
Am 4: 8 for *w* that did not quench their thirst;
5:24 holocausts, then let justice surge like *w*,
8:11 Not a famine of bread, or thirst for *w*,
Jon 3: 7 they shall not eat, nor shall they drink *w*.
Mi 1: 4 the fire, like *w* poured down a slope.
Na 3: 8 the flood for her rampart and *w* her wall?
3:14 Draw *w* for the siege,
Hb 2:14 of the LORD's glory as *w* covers the sea.
Mt 3:11 I baptize you in *w* for the sake of reform,
3:16 baptized, he came directly out of the *w*.
10:42 that whoever gives a cup of cold *w* to one
14:26 the disciples saw him walking on the *w*,
14:28 you, tell me to come to you across the *w*."
14:29 out of the boat and began to walk on the *w*,
17:15 into the fire and frequently into the *w*.
27:24 He called for *w* and washed his hands in
Mk 1: 8 I have baptized you in *w*;
1:10 Immediately on coming up out of the *w* he
4: 1 that he went and sat in a boat on the *w*,
4:37 over the boat and it began to ship *w* badly.
6:48 he came walking toward them on the *w*;
9:22 "Often it throws him into fire and into *w*.
9:41 of *w* because you belong to Christ will not,
14:13 you will come upon a man carrying a *w* jar.
Lk 3:16 "I am baptizing you in *w*,
5: 4 deep *w* and lower your nets for a catch."
7:44 and you provided me with no *w* for my feet.
8:23 they began to ship *w* and to be in danger.
13:15 out of the stall on the sabbath to *w* it?
16:24 of his finger in *w* to refresh my tongue,
22:10 you will come upon a man carrying a *w* jar.
Jn 1:26 "I baptize with *w*.
1:31 *w* was that he might be revealed to Israel."
1:33 one who sent me to baptize with *w* told me,
2: 6 there were at hand six stone *w* jars,
2: 7 "Fill those jars with *w*,"
2: 9 waiter in charge tasted the *w* made wine,
2: 9 waiters knew, since they had drawn the *w*.
3: 5 without being begotten of *w* and Spirit.
3:23 at Aenon near Salim where *w* was plentiful,
4: 7 When a Samaritan woman came to draw *w*,
4:10 and he would have given you living *w*."

4:11 Where do you expect to get this flowing *w*?
4:13 who drinks this *w* will be thirsty again.
4:14 the *w* I give him will never be thirsty;
4:14 the *w* I give shall become a fountain
4:15 The woman said to him, "Give me this *w*,
4:15 and have to keep coming here to draw *w*."
4:28 left her *w* jar and went off into the town.
4:46 once more, where he had made the *w* wine.
5: 4][waiting for the movement of the *w*.
5: 7 the pool once the *w* has been stirred up.
6:19 approaching the boat, walking on the *w*.
7:38 within him rivers of living *w* shall flow.'"
13: 5 Then he poured *w* into a basin and began to
19:34 and immediately blood and *w* flowed out.
21: 7 and jumped into the *w*.
Acts 1: 5 John baptized with *w*,
8:36 moved along the road they came to some *w*,
8:37 said, "Look, there is some *w* right there.
8:38 the *w* with the eunuch and baptized him.
8:39 When they came out of the *w*,
10:47 as we have, from being baptized with *w*?"
11:16 'John baptized with *w* but you will be
Eph 5:26 in the bath of *w* by the power of the word,
1Tm 5:23 Stop drinking *w* only.
Heb 9:19 with *w* and crimson wool and hyssop,
10:22 conscience and our bodies washed in pure *w*.
Jas 3:11 fresh *w* and foul from the same outlet?
3:12 more can a brackish source yield fresh *w*.
1Pt 3:20 in all, escaped in the ark through the *w*.
2Pt 3: 6 By *w* that world was then destroyed;
1Jn 5: 6 Christ it is who came through *w* and blood
5: 6 not in water only, but in *w* and in blood.
5: 8 the Spirit and the *w* and the blood
Rv 7:17 will lead them to springs of life-giving *w*.
8:11 third part of all the *w* turned to wormwood.
8:11 Many people died from this polluted *w*.
11: 6 They also have power to turn *w* into blood
12:15 spewed a torrent of *w* out of his mouth to
16:12 Its *w* was dried up to prepare the way for
21: 6 cost from the spring of life-giving *w*.
22: 1 then showed me the river of life-giving *w*,
22:17 desire it accept the gift of life-giving *w*.

WATER-CITY (1)

2Sm 12:27 fought against Rabbah and have taken the *w*.

WATERCOURSES (3)

Jb 6:15 a brook, as *w* that run dry in the wadies;
Ps(s) 65:10 God's *w* are filled;
104:10 into the *w* that wind among the mountains,

WATERDROPS (1)

Jb 36:27 *w* that filter in rain through his mists,

WATERED (15)

Gn 13:10 Lot looked about and saw how well *w* the
24:46 So I drank, and she *w* the camels also.
29: 2 near it, for droves were *w* from that well.
29:10 mouth of the well, and *w* his uncle's sheep.
Ex 2:17 up and defended them and *w* their flocks.
2:19 He even drew water for us and *w* the flock!"
Dt 29:18 both the *w* soil and the parched ground,
Ps(s) 65:10 You have visited the land and *w* it;
104:16 Well *w* are the trees of the LORD,
Is 55:10 return there till they have *w* the earth,
58:11 strength, and you shall be like a *w* garden,
Jer 31:12 They themselves shall be like *w* gardens,
Ez 47:12 shall be *w* by the flow from the sanctuary.
Am 4: 7 One field was *w* by rain,
1Cor 3: 6 I planted the seed and Apollos *w* it,

WATERING (3)

Gn 2: 6 and was *w* all the surface of the ground
30:38 he then set upright in the *w* troughs,
Ps(s) 72: 6 on the meadow, like showers *w* the earth.

WATERLESS (3)

Dt 8:15 and scorpions, its parched and *w* ground;
Ps(s) 107:35 pools of water, *w* land into water springs.
2Pt 2:17 These men are *w* springs,

WATERS (189)

Gn 1: 2 while a mighty wind swept over the *w*.
1: 6 there be a dome in the middle of the *w*,
6:17 am about to bring the flood *w* on the earth,
7: 6 old when the flood *w* came upon the earth.
7: 7 the ark because of the *w* of the flood.
7:10 the *w* of the flood came upon the earth.
7:17 As the *w* increased, they lifted the ark,
7:18 The swelling *w* increased greatly,
7:18 the ark floated on the surface of the *w*.
7:19 and higher above the earth rose the *w*.
7:24 The *w* maintained their crest over the
8: 1 over the earth, and the *w* began to subside.
8: 3 Gradually the *w* receded from the earth.
8: 3 fifty days, the *w* had so diminished that,
8: 5 The *w* continued to diminish until the
8: 7 to see if the *w* had lessened on the earth.
8: 7 forth until the *w* dried off from the earth.
8: 8 to see if the *w* had lessened on the earth.
8:11 knew that the *w* had lessened on the earth.
9:11 creatures be destroyed by the *w* of a flood;
9:15 so that the *w* shall never again become a
Ex 7:19 stretch out your hand over the *w* of Egypt
7:20 Aaron raised his staff and struck the *w* of
8: 2 stretched out his hand over the *w* of Egypt,
15: 5 The flood *w* covered them.
15: 8 *w* piled up, the flowing *w* stood like a mound,
15: 8 flood *w* congealed in the midst of the sea.
15:10 like lead they sank in the mighty *w*.
15:19 made the *w* of the sea flow back upon them,
20: 4 earth below or in the *w* beneath the earth;
Lv 11: 9 *w* has both fins and scales you may eat.
Nm 20: 8 presence order the rock to yield its *w*.
20:13 These are the *w* of Meribah,
20:24 against my commandment at the *w* of Meribah.
24: 7 His wells shall yield free-flowing *w*,
Dt 4:18 or of any fish in the *w* under the earth.
5: 8 earth below or in the *w* beneath the earth;
32:51 with me among the Israelites at the *w*
33: 8 you contended with him at the *w* of Meribah.
Jos 2:10 the LORD dried up the *w* of the Red Sea
3: 8 Jordan when they reach the edge of the *w*."
3:15 waded into the *w* at the edge of the Jordan,
3:16 than the *w* flowing from upstream halted,
4: 7 'The *w* of the Jordan ceased to flow before
4:18 the *w* of the Jordan resumed their course
4:23 dried up the *w* of the Jordan in front of
5: 1 LORD had dried up the *w* of the Jordan
11: 5 forces and marched to the *w* of Merom,
11: 7 at the *w* of Merom in a surprise attack.
15: 7 *w* of En-shemesh and emerged at En-rogel.
15: 9 it ran to the fountain of *w* of Nephtoah,
16: 1 to the *w* of Jericho east of the desert;
Jgs 5:19 of Canaan, At Taanach by the *w* of Megiddo;
2Sm 5:20 before me like *w* that have broken free."
22:17 he drew me out of the deep *w*.
2Kgs 5:12 Pharpar, better than all the *w* of Israel?
2Chr 32: 3 stop the *w* of the springs outside the city.
Neh 9:11 the depths, like a stone into the mighty *w*.
Jdt 9:12 of heaven and earth, Creator of the *w*,
Est F: 3 a river, the light of the sun, the many *w*.
1Mc 9:33 and camped by the *w* of the pool of Asphar.
9:45 us are the *w* of the Jordan on one side,
11:67 their camp near the *w* of Gennesaret,
Jb 11:16 or recall it like *w* that have ebbed away.
12:15 He holds back the *w* and there is drought;
12:19 and lets their never-failing *w* flow away.
14:11 As when the *w* of a lake fail,
14:19 As *w* wear away the stones and floods wash
20:28 *w* that run off in the day of God's anger.
22:11 a deluge of *w* covers you.
26: 5 The shades beneath writhe in terror, the *w*,
26: 8 He binds up the *w* in his clouds,
26:13 With his angry breath he scatters the *w*,
28:25 the wind, and fixed the scope of the *w*;
29:19 My root is spread out to the *w*;
37:10 frost, and the broad *w* become congealed.
38:30 When the *w* lie covered as though with
38:34 or veil yourself in the *w* of the storm?
Ps(s) 18:17 he drew me out of the deep *w*.
23: 2 Beside restful *w* he leads me;
29: 3 The voice of the LORD is over the *w*,
29: 3 of glory thunders, the LORD, over vast *w*.
32: 6 Though deep *w* overflow,
33: 7 He gathers the *w* of the sea as in a flask;
42: 2 As the hind longs for the running *w*,
46: 4 Though its *w* rage and foam and the
69: 2 Save me, O God, for the *w* threaten my life;
74:13 smashed the heads of the dragons in the *w*.
74:15 you brought dry land out of the primeval *w*.
77:17 The *w* saw you, O God; the waters saw you
77:20 your way, and your path through the deep *w*,
78:13 and he made the *w* stand as in a mound.
78:16 the crag and brought the *w* forth in rivers.
78:20 when he struck the rock, *w* gushed forth,
81: 8 I tested you at the *w* of Meribah.
93: 4 More powerful than the roar of many *w*,
104: 3 have constructed your palace upon the *w*.
104: 6 above the mountains the *w* stood.
105:29 their *w* into blood and killed their fish.
106:11 The *w* covered their foes;
106:32 They angered him at the *w* of Meribah,
107:23 the sea in ships, trading on the deep *w*,
124: 4 us, then would the *w* have overwhelmed us;
124: 5 us then would have swept the raging *w*.
136: 6 Who spread out the earth upon the *w*,
144: 7 Deliver me and rescue me from many *w*,
147:17 before his cold the *w* freeze.
147:18 he lets his breeze blow and the *w* run.
148: 4 heavens, and you *w* above the heavens.
Prv 8:29 the *w* should not transgress his command;
18: 4 The words from a man's mouth are deep *w*,
30: 4 Who has bound up the *w* in a cloak
Eccl 11: 1 Cast your bread upon the *w*;
Sg 5:12 His eyes are like doves beside running *w*,
8: 7 Deep *w* cannot quench love,
Wis 10:18 Sea and brought them through the deep *w*—
Sir 18:29 sound proverbs like life-giving *w*.
24:28 her stream, channeling the *w* into a garden,
39:13 petals, like roses planted near running *w*;
39:17 his word the *w* become still as in a flask;
43:10 weapon against the flood *w* stored on high,
Is 8: 6 rejected the *w* of Shiloah that flow gently,
8: 7 raises against them the *w* of the River,
15: 6 The *w* of Nimrim have become a waste;
15: 9 The *w* of Dimon are filled with blood,
18: 2 by sea, in papyrus boats on the *w*!
19: 5 The *w* shall be drained from the sea,
23: 3 crossed the sea over the deep *w*.
28:17 lies, and *w* shall flood the hiding place.
40:12 has cupped in his hand the *w* of the sea,
43:16 way in the sea and a path in the mighty *w*,
44: 4 verdure like poplars beside the flowing *w*.
48:21 he cleft the rock, and *w* welled forth."
51:10 dried up the sea, the *w* of the great deep,
54: 9 when I swore that the *w* of Noah should
57:20 be calmed, And its *w* cast up mud and filth.
63:12 Who divided the *w* before them,
Jer 2:13 have forsaken me, the source of living *w*;
2:18 go to Egypt, to drink the *w* of the Nile?
2:18 Assyria, to drink the *w* of the Euphrates?
6: 7 As the well gushes out its *w*,
10:13 he thunders, the *w* in the heavens roar,
15:18 a treacherous brook, whose *w* do not abide!
17: 8 He is like a tree planted beside the *w*
17:13 forsaken the source of living *w* [the LORD].
18:14 Do the gushing *w* dry up that flow fresh
41:12 They overtook him at the Great *W* in Gibeon.
46: 7 like the Nile, like rivers of billowing *w*?
46: 8 like the Nile, like rivers of billowing *w*.
47: 2 *w* are rising from the north,
48:34 even the *w* of Nimrim turn into a desert.
50:38 A sword upon her *w*,
51:13 You who dwell by mighty *w*,
51:16 he thunders, the *w* in the heavens roar,
51:55 her waves were roaring like mighty *w*,
Lam 3:54 The *w* flowed over my head,
Ez 1:24 their wings, like the roaring of mighty *w*,
17: 5 A shoot by plentiful *w*,
17: 8 field by plentiful *w* it was planted,
26:19 against you, and its mighty *w* cover you,
27:26 the deep *w* your oarsmen brought you home,
31: 4 *W* made it grow,
31:15 streams so that the deep *w* were held back.
32:13 her animals perish beside her abundant *w*;
32:14 Then will I make their *w* clear,
43: 2 I heard a sound like the roaring of many *w*,
47: 8 and empties into the sea, the salt *w*,
47:19 from Tamar to the *w* of Meribath-kadesh,
48:28 from Tamar to the *w* of Meribath-kadesh,
Dn 3:60 All you *w* above the heavens,
Hos 6: 3 rain, like spring rain that *w* the earth."
10: 7 shall disappear, like foam upon the *w*.
Am 5: 8 Who summons the *w* of the sea,
9: 6 I summon the *w* of the sea and pour them
Jon 2: 6 The *w* swirled about me,
Na 2: 9 Nineveh is like a pool whose *w* escape;
3: 8 set among the streams, Surrounded by *w*,
Hb 3:15 steeds amid the churning of the deep *w*.
Zec 14: 8 day, living *w* shall flow from Jerusalem,
1Cor 3: 7 nor he who *w* is of any special account,
3: 8 plants and he who *w* work to the same end.
2Pt 3: 5 of the waters and standing between the *w*,
Rv 1:15 voice sounded like the roar of rushing *w*.
16: 5 heard the angel in charge of the *w* cry out:
17: 1 great harlot who sits by the *w* of the deep.
17:15 "The *w* on which you saw the harlot

WATERY (3)

Ps(s) 69: 3 I have reached the *w* depths;
69:15 from my foes, and from the *w* depths.
Ez 27:34 are wrecked in the sea, in the *w* depths;

WAVE (37)

Ex 29:24 wave them as a *w* offering before the LORD.
29:26 *w* it as a wave offering before the LORD;
29:27 the breast of whatever *w* offering is waved,
Lv 7:30 be waved as a *w* offering before the LORD.
8:27 *w* them as a wave offering before the LORD.
8:29 waved it as a *w* offering before the LORD;
9:21 right legs as a *w* offering before the LORD,
10:14 you shall also eat the breast of the *w* offering
10:15 raised offering and the breast of the *w*
10:15 be waved as a *w* offering before the LORD.
14:12 them as a *w* offering before the LORD.
14:21 as a *w* offering in atonement for himself,
14:24 *w* them as a wave offering before the LORD.
23:11 who shall *w* the sheaf before the LORD that
23:17 For the *w* offering of your first fruits to
23:20 The priest shall *w* the bread of the first
23:20 two lambs as a *w* offering before the LORD;
Nm 6:20 *w* them as a *w* offering before the LORD.
6:20 along with the breast of the *w* offering
8:11 LORD as a *w* offering from the Israelites,
8:13 to be offered as a *w* offering to the LORD.
8:15 purify them and offer them as a *w* offering;
8:21 them as a *w* offering before the LORD,
18:11 gift in every *w* offering of the Israelites;
18:18 right leg of the *w* offering belong to you.
Jgs 9: 9 are honored, and go to *w* over the trees?'
9:11 my good fruit, and go to *w* over the trees?'
9:13 gods and men, and go to *w* over the trees?'
1Sm 10: 4 you and offer you two *w* offerings of bread,
Is 11:15 and *w* his hand over the Euphrates in his

WAVE (cont.)

13: 2 *W* for them to enter the gates of the
Zec 2:13 See, I *w* my hand over them;

WAVE-OFFERING (1)

Lv 23:15 the day on which you bring the *w* sheaf,

WAVED (9)

Ex 29:27 the breast of whatever wave offering is *w*,
Lv 7:30 to be *w* as a wave offering before the LORD.
7:34 that is *w* and the leg that is raised up,
8:29 *w* it as a wave offering before the LORD;
9:21 having first *w* the breasts and the right
10:15 to be *w* as a wave offering before the LORD.
23:12 On this day, when your sheaf is *w*,
Nm 5:25 and having *w* this offering before the LORD,
Acts 22:23 They yelled and *w* their cloaks and flung

WAVERING (1)

Ps(s) 26: 1 and in the LORD I trust without *w*,

WAVES (29)

2Mc 9: 8 thought he could command the *w* of the sea,
Jb 10:17 in *w* your troops come against me.
30:14 Amid the uproar they come on in *w*;
38:11 and here shall your proud *w* be stilled!
41:17 the *w* of the sea fall back.
Ps(s) 65: 8 of their *w* and the tumult of the peoples.
89:10 you still the swelling of its *w*.
107:25 up a storm wind which tossed its *w* on high.
Wis 5:10 can be found, no path of its keel in the *w*.
14: 1 about to traverse the wild *w* cries out
14: 3 a road, and through the *w* a steady path,
Sir 24: 6 Over *w* of the sea,
29:17 and tossed them about like *w* of the sea,
Is 17:12 that surge like the surging of mighty *w*!
21: 1 whirlwinds sweeping in *w* through the Negeb,
48:18 and your vindication like the *w* of the sea;
51:15 who stirs up the sea so that its *w* roar;
Jer 31:35 Who stirs up the sea till its *w* roar,
51:42 rises, she is overwhelmed by the roaring *w*!
51:55 her *w* were roaring like mighty waters,
Ez 26: 3 nations, even as the sea churns up its *w*;
Zec 10:11 smite the *w* of the sea and all the depths
Mt 8:24 and the boat began to be swamped by the *w*.
14:24 about in the *w* raised by strong head winds.
Mk 4:37 The *w* were breaking over the boat and it
Lk 8:24 and rebuked the wind and the tumultuous *w*.
8:24 The *w* subsided and it grew calm.
21:25 at the roaring of the sea and the *w*.
Jude 1:13 They are wild ocean *w*,

WAVING (2)

Lv 14:12 *w* them as a wave offering before the LORD.
1Mc 13:51 shouts of jubilation, *w* of palm branches,

WAX (5)

Jdt 16:15 the rocks, like *w*,
Ps(s) 22:15 become like *w* melting away within my bosom.
68: 3 as *w* melts before the fire,
97: 5 The mountains melt like *w* before the LORD,
Mi 1: 4 valleys split open, Like *w* before the fire,

WAY (724)

Gn 3:24 sword, to guard the *w* to the tree of life.
9:23 since their faces were turned the other *w*,
10:19 extended from Sidon all the *w* to Gerar,
10:19 Gerar, near Gaza, and all the *w* to Sodom,
10:30 settlements extended all the *w* to Sephar,
12:20 him, and they sent him on his *w*,
14:11 Sodom and Gomorrah and then went their *w*,
18: 5 and afterward you may go on your *w*."
18:16 walking with them, to see them on their *w*.
18:19 to keep the *w* of the LORD by doing what
19:15 angels urged Lot on, saying, "On your *w*!
20: 9 You have treated me in an intolerable *w*.
24: 1 and the LORD had blessed him in every *w*.
24:10 *w* to the city of Nahor in Aram Naharaim.
24:14 In this *w* I shall know that you have dealt
24:61 the servant took Rebekah and went on his *w*.
25:18 the border of Egypt, all the *w* to Asshur;
25:34 Esau ate, drank, got up, and went his *w*.
28: 5 Then Isaac sent Jacob on his *w*;
32: 2 home, while Jacob continued on his own *w*.
33:12 said, "Let us break camp and be on our *w*;
35:16 some distance to go on the *w* to Ephrath,
36: 6 of Seir, out of the *w* of his brother Jacob.
38:13 on his *w* up to Timnah to shear his sheep,
38:14 to Enaim, which is on the *w* to Timnah;
43: 8 that we may be off and on our *w* if you and
43:13 too, and be off on your *w* back to the man.
43:15 were off on their *w* down to Egypt to
45:19 transport your father on your *w* back here.
45:24 As he sent his brothers on their *w*,
45:24 "Let there be no recriminations on the *w*."
45:25 So they left Egypt and made their *w* to
48: 7 her there on the *w* to Ephrath [that is,
Ex 3:16 about the *w* you are being treated in Egypt;
4:14 Besides, he is now on his *w* to meet you.
9:17 *w* for my people by refusing to let them go?
13:17 lead them by *w* of the Philistines' land,
13:18 the Red Sea by *w* of the desert road.
13:21 of a column of cloud to show them the *w*,
23:20 to guard you on the *w* and bring you to the
23:28 Canaanites and Hittites out of your *w*.
23:31 over to you to be driven out of your *w*.
26:17 In this *w* all the boards of the Dwelling
28:37 *w* that it rests on the front of the miter,
32: 8 aside from the *w* I pointed out to them,
33: 3 otherwise I might exterminate you on the *w*."
36:22 *w* all the boards of the Dwelling were made.
Lv 5:10 be offered as a holocaust in the usual *w*.
16: 3 in this *w* may Aaron enter the sanctuary.
18:24 out of your *w* have defiled themselves.
20:23 nations whom I am driving out of your *w*,
22:23 An ox or a sheep that is in any *w*
Nm 11:15 If this is the *w* you will deal with me,
13:22 Going up by *w* of Negeb,
15:13 shall make these offerings in the same *w*,
17: 3 In this *w* they shall serve as a sign to
21: 1 were coming along the *w* of Atharim,
22:30 in the habit of treating you this *w* before?"
24:25 and Balak also went his *w*.
32:21 his *w* and the land is subdued before him,
Dt 1: 2 by *w* of the highlands of Seir].
1:33 in the fire, to show the *w* you must go.
2:12 them out of the *w* and taking their place,
2:21 cleared out of the *w* for the Ammonites,
2:22 by clearing the Horites out of their *w*,
4:38 *w* nations greater and mightier than you,
5:33 the *w* prescribed for you by the LORD,
6:19 thrusting all your enemies out of your *w*.
9: 4 your God, has thrust them out of your *w*,
9:12 turned aside from the *w* I pointed out
9:16 you had already turned aside from the *w*
11:23 drive all these nations out of your *w*,
11:28 aside from the *w* I ordain for you today,
12:29 your *w* as you advance to dispossess them,
13: 6 lead you astray from the *w* which the LORD,
15:17 slave, also, you shall treat in the same *w*.
17:16 that you must never go back that *w* again.
18:12 is driving these nations out of your *w*.
25:18 of any god he harassed you along the *w*,
27:18 be he who misleads a blind man on his *w*!'
28:29 man in the dark, unable to find your *w*.
31:29 from the *w* along which I directed you,
33:27 out of your *w* and the Amorite he destroyed.
Jos 2: 7 out along the *w* to the fords of the Jordan,
2:16 then you may proceed on your *w*."
3: 4 follow it, that you may know the *w* to take,
10:11 the sky above them all the *w* to Azekah,
23:13 longer drive these nations out of your *w*.
23:14 as you see, I am going the *w* of all men.
24:12 Hivites and Jebusites] out of your *w*;
Jgs 1:24 said to him, "Show us a *w* into the city,
1:25 He showed them a *w* into the city,
2: 3 you, I will not clear them out of your *w*;
2:17 stray from the *w* their fathers had taken,
2:22 they would keep to the *w* of the LORD
5:10 seated on saddlecloths as they go their *w*;
9:37 company is coming by *w* of Elon-Meonenim."
11:23 the Amorites out of the *w* of his people,
17: 9 my *w* to find some other place of residence."
18:26 The Danites then went on their *w*,
19:14 So they continued on their *w* till the sun
1Sm 6: 8 Start it on its *w*, and let it go.
9: 8 to the man of God, he will tell us our *w*."
9:14 toward them on his *w* to the high place.
12:23 you and to teach you the good and right *w*.
13:15 set out from Gilgal and went his own *w*;
15: 2 his *w* as he was coming up from Egypt.
16: 1 Fill your horn with oil, and be on your *w*.
16:10 *w* Jesse presented seven sons before Samuel,
17:20 the army, on their *w* to the battleground,
18:25 Saul intended in this *w* to bring about
20:13 you of it and send you on your *w* in peace.
21: 1 Then David departed on his *w*,
24: 4 he came to the sheepfolds along the *w*,
24: 8 Saul then left the cave and went on his *w*.
26:11 and the water jug, and let us be on our *w*."
26:25 David went his *w*, and Saul returned
28:22 may have strength when you go on your *w*."
29:10 soon as it grows light, and be on your *w*."
30:22 them take those along and be on their *w*."
2Sm 3:22 him in Hebron but had gone his *w* in peace.
3:23 he has been sent on his *w* in peace."
3:24 Why did you let him go peacefully on his *w*?
5: 6 which was their *w* of saying,
7:23 and their gods out of the *w* of your people,
10:18 But the Arameans gave *w* before Israel,
14:20 to come at the issue in a roundabout *w*.
15: 6 By behaving in this *w* toward all the
15:23 ahead of him by *w* of the Mount of Olives,
17:18 They sped on their *w* and reached the house
18:14 "I will not waste time with you in this *w*."
18:23 Ahimaaz sped off by *w* of the Jordan plain
22:31 God's *w* is unerring;
22:33 me with strength and kept my *w* unerring;
1Kgs 1:49 left in terror, each going his own *w*.
2: 2 "I am going the *w* of all mankind.
7:24 it, ten to the cubit all the *w* around;
8:36 teaching them the right *w* to live and
13: 9 water and not to return by the *w* I came."
13:10 not go back the *w* he had come to Bethel.
13:12 the father asked them, "Which *w* did he go?"
13:17 here, and not to go back the *w* I came,"
14:24 LORD had cleared out of the Israelites' *w*.
18: 6 one *w* by himself, Obadiah another *w*
18: 7 As Obadiah was on his *w*, Elijah met him.
21:16 Ahab started off on his *w* down to the
2Kgs 2: 1 he and Elisha were on their *w* from Gilgal.
2:23 While he was on the *w*,
5:24 the house, and sent the men on their *w*.
10:12 Samaria, and at Beth-eked-haroim on the *w*,
15:16 his *w* from Tirzah they did not let him in.
16: 3 cleared out of the *w* of the Israelites.
17: 8 whom the LORD had cleared out of the *w*
18: 8 all the *w* to Gaza and its territory.
19:28 mouth, and make you return the *w* you came.
19:33 He shall return by the same *w* he came,
21: 2 had cleared out of the *w* of the Israelites.
1Chr 5:25 land, whom God had cleared out of their *w*.
11: 8 all sides, from the Millo all the *w* around,
18: 3 when the latter was on his *w* to set up his
24:31 so in the same *w* as the less important one.
26:12 of the LORD, for each group in the same *w*.
28:12 by *w* of courts for the house of the LORD,
2Chr 4: 3 sea, ten to the cubit, all the *w* around;
6:27 But teach them the right *w* to live,
11:17 in the *w* of David and Solomon three years.
18:23 "Which *w* did the spirit of the LORD go
21:13 but instead have walked in the *w* of the
22:11 In this *w* Jehosheba, who was the daughter
28:19 *w* and proved utterly faithless to the LORD.
32:15 you further and deceive you in any such *w*.
33: 2 had cleared out of the *w* of the Israelites.
Ezr 1: 6 their neighbors gave them help in every *w*,
8:22 to protect us against enemies along the *w*,
8:31 us from enemies and bandits along the *w*.
Neh 9:12 of fire, To light the *w* of their journey.
9:12 the *w* in which they must travel.
9:19 them the *w* by which they were to travel.
13:18 Did not your fathers act in this same *w*,
Tb 4: 3 her, and do not grieve her spirit in any *w*.
4:15 let drunkenness accompany you on your *w*.
5: 5 Tobiah said, "Do you know the *w* to Media?"
5:10 Can you go with him to show him the *w*?
5:16 we shall return to you, for the *w* is safe."
5:17 *w* and bring you back to me safe and sound;
11: 3 the rest of the party are still on the *w*."
12: 7 good, and evil will not find its *w* to you.
Jdt 4: 6 which is on the *w* to Esdraelon,
5: 8 they abandoned the *w* of their ancestors,
5:18 deviated from the *w* he prescribed for them,
7:19 was no *w* of slipping through their lines.
8:27 It is by *w* of admonition that he chastises
12: 8 direct her *w* for the triumph of his people.
Est A:11 He kept it in mind, and tried in every *w*,
4:16 and my maids will also fast in the same *w*.
1Mc 1:13 introduce the *w* of living of the Gentiles.
4:35 Lysias saw his ranks beginning to give *w*,
5:46 and strongly fortified city along the *w*,
5:53 and encouraging the people the whole *w*,
6:32 on the *w* to the king's camp.
7:42 In the same *w*, crush this army before us
8:27 In the same *w*, if war is made first on
9:45 on the other, and there is no *w* of escape.
10:63 grounds or be troublesome to him in any *w*."
12:40 Looking for a *w* to seize and kill him.
13:21 him to come to them by *w* of the desert,
14:35 In every *w* he sought to exalt his people.
2Mc 1:14 to get its great treasures by *w* of dowry.
2:12 the feast in the same *w* for eight days.
3:24 manifested himself in so striking a *w*
4:10 his countrymen into the Greek *w* of life.
6: 3 in an intolerable and utterly disgusting *w*.
6: 8 to act in the same *w* against the Jews:
6:22 this *w* he would escape the death penalty,
7:13 the fourth brother in the same *w*.
7:28 same *w* the human race came into existence.
8:17 subversion of their ancestral *w* of life.
10:36 the same *w* swung around on the defenders,
11:24 customs but prefer their own *w* of life.
11:31 *w* for faults committed through ignorance.
11:36 advantage, for we are on our *w* to Antioch.
12:11 cattle and to help them in every other *w*.
12:43 he acted in a very excellent and noble *w*,
14: 3 realized that there was no *w* for him to
14:22 the conference was held in the proper *w*.
14:29 there was no *w* of opposing the king,
15: 2 pleaded, "Do not massacre them in that *w*,
15:13 Then in the same *w* another man appeared,
15:37 Since Nicanor's doings ended in this *w*,
Jb 17: 9 Yet the righteous shall hold to his *w*,
18:10 the ground, and the toils for him on the *w*.
19: 8 He has barred my *w* and I cannot pass;
22:15 to the ancient *w* trodden by worthless men,
23:10 Yet he knows my *w*; if he proved me,
23:11 *w* I have kept and have not turned aside.
27:11 the *w* of the Almighty I will not conceal.
28: 8 trodden it, nor has the lion gone that *w*.
28:23 God knows the *w* to it;
29:25 I chose out their *w* and presided;
31: 7 If my steps have turned out of the *w*,
34:11 and brings home to a man his *w* of life.
38:19 is the *w* to the dwelling place of light,

38:24 Which *w* to the parting of the winds,
38:35 you send forth the lightnings on their *w.*
Ps(s) 1: 1 the wicked Nor walks in the *w* of sinners,
1: 6 *w* of the just, but the *w* of the wicked vanishes.
2:12 Lest he be angry and you perish from the *w,*
5: 9 make straight your *w* before me.
18:31 God's *w* is unerring,
18:33 me with strength and kept my *w* unerring;
25: 8 thus he shows sinners the *w.*
25: 9 to justice, he teaches the humble his *w.*
25:12 LORD, he shows him the *w* he should choose.
27:11 Show me, O LORD, your *w,*
32: 8 you and show you the *w* you should walk;
35: 3 and block the *w* in the face of my pursuers;
35: 6 Let their *w* be dark and slippery,
36: 5 he sets out on a *w* that is not good,
37: 5 Commit to the LORD your *w;*
37:23 of a man made firm, and he approves his *w.*
37:34 Wait for the LORD, and keep his *w;*
49: 8 Yet in no *w* can a man redeem himself,
49:14 is the *w* of those whose trust is folly,
50:23 right *w* I will show the salvation of God."
67: 3 So may your *w* be known upon earth;
77:14 O God, your *w* is holy;
77:20 Through the sea was your *w,*
85:14 and salvation, along the *w* of his steps.
86:11 LORD, your *w* that I may walk in your truth;
89:42 All who pass by the *w* have plundered him;
89:52 they have reviled your anointed on his *w!*
101: 2 I will persevere in the *w* of integrity;
101: 6 the *w* of integrity shall be in my service.
102:24 He has broken down my strength in the *w;*
106:14 They gave *w* to craving in the desert and
107: 4 *w* to an inhabited city they did not find.
107: 7 by a direct *w* to reach an inhabited city.
119: 1 Happy are they whose *w* is blameless,
119: 9 shall a young man be faultless in his *w?*
119:14 In the *w* of your decrees I rejoice,
119:27 Make me understand the *w* of your precepts,
119:29 Remove from me the *w* of falsehood,
119:30 The *w* of truth I have chosen;
119:32 I will run the *w* of your commands when you
119:33 me, O LORD, in the *w* of your statutes,
119:37 by your *w* give me life.
119:101 From every evil *w* I withhold my feet,
119:104 therefore I hate every false *w.*
119:128 every false *w* I hate.
139:24 *w* is crooked, and lead me in the *w* of old.
142: 4 In the *w* along which I walk they have
143: 8 Show me the *w* in which I should walk,
146: 9 but the *w* of the wicked he thwarts.
Prv 1:15 My son, walk not in the *w* with them,
1:31 they must eat the fruit of their own *w,*
2: 8 protecting the *w* of his pious ones.
2:12 Saving you from the *w* of evil men,
2:13 paths to walk in the *w* of darkness,
2:20 Thus you may walk in the *w* of good men,
3:23 Then you may securely go your *w;*
4:11 On the *w* of wisdom I direct you,
4:14 enter not, walk not on the *w* of evil men;
4:19 The *w* of the wicked is like darkness;
5: 8 Keep your *w* far from her,
6:23 a *w* to life are the reproofs of discipline;
8:13 Pride, arrogance, the evil *w,*
8:20 On the *w* of duty I walk,
9: 6 advance in the *w* of understanding.
9:15 passers-by as they go on their straight *w:*
11: 5 honest man's virtue makes his *w* straight,
11:15 in a bad *w* who becomes surety for another,
12:15 *w* of the fool seems right in his own eyes,
12:26 but the *w* of the wicked leads them astray.
12:28 life, but the abominable *w* leads to death.
13:15 but the *w* of the faithless is their ruin.
14: 8 man's wisdom gives him knowledge of his *w,*
14:12 Sometimes a *w* seems right to a man,
15: 9 The *w* of the wicked is an abomination to
15:19 The *w* of the sluggard is hemmed in as with
15:21 man of understanding goes the straight *w.*
16:17 attention to his *w* safeguards his life.
16:25 Sometimes a *w* seems right to a man,
16:29 and leads him into a *w* that is not good.
18:16 A man's gift clears the *w* for him,
19: 3 A man's own folly upsets his *w,*
20:14 but once he has gone his *w,*
20:24 how, then, can a man understand his *w?*
21: 8 The *w* of the culprit is crooked,
21:16 The man who strays from the *w* of good
22: 6 Train a boy in the *w* he should go;
23:19 wise, and guide your heart in the right *w.*
25:26 a just man who gives *w* before the wicked.
28:10 evil *w* will himself fall into his own pit.
30:19 *w* of an eagle in the air, the *w* of a serpent
30:19 a rock, The *w* of a ship on the high seas,
30:19 seas, and the *w* of a man with a maiden.
30:20 Such is the *w* of an adulterous woman:
30:28 yet they find their *w* into king's palaces.
Eccl 3:18 it is God's *w* of testing them and of
10:15 labor, he who knows not the *w* to the city?
Wis 1:12 Court not death by your erring *w* of life,
5: 6 We, then, have strayed from the *w* of truth,
5: 7 deserts, but the *w* of the Lord we knew not.
5:12 that none discerns the *w* it went through
7: 6 and in one same *w* they leave it.

11: 7 them abundant water in an unhoped-for *w,*
15:12 one must," says he, "make profit every *w,*
18: 3 pillar which was a guide on the unknown *w,*
18:23 the anger, and cut off the *w* to the living.
19: 2 and had anxiously sent them on their *w,*
19:22 For every *w,* O Lord!
Sir 8:15 For he will go his own *w* straight,
11:12 goes his *w* a weakling and a failure,
14:22 a scout, and lies in wait at her entry *w;*
17:19 But to the penitent he provides a *w* back,
20:25 A liar's *w* leads to dishonor,
30:11 Give him not his own *w* in his youth,
32:20 Go not on a *w* that is set with snares,
32:23 in this *w* you will keep the commandments.
37: 7 Every counselor points out a *w,*
37: 9 He may tell you how good your *w* will be,
40:25 Gold and silver make one's *w* secure,
46: 9 he won his *w* onto the summits of the land;
51: 7 I turned every *w,*
51:17 Since in this *w* I have profited,
Is 8:11 me not to walk in the *w* of this people:
15: 5 the *w* to Horonaim they utter rending cries.
19: 1 riding on a swift cloud on his *w* to Egypt;
22:25 the peg fixed in a sure spot shall give *w,*
26: 7 The *w* of the just is smooth;
26: 8 Yes, for your *w* and your judgments,
30:11 Out of the *w!*
30:21 "This is the *w;* walk in it," when you
35: 8 highway will be there, called the holy *w;*
37:29 mouth, and make you return the *w* you came.
37:34 He shall return by the same *w* he came,
40: 3 In the desert prepare the *w* of the LORD!
40:14 or showed him the *w* of understanding?
40:27 O Israel, "My *w* is hidden from the LORD,
43:16 who opens a *w* in the sea and a path in the
43:19 In the desert I make a *w,*
47:15 Each wanders his own *w,*
48:15 I have brought him, and his *w* succeeds!
48:17 good, and lead you on the *w* you should go.
51:10 sea into a *w* for the redeemed to pass over?
53: 6 like sheep, each following his own *w;*
55: 7 Let the scoundrel forsake his *w,*
56:11 Each of them goes his own *w,*
57:14 Build up, build up, prepare the *w,*
57:17 wrath, as they went their own rebellious *w.*
59: 8 The *w* of peace they know not,
59:10 like people without eyes we feel our *w.*
62:10 the gates, prepare the *w* for the people;
Jer 2:33 How well you pick your *w* when seeking love!
5: 4 For they know not the *w* of the LORD,
5: 5 For they know the *w* of the LORD,
5:28 They go their wicked *w;*
6:16 the pathways of old Which is the *w* to good,
6:27 appointed you, to search and test their *w.*
10:23 O LORD, that man is not master of his *w;*
12: 1 Why does the *w* of the godless propser,
18:11 Return, each of you, from, his evil *w;*
22:21 This has been your *w* from your youth,
23:12 *w* shall become for them slippery ground.
25: 5 from your evil *w* and from your evil deeds;
26: 3 and turn back, each from his evil *w,*
31:36 these natural laws give *w* in spite of me,
32:39 One heart and one *w* I will give them,
35:15 turn back, all of you, from your evil *w;*
36: 3 they will turn back each from his evil *w,*
36: 7 and will all turn back from their evil *w;*
41:10 set out to make his *w* to the Ammonites.
42: 3 *w* we should take and what we should do."
50: 5 their goal in Zion they shall ask the *w.*
50: 6 they wandered, losing the *w* to their fold.
Lam 1:12 "Come, all you who pass by the *w,*
Bar 3:13 Had you walked in the *w* of God,
3:20 the *w* to understanding they have not known,
3:21 their offspring were far from the *w* to her.
3:23 These have not known the *w* to wisdom,
3:27 did he give them the *w* of understanding;
3:31 None knows the *w* to her,
3:37 has traced out all the *w* of understanding,
6:68 no *w* is it clear to us that they are gods;
Ez 11: 5 This is the *w* you talk,
12:27 "The vision he sees is a long *w* off;
18:23 he turns from his evil *w* that he may live?
18:25 You say, "The LORD's *w* is not fair!"
18:25 Is it my *w* that is unfair,
18:29 Israel says, "The LORD's *w* is not fair!"
18:29 Is it my *w* that is not fair,
20:27 In this *w* also your fathers blasphemed me,
33: 8 out to dissuade the wicked man from his *w,*
33: 9 way, and he refuses to turn from his *w,*
33:17 say, "The *w* of the LORD is not fair!";
33:17 but it is their *w* that is not fair.
33:20 you say, "The *w* of the LORD is not fair"?
41: 5 which extended all the *w* around the temple,
41: 7 all the *w* around and all the wayupward;
41: 7 therefore the temple had a broad *w* running
41:21 The *w* into the nave was a square doorframe.
42: 9 chambers there was the *w* in from the east,
42:12 of the *w* which led to the back wall,
42:15 he brought me out by *w* of the gate which
43: 4 by *w* of the gate which faces the east,
44: 3 enter by *w* of the vestibule of the gate,
44: 3 of the gate, and leave by the same *w.*
44: 4 Then he brought me by *w* of the north gate

46: 2 The prince shall enter from outside by *w*
46:23 built beneath the stones all the *w* around.
Dn 3:50 *w* touched them or caused them pain or harm.
6: 6 Daniel unless by *w* of the law of his God."
10:13 Persia stood in my *w* for twenty-one days,
Hos 2: 8 *w* with thorns and erect a wall against her,
6: 9 a band of priests slay on the *w* to Shechem,
Am 2: 7 earth, and force the lowly out of the *w.*
4: 3 breached walls each by the most direct *w,*
4:12 So now I will deal with you in my own *w,*
Jon 3: 8 *w* and from the violence he has in hand.
3:10 actions how they turned from their evil *w,*
Mi 2: 8 Of those who go their *w* in confidence,
Zec 1: 7 Berechiah, son of Iddo, in the following *w:*
Mal 2: 8 But you have turned aside from the *w,*
3: 1 my messenger to prepare the *w* before me;
Mt 2:23 In this *w* what was said through the
3: 3 'Prepare the *w* of the Lord,
5:12 the prophets before you in the very same *w.*
5:16 In the same *w,*
5:25 opponent while on your *w* to court with him.
6:18 In that *w* no one can see you are fasting
6:28 a lesson from the *w* the wild flowers grow.
6:33 his kingship over you, his *w* of holiness,
7:12 others the *w* you would have them treat you:
8:25 they made their *w* toward him and woke him:
9:17 and in that *w* both are preserved."
11:10 ahead of you, to prepare your *w* before you.'
12:14 against him to find a *w* to destroy him.
15:14 "Let them go their *w;*
15:32 for fear they may collapse on the *w.*"
17:12 will suffer at their hands in the same *w.*"
18:25 As he had no *w* of paying it,
18:35 will treat you in exactly the same *w* unless
19: 8 "but at the beginning it was not that *w.*
21:29 The son replied, 'I am on my *w,*
21:32 When John came preaching a *w* of holiness,
21:36 before, but they treated them the same *w.*
22: 5 ignored the invitation and went their *w,*
22:16 a truthful man and teach God's *w* sincerely.
24:44 You must be prepared in the same *w.*
25:17 In the same *w,* the man who received
26:46 Let us be on our *w!*
26:54 fulfilled which say it must happen this *w?*"
27:32 *w* out they met a Cyrenian named Simon.
27:44 with him kept taunting him in the same *w.*
28:16 eleven disciples made their *w* to Galilee,
Mk 1: 3 crying, 'Make ready the *w* of the Lord,
1:16 As he made his *w* along the Sea of Galilee,
1:43 him a stern warning and sent him on his *w.*
2: 7 "Why does the man talk in that *w?*
3:23 began to speak to them by *w* of examples:
4:33 the message in a *w* they could understand.
4:34 To them he spoke only by *w* of parable,
6: 2 in a *w* that kept his large audience amazed.
7:13 That is the *w* you nullify God's word in
7:31 by *w* of Sidon to the Sea of Galilee,
8: 3 home hungry, they will collapse on the *w.*
8:27 the *w* he asked his disciples this question:
9:33 "What were you discussing on the *w* home?"
9:34 for on the *w* they had been arguing about
10:33 "We are on our *w* up to Jerusalem,
10:52 Jesus said in reply, "Be on your *w.*
11:18 and began to look for a *w* to destroy him.
12:14 but teach God's *w* of life sincerely.
13: 1 he was making his *w* out of the temple area,
13:29 In the same *w,* when you see these things
14: 1 *w* to arrest him by some trick and kill him.
14:11 for an opportune *w* to hand him over.
14:21 is going the *w* the Scripture tells of him.
14:29 in faith, it will not be that *w* with me."
16: 8 They made their *w* out and fled from the
16:12 walking along on their *w* to the country,
Lk 1:79 to guide our feet into the *w* of peace."
3: 4 crying, 'Make ready the *w* of the Lord,
5:19 but they found no *w* of getting him through
6:26 treated the false prophets in just this *w.*
7: 8 I say to one, 'On your *w,*'
7:27 ahead of you to prepare your *w* before you.'
9:53 him because he was on his *w* to Jerusalem.
9:57 As they were making their *w* along,
10: 3 Be on your *w,* and remember:
10: 4 no sandals and greet no one along the *w.*
10:32 there was a Levite who came the same *w;*
10:35 expense I will repay you on my *w* back.'
11:45 in speaking this *w* you insult us too."
12:21 That is the *w* it works with the man who
12:58 the *w* lest he turn you over to the judge,
13:22 the while making his *w* toward Jerusalem.
13:31 "Go on your *w!*"
14: 4 the man, healed him, and sent him on his *w.*
14:33 same *w,* none of you can be my disciple
15:20 While he was still a long *w* off,
15:25 As he neared the house on his *w* home,
16: 4 Here is a *w* to make sure that people will
16:16 of every sort are forcing their *w* in.
17:14 On their *w* there they were cured.
17:19 said to the man, "Stand up and go your *w;*
19:47 were looking for a *w* to destroy him,
20:21 of persons but teach the *w* of God in truth.
22: 2 began to look for some *w* to dispose of him;
22: 4 about a *w* to hand him over to them.
22:26 Yet it cannot be that *w* with you.

WAY (cont.)

22:39 Then he went out and made his *w*,
24:13 same day were making their *w* to a village
24:17 "What are you discussing as you go your *w?*"
Jn 1:23 Make straight the *w* of the Lord!'"
4:51 He was on his *w* there when his servants
8:30. Because he spoke this *w*,
10: 1 in some other *w* is a thief and a marauder.
10:15 my sheep know me in the same *w*
14: 4 You know the *w* that leads where I go."
14: 5 How can we know the *w?*"
14: 6 "I am the *w*, and the truth, and the life;
14:31 Let us be on our *w*.
16:22 In the same *w*, you are sad for a time,
16:32 will be scattered and each will go his *w*,
18:22 "Is that the *w* to answer the high priest?"
20: 3 started out on their *w* toward the tomb.
Acts 1:25 cause and went the *w* he was destined to go."
3: 3 When he saw Peter and John on their *w* in,
4:21 no *w* to punish them because of the people,
5:27 priest began the interrogation in this *w*:
6:12 God, and in this *w* they incited the people,
8:22 may pardon you for thinking the *w* you have.
8:25 news to many villages of Samaria on the *w*.
8:39 the man went on his *w* rejoicing.
9: 2 or woman, living according to the new *w*.
9:17 Jesus who appeared to you on the *w* here,
10:38 of the *w* God anointed him with the Holy
12:10 and made their *w* down a narrow alley,
13:50 and in that *w* got a persecution started
14: 1 spoke in such a *w* as to convince a good
14:16 past ages he let the Gentiles go their *w*.
15: 3 their *w* through Phoenicia and Samaria,
15:30 representatives sent on their *w* to Antioch;
16: 4 As they made their *w* from town to town,
16:16 It was while we were on our *w* out to the
16:17 will make known to you a *w* of salvation."
16:36 Get started, now. On your *w!*"
16:40 two first made their *w* to Lydia's house,
17: 8 In this *w* they stirred up the crowd.
17:14 sent Paul off directly on his *w* to the sea,
18:25 and instructed in the new *w* of the Lord.
18:26 to him God's new *w* in greater detail.
19: 9 the new *w* in the presence of the assembly,
19:23 disturbance broke out concerning the new *w*.
20: 3 so he decided to return by *w* of Macedonia.
20:19 my *w* from the plottings of certain Jews.
20:22 now, as you see, I am on my *w* to Jerusalem,
20:33 silver or gold or envy the *w* he dressed.
21:13 you crying and breaking my heart in this *w?*
21:24 In that *w*, everyone will know that there
22: 4 this new *w* to the point of death.
22:21 'Be on your *w*.
23:29 in no *w* guilty of anything deserving death
24:14 to you that it is according to the new *w*—
24:22 was rather well informed about the new *w*,
25: 3 Their plot was to kill him on the *w*.
26: 4 "The *w* I have lived since my youth,
26: 9 of Jesus the Nazorean in every *w* possible.
26:24 Paul went on defending himself in this *w*,
27:44 In this *w* all came safely ashore.
Rom 1:10 I may at last find my *w* clear to visit you.
3: 5 (I speak in a merely human *w*.)
3:26 in the present, by *w* of forebearance,
5:21 by *w* of justice leading to eternal life,
6:11 same *w*, you must consider yourselves
7: 4 In the same *w*, my brothers, you died to
14:13 block or hindrance in your brother's *w*.
14:18 *w* pleases God and wins the esteem of men.
14:21 or scandal, or that weakens him in any *w*.
15:15 in parts of this letter by *w* of reminder.
15:19 from Jerusalem all the *w* around to Illyria.
15:28 Spain, passing through your midst on the *w*.
1Cor 2:14 it must be appraised in a spiritual *w*.
3:18 of you thinks he is wise in a worldly *w*,
3:18 In that *w* he will really be wise,
4: 6 Apollos by *w* of example for your benefit.
4:12 Persecution comes our *w*;
4:14 I am writing you in this *w* not to shame
7: 6 I say this by *w* of concession,
9:12 obstacle in the *w* of the gospel of Christ.
10:13 Along with the test he will give you a *w*
10:33 to please all in any *w* I can by seeking,
11:12 In the same *w* that woman was made from man,
11:25 same *w*, after the supper, he took the cup,
11:31 not be falling under judgment in this *w*;
16:11 to me by sending him on his *w* in peace.
2Cor 1:16 both on my *w* to Macedonia and on my return,
2:15 saved and those on the *w* to destruction;
4: 8 We are afflicted in every *w* possible,
7:11 In every *w* you have displayed your
9:11 In every *w* your liberality is enriched;
11: 6 this evident to you in every conceivable *w*.
11: 9 In every *w* possible I kept myself from
11:16 all the *w* and let me do a little boasting.
12:11 in no *w* inferior to the "super-apostles."
12:13 In what *w* are you inferior to the other
12:18 Did Titus take advantage of you in any *w?*
13:10 I am writing in this *w* while away from you,
Gal 1:13 story of my former *w* of life in Judaism.
2: 4 they wormed their *w* into the group to spy
3: 8 Scripture saw in advance that God's *w*
3:18 Yet it was by *w* of promise that God
4: 3 In the same *w*,
5:12 who are troubling you might go the whole *w*.
6: 2 that *w* you will fulfill the law of Christ.
Eph 4:22 you must lay aside your former *w* of life
4:23 acquire a fresh, spiritual *w* of thinking.
5: 2 Follow the *w* of love,
6: 9 act in a similar *w* toward your slaves.
Phil 1: 5 at the *w* you have all continually helped
1:18 that matters is that in any and every *w*,
1:27 in a *w* worthy of the gospel of Christ.
3:15 If you see it another *w*,
3:18 many go about in a *w* which shows them to
4:19 in a *w* worthy of his magnificent riches
Col 1:10 of the Lord and pleasing to him in every *w*.
3:20 everything as the acceptable *w* in the Lord.
1Thes 1: 3 Father of the *w* you are proving your faith,
2: 9 you in order not to impose on you in any *w*.
2:18 but Satan blocked the *w*.
4: 1 conduct yourselves in a *w* pleasing to God
4:15 will in no *w* have an advantage over those
2Thes 1:12 In this *w* the name of our Lord Jesus may
3:16 you continued peace in every possible *w*.
1Tm 1: 3 I gave you when I was on my *w* to Macedonia:
1: 8 it in the *w* law is supposed to be used
2:12 or in any *w* to have authority over a man;
3: 8 In the same *w*, deacons must be serious,
5: 4 this is the *w* God wants it to be.
6: 3 Whoever teaches in any other *w*,
2Tm 3: 6 It is such as these who worm their *w* into
Ti 2: 9 They should try to please them in every *w*,
2:10 *w* possible the doctrine of God our Savior.
3: 3 We went our *w* in malice and envy,
Heb 2:17 to become like his brothers in every *w*,
4:15 one who was tempted in every *w* that we are,
6: 9 Beloved, even though we speak in this *w*,
9: 8 the *w* into the sanctuary had not yet been
9:23 the heavenly models be purified in this *w*,
13: 4 *w* and the marriage bed be kept undefiled,
Jas 5:12 In this *w* you will not incur condemnation.
5:20 who brings a sinner back from his *w*
1Pt 1:18 *w* of life your fathers handed on to you,
2:21 you in just this *w* and left you an example,
3: 2 the reverent purity of your *w* of life.
3: 5 ages used to adorn themselves in this *w*,
3:16 your *w* of life in Christ may be shamed.
4:17 If it begins this *w* with us,
5: 5 same *w*, you younger men must be obedient
2Pt 1:16 It was not by *w* of cleverly concocted
2: 2 true *w* will be made subject to contempt.
3:11 everything is to be destroyed in this *w*,
1Jn 2: 3 The *w* we can be sure of our knowledge of
2: 5 The *w* we can be sure we are in union with
3:10 is the *w* to see who are God's children,
3:16 The *w* we came to understand love was that
3:19 This is our *w* of knowing we are committed
4: 9 love was revealed in our midst in this *w*:
4:13 The *w* we know we remain in him and he in
2Jn 1: 6 is the *w* in which you should walk.
3Jn 1: 6 a good thing if, in a *w* that pleases God,
Jude 1: 4 recently wormed their *w* into your midst,
Rv 2:14 Balak to throw a stumbling block in the *w*
3: 9 will learn of my love for you in that *w*.
11: 5 harm them will surely be slain in this *w*.
16:12 to prepare the *w* for the kings of the East.
17:11 one of the seven and is on its *w* to ruin.

WAYFARER (5)

Gn 47: 9 as a *w* amount to a hundred and thirty.
2Sm 12: 4 a meal for the *w* who had come to him.
Ps(s) 39:13 For I am but a *w* before you,
119:19 I am a *w* of earth;
Sir 10:21 Be it tenant or *w*,

WAYFARERS (4)

Gn 47: 9 the years that my ancestors lived as *w*."
Jb 21:29 *w* and do you not recognize their monuments?
31:32 in the street, but I opened my door to *w*—
Jer 35: 7 may live long on the earth where you are *w*.'

WAYLAID (1)

Lam 4:19 us on the mountains and *w* us in the desert.

WAYLAYS (1)

Wis 14:24 but each either *w* and kills his neighbor,

WAYS (179)

Gn 48:15 *w* my fathers Abraham and Isaac walked,
Ex 33:13 with you, do let me know your *w* so that,
Lv 2: 8 any of these *w* you shall bring to the LORD,
20: 6 fortune-tellers and follow their wanton *w*,
Dt 8: 6 God, by walking in his *w* and fearing him.
10:12 LORD, your God, and follow his *w* exactly,
11:22 your God, and following his *w* exactly,
19: 9 LORD, your God, and ever walking in his *w*:
26:17 to walk in his *w* and observe his statutes,
28: 9 of the LORD, your God, and walk in his *w*,
30:16 today, loving him, and walking in his *w*,
32: 4 how right all his *w!*
2Sm 22:22 For I kept the *w* of the LORD and was not
1Kgs 2: 3 following his *w* and observing his statutes,
11:33 he has not followed my *w* or done what is
11:38 heed all that I command you, follow my *w*,
13:33 not give up his evil *w* after this event,
22:43 all the *w* of his father Asa unswervingly,
2Kgs 17:13 *w* and keep my commandments and statutes,
2Chr 6:31 So may they fear you and walk in your *w* as
7:14 my presence and turn from their evil *w*,
17: 3 *w* his father had pursued in the beginning,
17: 6 he was encouraged to follow the LORD's *w*,
22: 3 too, followed the *w* of the house of Ahab,
Tb 3: 2 All your *w* are mercy and truth;
Jdt 9: 6 All your *w* are in readiness,
2Mc 12:41 all therefore praised the *w* of the Lord,
Jb 21:14 us, for we have no wish to learn your *w!*
22: 3 a gain to him if you make your *w* perfect?
22:28 you, and upon your *w* the light shall shine.
24:13 they know not its *w*;
24:23 his strength, and his eyes are on their *w*.
26:14 Lo, these are but the outlines of his *w*,
31: 4 Does he not see my *w*,
33:11 he watches all my *w!*"
34:21 For his eyes are upon the *w* of man,
34:27 away from him and heeded none of his *w*,
40:19 He came at the beginning of God's *w*,
Ps(s) 10: 5 His *w* are secure at all times;
17: 4 of your lips I have kept the *w* of the law.
18:22 For I kept the *w* of the LORD and was not
25: 4 Your *w*,
39: 2 I said, "I will watch my *w*,
39: 7 A phantom only, man goes his *w*;
51:15 I will teach transgressors your *w*,
81:14 would hear me, and Israel walk in my *w*,
91:11 you, that they guard you in all your *w*.
95:10 of erring heart, and they know not my *w*.
103: 7 He has made known his *w* to Moses,
107:17 *w* and afflicted because of their sins,
119: 3 heart, And do no wrong, but walk in his *w*.
119: 5 be firm in the *w* of keeping your statutes!
119:15 on your precepts and consider your *w*.
119:26 I declared my *w*, and you answered me;
119:59 my *w* and turned my feet to your decrees.
119:168 your decrees, for all my *w* are before you.
125: 5 But such as turn aside to crooked *w* may
128: 1 you who fear the LORD, who walk in his *w!*
138: 5 And they shall sing of the *w* of the LORD:
139: 3 scrutinize, with all my *w* you are familiar.
145:17 in all his *w* and holy in all his works.
Prv 1:21 Down the crowded *w* she calls out,
2:15 Whose *w* are crooked,
3: 6 In all your *w* be mindful of him,
3:17 Her ways are pleasant *w*,
3:31 the lawless man and choose none of his *w*:
4:26 for your feet, and let all your *w* be sure.
5:21 each man's *w* are plain to the LORD's sight;
6: 6 O sluggard, study her *w* and learn wisdom;
7:25 Let not your heart turn to her *w*,
7:27 house is made up of *w* to the nether world,
8:22 LORD begot me, the first-born of his *w*,
8:33 obeys me, and happy those who keep my *w*,
10: 9 but he whose *w* are crooked will fare badly.
14: 2 but he who is devious in his *w* spurns him.
14:14 suffers the consequences of his *w*,
16: 2 the *w* of a man may be pure in his own eyes,
16: 7 When the LORD is pleased with a man's *w*,
19: 1 than he who is crooked in his *w* and rich.
21: 2 *w* of a man may be right in his own eyes,
21:29 but the upright man pays heed to his *w*.
22:25 of a wrathful man, Lest you learn his *w*,
23:26 your heart, and let your eyes keep to my *w*.
28: 6 than he who is crooked in his *w* and rich.
28:18 he whose *w* are crooked falls into the pit.
Eccl 11: 9 Follow the *w* of your heart,
Wis 2:15 like other men's, and different are his *w*.
5: 7 our fill of the *w* of mischief and of ruin;
6:16 and graciously appears to them in the *w*,
10:10 brother's anger, guided him in direct *w*,
16:25 very time, transformed in all sorts of *w*,
Sir 2: 6 make straight your *w* and hope in him.
2:15 those who love him keep his *w*.
6:27 with all your strength keep her *w*.
13: 1 with an impious man learns his *w*.
14:21 Who ponders her *w* in his heart,
16:18 with my *w* who will concern himself?
17:13 Their *w* are ever known to him,
17:15 sun to him, his eyes are ever upon their *w*.
37: 7 out a way, but some counsel *w* of their own;
Is 2: 3 of Jacob, That he may instruct us in his *w*,
42:16 before them, and make crooked *w* straight.
42:24 In his *w* they refused to walk,
45:13 all his *w* I make level.
49: 9 Along the *w* they shall find pasture,
55: 8 not your thoughts, nor are your *w* my ways,
55: 9 so high are my *w* above your ways and my
57:18 I saw their *w*, but I will heal them
58: 2 me day after day, and desire to know my *w*,
58:13 If you honor it by not following your *w*,
59: 8 Their *w* they have made crooked,
63:17 do you let us wander, O LORD, from your *w*,
64: 4 that we were mindful of you in our *w!*
66: 3 Since these have chosen their own *w* and
Jer 2:33 in your wickedness, have gone by *w* unclean!
3:21 perverted their *w* and forgotten the LORD,
7: 3 Reform your *w* and your deeds,

7: 5 thoroughly reform your *w* and your deeds;
7:23 Walk in all the *w* that I command you,
12: 4 because they say, "God does not see our *w*."
15: 7 they returned not from their evil *w*.
16:17 For my eyes are upon all their *w*;
17:10 To reward everyone according to his *w*,
18:11 reform your *w* and your deeds.
18:15 They stumble out of their *w*,
23:22 from evil *w* and from their wicked deeds.
26:13 therefore, reform your *w* and your deeds;
32:19 whose eyes are open to all the *w* of men,
32:19 of men, giving to each according to his *w*,
Lam 3: 9 He has blocked my *w* with fitted stones,
3:11 He deranged my *w*,
3:40 our *w* that we may return to the LORD!
Bar 4:13 *w* of God's commandments they did not walk,
Ez 16:47 Yet not only in their *w* did you walk,
16:47 more corrupt in all your *w* than they.
18:25 unfair, or rather, are not your *w* unfair?
18:29 rather, is it not that your *w* are not fair?
18:30 of Israel, each one according to his *w*,
33:11 Turn, turn from your evil *w*!
33:20 judge every one of you according to his *w*,
Dn 3:27 your deeds are faultless, all your *w* right,
4:34 all his works are right and his *w* just;
Hos 4: 9 I will punish them for their *w*,
9: 8 God, yet a fowler's snare is on all his *w*,
Mi 4: 2 of Jacob, That he may instruct us in his *w*,
Hb 3: 6 age-old hills bow low along his ancient *w*.
Hg 1: 5 Consider your *w*!
1: 7 Consider your *w*!
Zec 1: 4 your evil *w* and from your wicked deeds.
1: 6 treated us according to our *w* and deeds,
3: 7 If you walk in my *w* and heed my charge,
Mal 2: 9 all the people, Since you do not keep my *w*,
Lk 3: 5 be made straight And the rough *w* smooth,
Jn 19:23 took his garments and divided them four *w*,
Acts 1: 3 in many convincing *w* that he was alive,
3:26 bless you by turning you from your evil *w*."
8:22 Reform your evil *w*.
18:13 worship God in *w* that are against the law."
Rom 11:33 his judgments, how unsearchable his *w*!
1Cor 4:17 He will remind you of my *w* in Christ,
13:11 When I became a man I put childish *w* aside.
2Cor 8:22 eagerness has been proved to us in many *w*.
13:11 Mend your *w*.
Gal 2:14 according to Gentile *w* rather than Jewish,
2:14 you force the Gentiles to adopt Jewish *w*?"
1Tm 1:10 and those who in other *w* flout the sound
Ti 2: 3 in *w* that befit those who belong to God.
2:12 us to reject godless *w* and worldly desires,
Heb 1: 1 *w* to our fathers through the prophets;
3:10 of erring heart, and have never known my *w*.'
2Pt 2: 2 Their lustful *w* will lure many away.
2:18 passion, with the lustful *w* of the flesh,
3Jn 1: 2 in all other *w* as you do in the spirit.
Rv 2:26 victory, who keeps to my *w* till the end,
15: 3 Righteous and true are your *w*,
22:11 Let the wicked continue in their wicked *w*,

WAYSIDE (3)

Ps(s) 110: 7 From the brook by the *w* he will drink;
140: 6 by the *w* they have laid snares for me.
Jer 48:19 Stand by the *w*,

WAYSIDES (1)

Jer 3: 2 By the *w* you waited for them like an Arab

WAYWARD (1)

Ps(s) 78: 8 fathers, a generation *w* and rebellious,

WEAK (66)

Lv 19:15 to the *w* nor deference to the mighty,
Nm 13:18 Are the people living there strong or *w*,
Dt 25:18 you along the way, *w* and weary as you were,
Jgs 16: 7 her, "I shall be as *w* as any other man."
16:11 her, "I shall be as *w* as any other man."
16:13 the pin, I shall be as *w* as any other man."
16:17 me, and I shall be as *w* as any other man."
1Sm 3: 2 lately grown so *w* that he could not see.
14:28 As a result the people are *w*."
2Sm 3:39 I am the anointed king, I am *w* this day,
2Chr 28:15 them, and all who were *w* they set on asses.
Jdt 9:11 of the oppressed, the supporter of the *w*,
1Mc 3:17 Besides, we are *w* today from fasting."
Ps(s) 69:21 Insult has broken my heart, and I am *w*,
Wis 9: 5 a man *w* and short-lived and lacking in
Sir 11:30 like a spy he will pick out the *w* spots.
35:13 Though not unduly partial toward the *w*,
41: 2 sentence to the *w* man of failing strength,
Is 14:10 to you, "You too have become *w* like us,
16:14 there shall be a remnant, very small and *w*.
35: 3 feeble, make firm the knees that are *w*,
38:14 My eyes grow *w*, gazing heavenward:
40:29 for the *w* he makes vigor abound.
44:12 He is hungry and *w*, drinks no water
Jer 22:16 he dispensed justice to the *w* and the poor,
Bar 6:27 do not share it with the poor and the *w*;
6:35 death, nor deliver the *w* from the strong.
Ez 34: 4 You did not strengthen the *w* nor heal the
34:21 and butt all the *w* sheep with your horns
Dn 8:27 I, Daniel, was *w* and ill for some days;
Jl 4:10 let the *w* man say,
Am 2: 7 heads of the *w* into the dust of the earth,
4: 1 You who oppress the *w* and abuse the needy;
5:11 the *w* and exacted of them levies of grain,
Mt 6:30 provide much more for you, O *w* in faith!
16: 8 How *w* your faith is!
26:41 The spirit is willing but nature is *w*."
Mk 14:38 The spirit is willing but nature is *w*."
Lk 12:28 more will he provide for you, O *w* in faith!
Acts 20:35 by such hard work that you must help the *w*.
Rom 4:19 *w* in faith he thought of his own body,
6:19 affairs because of your *w* human nature.)
7:14 I am *w* flesh sold into the slavery of sin.
14: 1 a kind welcome to those who are *w* in faith.
14: 2 one who is *w* in faith eats only vegetables.
15: 1 the scruples of those whose faith is *w*;
1Cor 1:27 the *w* of this world to shame the strong.
4:10 We are the *w* ones, you the strong!
8: 7 and because their conscience is *w*,
8: 9 you become an occasion of sin to the *w*.
8:10 may not his conscience in its *w* state be
8:11 of your "knowledge" the *w* one perishes,
8:12 brothers and wound their *w* consciences,
9:22 To the *w* I became a weak person with a
9:22 a *w* person with a view to winning the weak.
2Cor 10: 2 ones who accuse us of *w* human behavior.
11:21 that we have been too *w* to do such things.
11:29 Who is *w* that I am not affected by it?
13: 3 He is not *w* in dealing with you,
13: 4 We too are *w* in him,
13: 9 rejoice when we are *w* and you are strong.
1Thes 5:14 support the *w*;
Heb 7:28 law sets up as high priests men who are *w*,
11:34 though *w* they were made powerful,
12:12 your drooping hands and your *w* knees.

WEAKEN (2)

1Mc 4:32 fear, *w* the boldness of their strength,
Is 57:10 strength you found, and so you did not *w*.

WEAKENED (2)

Jdt 8:31 our cisterns, lest we be *w* still further."
Jer 49:24 Damascus is *w*,

WEAKENING (1)

Rom 8: 3 powerless because of its *w* by the flesh.

WEAKENS (1)

Rom 14:21 or scandal, or that *w* him in any way.

WEAKER (5)

Gn 30:42 *w* animals he would not put the rods there.
2Sm 3: 1 grew stronger, but the house of Saul *w*.
1Mc 6:57 "We are growing *w* every day,
1Pt 3: 7 Treat women with respect as the *w* sex,
2Pt 2:14 They lure the *w* types.

WEAKHEARTED (2)

Dt 20: 3 Be not *w* or afraid; be neither alarmed
20: 8 'Is there anyone who is afraid and *w*?

WEAKLING (3)

Ps(s) 105:37 and gold, with not a *w* among their tribes.
Sir 11:12 Another goes his way a *w* and a failure,
Zec 12: 8 and the *w* among them shall be like David

WEAKLINGS (1)

Jdt 16:11 when my *w* cried out,

WEAKLY (2)

Lv 21:20 or who is humpbacked or *w* or walleyed,
Est D: 7 and leaned *w* against the head of the maid

WEAKNESS (12)

Jb 31:33 Had I, out of human *w*,
Wis 2:11 for *w* proves itself useless.
Rom 8:26 The Spirit too helps us in our *w*,
1Cor 1:25 than men, and his *w* more powerful than men.
2: 3 I came among you it was in *w* and in fear,
15:43 *W* is sown, strength rises up.
2Cor 12: 9 for you, for in *w* power reaches perfection."
12:10 Therefore I am content with *w*,
13: 4 It is true he was crucified out of *w*,
Heb 4:15 who is unable to sympathize with our *w*,
5: 2 for he himself is beset by *w* and so must
7:18 annulled because of its *w* and uselessness,

WEAKNESSES (3)

2Cor 11:30 I must boast, I will make a point of my *w*.
12: 5 about myself unless it be about my *w*.
12: 9 And so I willingly boast of my *w* instead,

WEALTH (115)

Gn 15:14 in the end they will depart with great *w*.
31: 1 *w* of his by using our father's property."
31:16 All the *w* that God reclaimed from our
34:29 They carried off all their *w*,
Nm 31: 9 all their herds and flocks and *w* as spoil,
Dt 8:17 own hand that has obtained for me this *w*.'
8:18 God, who gives you the power to acquire *w*,
Jos 22: 8 returning to your own tents with great *w*,
1Sm 17:25 kill him, the king would give him great *w*,
1Chr 29:16 all this *w* that we have brought together
29:28 old age, rich in years and *w* and glory,
2Chr 17: 5 so that he enjoyed great *w* and glory.
18: 1 therefore had *w* and glory in abundance;
21:17 away all the *w* found in the king's palace,
31: 3 From his own *w* the king allotted a portion
32:27 Hezekiah possessed very great *w* and glory.
Tb 4: 8 If you have great *w*, give alms out
12: 2 half of all the *w* he brought back with me.
Est 1: 4 and the resplendent *w* of his royal estate.
1Mc 6: 1 famous for its *w* in silver and gold,
2Mc 3: 7 to expropriate the aforesaid *w*.
Jb 20:18 though his *w* increases,
31:25 Or had I rejoiced that my *w* was great,
Ps(s) 37:16 of the just than the great *w* of the wicked,
49: 7 They trust in their *w*;
49:11 pass away, leaving to others their *w*.
49:17 when the *w* of his house becomes great,
49:18 his *w* shall not follow him down.
52: 9 strength, But put his trust in his great *w*,
62:11 though *w* abound,
73:12 always carefree, while they increase in *w*.
112: 3 *W* and riches shall be in his house;
Prv 1:13 All kinds of precious *w* shall we gain,
3: 9 Honor the LORD with your *w*,
5:10 Lest strangers have their fill of your *w*,
6:31 all the *w* of his house he may yield up.
8:18 and honor, enduring *w* and prosperity.
8:21 justice, Granting *w* to those who love me,
10:15 The rich man's *w* is his strong city;
10:22 It is the LORD's blessing that brings *w*,
11: 4 *W* is useless on the day of wrath,
11:16 but the diligent gain *w*
12:27 but the *w* of the diligent man is great.
13: 7 pretends to be poor, yet has great *w*.
13:11 *W* quickly gotten dwindles away,
13:22 *w* of the sinner is stored up for the just.
18:11 The rich man's *w* is his strong city;
19: 4 *W* adds many friends,
20:15 Like gold or a *w* of corals,
23: 4 Toil not to gain *w*,
24: 6 the victory is due to a *w* of counselors.
27:24 For *w* lasts not forever,
28: 8 He who increases his *w* by interest and
28:22 avaricious man is perturbed about his *w*,
29: 3 who consorts with harlots squanders his *w*.
Eccl 2: 8 and gold, and the *w* of kings and provinces.
5: 9 and the lover of *w* reaps no fruit from it;
10: 1 weighty than wisdom or *w* is a little folly!
Wis 5: 8 have *w* and its boastfulness afforded us?
Sir 5: 1 Rely not on your *w*; say not:
5:10 Rely not upon deceitful *w*,
10:29 as the rich man is honored for his *w*;
10:30 Honored in poverty, how much more so in *w*!
10:30 Dishonored in *w*,
11:10 he who is avid for *w* will not be blameless?
13:23 *W* is good when there is no sin;
14: 3 *W* ill becomes the mean man;
18:25 plenty, poverty and want in the day of *w*.
21: 4 Violence and arrogance wipe out *w*;
25:20 a woman's beauty, nor be greedy for her *w*;
27: 1 and the struggle for *w* blinds the eyes.
29: 5 speaks with respect of his creditor's *w*;
29: 6 *w* and acquires an enemy at no extra charge;
31: 1 flesh, and the care of *w* drives away rest.
31: 3 The rich man labors to pile up *w*,
31: 5 for he who pursues *w* is led astray by it.
33:21 Give not to another your *w*,
40:13 *W* out of wickedness is like a wadi in spate:
40:17 *W* or wages can make life sweet,
40:26 *W* and vigor build up confidence,
44:11 Their *w* remains in their families,
Is 8: 4 the *w* of Damascus and the spoil of Samaria
10: 3 Where will you leave your *w*,
60: 5 the *w* of nations shall be brought to you.
60:11 But shall admit to you the *w* of nations,
61: 6 You shall eat the *w* of the nations and
66:12 and the *w* of the nations like an
Jer 17: 3 Your *w* and all your treasures I will give
17:11 her own is the man who acquires *w* unjustly:
20: 5 All the *w* of this city,
48:36 the *w* they acquired has perished.
Ez 22:25 seizing their *w* and precious things,
26: 2 now that it is ruined, its *w* reverts to me!"
26:12 Your *w* shall be plundered,
27:12 traded with you, so great was your *w*,
27:18 traded with you, so great was your *w*,
27:27 Your *w*, your goods, your wares,
27:33 With your great *w* and merchandise you
Na 2:10 their *w* in precious things of every kind!
Hb 2: 4 *W*, too, is treacherous:
Zep 1:13 Their *w* shall be given to pillage and
Zec 9:17 For what *w* is theirs, and what beauty!
Mk 4:19 over life's demands, and the desire for *w*,
12:44 They gave from their surplus *w*,
Lk 12:20 whom will all this piled-up *w* of yours go?'
16:11 If you cannot be trusted with elusive *w*,

WEALTH (cont.)

Eph 1:18 the *w* of his glorious heritage to be
2: 7 he might display the great *w* of his favor,
Phil 1: 9 both in understanding and *w* of experience.
3: 8 Christ may be my *w* and I may be in him,
1Tm 6:17 not to rely on so uncertain a thing as *w*.
Jas 5: 2 Your *w* has rotted,
Rv 18: 3 grew rich from her *w* and wantonness."
18:17 hour this great *w* has been destroyed!"
21:26 *w* of the nations shall be brought there,

WEALTHIER (1)

Sir 13: 2 go with no one greater or *w* than yourself.

WEALTHY (12)

Gn 24:35 so abundantly that he has become a *w* man;
26:13 all the time, until he was very *w* indeed.
Lv 25:47 such poverty that he sells himself to a *w* alien
1Sm 25: 2 he was very *w*,
2Sm 19:33 very old man of eighty and very *w* besides,
Sir 26:19 A *w* man reduced to want;
Mt 27:57 fell, a *w* man from Arimathea arrived,
Mk 12:41 Many of the *w* put in sizable amounts;
Lk 12:15 A man may be *w*,
14:12 or brothers or relatives or *w* neighbors.
19: 2 the chief tax collector and a *w* man.
Rv 6:15 and those in command, the *w* and powerful,

WEANED (8)

1Sm 1:22 to her husband, "Once the child is *w*,
1:23 wait until you have *w* him.
1:23 and nursed her son until she had *w* him.
1:24 Once he was *w*,
Ps(s) 131: 2 stilled and quieted my soul like a *w* child.
131: 2 Like a *w* child on its mother's lap,
Is 28: 9 To those just *w* from milk,
Hos 1: 8 After she *w* Lo-ruhama,

WEANING (2)

Gn 21: 8 grew, and on the day of the child's *w*,
1Kgs 11:20 After his *w*,

WEAPON (13)

Lv 26:37 over one another as if to escape a *w*,
2Sm 2:23 javelin, and the *w* protruded from his back.
1Chr 12:34 battle array with every kind of *w* for war:
12:38 men equipped with every kind of *w* of war:
2Chr 23: 7 king on all sides, each with his *w* drawn.
Neh 4:11 with one hand and held a *w* with the other.
4:17 everyone kept his *w* at his right hand.
Jb 20:24 Should he escape the iron *w*,
Wis 18:21 bearing the *w* of his special office,
Sir 43:10 *w* against the flood waters stored on high,
Is 54:17 No *w* fashioned against you shall prevail;
Jer 51:20 You are my hammer, my *w* for war;
Ez 9: 2 each with a destroying *w* in his hand.

WEAPONS (42)

Gn 49: 5 indeed, *w* of violence are their knives.
Dt 1:41 And each of you girded on his *w*,
Jgs 14: 6 upon Samson, and although he had no *w*,
18:11 of the Danites, fully armed with *w* of war,
18:16 The six hundred men girt with *w* of war,
1Sm 20:40 his *w* to this boy of his and said to him,
21: 9 I brought along neither my sword nor my *w*,
2Sm 1:27 have fallen, the *w* of war have perished!"
1Kgs 10:25 silver or gold articles, garments, *w*,
2Kgs 10: 2 the horses, a fortified city, and the *w*,
11: 8 surround the king, each with drawn *w*,
11:11 And the guards, with drawn *w*,
2Chr 9:24 silver and gold articles, garments, *w*,
Jdt 6:12 they seized their *w* and ran out of the
7: 5 Yet they all seized their *w*,
14: 2 on the earth, let each of you seize his *w*,
1Mc 1:35 inside it, storing up *w* and provisions,
3: 3 He armed himself with *w* of war;
6: 2 and *w* left there by Alexander,
14:42 the country, its *w* and strongholds,
15: 7 All the *w* you have prepared
16:16 Ptolemy and his men sprang up, *w* in hand,
2Mc 8:18 "They trust in *w* and acts of daring,"
8:31 They collected the enemies' *w* and
11: 8 in white garments and brandishing gold *w*.
Jb 39:21 and rushes in his might against the *w*.
Ps(s) 7:14 bow, Prepare his deadly *w* against them,
76: 4 of the bow, shield and sword, and *w* of war.
Is 22: 8 looked to the *w* in the House of the Forest;
54:16 the burning coals and forges *w* as his work;
Jer 21: 4 I will turn back in your hands the *w* with
21: 4 *w* I will pile up in the midst of this city,
50:25 armory and brings forth the *w* of his wrath;
Ez 26: 9 and break down your towers with his *w*.
32:27 to the nether world with their *w* of war,
39: 9 in the cities of Israel go out and burn *w*:
39:10 for they shall make fires with the *w*.
Jn 18: 3 came there with lanterns, torches and *w*.
Rom 6:13 members of your body to sin as *w* for evil.
6:13 and your bodies to God as *w* for justice.
2Cor 6: 7 wielding the *w* of righteousness with right
10: 4 The *w* of our warfare are not merely human.

WEAR (47)

Gn 27:15 gave them to her younger son Jacob to *w*;
28:20 me enough bread to eat and clothing to *w*,
Ex 18:18 "You will surely *w* yourself out,
28: 4 his sons are to *w* in serving as my priests,
28:35 Aaron shall *w* it when ministering,
28:43 Aaron and his sons shall *w* them whenever
Lv 16: 4 He shall *w* the sacred linen tunic,
16:32 He shall *w* the linen garments,
21:10 been ordained to *w* the special vestments,
Dt 22: 5 shall not *w* an article proper to a man,
22:11 *w* cloth of two different kinds of thread,
1Sm 2:28 burn incense, and to *w* the ephod before me;
2:33 to *w* out their eyes in consuming greed;
Est C:27 a polluted rag, and do not *w* it in private.
1Mc 11:58 in royal purple, and to *w* a gold buckle.
14:43 right to *w* royal purple and gold ornaments.
14:44 royal purple or *w* an official gold brooch.
2Mc 4:12 the noblest young men to *w* the Greek hat.
12:40 which the law forbids the Jews to *w*.
Jb 14:19 As waters *w* away the stones and floods
27:17 What he has stored the just man shall *w*,
31:36 I should *w* it on my shoulder or put it on
Ps(s) 109:29 and let them *w* their shame like a mantle.
Wis 5:18 and shall *w* sure judgment for a helmet;
Sir 6:31 You will *w* her as your robe of glory,
6:36 let your feet *w* away his doorstep!
11: 5 some that none would consider *w* a crown.
Is 4: 1 eat our own food and *w* our own clothing;
15: 3 In the streets they *w* sackcloth,
50: 9 Lo, they will all *w* out like cloth,
Jer 13: 1 *w* it on your loins,
Ez 16:10 you a fine linen sash and silk robes to *w*.
44:17 inner court, they shall *w* linen garments;
Dn 5: 7 purple, *w* a golden collar about his neck,
5:16 in purple, *w* a gold collar about your neck,
Mt 6:31 what are we to drink, or what are we to *w?*'
23: 5 their phylacteries and *w* huge tassels.
Mk 6: 9 They were, however, to *w* sandals.
Lk 10: 4 *w* no sandals and greet no one along the
12:22 eat, or for your body, what you are to *w*.
12:33 purses for yourselves that do not *w* out,
Acts 28:20 I *w* these chains solely because I share
1Cor 11: 6 Indeed, if a woman will not *w* a veil,
11: 6 it is clear that she ought to *w* a veil.
11:14 dishonorable for a man to *w* his hair long,
Jas 2:15 has nothing to *w* and no food for the day,
Rv 19: 8 given a dress to *w* made of finest linen,

WEARIED (11)

Ps(s) 6: 7 I am *w* with sighing; every night I flood
69: 4 I am *w* with calling,
Sir 22:13 rest and not be *w* by his lack of sense.
Is 33: 1 when *w* with betraying you will be betrayed.
43:24 with your sins, and *w* me with your crimes.
47:13 You *w* yourself with many consultations,
Jer 12: 5 If running against men has *w* you,
Mi 6: 3 have I done to you, or how have I *w* you?
Zec 11: 8 I *w* of them, and they behaved badly
Mal 2:17 You have *w* the LORD with your words,
2:17 words, yet you say, "How have we *w* him?"

WEARINESS (3)

Eccl 12:12 and in much study there is *w* for the flesh.
Is 5:27 None of them will stumble with *w*,
Lam 3: 5 beset me round about with poverty and *w*;

WEARING (23)

Ex 32: 2 take off the golden earrings they are *w*,
Lv 6: 3 linen robe and *w* linen drawers on his body,
1Sm 14: 3 of the LORD at Shiloh, was *w* the ephod.)
14:18 (Ahijah was *w* the ephod in front of the
18: 4 the mantle he was *w* and gave it to David,
1Kgs 11:29 area, and the prophet was *w* a new cloak.
20:32 the waist, and *w* cords around their heads,
2Kgs 1: 8 *W* a hairy garment," they replied,
6:30 saw that he was *w* sackcloth underneath,
1Chr 15:27 David was also *w* a linen ephod.
Jdt 9: 1 her head, and *w* nothing over her sackcloth.
15:13 their armor, *w* garlands and singing hymns.
Est 1:11 Vashti into his presence *w* the royal crown,
2Mc 3:25 The rider was seen to be *w* golden armor.
6: 7 march in his procession, *w* wreaths of ivy.
Sir 50:11 robes, and *w* his garments of splendor,
Jer 2:25 *w* out your shoes and parching your throat!
13: 4 the loincloth which you bought and are *w*,
Lk 18: 5 for God or man, but this widow is *w* me out.
Jn 19: 5 *w* the crown of thorns and the purple cloak,
1Pt 3: 3 hairdress, the *w* of golden jewelry,
Rv 1:13 like a Son of Man *w* an ankle-length robe,
14:14 sat One like a Son of Man *w* a gold crown

WEARISOME (1)

Jb 16: 2 *W* comforters are you all!

WEARS (3)

Jb 13:28 Though he *w* out like a leather bottle,
Sir 18:17 a grudging gift *w* out the expectant eyes.
Is 51: 6 the earth *w* out like a garment and its

WEARY (35)

Dt 25:18 you along the way, weak and *w* as you were,
Jgs 8:15 we should give food to your *w* followers?'"
16:16 complaints till he was deathly *w* of them.
2Sm 16: 2 for those to drink who are *w* in the desert."
17: 2 come upon him when he is *w* and discouraged,
2Mc 12:36 been fighting for a long time and were *w*,
Jb 3:17 from troubling, there the *w* are at rest.
Prv 26:15 he is too *w* to lift it to his mouth.
Eccl 10:15 When will the fool be *w* of his labor,
Sir 16:25 They were not to hunger, nor grow *w*,
43:32 Extol him with renewed strength, and *w* not,
51:19 with her, never *w* of extolling her.
Is 7:13 Is it not enough for you to *w* men,
7:13 you to weary men, must you also *w* my God?
16:12 When Moab grows *w* on the high places,
28:12 is the resting place, give rest to the *w*;
40:28 He does not faint nor grow *w*,
40:30 Though young men faint and grow *w*,
40:31 They will run and not grow *w*,
43:22 upon me, O Jacob, for you grew *w* of me,
43:23 of offerings, nor *w* you for frankincense.
46: 1 on shoulders, carried as burdens by the *w*.
50: 4 speak to the *w* a word that will rouse them.
Jer 6:11 up within me, I am *w* of holding it in;
15: 6 to destroy you, I was *w* of sparing you.
20: 9 I grow *w* holding it in,
31:25 For I will refresh the *w* soul;
45: 3 I am *w* from groaning,
51:58 for the flames the peoples *w* themselves.
51:64 *w* themselves" are the words of Jeremiah.]
Hb 2:13 the flames, and nations grow *w* for nought!
Mt 11:28 all you who are *w* and find life burdensome,
Gal 6: 9 Let us not grow *w* of doing good;
2Thes 3:13 must never grow *w* of doing what is right,
Heb 8: 9 broke my covenant and I grew *w* of them,

WEATHER (2)

Sir 18:26 Between morning and evening the *w* changes;
Dn 13:15 She decided to bathe, for the *w* was warm.

WEAVE (4)

Jgs 16:13 "If you *w* my seven locks of hair into the
Is 30: 1 who *w* webs that are not inspired by me,
59: 5 hatch adders' eggs, and *w* spiders' webs:
Lk 12:27 they do not spin, they do not *w*;

WEAVER (3)

Ex 38:23 and a *w* of variegated cloth of violet,
Sir 45:11 with scarlet yarn, the work of the *w*;
Is 38:12 life, like a *w* who severs the last thread.

WEAVERS (8)

Jgs 16:14 he pulled out both the *w* pin and the web.
1Sm 17: 7 of his javelin was like a *w* heddle-bar,
2Sm 21:19 a spear with a shaft like a *w* heddle-bar.
1Chr 4:21 clans of the linen *w*' guild in Bethashbea,
11:23 a spear that was like a *w* heddle-bar,
20: 5 whose spear shaft was like a *w* heddle-bar.
Jb 7: 6 My days are swifter than a *w* shuttle;
Is 19: 9 the combers and *w* shall turn pale;

WEAVING (4)

Ex 35:35 and scarlet yarn and fine linen thread, *w*,
Tb 2:11 my wife Anna worked for hire at *w* cloth,
Est E:13 and by *w* intricate webs of deceit,
Mt 27:29 *W* a crown out of thorns they fixed it on

WEB (5)

Jgs 16:13 into the *w* and fasten them with the pin,
16:14 wove his seven locks of hair into the *w*,
16:14 pulled out both the weaver's pin and the *w*.
Jb 8:14 thread and his trust is a spider's *w*.
Is 25: 7 The *w* that is woven over all nations;

WEBS (4)

Est E:13 and by weaving intricate *w* of deceit,
Is 30: 1 who weave *w* that are not inspired by me,
59: 5 hatch adders' eggs, and weave spiders' *w*:
59: 6 Their *w* cannot serve as clothing,

WED (2)

Dt 24: 5 "When a man is newly *w*,
Prv 30:23 Under an odious woman when she is *w*,

WEDDING (25)

Jgs 14:20 to the one who had been best man at his *w*.
Tb 6:13 Rages, we will hold the *w* feast for her.
9: 2 him along with you to the *w* celebration.
9: 5 and was inviting him to the *w* celebration.
9: 6 start and traveled to the *w* celebration.
10: 7 Now at the end of the fourteen-day *w*
11:18 Tobiah's *w* feast for seven happy days,
12: 1 When the *w* celebration came to an end,
1Mc 9:37 sons of Jambri are celebrating a great *w*,
9:41 Thus the *w* was turned into mourning,
10:58 Their *w* was celebrated at Ptolemais with
Mt 9:15 "How can *w* guests go in mourning so long

22: 2 to a king who gave a *w* banquet for his son.
22: 3 to summon the invited guests to the *w*,
22: 9 'and invite to the *w* anyone you come upon.'
22:10 This filled the *w* hall with banqueters.
22:11 a man not properly dressed for a *w* feast.
25:10 who were ready went in to the *w* with him.
Mk 2:19 "How can the guests at a *w* fast as long
Lk 12:36 awaiting their master's return from a *w*,
14: 8 you are invited by someone to a *w* party,
Jn 2: 1 third day there was a *w* at Cana in Galilee,
Rv 19: 7 For this is the *w* day of the Lamb;
19: 7 his bride has prepared herself for the *w*.
19: 9 been invited to the *w* feast of the lamb."

WEDGED (1)

Sir 27: 2 between buying and selling sin is *w* in.

WEDLOCK (1)

Wis 14:24 longer safeguard either lives or pure *w*;

WEEDS (12)

Jdt 8: 5 about her loins and wore widow's *w*.
1Mc 4:38 *w* growing in the courts as in a forest or
Jb 31:40 of wheat and noxious *w* instead of barley!
Hos 9: 6 *W* shall overgrow their silver treasures,
Mt 13:25 enemy came and sowed *w* through his wheat,
13:26 grain, the *w* made their appearance as well.
13:27 Where are the *w* coming from?'
13:29 'pull up the *w* and you might take the
13:30 collect the *w* and bundle them up to burn,
13:36 to us the parable of the *w* in the field."
13:38 The *w* are the followers of the evil one
13:40 Just as *w* are collected and burned,

WEEK (25)

Gn 29:27 Finish the bridal *w* for this one,
29:28 He finished the bridal *w* for Leah,
Lv 23:16 and then on the day after the seventh *w*,
23:39 a pilgrim feast of the LORD for a whole *w*.
23:40 a *w* you shall make merry before the LORD,
23:41 whole *w* in the seventh month of the year.
23:42 During this *w* every native Israelite among
2Kgs 11: 7 divisions who are going off duty that *w*
11: 9 sabbath and those going off duty that *w*,
2Mc 12:38 As the *w* was ending,
Dn 9:27 For one *w* he shall make a firm compact
9:27 *w* he shall abolish sacrifice and oblation;
Mt 28: 1 as the first day of the *w* was dawning,
Mk 16: 2 first day of the *w* they came to the tomb.
16: 9 the dead early on the first day of the *w*.
Lk 18:12 I fast twice a *w*.
24: 1 On the first day of the *w*,
Jn 20: 1 in the morning on the first day of the *w*,
20:19 On the evening of that first day of the *w*,
20:26 A *w* later, the disciples were once more
Acts 20: 6 joined them in Troas, where we spent a *w*.
20: 7 On the first day of the *w* when we gathered
21: 4 there and stayed with them for a *w*.
28:14 who urged us to stay on with them for a *w*.
1Cor 16: 2 On the first day of each *w* everyone should

WEEKS (17)

Ex 34:22 of *W* with the first of the wheat harvest;
Lv 23:15 sheaf, you shall count seven full *w*,
25: 8 "Seven *w* of years shall you count
Nm 28:26 day of first fruits, on your feast of *W*,
Dt 16: 9 "You shall count off seven *w*,
16:10 keep the feast of *W* in honor of the LORD,
16:16 of Unleavened Bread, at the feast of *W*,
2Chr 8:13 the feast of *W* and the feast of Booths.
Tb 2: 1 our festival of Pentecost, the feast of *W*,
2Mc 12:31 Jerusalem, shortly before the feast of *W*.
Jer 5:24 for us over the appointed *w* of harvest."
Dn 9:24 "Seventy *w* are decreed for your people
9:25 and a leader, there shall be seven *w*.
9:25 During sixty-two *w* it shall be rebuilt,
9:26 After the sixty-two *w* an anointed shall be
10: 2 days, I, Daniel, mourned three full *w*.
10: 3 myself at all until the end of the three *w*.

WEEP (53)

1Sm 1: 7 her, and Hannah would *w* and refuse to eat.
1: 8 "Hannah, why do you *w*,
30: 4 him wept aloud until they could *w* no more.
2Sm 1:24 Women of Israel, *w* over Saul,
3:34 And all the people continued to *w* for him.
19: 1 up to the room over the city gate to *w*.
Neh 1: 4 *w* and continued mourning for several days;
8: 9 Do not be sad, and do not *w*—
Tb 5:18 But his mother began to *w*.
7: 7 to *w* in the arms of his kinsman Tobiah.
7: 8 and even their daughter Sarah began to *w*.
10: 4 began to *w* aloud and to wail over her son:
Jb 2:12 not recognize him, they began to *w* aloud;
Eccl 3: 4 A time to *w*, and a time to laugh;
Sir 7:34 Avoid not those who *w*,
22: 9 *W* over the dead man,
22: 9 *w* over the fool,
22:10 *W* but a little over the dead man,
Is 15: 2 daughter Dibon to the high places to *w*;
16: 9 I *w* with Jazer for the vines of Sibmah;
22: 4 Turn away from me, let me *w* bitterly;
22:12 GOD of hosts, called on you To *w* and mourn,
30:19 dwell in Jerusalem, no more will you *w*;
33: 7 the messengers of Shalem *w* bitterly.
Jer 8:23 That I might *w* day and night over the
13:17 your pride, I will *w* in secret many tears;
22:10 *W* not for him who is dead,
22:10 *W* rather for him who is going away;
48:32 More than for Jazer I *w* over you,
Lam 1:16 "At this I *w*, my eyes run with tears:
Ez 24:16 but do not mourn or *w* or shed any tears.
24:23 You shall not mourn or *w*,
27:31 on sackcloth, For you they *w* in anguish,
Jl 1: 5 Wake up, you drunkards, and *w*;
1:13 Gird yourselves and *w*, O priests!
2:17 the priests, the ministers of the LORD *w*,
Mi 1:10 Publish it not in Gath, *w* not at all;
Mt 26:75 He went out and began to *w* bitterly.
Lk 6:25 you shall *w* in your grief.
23:28 "Daughters of Jerusalem, do not *w* for me.
23:28 *W* for yourselves and for your children.
Jn 11:31 she was going to the tomb to *w* there.
11:35 Jesus began to *w*,
16:20 will *w* and mourn while the world rejoices;
Acts 20:37 They began to *w* without restraint,
Rom 12:15 those who rejoice, *w* with those who weep.
12:15 those who rejoice, weep with those who *w*.
1Cor 7:30 those who *w* should live as though they
Jas 4: 9 Begin to lament, to mourn, and to *w*;
5: 1 *w* and wail over your impending miseries.
Rv 5: 5 "Do not *w*.
18: 9 wallowed in her sensuality will *w* and lament
18:11 of the world will *w* and mourn over her too,

WEEPING (49)

Nm 25: 6 were *w* at the entrance of the meeting tent.
1Sm 1:10 she prayed to the LORD, *w* copiously,
11: 5 "Why are the people *w*?"
2Sm 3:16 who followed her *w* as far as Bahurim.
13:36 than the princes came in, *w* aloud.
15:30 heads covered and were *w* as they went.
19: 2 the king was *w* and mourning for Absalom;
2Kgs 8:12 wept, and Hazael asked, "Why are you *w*,
13:14 he exclaimed, *w* over him.
Ezr 3:13 from the sound of those who were *w*;
10: 1 *w* and prostrate before the house of God,
Neh 8: 9 were *w* as they heard the words of the law.
Tb 6: 1 Then she stopped *w*.
Jdt 14:16 He broke into a loud clamor of *w*,
Est 4: 3 went into deep mourning, with fasting, *w*,
2Mc 13:12 LORD continuously with *w* and fasting
Jb 16:16 with *w* and there is darkness over my eyes,
30:31 mourning, and my reed pipe to sounds of *w*.
Ps(s) 6: 7 every night I flood my bed with *w*;
6: 9 for the LORD has heard the sound of my *w*;
30: 6 At nightfall, *w* enters in,
39:13 to my *w* be not deaf!
126: 6 Although they go forth *w*,
Sir 38:17 *W* bitterly, mourning fully,
Is 15: 3 they wear sackcloth, lamenting and *w*;
15: 5 The ascent of Luhith they climb *w*;
65:19 longer shall the sound of *w* be heard there,
Jer 3:21 the plaintive *w* of Israel's children,
9:17 for us, That our eyes may be wet with *w*,
31:15 is heard the sound of moaning, of bitter *w*!
41: 6 out from Mizpah to meet them, *w* as he went.
48: 5 The ascent of Luhith they climb *w*;
50: 4 and of Judah shall come, *W* as they come,
Lam 2:11 Worn out from *w* are my eyes,
Ez 8:14 there the women who were *w* for Tammuz.
Dn 13:33 All her relatives and the onlookers were *w*.
Jl 2:12 your whole heart, with fasting, and *w*,
Mal 2:13 LORD you cover with tears, *w* and groaning,
Mk 16:10 his followers, who were now grieving and *w*.
Lk 6:21 Blest are you who are *w*; you shall laugh.
7:38 *w* so that her tears fell upon his feet.
Jn 11:33 When Jesus saw her *w*,
11:33 the Jews who had accompanied her also *w*,
20:11 Meanwhile, Mary stood *w* beside the tomb.
20:13 "Woman," they asked her, "why are you *w*?"
20:15 "Woman," he asked her, "why are you *w*?
1Cor 7:30 should live as though they were not *w*,
Rv 18:15 *W* and mourning, they cry out:
18:19 their heads and cried out, *w* and mourning:

WEEPS (3)

Ps(s) 119:28 My soul *w* for sorrow;
Sir 31:13 therefore it *w* for any cause.
Lam 1: 2 Bitterly she *w* at night,

WEIGH (15)

1Kgs 7:47 Solomon did not *w* all the articles because
2Kgs 12:11 were in the temple of the LORD, and *w* them.
1Chr 20: 2 It was found to *w* a talent of gold;
Ezr 8:29 Keep good watch over them till you *w* them
2Mc 9: 8 he could *w* the mountaintops in his scales,
Jb 31: 6 Let God *w* me in the scales of justice;
33: 7 nor should my presence *w* heavily upon you.
Sir 8:15 man, lest he *w* you down with calamity;
28:25 and gold, so balance and *w* your words.
Is 1:14 they *w* me down,
24:20 Its rebellion will *w* it down,
40:15 the coastlands *w* no more than powder.
46: 6 a purse and *w* out silver on the scales;
Ez 33:10 say, "Our crimes and our sins *w* us down;
Zep 1:11 will be destroyed, all who *w* out silver,

WEIGHED (30)

Gn 23:16 he *w* out to him the silver that Ephron had
Nm 7:85 plate *w* a hundred and thirty shekels,
7:86 filled with incense *w* ten shekels apiece,
Jgs 4:24 their power *w* ever heavier upon him,
8:26 requested *w* seventeen hundred gold shekels,
1Sm 17: 7 and its iron head *w* six hundred shekels.
2Sm 12:30 *w* a talent, of gold and precious stones;
14:26 the hair *w* two hundred shekels according
21:16 whose bronze spear *w* three hundred shekels,
1Kgs 10:14 *w* six hundred and sixty-six gold talents,
1Chr 22: 3 with so much bronze that it could not be *w*,
22:14 great quantities that they cannot be *w*.
2Chr 9:13 *w* six hundred and sixty-six gold talents,
Ezr 8:25 and I *w* out before them the silver and the
8:30 gold, and the utensils that had been *w* out,
8:33 and the utensils were *w* out in the house
Jb 28:25 He has *w* out the wind,
Ps(s) 105:18 They had *w* him down with fetters,
Eccl 12: 9 taught the people knowledge, and *w*,
Sir 21:25 the words of the prudent are carefully *w*.
Is 33:18 is he who counted, where is he who *w*?
40:12 *w* the mountains in scales and the hills in
Jer 32:10 and *w* out the silver on the scales,
52:20 of all these furnishings could not be *w*.
Lam 3: 7 with no escape and *w* me down with chains;
Ez 4:16 eat bread which they have *w* out anxiously,
Dn 5:27 been *w* on the scales and found wanting;
Jn 19:39 and aloes which *w* about a hundred pounds.
Acts 27:13 for, so they *w* anchor and proceeded,
2Cor 5: 4 we are *w* down because we do not wish to be

WEIGHING (28)

Gn 24:22 man took out a gold ring *w* half a shekel,
24:22 nose, and two gold bracelets *w* ten shekels,
Nm 7:13 silver plate *w* a hundred and thirty shekels
7:13 and one silver basin *w* seventy shekels,
7:19 silver plate *w* a hundred and thirty shekels
7:19 and one silver basin *w* seventy shekels,
7:25 silver plate *w* a hundred and thirty shekels
7:25 and one silver basin *w* seventy shekels,
7:31 silver plate *w* a hundred and thirty shekels
7:31 and one silver basin *w* seventy shekels,
7:37 silver plate *w* a hundred and thirty shekels
7:37 and one silver basin *w* seventy shekels,
7:43 silver plate *w* a hundred and thirty shekels
7:43 and one silver basin *w* seventy shekels,
7:49 silver plate *w* a hundred and thirty shekels
7:49 and one silver basin *w* seventy shekels,
7:55 silver plate *w* a hundred and thirty shekels
7:55 and one silver basin *w* seventy shekels,
7:61 silver plate *w* a hundred and thirty shekels
7:61 and one silver basin *w* seventy shekels,
7:67 silver plate *w* a hundred and thirty shekels
7:67 and one silver basin *w* seventy shekels,
7:73 silver plate *w* one hundred and thirty shekels
7:73 and one silver basin *w* seventy shekels,
7:79 silver plate *w* a hundred and thirty shekels
7:79 and one silver basin *w* seventy shekels,
1Sm 17: 5 of scale armor *w* five thousand shekels,
1Mc 14:24 a great gold shield *w* a thousand minas,

WEIGHS (3)

Prv 15:28 The just man *w* well his utterance,
Eccl 6: 1 under the sun, and it *w* heavily upon man:
Wis 9:15 the earthen shelter *w* down the mind

WEIGHT (37)

Lv 19:35 using measures of length or *w* or capacity.
Nm 7:14 cup of ten shekels' *w* filled with incense;
7:20 cup of ten shekels' *w* filled with incense,
7:26 cup of ten shekels' *w* filled with incense,
7:32 cup of ten shekels' *w* filled with incense;
7:38 cup of ten shekels' *w* filled with incense;
7:44 cup of ten shekels' *w* filled with incense;
7:50 cup of ten shekels' *w* filled with incense;
7:56 cup of ten shekels' *w* filled with incense;
7:62 cup of ten shekels' *w* filled with incense;
7:68 cup of ten shekels' *w* filled with incense;
7:74 cup of ten shekels' *w* filled with incense;
7:80 cup of ten shekels' *w* filled with incense;
Dt 15:14 but shall *w* him down with gifts from your
25:15 But use a true and just *w*,
Jos 7:21 and a bar of gold fifty shekels in *w*;
1Kgs 7:47 the *w* of the bronze,
2Kgs 25:16 The *w* in bronze of the two pillars,
1Chr 28:14 He specified the *w* of gold to be used in
28:14 *w* of silver to be used in the silver vessels
28:15 *w* of gold for each lampstand and its lamps,
28:15 specified the *w* of silver for each lampstand
28:16 He specified the *w* of gold for each table
28:18 the refined gold, and its *w*,
2Chr 3: 9 The *w* of the nails was fifty gold shekels.
4:18 the *w* of the bronze was not ascertained.

WEIGHT (cont.)

Ezr	8:34	was in order as to number and *w*,
	8:34	and weight, and the total *w* was registered.
Jb	26: 8	yet the cloud is not rent by their *w*;
Prv	11: 1	to the LORD, but a full *w* is his delight.
Wis	11:20	all things by measure and number and *w*.
Is	22:25	*w* that hung on it shall be done away with;
Jer	15:17	Under the *w* of your hand I sat alone
Ez	4:10	you eat shall be twenty shekels a day by *w*;
2Cor	2: 7	not be crushed by too great a *w* of sorrow.
	4:17	eternal *w* of glory beyond all comparison.
Ti	3: 8	great *w* on the things I have been saying,

WEIGHTIER (1)

Mt	23:23	while neglecting the *w* matters of the law,

WEIGHTS (8)

Lv	19:36	You shall have a true scale and true *w*,
Dt	25:13	shall not keep two differing *w* in your bag,
Prv	16:11	all the *w* used with them are his concern.
	20:10	Varying *w*,
	20:23	Varying *w* are an abomination to the LORD,
Sir	42: 4	and balances, or of tested measures and *w*;
Mi	6:11	acquit criminal balances, bags of false *w*?
Rv	16:21	Giant hailstones like huge *w* came crashing

WEIGHTY (3)

Ps(s)	139:17	How *w* are your designs,
Eccl	10: 1	*w* than wisdom or wealth is a little folly!
Zec	12: 3	make Jerusalem a *w* stone for all peoples.

WELCOME (36)

Jgs	19: 3	him, the girl's father joyfully made him *w*.
	19:20	"You are *w*,"
1Sm	29: 6	But you are not *w* to the lords.
Tb	5:14	*W*! God save you, brother!
	5:14	You are certainly of good lineage, and *w*!"
	7: 1	Good health to you, and *w*!"
	11:17	*W*, my daughter!
	11:17	*W* to your home with blessing and joy.
Est	5: 2	and made her *w* by extending toward her the
1Mc	11: 2	in the cities opened their gates to *w* him,
	16:15	The son of Abubus gave them a deceitful *w*
Sg	8:14	boasts of having found *w* from her lover.
Sir	14:25	beside her, and lives as her *w* neighbor;
	35:24	*W* is his mercy in time of distress as rain
	41: 2	how *w* your sentence to the weak man of
Mal	1: 8	see if he will accept it, or *w* you,
	1: 9	have done the like Will he *w* any of you?
Mt	25: 1	their torches and went out to *w* the groom.
	25:38	When did we *w* you away from home or clothe
	25:43	I was away from home and you gave me no *w*,
Lk	9:53	but the Samaritans would not *w* him because
	10: 8	whatever city you go, after they *w* you,
	10:10	people of any town you enter do not *w* you,
Acts	18:27	by writing the disciples there to *w* him.
	21:17	the brothers there gave us a warm *w*.
Rom	14: 1	a kind *w* to those who are weak in faith.
	14: 3	After all, God himself has made him *w*.
	16: 2	Please *w* her in the Lord,
2Cor	6:18	I will *w* you and be a father to you and
	8:17	Not only did he *w* our appeal,
Phil	2:29	*W* him joyously in the Lord and hold men
Col	4:10	if he comes to you, make him *w*.
Phlm	1:17	me as a partner, *w* him as you would me.
Jas	1:21	*w* the word that has taken root in you,
3Jn	1:10	Not only does he refuse to *w* the brothers
Jude	1:21	and *w* the mercy of our Lord Jesus Christ

WELCOMED (13)

Jdt	13:13	They opened the gate and *w* the two women.
1Mc	11:60	at Ashkalon, the citizens *w* him with pomp.
	12: 8	Onias *w* the envoy with honor and received
2Mc	10:15	they *w* fugitives from Jerusalem and
Ps(s)	21: 4	For you *w* him with goodly blessings,
Sg	8:10	now in his eyes I have become one to be *w*.
Mt	25:35	I was a stranger and you *w* me,
Lk	8:40	On his return, Jesus was *w* by the crowd;
	10:38	a woman named Martha *w* him to her home.
	19: 6	quickly descended, and *w* him with delight.
Jn	4:45	arrived in Galilee, the people there *w* him.
Acts	15: 4	in Jerusalem they were *w* by that church,
	17:11	and *w* the message with great enthusiasm.

WELCOMES (17)

Mt	10:40	"He who *w* you welcomes me,
	10:40	and he who *w* me welcomes him who sent me.
	10:41	He who *w* a prophet because he bears the
	10:41	he who *w* a holy man because he is known to
	18: 5	*w* one such child for my sake welcomes me.
Mk	9:37	"Whoever *w* a child such as this for my sake *w*
	9:37	And whoever welcomes me *w*,
Lk	9:48	"Whoever *w* this little child on my account *w*
	9:48	and whoever *w* me welcomes him who sent me;
	15: 2	"This man *w* sinners and eats with them."

WELCOMING (2)

Wis	19:16	Yet these, after *w* them with festivities,
Acts	28:30	his rented lodgings, *w* all who came to him.

WELFARE (15)

Neh	2:10	had come to seek the *w* of the Israelites.
Est	10: 3	as the promoter of his people's *w*
1Mc	12:22	this, kindly write to us about your *w*.
2Mc	9:21	to form plans for the general *w* of all.
	13: 3	Antiochus on, not for the *w* of his country,
Jb	30:15	the wind, and my *w* vanishes like a cloud.
Ps(s)	119:122	Be surety for the *w* of your servant;
Sir	45:26	Lest their *w* should ever be forgotten,
Jer	15: 5	Who will stop to ask about your *w*?
	29: 7	*w* of the city to which I have exiled you;
	29: 7	the LORD, for upon its *w* depends your own.
	29:11	for you, says the LORD, plans for your *w*,
	38: 4	is not interested in the *w* of our people,
	40: 9	to the king of Babylon, for their own *w*;
Bar	4:22	trusted in the Eternal God for your *w*,

WELL (479)

Gn	3: 5	God knows *w* that the moment you eat of it
	4: 7	If you do *w*,
	6: 4	Nephilim appeared on earth (as *w* as later),
	7:21	swarmed on the earth, as *w* as all mankind.
	10:12	Rehoboth-Ir, and Calah, as *w* as Resen,
	12:11	"I know *w* how beautiful a woman you are.
	12:13	so that it may go *w* with me on your
	12:16	On her account it went very *w* with Abram,
	13:10	Lot looked about and saw how *w* watered the
	14:12	living in Sodom, as *w* as his possessions.
	16:14	That is why the *w* is called Beer-lahai-roi.
	18: 5	"Very *w*," they replied, "do as you have
	18: 8	as *w* as the steer that had been prepared,
	19: 9	*W* treat you worse than them!"
	19:21	*W*, then," he replied, "I will also grant you
	21:19	opened her eyes, and she saw a *w* of water.
	21:25	*w* that Abimelech's men had seized by force.
	21:30	acknowledgment that the *w* was dug by me."
	22: 3	son Isaac, and two of his servants as *w*.
	24:11	the camels kneel by the *w* outside the city.
	24:20	and ran back to the *w* to draw more water,
	24:31	for you, as *w* as a place for the camels?"
	26:19	wadi and reached spring water in their *w*,
	26:20	So the *w* was called Esek,
	26:21	Then they dug another *w*,
	26:22	on from there, he dug still another *w*;
	26:25	his servants began to dig a *w* nearby.
	26:32	him news about the *w* they had been digging;
	27:20	your God, let things turn out *w* with me."
	27:36	exclaimed, "He has been *w* named Jacob!
	29: 2	about, he saw a *w* in the open country,
	29: 2	it, for droves were watered from that *w*.
	29: 2	A large stone covered the mouth of the *w*.
	29: 3	the mouth of the *w* and water the flocks.
	29: 3	stone back again over the mouth of the *w*.
	29: 6	He inquired further, "Is he *w*?"
	29: 8	the stone away from the mouth of the *w*;
	29:10	the stone away from the mouth of the *w*,
	29:17	but Rachel was *w* formed and beautiful.
	30:15	"Very *w*, then!"
	30:26	*w* the service that I have rendered you."
	30:29	how *w* your livestock fared under my care;
	30:30	now do something for my own household as *w*.
	30:34	"Very *w*," agreed Laban.
	30:35	them, as *w* as the fully dark-colored sheep;
	31: 6	You *w* know what effort I put into serving
	31:12	'Note *w*. All the he-goats in the flock,
	31:33	as *w* as the tents of the two maidservants;
	32: 6	sheep, as *w* as male and female servants.
	32: 8	who were with him, as *w* as his flocks,
	36: 6	as *w* as his livestock comprising various
	37:14	"see if all is *w* with your brothers and
	38:17	"Very *w*," she said, "provided you leave
	39: 2	Joseph got on very *w* and was assigned to
	40:14	still remember, when all is *w* with you,
	43:14	your other brother go, as *w* as Benjamin.
	46:32	herds, as *w* as everything else they own.
	48:10	were dim from age, and he could not see *w*.)
	48:11	allowed me to see your descendants as *w*!"
	50: 8	of Egypt, as *w* as Joseph's whole household,
Ex	1:20	Therefore God dealt *w* with the midwives.
	2:15	As he was seated there by a *w*,
	3: 7	so I know *w* what they are suffering.
	8:24	*W*, then," said Pharaoh, "I will let you go
	10: 5	as *w* as all the foliage that has since
	10: 9	"our sons and daughters as *w* as our
	10:29	Moses replied, *W* said!
	11: 5	as *w* as all the first-born of the animals.
	12:29	as *w* as all the first-born of the animals.
	21:35	*w* as the dead animal equally between them.
	23: 9	you *w* know how it feels to be an alien,
	25:29	as *w* as its pitchers and bowls for pouring
	25:38	as *w* as the trimming shears and trays,
	27: 3	for removing the ashes, as *w* as shovels,
	27:19	as *w* as all its tent pegs and all the tent
	28:14	of gold, as *w* as two chains of pure gold,
	29:13	as *w* as the lobe of its liver and its two
	29:21	as *w* as on his sons and their vestments,
	29:27	as *w* as the thigh of whatever raised
	32:22	*w* enough how prone the people are to evil.
	35:28	as *w* as spices,
	36:38	hooks as *w* as their capitals and bands,
	37:16	as *w* as its pitchers and bowls for pouring
	37:17	its shaft and branches as *w* as its cups
	37:23	as *w* as its trimming shears and trays,
	39: 1	as *w* as the sacred vestments for Aaron,
Lv	3: 4	adheres to them, as *w* as the two kidneys,
	3:10	adheres to them, as *w* as the two kidneys,
	3:15	adheres to them, as *w* as the two kidneys,
	4: 9	adheres to them, as *w* as the two kidneys,
	6:14	It shall be *w* kneaded and fried in oil on
	7: 4	as *w* as the two kidneys with the fat on
	7:12	of fine flour mixed with oil and *w* kneaded.
	8:16	as *w* as the lobe of the liver and the two
	8:30	as *w* as his sons and their vestments,
	14: 4	live, clean birds, as *w* as some cedar wood,
	14:11	purified, as *w* as all these offerings,
	14:49	shall take two birds, as *w* as cedar wood,
	14:56	of garments and houses, as *w* as for scabs,
	15:33	as *w* as for the woman who has her
	16:12	as *w* as a double handful of finely ground
	16:17	as *w* as for the whole Israelite community,
	16:33	as *w* as for the priests and all the people
	17: 2	his sons, as *w* as to all the Israelites,
	20:14	the man and the two women as *w* shall be
	21:22	is most sacred as *w* as of what is sacred.
Nm	3:37	as *w* as the columns of the surrounding
	3:41	as *w* as their cattle in place of all the
	4: 7	*w* as the bowls and pitchers for libations;
	4: 9	as *w* as the various containers of oil from
	5:17	as *w* as some dust that he has taken from
	6:19	as *w* as one unleavened cake and one
	7: 1	(as *w* as the altar with all its equipment),
	11:18	Oh, how *w* off we were in Egypt!'
	13:23	a pole, as *w* as some pomegranates and figs.
	15: 5	as *w* as a libation of a fourth of a hin of
	15:24	as *w* as one he-goat as a sin offering.
	17:23	forth not only shoots, but blossoms as *w*,
	18: 1	"You and your sons as *w* as the other
	18:15	of man, as *w* as of unclean animals,
	18:31	Your families, as *w* as you,
	19:14	the tent, as *w* as everyone already in it,
	20:17	or vineyards, nor drink of any *w* water,
	21:16	was the *w* of which the LORD said to Moses,
	21:17	"Spring up, O *w*— so
	21:18	The *w* that was the princes sank,
	21:22	or vineyard, nor will we drink any *w* water,
	22:38	Balaam answered him, *W*, I have come to
	29:19	as *w* as one goat for a sin offering,
	29:22	as *w* as one goat for a sin offering,
	29:25	as *w* as one goat for a sin offering,
	29:28	as *w* as one goat for a sin offering,
	29:31	as *w* as one goat for a sin offering,
	29:34	as *w* as one goat for a sin offering,
	29:38	as *w* as one goat for a sin offering,
	30:17	as *w* as between a father and his daughter
	32:33	as *w* as half the tribe of Manasseh,
	34:14	Gad, as *w* as half of the tribe of Manasseh,
	35: 2	as *w* as pasture lands around the cities.
Dt	1:31	very eyes in Egypt, as *w* as in the desert,
	2: 6	the food you eat and the *w* water you drink.
	2:36	no city was too *w* fortified for us to whom
	3:17	as *w* as the Arbah with the Jordan and its
	3:19	wives and children, as *w* as your livestock,
	3:20	the LORD has settled your kinsmen as *w*,
	3:27	Look *w*,
	4:47	and the land of Og, king of Bashan, as *w*—
	5:28	have spoken to you, which are all *w* said.
	10:14	as *w* as the earth and everything on it.
	12:12	as *w* as with the Levite who belongs to
	12:15	the unclean as *w* as the clean may eat it,
	14:23	*w* as the firstlings of your herd and flock,
	15:16	your household, since he fares *w* with you,
	16:11	to your community, as *w* as the alien,
	18: 4	as *w* as the first fruits of the shearing
	18:17	And the LORD said to me, 'This was *w* said.
	29:21	as *w* as the foreigners who will come here
	31:12	as *w* as the aliens who live in your
	32:25	the nursing bade as *w* as the hoary old man.
Jos	6:21	men and women, young and old, as *w* as oxen,
	10:39	to Hebron, as *w* as to Libnah and its king.
	11:16	as *w* as the mountain regions and foothills
	12: 3	as *w* as the Arabah from the eastern side
	13: 8	as *w* as the Reubenites and Gadites,
	23: 4	[as *w* as those I destroyed]
Jgs	7:24	as far as Beth-barah, as *w* as the Jordan."
	7:24	as far as Beth-barah, and the Jordan as *w*.
	8: 7	Gideon said, "Very *w*;
	9:16	dealt *w* with Jerubbaal and with his family,
	11:29	Manasseh, and through Mizpah-Gilead as *w*,
	15: 5	and the vineyards and olive orchards as *w*.
	18:24	and have gone off with my priest as *w*,"
Ru	2:22	"You would do *w*,
	4:11	*w* in Ephrathah and win fame in Bethlehem.
1Sm	8:16	as *w* as your best oxen and your asses,
	9:10	Saul then said to his servant, *W* said!
	12: 5	you this day, and his anointed as *w*,
	12:14	you follow the LORD your God *w* and good.
	17:12	the days of Saul was old and *w* on in years.
	17:25	him great wealth, and his daughter as *w*,
	19: 4	then spoke *w* of David to his father Saul,
	20: 3	"Your father is *w* aware that I am favored
	20: 7	If he says, 'Very *w*,'
	20:12	he is *w* disposed toward David or not,
	20:29	Now, therefore, if you think *w* of me,
	22:10	the sword of Goliath the Philistine as *w*."
	28:19	the LORD will deliver Israel, and you as *w*,

2Sm 3:13 "Very w, I will make an agreement with
5:11 cedar wood, as w as carpenters and masons,
10: 6 as w as the king of Maacah with one
11: 7 going, and Uriah answered that all was w.
14:16 me and my son as w from God's inheritance.
17:28 basins and earthenware, as w as wheat,
18:23 Joab said to him, "Very w."
1Kgs 2:18 "Very w," replied Bathsheba, "I will speak
2:22 "Ask the kingdom for him as w,
4:10 son of Hesed in Arubboth as w as in Socoh
7:36 were carved, as w as wreaths all around.
8:18 to build a temple to my honor, you do w.
14:26 as w as all the gold shields made under
17:15 eat for a year, and he and her son as w;
18:19 as w as the four hundred and fifty
20:22 Mark w what you do,
22: 4 my people, your horses and my horses as w."
2Kgs 3: 7 and mine, and your horses and mine as w."
4:26 to meet her, and ask if all is w with her,
9:11 servants, they asked him, "Is all w?
9:17 to meet them and to ask whether all is w."
9:18 "The king asks whether all is w."
9:19 and said, "The king asks whether all is w."
9:22 recognized Jehu, he asked, "Is all w,
9:22 "How can all be w," Jehu replied,
9:31 the gate, she cried out, "Is all w,
10:11 as w as all his powerful supporters,
10:30 you have done w what I deem right,
12:19 Ahaziah, kings of Judah, as w as his own,
14:14 of the palace, and hostages as w.
16:15 cereal-offering, as w as the holocausts,
17: 9 the watchtowers as w as the walled cities.
23: 5 as w as those who burned incense to Baal,
25:24 of Babylon, and all will be w with you."
1Chr 4: 8 Zobebah, as w as of the clans of Aharhel,
9:29 the sacred vessels, as w as the fine flour,
18:10 his son Hadoram to wish King David w
28:13 as w as for the divisions of the priests
2Chr 3: 7 as w as its walls and its doors,
4:22 of holies, as w as the doors to the nave,
6: 8 to build a temple to my honor, you do w.
9: 9 of spices, as w as precious stones.
9:22 of the earth in riches as w as in wisdom.
9:29 first and last, are written, as is w known,
12:15 first and last, are written, as is w known,
18: 3 "your people and my people as w.
23: 8 who were to come in on the sabbath as w
25:24 treasures of the palace, and hostages as w.
25:26 last, can be found written, as is w known,
30:22 w skilled in the service of the LORD.
30:25 as w as the sojourners from the land of
34: 8 to cleanse the temple as w as the land,
34: 9 of Israel, as w as from all of Judah,
Ezr 7:16 as w as all the silver and gold which you
Neh 5:17 as w as those who came to us from the
6:14 keep in mind as w Noadiah the prophetess
9:24 kings as w as the peoples of the land,
10:32 seventh year, as w as every kind of debt.
Tb 1: 5 as w as to the young bull which Jeroboam,
5: 6 know the place w and I know all the routes.
5: 8 Raphael replied, "Very w, I will wait for
5:10 so I know every road w."
7: 4 She asked, "Is he w?"
7: 5 They answered, "Yes, he is alive and w."
14:11 my children, note w what almsgiving does,
14:13 estate as w as that of his father Tobit.
Jdt 6:16 and all their young men, as w as the women,
10:16 you speak of, and he will treat you w."
11: 4 Rather, you will be w treated,
11:22 done w in sending you ahead of your people,
11:23 to behold, and your words are w spoken.
16:19 as w as the canopy that she herself had
Est 4: 7 as w as the exact amount of silver Haman
E:17 "You will do w,
9:12 hundred men, as w as the ten sons of Haman.
10: 2 as w as a detailed account of the
1Mc 8:23 "May it be w with the Romans and the
9:50 the Jericho fortress, as w as Emmaus,
12:45 and their garrisons, as w as the officials,
13: 6 sanctuary, as w as your wives and children,
13:39 to now, as w as the crown tax that you owe.
2Mc 2:25 as w as to make it easy for the studious
4: 8 as w as eighty talents from another source
4:35 but many people of other nations as w,
6:30 in his holy knowledge knows full w that,
8:17 as w as the subversion of their ancestral
9:20 w and your affairs are going as you wish,
11:20 my representatives, as w as your envoys,
11:28 If you are w, it is what we desire.
12:21 women and children, as w as the baggage,
12:31 exhorted them to be w disposed
13:26 defended the treaty as w as he could and
14: 4 as w as some of the customary olive
15:38 If it is w written and to the point,
Jb 3:24 food, and my groans w forth like water.
9: 2 I know w that it is so;
12: 3 But I have intelligence as w as you;
13: 9 Will it be w when he shall search you out?
35: 4 to you and your three companions as w.
Ps(s) 49:19 will praise you for doing w for yourself,"
104:16 W watered are the trees of the LORD,
112: 5 W for the man who is gracious and lends,
139:14 My soul also you knew full w;
144:14 may our oxen be w laden.
Prv 5:15 own cistern, running water from your own w.
10:19 but he who restrains his lips does w.
15:28 The just man weighs w his utterance,
22:18 will be w if you keep them in your bosom,
24:25 who convict the evildoer will fare w,
27: 6 from a friend may be accepted as w meant,
Eccl 2:16 it that the wise man dies as w as the fool!
3:12 than to be glad and to do w during life.
3:19 the one dies as w as the other.
5:17 it is w for a man to eat and drink and
8:12 that it shall be w with those who fear God,
8:13 that it shall not be w with the wicked man,
11: 6 or whether both alike will turn out w.
12: 6 and the broken pulley falls into the w,
Sg 4:15 a w of water flowing fresh from Lebanon.
Wis 6: 7 himself made the great as w as the small,
7:16 w as all prudence and knowledge of crafts.
8: 1 to end mightily and governs all things w.
8: 9 she would be my counselor while all was w,
14: 8 idol is accursed, and its maker as w:
15: 3 For to know you w is complete justice,
Sir 4:20 Use your time w; guard yourself from evil
6:11 When things go w,
10: 1 government of a prudent man is w ordered.
14:16 Give, take, and treat yourself w,
17:23 they glorify the LORD who are alive and w.
27:24 hate so much, and the LORD hates him as w.
37:26 My son, while you are w,
41:14 For it is not always w to be ashamed,
Is 3:10 Happy the just, for it will be w with them,
30:16 —Very w, flee!
46: 8 this and be firm, bear it w in mind,
55: 2 Heed me, and you shall eat w,
65: 7 crimes and the crimes of your fathers as w,
Jer 1:12 W have you seen,
2:33 How w you pick your way when seeking love!
6: 7 As the w gushes out its waters,
6:12 their fields and their wives as w;
9: 9 Birds of the air as w as beasts,
22:15 right and just, and it went w with him.
22:16 the weak and the poor, it went w with him.
26:15 But mark w: if you put me to death,
29:11 I know w the plans I have in mind for you,
31:13 and dance, and young men and old as w.
34: 1 subject to him, as w as the other peoples,
38:20 then it shall go w with you,
40: 4 I will look after you w.
42: 2 now few who once were many, as you w see.
42: 4 Very w! the prophet Jeremiah answered
42: 6 so that it will go w with us for obeying
44:17 had enough food to eat and we were w off;
44:25 Very w! Keep your vows,
48:17 his neighbors, all you who knew him w!
52:10 as w as all the princes of Judah at Riblah.
52:20 guard carried off, as w as the two pillars,
Bar 1: 3 as w as all the people who came to the
6:21 and cats as w as birds.
6:33 they are treated w or ill by anyone,
Ez 3:10 hear them w.
4:15 Very w, he replied, I allow your cow's
11: 5 Israel, and what you are plotting I w know.
21: 3 all trees, the green as w as the dry.
41:17 part of the temple as w as outside,
Dn 4:32 as w as with those who live on the earth.
6:29 So Daniel fared w during the reign of
8:12 sanctuary it cast down, as w as the host,
Mt 5:40 over your shirt, hand him your coat as w.
7:22 we not do many miracles in your name as w?'
9:21 his cloak," she thought, "I shall get w."
9:22 That very moment the woman got w.
11:13 All the prophets as w as the law spoke
12:12 W, think how much more precious a human
13:18 "Mark w, then, the parable of the sower.
13:26 the weeds made their appearance as w.
21: 9 as w as those following kept crying out:
22:10 up everyone they met, bad as w as good.
22:40 whole law is based, and the prophets as w."
25: 4 took flasks of oil as w as their torches.
25:21 His master said to him, W done!
Mk 5:23 on her so that she may get w and live."
5:28 clothing," she thought, "I shall get w."
6:56 All who touched him got w.
7:37 "He has done everything w!
11: 9 him as w as those who followed cried out:
12:12 (They knew w enough that he meant the
Lk 5:10 all his shipmates, as w as James and John,
6:26 "Woe to you when all speak w of you.
6:29 your coat, let him have your shirt as w.
12:19 Eat heartily, drink w.
12:37 It will go w with those servants whom the
12:38 find them prepared, it will go w with them.
12:39 You know as w as I that if the head of the
16:25 that you were w off in your lifetime,
20:19 They were w aware that he had told the
20:39 Some of the scribes responded, W said,
23:33 him there and the criminals as w,
Jn 2:25 He was w aware of what was in man's heart.
4: 6 This was the site of Jacob's w.
4: 6 tired from his journey, sat down at the w.
4:11 do not have a bucket and this w is deep.
4:12 who gave us this w and drank from it with
5:17 at work until now, and I am at work as w."
6: 6 (He knew w what he intended to do but he
7: 4 w display yourself to the world at large."
8:55 Yes, I know him w, and I keep his word.
9:30 W, this is news!
13: 9 only my feet, but my hands and head as w."
15:27 You must bear witness as w,
18: 2 The place was familiar to Judas as w (the
18: 3 Judas took the cohort as w as guards
20:30 performed many other signs as w—
21:17 You know w that I love you."
Acts 2:22 through him in your midst, as you w know.
3:16 limbs of this man whom you see and know w.
10:22 w thought of in the whole Jewish community,
15: 4 as w as by the apostles and the presbyters,
15: 7 you know w enough that from the early days
15:29 will be w advised to avoid these things.
16:23 was given instructions to guard them w.
17:17 as w as daily debates in the public square
17:21 as w as the foreigners who live there,
17:30 God may w have overlooked bygone periods
19: 3 W, how were you baptized?"
22:12 devout observer of the law and w spoken of
24:22 was rather w informed about the new way,
26: 4 later at Jerusalem, is w known to all Jews.
26:26 here is w acquainted with these matters.
27:10 ship and cargo, but to our own lives as w."
28:22 w that this sect is denounced everywhere."
28:25 "The Holy Spirit stated it w when he said
Rom 1:15 to preach the gospel to you Romans as w.
2:25 break it you might as w be uncircumcised!
3: 9 W, then, do we find ourselves in a position
4: 9 circumcised, or to the uncircumcised as w?
4:12 as w as the father of those circumcised
8:17 But if we are children, we are heirs as w:
11:20 W and good. They were cut off
15:31 may be w received by the saints there;
16:13 mother, who has been a mother to me as w.
1Cor 7: 8 It would be w if they remain as they are,
13: 1 speak with human tongues and angelic as w,
14:15 sing with my spirit and with my mind as w.
14:17 You will be uttering praise very w indeed,
14:26 All w and good, so long as everything
2Cor 1:13 you will in time come to know us w,
2: 3 I know you all w enough to be convinced
2:11 whose guile we know too w—
3: 1 Am I beginning to speak w of myself again?
6: 8 honored or dishonored, spoken of w or ill.
6: 9 no bodies who in fact are w known;
8: 9 You are w acquainted with the favor shown
10:11 W, let such people give this some thought,
11: 4 accepted, you seem to endure it quite w.
Gal 4:18 It would be w for you to be courted for
5: 7 You were progressing so very w;
Eph 5: 8 W, then, live as children of light.
5:23 of his body the church, as w as its savior.
6: 3 "that it may go w with you,
Phil 1:13 w known throughout the praetorium here,
1:13 the praetorium here, and to others as w;
3:20 As you w know,
4:12 how to eat w or go hungry, to be w provided
4:18 I am w supplied because of what I received
Col 3:24 since you know full w you will receive an
4:16 in the assembly of the Laodiceans as w,
1Thes 1: 5 w as we do what we proved to be like when,
2: 1 You know w enough, brothers,
2: 5 We were not guilty, as you w know,
2: 8 So w disposed were we to you,
3: 3 You know w enough that such trials are our
5: 2 you know very w that the day of the Lord
2Thes 1: 7 to you who are sorely tired, as w as to us,
1Tm 3: 7 w thought of by those outside the church,
3:13 Those who serve w as deacons gain a worthy
5:13 but gossips and busybodies as w,
5:17 do w as leaders deserve to be paid double,
2Tm 2:23 As you w know, they only breed quarrels,
Heb 5: 3 for himself as w as for the people.
Jas 2:16 Keep warm and w fed,"
2Pt 2:22 How w the proverb fits them:
3: 2 as w as the new command of the Lord and
1Jn 2:23 the Son can claim the Father as w.
3: 5 You know w that the reason he revealed
3Jn 1:12 We give our testimonial as w,
Jude 1: 5 you may already be very w aware of them.
Rv 2:19 as w as your patient endurance;
13: 6 the members of his heavenly household as w.

WELL-AIMED (1)

Wis 5:21 W shafts of lightnings shall go forth and

WELL-BEING (6)

1Mc 8:15 all that concerned the people and their w.
Ps(s) 14: 7 When the LORD restores the w of his people,
53: 7 When God restores the w of his people,
85: 2 you have restored the w of Jacob.
Sir 30:15 More precious than gold is health and w,
Is 45: 7 the darkness, I make w and create woe:

WELL-BORN (1)

1Cor 1:26 and surely not many are w.

WELL-BRED (2)

Sir 21:22 a house, while the *w* man remains outside;
31:19 Does not a little suffice for a *w* man?

WELL-DISPOSED (5)

Gn 39:21 by making the chief jailer *w* toward him.
Ex 3:21 the Egyptians so *w* toward this people that,
11: 3 made the Egyptians *w* toward the people;
12:36 made the Egyptians so *w* toward the people
Lk 1:17 and to prepare for the Lord a people *w*."

WELL-DRAWN (1)

Wis 5:21 as from a *w* bow shall leap to the mark;

WELL-DRESSED (1)

Jas 2: 3 were to take notice of the *w* man and say,

WELL-FAVORED (1)

Wis 8:19 Now, I was a *w* child,

WELL-FED (1)

1Sm 2: 5 The *w* hire themselves out for bread,

WELL-FLOGGED (1)

2Mc 3:38 there, and you will receive him back *w*,

WELL-FORMED (2)

Gn 41:18 from the Nile came seven cows, fat and *w*;
Lam 2:20 eat their offspring, their *w* children?

WELL-FORTIFIED (1)

2Mc 10:32 fled to a *w* stronghold called Gazara,

WELL-INSTRUCTED (1)

Ezr 8:18 a *w* man, one of the sons of Mahli,

WELL-KNOWN (1)

Ez 39:11 give Gog for his tomb a *w* place in Israel,

WELL-NURTURED (1)

Ps(s) 144:12 our sons be like plants *w* in their youth,

WELL-TRAINED (1)

Is 50: 4 The Lord GOD has given me a *w* tongue,

WELL-VERSED (2)

Ezr 7: 6 *w* in the law of Moses which was given by
2Mc 8: 9 military commander, *w* in the art of war.

WELL-WROUGHT (1)

Nm 31:51 gold from them, all of it in *w* articles.

WELLED (1)

Is 48:21 he cleft the rock, and waters *w* forth."

WELLING (2)

Gn 2: 6 but a stream was *w* up out of the earth
Dt 8: 7 fountains *w* up in the hills and valleys,

WELLS (7)

Gn 26:15 filled with dirt all the *w* that his father's
26:18 (Isaac reopened the *w* which his father's
Nm 24: 7 His *w* shall yield free-flowing waters,
Jgs 5:11 to the strains of the harpers at the *w*,
2Kgs 19:24 I dug *w* and drank water in foreign lands;
Sir 21:13 A wise man's knowledge *w* up in a flood,
Is 37:25 I dug *w* and drank water in foreign lands;

WELLSPRING (1)

Ps(s) 68:27 bless the Lord, you of Israel's *w*!

WELLSPRINGS (3)

2Sm 22:16 Then the *w* of the sea appeared,
Jb 28:11 He probes the *w* of the streams,
Is 44:27 Be dry; I will dry up your *w*.

WELT (2)

Sir 28:17 A blow from a whip raises a *w*,
Is 1: 6 Wound and *w* and gaping gash,

WELTERING (2)

Ez 16: 6 I passed by and saw you *w* in your blood.
16:22 a girl, stark naked and *w* in your blood.

WELTS (1)

Sir 23:10 under scrutiny will not be without *w*,

WEPT (52)

Gn 27:38 and Esau *w* aloud.
33: 4 himself on his neck, kissed him as he *w*.
42:24 But turning away from them, he *w*.
43:30 He went into a private room and *w* there.
45:14 and wept, and Benjamin *w* in his arms.
46:29 on his neck and *w* a long time in his arms.
50: 1 face and *w* over him as he kissed him.
Dt 1:45 On your return you *w* before the LORD,
34: 8 *w* for Moses in the plains of Moab,
Jgs 2: 4 to all the Israelites, the people *w* aloud,
14:16 At Samson's side, his wife *w* and said,
14:17 But she *w* beside him during the seven days
20:22 up and *w* before the LORD until evening.
20:26 where they *w* and remained fasting before
Ru 1: 9 them good-bye, but they *w* with loud sobs,
1:14 Again they sobbed aloud and *w*;
1Sm 11: 4 news to the people, all of whom *w* aloud.
20:41 kissed each other and *w* aloud together.
24:17 And he *w* aloud.
30: 4 him *w* aloud until they could weep no more.
2Sm 1:12 They mourned and *w* and fasted until
3:32 the king *w* aloud at the grave of Abner,
3:32 the grave of Abner, and the people also *w*.
12:21 living, you fasted and *w* and kept vigil;
12:22 the child was living, I fasted and *w*,
13:36 too, and all his servants *w* very bitterly.
15:23 Everyone in the countryside *w* aloud as the
15:30 the Mount of Olives, he *w* without ceasing.
19: 1 He said as he *w*, "My son Absalom!
2Kgs 8:11 The man of God *w*,
20: 3 And Hezekiah *w* bitterly.
22:19 you tore your garments and *w* before me;
2Chr 34:27 torn your garments, and have *w* before me,
Ezr 10: 1 and the people *w* profusely.
Tb 2: 7 And I *w*.
3: 1 in spirit, I groaned and *w* aloud.
7: 7 his eyesight, he was grieved and *w* aloud.
7: 8 His wife Edna also *w* for Tobit;
9: 6 greeted Gabael, who *w* and blessed him,
11:14 son, he threw his arms around him and *w*.
1Mc 7:36 They *w* and said:
2Mc 4:37 he *w* as he recalled the prudence and noble
Jb 30:25 have I not *w* for the hardships of others;
Ps(s) 137: 1 we sat and *w* when we remembered Zion.
Is 38: 3 And Hezekiah *w* bitterly.
Bar 1: 5 *w* and fasted and prayed before the Lord,
Lk 8:52 While everyone *w* and lamented her,
19:41 sight of the city, he *w* over it and said:
22:62 He went out and *w* bitterly.
Jn 20:11 Even as she *w*,
Rv 5: 4 I *w* bitterly because no one could be found

WEST (77)

Gn 12: 8 with Bethel to the *w* and Ai to the east.
13:14 gaze to the north and south, east and *w*;
28:14 them you shall spread out east and *w*,
Ex 10:19 changed the wind to a very strong *w* wind,
26:22 for the rear of the Dwelling, to the *w*;
26:27 five for those at the rear, toward the *w*.
27:12 On the *w* side,
36:27 at the rear of the Dwelling, to the *w*;
36:32 and five for those at the rear, to the *w*.
38:12 On the *w* side there were hangings,
Nm 2:18 "On the *w* side shall be the divisional
3:23 camped behind the Dwelling, to the *w*.
10: 6 those encamped on the *w* side shall set out;
35: 5 east, south, *w* and north
Dt 3:27 the top of Pisgah and look out to the *w*,
Jos 1: 4 river Euphrates and *w* to the Great Sea.
5: 1 Amorites to the *w* of the Jordan
8: 9 taking up their position to the *w* of Ai,
8:12 between Bethel and Ai, *w* of the city.]
8:13 north of the city and the ambush *w* of it,
9: 1 the news reached the kings *w* of the Jordan,
11: 2 the foothills, and in Naphath-dor to the *w*.
11: 3 These were Canaanites to the east and *w*,
12: 7 conquered *w* of the Jordan and whose land,
15: 8 which bounds the Valley of Hinnom on the *w*.
19:11 Their boundary went up *w* . . .
19:26 and Mishal, and reached Carmel on the *w*,
19:34 Zebulun on the south, Asher on the *w*,
22: 7 along with their kinsmen *w* of the Jordan.)
23: 4 the Jordan and the Great Sea in the *w*.
Jgs 18:12 the place, which lies *w* of Kiriath-jearim,
20:33 ambush rushed from their place *w* of Gibeah,
1Kgs 5: 4 ruled over all the land *w* of the Euphrates,
7:25 oxen, three facing north, three facing *w*,
1Chr 7:28 to the east, Gezer and its towns to the *w*,
9:24 at the four sides, to the east, the *w*,
12:16 in the valleys to the east and to the *w*.
26:16 To Hosah fell the *w* side with the
26:18 as for the large building on the *w*,
2Chr 4: 4 twelve oxen, three facing north, three *w*,
33:14 of David to the *w* of Gihon in the valley,
Tb 1: 2 upper Galilee, above and to the *w* of Asser,
Jdt 1: 7 and to all those who dwelt in the *W*:
1: 9 and *w* of the Jordan as far as Jerusalem,
2: 6 and proceed against all the land of the *W*,
5: 4 with all the other inhabitants of the *W*?"
Jb 23: 8 or to the *w*,
Ps(s) 65: 9 east and *w* you make resound with joy.
75: 7 For neither from the east nor from the *w*,
103:12 As far as the east is from the *w*,
107: 3 from the lands, from the east and the *w*,
Is 8:23 the seaward road, the land *w* of the Jordan,
9:11 on the *w* devour Israel with open mouth.
11:14 the foothills of the Philistines to the *w*,
43: 5 descendants, from the *w* I will gather you.
49:12 from afar, others from the north and the *w*,
59:19 in the *w* shall fear the name of the LORD,
Bar 4:37 and from the *w* By the word of the Holy One,
5: 5 east and the *w* at the word of the Holy One,
Ez 41:12 *w* side was seventy cubits front to back;
42:19 Then he turned to the *w* and measured five
46:19 There, at their *w* end,
48:10 on the north, ten thousand on the *w*,
48:16 and the *w* side,
48:17 cubits, and *w* two hundred and fifty cubits.
48:18 to the east and ten thousand to the *w*,
48:34 On the *w* side, measuring forty-five
Dn 8: 4 I saw the ram butting toward the *w*,
8: 5 its forehead suddenly came from the *w*
Hos 11:10 his sons shall come frightened from the *w*,
Zec 14: 4 two from east to *w* by a very deep valley,
Mt 8:11 Many will come from the east and the *w* and
24:27 lightning from the east flashes to the *w*,
Mk 16:20 Jesus himself sent out from east to *w*
Lk 12:54 "When you see a cloud rising in the *w*,
13:29 People will come from the east and the *w*,
Rv 21:13 three north, three south, and three *w*.

WEST-OF-EUPHRATES (20)

Ezr 4:10 of Samaria and elsewhere in the province *W*.
4:11 Artaxerxes, your servants, the men of *W*,
4:16 fact you will no longer own any part of *W*."
4:17 in Samaria and elsewhere in the province *W*,
4:20 once in Jerusalem who ruled over all *W*,
5: 3 came to them Tattenai, governor of *W*,
5: 6 to King Darius by Tattenai, governor of *W*,
5: 6 and their fellow officials from *W*;
6: 6 "Now, therefore, Tattenai, governor of *W*,
6: 6 and you, their fellow officials in *W*,
6: 8 From the royal revenue, the taxes of *W*,
6:13 Then Tattenai, the governor of *W*,
7:21 this decree to all the treasurers of *W*:
7:25 administer justice to all the people in *W*,
8:36 king's satraps and to the governors in *W*
Neh 2: 7 be given to me for the governors of *W*,
2: 9 *W* and presented the king's letters to them.
3: 7 the jurisdiction of the governor of *W*.
1Mc 7: 8 one of the King's Friends, governor of *W*,
11:60 out and traveled through *W* and its cities,

WESTERLY (1)

Jos 19:34 In the opposite direction, *w*,

WESTERN (32)

Nm 34: 6 "For your *w* boundary you shall have the
34: 6 this shall be your *w* boundary.
Dt 11:24 from the Euphrates River to the *W* Sea,
11:30 on the other side of the *w* road in the
34: 2 all the land of Judah as far as the *W* Sea,
Jos 15:12 *w* boundary was the Great Sea and its coast.
18:14 For the *w* border,
18:14 This was the *w* boundary.
1Chr 26:30 administration of Israel on the *w* side
Jdt 2:19 to cover all the *w* region with their
Ez 45: 7 *w* side and eastward on the eastern side,
45: 7 tribal portions from the *w* boundary
47:20 The *w* boundary: the Great Sea forms
47:20 This is the *w* boundary.
48: 1 from the eastern to the *w* boundary.
48: 2 of Dan, from the eastern to the *w* boundary.
48: 3 Asher, from the eastern to the *w* boundary.
48: 4 from the eastern to the *w* boundary.
48: 5 from the eastern to the *w* boundary.
48: 6 from the eastern to the *w* boundary.
48: 7 Reuben, from the eastern to the *w* boundary.
48: 8 from the eastern to the *w* boundary there
48: 8 from the eastern to the *w* boundary.
48:21 line to the *w* boundary,
48:23 from the eastern to the *w* boundary.
48:24 from the eastern to the *w* boundary.
48:25 Simeon, from the eastern to the *w* boundary.
48:26 from the eastern to the *w* boundary.
48:27 from the eastern to the *w* boundary.
48:35 o the *w* boundary.
Jl 2:20 eastern sea, and his rear toward the *w* sea;
Zec 14: 8 to the eastern sea, and half to the *w* sea,

WESTWARD (7)

Jos 15:10 From Baalah the boundary curved *w* to Mount
16: 3 *w* to the border of the Japhletites,
16: 8 *w* to the Wadi Kanah and ended at the sea.
18:12 flank of Jericho, up *w* into the mountains,
2Chr 32:30 led it underground *w* to the City of David.
Ez 45: 7 extending *w* on the western side and
48:21 and *w* along the twenty-five-thousand-cubit

WET (2)

Sg 5: 2 For my head is *w* with dew,
Jer 9:17 us, That our eyes may be *w* with weeping,

WHALE (1)

Mt 12:40 and three nights in the belly of the *w*,

WHATEVER (216)

Gn 2:19 *w* the man called each of them would be its
11: 6 stop them from doing *w* they presume to do.
16: 6 Do to her *w* you please."
20:13 In *w* place we come to,
34:11 favor, and I will pay *w* you demand of me.
34:12 the bridal price, I will pay you *w* you ask;
34:28 *w* was in the city and in the country
34:29 and took for loot *w* was in the houses.
39: 3 him and brought him success in *w* he did,
41:55 to go to Joseph and do *w* he told them.
Ex 9:19 order all your livestock and *w* else you
9:19 *W* man or beast remains in the fields and
10:12 all the vegetation and *w* the hail has left."
10:15 the fruit of *w* trees the hail had spared.
12:10 *w* is left over in the morning shall be
12:36 that they let them have *w* they asked for.
16:23 but *w* is left put away and keep for the
18:19 God, bringing to him *w* they have to say.
20:24 In *w* place I choose for the remembrance of
21:30 for his life *w* amount is imposed on him.
27:19 fittings of the Dwelling, *w* be their use,
28:38 Since Aaron bears *w* guilt the Israelites
29:27 the breast of *w* wave offering is waved,
29:27 thigh of *w* raised offering is raised up,
29:37 and *w* touches it will become sacred.
30:29 *w* touches them shall be sacred.
Lv 5: 3 *w* kind of uncleanness this may be,
5:24 he found or *w* else he swore falsely about;
5:26 be forgiven *w* guilt he may have incurred."
6:11 *W* touches the oblations becomes sacred."
6:20 *W* touches its flesh shall become sacred.
11: 9 *w* in the seas or in river waters has both
13:51 material, or on the leather, *w* be its use,
13:52 linen, or the leather article, *w* it may be,
19: 6 *W* is left over until the third day shall
21:17 None of your descendants, of *w* generation,
22: 5 man whose uncleanness, of *w* kind it may be,
Nm 3:25 had charge of *w* pertained to the Dwelling,
3:31 They had charge of *w* pertained to the ark,
3:36 *w* pertained to the boards of the Dwelling,
4:26 *W* is to be done with these things shall be
15:12 *W* the number you offer,
18: 7 priestly functions in *w* concerns the altar
18: 9 in *w* they offer me as cereal offerings or
18:13 and likewise, of *w* grows on their land,
18:14 *W* is doomed in Israel shall be yours.
19:22 *w* the unclean person touches becomes
22: 8 I will give you *w* answer the LORD gives me."
23: 3 and then I will tell you *w* he lets me see."
24:13 *W* the LORD says I must repeat.
29:39 on your festivals, besides *w* holocausts,
30:13 then *w* she has expressly promised in her
31:22 *W* can stand fire, such as gold, silver,
31:23 But *w* cannot stand fire you shall put into
Dt 12:14 shall make *w* offerings I enjoin upon you.
14: 9 *w* has both fins and scales you may eat,
14:26 then exchange the money for *w* you desire,
21:17 him a double share of *w* he happens to own,
29: 8 them, that you may succeed in *w* you do.
30: 1 in you, and from among *w* nations the LORD,
Jgs 2:15 *W* they undertook, the LORD turned
10:15 Do to us *w* you please.
19:24 Ravish them, or do *w* you want with them;
Ru 3: 5 "I will do *w* you advise," Ruth replied.
3:11 daughter, I will do for you *w* you say;
1Sm 2:14 *W* the fork brought up,
2:16 as is the custom, then take *w* you wish,"
9:19 dismissing you, I will tell you *w* you wish.
10: 7 signs fulfilled, do *w* you judge feasible,
11:10 you, and you may do *w* you please with us."
14: 7 replied, "Do *w* you are inclined to do;
14:34 brought to the LORD *w* ox he had seized,
20: 4 then said to David, "I will do *w* you wish."
21: 4 Give me five loaves, or *w* you can find."
25: 8 and your son David *w* you can manage.'"
26:25 shall certainly succeed in *w* you undertake."
2Sm 7: 3 the king, "Go do *w* you have in mind,
15:15 ready, *w* our lord the king chooses to do."
15:36 them you shall send on to me *w* you hear."
19:19 household over and to do *w* he wished.
19:38 Do for him *w* you will."
21: 4 he said, "I will do for you *w* you propose."
24:22 the king take and offer up *w* he may wish.
1Kgs 2: 3 of Moses, that you may succeed in *w* you do,
5:20 you *w* you say for your servants' salary."
8:37 *w* plague or sickness there may be,
8:44 *W* the direction in which you may send your
9:19 and *w* else Solomon decided should be built
20: 6 and take away *w* they consider valuable.'"
22:14 "I shall say *w* the LORD tells me."
2Kgs 2: 9 "Ask for *w* I may do for you before I am
10: 5 do *w* you think best."
11: 8 stay with the king, *w* he may do."
12: 5 and *w* funds are freely brought to the
12: 6 they must make *w* repairs on the temple may
18:14 and I will pay *w* tribute you impose on me."
1Chr 17: 2 to David, "Do, therefore, *w* you desire,
26:28 Also, *w* Samuel the seer,
2Chr 6:33 place, and do *w* the foreigner entreats you,
8: 6 and *w* else Solomon decided should be built
29:16 and *w* they found in the LORD's temple that
Ezr 1: 4 has survived, in *w* place he may have dwelt,
6: 9 *W* else is required—young bulls,
7:18 You and your brethren may do *w* seems best
7:20 *W* else you may be required to supply for
7:21 *W* Ezra the priest, scribe of the law
Neh 6:19 in my presence and relate to him *w* I said;
10:36 fields and of our fruit trees, of *w* kind;
Tb 4: 3 Do *w* pleases her, and do not grieve her
4:16 *W* you have left over, give away as alms
5:17 son, prepare *w* you need for the journey,
8:21 half of *w* I own when you go back in good
14: 4 indeed, *w* was said by Israel's prophets,
14: 4 that *w* God has spoken will be accomplished.
Jdt 9: 5 *W* you devise comes into being;
12:14 *W* is pleasing to him I will promptly do.
Est 2:13 the harem to the royal palace *w* she chose.
3:11 for this people, do with them *w* you please."
5: 6 *W* you ask for shall be granted, and *w*
7: 2 wine, the king said to Esther, *W* you ask,
7: 2 *W* request you make shall be honored,
8: 8 For *w* is written in the name of the king
9:12 *w* you ask, and *w* you request
1Mc 3:59 *W* Heaven wills, he will do."
8:30 and *w* they shall add or take away shall be
13:38 *W* we have guaranteed to you remains in
15: 5 *w* other privileges they conferred on you.
2Mc 11:18 *W* had to be referred to the king I called
11:35 *W* Lysias, kinsman of the king,
Ps(s) 1: 3 *W* he does, prospers.]
8: 9 sea, and *w* swims the paths of the seas.
50:11 of the air, and *w* stirs in the plains,
69:35 praise him, the seas and *w* moves in them!"
115: 3 Our God is in heaven; *w* he wills, he does.
Eccl 2:26 For to *w* man he sees fit he gives wisdom
2:26 to be given to *w* man God sees fit.
3:14 that *w* God does will endure forever;
6:10 *W* is, was long ago given its name,
8: 3 with a base plot, for he does *w* he pleases,
Wis 16:21 was blended to *w* flavor each one wished,
Sir 2: 4 Accept *w* befalls you,
7:36 In *w* you do, remember your last days,
8:12 and *w* you lend,
14:11 *w* you have and enjoy it as best you can;
31:22 In *w* you do, be moderate,
32:23 *W* you do, be on your guard,
41:10 *W* is of nought returns to nought,
Is 15: 7 So now *w* they have acquired or stored away
19:14 they have made Egypt stagger in *w* she does,
Jer 1: 7 *w* I command you, you shall speak
11:12 them no help *w* when misfortune strikes.
17:22 Do no work *w*, but keep holy the sabbath
18: 4 clay another object of *w* sort he pleased.
26: 2 *w* I command you,
42: 4 *w* the LORD answers you,
Ez 12:25 *W* I speak is final, and it shall be done
12:25 house, *w* I speak I will bring about,
12:28 *w* I speak is final,
44:29 *w* is under the ban in Israel shall be
46: 5 for the ram, *w* he pleases for the lambs,
47:23 In *w* tribe the alien may be resident,
Mt 12:34 The mouth speaks *w* fills the mind.
16:19 *W* you declare bound on earth shall be
16:19 *w* you declare loosed on earth shall be
18:18 *w* you declare bound on earth shall be held
18:18 and *w* you declare loosed on earth shall be
18:19 voices on earth to pray for anything *w*,
19: 3 a man divorce his wife for any reason *w*?"
20: 4 my vineyard and I will pay you *w* is fair.'
Mk 3:20 it impossible for them to get any food *w*.
6:10 *W* house you find yourself in,
6:23 "I will grant you *w* you ask,
11:24 you will receive *w* you ask for in prayer,
14:14 *W* house he enters, say to the owner,
Lk 9: 4 *w* house you enter and proceed from there.
10: 8 "Into *w* city you go,
21:36 the strength to escape *w* is in prospect,
Jn 1: 4 *W* came to be in him, found life,
2: 5 waiting on table, "Do *w* he tells you."
5:19 For *w* the Father does,
10:41 "but *w* John said about this man was true."
11:22 that God will give you *w* you ask of him."
11:49 "You have no understanding *w*!
12:50 *w* I say is spoken just as he instructed me."
14:13 and *w* you ask in my name I will do,
16:23 you my assurance, *w* you ask the Father,
19:11 me *w* unless it were given you from above.
Acts 10:33 hear *w* directives the Lord has given you."
13:45 countered with violent abuse *w* Paul said.
24:19 you to make *w* charge they have against me.
28:31 assurance, and without any hindrance *w*,
Rom 1:19 *w* can be known about God is clear to them;
4:21 that God could do *w* he had promised.
14:23 *W* does not accord with one's belief is
1Cor 10:25 Eat *w* is sold in the market without
10:27 you want to go, eat *w* is placed before you,
16: 2 put aside *w* he has been able to save,
2Cor 1:20 *W* promises God has made have been
Eph 6: 8 be repaid by the Lord for *w* good he does.
Phil 2:20 him for genuine interest in *w* concerns you.
4:11 for *w* the situation I find myself in I
Col 1:11 fast, even to endure joyfully *w* may come,
3: 5 death *w* in your nature is rooted in earth;
3:13 *w* grievances you have against one another.
3:17 *W* you do, whether in speech or in action,
3:23 *W* you do, work at it with your whole
4:12 conviction about *w* pertains to God's will.
2Thes 3: 4 doing and will continue to do *w* we enjoin.
Jas 1:25 Blest will this man be in *w* he does.
3: 4 *w* course the steerman's impulse may select.
2Pt 2:10 the flesh in their desire for *w* corrupts,
2:10 qualms *w* about reviling celestial beings,
1Jn 3:22 that we will receive at his hands *w* we ask.
Rv 1:19 down, therefore, *w* you see in visions

WHATSOEVER (1)

Dt 4:23 against his command an idol in any form *w*.

WHEAT (54)

Gn 30:14 One day, during the *w* harvest,
Ex 9:32 But the *w* and the spelt were not ruined,
29: 2 With fine *w* flour make unleavened cakes
34:22 of Weeks with the first of the *w* harvest;
Dt 8: 8 hills and valleys, a land of *w* and barley,
32:14 its goats, with the cream of its finest *w*;
Jgs 6:11 While his son Gideon was beating out *w* in
15: 1 some time, in the season of the *w* harvest,
Ru 2:23 until the end of the barley and *w* harvests.
1Sm 6:13 were harvesting the *w* in the valley.
12:17 Are we not in the harvest time for *w*?
2Sm 4: 6 of the house had dozed off while sifting *w*,
17:28 basins and earthenware, as well as *w*,
24:15 Now it was the time of the *w* harvest when
24:20 coming toward him while he was threshing *w*.
1Kgs 5:25 kors of *w* to provide for his household,
1Chr 21:20 While Ornan was threshing *w*,
21:23 wood, and the *w* for the cereal offering.
2Chr 2: 9 cut the wood, twenty thousand kors of *w*,
2:14 let my lord send to his servants the *w*,
27: 5 kors of *w* and ten thousand of barley.
Ezr 6: 9 for holocausts to the God of heaven, *w*,
7:22 *w*,
Jdt 2:27 of Damascus at the time of the *w* harvest,
3: 3 Our dwellings and all our *w* fields,
Jb 31:40 of *w* and noxious weeds instead of barley!
Ps(s) 81:17 Israel I would feed with the best of *w*,
147:14 with the best of *w* he fills you.
Sg 7: 3 body is a heap of *w* encircled with lilies.
Sir 39:26 fire, iron and salt, The heart of the *w*,
Is 28:25 gith and sow cumin, Put in *w* and barley,
30:23 And the *w* that the soil produces will be
Jer 12:13 They have sown *w* and reaped thorns,
23:28 What has straw to do with the *w*?
41: 8 *w* and barley, oil and honey."
Ez 4: 9 Again, take *w* and barley,
27:17 trafficked with you, exchanging Minnith *w*,
45:13 sixth of an ephah from each homer of *w*,
Hos 7:14 For *w* and wine they lacerated themselves,
Jl 1:11 Over the *w* and the barley,
Am 8: 5 and the sabbath, that we may display the *w*?
8: 6 even the refuse of the *w* we will sell!"
Mt 13:25 enemy came and sowed weeds through his *w*,
13:29 and you might take the *w* along with them.
13:30 up to burn, then gather the *w* into my barn.'"
Mk 4:28 the ear, finally the ripe *w* in the ear.
Lk 3:17 floor and gather the *w* into his barn;
16: 7 The answer came, 'A hundred measures of *w*,'
22:31 has asked for you, to sift you all like *w*.
Jn 12:24 the grain of *w* falls to the earth and dies,
12:24 and dies, it remains just a grain of *w*.
Acts 27:38 ship further by throwing the *w* overboard.
1Cor 15:37 but a kernel of *w* or some other grain.
Rv 6: 6 of *w* and the same for three of barley!

WHEEL (9)

1Kgs 7:32 Each *w* was a cubit and a half high.
Sir 33: 5 Like the *w* of a cart is the mind of a fool;
38:29 his labor, revolving the *w* with his feet.
Jer 18: 3 house and there he was, working at the *w*.
Ez 1:16 as though one *w* were within another.
10: 9 beside them, one *w* beside each cherub;
10:10 as though they were a *w* within a wheel.
Na 2: 5 through the streets And *w* in the squares,

WHEELED (6)

Jgs 20:39 the Israelites *w* about to resist as the
20:41 the sky that the men of Israel *w* about.
2Kgs 25:13 and the *w* carts and the bronze sea in the
25:16 pillars, the bronze sea, and the *w* carts,
Jer 52:17 and the *w* carts and the bronze sea in the
52:20 and the *w* carts which King Solomon had

WHEELING (1)

Mk 5:30 *W* about in the crowd,

WHEELS (29)

Ex 14:25 chariot *w* that they could hardly drive.
1Kgs 7:30 stand had four bronze *w* and bronze axles.
7:32 The four *w* were below the paneling,
7:32 axletrees of the *w* and the stand were of one
7:33 The *w* were constructed like chariot wheels;
Is 5:28 and their chariot *w* like the hurricane.
Jer 47: 3 the rattling chariot, the rumbling *w*.
Ez 1:15 living creatures, I saw *w* on the ground,

WHEELS (cont.)

1:16 The *w* had the sparkling appearance of
1:19 creatures moved, the *w* moved with them;
1:19 from the ground, the *w* also were raised.
1:20 the spirit wished to go, there the *w* went,
1:20 of the living creatures was in the *w*.
3:13 one another, and by the *w* alongside them,
10: 6 the man entered and stood by one of the *w*.
10: 9 I also saw four *w* beside them,
10: 9 the *w* appeared to have the luster of
10:12 of the four *w* were full of eyes all around.
10:13 I heard the *w* given the name "wheelwork."
10:16 the cherubim moved, the *w* went beside them;
10:16 even then the *w* did not leave their sides.
10:17 When they stood still, the *w* stood still;
10:17 when they rose, the *w* rose with them;
10:19 the earth, the *w* rising along with them.
11:22 wings, and the *w* went along with them,
26:10 the noise of steeds, of *w* and of chariots.
Dn 7: 9 was flames of fire, with *w* of burning fire.
Na 3: 2 of the whip, the rumbling sound of *w*;

WHEELWORK (3)

Ez 10: 2 Go within the *w* under the cherubim;
10: 6 in linen to take fire from within the *w*,
10:13 I heard the wheels given the name *w*."

WHELP (3)

Gn 49: 9 Judah, like a lion's *w*, you have grown up
Dt 33:22 "Dan is a lion's *w*, that springs forth
Ez 19: 3 One *w* she raised up, a young lion

WHELPS (3)

Is 5:29 of the lion, like the lion's *w* they roar;
Ez 19: 2 young lions she couched to rear her *w*.
19: 5 She took another of her *w*,

WHENCE (10)

Jgs 19:17 where he was going, and *w* he had come.
2Chr 2:15 Joppa, *w* you may take them up to Jerusalem."
Jb 1: 7 the LORD said to Satan, *W* do you come?"
2: 2 the LORD said to Satan, *W* do you come?"
10:21 a little Before I go *w* I shall not return,
28:12 But *w* can wisdom be obtained,
28:20 *W*, then, comes wisdom,
38:24 *w* the east wind spreads over the earth?
Ps(s) 121: 1 *w* shall help come to me?
Wis 15: 8 after a little, is to go *w* he was taken,

WHENEVER (57)

Gn 30:33 future, *w* you check on these wages of mine,
30:41 *w* the hardier animals were in heat,
31: 8 *W* your father said, 'The speckled animals
31: 8 *w* he said,
38: 9 so *w* he had relations with his brother's
Ex 18:16 *W* they have a disagreement,
28:29 *W* Aaron enters the sanctuary,
28:30 heart *w* he enters the presence of the LORD.
28:43 Aaron and his sons shall wear them *w* they
33: 8 *W* Moses went out to the tent,
34:34 *W* Moses entered the presence of the LORD
40:32 for they washed themselves *w* they went
40:36 *W* the cloud rose from the Dwelling,
Lv 16: 2 to come *w* he pleases into the sanctuary,
22:29 *W* you offer a thanksgiving sacrifice to
Nm 9:17 *W* the cloud rose from the tent,
10:35 *W* the ark set out,
15:13 *w* they present a sweet-smelling oblation
21: 9 and *w* anyone who had been bitten by a
35:30 *W* someone kills another,
Dt 4: 7 LORD, our God, is to us *w* we call upon him?
Jgs 2:18 *W* the LORD raised up judges for them,
1Sm 16:23 *W* the spirit from God seized Saul,
17:34 and *w* a lion or bear came to carry off a
21: 6 *W* I go on a journey,
23:20 Therefore, *w* the king wishes to come down,
2Sm 15: 5 *W* a man approached him to show homage,
1Kgs 8:52 Hear them *w* they call upon you,
14:28 *W* the king visited the temple of the LORD,
2Kgs 4: 8 Afterward, *w* he passed by,
21:12 and Judah that, *w* anyone hears of it,
2Chr 6:28 *w* there is a plague or sickness of any
12:11 *W* the king visited the temple of the LORD,
24:11 *W* the chest was brought to the royal
Jdt 11:11 of their God upon them *w* they do wrong;
2Mc 9:23 *w* he went on campaigns in the hinterland,
Wis 12:18 for power, *w* you will,
Is 28:19 *W* it passes, it shall take you;
Jer 18: 4 *W* the object of clay which he was making
20: 8 *W* I speak, I must cry out, violence
48:27 you shake your head *w* you speak of her?
Bar 6:43 and *w* one of them is drawn aside by some
Ez 44:17 *W* they enter the gates of the inner court,
Dn 3:15 made, *w* you hear the sound of the trumpet,
Mt 5:31 was also said, *W* a man divorces his wife,
6: 6 *W* you pray, go to your room
Mk 9:18 *W* it seizes him it throws him down;
14: 7 and you can be generous to them *w* you wish,
Lk 14:12 *W* you give a lunch or dinner,
1Cor 11:25 Do this, *w* you drink it,
2Cor 3:16 "But *w* he turns to the Lord,
2Tm 1: 3 conscience, *w* I remember you in my prayers
1Pt 3:16 clear, so that, *w* you are defamed,
1Jn 5:14 that he hears us *w* we ask for anything
5:15 since we know that he hears us *w* we ask,
Jude 1:16 *W* it is expedient,
Rv 4: 9 *W* these creatures give glory and honor and

WHEREAS (23)

Gn 25:27 *w* Jacob was a simple man,
28:19 *w* the former name of the town had been Luz.
Ex 40:38 *w* at night,
Lv 7:10 *w* all cereal offerings that are offered up
1Kgs 12:11 *W* my father put a heavy yoke on you,
2Chr 10:11 *W* my father put a heavy yoke on you,
1Mc 10:81 *w* the enemy's horses became tired out.
15: 3 *W* certain villains have gained control of
2Mc 15:38 *w* mixing wine with water makes a more
Sir 34:10 *w* with travel a man adds to his
Hos 2: 1 *W* they were called, "Lo-ammi,"
Zec 1:15 *w* I was but a little angry,
Mt 10:39 *w* he who brings himself to nought for me
Lk 12:48 *w* the one who did not know them and who
20: 6 *w* if we say, 'From men,' the people will
Jn 7: 6 for me, *w* the time is always right for you.
16: 7 will never come to you, *w* if I go,
Rom 7:14 *w* I am weak flesh sold into the slavery of
15: 9 *w* the Gentiles glorify God because of his
1Cor 8: 1 But *w* "knowledge" inflates,
2Cor 7:10 salvation, *w* worldly sorrow brings death.
Heb 7: 8 And *w* men subject to death receive tithes,
Jas 2: 3 *w* you were to say to the poor man,

WHEREBY (2)

Jgs 9: 9 up my rich oil, *w* men and gods are honored,
Jn 18:39 Recall your custom *w* I release someone to

WHEREFORE (5)

Jb 3:12 *W* did the knees receive me?
Heb 3: 7 *W*, as the Holy Spirit says:
10: 5 *W*, on coming into the world, Jesus said:
11:16 *W* God is not ashamed to be called their God,
12:28 *W*, we who are receiving the unshakable

WHEREIN (4)

Dt 30: 3 all the nations *w* he has scattered you.
Jdt 5:19 from the Dispersion *w* they were scattered,
Jb 6:24 prove to me *w* I have erred.
34:32 Teach me *w* I have sinned;

WHEREUPON (3)

2Chr 35:11 *w* the priests sprinkled some of the blood
Lk 8:55 *w* he told them to give her something to
24:31 *w* he vanished from their sight.

WHEREVER (72)

Gn 20:15 settle *w* you please."
26: 2 continue to camp *w* in this land I tell you.
28:15 I will protect you *w* you go,
35: 3 and who has been with me *w* I have gone."
Ex 5:11 the straw yourselves, *w* you can find it.
12:20 *w* you dwell you may eat only unleavened
Lv 3:17 for your descendants *w* they may dwell.
7:26 *W* you dwell, you shall not partake
23: 3 shall belong to the LORD *w* you dwell.
23:14 for you and your descendants *w* you dwell.
23:17 you shall bring with you from *w* you live
23:21 be a perpetual statute for you *w* you dwell.
23:31 for you and your descendants *w* you dwell:
Nm 9:17 *w* the cloud came to rest,
33:54 *W* anyone's lot falls,
35:29 you and all your descendants, *w* you live,
Dt 23:17 Let him live with you *w* he chooses,
Jos 1: 7 to the left, that you may succeed *w* you go.
1: 9 the LORD, your God, is with you *w* you go."
1:16 Joshua, "and we will go *w* you send us.
Ru 1:16 for *w* you go I will go, wherever you lodge
1:17 *W* you die I will die, and there be buried.
1Sm 14:47 *W* he turned, he was successful
2Sm 7: 9 I have been with you *w* you went,
15:20 wander about with us today, *w* I have to go?
15:21 servant shall be *w* my lord the king may be,
17:12 We can then attack him *w* we find him,
1Kgs 2: 3 may succeed in whatever you do, *w* you turn,
5:23 rafts in the sea and bring them *w* you say.
7:36 on the panels, *w* there was a clear space,
2Kgs 8: 1 with your family and settle *w* you can,
1Chr 17: 8 I was with you *w* you went,
2Chr 6:34 war against their enemies, *w* you send them,
23: 7 Stay with the king *w* he goes."
Neh 4:14 *w* you hear the trumpet sound,
12:27 the Levites were sought out *w* they lived
Jdt 8:22 *W* we shall be enslaved among the nations,
Est 4: 3 *w* the king's legal enactment reached,
8:17 and every city, *w* the king's order arrived,
1Mc 1:53 hiding, *w* places of refuge could be found.
5:63 all the Gentiles, *w* their name was heard;
6:36 anticipated the beast *w* it was; and *w*
Prv 6:22 *w* you turn, she will guide you.
21: 1 *w* it pleases him, he directs it.
Eccl 11: 3 to the south or to the north, *w* it falls.
Sir 4:13 *w* he dwells, the LORD bestows blessings.
38:32 no city could be lived in, and *w* they stay,
Jer 40: 4 go *w* you think good and proper";
40: 5 him among the people, or go *w* you please."
45: 5 I will leave you as booty, *w* you may go.
Ez 1:12 *w* the spirit wished to go,
1:20 *W* the spirit wished to go,
6:13 *w* they offered appeasing odors to any of
6:14 and *w* they live I will make the land a
21:21 *w* your edge is turned.
36:20 they came among the nations *w* they came],
47: 9 *W* the river flows,
47: 9 for *w* this water comes the sea shall be
Dn 2:38 and birds of the air, *w* they may dwell,
3:98 of every language, *w* they dwell on earth:
6:26 every language, *w* they dwell on the earth:
Mt 8:19 "Teacher, *w* you go I will come after you."
26:13 *w* the good news is proclaimed throughout
Mk 6:56 *W* he put in an appearance, in villages,
14: 9 *w* the good news is proclaimed throughout
Lk 9:57 to him, "I will be your follower *w* you go."
12:34 *W* your treasure lies, there your heart will
17:37 him, and he answered, *W* the carcass is,
1Cor 1: 2 people, as to all those who, *w* they may be,
Rv 14: 4 are pure and follow the Lamb *w* he goes.

WHET (1)

Wis 5:20 shield and *w* his sudden anger for a sword,

WHETHER (148)

Gn 17:23 *w* born in his house or acquired with his
18:21 that I must go down and see *w* or not their
24:21 silently waiting to learn *w* or not the
27:21 learn *w* you really are my son Esau or not."
37:32 See *w* it is your son's tunic or not."
Ex 4:18 in Egypt, to see *w* they are still living."
16: 4 see *w* they follow my instructions or not.
21:16 *w* he sells his victim or still has him
22: 8 appropriation, *w* it be about an ox,
29:27 *w* this be the ordination ram or anything
34:19 livestock, *w* in the herd or in the flock.
Lv 7:21 *w* the uncleanness be of human or of animal
11:10 the water, *w* in the sea or in the rivers,
11:32 that men use, *w* it be an article of wood,
11:42 *W* it crawls on its belly,
13:59 to determine *w* it is clean or unclean."
15: 3 *w* the flow drains off or is blocked up;
16:29 of you, *w* a native or a resident alien,
17: 3 or goat, *w* in the camp or outside of it,
17: 8 *w* of the house of Israel or of the aliens
17:10 *w* of the house of Israel or of the aliens
17:13 *w* of the Israelites or of the aliens
17:15 "Everyone, *w* a native or an alien,
18: 9 *w* she was born in your own household or
18:26 You, however, *w* natives or resident aliens,
20: 2 *w* an Israelite or an alien residing in
27:28 *w* it is a human being or an animal or a
27:30 *w* in grain from the fields or in fruit
27:33 *w* good ones or bad ones are thus chosen,
Nm 5:14 his wife, *w* she was actually impure or not:
9:22 *W* the cloud tarried over the Dwelling for
11:23 You shall see now *w* or not what I have
15:29 *w* he be a native Israelite or an alien
15:30 defiantly, *w* he be a native or an alien,
18:15 that opens the womb, *w* of man or of beast,
19:16 *w* he was slain by the sword or died
Dt 4:16 *w* it be in the form of a man or a woman,
5:14 No work may be done then, *w* by you,
6: 7 home and abroad, *w* you are busy or at rest.
8: 2 test you by affliction and find out *w* or not
11:19 home and abroad, *w* you are busy or at rest.
13: 4 is testing you to learn *w* you really love
18: 3 *w* the victim is from the herd or from the
24:14 *w* he be one of your own countrymen or one
Jos 14:11 less vigor *w* for war or for ordinary tasks.
Jgs 2:22 prove *w* or not they would keep to the way
3: 4 to determine *w* they would obey the
18: 5 that we may know *w* the undertaking we are
21: 8 And when they asked *w* anyone among the
Ru 3:10 going after the young men, *w* poor or rich.
1Sm 11:12 questioned *w* Saul should rule over us?
20:12 *W* he is well disposed toward David or not,
26:10 him, *w* the time comes for him to die,
28: 6 *w* in dreams or by the Urim or through
2Sm 15:21 the king may be, *w* for death or for life."
20:19 *w* loyalty is finished or ended in Israel.'
1Kgs 14:10 line, *w* slave or freeman in Israel,
20:18 *W* they have come out for peace or for war,
21:21 male in Ahab's line, *w* slave or freeman,
2Kgs 1: 2 Ekron, *w* I shall recover from this injury."
8: 8 as to *w* I shall recover from this sickness."
8: 9 you *w* he will recover from his sickness."
9: 8 Ahab's line, *w* slave or freeman in Israel.
9:17 him to meet them and to ask *w* all is well."
9:18 "The king asks *w* all is well."
9:19 and said, "The king asks *w* all is well."
19:27 *w* you stand or sit; I know whether you
1Chr 25: 6 All these, *w* of Asaph,
2Chr 15:13 *w* small or great, whether man or woman.
19:10 *w* it concerns bloodguilt or questions of
31: 2 *w* in regard to holocausts or peace

Ezr 5:17 to discover *w* a decree really was issued
7:26 upon him, *w* death or corporal punishment,
Tb 5: 9 and *w* he is trustworthy enough to travel
8:12 maids in to see *w* Tobiah is alive or dead,
Est 3: 4 *w* Mordecai's explanation was acceptable,
2Mc 6:26 of men, I shall never, *w* alive or dead,
Jb 37:13 of the earth, *w* for punishment or mercy,
Prv 20:11 *w* his conduct is innocent and right.
Eccl 2:19 knows *w* he will be a wise man or a fool?
5:11 the laboring man, *w* he eats little or much,
11: 3 *W* a tree falls to the south or to the north,
11: 6 or *w* both alike will turn out well.
12:14 all its hidden qualities, *w* good or bad.
Wis 2:17 Let us see *w* his words be true;
17:17 For *w* one was a farmer,
Sir 40: 3 *W* he sits on a lofty throne or grovels in
40: 4 *W* he bears a splendid crown or is wrapped
41: 4 *W* one has lived a thousand years,
Is 37:28 whether you stand or sit; I know *w* you
Jer 37:17 *w* there was any message from the LORD.
40:14 asked him *w* he did not know that Baalis,
42: 6 *W* it is pleasant or difficult,
Lam 1:12 *W* there is any suffering like my suffering,
3:38 the Most High, *w* the thing be good or bad!
3:63 *W* they sit or stand,
Bar 6:33 *W* they are treated well or ill by anyone,
6:62 not their equal, *w* in beauty or in power;
Ez 2: 5 And *w* they heed or resist
2: 7 my words to them, *w* they heed or resist,
3:11 *w* they heed or resist!
16:37 please, *w* you loved them or loved them not;
44:31 shall not eat anything, *w* flesh or fowl,
46:12 the LORD, *w* holocausts or peace offerings,
Mt 26:63 the living God *w* you are the Messiah,
27:49 Let's see *w* Elijah comes to his rescue."
Mk 3: 2 to see *w* he would heal him on the sabbath,
10: 2 ask him *w* it was permissible for a husband
13:35 master of the house is coming, *w* at dusk,
15:36 let's see *w* Elijah comes to take him down."
15:44 and inquired *w* Jesus was already dead.
Lk 3:15 their hearts *w* John might be the Messiah.
14:31 will he not sit down first and consider *w*,
Jn 7:17 *w* it comes from God or is simply spoken on
9:25 "I do not know *w* his is a sinner or not,"
Acts 4:19 "Judge for yourselves *w* it is right in
7: 1 high priest asked *w* the charges were true.
10:18 to inquire *w* Simon Peter was a guest there.
17:11 Scriptures to see *w* these things were so.
25:20 I asked *w* the prisoner was willing to go
26:29 Paul replied, *W* little more or much more,
Rom 6:16 you obey, *w* yours is the slavery of sin,
14: 4 alone can judge *w* he stands or falls.
1Cor 3:22 All things are yours, *w* it be Paul,
4: 3 It matters little to me *w* you or any human
10:31 The fact is that *w* you eat or drink
12:13 one Spirit that all of us, *w* Jew or Greek,
15:11 In any case, *w* it be I or they,
2Cor 2: 9 learn *w* you are obedient in all matters.
5: 9 him *w* we are with him or away from him.
6: 8 hand and left, *w* honored or dishonored,
12: 2 *w* he was in or outside his body I cannot
12: 3 man *w* in or outside his body I do not know,
13: 5 to see *w* you are living in faith;
Gal 6:15 means nothing *w* one is circumcised or not.
Eph 6: 8 You know that each one, *w* slave or free,
Phil 1:18 *w* from specious motives or genuine ones,
1:20 be exalted through me, *w* I live or die.
1:27 *w* I come and see you myself or hear about
Col 1:16 and invisible, *w* thrones or dominations,
3:17 Whatever you do, *w* in speech or in action,
1Thes 5:10 for us, that all of us, *w* awake or asleep,
2Thes 2: 2 or terrified, *w* by an oracular utterance,
2Tm 4: 2 this task *w* convenient or inconvenient
1Pt 2:13 *w* to the emperor as sovereign or to the

WHETTED (1)

Is 21:15 They flee from the sword, from the *w* sword;

WHICHEVER (4)

Sir 15:16 to *w* you choose,
15:17 and death, *w* he chooses shall be given him.
Ez 10:11 for in *w* direction they were faced,
Dn 8:13 another said to *w* one it was that spoke,

WHIFF (2)

Jgs 16: 9 a thread of tow is severed by a *w* of flame;
Jb 14: 9 Yet at the first *w* of water it may

WHIM (2)

Sir 8:14 for he will settle it according to his *w*.
Eph 2: 3 of the flesh, following every *w* and fancy,

WHIMS (1)

Prv 29:15 a boy left to his *w* disgraces his mother.

WHINERS (1)

Jude 1:16 These men are grumblers and *w*.

WHIP (5)

Prv 26: 3 The *w* for the horse,
Sir 28:17 A blow from a *w* raises a welt,
33:25 Fodder and *w* and loads for an ass;
Na 3: 2 The crack of the *w*,
Jn 2:15 He made a [kind of] *w* of cords and drove

WHIPPED (2)

Acts 5:40 called in the apostles and had them *w*.
2Pt 2:17 are waterless springs, mists *w* by the gale.

WHIPS (5)

1Kgs 12:11 My father beat you with *w*,
12:14 My father beat you with *w*,
2Chr 10:11 My father beat you with *w*,
10:14 My father beat you with *w*,
2Mc 7: 1 tortured with *w* and scourges by the king,

WHIRL (1)

Wis 4:12 *w* of desire transforms the innocent mind.

WHIRLING (2)

Jer 23:19 His wrath breaks forth In a *w* storm that
30:23 His wrath breaks forth In a *w* storm that

WHIRLWIND (12)

2Kgs 2: 1 about to take Elijah up to heaven in a *w*,
2:11 them, and Elijah went up to heaven in a *w*.
Ps(s) 58:10 like thistles, let the *w* carry them away.
77:19 Your thunder resounded in the *w*;
83:14 O my God, make them like leaves in a *w*,
Prv 1:27 a storm, and your doom approaches like a *w*;
Sir 48: 9 You were taken aloft in a *w*,
48:12 he dies, O Elijah, enveloped in the *w*!
Is 29: 6 thunder, earthquake, and great noise, *w*,
66:15 come in fire, his chariots like the *w*,
Hos 8: 7 they sow the wind, they shall reap the *w*;
Zec 7:14 but would scatter them with a *w* among all

WHIRLWINDS (1)

Is 21: 1 Like *w* sweeping in waves through the Negeb,

WHISPER (2)

Jb 4:12 brought to me, and my ear caught a *w* of it.
Ps(s) 41: 8 All my foes *w* together against me;

WHISPERED (4)

1Sm 26: 8 Abishai *w* to David:
Lam 3:62 against me], The *w* murmurings of my foes,
Lk 12: 3 what you have *w* in locked rooms will be
Jn 11:28 Teacher is here, asking for you," she *w*.

WHISPERING (2)

2Sm 12:19 But David noticed his servants *w* among
1Kgs 19:12 After the fire there was a tiny *w* sound.

WHISPERINGS (1)

Jer 20:10 Yes, I hear the *w* of many:

WHISPERS (1)

Ps(s) 31:14 I hear the *w* of the crowd,

WHISTLE (3)

Is 5:26 and *w* to them from the ends of the earth;
7:18 On that day The LORD shall *w* for the fly
Zec 10: 8 I will *w* for them to come together,

WHISTLING (1)

Wis 17:18 And were it only the *w* wind,

WHITE (62)

Gn 30:35 she-goats, all those with some *w* on them,
30:37 and he made *w* stripes in them by peeling
30:37 the bark down to the *w* core of the shoots.
42:38 *w* head down to the nether world in grief."
44:29 *w* head down to the nether world in grief.'
44:31 will thus send the *w* head of our father
Ex 16:31 It was like coriander seed, but *w*,
Lv 13: 3 If the hair on the sore has turned *w* and
13: 4 If, however, the blotch on the skin is *w*,
13: 4 below the skin, nor has the hair turned *w*,
13:10 find that there is a *w* scab on the skin
13:10 hair *w* and that there is raw flesh in it,
13:13 since it has all turned *w*,
13:16 If, however, the raw flesh again turns *w*,
13:17 find that the sore has indeed turned *w*,
13:19 of the boil have a *w* scab or a pink blotch,
13:20 the skin and that the hair has turned *w*,
13:21 finds that there is no *w* hair in it and
13:24 the burn now becomes a pink or a *w* blotch,
13:25 If the hair has turned *w* on the blotch and
13:26 finds that there is no *w* hair on the
13:38 man or a woman is spotted with *w* blotches,
13:39 on the skin are *w* and already dying out,
Jgs 5:10 They who ride on *w* asses,
2Kgs 5:27 And Gehazi left Elisha, a leper *w* as snow.
Est 1: 6 *w* cotton draperies and violet hangings,
8:15 in a royal robe of violet and of *w* cotton,
2Mc 11: 8 in *w* garments and brandishing gold weapons.
15:13 distinguished by his *w* hair and dignity,
Jb 6: 6 Is there flavor in the *w* of an egg?
Eccl 9: 8 At all times let your garments be *w*,
Wis 2:10 the old man for his hair grown *w* with time.
Is 1:18 be like scarlet, they may become *w* as snow;
1:18 be crimson red, they may become *w* as wool.
Dn 7: 9 and the hair on his head as *w* as wool;
Jl 1: 7 its branches are made *w*.
Zec 1: 8 behind him were red, sorrel, and *w* horses.
6: 3 black horses, the third chariot *w* horses,
6: 6 the red and the *w* horses went after them,
Mt 5:36 (you cannot make a single hair *w* or black).
Mk 9: 3 eyes and his clothes became dazzlingly *w*—
16: 5 sitting at the right, dressed in a *w* robe.
Lk 9:29 and his clothes became dazzlingly *w*.
Acts 1:10 two men dressed in *w* stood beside them.
Rv 1:14 The hair of his head was as *w* as
2:17 *w* stone upon which is inscribed a new name,
3: 4 walk with me in *w* because they are worthy.
3: 5 " 'The victor shall go clothed in *w*.
3:18 Buy *w* garments in which to be clothed,
4: 4 they were clothed in *w* garments and had
6: 2 To my surprise, I saw a *w* horse;
6:11 of the martyrs was given a long *w* robe,
7: 9 dressed in long *w* robes and holding palm
7:13 "Who are these people all dressed in *w*?
7:14 and made them *w* in the blood of the Lamb.
14:14 Then, as I watched, a *w* cloud appeared,
15: 6 The angels were dressed in pure *w* linen,
19: 8 to wear made of finest linen, brilliant *w*."
19:11 and as I looked on, a *w* horse appeared;
19:14 riding *w* horses and dressed in fine linen,
19:14 and dressed in fine linen, pure and *w*.
20:11 a large *w* throne and the One who sat on it.

WHITE-HOT (8)

Dn 3: 6 shall be instantly cast into a *w* furnace."
3:11 did not was to be cast into a *w* furnace.
3:15 shall be instantly cast into the *w* furnace;
3:17 us from the *w* furnace and from your hands,
3:20 Abednego and cast them into the *w* furnace.
3:21 cast into the *w* furnace with their coats,
3:23 bound, into the midst of the *w* furnace.
3:93 of the *w* furnace and called to Shadrach,

WHITENESS (1)

Sir 43:19 Its shining *w* blinds the eyes,

WHITER (4)

Gn 49:12 than wine, and his teeth are *w* than milk.
Ps(s) 51: 9 wash me, and I shall be *w* than snow.
Lam 4: 7 than snow were her princes, *w* than milk,
Mk 9: 3 became dazzlingly white *w* than the work

WHITEWASH (3)

Ez 13:10 built a wall, they would cover it with *w*,
13:12 Where is the *w* you spread on?
22:28 Her prophets cover them with *w*,

WHITEWASHED (3)

Ez 13:14 that you have *w* and level it to the ground,
Mt 23:27 You are like *w* tombs,
Acts 23: 3 are the one God will strike, you *w* wall!

WHITEWASHERS (3)

Ez 13:11 cover it with whitewash, say then to the *w*:
13:15 have spent my fury on the wall and its *w*,
13:15 shall be no wall, nor shall there be *w*—

WHITHER (1)

Ex 32:34 go and lead the people *w* I have told you.

WHOEVER (164)

Ex 12:15 *W* eats leavened bread from the first day
21:12 *W* strikes a man a mortal blow must be put
21:15 *W* strikes his father or mother shall be
21:17 *W* curses his father or mother shall be put
22:19 *W* sacrifices to any god,
30:33 *W* prepares a perfume like this,
30:33 this, or *w* puts any of this on a layman,
30:38 *W* makes an incense like this for his own
31:14 *W* desecrates it shall be put to death.
32:26 of the camp and cried, *W* is for the LORD,
35:24 *W* could make a contribution of silver or
Lv 5: 5 then *w* is guilty in any of these cases
11:36 *w* touches the dead body becomes unclean.
14:46 *W* enters a house while it is quarantined
14:47 *W* sleeps or eats in such a house shall
15: 6 *W* sits on a piece of furniture on which
15: 7 *W* touches the body of the afflicted man
15:10 *W* touches anything that was under him
15:10 *w* lifts up any such thing shall wash his
15:22 *W* touches any article of furniture on
19: 8 *w* eats of it then shall pay the penalty
20:19 *w* does so shall pay the penalty of incest.
24:16 *w* blasphemes the name of the LORD shall be
24:17 *W* takes the life of any human being shall
24:18 *w* takes the life of an animal shall make
24:21 *W* slays an animal shall make restitution,

WHOEVER (cont.)

24:21 but w slays a man shall be put to death.
Nm 15: 4 w does so shall also present to the LORD a
19:11 W touches the dead body of any human being
22: 6 whoever you bless is blessed and w you
Jos 7:12 from among you w has incurred the ban.
7:13 from among you w has incurred the ban.
Jgs 11:31 w comes out of the doors of my house to
1Sm 2:36 Then w is left of your family will come to
2Sm 17: 9 the first attack, w hears of it will say,
1Kgs 13:33 W desired it was consecrated and became a
2Kgs 10:19 W is absent shall not live."
1Chr 11: 6 W strikes the Jebusites first shall be
2Chr 23: 7 W tries to enter the house must be slain.
36:23 W, therefore, among you belongs to any
Ezr 1: 3 W, therefore, among you belongs to any
7:26 W does not obey the law of your God and
10: 8 w failed to appear within three days would,
1Mc 1:50 W refused to act according to the command
1:57 W was found with a scroll of the covenant,
1:57 of the covenant, and w observed the law,
10:43 W takes refuge in the temple of Jerusalem
14:45 W acts otherwise or violates any of these
2Mc 3:16 W saw the appearance of the high priest
Jb 29:11 W heard of me blessed me;
41: 1 W might vainly hope to do so need only see
Ps(s) 101: 5 W slanders his neighbor in secret,
Prv 9: 4 "Let w is simple turn in here;
9:16 "Let w is simple turn in here,
Wis 17:16 w was there fell into that unbarred prison
Sir 6:34 w is wise,
16:14 W does good has his reward,
22: 2 w touches him wipes his hands.
27:27 W does harm will be involved in it without
28:16 W heeds it has no rest,
38:24 w is free from toil can become a wise man.
Is 54:15 w attacks you shall fall before you.
59: 5 W eats their eggs will die,
59: 8 made crooked, w treads them knows no peace.
Jer 15: 2 W is marked for death, to death; whoever
15: 2 w is marked for famine,
15: 2 w is marked for captivity,
21: 9 W remains in this city shall die by the
21: 9 But w leaves and surrenders to the
43:11 with death, w is marked for death;
50: 7 W came upon them devoured them,
Dn 3: 6 W does not fall down and worship shall be
3:11 w did not was to be cast into a white-hot
3:96 that w blasphemes the God of Shadrach,
5: 7 W reads this writing and tells me what it
11:39 W acknowledges him he shall provide with
Zep 2:15 W passes by her hisses,
Zec 2:12 W touches you touches the apple of my eye.
Mt 5:19 That is why w breaks the least significant
5:19 W fulfills and teaches these commands
10:22 w holds out till the end will escape death.
10:32 W acknowledges me before men I will
10:33 W disowns me before men I will disown
10:37 W loves father or mother,
10:42 And I promise you that w gives a cup of
12:32 W says anything against the Son of Man
12:32 but w says anything against the Holy
12:50 W does the will of my heavenly Father is
15: 4 W curses father or mother shall be put to
15: 5 W says to his father or his mother,
16:25 W would save his life will lose it, but w
18: 4 W makes himself lowly,
18: 5 W welcomes one such child for my sake
19: 9 w divorces his wife (lewd conduct is a
20:27 and w wants to rank first among you must
23:12 W exalts himself shall be humbled, but w
Mk 3:29 but w blasphemes against the Holy Spirit
3:35 W does the will of God is brother and
7:10 W curses father or mother shall be put to
8:35 W would preserve his life will lose it, but w
9:37 W welcomes a child such as this for my
9:37 And w welcomes me welcomes,
10:11 W divorces his wife and marries another
10:15 I assure you that w does not accept the
10:44 w wants to rank first among you must serve
11:23 assure you, w says to this mountain,
Lk 8:16 a lampstand so that w comes in can see it.
9:23 W wishes to be my follower must deny his
9:24 W would save his life will lose it, but w
9:48 W welcomes this little child on my account
9:48 and w welcomes me welcomes him who sent
9:62 W puts his hand to the plow but keeps
11:10 w asks, receives; whoever seeks, finds; w
12: 8 "I tell you, w acknowledges me before men
12:10 but w blasphemes the Holy Spirit will
17:33 W tries to preserve his life will lose it; w
18:17 Trust me when I tell you that w does not
19:26 w has will be given more,
Jn 3:16 that w believes in him may not die but may
3:18 W believes in him avoids condemnation, but w
3:33 W does accept this testimony certifies
3:36 W believes in the Son has life eternal.
3:36 W disobeys the Son will not see life,
4:14 But w drinks the water I give him will
7:18 w speaks on his own is bent
8:47 W is of God hears every word God speaks.
10: 1 W does not enter the sheepfold through the
10: 9 W enters through me will be safe.
11:26 w believes in me,
11:26 and w is alive and believes in me will
12:44 W puts faith in me believes not so much in
12:45 w looks on me is seeing him who sent me.
12:48 W rejects me and does not accept my words
14: 9 W has seen me has seen the Father.
Rom 14:18 W serves Christ in this way pleases God
1Cor 6:17 But w is joined to the Lord becomes one
11:27 This means that w eats the bread or drinks
Gal 3:12 W does these things shall live by them."
5:10 fall on w it is that is unsettling you!
Col 3:25 W acts unjustly will be repaid for the
1Thes 4: 8 w rejects these instructions rejects,
1Tm 3: 1 w wants to be a bishop aspires to a noble
6: 3 W teaches in any other way,
Jas 2:10 W falls into sin on one point of the law,
1Jn 2: 5 But w keeps his word,
4:21 w loves God must also love his brother.
5:10 W believes in the Son of God possesses
5:10 W does not believe God has made God a liar
5:12 W possesses the Son possesses life; w
2Jn 1:11 w greets him shares in the evil he does.
3Jn 1:11 W does what is good belongs to God; w
Rv 3:19 W is dear to me I reprove and chastise.

WHOLE (510)

Gn 2:11 that winds through the w land of Havilah,
5: 5 The w lifetime of Adam was nine hundred
5: 8 The w lifetime of Seth was nine hundred
5:11 The w lifetime of Enosh was nine hundred
5:14 The w lifetime of Kenan was nine hundred
5:17 The w lifetime of Mahalalel was eight
5:20 The w lifetime of Jared was nine hundred
5:23 The w lifetime of Enoch was three hundred
5:27 The w lifetime of Methuselah was nine
5:31 The w lifetime of Lamech was seven hundred
9:19 and from them the w earth was peopled.
9:29 The w lifetime of Noah was nine hundred
11: 1 The w world spoke the same language,
13: 9 Is not the w land at your disposal?
13:10 the w Jordan Plain was as far as Zoar,
13:11 the w Jordan Plain and set out eastward.
14: 7 and they subdued the w country both of the
17: 8 you are now staying, the w land of Canaan,
18:26 I will spare the w place for their sake."
18:28 destroy the w city because of those five?"
19:25 He overthrew those cities and the w Plain,
19:28 and Gomorrah and the w region of the Plain,
24:21 The man watched her the w time,
25: 7 The w span of Abraham's life was one
25:25 and his w body was like a hairy mantle;
30:32 go through your w flock today and remove
33:13 for a single day, the w flock will die.
41:41 place you in charge of the w land of Egypt."
41:43 Joseph installed over the w land of Egypt.
41:57 grain, for famine had gripped the w world.
45: 8 and ruler over the w land of Egypt.
45:20 best in the w land of Egypt shall be yours.'"
47:12 father's w household down to the youngest,
50: 8 of Egypt, as well as Joseph's w household,
Ex 1: 6 his brothers and that w generation died.
1:14 the w cruel fate of slaves.
9: 9 turn into fine dust over the w land of Egypt
10:14 They swarmed over the w land of Egypt and
10:15 They covered the surface of the w land,
12: 3 Tell the w community of Israel:
12: 4 If a family is too small for a w lamb,
12: 6 with the w assembly of Israel present,
12: 9 not be eaten raw or boiled, but roasted w,
12:47 w community of Israel must keep this feast.
14: 9 Pharaoh's w army,
14:28 and the charioteers of Pharaoh's w army
16: 1 the w Israelite community came into the
16: 2 Here in the desert the w Israelite
16: 3 to make the w community die of famine!"
16: 9 to Aaron, "Tell the w Israelite community:
16:10 this to the w Israelite community,
17: 1 w Israelite community journeyed by stages,
19:18 and the w mountain trembled violently.
25:36 that the w will form but a single piece of
26: 6 sheets, so that the Dwelling forms one w.
26:11 the loops, to join the tent into one w.
35: 1 the w Israelite community and said to them,
35: 4 Moses told the w Israelite community,
35:20 w Israelite community left Moses' presence,
36:13 joined so that the Dwelling formed one w.
36:18 tent was joined so that it formed one w.
37:22 that the w formed but a single piece of pure
38: 2 The w was plated with bronze.
40:38 seen in the cloud by the w house of Israel
Lv 1: 9 the w offering on the altar as a holocaust,
1:13 the w offering on the altar as a holocaust,
3: 9 the w fatty tail,
4:12 organs, and offal, in short, the w bullock,
4:13 "If the w community of Israel
6:15 the LORD the w offering shall be burned.
6:16 of a priest shall be a w burnt offering;
8: 3 Then assemble the w community at the
9: 5 When the w community had come forward and
10: 6 but God's wrath also on the w community.
13:13 that the leprosy does cover his w body,
14:41 The w inside of the house shall then be
15:16 he shall bathe his w body in water and be
16:17 as well as for the w Israelite community,
19: 2 to the w Israelite community and tell them:
23:39 a pilgrim feast of the LORD for a w week.
23:41 w week in the seventh month of the year.
24:14 on his head, let the w community stone him.
24:16 The w community shall stone him;
Nm 1: 2 of the w community of the Israelites,
1:18 and assembled the w community on the first
3: 7 his obligations and those of the w community
4:16 He shall be in charge of the w Dwelling
8: 7 their w bodies and wash their clothes,
8: 9 also the w community of the Israelites.
8:20 did Moses and Aaron and the w community of
10: 3 the w community shall gather round you at
11:20 or ten, or twenty days, but for a w month
11:21 will give them meat to eat for a w month.'
13:26 met Moses and Aaron and the w community of
14: 1 the w community broke out with loud cries,
14: 2 and Aaron, the w community saying to them,
14: 5 w assembled community of the Israelites;
14: 7 said to the w community of the Israelites,
14:10 the w community threatened to stone them.
14:15 If now you slay this w people,
14:21 the LORD's glory that fills the w earth,
14:36 set the w community grumbling against him
15:24 the w community shall offer the holocaust
15:25 atonement for the w Israelite community;
15:26 Not only the w Israelite community,
15:33 him to Moses and Aaron and the w assembly.
15:35 the w community stone him outside the camp."
15:36 So the w community led him outside the
16: 3 The w community,
16:22 sin make you angry with the w community?"
17: 6 The next day the w Israelite community
18: 3 look after your persons and the w tent;
20: 1 The w Israelite community arrived in the
20:22 w Israelite community came to Mount Hor.
20:27 Mount Hor in view of the w community,
20:29 days the w house of Israel mourned him.
25: 6 of Moses and of the w Israelite community,
27: 2 and the w community at the entrance of the
27:19 the priest Eleazar and of the w community,
27:20 the w Israelite community may obey him.
27:21 as a w shall perform all their actions."
27:22 the priest Eleazar and of the w community,
32:13 until the w generation that had done evil
32:15 will bring about the ruin of this w nation."
Dt 1:19 Horeb and journeyed through the w desert,
2:14 in the meantime the w generation of
3: 4 eluding our grasp, the w region of Argob,
3:13 the kingdom of Og, the w Argob region,
4: 8 w law which I am setting before you today?
4:29 him with your w heart and your whole soul.
6:22 Egypt and against Pharaoh and his w house.
13:17 spoils as a w burnt offering to the LORD,
18: 1 "The w priestly tribe of Levi shall have
31:30 end, for the w assembly of Israel to hear:
Jos 3:11 w earth will precede you into the Jordan.
3:13 ark of the LORD, the Lord of the w earth,
3:17 the w nation had completed the passage.
4:14 and thenceforth during his w life they
5: 8 w nation remained in camp where they were,
10:13 for a w day did it resume its swift course.
11: 7 Joshua with his w army came upon them at
11:23 Thus Joshua captured the w country,
18: 1 the w community of the Israelites
22: 5 and serve him with your w heart and soul."
22:12 they assembled their w community at Shiloh
22:16 w community of the LORD sends this message:
22:18 be angry with the w community of Israel!
23:14 So now acknowledge with your w heart and
Jgs 1:25 they let the man and his w clan go free.
7:21 while the w camp fell to running and
8:10 all who were left of the w Kedemite army,
9: 1 and said to them and to the w clan to
11:22 w territory from the Arnon to the Jabbok,
20:37 it, and put the w city to the sword.
20:40 Benjamin looked back and saw the w city
21:13 Then the w community sent a message to the
Ru 1:19 there, the w city was astir over them,
1Sm 4:13 news, which put the w city in an uproar.
5:11 A deadly panic had seized the w city,
7: 2 w Israelite population turned to the LORD.
7: 3 with your w heart to return to the LORD,
12:20 but must worship him with your w heart.
12:24 worship him faithfully with your w heart;
13:19 was to be found in the w land of Israel,
14:24 the w people, about ten thousand combatants,
17:46 w land shall learn that Israel has a God.
18: 5 and this was agreeable to the w army,
19: 7 and repeated the w conversation to him.
20: 6 because his w clan is holding its seasonal
22:15 at all, great or small, about the w matter."
25:16 like a rampart night and day the w time
25:17 store for our master and for his w family.
25:28 evil to be found in you your w life long.
2Sm 3:19 to Israel and to the w house of Benjamin.
3:23 and the w force he had with him arrived,
6:11 the LORD blessed Obed-edom and his w house.
6:21 preferred me to your father and his w family
13:21 King David, who got word of the w affair,
14: 7 Then the w clan confronted your servant

15:18 while the *w* army marched past him.
18:13 the *w* matter would have come to the
19: 3 was turned into mourning for the *w* army
19:21 have been the first of the *w* house of Joseph
20:23 was in command of the *w* army of Israel.
24: 8 Thus they toured the *w* country,
1Kgs 2: 4 their *w* heart and with their whole soul,
4:10 as in Socoh and the *w* region of Hepher;
6:22 the *w* altar before the sanctuary was also
8:14 the *w* community of Israel as they stood.
8:22 the presence of the *w* community of Israel,
8:23 who are faithful to you with their *w* heart.
8:48 if with their *w* heart and soul they turn
8:55 and blessed the *w* community of Israel,
10:24 the *w* world sought audience with Solomon,
11:13 Nor will I take away the *w* kingdom.
14: 8 and followed me with his *w* heart,
16:11 he killed off the *w* house of Baasha,
22:19 with the *w* host of heaven standing by to
2Kgs 5:15 with his *w* retinue to the man of God.
6:24 his *w* army and laid siege to Samaria.
7: 7 and their asses, the *w* camp just as it was,
7:15 and the *w* route was strewn with garments
11: 1 she began to kill off the *w* royal family.
15:16 of the town and of its *w* district,
17: 5 occupied the *w* land and attacked Samaria,
17:20 So the LORD rejected the *w* race of Israel.
20:13 showed the messengers his *w* treasury,
21: 3 worshiped and served the *w* host of heaven.
21: 5 altars for the *w* host of heaven,
23: 3 and decrees with their *w* hearts and souls,
23: 4 Baal, Asherah, and the *w* host of heaven.
23: 5 of the Zodiac, and to the *w* host of heaven.
23:25 *w* heart, his whole soul, and his *w* strength,
25: 1 and his *w* army advanced against Jerusalem,
25: 5 near Jericho, abandoned by his *w* army.
1Chr 10: 3 the *w* fury of the battle descended upon Saul.
10: 6 three sons, his *w* house died at one time.
13: 2 he said to the *w* assembly of Israel:
13: 4 And the *w* assembly agreed to do this,
17:15 *w* vision Nathan related exactly to David.
19: 8 and his *w* army of warriors against them.
20: 3 he and his *w* army returned to Jerusalem.
29: 1 King David then said to the *w* assembly:
29:10 the LORD in the presence of the *w* assembly,
29:20 Then David besought the *w* assembly,
29:20 And the *w* assembly blessed the LORD,
2Chr 1: 3 and, accompanied by the *w* assembly,
6: 3 the *w* community of Israel as they stood.
6:12 LORD in the presence of the *w* community
6:13 knelt in the presence of the *w* of Israel
6:38 with their whole heart and with their *w* soul
15: 8 detestable idols from the *w* land of Judah
15:15 for they had sworn with their *w* heart and
16: 9 The eyes of the LORD roam over the *w* earth,
18:18 with the *w* host of heaven standing by to
22: 9 who sought the LORD with his *w* heart."
23: 3 the *w* assembly made a covenant with the
28:14 before the princes and the *w* assembly.
30:23 the *w* assembly agreed to celebrate another
30:25 and the *w* assembly of Judah rejoiced,
33: 3 the *w* host of heaven and worshiped them.
33: 5 he built altars to the *w* host of heaven in
33: 8 keeping the *w* law and the statutes and the
34:31 and statutes with his *w* heart and soul,
Ezr 10:12 the *w* assembly cried out with a loud voice:
10:14 Let our leaders represent the *w* assembly;
Neh 4:10 *w* house of Judah as they rebuilt the wall.
5:13 And the *w* assembly answered,
8: 1 the *w* people gathered as one man in the
8:13 the family heads of the *w* people and also
Tb 10: 7 home to wail and cry the *w* night through,
12:11 "I will now tell you the *w* truth;
Jdt 1:12 inhabitants of Moab, Ammon, the *w* of Judea,
1:13 He routed the *w* force of Arphaxad,
2: 1 about taking revenge on the *w* world,
2:19 Then he and his *w* army proceeded on their
2:22 From there Holofernes took his *w* force,
3: 8 he devastated their *w* territory and cut
3:10 and stayed there a *w* month to refurbish
4: 4 they sent word to the *w* region of Samaria,
4: 8 and the senate of the *w* people of Israel,
4:15 look with favor on the *w* house of Israel.
5:10 famine had gripped the *w* land of Canaan,
5:15 took possession of the *w* mountain region.
5:21 become the laughing stock of the *w* world."
6: 1 of the *w* throng of coastland peoples,
6:21 That *w* night they called upon the God of
7: 1 day Holofernes ordered his *w* army,
7: 4 "Soon they will devour the *w* country.
7:18 in the plain, covering the *w* countryside.
7:20 The *w* Assyrian camp,
7:26 summon them and deliver the *w* city as
9:14 Let your *w* nation and all the tribes know
10:13 take possession of the *w* mountain district
10:19 be spared they could beguile the *w* world."
11: 7 live for Nebuchadnezzar and his *w* house.
11:18 so that you may go out with your *w* force,
14: 4 other inhabitants of the *w* territory of Israel
15: 4 and to the *w* country of Israel to report
15:11 days the *w* populace plundered the camp,
Est A: 8 The *w* race of the just were dismayed with
B: 2 peoples and to hold sway over the *w* world,
E:13 royal consort, together with their *w* race.
10: 3 and the herald of peace for his *w* race.
1Mc 1:41 *w* kingdom that all should be one people,
4:15 Their *w* rearguard fell by the sword,
4:37 So the *w* army assembled,
5:15 and the *w* of Gentile Galilee had joined
5:53 and encouraging the people the *w* way,
6:14 and put him in charge of his *w* kingdom.
6:25 us, but throughout their *w* territory.
8: 4 persistence had conquered the *w* country,
9:63 he gathered together his *w* force and sent
12:32 on to Damascus and traversed that *w* region.
2Mc 2:21 few as they were, they seized the *w* land,
2:29 must give his attention to the *w* structure,
3:28 his *w* bodyguard was carried away helpless,
4: 1 and instigated the *w* miserable affair.
4:38 and had him led through the *w* city to the
6:31 only for the young but for the *w* nation.
7:38 that has justly fallen on our *w* nation."
8:18 only those who attack us, but the *w* world."
10: 8 *w* Jewish nation should celebrate these days
15:12 arms for the *w* Jewish community.
15:30 ordered Nicanor's head and *w* right arm to
Ps(s) 72:19 may the *w* earth be filled with his glory.
139: 4 behold, O LORD, you know the *w* of it.
Prv 4:22 them, to man's *w* being they are health.
Wis 5:23 Thus lawlessness shall lay the *w* earth
11:22 *w* universe is as a grain from a balance.
17:20 Darkness Afflicts Egyptians For the *w*
18:24 on his full-length robe was the *w* world,
19: 8 the *w* nation sheltered by your hand,
Sir 7:27 With your *w* heart honor your father;
22:11 dead, but for the wicked fool a *w* lifetime.
47: 8 With his *w* being he loved his Maker and
47:15 Your understanding covered the *w* earth,
49: 3 He turned to God with his *w* heart,
50:13 the presence of the *w* assembly of Israel.
50:25 My *w* being loathes two nations,
51:21 *w* being was stirred as I learned about her;
Is 1: 5 The whole head is sick, the *w* heart faint.
4: 5 over the *w* site of Mount Zion and over her
10:23 of hosts, will carry out within the *w* land.
14: 7 The *w* earth rests peacefully,
14:26 This is the plan proposed for the *w* earth,
25: 8 his people he will remove from the *w* earth;
27: 9 this the *w* fruit of the removal of his sin:
28:22 the destruction decreed for the *w* earth.
39: 2 the spices and fine oil, his *w* armory,
39: 2 in his *w* realm that he did not show them.
53: 5 him was the chastisement that makes us *w*,
Jer 1:18 iron, a wall of brass, against the *w* land:
4:20 the *w* earth is laid waste.
4:27 Waste shall the *w* land be;
8: 2 sun and the moon and the *w* army of heaven,
8:16 of his stallions shakes the *w* land.
9:25 these nations, like the *w* house of Israel,
12: 4 the green of the *w* countryside wither?
13:11 whole house of Israel and the *w* house
19:13 they burnt incense to the *w* host of heaven
23:15 ungodliness has gone forth into the *w* land.
24: 7 they shall return to me with their *w* heart.
25:11 This *w* land shall be a ruin and a desert.
31:37 Then will I cast off the *w* race of Israel
31:40 The *w* valley of corpses and ashes,
35: 3 his sons, the *w* company of the Rechabites,
37:10 the *w* Chaldean army now attacking you,
40: 4 See, the *w* land is before you;
43: 5 leaders took along the *w* remnant of Judah
44:26 in the *w* land of Egypt no man of Judah
44:28 The *w* remnant of Judah who came to settle
45: 4 even the *w* land.
50:23 of the *w* earth been broken and shattered!
51: 7 of the LORD which made the *w* earth drunk;
51:41 made captive, the glory of the *w* world!
51:47 her *w* land shall be put to shame,
51:52 and in her *w* land the wounded will groan.
52: 4 and his *w* army advanced against Jerusalem,
52: 8 Jericho, while his *w* army fled from him.
Lam 2: 3 the horn that was Israel's *w* strength;
2:15 all-beautiful city, the joy of the *w* earth?"
Bar 1: 4 kings' sons, the elders, and the *w* people,
1: 7 *w* people who were with him in Jerusalem.
2:15 the *w* earth may know that you are the Lord,
6:61 by God to proceed across the *w* world,
Ez 3: 7 For the *w* house of Israel is stubborn of
5: 4 Say to the *w* house of Israel:
11:15 and the *w* house of Israel that the
12:10 and the *w* house of Israel within it.
15: 5 even when it was *w* it was good for nothing;
20:40 there the *w* house of Israel without
34: 6 my sheep were scattered over the *w* earth,
35:15 you be, Mount Seir, you and the *w* of Edom.
36:10 of men upon you, the *w* house of Israel;
37:11 these bones are the *w* house of Israel.
39:25 and have pity on the *w* house of Israel,
41:19 on every side throughout the *w* temple.
43:12 its *w* surrounding area on the mountain top
45: 1 its *w* area shall be sacred.
45: 6 this shall belong to the *w* house of Israel.
48:13 The *w* tract shall be twenty-five thousand
Dn 2:35 a great mountain and filled the *w* earth.
2:39 bronze, which shall rule over the *w* earth.
2:48 made him ruler of the *w* province of
3:41 And now we follow you with our *w* heart,
3:45 the Lord God, glorious over the *w* world."
4:17 heavens, that could be seen by the *w* earth,
4:19 and your rule extends over the *w* earth.
5:23 life breath and the *w* course of your life,
7:23 It shall devour the *w* earth,
8: 5 the *w* earth without touching the ground.
13:60 The *w* assembly cried aloud,
14:14 which they scattered through the *w* temple;
Jl 2:12 the LORD, return to me with your *w* heart,
Am 1: 6 took captive *w* groups to hand over to Edom,
1: 9 they delivered *w* groups captive to Edom,
3: 1 over the *w* family that I brought up from
Mi 4:13 their riches to the Lord of the *w* earth.
Zec 1:11 see, the *w* earth is tranquil and at rest!"
4:10 of the LORD that range over the *w* earth.
4:14 who stand by the LORD of the *w* earth."
5: 3 which is to go forth over the *w* earth;
14: 9 LORD shall become king over the *w* earth;
Mal 3: 9 are indeed accursed, for you, the *w* nation,
3:10 Bring the *w* tithe into the storehouse,
Mt 3: 5 and the *w* region around the Jordan were
8:32 The *w* herd went rushing down the bluff
9:31 and spread word of him through the *w* area.
13:33 the *w* mass of dough began to rise."
16:26 *w* world and destroy himself in the process?
18:31 to their master to report the *w* incident.
21:10 the *w* city was stirred to its depths,
22:37 love the Lord your God with your *w* heart,
22:37 with your whole heart, with your *w* soul,
22:40 these two commandments the *w* law is based,
26:59 The chief priests, with the *w* Sanhedrin,
27:25 The *w* people said in reply,
27:27 and collected the *w* cohort around him.
27:45 over the *w* land until midafternoon.
Mk 1:33 the *w* town was gathered outside the door.
1:39 demons throughout the *w* of Galilee.
1:45 and began to proclaim the *w* matter freely,
5:29 of her affliction ran through her *w* body.
5:33 in front of him and told him the *w* truth.
8:36 who gains the *w* world and destroys himself
9:15 Jesus, the *w* crowd was overcome with awe.
11:18 because the *w* crowd was under the spell
14:55 The chief priests with the *w* Sanhedrin
15: 1 and scribes (that is, the *w* Sanhedrin),
15:16 the same time they assembled the *w* cohort.
15:33 darkness fell on the *w* countryside and
16:15 "Go into the *w* world and proclaim the
Lk 1: 3 *w* sequence of events from the beginning,
2: 1 a decree ordering a census of the *w* world.
2:10 of great joy to be shared by the *w* people.
4:28 At these words the *w* audience in the
6:19 the *w* crowd was trying to touch him
8:47 she related before the *w* assemblage why
9:25 What profit does he show who gains the *w*
11:34 is sound, your *w* body is lighted up,
11:36 If your *w* body is lighted up and not
13:21 until the *w* mass of dough began to rise."
17:17 occasion to say, "Were not all ten made *w*?
23: 5 by his teaching throughout the *w* of Judea,
23:18 The *w* crowd cried out,
23:44 and darkness came over the *w* land until
Jn 4:53 his *w* household thereupon became believers.
7:23 with me for curing a *w* man on the sabbath?
11:48 like this, the *w* world will believe in him.
11:50 than to have the *w* nation destroyed?"
12:19 The *w* world has run after him."
Acts 2: 7 The *w* occurrence astonished them.
2:36 Therefore let the *w* house of Israel know
3: 5 The cripple gave them his *w* attention,
3:11 the *w* crowd rushed over to them excitedly
4:12 for there is no other name in the *w* world
5:11 on the *w* church and on all who heard of it.
10: 1 The same was true of his *w* household.
10:22 well thought of in the *w* Jewish community,
11: 4 Peter then explained the *w* affair to them
11:26 For a *w* year they met with the church and
12: 9 The *w* thing seemed to him a mirage.
13: 6 over the *w* island as far as Paphos,
15:12 At that the *w* assembly fell silent.
15:22 in agreement with the *w* Jerusalem church,
16:33 then he and his *w* household were baptized.
16:34 his *w* family his newfound faith in God.
17: 8 the town's magistrates heard the *w* story,
18: 8 Crispus, along with his *w* household,
19:32 with the *w* assembly in chaos and the
20:28 and over the *w* flock the Holy Spirit has
21:27 and began to stir up the *w* crowd there.
21:30 Before long the *w* city was in turmoil.
22: 5 *w* council of elders can bear me witness,
22:30 priests and the *w* Sanhedrin to a meeting;
23: 7 and Sadducees which divided the *w* assembly.
25:24 The *w* Jewish community,
Rom 3:19 the *w* world stands convicted before God,
8:19 the *w* created world eagerly awaits the
10:18 "their voice has sounded over the *w* earth,
11:16 consecrated, so too is the *w* mass of dough,
16:23 who is host to me and to the *w* church.
1Cor 14:23 come in when the *w* church is assembled
Gal 5:12 who are troubling you might go the *w* way,
5:14 The *w* law has found its fulfillment in
Eph 2:21 Through him the *w* structure is fitted
4:16 Through him the *w* body grows,

WHOLE (cont.)

6: 6 will with your *w* heart as slaves of Christ.
Col 2:19 The *w* body,
3:23 you do, work at it with your *w* being.
1Thes 5:23 May he preserve you *w* and entire,
Ti 1:11 They are upsetting *w* families by teaching
Heb 2:15 had been slaves their *w* life long.
Jas 3: 6 our members as a *w* universe of malice.
1Jn 2: 2 sins only, but for those of the *w* world.
5:19 while the *w* world is under the evil one.
Rv 3:10 of trial which is coming on the *w* world,
12: 9 devil or Satan, the seducer of the *w* world,
13: 3 the *w* world followed after the beast.
14: 6 of everlasting good news to the *w* world,
20: 9 They invaded the *w* country and surrounded

WHOLE-BURNT (1)

Is 1:11 had enough of *w* rams and fat of fatlings;

WHOLEHEARTED (11)

2Sm 22:24 But I was *w* toward him,
22:26 toward the wholehearted you are *w*;
1Chr 29:19 a *w* desire to keep your commandments,
Tb 1:12 Because of this *w* service of God,
Ps(s) 18:24 I put not from me, But I was *w* toward him,
18:26 toward the wholehearted you are *w*,
37:18 The LORD watches over the lives of the *w*;
37:37 Watch the *w* man
Ez 36: 5 who with *w* joy and utter contempt

WHOLEHEARTEDLY (12)

2Kgs 10:31 careful to observe *w* the law of the LORD,
20: 3 and *w* I conducted myself in your presence,
1Chr 29: 9 which had been contributed to the LORD *w*.
2Chr 6:14 to your servants who are *w* faithful to you.
16: 9 encourage those who are devoted to him *w*.
19: 9 faithfully and *w* in the fear of the LORD.
25: 2 in the sight of the LORD, though not *w*.
31:21 He did this *w*, and he prospered.
1Mc 8:25 the Jewish nation will help them *w*,
Is 38: 3 and *w* I conducted myself in your presence,
Jer 3:10 Judah did not return to me *w*
17:24 If you obey me *w*, says the LORD,
Dn 13:35 to heaven, for she trusted in the Lord *w*.

WHOLENESS (1)

Ps(s) 38: 4 is no *w* in my bones because of my sin,

WHOLESOME (1)

Wis 1:14 and the creatures of the world are *w*,

WHOLLY (17)

1Sm 14:20 fight, where the Philistines, *w* confused,
1Kgs 7:19 columns were finished *w* in a lotus pattern
8:61 You must be *w* devoted to the LORD,
Est C:13 put aside, and her hair was *w* disheveled.
Jb 19:13 from me, and my friends are *w* estranged.
21:23 in his full vigor, *w* at ease and content;
Ps(s) 48: 2 and *w* to be praised in the city of our God.
78:29 So they ate and were *w* surfeited;
Wis 13:18 And for aid he beseeches the *w* incompetent,
Sir 45:14 His cereal offering is *w* burnt with the
Is 9:16 They are *w* profaned and sinful,
Jer 3: 1 Would not the land be *w* defiled?
4:27 I will [not] *w* destroy it.
5:10 and ravage them, destroy them [not] *w*.
5:18 says the LORD, I will not *w* destroy you.
44:12 Egypt, so that they shall be *w* destroyed.
Phil 4: 8 should be *w* directed to all that is true,

WHOMEVER (7)

Jer 1: 7 To *w* I send you,
27: 5 and I can give them to *w* I think fit.
Dn 5:19 *W* he wished, he killed or let live; *w*
5:19 *w* he wished,
Lk 4: 6 given to me and I give it to *w* I wish.
Rom 9:15 *w* I choose; I will have pity on whomever

WHOREDOM (1)

Ez 23:43 Now they will commit *w* with her,

WICK (3)

Is 42: 3 and a smoldering *w* he shall not quench,
43:17 to rise, snuffed out and quenched like a *w*.
Mt 12:20 the smoldering *w* he will not quench until

WICKED (383)

Gn 13:13 Now the inhabitants of Sodom were very *w*
19: 7 you my brothers, not to do this *w* thing.
Ex 23: 1 Do not join the *w* in putting your hand,
Nm 14:27 will this *w* community grumble against me?
14:35 this *w* community that conspired against me:
16:26 "Keep away from the tents of these *w* men
Jgs 19:23 do not be so *w*.
1Sm 2: 9 but the *w* shall perish in the darkness.
2:12 Now the sons of Eli were *w*;
24:14 says, 'From the *w* comes forth wickedness.'
2Sm 3:34 as men fall before the *w*,
4:11 when *w* men have slain an innocent man in
7:10 Neither shall the *w* continue to afflict
16: 7 "Away, away, you murderous and *w* man!
23: 6 the *w* are all like thorns to be cast away;
1Kgs 8:32 the *w* and punish him for his conduct,
8:47 we have been *w*';
1Chr 2: 3 Er, was *w* in the sight of the LORD,
17: 9 nor shall *w* men ever again oppress them,
21:17 am the one who sinned, I did this *w* thing.
2Chr 6:23 requiting the *w* man and holding him
6:37 we have been *w*,'
19: 2 the *w* and love those who hate the LORD?
24: 7 For the *w* Athaliah and her sons had
Ezr 9: 6 for our *w* deeds are heaped up above our
9: 7 our *w* deeds we have been delivered over,
Tb 3: 8 but the *w* demon Asmodeus killed them off
3:17 then drive the *w* demon Asmodeus from her.
Est 4:30 Save us from the power of the *w*,
7: 6 "The enemy oppressing us is this *w* Haman."
E: 7 when one considers the *w* deeds perpetrated
9:25 ordered in writing that the *w* plan Haman
1Mc 1:36 and a *w* adversary to Israel at all times.
3: 5 He pursued the *w*,
14:14 he suppressed all the lawless and the *w*.
2Mc 1:17 be our God, who has thus punished the *w*!
8:32 of Timothy's forces, a most *w* man,
8:33 received the reward his *w* deeds deserved.
Jb 3:17 There the *w* cease from troubling,
8:20 neither will he take the hand of the *w*.
8:22 and the tent of the *w* shall be no more.
9:22 Both the innocent and the *w* he destroys.
9:24 The earth is given into the hands of the *w*;
10: 3 hands, and smile on the plan of the *w*?
10: 7 Even though you know that I am not *w*,
10:15 If I should be *w*, alas for me!
11:20 shall entreat your favor, but the *w*,
15:20 The *w* man is in torment all his days,
16:11 into the clutches of the *w* he has cast me.
17: 8 and the innocent aroused against the *w*.
18: 5 Truly, the light of the *w* is extinguished;
20: 5 That the triumph of the *w* is short and the
20:29 This is the portion of a *w* man,
21: 7 Why do the *w* surive, grow old,
21:16 the counsel of the *w* is repulsive to God,
21:17 How often is the lamp of the *w* put out?
21:28 and where the dwelling place of the *w*?"
24: 2 The *w* remove landmarks;
24:11 they glean in the the vineyard of the *w*.
27: 7 be as the *w* and my adversary as the unjust!
27:13 This is the portion of a *w* man from God,
29:17 studied, And I broke the jaws of the *w* man;
34: 8 with evildoers and goes along with *w* men,
34:18 and to nobles, "You are *w*!"
35:12 he answers not against the pride of the *w*.
36: 5 he preserves not the life of the *w*.
38:13 till the *w* are shaken from its surface?
38:15 But from the *w* the light is withheld,
40:12 tear down the *w* and shatter them.
Ps(s) 1: 1 of the *w* Nor walks in the way of sinners,
1: 4 Not so the *w*, not so; they are like chaff
1: 5 in judgment the *w* shall not stand,
1: 6 of the just, but the way of the *w* vanishes.
3: 8 the teeth of the *w* you break.
7:10 Let the malice of the *w* come to an end,
9: 6 rebuked the nations and destroyed the *w*;
9:17 the *w* are trapped by the work of their own
9:18 To the nether world the *w* shall turn back,
10: 2 Proudly the *w* harass the afflicted,
10: 2 caught in the devices the *w* have contrived.
10: 3 For the *w* man glories in his greed,
10: 4 The *w* man boasts,
10:13 Why should the *w* man despise God,
10:15 the strength of the *w* and of the evildoer;
11: 2 For, see, the *w* bend the bow;
11: 5 The LORD searches the just and the *w*;
11: 6 rains upon the *w* fiery coals and brimstone;
12: 9 While about us the *w* strut and in high
17: 9 from the *w* who use violence against me.
17:13 rescue me by your sword from the *w*,
26: 5 evildoers, and with the *w* I will not stay.
28: 3 Drag me not away with the *w*,
31:18 let the *w* be put to shame;
32:10 Many are the sorrows of the *w*,
34:22 Vice slays the *w*,
36: 2 Sin speaks to the *w* man in his heart;
36:12 me nor the hand of the *w* disquiet me.
37:10 while, and the *w* man shall be no more;
37:12 The *w* man plots against the just and
37:14 A sword the *w* draw;
37:16 the just than the great wealth of the *w*,
37:17 For the power of the *w* shall be broken,
37:20 But the *w* perish,
37:21 The *w* man borrows and does not repay;
37:28 and the posterity of the *w* is cut off.
37:32 The *w* man spies on the just,
37:34 when the *w* are destroyed,
37:35 I saw a *w* man, fierce, and stalwart as a
37:38 the future of the *w* shall be cut off.
37:40 he delivers them from the *w* and saves them,
39: 2 While the *w* man was before me
49: 6 days when my *w* ensnarers ring me round?
50:16 But to the *w* man God says:
55: 4 voice of the enemy and the clamor of the *w*.
58: 4 From the womb the *w* are perverted;
58:11 shall bathe his feet in the blood of the *w*.
64: 6 They resolve on their *w* plan;
64: 7 They devise a *w* scheme,
65: 4 all flesh must come because of *w* deeds.
68: 3 the fire, so the *w* perish before God.
71: 4 my God, rescue me from the hand of the *w*,
73: 3 when I saw them prosper though they were *w*.
73:12 Such, then, are the *w*;
75: 5 Boast not; and to the *w*:
75: 9 all the *w* of the earth shall drink.
75:11 I will break off the horns of all the *w*;
82: 2 unjustly and favor the cause of the *w*?
82: 4 from the hand of the *w* deliver them.
84:11 of my God than dwell in the tents of the *w*.
89:23 deceive him, nor shall the *w* afflict him.
91: 8 you behold and see the requital of the *w*,
92: 8 Though the *w* flourish like grass and all
92:12 have heard of the fall of my *w* adversaries.
94: 3 the wicked, how long shall the *w* glory,
94:13 evil days, till the pit be dug for the *w*.
94:16 Who will rise up for me against the *w*?
97:10 from the hand of the *w* he delivers them.
101: 8 I will destroy all the *w* of the land,
104:35 from the earth, and may the *w* be no more.
106:18 a flame consumed the *w*.
107:17 *w* ways and afflicted because of their sins,
109: 2 opened *w* and treacherous mouths against me.
109: 6 Raise up a *w* man against him,
112:10 The *w* man shall see it and be vexed;
112:10 the desire of the *w* shall perish.
119:53 me because of the *w* who forsake your law.
119:61 Though the snares of the *w* are twined
119:110 The *w* have laid a snare for me,
119:119 account all the *w* of the earth as dross;
125: 3 For the scepter of the *w* shall not
129: 4 just LORD has severed the cords of the *w*.
139:19 If only you would destroy the *w*,
140: 5 Save me, O LORD, from the hands of the *w*;
140: 9 Grant not, O LORD, the desires of the *w*;
140:12 of *w* tongue shall not abide in the land;
141:10 Let all the *w* fall,
145:20 love him, but all the *w* he will destroy.
146: 9 sustains, but the way of the *w* he thwarts.
147: 6 the *w* he casts to the ground.
Prv 2:22 But the *w* will be cut off from the land,
3:25 terror, of the ruin of the *w* when it comes;
3:33 of the LORD is on the house of the *w*,
4:14 The path of the *w* enter not,
4:19 The way of the *w* is like darkness;
5:22 own iniquities the *w* man will be caught,
6:18 A heart that plots *w* schemes,
9: 7 he who reproves a *w* man incurs opprobrium.
10: 3 but the craving of the *w* he thwarts.
10: 7 be blessed, but the name of the *w* will rot.
10:11 but the mouth of the *w* conceals violence.
10:13 [but the mouth of the *w* conceals violence].
10:16 leads to life, the gains of the *w*,
10:20 the heart of the *w* is of little worth.
10:24 What the *w* man fears will befall him,
10:25 the tempest passes, the *w* man is no more;
10:27 life, but the years of the *w* are brief.
10:28 the expectation of the *w* comes to nought.
10:30 but the *w* will not abide in the land.
10:32 know how to please, but the mouth of the *w*,
11: 5 but by his wickedness the *w* man falls.
11: 7 When a *w* man dies his hope perishes,
11: 8 and the *w* man falls into it in his stead.
11:10 when the *w* perish, there is jubilation.
11:11 the mouth of the *w* it is overthrown.
11:18 The *w* man makes empty profits,
11:23 the expectation of the *w* is wrath.
11:31 earth, how much more the *w* and the sinner!
12: 5 the designs of the *w* are deceitful.
12: 6 The words of the *w* are a deadly ambush,
12: 7 The *w* are overthrown and are no more,
12:10 beast, but the heart of the *w* is merciless.
12:21 but the *w* are overwhelmed with misfortune.
12:26 but the way of the *w* leads them astray.
13: 5 hates, but the *w* brings shame and disgrace.
13: 6 honestly, but the downfall of the *w* is sin.
13: 9 gaily, but the lamp of the *w* goes out.
13:17 A *w* messenger brings on disaster,
13:25 but the belly of the *w* suffers want.
14:11 The house of the *w* will be destroyed,
14:19 must bow down before the good, and the *w*,
14:32 The *w* man is overthrown by his wickedness,
15: 6 but the earnings of the *w* are in turmoil.
15: 8 of the *w* is an abomination to the LORD,
15: 9 way of the *w* is an abomination to the LORD,
15:26 The *w* man's schemes are an abomination to
15:28 but the mouth of the *w* pours out evil.
15:29 The LORD is far from the *w*,
16: 4 his own ends, even the *w* for the evil day.
17: 4 The evil man gives heed to *w* lips,
17:11 On rebellion alone is the *w* man bent,
17:15 He who condones the *w*,
17:23 The *w* man accepts a concealed bribe to
19:28 and the mouth of the *w* pours out iniquity.
20:26 A wise king winnows the *w*,

21: 4 the tillage of the *w* is sin.
21: 7 oppression of the *w* will sweep them away,
21:10 The soul of the *w* man desires evil;
21:12 The just man appraises the house of the *w*:
21:12 there is one who brings down the *w* to ruin.
21:18 The *w* man serves as ransom for the just,
21:27 The sacrifice of the *w* is an abomination,
21:29 The *w* man is brazenfaced,
24:16 and rises again, but the *w* stumble to ruin.
24:19 with evildoers, nor envious of the *w*;
24:20 future, the lamp of the *w* will be put out.
24:24 He who says to the *w* man,
25: 5 Remove the *w* from the presence of the king,
25:26 is a just man who gives way before the *w*.
26:23 earthenware are smooth lips with a *w* heart.
28: 1 *w* man flees although no one pursues him;
28: 4 Those who abandon the law praise the *w* man,
28:12 but when the *w* gain pre-eminence,
28:15 bear is a *w* ruler over a poor people.
28:28 When the *w* gain pre-eminence,
29: 2 but when the *w* rule,
29: 6 The *w* man steps into a snare,
29: 7 the *w* man has no such concern.
29:12 to lying words, his servants all become *w*.
29:16 When the *w* prevail,
29:27 walks uprightly is an abomination to the *w*.
Eccl 3:17 both the just and the *w* God will judge,
4: 3 seen the *w* work that is done under the sun.
7:15 and a *w* one surviving in his wickedness.
7:17 Be not *w* to excess, and be not foolish.
8: 8 nor are the *w* saved by their wickedness.
8:10 Meanwhile I saw *w* men approach and enter;
8:13 that it shall not be well with the *w* man,
8:14 *w* men treated as though they had done justly.
9: 2 same lot for all, for the just and the *w*,
Wis 1: 8 one who utters *w* things can go unnoticed,
1: 9 devices of the *w* man shall be scrutinized,
1:16 *w* who with hands and words invited death,
3:10 But the *w* shall receive a punishment to
3:12 wives are foolish and their children *w*;
3:14 who held no *w* thoughts against the Lord
3:19 for dire is the end of the *w* generation.
4: 3 progeny of the *w* shall be of no avail;
4:16 the many years of the *w* man grown old.
5:14 *w* is like thistledown borne on the wind,
10: 6 from among the *w* who were being destroyed,
10:20 Therefore the just despoiled the *w*;
11: 9 chastised, they recognized how the *w*,
11:15 in return for their senseless, *w* thoughts,
12: 9 the *w* vanquished in battle by the just,
12:10 race was *w* and their malice ingrained,
14:31 follows upon the transgression of the *w*.
16:16 For the *w* who refused to know you were
16:18 not be burnt up that were sent upon the *w*,
16:19 so as to consume the produce of the *w* land.
16:24 grows tense for punishment against the *w*,
19: 1 *w*, merciless wrath assailed until the end.
Sir 5: 7 upon the *w* alights his wrath.
11:33 Avoid a *w* man,
12: 3 comes to him who gives comfort to the *w*,
12: 7 sinners, and upon the *w* he takes vengeance.
15:12 for he has no need of *w* man.
16: 1 children, nor rejoice in *w* offspring.
16:11 though on the *w* alights his wrath.
19:22 There is the *w* man who is bowed in grief,
20:17 why the downfall of the *w* comes so quickly.
22:11 dead, but for the *w* fool a whole lifetime.
27:13 The conversation of the *w* is offensive,
29:16 The *w* turn a pledge on their behalf into
33:27 and for a *w* slave,
35:21 branch, and smashes the scepter of the *w*;
39:25 but for the *w* good things and bad.
39:27 are good, but for the *w* they turn out evil.
39:30 the avenging sword to exterminate the *w*;
40:10 For the *w*,
41: 5 offspring are in the homes of the *w*.
41: 7 Children curse their *w* father,
46: 7 the people and suppressed the *w* complaint
49: 4 Hezekiah and Josiah, they all were *w*;
Is 3:11 Woe to the *w* man!
11: 4 the breath of his lips he shall slay the *w*.
13:11 for its evil and the *w* for their guilt.
14: 5 The LORD has broken the rod of the *w*,
26:10 The *w* man, spared, does not learn justice;
31: 2 the *w* and against those who help evildoers.
32: 7 And the trickster uses *w* trickery,
48:22 [There is no peace for the *w*,
53: 9 the *w* and a burial place with evildoers,
53:12 to death and was counted among the *w*;
55: 7 his way, and the *w* man his thoughts;
57:17 Because of their *w* avarice I was angry,
57:20 But the *w* are like the tossing sea which
57:21 No peace for the *w*!
58: 4 and fighting, striking with *w* claw.
63:18 Why have the *w* invaded your holy place,
Jer 3: 2 You defiled the land by your *w* harlotry.
5:28 They go their *w* way;
6:29 smelter refined, the *w* are not drawn off.
8: 3 to life by all the survivors of this *w* race
13:10 This *w* people who refuse to obey my words,
15:21 I will free you from the hand of the *w*,
20:13 life of the poor from the power of the *w*!
23:14 living in lies, siding with the *w*,
23:19 storm that bursts upon the heads of the *w*.
23:22 back from evil ways and from their *w* deeds.
30:23 storm that bursts upon the heads of the *w*.
Bar 1:22 off after the devices of our own *w* hearts,
Ez 3:18 If I say to the *w* man,
3:18 him from his *w* conduct so that he may live:
3:18 that *w* man shall die for his sin,
3:19 the other hand, you have warned the *w* man,
3:19 away from his evil nor from his *w* conduct,
7:21 spoiled and defiled by the *w* of the earth.
11: 2 evil and giving *w* counsel in this city.
13:22 and have encouraged the *w* man not to turn
18:20 as the *w* man's wickedness shall be his.
18:21 But if the *w* man turns away from all the
18:23 any pleasure from the death of the *w*?
18:24 of abominable things that the *w* man does,
18:27 But if a *w* man,
21: 8 cut off from you the virtuous and the *w*.
21:29 bare and your sinfulness in all your *w* deeds
21:30 for you, depraved and *w* prince of Israel,
21:34 lay it on the necks of depraved and *w* men
30:12 sell the land over to the power of the *w*.
33: 8 I tell the *w* man that he shall surely die,
33: 8 wicked man from his way, he [the *w* man]
33: 9 But if you warn the *w* man,
33:11 the wicked man, but rather the *w* man's
33:14 say to the *w* man that he shall surely die,
33:19 But when a *w* man turns away from
Dn 9: 5 We have sinned, been *w* and done evil;
12:10 and tested, but the wicked shall prove *w*;
13:28 the next day, the two *w* elders also came,
13:32 but those *w* men ordered her to uncover her
13:43 with which these *w* men have charged me."
Hos 9:15 *w* deeds I will drive them out of my house.
Hb 1: 4 Because the *w* circumvent the just;
1:13 *w* man devours one more just than himself?
3:13 You crush the heads of the *w*,
Zep 1: 3 I will overthrow the *w*;
Zec 1: 4 from your evil ways and from your *w* deeds.
Mal 3:18 distinction between the just and the *w*;
3:21 out of the stall and tread down the *w*;
Mt 13:49 Angels will go out and separate the *w* from
13:50 just and hurl the *w* into the fiery furnace,
21:41 "He will bring that *w* crowd to a bad end
23:15 a devil of him twice as *w* as yourselves.
Mk 7:21 *W* designs come from the deep recesses of
Lk 6:35 is good to the ungrateful and the *w*.
22:37 in Scripture, 'He was counted among the *w*,'
Jn 3:19 than light because their deeds were *w*.
Acts 24:15 a resurrection of the good and the *w* alike.
1Cor 5:13 "Expel the *w* man from your midst."
6: 1 to the *w* and not to God's holy people?
10: 6 to keep us from *w* desires such as theirs.
2Thes 2:10 by every seduction the *w* can devise for
1Tm 1: 9 and the sinful, the *w* and the godless,
2Pt 2: 9 of the *w* up to the day of judgment.
3:17 you be led astray by the error of the *w*,
1Jn 3:12 deeds were *w* while his brother's were just.
Rv 2: 2 I know you cannot tolerate *w* men;
16:11 they did not turn away from their *w* deeds.
22:11 Let the *w* continue in their wicked ways,

WICKEDLY (4)

1Mc 7:42 Nicanor spoke *w* against your sanctuary;
Jb 34:12 Surely, God cannot act *w*,
Ps(s) 139:20 *W* they invoke your name;
Ez 5: 6 my ordinances more *w* than the nations,

WICKEDNESS (129)

Gn 6: 5 LORD saw how great was man's *w* on earth,
15:16 the *w* of the Amorites will not have
Ex 20: 5 *w* on the children of those who hate me,
34: 7 and forgiving *w* and crime and sin;
34: 7 and fourth generation for their fathers' *w*!"
34: 9 yet pardon our *w* and sins,
Lv 18:25 defiled, I am punishing it for its *w*,
Nm 14:18 rich in kindness, forgiving *w* and crime;
14:18 and fourth generation for their fathers' *w*.'
14:19 the *w* of this people in keeping with your
Dt 5: 9 *w* on the children of those who hate me,
9: 4 for it is really because of the *w* of these
9: 5 out before you on account of their *w*
9:27 of this people nor upon their *w* and sin,
Jgs 9:57 all their *w* home to the Shechemites,
1Sm 24:14 says, 'From the wicked comes forth *w*.'
1Kgs 2:44 Now the LORD requites you for your own *w*.
Tb 12: 8 is better than abundance with *w*.
14:10 commit all sorts of *w* and treachery.
14:11 what almsgiving does, and also what *w* does
Jdt 5:17 they prospered, for their God, who hates *w*,
1Mc 7:42 judge him according to his *w*."
2Mc 4: 4 and Phoenicia, was abetting Simon's *w*.
4:13 *w* of the ungodly pseudo-high-priest Jason,
4:50 where he grew in *w* and became the chief
Jb 15: 5 God, Because your *w* instructs your mouth,
20:12 Though *w* is sweet in his mouth,
22: 5 Is not your *w* manifold?
24:20 accursed, and *w* is splintered like wood.
34:10 far be it from God to do *w*;
35: 8 Your *w* can affect only a man like yourself;
Ps(s) 5: 5 For you, O God, delight not in *w*;
10:15 punish their *w*;
36: 5 He plans *w* in his bed;
45: 8 You love justice and hate *w*;
56: 8 because of their *w* keep them in view:
66:18 Were I to cherish *w* in my heart,
94:20 the tribunal of *w* be leagued with you,
94:23 and for their *w* he will destroy them;
107:34 marsh, because of the *w* of its inhabitants.
107:42 and rejoice, and all *w* closes its mouth.
125: 3 Lest the just put forth to *w* their hands.
141: 4 in deeds of *w* With men who are evildoers;
Prv 4:17 bread of *w* and drink the wine of violence.
8: 7 my mouth recounts, but the *w* my lips abhor.
11: 5 but by his *w* the wicked man falls.
12: 3 No man is built up by *w*,
14:32 The wicked man is overthrown by his *w*.
18: 3 With *w* comes contempt,
Eccl 3:16 the sun in the judgment place I saw *w*,
7:15 and a wicked one surviving in his *w*.
7:25 that *w* is foolish and folly is madness.
8: 8 nor are the wicked saved by their *w*.
Wis 2:21 for their *w* blinded them,
4: 6 give evidence of the *w* of their parents,
4:11 lest *w* pervert his mind or deceit beguile
4:14 he sped him out of the midst of *w*.
5:13 to display, but were consumed in our *w*."
7:30 supplants, but *w* prevails not over Wisdom.
10: 5 when the nations were sunk in universal *w*,
10: 7 Where as a testimony to its *w*,
12: 2 may abandon their *w* and believe in you,
12:20 time and opportunity to abandon *w*,
17:11 For *w*, of its nature cowardly, testifies in
Sir 7: 2 avoid *w*, and it will turn aside from you.
12:10 for his *w* is like corrosion in bronze.
15:13 Abominable *w* the LORD hates,
17:16 Their *w* cannot be hidden from him;
19:18 The knowledge of *w* is not wisdom,
25:16 *W* changes a woman's looks,
38:10 Flee *w*; let your hands be just,
40:13 Wealth out of *w* is like a wadi in spate:
46:20 his voice as a prophet, to put an end to *w*.
Is 1: 4 sinful nation, people laden with *w*,
1:13 calling of assemblies, octaves with *w*:
6: 7 has touched your lips, your *w* is removed,
9:17 For *w* burns like fire,
22:14 shall not be pardoned this *w* till you die,
26:21 to punish the *w* of the earth's inhabitants;
32: 6 How to do *w*, to speak perversely against
47:10 Because you felt secure in your *w*,
58: 1 Tell my people their *w*,
Jer 1:16 them for all their *w* in forsaking me,
2:19 Your own *w* chastises you,
2:33 You who, in your *w*,
3:17 will walk no longer in their hardhearted *w*.
6: 7 out its waters, so she gushes out her *w*.
7:12 to it because of the *w* of my people Israel.
8: 6 No one repents of his *w*,
9: 6 how else should I deal with their *w*?
12: 4 For the *w* of those who dwell in it beasts
14:16 for I will pour out upon them their own *w*.
14:20 We recognize, O LORD, our *w*,
22:22 and confounded because of all your *w*.
23:11 In my very house I find their *w*,
32:32 for all the *w* the Israelites and Judeans,
33: 5 my face from this city for all their *w*.
36: 3 that I may forgive their *w* and their sin.
36:31 descendants and his ministers for their *w*;
Lam 4:22 But your *w*,
Bar 2:26 for the *w* of the kingdom of Israel and the
3: 7 *w* of our fathers who sinned against you.
Ez 7:11 violence has risen to support *w*.
16:57 of yourself, before your *w* became evident?
18:20 own, as the wicked man's *w* shall be his.
18:27 man, turning from the *w* he has committed,
31:11 has dealt with it in keeping with its *w*.
33:12 neither will the *w* that a man has done
33:12 turns from his *w* [nor can the virtuous man,
33:19 from *w* and does what is right and just,
Dn 9:13 from our *w* and recognizing his constancy,
13: 5 the Lord said, *W* has come out of Babylon:
13:57 daughter of Judah did not tolerate your *w*.
Hos 5: 2 In their perversity they have sunk into *w*,
7: 1 of Ephraim stands out, the *w* of Samaria;
7: 2 themselves that I remember all their *w*.
7: 3 In their *w* they regale the king,
9:15 All their *w* is in Gilgal;
10:13 But you have cultivated *w*,
10:15 to you, Bethel, Because of your utter *w*:
Jon 1: 2 their *w* has come up before me."
Mi 3:10 Zion with bloodshed, and Jerusalem with *w*!
Hb 2:12 by bloodshed, and establishes a town by *w*!
Zec 5: 8 "This is *W*," he said; and he thrust her
Rom 1:29 They are filled with every kind of *w*:
2: 8 who selfishly disobey the truth and obey *w*.
1Cor 5: 8 the old yeast, that of corruption and *w*,
Heb 1: 9 You have loved justice and hated *w*,
2Pt 2:12 destroyed, suffering the reward of their *w*.

WICKER (2)

Gn 40:16 In it I had three *w* baskets on my head;
Mk 8: 8 gathered up seven *w* baskets of leftovers.

WIDE (89)

Ex 25:10 half cubits long, one and a half cubits *w*,
25:17 a half long, and one and a half cubits *w*.
25:23 of acacia wood, two cubits long, a cubit *w*,
27: 1 square, five cubits long and five cubits *w*;
27:18 be one hundred cubits long, fifty cubits *w*,
28:16 folded double, a span high and a span *w*.
30: 2 a square surface, a cubit long, a cubit *w*,
37: 1 half cubits long, one and a half cubits *w*,
37: 6 cubits long and one and a half cubits *w*.
37:10 wood, two cubits long, and one cubit *w*,
37:25 on a square, a cubit long, a cubit *w*,
38: 1 square, five cubits long and five cubits *w*;
38:18 twenty cubits long and five cubits *w*,
39: 9 span high and a span *w* in its folded form.
Dt 3:11 iron, nine regular cubits long and four *w*,
1Kgs 6: 2 the LORD was sixty cubits long, twenty *w*,
6: 6 cubits wide, the middle one six cubits *w*,
6: 6 six cubits wide, the third seven cubits *w*,
6:20 covenant, twenty cubits long, twenty *w*,
6:27 of the temple, with their wings spread *w*,
7: 2 Lebanon one hundred cubits long, fifty *w*,
7: 6 he made fifty cubits long and thirty *w*.
7:27 of bronze, each four cubits long, four *w*,
2Chr 4: 1 long, twenty cubits *w* and ten cubits high.
6:13 platform five cubits long, five cubits *w*,
26:15 His fame spread far and *w*,
Neh 7: 4 Now the city was quite *w* and spacious but
9:35 in the *w* and fertile land that you
Jdt 1: 4 with an opening forty cubits *w* for the
4: 7 defile was only *w* enough for two abreast.
2Mc 12:16 which was about a quarter of a mile *w*,
Jb 30:14 as through a *w* breach they advance.
Ps(s) 35:21 And they open *w* their mouths against me,
81:11 open *w* your mouth,
104:25 The sea also, great and *w*,
110: 6 he will crush heads over the *w* earth.
Prv 13: 3 to open *w* one's lips brings downfall.
20:13 eyes *w* open mean abundant food.
Sir 25: 6 The crown of old men is *w* experience;
34: 9 A man with training gains *w* knowledge;
Is 33:21 and *w* streams on which no boat is rowed,
57: 4 sport, at whom do you open *w* your mouth,
57: 8 me, you spread out your high, *w* bed;
Jer 8:19 of my people, far and *w* in the land!
Ez 23:32 your sister you shall drink, so *w* and deep,
40: 6 threshold, which was found to be a rod *w*.
40: 7 The cells were a rod long and a rod *w*,
40:11 gate's entrance, which was ten cubits *w*,
40:18 the gates, as *w* as the gates were long;
40:21 fifty cubits long and twenty-five cubits *w*.
40:25 fifty cubits long and twenty-five cubits *w*.
40:29 fifty cubits long and twenty-five cubits *w*.
40:33 fifty cubits long and twenty-five cubits *w*.
40:36 fifty cubits long and twenty-five cubits *w*.
40:42 half cubits long, one and a half cubits *w*,
40:43 The ledges, a handbreadth *w*,
40:47 hundred cubits long and a hundred cubits *w*,
40:49 was twenty cubits *w* and twelve cubits deep;
41: 4 twenty cubits long and twenty cubits *w*,
41:10 cubits *w* going all around the temple.
41:14 on the east side, was one hundred cubits *w*.
41:22 height, two cubits long, and two cubits *w*.
42: 2 north side, and they were fifty cubits *w*,
42:11 to the north, just as long and just as *w*,
42:20 cubits long and five hundred cubits *w*.
43:16 twelve cubits long and twelve cubits *w*.
43:17 fourteen cubits long and fourteen cubits *w*.
43:17 sixteen cubits long and sixteen cubits *w*,
45: 1 thousand cubits long and twenty thousand *w*;
45: 3 thousand cubits long and ten thousand *w*,
45: 5 ten thousand *w* as property for the Levites,
45: 6 cubits *w* and twenty-five thousand long,
46:22 courts, forty cubits long and thirty *w*,
48: 8 and as *w* as one of the tribal portions
Dn 3: 1 made, sixty cubits high and six cubits *w*,
Na 3:13 foes the gates of your land are open *w*,
Hb 2: 5 opens *w* his throat like the nether world,
Zec 5: 2 it is twenty cubits long and ten cubits *w*."
Mt 7:13 The gate that leads to damnation is *w*,
Lk 12:37 whom the master finds *w* awake on his
Acts 1:18 His body burst *w* open,
16:27 woke up to see the prison gates *w* open.
1Cor 16: 9 A door has been opened *w* for my work,
2Cor 2:12 was opened *w* for me by the Lord.
6:11 you frankly, opening our hearts *w* to you.
6:13 to his children), open *w* your hearts!
2Tm 2:18 who have gone far *w* of the truth in saying
Rv 16:15 Happy the man who stays *w* awake and fully

WIDELY (2)

Neh 4:13 and we are *w* separated from one another
Sir 21: 7 *W* known is the boastful speaker but the

WIDEN (1)

Mt 23: 5 *w* their phylacteries and wear huge tassels.

WIDER (1)

Am 6: 2 or is your territory *w* than theirs?

WIDESPREAD (1)

Mk 6:14 had become *w* and people were saying,

WIDOW (63)

Gn 38: 8 to Onan, "Unite with your brother's *w*,
38: 9 he had relations with his brother's *w*,
38:11 "Stay as a *w* in your father's house until
Ex 22:21 You shall not wrong any *w* or orphan.
Lv 21:14 Not a *w* or a woman who has been divorced
Nm 30:10 The vow of a *w* or of a divorced woman,
Dt 10:18 executes justice for the orphan and the *w*,
14:29 and the *w* who belong to your community,
16:11 the alien, the orphan and the *w* among you.
16:14 and the *w* who belong to your community.
24:17 nor take the clothing of a *w* as a pledge.
24:19 it be for the alien, the orphan or the *w*,
24:20 be for the alien, the orphan and the *w*.
24:21 be for the alien, the orphan, and the *w*.
25: 5 the *w* of the deceased shall not marry
26:12 Levite, the alien, the orphan and the *w*,
26:13 Levite, the alien, the orphan and the *w*,
27:19 rights of the alien, the orphan or the *w*!'
Ru 4: 5 Ruth the Moabite, the *w* of the late heir,
4:10 take Ruth the Moabite, the *w* of Mahlon,
1Sm 27: 3 and Abigail, the *w* of Nabal from Carmel.
30: 5 and Abigail, the *w* of Nabal from Carmel,
2Sm 2: 2 and Abigail, the *w* of Nabal of Carmel.
3: 3 of Abigail the *w* of Nabal of Carmel;
14: 5 "Alas, I am a *w*; my husband is dead.
1Kgs 7:14 the son of a *w* from the tribe of Naphtali;
17: 9 designated a *w* there to provide for you."
17:10 the city, a *w* was gathering sticks there;
17:20 will you afflict even the *w* with whom I am
2Kgs 4: 1 woman, the *w* of one of the guild prophets,
1Chr 2:24 with Ephrathah, the *w* of his father Hezron,
Jdt 9: 5 "O God, my God, hear me also, a *w*.
9: 9 Give me, a *w*,
Jb 29:13 me, and the heart of the *w* I made joyful.
31:16 or allowed the eyes of the *w* to languish
Ps(s) 94: 6 *W* and stranger they slay,
109: 9 children be fatherless, and his wife a *w*.
146: 9 the fatherless and the *w* he sustains,
Wis 2:10 let us neither spare the *w* nor revere the
Sir 35:14 to the *w* when she pours out her complaint;
Is 1:17 hear the orphan's plea, defend the *w*.
47: 8 I shall never be a *w*,
Jer 7: 6 residential alien, the orphan, and the *w*;
22: 3 the resident alien, the orphan, or the *w*,
Bar 4:12 Let no one gloat over me, a *w*,
6:37 neither pity the *w* nor benefit the orphan.
Zec 7:10 Do not oppress the *w* or the orphan,
Mk 12:42 but one poor *w* came and put in two small
12:43 "I want you to observe that this poor *w*
Lk 2:37 and then as a *w* until she was eighty-four.
4:26 sent, but to a *w* of Zarephath near Sidon.
18: 3 A *w* in that city kept coming to him saying,
18: 5 God or man, but this *w* is wearing me out.
20:28 the *w* and raise posterity to his brother.
20:31 Next, the second brother married the *w*,
20:32 Finally the *w* herself died.
21: 2 also a poor *w* putting in two copper coins.
21: 3 poor *w* has put in more than all the rest.
1Tm 5: 4 If a *w* has any children or grandchildren,
5: 5 The real *w*, left destitute, is one who has
5: 6 A *w* who gives herself up to selfish
5: 9 a *w* should be not less than sixty years of
Rv 18: 7 No *w* am I, and never will I go

WIDOWED (7)

Lv 22:13 a priest's daughter is *w* or divorced and,
1Kgs 11:26 an Ephraimite from Zeredah with a *w* mother,
Jdt 8: 4 The *w* Judith remained three years and four
Jer 51: 5 Israel and Judah are not *w* of their God,
Lam 1: 1 *W* is she who was mistress over nations;
5: 3 *w* are our mothers.
Lk 7:12 carried out, the only son of a *w* mother.

WIDOWHOOD (4)

Jdt 8: 6 She fasted all the days of her *w*,
10: 3 had on, laid aside the garments of her *w*,
Is 47: 9 Complete bereavement and *w* shall come upon
54: 4 the reproach of your *w* no longer remember.

WIDOWS (44)

Gn 38:14 shear his sheep, she took off her *w* garb,
38:19 off her shawl and put on her *w* garb again.
Ex 22:23 then your own wives will be *w*,
2Sm 20: 3 to the day of their death, lifelong *w*.
Tb 1: 8 The third tithe I gave to orphans and *w*,
Jdt 8: 5 sackcloth about her loins and wore *w* weeds.
16: 7 *w* garb to raise up the afflicted in Israel.
2Mc 3:10 money was a care fund for *w* and orphans,
8:28 to the persecuted and to *w* and orphans;
8:30 the rest to the persecuted, to orphans, *w*,
Jb 22: 9 You have sent *w* away empty-handed,
24: 3 they take the *w* ox for a pledge.
27:15 burial, and their *w* shall not be mourned.
Ps(s) 68: 6 defender of *w* is God in his holy dwelling.
78:64 by the sword, and their *w* sang no dirges.
Prv 15:25 but he preserves intact the *w* landmark.
Is 1:23 not, and the *w* plea does not reach them.
9:16 and their orphans and *w* he does not pity;
10: 2 of their rights, Making *w* their plunder,
Jer 15: 8 Their *w* were more numerous before me than
18:21 Let their wives be made childless and *w*;
49:11 your *w*,
Bar 4:16 They have led away this *w* cherished sons,
Ez 22: 7 within you, they oppress orphans and *w*.
22:25 things, and make *w* of many within her.
44:22 for their wives either *w* or divorced women,
44:22 may marry women who are the *w* of priests.
Mal 3: 5 Against those who defraud *w* and orphans;
Mk 12:40 These men devour the savings of *w* and
Lk 4:25 there were many *w* in Israel in the days of
20:47 men are going through the savings of *w*
Acts 6: 1 that their *w* were being neglected in the daily
6: 1 with the *w* of those who spoke Hebrew.
9:39 All the *w* came to him in tears and showed
9:41 and the *w* to show them that she was alive.
1Cor 7: 8 not married and to *w* I have this to say:
1Tm 5: 3 Honor the claims of *w* who are real widows
5: 7 Make the following rules about *w*,
5: 9 To be on the church's roll of *w*,
5:11 Refuse to enroll the younger *w*,
5:16 church member has relatives who are *w*,
5:16 give help to the *w* who are really in need.
Jas 1:27 Looking after orphans and *w* in their

WIDTH (32)

Gn 6:15 three hundred cubits, its *w* fifty cubits,
Ex 26: 2 twenty-eight cubits, and the *w* four cubits;
26: 8 be thirty cubits, and the *w* four cubits:
26:16 cubits, and its *w* one and a half cubits.
27:12 the *w* of the court there shall be hangings,
27:13 The *w* of the court on the east side shall
36: 9 twenty-eight cubits and the *w* four cubits;
36:15 was thirty cubits and the *w* four cubits;
36:21 cubits, and the *w* one and a half cubits.
1Kgs 6: 3 from side to side, along the *w* of the nave,
7: 6 porch extended the *w* of the columned hall,
2Chr 3: 3 old measure, and the *w* was twenty cubits;
3: 4 the *w* of the house was also twenty cubits,
3: 8 of the house, twenty cubits, and its *w*
Ezr 6: 3 to be sixty cubits and its *w* sixty cubits.
Is 8: 8 spread its wings the full *w* of your land,
Ez 40: 5 the *w* and the height of the structure,
40:11 while the *w* of the gate's passage itself
40:13 the *w* was twenty-five cubits.
40:19 He measured the *w* of the court from the
40:20 north, whose length and *w* he measured.
40:48 The *w* of the doorway was fourteen cubits,
41: 2 The *w* of the entrance was ten cubits,
41: 2 to be forty cubits, while its *w* was twenty.
41: 3 the *w* of the entrance was six cubits,
41: 5 around the temple, had a *w* of four cubits.
41: 9 The *w* of the outside wall which enclosed
41:11 The *w* of the wall surrounding the open
Zec 2: 6 great is its *w* and how great its length."
Rv 21:16 its length and its *w* being the same.
21:16 twelve thousand furlongs in length, in *w*,

WIELD (4)

2Chr 22: 9 no one powerful enough to *w* the kingship.
Jer 6:23 Bow and javelin they *w*;
50:42 Bow and javelin they *w*,
Ez 30:25 for him to *w* against the land of Egypt.

WIELDED (3)

Is 31: 8 Assyria shall fall by a sword not *w* by man,
Rv 14:16 So the one sitting on the cloud *w* his
14:19 So the angel *w* his sickle over the earth

WIELDERS (1)

Jgs 5:14 from Zebulun *w* of the marshal's staff.

WIELDING (4)

2Kgs 2:14 *W* the mantle which had fallen from Elijah,
1Chr 21: 5 of men capable of *w* a sword,
Sir 38:25 who thrills in *w* the goad like a lance,
2Cor 6: 7 *w* the weapons of righteousness with right

WIELDS (5)

Gn 39: 9 He *w* no more authority in this house than
Is 10:15 the saw exalt itself above him who *w* it?
Jer 50:16 and him who *w* the sickle in harvest time!
Mk 4:29 When the crop is ready he *w* the sickle,
Rv 3: 7 holy One, the true, who *w* David's key,

WIFE (392)

Gn 2:24 his father and mother and clings to his *w*,
2:25 The man and his *w* were both naked,
3: 8 the man and his *w* hid themselves from the
3:17 "Because you listened to your *w* and ate
3:20 The man called his *w* Eve,
3:21 his *w* the LORD God made leather garments,
4: 1 The man had relations with his *w* Eve,
4:17 Cain had relations with his *w*,

4:25 Adam again had relations with his *w*,
6:18 and your sons, your *w* and your sons' wives,
7: 7 Together with his sons, his *w*,
7:13 sons Shem, Ham, and Japheth, and Noah's *w*,
8:16 your *w* and your sons and your sons' wives.
8:18 his *w* and his sons and his sons' wives;
11:29 wife was Sarai, and the name of Nahor's *w*
11:31 Sarai, the *w* of his son Abram,
12: 5 Abram took his *w* Sarai,
12:11 to enter Egypt, he said to his *w* Sarai:
12:12 see you, they will say, 'She is his *w*';
12:17 severe plagues because of Abram's *w* Sarai.
12:18 Why didn't you tell me she was your *w?*
12:19 is my sister,' so that I took her for my *w?*
12:19 Here, then, is your *w*.
12:20 with his *w* and all that belonged to him.
13: 1 with his *w* and all that belonged to him,
16: 1 Abram's *w* Sarai had borne him no children.
16: 3 land of Canaan, his *w* Sarai took her maid,
17:15 "As for your *w* Sarai,
17:19 your *w* Sarah is to bear you a son,
18: 9 "Where is your *w* Sarah?"
19:15 your *w* and your two daughters who are here,
19:16 seized his hand and the hands of his *w*
19:26 But Lot's *w* looked back,
20: 2 he stayed in Gerar, he said of his *w* Sarah,
20: 7 Therefore, return the man's *w*—
20:11 so they would kill me on account of my *w*.
20:12 and so she became my *w*.
20:14 and after he restored his *w* Sarah to him,
20:17 that is, to his *w* and his maidservants,
20:18 household on account of Abraham's *w* Sarah.
21:21 got a *w* for him from the land of Egypt.
23: 4 a burial ground, that I may bury my dead *w*."
23:19 Abraham buried his *w* Sarah in the cave of
24: 3 that you will not procure a *w* for my son
24: 4 to my kindred to get a *w* for my son Isaac."
24: 7 and you will obtain a *w* for my son there.
24:15 the *w* of Abraham's brother Nahor) came out
24:36 My master's *w* Sarah bore a son to my
24:37 'You shall not procure a *w* for my son
24:38 to my own relatives, to get a *w* for my son.'
24:40 and so you will get a *w* for my son from my
24:51 she may become the *w* of your master's son,
24:67 he married her, and thus she became his *w*.
25: 1 Abraham married another *w*,
25:10 there he was buried next to his *w* Sarah.
25:21 entreated the LORD on behalf of his *w*,
26: 7 of the place asked questions about his *w*,
26: 7 He was afraid, if he called her his *w*,
26: 8 to see Isaac fondling his *w* Rebekah.
26: 9 "She must certainly be your *w!*
26:10 for one of the men to lie with your *w*,
26:11 or his *w* shall forthwith be put to death."
28: 2 and there choose a *w* for yourself from
28: 6 to Paddan-aram to get himself a *w* there,
29:21 Then Jacob said to Laban, "Give me my *w*,
34: 4 father Hamor, "Get me this girl for a *w*."
36:10 wife Adah; and Reuel, son of Esau's *w*
36:12 These are the descendants of Esau's *w* Adah.
36:13 are the descendants of Esau's *w* Basemath.
36:14 The descendants of Esau's *w* Oholibamah
36:17 they are descended from Esau's *w* Basemath.
36:18 The descendants of Esau's *w* Oholibamah:
36:18 These are the clans of Esau's *w* Oholibamah,
38: 6 got a *w* named Tamar for his first-born,
38:12 Years passed, and Judah's *w*,
39: 7 *w* began to look fondly at him and said,
39: 9 nothing but yourself, since you are his *w*.
44:27 to us, 'As you know, my *w* bore me two sons.
46:19 The sons of Jacob's *w* Rachel:
49:31 There Abraham and his *w* Sarah are buried,
49:31 buried, and so are Isaac and his *w* Rebekah,
Ex 4:20 So Moses took his *w* and his sons,
18: 2 Jethro took along Zipporah, Moses' *w*,
18: 5 Together with Moses' *w* and sons,
18: 6 to you, along with your *w* and her two sons."
20:17 You shall not covet your neighbor's *w*,
21: 3 with a wife, his *w* shall leave with him.
21: 4 a *w* and she bears him sons or daughters,
21: 5 devoted to my master and my *w* and children;
21:10 If he takes another *w*,
Lv 18: 8 not have intercourse with your father's *w*,
18:11 daughter whom your father's *w* bore to him,
18:14 brother by being intimate with his *w*,
18:15 she is your son's *w*,
18:16 have intercourse with your brother's *w*,
18:18 While your *w* is still living you shall not
18:18 for thus you would disgrace your first *w*.
18:20 carnal relations with your neighbor's *w*,
20:10 commits adultery with his neighbor's *w*,
20:11 his father by lying with his father's *w*,
20:20 by having intercourse with his uncle's *w*,
20:21 brother's *w* and thus disgraces his brother,
Nm 5:12 If a man's *w* goes astray and becomes
5:14 of jealousy that makes him suspect his *w*,
5:15 he shall bring his *w* to the priest and
5:30 a man that he becomes suspicious of his *w*,
26:59 was Amram, whose *w* was named Jochebed.
30:17 relationship between a husband and his *w*,
Dt 5:21 'You shall not covet your neighbor's *w*.
13: 7 your son or daughter, or your beloved *w*,
20: 7 a woman and not yet taken her as his *w?*
20: 7 he die in battle and another take her to *w*.'
21:11 of her that you wish to have her as *w*,
21:13 be her husband and she shall be your *w*.
21:16 his first-born the son of the *w* he loves,
21:16 the son of the *w* whom he dislikes.
22:19 Moreover, she shall remain his *w*,
22:24 man because he violated his neighbor's *w*.
22:29 fifty silver shekels and take her as his *w*,
23: 1 "A man shall not marry his father's *w*,
24: 2 she goes and becomes the *w* of another man,
24: 4 her as his *w* after she has become defiled.
24: 5 to bring joy to the *w* he has married.
25: 7 does not care to marry his brother's *w*,
25:11 "When two men are fighting and the *w* of
27:20 he who has relations with his father's *w*,
28:30 Though you betroth a *w*,
28:54 his beloved *w* and his surviving children,
Jgs 4: 4 the prophetess Deborah, *w* of Lappidoth,
4:17 to the tent of Jael, *w* of the Kenite Heber,
4:21 Instead Jael, *w* of Heber,
11: 2 Gilead's *w* had also borne him sons,
11: 2 the sons of the *w* had driven Jephthah away,
13: 2 His *w* was barren and had borne no children.
13:11 so Manoah got up and followed his *w*.
13:11 him, "Are you the one who spoke to my *w?*"
13:13 "Your *w* is to abstain from all the things
13:19 While Manoah and his *w* were looking on,
13:20 When Manoah and his *w* saw this,
13:21 LORD was seen no more by Manoah and his *w*.
13:22 was the angel of the LORD, said to his *w*,
13:23 But his *w* pointed out to him,
14: 2 whom I wish you to get as a *w* for me."
14: 3 "Can you find no *w* among your kinsfolk or
14: 3 a *w* from the uncircumcised Philistines?"
14:15 they said on the fourth day to Samson's *w*,
14:16 At Samson's side, his *w* wept and said,
14:20 and Samson's *w* was married to the one who
15: 1 of the wheat harvest, Samson visited his *w*,
15: 1 he said, "Let me be with my *w* in private,"
15: 6 his *w* was taken and given to his best man."
21:21 seize one of the girls of Shiloh for a *w*,
21:23 they carried off a *w* for each of them from
Ru 1: 1 departed with his *w* and two sons to reside
1: 2 The man was named Elimelech, his *w* Naomi,
4:10 the Moabite, the widow of Mahlon, as my *w*,
4:11 May the LORD make this *w* come into your
4:13 When they came together as man and *w*,
1Sm 1: 4 he used to give a portion each to his *w*
1:19 Elkanah had relations with his *w* Hannah,
2: 5 The barren *w* bears seven sons,
2:20 And Eli would bless Elkanah and his *w*,
4:19 His daughter-in-law, the *w* of Phinehas,
14:50 Saul's *w*,
19:10 David's *w* Michal informed him,
25: 3 The man was named Nabal, his *w* Abigail.
25:14 But Nabal's *w* Abigail was informed of this
25:37 sober, his *w* told him what had happened.
25:40 us to you that he may take you as his *w*."
25:42 She became his *w*, and David also married
25:43 but Saul gave David's *w* Michal,
30:22 except to each man his *w* and children.
2Sm 3: 5 and the sixth, Ithream, of David's *w* Eglah.
3:14 son of Saul, to say, "Give me my *w* Michal,
11: 3 and *w* of [Joab's armor-bearer] Uriah the
11:11 to eat and to drink and to sleep with my *w?*
11:26 *w* of Uriah heard that her husband had died,
11:27 She became his *w* and bore him a son.
12: 9 you took his *w* as your own,
12:10 have taken the *w* of Uriah to be your wife.'
12:15 that the *w* of Uriah had borne to David,
12:24 Then David comforted his *w* Bathsheba.
1Kgs 2:17 to give me Abishag the Shunamite for my *w*."
2:21 given to your brother Adonijah for his *w*."
9:16 it as dowry to his daughter, Solomon's *w*;
11:19 the sister of Queen Tahpenes, his own *w*.
14: 2 So Jeroboam said to his *w*,
14: 2 none will recognize you as Jeroboam's *w*.
14: 4 The *w* of Jeroboam obeyed.
14: 5 *w* is coming to consult you about her son,
14: 6 the door, said, "Come in, *w* of Jeroboam.
14:17 So Jeroboam's *w* started back;
21: 5 His *w* Jezebel came to him and said to him.
21: 7 his *w* Jezebel said to him.
21:25 as did Ahab, urged on by his *w* Jezebel.
2Kgs 5: 2 girl, who became the servant of Naaman's *w*.
8:18 Ahab, since the sister of Ahab was his *w*;
22:14 She was the *w* of Shallum,
1Chr 2:18 By his *w* Azubah, Caleb, son of Hezron,
2:26 Jerahmeel also had another *w*,
2:29 Abishur's *w*, who was named Abihail,
3: 3 the sixth, Ithream, by his *w* Eglah.
4:18 His (Mered's) Egyptian *w* bore Jered,
4:19 The sons of his Jewish *w*,
7:15 Machir took a *w* whose name was Maacah;
7:16 Maacah, Machir's *w*, bore a son
7:23 come and comforted him, he visited his *w*,
8: 9 his *w* Hodesh he became the father of Jobab,
2Chr 8:11 "No *w* of mine shall dwell in the house of
11:18 Rehoboam took to himself as *w* Mahalath,
21: 6 because one of Ahab's daughters was his *w*.
22:11 of Ahaziah, and *w* of Jehoiada the priest,
25:18 'Give your daughter to my son for his *w*.'
34:22 to the prophetess Huldah, the *w* of Shallum,
Tb 1:20 except for my *w* Anna and my son Tobiah.
2: 1 and my *w* Anna and my son Tobiah were
2:11 my *w* Anna worked for hire at weaving cloth,
2:13 I called to my *w* and said:
4:13 to take a *w* for yourself from among them.
6:16 that tonight you shall have her for your *w!*
7: 2 them into his home, he said to his *w* Edna,
7: 8 His *w* Edna also wept for Tobit;
7:12 written in the Book of Moses she is your *w*.
7:13 he gave Sarah to Tobiah as his *w*
7:15 Later Raguel called his *w* Edna and said,
8: 4 Tobiah arose from bed and said to his *w*,
8: 6 him his *w* Eve to be his help and support;
8: 7 I take this *w* of mine not because of lust,
8:11 went back into the house and called his *w*,
8:19 asked his *w* to bake many loaves of bread;
8:21 half will be yours when I and my *w* die.
9: 6 heavenly blessing to you and to your *w*,
10: 4 His *w* Anna said,
10:10 handed over to Tobiah Sarah his *w*,
10:11 prosperity to you and to your *w* Sarah.
10:14 he said good-bye to Raguel and his *w* Edna,
11: 3 Let us hurry on ahead of your *w* to prepare
11:17 reached Sarah, the *w* of his son Tobiah,
12: 3 he cured my *w*;
14:12 departed with his *w* and children for Media,
Est 5:10 he summoned his friends and his *w* Zeresh.
5:14 *w* Zeresh and all his friends said to him,
6:13 When he told his *w* Zeresh and all his
6:13 his advisers and his *w* Zeresh said to him,
1Mc 10:54 Give me your daughter for my *w*;
Jb 2: 9 Then his *w* said to him,
19:17 My breath is abhorred by my *w*;
31:10 Then may my *w* grind for another,
Ps(s) 109: 9 children be fatherless, and his *w* a widow.
113: 9 barren *w* as the joyful mother of children.
128: 3 Your *w* shall be like a fruitful vine in
Prv 2:16 Saving you from the *w* of another,
5:18 And have joy of the *w* of your youth,
5:20 *w* and accept the embraces of an adulteress?
6:24 To keep you from your neighbor's *w*,
6:29 with him who goes in to his neighbor's *w*—
7: 5 That they may keep you from another's *w*,
12: 4 A worthy *w* is the crown of her husband,
18:22 He who finds a *w* finds happiness;
19:13 the nagging of a *w* is a persistent leak.
19:14 parents, but a prudent *w* is from the LORD.
21:19 than with a quarrelsome and vexatious *w*.
31:10 When one finds a worthy *w*,
31:13 The Ideal *W* Like merchant ships,
Eccl 9: 9 Enjoy life with the *w* whom you love,
Sir 7:19 Dismiss not a sensible *w*; a gracious wife
7:26 If you have a *w*, let her not seem odious
9: 1 Be not jealous of the *w* of your bosom,
9: 8 gaze not upon the beauty of another's *w*—
25: 1 and the mutual love of husband and *w*.
25: 8 Happy is he who dwells with a sensible *w*,
25:19 to aged feet is a railing *w* to a quiet man.
25:21 and shame, when a *w* supports her husband.
25:22 this from an evil *w*.
25:22 a *w* who brings no happiness to her husband.
25:24 and be not indulgent to an erring *w*.
26: 1 Happy the husband of a good *w*,
26: 2 A worthy *w* brings joy to her husband,
26: 3 A good *w* is a generous gift bestowed upon
26: 6 A jealous *w* is heartache and mourning and
26: 7 A bad *w* is a chafing yoke;
26: 8 A drunken *w* arouses great anger,
26: 9 stare an unchaste *w* can be recognized.
26:10 Keep a strict watch over an unruly *w*,
26:13 A gracious *w* delights her husband,
26:15 Choicest of blessings is a modest *w*,
26:16 a virtuous *w* is the radiance of her home.
33:20 Let neither son nor *w*,
36:24 A *w* is her husband's richest treasure,
36:25 man with no *w* becomes a homeless wanderer.
40:19 but better than either, a devoted *w*;
40:23 but better than either, a prudent *w*.
41:21 entertaining thoughts about another's *w*;
42: 6 Of a seal to keep an erring *w* at home,
42:10 lest she be seduced, or, as a *w*,
Is 54: 1 are the children of the deserted *w*
54: 6 *w* forsaken and grieved in spirit, A wife
Jer 3: 1 If man sends away his *w* and,
5: 8 they are, each neighs after another's *w*.
6:11 Yes, all will be taken, husband and *w*,
44: 7 Will you root out from Judah man and *w*,
51:22 With you I shatter man and *w*,
Ez 16:32 The adulterous *w* receives,
18: 6 if he does not defile his neighbor's *w*,
18:11 mountains, defiles the *w* of his neighbor,
18:15 of Israel, or defile his neighbor's *w*;
24:18 That evening my *w* died,
33:26 each one of you defiles his neighbor's *w*—
Dn 13:29 the daughter of Hilkiah, the *w* of Joakim."
13:63 *w* praised God for their daughter Susanna,
Hos 1: 2 Go, take a harlot *w* and harlot's children,
2: 4 for she is not my *w*,
12:13 for a wife; for a *w* Israel tended sheep.
Am 7:17 Your *w* shall be made a harlot in the city,
Mal 2:14 between you and the *w* of your youth,
2:14 she is your companion, your betrothed *w*.
2:15 not break faith with the *w* of your youth.

WIFE (cont.)
Mt 1: 6 whose mother had been the *w* of Uriah.
1:20 have no fear about taking Mary as your *w*.
1:24 and received her into his home as his *w*.
5:31 also said, 'Whenever a man divorces his *w*,
5:32 everyone who divorces his *w*—
14: 3 of Herodias, the *w* of his brother Philip.
18:25 ordered him to be sold, along with his *w*,
19: 3 man divorce his *w* for any reason whatever?"
19: 5 his father and mother and cling to his *w*,
19: 9 whoever divorces his *w* (lewd conduct is a
19:10 "If that is the case between man and *w*,
19:29 *w* or children or property for my sake will
22:24 *w* and produce offspring for his brother.'
22:25 had no children, left his *w* to his brother.
22:28 At the resurrection, whose *w* will she be,
27:19 on the bench, his *w* sent him a message:
Mk 6:17 of Herodias, the *w* of his brother Philip,
6:18 for you to live with your brother's *w*."
10: 2 permissible for a husband to divorce his *w*.
10:11 "Whoever divorces his *w* and marries
12:19 *w* but no child, his brother must take the *w*
12:20 The eldest took a *w* and died,
12:23 all come back to life, whose *w* will she be?
Lk 1: 5 his *w* was a descendant of Aaron named
1:13 Your *w* Elizabeth shall bear a son whom you
1:18 my *w* too is advanced in age."
1:24 Afterward, his *w* Elizabeth conceived.
2: 5 to register with Mary, his espoused *w*,
3:19 the subject of Herodias, his brother's *w*,
8: 3 Joanna, the *w* of Herod's steward Chuza,
14:26 father and mother, his *w* and his children,
16:18 his *w* and marries another commits adultery.
17:32 Remember Lot's *w*.
18:29 no one who has left home or *w* or brothers,
20:28 brother dies leaving a *w* and no child,
20:33 At the resurrection, whose *w* will she be?
Jn 19:25 his mother's sister, Mary the *w* of Clopas,
Acts 5: 1 Another man named Ananias and his *w*
5: 2 With the connivance of his *w* he put aside
5: 7 Three hours later Ananias' *w* came in,
18: 2 arrived from Italy with his *w* Priscilla.
24:24 days later Felix came with his Jewish *w*,
1Cor 5: 1 a man living with his father's *w*.
7: 2 his own *w* and every woman her own husband.
7: 3 his wife, the *w* hers toward her husband.
7: 4 A *w* does not belong to herself but to her
7: 4 does not belong to himself but to his *w*.
7:10 a *w* must not separate from her husband.
7:11 a husband must not divorce his *w*.
7:12 If any brother has a *w* who is an
7:14 by his believing *w*; the unbelieving wife
7:15 husband or *w* is not bound in such cases.
7:16 *W*, how do you know that you will not save
7:16 husband, that you will not save your *w*?
7:27 Are you bound to a *w*?
7:27 Are you free of a *w*?
7:33 demands and occupied with pleasing his *w*.
7:39 A *w* is bound to her husband as long as he
Gal 4:22 girl, and the other by his freeborn *w*.
4:27 many are the children of the *w* deserted
Eph 5:23 Lord because the husband is head of his *w*
5:28 He who loves his *w* loves himself.
5:31 and mother, and shall cling to his *w*,
5:33 his *w* as he loves himself, the wife for her

WIFE'S (6)
Gn 36:39 (His *w* name was Mehetabel;
39:19 As soon as the master heard his *w* story
1Chr 1:50 city was Pai, and his *w* name was Mehetabel.
8:29 founder of Gibeon whose *w* name was Maacah;
9:35 founder of Gibeon, whose *w* name was Maacah.
Tb 9: 6 your wife, and to your *w* father and mother.

WILD (119)
Gn 1:24 things, and *w* animals of all kinds."
1:25 God made all kinds of *w* animals,
1:26 and over all the *w* animals and all the
2:19 *w* animals and various birds of the air,
2:20 birds of the air, and all the *w* animals;
3:14 the animals and from all the *w* creatures;
7:14 ark, together with every kind of *w* beast,
7:21 birds, cattle, *w* animals,
8: 1 Noah and all the animals, *w* and tame,
8:19 and all the animals, *w* and tame,
9:10 and the various tame and *w* animals that
16:12 He shall be a *w* ass of a man,
31:39 brought you an animal torn by *w* beasts;
37:20 we could say that a *w* beast devoured him.
37:33 A *w* beast has devoured him!
44:28 must have been torn to pieces by *w* beasts;
49:22 wild colt, a *w* colt by a spring, a wild ass
Ex 22:12 If it has been killed by a *w* beast,
23:29 the *w* beasts will multiply against you.
32:25 foes, Aaron had let the people run *w*,
Lv 5: 2 as the carcass of an unclean *w* animal,
7:24 by *w* beasts may be put to any other use,
17:15 died of itself or was killed by a *w* beast,
22: 8 of itself or has been killed by *w* beasts.
25: 7 and for the *w* animals on your land.
26:22 I will unleash the *w* beasts against you,
Nm 23:22 out of Egypt, a *w* bull of towering might.
24: 8 out of Egypt, a *w* bull of towering might.
Dt 7:22 the *w* beasts become too numerous for you.
32:24 teeth of *w* beasts I will send among them,
33:17 of the *w* ox With which to gore the nations,
1Sm 24: 3 men in the direction of the *w* goat crags.
2Sm 17: 8 as a bear in the *w* robbed of her cubs.
21:10 on them by day, and the *w* animals by night.
2Kgs 4:39 field to gather herbs and found a *w* vine,
4:39 which he picked a clothful of *w* gourds.
6:25 a kab of *w* onion for five pieces of silver.
2Chr 25:18 But the *w* beasts of the Lebanon passed by
Jdt 11: 7 but even the *w* beasts and the cattle and
Est E:24 even shunned by *w* beasts and birds forever."
2Mc 4:25 a cruel tyrant and the rage of a *w* beast.
4:41 in *w* confusion at Lysimachus and his men.
5:11 Raging like a *w* animal,
5:27 lived like *w* animals in the hills,
5:27 grew *w* to avoid sharing the defilement.
9:15 to be eaten by vultures and *w* animals;
10: 6 like *w* animals in caves on the mountains.
Jb 5:23 the *w* beasts shall be at peace with you.
6: 5 Does the *w* ass bray when he has grass?
11:12 and the *w* jackass be made docile?
24: 5 Like *w* asses in the desert,
37: 8 the *w* beasts take to cover and remain
39: 5 Who has given the *w* ass his freedom,
39: 9 Will the *w* ox consent to serve you,
39:15 them, that the *w* beasts may trample them,
40:20 him, and of all *w* animals he makes sport.
Ps(s) 22:22 from the horns of the *w* bulls,
68:31 Rebuke the *w* beast of the reeds,
92:11 You have exalted my horn like the *w* bull's;
104:11 till the *w* asses quench their thirst.
104:18 The high mountains are for *w* goats;
148:10 You *w* beasts and all tame animals,
Wis 14: 1 to traverse the *w* waves cries out to wood
Sir 12:13 bitten, or anyone who goes near a *w* beast?
13:18 Lion's prey are the *w* asses of the desert;
Is 5: 2 grapes, but what it yielded was *w* grapes.
5: 4 of grapes, did it bring forth *w* grapes?
32:19 wasteland forever for *w* asses to frolic in,
34: 7 *W* oxen shall be struck down with fatlings,
43:20 *W* beasts honor me, jackals and ostriches,
56: 9 All you *w* beasts of the field,
Jer 14: 6 The *w* asses stand on the bare heights,
48: 6 to survive like the *w* ass in the desert!"
Bar 3:16 lorded it over the *w* beasts of the earth,
Ez 4:14 carrion flesh or that torn by *w* beasts;
5:17 and *w* beasts that shall rob you of your
14:15 I were to cause *w* beasts to prowl the land,
14:15 traversed by none because of the *w* beasts,
14:21 punishments, the sword, famine, *w* beasts,
16:30 How *w* your lust!
33:27 I have given to the *w* beasts for food;
34: 5 and became food for all the *w* beasts.
34: 8 sheep have become food for every *w* beast,
35:13 and *w* words you have spoken against me.
39: 4 the *w* beasts I am giving you to be eaten.
39:17 of every kind and to all the *w* beasts:
44:31 of itself or has been killed by *w* beasts.
Dn 2:38 men, *w* beasts,
3:81 All you beasts, *w* and tame,
4: 9 Under it the *w* beasts found shade,
4:18 for all, under which the *w* beasts lived,
4:20 and let his lot be among *w* beasts till
4:22 out from among men and dwell with *w* beasts;
4:29 among men, and shall dwell with *w* beasts;
5:21 he lived with *w* asses,
Hos 2:14 rank growth and *w* beasts shall devour them.
8: 9 a *w* ass off on its own
10: 4 grows *w* like wormwood in a plowed field!
13: 8 as though a *w* beast were to rend them.
Zep 2:14 in droves all the *w* life of the hollows;
2:15 she become a waste, a lair for *w* beasts?
Mt 3: 4 Grasshoppers and *w* honey were his food.
6:28 a lesson from the way the *w* flowers grow.
Mk 1: 6 His food was grasshoppers and *w* honey.
1:13 He was with the *w* beasts,
Acts 11: 6 of the earth, *w* beasts and reptiles,
19:40 no valid excuse for this *w* demonstration."
26:11 so *w* was my fury against them that I
Rom 11:17 off and you, a branch of the *w* olive tree,
11:24 were cut off from the natural *w* olive and,
Ti 1: 6 are known not to be *w* and insubordinate.
Jude 1:13 They are *w* ocean waves,
Rv 6: 8 and plague and the *w* beasts of the earth.
11: 7 the *w* beast that comes up from the abyss
13: 1 Then I saw a *w* beast come out of the sea
13:11 another *w* beast come up out of the earth;
13:15 The second *w* beast was then permitted to

WILDCATS (3)
Is 13:21 But *w* shall rest there and owls shall fill
34:14 *W* shall meet with desert beasts,
Jer 50:39 *w* and desert beasts shall dwell there,

WILDERNESS (23)
Gn 14: 6 Seir, as far as El-paran, close by the *w*.
16: 7 messenger found her by a spring in the *w*,
21:14 roamed aimlessly in the *w* of Beer-sheba,
21:20 lived in the *w* and became an expert bowman,
21:21 bowman, with his home in the *w* of Paran.
Lv 7:38 commanded the Israelites in the *w* of Sinai
Dt 32:10 He found them in a *w*,
1Chr 12: 9 when he was at the stronghold in the *w*.
2Chr 20:16 of the wadi which opens on the *w* of Jeruel.
20:20 they hastened out to the *w* of Tekoa.
1Mc 1:39 Her sanctuary was as desolate as a *w*;
2Mc 5:27 and about nine others withdrew to the *w*,
Jb 38:26 rain to no man's land, the unpeopled *w*;
39: 6 *w* his home and the salt flats his dwelling.
Ps(s) 29: 8 desert, the LORD shakes the *w* of Kadesh.
55: 8 I would lodge in the *w*.
68: 8 people, when you marched through the *w*,
78:40 him in the desert and grieved him in the *w*!
106:14 in the desert and tempted God in the *w*.
107: 4 They went astray in the desert *w*;
136:16 Who led his people through the *w*,
Prv 21:19 It is better to dwell in a *w* than with a
Is 27:10 an abandoned pasture, a forsaken *w*,

WILDLY (1)
Jer 4:19 My heart beats *w*,

WILES (1)
Sir 9: 4 not familiar, lest you be caught in her *w*.

WILLED (8)
2Chr 22: 7 Now it was *w* by God for Ahaziah's downfall
Wis 11:25 how could a thing remain, unless you *w* it;
12: 6 *w* to destroy by the hands of our fathers,
Mt 11:26 You have graciously *w* it so.
Lk 10:21 "Yes, Father, you have graciously *w* it so.
Gal 1: 4 present evil age, as our God and Father *w*—
Col 1:27 God has *w* to make known to them the glory
Heb 2: 4 of the gifts of the Holy Spirit as he *w*.

WILLFULLY (3)
Nm 22:29 "You have acted so *w* against me,"
2Mc 14: 3 who had *w* incurred defilement at the time
Heb 10:26 If we sin *w* after receiving the truth,

WILLFULNESS (1)
Gn 49: 6 they slew men, in their *w* they maimed oxen.

WILLING (27)
Gn 43: 4 If you are *w* to let our brother go with us,
43: 5 But if you are not *w*,
Dt 25: 8 in saying, 'I am not *w* to marry her,'
1Chr 28: 9 him with a perfect heart and a *w* soul,
29: 5 who else is *w* to contribute generously
2Chr 29:34 *w* than the priests to sanctify themselves.
Neh 1:11 all your *w* servants who revere your name.
1Mc 13:37 We are *w* to be on most peaceful terms with
15:35 we are *w* to pay you a hundred talents for
Ps(s) 51:14 salvation, and a *w* spirit sustain in me.
Sir 6:33 If you are *w* to listen,
Is 1:19 If you are *w*,
Hos 10:11 Ephraim was a trained heifer, *w* to thresh;
Mt 26:15 you *w* to give me if I hand him over to you?"
26:41 The spirit is *w* but nature is weak."
Mk 14:38 The spirit is *w* but nature is weak."
Jn 1:13 nor by carnal desire, nor by man's *w* it,
Acts 18:21 goodbye he gave them his promise, "God *w*,
25: 9 "Are you *w* to go up to Jerusalem and
25:20 I asked whether the prisoner was *w* to go
Rom 9:16 of man's *w* or doing but of God's mercy.
15:32 so that, God *w*,
1Cor 4:19 But I shall come to you soon, the Lord *w*,
7:12 is an unbeliever but is *w* to live with him,
7:13 is an unbeliever but is *w* to live with her,
Gal 4: 9 you seem *w* to enslave yourselves once more?
2Pt 1:21 has never been put forward by man's *w* it.

WILLINGLY (18)
1Chr 29: 6 forward *w* and contributed for the service
29:17 With a sincere heart I have *w* given all
2Chr 26:20 He himself fled *w*,
Neh 11: 2 *w* agreed to take up residence in Jerusalem.
1Mc 8:27 nation, the Romans will help them *w*,
2Mc 6:28 young a noble example of how to die *w*
Ps(s) 58: 3 Nay, you *w* commit crimes;
Sir 35:16 He who serves God *w* is heard;
Ez 13:19 live, lying to my people who *w* hear lies.
Hos 5:11 No, he has *w* gone after filth!
Jn 5:35 and for a while you exulted *w* in his light.
8:44 the devil, and *w* you carry out his wishes.
1Cor 9:17 If I do it *w*, I have my recompense;
2Cor 8:10 only to carry it through, but to do so *w*.
8:19 as we *w* carry on this work of charity for
12: 9 And so I *w* boast of my weaknesses instead,
Eph 6: 7 Give your service *w*, doing it for the Lord
1Pt 5: 2 Watch over it *w* as God would have you do,

WILLINGNESS (2)
2Cor 8:12 *w* to give should accord with one's means,
9: 2 I already know your *w*,

WILLOW (1)
Ez 17: 5 by plentiful waters, like a *w* he placed it,

WILLS (8)

1Mc 3:59 Whatever Heaven *w,* he will do."
Ps(s) 35:27 he *w* the prosperity of his servant!"
115: 3 whatever he *w,* he does.
135: 6 the LORD *w* he does in heaven and on earth,
Rom 8:27 intercedes for the saints as God himself *w.*
1Cor 12:11 gifts, distributing them to each as he *w.*
Jas 1:18 He *w* to bring us to birth with a word
4:15 Instead of saying, "If the Lord *w* it,

WILT (1)

Ps(s) 37: 2 wither, and like green herbs they *w.*

WILTS (5)

Ps(s) 90: 6 up anew, but by evening *w* and fades.
Is 34: 4 wither away, As the leaf *w* on the vine,
40: 7 The grass withers, the flower *w,*
40: 8 Though the grass withers and the flower *w,*
1Pt 1:24 The grass withers, the flower *w,*

WILY (2)

Nm 25:18 have been your enemies by their *w* dealings
Prv 8: 8 my mouth, no one of them is *w* or crooked;

WIN (34)

Gn 34: 3 the girl, he endeavored to *w* her affection.
Ex 14:13 the victory the LORD will *w* for you today.
Lv 7:18 it shall not *w* favor for him nor shall it
Ru 4:11 well in Ephrathah and *w* fame in Bethlehem.
1Sm 29: 4 how else can he *w* back his master's favor,
1Mc 2:51 *w* great glory and an everlasting name.
3:14 will make a name for myself and *w* glory
6:44 and *w* an everlasting name for himself.
2Mc 2:27 to *w* the gratitude of many we will gladly
4:45 sum of money if he would *w* the king over.
Prv 3: 4 *w* favor and good esteem before God and man.
Eccl 7:18 who fears God will *w* through at all events.
10:12 Words from the wise man's mouth *w* favor,
Wis 7:14 gain this treasure *w* the friendship of God,
Sir 4:12 those who seek her out *w* her favor.
13: 5 and with smiles he will *w* your confidence;
32: 2 joy and *w* praise for your hospitality.
34:18 from the lawless *w* not God's favor.
46: 1 enemy and to *w* the inheritance for Israel.
51:28 you will *w* silver and gold through her.
Is 53:12 of many, and *w* pardon for their offenses.
Jer 32: 5 in fighting the Chaldeans, you cannot *w!*"
Mt 6: 7 They think they will *w* a hearing by the
Lk 14:10 *w* you the esteem of your fellow guests.
Rom 3: 4 you say, and *w* out when you are judged."
15:18 Christ has done through me to *w* the Gentiles
1Cor 9:19 of all so as to *w* over as many as possible.
9:20 a Jew to the Jews in order to *w* the Jews.
9:20 it), that I might *w* those bound by the law.
9:21 I might *w* those not subject to the law.
9:24 In that case, run so as to *w!*
9:25 this to *w* a crown of leaves that withers,
Gal 1:10 If I were trying to *w* man's approval,
1Pt 5: 4 *w* for yourselves the unfading crown of glory.

WIND (133)

Gn 1: 2 while a mighty *w* swept over the waters.
8: 1 So God made a *w* sweep over the earth,
41: 6 of grain, thin and blasted by the east *w;*
41:23 and thin and blasted by the east *w,*
Ex 10:13 and the LORD sent an east *w* blowing over
10:13 At dawn the east *w* brought the locusts.
10:19 changed the wind to a very strong west *w,*
14:21 LORD swept the sea with a strong east *w*
15:10 When your *w* blew,
Nm 11:31 There arose a *w* sent by the LORD,
Dt 28:22 fiery drought, with blight and searing *w,*
2Sm 22:11 and flew, borne on the wings of the *w.*
22:16 LORD, at the blast of the *w* of his wrath.
1Kgs 18:45 trice, the sky grew dark with clouds and *w,*
19:11 A strong and heavy *w* was rending the
19:11 but the LORD was not in the *w.*
19:11 After the *w* there was an earthquake
2Kgs 3:17 'Though you will see neither *w* nor rain,
Jb 1:19 when suddenly a great *w* came across the
6:26 but the sayings of a desperate man as *w?*
7: 7 Remember that my life is like the *w;*
8: 2 words from your mouth are like a mighty *w!*
15: 2 airy opinions, or puff himself up with *w?*
15:30 with the *w* his blossoms shall disappear.
21:18 Let them be like straw before the *w,*
27:21 The storm *w* seizes him and he disappears;
28:25 He has weighed out the *w,*
30:15 My dignity is borne off on the *w,*
30:22 You raise me up and drive me before the *w;*
37:21 the *w* comes by and sweeps the clouds away.
38:24 whence the east *w* spreads over the earth?
Ps(s) 1: 4 are like chaff which the *w* drives away.
18:11 and flew, borne on the wings of the *w.*
18:16 LORD, at the blast of the *w* of his wrath.
18:43 ground them fine as the dust before the *w;*
35: 5 Let them be like chaff before the *w,*
48: 8 As though a *w* from the east were
78:26 He stirred up the east *w* in the heavens,
78:26 and by his power brought on the south *w.*
83:14 in a whirlwind, like chaff before the *w.*
103:16 The *w* sweeps over him and he is gone,
104: 3 you travel on the wings of the *w.*
104:10 watercourses that *w* among the mountains,
107:25 a storm *w* which tossed its waves on high.
Prv 25:14 Like clouds and *w* when no rain follows is
25:23 The north *w* brings rain,
30: 4 who has cupped the *w* in his hands?
Eccl 1: 6 the north, the *w* turns again and again,
1:14 behold, all is vanity and a chase after *w.*
1:17 learned that this also is a chase after *w.*
2:11 all was vanity and a chase after *w,*
2:17 for all is vanity and a chase after *w.*
2:26 This also is vanity and a chase after *w.*
4: 4 This also is vanity and a chase after *w.*
4: 6 than two with toil and a chase after *w!*
4:16 This also is vanity and a chase after *w.*
5:15 What then does it profit him to toil for *w?*
6: 9 This also is vanity and a chase after *w.*
11: 4 One who pays heed to the *w* will not sow,
Sg 4:16 Arise, north *w!*
4:16 Come, south *w!*
Wis 4: 4 unsteady and shall be rocked by the *w* and,
5:14 wicked is like thistledown borne on the *w,*
5:14 Like smoke scattered by the *w,*
5:23 A mighty *w* shall confront them and a
13: 2 But either fire, or *w,* or the swift air,
17:18 And were it only the whistling *w,*
Sir 5:11 Winnow not in every *w,*
18:15 Like dew that abates a burning *w,*
22:18 height will not remain when the *w* blows;
34: 2 man who catches at shadows or chases the *w,*
43:17 on the south wind, the angry north *w,*
Is 7: 2 the trees of the forest tremble in the *w.*
26:18 and writhed in pain, giving birth to *w;*
27: 8 them off with my cruel *w* in time of storm.
32: 2 Each of them will be a shelter from the *w,*
41:16 the *w* shall carry them off and the storm
41:29 works are nought, their idols are empty *w!*
49:10 the scorching *w* or the sun strike them;
57:13 All these the *w* shall carry off,
64: 5 and our guilt carries us away like the *w.*
Jer 2:24 the desert, Snuffing the *w* in her ardor
4:11 a *w* comes toward the daughter of my people."
4:12 this *w* from the heights come at my bidding;
5:13 The prophets have become *w,*
13:24 chaff that flies when the desert *w* blows.
18:17 Like the east *w,* I will scatter them
22:22 The *w* shall shepherd all your shepherds,
51: 1 those who live in Chaldea, a destroying *w.*
Bar 6:60 and the same *w* blows over all the land.
Ez 5: 2 the final third strew in the *w,*
17:10 rather wither, when touched by the east *w,*
19:12 The east *w* withered her up,
27:26 east *w* smashed you in the heart of the sea.
Dn 2:35 *w* blew them away without leaving a trace.
14:36 with the speed of the *w,*
Hos 4:19 The *w* has bound them up in its pinions;
8: 7 When they sow the *w,* they shall reap
12: 2 Ephraim chases the *w,* ever pursuing
13:15 an east wind shall come, a *w* from the LORD,
Am 4: 9 I struck you with blight and searing *w;*
4:13 formed the mountains, and created the *w,*
Jon 1: 4 however, hurled a violent *w* upon the sea,
4: 8 the sun arose, God sent a burning east *w;*
Hb 1:11 Then he veers like the *w* and is gone
Hg 2:17 of your hands with blight, searing *w,*
Zec 5: 9 coming forth with a *w* ruffling their wings,
Mt 11: 7 a reed swaying in the *w?*
14:30 But when he perceived how strong the *w* was,
14:32 had climbed into the boat, the *w* died down.
Mk 4:39 and rebuked the *w* and said to the sea:
4:39 The *w* fell off and everything grew calm.
4:41 this be that the *w* and the sea obey him?"
6:48 they tried to row with the *w* against them,
6:51 the boat with them and the *w* died down.
Lk 7:24 a reed swayed by the *w?*
8:24 and rebuked the *w* and the tumultuous waves.
12:55 When the *w* blows from the south,
Jn 3: 8 The *w* blows where it will.
6:18 moreover, with a strong *w* blowing,
Acts 2: 2 driving *w* which was heard all through the
27:13 When a gentle south *w* began to blow,
27:15 up in it and could not head into the *w,*
27:40 rudders, hoisted the foresail into the *w,*
28:13 A day later a south *w* began to blow which
Eph 4:14 carried about by every *w* of doctrine that
Jas 1: 6 like the surf tossed and driven by the *w.*
Jude 1:12 on the *w* like clouds that bring no rain.
Rv 6:13 earth like figs shaken loose by a mighty *w.*
7: 1 *w* blew on land or sea or through any tree.

WIND-BLASTED (1)

Gn 41:27 seven years, as are the seven thin, *w* ears;

WIND-BORNE (1)

Nm 23:10 of Jacob, or numbered Israel's *w* particles?

WIND-DRIVEN (1)

Jb 13:25 Will you harass a *w* leaf,

WINDINGS (1)

Lk 3: 5 The *w* shall be made straight And the rough

WINDOW (17)

Gn 26: 8 happened to look out of a *w* and was
Jos 2:15 let them down through the *w* with a rope;
2:18 *w* through which you are letting us down;
2:21 gone, she tied the scarlet cord in the *w.*
Jgs 5:28 From the *w* peered down and wailed the
1Sm 19:12 Then Michal let David down through a *w,*
2Sm 6:16 daughter Michal looked down through the *w*
1Kgs 7: 4 There were three *w* frames at either end,
2Kgs 9:30 her hair, and looked down from her *w.*
9:32 Jehu looked up to the *w* and shouted,
13:17 and said, "Open the *w* toward the east."
1Chr 15:29 daughter of Saul, looked down from her *w,*
Tb 3:11 she spread out her hands, and facing the *w,*
Prv 7: 6 For at the *w* of my house,
Hos 13: 3 threshing floor or like smoke out of the *w.*
Zep 2:14 Their call shall resound from the *w,*
2Cor 11:33 a *w* in the wall and escaped his hands.

WINDOW-SILL (1)

Acts 20: 9 on the *w* became drowsier and drowsier.

WINDOWS (25)

1Kgs 6: 4 *w* with trellises were made for the temple,
7: 4 at either end, with *w* in strict alignment.
2Kgs 7: 2 if the LORD were to make *w* in heaven,
7:19 if the LORD were to make *w* in heaven,
2Mc 3:19 to the walls, others peered through the *w,*
Eccl 12: 3 and they who look through the *w* grow blind;
Sg 2: 9 behind our wall, gazing through the *w,*
Sir 14:23 Who peeps through her *w,*
Is 24:18 For the *w* on high will be opened,
Jer 9:20 Death has come up through our *w,*
22:14 with airy rooms," Who cuts out *w* for it,
Ez 40:16 on both sides there were splayed *w*
40:16 the vestibule on both sides there were *w.*
40:22 Its windows, the *w* of its vestibule,
40:25 windows on both sides, like the other *w.*
40:29 gate and its vestibule had *w* on both sides;
40:33 gate and its vestibule had *w* on both sides;
40:36 gate and its vestibule had *w* on both sides;
41:16 around, covered from the ground to the *w.*
41:16 There were splayed *w* with trellises about
41:26 There were splayed *w* [and palmtrees] on
Dn 6:11 a day, with the *w* open toward Jerusalem.
Jl 2: 9 In at the *w* they come like thieves.

WINDS (32)

Gn 2:11 that *w* through the whole land of Havilah,
2:13 one that *w* all through the land of Cush.
Jb 37: 9 from the north *w,*
38:24 parting of the *w,* whence the east winds
Ps(s) 104: 4 You make the *w* your messengers,
135: 7 he brings forth the *w* from his storehouse.
148: 8 and mist, storm *w* that fulfill his word;
Wis 4: 4 by the wind and, by the violence of the *w,*
7:20 Powers of the *w* and thoughts of men,
Sir 39:28 There are storm *w* created to punish,
Jer 49:32 to the *w* those who shave their temples,
49:36 four *w* from the four ends of the heavens:
49:36 I will scatter them to all these *w,*
Ez 37: 9 From the four *w* come,
Dn 3:65 All you *w,* bless the Lord;
7: 2 four *w* of heaven stirred up the great sea,
8: 8 four others, facing the four *w* of heaven.
Zec 2:10 for I scatter you to the four *w* of heaven,
6: 5 "These are the four *w* of the heavens,
Mt 7:25 came and the *w* blew and buffeted his house.
7:27 the *w* blew and lashed against his house.
8:26 up and took the *w* and the sea to task.
8:27 "that even the *w* and the sea obey him?"
14:24 about in the waves raised by strong head *w.*
24:31 will assemble his chosen from the four *w,*
Mk 13:27 and assemble his chosen from the four *w,*
Lk 8:25 even the *w* and the sea and they obey him?"
Acts 27: 7 Since the *w* would not permit us to
Heb 1: 7 angels he says, "He makes his angels *w,*
Jas 3: 4 the fact that they are driven by fierce *w,*
Rv 7: 1 they held in check the earth's four *w*

WINDSTORM (1)

Lk 8:23 A *w* descended on the lake,

WINDSWEPT (1)

Is 17:13 *W,*

WINDY (1)

Jb 16: 3 Is there no end to *w* words?

WINE (260)

Gn 9:21 When he drank some of the *w,*
14:18 king of Salem, brought out bread and *w,*
19:32 our father with *w* and then lie with him,
19:33 that night they plied their father with *w,*
19:34 Let us ply him with *w* again tonight,
19:35 too, they plied their father with *w,*

WINE (cont.)
27:25 he brought him *w*,
27:28 of the earth abundance of grain and *w*.
27:37 I have enriched him with grain and *w*.
49:11 In *w* he washes his garments,
49:12 His eyes are darker than *w*,
Ex 29:40 as its libation, a fourth of a hin of *w*.
Lv 10: 9 to drink any *w* or strong drink.
23:13 libation shall be a fourth of a hin of *w*.
Nm 6: 3 *w* and strong drink; he may neither drink *w*
6:20 Only after this may the nazirite drink *w*.
15: 5 as a libation of a fourth of a hin of *w*,
15: 7 and a libation of a third of a hin of *w*,
15:10 of oil, and a libation of half a hin of *w*,
18:12 the best of the new oil and of the new *w*
18:27 threshing floor or new *w* from the press.
18:30 of the threshing floor or of the *w* press.
28: 7 in the sanctuary a fourth of a hin of *w*.
28:14 shall be half a hin of *w* for each bullock,
Dt 7:13 of your soil, your grain and *w* and oil,
11:14 have your grain, *w* and oil to gather in;
12:17 partake of your tithe of grain or *w* or oil,
14:23 your tithe of the grain, *w* and oil,
14:26 desire, oxen or sheep, *w* or strong drink,
15:14 your flock and threshing floor and *w* press,
16:13 from your threshing floor and *w* press.
18: 4 first fruits of your grain and *w* and oil,
28:39 you will not drink or store up the *w*,
28:51 they will leave you no grain or *w* or oil,
29: 5 not your food, nor *w* or beer your drink.
32:33 Their *w* is the venom of dragons and the
32:38 sacrifices and drank the *w* of your libations
33:28 been undisturbed In a land of grain and *w*,
Jgs 6:11 the *w* press to save it from the Midianites,
7:25 of Oreb and Zeeb at the *w* press of Zeeb.
9:13 I give up my *w* that cheers gods and men,
13: 4 be careful to take no *w* or strong drink
13: 7 So take neither *w* nor strong drink,
13:14 from the vine, nor take *w* or strong drink,
19:19 and bread and *w* for the woman and myself
1Sm 1:11 neither *w* nor liquor shall he drink,
1:14 Sober up from your *w*!"
1:15 I have had neither *w* nor liquor;
1:24 bull, an ephah of flour and a skin of *w*,
10: 3 loaves of bread, and the third a skin of *w*.
16:20 took five loaves of bread, a skin of *w*,
25:11 Must I take my bread, my *w*,
25:18 two hundred loaves, two skins of *w*,
2Sm 13:28 Amnon is merry with *w* and I say to you,
16: 1 an ephah of summer fruits, and a skin of *w*.
16: 2 and the *w* for those to drink who are weary
2Kgs 18:32 land like your own, a land of grain and *w*,
1Chr 9:29 vessels, as well as the fine flour, the *w*,
12:41 of meal, pressed figs, raisins, *w* oil,
27:27 for the *w* cellars was Zabdi the Shiphmite.
2Chr 2: 9 of barley, twenty thousand measures of *w*,
2:14 barley, oil and *w* which he has promised.
11:11 in them, with supplies of food, oil and *w*.
31: 5 quantities, the best of their grain, *w*,
32:28 for the harvest of grain, for *w* and oil,
Ezr 6: 9 to the God of heaven, wheat, salt, *w*,
7:22 *w*, one hundred baths;
Neh 2: 1 Artaxerxes, when the *w* was in my charge,
5:11 interest on the money, the grain, the *w*,
5:18 all kinds of *w* in abundance every ten days,
10:38 the fruit of every tree, of *w* and of oil,
10:40 Levites bring the offerings of grain, *w*,
13: 5 and utensils, the tithes in grain, *w*,
13:12 more brought in the tithes of grain, *w*,
13:15 them on their asses, together with *w*,
Tb 1: 7 I would give the tithe of grain, *w*,
4:15 Do not drink *w* till you become drunk,
4:17 bread and *w* at the burial of the virtuous,
Jdt 10: 5 a leather flask of *w* and a cruse of oil.
11:13 first fruits of grain and the tithes of *w*
12: 1 delicacies to eat and his own *w* to drink.
12:13 by him, to enjoy drinking *w* with us,
12:20 by her, drank a great quantity of *w*,
13: 2 on his bed, for he was sodden with *w*.
Est 1: 7 golden cups, and the royal *w* flowed freely,
1:10 day, when the king was merry with *w*,
C:28 of the king or drunk the *w* of libations.
5: 6 During the drinking of the *w*,
7: 2 second day, during the drinking of the *w*,
2Mc 15:38 *w* alone or water alone, whereas mixing *w*
Jb 1:13 *w* in the house of their eldest brother,
1:18 *w* in the house of their eldest brother,
24:11 They tread the *w* presses,
32:19 Like a new wineskin with *w* under pressure,
Ps(s) 4: 8 heart, more than when grain and *w* abound.
60: 5 you have given us stupefying *w*.
75: 9 LORD's hand, full of spiced and foaming *w*,
78:65 from sleep a champion overcome with *w*;
104:15 the earth, and *w* to gladden men's hearts,
Prv 3:10 grain, with new *w* your vats will overflow.
4:17 of wickedness and drink the *w* of violence.
9: 2 She has dressed her meat, mixed her *w*,
9: 5 my food, and drink of the *w* I have mixed!
20: 1 *W* is arrogant,
21:17 who loves *w* and perfume will not be rich.
23:30 *w*, those who engage in trials of blended *w*.
23:31 Look not on the *w* when it is red,
23:35 When shall I awake to seek *w* once again?"
31: 4 kings, O Lemuel, not for kings to drink *w*;
31: 6 perishing, and *w* to the sorely depressed,
Eccl 2: 3 I thought of beguiling my senses with *w*,
9: 7 joy and drink your *w* with a merry heart,
10:19 merriment and *w* makes the living glad,
Sg 1: 2 More delightful is your love than *w*!
4:10 much more delightful is your love than *w*,
5: 1 my sweetmeats, I drink my *w* and my milk.
7: 3 bowl that should never lack for mixed *w*.
7:10 And your mouth like an excellent *w*—
8: 2 spiced *w* to drink and pomegranate juice.
Wis 2: 7 us have our fill of costly *w* and perfumes,
Sir 9:10 A new friend is like new *w* which you drink
19: 2 *W* and women make the mind giddy,
31:25 strength, for *w* has been the ruin of many.
31:26 so does *w* the hearts of the insolent.
31:27 *W* is very life to man if taken in
31:27 lacks the *w* which was created for his joy?
31:28 are *w* drunk freely at the proper time.
31:29 disgrace is *w* drunk amid anger and strife.
31:30 More and more *w* is a snare for the fool;
31:31 Rebuke not your neighbor when *w* is served,
32: 4 When *w* is present, do not pour out
32: 5 of gold is a concert when *w* is served.
32: 6 seal is string music with delicious *w*.
40:20 *W* and music delight the soul,
Is 1:22 to dross, your *w* is mixed with water.
5: 2 a watchtower, and hewed out a *w* press.
5:11 into the night while *w* inflames them!
5:12 lyre, timbrel and flute, they feast on *w*;
5:22 Woe to the champions at drinking *w*,
16:10 In the *w* presses no one treads grapes,
22:13 butcher sheep, You eat meat and drink *w*:
24: 7 The *w* mourns, the wine languishes,
24: 9 They cannot sing and drink *w*;
24:11 In the streets they cry out for lack of *w*;
28: 1 on the head of him who is stupefied with *w*.
28: 7 from *w* and stumble from strong drink:
28: 7 from strong drink, overpowered by *w*;
29: 9 Be drunk, but not from *w*,
36:17 land like your own, a land of grain and *w*,
51:21 O afflicted one, drunk, but not with *w*,
55: 1 paying and without cost, drink *w* and milk!
56:12 "Come, I will fetch some *w*;
62: 8 Nor shall foreigners drink your *w*,
62: 9 drink the *w* in the courts of my sanctuary.
63: 2 your garments like those of the *w* presser?
63: 3 "The *w* press I have trodden alone,
65:11 and fill cups of blended *w* for Destiny,
Jer 13:12 wineflask is meant to be filled with *w*.
13:12 wineflask is meant to be filled with *w*?"
23: 2 am like a man who is drunk, overcome by *w*,
25:15 Take this cup of foaming *w* from my hand,
31:12 The grain, the *w*, and the oil, the sheep
35: 2 one of the rooms, and give them *w* to drink.
35: 5 *w* and offered them cups to drink the wine.
35: 6 "We do not drink *w*," they said to me:
35: 6 you nor your children shall ever drink *w*.
35: 8 All our lives we have not drunk *w*,
35:14 which he forbade his children to drink *w*,
40:10 They were to collect the *w*,
40:12 and had a rich harvest of *w* and fruit.
48:33 I drain the *w* from the wine vats,
51: 7 The nations drank its *w*,
Lam 1:15 in the *w* press virgin daughter Judah.
Ez 27:18 wealth, exchanging Helbon *w* and Zahar wool.
44:21 *w* when he is to enter the inner court.
Dn 1: 5 portion of food and *w* from the royal table.
1: 8 defile himself with the king's food or *w*;
1:16 away the food and *w* they were to receive,
5: 2 Under the influence of the *w*,
5: 4 his entertainers were drinking *w* from them,
5:23 your entertainers, might drink *w* from them;
10: 3 I ate no savory food, I took no meat or *w*,
14: 3 flour, forty sheep, and six measures of *w*.
14:11 king, set out the food and prepare the *w*;
Hos 2:10 it was I who gave her the grain, the *w*,
2:11 grain in its time, and my *w* in its season;
2:24 earth shall respond to the grain, and *w*,
4:11 Old *w* and new deprive my people of
7: 5 princes are overcome with the heat of *w*.
7:14 For wheat and *w* they lacerated themselves,
9: 2 *w* press shall not nourish them, the new *w*
9: 4 shall not pour libations of *w* to the LORD,
14: 8 his fame shall be like the *w* of Lebanon.
Jl 1: 5 wail, all you drinkers of *w*,
2:19 See, I will send you grain, and *w*,
2:24 and the vats shall overflow with *w* and oil.
4: 3 and sold a girl for the *w* they drank.
4:13 Come and tread, for the *w* press is full;
4:18 that day, the mountains shall drip new *w*,
Am 2: 8 And the *w* of those who have been fined
2:12 But you gave the nazirites *w* to drink,
5:11 vineyards, you shall not drink their *w*!
6: 6 They drink *w* from bowls and anoint
9:14 cities, Plant vineyards and drink the *w*,
Mi 2:11 pour you *w* and strong drink as my prophecy,"
6:15 no oil, and the grapes, yet drink no *w*.
Zep 1:13 plant vineyards, but not drink their *w*,
Hg 1:11 Upon the grain, and upon the *w*,
2:12 the fold touches bread, or pottage, or *w*,
Zec 9:15 They shall drink blood like *w*,
9:17 that makes the youths flourish, and new *w*,
10: 7 and their hearts shall be cheered as by *w*.
14:10 Tower of Hananel to the king's *w* presses,
Mt 9:17 do not pour new *w* into old wineskins.
9:17 they do, the skins burst, the *w* spills out,
9:17 No, they pour new *w* into new wineskins,
27:34 gave him a drink of *w* flavored with gall,
27:48 He soaked it in cheap *w*,
Mk 2:22 no man pours new *w* into old wineskins.
2:22 the *w* will burst the skins and both wine
2:22 No, new *w* is poured into new skins."
15:23 tried to give him *w* drugged with myrrh,
15:36 ran off, and soaking a sponge in sour *w*,
Lk 1:15 He will never drink *w* or strong drink,
5:37 no one pours new *w* into old wineskins.
5:37 *w* will burst the old skins, the wine will
5:38 New *w* should be poured into fresh skins.
5:39 No one, after drinking old *w*, wants new.
5:39 He says, 'I find the old *w* better.'"
7:33 came neither eating bread nor drinking *w*,
10:34 dressed his wounds, pouring in oil and *w*.
23:36 to offer him their sour *w* and saying,
Jn 2: 3 At a certain point the *w* ran out,
2: 3 mother told him, "They have no more *w*."
2: 9 waiter in charge tasted the water made *w*,
2:10 "People usually serve the choice *w* first;
2:10 have done is keep the choice *w* until now."
4:46 once more, where he had made the water *w*.
19:29 There was a jar there, full of common *w*.
19:29 *w* on some hyssop and raised it to his lips.
19:30 When Jesus took the *w*,
Acts 2:13 a sneer, "They have had too much new *w*!"
Rom 14:21 abstained from eating meat, or drinking *w*.
Eph 5:18 Avoid getting drunk on *w*;
1Tm 5:23 a little *w* for the good of your stomach,
Rv 6: 6 But spare the olive oil and the *w*!"
14: 8 drink the poisoned *w* of her lewdness!"
14:10 he too will drink the *w* of God's wrath,
16:19 cup filled with the blazing *w* of his wrath.
17: 2 have grown drunk on the *w* of her lewdness."
18: 3 drink the poisoned *w* of her lewdness.
18:13 *w* and olive oil, fine flour and grain;

WINE-DRINKING (1)
Sir 31:25 Let not *w* be the proof of your strength,

WINEBIBBER (1)
Sir 18:33 glutton and a *w* with nothing in your purse.

WINEBIBBERS (1)
Prv 23:20 Consort not with *w*,

WINEFLASK (2)
Jer 13:12 Every *w* is meant to be filled with wine.
13:12 every *w* is meant to be filled with wine?"

WINEPRESS (6)
2Kgs 6:27 from the threshing floor or the *w*?"
Sir 33:17 till like a vintager I have filled my *w*,
Rv 14:19 threw them into the huge *w* of God's wrath.
14:20 The *w* was trodden outside the city,
14:20 of the *w* that for two hundred miles around,
19:15 *w* the blazing wrath of God the Almighty.

WINEPRESSES (1)
Neh 13:15 Judah were treading the *w* on the sabbath;

WINES (2)
Is 25: 6 wines, juicy, rich food and pure, choice *w*.

WINESKIN (1)
Jb 32:19 Like a new *w* with wine under pressure,

WINESKINS (6)
Jos 9: 4 of old sacks for their asses, and old *w*,
9:13 here are our *w*, which were new when we
Mt 9:17 People do not pour new wine into old *w*.
9:17 No, they pour new wine into new *w*,
Mk 2:22 no man pours new wine into old *w*.
Lk 5:37 Moreover, no one pours new wine into old *w*.

WING (18)
1Kgs 6:24 Each *w* of a cherub measured five cubits so
6:24 *w* tip to wing tip of each was ten cubits.
6:27 so that one *w* of each cherub touched a
6:27 touched a side wall while the other *w*,
6:27 the corresponding *w* of the second cherub.
2Chr 3:12 one *w* of each cherub,
3:12 a wall of the building, while the other *w*,
3:12 the corresponding *w* of the second cherub.
1Mc 9: 1 Judah, along with the right *w* of his army.
9:12 Bacchides was on the right *w*.
9:15 drove back the right *w* and pursued them as
9:16 *w* saw that the right wing was driven back,
Is 8:23 Anguish has taken *w*, dispelled is darkness:
10:14 No one fluttered a *w*,
Ez 17: 7 there was another great eagle, great of *w*,
Dn 9:27 On the temple *w* shall be the horrible

WINGED (12)

Gn 1:21 the water teems, and all kinds of *w* birds.
Lv 11:20 "The various *w* insects that walk on all
11:21 But of the various *w* insects that walk on
11:23 All other *w* insects that have four legs
Dt 14:19 All *w* insects, too, are unclean for you
14:20 But you may eat any clean *w* creatures.
Ps(s) 78:27 and, like the sand of the sea, *w* fowl,
148:10 you creeping things and you *w* fowl.
Eccl 10:20 voice, a *w* creature may tell what you say.
Sir 11: 3 Least is the bee among *w* things,
Ez 17:23 every *w* thing in the shade of its boughs.
Jas 3: 7 Every form of life, four-footed or *w*,

WINGS (63)

Ex 19: 4 on eagle *w* and brought you here to myself.
25:20 shall have their *w* spread out above,
37: 9 The cherubim had their *w* spread out above,
Dt 32:11 So he spread his *w* to receive them and
Ru 2:12 under whose *w* you have come for refuge."
2Sm 22:11 and flew, borne on the *w* of the wind.
1Kgs 6:27 of the temple, with their *w* spread wide,
8: 6 the *w* of the cherubim in the sanctuary,
8: 7 *w* spread out over the place of the ark,
1Chr 28:18 the cherubim that spread their *w* and
2Chr 3:11 *w* of the cherubim spanned twenty cubits:
5: 7 the *w* of the cherubim in the sanctuary,
5: 8 *w* spread out over the place of the ark,
Jb 39:13 The *w* of the ostrich beat idly;
39:26 that he spreads his *w* toward the south?
Ps(s) 17: 8 hide me in the shadow of your *w* 9 from
18:11 and flew, borne on the *w* of the wind.
36: 8 of men take refuge in the shadow of your *w*.
55: 7 me, And I say, "Had I but *w* like a dove,
57: 2 In the shadow of your *w* I take refuge,
61: 5 take refuge in the shelter of your *w*!
63: 8 in the shadow of your *w* I shout for joy.
68:14 the *w* of the dove shone with silver,
91: 4 you, and under his *w* you shall take refuge;
104: 3 you travel on the *w* of the wind.
139: 9 If I take the *w* of the dawn,
Prv 23: 5 for assuredly it grows *w*,
Wis 5:11 cleft by the rushing force Of speeding *w*,
Is 6: 2 each of them had six *w*:
8: 8 spread its *w* the full width of your land,
40:31 they will soar as with eagles' *w*;
Jer 48:40 an eagle he soars, spreads his *w* over Moab.
49:22 soars aloft, and spreads his *w* over Bozrah;
Ez 1: 6 human, but each had four faces and four *w*,
1: 8 hands were under their wings, and the *w*
1: 9 their *w* looked out on all their four sides;
1:11 Each had two *w* spread out above so that
1:11 the other two *w* of each covered his body.
1:23 the firmament their *w* were stretched out,
1:24 Then I heard the sound of their *w*,
1:24 they lowered their *w*
3:13 the noise made by the *w* of the living
10: 5 The noise of the *w* of the cherubim could
10: 8 could be seen under the *w* of the cherubim.]
10:16 lifted their *w* to rise from the earth,
10:19 These lifted their *w*, and I saw them rise
10:21 Each had four faces and four *w*;
10:21 like human hands were under their *w*.
11:22 Then the cherubim lifted their *w*,
17: 3 The great eagle, with great *w*,
Dn 7: 4 first was like a lion, but with eagle's *w*.
7: 4 While I watched, the *w* were plucked;
7: 6 its back were four *w* like those of a bird,
Na 3:17 grasshoppers will spread their *w* and fly,
Zec 5: 9 their wings, for they had *w* like the wings
Mt 23:37 mother bird gathers her young under her *w*,
Lk 13:34 mother bird collects her young under her *w*,
Rv 4: 8 creatures had six *w* and eyes all over,
9: 9 Their *w* made a sound like the roar of many
12:14 But the woman was given the *w* of a

WINGSPREAD (1)

2Chr 3:13 The combined *w* of the two cherubim was

WINK (1)

Ps(s) 35:19 let not my undeserved foes *w* knowingly.

WINKS (3)

Prv 6:13 He *w* his eyes,
10:10 He who *w* at a fault causes trouble,
16:30 He who *w* his eye is plotting trickery;

WINNERS (1)

2Tm 2: 5 the *w* crown unless he has kept the rules.

WINNING (6)

2Mc 5: 6 that he was *w* a victory over his enemies,
Prv 22:11 of *w* speech has the king for his friend.
Is 63:12 before them, *w* for himself eternal renown;
Jn 4: 1 he was *w* over and baptizing more disciples
Acts 2:47 God and *w* the approval of all the people.
1Cor 9:22 a weak person with a view to *w* the weak.

WINNOW (6)

Wis 5:23 confront them and a tempest *w* them out;
Sir 5:11 *W* not in every wind,
Is 30:28 Will *w* the nations with a destructive
41:16 When you *w* them,
Jer 4:11 Not to *w*,
51: 2 winnowers to *w* her and lay waste her land;

WINNOWED (2)

Wis 11:20 and *w* out by your mighty spirit;
Jer 15: 7 I *w* them with the fan in every city gate.

WINNOWERS (1)

Jer 51: 2 *w* to winnow her and lay waste her land;

WINNOWING (2)

Ru 3: 2 he will be *w* barley at the threshing floor.
Is 30:28 winnow the nations with a destructive *w*,

WINNOWING-FAN (2)

Mt 3:12 His *w* is in his hand.
Lk 3:17 His *w* is in his hand to clear his

WINNOWINGS (1)

Is 30:28 and with repeated *w* will he battle against

WINNOWS (1)

Prv 20:26 A wise king *w* the wicked,

WINS (10)

Prv 7:21 She *w* him over by her repeated urging,
8:35 me finds life, and *w* favor from the LORD;
11:16 A gracious woman *w* esteem,
12: 2 The good man *w* favor from the LORD,
Sir 13:21 what he says is odious, it *w* approval.
19:21 dishonest, which by duplicity *w* a judgment.
37:25 wise for his people *w* a heritage of glory,
Rom 14:18 way pleases God and *w* the esteem of men.
Rv 2:26 " 'To the one who *w* the victory,
21: 7 *w* the victory shall inherit these gifts;

WINTER (18)

Gn 8:22 heat, seedtime and harvest, Summer and *w*,
Tb 2:12 Late in *w* she finished the cloth and sent
Ps(s) 74:17 summer and *w* you made.
Sg 2:11 "For see, the *w* is past,
Is 18: 6 them all the beasts of the earth shall *w*.
Jer 36:22 Now the king was sitting in his *w* house,
Am 3:15 I strike the *w* house and the summer house;
Zec 14: 8 sea, and it shall be so in summer and in *w*.
Mt 24:20 will not have to flee in *w* or on a sabbath,
Mk 13:18 praying that none of this happens in *w*.
Jn 10:22 It was *w*, and the time came for the feast
Acts 27:12 the harbor was not fit to pass the *w* in,
27:12 of making Phoenix and spending the *w* there.
28:11 ship which had passed the *w* at the island.
1Cor 16: 6 even to spend the *w* with you
2Tm 4:21 Get here before *w* if you can.
Ti 3:12 I have decided to spend the *w* there.
Jas 5: 7 soil receives the *w* and the spring rains.

WINTRY (1)

Wis 16:29 a *w* frost and runs off like useless water.

WIPE (25)

Gn 6: 7 "I will *w* out from the earth the men whom
7: 4 and so I will *w* out from the surface of
18:24 would you *w* out the place,
Ex 9:15 pestilence as would *w* you from the earth.
23:23 and I will *w* them out.
Lv 26:22 of your children and *w* out your livestock,
Nm 14:12 strike them with pestilence and *w* them out.
2Kgs 21:13 will *w* Jerusalem clean as one wipes a dish,
Est 8:11 their lives, and to kill, destroy, *w* out,
1Mc 3:42 to destroy and utterly *w* out the people.
12:53 them and *w* out their memory from among
2Mc 8: 9 nations to *w* out the entire Jewish race.
12: 7 and *w* out the entire population of Joppa.
Ps(s) 51: 3 of your compassion *w* out my offense.
Sir 21: 4 Violence and arrogance *w* out wealth;
Is 25: 8 GOD will *w* away the tears from all faces;
43:25 It is I, I, who *w* out,
Jer 31:16 of mourning, *w* the tears from your eyes.
Bar 6:12 They *w* their faces clean of the house dust
Ez 9: 6 and maidens, women and children *w* them out!
11:13 you utterly *w* out what remains of Israel?"
25:16 and *w* out the remnant on the seacoast.
Lk 19:44 They will *w* you out,
Rv 7:17 and God will *w* every tear from their eyes."
21: 4 He shall *w* every tear from their eyes,

WIPED (18)

Gn 7:23 The LORD *w* out every living thing on earth:
7:23 all were *w* out from the earth.
34:30 attack me, I and my family will be *w* out."
Dt 2:15 till he *w* them out of the camp completely.
4:26 length of time but shall be promptly *w* out.
12:29 once they have been *w* out before you and
Jgs 21:17 one of the Israelite tribes will be *w* out.
Tb 7:16 over her, she *w* away the tears and said:
Est 3:13 be killed, destroyed, *w* out in one day,
Prv 6:33 get, and his disgrace will not be *w* away;
Wis 12: 9 or *w* out at once by terrible beasts or by
Sir 40:12 from bribes or injustice will be *w* out,
47: 4 the giant and *w* out the people's disgrace,
Is 26:14 them, and *w* out all memory of them.
Lk 7:38 Then she *w* them with her hair,
7:44 with her tears and *w* them with her hair.
11:41 have as alms, all will be *w* clean for you.
Acts 3:19 Turn to God, that your sins may be *w* away!

WIPES (4)

2Kgs 21:13 will wipe Jerusalem clean as one *w* a dish,
Prv 30:20 she eats, *w* her mouth,
Sir 22: 2 whoever touches him *w* his hands.
Bar 6:23 unless someone *w* away the corrosion,

WIPING (2)

Lv 26:44 reject or spurn them, lest, by *w* them out,
2Kgs 21:13 as one wipes a dish, *w* it inside and out.

WISDOM (303)

Gn 3: 6 to the eyes, and desirable for gaining *w*.
Dt 4: 6 of your *w* and intelligence to the nations,
34: 9 of Nun, was filled with the spirit of *w*,
1Kgs 2: 6 Act with the *w* you possess;
3:28 in him the *w* of God for giving judgment.
5: 9 God gave Solomon *w* and exceptional
5:10 the Cedemites and all the Egyptians in *w*.
5:14 came to hear Solomon's *w* from all nations,
5:14 kings of the earth who had heard of his *w*.
5:26 gave Solomon *w* as he promised him,
10: 4 of Sheba witnessed Solomon's great *w*,
10: 6 about your deeds and your *w* is true,"
10: 7 Your *w* and prosperity surpass the report I
10: 8 before you always and listen to your *w*.
10:23 in riches and *w* all the kings of the earth.
10:24 him the *w* which God had put in his heart.
11:41 of Solomon, with all his deeds and his *w*,
2Chr 1:10 *w* and knowledge to lead this people,
1:11 but have asked for *w* and knowledge in
1:12 you king, *w* and knowledge are given you;
9: 3 the queen of Sheba witnessed Solomon's *w*,
9: 5 about your deeds and your *w* is true,"
9: 6 did not tell me the half of your great *w*;
9: 7 before you always and listen to your *w*.
9:22 of the earth in riches as well as in *w*.
9:23 him the *w* which God had put in his heart.
Ezr 7:25 *w* of your God which is in your possession,
Jdt 8:29 Not today only is your *w* made evident,
11: 8 we have heard of your *w* and sagacity,
11:20 they marveled at her *w* and exclaimed,
Est B: 3 Haman, who excels among us in *w*,
2Mc 2: 9 It is also related how Solomon in his *w*
Jb 4:21 they die without knowing *w*."
11: 6 the secrets of *w* are twice as effective:
12: 2 intelligent folk, and with you *w* shall die!
12:12 So with old age is *w*,
12:13 With him are *w* and might;
13: 5 This for you would be *w*.
15: 8 of God, and do you restrict *w* to yourself?
26: 3 How you counsel, as though he had no *w*;
28:12 But whence can *w* be obtained,
28:20 Whence, then, comes *w*,
28:27 Then he saw *w* and appraised it,
28:28 Behold, the fear of the LORD is *w*;
32: 7 speak, I thought, and many years teach *w*!
32:13 Yet do not say, "We have met *w*.
33:33 be silent while I teach you *w*.
38:36 Who puts *w* in the heart,
38:37 Who counts the clouds in his *w*?
39:17 For God has withheld *w* from her and has
Ps(s) 19: 8 is trustworthy, giving *w* to the simple.
37:30 of *w* and his tongue utters what is right.
49: 4 My mouth shall speak *w*;
51: 8 and in my inmost being you teach me *w*.
90:12 days aright, that we may gain *w* of heart.
104:24 In *w* you have wrought them all
105:22 to be like him and teach his elders *w*.
111:10 The fear of the LORD is the beginning of *w*;
119:66 Teach me *w* and knowledge,
136: 5 Who made the heavens in *w*,
147: 5 to his *w* there is no limit.
Prv 1: 2 That men may appreciate *w* and discipline,
1: 7 *w* and instruction fools despise.
1:20 *W* cries aloud in the street,
2: 2 my commands, Turning your ear to *w*,
2: 6 For the LORD gives *w*,
2:10 For *w* will enter your heart,
3:13 Happy the man who finds *w*,
3:19 The LORD by *w* founded the earth,
4: 5 "Get *w*, get understanding!
4: 7 The beginning of *w* is:
4: 7 get *w*; at the cost of all you have,
4:11 On the way of *w* I direct you,
5: 1 My son, to my *w* be attentive,
6: 6 O sluggard, study her ways and learn *w*;
7: 4 Say to *W*, "You are my sister!"

WISDOM (cont.)
8: 1 Does not *W* call,
8:11 [For *W* is better than corals,
8:12 "I, *W*, dwell with experience,
8:33 instruction and *w* do not reject!
9: 1 *W* has built her house,
9:10 The beginning of *w* is the fear of the LORD,
10:13 On the lips of the intelligent is found *w*,
10:23 so is *w* for the man of sense.
10:31 The mouth of the just yields *w*,
11: 2 but with the humble is *w*.
13:10 but with those who take counsel is *w*.
14: 1 *W* builds her house,
14: 6 The senseless man seeks in vain for *w*,
14: 8 man's *w* gives him knowledge of his way,
14:33 In the heart of the intelligent *w* abides,
15:33 The fear of the LORD is training for *w*,
16:16 How much better to acquire *w* than gold!
17:16 in the fool's hand are the means to buy *w*,
17:24 man of intelligence fixes his gaze on *w*,
18: 4 but the source of *w* is a flowing brook.
21:30 There is no *w*,
23: 9 he will despise the *w* of your words.
23:23 *w*,
24: 3 By *w* is a house built,
24: 7 For a fool, to be silent is *w*;
24:14 Such, you must know, is *w* to your soul.
28:26 is a fool, but he who walks in *w* is safe.
29: 3 He who loves *w* makes his father glad,
29:15 The rod of correction gives *w*,
30: 3 Neither have I learned *w*,
31:26 She opens her mouth in *w*,
Eccl 1:13 *w* all things that are done under the sun.
1:16 I have become great and stored up *w*
1:16 has broad experience of *w* and knowledge";
1:17 I applied my mind to know *w* and knowledge,
1:18 For in much *w* there is much sorrow,
2: 3 wine, though my mind was concerned with *w*,
2: 9 my *w*,
2:12 I went on to the consideration of *w*,
2:13 And I saw that *w* has the advantage over
2:21 has labored with *w* and knowledge and skill,
2:26 sees fit he gives *w* and knowledge and joy;
7:10 For it is not in *w* that you ask about this.
7:11 *W* and an inheritance are good,
7:12 of *w* is as the protection of money;
7:12 is that *w* preserves the life of its owner.
7:19 *W* is a better defense for the wise man
7:22 All these things I probed in *w*.
7:23 I said, "I will acquire *w*";
7:25 I sought and pursued *w* and reason,
8: 1 A man's *w* illumines his face,
8:16 *w* and to observe what is done on earth,
9:10 *w* in the nether world where you are going.
9:15 wise, and he delivered it through his *w*.
9:16 *W* is better than force," yet the wisdom
10: 1 weighty than *w* or wealth is a little folly!
Wis 1: 4 into a soul that plots evil *w* enters not,
1: 6 For *w* is a kindly spirit,
3:11 who despises *w* and instruction is doomed.
6: 9 you may learn *w* and that you may not sin.
6:12 Resplendent and unfading is *W*,
6:20 the desire for *W* leads up to a kingdom.
6:21 you princes of the peoples, honor *W*,
6:22 Now what *w* is, and how she came
6:23 because that can have no fellowship with *W*.
7: 7 I pleaded and the spirit of *W* came to me.
7:12 in them all, because *W* is their leader,
7:15 guide of *W* and the director of the wise.
7:22 for *W*,
7:24 For *W* is mobile beyond all motion,
7:28 God loves, be it not one who dwells with *W*.
7:30 but wickedness prevails not over *W*.
8: 5 in life, what is more rich than *W*,
8:17 there is immortality in kinship with *W*,
9: 2 in your *w* have established man to rule
9: 4 Give me *W*, the attendant at your throne,
9: 6 be perfect among the sons of men, if *W*,
9: 9 Now with you is *W*,
9:17 *W* and sent your holy spirit from on high?
9:18 was your pleasure, and were saved by *W*.
10: 4 the earth was flooded, *W* again saved it,
10: 8 For those who forsook *W* first were bereft
10: 9 But *W* delivered from tribulations those
10:21 Because *W* opened the mouths of the dumb,
14: 2 latter, and *W* the artificer produced it.
14: 5 that the products of your *W* be not idle;
Sir 1: 1 All *w* comes from the LORD and with him it
1: 4 Before all things else *w* was created;
1:12 The beginning of *w* is fear of the LORD,
1:14 Fullness of *w* is fear of the LORD;
1:18 The root of *w* is fear of the LORD;
1:21 words, then the lips of many herald his *w*.
1:23 If you desire *w*, keep the commandments,
1:24 For fear of the LORD is *w* and culture;
3:24 where there is no knowledge, there is no *w*.
4:11 *W* instructs her children and admonishes
4:23 the proper time, and hide not away your *w*;
4:24 it is through speech that *w* becomes known,
6:18 thus will you find *w* with graying hair.
6:37 mind, and the *w* you desire he will grant.
7: 5 and before the king flaunt not your *w*.
10: 3 a city grows through the *w* of its princes.
10:25 Flaunt not your *w* in managing your affairs,
10:29 The poor man is honored for his *w* as the
11: 1 The poor man's *w* lifts his head high and
11:15 *W* and understanding and knowledge of
13:22 are silent, his *w* they extol to the clouds.
14:20 Happy the man who meditates on *w*,
15: 1 who is practiced in the law will come to *w*.
15:18 Immense is the *w* of the LORD;
16:23 to my words, While I propose measured *w*,
17: 6 With *w* and knowledge he fills them;
18:28 Any learned man should make *w* known,
18:29 trained in her words must show their *w*,
19:17 *w* is fear of the LORD; perfect wisdom
19:18 The knowledge of wickedness is not *w*,
20:29 Hidden *w* and unseen treasure
20:30 his folly than the one who hides his *w*.
21:11 who is perfect in fear of the LORD has *w*.
21:15 When an intelligent man hears words of *w*,
21:18 Like a house in ruins is *w* to a fool;
22: 6 lashes and discipline are at all times *w*.
24: 1 *W* sings her own praises,
24:23 It overflows like the Pishon, with *w*—
24:26 first man never finished comprehending *w*,
25: 5 How becoming to the aged is *w*,
25:10 He who finds *w* is great indeed,
32: 3 that is only your right, but temper your *w*,
32: 4 and flaunt not your *w* at the wrong time.
33: 2 He who hates the law is without *w*,
33: 8 It is due to the LORD's *W* that they differ;
33:18 I toiled, but for every seeker after *w*.
34: 8 and perfect *w* is found in the mouth of
38: 2 From God the doctor has his *w*,
38:24 The scribe's profession increases his *w*;
39: 1 He explores the *w* of the men of old and
39: 6 of *w* and in prayer give thanks to the LORD,
39: 8 He will show the *w* of what he has learned
39:10 Peoples will speak of his *w*,
40:18 name, but better than either, attaining *w*.
42:21 Perennial is his almighty *w*;
43:35 and to those who fear him he gives *w*.
44:15 At gatherings their *w* is retold,
45:26 *w* of heart to govern his people in justice,
51:13 When I was young and innocent, I sought *w*.
51:25 gain, at no cost, *w* for yourselves.
Is 10:13 my own power I have done it, and by my *w*,
11: 2 a spirit of *w* and of understanding,
28:29 wonderful is his counsel and great his *w*.
29:14 The *w* of its wise men shall perish and the
33: 6 riches that save her, are *w* and knowledge;
47:10 Your *w* and your knowledge led you astray,
Jer 8: 9 word of the LORD, of what avail is their *w*?
9:22 Let not the wise man glory in his *w*,
10:12 his power, established the world by his *w*,
49: 7 Is there no more *w* in Teman,
49: 7 the prudent, has their *w* become corrupt?
51:15 power, and established the world by his *w*,
Bar 3:12 You have forsaken the fountain of *w*!
3:15 Who has found the place of *w*,
3:23 These have not known the way to *w*,
Ez 28: 4 By your *w* and your intelligence you
28: 5 By your great *w* applied to your trading
28: 7 their swords against your beauteous *w*,
28:12 of complete *w* and perfect beauty,
28:17 the sake of splendor you debased your *w*.
Dn 1:20 *w* or prudence which the king put to them,
2:20 forever and ever, for *w* and power are his.
2:21 He gives *w* to the wise and knowledge to
2:23 because you have given me *w* and power.
5:11 to have brilliant knowledge and god-like *w*.
5:14 brilliant knowledge and extraordinary *w*.
Mi 6: 9 [It is *w* to fear your name!]
Mt 11:19 Yet time will prove where *w* lies."
12:42 of the earth to listen to the *w* of Solomon;
13:54 this man get such *w* and miraculous powers?
Mk 6: 2 What kind of *w* is he endowed with?
Lk 1:17 and the rebellious to the *w* of the just,
2:40 grew in size and strength, filled with *w*,
2:52 in *w* and age and grace before God and men.
7:35 God's *w* is vindicated by all who accept it."
11:31 of the world to listen to the *w* of Solomon,
11:49 That is why the *w* of God has said,
21:15 for I will give you words and a *w*
Acts 6:10 for the *w* and spirit with which he spoke.
7:10 favor and *w* in the court of the Pharaoh,
Rom 11:33 riches and the *w* and the knowledge of God!
1Cor 1:17 not with wordy *w*,"
1:19 says, "I will destroy the *w* of the wise,
1:20 God turned the *w* of this world into folly?
1:21 Since in God's *w* the world did not come to
1:21 world did not come to know him through *w*,"
1:22 demand "signs" and Greeks look for *w*,"
1:24 Christ the power of God and the *w* of God.
1:26 many of you are wise, as men account *w*;
1:30 He has made him our *w* and also our justice,
2: 1 with any particular eloquence or *w*."
2: 5 on the *w* of men but on the power of God.
2: 6 a certain *w* which we express among the
2: 6 It is not a *w* of this age,
2: 7 No, what we utter is God's *w*:
2: 7 a mysterious, a hidden *w*.
2: 9 Of this *w* it is written:
2:10 revealed this *w* to us through the Spirit.
2:13 human *w* but in words taught by the Spirit,
3:19 the *w* of this world is absurdity with God.
12: 8 To one the Spirit gives *w* in discourse,
2Cor 1:12 has been prompted, not by debased human *w*,
Eph 1: 9 us the *w* to understand fully the mystery,
1:17 of *w* and insight to know him clearly.
3:10 God's manifold *w* is made known to the
Col 1: 9 through perfect *w* and spiritual insight.
1:28 and teach them in the full measure of *w*,
2: 3 treasure of *w* and knowledge is hidden.
2:23 certain show of *w* in their affected piety,
3:16 In *w* made perfect,
2Tm 3:15 the source of the *w* which through faith in
Jas 1: 5 If any of you is without *w*,
3:15 *W* like this does not come from above.
3:17 *W* from above,
2Pt 3:15 you this in the spirit of *w* that is his,
Rv 5:12 receive power and riches, *w* and strength,
7:12 and glory, *w* and thanksgiving and honor,
13:18 A certain *w* is needed here;
17: 9 Here is the clue for one who possesses *w*!

WISDOM'S (4)
Sir 1: 5 To whom has *w* root been revealed?
1:16 *W* garland is fear of the LORD,
1:22 *w* treasures is the paragon of prudence;
51:24 How long will you be deprived of *w* food,

WISE (213)
Gn 41:33 let Pharaoh seek out a *w* and discerning
41:39 one can be as *w* and discerning as you are.
Ex 7:11 in turn, summoned *w* men and sorcerers,
Dt 1:13 *w*, intelligent and experienced men
1:15 men of your tribes, *w* and experienced,
4: 6 nation is truly a *w* and intelligent people.'
16:19 *w* and twists the words even of the just.
2Sm 14:20 But my lord is as *w* as an angel of God,
20:16 Then a *w* woman from the city stood on the
1Kgs 3:12 I give you a heart so *w* and understanding
5:21 David a *w* son to rule this numerous people."
2Chr 2:11 a *w* son of intelligence and understanding,
Ezr 8:16 Zechariah, and Meshullam, *w* leaders,
Tb 4:18 "Seek counsel from every *w* man,
Jdt 10:19 It is not *w* to leave one man of them alive,
Est 1:13 conferred with the *w* men versed in the law,
1Mc 2:65 your brother Simeon who I know is a *w* man;
Jb 5:13 He catches the *w* in their own ruses,
9: 4 God is *w* in heart and mighty in strength;
15: 2 Should a *w* man answer with airy opinions,
15:18 What *w* men relate and have not
17:10 for I shall not find a *w* man among you!
22: 2 Though to himself a *w* man be profitable!
32: 9 It is not those of many days who are *w*,
34: 2 Hear, O *w* men, my discourse,
34:34 say to me, every *w* man who hears my views:
35:11 us *w* rather than the birds of the heavens?"
37:24 none can see him, however *w* their hearts.
Ps(s) 14: 2 see if there be one who is *w* and seeks God.
49:11 For he can see that *w* men die,
53: 3 see if there be one who is *w* and seeks God.
94: 8 and, you fools, when will you be *w*?
107:43 Who is *w* enough to observe these things
Prv 1: 3 May receive training in *w* conduct,
1: 5 A *w* man by hearing them will advance in
1: 6 the words of the *w* and their riddles.
3: 7 Be not *w* in your own eyes.
3:35 Honor is the possession of *w* men,
9: 8 reprove a *w* man,
9: 9 Instruct a *w* man,
9:12 If you are *w*, it is to your own advantage;
10: 1 A *w* son makes his father glad,
10: 8 A *w* man heeds commands,
10:14 *W* men store up knowledge,
11:29 the fool will become slave to the *w* man.
12:15 eyes, but he who listens to advice is *w*.
12:18 but the tongue of the *w* is healing.
13: 1 A *w* son loves correction,
13:14 teaching of the *w* is a fountain of life,
13:20 Walk with wise men and you will become *w*,
14: 3 back, but the lips of the *w* preserve them.
14:16 The *w* man is cautious and shuns evil;
14:24 The crown of the *w* is resourcefulness;
15: 2 The tongue of the *w* pours out knowledge,
15: 7 The lips of the *w* disseminate knowledge,
15:12 to *w* men he will not go.
15:20 A *w* son makes his father glad,
15:31 to salutary reproof will abide among the *w*.
16:14 of death, but a *w* man can pacify it.
16:21 The *w* man is esteemed for his discernment,
16:23 The mind of the *w* man makes him eloquent,
17:27 He who spares his words is truly *w*,
17:28 fool, if he keeps silent, is considered *w*;
18:15 and the ear of the *w* seeks knowledge.
19:20 that you may eventually become *w*.
20: 1 none who goes astray for it is *w*.
20:15 of corals, *w* lips are a precious ornament.
20:18 so with *w* guidance wage your war.
20:26 A *w* king winnows the wicked,
21:11 when the *w* man is instructed,
21:20 treasure remains in the house of the *w*,
21:22 The *w* man storms a city of the mighty,
22:17 The sayings of the *w*:
23:15 My son, if your heart be *w*,

23:19 Hear, my son, and be *w*,
23:24 he who begets a *w* son will have joy in him.
24: 5 A *w* man is more powerful than a strong man,
24: 6 it is by *w* guidance that you wage your war,
24:23 These also are Sayings of the *w*;
25:12 gold, is a *w* reprover to an obedient ear.
26: 5 folly, lest he become *w* in his own eyes.
26:12 You see a man *w* in his own eyes?
27:11 If you are *w*, my son, you will gladden my
28: 7 He who keeps the law is a *w* son,
28:11 The rich man is *w* in his own eyes,
29: 8 the city ablaze, but *w* men calm the fury.
29: 9 If a *w* man disputes with a fool,
29:11 but by biding his time, the *w* man calms it.
30:24 on the earth, and yet are exceedingly *w*:
Eccl 2:14 The *w* man has eyes in his head,
2:15 to befall me also, why then should I be *w*?
2:16 Neither of the *w* man nor of the fool will
2:16 it that the *w* man dies as well as the fool!
2:19 knows whether he will be a *w* man or a fool?
2:19 all the fruits of my *w* labor under the sun.
4:13 Better is a poor but *w* youth than an old
6: 8 what advantage has the *w* man over the fool,
7: 4 heart of the *w* is in the house of mourning,
7: 5 It is better to hearken to the *w* man's
7: 7 For oppression can make a fool of a *w* man,
7:19 Wisdom is a better defense for the *w* man
8: 1 Who is like the *w* man,
8: 5 *w* man's heart knows times and judgments;
8:17 and even if the *w* man says that he knows,
9: 1 the just, the *w*,
9:11 by the valiant, nor a livelihood by the *w*,
9:13 other hand I saw this *w* deed under the sun,
9:15 city lived a man who, though poor, was *w*,
9:17 "The quiet words of the *w* are better
10: 2 The *w* man's understanding turns him to his
10:12 Words from the *w* man's mouth win favor,
12: 9 Besides being *w*, Qoheleth taught
12:11 The sayings of the *w* are like goads;
Wis 4:17 For they see the death of the *w* man and do
6:24 number of *w* men is the safety of the world,
7:15 guide of Wisdom and the director of the *w*.
Sir 1: 6 is but one, *w* and truly awe-inspiring,
3:28 and an attentive ear is the *w* man's joy.
6:33 if you give heed, you will be *w*.
6:34 whoever is *w*,
6:35 let no *w* saying escape you.
7:21 *w* servant be dear to you as your own self;
8: 8 Spurn not the discourse of the *w*,
9:14 measure, and associate with the *w*.
10: 1 *w* magistrate lends stability to his people,
10:22 just to despise a man who is *w* but poor,
10:24 prudent slave, the *w* man does not complain.
15:10 praise is offered by the *w* man's tongue;
16: 4 Through one *w* man can a city be peopled;
18:27 A *w* man is circumspect in all things;
19:25 a *w* man is known as such when first met.
20: 1 and a man may be *w* to hold his peace.
20: 4 One man is silent and is thought *w*,
20: 6 *w* man is silent till the right time comes,
20:12 *w* man makes himself popular by a few words,
20:26 A *w* man advances himself by his words,
21: 7 speaker but the *w* man knows his own faults.
21:13 A *w* man's knowledge wells up in a flood,
21:16 charm to be found upon the lips of the *w*.
21:21 a chain of gold is learning to a *w* man,
21:26 mouths, *w* men's words are in their hearts.
27:11 Ever *w* are the discourses of the devout,
32: 8 in those few words, be like the *w* man,
37:19 A man may be *w* and benefit many,
37:20 Though a man may be *w*,
37:21 When a man is *w* to his own advantage,
37:22 When a man is *w* to his people's advantage,
37:24 One *w* for himself has full enjoyment,
37:25 *w* for his people wins a heritage of glory,
38:24 is free from toil can become a *w* man.
47:12 his merits he had as his successor a *w* son,
47:14 How *w* you were when you were young,
50:27 *W* instruction, appropriate proverbs,
50:28 things, *w* the man who takes them to heart!
Is 5:21 Woe to those who are *w* in their own sight,
19:11 say to Pharaoh, "I am a disciple of *w* men,
19:12 Where then are your *w* men?
29:14 The wisdom of its *w* men shall perish and
31: 2 Yet he too is *w* and will bring disaster;
32: 4 The flighty will become *w* and capable,
44:25 I turn *w* men back and make their knowledge
Jer 4:22 They are *w* in evil,
8: 8 How can you say "We are *w*,
8: 9 The *w* are confounded,
9:11 Who is so *w* that he can understand this?
9:22 Let not the *w* man glory in his wisdom,
18:18 the priests, nor of counsel from the *w*,
50:35 Babylon's people, her princes and *w* men!
51:57 will make her princes and her *w* men drunk,
Dn 1: 4 any defect, handsome, intelligent and *w*,
2:12 the *w* men of Babylon to be put to death.
2:13 was issued that the *w* men should be slain,
2:14 had set out to kill the *w* men of Babylon:
2:18 with the rest of the *w* men of Babylon.
2:21 *w* and knowledge to those who understand.
2:24 appointed to destroy the *w* men of Babylon,
2:24 "Do not put the *w* men of Babylon to death.
2:27 which the king has inquired, the *w* men,
2:48 prefect over all the *w* men of Babylon.
4: 3 So I issued a decree that all the *w* men of
4:15 Although none of the *w* men in my kingdom
5: 7 means," he said to the *w* men of Babylon,
5: 8 But though all the king's *w* men came in,
5:15 the *w* men and enchanters were brought in
11:33 The nation's *w* men shall instruct the many;
11:35 Of the *w* men, some shall fall,
12: 3 But the *w* shall shine brightly like the
12:10 understanding, but the *w* shall have it.
Hos 14:10 Let him who is *w* understand these things;
Ob 1: 8 day make the *w* men disappear from Edom,
Zec 9: 2 Tyre too, and Sidon, however *w* they be.
Mt 7:24 like the *w* man who built his house on rock.
23:34 send you prophets and *w* men and scribes.
Rom 1:22 They claimed to be *w*,
12:16 Do not be *w* in your own estimation.
16:19 I want you to be *w* in regard to what is
16:27 to him, the God who alone is *w*,
1Cor 1:19 "I will destroy the wisdom of the *w*,
1:20 Where is the *w* man to be found?
1:26 Not many of you are *w*,
1:27 the world considers absurd to shame the *w*;
2: 4 the persuasive force of *w*" argumentation,
3:10 foundation as a *w* master-builder might do,
3:18 of you thinks he is *w* in a worldly way,
3:18 In that way he will really be *w*,
3:19 "He catches the *w* in their craftiness";
3:20 knows how empty are the thoughts of the *w*."
4:10 Ah, but in Christ you are *w*!
6: 5 there is no one among you *w* enough
2Cor 11:19 *w* yourselves, you gladly put up with fools.
2Tm 1: 7 one that makes us strong, loving, and *w*.
Jas 3:13 If one of you is *w* and understanding,

WISELY (5)

Ex 18:17 "You are not acting *w*,"
Jdt 11:21 other looks so beautiful and speaks so *w*!"
Sir 13:21 he speaks *w* and no attention is paid him.
Jer 3:15 who will shepherd you *w* and prudently.
23: 5 As king he shall reign and govern *w*,

WISER (9)

1Kgs 5:11 He was *w* than all other men
Ps(s) 119:98 Your command has made me *w* than my
Prv 9: 9 a wise man, and he becomes still *w*;
21:11 man is punished, the simple are the *w*;
26:16 The sluggard imagines himself *w* than seven
Eccl 7: 3 when the face is sad the heart grows *w*.
Ez 28: 3 Oh yes, you are *w* than Daniel,
Dn 2:30 that I am *w* than any other living person,
1Cor 1:25 For God's folly is *w* than men,

WISEST (3)

Jgs 5:29 The *w* of her princesses answers her,
Is 19:11 the *w* of Pharaoh's advisers give stupid
Jer 10: 7 Among all the *w* of the nations,

WISH (105)

Gn 24:58 asked her, "Do you *w* to go with this man?"
47:29 "If you really *w* to please me,
Ex 12:48 *w* to celebrate the Passover of the LORD,
25:22 that I *w* you to give the Israelites.
Lv 19: 5 to the LORD, if you *w* it to be acceptable,
Nm 32: 7 Why do you *w* to discourage the Israelites
32:16 "We *w* only to build sheepfolds here for
Dt 12:20 he promised you, when you *w* meat for food,
15:16 tells you that he does not *w* to leave you,
21:11 of her that you *w* to have her as wife,
23:25 you may eat as many of his grapes as you *w*,
Jos 24:27 against you, should you *w* to deny your God."
Jgs 9:15 'If you *w* to anoint me king over you in
14: 2 whom I *w* you to get as a wife for me."
Ru 3:13 But if he does not *w* to claim you,
3:17 because he did not *w* me to come back
4: 4 it if you *w* to acquire it as next of kin.
4: 4 But if you do not *w* to claim it,
1Sm 2:16 is the custom, then take whatever you *w*,"
7: 3 "If you *w* with your whole heart to return
9:19 you, I will tell you whatever you *w*.
20: 4 said to David, "I will do whatever you *w*."
21:10 If you *w* to take that,
2Sm 3:21 then be king over all whom you *w* to rule."
5: 8 "All who *w* to attack the Jebusites must
19:39 me, and I will do for him as you would *w*.
20:19 *w* to destroy the inheritance of the LORD?"
20:20 I do not *w* to destroy or to ruin anything.
24:22 king take and offer up whatever he may *w*.
1Kgs 1:16 the king, who said to her, "What do you *w*?"
5:22 provide all the cedars and fir trees you *w*.
2Kgs 2:10 taken up from you, your *w* will be granted;
1Chr 18:10 he sent his son Hadoram to *w* King David
2Chr 1:11 your *w* and you have not asked for riches,
Neh 2: 4 asked me, "What is it, then, that you *w*?"
Tb 3:17 before any other who might *w* to marry her.
4:20 I *w* to inform you that I have deposited a
5:12 "I *w* to know truthfully whose son you are,
Jdt 5: 7 for they did not *w* to follow the gods of
8:15 *w* to come to our aid within the five days,
Est 5: 5 make haste to fulfill the *w* of Esther."
6: 6 the king more probably *w* to reward than me?"
1Mc 5:48 "We *w* to cross your territory in order to
11:57 and *w* you to be one of the King's Friends."
12:14 We did not *w* to be troublesome to you and
2Mc 1: 1 the Jews in Egypt, and *w* them true peace!
2:24 encountered by those who *w* to plunge
2:25 studious who *w* to commit things to memory,
9:20 well and your affairs are going as you *w*,
11:23 we *w* the subjects of our kingdom to be
11:29 Menelaus has told us of your *w* to return
Jb 9: 3 Should one *w* to contend with him,
13: 3 I *w* to reason with God.
21:14 us, for we have no *w* to learn your ways!
Ps(s) 21: 3 you refused not the *w* of his lips.
40: 6 Should I *w* to declare or to tell them,
Prv 13:12 sick, but a *w* fulfilled is a tree of life.
Wis 13: 6 though they seek God and *w* to find him.
Sir 6:32 My son, if you *w*,
32:12 your ease, And there enjoy doing as you *w*,
Is 30:15 But this you did not *w*.
44:28 My shepherd, who fulfills my every *w*;
58: 5 Is this the manner of fasting I *w*,
58: 6 This, rather, is the fasting that I *w*:
Jer 4: 1 If you *w* to return,
5:31 falsely, and the priests teach as they *w*;
42:22 in the place where you *w* to go and settle.
Bar 6:45 than what these craftsmen *w* them to be.
Ez 2: 1 I *w* to speak with you.
13:22 man with lies when I did not *w* him grieved,
Mt 12:47 out there and they *w* to speak to you."
15:28 Your *w* will come to pass."
15:32 I do not *w* to send them away hungry,
19:17 If you *w* to enter into life,
26:17 "Where do you *w* us to prepare the
27:17 "Which one do you *w* me to release for you,
27:21 "Which one do you *w* me to release for you?"
Mk 14: 7 you can be generous to them whenever you *w*,
14:12 "Where do you *w* us to go to prepare the
Lk 4: 6 given to me and I give it to whomever I *w*.
8:20 are standing outside and they *w* to see you."
12:49 How I *w* the blaze were ignited!
16:26 *w* to cross from here to you cannot do so,
Acts 13:22 my own heart who will fulfill my every *w*.'
26: 5 a long time and can testify, if they *w*,
Rom 1:12 what I *w* is that we may be mutually
9: 3 I could even *w* to be separated from Christ
9:15 I will have pity on whomever I *w*."
13: 3 *w* to be free from the fear of authority?
16:24 brother Quartus *w* to be remembered to you.
1Cor 16:12 but he did not *w* to go at this time.
2Cor 1: 8 we do not *w* to leave you in the dark about
5: 4 because we do not *w* to be stripped naked
8:20 There is one thing I *w* to avoid,
10: 9 do not *w* to intimidate you with my letters.
Gal 1: 3 We *w* you the favor and peace of God our
1: 7 Some who *w* to alter the gospel of Christ
Phil 1:11 It is my *w* that you may be found rich in
3:10 I *w* to know Christ and the power flowing
Col 2: 2 I *w* their hearts to be strengthened and
1Tm 2: 8 is my *w*, then, that in every place the men
3Jn 1:10 *w* to do so and expels them from the church!
1:13 do not *w* to write it out with pen and ink.
Jude 1: 5 I *w* to remind you of certain things,
Rv 3:15 How I *w* you were one or the other

WISHED (29)

Ex 33: 7 Anyone who *w* to consult the LORD would go
Jgs 15: 2 thought it certain you *w* to repudiate her;
2Sm 15: 9 The king *w* him a safe journey,
19:19 household over and to do whatever he *w*.
1Kgs 5:24 with all the cedars and fir trees he *w*;
8:17 When my father David *w* to build a temple
9:11 the cedar wood, fir wood, and gold he *w*—
2Chr 6: 7 My father David *w* to build a temple to the
Jdt 16:22 Many *w* to marry her,
1Mc 4: 6 such armor and swords as they would have *w*.
8:13 those whom they *w* to depose they deposed;
2Mc 1:35 To those on whom the king *w* to bestow
Ps(s) 40: 7 III Sacrifice or oblation you *w* not,
Wis 14:17 made a public image of him they *w* to honor,
16:21 was blended to whatever flavor each one *w*,
Ez 1:12 wherever the spirit *w* to go,
1:20 Wherever the spirit *w* to go,
Dn 5:19 he *w*, he killed or let live; whomever he *w*,
7:19 I *w* to make certain about the fourth beast,
Hos 7:13 Though I *w* to redeem them,
Mk 15:15 So Pilate, who *w* to satisfy the crowd,
Lk 1:62 the father what he *w* him to be called.
10:24 *w* to see what you see but did not see it,
10:29 he *w* to justify himself he said to Jesus,
11:52 yet you have stopped those who *w* to enter!"
Acts 14:13 because he *w* to offer sacrifice to them
Rom 11:31 since God *w* to show you mercy
Heb 11:25 he *w* to be ill-treated along with God's

WISHES (40)

Lv 1: 2 *w* to bring an animal offering to the LORD,
2: 1 *w* to bring a cereal offering to the LORD,
22:18 in Israel, who *w* to offer a sacrifice,
27:13 If the offerer *w* to redeem the animal,
27:15 one who dedicated his house *w* to redeem it,
27:19 one who dedicated his field *w* to redeem it,

WISHES (cont.)
27:31 If someone *w* to buy back any of his tithes,
Nm 9:14 among you *w* to keep the LORD's Passover,
Dt 21:14 shall give her her freedom, if she *w* it;
Ru 3:13 and tomorrow, if he *w* to claim you,
1Sm 23:20 whenever the king *w* to come down,
2Sm 23: 7 He who *w* to touch them must arm himself
Ezr 5: 7 "To King Darius all good *w*!
Tb 6:15 slay any man who *w* to come close to her.
Est 6: 6 done for the man whom the king *w* to reward?"
6: 7 "For the man whom the king *w* to reward
6: 9 must clothe the man the king *w* to reward,
6: 9 done for the man whom the king *w* to reward!'
6:11 done for the man whom the king *w* to reward!"
2Mc 1:10 send greetings and good *w* to Aristobulus,
9:19 and best *w* for their health and happiness.
Ps(s) 27:12 Give me not up to the *w* of my foes;
Is 50: 8 if anyone *w* to oppose me,
Mt 11:27 and anyone to whom the Son *w* to reveal him.
16:24 "If a man *w* to come after me,
Mk 8:34 "If a man *w* to come after me,
9:35 him and said, "If anyone *w* to rank first,
Lk 9:23 "Whoever *w* to be my follower must deny
10:22 and anyone to whom the Son *w* to reveal him."
12:47 The slave who knew his master's *w* but did
23:25 murder, and delivered Jesus up to their *w*.
Jn 5:21 the Son grants life to those to whom he *w*.
7: 4 No one who *w* to be known publicly keeps
8:44 devil, and willingly you carry out his *w*.
Rom 9:18 In other words, God has mercy on whom he *w*,
9:18 he wishes, and whom he *w* he makes obdurate.
1Cor 7:15 If the unbeliever *w* to separate,
7:36 should be done, let him do as he *w*.
Col 4:15 Give our best *w* to the brothers at
Rv 1: 4 John *w* you grace and peace

WISHING (8)
1Kgs 8:18 him, 'In *w* to build a temple to my honor,
2Chr 6: 8 'In *w* to build a temple to my honor,
2Mc 12: 4 treachery and *w* to live on friendly terms,
Sir 23:14 By *w* you had never been born or cursing
Acts 25: 9 But Festus, *w* to please the Jewish people,
Rom 9:22 *w* to show his wrath and make known his
Heb 6:17 *w* to give the heirs of his promise even
13:18 that we have a good conscience, *w*,

WITCHCRAFT (3)
Wis 12: 4 Works of *w* and impious sacrifices;
Na 3: 4 fair and charming, a mistress of *w*,
3: 4 with her harlotries, and peoples by her *w*:

WITCHCRAFTS (1)
2Kgs 9:22 and *w* of your mother Jezebel continue?"

WITCHERY (1)
Wis 4:12 For the *w* of paltry things obscures what

WITHAL (1)
Jer 2:35 Yet *w* you say,

WITHDRAW (38)
Gn 45: 1 so he cried out, "Have everyone *w* from me!"
Nm 16:24 *W* from the space around the Dwelling" [of
Jgs 3:22 he did not *w* the dagger from his body.
1Sm 14:19 So he said to the priest, *W* your hand."
15: 6 Leave Amalek and *w*,
20:15 I die, never *w* your kindness from my house.
29: 7 *W* peaceably,
2Sm 7:15 but I will not *w* my favor from him as I
20:21 him alone, and I will *w* from the city."
1Kgs 9: 6 if you and your descendants ever *w* from me,
13: 6 for me that I may be able to *w* my hand."
15:19 king of Israel, that he may *w* from me."
1Chr 17:13 and I will not *w* my favor from him as I
2Chr 6:26 they *w* from sin because you afflict them,
16: 3 king of Israel, that he may *w* from me."
29:10 that his burning anger may *w* from us.
35:22 But Josiah would not *w* from him,
1Mc 6:57 So he hastily resolved to *w*.
11:41 sent the request to King Demetrius to *w*
Jb 9:34 hand upon us both and *w* his rod from me.
13:21 *W* your hand far from me,
34:14 spirit to himself, *w* to himself his breath,
Ps(s) 73:27 For indeed, they who *w* from you perish;
80:19 Then we will no more *w* from you;
104:22 sun rises, they *w* and couch in their dens.
132:11 a firm promise from which he will not *w*:
Prv 24:11 from those tottering to execution *w* not.
24:18 with you, and *w* his wrath from your enemy.
Eccl 8: 3 to God, be not hasty to *w* from the king;
Sir 35:18 Nor will it *w* till the Most High responds,
47:22 But God does not *w* his mercy,
Is 60:20 shall your sun go down, or your moon *w*,
Jer 21: 2 wonderful works, so that he will *w* from us.
Ez 21:15 Why should I now *w* it?
Dn 11:10 which shall advance like a flood, then *w*.
Mi 2: 3 evil from which you shall not *w* your necks;
2: 6 The shame will not *w*.
Lk 19:21 You *w* what you never deposited.

WITHDRAWAL (1)
2Mc 13:26 That is how the king's attack and *w* went.

WITHDRAWING (4)
2Mc 4:33 *w* to the inviolable sanctuary at Daphne,
Sir 10:12 *w* his heart from his Maker;
Mt 26:42 *W* a second time, he began to pray:
Lk 19:22 I was a hard man, *w* what I never deposited,

WITHDRAWN (16)
Ex 25:15 in the rings of the ark and never be *w*.
Nm 27: 4 But why should our father's name be *w* from
36: 3 their heritage will be *w* from our
36: 4 will be *w* from that of our ancestral tribe."
36:13 will be *w* from that of our ancestral tribe."
2Sm 2:27 would not have been *w* from the pursuit
2Kgs 19: 8 the king of Assyria had *w* from Lachish,
Jdt 13:14 not *w* his mercy from the house of Israel,
Jb 19:13 My brethren have *w* from me,
Ps(s) 85: 4 You have *w* all your wrath;
Sir 13:25 *w* and perplexed is the laborious schemer.
Jer 16: 5 I have *w* my friendship from this people,
34:21 of Babylon who have at present *w* from you.
Bar 1:13 not yet been *w* from us at the present day.
2:13 Let your anger be *w* from us,
Hos 5: 6 he has *w* himself from them.

WITHDRAWS (2)
2Mc 6:16 He never *w* his mercy from us.
Wis 1: 5 flees deceit and *w* from senseless counsels;

WITHDREW (38)
Gn 38:29 But as he *w* his hand,
47:10 Pharaoh farewell and *w* from his presence.
Ex 4: 6 He put it in his bosom, and when he *w* it,
4: 7 hand back in his bosom, and when he *w* it,
Nm 12:10 he departed, and the cloud *w* from the tent,
16:35 So they *w* from the space around the
Jgs 20:48 The men of Israel *w* through the territory
2Sm 7:15 him as I *w* it from your predecessor Saul,
10:14 also fled from Abishai and *w* into the city.
2Kgs 15:20 did not remain in the country but *w*.
1Chr 17:13 him as I *w* it from him who preceded you;
Jdt 8:36 Then they *w* from the tent and returned to
13: 1 When it grew late, his servants quickly *w*.
1Mc 4:35 he *w* to Antioch and began to recruit
6: 4 dismay *w* from there to return to Babylon.
7:19 Bacchides *w* from Jerusalem and pitched his
9:62 companions *w* to Bethbasi in the desert;
12:28 They lighted fires and then *w*.
2Mc 5:27 and about nine others *w* to the wilderness,
9:29 Antiochus' son, he later *w* into Egypt,
12: 7 the gates of the town were shut, he *w*,
12:12 exchanged, the Arabs *w* to their tents.
13:16 Finally they *w* in triumph,
13:22 he *w* and attacked Judas and his men.
Jb 29: 8 Then the young men saw me and *w*,
Wis 10: 3 the unjust man *w* from her in his anger,
Jer 2: 5 fathers find in me that they *w* from me,
Bar 3: 8 of our fathers, who *w* from the Lord,
Ez 31:12 the peoples of the land *w* from its shade,
Mt 4:12 John had been arrested, he *w* to Galilee.
12:15 aware of this, and so he *w* from that place.
14:13 he *w* by boat from there to a deserted
15:21 and *w* to the district of Tyre and Sidon.
26:44 He left them again, *w* somewhat,
Mk 3: 7 Jesus *w* toward the lake with his disciples.
Lk 22:41 He *w* from them about a stone's throw,
Jn 11:54 He *w* instead to a town called Ephraim in
Acts 18: 7 Paul *w* and went to the house of a Gentile

WITHER (20)
Jb 15:30 A flame shall *w* him up in his early growth,
15:32 His stalk shall *w* before its time,
18:16 roots dry up, and above, his branches *w*.
Ps(s) 37: 2 For like grass they quickly *w*,
102:12 a lengthening shadow, and I *w* like grass.
Wis 2: 8 crown ourselves with rosebuds ere they *w*.
Is 19: 6 Reeds and rushes shall *w* away,
27:11 its branches shall *w* and be broken off,
34: 4 a scroll, and all their host shall *w* away,
40:24 When he breathes upon them and they *w*,
Jer 12: 4 the green of the whole countryside *w*?
Ez 17: 9 will *w* when he pulls it up by the roots?
17:10 Will it not rather *w*,
17:24 high the lowly tree, *W* up the green tree,
Am 1: 2 will languish, and the summit of Carmel *w*.
Zec 11:17 Let his arm *w* away entirely,
Mt 13: 6 it, it began to *w* for lack of roots.
21:20 "Why did the fig tree *w* up so quickly?"
Mk 4: 6 it, it began to *w* for lack of roots.
Jas 1:11 the rich man *w* away amid his many projects.

WITHERED (22)
Gn 18:12 that I am so *w* and my husband is so old,
1Kgs 13: 4 the hand he stretched forth against him *w*,
Jb 13:25 a wind-driven leaf, or pursue a *w* straw?
Ps(s) 102: 5 *W* and dried up like grass is my heart;
Sir 40:16 the riverbank, *w* before all other plants;
Is 15: 6 The grass is *w*,
64: 5 We have all *w* like leaves,
Jer 8:13 vine, No figs on the fig trees, foliage *w*!
Ez 17:24 the green tree, and make the *w* tree bloom.
19:12 The east wind *w* her up,
19:12 Then her strong branch *w* up,
Jl 1:12 The vine has dried up, the fig tree is *w*;
1:12 Yes, joy has *w* away from among mankind.
Jon 4: 7 which attacked the plant, so that it *w*.
Na 1: 4 *W* are Bashan and Carmel,
Mt 21:19 and it *w* up instantly.
Mk 11:20 they saw the fig tree *w* to its roots.
11:21 The fig tree you cursed has *w* up."
Lk 6: 6 there was a man whose right hand was *w*.
6: 8 and said to the man whose hand was *w*,
8: 6 up, then *w* through lack of moisture.
Jn 15: 6 A man who does not live in me is like a *w*,

WITHERS (8)
Jb 8:12 and uncut, it *w* quicker than any grass.
Ps(s) 129: 6 housetops, which *w* before it is plucked;
Is 33: 9 in mourning, Lebanon *w* with shame;
34: 4 on the vine, or as the fig *w* on the tree.
40: 7 The grass *w*, the flower wilts,
40: 8 Though the grass *w* and the flower wilts,
1Cor 9:25 do this to win a crown of leaves that *w*,
1Pt 1:24 The grass *w*, the flower wilts, but the word

WITHHELD (12)
Gn 39: 9 and he has *w* from me nothing but yourself,
Lv 5:16 what he has sinfully *w* from the sanctuary,
Nm 24:11 but the LORD has *w* the reward from you!"
Jb 22: 7 and from the hungry you have *w* bread;
38:15 But from the wicked the light is *w*,
39:17 For God has *w* wisdom from her and has
Jer 3: 3 Therefore the showers were *w*,
Lam 2: 3 He *w* the support of his right hand when
Jl 1: 5 of the grape will be *w* from your mouths.
Am 4: 7 Though I also *w* the rain from you when the
Hg 1:10 Therefore the heavens *w* from you their dew,
Jas 5: 4 are the wages you *w* from the farmhands who

WITHHOLD (14)
Gn 22:12 you did not *w* from me your own beloved son."
Ex 21:10 another wife, he shall not *w* her food,
Lv 19:13 *w* overnight the wages of your day laborer.
Neh 9:20 your manna you did not *w* from their mouths,
Ps(s) 40:12 *W* not, O LORD, your compassion
77:10 Does he in anger *w* his compassion?"
119:101 From every evil way I *w* my feet,
Prv 23:13 *W* not chastisement from a boy;
Wis 1:11 grumbling, and from calumny *w* your tongues;
Sir 7:33 and *w* not your kindness from the dead.
Jer 42: 4 I will *w* nothing from you.
Jl 2:10 darkened, and the stars *w* their brightness.
4:15 darkened, and the stars *w* their brightness.
Jon 3: 9 and forgive, and *w* his blazing wrath,

WITHHOLDING (1)
Gn 22:16 you did in not *w* from me your beloved son,

WITHHOLDS (5)
Jb 27: 2 As God lives, who *w* my deserts,
33:18 He *w* his soul from the pit and his life
36: 6 He *w* not the just man's rights,
Ps(s) 84:12 The LORD *w* no good thing from those who
Sir 34:21 he who *w* it is a man of blood.

WITHSTAND (21)
Jos 1: 5 No one can *w* you while you live.
10: 8 Not one of them will be able to *w* you."
21:44 Not one of their enemies could *w* them;
Jgs 2:14 about whom they were no longer able to *w*.
2Kgs 10: 4 and said, "If two kings could not *w* him,
2Chr 20: 6 is power and might, and no one can *w* you.
Jdt 6: 3 be unable to *w* the force of our cavalry.
11:18 and not one of them will be able to *w* you.
Est 9: 2 to do them harm, and no one could *w* them,
1Mc 10:73 Now you too will be unable to *w* our
14: 7 there was no one to *w* him.
2Mc 8: 5 organized, the Gentiles could not *w* him,
Ps(s) 76: 8 who can *w* you for the fury of your anger?
Sir 22:18 based on foolish plans *w* fear of any kind.
46: 3 And who could *w* him when he fought the
Dn 8: 4 could *w* it or be rescued from its power;
8: 7 the ram, which had not the force to *w* it,
11:15 The power of the south shall not *w* him,
11:16 and do as he pleases, with no one to *w* him.
Lk 14:31 he can *w* an enemy coming against him with
Rv 6:17 Who can *w* it?

WITHSTOOD (8)
Jos 23: 9 nations, and to this day no one has *w* you.
Jb 9: 4 who has *w* him and remained unscathed?
Ps(s) 106:23 *W* him in the breach to turn back his
Wis 10:16 *w* fearsome kings with signs and portents;
11: 3 *w* enemies and took vengeance on their foes.
16:22 snow and ice *w* fire and were not melted,
18:21 *w* the wrath and put a stop to the calamity,
Gal 2:11 Cephas came to Antioch I directly *w* him,

WITLESS (1)

Sir 41: 5 *w* offspring are in the homes of the wicked.

WITNESS (127)

Gn 31:44 the LORD shall be a *w* between us."
31:48 be a *w* from now on between you and me."
31:50 is about, God will be *w* between you and me."
31:52 *w*, and this memorial stone shall be *w*,
Ex 20:16 not bear false *w* against your neighbor.
23: 1 in putting your hand, as an unjust *w*,
Lv 5: 1 as a *w* of something he has seen or learned,
Nm 5:13 a *w* who might have caught her in the act;
35:30 The evidence of a single *w* is not
Dt 4:26 heaven and earth this day to *w* against you,
5:20 not bear dishonest *w* against your neighbor.
17: 6 to death on the testimony of only one *w*.
19:15 "One *w* alone shall not take the stand
19:16 "If an unjust *w* takes the stand against a
19:18 witness is a false *w* and has accused
30:19 heaven and earth today to *w* against you:
31:19 may be a *w* for me against the Israelites.
31:21 to recite, will bear *w* against them.
31:26 God, that there it may be a *w* against you.
31:28 call heaven and earth to *w* against them.
Jos 22:28 sacrifices, but to *w* between you and us.'
22:34 as a *w* among them that the LORD is God.
24:27 the people, "This stone shall be our *w*,
24:27 It shall be a *w* against you,
Jgs 11:10 is *w* between us that we will do as you say."
Ru 4:10 Do you *w* this today?"
1Sm 2:32 You shall *w* as a disappointed rival all
12: 5 them, "The LORD is *w* against you this day,
12: 5 "He is *w*," they agreed.
12: 6 "The LORD is *w*, who appointed Moses
12:16 stand ready to *w* the great marvel the LORD
Neh 6: 6 Geshem is *w* to this
9:26 they slew your prophets who bore *w* against
9:29 You bore *w* against them,
9:30 bearing *w* against them through your spirit,
Est 8: 6 I *w* the evil that is to befall my people,
1Mc 2:56 Caleb, for bearing *w* before the assembly,
3:59 *w* the ruin of our nation and our sanctuary.
2Mc 3:36 Before all men he gave *w* to the deeds of
Jb 16: 8 As a *w* there rises up my traducer,
16:19 Even now, behold, my *w* is in heaven,
Ps(s) 89:38 a faithful *w* in the sky."
Prv 6:19 to evil, The false *w* who utters lies,
12:17 sure of, but a lying *w* speaks deceitfully.
14: 5 truthful witness does not lie, but a false *w*
14:25 The truthful *w* saves lives,
19: 5 The false *w* will not go unpunished,
19: 9 The false *w* will not go unpunished,
19:28 An unprincipled *w* perverts justice,
21:28 The false *w* will perish,
24:28 *w* against your neighbor without just cause,
25:18 man who bears false *w* against his neighbor.
Wis 1: 6 Because God is the *w* of his inmost self
Is 3: 9 Their very look bears *w* against them;
19:20 It shall be a sign and a *w* to the LORD of
30: 8 That it may be in future days an eternal *w*:
44: 9 are of no avail, as they themselves give *w*.
55: 4 As I made him a *w* to the peoples,
59:12 you are many, our sins bear *w* against us.
Jer 12:20 Let me *w* the vengeance you take on them,
14: 7 Even though our crimes bear *w* against us,
20:12 Let me *w* the vengeance you take on them,
29:23 I know, I am *w*, says the LORD.
42: 5 said to Jeremiah, "May the LORD be our *w*:
Dn 13:54 Now, then, if you were a *w*,
Hos 5: 5 arrogance of Israel bears *w* against him;
7:10 arrogance of Israel bears *w* against him;
Am 3:13 Hear and bear *w* against the house of Jacob,
Mi 1: 2 Let the Lord GOD be *w* against you,
Mal 2:12 *w* and advocate out of the tents of Jacob,
2:14 *w* between you and the wife of your youth,
3: 5 be swift to bear *w* Against the sorcerers,
Mt 10:18 to give *w* before them and before the
11:19 Christ's *W* to JohnHe began to reproach
15:19 conduct, fornication, stealing, false *w*,
19:18 'You shall not bear false *w*';
24:14 the world as a *w* to all the nations.
Mk 10:19 You shall not bear false *w*;
Lk 18:20 You shall not bear dishonest *w*.
21:13 will be brought to give *w* on account of it.
Jn 1: 7 who came as a *w* to testify to the light,
5:31 "If I *w* on my own behalf,
8:13 "You are your own *w*.
8:14 "What if I am my own *w*?
10:25 do in my Father's name give *w* in my favor,
15:26 he will bear *w* on my behalf.
15:27 You must bear *w* as well,
21:24 same disciple who is the *w* to these things;
Acts 1:22 be named as *w* with us to his resurrection."
4:33 *w* to the resurrection of the Lord Jesus,
10:42 bear *w* that he is the one set apart by God
20:24 bearing *w* to the gospel of God's grace.
22: 5 the whole council of elders can bear me *w*,
22:15 be his *w* to what you have seen and heard.
22:20 the blood of your *w* Stephen was being shed,
26:16 as a *w* to what you have seen of me
28:23 bearing *w* to the reign of God among men.
Rom 1: 9 *w* that I constantly mention you in prayer,
2:15 conscience bears *w* together with that law,
3:21 though both law and prophets bear *w* to it
8:16 The Spirit himself gives *w* with our spirit
9: 1 My conscience bears me *w* in the Holy
1Cor 1: 6 the *w* I bore to Christ has been so
15:15 *w* before him that he raised up Christ;
2Cor 1:23 I call on God as my *w* that it was out of
1Thes 2: 5 greed under any pretext, as God is our *w*!
2Thes 1:10 for you already have our *w* to you.
1Tm 6:13 who in bearing *w* made his noble profession
Heb 2: 4 God then gave *w* to it by signs,
11: 4 borne *w* to him on account of his gifts;
1Pt 5: 1 a *w* of Christ's sufferings and sharer in
1Jn 1: 1 we have seen and bear *w* to it,
3Jn 1: 3 bear *w* to how truly you walk in the path
Rv 1: 2 who in reporting all he saw bears *w* to the
1: 5 and from Jesus Christ the faithful *w*,
1: 9 proclaimed God's word and bore *w* to Jesus.
2:13 at the time when Antipas, my faithful *w*,
3:14 "'The Amen, the faithful *W* and true,
6: 9 of the *w* they bore to the word of God.
12:17 God's commandments and give *w* to Jesus.
15: 5 sanctuary which is the tent of *w* opened up,
19:10 you and your brothers who give *w* to Jesus.
20: 4 for their *w* to Jesus and the word of God,
22:18 I myself give *w* to all who hear the

WITNESSED (13)

Ex 2:11 his kinsmen and *w* their forced labor,
3: 7 "I have *w* the affliction of my people in
20:18 the people *w* the thunder and lightning,
Jos 24: 7 After you *w* what I did to Egypt,
1Sm 9:16 for I have *w* their misery and accept their
1Kgs 10: 4 queen of Sheba *w* Solomon's great wisdom,
2Chr 9: 3 When the queen of Sheba *w* Solomon's wisdom,
Tb 9: 3 You *w* the oath that Raguel has sworn;
14:15 He *w* the exile of the city's inhabitants
Est 9:26 they had *w* and experienced in this affair,
Lk 2:30 For my eyes have *w* your saving deed
18:43 *w* it and they too gave praise to God.
Acts 7:34 I have *w* the affliction of my people in

WITNESSES (45)

Nm 35:30 the evidence of *w* is required for the
Dt 17: 6 The testimony of two or three *w* is
17: 7 the *w* are to be the first to raise their
19:15 only on the testimony of two or three *w*.
Jos 24:22 *w* that you have chosen to serve the LORD."
Ru 4: 9 "You are *w* today that I have acquired
1Mc 2:37 are our *w* that you destroy us unjustly."
Ps(s) 27:12 for false *w* have risen up against me,
35:11 Unjust *w* have risen up;
Is 8: 2 And I took reliable *w*, Uriah the priest,
43: 9 them produce *w* to prove themselves right,
43:10 You are my *w*, says the LORD,
43:12 You are my *w*,
44: 8 You are my *w*!
Jer 32:10 called *w* and weighed out the silver on the
32:12 and of the *w* who had signed the deed,
32:25 Buy the field with money, call in *w*.
32:44 *w* shall be used in the land of Benjamin,
Mt 18:16 may stand on the word of two or three *w*.
26:60 the many false *w* who took the stand.
26:65 What further need have we of *w*?
Mk 14:63 "What further need do we have of *w*?
Lk 8:36 by *w* how the possessed man had been cured.
22:71 They said, "What need have we of *w*?
24:48 You are *w* of this.
Jn 3:28 yourselves are *w* to the fact that I said:
Acts 1: 8 then you are to be my *w* in Jerusalem,
2:32 Jesus God has raised up, and we are his *w*.
3:15 raised him from the dead, and we are his *w*.
6:13 There they brought in false *w*, who said:
7:58 The *w* meanwhile were piling their cloaks
10:39 We are *w* to all that he did in the land of
10:41 *w* as had been chosen beforehand by God
13:31 These are his *w* now before the people.
1Cor 15:15 should then be exposed as false *w* of God,
2Cor 13: 1 only on the testimony of two or three *w*."
1Thes 2:10 You are *w*,
1Tm 5:19 unless it is supported by two or three *w*.
6:12 called when, in the presence of many *w*,
2Tm 2: 2 you have heard from me through many *w*
Heb 10:28 mercy on the testimony of two or three *w*.
12: 1 part are surrounded by this cloud of *w*,
Rv 11: 3 I will commission my two *w* to prophesy for
11: 5 mouths of these *w* to devour their enemies.
11: 6 These *w* have power to close up the sky so

WITNESSING (4)

Ex 22: 9 snatched away, without anyone *w* the fact,
1Sm 6:16 After *w* this,
Heb 3: 5 with the task of *w* to what would be spoken;
Rv 19:10 spirit proves itself by *w* to Jesus."

WITS (1)

Acts 12:15 "You're out of your *w*,"

WIVES (151)

Gn 4:19 Lamech took two *w*;
4:23 Lamech said to his *w*:
4:23 *w* of Lamech,
6: 2 for their *w* as many of them as they chose.
6:18 and your sons, your wife and your sons' *w*,
7: 7 with his sons, his wife, and his sons' *w*,
7:13 three *w* of Noah's sons had entered the ark,
8:16 your wife and your sons and your sons' *w*.
8:18 his wife and his sons and his sons' *w*;
11:29 Abram and Nahor took *w*;
28: 9 Ishmael, and in addition to the *w* he had,
30:26 Let me have my *w*,
31:17 to put his children and *w* on camels,
31:50 or take other *w* besides my daughters,
32:23 however, Jacob arose, took his two *w*,
36: 2 took his *w* from among the Canaanite women:
36: 6 Esau took his *w*, his sons, his daughters,
37: 2 sons of his father's *w* Bilhah and Zilpah,
45:19 your children and your *w* and to transport
46: 5 *w* and children on the wagons that Pharaoh
46:26 not counting the *w* of Jacob's sons
Ex 22:23 then your own *w* will be widows,
32: 2 "Have your *w* and sons and daughters take
34:16 take their daughters as *w* for your sons;
Nm 14: 3 *w* and little ones will be taken as booty.
16:27 with their *w* and sons and little ones,
32:26 While our *w* and children,
32:30 you shall bring their *w* and children and
Dt 3:19 Only your *w* and children,
17:17 Neither shall he have a great number of *w*,
21:15 two *w* loves one and dislikes the other;
29:10 together with your *w* and children and the
Jos 1:14 Your *w*,
Jgs 8:30 his direct descendants, for he had many *w*.
12: 9 and he brought in as *w* for his sons thirty
21: 7 What can we do about *w* for the survivors,
21:14 they gave them as *w* the women of
21:16 "What shall we do for *w* for the survivors?
21:22 Had you yourselves given them these *w*,
1Sm 1: 2 He had two *w*, one named Hannah,
25:43 Thus both of them were his *w*;
27: 3 had his family, and David had his two *w*,
30: 3 find it burned to the ground and their *w*,
30: 5 David's two *w*, Ahinoam of Jezreel
30:18 had taken, and rescued his two *w*.
2Sm 2: 2 went up there accompanied by his two *w*,
5:13 David took more concubines and *w* in
12: 8 house and your lord's *w* for your own.
12:11 will take your *w* while you live to see it,
12:11 He shall lie with your *w* in broad daylight.
19: 6 of your *w* and those of your concubines,
1Kgs 11: 3 He had seven hundred *w* of princely rank
11: 3 concubines, and his *w* turned his heart.
11: 4 his *w* had turned his heart to strange gods,
11: 8 He did the same for all his foreign *w* who
20: 3 your *w* and your promising sons are mine.'"
20: 5 your silver and gold, your *w* and your sons.
20: 7 When he sent to me for my *w* and sons,
2Kgs 24:15 to Babylon the king's mother and *w*,
1Chr 4: 5 Ashbur, the father of Tekoa, had two *w*,
7: 4 *w* and sons than their fellow tribesmen.
8: 8 he had put away his *w* Hushim and Baara.
14: 3 David took other *w* in Jerusalem and became
2Chr 11:21 than all his other *w* and concubines;
11:21 had taken eighteen *w* and sixty concubines,
11:23 and sought an abundance of *w* for them.
13:21 He took to himself fourteen *w* and fathered
20:13 the LORD, with their little ones, their *w*,
21:14 strike your people, your children, your *w*,
21:17 palace, along with his sons and his *w*;
24: 3 Jehoiada provided him with two *w*,
28: 8 hundred thousand of their brethren's *w*,
29: 9 *w* have been taken captive because of this.
31:18 family records, for their little ones, *w*,
Ezr 9: 2 as *w* for themselves and their sons,
10: 2 by taking as *w* foreign women
10: 3 foreign *w* and the children born of them,
10:10 women as *w* has added to Israel's guilt.
10:14 women for *w* appear at appointed times,
10:17 the men who had taken foreign women for *w*.
10:18 found to have taken foreign women for *w*:
10:19 pledged themselves to dismiss their *w*,
10:44 All these had taken foreign *w*;
Neh 4: 8 sons and daughters, your *w* and your homes."
5: 1 *w* against certain of their fellow Jews.
10:29 in favor of the law of God, with their *w*,
13:23 married Ashdodite, Ammonite, or Moabite *w*.
Tb 3: 8 with her, as it is prescribed for *w*.
4:12 all of them took *w* from among their own
Jdt 4:10 they, along with their *w*,
4:12 to be seized, their *w* to be taken captive,
7:14 *w* and children will languish with hunger,
7:27 *w* and children breathing out their souls.
9: 4 Their *w* you handed over to plunder,
Est 1:20 as it is, all *w* will honor their husbands,
B: 6 shall, together with their *w* and children,
8:11 wipe out, along with their *w* and children,
1Mc 2:30 and their sons, their *w* and their cattle,
2:38 the sabbath, and they died with their *w*,
3:20 and our *w* and children and to despoil us;
5:13 away their *w* and children and their goods,
5:23 their *w* and children and all that they had,
5:45 with their *w* and children and their goods,
8:10 Romans took their *w* and children captive.

WIVES (cont.)

13: 6 sanctuary, as well as your *w* and children,
13:45 the city, joined by their *w* and children,
2Mc 12: 3 them, together with their *w* and children,
15:18 were not so much concerned about their *w*
Wis 3:12 *w* are foolish and their children wicked;
Is 13:16 shall be plundered and their *w* ravished.
Jer 6:12 their fields and their *w* as well;
8:10 I will give their *w* to strangers,
14:16 No one shall bury them, their *w*,
18:21 Let their *w* be made childless and widows;
29: 6 Take *w* and beget sons and daughters;
29: 6 find *w* for your sons and give your
29:23 adultery with their neighbors' *w*,
35: 8 have not drunk wine, neither we, nor our *w*,
38:23 All your *w* and sons shall be led forth to
44: 9 their *w*, and you yourselves and your wives
44:15 *w* were burning incense to strange gods,
44:25 You and your *w* have stated your intentions,
Lam 5:11 The *w* in Zion were ravished by the enemy,
Bar 6:27 Even their *w* cure parts of the meat,
6:32 and put it on their *w* and children.
Ez 22:11 things with the *w* of their neighbors,
44:22 their *w* either widows or divorced women,
Dn 5: 2 his *w* and his entertainers might drink
5: 3 his *w* and his entertainers were drinking
5:23 your nobles, your *w* and your entertainers,
6:25 along with their children and their *w*,
14:10 of Bel, besides their *w* and children.
14:15 night as usual, with their *w* and children,
14:21 angry king arrested the priests, their *w*,
Zec 12:12 family of the house of David, and their *w*;
12:12 of the house of Nathan, and their *w*;
12:13 *w*; the family of Shemei, and their wives;
12:14 each family apart, and the *w* apart.
Mt 19: 8 stubbornness Moses let you divorce your *w*,"
Lk 17:27 ate and drank, they took husbands and *w*,
Acts 21: 5 All of them *w* and children included
1Cor 7:29 with *w* should live as though they had none;
Eph 5:22 *W* should be submissive to their husbands
5:24 so *w* should submit to their husbands in
5:25 Husbands, love your *w*,
5:28 love their *w* as they do their own bodies.
Col 3:18 You who are *w*, be submissive
3:19 Husbands, love your *w*.
1Tm 4: 7 to do with profane myths or old *w*' tales.
1Pt 3: 1 from preaching, through their *w*' conduct.

WIZARDS (1)

Is 47:15 Thus do your *w* serve you with whom you

WOE (101)

Nm 21:29 *W* to you, O Moab!
Dt 32:23 I will spend on them *w* upon woe and
1Sm 4: 7 They said also, *W* to us!
4: 8 *W* to us! Who can deliver us
Jdt 16:17 *W* to the nations that rise against my
1Mc 2: 7 *W* is me! Why was I born
Jb 31: 3 for the unrighteous, and *w* for evildoers?
Ps(s) 44:25 forgetting our *w* and our oppression?
120: 5 *W* is me that I sojourn in Meshech,
Eccl 4:10 *W* to the solitary man!
10:16 *W* to you, O land, whose king was
Sir 2:12 *W* to craven hearts and drooping hands,
2:13 *W* to the faint of heart who trust not,
2:14 *W* to you who have lost hope!
41: 8 *W* to you, O sinful men, who forsake
Is 3: 9 *W* to them! they deal out evil
3:11 *W* to the wicked man!
5: 8 *W* to you who join house to house who
5:11 *W* to those who demand strong drink as soon
5:18 *W* to those who tug at guilt with cords of
5:20 *W* to those who call evil good,
5:21 *W* to those who are wise in their own sight,
5:22 *W* to the champions at drinking wine,
6: 5 Then I said, *W* is me, I am doomed!
10: 1 *W* to those who enact unjust statutes and
10: 5 *W* to Assyria! My rod in anger
24:16 *W* is me! The traitors betray:
28: 1 *W* to the majestic garland of the drunkard
29: 1 *W* to Ariel, Ariel, the city where David
29:15 *W* to those who would hide their plans too
30: 1 *W* to the rebellious children,
31: 1 *W* to those who go down to Egypt for help,
33: 1 *W*, O destroyer never destroyed,
45: 7 darkness, I make well-being and create *w*:
45: 9 *W* to him who contends with his Maker;
45:10 *W* to him who asks a father,
Jer 4:13 *W* to us! we are ruined."
4:31 "Ah, *w* is me! I sink exhausted
6: 6 *W* to the city marked for punishment;
10:19 *W* is me! I am undone
13:27 *W* to you, Jerusalem,
15:10 *W* to me, mother, that you gave me birth!
21:10 this city, for its *w* and not for its good,
22:13 *W* to him who builds his house on wrong,
23: 1 *W* to the shepherds who mislead and scatter
28: 8 were before you and me prophesied war, *w*,
29:11 LORD, plans for your welfare, not for *w*!
48: 1 *W* to Nebo, it is laid waste;
48:46 *W* to you, O Moab, you are ruined,
50:27 *W* to them!
Lam 5:16 *w* to us, for we have sinned!
Ez 2:10 Lamentation and wailing and *w*!
13: 3 *W* to those prophets who are fools,
13:18 *W* to those who sew bands for everyone's
16:23 woe, *w* to you!
22: 3 *W* to the city which sheds blood within
24: 6 *W* to the bloody city,
34: 2 *W* to the shepherds of Israel who have been
Hos 7:13 *W* to them, they have strayed from me!
9:12 *W* to them when I turn away from them!
Am 5: 7 *W* to those who turn judgment to wormwood
5:18 *W* to those who yearn for the day of the
6: 1 *W* to the complacent in Zion,
Mi 2: 1 *W* to those who plan iniquity,
Na 3: 1 *W* to the bloody city,
Hb 2: 6 *W* to him who stores up what is not his:
2: 9 *W* to him who pursues evil gain for his
2:12 *W* to him who builds a city by bloodshed,
2:15 *W* to you who give your neighbors a flood
2:19 *W* to him who says to wood, "Awake!"
Zep 2: 5 *W* to you who dwell by the seacoast,
3: 1 *W* to the city, rebellious and polluted,
Zec 11:17 *W* to my foolish shepherd who forsakes the
Mt 18: 7 *w* to that man through whom scandal comes!
23:13 *W* to you scribes and Pharisees,
23:15 *W* to you scribes and Pharisees,
23:23 *W* to you scribes and Pharisees,
23:25 *W* to you scribes and Pharisees,
23:27 *W* to you scribes and Pharisees,
23:29 *W* to you scribes and Pharisees,
26:24 but *w* to that man by whom the Son of Man
Lk 6:24 "But *w* to you rich,
6:25 *W* to you who are full;
6:25 *W* to you who laugh now;
6:26 *W* to you when all speak well of you.
11:42 *W* to you Pharisees! You pay tithes
11:43 *W* to you Pharisees! You love the front
11:44 *W* to you! You are like hidden tombs
11:46 *W* to you lawyers also!
11:47 *W* to you! You build the tombs
11:52 *W* to you lawyers! You have taken away
17: 1 arise, but *w* to him through whom they come.
22:22 but *w* to that man by whom he is betrayed."
Rv 8:13 "Woe, woe, and again *w* to the inhabitants
9:12 The first *w* is past, but beware!
11:14 The second *w* is past, but beware!
12:12 But *w* to you, earth and sea, for the devil

WOES (1)

Lv 26:16 I will punish you with terrible *w*—

WOKE (10)

Gn 9:24 When Noah *w* up from his drunkenness and
41: 4 Then Pharaoh *w* up.
41: 7 Then Pharaoh *w* up,
41:21 Then I *w* up.
Jgs 16:20 and he *w* from his sleep,
Mt 8:25 they made their way toward him and *w* him:
25: 7 virgins *w* up and got their torches ready.
Mk 4:38 They finally *w* him and said to him,
Acts 12: 7 He tapped Peter on the side and *w* him.
16:27 *w* up to see the prison gates wide open.

WOLF (6)

Gn 49:27 "Benjamin is a ravenous *w*;
Sir 13:16 Is a *w* ever allied with a lamb?
Is 11: 6 Then the *w* shall be a guest of the lamb,
65:25 The *w* and the lamb shall graze alike,
Jn 10:12 sight of the *w* coming and runs away,
10:12 to be snatched and scattered by the *w*.

WOLVES (8)

Jer 5: 6 slay them, *w* of the desert ravage them,
Ez 22:27 within her are like *w* that tear prey,
Hb 1: 8 his horses, and keener than *w* at evening.
Zep 3: 3 Her judges are *w* of the night that have
Mt 7:15 clothing but underneath are *w* on the prowl.
10:16 is sending you out like sheep among *w*.
Lk 10: 3 am sending you as lambs in the midst of *w*.
Acts 20:29 savage *w* will come among you who will not

WOMAN (373)

Gn 2:22 a *w* the rib that he had taken from the man.
2:23 This one shall be called *w*,'
3: 1 The serpent asked the *w*,
3: 2 The *w* answered the serpent:
3: 4 But the serpent said to the *w*:
3: 6 The *w* saw that the tree was good for food,
3:12 replied, "The *w* whom you put here with me
3:13 The LORD God then asked the *w*,
3:13 The *w* answered,
3:15 I will put enmity between you and the *w*,
3:16 To the *w* he said: "I will intensify
12:11 "I know well how beautiful a *w* you are.
12:14 the Egyptians saw how beautiful the *w* was;
20: 3 to die because of the *w* you have taken,
21:12 about the boy or about your slave *w*.
21:13 As for the son of the slave *w*,
24: 5 *w* is unwilling to follow me to this land?
24: 8 If the *w* is unwilling to follow you,
24:39 master, 'What if the *w* will not follow me?,'
24:43 to a young *w* who comes out to draw water,
24:44 let her be the *w* whom the LORD has decided
27:46 If Jacob also should marry a Hittite *w*,
28: 1 "You shall not marry a Canaanite *w*!
28: 6 his blessing, not to marry a Canaanite *w*,
38:20 to recover the pledge from the *w*;
46:10 Zohar, and Shaul, son of a Canaanite *w*.
Ex 2: 1 of the house of Levi married a Levite *w*,
2: 9 *w* therefore took the child and nursed it.
3:22 Every *w* shall ask her neighbor and her
6:15 Shaul, who was the son of a Canaanite *w*;
11: 2 ask his neighbor, and every *w* her neighbor,
19:15 Have no intercourse with any *w*."
21: 4 the *w* and her children shall remain the
21:22 men have a fight and hurt a pregnant *w*,
21:28 "When an ox gores a man or a *w* to death,
21:29 should it then kill a man or a *w*,
23:26 *w* in your land will be barren or miscarry;
35:29 Every Israelite man and *w* brought to the
36: 6 "Let neither man nor *w* make any more
Lv 12: 2 a *w* has conceived and gives birth to a boy,
12: 7 *w* who gives birth to a boy or a girl child.
13:29 man or a *w* has a sore on the head or cheek,
13:38 man or a *w* is spotted with white blotches,
15:18 "If a man lies carnally with a *w*,
15:19 "When a *w* has her menstrual flow,
15:25 "When a *w* is afflicted with a flow of
15:33 as for the *w* who has her menstrual period,
15:33 for the man who lies with an unclean *w*."
18:17 with a *w* and also with her daughter,
18:19 "You shall not approach a *w* to have
18:22 You shall not lie with a male as with a *w*;
18:23 nor shall a *w* set herself in front of an
20:13 If a man lies with a male as with a *w*,
20:14 If a man marries a *w* and her mother also,
20:16 a *w* goes up to any animal to mate with it,
20:16 it, the *w* and the animal shall be slain;
20:18 with a *w* during her menstrual period,
20:27 "A man or a *w* who acts as a medium or
21: 7 "A priest shall not marry a *w* who has
21: 7 a *w* who has been divorced by her husband;
21:14 a *w* who has been divorced or a woman
27: 4 for a man, and thirty shekels for a *w*;
27: 7 shekels for a man, and ten for a *w*.
Nm 5: 6 If a man (or a *w*) commits a fault against
5:16 *w* come forward and stand before the LORD.
5:18 Then, as the *w* stands before the LORD,
5:19 Then he shall adjure the *w*,
5:21 adjure the *w* with this oath of imprecation
5:22 And the *w* shall say, 'Amen, amen!'
5:24 water, which he is to have the *w* drink,
5:26 then shall he have the *w* drink the water.
5:28 If however, the *w* has not defiled herself,
5:29 When a *w* goes astray while under the
5:31 *w* shall bear such guilt as she may have."
6: 2 When a man (or a *w*) solemnly takes the
12: 1 he had contracted with a Cushite *w*.
25: 6 came and brought in a Midianite *w*
25: 8 the pair of them, the Israelite and the *w*.
25:14 slain with the Midianite *w* was Zimri,
25:15 The slain Midianite *w* was Cozbi,
30: 4 "When a *w*, while still a maiden in her
30:10 woman, or any pledge to which such a *w*
31:17 every *w* who has had intercourse with a man.
Dt 4:16 whether it be in the form of a man or a *w*,
7:14 no man or *w* among you shall be childless
15:12 "If your kinsman, a Hebrew man or *w*,
17: 2 a *w* who does evil in the sight of the LORD,
17: 5 you shall bring the man (or *w*) who has
20: 7 a *w* and not yet taken her as his wife?
21:11 if you see a comely *w* among the captives
22: 5 "A *w* shall not wear an article proper to
22:13 marrying a *w* and having relations with her,
22:14 defames her by saying, 'I married this *w*,
22:22 with a *w* who is married to another,
22:22 *w* with whom he has had relations shall die.
24: 1 marrying a *w* and having relations with her,
28:56 The most refined and delicate *w* among you,
29:17 Let there be, then, no man or *w*,
Jos 2: 4 *w* had taken the two men and hidden them,
6:22 house and bring out the *w* with all her kin,
Jgs 4: 9 have Sisera fall into the power of a *w*."
9:53 But a certain *w* cast the upper part of a
9:54 me, lest they say of me that a *w* killed me."
11: 2 family, for you are the son of another *w*."
13: 3 the LORD appeared to the *w* and said to her,
13: 6 The *w* went and told her husband,
13: 9 to the *w* as she was sitting in the field.
13:10 the *w* ran in haste and told her husband.
13:24 The *w* bore a son and named him Samson.
14: 2 "There is a Philistine *w* I saw in Timnah
14: 7 on the journey to speak for the *w*,
14: 8 he returned to marry the *w* who pleased him,
14:10 His father also went down to the *w*,
16: 4 *w* in the Wadi Sorek whose name was Delilah.
19:19 for the *w* and myself and for our servant;
19:26 Then at daybreak the *w* came and collapsed
19:27 out again on his journey, there lay the *w*,
20: 4 the Levite, the husband of the murdered *w*,
21:11 and every *w* who was not still a virgin.
21:16 every *w* in Benjamin has been put to death."
21:18 'Cursed be he who gives a *w* to Benjamin!'"

21:22 we did not take a *w* apiece in the war.
Ru 1: 5 and the *w* was left with neither her two
3: 8 around to find a *w* lying at his feet.
3:11 all my townspeople know you for a worthy *w*.
3:14 that this *w* came to the threshing floor."
1Sm 1:15 "I am an unhappy *w*.
1:26 lord, I am the *w* who stood near you here,
2:20 *w* for the gift she has made to the LORD!"
20:30 "Son of a rebellious *w*,
25: 3 The *w* was intelligent and attractive,
27: 9 David would not leave a man or *w* alive,
27:11 a man or *w* alive to be brought to Gath,
28: 7 servants, "Find me a *w* who is a medium,
28: 7 "There is a *w* in Endor who is a medium."
28: 8 They came to the *w* by night,
28: 9 *w* answered him, "You are surely aware
28:11 *w* asked him, "Whom do you want me
28:12 When the *w* saw Samuel,
28:13 *w* answered Saul, "I see a preternatural
28:21 Then the *w* came to Saul,
28:23 his servants joined the *w* in urging him,
28:24 The *w* had a stall-fed calf in the house,
2Sm 3: 8 you charge me with a crime involving a *w*!
6:19 each *w* in the entire multitude of Israel,
11: 2 From the roof he saw a *w* bathing,
11: 3 inquiries made about the *w* and was told,
11: 5 But the *w* had conceived,
11:21 Was it not a *w* who threw a millstone down
14: 2 to Tekoa and brought from there a gifted *w*,
14: 2 that you may appear to be a *w* who has been
14: 4 So the *w* of Tekoa went to the king and
14: 8 The king then said to the *w*:
14: 9 The *w* of Tekoa answered him,
14:12 The *w* continued, "Please let your servant
14:13 So the *w* said: "Why then, do you think
14:17 *w* concluded: "Let the word of my lord
14:18 The king answered the *w*,
14:18 The *w* said,
14:19 And the *w* answered: "As you live, my lord
14:27 named Tamar, who was a beautiful *w*.
17:20 servants came to the *w* at the house,
17:20 The *w* replied,
20:16 Then a wise *w* from the city stood on the
20:17 When Joab had come near her, the *w* said,
20:21 Then the *w* said to Joab,
1Kgs 3:17 One *w* said: "By your leave, my lord
3:17 lord, this *w* and I live in the same house,
3:18 after I gave birth this *w* also gave birth.
3:22 The other *w* answered, "It is not so!
3:23 "One *w* claims, 'This, the living one,
3:25 give half to one *w* and half to the other."
3:26 The *w* whose son it was,
17:24 a man of God," the *w* replied to Elijah.
2Kgs 4: 1 A certain *w*, the widow of one of the guild
4: 8 Shunem, where there was a *w* of influence,
4:12 servant Gehazi, "Call this Shunammite *w*."
4:17 Yet the *w* conceived, and by the same time
6:26 on the city wall, a *w* cried out to him,
6:28 "This *w* said to me, 'Give up your son
8: 1 to the *w* whose son he had restored to life:
8: 2 *w* got ready and did as the man of God said,
8: 3 the *w* returned from the land of the
8: 5 the very *w* whose son Elisha had restored
8: 5 lord king," Gehazi said, "this is the *w*,
8: 6 The king questioned the *w*,
9:34 "Attend to that accursed *w* and bury her;
1Chr 2: 3 born to him of Bathshua, a Canaanite *w*.
16: 3 every Israelite, to every man and every *w*,
2Chr 2:13 of a Danite *w* and of a father from Tyre;
15:13 whether small or great, whether man or *w*.
Tb 1: 9 I married Anna, a *w* of our own lineage.
4:12 a *w* of the lineage of your forefathers.
6: 8 a man or a *w* who is afflicted by a demon
6:14 *w* has already been married seven times,
6:16 you to marry a *w* from your own family.
Jdt 8: 8 her, for she was a very God-fearing *w*.
8:31 But now, God-fearing *w* that you are,
9:10 crush their pride by the hand of a *w*.
11:17 Your handmaid is, indeed, a God-fearing *w*,
11:21 "No other *w* from one end of the world to
12:11 "Go and persuade this Hebrew *w* in your
12:12 a *w* with us without enjoying her company.
13:15 Lord struck him down by the hand of a *w*.
14:18 A single Hebrew *w* has brought disgrace on
Est 4:11 that any man or *w* who goes to the king
Jb 14: 1 of *w* is short-lived and full of trouble,
15:14 one born of *w* that he should be righteous?
31: 9 If my heart has been enticed toward a *w*,
Prv 6:26 a loose *w* may be scarcely a loaf of bread,
7:10 the *w* comes to meet him,
9:13 The *w* Folly is fickle,
11:16 A gracious *w* wins esteem,
11:22 beautiful *w* with a rebellious disposition.
21: 9 than in a roomy house with a quarrelsome *w*.
25:24 than in a roomy house with a quarrelsome *w*.
27:15 a rainy day the match is a quarrelsome *w*.
30:20 Such is the way of an adulterous *w*:
30:23 Under an odious *w* when she is wed,
31:30 the *w* who fears the LORD is to be praised.
Eccl 7:26 death I find the *w* who is a hunter's trap,
7:28 but a *w* among them all I have not found.
Sir 9: 2 Give no *w* power over you to trample upon
9: 3 Be not intimate with a strange *w*,
9: 8 Avert your eyes from a comely *w*;
9: 9 With a married *w* dine not,
10:18 a man, nor stubborn anger to one born of *w*.
19:10 in labor, like a *w* giving birth to a child.
23:22 So also with the *w* who is unfaithful to
23:24 a *w* will be dragged before the assembly,
25:12 heart, worst of all evils is that of a *w*.
25:14 serpent, no venom greater than that of a *w*.
25:15 rather dwell than live with an evil *w*.
25:18 There is scarce any evil like that in a *w*;
25:23 In *w* was sin's beginning,
37:11 Speak not to a *w* about her rival,
41:21 Of gazing at a married *w*,
Is 13: 8 of them, like a *w* in labor they writhe;
21: 3 have seized me like those of a *w* in labor;
26:17 As a *w* about to give birth writhes and
42:14 But now, I cry out as a *w* in labor,
45:10 or a *w*, "What are you giving birth to?"
Jer 3:20 But like a *w* faithless to her lover,
4:31 I hear the moaning, as of a *w* in travail,
13:21 seize you like those of a *w* giving birth?
16: 2 Do not marry any *w*;
22:23 upon you, like the pangs of a *w* in travail!
31:22 *w* must encompass the man with devotion.
48:19 man who flees, the *w* who tries to escape:
48:41 are like the heart of a *w* in travail.
49:22 shall be like the heart of a *w* in travail.
49:24 hold of her, like those of a *w* in travail.
Ez 18: 6 relations with a *w* in her menstrual period;
23:43 "Oh, this *w* jaded with adulteries!
36:17 was like the defilement of a menstruous *w*.
Dn 13: 2 a very beautiful and God-fearing *w*,
13:36 this *w* entered with two girls and shut the
13:46 will have no part in the death of this *w*."
13:48 To condemn a *w* of Israel without
Hos 3: 1 your love to a *w* beloved of a paramour,
Mi 4: 9 are seized with pains like a *w* in travail?
4:10 O daughter Zion, like a *w* in travail;
Zec 5: 7 there was a *w* sitting inside the bushel.
Mal 2:11 loves, and has married an idolatrous *w*.
Mt 5:28 anyone who looks lustfully at a *w* has
5:32 a divorced *w* likewise commits adultery.
9:20 a *w* who had suffered from hemorrhages for
9:22 That very moment the *w* got well.
11:11 born of *w* greater than John the Baptizer.
13:33 like yeast which a *w* took and kneaded
15:22 It happened that a Canaanite *w* living in
15:28 Jesus then said in reply, *W*,
19: 9 who marries a divorced *w* commits adultery."
22:27 Last of all the *w* died too.
26: 7 a *w* carrying a jar of costly perfume came
26:10 "Why do you criticize the *w*?
Mk 5:25 There was a *w* in the area who had been
5:32 around to see the *w* who had done it.
5:33 the *w* came and fell in front of him and
7:25 Soon a *w*,
7:26 The *w* who was Greek
10:12 and the *w* who divorces her husband and
12:21 The second took the *w*,
12:22 Last of all, the *w* also died.
14: 3 a *w* entered carrying an alabaster jar of
Lk 7:28 is no man born of *w* greater than John.
7:37 A *w* known in the town to be a sinner
7:39 what sort of *w* this is that touches him
7:44 Turning then to the *w*, he said to Simon:
7:44 "You see this *w*?
7:50 Meanwhile he said to the *w*,
8:43 A *w* with a hemorrhage of twelve years'
8:47 *w* saw that her act had not gone unnoticed,
10:38 a *w* named Martha welcomed him to her home.
11:27 saying this a *w* from the crowd called out,
13:11 There was a *w* there who for eighteen
13:12 saw her, he called her to him and said, *W*,
13:21 It is like yeast which a *w* took to knead
15: 8 "What *w*,
16:18 The man who marries a *w* divorced from her
22:57 He denied it, saying, *W*,
Jn 2: 4 Jesus replied, *W*,
4: 7 When a Samaritan *w* came to draw water,
4: 9 The Samaritan *w* said to him,
4: 9 How can you ask me, a Samaritan and a *w*,
4:15 The *w* said to him,
4:17 "I have no husband," replied the *w*.
4:19 "Sir," answered the *w*,
4:21 "Believe me, *w*,
4:25 The *w* said to him: "I know there is
4:27 surprised that Jesus was speaking with a *w*.
4:28 The *w* then left her water jar and went off
4:42 they told the *w*: "No longer does our faith
8: 3 *w* forward who had been caught in adultery.
8: 4 *w* has been caught in the act of adultery.
8: 9 This left him alone with the *w*,
8:10 finally straightened up and said to her, *W*,
16:21 When a *w* is in labor she is sad that her
18:16 came out and spoke to the *w* at the gate,
19:26 whom he loved, Jesus said to his mother, *W*,
20:13 *W*," they asked her,
20:15 *W*," he asked her, "why are you weeping?
Acts 9: 2 Jerusalem anyone he might find, man or *w*,
9:36 *w* convert named Tabitha (in Greek Dorcas,
16:14 One who listened was a *w* named Lydia,
17:34 court of the Areopagus, a *w* named Damaris,
Rom 7: 2 a married *w* is bound to her husband by law
1Cor 7: 1 is better off having no relations with a *w*.
7: 2 his own wife and every *w* her own husband.
7:13 And if any *w* has a husband who is an
7:34 indeed, any unmarried *w*—
7:34 The married *w*,
9: 5 not have the right to marry a believing *w*
11: 3 the head of a *w* is her husband;
11: 5 any *w* who prays or prophesies with her
11: 6 Indeed, if a *w* will not wear a veil,
11: 6 If it is shameful for a *w* to have her hair
11: 7 *W*, in turn,
11: 8 was not made from *w* but woman from man.
11: 9 was man created for *w* but woman for man.
11:10 For this reason a *w* ought to have a sign
11:11 *w* is not independent of man nor man
11:11 of man nor man independent of *w*.
11:12 In the same way that *w* was made from man,
11:12 was made from man, so man is born of *w*;
11:13 it proper for a *w* to pray to God unveiled?
11:14 while the long hair of a *w* is her glory?
14:35 a disgrace when a *w* speaks in the assembly.
Gal 4: 4 come, God sent forth his Son born of a *w*,
4:23 of the free *w* was the fruit of the promise.
1Thes 5: 3 of pains overtaking a *w* in labor,
1Tm 2:11 A *w* must listen in silence and be
2:12 I do not permit a *w* to act as teacher,
2:14 it was not Adam who was deceived but the *w*.
5:16 If a *w* church member has relatives who are
2Pt 2:14 Constantly on the lookout for a *w*,
Rv 12: 1 in the sky, a *w* clothed with the sun,
12: 4 stood before the *w* about to give birth,
12: 6 The *w* herself fled into the desert,
12:13 the *w* who had given birth to the boy.
12:14 But the *w* was given the wings of a
12:15 to search out the *w* and sweep her away.
17: 3 where I saw a *w* seated on a scarlet beast
17: 4 The *w* was dressed in purple and scarlet
17: 6 I saw that the *w* was drunk with the blood
17: 7 explain to you the symbolism of the *w*
17: 9 seven hills on which the *w* sits enthroned.
17:18 The *w* you saw is the great city which has
21: 9 you the *w* who is the bride of the Lamb."

WOMANLY (2)

Gn 18:11 and Sarah had stopped having her *w* periods.
2Mc 7:21 stirred her *w* heart with manly courage,

WOMAN'S (16)

Gn 31:35 a *w* period is upon me."
Ex 21:22 as much as the *w* husband demands of him,
Nm 5:25 offering of jealousy from the *w* hand,
Dt 22: 5 to a man, nor shall a man put on a *w* dress;
1Kgs 3:19 This *w* son died during the night;
2Kgs 6:30 When the king heard the *w* words,
Jdt 16: 5 them, by a *w* hand he confounded them.
Jb 25: 4 sight, or how can any *w* child be innocent?
Ps(s) 48: 7 anguish, like a *w* in labor,
Sir 9: 8 Through *w* beauty many perish,
25:16 Wickedness changes a *w* looks,
25:20 Stumble not through a *w* beauty,
36:22 *w* beauty makes her husband's face light up,
42:14 a man's harshness than a *w* indulgence,
Jn 4:39 on the strength of the *w* word of testimony:
Rv 12:16 The earth then came to the *w* rescue by

WOMB (75)

Gn 20:18 for God had tightly closed every *w*
25:22 But the children in her *w* jostled each
25:23 "Two nations are in your *w*,
25:24 delivery came, there were twins in her *w*.
30: 2 God, who has denied you the fruit of the *w*?"
38:27 came, she was found to have twins in her *w*.
49:25 below, The blessings of breasts and *w*,
Ex 13: 2 that opens the *w* among the Israelites,
13:12 to the LORD every son that opens the *w*;
13:15 of the male sex that opens the *w*,
34:19 that opens the *w* among all your livestock,
Nm 3:12 that opens the *w* among the Israelites.
8:16 that opens the *w* among the Israelites.
12:12 mother's *w* with its flesh half consumed."
18:15 Every living thing that opens the *w*,
Dt 7:13 of your *w* and the produce of your soil,
28: 4 "Blessed be the fruit of your *w*,
28:11 than goodly measure the fruit of your *w*,
28:18 "Cursed be the fruit of your *w*,
28:53 you, you will eat the fruit of your *w*,
28:57 the afterbirth that issues from her *w*
30: 9 from all your labors, the fruit of your *w*,
Jgs 13: 5 boy is to be consecrated to God from the *w*.
13: 7 boy shall be consecrated to God from the *w*,
16:17 been consecrated to God from my mother's *w*.
Ru 1:11 sons in my *w* who may become your husbands?
Tb 4: 4 for your sake while you were in her *w*.
2Mc 7:22 know how you came into existence in my *w*;
7:27 who carried you in my *w* for nine months,
Jb 1:21 "Naked I came forth from my mother's *w*,
3:10 of the *w* to shield my eyes from trouble!
3:11 at birth, come forth from the *w* and expire?
10:18 Why then did you bring me forth from the *w*?
10:19 have been taken from the *w* to the grave.
31:15 Did not he who made me in the *w* make him?

WOMB (cont.)

31:18 guiding me even from my mother's w—
38: 8 the sea, when it burst forth from the w;
38:29 Out of whose w comes the ice,
Ps(s) 22:11 birth, From my mother's w you are my God.
58: 4 From the w the wicked are perverted;
71: 6 from my mother's w you are my strength;
127: 3 the fruit of the w is a reward.
139:13 you knit me in my mother's w.
Prv 30:16 The nether world, and the barren w;
31: 2 what, O son of my w;
Eccl 5:14 As he came forth from his mother's w,
11: 5 the human frame in the mother's w,
Wis 7: 1 And in my mother's w I was molded into
Sir 1:12 which is formed with the faithful in the w.
40: 1 From the day one leaves his mother's w
46:13 his Maker, dedicated from his mother's w,
49: 7 who even in the w had been made a prophet,
50:22 men's growth from their mother's w,
Is 13:18 The fruit of the w they shall not spare,
44: 2 your help, who formed you from the w:
44:24 your redeemer, who formed you from the w:
49: 1 from my mother's w he gave me my name.
49: 5 who formed me as his servant from the w,
49:15 without tenderness for the child of her w?
66: 9 who allow her to conceive, yet close her w?
Jer 1: 5 Before I formed you in the w I knew you,
20:17 because he did not dispatch me in the w!
20:17 been my grave, her w confining me forever.
20:18 Why did I come forth from the w,
Hos 9:11 no birth, no carrying in the w,
9:11 I would slay the darlings of their w.
9:14 Give them an unfruitful w,
12: 4 In the w he supplanted his brother,
Lk 1:15 with the Holy Spirit from his mother's w.
1:41 Mary's greeting, the baby leapt in her w.
1:42 women and blest is the fruit of your w.
1:44 in my ears, the baby leapt in my w for joy.
11:27 "Blest is the w that bore you and the
Jn 3: 4 to his mother's w and be born over again?"
Rom 4:19 years old), and of the dead w of Sarah.

WOMBS (1)

Lk 23:29 the w that never bore and the breasts that

WOMEN (222)

Gn 14:16 along with the w and the other captives.
24:11 at the time when w go out to draw water,
27:46 with life because of the Hittite w.
27:46 woman, a native of the land, like these w,
28: 8 the Canaanite w were to his father Isaac,
30:13 W call me fortunate."
31:43 "The w are mine,
31:43 But since these w are my daughters,
33: 5 looked about, he saw the w and children.
34: 1 out to visit some of the w of the land.
34:29 carried off all their wealth, their w,
36: 2 took his wives from among the Canaanite w:
Ex 1:16 for the Hebrew w and see them giving birth,
1:19 Hebrew women are not like the Egyptian w.
2: 7 of the Hebrew w to nurse the child for you?"
15:20 the w went out after her with tambourines,
35:22 Both the men and the w
35:25 All the w who were expert spinners brought
35:26 thread, All the w who possessed the skill,
38: 8 was made from the mirrors of the w who
Lv 20:14 the man and the two w as well shall be
26:26 ten w will need but one oven for baking
Nm 25: 1 illicit relations with the Moabite w.
31: 9 But the Israelites kept the w of the
31:15 "So you have spared all the w!"
36: 4 the heritage of these w will be
Dt 2:34 them all, with their men, w and children;
3: 6 the cities, with their men, w and children;
20:14 but the w and children and livestock and
23:18 be no temple harlot among the Israelite w,
31:12 men, w and children,
Jos 6:21 men and w, young and old,
8:25 day a total of twelve thousand men and w,
8:35 community, including the w and children,
Jgs 5:24 w be Jael, blessed among tent-dwelling w.
9:49 Migdal-shechem, about a thousand men and w,
9:51 middle of the city, and all the men and w,
11:40 w to go yearly to mourn the daughter
12: 9 thirty young w from outside the family.
14: 1 and saw there one of the Philistine w.
16:27 The temple was full of men and w:
16:27 w looked on as Samson provided amusement.
21:10 to the sword, including the w and children.
21:14 w of Jabesh-gilead whom they had spared;
Ru 1: 4 with her two sons, who married Moabite w,
1:19 city was astir over them, and the w asked,
2: 8 Stay here with my w servants.
4:14 Then the w said to Naomi,
4:17 And the neighbor w gave him his name,
1Sm 2:22 they were having relations with the w
4:20 when the w standing around her said to her,
15: 3 Do not spare him, but kill men and w,
15:33 "As your sword has made w childless,
15:33 so shall your mother be childless among w."
18: 6 w came out from each of the cities of
18: 7 The w played and sang:
21: 5 if the men have abstained from w,
21: 6 segregated from w as on previous occasions.
22:19 of Nob to the sword, including men and w,
30: 2 captive the w and all who were in the city,
2Sm 1:24 W of Israel, weep over Saul,
1:26 have I held love for you than love for w.
1Kgs 11: 1 King Solomon loved many foreign w besides
2Kgs 8:12 you will rip open their pregnant w."
15:16 even to ripping open all the pregnant w.
23: 7 which the w wove garments for the Asherah.
Ezr 10: 1 of Israelites gathered about him, men, w,
10: 2 foreign w of the peoples of the land.
10:10 w as wives has added to Israel's guilt.
10:11 of the land and from these foreign w."
10:14 w for wives appear at appointed times,
10:17 the men who had taken foreign w for wives.
10:18 found to have taken foreign w for wives:
10:44 them away, both the w and their children.
Neh 8: 2 the assembly, which consisted of men, w,
8: 3 midday, in the presence of the men, the w,
12:43 The w and the children joined in,
13:26 yet even he was made to sin by foreign w.
13:27 betraying our God by marrying foreign w?"
Tb 2:11 at weaving cloth, the kind of work w do.
Jdt 4:11 w and children who lived in Jerusalem
6:16 and all their young men, as well as the w,
7:22 and the w and youths were consumed with
7:23 people, therefore, including youths, w,
7:32 the w and children he sent to their homes.
10:19 this people that has such w among them?
12:13 and to be like one of the Assyrian w who
13:13 opened the gate and welcomed the two w.
13:18 Most High God, above all the w on earth;
15:12 w around her, and she and the other w
15:13 women around her and she and the other w
Est 1: 9 Queen Vashti also gave a feast for the w
1:17 conduct will become known to all the w,
2: 3 the royal eunuch Hegai, custodian of the w,
2: 8 the care of Hegai, custodian of the w.
2:12 months' preparation decreed for the w.
2:15 the royal eunuch Hegai, custodian of the w,
2:17 king loved Esther more than all other w,
3:13 young and old, including w and children,
1Mc 1:26 and the beauty of the w was disfigured.
1:32 walls, took captive the w and children,
1:60 W who had had their children circumcised
2Mc 3:19 W, girded with sackcloth below their
5:13 young and old, a killing of w and children,
5:24 and sell the w and young men into slavery.
6: 4 with w even in the sacred court.
6:10 two w who were arrested for having
12:21 he sent on ahead of him the w and children,
Jb 2:10 even you going to speak as senseless w do?
42:15 In all the land no other w were as
Ps(s) 68:12 w bear the glad tidings,
Prv 31: 3 Give not your vigor to w,
31:29 "Many are the w of proven worth,
Sg 1: 8 you do not know, O most beautiful among w,
2: 2 among thorns, so is my beloved among w.
5: 9 from any other, O most beautiful among w?
6: 1 your lover gone, O most beautiful among w?
Sir 19: 2 Wine and w make the mind giddy,
28:15 A meddlesome tongue can drive virtuous w
42:12 men, or spend her time with married w;
42:13 garments, so harm to w comes from women:
47: 6 Therefore the w sang his praises and
47:19 to w and gave them dominion over your body.
Is 3:12 will be their tyrant, and w will rule them!
4: 1 w will take hold of one man on that day,
19:16 On that day the Egyptians shall be like w,
27:11 and w shall come to build a fire with them.
32: 9 rise up and hear my voice, overconfident w,
Jer 7:18 and the w knead dough to make cakes for
9:16 tell the wailing w to come,
9:19 Hear, you w, the word of the LORD,
30: 6 hands on their loins like w in childbirth?
38:22 All the w left in the house of Judah's
40: 7 of Ahikam, charge of the land, of men, w,
41:16 the w and children with their guardians,
43: 6 men, w, and children, the princesses and
44:15 w who were present in the immense crowd,
44:20 To all the people, men and w,
44:24 further to all the people, including the w:
50:37 her motley throng, that they may become w!
51:30 up is their strength, they have become w.
Lam 2:20 Must w eat their offspring,
4:10 compassionate w boiled their own children,
Bar 6:28 and w in childbed handle their sacrifices.
6:29 For w bring the offerings to these gods of
6:42 And their w, girt with cords,
Ez 8:14 there the w who were weeping for Tammuz.
9: 6 men, youths and maidens, w and children
16:34 you were different from all other w.
16:41 punishments on you while many w look on.
22:10 who coerce w in their menstrual period.
23: 2 Son of man, there were two w,
23:10 Thus she became a byword for w,
23:44 came to Oholah and Oholibah, the lewd w.
23:48 and all the w will be warned not to
44:22 their wives either widows or divorced w
44:22 may marry w who are the widows of priests.
Dn 11:37 ancestors or for the one in whom w delight;
14:20 "I see the footprints of men, w,
Am 4: 1 this word, w of the mountain of Samaria,
Mi 2: 9 The w of my people you drive out from
Na 3:13 See, the troops are w in your midst;
Zec 5: 9 Then I raised my eyes and saw two w coming
8: 4 Old men and old w, each with staff in hand
14: 2 be taken, houses plundered, w ravished;
Mt 14:21 five thousand, not counting w and children.
15:38 four thousand, apart from w and children.
24:41 Two w will be grinding meal;
27:55 w were present looking on from a distance.
28: 5 Then the angel spoke, addressing the w:
28: 9 The w came up and embraced his feet and
28:11 As the w were returning,
Mk 13:17 with pregnant and nursing w in those days.
15:40 also w present looking on from a distance.
15:41 These w had followed Jesus when he was in
Lk 1:28 Blessed are you among w."
1:42 w and blest is the fruit of your womb.
8: 2 and also some w who had been cured of evil
15:30 gone through your property with loose w,
17:35 Two w will be grinding grain together;
21:23 "The w who are pregnant or nursing at the
23:27 including w who beat their breasts and
23:49 All his friends and the w who had
23:55 The w who had come with him from Galilee
24: 1 the w came to the tomb bringing the spices
24: 5 Terrified, the w bowed to the ground.
24:10 The w were Mary of Magdala,
24:10 other w with them also told the apostles,
24:22 some w of our group have just brought us
24:24 tomb and found it to be just as the w said;
Jn 8: 5 the law, Moses ordered such w to be stoned.
Acts 1:14 There were some w in their company,
5:14 more believers, men and w in great numbers,
8: 3 house after house, dragged men and w out,
8:12 Christ, men and w alike accepted baptism.
13:50 stirred up their influential w sympathizers
16:13 and spoke to the w who were gathered there.
17: 4 to Judaism, and numerous prominent w.
17:12 did numerous influential Greek w and men.
22: 4 I arrested and imprisoned both men and w.
Rom 1:26 Their w exchanged natural intercourse for
1:27 w and burned with lust for one another.
1Cor 14:34 w should keep silent in such gatherings.
Gal 4:24 the two w stand for two covenants.
1Tm 2: 9 the w must deport themselves properly.
2:10 as becomes w who profess to be religious,
3:11 The w, similarly, should be serious,
5: 2 women as mothers, and younger w as sisters,
2Tm 3: 6 captives of silly w burdened with sins
Ti 2: 3 the older w must behave in ways that befit
2: 4 w to love their husbands and children,
Heb 11:35 W received back their dead through
1Pt 3: 1 You married w must obey your husbands,
3: 5 The holy w of past ages used to adorn
3: 7 Treat w with respect as the weaker sex,
Rv 14: 4 never been defiled by immorality with w.

WOMEN'S (2)

Ez 23:42 w arms and splendid diadems on their heads.
Rv 9: 8 men's faces but they had hair like w hair.

WON (28)

Dt 32:27 boast, 'Our own hand w the victory;
2Sm 19:15 He w over all the Judahites as one man,
1Kgs 11:19 Hadad w great favor with Pharaoh,
1Chr 17:21 You w for yourself a name for great and
2Chr 33:13 The LORD let himself be w over:
Est 2: 9 The girl pleased him and w his favor.
2:15 she w the admiration of all who saw her.
2:17 virgins she w his favor and benevolence.
1Mc 1:30 in peaceful terms, and w their trust.
10:60 gold and many gifts and thus w their favor.
2Mc 13:26 as he could and w them over by persuasion.
15: 9 them of the battles they had already w,
15:21 that victory is w by those who deserve it.
Ps(s) 78:54 to the mountains his right hand had w.
98: 1 His right hand has w victory for him,
106:46 And he w for them compassion from all who
111: 4 He has w renown for his wondrous deeds;
Eccl 9:11 sun that the race is not w by the swift,
Sir 45: 1 to spring the man who w the favor of all:
46: 9 he w his way onto the summits of the land;
Is 19:22 LORD and he shall be w over and heal them.
Mt 18:15 to you, you have w your brother over.
Acts 12:20 They w over his royal chamberlain Blastus
14:19 and Iconium arrived and w the people over.
1Pt 3: 1 gospel may be w over apart from preaching,
Rv 3:21 as I myself w the victory and took my seat
5: 5 has w the right by his victory to open the
15: 2 w the victory over the beast and its image,

WONDER (11)

Gn 28:17 In solemn w he cried out:
Ex 7: 9 Pharaoh demands that you work a sign or w,
Dt 13: 2 or a dreamer who promises you a sign or w,
13: 3 or w he has foretold you comes to pass,
28:46 descendants as a sign and a w for all time.
Tb 10: 2 appear, he said, "I w what has happened.
Jdt 10:19 the Israelites with w because of her,
Sir 16:11 man, it were a w had he gone unpunished.

Lk 24:41 still incredulous for sheer joy and w,
2Cor 11:14 And little w!
1Pt 4: 4 It is no w that those blasphemers are

WONDER-COUNSELOR (1)

Is 9: 5 They name him W,

WONDERED (1)

Lk 1:29 his words, and w what his greeting meant.

WONDERFUL (17)

2Chr 2: 8 I intend to build must be lofty and w.
Jdt 16:13 glorious, w in power and unsurpassable.
Est C: 3 earth and every w thing under the heavens.
Jb 42: 3 things too w for me,
Ps(s) 118:23 it is w in our eyes.
119:129 W are your decrees;
139: 6 Such knowledge is too w for me;
139:14 w are your works.
Prv 30:18 Three things are too w for me,
Sir 43: 2 what a w work of the Most High!
43:30 is the LORD's majesty, and w is his power.
Is 25: 1 For you have fulfilled your w plans of old,
28:29 w is his counsel and great his wisdom.
Jer 21: 2 deal with us according to all his w works,
Mi 7:15 from the land of Egypt, show us w signs.
1Tm 3:16 W, indeed, is the mystery of our faith,
Rv 15: 3 "Mighty and w are your works,

WONDERFULLY (2)

Ps(s) 16: 3 How w has he made me cherish the holy
139:14 you thanks that I am fearfully, w made;

WONDERING (2)

Lk 1:21 Zechariah, w at his delay in the temple.
3:15 w in their hearts whether John might be

WONDERMENT (3)

Mk 10:32 Their mood was one of w,
Jn 5:20 Yes, to your great w,
Rv 13: 3 w, the whole world followed after the beast.

WONDERS (63)

Ex 4:21 Pharaoh all the w I have put in your power.
7: 3 w that I will work in the land of Egypt,
11: 9 w may be multiplied in the land of Egypt."
11:10 these various w in Pharaoh's presence,
15:11 O terrible in renown, worker of w,
Dt 4:34 nation, by testings, by signs and w,
6:22 and wrought before our eyes signs and w,
7:19 your own eyes have seen, the signs and w,
26: 8 with terrifying power, with signs and w;
29: 2 have seen, and those great signs and w.
34:11 He had no equal in all the signs and w the
Jos 3: 5 tomorrow the LORD will perform w among
Neh 9:10 You worked signs and w against Pharaoh,
Est F: 6 God worked signs and great w,
Jb 37: 5 w past our searching out.
Ps(s) 4: 4 that the LORD does w for his faithful one;
77:12 yes, I remember your w of old.
77:15 You are the God who works w;
78: 4 and his strength and the w that he wrought.
78:11 forgot his deeds, the w he had shown them.
78:32 still more and believed not in his w.
88:11 Will you work w for the dead?
88:13 Are your w made known in the darkness,
89: 6 The heavens proclaim your w,
105:27 signs among them, and w in the land of Ham.
106: 7 fathers in Egypt considered not your w;
107:24 works of the LORD and his w in the abyss.
119:18 that I may consider the w of your law.
135: 9 He sent signs and w into your midst,
136: 4 I Who alone does great w,
Wis 8: 8 signs and w she knows in advance and the
19: 8 your hand, after they beheld stupendous w.
Sir 17: 8 w of his deeds and praise his holy name.
18: 4 increase, nor penetrate the w of the LORD.
31: 9 he, of all his kindred, has done w,
36: 5 Give new signs and work new w;
42:17 must fail in recounting the w of the LORD,
48:14 In life he performed w,
Jer 32:20 and w in the land of Egypt and to this day,
32:21 of Egypt amid signs and w and great terror.
Bar 2:11 hand, with signs and w and great might,
Dn 3:43 Deliver us by your w,
3:99 good to me to publish the signs and w
3:100 How great are his signs, how mighty his w;
6:28 working signs and w in heaven and on earth,
Jl 3: 3 work w in the heavens and on the earth,
Mt 21:15 when they observed the w he worked,
24:24 performing signs and w so great as to
Mk 13:22 appear performing signs and w to mislead,
Jn 3: 2 for no man can perform signs and w such as
4:48 "Unless you people see signs and w,
Acts 2:19 I will work w in the heavens above and
2:22 man whom God sent to you with miracles, w,
2:43 w and signs were performed by the apostles.
4:30 and w to be worked in the name of Jesus,
5:12 many signs and w occurred among the people.
6: 8 worked great w and signs among the people.
7:36 w and signs in the land of Egypt,
14: 3 signs and w to be done at their hands.
15:12 all the signs and w God had worked among
2Cor 12:12 apostle, signs and w and deeds of power.
Gal 3: 5 Spirit on you and works w in your midst?
2Thes 2: 9 signs and w at the disposal of falsehood

WONDROUS (35)

Ex 3:20 Egypt by doing all kinds of w deeds there.
Jgs 6:13 Where are his w deeds of which our fathers
1Chr 16: 9 sing his praise, proclaim all his w deeds.
16:12 Recall the w deeds that he has wrought,
16:24 among all peoples, his w deeds.
Jb 10:16 you show your w power against me,
37:14 Stand and consider the w works of God!
37:16 w work of him who is perfect in knowledge?
Ps(s) 9: 2 I will declare all your w deeds.
17: 7 Show your w kindness,
26: 7 my thanks, and recounting all your w deeds.
31:22 Blessed be the LORD whose w kindness he
40: 6 you made, O LORD, my God, your w deeds!
45: 5 and may your right hand show you w deeds.
71:17 till the present I proclaim your w deeds;
72:18 the God of Israel, who alone does w deeds.
75: 2 we declare your w deeds.
78:12 Before their fathers he did w things,
86:10 For you are great, and you do w deeds;
96: 3 among all peoples, his w deeds.
98: 1 LORD a new song, for he has done w deeds;
105: 2 sing his praise, proclaim all his w deeds.
105: 5 Recall the w deeds that he has wrought,
106:22 deeds in Egypt, W deeds in the land of Ham,
107: 8 and his w deeds to the children of men,
107:15 and his w deeds to the children of men,
107:21 and his w deeds to the children of men.
107:31 and his w deeds to the children of men.
111: 4 He has won renown for his w deeds;
119:27 and I will meditate on your w deeds.
145: 5 glorious majesty and tell of your w works.
Wis 10:17 their labors, Conducted them by a w road,
Sir 43: 8 how w in this change!
50:22 God of all, who has done w things on earth;
Is 29:14 this people in surprising and w fashion:

WONDROUSLY (2)

Jdt 10:14 face, which appeared w beautiful to them,
Jl 2:26 your God, Because he has dealt w with you;

WONT (1)

Est C:16 As a child I was w to hear from the people

WOOD (160)

Gn 22: 3 the w that he had cut for the holocaust,
22: 6 Thereupon Abraham took the w for the
22: 7 continued, "Here are the fire and the w,
22: 9 an altar there and arranged the w on it.
22: 9 and put him on top of the w on the altar.
Ex 15:25 pointed out to him a certain piece of w.
25: 5 acacia w;
25:10 "You shall make an ark of acacia w,
25:13 poles of acacia w and plate them with gold.
25:23 "You shall also make a table of acacia w,
25:28 shall make of acacia w and plate with gold.
26:15 of acacia w as walls for the Dwelling.
26:26 Also make bars of acacia w:
26:32 on four gold-plated columns of acacia w,
26:37 five columns of acacia w for this curtain;
27: 1 "You shall make an altar of acacia w,
27: 6 also make poles of acacia w for the altar,
30: 1 you shall make an altar of acacia w,
30: 5 too, of acacia w and plate them with gold.
31: 5 and mounting precious stones, in carving w,
35: 7 acacia w;
35:24 to have acacia w for any part of the work,
35:33 and mounting precious stones, in carving w,
36:20 w were made as walls for the Dwelling.
36:31 Bars of acacia w were also made,
36:36 Four gold-plated columns of acacia w,
37: 1 Bezalel made the ark of acacia w,
37: 4 of acacia w were made and plated with gold;
37:10 The table was made of acacia w,
37:15 were made of acacia w and plated with gold.
37:25 The altar of incense was made of acacia w,
37:28 were made of acacia w and plated with gold.
38: 1 altar of holocausts was made of acacia w,
38: 6 made of acacia w and plated with bronze.
Lv 1: 7 on the altar and laid some w on them,
1: 8 on top of the w and embers on the altar.
1:12 on top of the w, and the fire on the altar.
1:17 it on the altar, over the w on the fire,
3: 5 with the holocaust, on the w over the fire,
4:12 and there be burned up in a w fire.
11:32 men use, whether it be an article of w,
14: 4 live, clean birds, as well as some cedar w,
14: 6 Taking the living bird with the cedar w,
14:49 shall take two birds, as well as cedar w,
14:52 along with the living bird, the cedar w,
Nm 15:32 discovered gathering w on the sabbath day.
19: 6 and the priest shall take some cedar w,
31:20 of cloth, leather, goats' hair, or w."
Dt 4:28 by the hands of man out of w and stone,
10: 1 Also make an ark of w.
10: 3 So I made an ark of acacia w,
16:21 any kind of w beside the altar of the LORD,
19: 5 with his neighbor to a forest to cut w,
28:36 you will serve strange gods of w and stone.
28:64 you will serve strange gods of w and stone,
29:10 down to those who hew w and draw water for
29:16 you saw the loathsome idols of w and stone,
Jos 9:21 as hewers of w and drawers of water for
9:23 [hewers of w and drawers of water]
9:27 hewers of w and drawers of water for the
Jgs 6:26 w from the sacred pole you have cut down."
1Sm 6:14 the w of the cart was split up and the
2Sm 5:11 he furnished cedar w,
24:22 sledges and the yokes of the oxen for w.
1Kgs 5:32 the w and stones for building the temple.
6:23 each ten cubits high, made of olive w.
6:31 the sanctuary, doors of olive w were made;
6:32 The two doors were of olive w,
6:33 the doorposts of olive w were rectangular.
6:34 The two doors were of fir w;
7:11 were fine stones hewn to size, and cedar w.)
9:11 Solomon with all the cedar wood, fir w,
10:11 quantity of cabinet w and precious stones.
10:12 With the w the king made supports for the
10:12 w was brought or seen to the present day.
18:23 into pieces, and place it on the w,
18:23 prepare the other and place it on the w,
18:33 When he had arranged the w,
18:33 cut up the young bull and laid it on the w.
18:34 pour it over the holocaust and over the w."
18:38 came down and consumed the holocaust, w,
2Kgs 12:13 and for the purchase of the w and hewn
19:18 but the work of human hands, w and stone.
22: 6 of w and hewn stone for the temple repairs.
1Chr 14: 1 and cedar w to build him a house.
21:23 the threshing sledges for the w,
22:14 I have also stored up w and stones,
29: 2 of iron, w for what will be made of wood,
2Chr 2: 7 cedar, cypress and cabinet w from Lebanon,
2: 7 know how to cut the w of the Lebanon.
2: 8 to prepare for me a great quantity of w,
2: 9 your servants, the hewers who cut the w,
2:13 silver, bronze and iron, with stone and w,
3: 5 cypress w which he covered with fine gold,
9:10 also brought cabinet w and precious stones.
9:11 With the cabinet w the king made stairs
16: 6 of Judah to carry away the stone and w
Neh 2: 8 that he may give me w for timbering the
10:35 by lot concerning the procurement of w:
13:31 w at stated times and for the first fruits.
2Mc 1:21 with the water the w and what lay on it.
4:41 people picked up stones or pieces of w
Jb 24:20 and wickedness is splintered like w.
41:19 iron as straw, and bronze as rotten w.
Prv 25:20 Like a moth in clothing, or a maggot in w,
26:20 For lack of w,
26:21 is to live coals, what w is to fire,
Eccl 10: 9 and he who chops w is in danger from it.
Sg 3: 9 made himself a carriage of w from Lebanon.
Wis 10: 4 it, piloting the just man on frailest w.
13:13 remnants, crooked w grown full of knots,
13:13 This w he models with listless skill,
14: 1 w more unsound than the boat that bears
14: 5 men trust their lives even to frailest w.
14: 7 is the w through which justice comes about;
Sir 8: 3 of railing speech, heap no w upon his fire.
28:10 The more w, the greater the fire,
50:12 while he stood before the sacrificial w,
Is 10:15 who lifts it, or a staff him who is not w!
30:33 is piled with dry grass and w in abundance,
37:19 but the work of human hands, w and stone.
40:20 Mulberry w, the choice portion which
44:15 With a part of their w he warms himself,
44:19 say, "Half of the w I burned in the fire,
44:19 out of the rest, or worship a block of w?"
60:17 In place of w,
Jer 2:27 They who say to a piece of w,
3: 9 land, committing adultery with stone and w.
5:14 this people is the w that it shall devour!—
7:18 The children gather w,
10: 3 nations are nothing, w cut from the forest,
Lam 4: 8 skin shrinks on their bones, as dry as w.
5: 4 we must buy, for our own w we must pay.
5:13 boys stagger under their loads of w;
Bar 6: 3 shoulders gods of silver and gold and w,
6:10 men, these gods of silver and gold and w;
6:29 to these gods of silver and gold and w;
Ez 15: 2 wood of the vine better than any other w?
15: 3 you use its w to make anything worthwhile?
15: 6 Like the w of the vine among the trees of
20:32 of foreign lands, serving w and stone."
24: 5 Then pile the w beneath it;
24:10 piling on w and kindling the fire,
27: 6 of cypress w from the coasts of Kittim.
27:15 and ebony w they gave you for payment.
39:10 They shall not have to bring in w from the
41:16 were paneled with precious w all around,
41:22 corners, and its base and sides were of w.
Dn 5: 4 silver, bronze and iron, w and stone.
5:23 and gold, bronze and iron, w and stone,
Hos 4:12 They consult their piece of w,
Hb 2:19 Woe to him who says to w, "Awake!"

WOOD (cont.)

Lk 23:31 If they do these things in the green *w*,
1Cor 3:12 with gold, silver, precious stones, *w*,
2Tm 2:20 of gold and silver but also of *w* and clay,
Rv 9:20 and silver, from bronze and stone and *w*,
18:12 fragrant *w* of every kind,

WOODCHOPPERS (1)

Jer 46:22 like *w*, they attack her with axes.

WOODED (1)

Nm 13:20 Is the soil fertile or barren, *w* or clear?

WOODEN (18)

Ex 7:19 blood, even in the *w* pails and stone jars."
Lv 15:12 every *w* article shall be rinsed with water.
Neh 8: 4 Ezra the scribe stood on a *w* platform that
1Mc 6:37 A strong *w* tower covering each elephant,
Sir 22:16 *w* beams is not loosened by an earthquake;
Is 45:20 *w* idols and pray to gods that cannot save.
Jer 10: 8 these idols they teach about are *w*:
28:13 By breaking a *w* yoke,
Bar 6:38 These gilded and silvered *w* statues are
6:50 They are *w*, gilded and silvered;
6:54 of these *w* or gilded or silvered gods,
6:56 these *w* and silvered and gilded gods;
6:58 or a *w* post in a palace,
6:69 patch, that is no protection, are their *w*,
6:70 are their silvered and gilded *w* gods.
Ez 41:22 was something that looked like a *w* altar,
41:25 the vestibule outside was a *w* lattice.
Rv 18:12 of ivory pieces and expensive *w* furniture;

WOODLAND (3)

Eccl 2: 6 myself reservoirs to water a flourishing *w*.
Mi 7:14 your inheritance, That dwells apart in a *w*,
Zec 12: 6 of Judah like a brazier of fire in the *w*,

WOODS (2)

2Kgs 2:24 Then two she-bears came out of the *w* and
Sg 2: 3 BAs an apple tree among the trees of the *w*,

WOODWORK (1)

Hb 2:11 out, and the beam in the *w* shall answer it!

WOODWORKERS (2)

Bar 6: 7 Their tongues are smoothed by *w*;
6:45 They are produced by *w* and goldsmiths,

WOOL (17)

Lv 13:47 infection is on a garment of *w* or of linen,
13:48 woven or knitted material of linen or *w*,
13:52 woven or knitted material of *w* or linen,
13:59 infection on a garment of *w* or linen,
Dt 22:11 two different kinds of thread, *w* and linen,
2Kgs 3: 4 lambs and the *w* of a hundred thousand rams.
Ps(s) 147:16 He spreads snow like *w*;
Prv 31:13 She obtains *w* and flax and makes cloth
Is 1:18 crimson red, they may become white as *w*.
51: 8 eaten by moths, like *w* consumed by grubs;
Ez 27:18 wealth, exchanging Helbon wine and Zahar *w*.
34: 3 You have fed off their milk, worn their *w*,
Dn 7: 9 and the hair on his head as white as *w*;
Hos 2: 7 me my bread and my water, my *w* and my flax,
2:11 I will snatch away my *w* and my flax,
Heb 9:19 with water and crimson *w* and hyssop,
Rv 1:14 snow-white *w* and his eyes blazed like fire.

WOOLEN (2)

Jgs 6:37 this *w* fleece on the threshing floor.
Ez 44:17 not put on anything *w* when they minister

WORD (555)

Gn 15: 1 *w* of the LORD came to Abram in a vision:
15: 4 Then the *w* of the LORD came to him:
31:22 day, *w* came to Laban that Jacob had fled.
37:14 brothers and the flocks and bring back *w*."
38:25 her out, she sent *w* to her father-in-law,
Ex 3:18 the God of the Hebrews, has sent us *w*.
5: 3 "The God of the Hebrews has sent us *w*.
18: 6 mountain of God, and he sent *w* to Moses,
Nm 15:31 Since he has despised the *w* of the LORD
30: 3 of abstinence, he shall not violate his *w*,
32:20 "If you keep your *w* to march as troops in
Dt 6:18 LORD, that you may, according to his *w*,
8: 3 but by every *w* that comes forth from the
23:24 But you must keep your solemn *w* and
28:58 *w* of the law which is written in this book,
32:46 carry out carefully every *w* of this law.
Jos 6:10 any noise or outcry until he gave the *w*:
8:35 Every single *w* that Moses had commanded,
Jgs 9:51 women, in a *w* all the citizens of the city,
Ru 1: 6 because *w* reached her there that the LORD
1Sm 3:19 any *w* of his to be without effect.
13: 3 in Gibeah, and the Philistines got *w* of it.
23:25 David got *w* of it and went down to the
2Sm 3:11 was no longer able to say a *w* to him.
7: 7 did I ever utter *w* to any one of the
10: 5 told of it, King Da-vid sent out *w* to them,
12:27 He sent messengers to David with the *w*:
13:21 King David, who got *w* of the whole affair,
14:10 the king said, "If anyone says a *w* to you,
14:12 say still another *w* to my lord the king."
14:17 "Let the *w* of my lord the king provide a
19:12 sent *w* to the priests Zadok and Abiathar:
23: 2 his *w* was on my tongue.
1Kgs 5:22 Hiram then sent *w* to Solomon,
6:11 This *w* of the LORD came to Solomon:
8:56 Not a single *w* has gone unfulfilled of the
13: 1 from Judah to Bethel by the *w* of the LORD,
13: 2 out against the altar the *w* of the LORD:
13: 5 man of God had given as the *w* of the LORD.
13: 9 For I was instructed by the *w* of the LORD
13:17 "for I was told by the *w* of the LORD
13:18 and an angel told me in the *w* of the LORD
13:32 For the *w* of the LORD which he proclaimed
17: 1 shall be no dew or rain except at my *w*."
17:24 *w* of the LORD comes truly from your mouth."
19: 9 But the *w* of the LORD came to him,
20: 5 sent you *w* to give me your silver and gold,
20:17 *w* that some men had marched out of Samaria.
20:33 the men quickly took him at his *w* and said,
22: 5 Israel, "Seek the *w* of the LORD at once."
22:13 Let your *w* be the same as any of theirs;
22:19 "Therefore hear the *w* of the LORD:
2Kgs 3:12 "He has the *w* of the LORD,"
4:13 Can we say a good *w* for you to the king or
5: 8 torn his garments, he sent *w* to the king:
5:14 seven times at the *w* of the man of God.
6: 9 of God would send *w* to the king of Israel,
6:10 So the king of Israel would send *w* to the
7: 1 "Hear the *w* of the LORD!
9:26 ground, in keeping with the *w* of the LORD."
10:10 Know that not a single *w* which the LORD
10:21 sent *w* of it throughout the land of Israel.
14: 9 of Lebanon sent *w* to the cedar of Lebanon,
18:36 silent and did not answer him one *w*,
19:21 the *w* the LORD has spoken concerning him:
20: 4 courtyard, the *w* of the LORD came to him.
20:16 "Hear the *w* of the LORD:
20:19 "The *w* of the LORD which you have spoken
23:16 defiled it in fulfillment of the *w* of the LORD
1Chr 11: 3 *w* of the LORD as revealed through Samuel.
15:15 ordained according to the *w* of the LORD.
17: 3 same night the *w* of God came to Nathan:
17: 6 Did I ever say a *w* to any of the judges of
22: 8 But this *w* of the LORD came to me:
2Chr 11: 2 the *w* of the LORD came to Shemaiah,
12: 7 the *w* of the LORD came to Shemaiah:
18: 4 Israel, "Seek the *w* of the LORD at once."
18:12 predict good for the king, let your *w*,
18:18 "Therefore hear the *w* of the LORD:
30:12 in accordance with the *w* of the LORD.
34:21 since our fathers have not kept the *w* of
35: 6 to the *w* of the LORD given through Moses."
36:12 Jeremiah, who spoke the *w* of the LORD.
36:21 the *w* of the LORD spoken by Jeremiah:
36:22 the *w* of the LORD spoken by Jeremiah,
36:22 kingdom, both by *w* of mouth and in writing:
Ezr 1: 1 the *w* of the LORD spoken by Jeremiah,
1: 1 kingdom, both by *w* of mouth and in writing:
Tb 13:12 are all who speak a harsh *w* against you;
14: 4 flee into Media for I believe God's *w*
14: 4 *w* of the prophecies shall prove false.
Jdt 4: 4 they sent *w* to the whole region of Samaria,
8: 8 No one had a bad *w* to say about her,
11:10 my lord and master, do not disregard his *w*,
16:14 no one can resist your *w*.
Est 9:26 days have been named Purim after the *w* pur.
1Mc 9:37 *w* was brought to Jonathan and his brother
9:55 a *w* to give orders concerning his house.
9:63 and sent *w* to those who were in Judea.
11:42 in turn, sent this *w* to Jonathan:
12:10 we have ventured to send *w* to you for the
16:21 But someone ran ahead and brought *w* to
2Mc 4:39 When *w* was spread that a large number of
8:11 immediately sent *w* to the coastal cities,
Jb 2:13 nights, but none of them spoke a *w* to him;
4: 2 If someone attempts a *w* with you,
4:12 For a *w* was stealthily brought to me,
26:14 his ways, and how faint is the *w* we hear!
42: 5 I had heard of you by *w* of mouth,
Ps(s) 15: 4 be to his loss, changes not his pledged *w*;
17: 6 hear my *w*.
19: 3 Day pours out the *w* to day,
19: 4 Not a *w* nor a discourse whose voice is not
33: 4 For upright is the *w* of the LORD,
33: 6 By the *w* of the LORD the heavens were made;
59:13 By the sin of their mouths and the *w* of
68:12 The Lord gives the *w*;
103:20 who do his bidding, obeying his spoken *w*.
105:19 pass and the *w* of the LORD proved him true.
105:42 his holy *w* to his servant Abraham.
106:24 they believed not his *w*.
107:20 He sent forth his *w* to heal them and to
119:25 give me life according to your *w*.
119:43 Take not the *w* of truth from my mouth,
119:49 Remember your *w* to your servant since
119:65 your servant, O LORD, according to your *w*.
119:74 me and be glad, because I hope in your *w*.
119:81 I hope in your *w*.
119:89 Your *w*, O LORD, endures forever;
119:105 A lamp to my feet is your *w*,
119:107 O LORD, give me life according to your *w*.
119:114 in your *w* I hope.
119:161 cause but my heart stands in awe of your *w*.
119:169 in keeping with your *w*,
130: 5 my soul trusts in his *w*.
139: 4 Even before a *w* is on my tongue,
147:15 swiftly runs his *w*!
147:18 He sends his *w* and melts them;
147:19 He has proclaimed his *w* to Jacob,
148: 8 and mist, storm winds that fulfill his *w*;
Prv 12:25 depresses it, but a kindly *w* makes it glad.
13:13 He who despises the *w* must pay for it,
15: 1 calms wrath, but a harsh *w* stirs up anger.
15:23 a *w* in season,
19:16 life, but the despiser of the *w* will die.
30: 5 Every *w* of God is tested;
Eccl 7:21 Do not give heed to every *w* that is spoken
8: 4 he pleases, because his *w* is sovereign,
12:13 The last *w*, when all is heard:
Wis 9: 1 you who have made all things by your *w*
12: 9 by terrible beasts or by one decisive *w*;
16:12 cured them, but your all-healing *w*,
16:26 *w* that preserves those who believe you!
18:15 *w* from heaven's royal throne bounded,
18:22 But by *w* he overcame the smiter,
Sir 3: 8 In *w* and deed honor your father that his
16:26 nor should they ever disobey his *w*.
18:15 a burning wind, so does a *w* improve a gift.
18:16 Sometimes the *w* means more than the gift;
27:23 honeyed talk, and admires your every *w*,
33: 3 prudent man trusts in the *w* of the LORD,
37:16 A *w* is the source of every deed;
39:17 *w* the waters become still as in a flask;
42:15 God's *w* were his works brought into being;
43:17 A *w* from him drives on the south wind,
43:28 let the last *w* be,
46:13 At God's *w* he established the kingdom and
48: 3 By God's *w* he shut up the heavens and
48:12 spirit, wrought many marvels by his mere *w*.
Is 1:10 Hear the *w* of the LORD, princes of Sodom!
2: 3 and the *w* of the LORD from Jerusalem.
5:24 scorned the *w* of the Holy One of Israel.
7: 2 When *w* came to the house of David that
9: 7 The Lord has sent *w* against Jacob,
16:13 This is the *w* of the LORD spoke against
28:13 So for them the *w* of the LORD shall be:
28:14 Therefore, hear the *w* of the LORD,
29:21 off, those whose mere *w* condemns a man,
30:12 Because you reject this *w*,
36:21 silent and did not answer him one *w*,
37:22 the *w* the LORD has spoken concerning him:
38: 4 Then the *w* of the LORD came to Isaiah:
39: 5 "Hear the *w* of the LORD of hosts:
39: 8 "The *w* of the LORD which you have spoken
40: 8 wilts, the *w* of our God stands forever."
45:23 my just decree and my unalterable *w*:
50: 4 to the weary a *w* that will rouse them.
55:11 my *w* be that goes forth from my mouth;
66: 2 and afflicted man who trembles at my *w*.
66: 5 word of the LORD, you who tremble at his *w*:
Jer 1: 2 The *w* of the LORD first came to him in the
1: 4 The *w* of the LORD came to me thus:
1:11 *w* of the LORD came to me with the question:
1:12 seen, for I am watching to fulfill my *w*.
1:13 *w* of the LORD came to me with the question:
2: 1 This *w* of the LORD came to me:
2: 4 Listen to the *w* of the LORD,
2:31 generation, take note of the *w* of the Lord:
2:35 I will judge you on that *w* of yours,
5:13 have become wind, and the *w* is not in them.
6:10 the *w* of the LORD has become for them an
7: 2 Hear the *w* of the LORD,
7:27 the *w* itself is banished from their speech.
8: 9 Since they have rejected the *w* of the LORD,
9:19 Hear, you women, the *w* of the LORD,
10: 1 Hear the *w* which the LORD speaks to you,
13: 3 time the *w* of the LORD came to me thus:
13:12 Now speak to them this *w*:
14: 1 The *w* of the LORD that came to Jeremiah
14:17 Speak to them this *w*:
17:15 say to me, "Where is the *w* of the LORD?
17:20 Hear the *w* of the LORD,
18: 1 This *w* came to Jeremiah from the LORD:
18: 5 Then the *w* of the LORD came to me.
18:18 let us carefully note his every *w*."
19: 3 Listen to the *w* of the LORD,
20: 8 The *w* of the LORD has brought me derision
21:11 Hear the *w* of the LORD, O house of David!
22: 2 Listen to the *w* of the LORD,
22:29 O land, land, land, hear the *w* of the LORD
23:17 say to those who despise the *w* of the LORD,
23:18 of the LORD, to see him and to hear his *w*?
23:18 Who has heeded his *w*,
23:28 him who has my *w* speak my word truthfully!
23:29 Is not my *w* like fire,
23:36 For each man his own *w* becomes the burden
24: 4 Thereupon this *w* of the LORD came to me:
25: 1 The *w* that came to Jeremiah concerning all
25: 2 This *w* the prophet Jeremiah spoke to all
25: 3 the *w* of the LORD has come to me and I
27:18 if the *w* of the LORD were with them,

28:12 the *w* of the LORD came to Jeremiah:
29:20 You, now, listen to the *w* of the LORD,
29:30 the *w* of the LORD came to Jeremiah:
31:10 Hear the *w* of the LORD,
32:26 Then this *w* of the LORD came to Jeremiah:
33: 1 The *w* of the LORD came to Jeremiah a
33:18 This *w* of the LORD also came to Jeremiah:
33:23 This *w* of the LORD came to Jeremiah:
34: 1 This *w* came to Jeremiah from the LORD
34: 4 But if you obey the *w* of the LORD,
34: 8 This is the *w* that came to Jeremiah from
34:12 Then this *w* of the LORD came to Jeremiah:
35: 1 This *w* came to Jeremiah from the LORD in
35:12 Then this *w* of the LORD came to Jeremiah:
36: 1 this *w* came to Jeremiah from the LORD.
36:27 This *w* of the LORD came to Jeremiah,
37: 6 This *w* of the LORD then came to the
39:15 the guard, the *w* of the LORD came to him:
40: 1 This *w* came to Jeremiah from the LORD,
42: 7 before the *w* of the LORD came to Jeremiah.
42:15 then listen to the *w* of the LORD,
43: 8 This *w* of the LORD came to Jeremiah in
44: 1 This *w* came to Jeremiah for all the people
44:24 Hear the *w* of the LORD,
44:26 But listen then to the *w* of the LORD,
44:28 settle in Egypt shall know whose *w* stands,
46: 1 This is the *w* of the LORD that came to the
47: 1 This is the *w* that came from the LORD to
49:34 The following *w* of the LORD against Elam
50: 1 The *w* which the LORD spoke against Babylon,
Bar 4:37 and from the west By the *w* of the Holy One,
5: 5 east and the west at the *w* of the Holy One,
Ez 1: 3 *w* of the LORD came to the priest Ezekiel,
3:17 Thus the *w* of the LORD came to me:
3:17 When you hear a *w* from my mouth,
6: 1 Thus the *w* of the LORD came to me:
6: 3 of Israel, hear the *w* of the Lord GOD.
7: 1 Thus the *w* of the LORD came to me:
11:14 Thus the *w* of the LORD came to me:
12: 1 Thus the *w* of the LORD came to me:
12: 8 the morning, the *w* of the LORD came to me:
12:17 Thus the *w* of the LORD came to me:
12:21 Thus the *w* of the LORD came to me:
12:26 Thus the *w* of the LORD came to me:
13: 1 Thus the *w* of the LORD came to me:
13: 2 Hear the *w* of the LORD:
13: 6 then they wait for him to fulfill their *w!*
14: 2 before me, the *w* of the LORD came to me:
14: 9 if he is beguiled into speaking a *w,*
14:12 Thus the *w* of the LORD came to me:
15: 1 Thus the *w* of the LORD came to me:
16: 1 Thus the *w* of the LORD came to me:
16:35 Therefore, harlot, hear the *w* of the LORD!
17: 1 Thus the *w* of the LORD came to me:
17:11 Thus the *w* of the LORD came to me:
18: 1 Thus the *w* of the LORD came to me:
20: 2 Then the *w* of the LORD came to me:
21: 1 Thus the *w* of the LORD came to me:
21: 3 Hear the *w* of the LORD!
21: 6 Then the *w* of the LORD came to me:
21:13 Thus the *w* of the LORD came to me:
21:23 Thus the *w* of the LORD came to me:
22: 1 Thus the *w* of the LORD came to me:
22:17 Thus the *w* of the LORD came to me:
22:23 Thus the *w* of the LORD came to me;
23: 1 Thus the *w* of the LORD came to me:
24: 1 ninth year, the *w* of the LORD came to me:
24:15 Thus the *w* of the LORD came to me:
24:20 Thus the *w* of the LORD came to me:
25: 1 Thus the *w* of the LORD came to me:
25: 3 Hear the *w* of the LORD!
26: 1 year, the *w* of the LORD came to me:
27: 1 Thus the *w* of the LORD came to me:
28: 1 Thus the *w* of the LORD came to me:
28:11 Thus the *w* of the LORD came to me:
28:20 Thus the *w* of the LORD came to me:
29: 1 tenth year, the *w* of the LORD came to me:
29:17 year, the *w* of the LORD came to me:
30: 1 Thus the *w* of the LORD came to me:
30:20 year, the *w* of the LORD came to me:
31: 1 year, the *w* of the LORD came to me:
32: 1 twelfth year, the *w* of the LORD came to me:
32:17 twelfth year, the *w* of the LORD came to me:
33: 1 Thus the *w* of the LORD came to me:
33:23 Thus the *w* of the LORD came to me:
33:30 hear the latest *w* that comes from the LORD."
34: 1 Thus the *w* of the LORD came to me:
34: 7 shepherds, hear the *w* of the LORD.
34: 9 of this, shepherds, hear the *w* of the LORD:
35: 1 Thus the *w* of the LORD came to me:
36: 1 of Israel, hear the *w* of the LORD!
36: 4 of Israel, hear the *w* of the LORD:
36:16 Thus the *w* of the LORD came to me:
37: 4 Dry bones, hear the *w* of the LORD!
37:15 Thus the *w* of the LORD came to me:
38: 1 Thus the *w* of the LORD came to me:
Dn 9:25 From the utterance of the *w* that Jerusalem
Hos 1: 1 The *w* of the Lord that came to Hosea,
4: 1 Hear the *w* of the LORD,
13: 1 Ephraim's *w* caused fear,
Jl 1: 1 The *w* of the LORD which came to Joel,
Am 1: 3 revoke my *w;* Because they threshed Gilead
1: 6 revoke my *w;* Because they took captive
1: 9 not revoke my *w;* Because they delivered
1:11 not revoke my *w;* Because he pursued
1:13 not revoke my *w;* Because they ripped
2: 1 not revoke my *w;* Because he burned to
2: 4 not revoke my *w;* Because they spurned
2: 6 not revoke my *w;* Because they sell the
3: 1 Hear the *w,* O men of Israel,
4: 1 Hear this *w,* women of the mountain
5: 1 Hear this *w* which I utter over you,
7:10 the priest of Bethel, sent *w* to Jeroboam,
7:16 Now hear the *w* of the LORD!"
8:11 water, but for hearing the *w* of the LORD.
8:12 to the east In search of the *w* of the LORD,
Jon 1: 1 is the *w* of the LORD that came to Jonah,
3: 1 *w* of the LORD came to Jonah a second time:
Mi 1: 1 The *w* of the LORD which came to Micah of
4: 2 and the *w* of the LORD from Jerusalem.
Zep 1: 1 The *w* of the LORD which came to Zephaniah,
2: 5 The *w* of the LORD is against you,
Hg 1: 1 the *w* of the LORD came through the prophet
1: 3 this *w* of the LORD came through Haggai,
2: 1 the *w* of the LORD came through the prophet
2:10 *w* of the LORD came to the prophet Haggai:
Zec 1: 1 the *w* of the LORD came to the prophet
1: 7 the *w* of the LORD came to the prophet
4: 8 The *w* of the LORD then came to me:
6: 9 This *w* of the LORD then came to me:
7: 1 king [the *w* of the LORD came to Zechariah],
7: 4 this *w* of the LORD of hosts came to me:
7: 8 [This *w* of the LORD came to Zechariah:
8: 1 This *w* of the LORD of hosts came:
8:18 This *w* of the LORD of hosts came to me:
9: 1 *w* of the LORD is upon the land of Hadrach,
11:11 understood that this was the *w* of the LORD.
12: 1 the *w* of the LORD concerning Israel.
Mal 1: 1 *w* of the LORD to Israel through Malachi.
3:13 You have defied me in *w,*
Mt 5:48 In a *w,* you must be made perfect
6: 5 I give you my *w,* they are already repaid.
9:31 and spread *w* of him through the whole area.
12:36 for every unguarded *w* they speak.
14:35 they spread the *w* throughout the region.
15: 6 your tradition you have nullified God's *w.*
15:23 He gave her no *w* of response.
18:16 stand on the *w* of two or three witnesses.
19:28 "I give you my solemn *w,*
21: 3 If anyone says a *w* to you,
26:34 Jesus said to him, "I give you my *w,*
28:14 If any *w* of this gets to the procurator,
Mk 1:44 "Not a *w* to anyone, now," he said.
2: 1 days and *w* got around that he was at home.
2: 3 While he was delivering God's *w* to them,
3:28 "I give you my *w,*
3:31 outside they sent *w* to him to come out.
4:14 What the sower is sowing is the *w.*
4:15 ones to whom, as soon as they hear the *w,*
4:16 to the *w* accept it joyfully at the outset.
4:17 overtakes them because of the *w,*
4:18 They have listened to the *w,*
4:20 soil are the ones who listen to the *w,*
5:13 He gave the *w,* and with it the unclean
7:13 That is the way you nullify God's *w* in
9:10 They kept this *w* of his to themselves,
10:29 "I give you my *w,* there is no one
11:24 I give you my *w,* if you are ready
14:18 of the meal Jesus said, "I give you my *w,*
Lk 1: 2 eyewitnesses and ministers of the *w.*
2:29 you have fulfilled your *w.*
3: 2 the *w* of God was spoken to John son of
5: 1 pressed in on him to hear the *w* of God,
7:18 their teacher *w* of all these happenings.
8:11 The seed is the *w* of God.
8:12 but the devil comes and takes the *w* out of
8:13 are the ones who, when they hear the *w,*
8:15 who hear the *w* in a spirit of openness,
8:21 who hear the *w* of God and act upon it."
11:28 are they who hear the *w* of God and keep it."
19:19 His *w* to him was,
22:61 the *w* that the Lord had spoken to him,
24:19 a prophet powerful in *w* and deed in the
Jn 1: 1 In the beginning was the *W;*
1: 1 *W* was in God's presence, and the Word
1:14 The *W* became flesh and made his dwelling
2:22 the Scripture and the *w* he had spoken.
4:39 the strength of the woman's *w* of testimony:
4:41 his own spoken *w* many more came to faith.
4:50 put his trust in the *w* Jesus spoke to him,
5:24 the man who hears my *w* and has faith in
5:38 neither do you have his *w* abiding in your
7:26 in public and they don't say a *w* to him!
8:37 me because my *w* finds no hearing among you.
8:43 It is because you cannot bear to hear my *w.*
8:47 Whoever is of God hears every *w* God speaks.
8:51 is true to my *w* he shall never see death."
8:52 shall never know death if he keeps my *w.*'
8:55 Yes, I know him well, and I keep his *w.*
10: 7 "My solemn *w* is this:
10:35 men gods to whom God's *w* was addressed
11: 3 The sisters sent *w* to Jesus to inform him,
12:38 was to fulfill the *w* of the prophet Isaiah:
12:48 has his judge, namely, the *w* I have spoken
14:23 who loves me will be true to my *w,*
14:24 Yet the *w* you hear is not mine;
15: 3 thanks to the *w* I have spoken to you.
17: 6 they have kept your *w.*
17:14 I gave them your *w,*
17:17 'Your *w* is truth.'
17:20 who will believe in me through their *w,*
Acts 4:31 continued to speak God's *w* with confidence.
5:21 They sent *w* to the jail that the prisoners
6: 2 the *w* of God in order to wait on tables.
6: 4 on prayer and the ministry of the *w.*"
6: 7 The *w* of God continued to spread,
7:22 He was a man powerful in *w* and deed.
8: 4 been dispersed went about preaching the *w.*
8:14 that Samaria had accepted the *w* of God,
8:25 and proclaiming the *w* of the Lord,
11: 1 Gentiles, too, had accepted the *w* of God.
12:24 Meanwhile the *w* of the Lord continued to
13: 5 the *w* of God in the Jewish synagogues,
13: 7 Saul and was anxious to hear the *w* of God.
13:44 entire city gathered to hear the *w* of God.
13:46 "The *w* of God has to be declared to you
13:48 responded to the *w* of the Lord with praise.
13:49 Thus the *w* of the Lord was carried
15:27 who will convey this message by *w* of mouth:
15:35 teaching and preaching the *w* of the Lord.
15:36 where we proclaimed the *w* of the Lord."
16:32 They proceeded to announce the *w* of God to
17:13 Jews of Thessalonica learned that the *w* of
18:11 and a half, teaching them the *w* of God.
19:10 and Greeks alike, heard the *w* of the Lord.
19:20 Thus did the *w* of the Lord continue to
19:31 Asiarchs who were friends of Paul sent *w*
20:17 Paul sent *w* from Miletus to Ephesus,
20:32 gracious *w* of his which can enlarge you,
28:25 Then Paul added one final *w:*
Rom 4:14 empty *w* and the promise loses its meaning.
9: 6 Not that God's *w* has failed.
10: 8 "The *w* is near you,
10: 8 (that is, the *w* of faith which we preach).
10:17 and what is heard is the *w* of Christ.
15:18 the Gentiles to obedience by *w* and deed,
15:21 who received no *w* of him will see him,
1Cor 14:36 preaching of God's *w* originate with you?
16:13 In a *w,* be strong.
2Cor 1:18 God keeps his *w,* I declare that my word
2:17 not like so many who trade on the *w* of God.
4: 2 resort to trickery or falsify the *w* of God.
10:10 and his *w* makes no great impact.
10:11 this some thought, that what we are by *w,*
Gal 6: 6 The man instructed in the *w* should share
Eph 1:13 glad tidings of salvation, the *w* of truth,
5:26 the bath of water by the power of the *w,*
6:17 and the sword of the spirit, the *w* of God.
6:19 for me that God may put his *w* on my lips,
Phil 1:14 to speak the *w* of God fearlessly.
2:16 sky while holding fast to the *w* of life.
Col 1:25 to preach among you his *w* in its fullness,
3:16 Let the *w* of Christ, rich as it is,
1Thes 1: 6 Lord, receiving the *w* despite great trials,
1: 8 The *w* of the Lord has echoed forth from
2:13 word of men, but as it truly is, the *w* of
4:16 come down from heaven at the *w* of command,
2Thes 2:15 from us, either by our *w* or by letter.
2:17 strengthen them for every good work and *w.*
3: 1 pray for us that the *w* of the Lord may
1Tm 4: 5 it is made holy by God's *w* and by prayer.
5:10 In a *w,* has she been eager to do every
6: 5 in a *w,*
2Tm 2: 9 but there is no chaining the *w* of God!
4: 2 power, I charge you to preach the *w,*
Ti 1: 3 manifested in his own good time as his *w,*
2: 5 the *w* of God will not fall into disrepute.
Heb 1: 3 he sustains all things by his powerful *w.*
2: 2 *w* spoken through angels stood unchanged,
4: 2 the *w* which they heard did not profit them,
4:12 Indeed, God's *w* is living and effective,
5:13 alone is ignorant of the *w* that sanctifies,
6: 5 *w* of God and the powers of the age to come,
7:28 but the *w* of the oath which came after the
11: 3 the worlds were created by the *w* of God,
13: 7 your leaders who spoke the *w* of God to you;
13:22 you to bear with this *w* of encouragement,
Jas 1:18 He wills to bring us to birth with a *w*
1:21 welcome the *w* that has taken root in you,
1:22 Act on this *w.*
1:23 A man who listens to God's *w* but does not
1Pt 1:23 through the living and enduring *w* of God.
1:24 but the *w* of the Lord endures forever."
1:25 Now this *w*" is the gospel which was
2: 8 and fall are the disbelievers in God's *w;*
2:16 In a *w,* live as servants of God.
3: 1 any of them who do not believe in the *w*
2Pt 3: 5 all brought into being by the *w* of God.
3: 7 earth are reserved by God's *w* for fire;
1Jn 1:10 him a liar and his *w* finds no place in us.
2: 5 But whoever keeps his *w,*
2: 7 now old, is the *w* you have already heard.
2:14 strong, and the *w* of God remains in you,
Jude 1:15 harsh *w* they have uttered against him."
Rv 1: 2 *w* of God and the testimony of Jesus Christ.
1: 9 God's *w* and bore witness to Jesus.
2: 7 ears heed the Spirit's *w* to the churches!
2:11 ears heed the Spirit's *w* to the churches!
2:17 ears heed the Spirit's *w* to the churches!

WORD (cont.)

2:29 ears heed the Spirit's *w* to the churches!'
3: 6 ears heed the Spirit's *w* to the churches!'
3: 8 fast to my *w* and have not denied my name.
3:13 ears heed the Spirit's *w* to the churches!
3:22 ears heed the Spirit's *w* to the churches.'"
6: 9 of the witness they bore to the *w* of God.
12:11 the Lamb and by the *w* of their testimony;
19:13 in blood, and his name was the *W* of God.
20: 4 their witness to Jesus and the *w* of God,

WORDED (1)

Acts 2:22 These God *w* through him in your midst,

WORDS (541)

Gn 11: 1 spoke the same language, using the same *w*.
14:18 Most High, he blessed Abram with these *w*:
24:15 *w* when Rebekah (who was born to Bethuel,
24:30 her *w* about what the man had said to her,
27:34 On hearing his father's *w*,
42:16 shall your *w* be tested for their truth;
42:20 Your *w* will thus be verified,
44: 6 overtook them and repeated these *w* to them,
44:24 we reported to him the *w* of my lord.
48:15 Then he blessed them with these *w*:
50:17 When they spoke these *w* to him,
Ex 4:15 to him, then, and put the *w* in his mouth.
5: 9 mind on it and pay no attention to lying *w*."
23: 8 and twists the *w* even of the just.
24: 3 all the *w* and ordinances of the LORD,
24: 4 then wrote down all the *w* of the LORD and,
24: 8 you in accordance with all these *w* of his."
34:27 LORD said to Moses, "Write down these *w*,
34:28 wrote on the tablets the *w* of the covenant,
Nm 12: 6 he said, "Now listen to the *w* of the LORD:
14:39 repeated these *w* to all the Israelites,
22: 5 the Amawites, summoning him with these *w*,
Dt 1: 1 These are the *w* which Moses spoke to all
1:34 When the LORD heard your *w*,
4:10 I will have them hear my *w*,
4:12 You heard the sound of the *w*,
5: 5 to announce to you these *w* of the LORD:
5:22 "These *w*, and nothing more, the LORD
5:28 "The LORD heard your *w* as you were
5:28 the *w* these people have spoken to you,
6: 6 heart these *w* which I enjoin on you today.
9:10 with a copy of all the *w* that the LORD
11:18 these *w* of mine into your heart and soul.
13: 4 to the *w* of that prophet or that dreamer;
16:19 the wise and twists the *w* even of the just.
17:19 all the *w* of this law and these statutes.
18:18 kinsmen, and will put my *w* into his mouth;
18:19 listen to my *w* which he speaks in my name,
27: 3 the time you cross, all the *w* of this law,
27: 8 all the *w* of this law very clearly."
28:69 These are the *w* of the covenant which the
29:18 person, upon hearing the *w* of this curse,
29:28 we may carry out all the *w* of this law.]
31: 1 finished speaking these *w* to all Israel,
31:12 carefully observe all the *w* of this law.
31:24 scroll the *w* of the law in their entirety,
31:28 that I may speak these *w* for them to hear,
31:30 the *w* of this song from beginning to end,
32: 1 let the earth hearken to the *w* of my mouth!
32:44 the *w* of this song for the people to hear.
32:45 speaking all these *w* to all Israel,
33: 9 Thus the Levites keep your *w*,
Jos 3: 9 here and listen to the *w* of the LORD,
8:34 Then were read aloud all the *w* of the law,
24:27 heard all the *w* which the LORD spoke to us.
Jgs 6:32 was called Jerubbaal, because of the *w*,
9: 3 kin repeated these *w* to them on his behalf,
13:17 we may honor you when your *w* come true?"
Ru 2:13 me, your servant, with your consoling *w*;
1Sm 17:27 They repeated the same *w* to him and said,
17:31 The *w* that David had spoken were overheard
24: 8 With these *w* David restrained his men and
25:24 you, and listen to the *w* of your handmaid.
26:19 the king listen to the *w* of his servant.
2Sm 3: 8 Enraged at the *w* of Ishbaal,
7:17 these *w* and this entire vision to David.
7:28 Lord GOD, you are God and your *w* are truth;
22: 1 David sang the *w* of this song to the LORD
23: 1 These are the last *w* of David:
1Kgs 5:21 When he had heard the *w* of Solomon,
13:11 father the *w* he had spoken to the king,
21:27 When Ahab heard these *w*,
2Kgs 6:12 the very *w* you speak in your bedroom."
6:30 When the king heard the woman's *w*,
18:20 *w* substitute for strategy and might in war?
18:27 you that my lord sent me to speak these *w*?
18:28 "Listen to the *w* of the great king,
19: 4 God, will hear all the *w* of the commander,
19: 4 will rebuke him for the *w* which the LORD,
19: 6 not be frightened by the *w* you have heard,
19:16 Hear the *w* of Sennacherib which he sent to
23:16 the man of God who had proclaimed these *w*,
1Chr 12:18 to meet them and addressed them in these *w*:
17:15 All these *w* and this whole vision Nathan
21: 9 spoke to Gad, David's seer, in these *w*:
29:10 of the whole assembly, praying in these *w*:
2Chr 13:22 of Abijah's acts, his deeds and his *w*,
15: 8 *w* and the prophecy [Oded the prophet],
29:15 the LORD's house in keeping with his *w*.
29:30 in the *w* of David and of Asaph the seer.
32: 6 the city and encouraged them with these *w*:
32: 8 from the *w* of King Hezekiah of Judah.
33:18 and the *w* of the seers who spoke to him in
34:19 When the king heard the *w* of the law,
34:21 the *w* of the book that has been found.
34:27 yourself before God on hearing his *w* spoken
35:22 *w* of Neco that came from the mouth of God,
Ezr 5: 9 elders, addressing to them the following *w*:
8:28 I addressed them in these *w*:
Neh 1: 1 The *w* of Nehemiah, the son of Hacaliah.
4: 8 then addressed these *w* to the nobles,
8: 9 weeping as they heard the *w* of the law.
8:12 the *w* that had been expounded to them.
8:13 and examined the *w* of the law more closely.
Tb 6:13 So heed my *w*,
7:10 Raguel overheard the *w*;
7:12 the hand and gave her to Tobiah with the *w*:
8: 5 He began with these *w*:
8:15 praised the God of heaven in these *w*:
Jdt 3: 1 to him to sue for peace in these *w*:
6: 4 and his *w* shall not remain unfulfilled.
6: 9 my *w* shall not prove false in any respect."
6:17 all his own *w* among the Assyrian officers,
7:16 *w* pleased Holofernes and all his ministers,
8: 9 heard of the harsh *w* which the people,
8:28 good sense, and no one can gainsay your *w*.
10:14 men heard her *w* and gazed upon her face,
11: 5 "Listen to the *w* of your servant,
11: 6 if you follow out the *w* of your handmaid,
11:20 *w* pleased Holofernes and all his servants;
11:23 fair to behold, and your *w* are well spoken.
14:19 of the Assyrian army heard these *w*,
Est 4:12 When Esther's *w* were reported to Mordecai,
C:24 persuasive *w* in the presence of the lion,
D: 8 and comforted her with reassuring *w*.
1Mc 2:22 We will not obey the *w* of the king nor
2:23 As he finished saying these *w*,
2:62 Do not fear the *w* of a sinful man,
7:11 But these paid no attention to their *w*,
10:24 *w* and offer dignities and gifts,
10:46 Jonathan and the people heard these *w*,
10:55 King Ptolemy answered in these *w*:
11: 2 He entered Syria with peaceful *w*,
13: 3 the people and exhorted them in these *w*:
13: 7 As the people heard these *w*,
14:23 a copy of their *w* in the public archives,
15:36 When he told him of Simon's *w*,
2Mc 2: 3 With other similar *w* he urged them not to
6:17 these *w* suffice for recalling this truth.
7: 5 to die bravely, saying such *w* as these:
7: 6 when he protested openly with the *w*,
7:11 out his hands, as he spoke these noble *w*:
7:21 language of their forefathers with these *w*:
7:24 Antiochus, suspecting insult in her *w*,
7:24 the king appealed to him, not with mere *w*,
8:21 With such *w* he encouraged them and made
9: 5 for scarcely had he uttered those *w* when
10:34 blasphemies and uttering abominable *w*.
14:34 With these *w* he went away.
14:34 defender of our nation in these *w*:
15: 9 them with *w* from the law and the prophets,
15:11 as with the encouragement of noble *w*,
15:17 Encouraged by Judas' noble *w*,
Jb 4: 4 Your *w* have upheld the stumbler;
6:25 How agreeable are honest *w*;
6:26 Do you consider your *w* as proof,
8: 2 *w* from your mouth are like a mighty wind!
8:10 you and utter their *w* of understanding?
9:16 not believe that he would hearken to my *w*;
11: 2 Should not the man of many *w* be answered,
12:11 the ear judge *w* as the mouth tastes food?
15: 3 avail, and in *w* which are to no profit?
15:13 God and let such *w* escape your mouth!
16: 3 Is there no end to windy *w*?
18: 2 When will you put an end to *w*?
19: 2 will you vex my soul, grind me down with *w*?
19:23 Oh, would that my *w* were written down!
21: 2 At least listen to my *w*,
22:22 his mouth, and lay up his *w* in your heart.
23: 5 learn the *w* with which he would answer,
23:12 the *w* of his mouth I have treasured in my
26: 4 With whose help have you uttered those *w*,
27:12 why then do you spend yourselves in idle *w*!
29:23 they drank in my *w* like the spring rains.
31:37 The *w* of Job are ended.
32:14 For had he addressed his *w* to me,
32:15 *w* fail them.
33: 1 hear my discourse, and hearken to all my *w*.
33: 2 my tongue and my voice form *w*.
33: 8 as I listened to the sound of your *w*:
34: 3 For the ear tests *w*,
34:16 Hearken to the *w* I speak!
34:35 intelligence, and his *w* are without sense."
34:37 our arguments and addressing many *w* to God.
35: 4 I have *w* for a reply to you and your three
35:16 mouth, and without knowledge multiplies *w*.
36: 2 are still *w* to be said on God's behalf.
38: 2 obscures divine plans with *w* of ignorance?
40:27 after time, or address you with tender *w*?
42: 7 after the LORD had spoken these *w* to Job,
Ps(s) 5: 2 Hearken to my *w*, O LORD,
17: 4 according to the *w* of your lips I have
18: 1 who sang to the Lord the *w* of this song
19:15 Let the *w* of my mouth and the thought of
22: 2 far from my prayer, from the *w* of my cry?
35:20 For civil *w* they speak not,
36: 4 The *w* of his mouth are empty and false;
50:17 hate discipline and cast my *w* behind you?
54: 4 hearken to the *w* of my mouth.
55:22 His *w* are smoother than oil,
64: 4 who aim like arrows their bitter *w*,
66:14 uttered and my *w* promised in my distress.
66:17 When I appealed to him in *w*,
78: 1 incline your ears to the *w* of my mouth.
105:28 grew dark, but they rebelled against his *w*.
106:12 they believed his *w* and sang his praises.
107:11 they had rebelled against the *w* of God
109: 3 and with *w* of hatred they have
119: 9 By keeping to your *w*.
119:16 I will not forget your *w*.
119:17 servant, that I may live and keep your *w*.
119:28 strengthen me according to your *w*.
119:42 who reproach me, for I trust in your *w*.
119:57 O LORD, that my part is to keep your *w*.
119:101 I withhold my feet, that I may keep your *w*.
119:130 The revelation of your *w* sheds light,
119:139 consumes me, because my foes forget your *w*.
119:147 I hope in your *w*.
119:160 Permanence is your *w* chief trait;
138: 1 [for you have heard the *w* of my mouth;]
138: 4 O LORD, when they hear the *w* of your mouth;
141: 6 and they heard how pleasant were my *w*.
145:13 in all his *w* and holy in all his works.
Prv 1: 2 may understand *w* of intelligence;
1: 6 the *w* of the wise and their riddles.
1:21 out, at the city gates she utters her *w*:
1:23 my spirit, I will acquaint you with my *w*.
2: 1 you receive my *w* and treasure my commands,
2:16 from the adulteress with her smooth *w*,
4: 4 "Let your heart hold fast my *w*:
4: 5 forget or turn aside from the *w* I utter.
4:10 Hear, my son, and receive my *w*,
4:20 My son, to my *w* be attentive,
5: 7 me, go not astray from the *w* of my mouth.
6: 2 your lips, caught by the *w* of your mouth;
7: 1 My son, keep my *w*,
7: 5 from the adulteress with her smooth *w*.
7:24 to me, be attentive to the *w* of my mouth!
8: 8 Sincere are all the *w* of my mouth,
10:19 Where *w* are many, sin is not wanting;
12: 6 The *w* of the wicked are a deadly ambush,
12:14 of his *w* a man has his fill of good things,
13: 2 the fruit of his *w* a man eats good things,
16:24 Pleasing *w* are a honeycomb,
17: 7 Fine *w* are out of place in a fool;
17: 7 how much more, lying *w* in a noble!
17:27 He who spares his *w* is truly wise,
18: 4 The *w* from a man's mouth are deep waters,
18: 8 The *w* of a talebearer are like dainty
19:27 he wanders from *w* of knowledge.
22:17 Incline your ear, and hear my *w*,
22:19 I make known to you the *w* of Amen-em-Ope.
23: 8 and you will have wasted your agreeable *w*.
23: 9 he will despise the wisdom of your *w*.
23:12 and your ears to *w* of knowledge.
25:11 settings are *w* spoken at the proper time.
26:22 The *w* of a talebearer are like dainty
29:12 If a ruler listens to lying *w*,
29:19 By *w* no servant can be trained;
29:20 Do you see a man hasty in his *w*?
30: 1 The *w* of Agur, son of Jakeh the Massaite:
30: 6 Add nothing to his *w*,
31: 1 The *w* of Lemuel, king of Massa.
Eccl 1: 1 The *w* of David's son,
5: 1 therefore let your *w* be few.
5: 2 cares, and a fool's utterance with many *w*.
5: 5 such *w* and destroy the works of your hands.
9:16 poor man is despised and his *w* go unheeded.
9:17 "The quiet *w* of the wise are better
10:12 *W* from the wise man's mouth win favor,
10:13 The beginning of his *w* is folly,
10:14 yet the fool multiplies *w*.
Wis 1: 9 the sound of his *w* shall reach the Lord,
1:16 wicked who with hands and *w* invited death,
2:17 Let us see whether his *w* be true;
2:20 for according to his own *w*,
6: 9 are my *w* addressed that you may learn
6:11 Desire therefore my *w*;
6:25 so take instruction from my *w*,
7:16 For both we and our *w* are in his hand,
Sir 1:21 For a while he holds back his *w*,
2:15 Those who fear the LORD disobey not his *w*;
5:12 steadfast be your *w*.
7:14 and repeat not the *w* of your prayer.
13: 5 have anything he will speak fair *w* to you,
13:11 discussion with him, trust not his many *w*;
16:22 take my advice, apply your mind to my *w*,
18:14 no reproach, nor spoil any gift by harsh *w*.
18:29 trained in her *w* must show their wisdom,
20:12 wise man makes himself popular by a few *w*,
20:26 A wise man advances himself by his *w*,
21:15 When an intelligent man hears *w* of wisdom,
21:17 and his *w* are considered with care.

21:18 stupid man knows it only as inscrutable w.
21:25 the w of the prudent are carefully weighed.
21:26 mouths, wise men's w are in their hearts.
23:12 There are w which merit death;
23:12 For all such w are foreign to the devout,
27:23 his tone and twists your w to your ruin.
28:25 and gold, so balance and weigh your w.
29:25 besides, you will hear these bitter w:
31:31 Use no harsh w with him and distress him
32: 8 Be brief, but say much in those few w,
32:12 you wish, but without sin or w of pride.
33: 4 Prepare your w and you will be listened to;
36:19 its savor, so does a keen mind insincere w.
37:20 if his w are rejected he will be deprived
39: 6 He will pour forth his w of wisdom and in
41:22 Of using harsh w with friends,
45: 3 w and sustained him in the king's presence.
46:15 out and his w proved him true as a seer.
47: 8 thanks to God Most High, in w of praise.
48: 1 prophet whose w were as a flaming furnace.
Is 16: 6 insolence that his empty w do not match.
29: 4 and from the base dust your w shall come.
29: 4 and your w like chirping from the dust.
29:11 has become like the w of a sealed scroll.
29:13 w only and honors me with their lips alone,
29:18 day the deaf shall hear the w of a book;
32: 9 overconfident women, give heed to my w.
36: 5 w substitute for strategy and might in war?
36:12 that my lord sent me to speak these w?
36:13 "Listen to the w of the great king,
37: 4 your God, will hear the w of the commander,
37: 4 will rebuke him for the w which the LORD,
37: 6 not be frightened by the w you have heard,
37:17 Hear all the w of the letter that
41: 1 you peoples, wait for my w!
44:26 It is I who confirm the w of my servants,
51:16 I have put my w into your mouth and
59:13 w of falsehood the heart has conceived.
59:21 My spirit which is upon you and my w that
Jer 1: 1 The w of Jeremiah,
1: 9 saying, See, I place my w in your mouth!
3:12 Go, proclaim these w toward the north,
5:14 Behold, I make my w in your mouth,
6:19 own schemes, Because they heeded not my w,
7: 4 Put not your trust in the deceitful w:
7: 8 your trust in deceitful w to your own loss!
7:27 When you speak all these w to them,
11: 6 Proclaim all these w in the cities of
11: 6 Hear the w of this covenant and obey them.
11:10 their forefathers who refused to obey my w.
12: 6 if they are friendly to you in their w.
13:10 wicked people who refuse to obey my w,
15:16 When I found your w,
16:10 these w to this people and they ask you:
19: 2 proclaim the w which I will speak to you:
19:15 their necks and have not obeyed my w.
23: 2 Because of the LORD, because of his holy w.
23:16 Listen not to the w of your prophets,
23:22 did they but proclaim to my people my w,
23:30 the LORD, who steal my w from each other.
23:36 that you pervert the w of the living God,
25: 8 Since you would not listen to my w, lo!
25:13 I will fulfill all the w I have spoken against
26: 5 to the w of my servants the prophets,
26: 7 speak these w in the house of the LORD.
26:21 and princes were informed of his w,
27:12 king of Judah, I spoke the same w:
27:14 listen to the w of those prophets who say,
27:16 the w of your prophets who prophesy to you:
29:19 For they did not listen to my w,
30: 2 all the w I have spoken to you in a book:
30: 4 These are the w which the LORD spoke to
35: 6 son, our father, forbade us in these w:
35:13 Will you not take correction and obey my w?
36: 2 the w I have spoken to you against Israel,
36: 4 all the w which the LORD had spoken to him.
36: 6 publicly in the LORD's house the LORD's w
36: 8 he read the LORD's w in the LORD's house.
36:10 read the w of Jeremiah from his book.
36:11 all the w of the LORD read from the book.
36:16 it to them, and when they heard all its w,
36:17 how you came to write down all these w."
36:18 "Jeremiah dictated all these w to me,"
36:24 Hearing all these w did not frighten the
36:32 w contained in the book which Jehoiakim,
37: 2 to the w of the LORD spoken by Jeremiah
38: 1 speaking these w to all the people:
38:27 them in the very w the king had commanded.
39:16 fulfilling the w I spoke against this city,
43: 1 to the people all these w of the LORD,
51:60 these w that were written against Babylon.
51:61 see that you read aloud all these w,
51:64 "weary themselves" are the w of Jeremiah.]
Bar 1: 1 these are the w of the scroll which Baruch,
1: 3 read the w of this scroll for Jeconiah,
1:21 all the w of the prophets whom he sent us,
Ez 2: 6 w when they contradict you and reject you,
2: 6 their w nor be dismayed at their looks,
2: 7 [But speak my w to them,
3: 4 house of Israel, and speak my w to them.
3: 6 language] whose w you cannot understand.
3:10 your heart all my w that I speak to you;
12:28 None of my w shall be delayed any longer;
20: 5 abominations of their ancestors in these w:
33:31 they sit down before you and hear your w,
33:32 They listen to your w,
34: 2 w prophesy to them [to the shepherds]:
35:13 and wild w you have spoken against me.
36: 3 [therefore prophesy in these w:
39: 1 of man, prophesy against Gog in these w:
Dn 4:28 these w were still on the king's lips,
5:15 but they could not say what the w meant.
5:25 These w mean:
7:11 of the arrogant w which the horn spoke,
9:22 He instructed me in these w:
10:11 the w which I am speaking to you;
12: 9 "because the w are to be kept secret and
13:61 own w Daniel had convicted them of perjury.
Hos 6: 5 prophets, I slew them by the w of my mouth;
14: 3 Take with you w,
Am 1: 1 The w of Amos,
7:10 the country cannot endure all his w.
Mi 2: 7 w promise good to him who walks uprightly?
Hg 1:12 God, and to the w of the prophet Haggai,
Zec 1: 6 But my w and my decrees,
1:13 me, the LORD replied with comforting w.
7: 7 Were not these the w which the LORD spoke
8: 9 hear these w spoken by the prophets
Mal 2:17 You have wearied the LORD with your w,
Mt 6: 7 hearing by the sheer multiplication of w.
7:24 "Anyone who hears my w and puts them into
7:26 Anyone who hears my w but does not put
9:13 Go and learn the meaning of the w,
11:18 In other w,
12:37 w you will be acquitted, and by your words
17:23 these w they were overwhelmed with grief.
19:22 Hearing these w,
23: 4 Their w are bold but their deeds are few.
24:35 will pass away but my w will not pass.
26:44 a third time, saying the same w as before.
28:18 came forward and addressed them in these w:
Mk 6:20 yet he felt the attraction of his w.
9:32 Though they failed to understand his w,
10:22 At these w the man's face fell.
10:24 The disciples could only marvel at his w.
13:31 will pass away but my w will not pass.
14:39 back again he began to pray in the same w.
Lk 1:20 place, because you have not trusted my w.
1:29 She was deeply troubled by his w,
1:45 the Lord's w to her would be fulfilled."
1:63 for a writing tablet and wrote the w,
2:28 him in his arms and blessed God in these w:
3: 4 in the book of the w of Isaiah the prophet:
4:28 At these w the whole audience in the
4:32 by his teaching, for his w had authority.
6:47 will hear my w and put them into practice.
6:49 anyone who has heard my w but not put them
8:39 with him, but he sent him away with the w,
8:54 He took her by the hand and spoke these w:
10:39 at the Lord's feet and listened to his w.
11:29 him he began to speak to them in these w:
12:16 He told them a parable in these w:
13:17 At these w, his opponents were covered
14:15 At these w one in the party said to him,
19:48 was listening to him and hanging on his w.
20: 2 In other w, who has authorized you?"
20:19 At these w the scribes and high priests
20:21 we know that your w and your doctrine are
21:15 for I will give you w and a wisdom which
21:33 will pass away, but my w will not pass.
22:41 down on his knees and prayed in these w:
22:65 directed many other insulting w at him.
24: 8 this reminder, his w came back to them.
24:44 w I spoke to you when I was still with you:
Jn 2:17 His disciples recalled the w of Scripture:
3:34 One whom God has sent speaks the w of God;
6:60 After hearing his w, many of his disciples
6:63 The w I spoke to you are spirit and life.
6:68 You have the w of eternal life.
7:40 the crowd who heard these w began to say,
8:20 w while teaching at the temple treasury.
10:19 Because of these w, the Jews were sharply
10:21 "These are not the w of a madman.
10:24 are the Messiah, tell us so in plain w."
10:39 At these w they again tried to arrest him,
11:11 After uttering these w,
12:34 The crowd objected to his w:
12:41 these w because he had seen Jesus' glory,
12:47 anyone hears my w and does not keep them,
12:48 does not accept my w already has his judge,
14:10 The w I speak are not spoken of myself;
14:24 He who does not love me does not keep my w.
15: 7 you live in me, and my w stay part of you,
15:20 your w as much as they respected mine.
17: 1 After he had spoken these w,
Acts 4:29 your servants, even as they speak your w,
5: 5 At the sound of these w,
7: 6 These are the w God used:
7:35 Moses whom they had rejected with the w,
7:54 listened to his w were stung to the heart;
10: 7 who spoke these w had disappeared,
10:34 Peter proceeded to address them in these w:
10:44 Peter had not finished these w when the
11:18 instead began to glorify God in these w:
13:27 they fulfilled the w of the prophets which
15:15 The w of the prophets agree with this,
19:40 These w of his broke up the meeting.
20: 2 providing as he went many w of
20:25 I know as I speak these w that none of you
20:35 to recall the w of the Lord Jesus himself,
22:29 At these w, those who were about to
23: 7 At these w, a dispute arose between
24:22 he heard these w he adjourned the trial,
Rom 3: 2 all, the Jews were entrusted with w of God.
4:23 The w, "It was credited to him," were not
9:18 In other w, God has mercy on whom he
10:18 and their w to the limits of the world."
15: 4 the w of encouragement in the Scriptures.
15:21 but rather to fulfill the w of Scripture,
1Cor 2:13 in words of human wisdom but in w taught
14:19 w to instruct others than ten thousand words
2Cor 12: 4 hear words which cannot be uttered, w
Gal 3:24 In other w, the law was our monitor until
Eph 4:31 bitterness, all passion and anger, harsh w,
1Thes 1: 5 mere matter of w for you but one of power;
2: 5 of flattering w or greed under any pretext,
1Tm 1: 7 not understanding the w they are using,
4: 6 reared in the w of faith and the sound
2Tm 2:14 before God to stop disputing about mere w.
Ti 2: 8 sound w to which no one can take exception.
Heb 4: 7 spoke through David the w we have quoted:
10: 9 other w, he takes away the first covenant
12: 5 the encouraging w addressed to you as sons:
12:19 nor a voice speaking w such that those who
Jude 1:17 w of the apostles of our Lord Jesus Christ;
Rv 13: 9 Let him who has ears heed these w!
19: 9 The angel continued, "These w are true;
21: 5 down, for the w are trustworthy and true!"
21: 6 "These w are already fulfilled!
22: 6 "These w are trustworthy and true;
22:10 not seal up the prophetic w of this book,
22:18 all who hear the prophetic w of this book.
22:18 If anyone adds to these w,
22:19 takes from the w of this prophetic book,

WORDY (1)

1Cor 1:17 not with w "wisdom,"

WORE (19)

Ex 33: 4 into mourning, and no one w his ornaments.
Jos 9: 5 They w old, patched sandals and shabby
Jgs 3:16 and w it under his clothes over his right
1Sm 17: 5 He had a bronze helmet on his head and w a
22:18 that day eighty-five who w the linen ephod.
1Chr 20: 2 stones, which David w on his own head.
Jdt 8: 5 about her loins and w widow's weeds.
Est 6: 8 brought the royal robe which the king w
1Mc 3:47 That day they fasted and w sackcloth;
8:14 crown or w purple as a display of grandeur.
11:13 he thus w two crowns on his head,
11:54 who became king and w the royal crown.
14: 9 young men w the glorious apparel of war.
Jb 29:14 I w my honesty like a garment;
Mt 3: 4 and w a leather belt around his waist.
Mk 1: 6 and w a leather belt around his waist.
Rv 9: 7 heads they w something like gold crowns;
9:17 The breastplates they w were fiery red,
19:13 He w a cloak that had been dipped in blood,

WORK (352)

Gn 2: 2 was finished with the w he had been doing,
2: 2 day from all the w he had undertaken.
2: 3 from all the w he had done in creation.
5:29 from our w and the toil of our hands."
26:14 flocks and herds, and so many w animals,
30:29 "You know what w I did for you and how
39:11 Joseph came into the house to do his w,
Ex 1:14 making life bitter for them with hard w
1:14 mortar and brick and all kinds of field w—
5: 4 by taking the people away from their w?
5: 9 Increase the w for the men,
5:11 not be the slightest reduction in your w."
5:13 driving them on, saying, "Finish your w,
5:18 'Off to w, then!
7: 3 wonders that I will w in the land of Egypt,
7: 9 demands that you w a sign or wonder,
12:16 these days you shall not do any sort of w,
20: 9 Six days you may labor and do all your w,
20:10 No w may be done then either by you,
23:12 "For six days you may do your w,
28:11 Israel and then mounted in gold filigree w.
28:20 are to be mounted in gold filigree w,
28:39 The sash shall be of variegated w.
31:14 If anyone does w on that day,
31:15 Six days there are for doing w,
31:15 w on the sabbath day shall be put to death.
34:10 of all your people I will w such marvels
34:21 "For six days you may w,
35: 2 On six days w may be done,
35: 2 does w on that day shall be put to death.
35:24 to have acacia wood for any part of the w,
35:29 for the various kinds of w which the LORD
35:35 them with skill to execute all types of w:
36: 1 will set to w with Oholiab and with all
36: 1 all the w for the service of the sanctuary,
36: 2 moved them to come and take part in the w.
36: 4 of work for the sanctuary, all left the w

WORK (cont.)
36: 5 *w* which the LORD has commanded us to do."
36: 7 than enough, to complete the *w* to be done.
36: 8 various experts who were executing the *w*,
39: 6 prepared and mounted in gold filigree *w*;
39:13 They were mounted in gold filigree *w*.
39:29 *w* made of fine linen twined and of violet,
39:32 Thus the entire *w* of the Dwelling of the
39:32 the *w* just as the LORD had commanded Moses.
39:42 the *w* just as the LORD had commanded Moses.
39:43 *w* was done just as the Lord had commanded,
40:33 Thus Moses finished all the *w*.
Lv 16:29 shall mortify himself and shall do no *w*.
23: 3 "For six days *w* may be done;
23: 3 assembly, on which you shall do no *w*.
23: 7 hold a sacred assembly and do no sort of *w*.
23: 8 hold a sacred assembly and do no sort of *w*."
23:21 assembly, and no sort of *w* may be done.
23:25 you shall then do no sort of *w*,
23:28 On this day you shall not do any *w*,
23:30 and if anyone does any *w* on this day,
23:31 you shall do no *w*,
23:35 assembly, and you shall do no sort of *w*.
23:36 solemn closing you shall do no sort of *w*.
25:39 his services, do not make him *w* as a slave.
Nm 8:25 from the required service and *w* no longer.
8:26 meeting tent, but he shall not do the *w*.
18: 4 all the *w* connected with the meeting tent.
28:18 a sacred assembly, and do no sort of *w*.
28:25 a sacred assembly, and do no sort of *w*.
28:26 a sacred assembly, and do no sort of *w*.
29: 1 a sacred assembly, and do no sort of *w*;
29: 7 mortify yourselves, and do no sort of *w*.
29:12 a sacred assembly, and do no sort of *w*;
29:35 hold a solemn meeting, and do no sort of *w*.
Dt 5:13 Six days you may labor and do all your *w*;
5:14 No *w* may be done then,
15:19 shall not *w* the firstlings of your cattle,
16: 8 on that day you shall not do any sort of *w*.
21: 3 put to *w* as a draft animal under a yoke,
Jgs 2: 7 great *w* which the LORD had done for Israel,
16:11 new ropes, with which no *w* has been done,"
19:16 an old man came from his *w* in the field;
Ru 2:19 Where did you go to *w*?
1Sm 6: 7 So now set to *w* and make a new cart.
8:16 and your asses, and use them to do his *w*.
2Sm 12:31 whom he assigned to *w* with saws,
12:31 iron axes, or put to *w* at the brickmold.
1Kgs 5:30 *w*, directing the people engaged in the *w*.
7:14 of how to produce any *w* in bronze.
7:14 to King Solomon and did all his metal *w*.
7:22 Thus the *w* on the columns was completed.
7:31 There was carved *w* at the opening,
7:40 he therewith completed all his *w* for King
7:51 When all the *w* undertaken by King Solomon
9:23 in the *w* numbered five hundred and fifty.
2Kgs 19:18 were not gods, but the *w* of human hands,
1Chr 9:13 the *w* of the service of the house of God.
20: 3 of the city and set them to *w* with saws,
22:16 Set to *w*, therefore, and the LORD be
23:24 They performed the *w* of the service of the
26:30 side of the Jordan in all the *w* of the LORD
28:10 Take courage and set to *w*."
28:13 *w* of the service of the house of the LORD,
28:20 go to *w* without fear or discouragement,
28:20 *w* for the service of the house of the LORD.
28:21 they will help you in all your *w* with all
29: 1 the *w*,
29: 5 for every *w* that is to be done by artisans.
2Chr 2: 6 Now, send me men skilled at *w* in gold,
2: 6 and who know how to do engraved *w*,
2:13 he knows how to *w* with gold,
2:13 *w* and to devise every type of artistic work
4:11 Huram thus completed the *w* he had to do
5: 1 When all the *w* undertaken by Solomon for
8:16 All of Solomon's *w* was carried out
15: 7 do not relax, for your *w* shall be rewarded."
16: 5 he stopped his *w*.
20:37 with Ahaziah, the LORD will shatter your *w*."
29:17 They began the *w* of consecration on the
29:31 "You have undertaken a *w* for the LORD.
32:19 peoples of the earth, a *w* of human hands.
Ezr 3: 8 supervise the *w* on the house of the LORD.
3: 9 were engaged in the *w* on the house of God.
4: 5 They also suborned counselors to *w*
4:21 that will stop the *w* of these men.
4:23 and stopped their *w* by force of arms.
4:24 Thus it was that the *w* on the house of God
5: 8 the *w* is being carried on diligently and
6: 7 Jews continue to *w* on that house of God;
6:22 them help in their *w* on the house of God,
Neh 2:18 And they undertook the good *w* with vigor.
3: 4 son of Hakkoz, carried out the *w* of repair;
3: 5 the Tekoites carried out the *w* of repair;
3: 8 the *w* of repair was carried out by Uzziel,
3: 9 *w* of repair was carried out by Rephaiah,
3:10 Hashabneiah, carried out the *w* of repair.
3:12 the *w* of repair was carried out by Shallum,
3:16 *w* of repair was carried out by Nehemiah,
3:17 the Levites carried out the *w* of repair:
3:18 their brethren carried out the *w* of repair:
3:22 *w* of repair was carried out by the priests,
3:25 carried out the *w* of repair opposite the
3:25 carried out the *w* of repair to a point
3:28 the priests carried out the *w* of repair,
3:31 carried out the *w* of repair as far as the
3:32 the merchants carried out the *w* of repair.
4: 5 midst, kill them, and put an end to the *w*."
4:10 half my able men took a hand in the *w*,
4:11 each did his *w* with one hand and held a
4:13 "Our *w* is scattered and extensive,
4:15 Thus we went on with the *w*,
5:16 own, I did my part in this *w* on the wall,
5:16 all my men were gathered there for the *w*.
6: 3 why should the *w* stop,
6: 9 "Their hands will slacken in the *w*,
6:16 God's help that this *w* had been completed.
Tb 2:11 at weaving cloth, the kind of *w* women do.
5: 5 I have come here to *w*."
Est F: 1 "This is the *w* of God.
1Mc 2:47 and the *w* prospered in their hands.
4:51 finished all the *w* they had undertaken.
9:54 thus destroying the *w* of the prophets.
9:55 he had a stroke, and his *w* was interrupted;
2Mc 5:25 then, finding the Jews refraining from *w*,
15:38 delights the ears of those who read the *w*.
Jb 1: 3 she-asses, and a great number of *w* animals,
1:10 You have blessed the *w* of his hands,
10: 3 to oppress, to spurn the *w* of your hands,
14:15 you would esteem the *w* of your hands.
34:19 For they are all the *w* of his hands:
36:24 Remember, you should extol his *w*,
37:16 *w* of him who is perfect in knowledge?
Ps(s) 8: 4 behold your heavens, the *w* of your fingers,
9:17 are trapped by the *w* of their own hands.
28: 4 For the *w* of their hands repay them;
28: 5 deeds of the LORD nor the *w* of his hands,
64:10 And all men fear and proclaim the *w* of God,
88:11 Will you *w* wonders for the dead?
90:16 Let your *w* be seen by your servants and
90:17 prosper the *w* of our hands for us!
90:17 [Prosper the *w* of our hands!]
102:26 and the heavens are the *w* of your hands.
104:23 his *w* and to his tillage till the evening.
111: 3 Majesty and glory are his *w*,
138: 8 forsake not the *w* of your hands.
Prv 12:14 *w* of his hands comes back to reward him.
18: 9 The man who is slack in his *w* is own
21:25 slays him, for his hands refuse to *w*.
22:29 You see a man skilled at his *w*?
24:27 tasks, and arrange your *w* in the field;
Eccl 2:17 the *w* that is done under the sun is evil;
3:11 beginning to end, the *w* which God has done.
3:17 for every affair and on every *w* a judgment.
3:22 better for a man than to rejoice in his *w*;
4: 3 the wicked *w* that is done under the sun.
4: 4 *w* is the rivalry of one man for another.
7:13 Consider the *w* of God.
8: 9 mind to every *w* that is done under the sun,
8:17 out all God's *w* that is done under the sun,
9:10 for there will be no *w*,
11: 5 So you know not the *w* of God which he is
12:14 God will bring to judgment every *w*,
Sg 5:14 is a *w* of ivory covered with sapphires.
Wis 9:10 her That she may be with me and *w* with me,
13:10 or useless stone, the *w* of an ancient hand.
Sir 4:30 lion at home, nor sly and suspicious at *w*.
31:26 As the furnace probes the *w* of the smith,
33:26 a slave *w* and he will look for his rest;
33:27 Food, correction and *w* for a slave;
33:28 Force him to *w* that he be not idle,
33:29 Put him to *w*, for that is what befits him;
36: 5 Give new signs and *w* new wonders;
37:11 man about mercy, to a lazy man about *w*,
38: 8 Thus God's creative *w* continues without
38:28 His care is to finish his *w*,
43: 2 what a wonderful *w* of the Most High!
45:11 with scarlet yarn, the *w* of the weaver;
45:11 in golden settings, the *w* of the jeweler,
51:30 *W* at your tasks in due season,
Is 1:31 to tow, and his *w* shall become a spark;
3:11 with the *w* of his hands he will be repaid.
5:12 not, the *w* of his hands they see not.
5:19 say, "Let him make haste and speed his *w*,
10:12 all his *w* on Mount Zion and in Jerusalem,
19:15 shall have no *w* to do for head or tail,
19:25 Egypt, and the *w* of my hands Assyria,
28:21 To carry out his *w*, his singular work,
29:15 Who *w* in the dark,
29:23 see the *w* of my hands in his midst,
37:19 were not gods but the *w* of human hands,
41:24 Why, you are nothing and your *w* is nought!
45:11 or prescribe the *w* of my hands for me!
54:16 burning coals and forges weapons as his *w*;
54:16 who have created the destroyer to *w* havoc.
64: 7 we are all the *w* of your hands.
Jer 8:17 which no charm will *w* when they bite you,
10: 9 The *w* of the craftsman and the handiwork
10: 9 all of them the *w* of artisans.
10:15 Nothingness are they, a ridiculous *w*;
17:22 Do no *w* whatever,
17:24 holy and abstaining from all *w* on it,
48:10 be he who does the LORD's *w* remissly,
50:25 has *w* to do in the land of the Chaldeans.
51:18 Nothingness are they, a ridiculous *w*,
Bar 3:18 money, but there is no trace of their *w*:
6:50 and that God's *w* is not in them.
Ez 21:15 To *w* slaughter has it been sharpened,
24: 8 To *w* up my wrath,
44:14 for all its *w* and for everything that is
Hos 8: 6 The *w* of an artisan no god at all
13: 2 their fancy, all of them the *w* of artisans.
14: 4 no more, 'Our god,' to the *w* of our hands;
Jl 3: 3 *w* wonders in the heavens and on the earth,
Mi 2: 1 iniquity, and *w* out evil on their couches;
Hb 1: 5 For a *w* is being done in your days that
3: 2 your renown, and feared, O LORD, your *w*.
Hg 1:14 set to *w* on the house of the LORD of hosts,
2: 4 people of the land says the LORD, and *w*!
Mt 6:28 They do not *w*, they do not spin.
12:10 "Is it lawful to *w* a cure on the sabbath?"
12:38 "Teacher, we want to see you *w* some signs."
13:58 And he did not *w* many miracles there
14: 2 such miraculous powers are at *w* in him!"
20: 3 standing around the marketplace without *w*,
20:12 'This last group did only an hour's *w*,
21:28 'Son, go out and *w* in the vineyard today.'
24:46 his master discovers at *w* on his return!
Mk 6: 5 He could *w* no miracle there,
6:14 why such miraculous powers are at *w* in him."
9: 3 than the *w* of any bleacher could make them.
13:19 any between God's *w* of creation and now,
16:20 The Lord continued to *w* with them
Lk 1:78 this is the *w* of the kindness of our God;
3:23 his *w* he was about thirty years of age,
14:29 and then not being able to complete the *w*;
23: 8 he was hoping to see him *w* some miracle.
Jn 4:34 bringing his *w* to completion is my food.
5:17 at work until now, and I am at *w* as well."
6:29 "This is the *w* of God:
6:30 What is the *w*' you do?
7:21 *w* and you profess astonishment over it.
9: 4 The night comes on when no one can *w*.
17: 4 earth by finishing the *w* you gave me to do.
Acts 2:19 I will *w* wonders in the heavens above and
13: 2 to do the *w* for which I have called them."
19:24 brought in no little *w* for his craftsmen.
19:25 know that our prosperity depends on this *w*.
20:35 by such hard *w* that you must help the weak.
27:25 it will all *w* out just as I have been told,
Rom 1:13 in order to do some fruitful *w* among you,
8:28 We know that God makes all things *w*
13: 4 ruler is God's servant to *w* for your good.
14:19 *w* for peace and to strengthen one another.
14:20 God's *w* for the sake of something to eat.
15:17 Christ Jesus for the *w* I have done for God.
15:23 I have no more *w* to do in these regions,
1Cor 3: 8 plants and he who waters *w* to the same end.
3:13 or straw, the *w* of each will be made clear.
3:13 fire will test the quality of each man's *w*.
4:12 We *w* hard at manual labor.
9: 1 And are you not my *w* in the Lord?
9: 6 Barnabas who are forced to *w* for a living?
9:13 Do you not realize that those who *w* in the
12:29 all *w* miracles or have the gift of healing?
15:58 fully engaged in the *w* of the Lord.
16: 9 A door has been opened wide for my *w*,
16:10 He does the Lord's *w* just as I do,
2Cor 1:24 prefer to *w* with you toward your happiness.
4:12 Death is at *w* in us, but life in you.
6: 5 as men familiar with hard *w*,
8: 6 already begun this *w* of charity among you,
8:10 help you who began this good *w* last year,
8:19 *w* of charity for the glory of the Lord.
8:22 this *w* because of his great trust in you.
10:15 not boast immoderately of the *w* of others;
10:16 without having to boast of *w* already done
11:12 ministry they *w* on the same terms as we do.
Gal 2: 8 Jews had been at *w* in me for the Gentiles),
Eph 2: 2 who is even now at *w* among the rebellious.
3:20 To him whose power now at *w* in us can do
4:27 do not give the devil a chance to *w* on you.
4:28 let him *w* with his hands at honest labor
Phil 1: 6 that he who has begun the good *w* in you
2:12 *w* with anxious concern to achieve your
2:16 run the race in vain or *w* to no purpose.
2:30 near to death for the sake of Christ's *w*.
Col 1:29 For this I *w* and struggle,
3:23 you do, *w* at it with your whole being.
1Thes 2:13 word of God at *w* within you who believe.
4:11 *W* with your hands as we directed you to do,
5:13 with the greatest love because of their *w*.
2Thes 1:11 every honest intention and *w* of faith.
2: 7 force of lawlessness is already at *w*,
2:17 strengthen them for every good *w* and word.
3:10 that anyone who would not *w* should not eat.
1Tm 4:10 explains why we *w* and struggle as we do;
5:10 she been eager to do every possible good *w*?
5:17 those whose *w* is preaching and teaching.
6: 2 their *w* are believers and beloved brothers.
2Tm 3:17 competent and equipped for every good *w*.
4: 5 hardship, perform your *w* as an evangelist,
Ti 3:14 *w* in order to take care of their needs,
Heb 1:10 and the heavens are the *w* of your hands.
2:10 *w* of salvation perfect through suffering.
4: 3 *w* was finished when he created the world,
4: 4 rested from all his *w* on the seventh day";
4:10 rests from his own *w* as God did from his.
6:10 he will not forget your *w* and the love you

1Pt 2:19 presence, this is the *w* of grace in him.
3Jn 1: 8 thus to have our share in the *w* of truth.

WORKED (40)

Nm 14:22 the signs I *w* in Egypt and in the desert,
Ru 2:19 told her mother-in-law with whom she had *w*.
2:19 man at whose place I *w* today is named Boaz,"
2Sm 9:12 tenants of Ziba's family *w* for Meribbaal.
2Chr 3:16 He *w* out chains in the form of a collar
34:12 The men *w* faithfully at their task;
Neh 3:38 The people *w* with a will.
4:12 Every builder, while he *w*,
9:10 You *w* signs and wonders against Pharaoh,
9:17 remembered the miracles you had *w* for them.
Tb 2:11 my wife Anna *w* for hire at weaving cloth,
Est F: 6 God *w* signs and great wonders,
1Mc 12:37 *w* together on building up the city,
Ez 23:29 you have *w* for and leaving you stark naked,
Dn 6:15 he *w* till sunset to rescue him.
Mt 11:20 where most of his miracles had been *w*,
11:21 *w* in you had taken place in Tyre and Sidon,
11:23 miracles *w* in you had taken place in Sodom,
20:12 have *w* a full day in the scorching heat.'
21:15 when they observed the wonders he *w*,
28:12 with the elders and *w* out their strategy,
Mk 6:13 the sick with oil, and *w* many cures.
Lk 10:13 If the miracles *w* in your midst had
Jn 4:38 I sent you to reap what you had not *w* for.
Acts 4:30 and wonders to be *w* in the name of Jesus,
6: 8 *w* great wonders and signs among the people.
9:21 "Isn't this the man who *w* such havoc in
15:12 God had *w* among the Gentiles through them.
18: 3 them and they *w* together as tentmakers.
19:11 Meanwhile God *w* extraordinary miracles at
Rom 7: 5 roused by the law *w* in our members
16: 6 greetings to Mary, who has *w* hard for you,
16:12 and Tryphosa, who have *w* hard for the Lord;
1Cor 15:10 I have *w* harder than all the others,
Gal 2: 8 for he who *w* through Peter as his apostle
Phil 1:12 has *w* out to the furtherance of the gospel.
1Thes 2: 9 how we *w* day and night all the time we
2Thes 3: 8 Rather, we *w* day and night,
2Jn 1: 8 yourselves do not lose what you have *w* for;
Rv 16:14 these spirits were devils who *w* prodigies.

WORKER (13)

Ex 15:11 O terrible in renown, *w* of wonders,
1Kgs 7:14 He was a bronze *w*,
Eccl 3: 9 What advantage has the *w* from his toil?
Wis 15: 7 of either class the *w* in clay is the judge.
17:17 shepherd, or a *w* at tasks in the wasteland,
Sir 10:26 Better the *w* who has plenty of everything
Rom 16: 9 our fellow *w* in the service of Christ;
16:21 Timothy, my fellow *w*,
2Cor 8:23 my companion and fellow *w* in your behalf;
Phil 4: 3 I ask you, too, my dependable fellow *w*,
1Thes 3: 2 fellow *w* in preaching the gospel of Christ,
1Tm 5:18 and also, "The *w* deserves his wages."
Phlm 1: 1 our beloved friend and fellow *w* Philemon,

WORKERS (14)

1Chr 27:26 the farm *w* who tilled the soil was Ezri,
2Chr 34:13 directed all the *w* in every kind of labor.
Jer 24: 1 of Judah, the artisans and the skilled *w*,
Bar 1: 9 and the princes, and the skilled *w*,
Ez 48:18 shall provide food for the *w* of the City.
48:19 The *w* in the City shall be taken from all
Lk 10: 2 "The harvest is rich but the *w* are few;
10: 2 harvest-master to send *w* to his harvest.
Acts 19:25 of these men and other *w* in the same craft.
Rom 16: 3 they were my fellow *w* in the service of
1Cor 12:28 prophets, third teachers, then miracle *w*,
2Cor 6: 1 As your fellow *w* we beg you not to receive
Phil 3: 2 Watch out for *w* of evil.
Phlm 1:24 Aristarchus, Demas, and Luke, my fellow *w*.

WORKING (13)

Lv 25:40 tenant, *w* with you until the jubilee year,
2Kgs 12:12 and builders *w* in the temple of the LORD,
2Chr 2:17 six hundred overseers to keep the people *w*.
Neh 4:16 as a guard by night and a *w* force by day.
Wis 15: 7 the potter, laboriously *w* the soft earth,
Jer 18: 3 house and there he was, *w* at the wheel.
Ez 46: 1 remain closed throughout the six *w* days,
Dn 6:28 *w* signs and wonders in heaven and on earth,
Lk 13:14 "There are six days for *w*.
Jn 6:27 You should not be *w* for perishable food
Eph 3:16 you inwardly through the *w* of his Spirit.
Col 4:11 who are *w* with me for the kingdom of God.
2Thes 3:12 to earn the food they eat by *w* quietly.

WORKINGS (2)

Jdt 8:14 heart or grasp the *w* of the human mind;
2Thes 2: 9 one will appear as part of the *w* of Satan,

WORKMAN (2)

Mt 10:10 The *w*, after all, is worth his keep.
2Tm 2:15 a *w* who has no cause to be ashamed,

WORKMAN'S (1)

Jgs 5:26 the peg, with her right, for the *w* mallet.

WORKMANSHIP (2)

2Chr 3:10 of holies he made two cherubim of carved *w*,
Wis 14:20 the masses drawn by the charm of the *w*,

WORKMEN (18)

Ex 28: 3 expert *w* whom I have endowed with skill,
1Kgs 5:27 thirty thousand *w* from all Israel.
2Kgs 12:12 to the master *w* in the temple of the LORD.
12:15 Instead, they were given to the *w*,
12:16 provided with the funds to give to the *w*,
22: 5 to the master *w* in the temple of the LORD,
22: 9 to the master *w* in the temple of the LORD."
1Chr 22:15 have available an unlimited supply of *w*,
2Chr 24:12 the king and Jehoiada gave it to the *w*
24:13 The *w* labored,
34:10 to the master *w* in the house of the LORD,
34:10 these in turn used it to pay the *w*
34:17 handed it over to the overseers and the *w*."
1Mc 10:11 He ordered the *w* to build the walls and
Jer 29: 2 and the skilled *w* had left Jerusalem.
39: 9 had deserted to him, and the rest of the *w*.
Mt 20: 1 out at dawn to hire *w* for his vineyard.
20: 8 'Call the *w* and give them their pay,

WORKS (162)

Dt 15:10 for this in all your *w* and undertakings.
Jgs 13:19 rock to the LORD, whose *w* are mysteries.
1Kgs 9:23 The supervisors of Solomon's *w* who policed
2Chr 8: 9 did not enslave the Israelites for his *w*.
17:13 carried out many *w* in the cities of Judah,
32:32 of Hezekiah's acts, including his pious *w*,
Tb 1: 3 I performed many charitable *w* for my
1:16 charitable *w* for my kinsmen and my people.
4: 5 Perform good *w* all the days of your life,
4: 6 service, your good *w* will bring success,
4:14 the wages of any man who *w* for you,
12: 7 *w* of God are to be declared and made known.
12:11 but the *w* of God are to be made known with
13: 9 he scourged you for the *w* of your hands,
2Mc 15:21 and called upon the LORD who *w* miracles;
Jb 34:25 Therefore he discerns their *w*;
37:14 Stand and consider the wondrous *w* of God!
Ps(s) 8: 7 given him rule over the *w* of your hands,
33: 4 of the LORD, and all his *w* are trustworthy.
33:15 heart of each, he who knows all their *w*.
66: 5 Come and see the *w* of God,
71:16 I will treat of the mighty *w* of the Lord;
73:28 *w* in the gates of the daughter of Zion.
77:13 And I meditate on your *w*;
77:15 You are the God who *w* wonders;
86: 8 O Lord, and there are no *w* like yours.
92: 5 at the *w* of your hands I rejoice.
92: 6 How great are your *w*, O LORD!
95: 9 they tested me though they had seen my *w*.
103:22 Bless the LORD, all his *w*,
104:13 earth is replete with the fruit of your *w*.
104:24 How manifold are your *w*, O LORD!
104:31 may the LORD be glad in his *w*!
106:13 But soon they forgot his *w*;
106:35 with the nations and learned their *w*.
106:39 They became defiled by their *w*,
107:22 and declare his *w* with shouts of joy.
107:24 *w* of the LORD and his wonders in the abyss.
111: 2 Great are the *w* of the LORD,
111: 6 known to his people the power of his *w*,
111: 7 The *w* of his hands are faithful and just;
118:17 but live, and declare the *w* of the LORD.
139:14 wonderful are your *w*.
143: 5 your doings, the *w* of your hands I ponder.
145: 4 praises your *w* and proclaims your might.
145: 5 majesty and tell of your wondrous *w*.
145: 9 to all and compassionate toward all his *w*.
145:10 Let all your *w* give you thanks,
145:13 in all his words and holy in all his *w*.
145:17 just in all his ways and holy in all his *w*.
Prv 16: 3 Entrust your *w* to the LORD,
26:28 enemy, and the flattering mouth *w* ruin.
31:31 and let her *w* praise her at the city gates.
Eccl 2: 4 I undertook great *w*;
2:11 to all the *w* that my hands had wrought,
5: 5 such words and destroy the *w* of your hands.
9: 7 because it is now that God favors your *w*.
Wis 1:12 destruction by the *w* of your hands.
3:11 their labors, and worthless are their *w*.
6: 3 probe your *w* and scrutinize your counsels!
8: 4 of God, the selector of his *w*.
8: 7 justice, the fruits of her *w* are virtues;
8:18 and unfailing riches in the *w* of her hands,
9: 9 *w* and was present when you made the world;
10:10 and made abundant the fruit of his *w*.
12: 4 *W* of witchcraft and impious sacrifices;
13: 1 studying the *w* did not discern the artisan:
13: 7 For they search busily among his *w*,
14:11 they have become abominable amid God's *w*,
17:20 and continued its *w* without interruption;
Sir 1: 8 He has poured her forth upon all his *w*,
11: 4 For strange are the *w* of the LORD,
14:19 All man's *w* will perish in decay,
16:24 When at the first God created his *w* and,
17: 7 hearts, and shows them his glorious *w*,
18: 2 Whom has he made equal to describing his *w*,
20:27 He who *w* his land has abundant crops,
33:15 See now all the *w* of the Most High:
35: 2 In *w* of charity one offers fine flour,
38: 6 the knowledge to glory in his mighty *w*,
39:16 The *w* of God are all of them good;
39:19 The *w* of all mankind are present to him;
39:33 The *w* of God are all of them good;
42:15 Now will I recall God's *w*;
42:15 God's word were his *w* brought into being;
42:16 so the glory of the LORD fills all his *w*;
42:23 How beautiful are all his *w*,
43:29 him, for greater is he than all his *w*;
43:34 only a few of his *w* have we seen.
Is 2: 8 they worship the *w* of their hands,
3:10 them, the fruit of their *w* they will eat.
29: 3 outposts and set up siege *w* against you.
41:29 of them are nothing, their *w* are nought,
44: 9 and their precious *w* are of no avail,
44:12 an iron image, *w* it over the coals,
57:12 I will expose your justice and your *w*;
59: 6 nor can they cover themselves with their *w*.
59: 6 Their works are evil *w*,
Jer 21: 2 with us according to all his wonderful *w*,
22:13 Who *w* his neighbor without pay,
32:30 but provoke me with the *w* of their hands,
44: 8 go on provoking me by the *w* of your hands,
48: 7 you trusted in your *w* and your treasures,
Bar 2: 9 is just in all the *w* he commanded us to do,
Dn 3:57 Bless the Lord, all you *w* of the Lord,
4:34 all his *w* are right and his ways just;
Mi 5:12 shall no longer adore the *w* of your hands.
6:16 Omri, and all the *w* of the house of Ahab,
Hg 2:14 And so are all the *w* of their hands;
2:17 you in all the *w* of your hands with blight,
Mt 11: 2 heard about the *w* Christ was performing,
23: 5 All their *w* are performed to be seen.
Lk 12:21 That is the way it *w* with the man who
Jn 5:20 he will show him even greater *w* than these.
5:36 *w* the Father has given me to accomplish.
5:36 These very *w* which I perform testify on my
6:28 "What must we do to perform the *w* of God?"
7: 3 there may see the *w* you are performing.
8:41 Indeed you are doing your father's *w*!"
9: 3 it was to let God's *w* show forth in him.
10:13 That is because he *w* for pay;
10:25 The *w* I do in my Father's name give
10:37 If I do not perform my Father's *w*,
10:38 put no faith in me, put faith in these *w*,
14:10 Father who lives in me accomplishing his *w*.
14:11 me, or else, believe because of the *w* I do.
14:12 man who has faith in me will do the *w* I do,
15:24 Had I not performed such *w* among them as
Acts 10:38 He went about doing good *w* and healing all
Rom 3:22 that justice of God which *w* through faith
3:27 By what law, the law of *w*?
4: 4 Now, when a man *w*,
9:12 by *w* but by the favor of him who calls"
9:32 justice comes from faith, not from *w*.
11: 6 is by grace, it is not because of their *w*—
12: 8 *w* of mercy should do so cheerfully.
1Cor 12: 6 there are different *w* but the same God who
2Cor 9: 8 everything and even a surplus for good *w*,
Gal 2:16 by *w* of the law no one will be justified.
3: 5 Spirit on you and *w* wonders in your midst?
Eph 4: 6 of all, who is over all, and *w* through all,
Col 1:10 You will multiply good *w* of every sort and
1Tm 6:18 do good, to be rich in good *w* and generous,
Heb 3: 9 and tried me, and saw my *w* for forty years.
6: 1 repentance from dead *w*,
9:14 from dead *w* to worship the living God!
Jas 2:18 might say, "You have faith and I have *w*—
2:18 Show me your faith without *w*,
2:18 show you the faith that underlies my *w*!
2:20 ignoramus, that without *w* faith is idle?
2:21 not our father Abraham justified by his *w*
2:22 his *w* and implemented by his works.
2:24 justified by his *w* and not by faith alone.
2:25 Was she not justified by her *w* when she
2:26 *w* is as dead as a body without breath.
1Pt 2: 9 for his own to proclaim the glorious *w*"
2:12 By observing your good *w* they may give
1Jn 3: 8 *w* that the Son of God revealed himself.
Rv 14:13 labors, for their good *w* accompany them."
15: 3 "Mighty and wonderful are your *w*,

WORLD (379)

Gn 10:25 Peleg, for in his time the *w* was divided;
11: 1 The whole *w* spoke the same language,
11: 9 the LORD confused the speech of all the *w*.
18:25 the judge of all the *w* act with justice?"
37:35 go down mourning to my son in the nether *w*."
41:57 all the *w* came to Joseph to obtain rations
41:57 grain, for famine had gripped the whole *w*.
42:38 white head down to the nether *w* in grief."
44:29 white head down to the nether *w* in grief.'
44:31 our father down to the nether *w* in grief.
Nm 16:30 them alive down into the nether *w*,
16:33 to the nether *w* with all belonging to them;
Dt 30: 4 driven to the farthest corner of the *w*,

WORLD (cont.)
32:22 shall rage to the depths of the nether *w*,
1Sm 2: 6 he casts down to the nether *w*;
2: 8 the LORD's, and he has set the *w* upon them.
2Sm 22: 6 The cords of the nether *w* enmeshed me,
1Kgs 10:24 the whole *w* sought audience with Solomon,
1Chr 1:19 Peleg (for in his time the *w* was divided),
16:30 he has made the *w* firm,
Neh 1: 9 driven to the farthest corner of the *w*,
Tb 3: 2 you are the judge of the *w*.
3:10 go down to the nether *w* laden with sorrow.
4:19 to the deepest recesses of the nether *w*.
6:18 was set apart for you before the *w* existed.
10:12 as the ones who brought you into the *w*.
13: 2 casts down to the depths of the nether *w*,
14: 6 All the nations of the *w* shall be
Jdt 2: 1 about taking revenge on the whole *w*,
5:21 become the laughing stock of the whole *w*."
10:19 be spared they could beguile the whole *w*."
11: 8 and all the *w* is aware that throughout
11:16 *w* will be astonished on hearing of them.
11:21 "No other woman from one end of the *w*
Est B: 2 and to hold sway over the whole *w*,
B: 4 in with all the races throughout the *w*,
B: 7 *w* by a violent death on a single day,
2Mc 3:12 of a temple venerated all over the *w*.
5:15 to enter the holiest temple in the *w*;
7: 9 *w* will raise us up to live again forever.
8:18 only those who attack us, but the whole *w*."
12:15 the aid of the great Sovereign of the *w*,
13:14 the outcome to the Creator of the *w*,
Jb 7: 9 down to the nether *w* shall come up no more.
11: 8 It is deeper than the nether *w*;
14:13 that you would hide me in the nether *w*
17:13 If I look for the nether *w* as my dwelling,
17:16 they descend with me into the nether *w*?
18:18 into darkness, and banished out of the *w*.
21:13 and tranquilly go down to the nether *w*.
26: 6 Naked before him is the nether *w*,
40:13 in the hidden *w* imprison them.
Ps(s) 6: 6 in the nether *w* who gives you thanks?
9: 9 He judges the *w* with justice;
9:18 To the nether *w* the wicked shall turn back,
16:10 will not abandon my soul to the nether *w*,
17:14 men whose portion in life is in this *w*,
18: 6 The cords of the nether *w* enmeshed me,
18:16 the foundations of the *w* were laid bare,
19: 5 voice resounds, and to the ends of the *w*,
24: 1 the *w* and those who dwell in it.
30: 4 LORD, you brought me up from the nether *w*;
31:18 them be reduced to silence in the nether *w*.
33: 8 let all who dwell in the *w* revere him.
49: 2 hearken, all who dwell in the *w*,
49:15 sheep they are herded into the nether *w*;
49:15 the nether *w* is their palace.
49:16 the power of the nether *w* by receiving me.
50:12 you, for mine are the *w* and its fullness.
55:16 let them go down alive to the nether *w*,
77:19 your lightning illumined the *w*;
86:13 rescued me from the depths of the nether *w*.
88: 4 and my life draws near to the nether *w*.
89:12 the *w* and its fullness you have founded;
89:49 himself from the power of the nether *w*?
90: 2 and the earth and the *w* were brought forth,
93: 1 with strength, And he has made the *w* firm,
96:10 He has made the *w* firm,
96:13 He shall rule the *w* with justice and the
97: 4 His lightnings illumine the *w*;
98: 7 resound, the *w* and those who dwell in it;
98: 9 *w* with justice and the peoples with equity.
116: 3 the snares of the nether *w* seized upon me;
139: 8 if I sink to the nether *w*,
141: 7 are strewn by the edge of the nether *w*.
Prv 1:12 us swallow them up, as the nether *w* does,
5: 5 to death, to the nether *w* her steps attain;
7:27 house is made up of ways to the nether *w*,
8:26 not made, nor the first clods of the *w*.
9:18 the depths of the nether *w* are her guests!
15:11 *w* and the abyss lie open before the LORD;
15:24 that he may avoid the nether *w* below.
23:14 and you will save him from the nether *w*.
27:20 nether *w* and the abyss are never satisfied;
30:16 The nether *w*,
Eccl 1: 4 and another comes, but the *w* forever stays.
9:10 wisdom in the nether *w* where you are going.
Sg 8: 6 relentless as the nether *w* is devotion;
Wis 1: 7 For the spirit of the Lord fills the *w*,
1:14 and the creatures of the *w* are wholesome,
1:14 nor any domain of the nether *w* on earth,
2: 1 known to have come back from the nether *w*.
2:24 envy of the devil, death entered the *w*,
6:24 number of wise men is the safety of the *w*,
8: 6 in the *w* is a better craftsman than she?
9: 3 To govern the *w* in holiness and justice,
9: 9 works and was present when you made the *w*;
10: 1 of the *w* when he alone had been created;
13: 2 of heaven, the governors of the *w*,
13: 9 that they could speculate about the *w*,
14: 6 raft, left to the *w* a future for his race,
14:14 by the vanity of men they came into the *w*,
16:13 you lead down to the gates of the nether *w*,
17:14 from the recesses of a powerless nether *w*,
17:20 For the whole *w* shone with brilliant light
18: 4 light of the Law was to be given to the *w*.
18:24 on his full-length robe was the whole *w*.
Sir 14:16 in the nether *w* there are no joys to seek.
16:15 what am I in the *w* of spirits?
17:22 Who in the nether *w* can glorify the Most
21:10 that end in the depths of the nether *w*.
23:27 and all who inhabit the *w* shall understand,
28:21 besides which even the nether *w* is a gain;
41: 4 in the nether *w* he has no claim on life.
48: 5 a dead man back to life from the nether *w*,
51: 2 of the nether *w* you have snatched my feet;
51: 5 from the deep belly of the nether *w*;
51: 6 was nearing the depths of the nether *w*;
51: 9 very earth, from the gates of the nether *w*,
Is 5:14 Therefore the nether *w* enlarges its throat
7:11 let it be deep as the nether *w*,
13:11 Thus I will punish the *w* for its evil and
14: 9 The nether *w* below is all astir preparing
14:11 Down to the nether *w* your pomp is brought,
14:15 nether *w* you go to the recesses of the pit!
14:17 Who made the *w* a desert,
14:21 and fill the breadth of the *w* with tyrants.
18: 3 All you who inhabit the *w*,
24: 4 and fades, the *w* languishes and fades;
26:18 inhabitants of the *w* cannot bring it forth.
27: 6 and blossom, covering all the *w* with fruit.
28:15 and with the nether *w* we have made a pact;
28:18 pact with the nether *w* shall not stand.
34: 1 fills it listen, the *w* and all it produces.
38:10 To the gates of the nether *w* I shall be
38:11 fellow men among those who dwell in the *w*."
38:18 is not the nether *w* that gives you thanks,
57: 9 far away, down even to the nether *w*.
Jer 10:12 his power, established the *w* by his wisdom,
31: 8 I will gather them from the ends of the *w*,
51:15 power, and established the *w* by his wisdom,
51:41 made captive, the glory of the whole *w*!
Bar 2:17 it is not the dead in the nether *w*,
3:11 with those destined for the nether *w*?
3:19 have vanished down into the nether *w*,
6:61 by God to proceed across the whole *w*,
Ez 31:15 *w* I made the abyss close up over him;
31:16 *w* with those who go down into the pit.
31:17 have come down with him to the nether *w*,
32:20 Then from the midst of the nether *w*,
32:27 to the nether *w* with their weapons of war,
Dn 3:32 to an unjust king, the worst in all the *w*.
3:37 in the *w* this day because of our sins.
3:45 the Lord God, glorious over the whole *w*."
3:88 For he has delivered us from the nether *w*,
4: 7 of great height at the center of the *w*.
Hos 13:14 them from the power of the nether *w*?
13:14 where is your sting, O nether *w*!
Am 9: 2 Though they break through to the nether *w*,
Jon 2: 3 the midst of the nether *w* I cried for help,
2: 7 nether *w* were closing behind me forever,
Na 1: 5 before him, the *w* and all who dwell in it.
Hb 2: 5 opens wide his throat like the nether *w*,
Mt 4: 8 kingdoms of the *w* in their magnificence,
5:14 "You are the light of the *w*.
13:35 lain hidden since the creation of the *w*."
13:38 the field is the *w*,
13:39 The harvest is the end of the *w*,
13:40 burned, so will it be at the end of the *w*.
13:49 That is how it will be at the end of the *w*.
16:26 whole *w* and destroy himself in the process?
17:25 of the *w* take tax or toll from their sons,
18: 7 things will come on the *w* through scandal!
24: 3 sign of your coming and the end of the *w*?"
24:14 the *w* as a witness to all the nations.
24:21 of the *w* until now or in all ages to come.
25:34 for you from the creation of the *w*.
26:13 good news is proclaimed throughout the *w*,
28:20 am with you always, until the end of the *w*!"
Mk 8:36 *w* and destroys himself in the process?
14: 9 good news is proclaimed throughout the *w*,
16:15 "Go into the whole *w* and proclaim the
Lk 2: 1 a decree ordering a census of the whole *w*.
4: 5 the kingdoms of the *w* in a single instant.
9:25 *w* and destroys himself in the process?
9:51 when he was to be taken from this *w*,
11:31 the *w* to listen to the wisdom of Solomon,
11:50 shed since the foundation of the *w*.
12:30 *w* are always running after these things.
Jn 1: 9 light to every man was coming into the *w*.
1:10 the world, and through him the *w* was made,
1:10 made, yet the *w* did not know who he was.
1:29 of God who takes away the sin of the *w*!
3:16 so loved the *w* that he gave his only Son,
3:17 *w* to condemn the *w*, but that the *w*
3:19 the light came into the *w*,
4:42 that this really is the Savior of the *w*."
6:14 the Prophet who is to come into the *w*."
6:33 down from heaven and gives life to the *w*."
6:51 give is my flesh, for the life of the *w*."
7: 4 as well display yourself to the *w* at large."
7: 7 The *w* is incapable of hating you,
8:12 "I am the light of the *w*.
8:23 You belong to this world—a *w* which
8:26 only tell the *w* what I have heard from him,
9: 5 I am in the world I am the light of the *w*."
9:39 "I came into this *w* to divide it,
10:36 the Father consecrated and sent into the *w*,
11: 9 because he sees the *w* bathed in light.
11:27 he who is to come into the *w*."
11:48 like this, the whole *w* will believe in him.
12:19 The whole *w* has run after him."
12:25 in this *w* preserves it to life eternal.
12:31 "Now has judgment come upon this *w*,
12:46 I have come to the *w* as its light,
12:47 not come to condemn the *w* but to save it.
13: 1 for him to pass from this *w* to the Father.
13: 1 He had loved his own in this *w*,
14:17 Spirit of truth, whom the *w* cannot accept,
14:19 while now and the *w* will see me no more;
14:22 reveal yourself to us and not to the *w*?"
14:27 do not give it to you as the *w* gives peace.
14:30 the Prince of this *w* is at hand.
14:31 He has no hold on me but the *w* must know
15:18 "If you find that the *w* hates you know it
15:19 If you belonged to the *w*,
15:19 you is that you do not belong to the *w*.
15:19 But I chose you out of the *w*.
16: 8 comes, he will prove the *w* wrong about sin,
16:11 the prince of this *w* has been condemned.
16:20 will weep and mourn while the *w* rejoices;
16:21 joy that a man has been born into the *w*.
16:28 I came into the *w*.
16:28 Now I am leaving the *w* to go to the Father."
16:33 You will suffer in the *w*.
16:33 I have overcome the *w*."
17: 5 a glory I had with you before the *w* began.
17: 6 known to those you gave me out of the *w*.
17: 9 for the *w* but for these you have given me,
17:11 *w* no more, but these are in the world
17:13 *w* that they may share my joy completely.
17:14 your word, and the *w* has hated them for it;
17:14 the world [any more than I belong to the *w*.
17:15 I do not ask you to take them out of the *w*,
17:16 the world, any more than I belong to the *w*.
17:18 world, so as I have sent them into the *w*;
17:21 that the *w* may believe that you sent me.
17:23 So shall the *w* know that you sent me,
17:24 of the love you bore me before the *w* began.
17:25 Just Father, the *w* has not known you,
18:36 "My kingdom does not belong to this *w*.
18:36 If my kingdom were of this *w*,
18:37 was born, the reason why I came into the *w*,
21:25 entire *w* to hold the books to record them.
Acts 2:27 will not abandon my soul to the nether *w*,
2:31 that he was not abandoned to the nether *w*,
4:12 no other name in the whole *w* given to men
11:28 going to be a severe famine all over the *w*.
17:24 God who made the *w* and all that is in it,
17:31 he is going to 'judge the *w* with justice'
19:27 she whom Asia and all the *w* revere may
24: 5 up sedition among the Jews all over the *w*.
Rom 1: 8 your faith is heralded throughout the *w*.
1:20 Since the creation of the *w*,
3: 6 If that were so, how could God judge the *w*?
3:19 the whole *w* stands convicted before God,
4:13 inherit the *w* did not depend on the law;
5:12 man sin entered the *w* and with sin death,
5:13 before the law there was sin in the *w*,
8:19 the whole created *w* eagerly awaits the
8:21 because the *w* itself will be freed from
10:18 and their words to the limits of the *w*."
11:12 have meant riches for the Gentile *w*,
11:15 has meant reconciliation for the *w*,
1Cor 1:20 God turned the wisdom of this *w* into folly?
1:21 Since in God's wisdom the *w* did not come
1:27 the *w* considers absurd to shame the wise;
1:27 out the weak of this *w* to shame the strong.
3:19 the wisdom of this *w* is absurdity with God.
3:22 be Paul, or Apollos, or Cephas, or the *w*,
5:10 with immoral people in this *w*,
5:10 avoid them, you would have to leave the *w*!
6: 2 know that the believers will judge the *w*?
6: 2 If the judgment of the *w* is to be yours,
7:31 of the *w* as though they were not using it,
7:31 for the *w* as we know it is passing away.
7:34 has the cares of this *w* to absorb her and
11:32 being condemned with the rest of the *w*.
14:10 in the *w* and all are marked by sound;
2Cor 5:19 Christ, was reconciling the *w* to himself,
Gal 4: 3 subordinated to the elements of the *w*;
6:14 *w* has been crucified to me and I to the *w*.
Eph 1: 4 God chose us in him before the *w* began,
2:12 were without hope and without God in the *w*.
3:21 through all generations, *w* without end.
6:12 powers, the rulers of this *w* of darkness,
Phil 3:19 who are set upon the things of this *w*.
Col 1: 6 your midst, as it has everywhere in the *w*.
2:21 were still living a life bounded by this *w*?
1Tm 1:15 Jesus came into the *w* to save sinners.
3:16 the Gentiles, Believed in throughout the *w*,
6: 7 We brought nothing into this *w*,
2Tm 1: 9 before the *w* began but now made manifest
4:10 soon, for Demas, enamored of the present *w*,
Heb 1: 6 when he leads his first-born into the *w*,
2: 5 not make the world to come—that *w* of
4: 3 work was finished when he created the *w*,
9:26 over and over from the creation of the *w*.
10: 5 Wherefore, on coming into the *w*,
11: 7 He thereby condemned the *w* and inherited
11:38 The *w* was not worthy of them.

Jas 1:27 keeping oneself unspotted by the *w*
2: 5 those who are poor in the eyes of the *w*
4: 4 aware that love of the *w* is enmity to God?
1Pt 5: 9 the same sufferings throughout the *w*.
2Pt 1: 4 you who have fled a *w* corrupted by lust
2: 5 Nor did he spare the ancient *w*—
2:20 When men have fled a polluted *w* by
3: 4 just as it was when the *w* was created."
3: 6 By water that *w* was then destroyed;
1Jn 2: 2 sins only, but for those of the whole *w*.
2:15 world, nor the things that the *w* affords.
2:15 If anyone loves the *w*,
2:16 that the *w* affords comes from the Father.
2:16 all these are from the *w*.
2:17 And the *w* with its seductions is passing
3: 1 The reason the *w* does not recognize us is
3:13 to be surprised if the *w* hates you.
4: 1 many false prophets have appeared in the *w*.
4: 3 in fact, it is in the *w* already.
4: 4 One greater in you than there is in the *w*.
4: 5 Those others belong to the *w*;
4: 5 of the *w* and why the world listens to them.
4: 9 the *w* that we might have life through him.
4:14 Father has sent the Son as savior of the *w*.
4:17 our relation to this *w* is just like his.
5: 4 Everyone begotten of God conquers the *w*,
5: 4 has conquered the *w* is the faith of ours.
5: 5 Who, then, is conqueror of the *w*?
5:19 while the whole *w* is under the evil one.
2Jn 1: 7 deceitful men have gone out into the *w*,
Rv 1:18 I hold the keys of death and the nether *w*.
3:10 of trial which is coming on the whole *w*,
5: 6 spirits of God, sent to all parts of the *w*.
6: 8 Death, and the nether *w* was in his train.
11:15 "The kingdom of the *w* now belongs to our
12: 9 or Satan, the seducer of the whole *w*,
13: 3 the whole *w* followed after the beast.
13:12 making the *w* and all its inhabitants worship
14: 3 thousand who had been ransomed from the *w*.
14: 6 of everlasting good news to the whole *w*,
17: 8 *w* shall be amazed when they see the beast,
18:11 of the *w* will weep and mourn over her too,
20:13 death and the nether *w* gave up their dead.
20:14 nether *w* were hurled into the pool of fire,
21: 4 or pain, for the former *w* has passed away."

WORLD-FAMOUS (1)

2Mc 2:22 regained possession of the *w* temple,

WORLDLY (9)

Mt 13:22 but then *w* anxiety and the lure of money
Lk 16: 8 Because the *w* take more initiative than
21:34 indulgence and drunkenness and *w* cares.
1Cor 1:20 Where is the master of *w* argument?
3:18 one of you thinks he is wise in a *w* way,
2Cor 7:10 salvation, whereas *w* sorrow brings death.
1Tm 6:20 Stay clear of *w*,
2Tm 2:16 Avoid *w*,
Ti 2:12 us to reject godless ways and *w* desires,

WORLD'S (18)

Is 23:17 the *w* kingdoms on the face of the earth.
26: 9 the earth, the *w* inhabitants learn justice.
Lam 4:12 not believe, nor any of the *w* inhabitants,
Lk 16: 9 through your use of this *w* goods,
Jn 12:31 now will this *w* prince be driven out,
1Cor 1:28 He chose the *w* lowborn and despised,
2:12 is not the *w* spirit but God's Spirit,
4:13 We have become the *w* refuse,
7:33 married man is busy with this *w* demands
1Tm 6:17 are rich in this *w* goods not to be proud,
Heb 11: 3 that the *w* were created by the word of God,
Jas 4: 4 enemy if he chooses to be the *w* friend.
1Pt 1:20 lamb chosen before the *w* foundation
1Jn 3:17 man who has enough of this *w* goods
Rv 13: 8 the *w* beginning in the book of the living,
17: 5 of harlots and all the *w* abominations."
18: 3 and the *w* merchants grew rich from her
18:23 Because your merchants were the *w* nobility,

WORM (8)

Jb 25: 6 a maggot, the son of man, who is only a *w*?
Ps(s) 22: 7 But I am a *w*,
Is 14:11 you is the maggot, your covering, the *w*."
41:14 Fear not, O *w* Jacob,
66:24 Their *w* shall not die,
Jon 4: 7 dawn God sent a *w* which attacked the plant,
Mk 9:48 where 'the *w* dies not and the fire is
2Tm 3: 6 It is such as these who *w* their way into

WORMED (2)

Gal 2: 4 they *w* their way into the group to spy on
Jude 1: 4 have recently *w* their way into your midst,

WORMS (9)

Jdt 16:17 He will send fire and *w* into their flesh,
1Mc 2:62 for his glory ends in corruption and *w*.
2Mc 9: 9 body of this impious man swarmed with *w*,
Jb 7: 5 My flesh is clothed with *w* and scabs;
21:26 down in the dust, and *w* cover them both.
Sir 7:17 what awaits man is *w*.
10:11 *w* and gnats and maggots.
19: 3 Rottenness and *w* will possess him,
Acts 12:23 the honor to God, and he died eaten by *w*.

WORMWOOD (11)

Dt 29:17 would bear such poison and *w* among you.
Prv 5: 4 But in the end she is as bitter as *w*,
Jer 9:14 give them *w* to eat and poison to drink.
23:15 Behold, I will give them *w* to eat,
Lam 3:15 bitter food, made me drink my fill of *w*.
3:19 of my homeless poverty is *w* and gall;
Hos 10: 4 grows wild like *w* in a plowed field!
Am 5: 7 to *w* and cast justice to the ground!
6:12 into gall, and the fruit of justice into *w*.
Rv 8:11 The star's name was *W*" because a third
8:11 a third part of all the water turned to *w*.

WORMY (2)

Ex 16:20 following morning, it became *w* and rotten.
16:24 commanded, it did not become rotten or *w*.

WORN (16)

Ex 35:19 vestments *w* by his sons in their ministry."
39:26 was to be *w* in performing the ministry
39:41 to be *w* by his sons in their ministry.
Nm 21: 4 with their patience *w* out by the journey,
Jos 9:13 which are *w* out from the very long journey."
Jgs 8:26 purple garments *w* by the kings of Midian,
Neh 9:21 their garments did not become *w*,
Jdt 10: 3 festive attire she had *w* while her husband,
Sir 11: 4 *w* cloak and jibe at no man's bitter day:
45:13 be *w* by any Except his sons and them alone,
Is 57:10 Though *w* out by your many misdeeds,
Lam 2:11 *W* out from weeping are my eyes,
3: 4 He has *w* away my flesh and my skin,
5: 5 we are *w* out,
Ez 34: 3 You have fed off their milk, *w* their wool,
Lk 8:27 For a long time he had not *w* any clothes;

WORRIED (2)

1Sm 10: 2 Your father is no longer *w* about the asses,
Jer 49:23 *W*,

WORRIES (1)

1Cor 7:32 I should like you to be free of all *w*.

WORRY (15)

Lv 25:19 so that you may live there without *w*.
1Sm 9:20 lost three days ago, do not *w* about them,
Tb 5:22 do not *w* about them,
6:18 So do not *w*."
10: 3 And he began to *w*.
10: 6 So do not *w* over him, my love.
2Mc 11:26 they may have nothing to *w* about but may
Sir 30:23 For *w* has brought death to many,
30:24 one's life, *w* brings on premature old age.
42: 9 wakeful, and *w* over her drives away rest:
Mt 6:25 do not *w* about your livelihood,
10:19 do not *w* about what you will say or how
Mk 13:11 do not *w* beforehand about what to say.
Lk 12:11 do not *w* about how to defend yourselves or
21:14 not to *w* about your defense beforehand,

WORRYING (5)

Mt 6:27 you by *w* can add a moment to his life-span?
6:31 Stop *w*, then, over questions like,
6:34 Enough, then, of *w* about tomorrow.
Lk 12:25 you by *w* can add a moment to his life-span?
12:29 Stop *w*.

WORSE (35)

Gn 19: 9 We'll treat you *w* than them!"
Lv 27:10 for a *w* one or a worse for a better one.
Jgs 2:19 would relapse and do *w* than their fathers,
2Sm 13:16 *w* than the first injury you have done me."
1Kgs 14: 9 You have done *w* than all who preceded you:
Tb 2:10 various salves, the *w* the cataracts became,
1Mc 6:27 they will do even *w* things than these,
2Mc 5:23 his fellow citizens *w* than the others did.
7:39 and treated him even *w* than the others,
13: 9 plans for inflicting on the Jews *w* things
Wis 15:14 senseless, and *w* than childish in mind,
15:18 as to folly, these are *w* than the rest,
17: 6 beholding these was *w* than the times when
Sir 22:10 but *w* than death is the life of a fool.
25:14 No poison *w* than that of a serpent,
Is 7:17 days *w* than any since Ephraim seceded
Jer 7:26 their necks and done *w* than their fathers.
16:12 And you have done *w* than your fathers.
Mt 9:16 the hole will pull, and the rip only get *w*.
12:45 state of that man becomes *w* than the first.
27:64 final imposture would be *w* than the first."
Mk 2:21 and the tear would get *w*.
5:26 on the contrary, she only grew *w*.
Lk 11:26 with seven other spirits far *w* than itself,
11:26 last state of the man is *w* than the first."
Jn 5:14 so that something *w* may not overtake you."
5:18 only was breaking the sabbath but, *w* still,
Acts 23:10 the dispute grew *w* and the commander
2Cor 11:23 *w* beatings and frequent brushes with death.
1Tm 5: 8 he is *w* than an unbeliever.
2Tm 3:13 men and charlatans will go from bad to *w*,
Heb 10:29 Do you not suppose that a much *w*
2Pt 2:20 their last condition is *w* than their first.
Jude 1:11 So much the *w* for them!

WORSHIP (171)

Gn 22: 5 We will *w* and then come back to you."
24:26 The man then bowed down in *w* to the LORD,
24:48 Then I bowed down in *w* to the LORD,
Ex 3:12 you will *w* God on this very mountain."
4:31 their affliction, they bowed down in *w*.
7:16 Let my people go to *w* me in the desert.
7:26 Let my people go to *w* me,
8:16 Let my people go to *w* me.
9: 1 Let my people go to *w* me.
9:13 Let my people go to *w* me,
10: 3 Let my people go to *w* me.
10: 7 Let the men go to *w* the LORD, their God.
10: 8 said to them, "You may go and *w* the LORD,
10:11 Just you men can go and *w* the LORD.
10:24 and Aaron and said, "Go and *w* the LORD.
12:27 Then the people bowed down in *w*,
12:31 Go and *w* the LORD as you said.
20: 5 shall not bow down before them or *w* them.
23:24 shall not bow down in *w* before their gods,
23:25 The LORD, your God, you shall *w*;
24: 1 You shall all *w* at some distance,
33:10 and *w* at the entrance of their own tents.
34: 8 at once bowed down to the ground in *w*.
34:14 You shall not *w* any other god,
34:15 *w* to their gods and sacrifice to them,
34:16 render their wanton *w* to their gods,
Lv 17: 7 to whom they used to render their wanton *w*.
20: 5 all who join him in his wanton *w* of Molech.
26: 1 set up a stone figure for *w* in your land;
Dt 5: 9 shall not bow down before them or *w* them.
11:16 away that you serve other gods and *w* them.
12: 2 nations you are to dispossess *w* their gods.
12: 4 is not how you are to *w* the LORD your God.
12:30 gods, 'How did these nations *w* their gods?
12:31 You shall not thus *w* the LORD,
31:16 people will take to rendering wanton *w*
Jos 5:14 Joshua fell prostrate to the ground in *w*,
22:27 that we have the right to *w* the LORD in
23: 7 or swear by them, or serve them, or *w* them,
23:16 on you, serve other gods and *w* them,
Jgs 2:12 by their *w* of the gods provoked the LORD.
2:17 themselves to the *w* of other gods.
2:19 following other gods in service and *w*,
1Sm 1: 3 pilgrimage from his city to *w* the LORD
7: 3 yourselves to the LORD, and *w* him alone.
12:10 power of our enemies, and we will *w* you.'
12:14 If you fear the LORD and *w* him,
12:20 LORD, but must *w* him with your whole heart.
12:24 and *w* him faithfully with your whole heart;
15:25 and return with me, that I may *w* the LORD."
15:30 with me that I may *w* the LORD your God."
2Sm 15: 8 back to Jerusalem, I will *w* him in Hebron.'"
15:32 reached the top, where men used to *w* God,
1Kgs 9: 6 and proceed to venerate and *w* strange gods,
16:31 went over to the veneration and *w* of Baal.
2Kgs 5:18 enters the temple of Rimmon to *w* there,
10:28 Jehu rooted out the *w* of Baal from Israel.
17:26 do not know how to *w* the God of the land,
17:26 do not know how to *w* the God of the land."
17:27 to teach them how to *w* the God of the land."
17:33 following the *w* of the nations from among
17:34 they *w* according to their ancient rites.
17:35 must not venerate other gods, nor *w* them,
17:36 him shall you venerate, him shall you *w*,
18:22 to *w* before this altar in Jerusalem?'
1Chr 16:29 *w* the LORD in holy attire.
21:30 But David could not go there to *w* God,
2Chr 7:19 you proceed to venerate and *w* strange gods,
20:18 Jerusalem fell down before the LORD in *w*.
Tb 5:14 to Jerusalem, where we would *w* together.
14: 6 be converted and shall offer God true *w*;
Jdt 3: 8 every nation might *w* Nebuchadnezzar alone,
5: 8 with divine *w* the God of heaven,
16:18 The people then went to Jerusalem to *w* God;
2Mc 1: 3 May he give to all of you a heart to *w* him
Ps(s) 5: 8 will *w* at your holy temple in fear of you,
31: 7 You hate those who *w* vain idols,
45:12 for he is your lord, and you must *w* him.
66: 4 Let all on earth *w* and sing praise to you,
81:10 among you nor shall you *w* any alien god.
86: 9 nations you have made shall come and *w* you,
95: 6 Come, let us bow down in *w*;
96: 9 *w* the LORD in holy attire.
97: 7 All who *w* graven things are put to shame,
99: 5 the LORD, our God, and *w* at his footstool;
99: 9 LORD, our God, and *w* at his holy mountain;
138: 2 I will *w* at your holy temple and give
Wis 14:27 For the *w* of infamous idols is the reason
15: 6 who make them and long for them and *w* them.
15:18 besides, they *w* the most loathsome beasts
Is 2: 8 they *w* the works of their hands,
2:20 of silver and gold which they made for *w*.
27:13 come and *w* the LORD on the holy mountain,

WORSHIP (cont.)

36: 7 Judah and Jerusalem to *w* before this altar?'
44:17 his idol, and prostrate before it in *w*,
44:19 out of the rest, or *w* a block of wood?"
46: 6 a god before which they fall down in *w*.
49:23 shall *w* you and lick the dust at your feet.
66:23 All mankind shall come to *w* before me,
Jer 7: 2 Judah who enter these gates to *w* the LORD!
26: 2 who come to *w* in the house of the LORD;
Bar 5: 4 the peace of justice, the glory of God's *w*.
6:25 who *w* them are put to confusion because,
Ez 20:40 of Israel without exception shall *w* me;
46: 2 he shall *w* at the threshold of the gate
46: 3 The people of the land shall *w* before the
46: 9 presence of the LORD to *w* on the festivals,
Dn 3: 5 ordered to fall down and *w* the golden statue
3: 6 Whoever does not fall down and *w* shall be
3:10 should fall down and *w* the golden statue;
3:12 or *w* the golden statue which you set up."
3:14 god, or *w* the golden statue that I set up?
3:15 to fall down and *w* the statue I had made,
3:18 or *w* the golden statue which you set up."
3:95 serve or *w* any god except their own God.
14: 5 "Because I *w* not idols made with hands,
Jon 1: 9 "I *w* the LORD,
2: 9 *w* vain idols forsake their source of mercy.
Zec 14:16 come up year after year to *w* the King,
14:17 not come up to Jerusalem to *w* the King,
Jn 4:20 is the place where men ought to *w* God."
4:21 an hour is coming when you will *w* the
4:22 You people *w* what you do not understand,
4:22 understand, while we understand what we *w*;
4:23 will *w* the Father in Spirit and truth.
4:24 who worship him must *w* in Spirit and truth."
9:38 he said, and bowed down to *w* him.
12:20 come up to *w* at the feast were some Greeks.
Acts 7: 7 after that they will *w* me in this place.
7:42 to the *w* of the galaxies in the heavens.
18:13 to *w* God in ways that are against the law."
24:11 since I went to Jerusalem to *w* there.
24:14 that I *w* the God of our fathers.
26: 7 twelve tribes of our people fervently *w* God
Rom 1: 9 The God I *w* in the spirit by preaching the
9: 4 the covenants, the law-giving, the *w*,
12: 1 and acceptable to God, your spiritual *w*.
1Cor 10:14 you, whom I love, to shun the *w* of idols,
10:28 say to you, "This was offered in idol *w*,"
14:25 Falling prostrate, he will *w* God,
2Cor 1:20 address our Amen to God when we *w* together.
Phil 3: 3 who *w* in the spirit of God and glory in
Col 2:18 insisting on servility in the *w* of angels.
2Thes 2: 4 above every so-called god proposed for *w*,
2Tm 1: 3 whom I *w* with a clear conscience,
Heb 1: 6 he says, "Let all the angels of God *w* him."
8: 5 They offer *w* in a sanctuary which is only
9: 1 regulations for *w* and an earthly sanctuary.
9: 6 These were the arrangements for *w*.
9:14 from dead works to *w* the living God!
9:21 and all the vessels of *w* with blood.
12:28 *w* acceptable to him in reverence and awe.
Jas 1:26 his *w* is pointless.
1:27 *w* without stain before our God and Father.
Rv 4:10 and *w* him who lives forever and ever.
7:11 fell down before the throne to *w* God.
9:20 They did not give up the *w* of demons,
11: 1 and altar, and count those who *w* there.
11:16 God's presence fell down to *w* God and said:
13:12 and all its inhabitants *w* the first beast,
13:15 to death anyone who refused to *w* it.
14: 7 *W* the Creator of heaven and earth,
14:11 for those who *w* the beast or its image
15: 4 nations shall come and *w* in your presence.
19:10 I fell at his feet to *w* him,
19:10 *W* God alone.
19:20 the mark of the beast and *w* its image.
22: 8 I heard and saw them I fell down to *w*
22: 9 *W* God alone!"

WORSHIPED (40)

Nm 25: 2 ate of the sacrifices and *w* their god.
Jgs 10:13 you still forsook me and *w* other gods.
1Sm 1:19 the next morning they *w* before the LORD,
2: 1 and as she *w* the LORD, she said:
7: 4 Baals and Ashtaroth, and *w* the LORD alone.
15:31 returned with him, and Saul *w* the LORD.
2Sm 12:20 he went to the house of the LORD and *w*.
1Kgs 1:47 And the king in his bed *w* God,
9: 9 strange gods which they *w* and served.
11:33 he has forsaken me and has *w* Astarte,
22:54 He served and *w* Baal,
2Kgs 17:16 a sacred pole and *w* all the host of heaven,
21: 3 He *w* and served the whole host of heaven.
2Chr 7:22 strange gods and *w* them and served them.
33: 3 before the whole host of heaven and *w* them.
33:22 his father Manasseh had made, and *w* them.
Jdt 6:18 this the people fell prostrate and *w* God;
13:17 They bowed down and *w* God,
Est C:18 of our enemies, because we *w* their gods.
Wis 14:16 graven things were *w* by princely decrees.
14:20 *w* who shortly before was honored as a man.
Jer 8: 2 which they followed, consulted, and *w*.
16:11 strange gods, which they served and *w*;
Bar 6: 5 in your hearts, "You, O Lord, are to be *w*!";
Dn 2:46 Then King Nebuchadnezzar fell down and *w*
3: 7 all fell down and *w* the golden statue
14: 4 king *w* it and went every day to adore it;
14:23 was a great dragon which the Babylonians *w*.
14:27 "This," he said, "is what you *w*."
Jn 4:20 Our ancestors *w* on this mountain,
Rom 1:25 the truth of God for a lie and *w* and served
Heb 11:21 each of the sons of Joseph, and *w* God,
Rv 5:14 "Amen," and the elders fell down and *w*.
11:13 so terrified that they *w* the God of heaven.
13: 4 Men *w* the dragon for giving his authority
13: 4 they also *w* the beast and said,
13: 8 The beast will be *w* by all those
16: 2 the mark of the beast or *w* its image.
19: 4 and *w* God seated on the throne and sang,
20: 4 those who had never *w* the beast or its

WORSHIPER (3)

2Kgs 10:23 there is no *w* of the LORD here with you,
Tb 2: 2 If he is a sincere *w* of God,
Heb 9: 9 make perfect the conscience of the *w*,

WORSHIPERS (12)

2Kgs 10:19 for me all Baal's prophets, all his *w*,
10:19 so that he might destroy the *w* of Baal.
10:21 All the *w* of Baal without exception came
10:22 out the garments for all the *w* of Baal."
10:23 temple of Baal and said to the *w* of Baal,
10:23 the LORD here with you, but only *w* of Baal."
Bar 6:26 to the ground, the *w* must raise them up.
6:38 and their *w* will be put to shame.
Jn 4:23 when authentic *w* will worship the Father
4:23 Indeed, it is just such *w* the Father seeks.
Heb 10: 1 it was never able to perfect the *w* by the
10: 2 have stopped offering them, for the *w*,

WORSHIPING (15)

Ex 23:33 me by ensnaring you into *w* their gods."
32: 8 for themselves a molten calf and *w* it,
Dt 8:19 and follow other gods, serving and *w* them,
17: 3 or by *w* the sun or the moon or any of the
1Sm 8: 8 this day, deserting me and *w* strange gods,
12:10 the LORD and *w* Baals and Ashtaroth;
2Kgs 19:37 he was *w* in the temple of his god Nisroch,
21:21 and *w* the idols his father had served.
Wis 11:15 into *w* dumb serpents and worthless insects,
Is 37:38 he was *w* in the temple of his god Nisroch,
Jer 22: 9 their God, by *w* and serving strange gods."
Bar 6: 5 the crowd before them and behind *w* them.
Lk 2:37 *w* day and night in fasting and prayer.
Acts 17:23 what you are thus *w* in ignorance I intend
Rv 15: 2 They were holding the harps used in *w* God,

WORSHIPS (4)

Jdt 8:18 or city of ours that *w* gods made by hands,
Wis 15:17 For he is better than the things he *w*;
Is 44:15 a god which he adores, an idol which he *w*.
Rv 14: 9 "If anyone *w* the beast or its image,

WORST (12)

Tb 12:10 guilty of sin are their own *w* enemies.
Est B: 5 to our interests, and commits the *w* crimes,
Ps(s) 41: 6 My enemies say the *w* of me:
41: 8 against me they imagine the *w*:
Eccl 9: 3 that happen under the sun, this is the *w*,
Sir 25:12 *W* of all wounds is that of the heart, worst
25:13 *W* of all sufferings is that from one's foes,
25:13 *w* of all vengeance is that of one's
Ez 7:24 I will bring in the *w* of the nations,
Dn 3:32 to an unjust king, the *w* in all the world.
1Tm 1:15 Of these I myself am the *w*.

WORTH (29)

Gn 23:15 of land *w* four hundred shekels of silver
Dt 15:18 six years was *w* twice a hired man's salary;
20:14 is *w* plundering you may take as your booty,
Ru 4:15 She is *w* more to you than seven sons!"
1Sm 2:26 *w* in the estimation of the LORD and of men.
1Kgs 1:42 are a man of *w* and must bring good news."
1Mc 15:18 with them a gold shield *w* a thousand minas.
Jb 28:17 it, nor can golden vessels reach its *w*.
Prv 10:20 the heart of the wicked is of little *w*.
31:29 "Many are the women of proven *w*,
Wis 7:15 and value these endowments at their *w*:
Sir 6:15 is beyond price, no sum can balance his *w*.
18: 6 What is man, of what *w* is he?
24: 2 presence of his hosts she declares her *w*:
26:14 and her firm virtue is of surpassing *w*.
39:34 for each shows its *w* at the proper time.
44:17 Because of his *w* there were survivors,
Is 2:22 for what is he *w*?
7:23 vines, *w* a thousand pieces of silver,
Lam 4: 2 Now *w* no more than earthen jars made by
Mt 10:10 The workman, after all, is *w* his keep.
10:31 *w* more than an entire flock of sparrows.
17:27 there a coin *w* twice the temple tax.
Mk 12:33 love our neighbor as ourselves' is *w* more
12:42 in two small copper coins *w* a few cents.
Lk 10: 7 they have, for the laborer is *w* his wage.
12: 7 You are *w* more than a flock of sparrows.
1Cor 14:29 let the rest judge the *w* of what they say.
16:18 You should recognize the *w* of such men.

WORTHLESS (36)

1Sm 10:27 But certain *w* men said,
15: 9 dooming only what was *w* and of no account.
25:25 my lord pay attention to that *w* man Nabal,
30:22 But all the stingy and *w* men among those
1Kgs 10:21 for in Solomon's time it was considered *w*.
2Chr 13: 7 *W* men, scoundrels, joined him
Jb 22:15 keep to the ancient way trodden by *w* men,
34:18 Just One, Who says to a king, "You are *w*!"
Ps(s) 26: 4 I stay not with *w* men,
59: 6 have no pity on any *w* traitors.
60:13 against the foe, for *w* is the help of men.
108:13 against the foe, for *w* is the help of men.
Prv 14:35 servant, but the *w* one incurs his wrath.
17: 2 intelligent servant will rule over a *w* son,
19:26 his mother, is a *w* and disgraceful son.
Eccl 4: 8 This also is vanity and a *w* task.
Wis 3:11 are their labors, and *w* are their works.
11:15 worshiping dumb serpents and *w* insects,
12:24 for gods the *w* and disgusting among beasts,
13:14 a man or makes it resemble some *w* beast.
15:10 more *w* than earth is his hope,
Sir 15: 7 *W* men will not attain to her,
16: 1 Desire not a brood of *w* children,
Is 1:13 Bring no more *w* offerings;
57: 4 Are you not rebellious children, a *w* race;
Lam 1:11 O LORD, and see how *w* I have become!
Mt 18:32 sent for him and said, 'You *w* wretch!
24:48 But if the servant is *w* and tells himself,
25:26 'You *w*, lazy lout!
25:30 this *w* servant into the darkness outside,
Lk 19:22 'You *w* lout!
Rom 3:12 the wrong course, all alike have become *w*;
1Cor 15:17 if Christ was not raised, your faith is *w*.
Gal 4: 9 can you return to those powerless, *w*,
Eph 5: 6 Let no one deceive you with *w* arguments.
Heb 6: 8 if it bears thorns and thistles, it is *w*;

WORTHLESSNESS (3)

Tb 4:13 *w* there is decay and dire poverty, for *w*
Jb 11:11 he knows the *w* of men and sees iniquity;

WORTHWHILE (4)

1Sm 15: 9 carry out the doom on anything that was *w*,
Ez 15: 3 Can you use its wood to make anything *w*?
Mt 13:48 sat down to put what was *w* into containers.
Jas 1:17 Every *w* gift,

WORTHY (62)

Ru 2:13 She said, "May I prove *w* of your kindness,
3:11 all my townspeople know you for a *w* woman.
1Kgs 1:52 Solomon answered, "If he proves himself *w*,
Tb 4:11 Alms are a *w* offering in the sight of the
Jdt 8:29 to the *w* dispositions of your heart.
Est 1:19 her royal dignity to one more *w* than she.
1Mc 10:19 a mighty warrior and *w* to be our friend.
10:54 will give to you and to her gifts *w* of you."
2Mc 4:25 that made him *w* of the high priesthood;
6:23 his mind in a noble manner, *w* of his years,
6:27 now, I will prove myself *w* of my old age,
7:20 Most admirable and *w* of everlasting
7:29 but be *w* of your brothers and accept death,
9:15 whom he had judged not even *w* of burial,
15:11 a dream, a kind of vision, *w* of belief.
Ps(s) 93: 5 Your decrees are *w* of trust indeed:
Prv 12: 4 A *w* wife is the crown of her husband,
20: 6 but who can find one *w* of trust?
31:10 When one finds a *w* wife,
Wis 3: 5 God tried them and found them *w* of himself.
6:16 her own rounds, seeking those *w* of her,
9:12 justly and be *w* of my father's throne.
12: 7 might receive a *w* colony of God's children.
12:26 were to experience a condemnation *w* of God.
15: 6 and *w* of such hopes are they who make them
Sir 2: 5 and *w* men in the crucible of humiliation.
7:25 but give her to a *w* man.
26: 2 A *w* wife brings joy to her husband,
29:27 Away, stranger, for one more *w*;
Mt 8: 8 "I am not *w* to have you under my roof.
10:11 "Look for a *w* person in every town or
10:37 or daughter, more than me is not *w* of me.
10:38 his cross and come after me is not *w* of me.
Lk 7: 6 for I am not *w* to have you enter my house.
20:35 but those judged *w* of a place in the age
Jn 1:27 of whose sandal I am not *w* to unfasten."
Acts 5:41 they had been judged *w* of ill-treatment
13:25 not *w* to unfasten the sandals on his feet.'
22:22 He isn't *w* to live!"
Eph 4: 1 a life *w* of the calling you have received,
Phil 1:27 then, in a way *w* of the gospel of Christ.
4: 8 decent, virtuous, or *w* of praise.
4:19 in a way *w* of his magnificent riches in
Col 1:10 Then you will lead a life *w* of the Lord
1:12 *w* to share the lot of the saints in light.
1Thes 2:12 to make your lives *w* of the God
2Thes 1: 5 in order to be found *w* of his kingdom
1:11 that our God may make you *w* of his call,

1Tm 1:15 can depend on this as *w* of full acceptance:
3:13 Those who serve well as deacons gain a *w*
4: 9 depend on this as *w* of complete acceptance.
6: 1 regard their masters as *w* of full respect;
2Tm 2:15 hard to make yourself *w* of God's approval,
Heb 3: 3 but Jesus is more *w* of honor than he,
11:11 who had made the promise was *w* of trust.
11:38 The world was not *w* of them.
Rv 3: 4 walk with me in white because they are *w*.
4:11 are *w* to receive glory and honor and power!
5: 2 *w* to open the scroll and break its seals?"
5: 4 be found *w* to open or examine the scroll.
5: 9 *W* are you to receive the scroll and break
5:12 *W* is the Lamb that was slain to receive

WOUND (20)

Ex 21:25 foot for foot, burn for burn, wound for *w*,
2Sm 1:10 for I knew that he could not survive his *w*.
1Kgs 22:35 his *w* flowed to the bottom of the chariot.
Jdt 9:13 Let my guileful speech bring *w* and wale on
Jb 34: 6 in my *w* the arrow rankles,
Sir 27:21 A *w* can be bound up,
Is 1: 6 *W* and welt and gaping gash,
58: 8 dawn, and your *w* shall quickly be healed;
Jer 8:22 over the *w* of the daughter of my people?
10:19 I am undone, my *w* is incurable;
10:19 if I make light of my *w*, I can bear it.
14:17 of my people, over her incurable *w*.
15:18 Why is my pain continuous, my *w* incurable,
30:12 Incurable is your *w*,
30:15 Why cry out over your *w*?
Na 3:19 no healing for your hurt, your *w* is mortal.
1Cor 8:12 your brothers and *w* their weak consciences,
Rv 13: 3 wounded, but this mortal *w* was healed.
13:12 beast, whose mortal *w* had been healed.

WOUNDED (29)

1Sm 17:52 and Philistines fell *w* along the road from
31: 1 and falling mortally *w* on Mount Gilboa,
2Sm 2:31 *w* three hundred and sixty men of Benjamin,
1Kgs 20:37 The man struck him a blow and *w* him.
2Kgs 8:28 Ramoth-gilead, where the Arameans *w* Joram.
1Chr 10: 3 found him, and *w* him with their arrows.
2Chr 22: 5 There Jehoram was *w* by the Arameans.
35:23 "Take me away, for I am seriously *w*."
1Mc 3:11 Many fell *w*, and the rest fled.
8:10 Many were *w* and fell,
9:17 desperately, and many on both sides fell *w*.
9:40 Many fell *w*,
16: 8 many of them fell *w*,
16: 9 was then that John's brother Judas fell *w*;
2Mc 4:42 they *w* many of them and even killed a few,
8:24 *w* and disabled the greater part of
10:30 their own armor, kept him from being *w*.
11:12 got away were *w* and stripped of their arms,
12:22 that in many cases they *w* one another,
Jb 24:12 and the souls of the *w* cry out [yet God
Ps(s) 69:27 smote, and added to the pain of him you *w*.
Sg 5: 7 They struck me, and *w* me,
Jer 37:10 now attacking you, and only the *w* remained,
51:52 and in her whole land the *w* will groan.
Lam 2:12 away like the *w* in the streets of the city,
Ez 26:15 of your fall, at the groaning of the *w*,
Zec 13: 6 these I was *w* in the house of my dear ones."
Rv 13: 3 heads seemed to have been mortally *w*,
13:14 that had been *w* by the sword and yet lived.

WOUNDING (2)

Gn 4:23 I have killed a man for *w* me,
Prv 26:10 Like an archer *w* all who pass by is he who

WOUNDS (26)

Dt 32:39 and life, I who inflict *w* and heal them,
2Kgs 8:29 *w* which the Arameans had inflicted on him
9:15 Jezreel to be healed of the *w* the Arameans
2Chr 22: 6 *w* he had received at Rama in his battle
2Mc 14:45 with blood gushing from his frightful *w*.
Jb 5:18 For he *w*, but he binds up; he smites,
9:17 me, and multiply my *w* without cause;
Ps(s) 147: 3 the brokenhearted and binds up their *w*.
Prv 23:29 Who have *w* for nothing?
27: 6 *W* from a friend may be accepted as well
Sir 25:12 Worst of all *w* is that of the heart,
30: 7 who spoils his son will have *w* to bandage,
31:30 lessens his strength and multiplies his *w*.
Is 30:26 day the LORD binds up the *w* of his people,
Jer 6: 7 ever before me are *w* and blows.
19: 8 Because of all its *w*,
30:17 of your *w* I will heal you,
33: 6 I will treat and assuage the city's *w*;
49:17 appalled and catch his breath at all her *w*.
50:13 and catch his breath, at all her *w*.
51: 8 Bring balm for her *w*,
Hos 6: 1 he has struck us, but he will bind our *w*.
Zec 13: 6 asks him, "What are these *w* on your chest?"
Lk 10:34 He approached him and dressed his *w*,
Acts 16:33 night he took them in and bathed their *w*;
1Pt 2:24 By his *w*, you were healed.

WOVE (4)

Jgs 16:14 *w* his seven locks of hair into the web,
2Kgs 23: 7 which the women *w* garments for the Asherah.
Mk 15:17 then *w* a crown of thorns and put it on him,
Jn 19: 2 The soldiers then *w* a crown of thorns and

WOVEN (33)

Ex 26: 1 *w* of fine linen twined and of violet,
26: 7 "Also make sheets *w* of goat hair,
26:31 "You shall have a veil *w* of violet,
27: 9 cubits long, *w* of fine linen twined,
27:16 curtain, twenty cubits long, *w* of violet,
28:32 a selvage, *w* as at the opening of a shirt,
28:33 you shall make pomegranates, *w* of violet,
36: 8 with its ten sheets *w* of fine linen twined,
36:14 were also *w* as a tent over the Dwelling.
36:35 The veil was *w* of violet,
36:37 linen twined, *w* in a variegated manner.
38: 9 were hangings, *w* of fine linen twined,
38:16 of the court were *w* of fine linen twined.
38:18 was a variegated curtain, *w* of violet,
39: 1 purple and scarlet yarn were *w* the service
39: 2 ephod was *w* of gold thread and of violet,
39: 3 into threads, which were *w* with the violet,
39:22 of the ephod was *w* entirely of violet yarn,
39:27 there were also *w* tunics of fine linen;
Lv 13:48 on *w* or knitted material of linen or wool,
13:49 or hide, or on the *w* or knitted material,
13:51 garment, or on the *w* or knitted material,
13:52 the *w* or knitted material of wool or linen,
13:53 garment, or on the *w* or knitted material,
13:56 the leather, or the *w* or knitted material.
13:57 garment, or on the *w* or knitted material,
13:58 the garment, or the *w* or knitted material,
13:59 wool or linen, or on *w* or knitted material,
19:19 *w* with two different kinds of thread.
Dt 22:11 of thread, wool and linen, *w* together.
Is 25: 7 The web that is *w* over all nations;
Ez 27:24 varicolored carpets, and firmly *w* cords.
Jn 19:23 but this tunic was *w* in one piece from top

WRANGLING (1)

Sir 27:15 *W* among the haughty ends in bloodshed,

WRAP (4)

Nm 4:12 they shall *w* them all in violet cloth and
Dt 22:12 corners of the cloak that you *w* around you."
Ps(s) 18:12 dark, misty rain-clouds his *w*.
Is 28:20 out in, and the cover too narrow to *w* in.

WRAPPED (25)

Ex 12:34 bowls *w* in their cloaks on their shoulders.
19:18 Mount Sinai was all *w* in smoke,
1Sm 21:10 is here *w* in a mantle] behind an ephod.
2Kgs 19: 1 tore his garments, *w* himself in sackcloth,
19: 2 the elders of the priests, *w* in sackcloth,
Jdt 10: 5 she *w* up and gave to the maid to carry.
Ps(s) 71:13 let them be *w* in ignominy and disgrace who
Sir 40: 4 crown or is *w* in the coarsest of cloaks
Is 37: 1 tore his garments, *w* himself in sackcloth,
37: 2 the elders of the priests, *w* in sackcloth,
59:17 vengeance, *w* himself in a mantle of zeal.
61:10 salvation, and *w* me in a mantle of justice,
Lam 3:44 You *w* yourself in a cloud which prayer
Bar 5: 2 *W* in the cloak of justice from God,
6:11 but though they are *w* in purple clothing,
Hos 13:12 The guilt of Israel is *w* up,
Mt 27:28 and *w* him in a scarlet military cloak.
27:59 Joseph *w* it in fresh linen and laid it in
Mk 15:46 Joseph took him down, *w* him in the linen,
Lk 2: 7 *w* him in swaddling clothes and laid him
2:12 will find an infant *w* in swaddling clothes."
23:53 He took it down, *w* it in fine linen,
Jn 11:44 with linen strips, his face *w* in a cloth.
Acts 5: 6 the young men came forward, *w* up the body,
Rv 10: 1 angel come down from heaven *w* in a cloud,

WRAPPING (1)

Nm 4:25 covering and the outer *w* of tahash skin,

WRAPPINGS (5)

Lk 24:12 down but could see nothing but the *w*.
Jn 19:40 it up in *w* of cloth with perfumed oils.
20: 5 peer in, and saw the *w* lying on the ground.
20: 6 He observed the *w* on the ground and saw
20: 7 had covered the head not lying with the *w*,

WRAPS (1)

Is 3:22 the court dresses, *w*,

WRATH (246)

Ex 15: 7 you loosed your *w* to consume them like
22:23 My *w* will flare up, and I will kill you
32:10 that my *w* may blaze up against them to
32:11 your *w* blaze up against your own people,
32:12 Let your blazing *w* die down;
32:19 With that, Moses' *w* flared up,
Lv 10: 6 but God's *w* also on the whole community.
Nm 1:53 *w* will strike the Israelite community.
11: 1 and when he heard it his *w* flared up so
11:33 the LORD's *w* flared up against the people,
17:11 for *w* has come forth from the LORD and the
18: 5 that *w* may not fall again upon the Israelites.
25: 4 blazing *w* may be turned away from Israel."
32:10 At that time the *w* of the LORD flared up,
32:14 LORD's blazing *w* against the Israelites.
Dt 6:15 nations, lest the *w* of the LORD,
7: 4 and then the *w* of the LORD would flare up
9:19 his *w* would destroy you.
11:17 For then the *w* of the LORD will flare up
13:18 that the blazing *w* of the LORD may die
29:19 the LORD'S *w* and jealousy will flare up
29:22 *w* they and all the nations will ask,
29:23 Why this fierce outburst of *w*?'
29:27 in his furious *w* and tremendous anger the
32:22 "For by my *w* a fire is enkindled that
33: 2 forth and his *w* devastated the nations.
Jos 22:20 *w* fall upon the entire community of Israel?
2Sm 22: 8 trembled and shook when his *w* flared up.
22:16 LORD, at the blast of the wind of his *w*.
2Kgs 3:27 The *w* against Israel was so great that
1Chr 15:13 the *w* of the LORD our God burst upon us,
27:24 it, for because of it *w* fell upon Israel.
2Chr 12: 7 and my *w* shall not be poured out upon
19: 2 this reason, *w* is upon you from the LORD.
19:10 and his *w* come upon you and your brethren.
24:18 of theirs, *w* came upon Judah and Jerusalem.
Ezr 5:12 provoked the *w* of the God of heaven,
7:23 that *w* may not come upon the realm of the
8:22 mighty *w* is against all who forsake him,
Neh 13:18 Would you add to the *w* against Israel by
Jdt 2: 7 for I will come against them in my *w*;
9: 8 might, and crush their force in your *w*;
9: 9 and send forth your *w* upon their heads.
11:11 by which they bring the *w* of their God
Est 1:12 At this the king's *w* flared up,
2: 1 this, when King Ahasuerus' *w* had cooled,
1Mc 2:44 in their anger and lawbreakers in their *w*,
3: 8 He turned away *w* from Israel 9and was
2Mc 7:38 may there be an end to the *w* of the
8: 5 for the Lord's *w* had now changed to mercy.
Jb 4: 9 by the blast of his *w* they are consumed.
14:13 and keep me sheltered till your *w* is past;
16: 9 I am the prey his *w* assails,
19:11 His *w* he has kindled against me;
20:23 shall send against him the fury of his *w*
21:20 and the *w* of the Almighty let him drink!
32: 5 of the three men, his *w* was inflamed.
40:11 Let loose the fury of your *w*;
Ps(s) 2: 5 he terrifies them in his *w*:
6: 2 in your anger, nor chastise me in your *w*.
18: 8 trembled and shook when his *w* flared up.
18:16 LORD, at the blast of the wind of his *w*.
37: 8 Give up your anger, and forsake *w*;
38: 2 punish me not, in your *w* chastise me not;
56: 8 in your *w* bring down the peoples, O God.
59:14 Consume them in *w*;
69:25 Pour out your *w* upon them;
78:38 his anger and let none of his *w* be roused.
78:49 his fierce anger, *w* and fury and strife,
79: 6 Pour out your *w* upon the nations that
85: 4 You have withdrawn all your *w*;
88: 8 Upon me your *w* lies heavy,
89:47 Will your *w* burn like fire?
90: 7 anger, and by your *w* we are put to rout.
102:11 tears, Because of your fury and your *w*;
103: 9 chide, nor does he keep his *w* forever.
106:23 the breach to turn back his destructive *w*.
110: 5 he will crush kings on the day of his *w*.
Prv 6:34 For vindictive is the husband's *w*,
11: 4 Wealth is useless on the day of *w*,
11:23 the expectation of the wicked is *w*.
14:35 but the worthless one incurs his *w*.
15: 1 A mild answer calms *w*,
16:14 The king's *w* is like messengers of death,
19:12 The king's *w* is like the roaring of a lion,
21:14 anger, and a concealed present, violent *w*.
24:18 you, and withdraw his *w* from your enemy.
27: 4 Anger is relentless, and *w* overwhelming
Eccl 5:16 under great vexation, sickness and *w*.
Wis 10: 3 he perished through his fratricidal *w*.
18:21 the *w* and put a stop to the calamity,
19: 1 wicked, merciless *w* assailed until the end.
Sir 5: 7 upon the wicked alights his *w*.
5: 9 For suddenly his *w* flames forth;
5:10 for it will be no help on the day of *w*.
7:16 remember, his *w* will not delay.
16: 6 upon a godless people *w* flames out.
16:11 though on the wicked alights his *w*.
18:24 Think of *w* and the day of death,
23:16 men multiply sins, a third draws down *w*;
27:30 *W* and anger are hateful things,
28: 5 If he who is but flesh cherishes *w*,
28:10 the greater his power, the greater his *w*.
28:19 from it, and has not endured its *w*;
36: 6 Rouse your anger, pour out *w*,
39:23 his *w* expels the nations and turns fertile
40: 5 Are of *w* and envy,
40: 9 Plague and bloodshed, *w* and the sword,
45:19 angry, he destroyed them in his burning *w*.
47:20 your marriage, *W* upon your descendants,
48:10 put an end to *w* before the day of the LORD,

WRATH (cont.)

Is 5:25 *w* of the LORD blazes against his people,
5:25 For all this, his *w* is not turned back,
9:11 For all this, his *w* is not turned back,
9:16 For all this, his *w* is not turned back,
9:18 the *w* of the LORD of hosts the land quakes,
9:20 For all this, his *w* is not turned back,
10: 4 For all this, his *w* is not turned back,
10: 5 My rod in anger, my staff in *w*.
10: 6 under my *w* I order him To seize plunder,
10:25 but them I will destroy in *w*.
13: 5 The LORD and the instruments of his *w*,
13: 9 LORD comes cruel, with *w* and burning anger;
13:13 At the *w* of the LORD of hosts on the day
14: 6 struck the peoples in *w* relentless blows;
26:20 for a brief moment, until the *w* is past.
30:27 of the LORD coming from afar in burning *w*,
42:25 So he poured out *w* upon them,
51:17 drank at the LORD's hand the cup of his *w*;
51:20 They are filled with the *w* of the LORD,
51:22 The bowl of my *w* you shall no longer drink.
54: 8 In an outburst of *w*,
57:17 angry, and struck them, hiding myself in *w*,
59:18 deserts, and requites his foes with *w*.
60:10 Though I struck you in my *w*,
63: 3 my anger, and trampled them down in my *w*;
63: 5 victory and my own *w* lent me its support.
63: 6 in my anger, I crushed them in my *w*,
65: 5 These things enkindle my *w*,
66:14 to his servants, but to his enemies, his *w*.
66:15 To wreak his *w* with burning heat and his
Jer 3: 5 "Will he keep his *w* forever,
3:12 the LORD, I will not continue my *w* forever.
4: 8 *w* of the LORD is not turned away from us."
4:26 before the LORD, before his blazing *w*.
6:11 Therefore my *w* brims up within me,
7:20 and my *w* will pour out upon this place,
7:29 off the generation that draws down his *w*.
10:10 quakes, whose *w* the nations cannot endure:
10:25 your *w* on the nations that know you not,
17: 4 kindled by my *w* that will burn forever.
18:20 behalf, to turn away your *w* from them.
21: 5 hand and mighty arm, in anger, and *w*,
23:19 His *w* breaks forth In a whirling storm
25:38 sword, by the burning *w* of the LORD.
30:23 His *w* breaks forth In a whirling storm
32:31 day, this city has excited my anger and *w*,
32:37 from all the lands to which in anger, *w*,
33: 5 of those whom I slay in my anger and *w*,
49:37 I will bring evil upon them, my burning *w*,
50:13 Because of the LORD's *w* she shall be empty,
50:25 and brings forth the weapons of his *w*;
51:45 himself from the burning *w* of the LORD.
Lam 1:12 afflicted me on the day of his blazing *w*.
2: 1 Lord in his *w* has detested daughter Zion!
2: 1 of his footstool on the day of his *w*.
2: 3 He broke off, in fiery *w*,
2: 4 Zion he poured out his *w* like fire.
2: 6 scorned in fierce *w* both king and priest.
2:21 You have slain on the day of your *w*,
2:22 There was not, on the day of your *w*,
3:43 You veiled yourself in *w* and pursued us,
3:66 *w* and destroy them from under your heavens!
4:11 spent his anger, poured out his blazing *w*;
5:22 in full measure turned your *w* against us.
Bar 1:13 and the *w* and anger of the Lord have not
2:20 have brought your *w* and anger down upon us,
Ez 7:12 mourn, for *w* shall be upon all the throng.
7:13 lives, for *w* shall be upon all the throng.
7:14 go to war, for my *w* is upon all the throng.
7:19 save them on the day of the LORD's *w*.
13:13 hailstones shall fall with destructive *w*.
20:33 and outstretched arm, with poured-out *w*,
20:34 and outstretched arm, with poured-out *w*,
21:36 breathing my fiery *w* upon you;
22:20 I will gather you together in my furious *w*,
22:31 with my fiery *w* I have consumed them;
24: 8 To work up my *w*, to excite my vengeance,
30:15 I will pour out my *w* on Pelusium,
38:19 my anger and in my jealousy, in my fiery *w*,
43: 8 therefore I consumed them in my *w*.
Dn 8:19 is to happen later in the period of *w*;
9:16 *w* be turned away from your city Jerusalem,
11:36 shall prosper only till divine *w* is ready,
Hos 5:10 Upon them I will pour out my *w* like water.
7: 4 are all kindled to *w* like a blazing oven,
8: 5 my *w* is kindled against them;
13:11 in my anger, and I take him away in my *w*.
14: 5 for my *w* is turned away from them.
Am 1:11 in his anger and kept his *w* to the end,
Jon 3: 9 and forgive, and withhold his blazing *w*,
Mi 5:14 *w* upon the nations that have not hearkened.
7: 9 The *w* of the LORD I will endure because I
Na 1: 2 adversaries, and lays up *w* for his enemies;
1: 6 Before his *w*, who can stand firm,
Hb 2:15 your neighbors a flood of your *w* to drink,
3: 2 in your *w* remember compassion!
3: 8 Is your *w* against the streams,
3:12 In *w* you bestride the earth,
Zep 1:15 A day of *w* is that day a day of anguish
1:18 to save them on the day of the LORD's *w*,
3: 8 In order to pour out upon them my *w*,
Zec 8: 2 for Zion, stirred to jealous *w* for her.
8:14 you when your fathers provoked me to *w*,
10: 3 My *w* is kindled against the shepherds,
Mt 3: 7 Who told you to flee from the *w* to come?
Lk 3: 7 Who told you to flee from the *w* to come?
21:23 the *w* against this people will be great.
Jn 3:36 not see life, but must endure the *w* of God."
Rom 1:18 The *w* of God is being revealed from heaven
2: 5 storing up retribution for that day of *w*
2: 8 *w* and fury to those who selfishly disobey
4:15 the law serves only to bring down *w*,
5: 9 that we shall be saved by him from God's *w*.
9:22 to show his *w* and make known his power,
9:22 with much patience vessels fit for *w*,
12:19 leave that to God's *w*,
13: 4 inflict his avenging *w* upon the wrongdoer.
Eph 2: 3 by nature deserved God's *w* like the rest.
4:26 The sun must not go down on your *w*;
5: 6 that bring God's *w* down on the disobedient;
Col 3: 6 These are the sins which provoke God's *w*.
1Thes 1:10 Jesus, who delivers us from the *w* to come.
2:16 but the *w* has descended upon them at last.
5: 9 God has not destined us for *w* but for
Heb 11:27 he left Egypt, not fearing the king's *w*,
Rv 6:16 on the throne and from the *w* of the Lamb!
11:18 day of *w* and the moment to judge the dead:
14:10 he too will drink the wine of God's *w*,
14:19 them into the huge winepress of God's *w*.
15: 1 which would bring God's *w* to a climax.
15: 7 *w* of the God who lives forever and ever.
16: 1 upon the earth the seven bowls of God's *w*!"
16:19 cup filled with the blazing wine of his *w*.
19:15 the blazing *w* of God the Almighty.

WRATHFUL (5)

Ps(s) 76:11 For *w* Edom shall glorify you,
Prv 22:24 man, nor the companion of a *w* man,
Wis 5:22 his sling, *w* hailstones shall be hurled.
11:18 or fierce lions, Or new-created, *w*,
Is 34: 2 nations and is *w* against all their host;

WREAK (8)

Is 66:15 To *w* his wrath with burning heat and his
Ez 5:13 *w* my fury upon them till I am appeased;
7:23 They shall *w* slaughter,
16:38 I will *w* fury and jealousy upon you.
21:22 one hand against the other and *w* my fury.
24:13 not be purified until I *w* my fury on you.
25:17 am the LORD, when I *w* my vengeance on
Mi 5:14 I will *w* vengeance in anger and wrath upon

WREAKED (1)

Ez 16:42 When I have *w* my fury upon you I will

WREAKS (1)

Sir 35:20 merciless and *w* vengeance upon the proud;

WREATHS (4)

1Kgs 7:29 the lions and oxen, there were *w* in relief.
7:33 they had *w* on each side.
7:36 trees were carved, as well as *w* all around.
2Mc 6: 7 march in his procession, wearing *w* of ivy.

WRECKED (4)

1Kgs 22:49 not go, because they were *w* at Eziongeber.
2Chr 20:37 were *w* and were unable to sail to Tarshish.
Ez 27:34 Now you are *w* in the sea,
Rv 8: 9 sea died, and a third of the ships were *w*.

WRENCHED (1)

Gn 32:26 that the hip socket was *w* as they wrestled.

WRESTED (3)

2Sm 23:21 and *w* the spear from the Egyptian's hand,
1Chr 11:23 *w* the spear from the Egyptian's hand,
Is 3:14 the loot *w* from the poor is in your house.

WRESTING (1)

2Sm 8: 1 the Philistines and conquered them, *w* . . .

WRESTLED (2)

Gn 32:25 man *w* with him until the break of dawn.
32:26 that the hip socket was wrenched as they *w*.

WRETCH (4)

2Mc 7:34 But you, *w*, vilest of all men!
12:35 intending to capture the vile *w* alive,
15: 3 At this the thrice-sinful *w* asked if there
Mt 18:32 sent for him and said, 'You worthless *w*!

WRETCHED (15)

Nm 20: 5 only to bring us to this *w* place which has
21: 5 We are disgusted with this *w* food!"
2Mc 15:32 *w* blasphemer's arm that had been boastfully
Jb 30:24 held out to help a *w* man in his calamity?
Ps(s) 22:22 the horns of the wild bulls, my *w* life.
22:25 nor disdained the *w* man in his misery,
109:16 the *w* and poor and the brokenhearted,
109:22 For I am *w* and poor,
Lam 1: 7 mindful of the days of her *w* homelessness,
Dn 1:10 If he sees that you look *w* by comparison
Hb 3:14 would be of devouring the *w* in their lair.
Zec 10: 2 This is why they wander like sheep, *w*.
Rom 7:24 What a *w* man I am!
Rv 3:17 Little do you realize how *w* you are,

WRETCHEDNESS (1)

Ezr 9: 5 of the evening sacrifice, I rose in my *w*,

WRINKLE (1)

Eph 5:27 stain or *w* or anything of that sort.

WRIST (4)

Dt 6: 8 Bind them at your *w* as a sign and let them
11:18 Bind them at your *w* as a sign,
Dn 5: 5 the king saw the *w* and hand that wrote,
5:24 By him were the *w* and hand sent,

WRISTS (4)

Gn 24:22 ten shekels, which he put on her *w*.
24:47 on her nose and the bracelets on her *w*.
Ez 13:18 to those who sew bands for everyone's *w*
Acts 12: 7 that, the chains dropped from Peter's *w*.

WRITE (71)

Ex 17:14 *W* this down in a document as something to
34: 1 that I may *w* on them the commandments
34:27 the LORD said to Moses, *W* down these words,
Dt 6: 9 *W* them on the doorposts of your houses and
10: 2 I will *w* upon the tablets the commandments
11:20 And *w* them on the doorposts of your houses
27: 3 Also *w* on them,
31:19 *W* out this song, then, for yourselves.
Tb 12:20 *w* down all these things that have happened
Est 8: 8 you in turn may *w* in the king's name what
1Mc 10:24 I too will *w* them conciliatory words and
12:22 this, kindly *w* to us about your welfare.
13:37 to *w* to our official to grant you release
13:42 began to *w* in their records and contracts,
15:19 to *w* to various kings and countries,
2Mc 2:32 it would be nonsense to *w* a long preface
Jb 31:35 that my accuser would *w* out his indictment!
Prv 7: 3 *w* them on the tablet of your heart.
Eccl 12:10 and to *w* down true sayings with precision.
Is 10: 1 statutes and who *w* oppressive decrees,
30: 8 Now come, *w* it on a tablet they can keep,
44: 5 Jacob, And this one shall *w* on his hand,
Jer 22:30 *W* this man down as one childless,
30: 2 *W* all the words I have spoken to you in a
31:33 within them, and *w* it upon their hearts;
36: 2 Take a scroll and *w* on it all the words I
36:17 how you came to *w* down all these words."
36:28 and *w* on it everything that the first
36:29 that scroll, saying, "Why did you *w* on it:
Bar 2:28 the day you ordered him to *w* down your law
Ez 24: 2 Son of man, *w* down this date today,
37:16 of man, take a single stick, and *w* on it:
37:16 Then take another stick and *w* on it:
37:20 you *w* you shall hold up before them to see.
43:11 *w* these down for them to see,
Hos 8:12 Though I *w* for him my many ordinances,
Hb 2: 2 *W* down the vision Clearly upon the tablets,
Jn 19:21 *W* instead, 'This man claimed to be King
Acts 15:20 We should merely *w* to them to abstain from
25:26 definite to *w* about him to our sovereign.
1Cor 9:15 nor do I *w* this now to see to it that
2Cor 1:13 We never *w* anything that you cannot read
9: 1 There is really no need for me to *w* you
Gal 6:11 I *w* to you in my own large handwriting!
1Thes 4: 9 love, there is no need for me to *w* you.
5: 1 moments, brothers, we do not need to *w* you;
2Thes 3:17 append this signature to every letter I *w*.
Phlm 1:19 I, Paul, *w* this in my own hand:
1:21 Confident of your compliance, I *w* you,
Heb 8:10 minds and I will *w* them upon their hearts;
10:16 hearts and I will *w* them on their minds,
1Jn 2: 7 it is no new commandment that I *w* to you,
2: 8 the commandment that I *w* you is new,
2Jn 1:12 there is much more that I could *w* you,
3Jn 1: 9 I did *w* to the church;
1:13 to write you, but I do not wish to *w* it
Jude 1: 3 But now I feel obliged to *w* and encourage
Rv 1:11 *W* on a scroll what you now see and send it
1:19 *W* down,
2: 1 spirit of the church in Ephesus, *w* this:
2: 8 spirit of the church in Smyrna, *w* this:
2:12 spirit of the church in Pergamum, *w* this:
2:18 spirit of the church in Thyatira, *w* this:
3: 1 spirit of the church in Sardis, *w* this:
3: 7 of the church in Philadelphia, *w* this:
3:14 spirit of the church in Laodicea, *w* this:
10: 4 thunders have spoken and do not *w* it down!"
14:13 *W* this down: Happy now are the dead
19: 9 *W* this down: Happy are they who have
21: 5 Then he said, *W* these matters down,

WRITERS (2)

Ez 9: 2 in linen, with a *w* case at his waist.

9: 3 in linen with the *w* case at his waist,

WRITES (3)

Dt 24: 1 and therefore he *w* out a bill of divorce
Est B: 1 "The great King Ahasuerus *w* to the
Rom 10: 5 *w* of the justice that comes from the law,

WRITHE (5)

Jb 26: 5 The shades beneath *w* in terror,
Sir 43:16 The thunder of his voice makes the earth *w*;
Is 13: 8 of them, like a woman in labor they *w*;
Ez 30:16 Syene shall *w* in anguish;
Mi 4:10 *W* in pain, grow faint,

WRITHED (1)

Is 26:18 We conceived and *w* in pain,

WRITHES (2)

Is 26:17 to give birth *w* and cries out in her pains,
Jer 51:29 The earth quakes and *w*,

WRITHING (1)

Na 2:11 and trembling knees, *W* in every frame,

WRITING (41)

Nm 5:23 priest shall put these imprecations in *w*
Dt 31:24 When Moses had finished *w* out on a scroll
Jos 18: 9 listed its cities in *w* in seven sections
1Kgs 21:11 did as Jezebel had ordered them in *w*,
1Chr 28:19 *w* the exact specifications of the pattern,
2Chr 36:22 kingdom, both by word of mouth and in *w*:
Ezr 1: 1 kingdom, both by word of mouth and in *w*:
Neh 10: 1 a firm pact, which we are putting into *w*.
Est A:15 Mordecai, too, put them into *w*.
9:25 the king ordered in *w* that the wicked plan
2Mc 2:16 we are *w* to you requesting you also to
Ez 2:10 It was covered with *w* front and back,
9:11 the *w* case at his waist make his report:
Dn 5: 5 *w* on the plaster of the wall in the king's
5: 7 reads this *w* and tells me what it means,"
5: 8 read the *w* or tell the king what it meant.
5:15 me to read this *w* and tell me its meaning,
5:16 to read the *w* and tell me what it means,
5:17 but the *w* I will read for you,
5:24 wrist and hand sent, and the *w* set down.
5:25 "This is the *w* that was inscribed:
Mt 27:37 they had put the charge against him in *w*:
Mk 10: 4 divorce and the *w* of a decree of divorce."
12:19 "Teacher, we were left this in *w* by Moses:
Lk 1: 3 and have decided to set it in *w* for you,
1:63 for a *w* tablet and wrote the words,
Acts 18:27 by *w* the disciples there to welcome him.
1Cor 4:14 I am *w* you in this way not to shame you
2Cor 3: 7 ministry of death, carved in *w* on stone,
7:12 my *w* to you was not intended for the man
13:10 I am *w* in this way while away from you,
Phil 3: 1 I find *w* you these things no burden,
1Tm 3:14 I am *w* you about these matters so that if
1Pt 5:12 I am *w* briefly through Silvanus,
2Pt 3: 1 I am *w* you this second letter,
1Jn 1: 4 our purpose in *w* you this is that our joy
2: 1 ones, I am *w* this to keep you from sin.
2Jn 1: 5 as if I were *w* you some new commandment;
Jude 1: 3 I was already fully intent on *w* you,
Rv 5: 1 It had *w* on both sides and was sealed with
10: 4 to start *w* when the seven thunders spoke,

WRITINGS (3)

2Mc 2:13 kings, the *w* of the prophets and of David,
Mt 26:56 in fulfillment of the *w* of the prophets."
Rom 16:26 manifested through the *w* of the prophets,

WRITTEN (167)

Ex 24:12 on which I have *w* the commandments
32:15 hands, tablets that were *w* on both sides,
32:32 strike me out of the book that you have *w*."
Dt 10: 4 then wrote on them, as he had *w* before,
24: 3 house by handing her a *w* bill of divorce;
28:58 word of the law which is *w* in this book,
30:10 that are *w* in this book of the law,
31: 9 When Moses had *w* down this law,
Jos 1: 8 may observe carefully all that is *w* in it;
8:32 the stones a copy of the law *w* by Moses.
8:34 exactly as *w* in the book of the law.
23: 6 that is *w* in the book of the law of Moses,
1Kgs 2: 3 decrees as they are *w* in the law of Moses,
15: 7 are *w* in the book of the chronicles of the
15:23 are *w* in the book of the chronicles of the
15:31 are *w* in the book of the chronicles of the
16: 5 are *w* in the book of the chronicles of the
16:14 are *w* in the book of the chronicles of the
16:20 are *w* in the book of the chronicles of the
16:27 are *w* in the book of the chronicles of the
2Kgs 10:34 are *w* in the book of the chronicles of the
14: 6 command *w* in the book of the law of Moses,
14:18 The rest of the acts of Amaziah are *w* in
20:20 are *w* in the book of the chronicles of the
21:17 are *w* in the book of the chronicles of the
21:25 The rest of the acts that Amon did are *w*
22:13 this book, nor fulfill our *w* obligations."
23: 3 of the covenant which were *w* in this book.
23:24 stipulations of the law *w* in the book
23:28 are *w* in the book of the chronicles of the
24: 5 are *w* in the book of the chronicles of the
1Chr 16:40 and to do all that is *w* in the law of the
29:29 found *w* in the history of Samuel the seer,
2Chr 9:29 acts of Solomon, first and last, are *w*,
12:15 acts of Rehoboam, first and last, are *w*,
13:22 are *w* in the midrash of the prophet Iddo.
20:34 can be found *w* in the chronicle of Jehu,
23:18 of the LORD, as is *w* in the law of Moses,
24:27 there is a *w* account in the midrash of the
25: 4 he acted according to what is *w* in the law,
25:26 Amaziah, first and last, can be found *w*,
27: 7 can be found *w* in the book of the kings of
28:26 can be found *w* in the book of the kings of
30: 6 the letters *w* by the king and his princes,
32:17 for he had *w* letters to deride the LORD,
32:32 *w* in the Vision of the Prophet Isaiah,
33:18 *w* in the chronicles of the kings of Israel.
33:19 found *w* down in the history of his seers.
34:21 have not done all that is *w* in this book."
34:24 all the curses *w* in the book that has been
34:31 the terms of the covenant *w* in this book.
35:25 and can be found *w* in the Lamentations.
35:26 regard to what is *w* in the law of the LORD,
35:26 can be found *w* in the book of the kings of
36: 8 can be found *w* in the book of the kings of
Ezr 2:62 but their names could not be found *w* there;
4: 6 they prepared a *w* accusation against
4: 7 The document was *w* in Aramaic and was
5: 5 to Darius and then a *w* order be sent back
5: 7 him a report in which was *w* the following:
Neh 7: 5 There I found the following *w*:
7:64 but their names could not be found *w* there;
8:14 They found it *w* in the law prescribed by
12:22 were *w* down in the Book of Chronicles,
12:23 were *w* down in the Book of Chronicles,
13: 1 it was found *w* there that "no Ammonite or
Tb 5: 3 signatures on a document *w* in duplicate;
7:12 *w* in the Book of Moses she is your wife.
Est 2:23 was *w* in the annals for the king's use.]
3:12 It was *w* in the name of King Ahasuerus and
4: 8 He also gave him a copy of the *w* decree
8: 8 For whatever is *w* in the name of the king
9:23 instituted at the *w* direction of Mordecai.
1Mc 8:31 has done to them, we have *w* to him thus:
10: 3 a letter to Jonathan *w* in peaceful terms,
10:17 he sent Jonathan a letter *w* in these terms:
10:56 I will do for you what you have *w*;
2Mc 9:25 I have *w* to him the letter copied below.
11:15 all the *w* requests of Maccabeus to Lysias.
15:38 If it is well *w* and to the point,
Jb 19:23 Oh, would that my words were *w* down!
Ps(s) 40: 8 in the *w* scroll it is prescribed for me,
102:19 Let this be *w* for the generation to come,
139:16 in your book they are all *w*;
149: 9 To execute on them the *w* sentence.
Prv 22:20 Have I not *w* for you the "Thirty,"
Sir 48:10 You are destined, it is *w*,
50:27 proverbs, I have *w* in this book,
Is 49:16 the palms of my hands I have *w* your name;
65: 6 Lo, before me it stands *w*;
Jer 17: 1 The sin of Judah is *w* with an iron stylus,
25:13 against it [all that is *w* in this book,
32:10 When I had *w* and sealed the deed,
32:44 bought with money, deeds *w* and sealed,
51:60 Jeremiah had *w* the misfortune that was to
51:60 these words that were *w* against Babylon.
Bar 2: 2 in Jerusalem, as was *w* in the law of Moses:
Ez 2: 9 was a *w* scroll which he unrolled before me.
2:10 writing front and back, and *w* on it was:
Dn 9:13 As it is *w* in the law of Moses,
10:21 tell you what is *w* in the truthful book.
12: 1 everyone who is found *w* in the book.
Mal 3:16 And a record book was *w* before him of
Mt 2: 5 "Here is what the prophet has *w*:
Mk 1: 2 In Isaiah the prophet it is *w*:
Lk 2:23 Lord, for it is *w* in the law of the Lord,
3: 4 as is *w* in the book of the words of Isaiah
4:17 and found the passage where it was *w*:
10:26 "What is *w* in the law?
18:31 so that all that was *w* by the prophets
21:22 when all that is *w* must be fulfilled.
22:37 It is *w* in Scripture, 'He was counted
24:44 everything *w* about me in the law of Moses
24:46 "Thus it is *w* that the Messiah must
Jn 6:45 It is *w* in the prophets:
10:34 "Is it not *w* in your law,
12:16 to him precisely what had been *w* about him.)
19:21 to tell Pilate, "You should not have *w*,
19:22 answered, "What I have written, I have *w*."
21:25 did, yet if they were *w* about in detail,
Acts 1:20 "It is *w* in the Book of Psalms.
7:42 we find it *w* in the Book of the Prophets:
13:29 brought about all that had been *w* of him,
13:33 according to what is *w* in the second psalm,
24:14 all that is *w* in the law and the prophets,
Rom 2:15 demands of the law are *w* in their hearts.
2:27 you who, with your *w* law and circumcision,
4:23 him," were not *w* with him alone in view;
12:19 leave that to God's wrath, for it is *w*:
14:11 It is *w*, "As surely as I live,
15: 4 Everything *w* before our time was written
15:15 Yet I have *w* to you rather boldly in parts
16:22 I, Tertius, who have *w* this letter,
1Cor 1:31 This is just as you find it *w*,
2: 9 Of this wisdom it is *w*:
9: 8 It is *w* in the law of Moses,
9:10 You can be sure it was *w* for us,
10:11 They have been *w* as a warning to us,
14:21 It is *w* in the law,
14:37 I have *w* you is the Lord's commandment.
2Cor 3: 2 and read by all men, *w* on your hearts.
3: 3 a letter *w* not with ink but by the Spirit
3: 6 a covenant not of a *w* law but of spirit.
3: 6 The *w* law kills,
8:15 It is *w*, "He who gathered much had no
9: 9 even a surplus for good works, as it is *w*:
Gal 1:20 before God that what I have just *w* is true.
3:10 It is *w*, "Cursed is he who does not abide
3:10 does not abide by everything *w* in the book
3:13 becoming a curse for us, as it is *w*:
4:22 There it is *w* that Abraham had two sons,
Heb 10: 7 Then I said, 'As is *w* of me in the book,
13:22 for I have *w* to you rather briefly.
Jas 4: 6 gift, for the sake of which it is *w*,
1Jn 2:21 My reason for having *w* you is not that you
2:26 I have *w* you these things about those who
5:13 I have *w* this to you to make you realize
Rv 1: 3 those who hear it and heed what is *w* in it,
13: 8 *w* at the world's beginning in the book
14: 1 name of his Father *w* on their foreheads.
17: 5 On her forehead was *w* a symbolic name,
17: 8 have not been *w* in the book of the living
19:16 A name was *w* on the part of the cloak that
21:12 Twelve names were *w* on the gates,
21:14 on which were *w* the names of the twelve

WRONG (84)

Gn 20: 9 What *w* did I do to you that you should
39: 9 a *w* and thus stand condemned before GOD?"
42:22 broke in Reuben, "not to do *w* to the boy?
44: 5 What you have done is *w*.'"
48:17 on Ephraim's head, this seemed *w* to him;
50:15 us back in full for all the *w* we did him!"
Ex 22:21 You shall not *w* any widow or orphan.
22:22 If ever you *w* them and they cry out to me,
23: 2 of the many as an excuse for doing *w*,
Lv 22: 9 keep my charge and not do *w* in this matter;
Nm 5: 7 LORD, he shall confess the *w* he has done,
14:40 for we were indeed doing *w*."
Jgs 11:27 you, but you *w* me by warring against me,
1Sm 24:12 I have done you no *w*,
26:21 "I have done *w*.
29: 6 for I have found nothing *w* with you from
2Sm 7:14 And if he does *w*,
19:20 take to heart the *w* that your servant did
19:21 For your servant knows that he has done *w*.
24:17 it is I, the shepherd, who have done *w*.
1Kgs 3: 9 people and to distinguish right from *w*.
8:47 and say, 'We have sinned and done *w*;
2Kgs 6:19 is the wrong road, and this is the *w* city.
18:14 "I have done *w*.
1Chr 12:18 my enemies though my hands have done no *w*,
2Chr 6:37 and say, 'We have sinned and done *w*;
Tb 8:14 was alive, and that there was nothing *w*.
Jdt 11:11 of their God upon them whenever they do *w*;
1Mc 7:14 with the army, and he will not do us any *w*."
2Mc 14:28 his agreement with a man who had done no *w*.
Jb 9:20 were I innocent, he might put me in the *w*.
10: 2 Do not put me in the *w*!
16:20 My friends it is who *w* me;
33:27 before men and say, "I sinned and did *w*,
34:10 far from the Almighty to do *w*!
34:32 if I have done *w*,
36:23 or who can say, "You have done *w*"?
Ps(s) 28: 3 away with the wicked, with those who do *w*,
37: 1 evildoers, nor jealous of those who do *w*;
92:16 the LORD, my Rock, in whom there is no *w*.
106: 6 we have done *w*.
119: 3 seek him with all their heart, And do no *w*,
Prv 17:26 It is *w* to fine an innocent man,
28:21 for even a morsel of bread a man may do *w*.
30:20 her mouth, and says, "I have done no *w*."
Wis 17: 1 therefore the unruly souls were *w*.
Sir 10: 6 No matter the *w*,
13: 3 The rich man does *w* and boasts of it,
32: 4 and flaunt not your wisdom at the *w* time.
Is 50: 9 who will prove me *w*?
53: 9 he had done no *w* nor spoken any falsehood.
Jer 22: 3 Do not *w* or oppress the resident alien,
22:13 Woe to him who builds his house on *w*,
Ez 3:20 does *w* when I place a stumbling block
33:13 he then presumes on his virtue and does *w*,
33:13 because of the *w* he has done,
33:15 statutes that bring life, and doing no *w*,
33:18 turns away from what is right and does *w*,
Zep 3: 5 LORD within her is just, who does no *w*;
3:13 They shall do no *w* and speak no lies;
Mt 6:12 *w* we have done as we forgive those who *w*
18:15 brother should commit some *w* against you,
27: 4 "I did *w* to deliver up an innocent man!"
Lk 11: 4 sins for we too forgive all who do us *w*;

WRONG (cont.)

17: 3 If your brother does *w*,
23:22 third time, "What *w* is this man guilty of?
23:41 done, but this man has done nothing *w*."
Jn 16: 8 comes, he will prove the world *w* about sin,
18:23 I said anything *w* produce the evidence,
Acts 25:10 I have done the Jews no *w*,
Rom 3:12 All have taken the *w* course,
13: 4 Only if you do *w* ought you to be afraid.
14:20 but it is *w* for a man to eat when the food
1Cor 13: 6 in what is *w* but rejoices with the truth.
2Cor 11: 7 Could I have done *w* when I preached the
Gal 2:11 him, because he was clearly in the *w*.
4:12 (Understand, you have not done me any *w*.)
Col 3:25 will be repaid for the *w* he has done.
1Pt 2:20 If you do *w* and get beaten for it,
2:22 He did no *w*; no deceit was found
1Jn 1: 9 our sins and cleanse us from every *w*.

WRONGDOER (1)

Rom 13: 4 to inflict his avenging wrath upon the *w*.

WRONGDOERS (1)

Ps(s) 119:115 Depart from me, you *w*,

WRONGDOING (10)

Gn 50:17 to forgive the criminal *w* of your brothers,
Tb 4: 5 your life, and do not tread the paths of *w*.
1Mc 1:15 with the Gentiles and sold themselves to *w*.
Prv 16:12 Kings have a horror of *w*,
Sir 18:27 when sin is rife he keeps himself from *w*.
Dn 6: 5 But they could accuse him of no *w*;
Rom 1:30 *w* and rebellious toward their parents.
3: 5 if our *w* provides proof of God's justice,
7:21 that leads to *w* is always ready at hand.
1Jn 5:17 True, all *w* sin

WRONGED (9)

Nm 5: 7 fifth of their value to the one he has *w*.
16:15 from them, nor have I *w* any one of them."
Est 1:16 "Queen Vashti has not *w* the king alone,
Wis 18: 2 who formerly had been *w* did not harm them,
Sir 13: 3 it, the poor man is *w* and begs forgiveness.
23:23 secondly, she has *w* her husband;
Is 1:17 redress the *w*,
Jer 37:18 In what have I *w* you, or your ministers,
Lam 3:59 You see, O Lord, how I am *w*;

WRONGFULLY (2)

Ps(s) 69: 5 my strength are they who *w* are my enemies.
119:86 they persecute me *w*;

WRONGING (1)

Acts 7:27 who was *w* his neighbor pushed Moses aside.

WRONGLY (1)

Jas 4: 3 and you do not receive because you ask *w*,

WRONGS (6)

Nm 5: 6 a fault against his fellow man and *w* him,
1Mc 2:67 and you shall avenge the *w* of your people.
8:31 the *w* that King Demetrius has done to them,
10: 5 remember all the *w* we have done to him,
Mt 18:21 asked him, "Lord, when my brother *w* me,
Rom 13:10 Love never *w* the neighbor,

WROTE (64)

Ex 24: 4 then *w* down all the words of the LORD and,
34:28 *w* on the tablets the words of the covenant,
Dt 4:13 which he *w* on two tablets of stone.
5:22 He *w* them upon two tablets of stone and
10: 4 The LORD then *w* on them,
31:22 So Moses *w* this song that same day,
1Sm 10:25 the law of royalty and *w* it in a book,
2Sm 11:14 *w* a letter to Joab which he sent by Uriah.
1Kgs 21: 8 So she *w* letters in Ahab's name and,
21: 9 This is what she *w* in the letters:
2Kgs 10: 2 your master's sons are with you," he *w*,
10: 6 So Jehu *w* them a second letter:
17:37 law and commandment, which he *w* for you,
2Chr 2:10 Tyre, *w* an answer which he sent to Solomon:
26:22 of Amos, *w* the rest of the acts of Uzziah,
30: 1 and even *w* letters to Ephraim and Manasseh
Ezr 4: 7 Mithredath *w* in concert with Tabeel and
4: 8 *w* the following letter against Jerusalem
Jdt 4: 6 *w* to the inhabitants of Bethulia [and
Est 3:12 thirteenth day of the first month they *w*,
8: 5 *w* for the destruction of the Jews in all
8: 9 they *w* to the Jews and to the satraps,
8:10 which he *w* in the name of King Ahasuerus
9:29 *w* to confirm with full authority this
1Mc 1:41 Then the king *w* to his whole kingdom that
10:59 also *w* to Jonathan to come and meet him.
11:22 He *w* to Jonathan to discontinue the siege
11:29 The king agreed and *w* the following letter
11:31 *w* to Lasthenes our kinsman concerning you.
11:57 Then young Antiochus *w* to Jonathan:
12: 5 the letter that Jonathan *w* to the Spartans:
16:18 Then Ptolemy *w* an account of this and sent
2Mc 1: 7 we Jews *w* to you during the trouble and
8: 8 becoming more frequent, he *w* to Ptolemy,
9:18 lost hope for himself and *w* the following
11:16 of the letter which Lysias *w* to the Jews:
14:27 He *w* to Nicanor,
Sir 39:32 I took my stand, and *w* down as my theme:
Jer 36: 4 son of Neriah, who *w* down on a scroll,
36: 6 from the scroll you *w* at my dictation;
36:18 "and I *w* them down with ink in the book."
36:32 he *w* on it at Jeremiah's dictation all the
45: 1 when he *w* in a book the prophecies that
Bar 1: 1 of Hasadiah, son of Hilkiah, *w* in Babylon,
Dn 5: 5 the king saw the wrist and hand that *w*,
6:26 Then King Darius *w* to the nations and
7: 1 Then he *w* down the dream;
Mt 18:27 let the official go and *w* off the debt.
Mk 7: 6 prophesied about you hypocrites when he *w*,
10: 5 "He *w* that commandment for you because of
Lk 1:63 for a writing tablet and *w* the words,
7:42 was able to repay, he *w* off both debts.
Jn 5:46 believe me, for it was about me that he *w*.
5:47 But if you do not believe what he *w*,
8: 8 time he bent down and *w* on the ground.
21:24 it is he who *w* them down and his testimony,
Acts 23:25 *w* the governor a letter to this effect:
1Cor 5: 9 I *w* you in my letter not to associate
5:11 What I really *w* about was your not
7: 1 Now for the matters you *w* about.
2Cor 2: 3 I *w* as I did so that when I come I may not
2: 4 is why I *w* you in great sorrow and anguish,
2: 9 The reason I *w* you was to test you and
2Pt 3:15 *w* you this in in the spirit of wisdom that

WROUGHT (32)

Gn 37:11 So his brothers were *w* up against him but
Ex 10: 2 Egyptians and what signs I *w* among them,
34:10 been *w* in any nation anywhere on earth,
Nm 23:23 and of Israel, "Behold what God has *w*!"
Dt 6:22 and *w* before our eyes signs and wonders,
11: 3 signs and deeds he *w* among the Egyptians,
Jos 24: 5 with the prodigies which I *w* in her midst.
Jgs 11:36 because the LORD has *w* vengeance for you
1Chr 16:12 Recall the wondrous deeds that he has *w*,
Jdt 15:10 and God is pleased with what you have *w*.
Ps(s) 46: 9 the astounding things he has *w* on earth:
78: 4 and his strength and the wonders that he *w*.
78:43 When he *w* his signs in Egypt and his
99: 4 justice and judgment in Jacob you have *w*.
104:24 In wisdom you have *w* them all
105: 5 Recall the wondrous deeds that he has *w*,
105:27 They *w* his signs among them,
111: 8 forever and ever, *w* in truth and equity.
144:12 Our daughters like *w* columns such as stand
Eccl 2:11 to all the works that my hands had *w*,
Wis 3:14 So also the eunuch whose hand *w* no misdeed,
Sir 45: 3 God *w* swift miracles at his words and
45:10 violet, and of crimson, *w* with embroidery;
45:12 its plate *w* with the insignia of holiness,
48:12 spirit, *w* many marvels by his mere word.
Is 64: 2 you *w* awesome deeds we could not hope for,
Jer 8:14 For the LORD has *w* our destruction,
10: 3 the forest, *W* by craftsmen with the adze,
32:20 you have *w* signs and wonders in the land
Lam 1:21 it is you who have *w* it.
Ez 27:19 Javan exchanged *w* iron,
Rom 3:24 through the redemption *w* in Christ Jesus.

WRUNG (1)

Jgs 6:38 next morning he *w* the dew from the fleece,

X

X (2)

Ez 9: 4 mark an *X* on the foreheads of those
9: 6 But do not touch any marked with the *X*;

XANTHICUS (3)

2Mc 11:30 those who return by the thirtieth of *X*
11:33 and forty-eight, the fifteenth of *X*.
11:38 and forty-eight, the fifteenth of *X*.

Y

YAD-ABSHALOM (1)

2Sm 18:18 for himself is called *Y* to the present day.

YAHWEH-NISSI (1)

Ex 17:15 built an altar there, which he called *Y*;

YAHWEH-SHALOM (1)

Jgs 6:24 there an altar to the LORD and called it *Y*.

YAHWEH-YIREH (1)

Gn 22:14 Abraham named the site *Y*;

YARDS (2)

Mt 14:24 already several hundred *y* out from shore,
Jn 21: 8 no more than a hundred *y*.

YARN (36)

Ex 25: 4 violet, purple and scarlet *y*;
26: 1 twined and of violet, purple and scarlet *y*,
26: 4 Make loops of violet *y* along the edge of
26:31 woven of violet, purple and scarlet *y*,
26:36 and scarlet *y* and of fine linen twined.
27:16 and scarlet *y* and of fine linen twined.
28: 5 purple and scarlet *y* and fine linen.
28: 6 and of violet, purple and scarlet *y*,
28: 8 thread, of violet, purple and scarlet *y*,
28:15 scarlet *y* on cloth of fine linen twined.
28:33 purple and scarlet *y* and fine linen twined,
35: 6 violet, purple and scarlet *y*;
35:23 to have violet, purple or scarlet *y*,
35:25 purple and scarlet *y* and fine linen thread,
35:35 purple and scarlet *y* and fine linen thread,
36: 8 on them with violet, purple and scarlet *y*.
36:11 Loops of violet *y* were made along the edge
36:35 woven of violet, purple and scarlet *y*,
36:37 was made of violet, purple and scarlet *y*,
38:18 and scarlet *y* and of fine linen twined,
38:23 purple and scarlet *y* and of fine linen.
39: 1 purple and scarlet *y* were woven the
39: 2 and scarlet *y* and of fine linen twined.
39: 3 purple and scarlet *y* into an embroidered
39: 5 thread, of violet, purple and scarlet *y*,
39: 8 scarlet *y* on cloth of fine linen twined.
39:22 the ephod was woven entirely of violet *y*,
39:24 and scarlet *y* and of fine linen twined;
39:29 twined and of violet, purple and scarlet *y*,
Lv 14: 4 as well as some cedar wood, scarlet *y*,
14: 6 cedar wood, the scarlet *y* and the hyssop,
14:49 birds, as well as cedar wood, scarlet *y*,
14:51 cedarwood, the hyssop and the scarlet *y*,
14:52 cedar wood, the hyssop, and the scarlet *y*.
Nm 19: 6 hyssop and scarlet *y* and throw them into
Sir 45:11 the ephod and cincture with scarlet *y*,

YAVAN (1)

Zec 9:13 *Y* and I will use you as a warrior's sword.

YAWNING (1)

Wis 19:17 When, surrounded by *y* darkness,

YEAR (355)

Gn 7:11 In the six hundredth *y* of Noah's life,
8:13 the six hundred and first *y* of Noah's life,
14: 4 but in the thirteenth *y* they rebelled.
14: 5 In the fourteenth *y* Chedorlaomer and the
17:21 shall bear to you by this time next *y*."
18:10 return to you about this time next *y*,
18:14 appointed time, about this time next *y*,
26:12 region and reaped a hundredfold the same *y*.
47:17 Thus he got them through that *y* with bread
47:18 When that *y* ended, they came to him
Ex 12: 2 shall reckon it the first month of the *y*.
13:10 rite at its appointed time from *y* to year.
21: 2 but in the seventh *y* he shall be given his
23:11 But the seventh *y* you shall let the land
23:14 "Three times a *y* you shall celebrate a
23:16 at the fruit harvest at the end of the *y*,
23:17 Thrice a *y* shall all your men appear
23:29 one *y* will I drive them all out before you;
30:10 Once a *y* Aaron shall perform the atonement
30:10 this atonement is to be made once a *y*
34:22 at the fruit harvest at the close of the *y*.
34:23 Three times a *y* all your men shall appear
34:24 three times a *y* to appear before the LORD,
40:17 of the second *y* the Dwelling was erected.
Lv 16:34 once a *y* atonement shall be made for all
19:24 In the fourth *y*, however, all of its fruit
19:25 until the fifth *y* may you eat its fruit.
23:41 whole week in the seventh month of the *y*.
25: 4 *y* the land shall have complete rest,
25: 5 in this *y* of sabbath rest for the land.
25:10 This fiftieth *y* you shall make sacred by
25:11 In this fiftieth year, your *y* of jubilee,
25:13 "In this *y* of jubilee,
25:20 say, 'What shall we eat in the seventh *y*,
25:21 such blessings on you in the sixth *y*
25:22 When you sow in the eighth *y*,
25:22 and even into the ninth *y*,
25:29 the time of one full *y* from its sale.
25:30 not been redeemed at the end of a full *y*,
25:40 working with you until the jubilee *y*,
25:52 years there are left before the jubilee *y*,
25:54 with his children, in the jubilee *y*.
27:18 of years left until the next jubilee *y*,
Nm 1: 1 In the *y* following that of the Israelites'
8:24 Each from his twenty-fifth *y* onward shall
9: 1 In the first month of the *y* following
10:11 In the second *y*, on the twentieth day
14:34 one *y* for each day.
28:14 moon holocaust for every new moon of the *y*.
33:38 and there he died in the fortieth *y*
36: 4 the Israelites celebrate the jubilee *y*,

Dt 1: 3 In the fortieth *y*,
11:12 from the beginning of the *y* to the end.
14:22 "Each *y* you shall tithe all the produce
14:28 "At the end of every third *y* you shall
14:28 *y* and deposit them in community stores,
15: 9 that the seventh year, the *y* of relaxation,
15:12 *y* you shall dismiss him from your service,
15:20 Year after *y* you and your family shall eat
16:16 "Three times a *y*, then, every male
24: 5 for one *y* for the sake of his family,
26:12 in the third year, the *y* of the tithes,
31:10 at the prescribed time in the *y* of
33:14 With the best of the produce of the *y*,
Jos 5:12 *y* ate of the yield of the land of Canaan.
Jgs 11:40 the Gileadite for four days of the *y*.
17:10 and I will give you ten silver shekels a *y*,
1Sm 1: 7 This went on year after *y*; each time
18:26 [Before the *y* was up,]
27: 7 David lived a *y* and four months in the
29: 3 He has been with me now for a *y* or two,
2Sm 11: 1 At the turn of the *y*, when kings go out
14:26 he used to do at the end of every *y*,
1Kgs 4: 7 having to provide for one month in the *y*.
5:25 while Solomon every *y* gave Hiram twenty
6: 1 In the four hundred and eightieth *y* from
6: 1 fourth *y* of Solomon's reign over Israel,
6:38 laid in the month of Ziv in the fourth *y*,
6:38 Bul, the eighth month, in the eleventh *y*.
9:25 Three times a *y* Solomon used to offer
10:14 The gold that Solomon received every *y*
14:25 In the fifth *y* of King Rehoboam,
15: 1 In the eighteenth *y* of King Jeroboam,
15: 9 In the twentieth *y* of Jeroboam,
15:25 In the second *y* of Asa,
15:28 Baasha killed him in the third *y* of Asa,
15:33 In the third *y* of Asa,
16: 8 In the twenty-sixth *y* of Asa,
16:10 killed him in the twenty-seventh *y* of Asa,
16:15 In the twenty-seventh *y* of Asa,
16:23 In the thirty-first *y* of Asa,
16:29 In the thirty-eighth *y* of Asa,
17:15 She was able to eat for a *y*,
18: 1 Long afterward, in the third *y*,
20:22 of the *y* the king of Aram will attack you."
20:26 At the beginning of the *y*,
22: 2 In the third *y*,
22:41 reign over Judah in the fourth *y* of Ahab,
22:52 in the seventeenth *y* of Jehoshaphat,
2Kgs 1:17 him as king, in the second *y* of Jehoram,
3: 1 [in the eighteenth *y* of Jehoshaphat,
4:16 next *y* you will be fondling a baby son."
4:17 following *y* she had given birth to a son,
8:16 In the fifth *y* of Joram,
8:25 became king in the twelfth *y* of Joram,
8:26 reign, and he reigned one *y* in Jerusalem.
9:29 king of Judah in the eleventh *y* of Joram,
11: 4 But in the seventh *y*,
12: 2 began to reign in the seventh *y* of Jehu,
12: 7 twenty-third *y* of the reign of King Joash,
13: 1 In the twenty-third *y* of Joash,
13:10 In the thirty-seventh *y* of Joash,
13:20 of Moabites used to raid the land each *y*.
14: 1 In the second *y* of Joash,
14:23 In the fifteenth *y* of Amaziah,
15: 1 king in the twenty-seventh *y* of Jeroboam,
15: 8 In the thirty-eighth *y* of Azariah,
15:13 king in the thirty-ninth *y* of Uzziah,
15:17 In the thirty-ninth *y* of Azariah,
15:17 began his ten *y* reign over Samaria.
15:23 In the fiftieth *y* of Azariah,
15:27 In the fifty-second *y* of Azariah,
15:30 in his place [in the twentieth *y* of Jotham,
15:32 In the second *y* of Pekah,
16: 1 In the seventeenth *y* of Pekah,
17: 1 In the twelfth *y* of Ahaz,
17: 6 In the ninth *y* of Hoshea,
18: 1 In the third *y* of Hoshea,
18: 9 In the fourth *y* of King Hezekiah,
18: 9 which was the seventh *y* of Hoshea,
18:10 year of Hezekiah, the ninth *y*
18:13 In the fourteenth *y* of King Hezekiah,
19:29 *y* you shall eat the aftergrowth, next *y*,
19:29 But in the third *y*, sow and reap,
22: 3 In his eighteenth *y*,
23:23 until the eighteenth *y* of king Josiah,
24:12 Babylon, who, in the eighth *y* of his reign,
25: 1 month of the ninth *y* of Zedekiah's reign,
25: 2 continued until the eleventh *y* of Zedekiah.
25: 8 was in the nineteenth *y* of Nebuchadnezzar,
25:27 *y* of the exile of Jehoiachin,
25:27 in the inaugural *y* of his own reign,
1Chr 20: 1 At the beginning of the following *y*,
26:31 *y* of David's reign search was made,
27: 1 and went month by month throughout the *y*.
2Chr 3: 2 second month of the fourth *y* of his reign.
8:13 and on the fixed festivals three times a *y*:
9:13 The gold that Solomon received each *y*
9:24 Year in and *y* out, each one would bring
12: 2 that in the fifth *y* of King Rehoboam,
13: 1 In the eighteenth *y* of King Jeroboam,
15:10 month of the fifteenth *y* of Asa's reign,
15:19 until the thirty-fifth *y* of Asa's reign.
16: 1 In the thirty-sixth *y* of Asa's reign,
16:12 In the thirty-ninth *y* of his reign,
16:13 he died in the forty-first *y* of his reign.
17: 7 *y* of his reign he sent his leading men,
22: 2 king, and he reigned one *y* in Jerusalem.
23: 1 In the seventh *y*, Jehoiada took courage
24:23 At the turn of the *y* a force of Arameans
27: 5 That *y* the Ammonites paid him one hundred
27: 5 to him also in the second and in the third *y*.
29: 3 first month of the first *y* of his reign,
34: 3 In the eight *y* of his reign,
34: 3 and in his twelfth *y* he began to purge
34: 8 In the eighteenth *y* of his reign,
35:19 It was in the eighteenth *y* of Josiah's
36:10 At the turn of the *y*, King Nebuchadnezzar
36:22 In the first *y* of Cyrus, king of Persia,
Ezr 1: 1 In the first *y* of Cyrus, king of Persia,
3: 8 In the *y* after their coming to the house
4:24 until the second *y* of the reign of Darius,
5:13 However, in the first *y* of Cyrus,
6: 3 In the first *y* of King Cyrus,
6:15 in the sixth *y* of the reign of King Darius.
7: 7 in the seventh *y* of King Artaxerxes.
7: 8 fifth month of that seventh *y* of the king.
Neh 1: 1 In the month Chislev of the twentieth *y*,
2: 1 of the twentieth *y* of King Artaxerxes,
5:14 from his twentieth to his thirty-second *y*—
10:32 We will forgo the seventh *y*,
10:33 *y* for the service of the house of our God,
10:35 our family houses at stated times each *y*,
10:36 We have agreed to bring each *y* to the
13: 6 for in the thirty-second *y* of Artaxerxes,
Tb 1: 7 *y* I would go and disburse in Jerusalem.
1: 8 third *y* I would bring them this offering,
Jdt 1: 1 twelfth *y* of the reign of Nebuchadnezzar,
1:13 In the seventeenth *y* he proceeded with his
2: 1 In the eighteenth *y*, on the twenty-second
Est A: 1 *y* of the reign of the great King Ahasuerus,
1: 3 of Susa, in the third *y* of his reign,
2:16 Tebeth, in the seventh *y* of his reign.
3: 7 Nisan, in the twelfth *y* of King Ahasuerus,
B: 6 the twelfth month, Adar, of the current *y*;
9:21 He ordered them to celebrate every *y* both
9:27 *y* in the manner prescribed by this letter,
1Mc 1:10 He became king in the *y* one hundred and
1:20 Egypt in the *y* one hundred and forty-three,
1:54 in the *y* one hundred and forty-five,
2:70 He died in the *y* one hundred and forty-six,
3:37 in the *y* one hundred and forty-seven;
4:28 So the following *y* he gathered together
4:52 in the *y* one hundred and forty-eight,
4:59 on the anniversary every *y* for eight days,
6:16 Persia in the *y* one hundred and forty-nine.
6:20 So in the *y* one hundred and fifty they
6:49 for that was a sabbath *y* in the land.
6:53 storerooms, because it was the seventh *y*,
7: 1 In the *y* one hundred and fifty-one,
7:49 observed every *y* on the thirteenth of Adar.
8: 4 and the rest paid tribute to them every *y*.
8:16 their government to one man every *y*,
9: 3 month of the *y* one hundred and fifty-two,
9:54 In the *y* one hundred and fifty-three,
10: 1 In the *y* one hundred and sixty,
10:21 vestments in the seventh month of the *y*
10:42 of the sanctuary every *y* shall be canceled,
10:57 in the *y* one hundred and sixty-two.
10:67 In the *y* one hundred and sixty-five,
11:19 king in the *y* one hundred and sixty-seven.
11:34 the king received from them each *y*
13:41 Thus in the *y* one hundred and seventy,
13:42 and contracts, "In the first *y* of Simon,
13:51 in the *y* one hundred and seventy-one,
13:52 be celebrated every *y* with rejoicing,
14: 1 In the *y* one hundred and seventy-two,
14:27 Elul, in the *y* one hundred and seventy-two,
14:27 *y* under Simon the high priest in Asaramel,
15:10 In the *y* one hundred and seventy-four
16:14 in the *y* one hundred and seventy-seven,
2Mc 1: 7 the *y* one hundred and sixty-nine,
1:10 in the *y* one hundred and eighty-eight.
10: 8 nation should celebrate these days every *y*.
11: 3 the high priesthood up for sale every *y*.
11:21 The *y* one hundred and forty-eight,
11:33 In the *y* one hundred and forty-eight,
11:38 In the *y* one hundred and forty-eight,
13: 1 In the *y* one hundred and forty-nine,
14: 4 So he went to King Demetrius in the *y* one
Jb 3: 6 let it not occur among the days of the *y*,
Ps(s) 65:12 You have crowned the *y* with your bounty,
Sir 47: 9 each *y* With string music before the altar,
Is 6: 1 In the *y* King Uzziah died,
14:28 In the *y* that King Ahaz died,
20: 1 In the *y* the general sent by Sargon,
21:16 In another *y*, like those of a hireling,
29: 1 Add *y* to year, let the feasts come round.
32:10 a *y* you overconfident ones will be shaken;
34: 8 a *y* of requital by Zion's defender.
36: 1 In the fourteenth *y* of King Hezekiah,
37:30 *y* you shall eat the aftergrowth, next year,
37:30 But in the third *y*,
61: 2 To announce a *y* of favor from the LORD and
63: 4 my heart, my *y* for redeeming was at hand.
Jer 1: 2 of Judah, in the thirteenth *y* of his reign,
1: 3 fifth month of the eleventh *y* of Zedekiah,
11:23 men of Anathoth, the *y* of their punishment.
17: 8 In the *y* of drought it shows no distress,
23:12 the *y* of their punishment, says the LORD.
25: 1 of Judah, in the fourth *y* of Jehoiakim,
25: 1 of Judah (the first *y* of Nebuchadnezzar,
25: 3 Since the thirteenth *y* of Josiah,
28: 1 That same *y*, in [the beginning of]
28: 1 Judah, in the fifth month of the fourth *y*,
28:16 this very *y* you shall die,
28:17 That same *y*, in the seventh month,
32: 1 from the LORD in the tenth *y* of Zedekiah,
32: 1 Judah, the eighteenth *y* of Nebuchadnezzar.
34:14 Every seventh *y* each of you shall set free
36: 1 In the fourth *y* of Jehoiakim,
36: 9 ninth month, in the fifth *y* of Jehoiakim,
39: 1 the tenth month of the ninth *y* of Zedekiah,
39: 2 month, in the eleventh *y* of Zedekiah,
45: 1 dictated in the fourth *y* of Jehoiakim,
46: 2 of Babylon, in the fourth *y* of Jehoiakim,
48:44 upon Moab in the *y* of their punishment,
51:46 this *y* the rumor comes,
51:59 in the fourth *y* of the reign of Zedekiah;
52: 4 tenth month of the ninth *y* of his reign,
52: 5 until the eleventh *y* of King Zedekiah.
52:12 the nineteenth *y* of Nebuchadnezzar,
52:28 in his seventh *y*,
52:29 in the eighteenth *y* of Nebuchadnezzar,
52:30 in the twenty-third *y* of Nebuchadnezzar,
52:31 *y* of the exile of Jehoiachin,
52:31 Babylon, in the inaugural *y* of his reign,
Bar 1: 2 fifth *y* [on the seventh day of the month,
Ez 1: 1 In the thirtieth *y*, on the fifth day
1: 2 the fifth day of the month, the fifth *y*,
4: 6 one day for each *y* I have allotted you.
8: 1 day of the sixth month, in the sixth *y*,
20: 1 In the seventh *y*, on the tenth day
24: 1 day of the tenth month, in the ninth *y*,
26: 1 in the eleventh *y*, the word of the LORD
29: 1 day of the tenth month in the tenth *y*,
29:17 of the first month in the twenty-seventh *y*,
30:20 day of the first month in the eleventh *y*,
31: 1 day of the third month in the eleventh *y*,
32: 1 day of the twelfth month in the twelfth *y*,
32:17 day of the first month in the twelfth *y*,
33:21 tenth month, in the twelfth *y* of our exile,
40: 1 beginning the twenty-fifth *y* of our exile,
46:17 to the latter only until the *y* of release,
Dn 1: 1 In the third *y* of the reign of Jehoiakim,
1:21 there until the first *y* of King Cyrus.
2: 1 In the second *y* of his reign,
7: 1 the first *y* of King Belshazzar of Babylon,
7:25 They shall be handed over to him for a *y*,
8: 1 third *y* of the reign of King Belshazzar.
9: 1 It was the first *y* that Darius,
9: 2 in the first *y* of his reign I,
10: 1 In the third *y* of Cyrus,
12: 7 lives forever that it should be for a *y*,
13: 5 That *y*, two elders of the people
Mi 6: 6 him with holocausts, with calves a *y* old?
Hg 1: 1 sixth month in the second *y* of King Darius,
2:10 month, in the second *y* of King Darius,
Zec 1: 1 In the second *y* of Darius,
1: 7 In the second *y* of Darius,
7: 1 In the fourth *y* of Darius the king [the
14:16 come up year after *y* to worship the King,
Lk 2:41 His parents used to go every *y* to
3: 1 fifteenth *y* of the rule of Tiberius Caesar,
4:19 To announce a *y* of favor from the Lord."
13: 8 the man said, 'Sir, leave it another *y*,
Jn 11:49 named Caiaphas, who was high priest that *y*,
11:51 It was rather as high priest for that *y*
18:13 of Caiaphas who was high priest that *y*.
Acts 11:26 For a whole *y* they met with the church and
18:11 ended by settling there for a *y* and a half,
27: 9 of the *y* sailing had become hazardous.
2Cor 8:10 help you who began this good work last *y*,
9: 2 that Achaia has been ready since last *y*.
Heb 9: 7 into the inner one, and that but once a *y*,
9:25 as the high priest enters *y* after year
10: 1 offered continually *y* after year.
Jas 4:13 to such and such a town, spend a *y* there,
Rv 9:15 and the *y* for which they had been prepared,
12:14 for a *y* and for two and a half years more.
22: 2 life which produce fruit twelve times a *y*,

YEAR-OLD (1)

Ex 12: 5 lamb must be a *y* male and without blemish.

YEARLING (52)

Ex 29:38 two *y* lambs as the sacrifice established
Lv 12: 6 a *y* lamb for a holocaust and a pigeon
14:10 male lambs, one unblemished *y* ewe lamb,
23:12 LORD for a holocaust an unblemished *y* lamb.
23:18 a holocaust of seven unblemished *y* lambs,
23:19 and two *y* lambs as a peace offering.
Nm 6:12 bringing a *y* lamb as a guilt offering.
6:14 one unblemished *y* lamb for a holocaust,
6:14 unblemished *y* ewe lamb for a sin offering,
7:15 one ram, and one *y* lamb for a holocaust:
7:17 and five *y* lambs for a peace offering.
7:21 one ram, and one *y* lamb for a holocaust;
7:23 and five *y* lambs for a peace offering.

YEARLING (cont.)

7:27 one ram, and one *y* lamb for a holocaust;
7:29 and five *y* lambs for a peace offering.
7:33 one ram, and one *y* lamb for a holocaust;
7:35 and five *y* lambs for a peace offering.
7:39 one ram, and one *y* lamb for a holocaust;
7:41 and five *y* lambs for a peace offering.
7:45 one ram, and one *y* lamb for a holocaust;
7:47 and five *y* lambs for a peace offering.
7:51 one ram, and one *y* lamb for a holocaust;
7:53 and five *y* lambs for a peace offering.
7:57 one ram, and one *y* lamb for a holocaust;
7:59 and five *y* lambs for a peace offering.
7:63 one ram, and one *y* lamb for a holocaust;
7:65 and five *y* lambs for a peace offering.
7:69 one ram, and one *y* lamb for a holocaust;
7:71 and five *y* lambs for a peace offering.
7:75 one ram, and one *y* lamb for a holocaust;
7:77 and five *y* lambs for a peace offering.
7:81 one ram, and one *y* lamb for a holocaust;
7:83 and five *y* lambs for a peace offering.
7:87 bulls, twelve rams, and twelve *y* lambs,
7:88 sixty rams, sixty goats, and sixty *y* lambs.
15:27 shall bring a *y* she-goat as a sin offering,
28: 3 two unblemished *y* lambs each day as the
28: 9 you shall offer two unblemished *y* lambs,
28:11 one ram, and seven unblemished *y* lambs,
28:19 *y* lambs that you are sure are unblemished,
28:27 *y* lambs that you are sure are unblemished,
29: 2 one ram, and seven unblemished *y* lambs,
29: 8 *y* lambs that you are sure are unblemished,
29:13 and fourteen *y* lambs that are unblemished,
29:17 two rams, and fourteen unblemished *y* lambs,
29:20 two rams, and fourteen unblemished *y* lambs,
29:23 two rams, and fourteen unblemished *y* lambs,
29:26 two rams, and fourteen unblemished *y* lambs,
29:29 two rams, and fourteen unblemished *y* lambs,
29:32 two rams, and fourteen unblemished *y* lambs,
29:36 one ram, and seven unblemished *y* lambs,
Ez 46:13 to the LORD an unblemished *y* lamb;

YEARLINGS (1)

Lv 9: 3 a calf and a lamb, both unblemished *y*,

YEARLY (7)

Jgs 11:40 in Israel for Israelite women to go *y*
21:19 of the *y* feast of the LORD at Shiloh,
1Sm 7:16 He made a *y* journey,
1Kgs 10:25 Each one brought his *y* tribute:
1Mc 10:40 I make a *y* personal grant of fifteen
Col 2:16 or what you do on *y* or monthly feasts,
Heb 10: 3 there came only a *y* recalling of sins,

YEARN (7)

Sir 24:18 Come to me, all you that *y* for me,
Jer 22:27 come back to the land for which they *y*.
44:14 though they *y* to return and live there.
Am 5:18 Woe to those who *y* for the day of the LORD!
2Cor 5: 2 even as we *y* to have our heavenly
2Tm 1: 4 tears when we parted, I *y* to see you again.
Rv 9: 6 will *y* to die but death will escape them.

YEARNED (2)

Ez 23:21 You *y* for the lewdness of your girlhood,
Mt 23:37 How often have I *y* to gather your children,

YEARNING (3)

Ps(s) 119:131 with open mouth in my *y* for your commands.
Wis 15: 5 of which arouses *y* in the senseless man,
Is 21: 4 My *y* for twilight has turned into dread.

YEARNS (4)

Ps(s) 84: 3 *y* and pines for the courts of the LORD.
Sg 7:11 I belong to my lover and for me he *y*.
Wis 8: 8 Or again, if one *y* for copious learning,
Is 26: 9 My soul *y* for you in the night,

YEARS (532)

Gn 1:14 mark the fixed times, the days and the *y*,
5: 3 *y* old when he begot a son in his likeness,
5: 4 eight hundred *y* after the birth of Seth,
5: 5 of Adam was nine hundred and thirty *y*;
5: 6 When Seth was one hundred and five *y* old,
5: 7 and seven *y* after the birth of Enosh,
5: 8 of Seth was nine hundred and twelve *y*;
5: 9 When Enosh was ninety *y* old,
5:10 and fifteen *y* after the birth of Kenan,
5:11 of Enosh was nine hundred and five *y*;
5:12 When Kenan was seventy *y* old,
5:13 and forty *y* after the birth of Mahalalel,
5:14 of Kenan was nine hundred and ten *y*;
5:15 When Mahalalel was sixty-five *y* old,
5:16 and thirty *y* after the birth of Jared,
5:17 was eight hundred and ninety-five *y*;
5:18 Jared was one hundred and sixty-two *y* old,
5:19 eight hundred *y* after the birth of Enoch,
5:20 of Jared was nine hundred and sixty-two *y*;
5:21 When Enoch was sixty-five *y* old,
5:22 hundred *y* after the birth of Methuselah,
5:23 Enoch was three hundred and sixty-five *y*.
5:25 was one hundred and eighty-seven *y* old,
5:26 and eighty-two *y* after the birth of Lamech,
5:27 was nine hundred and sixty-nine *y*;
5:28 was one hundred and eighty-two *y* old,
5:30 and ninety-five *y* after the birth of Noah,
5:31 was seven hundred and seventy-seven *y*;
5:32 When Noah was five hundred *y* old,
6: 3 shall comprise one hundred and twenty *y*."
7: 6 Noah was six hundred *y* old when the flood
9:28 three hundred and fifty *y* after the flood.
9:29 of Noah was nine hundred and fifty *y*;
11:10 When Shem was one hundred *y* old,
11:10 of Arpachshad, two *y* after the flood.
11:11 hundred *y* after the birth of Arpachshad,
11:12 When Arpachshad was thirty-five *y* old,
11:13 and three *y* after the birth of Shelah,
11:14 When Shelah was thirty *y* old,
11:15 and three *y* after the birth of Eber,
11:16 When Eber was thirty-four *y* old,
11:17 and thirty *y* after the birth of Peleg,
11:18 When Peleg was thirty *y* old,
11:19 hundred and nine *y* after the birth of Reu,
11:20 When Reu was thirty-two *y* old,
11:21 and seven *y* after the birth of Serug,
11:22 When Serug was thirty *y* old,
11:23 two hundred *y* after the birth of Nahor,
11:24 When Nahor was twenty-nine *y* old,
11:25 and nineteen *y* after the birth of Terah,
11:26 When Terah was seventy *y* old,
11:32 of Terah was two hundred and five *y*;
12: 4 was seventy-five *y* old when he left Haran.
14: 4 *y* they had been subject to Chedorlaomer,
15:13 enslaved and oppressed for four hundred *y*.
16: 3 had lived ten *y* in the land of Canaan,
16:16 *y* old when Hagar bore him Ishmael.
17: 1 When Abram was ninety-nine *y* old,
17:17 be born to a man who is a hundred *y* old?
17:24 Abraham was ninety-nine *y* old when the
17:25 and his son Ishmael was thirteen *y* old
18:11 Abraham and Sarah were old, advanced in *y*,
21: 5 *y* old when his son Isaac was born to him.
21:34 in the land of the Philistines for many *y*.
23: 1 life was one hundred and twenty-seven *y*.
25: 7 life was one hundred and seventy-five *y*.
25:17 life was one hundred and thirty-seven *y*.
25:20 was forty *y* old when he married Rebekah,
25:26 Isaac was sixty *y* old when they were born.
26:34 When Esau was forty *y* old,
29:18 seven *y* for your younger daughter Rachel."
29:20 So Jacob served seven *y* for Rachel,
29:27 for another seven *y* of service with me."
29:30 in Laban's service another seven *y*.
31:38 "In the twenty *y* that I was under you,
31:41 *y* that I have now spent in your household,
31:41 *y* for your two daughters and six years
35:28 of Isaac was one hundred and eighty *y*;
37: 2 When Joseph was seventeen *y* old,
38:12 *Y* passed, and Judah's wife,
41: 1 After a lapse of two *y*,
41:26 *y*, and the seven healthy ears are seven *y*—
41:27 cows that came up after them are seven *y*,
41:27 they are seven *y* of famine.
41:29 Seven *y* of great abundance are now coming
41:30 will be followed by seven *y* of famine,
41:34 the land during the seven *y* of abundance.
41:35 husband all the food of the coming good *y*,
41:36 seven *y* of famine that are to follow
41:46 Joseph was thirty *y* old when he entered
41:47 During the seven *y* of plenty,
41:48 husbanded all the food of these *y* of plenty
41:50 Before the famine *y* set in,
41:53 When the seven *y* of abundance enjoyed by
41:54 to an end, the seven *y* of famine set in,
45: 6 two *y* now the famine has been in the land,
45: 6 five more *y* tillage will yield no harvest.
45:11 Since five *y* of famine still lie ahead,
47: 8 asked him, "How many *y* have you lived?"
47: 9 "The *y* I have lived as a wayfarer amount
47: 9 Few and hard have been these *y* of my life,
47: 9 the *y* that my ancestors lived as wayfarers."
47:28 in the land of Egypt for seventeen *y*;
47:28 life came to a hundred and forty-seven *y*.
50:22 He lived a hundred and ten *y*.
Ex 6:16 Levi lived one hundred and thirty-seven *y*.
6:18 lived one hundred and thirty-three *y*.
6:20 Amram lived one hundred and thirty-seven *y*.
7: 7 Moses was eighty *y* old and Aaron
12:40 in Egypt was four hundred and thirty *y*.
12:41 At the end of four hundred and thirty *y*,
16:35 The Israelites ate this manna for forty *y*,
21: 2 slave, he is to serve you for six *y*,
23:10 "For six *y* you may sow your land and
30:14 Everyone of twenty *y* or more who enters
38:26 *y* or more who entered the registered group;
Lv 19:23 For three *y*, while its fruit remains
25: 3 *y* you may sow your field, and for six *y*
25: 8 *y* shall you count seven times seven *y*—
25: 8 the seven cycles amount to forty-nine *y*.
25:15 On the basis of the number of *y* since the
25:15 on the basis of the number of *y* for crops,
25:16 When the *y* are many,
25:16 when the *y* are few,
25:21 there will then be crop enough for three *y*.
25:27 to the number of *y* since the sale,
25:50 compute the *y* from the sale to the jubilee,
25:50 distributing the sale price over these *y*
25:51 The more such *y* there are,
25:52 *y* there are left before the jubilee year,
25:52 his *y* of service shall he pay his ransom.
27: 6 between the ages of one month and five *y*,
27:18 of *y* left until the next jubilee year,
27:23 to the number of *y* until the next jubilee,
Nm 1: 3 *y* or more who are fit for military service.
1:18 Every man of twenty *y* or more then
1:20 when all the males of twenty *y* or more who
1:22 when all the males of twenty *y* or more who
1:24 when all the males of twenty *y* or more who
1:26 when all the males of twenty *y* or more who
1:28 when all the males of twenty *y* or more who
1:30 when all the males of twenty *y* or more who
1:32 when all the males of twenty *y* or more who
1:34 when all the males of twenty *y* or more who
1:36 when all the males of twenty *y* or more who
1:38 when all the males of twenty *y* or more who
1:40 when all the males of twenty *y* or more who
1:42 when all the males of twenty *y* or more who
1:45 number of the Israelites of twenty *y*
4: 3 between thirty and fifty *y* of age;
4:23 the men between thirty and fifty *y* of age;
4:30 men between thirty and fifty *y* of age;
4:31 the *y* of their service in the meeting tent:
4:35 the men between thirty and fifty *y* of age.
4:39 the men between thirty and fifty *y* of age.
4:43 the men from thirty up to fifty *y* of age.
4:47 men between thirty and fifty *y* of age
8:25 When he is fifty *y* old,
13:22 been built seven *y* before Zoan in Egypt.]
14:29 Of all your men of twenty *y* or more,
14:33 your children must wander for forty *y*,
14:34 forty *y* shall you suffer for your crimes:
26: 2 Israelites of all those of twenty *y* or more
26: 4 registered those of twenty *y* or more,
32:11 none of these men of twenty *y* or more
32:13 made them wander in the desert forty *y*,
33:39 *y* old when he died on Mount Hor.
Dt 2: 7 is now forty *y* that he has been with you,
2:14 Thirty-eight *y* had elapsed between our
8: 2 Remember how for forty *y* now the LORD,
8: 4 nor did your feet swell these forty *y*.
15:12 to you, he is to serve you for six *y*,
15:18 six *y* was worth twice a hired man's salary;
29: 4 'I led you for forty *y* in the desert.
31: 2 "I am now one hundred and twenty *y* old
32: 7 of old, reflect on the *y* of age upon age.
34: 7 one hundred and twenty *y* old when he died,
Jos 5: 6 had wandered forty *y* in the desert,
13: 1 When Joshua was old and advanced in *y*,
13: 1 now you are old and advanced in *y*,
14: 7 forty *y* old when the servant of the LORD,
14:10 *y* since the LORD spoke thus to Moses;
14:10 and although I am now eighty-five *y* old,
22: 3 For many *y* now you have not once abandoned
23: 1 Many *y* later, after the LORD had given
23: 1 and when Joshua was old and advanced in *y*,
23: 2 "I am old and advanced in *y*.
Jgs 2: 8 was a hundred and ten *y* old when he died;
3: 8 Naharaim, whom they served for eight *y*.
3:11 The land then was at rest for forty *y*,
3:14 served Eglon, king of Moab, for eighteen *y*.
3:30 and the land had rest for eighty *y*.
4: 3 oppressed the Israelites for twenty *y*.
5:31 And the land was at rest for forty *y*.
6: 1 them into the power of Midian for seven *y*,
8:28 And the land had rest for forty *y*,
9:22 Abimelech had ruled Israel for three *y*,
10: 2 When he had judged Israel twenty-three *y*,
10: 3 after him and judged Israel twenty-two *y*.
10: 8 For eighteen *y* they afflicted and
11:26 Three hundred *y* have passed;
12: 7 After having judged Israel for six *y*,
12: 9 After having judged Israel for seven *y*,
12:11 When he had judged Israel for ten *y*,
12:14 After having judged Israel for eight *y*,
13: 1 the power of the Philistines for forty *y*.
15:20 twenty *y* in the days of the Philistines.
16:31 He had judged Israel for twenty *y*.
Ru 1: 4 When they had lived there about ten *y*,
1Sm 4:15 (Eli was ninety-eight *y* old,
4:18 He had judged Israel for forty *y*.
7: 2 twenty *y*—
13: 1 *y* old when he became king and he reigned . . .
13: 1 (two) *y* over Israel.]
17:12 the days of Saul was old and well on in *y*.
2Sm 2:10 *y* old when he became king over Israel,
2:10 king over Israel, and he reigned for two *y*.
2:11 David spent seven *y* and six months in
4: 4 He was five *y* old when the news about Saul
5: 4 David was thirty *y* old when he became king,
5: 4 he became king, and he reigned for forty *y*:
5: 5 *y* and six months in Hebron over Judah,
5: 5 *y* in Jerusalem over all Israel and Judah.
13:23 After a period of two *y*,
13:38 Geshur, and stayed in Geshur for three *y*.
14:28 two *y* without appearing before the king.
15: 7 After a period of four *y*,
19:36 I am now eighty *y* old.
21: 1 there was a famine for three successive *y*.

24:13 a three *y'* famine to come upon your land,
1Kgs 1: 1 When King David was old and advanced in *y*,
2:11 of David's reign over Israel was forty *y*:
2:11 seven *y* in Hebron and thirty-three years
2:39 But three *y* later,
6:38 Thus it took Solomon seven *y* to build it.
7: 1 completed after thirteen *y* of construction.
9:10 After the twenty *y* during which Solomon
10:22 Once every three *y* the fleet of Tarshish
11:42 in Jerusalem over all Israel was forty *y*.
14:20 of Jeroboam's reign was twenty-two *y*.
14:21 He was forty-one *y* old when he became king,
14:21 and he reigned seventeen *y* in Jerusalem,
15: 2 He reigned three *y* in Jerusalem.
15:10 he reigned forty-one *y* in Jerusalem.
15:25 he reigned over Israel two *y*.
16:23 he reigned over Israel twelve *y*,
16:29 over Israel in Samaria for twenty-two *y*.
17: 1 during these *y* there shall be no dew or
22: 1 Three *y* passed without war between Aram
22:42 thirty-five *y* old when he began to reign,
22:42 and he reigned twenty-five *y* in Jerusalem.
22:52 he reigned two *y* over Israel.
2Kgs 3: 1 king of Judah, and he reigned for twelve *y*.
4:14 no son, and her husband is getting on in *y*."
8: 2 in the land of the Philistines for seven *y*.
8: 3 At the end of the seven *y*,
8:17 thirty-two *y* old when he began to reign,
8:17 reign, and he reigned eight *y* in Jerusalem.
8:26 twenty-two *y* old when he began his reign,
10:36 Israel in Samaria was twenty-eight *y*.
11: 3 For six *y* he remained hidden in the temple
12: 1 Joash was seven *y* old when he became king.
12: 2 Jehu, and he reigned forty *y* in Jerusalem.
14: 2 was twenty-five *y* old when he became king,
14: 2 and he reigned twenty-nine *y* in Jerusalem.
14:17 of Jehoahaz, king of Israel, by fifteen *y*.
15: 2 was sixteen *y* old when he began to reign,
15: 2 and he reigned fifty-two *y* in Jerusalem.
15:33 was twenty-five *y* old when he became king,
15:33 and he reigned sixteen *y* in Jerusalem.
16: 2 Ahaz was twenty *y* old when he became king,
16: 2 and he reigned sixteen *y* in Jerusalem.
17: 5 Samaria, which he besieged for three *y*.
18: 2 was twenty-five *y* old when he became king,
18: 2 and he reigned twenty-nine *y* in Jerusalem.
18:10 siege to it, and after three *y* captured it.
20: 6 I will add fifteen *y* to your life.
21: 1 was twelve *y* old when he began to reign,
21: 1 and he reigned fifty-five *y* in Jerusalem.
21:19 twenty-two *y* old when he began to reign,
21:19 reign, and he reigned two *y* in Jerusalem.
22: 1 was eight *y* old when he began to reign,
22: 1 and he reigned thirty-one *y* in Jerusalem.
23:31 twenty-three *y* old when he began to reign,
23:36 twenty-five *y* old when he began to reign,
23:36 and he reigned eleven *y* in Jerusalem.
24: 1 Jehoiakim became his vassal for three *y*.
24: 8 was eighteen *y* old when he began to reign,
24:18 was twenty-one *y* old when he became king,
24:18 king, and he reigned eleven *y* in Jerusalem.
1Chr 2:21 having married her when he was sixty *y* old.
3: 4 where he reigned seven *y* and six months.
3: 4 he reigned thirty-three *y* in Jerusalem,
21:12 will it be three *y* of famine;
23: 3 thirty *y* old and above were counted,
23:24 of the LORD from twenty *y* of age upward,
23:27 from the time they were twenty *y* old.
27:23 those who were twenty *y* of age or younger,
29:27 that he reigned over Israel was forty *y*:
29:27 in Hebron he reigned seven *y*,
29:28 old age, rich in *y* and wealth and glory,
2Chr 8: 1 After the twenty *y* during which Solomon
9:21 Once every three *y* the fleet of Tarshish
9:30 in Jerusalem over all Israel for forty *y*.
11:17 son of Solomon, prevail for three *y*;
11:17 in the way of David and Solomon three *y*.
12:13 he was forty-one *y* old when he became king,
12:13 and he reigned seventeen *y* in Jerusalem,
13: 2 he reigned three *y* in Jerusalem.
13:23 time, ten *y* of peace began in the land.
14: 5 war was waged against him during these *y*,
18: 2 some *y* he went down to Ahab at Samaria;
20:31 was thirty-five *y* old when he became king,
20:31 and he reigned twenty-five *y* in Jerusalem.
21: 5 was thirty-two *y* old when he became king,
21: 5 king, and he reigned eight *y* in Jerusalem.
21:19 on until a period of two *y* had elapsed,
21:20 was thirty-two *y* old when he became king,
21:20 king, and he reigned eight *y* in Jerusalem.
22: 2 was twenty-two *y* old when he became king,
22:12 For six *y* he remained hidden with them in
24: 1 Joash was seven *y* old when he became king,
24: 1 king, and he reigned forty *y* in Jerusalem.
24: 5 repair the house of your God over the *y*.
24:15 a hundred and thirty *y* old when he died.
25: 1 was twenty-five *y* old when he became king,
25: 1 and he reigned twenty-nine *y* in Jerusalem.
25: 5 he had counted those of twenty *y* and over,
25:25 of Jehoahaz, king of Israel, by fifteen *y*.
26: 1 Uzziah, though he was but sixteen *y* of age,
26: 3 was sixteen *y* old when he became king,
26: 3 and he reigned fifty-two *y* in Jerusalem.
27: 1 was twenty-five *y* old when he became king,
27: 1 and he reigned sixteen *y* in Jerusalem.
27: 8 was twenty-five *y* old when he became king,
27: 8 and he reigned sixteen *y* in Jerusalem.
28: 1 Ahaz was twenty *y* old when he became king,
28: 1 and he reigned sixteen *y* in Jerusalem.
29: 1 was twenty-five *y* old when he became king,
29: 1 and he reigned twenty-nine *y* in Jerusalem.
31:16 houses of males thirty *y* of age and over,
31:17 and the Levites of twenty *y* and over
33: 1 was twelve *y* old when he became king,
33: 1 and he reigned fifty-five *y* in Jerusalem.
33:21 was twenty-two *y* old when he became king,
33:21 king, and he reigned two *y* in Jerusalem.
34: 1 Josiah was eight *y* old when he became king,
34: 1 and he reigned thirty-one *y* in Jerusalem.
36: 2 was twentythree *y* old when he became king,
36: 5 was twenty-five *y* old when he became king,
36: 5 king, and he reigned eleven *y* in Jerusalem.
36: 9 was eighteen *y* old when he became king,
36:11 was twenty-one *y* old when he became king,
36:11 king, and he reigned eleven *y* in Jerusalem.
36:21 have rest while seventy *y* are fulfilled."
Ezr 3: 8 by appointing the Levites twenty *y* of age
4: 5 plans during the remaining *y* of Cyrus,
5:11 rebuilding the house built here long *y* ago,
Neh 5:14 during these twelve *y* neither I nor my
9:21 Forty *y* in the desert you sustained them:
9:30 You were patient with them for many *y*,
Tb 1: 7 And except for sabbatical *y*,
2:10 For four *y* I was deprived of eyesight,
2:10 Ahiqar, however, took care of me for two *y*,
5: 3 twenty *y* have already passed since I
14: 2 sixty-two *y* old when he lost his eyesight,
Jdt 8: 4 remained three *y* and four months at home,
8:29 but from your earliest *y* all the people
1Mc 1: 7 had reigned twelve *y* when he died.
1: 9 so did their sons after them for many *y*,
1:29 Two *y* later, the king sent the Mysian
3:28 treasure chests, gave his soldiers a *y* pay,
9:57 and the land of Judah was quiet for two *y*.
10:41 hand over as they had done in the first *y*,
2Mc 1: 7 violence that overtook us in those *y*
1:20 Many *y* later, when it so pleased God,
4:23 Three *y* later Jason sent Menelaus,
4:40 a man as advanced in folly as he was in *y*.
6:23 mind in a noble manner, worthy of his *y*,
7:27 for nine months, nursed you for three *y*,
10: 3 sacrifice for the first time in two *y*,
14: 1 Three *y* later, Judas and his men learned
Jb 10: 5 and are your *y* as a man's lifetime,
15:10 us more advanced in *y* than your father.
15:20 and limited *y* are in store for the tyrant;
16:22 For my *y* are numbered now,
29:18 I shall multiply *y* like the phoenix.
30: 1 me in derision who are younger in *y* than I;
32: 7 speak, I thought, and many *y* teach wisdom!
36:11 days in prosperity, their *y* in happiness.
36:26 the number of his *y* is past searching out.
38:21 them, and the number of your *y* is great!
42:16 this, Job lived a hundred and forty *y*;
42:17 Then Job died, old and full of *y*.
Ps(s) 23: 6 in the house of the LORD for *y* to come.
31:11 is spent with grief and my *y* with sighing;
61: 7 let his *y* be many generations;
77: 6 the *y* long past I remember.
78:33 days and their *y* with sudden destruction.
90: 4 thousand *y* in your sight are as yesterday,
90: 9 we have spent our *y* like a sigh.
90:10 Seventy is the sum of our *y*,
90:15 afflicted us, for the *y* when we saw evil.
95:10 Forty *y* I loathed that generation,
102:25 through all generations your *y* endure.
102:28 you are the same, and your *y* have no end.
Prv 3: 2 For many days, and *y* of life,
4:10 and the *y* of your life shall be many.
5: 9 to others, and your *y* to a merciless one;
9:11 and the *y* of your life increased."
10:27 life, but the *y* of the wicked are brief.
Eccl 6: 3 have a hundred children and live many *y*,
6: 6 twice a thousand *y* and not enjoy his goods,
11: 8 However many *y* a man may live,
12: 1 And the *y* approach of which you will say,
Wis 4: 8 time, nor can it be measured in terms of *y*.
4:16 the many *y* of the wicked man grown old.
7:19 Cycles of *y*, positions of the stars,
Sir 18: 7 days is great if it reaches a hundred *y*:
18: 8 are these few *y* among the days of eternity.
25: 4 a knowledge of counsel to those on in *y*!
41: 4 Whether one has lived a thousand *y*,
Is 7: 9 But within sixty *y* and five,
16:14 In three *y*, like those of a hireling,
20: 3 has gone naked and barefoot for three *y*
23:15 day, Tyre shall be forgotten for seventy *y*.
23:15 of another king, at the end of seventy *y*,
23:17 of the seventy *y* the LORD shall visit Tyre.
38: 5 I will add fifteen *y* to your life.
38:10 I shall be consigned for the rest of my *y*."
38:15 all my *y* despite the bitterness of my soul.
65:20 a mere youth who reaches but a hundred *y*,
65:22 the years of a tree, so the *y* of my people;
Jer 25: 3 these three and twenty *y*—
25:11 Seventy *y* these nations shall be enslaved
25:12 but when the seventy *y* have elapsed,
28: 3 Within two *y* I will restore to this place
28:11 *y* I will break the yoke of Nebuchadnezzar,
29:10 Only after seventy *y* have elapsed for
34:14 six *y* he shall serve you,
52: 1 was twenty-one *y* old when he became king,
52: 1 king, and he reigned eleven *y* in Jerusalem.
Bar 6: 2 reach Babylon you will be there many *y*,
Ez 4: 5 For the *y* of their sins I allot you the
22: 4 day, so that the end of your *y* has come.
29:11 it, and it will be uninhabited for forty *y*.
29:12 the most deserted of cities for forty *y*;
29:13 At the end of forty *y* I will gather the
38: 8 [in the last *y* you will come]
39: 9 seven *y* they shall make fires with them.
40: 1 exile, fourteen *y* after the city was taken,
Dn 1: 5 after three *y'* training they were to enter
4:13 of a beast, till seven *y* pass over him.
4:20 wild beasts till seven *y* pass over him'
4:22 seven *y* shall pass over you,
4:29 an ox, and seven *y* shall pass over you,
7:25 be handed over to him for a year, two *y*,
9: 2 counting of the *y* of which the LORD spoke
9: 2 of Jerusalem seventy *y* must be fulfilled.
11: 6 After some *y* they shall become allies:
11: 8 For *y* he shall have nothing to do with the
11:13 after some *y* he shall attack with this
12: 7 that it should be for a year, two *y*,
Jl 2: 2 them, even to the *y* of distant generations.
2:25 you for the *y* which the locust has eaten,
Am 1: 1 of Israel, two *y* before the earthquake:
2:10 who led you through the desert for forty *y*,
5:25 and offerings for forty *y* in the desert,
Hb 3: 2 the *y* revive it, in the course of the years
Zec 1:12 that have felt your anger these seventy *y*?"
7: 3 month as I have been doing these many *y*?"
7: 5 and in the seventh month these seventy *y*,
Mt 2:16 the massacre of all the boys two *y* old
9:20 suffered from hemorrhages for twelve *y*
Mk 5:25 afflicted with a hemorrhage for a dozen *y*.
16:20 the *y* of Satan's power has been fulfilled,
Lk 1: 7 moreover, both were advanced in *y*.
2:36 having lived seven *y* with her husband
3:23 his work he was about thirty *y* of age,
4:25 *y* and a great famine spread over the land.
8:43 with a hemorrhage of twelve *y'* duration,
12:19 have blessings in reserve for *y* to come.
13: 7 For three *y* now I have come in search of
13:11 was a woman there who for eighteen *y* had
13:16 in the bondage of Satan for eighteen *y*
15:29 'For *y* now I have slaved for you.
Jn 2:20 "This temple took forty-six *y* to build,
5: 5 man who had been sick for thirty-eight *y*.
Acts 4:22 cured was more than forty *y* of age.
7: 6 to slavery and oppressed four hundred *y*.
7:30 "Forty *y* later an angel appeared to him
7:36 the Red Sea, and for forty *y* in the desert.
7:42 and offerings for forty *y* in the desert,
9:33 who had been bedridden for eight *y*.
13:18 forty *y* he put up with them in the desert:
13:20 the end of some four hundred and fifty *y*.
13:21 tribe of Benjamin, who ruled for forty *y*.
19:10 This continued for two *y*,
20:31 Do not forget that for three *y*,
24:10 been a judge over this nation for many *y*.
24:17 "After several *y'* absence,
24:27 Two *y* passed,
28:30 *y* Paul stayed on in his rented lodgings,
Rom 4:19 dead (for he was nearly a hundred *y* old),
15:23 to visit you which I have had for many *y*.
2Cor 12: 2 I know a man in Christ who, fourteen *y* ago,
Gal 1:18 Three *y* after that I went up to Jerusalem
2: 1 Then, after fourteen *y*, I went up
3:17 into being four hundred and thirty *y* later,
4:10 of days and months, seasons and *y*!
1Tm 5: 9 should be not less than sixty *y* of age.
Heb 1:12 are the same, and your *y* will have no end."
3:10 and tried me, and saw my works for forty *y*.
3:17 With whom was God angry for forty *y*?
Jas 5:17 on the land for three *y* and six months.
2Pt 3: 8 years and a thousand *y* are as a day.
Jude 1:12 Like trees at the *y* end they bear no fruit,
Rv 12:14 for a year and for two and a half *y* more.
20: 2 Satan, and chained him up for a thousand *y*.
20: 3 astray until the thousand *y* are over.
20: 4 and reigned with Christ for a thousand *y*.
20: 5 come to life till the thousand *y* were over.
20: 6 and shall reign with him for a thousand *y*.
20: 7 When the thousand *y* are over,

YEAST (12)

Mt 13:33 "The reign of God is like *y* which a woman
16: 6 the *y* of the Pharisees and Sadducees,"
16:11 warning you against the *y* of the Pharisees?"
16:12 he was not issuing a warning against *y*
Mk 8:15 yeast of the Pharisees and the *y* of Herod,"
Lk 12: 1 on guard against the *y* of the Pharisees,
13:21 It is like *y* which a woman took to knead
1Cor 5: 6 *y* has its effect all through the dough?
5: 7 old *y* to make of yourselves fresh dough,
5: 8 us celebrate the feast not with the old *y*,
Gal 5: 9 "A little *y* can affect the entire dough."

YELLED (1)

Acts 22:23 They *y* and waved their cloaks and flung

YELLOW (4)

Lv 13:30 skin and that there is fine *y* hair on it,
13:32 If the scall has not spread and has no *y*
13:36 on the skin he need not look for *y* hair;
Rv 9:17 wore were fiery red, deep blue, and pale *y*.

YES (164)

Gn 17:13 *Y*, both the houseborn slaves and those
18:15 But he said, *Y* you did."
20: 6 *Y*, I know you did it in good faith.
22: 7 *Y*, son," he replied.
22:11 *Y*, Lord," he answered.
27: 1 *Y*, father!"
27:18 *Y*?" replied Isaac. "Which of my sons
Ex 2: 8 *Y*, do so," she answered.
Jgs 13:11 *Y*," he answered.
1Sm 2:31 *Y*, the time is coming when I will break
9:12 The girls answered, *Y*,
16: 5 *Y*! I have come to sacrifice
22:12 He replied, *Y*, my lord."
23:12 And the LORD answered, *Y*."
26:17 David answered, *Y*, my lord the king."
2Sm 2: 1 The LORD replied to him, *Y*."
2:20 He replied, *Y*."
12:19 They replied, *Y*, he is."
20:17 And he replied, *Y*."
1Kgs 2:13 *Y*," he answered,
13:14 he answered, *Y*."
18: 8 *Y*," he answered.
21:20 *Y*," he answered.
2Kgs 2: 3 *Y*, I know it," he replied.
2: 5 *Y*, I know it," he replied.
4:14 *Y*!" Gehazi answered.
5:22 *Y*," Gehazi replied,
6: 3 *Y*, I will come," he replied.
10:15 *Y*," replied Jehonadab.
Ezr 10:12 *Y*, it is our duty to do as you say!
Neh 9:34 *Y*, our kings,
Tb 3: 5 *Y*, your judgments are many and true in
5: 6 *Y*, I have been there many times.
5:10 *Y*, I can go with him,
6:11 He answered, *Y*, what is it?"
7: 5 They answered, *Y*, he is alive and well."
14: 5 *y*, it will be rebuilt for all generations
2Mc 11: 9 only men, but the most savage beasts, *y*,
Jb 23:17 *Y*, would that I had vanished in darkness,
32:12 *Y*, I followed you attentively as you
Ps(s) 8: 8 All sheep and oxen, *y*,
56: 3 *y*, many fight against me.
59:14 know that God is the ruler of Jacob, *y*,
77:12 *y*, I remember your wonders of old.
78:19 *Y*, they spoke against God,
83: 6 *Y*, they consult together with one mind,
116: 5 *y*, our God is merciful.
119:24 *Y*, your decrees are my delight;
Prv 2: 3 *Y*, if you call to intelligence,
4: 2 *Y*, excellent advice I give you;
6:16 There are six things the LORD hates, *y*,
8: 7 *Y*, the truth my mouth recounts,
8:19 My fruit is better than gold, *y*,
9: 2 has dressed her meat, mixed her wine, *y*,
23:28 *Y*, she lies in wait like a robber,
30:18 Three things are too wonderful for me, *y*,
30:21 Under three things the earth trembles, *y*,
30:29 things are stately in their stride, *y*,
Sg 1:16 *y*, you are lovely.
Wis 3:13 *Y*, blessed is she who,
4:16 *Y*, the just man dead condemns the sinful
5:14 *Y*, the hope of the wicked is like
Is 2:13 *Y*, against all the cedars of Lebanon
3: 5 the people shall oppress one another, *y*,
5: 6 *Y*, I will make it a ruin:
8:17 *y*, I will wait for him.
10:23 *Y*, the destruction he has decreed,
26: 8 *Y*, for your way and your judgments,
26: 9 My soul yearns for you in the night, *y*,
28: 8 *Y*, all the tables are covered with filthy
28:11 *Y*, with stammering lips and in a strange
32:14 *Y*, the castle will be forsaken,
33:22 *y*, the LORD our judge,
41:11 *Y*, all shall be put to shame and disgrace
43:13 I am God, *y*,
46:11 *Y*, I have spoken, I will accomplish it;
48: 8 *Y*, I know you are utterly treacherous,
48:13 *Y*, my hand laid the foundations of the
49:25 *Y*, captives can be taken from a warrior,
51: 3 *Y*, the LORD shall comfort Zion and have
55:12 *Y*, in joy you shall depart,
58: 4 *Y*, your fast ends in quarreling and
59:12 *Y*, our offenses are present to us,
Jer 2:16 *Y*, the people of Memphis and Tahpanhes
4:31 *Y*, I hear the moaning,
6:11 *Y*, all will be taken,
8:17 *Y*, I will send against you poisonous snakes,
10:21 *Y*, the shepherds were stupid as cattle,
20:10 *Y*, I hear the whisperings of many:
23:31 *Y*, I am against the prophets,
23:32 *Y*, I am against the prophets who prophesy
24: 8 are bad, so bad they cannot be eaten *y*,
27:21 all the nobles of Judah and Jerusalem *y*,
29:13 *Y*, when you seek me with all your heart,
31: 6 *Y*, a day will come when the watchmen will
35:16 *Y*, the children of Jonadab,
37:17 *Y*! Jeremiah answered:
46:22 *Y*, they come in force;
47: 4 *Y*, the LORD is destroying the Philistines,
48:20 Moab is disgraced, *y*, destroyed, howl
50:11 *Y*, rejoice and exult,
51:11 *Y*, it is the vengeance of the LORD,
Ez 16:45 *Y*, you are the true daughter of the mother
16:55 *Y*, your sisters, Sodom and her daughters,
28: 3 Oh *y*, you are wiser than Daniel,
39: 8 *Y*, it is coming and shall be fulfilled,
Hos 2: 7 *Y*, their mother has played the harlot;
9:15 *y*, there they incurred my hatred.
Jl 1:12 *Y*, joy has withered away from among
2: 2 *Y*, it is near, a day of darkness
2:11 For immense indeed is his camp, *y*,
4: 1 *Y*, in those days, and at that time,
Am 5:12 *Y*, I know how many are your crimes,
8:11 *Y*, days are coming, says the Lord GOD,
9:13 *Y*, days are coming, says the LORD,
Ob 1:16 *Y*, they shall drink and swallow,
Zep 1: 7 for near is the day of the LORD, *Y*,
1:18 For he shall make an end, *y*,
3:19 *Y*, at that time I will deal with all who
Zec 3: 8 *Y*, I will bring my servant the Shoot.
6:13 *Y*, he shall build the temple of the LORD,
8:23 different tongues, shall take hold, *y*,
11: 6 *Y*, I will deliver each of them into the
Mal 1:13 *y*, you bring it as a sacrifice.
2: 2 *Y*, I have already cursed it,
3: 1 *Y*, he is coming, says the LORD of hosts.
Mt 5:37 *Y*' when you mean 'Yes' and 'No' when you
9:28 *Y*, Lord," they told him.
13:51 *Y*," they answered:
Mk 12:33 *Y*, 'to love him with all our heart,
14:18 word, one of you is about to betray me, *y*,
Lk 10:21 *Y*, Father,
11:51 *Y*, I tell you,
12: 5 *Y*, I tell you, fear him.
19:25 *Y*, but he already has ten,' they said.
Jn 3:16 *Y*, God so loved the world that he gave his
5:20 *Y*, to your great wonderment,
8:55 *Y*, I know him well, and I keep his word.
11:27 *Y*, Lord," she replied.
21:15 *Y*, Lord," he said, "you know that I love
21:16 *Y*, Lord," Peter said, "you know that
Acts 1: 8 Jerusalem, throughout Judea and Samaria, *y*,
2:18 *Y*, even on my servants and handmaids I
5: 8 She answered, *Y*, that was the sum."
17:27 *y* to grope for him and perhaps eventually
26:20 *y*, even to the Gentiles.
Rom 2: 9 *Y*, affliction and anguish will come upon
3:29 *Y*, of the Gentiles too.
4:17 *Y*, he is our father in the sight of God in
8:22 *Y*, we know that all creation groans and is
15: 8 *Y*, I affirm that Christ became the servant
1Cor 1:22 *Y*, Jews demand "signs" and Greeks look
2Cor 1:18 is not *y*" one minute and "no" the next.
1:19 of God, was not alternately *y*" and "no";
1:19 he was never anything but *y*."
Phil 4: 3 *Y*, and I ask you, too, my dependable
Phlm 1: 9 *Y*, I, Paul, ambassador of Christ
Jas 5:12 let it be *y*" if you mean yes and "no"
Rv 2:15 *Y*, you too have those among you who hold
14:13 The Spirit added, *Y*, they shall find rest
16: 7 *Y*, Lord God Almighty, your judgments
22:20 The One who gives this testimony says, *Y*,

YESTERDAY (11)

Ex 5:14 prescribed amount of bricks *y* and today,
1Sm 20:27 son of Jesse not come to table *y* or today?"
2Sm 15:20 You came only *y*,
2Kgs 9:26 'As surely as I saw *y* the blood of Naboth
1Mc 9:44 for today is not like *y* and the day before.
Jb 8: 9 (As we are but of *y* and have no knowledge,
Ps(s) 90: 4 a thousand years in your sight are as *y*,
Sir 38:22 for him it was *y*,
Jn 4:52 "The fever left him *y* afternoon about one."
Acts 7:28 of killing me as you killed the Egyptian *y*?'
Heb 13: 8 Jesus Christ is the same *y*,

YIELD (54)

Gn 3:17 you eat its *y* all the days of your life.
45: 6 five more years tillage will *y* no harvest.
Lv 19:25 Thus it will continue its *y* for you.
25:19 The land will *y* its fruit and you will
Nm 20: 8 presence order the rock to *y* its waters.
24: 7 His wells shall *y* free-flowing waters,
Dt 11:17 fall, and the soil will not *y* its crops,
13: 9 do not *y* to him or listen to him,
22: 9 you have sown and the *y* of the vineyard.
32:22 world, Consuming the earth with its *y*,
Jos 5:12 year ate of the *y* of the land of Canaan.
1Mc 10:32 I also *y* my authority over the citadel in
Jb 20:10 and his hands shall *y* up his riches.
39:12 gather in the *y* of your threshing floor?
Ps(s) 65:11 Softening it with showers, blessing its *y*.
72: 3 The mountains shall *y* peace for the people,
85:13 our land shall *y* its increase.
107:37 vineyards, And they obtained a fruitful *y*.
Prv 6:31 all the wealth of his house he may *y* up.
18:20 with the *y* of his lips he sates himself.
20:16 for another, and for strangers *y* it up!
22:16 *y* up his gains to the rich as sheer loss.
27:13 and for the sake of a stranger, *y* it up!
Sir 38: 4 God makes the earth *y* healing herbs which
Is 5:10 of vineyard shall *y* but one liquid measure,
5:10 And a homer of seed shall *y* but an ephah.
7:22 abundant *y* of milk he shall live on curds:
47: 3 take vengeance, I will *y* to no entreaty,
Dn 13:22 "If I *y*, it will be my death;
Hos 8: 7 of grain that forms no ear can *y* no flour;
Jl 2:22 the fig tree and the vine give their *y*.
Hb 3:17 Though the *y* of the olive fail and the
Hg 2:16 for twenty measures, it would *y* but ten;
Zec 8:12 the vine shall *y* its fruit,
Mt 13:22 Such a one produces no *y*.
13:23 a *y* of a hundred- or sixty- or thirtyfold."
13:26 When the crop began to mature and *y* grain,
21:43 to a nation that will *y* a rich harvest.
Mk 4: 7 choked it off, and there was no *y* of grain.
4:19 it bears no *y*.
4:20 *y* at thirty- and sixty- and a hundredfold."
13: 7 wars and threats of war, do not *y* to panic.
Lk 6:44 Each tree is known by its *y*.
Jn 4:36 his wages and gathers a *y* for eternal life,
15: 2 ones he trims clean to increase their *y*.
1Cor 9: 7 a vineyard and does not eat of its *y*?
2Cor 9:10 seed you sow and increase your generous *y*.
Gal 5: 5 we hope for, and only faith can *y* it.
5:16 will not *y* to the cravings of the flesh.
1Thes 4:13 otherwise you might *y* to grief,
Ti 2: 8 about us, and hostility will *y* to shame.
Jas 3:12 more can a brackish source *y* fresh water.
5: 7 farmer awaits the precious *y* of the soil.
1Pt 1:14 do not *y* to the desires that once shaped

YIELDED (11)

1Mc 14: 8 the land *y* its produce and the trees of
Ps(s) 67: 7 The earth has *y* its fruits;
Wis 18:25 To these names the destroyer *y*,
Sir 51:15 As the blossoms *y* to ripening grapes,
Is 5: 2 of grapes, but what it *y* was wild grapes.
Dn 3:95 *y* their bodies rather than serve or worship
13:57 of Israel, and in their fear they *y* to you;
Mt 13: 8 *y* grain a hundred- or sixty- or thirtyfold.
Mk 4: 8 landed on good soil and *y* grain that
Lk 8: 8 soil, grew up, and *y* grain a hundredfold."
Acts 27:15 head into the wind, we *y* and ran before it.

YIELDS (3)

Ps(s) 1: 3 water, That *y* its fruit in due season,
Prv 10:31 The mouth of the just *y* wisdom,
Wis 7:10 the splendor of her never *y* to sleep.

YIRON (1)

Jos 19:38 Ramah, Hazor, Kedesh, Edrei, En-hazor, *Y*,

YOKE (70)

Gn 27:40 you shall throw off his *y* from your neck."
Lv 26:13 breaking the *y* they had laid upon you and
Nm 19: 2 and on which no *y* has ever been laid.
Dt 21: 3 put to work as a draft animal under a *y*,
28:48 He will put an iron *y* on your neck,
1Sm 6: 7 two milch cows that have not borne the *y*;
11: 7 Taking a *y* of oxen,
1Kgs 12: 4 "Your father put on us a heavy *y*.
12: 4 and the heavy *y* your father imposed on us,
12: 9 to lighten the *y* my father imposed on them?"
12:10 to lighten the *y* your father put on them:
12:11 Whereas my father put a heavy *y* on you,
12:14 "My father put on you a heavy *y*,
19:19 as he was plowing with twelve *y* of oxen;
19:21 Elisha left him and, taking the *y* of oxen,
2Chr 10: 4 "Your father laid a heavy *y* upon us.
10: 4 the heavy *y* that your father imposed on us,
10: 9 to lighten the *y* my father imposed on them?"
10:10 you, 'Your father laid a heavy *y* upon us,
10:10 yoke upon us, but do you lighten our *y*';
10:11 Whereas my father put a heavy *y* on you,
10:14 "My father laid a heavy *y* on you,
1Mc 8:18 He did this to get rid of the *y*,
8:31 'Why have you made your *y* heavy upon our
13:41 *y* of the Gentiles was removed from Israel,
Jb 1: 3 thousand camels, five hundred *y* of oxen,
42:12 six thousand camels, a thousand *y* of oxen,
Sir 6:25 her fetters, and your neck under her *y*.
26: 7 A bad wife is a chafing *y*;
28:19 its *y* nor been fettered with its chain;
28:20 For its *y* is a yoke of iron and its chains
30:12 Bend him to the *y* when he is young,
30:13 Discipline your son, make heavy his *y*,
33:25 *y* and harness and the rod of his master.
40: 1 anxiety has God allotted, and a heavy *y*,
51:26 Submit your neck to her *y*,
Is 9: 3 For the *y* that burdened them,
10:27 and his *y* shattered from your neck.
14:25 Then his *y* shall be removed from them,
47: 6 And upon old men you laid a very heavy *y*.

58: 6 unjustly, untying the thongs of the *y;*
58: 6 free the oppressed, breaking every *y;*
Jer 2:20 Long ago you broke your *y,*
5: 5 But, one and all, they had broken the *y,*
27: 2 *y* bars and put them over your shoulders.
27: 8 neck under the *y* of the king of Babylon,
27:11 The people that submits its neck to the *y*
27:12 your necks to the *y* of the king of Babylon;
28: 2 'I will break the *y* of the king of Babylon.
28: 4 I will break the *y* of the king of Babylon.' "
28:10 *y* from the neck of the prophet Jeremiah,
28:11 years I will break the *y* of Nebuchadnezzar,
28:12 had broken the *y* from off the neck
28:13 a wooden yoke, you forge an iron *y!*
28:14 A *y* of iron I will place on the necks of
30: 8 *y* from off your necks and snap your bonds."
Lam 3:27 for a man to bear the *y* from his youth.
5: 5 our necks is the *y* of those who drive us;
Ez 34:27 LORD when I break the bonds of their *y*
Hos 10:11 I myself laid a *y* upon her fair neck;
Na 1:13 Now will I break his *y* from off you,
Mt 11:29 my *y* upon your shoulders and learn from me,
11:30 rest, for my *y* is easy and my burden light."
Lk 14:19 *y* of oxen and I am going out to test them.
Acts 15:10 on the shoulders of these converts a *y*
2Cor 6:14 Do not *y* yourselves in a mismatch with
Gal 5: 1 yourselves the *y* of slavery a second time!
1Tm 6: 1 All under the *y* of slavery must regard

YOKED (1)

Sir 25: 8 who plows not like a donkey *y* with an ox.

YOKES (1)

2Sm 24:22 sledges and the *y* of the oxen for wood.

YON (1)

Jer 3:13 How you ran hither and *y* to strangers

YONDER (1)

Gn 22: 5 donkey, while the boy and I go on over *y.*

YOUNG (261)

Gn 15: 9 ram, a turtledove, and a *y* pigeon."
19: 4 all the townsmen of Sodom, both *y* and old
24:43 to a *y* woman who comes out to draw water,
31: 8 the entire flock would bear speckled *y;*
31: 8 the entire flock would bear streaked *y.*
32:16 thirty milch camels and their *y;*
34:19 *y* man lost no time in acting in the matter,
44:20 'We have an aged father, and a *y* brother,
Ex 10: 9 *Y* and old must go with us,"
24: 5 having sent certain *y* men of the
24: 5 *y* bulls as peace offerings to the LORD,
29: 1 Procure a *y* bull and two unblemished rams.
33:11 return to the camp, but his *y* assistant,
Lv 4: 3 guilty, he shall present to the LORD a *y,*
4:14 shall present a *y* bull as a sin offering.
16: 3 He shall bring a *y* bullock for a sin
22:28 a sheep on one and the same day with its *y.*
23:18 unblemished yearling lambs, one *y* bull,
Nm 7:15 one *y* bull,
7:21 weight filled with incense, one *y* bull,
7:27 one *y* bull,
7:33 one *y* bull,
7:39 one *y* bull,
7:45 one *y* bull,
7:51 one *y* bull,
7:57 one *y* bull,
7:63 one *y* bull,
7:69 one *y* bull,
7:75 one *y* bull,
7:81 one *y* bull,
7:87 holocausts were, in all, twelve *y* bulls,
8: 8 They shall take a *y* bull,
8: 8 take another *y* bull for a sin offering.
11:27 So, when a *y* man quickly told Moses,
15:24 shall offer the holocaust of one *y* bull
Dt 7:13 of your herds and the *y* of your flocks,
22: 6 a bird's nest with *y* birds or eggs in it,
28: 4 of your herds and the *y* of your flocks!
28:18 of your herds and the *y* of your flocks!
28:50 respect for the aged nor pity for the *y.*
28:51 no issue of your herds or *y* of your flocks,
Jos 6:21 men and women, *y* and old,
Jgs 8:14 He captured a *y* man of Succoth,
12: 9 thirty *y* women from outside the family.
14: 5 Timnah, a *y* lion came roaring to meet him.
14:10 it was customary for the *y* men to do this.
17: 7 There was a *y* Levite who had resided
17:11 the *y* Levite decided to stay with the man,
17:12 Micah consecrated the *y* Levite,
18: 3 the *y* Levite and turned in that direction.
18:15 they went to the house of the *y* Levite
21:12 of Jabesh-gilead four hundred *y* virgins,
Ru 2: 9 have commanded the *y* men to do you no
2: 9 from the vessels the *y* men have filled."
3:10 than before in not going after the *y* men,
1Sm 1:25 the boy's father had sacrificed the *y* bull,
2:17 Thus the *y* men sinned grievously in the
2:21 while *y* Samuel grew up in the service of
2:26 *y* Samuel was growing in stature and in
3: 1 During the time *y* Samuel was minister to
5: 9 he afflicted its inhabitants, *y* and old,
9: 2 a son named Saul, who was a handsome *y* man.
16:12 sent and had the *y* man brought to them.
17:58 then asked him, "Whose son are you, *y* man?"
21: 6 a journey, all the *y* men are consecrated
25: 5 was shearing his flock, he sent ten *y* men,
25: 8 Look kindly on these *y* men,
25: 9 When David's *y* men arrived,
25:12 So David's *y* men retraced their steps and
25:25 did not see the *y* men whom my lord sent.
25:27 be given to the *y* men who follow my lord.
30: 2 and all who were in the city, *y* and old,
30:17 none escaped except four hundred *y* men,
2Sm 1:13 *y* man who had brought him the information,
2:14 "Let the *y* men rise and perform for us."
2:21 seize one of the *y* men and take what you
4:12 the *y* men killed them and cut off their
9:12 Meribbaal had a *y* son whose name was Mica;
13:32 that all the *y* princes have been killed!
14:21 Go, therefore, and bring back *y* Absalom."
18: 5 "Be gentle with *y* Absalom for my sake."
18:15 *y* armor-bearers closed in on Absalom,
18:32 asked the Cushite, "Is *y* Absalom safe?"
18:32 you with evil intent be as that *y* man!"
1Kgs 1: 2 "Let a *y* virgin be sought to attend you,
11:28 saw that he was also an industrious *y* man,
12: 8 and consulted the *y* men who had grown up
12:10 *y* men who had grown up with him replied,
12:14 He said to them, as the *y* men had advised:
18:23 Give us two *y* bulls.
18:25 "Choose one *y* bull and prepare it first,
18:26 the *y* bull that was turned over to them,
18:33 cut up the *y* bull and laid it on the wood.
2Kgs 5:22 me to say, 'Two *y* men have just come to me,
9: 4 The *y* man (the guild prophet) went to
9: 6 *y* man poured the oil on his head and said,
9:12 told them what the *y* man had said to him,
1Chr 12:29 seven hundred, and Zadok, a *y* warrior,
22: 5 "My son Solomon is *y* and immature:
25: 8 for their functions equally, *y* and old,
29: 1 God has chosen, is still *y* and immature;
2Chr 10: 8 consulted the *y* men who had grown up
10:10 *y* men who had grown up with him replied:
10:14 them according to the advice of the *y* men:
13: 7 when Rehoboam was *y* and unthinking,
13: 9 comes to consecrate himself with a *y* bull
20:13 little ones, their wives, and their *y* sons.
36:17 *y* men in their own sanctuary building,
36:17 building, sparing neither *y* man nor maiden,
Ezr 6: 9 Whatever else is required *y* bulls,
Tb 1: 4 When I lived as a *y* man in my own country,
1: 5 as well as to the *y* bull which Jeroboam,
2:12 and also gave her a *y* goat for the table.
5: 5 Tobiah said to him, "Who are you, *y* man?"
5: 7 Tobiah said to him, "Wait for me, *y* man,
5: 9 went out to summon the man, saying, *Y* man,
7: 2 *y* man looks just like my kinsman Tobit!"
8: 1 They brought the *y* man out of the dining
Jdt 6:16 and all their *y* men,
Est 2: 2 beautiful *y* virgins be sought for the king.
2: 3 realm to bring together all beautiful *y* virgins
3:13 provinces, that all the Jews, *y* and old,
1Mc 1:26 Virgins and *y* men languished,
2: 9 her *y* men by the sword of the enemy.
3: 4 a lion, like a *y* lion roaring for prey.
11:39 bringing up Alexander's *y* son Antiochus.
11:54 and brought with him the *y* boy Antiochus,
11:57 Then *y* Antiochus wrote to Jonathan:
13:31 treacherously with the *y* King Antiochus.
14: 9 the *y* men wore the glorious apparel of war.
2Mc 3:26 Then two other *y* men,
3:33 the same *y* men in the same clothing again
4:12 the noblest *y* men to wear the Greek hat.
5:13 There was a massacre of *y* and old,
5:24 and sell the women and *y* men into slavery.
6:24 many *y* men would think the ninety-year-old
6:28 and I will leave to the *y* a noble example
6:31 only for the *y* but for the whole nation.
7:12 attendants marveled at the *y* man's courage,
10:35 twenty *y* men in the army of Maccabeus,
12:27 Robust *y* men took up their posts in
13:15 with a picked force of the bravest *y* men
15:17 instill valor and stir *y* hearts to courage,
Jb 1:19 fell upon the *y* people and they are dead;
4:10 yet the teeth of the *y* lions are broken;
14: 9 and put forth branches like a *y* plant.
19:18 The *y* children,
24: 5 steppe provides food for the *y* among them;
29: 8 Then the *y* men saw me and withdrew,
32: 6 I am *y* and you are very old;
38:41 ravens when their *y* ones cry out to God,
39: 3 They crouch down and bear their *y;*
39:16 *y* and ruthlessly makes nought of her brood;
39:30 His *y* ones greedily drink blood;
Ps(s) 17:12 for prey, like *y* lions lurking in hiding.
29: 6 leap like a calf and Sirion like a *y* bull.
78:31 best men, and laid low the *y* men of Israel.
78:63 Fire consumed their *y* men,
84: 4 swallow a nest in which she puts her *y*—
104:21 *Y* lions roar for the prey and seek their
119: 9 shall a *y* man be faultless in his way?
147: 9 and to the *y* ravens when they cry to him.
148:12 and all the judges of the earth, *Y* men too,
Prv 1: 4 to the *y* man knowledge and discretion.
7: 7 simple ones, I observed among the *y* men,
20:29 The glory of *y* men is their strength,
30:17 the *y* eagles will devour it.
Eccl 11: 9 O young man, while you are *y* and let
Sg 1: 8 the *y* ones near the shepherds' camps.
2: 9 My lover is like a gazelle or a *y* stag.
2:17 or a *y* stag upon the mountains of Bether.
4: 5 the *y* of a gazelle that browse among the
7: 4 are like twin fawns, the *y* of a gazelle.
8:14 or a *y* stag on the mountains of spices!
Wis 19:10 *y* of animals the land brought forth gnats,
Sir 15: 2 him, like a *y* bride she will embrace him,
30:12 Bend him to the yoke when he is *y,*
32: 7 *Y* man, speak only when necessary,
47:14 How wise you were when you were *y,*
51:13 When I was *y* and innocent,
Is 9:16 the Lord does not spare their *y* men,
11: 6 calf and the *y* lion shall browse together,
11: 7 be neighbors, together their *y* shall rest;
13: 7 bows of the *y* men fall from their hands.
20: 4 Egypt, and exiles from Ethiopia, *y* and old,
23: 4 labor, nor given birth, nor raised *y* men,
31: 8 his *y* men shall be impressed as laborers.
40:30 Though *y* men faint and grow weary,
62: 5 As a *y* man marries a virgin,
Jer 1: 6 I am too *y.*"
1: 7 LORD answered me, Say not, "I am too *y.*"
6:11 street, upon the *y* men gathered together.
9:20 in the street, *y* people in the squares.
11:22 The *y* men shall die by the sword;
18:21 *y* men be slain by the sword in battle.
31:13 merry and dance, and *y* men and old as well.
49:26 now her *y* men shall fall in her streets,
50:30 her *y* men shall fall in her streets,
51: 3 Spare not her *y* men,
51:22 and wife, with you I shatter old and *y,*
Lam 1:15 an army against me to crush my *y* men;
2:21 lie *y* and old; My maidens and young
4: 3 bare their breasts and suckle their *y;*
5:14 abandoned the gate, the *y* men their music.
Ez 19: 2 *y* lions she couched to rear her whelps.
19: 3 whelp she raised up, a *y* lion he became;
19: 5 of her whelps, him she made a *y* lion.
19: 6 among the lions, a *y* lion he became;
23: 3 even as *y* girls played the harlot in Egypt.
23: 6 and officers, all of them attractive *y* men,
23: 8 when they had lain with her as a *y* girl,
23:12 on horses, all of them attractive *y* men.
23:23 all those of Assyria, attractive *y* men,
30:17 The *y* men of On and of Pibeseth shall fall
38:13 Tarshish and all her *y* lions shall ask you:
43:19 a *y* bull as a sin offering to the priests,
43:23 bring an unblemished *y* bull and an
43:25 and a *y* bull and a ram from the flock,
45:18 you shall use an unblemished *y* bull
46: 6 he shall provide an unblemished *y* bull,
Dn 1: 4 of the nobility, *y* men without any defect,
1:10 with the other *y* men of your age,
1:13 other *y* men who eat from the royal table,
1:15 of the *y* men who ate from the royal table.
1:17 To these four *y* men God gave knowledge and
13:21 maids because a *y* man was here with you,""I
13:37 A *y* man, who was hidden there,
13:40 this one and asked who the *y* man was,
13:45 up the holy spirit of a *y* boy named Daniel,
Hos 5:14 like a *y* lion to the house of Judah;
13: 8 attack them like a bear robbed of its *y,*
Jl 3: 1 dream dreams, your *y* men shall see visions;
Am 2:11 your sons, and nazirites among your *y* men.
3: 4 Does a *y* lion cry out from its den unless
4:10 and with the sword I slew your *y* men;
8:13 virgins and *y* men shall faint from thirst;
Mi 5: 7 like a *y* lion among flocks of sheep;
Na 2:12 Where is the lions' cave, the *y* lions' den,
2:14 and the sword shall devour your *y* lions;
Zec 2: 8 to him, "Run, tell this to that *y* man:
11: 3 the roaring of the *y* lions,
Mt 19:20 The *y* man said to him,
19:22 these words, the *y* man went away sad,
23:37 mother bird gathers her *y* under her wings,
Mk 14:51 There was a *y* man following him who was
16: 5 tomb they saw a *y* man sitting at the right,
Lk 2:24 "a pair of turtledoves or two *y* pigeons,"
7:14 He said, *Y* man, I bid you get up."
13:34 mother bird collects her *y* under her wings,
Jn 21:18 as a *y* man you fastened your belt and went
Acts 2:17 your *y* men shall see visions and your old
5: 6 Some of the *y* men came forward,
5:10 The *y* men came in,
7:58 cloaks at the feet of a *y* man named Saul.
20: 9 and a certain *y* lad named Eutychus who was
23:17 said, "Take this *y* man to the commander;
Ti 2: 6 Tell the *y* men to keep themselves
1Jn 2:13 *Y* men, I address you,
2:14 from the beginning, I address you, *y* men,

YOUNGER (31)

Gn 19:31 The older one said to the *y:*
19:34 Next day the older one said to the *y:*

YOUNGER (cont.)

19:35 then the *y* one went in and lay with him;
19:38 The *y* one,
25:23 the other, and the older shall serve the *y.*"
27:15 and gave them to her *y* son Jacob to wear;
27:42 she called her *y* son Jacob and said to him:
29:16 the older was called Leah, the *y* Rachel.
29:18 you seven years for your *y* daughter Rachel."
29:26 marry off a *y* daughter before an older one.
48:14 head of Ephraim, although he was the *y,*
48:19 his *y* brother shall surpass him,
Jgs 1:13 Othniel, son of Caleb's *y* brother Kenaz,
3: 9 Othniel, son of Caleb's *y* brother Kenaz,
15: 2 Her *y* sister is more beautiful than she;
1Sm 14:49 were named, the elder, Merob, and the *y,*
1Chr 27:23 those who were twenty years of age or *y,*
Ezr 8:13 of the sons of Adonikam, *y* sons,
Jb 30: 1 me in derision who are *y* in years than I;
Ez 16:46 and your *y* sister,
16:61 your sisters, those older and *y* than you,
Mk 15:40 Mary the mother of James the *y* and Joses,
Lk 15:12 The *y* of them said to his father,
15:13 Some days later this *y* son collected all
Rom 9:12 said to her, "The older shall serve the *y.*"
1Tm 5: 1 You should treat *y* men as brothers,
5: 2 women as mothers, and *y* women as sisters,
5:11 Refuse to enroll the *y* widows,
5:14 why I should like to see the *y* ones marry,
Ti 2: 4 they must teach the *y* women to love
1Pt 5: 5 you *y* men must be obedient to your elders.

YOUNGEST (24)

Gn 9:24 and learned what his *y* son had done to him,
42:13 the *y* one is at present with our father,
42:15 unless your *y* brother comes here,
42:20 must come back to me with your *y* brother.
42:32 and the *y* one is at present with our
42:34 you come back to me with your *y* brother,
43:29 he asked, "Is this your *y* brother,
43:33 to their age, from the oldest to the *y,*
44: 2 the *y* one's bag put also my silver goblet,
44:12 with the oldest and ending with the *y,*
44:23 'Unless your *y* brother comes back with you,
44:26 only if our *y* brother is with us can we go,
44:26 the man if our *y* brother is not with us.
47:12 his father's whole household down to the *y,*
Jos 6:26 lose his *y* son when he sets up its gates.
Jgs 9: 5 Only the *y* son of Jerubbaal,
1Sm 16:11 Jesse replied, "There is still the *y,*
17:14 David was the *y.*
1Kgs 16:34 when he laid the foundation, and his *y* son,
2Chr 21:17 left to him only one son, Jehoahaz, his *y.*
22: 1 of Jerusalem made Ahaziah, his *y* son,
2Mc 7:24 As the *y* brother was still alive,
Ps(s) 68:28 There is Benjamin, the *y,*
Is 60:22 smallest shall become a thousand, the *y,*

YOURSELF (234)

Gn 6:14 "Make *y* an ark of gopherwood,
6:21 *y* with all the food that is to be eaten,
28: 2 and there choose a wife for *y* from among
32:13 You *y* said, 'I will be very good to you,
37: 8 you really going to make *y* king over us?"
38:29 said, "What a breach you have made for *y!*"
39: 9 and he has withheld from me nothing but *y,*
Ex 7:15 water, go and present *y* by the river bank,
8:16 "Early tomorrow morning present *y* to
9:13 present *y* to Pharaoh and say to him:
18:18 surely wear *y* out, and not only yourself
19:23 for you *y* warned us to set limits around
33:15 Moses replied, "If you are not going *y,*
33:21 me where you shall station *y* on the rock.
34: 2 present *y* to me on the top of the mountain.
Lv 9: 7 in atonement for *y* and for your family;
18:20 your neighbor's wife, defiling *y* with her.
18:23 with an animal, defiling *y* with it;
19:18 You shall love your neighbor as *y.*
19:34 have the same love for *y;*
25: 6 you *y* and for your male and female slaves,
Nm 11:17 You will then not have to bear it by *y.*
14:14 you, LORD, who plainly reveal *y!*
Jos 14:12 LORD promised me that day, as you *y* heard.
Jgs 8:21 and Zalmunna said, "Come, kill us *y,*
9:32 Now rouse *y;*
19: 5 son-in-law, "Fortify *y* with a little food;
19: 6 decide to spend the night here and enjoy *y?*"
19: 8 "Fortify *y* and tarry until the afternoon."
19: 9 Spend the night here and enjoy *y.*
Ru 3: 3 So bathe and anoint *y;*
3: 3 Do not make *y* known to the man before he
4: 6 Put in a claim *y* in my stead,
4: 8 in saying to Boaz, "Acquire it for *y,*"
1Sm 1:14 long will you make a drunken show of *y?*
9:27 of us, but stay here *y* for the moment,
19:10 informed him, "Unless you save *y* tonight,
20: 8 if I am guilty, kill me *y!*
24:11 You see for *y* today that the LORD just now
25:26 blood and from avenging *y* personally.
25:31 for having avenged *y* personally.
25:33 your good judgment and blessed be you *y,*
2Sm 1:16 for you testified against *y* when you said,
3:13 daughter, when you come to present *y* to me."
7:23 *y* renowned by doing this magnificent deed,
7:23 which you redeemed for *y* from Egypt?
7:24 for *y* your people Israel as yours forever,
13:26 then said, "If you will not come *y,*
14: 2 apparel and do not anoint *y* with oil,
16:21 how odious you have made *y* to your father,
17:11 and go with them *y.*
20: 4 Then present *y* here."
1Kgs 2: 5 You *y* know what Joab,
2:36 *y* a house in Jerusalem and live there.
3:11 not for a long life for *y,*
11:31 "Take ten pieces for *y;*
14: 2 "Get ready and disguise *y* so that none
14: 9 you have gone and made for *y* strange gods
17:13 can prepare something for *y* and your son.
18: 1 spoke to Elijah, "Go, present *y* to Ahab,"
20:34 and you may make *y* bazaars in Damascus,
20:40 You have decided it *y.*"
21:20 *y* up to doing evil in the LORD'S sight,
2Kgs 2: 2 "As the LORD lives, and as you *y* live,"
2: 4 "As the LORD lives, and as you *y* live,"
2: 6 "As the LORD lives, and as you *y* live,"
4: 4 and close the door on *y* and your children;
4:30 "As the LORD lives and as you *y* live,
14:10 Why involve *y* and Judah with you in
22:19 have humbled *y* before the LORD
1Chr 17:21 You won for *y* a name for great and awesome
2Chr 1:11 hate you, nor even for a long life for *y,*
25:19 Why involve *y,*
34:27 have humbled *y* before God on hearing
34:27 because you have humbled *y* before me,
Neh 9:10 you made for *y* a name even to this day.
Tb 4: 9 for *y* against the day of adversity.
4:13 to take a wife for *y* from among them.
4:14 Keep a close watch on *y,*
4:14 do, and discipline *y* in all your conduct.
4:15 Do to no one what you *y* dislike.
5: 3 find *y* a trustworthy man who will make the
Est C: 9 which you redeemed for *y* out of Egypt.
C:23 Manifest *y* in the time of our distress and
1Mc 5:17 "Choose men for *y,*
2Mc 7:34 insolence, concern *y* with unfounded hopes,
14: 9 have informed *y* in detail on these matters,
Jb 4: 5 when it touches *y,*
8: 5 if you *y* have recourse to God and make
15: 8 of God, and do you restrict wisdom to *y?*
18: 4 You who tear *y* in your anger,
33: 6 Behold I, like *y,*
35: 8 wickedness can affect only a man like *y;*
38:34 or veil *y* in the waters of the storm?
40:10 *y* with grandeur and majesty, and array *y*
Ps(s) 49:19 will praise you for doing well for *y,*"
50:21 Or do you think that I am like *y?*
59: 5 Rouse *y* to see it,
80:16 [the son of man whom you *y* made strong].
80:18 with the son of man whom you *y* made strong.
89:47 Will you hide *y* forever?
94: 1 vengeance, LORD, God of vengeance, show *y.*
Prv 6: 3 So do this, my son, to free *y,*
6: 5 Free *y* as a gazelle from the snare,
22:25 you learn his ways, and get *y* into a snare.
Sir 1:27 Exalt not *y* lest you fall and bring upon
2: 1 to serve the LORD, prepare *y* for trials.
3:18 Humble *y* the more,
4: 7 Endear *y* to the assembly;
4:20 *y* from evil, and bring upon yourself
4:27 Do not abase *y* before an impious man,
6:32 if you apply *y,*
7: 7 nor disgrace *y* before the assembly.
7:14 not *y* into the deliberations of princes,
7:16 Do not esteem *y* better than your fellows;
8: 8 wise, but acquaint *y* with their proverbs;
8:12 Lend not to one more powerful than *y;*
9: 6 Give not *y* to harlots,
10:27 prize *y* as you deserve.
11:20 hold fast to your duty, busy *y* with it,
12: 5 you give him, lest he use them against *y;*
13: 2 go with no one greater or wealthier than *y.*
14:14 Deprive not *y* of present good things,
14:16 Give, take, and treat *y* well,
18:19 Before you are judged, seek merit for *y,*
18:20 Before you have fallen, humble *y;*
30:21 in to sadness, torment not *y* with brooding;
30:23 Distract *y,* renew your courage,
31:17 gorge not *y,* lest you give offense.
33:31 you have but one slave, treat him like *y,*
37:12 with *y* and will feel for you if you fall.
38:16 the body, absent not *y* from his burial:
38:18 then compose *y* after your grief,
47:19 But you abandoned *y* to women and gave them
Is 22:16 here, that here you have hewn for *y* a tomb?"
37:11 You *y* have heard what the kings of Assyria
47: 8 one, enthroned securely, Saying to *y,*
47:10 led you astray, And you said to *y,*
47:13 You wearied *y* with many consultations,
49:21 You shall ask *y:*
Jer 2:20 every green tree, you gave *y* to harlotry.
4:30 putting on purple, bedecking *y* with gold,
4:30 eyes with cosmetics, beautifying *y* in vain?
13: 1 Go buy *y* a linen loincloth;
27: 2 Make for *y* bands and yoke bars and put
32: 7 "Buy for *y* my field in Anathoth,
32:24 you threatened has happened, you see it *y;*
45: 5 And do you seek great things for *y?*
47: 5 their strength, how long will you gash *y?*
50:24 You ensnared *y,*
51:62 you *y* threatened to destroy this place,
Lam 3:43 You veiled *y* in wrath and pursued us,
3:44 *y* in a cloud which prayer could not pierce.
Bar 2:11 made for *y* a name till the present day:
Ez 3:24 Go shut *y* up in your house.
16:15 you used your renown to make *y* a harlot,
16:16 gowns and made for *y* gaudy high places,
16:17 I had given you and made for *y* male images,
16:24 you raised for *y* a platform and a dais in
16:25 a dais for *y* to use your beauty obscenely,
16:56 repute by you while you felt proud of *y,*
21:24 make for *y* two roads over which the sword
23:30 the nations by defiling *y* with their idols.
23:40 and for them you bathed *y,*
24:13 Because you have sullied *y* with lewdness
24:26 come to you, that you may hear it for *y;*
28: 2 a god, however you may think *y* like a god.
28: 4 intelligence you have made riches for *y;*
28: 6 have thought *y* to have the mind of a god,
33: 9 die for his guilt, but you shall save *y.*
38: 7 Prepare *y,* be ready, you and all your
38:14 will you not bestir *y* and come from your
Dn 9:15 and made a name for *y* even to this day,
10:12 understanding and humble *y* before God,
Am 7:17 and you *y* shall die in an unclean land;
Mi 1:16 Make *y* bald,
4:14 Now fence *y* in, Bat-gader!
Zep 3:11 no longer exalt *y* on my holy mountain.
Mt 4: 6 "If you are the Son of God, throw *y* down.
4: 9 you if you prostrate *y* in homage before me."
6:24 You cannot give *y* to God and money.
8: 4 Go and show *y* to the priest and offer the
19:19 and 'Love your neighbor as *y.*'"
22:39 'You shall love your neighbor as *y.*'
27:40 Save *y,* why don't you?
Mk 1:44 "Go off and present *y* to the priest and
6:10 "Whatever house you find *y* in,
12:31 second, 'You shall love your neighbor as *y.*'
15:30 Save *y* now by coming down from that cross!"
Lk 2:35 and you *y* shall be pierced with a sword
4: 7 Prostrate *y* in homage before me,
4: 9 are the Son of God, throw *y* down from here,
4:23 quote me the proverb, 'Physician, heal *y,*'
5:14 no one, but go and show *y* to the priest.
6:42 fail *y* to see the plank lodged in your own?
7: 6 "Sir, do not trouble *y,*
10:27 and your neighbor as *y.*"
12:19 Enjoy *y.*'
16:13 You cannot give *y* to God and money."
19:17 'You showed *y* capable in a small matter.
23:37 "If you are the king of the Jews, save *y.*"
23:39 Then save *y* and us."
Jn 1:22 What do you have to say for *y?*"
1:46 and Philip replied, "Come, see for *y.*"
7: 4 as well display *y* to the world at large."
8:53 Whom do you make *y* out to be?"
10:33 You who are only a man are making *y* God."
14:22 will reveal *y* to us and not to the world?"
Acts 5: 3 for *y* some of the proceeds from that field?
16:28 "Do not harm *y!*
21:24 you follow the law *y* with due observance.
23: 3 the law *y* by ordering me to be struck!"
24: 8 and learn for *y* why we are accusing him."
25:10 done the Jews no wrong, as you *y* realize.
Rom 2: 1 By your judgment you convict *y,*
2: 3 these things in others yet do them *y?*
2:17 rely firmly on the law and pride *y* on God.
2:21 of others, are you failing to teach *y?*
2:23 You who pride *y* on the law,
13: 9 this, "You shall love your neighbor as *y.*"
Gal 5:14 "You shall love your neighbor as *y.*"
1Tm 4: 7 Train *y* for the life of piety,
4:13 devote *y* to the reading of Scripture,
4:16 Watch *y* and watch your teaching.
4:16 bring to salvation *y* and all who hear you.
5:22 Keep *y* pure.
2Tm 2:15 hard to make *y* worthy of God's approval,
Ti 2: 1 As for *y,* let your speech be consistent
2: 7 may you *y* fail to set them good example.
Jas 2: 8 it, "You shall love your neighbor as *y.*"

YOURSELVES (232)

Gn 18: 4 your feet, and then rest *y* under the tree.
18: 5 you a little food, that you may refresh *y;*
34: 9 to us, and take our daughters for *y.*
35: 2 then purify *y* and put on fresh clothes.
45: 5 do not reproach *y* for having sold me here.
45:12 Surely, you can see for *y,*
47:24 fields and as food for *y* and your families
Ex 5:11 Go and gather the straw *y,*
12:24 ordinance for *y* and your descendants.
16: 9 Present *y* before the LORD,
19: 4 you have seen for *y* how I treated the
20: 4 You shall not carve idols for *y* in the
20:22 *y* that I have spoken to you from heaven.
20:23 nor gods of gold shall you make for *y.*
22:20 were once aliens *y* in the land of Egypt.
23: 9 were once aliens *y* in the land of Egypt.
30:37 not make incense of a like mixture for *y;*

32:29 to bring a blessing upon *y* this day."
34:17 "You shall not make for *y* molten gods.
Lv 10: 6 bring not only death on *y* but God's wrath
11:43 Do not make *y* loathsome or unclean with
11:44 and you shall make and keep *y* holy,
11:44 You shall not make *y* unclean,
16:31 for you, on which you must mortify *y*.
18:24 "Do not defile *y* by any of these things
18:30 not to defile *y* by observing the
19: 4 aside to idols, nor make molten gods for *y*.
19:28 bodies for the dead, and do not tattoo *y*.
20: 7 Sanctify *y*, then, and be holy;
23:27 *y* and offer an oblation to the LORD.
23:32 a sabbath of complete rest and mortify *y*.
26: 1 "Do not make false gods for *y*.
26: 1 erect an idol or a sacred pillar for *y*,
26:33 You *y* I will scatter among the nations at
Nm 11:18 Sanctify *y* for tomorrow,
15:16 for the alien residing among you as for *y*."
16: 3 you set *y* over the LORD's congregation?"
18:32 of the Israelites and so bring death on *y*."
28:22 goat as a sin offering in atonement for *y*.
28:30 as a sin offering in atonement for *y*.
29: 5 as a sin offering in atonement for *y*.
29: 7 hold a sacred assembly, and mortify *y*,
31:18 But you may spare and keep for *y* all girls
31:19 *y* on the third and on the seventh day.
33:54 shall apportion the land among *y* by lot,
35:11 for *y* cities to serve as cities of asylum,
Dt 1:40 But as for *y*: turn about and proceed
4:16 not to degrade *y* by fashioning an idol to
4:23 you fashion for *y* against his command an
4:25 should you then degrade *y* by fashioning an
5: 8 You shall not carve idols for *y* in the
7:17 Perhaps you will say to *y*,
7:25 silver or gold on them, nor take it for *y*,
8:17 Otherwise, you might say to *y*,
9: 1 nations greater and stronger than *y*,
9: 4 them out of your way, do not say to *y*,
9:16 out to you by making for *y* a molten calf!
10:19 were once aliens *y* in the land of Egypt.
11: 2 but you *y* who must now understand the
11:23 nations greater and mightier than *y*.
14: 1 You shall not gash *y* nor shave the hair
18:21 "If you say to *y*,
23:10 you shall keep *y* from everything offensive.
28:68 and there you will offer *y* for sale to
31:14 and present *y* at the meeting tent that I
31:19 Write out this song, then, for *y*.
Jos 3: 5 also said to the people, "Sanctify *y*,
7:14 the morning you must present *y* by tribes.
10:19 But do not remain there *y*.
17:15 clear out a place for *y* there in the land
23:12 For if you ever abandon him and ally *y*
Jgs 15:12 "Swear to me that you will not kill me *y*."
21:22 Had you *y* given them these wives,
Ru 1:13 *y* of husbands until those sons grew up?
1Sm 2:29 fattening *y* with the choicest part of
7: 3 and your Ashtaroth, devote *y* to the LORD,
8:17 flocks and you *y* will become his slaves.
16: 5 *y* and join me today for the banquet."
2Sm 2: 7 therefore, and prove *y* valiant men,
3:31 your garments, gird *y* with sackcloth,
1Chr 15:12 must sanctify *y* along with your brethren
2Chr 13: 9 and made for *y* priests like the peoples of
28:10 Are not you *y*, therefore, guilty of a crime
29: 5 *y* now and sanctify the house of the LORD,
30: 7 them over to desolation, as you *y* now see.
32:12 shall prostrate *y* before one altar only,
35: 4 Prepare *y* in your ancestral houses and
35: 6 Slay the Passover sacrifice, sanctify *y*,
Ezr 10:11 separate *y* from the peoples of the land
Neh 13:25 of their daughters for your sons or for *y*!
Jdt 8:11 between God and *y* this oath which you took.
8:12 *y* in the place of God in human affairs?
1Mc 3:58 "Arm *y* and be brave;
2Mc 7:23 now disregard *y* for the sake of his law."
Jb 19: 5 if you would vaunt *y* against me and cast
19:29 Be afraid of the sword for *y*,
27:12 Behold, you *y* have all seen it;
27:12 why then do you spend *y* in idle words!
42: 8 Job, and offer up a holocaust for *y*;
Wis 1:12 *y* destruction by the works of your hands.
Sir 51:25 gain, at no cost, wisdom for *y*.
51:27 See for *y*! I have labored
Is 1:16 Wash *y* clean!
26:20 Hide *y* for a brief moment,
29: 9 blind *y* and stay blind!
32:11 Strip *y* bare,
49: 9 Show *y*! Along the ways
52:11 Purify *y*, you who carry the vessels
61: 6 You *y* shall be named priests of the LORD,
Jer 2:28 Where are the gods you made for *y*?
4: 8 So gird *y* with sackcloth, mourn and wail:
26:15 death, it is innocent blood you bring on *y*,
29: 8 Do not let *y* be deceived by the prophets
37: 9 Do not deceive *y* with the thought that the
44: 7 Why do you inflict so great an evil upon *y*?
44: 7 nursling, and not leave *y* even a remnant?
44: 9 and you *y* and your wives have done in the
46:14 Take your stand, prepare *y*,
49: 3 and mourn, run to and fro, gashing *y*;
Bar 6: 4 Take care that you *y* do not imitate their

Ez 13:18 the lives of my people, yet keep *y* alive?
14: 6 turn *y* away from all your abominations.
18:31 make for *y* a new heart and a new spirit.
20: 7 do not defile *y* with the idols of Egypt:
20:18 do not defile *y* with their idols.
20:29 To what sort of high place do you betake *y*—
20:30 will you defile *y* like your fathers?
20:31 *y* with all your idols even to this day.
20:43 defiled *y*; and you shall loathe yourselves
36:31 *y* for your sins and your abominations.
47:21 among *y* according to the tribes of Israel.
47:22 You shall allot it as inheritances for *y*
Hos 4:14 You *y* consort with harlots,
10:12 Sow for *y* justice
10:12 Break up for *y* a new field,
Jl 1:13 Gird *y* and weep, O priests!
Am 5:26 god, the images that you have made for *y*;
Zep 2: 1 Gather, gather *y* together,
Hg 1: 6 have clothed *y*,
Zec 7: 6 for *y* that you ate, and for yourselves
Mt 3: 9 Do not pride *y* on the claim,
6:19 "Do not lay up for *y* an earthly treasure.
10: 9 Provide *y* with neither gold nor silver nor
10:20 You *y* will not be the speakers;
14:16 Give them something to eat *y*."
14:27 "Get hold of *y*!
23:13 neither entering *y* nor admitting those who
23:15 make a devil of him twice as wicked as *y*.
25: 9 better go to the dealers and buy *y* some.'
Mk 6:31 "Come by *y* to an out-of-the-way place and
6:50 "Get hold of *y*!
9:16 them, "What are you discussing among *y*?"
13:11 will not be *y* speaking but the Holy Spirit.
14:42 Rouse *y* and come along.
Lk 3: 8 Do not begin by saying to *y*,
9:13 do you not give them something to eat *y*?"
11:52 You *y* have not gained access,
12:11 worry about how to defend *y* or what to say.
12:33 Get purses for *y* that do not wear out,
12:57 why do you not judge for *y* what is just?
13:28 in the kingdom of God, and you *y* rejected.
16: 9 *y* through your use of this world's goods,
16:15 "You justify *y* in the eyes of men,
17:14 responded, "Go and show *y* to the priests."
21:30 and know for *y* that summer is near.
23:28 Weep for *y* and for your children.
Jn 3:28 *y* are witnesses to the fact that I said:
7: 8 Go up *y* to the festival.
19: 6 Pilate said, "Take him and crucify him *y*;
Acts 2:40 "Save *y* from this generation which has
4:19 "Judge for *y* whether it is right in God's
13:46 convict *y* as unworthy of everlasting life,
18:15 and your own law, you must see to it *y*.
19:26 But as you can see and hear for *y*,
19:36 you must calm *y* and not do anything rash.
20:28 "Keep watch over *y*,
20:34 You *y* know that these hands of mine have
Rom 6:11 you must consider *y* dead to sin but alive
6:13 offer *y* to God as men who have come back
6:16 you offer *y* to someone as obedient slaves,
12: 2 Do not conform *y* to this age but be
12:19 Beloved, do not avenge *y*;
1Cor 1:11 household that you are quarreling among *y*.
5: 7 of the old yeast to make of *y* fresh dough,
6: 7 up with injustice, and let *y* be cheated?
6: 8 *y* injure and cheat your very own brothers.
6: 9 Do not deceive *y*:
7: 5 consent for a time, to devote *y* to prayer.
7:23 Do not enslave *y* to men.
7:35 help you to devote *y* entirely to the Lord.
10:15 You may judge for *y* what I am saying.
11:13 I will let you judge for *y*.
2Cor 6:14 not yoke *y* in a mismatch with unbelievers.
6:17 from among them and separate *y* from them,'
7:11 you, not to speak of readiness to defend *y*!
11:19 Being wise *y*, you gladly put up with fools.
13: 5 *y* to see whether you are living in faith;
13: 5 examine *y*.
13: 5 Perhaps you *y* do not realize that Christ
Gal 3:27 into Christ have clothed *y* with him.
4: 9 you seem willing to enslave *y* once more?
4:14 you took me to *y* as an angel of God,
5: 1 on *y* the yoke of slavery a second time!
5: 2 I tell you that if you have *y* circumcised,
5: 4 *y* from Christ and fallen from God's favor!
5:13 of love, place *y* at one another's service.
Phil 1:27 Conduct *y*, then, in a way worthy
1:27 exerting *y* with one accord for the faith
2:15 prove *y* innocent and straightforward,
4:15 You *y* know,
4:15 not a single congregation except *y* shared
Col 1:21 You *y* were once alienated from him;
3:12 and beloved, clothe *y* with heartfelt mercy,
3:15 Dedicate *y* to thankfulness.
4:16 and that you *y* read the letter that is
1Thes 4: 1 how to conduct *y* in a way pleasing to God
Heb 10:33 *y* with those who were being so dealt with.
13: 3 and of the ill-treated as of *y*,
Jas 1:22 do is listen to it, you are deceiving *y*.
2: 4 Have you not set *y* up as jugdes handing
5: 3 have stored up for *y* against the last days.
5: 5 you fattened *y* for the day of slaughter.
1Pt 1:15 holy *y* in every aspect of your conduct,

1:17 conduct *y* reverently during your sojourn
1:22 *y* for a genuine love of your brothers;
2:12 conduct *y* blamelessly among them.
4: 1 therefore, arm *y* with his same mentality.
5: 4 will win for *y* the unfading crown of glory.
5: 5 with one another, clothe *y* with humility,
2Jn 1: 8 you *y* do not lose what you have worked for;
Rv 3: 3 rouse *y* I will come upon you like a thief,

YOUTH (84)

Gn 41:12 There with us was a Hebrew *y*,
Lv 22:13 then eat of her father's food as in her *y*.
27: 5 fixed sum shall be twenty shekels for a *y*,
Nm 11:28 Nun, who from his *y* had been Moses' aide,
Dt 32:25 home Shall be the *y* and the maiden alike,
1Sm 3: 8 understood that the LORD was calling the *y*.
12: 2 with you from my *y* to the present day.
16:12 a *y* handsome to behold and making a
17:33 and fight with him, for you are only a *y*;
17:33 while he has been a warrior from his *y*."
17:55 Abner, "Abner, whose son is that *y*?"
2Sm 1: 5 said to the *y* who was reporting to him,
1:15 and the *y* struck him a mortal blow.
13:17 the *y* who was his attendant and said,
18:12 to protect the *y* Absalom for his sake.
18:29 the king asked, "Is the *y* Absalom safe?"
19: 8 has afflicted you from your *y* until now."
1Kgs 3: 7 but I am a mere *y*,
18:12 servant has revered the LORD from his *y*.
18:44 And the seventh time the *y* reported,
2Kgs 8:12 you will slay their *y* with the sword,
2Chr 34: 3 year of his reign, while he was still a *y*,
1Mc 1: 6 had been brought up with him from his *y*,
2:66 And Judas Maccabeus, a warrior from his *y*,
16: 2 battles of Israel from our *y* until today,
2Mc 4: 9 to establish a gymnasium and a *y* club
7:25 When the *y* paid no attention to him at all,
7:30 scarcely finished speaking when the *y* said:
15:30 from *y* his affection for his countrymen,
Jb 13:26 me, and punish in me the faults of my *y*.
31:18 like a father God has reared me from my *y*.
33:25 he shall be again as in the days of his *y*.
36:14 Therefore they expire in *y*,
Ps(s) 25: 7 sins of my *y* and my frailties remember not;
37:25 Neither in my *y*,
71: 5 my trust, O GOD, from my *y*.
71:17 O God, you have taught me from my *y*,
88:16 I am afflicted and in agony from my *y*;
89:20 over the people I have set a *y*.
89:46 You have shortened the days of his *y*;
103: 5 your *y* is renewed like the eagle's.
127: 4 hand of a warrior are the sons of one's *y*.
129: 1 Much have they oppressed me from my *y*,
129: 2 Much have they oppressed me from my *y*;
144:12 be like plants well-nurtured in their *y*,
Prv 2:17 of her *y* and forgets the pact with her God;
5:18 And have joy of the wife of your *y*,
7: 7 among the young men, a *y* with no sense,
Eccl 4:13 Better is a poor but wise *y* than an old
11: 9 your heart be glad in the days of your *y*.
11:10 presence, though the dawn of *y* is fleeting.
12: 1 your Creator in the days of your *y*,
Wis 4:16 and *y* swiftly completed condemns the many
8: 2 Her I loved and sought after from my *y*;
8:10 esteem from the elders though I be but a *y*.
Sir 6:18 My son, from your *y* embrace discipline;
25: 3 What you have not saved in your *y*,
30:11 Give him not his own way in his *y*,
47: 4 As a *y* he slew the giant and wiped out the
51:15 from earliest *y* I was familiar with her.
Is 47:13 at which you toiled from your *y*;
47:15 you with whom you have toiled from your *y*;
54: 4 The shame of your *y* you shall forget,
56: 4 A wife married in *y* and then cast off,
65:20 a mere *y* who reaches but a hundred years,
Jer 2: 2 I remember the devotion of your *y*,
3: 4 you who are the bridegroom of my *y*"?
3:24 has devoured our fathers' toil from our *y*,
3:25 the LORD, our God, From our *y* to this day,
22:21 This has been your way from your *y*,
31:19 with shame, I bear the disgrace of my *y*.
32:30 *y* have done only what is evil in my eyes;
48:11 Moab has been tranquil from his *y*,
48:15 of his *y* goes down to be slaughtered,
51:22 young, with you I shatter the *y* and maiden.
Lam 3:27 good for a man to bear the yoke from his *y*.
Ez 4:14 been made unclean, and from my *y* till now,
Hos 2:17 respond there as in the days of her *y*,
Jl 1: 8 with sackcloth for the spouse of her *y*.
Zec 13: 5 the soil, for I have owned land since my *y*."
Mal 2:14 between you and the wife of your *y*,
2:15 not break faith with the wife of your *y*.
Acts 26: 4 "The way I have lived since my *y*,
1Tm 4:12 no one look down on you because of your *y*,

YOUTHFUL (4)

1Sm 17:42 sized David up, and seen that he was *y*,
2Sm 1: 6 The *y* informant replied: It was by chance
Jb 20:11 Though his frame is full of *y* vigor,
2Tm 2:22 turn from *y* passions and pursue integrity,

YOUTHS (12)

Jdt 2:27 plains, and put all their *y* to the sword.
7:22 and the women and *y* were consumed with
7:23 All the people, therefore, including *y*,
10: 9 So they ordered the *y* to open the gate for
16: 4 to burn my land, put my *y* to the sword,
16: 6 Not by *y* was their mighty one struck down,
Is 40:30 and grow weary, and *y* stagger and fall,
Jer 15: 8 the mother of *y* the spoiler at midday;
Lam 1:18 maidens and my *y* have gone into captivity.
5:13 The *y* carry the millstones,
Ez 9: 6 Old men, *y* and maidens,
Zec 9:17 grain that makes the *y* flourish,

Z

ZAANAN (1)

Mi 1:11 of *Z* come not forth from their city.

ZAANANNIM (2)

Jos 19:33 from Heleph, from the oak at *Z* to Lakkum,
Jgs 4:11 had pitched his tent by the terebinth of *Z*,

ZAAVAN (2)

Gn 36:27 The descendants of Ezer were Bilhan, *Z*,
1Chr 1:42 The sons of Ezer were Bilhan, *Z*,

ZABAD (8)

1Chr 2:36 Nathan became the father of *Z*.
2:37 *Z* became the father of Ephlal.
7:21 whose son was Tahath, whose son was *Z*.
11:41 *Z*, son of Ahlai,
2Chr 24:26 *Z*, son of Shimeath from Ammon,
Ezr 10:27 Elioenai, Eliashib, Mattaniah, Jeremoth, *Z*,
10:33 Mattenai, Mattattah, *Z*,
10:43 Jeiel, Mattithiah, *Z*,

ZABADEANS (1)

1Mc 12:31 aside against the Arabs who are called *Z*,

ZABAD'S (1)

1Chr 7:25 *Z* son was Rephah,

ZABBAI (2)

Ezr 10:28 Jehohanan, Hananiah, *Z*,
Neh 3:20 After him, Baruch, son of *Z*,

ZABDI (5)

Jos 7:17 forward by families, and *Z* was designated.
7:18 by one, and Achan, son of Carmi, son of *Z*,
1Chr 8:19 Jakim, Zichri, *Z*,
27:27 for the wine cellars was *Z* the Shiphmite.
Neh 11:17 son of *Z*,

ZABDIEL (3)

1Chr 27: 2 the first month was Ishbaal, son of *Z*,
Neh 11:14 Their commander was *Z*, son of Haggadol.
1Mc 11:17 when the Arab *Z* cut off Alexander's head

ZABUD (1)

1Kgs 4: 5 *Z*, son of Nathan,

ZACCAI (2)

Ezr 2: 9 sons of *Z*,
Neh 7:14 sons of *Z*,

ZACCHAEUS (4)

2Mc 10:19 Simon and Joseph, along with *Z* and his men,
Lk 19: 2 There was a man there named *Z*,
19: 5 came to the spot he looked up and said, *Z*,
19: 8 *Z* stood his ground and said to the Lord:

ZACCUR (9)

Nm 13: 4 Shammua, son of *Z*,
1Chr 4:26 were his son Hammuel, whose son was *Z*,
24:27 Shoham, *Z*, and Ibri.
25: 2 *Z*, Joseph,
25:10 The third was *Z*,
Neh 3: 2 were rebuilding, and next to them was *Z*,
10:13 Pelaiah, Hanan, Mica, Rehob, Hashabiah, *Z*,
12:35 of Mattaniah, son of Micaiah, son of *Z*,
13:13 Levites, together with Hanan, son of *Z*,

ZACHAI (1)

Ezr 10:40 of the sons of *Z*:

ZADOK (49)

2Sm 8:17 *Z*, son of Ahitub,
15:24 *Z*, too [with all the Levite bearers of the
15:25 Then the king said to *Z*:
15:27 The king also said to the priest *Z*:
15:29 So *Z* and Abiathar took the ark of God back
15:35 the priests *Z* and Abiathar there with you.
15:35 report it to the priests *Z* and Abiathar,
17:15 Hushai said to the priests *Z* and Abiathar:
18:19 Then Ahimaaz, son of *Z*,
18:22 But Ahimaaz, son of *Z*,
18:27 the first one runs like Ahimaaz, son of *Z*."
19:12 sent word to the priests *Z* and Abiathar:
20:25 *Z* and Abiathar were priests.
1Kgs 1: 8 However, *Z* the priest,
1:26 nor *Z* the priest,
1:32 Then King David summoned *Z* the priest,
1:34 There *Z* the priest and Nathan the prophet
1:38 So *Z* the priest,
1:39 Then *Z* the priest took the horn of oil
1:44 The king sent with him *Z* the priest,
1:45 *Z* the priest and Nathan the prophet
2:35 and put *Z* the priest in place of Abiathar.
4: 2 Azariah, son of *Z*,
4: 4 *Z* and Abiathar,
2Kgs 15:33 mother's name was Jerusha, daughter of *Z*.
1Chr 5:34 Ahitub became the father of *Z*.
5:34 *Z* became the father of Ahimaaz.
5:38 Ahitub became the father of *Z*.
5:38 *Z* became the father of Shallum.
6:38 whose son was Ahitub, whose son was *Z*,
9:11 of Hilkiah, son of Meshullam, son of *Z*,
12:29 three thousand seven hundred, and *Z*,
15:11 David summoned the priests *Z* and Abiathar,
16:39 But the priest *Z* and his priestly brethren
18:16 *Z*, son of Ahitub,
24: 3 David, with *Z*,
24: 6 king, and of the leaders, of *Z* the priest,
24:31 lots in the presence of King David, *Z*,
27:17 for Aaron, *Z*:
29:22 him as the LORD'S prince, and *Z* as priest.
2Chr 27: 1 His mother was named Jerusa, daughter of *Z*.
31:10 priest Azariah, head of the house of *Z*
Ezr 7: 2 son of Shallum, son of *Z*,
Neh 3: 4 and next to him was *Z*,
3:29 After them *Z*,
10:22 Magpiash, Meshullam, Hezir, Meshezabel, *Z*,
11:11 of Hilkaiah, son of Meshullam, son of *Z*,
13:13 the priest Shelemiah, *Z* the scribe,
Ez 43:19 the Levites who are of the line of *Z*,
Mt 1:14 Azor was the father of *Z*,
1:14 the father of Zadok, *Z* the father of Achim,

ZADOKITES (3)

Ez 40:46 These are the *Z*,
44:15 the *Z* who cared for my sanctuary when the
48:11 The consecrated priests, the *Z*,

ZADOK'S (1)

2Sm 15:36 *Z* son Ahimaaz and Abiathar's son Jonathan.

ZAHAM (1)

2Chr 11:19 Jeshush, Shemariah and *Z*.

ZAHAR (1)

Ez 27:18 wealth, exchanging Helbon wine and *Z* wool.

ZAIR (1)

2Kgs 8:21 with all his chariots crossed over to *Z*.

ZAKKUR (2)

Ezr 8:14 of the sons of Bigvai, Uthai, son of *Z*,
10:24 Eliashib and *Z*; of the gatekeepers:

ZALAPH (1)

Neh 3:30 Shelemiah, and Hanun, the sixth son of *Z*,

ZALMON (3)

Jgs 9:48 he went up Mount *Z* with all his soldiers,
2Sm 23:28 *Z* from Ahoh;
Ps(s) 68:15 dispersed the kings there, snow fell on *Z*."

ZALMONAH (2)

Nm 33:41 They camped at *Z*.
33:42 Setting out from *Z*, they camped at Punon.

ZALMUNNA (12)

Jgs 8: 5 exhausted, and I am pursuing Zebah and *Z*,
8: 6 of Zebah and *Z* already in your possession,
8: 7 has delivered Zebah and *Z* into my power,
8:10 Now Zebah and *Z* were in Karkor with their
8:12 Zebah and *Z* fled.
8:12 took the two kings of Midian, Zebah and *Z*,
8:15 Succoth and said, "Here are Zebah and *Z*,
8:15 of Zebah and *Z* already in your possession,
8:18 Then he said to Zebah and *Z*,
8:21 Zebah and *Z* said,
8:21 stepped forward and killed Zebah and *Z*.
Ps(s) 83:12 all their chiefs like Zebah and *Z*,

ZAMZUMMIM (1)

Dt 2:20 inhabitants, whom the Ammonites called *Z*,

ZANOAH (5)

Jos 15:34 Eshtaol, Zorah, Ashnah, *Z*,
15:56 Carmel, Ziph, Juttah, Jezreel, Jokdeam, *Z*,
1Chr 4:18 of Soco, and Jekuthiel, the father of *Z*.
Neh 3:13 by Hanun and the inhabitants of *Z*;
11:30 in En-rimmon, Zorah, Jarmuth, *Z*,

ZAPHANIAH (1)

1Chr 6:21 son of Joel, son of Azariah, son of *Z*,

ZAPHENATH-PANEAH (1)

Gn 41:45 also bestowed the name of *Z* on Joseph,

ZAPHON (2)

Jos 13:27 Beth-haram, Bethnimrah, Succoth, *Z*,
Jgs 12: 1 gathered together and crossed over to *Z*.

ZARA (1)

Jos 7: 1 of Zerah, son of *Z* of the tribe of Judah,

ZAREPHATH (4)

1Kgs 17: 9 "Move on to *Z* of Sidon and stay there.
17:10 He left and went to *Z*.
Ob 1:20 occupy the Canaanite land as far as *Z*,
Lk 4:26 was sent, but to a widow of *Z* near Sidon.

ZARETHAN (4)

Jos 3:16 from Adam, a city in the direction of *Z*;
Jgs 7:22 far as Beth-shittah in the direction of *Z*,
1Kgs 4:12 and in the country around *Z* below Jezreel
7:46 in the clayey ground between Succoth and *Z*.

ZATTU (5)

Ezr 2: 8 sons of *Z*,
8: 5 of the sons of *Z*,
10:27 of the sons of *Z*:
Neh 7:13 sons of *Z*,
10:15 Parosh, Pahath-moab, Elam, *Z*,

ZAZA (1)

1Chr 2:33 The sons of Jonathan were Peleth and *Z*.

ZEAL (28)

Nm 25:11 by his *z* for my honor among them;
2Sm 21: 2 in his *z* for the men of Israel and Judah.)
2Kgs 10:16 me," he said, "and see my *z* for the LORD."
19:31 The *z* of the LORD of hosts shall do this.'
Jdt 9: 4 favored sons, who burned with *z* for you,
1Mc 2:24 Mattathias saw him, he was filled with *z*;
2:26 Thus he showed his *z* for the law,
2:54 Phinehas our father, for his burning *z*,
2:58 Elijah, for his burning *z* for the law,
2Mc 14:38 body and life in his ardent *z* for it.
Ps(s) 69:10 sons, Because *z* for your house consumes me,
119:139 My *z* consumes me,
Prv 19: 2 Without knowledge even *z* is not good;
Wis 5:17 He shall take his *z* for armor and he shall
14:17 honor, out of *z* to flatter him when absent,
Sir 48: 2 in his *z* he reduced them to straits;
Is 9: 6 The *z* of the LORD of hosts will do this!
26:11 when they see your *z* for your people:
37:32 The *z* of the LORD of hosts shall do this.
59:17 wrapped himself in a mantle of *z*.
Jn 2:17 *Z* for your house consumes me."
Rom 10: 2 for God though their *z* is unenlightened.
2Cor 7:11 a measure of holy *z* it has brought you,
8:16 an equal *z* for you in the heart of Titus!
9: 2 Your *z* has stirred up most of them.
Gal 1:14 in my excess of *z* to live out all the
Eph 6:15 and *z* to propagate the gospel of peace as
Heb 6:11 each of you show the same *z* till the end,

ZEALOT (4)

Mt 10: 4 Simon the *Z* Party member,
Mk 3:18 Thaddaeus, Simon of the *Z* Party,
Lk 6:15 son of Alphaeus, and Simon called the *Z*,
Acts 1:13 Simon, the *Z* party member,

ZEALOUS (14)

Nm 25:13 because he was *z* on behalf of his God and
1Kgs 18: 4 vizier, who was a *z* follower of the LORD.
19:10 "I have been *z* for the LORD, the
19:14 replied, "I have been most *z* for the LORD,
1Mc 2:27 "Let everyone who is *z* for the law and
2:50 be *z* for the law and give your lives for
14:14 among his people and was *z* for the law;
2Mc 4: 2 compatriots, and a *z* defender of the laws.
Prv 23:17 but be *z* for the fear of the LORD always;
29:14 If a king is *z* for the rights of the poor,
Sir 45:23 of his line When, *z* for the God of all,
Is 63:15 Where is your *z* care and your might,
Rom 10: 2 I can testify that they are *z* for God
Phil 3: 6 and so *z* that I persecuted the church.

ZEBADIAH (9)

1Chr 8:15 *Z*, Arad,
8:17 *Z*, Meshullam,
12: 8 Joelah, finally, and *Z*,
26: 2 first-born, Jediael, the second son, *Z*,

27: 7 brother of Joab, and after him his son *Z*,
2Chr 17: 8 sent the Levites, Shemaiah, Nethaniah, *Z*,
19:11 that pertains to the LORD, and *Z*,
Ezr 8: 8 of the sons of Shephatiah, *Z*,
10:20 Hanani and *Z*; of the sons of Harim:

ZEBAH (12)

Jgs 8: 5 and I am pursuing *Z* and Zalmunna,
8: 6 *Z* and Zalmunna already in your possession,
8: 7 has delivered *Z* and Zalmunna into my power,
8:10 Now *Z* and Zalmunna were in Karkor with
8:12 *Z* and Zalmunna fled.
8:12 the two kings of Midian, *Z* and Zalmunna,
8:15 and said, "Here are *Z* and Zalmunna,
8:15 *Z* and Zalmunna already in your possession,
8:18 Then he said to *Z* and Zalmunna,
8:21 *Z* and Zalmunna said,
8:21 stepped forward and killed *Z* and Zalmunna.
Ps(s) 83:12 all their chiefs like *Z* and Zalmunna,

ZEBEDEE (3)

Mt 4:21 their nets in order with their father, *Z*.
Mk 1:20 They abandoned their father *Z*,
3:17 James, son of *Z*;

ZEBEDEE'S (9)

Mt 4:21 sight of two other brothers, James, *Z* son,
10: 2 James, *Z* son,
20:20 The mother of *Z* sons came up to him
26:37 He took along Peter and *Z* two sons,
27:56 and Jo-seph, and the mother of *Z* sons.
Mk 1:19 along, he caught sight of James, *Z* son,
10:35 *Z* sons, James and John, approached him.
Lk 5:10 as well as James and John, *Z* sons,
Jn 21: 2 Nathanael (from Cana in Galilee), *Z* sons,

ZEBIDAH (1)

2Kgs 23:36 His mother's name was *Z*,

ZEBINA (1)

Ezr 10:43 Jeiel, Mattithiah, Zabad, *Z*,

ZEBOIIM (5)

Gn 10:19 the way to Sodom, Gomorrah, Admah and *Z*,
14: 2 Shinab king of Admah, Shemeber king of *Z*,
14: 8 the king of Admah, the king of *Z*,
Dt 29:22 like Sodom and Gomorrah, Admah and *Z*,
Hos 11: 8 I treat you as Admah, or make you like *Z*?

ZEBOIM (1)

Neh 11:34 Hadid, *Z*, Neballat,

ZEBUL (6)

Jgs 9:28 *Z* once subject to the men of Hamor,
9:30 of what Gaal, son of Ebed, had said, *Z*,
9:36 of ambush, Gaal saw them and said to *Z*,
9:36 But *Z* answered him,
9:38 *Z* said to him,
9:41 *Z* drove Gaal and his kinsmen from Shechem,

ZEBULUN (42)

Gn 30:20 so she named him *Z*.
35:23 Simeon, Levi, Judah, Issachar, and *Z*;
46:14 The sons of *Z*: Sered, Elon,
49:13 *Z* shall dwell by the seashore [This means
Ex 1: 2 3 Issachar, *Z* and Benjamin;
Nm 1: 9 Nethanel, son of Zuar; from *Z*:
1:30 Of the descendants of *Z*,
1:31 hundred were enrolled in the tribe of *Z*.
2: 7 and the tribe of *Z*.
10:16 of Helon, over the host of the tribe of *Z*.
13:11 son of Sodi; of the tribe of *Z*
34:25 the tribe of *Z*:
Dt 27:13 the people, while Reuben, Gad, Asher, *Z*,
33:18 Of *Z* he said:
33:18 "Rejoice, O *Z*,
Jos 19:27 reached *Z* and the valley of Iphtahel;
19:34 it touched *Z* on the south,
21: 7 from the tribes of Reuben, Gad and *Z*.
21:34 received from the tribe of *Z* the four
Jgs 1:30 *Z* did not dislodge the inhabitants of
4:10 Barak summoned *Z* and Naphtali to Kedesh,
5:14 from *Z* wielders of the marshal's staff.
5:18 *Z* is the people defying death;
6:35 through Asher, *Z* and Naphtali,
12:12 and was buried in Elon in the land of *Z*.
1Chr 2: 1 Reuben, Simeon, Levi, Judah, Issachar, *Z*,
6:48 lot from the tribes of Reuben, Gad, and *Z*.
6:62 the Merarites received from the tribe of *Z*:
12:34 From *Z*, men fit for military service,
12:41 neighbors from as far as Issachar, *Z*,
27:19 for *Z*,
2Chr 30:10 of Ephraim and Manasseh and as far as *Z*,
30:11 *Z* humbled themselves and came to Jerusalem.
30:18 from Ephraim, Manasseh, Issachar and *Z*,
Ps(s) 68:28 of Judah in a body, the princes of *Z*,
Is 8:23 the land of *Z* and the land of Naphtali;
Ez 48:26 *Z*: on the frontier of Issachar
48:27 on the frontier of *Z*,
48:33 the gate of Issachar, and the gate of *Z*.
Mt 4:13 sea near the territory of *Z* and Naphtali,
4:15 "Land of *Z*,
Rv 7: 8 twelve thousand from the tribe of *Z*,

ZEBULUNITE (2)

Jgs 12:11 After him the *Z* Elon judged Israel.
12:12 the *Z* Elon died and was buried in Elon in

ZEBULUNITES (6)

Nm 7:24 of Eliab, son of Helon, prince of the *Z*.
26:26 The *Z* by clans were:
26:27 These were the clans of the *Z*,
Jos 19:10 The third lot fell to the clans of the *Z*.
19:16 the heritage of the clans of the *Z*.
Jgs 4: 6 with you ten thousand Naphtalites and *Z*.

ZECHARIAH (56)

2Kgs 14:29 and his son *Z* succeeded him as king.
15: 8 year of Azariah, king of Judah, *Z*,
15:10 son of Jabesh, conspired against *Z*,
15:11 The rest of the acts of *Z* are recorded in
18: 2 His mother's name was Abi, daughter of *Z*.
1Chr 5: 7 Jeiel, the chief, and *Z*,
9:21 *Z*, son of Meshelemiah,
9:37 Kish, Baal, Ner, Nadab, Gedor, Ahio, *Z*,
15:18 the gatekeepers *Z*,
15:20 *Z*, Uzziel,
15:24 Shebaniah, Joshaphat, Nethanel, Amasai, *Z*,
16: 5 was their chief, and second to him were *Z*,
24:25 and *Z*, a descendant of Isshiah.
26: 2 *Z*, the first-born,
26:11 the second son, Tebaliah, the third, *Z*,
26:14 Then they cast lots for his son *Z*,
27:21 of Manasseh in Gilead, Iddo, son of *Z*;
2Chr 17: 7 his leading men, Ben-hail, Obadiah, *Z*,
20:14 of the LORD came upon Jahaziel, son of *Z*,
21: 2 of Jehoshaphat, were Azariah, Jehiel, *Z*,
24:20 Then the spirit of God possessed *Z*,
26: 5 prepared to seek God as long as *Z* lived,
29: 1 His mother was named Abia, daughter of *Z*.
29:13 *Z* and Mattaniah; of the sons of Heman:
34:12 of the line of Merari, and *Z* and Meshullam,
35: 8 Hilkiah, *Z* and Jehiel,
Ezr 5: 1 Then the prophets Haggai and *Z*,
6:14 the message of the prophets, Haggai and *Z*,
8: 3 of the sons of Parosh, *Z*,
8:11 of the sons of Bebai, *Z*,
8:16 Shemaiah, Jarib, Elnathan, Nathan, *Z*,
10:26 Mattaniah, *Z*,
Neh 8: 4 Hashum, Hashbaddanah, *Z*,
11: 4 Athaiah, son of Uzziah, son of *Z*,
11: 5 son of Adaiah, son of Joiarib, son of *Z*,
11:12 son of Pelaliah, son of Amzi, son of *Z*,
12:16 for Iddo, *Z*;
12:35 priests with the trumpets, and also *Z*,
12:41 Maaseiah, Minjamin, Micaiah, Elioenai, *Z*,
1Mc 5:18 In Judea he left Joseph, son of *Z*,
5:56 opposite Ptolemais, Joseph, son of *Z*,
Is 8: 2 witnesses, Uriah the priest, and *Z*,
Zec 1: 1 the word of the LORD came to the prophet *Z*,
1: 7 word of the LORD came to the prophet *Z*,
7: 1 the king [the word of the LORD came to *Z*,
7: 8 [This word of the LORD came to *Z*:
Mt 23:35 Abel to the blood of *Z* son of Barachiah,
Lk 1: 5 named *Z* of the priestly class of Abijah;
1:12 *Z* was deeply disturbed upon seeing him,
1:13 "Do not be frightened, *Z*:
1:18 *Z* said to the angel: "How am I to know
1:21 Meanwhile, the people were waiting for *Z*,
1:59 intended to name him after his father *Z*.
1:67 Then *Z* his father,
3: 2 was spoken to John son of *Z* in the desert.
11:51 from the blood of Abel to the blood of *Z*,

ZECHARIAH'S (3)

2Chr 24:22 devotion shown him by Jehoiada, *Z* father,
Lk 1: 8 when it was the turn of *Z* class and he was
1:39 Judah, where she entered *Z*

ZECHER (1)

1Chr 8:31 Kish, Baal, Ner, Nadab, Gedor, Ahio, *Z*,

ZEDAD (2)

Nm 34: 8 with the boundary extending through *Z*.
Ez 47:15 of Hethlon, past Labo of Hamath, to *Z*,

ZEDEKIAH (64)

1Kgs 22:11 *Z*, son of Chenaanah,
22:24 Thereupon *Z*,
2Kgs 24:17 Mattaniah king, and changed his name to *Z*.
24:18 *Z* was twenty-one years old when he became
24:20 *Z* rebelled against the king of Babylon.
25: 2 continued until the eleventh year of *Z*.
25: 7 Then he blinded *Z*,
1Chr 3:15 the third, *Z*;
3:16 Jeconiah, his son; *Z*, his son.
2Chr 18:10 *Z*, son of Chenaanah,
18:23 Thereupon *Z*,
36:10 brother *Z* king over Judah and Jerusalem.
36:11 *Z* was twenty-one years old when he became
Neh 10: 2 Nehemiah, son of Hacaliah, and *Z*.
Jer 1: 3 the fifth month of the eleventh year of *Z*,
21: 1 from the LORD when King *Z* sent him Pashhur,
21: 3 This is what you shall report to *Z*:
21: 7 that, says the LORD, I will hand over *Z*,
24: 8 even so will I treat *Z*,
27: 3 who have come to Jerusalem to *Z*,
27:12 To *Z*, king of Judah,
28: 1 in [the beginning of] the reign of *Z*,
29: 3 and by Gemariah, son of Hilkiah, whom *Z*,
29:21 in my name, Ahab, son of Kolaiah, and *Z*,
29:22 "May the LORD make you like *Z* and Ahab,
32: 1 from the LORD in the tenth year of *Z*,
32: 3 *Z*, king of Judah,
32: 4 Neither shall *Z*,
32: 5 to face, and *Z* shall be taken to Babylon.
34: 2 Go to *Z*, king of Judah, and tell him:
34: 4 But if you obey the word of the LORD, *Z*,
34: 6 Jeremiah told all these things to *Z*,
34: 8 *Z* had made an agreement with all the people
34:21 *Z*, too, king of Judah, and his princes,
36:12 of Achbor, Gemariah, son of Shaphan, *Z*,
37: 1 son of Jehoiakim, was succeeded by King *Z*,
37: 3 Yet King *Z* sent Jehucal,
37:17 Once King *Z* had him brought to his palace
37:18 Jeremiah then asked King *Z*:
37:21 King *Z* ordered that Jeremiah be confined
38: 5 King *Z* answered: "He is in your power"
38:14 Once King *Z* summoned the prophet Jeremiah
38:14 Jeremiah answered *Z*:
38:16 But King *Z* swore to Jeremiah secretly:
38:17 Thereupon Jeremiah said to *Z*;
38:19 King *Z* however,
38:24 Then *Z* said to Jeremiah,
39: 1 In the tenth month of the ninth year of *Z*,
39: 2 fourth month, in the eleventh year of *Z*,
39: 4 When *Z*, king of Judah saw them,
39: 5 and captured *Z* in the desert near Jericho.
39: 6 As *Z* looked on,
39: 7 He then blinded *Z*,
44:30 seek his life, just as I handed over *Z*,
49:34 at the beginning of the reign of *Z*,
51:59 king in the fourth year of the reign of *Z*;
52: 1 *Z* was twenty-one years old when he became
52: 3 *Z* rebelled against the king of Babylon.
52: 5 until the eleventh year of King *Z*.
52: 8 and overtook *Z* in the desert near Jericho,
52:10 As *Z* looked on, the king of Babylon
52:11 Then he blinded *Z*,
Bar 1: 1 son of Neriah, son of Mahseiah, son of *Z*,
1: 8 These silver vessels *Z*,

ZEDEKIAH'S (2)

2Kgs 25: 1 tenth month of the ninth year of *Z* reign,
25: 7 He had *Z* sons slain before his eyes.

ZEEB (6)

Jgs 7:25 *Z*, killing Oreb at the rock of Oreb and *Z*
7:25 of Oreb and Zeeb at the wine press of *Z*.
7:25 of Oreb and *Z* to Gideon beyond the Jordan.
8: 3 the princes of Midian, Oreb and *Z*.
Ps(s) 83:12 Make their nobles like Oreb and *Z*;

ZELA (2)

Jos 18:28 Mozah, Rekem, Irpeel, Taralah, *Z*,
2Sm 21:14 Kish at *Z* in the territory of Benjamin.

ZELEK (2)

2Sm 23:37 *Z* the Ammonite;
1Chr 11:39 *Z* the Ammonite;

ZELOPHEHAD (8)

Nm 26:33 *Z*, son of Hepher,
27: 1 *Z*, son of Hepher,
36: 2 heritage of our kinsman *Z* to his daughters.
36: 6 commands with regard to the daughters of *Z*:
36:10 The daughters of *Z* obeyed the command
Jos 17: 3 Furthermore, *Z*, son of Hepher,
1Chr 7:15 was named Zelophehad, but to *Z* only

ZELOPHEHAD'S (2)

Nm 27: 7 to him, "The plea of *Z* daughters is just;
36:11 Hoglah, Milcah and Noah, *Z* daughters,

ZELZAH (1)

1Sm 10: 2 tomb at *Z* in the territory of Benjamin,

ZEMARAIM (1)

Jos 18:22 Beth-hoglah, Emek-keziz, Beth-arabah, *Z*,

ZEMARIAM (1)

2Chr 13: 4 Abijah stood on Mount *Z*,

ZEMARITE (1)

1Chr 1:16 Arkite, the Sinite, the Arvadite, the *Z*,

ZEMARITES (1)
Gn 10:18 the Sinites, the Arvadites, the Z,

ZEMER (1)
Ez 27: 8 men of Z were in you to be your mariners;

ZEMIRAH (1)
1Chr 7: 8 The sons of Becher were Z,

ZENAN (1)
Jos 15:37 Z, Hadashah,

ZENAS (1)
Ti 3:13 Z the lawyer and Apollos on their journey,

ZEPHANIAH (9)
2Kgs 25:18 the high priest, Z the second priest,
Jer 21: 1 Pashhur, son of Malchiah, and the priest Z,
29:25 of Jerusalem, to all the priests and to Z,
29:29 priest Z read this letter to the prophet,
37: 3 sent Jehucal, son of Shelemiah, and Z,
52:24 also took Seraiah, the high priest, Z,
Zep 1: 1 The word of the LORD which came to Z,
Zec 6:10 son of Z (these had come from Babylon).
6:14 Heldai, Tobijah, Jedaiah, and the son of Z.

ZEPHATH (1)
Jgs 1:17 defeated the Canaanites who dwelt in Z.

ZEPHATHAH (1)
2Chr 14: 9 himself in battle array in the valley of Z,

ZEPHI (1)
1Chr 1:36 The sons of Eliphaz were Teman, Omar, Z,

ZEPHO (2)
Gn 36:11 The sons of Eliphaz were Teman, Omar, Z,
36:15 the clans of Teman, Omar, Z,

ZEPHON (2)
Gn 46:16 Z, Haggi,
Nm 26:15 through Z the clan of the Zephonites,

ZEPHONITES (1)
Nm 26:15 through Zephon the clan of the Z,

ZER (1)
Jos 19:35 The fortified cities were Ziddim, Z,

ZERAH (25)
Gn 36:13 The sons of Reuel were Nahath, Z,
36:17 the clans of Nahath, Z,
36:33 When Bela died, Jobab, son of Z,
38:30 he was called Z.
46:12 Er, Onan, Shelah, Perez, and Z—
Nm 26:20 through Z the clan of the Zerahites.
Jos 7: 1 Achan, son of Carmi, son of Z,
7:17 forward, and the clan of Z was designated.
7:17 had the clan of Z come forward by families,
7:18 of Zabdi, son of Z of the tribe of Judah,
7:24 and all Israel took Achan, son of Z,
22:20 When Achan, son of Z,
1Chr 1:37 The sons of Reuel were Nahath, Z,
1:44 When Bela died, Jobab, son of Z,
2: 4 daughter-in-law Tamar bore him Perez and Z,
2: 6 The sons of Z were Zimri,
4:24 of Simeon were Nemuel, Jamin, Jachin, Z,
6: 6 Joah, whose son was Iddo, whose son was Z,
6:26 son of Malchijah, son of Ethni, son of Z,
27: 8 the commander Shamhuth, a descendant of Z,
27:11 the Hushathite, a descendant of Z,
27:13 Maharai from Netophah, a descendant of Z,
2Chr 14: 8 Z the Ethopian moved against them with a
Neh 11:24 son of Meshezabel, a descendant of Z,
Mt 1: 3 Jesus Judah was the father of Perez and Z,

ZERAHIAH (5)
1Chr 5:32 Uzzi became the father of Z.
5:32 Z became the father of Meraioth.
6:36 whose son was Uzzi, whose son was Z,
Ezr 7: 4 son of Azariah, son of Meraioth, son of Z,
8: 4 sons of Pahathmoab, Eliehoenai, son of Z,

ZERAHITES (2)
Nm 26:20 Perezites, through Zerah the clan of the Z.
1Chr 9: 6 Among the Z were Jeuel and six hundred and

ZERED (2)
Nm 21:12 from there, they encamped in the Wadi Z.
Dt 2:13 Get ready, then, to cross the Wadi Z.'

ZEREDAH (2)
1Kgs 11:26 an Ephraimite from Z with a widowed mother,
2Chr 4:17 in the clayey ground between Succoth and Z.

ZERESH (4)
Est 5:10 he summoned his friends and his wife Z.
5:14 His wife Z and all his friends said to him,
6:13 When he told his wife Z and all his
6:13 his advisers and his wife Z said to him,

ZERETH (1)
1Chr 4: 7 The sons of Helah were Z,

ZERETH-SHAHAR (1)
Jos 13:19 Sibmah, Z on the knoll within the valley,

ZERI (1)
1Chr 25: 3 Gedaliah, Z,

ZEROR (1)
1Sm 9: 1 Kish, who was the son of Abiel, son of Z,

ZERUAH (1)
1Kgs 11:26 from Zeredah with a widowed mother, Z,

ZERUBBABEL (27)
1Chr 3:19 The sons of Pedaiah were Z and Shimei.
3:19 The sons of Z were Meshullam and Hananiah;
Ezr 2: 2 his own city (those who returned with Z,
3: 2 with his brethren the priests, and Z,
3: 8 God in Jerusalem, in the second month, Z,
4: 2 Z and the family heads and said to them,
4: 3 But Z, Jeshua, and the rest of the family
5: 2 Thereupon Z, son of Shealtiel,
Neh 7: 7 his own city (those who returned with Z,
12: 1 priests and Levites who returned with Z,
12:47 days of Z [and in the days of Nehemiah],
Sir 49:11 How can we fittingly praise Z,
Hg 1: 1 Haggai to the governor of Judah, Z,
1:12 Then Z, son of Shealtiel, and the high priest
1:14 up the spirit of the governor of Judah, Z,
2: 2 Tell this to the governor of Judah, Z,
2: 4 But now take courage, Z,
2:21 Tell this to Z, the governor of Judah:
2:23 the LORD of hosts, I will take you, Z,
Zec 4: 6 to me, "This is the LORD's message to Z:
4: 7 Before Z you are but a plain.
4: 9 Z have laid the foundations of this house,
4:10 to see the select stone in the hands of Z.
6:11 son of Jehozadak, the high priest] Z.
Mt 1:12 of Shealtiel, Shealtiel the father of Z.
1:13 Z was the father of Abiud,
Lk 3:27 son of Joanan, son of Rhesa, son of Z,

ZERUIAH (26)
1Sm 26: 6 and Abishai, son of Z and brother of Joab,
2Sm 2:13 Joab, son of Z,
2:18 The three sons of Z were there
3:39 this day, and these men, the sons of Z,
8:16 Joab, son of Z,
14: 1 When Joab, son of Z,
16: 9 Abishai, son of Z, said to the king:
16:10 is it of mine or of yours, sons of Z,
17:25 of Jesse and sister of Joab's mother Z.
18: 2 of Abishai, son of Z and brother of Joab,
19:22 But Abishai, son of Z, countered:
19:23 has come between you and me, sons of Z,
21:17 to kill David, but Abishai, son of Z,
23:18 Abishai, brother of Joab, son of Z,
23:37 Beeroth, armor-bearer of Joab, son of Z;
1Kgs 1: 7 He conferred with Joab, son of Z,
2: 5 You yourself know what Joab, son of Z,
2:22 him Abiathar the priest and Joab, son of Z."
1Chr 2:16 Their sisters were Z and Abigail.
2:16 Z had three sons:
11: 6 Joab, the son of Z,
11:39 the armor-bearer of Joab, son of Z;
18:12 Abishai, the son of Z,
18:15 Joab, son of Z,
26:28 Kish, Abner, son of Ner, Joab, son of Z,
27:24 Joab, son of Z,

ZETHAM (2)
1Chr 23: 8 Jehiel the chief, then Z and Joel;
26:22 of Jehiel, Z and his brother Joel,

ZETHAN (1)
1Chr 7:10 were Jeush, Benjamin, Ehud, Chenaanah, Z,

ZETHAR (1)
Est 1:10 Biztha, Harbona, Bigtha, Abagtha, Z,

ZEUS (4)
2Mc 6: 2 Zeus, and that on Mount Gerizim to Z
Acts 14:12 They named Barnabas Z;
14:13 Even the priest of the temple of Z,

ZIA (1)
1Chr 5:13 Michael, Meshullam, Sheba, Jorai, Jacan, Z,

ZIBA (14)
2Sm 9: 2 a servant of the family of Saul named Z.
9: 2 David, and the king asked him, "Are you Z?"
9: 3 Z answered the king,
9: 4 and Z answered,
9: 9 The king then called Z,
9:10 Z, who had fifteen sons and twenty servants,
16: 1 had gone a little beyond the top when Z,
16: 2 The king said to Z,
16: 2 Z replied: "The asses are for the king's
16: 3 Z answered the king,
16: 4 The king therefore said to Z, "So!
16: 4 Then Z said: I pay you homage
19:18 Z, too, the servant of the house of Saul,
19:30 say, 'You and Z shall divide the property.'"

ZIBA'S (1)
2Sm 9:12 tenants of Z family worked for Meribbaal.

ZIBEON (7)
Gn 36: 2 granddaughter through Anah of Z the Hivite;
36:14 through Anah of Z—
36:20 Lotan, Shobal, Z,
36:24 he was pasturing the asses of his father Z.)
36:29 the clans of Lotan, Shobal, Z,
1Chr 1:38 descendants of Seir were Lotan, Shobal, Z,
1:40 The sons of Z were Aiah and Anah.

ZIBEON'S (1)
Gn 36:24 Z descendants were Aiah and Anah.

ZIBIA (1)
1Chr 8: 9 Hodesh he became the father of Jobab, Z,

ZIBIAH (2)
2Kgs 12: 2 His mother, who was named Z,
2Chr 24: 1 His mother, named Z, was from Beer-sheba.

ZICHRI (12)
Ex 6:21 sons of Izhar were Korah, Nepheg, and Z.
1Chr 8:19 Jakim, Z,
8:23 of Shimei, Ishpan, Eber, Eliel, Abdon, Z,
8:27 Elijah, and Z were the sons of Jeroham.
9:15 Mattaniah, son of Mica, son of Z,
26:25 whose son was Joram, whose son was Z,
27:16 the leader was Eliezer, son of Z;
2Chr 17:16 Next to him, Amasiah, son of Z,
23: 1 and Elishaphat, son of Z.
28: 7 Z, an Ephraimite warrior,
Neh 11: 9 Joel son of Z,
12:17 for Abijah, Z;

ZIDDIM (1)
Jos 19:35 The fortified cities were Z,

ZIHA (3)
Ezr 2:43 sons of Z,
Neh 7:46 sons of Z,
11:21 Z and Gishpa were in charge of the temple

ZIKLAG (13)
Jos 15:31 Iim, Ezem, Eltolad, Chesil, Hormah, Z,
19: 5 Balah, Ezem, Eltolad, Bethul, Hormah, Z,
1Sm 27: 6 That same day Achish gave him Z,
30: 1 and his men reached Z on the third day,
30: 1 the Amalekites had raided the Negeb and Z,
30:14 and we set Z on fire."
30:26 When David came to Z,
2Sm 1: 1 of the Amalekites and spent two days in Z.
4:10 in Z I seized and put to death the man who
1Chr 4:30 Bilhah, Ezem, Tolad, Bethuel, Hormah, Z,
12: 1 The following men came to David in Z while
12:21 As he was returning to Z,
Neh 11:28 in Beer-sheba and its dependencies, in Z,

ZILLAH (3)
Gn 4:19 was Adah, and the name of the second Z.
4:22 Z, on her part,
4:23 "Adah and Z,

ZILLETHAI (2)
1Chr 8:20 Jakim, Zichri, Zabdi, Elienai, Z,
12:21 Jediael, Michael, Jozabad, Elihu, and Z,

ZILPAH (7)
Gn 29:24 Z to his daughter Leah as her maidservant.)
30: 9 her maidservant Z to Jacob as a consort.
30:10 So Jacob had intercourse with Z,
30:12 maidservant Z bore a second son to Jacob;
35:26 the sons of Leah's maid Z:
37: 2 sons of his father's wives Bilhah and Z,
46:18 These were the descendants of Z,

ZIMMAH (3)
1Chr 6: 5 whose son was Jahath, whose son was Z,
6:27 son of Adaiah, son of Ethan, son of Z,

2Chr 29:12 Joah, son of Z,

ZIMRAN (2)

Gn 25: 2 She bore him Z,
1Chr 1:32 she bore Z,

ZIMRI (17)

Nm 25:14 slain with the Midianite woman was Z,
1Kgs 16: 9 His servant Z,
16:10 of his palace in Tirzah, Z entered;
16:12 Z destroyed the entire house of Baasha,
16:15 of Judah, Z reigned seven days in Tirzah.
16:16 they heard that Z had formed a conspiracy
16:18 When Z saw the city was captured,
16:20 The rest of the acts of Z,
2Kgs 9:31 the gate, she cried out, "Is all well, Z,
1Chr 2: 6 The sons of Zerah were Z,
2: 7 The sons of Z:
8:36 the father of Alemeth, Azmaveth, and Z.
8:36 Z became the father of Moza.
9:42 the father of Alemeth, Azmaveth, and Z.
9:42 Z became the father of Moza.
1Mc 2:26 for the law, just as Phinehas did with Z,
Jer 25:25 all the kings of Z,

ZIN (9)

Nm 13:21 desert of Z as far as where Rehob adjoins
20: 1 in the desert of Z in the first month,
27:14 Z you both rebelled against my order
27:14 Meribah of Kadesh in the desert of Z
34: 3 the desert of Z along the border of Edom;
34: 4 of the Akrabbim Pass, it shall cross Z,
Dt 32:51 of Meribath-kadesh in the desert of Z
Jos 15: 1 of Edom, the desert of Z in the Negeb.
15: 3 the pass of Arkrabbim, across through Z,

ZION (170)

2Sm 5: 7 But David did take the stronghold of Z,
1Kgs 8: 1 from the city of David [which is Z,
2Kgs 19:21 laughs you to scorn, the virgin daughter Z!
19:31 shall come a remnant, and from Mount Z,
1Chr 11: 5 nevertheless captured the fortress of Z,
2Chr 5: 2 from the City of David (which is Z).
Jdt 9:13 your covenant, your holy temple, Mount Z,
1Mc 4:37 army assembled, and went up to Mount Z.
4:60 walls and strong towers around Mount Z,
5:54 They ascended Mount Z in joy and gladness
6:48 established camps in Judea and at Mount Z.
6:62 Z and saw how the place was fortified,
7:33 After this, Nicanor went up to Mount Z.
10:11 Z with square stones for its fortification,
14:26 which they affixed to pillars on Mount Z.
Ps(s) 2: 6 "I myself have set up my king on Z,
9:12 Sing praise to the LORD enthroned in Z;
9:15 and, in the gates of the daughter of Z,
14: 7 of Z would come the salvation of Israel!
20: 3 the sanctuary, from Z may he sustain you.
48: 3 Mount Z,
48:12 let Mount Z be glad,
48:13 Go about Z, make the round;
50: 2 From Z, perfect in beauty,
51:20 to Z in your kindness by rebuilding the
53: 7 of Z would come the salvation of Israel!
65: 2 we owe our hymn of praise, O God, in Z;
69:36 save Z and rebuild the cities of Judah.
73:28 works in the gates of the daughter of Z.
74: 2 Mount Z, where you took up abode
76: 3 his dwelling is in Z.
78:68 the tribe of Judah, Mount Z which he loved.
84: 8 they shall see the God of gods in Z.
87: 2 The gates of Z,
87: 5 And of Z they shall say:
97: 8 Z hears and is glad,
99: 2 The LORD in Z is great,
102:14 You will arise and have mercy on Z,
102:17 has rebuilt Z and appeared in his glory;
102:22 the name of the LORD may be declared in Z;
110: 2 power the LORD will stretch forth from Z:
125: 1 who trust in the LORD are like Mount Z,
126: 1 the LORD brought back the captives of Z,
128: 5 The LORD bless you from Z:
129: 5 be put to shame and fall back that hate Z.
132:13 For the LORD has chosen Z;
132:14 Z is my resting place forever;
133: 3 which come down upon the mountains of Z;
134: 3 May the LORD bless you from Z,
135:21 Blessed from Z be the LORD,
137: 1 we sat and wept when we remembered Z.
137: 3 "Sing for us the songs of Z!"
146:10 your God, O Z,
147:12 praise your God, O Z.
149: 2 the children of Z rejoice in their king.
Sir 24:10 before him, and in Z I fixed my abode.
36:13 Fill Z with your majesty,
48:18 fist at Z and blasphemed God in his pride.
48:24 the future and consoled the mourners of Z;
Is 1: 8 Z is left like a hut in a vineyard,
1:27 Z shall be redeemed by judgment,
2: 3 For from Z shall go forth instruction,
3:16 Because the daughters of Z are haughty,
4: 3 He who remains in Z and he that is left in
4: 4 away the filth of the daughters of Z,
4: 5 of Mount Z and over her place of assembly,
8:18 the LORD of hosts who dwells on Mount Z.
10:12 all his work on Mount Z and in Jerusalem,
10:24 O my people, who dwell in Z,
10:32 shake his fist at the mount of daughter Z,
12: 6 Shout with exultation, O city of Z,
14:32 "The LORD has established Z,
16: 1 the desert, to the mount of daughter Z.
18: 7 to Mount Z where dwells the name of the
24:23 will reign on Mount Z and in Jerusalem,
28:16 See, I am laying a stone in Z,
29: 8 all the nations be, who make war against Z.
30:19 O people of Z,
31: 4 wage war upon the mountain and hill of Z.
31: 9 has a fire in Z and a furnace in Jerusalem.
33: 5 he fills Z with right and justice.
33:14 On Z sinners are in dread,
33:20 Look to Z, the city of our festivals;
35:10 ransomed will return and enter Z singing,
37:22 you to scorn, the virgin daughter Z;
37:32 shall come a remnant, and from Mount Z,
40: 9 Go up onto a high mountain, Z,
41:27 one heard you say, "The first news for Z:
46:13 I will put salvation within Z,
49:14 But Z said, "The LORD has forsaken me;
51: 3 comfort Z and have pity on all her ruins;
51:11 ransomed will return and enter Z singing,
51:16 the foundations of the earth, who say to Z:
52: 1 Put on your strength, O Z:
52: 2 bonds from your neck, O captive daughter Z!
52: 7 announcing salvation, and saying to Z,
52: 8 before their eyes, the LORD restoring Z.
59:20 He shall come to Z a redeemer to those of
60:14 of the LORD," Z of the Holy One of Israel."
61: 3 who mourn in Z a diadem instead of ashes,
62:11 Say to daughter Z, your savior comes!
64: 9 cities have become a desert, Z is a desert,
66: 8 Yet Z is scarcely in labor when she gives
Jer 3:14 city, two from a clan, and bring you to Z.
4: 6 Bear the standard to Z,
4:31 The cry of daughter Z gasping,
6: 2 O lovely and delicate daughter Z,
6:23 place, for battle against you, daughter Z.
8:19 Is the LORD no longer in Z,
9:18 The dirge is heard from Z:
14:19 Is Z loathsome to you?
26:18 Z shall become a plowed field,
31: 6 "Rise up, let us go to Z,
31:12 they shall mount the heights of Z,
50: 5 to their goal in Z they shall ask the way.
50:28 announce in Z the vengeance of the LORD,
51:10 come, let us tell in Z what the LORD,
51:24 in Chaldea All the evil they did to Z,
51:35 flesh be upon Babylon, says the city on Z;
Lam 1: 4 The roads to Z mourn for lack of pilgrims
1: 6 Gone from daughter Z is all her glory:
1:17 Z stretched out her hands,
2: 1 Lord in his wrath has detested daughter Z!
2: 4 Z he poured out his wrath like fire.
2: 6 In Z the LORD has made feast and sabbath
2: 8 for destruction the wall of daughter Z:
2:10 in silence sit the old men of daughter Z;
2:13 you for your comfort, virgin daughter Z?
2:18 Cry out to the LORD; moan, O daughter Z!
4:11 in Z that has consumed her foundations.
4:22 chastisement is completed, O daughter Z,
5:11 The wives in Z were ravished by the enemy,
5:18 That Mount Z should be desolate,
Bar 4: 9 "Hear you neighbors of Z!
Jl 2: 1 Blow the trumpet in Z,
2:15 Blow the trumpet in Z!
2:23 And do you, O children of Z,
3: 5 For on Mount Z there shall be a remnant,
4:16 The LORD roars from Z,
4:17 I, the LORD, am your God, dwelling on Z,
4:21 The LORD dwells in Z.
Am 1: 2 The LORD will roar from Z,
6: 1 Woe to the complacent in Z,
Ob 1:17 on Mount Z there shall be a portion saved;
1:21 ascend Mount Z to rule the mount of Esau,
Mi 1:13 the beginning of sin for daughter Z,
3:10 Who build up Z with bloodshed,
3:12 of you, Z shall be plowed like a field,
4: 2 For from Z shall go forth instruction,
4: 7 LORD shall be king over them on Mount Z,
4: 8 you, O Magdal-eder, hillock of daughter Z!
4:10 Writhe in pain, grow faint, O daughter Z,
4:13 Arise and thresh, O daughter Z;
Zep 3:14 Shout for joy, O daughter Z!
3:16 Fear not, O Z, be not discouraged!
Zec 1:14 moved for the sake of Jerusalem and Z,
1:17 the LORD will again comfort Z,
2:11 Up, escape to Z!
2:14 Sing and rejoice, O daughter Z!
8: 2 I am intensely jealous for Z,
8: 3 I will return to Z,
9: 9 Rejoice heartily, O daughter Z,
9:13 I will arouse your sons, O Z,
Mt 21: 5 "Tell the daughter of Z,
Jn 12:15 "Fear not, O daughter of Z!
Rom 9:33 I am placing in Z a stone to make men
11:26 "Out of Z will come the deliverer who
Heb 12:22 to Mount Z and the city of the living God,
1Pt 2: 6 "See, I am laying a cornerstone in Z,
Rv 14: 1 He was standing on Mount Z,

ZION'S (7)

Is 3:17 cover the scalps of Z daughters with scabs,
34: 8 a year of requital by Z defender.
62: 1 For Z sake I will not be silent,
Lam 4: 2 Z precious sons,
Bar 4:14 "Let Z neighbors come,
4:24 Z neighbors lately saw you taken captive,
Mi 4:11 be profaned, let our eyes see Z downfall!"

ZIOR (1)

Jos 15:54 Kiriath-arba (that is, Hebron), and Z;

ZIPH (11)

Jos 15:24 Z, Telem, Bealoth,
15:55 Maon, Carmel, Z,
1Sm 23:14 or in the barren hill country near Z.
23:15 he was at Horesh in the barrens near Z,
23:24 So they went off to Z ahead of Saul.
26: 1 Men from Z came to Saul in Gibeah
26: 2 Z with three thousand picked men of Israel,
26: 2 to search for David in the desert of Z.
1Chr 2:42 his first-born, who was the father of Z.
4:16 The sons of Jehallelel were Z,
2Chr 11: 8 Soco, Adullam, Gath, Mareshah, Z,

ZIPHAH (1)

1Chr 4:16 The sons of Jehallelel were Ziph, Z,

ZIPHITES (1)

1Sm 23:19 the Z went up to Saul in Gibeah and said,

ZIPHRON (1)

Nm 34: 9 reach to Z and terminate at Hazar-enan.

ZIPPOR (6)

Nm 22: 2 Now Balak, son of Z,
22:10 Balaam answered God, "Balak, son of Z,
22:16 told him, "This is what Balak, son of Z,
23:18 give ear to my testimony, O son of Z!
Jos 24: 9 Then Balak, son of Z,
Jgs 11:25 are you any better than Balak, son of Z,

ZIPPORAH (3)

Ex 2:21 man gave him his daughter Z in marriage.
4:25 But Z took a piece of flint and cut off
18: 2 So his father-in-law Jethro took along Z,

ZIPPOR'S (1)

Nm 22: 4 Z son who was king of Moab at that time,

ZIV (2)

1Kgs 6: 1 reign over Israel, in the month of Z,
6:37 laid in the month of Z in the fourth year,

ZIZ (1)

2Chr 20:16 see them coming up by the ascent of Z,

ZIZA (2)

1Chr 4:37 Asaiah, Adiel, Jesimiel, Benaiah, Z,
2Chr 11:20 bore him Abijah, Attai, Z and Shelomith.

ZIZAH (2)

1Chr 23:10 The sons of Shimei were Jahath, Z,
23:11 was the chief and Z was second to him;

ZOAN (7)

Nm 13:22 been built seven years before Z in Egypt.]
Ps(s) 78:12 in the land of Egypt, in the plain of Z.
78:43 Egypt and his marvels in the plain of Z,
Is 19:11 Utter fools are the princes of Z!
19:13 The princes of Z have become fools,
30: 4 are at Z and their messengers reach Hanes,
Ez 30:14 I will set fire to Z,

ZOAR (12)

Gn 13:10 the whole Jordan Plain was as far as Z,
14: 2 Zeboiim, and the king of Bela (that is, Z).
14: 8 the king of Bela (that is, Z) marched out,
19:22 That is why the town is called Z.
19:23 rising over the earth as Lot arrived in Z,
19:30 Since Lot was afraid to stay in Z,
19:30 up from Z and settled in the hill country,
Dt 34: 3 at Jericho, city of palms, and as far as Z.
34:12 at Jericho, city of palms, and as far as Z.
Is 15: 5 his fugitives reach Z [Eglath-shelishiyah].
Jer 48: 4 is crushed, their outcry is heard in Z.
48:34 they call from Z to Horonaim,

ZOBA (1)

2Chr 8: 3 went to Hamath of Z and conquered it.

ZOBAH (12)

1Sm 14:47 Ammonites, Aram, Beth-rehob, the king of *Z*,
2Sm 8: 3 Hadadezer, son of Rehob, king of *Z*,
8: 5 came to the aid of Hadadezer, king of *Z*,
8:12 of Hadadezer, son of Rehob, king of *Z*.
10: 6 foot soldiers from Beth-rehob and *Z*,
10: 8 while the Arameans of *Z* and Rehob and the
23:36 Igal, son of Nathan, from *Z*;
1Kgs 11:23 fled from his lord, Hadadezer, king of *Z*,
1Chr 18: 3 Hadadezer, king of *Z* toward Hamath,
18: 5 came to the aid of Hadadezer, king of *Z*,
18: 9 the entire army of Hadadezer, king of *Z*,
19: 6 Naharaim, from Aram-maacah, and from *Z*.

ZOBEBAH (1)

1Chr 4: 8 Koz became the father of Anub and *Z*,

ZODIAC (1)

2Kgs 23: 5 Baal, to the sun, moon, and signs of the *Z*,

ZOHAR (4)

Gn 23: 8 Intercede for me with Ephron, son of *Z*,
25: 9 the field of Ephron, son of *Z* the Hittite,
46:10 Nemuel, Jamin, Ohad, Jachin, *Z*,
Ex 6:15 Jenuel, Jamin, Ohad, Jachin, *Z* and Shaul,

ZOHELETH (1)

1Kgs 1: 9 sheep, oxen, and fatlings at the stone *Z*,

ZOHETH (2)

1Chr 4:20 son of Ishi was *Z* and the son of Zoheth. . . .

ZOPHAH (2)

1Chr 7:35 The sons of his brother Hotham were *Z*,
7:36 The sons of *Z* were Suah,

ZOPHAI (1)

1Chr 6:11 whose son was Elkanah, whose son was *Z*,

ZOPHAR (4)

Jb 2:11 Bildad from Shuh, and *Z* from Naamath.
11: 1 And *Z* the Naamathite spoke out and said:
20: 1 Then *Z* the Naamathite spoke and said:
42: 9 Bildad the Shuhite, and *Z* the Naamathite,

ZORAH (11)

Jos 15:33 Eshtaol, *Z*,
19:41 Their heritage was the territory of *Z*,
Jgs 13: 2 There was a certain man from *Z*,
13:25 which is between *Z* and Eshtaol.
16:31 of his father Manoah between *Z* and Eshtaol.
18: 2 of five valiant men of *Z* and Eshtaol,
18: 8 *Z* and Eshtaol and were asked for a report,
18:11 out from where they were in *Z* and Eshtaol,
1Chr 2:53 people of *Z* and the Eshtaolites derived.
2Chr 11:10 Ziph, Adoraim, Lachish, Azekah, *Z*,
Neh 11:29 and its dependencies, in En-rimmon, *Z*,

ZORATHITES (1)

1Chr 4: 2 These were the clans of the *Z*.

ZORES (1)

Jos 15:59 Bethlehem), Peor, Etam, Kulom, Tatam, *Z*,

ZORITES (1)

1Chr 2:54 half the Manahathites, and the *Z*.

ZUAR (5)

Nm 1: 8 Nethanel, son of *Z*;
2: 5 Their prince was Nethanel, son of *Z*,
7:18 On the second day Nethanel, son of *Z*,
7:23 was the offering of Nethanel, son of *Z*.
10:15 over their host, and Nethanel, son of *Z*,

ZUPH (2)

1Sm 1: 1 son of Elihu, son of Tohu, son of *Z*,
9: 5 When they came to the land of *Z*,

ZUPHITE (1)

1Sm 1: 1 name, a *Z* from the hill country of Ephraim.

ZUR (5)

Nm 25:15 Midianite woman was Cozbi, daughter of *Z*,
31: 8 Evi, Rekem, *Z*,
Jos 13:21 Evi, Rekem, *Z*,
1Chr 8:30 also his first-born son, Abdon, and *Z*,
9:36 then came *Z*,

ZURIEL (1)

Nm 3:35 house of the clans of Merari was *Z*,

ZURISHADDAI (5)

Nm 1: 6 Shelumiel, son of *Z*;
2:12 [Their prince was Shelumiel, son of *Z*,
7:36 day it was the turn of Shelumiel, son of *Z*,
7:41 was the offering of Shelumiel, son of *Z*.
10:19 over their host, and Shelumiel, son of *Z*,

ZUTH (1)

1Chr 6:20 son of Eliel, son of Toah, son of *Z*,

ZUZIM (1)

Gn 14: 5 Rephaim in Ashteroth-karnaim, the *Z* in Ham,